PENGUIN BOOKS

The Penguin Guide to Jazz on CD

Praise for the previous editions

'It must be one of the most elegantly written and useful books ever to have appeared about jazz'
Adam Lively, *Mail on Sunday*

'Suitably monumental . . . admirably thorough . . . an impressive achievement – any serious collector of jazz recordings ought to have it on his or her shelf'
James Maxfield, *Cadence*

'A volume whose scholarship is matched by its sassy wit . . . you find something new on every read'
Christopher Hawtree, *The Times*

'Discerning and conscientious . . . a splendid source of information at a bargain price'
Jazz Times

'Highly recommended . . . the book is a valuable reference tool, a thorough catalogue, and a credible guide through the ocean of discs that flood the stores'
Fanfare

'Comprehensive, endlessly fascinating and informative . . . I was lost in admiration'
Literary Review

'This masterpiece of compilation . . . provides the newcomer with an easy to use and accessible introduction . . . for the regular jazz collector it is the first truly comprehensive and critical reference source (of its kind)'
Sinan Carter Savaskan,
The Times Educational Supplement

About the Authors

Richard Cook was born in Kew. He solved the early problem of choosing between The Rubettes and Pink Floyd by settling on Charlie Parker (mind you, he does have a copy of *Meddle*). He began writing about music with some element of professionalism in 1979. He spent seven years editing *The Wire* and is now back in another editorial chair at *Jazz Review*. He has also turned up in the pages of many other periodicals, welcome or otherwise, and currently pens some lines in *New Statesman*. Novice hurdles at Fakenham and glasses of Springbank account for the rest of the week.

Brian Morton has been a university lecturer, journalist and broadcaster, with briefer episodes as a semi-professional footballer and organic smallholder. Morton's home-grown garlic is now almost as pungent as his tackling used to be. He is currently presenter of BBC Radio Scotland's daily arts programme which, by a remarkable coincidence, is called The Brian Morton Show. He has written and broadcast extensively on jazz and classical music, and is the author of biographies of Sir David Wilkie (the artist, not the swimmer) and painters Robert Colquhoun and Robert MacBryde. His saxophone playing was once described as 'quite like Charles McPherson'; unfortunately, this was the Charlie McPherson who used to play in the house band at the Glenmorag Hotel in Dunoon.

The Penguin Guide to **Jazz** on CD

Richard Cook and Brian Morton

PENGUIN BOOKS

PENGUIN BOOKS

Published by the Penguin Group
Penguin Books Ltd, 27 Wrights Lane, London W8 5TZ, England
Penguin Putnam Inc., 375 Hudson Street, New York, New York 10014, USA
Penguin Books Australia Ltd, Ringwood, Victoria, Australia
Penguin Books Canada Ltd, 10 Alcorn Avenue, Toronto, Ontario, Canada M4V 3B2
Penguin Books India (P) Ltd, 11, Community Centre, Panchsheel Park, New Delhi – 110 017, India
Penguin Books (NZ) Ltd, Private Bag 102902, NSMC, Auckland, New Zealand
Penguin Books (South Africa) (Pty) Ltd, 5 Watkins Street, Denver Ext 4, Johannesburg 2094, South Africa

Penguin Books Ltd, Registered Offices: Harmondsworth, Middlesex, England

First published 1992
Second edition 1994
Third edition 1996
Fourth edition 1998
Fifth edition, completely revised and updated, first published 2000
2

Set in Linotype Minion and Linotype ITC Officina
Typeset by Rowland Phototypesetting Ltd, Bury St Edmunds, Suffolk
Printed in Finland by WS Bookwell Ltd

Contents

Introduction

Jelly Roll Morton always said he started it; so did Nick LaRocca. Perhaps it was born in New Orleans; maybe it just sort of drifted that way and bloomed there. Either way, jazz has been around since the beginning of the last century, even if it didn't start being recorded until about 1917, when the Original Dixieland Jazz Band first went into a studio. We shall never know what Buddy Bolden, the first 'king' of New Orleans cornet playing, sounded like, since he never recorded; and many other opportunities were also missed by the American industry. King Oliver and Jelly Roll Morton, both prominent figures before 1917, didn't arrive in the studios until the 1920s; Freddie Keppard, whose band was a sensation in the 1910s, allegedly refused to make records lest anyone steal his sound. In fact, very little significant recording was done in New Orleans, the supposed birthplace of jazz, until the 1940s. So a white band in New York made 'Darktown Strutters' Ball' in January 1917: at that time, they were described on the record labels as 'Original Dixieland Jass Band'.

Jazz (or jass) has become as widely documented on record as any music. It has rushed through its history – from traditional jazz to swing to bebop to free jazz and back again – in less than a century, and the gramophone has enjoyed the unique position of being able to document it at almost every step along the way. Although many will always hold that jazz is primarily a live music, at its best created in the immediacy of a concert setting of some kind, it has long been disseminated, listened to and argued about via the medium of records. Jazz was, indeed, the first music to be dramatically affected *by* records. As the 78-r.p.m. medium gave way to the LP format, the confining bonds of the three-minute disc were abandoned and jazz performance became longer, less contained, more multifarious.

It is one of the paradoxes of the jazz life that, although the musicians who play the music are seldom as financially rewarded as their counterparts in rock and classical music, they often get to make many more records. Jazz recordings are relatively economical to produce compared with the studio time which rock and classical records seem to demand. Starting your own label has often been the way by which musicians themselves disseminate their work, and there are many, many entrepreneurial spirits whose eagerness to record and distribute the music has helped to keep the jazz record scene a burgeoning phenomenon. Today, more jazz records than ever are recorded and released, despite its allegedly marginal status.

There is also the matter of some eight decades of 'catalogue' to be reissued. The advent of the compact disc brought new life to many a neglected jazz archive. Most of the major catalogues of the past – RCA's Bluebird, Warner Bros' Atlantic, the great modern archives of Blue Note, Verve and Prestige – have been restored to circulation via CD. As many of the earlier recordings have fallen out of copyright, independent enterprises such as Classics, Frog and Retrieval have embarked on extensive CD reissues of the jazz of the 1920s and '30s. This has now extended to the 1940s. Before long – unless the industry forces a change in copyright laws – it may begin to apply to the LP era.

Our aim in this book has been to try to provide as comprehensive an overview as possible of this vast and bewilderingly diverse area of recorded music. Newcomers to jazz are always hard-pressed to know both where to start and where to proceed from there. Most will have heard of Miles Davis's *Kind Of Blue* or John Coltrane's *Giant Steps*, two of the most famous jazz albums ever released. But both those musicians have enormous discographies, and this presents a formidable problem to collectors on a limited budget or to those who wish to acquire just a few examples of Davis or Coltrane on record. At the same time, more experienced fans and collectors deserve a detailed summary and evaluation of what exactly is available by both major and minor figures in the jazz field. That is what we've tried to do here.

As in the areas routinely defined by the terms 'rock' or 'classical', the diversity of music covered by the term 'jazz' is extraordinary. Our aim is to list and discuss as many records currently available in the field as possible – but, since jazz itself remains a difficult area to define, this has inevitably led to problems over what to include and what to leave out. Although jazz and blues are inextricably bound up in each other, we have omitted such musicians as Bessie Smith and Joe Turner, even though their records are listened to and enjoyed by countless numbers of 'jazz fans': the blues demands a volume to itself, which should be documented by safer hands than ours (and we are delighted to hear that a *Penguin Guide To Blues* is at last in preparation). Singers, too, are difficult to make clear judgement-calls on: the old argument as to what is a jazz singer has never been resolved, and it could be contended that, if we have included Mel Torme (as we have), then why not Peggy Lee, or Bing Crosby, or Frank Sinatra, all of whom made records of a jazz inclination? Often we have been guided by the nature of the accompaniments, and in some cases we have chosen to include only the jazz-directed output of a particular artist. In the case of Nat Cole, for instance, we've omitted the bulk of his vocal recordings, while his instrumental ones have remained; much the same applies to George Benson. We don't wish to discriminate against an artist seeking pop status, but we try to stick to discussing jazz records.

The advent of 'free music' placed a further strain on jazz classification: the work of such musicians as Derek Bailey and Billy Jenkins may, often at their own insistence, have little to do with any jazz tradition. But the connections between jazz and improvised music are indisputable, and there is no feasible reason to discriminate against free music by excluding it from this book.

It hardly needs saying that it's impossible to include every jazz record from every part of the globe. This was already a big book before we started preparing this edition, and thousands of new discs have been considered for inclusion. Since the

Guide can only get so big, we've had to be more selective in our approach, much as we try to offer a genuinely comprehensive overview. Another factor is the increasing bulk of the jazz back-catalogue. While many records have disappeared from circulation since last time, it is increasingly the practice of major jazz labels such as ECM and Black Saint/Soul Note to keep their entire catalogues in print. We still try to cover as much of significance as we can of what was available at the time of our cut-off point (early summer 2000).

We continue to omit budget-priced collections of dubious provenance. Readers who think they've found a bargain in some nefarious-looking release of unidentified origin may care to remember that the musicians involved probably aren't benefiting from the issue in any way. In situations where there is a big overlap in the reissues of early material, as is now the case with some major artists, we've simply tried to choose the best records to list. Compilations, either of a single artist or of some style of jazz genre, have been flooding out in recent years, as major labels seek to put a bit of fresh life (as they see it) into comparatively quiescent areas of their catalogue. We've omitted many of these, unless they're a really effective piece of cherrypicking.

We have again decided to dismiss many records which amount to little more than easy-listening, instrumental or vocal music with only the vaguest of jazz connotations. The radio format in America known as 'smooth jazz' includes a great deal of this kind of thing. Many such records have little to do with what we (and most of our readers) understand as jazz – and if that seems an élitist view, we prefer to see it as a pragmatic one. There's a substantial grey area between jazz and contemporary composition: some musicians, such as Fred Rzewski or John Lewis, move freely between these genres, and there are many records – particularly from such companies as Bvhaast – which count jazz as an element (though not perhaps the defining one) in their make-up. On this issue, we've used our discretion here as best we can.

How do we get the records we review? Many companies and indeed the artists themselves are kind enough to send us review copies – although they can all vouch for the fact that this has no bearing on what we think of the music we listen to! Some may be astonished to hear that many, many records were also purchased, across the counter, by ourselves – just as most of our readers do. We like to think that we haven't entirely lost touch with how collectors and fans approach building their personal library of music. But if nobody has sent us a disc, and we haven't been able to lay our hands on a copy, it won't be listed here. If a disc is literally impossible to find, even if theoretically available, it does no kind of service to collectors to give it coverage.

Other discs may have arrived too late for inclusion. Some we have deemed too poor to be even worth listing. Some we may have simply missed altogether. A few of our correspondents take obvious delight in pointing out discs which we've omitted, to which we can only say . . . excuse us, but no one's perfect.

One trend of late has been for some of the major labels to issue limited-edition releases – Blue Note with their Connoisseur series, Verve with their Elite Editions. Here and there we have listed a few of these titles, where we think the release is of particular significance and the reader stands a good chance finding a copy: some 'limited editions' seem to last a long time.

This is designed to be a practical book, to assist our readership in putting together a fine and enjoyable collection of jazz music. None of the judgements herein is set in stone: further listening and pondering on the music may yield different opinions in the fullness of time, and – as always – here and there assiduous readers may again spot a slight change of opinion from our previous editions. In that respect, we share a characteristic that is surely common to all jazz listeners: that of living and developing with this music as it continues to evolve and grow. We have tried not to be sentimental about our evaluations: it is all too tempting to overrate some records on the basis that the jazz musician's lot is trying enough without having to endure negative criticism. But the first responsibility of a *Guide* such as this is to the listeners and record-buyers. Building a comprehensive library of jazz CDs is an expensive business, and most enthusiasts will be able to invest in only a fraction of what is available to them in the current record marketplace. Our primary aim has been to assist in deciding how best to make that choice and to suggest areas of the music which may yield hitherto unrealized pleasures.

Evaluation

While some may consider it iniquitous to define the merits of a record using a star-system, we feel that it's simply the most useful shorthand as a starting point for discussing the disc in question. But we cannot stress too strongly that the reader should consult the text in addition to the star rating for our overall evaluation of the record. We have chosen to make use of between one and four stars: parentheses round a single star indicate that some small reservation prevents our placing it in the higher category. Parentheses round all the stars indicate that some more fundamental reservation exists which prevents us giving a wholehearted recommendation: usually this will relate to some aspect of the recording or presentation of the disc in question, but again we advise the reader to consult the text.

**** Very fine: an outstanding record that yields consistent pleasure and is a splendid example of the artist's work.

***(*) A fine record, with some exceptional music. Only kept out of the front rank by some minor reservations.

*** A good if middleweight set; one that lacks the stature or consistency of the finest records, but which is certainly rewarding on its own terms.

**(*) There are worthwhile things here, but some significant flaws in either performance or presentation tell against it. Probably for completists of the artist in question only.

** Perhaps some good points, but there are many better records to listen to.

*(*) Seriously flawed; not worth bothering with.

* Who authorized this outrage?

In a *very* few cases we have chosen to award a special token of merit; in our *Guide*, it takes the form of a crown. This is to denote records we feel a special admiration or affection for: a purely personal choice, which we hope our readers will deem as such. It is by no means something of the order of an 'All-Time Top 100', or whatever; more a personal indulgence.

Recording Quality

Our first concern is with the music itself, and most contemporary jazz records are engineered to the customary high standards which are the norm for the industry; they therefore require little further comment – although, whenever there is some particular felicity or problem with the production, we have noted it as such. Far more important, however, is the question of the remastering of older material for CD reissue. We have to report that there are still erratic and unreliable standards of remastering for CD, among major and independent companies alike. Remastering from 78s continues to be an area which excites controversy, just as it was in the LP era, and numerous issues have caused us disappointment in this regard. Set against this is the magnificent work which has been done by, in particular, John R.T. Davies, the doyen of the field, and Robert Parker, some of whose stereo re-creations have been outstanding. We have attempted to be as scrupulous as possible in our evaluation of this issue. We might also mention that we have frequently discovered many instances when the CD version of even a relatively modern record offers no noticeable improvement over the LP issue. Overall, however, we are glad to note that, as the CD era has matured, standards of remastering have become much more consistent, and more often than not there is evidence of real craftsmanship in a typical CD reissue.

Running Time: Never Mind the Width ...

Our decision to ignore the question of CD running-time may vex some readers, since it continues to bother a number of pundits. The compact disc can comfortably accommodate some 80 minutes of music, yet most jazz CDs fail to use the full capacity of the disc and, in the case of many reissues, no attempt is made to beef up the running-time of the original LP by adding extra material. That said, a considerable number of issues *do* include extra tracks by way of alternative takes or previously rejected pieces. But such material is often of dubious value, and an ordinary LP is unlikely to become an extraordinary CD by the addition of three or four more-of-the-same tunes. Our criterion continues to be that the quality of the music determines the desirability of the disc, not its running-time. An outstanding 40-minute record remains outstanding, even if it does run to only half of what could be put on the CD. The mysterious means-test of 'value for money' is not worth addressing here. In our experience, most CDs are too long, not too short.

Pricing

The jazz record business is a global one and, with the rise in internet commerce and international retailing, CD pricing is a far from static issue: the price of a disc in one territory may conflict with its cost as an import in another. As usual, we do not denote whether an issue is full- or mid-price, or indeed at budget. The latter bracket is still a rarity among jazz CDs but, with Naxos launching their own series and with many of the major companies releasing compilation series which are at least close to the budget point, it's an increasingly populated area.

Layout of Text

Musician entries are listed alphabetically. Here is a typical record-entry:

***(*) **The Return Of Tal Farlow**
Original Jazz Classics OJC 356 *Farlow; John Scully (p); Jack Six (b); Alan Dawson (d). 9/69.*

The star-rating is followed by the title of the record; its label and catalogue number follow. Next we list the musicians who are playing on the disc, together with their instrumental credits, and – where available – the date of the recording (month/year). All personnel are listed collectively – that is, it shouldn't be implied that every musician listed for a record is featured on every track. A full list of instrument abbreviations follows this introduction. Where there are multiple records in an entry, each change in personnel is duly noted – although, rather than listing the same musicians over again, subsequent details may begin with 'As above, except . . .'. Sometimes, where there may be some minor changes between complex lists of personnel, we have chosen to say 'similar to above' or suchlike. Where the recording dates span a number of different sessions, as is the case for many compilations, they are listed as, for example, 5/74–10/80. While we've tried to present the clearest possible picture of who recorded what and when, this is a guide, not a discography, and we've attempted to be sensible over the listing of minutiae. We hope our readers will indulge any slight discrepancies of style which may result.

We have tried to be as accurate as possible over listing catalogue numbers, but neither we nor our publishers can be held responsible for mistakes which may have eluded our checking. By and large, we have attempted to simplify the situation as far as possible by concentrating on the 'core' number which most records are assigned. Many CDs now show a seemingly baffling array of digits, but often these refer to bar-code configurations as well as the core number. It has become an industry standard to use the suffix -2 to denote a CD issue. Independent companies often use very simple systems of cataloguing – which we wish the major companies would avail themselves of! Most record companies are seeking to standardize their catalogue-number system to ensure that a world-wide release uses the same central number.

We always advise that, when ordering records, readers state in full the title and artist and desired format, as well as the catalogue numbers. Experienced dealers will be able to spot any possible confusion over the number when furnished with these extra details.

Biography

For the first time, we've chosen to preface each artist's entry with a few lines – in some cases, no more than a few words – which offer some biographical information, or frequently a simple pointer to the kind of player he or she is. We've no wish to charge into the sort of territory inhabited by the several excellent biographical A–Z jazz works which are already out there; this is more of a 'sighter' on the artist in question.

Formats: CD and Nothing But?

The compact disc is still king in the music marketplace, although we hear, with amusing regularity, young internet entrepreneurs boasting that it will soon be an obsolete format. DCC has disappeared; the Minidisc has made a slight comeback but remains a minority interest; and high-quality audiophile vinyl still has its legion of admirers. So far, though, the propensity to scratch such discs has not been eliminated by frail human beings. Downloading music off the World Wide Web has become a fascination of internet users, and jazz is taking its place in the roll-call of musics that are available in this way. But what kind of real impact it will have on the global CD market is something which, as in most areas of the internet, is a matter of speculation. At present, most jazz musicians still seem to be thinking in terms of recording 'albums' (that delightfully old-fashioned word).

Deletions

A book like this can never be as up to date as we would wish. Many records will have appeared since our manuscript went to press, and a number of those listed here may have fallen victim to the deletions axe. Records often stay in circulation even after they have been officially deleted: dealers and independent distributors may hold stocks, and a diligent search can often locate a supposedly extinct item. All this will be familiar to experienced collectors, who know how difficult it can be to locate a particular record; but we counsel that a patient reader should try more than one source if confronted with an initial response that a record is deleted and therefore impossible to obtain. For that purpose we have included a list of distributors at the end of this introduction.

Mosaic Records

The programme of high-quality reissues run by Mosaic Records of Stamford, Connecticut, has continued since our last edition. Once again, we have omitted editions from our listing since they are specialist items available only from the company itself or from the small number of retailers who stock them. However, we again applaud Mosaic's work and would suggest that interested parties get in touch with the company direct for information regarding current releases. Their address is 35 Melrose Place, Stamford, CT 06902, USA (Tel.: 06902-7533; www.mosaicrecords.com).

Market Overview: 2000–2001

A fascinating period for the music, on and off record. A small number of ill-informed writers claimed at the end of 1999 that jazz was a spent force and was ending with the century, but readers will be aware that such nonsense has been said many times before in the music's history. Instead, jazz seems to be entering a dramatic new phase, in which a period of retrenchment and pondering on the music's resources is beginning to yield some surprising results. The size and nature of the jazz ensemble has never been more diverse, with even a basic small-group configuration of one or two horns and a rhythm section open to multiple variations. New instruments are coming on to the jazz bandstand and old instruments are being used in new ways. The rhythmic language of jazz has expanded further. Even the oldest or the most familiar parts of 'the tradition', from Dixieland to the swing-mainstream, are being enlivened by new voices and new audiences.

This is not the same thing as the forced 'crossover' concepts which some companies have been assigning to their artists. Jazz is peculiarly responsive to change from within but rarely accommodates the imposition of business-driven 'creativity'. Indeed, there is evidence to suggest that the major record companies are losing interest in jazz at present. Unfortunately, 'smooth jazz', which has very little to do with the music discussed in this book, continues to make money for the industry and diverts resources which could be used to support more challenging music. But there should be no surprise in that.

If major labels are faltering, there is no shortage of independent interest in recording the music. Veteran operations such as ECM as well as comparative newcomers like Fresh Sound's New Talent imprint continue to document music which is deemed unworthy of business interest by larger outfits. The Naxos label has made an impressive start as the first budget-price new jazz operation. As in most other walks of life, the internet is having an impact, making smaller labels more 'available' than ever before to a global audience via their own websites and through e-commerce. We are confident that more jazz is being recorded and listened to than ever before, and what's heartening is that so much of it affirms that the music remains individual and fresh, even with so much already said and done. As with the novel, or the symphony, something new keeps turning up.

Acknowledgements

Our burden in compiling the fifth edition of this overweight tome has, as always, been greatly lightened by the kindness and affable co-operation of many friends involved in the jazz business, both in the UK and abroad. Our special thanks in this regard go to (alphabetically this time!) Derek 'Templegate' Day, Wendy Day, Carl Ericson, Mark Gillinson, Nathan Graves, Terri Hinte, John Jack, Sharon Kelly, Kerstan Mackness, Trevor Manwaring, Gaylene Martin, Leonard Newman, Danielle Richards, Steve Sanderson, Adam Sieff, Laurie Staff, Becky Stevenson, Bill Trythall, Clare Tyler, Oliver Weindling and Eddie Wilkinson. We should also thank the many readers who have written to us with suggestions or corrections: always gratefully received. As ever, the incomparable Roger Wells ('Good morning, R.D.!') has been our unflappable copy editor. Nigel Wilcockson ('I think you should think about doing it this way') has undertaken his new role of Our Man At Penguin with finesse and charm. Mark Handsley ('The typesetters have assured me that it was') has been the master technocrat.

The other great contributors have been, in the Morton household, Pam, Fiona and Alice; at chez Cook, Lee Ellen. Their fortitude in the face of many a Peter Brötzmann or Kenny Ball record has been extraordinary, and our love and admiration for them abides.

Richard Cook
Brian Morton

Distributors

The following UK distributors may be able to help in obtaining records. We have appended the names of some of the labels they deal with, where appropriate.

New Note Distribution, Electron House, Cray Avenue, Orpington, Kent BR5 3RJ
(Tel.: 01689 877884; Fax: 01689 877891)
Astor Place, Concord, ECM, Enja, GoJazz, Hep, Label Bleu, N2K, Stretch, Timeless, Tutu, Zephyr

Harmonia Mundi Ltd, 19–21 Nile St, London N1 7LR
(Tel.: 0207 253 0863; Fax: 0207 253 3237)
Avant, Black Saint, Chronoscope, DIW, Flapper, hatOLOGY, Philology, PSF, Red, Soul Note

Cadillac Distribution, 61–71 Collier Street, London N1 9DF
(Tel.: 0207 278 7391; Fax: 0207 278 7394)
Arbors, Bvhaast, Cadillac, Collector's Classics, Dragon, 504, FMP, Frog, Geestgronden, Gemini, ICP, Incus, Jazz Hour, Moers, Nagel Heyer, Ogun, Olufsen, Phono Suecia, Phontastic, Reservoir, Storyville

Spotlite, 103 London Road, Sawbridgeworth, Herts CM21 9JJ
(Tel.: 01279 724572)
Sackville, Spotlite

Discovery Records, Old Church Mission Room, Kings Corner, Pewsey, Wilts SN9 5BS
(Tel.: 01672 63931; Fax: 01672 563934)
Classics, Cool N Blue, Fresh Sound, Steeplechase, Sunnyside

Impetus Distribution, 10 High Street, Skigersta Ness, Isle of Lewis, Outer Hebrides HS2 0TS
(Tel.: 01851 810808; Fax: 01851 810809)
Impetus, Jazz, Nine Winds, Splasc(h)

Proper Distribution, 6 Forest Hill Industrial Estate, Forest Hill, London SE23 2LX
(Tel: 0208 699 8100; Fax: 0208 699 5111)
A, Black Lion, Challenge, Chesky, Criss Cross, Delmark, High Note, Lake, Retrieval, Savant

Via Distribution UK, Truman Brewery Building, Brick Lane London E1 6QB
(Tel.: 0207 377 6515; Fax: 0207 377 5841)
Dreyfus, ESP, Jazz In Motion, Palmetto, Provocateur, Via.

Support your local record shop! However, since mail order is often the only available option for many, we recommend: Crazy Jazz, 1 Hearn Road, Romford RM1 2DP (Tel.: 01992 625436; Fax: 01992 640644).

Artists or companies who have records which they feel should be heard by the authors for the next edition are invited to contact Richard Cook via email at : RDCookJazz@aol.com.

Abbreviations

acc	accordion	Cmel	C-melody saxophone	p	piano
acl	alto clarinet	comp	composer	perc	percussion
af	alto flute	cond	conductor	picc	piccolo
ahn	alto horn	cor	cor anglais	picc t	piccolo trumpet
arr	arranger	d	drums	pkt-t	pocket-trumpet
as	alto saxophone	elec	electronics	sno	sopranino saxophone
b	bass	eng hn	english horn	sou	sousaphone
ban	bandoneon	euph	euphonium	srspn	sarrusophone
bb	brass bass	f	flute	ss	soprano saxophone
bcl	bass clarinet	flhn	flugelhorn	syn	synthesizer
bf	bass flute	frhn	french horn	t	trumpet
bhn	baritone horn	g	guitar	tb	trombone
bj	banjo	gfs	goofus	tba	tuba
bs	baritone saxophone	g-syn	guitar synthesizer	thn	tenor horn
bsn	bassoon	hca	harmonica	ts	tenor saxophone
bsx	bass saxophone	hn	horn	uke	ukulele
b-t	bass trumpet	hp	harp	v	vocal
btb	bass trombone	hpd	harpsichord	vib	vibraphone
c	cornet	ky	keyboards	vla	viola
cbcl	contrabass clarinet	kz	kazoo	vn	violin
cbsx	contrabass saxophone	mand	mandolin	vtb	valve trombone
cbsrspn	contrabass sarrusophone	mar	marimba	wbd	washboard
cel	celeste	mel	mellophone	xy	xylophone
cl	clarinet	ob	oboe		
clo	cello	org	organ		

AALY Trio

GROUP

Swedish improv power trio, on both occasions abetted by guest, Ken Vandermark.

***** Stumble**

Wobbly Rail 002 *Mats Gustafsson (ts, f, fluteophone); Ken Vandermark (ts, cl, bcl); Peter Janson (b); Kjell Nordeson (d).* 1/98.

*****(*) Live At The Glenn Miller Café**

Wobbly Rail 008 *As above.* 3/99.

Gustafsson, Janson and Nordeson are a formidable team in their own right, starting off from loose but palpable structures and charging into black, unlit space. But this is not all blood and iron. There is a rather beautiful and affecting version of Charlie Haden's 'Song For Che' on the earlier disc, with a long and superbly accomplished bass improvisation by Nordeson. Nevertheless, it's the cathartic sequences on both discs that make the most impact. Both sets were cut live, and the somewhat remote sound on *Stumble*, set down at a Chicago concert on an American tour, detracts from the group's viscerality. Vandermark and Gustafsson are formidably like-minded, at least in the way they want the band to make its impression, and the sound of the quartet in full flight has a harsh, narcotic edge to it. The Glenn Miller café in Stockholm hosted the second event, and this one is a twist more immediate and – in its way – sensual. There is an absolutely overwhelming treatment of Albert Ayler's 'Ghosts' and a vibrant one of Joe Harriott's 'Idioms', which sounds better than anything on Vandermark's own Joe Harriott Project record.

Eivind Aarset

GUITAR, COMPUTERS

The talented young Norwegian has previously collaborated with trumpeter Nils Petter Molvaer and the multi-talented Bugge Wesseltoft, between them the advance guard of a vital new Scandinavian movement to unite jazz and contemporary popular forms.

***** Electronique Noir**

Jazzland 558 128-2 *Aarset; Nils Petter Molvaer (t); Vidar Johannesen (bcl); Ketil Bjerkestrand, Kjetil Saunes, Bugge Wesseltoft (ky); Bjørn Kjellemyr, Jonny Sjo (b); Kim Ofstad (d).* 97.

Rarely has the guitar gone through quite so many transformations: flanged, reverbed, echoed, tweaked, distorted. Rarely, too, has jazz danced so promiscuously with other styles and genres. Aarset has assembled a technically ingenious, technologically astute montage of techno, ambient, drum'n'bass with blues-based jazz.

How far it is effective rather depends on attitudes to the source material. American attempts to work similar syntheses – the legacy of M-Base and like-minded musicians – have rarely sounded as innocent or as whole-hearted. Aarset is perhaps too enamoured of his gadgets and widgets to be entirely engaging. There is a hint of muso self-indulgence, and yet the very enthusiasm carries the day and *Electronique Noir* is wonderfully infectious and enjoyable.

Abash

GROUP

Swedish trio moving between post-bop structure and free playing.

*****(*) Abash**

Dragon DRCD 249 *Anders Ekholm (ts); Tommy Skotte (b); Nils Danell (d).* 6/93.

This trio approaches an open canvas with a fine blend of fresh ideas and hard-won acumen. Skotte and Danell are the more experienced pair, and the drummer's noisily swinging style merges handsomely with Skotte's fundamentally lyrical free playing. Ekholm, though sometimes a bit diffident, usually plays with a brimming energy that his attractively scratchy tone tempers and scales down to the intimacy of the setting. He is responsible for 6 of the 11 themes and there's plenty of ingenuity here, as in the endless melody of 'P1', to take a single example. Humour, too – 'Caravan' is a surprising, funny rendition of the Ellington chestnut that contrasts nicely with the hard-bitten, rather bleak handling of 'Out Of Nowhere'.

****** Jazz**

Dragon DRCD 295 *As above, except Ekholm also plays Cmel.* 11/95.

The gnomic title hides a quite extraordinary record. If Ekholm sounded a little reserved on *Abash*, he's magnificent here. Amazingly, four of the six pieces are done on C-melody saxophone. He gets a piercing wail out of the horn that goes with an improvised line of superb inventiveness, phrase shapes never coming out as expected, tempos decelerated and altered at will, the dynamic intensity under constant scrutiny. Next to these, the tenor solos are almost conventional, but they're equally accomplished. Skotte plays with Haden-like gravitas, and Danell takes an almost minimalist role at the kit, which makes every stick-stroke count. Not for nothing is Rollins evoked in the sleeve-notes: this is as impressive sax trio music as anything since Sonny's golden days. Recorded at two live shows, one in Umeå and one at Club Fasching in Stockholm: a superlative disc.

Greg Abate

ALTO, SOPRANO AND TENOR SAXOPHONES, FLUTE

From New England, Abate has vast big-band section experience and he began recording as a leader, mostly in a straight-ahead bebop style, in the 1990s.

***** Bop City – Live At Birdland**

Candid CCD 79513 *Abate; James Williams (p); Rufus Reid (b); Kenny Washington (d).* 7/91.

***** Straight Ahead**

Candid CCD 79530 *Abate; Claudio Roditi (t, flhn); Hilton Ruiz (p); George Mraz (b); Kenny Washington (d).* 9/92.

****(*) Dr Jekyll And Mr Hyde**

Candid CCD 79715 *Abate; Richie Cole (as); Chris Neville (p); Paul Del Nero (b); Artie Cabral (d).* 11/94.

Abate worked as a section player in big bands for nearly 20 years before making these small-group albums for Candid. *Bop City* is a breezy session which affirms a basic interest in bebop saxophone, since the leader is apparently at home on any of the models. Alto is his main preoccupation, but his tenor features on 'Peaks Beaks' and 'Gemini Mood' are convincing, and the soprano on 'Opportunity' reveals a lesson absorbed from Coltrane. It's a pick-up rhythm section, but they know exactly what they're doing. *Straight Ahead* re-runs the formula with Roditi as sparring partner, but his sometimes anonymous facility is more of a distraction than a counterweight: the best music is created between Abate and another heavyweight rhythm section. *Dr Jekyll And Mr Hyde* offers a second repeat of the formula, with Cole on board, but this time it's starting to wear thin and the impression at the end is of nothing much at all except facility.

***** My Buddy**

Seaside 132 *Abate; Paul Fontaine (t); Mac Chrupcala (p); Al Bernstein (b); John Anter (d); Donna Byrne (v).* 3–12/94.

*****(*) Bop Lives!**

Blue Chip Jazz 4001 *Abate; Claudio Roditi (t, flhn); Kenny Barron (p); Rufus Reid (b); Ben Riley (d).* 5/96.

My Buddy is an honest and direct set of originals and a couple of standards, played by a band based largely around Abate's frequent stamping-ground of Rhode Island. Unfussy but cogent, this won't turn heads but it's a satisfying show of playing it by bebop's rules.

As is *Bop Lives!*, but the excellent band and, above all, Mark Morganelli's sympathetic and pointed production get the very best out of the situation. The studio sound is beautifully clear and punchy, with very little reverb, and it suits the lean and wasteless playing. Abate has never sounded tougher or more direct on record (for once he plays alto exclusively here) and Roditi, on five of the nine tracks, is a willing partner. It might be no more than another solid bebop date, but it's surely Abate's best.

Ahmed Abdul-Malik (1927–93)

DOUBLE BASS, OUD

Originally Sam Gill, a New Yorker with Sudanese parents, Abdul-Malik worked with Randy Weston and Thelonious Monk as a bassist, but he turned to his education in African music and made the lute-like oud a viable jazz instrument. His rare excursions as leader are interesting but by no means essential.

****(*) Jazz Sahara**

Original Jazz Classics OJCCD 1820 *Abdul-Malik; Johnny Griffin (ts); Naim Karacand (vn); Jack Ghanaim (kanon); Al Harewood (d); Bilal Abdurrahman, Mike Hamway (perc).* 10/58.

***** East Meets West: Musique of Ahmed Abdul-Malik**

RCA 74321 25723 *As above, except add Lee Morgan (t); Curtis Fuller (tb); Benny Golson (ts); Jerome Richardson (f); replace Ghanaim with Ahmed Yetman (kanon).* 3/59.

Abdul-Malik was briefly touted at the end of the 1950s as the cutting edge of East–West crossover music. As a bass player, he saw service in some of the most innovative jazz groups of the time, including Thelonious Monk's, and the presence of Griffin, Golson and Fuller on these albums attests to his mainstream acceptance. However, he tended to gravitate towards leaders who were similarly interested in investigating some sort of rapprochement between Asian or African musics and American jazz; hence his engagements with Randy Weston and, more briefly, John Coltrane. As with so many such experiments, one sometimes feels that Eastern and Western elements are juxtaposed rather than properly synthesized. That is certainly true of the opening tracks on both these interesting records. On the long 'Ya Annas (Oh, People)' which launches *Jazz Sahara*, he begins on the lute-like *oud*, before switching to bass to set up a rhythmic pattern for Griffin's first entrance. Much the same happens on 'E-Lail (The Night)' on the later album, eighty seconds of 'ethnic' ostinati with an unfamiliar scalar feel, except that Lee Morgan doesn't seem to need a 'jazz' context, playing comfortably and often inspirationally even without conventional changes and showing some understanding in his slides and growls of the microtonal basis of Abdul-Malik's music. Even without a settled tonality, the music has a minor key feel which affords the jazz players – and particularly the brass players – room for manoeuvre, though Griffin (a partner in the 1958 Monk quartet) and Golson both respond positively. The only straightforward jazz writing on either disc is 'Searchin'' on *East Meets West*, a relatively conventional blowing theme that highlights Abdul-Malik's slightly fruity bass sound (something of a cross between Wilbur Ware and a camp Paul Chambers) and his interesting approach to textures. Arranged for trombone, flute, tenor and rhythm, and stripped of the shimmering 72-stringed *kanon* and the Middle Eastern percussion, it manages to sound both familiar and alien. Though he was perhaps something of a singleton, an isolated experimenter who happened to chime with aspects of a wider musical environment, Abdul-Malik still repays attention.

Ahmed Abdullah (born 1947)

TRUMPET, FLUGELHORN, VOCAL

A rarely sighted free player of the '70s and '80s, recently active again.

****(*) Liquid Magic**

Silkheart SHCD-104 *Abdullah; Charles Brackeen (ts); Malachi Favors (b); Alvin Fielder (d).* 2/87.

***** Ahmed Abdullah And The Solomonic Quintet**

Silkheart SHCD-109 *Abdullah; David S Ware (ts); Masujaa (g); Fred Hopkins (b); Charles Moffett (d).*

***** Dedication**

CIMP 152 *Abdullah; Carlos Ward (as, f); Masujaa (g); Alex Blake (b); Cody Moffett (d).* 6/97.

***** Actual Proof**

CIMP 192 *Abdullah; Alex Harding (bs, bcl); Masa Kamaguchi (b); Jimmy Weinstein (d).* 1/99.

Abdullah's original inspiration was Louis Armstrong, but his main areas of activity have more to do with the free playing of the 1970s and '80s. The two Silkheart albums are interesting if inconclusive. Tersely organized, the six tunes on *Liquid Magic* reflect a Colemanesque feel which suits the folk-like melodies. But the trumpeter is, frankly, the least impressive player here: Brackeen's fierce yet lightly shaded solos make a more powerful impression, and Favors and Fielder generate a loose yet convincingly swinging pulse. The second disc has a similar problem: the leader is outclassed by his own band. The rhythm section is wonderfully alert and inventive, with Masujaa's guitar an especially individual presence, and Ware is a gritty improviser. Abdullah's writing is at its best in the Latin lope of 'El Canto II'.

Dedication is his first record in a while. The music tends to be dominated by Cody Moffett (playing his father's kit), and he creates a fine, swinging drive for the big pieces, 'Amanpondo' and 'Song Of The Holy Warrior'. Ward seems a little sidelined and Abdullah again lacks authority as a player; but the music has a cheerful, celebratory feel, old-fashioned like a free-bop date of 25 years before, and it's quite a warming experience, though Abdullah's singing on 'La Vie en Rose' is one track that many will prefer to skip.

The spirit of Charles Moffett hangs over *Actual Proof* as well. Drummer Jimmy Weinstein met the veteran in a Brooklyn store, and then heard Abdullah at Moffett's funeral service. Through a sequence of circumstances, NAM was formed and this record, whose title refers to the Buddhist belief in something like synchronicity, is the result. Abdullah is in stronger voice than on previous records and the group is altogether better balanced than on *Dedication*. A long 'Naima' and Gunter Hampel's 'Serenade For Marion Brown' occupy the heart of the set, though once again Abdullah's interest in the nexus of New Orleans and Africa is a dominant concern. The final 'Song Of Time/Shaka Zulu' is dedicated to the late Fred Hopkins, but the most straightforwardly moving cut is Abdullah's own 'Song Of Tenderness', on which his muted solo floats over a bass line that old Fred would have loved.

Kaoru Abe (1948–78)

ALTO AND SOPRANINO SAXOPHONES, HARMONICA, GUITAR, PIANO

A minor legend in his field, Abe was one of the central figures in the small but intensely committed group of Japanese free improvisers at work during the 1970s. In recent years almost all of his legacy has been released on CD, reaching a larger audience for the first time.

***** Duo**

1971 PSFD-67 *Abe; Huiroshi Yamazaki (d).* 1/71.

*****(*) Solo**

PSFD-66 *Abe (as solo).* 7/72.

***** Live At Gaya Vol. 1**

DIW 371 *Abe (sno, as solo).* 9–12/77.

***** Live At Gaya Vol. 2**

DIW 372 *Abe (sno, as, p solo).* 1/78.

***** Live At Gaya Vol. 3**

DIW 373 *Abe (as solo).* 3/78.

***** Live At Gaya Vol. 4**

DIW 374 *Abe (sno, as solo).* 4/78.

**** Live At Gaya Vol. 5**

DIW 375 *Abe (sno, hca, p solo).* 5/78.

****(*) Live At Gaya Vol. 6**

DIW 376 *Abe (sno, as, hca solo).* 5–6/78.

***** Live At Gaya Vol. 7**

DIW 377 *Abe (sno, as solo).* 6/78.

***** Live At Gaya Vol. 8**

DIW 378 *Abe (as solo).* 7/78.

***** Live At Gaya Vol. 9**

DIW 379 *Abe (as solo).* 7/78.

****(*) Live At Gaya Vol. 10**

DIW 380 *Abe (sno, g solo).* 8/78.

****(*) Last Date**

DIW 335 *Abe (as, g, hca solo).* 8/78.

Abe is scarcely known outside Japan, in part due to his early death, and until recently there was nothing accessible on CD. This remarkable burst of releases from DIW and PSFD quite suddenly placed him in a far wider currency: 12 solo albums of mostly saxophone improvisation, plus one duo recording with drummer Yamazaki. Abe's style is one of near-total extremes, and he may well earn an honoured place in the affections of today's generation of Japanese noise-makers such as The Boredoms. The first *Solo* disc consists of three mouth-splitting exercises on alto, phrases that sound scalded on his own lips, and though he actually resorts to overblowing only infrequently his phrasing is gnarled, squalling, of indeterminate shape. Sometimes he starts with an actual melody: though uncredited, the second piece on *Solo* is based on 'Fly Me To The Moon', and the Gaya series includes a savage sopranino disquisition on 'Chim Chim Cheree' (Volume 4), while Volume 9 consists of a single alto improvisation on 'Lover Come Back To Me'. Abe is quite unafraid to use space: some solos contain huge chunks of silence, others seem to crawl along at a tempo that suggests a music of no momentum at all and, though he seems unaware of imperatives such as beginning, middle and end, one finds oneself adjusting to his peculiar timelessness when sitting through long sections of this music. Of less interest are the pieces on guitar (scratchy and home-made-sounding), piano (bass-chord thunder, of no discernible consequence) and harmonica (which seems like nothing more than mere sucking and blowing). But his alto and sopranino pieces have their own strange vocabulary, and it is surely not fanciful to place them in a Japanese tradition of spare, intensely refined music-making. Even as they exist in a parallel universe to Albert Ayler.

Of these 13 discs, we would cautiously recommend *Solo*, Volumes 1, 4, 7 and 9 of the *Gaya* sequence, and (for a little variety) the duos with Yamazaki, a conventional but energetic free drummer. *Last Date* has its own poignancy in view of the circumstances, but the guitar and harmonica pieces which take up 40 minutes or so are of very modest interest.

***** Aida's Call**

Starlight Furniture Company 9 *Abe; Toshinori Kondo (t); Derek Bailey (g); Motoharu Yoshizawa (b).* 5/78.

A postscript, and a fascinating one, although we should warn that the recording is very poor by modern standards. This catches three of the major Japanese players of their era, plus their distinguished western visitor, at a gig at Michada-Kavalinka in May 1978. One long improvisation and two shorter ones. The group situation finds Abe reining himself in more than usual perhaps, but nevertheless there are some thrilling sparks with Kondo and Bailey.

Chris Abelen

TROMBONE

Young Dutch trombonist, working in the local free-bop music.

*****(*) Dance Of The Penguins**

Bvhaast 9608 *Abelen; Tobias Delius (ts); Corrie Van Binsbergen (g); Wilbert De Joode (b); Charles Huffstadt (d). n.d.*

Abelen is a great believer in less-is-more: this is a refreshingly short CD, leaving one wanting more, and the band seem reluctant to play as a group, one or other musician always dropping out to listen to the others, the quirky little tunes laid skeletally bare by their delivery, the cranky rhythms and rising-falling dynamics constantly pulling the rug out from under. Abelen himself plays a patrician-type role, his horn making melodic statements and using his rather starchy delivery to deadpan the group's more cartoonish moments. Delius, who can play in any style, is the singular voice, and the others play with a conspiratorial, behind-the-hand stealth. Hard to pin down but surprisingly engrossing.

John Abercrombie (born 1944)

GUITAR, GUITAR SYNTHESIZER, ELECTRIC MANDOLIN, GUITAR MANDOLIN, PIANO

Like several gifted young guitarists, Abercrombie got a professional start – after four years at Berklee – with Chico Hamilton's group, before going on to record with drummer Billy Cobham. His characteristic style, which some would regard as definitive of the ECM label, is limpid and evocative and makes imaginative use of electronic sweetening and extensions. It's hard to pin down obvious influences; Abercrombie is very much his own man.

****** Timeless**

ECM 829114-2 *Abercrombie; Jan Hammer (p, ky); Jack DeJohnette (d).* 6/74.

***** Sargasso Sea**

ECM 835015-2 *Abercrombie; Ralph Towner (g, p).* 5/76.

*****(*) Characters**

ECM 829372-2 *Abercrombie (g solo).* 11/77.

All credit to ECM for spotting and signing up the often understated Abercrombie. There's more filigree than flash on the early *Timeless*, and it's left to DeJohnette (the first of several tough-minded drummers Abercrombie has used as foils) and the underrated Hammer to give the set the propulsion it calls for. It would be unfair, though, to suggest that the guitarist doesn't punch his weight. There is always more to his playing than hits the ear first time around, and this is a session that has grown in stature with familiarity, an altogether tougher and more resilient label debut than anyone remembers. (And if anyone is wondering where *Gateway* and its successors have gone, may we recommend a quick flip to the G-spot, where this properly collaborative group is now listed separately.)

Sargasso Sea is a very different pile of weed, a winsome, diffident affair on which only the timbral variation of Towner's 12-string and piano figures sustains interest. This is the sort of thing that gave ECM its (mostly) undeserved reputation for unfunky pastel-jazz and, though the album still has its advocates, it's less than representative of Abercrombie's real strengths. If American popular music can be seen as a long struggle between 3/4 and 4/4, then Abercrombie is squarely on the side of the waltzers; 6/8 and 12/8 are actually his most effective settings, but he rations both.

Though an eponymous album was still, for some unexplained reason, some years off, *Characters* was Abercrombie's most overt manifesto and calling-card, a demonstration of styles and moods and, even at this point in his career, influences too. If they weren't obvious before, Jim Hall and Tal Farlow are evident in the mix, and there's a touch of Wes Montgomery that was to come out again in the '90s trio with Dan Wall and Adam Nussbaum.

***** Upon A Time**

New Albion NA 020 *Abercrombie; Mel Graves (b); George Marsh (d, perc, thumb p).* 82.

This isn't, strictly speaking, an Abercrombie album at all. It consists of ten duos with percussionist Marsh, who then partners the interesting Graves for the remainder, material drawn from an album called *Marshland*. The guitar/percussion tracks are beautifully crafted, meditative and personal, musical short stories without stings in the tail. The record features a rare Abercrombie appearance on piano, but also a highly effective feature for the mandolin guitar which serves his more folky and homely side.

***** Night**

ECM 823212-2 *Abercrombie; Michael Brecker (ts); Jan Hammer (p, ky); Jack DeJohnette (d).* 4/84.

*****(*) Current Event**

ECM 827770-2 *Abercrombie; Marc Johnson (b); Peter Erskine (d).* 9/85.

***** Getting There**

ECM 833494-2 *As above, except add Michael Brecker (ts).* 4/87.

***** John Abercrombie**

ECM 837756-2 *As above, except omit Brecker.* 4/88.

****** Animato**

ECM 841779-2 *Abercrombie; Vince Mendoza (syn); Peter Erskine (d).* 10/89.

By the later '80s, Abercrombie had something of an image problem. In terms of sheer bankability, he had been overtaken by John Scofield, and Bill Frisell's bag of tricks was significantly more capacious. Mercifully, whatever was discussed across the table at

ECM (or, more realistically, whatever went on in Manfred Eicher's or Abercrombie's own head), there were to be no career-boosting gimmicks. These albums mark a period of consolidation during which Abercrombie simply dug in and got on with what he was good at. The self-titled record says nothing other than 'Here I am; this is what I do; hope you like it', and if it doesn't quite come up to the strength of *Current Event*, which introduces two of the guitarist's most sympathetic and responsive partners, it is still a very strong statement. The decision to include standard material – in particular a truly beautiful 'Stella By Starlight' and an unexpected reading of 'Haunted Heart' – was a good one at this point.

Night demonstrated two things: first, that Abercrombie had outgrown the association with Hammer in particular, probably because increasingly he could give those evocative keyboard figures his own spin, using pedals and, later, guitar synth; and secondly, that he never sounds entirely easy in the company of a horn player whose main strength is rapid-fire changes work. Brecker comes on like the hired gun who takes over the whole show, as he always does, and there's perhaps too generous an allocation of space to both Johnson and Erskine on *John Abercrombie*, a further hint that the guitarist isn't quite selfish enough to stamp himself on the music (though, to be fair, these albums are among the first to feature ECM's later habit of giving individual group members an opportunity to develop their own thing; it sometimes works, sometimes not).

Animato is interesting in this regard. Though it seems to contradict the point about not needing an effects man any more, it includes in Mendoza a synthesizer player very like Hammer in general conception and it gives considerable (and justified) prominence to the drummer. However, longer retrospect reveals this as one of Abercrombie's most cohesive and swinging sets. He sounds completely in control of the music, and it is almost axiomatic, given the label concerned, that the production is flawless. This probably wouldn't be most people's desert island choice, but time and the sea-change that followed have given it a new gloss and urgency.

*****(*) Now It Can Be Played**

Steeplechase SCCD 31314 *Abercrombie; Andy LaVerne (p); Steve LaSpina (b); Jeff Hirshfield (d).* 4/92.

***** Farewell**

Musidisc 500462 *Abercrombie; Andy LaVerne (p); George Mraz (b); Adam Nussbaum (d).* 4/93.

During the '90s Abercrombie flirted with a couple of other labels. The knee-jerk was to turn Jewish mother and declare that he wouldn't get the Eicher and Kongshaug treatment from anyone else, but in fact the rather more homecooked sound on the Steeplechase serves him very well indeed. 'Cat Nap' and 'Waltz King' are both exceptional performances, with LaVerne strongly featured as co-leader.

The Musidisc record is less satisfactory, though admirers of jazz bass can always turn up the appropriate dial and marvel at the genius of George Mraz. His contribution aside, the version of 'Ralph's Piano Waltz' (a long-established favourite) is pretty ineffectual. Abercrombie had by this time written his own eponymous waltz. It turns up again on *November* ...

****** November**

ECM 519073-2 *Abercrombie; John Surman (ss, bs, bcl); Marc Johnson (b); Peter Erskine (d).* 11/92.

Reconvening the trio with Johnson and Erskine was a masterstroke. Teaming them with stablemate Surman was little short of genius. In keeping with ECM's later policy, this isn't so much an Abercrombie record as a collaborative set that allows all four players to develop ideas. The title-track, though, is for the trio and it is one of the very best things Abercrombie has ever done: moody, faintly bleak but undeniably hard-edged and without sentiment. Johnson's 'Right Brain Patrol', which on his own projects has always seemed slightly winsome and out-of-focus, emerges here as a compelling addition to the modern repertory, while Surman's contribution to the freely improvised opening number, 'The Cat's Back', suggests strongly that he had familiarized himself with at least some of Abercrombie's back-catalogue before turning up to play. The retread of 'John's Waltz' suggests it's a theme we will be hearing again and, unexpectedly in this context, there is an arrangement of a standard, 'Come Rain Or Come Shine'. Superb, evocative modern jazz. One day, we'll get the out-takes as well.

*****(*) While We're Young**

ECM 517352-2 *Abercrombie; Dan Wall (org); Adam Nussbaum (d).* 6/92.

***** Speak Of The Devil**

ECM 849648-2 *As above.* 7/93.

*****(*) Tactics**

ECM 533680-2 *As above.* 7/96.

No one expected this to last. It was widely assumed in 1992 that Abercrombie's organ trio – poised somewhere between Wes Montgomery and Lifetime – was a one-off idea, a forgivable selfindulgence that actually worked better than anyone had any right to expect. In fact, its great success has largely defined Abercrombie's recent career and has very significantly kick-started his playing. The most recent of the trio was recorded live at Visiones in New York and it represents a working band who have come to understand each other's needs very well. Nussbaum, like Christensen and Erskine before him, doesn't so much drive the thing along as provide injections of fuel when they are needed. There are signs that much of the material on the second album was written especially for the trio, but perhaps with some pragmatic haste. It must have been fun to play, but there is too little for the listener to get a purchase on. The live album, *Tactics*, is much stronger: churning but still delicate Hammond shapes, a rock-steady bass, and some of Abercrombie's lightest and most dancing jazz-playing.

*****(*) Open Land**

ECM 557652 *As above, except add Kenny Wheeler (t, flhn), Joe Lovano (ts), Mark Feldman (vn).* 99.

There was no particular need to augment or spice up the existing trio, which still had lots of mileage, but this was an intriguing collaboration. The revelation of the set is Feldman, who is as fiery and antagonistic in places as Leroy Jenkins or Billy Bang, and he blends brilliantly with both organ and guitar. Wheeler, as ever, has more sinew in his playing than at first appears, and his attack is notably sharper and more plosive here than in his usual guest-musician mode. The slight disappointment is Lovano who very much sounds as though he's around for a casual sit-in; Joe never plays badly or with less than imagination, but there's no fire to his work. Both the title-track and 'Free Piece Suite' are quite free in conception, and Wall's open-ended dissonances leave any amount of room for imaginative improvisation. Like most current ECM sets, this feels very much like a collaborative project rather than leader-plus-group; but Abercrombie does seem firmly, quietly in charge here, steering the performances in his distinctive, hard to define way.

*****(*) The Hudson Project**

Stretch 9024 *Abercrombie; John Patitucci (b); Peter Erskine (d).* 99.

Classic trio jazz from three masters, sensitively produced by Paul Siegel and label boss Chick Corea. Our only reservation is that the record somewhat lacks light and shade. Abercrombie's two compositions are the most upbeat and buoyant on the set, bracketed by Bob Mintzer's 'Runferyerlife' and 'Modern Day Tuba'. John's 'Little Swing' shows how comfortably he remains in possession of a classic jazz guitar idiom, while his solos on 'Cats & Kittens' and 'Well', composed by Erskine and Patitucci respectively, suggest once again how much wit and humour there is in his playing.

Rabih Abou-Khalil

OUD, FLUTE

Abou-Khalil is a young Lebanese master forced into exile in 1978 by the increasingly chaotic civil war. A follower of the great Wadih Al-Safi, he has maintained a passionate commitment to the 'new music' while taking account of the singing and playing traditions of Western jazz. His playing is as fleet and rhythmic as that of any jazz guitarist.

****** Between Dusk And Dawn**

MMP 170886 *Abou-Khalil; Charlie Mariano (as, ss); Christian Burchard (mar); Michael Armann (p); Glen Moore (b); Glen Velez (frame d, bodhran, darabukka, perc); Ramesh Shotham (tavil, ghatam, mouth hp, dholak, kanjira, perc).* 86.

*****(*) Nafas**

ECM 835781-2 *Abou-Khalil; Selim Kusur (nay, v); Glen Velez (frame d); Setrak Sarkissian (darabukka).* 2/88.

****** Bukra**

MMP 170889 *Abou-Khalil; Sonny Fortune (as); Glen Moore (b); Glen Velez (frame d, perc, v); Ramesh Shotham (South Indian d, perc).* 3/88.

*****(*) Al-Jadida**

Enja 6090 *Abou-Khalil; Sonny Fortune (as); Glen Moore (b); Ramesh Shotham (South Indian d, perc); Nabil Khaiat (frame d, perc).* 10/90.

***** Roots And Sprouts**

MMP 170890 *Abou-Khalil; Selim Kusur (nay); Yassin El-Achek (v); Glen Moore (b); Glen Velez (frame d); Mohammad Al-Sous (darabukka).* 11/90.

****** Blue Camel**

Enja 7053 *Abou-Khalil; Charlie Mariano (as); Kenny Wheeler (t, flhn); Steve Swallow (b); Milton Cardona (perc); Nabil Khaiat (frame d); Ramesh Shotham (Indian d, perc).* 5/92.

*****(*) Tarab**

Enja 7083 *Abou-Khalil; Selim Kusur (nay); Glen Moore (b); Nabil Khaiat (frame d, perc); Ramesh Shotham (Indian d, perc).* 2–3/92.

***** The Sultan's Picnic**

Enja 8078 *Abou-Khalil; Kenny Wheeler (t, flhn); Charlie Mariano (as); Howard Levy (hca); Michel Godard (tba, serpent); Steve Swallow (b); Mark Nauseef (d); Milton Cardona, Nabil Khaiat (perc).* 3/94.

***** Odd Times**

Enja ENJ 9330 *Similar to above.* 96.

Jazz is only one of the world's great improvising traditions. Within Arab music, there has always been a substantial area of freedom for the virtuoso performer, and the 11-string *oud* has occupied a role in classical and more popular forms roughly analogous to that of the piano and guitar in the West. The 'new' music of which he is an exponent – *al-Jadida* – is new not just in the sense of modern, but also in the sense that Western homophony was once dubbed 'new'. From the point of view of a jazz-literate listener, it is clear that the first and last items above are likely to be the least familiarly accessible and their ratings reflect that rather than their perceived quality. One of the main points of contact on the middle three items is the presence of jazz improvisers Charlie Mariano, Sonny Fortune and Oregon bassist, Glen Moore, all of whom have made the same cultural journey as Abou-Khalil, but in reverse, west to east. There is an impressive absence of pastiche or self-conscious eclecticism. A composition like 'Ornette Never Sleeps' (*Al-Jadida*) gives off no obvious irony; like much of Abou-Khalil's work, it is intended as sincere *hommage*. Those well disposed towards Oregon's proto-'world music' will feel most comfortable with the magnificent *Between Dusk And Dawn*, but *Bukra* is in some regards more challenging. Like early jazz, much of the emphasis is on ensemble improvisation rather than more obviously virtuosic soloing. Apart from the leader's cleanly picked multi-directional lines, it's also worth mentioning Moore's marvellously sonorous bass and Mariano's familiarly 'Eastern' mode. Fortune is more of a revelation; staying mainly with the alto saxophone, which is perhaps a more promising choice in this harmonic context, he sounds absolutely familiar with the idiom, and it's the saxophonist who gives *Bukra* much of its compelling power; his unaccompanied introduction to 'Kibbe' is breathtaking, matched for sheer surprise only by Glen Velez's perfectly controlled overtone singing on 'Remember … The Desert'.

Restored to the catalogue just as the early *Bitter Harvest* on MMP was disappearing, *Nafas* is most notable for a brilliant performance by Selim Kusur, a leading performer on the bamboo *nay* flute. Recent sets have also leant heavily on guest players, as Abou-Khalil's own playing increasingly takes a back seat to a more ensemble approach with occasional vivid highlighting. *Blue Camel*, with Wheeler, Swallow and Mariano again all guesting, might on the surface appear to be his 'jazz' album, but the mix is very much as usual. *Tarab* returns unequivocally to a highly traditional style, as if to refute any suspicion of commercial sell-out, but again the slightly disappointing *Sultan's Picnic* looks to be aimed at a crossover audience, as is the more recent *Odd Times*. Even so, because it is so uncompromised, it is hard to see this music ever reaching a mass audience; but it is highly attractive none the less, and the laminated digipacks Enja have now seemingly reserved for Abou-Khalil are among the most attractive around.

Muhal Richard Abrams (born 1930)

PIANO, SYNTHESIZER, CLARINET, COMPOSER

Abrams's contribution to the new music goes back all the way to 1961 when he formed the Experimental Band. Unlike the scorched-earth philosophers who followed him, Abrams was deeply versed in jazz history and he regarded the work of the legendary Association for the Advancement of Creative Musicians as a combination of lab work and archive. His enormous influence outweighs his recorded output.

***** Levels And Degrees Of Light**

Delmark DD 413 *Abrams; Anthony Braxton (as); Maurice McIntyre (ts); Leroy Jenkins (vn); Gordon Emmanuel (vib); Charles Clark, Leonard Jones (b); Thurman Barker (d); David Moore, Penelope Taylor (v).* 1–7/67.

*****(*) Young At Heart / Wise In Time**

Delmark DD 423 *Abrams; Leo Smith (t, flhn); Henry Threadgill (as); Lester Lashley (b); Thurman Barker (d).* 68.

There is no absolute or reliable means of measuring artistic influence. If there were, Muhal Richard Abrams would surely stand higher in the canon of recent American jazz than he does or seems to in the hearts of jazz fans. Like any physical catalyst, he seems curiously unchanged by the forces he has set in motion, as composer, performer and educator. In a curious way, he has no 'style' of his own; that is his strength. In its place, a free array of Black and European idioms, everything from stride to serialism, deployed within an intensely rhythmic but often quite complex framework.

Levels And Degrees Of Light would be a slightly difficult record to place in a blindfold test. It is certainly not untypical of the Chicago experimentalism of the period, except that it seems much less chaotic, much more responsive to European models. It opens in almost prayerful mood, with Penelope Taylor's wavering vocalize giving way to Abrams's unvirtuosic but strangely effective clarinet (which bears much the same relation to his keyboard work as Keith Jarrett's occasional soprano outbreaks to his piano playing). The lyrical content of the very long 'Bird Song' is much less effective, though the inclusion of Jenkins and Jones gives the music an almost orchestral depth of focus, and Barker too contributes enormously, as he does on both records; one of the most musical drummers of his generation.

Young/Wise combines the definitive Abrams solo performance of the period with a group of tracks of burning intensity. 'Wise In Time', the piano piece, is both a good representation of Abrams's strengths and the clearest indication of his limits as a solo performer. It's packed with powerful striding metres and wonderful left-hand geometries that recall the greats of the piano, Tatum, James P. Johnson and Bud, but overlaid with ideas that come from a very different tradition altogether.

***** 1-OQA+19**

Black Saint 120017 *Abrams; Anthony Braxton (as, sno, f, cl, v); Henry Threadgill (as, ts, f, v); Leonard Jones (b, v); Steve McCall (d, perc, v).* 11–12/77.

***** Spihumonesty**

Black Saint 120032 *Abrams; George Lewis (tb, sou, syn); Roscoe Mitchell (as, f); Amina Claudine Myers (p, electric p, org); Youssef Yancey (theremin); Leonard Jones (b); Jay Clayton (v).* 7/79.

Like other American radicals (Bill Dixon and George Lewis are other good examples) Abrams has had to rely on European labels – and in particular on the Italian-based Black Saint – to make his music heard. These two discs underline how early Giovanni Bonandrini's adventurous imprints actually were. This is music that still retains the experimental edge of earlier years, but with a much more settled approach and a highly sophisticated group sound.

Myers's contribution to *Spihumonesty* (a typically punning title that recalls the gnomic titles of bebop, like 'Klactoveeseedstene') is much more focused than on the duo set. This drummerless band moves through the charts like information through a printed circuit, and there is an impressive simultaneity to some of the cues which suggests that at least some of this music was predetermined and meticulously rehearsed. Abrams still isn't a great soloist in any conventional sense but, like Ellington, he has a rare gift for taking and retaining strong personalities and yet making them part of an overall sound which is very much greater than the parts.

The earlier record has on the face of it a more impressive starting line-up, though also a much more conventionally jazz-based sound. Though Threadgill is a much less demanding player than Roscoe Mitchell, Anthony Braxton is one of the certain masters of modern jazz and perhaps Abrams's most gifted pupil. The music they make together is complex, scurryingly allusive and seldom directly appealing. Braxton's title-composition is handled with great intelligence and reserve and so is 'Charlie In The Parker', but there are question marks elsewhere.

***** Mama And Daddy**

Black Saint 120041 *Abrams; Baikida Carroll (t, flhn); George Lewis (tb); Bob Stewart (tba); Vincent Chauncey (hn); Wallace McMillan (as, bs, ts, f, perc); Leroy Jenkins (vn); Brian Smith (b); Andrew Cyrille (d, perc).* 12/79.

***** Rejoicing With The Light**

Black Saint 120071 *Abrams; Baikida Carroll (t, flhn); Vincent Chauncey (hn); Wallace McMillan (as, bs, ts, f, perc); Marty Ehrlich (as, f, cl); Patience Higgins (cl, acl, bs); Jean-Paul Bourelly (g); Abdul Wadud (clo); Rick Rosie (b); Warren Smith (vib, timp, perc).* 1/83.

If there is a 'transitional' period in the career of a musician as doggedly exploratory as Abrams, then this has to be it. These albums seem more compelling now than they did at the time, because it is clear where the leader's ideas are going, even if it wasn't (yet) to some of even his most devoted followers. The addition of the powerful Carroll (who sounds like Leo Smith cross-matched with Fats Navarro), the estimable Lewis and, to be an Abrams regular after *Rejoicing*, Patience Higgins gives these records a sonic authority which isn't yet matched by either writing or playing. (In a previous edition, we mistakenly identified Higgins as female. We are pleased to confirm that he is a man and, since he hasn't sent the lads round to sort us out, a gentleman as well.)

****(*) Duet**

Black Saint 120051 *Abrams; Amina Claudine Myers (p).* 5/81.

*****(*) Duets And Solos**

Black Saint 120133 *Abrams; Roscoe Mitchell (reeds, f).* 3/90.

Unfortunately still missing is the 1975 *Sightsong*, a duo album with Malachi Favors, a richly textured meditation on the bass tradition of Wilbur Ware, another great Chicagoan. The encounters with Mitchell and Myers are both somewhat later, dating from a time when Abrams's interests seem to be settling down to composition rather than improvised structures. Retrospect hasn't changed our view that the two pianists simply get in each other's way on the earlier record. Mitchell, though, is a consummate duo performer, a listening musician who delivers a telling statement every time he allows himself to step forward. His flute playing is perhaps less well documented than his other reeds, and it is that frail but hard-edged sound which is most to be treasured here.

***** View From Within**

Black Saint 120081 *Abrams; Stanton Davis (t, flhn); John Purcell (as, ss, f, ts, bcl); Marty Ehrlich (picc, f, as, ts, cl, bcl); Warren Smith (vib, mar, perc); Rick Rosie (b); Thurman Barker (d, perc); Ray Mantilla (perc).* 9/84.

***** Colors In Thirty-Third**

Black Saint 120091 *Abrams; John Purcell (ts, ss, bcl); John Blake (vn); Dave Holland (b, clo); Fred Hopkins (b); Andrew Cyrille (d).* 12/86.

Like the slightly later *Colors In Thirty-Third*, *View* sounds like a thoroughly personal statement. The multi-instrumental approach lends it a fluid, unsettled quality, but with a huge timbral and textural range. Again much of the energy transfers between Abrams, articulating patiently and without overt drama, and the estimable Barker.

The later record continues the experiment with texture and harmonic depth by building in string lines, Holland on cello an obvious asset on a set like this. This might be thought to be Purcell's finest hour, but everyone contributes. The basic personnel divides into trio, quartet, quintet and, for the title-piece and the significantly named 'Introspection', full sextet. Cyrille matches Thurman Barker for sheer strength and personality, and richly deserves the dedication of 'Drumman'.

*****(*) The Hearinga Suite**

Black Saint 120103 *Abrams; Cecil Bridgewater, Frank Gordon, Ron Tooley, Jack Walrath (t); Clifton Anderson, Dick Griffin (tb); Jack Jeffers, Bill Lowe (btb); John Purcell (ts, f, cl); Marty Ehrlich (as, picc, f, cl); Patience Higgins (ts, bcl); Courtney Wynter (bsn, bcl, ts); Charles Davis (bs, ss); Dierdre Murray (clo); Fred Hopkins (b); Andrew Cyrille (d).* 1/89.

This marks something of a quantum shift, a move towards something larger and more cohesive. The spirit of Ellington isn't far away here. Pieces like 'Hearinga' itself, 'Seesall' and 'Bermix' are self-contained and robustly structured, though one finds oneself wishing now and again for a more relaxed and open-ended performance. Ehrlich, Higgins, Wynter and Davis might have been given a bit more room to expand, though this time out the rhythm section could hardly be bettered. Hopkins is still underrated, though this is one of Cyrille's very best recorded performances.

****** Blu Blu Blu**

Black Saint 120117 *Abrams; Joel Brandon (whistle); Jack Walrath (t); Alfred Patterson (tb); Mark Taylor (frhn); Joe Daley (tba); John Purcell (as, f, bcl); Bob DeBellis (as, cl, bcl); Eugene Ghee (ts, cl, bcl); David Fiuczynski (g); Lindsey Horne, Brad Jones (b); Warren Smith (vib, tim); Thurman Barker (d).* 11/90.

Abrams's best album for some time is almost hi-jacked by the extraordinary Brandon, who has also worked with David Murray. His high, bird-like tones could almost be produced by a synth, were they not so rapidly and naturally articulated. 'One For The Whistler' is a *tour de force*, and elsewhere on the record Brandon demonstrates his own and his overlooked instrument's viability as an improvising voice; he should be picking up 'miscellaneous instrument' citations like litter.

Abrams really gets going as a pianist only on the final 'Stretch Time', leaving most of the foreground to a tonally varied and adventurous band. The title-track is a dedication to McKinley Morganfield (better known as Muddy Waters). Fiuczynski's howling guitar initially sounds out of place, but it settles back into a sophisticated chart in which Abrams brings together much of the continuum of recent black music. Of the brasses, Walrath is the unchallenged star: punchy, accurate and full of droll wit. As ever, Barker takes control of the engine room. To be set alongside Sun Ra's later work and the better of Butch Morris's 'Conduction' experiments, this is among the most important contemporary big-band records.

*****(*) Family Talk**

Black Saint 120132 *Abrams; Jack Walrath (t); Patience Higgins (ts, bcl, eng hn); Warren Smith (vib, timp, mar, gongs); Brad Jones (b); Reggie Nicholson (d, mar, bells).* 3/93.

A fine record which transcends individual contributions. Higgins is a somewhat limited soloist, probably best deployed as a colourist on a session like this. His tenor solo on 'Illuso' is so forcedly naïve, we begin to wonder if he is putting us on. By contrast, Walrath this time out sounds too knowing and technically assured, as if trying to distance himself from his confrères. On the long 'DizBirdMonkBudMax' he sounds poised and at ease, but he's the wrong man for the moodier and more complex tracks like 'Drumbutu', where he simply reworks the cod-Gothick effects he has patented on his own records.

As on a couple of occasions before, *Family Talk* really belongs to the rhythm section. Abrams is securely anchored and the addition of tuned percussion allows him to play quite abstractly when he feels the need. His synthesizer work, which goes in and out of focus, is mainly reserved here for introductory sketches and background washes, but it adds an important element to the overall sound. Smith is excellent on vibes and marimba. The woodier tones mix well with Jones's bass, and overall the album has a lovely rich sound.

***(*) **Think All, Focus One**

Black Saint 120141-2 *Abrams; Eddie Allen (t); Alfred Patterson (tb); Eugene Ghee (ts, bcl); David Gilmore (g); Brad Jones (b); Reggie Nicholson (d).* 7/94.

Henry Threadgill's liner-notes come in the form of a poem, a free-form rhapsody that invokes hunger, fear, delight, pursuit and the sheer playful exuberance of language. The music doesn't quite come up to the level of Threadgill's emotive response, but it's fine, toughly thought jazz all the same.

Abrams's own playing is still relatively unemphatic but, by this stage in the game, his 'instrument' is the whole band, and these musicians understand exactly what he is about. 'The Harmonic Veil' and 'Scaledance' are relatively technical opuses, and Abrams has interspersed these with more associative pieces like 'Crossbeams' and 'The Junction', both of which seem to strike specific chords in Threadgill. The title-track, which comes right at the end, is a small-scale classic, a piece of jazz writing which manages to collapse a whole lifetime of experience into just five and a half minutes.

That said, there is something almost routine about the playing, almost as if this repertoire had been rehearsed and workshopped to the point where all spontaneity ceased.

***(*) **Song For All**

Black Saint 120161 *Abrams; Eddie Allen (t); Craig Harris (tb); Aaron Stewart (ts, ss); Bryan Carrott (vib, perc); Brad Jones (b); Reggie Nicholson (d).* 95.

Again, the presence of a vibist makes a significant difference to Abrams's own approach. He sounds more concerned with colours and shapes than with the forward momentum of a piece, and this is all to the good. The group has a somewhat unfamiliar aspect. Allen is a bouncy, often provocative player, sounding almost as if he comes from an earlier generation. Harris is a star, of course, and cannot keep his light under even a row of bushels, beaming out of the ensembles like the boy who habitually sticks out his tongue in the school photo. Stewart is not so much anonymous as easily overlooked, but he makes an attractive noise.

The two long tracks, 'GMBR' and 'Over The Same Over', are richly constructed and intelligently paced. The opening 'Song For All' and 'Dabba Dabba Doo' which follows it are probably the best on the record, though. One of those sets which palls a little over the full length and which is probably better sampled a track at a time.

**** **One Line, Two Views**

New World 80469 *Abrams; Eddie Allen (t, perc, v); Marty Ehrlich (as, bcl, perc, v); Patience Higgins (ts, bcl, perc, v); Mark Feldman (vn, perc, v); Tony Cedras (acc, perc, v); Anne LeBaron (hp, perc, v); Bryan Carrott (vib, perc, v); Lindsey Horner (b, perc, v); Reggie Nicholson (d, perc, v).* 6/95.

This is the record Abrams has been promising for years, and it is perhaps ironic that it should appear other than on Black Saint, who have kept faith with the man for a decade and a half. As expected, it's characterized by tight, intelligent charts, an imaginative approach to timbre, and a headlong freedom that remains intact from early days. Higgins still isn't an impressive soloist – neither Hodges nor Gonsalves – but he does fit this music very well. Ehrlich's reappearance brings in a whole range of sounds, and Abrams finds key roles for harpist LeBaron (herself an important composer) and accordionist Cedras. At the heart of the set, a brief, heartfelt threnody to Julius Hemphill and Don Pullen, fellow-composers who left in a hurry with much undone. The longer pieces never drag, though there are moments in the closing 'Ensemble Song' which border on self-indulgence. A triumph, and an essential purchase for Abrams enthusiasts.

***(*) **The Open Air Meeting**

New World 80512 *Abrams; Marty Ehrlich (as, cl).* 8/96.

Recorded at the Brooklyn Museum, outdoors and in high summer, this is a fresh, mostly sunlit performance from two old friends whose association isn't always easy to unpick from a larger group performance. Two Ehrlich compositions – 'Dark Sestina' and 'Bright Canto' – set the expressive parameters of the set, the latter a glorious example of duo playing at the very highest level. Ehrlich's clarinet stands out strongly: vigorous, reedy and oddly traditional in articulation. Abrams deals with a less than wonderful piano with his usual lack of fuss, dodging round what sound like a couple of slightly dead keys. Good stuff, and a welcome return to the duet experiments of the early '80s.

Bruce Ackley

SOPRANO SAXOPHONE

The treble voice in the innovative saxophone quartet, ROVA, Ackley is one of that brave band who specialize in the treacherous soprano saxophone. Influences range from Johnny Hodges and Lucky Thompson to Coltrane and Evan Parker.

**** **The Hearing**

Avant AVAN 069 *Ackley; Greg Cohen (b); Joey Baron (d).* 5/97.

The rhythm section of exec. producer John Zorn's Masada make an unmistakable sound, and it's one that suits ROVA man Ackley's long-cherished ambition to make a trio record with soprano saxophone, but *sans* a harmony instrument. The idiom is established from the very outset with a reworking of melodic cells by Herbie Nichols as 'Out Of The Box', which is just the first in a sequence of cleverly conceived and executed originals that highlight Ackley's peerless technique and witty delivery. Baron is an ideal partner on a project like this, a musician who drums like a tap-dancer, anti-gravity shoes and a big smile.

'Syndrome' is dedicated to Anthony Braxton, whose work with Dave Holland and Barry Altschul is a useful reference-point for these tracks. 'Juggernaut' is for Sonny Simmons, and one can imagine him gobbling up its light, fast transitions. 'Mr Mood' is dominated by the spirit of Billy Strayhorn, and if the listener knows Steve Lacy's Strayhorn essays with Mal Waldron, this adds a further gloss. The final track, 'Ivan's Bell', plays Bill Evans's anagrammatical trick back at him, a sweet and tender love-song for Ackley's five-year-old son, Ivan, done in something like the spirit of Evans's more free-floating compositions.

ROVA are something of an acquired taste, so musicianly as to exclude all but the most sympathetic of listeners. Ackley's solo debut – we're unaware of any earlier venture – is as inviting as it is accomplished.

Clifford Adams

TROMBONE

American post-bop trombonist with strong sideman credits.

***** The Master Power**

Naxos 86015-2 *Adams; Antonio Hart (as); Kenny Barron (p); Ray Drummond (b); Lewis Nash (d); (perc).* 2/98.

Adams has previously recorded with Vincent Herring, Charles Earland and others, and the only wonder is that he has taken so long to record under his own name. It's probably no bad thing that he waited till a band of this quality was on offer. With a sound that is closer to that of the swing masters than to J.J. Johnson's saxophone-derived phrasing, he can sound old-fashioned until the sophistication and complexity of what he does start to impinge.

The band is terrific, with Hart in great form and Barron doing his usual unflappable thing. Even so, this isn't the kind of record that sets the world on fire, and repeated hearings haven't yielded up any further revelations. Perhaps Adams will have to serve a further apprenticeship or hope for a more cushioned recording contract in order to develop. Two cheers only.

George Adams (1940–92)

TENOR SAXOPHONE, FLUTE, BASS CLARINET, VOCAL

The much-missed Georgian worked with Charles Mingus, Gil Evans and McCoy Tyner but had his first and major starring role in a collaborative group with Don Pullen. His saxophone style was deep and earthy, with many modernist elements but also a deep awareness of the blues.

*****(*) Sound Suggestions**

ECM 517755-2 *Adams; Kenny Wheeler (t, flhn); Heinz Sauer (ts); Richie Beirach (p); Dave Holland (b); Jack DeJohnette (d).* 5/79.

***** Don't Loose Control**

Soul Note 121104-2 *Adams; Don Pullen (p); Cameron Brown (b); Dannie Richmond (d).* 11/79.

***** Hand To Hand**

Soul Note 121107-2 *Adams; Jimmy Knepper (tb); Hugh Lawson (p); Mike Richmond (b); Dannie Richmond (d).* 2/80.

What an irony that George Adams should have inspired one of the most heartfelt personal memorials of recent times, a tune almost on a par with 'Goodbye Pork Pie Hat', from a friend and partner who was fated to survive him for no more than three short years. Don Pullen's 'George, We Hardly Knew Ya' celebrated a working relationship that was close and instinctive and produced some of the fieriest small-group jazz of the 1980s. Pullen was perhaps the dominant partner in terms of compositional ideas, but it was big George's hot, fruity tone that dominated the groups. An essentially melodic player in the tradition of Sonny Rollins, Adams had listened to enough of the avant-garde to bring in aspects of Coltrane's harmonic revolution and of Albert Ayler's unfettered testifying. If the elements weren't always comfortably blended – and the reissued *Sound Suggestions* conveys a man in search of his creative identity – the results were always exciting. Listening to the solitary ECM (an association which doesn't seem to have satisfied either side) alongside the first of the Soul Notes, recorded six months later, boldly underlines Pullen's role in Adams's emergence. He thrives on the big, vamped chords and gospelly runs and, though the duos on *Melodic Excursions* (below) are disappointing, the basic vocabulary is all in place. The strengths of the ECM lie in Adams's interplay with Holland and DeJohnette. Beirach and Wheeler are scarcely sympathetic partners and there is no need for a second saxophonist, especially when the horns are panned hard right and left. Only two compositions are credited to the leader, the remainder to Wheeler and, inexplicably, to the anonymous Sauer, reinforcing the sense that this was an uneasy collaboration, not really Adams's own session. Only on his own 'Imani's Dance' and 'Got Somethin' Good For You' does he feel confident enough to let rip.

Hand To Hand was another co-led session, cementing what was to be another important association, with Mingus's favourite drummer, Dannie Richmond. The trombonist is much more like the thing than Wheeler, a raw, regressive player who sounds as if he has completely missed out on J.J. Johnson's revisionist teachings.

***** Earth Beams**

Timeless SJP 147 *As for Don't Loose Control.* 4/81.

*****(*) Life Line**

Timeless SJP 154 *As above.* 81.

Someone once commented that the success of the Adams/Pullen quartet was that it united the musical sensibilities of North and South, the two leaders coming from Georgia and Virginia respectively, Brown and Richmond from Detroit and New York. Though it's seldom possible to trade on origins, these are the albums that give the argument some weight. A tune like Pullen's 'The Great Excape, or Run John Henry Run', which kicks off the better of the pair, is an overt attempt to blend a Southern folk sensibility with the angularity of the New Thing, and Adams's own 'Nature's Children' works in much the same direction, only backwards. The real pay-off on this fine record is Pullen's closer, 'Newcomer: Seven Years Later', a terse, abrasive idea which gives Adams some of his best recorded moments to date.

***** Melodic Excursions**

Timeless SJP 166 *Adams; Don Pullen (p).* 6/82.

The premature loss of both men makes this album seem more precious now than when they were still around. It still sounds as if they were working in parallel rather than fully responsively, and it sounds very much as though it was the pianist who was pushing the pace, ideas-wise, leaving Adams to bluster and bluff on occasion. However, George does contribute three tunes, including the intriguing 'Reflexions Inward', and he declaims with all the passion of a storefront preacher.

***** Gentlemen's Agreement**

Soul Note 121057-2 *As for Hand To Hand.* 2/83.

An interesting reunion of the Adams/Richmond unit which suggests that both men might have been looking for alternative directions and a much broader tonal and timbral range. 'Prayer For A Jitterbug' and 'Symphony For Five' are redolent of Eric Dolphy's work on *Iron Man*, and Lawson (who registers more strongly with each return visit) combines lyricism with a blunt strength, almost like a selected hybrid of Beirach and Pullen. Less sheerly exciting than the quartets, but not to be overlooked.

***** City Gates**
Timeless SJP181 *As for Don't Loose Control.* 3/83.

***** Live At The Village Vanguard**
Soul Note 121094-2 *As above.* 8/83.

***** Live At The Village Vanguard: Volume 2**
Soul Note 121144-2 *As above.* 8/83.

*****(*) Decisions**
Timeless SJP 205 *As above.* 2/84.

****(*) Live at Montmartre**
Timeless SJP 219 *As above, except add John Scofield (g).* 4/85.

The working band *in excelsis*, rounding off a half-decade of concentrated activity with four heated – sometimes overheated – sets. Perhaps oddly, given the chemistry, this is a band that always sounded better in the studio. The Village Vanguard sets are slightly ramshackle (compare the live version of 'Thank You Very Much, Mr Monk' with the one on *City Gates*), and much of the interest now lies in hearing how much Adams anticipates what David Murray was going to be doing (sambas, spirituals) at the end of the decade.

By the narrowest of necks and the benefit of much hindsight, *Decisions* just wins the ears-and-tail for a brashly thoughtful set which combines New Wave things like the title-piece with Pullen's Janus-faced 'Trees And Grass And Thangs', the traditional 'His Eye Is On The Sparrow', and the familiar roarers from Adams, 'Message Urgent' and 'I Could Really For You' (*what* isn't specified). A powerful set, sympathetically produced as ever by Wim Wigt.

Pepper Adams (1930–86)

BARITONE SAXOPHONE

Park Adams III was touring with Lionel Hampton in his teens and, after army duty, he worked in Detroit during the early 1950s. From 1958 he based himself in New York, and among his principal associations were spells with Charles Mingus, a co-led quintet with Donald Byrd, and the Thad Jones–Mel Lewis Orchestra, as well as many dates under his own leadership.

***** 10 To 4 At The 5-Spot**
Original Jazz Classics OJC 031 *Adams; Donald Byrd (t); Bobby Timmons (p); Doug Watkins (b); Elvin Jones (d).* 4/58.

The baritone sax was as unpopular with hard-bop musicians as it was with the original boppers and, come to that, with the swing-era saxophonists. Pepper Adams, more than anyone, came close to making it a congenial instrument in the hot-house environment of hard bop. He had a dry, unsentimental tone – very different from either Serge Chaloff or Gerry Mulligan – and a penchant for full-tilt solos that gave no shred of concession to the horn's 'cumbersome' reputation. The live session, made with a frequent partner at the time, Donald Byrd, is typical of Adams's kind of date, with muscular blow-outs of the order of 'Hastings Street Bounce' sitting next to a clear-headed ballad reading of 'You're My Thrill'. That said, it's sometimes only the novelty value of hearing a baritone in the ensembles that lifts the music out of a professional hard-bop routine.

***** Stardust**
Bethlehem 6018-2 *Adams; Donald Byrd (t); Tommy Flanagan (p); Kenny Burrell (g); Paul Chambers (b); Louis Hayes (d).* 60.

***** Out Of This World**
Fresh Sound FSR-CD 137 *Adams; Donald Byrd (t); Herbie Hancock (p); Teddy Charles (vib); Laymon Jackson (b); Jimmy Cobb (d).* 61.

Though sometimes listed under either Byrd's name or Adams's, we have elected to include these albums under the saxophonist's entry. Though one might expect a bluff, no-nonsense kind of hard bop, these sessions tend to spotlight the gentler side of the two leaders. The Fresh Sound date, tracks originally released on Warwick and produced by Teddy Charles, is the better bet since it has more music and some genuinely lyrical touches: Adams's solo turn on 'Day Dream', for instance, with a pleasing early solo by Hancock. But the Bethlehem set isn't far behind, in the same mould.

***** Pepper Adams Plays Charlie Mingus**
Fresh Sound FSR-CD 177 *Adams; Thad Jones (t); Bennie Powell (tb); Charles McPherson (as); Zoot Sims (ts); Hank Jones (p); Paul Chambers, Bob Cranshaw (b); Dannie Richmond (d).* 9/63.

Adams led this date with his usual unfussy authority. There are nine Mingus tunes and a mixture of Mingusians and – in the case of Zoot Sims – at least one musician about as far removed from being a Mingus sideman as one could imagine, though Zoot deals with the situation as imperturbably as always. The results, split between a quintet and an octet, are akin to a pocket-size edition of a typical Mingus band: 'Haitian Fight Song' and 'Fables Of Faubus' are as swinging as any Mingus version (Chambers is at the top of his game), but 'Better Git In Your Soul' (*sic*) is comparatively watery, and Jones is a lot more dapper than a Mingus pianist might have been.

*****(*) Encounter!**
Original Jazz Classics OJC 892 *Adams; Zoot Sims (ts); Tommy Flanagan (p); Ron Carter (b); Elvin Jones (d).* 12/68.

A very good one. The band is absolutely stellar, full of Detroit homeboys, and Sims was a fail-safe choice for the front-line partner. If anything, Jones overdoes the bashing, and the up-tempo pieces are a battle, but the saxophonists don't falter at any point. There is a fine Adams ballad in 'I've Just Seen Her', as well as a choice arrangement of 'Star-Crossed Lovers'.

***** Live**
Culture Press/That's Jazz CP 2003 *Adams; John Marabuto (p); Bob Maize (b); Ron Marabuto (d).* 9/77.

A snapshot of Pepper at work in California in the '70s, at the celebrated Douglas Beach House. Nothing outstanding, and Ron

Marabuto's drums are too busy in a pretty rough sound-mix, but the energy of the leader is as unstinting as ever, and 'Body And Soul' is particularly dark.

*****(*) Conjuration: Fat Tuesday's Session**
Reservoir RSR 113 *Adams; Kenny Wheeler (t, flhn); Hank Jones (p); Clint Houston (b); Louis Hayes (d).* 8/83.

This live set emphasizes Pepper's virtues – the muscularity of sound, oversized tone and plangent phrasing – so decisively that one overlooks any scent of routine in the playing. Kenny Wheeler, an unlikely partner, adds sparkle and some good material, and Hank Jones is sublimely buoyant, as are Houston and Hayes.

***** Pepper**
Enja 9079-2 *Adams; Walter Norris (p); George Mraz (b); Makaya Ntoshko (d); Denny Christianson Big Band.* 8/75–2/86.

Although rather scrappy as a CD, this valedictory reissue stands as a final testament to Adams's art. There are four tracks from an on-the-hoof live date at a Munich club from 1975 with Norris, Mraz and Ntshoko which include a good blues, a decent 'Well You Needn't' and a gentle 'When A Child Is Born'; but the moving moments come with the bonus 'My Funny Valentine', done with the Denny Christianson band when Pepper was only months away from his death. The baritone sounds dry and cracked but the spirit is indomitable, and it's a moving interpretation which survives the rather curious studio sound (the original album, *Suite Mingus*, was listed in a previous edition under Christianson's name).

Steve Adams

SOPRANINO, SOPRANO, ALTO, TENOR AND BARITONE SAXOPHONES, PICCOLO, FLUTE, ALTO FLUTE, PERCUSSION

Contemporary multi-instrumentalist and improviser, based in California.

*****(*) In Out Side**
Nine Winds NWCD 0156 *Adams; Ken Filiano (b, chimes).* 7/91–1/92.

Adams and Filiano have previous records to their name – two excellent back-numbers in the Nine Winds vinyl catalogue – and this duo set continues a thoughtful body of work. There's none of the usual pale impressionism which sometimes attends this kind of situation: the recording emphasizes the muscularity and power of the playing. Several of the pieces use multiple over-dubbing, superbly effective on 'Throb', 'Myself See Three' and 'Tag' in particular, where the reeds are plaited round intensely delivered bass-lines. There are five 'Haiku' tracks, 'pieces that are only one thought long', a tough and raw-edged blues and a final flutes-and-bass piece called 'Signal Buoys' which eventually nods towards ECM territory. A 'free' record that nevertheless takes much of its merit from rigorous arrangement and careful preparation.

Julian 'Cannonball' Adderley (1928–75)

ALTO SAXOPHONE

Born in Tampa, Florida, he taught music and led groups only part-time but was persuaded to try his luck in New York in 1955. Joined Miles Davis, 1957–9, then re-formed band with brother Nat, touring and recording more or less continuously thereafter until his death from a stroke. A great popularizer, and a leader in the soul-jazz style of the '60s, Cannon was a much-loved figure who helped keep jazz before an audience at a time when it was losing listeners.

*****(*) Sophisticated Swing**
Verve 528408-2 2CD *Adderley; Nat Adderley (c); Junior Mance (p); Sam Jones, Al McKibbon (b); Specs Wright, Jimmy Cobb (d).* 7/56–3/58.

***** Jump For Joy**
Verve 528699-2 *Adderley; Emmett Berry (t); Bill Evans (p); Barry Galbraith (g); Milt Hinton (b); Jimmy Cobb (d).* 10/55–8/58.

****** Somethin' Else**
Blue Note 95392-2 *Adderley; Miles Davis (t); Hank Jones (p); Sam Jones (b); Art Blakey (d).* 3/58.

***** Portrait Of Cannonball**
Original Jazz Classics OJC 361 *Adderley; Blue Mitchell (t); Bill Evans (p); Sam Jones (b); Philly Joe Jones (d).* 7/58.

*****(*) Things Are Getting Better**
Original Jazz Classics OJC 032 *Adderley; Wynton Kelly (p); Milt Jackson (vib); Percy Heath (b); Art Blakey (d).* 10/58.

***** Quintet In Chicago**
Verve 559770-2 *Adderley; John Coltrane (ts); Wynton Kelly (p); Paul Chambers (b); Jimmy Cobb (d).* 2/59.

***** Ultimate Cannonball Adderley**
Verve 559710-2 *As Verve albums listed above.* 58–62.

Long a critically undervalued figure, Cannonball Adderley's status as a master communicator in jazz has increased since his sadly early death. The blues-soaked tone and hard, swinging delivery of his alto lines are as recognizable a sound as anything in the aftermath of bebop and, while many have been quick to criticize his essentially derivative manner – Cannonball frequently fell back on clichés, because he just liked the sound of them – there's a lean, hard-won quality about his best playing that says a lot about one man's dedication to his craft. When he joined Miles Davis, Adderley's cameo appearances on *Milestones* and *Kind Of Blue* were somewhat outclassed by the leader's returning-the-favour guest spot on *Somethin' Else*, which features some of Davis's most pithy improvising. But something else distinguishes the Adderley sessions of this period: the superb line-up of supporting players. There is marvellous sparring with Milt Jackson on *Things Are Getting Better* and with Kelly, Heath and Blakey also in great form; and 'The Sidewalks Of New York' is an inspired revision which only Ellington's incomparable 1940 version can surpass. *Portrait Of Cannonball* (which includes three alternative takes on the CD issue) finds Blue Mitchell taking some welcome limelight – though he sounds no more facile than the oft-maligned Nat – and an early glimpse of Bill Evans feeling his way through 'Nardis'. The session with Coltrane is really the Miles Davis band without Miles, and it's a bit of good fun, both hornmen flexing their muscles on the blues and a ballad feature apiece. There really isn't a dud record in this batch.

Verve have filled in the picture of this period by putting together Cannonball's Emarcy sessions. *Sophisticated Swing* pulls together all the LPs *Sophisticated Swing*, *Cannonball En Route* and *Cannonball's Sharpshooters*, plus Nat's date, *To The Ivy League From Nat*, in a double-disc reissue. The clipped, punchy format of most of the tracks suits the playing, and there is some of the altoist's freshest music hidden in some otherwise unpromising songs. *Jump For Joy* puts Cannonball with Richard Hayman's strings for the first half, and it's not the happiest of combinations, though the sheer alacrity of Adderley's sound energizes some otherwise tepid writing. The second half, arranged by Bill Russo to accommodate a string quartet beside a familiar rhythm section, works better, and there is some felicitous work by all hands. Excellent remastering of both discs.

It was a gracious touch to have Joe Zawinul select favourites by his old boss for the *Ultimate* compilation. No surprises here, although since there's nothing from the period when Joe himself was in the band (because none of that music belongs to Verve) there's a degree of pointlessness about it too.

***** In San Francisco**
Original Jazz Classics OJC 035 *Adderley; Nat Adderley (c); Bobby Timmons (p); Sam Jones (b); Louis Hayes (d).* 10/59.

***** What Is This Thing Called Soul**
Original Jazz Classics OJC 801 *Adderley; Nat Adderley (c); Victor Feldman (p); Sam Jones (b); Louis Hayes (d).* 11/60.

***** Paris 1960**
Pablo PACD-5303-2 *As above.* 11/60.

Adderley's regular quintet has often been damned with such faint praise as 'unpretentious' and 'soulful'. This was a hard-hitting, rocking band which invested blues and blowing formulae with an intensity that helped to keep one part of jazz's communication channels open at the time of Ornette Coleman, Eric Dolphy and other seekers after new forms. The earlier live album is a memorably rowdy and exciting session. *In San Francisco* is a little overstretched, with four tracks nudging the 12-minute mark and some of the solos running out of steam too soon. *What Is This Thing Called Soul* is taken from European concerts: the band is on cracking form on Jimmy Heath's 'Big P', and the rest of the set is up to scratch. *Paris 1960* is a recent discovery with six favourites from the band's book: scarcely essential, given the several versions of titles like 'Dis Here' in the discography, but no disappointments about the form of the band.

***** African Waltz**
Original Jazz Classics OJC 258 *Adderley; Clark Terry, Ernie Royal, Joe Newman, Nick Travis (t); Nat Adderley (c); Bob Brookmeyer (vtb); Melba Liston, Arnette Sparrow, George Matthews, Jimmy Cleveland, Paul Faulise (tb); George Dorsey (as, f); Jerome Richardson, Oliver Jackson (ts, f); Arthur Clarke (bs); Wynton Kelly (p); Sam Jones (b); Don Butterfield (tba); Louis Hayes, Charli Persip (d); Ray Barretto, Olatunji (perc).* 2–5/61.

A departure from and an extension of what the Adderleys were doing in their small groups. Ernie Wilkins arranges a set of fulsome, top-heavy charts which Adderley has to jostle with to create their own space, and the music's worth hearing for its sheer brashness and impact. But the simple clarity of the Adderley small groups is a casualty of the setting, and the altoman isn't as convincingly at home here as he is in the *Great Jazz Standards* album with Gil Evans, one of his finest hours.

***** Know What I Mean?**
Original Jazz Classics OJC 105 *Adderley; Bill Evans (p); Percy Heath (b); Connie Kay (d).* 1–3/61.

***** Cannonball Adderley Quintet Plus**
Original Jazz Classics OJC 306 *Adderley; Nat Adderley (c); Victor Feldman (p, vib); Wynton Kelly (p); Sam Jones (b); Louis Hayes (d).* 5/61.

****(*) In New York**
Original Jazz Classics OJC 142 *Adderley; Nat Adderley (c); Yusef Lateef (ts, ob); Joe Zawinul (p); Sam Jones (b); Louis Hayes (d).* 1/62.

***** Cannonball's Bossa Nova**
Capitol 22667-2 *Adderley; Pedro Paulo (t); Paulo Moura (as); Sergio Mendes (p); Durval Ferreria (g); Octavio Bailly Jr (b); Dom Um Romao (d).* 12/62.

***** Nippon Soul**
Original Jazz Classics OJC 435 *Adderley; Nat Adderley (c); Yusef Lateef (ts, ob, f); Joe Zawinul (p); Sam Jones (b); Louis Hayes (d).* 7/63.

***** Dizzy's Business**
Milestone MCD-47069-2 *As above.* 9/62–7/63.

***** Lugano 1963**
TCB TDE 02032 *As above.* 3/63.

Cannonball continued to turn out records for Riverside at a cracking pace and, while there are no classics here, his own big-hearted playing seldom falters. At this point, though, the regimen of tours and records begins to fossilize some aspects of his own playing. Having stratified bop licks and set the pace for so-called 'soul jazz', Adderley found there wasn't much left to do but play them over again. If he plays with undiminished verve, the power of his improvising declines. The quartet date with Bill Evans was one of the last chances to hear him as sole horn, and he sounds fine; *Plus* brings in Wynton Kelly on a few tracks, enabling Feldman to play some more vibes, but it's otherwise a routine Adderley band date. Bringing in Joe Zawinul and Yusef Lateef energized the band anew, but the records are all vaguely disappointing. Zawinul is still no more than a good bandsman, and Lateef's touches of exotica – such as the oboe solo on 'Brother John' (*Nippon Soul*) or his furry, Roland Kirk-like flute improvisations – are an awkward match for the sunnier disposition of the customary material. Nevertheless *Nippon Soul* is perhaps the best of this bunch. *Dizzy's Business* patches together some out-takes from the sessions for *Jazz Workshop Revisited* and *Nippon Soul*: not bad, with the title-track a solidly turned cooker. The Lugano date is another characteristic concert from one of the hardest-working bands of their era: familiar songs, though done as well as anywhere, and one nice note with 'Jessica's Birthday'. Recorded by Swiss Radio and in good fidelity. The men who earn exemption from criticism on all these records are Sam Jones and

Louis Hayes: seldom remembered as a major rhythm section, their unflagging tempos and generosity of spirit centre the music at all times.

Cannonball's Bossa Nova finds Adderley on a Brazilian vacation, with some of the local talent. Little more than a sweet-natured excursion into some of the indigenous music, it's a pleasing diversion.

**** Cannonball In Japan**

Capitol 93560-2 *Adderley; Nat Adderley (c); Joe Zawinul (p); Victor Gaskin (b); Roy McCurdy (d).* 8/66.

***** Mercy, Mercy, Mercy**

Capitol 29915-2 *As above.* 10/66.

***** Inside Straight**

Original Jazz Classics OJC 750 *Adderley; Nat Adderley (c); Hal Galper (p); Walter Booker (b); Roy McCurdy (d); King Errisson (perc).* 6/73.

****(*) Pyramid**

Original Jazz Classics OJC 952 *As above, except add George Duke (ky), Jimmy Jones (p), Phil Upchurch (g); omit Errisson.* 74.

Adderley kept on recording regularly until his death, but many of his later albums are currently in limbo so far as the catalogues are concerned. Close to 20 Capitol albums have been boiled down to what's on offer here. Given that many of the later records were misfire attempts at fusion of one sort or another, maybe it's not such a bad thing. *Cannonball In Japan* is another live show in a favourite location: the group play well enough, but it won't enrich any who already have other Adderley records. The Capitol best-of is short on surprise and concentrates mostly on Zawinul's additions to the band's book, including their hit, 'Mercy, Mercy, Mercy', and 'Country Preacher', which has a rare glimpse of the leader on soprano. But the most interesting thing is the lengthy '74 Miles Away', which suggests the distant influence of late Coltrane, with Cannonball's solo straying into what are for him very remote regions. That the group finally don't know what to do with the situation says something about the limits of their ambitions. *Mercy, Mercy, Mercy* is a hard-swinging live album with one of Cannon's hottest outings in 'Sticks'.

Inside Straight is a welcome addition to latter-day Cannon on CD. This was one of his live-in-the-studio sessions with a late edition of the band: Galper plays smart, probing electric piano, and Booker and McCurdy generate considerable heat. The tunes are a little more severe than before: only the title-track can be called a typical Adderley slice of soul-jazz. 'Inner Journey', 'Snakin' The Grass' and 'Second Son' are more sidelong looks at the band's playing methods, and more interesting for it. No masterpiece, but a hint of other paths the group might have explored. Less valuable is *Pyramid*, which imports Duke and Upchurch for some modish touches and gets righteous mostly with a more traditionally inclined 'Bess, Oh Where's My Bess'.

Nat Adderley (1931–2000)

CORNET, TRUMPET

One of the few modern brass players to have specialized on cornet, Nat had a sharp, staccato tone in melody statements which could give way to the most unctuous and syrupy of deliveries when he played ballads. He worked with J.J. Johnson and Woody Herman and, most famously, with his older brother Cannonball, to whom he was an ideal foil.

***** Branching Out**

Original Jazz Classics OJC 255 *Adderley; Johnny Griffin (ts); The Three Sounds (Gene Harris (p); Andy Simpkins (b); Bill Dowdy (d)).* 58.

****** Work Song**

Original Jazz Classics OJC 363 *Adderley; Bobby Timmons (p); Wes Montgomery (g); Keter Betts, Sam Jones (b); Louis Hayes, Percy Heath (d).* 60.

The Adderley brothers helped keep a light burning for jazz when rock'n'roll was dominating the industry 'demographics'. Neither was ever particularly revolutionary or adventurous in style, but saxophonist Cannonball's enormous personality and untimely death, together with his participation in such legendary dates as Miles's *Kind Of Blue*, have sanctified his memory with young fans who would have found his live performances rather predictable.

Nat was always the more incisive soloist, with a bright, ringing tone that most obviously drew on the example of Dizzy Gillespie but in which could be heard a whole raft of influences from Clark Terry to Henry 'Red' Allen to the pre-post-modern Miles of the 1950s.

In the late 1950s the cornetist was playing at his peak, and these sessions do genuinely merit the 'classic' tag, though 'original' is probably stretching things a bit. *Branching Out* is an attractive enough set, but Griff doesn't seem to be the right saxophone player for the gig, too noisy and rapid-fire on things like 'I Got Plenty of Nuthin''. *Work Song* is the real classic, of course, laced with a funky blues feel but marked by some unexpectedly lyrical playing (on 'Violets For Your Furs' and 'My Heart Stood Still') from the leader. Montgomery manages to produce something more enterprising than his trademark octave-runs and hits a tense, almost threatening groove. Timmons is more predictable, but just right for this sort of set; compare *In San Francisco* (OJC 035), which was made under Cannonball's name.

***** Much Brass**

Original Jazz Classics OJCCD 848 *Adderley; Slide Hampton (tb); Wynton Kelly (p); Laymon Jackson, Sam Jones (b); Albert 'Tootie' Heath (d).* 3/59.

Some interesting arrangements here, presumably largely the work of Hampton, and some delicately interwoven playing which largely belies the bluster implied in the title. 'Israel' is gorgeous, as is the closing 'Sometimes I Feel Like A Motherless Child'. Not immediately identifiable as a 'typical' Nat Adderley record, but a beautiful statement all the same.

*****(*) That's Right**

Original Jazz Classics OJC 791 *Adderley; Julian 'Cannonball' Adderley (as); Yusef Lateef (ts, f, ob); Jimmy Heath, Charlie Rouse (ts); Tate Houston (bs); Wynton Kelly (p); Jim Hall, Les Spann (g); Sam Jones (b); Jimmy Cobb (d).* 9/60.

*****(*) In The Bag**

Original Jazz Classics OJC 648 *Adderley; Julian 'Cannonball' Adderley (as); Nat Perrilliat (ts); Ellis Marsalis (p); Sam Jones (b); James Black (d).* 62.

That's Right is a bit of an oddity, with Nat's cornet placed in front of what was billed, quite accurately, as the Big Sax Section. Lateef's multi-instrumentalism is kept to a minimum. He leads the ensemble on flute for 'My Old Country' but switches back to tenor for a rich, folksy solo. His oboe doesn't quite work out on 'Night After Night'; back in 1960 there weren't that many soprano specialists around to take a part made for one of them. Heath and Rouse are well featured, taking fine solos either side of Nat and the pianist on Heath's own 'Chordnation'. One of the high points of a thoroughly enjoyable record.

In The Bag is welcome for a further glimpse of the brothers playing together but isn't specially exciting. Watch out for the little-known Perrilliat, who plays a firm-toned and steady tenor with some interesting quirks. The CD has added a couple of rather inconsequential bonus tracks.

****** Little Big Horn!**

Original Jazz Classics OJCCD 1001 *Adderley; Junior Mance (p); Kenny Burrell, Jim Hall (g); Bob Cranshaw (b); Mickey Roker (d).* 9 & 10/63.

Nat was still working with his brother's group when this was recorded, and it disappeared from sight surprisingly quickly after first release. Restored, it suggests again what a fine writer the wee man was. There's nothing as powerful as 'Work Song', but 'Loneliness' is an almost archetypal Nat tune and solo, and the penultimate track, 'Roses For Your Pillow', one of eight composed by the leader, is beautifully pitched and harmonized, a ballad worthy of frequent revival. Listening to this after a gap of – in our case – 15 years, it's hard to understand why such a quiet gem has slipped through the net.

*****(*) Sayin' Somethin'**

Atlantic 1221 *Adderley; Joe Henderson (ts); Herbie Hancock (p); Bob Cranshaw (b); Mickey Roker (d).* 2/66.

Hearing Nat in the presence of both Joe Henderson and Herbie Hancock provides ample reminder that his approach to hard bop and soul-jazz was one that very much stayed up with the times. His solo on Herbie's 'Canteloupe Island' is simplicity itself, but none the less effective for avoiding over-elaboration. 'Hippodelphia' and 'Manchild' are funky treatments and even the pop tune, 'Call Me', seems to fit the setting comfortably enough. Very dated sound, which remastering hasn't smoothed out.

****(*) Don't Look Back**

Steeplechase SCCD 31059 *Adderley; Ken McIntyre (as, bcl, ob, f); John Stubblefield (ts, ss); Onaje Allan Gumbs (p, ky); Fernando Gumbs (b); Ira Buddy Williams (d); Victor See Yuen (perc).* 8/76.

Adderley's reputation as a mainstream traditionalist takes a knock with sets like these. Unfortunately, the results aren't by any means commensurate with the daring of the line-up. McIntyre is an important catalyst in the re-voicing of jazz horns but, like a true catalyst, he remains largely untouched by what is going on round him and he solos as if alone. Stubblefield is fierier and provokes some of the leader's best returns of fire. Whatever Onaje Allen Gumbs's qualities, he's patently wrong for this gig, and the rest of the group circle round him somewhat uneasily. A bold effort, but not quite there.

***** A Little New York Midtown Music**

Original Jazz Classics OJCCD 1008 *Adderley; Johnny Griffin (ts); Victor Feldman (p); Ron Carter (b); Roy McCurdy (d).* 9/78.

A resilient and tough-minded hard-bop session, this late-'70s set is distinguished by some expert accompaniment from Victor Feldman and by superb solos from Nat and Johnny Griffin. Vic chips in with an original theme, 'Whipitup', but the bulk of the material, as ever, comes from Nat himself, and of his four compositions the title-track and 'Fortune's Child' are the best. Which means it's an album that peaks too soon, waning in interest after the first few cuts. Very much of its day, it has a brittle register which pervades the playing as well as the recording. Carter is poorly recorded, suggesting that even producer Orrin Keepnews could have an off-day.

***** On The Move**

Evidence ECD 22064 *Adderley; Sonny Fortune (as); Larry Willis (p); Walter Booker (b); Jimmy Cobb (d).* 83.

*****(*) Blue Autumn**

Evidence ECD 22035 *As above.* 83.

***** Mercy, Mercy, Mercy**

Evidence 22087 *As above.* 83.

A fair proportion of listeners who played any of these cold would plump for Cannonball as the altoist, which suggests it may have been an attempt to re-create that cheerfully bouncing sound. In many respects Fortune is a more interesting player, inserting oddly angular ideas and figures into relatively innocuous contexts, stretching out with ideas that Cannonball would have dismissed with the back of his hand. The group as a whole is very strong and, while there might be quibbles about the sound-quality on the first of the trio (which was formerly listed as a Theresa release), there are none whatsoever about the music.

At just 40 minutes, *Blue Autumn* gives slightly short measure, but there's plenty packed in. Sonny Fortune's 'For Duke And Cannon' is a great opener and Adderley responds warmly to it. Larry Willis claims the lion's share of writing credits with both 'Blue Autumn' and 'Tallahassee Kid', but these are not much more than blowing ideas and they're treated accordingly, with Fortune in particular offering his own perspective on them.

*****(*) Autumn Leaves**

Evidence ECD 22102 *Adderley; Sonny Fortune, Vincent Herring (as); Rob Bargad (p); Walter Booker (b); Jimmy Cobb (d).* 5/90.

*****(*) Work Song: Live At Sweet Basil**

Peter Pan 7312 *As above.* 5/90.

*****(*) Thinkin' About Ya**

32 Records 32082 *As above, except omit Fortune.* 11/90.

The switch from Willis to Bargad is probably less significant at a superficial level than changes to the saxophone incumbency. Nat's decision to add another horn may have been a tacit acknowledgement of his own waning powers, or it may simply have been another way of suggesting that it would take two gifted youngsters to fill Cannonball's shoes. The cornetist is pretty much overshadowed by Herring and Fortune on both these live sessions from a Sweet Basil residency, but he is still blowing sweetly and with strength when he needs it. Long versions of 'Autumn Leaves' and 'Yesterdays' follow Jimmy Heath's 'Big P.' on the Evidence disc and they pretty much dominate it. There's room at the end for Fortune's intense and heartfelt 'For Duke And Cannon', just one of his many tributes to other players, a twinned theme that manages to suggest a blues feel while not falling strictly into conventional blues form.

The other live set is less well recorded, though in some respects it is more challenging musically. Opening with 'Work Song' is a pretty disarming tactic and, by the time Randy Weston's 'Hi Fly' kicks in, you're hooked. Again, the solos are long and impressively well developed, and Nat delivers two superb solos, on 'In A Sentimental Mood', paying his own tribute to Duke, and on the closing 'Jive Samba'. Both are good-value sets and hard for the enthusiast to separate. Anyone tempted to dabble might start with the Evidence, just because the mix is cleaner and the playing more varied.

Fortune was absent from the November session for Landmark, which has reappeared in catalogue under the estimable 32 imprint. It's a pretty basic set from what sounds like a very settled band, combining original ideas and standard fare. A good point at which to pick up the later Nat, and certainly a much cleaner sound than on the live discs.

*****(*) Good Company**
Challenge 70009 *Adderley; Antonio Hart (as); Rob Bargad (p); Walter Booker (b); Jimmy Cobb (d).* 6/94.

***** Live At The Floating Jazz Festival 1994**
Chiaroscuro 334 2CD *As above, except omit Hart; add Vincent Herring (as).* 10/94.

By the mid-'90s, Nat had become something of an elder statesman of the music and one of its living historians. As the chops faltered, the monologues between numbers tended to get longer, and on the double festival CD the chat outweighs solo playing from the leader at least. His account of the origins of Sam Jones's 'Unit Seven' (heard to good effect on *Good Company*) has already entered jazz mythology, a hilarious performance, even if after a first hearing one starts to wish for a little more jazz. Most of the serious solo honours now fall to young Herring and to Bargad, both of whom sound poised and confident in such senior company.

Opening with Hank Mobley's 'This I Dig Of You' and Walter Booker's 'Soudade', the Floating Jazz set soon moves in more familiar directions, with fine versions of 'Work Song' and, rather briefly, 'Mercy, Mercy, Mercy'. Nat's most effective feature is his solo on 'Once I Had A Secret Love', on which the tone of the old days comes back ripe and fat and buttery. Bargad is excellent on the Chiaroscuro disc and he is rewarded with inclusion of two new compositions, 'War Zone' and 'Rob's New Tune'. Hart is a more intuitive soloist than Herring, and his ensemble work is tighter and more obviously integrated with the leader's idiom, and yet he lacks his fellow-altoist's simplicity of tone. Producer Hein Van De Geyn goes for a plain but resonant sound and he seems to have boosted Nat in places, which is no more than his due.

Ron Affif (born 1965)

GUITAR

Post-bop guitarist, tougher than the average while working from a fundamentally conventional jazz viewpoint.

***** Ron Affif**
Pablo 2310-949-2 *Affif; Brian O'Rourke (p); Andy Simpkins (b); Colin Bailey (d).* 10/92.

*****(*) Vierd Blues**
Pablo 2310-954-2 *As above, except add Ron Anthony (g), Brian Kilgore (d).* 12/93–2/94.

****** 52nd Street**
Pablo 2310-958-2 *Affif; Essiet Essiet (b); Jeff Tain Watts (d).* 10/95.

*****(*) Ringside**
Pablo 2310-962-2 *Affif; Essiet Essiet (b); Colin Bailey (d).* 2/97.

***** Solotude**
Pablo 2310-965-2 *Affif (g solo).* 99.

Guitar fans should be following Affif. It's a little surprising at first to read that he was never a rock player, since his hard tone is at odds with the sweeter, warmer jazz feel of Montgomery, Pass or Hall, three clear role-models to judge from the interesting debut set, *Ron Affif*. There's something of a pull between the guitarist's obvious chopsmanship and his reluctance to take all the limelight: O'Rourke is just as readily featured, and nothing Affif does takes up too much space. Nevertheless this is still a fundamentally traditional-modern guitar programme, with standards the main bill of fare. *Vierd Blues* is a surprising advance. The programme is all Miles Davis tunes or dedications, and Affif goes at it with a startling blend of irreverence and homage. 'Solar' is turned into a helter-skelter samba tune; 'So What' is genuinely hard-bitten, a striking antidote to the many softer versions of the past 30 years. Affif puts some fresh light on most of the tunes, and his gutsy playing is capable enough to silence any talk of mere disrespect.

52nd Street is mostly bebop, but done with such skill and intensity that one never thinks of revivalism. On pure bop tunes such as 'Bohemia After Dark' Affif goes at it like a terrier, reeling off lines without relinquishing a finesse which is clearly his trademark. Yet there are subtle performances here too, especially the remarkable treatment of 'You Don't Know What Love Is', which starts out as a straightforward ballad and gets tougher and darker as it proceeds. There is superb support from Essiet and Watts, and they're all granted a wonderful sound in the studio. That pristine focus softens a little on *Ringside*, which has a frisson of excitement provided by a live-in-the-studio audience. If this one seems a shade more prosaic than before, there's no dimming of Affif's intensity or his capacity to build big-scale solos.

Perhaps the solo album was inevitable but, for a player who seems to thrive on interaction, this is a predictably quiescent and so-so situation. The music offers all the virtues of the earlier records, minus the intensity, and to that extent it's a viable but ultimately directionless continuation.

Affinity

GROUP

West Coast band of players dedicated to the kind of free bop associated with Eric Dolphy.

*****(*) Plays Modern Jazz Classics**

Music & Arts CD 834 *Joe Rosenberg (ss); Rob Sudduth (ts); Richard Sanders (b); Bobby Lurie (d).* 93.

****** A Tribute To Eric Dolphy**

Music & Arts CD 939 *As above, except omit Sanders; add Buddy Collette (as, f), Michael Silverman (b).* 3/95.

*****(*) This Is Our Lunch**

Music & Arts CD 940 *As above, except omit Collette.* 4/95.

*****(*) A Tribute To Ornette Coleman**

Music & Arts CD 938 *As above, except omit Sudduth.* 5/95.

Heart-on-sleeve stuff from soprano specialist Rosenberg's dedicated modernists. Originally a limited-edition release, the 1993 record establishes the group sound quite emphatically. There is a burning version of Lee Morgan's 'Afrique', a fine version of Ornette's rarely covered 'Little Symphony' and an unexpectedly mainstream turn for Ellis Marsalis's 'After'. This, plus material by Dolphy ('Miss Ann') and Anthony Braxton, paves the way for future *hommages*. The Dolphy record is a delight, and the presence of old chum Collette lifts it more than a notch. Having already covered the most distinctive Dolphy original, the choice of material is slightly unexpected, mostly material associated with the great saxophonist (Booker Little's 'Bee Vamp', Jaki Byard's 'Ode To Charlie Parker', Mingus's 'So Long Eric') rather than written by him. As before, Sudduth is the linchpin harmonically, tying together themes and ideas that are as wilful and wayward as anything that's been attempted by the so-called avant-garde since. On the Coleman disc, Redman fulfils the same role (Sudduth is absent) as he did on Ornette sessions in the late 1960s and early '70s. 'Little Symphony' is here, as are 'Blues Connotation', 'Peace', 'Face Of The Bass', 'The Sphinx' and 'Beauty Is A Rare Thing'. One almost waits at the end for an encore of 'Lonely Woman', but it fails to materialize. The other album of the group is mostly Rosenberg originals (Dolphy's 'Hat And Beard' is the exception), strongly written themes which seem to encapsulate much of what has gone on in jazz post-Parker. The playing on this studio recording is terse, urgent and always very immediate. Rosenberg leads from the front as ever, a strident voice with more control than most soprano specialists can muster and a very distinctive approach to soloing. Wonderful stuff. Nothing will ever take the place of Dolphy or Ornette doing their own thing, but in spirit and in execution this runs them very close.

Afro Blue Band

GROUP

A one-off group collected for this record.

****(*) Impressions**

Milestone MCD-9237-2 *Melton Mustafa (t); Mario Rivera (c, f); Papo Vasquez (tb); Dave Liebman (ss); Mel Martin (as, ts, bcl, f, picc); Arthur Barron (as, ts); Hilton Ruiz, Mark Levine (p); Nicole Yarling (vn, v); Steve Neil (b); Phoenix Rivera (d); Jerry Gonzalez, Glen Cronkhite, Steve Berrios (perc).* 12/94–5/95.

This three-way one-off, put together in New York, San Francisco and Fort Lauderdale, features players from three distinct musical scenes and blends a particular kind of metropolitan jazz with an Afro-Cuban base. Problematically, though, a good idea is often squandered through poor preparation and plain lack of finesse. The title-track is an impassioned but unconvincing mess, Yarling's inadequate vocals spoil 'Lonnie's Lament' and it's only when the more demanding contributions of Liebman and Ruiz – easily the most authoritative voices here – are thrown into relief that the undoubted energy and exuberance assume any genuine stature. This comes out best in 'Latin Jazz Dance', though Horace Silver's 'Senor Blues' isn't a bad effort.

Air / New Air

GROUP

Almost definitive of the experimental Chicago sound of the '70s, Air and New Air combined radical free improvisation with the democratic levelling of so-called 'little instruments'.

***** Live Air**

Black Saint 120034 *Henry Threadgill (as, ts, f, bf, hubkaphone); Fred Hopkins (b); Steve McCall (d, perc).* 10/77.

****** Air Time**

Nessa NCD 12 *As above.* 11/77.

***** Air Mail**

Black Saint 120049 *As above.* 12/80.

****(*) New Air: Live At The Montreal International Jazz Festival**

Black Saint 120084 *As above, except add Pheeroan akLaff (d, perc).* 7/83.

Air's first ever gig was a theatre performance of Scott Joplin themes, played as rags and as a basis for jazz improvisation. It has remained a key source. The group has always placed great emphasis on tightly co-ordinated ensemble work while at the same time exploring the kind of sonic *terra incognita* represented by Threadgill's hubkaphone, which is exactly what it says, an array of auto accessories yielding a sound that is neither urban nor 'ethnic', but profoundly strange. It figures in the improvised conclusion to Threadgill's long 'Subtraction' (*Air Time*), almost the only non-scored element of the piece, except for some of Hopkins's bass embellishments behind the flute, and it's put to good effect on the first of the Black Saints.

Air were capable of riveting live performance, but one suspects that the intimate, almost hermetic atmosphere of the studio usually brought out their most characteristic work. Twenty years on, *Air Time* is a particularly valuable return to catalogue, and we've no hesitation in giving it the nod ahead of the others. Listening in detail to its five tracks – two of them very short indeed and one, Threadgill's 'Keep Right On Playing Through The Mirror Over

The Water', developing so seamlessly out of 'Subtraction' as to appear to be the same piece – helps illuminate much of the group's language, its vivid exploitation of splintered tempi, deliberately awkward and raucous phrasing, devices from other musical traditions (like the Burundi music which lies behind Hopkins's 'G.v.E.'), and most particularly the use of percussion as another voiced and pitched instrument.

It also clarifies some unresolved aspects to the other albums listed in which the improvisational component became dominant over fixed forms. *Live Air*, recorded a month earlier, almost sounds like a dry run and it benefits enormously from a hearing in tandem. McCall is immense, probably the only player of his generation (and that includes Sunny Murray, Andrew Cyrille and Milford Graves) who can sound this far out and at the same time so firmly anchored in tradition. Such a rating inevitably damns the born-again New Air. Pheeroan akLaff acquits himself well but rather conventionally. He works closer to the motoric drive Cyrille and Murray brought to Cecil Taylor's music and lacks McCall's ability to work melodically around the saxophonist, subtilizing his powerful, shouting lines. Hopkins is uneasily placed in the live recordings and reasserts himself only on *Air Mail* which, along with the Morton and Joplin arrangements on the now-deleted RCA *Air Lore*, is the most instantly approachable of the group's records. For sheer impact, Air have seldom been equalled. If it seemed for a time that their musical language belonged in the past, the re-emergence of *Air Time* forces a rethink, and a very welcome one.

Noël Akchoté (born 1968)

GUITAR

The young Parisian studied with Chet Baker and Barney Wilen, as well as with fellow guitarists John Abercrombie and Philip Catherine. He has emerged as the European Bill Frisell, a player with a gift for atmosphere and an iron-clad musical understanding.

*****(*) Lust Corner**

Winter & Winter 910 019-2 *Akchoté; Eugene Chadbourne (g, bjo, v); Marc Ribot (g). 6/96–7/97.*

It's no great surprise to find this debut album from the young Frenchman dominated by Ornette Coleman compositions. Ornette's liberation of the guitar must have figured prominently in Akchoté's musical education, and he takes to 'New York' (with Ribot), 'Street Woman', 'Peace Warriors' and that magnificent dirge, 'Broken Shadows' (with the more abrasive Chadbourne), as if they had been written for him.

The impressive thing about Akchoté is how comfortably he has synthesized the clean-picked single lines of classic jazz with a more contemporary, noise-based approach. A piece like 'Chadology' recalls Frisell's duets with Living Color frontman Vernon Reid on *Smash And Scatteration*, but with a more graceful and laid-back quality.

Akchoté has greatly impressed as a member of drummer Steve Arguëlles's Recyclers group and with Tim Berne's touring band. Striking out on his own, he suggests he's not going to be a sideman for long. *Lust Corner* is an impressive and confidently understated coming-out.

Ola Akerman

TROMBONE

Contemporary Swedish trumpeter in a post-bop idiom.

***** Ola Akerman**

Four Leaf Clover FLC CD 164 *Akerman; Vincent Nilsson, Ola Nordqvist, Bjorn Hangsel (tb); Jacob Karlzon (p); Johan Leijonhufvud (g); Matthias Hjorth (b); Peter Nilsson (d); Anders Vestergard (perc). 6–7/98.*

An entertaining debut as leader by this ebullient and humorous trombonist. He gets a good brassy rip out of the horn, shown off to a 't' on the opening 'F&M', which is attractively offset by the sparse textures of the basic quintet (trombone, guitar, bass, drums and percussion). There's apparently as much rock as jazz in Akerman's listening and he pays two tributes to Stevie Wonder, but it's arguably on the two ballads, 'Cry Me A River' and 'The Gentle Rain' – each actually set to an unusual walking beat – that he plays his most persuasive solos. The other horns step in for some written parts on two tracks and Karlzon turns up twice, but it's the quick-fingered Leijonhufvud, as ever, who is perhaps the star turn, supportive but always taking the ear with what he's playing. Some of the writing is lightweight and it may not be a disc to return to often.

Toshiko Akiyoshi (born 1929)

PIANO, COMPOSER

Akiyoshi was born in Manchuria and managed to study classical piano before the militaristic ethos of pre-war Japan imposed restrictions on what musicians might listen to and play. Already a formidable presence in her native Japan, Akiyoshi went to the United States in 1956 under the tutelage of Oscar Peterson. She met Charlie Mariano while a student at Berklee and the couple married in 1959. Her style combines a historically aware jazz feel, an unfailing swing, and a still unexpected admixture of non-Western harmonies.

***** Live At Birdland**

Fresh Sound FSRCD 1021 *Akiyoshi; Charlie Mariano (as); Gene Cherico (b); Eddie Marshall (d). 4/60–10/61.*

*****(*) Toshiko–Mariano Quartet**

Candid 79012 *As above. 12/60.*

Akiyoshi's playing was based closely but not slavishly on Bud Powell's, an influence that was to surface from time to time over the years. The Candid session, made with new husband Mariano, is forceful and intelligent, and the only sign of 'orientalism' in the small-group playing (there have always been engaging oddities of scoring in the big-band arrangements) is a willingness to mix modes, as on the Mariano-composed 'Little T', dedicated to her, and on the closing 'Long Yellow Road'.

Recorded with an established band (the excellent Eddie Marshall had signed up a few months before), the set has a coherence of tone and enthusiasm which provides Mariano with the impetus for some of his best recorded playing. Supervised by Nat Hentoff, the balances and registrations are ahead of their time.

The Birdland sets, one before and one after the studio recording, are worthwhile in themselves, but they also offer a useful way of judging how much the band developed in its short life. A later version of 'Blues For Father' (introduced by stand-in compère Maynard Ferguson on the April 1960 date as a new composition) is taken rather slower and Mariano's solo opens on a sequence of held notes that feed directly off Akiyoshi's accompaniment, rather than varying the melody. Unfortunately, the sound is much poorer on the later session, roughening his tone and significantly muting the piano and bass.

*****(*) Toshiko Mariano And Her Big Band: Recorded In Tokyo**

Vee Jay VJ 023 *Akiyoshi; Tetsuo Fushimini, Terumaso Hino, Hisao Mori, Shigeru (t); Taleshi Aoki, Teruhiko Kataoka, Mitsuhiko Matsumoto, Hiroshi Suzuki (tb); Hiroshi Ozazaki, Shigeo Suzuki (as); Sleepy Matsumoto, Akira Mayazawa (ts); Tadayuki Harada (bs); Paul Chambers (b); Jimmy Cobb (d).* 65.

The war was only twenty years over when this remarkable record was cut in Tokyo. Never before had a basically Japanese unit – albeit driven by two powerful American rhythm-players – come together to create such music. Even so, the arrangements are definitely home-grown. The opening 'Kisrazu Jink' is traditional, a theme cast in 5/4 and dominated by the pianist. It's followed by J.J. Johnson's 'Lament', done by the trio and a theme which sits very comfortably for Akiyoshi's approach; after that, there is a version of Mariano's 'The Shout', John Carisi's 'Israel' and, arranged for tenors and trio, the blues 'Walkin'', a Miles Davis staple. Sleepy Matsumoto, who seems to have stayed awake for whatever was going on in the States, switches to soprano and manages to sound both like Trane and like no one you ever heard before, all in one track.

The other tracks are Mariano's 'Santa Barbara' and, placed just after Mariano's arrangement of 'Israel', a version of 'Land Of Peace' by Leonard Feather, who supervised the original recording. There may come a moment when Akiyoshi's music is fully assimilated. For the moment, though, it's the underlying hint of strangeness that makes her so compelling. These are marvellous cuts; a valuable reissue.

***** Finesse**

Concord CCD 4069 *Akiyoshi; Monty Budwig (b); Jake Hanna (d).* 5/78.

***** Interlude**

Concord CCD 4324 *Akiyoshi; Dennis Irwin (b); Eddie Marshall (d).* 2/87.

It's a pity that Akiyoshi should have cluttered herself with a rhythm section for at least the second of these sets. She is such an interesting player that she barely needs an external context – even one as sympathetic as that provided by Irwin and Marshall.

The earlier set is marginally the more impressive and there is a slightly perfunctory quality to the 1987 cuts. Working an unpromising theme like 'Solveig's Song', which can turn to mush without undue trouble, her harmonic rigour is impressive. Nor is she troubled by the demands of such very different standards as 'Mr Jelly Lord' and 'You Go To My Head'. 'American Ballad' is one of her best performances, beautifully judged. The later trio seems tighter but much less conscious, as if the whole business had become second nature. The closing 'You Stepped Out Of A Dream' is the high spot. Some doubts about the recording levels on both sets, but no loss of clarity.

*****(*) Remembering Bud / Cleopatra's Dream**

Evidence ECD 22034 *Akiyoshi; George Mraz, Ray Drummond (b); Lewis Nash, Al Harewood (d).* 7 & 8/91.

Bud Powell played a significant role in Akiyoshi's development as a jazz pianist. They met in New York in 1964, in the last phase of the great pianist's life, and there are echoes of Powell's classic trios all through her work. In 1990 she recorded this tribute album, a mixture of Powell tunes – 'Tempus Fugit', 'Parisian Thoroughfare', 'Budo' and 'Dance Of The Infidels' – along with her own composition, 'Remembering Bud', which had already been recorded by Akiyoshi's orchestra.

Throughout the session, she maintains strong rhythmic patterns which sometimes seem to rule out the need for a bassist and drummer altogether. The most successful permutations of personnel (all the tracks are for trio) would seem to be those involving Mraz, who adds intriguing middle-register fills to Akiyoshi's forceful solos, and a magnificent solo on 'I'll Keep Loving You'. The only negative points relate to a certain predictability around the beginnings and ends of Akiyoshi's solos, almost as if she needs a nudge and then a safety net. But these are minor quibbles. A lovely set that Budophiles can also listen to with profit.

*****(*) At Maybeck**

Concord CCD 4635 *Akiyoshi (p solo).* 7/94.

For piano players, the Maybeck recital has become a sort of professional milestone. Akiyoshi comes 36th in the series that began with another female musician, JoAnne Brackeen, and tackles the challenge with similar *savoir faire* and a slightly muted self-confidence. Hearing her without a rhythm section and outside her more familiar role as a bandleader, Akiyoshi still sounds startlingly original. Almost as a signal of intent, she opens with an original, 'The Village', that establishes her voice and stylistic mannerisms. The trajectory from there to the staple, 'Quadrille, Anyone?', and a closing interpretation of Bud Powell's 'Tempus Fugit' is more conventional and standards-based than expected. She finds room for Diz's 'Con Alma', on which she manages to avoid the usual horn-derived clichés, and two Duke tunes – 'Come Sunday' and 'Sophisticated Lady' – are particularly suited to her delivery. For the most part, though, this is a very straightforward, perhaps even slightly diffident, set; there are intimations that, even at this point in her career, Akiyoshi isn't entirely happy with this degree of exposure.

Joe Albany (1924–88)

PIANO, VOCAL

Somewhat of a bebop legend, Albany was Charlie Parker's roommate and worked with him and in the Boyd Raeburn orchestra, also recording with Lester Young. But his career was constantly interrupted by drug addiction and spells in prison. He was hardly recorded until his rediscovery in the 1970s.

*****(*) The Right Combination**

Original Jazz Classics OJC 1749 *Albany; Warne Marsh (ts); Bob Whitlock (b). 57.*

Albany remains a frustrating enigma. Legendary in his time, as the sleeve to this album proclaims, he was allegedly one of Parker's favourite accompanists but never made a studio recording with him. In fact he didn't make any kind of studio sessions until the 1970s. This reissue was spliced together from an impromptu session at engineer Ralph Garretson's home which caught Albany and Marsh jamming together on seven standards (the last of which, 'The Nearness Of You', is only a fragment). While the sound is very plain and the piano in particular is recessed, the music is intermittently remarkable. Albany's style is a peculiar amalgam of Parker and Art Tatum: the complexity of his lines suggests something of the older pianist, while the horn-like figures in the right hand might suggest a bop soloist. Yet Albany's jumbled, idiosyncratic sense of time is almost all his own, and his solos are cliff-hanger explorations. Marsh is at his most fragmentary, his tone a foggy squeal at some points, yet between them they create some compelling improvisations: 'Body And Soul', done at fast and slow tempos, is as personal as any version, and a dreamy, troubled 'Angel Eyes' shows off Albany's best work. No wonder, with the next 25 years spoiled by narcotic and personal problems, that Albany seemed like a wasted talent.

**** Birdtown Birds**

Steeplechase SCCD 1003 *Albany; Hugo Rasmussen (b); Hans Nymand (d). 4/73.*

****(*) Two's Company**

Steeplechase SCCD 1019 *Albany; Niels-Henning Orsted Pedersen (b). 2/74.*

Once rediscovered, first through a home-made tape which forms the basis of *Joe Albany At Home*, a now-deleted comeback album on Spotlite, and then on subsequent European sojourns and New York appearances, Albany made a dozen or so albums during the 1970s. While much talked-up at the time, none of them has worn at all well. The best music comes on *Two's Company*, where the duets with bassist NHOP are elaborately conceived and confidently dispatched. But many of Albany's ideas are beset by misfingerings, and the famously off-kilter conception of time can sometimes sound more like clumsiness than anything else.

****(*) Live In Paris**

Fresh Sound FSCD-1010 *Albany; Alby Cullaz (b); Aldo Romano (d). 77.*

This recent discovery sheds no special new light on Albany, but there are some rather more impressive things here: the long Jerome Kern medley which opens the solo section (six titles; there are five more with the trio) shows the pianist's dense, heavily allusive style at its best, and it's a severe disappointment when he follows this with a terribly maudlin vocal treatment of 'Lush Life' (he also sings 'The Christmas Song'). Cullaz and Romano accompany as best they can, but this was clearly a trio that needed more work. The sound is a bit flat, but not too bad, for what seems to be a private club recording.

***** Bird Lives**

Storyville STCD 4164 *Albany; Art Davis (b); Roy Haynes (d). 1/79.*

Davis and Haynes play particularly well and ensure that there's no loss of focus on what is one of the best sets that Albany laid down. The strong emphasis on blues lines – most of the songs are Parker originals, but most are based on the blues – might have led to a lack of variety, but they're more useful in keeping Albany's mind on the job, perhaps. A decent piano and respectable sound.

Albion Jazz Band

GROUP

Veteran British tradsters, on their holidays.

**** One For The Guv'nor**

Stomp Off 1206 *Tony Pringle (c, v); Jim Klippert (tb, v); Gerry Green (cl); Bob Pelland (p); Mike Cox (bj, v); Mike Fay (b); Mike McCombe (d). 3/90.*

****(*) They're All Nice Tunes**

Stomp Off 1249 *As above. 3/92.*

A couple of waggish trad sessions by a troupe of cheerful British Luddites, transported to Vancouver for the occasion (both times!). The first album is a tribute to Ken Colyer and is pretty effortful stuff, with Colyer's dogged primitivism overshadowing their more sprightly moments. The subsequent *They're All Nice Tunes* is a smidgeon more lively and gets an extra notch for the sheer cheek of turning the Beatles' 'I'll Follow The Sun' into a George Lewis-like dirge. Some of the horn playing is stunningly ham-fisted, but the band have a knack of sticking an extra chorus on to the end of most of the tunes, which always seem to pick up a ragged second wind as a result.

Alvin Alcorn (born 1912)

TRUMPET

Alcorn was leading groups in his native New Orleans when still a teenager. He toured with Don Albert in the 1930s, based himself in his home town in the '40s, and had a very successful stint with the Kid Ory band of the '50s. Thereafter he performed back at home and on European tours, one with the Chris Barber band.

***** Sounds Of New Orleans Vol. 6**

Storyville STCD 6012 *Alcorn; Jack Delaney, Bill Matthews (tb); Raymond Burke (cl); Stanley Mendelson (p); Lawrence Marrero (bj); Chink Martin, Sherwood Mangiapane, Alcide 'Slow Drag' Pavageau (b); Abbie Brunies (d). 12/52–11/53.*

***** Live At Earthquake McGoon's Vol. 1**

GHB BCD-238 *Alcorn; Big Bill Bissonnette (tb); Paul 'Polo' Barnes (cl, as); James 'Sing' Miller (p); Jim Tutunjian (b); Alex Bigard (d). 7/69.*

****(*) Live At Earthquake McGoon's Vol. 2**
GHB BCD-239 *As above.* 7/69.

Alcorn was lightly recorded as a leader, and he might almost be termed a cool hornman in comparison with some of his New Orleans peers. His contribution to Storyville's archive series of sessions consists of two live dates from Joe Mares's Place and an informal studio session by the Alcorn Jazz Babies, all using largely the same personnel. As so often, the group plays with more spirit than finesse, but Alcorn's controlled lead (he is never much of a soloist) settles a certain steady-rolling fluency on much of the playing.

In 1969, at Turk Murphy's club, four New Orleanians sat down with Bissonnette and played through a stack of old numbers. The music has its ragged edges, but what compensates is a gentlemanly camaraderie that is rather different from the fierceness of much authentic New Orleans playing. Alcorn still sounds better as ensemble man than as improviser, and Bissonnette's barking trombone can sound overly heated; it's Barnes's charmingly old-fashioned alto playing which is the most distinctive thing. History may be glad that there are two volumes, but most will settle for the first. Bissonnette has cleaned up the original tapes quite respectably.

Howard Alden (born 1958)

GUITAR

A classic example of the jazz 'young fogey', Alden is a Californian who began playing banjo in pizza parlours before working in numerous swing-to-mainstream outfits. His Concord records began in a conservative vein and have since diversified into a sophisticated and personal take on jazz history. He remains much in demand for record session-work in several styles.

***** Swing Street**
Concord CCD 4349 *Alden; Dan Barrett (tb); Chuck Wilson (as, cl); Frank Tate (b); Jackie Williams (d).* 9/86.

***** The A.B.Q. Salutes Buck Clayton**
Concord CCD 4395 *As above.* 6/89.

Alden has grown into an artist of formidable stature, and his early records for Concord now seem comparatively lightweight in view of the more recent ones; but on their own terms they're still very enjoyable. The guitarist's polished manner placed him in the swing-to-modern lineage of Herb Ellis, and he has mastered the style as well as anybody. In this band of young fogeys, the musicians don't so much re-create swing styles as reinvigorate them, adding a modern lick or two to classic material and classy arrangements, and throwing the occasional curve, such as a lucid treatment of Monk's 'Pannonica', into the game-plan. Barrett, a superbly accomplished player, is the star of these sessions, but the group is uniformly commanding and relaxed. The session devoted to material associated with Buck Clayton is marginally superior, if only because of the interesting concept.

***** The Howard Alden Trio Plus Special Guests**
Concord CCD 4378 *Alden; Warren Vaché (c); Ken Peplowski (ts, cl); Lynn Seaton (b); Mel Lewis (d).* 1/89.

***** Snowy Morning Blues**
Concord CCD 4424 *Alden; Monty Alexander (p); Lynn Seaton (b); Dennis Mackrel (d).* 4/90.

Vaché sits in with Alden's trio for five tracks, Peplowski for three, and the music has less cohesion than the ABQ record, although no less freshness. Vaché rewards Ellington's 'Purple Gazelle' with special radiance. Alexander's customary enthusiasm puts a little more obvious pep into Alden's music, though not enough to coarsen the guitarist's smoothly effective approach. The programme is well chosen to include some lesser-known Ellington and Monk tunes, a hint of the ingenious programming of the later records.

***** Misterioso**
Concord CCD 4487 *Alden; Frank Tate (b); Keith Copeland (d).* 4/91.

*****(*) A Good Likeness**
Concord CCD 4544 *Alden; Michael Moore (b); Alan Dawson (d).* 8/92.

Like such older Concord hands as Scott Hamilton and Warren Vaché, Alden began to assume his methods so convincingly that the prettiness and formal grace of his playing took on an iron-clad quality. *Misterioso* was certainly his most effective record to date: 'We See' and 'Misterioso' don't so much simplify Monk as put the crusty elegance of his tunes in the forefront, and everything else – including such bedfellows as 'Flying Down To Rio' and Jelly Roll Morton's 'The Pearls' – is delivered with the same fine touch. But it's outdone by *A Good Likeness*, which finds Alden brimming with ideas and drive. The tunes are another surprising bunch – Bud Freeman's 'The Eel's Nephew', Monk's 'Crepuscule With Nellie', Willie Smith's 'Echoes Of Spring' – and this time Alden lets rip at fast tempos as he never has before on record, with the rippling grace of a solo 'Single Petal Of A Rose' as the other side of the coin.

***** 13 Strings**
Concord CCD 4464 *Alden; George Van Eps (g); Dave Stone (b); Jake Hanna (d).* 2/91.

****(*) Hand-Crafted Swing**
Concord CCD 4513 *As above.* 6/91.

**** Seven & Seven**
Concord CCD 4584 *As above, except omit Stone and Hanna.* 12/92.

It's interesting to hear Alden playing alongside a man who himself played alongside Eddie Lang more than 60 years ago. Van Eps prefers stately chord-based playing and, while it might not inhibit the younger man, Alden certainly scales down his approach to accommodate his senior (he also had a seven-string guitar made in the fashion of van Eps's instrument). The first record is nice and the second pleasant, but the third is dull: without any rhythm players to egg them on, they're too slow and quiet, and the sluggish tempos tend to push the music into the background.

****** Your Story – The Music Of Bill Evans**
Concord CCD 4621 *Alden; Frank Wess (ts, f); Michael Moore (b); Al Harewood (d).* 5/94.

***** Encore!**

Concord CCD 4654 *Alden; Ken Peplowski (cl, ts); Jeff Chambers (b); Colin Bailey (d). 8/94.*

Alden continued to expand his range and ambition with these sets. The Evans album is quite beautifully done, a considerably more involving record than John McLaughlin's tribute album. The bluesier side of Evans's playing isn't neglected, with the surprise choice of Frank Wess sitting in on three tracks; but, for touch, line and texture, it's hard to top the exquisite way the trio has with 'Time Remembered' and 'Your Story', with a bass/guitar duet on 'Two Lonely People' as a charming coda.

Encore! is slighter stuff, a concert in which Peplowski and Alden josh around on a catholic set of material – 'It All Depends On You', Konitz's 'Palo Alto', 'The Dolphin'. When bass and drums come in, as on the closing romp through 'You', it's close to burning.

****** Take Your Pick**

Concord CCD 4743 *Alden; Lew Tabackin (ts, f); Renee Rosnes (p); Michael Moore (b); Bill Goodwin (d). 5/96.*

Is anyone making better mainstream-to-modern records than Alden? Another impeccable choice of tunes sets Ellington and Herbie Nichols alongside Berlin and Porter, and Alden's masterstroke is to treat them all on the same terms: when he does Nichols's 'The Gig' and follows it with a gorgeous (yet unsentimental) 'My Funny Valentine', it's clear how thoroughly and effectively he's developed his own idiom out of jazz's compositional history. The band could hardly be better: Tabackin's gruff, swinging intensity (he gets the flute out only for 'U.M.M.G.') sits perfectly next to Rosnes's crackling solos and accompaniments and, with Moore and Goodwin both flawless, this is music that thrills with its own calm intensity.

*****(*) Full Circle**

Concord CCD2-4788-2 2CD *Alden; Jimmy Bruno (g); Michael Moore (b); Alan Dawson (d). 3/95.*

Recorded before *Take Your Pick* but not released until 1998, this mellifluous but steely series of duets with fellow stringsman Bruno will appeal most to guitar followers. Compared to the albums that came before, this seems like lightweight stuff, but the beautifully measured touch of both men is a pleasure in itself on the likes of 'Polka Dots And Moonbeams'. Played softly, it makes for very hip easy listening. There is a bonus CD of the *Jazz/Concord* album cut in 1973 by a quartet with Herb Ellis and Joe Pass, making this a particularly attractive package.

Terrie Richards Alden

VOCAL

Debut appearance for American singer, wife of guitarist Howard Alden.

***** Voice With Heart**

Nagel-Heyer 048 *Alden; Warren Vaché (c, flhn, v); Howard Alden (g); Michael Moore (b); Jackie Williams (d). 8/96.*

A sexy voice, and the heart's certainly in the right place. She covers some tunes that are probably a shade too familiar, but she does get a sting or a twist out of several of them that isn't so obvious: try the bluesy tang in 'Comes Love' or the *a cappella* intro to 'Dindi'. That isn't an especially successful treatment of the Jobim tune, though, and she sounds happier on old-fashioned standards with a jazz legacy, such as 'Gee Baby Ain't I Good To You' or the delicious stroll through 'Please Don't Talk About Me When I'm Gone', which opens the record. The backings are surprisingly sparse, and a courageous thing for a singer to try on her debut. Vaché and Mr Alden play some ear-tickling cameos throughout.

Eric Alexander (born 1968)

TENOR SAXOPHONE

He grew up in Washington State and studied in Indiana, moving to Chicago and playing on the club scene there. He moved to New York in 1992 and has since freelanced.

***** Straight Up**

Delmark 461 *Alexander; Jim Rotondi (t); Harold Mabern (p); John Webber (b); George Fludas (d). 8/92.*

***** New York Calling**

Criss Cross 1077 *Alexander; John Swana (t, flhn); Richard Wyands (p); Peter Washington (b); Kenny Washington (d). 12/92.*

***** Up, Over And Out**

Delmark 476 *Alexander; Harold Mabern (p); John Ore (b); Joe Farnsworth (d). 8/93.*

***** Full Range**

Criss Cross 1098 *Alexander; John Swana (t); Kenny Barron (p); Peter Bernstein (g); Peter Washington (b); Carl Allen (d). 1/94.*

***** Stablemates**

Delmark DE-488 *Alexander; Lin Halliday (ts); Jodie Christian (p); Dan Shapera (b); Wilbur Campbell (d). 95.*

In his early records, Alexander stands four-square in the tradition of big Chicago tenors: the first disc was made on local turf, the second in the city of the title, and in either milieu he sounds completely assured. This is old-fashioned tenor playing: fat, bruising, wide-bodied, but limber enough to handle bebop tempos and inner complexities, even if Alexander prefers a more seasoned tradition. His laggardly way with the beat makes one think of Dexter Gordon. Still, neither of these records is a world-beater, and the next two – again, one from Chicago, one from New York – show no specific advance. Each of the Delmark albums includes some professorial work from Mabern, even while the other players are unexceptional: *Up, Over And Out* is arguably the best of the three for its tough, uncompromising take on Monk's 'Eronel' and – the other side of Alexander's persona – the tender trap of 'The Nearness Of You'. Both the Criss Cross dates are good value yet neither really lifts itself out of the blowing-session convention that is wearing after a few tracks. Alexander's writing shows only modest promise and he sounds more like an executant than a leader; but it will be interesting to hear him marshal a properly prepared record. *Stablemates* is more an off-the-cuff interlude than anything. Alexander shares front-and-centre with veteran tenorman Halliday in a specific attempt to revitalize the two-tenor fisticuffs of yore. They certainly strike sparks on the up-tempo pieces and there is a fetching ballad medley of 'Polka Dots And Moonbeams' and 'Old Folks', but otherwise this goes down as little more than a good potboiler.

***** Eric Alexander In Europe**
Criss Cross 1114 *Alexander; Melvin Rhyne (org); Bobby Broom (g); Joe Farnsworth (d).* 4/95.

*****(*) 2 Soon 2 Tell**
Sharp Nine 1006 *Alexander; Jim Rotondi (t, flhn); Steve Davis (tb); David Hazeltine (p); Peter Washington (b); Joe Farnsworth (d).* 2/97.

Cut in the Netherlands following a tour, *In Europe* features a format which Alexander already has plenty of experience of, and he sounds very comfortable. The date still falls prey to its essentially conservative programme – blues, ballads and a couple of mildly engaging originals – but Alexander and Broom in particular settle themselves into long solos which they can carry off with aplomb. Broom's 'The Edge' is a particularly well-cast original.

The Sharp Nine album was made live at a New York club where the band had already been working for a while, and here Alexander comes into his own in a band of strong spirits. The Messengers format is adapted and surpassed: there are several impressive originals, Rotondi and Davis are executants who want to go their own way too, and Alexander sounds transfigured by the situation – he's probably never played a better solo than the one on 'Visionary'.

****** Man With A Horn**
Milestone 9293-2 *Alexander; Jim Rotondi (t); Steve Davis (tb); Cedar Walton (p); Dwayne Burno (b); Joe Farnsworth (d).* 1/97.

***** Mode For Mabes**
Delmark 500 *Alexander; Jim Rotondi (t); Steve Davis (tb); Harold Mabern (p); John Webber (b); George Fludas (d).* 5/97.

***** Alexander The Great**
High Note HCD 7013 *Alexander; Jim Rotondi (t); Charles Earland (org); Peter Bernstein (g); Joe Farnsworth (d).* 5/97.

*****(*) Solid!**
Milestone 9283-2 *Alexander; Jim Rotondi (t); John Hicks (p); Joe Locke (vib); George Mraz (b); Idris Muhammad (d).* 4–5/98.

Alexander's patient but inexorable progress is enjoyable to watch. In the course of a few years, he's bloomed into a tenorman of formidable authority and adaptability: the only danger now is that, via sideman and leadership work, he might be over-recorded. The High Note and Delmark albums are sound, foot-perfect hard-bop dates, *Alexander The Great* (ahem!) nudges just ahead for the splendid work by Earland on one of his last sessions. But the Milestone albums suggest something of the eminence which Alexander is working towards. Beautifuly recorded, *Man With A Horn* is a quartet date (Rotondi and Davis play on three tracks) where the saxophonist luxuriates in the rhythm section (Walton on top form) and peels off some of his most expansive and full-blooded improvising. Years of working on his sound have developed a quite magisterial voice on the tenor, massive in the mid-register and smoothly convincing when he goes towards the top. *Solid!* is in some ways more ambitious, since the programme features hard-bop nuggets like 'Solid' (Rollins), 'Little Melonae' (McLean), 'My Conception' (Sonny Clark) and 'Straight Street' (Coltrane), the leader apparently out to settle his credentials in the heaviest company. This is a slightly less convincing rhythm section – Muhammad plays well but never as capably as Farnsworth on the other date – and to that degree it's a less imposing record, but Alexander's sound is again tremendous; some of his most precocious solos, vaulting into double-time, are enough to have one reaching for the repeat button. Look for this man to be one of the major saxophonists of the decade ahead.

Monty Alexander (born 1944)

PIANO

There have been many attempts to hybridize jazz and Afro-Cuban music, but relatively few to bring the rhythms of reggae, ska and mento into a jazz context. Jamaican-born Alexander remains the prime exponent, using steel pans in his Ivory and Steel group and exploiting Caribbean backbeats to a jazz idiom influenced by Nat Cole and Oscar Peterson.

*****(*) Live At The Montreux Festival**
MPS 817 487 *Alexander; John Clayton (b); Jeff Hamilton (d).* 6/76.

Only Tommy Smith has a more variable accent. Kingston-born, Alexander has never quite decided whether he is a Jamaican homeboy, an enthusiastic *norteamericano*, or indeed a European. He has fronted a style of jazz in which swing is recast in Caribbean rhythms, signalled by the steel pans, but also marked out by great formal control. Alexander now has an impressive back-catalogue of (mostly trio) recordings which reveal an exuberant sensibility schooled – sometimes a little too doctrinairely – in the School of Oscar Peterson. Typical of that tendency, he has a tone which is both percussive and lyrical, heavy on the triplets and arpeggiated chords, melodically inspired in the main (i.e. no long, chordal ramblings), maximal but controlled.

The trio is the ideal context for Alexander's playing. The best of this bunch is the earliest, recorded at a vintage Montreux Festival. Alexander opens with Ahmad Jamal's 'Nite Mist Blues' and closes with the 'Battle Hymn Of The Republic', and he doesn't put a foot wrong in between. Clayton is the only weak link – but only relative to the astonishingly high standard of bass playing the pianist has usually been able to call on. Brown, where he appears, is so beyond reproach as to be *sui generis*.

The *Reunion* set, recorded live in Germany, breaks the chronology somewhat, but it belongs with the work of this particular trio. Monty is in very good form and more or less hogs the foreground, though Clayton has come on in leaps and bounds and shapes a few lovely choruses, not least an *arco* interpretation of Charlie Chaplin's 'Smile'. He also has a composition in the programme, which is otherwise dominated by standards. His 'Blues For Stephanie' and Monty's 'Eleuthera' and 'That's Why' (which has some relation to both 'Dat Dere' and 'So What') are the only originals. Nice sound, with lots of unobtrusive atmosphere.

*****(*) Jamento**

Original Jazz Classics OJCCD 904 *Alexander; Ernest Ranglin (g); Andy Simpkins (b); Roger Bethelny, Duffy Jackson (d); Vince Charles (steel d); Larry McDonell (perc).* 6/78.

Recorded in Hollywood, this is one of the best of Alexander's synoptic essays in jazz-plus-reggae/merengue/mento. The presence of the irrepressible Ranglin is some sort of guarantee and the groove the guitarist lays down on 'Sugar Loaf At Twilight' and the closing 'Mango Rengue' is deep and wide enough to ride a bus down. Alexander produced the session himself, and if we have quibbles they have to do with the balance of sound, which is less than faithful to the component parts. Much of the percussion sounds off-stage, and the piano is oddly located in the mixing, seeming to phase across its range. Good stuff of its kind, though.

***** Just In Time**

EJ 605 2CD *Alexander; Bob Maize (b); Frank Gant (d).* 79.

E.J.'s closed its doors for business in 1982, but this must have been a long-cherished night at the Atlanta club. Monty is in crackling form, though some of the individual performances do outstay their welcome a little. The title-piece sums up the best and worst of the record, brilliantly conceived and pungently played, but way too long for comfort. 'Work Song' is as sharp as any of the composer's versions of it, and 'On Green Dolphin Street' is dispatched with a cool insouciance. The rather distant recording doesn't help, but what must have been a great club night communicates pretty well down the years.

***** Facets**

Concord CCD 4108 *Alexander; Ray Brown (b); Jeff Hamilton (d).* 8/79.

**** Full Steam Ahead**

Concord CCD 4287 *Alexander; Ray Brown (b); Frank Gant (d).*

***** Trio**

Concord CCD 4136 *Alexander; Herb Ellis (g); Ray Brown (b).* 8/80.

****(*) Triple Treat**

Concord CCD 4193 *As above.* 3/82.

***** Overseas Special**

Concord CCD 4253 *As above.* 82.

****(*) Triple Treat II**

Concord CCD 4338 *As above, except add John Frigo (vn).* 6/87.

***** Triple Treat III**

Concord CCD 4394 *As for II.* 6/87.

Alexander worked with both Ray Brown and Milt Jackson before breaking through as a solo artist. The vibes were close enough to the steel drums to be familiar, but his approach to the lower end is interesting and untypical and Alexander bassists are often found playing *arco*, favouring big-toned pedals against which he can punch out sometimes surprisingly complex augmented chords. In the drummerless *Triple Treat II*, he used the violinist, John Frigo, alongside Brown and Herb Ellis, to similar effect. Though they were recorded at the same time, *III* is a more interesting record, and the quartet interpretation of 'My One And Only Love' stands out. The rather lowly rating largely stems from a very poor sound, with everything jumbled together towards the middle.

There are wonderful things on *Trio* (the opening 'I'm Afraid The Masquerade Is Over') and *Triple Treat* ('Body And Soul' and, ahem, the 'Flintstones' theme). The sequel is a shade disappointing, given the weight of campaign medals, but there is a gorgeous quartet reading of 'Smile' and a fine trio 'It Might As Well Be Spring'.

Overseas Special was recorded live in Tokyo and is, if nothing else, an object lesson in how well Japanese engineers have mastered live engineering. The sound, of the bass in particular, is pristine, almost studio quality, but with a warmth and spaciousness that comes only from a club acoustic. 'But Not For Me', Johnny Mandel's 'A Time For Love', 'For All We Know' and 'C.C. Rider' are the outstanding cuts. A welcome reappearance on CD.

***** Ivory And Steel**

Concord CCD 4124 *Alexander; Othello Molineaux (steel d); Gerald Wiggins (b); Frank Gant (d); Robert Thomas Jr (perc).* 3/80.

***** Jamboree**

Concord CCD 4359 *Alexander; Othello Molineaux, Len 'Boogsie' Sharpe (steel d); Marshall Wood, Bernard Montgomery (b); Robert Thomas Jr (perc); Marvin 'Smitty' Smith (d).* 2–3/88.

One of the most interesting aspects of Alexander's career has been his attempt to assimilate the steel-drum sound of his native Jamaica to the conventional jazz rhythm section. In the earlier disc, the new sound is still a little tacked-on and Gant in particular seems slightly uneasy, but the balance of instrumentation is good and Alexander finds sufficient space on *Ivory And Steel* to rattle off some of his most joyous solos.

Jamboree is a marvellous record, partly because the playing is so good, but also because of the imaginative selection of covers. Bob Marley's 'No Woman, No Cry' and Joni Mitchell's 'Big Yellow Taxi' have not previously figured too prominently in the average fake book; indeed, with the very considerable exception of avant-garde trumpeter Leo Smith, reggae has made remarkably little impact on contemporary jazz. 'Smitty' Smith was an inspired addition on the later date, and he lifts the energy level a further notch. Both are highly recommended, but go for *Jamboree*. One–love.

*****(*) The River**

Concord CCD 4422 *Alexander; John Clayton (b); Ed Thigpen (d).* 10/85.

No confusing this with the Bruce Springsteen product of the same name. This is the unsentimental one, played largely in key. Alexander's reading of hymn tunes (all except the title-track and Ellington's 'David Danced') is as bold as anything he has tried since the 'Ivory and Steel' sets. Mostly played with a rolling, gospelly fervour, there is space for a little schmaltz on 'Ave Maria' (aching bowed bass from Clayton) and some surprisingly abstract drum and piano effects on the closing traditional 'How Great Thou Art'. Thigpen is magnificent throughout. A really beautiful record.

***** Threesome**

Soul Note 121152 *Alexander; Niels-Henning Orsted Pedersen (b); Grady Tate (d, v).* 11–12/85.

Well used to top-drawer rhythm sections, Alexander makes the most of this one, turning in a sparkling set with sufficient variety to suggest his responsiveness to others. The version of 'All Blues' is interesting, but the material is otherwise a little lack-lustre.

***** Caribbean Circle**

Chesky JD 80 *Alexander; Jon Faddis, E Dankworth (t); Slide Hampton (tb); Frank Foster (ts); Dave Glasser (as); Ira Coleman, Anthony Jackson (b); Othello Molineaux (steel d); Herlin Riley, Steve Ferrone (d); Robert Thompson Jr, Marjorie Whylie (perc).* 6/92.

An extension of his work with Ivory and Steel and the nearest thing to a big band Alexander has mustered so far, this is a jolly, romping session that slightly overplays the Jamaican accent that Alexander jokingly phoneticizes in his sleeve-notes. Credit for the arrangements goes to Hampton. They're characteristically bright and uncluttered, and features like Dankworth's solo on a bluebeat version of 'When The Saints' or Marjorie Whylie's one-woman-band percussion-breaks fit neatly into them. What don't are Alexander's own solos, which tend to go off in odd directions, a bit like his jivey monologues, which you'll find either charming or plain irritating, like the 'Cowboy Ska Melody'. A tribute to Miles called 'Oh Why?' shows the pianist still capable of writing and playing feelingly, but it's exceptional.

*****(*) Maybeck Recital Hall Series: Volume 40**

Concord CCD 4689 *Alexander (p solo).* 94.

The series may have been tiring by this point, but Alexander was determined to make it clear that he wasn't. Perhaps he responds to the surroundings with a little more reserve and solemnity than one might usually expect of him, but that is not to detract one jot from a fine, forceful performance that will delight his fans and satisfy anyone putting together a piano library on the strength of this series.

***** Steamin'**

Concord CCD 4636 *Alexander; Ira Coleman (b); Dion Parson (d).* 9/94.

A most unusual selection of material as Alexander continues his eclectic progress. Quincy Jones (the *Pawnbroker* theme) rubs shoulders with Anthony Newley, 'Young At Heart' is given the same treatment as 'Lively Up Yourself', a relatively early cover of a Bob Marley tune that would later yield the rather less-than-successful *Stir It Up* album. Varied though the choice of material is, the pace of the album is rather uniform, unhurried, melodic and rarely too stretching. Coleman lopes along, untroubled and without urgency, and it's left to Parson to up the ante in occasional flurries and double-times. An odd record, hard to categorize and resistant to straightforward assessment; worth sampling, though.

***** Yard Movement**

Island 524 232 *Alexander; Dwight Dawes (ky); Ernest Ranglin (g); Robert Thomas Jr, Roland Wilson (d).* 7/95.

During the '90s, Alexander started to explore a rootsier and less sun-kissed aspect of Jamaican music. *Yard Movement* is a flawed but powerful record with a punchy, electric sound that suits Monty surprisingly well, especially when he is mixed forward and gated quite sharply on the recording. The legendary Ernest Ranglin is part of the group, chuffing out shuffle rhythms and reggae chords with no apparent effort, and every now and then punctuating a line with what seems to be pure sound, harmonically unrelated to what he's playing. It would be fascinating to hear the rehearsal tapes and alternatives from these sessions; our assumption is that they must be much rougher (in an entirely positive sense) and more exploratory than the rather polished final product. *Yard Movement* is a more compelling and authentic record than the later tribute to the music of Bob Marley, but it does rely on uneasy stylistic compromise.

****(*) To The Ends Of The Earth**

Concord CCD 4221 *Alexander; Antonio Hart (as); Bernard Montgomery (hca); Ira Coleman (b); Idris Muhammad (d); Derek Oscenzo (steel d, g).* 96.

A curious *mésalliance*, with Hart going off on his own thang, seemingly impervious to the groove established by the pianist and his Caribbean cohorts. The Ivory and Steel concept now sounds a little dated, and Alexander's attempts to keep it fresh with new infusions of jazz juice are not quite working.

*****(*) Echos Of Jilly's**

Concord CCD 4769 *Alexander; John Patitucci (b); Troy Davis (d).* 97.

Thirty years after he first moved to New York from his first exile in Miami, Alexander meditates on the legacy of Jilly's most famous habitué. By the start of the last year of his life, jazz tributes to Frank Sinatra were becoming more frequent. Having played at the club himself, Alexander could claim a closeness of connection few others had and there is something about this session which recalls those years with exceptional vividness. It's partly the nicotine blue of the piano lines, partly the choice of Sinatra-connected material; but more importantly it's an attitude that hovers between aggression and devil-may-care relaxation. 'Strangers In The Night' comes from later in Frank's career, but it's full of that dry, threatening spirit. An exceptional record, from a musician whose shifts of identity and changeable solidarities have done him no favours. This is his most effective turf.

*****(*) Concord Jazz Heritage Series: Monty Alexander**

Concord CCD 4812 *As above.* 79–97.

A useful sampling of Monty's Concord years, with an emphasis on mid-paced swingers and familiar themes. A good introduction to the artist's work.

***** Stir It Up: The Music Of Bob Marley**

Telarc 83469 *Alexander; Steve Turre (tb); Dwight Dawes (ky); Robert Angus, Daniel Dicenzo (g); Glen Browne, Tony MacKenzie, Hassan J.J Wiggins (b); Troy Davis, Sly Dunbar, Rolando Wilson (d).* 99.

This is one of those rare jazz albums that simply flew off the shelves, thanks largely to the composer. It's not, to be frank, particularly strong, though there are some excellent set-pieces, like Steve Turre's solos on 'I Shot The Sheriff', which is taken at real high-speed pursuit pace and 'Running Away' (ditto). The title-track is very good, and more than one critic has rightly pointed out the debt to Ahmad Jamal. Indeed, the whole set smacks of the pop covers of an earlier day. Pointless to be snobbish about it, but Alexander has created a rod for his own back by combining a jazz trio with the Jamaican members of the Gumption Band, who know this stuff like the back of their hands and aren't going to let some bunch of jazzers steal it away from them.

The acid test was always going to be 'No Woman, No Cry' and it is a very strong performance, with Monty turning in some of his most compelling playing on an otherwise rather anonymous set. Mostly, though, the two rhythm sections cancel one another out and Monty is left to pick over rather unadorned melody lines. The album also includes a reworking of 'Could You Be Loved' by the legendary Sly Dunbar who, to his credit, puts heart and soul into his cameo.

Rashied Ali (born 1935)

DRUMS

The former Robert Patterson played R&B in his native Philadelphia before moving to New York, where he became involved in the avant-garde and came within the orbit of John Coltrane, in whose group he succeeded his own greatest influence, Elvin Jones. After Trane's death, Ali continued to work in the master's shadow, developing his little-understood rhythmic ideas. Ali founded his own record label and started his own jazz club.

*****(*) New Directions In Modern Music**

Knit Classics KCR 3022 *Ali; Carlos Ward (as, f); Fred Simmons (p); Stafford James (b).* 71.

***** Duo Exchange**

Knit Classics KCR3022 *Ali; Frank Lowe (ts).* 72.

*****(*) Swift Are The Winds Of Life**

Knit Classics KCR 3026 *Ali; Leroy Jenkins (vn).* 73.

Ali's Survival records was shorter-lived in the event than his club, Ali's Alley, but, thanks to the offices of Knit Media, an offshoot of Knitting Factory, the label's catalogue is available again. *New Directions* is curiously reminiscent of some of Paul Motian's earlier projects, except that the musical temperature is very much higher. Simmons was a spectacularly good pianist in those days and his interaction with Ward is worth listening to. Rashied is in cracking form, as he is in duet with Lowe, one of a number of occasions when he tried to recapture the dynamic of his *Interstellar Space* dialogues with John Coltrane. Lowe is more angular and harmonically less sophisticated, but the dynamics are imaginatively handled throughout.

The duets with Jenkins are more richly textured, and Leroy's biting tone and ability to slide at incredible speed between pitches even more forcefully recalls the Coltrane duos. The sound is better on this record than on the collaboration with Lowe, with the drums miked well forward but not so dominantly as to overpower the strings.

*****(*) Rashied Ali Quintet**

Knit Classics KCR 3021 *Ali; Earl Cross (t); Bob Ralston (ts); James Blood Ulmer (g); John Dana (b).* 73.

Leaving Blood Ulmer to fill in the middle and bottom on their first encounter, Ali goes for glory on a packed set of fierce free jazz. The guitarist's R&B and funk background is turned to signal advantage when Ali goes entirely outside the pulse, leaving guitar and horns to accompany him.

*****(*) Peace On Earth**

Knitting Factory 158 *Ali; Allan Chase (ss, as); John Zorn (as); Louis Belogenis (ts); Joe Gallant, William Parker (b).* 94.

***** Meditations**

Knitting Factory 180 *As above, except omit Parker, Zorn; add Greg Murphy (p).* 6/95.

***** Bells**

Knitting Factory 190 *As above.* 5/96.

This is the band which went out as Prima Materia, but on these records there is no doubting that it is Ali's project and that once again it is devoted to the memory and music of John Coltrane. Five of Trane's themes – 'Spiritual', 'Peace On Earth', 'Brazilia', 'Alabama' and 'India' – are treated at some length on the 1994 disc, and another five on *Meditations*, which even reduplicates the title of one of Trane's finest Impulse! sets. As ever, Zorn is revelatory on saxophone and it is a pity that he was not heard throughout the session. Parker and Gallant do their damnedest to sound like Garrison and Workman, and the two main saxophonists more than hold their own in territory which must instil as much anxiety as excitement in reed players.

Chase and Belogenis are not so comfortable on the second album, which digs into some of Trane's darker and more spiritually troublesome compositions, 'The Father And The Son And The Holy Ghost', 'Consequences' and 'Compassion'. Ali is as exciting as ever, but there is a thinness of conception that will trouble Coltrane loyalists.

With *Bells*, attention shifted to the even more discomfiting legacy of Albert Ayler. There was a huge market for this kind of retrospective avant-gardism in the mid-'90s and it's hard to avoid the feeling that the music has been stretched out and diluted for a less adventurous generation of listeners for whom the frissons of the avant-garde contain more recognition than surprise. That said, the band play very well and there is no mistaking the raw excitement of Ayler's original themes, which are all preserved more or less intact. As was to be the case three years later on their duo record, most of the excitement is generated between Ali and Belogenis, but Murphy is a compelling player in a Cecil Taylor mould, and Chase has a convincingly abrasive attack.

***** Rings Of Saturn**

Knitting Factory 232 *Ali; Louis Belogenis (ts).* 5/99.

Yet another attempt to capture the magic of *Interstellar Space*, but this time with the added fillip of one of the themes – 'Saturn' – from that modern classic as well as another Coltrane composition, 'Seraphic Light'. Belogenis is little known outside New York, but his discipleship to Coltrane is tempered by a hard, dry and very individual sound that perhaps owes even more to Ornette Coleman. Long originals like 'Mahakala' and 'Takedawitcha' are consistently compelling and the studio sound, reminiscent of CIMP's warts-and-all approach, gives the album an involving physicality.

Beppe Aliprandi

ALTO AND TENOR SAXOPHONES, FLUTE

Based in Milan, Aliprandi is by now a veteran of Italy's post-bop movement with occasional recordings as a leader.

***** Jazz Academy Trio**

Splasc(h) 397-2 *Aliprandi; Roberto Piccolo (b); Ferdinando Farao (d).* 10/91.

***** Blue Flowers**

Splasc(h) 470-2 *Aliprandi; Karl Berger (vib, p); Piero Leveratto (b); Aldo Romano (d).* 6/95.

Aliprandi's dry sound on the alto has a hollow-eyed quality that seems to impart a ghostly feel to his playing. *Jazz Academy Trio* puts him in front of a sympathetic rhythm section that do little more than sketch out a gently swinging background for his small tunes and puckish melodies. He is one of the few saxophonists who seem to draw a direct inspiration from the sound and stylings of Ornette Coleman: 'Dove Ti Ho Incontrata' sounds like the son of 'Ramblin'', and his legato wail and forlorn twists of melody seem born from Ornette's own meanderings. This is a pleasing set that speaks its unorthodox ways very quietly.

Blue Flowers puts him to work with a more renowned group, yet the results have the same quality of introspection and slightly querulous invention. Berger is an old acquaintance and they make a rather good team. When Aliprandi picks up the tenor (or the wood flute) he seems a lot less distinctive; but he sticks mostly to the alto and creates another group of odd, fidgety solos out of his material.

Jan Allan (born 1934)

TRUMPET

Began as a pianist but switched to trumpet as his main instrument in the 1950s. Worked in the Carl-Henrik Norin orchestra, then in numerous small groups with his contemporaries. Also holds a doctor's degree in particle physics.

♛ ** Jan Allan – 70**

Phono Suecia PSCD 130 *Allan; Lennart Axelsson, Weine Renliden, Bertil Lövgren, Rolf Ericson (t); Olle Holmqvist, George Vernon, Jörgen Johansson (tb); Olle Lind (btb); Sven-Ake Landström, Bengt Belfrage (frhn); Arne Domnérus (as); Lennart Aberg (ts, ss, f); Claes Rosendahl (ts, f); Bern Rosengren (ts); Bengt Christianson, Jerker Halldén (f, picc); Nils Lindberg, Bobo Stenson (p); Rune Gustafsson (g); Palle Danielsson, Roman Dylag (b); Egil Hohansen, Jon Christensen (d); Rupert Clemendore (perc).* 12/68–9/69.

*****(*) Sweet And Lovely**

Dragon DRCD 254 *Allan; Rune Gustafsson (g); Georg Riedel (b).* 3/92.

Allan's small number of records as a leader is an inadequate showing for one of the most eminent Swedish modernists: poised between a cool lyricism and a bashful affection for the long melodic line, the trumpeter's unfussy and effortless playing refuses to draw attention to itself.

His finest hour stretches back more than 30 years, to the marvellous *Jan Allan – 70*, released at last on CD. There are two small-group scores by Carl-Axel Dominique and one piece by Palle Danielsson, but the main focus of the record is on the three superlative scores by Nils Lindberg, 'Polska With Trumpet', 'Ballad For Trumpet' and 'Rolf Billberg In Memoriam'. Lindberg's writing is full of almost Byzantine detail at times, yet the music flows along without any difficulty and the sonorities of brass and woodwind are richly compelling. 'Polska With Trumpet' sparkles with rhythmic and harmonic invention and the 'Ballad' is serenely beautiful, but it's the deeply felt and profoundly moving dedication to Rolf Billberg that brings out the best in composer, soloist and orchestra. In what might almost be an answer record to the likes of *Miles Ahead*, Allan refuses to preen or overplay: his solos are part of a genuine dialogue with the orchestra, and he never loses his way or seems unsettled by such a demanding opportunity. A record that should be in every collection.

A long jump from there to *Sweet And Lovely*. Here, with two very old friends, he sketches a sequence of wonderful miniatures. Since Lars Gullin, Reinhold Svensson and Jan Johansson – three major contemporaries of Allan's – are all represented as composers, the record also stands as a meditation on the achievements (still sorely undervalued) of one of the great schools of modern jazz in Europe. Some may be reminded of many of Chet Baker's later sessions; but Allan, Gustafsson and Riedel, all in prime, easy-going form, sustain the flow of these 14 tunes with few difficulties.

Carl Allen (born 1958)

DRUMS

Born in Milwaukee, Allen began working with such experienced leaders as Freddie Hubbard and Jackie McLean before freelancing as a New York-based drummer.

***** Piccadilly Square**

Timeless SJP 406 *Allen; Roy Hargrove, Freddie Hubbard (t); Vincent Herring (ss, as, f); Donald Brown (p); Ira Coleman (b).* 12/89.

*****(*) The Dark Side Of Dewey**

Evidence ECD 22138-2 *Allen; Nicholas Payton (t); Vincent Herring (ss, as); Mulgrew Miller (p); Dwayne Burno (b).* 1/92.

***** The Pursuer**

Atlantic 82572-2 *Allen; Marcus Printup (t); Steve Turre (tb, shells); Vincent Herring (ss, as); Teodross Avery (ss, ts); George Coleman (ts); Ed Simon (p); Ben Wolfe (b).* 9/93.

***** Testimonial**

Atlantic 82755-2 *Allen; Nicholas Payton (t); Vincent Herring (ss, as); Cyrus Chestnut (p, org); Anthony Wonsey (p); Mark Whitfield (g); Christian McBride, Reuben Rogers (b); Daniel Sadownick (perc); Kevin Mahogany (v).* 12/94.

Polished, inventive music from drummer Allen and a stellar personnel mustered across all four discs. *Piccadilly Square* is a muscle-flexing show by all hands: Hubbard sits in on two tunes (to no great effect) and it's Hargrove and Herring who light the flares on chestnuts like 'What's New' and 'Lullaby Of Birdland'. Nothing extraordinary here, but there's some exciting music. Better still is *The Dark Side Of Dewey*, since it catches the young Payton at an undecided stage of his development – the more traditional side of his style gets eschewed here in favour of a boppish delivery – and the subtext of a Miles Davis tribute throws up some interestingly dark performances in 'All Blues' and the title-piece. Miller, always a guarantee of gravitas, is typically regal at the keyboard.

The Pursuer is modern bop delivered with a steely, notably aggressive stance: the title-piece, 'Hidden Agenda' and 'A Difference Of Opinion' are bruisers, though Herring's soprano feature, 'Alternative Thoughts', settles things down and the horn arrangements are thoughtfully prepared. Avery is good, but everyone is smoked by the tremendous Coleman on his one appearance. *Testimonial* is much more good-humoured and to that degree a little less exciting. 'Foot Pattin'' and 'Storefront Revival' are sanctified interludes in which Allen duets with Chestnut on organ, and 'Tuesday Night Prayer Meeting' and 'A City Called Heaven' continue the theme with mixed results. Nothing tops the opener, a leisurely but handsomely realized version of 'Come Sunday' where everyone shines. Allen himself throttles back a little at the drums. Enjoyable stuff.

Geri Allen (born 1957)

PIANO, SYNTHESIZER

Studied piano as a child, then later taught in Washington, DC, before moving to New York in 1980. Associated with the M-Base Collective early on, but came to work in a broad variety of contexts and has recorded for Blue Note and Verve as a leader.

***** The Printmakers**

Minor Music 8001 *Allen; Anthony Cox (b); Andrew Cyrille (d).* 2/84.

*****(*) Home Grown**

Minor Music 8004 *Allen (p solo).* 1/85.

To suggest that Geri Allen is something of an enigma is not to withdraw our earlier enthusiasm for her work. She is a formidable technician, drawing elements from all over the modern piano tradition – Bud Powell, Monk, tinges of Cecil Taylor, less celebrated figures like Herbie Nichols and Mary Lou Williams – and from non-pianists like Eric Dolphy, whose spiky, restless ideas are also reflected in her writing. And yet, for all this creative weaponry, there is something unaccountably soft-centred, almost whimsical about much of Allen's work under her own name. And therein lies the puzzle, for Allen has often seemed a more confident and accomplished performer on other leaders' dates than on her own.

Though she hasn't documented much solo performance, *Home Grown* is by far the more interesting of the two early discs. Minor is not just the label, but also a clue to the basic tonality; not much light to go with the shade, but certainly the most revealing and unselfconscious homage to Allen's influences, with two Monk tunes and a rather poignant version of 'Alone Together'. *The Printmakers* had been more ambitious, in terms both of structure and of integration of avant-garde gestures, but, Cyrille's vigorous presence aside, gestures they remain. The album has a slightly faded quality, as if it were itself a thinly inked print of something much more definite and emphatic. The talent and the urgency are both unquestionable. The execution is not quite convincing.

*****(*) Etudes**

Soul Note 121162 *Allen; Charlie Haden (b); Paul Motian (d).* 9/87.

***** Segments**

DIW 833 *As above.* 4/89.

****** Live At The Village Vanguard**

DIW 847 *As above.* 90.

These are the records which seem to confirm, both positively and negatively, our feeling that Allen fares better when relieved of leadership. She was officially guest soloist with the veteran Haden/Motian team, but hogged the praise for *Etudes* so completely that she was officially inducted into the freemasonry, immediately losing the freshness and the spontaneity that had made the 1987 record so striking. *Segments* was in every way a disappointment, and all too appropriately titled, a collection of bits rather than a convincing whole. The title-piece, 'Segment', is a Charlie Parker tune from 1949, and it's probably the best thing on the set because it gets the same unfussy treatment as nearly all the pieces on the Village Vanguard set.

Allen's approach to bebop is sufficiently original to carry the day, tinged with sardonic humour and a great sense of fun. It shines through on the live album, on which she's rather better recorded than her partners, and on tunes like Herbie Nichols's 'Shuffle Montgomery', an Allen favourite and the stand-out track on *Etudes*.

***** Some Aspects Of Water**

Storyville STCD 4212 *Allen; Johnny Coles (flhn); Henrik Bolberg Pedersen (t, flhn); Kjeld Ipsen (tb); Axel Windfeld (tba); Michael Hove (as, f, cl); Uffe Markussen (ts, ss, bcl, f); Palle Danielsson (b); Lenny White (d).* 3/96.

The Danish Jazz Centre gave Allen the 1996 Jazzpar Prize, a striking acknowledgement of her growing international reputation. The payback was a pair of concerts which were to include a commissioned work – the long title-piece here – and to involve a contingent of Scandinavian players.

The Copenhagen performance included long trio versions of Allen compositions, 'Skin' and 'Feed The Fire', with a flowing rendition of the Jules Styne and Sammy Cahn classic, 'A Beautiful Friendship', once again underlining how insecure Allen can still be on standards; she plays as if she understands the chords but has only recently heard the melody for the first time. Danielsson and White are both excellent. Wallace Roney was supposed to have guested with the trio but was detained on his own tour. Taking his place, the veteran Johnny Coles hijacks 'Old Folks' with his warm, buttery tone and unhurryable approach. To her credit, Allen enjoys the moment for what it is and shows no signs of wanting to recapture the spotlight.

The commissioned piece is a multi-part suite that sounds as if it had been assembled out of a good many sketchy ideas in Allen's workbasket. It certainly isn't incoherent (Allen is now far too consistent a stylist for that) but the title gives away the essentially episodic character. Coles is again the star and there is an excellent bass clarinet passage from Uffe Markussen, who is also a featured soloist on 'Smooth Attitudes', a piece commissioned for the nonet from Jens Winther, an earlier Jazzpar artist.

Allen's own contributions are gracefully Ellingtonian, but not quite arresting enough to secure ownership in a competent group performance, not quite note-perfect but accomplished enough, given limited rehearsal time and unfamiliar charts.

****** The Gathering**

Verve 557642-2 *Allen; Wallace Roney, Wallace Roney Jr (t); Robin Eubanks (tb); Dwight Andrews (picc, af, bf, bcl); Vernon Reid (g); Ralphe Armstrong, Buster Williams (b); Lenny White (d); Mino Cinelu (perc); Laila Roney (v).*

Touched by the hand of Teo Macero, *The Gathering* is Allen's most completely satisfying record to date. The writing is a synthesis of many of the ideas that have fed into her work over the past decade and some that seem to have been almost deliberately excluded. It is certainly the most textural album she has attempted, marked by wonderful things from Reid and multi-instrumentalist Andrews. The real revelation, though, is White, who creates a crisp and urgent pulse from the opening track. On the trio cuts with Allen and the bassist, he generates a com-plex signature that suggests the presence of another Williams altogether, the late, lamented Tony, but overall the approach is closer to that of Paul Motian.

Allen's phrasing has never been more relaxed or suffused with greater feeling. On 'Sleepin' Pretty', she glides over an evocative landscape of bass and bass clarinet, quoting Mary Lou Williams in passing. 'Ray' varies the line-up by substituting Reid and Cinelu for the more orthodox rhythm section. Roney and Eubanks are deployed quite sparingly but to maximum effect. The trumpeter grows mellower by the session and these days favours a burnished middle register and patiently articulated statements in place of the fire and vim of his own early records. There is even time for a family session on 'Angels', with Wally Jr making his trumpet debut and the charming Laila contributing a sweet vocal. This is the record Allen has threatened to make for some years. Underneath the gentleness one detects a fine musical mind which is only just limbering up for a new stage of development.

Harry Allen (born 1966)

TENOR SAXOPHONE

Born in Washington, DC, Allen studied at Rutgers in New Jersey and was soon hanging out in jazz clubs. He has been lionized as a young mainstreamer and plays in the manner of the swing masters rather than in the post-Coltrane idiom of his contemporaries.

****(*) How Long Has This Been Going On?**

Progressive 7082 *Allen; Keith Ingham (p); Major Holley (b); Oliver Jackson (d).* 6/88.

***** Someone To Light Up My Life**

Mastermix CHECD 00100 *Allen; John Horler (p); Peter Morgan (b); Oliver Jackson (d).*

***** I Know That You Know**

Mastermix CHECD 00104 *Allen; John Colianni (p); Michael Moore (b).* 1/92.

***** I'll Never Be The Same**

Mastermix CHECD 00106 *Allen; Howard Alden (g); Simon Woolf (b).* 11/92.

*****(*) Jazz Im Amerika Haus Vol. 1**

Nagel-Heyer 011 *Allen; John Bunch (p); Dennis Irwin (b); Duffy Jackson (d).* 5/94.

Allen has been acclaimed by an audience waiting for the Four Brothers to come back, if not the big bands. His full-blooded tenor sound offers countless tugs of the forelock to Zoot, Lester, Hawkins and whichever other standard-issue swing tenor one can think of; and it's hardly surprising that these enjoyable records have been given the kind of approbation that was heaped on the early Scott Hamilton albums. Allen plays nothing but standards, delivers them with a confidence and luxuriance that belie his then twenty-something age, and generally acts as if Coltrane and Coleman had never appeared at all. On their own terms, there is much to enjoy in all these records: the two earlier discs are a little too stratified by tenor-and-rhythm clichés but, by cannily removing any sign of a drummer on the later records, Allen frees himself up just enough to suggest that he might eventually do more than act the young fogey. Certainly the interplay with Alden, who has also found a way of investing more of himself into mainstream vocabulary, offers some piquant moments.

Allen has been doing some solid sideman duty of late, but his entry in the *Jazz Im Amerika Haus* series suggests that he's getting more authoritative all the time. His improvisation on 'Deed I Do' has a steamrollering sense of swing, and he's sewing phrases and licks together with the kind of assurance once associated with Zoot Sims. Since the rhythm section goes along with the same ineluctable purpose, this has to go down as Allen's best to this point.

***** A Night At Birdland Vol. 1**

Nagel-Heyer 007 *Allen; Randy Sandke (t); Brian Dee (p); Len Skeat (b); Oliver Jackson (d).* 11/93.

***** A Night At Birdland Vol. 2**

Nagel-Heyer 010 *As above.* 11/93.

***** Live At Renouf's**

Mastermix CHECD 00117 *Allen; John Colianni (p); Phil Flanigan (b); Duffy Jackson (d).* 8/96.

***** The Music Of The Trumpet Kings**

Nagel-Heyer 037 *Allen; Randy Sandke, Greg Bowen, Dieter Bilsheim, Till Bronner, Christian Grabandt (t); Thomas Loup, John Marshall, Soren Fischer, Andy Grossman (tb); Norbert Nagel, Klaus Marmulla (as); Walter Gauchel, Gregoire Peters (ts); Helmut Wenzel (bs); Ingo Cramer (g); Kai Rautenberg (p); Hajo Lange (b); Holger Nell (d).* 11/96.

*****(*) A Little Touch Of Harry**

Mastermix CHECD 00118 *Allen; Kenny Barron (p); George Mraz (b); Al Foster (d).* 97.

At this rate, Allen will have more albums even than Scott Hamilton to his name. He is clearly a favourite of the Nagel-Heyer set-up, and the two Birdland (Hamburg, not New York) sessions will be snapped up by the label's genre devotees. The rhythm section is perhaps no more than adequate, though Jackson, on some of his final recordings, seems enlivened by the situation, and interest centres on the two principals: Allen doesn't quite have Sandke's catholicity of taste, but they strike some pleasing sparks. The second shades out the first, though one disc from two might have been a better bet anyway. The *Trumpet Kings* session is really more Sandke's than Allen's, even though the tenorman's name comes first on the sleeve. Sandke arranged nearly all the charts for the RIAS Big Band of Berlin, and he and Allen are the featured soloists. It's intriguing to hear a discovery attributed to Beiderbecke, 'Cloudy', on which Allen rather than Sandke solos; and 'The Moontrane' and 'All Blues' are more modern pieces that go well enough, though the Band sound over-bright and over-eager in their delivery.

The quartet format is where Allen's destiny lies. *Live At Renouf's* is blemished by a very thin and clinky-sounding piano, and there's too much space for bass solos. But Allen himself, though he takes some of his ballad statements far too slowly, sounds imperious. The way he flies through 'The Man I Love' is almost boppish in its fleet intensity. He likes to stretch out, and he can make it work for him. The studio date is more contained in that respect. It also has far and away the best rhythm section he's ever worked with, and a thoughtful blend of familiar and more elusive standards. One point away from the masterpiece he may have in him.

*****(*) Harry Allen Meets The John Pizzarelli Trio**
BMG Novus 74321 37397-2 *Allen; Ray Kennedy (p); John Pizzarelli (g); Martin Pizzarelli (b).* 12/95.

*****(*) Tenors Anyone?**
BMG Novus 74321 50684-2 *As above.* 11/96.

Recorded by Ikuyoshi Hirakawa, initially for Japanese release, these meetings with the Pizzarelli trio are so affably swinging that they play through without a murmur of dissent from us. The impression they offer is of smart young professionals, absolutely in love with this music but unafraid to stamp themselves on what's often deemed to be a conservative idiom. To pick one instance, listen to the joyful romp through 'I Want To Be Happy' on the first disc. Allen's tone isn't always as conventionally lovely as you'd expect – he isn't really a breathy Webster type, and his ballads are leaner and a little quirkier than is at first noticeable. Pizzarelli is temperamentally akin, and his trio are a great team to have comping behind you. Soundwise, the second date is that bit fuller and livelier.

*****(*) Night Birds**
Gemini GMCD 95 *Allen; George Masso (tb); Totti Bergh (ss, ts); Per Husby (p); Bjørn Alterhaug (b); Per Hulten (d).* 8/97.

Recorded on a stopover in Oslo, Allen guests with some distinguished locals, as well as fellow visitor George Masso. Light and polite, but very pleasantly done, and there are some nice features – above all, Bergh's treatment of 'Don't Explain', with a quite superb introduction from Husby.

*****(*) Eu Não Quero Dança – I Won't Dance**
RCA Victor 74321 58126-2 *Allen; Larry Goldings (p); Dori Caymmi (g, v); Joe Cohn (g); Dennis Irwin (b); Duduka Fonseca (d); Maucha Adnet (v).* 12/97.

****** Day Dream**
RCA Victor 74321 67152-2 *Allen; Tommy Flanagan (p); Peter Washington (b); Lewis Nash (d).* 9/98.

For a change of pace, Allen did a sort of bossa nova album in *I Won't Dance* – sort of, because he swings it a lot harder than Getz chose to. Instead of the melodies billowing off balmy breezes, there's the odd tropical storm along the way, and it's an agreeable variation on what might have been expected. 'Desafinado', for instance, is given the office by Fonseca, and Adner's vocal is darker than Astrud Gilberto ever sounded. A good record, but *Day Dream* looks like the one set up to be a definitive statement, and it's hard to argue with the results. Flanagan is still one of the best people to have in this situation, and the unfussy elegance of his style is a handsome fit with Allen's own demeanour. Bass and drums sit out on every other selection through the programme, and the five duets are beautifully handled by both men, measured and unsentimental. Washington and Nash lend a snap and immediacy that has been missing from some of Allen's other rhythm sections, and the sheer classy ebullience of 'I'm Checking Out, Goombye' hits a peak that Harry's often even-tempered records rarely find. In other words, four stars.

Henry 'Red' Allen (1908–67)

TRUMPET, VOCAL

Born in New Orleans, Allen's father ran a renowned brass band and he became a trumpeter himself. Joined King Oliver in 1927, then (in New York) Luis Russell in 1929 and Fletcher Henderson in 1933. He recorded extensively as a small-group leader in the 1930s and '40s, and managed to work through the '50s and early '60s in the same format, despite the depressed state of traditional jazz. He remained an idiosyncratic, unique stylist and was fêted as an avant-garde player by the young trumpeter, Don Ellis. He died from cancer in 1967, following a final European tour.

****** Henry 'Red' Allen & His Orchestra 1929–1933**
Classics 540 *Allen; Otis Johnson (t); J.C Higginbotham, Jimmy Archey, Dicky Wells, Benny Morton (tb); Charlie Holmes (cl, ss, as); Russell Procope, Edward Inge, Albert Nicholas, William Blue (cl, as); Hilton Jefferson (as); Teddy Hill (cl, ts); Coleman Hawkins, Greely Walton (ts); Luis Russell (p, cel); Don Kirkpatrick, Horace Henderson (p); Will Johnson (bj, g, v); Bernard Addison (g); Bob Ysaguirre, Pops Foster (bb, b); Ernest Hill (bb); Walter Johnson, Manzie Johnson, Paul Barbarin (d); Victoria Spivey, The Four Wanderers (v).* 7/29–11/33.

*****(*) Henry Allen Collection Vol. 1**
Collector's Classics COCD 1 *Allen; Jimmy Lord (cl); Pee Wee Russell (cl, ts); Joe Sullivan, Fats Waller (p); Eddie Condon (bj); Jack Bland (g); Al Morgan, Pops Foster (b); Zutty Singleton (d); Billy Banks (v).* 4–10/32.

***** Henry 'Red' Allen–Coleman Hawkins 1933**
Hep 1028 *As above, except add Russell Smith, Bobby Stark (t), Claude Jones (tb), John Kirby (b); omit Blue, Johnson, Higginbotham, Archey, Russell, Holmes, Walton, Johnson, Foster, Barbarin, Spivey.* 3–10/33.

****** Henry 'Red' Allen 1929–1936**

Jazz Classics In Digital Stereo RPCD 610 *Allen; plus groups led by Fats Waller, Luis Russell, Billy Banks, Walter Pichon, Spike Hughes, Horace Henderson, Benny Morton, Mills Blue Rhythm Band.* 29–36.

Henry Allen was once described as 'the last great trumpet soloist to come out of New Orleans', but that was before Wynton Marsalis and his followers. He was, though, the last to make a mark on the 1920s, recording his astonishing debut sessions as a leader for Victor in the summer of 1929 and immediately causing a stir. The four tracks are 'It Should Be You', 'Biff'ly Blues', 'Feeling Drowsy' and 'Swing Out', magnificently conceived and executed jazz, with the whole band – actually the nucleus of the Luis Russell Orchestra, where Allen had already set down some superb solos – playing with outstanding power and finesse, while Allen's own improvisations outplay any trumpeter of the day aside from Louis Armstrong. While his playing is sometimes a little unfocused, Allen's ideas usually run together with few seams showing, and the controlled strength of his solo on 'Feeling Drowsy' is as impressive as the more daring flights of 'Swing Out'. The beautifully sustained solo on 'Make A Country Bird Fly Wild' sees him through a tricky stop-time passage and shows how he was both like and unlike Armstrong: there's the same rhythmic chance-taking and nobility of tone, but Allen is often less predictable than Armstrong and can shy away from the signalled high notes which Louis always aimed at. He can even suggest a faintly wistful quality in an otherwise heated passage. The tracks for Victor, though, are abetted by his choice of companions: Higginbotham is wonderfully characterful on trombone, agile but snarlingly expressive, and the vastly underrated Charlie Holmes matches the young Johnny Hodges for a hard-hitting yet fundamentally lyrical alto style. Foster and Barbarin, too, are exceptionally swinging. This was an outstanding band which should have made many more records than it did.

The Classics CD omits the alternative takes which filled up the earlier edition on JSP (currently deleted) and carries on through the first sessions by the Allen–Coleman Hawkins Orchestra. Both men were then working with Fletcher Henderson, and this could have been an explosive combination, but their records are comparatively tame, with pop-tune material and Allen's admittedly engaging vocals taking up a lot of space. The Hep CD includes all the Allen–Hawkins tracks (the final three are on the next Classics disc) and adds the 1933 session under Horace Henderson's leadership, which includes what might be the most swinging 'Ol' Man River' on record and a splendid feature for Hawkins in 'I've Got To Sing A Torch Song'. Excellent remastering here: the Classics CD is patchy in comparison but most will find it very listenable. The first volume of the Collector's Classics edition brings together all the tracks released under the nominal leadership of Billy Banks and Jack Bland; if you can stomach Banks's singing, there's some very hot playing from what is basically an Eddie Condon group. Superb transfers.

Robert Parker's Jazz Classics compilation fills in some useful gaps – the very obscure session with the vaudeville singer Walter Pichon, for instance, and a date under Benny Morton's leadership – and picks some favourites by the Luis Russell band and Allen's own groups. A useful supplement to the Classics series, although concentrating on all the otherwise unavailable titles would have made it even more collectable. Parker's resonant transfers may not appeal to all, but they're very wide-ranging in their sonic detail.

***** Henry 'Red' Allen 1933–1935**

Classics 551 *Allen; Pee Wee Irwin (t); J.C Higginbotham, Dicky Wells, Benny Morton, Keg Johnson, George Washington (tb); Buster Bailey, Cecil Scott, Albert Nicholas (cl); Edward Inge (cl, as); Hilton Jefferson (as); Coleman Hawkins, Chu Berry (ts); Horace Henderson (p); Bernard Addison (bj, g); Lawrence Lucie (g); Bob Ysaguirre (bb); John Kirby (b, bb); Elmer James, Pops Foster (b); Manzie Johnson, Kaiser Marshall, Walter Johnson, Paul Barbarin, George Stafford (d).* 11/33–7/35.

***** Henry Allen Collection Vol. 2**

Collector's Classics COCD 2 *Similar to above.* 10/32–7/35.

***** Henry 'Red' Allen 1935–1936**

Classics 575 *Allen; J.C Higginbotham (tb); Albert Nicholas (cl); Rudy Powell, Hildred Humphries (cl, as); Cecil Scott (cl, ts); Pete Clark, Tab Smith (as); Happy Caldwell, Joe Garland, Ted McRae (ts); Edgar Hayes, Norman Lester, Jimmy Reynolds, Clyde Hart (p); Lawrence Lucie (g); Elmer James, John Kirby (b); O'Neil Spencer, Cozy Cole, Walter Johnson (d).* 11/35–8/36.

***** Henry Allen Collection Vol. 3**

Collector's Classics COCD 10 *Similar to above.* 35–36.

***** Henry 'Red' Allen 1936–1937**

Classics 590 *Allen; Gene Mikell, Buster Bailey, Glyn Paque (cl); Tab Smith (as); Ted McRae, Sonny Fredericks, Harold Arnold (ts); Clyde Hart, Billy Kyle, Luis Russell (p); Danny Barker (g); John Kirby, John Williams (b); Cozy Cole, Alphonse Steele, Paul Barbarin (d).* 10/36–4/37.

***** Henry Allen Collection Vol. 4**

Collector's Classics COCD 15 *Similar to above.* 10/36–6/37.

*****(*) Henry 'Red' Allen 1937–1941**

Classics 628 *Allen; Benny Morton, J.C Higginbotham (tb); Glyn Paque, Edmond Hall (cl); Tab Smith (as); Harold Arnold, Sammy Davis (ts); Luis Russell, Billy Kyle, Lil Armstrong, Kenny Kersey (p); Danny Barker, Bernard Addison (g); John Williams, Pops Foster, Billy Taylor (b); Paul Barbarin, Alphonse Steele, Zutty Singleton, Jimmy Hoskins (d).* 6/37–7/41.

*****(*) Henry Allen Collection Vol. 5**

Collector's Classics COCD 23 *As above.* 9/37–7/41.

***** Henry Allen Collection Vol. 6**

Collector's Classics COCD 24 *Allen; J.C Higginbotham (tb); Edmond Hall (cl); Don Stovall (as); Kenny Kersey, Al Williams, Bill Thompson (p); Billy Taylor, Clarence Moten (b); Jimmy Hoskins, Alvin Burroughs, Eddie Bourne (d).* 4/41–7/46.

***** Henry 'Red' Allen 1944–1947**

Classics 1067 *As above, except add Buster Bailey (cl), Johnny Guarnieri (p), Roy Ross (acc).* 5/44–3/47.

***** Original 1933–1941 Recordings**

Tax S-3-2 *As above Classics discs.* 33–41.

****** Swing Out**

Topaz TPZ 1037 *As above discs, plus tracks with Luis Russell, Spike Hughes, King Oliver and Fletcher Henderson.* 29–35.

Maybe Allen was a man out of his time: he arrived just too late to make a significant impact on the first jazz decade, and he had to work through the Depression – and the early part of the swing era – recording what were really novelty small-group sessions, most of which are little-known today. Like Armstrong and Waller, he had to record at least as many bad songs as good ones and, though he was an entertaining singer, he couldn't match either Fats or Louis as master of whatever material came his way. Still, the chronological Classics and Collector's Classics sequences are a valuable and pretty consistent documentation. The groups tend to be rough-and-ready but, whenever he's partnered by the superb Higginbotham, Allen comes up with marvellously exuberant jazz. And sometimes unpromising material releases a classic performance: hear, for instance, the completely wild version of 'Roll Along, Prairie Moon' on Classics 551/COCD 2, in which the trombonist blows such a fine solo that Allen insists on handing over his own solo space. The CDs in the middle of the sequence have too many duff tunes on them, but the 1937–41 set is stronger, since Allen switched labels (to Decca) in 1940 and started recording uncompromised jazz again. Sessions with Ed Hall, Zutty Singleton and Benny Morton are a little too brash, perhaps, but Allen's own playing is stirring throughout.

The Tax CD offers a somewhat mystifying selection of tracks from the period. The sound on all five Classics CDs is mostly very good, with just a few transfers suffering from noticeable blemishes, but they are outdone by the excellent new Collector's Classics edition, which gets our first choice. This has now been extended to six discs. Volume Six is a very erratic set: there's some dispiritingly bad music, such as 'Get The Mop' and 'Drink Hearty', and in general Allen seems a little lost for direction, but a few excellent pieces salvage everything: 'The Crawl', two takes of 'Indiana' and the blues 'Let Me Miss You Baby' which Allen turned into a great set-piece on his 1957 Victor date. Classics 1067 covers much the same ground but adds three tracks from a Saturday Night Swing Session and a sextet date for Apollo from 1947. 'Dark Eyes' and 'Sweet Lorraine' are almost extended trumpet solos by themselves and Bailey gets to do his extravagant thing on 'Indiana'. The Apollo tracks are restrained jump-band music with a lot of mugging on 'Old Fool Do You Know Me?'

The Topaz compilation is a very sensible selection of tracks from Allen's Victors, the Luis Russell band, Oliver, Henderson and Spike Hughes's 'Firebird'. A rounded and exciting portrait of the great stylist, and the transfers are fastidiously done.

****(*) Live, 1965**
Storyville STCD 8290 *Allen; Sam Price, Lannie Scott (p); Clarence Moten (b); George Reed (d).* 6/65.

Allen's best latter-day recordings are out of print, and unless they are restored to CD he will soon be a very distant player. This set from an engagement at a Long Island lounge finds him in good enough late form, but the recording is pretty awful, dropping in and out all the way through, and the group isn't exactly performing with distinction. Better to wait for some of his records for Columbia, RCA and Prestige to return to circulation.

Rex Allen (born 1952)

TROMBONE, VIBES

Born in Pittsburgh, Allen plays the rare double of vibes and trombone. He has led big bands in tribute to Tommy Dorsey, Glen Miller and Gene Krupa.

***** Keep Swingin'**
Nagel-Heyer CD 016 *Allen; Dan Barrett (t); Jim Rothermel (cl, ss, as); Harry Allen (ts); Mark Shane (p); Bucky Pizzarelli (g); Frank Tate (b); Gregor Beck (d); Terrie Richards (v).* 10/94.

Volume Five in Hans Nagel-Heyer's sequence of CDs recorded at Hamburg's Musikhalle features a man who must be one of the few musicians to double on trombone and vibes. Allen leads a group called the Swing Express, and with material like 'Back Bay Shuffle' and 'Opus 1' it's not hard to figure out where his tastes lie. The amazingly versatile Barrett forsakes his more customary trombone for trumpet, Allen is urbanity personified, and Rothermel does equally well on his three horns. There are one or two nice ideas for a tune – Quincy Jones's 'Pleasingly Plump', unheard since Basie days, is one – and if the audience is sometimes a little intrusive, well, everybody was swinging, after all.

Ben Allison

BASS

Bassist at work in the contemporary New York scene.

***** Seven Arrows**
Koch 3-7832-2 *Allison; Ron Horton (t, flhn); Ted Nash (ts, cl, f); Frank Kimbrough (p); Tim Horner (d).* 6/95–4/96.

A few catchy twists make tunes like 'Dragzilla' and 'Cosmic Groove Slinky' stand out from the run of post-bop writing and, though Allison's band of New Yorkers sound less comfortable with the abstract opening of 'Little Boy', this is a thoughtful programme. Nash and Horton are effective without springing any surprises, which is perhaps what the record needs in the end. Allison himself only rarely succumbs to the temptation of featuring himself too strongly.

Mose Allison (born 1927)

PIANO, VOCAL, TRUMPET

The quintessential Mississippi jazzman, Allison learned both piano and trumpet as a child, and soaked up the local black music as well as bebop. He played countless southern gigs before moving to New York in 1956. Though he is a good band pianist and played with Getz, Mulligan and Sims, his principal setting is the piano trio, where he sings the most knowingly world-weary songs over idiosyncratic, bumpy rhythms. A huge influence on many singers, players and songwriters alike, and a special favourite in England.

*****(*) Back Country Suite**
Original Jazz Classics OJC 075 *Allison; Taylor LaFargue (b); Frank Isola (d).* 3/57.

***** Local Color**
Original Jazz Classics OJC 457 *Allison; Addison Farmer (b); Nick Stabulas (d).* 11/57.

*****(*) Autumn Song**
Original Jazz Classics OJC 894 *Allison; Addison Farmer (b); Ronnie Free (d).* 58.

***** Down Home Piano**

Original Jazz Classics OJC 922 *Allison; Addison Farmer (b); Nick Stabulas, Ronnie Free (d).* 58.

*****(*) Creek Bank**

Prestige PRCD-24055-2 *As above.* 1–8/58.

***** Greatest Hits**

Original Jazz Classics OJC 6004 *As above five records.* 3/57–2/59.

****** Sings And Plays**

Prestige CDJZD 007 *As above.* 3/57–2/59.

By the time Mose Allison came to listen to bebop, a little of which creeps into his playing, he was already hooked on the light and steady kind of swing playing that Nat Cole's trio exemplified. Mose has always been a modernist: his hip fatalism and mastery of the wry put-down ('When you're walking your last mile / Baby, don't forget to smile') have always been paired with a vocal style that is reluctantly knowing, as though he tells truths which he has to force out. Coupled with a rhythmically juddering, blues-directed piano manner, he's made sure that there's been no one else quite like him, as influential as he's been.

Back Country Suite, his debut, remains arguably his best record as an instrumentalist and composer: the deft little miniatures which make up the 'suite' are winsome and rocking by turns, and LaFargue and Isola read the leader's moves beautifully. *Local Color* is nearly as good, with a rare glimpse of Allison's muted trumpet on 'Trouble In Mind', an unusual Ellington revival in 'Don't Ever Say Goodbye' and his first and best treatment of Percy Mayfield's 'Lost Mind'. *Autumn Song* is nicely balanced between his vocal set-pieces ('Eyesight To The Blind', one of his classic one-liners) and his 'serious' stuff, with a rare piece of straight bebop in 'Groovin' High'. *Down Home Piano* returns to the countrified feel of *Back Country Suite*, with 'Crepuscular Air', 'Devil In The Cane Field' and 'Mojo Woman' collating another suite's worth of impressionism. *Creek Bank* couples the album of that name with the slightly earlier *Young Man Mose* and is an excellent package: more standards, blues and Allison vignettes in generous playing time. *Greatest Hits* concentrates on Allison the singer/recitalist rather than the pianist/composer: a well-planned selection, but it bows to John Crosby's excellent compilation, *Sings And Plays*, which brings together all his vocal cuts for Prestige as well as ten instrumentals on an excellent-value 23-track CD. It's hard to go wrong with Allison in this period: any of these records will give much pleasure.

*****(*) High Jinks**

Columbia/Epic/Legacy J3K 64275 3CD *Allison; Addison Farmer, Henry Grimes, Aaron Bell, Bill Crow (b); Paul Motian, Jerry Segal, Osie Johnson, Gus Johnson (d).* 12/59–9/60.

Recorded across four different sessions, this three-disc set collects three original LPs – *I Love The Life I Live*, *V-8 Ford Blues* and *The Transfiguration Of Hiram Brown* – and adds a smattering of unreleased extras to each disc. The 'Hiram Brown' suite which takes up half of one of the discs is Allison's best instrumental work outside of the 'Back Country Suite', another tough, charming evocation of country-meets-the-city, while each of the other discs has its share of gems: 'A Pretty Girl Is Like A Melody', 'Life Is Suicide', 'Make Yourself Comfortable'. Nice remastering, a reminiscent note by Mose on each one, and some neat packaging.

****** I Don't Worry About A Thing**

Rhino/Atlantic R2 71417 *Allison; Addison Farmer (b); Osie Johnson (d).* 3/62.

No real change or advance, but this is perhaps the classic Allison album. Here are the first versions of two of his sharpest pieces, 'Your Mind Is On Vacation' and the title-song; one of his best Nat Cole treatments, 'Meet Me At No Special Place'; and three of his own oblique pieces of Americana for piano, bass and drums. Short shrift on playing time, but extra tracks would have spoiled the balance of a marvellous record.

****** The Sage Of Tippo**

32 Jazz 32068 2CD *Allison; Jimmy Knepper (tb); Jimmy Reider (ts); Addison Farmer, Ben Tucker, Earl May, Red Mitchell (b); Frankie Dunlop, Ron Lundberg, Paul Motian, Bill Goodwin (d).* 11/62–7/68.

Bringing together four vintage Atlantics – *Swingin' Machine*, *The Word From Mose*, *Wild Man On The Loose* and *I've Been Doin' Some Thinkin'* – this is an irresistible package for Allison addicts. The earliest session has a surprise bonus in the presence of Knepper and the little-known Reider, both of whom play with just the right measure of mournful drollery that suits the Mose situation. Four different rhythm-sections are all great, and several all-time Mose classics – 'Don't Forget To Smile', 'Your Molecular Structure', 'I'm Not Talking', 'Stop This World' – add up to a must-buy.

***** Middle Class White Boy**

Discovery 71011 *Allison; Joe Farrell (ts, f); Phil Upchurch (g); Putter Smith (b); John Dentz (d); Ron Powell (perc).* 82.

From the first of several 'comebacks', if one can be so impertinent to a timeless warrior. Spoilt by the clanky sound of the Yamaha piano he plays on most of the tracks, perhaps, but this is still buoyed up by some terrific Allisonisms – 'How Does It Feel (To Be Good Looking)?' and 'Hello There, Universe' are but two – and the music is consistently chipper.

***** Ever Since The World Ended**

Blue Note 48015 *Allison; Bob Malach (as, ts); Arthur Blythe (as); Bennie Wallace (ts); Kenny Burrell (g); Dennis Irwin (b); Tom Whaley (d).* 5–6/87.

***** My Backyard**

Blue Note 93840 *Allison; Tony Dagradi (ts); Steve Masakowski (g); Bill Huntington (b); John Vidacovich (d).* 12/89.

***** The Earth Wants You**

Blue Note 827640-2 *Allison; Randy Brecker (t); Joe Lovano (as); Bob Malach (ts); Hugh McCracken (hca); John Scofield (g); Ratzo Harris (b); Paul Motian (d); Ray Mantilla (perc).* 94.

After 30-plus years in the studios, some of Mose's world-view has become institutionalized, and his slip-on brand of fatalism might seem old hat to some. These are good, solid Allison albums, nevertheless. Blue Note's efforts to update him a little aren't especially successful: the guest-star turns on *Ever Since The World Ended* add weight but no special substance to the music, and the New Orleans team that supports him on *My Backyard* has its own agenda as well as following the leader. Allison's distinctive touch still comes through on 'The Gettin' Paid Waltz' and 'I Looked In The Mirror'.

After a further break came *The Earth Wants You*. Another cast of Blue Note heavies make themselves useful, none more so than the unerringly versatile Scofield, whose blues fills on 'You Can't Push People Around' and 'Natural Born Malcontent' make solid sense. Motian's return to the Allison fold after 30-odd years is another pleasure, and 'Certified Senior Citizen' is as canny a lyric as Mose has ever come up with. Excellent fun.

*****(*) Gimcracks And Gewgaws**

Blue Note 823211-2 *Allison; Mark Shim (ts); Russell Malone (g); Ratzo Harris (b); Paul Motian (d).* 5/97.

It seems boring to say it, but here's another great one from Mose. Some of his targets are a mite too easy, such as folks who live by their faxes and cellular phones ('The More You Get'), but Ben Sidran's production has sharpened up the music: new guy on the label Mark Shim is keen to please, and he does; Malone is right on it; Motian loves this gig; Ratzo's right there; and if the old guy's voice is shakier than it used to be, he's holding on tight.

Bill Allred (born 1936)

TROMBONE

Allred played Dixieland as a teenager and spent much of his later years working in tourist bands in Disney theme parks. He currently leads a swing-mainstream band out of Florida and tours as a festival guest.

****(*) Swing That Music**

Big Bear ESJCD 593 *Allred; Don Lord (c); J.J Argenziano (t); Terry Myers (cl, ts); Jim Maihack (p, tb); Boyd Bergeson (g, bj); Sam Noto (b, tba); Warren Sauer (d).* 7/89.

A somewhat belated appearance of a Birmingham Festival set by Allred's 'day-job' band. If there's such a thing as precision-tooled Dixieland, this is probably it, and it's no different in spirit and execution from, say, a Buddy Rich or Count Basie ghost band set. Allred is the one player of genuine individual style, and when he steps forward the music changes in character; otherwise it's impressive on a certain level. Big Bear's rather shrill recording probably suits them.

*****(*) Absolutely**

Nagel-Heyer 024 *Allred; Roy Williams (tb); Johnny Varro (p); Isla Eckinger (b); Butch Miles (d).* 9/95.

Plenty of fun here, and a rare addition to the tiny canon of two-trombone records. Allred has spent much of his playing career in Florida away from strict jazz situations, but his chops are impeccable and he cedes nothing to the more renowned Williams here. The tunes are an interesting lot, with a warhorse like 'It's Only A Paper Moon' pepped up with a brusque Latin arrangement, and although the rhythm section play well – even Miles, as boisterous as ever, behaves himself – it's all about the 'bones. While this isn't a cutting contest, and xenophobic British fans will disagree, Allred assuredly takes the honours on this occasion.

Karin Allyson

VOCAL, PIANO

Born in Kansas, Allyson studied piano at Nebraska University and worked around the Mid-West. She is again based in Kansas.

*****(*) I Didn't Know About You**

Concord CCD 4543 *Allyson; Gary Sivils (c); Mike Metheny (flhn); Joe Cartwright, Russ Long, Paul Smith (p); Rod Fleeman, Danny Embrey (g); Bob Bowman, Gerald Sparts (b); Todd Strait (d); Doug Auwarter (perc); Bryan Hicks (v).* 92.

***** Sweet Home Cookin'**

Concord CCD 4593 *Allyson; Randy Sandke (t); Bob Cooper (ts); Alan Broadbent, Paul Smith (p); Rod Fleeman (g); Putter Smith, Bob Bowman (b); Sherman Ferguson, Todd Strait (d).* 6–9/93.

***** Azure-Te**

Concord CCD 4641 *Allyson; Stan Kessler (t, flhn); Mike Metheny (flhn); Kim Park (as, ts); Randy Weinstein (hca); Paul Smith, Laura Caviani (p); Claude Williams (vn); Rod Fleeman, Danny Embrey (g); Bob Bowman, Gerald Sparts (b); Todd Strait (d).* 11/94.

The debut album established Allyson's sexy, fresh-faced delivery as something different in the small group of new jazz singers. With a background rather vaguely rooted in rock, she doesn't feel uptight about including material from writers like Randy Newman or Janis Ian, but her zestful rhythmic sense and solid scat capabilities let her walk in the tradition when she wants. A small-hours blues such as Newman's 'Guilty' sounds terrific here, but all the standards she tackles come off well, and her large cast of supporting players creates a wide variation of settings. If *Sweet Home Cookin'* was a slight disappointment as a follow-up, it's because it's that much more homogeneous, with Alan Broadbent's arrangements and horn charts fashioning a more familiar West Coast feel to the situations. Allyson herself still sounds fine. The same with *Azure-Te*, though again the material seems less catholic and more classic, with standards and bop tunes making up the programme. Heartbreaker: the slowly sighing 'Some Other Time'.

***** Collage**

Concord CCD 4709 *Allyson; Mike Metheny (flhn); Kim Park (as); Claude Williams (vn); Randy Weinstein (hca); Laura Caviani, Paul Smith (p); Rod Fleeman, Danny Embrey (g); Bob Bowman (b); Todd Strait (d).* 1/96.

***** Daydream**

Concord CCD4773 *As above, except add Randy Brecker (flhn), Gary Burton (vib); omit Metheny, Williams.* 1/96–3/97.

Allyson is edging away from jazz and further into a kind of adult pop – which, given her broad sympathies, doesn't hurt. Neither of these discs will convert any sceptics, but they're coolly effective, the lilt in her voice and the slight crack in it when she does a wistful line both working in her favour. *Collage* puts Billy Joel next to Clifford Brown next to Monk next to 'Cherokee' next to the Beatles, and her lack of pretension somehow carries it off. *Daydream* has more Monk and 'Donna Lee', which suggests that she isn't leaving jazz at all, although the show tune, 'Show Me', and a lovely 'Everything Must Change' come from somewhere else.

****(*) From Paris To Rio**

Concord CCD 4865-2 *Allyson; Kim Park (as, f); Paul Smith (ky); Gil Goldstein (acc); Rod Fleeman, Danny Embrey (g); Bob Bowman (b); Todd Strait, Doug Auwarter (d); strings.*

This feels like a disappointing misfire, which is a surprise given that Allyson has been performing a lot of this kind of material in live situations. She doesn't seem to characterize such widely different composers as Caetano Veloso, Ivan Lins, Ennio Morricone and Jacques Brel with enough distinctiveness to make the songs stand out from each other; Brel's 'Ne Me Quitte Pas' is entirely wrong. It's an amenable record, but for once in her discography she sounds little more than bland.

Peter Almqvist (born 1957)

GUITAR

Danish guitarist. In the '70s he followed rock, but moved into more straight-ahead jazz in the '80s and worked in a duo, Guitars Unlimited, with Ulf Wakenius.

***** Dig, Myself And I**

Storyville STCD 4201 *Almqvist; Yasuhitu Mori (b); Raymond Karlsson (d).* 10/94.

***** Peter Almqvist Trio With Horace Parlan**

Storyville STCD 4205 *As above, except add Horace Parlan (p).* 10/96.

A couple of sturdy if unremarkable straight-ahead guitar dates. Almqvist does nothing startling, but he seems entirely at ease on bebop tempos or blues grooves. He doesn't write much (and when he does, it's things like 'Minor Groove') and the best thing about the dates is the swinging interplay with the excellent Mori and Karlsson. Parlan sits in on the second disc, though he doesn't bring much bar his old-pro gravitas.

Mikhail Alperin

PIANO, MELODICA, VOICE

Russian pianist-bandleader with a sorrowful European aesthetic.

****(*) Waves Of Sorrow**

ECM 839621-2 *Alperin; Arkady Shilkloper (frhn, flhn, v).* 7/89.

***** Folk Dreams**

Jaro 4187 *As above, except add Sergey Starostin (v, reeds); Russkaja Pesnja Folk Choir.* 92.

***** North Story**

ECM 531022-2 *As above, except add Tore Brunborg (ts); Terje Gewelt (b); Jon Christensen (d).* 9/95.

*****(*) First Impression**

ECM 557650-2 *Alperin; Arkady Shilkloper (frhn, flhn); John Surman (ss, bs); Terje Gewelt (b); Jon Christensen (d); Hans-Kristian Kjos Sørenson (mar, perc).* 12/97.

'I saw a group of Moldavian square-dance musicians at a countryside wedding, performing a Beethoven sonata, dressed in studded leather jackets.' Misha Alperin's musical vision is attractively unconstrained but it only rarely breaks out of its own charmed and charming circle. Along with Shilkloper, who is wedded to melancholy by his choice of instrument, he has carved out a corner of world jazz and made it his own, a gentle, folksy idiom which never quite sounds so much improvised as tentatively remembered from long ago.

Reverie is the abiding characteristic of *North Story*. It's a sequence of eight impressionistic compositions filled out by the late Norwegian composer Harald Saeverud's chorale 'Kristi-Blodsdraper'. Why 'Ironical Evening' should come between 'Morning' and the long, slow 'Afternoon' isn't clear, but there is a coherent logic to the sequence, which deserves to be heard entire. Brunborg and the redoubtable Christensen provide an attractive range of variations on the rather limited range of sound offered by French horn and piano, as do the voices on *Folk Dreams*, an album which seems pretty remote from any jazz sensibility but for Alperin's occasional – and perhaps unconscious – echoes of Bill Evans.

The recent *First Impression* is readily mistakable as a John Surman record, perhaps some anachronistic hybrid of his solo *Westering Home* experiment and some of the more recent group recordings. Alperin's hand takes a moment or two to detect, but once one starts to hear his delicately folksy/classical approach, it is clear who is in charge. The title-track, which follows a deceptively naïve 'Overture', has the limpid inconsequence of one of Satie's 'Gnossiennes'. Later 'Impressions' and other tracks involve Surman and the group and are more grabbing and alert. Alperin is most convincingly an improviser in his responsiveness to nuance. 'Twilight Hour', 'City Dance' and 'Movement' represent a suite-within-a-suite, a quietly dancing interlude dropped into the quiet spaces Alperin likes to leave between notes and ideas. One of the quietest and most contemplative records you could ever hope to encounter.

Barry Altschul (born 1943)

DRUMS, PERCUSSION

A New Yorker, Altschul played in Paul Bley's trio for much of the '60s, then in Circle and the Anthony Braxton group of the early '70s. Recorded occasionally as a leader in the '80s, but since then more involved in teaching and only rarely sighted.

***** For Stu**

Soul Note 121015 *Altschul; Ray Anderson (tb); Anthony Davis (p); Rick Rozie (b).* 2/79.

***** Irina**

Soul Note 121106 *Altschul; Enrico Rava (t); John Surman (ss, bs); Mark Helias (b).* 2/83.

****(*) That's Nice**
Soul Note 121115 *Altschul; Glenn Ferris (tb); Sean Bergin (as, ts); Mike Melillo (p); Andy McKee (b).* 11/85.

Altschul is an intelligent, analytical man who has moved from an early free-form and avant-garde idiom to embrace virtually all the major world traditions (except, interestingly, the unaccented musics of East Asia). He has written persuasively about drumming; but, if there is anything that mars his recorded output, it is a slightly didactic insistence and a touch of stiffness in his solo work.

Dedicated to the late Stu Martin, the 1979 record is attractively boisterous, dominated by Anderson's old-fashioned brass sound and very contemporary concept, and wholly in command of its material. Davis is one of the few piano players likely to sound good in this context, able to balance free abstraction against a more settled jazz groove.

On *Irina*, the pianoless line-up offers an interestingly open-ended harmonic context which the two horn players exploit to the maximum. Surman is in somewhat muted form, never as ebullient or as thoughtful as a sideman as he tends to be on his own projects. Rava, by contrast, soars away with considerable dash and abandon, tinged with just a hint of melancholy. Hearing the record after a gap of some years – it has been absent since our first edition – the most immediate impact is made by Helias. His double-stopped figures and richly evocative strum chords come through very strongly.

That's Nice labours under the weight of too many 'drummer's album' peccadilloes. A longish tribute 'For "Papa" Jo, "Klook" And "Philly", Too' gets to grips with the ancestors but turns into a succession of licks and pastiches. The addition of Melillo for the title-track and one other softens the rather barking sound that Ferris and Bergin go in for, but the damage is already done.

Altschul's career seems to have marked time for much of the last decade. Given his talents, one would have expected more of a show than this, and there is enough writing on a broader scale here to suggest that he would make a convincing big-band leader. Perhaps just such a commission waits in the wings.

Ari Ambrose (born 1973)

TENOR SAXOPHONE

Studied sax in Washington, DC, and played in the local scene, then studied at Manhattan School from 1991. Played and recorded in sundry sideman situations before these leadership dates.

***** Introducing Ari Ambrose**
Steeplechase SCCD 31450 *Ambrose; Dennis Irwin (b); Billy Hart (d).* 4/98.

*****(*) Cyclic Episode**
Steeplechase SCCD 31472 *Ambrose; George Colligan (p); Joe Martin (b); Billy Drummond (d).* 12/98.

The gruff, almost barking sound suggests a lineage back through Rollins to Jacquet and early Webster, even if Ambrose does start the debut CD with a Coltrane tune. He says he wanted to make a three-man date that sounded more like a piano trio than a sax burn-out session, and the splendid playing of Irwin and Hart certainly helps in that direction. The awkwardness of Monk's 'Ugly Beauty' is smoothed away without sacrificing any grittiness of tone. But Ambrose is not quite imaginative enough to carry the slow tempo convincingly, and the playing ends up as a string of bits and pieces. That sense of disjunction afflicts all of these tracks to some degree. While it's a relief to find a tenorman not bent on flying past each harmonic hurdle, it's still only intermittently effective.

The quartet session benefits from Colligan's astuteness, which immediately cools off the excessive heat: this time Ambrose seems determined to tear 'Gingerbread Boy' limb from limb, but actually the opener is the only piece to divert from what's essentially a rather inscrutable set of interpretations. Although themes like Sam Rivers's title-track or Bobby Hutcherson's 'Roses Poses' are turned over and over by the quartet, they're made to seem like excerpts from even longer pieces. Ambrose never quite presents conclusive evidence that he knows where his improvising's going, but there are surprising and often fascinating passages in all his solos here. Ambitious and worth following.

Franco Ambrosetti (born 1941)

TRUMPET, FLUGELHORN

Ambrosetti's family business, in industrial management, takes up much of his time, but he learned piano as a child and began playing trumpet, often leading his own groups, working with his saxophonist father, or playing in the George Gruntz Band.

*****(*) Gin And Pentatonic**
Enja 4096-2 *Ambrosetti; Lew Soloff, Mike Mossman (t); Steve Coleman (as); Michael Brecker (ts); Howard Johnson (bs, tba); Alex Brofsky, John Clark (frhn); Tommy Flanagan, Kenny Kirkland (p); Dave Holland, Buster Williams (b); Daniel Humair (d).* 12/83–3/85.

***** Movies**
Enja 5035-2 *Ambrosetti; Geri Allen (p); John Scofield (g); Michael Formanek (b); Daniel Humair (d); Jerry Gonzalez (perc).* 11/86.

****(*) Music For Symphony And Jazz Band**
Enja 6070-2 *Ambrosetti; Daniel Schnyder (ss); Greg Osby (as); Simon Nabatov, Vladislaw Sendecki (p); Ed Schuller (b); Alfredo Glino (d); NDR Radio-Orchestra, Hannover.* 10/90.

*****(*) Live At The Blue Note**
Enja 7065-2 *Ambrosetti; Seamus Blake (ts); Kenny Barron (p); Ira Coleman (b); Victor Lewis (d).* 7/92.

Ambrosetti divides his time between corporate work and jazz – 'after a couple of days of intense industrial management I look for a jazz gig'. He seems to prefer flugelhorn to trumpet and holds his ground impressively with some distinguished musicians on all these dates. *Gin And Pentatonic* conflates the best of two albums, *Wings* and *Tentets*, into a fat-free single disc, all concerned playing with real enthusiasm. *Movies* is film music, treated with amused and slightly irreverent hospitality by Ambrosetti and some American friends. It's hardly as dramatic a disintegration as a John Zorn session but the players have fun, and Ambrosetti again impresses as an inventive soloist. The meeting with the NDR Orchestra is about as successful as most such things, which is to say not very. The most striking record is perhaps the live session at New York's Blue Note. This kind of venture – visitor pals up with American hirelings, makes solid and forgettable live date – is old hat, but Ambrosetti plays with real authority, and there are other virtues: Blake, making one of his first appearances on record, is far from the usual hard-bop fledgeling, taking some baroque, surprising solos; Coleman and Lewis are unbeatable, and Barron, who contributes two tunes, is a notch above his normal professional self. His unforgettable theme, 'Phantoms', receives an outstandingly fine reading, even at nearly 20 minutes in length.

***** Light Breeze**
Enja 9331-2 *Ambrosetti; Antonio Farao (p); John Abercrombie (g); Miroslav Vitous (b); Billy Drummond (d).* 4/97.

His first for some time and deliberately spontaneous, with the players allowed only one rehearsal – not that it seems to have hindered such an accomplished team, each of whom is also permitted a solo 'interlude'. The disappointing aspect, though, is in Ambrosetti's own playing. Remaining with flugelhorn once again, his solos tend to sputter out or take overworn paths, and with the other four each in full command – particularly fine to hear Vitous in this kind of context again – he seems uncomfortably exposed. That said, the record has much to offer if only in the calibre of what the others are doing.

American Jazz Orchestra

GROUP

A brief initiative from the late 1980s to create a New York-based jazz repertory orchestra.

***** Ellington Masterpieces**
East-West 7567-91423-2 *John Eckert, Virgil Jones, Bob Millikan, Marvin Stamm (t); Eddie Beret, Jimmy Knepper, Benny Powell (tb); Norris Turney (ss, as, cl); John Purcell (as cl); Bill Easley (ts, cl); Loren Schoenberg (ts); Danny Bank (bs, cl); Dick Katz, John Lewis (p); Howard Collins (g); John Goldsby (b); Mel Lewis (d).* 11/88.

A repertory orchestra that never seems to have progressed beyond this record, the AJO made a decent fist out of this Ellington programme, without persuading anyone that the record had much reason to exist. If the subsequent adventures by the Lincoln Center Orchestra in similar repertoire have had their faults, at least they weren't as rote as this band turned out to be. On their own terms, these treatments of 15 Ellington classics (all bar one from the great 1940–43 period) are entertaining enough and, in good sound, one can hear what might be a clear-toned echo of what Ellington was originally after. But, for all its fine players, the Orchestra seems characterless and, since they effectively follow the originals to the letter, they're inevitably found wanting: Bill Easley is no match for Barney Bigard on 'The Sidewalks Of New York', say, or Virgil Jones for Cootie Williams on 'Concerto For Cootie'.

AMM

IMPROVISING ENSEMBLE

AMM's 35-year history is one of the most extraordinary and disciplined in improvised music. It is also completely sui generis. The group's membership has changed over the years, with only Eddie Prévost and Keith Rowe remaining from the original configuration; what has remained consistent is the members' devotion to engaged music-making that is neither abstract nor conventionally expressive but always intensely beautiful.

*****(*) AMMusic 1966**
Matchless/rer no number *Cornelius Cardew (p, transistor radio); Lou Gare (ts, vn); Eddie Prévost (d); Keith Rowe (g, transistor radio); Lawrence Sheaff (cl, acc, transistor radio).* 6/66.

****** The Crypt – 12 June 1968**
Matchless MRCD 05 2CD *Cornelius Cardew (p, clo); Lou Gare (ts, vn); Christopher Hobbs, Eddie Prévost (perc); Keith Rowe (g, elec).* 6/68.

****** Laminal**
Matchless MRCD 31 3CD *As above, except add John Tilbury (p).* 12/69, 2/82, 5/94.

In a rather dense and difficult book called *Noise* (*Bruits*), the French cultural theorist Jacques Attali identifies four main stages in the political economy of music. It is a process that culminates in a final utopian phase which Attali calls composition. This is a music 'beyond exchange ... performed for the musician's own enjoyment, as self-communication, fundamentally outside all other communication, as self-transcendence, a solitary, egotistical, noncommercial act'. It's an argument and a model that applies very cogently, though not always entirely accurately, to the music of AMM, who for three decades have stood outside every commercial and critical nexus and continued to make rich, astonishing music. One would have to quibble with 'egotistical', for it is almost axiomatic of 'AMMusic' (no other category exists) that ego is effectively suspended. AMM's origin lies in the British free-jazz movement, but the political and philosophical instincts of the founding members quickly dictated its transformation into an improvising collective in which process rather than gesture was important and which redefined the growing division in new music between performers and audience. Early AMM performances were conducted in the dark – *The Crypt* seems an entirely appropriate setting – and often deliberately blurred starting and finishing times.

Though 'beyond exchange' and defined entirely by the context and the collective understanding of the changing membership, the music has begun to enjoy a second life on record. The advent of CD meant that for the first time whole performances could be issued without breaks or editing, and founder member Eddie Prévost has used his own Matchless imprint to document the group's early and ongoing history. *The Crypt* was previously available in a two-LP boxed set, but the improvement in sound-quality, a richness of texture and of detail in quieter passages, is revelatory, here and throughout the older catalogue. In a superb liner-note to the earliest performance, Prévost points out that the *Jazz Journal* once identified the group as the 'Cornelius Cardew

Quartet', a nonsensical and ironic attribution on all sorts of counts.

This is a music which rejects instrumentalism. It matters very little after a few minutes who is playing what, particularly when conventional technique is almost entirely overthrown. In later years, as can be heard in the later performances on *Laminal*, Prévost was to return to something that demonstrated at least a kinship with jazz drumming, and Tilbury's piano playing is more conventionally expressive than Cardew's. Rowe is perhaps the key to the sound-world. He is credited as 'guitarist', but only in the most deconstructionist sense, laying the instrument flat on a table and manipulating feedback, overtones, percussive effects and accidentals, using the instrument as a sound source without a playing history. Veterans will insist that the 1966 record and *The Crypt* are essential texts, but the newcomer should certainly settle on *Laminal*, which documents an early overseas performance (in Aarhus, Denmark) with much later work from what was to become the 1990s version of the group. There is much more (and perhaps better) from them below, but the juxtaposition of their intent, uneffusive music with the turbulent swirl of the late-1960s group is instructive.

***** To Hear And Back Again**

Matchless MRCD 03 *Lou Gare (ts); Eddie Prévost (d).* 6/73–4/75.

Like the similarly convened Spontaneous Music Ensemble, AMM functioned for a time as a duo. What's odd about these early-to-mid-'80s tracks and what distinguishes them most clearly from the Trevor Watts/John Stevens version of SME is the extent to which Gare and Prévost seem to have reverted to the free-jazz idiom they were presumed to have left behind more than a decade before. To be fair, the two long studio tracks which occupied sides one and two of the original LP, 'To Hear' and 'Back Again', are very much more abstract than the half-hour's worth of live performances from London and Berlin that fill out the CD reissue. It's the additional material, and particularly the opening item, 'Unity First', which reminds the listener that Gare and Prévost started out as Sonny Rollins and Max Roach acolytes and retained a good measure of that basic sound feel, that sense of musical organization in even their most 'out' performances. Three stars may seem diffident, or even damning. It's simply that this disc is far from representative of AMM and, while Prévost could doubtless point up some quite obvious continuities, this is probably better grouped with the recordings made under his own name.

***** Generative Themes**

Matchless MRCD 06 *John Tilbury (p); Keith Rowe (g, elec); Eddie Prévost (d).* 12/82.

***** Combine + Laminates + Treatise '84**

Matchless MRCD 26 *As above.* 84.

*****(*) The Inexhaustible Document**

Matchless MRCD 13 *As above, except add Rohan De Saram (clo).* 87.

****** The Nameless Uncarved Block**

Matchless MRCD 20 *As above, except replace De Saram with Lou Gare (ts).* 4/90.

The trio represented on *Generative Themes* and *Combine + Laminates* was to be the basic AMM line-up thereafter. Interestingly, the early '80s saw the group rethinking and in some respects greatly simplifying the approach of the Cardew years. Tilbury is a more conventionally expressive, but by no means a conventional, player. His use of space, light and shade is extraordinary, constantly suggesting (as does Prévost) the *possibility* of linear development without ever allowing it to emerge. That is particularly clear on *Generative Themes*, which can be heard as a sequence of five potential compositions in which the transformational rules and functions are laid out but given no straightforwardly meaningful substance. On reflection, this is perhaps the most abstract record AMM has issued. That is an attempt at description, not criticism. The third item on the 1984 album (originally a Pogus LP of a performance at the Arts Club in Chicago) introduced material which drew on Cardew's theoretical/conceptual work, suggesting that, just a year or two after his untimely death, his partners were working through ideas and procedures which it had not been possible hitherto to accommodate in AMM terms. The addition of cellist Rohan de Saram, who appears on *The Inexhaustible Document*, was a reminder of Cardew's other instrumental voice, except that de Saram, a member of the blue-chip new music group, the Arditti Quartet, is probably closer in instinct to a philosophical tradition in which suspension of the self is a premiss rather than a problematic goal. He certainly fits into the music seamlessly.

Gare, who reappears on the 1990 album, is a more problematic presence. Critics gleefully queued up to nominate *The Nameless Uncarved Block* as AMM's 'rock' record – ironically enough, given Prévost's very fruitful association with high-octane outfit God and other groups later in the decade when AMM began to receive paternity suits as progenitors of the new ambient and process-driven music. Again, the saxophonist doesn't sound quite in context. There are moments in the huge 'Igneous' (there are many longer AMM tracks, but this one feels burstingly oversized) when the whole thing seems poised on the brink of a catastrophic finale, much as John Coltrane's long-form improvisations with Pharoah Sanders did. There the similarities end, of course. This is music which is not exhausted by repetition, and even seasoned AMM admirers (ourselves included), who might once have rejected the very idea of 'mechanical reproduction', have begun to accept the importance of documentation. This is music which transcends its moment. It does make sense to listen to it many times. It is never the same, always fresh, always developing, or developing new pathways in the listener.

****** Newfoundland**

Matchless MRCD 23 *Keith Rowe (g, elec); John Tilbury (p); Eddie Prévost (d).* 7/92.

****** Live In Allentown USA**

Matchless MRCD 30 *As above.* 4/94.

*****(*) From A Strange Place**

Modern Music PSFD 80 *As above.* 10/95.

*****(*) Before Driving To The Chapel We Took Coffee With Rick And Jennifer Reed**

Matchless MRCD 35 *As above.* 4/96.

Composer Howard Skempton's sleeve-note for the marvellous *Newfoundland* makes salutary reading. 'It is surely easy to resort to adjectives' – we have tried to resist – 'this music is so stunningly immediate, so palpable, that it makes a nonsense of such musings.' Emphatically, yes, but it still demands some kind of response, and reactions to AMM are notoriously difficult to verbalize. Comparison is perhaps the safest resort. In purely timbral, textural terms, recent performances have been gentler, less confrontational than of yore. Some of this may be explained by passing years, some by changing expectations. In the 1990s AMM have been hailed as the progenitors of a whole slew of post-rock idioms, and there may be some subconscious attempt to build bridges to a younger generation. The dynamics of a trio are always intriguing. Prévost continues to suggest and imply a pulse even when it cannot be securely quantified. Tilbury is delicacy itself, somewhere between Satie and Bill Evans, but filtered through gauze. It's Rowe who is the anarchist, the deconstructor, splashing colours across the Allentown set and providing the most significant estrangements on *From A Strange Place*, a rare AMM appearance on another label. It is extraordinarily hard to separate these sessions. Different as they are, each has its beauties, and all three have their longueurs. The most recent of the bunch – and if there's a longer or worse album-title in the book you should probably claim discount – is curiously formulaic, cast in a language that often seems to be striving after effect rather than going straight for the unfettered *jouissance* that makes this music so absolute and so exceptional.

Albert Ammons (1907–49)

PIANO

Played in Chicago from the mid-'20s but didn't start recording until 1936. Made much success during the boogie-woogie craze of the late '30s and persisted through the '40s, but a final illness ended his career.

*****(*) Albert Ammons 1936–1939**
Classics 715 *Ammons; Guy Kelly (t); Dalbert Bright (cl, as); Ike Perkins (g); Israel Crosby (b); Jimmy Hoskins (d).* 2/36–10/39.

*****(*) Boogie Woogie Man**
Topaz TPZ 1067 *As above, except add Harry James, Frankie Newton, Hot Lips Page (t), J.C Higginbotham, Vic Dickenson (tb), Meade Lux Lewis, Pete Johnson (p), Teddy Bunn (g), Johnny Williams (b), Eddie Dougherty, Big Sid Catlett, James F Hoskins (d).* 2/36–2/44.

***** The Boogie Woogie Man**
ASV AJA 5305 *Similar to above.* 2/36–2/46.

One-third of the great boogie-woogie triumvirate (with Pete Johnson and Meade Lux Lewis), Albert Ammons was arguably the least individual of the three, though he lacked nothing in power and swinging. The Classics CD usefully rounds up all his tracks from the 1930s: there are two Decca sessions by his Rhythm Kings, but the meat is in the 18 piano solos, cut for Vocalion, Solo Art and Blue Note, with a session of airshots from Chicago making up the balance. 'Shout For Joy' and 'Boogie Woogie Stomp' are classics of boogie-woogie exuberance, but his 1939 Solo Art session proved he was also a considerable blues piano man: 'Chicago In Mind' contemplates the form with genuine insight. The CD offers mixed reproduction, mostly not bad.

Topaz have assembled 22 tracks, which include two of the startling pieces with Harry James from 1939, two by the Port Of Harlem Jazzmen with Newton and Higginbotham, and four by the 1944 Rhythm Kings for Commodore, as well as duos and trios with Pete Johnson and Meade Lux Lewis. 'Suitcase Blues' and 'Bass Goin' Crazy' are solos for Blue Note that suggest the extent of his range. As a rounded portrait of the man this beats the Classics disc, although remastering again seems rather mixed. ASV's set duplicates both discs and underlines the needless piling-up of reissues that deal with basically the same material.

Gene Ammons (1925–74)

TENOR SAXOPHONE

Son of pianist Albert, 'Jug' Ammons worked with Billy Eckstine and Woody Herman before leading his own bands through the 1950s and '60s, although prison terms for drug offences blighted his career. Despite that, he recorded a huge number of albums and continued to work until his death from pneumonia. A swing-to-bop stylist, his playing was one of the models for the soul-jazz movement of the '60s.

****(*) The Gene Ammons Story: The 78 Era**
Prestige PRCD-24058-2 *Ammons; Bill Massey, Nat Woodyard (t); Matthew Gee, Eli Dabney, Benny Green, Henderson Chambers (tb); Sonny Stitt, Rudy Williams, McKinley Easton (bs); Duke Jordan, Charlie Bateman, Junior Mance, Clarence Anderson, John Houston (p); Gene Wright, Earl May, Ernie Shepard, Ben Stuberville, Tommy Potter (b); Art Blakey, Wes Landers, Teddy Stewart, George Brown (d); Earl Coleman (v).* 4/50–2/55.

****(*) All Star Sessions**
Original Jazz Classics OJC 014 *Ammons; Art Farmer, Bill Massey (t); Al Outcalt (tb); Lou Donaldson (as); Sonny Stitt (ts, bs); Duke Jordan, Junior Mance, Charles Bateman, Freddie Redd (p); Tommy Potter, Gene Wright, Addison Farmer (b); Jo Jones, Wes Landers, Teddy Stewart, Kenny Clarke (d).* 3/50–6/55.

***** The Happy Blues**
Original Jazz Classics OJC 013 *Ammons; Art Farmer, Jackie McLean (as); Duke Jordan (p); Addison Farmer (b); Art Taylor (d); Candido Camero (perc).* 4/56.

****(*) Jammin' With Gene**
Original Jazz Classics OJC 211 *Ammons; Donald Byrd (t); Jackie McLean (as); Mal Waldron (b); Doug Watkins (b); Art Taylor (d).* 7/56.

***** Funky**
Original Jazz Classics OJC 244 *As above, except Art Farmer (t) replaces Byrd; add Kenny Burrell (g).* 1/57.

**** Jammin' In Hi Fi**
Original Jazz Classics OJC 129 *Ammons; Idrees Sulieman (t); Jackie McLean (as); Mal Waldron (p); Kenny Burrell (g); Paul Chambers (b); Art Taylor (d).* 4/57.

***** The Big Sound**
Original Jazz Classics OJC 651 *Ammons; John Coltrane (as); Paul Quinichette (ts); Pepper Adams (bs); Jerome Richardson (f); Mal Waldron (p); George Joyner (b); Art Taylor (d).* 1/58.

***** Groove Blues**

Original Jazz Classics OJC 723 *As above.* 1/58.

****(*) Blue Gene**

Original Jazz Classics OJC 192 *Ammons; Idrees Sulieman (t); Pepper Adams (bs); Mal Waldron (p); Doug Watkins (b); Art Taylor (d); Ray Barretto (perc).* 5/58.

Gene Ammons made a lot of records, and a surprising number are now in print on CD, thanks mainly to the extensive OJC/Prestige reissue programme. The earlier discs deal mainly with his jamming sessions of the mid- and late-1950s; they are entertaining but often flabby blowing dates that number as many clichés as worthwhile ideas in the playing. The leader's own style had been forged as a first-generation bopper, first with Billy Eckstine, then under his own name, but his early records find him walking a line between bop and R&B honking: the first disc listed above, *The 78 Era*, is rough-and-ready music, and listening to it is like thumbing coins into a jukebox of the day. Jug liked to enjoy his music, and perhaps the darker passions of a Parker were beyond him. The earliest tracks on *All Star Sessions* are also typical of the kind of stuff he recorded prior to the LP era, roistering through two-tenor battles with Sonny Stitt, a close kindred spirit. A later date with Farmer and Donaldson is more restrained until the collective whoop of 'Madhouse'.

The next six records all follow similar patterns: long, expansive tracks – at most four to a record – and variations on the blues and some standards for the material. Ammons himself takes the leading solos, but he so often resorts to quotes and familiar phrases that one is left wishing for a less open-ended environment; of the other players involved, McLean and Waldron are the most reliably inventive. *Jammin' In Hi Fi* is the weakest of the six, the whole session sounding like a warm-up, while *Jammin' With Gene* has a very long and overcooked 'Not Really The Blues' balancing two superior slow pieces. *Funky* and *Blue Gene* are decent if unremarkable, but the session that makes up both *The Big Sound* and *Groove Blues* has a couple of interesting points in featuring one of John Coltrane's few appearances on alto (undistinguished though it is) and some unexpectedly piquant flute solos by Richardson to vary the palette a little. These all count as playable but unexceptional discs.

***** The Gene Ammons Story: Organ Combos**

Prestige PRCD-24071-2 *Ammons; Joe Newman (t); Frank Wess (ts, f); Jack McDuff, Johnny 'Hammond' Smith (org); Wendell Marshall, Doug Watkins (b); Art Taylor, Walter Perkins (d); Ray Barretto (perc).* 6/60–11/61.

***** Boss Tenor**

Prestige 7180 *Ammons; Tommy Flanagan (p); Doug Watkins (b); Art Taylor (d); Ray Barretto (perc).* 6/60.

***** Jug**

Original Jazz Classics OJC 701 *Ammons; Richard Wyands (p); Clarence 'Sleepy' Anderson (org); Doug Watkins (b); J.C Heard (d).* 1/61.

*****(*) The Gene Ammons Story: Gentle Jug**

Prestige PRCD-24079-2 *Ammons; Richard Wyands, Patti Bown (p); George Duvivier, Doug Watkins (b); J.C Heard, Ed Shaughnessy (d).* 1/61–4/62.

****(*) Live! In Chicago**

Original Jazz Classics OJC 395 *Ammons; Eddie Buster (org); Gerald Donovan (d).* 8/61.

***** Up Tight!**

Prestige PRCD-24140-2 *Ammons; Walter Bishop Jr, Patti Bown (p); Arthur Davis, George Duvivier (b); Art Taylor (d); Ray Barretto (perc).* 10/61.

**** Preachin'**

Original Jazz Classics OJC 792 *Ammons; Clarence 'Sleepy' Anderson (org); Sylvester Hickman (b); Dorral Anderson (d).* 5/62.

***** Jug And Dodo**

Prestige PRCD-24021-2 *Ammons; Dodo Marmarosa (p); Sam Jones (b); Marshall Thompson (d).* 5/62.

****(*) Bad! Bossa Nova**

Original Jazz Classics OJC 351 *Ammons; Hank Jones (p); Bucky Pizzarelli, Kenny Burrell (g); Norman Edge (b); Oliver Jackson (d); Al Hayes (perc).* 9/62.

****(*) We'll Be Together Again**

Original Jazz Classics OJC 708 *Ammons; Sonny Stitt (as, ts); John Houston (p); Buster Williams (b); George Brown (d).* 68.

****(*) The Boss Is Back!**

Prestige PRCD-24129-2 *Ammons; Prince James, Houston Person (ts); Junior Mance (p); Sonny Phillips (org); Billy Butler (g); Buster Williams, Bob Bushnell (b); Frankie Jones, Bernard Purdie (d); Candido Camero (perc).* 11/69.

There is a lot of Gene Ammons available again. It's sad that the albums are so spotty and inconsistent, but that seemed to be his way: great performances can follow weary ones, even on the same record, and there doesn't seem to be a particular setting that turns him on to his best form. The clinkers here are *Preachin'*, a set of gospel tunes that he can barely be bothered to blow through, and *The Boss Is Back!*, which combines the original *Boss Is Back* (not bad) and *Brother Jug* (rotten). *We'll Be Together Again* should have been an incendiary meeting with Sonny Stitt, but it leaves a trail of smoke rather than any fire – the tracks are cut off short before they can really work up steam. *Bad! Bossa Nova* sounds like a duff corporate idea, setting him to work on bossa nova rhythms, but he blows hard enough to make it worthwhile. *Boss Tenor*, *Jug* and especially *Organ Combos* (which combines the original albums, *Twisting The Jug* and the fine *Angel Eyes*) are solid and worth the shelf-space. The best records, though, are probably *Jug And Dodo*, an unlikely, sometimes compelling meeting with Dodo Marmarosa in one of the pianist's rare recordings, and the splendid *Gentle Jug*. This at last puts on CD one of his very best Prestige dates, *The Soulful Moods Of Gene Ammons*, where he plays with Hawkins-like authority, and adds the similarly inclined *Nice An' Cool* session from a year earlier. *Up Tight!* is the most recent addition to the sequence, collecting the contents of two 1961 LPs, *Up Tight* and *Boss Soul*. A couple of good ones, too, though if anyone feels confused by the similarity of all these titles, much the same can be said about a lot of the music.

***** The Chase!**

Prestige 24166 *Ammons; Dexter Gordon (ts); John Young, Jodie Christian (p); Cleveland Eaton, Rufus Reid (b); Steve McCall, Wilbur Campbell (d); Vi Redd (v).* 7/70.

Not exactly a rekindling of the old two-tenor team, since either Ammons or Gordon sits out a lot of the time. But there are a few entertaining sparks struck off some old (and much-saddled) bebop warhorses and, with two down-home Chicagoan rhythm sections in attendance, there's plenty of fun.

***** Legends Of Acid Jazz**

Prestige 24188 *Ammons; Sonny Stitt (ts); Leon Spencer, Don Patterson (org); Harold Mabern (p); George Freeman, Paul Weeden (g); Ron Carter (b); Idris Muhammad, Bill James (d); strings.*

This is a useful sampling of Jug's music, since it combines the albums *The Black Cat* and *You Talk That Talk* and adds two tracks from a 1962 date with Don Patterson. The later disc offers some typical fisticuffs with Sonny Stitt while the *Black Cat* tracks include a couple of pieces with strings, some blues and a 'Piece To Keep Away Evil Spirits'. Ammons blows on regardless.

****(*) Greatest Hits, Vol. 1: The Sixties**

Original Jazz Classics OJC 6005 *Ammons; Joe Newman (t); Frank Wess (ts); Jack McDuff, Johnny Hammond Smith (org); Richard Wyands, Hank Jones, Tommy Flanagan (p); Kenny Burrell, Bucky Pizzarelli (g); Doug Watkins, Norman Edge, Wendell Marshall (b); Art Taylor, Oliver Jackson, Walter Perkins (d); Ray Barretto, Al Hayes (perc).* 61–69.

***** Soul Summit**

Prestige PRCD-24118-2 *Ammons; various others.* 6/61–4/62.

Two useful if sometimes frustrating compilations. The *Hits* collection isn't a bad trawl through some of his 1960s sessions, though any of the better albums listed above would do just as well as a sampling of Ammons in this decade. *Soul Summit* is shared with Sonny Stitt and Jack McDuff, and Jug turns up on a couple of tracks with a big band as well as sparring with Stitt.

****(*) Gene Ammons And Friends At Montreux**

Original Jazz Classics OJC 1023 *Ammons; Nat Adderley (c); Cannonball Adderley (as); Dexter Gordon (ts); Hampton Hawes (p); Bob Cranshaw (b); Kenny Clarke (d); Kenneth Nash (perc).* 7/73.

Almost the end of the line for Jug (although actually he still made another five albums after this one). He plays 'Yardbird Suite' and 'Sophisticated Lady' as if nothing had changed, but his era was almost over and what looks on paper like a classic live session feels tired. Nat, Dexter and Cannon join in only on the final 'Treux Blues'. It's sad to think that they're all now gone, as are Hawes and Clarke.

Franck Amsallem (born 1961)

PIANO

Algerian-born, Amsallem went to the USA two decades ago after graduating from Nice Conservatory. His list of credits since then includes gigs with A-list names like Gerry Mulligan, Charles Lloyd and Bobby Watson. He has also been MD at the Grand Casino in Monte Carlo.

****** Another Time**

Challenge A 73117 *Amsallem; Gary Peacock (b); Bill Stewart (d).* 7/90.

***** Regards**

Freelance 020 *Amsallem; Tim Ries (ts); Scott Colley (b); Bill Stewart (d).* 92.

*****(*) Is That So**

Sunnyside SSC 1071 *Amsallem; Tim Ries (ts); Leon Parker (d, perc).* 97.

***** Years Gone By**

Challenge A 73129 *Amsallem; Tim Ries (ts); Riccardo Del Frà (b); Daniel Humair (d).* 98.

Amsallem comes from Oran, the city that was home to Albert Camus, and, though no outsider and lacking all the usual symptoms of alienation and estrangement, he has certainly cut his own distinctive furrow. Periods of study in Nice, at Berklee, and at the Manhattan School of Music refined what was already an obvious talent, and Amsallem quickly became a first-call player. His debut recording was originally released on OMD as *Out A Day*. The writing is exquisite. '... And Keep This Place In Mind For A Better One Is Heart [*sic*] To Find' and the following two tracks, 'Running After Eternity' and 'Dee', are among the best things we have heard for piano trio in a long time. Peacock's huge sound and Bill Stewart's now widely recognized delicacy and grace contribute substantially.

The follow up record introduces a partnership with Tim Ries that has remained in place ever since. It's obviously a *simpatico* relationship, but we remain unpersuaded by the saxophonist, who always seems to be trying too hard to impress. The trio with saxophonist Parker is more effective and there are very good things on the most recent disc, where Ries sounds brisker and less cluttered.

It's still hard to go past the debut record but, as he rises forty, Amsallem has started to experiment with big-band arrangements, and every instinct suggests this may yet be his forte. As a soloist, he is impressive rather than totally engaging; too many notes, sometimes not enough reflection, and yet the outline of something grander is always evident.

Amsterdam Jazz Quintet

GROUP

The brainchild of keyboard man Vermeulen, the AJQ is an ensemble that combines real jazz feel with a genuinely offbeat compositional style.

***** Pictures Of Amsterdam**

A Records AL 73042 *Robert Van Vermeulen (p, org); David Rockefeller (t, flhn, vtb); Paul Berner (b); Jo Krause (d).* 7/95.

***** Portraits**

Challenge CHR 70048 *Robert Van Vermeulen (p, org); Bert Joris (t, flhn); Toon Roos (ts, ss); Paul Berner (b); Joost Van Schaik (d).* 4/97.

Brigitte Bardot, Gary Kasparov, Nick Leeson, Superbarrio, Pelé, the Dalai Lama, John Cleese, Nobel Peace Prizewinner Rigoberta Menchu, and M.C. Escher ... Not some kind of ultimate dinner party but the dedicatees of nine intimate *Portraits* by this gifted and multi-talented group. Roos is an interesting player and Joris has some nice moments, standing somewhere between Clifford Brown and Chet Baker. Rockefeller is a key presence on the earlier record; not so much a strong soloist as a textures man; horses for courses, for this is very much a textures record. It isn't clear whether the tunes are intended as aural soundscapes or evocations of places, or whether they have simply been attached to locations after the fact. Either way, it's an effective mix-and-match, and there is some lovely, if rather formal playing. Catch them live if you get the chance. That, rather than the studio, is their natural turf.

Curtis Amy (born 1927)

TENOR AND SOPRANO SAXOPHONES

A Texas tenorman, Amy learned saxophone in an army band and based himself in Los Angeles from 1955, playing in many hard-bop and soul-jazz groups in the area.

***(*) **Katanga**

Pacific Jazz 94850-2 *Amy; Dupree Bolton, Marcus Belgrave (t); Roy Brewster (vtb); John Houston, Jack Wilson (p); Roy Ayers (vib); Ray Crawford (g); Victor Gaskin, George Morrow (b); Doug Sides, Tony Bazley (d).* 62–63.

*** **Peace For Love**

Fresh Sound FSR 5004 *Amy; Steve Huffsteter (t, flhn); Bob McChesney (b); Frank Strazzeri (p); Donn Wyatt (ky); John B Williams (b); Leon Ndugu Chancler (d); Merry Clayton, Jessie Williams (v).* 6/94.

The reissue of *Katanga* will be welcomed by collectors not so much for Amy's work as for the glimpse of a semi-legendary figure, Dupree Bolton, who made hardly any other records yet was a fascinating stylist: his solos have a headlong momentum that is buoyed up by a poise which keeps the logic of the playing intact. The rest of the playing and the tunes are more ordinary, but these surviving fragments of a lost talent (Bolton served a prison sentence not long afterwards) are fascinating. Amy's own big-bodied Texas tenor is reliable and likeable, but none of his early records ever really stand out from each other, and there are several more Pacific Jazz albums yet to reappear. The CD has a bonus of three tracks from the earlier *Way Down*.

The Fresh Sound set is a rare recent record from the old pro. This easy-going date, while never striking more than a few sparks, is the jazz equivalent of comfort food. Amy's thick, soft tenor lines and insinuating tone are fine, but the best features are the astute writing for the three-horn front line and the slowly unfolding groove which the splendid rhythm section put together for most of the tunes. Mrs Amy, Merry Clayton, adds wordless vocals to track one.

Arild Andersen (born 1945)

DOUBLE BASS

Like many players of his generation in Scandinavia, Andersen was much influenced by exiled guru George Russell's Lydian Chromatic approach to harmony. The bassist has worked in a wide range of contexts and was leader of Masqualero. His characteristic manner is resonant and fleet, with much of the harmonic complexity Russell's influence imbued.

***(*) **Sagn**

ECM 849647-2 *Andersen; Bendik Hofseth (ts, ss); Bugge Wesseltoft (ky); Frode Alnaes (g); Nana Vasconcelos (perc, v); Kirsten Braten Berg (v).* 8/90.

*** **If You Look Far Enough**

ECM 513902-2 *Andersen; Ralph Towner (g); Audun Kleive (d); Nana Vasconcelos (perc).* 88, 7/91, 2/92.

**** **Hyperborean**

ECM 537342-2 *Andersen; Bendik Hofseth (ts); Tore Brunborg (ts, ss); Kenneth Knudsen (ky); Paolo Vinaccia (d, perc); Cikada String Quartet.* 12/96.

***(*) **Achirana**

ECM 1728 *Andersen; Vassilis Tsabropoulos (p); John Marshall (d).* 98.

No one has yet come up with a satisfactory explanation. Why does Scandinavia produce so many fine bass players: Niels-Henning Orsted Pedersen, Palle Danielsson, Lars Danielsson and, second only to NHOP for sheer inventiveness and beauty of tone, Arild Andersen?

Andersen's music is an intriguingly unstable amalgam of Miles Davis (an influence evident in the bassist's group, Masqualero) and Norwegian folk forms. *Sagn* is weighted towards the latter, an early shot in ECM's effort to integrate the Nordic tradition and American jazz and one of the most successful, though Berg is not as compelling a presence as her countrywomen, Agnes Buen Gårnas or Mari Boine. She is the weak link in an otherwise splendid record.

If You Look Far Enough is constrained by its origins – recorded over nearly four years – and by the original purpose of much of the material. Written as a soundtrack for the film *Blucher*, it limps along for lack of supporting images, and some of the playing is notably limp, too. It does, however, feature Andersen prominently as soloist, sometimes unadorned, sometimes making use of real-time delay and a cathedral-proportioned reverb. The lines positively sing.

Hyperborean is a reference to the cool, ageless land the Greeks believed lay beyond the northern mountains. The music is disciplined, unromantic and timeless. Andersen dispenses with effects pedals, combining his increasingly elaborate improvisations in real time with keyboards and string quartet, lending the whole – ironically enough – a jazzier feel than anything he has done since Masqualero. Hofseth and Brunborg are reduced to supporting cast and it's the Cikada Quartet that dominates the first half. Things loosen up later, albeit leaving an uneasy sense that Andersen has delivered his main ideas upfront and is then struggling to fill the slot. Though structurally less elaborate than *Sagn*, which is organized as a three-part suite, *Hyperborean* has a unity of tone and an overall sense of direction lacking on the earlier discs. Andersen dominates completely. His sound is immense and his soloing involved and compelling, once again prompting the question why he hasn't yet recorded unaccompanied.

The new record resembles nothing more than Paul Bley's trios of the early '70s with Kent Carter and Barry Altschul. Tsabropoulos favours tiny, disengaged phrases strung together into long, long lines. Marshall has long been an unsung hero – why *is* he heard so little of on record? – and Andersen is in top form on 'The Spell' and 'She's Gone'. Lovely, delicately cadenced jazz.

Clifton Anderson (born 1957)

TROMBONE

Trombonist best known as a sideman in the Sonny Rollins group.

****(*) Landmarks**
Milestone MCD-9266-2 *Anderson; Wallace Roney (t); Kenny Garrett (as); Monty Alexander (p); Bob Cranshaw (b); Al Foster (d).* 1/95.

It was both brave and sensible for Anderson to enlist such a blue-chip band for his leadership debut. The trombonist, who remains known primarily as a sideman in the Sonny Rollins group, is used to heavy company, and they don't come much more serious than this. The result is a capable record, although the leader really has little to offer other than a pleasing tone and a decent facility. He tends to alternate double-time and long-note passages with unvarying insistency, and after a couple of tracks one can guess where everything is going several beats before it gets there. Roney and Garrett take walk-on roles rather than full-fledged parts, but they play like the pros they are and superimpose some useful muscle on an otherwise unremarkable affair.

Ernestine Anderson (born 1928)

VOCAL

Sang with the Johnny Otis road show in the late '40s and early '50s, then in clubs, and made five albums for Mercury during 1958–60, most of which have never been reissued on CD. In the '80s she made many albums for Concord, moving between torch-song and R&B styles.

***** Hello Like Before**
Concord CCD 4031 *Anderson; Hank Jones (p); Ray Brown (b); Jimmie Smith (d).* 76.

****(*) Live From Concord To London**
Concord CCD 4054 *As above, except add John Horler (p), James Richardson (b), Jake Hanna, Roger Sellers (d), Bill Berry Big Band; omit Smith.* 8/76–10/77.

***** Sunshine**
Concord CCD 4109 *Anderson; Monty Alexander (p); Ray Brown (b); Jeff Hamilton (d).* 8/79.

***** Never Make Your Move Too Soon**
Concord CCD 4147 *Anderson; Monty Alexander (p); Ray Brown (b); Frank Gant (d).* 8/80.

***** Big City**
Concord CCD 4214 *Anderson; Hank Jones (p); Monty Budwig (b); Jeff Hamilton (d).* 2/83.

****(*) When The Sun Goes Down**
Concord CCD 4263 *Anderson; Red Holloway (ts); Gene Harris (p); Ray Brown (b); Gerryck King (d).* 8/84.

***** Be Mine Tonight**
Concord CCD 4319 *Anderson; Benny Carter (as); Marshall Otwell (p); Ron Eschete (g); Ray Brown (b); Jimmie Smith (d).* 12/86.

***** Boogie Down**
Concord CCD 4407 *Anderson; Clayton–Hamilton Jazz Orchestra.* 9/89.

***** Live At The 1990 Concord Jazz Festival – Third Set**
Concord CCD 4454 *Anderson; Marshal Royal (as); Frank Wess (ts); Gene Harris (p); Ed Bickert (g); Lynn Seaton (b); Harold Jones (d).* 8/90.

Ernestine Anderson isn't the kind of singer one expects to find on Concord: she's more of a rhythm-and-blues shouter, and her 1958 debut for Mercury (now back in limbo) was a typical girl-singer date in which she sounded fine on the belters and less sure with the ballads. The suave situations she's been placed in at Concord may on the face of it seem to be inappropriate. Yet the least satisfying session here is the most 'bluesy', *When The Sun Goes Down*, which wastes the subtleties in Anderson's voice on lesser material, with Holloway and Harris also sounding stuck in routine. None of these records counts as a classic but each has its own particular interest. The two with Hank Jones benefit from the pianist's ingenious accompaniments, although *Hello Like Before* suffers from a couple of weak song choices. *Never Make Your Move Too Soon* also has too many familiar tunes on it, but Alexander's knowing vivacity is a tonic. Benny Carter's stately appearance on *Be Mine Tonight* adds some extra interest, and here the songs are chosen perfectly, including 'Christopher Columbus', 'London By Night' and 'Sack Full Of Dreams'. Anderson's voice isn't the strong, smoky instrument it was on her Mercury album, but she often takes hold of a song with a kind of infectious intensity that is exciting; her ballads, by contrast, are either compelling or heavy-going. *Boogie Down*, with a full big band behind her, is suitably rollicking music, and she can show Diane Schuur, for one, how to make such a situation work best for a singer. The Concord Festival set from 1990 is par for this particular course – Royal and Wess make statesman-like guest appearances, and there is a lot of applause.

Fred Anderson (born 1929)

TENOR SAXOPHONE

Anderson wasn't the first and won't be the last musician to give up active playing to run a joint of his own. Fortunately the Chicagoan has resurfaced in the 1990s to re-establish a recording career that was late enough in starting but which even then seemed to stall prematurely.

*****(*) The Missing Link**

Nessa NCD 23 *Anderson; Larry Hayrod (b); Hamid Drake (d); Adam Rudolph (perc).* 9/79.

***** Vintage Duets: 1.11.1980**

Okkadisk OD 12001 *Anderson; Steve McCall (d).* 1/80.

***** Birdhouse**

Okkadisk OD 12007 *Anderson; Jim Baker (p); Harrison Bankhead (b); Hamid Drake (d).* 4/94, 2/95.

It's irritating to hear people talk about having *seen* a musician when they really mean they've *heard* him. With Fred Anderson, as with a few others, the two are more than usually connected. Not for him the upright stance and relaxed shoulders the manuals suggest. The veteran Chicagoan dips, stoops and crouches and, what's more, you can hear him do it. Anderson always sounds in pursuit of what he has to say, in struggle with the sheer intransigence of the music. If he is a missing link, as the title of the very welcome Nessa reissue suggests, what he's bridging is the gap between the spare, blues-soaked sound of early Ornette and the clean-sweep radicalism of AACM.

Anderson first made his presence felt three decades ago on fellow-saxophonist Joseph Jarman's ground-breaking Delmark record, *Song For*. Thereafter he disappeared for a decade and more, so far as a wider record-buying public was concerned, concentrating on running his South Side jazz joint, the Velvet Lounge. It was only in the '80s, and then again more securely in the '90s that he became a presence on the scene. He shares with Von Freeman a knack for sounding absolutely contemporary and completely steeped in the tradition. There is an excellent Okkadisk release called *Destiny* with Hamid Drake and under Marilyn Crispell's nominal leadership. It underlines the point perfectly.

If there is a single reference-point for his playing, it has to be Gene Ammons; it's in the phrasing and in the shape of almost every solo. Anderson is raw and spare, feeding directly off the percussion rather than the chords, which is why he never sounds quite as focused working with a piano player. Like Jug, he doesn't rush to make his point. The duets with McCall (the only other percussionist on the planet who really taps into what he's about) are as laid back and unhurried as could ever be, sometimes to the point where the listener feels excluded. It isn't so much a dialogue as two overlapping soliloquies, with McCall relying on the sheer suppleness of his deceptively straightforward count to keep Fred on his toes.

The Missing Link catches him early enough for all the components – Jug, Ornette, the AACM experiment – to be severally audible. It now reappears with a long extra track, Hamid Drake's composition, 'Tabla Peace', and is certainly the disc of choice. *Birdhouse* never quite fires, perhaps because the pianist is so restrictive, though 'Like Sonny', a tribute to Sonny Stitt, is worth the wait, done without a hint of pastiche. The duets suffer from a poor transfer which leaves the splendid McCall sounding as if he's in another place.

*****(*) Live At The Velvet Lounge**

Okkadisk OD 12023 *Anderson; Peter Kowald (b); Hamid Drake (d).* 6/98.

The live session comes from Anderson's own club, and it has the self-indulgent relaxation of focus that comes with a home gig. Kowald is a master, but even he seems to be taking a night off and, apart from the emotionally driven 'To Those Who Know', barely registers as anything more than an accompanist. Drake is more forceful, but he drifts into an over-emphatic grandstanding which doesn't suit the occasion. The opening track, 'Straight, But Not Straight', may well be a homage to Monk, but without the master's wry refusal of self-importance. Anderson is more of a stalwart than an innovator. His impact on the Chicago scene has been considerable and he's affectionately spoken of by two generations of players there. Not quite a players' player, but not quite defined enough for stardom.

Ray Anderson (born 1952)

TROMBONE, ALTO TROMBONE, OTHER BRASS AND PERCUSSION, VOCALS

Anderson came to New York in 1972 and five years later joined Anthony Braxton's quartet, replacing his teacher, George Lewis. His work encompasses the avant-garde, jazz and funk, all of it handled in an old-fashioned tailgating style that is usually irresistible.

***** Right Down Your Alley**

Soul Note 121087 *Anderson; Mark Helias (b); Gerry (d).* 2/84.

*****(*) Old Bottles – New Wine**

Enja 4098 *Anderson; Kenny Barron (p); Cecil McBee (b); Dannie Richmond (d).* 6/85.

Ray Anderson always gives the impression that he goes to work with a smile. Whether playing in a – more or less – straight jazz context, or with the relative freedom of the BassDrumBone group with Mark Helias and Gerry Hemingway, or most obviously with his R&B unit, Slickaphonics, there is an exuberance and verve about his playing which is impossible to resist. The early *Old Bottles – New Wine* was recorded by a player who had just begun to pull down poll awards. It's pretty clear what Anderson means by his title. This is very much in the tradition, but with some fresh wrinkles, and he could hardly have hoped for a more responsive band.

By contrast, the trio with Helias and Hemingway is much freer and more open-ended, with a greater emphasis on blurts, smears and huge portamento effects. Like George Lewis, Anderson favours a horn with an F-key, a thumb-operated valve which allows him to drop the sound a fourth as required, and there's a depth to the sound that here and there almost suggests a bass instrument. Timbrally, it's engaging enough, but *Right Down Your Alley* is a drier and more demanding listen than the Enja record.

***** It Just So Happens**

Enja 5037 *Anderson; Stanton Davis (t); Bob Stewart (tba); Perry Robinson (cl); Mark Dresser (b); Ronnie Burrage (d).* 86.

***** Blues Bred In The Bone**

Enja 5081 *Anderson; John Scofield (g); Anthony Davis (p); Mark Dresser (b); Johnny Vidacovich (d).* 3/88.

Not the least of Anderson's great strengths is an instinctive feeling for the blues, one honed by a stint in saxophonist Bennie Wallace's revivalist project. *Blues Bred In The Bone* is a less strikingly individual record than its immediate predecessor, which is fascinating for the ever-broadening range of colours Anderson calls on, not just from the trombone, but from his sidemen as well. The pairing of Davis and the still-marginalized Robinson was an inspired one, however it came about, and the addition of another low brass horn gives the sound a rounded quality, full and resonant, but by no means lacking in attack.

The blues were indeed bred in the 'bone and the 1988 session finds Anderson exploiting his instrument's vocal qualities, passages that sound like common speech leading into preacherly soliloquies and hot gospel choruses. The partnership with Scofield is a fruitful one, especially on the original '53rd and Greenwood' and on a marvellous version of 'A Flower Is A Lovesome Thing', which sounds just about ready to drop its petals and fade, but is held together by Anderson's sheer presence.

*****(*) Don't Mow Your Lawn**

Enja ENJ 8070 *Anderson; Lew Soloff (t); Jerome Harris (g); Gregory Jones (b, v); Tommy Campbell (d); Frank Colon (perc).* 3/94.

****** Heads and Tales**

Enja ENJ 9055 *As above.* 5/95.

Enter the Alligatory Band. Anderson's most settled recent outfit is closer in spirit to Slickaphonics than to the other small groups, but it marks a significant step for him, both as player and as writer. Our shaky purchase on the pun may be judged from the mis-spelling of the later title as 'Heads and Tails' in a previous edition. It might restore credibility if we explain that 'alligatory' music is the lyrical expression of 'swamp-infested rug-cutters from the bayous of the mind with allegorical twists and an aleatoric joie-de-vivre' (R. Anderson, 1995).

Despite the sometimes rather flip approach, these are the most personal and expressive sessions the trombonist has yet consigned to record. The opening suite, 'The Four Reasons', is deceptively powerful, beginning and ending with two of Anderson's strongest tunes, 'Hunting And Gathering' and 'Unsung Songs'. Wife Jackie Raven's lyric for 'Tough Guy' might have sold the music short if it weren't for the old man's bravura delivery. The freewheeling stuff is saved for the closing 'Road Song' and 'Drink And Blather', and Soloff's high-register approach is significantly kept in check for much of the record.

Don't Mow Your Lawn is pretty much hi-jacked by the trumpeter, evidence of Anderson's occasional difficulty in producing his best playing when also juggling leadership duties. He also indulges in more singing than usual, which wasn't a good idea. As before, production is by bassist Mark Helias, and the sound is absolutely first rate, big and brash but by no means lacking in subtlety.

*****(*) Funkorific**

Enja ENJ 9340-2 *Anderson; Amina Claudine Myers (p, org, v); Jerome Harris (g); Lonnie Plaxico (b); Tommy Campbell (d).* 1/98.

****** Where Home Is**

Enja ENJ 9366-2 *Anderson; Lew Soloff (t); Matt Perine (sou); Bobby Previte (d).* 11/98.

The disappearance of Anderson's hat ART albums, *Azurety*, *Cheer Up* and *Slide Ride*, leave a hole in the catalogue; who knows when and whether any of these will reappear? These recent sessions don't quite plug the gap, but they do go some way towards it.

What colour is lapis lazuli? Blue, blue, blue. *Funkorific* is blue to its core, a blues album of the fastest and most evocative dye. Signing up Amina Claudine Myers was a brilliant notion. She is the key element in the new Lapis Lazuli band, creating funky but edgy accompaniments for Anderson's latest extension of the Slickaphonics concept, a roots band with a toe dipped in the avant-garde. 'Hammond Eggs' and 'Willie & Muddy' are as down-home as it gets, while the opening 'Pheromonical' shows how much Anderson and Myers have drawn from stylistically more experimental settings.

The Pocket Brass Band featured on *Where Home Is* consciously closes the distance between the early days of jazz and the contemporary, saxophone-haunted scene. Moving on from the all-trombone front line which made *Slideride* for hat ART, this line- up calls on the fierce, stabbing attack of Lew Soloff and the eclectic bass lines of Matt Perrine, who has worked in every genre from straight brass to reggae. 'The Alligatory Abagua' recalls previous bands, a strutting, confident performance that is deeply rooted in brass-band idiom. There are absences to regret in Anderson's discography but, as long as he turns out albums as strong as these, there is going to be little time to mourn them.

Reid Anderson

BASS

Contemporary bassist at work on the current New York scene.

*****(*) Dirty Show Tunes**

Fresh Sound FSNT 030 *Anderson; Mark Turner (ts); Ethan Iverson (p); Jorge Rossy (d).* 5/97.

****** Abolish Bad Architecture**

Fresh Sound FSNT 062 *As above, except Jeff Ballard (d) replaces Rossy.* 5/99.

Despite the title of the first disc (also Anderson's publishing name), no show tunes, dirty or otherwise, and not a lot to bed these down among the conventions of tenor-and-rhythm either. Anderson writes material that continually changes its shape as it goes forward. The harmonic structure of each piece is elusive: it never seems to be made particularly manifest, and there's a feeling of clear freedom even as each component seems to lead inevitably to the next. Tempos evolve out of the collective playing, slowing or accelerating as the internal dynamics demand. The music is more melodious than tied to set lines of melody. It's at least fascinating, often utterly compelling: listen to the absolutely extraordinary 'Mystery Girl' on *Abolish Bad Architecture*, which is not a ballad in feel but is as serenely contemplative as any conventional bit of post-bop lyricism, yet from another, oblique world. It helps Anderson that he has two magnificent contributors in Turner and Iverson, players who are themselves very out of the ordinary, as their own discs suggest. The second disc is the superior one because the empathy seems even more attuned, and Ballard is a less conventionally swinging drummer than Rossy, and he suits this unconventional music better (Ballard even uses relatively simple rock patterns at times, as on 'Hommage; Mahler'). This is one place jazz is going next.

Wessell Anderson (born 1964)

ALTO AND SOPRANINO SAXOPHONES

Alto saxophonist of today, best known as a sideman in the Wynton Marsalis group.

*** Warmdaddy In The Garden Of Swing

Atlantic 82657-2 *Anderson; Eric Reed (p); Ben Wolfe (b); Donald Edwards (d).* 5/94.

*** The Ways Of Warmdaddy

Atlantic 82860-2 *Anderson; Antoine Drye (t); Ellis Marsalis (p); Tarus Mateen (b); Donald Edwards (d).* 6–7/95.

'Warmdaddy' Anderson's big, oleaginous sound spreads like molasses over the rhythms on the first record. It's a surprise that he starts the disc with a sopranino outing, 'The Black Cat', but the title blues tells more of what he's about. For the most part, the record is a dialogue between himself and Reed (a fellow bandmate in the Wynton Marsalis group), since Wolfe and Edwards play a very subsidiary role; and the problem here is the pianist's sometimes irritating manner of taking the trickiest path he can possibly find on an otherwise simple sequence. When they set down an actual duet, 'Go Slow For Mo'', they sound deadly serious.

The Ways Of Warmdaddy is a step forward. The material seems more focused, less wound up: 'Change Of Heart' is a boppish blues executed with a fine bounce, 'Rockin' In Rhythm' is done with some panache, and the trio tracks in which Ellis Marsalis sits out are shouldered to good effect by the leader – 'Desimonae' sounds particularly fine. But so far Anderson hasn't solved a problem that seems to beset a number of Marsalis associates: he wants to play with the kind of unfettered, rocking swing that was second nature to pre-boppers, but he can't throw off the self-consciousness which that approach has built into it today.

Krister Andersson

TENOR SAXOPHONE, CLARINET

Contemporary Swedish saxman in the post-bop idiom.

***(*) About Time

Flash Music FLCD 1 *Andersson; Ion Baciu (p); Torbjørn Hultcrantz, Markus Wikstrom (b); Leif Wennerstrom, Jan Robertson (d); Malando Gassama (perc).* 93.

A rare outing as leader for this very accomplished Swedish tenorman. One of his models is Joe Henderson: the long, looping phrases and faintly querulous tone are familiar from the American's music. But Andersson is his own man. He thinks a long way ahead, mapping out improvisations with shrewd foresight so that they feel all of a piece, as spontaneous as they sound. 'How High The Moon' is coolly dismantled, an old bop blowing vehicle with all the clichés cleared away. The rhythm sections add anonymous support, somewhat in the manner of Tristano-school players, and it would be interesting to hear Andersson in the company of more assertive musicians. Gassama's guest presence on one track is also a mistake, since he sounds entirely wrong. Otherwise a fine record.

Apaturia Quintet

GROUP

Modern Italian small group organized by Giuseppe Bassi.

**** Apaturia

YVP 3054 *Flavio Boltro (t, flhn); Roberto Ottaviano (ss); Nico Morelli (p); Giuseppe Bassi (b); Marcello Magliocchi (d).* 11/94–2/95.

A pristine example of contemporary Italian jazz. The date belongs to Bassi, who co-produced and wrote five of the eight pieces, but it's a beautiful display of co-operative playing, concentration, finesse and elegance. This is a relatively straightforward setting for Ottaviano, and the staunchless flow of ideas he comes up with, melodies streaming out of the horn, compel the attention. Boltro seems slightly more reserved in comparison, yet they work together beautifully, as the dovetailing on 'Love From Tango' displays. Bassi offers them some charming material and an hour of music passes without a blemish.

Peter Apfelbaum

TENOR SAXOPHONE, PIANO, ORGAN

Apfelbaum and his circle are California-based eclectics, with an ambitious take on various jazz and other-musical strands.

**(*) Luminous Charms

Gramavision GCD 79511 *Apfelbaum; Jeff Cressman (tb, b); Will Bernerd (g); Jai Uttal (harmonium); John Shifflet (b); Deszon X Claiborne (d); Josh Jones (d, perc).* 1/96.

Not surprisingly, this is dedicated to the late Don Cherry, who died in 1995. Cherry – and particularly the *Multi-Kulti* project – was the inspiration behind Apfelbaum's highly idiosyncratic (if too self-consciously eclectic) Hieroglyphics Ensemble. Their Antilles albums, *Signs Of Life* and *Jodoji Brightness*, intrigued and frustrated by turns. It was quite difficult to say what the group was about, because it was about something different almost every track. That may not have helped build a market profile. Either way, the Antilles contract is at an end.

The unit on *Luminous Charms* is now unambiguously Apfelbaum's group rather than a collective and, though some of the personnel remain the same, he is definitely the driving force. His tenor playing is quite conventional, blues-driven and attractively soft-edged, with a generous vibrato. Jeff Cressman's trombone is not perhaps the ideal foil, but they negotiate agree-to-differ terms in the arrangements, perhaps because Apfelbaum plays slightly sharp.

'Luminous Charms' opens on saxophone over a still bass pedal, before guitar, bass and drums successively kick in. It isn't a number that seems destined to go anywhere particular and, though there are unexpected changes of tempo and key here and there, they don't seem to have too much to do with the basic idea.

'Chimes', for Roscoe Mitchell, is a more coherent idea and 'Song Of Corrosion' is both sweet and faintly disturbing.

Apfelbaum isn't strong enough either as a writer or as a soloist. He needs many more hours spent bashing away at someone else's charts, unpicking them, tripping on their hard places, before he arrives at a genuinely distinctive sound. The Hieroglyphics Ensemble managed to keep ahead of its own limitations; with *Luminous Charms*, Apfelbaum has just come across his. Like they say, it's a learning curve.

Arc

GROUP

The String Trio of New York proved that it was possible to make vivid jazz with no horns, piano or percussion. This British trio has carved its own course, quirky and effective.

***** Out Of Amber**

Slam CD 025 *Sylvia Hallett (vn); Danny Kingshill (clo); Gus Garside (b).* 10/92, 1/93.

Not to be confused with the American string group, Arcado, Garside, Hallett and Kingshill operate in a territory that embraces the fringes of composition and the more idiosyncratic end of British improvisation. Hallett is also a member of the cult group, British Summertime Ends, and he brings to Arc something of the same blend of enigmatic melody and sheer whimsy. Kingshill's orientation is more obviously settled towards composed forms and he occasionally sounds as if he is trying to impose form on otherwise improvised pieces. An atmospheric player with a beautiful big tone, he provides a bridge between his two colleagues. Garside is unmistakably a jazz player, and he frequently introduces a rhythmic groove that would otherwise be lacking. Where he differs from the average jazz bassist is in the range of tones he extracts from his instrument. 'Circadian Rhythms' and 'Snow Dance' are both lovely, but the whole album is well worth sampling, even at this late date.

Arcana

GROUP

A supergroup of improvisers, in two incarnations.

****** The Last Wave**

DIW 903 *Derek Bailey (g); Bill Laswell (b); Tony Williams (d).* 4/95.

*****(*) Arc Of The Testimony**

Axiom 524431-2 *Graham Haynes (c); Byard Lancaster (as, bcl); Pharoah Sanders (ts); Buckethead, Nicky Skopelitis (g); Bill Laswell (b); Tony Williams (d).* 97.

As power trios go, the original Arcana packed interstellar power. The prospect of Bailey, godfather of the British free scene, recording with the most creative and open-minded drummer of his generation (and erstwhile leader of Lifetime) was irresistible. The results were well up to expectation, clangorous, dark-toned music from territory out beyond either jazz or rock, or any conceivable industry hybrid. Laswell was inevitably the junior partner, but it's his instinctive production skill, as well as the cementing breadth of his eight-string bass, that holds the set together. It's very clear that, for all his recent experiments with drum'n'bass, with flat-out power merchants like Keiji Haino, and with rappers and scratchers, Bailey is not on familiar ground; he isn't so much uneasy as unbending, an Englishman abroad speaking louder in order to be understood. The opening 'Broken Circle' could almost be a Lifetime piece, if there were churning organ chords in place of Laswell's fat but quick-footed sounds. 'Pearls And Transformation' is the key track, more than a quarter of an hour of stark beauty which features Williams's subtlest drumming. By contrast, the shorter 'Rattle Of Bones' and 'Tears Of Astral Rain' seem a bit on the light side, ideas-wise.

The follow-up album was entirely overshadowed by the death of Tony Williams shortly before its release. The addition of saxophonists squared with our desire to see Peter Brötzmann guesting with the original trio, but what an interesting choice in the event. Sanders was no great surprise; he has trodden this turf before. Lancaster, though, remains poorly recognized and it's his taut alto, doubled with bass clarinet on 'Into The Circle' and 'Calling Out The Blue Light', which lifts those tracks. Graham Haynes is heard on the former and also on 'Gone Tomorrow', seemingly playing from distant, cavernous space that turns his horn into a plangent, lost-soul voice. No Bailey this time out, of course. One immediately misses the sheer oddity of that sound. Skopelitis is a fine player, controlled but relentlessly in the groove. However, it's an approach that palls over the distance. The eccentric Buckethead brings his cartoon style to three tracks, somewhere between odd and irritating, with occasional flashes of graphic brilliance. As a memorial to Williams, this probably isn't as typical as some of the last albums with acoustic groups, but it serves as a forceful reminder of the immense power he was holding in check even when he was playing straight fours and quiet ballad figures.

Jimmy Archey (1902–67)

TROMBONE

In New York from 1927 and played in many of the major big bands in the '30s. Later, he was more familiarly seen in revivalist bands but could always move easily between trad, swing and mainstream styles.

***** Dr Jazz Vol. 4**

Storyville STCD 6044 *Archey; Henry Goodwin (t); Benny Waters (cl, ss, as); Dick Wellstood (p); Pops Foster (b); Tommy Benford (d).* 1–4/52.

**** Reunion**

GHB BCD-310 *Archey; Punch Miller (t); Albert Burbank (cl); Dick Griffith (bj); Dick McCarthy (b); Sammy Penn (d).* 2/67.

Rare examples of this redoubtable 'bone man as leader. The Storyville disc is from the *Dr Jazz* series of radio broadcasts, and though as usual the band was encouraged to play overheated Dixieland, some excellent moments survive. Waters, not often in the limelight at this stage of his career, is in top form, and the rarely heard Goodwin stands comfortably beside the leader.

Archey was from Virginia, but the *Reunion* with a group of New Orleans players actually took place in Connecticut. The material is bedraggled – and so, alas, is much of the playing: Burbank's agile phrasing is flawed by his terribly squeaky tone, and Punch Miller was having an indifferent day. Archey's spirited, melodic solos are much more encouraging, though, and the rhythm players make sure that the music clatters along.

Julian Arguëlles (born 1966)

TENOR SAXOPHONE

Emerged from the Loose Tubes collective as a singular musician in his own right. Has often worked with brother Steve but is asserting himself as a group leader and recording artist.

*** Phaedrus

Ah Um 010 *Arguëlles; John Taylor (p); Mick Hutton (b); Martin France (d).* 91.

*** Home Truths

Babel BDV 9503 *Arguëlles; Mike Walker (g); Steve Swallow (b); Martin France (d).* 5/95.

The Arguëlles brothers – Julian and Steve – are, along with the Mondesirs, the Traceys and the Bancrofts in Scotland, the closest thing to a significant family dynasty in British jazz. Both are richly talented; both have created music of considerable individuality. *Home Truths* is an encouragingly personal sax-and-rhythm date for the young British saxophonist. Abjuring obvious role-models has apparently led him in the direction of such players as Warne Marsh and some of the modern European masters, but on *Phaedrus* he tempers any danger of humourless expertise with some typically off-kilter melodies which Taylor, in particular, underlines with harmonic and textural strength. While there are hints of deliberate foolishness in some of the writing – a trait that continues to be a besetting sin among many British players – it livens up the sometimes portentous Taylor no end, and Hutton and France play with plenty of enjoyment too.

If Arguëlles is a Good Thing, then so, too, is Oliver Weindling's Babel label, which has dedicated itself to some of the most creative music around. It is a measure of the reputation of young Brits like Arguëlles and guitarist Mike Walker that Steve Swallow should find time in a busy schedule to come and record a session like this. To be frank, he makes it. Weaving in and around both Walker and Arguëlles, he creates a skein of sound that is almost too beguiling, and the listener may end up pulled away from the main action.

***(*) Scapes

Babel BDV 9674 *Arguëlles; Steve Arguëlles (d, perc).* 95.

The duos on *Scapes* are brief, clever, funny and thoroughly musical. Julian's multi-instrumentalism has never been a pose, and increasingly he has developed a definite character on all his instruments. Steve's contributions are more than functional. He inhabits the music and propels it at the same time, turning the shortest tracks into mini-odysseys that go in unexpected directions. A fine, comradely album.

*** Skull View

Babel BDV 9719 *Arguëlles; Mark Bassey (tb); Django Bates (thn); Iain Dixon (ts, bcl, cl); Mario Laginha (p); Mike Walker (g); Steve Watts (b); Martin France (d).* 96.

Skull View is ambitiously conceived and contoured, an album that suggests Arguëlles will develop into a fine composer for larger units. His command of small detail is matched by a generous musical sweep, and there is a mature exuberance even to pieces which seem to flirt with the macabre humour that one thought was left behind in Loose Tubes days.

**** Escapade

Provocateur PVC 1019 *Arguëlles; Django Bates (thn); Iain Dixon (ts, cl, bcl); Mario Laginha (p); Mike Walker (g); Steve Watts (b); Martin France (d).* 6/99.

This is one of the best British jazz albums of recent memory, a subtle, compelling record which repays the closest attention or one that can be put on simply for the groove. 'The Pow Wow' is reminiscent of things John Surman and John McLaughlin were doing at the time of *Extrapolation*, and the whole album has all the serious, insouciant perversity of those days, locked into a compelling groove but also brimming over with ideas.

Guitarist Walker has a hefty reputation on the scene but one which, until now, has not seemed to transfer easily to record. The delicacy of his understated chordal introduction to the brief '9 Grammes Of Lead' is a measure of how subtle he can be. Mark Bassey's mournful brass-band trombone and Django's now familiar peckhorn lines are singularly adapted to Arguëlles's slower compositions, but even when the tempo is frenetic, as on the scratch 'Coffee And Diesel' (which might almost be a Tim Berne out-take), the band is ideally attuned to the material. Pianist Laginha is a revelation, though occasionally he and Walker seem to have each other's charts. There will be no better British jazz album this year.

Steve Arguëlles (born 1963)

DRUMS

British drummer/percussionist, brother of saxophonist Julian, who emerged as part of the Loose Tubes collective in the '80s and has latterly based himself in Paris; numerous projects include The Recyclers.

*** Blue Moon In A Function Room

Babel BDV 9402 *Arguëlles; Stuart Hall (g, v); Billy Jenkins (g); Steve Watts (b).* 90.

*** Busy Listening

Babel BDV 9406 *Arguëlles; Julian Arguëlles (as); Stuart Hall (g, v); Huw Warren (acc); Mick Hutton (b).* 9/93.

So richly and sympathetically has Britain nourished and nurtured talent like Arguëlles's that he has had to move to France to find an acceptable amount of paid work. A familiar story, and a very galling one. Fortunately, though he is less often to be heard at home, Arguëlles has established a recording career as well. The earliest of these goes back some way and is still a little self-conscious, bearing the stamp of Jenkins's maverick genius. Items like 'Vision On', theme music to a British television programme for deaf children, seem unlikely in a jazz context, alongside 'Tiger Rag', 'Lady Be Good' (which is segued with 'Johnny B. Goode') and 'Ruby (Don't Take Your Love To Town)'. Hugely entertaining, but not by any means as interesting as what Arguëlles has done more recently with The Recyclers (who are reviewed separately) and on *Busy Listening*, both of which are splendidly mature but not solemn, and packed with ideas without becoming po-faced. Arguëlles lays down a crackling groove for his colleagues on both sets. Some of the laddishness has worn off, and the music is all the better for it.

Lil Hardin Armstrong (1898–1971)

PIANO, VOCAL

Born in Memphis, Lillian Hardin demonstrated pianos at a Chicago store before working with some of the best bands in the city, eventually joining King Oliver and meeting her future husband, Louis Armstrong. She helped drive his career early on, but they eventually divorced in 1938. She led groups of her own and was house pianist at Decca for a spell. From the '40s onwards she was a familiar presence once again on the Chicago club scene.

***** Lil Hardin Armstrong And Her Swing Orchestra 1936–1940**

Classics 564 *Armstrong; Joe Thomas, Shirley Clay, Ralph Muzillo, Johnny McGee, Reunald Jones, Jonah Jones (t); Al Philburn, J.C Higginbotham (tb); Buster Bailey, Tony Zimmers (cl); Don Stovall (as); Russell Johns, Prince Robinson, Robert Carroll, Chu Berry (ts); Frank Froeba, James Sherman, Teddy Cole (p); Arnold Adams, Huey Long, Dave Barbour (g); John Frazier, Wellman Braud, Haig Stephens (b); O'Neil Spencer, Sam Weiss, George Foster, Manzie Johnson (d); Midge Williams, Hilda Rogers (v).* 10/36–3/40.

Although she was a real modernist in her youth, the former Mrs Armstrong never advanced very much as a piano player, which may be why keyboard duties were entrusted to others on most of these sessions. But her vocal talents are still likeable, and on these now largely forgotten sides she comes on like a precursor of Nellie Lutcher and other, vaguely racy, post-war singers. The accompaniments offer a rough distillation of small-band swing and rather older styles, suggested by the presence of such veterans of the 1920s as Robinson and Clay, alongside the more modernistic Thomas and Berry. Titles such as '(I'm On A) Sit-down Strike For Rhythm' have a self-explanatory charm, and there's a more distinctive jazz content in the typically hot and fluent playing of Bailey. On the final, 1940 date, Mrs Armstrong returns to the piano and leaves the singing to others. A mixed bag as far as reproduction goes, but mostly dubbed from decent originals.

***** Lil Hardin Armstrong – Chicago: The Living Legends**

Original Jazz Classics OJC 1823 *Armstrong; Bill Martin, Roi Nabors, Eddie Smith (t); Preston Jackson, Al Wynn (tb); Darnell Howard, Franz Jackson (cl); Pops Foster (b); Booker Washington (d).* 9/61.

This group of old-timers plays with astonishing vitality, even mania, on some of these tracks. 'Royal Garden Blues' has seldom had such a shaking-down as it gets here: Howard's clarinet goes from a woody moan to a near-shriek, and the trumpeters all take their turn to rattle the roof. There is also some solid blues, an enjoyable feature for Lil's singing on 'Clip Joint', and 'Boogie Me', where she duets with Washington and makes one wonder why she didn't play piano like that with the Hot Five. Hardly subtle, but much merriment.

Louis Armstrong (1901–71)

TRUMPET, CORNET, VOCAL

Born in New Orleans, Armstrong learned the cornet after being sent to a waifs' home in 1913. By 1919 he was already a formidable player, and he began recording with King Oliver in 1923, as second cornet. He went to New York a year later and joined the Fletcher Henderson orchestra, then he began recording under his own name in 1925 with the Hot Five and Hot Seven for Okeh Records in Chicago. By the end of the 1920s he was a great star as a soloist, and his playing had influenced everybody in jazz, shifting the emphasis from group playing to solo improvising. He also created a vocal style for all jazz singers. In the 1930s he worked in a big-band context and began touring with what had been the Luis Russell Orchestra in 1935. In 1947, his career at a comparatively low ebb despite Hollywood appearances and an invincible personality, he switched to small groups and began leading his All Stars, a sextet format he remained with for the rest of his touring career. In the '60s he had worldwide pop hits with the likes of 'Hello Dolly' and 'What A Wonderful World'. Though illness left him faltering at times in his later years, he was always the greatest ambassador in jazz and he remains its best-loved individual figure.

****** Hot Fives & Sevens Vol. 1**

JSP CD 312 *Armstrong; Kid Ory (tb); Johnny Dodds (cl, as); Lil Armstrong (p); Johnny St Cyr (bj); Butterbeans & Susie, May Alix (v).* 11/25–11/26.

****** Louis Armstrong 1925–1926**

Classics 600 *As above.* 11/25–11/26.

****** Hot Fives And Hot Sevens Vol. 2**

JSP CD 313 *As above, except add Bill Wilson (c), Honore Dutrey, John Thomas (tb), Boyd Atkins (cl, ss, as), Albert Washington (ts), Earl Hines (p), Lonnie Johnson (g), Rip Bassett (bj, g), Pete Briggs (bb), Baby Dodds, Tubby Hall (d).* 5–12/27.

****** Hot Fives And Hot Sevens Vol. 3**

JSP CD 314 *Armstrong; Homer Hobson (t); Fred Robinson, Jack Teagarden (tb); Jimmy Strong (cl, ts); Don Redman (cl, as); Bert Curry, Crawford Wetherington (as); Happy Caldwell (ts); Earl Hines, Joe Sullivan (p); Carroll Dickerson (vn); Eddie Lang (g); Mancy Cara (bj, v); Dave Wilborn (bj, g); Pete Briggs (tba); Zutty Singleton, Kaiser Marshall (d).* 5–12/27.

****** Louis Armstrong 1926-1927**

Classics 585 *As above.* 11/26–12/27.

****** Hot Fives & Sevens Vol 4**

JSP CD 315 *Armstrong; Homer Hobson, Henry Allen, Otis Johnson (t); J.C Higginbotham, Fred Robinson (tb); Jimmy Strong (cl, ts); Charlie Holmes, Albert Nicholas, William Blue (cl, as); Bert Curry, Crawford Wetherington (as); Teddy Hill (ts);*

Carroll Dickerson (vn); Gene Anderson (p, cel); Luis Russell, Buck Washington (p); Lonnie Johnson, Will Johnson (g); Eddie Condon, Mancy Cara (bj); Pete Briggs (tba); Pops Foster (b); Zutty Singleton, Paul Barbarin (d); Hoagy Carmichael (v). 3/29–4/30.

♛ ** Hot Fives & Sevens**

JSP LOUISBOX 100 *As above four JSP discs.* 25–30.

****** The 25 Greatest Hot Fives And Hot Sevens**

ASV AJA 5171 *Basically as above.* 25–29.

Armstrong's music is one of the cornerstones of jazz and, while his most famous records – principally, the small-group sides made under the names The Hot Five and The Hot Seven – are now antiquarian in terms of their place in the jazz chronology, his playing remains a marvel. While we are envious of any who are discovering the likes of 'Wild Man Blues' or 'Tight Like This' for the first time, we acknowledge that the sound of the records – particularly the earliest, acoustic dates by The Hot Five from 1925 – can seem as 'difficult' to ears raised on digital sound as anything from the pre-LP era. Considering he was playing with his peers – Kid Ory and Johnny Dodds were two of the most respected performers in their field – the group's basic sound seems unexpectedly rough and unsophisticated, at least on the earlier sessions. Yet when one focuses on Armstrong himself, shortcomings seem to fall away in the face of his youthful mastery. Not yet 25 and still playing cornet when the sessions for OKeh started, he is still trying out for greatness, even if his spell with Fletcher Henderson a year earlier had already alerted the growing jazz community to his incipient greatness. Earlier pieces like 'Jazz Lips' or 'Cornet Chop Suey' have a rough-and-ready quality which Armstrong's blossoming power either barges past or transcends, and although there is a degree of vaudeville in his music already – exemplified by pieces like 'Heebie Jeebies' and 'Muskrat Ramble', with their comic studio routines – a lot of the time he elevates his surroundings through sheer charisma. By the time of the Hot Seven dates, beginning in 1927, with Dodds assuming a second-voice role that has even Armstrong compelled to play at his best, the music seems mystical in its poetry and majesty. 'Potato Head Blues', with its incredible stop-time solo, the astounding improvisation on 'Wild Man Blues' and the glittering blues playing on 'Willie The Weeper' are but three examples of the artistry that at that moment was reducing everyone else in jazz to a bit-player. By the time of the 'second' series of Hot Fives, with Earl Hines arriving on piano, Armstrong was already approaching the stature of a concerto soloist, a role he would play more or less throughout the next decade, which makes these final small-group sessions something like a reluctant farewell to jazz's first golden age. Since Hines is also magnificent on these discs (and their insouciant exuberance is a marvel on the duet showstopper, 'Weather Bird'), the results seem like eavesdropping on great men speaking almost quietly among themselves. There is nothing in jazz finer or more moving than the playing on 'West End Blues', 'Tight Like This', 'Beau Koo Jack' and 'Muggles'.

It should go almost without saying that we consider these tracks indispensable in any jazz collection. They have been reissued many times over the years, and OKeh's excellent studio sound has been faithfully transferred to a number of LP editions from the 1960s onwards. We are delighted to welcome back the superlative four-disc edition remastered by John R.T. Davies for JSP which should be generally available (although we are advised that it is to some extent a limited edition). Besides the basic Hot Five and Seven library, they also include such pieces as a Butterbeans and Susie duet which the group play behind, two tracks with Carroll Dickerson's Savoyagers, the classic 'Knockin' A Jug' date with Jack Teagarden and Eddie Lang, and the first 1929–30 sessions where Armstrong plays in front of the Luis Russell band. The four discs are available separately, but they can be bought in a four-disc slipcase to which we must inevitably accord a crown rating. Columbia have been mystifyingly neglectful of these great recordings, and currently their previous editions seem to have disappeared, although it seems likely that a new edition will be prepared for Armstrong's centenary in 2001. Classics have done their usual job, but their editions pale next to the JSP set.

The ASV disc isn't far behind the best in terms of sound and, as a single-disc representation of some of the best in the series, this works pretty well.

****** Louis Armstrong & His Orchestra 1928–1929**

Classics 570 *Personnel as listed under appropriate dates above.* 6/28–3/29.

****** Louis Armstrong & His Orchestra 1929–1930**

Classics 557 *Armstrong; Homer Hobson (t); Fred Robinson, Jack Teagarden, J.C Higginbotham (tb); Jimmy Strong (cl, ts); Albert Nicholas, Charlie Holmes, Bert Curry, William Blue, Crawford Wethington (as); Happy Cauldwell (ts); Joe Sullivan, Luis Russell, Buck Washington (p); Eddie Lang, Lonnie Johnson (g); Eddie Condon (bj); Pops Foster (b); Paul Barbarin, Kaiser Marshall (d); Hoagy Carmichael (v).* 3/29–5/30.

****** Louis Armstrong & His Orchestra 1930–31**

Classics 547 *Armstrong; Leon Elkins, George Orendorff, Harold Scott (t); Lawrence Brown, Luther Graven (tb); Leon Herriford, Willie Stark, Marvin Johnson (as); Les Hite (as, bs); Charlie Jones (cl, ts); Wiliam Franz (ts); Harvey Brooks, Henry Prince (p); Bill Perkins, Ceele Burke (bj, g); Reggie Jones (tba); Joe Bailey (b); Lionel Hampton (d, vib).* 7/30–4/31.

****** Louis Armstrong & His Orchestra 1931–32**

Classics 536 *Armstrong; Zilmer Randolph (t); Preston Jackson (tb); George James (cl, ss, as); Lester Boone (cl, as); Albert Washington (cl, ts); Charlie Alexander (p); Mike McKendrick (g, bj); John Lindsay (b); Tubby Hall (d).* 4/31–3/32.

Following the final Hot Five records, Armstrong recorded almost exclusively as a soloist in front of big bands, at least until the formation of the All Stars in the 1940s. Although the records became much more formal in shape – most of them are recordings of contemporary pop tunes, opened by an Armstrong vocal and climaxing in a stratospheric solo – the finest of them showcase Louis as grandly as anything he'd already recorded, and they certainly provide him with his best opportunities to sing. Since his vocal stylings were becoming at least as influential as his trumpet playing, it was critical that he get some of the best tunes of the day – and at this stage in his career, he did. Classics 557 covers the period when Armstrong was fronting the Luis Russell band. 'Black And Blue', 'Dallas Blues' and 'After You've Gone' offer superb improvisations against bland but functional backdrops and, while some of the sheer daring has gone out of Armstrong's playing, he's become more poised, more serenely powerful than before. Finer still, though, are the records made in Los Angeles in 1930 with, among others, the young Lionel

Hampton. There are few Armstrong performances superior to 'Body And Soul', 'I'm A Ding Dong Daddy From Dumas' and 'Memories Of You', where his singing is as integral and inventive as his trumpet-playing, and the sequence culminates in the moving and transcendent performance of 'Sweethearts On Parade'. The 1931–2 sessions find him in front of another anonymous orchestra and, although arrangements and performances are again merely competent, they serve to throw the leader's own contributions into sharper relief, with 'Star Dust', 'Lawd, You Made The Night Too Long' and 'Chinatown, My Chinatown' among the outstanding tracks. These were his final recordings for OKeh before a move to Victor in 1933.

The Classics sequence has the merit of uninterrupted chronological presentation at an attractive price and, while their transfers aren't always of the finest, there are no serious problems with the overall sound. As noted above, some of the earlier tracks are on the fourth disc in the JSP edition.

****** Louis Armstrong & His Orchestra 1932–33**

Classics 529 *Armstrong; Louis Bacon, Louis Hunt, Billy Hicks, Charlie Gaines, Elmer Whitlock, Zilmer Randolph (t); Charlie Green, Keg Johnson (tb); Pete Clark, Scoville Brown, George Oldham (cl, as); Edgar Sampson (as, vn); Louis Jordan, Arthur Davey (as); Budd Johnson (cl, ts); Elmer Williams, Ellsworth Blake (ts); Don Kirkpatrick, Wesley Robinson, Teddy Wilson (p); Mike McKendrick (bj, g); John Trueheart (g); Edgar Hayes, Bill Oldham (bb, b); Elmer James (b); Chick Webb, Benny Hill, Yank Porter (d).* 12/32–4/33.

Armstrong's Victor records of 1932–3 are among his most majestic statements. If he had simplified his style, the breadth of his tone and seeming inevitability of timing and attack have been fashioned into an invincible creation: the way he handles 'I Gotta Right To Sing The Blues' or 'Basin Street Blues' makes them seem like conclusive offerings from jazz's greatest virtuoso. Even so, weaker material was already starting to creep into his repertoire, and it planted the seeds for the often unfortunate choices of tune that would beset his years at Decca. The Classics series continues apace and gathers in most of the Victor material on to one CD.

****** Louis Armstrong & His Orchestra 1934–36**

Classics 509 *Armstrong; Jack Hamilton, Leslie Thompson, Leonard Davis, Gus Aiken, Louis Bacon, Bunny Berigan, Bob Mayhew (t); Lionel Guimaraes, Harry White, Jimmy Archey, Al Philburn (tb); Pete Duconge (cl, as); Sid Trucker (cl, bs); Henry Tyre, Henry Jones, Charlie Holmes, Phil Waltzer (as); Alfred Pratt, Bingie Madison, Greely Walton, Paul Ricci (ts); Herman Chittison, Luis Russell, Fulton McGrath (p); Maceo Jefferson, Lee Blair, Dave Barbour (g); German Artango, Pops Foster, Pete Peterson (b); Oliver Tynes, Paul Barbarin, Stan King (d).* 10/34–2/36.

*****(*) Rhythm Saved The World**

GRP 051602-2 *Largely as above.* 10/35–2/36.

*****(*) Louis Armstrong & His Orchestra 1936–37**

Classics 512 *As above, except add Snub Mosley, Bobby Byrne, Joe Yukl, Don Mattison (tb), Jimmy Dorsey, Jack Stacey (cl, as), Fud Livingston, Skeets Herfurt (cl, ts), Bobby Van Eps (p), George Archer, Harry Baty (g, v), Roscoe Hillman (g), Sam Koki (stg), Andy Iona (uke, v), Jim Taft, Joe Nawahi (b), Ray McKinley, Lionel Hampton (d), Bing Crosby, Frances Langford, The Mills Brothers (v).* 2/36–4/37.

****** Louis Armstrong & His Orchestra 1937–38**

Classics 515 *Armstrong; Shelton Hemphill, Louis Bacon, Henry Allen (t); George Matthews, George Washington, J.C Higginbotham, Wilbur De Paris (tb); Pete Clark, Charlie Holmes, Rupert Cole (as); Albert Nicholas, Bingie Madison (cl, ts); Luis Russell (p); Lee Blair (g); Pops Foster, Red Callender (b); Paul Barbarin (d); The Mills Brothers (v).* 6/37–5/38.

*****(*) Louis Armstrong & His Orchestra 1938–39**

Classics 523 *As above, except add Bob Cusamano, Johnny McGee, Otis Johnson, Frank Zullo, Grady Watts, Sonny Dunham (t); Al Philburn, Murray McEachern, Russell Rauch, Pee Wee Hunt (tb); Sid Stoneburn (cl); Art Ralston, Clarence Hutchenrider (as); Pat Davis, Dan D'Andrea, Joe Garland (ts); Kenny Sargent (bs); Nat Jaffe, Howard Hall (p); Jack Blanchette, Dave Barbour (g); Haig Stephens, Stan Dennis (b); Sam Weiss, Big Sid Catlett, Tony Briglia (d).* 5/38–4/39.

***** Vol. 2 – Heart Full Of Rhythm**

GRP 051620-2 *As above discs.* 4/36–12/38.

***** Louis Armstrong 1939–1940**

Classics 615 *Armstrong; Shelton Hemphill, Otis Johnson, Henry Allen, Bernard Flood (t); Wilbur De Paris, George Washington, J.C Higginbotham (tb); Charlie Holmes, Rupert Cole (cl, as); Joe Garland, Bingie Madison (ts); Luis Russell (p); Lee Blair (g); Pops Foster (b); Big Sid Catlett (d); The Mills Brothers (v).* 4/39–4/40.

*****(*) Louis Armstrong 1940–1942**

Classics 685 *As above, except add Gene Prince, Frank Galbreath (t), Claude Jones, Norman Greene, Henderson Chambers, James Whitney (tb), Sidney Bechet (cl, ss), Carl Frye (as), Prince Robinson (cl, ts), Bernard Addison, Lawrence Lucie (g), John Simmons, Hayes Alvis, Wellman Braud (b), Zutty Singleton (d).* 5/40–4/42.

Armstrong's Decca recordings in the 1930s have been a maligned group of records, always the least favoured part of his career. This is both a right and a wrong view. While there are many throwaway songs and plain bad ideas – even Louis couldn't do much with 'She's The Daughter Of A Planter From Havana' and its sorry ilk – he does rise above the circumstances much as Fats Waller and Billie Holiday do in the same period: the sheer *sound* of Armstrong, whether singing or playing trumpet, is exhilarating, and there are merits in these sessions which have often been overlooked. Decca's studio sound is often very handsome and they caught a silvery quality in Armstrong's tone which is not often apparent on his other records. He was playing with a particularly steely finesse at this point, far from the bubbling genius of a decade earlier but not yet the benign maestro of a decade hence. There is also his singing: whatever the lyric, Pops gives it his full measure.

The sequential Classics issues have to compete with the GRP reissues, which collectors will want for some rare alternative takes. The 1934–5 Classics disc includes a memorable session made in Paris with a local band including the very fine pianist, Herman Chittison, with a terrific 'St Louis Blues'; from there, Armstrong is backed mostly by a Luis Russell band, and it performs very creditably, with some members stepping forward for occasional solos. 1936–7 includes two tremendous pieces in 'Swing That Music' and 'Mahogany Hall Stomp' as well as a peculiar meeting with a Hawaiian group and two dates with the Mills Brothers. The fine session from January 1938 is on the next disc, with Albert Nicholas almost stealing the occasion on 'Struttin' With Some Barbecue' until Louis's own solo. The 1938–9 record has a session with the Casa Loma Orchestra, another with a rather white-toned gospel group, the lovely 'My Walking Stick' with the Mills Brothers and a concluding date which remakes 'West End Blues' and Don Redman's 'Save It, Pretty Mama'. Classics 615 has some miserable stuff of the order of 'Me And Brother Bill' but peaks on a new 'Confessin'', a fine 'Wolverine Blues' and a stunning new 'Sweethearts On Parade'. The final disc in the sequence, Classics 685, is again rather dated, although it includes the complete reunion date with Bechet from May 1940 and has a majestic 'When It's Sleepy Time Down South' – not the last track, but a suitable climax. We must award all these high marks, if only for the occasions when the material, music and Armstrong himself are all strong. The transfers are consistent enough.

The first GRP compilation takes a look at one of the most enjoyable of this run of sessions, from 1935–6, with 'I've Got My Fingers Crossed', 'Solitude' and 'I'm Putting All My Eggs In One Basket' among the standouts. Having creamed off the best of those, the second disc, *Heart Full Of Rhythm*, is a little less consistent, though there are still half a dozen tracks that any Armstrong collector should have; together, these two make a good sampler of the period. Some may prefer the highly cleaned-up sound of these transfers using the NoNoise system. See also the two-disc *Highlights* set, which we have listed below.

***** On The Sunny Side Of The Street**

Jazz J-CD-19 *Armstrong; Shelton Hemphill, Frank Galbreath, Bernard Flood, Robert Butler, Louis Gray, Fats Ford (t); George Washington, Henderson Chambers, James Whitney, Russell Moore, Waddet Williams, Nat Allen, James Whitney (tb); Don Hill, Amos Gordon, Rupert Coile (as); Dexter Gordon, Budd Johnson, John Sparrow (ts); Ernest Thompson (bs); Prince Robinson, Joe Garland, Carl Frye (saxes); Luis Russell, Earl Mason, Gerald Wiggins (p); Elmer Warner, Lawrence Lucie (g); Art Simmons, Arvell Shaw (b); Chick Morrison, Edward McConney, Jesse Price (d); The Mills Brothers, Velma Middleton, Jimmy Anderson, Ann Baker, Bea Booze (v).* 6/38–8/46.

A very entertaining compilation of broadcast and soundtrack material. Three shows for Forces Radio feature plenty of mugging and a degree of great trumpet, though a soundtrack reading of 'Jeepers Creepers' also has a strong solo, and a closing and very frantic 'Hot Chestnuts' is surprisingly wild. Sound-quality is very clean for all except two tracks, which suffer from some distortion.

****** Louis Armstrong 1944–1946**

Classics 928 *Armstrong; Roy Eldridge, Billy Butterfield, Jesse Brown, Fats Ford, Sleepy Grider, Lester Currant, Charlie Shavers, Moons Mullens, Neal Hefti, Chieftie Scott (t); Bobby Hackett (c); Jack Teagarden (tb, v); Russell Moore, Adam Martin, Norman Powe, Al Cobbs, Taswell Baird, Larry Anderson, Lou McGarity (tb); Barney Bigard, Ernie Caceres, Jimmy Hamilton (cl); Bill Stegmeyer (as, ts, cl); John Brown, Willard Brown, Johnny Hodges, Sid Stoneburn, Jules Rubin, George Koenig, Donald Hill, Amos Gordon (as); Don Byas, Jack Greenberg, Art Drelinger, Coleman Hawkins, Joe Garland, Johnny Sparrow, Ted McRae, Dexter Gordon, Nick Caiazza, Arthur Rollini (ts); Ernest Thompson, Paul Ricci, Milton Shatz (bs); Duke Ellington, Billy Strayhorn, Ed Swanston, Joe Bushkin, Art Tatum, Dave Bowman, Johnny Guarnieri (p); Al Casey, Emmitt Slay, Herb Ellis, Carl Kress, Remo Palmieri, Danny Perri, Elmer Warner (g); Trigger Alpert, Chubby Jackson, Arvell Shaw, Oscar Pettiford, Alfred Moore, Al Hall, Bob Haggart (b); Big Sid Catlett, James Harris, Cozy Cole, Johnny Blowers, Sonny Greer, Butch Ballard (d); Ella Fitzgerald, Velma Middleton, Dorothy Dandridge (v).* 1/44–4/46.

A very fine cross-section of Armstrong as guest star and bandleader during this period. The five tracks from the Esquire Metropolitan Opera House Jam Session are by a peerless supergroup – Pops, Teagarden, Tatum, Eldridge, Hawkins, Bigard and more – and despite scrappy ensembles the music lives up to the billing. Two sessions for Decca bookend two V-Discs, including a superb 'Jack-Armstrong' Blues, where for once Tea duets with Lou McGarity and Armstrong solos by himself. Another Esquire date has Louis with Ellington and others on a lovely 'Long Long Journey', before two sweet duets with Ella and a Bob Haggart band; then a final big-band session for Decca with Armstrong playing excellently on five titles. A delightful pot-pourri in mostly excellent sound.

*****(*) Louis Armstrong 1946–1947**

Classics 992 *Armstrong; Bob Butler, Sleepy Grider, Ed Mullens, William Scott, Louis Gray, Fats Ford (t); Vic Dickenson, Alton Moore, Russell Moore, Waddet Williams, Nathaniel Allen, James Whitney, Jack Teagarden (tb); Edmond Hall, Barney Bigard (cl); Don Hill, Amos Garden, Arthur Dennis (as); Joe Garland, Johnny Sparrow, Lucky Thompson, Flip Phillips (ts); Ernest Thompson (bs); Charlie Beal, Leonard Feather, Earl Mason, Charlie Bateman (p); Allen Reuss, Bud Scott, Elmer Warner (g); Red Callender, Johnny Williams, Arvell Shaw (b); Big Sid Catlett, Zutty Singleton, Minor Hall, Jimmy Crawford, James Harris (d); Billie Holiday (v).* 9/46–4/47.

****** Louis Armstrong 1947**

Classics 1072 *Armstrong; Bobby Hackett (c); Jack Teagarden, Tommy Dorsey (tb); Benny Goodman, Peanuts Hucko, Barney Bigard (cl); Ernie Caceres (cl, bs); Charlie Barnet (as); Lionel Hampton (vib); Dick Cary, Mel Powell (p); Al Casey, Al Hendrickson (g); Bob Haggart, Harry Babasin, Arvell Shaw, Al Hall (b); Big Sid Catlett, George Wettling, Cozy Cole, Louie Bellson (d); Jeri Sullivan, Golden Gate Quartet (v).* 5–11/47.

After some years of comparative neglect, Armstrong bounced back via the film *New Orleans*, which was made during the period covered by the earliest tracks here, and the formation of the All Stars, a move initiated by the celebrated 1947 New York Town Hall concert. Classics 992 starts with four little-known tracks cut for the French Swng label, excellent sides, and has three final big-band sessions for RCA, including the fine 'The Blues Are Brewin'', and some stray V-Disc material, including 'Do You Know What It Means To Miss New Orleans' alongside Holiday and an interview with Louis. Mixed stuff, but entertaining.

Although the complete RCA editions seem to have gone for now, Classics have their own six tracks from the Town Hall event, all of the four-title session for Victor cut a month later, two jam-session tracks with an all-star band for Capitol and the first ten tracks by the 'original' All Stars. Throughout all this material Armstrong sounds like a maestro ready to resume his eminence: his playing here on 'Back O'Town Blues' and 'Jack-Armstrong

Blues' has riveting intensity. Teagarden matches him with his own playing. Indispensable.

*****(*) Satchmo At Symphony Hall**

GRP 051661-2 *Armstrong; Jack Teagarden (tb, v); Barney Bigard (cl); Dick Cary (p); Arvell Shaw (b); Big Sid Catlett (d); Velma Middleton (v).* 11/47.

Live from Boston with some 70 minutes of music, this is a re-run of the Town Hall situation with some bonus points. One is hearing Sid Catlett at some length on two titles, a rarity in that this master drummer seldom has more than ensemble work to show in his recorded career. Another is the interplay between Armstrong and Teagarden, if anything even more affectionate than it was in New York. Valuable.

***** Live At Winter Garden New York And Blue Note Chicago**

Storyville STCD 8242 *Armstrong; Bobby Hackett (c); Jack Teagarden (tb, v); Barney Bigard, Peanuts Hucko (cl); Ernie Caceres (bs); Dick Cary, Earl Hines (p); Jack Lesberg, Arvell Shaw (b); George Wettling, Big Sid Catlett (d).* 6/47–12/48.

Two brief broadcasts by two editions of the All Stars – though the group wasn't formally in existence at the time of the first (June 1947). This is comparatively scrappy material, and even Pops and Hines sound in less than their best form, but as a survival it's worthwhile.

*****(*) Plays W.C. Handy**

Columbia CK 64925 *Armstrong; Trummy Young (tb); Barney Bigard (cl); Billy Kyle (p); Arvell Shaw (b); Barrett Deems (d); Velma Middleton (v).* 6/54.

***** Satch Plays Fats**

Columbia 450980-2 *As above.* 4–5/55.

The new edition of *Plays W.C. Handy* includes a brief, rather touching interview with Handy himself and a sequence of rehearsal tracks by the group who show how seriously they were taking this project. It still sounds like one of the very best of Armstrong's latter-day records. If he is most himself on the slower tunes, there's still a geniality about 'The Memphis Blues' and even in 'Loveless Love' which is comparatively rare. The Waller collection is nearly as good, although here the showbiz characteristics which stick to many of the tunes renege on their jazz content. The All Stars were playing well enough, but Young is scarcely a strong replacement for Teagarden, no matter how lax the latter might become, and the ratings for almost all the All Stars records from this point refer only to Louis himself: without him, the band would amount to nothing at all.

****** The California Concerts**

GRP 050613-2 4CD *Armstrong; Jack Teagarden, Trummy Young (tb, v); Barney Bigard (cl, v); Earl Hines, Billy Kyle (p); Arvell Shaw (b); Barrett Deems, Cozy Cole (d); Velma Middleton (v).* 1/51–1/55.

*****(*) The Great Chicago Concert 1956**

Columbia C2K 65119 2CD *As above, except add Edmond Hall (cl), Dale Jones (b); omit Teagarden, Bigard, Hines, Shaw, Cole and Middleton.* 6/56.

Armstrong's period with the All Stars has often been treated unfairly over the years. While there have been many indifferent and low-fi concert recordings floating around on dubious labels, these well-packaged and handsomely remastered collections call for a new appraisal of the group. The superb MCA set, spread across four CDs, covers two dates four years apart: the original All Stars with Teagarden and Hines, and the more familiar later group with Young and Kyle. Pops is in good form throughout and, though the vaudevillian aspects of the group often take precedence, there is always some piece of magic from the leader that transforms routine; his singing, as nearly always, is beyond reproof. There are many previously unreleased tracks and a good deal of straight-ahead jazz. The *Chicago Concert* date is slighter stuff, but there are still memorable takes of 'Black And Blue', 'Tenderly' and 'Struttin' With Some Barbecue' – not exactly revisionist, more the master shedding new light on old favourites via a few inflexions.

***** Satchmo A Musical Autobiography Vol. 1**

Jazz Unlimited JUCD 2003 *Armstrong; Yank Lawson (t); Jack Teagarden, Trummy Young (tb); Edmond Hall, Barney Bigard (cl); Dick Cary, Earl Hines, Billy Kyle (p); Everett Barksdale, George Barnes (g); Squire Gersh, Arvell Shaw (b); Cozy Cole, Big Sid Catlett, Barrett Deems (d); Velma Middleton (v).* 11/47–1/57.

***** Satchmo A Musical Autobiography Vol. 2**

Jazz Unlimited JUCD 2004 *As above, except add Lucky Thompson (ts), George Dorsey (as, f), Dave McRae (bs, bsx), Kenny John (d); omit Teagarden, Cary, Hines, Catlett, Bigard.* 1/51–1/57.

***** Satchmo A Musical Autobiography Vol. 3**

Jazz Unlimited JUCD 2005 *As above, except omit Lawson and John.* 1/55–1/57.

Armstrong tells something of his life and career in the spoken intros to most of the tracks on these three CDs. This should have been some of the most worthwhile Armstrong of the period, with the material including plenty of tunes he hadn't returned to for many years, but the arrangements by Bob Haggart or Sy Oliver are a bit tight and Dixielandish, with the tempos a shade too taut to suit him. That said, it's still a pleasure to hear him go back to the likes of 'Knockin' A Jug'. The remastered sound is a little thin compared with that of the Columbia discs of the period.

*****(*) Highlights From His Decca Years**

GRP 052638-2 2CD *Armstrong; various groups as above.* 24–57.

Starting with Fletcher Henderson and going as far as the *Musical Autobiography* sessions, this is something of a hotchpotch round the edges, although the core of it rests with the Decca sessions of the 1930s. The second disc covers much of the All Stars period and includes some showbiz set-pieces with the likes of Louis Jordan and Bing Crosby. Little that isn't purely enjoyable, and a decent sweep through a large part of Armstrong's career.

***** Louis And The Angels / Louis And The Good Book**

Universal MLCD 19379 *Armstrong; Trummy Young (tb); Hank D'Amico, Edmond Hall (cl); George Dorsey, Phil D'Urso (as, f); Lucky Thompson (ts); Dave Macrae (bs); Billy Kyle (p); Nick Tragg (org); Everett Barksdale, George Barnes (g); Mort Herbert, Joe Benjamin, Sid Block (b); Rudy Taylor, Barrett Deems (d); strings, choir.* 1/57–2/58.

Armstrong's two 'sacred' albums for Decca are about as secular as one can imagine. *Louis And The Angels* is more arranged and dependent on the strings, with chestnuts like 'A Sinner Kissed An Angel' alongside 'Angela Mia'; *Louis And The Good Book* is more fun, Armstrong swapping notes with his very white-sounding choir, although there's a surprisingly feelingful 'Nobody Knows The Trouble I've Seen' along the way. If this is all a bit light and obvious, it's still hugely enjoyable, and Louis himself is in great singing voice.

****(*) Louis Armstrong: The Silver Collection**
Verve 823446-2 *Armstrong; Russell Garcia Orchestra.* 8/57.

***** Louis Armstrong Meets Oscar Peterson**
Verve 539060-2 *Armstrong; Oscar Peterson (p); Herb Ellis (g); Ray Brown (b); Louie Bellson (d).* 7–10/57.

***** Verve Jazz Masters: Louis Armstrong**
Verve 519818-2 *Armstrong; Trummy Young (tb); Edmond Hall (cl); Billy Kyle, Oscar Peterson (p); Herb Ellis (g); Ray Brown, Dale Jones (b); Louie Bellson, Barrett Deems (d); Ella Fitzgerald (v); Russell Garcia Orchestra.* 8/56–10/57.

***** Jazz Around Midnight: Louis Armstrong**
Verve 843422-2 *As above, except add Tyree Glenn (tb), Buster Bailey (cl), Marty Napoleon (p), Alfred Di Lernia (bj), Buddy Catlett (b), Danny Barcelona (d).* 7/57–5/66.

*****(*) Let's Do It**
Verve 529017-2 2CD *As above discs, except add Big Chief Russell Moore (tb), Joe Darensbourg (cl), Everett Barksdale (g), Arvell Shaw (b).* 8/57–9/64.

Verve recorded Armstrong with a little more initiative as regards concepts, but it didn't always work out. *The Silver Collection* finds Armstrong fronting Russell Garcia's hearty though not graceless orchestra with his usual aplomb; comparing, say, 'I Gotta Right To Sing The Blues' with his version of some 25 years earlier isolates the maturity of Armstrong's later art: he hasn't the chops for grandstand improvisations any more, but his sense of timing and his treatment of pure melody are almost as gratifying. Yet some of the songs end up as merely dull.

The meeting with Oscar Peterson's trio, now reissued in one of Verve's Master Edition series, is perhaps a mixed success but nevertheless an intriguing disc. Peterson can't altogether avoid his besetting pushiness, yet he's just as often *sotto voce* in accompaniment, and on the slower tunes especially – 'Sweet Lorraine' and 'Let's Fall In Love' – the chemistry works, and Louis is certainly never intimidated. It's good to hear him on material more obviously 'modern' than he normally tackled and, although he sometimes gets the feel of a song wrong, he finds a surprising spin for several of the lyrics. Both of the two compilations are quite thoughtfully chosen and, with the spotlight primarily on Louis's singing, the VJM disc is a good sampler of the period.

Dan Morgenstern's selection and notes for *Let's Do It*, a comprehensive overview of Louis with Verve, make a good case for reconsidering this period. If one wants a single selection here, this is certainly the one to go for, with some of his very best moments with Ella, Russ Garcia and Peterson carefully sequenced.

*****(*) I've Got The World On A String + Louis Under The Stars**
Verve 559831-2 2CD *Armstrong; Paul Smith (p); Russell Garcia Orchestra.* 8/57.

In this very fine remastering it's the sheer grandeur of Pops the vocalist and interpreter that comes off this double-disc set. His voice sounds huge. Some of the songs, such as 'Little Girl Blue', don't really suit him, and there is very little trumpet to offset Russell Garcia's swooning strings, but the magnetism of the man is sometimes awe-inspiring. There are a lot of alternative takes to pad out the two discs, but most of them offer little but extra weight.

***** Mack The Knife**
Pablo 2310941 *Armstrong; Trummy Young (tb, v); Edmond Hall (cl); Billy Kyle (p); Squire Gersh (b); Barrett Deems (d).* 7/57.

****(*) Basin Street Blues**
Black Lion BLCD 760128 *As above, except add Dale Jones (b).* 8/56–10/57.

There seem to be many, many All Stars concerts which have survived on tape, and these two are no better or worse than any for the period. They're also all pretty much the same, song-wise and treatment-wise. But the Pablo set, which includes a slightly more concentrated amount of jazz material, is marginally the better, with certainly the better sound.

*****(*) Porgy And Bess**
Verve 827475-2 *Armstrong; Ella Fitzgerald (v); Russell Garcia Orchestra.* 8/57.

*****(*) Ella And Louis**
Verve 543304-2 *Armstrong; Oscar Peterson (p); Herb Ellis (g); Ray Brown (b); Louie Bellson (d); Ella Fitzgerald (v).* 57.

*****(*) Ella And Louis Again**
Verve 825374-2 *As above.* 57.

***** Verve Jazz Masters 24: Ella Fitzgerald & Louis Armstrong**
Verve 521851-2 *As above discs.* 56–57.

*****(*) The Complete Ella Fitzgerald & Louis Armstrong On Verve**
Verve 537284-2 3CD *As above.* 56–57.

We have been dismissive of these sessions in the past and perhaps they *are* disappointing: the two greatest voices in jazz ought to have been a dream pairing, but with Pops used to trading innuendo with Velma Middleton and Ella always going her own queenly way, maybe it was never a match made in jazz heaven. But there are compensations which make a lot of the music hard to resist. *Porgy And Bess* has never been highly regarded among the numerous jazz versions of Gershwin's opera, yet though Russell Garcia's orchestra tends to loom over the music, there are a handful of sublime moments which make up for the stiffness: 'Summertime', in particular, is turned into a profoundly moving meditation, and the closing bars of this version are as transcendent as anything in the work of Ella and Louis. The two small-group dates have material that suits Fitzgerald rather than her partner, and some of the tunes end up either bland or merely workmanlike; yet others are a delight, especially 'I Won't Dance' and 'Isn't This A Lovely Day', and there is the deftest support from Peterson and his team. The *Jazz Masters* compilation isn't bad, but we would quarrel with some of the tune choices. *The Complete* puts the whole lot in one place, though the concertina packaging is somewhat eccentric.

****(*) Americans In Sweden**
Tax CD 3712-2 *Armstrong; Trummy Young (tb, v); Peanuts Hucko (cl); Billy Kyle (p); Mort Herbert (b); Danny Barcelona (d); Velma Middleton (v).* 1/59.

The Stockholm concert is an unusually crisp and forthright example of a latter-day All Stars performance: the sound is clear and well balanced, and Louis's singing is impeccable, although most of the instrumental spots are given over to the band.

****** Louis Armstrong & Duke Ellington: The Complete Sessions**
Roulette 793844-2 *Armstrong; Trummy Young (tb); Barney Bigard (cl); Duke Ellington (p); Mort Herbert (b); Danny Barcelona (d).* 4/61.

These sessions have never been highly regarded: Ellington is more or less slumming it with the All Stars, and some of his piano parts do sound eccentrically isolated. Yet this is Armstrong's date, not his, even with all the material composed by Duke: Louis stamps his imprimatur on it from the first vocal on 'Duke's Place'. His occasional frailties and the sometimes tired tempos only personalize further his single opportunity to interpret his greatest contemporary at length. On the extraordinarily affecting 'I Got It Bad And That Ain't Good' or the superbly paced 'It Don't Mean A Thing', Louis reflects on a parallel heritage of tunes which his traditional proclivities perhaps denied him; and the results are both moving and quietly eloquent.

**** Masters Of Jazz: Louis Armstrong**
Storyville SLP 4101 *Armstrong; Trummy Young (tb); Joe Darensbourg (cl); Billy Kyle (p); Billy Cronk (b); Danny Barcelona (d).* 8/62.

*** Louis Armstrong & The All Stars 1965**
EPM Musique FDC 5100 *As above, except Eddie Shu (cl) and Arvell Shaw (b) replace Darensbourg and Cronk; add Jewel Brown (v).* 3/65.

By the mid-1960s, Armstrong's powers as a trumpeter were finally in serious decline, and there are sad moments among the glimmers of greatness which remain. The Storyville date isn't bad, but the band sound overcome by ennui, while the other disc, recorded at concerts in Prague and the former East Berlin, is poorly recorded and, aside from a moving version of Fats Waller's 'Black And Blue', scarcely worth hearing.

****(*) What A Wonderful World**
MCA 811876-2 *Armstrong; strings.* 68.

The spirit abides in this late set, but the showbiz material hurts, and only his great heart gets him through it to any effectiveness.

Bernhard Arndt

PIANO, ELECTRONICS

German piano experimenter.

***** Inside Insight**
FMP OWN 90005 *Arndt (p, elec solo).* 7/92–10/95.

Ah, the piano! There's nothing you can't do with it. That seems to be Arndt's point of view, at least, and he has the record to prove it. Playing inside and out, using delay devices, octave dividers, hunks of glass on the strings (none of this is specified, but this is what it sounds like), Arndt comes up with 70 minutes of abstraction which is absorbing enough, although listeners experienced in the avant-garde composition of 30 or 40 years ago may find a lot of this old hat. The two pieces which use delay create some textures which will either grate or entrance, but 'Metropolis' is ten minutes of dead space – what's he doing?

Dag Arnesen

PIANO

Norwegian post-bop pianist of affable style.

**** The Day After**
Taurus TRCD 829 *Arnesen; Odd Riisnaes (ss, ts); Bjorn Kjellemyr (b); Sven Christiansen (d); Wenche Gausdal (v).* 2/90.

**** Photographs**
Taurus TRCD 830 *As above, except Terje Gewelt (b) replaces Kjellemyr and Riisnaes.*

***** Movin'**
Taurus TRCD 832 *As above, except omit Gausdal.* 1–2/94.

Arnesen's romantic kind of post-bop falls easily on the ear. His 1980s recordings seem to be out of print, which is a pity since they're some of his most assured. The Taurus albums take a different route with the arrival of vocalist Gausdal, who co-writes much of the material. Despite some fine work by the players on both records, Gausdal's studied pronunciation, flimsy lyrics and plain lack of authority are deeply unfortunate. *Movin'* gets the pianist back on the track: this is a strong trio and, though Arnesen's composing is no more than functional, the calibre of the playing engages the ear. Gewelt also contributes the most interesting tune, 'Maybe'.

Thomas Arnesen

GUITAR, VOCAL

Born in Dalarna, Sweden, Arnesen studied music at Uppsala University. He was playing rock with Panta Rei in the early 1970s, but the Sittel album is the first under his own leadership.

***** Backwater Blues**

Sittel 9227 *Arnesen; John Högman (bs); Anders Widmark (p); Anders Johansson (g); Hans Backenroth (b); Egil Johansen (d).* 4/95.

Arnesen seldom does the obvious on this pleasing and belated debut. He starts with the title blues played on an acoustic. Standard ballads such as 'Stella By Starlight' are played with a swirling electric tone. There are three duets with Johansson, mood pieces and the droll anti-evolutionary 'All The Things You Are', which starts like a Hendrix-styled rock-out before reversing into bebop rhythms and ending up with Högman (under-used, as he's only on two tracks) back on 52nd Street with Arnesen apparently having packed up and gone. The guitarist has a good tone and a fine touch.

Unfortunately, the follow-up *Tillbaks Igen* (Sittel 9244) is entirely different, a blues-rock record which Arnesen leads with his voice as much as his guitar. A listing for this one would be inappropriate.

Kenneth Arnström (born 1946)

ALTO, TENOR AND BARITONE SAXOPHONES, CLARINET, BASS CLARINET

Having made a name for himself in Sweden as a prodigious saxophonist in a trad-to-mainstream style, the enigmatic Arnström disappeared from the scene for 15 years and worked as a carpenter. In the '90s he returned to more active duty, picking up where he left off. He also founded the Kenneth jazz label.

***** Saxcess**

Phontastic NCD 8836 *Arnström; Jan Stolpe (t); Pelle Larsson (p); Dan Berglund (b); Hasse Linskog (d); Sabina Have (v).* 1–7/95.

***** Rhythm King**

Opus 3 19502 *Arnström; Bent Persson (c, t); Tomas Ornberg (cl, ss); Keith Durston (p); Olle Nyman (g, bj); Goran Eriksson (bj); Bo Juhlin (sou); Tomas Ekstrom (b).* 4–5/95.

****(*) Hittin' The Roots**

Phontastic PHONTCD 8849 *Arnström; Peter Kjellin (t); Fredrik John (tb): Per Notini (p); Rune Gustafsson (g); Christian Franck (b); Sven Stahlberg, Peter Ostlund (d).* 3/95–2/96.

Arnström originally impressed as a big-toned tenorman in the classic manner. *Saxcess* seems to be the first album under his own name, tempted back to playing after a long sabbatical, and only the cursory support and off-the-cuff tune-choices withhold a higher commendation: his own playing is in the top class. He musters a fluent delivery, but it's edged by a black tone that intensifies when his phrases turn vehement – scarcely a solo goes by without some seemingly angry turn of expression. Partnered by Stolpe, who comes on as if Louis Armstrong was still everybody's main influence on the horn, this gives the front line a rare virility.

Rhythm King is quite different, a set of mostly very old tunes (one surprise: Paul Gonsalves's 'Solitariness') given a rather steely recitation by a small group. Minus any drums, the sparse setting grants an odd, almost metallic feel to the sound and, when they handle pieces like 'Funny Feathers' or 'Forty And Tight' (or 'Somebody Stole My Gal', done as a duet for banjo and bass clarinet!), it seems more like an essay on traditional forms than anything. A charismatic but rather rarefied date. *Hittin' The Roots* seems much more prosaic and rather less successful, the rhythm section tying down the horns and the result a playable if unremarkable session. Arnström himself remains an enigma.

ARP

GROUP

Group led by drummer Dahlback and playing in a sort of post-modern Swedish style.

***** Muskel Svan Gunga**

Dragon DRCD 271 *Anders Ekholm (ts, cl); Erik Norstrom (ky); Jan Johansson (g, vn); Peter Janson (b); Erik Dahlback (d).* 4/94.

It starts like chamber music going into a ridiculous burn-out blues, and from there ARP set out to subvert every expectation. Dahlback's group enjoy themselves enormously across this CD, cheerfully throwing together styles that start with modal playing, go past old-fashioned jazz-rock, and even take a sly dig at the likes of M-Base rhythms. Ekholm, Johansson and Norstrom all get in plenty of blows and, just as things seem to gel, the piece either comes to an end or somebody else blows it open. Some of it seems like a misfire, but it hardly matters.

Art Ensemble Of Chicago

GROUP

Born out of Chicago's Association for the Advancement of Creative Musicians, this co-operative grew out of a Roscoe Mitchell small group. Philip Wilson drummed for them early on, but it was the quartet of Mitchell, Lester Bowie, Joseph Jarman and Malachi Favors which went to live and play in Europe in 1969. They returned to US work in 1972 and were joined by drummer Famoudou Don Moye. They became a leading concert attraction during the late '70s, '80s and '90s, but as a group they recorded only occasionally, each member often busy with other projects. Nevertheless, they symbolize the creative spirit of Chicago's black avant-gardists of the '60s.

****** Art Ensemble 1967–68**

Nessa NCD-2500 5CD *Lester Bowie (t, flhn, perc); Roscoe Mitchell (saxes, perc); Joseph Jarman (saxes, bsn, cl); Malachi Favors (b, zith, perc); Charles Clark (b); Phillip Wilson, Thurman Barker, Robert Crowder (d).* 67–68.

***** Tutankhamun**

Black Lion BLCD 760199 *As above, except omit Clark, Wilson, Barker and Crowder.* 6/69.

***** The Spiritual**

Black Lion BLCD 760219 *As above.* 6/69.

***** A Jackson In Your House / Message To Our Folks**

Charly CDGR 293 *As above.* 6–8/69.

Those who know the Art Ensemble of Chicago only by their considerable reputation may be disappointed by their work as it's been documented on record. Bowie, Jarman, Favors and Mitchell, later joined by percussionist Famoudou Don Moye, have been celebrated as among the most radical and innovative musicians in the intensely creative environment which was centred on Chicago's AACM movement in the 1960s. Not surprisingly, they had to uproot and head for Europe in order to find work and recording opportunities at the time, and most of their music remains on European labels. As a mix of personalities, the Ensemble has always been in a crisis of temperament, with Bowie's arsenal of sardonic inflexions pitched against Mitchell's schematic constructions, Jarman's fierce and elegant improvising and Favors's other-worldly commentaries from the bass. Satire, both musical and literal, has sustained much of their music; long- and short-form pieces have broken jazz structure down into areas of sound and silence. At their best, they are as uncompromisingly abstract as the most severe European players, yet their materials are cut from the heart of the traditions of black music in Chicago and St Louis.

The Nessa five-disc set (which is a limited though very expensive edition) compiles three previously issued LPs – Mitchell's *Congliptious* and *Old/Quartet*, and Bowie's *Numbers 1 & 2* – along with some two and a half hours of previously unreleased workshop tapes, alternative takes and some demos. Historically, with relatively little of the Chicago free masters having been documented at the time, this is of great importance and, while the best music is probably that heard on those original albums, there are some fascinating things in the sometimes messy alternative tracks and rehearsals, with the legendary Clark and drummers Crowder and Barker making rare appearances. For specialists, arguably, but there is much here that deserves wider circulation.

Their French recordings of 1969 have made their way back into print, spasmodically. The two Black Lion reissues, *Tutankhamun* and *The Spiritual*, are typical of the Ensemble's hit-and-miss results and are like samplers of their strategies. *Tutankhamun* collects three noisy, reflective, ambitious pieces. *The Spiritual* starts with eight minutes of percussion, passes through two brief and mysterious pieces, and winds up in the 20-minute title-piece with its hooting horns, Stepin Fetchit voices and sardonic, Deep South fantasia. Indulgent and sketchy as well as powerful and surprising, these records haven't endured as well as the American discs (*Reese And The Smooth Ones*, probably the best of their French records, is still in limbo). *A Jackson In Your House/Message To Our Folks* follows a similar pattern, although the dedication to Charles Clark, 'Song For Charles', has a poignancy in it which the Ensemble didn't always allow themselves.

***** Live**

Delmark DE-432 *As above, plus Famoudou Don Moye (d).* 1/72.

*****(*) Bap-Tizum**

Atlantic 7567-80757-2 *As above.* 9/72.

*****(*) Fanfare For The Warriors**

Koch 8501/Atlantic 8122-7235-2 *As above, except add Muhal Richard Abrams (p).* 9/73.

***** Nice Guys**

ECM 827876-2 *As above, except omit Abrams.* 5/78.

***** Full Force**

ECM 829197-2 *As above.* 1/80.

*****(*) Urban Bushmen**

ECM 829394-2 2CD *As above.* 5/80.

The Ensemble made only a handful of discs in the 1970s, and most are now back in circulation. The live session, recorded at Chicago's Mandel Hall in 1972, has been remastered by Delmark. This was something of a homecoming affair and there is much jubilation in the playing, but the recording remains imperfect, the detail skimped, and in a continuous 76-minute performance there are inevitable dead spots which the Ensemble have never truly found a way of avoiding. *Bap-Tizum* is another concert set, from the 1972 Ann Arbor Festival, and is better – more coherent, more purposeful. The studio *Fanfare For The Warriors* is one of their most finished efforts, with Mitchell's 'Nonaah' and 'Tnoona' among their most challenging original structures and Jarman's fierce title-piece delivered with real, concentrated force. As guest, Abrams thickens the stew and acts as something of a binding force: no theatre, just hard music. Even here, though, the production isn't really up to evoking a true picture of the Ensemble's sound.

It wasn't until they secured a deal with ECM that they were finally given the opportunity to record in the sonic detail which their work has always demanded. Even so, the two studio albums were good yet unexceptional instances of the group at work. *Nice Guys* has two absorbing Jarman pieces in '597-59' and 'Dreaming Of The Master', but the attempt at a ska beat in 'JA' is unconvincing and much of the music seems almost formulaic, the improvisation limited. *Full Force* is a little more outgoing without cutting loose, and the lengthy 'Magg Zelma' seems long-winded rather than epic in its movement. The Ensemble's concert appearances could still generate music of blistering power, which made their apparently desultory records all the more frustrating. So the live *Urban Bushmen*, while still somewhat muted and inevitably deprived of the theatrical impact of the Ensemble's in-person charisma, proved to be their most worthwhile record for many years. Spread over 90 minutes, the group displayed their virtuosity on a vast panoply of devices (Jarman alone is credited with playing 14 different wind instruments, along with sundry items of percussion) and the patchwork of musics adds up to a tying together of their many endeavours in form and content. Revisiting it recently, it does not seem to have worn as well as we remembered, but it remains a useful introduction to their work.

****(*) The Third Decade**

ECM 823213-2 *As above.* 6/84.

A dispiriting continuation after another longish absence from the studios. Embarking on their third decade together suggested nothing so much as the atrophy of a once-radical band. The horn players are as spikily creative as ever in those moments when the Ensemble parts to reveal them, but the crucial decline is in the quality of interaction: several of these pieces dispel the collective identity of the group rather than binding it together.

***** Live In Japan**

DIW 8005 *As above.* 4/84.

***** The Complete Live In Japan**

DIW 8021/2 2CD *As above.* 4/84.

The AEOC commenced a new contract with the Japanese DIW company with this worthwhile though hardly enthralling live set (the first record is a distillation of the concert, which appears in its totality on the subsequent double-CD). Some of the earlier ECM material reappears in concert form: the differences in emphasis are interesting, if little more. Acceptable rather than outstanding sound.

***** Naked**

DIW 8011 *As above.* 11/85–7/86.

****(*) Vol. I: Ancient To The Future**

DIW 8014 *As above, plus Bahnamous Lee Bowie (ky).* 3/87.

The group's recording for DIW continued with records which, because of their limited distribution, caused little excitement. But the music continued to be a revisiting of old haunts rather than anything strikingly new; Mitchell and Bowie were, in any case, more active elsewhere. A taste for fanciful, zig-zagging hard bop lightens some of *Naked*, and the impeccable recording affords some pleasure in just listening to the sound of Jarman, Mitchell and Favors in particular. But the attempts at rounding up 'the tradition' on DIW 8014 include poorly conceived stabs at 'Purple Haze' and 'No Woman No Cry' which mock their mastery.

****** The Alternate Express**

DIW 8033 *As above.* 1/89.

A remarkable record from a period when it seemed that the Ensemble's powers were all but spent. The huge, blustering 'Kush' rekindles the wildness of their best improvising; 'Imaginary Situations' is a ghostly collective sketch; 'Whatever Happens' catches Bowie at his melancholy best, while Mitchell's title-piece is a fine tribute to the group's survivalist spirit. A valuable and welcome document that might be called a comeback.

****(*) Art Ensemble Of Soweto**

DIW 837 *As above, plus Elliot Ngubane (v, ky, perc); Joe Leguabe (v, perc); Zacheuus Nyoni, Welcome Max Bhe Bhe, Kay Ngwazene (v).* 12/89–1/90.

This might have seemed like a logical collaboration, between the Ensemble and the African male chorus Amabutho, but the results tend to declare the differences between the two groups rather than their allegiances. The harmonic dignity of Amabutho stands alone on the three tracks they're featured on, while the best instrumental music comes on Mitchell's 'Fresh Start', an invigorating blast of free bop. Worth hearing, but not the grand encounter which must have been intended.

***** Live At The Eighth Tokyo Music Joy 1990**

DIW 842 *Lester Bowie, Stanton Davis, E.J Allen, Gerald Brazel (t); Vincent Chancey (frhn); Steve Turre, Clifton Anderson (tb); Roscoe Mitchell, Joseph Jarman (reeds); Bob Stewart (tba); Malachi Favors (b); Famoudou Don Moye, Vinnie Johnson (d).* 2/90.

A meeting between two great ensembles, the AEOC and Bowie's Brass Fantasy. Each has three tracks of its own and there are four collective pieces, of which Steve Turre's arrangement of 'The Emperor' seems to prove the idea that he is the real leader of Brass Fantasy – or, at least, the one who knows how to make it work for the best. A celebratory meeting but not an altogether successful one.

***** Dreaming Of The Masters Vol. 2: Thelonious Sphere Monk**

DIW 846 *Lester Bowie (t); Roscoe Mitchell, Joseph Jarman (reeds); Cecil Taylor (p, v); Malachi Favors (b); Famoudou Don Moye (d).* 1–3/90.

***** Dreaming Of The Masters Suite**

DIW 854 *As above, except omit Taylor.* 1–3/90.

It seems a curiously neo-classic device for the Ensemble to be so specifically paying tribute to senior spirits, which was on the face of it the kind of laborious dues-paying which Bowie in particular was critical of in many of today's younger players. Their approach is, of course, different: the colouristic interchanges between Mitchell and Jarman, Bowie's now inimitable irreverence and the patient, other-worldly bass of Favors all ensure that. But neither of these records is anything much more than a reminder of the AEOC's existence; certainly no specific new ground is broken, and in that sense the encounter with Cecil Taylor is a disappointment, although Taylor's singing is actually a fascinating embellishment of the Ensemble's own tradition. When he plays piano, the two sides – perhaps inevitably – don't really meet. Oddly, neither record is much about its respective dedicatees: there are only two Monk tunes and three by Coltrane here, though 'Impressions' is a fine repertory performance. The Ensemble still exists as a performing unit but its status as an ongoing contributor is in doubt: it now seems to belong to the past.

***** Coming Home Jamaica**

Birdology/Atlantic 3984-24792-2 *As above, except omit Jarman; add Bahnamous Bowie (ky).* 12/95–1/96.

With Jarman retiring from active duty and Bowie now gone, this is surely the final AEOC album. From the R&B shuffle of 'Grape Escape' to the portly ska of 'Strawberry Mango', it's a good-natured farewell. All the real electricity went out of the group some time ago, but as a kind of repertory exercise this has its share of moments: Bowie plays well and, if Jarman's elegance is sadly missed, Mitchell's deadpan aggression still has its say.

Joe Ascione (born 1961)

DRUMS

An Italian-American from Long Island, Ascione started by worshipping Krupa and Rich. His CV has since stretched from Cab Calloway to Donald Fagen, and he seems at home in any style from swing onwards.

***** My Buddy**

Nagel-Heyer 036 *Ascione; Randy Sandke (t); Dan Barrett (tb); Brian Ogilvie (cl, as, ts); Billy Mitchell (ts); Mark Shane (p); James Chirillo (g); Bob Haggart (b).* 11/96.

***** Post No Bills**

Arbors ARCD 19174 *Ascione; Jerry Weldon (ts); Dave LaLama (p); Ron Affif (g); Tim Givens (b).* 12/96.

Ascione idolized Buddy Rich; *My Buddy* is a set of tunes associated with the man and is a worthy homage. The band is drawn from what is now the Nagel-Heyer repertory crew and is none the worse for that, though it's nice to welcome the gruff, booting tenor of Billy Mitchell – frayed round the edges, but more distinctive than many a saxophonist of today – back to the studios. The trumpet–drums duet of 'Nica's Dream' and the floating tempo on 'Soft Winds', deliciously set up by Barrett, are useful changes of pace, even if much of the music is the kind of thing we've heard many times before. The closing blues is a bit of a marathon.

Post No Bills takes some similar cues, but it is generally much more boppishly inclined and is built round the trio of Ascione, LaLama and Givens. The pianist's neat touch finds some soft light on 'Chelsea Bridge', played at a very quiescent pace, and, with Weldon adding muscular tenor to the likes of 'Moment's Notice', this is about as modern a record as Arbors seems likely to deliver.

Dorothy Ashby (1932–86)

HARP

The first jazz harpist? Not quite – Casper Reardon got there first.

*****(*) In A Minor Groove**

Prestige PCD 24120 *Ashby; Frank Wess (f); Eugene Wright, Herman Wright (b); Roy Haynes, Art Taylor (d).* 3–12/58.

The New Grove Dictionary of Jazz describes Ashby as 'the only important bop harpist', which might seem a rather empty accolade, given a rather scant subscription to the instrument in this music. On balance, though, it's fair comment. Ashby came to notice in her early twenties, playing with no less a man than Louis Armstrong. Remarkably, she saw a place for herself in the new idiom and managed to fit her seemingly unwieldy instrument to the contours of an essentially horn-dominated style. There are affinities between her harp playing and some contemporary guitar stylings, notably Wes Montgomery's, but she also learned something from bebop pianists like Bud Powell, bringing an unusually dark tonality and timbre to a notoriously soft-voiced instrument. Ashby's determination to lead her own groups allowed her to develop a personal language and style. Although she recruited such fine players as Roy Haynes and Jimmy Cobb, her most fruitful association was with Frank Wess, whose flute playing (still much undervalued) was perfect for her. The best of their partnership can be sampled on the Prestige. This found her working with two equally good rhythm-sections, Haynes and Gene Wright, Art Taylor and Herman Wright, against which Jones and Thigpen didn't quite match up. The absence of a more familiar piano or guitar left some of the harmonies quite open, and there are unexpected chromatic sweeps in some of these tracks – 'It's A Minor Thing' and 'Alone Together' – which seem ahead of their time.

Harold Ashby (born 1925)

TENOR SAXOPHONE

Ashby was born in Kansas and worked in relative obscurity in the Mid-West until moving to New York in the late 1950s. He worked with Duke Ellington on and off until joining permanently in 1968. His records represent an Indian summer in the recording studios.

***** The Viking**

Gemini GM 60 *Ashby; Norman Simmons (p); Paul West (b); Gerryck King (d).* 8/88.

***** What Am I Here For?**

Criss Cross 1054 *Ashby; Mulgrew Miller (p); Rufus Reid (b); Ben Riley (d).* 11/90.

***** I'm Old Fashioned**

Stash ST-CD-545 *Ashby; Richard Wyands (p); Aaron Bell (b); Connie Kay (d).* 7/91.

***** On The Sunny Side Of The Street**

Timeless SJP 385 *Ashby; Horace Parlan (p); Wayne Dockery (b); Steve McCraven (d).* 1/92.

A late arrival in the Duke Ellington orchestra, Harold Ashby was really Ben Webster's replacement: he still has the Webster huff on ballads and the grouchy, just-woke-up timbre on up-tempo tunes. Quicker tempos don't bother him as much as they did Ben, but he likes to take his own time, and he fashions storytelling solos which can freshen up the material. It's all done consistently enough to ensure that there's little to choose between these four records for four labels. *What Am I Here For?* is an ideal programme of Ellingtonia and, though the disc is a little too long to sustain interest, the playing is jauntily assured from track to track. The Gemini set sounds perkier, perhaps because the rhythm section is less of a signed-up star group and because Ashby sounds expansive and happy with the four original lines he came up with for the date ('Hash' sounds unsurprisingly like 'Dash', which is on the Stash record). The Timeless album revisits some more Ellington and a handful of failsafe standards: 'It's The Talk Of The Town' is a favourite tenorman's set-piece. Horace Parlan, imperturbable as ever, beds everything down with a hint of the blues.

Mickey Ashman (born 1927)

BASS

A veteran mainstay of British trad rhythm sections, Ashman has worked with Barber, Colyer, Lyttelton, Lightfoot and Sunshine, among others.

***** Through Darkest Ashman**

Lake LACD86 *Ashman; Stan Sowden, Sonny Morris (t); Peter Jamieson, Brian Cotton (tb); Gerry Turnham (cl); Dickie Bishop, Martin Boorman (bj); Trevor Glenroy, Billy Loch (d).* 8/58–1/61.

Mickey Ashman is still playing the kind of absolute bass heard on these tracks – turn to the Neville Dickie entry for details. This is a reissue of a fondly remembered Pye LP by a good trad outfit:

Turnham's woodsy clarinet and Morris's brisk trumpet stand out on a set of tunes all with some kind of jungle connection, the standout arguably a surprisingly fine treatment of Ellington's 'Jungle Nights In Harlem'. As a bonus, there are four tracks from a rare 1958 EP of old-time tunes, which goes out on an astonishingly full-tilt 'If Those Lips Could Only Speak'. Those were remastered off vinyl and sound a bit rough, but the Pye tracks are beautifully clear and Mickey's bass comes through mightily.

Svend Asmussen (born 1916)

VIOLIN, VIBRAPHONE, VOCAL

Asmussen has been working professionally since the 1930s, although much of his post-war output was closer to salon music than to jazz. His celebrated LP with John Lewis, European Encounter, has yet to appear on CD.

*** Musical Miracle 1935–1940

Phontastic PHONTCD 9306 *Asmussen; Svend Hauberg (t, cl, g); Olaf Carlson (t); Kai Ewans (cl); Aage Voss, Kai Moller, Johnny Campbell (as); Henry Hagemann, Banner Jansen, Valdemar Nielsen (ts); Kjeld Bonfils (p, vib); Kjeld Norregaard (p); Hans Ulrik Neumann, Helge Jacobsen, Jimmy Campbell, Borge Ring, Oscar Aleman (g); Niels Foss, Christian Jensene, Alfred Rasmussen (b); Bibi Miranda, Erik Frederiksen, Rik Kragh (d).* 11/35–12/40.

Asmussen should be celebrated as one of the major jazz violinists, yet he remains relatively little-known outside his native Denmark. Like, say, Bengt Hallberg, his musical tastes stretch to areas of music remote from jazz and have led him into light-music byways that have perhaps not done his reputation much good. Nevertheless he remains preposterously neglected by CD reissues, and a listen to some of the tracks on this early collection will make one wonder why: he is at least as fluent as Grappelli or South, and with little of the sweetness or strictness that sometimes mars their work. Try, for example, the rigorous variation on the theme of 'Limehouse Blues' (1938), or the flawless impetus of 'After You've Gone' (1940). The earliest tracks feature him as sideman, but the majority are by small groups designed to feature him as violinist, occasional vibesman and an agreeable if Armstrong-derived vocalist. Aside from Aleman, present on only two tracks, none of the guitarists really challenges him the way Reinhardt did Grappelli, and there's a hint of café society kitsch here and there; otherwise, this is an excellent programme. Remastering is a little tubby in the bass and 'Jazz Potpourri 2' is from a swishy original 78, but the sound is fine in most respects.

*** Fiddling Around

Imogena IGCD 039 *Asmussen; Jacob Fischer (g); Jesper Lundgaard (b); Aage Tanggaard (d).* 3/93.

Interesting, but Asmussen's originals here are insubstantial and the arrangements of the more familiar material are inconsistent: a slow, thoughtful 'Cherokee' is set beside a merely silly 'Alabama Barbecue'. Still, the rest of the group are in fine fettle and the violinist has lost none of his panache.

Peter Asplund (born 1969)

TRUMPET, FLUGELHORN

Studied in Stockholm's Royal College of Music, then played big-band gigs and led his own group.

*** Open Mind

Dragon DRCD281 *Asplund; Johan Hörlén (ss, as); Ion Baciu (p); Christian Spering (b); Johan Löfcrantz (d).* 95.

*** Melos

Sittel SITCD 9260 *Asplund; Johan Hörlen (ss, as, f); Anders Holtz (ky); Jacob Karlzon (p); Dan Berglund (b); Johan Löfcrantz (d); Rigmor Gustafsson (v).* 1/99.

Asplund is a post-bop trumpeter who likes to push hard – there's nothing laid-back or very impressionistic about his view of the modern mainstream. He's focused on a result in every track. Löfcrantz is a drummer who picks up and carries the rest of the band if he feels they're lagging behind, and that sense of urgency carries over into all but the most sedate pieces. *Open Mind* benefits from the decisiveness, since in and of itself it's not an especially individual programme of material. Some attractively resolved melodies, and the horns have sufficient to chew on, but nothing leaves an indelible mark. Asplund saves some of his best for a very long and detailed look at 'Stardust'.

Melos is a shade different, though perhaps not quite as removed from orthodoxy as the leader's notes imply. He claims that the use of a female voice and occasional synths introduce a romantic element which he's been moving towards in his writing. Gustafsson is used both in a wordless role and as a lyric interpreter and, if anything, this brings the record closer to the cool lyricism that is a Swedish strain which followers of that music will readily identify. Oddly enough, Asplund himself seems to take a less forthright role as soloist here, leaving Karlzon in particular to make the most distinctive impression.

Astreja

GROUP

Gubaidulina and Suslin are both composers; Pekarsky leads one of Russia's most distinguished percussion ensembles; Ponomareva is a dramatic singer of gypsy extraction. The latter pair are here guesting with a group which began in the underground improvisation scene of the mid-1970s.

(***) Music From Davos

Leo CDLR 181 *Sofia Gubaidulina, Viktor Suslin, Mark Pekarsky (various inst); Valentina Ponomareva (v).* 8/91.

Astreja originally functioned as a composition workshop, allowing the composers to free themselves from the tyranny of notation. Since they have also been freed from the tyranny of state control, the music has begun to sound a little self-indulgent. However, their intense interest in the nature of sound and its spiritual implications gives these performances an impact that fully compensates for the appalling recording-quality. An unfortunate return, this, to the good old days of smuggled tapes and *samizdat* imprints; odd, though, because Davos in 1991 was scarcely inaccessible.

Eden Atwood (born 1969)

VOCALS

The daughter of composer Hubbard Atwood, Eden Atwood was raised in Montana and now works in the Chicago area as a singer caught up in the American songbook and a swing-styled approach.

***** No One Ever Tells You**

Concord CCD 4560 *Atwood; Rob Parton, Steve Smyth (t); Paul McKee (tb); Steve Zoloto (as); Brian Budzik, Von Freeman, Edward Petersen (ts); Linda Van Dyke (bs); Laurence Hobgood, Bradley Williams (p); Dave Onderdonk, Akio Sasajima (g); El Dee Young (b, v); John Whitfield, Doug Hayes (b); Michael Raynor, Redd Holt (d); Mark Walker (perc).* 91.

***** Cat On A Hot Tin Roof**

Concord CCD 4599 *Atwood; Ken Peplowski (cl, as); Jesse Davis (as); Allen Farnham (p); John Goldsby (b); Alan Dawson (d).* 2–10/93.

***** There Again**

Concord CCD-4645 *Atwood; Chris Potter (ts); Dave Berkman, Marian McPartland (p); Michael Moore (b); Ron Vincent(d).* 12/94–1/95.

***** A Night In The Life**

Concord CDD-4730 *Atwood; Chris Potter (ts); Jeremy Kahn (p); Larry Koghut (b); Joel Spencer (d).* 4/96.

Atwood has a pleasing, limber voice that can make its way round a lyric with a sexy aplomb. The debut record, originally released on the Chicago label Southport, is an enthusiastic start for a young artist, backed with some of the best of the city's talent: Freeman dons his ballad shoes for the touching treatment of her father's song, 'I Was The Last One To Know'. But the record is a bit muddled, stylistically, with the singer unsure of mixing small-combo jazz singing with bigger groups and pop leanings. *Cat On A Hot Tin Roof* has a smoother, more unified feel, with a characteristic Concord team on hand, although when Atwood tries too hard to be a vamp – as on the title-track – it doesn't really work. She's better on a quieter approach to a ballad, as with 'You've Changed' and 'Never Let Me Go'.

There Again and *A Night In The Life* continue the pattern but, while both are entirely agreeable on their own terms, they miss the distinction of being great records: there are too many too-familiar songs, and Atwood does nothing with them to make them stand out from many another version. Some of her ballads end up going by so slowly that they almost drag. But given an unhackneyed tune – 'In The Days Of Our Love', which McPartland wrote and plays on, 'Why Did I Choose You?', 'When The Sun Comes Out' – she delivers her best performances.

Georgie Auld (1919–90)

SOPRANO, ALTO AND TENOR SAXOPHONES

Canadian born Auld – originally John Altwerger – took over the Artie Shaw band in 1939, led his own outfit for a while, and kept his identity all through the bebop era. Still playing in the 1970s, with a richly romantic tone, Georgie was the featured artist in the movie, New York, New York.

***** Jump, Georgie, Jump**

Hep 27 *Auld; Sonny Berman, John Best, Norman Faye, Manny Fox, Art House, Tony Pastor, Chuck Peterson, Al Porcino, Bernie Privin, George Schwartz (t); Tracy Allen, Jerry Dorn, Gus Dixon, Harry Rodgers (tb); Lou Prisby, Les Robinson, Gene Zanoni (as); George Arus, Al Cohn, Ron Perry, Irving Roth, Jack Schwartz (ts); Manny Albam, Ed Cunningham, Morris Rayman (bs); Harry Biss, Bob Kitsis (p); Dave Barbour (g); Buddy Christian, Lou Fromm, Ralph Hawkins (d); Patti Powers (v).* 40, 44.

***** Handicap**

Discovery 70062 *As above, except add George Schwartz (t), Johnny Mandel, Roger Smith (tb), Musko Ruffo, Sam Zittman (as), Joe Megro, Hy Rubenstein, Jackson Schwartz (ts), Turk Van Lake (g), Joe Pellicane, Iggy Shevak (b), Patti Powers (v).* 45–47.

Auld's career was long and relatively undramatic but packed with thoroughly entertaining music. Having assumed leadership of the Shaw band, Auld turned out professional swing without creating too many surprises. The Hep release brings together studio recordings from 1940 with airshots from 1944 which feature the astonishing talent of Sonny Berman, who died at the absurdly early age of 22. After the war, Auld worked with Sarah Vaughan and recorded the classic 'A Hundred Years From Today' with her. The line-ups on these sessions were very strong indeed and mark the beginnings of a shift towards what would be a moderately successful flirtation with bebop. Here and there one can pick up signs of the lush romanticism of Georgie's later years, but tempered here by an unexpectedly spikey modernism. His solo spots are for the most part sparse and functional, and there is certainly no sign that he wants to hog the spotlight. 'I've Got A Right To Know', 'Mo Mo' and 'Co-Pilot' are strong if somewhat generic originals, but Georgie was never a significant composer.

Lovie Austin (1887–1972)

PIANO

Born in Chattanooga, Austin was an educated musician who ran her own vaudeville show, before settling in Chicago and leading pit bands and record dates as a Paramount house-pianist. She later worked in munitions and, after the war, played in dance instruction classes, recording again in the early '60s.

***** Lovie Austin 1924–1926**

Classics 756 *Austin; Tommy Ladnier, Bob Shoffner, Natty Dominique (c); Kid Ory (tb); Jimmy O'Bryant, Johnny Dodds (cl); Eustern Woodfork (bj); W.E Burton (d); Ford & Ford,*

Edmonia Henderson, Viola Bartlette, Henry Williams (v). 9/24–8/26.

A remarkable woman, and one of the first female musicians to make a significant contribution to jazz, the Tennessee-born Austin became house-pianist at Paramount in the early 1920s. She settled in Chicago, but after the end of the decade she scarcely recorded again until the early '60s. There are 17 surviving sides by her Blues Serenaders, plus various accompaniments to blues and vaudeville singers, and they're all on this valuable CD. Austin's music was a tight, sophisticated variation on the barrel-house style that was prevalent in Chicago at the time. The two sides by the trio of Austin, Ladnier and O'Bryant create a densely plaited counterpoint which seems amazingly advanced for its time. The quartet and quintet sides are harsher, with Burton's clumping drumming on what sounds like a military side-drum taking unfortunate precedence, but the simple breaks and stop-time passages have a rough poetry about them that transcends the very grimy recording. This CD adds to the old Fountain LP by including nine tracks in which Austin and some of her colleagues accompany various blues singers. The transfers are a very mixed bag, as usual with Classics: two tracks by Edmonia Henderson are terribly noisy, and none of the original Paramount recordings are better than average; but practised ears will listen through the noise to some classic Chicago jazz of its day.

In 1961, when in her seventies, Austin was persuaded to record again, as accompanist to Alberta Hunter. The results are available on Original Blues Classics OBC-510.

Available Jelly

GROUP

A Netherlands-based group under the direction of Eric Boeren and Michael Moore, performing free-bop jazz of its own making.

*** In Full Flail

Ear-rational ECD 1013 *Eric Boeren (t, c); Michael Moore (cl, bcl, as, p, mar, hca, bells); Gregg Moore (tb, tba, b, mand); Michael Vatcher (d, dulc, mar).* 6/88.

***(*) Al(l)ways

NOM CD00110 *As above, except add Tobias Delius (ts, hca), Eric Calmes (b, perc).* 11/89.

*** Monuments

Ramboy 07 *As above, except add Jimmy Sernesky (t), Alexei Levin (p, org, acc).* 8–10/93.

*** Happy Camp

Ramboy 10 *Eric Boeren (c, melodica); Wolter Wierbos (tb); Michael Moore (as, cl, bcl); Tobias Delius (ts); Ernst Glerum (b); Michael Vatcher (d).* 6/96.

Michael Moore and Eric Boeren mastermind most of the material for this band, which grew out of a group that worked as accompanists to a mime troupe in the 1970s. *In Full Flail* has a theatrical feel to it, with 11 of the 21 pieces done and dusted in less than three minutes, some of them tossed out like a spontaneous idea. Yet most of it is impeccably organized, especially the pair of sad, funny, faintly satirical tunes at the heart of the disc, Boeran's 'Waggery' and Moore's 'Beauty'. Boeren plays with a fat, brassy intensity that can crack into a chuckling aside, while Moore can play any style, anywhere. Gregg Moore and Vatcher follow them with wit and guile. But it remains a tad arch. *Al(l)ways* is arguably their best record, though it's on the hard-to-find NOM label. The expanded personnel has a number of consequences: it takes the arrangements a step away from jazz and towards the kind of art-rock espoused by Frank Zappa and Henry Cow, it frees up Gregg Moore to play more trombone, and it allows brother Michael to include perfectly logical tributes to Steve Lacy and Thelonious Monk (in the shape of three seldom-played Monk tunes). Some of the short tracks seem like space-wasters, and three melodica players is two too many; but there are many lovely, tart moments. Special highlight: a drowsy treatment of Neal Hefti's 'Girl Talk'.

Monuments overdoes it. The new members add extra weight but they sometimes seem like excess baggage. The firecracker playing that Boeren contributed to the first disc seems to have been swamped by the arrangements, some of which are merely lugubrious, and the concert-hall ambience of the sound-mix doesn't suit them. But there are still some moments to savour, such as Moore's doleful 'Shotgun Wedding', a classic sad-sack dirge, and a couple of Boeren's neatest miniatures. *Happy Camp* is the loosest and liveliest of their records, recorded live at the BIM-Huis. Here the band seem ready to go back to jazz, what with two Ellington tunes (a lovely version of 'The Feeling Of Jazz') and the extra weight lost as the instrumentation goes back to six. Glerum makes the band swing more, and he fits well with Vatcher. Moore does most of the writing and he savours the counterpoint as it proceeds. A nice run of records.

Bent Axen (born 1925)

PIANO

Studied Charlie Parker's music as it appeared in Denmark, and began playing regularly at Copenhagen's Vingaarden club in the late '50s. Backed many visiting Americans during this period, but eventually moved into theatre and TV work and left jazz behind.

**(*) Axen

Steeplechase SCCD 36003 *Axen; Allan Botschinsky (t); Bent Jaedig, Frank Jensen (ts); Niels-Henning Orsted Pedersen, Ole Laumann, Erik Molbach (b); Finn Frederiksen, Jorn Elniff (d).* 12/59–10/60.

The back pages of Danish jazz history. Axen subsequently left the music, but he helped pioneer modern jazz on record in Denmark and this documents some early steps. The CD gathers in three sessions, two quintets and a trio, for what are rough-and-ready approximations of the American bebop model, refracted through the Scandinavian affection for Getzian cool. NHOP was still only fourteen when he made the trio tracks and Botschinsky was barely out of his teens. Nothing startling here, really: Axen's tunes follow familiar models and his own playing is decent if unexceptional. The most interesting player is probably Jaedig, who was as close to a genuine hard-bopper in delivery as anyone in that scene at the time. The sound is rather rough and tends to distort on volume peaks.

Albert Ayler (1936–70)

TENOR SAXOPHONE, ALTO SAXOPHONE, SOPRANO SAXOPHONE

Born in Cleveland, Ayler played R&B on alto as a teenager, then switched to tenor during army service. Left for Sweden in 1962, recording in Europe, and returned to the USA in 1963, recording for ESP and later Impulse! through the rest of the decade. The most intense of avant-gardists, his recordings map out much of what happened to jazz in the '60s, including its decline into attempted populism. Found dead in New York's East River in 1970.

****(*) The First Recordings: Volume 2**
DIW 349 *Ayler; Torbjørn Hultcrantz (b); Sune Spangberg (d).* 10/62.

***** My Name Is Albert Ayler**
Black Lion BLCD 760211 *Ayler; Niels Bronsted (p); Niels-Henning Orsted Pedersen (b); Ronnie Gardiner (d).* 1/63.

***** Goin' Home**
Black Lion BLCD 760197 *Ayler; Call Cobbs (p); Henry Grimes (b); Sunny Murray (d).* 2/64.

Ayler's style has been subjected to just as many conspiracy theories as the life and death but is now generally considered to be a highly personal amalgam of New Orleans brass, rhythm and blues (to which Ayler unapologetically returned in his last two years) and some of the more extreme timbral innovations of the '60s New Thing.

The first recordings, made in Denmark, are astonishingly sparse. With no harmony instrument and a concentration on stark melodic variations in and out of tempo, they sound influenced by early Ornette Coleman; but what is immediately distinctive about Ayler is the almost hypnotic depth of his concentration on a single motif, which he repeats, worries, splinters into constituent harmonics, until even familiar standards are virtually unrecognizable. Ayler's impatience with bebop is evident throughout and, for all their unrelieved starkness, these rather solitary experiments are still remarkably refreshing. Not called on to keep time, Hultcrantz and Spangberg occasionally resort to marking it, but they seem unfazed by Ayler's primitivism. Why a regular working band should be so lackadaisical about music as unexpected as this remains mysterious. There is some evidence that Ayler didn't want these sessions to be released, or at the very least he was sceptical about their merits. The second batch of material from October 1962 consists of four disjointed repertory pieces – 'Moanin'', 'Good Bait', 'I Didn't Know What Time It Was' and a take of 'Softly, As In A Morning Sunrise' – which see Albert effectively ignore the harmonic structure of the song and simply follow the logic of his own invention. Not once, though, does the rhythm section follow him 'out', and it is already clear that the saxophonist needs not only sympathetic interpreters but also a new body of material. John Coltrane's dismantling and reconfiguration of the popular song was not to be Ayler's recourse.

Back in the USA, Ayler cut a session for Debut Records' Ole Vestergaard Jensen; it was released as *My Name Is Albert Ayler* and, like much of the saxophonist's output, has enjoyed only rather uncertain circulation. The opening track is a short, spoken introduction by the saxophonist. Couched in terms of great modesty, which hint at near if not actual poverty, they convey a man of humble and unemphatic character (sounding a little like Eric Dolphy) but certainly not a man capable of the ferocious saxophone outbursts of subsequent years, nor indeed the man who was to fall prey to such corrosive depression. With the exception of the closing 'C.T.' all the tunes are standards: 'Bye Bye Blackbird', 'Billie's Bounce', 'Summertime' and a fine version of 'On Green Dolphin Street'. *Goin' Home* contains the rest of the session. It finds Ayler at his most 'primitive', digging deep into traditional Americana for themes like 'Down By The Riverside' and 'Swing Low, Sweet Chariot' and 'When The Saints Go Marchin' In', with 'Old Man River' thrown in; all but 'Saints' are offered in two versions, forgivable padding for such an important document. Working with a pianist constrained Ayler a touch, though later Cobbs was to contribute a distinctive harpsichord part to *Love Cry*. The saxophone lines are gloriously unadorned and *Goin' Home* is doubly valuable for a rare glimpse of Ayler's soprano sound.

*****(*) Witches And Devils**
Freedom 741018 *Ayler; Norman Howard (t); Henry Grimes, Earl Henderson (b); Sunny Murray (d).* 2/64.

On his return from Europe, where he had moved to find work and cut that tentative debut, Ayler bunked for a time with the trumpeter Norman Howard, who had been a friend since schooldays. There he met Earl (or Errol) Henderson, a sax player who had turned, it seems wisely, to playing bass. Jensen arranged a recording in New York City. This might be seen as Albert's real debut, but Howard was more of a sympathetic friend than a genuinely challenging musician, and he seems no more certain of Ayler's direction than the Scandinavian sidemen on the early records. However, he had the basic chops and a sufficient measure of respect for his friend to throw himself into the project, and he plays more than competently on 'Saints' (which is a version of a theme listed on *Spiritual Unity* as 'Spirits'), 'Witches And Devils', 'Holy Holy' and, the track that gave the original release its title, 'Spirits'.

A bare three months before the mammoth achievement of *Spiritual Unity*, Ayler sounds poised and confident, the Sonny Rollins mannerisms of the first record still evident. Henderson and Grimes combine for 'Witches And Devils', giving the saxophonist the weight of sound he was looking for and was to get from Gary Peacock. The recording quality was surprisingly good, with the two horns well balanced and the rhythm section spread across the background.

♛ ** Spiritual Unity**
ESP Disk 1002 *Ayler; Gary Peacock (b); Sunny Murray (d).* 7/64.

The poet Ted Joans likened the impact of this trio to hearing someone scream the word 'fuck' in St Patrick's Cathedral. Subjectively, there may be some validity in this, but it makes a nonsense of what was actually going on in this group. The intensity of interaction among the three individuals, their attentiveness to what the others were doing, ruled out any such gesture. Even amid the noise, the 1964 Ayler trio was quintessentially a listening band, locked in a personal struggle which it is possible only to observe, awe-struck, from the side-lines.

Prophecy catches a group poised on the brink of greatness. The music was recorded at the Cellar Café in New York by the writer Paul Haines, best known as the librettist on Carla Bley's *Escalator Over The Hill*. The recording seems to have been done with Ayler's permission, but it was released only in 1976. As so often with Ayler's discography, there is no consensus as to whether the themes performed are those listed. 'Wizard' has close links to 'Holy Holy' and a supposed version of 'Ghosts' is actually a further version of 'Spirits'. Murray is torrential throughout, and Peacock, seemingly recorded quite close, is much sharper than most of Ayler's bassists.

***** Vibrations**

Freedom 741000 *Ayler; Don Cherry (t); Gary Peacock (b); Sunny Murray (d).* 9/64.

***** The Hilversum Session**

Coppens CCD 6001 *As above.* 11/64.

The chief problem with the Ayler discography – quite apart from the record companies' unwillingness until recently to keep it up to date – is his remarkably slender basic repertoire; there was not much of it and what there was tended to be melodically skeletal, almost folkish. Versions of 'Ghosts' turn up on this pair, played pretty much straight and in line with his growing sense that the exact notes mattered considerably less than the amount of emotional charge that could be put across the poles of a melody.

Cherry was, as with Ornette, his most sympathetic interpreter, a more responsive and clear-sighted musician than the saxophonist's brother, trumpeter Donald Ayler, with whom he was to form his next band, this time in the USA. Both 1964 sessions are well recorded and transfer well to CD (the shift of medium is particularly advantageous to Peacock, whose critical contribution tends to get lost on vinyl).

****** Live In Greenwich Village: The Complete Impulse Recordings**

Impulse! IMP 12732 2 CD *Ayler; Donald Ayler (t); George Steele (tb); Michel Sampson (vn); Joel Freedman (clo); William Folwell, Henry Grimes, Alan Silva (b); Beaver Harris, Sunny Murray (d).* 3/65–2/67.

Whatever technical and aesthetic shortcomings the Lörrach and Paris sessions may have had (there is a nihilistic, fragmentary quality to the latter), the Village Theater and Village Vanguard sessions are hugely affirmative and satisfyingly complete without losing a jot of Ayler's angry and premonitory force. These are some of the essential post-war jazz recordings, and they include some of Ayler's best playing on both alto ('For John Coltrane', ironically or self-protectively) and tenor (the apocalyptic 'Truth Is Marching In'). For comparison, try the closing version of 'Our Prayer' here, with the version recorded in Germany, above. The addition of a second bass, in addition to either violin or cello, actually sharpens the sound considerably, producing a rock-solid foundation for Ayler's raw witness.

This splendid reissue continues the progress towards a new sound. It supersedes *In Greenwich Village* and *The Village Concerts* without adding very much of significance towards what was already a remarkable record. There is a single track ('Holy Ghost') from March 1965, originally issued on the Impulse! compilation, *The New Wave In Jazz*. One other track, 'Universal Thoughts', is incomplete, presumably because the tape ran out. However, having these performances together on one set is of value. John Coltrane was present, ailing and tired, when 'Truth Is Marching In' and 'Our Prayer' were recorded at the Village Vanguard. John was to die in the summer of the following year, but his spirit is everywhere here, even though Ayler was firmly in command of his own style and approach. These are Don Ayler's finest moments. Always an approximate technician, but driven by loyalty to his brother, he produces a stream of pure sound which is unique in jazz. Not even Ornette Coleman on brass sounds so alien. A remarkable record, to be prized by anyone who shares Ayler's lonely vigil on the planet.

Azimuth

GROUP

The trio of Taylor, Wheeler and Winstone, subsequently built on but as basic an improvising chamber-jazz group as can be thought of.

*****(*) Azimuth / The Touchstone / Départ**

ECM 523010-2 3CD *Kenny Wheeler (t, flhn); John Taylor (ky); Norma Winstone (v); Ralph Towner (g on Départ only).* 3/77–12/79.

****(*) Azimuth '85**

ECM 827520-2 *As above, except omit Towner.* 3/85.

***** 'How It Was Then ... Never Again'**

ECM 523820-2 *As above.* 4/94.

The repackaging of Azimuth's first three records, and the appearance of a new disc after a break of some years, offered a chance to reassess the work of a notably understated trio whose live appearances (at least one gig every year since 1977; no mean achievement in this branch of music) are often far more rugged and sharply inflected than the recorded product would suggest. Initially, the group was a duo format for the then-married Taylor and Winstone. On the debut album, her voice floats with a characteristic balance between freedom and control over Taylor's minimalistic piano figures. Any doubts that these are jazz-trained and jazz-centred performers are immediately dispelled, and the second track, called simply 'O', is not much more than a blowing shape, over which Winstone and Wheeler (whose inclusion was suggested by ECM producer and demiurge, Manfred Eicher, with a characteristic instinct for the appropriate touch) improvise freely. The very next track, significantly the title-cut, is the first to use the studio as a compositional device, building up layers of keyboard, voice and trumpets into a grand acoustic edifice that constantly reveals new areas of interest.

The most obvious difference between the first and third albums and the middle one of the original group is that on *Touchstone* there is no lyric component as such. Here Winstone vocalizes, turning her voice into a third and equal part in the mix. Taylor abandons the synthesizer swirls of *Azimuth* in favour of the organ's richly *breathing* sound. The result is perhaps the group's masterpiece, combining jazz, classical and contemporary composition, and sheer sound in a mix that is as invigorating as it is thought-provoking. The outstanding track is without a doubt the glorious 'See'.

Azimuth and Ralph Towner met at ECM's Oslo studios, where the guitarist was finishing an album of his own. The end of the 1970s probably marked the high-water mark of the label's more experimental ethos, with Eicher encouraging previously untried permutations. Much as he does on Weather Report's *I Sing The Body Electric*, Towner sounds as if he comes from outside the basic conception of the group, but with a genuine understanding and appreciation of what it's all about. His contribution is perhaps most emphatic on 'Arrivée', which is a companion-piece to the title-track, linking the whole disc into a continuous suite. As such, it's perhaps slightly too mannered and deliberate, but none the less effective for that.

Succeeding years presented fewer opportunities to record as a unit, presumably to some extent because Wheeler in particular was busy on projects of his own. Azimuth's return to the studio was the pretty disappointing '85. With '85, Azimuth fell into the trap Towner's Oregon has always avoided: that of making style an end in itself. There is no fixed requirement that musicians or bands 'develop' stylistically, but, for all the quality of writing and performance, *Azimuth '85* did seem to be an unconfident step back.

It was then nearly a decade before the group recorded again, an awkward gap of time in critical and commercial terms. The signs are, though, that the energies of the first record have been significantly re-channelled and re-directed. '*How It Was Then ... Never Again*' suggests a backward-looking and even nostalgic subtext; the music within is as progressive and empirical as anything the group had done in 20 years. Taylor restricts himself to piano and to a compositional style that has acquired a new, though entirely non-linear, logic. Titles like 'Whirlpool' and 'Full Circle' very accurately convey his ability to infuse harmonic and melodic stasis with hints of tremendous energy. Winstone's voice is as pure and reed-like as ever, and the only question marks relate to Wheeler, who increasingly seems to be speaking in a different musical language.

Ab Baars

CLARINET, SOPRANO, TENOR AND BARITONE SAXOPHONES

Dutch improviser specializing in the reed family, a sideman with Maarten Altena.

**** Krang**
Geestgronden 2 *Baars (solo).* 12/87–6/89.

****(*) 3900 Carol Court**
Geestgronden 12 *Baars; Wilbert De Joode (b); Martin Van Duynhoven (d).* 3–6/92.

***** Sprok**
Geestgronden 14 *As above.* 2–5/94.

****(*) Verderame**
Geestgronden 17 *Baars (solo).* 1/95.

Baars makes very heavy weather of *Krang*. Rather than improvising in any specific direction, his solos tend to circle in on themselves or to reach a spurious climax of increasingly harsh repetitions. This makes the soprano solo, 'Geel en Rood', barely listenable, a different application of Steve Lacy's methods to sometimes grisly ends. But the blustering weight of the baritone on 'Spaat' or the false pathos of the tenor on the title-track are more interesting.

There's another version of 'Krang' on the first trio album. After the abstractions of the solo record, it comes as a mild shock to hear him with an almost conventionally swinging rhythm section on John Lewis's 'Plastic Dreams'. But the other pieces, revolving round remote kinds of interplay among the three players, are more typical of what Baars is after. The leader's solos still tend to grind through curtly defined areas of timbre and phrasing, but at least they're leavened by the inquiring bass and drum parts.

Sprok seems like a loosening-up and a further clarifying at the same time. Baars makes his clarinet and tenor sound more dry and stone-faced than ever, but bass and drums shift smoothly between free playing and courtly, strict time. Not bad at all.

His second solo disc, though, isn't much less drear and mirthless than the first one. Various dedications – to Han Bennink, Misha Mengelberg, Pee Wee Russell, John Carter – are writ intimidatingly large, as if he wants to express only the starkest and most harsh aspects of his influences. He sticks to clarinet and tenor, and several of the pieces have a morse-code brevity of layout. Taken one or two at a time it is quite powerful, but a whole disc (even at only 40 minutes) is pretty hard going.

Babkas

GROUP

Three young American free-bop players in a power trio, of sorts.

***** Babkas**
Songlines 1502-2 *Briggan Krauss (as); Brad Schoeppach (g); Aaron Alexander (d).* 1/93.

***** Ants To The Moon**
Songlines 1505-2 *As above.* 2/94.

***** Fratelli**
Songlines 1513-2 *As above.* 3–5/96.

Entertaining variations on the power trio by the not-quite-splenetic Babkas. Schoeppach is the principal writing force and the major musical personality: he tends to set the tone for each of their pieces, with decoration by Krauss and pulse and splashing rhythm from Alexander. The earliest disc is less unified, more diverse. 'Czugy Stodel' sounds like a Hungarian dance, and they then proceed to cover a genuine one, No. 20 by Brahms. Punky outbursts like 'Piglet' are measured against long, dense explorations. Schoeppach favours lots of thick-toned fuzz on this disc; he prefers a more open tone on the next disc, which is more composed and poised, though not necessarily superior – some of the pieces go on a bit, and Krauss's squalling delivery has its limitations exposed. *Fratelli* is the gentlest of the three, chamberish for much of the time, with Alexander often just sitting and listening as Krauss and Schoeppach intertwine. Much of this one relies on texture, but they end with a blowout of sorts on 'Seaweed Crunch'. A progressive group.

Alice Babs (born 1924)

VOCAL, PIANO

Born in Kalmar, Babs was more of a pop-MOR singer in her native Sweden, but her affiliations with jazz were recognized by Duke Ellington, who featured her with the band on several occasions from 1963.

***** Swing It!**

Phontastic PHONTCD 9302 *Babs; Thore Ehrling, Gosta Redlig, Gosta Torner, Rolf Ericson, Rune Ander, Olle Jacobson, Nisse Skoog, Anders Sward (t); George Vernon, Bertil Jacobson, Sven Bohman, Karl-Erik Lennholm, Sverre Oredsson (tb); Sven Gustafsson, Ove Lind, Putte Wickman, Charlie Redland (cl); Casper Hjukstrom (cl, as); John Bjorling, Ove Ronn, Arne Domnérus, O Thalen (as); Carl-Henrik Norin, Gunnar Lunden-Velden, Gosta Theselius, Curt Blomqvist (ts); Lars Schonning (bs); Stig Holm, Allan Johansson, Rolf Larsson, Charles Norman, Rolf Svensson (p); Bosse Callstrom (vib); Erik Frank, Nisse Lind (acc); Rolf Berg, B Larsson, Folke Eriksberg, Sven Stiberg, Jonny Bossman, Nils-Erik Sandell, Sten Carlberg, Kalle Lohr (g); Thore Jederby, Henry Lundin, Gunnar Almstedt, Romeo Sjoberg, Simon Brehm, Rolf Bengtsson (b); Ake Brandes, Andrew Burman, Henry Wallin, Gosta Heden, Thord Waerner, Gosta Oddner (d).* 5/39–4/53.

****(*) Metronome-Aren 1951–1958**

Metronome 4509-93189-2 2CD *Babs; orchestras of Charlie Norman, Harry Arnold, Gunnar Lunden-Velden, Anders Burman, Ernie Englund.* 51–58.

***** Far Away Star**

Bluebell ABCD 005 *Babs; Money Johnson, Johnny Coles, Barry Lee Hall, Willie Cook, Mercer Ellington, Americo Bellotto, Bertil Lövgren, Jan Allan, Håkan Nyqvist (t); Vince Prudente, Chuck Connors, Art Baron, Torgny Nilsson, Lars Olofsson, Bertil Strandberg, Sven Larsson (tb); Harry Carney, Russell Procope, Harold Minerve, Harold Ashby, Parcy Marion, Arne Domnérus, Claes Rosendahl, Lennart Aberg, Ulf Andersson, Erik Nilsson (reeds); Duke Ellington, Nils Lindberg (p); Rune Gustafsson (g); Joe Benjamin, Red Mitchell (b); Quentin White Jr, Nils-Erik Slorner (d).* 6/73–5/76.

***** There's Something About Me ...**

Bluebell ABCD 052 *As above, except omit Ellington personnel; add Jan Allan (t), Anders Lindskog (ts), Erik Nilsson (bs), Davor Kajfes (ky), Rune Carlsson (d).* 5/73–9/78.

Along with the very different stylist, Monica Zetterlund, Alice 'Babs' Nilsson is Sweden's most renowned vocalist in the jazz world – although, like Zetterlund, she has often touched only peripherally on jazz surroundings. Her early tracks feature on the useful compilation, *Swing It!*, which is in many ways the most jazz-orientated of all four discs. She tackles everything from 'Some Of These Days' and 'Darktown Strutters Ball' to 'Yodel In Swing' and 'Opus In Scat', in settings that range from accordion trios to impressive big bands. Three airchecks with a small group including Rolf Ericson (terrific on 'Truckin'') offer some of the best music, but the entire disc has much to enjoy, not least Babs's light but amazingly confident handling of the English lyrics. The earliest track dates from before her sixteenth birthday, yet she seems fearless in all this music. The Metronome two-disc set is of much more limited appeal. Sung mainly in Swedish, this includes a lot of pop material which has marginal jazz content and, though Babs is unfailingly charming, in parts it can be a struggle.

She first worked with Ellington in 1963, and she remained a favourite with Duke: the four 1973 tracks with the band on *Far Away Star* are a souvenir of one of their final collaborations, though the tracks from an Ellington memorial concert the following year with a Swedish group are actually rather better. So is *There's Something About Me* ..., which has some more Ellington material – 'Checkered Hat', 'Me And You' and the title-piece – but which is most interesting for five songs co-written by John Lewis. Babs, whose cool, slightly impassive but fundamentally emotional delivery seems well suited to this material, produces some of her best work here. There is much more still awaiting reissue.

Back Bay Ramblers

GROUP

An 'occasional' American repertory group playing the hot dance music of the 1920s.

***** 'Leven Thirty Saturday Night**

Stomp Off CD 1262 *Peter Ecklund (c); Bob Connors (tb); Steve Wright (cl, as, ts, bs, bsx); Bill Novick (cl, as); Butch Thompson (p); Peter Bullis (g, bj); Stu Gunn (tba, b); Bill Reynolds (d); Karen Cameron (v).* 1/93

***** My Mamma's In Town!**

Stomp Off CD 1279 *As above, except Mark Shane, Bob Pilsbury (p), Vince Giordano (tba, bsx, b) replace Thompson and Gunn; add Andy Stein (vn), Jimmy Mazzy (v).* 1/94.

Of the many repertory bands recording for Stomp Off, the Ramblers pay some of the most dutiful homage to their inspirations – usually the hot dance music of the 1920s rather than the out-and-out jazz of the period. So the first CD includes arrangements drawn from the books of Bob Haring, Jack Pettis and Spike Hughes, while the second relies heavily on the work of Jean Goldkette, Annette Hanshaw and Ted Lewis. None of the players makes a special impression by himself – they're playing for the band, and the lilt and deferential swing of this music is its reason to exist. Ecklund has some agreeable 16-bar interludes, Connors is splendidly versatile, and Novick and Wright are skilled interpreters of the old-time reedsman's role. That said, the music can seem almost airlessly polite at times. Cameron sings sweetly, Mazzy with a bit more gusto on the second disc. Little to choose between the two discs, and it's a churl who would deny that it's pleasant to find a group ready to perform something like Phil Napoleon's 'You Can't Cheat A Cheater' in the godless '90s.

Badland

GROUP

British improvising trio working from a game-plan of 'real' compositions.

*** Badland

Bruce's Fingers BF 14 *Simon Rose (as, ss); Simon H Fell (b); Mark Sanders (d).* 5/95.

Vivid free-bop from a highly accomplished trio who venture gamely out into new and lawless territory. Bracketed by two versions of Ornette's 'Sadness' and with an unexpected version of Duke's 'Come Sunday' in the middle, it's a record that repays close and repeated attention. Firmly in the line of earlier British groups like Amalgam, it nevertheless brings new ideas and a freshness of diction to this challenging idiom.

Baecastuff

GROUP

Australian bop-to-fusion band of distinctive calibre.

*** Big Swell

Rufus RF033 *Phil Slater (t); Rick Robertson (ts, ss); Matt McMahon (p); Alex Hewelson (b); Simon Barker (d); Nick McBride (perc).* 11/96.

In their modest way, this Australian group get a lot more out of jazz, funk and rock and their various crossing-points than many a more renowned band. Barker and McBride tend to lay down a tough, funky beat that the horn players (including Rick Robertson of the excellent Directions In Groove) have time to decorate or spin off more or less at their own pleasure. McMahon plays elliptical Fender Rhodes in the style of the early Weather Report Zawinul, and the tunes are a bright, precocious lot that the players find very suitable.

Benny Bailey (born 1925)

TRUMPET, FLUGELHORN

Bailey won his spurs in three of the most important big bands of his day, Jay McShann's, Dizzy Gillespie's and Lionel Hampton's, with which he stayed for almost five years. His bright, hard-edged tone softens markedly in small-group settings, but without losing its burnish. Bailey spent a considerable time in Europe, where he worked with Eric Dolphy and where he has sustained a regular recording schedule.

*** Big Brass

Candid CCD 79011 *Bailey; Julius Watkins (hn); Phil Woods (as, b cl); Les Spann (f, g); Tommy Flanagan (p); Buddy Catlett (b); Art Taylor (d).* 11/60.

Bailey is probably best known as first trumpet in the Kenny Clarke/Francy Boland big bands of the 1960s, but he is also an impressive and entertaining soloist, with a number of distinguishing marks on his musical passport, noticeably his much-commented-upon octave plummets and his attraction to enigmatic lines that seem from moment to moment to have neither melodic nor harmonic significance, just a strangely specific logic all their own. His bebop background is still evident on *Big Brass*, certainly his finest available record (though the deleted *Serenade To The Planet* is considered essential documentation). The themes have begun to stretch out, though, into long, quasi-modal strings that contain any number of potential resolutions. Flanagan is a sympathetic accompanist. Woods and Rouse could hardly be more different, but Bailey responds magnanimously to the challenge posed by each.

** Islands

Enja 2082 *Bailey; Sigi Schwab (g, sitar); Eberhard Weber (b); Lala Kovacev (d).* 5/76.

Islands bumps the story along a decade and a half, during which time Bailey devoted most of his energies to the Clarke–Boland band. Trying to restart his solo career, he seemed rather too deliberate and mannered, and certainly long exposure to European music and musicians had a curious effect on his approach, cooling it almost to the point of stasis and replacing pace and fire with atmospherics. Weber's bass is not quite right, and Schwab's guitar and sitar seem almost surplus to the more straightforward themes.

***(*) Grand Slam

Storyville 8271 *Bailey; Charlie Rouse (ts); Richard Wyands (p); Sam Jones (b); Billy Hart (d).* 10/78.

Originally released on Jazzcraft, this pungent set is one of Bailey's very best. The inclusion of three tunes by arranger Fritz Pauer is a bit over the top, but there are also fine originals by Benny, 'Theloniousassault' and 'Who's Bossa Now?', which cover a good bit of his range, from fiery bebop to a more gently swinging sound. An alternative take of Pepper Adams's 'Reflectory' is less emphatic than the issued version, but Rouse's two solos and Wyands's generous accompaniment make the track a welcome addition. Bailey sounded capable of anything in these years. He has always quoted classic recordings – almost unconsciously, one suspects – and it's interesting here to see how often he seems to make reference to Dizzy, Fats and Howard McGhee in the course of his solos, even when the material is far removed from orthodox bebop or Afro-Cuban. A fine album, recommended to Bailey newcomers and established fans alike.

*** For Heaven's Sake

Hot House HHCD 1006 *Bailey; Tony Coe (ts, cl); Horace Parlan (p); Jimmy Woode (b); Idris Muhammad (d).* 88.

Like Bailey, Tony Coe is more widely appreciated in Continental Europe than in his homeland. This is a diaspora record, a meeting between five gifted and passionate musicians for whom Europe has proved to be a refuge and a challenge. British-made on this occasion, the record is perhaps the best showcase in recent times of Bailey's straight jazz playing, albeit too closely miked. The solos are without exception intelligent, elegant and finely crafted, and it's possible to hear the man from Cleveland running through and reminiscing about some of the styles he would have heard back home earlier in his career: Roy, Dizzy, Fats, a hint of Miles in the ballads, and here and there an echo of Booker Little who, like Bailey himself, had worked with Eric Dolphy.

***** Live At Grabenhalle, St Gallen**

TCB 8940 *Bailey; Carlo Schoeb (as); Peter Eigenmann (g); Reggie Johnson (b); Peter Schmidlin (d).* 4/89.

***** Peruvian Nights**

TCB 96102 *As above.* 4/89.

*****(*) While My Lady Sleeps**

Gemini GMCD 69 *Bailey; Harald Gundhus (ts); Emil Viklický (p); František Uhlírš (b); Ole-Jacob Hansen (d).* 4/90.

****** No Refill**

TCB 94202 *As for Live At Grabenhalle, except omit Johnson; add Jesper Lundgaard (b).* 2/92.

In contrast to the group on *Islands*, the quartet on *While My Lady Sleeps* is completely attuned to Bailey's music, combining an attractive obliqueness with some wonderfully concentrated ballad playing on 'While My Lady Sleeps'; Gundhus solos impressively and the rhythm section sustain a long, throbbing accompaniment. Two originals by Viklický (the disappointing opening 'Vino, Oh Vino!') and Uhlír ('Expectation') are redeemed by Bailey's thoughtful commentaries; but the meat of the album is kept till last with the long version of the title-track and a tight reading of Benny Golson's 'Along Came Betty'. Recording was done at the Rainbow Studio in Oslo by Jan Erik Kongshaug, both associated with ECM; the quality is exactly what you'd expect. Recommended.

No Refill and the live TCBs preserve a group that was Bailey's working outfit for several years, providing him with a solid platform for fresh adventures and quietly indulgent reverie. In the studio they sound absolutely top notch, and this is without question the record of choice, along with *Big Brass*. It includes a reprise of Bailey's own 'Serenade To A Planet' (as it is called here) and a long version of 'Surinam'. Other high spots are Carlo Schoeb's original 'Gryce's Grace' and the Thad Jones title-track, which brings a hugely satisfying record to a close. *Peruvian Nights* is distinguished by a long version of Isla Eckinger's 'Blues East', on which Benny stretches out more than usual, drifting across the bar lines in a manner oddly reminiscent of 1950s Miles, but with a tighter and more acid tone.

Buster Bailey (1902–67)

CLARINET

Bailey learned from a noted classical teacher in college in Chicago and was already a virtuoso by the time he joined Fletcher Henderson in 1924, staying until 1937. In the '50s he often played with Henry Allen, then freelanced until ending his career back with his Henderson colleague, Louis Armstrong, in the All Stars.

****(*) Buster Bailey 1925–1940**

Classics 904 *Bailey; Henry 'Red' Allen, Charlie Shavers, Frankie Newton (t); J.C Higginbotham (tb); Pete Brown, Benny Carter, Russell Procope (as); Clarence Todd, Charlie Beal, Don Frye, Billy Kyle (p); Danny Barker, James McLin (g); Buddy Christian (bj); Elmer James, Johnny Williams, John Kirby (b); Walter Johnson, O'Neil Spencer, Zutty Singleton (d); Jerry Kruger, Judy Ellington (v).* 5/25–6/40.

Bailey's many records with Fletcher Henderson are probably his best legacy. Certainly these sessions under his own name are a disappointing lot. His single coupling for Banner in 1925, with Clarence Todd and the vigorous Buddy Christian, is rather good, but it's dubbed from a very rough 78 and 'Squeeze Me' has some outrageous artificial echo. A 1934 session with Allen, Higginbotham and Carter is good if restrained, but most of the remaining dates – many with variations of the John Kirby line-up in which Bailey was a regular – are drearily bouncy light music, with the ludicrous tea-dance version of 'Pine Top's Boogie Woogie' a low point and the endearing if ridiculous 'Man With A Horn Goes Berserk' making one wonder what kind of musician Bailey saw himself as. The transfers, after the disastrous start, are just about acceptable.

Craig Bailey (born 1960)

ALTO SAXOPHONE, FLUTE

A contemporary hard-bopper with much sideman experience before making this debut as leader.

***** A New Journey**

Candid CCD 79725 *Bailey; Derrick Gardner, Terell Stafford (t, flhn); Patrick Face Rickman (t); Dupor Georges (tb); Jim Hartog (bs); Mark Feldman (vn); George Caldwell, Eric Lewis, Enos Payne (p); Eric Lemon (b); Bruce Cox, Kenny Washington (d); Jeffrey Haynes (perc).* 3/95.

As his birthdate suggests, Bailey has waited for some time to make his debut as leader. The Cincinnatian has worked extensively with Charlie Persip, Ray Charles, Slide Hampton, Jimmy Heath, Panama Francis, and with *A New Journey*'s producer, Bobby Watson, before taking the plunge. Doubtless he could have called on a heavyweight supporting cast, but it's interesting that he has preferred to assemble a large pool of mainly (and with the obvious exception of Washington, Hartog, Feldman and the up-and-coming Stafford) unknown players. Past allegiances are not difficult to identify. Though seemingly intended as a tribute to Art Blakey, the opening 'C.B. #1' could be something out of Watson's book, while the blues, 'What Would I Do Without You', is a Ray Charles favourite. The first indication of a more ambitious range of sound comes on 'Laura', a performance inspired by *Charlie Parker With Strings* records and combining Bailey's flute with Feldman (playing straight, for him) and Latin-tinged percussion from Haynes. 'Bells' is an original with an arresting tintinnabulatory opening theme; 'No Hip Hop' sounds like a declaration of intent; and 'Soul Flower' is the big love ballad. Here and there, Bailey shows signs of pushing out into more ambitious territory, as when he tackles 'Cherokee' without harmony instruments. A curious mix of mainstream, retro and outside notions, *A New Journey* doesn't quite gel as an album. It calls out for a more unfettered and confrontational approach, and for a less unctuous sound-mix.

Derek Bailey (born 1930)

GUITAR

A figure of immeasurable importance in contemporary music, Bailey has remained true to a radical philosophy of improvisation which dispenses with all the conventional parameters of music: line, rhythm, vertical harmony. The Yorkshireman was a key figure in the development of free jazz and in groups like Josef Holbrooke, Iskra 1903 and the Spontaneous Music Ensemble; other key associations were with drummer Tony Oxley and saxophonist Evan Parker, with whom he founded Incus records. Bailey was also for many years ringmaster of the annual Company week of free improvisation.

*** Fairly Early With Postscripts

Emanem 4027 *Bailey; Anthony Braxton (reeds, f); Kent Carter (b); John Stevens (d).* 7/71–10/98.

*** Solo Guitar: Volume 1

Incus CD10 *Bailey (g solo, syn).* 2/71.

*** Improvisation

Cramps 62 *Bailey (g solo).* 75.

**** Domestic & Public Pieces

Emanem 4001 *As above.* 75–77.

Bailey's sometimes forbidding but always challenging music illuminates certain important differences between European and American improvisers. Whereas American free jazz and improvisation have tended to remain individualistic – the most convenient image is the soloist stepping forward from the ensemble – European improvisers have tended to follow a broadly collectivist philosophy which downplays personal expression in favour of a highly objectified or process-dominated music. Perhaps the best concrete illustration of the difference can be found in Bailey's duo performances with the multi-instrumentalist, Anthony Braxton. Despite considerable mutual admiration, these confirm the old saw about Europeans and Americans being divided by a common language; Braxton's formulations are still conditioned by the deep structures of jazz, Bailey's according to a mysterious metalanguage by which a performance offers few guidelines as to its presumed origins and underlying processes. (The guitarist did once record a splendidly ironic version of 'The Lost Chord'.)

Like a good many European improvisers, Bailey underwent an accelerated and virtually seamless transition from jazz to free jazz to free music. He has performed with such innovative groups as Josef Holbrooke and Iskra 1903, but since 1976 his activities have centred on solo and duo work (where he is most influential as a performer) and on his loosely affiliated collective, Company, locus of some of the most challenging musical and para-musical performance of recent years. Company has been sufficiently unlimited to draw in musicians from a 'straight' jazz background (most strikingly Lee Konitz), avant-garde composer-performers such as trombonist Vinko Globokar, and even dancer Katie Duck, as well as long-standing associates Evan Parker, Jamie Muir, Barre Phillips, Han Bennink and Tristan Honsinger, with all of whom Bailey has made significant duo recordings.

Bailey's music resists exact description and evaluation. Eschewing special effects (apart from a swell pedal on his amplified performances and a one-off use of VCS3 synthesizer on *Solo Guitar: Volume One*), he plays intensely and abstractly. The early solo records are still the best place to start with Bailey, though the release of *Fairly Early* offers a glimpse of Derek playing solo and with other musicians who share his philosophy. It also offers a rare insight into his political view, as he discusses current affairs to a free-form accompaniment in a series of 'cassette letters' to label-owner Martin Davidson. The CD has the additional advantage of offering material from a nearly 30-year span, valuable if you want a quick introduction.

But a word of warning. If you don't open yourself without prejudice to what is happening on these tight, intense and dynamic numbers and on the three solo guitar records, it seems improbable to unlikely that you will respond to anything else that Bailey has recorded. The playing is, as even classical players have admitted, entirely idiomatic. It owes nothing to any existing style, though Bailey did make one BBC interviewer's jaw drop when (though famously resistant to any discussion of 'influence') he mentioned Teddy Bunn of the Spirits of Rhythm as a major source. In the most curious way, *Solo Guitar* now sounds quite old-fashioned – not anachronistic, but redolent of an earlier, more innocent phase in the free movement when the moment was everything.

This is still the spirit that governs *Domestic & Public Pieces* which, as the title suggests, brings performance material together with what can't be described as 'rehearsal' in this context but is closer to a process of private musing, diary-keeping, monologue. Some of these acoustic guitar pieces have spoken commentaries, which are, as ever, wry if mostly unenlightening. The amplified concert-pieces are more familiar in nature but no less appealing to the Bailey enthusiast. As ever, Martin Davidson has done a meticulous job.

*** Cyro

Incus CD01 *Bailey; Cyro Baptista (perc).* 86.

*** 1972

Cortical CD14 *Bailey; Han Bennink (perc).* 72.

***(*) Han

Incus CD02 *As above.* 3/86.

Bailey has generally preferred to work in the company of percussionists, and a quick comparison of his recordings with the elegant Baptista and the forceful and witty Bennink demonstrates how thoughtfully contextualized all his work is. The best point of comparison between these sets is illustrated on a much later album, *Village Life*, with the African percussionists Louis Moholo and the younger Thebe Lipere. Like Thebe, Cyro Baptista seems content to gloss and embellish Derek's ideas rather than taking a proactive stance. Bennink is much more like Moholo, driving the music along not in a rhythmic groove but by the sheer force and intensity of his sound. Bennink can sound like one of the great swing drummers of the 1930s, or like a Jean Tinguely sculpture, deconstructing itself. It is a relationship that has lasted many years and, apart from Tony Oxley, no other musician has ever shown a closer appreciation of what Bailey is about.

***** Drops**

Ictus/New Tone rdc 5037 *Bailey; Andrea Centazzo (perc).* 4/76.

Presumably mis-dated on the sleeve (which suggests 1967), this was originally released on Centazzo's own vinyl label, Ictus, which is now being reissued in some bulk. As often when working with percussionists, Bailey is in exceptional form, negotiating nine relatively short pieces on both acoustic and electric, spinning out his dry, unemphatic lines with characteristic authority and esprit. Centazzo might almost be confused with Paul Lovens on this showing, playing abstractly but with an undercurrent of melody never far from breaking surface. 'How Long Has This Been Going On?' bears no discernible relation to the standard, lest anyone picks it up in the hope that Bailey has been caught out doing some swing; there are better reasons for buying this unusual, original record.

***** Dynamics Of The Impromptu**

Entropy 4 *Bailey; Trevor Watts (ss, as); John Stevens (d, c).*

Though the Spontaneous Music Ensemble was co-led by John Stevens and Trevor Watts, Bailey was a core member and the perfect embodiment of the group's stance on radical abstraction. These self-title improvisations are cast in a language which will be immediately familiar to anyone who came up with the British improvised scene in the early '70s. Once heard, Watts's plangent alto and Stevens's rushing, almost swing-inspired percussion are unforgettable and Bailey seems to hold the balance of forces here. More than 70 minutes of music, played with absolute concentration and balance.

***** Aida**

Incus 40 *Bailey (g solo).* 8/80.

Miles Davis was much drawn to *Aida* as a source of rich funkable tunes. Bailey, almost needless to say, isn't thinking along those lines at all on this remarkable set, with its three broad slabs of guitar sound. As ever, Bailey keeps the effects and articulation devices pared to the bone, and his fretting and fingering have an unexpected softness and precision which occasionally suggest something graspable amid the abstraction. Even without reference points, this is intensely involving music.

***** Arch Duo**

Rastascan 45 *Bailey; Evan Parker (ss, ts).* 82.

A recent 'archive' release from old associates who have been making this kind of music for decades, and yet they still find new means of communication each time they meet. Parker utilizes ever higher harmonics and extremes of tone; Bailey's characteristic idiom is still a furious hardscrabble. Together, they create a unique language, not so much unintelligible to others as beyond simple decipherment.

*****(*) Yankees**

Charly CDGR 221 *Bailey; George Lewis (tb); John Zorn (as, ss, cl, game calls).* 83.

Originally released on Jean Karakos's innovative Celluloid label, this is a hugely welcome reissue of an almost forgotten classic. A collaborative trio no doubt this was, but both Zorn and Lewis have made clear their admiration and debt to Bailey and it is the guitarist who as often as not defines the parameters of these five excellent tracks. The two long items, 'The Legend Of Enos Slaughter' and 'On Golden Pond', are both indicative of Zorn's great skills as an improviser; not just a pasticheur or ironist, he is also a first-rate saxophone player, an aspect of his artistic personality that tended to be overlooked in the period between this record and the later, Masada project. Lewis is a giant, a player with a huge tone, a complex grasp of higher harmonics and, like Zorn, a dedicated deconstructor of his instrument, constantly experimenting with its component elements: mouthpiece, bell and slides. It's Bailey, though, who makes things happen. His acoustic and amplified playing is tight marshalled, fierce and never less than expressive. His first entrances on the opening 'City City City' are breathtaking, and anyone who takes the plunge and samples this (now mid-price) disc could well find it a taste-altering experience.

****** Figuring**

Incus CD05 *Bailey; Barre Phillips (b).* 5/87–9/88.

Dialogue in the conventional musical sense rarely occurs (with Braxton it sounds like a dialogue of the deaf), and there have been charges that Bailey is not a listening player, unwilling to compromise his own very driven and focused approach by having to respond to what anyone else is doing. With Phillips, interestingly, he seems to be doing just that, throwing back jagged and sometimes almost hostile reshapings of the bassist's typically complex and volatile ideas. This is perhaps the most accessible of the duo records, and is certainly of the highest musical standard.

****** Drop Me Off At 96th**

Scatter 02 *Bailey (g solo).* 5/86.

*****(*) Lace**

Emanem 4013 *As above.* 12/89.

*****(*) Solo Guitar: Volume 2**

Incus CD11 *Bailey (g solo).* 6/91.

It's still Bailey's solo performances that afford the clearest impression of his pitchless, metreless playing, and these examples are among the best of their kind. Twenty years on from the first *Solo Guitar*, the basic premisses seem not to have changed one iota, though by this time in his career Bailey was opening up to all sorts of unexpected influences and associations. The sound is less dry, but that may simply be because recording technology has moved on a step.

Drop Me Off, issued by the Glasgow-based Scatter label, is a very strong statement indeed, and one of the toughest sets Bailey had released for many years, unexpectedly so in some respects. Though it isn't a particularly sophisticated recording, it picks up a lot of low-level detail and sounds very true to the dynamics of live performance. *Lace* was recorded in Los Angeles (hence the acrostic title) and consists of just two long pieces and a short encore, 'Which bit would you like again?' a characteristic Bailey comment to the audience. Bailey had worked in LA a few times before and is regarded there as something of a visiting celebrity. Certainly, this concert seems to have been a prodigal homecoming and the playing is as warm and committed as ever, Bailey's pre-war Epiphone Triumph sounding full-voiced and hugely atmospheric.

***(*) **Village Life**

Incus CD09 *Bailey; Thebe Lipere (perc, v); Louis Moholo (d, perc, v).* 9/91.

As ever, Bailey is inspired and inspirational in the company of inventive percussionists, here two African modernists with very different musical styles. The young Lipere is more obviously decorative and takes what is basically an associate's role, leaving the main dialogue to take place between Bailey, who rips and tugs at his strings with delightful abandon, and the astonishing Moholo. The latter is much closer to Bailey's aesthetic than initially appears. An Afro-modernist, he moves freely between the most joyously groove-driven of township sounds to the most outside evasion of pulse. An exhilarating album.

***(*) **Playing**

Incus CD14 *Bailey; John Stevens (d, mini-t).* 8/92.

Despite a long association with Stevens, there was almost no duo material featuring the two together until *Playing* was recorded. Concentrated and flowing, it offers an ideal opportunity, as Steve Beresford points out in his liner-note, to examine at close quarters how this music works. Beresford's analogy to the 'butterfly effect', in which tiny events have disproportionately significant outcomes at considerable physical or temporal distances, is completely apt.

*** **Wireforks**

Shanachie 5011 *Bailey; Henry Kaiser (g).* 95.

***(*) **Banter**

O0 Discs 20 *Bailey; Gregg Bendian (perc).* 95

***(*) **Harras**

Avant AVAN 056 *Bailey; John Zorn (as); William Parker (b).* 95.

**** **The Last Wave**

DIW 903 *Bailey; Bill Laswell (b); Tony Williams (d).* 95

Typically, Bailey celebrated his 65th birthday with a fresh challenge rather than a comfortable downshift. The last few years have been extremely productive ones in Bailey's life, though a spell of bad health did seem to throw additional emphasis on the CD output. The duets with Kaiser and Bendian are interesting in the context of our earlier comments about the difficulties he has sometimes had squaring his very radical conception with the more groove-based work of American players. With neither of these players does he have any problem, nor with the self-aware but cartoonish post-bop of Zorn on the apparently big-selling *Harras* CD, which is a recommended place for newcomers to approach the later work. Of the others, Bendian is a fantastically open-minded musician whose interests embrace straight composition, folk forms, free jazz and more straight-ahead, pulse-driven things, while Kaiser is an eccentric (in the strict sense) who is always able to put his instincts out on the line and take chances. On all three of these discs it is the absolute *concentration* of Bailey's playing that compels attention.

The real shocker is *The Last Wave*, which can be described as a post-modern revenant of Williams's notorious Lifetime by a group officially known as Arcana. One simply isn't used to hearing Derek Bailey in a context like this. It is both exhilarating and rather unsettling, like seeing a favourite uncle give up chitting seed potatoes and debudding chrysanthemums in order to take up ju-jitsu.

*** **Drawing Close, Attuning**

Tokuma T34 *Bailey; Keiji Haino (g, v).*

The Japanese Derek Bailey? Whether playing guitar (or, indeed, hurdy gurdy) or singing, Haino is a formidable musician who seems to fill the space he occupies with sound. It is virtually impossible to categorize this music, and it is often difficult to judge whether what one is hearing is a genuine meeting of minds or an irreconcilable clash of aesthetic personalities. Interestingly, listening to Bailey in conjunction with Haino here, one realizes that what makes him so special is his immediacy, the sense he gives of real presence, as opposed to the cosmic remoteness and diffidence of the Japanese man. A fascinating encounter, but not a wholly engaging one.

**** **Soho Suites**

Incus CD CD 26/27 2CD *Bailey; Tony Oxley (d, perc).* 2/77–9/95.

Bailey's contribution to Tony Oxley's 1960s work was definitive: clangorous guitar chords which echoed the amplified strings and metal percussion the drummer added to his kit in those days. Latter-day Oxley is still utterly unmistakable and these extraordinary sides roll back the years like nobody's business. Bailey always sounds relaxed, almost conversational in the company of his old friend, and these two discs seem to pass by in moments, when in fact they are among the most substantial performances from either man in recent years. The sound could be better, but the quality of playing and the sense of mutual involvement are beguiling enough to overcome that.

***(*) **Takes Fakes And Dead She Dances**

Incus 31 *Bailey (g, v).* 9/95–5/97.

A mixture of studio improvisations and a quite extraordinary concert performance of Bailey accompanying his own recitation of Peter Riley's poem, 'Dead She Dances', a bleak work of verse that might have come from one of the neglected corners of a Paul Haines opera. Derek manipulates what might become melodic figures into dark, mutant shapes, spattering atonal sound all over the room.

*** **Saisoro**

Tzadik 7205 *Bailey; Masuda Ryuishi (b); Yoshida Tatsuya (d).* 95.

***(*) **Tohjinbo**

Paratactile PLE 1101 *As above, except omit Ryuishi; add Sasaki Hisashi (b).* 4/97.

After Derek and the Dominoes, this is Derek and the Ruins, further evidence of Bailey's fruitful association with Japanese performers. The surprise is how much of the music recalls the free jazz of the 1960s, and again how completely at ease Bailey sounds, without having to alter his usual attack and trajectory one whit. Tatsuya is the key element, a bright, lateral-thinking percussionist whose stop–start playing and use of vocals irresistibly recall the Scottish-born but Asian-influenced Ken Hyder. The earlier album, which apparently represented the Ruins' first attempt at live improvisation in the studio, has a freshness and candour that don't carry over into the second, which seems by contrast rather deliberate and mannered. Item by item, it's difficult to be greatly enthused by *Tohjinbo* but, like most of Bailey's projects with young Japanese rockers, it has a certain cumulative impact.

*****(*) Guitar, Drums'N'Bass**
Avant AVAN 060 *Bailey; DJ Ninj (d prog).* 96.

Guitar, Drums & Bass became one of the most talked-about records of recent years, and further proof of Bailey's extraordinary adaptability and willingness to experiment with new genres. As so often before, though, what one hears isn't a synthesis so much as an intriguing conjunction of almost entirely unconnected elements. Bailey certainly doesn't accommodate himself to drum'n'bass but simply carries on doing his own thing against a sequence of backgrounds which become ever less relevant to his spasmodic and abrasive discourse as the record proceeds. By the end, the exercise seems almost entirely played out, and many listeners have reported rapidly diminishing returns. We're inclined to think better of it than that, but lengthening retrospect suggests this may soon seem like an amusing sidebar rather than the revelatory change of direction that was hailed on first release, and Bailey's own comments on the project tend to reinforce that impression.

***** Duo**
Revenant CD 023 *Bailey; Min Tanaka (dance).* 96.

A strange one, with Bailey supplying accompaniment – though not of course literally so – to the Kundalini posturing and physical kinetics of one of his most sympathetic Japanese collaborators. As an aural experience, it isn't one of Bailey's most effective performances, but it has its strengths.

****** The Sign Of Four**
Knitting Factory KFW 197 3CD *Bailey; Pat Metheny (g); Gregg Bendian, Paul Wertico (perc).* 12/96.

Dear old Pat Metheny continues to throw himself into the roughest, toughest playing situations, like the boy at school who gets cheerfully creamed game after game just so no one will think he's wimping out. This specially priced three-CD set was recorded live and in studio during Bailey's pre-Christmas '96 visit to New York. Apart from the short studio track, 'The Rule Of Three', on which Wertico bows out, all the material is for twinned guitars and percussion, with Bailey and Wertico sharing the right channel, Metheny and Bendian the left. Most of the material is for amplified instruments, though both guitarists play acoustically on 'The Rule Of Three', which features Pat's sitar-guitar. The whole of the first disc is taken up with the live 'A Study In Scarlet', which sounds like an edited live performance. The Sherlock Holmes titling doesn't seem to have any particular significance, for the music is as resolutely abstract as ever. Bendian plays wonderfully, conjuring a huge range of sound from his 'arco disc' and other percussion, often vying with the guitarists for the foreground.

****** No Waiting**
Potlatch P 198 *Bailey; Joelle Léandre (b).* 5/97.

In anthropology, a potlatch is an extreme form of conspicuous consumption, a gift-giving splurge intended to show how generously funded the giver is. That's almost the opposite of what is going on in these quiet, grave interchanges. Léandre has, of course, worked with Bailey before, only most obviously under the aegis of his Company project. Like Barre Phillips, she is one of the few players with whom he seems prepared to exchange ideas and challenges, rather than galloping along on his own course. There are moments on the second and third improvisations (all of which were recorded at Les Instants Chavires), when *he* almost seems to be accompanying *her*; Léandre's low, sonorous line is reminiscent of the jazz bass of people like Scott LaFaro, Eddie Gomez and Marc Johnson, and here and there Bailey willy-nilly strays into quasi-harmonic territory that wouldn't have startled Bill Evans had he still been around. More than ever, we are convinced that the guitarist absorbs historical influences without even being aware of it. On this occasion, the results are absolutely fascinating.

****** Trio Playing**
Incus CD 28 *Bailey; John Butcher (ts, ss); Oren Marshall (tba).* 97.

With the exception of 'I'd Love A Key', which is almost a quarter of an hour in length, these are all relatively short pieces, seven expansive and almost jazz-like trios that recall nothing more than Jimmy Giuffre's early groups with Paul Bley and Steve Swallow; though the idiom is very different, there is the same lightness of touch and something of Giuffre's folksy abstraction. Marshall has established himself as a very considerable improviser on an improbable instrument, and Butcher is now quite simply one of the most effective free players in Europe: exact, unfussy and full of ideas. The studio sound is very good, but one can't help wanting to see this group in a live setting as well.

***** Play Backs**
Bingo 4 *Bailey; Henry Kaiser, Jim O'Rourke (g); Bundy K Brown, John French, Sasha Frere-Jones, John Herndon, Darryl Moore, John Oswald, Casey Rice, Ko Thein, Tied and Tickled Trio (various).* 98.

****(*) Viper**
Avant AVAN 50 *Bailey; Min Xiao-Fen (pipa).* 98.

More explorations of sound, in the company of more recent collaborators. The guitar/pipa duets on *Viper* are as close as it will ever get to Derek Bailey Lite, an oddly unsatisfying experience and somewhat grating over the span of a whole CD. The associations on *Play Backs* are more various, but hard to pin down verbally. We've found it to be one of his oddest records of recent years, without being able to describe its elusive essence.

***** Mirakle**
Tzadik 7603 *Bailey; Jamaaladeen Tacuma (b); Calvin Weston (d).* 99.

Derek's involvement with the kind of hard-edged noise-funk one associates with John Zorn and the Tzadik label has been one of his most fruitful directions over the last few years. As ever, he refuses to hook his usual claim on radical freedom on to fixed energy lines. The guitarist skates ahead of his companions, often playing with flashing speed, but equally often delivering sounds that have no reference to context. Not quite as startling as *Guitar, Drums & Bass* seemed on first appearance, five years ago, but a wallopingly unexpected album nevertheless.

Mildred Bailey (1904–51)

VOCAL

Mildred Rinker sent a demo record to Paul Whiteman, who hired her in 1929. After four years (and a signature hit, 'Rockin' Chair') she went solo on record and sang with husband Red Norvo's group. She was a star for the rest of the '30s, but a tempestuous personality and health problems saw her decline in the '40s, and she was hospitalized in 1949, dying after a brief comeback in 1951.

*****(*) That Rockin' Chair Lady**

Topaz TPZ 1007 *Bailey; Bunny Berigan, Jimmy Jake, Zeke Zachery, Barney Zudecoff, Manny Klein, Charlie Marhulis, Gordon Griffin, Bill Hyland, Stew Pletcher, Eddie Meyers, Eddie Sauter, Jimmy Blake (t); Tommy Dorsey, Sonny Lee, Leo Moran, Al Mastren, Wes Hein (tb); Jimmy Dorsey, Hank D'Amico, Benny Goodman (cl); Slats Long (cl, as); Frank Simeone, Len Goldstein, Johnny Hodges (as); Charles Lanphere (as, ts); Larry Binyon, Coleman Hawkins, Herbie Heymer, Jerry Jerome, Chu Berry (ts); Fulton McGrath, Arthur Schutt, Teddy Wilson, Joe Liss, Bill Miller, Mary Lou Williams (p); Red Norvo (xy); Dick McDonough, Alan Hanson, Allan Reuss, Floyd Smith (g); Artie Bernstein, Grachan Moncur, Pete Peterson, John Williams (b); Stan King, Eddie Dougherty, Maurice Purtill, George Wettling, Dave Tough (d).* 11/31–3/39.

***** Mildred Bailey 1929–1932**

Classics 1061 *Bailey; Andy Secrest, Charlie Margulis, Harry Goldfield, Nat Natoli, Joe Hostetter, Bo Ashford, Bobby Jones (t); Bill Rank, Jack Fulton, Fritz Hummel, Pee Wee Hunt, Billy Ruach (tb); Bernard Dalky, Charles Strickfadden, Izzy Friedman, Min Leibrook, Chester Hazlett, Frankie Trumbauer, Ray McDermott, Glen Gray, Clarence Hutchenrider, Kenny Sargent, Pat Davis (reeds); Mel Jenssen, Henry Whiteman, Joe Venuti, Matt Malneck, Mischa Russell, Kurt Dieterle, John Bowman (vn); Hoagy Carmichael, Roy Bargy, Joe Hall (p); Eddie Lang, Fritz Ciccone, Gene Gifford (g); Mike Trafficante, Pierre Olker, Art Miller, Stanley Dennis (b); George Marsh, Tony Briglia (d).* 10/29–8/32.

*****(*) Mildred Bailey 1932–1936**

Classics 1080 *Bailey; Bunny Berigan, Sonny Dunham, Grady Watts, Bobby Jones, Gordon Griffin, Ziggy Elman, Manny Klein (t); Tommy Dorsey, Pee Wee Hunt, Billy Rauch (tb); Artie Shaw (cl); Jimmy Dorsey, Clarence Hutchenrider (cl, as); Johnny Hodges, Kenny Sargent (as); Larry Binyon, Pat Davis, Chu Berry, Francis Lowe (ts); Luton McGrath, Joe Hall, Teddy Wilson (p); Red Norvo (xy); Mel Jenssen, Matt Malneck (vn); Dick McDonough, Gene Gifford, Dave Barbour (g); Artie Bernstein, Stanley Dennis, John Kirby (b); Stan King, Tony Briglia, Eddie Dougherty, Cozy Cole (d).* 8/32–11/36.

Mildred Bailey has secured some decent representation on CD, although some CDs we've previously listed have slipped from sight again. She had claims to be fêted on a par with Holiday and Fitzgerald – and she started recording well before either of them, with her first version of her signature, 'Rockin' Chair', dating back to 1931 – yet she was more of a transitional figure than either of those giants. Her early records suggest a singer struggling, gently, with the old style of Broadway belting (difficult enough for someone with a small voice), while some of the later ones are almost too placid and formal; yet she never lost the vaudevillian tang of the classic blues singers of the 1920s, which helped her put over risqué numbers like 'Jenny' or the wartime novelty, 'Scrap Your Fat'. Lacking either Holiday's modern pathos or Fitzgerald's monumental swing, her art is modest, stylized and innately graceful.

Classics is now competing with the Topaz collection (ASV have their own compilation, *Harlem Lullaby*, which is somewhat less effective). The Topaz collection concentrates on the 1930s and covers some strong sessions with the Dorsey Brothers (including Berigan in fine form), the superb 'Junk Man' with Benny Goodman, several tracks with then-husband Red Norvo and two rather muffled and low-fi tracks with a Mary Lou Williams group. Transfers are patchy – the Brunswicks sound excellent, the Columbias and Vocalions are boomy in the bass – but mostly acceptable.

Classics 1061 starts with Bailey as the unlisted vocalist on sides by Eddie Lang, Frankie Trumbauer and Paul Whiteman, plus a featured date with the Casa Loma Orchestra. Thereafter she gets top billing, mostly with rather schmaltzy and often unidentified bands. Most of her material seems to be songs of longing or regret, and the disc has a rather weepy feel to it. Classics 1080 sees her hitting her stride in earnest. Sessions with Berigan and the Dorsey brothers are assured, fun on 'Is That Religion?', sweet on 'Harlem Lullaby', hot on 'Doin' The Uptown Lowdown'. Sessions for Vocalion and Decca include four tracks with Berigan, Hodges and Wilson, and throughout Bailey's voice keeps its appeal while swinging the material: she was selling plenty of records. Transfers generally seem good enough.

Chet Baker (1929–88)

TRUMPET, FLUGELHORN, VOCAL

Baker was the archetypal, some would say stereotypical, 'young man with the horn', brilliant, inward, self-destructive. He grew up in Oklahoma but was in New York to witness the birth of bebop. He played briefly with Charlie Parker and developed a sound that was similar to Miles Davis's: quiet, restricted in range, and melodic rather than harmonically virtuosic. The famous pianoless quartet with Gerry Mulligan and Chet's keynote performance of 'My Funny Valentine' were important moments in the development of cool jazz. Chet's heroin habit led not so very indirectly to the loss of his teeth; the film star looks gave way to a sunken and haunted image that was all too easily projected on to the music. However low he sank – and, in later years, Chet was playing only to cover his drug bill – his technique was precise and his range of expression, whether playing trumpet or singing, remained unaffected.

**** Live At The Trade Winds 1952**

Fresh Sound FSCD-1001 *Baker; Ted Ottison (t); Sonny Criss (as); Wardell Gray, Jack Montrose, Dave Pell (ts); Les Thompson (hca); Jerry Mandell, Al Haig (p); Harry Babasin (clo); Bob Whitlock, Dave Bryant (b); Lawrence Marable, Larry Bunker (d).* 3–8/52.

***** LA Get Together**

Fresh Sound FSRCD 1022 *Baker; Stan Getz (ts); Russ Freeman (p); Joe Mondragon, Carson Smith (b); Larry Bunker, Shelly Manne (d).* 6 & 12/53.

***** Witch Doctor**

Original Jazz Classics OJC 609 *Baker; Rolf Ericson (t); Bud Shank (as, bs); Jimmy Giuffre, Bob Cooper (ts); Russ Freeman, Claude Williamson (p); Howard Rumsey (b); Max Roach, Shelly Manne (d).* 9/53.

***** Ensemble And Sextet**

Fresh Sound FSRCD 175 *Baker; Bob Brookmeyer (tb); Jack Montrose, Phil Urso (ts); Herb Geller (as, ts); Bob Gordon, Bud Shank (bs); Russ Freeman, Bobby Timmons (p); Jimmy Bond, Joe Mondragon, Carson Smith (b); Peter Littman, Shelly Manne (d).* 12/53, 9/54, 7/56.

***** Big Band**

Pacific Jazz 781202 *Baker; Norman Raye, Conte Candoli (t); Bob Burgess, Frank Rosolino (tb); Bob Brookmeyer (vtb); Art Pepper, Fred Waters (as); Bud Shank (as, bs); Phil Urso (ts, bs, as); Bob Graf, Bill Perkins (ts); Bill Hood (bs); Russ Freeman, Bobby Timmons (p); Jimmy Bond, Carson Smith (b); Peter Littman, James McLean, Shelly Manne, Lawrence Marable (d).* 9/54, 10/56.

***** Young Chet**

Pacific Jazz 36194 *Baker; Bob Brookmeyer (vtb); Bud Shank (f); Herb Geller (as, ts); Jack Montrose (ts); Bob Gordon (bs); Russ Freeman, Pete Jolly (p); Corky Hale (hp); Jimmy Bond, Red Mitchell, Joe Mondragon, Carson Smith, Leroy Vinnegar, Bob Whitlock (b); Larry Bunker, Stan Levey, Peter Littman, Shelly Manne, Lawrence Marable, Bob Neel, Bobby White (d).* 7/53–7/56.

There was considerable surprise first time around at the sheer size of Chet Baker's discography. It has altered very little since then. Some later items have disappeared (the material on Philology, for instance, has rather intermittent currency); some more live material has turned up, and will continue to do so. The most important initiative has been Pacific's rationalization of some of the mid-'50s material. Compilations will doubtless continue to proliferate. Newcomers may want to start with the better of them, or else to work their way through some of the more positively reviewed discs listed below.

Chet's crucial years came right at the beginning of his career, 1952–3, when he played with Charlie Parker (undocumented in the studios) and in Gerry Mulligan's pianoless quartet; Stan Getz joined Chet in a similar group at The Haig in LA in June 1953 (recorded on *LA Get Together*), returning that Christmas for a more conventional, piano-driven quintet. Some of the Monday-night jam sessions at the Trade Winds Club in Inglewood, California, produced the music collected on the first Fresh Sound CD: scrappily recorded, it doesn't make much of an album, but Baker already sounds like himself – cool, restrained, diffidently lyrical – and Criss is very much himself, a fire-engine next to Baker's roadster. Gray, Montrose and the mysterious Les Thompson garner other features, but it's nothing special. *Witch Doctor* was recorded at the Lighthouse and sounds superior, though again the diffuseness of the jam-session atmosphere tends to militate against it standing up as a record in its own right.

Ensemble And Sextet cobbles a bunch of Jack Montrose and Bill Holman arrangements, recorded in Hollywood in 1953 and 1954 (and originally released on a 10-inch LP), with a single track from a later Forum Theatre engagement which is reviewed below. The September 1954 material also appears on the Pacific *Big Band* CD, which pairs it with the ensemble tracks from an October 1956 band recording. It's unfortunate that the material falls the way it does, because collectors will certainly want to have all these sessions, irrespective of the overlap. Both are mono sets, but the Pacific probably has a shade more oomph.

Young Chet is one of a proliferating sub-genre of (mainly) vocal compilations. Individual sessions can probably be identified by reference to dates, but this is unlikely to be of interest to serious collectors. Insomniac romantics may well find it pleasing.

*****(*) The Best Of Chet Baker Plays**

Pacific Jazz 97161 *Baker; Conte Candoli, Norman Faye (t); Frank Rosolino (tb); Bob Brookmeyer (vtb); Bud Shank (as, bs); Herb Geller, Art Pepper (as); Richie Kamuca, Jack Montrose, Phil Urso, Bill Perkins (ts); Russ Freeman, Bobby Timmons, Pete Jolly, Carl Perkins (p); Carson Smith, Joe Mondragon, Curtis Counce, Leroy Vinnegar, Jimmy Bond (b); Larry Bunker, Lawrence Marable, Shelly Manne, Stan Levey, Peter Littman (d); Bill Loughborough (perc).* 7/53–10/56.

****** Let's Get Lost: The Best Of Chet Baker Sings**

Pacific Jazz 92932 *Baker; Russ Freeman (p); Carson Smith, Jimmy Bond, Joe Mondragon (b); Shelly Manne, Bob Neel, Lawrence Marable, Peter Littman (d).* 2/53–10/56.

***** The Route**

Pacific Jazz 92931 *Baker; Art Pepper (as); Richie Kamuca (ts); Pete Jolly (p); Leroy Vinnegar (b); Stan Levey (d).* 7/56.

***** At The Forum Theater**

Fresh Sound FSRCD-168 *Baker; Phil Urso (ts); Bobby Timmons (p); Jimmy Bond (b); Peter Littman (d).* 7/56.

*****(*) Chet Baker And Crew**

Pacific Jazz 781205 *As above.* 7/56.

***** Chet Baker Cools Out**

Boplicity CDBOP 013 *As above, except add Art Pepper (as), Richie Kamuca (ts), Pete Jolly (p), Leroy Vinnegar (b), Stan Levey (d).* 7/56.

Richard Bock began recording Baker as a leader when the quartet with Mulligan began attracting rave notices and even a popular audience, and the records the trumpeter made for Pacific Jazz remain among his freshest and most appealing work. The material is currently a little scattered across the seven releases listed above, two of which are best-ofs, and one – *The Route* – which was subsequently put together from tracks strewn across various compilations over the years. *The Route* is effective: Kamuca is strong enough to match the other horns, and the rhythm section does a surprisingly better job on what are mostly standards. On *Forum Theater* and *Cools Out*, Urso's almost mentholated tenor is an apposite foil, but the music is rather under-achieved and all too similar to many of the sessions being cut in the city in this period. A couple of tracks duplicate each other on these two CDs (not all the tracks were made for Pacific), and the Boplicity disc includes a single item from the *Route* band. The appearance in 1993 of *And Crew*, with two previously unissued tracks and material formerly issued on Jazz West Coast and Crown, offers pretty definitive coverage of this material, and there's no earthly reason to plump for the Fresh Sound instead.

To hear the best of Baker himself, one must turn to the other records. Controversy has simmered over the extent of Baker's powers: a poor reader, a restrained technician, he sticks to the horn's middle range and picks at bebop lines as if they were something that might do him harm; yet he can play with sometimes amazing accomplishment. The blues 'Bea's Flat' (on *The Best Of Chet Baker Plays*), a scintillating line by Russ Freeman, provokes a solo of agility enough to dismiss charges of Baker's incompetence as ludicrous. It was on the various quartet sessions with Freeman that Baker did most of his best work for Pacific, and it's a pity that they are currently available only in the excellent Mosaic boxed set (see Introduction). The five tracks on *Plays* will have to suffice. The rest of the compilation makes an intelligent choice from the trumpeter's other sessions, and – as the title suggests – it's all trumpet and no vocals.

The other disc contains what are still Baker's most popular recordings, his first vocal sessions for Pacific. The 20 tracks include all of the original *Chet Baker Sings* LP, which is a modest classic in its way. Baker's soft, pallidly intimate voice retained its blond timbre to the end of his life, but here – with his phrasing and tone uncreased by any trace of hard living – it sounds as charming as it ever would, and a song such as 'There Will Never Be Another You' is so deftly organized for voice, trumpet and rhythm section (Freeman's role here is as crucial as it is on the instrumental sessions) that it is very hard not to enjoy the music, even if it has become as buttressed by glamorous legend as much of Billie Holiday's later output.

*****(*) Chet Baker In Paris Volume 1**

Emarcy 837474-2 *Baker; Richard Twardzik, Gerard Gustin (p); Jimmy Bond (b); Peter Littman, Bert Dale (d).* 10/55.

*****(*) Chet Baker In Paris Volume 2**

Emarcy 837475-2 *As above, except add Benny Vasseur (tb), Jean Aldegon (as), Armand Migiani (ts), William Boucaya (bs), René Urtreger (p).* 10/55.

*****(*) Chet Baker In Paris Volume 3**

Emarcy 837476-2 *Baker; Benny Vasseur (tb); Reddy Ameline (as); Bobby Jaspar, Jean-Louis Chautemps, Armand Migiani (ts); William Boucaya (bs); René Urtreger, Francy Boland (p); Eddie De Haas, Benoît Quersin (b); Jean-Louis Viale, Charles Saudrais, Pierre Lemarchand (d).* 12/55–3/56.

***** Chet Baker In Paris Volume 4**

Emarcy 837477-2 *As above three discs.* 10/55–3/56.

***** Live In Europe, 1956**

Accord 556622 *Baker; Jean-Louis Chautemps (ts); Francy Boland (p); Eddie De Haas (b); Charles Saudrais (d).* 1/56.

*****(*) Verve Jazz Masters 32**

Verve 840632-2 *Baker; Benny Vasseur (tb); Jean Aldegon (as); Frank Strozier (as, f); Stan Getz, Armand Migiani, Jean-Louis Chautemps, Phil Urso (ts); William Boucaya (bs); Leon Cohen, Wilford Holcombe, Henry Freeman, Seldon Powell, Alan Ross (reeds); Francy Boland, Jodie Christian, Dick Twardzik, Hank Jones, Hal Galper, Gerard Goustin, Bob James, René Urtreger (p); Everett Barksdale (g); Caterina Valente (g, v); Jimmy Bond, Eddie De Haas, Richard Davis, Michael Fleming, Victor Sproles (b); Nils-Bertil Dahlander, Connie Kay, Charlie Rice, Charles Saudrais, Marshall Thompson (d).* 10/55–6/65.

Baker's Parisian sessions are among his finest and most considered work. The celebrated association with Richard Twardzik – abruptly terminated by the latter's ugly narcotics death – is followed on Volume 1, with tantalizing Twardzik originals such as 'The Girl From Greenland' and almost equally interesting writing from Bob Zieff to engage Baker's interest. The drift of the sessions varies from spare and introspective quartet music to more swinging larger groups, and it's by no means all pale and melancholic: what's striking is the firmness of Baker's lines and his almost Tristano-like logic on occasion. There is some very downcast music in the session immediately following Twardzik's death, but otherwise lyricism and energy usually combine to high effect. Of the four Emarcys, only the last, which is a supplemental set of alternative takes, is comparatively inessential. For non-specialists, though, the *Jazz Masters* compilation is good value for money. It includes a track from the October '55 sessions, with later European material and a group of tracks recorded back in America in 1964 and 1965; the best of these are probably the four songs recorded with Urso and Strozier in New York, November 1964, a highlight for that period. The Accord is unexpectedly bright and precise for its time and place and contains excellent (if not classic Chet) solos on 'Stella By Starlight' and 'You Don't Know What Love Is'.

***** Chet Baker Introduces Johnny Pace**

Original Jazz Classics OJCCD 433 2 *Baker; Herbie Mann (ts, f); Joe Berle (p); Jimmie Burke (b); Philly Joe Jones, Ed Thigpen (d); Johnny Pace (v).* 58.

By rights this should have been the baritone's album, and there is something very attractive about Pace's Sinatra-influenced delivery, but it's Chet's relaxed fills and solos which really command attention. On 'All Or Nothing At All', he strays outside the bar-lines to deliver a passionate declaration, while on 'We Could Make Such Beautiful Music', 'It Might As Well Be Spring' and 'Yesterdays' horn and voice combine in three seductive duets.

***** It Could Happen To You**

Original Jazz Classics OJC 303 *Baker; Kenny Drew (p); George Morrow, Sam Jones (b); Dannie Richmond, Philly Joe Jones (d).* 8/58.

***** Chet Baker In New York**

Original Jazz Classics OJC 207 *Baker; Johnny Griffin (ts); Al Haig (p); Paul Chambers (b); Philly Joe Jones (d).* 9/58.

***** Chet**

Original Jazz Classics OJC 087 *Baker; Herbie Mann (ts, f); Pepper Adams (bs); Bill Evans (p); Kenny Burrell (g); Paul Chambers (b); Connie Kay, Philly Joe Jones (d).* 3/59.

***** Plays The Best Of Lerner & Loewe**

Original Jazz Classics OJC 137 *Baker; Herbie Mann (ts, f); Zoot Sims (ts, as); Pepper Adams (bs); Bill Evans, Bob Corwin (p); Earl May (b); Clifford Jarvis (d).* 7/59.

Perhaps Baker wanted nothing more than to be a part of the modern-jazz mainstream; certainly, after his earlier adventures, his records were taking on the appearance of another bebop trumpeter wandering from session to session. These are all worthwhile records, but without any regular cast of players Chet sounds like a man trying to be one of the boys. He has no problem with the assertiveness of the group on *In New York*, which shows how far he'd come from the supposed early fumblings (never very apparent from the actual records). But this set, and the Lerner & Loewe collection and the similarly directed *Chet*, aren't very different from the standard bop outings of the time: good, but working off a solid routine. *It Could Happen To You* is more of a singing record, and it includes a couple of his most charming efforts on 'Do It The Hard Way' and 'I'm Old Fashioned'.

***** Italian Movies**

Liuto LRS 0063 *Baker; Piero Umiliani Band.* 58–62.

No revelations or stylistic jumps of the sort effected by Miles Davis in his score for *L'Ascenseur pour l'échafaud* but excellent and idiomatic music nevertheless. All the pieces are written by pianist Umiliani for a variety of settings, from small group to orchestra. The recordings are soaked in atmosphere, sometimes at the expense of hearing Chet correctly, but this does not significantly diminish the impact of these attractive sessions.

***** With Fifty Italian Strings**

Original Jazz Classics OJC 492 *Baker; Mario Pezzotta (tb); Glauco Masetti (as); Gianni Basso (ts); Fausto Papetti (bs); Giulio Libano (p, cel); Franco Cerri (b); Gene Victory (d); strings.* 9/59.

****(*) In Milan**

Original Jazz Classics OJC 370 *As above, except add Renato Sellani (p); omit Pezzotta, Papetti, Libano.* 9–10/59.

Back in Europe, Baker lived in Italy, where he eventually ended up in jail. The strings album is a rather good one of its kind: it was inevitable that Baker would go with this treatment eventually, and by now he was assured enough not to let the horn solos blow away on the orchestral breeze. 'Violets For Your Furs', for instance, makes the most of both the melody and the changes. *In Milan* features a good band – Basso was one of the leading Italians of the day – but it's an uneventful session.

***** The Italian Sessions**

RCA Bluebird 82001 *Baker; Bobby Jaspar (ts, f); Amadeo Tommasi (p); René Thomas (g); Benoît Quersin (b); Daniel Humair (d).* 62.

***** Somewhere Over The Rainbow**

RCA Bluebird 90640 *As above.* 62.

A fine group – it was mostly Bobby Jaspar's, with local man Tommasi sitting in – and Baker has to work hard to get some room. Quersin and Humair are a grooving rhythm section, Thomas gets in some voluble solos, and Jaspar is his usual mix of detachment and intensity; Baker, though, seems undecided whether to play hot or cool. *Somewhere Over The Rainbow* offers a budget-price version of the same music, minus two tracks.

***** Baker's Holiday**

Emarcy 838 204 *Baker; Alan Ross, Henry Freeman, Seldon Powell, Leon Cohen, Wilford Holcombe (reeds); Everett Barksdale (g); Hank Jones (p); Richard Davis (b); Connie Kay (d).* 65.

Chet on flugelhorn and as a vocalist obeying what he thought was the most impressive aspect of Billie Holiday's singing, that she never raised her voice. It's a warm, swinging session that is kept quite deliberately low-key. On the bigger horn, Chet actually doesn't sound so very different, a little broader, a little less clipped in faster passages, but essentially the same. Richard Davis emerges much more clearly than on the LP, and he and Jones provide the springboard for graceful solos on 'Travelin' Light' and 'That Ole Devil Called Love', our personal favourites from an album with a box-of-chocolates flavour.

***** Groovin' With The Chet Baker Quintet**

Prestige PR20 7460-2 *Baker; George Coleman (ts); Kirk Lightsey (p); Herman Wright (b); Roy Brooks (d).* 8/65.

***** Comin' On With The Chet Baker Quintet**

Prestige PR20 7478-2 *As above.* 8/65.

***** Cool Burnin' With The Chet Baker Quintet**

Prestige PR20 7496-2 *As above.* 8/65.

***** Boppin' With The Chet Baker Quintet**

Prestige PR20 7512-2 *As above. 8/65*

The pairing with Coleman might at first seem like *la belle et la bête*, except that Big George has always had a more sophisticated harmonic awareness than seems obvious at first hearing and an ability to enunciate a soft and unemphatic melody line with absolute directness of purpose. Factor in the magnificent Lightsey, and these sessions begin to make sense. There is certainly too much material spread too thinly, and it might have been just about possible to make one very strong or two very decent records out of the tracks available. As things stand, the quality is spread rather thin.

These records have previously been available under other names, but this restores the sequence to its original set of titles and to completion. The parallel with the classic Miles Davis discs, *Relaxin'*, *Cookin'*, and so on, was conscious and deliberate, designed to enhance Chet's reputation as the 'white Miles'. The main audible difference was that Baker played on flugelhorn throughout, getting a broad, 'fat' tone that worked superbly on ballads. There is scarcely a dud track in the sequence, but one or two inevitably stand out. 'On A Misty Night' (*Boppin'*) is wonderful, there is an unexpected reading of Tadd Dameron's 'The 490' on *Cool Burnin'* and that record also closes with a delicious interpretation of Jimmy Mundy's 'Sleeping Susan'. If you really can afford only one of the discs, it's the one to go for, but these have been reissued at an attractive budget price and Chetophiles can indulge their completism without breaking the bank.

***** You Can't Go Home Again**

Verve 543516-2 2CD *Baker; Paul Desmond (as); Michael Brecker (ts); Hubert Laws (f, bf, picc); John Scofield (g); Richie Beirach (p, ky); Kenny Barron, Don Sebesky (ky); Ron Carter (b); Alphonso Johnson, Tony Williams (d); Ralph McDonald (perc); strings.* 5/72.

(****) My Funny Valentine

Philology W 30 2 *Baker; Stan Getz (ts); Nicola Stilo (f); Philip Catherine (g); Nino Bisceglie, Kenny Drew, Gil Goldstein, Michel Graillier, Mike Melillo, Enrico Pieranunzi (p); Furio Di Castri, George Mraz, Edy Olivieri, Jean-Louis Rassinfosse, Larry Ridley (b); David Lee, Victor Lewis, Ilario De Marinis (d).* 80–87.

In 1968, having moved to San Francisco, Baker was attacked and severely beaten, suffering the kind of injuries to his mouth that horn players dread. The incident has been explained as a random mugging, and as a 'reminder' of defaulted drug payments by a local supplier. Whatever the explanation, the loss of several teeth and a nearly unbreakable narcotics habit gave his face that caved-in, despairing look that it wears on a score of album covers from the 1980s. If Chet began as a golden youth, he ended his days as a death's-head.

F. Scott Fitzgerald wrote that there were no second acts in American lives. To an extent, Chet bore that out. The years between 1970 and his rather mysterious death in 1988 were a prolonged curtain. What they did confirm was the truth of another literary tag, Thomas Wolfe's 'You can't go home again', which was used for a wonderful quartet piece, recorded by the slowly rehabilitating trumpeter in 1972 with Paul Desmond, by far the best thing on the A&M album, though by no means representative of its rather slick, fusion-tinged product. America really didn't know what to do with him, other than wrap him up in no-substance parcels like this, and he left for Europe again in 1975.

For the remainder of his life, Chet lived out of a suitcase. He enjoyed cult status in Europe and followed an exhausting and seemingly futile itinerary, 'going single' with local musicians. Having moved over to flugelhorn after his beating, he gradually restored his lip. The late sound is frail, airy, almost ethereal. Usually assumed to be a development of Miles Davis's style (and Chet followed a similar repertoire of standards), it was actually more reminiscent of Fats Navarro at his most delicate and attenuated. Unlike Miles, Chet did not favour mutes but developed a quiet, breathy delivery that made such accessories irrelevant.

His singing voice, which took on an increasingly significant role in his work, was a perfect match for his playing, a slight, hurt tenor, with a wistful vibrato. Though his singing was valued out of all proportion to its real worth, it served as a reminder of how important an understanding of the lyrics was to Chet, who often sounds as if he is softly enunciating the words through his horn. No song characterized his last years more fully than 'My Funny Valentine', another Miles-associated tune that he played and sang at almost every concert he gave. It appears with absolute predictability on the majority of the live albums and was the encore to the last full-scale concert he gave.

The Philology compilation brings together seven different performances of the song and illustrates a significant point about 'late Chet'. Though the material was increasingly repetitive, Chet's treatment of it was rarely formulaic but adapted itself to the demands of particular contexts and moods. There is, then, a dramatic difference between the all-star confrontation with Stan Getz at the Jazzhus Montmartre in 1983 and the very long version recorded with a drummerless quartet in Senigallia the year before he died. In contrast to its nearly 16 minutes, a July 1975 performance with Kenny Drew and a bebop-based rhythm section at Pescara is untypically boiled down. Performances range from the straightforward and melodic to the near abstract, and this is characteristic of the late years. There is a huge mass of material, but it is more various than initially appears. There is almost always something of interest, and only patient sampling will separate the corn from the chaff, the tough-minded music from the sentimental corn.

***** In Concert**
India Navigation IN 1052 *Baker; Lee Konitz (as); Michael Moore (b); Beaver Harris (d).* 74.

Not a label on which one would expect to find either of the two frontmen, concentrating as it did largely on avant-garde music. This set, apparently Baker's first in America for some time, was recorded at Ornette Coleman's New York City loft. It's standard bop fare, freeze-dried and then set to the quite demanding rhythm set up by Moore and Harris. Sonny Rollins's 'Airegin' gets things moving, followed by a long 'Au Privave'. Later tracks are more representative of Chet's style, and he shapes some lovely solos on 'Body And Soul' (demonstrating that it's not just a tenor saxophonist's number), 'Willow Weep For Me' and 'Walkin''. The sound is rather poor but the music is interesting enough and fills in an awkward gap in the current discography.

*****(*) Once Upon A Summertime**
Original Jazz Classics OJC 405 *Baker; Greg Herbert (ts); Harold Danko (p); Ron Carter (b); Mel Lewis (d).* 2/77.

Originally released on Galaxy, this is a fine, straightforward jazz session. Herbert isn't particularly well known, but he acquits himself with honour in a no-frills ballad style, with occasional glimpses of a tougher, hard-bop diction peeking through. Chet plays very cleanly and sounds in better lip than at any time in the previous ten years. The rhythm section can't be faulted. Good versions of 'E.S.P.' and 'The Song Is You', with Danko well to the fore on the latter.

****** The Best Thing For You**
A&M 397 050 *Baker; Paul Desmond (as); Michael Brecker (ts); Hubert Laws (f); Kenny Barron, Richie Beirach (p); John Scofield (g); Ron Carter (b); Tony Williams (d); Arto Tuncboyaciyan (perc).* 2 & 5/77.

Part of the intention here was to demonstrate that Chet was not merely a ballad player but also a swinger, so producer and arranger Don Sebesky pitched him into a top-flight band with an emphasis on upbeat measures and brisk solos. Hearing Chet in front of Ron Carter and Tony Williams (as Miles had been) is completely absorbing, and it is astonishing that it has taken so long for these superb tracks to resurface. Sebesky sticks to standard material for the most part but throws in his own 'El Morro' at the end, providing Baker with a stimulating, startling curtain-call that calls on guest appearances by Sco, Richie Beirach, Mike Brecker, Hubert Laws and Arto Tuncboyaciyan. All the other tracks are co-led by Paul Desmond, who is taste personified on 'How Deep Is The Ocean?' and the medley of 'I'm Getting Sentimental Over You' and 'You've Changed'. The big-band track is the most exciting item, but it is untypical of a well-crafted, generally low-key record.

****** Live At Nick's**
Criss Cross Jazz 1027 *Baker; Phil Markowitz (p); Scott Lee (b); Jeff Brillinger (d).* 11/78.

****(*) Two A Day**
Dreyfus Jazz Line FDM 365092 *As above, except Jean-Louis Rassinfosse (b) replaces Lee.* 12/78.

Distinguished by a notably fresh choice of material, the Criss Cross is another fine jazz set. Richie Beirach's 'Broken Wing' was written specially for Chet, but the long version of Wayne Shorter's 'Beautiful Black Eyes' (it can also be heard on the later France's Concert session) is the product of an unexpected enthusiasm that fed the trumpeter with new and relatively untried material. Markowitz is an admirably responsive accompanist and fully merits 'featured' billing on the sleeve. The Shorter track is by far the longest thing on the session, though two CD bonuses, the relatively predictable standards, 'I Remember You' and 'Love For Sale', are both over ten minutes. Gerry Teekens is too sophisticated and demanding a producer to have settled for just another ballad album and, with the exception of the last two tracks, this is extremely well modulated, one of a mere handful of records from the last two decades of Chet's career that have to be considered essential.

By contrast, the live session from Hérouville, France, is pretty nondescript, though recorded only a month later and with essentially the same band. Those who saw Baker on this trip will confirm that 'two a day' wasn't the reality of the situation at all, and it shows in the playing. Where *Live At Nick's* finds him crisp and pointed (albeit according to his own laid-back standard), the later session is merely messy and not helped by a cack-handed recording.

*****(*) The Touch Of Your Lips**

Steeplechase SCCD 31122 *Baker; Doug Raney (g); Niels-Henning Orsted Pedersen (b).* 6/79.

***** Daybreak**

Steeplechase SCCD 31142 *As above.* 10/79.

***** This Is Always**

Steeplechase SCCD 31168 *As above.* 10/79.

***** Someday My Prince Will Come**

Steeplechase SCCD 31180 *As above.* 10/79.

Chet greatly relished this format (and returned to it to even greater effect with Philip Catherine and Jean-Louis Rassinfosse in the mid-1980s). The absence of a drummer allowed him to develop long, out-of-tempo lines that were reminiscent of Miles Davis's ballad experiments in the 1950s in which bar-lines were largely ignored and phrases were overlapped or elided. This broke down the conventional development of a solo, replacing it with a relatively unstructured sequence of musical incidents, all of them directly or more obliquely related to the main theme. This was easier to do on ballads, and Chet's dynamics became increasingly restrictive in the last few years. *Chet's Choice*, below, is more varied in pace, but in 1979 Baker was still suffering some intonation problems, presumably as a result of losing teeth, and he fluffs some of the faster transitions. On slower material he sounds masterful and is ably accompanied by Raney's soft-bop guitar and NHOP's towering bass (a studio duo album with the great Dane would have been something to hear). Steeplechase are often guilty of issuing poorly recorded *audio vérité* sessions with little adjustment of balance or volume. *The Touch Of Your Lips*, though, is admirably done, though there's more than an element of overkill in the other three sessions, apparently from later that same year, in which there really isn't enough good material for more than one carefully edited CD, a double at most.

***** All Blues**

Arco 3 ARC 102 *Baker; Jean-Paul Florence (g); Henri Florence (p); James Richardson (b); Tony Mann (d); Rachel Gould (v).* 9/79.

Chet recorded surprisingly rarely with other singers. The tracks with Rachel Gould would be more interesting if she had a more appealing voice. There are two versions of 'Valentine' and two takes of 'Round About Midnight', a tune he tackled only rather rarely despite a considerable affection for the more lyrical side of Monk. The Florences play effectively, but they are not kindly served by a very dry acoustic. Generally good.

***** No Problem**

Steeplechase SCCD 31131 *Baker; Duke Jordan (p); Niels-Henning Orsted Pedersen (b); Norman Fearrington (d).* 10/79.

A more-than-usually boppish set for this vintage. Though none of the material is orthodox bebop, there is something about Chet's phrasing and Jordan's tight, unelaborate comping that looks back to a much earlier period. That may recommend the session to those who find the later material too far removed from the blues. Others may feel that Baker had moved too far beyond this kind of approach to be able to return to it comfortably.

*****(*) Burnin' At Backstreet**

Fresh Sound FSR CD 128 *Baker; Drew Salperto (p); Mike Formanek (b); Art Frank (d).* 2/80.

Unconsciously or no, this turns into a tribute by the white Miles Davis to the original and only Miles Davis. Three Davis compositions – 'Tune Up', 'Milestones' and 'Four' – and a version of 'Stella By Starlight' that twice quotes from the classic version. Baker often did these tunes, but seldom with this concentration. He had behind him a very good young band, including the excellent Formanek, and he had at the time (so it is said) a belief that every date could be his last. There was to be nearly a decade more of last dates and missed deadlines, but there were few better nights than this. The sound is our only problem with it. Recorded in the Backstreet Club in New Haven, it is no better than it might be, and there are a few off-mike moments that disturb the flow of solos. Strongly recommended, all the same.

**** And The Boto Brasilian Quartet**

Dreyfus Jazz Line 849228 *Baker; Richard Galliano (acc); Riqué Pentoja (p); Michel Peyratoux (b); José Boto (d, perc).* 7/80.

The combination of electric piano and bass guitar gives this a very dated sound, and Baker sounds rather diffident on a programme of unfamiliar Brazilian themes. Nevertheless the session does emphasize once again the number of very different settings in which either inclination or circumstance found him in these years.

*****(*) Live At Fat Tuesday's**

Fresh Sound FSR CD 131 *Baker; Bud Shank (as); Hal Galper, Phil Markowitz (p); Ron Carter (b); Ben Riley (d).* 4/81.

A great shame that Shank wasn't able to sit in on 'You Can't Go Home Again', thus wakening memories of the superb Baker–Desmond version; but there's no doubt that the altoist gives Chet a shot in the arm on their two tracks together. 'In Your Own Sweet Way' is handled with more fire than normal. Shank's tone (well captured on CD) is clear and bright, and Chet sounds more pungent and full-bodied than usual. Warmly recommended.

****** Peace**

Enja CD 4016 *Baker; David Friedman (vib, mar); Buster Williams (b); Joe Chambers (d).* 82.

By far the most interesting of the later studio sessions, *Peace* consists mainly of David Friedman originals. The exceptions are 'The Song Is You' and a feeling interpretation of the title-piece, a Horace Silver composition. 'Lament For Thelonious' has an elaborate-sounding melody, built up out of very simple elements. As on 'Peace', it's Williams rather than Friedman who takes responsibility for sustaining the chord progression, leaving the vibraharpist to elaborate the theme. His response to Chet's first couple of choruses is softly ambiguous. Chambers also takes a simple but effective solo. The CD has an alternative take of the opening '3 + 1 = 5', a confident post-bop structure that deserves to be covered more frequently. Remixed in 1987, the album sounds sharp and uncluttered.

***** Everything Happens To Me**
Timeless SJP 176 *Baker; Kirk Lightsey (p); David Eubanks (b); Eddie Gladden (d).* 3/83.

Stars for Lightsey, who has a good proportion of the album to himself, and his characteristically respectful readings of Wayne Shorter themes. Baker comes in for 'Ray's Idea' and the title-piece, making more of an impact than he does on many a longer set. Worth buying for Lightsey alone, but collectors will welcome Chet's trumpet and vocal contributions.

***** Mister B**
Timeless SJP 192 *Baker; Michel Graillier (p); Philip Catherine (g); Riccardo Del Frà (b).*

***** Sings Again**
Timeless SJP 238 *As above, except add John Engels (d); omit Catherine.* 5/83.

Catherine unfortunately shows up on only a single track, the far from typical 'Father Christmas'. However, the trio sessions on *Mister B* are good enough. Graillier was a sympathetic pianist in the lush, romantic manner (Danko, Beirach, Galper, Lightsey) that Chet preferred and which one associates with pianists who accompany singers. The absence of a drummer on the first album is more than made up for by Del Frà, who is brought through very strongly on this remixed issue, which also includes the bonus 'White Blues' and the Catherine track. All the same points apply to the *Sings Again* session, except that Del Frà has been relegated to the background in favour of Engels's notably soft touch, largely on brushes.

*****(*) Chet Baker At Capolinea**
Red CD 123206 *Baker; Diane Varvra (ss); Nicola Stilo (f); Michel (p); Riccardo Del Frà (b); Leo Mitchell (d).* 10/83.

***** A Night At The Shalimar**
Philology W 59 2 *Baker; Nicola Stilo (f); Mike Melillo (p); Furio Di Castri (b).* 5/87.

Flute was an integral feature of many of the 1980s groups, and Stilo had a particular facility for the long, slightly shapeless lines that the trumpeter was looking for. These are attractive sets in a rather lightweight way, but only the Red offers much challenge. Varvra's soprano is used, like the flute, to filigree the backgrounds, allowing Graillier to play slightly more percussively than usual. Of the two the Red is the one to go for. The opening 'Estate' is one of the most imaginative available readings of the Bruno Martino tune and (typical of Baker's unflagging ability to pull out unexpected themes) there is an excellent version of J.J. Johnson's little-heard 'Lament'.

****** Blues For A Reason**
Criss Cross Jazz 1010 *Baker; Warne Marsh (ts); Hod O'Brien (p); Cecil McBee (b); Eddie Gladden (d).* 9/84.

It has always been a matter of considerable debate whether or not Chet belongs in the 'Cool School', is a Tristano disciple, or has the authentic 'West Coast sound'. Just as it's now recognized in most quarters that Tristano was a much more forceful and swinging player than the conventional image allows, so it's clear that the near-abstraction and extreme chromaticism of Chet's last years were a perfectly logical outgrowth of bebop. Warne Marsh's style has been seen as equally problematic, 'cold', 'dry', 'academic', the apparent antithesis of Chet's romantic expressionism. When the two are put together, as on this remarkable session, it's clear that unsubstantiated generalizations and categorizations quickly fall flat. While Baker is quite clearly no longer an orthodox changes player, having followed Miles's course out of bop, he's still able to live with Marsh's complex harmonic developments. *Blues For A Reason* stands out from much of the work of the period in including relatively unfamiliar original charts, including three by Chet himself. The best of these, 'Looking Good Tonight', is heard in two versions, demonstrating how the trumpeter doesn't so much rethink his whole strategy on a solo as allow very small textural changes to dictate a different development. Marsh, by contrast, sounds much more of a *thinking* player and, to that extent, just a little less spontaneous. The saxophonist's 'Well Spoken', with which the set begins, is perhaps the most challenging single item Baker tackled in his final decade, and he sounds as confident with it as with the well-worn 'If You Could See Me Now' and 'Imagination'. This is an important and quietly salutary album that confounds the more casual dismissals of the trumpeter's latter-day work.

*****(*) Diane**
Steeplechase 1207 *Baker; Paul Bley (p).* 2/85.

Considerably undervalued as a standards player, Bley is exactly the right duo partner for Chet. His accompaniments frequently dispense with the chords altogether, holding on to the theme with the lightest of touches and allowing the basic rhythm to stretch out and dismantle itself. Typically of this period, the material is quite straightforward, but the treatments are far from orthodox and *Diane* would certainly merit an unqualified fourth star were it not for rather murky sound.

***** The Legacy: Volume 1**
Enja ENJ 9021 *Baker; Doug Raney (g); Jesper Lundgaard (b); Aage Tanggaard (d).* 2/85.

*****(*) I Remember You – The Legacy: Volume 2**
Enja ENJ 9077 *As above.* 2/85.

The heroism of Baker's final years continues to unfold. It has long been our conviction that the received image of a broken man continuing to play long past all logic and real creative intent merely to feed an out-of-control habit has to be done away with. Three years from the end of his life, Chet is playing with exquisite grace and control, and if one were told that the performer were a lovelorn youth who worked out every morning and went home to a cold and unruffled bed every night, who would be the wiser?

There was always a cool reserve about Chet's playing. It is only in the knowing what the circumstances were that one begins to erect fantasies around it. These performances are a perfect instance. Volume Two is very much the better. Raney gives a splendid performance and, as so often, the more open chords of a guitar player suit Chet's conception perfectly, even on the pianistic 'Broken Wing', Richie Beirach's wonderful tune for Baker. 'Nardis' is a well-worked groove for the band and Chet's Miles-referenced solo is one of his most obvious tributes to his predecessor and *alter ego*. Engineers always seem to get a good sound in the Café Montmartre, and there are no technical quibbles. A fine pairing.

****** Chet's Choice**

Criss Cross 1016 *Baker; Philip Catherine (g); Jean-Louis Rassinfosse, Hein Van Der Geyn (b).* 6/85.

*****(*) Strollin'**

Enja 5005 *As above, except omit Van Der Geyn.* 85.

****(*) Live In Bologna**

Dreyfus Jazz Line 36558-9 *As above.* 85.

This was the most productive year of Chet's last decade, and in the association with Catherine he hit a purple patch. It was a format he liked and had used to great effect in the 1979 sessions with Doug Raney and NHOP. The Criss Cross session is the most completely satisfying studio record of the period. Playing a basic standards set, he sounds refocused and clear-voiced, with a strength and fullness of tone that is undoubtedly helped by Gerry Teeken's typically professional production job. All three players are recorded in tight close-up, but with excellent separation.

The Enja performances are equally good, but the live sound isn't quite so distinct and it's a very much shorter set. One interesting link reflects Baker's outwardly unlikely enthusiasm for Horace Silver compositions, 'Doodlin'' on *Choice*, the title-piece on *Strollin'*. Their built-in rhythmic quality is ideal for players like Baker and Catherine who tend to drift out of metre very quickly, developing long, carefully textured improvisations with only a very basic pulse. Both of these sessions are strongly recommended.

The Bologna session is the weakest of the three. The trio doesn't sound comfortably played in, Chet seems to be having intonation problems, even on familiar stuff like 'Valentine' and 'My Foolish Heart', and the sound-balance is frequently awry. Completists only.

**** Symphonically**

Soul Note 121134 *Baker; Mike Melillo (p); Massimo Moriconi (b); Giampaola Ascolese (d); Orchestra Filarmonica Marchigiana.* 7/85.

Baker often performed well in front of big orchestras, but this was an over-produced and rather heavy-handed session and contains little of interest. The sound is very slushy and Chet is made to sound rather cavernous.

*****(*) Live From The Moonlight**

Philology W 10/11 2 2CD *Baker; Michel Graillier (p); Massimo Moriconi (b).* 11/85.

More than two and a half hours (on CD) from a single night at the Moonlight Club, Macerata. The extra material comprises three tracks from a third, presumably later, set and a long rehearsal performance of 'Polka Dots And Moonbeams'. Chet is in good lip and reasonable voice. There isn't a track under ten minutes and most are longer than a quarter of an hour. This, depending on the trumpeter's state of mind, was either his most serious vice or, as here, his most underrated virtue, for he was capable of remarkable concentration and, ironically, compression of ideas, and his up-close examination of themes like 'Estate' and Richie Beirach's 'Night Bird' (CD only) is extremely impressive. As an insight into how Baker worked over an entire evening, this is hard to beat. Without a drummer, the music can start to sound a little rarefied, and Moriconi often isn't clearly audible. A fine document, nevertheless. For a change the liner document includes something more useful than the usual over-emotional '*ciao*, Chet, *mille grazie*', a discography from 1952 to 1988 that lists a sobering 198 items; specialists will doubtless be able to add more to that.

***** Silent Nights**

Dinemec CD CD 04 *Baker; Christopher Mason (as); Mike Pellera (p); Jim Singleton (b); Johnny Vidacovich (d).* 1/86.

Given the sheer profusion and range of this discography, it would be more surprising if Baker *hadn't* made a Christmas album. This session was put together as a favour to the young Mason (and one of the authors once had similar reason to be grateful to Chet's generosity in this respect). The trumpeter's only proviso was that the music should be reverent ... and, lo and behold, another side to Chet revealed. After the Roland Kirk version of 'We Three' – or 'Free' – 'Kings', it might seem difficult to treat it with any sort of reverence in a jazz context but Chet and the young group manage without a blush, and the two versions of 'Silent Night' are quite breathtaking. A backwater project, of course, but one to be enjoyed.

*****(*) When Sunny Gets Blue**

Steeplechase SCCD 31121 *Baker; Butch Lacy (p); Jesper Lundgaard (b); Jukkis Uotila (d).* 2/86.

A rather melancholic session, but one of the better ones from the period. Lacy is a much-underrated piano player. He gives Baker a great deal of room, leaving chords suspended in unexpected places and rarely resorting to predetermined structures even on very familiar tunes. Indeed, he sets up conventional expectations on 'Here's That Rainy Day' and 'You'd Be So Nice To Come Home To' and then confounds them utterly with altered tonalities and out-of-tempo figures. Lundgaard and Uotila are both thoroughly professional and contribute to a fine, unpredictable set.

****(*) As Time Goes By**

Timeless SJP 251/2 *Baker; Harold Danko (p); Jon Burr (b); Ben Riley (d).* 12/86.

****(*) Cool Cat**

Timeless SJP 262 *As above.*

**** Heartbreak**

Timeless SJP 366 *As above, except add Michel Graillier (p), Riccardo Del Frà (b), John Engels (d), strings.* 86–91.

The first two were recorded at a single session, with considerable emphasis on Chet's singing. Given that his chops sound in very poor shape, this may not have been a matter of choice. Posthumously adding strings to a selection of tunes from the Timeless catalogue clearly was. The editing on *Heartbreak* hasn't been well done and there are joins all over the place, particularly obvious to anyone who knows the original sessions. These are slight enough, though Danko is a fine, lyrical player. Further sweetening doesn't redeem or enliven some very weary material.

***** Naima**

Philology W 52 2 *Baker; Mario Concetto Andriulli, Pino Caldarola, Martino Chiarulli, Tom Harrell, Mino Lacirignola (t); Nino Besceglie, Nucci Guerra, Giovanni Pellegrini, Muzio Petrella (tb); Giovanni Congedo, Franco Lorusso, Silvano Martina, Nicola Nitti, Pino Pichierri (reeds); Hal Galper, Hank Jones, Kirk Lightsey, Edy Olivieri, Enrico Pieranunzi (p); Steve Gilmore, Rocky Knower, Ilario De Marinis, Red Mitchell, Massimo Moriconi (b); John Arnold, Bill Goodwin, Shelly Manne, Vicenzo Mazzone (d).* 6/83–11/87.

Billed as Volume 1 of a sequence called 'Unusual Chet', this certainly has some unusual discographical quirks. Two tracks, valuable big-band readings of Benny Golson's 'Killer Joe', 'Lover Man' and Thad Jones's 'A Child Is Born' from 1985 are identified as 'never on record'. Two others, though, including a long version of the Coltrane title-piece with Lightsey, are described as 'never recorded', which presents a philosophical problem or suggests that they're coming from the Other Side. Essentially, this grab-bag set brings together live tapes of compositions that Chet rarely played or hadn't put on official releases. The big-band tracks are surprisingly strong, though the tone suggests he might be playing a flugelhorn. Much of the rest, like the opening blues scat with Jones, Mitchell and Manne, is rather scrappy. Despite its length, 'Naima' seems rather attenuated. A collector's set, but an interesting sidelight on Chet for non-specialists as well.

***** The Heart Of The Ballad**

Philology W 20 2 *Baker; Enrico Pieranunzi (p).* 2/88.

*****(*) Little Girl Blue**

Philology W 21 2 *Baker; Enrico Pieranunzi (p); Enzo Pietropaoli (b); Fabrizio Sferra (d).* 3/88.

Billed as Chet's last studio recordings, these encounters with Pieranunzi and his thoroughly professional Space Jazz Trio were recorded less than a week apart. Predictably, there are no late reversals or epiphanies, just a straightforward reading of some uncontroversial charts. On the group session, Baker counts each tune in but slows up progress after the theme in almost every case, not so much out of hesitancy as an apparent desire to linger over the melody. There are exceptions: 'Old Devil Moon' is quite upbeat and Wayne Shorter's 'House Of Jade', which had been a regular item in Chet's book for a long time, is given a smoothly swinging reading. Pieranunzi brings a crisp formality to his solos. The CD bonus is a long (presumably rehearsal) meditation on 'I Thought About You', which is placed first. It's slightly shapeless but includes some fine passages from Chet that one wouldn't like to have missed. The duos aren't particularly compelling, but Pieranunzi is a careful, quietly challenging accompanist and leaves a sufficient number of chords hanging or incompletely resolved to generate a measure of tension that's largely missing on the group set. It's unfortunate that there are no tunes in common with the Paul Bley duets, above. Pieranunzi certainly lacks the Canadian's brittle sensitivity and rarely risks anything like Bley's departures from conventional tonality. Generally, though, he shapes up pretty well.

****(*) Live In Rosenheim**

Timeless SJP 233 *Baker; Nicola Stilo (g, f); Marc Abrams (b); Luca Flores (d).* 4/88.

There's a slightly distasteful but commercially understandable desire among record labels to be able to release the last word from a great artist. This, following the final studio session, was billed as the last *quartet* recording. It's pretty thin stuff. Baker takes a turn at the piano, quite inconsequentially, and though the material is reasonably enterprising ('Funk In Deep Freeze', 'Arborway', 'Portait In Black And White') it's played with an almost total lack of conviction. The sound is respectable, though Stilo's flute, long a feature of Chet's groups, is sometimes overpoweringly vibrant.

***** My Favourite Songs**

Enja 5097 *Baker; L Axelsson, H Habermann, B Lanese, M Moch (t); W Ahlers, E Christmann, M Grossman, P Plato (tb); Herb Geller (as); A Boether, H Ende, K Nagurski, Emil Wurster, John Schröder (g); Walter Norris (p); Wolfgang Schluter (vib); Lucas Lindholm (b); Aage Tanggaard (d); Radio Orchestra Hannover.* 4/88

***** Straight From The Heart**

Enja 6020 *As above.* 4/88.

***** The Last Concert: Volume I & II**

Enja 6074 2CD *As above.* 4/88.

Billed as 'The last great concert' (Volume 1) and 'The great last concert' and only quibbles about one word. This was certainly something more than just another small-group recording, but by no stretch of the imagination does it merit any imputation of greatness. The photograph on the sleeve, repeated in reverse on Volume 2, is quite ghastly, a shrunken, pucker-mouthed shell of a man who looks ten years older than his actual 59 everywhere but the eyes, which still have the soft, faraway look they had back in the 1950s when Chet seemed like the freshest thing out. The horn with the big mouthpiece (pictured dewed with water on the cover of *Naima*, above) still looks burnished and pristine, but it only takes a track or two to realize that by the last year of his life Baker was trading on nothing more than pure sound and reputation. There are no new ideas any more, and the old ones lack the morning freshness that was their greatest lasting stock-in-trade.

There are small-group, big-band and orchestra tracks. There isn't much to choose among them, but for the fact that on the few quintet sessions one listens more attentively to Geller and Walter Norris than to Chet. The run of material is pretty standard, with Miles's 'All Blues', John Lewis's 'Django', 'Summertime', Brubeck's 'In Your Own Sweet Way', Monk's 'Well, You Needn't' and the inevitable 'Valentine' all on Volume 1; the sequel covers slightly less familiar ground, but, yes, the encore is 'My Funny Valentine' again. There's no obvious reason why the two single discs are still listed when a double-CD of the whole event (with no bonus tracks) is now in catalogue – but, as will be obvious from the pages above, unnecessary profusion seems to be the order of the day with this artist and, one way and another, it was the impossibility of maintaining the precarious balance between profusion and empty lack that killed him. Two weeks after the

Hannover concert, Chet Baker fell from an Amsterdam hotel window. The exact circumstances of his death have never been satisfactorily explained.

Ginger Baker (born 1940)

DRUMS

Began as a trad drummer, moved to R&B, attained superstar status with rock trio, Cream, dissipated his success in the '70s, re-emerged in the '80s as a ginger-greybeard master-drummer/bandleader and now firmly ensconsed as a paterfamilias.

***** Horses & Trees**

Terrascape TRS 4123 *Baker; Robert Musso, Bernie Worrell (org); Nicky Skopelitis (g); Shankar (vn); Foday Musa Suso (douss'n gouni); Nana Vasconcelos (berimbau, perc); Bill Laswell (b); Aiyb Dieng, Daniel Ponce (perc).* 86.

*****(*) Going Back Home**

Atlantic 7567 82652 *Baker; Bill Frisell (g); Charlie Haden (b).* 3/94.

*****(*) Falling Off The Roof**

Atlantic 7567 82900 *As above, except add Bela Fleck (bj); Jerry Hahn (g).* 12/95, 3/96.

****** Coward Of The County**

Atlantic 7567 83168-2 *Baker; Ron Miles (t); Fred Hess (ts); James Carter (bs, bcl); Eric Gunnison (p); Shamie Royston (org); Todd Ayers (g); Glenn Taylor (pedal steel g); Artie (b).* 9/98.

Ginger Baker made his professional debut playing in Dixieland groups. Even with rock supergroup Cream, even – dare we say it? – amid the confused eclecticism and sheer overload of later projects like Airforce and the ill-fated Baker–Gurvitz Army, he has remained loyal to his jazz roots. Perhaps the main model was Phil Seamen, who was briefly recruited to Airforce towards the end of his playing life, but Baker has a sound very much his own, superficially reminiscent of Paul Motian, but with heavier emphases and with a less delicate cadence.

Horses & Trees sounds like the work of a man who has still to unload a lot of baggage from years gone by. It's a clotted, overwrought album which affords tiny glimpses of something extraordinary but never manages to rise above a drab, rock-inflected production. One might almost be listening to a less-than-compelling jazz-rock record from a decade earlier, basically an augmented organ/guitar trio with overmixed drums.

Anyone sharp-eared enough to recognize either Frisell or Haden on the excellent Atlantics might well guess that Motian is the drummer, but Motian has never done anything as direct and resolute as the 'Straight, No Chaser' on *Goin' Back Home*, nor has he ever matched the sheer ferocity of Ginger's own anti-colonialist 'East Timor' on the same record. If anything, the follow-up is better. 'Bemsha Swing' is absolutely on the money and there is a totally unexpected version of 'Au Privave' with Bela Fleck guesting on banjo. Startling there, more obviously idiomatic on something like Haden's country-tinged 'Taney County' and Frisell's softly swinging 'Amarillo Barbados'. Jerry Hahn doubles up on just one track, Haden's 'Sunday At The Hillcrest', an appearance brief enough to wonder why Frisell wasn't simply double-tracked.

Unlike the Stones' Charlie Watts, who can afford to indulge his own bebop passions from time to time, Ginger is rooted in this music with the kind of imperative commitment that guarantees it keeps changing. *Coward Of The County* is a cracking record. The band is credited as the DJQ2O – the Denver Jazz Quintet-To-Octet – but the key relationship is that between Ginger and the album's main composer. Baker seems to have got involved with trumpeter, composer and educator Ron Miles and put on some polo and jazz evenings. Shoulder surgery and a set of cracked ribs (courtesy of a ballsy gelding called Clyde) put him out of action for a while, but he and Miles struck up an instantly sympathetic relationship and the trumpeter wrote some strong material with Ginger in mind. 'Daylight' is a storming idea, bleak and intense and full of scope for improvisation. 'Ginger Spice' was apparently written by Miles in complete ignorance of Ms Geri Halliwell, though we beg leave to doubt this, citing an unmistakable though momentary quote from the Girls' 'Spice Up Your Life'. One thing is sure. The Spices were never asked to sing and dance to a hybrid of 9/8 and 12/8.

The other key presence on the album is saxophonist Carter, who restricts himself to the lower end of his range, on baritone and bass clarinet. He honks righteously through 'Cyril Davies', a dedication to the harmonica player in Alexis Korner's Blues Incorporated and weaves a prayerful bass clarinet sound on 'Jesus Loves Me' and 'Jesus, I Just Want To Go To Sleep'. The first of these is a mazy rhythmic exercise; the latter – which has also featured on a Miles record – a moody and graceful farewell on which bassist Artie Moore also features. The title-track has nothing to do with the Johnny Cash song of that name, though it shares something of its down-home stoicism. With this beautiful collaborative album, Baker's reinvention seems complete.

Kenny Baker (1921–99)

TRUMPET

A Yorkshireman who learned to play in brass bands, Baker played lead in the Ted Heath band of the 1940s and helped cement its reputation for precision. Led his Baker's Dozen band in the '50s and recorded much sweet as well as hot music. Countless (anonymous) studio dates from the '60s onwards, abetted by frequent club appearances, and finally a starring role in both the posthumous Ted Heath Orchestra and the London Big Band. A musician's musician, regarded with much affection by his community.

***** Birth Of A Legend '41–'46**

Hep CD 58 *Baker; David Wilkins, Tommy McQuater, Stan Roderick, Alfie Noakes, Harry Letham, Alan Franks (t); Lad Busby, George Chisholm, Don McCaffer, Harry Roche, Jock Bain, Eric Breeze, Bruce Campbell, George Flynn, Jack Bentley, Jimmy Coombes, Woolf Phillips (tb); Harry Parry, Carl Barriteau (cl); Harry Hayes, Duggie Robinson, Reg Owen, Les Gilbert (as); Buddy Featherstonehaugh (cl, ts); George Evans, Reggie Dare, Aubrey Franks, Andy McDevitt, Jimmy Skidmore, Johnny Gray, Frank Reidy (ts); Bill Lewington, Charles Granville, Phil Goody, Jimmy Durant (bs); George Shearing, Dick Katz, Harry Rayner, Billy Munn, Ralph Sharon, Norman Stenfalt (p); Frank Deniz, Joe Deniz, Vic Lewis, Ivor Mairants, Archie Slavin, Dave*

Goldberg (g); Tommy Bromley, Charlie Short, Jack Collier (b); George Fierstone, Jock Cummings, Jack Parnell, Carlo Krahmer, Bobby Midgley (d). 11/41–1/46.

***** The Half Dozen / After Hours**

Lake LACD88 *Baker; George Chisholm (tb); Bruce Turner (cl, as); Derek Collins (cl, ts); Harry Smith, Dill Jones (p); Jack Fallon, Frank Clarke (b); Lennie Hastings, Derek Price (d).* 5/55–4/57.

***** Ain't Misbehavin'**

Zephyr ZECD 17 *Baker; Warren Vaché (c); Brian Lemon (p); Howard Alden (g); Dave Green (b); Allan Ganley (d).* 9/96–7/97.

Baker has left a vast legacy on record but little under his own name. Hep's fascinating compilation rounds up tracks by the likes of the Melody Maker Competition Band and First English Public Jam Session, as well as sessions under the leadership of Chisholm, Featherstonehaugh and Shearing, and early Ted Heath tracks. It's clear that from the start Baker was a tough nut and a pro's pro, his solos needle-fine in their precision and standing out among bands that were dance orchestras rather than jazz outfits. Harking back to a time when saxophone players had names like Aubrey Franks and Reggie Dare, the few enlightened souls – Baker, Shearing, Chisholm and Featherstonehaugh – sound like radicals. None of this is deathless music but it steps out of history well enough.

Baker's Dozen were more renowned for their regular broadcasts than for any records, and the legacy is disappointingly slight. Lake's CD gathers together tracks from one Pye and one Polygon LP. A mix of swing, jump-band music and a more relaxed mainstream, the music has a faceless feel which the solos at least put some colour into, and Baker remains impeccable.

John Bune should take credit for organizing the sessions for *Ain't Misbehavin'*, since this will probably turn out to be Baker's last featured recording. In his seventies, he was still turning in generous and enthusiastic playing, and it is hard to envisage that there is a 30-year difference in age between him and Vaché, who is enjoying himself just as much: the bubbling treatment of 'Who's Sorry Now' is marvellous. Alden slips in a few typically astute remarks along the way.

Kenny Ball (born 1930)

TRUMPET, VOCAL

Born in Ilford, Ball worked in dance-band small groups before leading his own trad-to-Dixie outfit from 1958. They introduced a new professionalism to the genre and their records for Pye were commercial enough to score several hits in the early '60s. Lip trouble interrupted his career in the later '60s, but since then Ball has been unstoppable as a touring attraction.

*****(*) Back At The Start**

Lake LACD114 *Ball; John Bennett (tb); Dave Jones (cl); Colin Bates, Ron Weatherburn (p); Dickie Bishop, Diz Disley, Paddy Lightfoot (bj); Vic Pitt (b); Tony Budd, Ron Bowden (d).* 6/59–3/62.

***** Great British Jazz Bands Vol. 8: Kenny Ball & His Jazzmen 1960–1961**

Lake LACD76 *As above, except add Lonnie Donegan (bj); omit Bishop, Budd.* 5/60–5/61.

****(*) Greensleeves**

Timeless TTD 505 *Ball; John Bennett (tb, v); Andy Cooper (cl, v); Duncan Swift (p); John Fenner (bj, g); John Benson (b); Ron Bowden (d).* 11/82.

**** The Very Best Of Kenny Ball**

Timeless TTD 598 *As above, except Hugh Ledigo (p) replaces Swift.* 91–95.

****(*) That's A Plenty**

Timeless TTD 629 *As above, except Nick Millward (d) replaces Bowden; omit Fenner.* 3-4/99.

Ball's early records may surprise any who only know his subsequent cabaret-styled jazz. He led a tough, hard-hitting outfit which his own powerful lead directed with great skill. John Bennett, one of the longest-serving sidemen in jazz, played urbane but gutsy trombone and the rhythm section had a tautness that evaded many lesser trad outfits. Ball's signing to Pye, engineered by Lonnie Donegan, was the commercial making of the band, and Ball was almost ruthless in pursuing a style of Dixieland that was disciplined enough to attract a popular audience (unthinkable today, but plausible in the chart environment of 1960). The two Lake discs bring together all of his early recordings and they're an impressive lot, particularly *Back At The Start*, which opens with three obscure 1959 tracks made for the Collector label and proceeds through the early Pye material. Ball's own playing is what stands out – unfussy, but surprisingly risk-taking at points. If his chops later bothered him, there's no evidence of it here. The second disc, while nearly as good, does sow the seeds of Ball's move towards trad as pop. 'Teddy Bear's Picnic' and 'I Got Plenty Of Nuthin'' are the kind of things that would later be the staple ingredients of his chicken-in-a-basket set.

There's a big jump from there to the latter-day output of The Jazzmen. *Greensleeves* isn't bad, but American revivalist bands can beat this kind of playing out of sight. The compilation of Ball's 1990s recordings is even less appealing since the front line sounds increasingly prone to either fluffs or fatigue, even as the rhythms sound bouncier than ever. A new recording of 'Midnight In Moscow' sounds more like next morning's hangover. *That's A Plenty* has an ounce more bounce thanks to new boy Nick Millward and, though they might have thought of one or two less obvious tunes to play, it's not bad as showbiz trad goes.

Iain Ballamy (born 1964)

TENOR SAXOPHONE, SOPRANO SAXOPHONE

Born in Guildford, Ballamy was a significant player in the new London jazz of the '80s. Since then he has worked steadily as a leader, and collected a lot of saxophones.

*****(*) Acme**

B & W BW101 *Ballamy; John Parricelli (g); Mike Mondesir (b); Mark Mondesir (d).* 5/96.

****** Food**

Feral Records ASFA 101 *Ballamy; Arve Henriksen (t, v, elec); Mat Eilertsen (b); Thomas Stronen (d, perc).* 7/98.

Though he had been leading bands since his late teens, it was only with the formation of Loose Tubes that Iain Ballamy came to wider notice. This shambolic collective – originally started by Graham Collier as a rehearsal band – became the talent pool for white British jazz in the '80s, but it also became something of a jail for those of its members who weren't prepared to sit their finals and move on. Ballamy always sounded like a man who wanted to learn as well as blow. He gravitated towards the Greenwich-based Voice of God Collective run by guitarist Billy Jenkins, and he became a member (with Django Bates, who'd been in his teenage group) of Bill Bruford's group, Earthworks. The end result, coupled with some personal misfortune, meant that his own career seemed to go on the back-burner for quite extended periods of time.

There was nothing wrong with Ballamy's debut album, *Balloon Man*, which is now deleted. It simply wasn't followed up quickly enough. When it came, *All Men Amen* (now also deleted) was far from sophomoric and every bit as good as hoped. A fair proportion of the tracks on the well-named *Acme* were written on a commission from Birmingham Jazz, a sign that Ballamy may need such a spur before he commits himself confidently to writing. Certainly the material on the album is very strong. The absence of Bates, and the replacement of piano with guitar gives the whole set a more abstract, less settled feel, and from 'Hermetology' and 'Egg Shells' onwards it intrigues, cajoles, puzzles and thoroughly entertains. 'Quandary' is a well-crafted idea, based on unusual intervals and possibly the germ of a standard which never quite declares itself. 'Bliss-Off' has a vague acid-jazz tinge but refuses to lapse into cliché.

The group is superlative, with the Mondesir brothers in particular reaffirming their status as Britain's premier contemporary rhythm pairing. Parricelli deserves to be better known. He's capable of playing clean-picked lines, either shadowing Ballamy or providing a counter-melody, and he's equally capable of laying down great squalls of sound (almost Frisell-like) which fit the harmonies only rather notionally but which make perfect musical sense every time. It's the saxophonist's gig, though.

The most recent album is a complete surprise, and this time the credit has to be shared a little more evenly. Ballamy's Norwegian colleagues create an entirely new environment for him: rich, tense and unfamiliarly abstract. It allows him to place his notes not with more care but with a more relaxed cadence. At moments, particularly on a track like 'Strange Burn', the music harks back to the British free jazz of the late '60s, which is another of Ballamy's sources. Recorded live to two-track at the Molde Jazz Festival, the sound is very raw and immediate, with Eilertsen's bass foregrounded and plenty of roomy ambience. The tracks are attractively spare and unindulgent, with a stark quality to the horns (Henriksen occasionally plays more than one trumpet simultaneously) that implies a much bigger sound-world than is actually present. Food for thought and, at its best, nourishment to the spirit as well.

Tom Bancroft

DRUMS

Brother of saxman Phil and a prominent force in the new Scottish jazz of the '90s and beyond, Bancroft also co-runs the 'local' jazz label, Caber.

***** Pieology**

Caber 001 *Bancroft; Claude Deppa, Eddie Severn, Colin Steele (t); Paul Jayasinha (t, clo); Rick Taylor (tb); Lindsay Cooper, Oren Marshall (tba); Phil (ts); Jorrit Dykstra (as, cl); Dick Lee (as, cl, bcl); John Burgess (as); Karen Wimhurst (cl, bcl); John Telfer (bs); Brian Kellock, Chick Lyall (p, ky); Kevin MacKenzie (g); Kenny Ellis (b); John Rae (d).* 2/93–2/97.

The first issue on the Bancrofts' own cottage – or should that be crofting? – label is a fairly random selection of live and broadcast cuts, but enough to show that Tom's desire to be the Scottish Basie and Ellington isn't so far off the pace. London's legendary Loose Tubes collective are the other obvious and more recent point of comparison, except that Bancroft's charts lack the wilful perversity that crept into the Tubes' act.

The opening 'Cat And Mouse' is a clever call-and-response theme, with a vocal line originally written for Fionna Duncan. It tees up the first of several superb solos from trumpeter Claude Deppa and Phil Bancroft. The tenor saxophonist is the dedicatee of the title-piece, 'Pieology', which was an early big-band effort by his brother, showing the joins here and there but still a generously proportioned blowing tune. 'Scottish Heart' was a bold synthesis of jazz and traditional Scottish ideas, dominated by Brian Kellock's Ellingtonian statement. 'The Piano Is A Dark Horse' features a fine duo between Phil Bancroft and Scotland's other ranking jazz pianist, Chick Lyall. 'Sleep Head' is an exquisite ballad with little or no solo play. The only non-Bancroft composition on the disc is Ennio Morricone's 'The Ballad Of Algiers', intended as a tribute to John Zorn and elevated by more wonderful playing from guitarist Kevin MacKenzie and tubist Oren Marshall. For much of the album, Bancroft cedes the drum stool to John Rae, head of another of Scotland's inventive musical families.

The economics of big-band jazz make it steadily more unlikely that the group will appear in this form again. For that reason alone, these cuts are valuable, but they also bespeak a generous talent. Forget what the worthier nutritionists say; eating all those pies seems to have done no harm.

Billy Bang (born 1947)

VIOLIN

Bang was born in Alabama, and served with the military in Vietnam, a combination of experiences which perhaps helps explain his passionate resistance to racial inequality. He began playing seriously relatively late, drawing inspiration from Ramsay Ameen and Leroy Jenkins, but also from the classic exponent of swing violin, Stuff Smith. His characteristic sound is combative, sometimes harsh, but always melodic.

****** Rainbow Gladiator**

Soul Note 121016 *Bang; Charles Tyler (as, bs); Michele Rosewoman (p); Wilber Morris (b); Dennis Charles (d).* 6/81.

***** Invitation**

Soul Note 121036 *As above, except Curtis Clark (p) replaces Rosewoman.* 4/82.

Rainbow Gladiator is a terrific record, bright, percussive and packed with ideas. The group has a unique and immediately identifiable sound, especially when Tyler is playing baritone, and this has to count as one of Rosewoman's best early recordings, reminiscent in places of Marilyn Crispell, with whom Bang recorded *Spirit Music*. The violinist's articulation is as precise as ever and ranges between a huge, raw vibrato and a lighter, dry, almost bleached effect. The title-track opens the album on a high; almost a quarter of an hour in length, it doesn't let up for a moment. Everything else is a good deal shorter. 'Ebony Minstrel Man', 'Broken Strings' and 'Bang's Bounce' are less than five minutes each, but they show how comfortable Bang is with song forms: a dedication to Laurel Van Horn, 'Yaa – Woman Born On Thursday', is extraordinary.

It's not clear why the second record is so disappointing. Certainly one misses the distinctiveness of Rosewoman's attack, but Clark is an excellent player and idiosyncratic enough not to leave a hole. It is simply that there is nothing very distinctive about any of the music, and Bang's own playing seems lacklustre and formulaic. The sound too is rather disappointing, though both these records gained immeasurably from transfer to CD.

***** Bangception, Willisau 1982**

hatOLOGY 517 *Bang; Dennis Charles (d).* 8/82.

Distinguished by an emotive reading of Ornette Coleman's 'Lonely Woman' and a thoughtfully respectful interpretation of Monk's 'Thelonious', this is a very welcome reissue. Recorded in concert at the Swiss new music festival, it opens with a freely improvised duet which allows both men to develop ideas at some length. Charles occasionally lapses into outbreaks of rather antagonistic sound, but these are few and far between and his sense of musical theatre is impeccable. Heavy tom-tom accents punctuate 'Lonely Woman' like a failing heart while the cymbals evoke helplessly falling tears.

Bang's interest in microtonality is less evident here than elsewhere, but it is fascinating to hear him slide across semitone shifts with expressive ease. A fine, well-recorded set from arguably Bang's strongest period.

*****(*) The Fire From Within**

Soul Note 121086 *Bang; Ahmed Abdullah (t); Oscar Sanders (g); William Parker (b); Thurman Barker (mar, perc); John Betsch (d); Charles Bobo Shaw (perc).*

***** Live At Carlos I**

Soul Note 121136 *As above, except omit Abdullah, Betsch, Shaw; add Roy Campbell (t); Zen Matsuura (d); Eddie Conde (congas).* 11/86.

The combination of trumpet, guitar and percussion makes a highly effective foil for Bang's grainy lines, especially when the splendid Barker turns to his marimba. The sheer woodiness of the sound – with Parker also making a strong contribution – is beguiling, and the melodic and rhythmic language very rich indeed. The live record underlines the distinctiveness of this group – by default, unfortunately. Campbell is a much less individual player than Abdullah, whose debt to Louis Armstrong is always evident, even when playing 'outside'. Betsch understands Bang's music as well as anyone and, Barker apart, seems the ideal sideman. The club date – Carlos I is an establishment in Greenwich Village – has a slightly plodding quality that even the mercurial William Parker can't quite mitigate.

****** Valve No. 10**

Soul Note 121186 *Bang; Frank Lowe (ts); Sirone (b); Dennis Charles (d).* 2/88.

A very definite high-point and Bang's most convincing performance since *Rainbow Gladiator*. The album was recorded on the eve of a long European tour which saw the violinist and his group cement a truly creative artistic relationship; some of the performances were uncanny and it would be fascinating to have a recording of these same tracks made a month later. Bang has always been drawn to bassists who think of their instruments as bass fiddles (William Parker frequently describes his in precisely those terms) and who try to accentuate the singing harmonies of violin and cello. The scandalously under-recorded Sirone (formerly Norris Jones) is just such a player; in Frank Lowe, Bang has a saxophonist who has managed to combine the freedoms and intensity of the avant-garde with a huge respect for tradition. Lowe himself cites Coleman Hawkins, Ben Webster and Lucky Thompson and dismisses his own sound as 'basic'; it is certainly unadorned, but it calls to mind nothing more than a latter-day Chu Berry.

The album opens very strongly with 'P.M.', an attention-grabber with its odd structure and tendency to begin solos in mid-chorus and allow them to leak over into the next. Charles is the featured soloist here, establishing a strong presence on the rest of the record as well. 'Bien Hoa Blues' is a reminiscence of Bang's Vietnam posting, and there are two tributes to John Coltrane, to mark the twentieth anniversary of his death; the disc closes with a searingly mournful 'Lonnie's Lament' on which Lowe's determination *not* to sound like Trane pays unexpected dividends. 'September 23rd' is less successful, a poem to Coltrane which draws on familiar album titles *and* the 'Love Supreme' chant.

***** A Tribute To Stuff Smith**

Soul Note 121216 *Bang; Sun Ra (p); John Ore (b); Andrew Cyrille (d).* 9/92.

Bang worked with Sun Ra's Intergalactic Arkestra for a time at the start of the 1980s. It was his first regular playing contact with standard material, and his first full exposure to large-ensemble playing. Sun Ra's presence on this record, a very rare appearance as a sideman, is the most remarkable thing about a set that never quite adds up to its promise or to more than the sum of its personnel. Cyrille is the key element, constantly suggesting new routes, changing the pace, lying back almost out of the picture, and then erupting in with another flurry of ideas. He and Sun Ra seem to be engaged in a constant dialogue, leaving the two strings to pick their way through some surprisingly conventional material.

The opening track is Stuff Smith's 'Only Time Will Tell', and there is one other tune by the great fiddler, 'Bugle Blues'. For the rest, slightly uneven, neither entirely authentic nor ironic readings of 'Satin Doll', 'Deep Purple', 'Foggy Day In London Town', 'April In Paris', a rather good 'Lover Man' and a weak 'Yesterdays'. A fascinating item in the Bang discography but, make no mistake, not a classic.

***** Spirits Gathering**

CIMP 109 *Bang; Brett Allen (g); Akira Ando (b); Dennis Charles (d).* 2/96.

This was a session beset with technical problems from the start, and they rebound on the music more than a little. CIMP pride themselves on a straight, unadorned recording technique; what is played is what you get. Bang seems to have had difficulties with his pickup from the start and, after various efforts to resolve them, was obliged to press ahead regardless. He sounds less open than usual and there are a few occasions when extraneous noise is evident, most obviously on the opening 'Tanko-bushi' and the following title-track.

This is a very strong group. As so often before, Bang doesn't seem to need or want a straightforward harmony instrument, using the guitar colouristically and for additional punctuation to the melody. The two standards – 'Softly, As In A Morning Sunrise' and 'My Funny Valentine' – are both excellent, idiomatic and original, but elsewhere there is little that startles, and the limitations of the sound become more and more evident as time passes. A fascinating session that doesn't quite transcend its circumstances.

****** Bang On!**

Justin Time JUST 105 *Bang; D.D Jackson (p); Akira Ando (b); Ronnie Burrage (d).* 4/97.

A complete surprise. This is by far the straightest and most mainstream sound Bang has ever committed to record, on the opening tracks at least. 'Sweet Georgia Brown' and then later 'Willow Weep For Me' and 'Yesterdays' are given light, sweet readings that concentrate heavily on the melody. 'Spirits Entering' is moodier and almost threatening, with Bang using drawn-out wails and glissandi to underpin a strong central idea.

Jackson is superb, almost hijacking the session with his rapid-fire delivery and invention. Burrage deserves to be better known and is particularly effective on the slower tunes, using his cymbals to great effect and constantly referring to the tune. An excellent record from a master craftsman who, at fifty, has learnt the virtues of a quieter approach.

*****(*) Commandment (For The Sculpture Of Alain Kirili)**

No More Records NO 5 *Bang (vn solo).*

The sheer physicality of this – recorded without sweetening in sculptor Kirili's loft – is astonishing. Bang sighs, stomps, taps his feet, *moves* to the music. The material is as eclectic as ever: Butch Morris's 'Music For The Love Of It', Sun Ra's 'They Plan To Leave', a gently busked 'Swing Low, Sweet Chariot', sounded pizzicato, and a performance of Bang's own quasi-classical 'Day-dreams'.

If you were never to hear another Billy Bang record, this would almost be enough. What's missing is his extraordinary ear, his ability to interact with other musicians and, to a large extent, his jazz sense. This should have the widest possible circulation; but, to get a true measure of the man, it will be necessary to look elsewhere.

Denys Baptiste

TENOR SAXOPHONE

London tenorman turned on to jazz by his father's record collection. Studied at Guildhall and joined Gary Crosby's Nu Troop. This debuts his quartet.

***** Be Where You Are**

Dune CD03 *Baptiste; Andrew McCormack (p); Larry Bartley (b); Daniel Crosby, Tom Skinner (d); Juliet Roberts, Sian Lord, Kevin Leo (v).* 99.

A skilful player with a big sound, Baptiste seems much in thrall to the obvious tenor forebears, and his original 'Rollinstone' and a blushing treatment of 'Naima' make that debt even more specific. His own writing seems rather green and it's the playing that counts – a sound, serious date which is enjoyable for its lack of pretension. There's a rousing version of Stevie Wonder's 'Have A Talk With God', voiced by Juliet Roberts, but it's hard to see why it's there, beyond a sense that it's trying to snare listeners who wouldn't care about a regular tenor-and-rhythm date.

Paul Barbarin (1899–1969)

DRUMS

Barbarin played in the New Orleans Young Olympian Brass Band as a teenager, and thereafter also worked in New York and Chicago with Oliver, Keppard and Henry Allen. From the 1930s he based himself in New Orleans but played frequent guest gigs in the northern cities. He died after leading his band in the hitherto segregated Proteus procession in 1969.

***** Streets Of The City**

504 CD 9 *Barbarin; Ernest Cagnolotti, John Brunious (t); Eddie Pierson, Worthia Thomas (tb); Albert Burbank, Willie Humphrey (cl); Lester Santiago (p); Edmond Souchon (bj, v); Richard McLean, Ricard Alexis (b).* 9/50–4/56.

***** Paul Barbarin And His Band**

Storyville STCD 6008 *As above, except add Johnny St Cyr (bj); omit Brunious, Thomas, Burbank, Souchon, Alexis.* 51.

***** Paul Barbarin And His New Orleans Band**

Atlantic 90977-2 *Barbarin; John Brunious (t); Bob Thomas (tb); Willie Humphrey (cl); Lester Santiago (p); Danny Barker (bj); Milt Hinton (b).* 55.

***** Oxford Series Vol. 15**

American Music AMCD-35 *As above, except Ricard Alexis (b) replaces Hinton.* 3/56.

One of the major New Orleans drummers, Paul Barbarin was most visibly active in the 1930s, when he played and toured with such leaders as Louis Armstrong and Luis Russell; but it was the revival of interest in New Orleans jazz which let him record as a leader. He had a hard yet restless manner of playing the beat, and his bands swing with a kind of relentlessness that can be very exciting. The Storyville disc catches his group at a peak: the horns are all excellent soloists as well as vivid ensemble players, with

Pierson a shouting trombonist, Burbank terrifically agile and Cagnolotti making light work of sounding tough and imaginative at the same time. There's an uproarious version of 'Clarinet Marmalade' and, though all the material is staple Dixieland repertoire, they play it all with seasoned rather than hackneyed dedication. The sound is a little flat but perfectly acceptable. *Streets Of The City* collects three sessions by two bands: with Cagnolotti and Burbank the music is more deeply traditional, with Brunious and the versatile Humphrey, a blend of looking back and glancing forward. Barbarin himself, a four-square traditionalist even though he worked on some very modern sessions two decades earlier, adds gravitas to every passage.

The 1955 edition of the group – which includes some major New Orleanians – is perhaps less exciting than the one which made the 1951 sessions. The music is otherwise much as before, though Hinton's flexible bass gives the underlying rhythms a more varied sense of swing, and this is certainly the clearest sound of Barbarin's available music. The Oxford session, by basically the same band, suffers from a wobbly balance, but the dominant musician here is certainly Humphrey, whose graceful lines are paradigmatic of New Orleans clarinet. All four discs are worth hearing and keeping.

Chris Barber (born 1930)

TROMBONE, BASS TRUMPET, VOCALS

Chris Barber has been playing jazz for half a century, which is also half the lifetime of the music itself. He was born in Welwyn Garden City and studied at the Guildhall in London. In the early '50s, he took over leadership of the Ken Colyer band and has been a leader ever since. The Barber band adapted its strategy to take account of the growing boom in blues, but otherwise has remained consistent in its approach to traditional jazz. Other soloists and vocalists have perhaps been more important to the band's sound and success, but Chris Barber's consistent presence has been the key to the band's longevity and high standard.

*****(*) Live In 1954/5**
Limelight 820878 *Barber; Pat Halcox (c); Monty Sunshine (cl); Lonnie Donegan (bj); Jim Bray (b, bb); Ron Bowden (d); Ottilie Patterson (v).* 10/54, 1/55.

***** The Original Copenhagen Concert**
Storyville STCD 5527 *As above.* 10/54.

*****(*) Ottilie Patterson With Chris Barber's Jazzband, 1955–1958**
Lake LACD 30 *As above, except add Eddie Smith (bj), Dickie Bishop (b).* 3/55–1/58.

****** The Chris Barber Concerts**
Lake LACD 55/56 2CD *As above, except omit Bray, Donegan; add Eddie Smith (bj), Graham Burbidge (d), Dick Smith (b).* 12/56, 1 & 3/58.

****** 30 Years Chris Barber: Can't We Get Together**
Timeless TTD 517/8 2CD *Barber; Pat Halcox (t, v); Monty Sunshine, Ian Wheeler (cl); John Crocker (ts); Dr John (Mac Rebennack) (p, v); Eddie Smith (bj); Roger Hill (g); Dick Smith (b); Vic Pitt (tba); Ron Bowden, Norman Emberson, Johnny McCallum (d).* 12/56–11/84.

***** The Traditional Jazz Scene: Volume 2**
Teldec 43997 *Barber; Pat Halcox (t); Monty Sunshine (cl); Eddie Smith (bj); Dick Smith (d); Graham Burbidge (d); Ottilie Patterson (v).* 1 & 9/59, 1/60.

*****(*) The Classic Concerts: 1959/1961**
Chris Barber Collection CBJBCD 4002 *Barber; Pat Halcox (t); Monty Sunshine (cl); Joe Harriott (as); Eddie Smith (bj); Dick Smith (b); Graham Burbidge (d); Ottilie Patterson (v).* 5/59, 3/61.

***** Hot Gospel**
Lake LACD 39 *Barber; Pat Halcox (t); Ian Wheeler (cl, as); Alex Bradford (p, v); Stu Morrison, Eddie Smith (bj); John Slaughter (g); Mickey Ashman, Dick Smith (b); Graham Burbidge (d); Alex Bradford Singers, Kenneth Washington (v).* 1/63, 66, 67.

***** Collaboration**
Jazzology BCD 40 *Barber; Pat Halcox (t); Ian Wheeler (cl, as); Graham Paterson (p); Stu Morrison (bj); Brian Turnock (b); Barry Martyn (d).* 9/66.

*****(*) Live In East Berlin**
Black Lion BLCD 760502 *Barber; Pat Halcox (t); John Crocker (as, cl); John Slaughter (g); Stu Morrison (bj); Jackie Flavelle (b, v); Graham Burbidge (d).* 11/68.

***** The Grand Reunion Concert**
Timeless TTD 553 *Barber; Pat Halcox (t, flhn, v); Monty Sunshine (cl); John Crocker (cl, as, v); Lonnie Donegan (bj, g, v); Johnny McCallum (bj, g); John Slaughter (g); Jim Bray (b); Ron Bowden, Graham Burbidge (d).* 6/75.

***** Echoes Of Ellington: Volume 1**
Timeless TTD 555 *Barber; Pat Halcox (t, flhn); John Crocker (cl, as, ts); Russell Procope (cl, as); Wild Bill Davis (p); John Slaughter (g); Johnny McCallum (g, bj); Jackie Flavelle (b); Pete York (d).* 6/76.

***** Echoes Of Ellington: Volume 2**
Timeless TTD 556 *As above.* 6/76.

***** Jazz Zounds: Chris Barber**
Zounds 2720008 2CD *Barber; Pat Halcox (t, v); John Crocker (cl, as, ts); Ian Wheeler (cl, as); John Slaughter (g); Johnny McCallum (bj, g); Vic Pitt (b); Norman Emberson (d); Rundfunkorchester Berlin.*

***** Concert For The BBC**
Timeless TTD 509/10 *Barber; Pat Halcox (t); Ian Wheeler (cl, as); John Crocker (cl, as, ts, hca); Johnny McCallum (g, bj); Roger Hill (g); Vic Pitt (b); Norman Emberson (d).* 6/82.

***** Live In '85**
Timeless TTD 527 *As above.* 11/85.

*****(*) Chris Barber Meets Rod Mason's Hot Five**
Timeless TTD 524 *Barber; Rod Mason (c, v); Klaus Dau (tb); Helm Renz (cl, as); Ansgar Bergmann (p); Udo Jagers (bj).* 8/85.

***** Stardust**
Timeless TTD 537 *Barber; Pat Halcox (t); Ian Wheeler (cl, as); John Crocker (cl, as, ts, hca); Johnny McCallum (g, bj); Roger Hill (g); Vic Pitt (b); Norman Emberson (d).* 5/88.

In his memoir, *Owning Up*, George Melly describes how Chris Barber 'prettified' the fundamentalist jazz of the 'holy fool', Ken Colyer. Colyer had been jailed in New Orleans, actually for overstaying his permit, but in the eyes of his acolytes for having dared to play with black musicians. In Melly's view, Colyer alone could never have brought about the British trad boom that lasted from the mid-1950s until rock and pop took a solid hold of the music industry a decade later. Melly presented the trad revolution as if it were the Reformation, purging jazz of solos and arrangements, bringing it back to the primitive collectivism of the Delta. 'It was [Ken] who established the totems and taboos, the piano-less rhythm section, the relentless four-to-the-bar banjo, the loud but soggy thump of the bass drum. Ken invented British traditional jazz. It wasn't exactly ugly' – as Picasso's primitivist canvases were thought to be ugly – 'on the contrary, it was quite often touchingly beautiful, but it was clumsy. It needed prettifying before it could catch on. Chris Barber was there to perform the function.'

Barber had been leading bands while still in his teens, but his first serious attempt was a co-operative group pulled together in 1953 during Colyer's extended 'vacation' in New Orleans. Colyer, who had some reason to feel that a *coup d'état* had taken place behind his back, was invited to join, and he did for a time, until he found himself out of tune with Lonnie Donegan's grandstanding (Donegan was soon to become a star in his own right) and what he thought of as the (gasp!) bebop mannerisms that were creeping in. Pat Halcox, who had declined the offer first time around, joined up and has grown in Barber's company from the slightly raw voice heard on *Live In 1954/5* into a first-rate performer with a ringing and occasionally vocalized tone of some power. The early live material on Limelight includes two skiffle features for Donegan, whose 'Rock Island Line' was to become a million-seller. The jazz material (which on *Echoes Of Ellington* takes in a little-known Ellington tune, 'Doin' The Crazy Walk') is not so much prettified as a 'middle way' between modern jazz (with accoutrements like solos and formal arrangements) and the grim, nonconformist Protestantism of Colyer's approach. It's hard to over-estimate the significance of Barber's contribution at this period, or that of Donegan's skiffle, which became the musical foundation for the Beatles and Herman's Hermits. Melly's description of the music holds good for *Live In 1954/5*. It's awkwardly recorded, the banjo chugs relentlessly and there's a plodding predictability to the bass drum beat.

Things are much better on the *Concerts* discs. The Lake documents what was, 45 years ago, the biggest musical draw in Britain, filling the Royal Festival Hall ten days before Christmas 1956 and packing venues elsewhere round the country with that full-hearted sound. Ottilie Patterson's occasional spots are uneven but tend to confirm her blues credentials. Not to question the sincerity of product like *Hot Gospel*, which is actually culled from often poorly documented or undated sessions, it provides an ideal example of Barber's adaptability. When rock and the British blues scene took off, he added electric basses and guitars to his band, rechristened it the Chris Barber Jazz & Blues Band and secured a haven between what already seemed to be irreconcilable musical tendencies. In the 1980s he has recorded very successfully with the New Orleans legend, Dr John, who (as 'The Night Tripper') was an icon of psychedelic blues in the later '60s; *Take Me Back To New Orleans* (Black Lion BLCD 760163), with Dr John and bass drummer Freddie Kohlman, is not currently in the catalogue, but Dr John can be heard on 'Good Queen Bess' on *30 Years Chris Barber*, a slightly misleading compilation that brings together material from 1956 (a film soundtrack for *Holiday*) and from 1984, but not from the intervening period; so it isn't a handy sampler.

Barber's groups were at their peak in the late 1950s, a period usefully and authentically caught on the Teldec compilation. At the end of the decade they became the first British group to play the blue-riband Ed Sullivan Show. There's no mistaking the raw authenticity of the May 1959 sell-out concert at the Deutschhalle in Berlin. There were allegedly 3,000 East Germans in the audience, and it's important to recognize with what respect and seriousness Barber's brand of jazz was regarded in the Eastern bloc; a measure of that respect is the collaboration with the Rundfunkorchester Berlin on the rather overcooked *Jazz Zounds*. In the communist countries, traditional jazz was the spontaneous music of an oppressed proletariat, uncomplicated by formalism or individualism, created collectively. Barber's later *Live In East Berlin* rarely reaches the heights of Ottilie Patterson's unaccompanied intro to 'Easy, Easy, Baby' or the rocking optimism of 'Gotta Travel On', but 'Royal Garden Blues' and 'Sweet As Bear Meat' have an authentic energy that highlights the leader's un-ironic populism. The East Berlin set also features a superb version of 'Revival' by Joe Harriott, the West Indian-born saxophonist who seemed able to play in any context, from trad to free. Harriott guests on 'Revival' at the 1961 London Palladium concert (*Classic Concerts*), which was a celebration of *Jazz News* poll winners. By 1968, Harriott was a forgotten figure, 'going single' round Britain, a reminder of the kind of suffering and neglect out of which jazz came.

Just because he was successful, Barber never forgot the origins of the music he loved. He has become an important practical historian of early 'hot' music in Britain and has constantly purified his own style, though not to the extent of shunning contact with other styles (witness the 1976 Ducal sessions, recorded in St Ives, with Ellingtonian Russell Procope), and he keeps a weather eye on shifts in public taste. In important essentials, though, Barber's approach has not changed in four decades; adaptability has never meant compromise. The later material, notably *Reunion* and *Live In '85*, albeit recorded a decade apart, betrays some signs of rote playing from some of the band, but Sunshine (who went off to make a career of his own on the back of 'Petite Fleur', a 1959 clarinet feature on which Barber did not solo but which became a major band hit) is an elegant and often moving performer, and Halcox has grown in stature with the years. The *Collaboration* with drummer Martyn is an interesting by-blow (taped by the late Doug Dobell, who was something of a legend on the British jazz scene), and the later record with Rod Mason's drummerless but piano'd Hot Five is also well worth checking out. Barber is one of the major figures in British popular music. His longevity is not that of a survivor but of a man whose roots go too deep to be disturbed by mere fashion.

*** New Orleans Symphony

Timeless TTD 610 2CD *Barber; Pat Halcox (t, v); John Crocker, Ian Wheeler (as, cl, v); John Slaughter (g); Johnny McCallum (bj, g); Vic Pitt (b); Norman Emberson (d); Grosse Rundfunk Orchester Berlin.* 10/86.

The most ambitious section of this capacious broadcast from Germany is Barber's 'Concerto for Jazz Trombone and Orchestra'. Not quite classically proportioned and defined by jazz styles rather than sonata form, it's still an impressive piece of musical organization. Barber's soloing is relaxed and thoughtful and doesn't sound too rigidly worked out in advance. The rest of the concert is more conventional, with an unusually large proportion of Barber themes – 'Lead Me On', 'Goin' Up The River' and 'Music From The Land Of Dreams' – included with the traditional material. The band are all playing well, Halcox especially, though there are a couple of moments when the sound is a touch fuzzy.

*****(*) In His Element**

Timeless CD TTD 572 2CD *Barber; Pat Halcox (t, c, flhn, v); John Crocker (as, ts, v); Ian Wheeler (as, cl); Johnny McCallum (bj, g); John Slaughter (g); Vic Pitt (b); Norman Emberson, Alan 'Sticky' Wickett (d).* 7/88, 5/90.

Live recordings from Berlin and Croydon, which are, you might say, both Barber heartland. The formula is by now tried and tested, with Barber material, 'Battersea Rain Dance and 'Crocker's Eleven' interspersed with traditional material. The Berlin disc opens with a definitive performance of collaborator Richard Hill's 'A New Orleans Overture' and then delivers a rousing, crowd-pleasing trad set that is as good as anything in the catalogue. We've some reservations about the balance of material, but if treated as two single CDs they make perfect sense individually.

(***) Under The Influence Of Jazz

Timeless TTD 569 *Barber; Bill Houghton, Mark Bennett (t); Chris Larkin (frhn); Jim Casey (tb); Steve Wick (tba).* 5 & 6/89.

****** Panama!**

Timeless CD TTD 568 *Barber; Wendell Brunious (t, v); Pat Halcox (t); Ian Wheeler (cl, as); John Crocker (cl, ts); Johnny McCallum (bj, g); John Slaughter (g); Vic Pitt (b); Russell Gilbrook (d).* 1/91.

***** Chris Barber And His New Orleans Friends**

Timeless TTD 573 *Barber; Percy Humphrey (t); Willie Humphrey (cl); Jeanette Kimball (p); Frank Fields (b); Barry Martyn (d).* 8/91.

****(*) Chris Barber With Zenith Hot Stompers**

Timeless TTD 582 *Barber; Tony Davis (c); Alan Bradley (tb); Roy Hubbard (cl); Ken Freeman (p); Brian Mellor (bj); Phil Matthews (b, tba); Derek Bennett (d).* 7/92.

Barber faced up to his fifth decade in the business with renewed energy and enterprise. Again, he was ever watchful for new wrinkles on the old routine. *Under The Influence*, with the Gabrieli Brass Ensemble, was an interesting one-off. Basically what happened was that Barber joined them for a jazz-tinged 'classical' piece, and then they played some trad arrangements. The results are predictably uneven, but Wick for one knows what jazz is all about and there's a convincing bounce to the whole thing.

The August 1991 meeting with members of the legendary Preservation Hall Band is as much of a disappointment as most of their activities. These may be the senior practitioners of the New Orleans style, but they make it sound a lot more pedestrian in the charmed air of New Orleans (albeit in a campus auditorium at Tulane University) than Barber's regular band can do in a small-town arts centre in the Home Counties, or in a school in Derby, in the case of the Zenith Hot Stompers. It's relatively unusual to hear him backed by a piano, but Jeanette Kimball isn't a particularly unusual player; indeed, she seems content to stay within reach of half a dozen trademark chords and runs at all times. There's certainly nothing more 'authentic' about the way the Preservation Hall laureates play the music than the Zenith Hot Stompers do it. Less accomplished than Barber's regular group and a bit heavy-handed when it comes to varying dynamics, they play with the enthusiasm that's almost essential for this game. The sound's average for a Barber production.

Panama! is really a showcase for the young New Orleanian trumpeter, who supplants the long-serving Halcox on most of the solo slots. Brunious builds a lovely solo on the extended 'Georgia On My Mind' and sings in a mournful, wavery mid-tenor. 'Careless Love' features clarinet before the vocal and then continues with a soft, cry-baby wah-wah chorus on trumpet (presumably from Brunious) that drops behind a delicate banjo and bass accompaniment; McCallum doubles the time on his own intriguingly jittery solo-line. Typically well crafted and intelligent, Barber's arrangements of 'Oh! Lady Be Good' and William Tyers's title-tune reflect traditional jazz at its best. Barber fans shouldn't miss it and trad enthusiasts should jump at the opportunity to hear Brunious in sympathetic company.

***** Forty Years Jubilee At The Opera House, Nürnberg**

Timeless TTD 590 *Barber; Pat Halcox (t); Monty Sunshine (cl); Ian Wheeler, John Crocker (cl, as); John Slaughter (g); Lonnie Donegan, Johnny McCallum (bj); Jim Bray, Vic Pitt (b); Ron Bowden, Russell Gilbrook (d).* 5/94.

The old gang's back in town. Two resurrected bands revisit one of their old stamping-grounds (and this corner of Europe is very much a hotbed of Barber loyalism), sounding in pretty good form. The chops, inevitably, aren't quite what they were, but the inclusion of Sunshine and a fit-sounding Donegan (who'd had cardiac problems) pushes the energy level well up. Delightful stuff from start to finish, though a better bet for collectors and nostalgia freaks than for newcomers, who might find it all a bit old-pals-ish.

***** Live In Munich**

Timeless CD TTD 600 *Barber; Pat Halcox (t, c, flhn); John Crocker (as, ts, cl); Ian Wheeler (as, cl); John Slaughter (g); Paul Sealey (bj, g); Vic Pitt (b); Alan 'Sticky' Wickett (d).* 2/95.

As so often, the Barber band goes down a storm in Germany, though this time in Bavaria where for a time there was a certain resistance to jazz. The line-up is familiar enough, and so is the programme. 'Tin Roof Blues' is stretched out long to give everybody a moment up in the sun. There's a fine if brief Duke Ellington medley which gives the saxophonists a nice lyrical feature, and the inclusion of 'Big Noise From Winnetka/Pitt's Extract' and 'Magnolia's Wedding Day' allows Barber to indulge some more ambitious material right in the middle of the set. A must for collectors and a good buy too for anyone who simply wants to sample later Barber work.

***** That's It Then!**

Timeless CD TTD619 *Barber; Pat Halcox (t); Acker Bilk (cl); John Crocker, Ian Wheeler (cl, sax, f); Paul Sealey (bj, g); John Slaughter (g); Vic Pett (b); Alan 'Sticky' Wickett (d).* 12/96.

Recorded in Manchester and Harrogate, these live dates are co-credited to Acker Bilk, whose 'Stranger On The Shore' dominates the first half of the CD, still haunting after all these years. The standard material ('Just A Closer Walk With Thee', 'Bugle Boy March', 'Wabash Blues', 'On The Sunny Side Of The Street' and 'High Society') is also high-calibre, with Barber in particular sounding very strong and convincing in his features. The ever-green Pat Halcox completes the horn line-up and shows no sign of ever changing his breezy, off-the-cuff approach. It may sound like an old act whose time has gone, but it is hard to argue with the musicianship all round.

Patricia Barber

PIANO, ORGAN, VOCAL

Studied psychology and classical piano in college and began piano and vocal work in clubs in the '80s. Recent work for Blue Note has brought her to prominence.

***** Café Blue**

Blue Note/Premonition 521810-2 *Barber; John McLean (g); Michael Arnopol (b); Mark Walker (d).* 6–7/94.

*****(*) Modern Cool**

Blue Note/Premonition 521811-2 *As above, except add Dave Douglas (t), Jeff Stitely (udu).* 1–2/98.

*****(*) Companion**

Blue Note/Premonition 522963-2 *As above, except add Eric Montzka (d), Jason Narducy (v); omit Douglas and Walker.* 7/99.

Barber made an album for Antilles in the early '90s which disappeared without trace, but her two Premonition records, subsequently licensed by Blue Note, have the feel of a cult sensation in the making. She uses pop material in a tough, unsparing way, and her own songwriting has a metropolitan wit that sits well beside the few standards that she tackles. *Café Blue* has some weaknesses: her piano playing is interesting, but she doesn't really sustain the very long 'Nardis' or 'Yellow Car III', and 'Too Rich For My Blood' is needlessly extended, but there are alternately sexy and troubling versions of 'A Taste Of Honey' and 'Ode To Billie Joe' and some smart originals. *Modern Cool* is the breakthrough record, with a string of the cleverest lyrics this side of Dave Frishberg and a delivery to match. She sounds best when she's using her contralto in its huskiest and most stand-offish tone, and that puts a proper erotic spin on 'Light My Fire', anti-coquette and all. Her band play slinky cool-cat combo music, with McLean outstanding and guest Douglas playing a little blues.

The quickie live album, *Companion*, is a fill-in release, but it has two of her most telling performances in covers of Sonny and Cher's 'The Beat Goes On' and Bill Withers's 'Use Me'. This could all get hung up in pure artifice, but Barber's been around, she keeps her distance in a very effective way and her method resists mere posturing. A name to follow.

Leandro 'Gato' Barbieri (born 1934)

TENOR SAXOPHONE, FLUTE, PERCUSSION, VOICE

Barbieri's intense, vocalized sound and upper-register screams can easily tip over into self-parody, but he remains a greatly underrated figure whose more radical and innovative work has been eclipsed by pop and film work. Born in Rosario, Argentina, Barbieri moved to Buenos Aires in his teens and began his professional career in Lalo Schifrin's orchestra as an altoist and clarinettist. He then switched to tenor and began to create his own distinctive hybrid of jazz and South American folk forms.

****** El Pampero**

RCA 6369 418 *Barbieri; Lonnie Liston Smith (p); Chuck Rainey (b); Bernard Pretty Purdie (d); Sonny Morgan, NaNa (perc, berimbau).* 71.

As we have noted before, Barbieri is also a classic victim of what is known as Rodin's Syndrome: being best known for your least representative work. Two decades before making it big with the *Last Tango* soundtrack, he had been one of the most innovative young horn players working in Europe, where he cut a classic set with Don Cherry, *Complete Communion*, and the intermittently available *In Search Of The Mystery* (which has also been reissued as *Obsession*, after one of the tracks) under his own name, before establishing himself in the Jazz Composers' Orchestra.

The good news on Barbieri is that some of his classic 1970s work is now being reissued on RCA, though it may be that some items are difficult to find outside continental Europe, where the Argentinian has always had a loyal following and a critically serious reputation.

El Pampero was recorded at the Montreux Jazz Festival, where Barbieri also guested with Oliver Nelson and Eddie Cleanhead Vinson as sax battlers in front of a United Nations big band. The small-group set with his regular band of the time is no less incendiary, with that extraordinary upper-register shriek kicking in less than a chorus into the title-track. 'Brasil' and 'Buenos Aires Querido' are both equally strong-voiced and Smith's electric piano, which had yet to slide into its egregious disco wobble, provides a strong harmonic base.

***** Fenix**

BMG 37506 *Barbieri; Lonnie Liston Smith (p); Joe Beck (g); Ron Carter (b); Lenny White (d); Nana Vasconcelos (berimbau, perc); Gene Golden (perc).* 4/71.

*****(*) Under Fire**

BMG 37507 *Barbieri; Lonnie Liston Smith (p); John Abercrombie (g); Stanley Clarke (b); Roy Haynes (d); Airto Moreira, Mtume (perc); Moulay Ali Hafid (dumbeq).* 71.

***** Bolivia**

BMG 22105 *As above, except add Jean-François Jenny-Clark (b).*

***** The Best Of The Early Years**

BMG 63523 2 *As above, except add Oliver Nelson (as, cond), Romeo Penque (afl, eng hn); Phil Bodner (f, af); Danny Bank (bcl); Hank Jones (p); David Spinozza (g); Bernard Purdie (d).* 71–73.

Fenix is one of the fieriest of the sessions Barbieri did for the Flying Dutchman label. It was one of a group of albums by the saxophonist which help deliver an audience previously largely uninterested even in the crossover style of Charles Lloyd and Miles Davis. The emphasis is laid pretty heavily on the saxophone throughout, and Barbieri's solos (still showing some of the influence of his avant-garde days) are raw and intense. His entry on 'Bahia' suggests an artist who is never going to surrender contentedly to mere prettiness.

Under Fire is, by contrast, the least incendiary of the Flying Dutchman albums. Abercrombie contributes significantly to a measured and lyrical approach, but the star player is Clarke. The material is heavily tinged with folk themes, and big Stanley's counter-melodies on 'Parana' and 'Maria Domingas' show how effortlessly he had assimilated similar material under Chick Corea's tutelage. Barbieri overdubs a second saxophone part on 'Antonico', a scaled-down version of the orchestrations he got from Nelson. A strong record from a vintage period.

The live *Bolivia* (like *El Pampero* before it) is a useful reminder of just how strong an improviser Barbieri was in live context as well as in the studio. The traditional 'Eclypse' and 'Vidala Triste' stand out, with the saxophone ranging restlessly over single-chord vamps from Smith on the Rhodes. Some of the best of the material is included on the compilation disc, which brings together 'Bolivia' and 'Eclypse', two tracks from *Under Fire*, two from *Fenix* and Oliver Nelson's 'El Gato'.

**** Last Tango In Paris

Rykodisc 10724 *Barbieri; Franco D'Andrea (p); Wolmer Beltrani, Franco Goldani (acc); Oliver Nelson (cond); strings.* 11/72.

We are in some doubt as to whether this astonishing soundtrack strictly belongs in a jazz guide, but it is the record which made and hijacked Barbieri's reputation, and it is still an invigorating listen. Bernardo Bertolucci's worked some pretty far-fetched variations on Rodin's 'The Kiss', but it was also accompanied by music of sensual grace, which always hinted at the darkness of passion and an almost nihilistic despair and self-concealment underlying the eroticism. The title-piece is intended to suggest thwarted climax, a steadily rising howl of desire and loss.

The focus is almost always on either the saxophonist or the accordions, but Oliver Nelson's lush arrangements are very much part of the mood of the film, velvety and intoxicated. This new issue is attractive for the inclusion of a 'Last Tango In Paris Suite', assembled by Barbieri from almost 30 cues from the original score. A plus for Barbieri fans and for collectors of film music.

**** Latino America

Impulse! IMP 22362 2CD *Barbieri; Helio Delmiro, Ricardo Lew, Quela Palacios, Lee Ritenour (g); Osvaldo Bellingieri (p); Dino Saluzzi (bandoneon); Isoca Fumero (charango); Daudeth De Azevado, Raul Mercado (quena); Amadeo Monges (hp); Adalberto Cevasco, Novelli (b); Pocho Lapuble, Paulinho (d); Domingo Cura (Indian d); Antonio Pantoja (various instruments); Jorge Padin, El Zurdo Roizner (perc); percussion section of Escola do Samba do Niteroi.* 73–74.

Having boosted his way to fame on the back of an (albeit controversial) film, and the quality of Barbieri's soundtrack was the one thing nobody disagreed about, it is no surprise that he, wife Michelle and producer Ed Michel should have been inclined to view the progress of his career cinematically. The two first albums for Impulse!, fulfilling the former Lalo Schifrin sideman's dream of recording for Coltrane's label, were called *Chapter One* and *Chapter Two* respectively, a practice that continued with their successors. This CD reissue puts them together, along with some previously unreleased material: a long version of 'Nunca Mas', a shorter 'single' version of the splendidly titled 'La China Leoncia Arreo La Correntinada Trajo Entre La Muchachada La Flore De La Juventud', and a single, 'Gato Gato', recorded with Lee Ritenour and an LA rhythm section. The pattern of almost all the music on both sets is a slow accretion of complex rhythm lines and very slowly shifting major–minor chord-patterns, over which Barbieri lifts steadily into the altissimo stratosphere. It is undeniably exciting stuff, even when it does lapse into histrionics. *Chapter One* ended, just to underline the filmic analogy, with 'To Be Continued', a two-minute curtain-call, in which Barbieri calls in the instruments one by one, like Vivian Stanshall on *Tubular Bells* or with the Bonzos.

Chapter Two also has additional tracks, the best of them being the alternative of 'Latino America' itself, and complete versions of 'Para Nostros' and 'Marissea', the latter minus the overdubbed flute part Gato added after the sessions, just one of several signs that these performances were both problematic and also an opportunity to experiment with collage effects. There is also an unreleased 'Mate', which is almost as stimulating as that beverage and which brings the set to a promising end. It seems clear that, between them, Michelle, Michel and engineer Baker Bigsby were Barbieri's Teo Macero, editing down sometimes cumbersomely long live performances to meet the exigencies of LP dimensions. Hearing these familiar tracks at full length isn't always as revelatory as one might have expected. There is, though, a trance-like quality to a Barbieri performance which comes across well and, for those who love his sound, more is very definitely better. The next item waiting for reissue is *Chapter Four: Alive In New York*, Barbieri's finest recorded appearance, with a wonderful band including Howard Johnson and the hugely underrated guitarist, Paul Metzke. We can't wait. In the meantime, this is a joy.

**** Priceless Jazz

GRP 98792 *As for the above, except add Osvaldo Bellingeri (p), Dino Saluzzi (bandoneon), Quelo Palacios (g), Adalberto Cevasco (b), Raul Mercado (quena), Amadeo Monges (Indian hp); Antonino Pantoja (anapa, erke, siku, quena, erkencho), Domingo Cura (bombo Indio).* 73, 74.

Like most of the *Priceless* series, this trawl through Barbieri's work for Impulse! is superb value and musically astute, covering everything from the folklorism of *Chapter 2*, recorded with local musicians in Buenos Aires, to later and more obviously jazz-centred material. Until the superb *Chapter 4, Alive In New York* becomes widely available again – it is currently a pricey Japanese import – this is the only way to get hold of material from Barbieri's successful residency at the Bottom Line Club in New York. There are just seven tracks, but well chosen to represent the range of styles in the *Chapters*. 'India' and 'Milonga Triste' are the best known, but there is a superb Latinized version of 'What A Difference A Day Makes' and a reprise of 'Nunca Mas'. At budget price this is an excellent buy, though bound to whet the appetite for more substantial investment, like the still available *Latino America*.

****(*) Caliente!**

A & M 394 597 *Barbieri; Marvin Stamm, Bernie Glow, Randy Brecker, Irvin Marvovitz (t); Wayne Andre, David Taylor, Paul Faulise (tb); Don Grolnick, Eddie Martinez (ky); Joe Beck, Eric Gale, David Spinozza (g); Gary King (b); Lenny White (d); Ralph MacDonald, Cachete Maldonado, Mtume (perc); strings.* 76.

Caliente! catches Barbieri halfway into his disco-god mode. There is some excellent playing, as usual, though oddly the upper-register stuff sounds far more overheated in this context than it ever did in the more way-out sessions, and the orchestrations (by Jay Chattaway) are as tight and crisp as anything that came out of the fusion movement. Whatever else, Herb Alpert knows how to produce this sort of thing, and there can be few quibbles on technical grounds. However, apart from the opening 'Fireflies' and the evocative 'Behind The Rain', which contains a tiny, almost subliminal reference to a similarly titled Coltrane piece, there is not much of any great substance here.

****(*) Ruby Ruby**

A & M 75021 3322 *Barbieri; Jon Faddis, Alan Rubin, Lew Soloff, Marvin Stamm (t, flhn); Wayne Andre, Paul Faulise, David Taylor (tb); John Gale, Peter Gordon, Tom Bones Malone (frhn); Don Grolnick (org); Ian Underwood (syn); Eddie Martinez (ky); Joe Caro, Lee Ritenour, David Spinozza (g); Eddie Guagua, Gary King (b); Steve Gadd, Steve Jordan, Bernard Pretty Purdie, Lenny White (d); Joe Clayton, Paulinho Da Costa, Mtume, Portinho (perc).* 78.

***** Tropico**

A & M 75021 3323 2 *Barbieri; John Barnes, Eddie Martinez (ky); Greg Poree, Carlos Santana, Wah Wah Watson (g); Eddie Watkins (b); Leon Ndugu Chancler (d); José Chepitó Areas, Armando Peraza, Bill Summers (perc); Lani Hall, Julia Tillman Waters, Luther Waters, Maxine Willard Waters, Oren Waters (v).* 78.

***** Fire And Passion**

A & M 75021 3029 2 *As above, except omit Santana; add Don Grolnick, Richard Tee (ky), Joe Beck, Lee Ritenour, David Spinozza (g), Leon Ndugu Chancler, Billy Cobham, Allan Schwartzberg, Lenny White (d), Ralph MacDonald, Mtume, Armando Peraza, Miguel Valdez (perc).*

In the 1970s, there was a huge constituency for albums like these from Herb Alpert's label and they became firm favourites on American college radio and in clubs. As pure listening experiences, Gato's pop-orientated records are fairly unsatisfying. This isn't to diminish their undoubted lustre and excitement, or indeed the leader's ability to invest chattering rhythms and some gruesome showboating with a subtler and more inventive edge. The love song, 'She Is Michelle', should probably be heard on a car radio within sight of midnight surf. On *Tropico* there is also a raunchy arrangement of Ravel's 'Bolero', which the conservative educationalist Allan Bloom said was the only classical piece American college students responded to, because it reminded them of sex. Gato is never less than convincingly raunchy, but – 'Bolero' apart – this is one of his airier and melodic records, and Carlos Santana fans will welcome his elegant, emotive contributions. *Ruby Ruby* is cloyingly produced and overcooked and likely to appeal only to firm fans.

Produced and arranged by Herb Alpert, whose career has described a similar trajectory to Barbieri's, *Fire And Passion* is the treacliest of the pop albums, so richly textured that the sheer force and strangeness of the saxophonist's delivery are largely nullified. The band is, as ever, as good as such units can be, and some of the players – Cobham, Tee, Ritenour – manage to make their presence known above the mix. Though he is not credited as such, the late Don Grolnick sounds as if he might have had a hand in some of the arrangements.

*****(*) Gato ... Para Los Amigos**

Columbia 488001 *Barbieri; Bernard Pretty Purdie (d); no other personnel specified.* 6/81.

And here Barbieri did manage to work with Teo Macero, who gives him a clear path through the potential clutter and confusion of a typically complex percussion picture and a range of sounds that might defeat a less adept producer. Michelle's touch as muse and dramaturge is also evident. The material is mostly familiar from the opening tango onwards, with 'Brasil', 'Viva Emiliano Zapata', 'Latino America' and 'Bolivia' all included. Barbieri collectors will cherish it, but they might wish for a little more detail about the group.

***** Que Pasa**

Columbia 01 067855 10 *Barbieri; Jim Hynes (t); Michael Davis (tb); Andy Snitzer (as); Philippe Saisse (ky, prog); Jeff Golub (g); Ron Jenkins, Mario Rodriguez (b); Dennis Chambers, Poogie Bell, Robbie Gonzalez (d); Cyro Baptista (perc); Vanessa Falabella (v).* 97.

It means 'what's happening'. This is Barbieri's *What's Going On?*, a meditation on life, violence, prejudice and the environment which manages to remain commercially astute. The key moment in Barbieri's recent life was the death of his wife, partner and helpmeet, Michelle. She is the dedicatee of 'The Woman I Remember', the strongest track on an album that is somewhat overpowered with something called 'sound design'. Barbieri has always been interested in the studio as a musical instrument in its own right, and he has always been able to find the appropriate techniques to match his conception. Here, though, he seems overwhelmed by the technology.

Interesting to hear him working with other horns on a couple of tracks. Barbieri has usually preferred to be sole front man, albeit in front of a huge range of percussion, but on 'Mystica' (dedicated to Jacques Tati) and 'Granada' (a poem to the bullfight) he brings in some solo brass and woodwind. Otherwise, producer Saisse is the main component of the sound on keyboards, and the range of percussion has been cut back dramatically. Not a classic record, but an intriguing one at this juncture. Almost 25 years after *Last Tango*, Barbieri is able to give his erotic soundtracking of the planet a very definite political spin.

Sam Bardfeld (born 1968)

VIOLIN

Violin still has a rather peripheral role in improvised music, but Bardfeld has devised a language which takes in classical models, jazz harmony and pure sound.

***** Taxidermy**

CIMP 195 *Bardfeld; Ken Wessel (g); Drew Gress (b); Mike Sarin (d).* 2/99.

CIMP had already experimented with improv violin in the shape of Billy Bang. Perhaps oddly, *until* you hear Bardfeld, he's not the first name in the young New Yorker's list of influences. These include Jean-Luc Ponty and Zbigniew Seifert – and we'd want to add the ill-fated Seifert's fellow-countryman, Michal Urbaniak, as well.

This line-up, which goes out as Cabal Fatale, had been around for some years before making a recording and there is obvious rapport between the players. The three string guys all have very different approaches and functions. Bardfeld favours a middle register and quite elaborate lines, however staccato the phrasing seems. Gress is reminiscent of the late David Izenzon and there are occasions when this might almost be an Ornette project.

'El Judio Demonstro Calidad' – 'the Jew demonstrated quality' – was a line about Bardfeld in a Colombian newspaper. 'One For Bill' is a tribute to the leader's teacher, saxophonist Bill Barron, while 'Curve' is a kind of abstract narrative, designed to feature the drummer over what is effectively a string ensemble. The title-piece, a protest against stuffed music, develops quite slowly, but actually has a rather sophisticated structure, revealing Bardfeld's interest in classical form.

Bardo State Orchestra

GROUP

Despite the name, a trio, studying on jazz in a context of several other musics.

****** The Ultimate Gift**

Impetus IMP CD 19425 *Jim Dvorak (t, perc, v); Marcio Mattos (b, clo, perc); Ken Hyder (d, perc, khoomei, v).* 10 & 11/94.

*****(*) Wheels Within Wheels**

Impetus IMP CD 19527 *As above, except add monks of the Schechen Tennyid Dhargyeling Monastery.* 5/95.

A rather grand name for such a small group, but what a range! All three men have studied Eastern musics in addition to jazz. This is what Jim Dvorak would call 'spirit music', dense, joyous sounds that seem to belong to no tradition exclusively. Hyder, who has led Talisker for many years, has worked extensively with shamans in Siberia, as well as studying Tuvan throat-singing. Dvorak has studied chanting under the Tibetan masters, and the Brazilian-born Mattos is a confirmed Buddhist. Lest this sound too other-worldly, there is a visceral physicality to the group's interaction, a toughness and humour which give long improvisations like 'On The Mend', 'Inside Out' and the opening 'No Harm Done' on *The Ultimate Gift* an almost matey, conversational quality. The inclusion of an ensemble of Buddhist monks on *Wheels Within Wheels* offers a fascinating and presumably authentic glimpse of one of BSO's main sources, but it tends to blunt the impact. They introduce sounds like the double-reeded *shenai*, the *thung-chen* (a Himalayan alp-horn), the conch and the *kangling* or thigh-bone trumpet, as well as additional percussion and voices. Their presence must have seemed blessing and confirmation to the trio, but it was hardly necessary. An extraordinary group, an extraordinary music.

Rob Bargad

PIANO

Played in rock and blues bands before more serious jazz work, with Nat Adderley and others.

***** Better Times**

Criss Cross 1086 *Bargad; Eddie Henderson (t, flhn); Tom Williams (t); Steve Wilson (as, ss); Donald Harrison (as); Peter Washington (b); Billy Drummond (d); Daniel G Sadownick (perc).* 12/92, 12/93.

There's something refreshingly simple but studied in Bargad's approach, and it's testimony to his powers as a writer of themes that the seven originals on *Better Times* all sound like things other bandleaders should pick up on. A duo performance of one of them, 'Is It Love?', on which he is partnered by Eddie Henderson, has the *déjà-écouté* quality of something that sounds as though it must have been around for years. Bargad has been singularly fortunate in his fellow-musicians on this debut recording. Henderson is a fierce and swinging trumpeter who manages to maintain beauty of tone even at full stretch. Wilson is an excellent partner. The two tracks from a December 1992 session – both standards, interestingly enough – feature Williams and Harrison instead and, while the former is in cracking form on 'When I Fall In Love', the partnership wouldn't be quite right for Bargad's own material. Of it, 'The Snake', 'Little J.J.' and 'Tears' are the most memorable themes, the last of them perfectly illustrating what the composer has learnt from rock. Some listeners may question Sadownick's role, which often does seem like one flavour too many. However, he does add a few angles to a rhythm section which – taking its cue from the composer/arranger, we tend to think – sounds uncharacteristically chunky and foursquare, even when the count is more complex.

Guy Barker (born 1957)

TRUMPET

The London-born trumpeter studied and worked in NYJO before making his mark as a sideman in local bands and taking countless sessionman credits. In the '90s he emerged as a forthright group leader and increasingly powerful composer, leading an international band and making a sequence of high-calibre studio dates.

*****(*) Isn't It?**

Spotlite SPJ-CD 545 *Barker; Jamie Talbot (ss); Nigel Hitchcock (as, ts); Peter King (as); Julian Joseph, Stan Tracey (p); Jim Mullen (g); Alec Dankworth (b); Clark Tracey (d).* 7–8/91.

Barker's standing as the doyen of Britain's younger trumpeters has scarcely resulted in a flood of recordings under his own name, but this belated effort as leader bristles with fine music. His own three originals suggest a witty composer as well as a polished musical mind, with the title-track a particularly lucid and clever line, while the trumpet-and-rhythm setting of 'Amandanita' strikes a measured balance between poise and tenderness. Some of his solos err on the side of self-consciousness, such as that on 'Sheldon The Cat', where both he and the garrulous saxman Hitchcock are outdone by Jim Mullen's flowing improvisation; but there is trumpet playing of sometimes awesome finesse scattered through the session. No complaints about anyone else's contribution, either. The sound is beautifully clear, if a little acidulous.

****** Into The Blue**

Verve 527656-2 *Barker; Sigurdur Flosason (as); Bernardo Sassetti (p); Alec Dankworth (b); Ralph Salmins (d).* 12/94, 2/95.

*****(*) Timeswing**

Verve 533029-2 *As above, except omit Flosason; add Perico Sambeat (as), Dale Barlow (ts).* 3/96.

Barker's debut for Verve was no rushed, back-of-an-envelope affair, put together with a band of safely bankable names. Instead, it's a carefully thought-out and patiently executed set, intended to introduce an artist whose personal style is deeply embedded in jazz history. Barker's thoughtful involvement with the tradition is reflected in cuts like 'Oh Mr Rex!', which takes as its starting-point phrases of Rex Stewart's, and 'Weather Bird Rag', an Oliver/Armstrong classic done here as a duo with bassist Dankworth. A more recent inspiration (and employer) is acknowledged in 'This Is The Life', a vigorous dedication to Stan Tracey. Barker's ballad playing has long been his trump suit, and on 'Low Down Lullaby' and the more familiar 'Ill Wind' he plays with poise and intelligence. These qualities are reflected in an intriguingly international band – Flosason is Icelandic, Sassetti Portuguese – which already sounds confidently seasoned and sure-footed. The saxophonist is perhaps inclined to dwell on pure tone for much of his impact, and Sassetti is occasionally tempted into puzzlement and riddling (as his composition, 'Enigma', might suggest) but together they give Barker just the blend he needs, and this is a band one can look forward to seeing develop and strengthen.

The follow-up is very far from being a disappointment, but it isn't a record that hangs together as comfortably. The production is drier and also more cluttered, perhaps because of the extra horn, and the sequencing of material is not as effective as it might be. That said, it marks a step on for Barker as a composer. The title-track and 'Sleeping In Iridium' both ooze with attitude, though Barker is often too reflective and thoughtful a player to add the requisite touch of aggression. 'Sometime Soon' is for quartet only, a dazzling exercise in dynamics and uneven time signatures. Whereas Sambeat fits in beautifully at all times, and especially on Latin-tinged 'The Whole Bit', ex-Messenger Barlow is too bustling and blustery a player for this music and, except on 'And All Of That', written with the late Art Blakey in mind, he doesn't come across well. The rhythm section are spot on, and Sassetti's own composition, 'O Subjectivo Objectivo', is worth exploring in detail, a densely compacted idea which nevertheless swings with abandon. There's only one standard, a throwaway trio for trumpet, piano and bass; but there is a full-blown version of Mingus's classic ballad, 'Duke Ellington's Sound Of Love', an interpretation that invites comparison (in Barker's favour, it has to be said) with his sometime boss Tommy Smith's nearly contemporary version.

****** What Love Is**

Emarcy 558331-2 *Barker; Perico Sambeat (as); Dave Hartley, Bernardo Sassetti (p); Geoff Gascoyne (b); Gene Calderazzo (d); Sting (v); London Metropolitan Orchestra.* 11/97.

Superbly orchestrated by Colin Towns, the third of the trumpeter's Universal releases has him in his most characteristic mood: romantic, thoughtful and exquisitely poised. Working without another horn casts him more clearly in focus than ever before; Sambeat appears only once, and he shakes up the pace, for the record isn't all relaxed and smoochy by any means. The saxophonist has his moment on an Ornette Coleman medley that's there to startle, coming just after a boisterous 'Monk's Mood' and just before 'The Things We Did Last Summer' and 'Angel Eyes'. What's also startling is that there are no originals this time out. Barker is perfectly capable of holding his own in company like this, though it may have been a good market decision to issue more familiar material at this point in his progress. Opening with a richly textured version of Jimmy Rowles's 'The Peacocks' was a masterstroke and, unlike *Timeswing*, the modulations of mood and harmonic profile are well observed throughout. Ellington's 'Star-Crossed Lovers' is perhaps the most sheerly perfect solo Barker has yet to record, a statement of touching simplicity and great emotional maturity. The strings and additional winds, courtesy of the London Metropolitan Orchestra, are tastefully balanced with the band, and Sting's vocal has a throaty intensity despite its bar-stool relaxation. (It's even more of a pleasure than a relief to one of the authors to be able to register so positive a response, since his colleague is credited as joint producer of all three records.)

Dale Barlow (born 1959)

TENOR SAXOPHONE

Born in Sydney, where he still lives for much of the year, Barlow is a no-nonsense hard-bop saxophonist. He lived and played in New York in the early '80s, including a brief stint with Art Blakey, then travelled the jazz world as an occasional leader or sideman with the likes of Guy Barker.

*****(*) Hipnotation**

Spiral Scratch 0009 *Barlow; Eddie Henderson (t); Kevin Hays (p); Essiet Okun Essiet (b); Billy Drummond (d).* 7/90.

***** Jazz Juice**

Hipnotation 001 *Barlow; Kenny Barron (p); Ray Drummond (b); Ben Riley (d).* 9/92.

An Australian who divides his time between Sydney and New York, Barlow's flexible style gets contrasting airings across these two discs. The earlier date, cut while he was still with the Jazz Messengers, is a grand and attacking session in which the players are all full-on from the first. Drummond and Essiet don't rush the tempos, but there's an abiding sense of bulldozing power about the playing that Barlow's appealing tunes mediate just sufficiently for the music not to overwhelm. 'Thick As Thieves', 'Hipnotation' and 'Bunyip' are all strong themes which both horns appropriate to their own ends: Barlow here sounds much in his adopted Blakey tradition, while Henderson's mix of grace and fire is especially effective. *Jazz Juice* seems almost laid-back in the comparison. It's oddly appropriate that Barlow should choose to cover Hank Mobley's 'This I Dig Of You', since this time his sound has some of the foggy lightness of Mobley's own. A charming 'Never Let Me Go' is also very fine, but at times the rest of the date sounds a trifle under-characterized, though that may be a consequence of the restrained studio mix.

Bob Barnard (born 1933)

CORNET, VOCAL

Born in Melbourne, he played in various Australian trad-mainstream groups, including the Graeme Bell group. He led his own groups to much acclaim in the 1970s and '80s, but only-occasional trips abroad have left him less widely known than he might be.

***** Cornet Chop Suey**

Opus 3 19503 *Barnard; Lars-Erik Eriksson, Tomas Ornberg (cl); Kalle Nygren, Johan Bijkerk (p); Olle Nyman (g, bj); Bjorn Hagerman (b).* 6–7/95.

***** New York Notes**

Sackville SKCD2-3061 *Barnard; Keith Ingham (p); Cal Collins (g); Earl May (b); Jackie Williams (d).* 12/95.

Barnard is an Australian whose occasional sojourns abroad have sometimes resulted in a record or two, as here. He admits to copying everything Armstrong did early on in his career, and that primary colour has since been assimilated into a modest style, marked by careful choices of notes, shaded dynamics and a clean melody-line. *Cornet Chop Suey* was done in Stockholm and is the more avowedly traditional record, with Barnard taking a notably reflective look at Armstrong staples such as 'West End Blues'. If there's such a thing as chamber-trad, this may be it, and the Swedes give him graceful support. *New York Notes* betrays the scholarly hand of Ingham at work, with many of the tracks resurrecting tunes unheard for decades. Barnard takes it in his stride and plays some of his most wistful horn. Comparatively uneventful but pleasing music.

Alan Barnes

CLARINET, ALTO AND BARITONE SAXOPHONES

Born in Altrincham, Barnes made waves as the saxophonist in the Tommy Chase band of the early '80s. Besides hard-bop gigs, he has also worked in the Humphrey Lyttelton band and the Pizza Express Modern Jazz Sextet. He can handle any swing-to-bop style, and virtually any member of the saxophone family, with the same facility.

***** Like Minds**

Fret FJCD 105 *Barnes; David Newton (p).* 7/93.

***** A Sleepin' Bee**

Zephyr ZECD7 *Barnes; Brian Lemon (p).* 12/95.

*****(*) Here Comes Trouble**

Fret FJCD 110 *Barnes; Steve Hamilton (p); Mick Hutton (b); Bryan Spring (d).* 1/96.

*****(*) Yesterdays**

Zephyr ZECD11 *Barnes; Brian Lemon (p); Dave Green (b).* 2/96.

***** Young Minds – Old Hands**

Zephyr ZECD13 *Barnes; Gerard Presencer (t); Iain Dixon (reeds); Andy Panayi (reeds, f); Brian Lemon (p); Anthony Kerr (vib); Dave Green, Alec Dankworth (b); Clark Tracey (d).* 3/96.

***** A Dotty Blues**

Zephyr ZECD26 *Barnes; Gerard Presencer (t, flhn); Mark Nightingale (tb); Andy Panayi (ts, f, picc); Iain Dixon (cl, ts); Brian Lemon (p); Anthony Kerr (vib); Dave Green (b); Steve Brown (d).* 1–6/97.

Barnes has been a stalwart saxophonist in all kinds of British jazz situations since the early 1980s. His recent rush of recording, thanks to the independent labels Fret and Zephyr, is a welcome testament by an unassuming yet significantly talented musician. Given the relative isolation of British musicians from the world jazz stage, it's sometimes difficult to get a handle on how good they really are. Barnes won't decimate any opposition, but he won't let anybody cut him either. He seems like a bopper by inclination – Phil Woods comes to mind as a possible model – who often ends up in mainstream situations, as happens on most of these records.

We have singled out two discs as the best examples of what he can do. *Here Comes Trouble* is a quartet date brimming with energy and chops. Barnes sticks to alto and baritone and handles what's almost an old Blue Note set-list (standards, Mobley, a Charlie Parker line) with ferocious aplomb. His principal activist in the group is the mercurial Spring, too rarely heard from these days, and it's a retro–hard-bop date of great character. The other one is the Zephyr set *Yesterdays*, with house pianist Lemon offering staunch support and bassist Green walking in here and there. It gets the nod over the similar *A Sleepin' Bee* if only for the quite sublime treatment of 'The Folks Who Live On The Hill'. Barnes and Lemon take few liberties with tunes and structure, and on a difficult one like 'Last Night When We Were Young' the embellishments are at the service of the song. *Like Minds* matches Barnes with the more introspective Newton: very good, if on a comparatively low flame. The one disappointment, arguably, is the octet date, *Young Minds – Old Hands*, which brings a splendid group rather deliberately to heel on nine tunes. Barnes himself plays with notable finesse and there are plenty of good solos to enjoy, but the music could use a jolt of something here and there, produced with too benign a hand to strike many sparks.

A Dotty Blues is his latest from the Zephyr stable. Panayi, Presencer and Lemon all take a turn, but it's mainly Alan's own arrangements that power the nine-strong band, of everything from 'Birdland' to Kid Ory's 'Savoy Blues'. All done with a nice sleight-of-hand, but the even-tempered nature of it all bespeaks a British reserve that to some may suggest indifference. There are, inevitably, some warming solos: Presencer, beautifully athletic on 'All The Things You Are', and the inextinguishable Lemon on 'It Had To Be You'.

Emil Barnes

CLARINET

A minor New Orleans legend who was taught by George Baquet, Barnes rarely recorded in the early days but figures in a number of location recordings from later in his life.

** Emil Barnes' Harmony Four The Very First Recordings 1946

American Music AMCD-102 *Barnes; De De Pierce, Charlie Love, Lawrence Tocca (t); Joe Avery, Harrison Brazlee (tb); Israel Gorman (cl); Billie Pierce, Emma Barrett (p); Albert Jiles, George Henderson, Willie Wilson (d).* 7/46–8/54.

Very rare recordings, the first four tracks from the dawn of New Orleans revivalism, with Barnes, Billie and De De Pierce and Willie Wilson in 1946. There's a 1954 session by Israel Gorman's band and two final tracks by a De De Pierce group. Rather peculiar that Barnes, under whose name this CD appears, is on only 4 of the 17 tracks, but that's American Music for you! While the performances have a certain dance-hall charm, this is ramshackle music that in all likelihood will appeal to diehard New Orleans campaigners only.

** Opening Night At Preservation Hall

American Music AMCD-86 *Barnes; George 'Kid Sheik' Cola (t); Eddie Summers (tb); Emanuel Sayles (bj); Alcide 'Slow Drag' Pavageau (b); Alex Bigard (d).* 6/61.

A little bit of history. These are rediscovered tapes of the very first night at the most famous shrine of the revival in New Orleans, Preservation Hall. Barnes was the nominal leader of a group of the old guys and they sound in good spirits, even if from time to time the music is sloppy to the point of a shambles. Soloists come across with gusto, including the vigorous Sayles, but the ensembles really are all over the place, and the sound is pretty dire. Still, scholars will welcome a valuable document of its kind, and the notes – by the Hall's real founder, Ken Mills – show how fiscal politics intruded even here.

Charlie Barnet (1913–91)

TENOR, ALTO AND SOPRANO SAXOPHONES

Born into a wealthy New York family, Barnet took up playing sax and was at work in Harlem – where he broke the colour bar – and everywhere in the city by the mid-'30s. But his band struggled until 1939, when he began making records for Bluebird, and broke big. He kept on through the '40s but disliked the way big-band music was going and quit bandleading in 1949, going into hotel management and leading groups only when he pleased, in the '50s, '60s and '70s. As an alto and soprano player, he idolized Johnny Hodges. He was married more times than even Dinah Washington.

*** The Transcription Performances 1941

Hep CD 53 *Barnet; Bernie Privin, Bob Burnet, George Esposito, Lyman Vunk (t); Spud Murphy, Don Ruppersberg, Bill Robertson, Ford Leary (tb); Leo White, James Lamare, Conn Humphries (as); Kurt Bloom (ts); Bill Miller (p); Bus Etri (g); Phil Stevens (b); Cliff Leeman (d); Lena Horne, Bob Carroll (v).* 1/41.

*** Swingsation

GRP 059952-2 *Barnet; Peanuts Holland, Lyman Vunk, Johnny Martel, Jack Mootz, Irving Berger, Chuck Zimmerman, Joe Ferrante, Ernie Figueroa, Roy Eldridge, Art House, Jimmy Pupa, Paul Webster, Al Killian, Everett Macdonald, Art Robey, Ed Stress (t); Russ Brown, Kahn Keene, Bill Robertson, Dave Hallett, Ed Fromm, Porky Cohen, Tommy Pederson, Walt Baron, Ben Pickering, Charles Coolidge, Gerald Foster, Dave Hallett, Burt Johnson (tb); Buddy DeFranco (cl); Harold Herzon, Joe Meisner, George Bohn, Murray Williams, Conn Humphries, Ray De Geer, Gene Kinsey (as); Kurt Bloom, Ed Pripps, James Lamare, Andy Pinot, Kenny Dehlin, Dave Matthews (ts); Bob Poland, Danny Bank, Bob Dawes (bs); Dodo Marmarosa, Bill Miller, Marty Napoleon, Sheldon Smith (p); Barney Kessel, Tommy Moore, Turk Van Lake, Dennis Sandole (g); Howard Rumsey, Bob Elden, John Chance, Andy Riccardi, Irv Lang (b); Harold Hahn, Cliff Leeman, Mickey Scrima (d).* 8/44–3/46.

Although a handful of Barnet's records – especially his big hits, 'Cherokee' and 'Skyliner' – stand as staples of the big-band era, he's generally been less than well served critically and by jazz collectors: there is nothing like enough available on CD at present. His own playing – which always points to Johnny Hodges as a first influence, and splendidly so – is usually restricted to a few telling bars, but he was an enthusiastic advocate of other, greater players, and he remains one of the few bandleaders to have virtually ignored racial distinctions. It may have cost him dear in career terms, too, though Barnet never seems to have cared very much.

A Lang–Worth transcription date fills the Hep CD, featuring a strong edition of Barnet's band, even if it lacks a little in star soloists. It's the gutsy ensemble playing that endured, even when the programme is biased towards the sweeter end of Barnet's repertoire, as it often is here. Carroll is a lugubrious crooner on his features but the young Lena Horne makes an impact in her two songs, and there are some useful Billy May arrangements, as well as several originals by 'Dale Bennett' (a Barnet *nom de plume* that he used to help him out with his alimony problems). Excellent remastering.

Barnet's allotment in the GRP *Swingsation* series is a miserly eight tracks on a CD shared with Jimmy Dorsey. 'Skyliner' and some other fine stuff is here, in very bright transfers, but this is short measure on a bandleader whose records are already suffering neglect.

***(*) The Capitol Big Band Sessions

Capitol 21258-2 *Barnet; Jack Hansen, Irv Lewis, Dave Nichols, Lamar Wright Jr, Dave Burns, Tony DiNardi, John Howell, Doc Severinsen, Rolf Ericson, Ray Wetzel, Maynard Ferguson, John Coppola, Carlton McBeath, Al Del Simone, Marvin Rosen (t);*

Karle De Karske, Herbie Harper, Phil Washburne, Dick Kenney, Obie Massingill, Kenny Martlock, Bob Burgess, Harry Betts, Dave Wells (tb); Frank Pappalardo, Walt Weidler, Vinnie Dean, Art Raboy, Ruben Leon, Dick Meldonian (as); Al Curtis, Bud Shank, Kurt Bloom, Dave Matthews, Dick Hafer, Bill Holman, Jack Laird (ts); Bob Dawes, Danny Bank, Manny Albam (bs); Claude Williamson, Don Trenner (p); Iggy Shevak, Eddie Safranski, Ed Mihelich (b); Dick Shanahan, Cliff Leeman, Tiny Kahn, John Markham (d); Carlos Vidal (perc, v); Francisco Alvarez, Diego Ibarra, Ivar Jaminez (perc); Trudy Richards (v); strings. 8/48–12/50.

This was Barnet's 'bebop' band. He knew he couldn't play the new jazz and that he didn't really want that kind of band, but he was shrewd enough to hire players who were adept enough to handle a really tough score such as 'Cu-ba', the sort of thing that was coming out of Dizzy Gillespie's book. Arrangers such as Manny Albam and Pete Rugolo posed plenty of challenges for the band, and here and there are pieces which pointed the Barnet men in the direction of Stan Kenton, which was the last thing their leader wanted. After he famously broke the band up in 1949, there came a new version, which cut the last four 1950 tracks here, with strings added. This is little-known jazz and it's a welcome addition to Barnet's CD showing, even if much of it is atypical of his best work.

**(*) Redskin Romp

RCA 74321 421292 *Barnet; Johnny Best, Pete Candoli, Conrad Gozzo, Buddy Childers, Maynard Ferguson (t); Milt Bernhart, Si Zentner, Tommy Pederson, Herbie Harper, Dick Nash (tb); Willie Smith (as); Georgie Auld, Fred Falensby (ts); Chuck Gentry, Bob Dawes (bs); Bob Harrington (p); Tony Rizzi (g); Sam Chiefetz, Joe Mondragon (b); Alvin Stoller (d); Jack Costanzo (perc).* 11–12/54.

An unlikely concept album of 'Indian' music, arranged by Billy May, although the linking of 'By The Waters Of Minnetonka' with 'Indian Summer' is a trifle far-fetched. Unfair that a potboiler like this is available when so much good Barnet is still out of print.

*** Cherokee

Evidence ECD 22065 *Barnet; Charlie Shavers, Marky Markowitz, Clark Terry, Al Stewart, Jimmy Nottingham (t); Bill Byers, Frank Sarroco, Bobby Byrne, Ed Price (tb); Vinnie Dean (as); Pete Mondello (as, ts, bs); Dick Hafer, Kurt Bloom (ts); Danny Bank (bs); Nat Pierce (p); Chubby Jackson (b); Terry Snyder (d); Bunny Briggs (v).* 8/58.

Full of pep and fizz. The arrangements, by Bill Holman, Jimmy Nottingham, Billy May and Billie Moore, emphasize swing energy over tonal sophistication and leave lots of room for soloing; with Shavers and Terry on hand, there's plenty to listen to. Barnet's own contributions reassert the Hodges influence, but there's a boppish edge, too, on 'Cherokee' and 'Skyliner'. Barnet didn't stand still.

Joey Baron (born 1955)

DRUMS, ELECTRONICS

One of the house-drummers for the New York downtown scene in the '80s and '90s, Baron also leads his own bands and now moves in wider, post-bop repertory circles.

*** RAIsedpleasuredot

New World 80449 *As above.* 2/93.

*** Crackshot

Avant 059 *As above.* 8/95.

Baron has a long list of credits by now, taking in sessions for Jim Hall and Toots Thielemans, as well as most of the leading lights of the downtown, post-Ornette school of noise-orientated sophisticates. *RAIsedpleasuredot* comes under New World's 'Counter Currents' rubric, and one can see why. The music is virtually uncategorizable, alternating thrashy punk-jazz outbreaks with longer and more thoughtful excursions. As the closing 'Girl From Ipanema Blues' perhaps suggests, the music is inclined to be arch, pointing to its own cleverness; but the point is that it is very clever indeed, and one somehow doesn't mind being reminded of it. Swell is a great ensemble player, but he also functions well in this outside-edge enterprise, staying out in front of Eskelin, who almost does accompanist's duties at some points.

Crackshot continues the fun in style, although in the end nothing Eskelin and Swell do betters the stuff on their own records, and Baron is left to simply swing things along from the back – which he does, on the likes of 'Dog' and 'Punt', to great effect. Not so much a power trio as a permanently argumentative one, they play with great chutzpah. But we doubt if many will want more than one of these records.

***(*) Down Home

Intuition INT 3503 2 *Baron; Arthur Blythe (as); Bill Frisell (g); Ron Carter (b).* 97.

Down Home is aptly titled, an earthy, blues-soaked journey back into the tradition in the company of four master musicians. Blythe's resurgent alto has rarely been heard in a more effective setting and Frisell thrives in contexts like these. The tempo is rarely faster than a mule on a hot day, and even when a 'Wide Load' has to be delivered, the urgency is kept pretty well damped down. Here and elsewhere Frisell plays straight, unadorned accompaniment, but he still manages, as does Baron himself, to make a straightforward count of four sound much more complicated.

Once or twice it sounds as though Carter may have gone back to Fender bass, though his articulation on the upright instrument is so powerful and resonant, it may be that that we're hearing. His walking intro to 'The Crock Pot' gives little hint of what is coming from Frisell and Blythe, who take a simple idea and turn it into something much more expansive without once departing from the basic changes.

Dan Barrett

TROMBONE, CORNET

Born in Pasadena, Barrett played in California revivalist groups before moving to New York in 1983 and working with Benny Goodman and Buck Clayton. He is a mainstream sideman par excellence.

***** Strictly Instrumental**

Concord CCD 4331 *Barrett; Warren Vaché (c); Chuck Wilson (as); Ken Peplowski (cl, ts); Howard Alden (g); Dick Wellstood (p); Jack Lesberg (b); Jackie Williams (d).* 6/87.

Dan Barrett is a formidably talented technician on the most problematic of jazz instruments, but he has a shrewd musical mind too. This session is perhaps a little too smoothly mainstream in the accredited Concord manner but, by mixing standards with surprise choices ('Quasimodo' and 'Minor Infraction'), Barrett tips one off that he doesn't think everything stops with swing. The band is a blend of youth and experience, too, with the leader, Vaché and Peplowski a strong front line and the dependable Wellstood underscoring the variations in texture. At the time it seemed Barrett would surely have more adventurous records ahead of him, but on the evidence below we're no longer so sure.

***** Jubilesta!**

Arbors ARCD 19107 *Barrett; Ray Sherman (p); David Stone (b); Jake Hanna (d).* 12/91–2/92.

***** Reunion With Al**

Arbors ARCD 19124 *As above, except add Al Jenkins (tb, v), Rick Fay (cl, ss, ts).* 3/93.

Barrett doesn't sound much like Teagarden, but his manner makes one think of the great man: he plays a melody with a singer's grace and vibrancy. This session is beautifully done, horn and rhythm section in simple, effective empathy; but the drowsy material takes the edge off, and even when he picks up the plunger mute Barrett doesn't really push himself. Or so one thinks. *Reunion With Al* seems meant primarily as a comeback showcase for octogenarian trombonist Jenkins. Despite the lavish praise in the sleeve-notes, Jenkins sounds unsurprisingly slow and careful in his playing, but the music still goes off at an agreeable lilt and, with Barrett sticking to cornet this time, the front line has a pleasing balance.

***** Two Sleepy People**

Arbors ARCD 19116 *Barrett; John Sheridan (p).* 2/94.

***** In Australia**

Arbors ARCD 19143 *Barrett; Bob Barnard (c); Tom Baker (ts, as, c); Chris Tapperell (p); Ian Date (g); Don Heap (b); Lynn Wallis (d).* 10/94.

Barrett has done so much sideman work lately that he seems to have left himself little time for his own records. These are both virtuous displays, though neither is a banner record. *Two Sleepy People* strolls good-naturedly through 13 standards and a Billie Holiday medley, Barrett dividing his time between trumpet and cornet, Sheridan a gentleman accompanist. They don't fail to please. It's just that the record could use a few peaks, and it's so even-tempered. Barrett and Baker were on a trip down under when they made *In Australia* with a local crew. Nothing amiss here either: Barnard sits in on only three tracks, which is a pity, though Baker's tenor gets nicely tough at quicker tempos. The rhythm section is fine, but they aren't blessed with a very friendly sound.

Kenny Barron (born 1943)

PIANO, CLARINET

The younger brother of saxophonist Bill Barron, Kenny was a phenomenally talented youngster who developed into a soloist of graceful and gracious presence, the perfect sideman, but also a leader of genuine presence and authority.

*****(*) First Half Highlights**

32 Jazz 32038 *Barron; Dizzy Gillespie (t); James Moody (as, ts, f); Stan Getz, Charlie Rouse (ts); Ray Bryant, Yusef Lateef (p, elp); Ted Dunbar (g); Warren Smith (vib, perc); Bob Cranshaw, Bob Cunningham, Sam Jones, George Mraz, Bill Salter, Chris White, Buster Williams, David Williams (b); Rudy Collins, Albert 'Tootie' Heath, Victor Lewis, Ben Riley, Freddie Waits (d); Ladzi Cammara, Richard Landrum (perc).* 62–74.

*****(*) Soft Spoken Here: Golden Lotus / Sunset To Dawn**

32 Jazz 32023 2CD *Barron; John Stubblefield (ts); Steve Nelson (vib); Buster Williams (b); Albert 'Tootie' Heath, Ben Riley, Freddie Waits (d); Richard Landrum, Sonny Morgan (perc).* 73.

*****(*) Peruvian Blue**

32 Records 32083 *Barron; Ted Dunbar (g); David Williams (b); Albert 'Tootie' Heath (d); Richard Landrum, Sonny Morgan (perc).* 3/74.

*****(*) Sunset**

Camden 610892 *As for Soft Spoken Here and Peruvian Blue.*

Barron came to notice during a short stint in 1961 with multi-instrumentalist Yusef Lateef, having previously played in R&B bands with his elder brother, Bill Barron. At nineteen, he replaced Lalo Schifrin in Dizzy Gillespie's group and worked with the trumpeter for nearly five years, subsequently rejoining Lateef and playing with Freddie Hubbard.

Barron has a funky, angular style that owes something to Monk but which is highly adept at lighter samba lines, romantic ballads and orthodox minor blues. His versatility is well attested in scores of recordings, mostly as sideman but with a substantial number under his own name. Of these records, it is possible to say only that the technical standard is high but that the performances often fall below the level of Barron's live appearances, and his work for other leaders.

As the title suggests, *First Half Highlights* is a good selection of Barron's early work as sideman and leader, including cuts under Dizzy Gillespie's name and one – a Barron composition – made in company with fellow-pianist Ray Bryant and first boss Yusef Lateef. Later material is culled from Verve, Muse and Black Hawk releases, albums such as *Four For All*, *Voyage*, Lucifer and *Sunset To Dawn*. The last of these is also packaged with *Golden Lotus* as *Soft Spoken Here*, which will be a delight for Barron enthusiasts.

Inevitably, there is some overlap of material, and only those same real enthusiasts may see the need to have *Peruvian* Blue as a separate item. Barron's debt to Bud Powell is evident on his unaccompanied exposition and development of 'Here's That Rainy Day', but the real stand-out track (unfortunately not included on the compilation) is a reading of 'Blue Monk' that involves him in some astonishing work with Dunbar. It is, though, included on the Camden compilation, of which more in a moment.

Partnerships with Stan Getz (on *Voyage*) and Charlie Rouse (on *Four For All*) produced some sympathetic playing, but Stubblefield was the most responsive colleague among the horns and some of the playing on *Soft Spoken Here* is as expressive as anything Barron has done. The recording quality was always good, and under Joel Dorn (to whom, respect) the presence of the originals has been preserved even as the sound has been sharpened attractively. Nelson and Barron himself are the main beneficiaries.

Camden and 32 seem to be tripping over each other at the moment. Before continuing their licensing arrangement, 32 might consider insisting that the BMG subsidiary spell artists' names correctly. Someone, perhaps conditioned by too many Rolling Stones records, has Freddie Waits's name as 'Watts'. Such niggles apart, this is an attractive compilation, bringing together *Peruvian Blue*, *Sunset To Dawn* and *Golden Lotus*. For sheer value, it is hard to beat.

*****(*) At The Piano**

Prevue CD PR 3 *Barron (p solo).* 2/81.

This fulfilled producer Don Schlitten's long-standing desire to create an album of Barron playing solo; to realize it, he booked the same room, RCA Studio C, and the same nine-foot Steinway on which the likes of Artur Rubinstein and Van Cliburn had recorded. This is certainly classic jazz, if not classical music. The opening bars of 'Bud-Like' are already too warped and subversive to sustain that categorization. It's the first of four Barron originals on the set. 'Calypso' sketches in an enthusiasm which has come out ever stronger in later years, while 'Enchanted Flower' builds on an idea first encountered on *Sunset To Dawn*, and an extra track, 'Wazuri Blues', suggests how much Barron had been influenced at this stage by the African rhythmic investigations of Tootie Heath, whose creative presence can readily be discerned here.

Monk and Ellington are the other tutelary presences, with versions of 'Misterioso', 'Rhythm-A-Ning' and 'The Star-Crossed Lovers', but it's the lyrical style of Billy Strayhorn that most profoundly influences the melody lines and improvisations. The sound, as one might expect, is very full and lush, and perhaps a little too curtained and veneered for some of the funkier material. An ideal place to follow Barron's procedures and take a measure on his expressive character.

****** Green Chimneys**

Criss Cross Jazz Criss 1008 *Barron; Buster Williams (b); Ben Riley (d).* 7/83.

*****(*) 1 + 1 + 1**

Black Hawk BKH 506-2 *Barron; Ron Carter, Michael Moore (b).* 4/84.

*****(*) Scratch**

Enja 4092 *Barron; Dave Holland (b); Daniel Humair (d).* 3/85.

***** What If**

Enja 5013 *Barron; Wallace Roney (t); John Stubblefield (ts); Cecil McBee (b); Victor Lewis (d).* 2/86.

***** Live At Fat Tuesday's**

Enja 5071 *Barron; Eddie Henderson (t); John Stubblefield (ts); Cecil McBee (b); Victor Lewis (d).* 1/88.

****(*) Rhythm-A-Ning**

Candid CCD 79044 *Barron; John Hicks (p); Walter Booker (b); Jimmy Cobb (d).* 9/89.

Barron's group work is always characterized by a sensitive balance of resources, and these records, which range from the stretching and unconventional piano-trio format of *Green Chimneys* and *Scratch* (which are by far his most adventurous recordings of this time) to outwardly more mainstream sets. However, the band on the Fat Tuesday's set is far from conventional and *What If* is a tough, uncompromising set that repays careful attention.

The piano/bass duets on *1 + 1 + 1* are exquisitely tasteful and largely devoted to familiar material – 'The Man I Love', 'C Jam Blues', 'Giant Steps' and 'Round Midnight' – but without cliché and without a hint of formulaic playing. Carter is a master, of course, but Moore stakes a claim for overdue recognition as well, and his presence on the Brubeck theme, 'In Your Own Sweet Way', is definitive of his forceful, unaggressive approach.

Hicks's presence on *Rhythm-A-Ning* is puzzling since he and Barron share so many strengths. Their collaboration doesn't quite strike sparks, largely because shared loyalties are less interesting than a degree of contention. Of the bunch, though, *Green Chimneys* is a neglected masterpiece with great character and a lovely balanced sound.

***** The Only One**

Reservoir RSR CD 115 *Barron; Ray Drummond (b); Ben Riley (d).* 90.

*****(*) The Artistry Of Kenny Barron**

Wave CD 34. *Barron; Peter Ind (b); Mark Taylor (d).* 3/90.

***** Invitation**

Criss Cross 1044 *Barron; Ralph Moore (ts); David Williams (b); Lewis Nash (d).* 12/90.

***** Live At Maybeck Recital Hall, Volume 10**

Concord CCD 4466 *Barron (p solo).* 12/90.

*****(*) Lemuria–Seascape**

Candid CCD 79508 *Barron; Ray Drummond (b); Ben Riley (d).* 1/91.

***** Quickstep**

Enja 6084 *Barron; Eddie Henderson (t); John Stubblefield (ts); David Williams (b); Victor Lewis (d).* 2/91.

Some of the 1980s work is disappointing but, like many musicians of his generation, Barron had a sudden boost at the start of the new decade. *Invitation* and the Maybeck solo recital were recorded within three weeks of each other, and both are well worth having. The only common track is Barron's own 'And Then Again' (that's the way he plays, setting out an idea, stating its converse, trying it out on the band if he has one, and then, as often as not, replacing it with the second subject or counter-melody rather than merely recapitulating). It's a brisk blues with the strong bebop overtones Barron brings to most of his work. The Maybeck recital has him playing three originals, but also looking back to influences earlier than Bud Powell, Tatum especially. There is much the same mix of inputs on the Wave CD, which was recorded on a memorable night at the Bass Clef club in London. Barron was in storming form and the long readings of 'Like Someone In Love', 'Body And Soul' and 'Lover Man' stand out in the work of recent years, suggesting that the only way to capture the quicksilver genius of this artist is to catch him in concert and unawares.

The trio on *Lemuria–Seascape* also features some good original material. The two title-tunes, at top and bottom of the programme, are more impressionistic than usual, though the rhythm section keeps the music driving forward. Riley's brushwork is prominently featured on 'Have You Met Miss Jones?'. The same 'and then again ...' effect transforms Monk's 'Ask Me Now' into an altogether less spiky number. *Lemuria–Seascape* is one of Barron's most attractively romantic sessions, a lighter and less rooted conception. Though none of them scales the heights, there are of course good things on almost all of these records, and Barron, who has suffered the kind of critical invisibility that comes with ubiquity, shouldn't be overlooked.

****** Other Places**

Verve 519699-2 *Barron; Ralph Moore (ss, ts); Bobby Hutcherson (vib); Rufus Reid (b); Victor Lewis (d); Mino Cinelu (perc).* 2/93.

This wipes out at a single stroke any problems the previous session might have had. Moore is in firm, probing voice, the rhythm section are wonderfully sharp and swinging, but it's the magnificent interplay between Hutcherson – still in absolutely prime shape – and Barron that marks this one down as a classic. The pianist saved some excellent writing for the date: 'Anywhere', 'Other Places' and 'Ambrosia' are deft, lyrical, unfussy themes that blossom into fine vehicles for improvising, and the chiming chord-structures set up by both piano and vibes ring long and loud in the memory. The duet between Hutcherson and Barron on 'For Heaven's Sake' is simply one of the most gorgeous ballad performances of recent times. Unmissable.

****** But Beautiful**

Steeplechase SCCD 31295 *Barron; Joe Locke (vib).*

The Steeplechase website refers to one of the tracks as 'Single *Pedal* Of A Rose', which makes a perverse kind of sense, for Barron's use of dynamics, damped notes and sustains is never more evident than on this lovely duo with vibist Locke. A set of romantic standards, played with authority and relaxed conviction. 'You Don't Know What Love Is' and the title-piece are almost symphonic in conception, with Locke's arpeggiated chords sounding like a whole string section. We've always had some doubts about piano/vibes combinations, but this one is exquisite.

*****(*) Wanton Spirit**

Verve 528634-2 *Barron; Charlie Haden (b); Roy Haynes (d).* 2/94.

Scarcely any less outstanding, and an affirmation of Barron's increasing stature as leader after countless sessions as loyal sideman. Ellington's sly blues, 'Take The Coltrane', gets a perfectly layered treatment, swung off its feet by Barron's attack, and from there the music opens out into alternately passionate and reflective settings. Haden and Haynes are a practised team by now, and they follow every line: they don't push Barron as a younger pair might, but it suits the wisdom inherent in the music. Haden and Barron have subsequently recorded *Night And The City*, which is reviewed under the bassist's entry.

***** Things Unseen**

Verve 537315-2 *Barron; Eddie Henderson (t); John Stubblefield (ts); John Scofield (g); Naoko Terai (vn); David Williams (b); Victor Lewis (d); Mino Cinelu (perc).* 3/95.

Released after *Swamp Sally*, but recorded six months earlier, this is a strangely unsatisfactory session. Reunited with Stubblefield, Williams and Lewis, Barron seems to be trying to rediscover some kind of expressive empathy that never reveals itself on *Things Unseen*. Were this a debut session by a young Turk or indeed a routine release by a more seasoned player, it would be a more than decent set, but, relative to Barron's remarkable contribution to modern jazz, it is a major disappointment.

'Christopher's Dance' teams Scofield and Terai and suggests a degree of adventure that is not so much lacking elsewhere on the album as abortive. The only exception is the long closing 'The Moment', an elegantly structured and agreeably contemplative tune that easily justifies its duration. The piano/violin duo, 'Rose Noire', is also of interest, but it seems a touch verbose at more than eight minutes.

Beautifully produced by Joanne Klein and entirely faithful to Barron's characteristic sound, this is one of those occasions when, for some indefinable reason, the group chemistry just doesn't work.

*****(*) Swamp Sally**

Verve 532268-2 *Barron; Mino Cinelu (g, bjo, mand, syn, perc, v).* 9/95.

Solos, duos, a rich tapestry of music woven into a complex understanding of two musical cultures. Cinelu's multi-instrumental approach, and his ability to give even solo percussion, as on 'Moon Dance', the richness and resonance of a whole group, offers Barron the freedom to range more widely than usual. Playing solo himself, he sounds liberated and relaxed, brimming over with ideas. An unusual record, but a very effective one.

Bruce Barth (born 1958)

PIANO

Unassuming post-bop pianist seeking to make his mark with a set of dates under his own name.

***** In Focus**

Enja 8010 *Barth; Scott Wendholt (t); Steve Wilson (as, ss); Robert Hurst (b); Lewis Nash (d).* 2/92.

*****(*) Morning Call**

Enja 8084 *As above, except Larry Grenadier (b), Leon Parker (d) replace Hurst and Nash.* 7/94.

***** Don't Blame Me**

Double-Time DTRCD129 *Barth; Ed Howard (b); Billy Drummond (d).* 6/97.

Barth balances an earnest pianism with a very fine touch. He doesn't exactly caress the keys, but he dislikes banging the piano, and each disc has a mellifluous quality that seems to emanate from the piano. The first group record is perhaps too consciously rounded between standards, originals and thinking man's jazz themes ('Pinocchio' and 'Wildflower'). We prefer *Morning Call*, which has a greater emphasis on his own writing – difficult music to play, and the more impressive for its apparent lightness of delivery. Wilson and Wendholt make a rather sombre sound as the front line, and their solos alternate between bluesiness and shafts of light. The trio record suffers slightly from Barth's touch of circumspection. When he plays Monk's 'Evidence', even though that composer is clearly an influence on his own writing, it comes out rather bland and forceless. The two ballads at the heart of the record, 'Song For Alex' and 'For Clara', are the best examples of his virtues as both composer and performer, and they're handled impeccably.

Gary Bartz (born 1940)

ALTO AND SOPRANO SAXOPHONES, SOPRANINO SAXOPHONE, CLARINET, FLUTE, WOOD FLUTE, PERCUSSION

Born in Baltimore, he studied at Juilliard and Peabody and played with hard-bop bands in the '60s before a stint with Miles Davis in 1970. Tried an increasingly dissipated fusion, but moved back to acoustic hard-bop in the '80s. Has lately taken to acting and production, and freelances as he pleases.

***** Libra / Another Earth**

Milestone MCD 47077 2 *Bartz; Jimmy Owens, Charles Tolliver (t, flhn); Pharoah Sanders (ts); Albert Dailey, Stanley Cowell (p); Richard Davis, Reggie Workman (b); Billy Higgins, Freddie Waits (d).* 5/67–6/68.

A slightly lumpy pairing of Bartz recording for Milestone, mismatched not just because the two groups are so very different but also that the saxophonist's growing interest in mystical science fiction never quite seems to blend with his raw blues phrasing. The second album, with its roster of avant-gardists, is a more satisfactory blend and Tolliver turns in some wonderful throaty horn. The version of 'Lost In The Stars' is well worth having, but also worth comparing with 'Cabin In The Sky' on the earlier half of the disc, where Bartz really doesn't seem to know quite what he's trying to do with this new hybrid sound.

***** Harlem Bush Music – Taifa / Uhuru**

BGP CD 108 *Bartz; Juni Booth (b); Harold White (d); Nat Bettis (perc); Andy Bey (v).* 70.

****(*) JuJu Street Songs**

Prestige PRCD 24181 *Bartz; Andy Bey (p, perc, v); Herbert Eaves (p); Herbert Centeno (g); Stafford James (b, perc, v); Howard King (d, perc, v).* 10/72–6/73.

Bartz's raw, intense sound reversed the usual tendency for other instrumentalists to be influenced by the dominant saxophone sound of the day. He was more obviously affected by brass players, mainly Lee Morgan and Grachan Moncur III, with whom he studied. His precocious talents won him a place in the Jazz Messengers, though by this time Bartz had already formed his Ntu Troop, a group which changed rapidly in style over succeeding years.

At the start of the 1970s he was recruited to Miles Davis's electric band, a prominent gig which did much to harden up what was already a strong interest in Afro-funk. Specializing, as he had from early years, in soprano, he developed an affecting if unadorned delivery which on the earlier disc (pairing two albums under the *Harlem Bush Music* title, *Taifa* and *Uhuru*) sounds unaffectedly original. *JuJu Street Songs* is much less clearly defined, a disappointing follow-up.

The years that followed were to be somewhat eclipsed. Bartz made a fairytale album for kids, called *Singerella*, and was active in politics and education, but there was no sign that he had much appetite for jazz activity and it was widely thought that his early promise (which had also included stints with Woody Shaw and Max Roach) would go no further.

****(*) Monsoon**

Steeplechase SCCD 31234 *Bartz; Butch Lacy (p); Clint Houston (b); Billy Hart (d).* 4/88.

****(*) Reflections Of Monk**

Steeplechase SCCD 31248 *Bartz; Eddie Henderson (t); Bob Butta (p); Geoff Harper (b); Billy Hart (d); Jenelle Fisher, Mekea Keith (v).* 11/88.

In the early 1970s, Bartz was collecting poll wins like beer mats. By the end of the decade he was playing drab pop, a shift of idiom legitimized to a degree by the sponsorship of Miles Davis, but lacking the boss's innate musicality.

Bartz had been picked out as a possible successor to Jackie McLean; while any such comparison went out of the window in the '70s, it was to return when, at near fifty, Bartz began to record jazz again. Both of these albums are a good deal more tentative than the run of live gigs at the time. There is a fine 'Soul Eyes' on *Monsoon*, but the Monk covers are slightly robotic despite strong contributions from Henderson. The superadded vocals on 'Monk's Mood' and 'Reflections' were a mistake (Jenelle Fisher is certainly no Abbey Lincoln). However, enough of the *Wunderkind* survives to guarantee Bartz listenability, if not much more than that.

*****(*) West 42nd Street**

Candid CCD 79049 *Bartz; Claudio Roditi (t, flhn); John Hicks (p); Ray Drummond (b); Al Foster (d).* 3/90.

Just occasionally, when a saxophone player climbs the stand at Birdland, a portly ghost in a pale suit wobbles out from the shadows and whispers in his ear. Bartz learned to be like Bird through Jackie McLean, but on this record he seems inclined to dig back deeper into the source material, and he plays like a man inspired. 'It's Easy To Remember' becomes a huge romantic edifice, from which he soars into 'Cousins' and a surprisingly Coltranish 'The Night Has A Thousand Eyes'. Hicks is the best piano player Bartz has come across in years, and Al Foster sends little whiplash figures along the line of the metre, coaxing the three main soloists on to even better things. Slightly exhausting, in the way a hot club set teeters between euphoria and growing weariness, but a more than welcome confirmation of Bartz's long-latent qualities. Strongly recommended.

****** There Goes The Neighbourhood!**

Candid CCD 79506 *Bartz; Kenny Barron (p); Ray Drummond (b); Ben Riley (d).* 11/90.

His finest hour. The opening 'Racism' is a boiling blues in double B flat minor, an original played with an increasingly noticeable Coltrane inflexion. The first of two Tadd Dameron compositions, 'On A Misty Night', was originally recorded in the mid-'50s in a band that included Coltrane; the mid-point of the set is a severe interpretation of 'Impressions'. Bartz's homage isn't limited to a growing repertoire of anguished cries and dissonant transpositions. He has also paid attention to how the younger Coltrane framed a solo; working against the trajectory of Dameron's theme, but sitting comfortably inside the beat, he constructs an ascending line that culminates each time in a beautifully placed false note. The result is as lovely as it is unsettling.

Johnny Mercer's 'Laura' receives a serene and stately reading, with Drummond featured. Bartz's coda restatement is masterful. He tackles 'Impressions' in the most boiled-down way, with only minimal rhythmic support, concentrating on the basics. Barron returns to the foreground for 'I've Never Been In Love' and the closing 'Flight Path', his own composition. Throughout, his touch is light but definite, freeing his accompaniments of any excess baggage.

Though previously Charles McPherson and Bobby Watson have laid claim to Parker's alto crown, Bartz appears to have come into his kingdom at last. A superb album that will grace and enliven any collection; recorded live at Birdland, it's well balanced and free from extraneous noise.

*****(*) Shadows**

Timeless CD SJP 379 *Bartz; Willie Williams (ts); Benny Green (p); Christian McBride (b); Victor Lewis (d).* 6/91.

The purple patch continues. No real complaints about this one, except that Bartz and the bustling Williams sometimes get in each other's way. The choice of material is also a bit questionable, with 'Holiday For Strings' not quite coming off as a curtain-piece. There is, to balance that, a riveting performance of Coltrane's 'Song Of The Underground Railroad'. McBride and Lewis are superlative, and Green makes his mark without fuss or histrionics. There are better moments, but this is well up to scratch.

***** Children Of Harlem**

Challenge CHR 70001 *Bartz; Larry Willis (p); Buster Williams (b); Ben Riley (d).* 1/94.

There's nothing on *Children Of Harlem* in terms of emotional urgency or social polemic that Bartz hadn't already done on *There Goes* ... The 1994 session is dedicated to Paul Laurence Dunbar, tagged with lines by Countee Cullen, another poet of the Harlem Renaissance, and kicked off with a version of the Amos'n'Andy theme. An unlikely parallel, maybe, but where Charlie Haden's Quartet West project works precisely because it is so determinedly unapologetic in its sentimentality, Bartz seems determined to throw in ironic nods and winks, quotes and antagonistic outbursts that don't really fit the mood of the thing. That said, the playing is generally very good (if recorded a bit crudely by Rudy Van Gelder's usual standard) and the long 'If This Isn't Love' stands upsides with anything Bartz has done in recent years.

***** The Red And Orange Poems**

Atlantic 7567 82720 *Bartz; Eddie Henderson (t, flhn); John Clark (frhn); Mulgrew Miller (p); Dave Holland (b); Greg Bundy (d); Steve Kroon (perc).*

Ambitious and rich, but the leader sounds slightly fettered by the format, and it is Henderson (whose critical reputation has had similar ups and downs to Bartz's) who steals the honours. Miller is a little busy and hyperactive compared to previous incumbents; and some of the bass lines, with Clark shadowing, are overdone, even given Bartz's preference for a very resonant sound. He's on a roll, for sure, but this one doesn't quite succeed.

***** The Blues Chronicles – Tales Of Life**

Atlantic 82893-2 *Bartz; Tom Williams (t); Cyrus Chestnut, George Colligan (p); Russell Malone (g); James King (b); Greg Bandy, Dennis Chambers (d); Maatkara Ali, Jon Hendricks, , Ransom (v).*

Bartz's latest attempt to update and upgrade the blues is framed by the veteran Jon Hendricks, who helps establish a lineage and a historical framework for these fresh-sounding but traditionally anchored themes. Bartz's writing is always best when simple, always most effective when sticking close to familiar tonalities and a basic count.

'One Million Blues' presumably refers to the Million Man March and draws on just about everyone from Ray Charles and Marvin Gaye to Duke and Mingus. 'Miss Otis Regrets' is a surprise, delicate and filigreed but with a deep sorrow hidden just under the surface. Raps and street hollers sit more comfortably than they might, and Hendricks's return on the closing 'Hustler's Holler: Song Of The Street' gives endearing shape to an album that might otherwise seem bitty and self-consciously eclectic.

Bartz's resurgence has probably peaked and declined a little. Going back to roots and consolidating is no bad thing at this stage in the game. Bartz has never been earthier and more unaffected.

Baseline

GROUP

A trio nominally led by bassist Van Der Geyn, playing a chamberish post-bop.

***** Why Really**

Challenge CHR 70002 *John Abercrombie (g); Hein Van Der Geyn (b); Joe LaBarbera (d); Dee Dee Bridgewater (v).* 2/94.

***** Standards**

Challenge CHR 70023 *As above, except omit Bridgewater.* 2/94.

*****(*) Baseline Returns**

Challenge CHR 70047 *As above, except add John Ruocco (cl).* 2/96.

Some three hours of impeccable jazz are spread across these three discs. The guiding hand belongs to Van Der Geyn, who wrote all the material on the first and third discs, but this is very much a three-way conversation, and Abercrombie and LaBarbera play a comparable role in setting the tone and creativity of the playing. Album two, which is made up of nine standards, is perhaps the best place to go if you want to hear three men plying their craft with superb integrity and suppleness; while nothing surprising comes out either from here or from the first disc (which features a somewhat oddly sited guest vocal by Bridgewater), this is one of those dates where the sheer calibre of the playing is its own reward. Abercrombie plays in his most relaxed, chamberish vein, often content to offer counterpoint to Van Der Geyn's bass parts, which leaves the splendid LaBarbera to step forward with drum passages that are a marvel of playing intensely without playing loudly.

The most compelling music is to be found on *Baseline Returns*. The surprise addition of Ruocco adds an unexpected colour to the group (though he isn't present on all tracks), and his woodsy sound adds an affecting patina to 'The Avenger' and 'Wheeling'. Abercrombie finally turns on some of his FX for 'Che Cha' but the superfine balance within the core trio is never endangered.

Count Basie (1904–84)

PIANO, ORGAN

Born in Red Bank, New Jersey, William Basie settled in Kansas City after experience in clubs and vaudeville. He joined the Bennie Moten band there in 1929, and eventually took over its leadership in 1935. His band moved to New York in 1936 and became one of the most eminent of its day, with many important soloists and with a uniquely swinging rhythm section characterized by Basie's own minimalist piano style. He also ran small groups within the big band, and cut back to an octet for a while (1950–51) when the big band proved too expensive to run. European tours in the 1950s and '60s restored the band's popularity; Basie's final period of recording, with the Pablo label, was the most prolific of his career, despite some spells of illness and finally having to lead the band from a motorized wheelchair. The band is still a working unit, now under the leadership of long-time Basieite Grover Mitchell.

♛ ** The Original American Decca Recordings**

MCA GRP 36112 3CD *Basie; Buck Clayton, Joe Keyes, Carl Smith, Ed Lewis, Bobby Moore, Karl George, Harry 'Sweets' Edison, Shad Collins (t); Eddie Durham (tb, g); George Hunt, Dan Minor, Benny Morton, Dicky Wells (tb); Jack Washington (as, bs); Caughey Roberts, Earl Warren (as); Lester Young, Herschel Evans (cl, ts); Chu Berry (ts); Claude Williams, Freddie Green (g); Walter Page (b); Jo Jones (d); Jimmy Rushing, Helen Humes (v).* 1/37–2/39.

****** Listen ... You Shall Hear**

Hep CD 1025 *As above.* 1–10/37.

****** Do You Wanna Jump ...?**

Hep CD 1027 *As above.* 1–11/38.

****** Basie Rhythm**

Hep CD 1032 *As above, except add Harry James (t), Jess Stacy (p).* 10/36–2/39.

****** Count Basie Volume One 1932–1938**

Jazz Classics In Digital Stereo RPCD 602 *As above, except add Hot Lips Page, Dee Stewart (t), Ben Webster (ts), Leroy Berry (g), Willie McWashington (d).* 12/32–6/38.

***** Jive At Five**

ASV AJA 5089 *As above.* 12/32–2/39.

****** Count Basie 1936–1938**

Classics 503 *As MCA disc, except omit Collins, Edison, Wells, Berry and Humes.* 10/36–1/38.

****** Count Basie 1938–39**

Classics 504 *As above, except omit Keyes, Smith, Hunt, Roberts and Williams; add Harry 'Sweets' Edison, Shad Collins (t), Dicky Wells (tb), Helen Humes (v).* 1/38–1/39.

(***) Lester–Amadeus

Phontastic CD 7639 *As above discs.* 10/36–9/38.

(***) Rock-A-Bye-Basie

Vintage Jazz Classics VJC-1033 *As above discs.* 38–39.

*****(*) Swingsation**

GRP 059920-2 *As above discs.* 37–39.

The arrival of the Count Basie band – on an East Coast scene dominated by Ellington, Lunceford and Henderson – set up a new force in the swing era, and hearing their records from the late 1930s is still a marvellous, enthralling experience. Basie's Kansas City band was a rough-and-ready outfit compared with the immaculate drive of Lunceford or Ellington's urbane mastery, but rhythmically it might have been the most swinging band of its time, based around the perfectly interlocking team of Basie, Green, Page and Jones, but also in the freedom of soloists such as Lester Young, Buck Clayton and Herschel Evans, in the intuitive momentum created within the sections (famously, Basie had relatively few written-out arrangements and would instead evolve head arrangements on the stand) and in the best singing team of any working with the big bands, Helen Humes and the incomparable Jimmy Rushing. There are paradoxical elements – the minimalism of the leader's piano solos that is nevertheless as invigorating as any chunk of fast stride piano, Green's invisible yet indispensable chording, the power of the band which still seems to drift rather than punch its way off the record. They all go to make up an orchestra unique in jazz.

There are too many great individual records to cite here, and instead we shall note only that there are two significant early periods covered by reissues, the Decca tracks (1937–9) and the subsequent recordings for Vocalion, OKeh and Columbia (1939–42). A contractual oddity is that Basie's first session – credited to Jones-Smith Inc., and marking the astonishing debut of Lester Young on record – was made for Columbia rather than Decca. Two of them are on the hotchpotch *Jive At Five*, but the first Classics CD has them all together. For a definitive study of the Decca sides, one must look to either the Hep or the MCA CDs. The Hep discs have been completed with *Basie Rhythm* and, besides having the four Jones-Smith Inc. tracks, the valuable thing here is the addition of eight tracks under the nominal leadership of Harry James but with Basie personnel dominating the line-up (also available under James's name on Classics). James himself sounds better than he does on most of his own records, but otherwise the outstanding figure is saxophonist Herschel Evans, always at least as interesting as Lester Young. The

MCA is complete to 1939 on three CDs. There is actually very little to choose between the transfers: the Hep remastering is sometimes a little more full-bodied, but the MCA is mostly smoother and often a little brighter. Given the completeness and the handsome packaging on the MCA discs, we have awarded them top marks for what is desert-island music. However, good though it is, we are confident that – in the ten years since it was remastered – techniques have improved to the extent that the Universal remastering team can now go back and do a better job.

The Classics CDs, as usual, ignore any 'label' boundaries and simply go through all the music chronologically, although no alternative takes are included. The transfers here are unpredictable. Some seem to have a lot of reverberation, which suggests second-hand tape transfers, and, while all the discs sound good enough, they can't compete with the Hep or MCA sets.

The Phontastic CD, though named for Lester Young, is nearly all Basie airshots and concert material. There are some rarities, such as two allegedly unreleased tracks from a 1938 Carnegie Hall concert, but sound-quality is often very poor; for fanatics only.

Rock-A-Bye-Basie, which is all airshots, also comes in very rough fidelity, but the standard of performances is high enough to warrant giving it an audition: if you can stand sound that seems to be crackling out of a pre-war receiver, this will be an exciting, surprising disc. There are some very fine treatments and individual spots by the usual stars, as well as undervalued performers such as Jack Washington. Edison especially gets a better shot in than on many of the studio sides: hear his chorus of trumpet on 'Moten Swing'.

Released to cash in on the (short-lived?) fad for swing music in the '90s, the *Swingsation* compilation is nevertheless an excellent choice of tracks from this vintage period.

*****(*) Count Basie 1939**

Classics 513 *Basie; Buck Clayton, Ed Lewis, Harry 'Sweets' Edison, Shad Collins (t); Dicky Wells, Benny Morton, Dan Minor (tb); Earl Warren (as); Jack Washington (as, bs); Chu Berry, Buddy Tate, Lester Young (cl, ts); Freddie Green (g); Walter Page (b); Jo Jones (d); Jimmy Rushing, Helen Humes (v).* 1–4/39.

*****(*) Count Basie 1939 Vol. 2**

Classics 533 *As above, except omit Berry.* 5–11/39.

***** Count Basie 1939–1940**

Classics 563 *As above, except add Al Killian (t), Tab Smith (ss, as); omit Collins.* 11/39–10/40.

***** Count Basie 1940–1941**

Classics 623 *As above, except add Ed Cuffee (tb), Paul Bascomb, Coleman Hawkins (ts).* 11/40–4/41.

***** Count Basie 1941**

Classics 652 *As above, except add Robert Scott, Eli Robinson (tb), Kenny Clarke (d), Paul Robeson, Lynne Sherman (v); omit Hawkins.* 5–11/41.

***** Count Basie 1942**

Classics 684 *As above, except add Jerry Blake (cl, as), Caughey Roberts (as), Henry Nemo (v); omit Minor, Cuffee, Robeson.* 5/41–7/42.

*****(*) Count Basie Volume 2**

Jazz Classics In Digital Stereo RPCD603 *As above discs.* 38–40.

The great change which commenced this Basie era was the sad death of Herschel Evans, 'the greatest jazz musician I ever played with in my life', as Jo Jones remembered him. In many ways the band was never the same again. Evans's partnership with Lester Young had given the reed section its idiosyncratic fluency, and perhaps his death marked the end of the original Basie era, when the band relied on its individual players to combine and create the instinctive Basie sound. That said, Chu Berry was a more than capable replacement for Evans, and the orchestra was still approaching a technical peak. Other arrivals – Shad Collins, Tab Smith (who also did some strong arrangements) and, later, Buddy Tate (when Berry also departed) – also had an impact on the band, and emerging arrangers (Andy Gibson, Buck Clayton) had a beneficial effect. But Basie was already steeped in a routine of riffs, conventional harmonies and familiar patterns which even the soloists (including the finally disenfranchised Young) couldn't really transcend, let alone transform. Taken a few at a time, these tracks are fine, but all together they can sometimes be dull as full-length records.

Highlights to listen for are 'Evil Blues', a memorable band performance, Lester Young's solo on 'Taxi War Dance' (both Classics 513), 'Clap Hands, Here Comes Charlie' and the Kansas City Seven date of September 1939 (all Classics 533), 'Blow Top' (Classics 563), Clayton's 'Love Jumped Out' and Helen Humes's delightful vocal on 'My Wanderin' Man' (both Classics 623). There are plenty of other interludes and solos to savour: this was too good a band to lack interest. Coleman Hawkins also makes a guest appearance on two tracks on Classics 623. But the paucity of genuinely memorable compositions and Basie's own leaning towards ensemble punch and exactness over personal flair sow the seeds of the band's decline.

There are also Basie's own piano 'solos' (actually with the rhythm section), ten of which were recorded in 1938–9 (they are split among Classics 503, 504 and 513). Basie had long since started to pare away the more florid and excitable elements of his early stride style and by now was cutting down to the bone. It works best on the elegance of 'How Long' and the almost playful feel accorded to 'Fare Thee Well, Honey, Fare Thee Well'. They also let the great rhythm section display itself away from the confines of the band, and one can hear how perfectly the team interlocks. But they also expose something of the repetitiousness and sometimes false economies of Basie's playing, even at the curtailed 78-r.p.m. length.

The next two Classics compilations take the story up to 1942. Classics 652 shows the band playing with unimpaired vitality, but the material is often grim: saving graces include 'Diggin' For Dex' and 'Platterbrains', and there is Paul Robeson's one jazz appearance on 'King Joe'. Classics 684 is considerably better: some excellent Rushing blues performances, eight titles by the Basie All-American Rhythm Section (all traditional blues), with Clayton and Byas featured on four of them, and a final date that produced a minor classic in Clayton's arrangement of 'It's Sand, Man!'.

Robert Parker's second volume of Basie (RPCD 603) is a strong selection in his customary superb sound. A fine companion-piece to his first.

*****(*) The Jubilee Alternatives**

Hep CD 38 *Basie; Harry 'Sweets' Edison, Al Killian, Ed Lewis, Snooky Young (t); Eli Robinson, Robert Scott, Louis Taylor, Dicky Wells (tb); Jimmy Powell, Earl Warren (as); Buddy Tate, Lester Young, Illinois Jacquet (ts); Rudy Rutherford (bs, cl); Freddie*

Green (g); Rodney Richardson (b); Jo Jones, Buddy Rich (d); Thelma Carpenter, Jimmy Rushing (v). 12/43–10/44.

***** Old Manuscripts: Broadcast Transcriptions 1944–45**
Music & Arts CD-844 *Similar to above.* 43–45.

***** Count Basie 1943–1945**
Classics 801 *Similar to above discs, except add Buck Clayton, Al Stearns, Joe Newman (t), Lucky Thompson (ts), Jack Washington (bs), Shadow Wilson (d).* 7/43–1/45.

Splendidly remastered in very crisp sound, these studio 'alternatives' to AFRS Jubilee show broadcasts give a useful impression of a transitional Basie band. Buddy Rich and Illinois Jacquet replace Jones and Young on some tracks, and the brass section is largely different from the previous commercial studio tracks. There are some good charts here – Andy Gibson's freshly paced 'Andy's Blues', Clayton's excellent 'Avenue C' and Tab Smith's 'Harvard Blues', one of the best of the later Columbias, with a repeat performance of the *tour de force* vocal by Jimmy Rushing – and many of the soloists sound in unusually lively form.

The Music & Arts disc collects another set of transcriptions. There is a handful of rarities, including 'Dance Of The Gremlins', but plenty of familiar things to please Basie's core audience. Reproduction varies rather wildly, but the best tracks sound clear and strong.

Classics pick up their story again with a group of V-Discs and one Columbia session. This covers some of the VJC material (below) and, as usual, no sources are listed for the transfers.

*****(*) Beaver Junction**
Vintage Jazz Classics VJC-CD-1018 *As above, except add Karl George (t), J.J Johnson (tb), Joe Marshall (d).* 44–46.

More Jubilee and V-Disc material, in excellent shape and featuring all the strengths of the mid-1940s band. Similar material to the above, but there are one or two previously unavailable tracks and, with all the remastering done from clean glass acetates, the sound is uncommonly bright and clear.

***** Count Basie And His Orchestra – 1944**
Circle CCD-60 *Similar to above.* 1/44.

Cut in a single three-hour session, these are 16 transcriptions from the Lang–Worth service. Another solid Basie session with staples from his then current book, three rather gooey ballads sung by Earl Warren and only two features for Rushing. Hardly essential, but the sound of the transcriptions is exceptionally clear and fresh.

****(*) Count Basie And His Orchestra 1944 & 1945**
Circle CCD-130 *Similar to above.* 1/44–2/45.

Another 17 transcriptions, remastered in very good sound. Too many vocals, perhaps, even though two of them are by Rushing, and jazz survives only in a couple of unremarkable Dicky Wells tunes, Earl Warren's predictable 'Rockin' The Blues' and Al Killian's boisterous 'Let's Jump'.

****(*) Count Basie 1945–1946**
Classics 934 *Basie; Harry 'Sweets' Edison, Al Killian, Joe Newman, Ed Lewis, Karl George, Emmett Berry, Snooky Young (t); Dicky Wells, Ed Donnelly, Eli Robinson, Louis Taylor, J.J Johnson (tb); Jimmy Powell, Earl Warren, Preston Love, George Dorsey (as); Buddy Tate, Illinois Jacquet, Lucky Thompson (ts); Rudy Rutherford (bs, cl); Freddie Green (g); Rodney Richardson (b); Shadow Wilson (d); Jimmy Rushing, Lynne Sherman, Taps Miller (v); strings.* 2/45–2/46.

Rather a thin bunch of Basie – one scratchy-sounding session for V-Disc, a misguided date for strings and three other Columbia with some particularly undistinguished titles among them. The studio version of Clayton's 'Avenue C' is the main point of interest.

***** Brand New Wagon**
RCA Bluebird ND 82292 *Basie; Harry 'Sweets' Edison, Ed Lewis, Emmett Berry, Snooky Young (t); Bill Johnson, Ted Donnelly, George Matthews, Dicky Wells, George Simon, George Washington, Eli Robinson (tb); Preston Love, Rudy Rutherford, C.Q Price (as); Paul Gonsalves, Buddy Tate (ts); Jack Washington (bs); Freddie Green (g); Walter Page (b); Jo Jones (d); Jimmy Rushing (v).* 1–12/47.

***** Count Basie 1947**
Classics 1018 *As above, except add Bob Bailey (v).* 5–12/47.

Basie signed a three-year contract with Victor in 1947, and the results have usually been regarded as something of a low point in his discography. But this set of 21 tracks from that initial year presents some good Basie performances, even if they show little sign of any marked change from the formula that had been enveloping the orchestra over the previous seven years. Gonsalves, seldom remembered as a Basieite, turns in some strong solos, 'Swingin' The Blues' and 'Basie's Basement' trim the band down to a small group without losing any impact, and there is the usual ration of features for Jimmy Rushing, always worth hearing. The sound hasn't been best served by the NoNoise process of remastering but will suffice.

The Classics disc covers the same ground but includes some tracks which the Bluebird set skips – not always to the listener's advantage, since they include fluff like Bob Bailey's feature on 'Blue And Sentimental'. But Basie collectors will welcome the complete approach, and the transfers seem respectable.

***** Shoutin' Blues**
RCA Bluebird 07863 66158 2 *Basie; Harry 'Sweets' Edison, Emmett Berry, Clark Terry, Gerald Wilson, Jimmy Nottingham (t); Ted Donnelly, Dicky Wells, George Matthews, Melba Liston (tb); C.Q Price, Earl Warren (as); Paul Gonsalves, Weasel Parker, George Auld (ts); Gene Ammons (ts, bs); Jack Washington (bs); Freddie Green (g); Singleton Palmer, Al McKibbon (b); Butch Ballard, Gus Johnson (d); Jimmy Rushing, Billy Valentine, Taps Miller, Google Eyes (v).* 4/49–2/50.

The final sessions before Basie disbanded the orchestra in 1950. Bop sidles into some of the arrangements here, notably 'Slider' and 'Normania', and it gives Basie's men no trouble – after all, this was one of the most accomplished of bands. There is some dreadful stuff as far as material is concerned, and it's only on the various permutations of the blues that the music settles down and grooves. Good moments for Wells, Edison and Rushing, as ever, and mostly fine remastering.

***** Count Basie**
Columbia 467143-2 *As appropriate discs above, plus Clark Terry (t), Buddy DeFranco (cl), Charlie Rouse, Wardell Gray (ts), Jimmy Lewis (b), Buddy Rich (d).* 8/39–11/50.

A solid compilation of Basie's Columbia years, although the later selections are a peculiar lot – 'For The Good Of Your Country' is a strange one, and the final four tracks by the 1950 small group with Terry, DeFranco, Rouse and Chaloff don't really belong, interesting though they are.

***** Americans In Sweden Vol. 1**
Tax CD 3701-2 *Basie; Reunald Jones, Joe Wilder, Wendell Culley, Joe Newman (t); Bill Hughes, Henry Coker, Benny Powell (tb); Marshal Royal (as, cl); Ernie Wilkins (as, ts); Frank Wess (ts, f); Frank Foster (ts); Charlie Fowlkes (bs); Freddie Green (g); Eddie Jones (b); Gus Johnson (d).* 3/54.

***** Americans In Sweden Vol. 2**
Tax CD 3702-2 *As above.* 3/54.

**** Class Of '54**
Black Lion BLCD 760924 *As above, except Thad Jones (t) replaces Wilder.* 9/54.

Basie had been obliged to work with an octet rather than a full band in 1950–51, but he put a new orchestra together the following year, and from then on he always remained in charge of a big band. It was the start of the 'modern' Basie era. By taking arrangements from a new team, of whom the most important was Neal Hefti, Basie made the most of a formidable new reed section, trumpets that streamlined the old Basie fire with absolute precision, and the first of a line of effusive drummers, Gus Johnson. The new soloists were showstoppers, but in a rather hard, sometimes brittle way, and Basie's belief in the primacy of the riff now led inexorably to arrangements that had screaming brass piled on top of crooning reeds on top of thunderous drums: it was a fearsome and in its way very exciting effect.

The two Tax CDs come from what was Basie's first European tour, and the sound is very good for the period, with only a few balance problems for the rhythm section: the brass and reeds come through very strikingly. In set-pieces like Foster's flag-waving solo on 'Jumpin' At The Woodside', Hefti's glittering charts for 'Fancy Meeting You' and 'Two Franks', and similarly punchy efforts by John Mandel and Buster Harding, all the gusto of the new Basie band comes powering through. The Black Lion CD mixed tracks by a nonet drawn from the band and others from a 1954 radio concert, though the sound is much less attractive on this disc, and the Tax CDs give a much better impression of the band as it then was.

***** April In Paris**
Verve 521402-2 *Basie; Reunald Jones, Thad Jones, Joe Newman, Wendell Culley (t); Benny Powell, Henry Coker, Matthew Gee (tb); Marshal Royal (cl, as); Bill Graham (as); Frank Wess (ts, f); Frank Foster (ts); Charlie Fowlkes (bs); Freddie Green (g); Eddie Jones (b); Sonny Payne (d); Joe Williams (v).* 1/56.

***** Basie In London**
Verve 833805-2 *As above.* 9/56.

****** Count Basie Swings, Joe Williams Sings**
Verve 519852-2 *As above, except Bill Hughes (tb) replaces Gee.* 7/55–6/56.

*****(*) The Greatest!!**
Verve 833774-2 *As above.* 57.

****(*) Count Basie At Newport**
Verve 833776-2 *As above, except add Roy Eldridge (t), Illinois Jacquet, Lester Young (ts), Jo Jones (d), Jimmy Rushing (v).* 7/57.

Facsimile editions of some of the most significant of Basie's Verve albums from the 1950s – *Dance Session No. 1* and *No. 2*, and *The Band Of Distinction* – have yet to appear. Of the three originals now on CD, *April In Paris* and *Basie In London* are typical Basie fare of the period: bustling charts, leathery solos and pinpoint timing. The new Master Edition of *April In Paris* has been quite handsomely restored in sonic terms and is lengthened by seven alternative takes – none of them especially revealing. *At Newport* is a fun reunion with some of Basie's old sidemen (though Young sounds as wayward as he usually then was) and features Eldridge going several miles over the top on 'One O'Clock Jump'. The outstanding albums are probably the two featuring Joe Williams. The debut appearance on 519852-2 is a classic of big-band singing: the original versions of 'Alright, OK, You Win', 'Every Day I Have The Blues' and 'In The Evening', material on which Williams made his name, still have terrific zip and élan, and the remastered sound has real clout. *The Greatest!!* concentrates on standards but is another faultless performance. Rich-toned, as oleaginous as Billy Eckstine could be, yet with a feeling for the blues which at least came some way near the irreplaceable Rushing, Williams's smoothness and debonair manner fitted the new Basie band almost perfectly.

****** The Complete Atomic Mr Basie**
Roulette 793273-2 *Basie; Joe Newman, Thad Jones, Wendell Culley, Snooky Young (t); Benny Powell, Henry Coker, Al Grey (tb); Marshal Royal, Frank Wess (as); Eddie 'Lockjaw' Davis, Frank Foster (ts); Charlie Fowlkes (bs); Freddie Green (g); Eddie Jones (b); Sonny Payne (d).* 10/57.

***** Basie Swings, Bennett Sings**
Roulette 93899-2 *As above, except add Ralph Sharon (p), Tony Bennett (v); George Duvivier (b) replaces Jones.* 1/59.

***** The Best Of Count Basie – The Roulette Years**
Roulette 97969 *Similar to above.* 57–62.

***** Atomic Swing**
Roulette 97871 *Similar to above.* 57–62.

Basie opened his contract for Roulette with the great show-stopping album that this band had in it, *The Atomic Mr Basie* (complete with mushroom cloud on the cover, a Cold War classic). It might be the last great Basie album. He had Neal Hefti (who already had scored most of the hottest numbers in the band's recent book) do the whole record, and Hefti's zesty, machine-tooled scoring reached its apogee in 'The Kid From Red Bank', 'Flight Of The Foo Birds', 'Splanky' and the rest. But it also had a guest soloist in the great Lockjaw Davis, whose splenetic outbursts gave just the right fillip to what might otherwise have been a too cut-and-dried effort. The record has been reissued in its full form, properly remastered (early pressings were flawed), with all the available extra tracks.

Thereafter, the Roulette albums become as prosaic and sensible as the rest of Basie's latter-day output. The meeting with Tony Bennett will please Bennett fans more than Basie admirers, but it's a very enjoyable record. The rest of the Roulette catalogue seems to have disappeared for now, but there are two different best-ofs available. *Atomic Swing* has 13 tracks, *The Best Of Count Basie* a more generous 20, though the former has the slightly superior sound. The original *Atomic* album, though, ought to suffice as a representative sample.

*****(*) Count On The Coast Vol. 1**

Phontastic PHONT CD 7574 *Basie; Snooky Young, Thad Jones, Wendell Culley, Joe Newman (t); Benny Powell, Henry Coker, Al Grey (tb); Frank Wess (as, f); Billy Mitchell, Frank Foster (ts); Charlie Fowlkes (bs); Freddie Green (g); Eddie Jones (b); Sonny Payne (d); Joe Williams (v).* 6–7/58.

*****(*) Count On The Coast Vol. 2**

Phontastic PHONT CD 7575 *As above.* 6–7/58.

***** Basie's Golden '58**

Phontastic PHONT NCD 8839 *As above.* 6–7/58.

***** Fresno, California**

Jazz Unlimited JUCD 2039 *As above.* 4/59.

*****(*) Live 1958–59**

Status STCD 110 *As above, except add John Anderson (t), Marshal Royal (as, cl).* 6/58–11/59.

These are exceptionally strong live recordings. The three Phontastic CDs and the Status disc are all in such clear and powerful sound that the recordings belie their age; and Basie's men sound in particularly muscular and good-humoured form, especially on the Status set, which includes a few uncommon parts of the Basie repertoire and some dry runs for the Roulette sessions that were coming up. Foster is a titan among the soloists, but Powell, Wess and Newman also have their moments, and Williams is very good on the Phontastic discs; *Basie's Golden '58* carries on the tradition of the two earlier discs. The date in Fresno caught another good one by the band, though the way the applause has been trimmed out you'd hardly know there was any encouragement for them. Sound is a little harsh, as if brightened from a dull master-tape, but listenable.

***** Count Basie And The Kansas City Seven**

Impulse! 12022 *Basie; Thad Jones (t); Eric Dixon (ts, cl, f); Frank Foster (ts, cl); Frank Wess (f); Eddie Jones (b); Sonny Payne (d).* 3/62.

A small-group one-off for Impulse!, this had the ingredients for a classic – Basie returning to a combo setting, the material ('Shoe Shine Boy', 'Lady Be Good') recalling the earliest recordings with Lester Young, and a congenial gathering of Basieites ready to give of their best. But Bob Thiele's overly cute production seems to have smothered all the spontaneity out of the date, there's too much flute and not enough saxophone, and apart from 'Lady Be Good' the music actually sounds formulaic. Still some nice moments, but a missed opportunity.

***** Lil' Ol' Groovemaker ... Basie!**

Verve 821799-2 *Basie; Don Rader, Sonny Cohn, Fip Ricard, Al Aarons (t); Benny Powell, Grover Mitchell, Henry Coker, Urbie Green (tb); Marshal Royal, Frank Wess, Frank Foster, Eric Dixon, Charlie Fowlkes (reeds); Freddie Green (g); Buddy Catlett (b); Sonny Payne (d).* 4/63.

**** This Time By Basie**

Reprise 45162 *As above, except add Edward Preston, Wallace Davenport, Sam Noto (t), Henderson Chambers, Al Grey, Bill Hughes, Gordon Thomas (tb), Eddie 'Lockjaw' Davis, Bobby Plater (reeds), Wyatt Ruther (b), Louie Bellson (d), Leon Thomas (v).* 1/63–12/64.

***** More Hits Of The Fifties And Sixties**

Verve 519849-2 *Similar to above discs.* 4/63–1/65.

***** Our Shining Hour**

Verve 837446-2 *Probably similar to above, except add Sammy Davis Jr (v).* 65.

**** Basie's Beatle Bag**

Verve 557455-2 *Similar to above.* 66.

Basie was at a low ebb in the mid-1960s, and record producers were probably asking themselves what to do with such a venerable and prolific recording artist. *This Time By Basie* is one of the misguided attempts to make the Count go pop. Competent, but any decent radio orchestra could have done just as good a job. *Our Shining Hour* is more showbiz in a collaboration with Sammy Davis, but the singer plays up to the occasion so much – and elevates the band in doing so – that it's hard not to enjoy. *Basie In Sweden* is a late Roulette disc and quite a good one. *Lil' Ol' Groovemaker* is another (and this time a rather better) set of Quincy Jones charts, with 'Pleasingly Plump' turning out to be a rather gracious ballad and the swingers taking off effectively. *More Hits* proves to be a series of covers of Frank Sinatra successes and, though the band is contained within precise arrangements and largely inflexible parts, the delivery is sometimes stunningly achieved. One of the better dates from a largely undistinguished period. We think that the less said about *Basie's Beatle Bag*, the better.

***** Verve Jazz Masters: Count Basie**

Verve 519819-2 *As appropriate discs above.* 8/54–10/65.

Old favourites and the obvious choices from Basie's Verve tenure – 'April In Paris', 'Shiny Stockings', 'Sent For You Yesterday' and 13 more.

***** Straight Ahead**

GRP Chessmates 051822-2 *Basie; Al Aarons, Oscar Brashear, Gene Coe, George Cohn (t); Dick Boone, Steve Galloway, Bill Hughes, Grover Mitchell (tb); Bobby Plater (as, f); Marshal Royal (as); Eddie 'Lockjaw' Davis (ts); Eric Dixon (ts, f); Charlie Fowlkes (bs); Freddie Green (g); Norman Kennan (b); Harold Jones (d).* 10/68.

Originally released on Dot, this is a stray entry from the late '60s, entirely written and arranged by Sammy Nestico. 'Everything he does fits the band so well,' says Basie in the sleeve-notes, and it's too true: in other words, Nestico comes out as just another faceless Basie hack. That said, the band seem to like the situation, and there are some spirited solos along with the usual machine-like playing.

***** Basie Jam**

Pablo 2310-718 *Basie; Harry 'Sweets' Edison (t); J.J Johnson (tb); Eddie 'Lockjaw' Davis (ts); Zoot Sims (ts); Irving Ashby (g); Ray Brown (b); Louie Bellson (d).* 12/73.

***** The Bosses**

Original Jazz Classics OJC 821 *Basie; Harry 'Sweets' Edison (t); J.J Johnson (tb); Eddie 'Lockjaw' Davis, Zoot Sims (ts); Irving Ashby (g); Ray Brown (b); Louie Bellson (d); Joe Turner (v).* 12/73.

***** For The First Time**

Pablo 2310-712 *Basie; Ray Brown (b); Louie Bellson (d).* 5/74.

***** For The Second Time**

Original Jazz Classics OJC 600 *As above.* 8/75.

***** Satch And Josh**

Original Jazz Classics OJC 959 *Basie; Oscar Peterson (p); Freddie Green (g); Ray Brown (b); Louie Bellson (d).* 12/74.

*****(*) Basie & Zoot**

Original Jazz Classics OJC 822 *Basie; Zoot Sims (ts); John Heard (b); Louie Bellson (d).* 4/75.

**** Jam Session At Montreux 1975**

Original Jazz Classics OJC 933 *Basie; Roy Eldridge (t); Johnny Griffin (ts); Milt Jackson (vib); Niels-Henning Orsted Pedersen (b); Louie Bellson (d).* 7/75.

***** Basie Big Band**

Pablo 2310-756 *Basie; Pete Minger, Frank Szabo, Dave Stahl, Bob Mitchell, Sonny Cohn (t); Al Grey, Curtis Fuller, Bill Hughes, Mel Wanzo (tb); Bobby Plater (as, f); Danny Turner (as); Eric Dixon, Jimmy Forrest (ts); Charlie Fowlkes (bs); Freddie Green (g); John Duke (b); Butch Miles (d).* 8/75.

****(*) Basie And Friends**

Pablo 2310-925 *Basie; Oscar Peterson (p); Freddie Green (g); Ray Brown, John Heard, Niels-Henning Orsted Pedersen (b); Louie Bellson (d).* 12/74–11/81.

Norman Granz signed Basie to his new Pablo label and began taking down albums more prolifically than ever before, some three dozen in the last ten years of the bandleader's life. The old wizard was effectively reborn as a recording artist. Eight new albums were set down in the first 18 months. *The Bosses* was a fine beginning, setting Basie alongside Joe Turner, who is in mellow but not reticent mood: there are too many remakes of his old hits here, but Turner and Basie make a magisterial combination, and the horns aren't too intrusive. *Basie Jam* was the first and perhaps the best of a series of studio jam sessions. The formula is, let it be said, predictable: fast blues, slow blues, fast blues, slow blues ... sort-of-fast blues. Basie plays as minimally as he ever has, but he presides grandly from the rear, and there are entertaining cameos from Johnson, Sims and Davis. The *Montreux Jam* is a bore, with Eldridge past his best and the others simply going on too long, while *Basie Big Band* was his first set for Pablo with the regular orchestra. This was a more than encouraging start. Sam Nestico, who wrote all nine charts, offered no radical departures from the Basie method, but at least he had had time to settle in since the *Straight Ahead* session and was starting to look for more interesting harmonies and section colours. There were some fine players in the band again: Jimmy Forrest, Bobby Mitchell, Curtis Fuller. Butch Miles, the least self-effacing of Basie's drummers, had also arrived, but was so far behaving, and Granz's dry studio sound suited the clean and direct lines rather well.

As far as Basie the pianist went, he made his first trio album in *For The First Time* (a formula repeated on *For The Second Time*) and traded licks with Oscar Peterson, his stylistic opposite, in the amusing *Satch And Josh*. Neither record was exactly a revelation, since Basie basically carried on in the style he'd played in for the last 40 years, but as fresh areas of work after 25 years of making the same kind of record, it must have been invigorating; and he plays as if it was. *Basie And Friends* is a collection of out-takes from various sessions, mainly made in this period, though a couple date from later on.

One of the best of all of Basie's Pablos is the meeting with Zoot Sims on *Basie & Zoot*. It's almost worth having just for the snorting blues choruses they put down on 'Hardav'. Basie gets a bit too ripe when he turns to the organ for a wallow through 'I Surrender Dear' but Sims always has a swinging line to put down, and this was a well-made match.

***** I Told You So**

Original Jazz Classics OJC 824 *As above, except John Thomas, Jack Feierman (t) replace Szabo and Stahl.* 1/76.

***** Basie Jam No. 2**

Original Jazz Classics OJC 631 *Basie; Clark Terry (t); Al Grey (tb); Benny Carter (as); Eddie 'Lockjaw' Davis (ts); Joe Pass (g); John Heard (b); Louie Bellson (d).* 5/76.

****(*) Basie Jam No. 3**

Original Jazz Classics OJC 687 *As above.* 5/76.

****(*) Prime Time**

Pablo 2310-797 *Basie; Pete Minger, Lyn Biviano, Bob Mitchell, Sonny Cohn (t); Al Grey, Curtis Fuller, Bill Hughes, Mel Wanzo (tb); Danny Turner, Bobby Plater (as); Jimmy Forrest, Eric Dixon (ts); Charlie Fowlkes (bs); Nat Pierce (p); Freddie Green (g); John Duke (b); Butch Miles (d).* 1/77.

**** Montreux '77**

Original Jazz Classics OJC 377 *As above, except Waymon Reed (t), Dennis Wilson (tb) replace Minger and Fuller.* 7/77.

***** Jam Montreux '77**

Original Jazz Classics OJC 379 *Basie; Roy Eldridge (t); Vic Dickenson, Al Grey (tb); Benny Carter (as); Zoot Sims (ts); Ray Brown (b); Jimmie Smith (d).* 7/77.

***** Kansas City Five**

Original Jazz Classics OJC 888 *Basie; Milt Jackson (vib); Joe Pass (g); John Heard (b); Louie Bellson (d).* 1/77.

***** Satch And Josh ... Again**

Original Jazz Classics OJC 960 *Basie; Oscar Peterson (p); John Heard (b); Louie Bellson (d).* 9/77.

Basie continued his Pablo run with a steady stream of solid, good or at least credible albums. The two further *Basie Jam* albums are lesser editions of the previous set, though, like all such records, they have a moment or two when things start happening. Carter and Davis are the most reliable soloists on hand. *I Told You So* and *Prime Time* were the second and third full-orchestra albums for Pablo and, while the first one is solid, the second misfires a few times: 'Bundle O'Funk' was exactly the kind of modishness that Basie's return to traditionalism should have eschewed, and some of the soloists sound tired. But it's better than the desperately routine live set from Montreux which wanders joylessly through a stale Basie set.

The small-band jam from the same year is much better: Carter's gorgeous solo on 'These Foolish Things', Sims wherever he plays, and even the by-now-unreliable Eldridge all make something good out of it. The second *Satch And Josh* album follows the same sort of pattern as the first and takes much of its energy from the grooving beat laid down by Heard and Bellson: 'Home Run', for instance, is deliciously spry and merry. *Kansas City Five* sets the unpretentious pairing of Basie and Jackson on their inevitable programme of blues and jazz chestnuts so old they ought to be roasted to a crisp by now. The veteran campaigners still find a wrinkle or two. Especially warm: 'Frog's Blues'.

***** Live In Japan '78**

Pablo 2308-246 *Basie; Pete Minger, Sonny Cohn, Nolan Smith, Waymon Reed (t); Mel Wanzo, Bill Hughes, Dennis Wilson, Alonzo Wesley (tb); Bobby Plater, Danny Turner (as); Eric Dixon (ts, f); Kenny Hing (ts); Charlie Fowlkes (bs); Freddie Green (g); John Clayton (b); Butch Miles (d).* 5/78.

***** Night Rider**

Original Jazz Classics OJC 688 *Basie; Oscar Peterson (p); John Heard (bb); Louie Bellson (d).* 2/78.

***** The Timekeepers**

Original Jazz Classics OJC 790 *As above.* 2/78.

***** Yessir, That's My Baby**

Pablo 2310-923 *As above.* 2/78.

***** On the Road**

Original Jazz Classics OJC 854 *Basie; Pete Minger, Sonny Cohn, Paul Cohen, Raymond Brown (t); Booty Wood, Bill Hughes, Mel Wanzo, Dennis Wilson (tb); Charlie Fowlkes, Eric Dixon, Bobby Plater, Danny Turner, Kenny Hing (reeds); Freddie Green (g); Keter Betts (b); Mickey Roker (d).* 7/79.

***** Get Together**

Pablo 2310-924 *Basie; Clark Terry (t, flhn); Harry 'Sweets' Edison (t); Budd Johnson (ts, bs); Eddie 'Lockjaw' Davis (ts); Freddie Green (g); John Clayton (b); Gus Johnson (d).* 9/79.

The Japanese concert must have been a happy experience for the band, since they sound in excellent spirits and familiar charts take on a springier life. The sound is unfortunately slightly constricted and certainly isn't as wide-bodied as the punchy crescendos secured on *On The Road*, which is another of the better live albums from this stage of Basie's career. The sheer wallop of 'Wind Machine' and 'Splanky' sums up the kind of unhindered and creaseless power that Basie's orchestra worked to secure and, while it says little of any personal nature, taken a few tracks at a time it certainly knocks the listener over. The three albums with Peterson are good enough on their own terms, but anyone who has either of the earlier discs won't find anything different here. Peterson carries most of the weight, and Basie answers with his patented right-hand fills and occasional brow-furrowing left-hand chords. If anything makes the music happen, though, it's again the exemplary swing of Heard and Bellson. *Get Together* is yet another small-group jam on a few old favourites, but the presence of the great Budd Johnson adds a few more felicitous moments than usual.

***** Kansas City Seven**

Original Jazz Classics OJC 690 *Basie; Freddie Hubbard (t); J.J Johnson (tb); Eddie 'Lockjaw' Davis (ts); Joe Pass (g); John Heard (b); Jake Hanna (d).* 4/80.

****(*) Kansas City Shout**

Pablo 2310-859 *Basie; Pete Minger, Sonny Cohn, Dale Carley, Dave Stahl (t); Booty Wood, Bill Hughes, Dennis Wilson, Grover Mitchell, Dennis Rowland (tb); Eddie Vinson (as, v); Eric Dixon, Bobby Plater (as); Danny Turner, Kenny Hing (ts); John Williams (bs); Freddie Green (g); Cleveland Eaton (b); Duffy Jackson (d); Joe Turner (v).* 4/80.

***** Warm Breeze**

Original Jazz Classics OJC 994 *As above, except add Bob Summers, Willie Cook, Harry 'Sweets' Edison, Frank Szabo (t), Harold Jones, Gregg Field (d); omit Rowland, Stahl, Minger.* 9/81.

***** Farmers Market Barbecue**

Original Jazz Classics OJC 732 *As above, except Chris Albert (t), James Leary (b) replace Eaton, Jackson, Vinson, Jones and Turner.* 5/82.

***** Me And You**

Original Jazz Classics OJC 906 *As above, except Steve Furtado, Frank Szabo (t), Eric Schneider (ts), Chris Woods (as), Dennis Mackrel (d) replace Albert, Hing, Dixon, Plater, Field.* 2/83.

****(*) 88 Basie Street**

Pablo 2310-901 *As above.* 5/83.

****(*) Fancy Pants**

Pablo 2310-920 *As above, except Jim Crawford (t) replaces Furtado.* 12/83.

***** Kansas City Six**

Original Jazz Classics OJC 449 *Basie; Willie Cook (t); Eddie Vinson (as, v); Joe Pass (g); Niels-Henning Orsted Pedersen (b); Louie Bellson (d).* 11/81.

***** Mostly Blues ... And Some Others**

Pablo 2310-919 *Basie; Snooky Young (t); Eddie 'Lockjaw' Davis (ts); Joe Pass, Freddie Green (g); John Heard (b); Roy McCurdy (d).* 6/83.

Basie carried on, regardless of encroaching arthritis, eventually working the stage from a wheelchair. The big-band records from this patch are some of his best Pablos, for the simple reason that Granz was recording the band to more telling effect: studio mixes had improved, the weight and balance of the orchestra came through more smoothly and arrived with a bigger punch and, since those virtues counted for more with Basie than did individual solos or any other idiosyncrasy, the band just sounded bigger and better. The arrangements on the final albums are shared among a number of hands. Sam Nestico was again responsible for most of *Warm Breeze* and *Fancy Pants*, while other bandmembers contributed to the other three discs, which also featured numbers by Ernie Wilkins and Basie himself. *Warm Breeze* is a particularly shapely album, with Willie Cook featured on a couple of tunes, Harry 'Sweets' Edison guesting on 'How Sweet It Is' and the themes standing among Nestico's more melodic efforts. *Me And You* and *Farmers Market Barbecue* are both split between full-band and some tracks by a smaller edition of the orchestra: the latter has a splendid 'Blues For The Barbecue' and fine tenor by Kenny Hing on 'St Louis Blues', while the former includes an overripe Booty Wood solo on a dead slow 'She's Funny That Way' as well as a look all the way back to 'Moten Swing'. *88 Basie Street* and *Fancy Pants* are a little more routine, even by Basie standards, but the slickness and precision are unfaltering. *Kansas City Shout* and *Six* are fun albums with Vinson and Turner vying for attention and Basie refereeing with stately calm at the piano. But the two best records from this closing period are probably *Kansas City Seven* and *Mostly Blues ... And Some Others.* The former features a cracking line-up and, though Hubbard sometimes goes too far and Hanna's cymbals are annoyingly over-busy, it makes for some steaming music. The latter is as slow, full-flavoured and hefty as Basie seemed to want his blues to be: Pass and the imperturbable Green make a memorable combination, and Young and Davis blow things that turn out just fine. The pianist, of course, does his usual.

***** Fun Time**

Pablo 2310-945 *Basie; Sonny Cohn, Frank Szabo, Pete Minger, Dave Stahl, Bob Mitchell (t); Al Grey, Curtis Fuller, Mel Wanzo, Bill Hughes (tb); Eric Dixon, Danny Turner, Bobby Plater, Jimmy Forrest, Charlie Fowlkes (reeds); Freddie Green (g); John Duke (b); Butch Miles (d); Bill Caffey (v).* 7/75.

The first of what could have been many more Basie records yet, although if Pablo has any kind of stockpile, it currently seems to be keeping quiet about it. This is the orchestra at Montreux in 1975, a very grand edition of the band, and delivering on all cylinders. Big and clear concert sound.

***** The Best Of Count Basie**

Pablo 2405-408

***** The Best Of The Count Basie Big Band**

Pablo 2405-422

Two solid compilations from a vast trove of recordings. The first concentrates on the small groups, the second on the orchestra, and either will serve as a sampler of the later Basie.

****** The Golden Years**

Pablo 4419-2 4CD *As Pablo and OJC albums listed above.* 73–83.

His last decade on record did little to challenge the memories of his (real) golden age, and none of the original albums really stands out as a classic. So this intelligent and smilingly prepared four-disc compilation is a welcome retrieval of many of the best moments from a very prolific Indian summer in the studios and on stage. Two discs of big bands, one of small groups and one where he assists various singers. Little to argue about in the choosing, either.

***** Live At El Morocco**

Telarc CD-83312 *Mike Williams, Melton Mustafa, Derrick Gardner, Bob Ojeda (t); Mel Wanzo, Clarence Banks, Robert Trowers, Bill Hughes (tb); Danny Turner (as, picc); Manny Boyd (as, f); Kenny Hing, Doug Miller (ts, f); Frank Foster (ts); John Williams (bs, bcl); George Caldwell (p); Charlie Johnson (g); Cleveland Eaton (b); David Gibson (d).* 2/92.

***** Basie's Bag**

Telarc CD-83358 *As above.* 11/92.

Given that the big band as it stood under Basie in the final years was as sleek and hard as polished steel, the idea of a ghost band seems more plausible than an Ellington, Goodman or Herman survival group. Frank Foster worked hard to maintain the standards of the group and these records are convincing reminders of Basie's legacy, even if they don't shake the earth. The live disc is warm enough to stir the blood a little. *Basie's Bag* has a grand set-piece in the 'Count Basie Remembrance Suite' and a few solid reshuffles from the band book: Foster, by now an eminence of Basie-esque stature himself, presides with fine authority. The band is now looked after by Grover Mitchell, and their anniversary concerts at Ronnie Scott's in 1999 were very warmly received. A great institution lives on.

Larry Baskett (born 1937)

TRUMPET, FLUGELHORN, VOCAL

Worked with Brew Moore and others in San Francisco at the end of the '50s, but he took a long time-out and didn't return to playing his cool style of bop until the '80s.

***** Chalice**

A Records AL 73047 *Baskett; Randy Vincent (g); Chris Amberger (d).* 4–6/95.

***** Poor Boy Blue**

A Records AL 73086 *As above, except add Frank Phipps (euph), Harold Jones (d).* 96.

Twenty-two years is a long sabbatical, but that's how long Colorado-born Baskett managed to stay away from the music he so palpably loves. Chet Baker is the main influence on both his playing and singing, a light, breathy sound in both cases, and one that lends itself most obviously to melodic ballad treatments. Of the two discs that are available, *Chalice* is far and away the more rewarding. Baskett has a nose for good repertoire, and the inclusion of two Wayne Shorter tunes, as well as J. J. Johnson's affecting 'Lament' and Victor Herbert's 'Indian Summer', lift this out of the ordinary. The vocals are nicely integrated, and the support from Vincent and Amberger could not be faulted.

Recorded live, and with a drummer in attendance, *Poor Boy Blue* attempts a more swinging approach and, lovely as it often is, doesn't quite pull off anything very different. The combination of trumpet, euphonium, guitar and string bass is highly effective and any album that kicks off with a Sam Rivers tune ('Beatrice') and then follows up with four intelligently thought-out originals can't be bad. Baskett is probably too securely hitched to Chet's flickering star to sound anything other than derivative, but there are excellent things on both discs.

Piero Bassini (born 1952)

PIANO, KEYBOARDS

Italian pianist working in the post-bop mainstream of the local music.

****(*) Into The Blue**

Red 123218-2 *Bassini; Flavio Boltro (t); Michele Bozza (ts); Riccardo Fioravanti (b); Giampiero Prina (b).* 11/87.

****(*) Lush Life**

Splasc(h) H 341-2 *Bassini (p solo); with Erminio Cella (ky).* 6/90.

Bassini's earlier records for Red are out of print, but he plays a useful role in the quintet session, which is otherwise under no single leader. All six tunes are based round the blues and, given the plain speaking of the group, the results are inevitably sound but unexceptional, with Boltro and Bozza sounding facile rather than involving. *Lush Life* is an energetic solo album that's let down somewhat by the hard piano-sound which accentuates Bassini's already percussive, almost belligerent manner – not much of his underlying romanticism comes through, though 'Night Moon' is a composition worth saving.

***** Intensity**

Red 123266-2 *Bassini; Luca Garlaschelli (b); Ettore Fioravanti, Massimo Pintori (d).* 2/95.

***** Portrait With In**

Splasc(h) 615 *As above, except omit Pintori.* 2/97.

These trio records are a stronger statement by Bassini, though they have a schematic flavour which sometimes gets in the way of the music making a deeper impact. The Red album has titles like 'Segment', 'Interval', 'Two Chords' and so on, while the Splasc(h) date relies on a similar distancing of emotion while attempting to plumb less obvious depths. The results are impressive in a somewhat detached way. The trio play with earnest concentration, and the music feels worked-through, thought-out, while missing a degree of spontaneity that might otherwise take these discs into the top bracket. The most exceptional moment comes in Bassini's solo 'Looking At The Hills' on the Splasc(h) album, a beautiful and less deliberate meditation.

Django Bates (born 1960)

PIANO, KEYBOARDS, TENOR HORN

After stints with London bands Borderline and Zila, Bates worked with his own Human Chain and was a central player in the big band, Loose Tubes. Became an international property in the '90s, with orchestral commissions, prizes and association with the Tim Berne circle of players.

*****(*) Like Life**

Storyville STCD 4221 *Bates; Palle Bolvig, Jan Kohlin, Henrik Bolberg Pederssen, Benny Rosenfeld, Jens Winther (t, flhn); Vincent Nilsson (tb, bhn); Steen Hansen, Kjeld Ipsen (tb); Klaus Lohrer (btb); Axel Windfeld (btb, tba); Terje Aadne (frhn); Nikolaj Schultz (f, bf); Iain Ballamy, Christina Von Bulow, Tomas Franck, Michael Hove, Flemming Madsen, Uffe Markussen, Jan Zum Vorde (reeds); Nikolaj Bentzon (ky); Anders Chico Lindvall (g); Michael Mondesir, Thomas Ovesen (b); Martin France, Jonas Johansen (d); Ethan Weisgard (perc).* 3/97.

Bates was the second Briton in three years to scoop the Jazzpar Prize. Coming as he did between Geri Allen and 1998 winner Jim Hall only reinforced the honour. As always, the prize provides for a recording with the winner's own group and with the Danish Radio Jazz Orchestra. It's the orchestra that tackles the three key compositions on the disc, a central section that must represent the most concentrated and effective music of Django's career to date.

The longest single item is 'The Strange Voyage Of Donald Crowhurst', a haunting, haunted evocation of the round-the-world yachtsman who pretended to be making potentially winning progress when in fact he was doing nothing more than sailing in circles and radioing in false bearings. It may be that Crowhurst took his own life rather than be exposed. Bates turns the story into a bitter-sweet epic, a feature for his own peckhorn and for Uffe Markussen's tenor. Bracketing it are two shorter pieces, 'Misplaced Swans', which sounds like scaled-up Loose Tubes, and the anarchic 'The Importance Of Boiling Water', another horn feature and a good example of Bates's fascination with the musicality, as he expatiates on the correct procedure for making tea.

The recording also featured a special Jazzpar version of Bates's band, Delightful Precipice, bringing in the estimable Ballamy, who solos beautifully on 'Tightrope' (on alto), 'The Loneliness Of Being Right' and the more skittish 'Armchair March' (both on soprano). Other Britons who made the trip were bassist Mondesir and drummer France. One suspects the DRJO may have found Bates's charts a little wayward; some of the playing is stiff and 'correct', and there is an immediate loosening of tension on the Delightful Precipice tracks. The writing is as extraordinary as ever, though, and it is that, and the Crowhurst piece in particular, which makes this such a special album.

*****(*) Quiet Nights**

Screwgun screwu 70007 *Bates; Iain Ballamy (sax, bass hca, lipo-sax); Michael Mondesir (b); Martin France (d, perc); Josefine Crønholm (v).* 98.

A standards album seemed a good bet at some point in the near future, but it was a racing certainty that a Django Bates solo album wasn't going to be a run-of-the-mill affair. 'Hi Lilli Hi Lo' segues into an abstract 'Solitude', with Ellington's opening chords played on a 'prepared' piano, accompanied by Martin France's wooden percussion and what we take to be Ballamy's lipo-sax. Two originals, 'And The Mermaid Laughed' and 'Is There Anyone Up There?', are idiosyncratic Batesian soundscapes. The opening 'Speak Low' reveals Crønholm's skills as a standards singer. Later, on Jobim's 'Quiet Nights Of Quiet Night Stars' and 'Solitude', she is required to sing in a deadened monotone. 'Like Someone In Love' begins with electronic squawks, settles into a version Jimmy Van Heusen might just have recognized, before exploding into a punkish thrash and then vanishing in a sad repetition of the hook down a phone line. Django is even further off-mike on 'Over The Rainbow', a faraway, offstage vocal amid the birdsong and Sibelius chords.

Weighing in light at less than 45 minutes, *Quiet Nights* is nevertheless near perfectly pitched, a clever, wry album full of unexpected twists and turns and some full-on beauty as well.

Alvin Batiste (born 1937)

CLARINET

A New Orleans man, Batiste is a modernist with deep roots. He played with Ornette Coleman in the 1950s but was little recorded, spending much of his time teaching in Baton Rouge. Not until the '80s was he given any serious opportunities to record. He was also part of the Clarinet Summit group organized by David Murray.

*****(*) Bayou Magic**

India Navigation IN1069 *Batiste; Emile Vinette, Maynard Batiste (p); Chris Severen (b); Herman Jackson (d).* 88.

Whatever attention Don Byron and others may have garnered, Batiste – along with John Carter – was the real architect of the clarinet in any avant-garde jazz environment. His mere handful of recordings have told against any wider reputation in the music, but this disc goes some way to establishing his name beyond the circles he teaches in. *Bayou Magic* is a rather extraordinary record which seems to come from nowhere as a manifesto. Batiste tackles a programme that covers bop, folk and even systems music: the uncredited synthesizer on 'Venus Flow' partners a clarinet line that sounds amazingly close to minimalist composition. The title-piece is a bebop fantasy of brilliant colour, but the exceptional piece is 'Picou', presumably a tribute to that clarinet master and an example of old roots flowering into an extremist improvisation. Batiste's sound is rather unlovely – he gets little of the woodiness of some players, bypasses the chalumeau timbres and prefers a pinched, exhortative approach – and that makes the standards 'I Want To Talk About You' and 'A Child Is Born' less impressive. But his playing has a baronial authority that invests his solos with compelling weight and intensity. Problematically, the studio sound is unacceptably flat, reducing Jackson's drums to mere boxes, and piano and bass are no more than competent. Otherwise, a remarkable record. Batiste has seemingly made only one disc since, a set for Columbia now out of print, and his absence is much regretted.

Milton Batiste (born 1934)

TRUMPET, FLUGELHORN, VOCAL

Another New Orleans man, Batiste played in R&B groups in the 1950s and has listened carefully to trumpet players of several jazz generations. But he remains primarily a traditional player.

***** Milton Batiste With The Rue Conti Jazz Band**

Lake LACD31 *Batiste; Mike Peters (t); Mick Burns (tb, v); George Berry (cl, as, ts); Andy Young (bj, d); Terry Knight (b); Jim Young (tba); Ron Darby (d); Paul Adams (perc).* 3/93.

Batiste is a New Orleans maverick. His repertoire is right in the New Orleans trad pocket but, with Clifford Brown as a major influence and an upbringing in R&B, he is scarcely a conventional Louisiana brassman. Unpredictable rips and squashed notes mark his style but he can also play controlled, severe trumpet, as on 'In The State Of Blues'. He was captured in the middle of a British tour with the local Rue Conti group and, while the band sometimes stumble more than is warranted, the playing is spirited and raffishly hot. There are one or two overworked pieces, fresh though Batiste sounds on them; but surprises like Dudu Pukwana's 'Tula Sana' take up the slack. At least British trad is far better served now by modern recording than it ever was in the past: the mix is tough and vibrant without losing that certain griminess which this music lives by.

Steffano Battaglia (born 1966)

PIANO

Born in Milan, Battaglia studied the classical piano literature before turning to jazz, moving between free playing and post-bop structure.

***** Auryn**

Splasc(h) H 161-2 *Battaglia; Paolino Dalla Porta (b); Manhu Roche (d).* 5/88.

*****(*) Explore**

Splasc(h) H 304-2 *Battaglia; Tony Oxley (d).* 2/90.

*****(*) Confession**

Splasc(h) H 344-2 *Battaglia; Paolino Dalla Porta (b); Roberto Gatto (d).* 3/91.

Battaglia is a formidable young player from Italy's impressive contemporary movement. His first album for Splasc(h), *Things Ain't What They Used To Be*, has yet to appear on CD, but the programme of original material on *Auryn* is a reasonable place to start: the rubato structure of 'The Real Meaning (Of The Blues)' and the Jarrett-like melodies elsewhere are vehicles for full-blooded and essentially romantic improvisations, though sometimes one feels they aren't really going anywhere much. The two later discs suggest a wider range of interests, starting with the unexpected meeting with Oxley. Most of the duo pieces on *Explore* are quite brief and contained, and structurally there's little sense of anything but careful preparation; yet spontaneity runs all through the music, whether in full-tilt, crashing interplay with the drummer or in small-voiced dialogue which shows great sensitivity. *Confession* is a much more closely developed trio music than that of his earlier releases, all three men taking virtually equal roles in a triologue that they sustain with few problems over the course of several very long tracks. These are distinctive and worth seeking out.

***** Bill Evans Compositions Vol. One**

Splasc(h) H 400-2 *Battaglia; Paolino Dalla Porta (b); Aldo Romano (d).* 12/92.

***** Bill Evans Compositions Vol. Two**

Splasc(h) 410-2 *As above.* 12/92.

The relatively small number of direct homages to Evans – as compared with the countless ones to Monk or Ellington – hints at the difficulty of getting inside the skin of his music, as opposed to decorating its surface. Battaglia looks to celebrate rather than scrutinize, and he sounds fully at ease on the likes of 'Five', 'Loose Bloose' and 'Nardis'. But when it comes to 'Time Remembered' or 'My Bells', the luminosity of the originals is what one thinks of, as charmingly as Battaglia plays.

***** Life Of A Petal**

Splasc(h) 422 *Battaglia (p solo).* 5/93.

*****(*) Baptism**

Splasc(h) 417 *Battaglia (p solo).* 12/93.

*****(*) Sulphur**

Splasc(h) 430 *Battaglia; Paolino Dalla Porta (b); Tony Oxley (d).* 10/93.

***(*) **Unknown Flames**

Splasc(h) 471/2 2CD *As above, except Roberto Gatto (d) replaces Oxley.* 7/95.

The solo records are interesting if rarefied. Battaglia doesn't amble unduly – a dozen pieces are dispatched inside an hour on the first set – but these miniatures often seem to be seeking an individual point that never arrives. There are some clever touches in 'Etude', 'Recitative' and 'Blowed' which would stand expansion within a trio format; but the title-piece is a particularly lyrical solo that stands on its own. *Baptism* pursues a similar path, and some of it offers a discrete viewpoint of the piano tradition, in pieces such as 'Tristano'. But the pyrotechnic cycles of 'Observe' and the stark spaces of 'Requiem Pour Renée Daumal' are the work of a very singular imagination altogether.

Sulphur is a rematch with Tony Oxley, this time with Dalla Porta also on hand. Battaglia meets Oxley on his own terms, and damping the strings or otherwise subverting his natural romanticism doesn't seem to trouble him, even if the blossoming 'Science Of The Heart' sounds more his sort of thing. Just as important here, though, is Dalla Porta, whose five compositions – particularly the dedications to Duchamp, Picasso and Klee – are the most striking and adventurous music on the record, with Oxley conspiring with characteristic unorthodoxy.

Unknown Flames offers an extravagant two hours of music from a Siena concert. Gatto is a much more conventional drummer and isn't favoured with ideal sound, but the trio work with an enthusiasm that overcomes most doubts. A second version of 'Lifebeat' and the Evans recollections of 'Orbit' and 'I've Grown Accustomed To Her Face' align the two faces of Battaglia's music, and the pianist continues to work on a blend of Bley, Jarrett and Evans which he can make into something entirely his own. Not there yet, but it's an absorbing journey.

*** **Gesti**

Splasc(h) 901 *Battaglia; Michael Gassmann (t); Mirco Mariottini (cl); Stefano Fanceschini, Dmitri Grechi Espinoza, Filiberto Palermini, Mirko Guerrini, Daniele Malvisi (reeds); Milko Ambrogini, Nino Pellegrini, Gianluca Renzi (b); Paolo Corsi, Riccardo Ienna, Alessio Riccio (d).* 6/97.

Two long pieces featuring players taught by Battaglia in his classes. These workshop pieces suggest the pianist's deftness in creating frameworks free enough for some uproar but ready to fall back into recognizable form. More experienced musicians might have given the music a bigger impact, but the enthusiasm of these musicians has merit in itself. A plausible interlude in his discography.

Conrad Bauer (born 1943)

TROMBONE, ELECTRONICS

Born in Halle, one of two trombonist brothers, Connie Bauer was a key player in the small group of East German improvisers at work from the end of the 1960s. Although only infrequently sighted on record, he is one of those who helped form the improvising vocabulary for free-jazz trombonists.

*** **Toronto Tone**

Victo CD017 *Bauer (tb, elec solo).* 10/91.

*** **Three Wheels – Four Directions**

Victo CD023 *Bauer; Peter Kowald (b); Gunter Sommer (d etc.).* 10/92.

***(*) **Bauer Bauer**

Intakt CD 040 *Bauer; Johannes Bauer (tb).*

**** **Plie**

Intakt CD 037 *Bauer; Ernst-Ludwig Petrowsky (as, cl, f); Ulrich Gumpert (p); Gunter Sommer (d).* 2/94.

Working out of the former East Germany for many years, Bauer is perhaps the least known of the great European trombone impressionists. Heard in successive years at Canada's Victoriaville Festival, he makes a good if less than outstanding account on these souvenirs of the occasions. The solo engagement finds him colouring his improvisations with a variety of electronics: chorus effects, loops, echo. Sometimes one feels that the FX are used for impressionistic rather than musical effect, although – as with similar projects by Bill Frisell or Eberhard Weber – the results can be entertaining enough to overcome doubts. As a plain soloist, Bauer can't match Paul Rutherford or Gunter Christmann for sheer inventiveness, but his folksy blares and long, sung tones have their own impact.

With Kowald and Sommer he uses the unadorned slide trombone. There are four group improvs and a solo apiece: Sommer's soliloquy is merely silly, and his lumpy kind of momentum can hold the group back, but there is some excellent stuff on 'Trio Goes East' and 'Trio Goes North'. Kowald, as usual, is beyond reproach, and his *arco* solo is intense enough to blister paint.

Bauer Bauer is a duo concert with his brother Johannes, recorded in the room inside Leipzig's Monument to the Battle of Nations, where there's a natural 20-second echo. The results are almost predictably beautiful, given the sonorities involved, and it must have been a temptation to remain with the long-held notes and counterpoint of 'Dialog 1' and 'Dialog 4' for the whole set; but there is some taut, snickering interplay elsewhere, and the senior Bauer uses some electronics to spare and judicious effect on his solo (there are six duets and a solo apiece).

Plie should properly be credited to the Zentralquartett, since this band of old cronies go under that name when working together. In the aftermath of free jazz (not to mention the DDR), the four players work through a bad-tempered kind of free bop that seems to blossom reluctantly into lyricism at the most unexpected moments. Fragments of blues piano, hard bop, hot solos and harsh ensemble-work permeate what turns out to be an absolutely engrossing record. Cantankerous and highly entertaining sleeve-notes by Christian Broecking fit the record perfectly.

***(*) **Reflections**

FMP CD 74 *Bauer; Johannes Bauer (tb); Uwe Kropinski, Joe Sachse (g).* 10/86.

***(*) **Aventure Québécoise**

Victo 065 *As above.* 5/98.

Strictly speaking, these are by the group Doppelmoppel. Although on the shelf for ten years before release, *Reflections* sounds fresh, and the interplay – at once skeletal and dense, with the spidery lines of the guitarists scuttling around the blurting, blaring horns – hasn't lost its wit and brightness. The tone sometimes comes down to the monochromatic, but these are imaginative players and they have a lot to say. Reconvening after a dozen years, the quartet seem invigorated by the occasion (a Victoriaville Festival set) and play with a matching intensity and cleverness.

Johannes Bauer

TROMBONE

Perhaps the slightly lesser-known of the Bauer brothers, Johannes is nevertheless a powerful trombone voice in European free playing.

***(*) Organo Pleno

FMP CD 56 *Bauer; Fred Van Hove (p, acc); Annick Nozati (v).* 7/92.

Not to be confused with Conrad 'Connie' Bauer (who plays the same instrument). Johannes is a blunter and less discursive player, these days wholly dedicated to free improvised music. The present trio is relatively long-standing by the usual measure of such things, and *Organo Pleno* bespeaks considerable understanding between the members. Van Hove is an enormously underrated player whose continued involvement in other areas of musical enterprise may be reflected in his patiently normative role, roping in the group's wilder excesses. As is the way of such things, the trio swing between spiky, open-form blasts that ruthlessly avoid anything resembling a groove and gentler, almost song-like patterns, such as 'Pars IV', on which piano gives way to organ, starbursts and broken-glass runs to soft, wheezy washes. In general the mood is fairly laid-back. There are plenty of sub-two-minute miniatures, and one mammoth work-out which approaches half an hour in length. Nozati tires and runs low on ideas here, and it is left to Bauer's post-Mangelsdorff phrase-making to give the thing a sense of direction. He is a wonderfully clean articulator with a very distinctive attack and a real dramatic presence.

Agneta Baumann

VOCAL

Swedish vocalist with much experience in theatre and cabaret music, here moving into a mainstream jazz idiom.

*** A Time For Love

Touché TMCCD 006 *Baumann; Anders Lindskog (ts); Staffan Hallgren (f); Carl Fredrik Orrje (p); Per-Ola Gadd (b); Bengt Stark (d).* 8/96.

***(*) Comes Love

Touché TMCCD 011 *Baumann; Bosse Broberg (t); Gösta Rundqvist (p); Hans Backenroth (b); Johan Löfcrantz (d).* 6/99.

Baumann's career in Sweden has been a mix of pop, jazz and cabaret singing, but she is at her slow-burning best on *A Time For Love*, a set of 15 standards, most of them delivered at a stately pace. She has a steady and soft-spoken way with a lyric that induces a sort of motionless drama into a song such as 'More Than You Know' (done with the verse complete) and, although this makes the album a bit tiring over 70 minutes, it's impressive taken a few tracks at a time. Playing honours mainly go to the rhythm section: Hallgren is pretty, and Lindskog comes on as a comatose Lester Young.

Comes Love repeats the trick, but just that bit better: familiar but very suitable tunes, the rhythm section scintillates, and Broberg keeps popping up to take brief, surprising solos, a bright, sharp light in an otherwise nocturnal sound. Baumann does what she did last time, but she's getting better, too.

Jim Beard

KEYBOARDS, PERCUSSION

Keyboard player and composer-arranger, Beard has also done extensive work as a producer on various jazz- and fusion-related projects.

*** Lost At The Carnival

Lipstick LIP 89027 *Beard; Bill Evans (ts, ss); Stan Harrison (cl, bcl, f, af); Jon Herington (g, hca, perc); Ron Jenkins, Steve Rodby (b); Scooter Warner, Mike Mecham, Billy Ward (d).* 94.

Beard has worked extensively with the Breckers, Sco and John McLaughlin, and a prejudiced eye wonders why he didn't try to get one or more of them in on his first solo project. The results are actually more interesting than they promise to be. The album has a rough concept, held together by fairground organ; the device allows Beard to wander, slightly distractedly, through the 'carnivalized' world of contemporary jazz, rock and funk, touching on styles and approaches, committing to none, discarding none. It's quite exhilarating in a headachey sort of way; but the voicings on 'Chunks And Chairknobs' are interesting enough to hear again, and 'Poke' has an insistent harmonic oddity that quickly overcomes its initial cheesy impression.

*** Truly ...

Escapade 03652-2 *As above, except add Aaron Heick (f, picc, cl, cor, ob), Todd Reynolds (vn), Erik Friedlander (clo), John Patitucci (b), Billy Ward (d), Mark Ledford (v, picc-t), David Blamires (v), Marc Quinones (perc); omit Jenkins, Rodby, Warner, Mecham.* 97.

Beard has, in the interim, become a rather ubiquitous figure in the world of electric, somewhat jazzed instrumental music. He's probably able to make a decent living at pop if he wants it, but his heart seems to be in these engagingly oddball projects which fashion a sophisticate's take on current trends in jazz-funk and its various offspring. Hiring Ledford and Blamires to sing their doo-doo-wop vocals on some tracks and directing a good if faceless team of studio players throughout, Beard (who dresses the part on the sleeve) seems like some court-composer to us gentrified patrons. Who else is going to buy this understated virtuosity, based around handsomely orchestrated keyboards, soufflé-light funk rhythms and a pasticheur's wittiest remarks on his chosen milieu? A lot of it passes uneventfully enough, but try the beautifully handled 'Gone Was, Gone Will Be'. If his next is that good all through, Beard will have more than won his spurs.

Sidney Bechet (1897–1959)

SOPRANO SAXOPHONE, CLARINET; ALSO TENOR AND BASS SAXOPHONES, PIANO, BASS, DRUM

Bechet is the first great soloist in jazz. Even before Louis Armstrong came along, he was playing vertical improvisations on the chords of a tune, rather than simple melodic breaks. Like Pops, Bechet grew up in New Orleans, transported his style north and then became the American star in Europe. A pioneer of the soprano saxophone, Sidney managed to combine its intense, sometimes treacherous tonality with the warm, woody sound of the clarinet.

***** Sidney Bechet: Complete Edition – Volume 1, 1923**
Media 7 MJCD 5 *Bechet; Thomas Morris (c); Charlie Irvis, John Mayfield (tb); Clarence Williams (p); Narcisse Buddy Christian (d, bj); Rosetta Crawford, Margaret Johnson, Sara Martin, Mamie Smith, Eva Taylor (v).* 7–10/23.

***** The Complete 1923–6 Clarence Williams Sessions: 1**
EPM Musique FDC 5197 *As above.*

***** Sidney Bechet, 1923–1936**
Classics 583 *Bechet; Clarence Brereton, Wendell Culley, Demas Dean, Tommy Ladnier (t); Billy Burns, Chester Burrill, Teddy Nixon (tb); Chauncey Haughton (cl, as); Ralph Duquesne, Rudy Jackson (cl, as, ss); Ramon Usera (cl, ts); Jerome Pasquall, Gil White (ts); Harry Brooks, Henry Duncan, Lloyd Pinckney, Clarence Williams (p); Oscar Madera (vn); Buddy Christian, Frank Ethridge (bj); Jimmy Miller (g); Wilson Myers (b, v); Edward Coles (bb); Jimmy Jones (b); Jack Carter, Wilbert Kirk, Morris Morland (d); Billy Banks, Lena Horne, Billy Maxey, Noble Sissle (v).* 10/23–3/36.

***** Young Sidney Bechet**
Timeless CBC 1-028 *Similar to above.* 23–25.

*****(*) Sidney Bechet, 1937–1938**
Classics 593 *Bechet; Clarence Brereton, Wendell Culley, Demas Dean, Charlie Shavers (t); Chester Burrill (tb); Chauncey Haughton (cl, as); Jerome Pasquall, Gil White (ts); Ernie Caceres (bs); Oscar Madera (vn); Dave Bowman, Harry Brooks, Erskine Butterfield, Sam Price (p); Teddy Bunn, Jimmy Miller, Leonard Ware (g); Richard Fulbright, Jimmy Jones, Henry Turner (b); Wilbert Kirk, Zutty Singleton (d); O'Neil Spencer (d, v); Billy Banks, The Two Fishmongers, Trixie Smith (v).* 4/37–11/38.

Bechet himself contributed to the heav'n-taught image surrounding his early days. His autobiography, *Treat It Gentle*, is a masterpiece of contrived ingenuousness – the opposite, one might say, of Charles Mingus's ruthlessly disingenuous rants in *Beneath the Underdog*. The fact is that Bechet was an exceptionally gifted and formally aware musician whose compositional skills greatly outshine those of Louis Armstrong, his rival for canonization as the first great jazz improviser. Armstrong's enormous popularity – abetted by his sky-writing top Cs and vocal performance – tended to eclipse Bechet everywhere except in France. Yet the musical evidence is that Bechet was an artist of equal and parallel standing. His melodic sense and ability to structure a solo round the harmonic sequence of the original theme (or with no theme whatsoever) have been of immense significance in the development of modern jazz. Bechet made a pioneering switch to the soprano saxophone (a stronger-voiced and more projective instrument than the clarinet) in the same year as Ansermet's essay, having found a second-hand horn in a London shop. Within a few years, his biting tone and dramatic tremolo were among the most distinctive sounds in jazz.

Bechet made a relatively slow start to his recording career. His first cuts as 'leader' are as accompanist on two tracks made in New York in October and credited to Rosetta Crawford & the King Bechet Trio. The early sessions with Clarence Williams and a variety of modestly talented singers (also available under Williams's name) include carefully annotated breaks and solos from Bechet, largely on soprano saxophone; but these sessions are of specialist interest in the main. His clarinet style (on tracks with Eva Taylor) is still strongly coloured by that of Alphonse Picou and Lorenzo Tio, who gave the precocious Bechet lessons, and is markedly less individual than his saxophone playing. The Timeless compilation is very attractive, and John R.T. Davies's remastering is pitch perfect, an appropriately flattering context for these marvellous early performances.

The Classics compilation is less detailed, but it includes material with Noble Sissle's orchestra not included on either of the other available options; in fact, only the two Rosetta Crawford tracks are in common. The sound is rather abrasive and these early sessions are essential only for a brief, brilliant soprano solo on 'Loveless Love'. According to John Chilton, Bechet is also responsible, on this and two other tracks (he solos only on the initially rejected 'In A Café On The Road To Calais'), for the bass saxophone parts, which are not credited in the Classics notes. The session of 15 September 1932 is one of Bechet's best yet, with superb solos on 'I Want You Tonight' and 'Maple Leaf Rag'. The later disc is generally more professional and every bit as compelling musically. Bechet reached a new high with two quintet tracks credited to Noble Sissle's Swingsters, an offshoot of the main band. His solos on 'Okey-Doke' and 'Characteristic Blues' are classic performances, full of extravagantly bent notes, trills and time-changes. Using both clarinet and soprano saxophone, Bechet creates an atmosphere of considerable tension that is discharged only during a phenomenal solo on 'Characteristic Blues'. Later, in 1938, there was controversy over the exact authorship of 'Hold Me Tight', which Bechet claimed was based on his earlier 'I Want Some Seafood, Mama', but which was declared obscene and withdrawn from radio stations. The real controversy, however, was directed towards what seemed to be a new way of playing jazz, and in that context the session of April 1937 is absolutely critical, not just to Bechet's development but to that of jazz itself.

*****(*) Sidney Bechet, 1938–1940**
Classics 608 *Bechet; Tommy Ladnier, Frankie Newton, Kenneth Roane (t); J.C Higginbotham (tb); Mezz Mezzrow (cl, ts); Meade Lux Lewis, Willie 'The Lion' Smith, Sonny White (p); Teddy Bunn, Charlie Howard (g); Elmer James, Olin Aderhold, Wilson Myers, John Williams (b); Big Sid Catlett, Kenny Clarke, Manzie Johnson, Leo Warney (d).* 11/38–40.

***** Sidney Bechet, 1940**
Classics 619 *Bechet; Sidney De Paris (t); Muggsy Spanier (c); Sandy Williams (tb); Cliff Jackson (p); Bernard Addison, Teddy Bunn, Carmen Mastren (g); Josh White (g, v); Wellman Braud, Pops Foster, Wilson Myers (b); Big Sid Catlett (d).* 3–6/40.

***(*) Sidney Bechet, 1940–1941

Classics 638 *Bechet; Gus Aiken, Henry 'Red' Allen, Henry Goodwin, Henry Levine, Charlie Shavers (t); Rex Stewart (c); Jack Epstein, Vic Dickenson, J.C Higginbotham, Sandy Williams (tb); Alfie Evans (cl); Rudolph Adler, Lem Johnson (ts); Don Donaldson, Earl Hines, Cliff Jackson, Mario Janarro, Willie 'The Lion' Smith, James Toliver (p); Everett Barksdale, Tony Colucci (g); Wellman Braud, John Lindsay, Wilson Myers, Harry Patent, Ernest Williamson (b); Baby Dodds, J.C Heard, Arthur Herbert, Manzie Johnson, Nat Levine (d); Herb Jeffries (v).* 9/40–10/41.

In April 1941 Bechet fulfilled the logic of his increasingly self-reliant musical conception (Hines suggested that his quietly 'evil' mood on the day of the 1940 sessions was characteristic of New Orleans players at the time when dealing with Northerners) by recording two unprecedented 'one-man-band' tracks, over-dubbing up to six instruments. 'Sheik Of Araby' is for the full 'band' of soprano and tenor saxophones, clarinet, piano, bass and drums; so time-consuming was the process that a second item, 'Blues For Bechet', had to be completed without bass or drums, leaving a fascinating fragment for RCA to release.

In September of the same year, Bechet made another classic trio recording, this time with Willie 'The Lion' Smith and the relative unknown, Everett Barksdale, on electric guitar. Though the two sidemen provide no more than incidental distractions, the trio sessions were more compelling than the full band assembled on that day (Charlie Shavers plays monster lines on 'I'm Coming Virginia', as on the October 'Mood Indigo', but is otherwise ill-suited); 'Strange Fruit' is one of Bechet's most calmly magisterial performances, and the two takes of 'You're The Limit' seem too good to have been dumped in the 'unreleased' bin, though perhaps the absence on either of a commanding solo from Bechet (who may not have liked Smith's uncomplicated tune) put the label off. But what did they know? A month later, in the same session that realized 'Mood Indigo', Bechet cut the utterly awful 'Laughin' In Rhythm', a New Orleans version of 'The Laughing Policeman' that, despite a taut soprano solo, hardly merits revival. Dickenson, whose humour was usually reliable, also plays beautifully on 'Blue In The Air', one of the finest of Bechet's recorded solos and one that merits the closest attention.

A lot of this material is available elsewhere: the Bluebirds from 1938, the Blue Notes, much of the Victor stuff. However, it's always good to have the simply and exactly documented Classics discs, and there are some useful inclusions and corrections, like the correct attribution of 'Ti Ralph' and 'Meringue D'Amour' from the Willie 'The Lion' Smith date of November 1939; these have been inverted on most reissues in recent times. The 'Original Haitian Music' with Smith is an oddity from a decidedly odd band, and one has a strong sense that Bechet was finding it harder over this period following his brief sabbatical in 1938 to set up completely sympathetic sessions. More and more often one finds him in bands where piano, not guitar, dominates the rhythm section, and he is paired with other saxophone players. It was always characteristic of Bechet's VSOP sound that it didn't marry well with sharper vintages, however potent they were in isolation. One would still want to recommend these discs, but with the proviso that they have their downs as well as ups.

Blues In Thirds is dominated by Sidney's somewhat hostile relationship with piano players. Earl Hines has spoken of the saxophonist's 'evil' mood on the day of their September 1940 encounter, when he refused to nominate which Hines tune was next on the programme. It turned out to be 'Blues In Thirds', and the trio with the pianist and Baby Dodds is a classic. So confused is the Bechet discography that it is becoming virtually impossible to offer reasoned preferences. Technically, these are sub-standard transfers, flat and unresonant.

*** Sidney Bechet, 1941–1944

Classics 860 *Bechet; Sidney De Paris, Charlie Shavers (t); Henry Goodwin (t, v); Vic Dickenson, Wilbur De Paris (tb); Gene Cedric (ts, cl); Don Donaldson, Art Hodes, Cliff Jackson, Willie 'The Lion' Smith (p); Everett Barksdale (g); Wellman Braud, Pops Foster, Wilson Myers, Ernest Williamson (b); Big Sid Catlett, Eddie Dougherty, Wilbert Kirk, Manzie Johnson (d).* 10/41.

This picks up where Classics 638 left off and overlaps with the RCA compilation at the point of 'Laughin' In Rhythm'. Better things were to follow later in October, but two other tracks from that session, 'Blues In The Air' and 'The Mooche', test the quality of this fine band. Duke was obviously on his mind at this time (unless it was Vic Dickenson who was pressing Ellington's suit), because he also includes 'Mood Indigo' on the 24 October session, and plays it quite beautifully. Willie The Lion is on top form and lets rip on 'Oh! Lady Be Good' and '12th Street Rag'. It was to be some time before Bechet recorded again; there were three V-Discs in December 1943, reworkings of jazz and blues classics, and then nothing for a further year, until the second of the saxophonist's contacts with Blue Note. This was the session that yielded 'Blue Horizon', a solo of structural perfection and exquisite grace, not very well transferred here but very welcome for all that. 'St Louis Blues' and 'Muskrat Ramble' aren't quite up to that quality, but the combination of Bechet, Sidney De Paris, Dickenson, Art Hodes, Pops Foster and Manzie Johnson was a potent one, and these sides are widely and rightly admired. The very next day, Bechet made a session as sideman with pianist Cliff Jackson's Village Cats, an artist whose work is shortly to be covered by Classics. Released on Black & White, these are agreeable enough sides, and Bechet is featured often enough to please his fans, but even 'Jeepers Creepers' and 'Quiet Please' don't do much more than fill out an otherwise thin disc.

*** Up A Lazy River

Good Time Jazz 12064 *Bechet; Muggsy Spanier (c); Henry Goodwin, Albert Snaer (t); Jimmy Archey, George Brunies, Wilbur De Paris, George Wettling (tb); Buster Bailey, Albert Nicholas, Bob Wilber (cl); James P Johnson, Dick Wellstood (p); Danny Barker, Carmen Mastren (g); Wellman Braud, Pops Foster, Walter Page (b); Tommy Benford (d).* 40–44.

*** Weary Blues

Jazz Hour 73553 *Bechet; Louis Armstrong, Clarence Brereton, Tommy Ladnier, Sidney De Paris (t); Claude Jones (tb); Albert Nicholas (cl); Mezz Mezzrow (cl, ts); Happy Caldwell, Gil White (ts); Ernie Caceres (bs); Dave Bowman, Harry Brooks, Cliff Jackson, Meade Lux Lewis, Jelly Roll Morton, Luis Russell (p); Bernard Addison, Teddy Bunn, Charlie Howard, Lawrence Lucie, Jimmy Miller, Leonard Ware (g); Wellman Braud, Pops Foster, Elmer James, Henry Turner (b); Big Sid Catlett, Kenny Clarke, Manzie Johnson, Zutty Singleton (d).*

Two attractive enough compilations of mostly familiar material, but with nothing to recommend them to anyone who wants more than a random sampling of Bechet material. There are enough chronological discs around which – even allowing for the technical shortcomings of the Classics format – tell the story in a reasonably logical fashion for the proliferation of career compilations to become simply confusing. Experienced Bechet listeners will be able to do their own chronologies based on personnel; more casual purchasers may not be concerned.

Weary Blues is very inconsistent in sound, with no attempt (laudably or laughably, depending on your point of view) to smooth out differences in source masters. On the other disc, the transfers are clean and unexceptionable and the only quibble might be a slightly artificial bass roll-off which isn't obvious elsewhere. The cover shows Sidney with a fishing rod rather than a saxophone.

***** Runnin' Wild**

Blue Note 21259 *Bechet; Wild Bill Davison (c); Jimmy Archey, Bob Diehl (tb); Art Hodes, Joe Sullivan (p); Pops Foster, Walter Page (b); Slick Jones, Freddie Moore (d).* 47.

Bechet was Blue Note's token traditionalist in the 1940s, a figure substantial enough to stand alongside the fierce hard-boppers. The partnership with Davison works well throughout the set, with Bill's punchy and ringing tone blending superbly with Bechet on 'Basin Street Blues' and 'Runnin' Wild' itself. There are alternative takes of it and of 'Ain't Gonna Give Nobody None Of My Jelly Roll', which is raunchy enough to merit a reprise.

*****(*) Jazz Classics: Volume 1**

Blue Note 789384 *Bechet; Bunk Johnson, Max Kaminsky, Frankie Newton, Sidney De Paris (t); Jimmy Archey, Vic Dickenson, J.C Higginbotham, George Lugg, Sandy Williams (tb); Albert Nicholas (cl); Art Hodes, Cliff Jackson, Meade Lux Lewis (p); Teddy Bunn (g); Pops Foster, John Williams (b); Big Sid Catlett, Manzie Johnson (d); Fred Moore (d, v).* 6/39–11/51.

***** Jazz Classics: Volume 2**

Blue Note 789385 *As above.* 6/39–11/51.

Bechet and Blue Note make an irresistible combination, but not an immediately obvious one. Though the label had its roots in earlier R&B and jazz, having recorded both Albert Ammons and Meade Lux Lewis, its stock-in-trade was to be hard bop and the more accommodating aspects of the avant-garde. Bechet had approached Alfred Lion, wanting to record a long version of 'Summertime' (*Volume 1*, also available on Classics, above), something he had not been able to do for another label. The session of June 1939, the earliest of the dates represented on these compilations, isn't vintage Bechet by any stretch of the imagination, but there are some striking moments. With Lewis all over the place, Bunn lays down a wonderfully simple accompaniment and, with no other horn to hand, Bechet plays a vivid solo that was to boost the original 78 into hit sales. The 1939 session came shortly after the death of Tommy Ladnier, and the full band recorded a less than morose 'Blues For Tommy' (*Volume 2*) on which only Bechet sounds as if he might honestly miss his old partner.

The association with Blue Note continued intermittently over the next few years. In March 1940, with the excellent Bunn again on hand, Bechet recorded 'Dear Old Southland' (*Volume 1*). The 1944 cuts with Sidney de Paris, Vic Dickenson and Art Hodes are less than wholly compelling; but the saxophonist's encounter with the enigmatic Bunk Johnson in March 1945 is a different matter. Bechet sounds cautiously respectful; Bunk sounds like a man whose mind is elsewhere. Nevertheless 'Milenberg Blues' and 'Days Beyond Recall' have a historic significance that goes well beyond their intrinsic value as performances.

The final Blue Note session was recorded a dozen years after the first, and it's a mellowing Bechet who plays the appropriately titled 'Changes Made' with de Paris again, and trombonist Jimmy Archey. Looked at objectively, these sides have taken on a certain sheen purely because of the label that recorded them. Technically, they're first class; historically, they're full of interest; but musically, they're second-order Bechet.

****** King Jazz: Volume 1**

GHB BCD 501/502 2CD *Bechet; Hot Lips Page (t); Mezz Mezzrow (cl); Sammy Price, Fritz Weston (p); Danny Barker (g); Pops Foster (b); Big Sid Catlett, Kaiser Marshall (d); Douglas Daniels, Pleasant Joseph (v).* 3–8/45.

*****(*) King Jazz: Volume 2**

GHB BCD 503/504/505 3CD *As above, except omit Page, Joseph, Daniels, Barker; add Sox Wilson (p), Coot Grant (v).* 9/46, 12/47.

The Bechet centenary came and went in 1997 with little more than a mild flurry of interest. Perhaps because there is no 'problematic' about Bechet, no need to rescue him from obscurity or debunk his undentable popularity, there was no real leverage for a reassessment. The one big event of the year, record-wise, was the appearance of the legendary King Jazz catalogue on CD. By rights, the label was the brainchild of Mezz Mezzrow, an extraordinary booster and self-promoter who managed to raise enough cash from a man who had made his pile in the war selling radar equipment to get the label under way. But Mezzrow was no better as a businessman than he was as a clarinettist, and he quickly got distracted into writing his (fictionalized) autobiography, *Really the Blues*, with the help of journalist Bernard Wolfe. However, the label's policy of recording much more than could be issued pays dividends now. The first sessions on the disc are of pianist Sammy Price with and without vocalist Pleasant Joseph. There follow, though, sessions from July and August with the Bechet–Mezzrow group. Some of these tracks – 'Revolutionary Blues', 'Perdido Street Stomp', 'The Sheik Of Araby' and 'Minor Swoon' – are classics of post-war Dixieland and, though Mezzrow's technical insufficiencies are in no way glossed over in the transfer, the brightness and unselfconscious ease of these performances warm the heart. For once Pops Foster and Danny Barker can be heard clearly, and the balance of the sound is as good as it is likely to get. Sammy Price plays on all the *Volume One* sides except those from the August sessions. He's a decent player, slightly florid and overcooked as a soloist, but he comes into his own as a group accompanist, bettered only by Art Hodes. Fritz Weston comes in for the later dates and isn't remotely as idiomatic or as good.

Volume Two doesn't reach the same heights but it does contain a generous amount of music and the chance to hear the basic band working at some length. 'Chicago Function' exists in alternative takes, as do several other tracks, and it's clear from these that, while Mezzrow has to plough pretty much the same furrow each time, Sidney throws off ideas like a meteor shower. The King Jazz story was a short one and, in the final analysis, no different from a thousand other small labels optimistically begun and naïvely mismanaged. Along the way, though, it threw up some wonderful music.

*** Bunk & Bechet In Boston

Jazz Crusade 3040 *Bechet; Bunk Johnson (t); Hank Duncan, Ray Parker (p); Pops Foster (b); Freddie Moore, George Thompson (d).* 4/45.

Like Louis Armstrong, Bunk Johnson did not like to share leadership with anyone. In 1945 he was something of a living legend, but he was also profoundly erratic and subject to drinking jags. On these radio sessions, Sidney backs him manfully and leaps in whenever the trumpeter loses the plot. Even allowing for such lapses and the rather shaky source material, the sessions are fascinating for the variation in personal styles. Johnson sounds like a man out on his back porch, while Bechet climbs all over the melody and, when things are not going disastrously wrong, merely proceeding at a pedestrian pace, he simply ignores what Bunk is doing and skyrockets off on his own. This material is also available on the Classics compilation below, but these transfers are very good indeed.

*** Sidney Bechet, 1945–1946

Classics 954 *Bechet; Bunk Johnson, Max Kaminsky, Frankie Newton (t); George Brunies, George Lugg, Sandy Williams (tb); Albert Nicholas (cl); Art Hodes, Cliff Jackson, Joe Sullivan (p); Pops Foster, Jack Lesberg (b); Danny Alvin, Manzie Johnson, George Wettling (d); Freddie Moore (d, v).* 45–46.

As inclusive and as muddy as ever, this further Classics volume takes the Bechet story on another step of the way, concentrating on sessions under his own name at the end of the war. The transfers seem uglier than ever here, but having this material, including such classic performances as the 1945 'Salty Dog' and 'Weary Blues', on just one CD is most welcome.

*** The Prodigious Bechet–Mezzrow Quintet & Septet

Musidisc 401172 *Bechet; Hot Lips Page (t); Mezz Mezzrow (cl); Sammy Price, Wesley Wilson(p); Danny Barker (g); Wellman Braud, Pops Foster (b); Big Sid Catlett, Baby Dodds, Kaiser Marshall (d).* 46, 47.

Sidney was in poor physical shape when the later of these sessions were recorded, but the great man rises above his gastric and dental problems and turns in some sterling performances. Mezzrow was very much in the saddle at this point, and tunes like 'Blues And Freud' and 'Chicago Function' are among Mezz's best moments on record.

*** In The Groove

Jazz Society (Vogue) 670506 *Bechet; Claude Luter (cl); Pierre Dervaux (t); Claude Philippe (cl, bj); Mowgli Jospin, Guy Longnon, Bernard Zacharias (tb); Christian Azzi (p); Roland Bianchini (b); François Moustache Galepides (d).* 10/49–1/52.

*** In New York, 1950–51

Storyville 6039 *Bechet; Vic Dickenson, Big Chief Russell Moore (tb); Ken Kersey, Red Richards (p); Herb Ward (b); Cliff Leeman, Art Trappier (d).* 50, 51.

***(*) Salle Pleyel: 31 January 52

Vogue 655001 *Bechet; Claude Luter (cl); Claude Rabanit (t); Guy Longnon, Bernard Zacharias (tb); Christian Azzi (p); Claude Philippe (bj); Roland Bianchini (b); François Moustache Galepides (d).* 1/52.

*** In Concert

Vogue 655625 *Bechet; Pierre Dervaux, Giles Thibaut (t); Benny Vasseur (tb); Claude Luter (cl); Yannick Singery (p); Claude Philippe (bj); Roland Bianchini (b); Marcel Blanche (d).* 12/54.

Luter was a surprisingly confident and self-assured partner for the newly emigrated Bechet, who regarded his move to France as the fulfilment of racial destiny rather than as escape from an unfeeling and unappreciative environment. Even so, Bechet's reputation in America never matched the adulation he received in France. With the exception of the leader, the French band give him an easy ride, offering *carte blanche* for either relatively pat solos or more developed excursions, as the mood took him. 'Ghost Of The Blues' and 'Patte De Mouche' (with Bechet taking over at the piano) are rare gems and 'Les Oignons' is a delight. Generally, though, quite low-key.

The live New York material contains some great moments, including a number of tracks, originally on Pumpkin, which modestly feature Russell Moore, a hugely affable player whose contribution to the music of the time is still not wholly valued. Bechet himself is in good form, with a harder than usual tone and some decidedly spikey moments.

The Salle Pleyel concert was a noisy, vociferous affair but also surprisingly inward-looking and musicianly. Introduced by Charles Delaunay, it features favourites like 'Les Oignons' again, 'Petite Fleur', 'St Louis Blues', 'Frankie And Johnny', 'Maryland My Maryland' and alternative versions of both 'Sweet Georgia Brown' and 'Royal Garden Blues' that are of more than incidental documentary interest. Recommended.

The later concert record has some interesting elements (Bechet's solos on 'Buddy Bolden Stomp' and 'On The Sunny Side Of The Street' are contrastingly good) but with a slightly bland air which isn't helped by a very skew-whiff recording that makes everyone sound as if they're moving around onstage.

***(*) Sidney Bechet At Storyville

Black Lion BLCD 760902 *Bechet; Vic Dickenson (tb); George Wein (p); Jimmy Woode (b); Buzzy Drootin (d).* 10/53.

A tight and professional set from mid-way through a residency at George Wein's Boston club. There is a slight sense of motions being gone through on some of Bechet's briefer breaks, but every now and then, as on 'Crazy Rhythm', he will make subtle changes of direction that Wein, for one, doesn't seem to have noticed. Sound-balances are erratic in places, but everyone can be heard and Woode in particular gains over his showing on the original Storyville LP release. Recommended.

**(*) Blues In My Heart

Intercontinental 1152 *Bechet; unknown personnel.*

We have been able to make few reliable guesses or cross-checks as to the provenance and date of these ten late blues performances. Certainly more than one band is involved and presumably different locations. Bechetphiles may be able to identify but probably won't much appreciate the rather boppish settings that a couple of tracks fight against; but the wholesale concentration on predominantly minor blues will undoubtedly suggest the early lineage of John Coltrane to listeners of a more modernist tendency.

Gordon Beck (born 1938)

PIANO, ELECTRIC PIANO, ELECTRONICS

A veteran British modernist, Beck drew attention in the Tubby Hayes group of the 1960s, as Ronnie Scott's house-pianist and with Phil Woods, 1969–72. Since then has freelanced, worked as an educator and helmed occasional albums.

**** Dreams**

JMS 049 *Beck; Rowanne Mark (v).* 5 & 6/89.

****** For Evans' Sake**

JMS 059 *Beck; Didier Lockwood (vn); Dave Holland (b); Jack DeJohnette (d).* 9/91.

Coming to jazz with a solid classical training and with the time-served draughtsman's sense of line and structure, Beck served further apprenticeships in the bands of Tubby Hayes and Phil Woods, as well as a stint as house pianist at Ronnie Scott's. In whatever context he is performing, whether unaccompanied, in small groups or large ensembles, acoustically or with electronics, he has a flowing, eloquent style, and an ability somewhat like Bill Evans's, to reveal the overall structure of a piece in almost every segment, without ever becoming diagrammatic.

It is little short of scandalous that Beck has been so poorly recognized in his native Britain and that the discography should be as thin as it is and so dependent on an overseas label. JMS have done well by him, producing a series of albums which, if they lack the sheer power of the 1968 *Gyroscope* (also the name of his group) or the elegance of *Seven Steps To Evans* a few years later, are nevertheless representative of his gifts.

A more recent tribute to his great predecessor, *For Evans' Sake* brings together a band worthy of his talents. Interestingly, Beck uses nothing by Evans himself. Miles's 'Blue In Green' is the only familiar piece, and that is an unaccompanied bass solo from Holland, in good form. Lockwood establishes a presence on the very first track, yawping away in overtones like a row of saxes. 'Re: Mister E' is Beck's own finest moment, a piece that refuses even to flirt with pastiche but sounds like the fullest-hearted tribute. 'He Is With Us Still' ends the set on exactly the right note, underlining not just Beck's mastery but that of the bassist and drummer as well.

Real-time acoustic playing is always going to be more satisfactory than electronic programming. *Dreams* sounds stiff and unresponsive because the keyboard-generated backgrounds are so unsubtle. Even when Beck experiments with unusual time-signatures the results are rather bland, and it would be good to hear some of the material on *Dreams* particularly reworked with a live band.

***** Once Is Never Enough**

FMR CD 28 *Beck; Stan Sulzmann (ts, f); Chris Laurence (b); Paul Clarvis (d, perc).* 2/96.

At long last, a British label recognizes Beck's brilliance. Unfortunately, the chemistry never quite fires and this remains a better record in potential than in fact. Sulzmann and Beck divide writing duties, and big Stan's three pieces, including the title-track, are impressive for their deceptive familiarity, almost as if each is drawn from a standard.

The piano at Gateway Studios sounds in excellent shape and Beck dwells more often than usual on richly sustained chords, allowing phrases to blend together, a change from his usual rather clean-edged delivery. Laurence provides a steady reference point, and the only serious quibble (beyond the rather tentative sound) is Clarvis, who always sounds disengaged from whichever band he's nominally in, pattering away in an undertone.

Harry Beckett (born 1935)

TRUMPET, FLUGELHORN

A Barbadian, he came to London in 1954, began playing in clubs and eventually rose to be a major presence on the British contemporary scene, working with all its major protagonists over decades. More recently lionized by Europe, with recordings in Germany and association with the French National Jazz Orchestra.

***** All Four One**

Spotlite SPJ CD 547 *Beckett; Chris Batchelor, Jon Corbett, Claude Deppa (flhn); Alistair Gavin (p); Fred T Baker (b); Tony Marsh (d); Jan Ponsford (v).* 91.

*****(*) Images Of Clarity**

Evidence EVCD 315 *Beckett; Didier Levallet (b); Tony Marsh (d).* 12/92.

Too vital a presence to be merely a father-figure, Beckett lent a rugged, avuncular blessing to the reintegration of young black musicians into post-free British jazz. Like many of the African- and Caribbean-born musicians who fell within the circle of Chris McGregor's Brotherhood of Breath, Beckett moves without strain between free and mainstream improvisation. His essential qualities are an untroubled romanticism and a brightly lyrical tone (to which he adds gruff asides and occasionally startling rhythmic punctuations). Though some of the best of Beckett's work is on sessions for other leaders, his re-emergence as a recording artist (no more than his deserts, albeit on small labels) finds him consolidating his strengths as an improviser. A pity he hasn't recorded more frequently in the sparse but richly contoured setting of *Images Of Clarity*. Levallet has a gorgeous touch (and chips in with two lovely themes it would be nice to hear again). Marsh is among the most musical of European drummers, embellishing softly without ever losing track of an already delicate pulse. Beckett sounds pensive and slightly wry, and he keeps a thread of humour running through the set, as he has throughout his career.

Beckett's All Four One project is based on a four-flugelhorn front line, an instrumentation capable of great richness but also, one fears and quickly hears confirmed, too little variety. There are some excellent moments. Mingus's 'Better Git It In Your Soul' is just right for this group and 'The Outstanding Light', a very Beckettian original, sits perfectly for the group, but it might have been better to have made an album on which this personnel appeared once or twice; they don't, alas, sustain the full distance.

A partially successful idea, then, that neverthless confirms this much-loved musician's continuing desire to experiment.

Bix Beiderbecke (1903–31)

CORNET

The quintessence of jazz legend, Leon 'Bix' Beiderbecke was born in Davenport, Iowa. He was mostly self-taught on both piano and cornet. He joined the Wolverine Orchestra and made his first records in 1923, but it was his periods with Jean Goldkette (St Louis, 1926–7) and Paul Whiteman (New York, 1928–30) which brought him to a wider attention, as well as his record dates with Frankie Trumbauer and under his own name. Alcoholism ruined his health and he died of pneumonia. Though comparatively little-known in his lifetime, he became idolized after his death as a unique figure – a cool stylist with a bell-like tone, the flip-side to Louis Armstrong's forthright playing.

***** Bix Beiderbecke And The Wolverines**

Timeless CBC 1-013 *Beiderbecke; Jimmy McPartland (c); Miff Mole, Tommy Dorsey, George Brunies, Al Gandee (tb); Don Murray (cl); Jimmy Hartwell (cl, as); Frankie Trumbauer (Cmel); George Johnson (ts); Dick Voynow, Rube Bloom, Paul Mertz (p); Bob Gillett, Howdy Quicksell (bj); Min Leibrook (tba); Vic Moore, Tom Gargano (d).* 2–12/24.

***** Bix Beiderbecke And The Chicago Cornets**

Milestone MCD-47019-2 *As above, except add Muggsy Spanier (c), Guy Carey (tb), Volly DeFaut (cl), Mel Stitzel (p), Marvin Saxbe (bj, g), Vic Berton (d).* 2–12/24.

Bix Beiderbecke, the cornetist from Davenport, Iowa, remains among the most lionized and romanticized of jazz figures, nearly 70 years after his death. Beiderbecke's understated mastery, his cool eloquence and precise improvising were long cherished as the major alternative to Louis Armstrong's clarion leadership in the original jazz age, and his records have endured remarkably well – even though comparatively few of them were in the uncompromised jazz vein of Armstrong's studio work. These CDs collect virtually everything he made in his first year in the studios, with the Wolverine Orchestra, the Sioux City Six and Bix's Rhythm Jugglers. With no vocalists to hinder them, these young white bands were following in the footsteps of the Original Dixieland Jazz Band and, although they sometimes seem rather stiff and unswinging, the ensembles are as daring as almost anything that was being recorded at the time. Yet despite the presence of such players as Mole, Dorsey and Murray, only Beiderbecke's solos have retained much independent life: the beautiful little contribution to 'Royal Garden Blues', for instance, shines through the dull recording and staid surroundings. The record also includes two tracks made after McPartland had replaced Bix in the Wolverines. Some of the original Gennett masters will never sound better than dusty and muffled, but John R.T. Davies has done his usual peerless job on the remastering for Timeless, and there is a fine essay by Beiderbecke scholar, Richard Sudhalter. Milestone's *Chicago Cornets* disc includes all this material but also adds five tracks by Chicago's Bucktown Five, fronted by the teenaged Muggsy Spanier – a not inconsiderable bonus, though overall the remastering isn't quite as good as that on the Timeless CD.

*****(*) Bix Beiderbecke 1924–1930**

Jazz Classics in Digital Stereo RPCD 620 *Beiderbecke; Ray Lodwig, Eddie Pinder, Charles Margulis, Bubber Miley (t); Andy Secrest (c); Jack Teagarden, Bill Rank, Tommy Dorsey (tb); Don Murray (cl); Benny Goodman, Jimmy Dorsey, Jimmy Hartwell, Issy Friedman, Frankie Trumbauer (cl, saxes); Arnold Brilhart (as); Bud Freeman, George Johnson, Charles Strickfadden (ts); Adrian Rollini (bsx); Irving Brodsky, Frank Signorelli, Lennie Hayton, Hoagy Carmichael, Roy Bargy, Tommy Satterfield (p); Joe Venuti, Matty Malneck (vn); Eddie Lang (g); Min Leibrook (tba, bsx); Harry Goodman (tba); Mike Trafficante (b); Chauncey Morehouse, Hal McDonald, Stan King, Gene Krupa, Harry Gale, Vic Moore (d); Irene Taylor, Hoagy Carmichael, The Rhythm Boys (v).* 24–30.

***** Bix Lives!**

Bluebird ND 86845 *Personnel largely as above; others present include Fred Farrar, Henry Busse (t), Boyce Cullen (tb), Pee Wee Russell (cl, as), Wes Vaughan, Jack Fulton (v).* 27–30.

***** The Beiderbecke File**

Saville CDSVL 201 *Personnel largely as above discs.* 10/24–9/30.

With Beiderbecke's recordings now out of copyright, reissues have recently emerged from several sources. Robert Parker's Jazz Classics compilation, taken from very fine originals, secures an admirable clarity of sound. The 16 tracks offer a somewhat hotchpotch collection of Beiderbecke, from the Wolverines up to his very last session with Hoagy Carmichael; it's a strong single-disc compilation, but it lacks such important sides as 'Singing The Blues' and 'I'm Coming Virginia'. The Bluebird collection, numbering 23 tracks, covers only his Victor sides with the Jean Goldkette and Paul Whiteman orchestras, along with the final date under his own name. Bix was rather buried amidst danceband arrangements of pop tunes of the day and has to be enjoyed in eight- and sixteen-bar solos, but the record does collect virtually everything important that he did with Whiteman, bar the *Show Boat* medley, which has yet to appear on CD. The sound is very clean, using BMG's NoNoise technique, although some may find the timbres a little too dry.

The Beiderbecke File mixes 1924–5 tracks with seven with Trumbauer, two with Whiteman and six of the Bix And His Gang titles. A sensible survey, and the sound is quite clean, though John Wadley's transfers seem a bit recessed and lacking in much spark.

****** Bix Beiderbecke Vol. I Singin' The Blues**

Columbia 466309-2 *Beiderbecke; Hymie Farberman (t); Bill Rank (tb); Don Murray (cl, bs); Jimmy Dorsey (cl, as); Frankie Trumbauer (Cmel); Red Ingle, Bobby Davis (as); Adrian Rollini (bsx); Paul Mertz, Itzy Riskin, Frank Signorelli (p); Joe Venuti (vn); Eddie Lang (g); John Cali (bj); Joe Tarto (tba); Chauncey Morehouse, Vic Berton (d); Sam Lanin (perc); Irving Kaufman, Seger Ellis (v).* 2–9/27.

This follows Beiderbecke chronologically through 1927, arguably his greatest year in the studios, and it also includes his curious piano solo, 'In A Mist'. Most of the tracks are under Frankie Trumbauer's leadership, and his own slippery, imaginative solos are often as inventive as Bix's, demonstrating why Lester Young named him as a primary influence. But most listeners will be waiting for the shining, affecting cornet improvisations on 'Singin' The Blues', 'Clarinet Marmalade', 'For No Reason At All In C' and the rest. The contributions of Lang and Dorsey are a further bonus. The Columbia sound seems quite light and clear.

****** Bix Beiderbecke Vol. II At The Jazz Band Ball**

Columbia 460825-2 *Beiderbecke; Charlie Margulis (t); Bill Rank (tb); Pee Wee Russell (cl); Jimmy Dorsey, Issy Friedman, Charles Strickfadden (cl, as); Don Murray (cl, bs); Frankie Trumbauer (Cmel); Adrian Rollini, Min Leibrook (bsx); Frank Signorelli, Arthur Schutt (p); Tom Satterfield (p, cel); Joe Venuti, Matty Malneck (vn); Carl Kress, Eddie Lang (g); Chauncey Morehouse, Harold MacDonald (d); Bing Crosby, Jimmy Miller, Charlie Farrell (v).* 10/27–4/28.

The survey of Beiderbecke's OKeh recordings has the advantage of eliminating the Whiteman material and concentrating on his most jazz-directed music; this disc includes some of the best of the Bix And His Gang sides, including the title-piece, 'Jazz Me Blues' and 'Sorry', plus further dates with Trumbauer. As a leader, Beiderbecke wasn't exactly a progressive – some of the material harks back to the arrangements used by the Original Dixieland Jazz Band – but his own playing is always remarkable: lean, bruised, a romantic's sound but one that feels quite at home in what were still rough and elementary days for jazz. Both sets of remastering sound good.

***** Bix Beiderbecke 1924–1927**

Classics 778 *As appropriate discs above.* 2/24–10/27.

***** Bix Beiderbecke 1927–1930**

Classics 788 *As appropriate discs above.* 10/27–9/30.

The world still waits for a fully comprehensive Beiderbecke collection, properly remastered and from a reputable source, and with Bix slipping further back into history one wonders how this young man's reputation is going to hold up over the next period of jazz appreciation. Classics entered the fray with two discs that start with the Wolverines' titles, go on through all of the Bix And His Gang tracks, and finish with the 1930 sessions for Hoagy Carmichael and Irving Mills, together with the final three Victors under his own name. As so often with this series, reproduction is rather up-and-down. While these are sound enough for those collecting the Classics titles in sequence, one should go to Timeless and then Columbia for the best edition of this music so far, while Parker's collection remains the best-sounding of the compilations. In the meantime, Bix slips further away from us. A complete edition of this remarkable man's work is now long overdue.

Richie Beirach (born 1947)

PIANO, KEYBOARDS

Studied at Berklee and in Manhattan before making a mark with Dave Liebman in the '70s, a continuing association. Only rarely leads his own groups on record, but he has many credits in his book and is much admired as a harmonic theoretician in particular.

***** Richie Beirach – Masahiko Togashi – Terumasa Hino**

Konnex KCD 5043 *Beirach; Terumasa Hino (t, flhn); Masahiko Togashi (d, perc).* 9/76–6/78.

This New Yorker's pianism is entirely unmistakable. Throughout his career, Beirach has attempted to blend jazz harmony with elements of European classical music: Chopin, Debussy's impressionism most obviously, and also the densely chromatic language of the Second Viennese School. He is most successful as a solo performer, but much of the early catalogue is currently out of circulation and it's quite difficult to get a fix on his development. Some of his best work has been with saxophonist Dave Liebman and in the context of groups like Quest and Lookout Farm, but these duos, made some five years after Beirach's real professional debut with Stan Getz, are full of interesting ideas. They're a little strange but they repay patient attention. Hino is better versed in jazz and gives a firm, Chet Baker-tinged account of 'What Is This Thing Called Love?'. The tracks with the drummer are more evanescent and non-Western; 'Tsunami' isn't quite as overwhelming as the title suggests it ought to be and there's a risible quality to the histrionics. 'Interesting' always sounds like damning with faint praise, but that's what we're stuck with.

***** Antarctica**

Evidence ECD 22086 *Beirach (p solo).* 9/85.

This made no impact at all on first appearance, a long, two-part suite inspired by the frozen continent, and pretty much locked up in its own chilly premisses. It's not entirely clear how the second part of the sequence, pieces like 'Mirage', 'Water Lilies (The Cloud)' and 'The Empress', have any bearing on the first. One assumes that they don't, except as contrast. The playing is stately and very clearly articulated on what sounds like a good-quality modern piano, but there's nothing to get a fix on, much like being caught in a blizzard or in an all-white environment. And because the ear has no reference points, the music drifts by without registering strongly.

****(*) Emerald City**

Evidence ECD 22079 *Beirach; John Abercrombie (g).* 87.

Formerly listed under the Core imprint, this has recently reappeared with a rather better sound. Though a very gifted duo player – with Dave Liebman, Frank Tusa and others – Beirach fails to gel with Abercrombie, leaving a sense of discontinuous textures and undeveloped ideas. They'd worked together almost a decade earlier on the guitarist's *Arcade* for ECM, but little of that empathy carries over to these pairings.

***** Some Other Time**

Triloka 180 *Beirach; Randy Brecker (t, flhn); Michael Brecker (ts); John Scofield (g); George Mraz (b); Adam Nussbaum (d).* 4/89.

Some Other Time is a tribute to Chet Baker, who hired Beirach in the early 1970s and recorded two of his compositions, 'Broken Wing' and 'Leaving', both of which are recorded here. The group is as good as the affection for Chet and his music is patently sincere. Randy Brecker never attempts to pastiche his fellow trumpeter, but allows hints and allusions to colour his own ideas. Michael is more circumspect than usual, tiptoeing round the originals as if not quite sure he's got the point. The real star of the group is Mraz. He anchors the music brilliantly with a technique that is ageless and individual. Apart from the Beirach originals, the material is fairly predictable, with a final flourish on 'My Funny Valentine'. No mush, jut a thoroughly professional performance all round.

*****(*) Convergence**

Triloka 185 *Beirach; George Coleman (ts, ss).* 11/90.

No one but the two participants could possibly have known how well this unlikely partnership would work. Beirach's interest in complex harmonies would not be alien or unfamiliar to Coleman, a much subtler stylist than his bruising tenorman manner would suggest. Equally, Beirach himself is capable of a more grounded and rootsy delivery when occasion demands. *Convergence* opens with a first glimpse of Coleman on soprano, a complex, polyrhythmic arrangement of Gordon Parish's 'The Lamp Is Low' that feeds into both players' considerable harmonic daring. They alternate four-bar sequences on an unusual and effective reading of Miles Davis's 'Flamenco Sketches', the most open-ended of the themes on *Kind Of Blue*. There are three excellent Beirach originals, of which the best is the blues, 'Rectilinear', Coleman on soprano again. He also completes the set on the higher horn, appropriately on a version of Wayne Shorter's 'Infant Eyes'.

*****(*) Maybeck Recital Hall Series: Volume 19**

Concord CCD 6014 *Beirach (p solo).* 1/92.

'Elm', the closing number and the only original on the Concord, is as floaty and abstract as any of his supposedly avant-garde pieces. Beirach's approach to standards is always a touch elaborated, with a grandmasterish gambit and a schoolmasterish portentousness, like one of those gowned figures who love to talk about 'pedal appendages' rather than feet. Coincidentally, he's a brilliant user of the piano pedals, damping off notes sharply and then letting the harmonics run under the next delicately etched phrase. It's the sort of device that can very rapidly become self-conscious and contrived, but it's lovely when it comes off.

***** Too Grand**

Steeplechase SCCD 31333 *Beirach; Andy LaVerne (p).* 11/92.

***** Universal Mind**

Steeplechase SCCD 31325 *As above.* 11/93.

Two fine duet albums, the second of which is unusual in jazz terms for being a four-hands project, using just one piano. The culminating part is 'The Town Hall Suite', four Bill Evans compositions, played with great freedom and inventiveness. For the rest, the dominating presence is Miles Davis, whose 'Solar' and 'Blue In Green' are both included. There is also a fresh outing for Beirach's 'Elm'. The earlier record also includes two Miles tunes, 'Milestones' and 'So What', as well as material by Monk, Brubeck, Tyner, Shorter and a lovely version of 'Nature Boy'. Andy and Richie swap treble and bass duties throughout the four-hands record, but they seem to do the same instinctively, even when there are two pianos. The performance of Brubeck's 'In Your Own Sweet Way' is particularly forceful in this regard, a huge spread of sound that might be from a much bigger ensemble were it not for the rich piano chording and the percussive off-accents.

*****(*) Trust**

Evidence ECD 22143 *Beirach; Dave Holland (b); Jack DeJohnette (d).* 2/93.

This is the setting that shows him to best advantage, allowing him all the subtleties and filigree effects he might ever want, but driving him along as well. Only a rather leaden sound prevents us going the whole hog with four stars. Apart from Shorter's 'Nefertiti' and a track apiece by Holland and fellow-bassist Gary Peacock, all the material is new. This significantly adds to the impact of the record, because for a few years Beirach seemed to be getting bogged down in a set repertoire. The challenge suits him very well and he responds magnificently to the vigorous pulse. A shame that there isn't a more evenly spread stereo. The mix is lumpy in all the wrong places.

***** The Snow Leopard**

Evidence ECD 22193 *Beirach; Gregor Huebner (vn); George Mraz (b); Billy Hart (d).* 6/96, 6/97.

*****(*) Round About Bartók**

ACT 9276 2 *As above, except omit Hart.* 12/99.

The Snow Leopard is a wonderfully varied trio set – Huebner appears on just three tracks – that covers material by Coltrane ('Expression' and 'Naima'), Bill Evans ('Peace Piece'), Billy Hart's wonderful 'Redemption' and classical themes by Mompou and Bartók. There is also a moving and profoundly effective 'In The Wee Small Hours Of The Morning', on which Mraz references Frank Sinatra's famous recording of the song. Beirach's own compositions are typically eclectic. 'The Snow Leopard' is as rarefied and elusive as the creature itself, and as beautiful. 'Citizen Code' and 'Elm' are more generic, but none the less effective.

The more recent, drummerless set is a further extension of Beirach's desire to synthesize jazz and the language of modern classical music. He draws on themes by Skryabin and Kodály as well as Bartók, and juxtaposes folk themes from Eastern Europe with his own 'Zal'. Working without percussion emphasizes the classical feel of the trio, and Mraz works much of the time down in cello range. The recording is flawless, warm and intimate, and impeccably balanced.

Bob Belden (born 1956)

TENOR AND SOPRANO SAXOPHONES, KEYBOARDS

Belden grew up in South Carolina and studied in Texas, before working with Woody Herman and Donald Byrd. His own large ensemble played and recorded in 1989–90 and secured a reputation which allowed him subsequently to work with high-profile names such as Sting and Herbie Hancock.

****(*) Treasure Island**

Sunnyside SSC 1041D *Belden; Jim Powell, Tim Hagans (t, flhn); John Fedchock (tb); George Moran (btb); Peter Reit (frhn); Tim Ries, Craig Handy (ss, ts); Chuck Wilson (cl, f); Mike Migliore (as, f, picc); Ron Kozak (bcl, f); Glenn Wilson (bs); Marc Cohen (ky); Carl Kleinsteuber (tba); Jay Anderson (b); Jeff Hirshfield (d).* 8/89.

***** La Cigale**

Sunnyside SSC 1097D *As above, except Larry Farrell (tb), Marc Copland (p) replace Fedchock and Cohen.* 10/90.

Belden's first record as a leader was belated, but it's not terribly exciting. His own 'Treasure Island Suite' is a cumbersome piece of scoring without anything compelling in it, and the rest of this well-recorded CD (which runs for nearly 80 minutes) offers an eclectic bunch of modern big-band workouts. Migliore and Wilson, at least, add purposeful improvising.

La Cigale was recorded live at the 1990 Paris Jazz Festival. The programme has a similar feel to the studio date, but it's looser-knit, and the soloists in the band get to show their paces with some aplomb. 'Psalm No. 1 (For The Heavens)' emerges as a rather attractive piece of mood music.

***** Straight To My Heart**

Blue Note 95137 *Belden; Jim Powell (t, flhn); Tony Kadleck, Tim Hagans (t); John Fedchock (tb); George Moran (btb); Peter Reit (frhn); Tim Ries (ss, ts, bf); Mike Migliore (as, f, bf, picc); Chuck Wilson (cl, f, af); Bobby Watson (as); Rick Margitza, Kirk Whalum (ts); Glenn Wilson (bs); Joey Calderazzo, Marc Copland, Benny Green, Kevin Hays (p); Doug Hall, Adam Holzman (ky); Pat Rebillot (org); Jim Tunnell (g, v); John Hart, John Scofield, Fareed Haque (g); Darryl Jones, Jay Anderson (b); Dennis Chambers, Jeff Hirshfield (d); Abraham Adzeneya, Ladji Camara, Jerry Gonzales, David Earle Johnson (perc); Dianne Reeves, Phil Perry, Mark Ledford (v).* 12/89–5/91.

Eleven compositions by Sting arranged by Belden and performed by an all-star cast drawn from the current Blue Note roster. The material is steeped in what might be called pop sophistication: simple tunes and constructions with underlying harmonic detail to make it interesting for superior players, and Belden utilizes the original structures in interesting ways. 'Roxanne', for instance, has its melody deconstructed and turned into a haunting concerto for Hagans, repetition used with mesmerizing effectiveness. But airplay-orientated touches let down parts of the project: the vocal tracks are tedious and, of the soloists, only Hagans and the superb Margitza (on 'They Dance Alone', easily the best track) make an individual impression.

While Belden's subsequent project, *When Doves Cry: The Music Of Prince* (Metro Blue 829515-2), has much engaging music, it probably stands *just* outside the borders of this book. One could also say the same about *Tapestry* (Blue Note 57891), which covers Carole King's singer–songwriter classic as some kind of jazz entity, with the usual Blue Note star cast. All very interesting, but both are a dilettante's idea of a jazz record. These were comparatively early examples of a jazz writer addressing himself to the heartland of rock repertoire, which is becoming an increasingly widespread phenomenon, and Belden may one day assume pioneer status in this regard. He is now much in demand as an arranger and he has taken on a consultancy role at Blue Note.

Louie Bellson (born 1924)

DRUMS

Born Luigi Paolino Balassoni, the drummer was working with Goodman, Dorsey and James in the 1940s, but his most famous early association was with Duke Ellington, whom he joined in 1951. He continued to work in big bands until the mid-'60s, whereupon he led his own groups of varying size, although his most authoritative work remains in the orchestral situation.

***** Live At Flamingo Hotel 1959**

Jazz Hour JH-1026 *Bellson; Guido Basso, Johnny Frock, Ralph Clark, Wally Buttogello, Fred Thompson (t); Juan Tizol, Earl Swope, Nick Di Maio (tb); Joe Di Angelis (frhn); Frank Albright, Herb Geller (as); Aaron Sachs, Nick Nicholas (ts); George Perry (bs); Ed Diamond (p); Lawrence Lucy (g); Truck Parham (b); Jack Arnold (vib, perc).* 6/59.

***** Louie In London**

DRG 8471 *Bellson; Stan Reynolds, Stan Roderick, Greg Bowen, Kenny Wheeler, Eddie Blair, Pete Winslow, Freddy Staff, Harry Rochie, Wally Smith, Don Lusher, Bobby Lamb, Bill Geldard, Ken Goldie (tb); Roy Willox, Peter Hughes, Dennis Walton, Bob Efford, Brian Ashe, Bernie George, Keith Bird, George Hunter (reeds); Frank Horrox (p); Ernie Shear (g); Frank Donnison, Arthur Watts (b); Derek Warne (perc).* 5/70.

****(*) Jam With Blue Mitchell**

Original Jazz Classics OJC 802 *Bellson; Blue Mitchell (t, flhn); Pete Christlieb (ts); Ross Tompkins (p); Bob Bain (g); Gary Pratt (b); Emil Richards (vib, perc).* 9/78.

**** Cool, Cool Blue**

Original Jazz Classics OJC 825 *Bellson; Ted Nash (ss, ts); Matt Catingub (ss, as); Frank Strazzeri (p); George Duvivier (b).* 11/82.

****(*) The Best Of Louie Bellson**

Pablo 2405-407 *Bellson; Blue Mitchell, Snooky Young, Bobby Shew, Dick Mitchell, Dick Cooper, Cat Anderson, Conte Candoli, Walter Johnson, Ron King (t); Nick Di Maio, Gil Falco, Ernie Tack, Mayo Tiana, Bob Payne, Alan Kaplan, Dana Hughes (tb); Don Menza, Pete Christlieb, Dick Spencer, Larry Covelli, Bill Byrne, Ted Nash, Andy Macintosh (reeds); Nat Pierce, Ross Tompkins (p); Emil Richards (vib, perc); Mitch Holder, Grant Geissman, Bob Bain (g); John Williams, Joel Dibartolo, Gary Pratt (b); Paulo Magalhaes, Dave Levine, John Arnold, Gene Estes (perc).* 5/75–9/78.

**** The Louie Bellson Explosion**

Original Jazz Classics OJC 728 *Similar to above.* 5/75.

Louie Bellson is one of the last survivors of a breed of tough and tirelessly energetic men who powered big bands and small groups with the same mix of showmanship and sheer muscle. His comprehensive work with the big-band élite – including Goodman, Basie, James and especially Ellington – gave him a nearly unrivalled experience, and his own groups are marked out by an authority which is often masked by Bellson's comparatively restrained style: virtuoso player that he is, he always plays for the band.

The Jazz Hour CD resurrects a typical hotel engagement by his band as it stood at the end of the 1950s. Location sound is excellent and the authentic whomp of the Bellson kit fires up the band, though soloists are left precious little space to shine: Basso and Geller get some time to themselves in 'Blast Off', but there isn't much more than that. *Louie In London* uncovers three days of recording with a British big band from 1970. Mostly co-written by Bellson and Jack Hayes, the titles are a tourist's notebook ('London Suite', 'Proud Thames' and so forth) and the playing is spick-and-span in the worthy way of British big bands, but Bellson sounds as if he must have enjoyed it.

Many of Bellson's records from the 1970s and '80s are blemished by a shallow attempt at crossover and unhappy eclecticism. Several have now returned on CD. The pick is probably the *Jam* date with Mitchell, even though Blue isn't his old self, and Christlieb supplies the most reliable solos. *Cool, Cool Blue* has very little going on. The *Best Of* is no great shakes, but it distils some of the superior moments from what were otherwise dispensable records. The 1975 *Explosion* has its moments, but the best of them are on the compilation.

****(*) Prime Time**

Concord CCD 4064 *Bellson; Blue Mitchell (t); Pete Christlieb (ts); Ross Tompkins (p); Bob Bain (g); John Williams (b); Emil Richards (perc).* 78.

***** Raincheck**

Concord CCD 4073 *Bellson; Blue Mitchell (t); Ted Nash (as, ts); Ross Tompkins (p); Joe DiBartolo (b).* 78.

***** Dynamite!**

Concord CCD 4105 *Bellson; Nelson Hatt, Bobby Shew, John Thomas, Walt Johnson, Ron King (t, flhn); Nick Di Maio, Alan Kaplan, Dana Hughes, Bob Payne (tb); Dick Spencer, Matt Catingub, Andrew Mackintosh, Gordon Goodwin, Don Menza (saxes); Frank Collett (p); John Chiodini (g); John Williams Jr (b); Jack Arnold (vib, perc).* 8/79.

****(*) Live At Joe Segal's Jazz Showcase**

Concord CCD 4350 *Bellson; Don Menza (f, ts); Larry Novak (p); John Heard (b).* 10/87.

Of Bellson's eight earlier albums for Concord, a much more consistent sequence than his Pablo records, half are currently in catalogue. *Prime Time* is polished, tough, unpretentious swing-to-bop, with some late-autumn Mitchell and excellent Christlieb for seasoning – at least for the first four tracks (including 'Cotton Tail' at a tempo Ben Webster wouldn't have enjoyed). Then it dissipates into a kind of tepidly funky jazz, typical for the era. *Raincheck* muscles up around the then-19-year-old Nash and is a superior bet, though the programme of standards is a bit brusque. The big-band date is solidly satisfying without living up to its title, and the main interest probably lies in the gripping section-work by the brass and reeds. The *Joe Segal's* date finds Louie with his trusted sideman and arranger, Don Menza, a hard-swinging and gruff tenor soloist whose amiable drive finds decent if unspectacular assignment here.

****** Hot**

Musicmasters 5008-2 *Bellson; Bob Millikan, Larry Lunetta, Danny Cahn, Glenn Drewes (t); Clark Terry (flhn); Don Mikkelsen, Hale Rood, Clinton Sharman, Keith O'Quinn (tb); Joe Roccisano (as, f); George Young (ss, as, f); Don Menza (ts); Jack Stuckey (bs, bcl); Kenny Hitchcock (ts, cl, f); John Bunch (p); Jay Leonhart (b).* 12/87.

*****(*) East Side Suite**

Musicmasters 5009-2 *As above.* 12/87.

A delightful pair of records which revitalized Bellson in the studios. Superbly engineered and produced, the sound gives the band both warmth and a sheen of top-class professionalism, and the arrangements – by Menza, Rood, Roccisano and Tommy Newsom – return the favour. There are storming features for the leader – 'Blues For Uncommon Kids', the opener on *East Side Suite*, is an absolute knockout – but just as memorable are the smooth changes of gear, the lovely section-work on 'Peaceful Poet' (*Hot*), the spots allotted to guest horn Clark Terry, the sense that the band always has something extra in its pocket.

*****(*) Jazz Giants**

Musicmasters 5035-2 *Bellson; Conte Candoli (t); Buddy DeFranco (cl); Don Menza (ts); Hank Jones (p); Keter Betts (b).* 4/89.

Bellson's records took such a turn for the better around this point that earlier discs (and, disappointingly, some of the later ones) seem like wasted opportunities. Here he's leading a top-flight sextet on a European tour at their Swiss stopover, and as a festival blowing date this is about as good as it gets. The soloists make a nicely contrasting front line – DeFranco's punctiliousness, Candoli's light fire, Menza's muscularity – and Louie fires them up with superb and never overbearing drumming.

***** Airmail Special**

Musicmasters 5038-2 *Bellson; Bob Millikan, Danny Cahn, Glenn Drewes, Joe Wilder, Joe Mosello, Marvin Stamm (t, flhn); Keith O'Quinn, James Pugh, Hale Rood, Dave Taylor (tb); George Young, Joe Roccisano, Don Menza, Ken Hitchcock, Scott Robinson (reeds); Derek Smith (p); Charlie Descarfino (vib, perc); Remo Palmieri (g); Jay Leonhart (b).* 2/90.

Just a shade disappointing after the last few. Bellson is still in commanding form and the band alternately steam and glide through these scores, but another tribute to other bandleaders' hits isn't the most striking notion in jazz at this point and only the handful of originals really get much above professional smarts.

***** Black, Brown & Beige**

Musicmasters 65096-2 *Bellson; Clark Terry, Marvin Stamm, Bob Millikan, Barry Lee Hall, Anthony Kadleck (t); Britt Woodman, Arthur Baron, Dave Bargeron (tb); Alan Ralph (btb); Frank Wess, Phil Bodner, Bill Easley, Scott Robinson, Ted Nash, Joe Temperley (reeds); Lesa Terry (vn); Harold Danko (p); Gene Bertoncini (g); John Beal (b).* 92.

***** Live From New York**

Telarc 83334 *Bellson; Clark Terry (flhn); Marvin Stamm, Bob Millikan, Danny Cahn, Glenn Drewes, Darryl Shaw (t); Larry Farrell, Mike Savis, Keith O'Quinn (tb); Herb Besson (btb); Joe Roccisano, Steve Wilson (as); Ted Nash, Scott Robinson (ts); Jack Stuckey (bs); Derek Smith (p); Harvie Swartz (b).* 12/93.

Recorded 50 years after the première, this *BB&B* is a tad disappointing. Despite the presence of several Ellingtonians in the cast, the orchestra – perhaps consciously – makes no attempt at Ducal impersonation. Problematically, though, it finds no real character as a substitute. The band plays a polished treatment of the score and, while Duke might have admired it, he would surely have been bothered that no maverick touches bring it properly to life. Bellson's original piece, 'Ellington–Strayhorn Suite', which acts as a makeweight, is similarly precise and unadventurous.

Live From New York features another set of Bellson originals played by a proficient team, with Terry guesting on two tracks. This is archetypal, big, bruising stuff, though never quite as overbearing as a typical Buddy Rich date.

****(*) Their Time Was The Greatest!**

Concord CCD 4683 *Bellson; Conte Candoli, Pete Candoli, Walt Johnson, Frank Szabo, Snooky Young (t); Thurman Green, Andy Martin, Jimmy Zito (tb); Mike Wimberley (btb); Sal Lozano, Ray Reed (as); Pete Christlieb, Tommy Newsom (ts); Bill Green (bs); Frank Strazzeri (p); Dave Carpenter (b); Jack Arnold (perc).* 8/95.

Paying homage to twelve 'super-drummers', from Chick Webb to Steve Gadd, this feels too worked-over. Bellson himself sounds anything but tired and his various nods to his peer group have impeccable élan. The band, though, seem unable to bring any special fizz to the occasion and one waits in vain for the kind of over-the-top attack which gives the Buddy Rich tribute albums their punch.

***** Air Bellson**

Concord CCD 4242 *Bellson; Conte Candoli (t); Andy Martin (tb); Sal Lozano (as, ss, f); Pete Christlieb (ts, f); Larry Novak (p); Dave Stone (b).* 8/96.

Louie invites some favourite team members back for a solid septet date. One hardly expects surprises from such a situation and this is more like an amiable jog round the track than anything, but with Candoli, Christlieb and the maverick Martin each playing himself to some effect, it's good-natured fun.

Gregg Bendian

PERCUSSION

An improvising drummer-percussionist, Bendian first played in art-rock situations but moved into free music and has been associated with many leading improvisers.

***** Definite Pitch**

Aggregate CD 001 *Bendian (perc solo).* 94.

*****(*) Counterparts**

CIMP 105 *Bendian; Paul Smoker (t, flhn); Vinny Golia (sno, cl, bcl); Mark Dresser (b).* 1/96.

*****(*) Interzone**

Eremite MTE 03 *Bendian; Nels Cline (g); Mark Dresser (b); Alex Cline (d, perc).* 8/96.

Like Gerry Hemingway, whom he in many ways resembles, Bendian was originally excited by rock music, before discovering the richness of percussion-aware composers like Edgard Varèse. Bendian has pointed out that the main influences on his development of a solo improvisational approach were not other percussionists but free players like Cecil Taylor (who has recorded some Bendian compositions) and Derek Bailey (with whom he has since recorded, see above). With one exception, the pieces on *Definite Pitch* are all written for tuned instruments, hence the title; Bendian uses chimes, timps, chromatic boobams, electronic keyboard percussion, vibes, but only on one track does he attempt to create an ensemble effect by moving among different instruments. This is a work-in-progress recording with an emphasis on repaying debts. There are tributes to Bailey associate Jamie Muir, one of the most extravagant contemporary percussion improvisers, to Captain Beefheart/Don Van Vliet, to filmmaker Stan Brakhage, physicist Richard Feynmann and others.

Brakhage and Beefheart are interesting figures to acknowledge because much of Bendian's work is surreal and associative, and this is very much the mood of his first group-recording, in which he takes a more conventional drummer's part but reinterprets it in that same, rather maverick way. Smoker, Golia and Dresser are very much kindred spirits in this. The pieces (rather dimly recorded, it should be said, on Caden magazine's own label) are for the most part long and open-formed and they integrate arranged themes with what sound like totally free passages. Precisely where one begins and the other ends remains unclear and there is a constant sense, as in Braxton's works, of multiple subjects being engaged, sometimes sequentially, sometimes overlapping slightly, sometimes simultaneous as in a palimpsest. CIMP's dedication to this music is admirable, but their as-it-happens approach to the sound is a little troubling and might be addressed in future issues. These are, after all, expensive items and not everyone wants the warts and all.

Interzone seems to be and sounds like a settled performing unit. Bendian concentrates on vibes and glockenspiel, leaving more conventional time-keeping to Alex Cline, and relying on the two string players for much of the texture and colour in the set, and there is no shortage of either. Most of the tracks are long and detailed and are structured round quite complex rhythmic ideas. 'I-Zones' is unembarrassedly abstract and uncompromisingly lateral in approach. 'Sunblade Strafe The Continent' is more obviously evocative (though it certainly doesn't have an identifiable programme) and the enigmatic 'Blood: Sassoon zi tavit' might almost be an offcut from some unreleased project of John Zorn's. This is a strong set, faithfully recorded and well engineered by Michael Ehlers and Jon Rosenberg. A tip of the hat to them, as well.

*****(*) Espiritu**

Truemedia D 98715 *Bendian; Alex Cline (perc).* 2/97.

*****(*) Trio Pianissimo**

Truemedia D 99205 *Bendian; Steve Hunt (p); John Lockwood (b).* 98.

Two beautifully inflected discs by a musician who grows more musical with every record. The piano trio is, of course, not a conventional piano trio at all, though Bendian does kick back here and there and settle into an accompanist's groove that suggests nothing more – however unlikely this sounds – than Paul Motian's work with Bill Evans. This is probably the closest the percussionist will ever come to a straight jazz setting, albeit a fractured and asymmetrical bebop.

The opening 'Doshi' is a bustling, urgent thing that shifts between two subtly differentiated time-counts. 'Silvia' is more of a pianist's feature, with drum and cymbal accents flawlessly placed. There is something of a sameness about later tracks, though it is Lockwood who sounds one-dimensional; properly, most of the interest rests with Bendian himself. The closing 'Hysteresis' redeems any shortcomings; opening with fruity bass chords, it develops into a free-flowing improvisation built round an idea that might have come straight from Bud Powell's notebooks. A strong, beautifully executed album that might have been improved only by the inclusion of more varied material.

The duets with Alex Cline are heart-liftingly good, percussion playing of the highest order and unfailingly musical. All the tracks were recorded over one convivial evening and, though seemingly not sequenced on the record as performed, they have the flow and logic of an actual performance. Bendian's rippling vibraphone has all the expressive character one would expect of masters like Milt Jackson and Bobby Hutcherson, and yet it probably comes from somewhere closer to the music of John Cage and Lou Harrison. The opening 'Breakthrough' is breathtaking, and the pace scarcely lags thereafter. A lovely record.

****** Interstellar Space: The Music Of John Coltrane**

Atavistic ALP 102 *Bendian; Nels Cline (g).* 2 & 4/98.

One of the most interesting of a whole shelfload of Coltrane anniversary records, this one appeared long after due date and was largely overlooked. Basically, it is a retread of Trane and Rashied Ali's experimental duets on *Interstellar Space*. Interestingly, Nels Cline, brother of Interzone's Alex, does not push his powerfully amped guitar up into the multiphonic and harmonically complex atmospheres which the great saxophonist claimed for jazz in the '60s, relying instead on much simpler lines and an almost delicate phrasing.

Bendian is so wholly besotted by free-jazz drumming that he adopts the mannerisms with absolute authenticity. As pastiche, this would be wonderful. As a tribute to the permanent revolution in modern music, it is very nearly grand, a superbly modulated performance from both players. The zodiacal themes from *Interstellar Space* would have been easy to overcook, but there is a plainness and humility to these *hommages* which refreshes the original more than we would have thought possible. Hard to listen to this contemporary pairing without returning to the source material. Hard to revisit that without wanting to hear Bendian and Cline again. The bonus live performance of 'Lonnie's Lament' is as good as anything Bill Frisell and Joey Baron have committed to record: atmospheric, moving, not a whit self-indulgent.

Sathima Bea Benjamin

VOCALS

A singer whose association with her husband, Dollar Brand (Abdullah Ibrahim), led to these somewhat by-chance recordings.

*****(*) A Morning In Paris**

Enja 9309-2 *Benjamin; Duke Ellington, Abdullah Ibrahim, Billy Strayhorn (p); Svend Asmussen (vn); Johnny Gertze (b); Mkaya Ntoshko (d).* 2/63.

****(*) Love Light**

Enja ENJ 6022-2 *Benjamin; Ricky Ford (ts); Larry Willis (p); Buster Williams (b); Billy Higgins (d).* 9/87.

***** Southern Touch**

Enja ENJ 7015-2 *As above, except omit Ford, Willis; add Kenny Barron (p).* 12/89.

Bea Benjamin has been scandalously overlooked. Apart from references in pieces about her husband Abdullah Ibrahim (Dollar Brand), she is barely noted in jazz reference books. *Grove* has no entry on her, and even the usually PC Linda Dahl omits her from her study of women in jazz, *Stormy Weather*. The appearance of *A Morning In Paris* changes the picture entirely, and not merely because of her remarkable sidemen and producer.

Inevitably, it eclipses the two later Enjas almost entirely. *Love Light* is unflatteringly recorded, lending her voice an odd, adenoidal character, but it does also expose a singer who, 25 years down the line, had lost much of the affecting freshness that marks her incredible debut. *Southern Touch* is rather better, despite starting uneasily with 'Loveless Love/Careless Love', which seems endless. Barron and Williams do their best for her, but for us these later albums will always be a lost cause.

They are pushed out of sight by the belated release of the 1963 album, a 'lost' session which has acquired a certain legend down the years. That it survives at all is due to the habit of the recording engineer, Gerhard Lehner, of keeping a private listening copy of every session he taped. Benjamin and her then boyfriend Dollar Brand had arrived in Zurich in 1962, part of a widespread exile from South Africa. When the Ellington orchestra visited Switzerland the following February, Bea went along and asked Duke to listen to Brand and his trio. Ellington (wrongly) assumed she was the manager. 'No. But I sing sometimes.' 'Then you must sing. Go and sing.' On the basis of an impromptu rehearsal, Ellington suggested – or, rather, commanded – that Benjamin, Brand and the other members of the trio attend Barclay Studios in Paris three days later.

The instrumental cuts made that day have been known for years as *Duke Ellington Presents The Dollar Brand Trio*, the start of a long admiration that once led to Brand standing in for Duke, but the Bea Benjamin sessions were lost until the mid-'90s. The recordings are rather casual, her intonation far from perfect in places, and there is little in the way of profound emotion in the singing or playing. What distinguishes these amazing survivals is the sheer simplicity she brings to a standard programme. It is almost as if she has never heard any other singer cover 'The Man I Love' or 'Lover Man'. On the former, she sings the whole song in a mournful murmur, before Johnny Gertze's driving bass and Ntoshko's weird offbeat accents push it into double time and a very different emotional cast.

Ellington insisted on playing piano himself on 'Solitude' (very beautifully crafted) and 'I Got It Bad And That Ain't Good', while Billy Strayhorn sat in for 'A Nightingale Sang In Berkeley Square' and his own 'Your Love Has Faded'. A key element of the session was the exact, strangely expressive pizzicato violin of Svend Asmussen, who seems to have been there by chance. In later years, Benjamin was guilty of over-emoting material, a tendency reinforced by or perhaps the result of her insufficiencies as a composer. This, though, documents a very special moment, one to treasure.

Don Bennett (born 1941)

PIANO

A picaresque career is detailed below, but Bennett is otherwise a swinging hard bopper of distinction.

*****(*) Chicago Calling!**

Candid CACD 79713 *Bennett; Arthur Hoyle, Steve Smyth (t); Art Porter (as, ss); Eddie Peterson (ts); Erich Hochberg (b); Paul Wertico, Darryl Ervin (d).* 5/90.

***** Solar**

Candid CACD 79723 *Bennett; James Long (b); Douglas Sides (d).* 8/94.

A fascinating story. Bennett gave up music for a decade and spent part of his off-time working as a private investigator. On his return, *Chicago Calling!* was released on the small Illinois label, Southport; it garnered positive notices and was picked up by Candid boss, Alan Bates. One wonders what a larger label would have done with Bennett, perhaps throwing him into a studio with a couple of celebrity horns and the house rhythm-section. The pianist has preferred to work with players who are known to him but little known outside the Windy City. Peterson heads the music department at the University of Illinois, and he turns out to be a persuasive soloist and tight ensemble player. Likewise, Arthur Hoyle, who didn't last out the session, having to retire with busted chops and cede his place to young Smyth. Before he went, though, he recorded the lovely bridge solo on Bennett's 'Sleeping Child'. The composer's own contribution is very striking, terse but not inexpressive, and leaning heavily on the melody. This is his great strength. On 'Love Found Me' he conjures the sort of song that sounds as though it must have been around for generations. Porter's avowed Lucky Thompson influence is very evident in his soprano solo. Though Parker's 'Au Privave' and the long bonus, 'All The Things You Are' (added for the CD), are intensely exciting, it is the highly personalized originals that attract attention on the comeback record. For the trio recording that followed, Bennett put considerably more emphasis on other people's writing. He takes a typically unpredictable route through Miles's title-piece and 'Tune Up', and he closes with vividly renewed versions of 'Blue Moon' and 'A Night In Tunisia'. Gorgeous as both are, they're still in danger of being eclipsed by 'In Search Of …' and 'Blues For Nikki'. Like 'Prayer For Sean' and 'Steven's Song' on *Chicago Calling!*, these are not politely bland dedications but profoundly felt pieces in which the personality and perhaps even the voice of the dedicatees can be heard. Our only reservation about *Solar* is the way the trio is recorded: very big and unsubtle, with a boxy bass sound and uncertain miking on the kit.

Han Bennink (born 1942)

DRUMS, PERCUSSION, ALLSORTS

Played behind many visiting Americans in Dutch clubs in the '60s, before co-forming the Instant Composers Pool and taking a key role in the free music of the '60s and beyond. As celebrated for his humour in performance as his drumming, but he is a master of both.

***** Serpentine**

Songlines SGL 1510 *Bennink; Dave Douglas (t).* 1/96.

Bennink is a showman whose clowning occasionally masks his formidable musical intelligence. One famous aspect of a live performance is his liking for beating out rhythm on the stage or floor with 'brushes' – not a drummer's usual set of wire, but janitor's brooms, often of considerable size. The payoff, of course, is that Bennink is always on the money, no matter what he happens to be playing. There is little around under his own name. A solo album made for FMP 20 years ago still hasn't reappeared. Many records with Brötzmann from the '70s are in the vinyl lost-and-found. There is a duo CD with Derek Bailey, another with Ellery Eskelin, and there are a good many appearances on jazz and improv records and with the Clusone 3.

The drummer is listed first on this disc and the ubiquitous Douglas has a quite large enough entry of his own, so it seems reasonable to treat *Serpentine* as a Bennink disc. Thirteen mostly short tracks, interspersing extemporized originals, a couple of tunes that sound as if they've had some preparatory work done on them, and a couple of standards, most startlingly 'Cherokee', which is a vividly comic but also deeply felt performance. 'Too Close For Comfort' is prefaced by 'Two Clogs For Comfort', but mostly the tone is quite sober. Both 'Serpentine' and 'Delft', the two most substantial pieces, are written by Douglas, but he does seem to defer to the drummer in performance. Han's sheer force of personality is always going to win the day, whatever the setting, whoever the partner.

George Benson (born 1943)

GUITAR, VOCAL

Sang from an early age and made R&B records as a teenager. Then focused on guitar, touring with Jack McDuff from 1962, his own albums from 1965, and sideman appearances with Miles Davis and others. Broke through to major crossover success in the '70s, first as a guitarist, then with a return to singing and upmarket soft-soul hits. Occasional forays back towards some kind of straight-ahead playing as his pop audience has waned.

***** The New Boss Guitar**

Original Jazz Classics OJC 460 *Benson; Red Holloway (ts); Jack McDuff (org); Ronnie Boykins (b); Montego Joe (d).* 5/64.

The huge success he earned in the 1970s and '80s as a light soul vocalist has obscured some of the impact of Benson's guitar playing. He is a brilliant musician. His first records were made when Wes Montgomery was alive and the acknowledged master of the style which Benson developed for his own ends: a rich, liquid tone, chunky chording which evolved from Montgomery's octave technique, and a careful sense of construction which makes each chorus tell its own story. At his best he can fire off beautiful lines and ride on a 4/4 rhythm with almost insolent ease; strain is never a part of his playing. Almost any record that he plays guitar on has its share of great moments, although this early date with his then-boss McDuff is comparatively routine, its short tracks and meagre playing-time very much in the organ-combo genre that churned out scores of records in the early and middle '60s. But it's still very good.

***** The Silver Collection**

Verve 823450-2 *Benson; Jimmy Owens (t, flhn); Clark Terry, Ernie Royal, Snooky Young (t); Garnett Brown (tb); Alan Raph (btb); Arthur Clarke, George Marge (ts, f); Pepper Adams (bs); Buddy Lucas (hca); Herbie Hancock, Paul Griffin (p); Jimmy*

Smith (org); Eric Gale (g); Jack Jennings (vib, perc); Bob Cranshaw, Ron Carter, Chuck Rainey (b); Billy Cobham, Jimmy Johnson Jr, Idris Muhammad, Donald Bailey (d); Johnny Pacheco (perc); strings. 1/67–11/68.

*** Talkin' Verve

Verve 553780-2 *Similar to above.* 2–11/68.

*** George Benson: Verve Jazz Masters 21

Verve 521861-2 *Similar to above discs.* 2/68–11/69.

After leaving McDuff, Benson cast around for success without really breaking through. His clean, funky but restrained style was hardly the thing in Hendrix's era, and the easy-listening option which Montgomery fell prey to had yet to envelop him while at Columbia and Verve. The *Silver Collection* and *Jazz Masters* sets are very similar, each an intelligent cross-section of Benson's small number of recordings in the period: a hot quintet with Hancock, Carter and Cobham glide through 'Billie's Bounce' and 'Thunder Walk', while 'I Remember Wes' is a sensitive tribute to the lately deceased Montgomery. The tracks with a larger band are ordinary; but this hints at Benson's growing versatility and suggests that he was already seen as Montgomery's natural successor. *Talkin' Verve* concentrates on tracks from the two original LPs, *Giblet Gravy* and *Goodies*, and to that extent is slightly more restricted in range. None of this is deathless music but it's begun to gather a period appeal to go with the virtues of Benson's playing.

*(*) Shape Of Things To Come

A&M CD-0803 *Benson; Joe Shepley, Marvin Stamm (t, flhn); Burt Collins (t); Wayne Andre (tb, bhn); Alan Raph (tb, vtb, tba); Buddy Lucas (ts, hca); George Marge, Romeo Penque, Stan Webb (f); Herbie Hancock, Hank Jones (p); Charles Covington (org); Jack Jennings (vib); Bernard Eichen, Charles Libove (vn); David Markowitz (vla); George Ricci (clo); Richard Davis, Ron Carter (b); Leo Morris (d); Johnny Pacheco (perc).* 8/67–10/68.

*** Beyond The Blue Horizon

CTI ZK 65130 *Benson; Clarence Palmer (org); Ron Carter (b); Jack DeJohnette (d); Michael Cameron, Albert Nicholson (perc).* 2/71.

** White Rabbit

Columbia 450555-2 *Benson; John Frosk, Alan Rubin (t, flhn); Wayne Andre (tb, bhn); Jim Buffington (frhn); Hubert Laws (f, picc); Phil Bodner (f, ob, cor); George Marge (f, cl, ob, cor); Romeo Penque (cl, bcl, ob, cor, f); Jane Taylor (bsn); Herbie Hancock (p); Gloria Agostini (hp); Phil Kraus (vib, perc); Jay Berliner, Earl Klugh (g); Ron Carter (b); Billy Cobham (d); Airto Moreira (perc, v).* 11/71.

Creed Taylor, who ran things at CTI, certainly thought Benson should carry on where Montgomery had left off. The A&M album, which quickly bogs down in Don Sebesky's typically ponderous arrangements, is a wet run for what came next, a sequence of strong-selling albums which found Benson gamely making the best of a near-hopeless situation. Given Taylor's proclivities for stupefying charts and tick-tock rhythms, it's surprising that there's as much decent music as there is here, although some of the original albums are currently (thankfully?) in limbo. The new edition of *Beyond The Blue Horizon* has claims on being Benson's best record in print. 'So What' and 'The Gentle Rain' are among the high points of Benson's CTI work, lyrical but quite hard-bitten in their handling, and with the excellent rhythm section behind him the guitarist finds plenty of room to stretch out. There are three alternative takes (none very revealing) on this new remastering. *White Rabbit* finds him ambling through pop material while reeds pipe soothingly behind him. Benson still finds interesting fills, but it's a terribly weak assignment for a man who was playing on *Miles In The Sky* a few years earlier. *Beyond The Blue Horizon* will do for anyone who wants to hear the pick of Benson's CTI work.

*** Breezin'

Warner Bros 256199 *Benson; Ronnie Foster, Jorge Dalto (ky); Phil Upchurch (g); Stanley Banks (b); Harvey Mason (d); Ralph McDonald (perc); strings.* 1/76.

** In Flight

Warner Bros 256327 *As above.* 8–11/76.

*** Weekend In L.A.

Warner Bros 3139-2 2CD *As above, except omit strings.* 2/77.

Breezin' was the first jazz album to go platinum and sell a million copies, but more important for the listener was its reconciliation of Taylor's pop-jazz approach with a small-group backing which Benson could feel genuinely at home in: Claus Ogerman's arrangements are still fluffy, and the tunes are thin if not quite anodyne, but Benson and his tightly effective band get the most out of them. It's a very pleasurable listen. *In Flight* reintroduces Benson as vocalist (he actually began as a singer in the 1950s), and 'Nature Boy' blueprints the direction he would take next, but the record is too patently a retread of the previous one. *Weekend In L.A.* is a live set that shows how the band can hit a groove outside the studio. Benson's treatment of 'On Broadway' is an infectious classic because he lives out the song; the session as a whole is a bit deodorized, but smoothness is the guitarist's trademark, and his solos are full of singing melodies, tied to their own imperturbable groove.

** Tenderly

Warner Bros 25907 *Benson; McCoy Tyner (p); Ron Carter (b); Louis Hayes, Al Foster (d).* 89.

** Big Boss Band

Warner Bros 26295 *Benson; Bob Ojeda, Byron Stripling, Randy Brecker, Jon Faddis, Lew Soloff, Larry Farrell (t); Paul Faulise, Earl Gardner, Keith O'Quinn, James Pugh (tb); David Glasser (as); Frank Foster (ts); Barry Eastmond, Richard Tee, Terry Burrus, David Witham (ky); Ron Carter (b); Carmen Bradford (v); Count Basie Orchestra; Robert Farnon Orchestra.* 90.

*** Best Of George Benson – The Instrumentals

Warners 946660-2 *As Warners albums above.*

Most of Benson's records after *Weekend In L.A.* fall outside the scope of this book, although many rate as high-calibre light-soul. But of late he's been investigating a return to more jazz-orientated material, possibly as a result of a somewhat waning general popularity. Guest appearances as a sideman with such friends as Earl Klugh and Jimmy Smith haven't yielded much, though, and these two sets must be counted great disappointments. *Tenderly* is far too relaxed: Benson's singing sounds tired, and his playing is as uneventful as that of the others involved, although such seasoned pros always deliver a few worthwhile touches. Weaker still is *Big Boss Band*, a collaboration with Frank

Foster's Count Basie band that runs aground on fussy arrangements, material Basie himself wouldn't have touched (the soporific 'How Do You Keep The Music Playing'), and one track with Robert Farnon's band ('Portrait Of Jennie') which suggests that a shot at Nat Cole's repertoire might have been the next thing on George's agenda (it wasn't, as it turned out). His guitar playing takes an entirely minor role. The new instrumental *Best Of* makes a game effort at distilling the jazz ingredients in Benson's pop albums, and it's agreeable enough, covering 1976–93 – even though several pieces sound like a master musician reduced to the sappiest of instrumental pop.

Benson has since signed to GRP for a couple of records that try to make his pop-jazz contemporary again. He has gone steadily back towards the hard stuff with the albums *That's Right* and *Standing Together*, and the 2000 release *Absolute Benson* comes close to his old form. Players like Joe Sample, Christian McBride and even Cindy Blackman are on hand to up the ante. But there is a distant veil of synthesizers on most tracks so as not to upset smooth-jazz radio, and by the end it's clear that George is long past the point of risking losing what remains of his easy-listening audience.

Alison Bentley

VOCALS

Vocalist and lyric-writer trying a jazz situation.

*** Alison Bentley Quartet

Slam SLAMCD 211 *Bentley; Mornington Lockett (ts); Jonathan Gee (p); Dave Jones (b); Paul Cavaciutti (d).* 12/94.

Alison Bentley is an elegant lyricist with an unspectacular but warm and subtle vocal delivery. Her songs are perhaps better than these particular performances of them. It's an oddity of the record that after it finishes one wants to hear it played again, but differently. It's no coincidence that the strongest tracks are those on which Lockett plays. At the mid-point of the set, 'Angels On A Pin' is a high point, reminiscent of Norma Winstone's 1970s' work, albeit with a folksier strain. Lockett's statement appears to chaff the song's ambiguities, before dissolving into its own. Gee, as always, is a sensitive and responsive accompanist, one of the best partners a singer could hope for.

Bob Berg (born 1951)

TENOR SAXOPHONE, SOPRANO SAXOPHONE

The New Yorker's career began early with Brother Jack McDuff, in whose group he played as a teenager. Technically less astute than Michael Brecker, whom he somewhat resembles, Berg has always overcome technical limitations by his sheer power and conviction, and his records have never quite had the authority of his live appearances. A complex man who has had his share of problems, Berg always has a story to tell, however haltingly.

***(*) Steppin'

Red RR123178-2 *Berg; Danilo Rea (p); Enzo Pietropaoli (b); Roberto Gatto (d).* 82.

A stint with Miles Davis, far from pushing Berg into the limelight, set his always-promising solo career back a good album or two. Miles, for reasons obvious from his earlier CV, has been less than generous to his latter-day reedmen, obviously looking on the sax as a regressive instrument *vis-à-vis* happening things like 'lead' bass guitars, synths and drum machines.

Berg is a hugely talented mainstream player with a well-assimilated Coltrane influence who could never realistically have been expected to fit into Miles's avant-disco conception. What he was expected to put in is now history, but what did he take away with him? Listening to him on *Steppin'*, which was recorded live in Europe with a decent but uninspiring band, the answer to that is as ambiguous as the question. In later years, Miles moved ever closer to the blues, and it's possible to hear Berg attempt the same simplification of idiom in almost every track on the Italian date, even when the material is reasonably complex. Tom Harrell's 'Terrestris' was an interesting composition to include; it isn't a tune that sits easily for the saxophone, but Bob turns it into a taut harmonic essay. His own 'Arja' is as lovely a thing as he's ever done but it is marred by a very distant recording. Another original, 'Luce di Fulvia', and an imaginative version of Stevie Wonder's 'Secret Life Of Plants' round out the record.

***(*) Enter The Spirit

Stretch GRS 00052 *Berg; Chick Corea, Jim Beard, David Kikoski (p); James Genus (b); Dennis Chambers (d).*

***(*) Riddles

Stretch GRS 00112 *Berg; Gil Goldstein (acc); Jim Beard (p, org, ky); Jon Herington (g, mand); Victor Bailey, John Patitucci (b); Steve Gadd (d); Arto Tuncboyaciyan (perc, v).* 94.

**** Another Standard

Stretch SCD 9013 *Berg; Randy Brecker (t); David Kikoski (p); Mike Stern (g); Ed Howard (b); Gary Novak (d).* 96.

Enter The Spirit was a more-than-welcome return to form, though it isn't clear from the record *when* this actually took place. Recorded on Chick Corea's label, it's far more musicianly and far less packaged than the earlier records. Berg lets his imagination take him along on the more extended themes – notably Chick Corea's enticing 'Snapshot' and 'Promise' – and dispatches more familiar repertoire like 'I Loves You, Porgy' and Rollins's 'No Moe' with great élan. Berg still doesn't write very appetizingly, and 'Blues For Béla' is hardly worthy of a jazz studies undergraduate. But his playing is getting there and, with this guy, that's what matters.

Riddles marks a step forward. There is turbulence that one doesn't detect on the more recent records and a power in the soloing that seems to come from deep within. Unlike, say, Michael Brecker, who always manages to sound completely in command of his material, Berg is best when he is on the brink of letting everything fall drastically apart.

Another Standard was the record some observers felt Berg should have made some years earlier, as a way of demonstrating that he could work someone else's turf convincingly and not just hide behind his own material. Not surprisingly, what transpires is an album that has Bob Berg written all over it: wry, witty, anarchic and sternly disciplined in one carefully assembled package. The outstanding performance is on 'It Was a Very Good Year', which Berg deconstructs from the bottom up, weaving a soprano line round Kikoski's piano. Adding Randy Brecker on two tracks

('My Man's Gone Now' and 'I Could Write A Book') suggests that Berg has absorbed himself in the work of Miles's quintet with Coltrane, while Mike Stern's walk-on part on 'No Trouble' is extremely effective, another Miles alumnus who has learnt to do things his way. Berg's desire to keep close to the original tunes is admirable, though more often honoured in the breach, for these are highly intelligent reinventions, packed with ideas and unflaggingly interesting.

Anders Bergcrantz (born 1961)

TRUMPET, CORNET, FLUGELHORN

Danish post-bop trumpeter with an increasing international reputation.

*** Live At Sweet Basil

Dragon DRCD 225 *Bergcrantz; Rick Margitza (ts); Richie Beirach (p); Ron McClure (b); Adam Nussbaum (d).* 2/92.

***(*) In This Together

Dragon DRCD 261 *As above, except omit Margitza.* 8/94.

Bergcrantz is a gifted hard-bop trumpeter whose fiery early days are settling into a more considered but still attacking manner. Some earlier records for Dragon have yet to make it to CD, and the enjoyable *Live At Sweet Basil* is unfortunately something of a pot-boiler. Bergcrantz is among peers for this New York visit, and he takes a firm lead with two interesting originals of his own and a striking recasting of 'Body And Soul' among other themes, but the sound of the group lacks the clear weave of his Swedish bands and the music isn't as tautly sustained as his earlier records. Margitza makes a useful partner – there's a nice touch of European bleakness about his tone – and Beirach, McClure and Nussbaum are this time dependable and classy rather than inspired. The sound is a little fuzzy when it ought to bite.

In This Together is very, very good. In the studio, the quartet comes together perfectly: Beirach plays in his most concentrated style, and McClure and Nussbaum swing mightily. Bergcrantz takes a more measured course than usual, pacing himself through his solos and finding a mellow, woodsmoked sound on flugelhorn. He comes up with tones and phrasings which no American trumpeter would play and, set against the strong yet thoughtful pulse of the others, the result is a rare kind of post-bop. Even so, it's difficult to sustain a trumpet quartet date for an hour, and just here and there one wishes for another horn for some piquancy, or to propel Bergcrantz in a fresh direction. Exemplary recording, done in New York.

**** C

Dragon DRCD 293 *As above.* 10/96.

It's a wonderful group, and this on-tour CD caught them at a playing peak. The 'C' is for Coltrane, and the four men give a pretty amazing impression of the great quartet on the title-track without resorting to mere copycat tricks. Beirach sounds bigger and stronger than he ever has, McClure is the epitome of the invisible, soulful bassman, and Nussbaum simply ransacks the kit for every bit of Elvin he can find. They do similar things on 'Footprints' and the rather more mysterious 'Renfield', but there's a lovely flugelhorn ballad on 'I Won Her Heart' and a quite thoughtful look at 'Stella By Starlight'. Interestingly, Bergcrantz chooses to play cornet more often than not, and it seems to put a bit of extra jab into his quicker phrases. His long solos have fire, ingenuity and elegance in as close to equality as one can hope. A great live one.

Karl Berger (born 1935)

VIBRAPHONE, PIANO

Born in Heidelberg, Berger learned to play jazz piano in the company of visiting Americans. After musical study at home and in Berlin, he switched his interest to free jazz and moved first to Paris (with Don Cherry) and then to the USA, where he and Ornette Coleman founded the Creative Music Studio at Woodstock, NY. This and similar educational activities have limited Berger's recorded output.

*** We Are You

Enja 6060 *Berger; Peter Kowald (b); Allen Blairman (d, perc); Ingrid Sertso (v).* 11/71.

The group with Kowald and Blairman finds him in free-ish mode, a vibes style that has more in common with fellow-European Gunter Hampel than with Bags or Hutcherson. Berger plays rather quietly, often with the electric fans on the vibraphone switched off, which renders the sound much purer and lighter. Sertso is an attractive enough singer but she lacks strength and presence, and one listens for a horn rather than a voice where she is placed in the group.

*** Just Play

Emanem 4037 *Berger; Ed Blackwell (d, perc).* 3/76.

Berger and Blackwell had worked together in Don Cherry's group and it was to be an important association for the vibist. This session was recorded in Albany, New York, by the estimable Martin Davidson. The 1979 Quark LP has long been out of circulation. Five of the tracks are for vibes (without fans) and drum kit, but the longest and most adventurous compositions are for African balafon and osi – or slit – drum. The two pieces, 'Balafon Samba' and 'Wood And Skin Works', occupy almost half the record between them. The shorter tracks are more dynamic but don't recapture the same, almost hypnotic, quality. Blackwell is in great form, perfectly in balance with Berger's own delicate touch.

***(*) Transit

Black Saint BSR 0092 *Berger; Dave Holland (b); Ed Blackwell (d).* 8/86.

*** Crystal Fire

Enja 7029 *As above.* 4/91.

The best of Berger's recorded output lies in the trio with Holland and Blackwell. 'Dakar Dance' and 'Ornette' on *Transit* are both open-hearted and expressive. The second record is much more inward-looking. Parts of the 'Crystal Fire Suite' are frankly boring and there's too much of Berger's alternately plonky and histrionically flowing piano (he sounds as though he spent his piano lessons skipping from 'Chopsticks' to 'Rustle Of Spring'). Holland is a completely sympathetic collaborator; this is very much his territory. One wonders about the choice of Blackwell rather than a European drummer better adapted to these abstractions. There's a sense that he's having to work harder than the others, giving the quieter tracks a rather tense quality that presumably isn't intentional.

***** Conversations**

In + Out IOR 77027 *Berger; Ray Anderson (tb); Carlos Ward (as, f); Mark Feldman (vn); James Blood Ulmer (g); Dave Holland (b); Ingrid Sertso (v).* 94.

Because of its relative lightness, the vibraphone makes an excellent duo instrument and the partnerships on *Conversations*, some long-standing, some new, show Berger off at his best. Inevitably, he only seems as good as his opposite number allows him to be, and Ulmer's contribution is (to say the least) unilluminating; but on balance this is a very fine album, up with his best.

***** No Man Is An Island**

Douglas Music ADC 4 *Berger; Enrico Rava (t); Arkady Shilkoper (frhn); Bernd Konrad (sax, cl); Jean Louis Maltinier (acc); Ernst Reijseger (clo); Marc Abrams (b); Billy Elgart (d, perc); Mutare String Trio; Ingrid Sertso (v).* 95.

No Man Is An Island was originally a radio commission for performance at the Donaueischingen Festival. John Donne's words (and the title is his most famous, overquoted line) give the work a coherence and a unity it would otherwise lack, for it is a rather scrappy structure, in nine rather fragmentary movements. Berger makes clear that the sixth of these is really a thing apart, a spontaneous memorial to the late Don Cherry. Even so, it's a little difficult to find a common thread in the rest. When it works, it works as a sequence of brilliant episodes. Rava's trumpet playing is as crystalline and gorgeous as ever and Reijseger's cello, quirky, oddly pitched and staccato, is the perfect foil to it. Berger himself once again alternates piano and vibraphone and always sounds much more convincing on the vibes.

Chuck Bergeron

BASS

Experienced sessionman–bassist with this rare leadership outing to his name.

***** Coast To Coast**

A Records AL 73107 *Bergeron; Randy Brecker (t); Rick Mandyk, Rick Margitza (ts); Charles Pillow (ts, bcl); John Hansen, Mike Holober (p); John Hart (g); John Bishop, Jeff Hirshfield, John Riley (d); Pat Ankrom (perc).* 1 & 7/97.

The title refers to the big bassist's removal from New York City to Seattle; *Coast To Coast* was recorded in both cities, a bright and varied set of originals. The basic section of Holober, Bergeron and Hirshfield is varied on the Seattle sessions by drummers Bishop and Riley and by a nicely judged permutation of horns. Brecker brings his usual pugnacious lyricism to 'The Spoiler', which might almost come from some lost Blue Note session, while the long 'Last Call', the centrepiece of the set, is distinguished by Pillow's elegant and moody bass clarinet. The album tails off with 'Last Tango In Gotham' and the only standard, 'I Only Have Eyes For You', but by then it has made its point with agreeable emphasis and, even shorn of a couple of tracks, it's still an impressive showing.

Totti Bergh (born 1935)

TENOR AND SOPRANO SAXOPHONES

Began on clarinet and later switched to tenor. Worked on cruise ships during the 1960s and since then has worked on a semi-pro basis. An exemplar of Norway's jazz mainstream.

*****(*) I Hear A Rhapsody**

Gemini GMCD 48 *Bergh; Per Husby, Egil Kapstad (p); Terje Venaas (b); Egil Johansen, Ole Jacob Hansen (d).* 8/85.

***** Tenor Gladness**

Gemini GMCD 53 *As above, except add Al Cohn (ts); omit Husby and Johansen.* 8/86.

***** On The Trail!**

Gemini GMCD 78 *As above, except Plas Johnson (ts) replaces Cohn.* 8/91.

*****(*) Remember**

Gemini GMCD 88 *Bergh; Joe Cohn (g); Erik Amundsen (b); Tom Olstad (d); Laila Dalseth (v).* 3/95.

***** Warm Valley**

Gemini GMCD 91 *Bergh; Einar Iversen (p); Kare Garnes (b); Eyvind Olsen (d).* 10/96.

Totti Bergh is a master saxophonist whose home-base of Norway has never managed to release him on to a wider audience. That shouldn't deter listeners from seeking out at least one of these handsome records. Bergh plays with the timeless authority of the mainstream saxman and there's scarcely a step out of place on any of these five sessions. *I Hear A Rhapsody* is a luscious set of ballads, the tenor curling round the melodies and huffing through solos that barely bother to move; lovely stuff, though, and the rhythm sections are good enough never to let the music bog down in treacle. Bergh's meeting with Al Cohn calls to mind the many Zoot-and-Al partnerships, perhaps slightly to Bergh's disadvantage, though Cohn (near the end of his life) was also taking things steady that day. The meeting with Plas Johnson is a bit livelier and there is some enjoyable banter on the likes of 'Smooth Sailing' and 'Tickle Toe'.

Bergh has never had a better sound in the studio than he has on the two most recent records. *Remember* is perhaps the best record the tenorman has made: Joe Cohn is a deft and encouraging partner who persuades the leader into his most beguiling form on 'Two Funky People' and 'Foolin' Myself'. Laila Dalseth (alias Mrs Bergh) sings five of her Merrillesque vocals and a long record never outstays its welcome. *Warm Valley* is another set of ballads which this time is just a shade too quiescent to hold the interest throughout, although any five minutes from the record will surely delight a casual listener. Bergh's grand tone and patient phrasing remain a steadfast pleasure.

Borah Bergman

PIANO

For a time, Borah Bergman concentrated exclusively on playing with his left hand in order to build up strength, suppleness and the kind of right-brain co-ordination that now underpin his formidable technique. Though most obviously of the Cecil Taylor school, his astonishing solo performances also recall the 'two pianists' illusion associated with Art Tatum, though in a fragmentary and disorderly sound-world far removed from Tatum's or that of the stride and ragtime pianists who are also part of Bergman's background.

****** A New Frontier**

Soul Note 121030 *Bergman (p solo).* 1/83.

***** The Fire Tale**

Soul Note 121252 *Bergman; Evan Parker (ss).*

*****(*) The Human Factor**

Soul Note 121212 *Bergman; Andrew Cyrille (d).* 6/92.

****** First Meeting**

Knitting Factory Works KFW 175 *Bergman; Roscoe Mitchell (as, ss); Thomas Buckner (v).* 12/94.

Record companies insist that no overdubs, multi-tracking or tape-speeding have been used on their records only when something rather special is going on inside. That is certainly the case with Borah Bergman, whose initial impact as a player can be likened – however lame a cliché this has become – only to that of Cecil Taylor. Bergman is both a composer and an improviser, and it is often difficult to draw lines between the two. What he has done is to break down any residual distinction between left- and right-hand functions in piano playing. On the two large-scale pieces which make up *A New Frontier* he sets up huge whirling shapes with each hand, which then engage in dialogue – often confrontational dialogue, at that. There is something slightly mechanistic about the playing on 'Night Circus' that makes one think of the player-piano pieces of Conlon Nancarrow, but this is eliminated on the remarkable 'Time For Intensity', a more richly coloured pair of contrasting pieces, the second of which, 'Webs And Whirlpools', must be one of the most purely astonishing piano performances of all time.

In contrast to these, the duos with Evan Parker are almost conventional, conforming to the basic idiomatic conventions of improvised music. Nevertheless there is a scope to 'The Fire Tale', a piece about the survival and extinction of creativity, and to 'Red Desert', which Bergman has recorded before, for which only classical parallels effectively apply. If some of the solo pieces are symphonic, the duos have to be heard as bizarre concertos in which the element of contention has once again taken over from simple concord.

The disc with Cyrille is both exhilarating and exhausting. Framed by two approaches to the title-theme and, more surprisingly, two takes of 'Chasin' The Trane' (why didn't he record that with Parker?), it is both visceral and intellectually challenging. 'Red Shadows' reappears from the earlier record, and Bergman enthusiasts must already be aware how doggedly and self-critically he pursues certain ideas. Even with Cyrille in harness, Ayler might perhaps be a more accurate analogy than Taylor, though for sheer thump there's not much in it.

Even given the variety of the foregoing, what a complete surprise *First Meeting* is. Coming to it with expectations based on the earlier records, on some knowledge of Mitchell's fierce saxophone poetry, or simply on reputation, one is astonished by the delicacy and precision, the sheer *quietness* of these pieces. 'Clear Blue' particularly has a limpid quality, as if every note had been gently diluted in water before being exposed to the air. Mitchell's breath-sounds are often louder than the actual reed-notes. Thomas Buckner was there as producer only, but it was decided that he should take part, and he did so, unrehearsed, on the suite, 'One Mind', bringing a further dimension to a riveting, gentle and perfectly centred hour of creative music.

****** Eight By Three**

Mixtery M00001 *Bergman; Anthony Braxton, Peter Brötzmann (reeds).* 4/96.

***** Exhilaration**

Soul Note 121330 *Bergman; Peter Brötzmann (as); Andrew Cyrille (d).* 9/96, 1/97.

Exhilaration consists of four stunning trio tracks and a further duo session with Bergman and Brötzmann, all recorded at the Knitting Factory. If the prevailing mood is exhilaration as in the first item, then it's of a particularly hectic and troubled sort. Bergman goes off like an express train, leaving nothing but sparks and cinders in his wake, and more or less abandoning Cyrille and even the normally sanguine Brötzmann standing in their tracks. Later tracks are quieter and more reserved, and with much more attention to structure. For the most part, though, this is a headlong set that demands much of the listener.

The set with Braxton is measured, cool and almost alien in its absence of expressionist dramas. The balance of two horns and piano is a hard one to sustain at length, but Bergman is a caustic enough player not to be troubled by it.

***** A New Organization**

Soul Note 121322 2 *Bergman; Oliver Lake (as).* 99.

Recorded live at the Knitting Factory, this is a fascinating encounter between two very different avant-gardists who have drawn on different and opposite aspects of twentieth-century music. Whether their work does represent a further step towards a new organization of musical language is more questionable, because much of this sounds like basic improv, stripped of its more schematic and abstract qualities. The intensity of 'I Kiss Your Eyes' and 'Forever Fervent' is not just a function of their titles, but something genuinely residing in the music, which toys with major–minor oppositions and slithers in and out of polytonality but which ultimately depends on melody, and melody alone, for its impact.

Jerry Bergonzi (born 1947)

TENOR AND SOPRANO SAXOPHONE

A Bostonian, Bergonzi studied at Berklee and went to New York in the early '70s, spending a period in the Dave Brubeck group, before returning home in 1981 to teach and play.

****(*) Jerry On Red**

Red 123224 *Bergonzi; Salvatore Bonafede (p); Dodo Goya (b); Salvatore Tranchini (d).* 5/88.

***** Inside Out**

Red 123230-2 *As above, except Bruce Gertz (b) replaces Goya.*

****(*) Lineage**

Red 123237 *Bergonzi; Mulgrew Miller (p); Dave Santoro (b); Adam Nussbaum (d).* 10/89.

***** Tilt**

Red 123245-2 *Bergonzi; Andy LaVerne, Salvatore Bonafede (p); Bruce Gertz (b); Salvatore Tranchini (d).* 5/90.

Bergonzi already had many years in jazz behind him before he made these dates: a quartet date from 1983 on the Plug label is worth seeking out as a vinyl rarity. The Red albums may disappoint those who've heard him in some excellent sideman situations, but the studio sound doesn't flatter him and we still find these to be unrepresentative of his talents; they suggest a tenor-man consistently in hock to Rollins and Coltrane and doing his best to struggle free of them. From moment to moment the records impress, but there isn't enough to make one much want to return. None of these is truly outstanding and Bergonzi's harshness and false-register cries are often more ugly than powerful. *Lineage* keeps up a high level of energy and inventiveness on its own terms. The best records, though, are *Inside Out* and *Tilt*. Gertz and Tranchini create a solid foundation with few distractions, and Bergonzi's rather spare writing works best in this context: 'Jones', from *Tilt*, makes the most of its simple bass motif, and the other tunes provide just enough material to keep the long, dissonant tenor solos on a particular track.

***** Etc Plus One**

Red 123249-2 *Bergonzi; Fred Hersch (p); Steve LaSpina (b); Jeff Hirshfield (d).* 3/91.

*****(*) Signed By**

Deux Z 84104 *Bergonzi; Joachim Kühn (p).* 10/91.

***** Peek A Boo**

Evidence 22119 *Bergonzi; Tiger Okoshi (t, flhn); Joachim Kühn (p); Dave Santoro (b); Daniel Humair (d).* 10/92.

Bergonzi's records have been growing in stature. *Etc Plus One* documents his meeting with Fred Hersch's trio, the pianist's elegance of line a shrewd counter to the saxophonist's spilling energy and hard sound. The result is a record that tends to drift between sensibilities, interesting if never quite compelling; and there are probably a few tracks where an extra take could have secured a higher result.

The duet with Kühn grips from the first, with 'Manipulations' asking Bergonzi to go as far out as he ever has over Kühn's vamping bass figure. One is reminded of both the Shepp/Parlan and Barbieri/Ibrahim duets, except that Bergonzi is a more accurate, specific executant than either of those saxophonists. His big tone has never been caught better than it is here and, though some of the pieces seem diffuse, the best of them act as both meditation and fierce interaction between the two men.

Peek A Boo, though Kühn is on board again, is more conventional. Bergonzi's command of the horn is one of the striking qualities here, and the expertise of this quintet can be enjoyed by itself, though again nothing in the set really stands out as unmissable.

*****(*) Vertical Reality**

Musidisc 500642 *Bergonzi; Mike Stern (g); Andy LaVerne (p); Mike Stern (g); George Mraz (b); Billy Hart (d).* 2/94.

***** Just Within**

Double-Time DTRCD 127 *Bergonzi; Dan Wall (org); Adam Nussbaum (d).* 12/96.

*****(*) Lost In The Shuffle**

Double-Time DTRCD-142 *As above.* 1/98.

Vertical Reality is one of Bergonzi's most appealing records. Stern's soft-toned electric guitar has an insinuating quality on the five tracks he appears on, which undercuts Bergonzi's usual grittiness, for the better. Mraz and Hart work so well together that they can be listened to by themselves: note Hart's textbook playing on 'Lover Man', subtle and evolved without drawing attention away from the soloists.

The Double-Time discs document a fruitful partnership with Wall, whose second-banana status to many a frontman can make one miss how good he is, and the skilful Nussbaum. Not quite an old-time bluesologist on the Hammond, there's no shortage of guts in Wall's playing, but the harmonic shading and soft melodic fills are a necessary counterweight to a musician like Bergonzi. Nussbaum is big and brawny at the kit, and the music has a quality of inexorable forward motion to go with the thoughtful aspects. Both of these dates are meritorious, and the second is that bit more expansive and substantial. Bergonzi has rarely been flattered by studio microphones and there's a hardness in his sound which some may find it difficult to warm to.

Gunnar Bergsten

BARITONE SAXOPHONE

Swedish baritone saxophonist, a Mulligan man from a young generation.

*****(*) The Good Life**

Arietta ADCD 5 *Bergsten; Peter Nordahl (p); Patrik Boman (b); Rune Carlsson (d).* 6/95.

*****(*) Somewhere**

Arietta ADCD 17 *As above, except Leif Wennerstrom (d) replaces Carlsson.* 1/98.

Gullin, Mulligan, Chaloff, Carney: Bergsten belongs in the highest company that this low instrument has kept. His light-bodied sound allows him a mobility which the big horn needs to get around a ballad without making it seem overweight and, while he prefers a steady mid-tempo, a quicker pace here and there gives him no difficulties. Listen to what he does with the old Gene Ammons chestnut, 'Ca Purange', on *Somewhere*: every idea is extracted from the theme, still kept in sight, but by the end Bergsten has been on a very long and masterfully navigated voyage. 'Ask Me Now' on *The Good Life* is that rarity, a Monk interpretation which has very little of Monk about it and a great deal of its interpreter. This is unambitious music in the way of its delivery – Bergsten pretends to nothing revolutionary, any more than the excellent Nordahl does – but in terms of poise and generosity these are wonderfully playable records.

Bunny Berigan (1908–42)

TRUMPET

He had college-band experience behind him when in 1931 he joined Fred Rich, then Paul Whiteman, though he disliked the music and took every chance at a hot solo on a studio session. He was a big hit when he joined Benny Goodman – and, later, Tommy Dorsey – but his own big bands were commercial disasters and he had to fight off bankruptcy. His greatest playing – with its huge sound, fascination with the low register and swinging poise – could cut most other players of his time, but chronic alcoholism and depression destroyed him, and he died in 1942.

***** Swingin' High**

Topaz TPZ 1013 *Berigan; Nate Kazebier, Joe Aguanno, John Fallstitch, Irving Goodman, George Johnston, Steve Lipkins, Ralph Muzillo, Jerry Neary, Charlie Spivak, Jimmy Welch, Carl Warwick, Joe Bauer, Bob Cusumano, Johnny Napton (t); Glenn Miller, Morey Samuel, Red Ballard, Jack Lacy, Marc Pasco, Al Jennings, Ray Conniff, Bob Jenny, Tommy Dorsey, Red Bone, Al George, Sonny Lee, Les Jenkins (tb); Johnny Mintz, Matty Matlock, Benny Goodman (cl); Fred Stulce, Clyde Rounds, Henry Saltman, Toots Mondello, Hymie Schertzer, Charlie DiMaggio, Jack Goldie (as); Gus Bivona, Murray Williams, Sid Pearlmutter, Joe Dixon (cl, as); Eddie Miller (cl, ts); Bud Freeman, Georgie Auld, Dick Jones, Don Lodice, Harry Walsh, Arthur Rollini, Dick Clark, Stewart Anderson (ts); Frank Froeba, Joe Lippman, Claude Thornhill, Fats Waller, Edwin Ross, Joe Bushkin (p); Eddie Condon, Larry Hall, Dick McDonough, Carmen Mastren, Tommy Moore, Tom Morgan, George Van Eps, Dick Wharton, Allan Reuss (g); Harry Goodman, Arnold Fishkind, Delmar Kaplan, Grachan Moncur, Pete Peterson, Mort Stuhlmaker, Gene Traxler, Hank Wayland (b); Ray Bauduc, Cozy Cole, Paul Collins, Eddie Jenkins, Gene Krupa, Dave Tough, George Wettling (d); Wingy Manone, Jack Leonard (v).* 4/35–11/39.

***** Portrait Of Bunny Berigan**

ASV Living Era AJACD 5060 *As above, except add Paul Hamilton and His Orchestra; Frankie Trumbauer and His Orchestra.* 32–37.

*****(*) Bunny Berigan 1935–1936**

Classics 734 *Berigan; Jack Lacey (tb); Joe Marsala, Slats Long, Artie Shaw, Paul Ricci (cl); Edgar Sampson (cl, as); Eddie Miller (cl, ts); Forrest Crawford, Art Drelinger, Bud Freeman, Herbie Haymer (ts); Joe Bushkin, Frank Froeba, Cliff Jackson (p); Dave Barbour, Bobby Bennett, Eddie Condon, Clayton Duerr (g); Artie Bernstein, Artie Shapiro, Mort Stuhlmaker, Grachan Moncur (b); Ray Bauduc, Maurice Purtill, Cozy Cole, Dave Tough (d); Chick Bullock, Tempo King, Midge Williams (v).* 12/35–8/36.

*****(*) Bunny Berigan And The Rhythm Makers: Volume 1 – Sing! Sing! Sing!**

Jass J-CD 627 *Berigan; Irv Goodman, Steve Lipkins, Ralph Muzillo, Harry Preble (t); Ray Conniff, Nat Lobovsky, George Mazza, Artie Foster (tb); Artie Shaw (cl); Joe Dixon, Mike Doty, Carl Swift (cl, as); Georgie Auld, Artie Drelinger, Clyde Rounds (ts); Joe Bushkin, Joe Lippman (p); Dick Wharton (g); Mort Stuhlmaker, Hank Wayland (b); Johnny Blowers, Bill Flanagan (d); Ruth Gaylor, Peggy , Bernie Mackey (v); other personnel unidentified.* 7/36–6/38.

*****(*) Bunny Berigan 1936–1937**

Classics 749 *Berigan; Irving Goodman, Harry Greenwald, L Brown, Cliff Natalie, Steve Lipkins (t); Morey Samuel, Sonny Lee, Frank D'Annolfo, Ford Leary, Red Jessup (tb); Matty Matlock (cl); Sid Pearlmutter, Joe Dixon, Slats Long, Henry Freling (cl, as); Toots Mondello, Hymie Schertzer (as); Artie Drelinger, Babe Russin, Clyde Rounds, Georgie Auld (ts); Joe Bushkin, Les Burness, Joe Lippman (p); Eddie Condon, Tom Morgan (g); Arnold Fishkind, Mort Stuhlmaker (b); Manny Berger, George Wettling (d); Art Gentry, Ruth Bradley, Johnny Hauser, Carol McKay, Sue Mitchell (v).* 11/36–6/37.

****** Bunny Berigan 1937**

Classics 766 *Berigan; Irving Goodman, Steve Lipkins (t); Morey Samuel, Sonny Lee, Al George (tb); Mike Doty, Sid Pearlmutter, Joe Dixon (cl, as); Clyde Rounds, Georgie Auld (ts); Joe Lippman (p); Tom Morgan (g); Arnold Fishkind, Hank Wayland (b); George Wettling (d); Ruth Bradley, Gail Reese (v).* 6–12/37.

****** Bunny Berigan 1937–1938**

Classics 785 *As above, except add Ray Conniff, Nat Lobovsky (tb), Graham Forbes, Fulton McGrath (p), Dick Wharton (g), Dave Tough (d), Ruth Gaylor (v).* 12/37–5/38.

*****(*) Bunny Berigan 1938**

Classics 815 *As above, except add John Napton (t), George Bohn, Gus Bivona, Milton Schatz, Murray Williams (cl, as), Buddy Rich (d), Jayne Dover, Kitty Lane, Bernie Mackey (v).* 6–11/38.

***** Gangbusters**

Hep CD 1036 *Berigan; Steve Lipkins, Irving Goodman, George Johnston, Jack Koven, Johnny Napton (t); Nat Lobovsky, Ray Conniff, Bob Jenney, Andy Russo (tb); Gigi Bohn, Milton Schatz, Hank Saltman, Murray Williams (as); Gus Bivona (cl, as); Georgie Auld, Don Lodice (ts); Clyde Rounds, Larry Walsh (ts, bs); Joe Bushkin (p); Dick Wharton, Allan Reuss (g); Hank Wayland (b); Eddie Jenkins, Buddy Rich (d); Jayne Dover, Kitty Lane, Bernie Mackey (v).* 9/38–3/39.

****(*) 1938 Broadcasts From The Paradise Restaurant**

Jazz Hour JH 1022 *Berigan; Georgie Auld (ts); Dave Tough (d); personnel unknown but probably from above.* 38.

***** Bunny Berigan And The Rhythm Makers: Volume 2 – Devil's Holiday!**

Jass JCD 638 *Berigan; Steve Lipkins, Irving Goodman (t); Ray Conniff, Nat Lobovsky (tb); Mike Doty, Joe Dixon (cl, as); Georgie Auld, Clyde Rounds (ts); Joe Bushkin (p); Dick Wharton (g); Hank Wayland (b); Johnny Blowers (d); Ruth Gaylor (v).* 6/38.

***** Bunny Berigan 1938–1942**

Classics 844 *Berigan; Joe Aguanno, John Fallstitch, Irving Goodman, Bobby Mansell, Arthur Mellor, Johnny Napton, Freddy Norton, Jack Koven, George Johnston, Carl Warwick (t); Ray Conniff, Max Smith, Charlie Stewart, Mark Pasco, Al Jennings, Bob Jenny (tb); Gus Bivona, Charlie DiMaggio, Jack Goldie, Henry Saltman, Walt Mellor, George Quinty, Murray Williams (cl, as); Georgie Auld, Stewart Anderson, Don Lodice, Neil Smith, Red Lang, Larry Walsh (ts); Joe Bushkin, Eugene*

Kutch, Edwin Ross (p); Tommy Moore, Allan Reuss (g); Mort Stuhlmaker, Tony Estren, Hank Wayland (b); Paul Collins, Eddie Jenkins, Buddy Rich, Jack Sperling (d); Kathleen Long, Danny Richards, Nita Sharon (v). 1/38–1/42.

Bunny Berigan's only flaw, in Louis Armstrong's opinion, was that he didn't live long enough. At the height of his career as an independent bandleader he was making impossible demands on an uncertain constitution. As a leader, he could be wildly exciting or beautifully lyrical, cutting solos like those on the concerto-like signature-piece, 'I Can't Get Started' (there are two versions, but the 1937 one is the classic); he was always one of the boys in the band but was utterly inept as an organizer. Stints with disciplinarians like Goodman and Tommy Dorsey (who valued his genius too much to pitch him out) didn't change his ways.

Though he died prematurely burnt out, Berigan left a legacy of wonderful music. The Topaz compilation is a pretty good introduction, basically chronological and nicely paced, better on the early years but not going quite as far back as the ASV Living Era package, which isn't so precisely documented; hard to pick between them. Converts, though, will certainly want the Classics documentation in full. Berigan's tone was huge and 'fat', a far cry from the tinny squawk with which he started out. The 1936 material on Jass was recorded for NBC's Thesaurus series of 16-inch electrical transcriptions. The arrangements are mostly very bland and the only thing that holds the attention is Berigan's horn, either open or muted, cutting through the pap with almost indecent ease. Typical devices are his use of 'ghost' notes and rapid chromatic runs that inject a degree of tension into music that often sounds ready to fall asleep.

By contrast, the small groups anthologized on the first Classics volume are sparky, tight and wholly inventive. Chick Bullock's vocals are no great asset, except on those occasions when they give Berigan the chance to mimic his singer's phrasing. The disc also includes six tracks under Frank Froeba's leadership and featuring Midge Williams, who later went on to make her own records. Pretty obscure stuff, this, but worth having for Berigan's buoyant fills.

That Berigan's time-sense and ability to play instant counter-melodies were God-given there is no doubt, but it's also clear that he studied Armstrong closely and learned a great deal from him. That's evident from the solos on 'Sing! Sing! Sing!' and 'On Your Toes'. The second volume continues with the June 1938 sessions and kicks off with the best track yet, a rousing 'Shanghai Shuffle' with Auld and Dixon bracketing Berigan himself; Dixon returns for another couple of choruses on alto at the end. Ray Conniff is featured on 'I Never Knew (I Could Love Anybody)' but it's not so much the solos that stand out as the section playing which often sounds like a much bigger band, yet is also marvellously detailed.

The Hep set is also an excellent buy. It covers the period between the two Jass dates with a detailed documentation of autumn 1938, which must be considered a final peak before Berigan's financial and alcoholic slide of the following year. There is a substantial mythology attached to Berigan's drinking. Looking at the 1938 recording schedule suggests he may have been as much a workaholic as an alcoholic. The falling away, perfectly evident on the final Classics volume, was doubtless tragic, but it came after a period of sustained excellence, a body of work attained by few who lived twice as long. The high point, undoubtedly, came in 1937 and 1938, and serious enthusiasts should make the relevant Classics volumes their priority. Long for its time at four minutes and forty seconds, 'I Can't Get Started' is exemplary jazz playing, with that mix of sheer bravura and pathos that was Berigan's signature. His solo on 'The Wearin' Of The Green' on the 1937–8 volume is a nod to Irish ancestry, blustering and demonstrative, but also touchingly guileless. Berigan's ability to sustain power throughout his impressive range was one of his most durable characteristics, and he retains the ability to say more in fewer notes than any of his rivals. His development is logical, and impressively simple; he tackles 'Russian Lullaby' without the onion-y emotion most players of the time brought to Irving Berlin's tune, and his deep-toned solo on 'A Serenade To The Stars' is as moving as trumpet gets before Miles Davis came along. These days, certainly among younger listeners and recent jazz converts, Berigan is little known. He should, rather, be remembered and heard as one of the great hornmen in the music. Almost any of the above discs will provide the evidence.

Dick Berk (born 1939)

DRUMS

Born in San Francisco, Berk was playing behind Billie Holiday and Anita O'Day when still a teenager. Moved east and studied at Berklee, returned to California (1968) and became a regular sessionman. Also leads own hard-bop-mainstream groups.

***(*) Bouncin' With Berk

Nine Winds NWCD 0142 *Berk; Andy Martin (tb); Mike Fahn (vtb); Tad Weed (p); Ken Filiano (b).* 6/90.

***(*) Let's Cool One

Reservoir RSR 122 *Berk; Andy Martin (tb); Jay Collins (ts); Tad Weed (p); Jeff Littlejohn (b).* 9/91.

*** East Coast Stroll

Reservoir RSR 128 *Berk; Jay Collins (ts); John Hicks (p); Dan Faehnle (g); Ray Drummond (b).* 2/93.

***(*) One By One

Reservoir RSR 143 *Berk; Andy Martin (tb); Mike Fahn (vtb); Tad Weed (p); Dan Faehnle (g); Phil Baker (b).* 10/95.

Berk, a strong drummer in the hard-bop manner, sometimes calls his bands The Jazz Adoption Agency. *Bouncin' With Berk* was an impressive start to a strong sequence of records. The two trombones are a telling match, both quiet virtuosos with a needling edge to their playing, and on thoughtfully revised bop set-pieces such as 'Lament' and 'Jive Samba' the quintet secure a real identity. Much of the credit goes to Weed, who acts as MD for the first two records and arranges the material in surprising ways. On *Let's Cool One*, he fashions a stop-go treatment of 'My Favorite Things', cools off the customary heat of 'A Night In Tunisia' and puts in a couple of smart originals in 'Judy, Judy' and 'Food Club'. Collins is a youthful saxophonist but he plays with grouchy maturity, and Martin repeats his fine turn from the previous disc. Sound on the Nine Winds album is regrettably thin and lacking in impact; on *Let's Cool One* it's congested but more full-bodied.

East Coast Stroll suffers a little from Weed's absence: Hicks and Drummond play with their usual skill, but they're doing session-man chores rather than being part of the band. Worthwhile, but something of a pressure drop. *One By One* brings back Martin, Fahn and Weed, and it's a winning result. Weed gets to show off his chops on 'Lester Left Town', and the other Shorter tune, 'One By One' itself, is beautifully voiced for the trombones. 'Blues For Dogs' is a tersely effective blues and perhaps only 'Lotus Blossom', where for once the horns sound a bit odd, is a misfire. Otherwise Fahn and Martin take plenty of head-turning solos. Berk himself, always a reluctant soloist, plays handsomely for the band.

Bernard Berkhout

CLARINET

Dutch clarinettist playing in an 'old-fashioned' mainstream style.

*** Airmail Special

Timeless SJP 360 *Berkhout; Frits Landesbergen (vib); Jeroen Koning (g); Frans Bouwmeester (b); Bob Dekker (d).* 7/90.

A group of young fogeys from Holland, centred round the swinging and stimulating partnership of Berkhout and Landesbergen, both of whom have a knack for taking not quite the expected route through their solos. The programme is Goodmanesque and the timbres of the group not very different from a classic B.G. line-up, yet Berkhout's variety of shadings – from a Getzian breathiness to dirty notes and sudden boppish flares – and Landesbergen's clear-headed virtuosity aim for something else. They don't always make it happen, since clarinet, vibes and soft-spoken rhythms will never move too far from the cocktail lounge, but it's interesting to hear them try. Beautiful studio sound.

**** Royal Flush

Timeless SJP 425 *Berkhout; Ian Cooper (vn); Ian Date, Horst Weber (g); Frans Van Geest (b).* 5/94.

Berkhout's gift is to take a jazz setting of foregone conclusion and resolve it in a wholly unexpected way. The opening track, 'Who?', is almost lubricious in its delivery, and throughout the disc the five players make deep, sensuous work out of what looks like a Palm Court programme and a hotel-lounge instrumentation. Berkhout's inspired playing – agile, yearning, without a hint of routine – is matched by Cooper's violin, which takes the Grappelli approach without overdoing the sweetness. Guitars and bass create a rich textural interplay below, as well as pushing the music forward when they have to. A memorable surprise for anyone who hears it.

Berlin Contemporary Jazz Orchestra

GROUP

The name tells the story, although this is only a very 'occasional' ensemble, with its participants usually busy with other matters.

**** Berlin Contemporary Jazz Orchestra

ECM 1409 *Benny Bailey, Thomas Heberer, Henry Lowther (t); Kenny Wheeler (t, flhn); Henning Berg, Hermann Breuer, Hubert Katzenbeier (tb); Ute Zimmermann (btb); Paul Van Kamenade, Felix Wahnschaffe (as); Gerd Dudek (ts, ss, cl, f); Walter Gauchel (ts); Ernst Ludwig Petrowsky (bs); Willem Breuker (bs, bcl); Misha Mengelberg, Aki Takase (p); Günter Lenz (b); Ed Thigpen (d); Alex von Schlippenbach (cond).* 5/89.

Much as Barry Guy's London Jazz Composers Orchestra has turned in recent years to large-scale composition, the Berlin Contemporary Jazz Orchestra presents its conductor/organizer with a more formal and structured resource for presentation of large-scale scored pieces with marked tempi for improvising orchestra. One outwardly surprising inclusion in the line-up is drummer Ed Thigpen, normally associated with conventional mainstream jazz. This superb set features one long piece by Canadian trumpeter Kenny Wheeler and two rather less melancholy pieces by Misha Mengelberg. Wheeler's 'Ana' is a long, almost hymnic piece whose mournful aspect nevertheless doesn't soften some powerful soloing; Thomas Heberer, Aki Takase and Gerd Dudek are just the most notable contributors, and the piece is held together as much by Thigpen's robust swing as by Wheeler's detailed score. Mengelberg's 'Reef Und Kneebus' and 'Salz' are very much in the line of a post-war Dutch style in which jazz is almost as dominant an element as serial procedures. Mengelberg's music is frequently satirical, then unexpectedly melancholy. Benny Bailey's bursting solo on 'Salz' prepares the way for some determined over-blowing on the second piece, which fits jazz themes into a 'Minuet', 'Rigaudon', 'Bourrée' matrix. (If the middle element is less familiar, it relates to another seventeenth-century dance-form with a sharp rhythmic hop at the opening and a central bridge passage which sharply changes the direction of both music and dancers. Of such turns are both of Mengelberg's compositions made.) Outstanding solos from Dudek again and van Kamenade, while, on 'Salz', Breuker almost matches Bailey for sheer brass – or, in this case, woodwind. Thoroughly enjoyable and thought-provoking music.

***(*) Live In Japan '96

DIW 922 *Axel Dorner, Thomas Heberer, Issei Igarashi, Henry Lowther (t); Marc Boukouya, Paul Rutherford, Haruki Sato, Wolter Wierbos (tb); Walter Gauchel (ts); Evan Parker (ts, ss); Gerd Dudek (ts, ss, f, cl); Eiichi Hayashi (as); Hiroaki Katayama (ts, bs); Alexander von Schlippenbach, Aki Takase (p); Nobuyoshi Ino (b); Paul Lovens (d).* 96.

Live, the BCJO is a formidable proposition. The opening 'Eric Dolphy Medley' ('The Prophet', 'Hat And Beard' and the blues, 'Serene') invites comparison with what the Vienna Art Orchestra has done with similar material. The German outfit, more realistically a League of Nations band, is unexpectedly more swinging and more true to the original thrust of the music, and yet at the same time more abstract as well. Alex von Schlippenbach is responsible for most of the remaining material, which includes his arrangement of Gordon Jenkins's 'Goodbye' and a fine version of his own 'The Morlocks'. The soloing is crisp, direct and to the point, and very well registered on this recording. An attractive and very enjoyable record, by no means as forbidding as might at first appear.

Tim Berne (born 1954)

ALTO SAXOPHONE, BARITONE SAXOPHONE, VOICE

Berne is never going to be considered one of the great instrumentalists of modern jazz, but his dogged self-determination and application to a starkly challenging idiom commend him as an experimenter who would surely have found a willing berth in the loft scene of the '60s. He is devoted to the music and the earthly philosophy of Julius Hemphill, a challenging guru for any musician.

*** Empire Box

Screwgun 700095 CD *Berne; Olu Dara (c); Glenn Ferris, James Harvey, John Rapson (tb); John Carter (cl); Vinny Golia (bs, picc, f, afl, bsn, khene); Mark Goldsbury (ss, ts); Nels Cline (g); John Lindberg, Roberto Miranda, Ed Schuller (b); Alex Cline (d).* 79–82.

Tim Berne called his first album *The Five Year Plan*. He released it himself, apparently unwilling to wait around for the bigger labels to get their heads together and totally unwilling to spend five or ten years hacking it as a sideman. *Empire Box* is a release on Berne's own label and it brings together the records he released as an unsigned independent between 1979 and 1981. This was a raw and in some respects unfocused period in Berne's development, and listening to these records after a gap of some years suggests a stash of rehearsal and workshop tapes that wouldn't otherwise have seen the light of day. This is not to decry them, because by 1979 genuine experimentation was at an appallingly low ebb in jazz. Berne's first release begins with a piece dedicated to Hemphill on his intense, squalling alto; it's a sound that was not to change significantly over the next couple of years. The Cline brothers were to be responsive partners, and Vinny Golia, a deft and clever instrumentalist, fills in a lot of ground that Berne himself is technically unable to cover. The material on *7X* was smoother and more harmonically centred, with trombone and guitar combining to give Berne's sour-toned forays a more settled foundation. The last of the bunch, *Songs And Rituals In Real Time*, was very stripped down – just two saxophones, bass and drums – but our favourite remains the 1981 *Spectres*, with its three-horn front line and stunningly inventive rhythm section of Alex Cline and either Ed Schuller or John Lindberg on bass.

Heard in bulk and after a lapse of nearly 20 (!) years, some of this sounds unbearably callow, and it might have been better to have filleted out a double CD of the strongest material: say 'The Glasco Cowboy' (that Hemphill posy from the debut disc), '7X' and 'Flies' from the second record; 'Grendel' and 'Stroll' from *Spectres*; and maybe the hugely ambitious 'The Ancient Ones' from *Songs And Rituals*. These, though, are subjective preferences and could change by tomorrow morning. Whatever, this reissue is too exhaustive to be entirely compelling.

*** The Ancestors

Soul Note 121061 *Berne; Herb Robertson (t, pkt-t, c, flhn); Ray Anderson (tb, tba); Mack Goldsbury (ts, ss); Ed Schuller (b); Paul Motian (d, perc).* 2/83.

*** Mutant Variations

Soul Note 121091 *As above, except omit Anderson, Goldsbury.* 3/83.

*** Fulton Street Maul

Koch Jazz 7826 *Berne; Bill Frisell (g); Hank Roberts (clo, v); Alex Cline (perc, v).* 86.

*** Sanctified Dreams

Koch 7825 *Berne; Herb Robertson (t, pkt-t, flhn, c); Hank Roberts (clo, v); Mark Dresser (b); Joey Baron (d).* 10/87.

The Ancestors was a first sign that Berne was willing to slow down, look about him and take stock. Recorded live, it's a measured, authoritative set, rhythmically more coherent than previous and later sessions, with passages of almost Asiatic beauty from Berne and some classic trombone from the still-developing Anderson. Berne's charts are increasingly adventurous, and ensemble passages are well played and registered in a typically professional Soul Note production. The set's coherence might be credited to the veteran Motian (he takes a fine solo on one piece and holds together the excellent *Mutant Variations*, with its leaner, punchier line-up), who makes a very effective rhythmic anchor with Schuller, a veteran of Berne albums.

Bizarrely, Berne was signed to Columbia in the mid-'80s – which was either a stroke of creative generosity on the corporation's part or a wooden horse operation, or a simple mistake. Certainly, the saxophonist does not appear to bow to major-label pressure, and he delivers a tough, antagonistic set that even after 15 years has a sandbagging power and thuggish authority. Like the leader, Frisell doesn't know his own strength. A bold reissue for Koch, who have rescued some valuable recordings over the last couple of years, though none as uncompromising as this.

Sanctified Dreams was originally released on Columbia in 1988 but, as at various stages in his career, Berne has regained control of the material and seen it reissued. After a decade it still sounds fresh, if a touch crude and over-eager, though that must be accounted a description rather than a criticism of what Berne does. The key players here are Robertson and Baron, always very forthright when they do appear, but relishing this setting and turning in career-best performances which make up for an occasionally lacklustre showing by the leader, who is also maddeningly, even perversely inconsistent.

*** Unwound

Screwgun SCREW U 70001 3CD *Berne; Chris Speed (ts, cl); Michael Formanek (b); Jim Black (d).* 3 & 4/96.

With the demise of JMT, Berne was once again thrown back on his own resources. He formed Screwgun and, with this unvarnished live recording, kicked off his own imprint. The performances, from Berlin and Ann Arbor, are raw, immediate and proudly unproduced, long versions of things like 'Blood Count' and 'What Are The Odds?', which on its own would have occupied the whole of an old-fashioned LP. Berne seems determined to go for the jugular with every tune, blazing away with an indiscriminate ferocity that alienates and attracts in equal proportion. Black is astonishingly good, clattering and riffing in a manner that suggests Joey Baron crossed with some fallen angel of percussion. Speed keeps his end up … just, but really isn't either passionate or charismatic enough for the material. Most of the attention is focused on the leader; never a virtuosic player, never a man who can move with a beautiful tone or a graceful phrase, he relies on a hectoring, abrasive sound that is less lovely than it is forceful.

***(*) **Visitation Rites**
Screwgun SCREW U 70002 *Berne; Drew Gress (b); Tom Rainey (d).* 96.

Sample three large, raw slabs of music, one composition by each of the three players, packaged with ugly artwork and unreadable texts, and still find yourself drawn in by Berne's other group of the moment. His own 'Piano Justice' is the longest piece of the set, a peculiar, almost perverse agglomeration of ideas. Rainey and Gress are heroic, making the best of what sounds like an unpromising acoustic and an unyielding crowd. Berne remains oblivious to everything except his own soapbox rant. It isn't pretty, but isn't it compulsive?

*** **Big Satan**
Winter & Winter 910 005 *Berne; Marc Ducret (g); Tom Rainey (d).* 5/96.

Much less rough and raw than the live sets on Screwgun – this was also recorded in concert, at *Instants chavires* in Montreuil – but music of relentless violence all the same. The closing 'Description du tunnel' is one of the most unrelieved pieces Berne has ever recorded. 'Dialectes' and 'Yes, Dear' are more subtle, the latter perhaps intended as some sort of nod in the direction of Thelonious Monk. Ducret emerges as the hero of the session, playing with a rare intensity, but subtilizing some of Berne's harsher passages and introducing small areas of calm here and there. Tim's baritone is becoming increasingly dominant, a broad, bludgeoning tone, but with a touch of warmth as well.

*** **Ornery People**
Little Brother 013 *Berne; Michael Formanek (b).* 98.

Recorded in the dry air of Arizona, these duo compositions and improvisations strip away some of the extraneous detail and highlight Berne's approach to melody. 'Emerger' was written by the bass player, but it's Berne who leads, with a blunt saxophone solo. The compliment is reversed on 'Byram's World', a Berne tune that provides Formanek with his most individual feature. The duo come together on the closing 'Brincident' which seems to be improvised and has Berne switch to baritone for a bruising and hostile encounter that will leave most listeners feeling a bit shell-shocked.

Peter Bernstein (born 1967)

GUITAR

A New Yorker who learned from several teachers in the city, Bernstein has been an increasingly ubiquitous presence during the 1990s as sideman and, more recently, as leader.

(*) **Somethin's Burnin'
Criss Cross 1079 *Bernstein; Brad Mehldau (p); John Webber (b); Jimmy Cobb (d).* 12/92.

*** **Signs Of Life**
Criss Cross 1095 *Bernstein; Brad Mehldau (p); Christian McBride (b); Gregory Hutchinson (d).* 12/94.

Bernstein's anonymous tone and easy fluency send the blameless *Somethin's Burnin'* on the way to mediocrity. Precious little here really burns – Mehldau's jabbing solos are a good deal more interesting than the leader's, who tends to come off the Grant Green axis without much to call his own. The follow-up is an improvement, though Bernstein has to lean very heavily on Mehldau and McBride to keep up the level of interest. Some promising signs of life, though.

*** **Brain Dance**
Criss Cross 1130 *Bernstein; Steve Davis (tb); Eric Alexander (ts); Larry Goldings (org); Billy Drummond (d).* 12/96.

*** **Earth Tones**
Criss Cross 1151 *Bernstein; Larry Goldings (org); Bill Stewart (d).* 12/97.

Bernstein has been racking up some impressive sideman credits recently and now there's little denying his fluency and wit in that role. As a leader, though, he tends to make agreeable records that frequently lose out in the battle for priority-plays. Nothing wrong with either *Brain Dance* or, especially, *Earth Tones*, the latter featuring a trio that has played together regularly (if on-and-off) since 1989. The sustained elegance of his improvising on 'The Acrobat' will delight guitar-followers. But the blowing formats of these discs don't find enough in them to transcend the occasion, so they end up in a bracket of nothing to disappoint but little to remember.

Bill Berry (born 1930)

TRUMPET, CORNET

Briefly with Ellington, from 1962, but mainly an LA studio musician in the '60s, then formed the LA Big band, which still occasionally performs, in 1971. Spotted in various mainstream situations.

(*) **Hello Rev
Concord CCD 4027 *Berry; Cat Anderson, Gene Goe, Blue Mitchell, Jack Sheldon (t); Britt Woodman, Jimmy Cleveland, Benny Powell, Tricky Lofton (tb); Marshal Royal, Lanny Morgan, Richie Kamuca, Don Menza, Jack Nimitz (saxes); Dave Frishberg (p); Monty Budwig (b); Frank Capp (d).* 8/76.

*** **Shortcake**
Concord CCD 4057 *Berry; Bill Watrous (tb); Marshal Royal (as, f); Lew Tabackin (ts, f); Mundell Lowe (g); Alan Broadbent, Dave Frishberg (p); Chuck Berghofer, Monty Budwig (b); Frank Capp, Nick Ceroli (d).* 78.

Berry presides over a big-band record that searches for an Ellingtonian feel and gets some of the way there. The group performs with cheerful swing on an effectively chosen programme, including such lesser-known Ducal pieces as 'Tulip Or Turnip', and the live recording is quite kind, but finally it resembles many another midstream big-band date too much to demand great attention. Berry himself did much better with the engaging small-group record, *Shortcake*, recently restored to the catalogue and certainly the best place to sample this engaging musician.

Chu Berry (1910–41)

TENOR SAXOPHONE

Leon Berry played with several New York bands before a spell with Fletcher Henderson, from 1935, then with Cab Calloway, from 1937. He also cut small-group sessions with Roy Eldridge and Lionel Hampton. A Hawkins follower, but with a character of his own, he was a popular man who was much mourned when he died after injuries received in a car crash.

****** Blowing Up A Breeze**

Topaz TPZ 124 *Berry; Henry 'Red' Allen, Mario Bauza, Emmett Berry, Buck Clayton, Leonard Davis, Harry Edison, Roy Eldridge, Dizzy Gillespie, Jonah Jones, Ed Lewis, Howard Scott, Russell Smith, Joe Thomas, Shad Collins, Dick Vance, Lamarr Wright (t); Fernando Arbello, Ed Cuffee, Tyree Glenn, J.C Higginbotham, Quentin Jackson, Claude Jones, Keg Johnson, Dicky Wells, Benny Morton, Dan Minor, Wilbur De Paris, George Washington, De Priest Wheeler (tb); Buster Bailey (cl); Benny Carter (cl, as, ss); Jerry Blake, Chauncey Haughton, Andrew Brown, Howard Johnson (cl, as); Scoops Carey, Hilton Jefferson, Earl Warren (as); Jack Washington (as, bs); Wayman Carver (cl, as, f); Coleman Hawkins, Walter Thomas, Ben Webster, Elmer Williams, Lester Young (ts); Count Basie, Clyde Hart, Fletcher Henderson, Benny Paine, Red Rodriguez, Teddy Wilson (p); Lionel Hampton (vib); Danny Barker, Albert Casey, Charlie Christian, Bob Lessey, Lawrence Lucie (g); Danny Barker, Israel Crosby, Freddie Green, Ernest Hill, Milt Hinton, John Kirby, Walter Page, Artie Shapiro (b); Big Sid Catlett, Cozy Cole, Walter Johnson, Jo Jones, Harry Jaeger (d).* 5/33–9/41.

*****(*) Chu Berry, 1937–1941**

Classics 784 *Berry; Roy Eldridge, Hot Lips Page, Irving Randolph (t); Keg Johnson, George Mathews (tb); Buster Bailey (cl); Charlie Ventura (ts); Horace Henderson, Clyde Hart, Benny Payne (p); Danny Barker, Al Casey (g); Israel Crosby, Milt Hinton, Al Morgan, Artie Shapiro (b); Big Sid Catlett, Cozy Cole, Leroy Maxey, Harry Yeager (d).* 3/37–9/41.

Sixty years after his premature death, Berry's reputation is still in eclipse. He died just a little too soon for the extraordinary revolution in saxophone playing that followed the end of the war. He had a big sound, not unlike that of Coleman Hawkins – who considered him an equal – with a curiously fey inflexion that was entirely his own and which appealed strongly to Young Turks like Frank Lowe, who began to listen to Berry again in the 1970s.

For someone who recorded a good deal, the catalogue has always been sparse. Classics have made some restitution, but it is the Topaz compilation which is more useful, going right back to Berry's apprenticeship with Spike Hughes as a 23-year-old. A self-effacing sort of character, Berry often found himself in the shadow of more celebrated figures such as Herschel Evans, Basie's right-hand man until his premature death. Berry was only ever a dep in the Basie orchestra, but he turned in one classic, 'Lady Be Good'. He had more prominence in the Calloway outfit, with whom he was employed at the time of his death; Berry came very much to the fore on ballad material like 'Ghost Of A Chance', another of the excellent things on *Blowing Up A Breeze*. Too often under other leaders he was restricted to brief excursions from the woodwind bench, and Berry was a player who needed time and space to have his say.

The partnership with Roy Eldridge was a matey, happy affair, and the 'Little Jazz' Ensembles of November 1938 (just three out of the four documented tracks on the Topaz, but rather better mastered) are among Chu's best small-group performances. The missing item is 'Body And Soul', a version which sits very well alongside the great ones. The opening number, 'Sittin' In', is introduced conversationally by the two principals. Talking or playing, they're both in rumbustious form, and the warmth of the partnership was equalled only by the late sessions with Hot Lips Page, made within weeks of the road accident which ended Chu's short life. 'On The Sunny Side Of The Street' had Page laying out, and it's an interesting place to study Berry as an improviser. Neither of the existing releases includes an alternative take, but these do exist, and here and elsewhere they expose a rather thin sense of structure; solos always seemed to follow much the same trajectory. Chu was a wonderfully complete player in every other regard, and with a strong band behind him he was up with the very best. When he died, they left his chair in the Cab Calloway band sitting empty.

Bob Bertles

ALTO, SOPRANO AND BARITONE SAXOPHONES

Australian bop-orientated saxman, in Britain for a spell in the 1970s.

***** Rhythm Of The Heart**

Rufus RF017 *Bertles; Warwick Alder (t, flhn); Dave Levy (p); Chris Qua (b); Ron Lemke (d).* 10/94.

*****(*) Cool Beans**

Rufus RF036 *As above.* 7/97.

British readers may remember Bertles as a member of Ian Carr's Nucleus in the early 1970s. This fine and adroit saxophonist has long since gone back to Australia, where he leads this impeccable quintet. They play fuss-free hard bop with few pretensions but a great deal of nous. Working far away from the expected models and history-mongering which this supposedly old-fashioned music entails, they deliver a buoyant treatise on the form that should delight a jazz listener of whatever pedigree. *Rhythm Of The Heart* is slightly bothered by the rather cavernous sound-mix, but it doesn't stand in the way of the writing and playing; and the subsequent *Cool Beans* gets closer and more immediate in its impact. Bertles, Alder and Levy share the writing between them and they have enough tunes in the book not to bother with any covers. Alder and Levy have plenty to say in their solos, but it's the leader's effortlessness which takes the ear: he can slip in and out of double time without any strain and, though he plays some soprano and baritone, it's his smooth, punchy way with the alto that takes the ear. Two very enjoyable discs.

Tony Bevan

TENOR SAXOPHONE, SOPRANO SAXOPHONE, BASS SAXOPHONE

Less well known than some of his saxophone-playing contemporaries in Britain, Bevan has carved his own quiet – or, rather, quietly abrasive – course. His use of overblowing and seemingly unmusical sound is very subtle and strangely elegant, in the way that primitive folksong has an unexpected elegance.

***** Original Gravity**

Incus CD 03 *Bevan; Greg Kingston (g, rec, tapes, toys); Matt Lewis (perc, bird calls).* 9/88.

****** Bigshots**

Incus CD 08 *Bevan; Paul Rogers (b); Steve Noble (perc).* 7/91.

****** Twisters**

Scatter 06CD *Bevan; Alexander Frangenheim (b); Steve Noble (perc).* 4 & 5/95.

***** Three Oranges**

Foghorn Records FOGCD001 *Bevan (bsx).* 7/98.

Bevan is a gritty British improviser who's managed to spell out an idiom sufficiently different from the dominant but hard-to-emulate Evan Parker style. The earliest of these sessions is engagingly spiny and good-humoured, with a few nods (Lewis's duck-calls most obviously) in the direction of John Zorn's free-style. The beery track-titles – '1044°–1050°', 'Original Gravity', 'Best Before End' – are a bit of a giveaway, for there's a boys'-night-out feel to the proceedings which makes you wonder if it wasn't a lot more fun for the participants than it could ever be for CD listeners.

That certainly isn't true of *Bigshots*, which is wonderfully controlled and dramatic, three absolutely compatible players working at full stretch, listening carefully to one another without surrendering a shred of autonomy. Rogers, as so often in these settings, is the dominant voice, and it's sometimes difficult not to home in exclusively on his rumbling lines. Bevan himself has started to play more smoothly, even lyrically in passages, and it suits him. Only on the long closing 'The Last Shot' does he appear to run out of ideas – though, listening to the track again, one almost wonders whether it wasn't actually an initial try-out rather than a curtain-call, so tentative are some of its components. The title-track is much more compelling. Noble comes into his own with a vengeance and Bevan truffles up ideas of real originality.

Noble is excellent again on *Twisters*: alternating long and short tracks, dense outbursts of sound with quieter and more spacious ideas. Closer to orthodox freebop – if there is such a thing as freebop orthodoxy – than on previous records, Bevan's own contribution is more linear and orderly, and 'Belly Of The Whale' might even be some mid-'60s group like Amalgam or Splinters. It, though, is an exception. This is fresh, undogmatic music, without a hint of retro styling or nostalgia.

Solo bass saxophone is a fairly recherché area of musical practice, and Bevan hasn't the depth of understanding which Roscoe Mitchell and Anthony Braxton have brought to such projects. The comfort is that the album is very short, more of an EP than an LP, and is played very expressively, with a nice modulation of mood. Even so, very much an acquired taste, and don't expect the echo of Prokofiev in the title to be reflected in the music.

Ed Bickert (born 1932)

GUITAR

Born in Manitoba, Bickert is based in Toronto, where he was playing in the 1950s, although he sometimes appears on the mainstream circuit in the USA.

***** I Wished On The Moon**

Concord CCD 4284 *Bickert; Rick Wilkins (ts); Steve Wallace (b); Terry Clarke (d).* 6/85.

Bickert's self-effacing style masks a keen intelligence. His deceptively soft tone is the front for a shrewd, unexpectedly attacking style that treats bebop tempos with the same equanimity as a swing-styled ballad. This was one of the best of several Concord albums (other earlier dates have drifted out of print). Although the music is rather too evenly modulated to sustain attention throughout, Bickert adds interest by choosing unhackneyed material, and this disc in particular has a fine programme of rare standards. Wallace and Clarke make useful foils.

***** Third Floor Richard**

Concord CCD 4380 *Bickert; Dave McKenna (p); Neil Swainson (b); Terry Clarke (d).* 1/89.

***** This Is New**

Concord CCD 4414 *Bickert; Lorne Lofsky (g); Neil Swainson (b); Jerry Fuller (d).* 12/89.

Bickert's subsequent records for the label continue the formula but, like so many other Concord artists, he's inhabiting the style so completely that the records are taking on a special elegance and grace. *Third Floor Richard* returns McKenna to a Bickert date, though he is in – for him – a quiescent mood, and the playing is sumptuously refined. The quartet with Lofksy, though, is a little sharper, with 'Ah-Leu-Cha' pacifying the contrapuntalism of the playing without surrendering all of the bebop fizz which underlines it. Very agreeable.

***** Mutual Street**

Jazz Alliance TJA-10003 *Bickert; Rob McConnell (tb).* 3/82–5/84.

A rare combination indeed, at least in this kind of jazz circle, but Bickert and McConnell make it sound easy. Since neither man is exactly a grandstander, the lack of aggression pushes the music into the background, which discourages hard listening – and yet there are interesting discoveries which repay close attention. As a pleasant, noodling dialogue between two modest personalities, it sounds fine as well – or at least better than much of today's easy-listening radio jazz. The unfussy studio sound is just what's needed.

Barney Bigard (1906–80)

CLARINET, TENOR SAXOPHONE

Born Albany Leon Bigard in New Orleans, his first major job was with King Oliver in Chicago, but he joined Duke Ellington at the start of his Cotton Club residency in 1927 and stayed till 1942. There followed five years with the Louis Armstrong All Stars, with a second brief stay in 1960, and general work as a freelance. He retired from full-time playing in 1965 but was a frequent guest and visitor to festivals.

***** Barney Bigard 1944**
Classics 896 *Bigard; Shorty Sherock, Norman Bowden, Joe Thomas (t); Shorty Haughton (tb); Les Robinson (as); Eddie Miller, Georgie Auld (ts); Stan Wrightsmann (p, cel); Pete Johnson, Leonard Feather, Fred Washington (p); Nappy Lamare, Bud Scott, Remo Palmieri, Chuck Wayne (g); Hank Wayland, Al Hall, Billy Taylor (b); Nick Fatool, Shelly Manne, Zutty Singleton, Stan Levey (d); Peggy Lee, Etta Jones (v); strings.* 1–12/44.

***** Barney Bigard 1944-1945**
Classics 930 *Bigard; Joe Thomas, Ray Linn (t); Vic Dickenson (tb); Willie Smith (as); Joe Thomas (ts, v); Georgie Auld (ts); Cyril Haynes, Leonard Feather, Calvin Jackson, Eddie Beal, Art Tatum, Johnny Guarnieri (p); Allan Reuss, Chuck Wayne (g); Billy Taylor, Red Callender (b); Zutty Singleton, Stan Levey, Cozy Cole (d); Wini Beatty, Claude Trenier, Monette Moore (v).* 12/44–12/45.

The conventional wisdom is that Bigard did all his best work with Ellington, and the rest isn't up to anything much. While some of the jazz on these two interesting compilations of his freelance work is less than immortal, his own playing is seldom less than fine. Classics 896 starts with four excellent titles by The Capitol International Jazzmen, including good work from Robinson and Miller as well as Bigard, and two charming vocals by Peggy Lee. A trio session for Signature is fluent and swinging and, though two dates with Zutty Singleton are less impressive and four titles with strings are unremarkable, the final four titles with Etta Jones and Joe Thomas include some excellent blues playing by Barney. Classics 930 brings together a string of largely less-than-classic dates, four of them accompanying singers, and some of these tracks are very obscure indeed: but there is an excellent quintet date for Keynote which offers Bigard at his best on 'Rose Room' and 'Bojangles', and a pair of titles for the Lamplighter label have some entertaining jousting with Vic Dickenson. Transfers are decent, especially considering that some of these tracks weren't exactly finessed by the microphones in the first place.

***** Bucket's Got A Hole In It**
Delmark DE-211 *Bigard; Nap Trottier (t); George Brunis (tb); Art Hodes (p); Rail Wilson (b); Barrett Deems (d).* 1/68.

A delightful reunion of old-timers, with the sextet ambling through this alternately rousing and bluesy date with evident enjoyment. The timing is rather off here and there, despite the reliable Deems, and Trottier and the engaging Brunis (who goes back almost to pre-history as far as jazz recording is concerned) aren't players of the stature of Bigard and Hodes, but the feeling is so warm and cheerful that the occasional frailties don't matter.

**** Barney Bigard And The Pelican Trio**
Jazzology JCD-228 *Bigard; Duke Burrell (p); Barry Martyn (d).* 76.

This one, though, should be left on the shelf. Bigard sounds well past his best and, though Burrell and Martyn play with great spirit, they tend to overpower the old man.

Acker Bilk (born 1929)

CLARINET

Best known, after nearly 40 years, for his 'Stranger On The Shore' hit, Bilk was the chart-topping star of British trad whose credentials – going as far back as the early Ken Colyer band – were actually impeccable. He has continued to perform, with strings, choirs and his own Paramount Jazzband, ever since.

****** Mr Acker Bilk And His Paramount Jazzband**
Lake LACD 48 *Bilk; Ken Sims (t); John Mortimer (tb); Jay Hawkins, Roy James (bj); Ernest Price (b); Ron McKay (d).* 3/58–1/59.

*****(*) The Traditional Jazz Scene: Volume 1**
Teldec 43996 *Bilk; Ken Sims, Colin Smith (t); John Mortimer (tb); Stan Greig (p); Roy James (bj); Ernest Price (b); Ron McKay (d).* 1/59–1/63.

*****(*) Stranger On The Shore / A Taste Of Honey**
Redial 546458-2 *Bilk; strings, choir, directed by Leon Young.* 61–65.

*****(*) Blaze Away**
Timeless TTD 543/4 2CD *Bilk; Mike Cotton (t); Campbell Burnap (tb); Colin Wood (p); Tucker Finlayson (b); Richie Bryant (d).* 1/87.

Barber, Ball and Bilk – the 'Three Bs' – were the heirs of Ken Colyer's trad revolution. If Barber 'prettified' Colyer's rough-edged approach, Bilk brought an element of showmanship and humour, speaking in a disconcerting Zummerzet accent, dressing his Paramount Jazzband in Edwardian waistcoats and bowlers, notching two enormous hits with 'Summer Set' (a further punning reference to the county of his birth) and 'Stranger On The Shore', a tune still much requested at autumnal wedding receptions. The idea had come from producer Dennis Preston, who wanted Bilk to record with strings. The clarinettist reworked a theme that was originally dedicated to his daughter, recorded it with the Leon Young String Chorale, saw it picked up as the signature-tune to a similarly titled television serial, and started counting the royalties. Bilk's success – 'Stranger' sold more than two million copies – and photogenic presentation attracted an inevitable mixture of envy and disdain, and it's often forgotten how accomplished and 'authentic' a musician he actually is. Working with Colyer in the mid-1950s, he played in a raw-edged George Lewis style very different from the silky, evocative vibrato he cultivated in later years.

The choice of a single Bilk album for a sample collection of British trad is made easier by the appearance on Lake of sessions from the Nixa 'Jazz Today' collection. These dates from 1958 and 1959 capture the Paramount Jazzband at its best, doing blues and rags with a raw, unembellished quality. 'Willie The Weeper' is pretty authentic, and things like 'Blaze Away' and 'Higher Ground' give the band plenty of scope for raucous to-and-froing. A hint of the rawer sound can be heard on the Teldec. It's more of a purist's sound, with many of the clichés of doctrinaire trad (like the banjo going *chung, chung, chung* exactly on the beat, as George Melly describes in *Owning Up*), and those not weaned on this kind of thing may well prefer the more varied instrumental spectrum of later years that found room for a piano and even (horrors!) a saxophone. The Redial reissue of the original *Stranger On The Shore* and *A Taste Of Honey* on a two-on-one CD will be greatly welcomed by admirers of the 'popular' Bilk. Whatever reservations one has about the setting, his own clarinet remains markedly individual and there are a few delightful surprises along the way, such as his own original 'Evening Shadows'.

The excellent Colin Smith was replaced first by Rod Mason (whose Hot Five was a fine revivalist outfit) and later by Mike Cotton, a more intense and subtle player who wasn't content to do Bunk Johnson impressions all night. The Timeless set highlights his talents and those of Campbell Burnap, who replaced John Mortimer. Bilk likens 'Stranger' to a pension plan and willingly keeps up payments on it. It appears on *Blaze Away*, as does the numbing 'Aria', another big hit; but that shouldn't detract from some rather less predictable fare, like 'Black And Tan Fantasy' which is played with impressive freshness and enough jazz 'feel' for anyone.

Bilk is an impressive middle-register player who seldom uses the coloratura range for spurious effect, preferring to work melodic variations on a given theme. Though he repeats certain formulae, he tends to do so with variations that stop them going stale. A major figure in British jazz, Bilk has to be separated from a carefully nurtured image. On record, he's consistently impressive and has continued to produce the goods right into the 1990s.

David Bindman

TENOR SAXOPHONE

East Coast American based in Brooklyn who works extensively around the New York–Connecticut axis.

***** Imaginings**

CIMP 151 *Bindman; Joe Fonda (b); Kevin Norton (d).* 7/97.

Bindman's style is energy-based but fundamentally conservative. He sometimes goes in for tonal distortions, but the more he pushes them, the less convincing he sounds. His full, brawny sound comes out best in the middle-lower register and many of his improvisations stick to that area and wring it out for inspiration. Some of these simple melodic themes suit him fine, and his bleak revamping of 'Jitterbug Waltz' is interesting, but ten shots of this music are a little wearing over CD length. Fonda and Norton, familiar partners, are noisily propulsive, and this is one occasion where CIMP's 'natural' sound detracts: the drums need extra width to accommodate Norton's brusque attack.

Walter Bishop Jr (1927–98)

PIANO

Swing-to-bop pianist who followed in the footsteps of a renowned swing-era musician.

***** Milestones**

Black Lion BLCD 760109 *Bishop; Jimmy Garrison (b); G.T Hogan (d).* 3/61.

Son-of-a-famous-dad syndrome loomed for a while – Bishop senior composed 'Swing, Brother, Swing' – but it was the lad who really made things happen, propelling some of the finest bebop sessions and sustaining a career as performer and teacher that ended only with Bish's death in 1998. If there was an obvious influence on his solo style, it was Erroll Garner but despite being widely regarded it was some time before he either felt confident enough or was deemed to be marketable enough to make a record of his own. There is nothing particularly startling or radical on *Milestones*. The title-theme is fresh and brightly played, though Garrison sounds a little flat in the mix. Alternative takes of 'Sometimes I'm Happy', 'Speak Low' and Oscar Pettiford's 'Blues In The Closet' all stand out, and there is a long version of 'On Green Dolphin Street' that is as good as anything in the piano literature on that overworked theme.

*****(*) Trio, 1965**

Original Jazz Classics OJC 1896 *Bishop; Butch Warren (b); Jimmy Cobb, Granville T Hogan (d).* 62, 10/63.

***** Summertime**

Fresh Sound FSCD 11 *As above, except omit Hogan.* 64.

We're slightly confused about the titling of the OJC set. The cover clearly reads 1965, which may have been the year of issue, but there are two references to sessions in spring 1962 and, with Cobb as drummer, autumn 1963, and this seems to be correct. Whatever the date, the playing is fine. Hogan plays on the four earlier selections only, and Cobb is certainly much more polished. A good deal of the material is co-credited to Bishop and supervisor Addison Amor, which suggests that it was run down in the studio. Fortunately, Bishop's improvisational skills are sufficient to sustain the quality. *Summertime* is marred only by poor sound. The playing is well up to scratch and it's a beautifully constructed set, evidence of Bishop's taste as a leader. Butch Warren is poorly served in the mastering and there is a fog over much of the music, though this is not serious enough to put off enthusiasts.

*****(*) What's New**

DIW 605 *Bishop; Peter Washington (b); Kenny Washington (d).* 90.

***** Midnight Blue**

Red RR 123251 *Bishop; Reggie Johnson (b); Doug Sides (d).* 12/91.

There is a huge gap in the available discography, with stuff on Xanadu – notably *Bish Bash* – unlikely to reappear on CD for the time being. The DIW set is fresh and unexpected, with an uncharacteristically virtuosic 'Crazy She Calls Me', on which bassist and drummer take a break. Bishop programmes Wayne

Shorter's 'Speak No Evil' and Kenny Dorham's 'Una Mas' and makes something personal out of both themes. The Red session includes more original material, including 'Lady Barbara', 'Farmer's Delight' and the eponymous 'Midnight Blue'. These sound uncomfortably like latter-day Bud Powell, just skirting pastiche. What redeems this session, like the other, is the uncomplicated and unfussy playing. Bishop articulates as cleanly as Al Haig, but he has also acquired a lyrical touch which can only have been influenced by Bill Evans. Four lovely records by a minor master whose real contribution was in other, more august company.

Michael Bisio

BASS

West Coast improviser and free-bop bassist, here given the opportunity to lead his own dates.

****(*) Covert Choreography**

Cadence CJR 1063 *Bisio; Rob Blakeslee (t); Eyvind Kang (vn); Bob Nell (p); Ed Pias (d).* 96.

***** Finger Wigglers**

CIMP 127 *Bisio; Joe McPhee (ts).* 9/96.

The quintet album offers some vigorous playing by a worthwhile group, but it comes across as a rather messily recorded document of a studio jam for much of its length. The title-piece runs for 40 minutes and fades from free to bop and back again with all too many desultory passages. The three remaining pieces are better focused, and Blakeslee is always worth hearing, but it's nothing special.

Bisio's duets with McPhee are harsh, even gruelling stuff: two takes of 'Lonely Woman' leave the tune almost unrecognizable, as is 'Blue Monk'; although 'Here's That Rainy Day' emerges into the light after a long bass introduction, McPhee is at his most intractable for much of this and everything else. Not without its rewards, and it has the merit of the saxophonist sticking to tenor for the whole date, which lets one examine his peculiarly cruel lyricism at length.

Ketil Bjørnstad

PIANO

Classically trained, but more interested in bringing that aesthetic into an area at least touched by jazz.

***** Water Stories**

ECM 519076-2 *Bjørnstad; Terje Rypdal (g); Bjorn Kjellemyr (b); Jon Christensen, Per Hillestad (d).* 1/93.

***** The Sea**

ECM 521718-2 *Bjørnstad; David Darling (clo); Terje Rypdal (g); Jon Christensen (d).* 9/94.

****(*) The Sea II**

ECM 537341-2 *As above.* 12/96.

***** Epigraphs**

ECM 543159-2 *Bjørnstad; David Darling (clo).* 9/98.

All those expensive lessons – wasted! Bjørnstad is a classically trained pianist who was turned on to jazz by *In A Silent Way* and hasn't looked back since. The debut album is a linked sequence of pieces inspired by the land- and seascape of Rosendal in western Norway. The first few sections evoke a glacier cutting its path through the mountains. Here at least it makes sense that the music is held in check, though one can almost hear Rypdal pumping the brakes. As things progress, the pace gradually increases, and Hillestad, who's played with underrated rockers A-Ha, replaces Christensen, bringing a more headlong sound.

Frankly, we find it difficult to distinguish between the two later records. Had they been recorded at the same time, and *Sea II* a set of offcuts, it would all make more sense, but to reconvene the same band 27 months on in order to record what sounds like the same material seems perverse in the extreme. To be fair to Bjørnstad, there has been some attempt to roughen up the textures a bit and to give the follow-up record a semblance of grit and fibre. Too late, though. Immaculate sound, thrown away on spindrift.

Epigraphs brings together two of the most pacific spirits on a label roster which isn't exactly brimming with warmongers. The settings of Dufay, Byrd, Gibbons and Aichinger are as gentle and sweetly voiced as the originals, all of it at a pace which rarely moves above slow motion. Beautiful – and goodbye to jazz.

Ed Blackwell (1929–92)

DRUMS

Born in New Orleans, he began playing in local R&B groups in the '40s and later moved to Los Angeles, working with Ornette Coleman, then, in the '60s, with Don Cherry, Coltrane, Dolphy and Coleman again. His playing was curtailed to some extent by his dependence on a dialysis machine, but he carried on through the '80s, always a dynamic member of a group.

***** What It Is?**

Enja ENJ 7089 *Blackwell; Graham Haynes (c); Carlos Ward (as, f); Mark Helias (b).* 8/92.

***** What It Be Like?**

Enja ENJ 8054 *As above, except add Don Cherry (t).* 8/92.

Like a lot of drummers, Blackwell appeared on a huge number of records, but very rarely indeed as leader. These are the only current releases bearing his name. They were recorded at a festival in Oakland, California, celebrating the life of another great drummer, Eddie Moore, who's played with Redman and many others. Blackwell was barely functioning at the date, suffering appallingly from the long-standing kidney ailment which had curtailed his activities for many years and which was to end his life only two months later. His contribution is inevitably a little muted, and at some points bordering on the embarrassing. The most straightforward feature for the drummer is on the first volume, Carlos Ward's 'Mallet Song', a ritualized sequence of drum-calls punctuated by horns and bowed bass. Helias's tunes, 'Beau Regard' and 'Thumbs Up', are more energetic but marked by free-ish singing lines from the bass, across which Blackwell plays his own melodies. 'Nette' is a tribute to the man whose work the drummer had explored in *Old And New Dreams*. Ward's theme has a typically African cast, his alto as fiery as his flute is softly lyrical on 'Beau Regard'. Haynes, the youngest of the group by a decade, has an almost quaintly old-fashioned sound on his cornet. Volume two is of even quality, certainly no sense that it was a second-choice afterthought. Ward's 'Lito', a three-part suite he has successfully recorded under his own name, is a fitting end to the whole thing, not least because it includes a guest slot from Don Cherry, himself now ailing but able to play with some of the old fire and commitment. In effect, this is a Carlos Ward record. He dominates the writing almost entirely and is the most prominent solo voice. 'Grandma's Shoes' is another featured outlet for the man they'd gathered to honour that evening at Yoshi's in Oakland, and just for a moment the old Blackwell, who'd played as an equal with some of the greats, surfaces and takes a bow.

Brian Blade

DRUMS, PERCUSSION

The talented drummer was part of Kenny Garrett's trio and had amassed an impressive array of credits before making his debut as lead.

****(*) Brian Blade Fellowship**

Blue Note 59417-2 *Blade; Myron Walden (as); Melvin Butler (ts, ss); Jon Cowherd (p, org); Daniel Lanois, Jeff Parker (g); Dave Easley (pedal steel g); Christopher Thomas (b).* 97.

***** Perceptual**

Blue Note 23571-2 *As above, except add Kurt Rosenwinkel (g), Joni Mitchell (v); omit Parker.* 99.

Blade's debut recording as leader is strikingly similar to early projects by fellow-percussionist Jack DeJohnette, and it shares some of their limitations. *Fellowship* is more impressionistic than dynamic, and the textures on the opening 'Red River Revel', an evocation of the annual festival in his home town of Shriveport, Louisiana, are surpassingly gentle, thanks largely to producer Lanois's mando-guitar and Dave Easley's pedal steel. The most obvious link with DeJohnette is 'Folklore', a collage of voices (apparently the Babenzele pygmies) and instrumental sounds. Whereas DeJohnette's world-music excursions almost always have a solid core, this has nothing but surface. The two saxophones pick up the pace here and there, and the basic group, with soul-brother Cowherd supplying 'Lifeline' and Thomas commanding the engine-room with old-fashioned string bass, has a coherence that suggests they probably sound great live. On this showing, though, not very forceful.

Blue Note's confidence in his talent is better borne out by the second record, which builds on the strengths of the debut and turns them in a more positive direction. Blade is rarely more than a subtle background presence, taking no solo spotlight and acting as a quiet dynamo to the guitar and saxophone front line, which is nicely balanced. The use of pedal steel has become a signature, enhanced this time by a further cameo from Daniel Lanois and a rather frail and plangent vocal from Joni Mitchell on 'Steadfast'. The most effective tracks are 'Evinrude Fifty (Trembling)' and the long, suite-like 'Variations Of A Bloodline', which might be influenced by the maverick Terry Allen of the Panhandle Mystery Band.

Ran Blake (born 1935)

PIANO, KEYBOARDS

Born in Springfield, Massachusetts, Blake studied at Bard and Lenox and was working as an accompanist-partner to Jeanne Lee from the late '50s. More renowned as an academic, at New England Conservatory, Blake's records arrive like unexpected lightning and are a mostly fascinating blend of his musical studies and what he's drawn from jazz tradition.

***** Duke Dreams**

Soul Note 121027 *Blake (p solo).* 5/81.

***** Suffield Gothic**

Soul Note 121077 *Blake (p solo); and with Houston Person (ts).* 6/81.

Since 1973 Blake has headed the Third Stream music department at the New England Conservatory. Cynics will say that only in the quieter backwaters of New England is Third Stream still considered a viable synthesis. Arguably only Blake and NEC president Gunther Schuller remain strict-constructionists. Blake is a scholar, and something of a gentleman, with an approach to the music very far removed from the seat-of-the-pants gigging mentality of most jazz musicians. His solo performances – and he has generally preferred to work without sidemen – are thoughtful, precisely articulated, but always intriguingly varied, combining jazz standards, original compositions of great interest, ethnic musics from all over the world (though Blake has a special interest in Spanish/Castilian Sephardic themes, as can be heard on *Painted Rhythms*, below). If he has a single influence from within jazz, it is Monk (though they seem temperamentally quite different), even if the Soul Note *Duke Dreams* has some wonderful treatments of Ellington and Strayhorn. Something of Monk's method of improvising on surprisingly limited motives can be heard even when Blake is working with standards, as on *Suffield Gothic*. His collaboration there with saxophonist Houston Person is intriguing but a little detached. Since his days with Arthur Blythe, though no one's suggesting any connection, Blake has tended to steer clear of saxophonists, and only his ex-NEC student, Ricky Ford, has worked out a viable *modus operandi*.

***** Improvisations**

Soul Note 121022 *Blake; Jaki Byard (p).* 6/81.

Piano duos can be messily unsatisfactory affairs; one thinks of the Cecil Taylor/Mary Lou Williams imbroglio in particular. This, though, is an exception. Blake and Byard don't so much share a common conception as an ecumenical willingness to meet each other half-way, a characteristic noted on Byard's remarkable Festival Hall, London, encounter with the British improviser, Howard Riley. The formalism of 'Sonata For Two Pianos' is mostly in the title; it's a limber, well-spaced piece with considerable harmonic interest. Almost inevitably, there is a taut, academic undercurrent to 'Tea For Two' and 'On Green Dolphin Street'. The pianos don't register quite as well as they might in some of the more exuberant passages but the sound is generally good, given the difficulties of recording this kind of music. A little more crispness in the bass might have helped, but the music is good enough to merit a sprinkle of stars.

****** Painted Rhythms: Volume 1**

GM 3007 *Blake (p solo).* 12/85.

****** Painted Rhythms: Volume 2**

GM 3008 *As above.* 12/85.

Like trumpeter Franz Koglmann, Blake takes a highly personal stance on the jazz tradition, reinterpreting classic material with a curious mixture of respectful precision and free-floating innovation. The most striking instances of that are the *four* versions of 'Maple Leaf Rag' that straddle these two remarkable discs. The third of them, bringing Volume One to a close, is dislocated, rediscovering Joplin's tune from a whirlpool of atonality and fractured rhythms. The second, by contrast, is played with a kind of sweet abandon that's the other side to Blake's sometimes rather severe approach. Volume One is largely concerned with jazz repertoire, originals like Duke's 'Azure' and 'Skrontch', Mary Lou Williams's 'What's Your Story, Morning Glory?', more recent things like George Russell's 'Ezzthetic' and the Stan Kenton tune that gives the set its name. Volume Two casts the net a lot wider, searching for that 'Spanish tinge' which Jelly Roll Morton thought was a constant in jazz. As noted above, Blake has long been interested in Sephardic music, and its distinctive harmonies (parallel to those familiar from the blues and jazz) provide this volume with new colours. Volume Two also features Blake the composer. 'Shoah!' and 'Storm Warning' both seem to hint at historical urgency, an impression heightened by the quotes from Shostakovich in the second, and by Blake's adaptation of Olshanetsky and Wolfson's *klezmer*-based 'Vilna', a mourning tune memorializing the victims of a Nazi massacre. 'Babbitt', presumably dedicated to the composer, is a more abstract exploration of sound and silence, each pushed to the limit in its power to communicate with the immediacy of images.

****** Short Life Of Barbara Monk**

Soul Note 121127 *Blake; Ricky Ford (ts); Ed Felson (b); Jon Hazilla (d).* 8/86.

This is a truly marvellous album, and it makes Blake's apparent unwillingness to work in ensemble settings all the more galling. The first part ends with the title-piece, dedicated to Thelonious Monk's daughter, Barbara, who died of cancer in 1984. It's a complex and moving composition that shifts effortlessly between a bright lyricism and an edgy premonition; Blake plays quite beautifully, and his interplay with the young but supremely confident rhythm section is a revelation. A death also lies behind the closing track on part two. 'Pourquoi Laurent?' expresses both a hurt need to understand and a calm desire to heal, written in the face of French jazz critic Laurent Goddet's suicide. 'Impresario Of Death' is equally disturbing but so intelligently constructed as to resolve its inner contradiction perfectly. 'Vradiazi' by the Greek composer, Theodorakis, is a favourite of Blake's, as is the Sephardic melody, 'Una Matica De Ruda' (two eye-blink takes), which also features on *Painted Rhythms 2* (above). To lighten the mix a little, there are astonishing versions of Stan Kenton's theme, 'Artistry In Rhythm', and, as an entirely unexpected opener, 'I've Got You Under My Skin'. Blake's Falcone Concert Grand sounds in perfect shape and the session – a single day of concentrated music-making – is superbly recorded and pressed.

*****(*) Epistrophy**

Soul Note 121177 *Blake (p solo).* 4/91.

Epistrophy is probably the most representative of Blake's records currently available. He touches bass with the title-tune no fewer than three times on the record and adopts characteristically acute angles on the others. Where Blake departs from Monk is in the regularity and precision of the pulse. There is not a trace of the original begetter's anarchic time-shifts and slippages. In their place an exactness which is admirable in its consistency, even if it seems alien to those who have spent most of their time in different cloisters.

***** Round About**

Music & Arts CD 807 *Blake; Christine Correa (v).* 12/92–8/93.

Some of the records on which Mal Waldron accompanies singers have made us think that Mal himself may prove to be a more expressive interpreter of a song than the lady (though not, of course, the Lady) herself. This project similarly. Correa has a strong and evocative voice, but she does rather diverge from the expected path of the lyric, and Blake seems too much involved in his own interpretations to steer her back. The top things are exactly those you'd expect: a reworking of 'Short Life Of Barbara Monk' and 'Blue Monk' ahead of it. Good as these are, they don't supersede Blake's earlier readings.

***** Memory Of Vienna**

hatOLOGY CD 6134 *Blake; Anthony Braxton (reeds).*

A pairing which is both predictable and full of surprises. Blake's moments of wildness are tempered by Braxton's cool precision and emphasis on control. The sound of the duo is very clear, very sharp, with the suffocating clarity one would find at two or three atmospheres, and this is where the set goes wrong. There is no spontaneity, just a clash of intellects communicating at a level above that of ordinary mortals. Slightly mandarin, and just a touch pointless.

*****(*) Unmarked Van**

Soul Note 121227 *Blake; Tiziano Tononi (d).* 12/94.

Blake's passion for singers has been well attested over the years, but no one was quite prepared for this astonishing tribute to the genius of Sarah Vaughan. Sassie's huge range and ability to texture and retexture a single tone made her one of the great instrumentalists of the music, and Blake has settled on that aspect of her singing, rather than its emotional components (arguable as these remain) in constructing his homage. The opening piece is an original composition which conjures up some of her most characteristic phrasing devices, including that famous deep roll up off the bottom of a chord. Sassie recorded Debussy's 'Reverie' more than once and Blake has attempted to capture the less obviously classical interpretation. That oscillation between more and less formal interpretations runs through the whole album, not least on four separate takes of 'Tenderly', the last of which closes the disc on a moment of romantic uncertainty, less definitive than the title-tune, a Blake original which quotes Vaughan's version of the Lord's Prayer. This is a record which demands and repays a little effort, not one which communicates immediately and straightforwardly. Nothing in Blake's previous output quite prepares the listener for it, and yet everything is absolutely characteristic.

***(*) **Something To Live For**

hatOLOGY 527 *Blake; Guillermo Gregorio (cl); David Fabris (g).* 3/98.

Unpredictable as ever in his choice of material and settings, Blake nevertheless delivers a characteristic record in this filigree recital. Nineteen tracks are dispatched in a little over 50 minutes, ten of them duets with either Gregorio or Fabris: many pieces are so cut back to the bone that they're little more than epigrams, and even when he indulges himself over five or six minutes, as in 'Memphis', each chord seems meticulously selected. Not that this is effete or even very introspective as a programme: Blake may be sparing, but he doesn't spare the keyboard, and every piece is defined and crisply delineated, however oblique the structures may seem. Gregorio and Fabris do their best to enter into the spirit, though at times they might be wondering where they are. If you're not a Blake believer, this set won't do anything to convert you, but its astringency will delight any of the already-hooked.

Seamus Blake (born 1969)

TENOR AND SOPRANO SAXOPHONES

Canadian-born, Blake made a mark as one of the crop of young saxophonists to enter the New York scene in the '90s.

*** **The Call**

Criss Cross 1088 *Blake; Kurt Rosenwinkel (g); Kevin Hays (p); Larry Grenadier (b); Bill Stewart (d).* 12/93.

***(*) **Four Track Mind**

Criss Cross 1126 *Blake; Tim Hagans (t); Mark Turner (ts); Kevin Hays (p, ky); Larry Grenadier (b); Billy Drummond (d).* 12/94.

*** **The Bloomdaddies**

Criss Cross 1110 *Blake; Chris Cheek (ts); Jesse Murphy (elec b); Jorge Rossy, Dan Reiser (d).* 12/95.

Blake has paid due respect to his masters – fellow-saxophonist Joe Lovano, fellow-Canadian Kenny Wheeler – without in any way standing in thrall to them. He has very quickly mapped out his own path, and the appearance of subsequent Criss Cross releases amply justifies label boss Gerry Teekens's confidence in giving the then-24-year-old a date as leader. For some reason, Blake's sessions for the label have been issued out of chronological sequence, as the issue numbers suggest. Perhaps Teekens wanted to highlight the 'other' side of his young signing, in the company of his electric band, The Bloomdaddies. Perhaps he had some doubts about the quality of *Four Track Mind*. If the latter, it's a surprising conclusion. The 1994 album is self-consciously a showcase, intended to demonstrate Blake's range and diversity. If there is a criticism, it is that the set has very little consistency. It opens with the funky title-track, and an off-the-peg blues, 'Dittee', before Blake shows any real originality either of conception or of execution. That comes with 'Jali', a tribute to former boss Victor Lewis, featuring Blake on soprano and Tim Hagans coming to the fore. The most striking piece on the album is 'In A Warring Absence', a jagged, almost serial piece written by Blake's violinist girlfriend, Farran, the same 'Miss James' who inspires the set's one romantic ballad and who probably bought young Seamus the Debussy discs he'd obviously been listening to.

Though there is an inevitable overlap of styles, *The Bloomdaddies* is a very different animal: loud, sometimes over-emphatic, and heavily processed, it's marked by rock and hip-hop sensibilities. Bass guitar, twinned drummers and, again, closely interwoven saxophone parts contribute to a dense, slightly programmed sound. Blake cedes some of the writing duties to partner Chris Cheek, specifically the last two tunes and the ballad feature, but by the time they come along the album has started to lose its way a little. A clangorous medley restores a forceful, upbeat feel after Cheek's 'Shelter', which is a lovely conception, and it might have been preferable to close proceedings at that point. Signs that Berklee-trained Blake hasn't yet got a comfortable range of material under his belt. He dabbles briefly with harmolodics on 'To Be Ornette To Be' and seems to decide he's a traditionalist – albeit a noisy one – after all, following up with Louis Prima's 'Sing, Sing, Sing'. Throughout, the emphasis is on tight ensemble playing, unlike the more open, blowing feel of *The Call*. It's often difficult to say which of the two saxophonists is to the fore, and how much is played as live and how much is a studio artefact.

*** **Stranger Things Have Happened**

Fresh Sound FSNT 063 *Blake; Kurt Rosenwinkel, Jesse Harris (g); Larry Grenadier (b); Jorge Rossy (d).* 3/99.

An interesting continuation, but the music feels rather shapeless, even melancholy: an uncredited vocalist (presumably Blake himself) sings on the doleful 'Northern Light' and, while Rosenwinkel's effects and free gestures leave the harmonic picture wide open, Blake tends to amble through it, focusing himself here and there, and just as often sounding unsure of quite where he is.

Rob Blakeslee

TRUMPET, CORNET, FLUGELHORN

Free-bop brassman, working in the community of improvisers and players associated with Vinny Golia's Nine Winds label in California.

(*) **Lifeline

Nine Winds NWCD 0147 *Blakeslee; Vinny Golia (ss, bs, f, bcl); Tad Weed (p); Ken Filiano (b); Billy Mintz (d).* 3/92.

*** **Long Narrows**

Nine Winds NWCD 0167 *As above, except Michael Bisio (b), Bob Meyer (d) replace Filiano and Mintz.* 7/94.

Blakeslee is the unassuming leader for two records that are effectively free-bop exercises by the repertory cast of Nine Winds. Both feature much food for thought, yet neither makes a very distinctive impact, sometimes through circumstances outside the playing. The sound on *Lifeline* is terribly thin and unfocused, and it tends to take all the sting out of the music, which suffers further from the longueurs of tracks which simply go on too long

('Absence Of Mallets' runs past 21 minutes). *Long Narrows* is better, more lucid and more decisive all round, without offering the rewards which these players have each managed to proffer up in other circumstances.

*****(*) Spirit Of The Times**
Nine Winds NWCD 0208 *Blakeslee; Vinny Golia (cl, bcl); Ken Filiano (b); Billy Mintz (d).* 5/97.

While there's still a suspicion that these performances sometimes outstay their welcome, this is otherwise a poised and inventive set of themes, and Blakeslee has never sounded better in a studio. 'Just Off The Avenue' is a worthy dedication to Bobby Bradford, the leader's playing finding the clarion pure tone which Bradford uses, and, with Golia restricting himself to two members of the clarinet family, there's a clear echo of the old Bradford–Carter quartet records for Revelation (missing from print and surely a candidate for revival on CD). A fine piece of work.

Art Blakey (1919–90)

DRUMS

Pittsburgh-born and self-taught as a pianist, Blakey was leading his own big band at fifteen, though he switched to drums when Erroll Garner came in. In New York he joined the powerhouse Billy Eckstine band and stayed for three years till it broke up in 1947. Freelancing and occasional bandleading followed until the 1954 Blue Note sessions which led to the formation of The Jazz Messengers (the name Blakey used for all his subsequent groups), the most famous academy in jazz, through which passed countless young and up-and-coming players. A master percussionist who investigated African and other styles along with his own swing-to-bop beginnings, he was peerless in support of soloists. He also loved to speak up on behalf of jazz, and he kept the standard unswervingly until his death in 1990.

****** A Night At Birdland Vol. 1**
Blue Note 46519-2 *Blakey; Clifford Brown (t); Lou Donaldson (as); Horace Silver (p); Curley Russell (b).* 2/54.

****** A Night At Birdland Vol. 2**
Blue Note 46520-2 *As above.* 2/54.

It was still called the 'Art Blakey Quintet', but this was the nexus of the band that became The Jazz Messengers, one of the most durable bywords in jazz, even if the name was first used on a Horace Silver album-cover. Blakey wasn't as widely acknowledged as Max Roach or Kenny Clarke as one of the leaders in establishing bop drumming, and in the end he was credited with working out the rhythms for what came after original bebop, first heard to significant effect on these records. Much of it is based on sheer muscle: Blakey played very loud and very hard, accenting the off-beat with a hi-hat snap that had a thunderous abruptness and developing a snare roll that possessed a high drama all its own. As much as he dominates the music, though, he always plays for the band, and inspirational leadership is as apparent on these early records as it is on his final ones. Both horn players benefit: Donaldson makes his Parkerisms sound pointed and vivacious, while Brown is marvellously mercurial, as well as sensitive on his ballad feature, 'Once In A While' from Volume 1 (Donaldson's comes on 'If I Had You' on the second record). Silver, too, lays down some of the tenets of hard bop, with his poundingly funky solos and hints of gospel melody. The sound has been capably transferred to CD, although owners of original vinyl needn't fear that they're missing anything extra.

*****(*) At The Café Bohemia Vol. 1**
Blue Note 46521-2 *Blakey; Kenny Dorham (t); Hank Mobley (ts); Horace Silver (p); Doug Watkins (b).* 11/55.

*****(*) At The Café Bohemia Vol. 2**
Blue Note 46522-2 *As above.* 11/55.

A very different band but results of equal interest to the Birdland session (the second volume of the Bohemia date was made 12 days after Volume 1). Hank Mobley is a somewhat unfocused stylist, and nothing quite matches the intensity which the Quintet secured at Birdland, yet the playing is finally just as absorbing. Dorham's elusive brilliance was seldom so extensively captured, his 'Yesterdays' ballad feature displaying a rare tenderness which faces off against the contentious dynamism of his fast solos which seem to forge a link between Dizzy Gillespie and Miles Davis. Long, mid-tempo pieces such as 'Soft Winds' and 'Like Someone In Love' find Silver and Blakey in reflective competition, but the drummer never slackens his grip: listen to what he does behind Dorham on 'Minor's Holiday'. The recording captures the atmosphere very truthfully, and there's some added charm in the announcements by Mobley and Dorham before their features.

*****(*) The Jazz Messengers**
Columbia CK 65265 *Blakey; Donald Byrd (t); Hank Mobley (ts); Horace Silver (p); Doug Watkins (b).* 4–5/56.

An expanded and revised version of the original Columbia date, with five extra tracks. Byrd and Mobley weren't the greatest front line Blakey had, and when McLean arrived shortly afterwards the group had a flash more fire about it; but these are still elegant and powerful tracks, and about as authentic as hard bop could be – tough, unfussy, swinging. It's a handsome new package with splendid photos and notes.

♛ ** Art Blakey's Jazz Messengers With Thelonious Monk**
Atlantic/Rhino R2 75598 *Blakey; Bill Hardman (t); Johnny Griffin (ts); Thelonious Monk (p); Spanky DeBrest (b).* 3/57.

Blakey appeared on several of Monk's seminal Blue Note sessions, and he had a seemingly intuitive knowledge of what the pianist wanted from a drummer. Griffin, volatile yet almost serene in his mastery of the horn, was another almost ideal yet very different interpreter of Monk's music. This set of five Monk tunes and one by Griffin is a masterpiece. If Hardman wasn't on the same exalted level as the other three, he does nothing to disgrace himself, and DeBrest keeps calm, unobtrusive time. The continuous dialogue between Blakey and Monk comes out most clearly in passages such as Monk's solo on 'In Walked Bud', but almost any moment on the session illustrates their unique empathy. Both use simple materials, which makes the music unusually clear in its layout, yet the inner complexities are astonishing, and as a result the music retains an uncanny freshness more than 40 years later; no passage is like another, and some of the tempos, such as those chosen for 'Evidence' and 'I Mean You', are almost unique in the annals of Monk interpretations. In its new Atlantic/Rhino edition, the music comes with three alternative takes, frankly inessential, but we welcome the superior sound of this remastering. Absolutely indispensable jazz.

*** Orgy In Rhythm

Blue Note 56586 *Blakey; Herbie Mann (f); Ray Bryant (p); Wendell Marshall (b); Jo Jones, Art Taylor, Specs Wright (d); Sabu Martinez (perc, v); Carlos Valdez, Jose Valiente, Ubal Nieto, Evilio Quintero (perc).* 3/57.

A good bash. The drummers get 'Split Skins' to themselves, and the rest is an entertaining if somewhat exhausting barrage of Latinesque licks provided by the massed percussionists, pepped up by Sabu's singing and Herbie's tootling flute. If the idea was to make a record that would fit in with the craze for exotic lounge music, Blakey was probably having little of that. The two original LPs have fitted on to a single CD.

***(*) Moanin'

Blue Note 95324-2 *Blakey; Lee Morgan (t); Benny Golson (ts); Bobby Timmons (p); Jymie Merritt (b).* 10/58.

*** 1958 Paris Olympia

Fontana 832659-2 *As above.* 11–12/58.

*** Des Femmes Disparaissent / Les Tricheurs

Fontana 834752-2 *As above.* 12/58.

*** Les Liaisons Dangereuses 1960

Fontana 812017-2 *Blakey; Lee Morgan (t); Barney Wilen (ss, ts); Duke Jordan, Bobby Timmons (p); Jymie Merritt (b); John Rodriguez, Willie Rodriguez, Tommy Lopez (perc).* 7/59.

Benny Golson wasn't a Jazz Messenger for very long – *Moanin'* was his only American album with the band – but he still contributed three of the most enduring themes to their book, all of them on *Moanin'*: the title-track, 'Blues March' and 'Along Came Betty'. These versions might seem almost prosaic next to some of the grandstand readings which other Blakey bands would later create, but Golson's own playing shows great toughness, and the ebullient Morgan, also making his Messengers debut, is a splendid foil. Another release in the Rudy Van Gelder Edition which is Blue Note's latest polishing of their catalogue. The set played at the Paris Olympia follows a similar pattern: Golson plays with riveting urgency (if imperfect control), and only the more distant sound keeps this one on the B-list of Messengers albums. The soundtrack for Eduardo Molinaro's *Des Femmes Disparaissent* is one of the least known of Blakey's albums, directed mainly by Golson: the album is made up of fragments of Messengers tunes, motifs, drum-rolls and blues. It scarcely hangs together as a Messengers session, but the components are impeccably conceived and finished, and the superb studio sound allows a close-up hearing of how this band worked.

Another soundtrack, *Les Liaisons Dangereuses*, offers a brief look at Barney Wilen in the band. The music is less than abundant in terms of material (most of it gets played twice for the purposes of the film) but Wilen acquits himself courageously, his tenor on 'Valmontana' and soprano on 'Prelude In Blue' both impressive.

***(*) At the Jazz Corner Of The World

Blue Note 28888-2 2CD *Blakey; Lee Morgan (t); Hank Mobley (ts); Bobby Timmons (p); Jymie Merritt (b).* 4/59.

A brief interlude with Hank Mobley returning to the tenor chair. He sounds comfortable enough – and gets to contribute three tunes of his own, even if they're hardly in the class set by the next tenorman to step in. Any live event with The Messengers in this period was worth saving, and this one sounds terrifically loud, up-front and spirited, with the master of the traps in imperious form. Originally on two separate LPs, now on a double-CD set.

*** The Big Beat

Blue Note 46400-2 *Blakey; Lee Morgan (t); Wayne Shorter (ts); Bobby Timmons (p); Jymie Merritt (b).* 3/60.

**** A Night In Tunisia

Blue Note 84049-2 *As above.* 8/60.

**** Roots And Herbs

Blue Note 21956-2 *As above, except add Walter Davis Jr (p).* 2–5/61.

***(*) The Freedom Rider

Blue Note 21287-2 *As above, except omit Davis.* 2–5/61.

***(*) The Witch Doctor

Blue Note 21957-2 *As above.* 3/61.

After Golson came Shorter, the most individual of composers and an invaluable source for The Messengers. *A Night In Tunisia* is a long-standing favourite among Messengers followers. Besides the wildly over-the-top version of the title-tune, there's Shorter's lovely 'Sincerely Diana' and two charming Lee Morgan themes. Shorter's playing had a dark, corrosive edge to it that turned softly beseeching when he played ballads, but some of his solos don't come off: that on 'The Chess Players' from the patchy *The Big Beat* never gets started. *The Freedom Rider* is beefed up with three extra tracks, including the Morgan themes 'Pisces' and 'Uptight'; this is a lesser-known Blakey album, but it still has Blakey's title-track drum solo (a celebration of the Freedom Ride anti-segregationists), Shorter's magnificent 'El Toro' (with a superb tenor improvisation) and the usual share of intensities. *The Witch Doctor* is a new arrival and a welcome one: Morgan's 'Afrique' and the title-tune are more New York than dark continent, but Shorter's mysterious 'Those Who Sit And Wait' was worth waiting for. Even more bountiful, though, is *Roots And Herbs*, which is arguably the great forgotten Blakey album. All six themes are by Shorter (and there are three alternative takes as a bonus) and from the ferocious 'Ping Pong' onwards the music hits a rare intensity, allied with the composer's enigmatic elegance. Davis sits in for Timmons on two titles.

*** Live In Stockholm 1959

DIW 313 *Blakey; Lee Morgan (t); Wayne Shorter (ts); Walter Bishop Jr (p); Jymie Merritt (b).* 11/59.

*** Live In Stockholm 1959

Dragon DRCD 182 *As above.* 11/59.

*** Live In Stockholm 1960

DIW 344 *As above, except Bobby Timmons (p) replaces Bishop.* 12/60.

*** Lausanne 1960 First Set

TCB 02058 *As above.* 12/60

***** Lausanne 1960 Second Set**
TCB 02062 *As above.* 12/60.

***** Unforgettable Lee!**
Fresh Sound FSCD-1020 *As above.* 4–6/60.

***** More Birdland Sessions**
Fresh Sound FSCD-1029 *As above, except add Walter Davis Jr (p).* 6–11/60.

Though one might imagine live Messengers recordings to be hotter than their studio counterparts, the band was able to generate the same intensity in both locations. Still, these live sessions from a couple of European visits are useful supplements to the Blue Note albums. There is little variation between the three Stockholm sets – although the 1959 Dragon issue includes some more interesting themes, recorded on the same day as the DIW disc but apparently using some different material. With the recordings probably emanating from radio tapes, the sound is consistently clear, if not as full-bodied as the studio sessions; in any event, Morgan and Shorter are always worth hearing as a youthful partnership, creating the kind of idiosyncratic front line that seems lost among today's more faceless technicians. The two *Lausanne* discs are from Swiss Radio archives and find the band on another European stopover – same tour, same calibre of playing, and probably for completists only.

The Fresh Sound disc sorts together nine tracks from various Birdland sessions in the spring of 1960 (it is nominally credited to Morgan and has his picture on the CD sleeve) and, although anyone who has the other discs listed here will have the material in other versions, this catches the Messengers on a very hot streak. A brief 'Justice' finds Morgan in explosive form on his solo, and he sounds particularly exciting on most of the tracks on a generously packed CD. The sound, though, is rather grainy and suffers from some drop-outs. *More Birdland Sessions* sweeps together some more offcuts from the same year: Shorter is at his most eccentric in the 'Lester Left Town' solo, but there is interesting stuff from both him and Morgan throughout. Indifferent sound, though.

****(*) Jazz Messengers**
Impulse! 051175-2 *Blakey; Freddie Hubbard (t); Curtis Fuller (tb); Wayne Shorter (ts); Cedar Walton (p); Jymie Merritt (b).* 6/61.

****** Mosaic**
Blue Note 46523-2 *As above.* 10/61.

****** Buhaina's Delight**
Blue Note 84104-2 *As above.* 11–12/61.

*****(*) Three Blind Mice Vol. 1**
Blue Note 84451 *As above.* 3/62.

*****(*) Three Blind Mice Vol. 2**
Blue Note 84452 *As above.* 3/62.

***** Caravan**
Original Jazz Classics OJC 038 *As above, except Reggie Workman (b) replaces Merritt.* 10/62.

*****(*) Ugetsu**
Original Jazz Classics OJC 090 *As above.* 6/63.

****** Free For All**
Blue Note 84170 *As above.* 2/64.

***** Kyoto**
Original Jazz Classics OJC 145 *As above.* 2/64.

Exit Morgan, enter Hubbard and Fuller. By now it was clear that Blakey's Jazz Messengers were becoming a dynasty unto themselves, with the drummer driving everything from his kit. As musical director, Shorter was still providing some startling material which Hubbard and Fuller, outstanding players but undercharacterized personalities, could use to fashion directions of their own. Cedar Walton was another significant new man: after the lightweight work of Bobby Timmons, Walton's deeper but no less buoyant themes added extra weight to the band's impact.

In some ways, this was the most adventurous of all Messengers line-ups. The three masterpieces are the amazingly intense *Free For All*, which reasserts Blakey's polyrhythmic firepower as never before and finds Shorter at his most ferocious on the title-tune and 'Hammer Head'; *Mosaic*, where the complex title-piece (by Walton) shows how the expanded voicings of the band added orchestral sonority to rhythmic power; and *Buhaina's Delight*, opening on the swaggering 'Backstage Sally' and leading to Shorter's stone-faced 'Contemplation' and vivid arrangement of 'Moon River'. Hubbard's feisty brightness and Fuller's sober, quickfire solos are a memorable counterweight to Shorter's private, dark improvisations. The tenorman is less evident on *Kyoto*, a breezier session dominated by Fuller and Hubbard, and although the live-at-Birdland *Ugetsu* is fine, it doesn't catch fire in quite the way the band might have been expected to in concert, though Shorter's feature on 'I Didn't Know What Time It Was' is ponderously impressive. More exciting are the two *Three Blind Mice* sets, mostly made at an engagement at the Renaissance in Los Angeles. Less finished than the studio recordings, but it's a thrill to hear Shorter and Hubbard tear into the likes of 'It's Only A Paper Moon' as well as the originals in the book. Walton is often rather remote in the mix.

Caravan is another solid though slightly less imposing set. The earliest date, for Impulse!, seems to have been organized more by the producer than by the musicians since it consists almost entirely of standards; though capably done, it's not what this edition of the band was about.

***** The African Beat**
Blue Note 22666-2 *Blakey; Yusef Lateef (ts, f, ob, cow horn, perc); Ahmed Abdul-Malik (b); Solomon G Ilori (v, whistle, perc); Chief Bey, Montego Joe, Garvin Masseaux, James Ola Folami, Robert Crowder, Curtis Fuller (perc).* 1/62.

A little more serious than *Orgy In Rhythm*, though the end result isn't all that different. No doubt Blakey was fascinated by the possibilities of African and American percussionists working together, and the recording is a starburst of energy, the master's kit-patterns surrounded by congas, telegraph drums, chekeres, maracas, bambara drums and more. Lateef is right at home in this setting, and there is the unique presence of Curtis Fuller as a tympanist. In the end, though, the music feels packaged for its surroundings, the hard bop of the Blue Note catalogue, with the various pieces either foreshortened or otherwise shaped to fit to an LP's needs.

****** The Best Of Art Blakey And The Jazz Messengers**
Blue Note 93205-2

***** The Best Of Art Blakey**

Emarcy 848245-2 *Blakey; Lee Morgan, Chuck Mangione, Valery Ponomarev (t); Bobby Watson (as); Benny Golson, Barney Wilen, Wayne Shorter, Frank Mitchell, David Schnitter (ts); Bobby Timmons, Walter Davis Jr, Keith Jarrett, James Williams (p); Jymie Merritt, Reggie Johnson, Dennis Irwin (b).* 12/58–2/79.

The Blue Note compilation is well chosen, with 'Moanin'', 'Blues March' and 'Dat Dere' covering the most popular Messengers tunes and 'Mosaic', 'Free For All' and 'Lester Left Town' their most challenging. 'A Night In Tunisia' is also here. Emarcy's collection includes four tracks with Barney Wilen opposite Morgan in the 1958–9 band, a 1966 reading of 'My Romance' which is included mainly for the presence of Keith Jarrett, and a somewhat desultory 1979 version of 'Blues March' by a less than distinguished line-up; a patchwork but worthwhile disc.

*****(*) A Jazz Message**

Impulse! 547964-2 *Blakey; Sonny Stitt (ts, as); McCoy Tyner (p); Art Davis (b).* 7/63.

Loose-limbed, flying, four great musicians having a high old time of it one day in the Van Gelder studios (though this wasn't a Blue Note date). It's just some blues and three standards, and it's no immortal statement, but Blakey sounds like he's enjoying himself hugely and, though Stitt rarely let himself go in the studios, he plays some of his most shining licks here. Tyner and the super-solid Davis go along for the ride.

****(*) Child's Dance**

Prestige 24130-2 *Blakey; Woody Shaw (t); Buddy Terry (ss); Ramon Morris (ts, f); Carter Jefferson (ts); Manny Boyd (f); George Cables, Cedar Walton, John Hicks, Walter Davis Jr (p); Essien Nkrumah (g); Stanley Clarke, Mickey Bass (b); Nathaniel Bettis, Sonny Morgan, Pablo Landrums, Emmanuel Rahid, Ray Mantilla, Tony Waters (perc).* 3/73.

***** Mission Eternal**

Prestige 24159-2 *Blakey; Woody Shaw (t); Steve Turre (tb); Carter Jefferson (ss, ts); Cedar Walton (p); Michael Howell (g); Mickey Bass (b); Tony Waters (perc); Jon Hendricks (v).* 3/73.

This Messengers period is scarcely represented in the catalogues at all at present. They cut three albums for Prestige at this time; the balance of two of them is presented on *Child's Dance*, with a long-unreleased track as a bonus. Musically, it's pretty poor stuff. The ramshackle percussion tracks, modish electric pianos, preponderance of flutes and generally rambling solos give little focus to a band that was stuck between past and future. The one figure of substance (aside from Blakey himself) is Shaw, who cuts out a few hard-edged solos and gives a slightly overcooked but mainly convincing reading of 'I Can't Get Started' as the anachronistic but solid centre of the disc.

Mission Eternal mops up the rest of the material and is a much better bet. Shaw again takes the honours, his solos full of snap but with a thoughtful, almost musing quality at times which militates against the volatility of the typical Messengers approach. Turre appears on three tracks and Hendricks guest-stars on a jolly treatment of 'Along Came Betty'. There is a worthwile bonus in the previously unheard 'Siempre Mi Amor'.

**** In My Prime Vol. 1**

Timeless SJP 114 *Blakey; Valery Ponomarev (t); Curtis Fuller (tb); Bobby Watson (as); David Schnitter (ts); James Williams (p); Dennis Irwin (b); Ray Mantilla (perc).* 12/77.

****(*) In This Korner**

Concord CCD 4068 *As above, except omit Fuller and Mantilla.* 5/78.

The long gap in Blakey's discography is symptomatic of the commercial decline of jazz in the 1960s and '70s. Some good Messengers line-ups, featuring Chuck Mangione, Woody Shaw, Bill Hardman and others, made only a few records in the period, and no studio dates are currently in print. This 1977 band was workmanlike rather than outstanding, although the redoubtable Fuller lends class and Watson lends firepower. The music, though, seems to have fallen into routine. There wasn't much improvement in the first of several live sessions Blakey was to cut at San Francisco's Keystone Korner: Watson's 'Pamela', later a staple in his repertoire, is engaging, but the rest is so-so.

***** Live At Montreux And Northsea**

Timeless SJP 150 *Blakey; Valery Ponomarev, Wynton Marsalis (t); Robin Eubanks (tb); Branford Marsalis (as, bs); Bobby Watson (as); Bill Pierce (ts); James Williams (p); Kevin Eubanks (g); Charles Fambrough (b); John Ramsey (d).* 7/80.

*****(*) Album Of The Year**

Timeless SJP 155 *Blakey; Wynton Marsalis (t); Bobby Watson (as); Bill Pierce (ts); James Williams (p); Charles Fambrough (b).* 4/81.

***** In Sweden**

Evidence ECD 22044 *As above.* 3/81.

*****(*) Straight Ahead**

Concord CCD 4168 *As above.* 6/81.

*****(*) Keystone 3**

Concord CCD 4196 *As above, except Branford Marsalis (as), Donald Brown (p) replace Watson and Williams.* 1/82.

Wynton Marsalis's arrival was a turning point for both Blakey and jazz in the 1980s. His peculiar assurance and whipcrack precision, at the age of nineteen, heralded a new school of Messengers graduates of rare confidence and ability. He plays only a minor role in the big-band album, which is devoted mainly to Watson's themes and is an exuberant round-robin of solos and blustering theme statements, with Eubanks appearing as the first guitarist in a Messengers line-up. Once Marsalis took over as MD, the ensembles took on a fresh bite and the soloists sound leaner, more pointed. The live set from Stockholm is solid stuff, if a notch behind *Album Of The Year*: Watson's feature on 'Skylark' is the best thing here, and a reminder that his time in the band has been unfairly eclipsed by Wynton's arrival. Both *Straight Ahead* and *Keystone 3* were recorded live at San Francisco's Keystone Korner (though on separate occasions) and both find a renewed involvement from Blakey himself, who's well served by the crisp recording. Watson's departure was a shade disappointing, given the tickle of creative confrontation between himself and Marsalis, but brother Branford's arrival, though he sounds as yet unformed, lends another edge of anxiety-to-please to the ensembles.

***** Oh – By The Way**

Timeless SJP 165 *Blakey; Terence Blanchard (t); Donald Harrison (as); Bill Pierce (ts); Johnny O'Neal (p); Charles Fambrough (b).* 5/82.

*****(*) New York Scene**

Concord CCD 4256 *Blakey; Terence Blanchard (t); Donald Harrison (as); Jean Toussaint (ts); Mulgrew Miller (p); Lonnie Plaxico (b).* 4/84.

****(*) Blue Night**

Timeless SJP 217 *As above.* 3/85.

***** Live At Kimball's**

Concord CCD 4307 *As above.* 4/85.

*****(*) Art Collection**

Concord CCD 4495 *As Concord albums above.* 78–85.

Even after Marsalis departed the band, The Messengers continued their winning streak. Blanchard, whom one might call the first post-Marsalis trumpeter, proved another inspiring MD, and his partnership with Harrison made the front line sizzle. Two trumpet solos on the *New York Scene* set, on 'Oh By The Way' and 'Tenderly', show off intelligence, fire and perfectly calculated risk in some abundance. Miller and Plaxico renewed the rhythm section with superlative technique, and the old man sounds as aggressive as ever. Only *Blue Night* is routine. Although all the live sessions are good, *New York Scene* is particularly hot. Toussaint's brawny solos are closely in the Messengers tradition, and only Williams sounds a little out of his depth. *Art Collection* is a best-of culled from five of the Concord albums, and the shrewd programming and sensible choice of tracks make this a useful one-disc introduction to what Blakey was doing in the early 1980s.

****(*) Not Yet**

Soul Note 121105-2 *Blakey; Philip Harper (t); Robin Eubanks (tb); Javon Jackson (ts); Benny Green (p); Peter Washington (b).* 3/88.

****(*) I Get A Kick Out Of Bu**

Soul Note 121550-2 *As above, except Leon Dorsey (b) replaces Washington.* 11/88.

Blakey's status as a bandmaster for all seasons was now as widely celebrated as anything in jazz, and taking a place in The Messengers was one of the most widespread ambitions among young players. Of those in this edition, only Jackson seems less than outstanding, with Eubanks splendidly peppery, Harper another Marsalis type with a silvery tone, and Green one of the funkiest pianists since the band's earlier days. Yet they never made a truly outstanding Messengers record together. By this time, much of the excitement about neo-classic jazz had subsided and the players had a hard time escaping the scent of technique-over-feeling which was beginning to invade a lot of precision-orientated young bands. Blakey's own playing remains thunderously powerful, and he makes a lot of things happen which might otherwise have slipped away, yet the Soul Note records seem made by rote, and there's an overall feeling of transition and that Blakey himself was too late in his career to move forward.

***** The Art Of Jazz**

In & Out 77028-2 *Blakey; Terence Blanchard, Freddie Hubbard, Brian Lynch (t); Curtis Fuller, Frank Lacy (tb); Jackie McLean (as); Wayne Shorter, Benny Golson, Javon Jackson (ts); Walter Davis Jr, Geoff Keezer (p); Buster Williams (b); Roy Haynes (d); Michelle Hendricks (v).* 10/89.

Probably the greatest Messengers line-up of all time – though this was for a one-off show on the occasion of Art's seventieth birthday. As with most such events, the music takes something of a second place to the general bonhomie and celebration, but there could hardly fail to be great moments with these players: an all-hands-in 'Along Came Betty' and Benny Golson's six-horn chart for 'Lester Left Town' among them. Twelve minutes of chat with Buhaina fill out the disc.

****(*) Chippin' In**

Timeless SJP 340 *Blakey; Brian Lynch (t); Frank Lacy (tb); Dale Barlow, Javon Jackson (ts); Geoff Keezer (p); Essiet Okun Essiet (b).* 4/90.

Keezer aside, the final Messengers line-up is a bit disappointing: Lynch, Barlow and Jackson are all in the front of the second division, but they can't strike sparks the way the best Messenger bands could. It's hard to avoid the feeling that Blakey, too, is slowing down, though he's trying his damnedest not to let anyone know it. Nevertheless, the Timeless session includes some strong new themes, and Lacy and Keezer have energy enough to stake places in the Messengers lineage.

Terence Blanchard (born 1962)

TRUMPET, PIANO

Came to prominence as a late-period Jazz Messenger and has since recorded as a leader and become heavily involved in film music, initially scoring several Spike Lee movies.

***** The Billie Holiday Songbook**

Columbia CK 57793 *Blanchard; Bruce Barth (p); Chris Thomas (b); Troy Davis (d); Jeanie Bryson (v); orchestra.* 10/93.

****** Romantic Defiance**

Columbia 480489 *Blanchard; Kenny Garrett (ts); Edward Simon (p); Chris Thomas (b); Troy Davis (d).* 12/94.

*****(*) The Heart Speaks**

Columbia 483638-2 *Blanchard; Ivan Lins (p, v); Edward Simon (p); Oscar Castro-Nueves (g); David Pulphus (b); Paulinho Da Costa (perc); Fred Zlotkin, David Bohanovich (v).* 95.

****** Jazz In Film**

Columbia SK 60671 *Blanchard; Steve Turre (tb); Donald Harrison (as); Joe Henderson (ts); Kenny Kirkland (p); Reginald Veal (b); Carl Allen (d).* 3 & 4/98.

Blanchard plays with a minimum of fuss and with admirable directness, simple and declarative: name, rank and number – though, if you're looking for a fancier way to describe what he does and how he sounds, 'romantic defiance' serves very well. If he looks more and more like Dizzy as the years go by, his sound seems to come from an earlier generation, 'Sweets' Edison and Buck Clayton foremost. An intriguing segue from the original

'Glass J' to 'Mo' Better Blues' and thence to Ornette's 'Lonely Woman' (on an earlier Columbia album, *Simply Stated*) serves as a brief but effective history lesson.

Blanchard took over Wynton Marsalis's chair in the Jazz Messengers (that was where he met sidekick, Donald Harrison, who'd stepped into Branford Marsalis's shoes) but though there are superficial similarities of approach he's a more open-hearted player, less hung up on self-defeating standards of authenticity. Earlier albums for Columbia are currently in the dead-letter office, but these more recent entries remain available. One wonders how exactly the Billie Holiday project was A&R'd. 'Songbook' albums are very popular again and, though Lady was no composer, she gave the material she sang such a highly personal cast that a whole raft of songs – not just 'Strange Fruit' – seem eternally associated with her. At what point, though, was Jeanie Bryson brought in as soloist? Whatever, it's the key to this extremely patchy session. Blanchard finds interesting things to do with 'Good Morning Heartache', a tune that sits comfortably for a brass player, and solos with some emotion on 'I Cover The Waterfront'. But the band trudges through the rest, and it's only on Bryson's five songs that things get seriously interesting. 'Strange Fruit' is always a bit of a gamble for other singers. Only Nina Simone has ever got a hold of its sheer weirdness, but Bryson takes it very simply and unaffectedly, unlike her dizzy reading of 'What A Little Moonlight Can Do'. Encouragingly, it's an album that gets better as it goes along. The closing 'Lady Sings The Blues' instrumental gets at the elements of Herbie Nichols's tune that are often overlooked, and Blanchard provides a nice coda.

Romantic Defiance remains his best to date. It sounds as though it was recorded by a seasoned working band. Garrett, who has been growing on his own account in recent years, plays with tremendous poise and conviction, and the rhythm section is subtly different in emphasis from the Marsalis-orbit players who have been round Blanchard up till now. A smashing record by any standard.

The Heart Speaks is very pleasing, if something of an interlude in the work of a musician who has progressed some way beyond mere gigging: his film-score work for Spike Lee (*Malcolm X*, *Mo' Better Blues* and *Clockers*) he may count among his most important work. This is nevertheless a charming and particularly warm set of interpretations of songs by Ivan Lins, the sometimes sappy melodiousness of Brazilian song firmed up by the trumpeter's gently assertive lines.

The recent *Jazz In Film* continues the interest in soundtrack music and confirms Blanchard's now substantial reputation. The material covered is as recent and close at hand as Blanchard's own score for *Clockers*, and as classic as Alex North's *A Streetcar Named Desire* and Elmer Bernstein's *The Man With The Golden Arm*. North's music for the Tennessee Williams play loses its *Suthuhn* feyness and comes out brisk and streetwise. Turre's solo is less shop-soiled than Blanche Dubois, but no less beguiling; the quote from 'It Don't Mean A Thing' is expertly timed. Blanchard's own intervention has none of the brutishness the theme might suggest. It's one of the most elegant he has committed to record.

The other material covered includes Jerry Goldsmith's theme for *Chinatown* (exquisitely introduced by the late lamented Kirkland), Duke's *Anatomy Of A Murder* and *Degas' Racing World*, Previn's *The Subterraneans* and Bernard Herrmann's chilling last work, the theme for *Taxi Driver*. Throughout, Blanchard is impeccably voiced, pitched just in front of an excellent band. Joe Henderson raises the ante whenever he plays, not content to let this lapse into easy filmic impressionism. His betting stubs are all on the table for the second of the Ellington pieces, a minor miracle of jazz impressionism.

Blanchard has found a convincing way of combining jazz performance with sound-pictures. It's to be hoped that he doesn't get lured too far from straight swinging.

****** Wandering Moon**

Sony Classics SK 89111 *Blanchard; Aaron Fletcher (as); Branford Marsalis, Brice Winston (ts); Edward Simon (p); Dave Holland (b); Eric Harland (d).* 6/99.

Under benign exile to Sony Classics, Blanchard goes for a long (over 75 minutes), ballad-orientated record which seems full of near-darkness. Originals such as 'Luna Viajera' and 'If I Could, I Would' distil a sense of melancholy which is mitigated by the serenity of the playing: even though there are one or two tear-ups, from Marsalis in particular, what one remembers about the record is its poise, its cool dedication to instrumental mastery. None are more masterful than the leader himself. The closing version of 'I Thought About You', taken at the slowest of tempos, is a definitive treatment which silences criticism and, in its final moments, leaves the listener dumbfounded.

Carla Bley (born 1938)

PIANO, ORGAN, SYNTHESIZERS, COMPOSER

Noted first as a composer and co-led Jazz Composers Orchestra in New York from 1964, some form of which is still her basic performing ensemble. Her label JCOA transformed into Watt, which releases most of her music. Also performs in small-group situations, mostly with Steve Swallow; her piano and organ playing, somewhat minimalist, seems to be progressing to a lead instrument of late.

*****(*) Escalator Over The Hill**

JCOA/ECM 839 310 2 2CD *Bley; Michael Mantler (t, vtb, p); Enrico Rava, Michael Snow (t); Don Cherry (t, f, perc, v); Sam Burtis, Jimmy Knepper, Roswell Rudd (tb); Jack Jeffers (btb); Bob Carlisle, Sharon Freeman (frhn); John Buckingham, Howard Johnson (tba); Peggy Imig, Perry Robinson (cl); Souren Baronian (cl, dumbec); Jimmy Lyons, Dewey Redman (as); Gato Barbieri (ts); Chris Woods (bs); Sam Brown, John McLaughlin (g); Karl Berger (vib); Don Preston (syn, v); Jack Bruce (b, v solo); Charlie Haden, Ron McClure, Richard Youngstein (b); Leroy Jenkins (vn); Nancy Newton (vla); Calo Scott (clo); Bill Morimando (bells); Paul Motian (d); Roger Dawson (perc); Jane Blackstone, Paul Jones, Sheila Jordan, Jeanne Lee, Timothy Marquand, Tod Papageorge, Linda Ronstadt, Bob Stewart, Viva (v solo); Jonathan Cott, Steve Gebhardt, Tyrus Gerlach, Eileen Hale, Rosalind Hupp (v).* 11/68–6/71.

Though initially influenced by the likes of Monk and Miles, with all that that implies, Carla Bley was profoundly influenced by European classical music and by the darker reaches of *chanson*. She quickly became disenchanted with free-form improvisation and, from the late 1960s onwards, began experimenting with large-scale composition. No jazz composition is as large and ungainly as the massive 'chronotransduction', *Escalator Over The Hill*. We fall in and out of love with this strange, perverse work. Like all genuinely original artistic experiments, it is an uneasy hybrid of genius – vivid and uplifting – and unbelievable tosh. Written to an impenetrable libretto by Paul Haines, it is more closely related to the non-linear, associative cinema of avant-garde film-makers Kenneth Anger, Stan Brakhage, Maya Deren and Jonas Mekas (at whose Cinemathèque some of the sessions were recorded) than to any musical parallel. The repetitious dialogue – 'again' is repeated *ad infinitum* – is largely derived from Gertrude Stein and it's perhaps best to take Stein's Alice-in-Wonderland advice and treat everything as meaning precisely what one chooses it to mean. Musically, it's a patchwork of raucous big-band themes like the opening 'Hotel Overture' (many of the events take place in Cecil Clark's Hotel with its pastiche Palm Court band), which has fine solos from Barbieri, Robinson, Haden and Rudd, heavy rock numbers like the apocalyptic 'Rawalpindi Blues' (McLaughlin, Bruce, Motian), ethnic themes from Don Cherry's Desert Band, and mysterious, ring-modulated 'dream sequences'. There is an element of recitative that, as with most opera recordings, most listeners will prefer to skip, since it doesn't advance understanding of the 'plot' one millimetre, and it's probably best to treat *Escalator* as a compilation of individual pieces with dispensable continuity. The slightly earlier *A Genuine Tong Funeral* is a genuine masterpiece on a slightly less ambitious scale and it, rather than *Escalator* (which was as much Paul Haines's work as Bley's), established her musical idiom of the 1970s.

Perhaps it's time now to re-record an edited version of *Escalator*, with a new cast. Or would that simply dispel the maddeningly chaotic magic of a flawed masterpiece?

*****(*) Tropic Appetites**

Watt/1 *Bley; Michael Mantler (t, vtb); Gato Barbieri (ts, perc); Howard Johnson (ss, bs, bsx, cl, bcl, tba, v); Dave Holland (b, clo) Toni Marcus (vn, vla); Paul Motian (d, perc); Julie Tippetts (v).* 9/73–2/74.

Tropic Appetites is the work that *Escalator* might have been with a little judicious editing. Its sheer strangeness is endlessly beguiling and the fact that this, unlike its bulky predecessor, has been out of circulation for some time lends the reissue a fizzy freshness. Haines's words are much more effective when not squeezed into a larger, quasi-narrative template and Julie Tippetts' voice is completely compelling; she is one of those rare creatures who would be worth hearing even if she were singing the phone book.

The instrumentation is gloriously cadenced. Howard Johnson is a complete horn section in himself, Barbieri was at his most freakishly expressionistic and Bley herself ranges over a whole spectrum of keyboards, doing her 'composer's piano' thing with a wry recognition of her own lack of virtuosity. The backgrounds she creates for 'What Will Be Left Between Us And The Moon Tonight?' and 'Song Of The Jungle Stream' are definitive of the Bley approach, correct but wacky, linear and perverse in the same breath. The latter track, dedicated to Tadd Dameron, reveals how much Bley owes to her predecessors and to the jazz tradition. Motian's drumming and Dave Holland's bass lines cement the astonishing architecture, while the horns create an illusion of scale that still surprises 25 years on.

***** Dinner Music**

Watt/6 *Bley; Michael Mantler (t); Roswell Rudd (tb); Bob Stewart (tba); Carlos Ward (as, ts); Richard Tee (p); Eric Gale, Cornell Dupree (g); Gordon Edwards (b); Steve Gadd (d).* 7–9/76.

***** European Tour 1977**

Watt/8 *Bley; Michael Mantler (t); Roswell Rudd (tb); John Clark (frhn); Elton Dean (as); Gary Windo (bs); Terry Adams (p); Hugh Hopper (b); Andrew Cyrille (d, perc).* 77.

***** Musique Mécanique**

Watt/9 *Bley; Michael Mantler (t); Roswell Rudd (tb); John Clark (frhn); Bob Stewart (tba); Alan Braufman (f, cl, as); Gary Windo (bcl, ts); Terry Adams (p, org); Eugene Chadbourne (g, radio); Steve Swallow (b); D Sharpe (d); Karen Mantler (glockenspiel).* 8–11/78.

This is an awkward period in Bley's and Watt's development, largely because there is no development. There was an understandable retreat from ambitious experimentation, and yet these records document a highly individual approach that draws on no obvious precedents. Something of a muchness, they are harmonically quirky, sometimes plain eccentric, song shapes delivered with a maximum of spin. The Brits on the European tour seemed to get the point straight away, paving a course for Carla's European bands of the '80s and after. Earlier editions give a more detailed breakdown of these records; time makes it harder to choose among them.

***** Social Studies**

Watt/11 *Bley; Michael Mantler (t); Gary Valente (tb); Joe Daley (euph); Earl McIntyre (tba); Carlos Ward (as, ss); Tony Dagradi (cl, ts); Steve Swallow (b); D Sharpe (d).* 12/80.

*****(*) Live!**

Watt/12 *Bley; Michael Mantler (t); Gary Valente (tb); Vincent Chancey (frhn); Earl McIntyre (tba, btb); Steve Slagle (as); Tony Dagradi (ts); Arturo O'Farrill (p, org); Steve Swallow (b); D Sharpe (d).* 8/81.

It's at this point that Bley's imagination makes a sharp left away from the European art-music models that haunted her throughout the 1970s and towards a more recognizable jazz idiom which may be less authentically individual but which gains immeasurably in sheer energy. *Live!* is a treat, representing one of the finest performances by her and Mantler on record. *Social Studies* shouldn't be missed; a bookish cover masks some wonderfully wry music.

**** I Hate To Sing**

Watt/12½ *Bley; Michael Mantler (t); Gary Valente (tb); Vincent Chancey (frhn); Earl McIntyre (tba, btb, v); Steve Slagle (as); Tony Dagradi (ts); Arturo O'Farrill (p, org, v); Steve Swallow (b, d); D Sharpe (d, v).* 8/81–1/83.

**** Heavy Heart**

Watt/14 *Bley; Michael Mantler (t); Gary Valente (tb); Earl McIntyre (tba); Steve Slagle (f, as, bs); Hiram Bullock (g); Kenny*

Kirkland (p); Steve Swallow (b); Victor Lewis (d); Manolo Badrena (perc). 9–10/83.

****(*) Night-Glo**

Watt/16 *Bley; Randy Brecker (t, flhn); Tom Malone (tb); Dave Taylor (btb); John Clark (frhn); Paul McCandless (ob, eng hn, ss, ts, bcl); Hiram Bullock (g); Larry Willis (p); Steve Swallow (b); Victor Lewis (d); Manolo Badrena (perc).* 6–8/85.

This is a disappointing vintage in Bley's music. Despite the undoubted popularity of *I Hate To Sing*, it is one of her least imaginative small-group albums, heavily reliant on a limited range of ideas that are far more heavily embellished than usual, with camouflaging percussion and timbral effects. *Heavy Heart* is similarly disappointing, though the arrangements and voicings transfer well to CD. *Night-Glo* is by far the best of the trio; Oregon's Paul McCandless produces some striking woodwind effects and Hiram Bullock's guitar, not yet promoted beyond 'other ranks' status, is used more sensibly than on the first item below. Completists – and there must be lots – will be happy enough. New listeners would do better elsewhere.

****(*) Sextet**

Watt/17 *Bley; Hiram Bullock (g); Larry Willis (p); Steve Swallow (b); Victor Lewis (d); Don Alias (perc).* 12/86–1/87.

***** Duets**

Watt/20 *Bley; Steve Swallow (b).* 7–8/88.

Towards the end of the 1980s, Bley's emphasis shifted towards smaller and more intimate units. Though never a virtuosic soloist, she grew in stature as a performer. *Sextet* was unusual in having no horns, but Bley's chords are so voiced as to suggest whole areas of harmonic interest that here and in the *Duets* with Swallow remain implicit rather than fully worked out. Bullock is perhaps too insistent a spokesman, though he takes his more promising cues from the veteran bass man. By this time there is an almost telepathic understanding between Bley and Swallow; the duets make an ironic but uncynical commentary on the cocktail-lounge conventions of piano-and-bass duos. It's an entertaining album and an ideal primer on Bley's compositional and improvising techniques.

*****(*) Fleur Carnivore**

Watt/21 839 662 *Bley; Lew Soloff, Jens Winther (t); Frank Lacy (frhn, flhn); Gary Valente (tb); Bob Stewart (tba); Daniel Beaussier (ob, f); Wolfgang Puschnig (as, f); Andy Sheppard (ts, cl); Christof Lauer (ts, ss); Roberto Ottini (bs, ss); Karen Mantler (hca, org, vib, chimes); Steve Swallow (b); Buddy Williams (d); Don Alias (perc).* 11/88.

This is something like a masterpiece. Having concentrated pretty much on small bands during the 1980s, Bley returned wholeheartedly to large-scale scoring and arranging, touring with a Big Band and a Very Big Band, working in an idiom that was not only unmistakably jazz but also plain unmistakable. The relation of parts to whole is far more confident than in times gone by and the solos are uniformly imaginative, with Lauer, Soloff and Mantler, K., deserving special commendation. The writing is acute and the concert recording manages to balance 'live' energy with studio precision and fullness of sound.

***** The Very Big Carla Bley Band**

Watt/23 *Bley; Guy Barker, Steven Bernstein, Claude Deppa, Lew Soloff (t); Richard Edwards, Gary Valente, Fayyaz Virji (tb); Ashley Slater (btb); Roger Jannotta (ob, f, cl, ss); Wolfgang Puschnig (as, f); Andy Sheppard (ts, ss); Pete Hurt (ts, cl); Pablo Calogero (bs); Karen Mantler (org); Steve Swallow (b); Victor Lewis (d); Don Alias (perc).* 10/90.

A stirring live outfit, the Very Big Band translates well to record, with plenty of emphasis on straightforward blowing from featured soloists Soloff, Valente, Puschnig and Sheppard. 'United States' opens with splashy percussion, low, threatening brass figures, with the theme only really hinted at in Lew Soloff's sensuous growl solo. The riff and horn voicings that follow are unmistakably Bley's, as is the sudden, swinging interpolation of an entirely new theme. 'Strange Arrangement' opens with an almost childish piano figure, which gives way to huge, shimmering harmonics that instantly explain its logic. 'Who Will Rescue You?' grows out of an almost gospelly vamp, but by this time the album has lost at least some of its initial impetus, and 'Lo Ultimo' is a rather limping curtain-piece.

***** Go Together**

Watt/24 *Bley; Steve Swallow (b).* 92.

An intriguingly relaxed and unhurried survey of (mostly) older material, this includes beautifully judged performances of 'Sing Me Softly Of The Blues', 'Mother Of The Dead Man' and 'Fleur Carnivore'. Students of Bley – and there are growing numbers, even in academia – will find much of interest in these slender, relatively unadorned arrangements. Everyone else can simply enjoy them.

***** Big Band Theory**

Watt/25 *Bley; Lew Soloff, Guy Barker, Claude Deppa, Steve Waterman (t); Gary Valente, Richard Edwards, Annie Whitehead (tb); Ashley Slater (btb); Roger Jannotta (ss, f); Wolfgang Puschnig (as, f); Andy Sheppard (ts, ss); Pete Hurt (ts); Julian Arguëlles (bs); Karen Mantler (org); Alex Balanescu (vn); Steve Swallow (b); Dennis Mackrel (d).* 7/93.

This never quite fulfils the promise of some exciting arrangements (notably of Mingus's 'Goodbye Pork Pie Hat') and a rash of hot soloists, including regulars Sheppard, Soloff, Puschnig and Swallow, and guest Alex Balanescu, who gets down to it with a will. 'Birds Of Paradise' was a commission for the Glasgow Jazz Festival and was a serious disappointment there. Typically, though, it has been reworked and sharpened up considerably, and it comes across much more forcefully on record.

The main reservation about *Big Band Theory* stems from the overall balance of the recording. Though in a warm, expansive analogue, it muffles and blurs some of the horn passages and exaggerates the rhythm tracks, often to the detriment of subtle voicings.

***** Songs With Legs**

Watt/26 *Bley; Andy Sheppard (ts, ss); Steve Swallow (b).* 5/94.

A matey trawl round Europe by three chums with a bag of songs. It isn't much more complicated than that, and just sometimes it conveys precisely that had-to-be-there feel that can be off-putting if you weren't. Carla's compositions have become modern classics and it is fascinating to hear 'Real Life Hits' and 'Wrong Key Donkey' given this stripped-down treatment. She doesn't put a foot wrong throughout, but then these performances were hand-picked from six different locations, so the selection process obviously played a part.

*****(*) The Carla Bley Big Band Goes To Church**

Watt/27 *Bley; Lew Soloff, Guy Barker, Claude Deppa, Steve Waterman (t); Gary Valente, Pete Beachill, Chris Dean (tb); Richard Henry (btb); Roger Jannotta (ss, as, f); Wolfgang Puschnig (as); Andy Sheppard, Jerry Underwood (ts); Julian Arguëlles (bs); Karen Mantler (org, hca); Steve Swallow (b); Dennis Mackrel (d).* 7/96.

Another episode from the road, so titled not just because of the gospelly, preaching tone that predominates but more immediately because these six cracking tracks were recorded in concert at the beautiful Chiesa San Francesco Al Prato, an important venue for the Umbria Jazz Festival. The acoustic is suprisingly dry and, but for occasional ripples of applause, *Goes To Church* might almost be a live studio recording.

The long (almost 25 minutes) opening piece, 'Setting Calvin's Waltz', was written on commission for the Berlin Jazz Festival. Opening on a soft, confessional dialogue between Bley and Swallow, it opens up into an episodic curtain-raiser featuring most of the major soloists: Sheppard, Soloff, Valente, Karen Mantler and Puschnig, who emerges as the favoured pupil this time with no fewer than five feature spots on the disc. The best of them come on the two closing tracks, 'Permanent Wave' and 'Who Will Rescue You?', on which his slightly dry tone and plangent delivery work to perfection.

As ever, Swallow's cleanly picked bass guitar lines are well to the fore, but Bley herself seems increasingly content on Big Band dates to disappear into the background, reserving herself for the occasional intro and, perhaps, for the small groups. Here and there, though, she provides some instinctive colours, and her quirky scales and chords are the thread on which Sheppard, Soloff and the highly accomplished Mackrel string their 'Beads'. The best Bley album since *Fleur Carnivore*?

***** Fancy Chamber Music**

Watt/28 *Bley; Alison Hayhurst (f); Sarah Lee (cl, glock); Steve Morris (vn); Andrew Byrt (vla); Emma Black (clo); Steve Swallow (b); Chris Wells (perc).* 12/97.

Bley is one of a small group of jazz composers who have attracted the admiring attention of conservatory and academic musicians. For a time, there was a Bley Band at Leicester Polytechnic (now de Montfort University) in England, dedicated to 'classical' performance of her repertoire. The material here, though, had its origins back in 1985 when Carla was asked to write some pieces for the Lincoln Center Chamber Music Society. A commission followed from avant-garde pianist Ursula Oppens and the Hamburg group, L'Art Pour L'Art. The first of these pieces, 'Copertone', for the LCCMS, seems to be lost to history, but 'Romantic Notions' and 'Tigers In Training', written for the latter pair, are included here.

The key work, though, is 'End Of Vienna' – and what a raft of associations is buried in that title! It was composed for the 300th jazz workshop conducted by North German Radio. The momentum continued with further work for the Guildhall in London, and the sequence ends with a moving piece called 'Jon Benet', the name of a little girl reported kidnapped by her family – involving the infamous '*War And Peace* of ransom notes' – and subsequently found murdered in the family cellar.

Bley's attraction to 'Fancy Chamber Music', ties and tails rather than jeans and trainers, was obvious from the first. What is immediately clear from these immaculately performed tracks is that there is very little in essence separating the fancy from the funky, except that well-brought-up music fans know not to applaud in the wrong places. It's a pity that this material wasn't recorded live and on the road. All it lacks is that fear of the mistimed cough or dropped programme. Otherwise, vintage Bley.

***** Are We There Yet?**

Watt/29 *Bley; Steve Swallow (b).* 10/98.

Just now and again, one wonders if having a 'home' recording label has done Carla Bley any real favours. While it's been an admirably disciplined imprint, without a hint of self-indulgence, there are moments like this when the output seems to require a level of editorial oversight which neither Carla nor Steve Swallow seems ready to bring.

The worst that can be said about *Are We There Yet?* is that it represents 80 minutes of self-indulgent noodling, recorded live on tour in Europe. The best that can be said of it is that Carla and Steve's public pillow talk is infinitely more interesting than anyone else's. Like *Duets* and *Go Together*, it plays on certain expectations and confounds them at the same time. A duo re-run of 'Musique Mécanique' apart, the bulk of the music here is written by Swallow, with a rather lovely version of 'Lost In The Stars' thrown in for good measure. Steve's cleanly articulated bass lines represent not just a second but in some respects the main lead instrument. He is awesome on 'A Dog's Life' and 'Satie For Two', two clever, witty compositions that (like Bley's recent chamber pieces) flout any distinction between 'jazz' and 'classical' forms.

Paul Bley (born 1932)

PIANO

The Canadian pianist is astonishingly prolific, having recorded over 100 discs down the years, by our reckoning. He is also extremely eclectic, ranging from free bop and ballads to electronic settings and larger groups. Consistently, though, he has produced vivid, vital jazz couched in an advanced and challenging idiom. Born in Montreal, he moved to New York, played in hard-bop groups and then crossed coasts to California, where he was nominal leader on one of Ornette Coleman's most important documented live dates. Bley then began to develop his own distinctive style, built on unexpected harmonic shifts, a steady but subtly varied pulse and powerful melodic statements.

*****(*) Introducing Paul Bley**

Original Jazz Classics OJC 201 *Bley; Charles Mingus (b); Art Blakey (p).* 11/53.

*****(*) The Fabulous Paul Bley Quintet**

Musidisc MU 500542 *Bley; Don Cherry (t); Ornette Coleman (as); Charlie Haden (b); Billy Higgins (d).* 7/58.

****** Touching**
Black Lion BLCD 760195 *Bley; Kent Carter, Mark Levinson (b); Barry Altschul (d).* 11/65, 11/66.

****** Open, To Love**
ECM 827751-2 *Bley (p solo).* 9/72.

***** Tango Palace**
Soul Note 121090 *As above.* 5/83.

*****(*) Solo**
Justin Time Just 28 *As above.* 87.

***** Solo Piano**
Steeplechase SCCD 31236 *As above.* 4/88.

***** Blues For Red**
Red Records RR 123238 *As above.* 5/89.

*****(*) Changing Hands**
Justin Time Just 40 *As above.* 2/91.

*****(*) Caravan Suite**
Steeplechase SCCD 31316 *As above.* 4/92.

***** Paul Bley At Copenhagen Jazz House**
Steeplechase SCCD 31348 *As above.* 11/92.

There is probably no other pianist currently active with a stylistic signature as distinctively inscribed as Paul Bley's – which is ironic, for he is a restless experimenter with an inbuilt resistance to stopping long in any one place. It is difficult to formulate exactly what unifies his remarkable body of work, beyond a vague sense that Bley's enunciation and accent are different from other people's, almost as if he strikes the keyboard differently. He favours curiously ambiguous diminuendo effects, tightly pedalled chords and sparse right-hand figures, often in challengingly different metre; working solo, he creates variety and dramatic interest by gradually changing note-lengths within a steady pulse (a device introduced to keyboard literature by a minor German improviser called Ludwig van Something) and generates considerable dramatic tension by unexpectedly augmenting chords, shifting the harmonic centre constantly.

Though he has played in a number of classic groups – notably with Jimmy Giuffre and Steve Swallow, that astonishing debut with Mingus and Blakey, on which he sounds edgy and a little cautious on the standards but absolutely secure in his technique, and, more recently, with John Surman and Bill Frisell – Bley is still perhaps best heard as a solo performer. The 1958 Hillcrest Club session has an almost legendary status, by no means hindered by the shaky recording. Though it is often discussed as if it were an Ornette Coleman record (and indeed the saxophonist dominates it), it was Bley's date. Having sacked vibraphonist Dave Pike to recruit Ornette and Cherry, Bley then had to absorb their radical new music at high speed; *Something Else* had been released a short time before and, though he was winning a critical following, Ornette was still considered a radical outsider. The first track was a version of 'Klactoveesedstene', which proceeds in a predictable bebop manner until the saxophonist takes off into his solo, at which point it is immediately obvious that something revolutionary is taking place. Bley audibly does his best to stick with it but, of course, even at this stage Ornette had very little use for an orthodox accompanist. The piano solo is a little spindly, but CD transfer has put a certain amount of meat on it. Bley's contributions to the two Ornette compositions, 'The Blessing' and 'Free', are much less assured. This is clearly an important record and, technical deficiencies aside, it should be in all modern collections. However, it isn't central to Bley's recorded output.

The earlier solo set neatly oversteps the most uncomfortably eclectic phase of Bley's career, when he turned to electronics in a largely unsuccessful bid to increase his tonal vocabulary. Bley claims that he only listens to his own records nowadays. Tongue in cheek or not, there are certainly enough of them on the backlist to occupy the bulk of his non-playing time (if bulk is the right word for a musician so promiscuously active). There are also signs that Bley listens to his past records in a quite constructive sense, constantly revising and modifying his thematic development (as in these intense reveries), constantly alluding to other melodies and performances. There is, perhaps, inevitably a hint of *déjà vu* here and there, but the terrain is always much too interesting for that to become a problem.

The 1965 sessions on Black Lion were once available on an Arista Freedom double-LP which featured one of the most unpleasant covers in the history of recorded music. The playing was superb, though, and it's a great shame that the whole disc hasn't been reproduced. Long tracks like 'Mister Joy' are missing, though other Annette Peacock and Carla Bley tracks are strongly in evidence, and Paul Bley's own 'Mazatalan' suggests that he's no slouch as a writer when he so chooses. Carter and Altschul offer solid support, but the focus is all on the piano.

Solo and *Changing Hands* are uniquely thoughtful piano solos, recorded back home in Montreal on a beautifully tempered instrument (and producer Jim West has to be congratulated for the immediacy and precision of the sound). Any suspicion that Bley may have become one-dimensionally meditative is allayed by the vigorous 'Boogie' on *Solo* and *Changing Hands*' remarkable interpretation of 'Summertime'. If it came down to a hard choice, the earlier album is marginally to be preferred; don't be seduced by the prettier cover.

Much of his recorded output has been on small-scale European labels, many of them in Italy, like the *Blues* set on Red. (See also *Lyrics*, below, on Splasc(h), which mixes vocal tracks by Tizia Ghiglioni with solo pieces.) *Blues For Red* is typical in all but content. Bley doesn't normally play as much in a blues mode as this, and it's pretty effective, though by no means orthodox. There are fine things on the Soul Note session (also recorded in Italy), but it is a mellow, after-dinner affair compared to the iced-vodka shocks of *Open, To Love*, one of Bley's finest-ever performances and the beginning of a productive relationship with ECM that really flowered only much later. Stand-out track is a fresh reading of ex-wife Carla Bley's uneasy 'Ida Lupino'. The 1988 Steeplechase has excellent sound and features the pianist in meditative mood; his reading of 'You Go To My Head' is so oblique as to suggest another tune entirely. Nevertheless there is little of the vapid meandering that afflicts so much piano improvisation; Bley is a tremendously disciplined improviser and this is one of his most intellectually rigorous albums.

Caravan Suite is an extended examination on Ellington. There's a long version of 'In My Solitude', notably sombre accounts of 'I Got It Bad And That Ain't Good' and 'I'm Beginning To See The Light', and an extended, four-part meditation on 'Caravan'. The Steeplechase piano (a new one, we believe) is very crisp and exact, suiting the material admirably. It's certainly a better instrument than the one at the Jazz House, which has a couple of unpleasant idiosyncrasies, not helped by the close-up recording of the top end. Good playing, though.

***** Paul Bley With Gary Peacock**
ECM 843162-2 *Bley; Gary Peacock (b); Paul Motian, Billy Elgart (d).* 4/63.

In November 1953, Bley had recorded a disc for Charles Mingus's Debut label, now available on a 12-CD compilation of all the Debut performances. A trio consisting of Charles Mingus and Art Blakey was a pretty decent coming-of-age present for a 21-year-old from Montreal, and it gave Bley a taste he was never to lose for strongly individual, not just blandly supportive sidemen. There are good things, too, from what was to be Bley's established trio. Up until that point, most of the trio's best work seems to have gone unrecorded. The ECM label's third release – following a superb Mal Waldron session and a thoroughly forgettable band led by the enigmatic Alfred Harth – highlighted 'When Will The Blues Leave'.

****(*) The Paul Bley Group**
Soul Note 121140 *Bley; John Scofield (g); Steve Swallow (b); Barry Altschul (d).* 3/85.

***** Fragments**
ECM 829280-2 *Bley; John Surman (ss, b cl, bs); Bill Frisell (g); Paul Motian (d).* 1/86.

***** The Paul Bley Quartet**
ECM 835250-2 *As above.*

Fragments is denied a further star only by the width of the band-book. As on the Soul Note session, recorded a year before, the writing and arranging are surprisingly below par and the recording isn't quite as clean as it might be. The Soul Note features a fine reading of Bley's staple 'Mazatalan', but little else of really compelling interest; Scofield and Swallow blend almost seamlessly, and Altschul has always been the perfect conduit for Bley's more advanced rhythmic cues. By contrast, the ECM band seems all texture, and much less structure; Frisell's almost apologetically discordant lines and reverberations blend unexpectedly well with Surman's almost equally introspective lines, and Motian – with whom Bley has duo'd to great effect – varies his emphases almost by the bar to accommodate whoever is in the forefront. The long 'Interplay' on the later, eponymous set, is disappointing enough to ease that album back a stellar notch. All three, though, are fine examples of a remarkable musician at work without preconceptions, doctrinaire stylistic theories or ego.

***** Questions**
Steeplechase SCCD 1205 *Bley; Jesper Lundgaard (b); Aage Tanggaard (d).* 2/85.

***** My Standard**
Steeplechase SCCD 1214 *As above, except replace Tanggaard with Billy Hart (d).* 12/85.

****(*) Live**
Steeplechase SCCD 1223 *As above, except omit Hart.* 3/86.

***** Live Again**
Steeplechase SCCD 1230 *As for Live.*

****** Indian Summer**
Steeplechase SCCD 31286 *Bley; Ron McClure (b); Barry Altschul (d).* 5/87.

The mid-'80s trios for Steeplechase mark a consistent high point in Bley's now capacious output. The Danish rhythm section isn't all that special on *Questions* but it functions more than adequately. The duos with Lundgaard are pretty dry; oddly, the best performances have been held over for the follow-up *Live Again*. Bley needs a bassist with a little more poke (step forward Swallow, Peacock and the better-known Dane, NHOP – see below) or a drummer who doesn't get swamped by the sheer profusion of Bley's notes. Hart tends to drive things along quite hard, and it's only really on *Indian Summer* that one feels the chemistry is just right. This is one of the pianist's periodic blues-based programmes. Engineered by Kazunori Sigiyama, who's responsible for DIW's output, it registers brightly, essential for music which is as softly pitched as much of this is. The high points are Bley's own 'Blue Waltz' and an ironic 'The More I See You', in which he works through variations in much the same way as he had on *Caravan Suite* for the same label, reconstructing the melodies rather than simply going through the changes. It's a fine record by any standards, but it stands out prominently among the later trios.

***** Paul Bley / NHOP**
Steeplechase SCCD 31005 *Bley; Niels-Henning Orsted Pedersen (b).*

***** Notes**
Soul Note 121190 *Bley; Paul Motian (d).* 7/87.

Years of standing behind Oscar Peterson did nothing to blunt NHOP's appetite for the job. He complements Bley's haunting chords perfectly, and on the inaugural 'Meeting' constructs an *arco* solo of great beauty over huge, ringing piano pedals (played on the electric instrument which reappears to good effect on the closing 'Gesture Without Plot' by Annette Peacock). 'Later' is perhaps the best-balanced duo performance; followed by the lively and intriguingly oblique 'Summer', it underlines once again Bley's sensitivity to his fellow-players and the emotional range of his playing. He is, nevertheless, absolutely distinctive. The opening notes of 'Meeting' could not be by anyone else, and a random sampling of any track uncovers his signature within half a dozen bars. The piano is appropriately well recorded and the bass is well forward with no flattening of the bottom notes (which is where NHOP works best) and no teeth-jangling distortion of his bridgework.

Motian is always wonderful, seeming to work in a time-scale all his own, conjuring tissues of sound from the kit that seem to have nothing to do with metal or skin. Their interplay in the most demanding of all improvisational settings is intuitive and perfectly weighted.

*****(*) Rejoicing**
Steeplechase SCCD 31274 *Bley; Michal Urbaniak (vn); Ron McClure (b); Barry Altschul (d).* 5/89.

The vibrant amplified sound of the Polish-born violinist works very effectively in the context of Bley's music. Add a rhythm section as sympathetic as McClure and Altschul, and you have a formula for something rather different and unpredictable. The Monk opening is certainly unexpected and leaves Urbaniak standing, but he recovers well enough to steal a couple of well-trodden standards – 'I Can't Get Started' and 'All The Things You Are' – and to make a dramatic contribution to 'Ictus', a tune that

Bley had recorded with Jimmy Giuffre and Steve Swallow back in 1961, and again on the ESP Disk. A slightly unusual item in Bley's list, this is nevertheless well worth sampling. Recorded live at Sweet Basil, it has a convincing live feel without too much dirt in the sound.

**** BeBopBeBopBeBopBeBop

Steeplechase SCCD 31259 *Bley; Bob Cranshaw (b); Keith Copeland (d).* 12/89.

There's a certain irony in the fact that the man who headed the palace coup that overthrew bebop at the Hillcrest Club in 1958 (the date is often credited to Ornette Coleman, but Bley was the nominal leader) should be the one to produce such an exacting and forward-looking variation on bop language in the last decade. Far from a nostalgia album, or an easy ride for soloist and sidemen, *BeBop* is a taxingly inventive and constantly surprising run through a dozen kenspeckle bop tunes, including (a circular tribute to the label) 'Steeplechase'. Bley's chording and lower-keyboard runs on 'My Little Suede Shoes' pull that rather banal theme apart; Cranshaw's solo is superb. 'Ornithology' and 'The Theme' receive equally extended attention; the closing '52nd Street Theme' is a suitably elliptical commentary on the whole era.

*** The Nearness Of You

Steeplechase SCCD 31246 *Bley; Ron McClure (b); Billy Hart (d).* 11/88.

For those who find Bley a shade too dry, 'Take The "A" Train' rousts along like it was trying to make up time between stops. By sharp contrast, the title-track is a long reverie punctuated by angry interpolations, almost as if a whole relationship is replaying on some inner screen. Compelling music as always, with an uncharacteristically laid-back rhythm section that on a couple of cuts might just as well have sat out and left the pianist to do his own remarkable thing. Good, well-rounded sound.

**** Memoirs

Soul Note 121240 *Bley; Charlie Haden (b); Paul Motian (d).* 7/90.

A dream line-up that promises much and delivers royally. If anything pricks the bubble of the concurrent trio featuring Geri Allen, it is this fine set. Bley's finely spun chromatic developments are now so well judged as to give an impression of being quite conventionally resolved. Given the title and the strategically placed 'Monk's Dream' and Ornette's 'Latin Genetics', it's tempting to read the set as an attempt to summarize Bley's career over the past three decades. Haden's 'Dark Victory' and 'New Flame' and Bley's own 'Insanity' suggest how far Bley, Haden and Motian have pushed the conventional piano trio. Tremendous stuff.

*** Lyrics

Splasc(h) H 348-2 *Bley; Tiziana Ghiglioni (v).* 3/91.

Ghiglioni's rather strained delivery does little more than point out the melody on the vocal tracks. These are interspersed by instrumental originals, which are a commentary (though recorded prior to the vocal track) on five otherwise uneventful standards. It's these re-readings which lift this rather low-key set. They're further testimony to Bley's remarkable harmonic imagination, and it may be that Ghiglioni felt constrained rather than inspired by them. The idea is an intriguing one, but one would like to hear him try it with a more sophisticated vocal artist, like Sheila Jordan.

***(*) In The Evenings Out There

ECM 517469-2 *Bley; John Surman (bs, bcl); Gary Peacock (b); Tony Oxley (d).* 9/91.

It's not clear quite how to attribute this one, since material from the same session has been released under Surman's name as *Adventure Playground*. The music is entirely collaborative and there are solo tracks, duos and trios, with only one substantial group track, so the emphasis is on intimate communications across small but significant musical distances. Oxley might not at first seem to be the ideal drummer for Bley, having played regularly with Cecil Taylor and in an almost antagonistic branch of the music. They play face to face only briefly, but it is enough to suggest that Bley's style is at least capable of re-incorporating some aspects of the free jazz he appeared to have left behind.

***(*) Paul Plays Carla

Steeplechase SCCD 31303 *Bley; Marc Johnson (b); Jeff Williams (d).* 12/91.

This contains a number of tunes by ex-wife Carla Bley that have criss-crossed Bley's playing career from the beginning. They still fall comfortably under his fingers. It's possible to trace through some of the tunes, 'Vashkar' and 'Ictus' particularly, how and where Bley's playing has changed over the years. His left-hand accents are now stronger and more insistently rhythmic than would once have been the case, and he has largely stripped away the grace notes and embellishments that once would have surrounded the solo line. It's all much cleaner and more exact, without in any way losing its romantic lilt.

**** Mindset

Soul Note 121213 *Bley; Gary Peacock (b).* 10/92.

Peacock's place in the history of modern jazz is less immediately obvious than Bley's but ironically is more secure because much of his career has been in the service of other visions. Increasingly in recent years, he has come out as a performer of absolute individuality, and the solo components of this remarkable record provide a primer to two men whose musical language – shared and several – is as rich and complex as any on the planet. They have worked together before, of course, not least in an early ECM session, and have always demonstrated a closeness of understanding that goes beyond basic stylistic similarities. The pattern is very straightforward: a solo from each and then a duet, repeated four times, with just a tiny coda of Ornette's 'Circle With The Hole In The Middle' to complete the engagement. As often as not, Bley is accompanying the bassist, as on 'Duality' and on parts of the long 'Mindset', and here he drifts easily into a flat-handed chording style that rolls back the years and demonstrates again how much he remains in touch with his own younger selves. On 'Duality' the pair explore just about every aspect of their stylistic changes from the 1950s to now, swing, bebop, cool, abstraction and resolute freedom. It's a hugely compelling performance. A shame that it lay around for five years before release – though, given the number of Bley records out there, one can hardly be surprised.

***(*) **If We May**

Steeplechase SCCD 31344 *Bley; Jay Anderson (b); Adam Nussbaum (d).* 4/93.

Not perhaps as successful as the slightly earlier Steeplechase trios (for which, see above) but a sterling performance all the same, and further testimony to Bley's willingness to reinvent himself and his repertoire. Nussbaum gives him a spacious rhythm, allowing him to stretch out on 'All The Things You Are' and 'Confirmation', two of his best-crafted solos of recent years. Once again the Steeplechase studio delivers the goods triumphantly, digital recording of marked sensitivity and warmth.

*** **Know Time**

Justin Time JUST 57 *Bley; Herbie Spanier (t, flhn); Geordie McDonald (d, perc).* 8/93.

A free session by three Canadians whose paths have crossed in different permutations over the years but who have never been able to preserve this type of gig on tape. McDonald is the wild card, a composer–improviser with a huge range of sounds at his disposal. Though the stated aim is the old one of finding a basis for improvisation that goes far beyond conventional song form, there is a persistent sense that this is exactly what lies behind these 13 shortish pieces. However, items like 'Seascape', 'Cave Painting' and 'Matrix' do suggest that the prevailing analogy is not musical at all but the visual arts, and that these are not so much songs as images. They are less static than this suggests, and it is possible to hear Bley in particular hesitate between linear logic (never something he has been wedded to) and a more impressionistic, flat-plane sound that generates very different patterns of sound. Though in some respects it sounds unresolved and even uncertain, in years to come this may be seen as one of Bley's most important later recordings, signalling yet another change of direction.

*** **Speechless**

Steeplechase SCCD 31363 *Bley; Jay Anderson (b); Victor Lewis (d).* 93.

Bley was to record again, and more convincingly, with this trio somewhat later. For some reason, it fails to fire on this occasion. Anderson is exactly the kind of bass he likes and needs, Haden-influenced, deep-toned and a reliable purveyor of root notes when the harmonics become complex, while Victor Lewis is one of the most musical drummers around. Whatever the reason, things failed to fire on the day. The later *Reality Check* is much better.

**** **Time Will Tell**

ECM 523819-2 *Bley; Evan Parker (ts, ss); Barre Phillips (b).* 1/94.

Superb. This is the kind of group that makes you wish you ran a festival or owned a club. The material is divided into seven trios, two duets pairing Bley with Phillips or Parker, and two excellent Parker/Phillips encounters. These are not apprentice players in a hurry but mature artists who can afford the time to let their music unfold organically. Every piece gives off a sense of having evolved spontaneously. The original intention was to create a setting very similar to the then recently reconvened Giuffre/Bley/Swallow trio (whose first two records had been reissued on ECM), but the strong personalities of three players who had not worked as a trio before very quickly asserted themselves. 'Poetic Justice' has a more restless quality than the rest, but the title-track is a near-perfect illustration of the way three senior players with yard-long CVs and utterly distinctive voices are still able to touch base with their own musical upbringing. Parker's Coltrane inflexions are only the most obvious example; Bley and Phillips dig deep into their own memories as well. A superb album, recommendable to anyone.

*** **Outside In**

Justin Time JUST 69 *Bley; Sonny Greenwich (g).* 7/94.

A very spontaneous and – apparently – unrehearsed studio session following one of the guitarist's relatively rare concert appearances at the Festival International de Jazz de Montréal in 1994. The aim was to explore a batch of songs from without and within, working in both directions simultaneously. The process is easier to follow on the standard and repertoire material, a very oblique interpretation of 'These Foolish Things' and versions of Eldridge's 'I Remember Harlem', Rollins's 'Pent Up House' and Charlie Parker's 'Steeplechase', a nod in the direction of Bley's other sponsoring label. Some of the material is clearly improvised on the spot or is based on material run down at the concert earlier. The playing is calm, detailed and resolutely un-intense. If improvising players now try to resist the 'conversational' analogy for what they do, this record seems to restore it. It's full of the elisions, repetitions, non-sequiturs and sheer playfulness found in any dialogue between friends, old or new.

***(*) **Synth Thesis**

Postcards POST 1001 *Bley (syn).* 8/94.

A year after *Know Time* and just six months after the triumph of *Time Will Tell*, Bley recorded this fascinating set of synth pieces. In the 1970s he had been one of the most accomplished and idiomatic electric piano players, but his association with what is after all an amplified clavichord and thus severely limiting did not last very long and he quickly re-established his commitment to the acoustic piano. In a sense, it was the technology that caught up with Bley. These tracks are subtle, imaginative and endlessly various, with not a cliché in sight. 'Poetic License' reappears from the *Time Will Tell* session, but transformed into a softly spoken electronic manifesto that, following 'Gentle Man' and preceding 'Augmented Ego', confirms the sense that Bley is searching for new ways of making the technology function – as another great Canadian put it – as 'extensions of the self'. Unless you're already committed to sounds of this persuasion, it's perhaps best to sample *Synth Thesis* a track or two at a time. No shortage of ideas, but the sound-world is still much less complex than that of a decent Steinway, or the spanking new piano at Steeplechase, and it would be easy and wrong to be put off by that.

**** **Reality Check**

Steeplechase SCCD 31379 *Bley; Jay Anderson (b); Victor Lewis (d).* 10/94.

Bley still jokes that he only listens to his own records these days. Such is the flow of material, it's all too possible, but the joke also contains a serious pointer, because he sounds like a man who inhabits his own musical world. It is now a very long time since it has been possible to say of him that he sounds like Monk, or Taylorish, or in the spirit of Bud Powell. Oddly, then, this is an album that seems to want to re-establish precisely some of those connections. Perhaps that is what he means by 'Reality Check', a stark, spare, stripped-down piece that builds up into a glorious abstract improvisation with a strictly limited palette and an unlimited range of ideas. Mark Gardner suggests that 'For George', exquisitely introduced on brushes by Victor Lewis, is dedicated to George Wallington, one of the lesser-known figures on the New York scene in the 1950s. Or it may simply be that memories of a friend have conjured up an older style of playing. There is certainly more than a whiff of Bill Evans throughout the record. In what would have been Bill's 75th year, perhaps his spirit was abroad again. Even Bley's approach to 'I Surrender, Dear' has an element of a more delicate and lyrical style in it, a softness of focus that balances the blunt, blocky chords and fierce stabs of colour. The trio is working as a unit, but with ample space for individual expression. Anderson's solo on 'Do Something' is good enough to cue back and play again, and Lewis doesn't put a foot wrong, often taking a forward role while Bley chords restlessly round an idea. A superb album, and one which stands out in a now crowded catalogue.

*****(*) Notes On Ornette**

Steeplechase SCCD 31437 *Bley; Jay Anderson (b); Jeff Hirshfield (d).* 9/97.

'Turnaround' has always been the Ornette theme that appeals to piano players. Hampton Hawes memorably recorded it with Charlie Haden, and now Bley, who worked with Ornette at the Hillcrest Club in California all those years ago, makes it his own in a long and deeply thoughtful reading. There are a couple of surprises on the set, the inclusion of 'Lorraine' and 'Crossroads', but the key inclusion, all too short, is 'When Will The Blues Leave', the composer's most rawly evocative work. Though only half the length of the other Ornette pieces (there is also a closing original 'AARP'), it's the defining cut on a heartfelt and very effective album.

Jane Ira Bloom (born 1954)

SOPRANO SAXOPHONE

Bloom went to Berklee and then Yale, before settling in New York and choosing to focus on the soprano sax. She began recording on her own Outline label in 1979 and had a brief spell at Columbia before going her own way.

***** Mighty Lights**

Enja 4044 807519 *Bloom; Fred Hersch (p); Charlie Haden (b); Ed Blackwell (d).* 11/82.

*****(*) Art And Aviation**

Arabesque AJ0107 *Bloom; Kenny Wheeler (t, flhn); Ron Horton (t); Kenny Werner (p); Rufus Reid, Michael Formanek (b); Jerry Granelli (d).* 7/92.

Bloom remains among the few musicians who play exclusively on the soprano sax. Recordings from the '80s – a pair of quickly deleted albums for Columbia, which found her dabbling with electronics – suggested she was becoming disenchanted with the possibilities of the instrument in a straight-ahead jazz format; but the earlier disc is a distinctive acoustic setting. She has a sparse, considered delivery, eschewing vibrato and sentimentality: Leroy Anderson's 'Lost In The Stars' is awarded an attractively tart reading. Particularly impressive are two tracks in which Hersch sits out and Bloom, Haden and Blackwell hit a propulsive groove.

After a quiet period, Bloom returned with the fine *Art And Aviation*. The seven originals are titled to suggest a concept of flying through dark, outer-space skies and, with the peripatetic Wheeler in wonderful form and spare, sharply attuned playing by the rhythm players, the music does indeed soar and glide when it wants to. The plangency of Wheeler's brass and Bloom's acerbic delivery grant a pleasingly frosty feel to much of the playing, as if they really were performing in a still, cold atmosphere. 'Hawkins' Parallel Universe' dovetails the two horns so acutely that they might be figure-skating the melodies. In context, the cover of Monk's 'Straight No Chaser' and the farewell of 'Lost In The Stars' work perfectly; and the occasional flicker of live electronics is much better adapted than on Bloom's earlier records.

****** The Nearness**

Arabesque AJ0120 *Bloom; Kenny Wheeler (t, flhn); Julian Priester (tb); Fred Hersch (p); Rufus Reid (b); Bobby Previte (d).* 95.

The surprise card is Priester and, with no electronics and several standards in the programme, this might have been an orthodox blowing record. Instead, Bloom recasts every melody and form in refreshing ways. Incredibly, she manages to find something new in 'Round Midnight', here done as a sober dance for the horns, and the ballads 'The Nearness Of You' and 'In The Wee Small Hours Of The Morning' are played – spoken, almost – with cadences of melody soft enough to suggest a music drifting down from the stars. Wheeler is his usual irresistible self, the rhythm section are marvellous, and an original such as 'It's A Corrugated World' stops the music becoming too navel-gazing. Very fine.

****** The Red Quartets**

Arabesque AJO144 *Bloom; Fred Hersch (p); Mark Dresser (b); Bobby Previte (d).* 5/97–1/99.

Another session with Hersch, and another marvellous record from Bloom. Though in other ways she is quite unlike him, she shares something of Steve Lacy's anti-virtuosity on the fish horn, often going aggravatingly against the grain of an otherwise busy dynamic which the rest of the group are involved in. She has stuck with her austere tone, which can at times seem baleful but at other moments – as in the extraordinary bittersweetness of 'Time After Time' – be uncommonly affecting. Without other horns to converse with, she forges an even closer alliance with Hersch and, for all the excellent work put in by Dresser and Previte, it's their dialogue which is the heartbeat of the record, Hersch's flowing lyricism filling out all the possibilities inherent in Bloom's themes. A record that stands apart from most modern-jazz releases.

Blue Notes

GROUP

A rare recording by the legendary South African group with their original line-up.

***** Live In South Africa, 1964**

Ogun OGCD 007 *Chris McGregor (p); Mongezi Feza (t); Dudu Pukwana (as); Nick Moyake (ts); Johnny Dyani (b); Louis Moholo (d).* 64.

The dateline tells you much of what you need to know. Two years after Sharpeville, a mixed-race group (Chris McGregor was white) playing jazz in Durban. Not long after this recording was made, the Blue Notes went to Europe to perform at the St Juan-les-Pins Jazz Festival and never returned. The early Blue Notes were more mixed stylistically than hindsight might have suggested. This is essentially a swing band, playing mostly in common time and with very few bebop accents. Moholo, later to be a fantastically lateral drummer, mainly keeps it straight, and the solos are delivered straight with none of the boiling dissonance that was to be a feature of later groups like Pukwana's Spear and Zila. They, of course, were founded amidst the agonies of exile and it would be idle to speculate how these six musicians (of whom only Moholo is still playing) might have developed – or not – had they lived untroubled in a liberal climate. As the set progresses, a mixture of McGregor and Pukwana tunes, with 'I Cover The Waterfront' featuring a Gonsalves-like Moyake, it becomes possible to hear some intimations of the later style. Pukwana's 'B My Dear' has a tender plangency that was to be reasserted when the piece was re-arranged for the Dedication Orchestra in 1993 (see below). Feza is less assertive than one expects, and the bulk of the solo space is devoted to alto and piano. Acoustically, the quality is no worse than one might expect, given the circumstances. Dyani is quite audible relative to McGregor, and the Kid's trumpet seems to be pointing away in another direction, which might offer some insight into the position of the mike. These are secondary issues, though. This is an important historical release for anyone interested in the development of the South African strain in British and European jazz. It conveys, particularly on the closing 'Dorkay House', something of the raw excitement of those extraordinary years.

Hamiet Bluiett (born 1940)

BARITONE SAXOPHONE, ALTO CLARINET

Settled in with the St Louis Black Artists Group in 1969, and in the '70s sparsely recorded before his association with World Saxophone Quartet. In the '90s he has been very active in the studios and is asserting his own career. Though the sound's been mollified by time, he can still make an elegant avant-garde roar on the big horn.

****** Birthright**

India Navigation IN 1030 *Bluiett (bs solo).* 77.

The baritone saxophone enjoyed a brief but historically unspecific boom in the 1950s. Why then? Harry Carney had turned it into a viable solo instrument; there were probably more good ensemble players around, conscious equally of the run-down on paying gigs with big bands and of the attractions of a little solo spotlight; lastly, the prevailing role-models on alto and tenor were, perhaps, a little too dominant. By contrast, no established baritone style developed; Gerry Mulligan was as different from Serge Chaloff as Chaloff was from Pepper Adams; and round the fringes there were players like Sahib Shihab and Nick Brignola doing very different things indeed.

Currently, the situation is much the same. The three most interesting baritonists all play in markedly different styles. The young Amerasian Fred Houn is very much a Carney disciple; Britain's John Surman blows baritone as if it were a scaled-up alto (which by and large it is); Hamiet Bluiett, on the other hand, gives the big horn and his 'double', alto clarinet, a dark, Mephistophelian inflexion, concentrating on their lower registers. A fine section-player – and his work with the World Saxophone Quartet is an extension of that – he is a highly distinctive soloist.

Heard unaccompanied on this set from The Kitchen, he is dark, rootsy and at moments almost unbearably intense. 'In Tribute To Harry Carney' is a deeply personal testimonial, redolent of the blues as the whole album is. The saxophonist's wife Ebu is the dedicatee of a short and heartful song which compresses much of his music to date. Other family members, including Hamiet Sr, are invoked in 'My Father's House', the longest single piece on the record.

Recorded without overdubbing or effects, but with multiple microphones to capture a sense of movement and of spatial relationships, the sound is very authentic and hauntingly present. As ever, it remains in the lower register for much of the duration of the concert, a vocalized sound that never becomes discursive but harks back to the most primitive of music making and the most sophisticated gestures of the avant-garde.

*****(*) Saying Something For All**

Just A Memory JAM 9134-2 *Bluiett; Muhal Richard Abrams (p).* 7/77, 79.

Justin Time has been very generous to Bluiett in recent years. These remarkable recordings are issued on the Canadian label's archive imprint. Abrams has always been a formidable duo player, endlessly challenging and responsive, hugely generous as well. His contribution, as writer and performer, to the two opening tracks – 'Night Dreams For Daytime Viewing' – calls for a separate credit. He is less in evidence later on when Bluiett compositions take over. The title-piece sounds like a spontaneous improvisation, but one which draws on both men's catalogues of work.

'Suite Pretty Tune' is a flute feature, light-toned and agreeably slight. 'Solo Flight' foregrounds the horn still more, but the real pay-off comes not from the duo's Environ gig – recorded in New York in 1977 – but from two years later when Bluiett was touring with the Sam Rivers band. 'Requiem For Kent State' was apparently recorded at the Ohio college where four anti-Vietnam protesters were shot dead by the National Guard. Emotionally it's a compelling piece, but it is also perhaps the best available sampling of Bluiett's technical resources on the big horn. Honks, slaps, vocalized overtones, toneless keying: all play their part in what is probably the definitive Bluiett performance. You can almost sense the silent band behind him watching in awe.

***(*) **Resolution**

Black Saint 120014 *Bluiett; Don Pullen (p); Fred Hopkins (b); Famoudou Don Moye (perc).* 11/77.

**** **Im/possible To Keep**

India Navigation IN 1072 2CD *As above.* 77.

*** **EBU**

Soul Note 121088 *Bluiett; John Hicks (p); Fred Hopkins (b); Marvin Smith (d).* 2/84.

Compared to the clutter (or exuberance – tastes vary) of the later, Africanized albums, the earlier recordings are stripped down (or downright sparse – ditto), muscular and sometimes chillingly abrasive. The *Resolution* quartet is perhaps heard to better effect on the deleted *SOS* (India Navigation IN 1039), a live New York set of near-identical vintage, but the studio cuts are still absolutely compelling. Bluiett, on baritone only, is in sterling form, relaxed in perhaps the most conducive company he has assembled on record. Pullen and Hopkins are masters of this idiom, and Moye curbs his occasionally foolish excesses. Production values aren't as hot as on the Soul Note sessions, but the music is way out in front.

The reappearance of the material on *Im/possible To Keep* is a huge bonus to this rather truncated discography. There is more than two and a quarter hours of concentrated music here, including a massive version of 'Sobre Una Nube' and a splendid reading of Miles's 'Tune Up'. The band sound is very authentic and unadorned, with a live ambience and no undue sweetening. Hopkins is in great shape throughout, sounding big and fast and unfailingly musical. Bluiett shifts from baritone to clarinet and flutes, playing fluently and with unmistakable passion. Strongly recommended.

A generous mix and better-than-average registration of the lead horn (the CD is first class) redeems *EBU*'s rather slack execution and raises it to the front rank. Hicks is a much lighter player than Pullen and is perhaps too much of an instinctive lyricist to combine well with Bluiett's increasingly declamatory responses. The rhythm section sometimes lacks incisiveness, fatally so on a rather odd 'Night In Tunisia'.

*** **Dangerously Suite**

Soul Note 121018 *Bluiett; Bob Neloms (p); Buster Williams (b); Billy Hart (d); Chief Bey (African perc); Irene Datcher (v).* 4/81.

*** **Nali Kola**

Soul Note 121188 *Bluiett; Hugh Masekela (t, flhn); James Plunky Branch (ss); Billy Spaceman Patterson (g); Donald Smith (b); Okyerema Asante, Chief Bey, Titos Sompa, Seku Tonge (perc); Quincy Troupe (poet).* 7/87.

Bluiett's pan-Africanism of the early 1980s opened up for him a whole book of new rhythmic codes that helped ease him out of the still impressive but palpably finite resources of his original post-bop orientation. *Dangerously* is a transitional exercise in that it merely grafts African percussion and voice on to the basic horn/piano/rhythm quartet. It is a fine album none the less, neither tentative nor blandly 'experimental'. *Nali Kola* is certainly not tentative, but it lacks the clearly methodological premisses someone like Marion Brown brings to projects of this type. The awkward instrumentation is intriguingly handled and well recorded – though the channel separation is a little crude – and Bluiett seems comfortable in his interplay with the still-adventurous Masekela and the little-known Branch and Smith, who are casual additions to the long title-track. It also features the 'verse' of Quincy Troupe, now better known for his ghosting of Miles's autobiography. As a whole, it is somewhat reminiscent of Archie Shepp's remarkable 1969 collaboration with Philly Joe Jones. And none the worse for that!

**** **The Clarinet Family**

Black Saint 120097 *Bluiett; Dwight Andrews (sno cl, s cl); Don Byron, Gene Ghee, John Purcell (s cl, bcl); Buddy Collette (s cl, acl); J.D Parran (sno cl, s cl, acl, contralto cl); Sir Kidd Jordan (cbcl); Fred Hopkins (b); Ronnie Burrage (d).* 11/84.

Utterly remarkable. The ten-minute egg of hard-boiled clarinet revivalism. Bluiett's inspired project may initially sound like a discursive guide to the woodwinds; in practice, it's a deeply celebratory, almost pentecostal rediscovery of the clarinet – once the jazz voice *par excellence* – and its preterite cousins and second cousins. Kidd Jordan's hefty contrabass instrument, hitherto associated only with Anthony Braxton, must count as a second cousin, twice removed; pitched at double B flat, it has an extraordinary tonality, as on 'River Niger', a Jordan composition that conjures up oddly disconnected echoes of Paul Robeson in *Sanders of the River*.

There's a strong sense of tradition through this fine live set, recorded in Berlin: two long tributes to Machito – a very different 'Macho' from the one credited to Steve Turre on the Brass Fantasy's ECM *Avant Pop* – and Duke Ellington, well-shared-out compositional credits, a startling bass solo from Hopkins, and, following it, a beautifully judged climax. After *Resolution* and the better of the WSQ albums, this is the essential Bluiett album, albeit one in which he plays a collective and slightly understated role.

**** **Live At Carlos I**

Just A Memory JAM 9129-2 *Bluiett; Don Pullen (p); Fred Hopkins (b); Idris Muhammad (d); Chief Bey (perc).* 8/86.

***(*) **Live At Carlos I: Another Night**

Just A Memory JAM 9136-2 *As above.* 8/86.

***(*) **Live At Carlos I: Last Night**

Just A Memory JAM 9192-2 *As above, except omit Pullen; add Mulgrew Miller (p).* 87.

Music from the much-missed New York club, a setting which always seemed to coax the best out of Bluiett. The last of the three has sometimes been reviewed as if it came from the same sessions, and with a sit-in guest. Miller took over from Don Pullen in the band called Concept. For our money, it was a mismatch, but Bluiett has a genius for selecting *simpatico* players and Mulgrew rises to the challenge, throwing his own 'Eastern Joy' into the pot and leading the way on Duke's 'Sophisticated Lady'.

Fine as he is, he doesn't really fill the shoes of Don Pullen, who was to Bluiett much what he had been to the late George Adams, a skilful and fiery co-leader. Don's instinct for the blues is nowhere better evident than on the Bluiett original, 'John', a performance which highlights the strengths and the shortcomings of *Another Night*. As a sequel to the original release from Carlos I it lacks focus but contains more free-hearted playing from the principals. Bluiett stretches out over nicely elastic changes and Pullen's response is every bit as creative. 'Sobra Una Nube', which follows, is a version of 'Nali Kola' on the earlier album. We are inclined to prefer the original release.

'The Mighty Dean' will be known to Bluiett followers from the solo *Birthright* record. With Pullen chording strongly behind and Hopkins pushing the pace along, it's a much tougher and more textured piece, leading directly into 'Full, Deep And Mellow', another repertory composition first heard on the *Dangerously Suite* album. 'Nali Kola' is reprised from the Black Saint record of that name, and the set closes with Bluiett's favourite bebop theme, 'A Night In Tunisia', a storming finish that belongs (as does the album as a whole) as much to the late Pullen as to the nominal leader.

There is nothing on the 1987 that matches up for sheer musicality and passion. *Last Night* is an excellent live document, but of a band playing at a different level of concentration from the dates with Pullen. These are consistently bold and inventive and will be appreciated by anyone who enjoys Bluiett's resonant delivery and toughly lyrical approach.

***** You Don't Need To Know ... If You Have To Ask**

Tutu CD 888 128 *Bluiett; Thomas Ebow Ansah (g, v); Fred Hopkins (b); Michael Carvin (d); Okyerema Asante (perc, v).* 2/91.

*****(*) Sankofa / Rear Garde**

Soul Note 121238 *Bluiett; Ted Dunbar (g); Clint Houston (b); Ben Riley (d).* 10/92.

The title refers to a celebrated riposte of Louis Armstrong's when asked what jazz really was. In the context of that his quotation of the celebrated waltz theme at the beginning of 'Black Danube', a tune described by drummer Carvin as 'James Brown in 3/4 time', has to be seen as slightly ironic in the context of Bluiett's now thoroughly Africanized approach to jazz performance. The rhythmic base, whether by Carvin or Asante, is in most cases the essence of the piece, over which Bluiett improvises with considerable freedom. His alto flute makes an effective opening to 'If Only We Knew', and Asante's percussion line bridges the piece with 'T.S. Monk, Sir' on which the baritone and bass punch out a respectful pastiche of the great pianist. Guitarist Thomas Ebow Ansah's vocal 'Ei Owora Befame-Ko' is built on a syncopated chord-sequence of the sort Bluiett instinctively heads for in his own compositions, and the two voices harmonize superbly, with Bluiett punctuating the melody with great bull-roar effects.

The last-but-one track of the session is perhaps the most straightforward and the most conventionally jazz-orientated. 'The Gift: One Shot From The Hip' has the kind of headlong, thunderous urgency that Bluiett can generate as a soloist, with Hopkins and Carvin tucked in behind like a three-man bob team. The bassist gets his big feature on 'Goodbye, Pork Pie Hat', but it's on 'The Gift' that his long-standing commitment to Bluiett's music pays its most generous dividends. Fred's untimely death is one of the shadows that hang over this edition of the *Guide*.

*****(*) Young Warrior, Old Warrior**

Mapleshade 02932 *Bluiett; Jack Walrath (t); Mark Shim (ts); Larry Willis (p); Keter Betts (b); Jimmy Cobb (d).* 3/95.

Astonishingly, the line-up here spans 50 years, young Turk Shim alongside the old masters Betts and Cobb, of whom more in a moment. Bluiett has an overlooked gift for constructing brilliant but unexpected bands. Calling up Walrath was a stroke of genius, because Jack falls into none of the stamped and addressed trumpet categories. Harmonically, Bluiett does service for both alto saxophone and trombone, and the group sound is huge.

Dizzy's 'Blue'N'Boogie' gets the album off to a roaring start, generously weighted in Shim's favour. He must have felt pretty good about himself, but when Bluiett comes in there's no doubt who's in charge and his high note coda is breathtaking. Betts responds with a solo straight out of the Jimmy Blanton yearbook. Pianist Willis is taste and precision personified and plays exquisitely on the slower tunes. 'Precious Moments For Right Now' seems to have been a rundown of a ballad idea, developed spontaneously in the studio. If so, it shows again how effectively Bluiett assembles his bands. 'Jimmy And Me' is a brief but dazzling duet for saxophone and drums, with Cobb quoting covertly from key moments in his long career. Just for the exercise, and possibly to scare the younger guys, the seniors end the day with Betts's 'Blues In F And G', again supposedly worked up on the spot, but way too acrobatic for that. Engineer Pierre Sprey says that all three takes were wildly different from one another, ranging between fiery bebop and Mulliganesque cool. Perhaps some day there will be room to release the alternatives, for the issued version is as intriguing a piece as Bluiett has released in years. The work of not one but of six masters, and a fitting conclusion to a remarkable, approachable album.

***** Bluiett's Barbeque Band**

Mapleshade Explorations 5 *Bluiett; Donald Blackman (ky); Kenny Davis, Calvin Jones (b); Ronnie Burrage (d, syn); Chief Bey (perc); Amba Hawthorne, Shirley LeFlore (v); Amidon Elementary Youth Group.* 6/95.

A joyous hour in the company of Bluiett and band, recorded up close and unvarnished. Oddly, despite the beer'n'ribs rhetoric surrounding this outwardly untypical release, it's much closer to Bluiett's avant-garde work than might appear; and yet, here he is again trying to inscribe himself across the broadest page of black American music. His version of the saxman's stalking horse, 'Body And Soul', is a glorious duet with electric pianist Blackman. At the opposite extreme, a kids' choir is called in to back Uncle Ham's song for his granddaughter's nanny.

Essentially a saxophone-plus-rhythm set, the Barbeque Band cooks along spicy and hot, with Bluiett to the fore throughout. The version of 'The Wind Beneath My Wings' could only have been improved had the pneumatic Bette Midler sashayed onstage for a couple of choruses. Shirley LeFlore's recitation on 'Give Me Rivers' – *not* Langston Hughes's 'I've Known Rivers', as suggested in some reviews – is genuinely moving, but oddly placed in the set. It might have been better as a coda.

*****(*) Libation For The Baritone Saxophone Nation**

Justin Time JTR 8470-2 *Bluiett; James Carter, Alex Harding, Patience Higgins (bs); Ronnie Burrage (d).* 97.

****** Live At The Knitting Factory**

Knitting Factory Records KFR 217 *As above.* 6/97.

This is what in certain circles is called turning up mob-handed. Bluiett first experimented with these forces in 1972 with the Baritone Saxophone Retinue, co-led with Pat Patrick and Charles Davis, and featuring Cecil Payne. Twenty years later, he revived the idea with the more anonymous International Baritone Conspiracy. The latest incarnation is the most convincingly idiomatic yet. Introducing the band at the 1997 Montreal Jazz Festival on *Libation*, Bluiett calls in his three baritone-wielding colleagues and the up-for-it Burrage as if he was warming up for James Brown on a funk revival tour. Bluiett is a master of upper-register playing and some of his top lines are light and fleet enough to sound like rootsy alto. On 'Discussion Among Friends' – otherwise the most prosaic performance on the record – he further extends the big horn's range with vocalized chord effects; but for the most part he sticks to the instrument's middle register, leaving the foundation work to Higgins and Harding.

Carter has, of course, carved his own path through this kind of repertoire; his composition, 'J.B. Groove', is a tribute to the master, but one cast in a version of Bluiett's own groovey hybrid of r'n'b and the avant-garde. The other material is splendidly varied, with a reading of Sam Rivers's 'Revival', a brassy version of trombonist Frank Lacy's 'Settegast Strut' and with E.J. Allen's 'Discussion Amongst Friends' used as a set exercise for the ensemble.

The Knitting Factory material is near identical – 'Lacy's 'Settagast Strut', 'Discussion Amongst Friends', 'Revival', 'J.B. Groove' and 'K.M.A./Q.B.' – with a few variations. In a club setting, and one which has a full-on reputation as an improvisers' hang-out, the set is a good deal more confrontational, freer in idiom and refreshingly caustic here and there. The Montreal set is politer and rather more measured and Bluiett keeps his more extravagant excursions to a minimum. New York air and a partisan, highly sussed crowd sitting just feet away presumably upped the ante considerably. Burrage is on ferociously good form. It has to be said that the sound isn't exactly pristine, but it's more than decent and more than made up for by the sheer vigour of the playing.

***** Makin' Whoopee: Tribute To the King Cole Trio**
Mapleshade 040932 *Bluiett; Ed Cherry (g); Keter Betts (b).* 97

Weird as this sometimes is, it's a model demonstration of how to record a small acoustic group in which one member – the saxophonist, natch – is always likely to overpower the rest of the group. Bluiett's devotion to Nat Cole seems improbable only until one thinks of his devotion to vocal jazz, soul and the vivid, harmonic swing that Nat bequeathed to American music. These cuts are not going to be to everyone's taste and there is an occasional mismatch of material and performance, but the overall effect is gorgeous and 'Route 66' is just about the boldest remake of an American classic that you'll ever hear.

*****(*) Same Space**
Justin Time JUST 109-2 *Bluiett; D.D Jackson (p, ky); Mor Thiam (v, djembe).* 97.

*****(*) Join Us**
Justin Time 124-2 *As above.* 10/98.

A rainbow coalition band, and a distinctive new sound for Bluiett. Initially, the emphasis seems to be firmly placed on vocal chants and dark, swampy rhythms, but there is a freedom as well which recalls nothing more strongly than legendary British group, The Trio, with baritonist John Surman, Barre Phillips and Stu Martin. For a change, Bluiett's baritone is at something of a discount, though his opening on 'Ayse' (*Join Us*) over djembe and piano is exquisitely thoughtful. Both records apportion writing credits very evenly; indeed Bluiett contributes only three atypical tunes to *Same Space*. African-born Mor Thiam and the rapidly developing Jackson, who won his spurs on the burgeoning Canadian scene, are unmistakably co-leaders. Serious Bluiett collectors should be aware that these are not headlining albums for the big man.

Jackson's funky organ might seem to pitch the music in the direction of jukebox r'n'b, but even here the initial impression is deceptive for, once the percussion kicks in, the count goes seriously wild. 'A Little Calypso' tips its hat to Sonny Rollins, but goes its own distinctive way. Both are studio recordings, although spoken introductions and vocal interjections, raps and poems give a strong impression of live immediacy. Apart from 'Mon Dieu' on the earlier record and D.D. Jackson's 'One Night' on *Join Us*, the tracks are mostly short and relaxedly conversational.

Larry Bluth

PIANO

A pianist, bassist and drummer working together in the Lennie Tristano idiom, the trio's records are all drawn from concerts played during the '90s.

***** Live At Orfeo**
Zinnia 105 *Bluth; Don Messina (b); Bill Chattin (d).* 11/91–1/92.

***** Five Concerts And A Landscape**
Zinnia 109 *As above.*

***** Formations**
Zinnia 114 *As above.* 10/96–2/98.

We are listing these records under Bluth's name purely for alphabetical convenience, since this is clearly a co-operative effort among three like-minded and accomplished thinkers in the Tristano tradition. Recorded in front of various small audiences at concerts in and around New York, the music consists of somewhat old-fashioned and deferential improvisations on some notable chord-sequences. The music will sound comfily familiar to those attuned to the Warne Marsh/Peter Ind sessions of the late 1950s or to anything by Sal Mosca (there is a dedication to Mosca on the third record). There's little to choose between the three discs, although the audiences were noisier in the early days of the trio, and the recording quality, which is hit and miss on the first two albums, has improved considerably by the time of *Formations*. There's a documentary feel, which results in, say, the music suddenly disappearing at the end of 'Shoals', on *Formations*, the kind of stroke which no major record label would allow. Bluth hints at melodies without quite realizing them, Messina plays a roving, modestly virtuosic line, and Chattin sets up the quietest of swinging grooves. There is always the fun of playing spot-the-standard, hidden under titles like 'Sundays At Elke's', although the later records own up to which tunes they're playing. Although the music spans seven years of work, there's no 'development' as such, more a sense that they're patiently working out directions that it will take them the rest of their performing lives to investigate. These are men playing for the music rather than for themselves, and the rarity of this kind of jazz makes these enjoyable sessions all the more satisfying.

Arthur Blythe (born 1940)

ALTO SAXOPHONE

Also known as Black Arthur, Blythe originally divided his career between relatively orthodox bebop and an innovative style of jazz that united the passionate immediacy of the early pioneers with non-Western harmonies and rhythms. Brilliant but erratic, he is still not well represented on record.

***(*) In Concert

India Navigation IN 1029 *Blythe; Ahmed Abdullah (t); Bob Stewart (tba); Abdul Wadud (clo); Steve Reid (d); Muhammad Abdullah (perc).* 2/77.

Arthur Blythe is a marvellous musician whose path has often seemed luckless. His India Navigation sets of the late 1970s were breathtakingly original and his form-sheet included demanding and chops-quickening stints with Gil Evans and Horace Tapscott, with whom he was a founding member of two radical co-operatives, Artists Ascension and Union of God's Musicians.

In Concert covers two major pieces, 'Metamorphosis' and 'The Grip'. The band has the sort of dark, experimental feel of Tapscott's West Coast collectives. The use of Stewart is brilliant and the absence of a string bassist irrelevant in face of his robust *legato* playing. Ahmed Abdullah is sharp and forceful, combining elements of Pops with Roy Eldridge and Charlie Shavers (and, frankly, nothing more contemporary than that). Blythe's solo formation isn't always entirely secure, but he is brimming over with ideas and he attempts to string them together at least logically.

♛ **** Lenox Avenue Breakdown

Koch KOC CD 7871 *Blythe; Bob Stewart (tba); James Newton (f); James Blood Ulmer (g); Cecil McBee (b); Jack DeJohnette (d); Guilermo Franco (perc).* 79.

In 1979 Blythe signed with Columbia and produced what became one of the lost masterpieces of modern jazz, reissued on CD only 20 years after its first appearance. *Lenox Avenue Breakdown* is a masterpiece of imaginative instrumentation, similar to the India Navigation set, but with the lighter and more complex sound of James Newton's flute backing the leader's extraordinary blues wail. There is scarcely a flat moment on the album, despite all four pieces being built round relatively static and repetitive ideas.

Stewart's long solo on the title-piece is one of the few genuinely important tuba statements in jazz, a nimble sermon that promises storms and sunshine. McBee has his moment on 'Slidin' Through' and Blythe himself saves his main contribution for the final track, the Eastern-sounding 'Odessa', on which he cries like a *muezzin*, a *cantor* and a storefront Salvationist, all in one impeccably structured arc. DeJohnette came of age with this record, playing with fire and authority, and with the sophisticated understanding of how rhythm and melody can combine which was to characterize his own later projects; *Special Edition*, which included Blythe, was recorded in the same year as this. His work behind Blythe on that final track deserves the closest attention. The other key element to the sound is Ulmer, who in those days was (like Blythe himself) moving comfortably between 'inside' and 'outside' projects.

There were more fine albums to come, but then Blythe's wind went, and he seemed lost. Much of his work in intervening years was in a pop vein, a watered-down version of the deep, urban groove he found on *Lenox Avenue Breakdown*. In recording terms, there is a long gap at this point. Worth dwelling just a moment longer with this extraordinary disc.

*** Hipmotism

Enja ENJ 6088-2 *Blythe; Hamiet Bluiett (bs); Kelvyn Bell (g); Gust William Tsilis (vib, mar); Bob Stewart (tba); Arto Tuncboyacian (perc, v); Famoudou Don Moye (d).* 3/91.

*** Retroflection

Enja ENJ 8046-2 *Blythe; John Hicks (p); Cecil McBee (b); Bobby Battle (d).* 6/93.

***(*) Calling Card

Enja ENJ 9051-2 *As above.* 6/93.

Blythe returned to jazz proper in the mid-'80s, seemingly unblunted by his dalliance with commercial music. For all the personal references and dedications, Blythe still betrays a lack of essential spirit on *Hipmotism*. There are also signs, most seriously on the opening trio and the concluding, unaccompanied 'My Son Ra', that a certain laziness of articulation had become second nature. The Village Vanguard session that makes up *Retroflection* finds him in better voice, technically speaking, but decidedly short of ideas. A more or less routine re-run of 'Lenox Avenue Breakdown' is relieved by crisp, sensitive playing from the group. Hicks is a total professional and McBee is absolutely on the spot, both harmonically and rhythmically. No complaints whatever there, but still an unsatisfyingly hollow centre.

The blend of instrumental voices on *Hipmotism* is intriguing enough to carry the day. There are only three all-in tracks, 'Matter Of Fact' and 'Bush Baby', both of them notably abstract, and the title-piece, which is simple and roistering. Blythe sounds good on them all, feeding off the deeper, darker sounds of Stewart's tuba and guest Bluiett's brassy baritone. The sparser settings expose him mercilessly and 'Miss Eugie', for alto saxophone, tuba and Tuncboyacian's percussion and voice, requires a more forceful performance.

Oddly enough, the second issue of material from the June 1993 Village Vanguard sessions is a good deal more satisfying than the first. There is the same stiltedness of delivery, but the material is looser and more expressive. Once again, Hicks's 'Naima's Love Song' is the crowning moment of a modern-jazz set, played feelingly and with lovely shifts of time and register throughout. 'Jitterbug Waltz' might almost be read as a nod to the example of Eric Dolphy. It isn't played on Eric's first choice of horn for this tune, but it has the same intriguing mix of familiarity and alienation. Battle is exceptionally good on these cuts, though here and there problems of registration surface on the two-track recording, which may have persuaded Enja to hold back these performances for later release. For our money, though, this is the better record.

***(*) Today's Blues

CIMP 158 *Blythe; David Eyges (clo).* 8/97.

One of those out-of-nowhere records that sends a thrill of excitement through the unprepared listener. The meeting with Eyges, playing amplified cello, rekindles memories of Blythe with Abdul Wadud, many years earlier, and the saxophonist's beautifully responsive and articulate lines are wonderful to hear. The lovely, ripe vibrato he puts on the end of some of his phrases, the rich, singing tone and speech-like reflexes all sound like Arthur at his best – and it's good to have him back on record sounding so strong. Eyges is no match for Wadud – much less Blythe – but he plays second fiddle to the alto master with a fine good humour.

Jimmy Blythe (1901–31)

PIANO

He arrived in Chicago around 1918 and over the next dozen years worked extensively in the South Side music business, recording from 1924 until shortly before his death. He recorded prolifically as soloist, accompanist and small-group leader, in a style that bridged the blues and the more rough-and-ready jazz of the area.

***** Jimmy Blythe 1924–1931**

RST JPCD-1510-2 *Blythe; Alfred Bell, Punch Miller (c); Darnell Howard (cl); Leroy Pickett (vn); Charlie Clark (p); William Lyle (b); W.E Burton (d, kz); Jimmy Bertrand (wbd); Viola Bartlette, Alexander Robinson, Frankie Jaxon (v).* 4/24–3/31.

***** State Street Ramblers 1927–1928**

RST JPCD-1512 *Blythe; Natty Dominique (c); Johnny Dodds, Baldy McDonald (cl); Bill Johnson (b); W.E Burton (wbd, kz, v); Baby Dodds (wbd); Marcus H Norman (d).* 8/27–7/28.

***** State Street Ramblers 1928–1931**

RST JPCD-1513 *As above, except add Alfred Bell (c, kz, v), Roy Palmer (tb), Darnell Howard (cl), Ed Hudson (bj, v), Cliff (d); omit Dominique, Dodds, Norman.* 7/28–3/31.

***** State Street Ramblers 1928–1931**

Cygnet CYG 1003 *As above, except add Charlie Clark (p), James 'Bat' Robinson, Ed 'Fats' Hudson (v).* 7/28–3/31.

Blythe was originally from Kentucky: Michael Moore's exemplary research has filled in many of the gaps in an elusive life, detailed in the notes to the first CD, but we still know little enough about him. The pianist should be remembered as an integral part of Chicago's South Side jazz in the 1920s, and his extensive work for Paramount, Gennett and Vocalion mixes a strong blues-piano approach with flakes of stride and boogie-woogie that show a determined and creative thinker. Many of the band sides collected on the State Street Ramblers CDs are relatively knockabout stuff: Blythe's driving piano parts have kept alive what are often jazz relics. Dodds appears on the earliest tracks and plays well, if not quite up to his best. The music shows no 'advance' by the later sessions, but the playing is more confident. For a good one-disc portrait of Blythe, though, either the first RST item or the Cygnet release will do. On the former, there are some doleful blues accompaniments and one or two items where Blythe's presence is dubious, but it includes all his piano solos, with 'Mr Freddie Blues' and 'Alley Rat' outstanding, a terrific coupling by Jimmy Bertrand's Washboard Wizards and two nimble duets with his cousin, Charlie Clark. The Cygnet release is generally in considerably better sound than the RST records and offers 15 tracks by the Ramblers, five with Fats Hudson and Bat Robinson singing, and the two Clark duets. Meningitis killed him only weeks after this final session.

Peter Bocage (1887–1967)

TRUMPET, VIOLIN

He started as a violinist but was taught cornet by Bunk Johnson. Worked with Fate Marable in New Orleans but left and recommended young Louis Armsrong as his replacement. Spent ten years with A.J. Piron's orchestra and was still playing in New Orleans at the end of a long life.

**** Peter Bocage With His Creole Serenaders And The Love–Jiles Ragtime Orchestra**

Original Jazz Classics OJC 1835-2 *Bocage; Charlie Love (t); Homer Eugene, Albert Warner (tb); Louis Cottrell, Paul Barnes (cl); Benjamin Turner (p); Sidney Pflueger (g); Emanuel Sayles (bj); McNeal Breaux, Auguste Lanoix (b); Alfred Williams, Albert Jiles (d).* 6/60–1/61.

One of the weakest entries in Riverside's *New Orleans: The Living Legends* series, and it does no justice to a brassman who first recorded with A.J. Piron in the early 1920s. Bocage sounds faltering and shaky on the tracks where he leads his Creole Serenaders and, though Cottrell provides some bright moments, this is pretty lame stuff. Bocage plays violin as a sideman in the Love–Jiles group, which handles five rags without a great deal of panache – Warner in particular plays some atrocious trombone. Definitely one for hardcore specialists only.

Eric Boeren (born 1959)

CORNET

Dutch brassman of the generation of improvisers that came after Mengelberg, Bennink and Breuker.

*****(*) Cross Breeding**

Bimhuis 005 *Boeren; Michael Moore (as, bcl); Jan Willem Van der Ham, Paul Termos (as); Ab Baars (cl, ts); Tobias Delius, Sean Bergin (ts); Wilbert De Joode, Ernst Glerum (b); Wim Janssen, Michael Vatcher (d).* 8/95.

***** Joy Of A Toy**

Bvhaast CD 9907 *Boeren; Michael Moore (cl, alto-cl, as); Wilbert De Joode (b); Han Bennink (d).* 6/97–3/99.

Boeren's sleeve-note to *Joy Of A Toy* confesses that he has often had his compositions described as sounding like those of Ornette Coleman (he took it as a compliment), so he has grasped the nettle by mixing his own originals with Coleman themes for both of these this tribute-cum-repertory exercises. The playing is strong and sensitively shaped, but, as with attempts to play the Hot Five or the Red Hot Peppers, the originals tend to cast an unflattering shadow on the new versions. Still, it's often very joyfully done. We prefer the earlier disc, cut over two nights at the Bimhuis. Boeren had been listening hard to each of Coleman's Atlantic sessions and had been presenting material from each album at individual concerts. 'Mapa' features Baars on tenor; the next four tracks include Moore on alto; then, most audaciously of all, Boeren revises Coleman's 'Free Jazz' as a double-quintet plus one (himself), mixing the theme of 'Free Jazz' itself and 'Happy House' alongside six of his own pieces. This is a striking adaptation of Coleman's music to Boeren's own. It's a pity that the sound is rather flat and lacking in detail.

On *Joy Of A Toy*, which was much more widely noticed on its appearance than the earlier disc, Boeren doesn't attempt to stray too far from the form of his models and, with Bennink his usual over-powerful self, too many of these pieces seem a fraction too fast; 'Joy Of A Toy' itself, for instance, has a clockwork feel to it. They do better on the gentler themes like 'Peace'. The opening track, 'A Fuzzphony', strays in from an earlier date, but the rest was recorded at a single 1999 concert, in slightly clattery sound.

Andres Boiarsky

TENOR AND SOPRANO SAXOPHONES

Argentinian saxophonist at work on the contemporary New York scene.

*** Into The Light

Reservoir RSR CD 149 *Boiarsky; Claudio Roditi (t); Paquito D'Rivera (as); George Cables (p); David Finck (b); Ignacio Berroa (d); Gabriel Machado (perc).* 9/96.

An Argentinian in New York. He's a big-toned, rather grand stylist, not quite the mercurial monster some South American jazzmen aspire to be – and all the better for it. This is a pleasing set of tunes: 'El Mono' is a very fetching melody over some nice changes, and the lustrous ballad, 'Saying Goodbye', abetted by a pearl of a solo from Cables, finds Andres at his most eloquent. Pals Roditi and D'Rivera turn up a few times without hijacking the date.

Paul Bollenback (born 1959)

GUITAR

Born in Hinsdale, Illinois, Bollenback listened to rock, fusion and jazz, apparently in that order, and studied jazz in Miami University. He spent several years in the Joey DeFrancesco group.

**(*) Original Visions

Challenge CHR 70022 *Bollenback; Gary Thomas (ts, f); Joey DeFrancesco (org); Ed Howard (b); Terri Lyne Carrington (d).* 2/95.

*** Double Gemini

Challenge CHR 70046 *Bollenback; Joey DeFrancesco (org); Jeff Tain Watts (d).* 3/97.

Bollenback has progressed from able sideman to leader comfortably enough, even if these records seldom stand out from the crowd. He seems divided, on *Original Visions*, between a harder, rockier route to catharsis and a more rigorous jazz achievement. He isn't helped by the bottom-heavy sound and an indifferent choice of material: his originals don't do much, and the standards are obvious. Thomas, who seldom does this kind of gig these days, does little of interest. Yet when guitar, organ and drums lock together and the groove toughens and intensifies, the music sometimes takes off.

Bollenback has worked often with DeFrancesco and they are clearly very simpatico. 'Breaking The Girl', which opens *Double Gemini*, is about as swinging and hard-hitting a guitar–organ blowout as one can imagine. The set this time blends four originals with six pop tunes (and we mean Hootie and the Blowfish, not Cole Porter) and Bollenback seems more at home here than he did on the other disc. Some if it sounds like merely engaging mood-music, even if Sting's 'Fields Of Gold' comes out pretty as a picture, but the burners are genuinely exciting. If Bollenback himself rarely impresses as a singular voice, he has some good moves.

Claudio Bolli

TRUMPET, FLUGELHORN

A regular on the contemporary Italian scene, Bolli has played many sideman roles, but this seems to be his only leadership date.

*** Empty Jazz Quintet & Octet

Splasc(h) H 371-2 *Bolli; Luca Begonia, Alessio Nava (tb); Claudio Chiara (as); Fulvio Albano (ts); Marco Visconti Prasea (bs); Paolo Brioschi (p); Roberto Piccolo (b); Ferdinando Farao (d).* 7–9/91.

The group name is asking for trouble, but this is light, bright post-bop from a mixed confederacy of old and young hands. Bolli himself plays an Art Farmer-like horn, reticent rather than pushy, and the other players all seem reluctant to take a firm lead. As far as co-operative spirit goes, though, it's amiably up to the mark.

Flavio Boltro

TRUMPET, BUGLE

Italian trumpeter working with a Franco-Italian alliance.

*** Road Runner

Blue Note 233422-2 *Boltro; Stefano Di Batista (ss); Daniele Scannapieco (ts); Eric Legnini (ky); Marcello Giuliani (g, b); Louis Winsberg (g); Pippo Matino (b); Stéphane Huchard, Paco Sery (d); Nantha Kumar (perc).* 99.

Boltro has been spotted in several sideman situations, but this Blue Note debut – a daring move for the label to go with such a musician, even if distribution is limited – is a confident and surprisingly effective nugget of modern fusion – even if much of it harks back to various phases of Miles Davis's electric music. Most of the mainly brief tracks pivot on an old-school groove of some sort, but the clarity of the sound, the individuality of each musician's contribution and the carefully judged shape of each piece is something rather more contemporary and skilful. Boltro gets good support from di Batista and Legnini in particular. We've heard it all before, but perhaps not quite in this way and this order.

Sharkey Bonano (1904–72)

TRUMPET, CORNET, VOCAL

Joseph Bonano was born in New Orleans and is associated mainly with NO revivalism. In the 1920s, though, he drifted around several musical jobs across America, and he was a hit with his own band in New York in the later 1930s. He had a second career with the revivalists of the 1940s and '50s and continued to work and play, although poor health wound down his career from the 1960s onwards.

*** Sharkey Bonano 1928–1937

Timeless CBC 1-001 *Bonano; Shorty Sherock (t); Santo Pecora, Moe Zudecoff, Julian Lane, George Brunies (tb); Meyer Weinberg (cl, as); Sidney Arodin (cl, tin whistle); Joe Marsala, Irving Fazola (cl); Hal Jordy (as, bs); Dave Winstein (ts); Johnnie Miller, Clyde Hart, Joe Bushkin, Stan Wrightman, Freddy Newman, Armand Hug (p); Joe Cupero, Frank Federico, Eddie Condon (g); Bill Bourjois (bj, g); Steve Brou (bj); Luther Lamar (tba, b); Chink Martin, Ray Bonitas, Thurman Teague, Artie Shapiro, Hank Wayland (b); Monk Hazel (d, mel, v); Leo Adde, Augie Schellange, Ben Pollack, George Wettling, Al Sidell, Riley Scott (d).* 4/28–4/37.

Bonano is conventionally placed as a New Orleans man, but though he was a native of the town his early career points elsewhere – he tried out as replacement for Beiderbecke with both The Wolverines and Jean Goldkette, for instance. The first two (little-known) sessions here, though, are among the very few home-grown New Orleans sessions of the 1920s – both showing an ironic New York influence, but with fine clarinet by Sidney Arodin and Bonano proving that he had a light but curiously engaging lead as a cornetist. A jump forward to 1936 brings a more Dixieland-orientated sound, and three further sessions from 1936–7 find him in New York with a band largely made up of Condonites. Four tracks by a Santo Pecora group with Shorty Sherock on trumpet round off the disc. Bonano's vaudevillian vocals dominate several tracks, but when his trumpet emerges he sounds in good fettle, and there are useful glimpses of the New Orleans clarinet of Fazola. A mixed but entertaining bag, and the remastering is fine.

*** Sharkey Bonano At Lenfant's Lounge

Storyville STCD 6015 *Bonano; Jack Delaney (tb); Bujie Centobie (cl); Stanley Mendelson (p); Arnold 'Deacon' Loyacano (b); Abbie Brunies, Monk Hazel (d); Lizzie Miles (v).* 8–9/52.

*** Sharkey Bonano And His Band

Storyville STCD 6011 *As above, except omit Hazel and Miles.* 12/52.

Bonano almost inevitably returned to New Orleans and spent most of the rest of his life there, working and recording frequently in the aftermath of the New Orleans revival of the 1940s and '50s. Location recordings catch his able band in lively form. The leader's own playing suggests that he was more convincing as a front man than as a soloist: if he tries to push too hard, his tone thins out and his phrases buckle. But Delaney and Centobie are both perfectly assured soloists, and Bonano sensibly gives them the lion's share of the attention. Lizzie Miles sings a couple of vocals on the first record and shouts encouragement too. The recordings are clear enough, though they don't have much sparkle, but the swing of the band stands up well: another valuable document of a genuine New Orleans outfit, playing to orders – the material is very familiar – but making the most of it.

Bone Structure

GROUP

A one-off album by a British team of trombonists.

**(*) Bone Structure

Calligraph CLG 020 *Mark Nightingale, Richard Edwards, Colin Hill, Andy Hutchinson (tb); Nigel Barr (btb); Pete Murray (p); Mike Eaves (g); Don Richardson (b); Chris Barron (d); Lorraine Craig (v).* 4–5/88.

There have been all-trombone front lines before, courtesy of J.J. Johnson, Slide Hampton and others, but this British group approaches the task with a flair and nicely deadpan wit that alleviate the built-in blandness of their sound. It's hard to make trombones sound interesting across the length of a record if they set out to avoid the expressionist approach, and Nightingale's team tend to impress through dexterity and timing. Nor do they truly sidestep the novelty aspects of the group, a trait which has plagued British trad and mainstream: Horace Silver's 'Doodlin'' is taken at a silly, ambling pace, and the sonorous treatment of 'Lush Life' seems designed more to elicit gee-whiz reactions than anything else. But their up-tempo pieces are delivered with a punch that overcomes doubts about musical integrity: if, at times, one longs to hear them loosen up, that may have more to do with the metronomic feel of the rhythm section.

Luis Bonilla

TROMBONE, BASS TROMBONE

A member of Lester Bowie's saxless Brass Fantasy and a seemingly indefatigable session player, Bonilla is a trombone revivalist who's nodded to J.J. Johnson and Ray Anderson as influences. He hasn't yet made much impact as a leader.

*** Pasos Gigantes

Candid CCD 79507 *Bonilla; Tony Lujan (t, flhn); Kenny Goldberg (as, bs, f); Justo Almario (ts, ss, f); Otmaro Ruiz (p, syn); Abe Laboriel (b); Alejandro Neciosup Acuna (d, perc); Michito Sanchez (perc).* 2/91.

Luis's solo debut is a lively Latin-jazz session without much in the way of surprise. The arrangement of 'Giant Steps', which provides the album's title, is nice, if a bit obvious; and it's clear that the trombonist knows his way round those graduation-class changes. Unfortunately the rest of the group doesn't quite match up. Except perhaps Laboriel, they sound a little as if they're trying to keep up with unfamiliar charts, and there's too much pointless time-filling on the straight Latin numbers. Anyone who's seen Bonilla with Brass Fantasy knows that he's capable of far, far more than he's been able to deliver on record until now.

Joe Bonner (born 1948)

PIANO

Easy at first hearing to dismiss Bonner as a rather watery disciple of McCoy Tyner. The truth is more individual and more challenging, a piano style that seems also to have drawn on some of the milder elements of Cecil Taylor's unique attempt to introduce an element of atonality into jazz.

*****(*) Parade**
Steeplechase SCCD 31116 *Bonner; Johnny Dyani (b); Billy Higgins (d).* 2/79.

***** Devotion**
Steeplechase SCCD 31182 *Bonner (p solo).* 2/83.

***** Suburban Fantasies**
Steeplechase SCCD 31176 *Bonner; Johnny Dyani (b).* 2/83.

***** Two & One**
Steeplechase SCCD 37033/34 2CD *As above.*

Bonner is an impressive modernist whose occasional resemblance to Thelonious Monk probably stems from the fact that he has listened and paid attention to the same swing-era players that Monk did. He has a surprisingly light touch (too light on some of the Steeplechases, where the miking sounds a bit remote) and he can seem a little diffident. He is, though, a fine solo performer, with a rolling, gospelly delivery, and an adventurous group leader. Much of his most distinctive work has been with the late Johnny Dyani, who has the same combination of dark strength and lyrical delicacy; over several albums they developed a rapport that seems to cement ever more strongly as they move outwards from settled bop progressions and into freer territory.

Suburban Fantasies is a lovely record, but oddly substanceless, as if worked up from scratch and on the spur of the moment. *Two & One* is a valuable mid-price compilation of Bonner's relationship with Dyani. It has the same rather slack-paced fascination of the single album but, over time, the sheer conversational magic of the relationship begins to work its spell.

*****(*) Suite For Chocolate**
Steeplechase SCCD 31215 *Bonner; Khan Jamal (vib); Jesper Lundgaard (b); Leroy Lowe (d).* 11/85.

***** New Life**
Steeplechase SCCD 31239 *Bonner; Hugo Rasmussen (b); Aage Tanggaard (d).* 8/86.

***** The Lost Melody**
Steeplechase SCCD 31227 *Bonner; Bob Rockwell (ts); Jesper Lundgaard (b); Jukkis Uotila (d).* 3/87.

***** Impressions Of Copenhagen**
Evidence ECD 22024 *Bonner; Eddie Shu (t); Gary Olson (tb); Holly Hoffman (f); Paul Warburton (b); J. Thomas Tilton (d); Carol Michalowski (vn); Carol Garrett (vla); Beverley Woolery (clo).*

The African elements also emerge in the lovely *Suite For Chocolate.* Working with the under-recorded Khan Jamal, who has had his own records issued on Steeplechase, gives Bonner a detailed stipple of sound over which to lay his discontinuous melody lines. A surprising record in many ways, it veers between experiment and conservatism, eventually coming down on the side of easy, unstressed swing.

The Lost Melody is a good group-session, marked by strong charts and just the right element of freedom for Rockwell, a fine soloist within his own square of turf, but apt to flounder beyond it. *Impressions Of Copenhagen* (formerly on Theresa) has been available for some time now on Evidence, with a bonus version of 'Lush Life'. There are some effectively impressionistic moments and the use of strings is quite original and uncluttered, but it's a bit of a by-blow and not really consistent in either tone or quality with Bonner's impressive jazz output. To the best of our knowledge, another Theresa LP, *New Beginnings*, with singer Laurie Antonioli, has not yet emerged on CD, leaving that aspect of the pianist's career, his gifts as an accompanist, still obscure.

Thomas Borgmann (born 1955)

SOPRANINO, SOPRANO AND TENOR SAXOPHONES, WHISTLES

Born in Münster, Borgmann is a free improviser in the grand tradition of European free playing, although so far his exposure on record has been compararively limited.

****(*) Orkestra Kith 'N Kin**
Cadence CJR 1081 *Borgmann; Martin Mayes (frhn); Lol Coxhill (ss); Erik Balke (as, sno); Dietmar Diesner (as, ss); Jonas Akerblom (bsx); Pat Thomas (p, elec); Hans Reichel (g, daxophon); Christoph Winckel (b); Mark Sanders (d).* 5/95.

****(*) Boom Swing**
Konnex KCD 5082 *Borgmann; Wilber Morris (b); Dennis Charles (d).* 97.

***** Stalker Songs**
CIMP 160 *As above, except add Peter Brötzmann (ts, cl tarogato).* 9/97.

***** BMN Trio ... You See What We're Sayin'?**
CIMP 188 *As above, except add Reggie Nicholson (d); omit Brötzmann and Charles.* 10/98.

Borgmann is no spring chicken as a free player, although he's made only a few records as a leader. The 1995 ensemble recording has a spirited hour-long piece (and a foolish ten-minute encore, which could profitably have been omitted). There are few 'solos' as such, more disparate lines drawn by different groupings, with the rousingly arranged finale raising the spirits. But the amateurish recording spoils much of the interest in what's going on.

Borgmann's trio with Morris and Charles was a regular working outfit in Europe and America. The Konnex album seems to be live (the documentation is a bit mysterious) and, though intense enough, it also suffers from a cloudy mix which obscures too much detail. *Stalker Songs* is much better. Brötzmann seems to be scaling himself down a bit for the occasion, and CIMP's 'truthful' sound isn't entirely adequate, but these two half-hour improvisations are good and gripping. Charles died a few months later, and a new trio convened to make the later *You See What We're Sayin'?*, which starts with a sombre dedication to the departed drummer before thundering forward through three more intense blows. Borgmann doesn't really impress as an individual voice: he synthesizes a lot of the familiar uproar of his forebears to ends which are intermittently dramatic. He puts his trust in an old-fashioned energy music. Not misplaced, though: such raw playing is always a welcome counter to the conventional language.

Pierre Boussaguet

DOUBLE BASS, PERCUSSION

French bassist of today, in a bebop lineage.

**** Trio Europa

Emarcy 538 468-2 *Boussaguet; Guy Lafitte (ts, v); Hervé Sellin (p); Alvin Queen (d).* 6/98.

France has always produced a healthy home-grown crop of fine, swinging bass players, as visiting Americans always attested. Boussaguet is very much in the line of Pierre Michelot and Henri Texier, favouring a rich but clearly etched sound that recalls the bassists of the bebop eara. There are lots of quotes and tags from bop tunes in the solos, though the basis of a mixed programme of originals and jazz standards is swing and mainstream jazz. His own composition, 'Le Chat Bebop Attendra', is a vivid caprice, multitracked and featuring the leader on hi-hat as well as pizzicato and *arco* basses. Even if he hadn't included a 'Hey, Raymond, thank you' at the end of the take, it would have been obvious he was thinking about Ray Brown.

Elsewhere, percussion duties are in safe hands. The real star of the trio is drummer Alvin Queen, a vividly unexpected player who has the same mixture of influences as the leader. Bizarre rhythmic 'bombs' punctuate a seemingly effortless rhythmic flow and even the most regular counts are embellished, pushed intriguingly off-centre. Pianist Hervé Sellin has a broad, emphatic touch and some skill as an arranger. His version of 'Body And Soul', with Boussaguet on Fender bass, has a rock feel which gives the old chestnut a fresher sound than it's had for years.

The most poignant dimension of the album is a last contribution from the dying Guy Lafitte, two solos of majestic calm and beauty and the recitation of a brief poem, a tribute to his friend Johnny Griffin. It all adds up to a beautifully balanced jazz album. You couldn't change a note.

Ralph Bowen

TENOR SAXOPHONE

Experienced post-bopper making a considered leadership debut for Criss Cross.

***(*) Movin' On

Criss Cross Criss 1066 *Bowen; Jim Beard (p); Jon Herington (g); Anthony Jackson (b); Ben Perowsky (d).* 12/92.

An able and in-demand sideman, Bowen took his time before recording a debut solo album. It was worth the wait. Bowen has been writing and putting by original themes since he was in his teens, and it's a symptom of his remarkable self-possession that he should have picked seven of them for *Movin' On* rather than opting for more familiar repertoire material. The title-piece is entirely characteristic, a lean but lyrical tune that propels him into the first of what is to be a batch of fine solos. Apprenticeship with Horace Silver has left an unmistakable mark on Bowen's writing, but it is Silver the melodist who predominates. Bowen rarely forces the pace, allowing each theme to dictate its own momentum. 'A Little Silver In My Pocket' is the most direct homage, and Jim Beard turns in a completely idiomatic solo with a brisk, bouncy left-hand part. Only on the longish 'Just Reconnoitering' does Bowen start to repeat himself. To some extent the piece draws on Coltrane's 'sheets of sound' approach, but this isn't a comfortable route, and the piece resolves itself much more conventionally. Mixed well up, the two guitars bring a soulful groove to 'Thru Traffic'; Herington draws heavily on Pat LaBarbera licks, but it's Jackson who impresses with a fluid legato. A pity that Bowen hasn't followed this one up at Criss Cross, but to find him in recent form go to the Orrin Evans entry.

Lester Bowie (1940–99)

TRUMPET, FLUGELHORN

Growing up in St Louis, though born in Maryland, Bowie based himself in Chicago in the mid-'60s and became a major force in both the AACM and the Art Ensemble Of Chicago, with whom he performed until the end of his life. He lived and worked in Jamaica and Africa for some spells, and he finally found his most popular niche with his nearly-all-brass band, Brass Fantasy. His 60-strong Sho' Nuff Orchestra was unfortunately never recorded. A pioneer of bringing expressionist playing into a modern vernacular, Bowie was a great renegade spirit in the music and fiercely critical of what he saw as the jazz conservatism of the 1980s and '90s. He died from liver cancer in 1999.

*** Mirage

RCA Camden 74321 610902 2CD *Bowie; Joseph Bowie (tb, perc); Julius Hemphill (as); John Stubblefield (ts); Raymond Chang (vn); John Hicks (p); Cecil McBee, Malachi Favors (b); Philip Wilson, Jerome Cooper, Charles Bobo Shaw, Don Moye (d).* 9/74–82.

This reissues three Muse albums: *Hello Dolly*, *Rope-A-Dope* and *Bugle Boy Bop*. It starts with an extraordinary version of Coleman's 'Lonely Woman', settled around moaning low brass and reeds, before a somewhat flatfooted feature for Hemphill, 'Banana Whistle'. Then a duet for trumpet and piano on 'Hello Dolly' which is so wittily done that it makes many of the later Brass Fantasy knees-ups sound clumsy in comparison (it helps that Hicks plays his part dead straight). The pianist is the unlikely member of this group and his romantic solos are a queer interpolation into what is otherwise a sour aesthetic.

Many of the other tracks are based around a dialogue for trumpet and drums: *Bugle Boy Bop* was an entire album of duets for Bowie and Shaw, and 'F Troop Rides Again' is a spectacular if chaotic blend of Bowie and three drummers. The *Rope-A-Dope* tracks are for trumpet, violin, bass, two drum sets and percussion: quite a bit of ramblin' around, but the music has its moments. These are an experimenter's notebook rather than anything more achieved, and they're rather typical documents of the avant-garde of the period. But Bowie's trumpet – brightly inventive, even in the midst of a lot of crashing noise – is worth focusing in on.

***** The Fifth Power**

Black Saint 120020-2 *Bowie; Arthur Blythe (as); Amina Claudine Myers (p, v); Malachi Favors (b); Phillip Wilson (d).* 4/78.

Bowie's 1970s band provides a more straightforward kind of post-Chicago jazz, but this quintet is loaded with expressive talent. Blythe and Myers are the outsiders here, yet their different kinds of playing – Blythe is swaggeringly verbose, Myers a gospelish spirit – add new flavours to Bowie's sardonic music. The 18 minutes of 'God Has Smiled On Me' are several too many, although the ferocious free-for-all in the middle is very excitingly done, while '3 In 1' finds a beautiful balance between freedom and form.

***** The Great Pretender**

ECM 829369-2 *Bowie; Hamiet Bluiett (bs); Donald Smith (ky); Fred Wilson (b); Phillip Wilson (d); Fontella Bass, David Peaston (v).* 6/81.

****(*) All The Magic!**

ECM 810625-2 2CD *As above, except Ari Brown (ss, ts), Art Matthews (p) replace Bluiett and Smith.* 6/82.

This was a disappointing band, at least on record: in concert, David Peaston's rendition of 'Everything Must Change' was astonishingly uplifting, but the version on *All The Magic!* is disarmingly tame. *The Great Pretender* began Bowie's exploration of pop standards as vehicles for extended free-jazz satire, but it tends to go on for too long. Perhaps the typically resplendent ECM recording didn't suit the group, although 'Rios Negroes' is a fine feature for the leader. The second half of *All The Magic!*, though, multitracks Bowie's trumpet into a gallery of grotesques: his style has matured into a lexicon of smears, growls, chirrups and other effects, and here he uses it as an expressionist cartoon.

****(*) I Only Have Eyes For You**

ECM 825902-2 *Bowie; Stanton Davis, Malachi Thompson, Bruce Purse (t); Steve Turre, Craig Harris (tb); Vincent Chancey (frhn); Bob Stewart (tba); Phillip Wilson (d).* 2/85.

****(*) Avant Pop**

ECM 829563-2 *As above, except Rasul Siddik (t), Frank Lacy (tb) replace Purse and Harris.* 3/86.

***** Serious Fun**

DIW 834/8035 *Bowie; Stanton Davis, E.J Allen, Gerald Brezel (t); Steve Turre, Frank Lacy (tb); Vincent Chancey (frhn); Bob Stewart (tba); Vinnie Johnson, Ken Crutchfield (d); Famoudou Don Moye (perc).* 4/89.

These records are by Bowie's group, Brass Fantasy, a band with an unprecedented instrumentation – at least, in modern jazz. The brass-heavy line-up has obvious echoes of marching bands and the oldest kinds of jazz, however, and one expects a provocative kind of neo-traditionalism with Bowie at the helm. But Brass Fantasy seldom delivers much more than a lightweight irreverence on record. The first two albums have some surprising choices of covers, including Whitney Houston's 'Saving All My Love For You' and Lloyd Price's 'Personality', but the studio seems to stifle some of the freewheeling bravado of the ensemble, and Bowie himself resorts to a disappointing self-parody. Just as one thinks it can go no further, though, the DIW disc displayed a fresh maturity: the brass voicing acquires a broader resonance, the section-work sounds funkier and, although the improvising is still too predictable, it suggests altogether that the group still has plenty left to play.

***** Works**

ECM 837274-2 *Bowie; various groups.* 81–86.

A respectable compilation from Bowie's four ECM records, plus one track ('Charlie M') from the AEOC's *Full Force*.

***** The Organizer**

DIW 821 *Bowie; Steve Turre (tb); James Carter (ts); Amina Claudine Myers (org); Famoudou Don Moye, Phillip Wilson (d).* 1/91.

Bowie stripped out the horns and added Amina Myers on organ: it's really an update of his Fifth Power band of the 1970s, and it works out fine, though the music trades the visceral punch of organ-soul jazz for a more rambling and discursive impact. Turre, as usual, gets in some of the best shots on trombone.

*****(*) My Way**

DIW 835 *Bowie; Stanton Davis, E.J Allen, Gerald Brazel, Earl Garner (t); Steve Turre (tb, conch); Frank Lacy (tb, v); Gregory Williams (frhn); Bob Stewart (tba); Vinnie Johnson, Ken Crutchfield (d); Famoudou Don Moye (perc).* 1/90.

In the past this project seemed like an amusing – if not especially productive – vehicle for Bowie to mess around with. This album brought a new focus to bear. The three originals which lead off *My Way* explore the sonorities of the band as never before; the playing glitters with a new finesse, and the improvising has real gravitas. 'My Way' itself should have been too cornball and obvious, but the superb central solo by Turre denies all that. 'I Got You' really is too obvious, but the closing 'Honky Tonk' is a good one.

*****(*) The Odyssey Of Funk And Popular Music Vol. 1**

Birdology/Atlantic 3984-23026-2 *Bowie; Joseph 'Mac' Gollehon, Ravi Best, Gerald Brazel (t); Joseph Bowie (tb, v); Luis Bonilla, Joshua Roseman, Gary Valente (tb); Vincent Chancey (frhn); Bob Stewart (tba); Victor See Yuen (d); Dean Bowman (v).* 9–10/97.

Bowie kept working until his illness overtook him, and this valedictory offering (unless there is an unreleased Volume Two waiting in the wings) is a splendid farewell. By this time, the Brass Fantasy had become a regular, showbiz gig, and there is no longer any shock value in hearing them tackle 'Don't Cry For Me Argentina' or 'Nessun Dorma', let alone Marilyn Mansun's 'Beautiful People' or the Spice Girls' (getting their first mention in the *Guide*) 'Two Become One'. To that extent, there's nothing surprising or essential about the record. But the ebullience, the fundamental panache of Bowie's own playing, and the braying impact of the group as a whole remain a pleasure. In itself his album title almost casts a snook at the Marsalis philosophy, to which Lester remained implacably opposed.

Michele Bozza

TENOR SAXOPHONE

Contemporary Italian tenorman in a rosy Neapolitan tradition.

***** Around**

Red 123271-2 *Bozza; Franco Ambrosetti (flhn); Marco Brioschi (p); Marco Micheli (b); Massimo Manzi (d).* 5/96.

Fat-free hard bop with, nevertheless, plenty of juice in it – notably Bozza's hefty, almost sentimental tone and Ambrosetti's melodious sound. They play this stuff big and bold, but they can't hide their fundamental faith in the lyricism of this kind of jazz. So even when Brioschi sits out, as he does on no fewer than five of the nine tunes, the horns work up a counterpoint to mollify the absent harmonies. Sam Rivers's 'Beatrice' gets a lush workout. Nothing goes wrong, even if nothing knocks you over.

Charles Brackeen (born 1940)

TENOR AND SOPRANO SAXOPHONES

Played a free-jazz variation in New York in the early '60s without much exposure and thereafter was seldom heard from, until a group of albums in the '80s; but he has since gone back into the shadows.

*****(*) Bannar**

Silkheart SH 105 *Brackeen; Dennis Gonzalez (t); Malachi Favors (b); Alvin Fielder (d).* 2/87.

***** Attainment**

Silkheart SH 110 *Brackeen; Olu Dara (c); Fred Hopkins (b); Andrew Cyrille (d, perc); Dennis Gonzalez (perc).* 11/87.

****** Worshippers Come Nigh**

Silkheart SH 111 *As above.* 11/87.

In 1986 the managing director of the recently founded Silkheart Records tracked down the reclusive Brackeen and persuaded him to record again. Over the following year, the saxophonist cut three splendid records for the label. If Coltrane was the over-determining presence for most saxophonists of the period, Brackeen seems virtually untouched, working instead in a vein reminiscent alternately of Ornette Coleman (as in the stop-start melodic stutter of 'Three Monks Suite' on *Bannar*) and Albert Ayler ('Allah' on the same album). He favours a high, slightly pinched tone; his soprano frequently resembles clarinet, and his tenor work is punctuated by Aylerish sallies into the 'false' upper register. The 'Three Monks Suite' is wholly composed and Brackeen really lets go as a soloist on *Bannar* only with 'Story', a limping melody with enough tightly packed musical information to fuel two superb solos from the horns.

The two November 1987 sessions are just as remarkable. Gonzalez is a fine, emotive trumpeter but he lacks the blowtorch urgency of Dara's more hotly pitched cornet. 'Worshippers Come Nigh' is as exciting a jazz piece as any in the catalogue, underpinned by Hopkins's fine touch (less spacious than Favors but generously responsive) and Cyrille's percussion. 'Bannar' confusingly finds its way on to this album rather than the one named after it, but all three have to be seen as a unit. *Attainment* is the least satisfying, but only because there are no solos on a par with 'Worshippers' and 'Story'. However, it does include the fascinating sax/bass/drums trio, 'House Of Gold'.

JoAnne Brackeen (born 1938)

PIANO

JoAnne Grogan grew up in California and moved to New York after divorcing the saxophonist Charles Brackeen. She worked with Art Blakey, Joe Henderson and Stan Getz, developing a muscular but harmonically limpid solo style.

***** New True Illusion**

Timeless SJP 103 *Brackeen; Clint Houston (b).* 7/76.

***** Invitation**

Black Lion 760218 *As above, except add Billy Hart (d).* 7/76.

***** AFT**

Timeless SJP 115 *As above, except add Ryo Kawasaki (g).* 12/77.

****** Havin' Fun**

Concord CCD 4280 *Brackeen; Cecil McBee (b); Al Foster (d).* 6/85.

***** Fi-Fi Goes To Heaven**

Concord CCD 4316 *As above, except add Terence Blanchard (t), Branford Marsalis (ss, as).* 10/86.

Always useful as a jazz trivia stumper: what white woman played piano for the Jazz Messengers? JoAnne Brackeen hung on to the piano chair with Blakey between 1969 and 1971; a poorly recorded spell, so, just to prove she could do it, she recorded *Fi-Fi Goes To Heaven*. Despite her formidable gifts, Brackeen has been shamefully overlooked by the critics. Since then, there's been some movement in her list, mainly new recording on Concord, for whom she debuted the now famous Maybeck Hall series, but also not least the reappearance of important back-catalogue items like *Invitation*, which is classic Brackeen: restless, wilful and endlessly thoughtful. If you've never heard a note of her work, her opening measures on 'Six Ate' and her solo on 'Canyon Lady' are definitive.

Brackeen has always gravitated towards strong, very melodic bass players. The two early discs with Houston expose some of his crudities – compare his playing on 'Solar' with the standard set by Eddie Gomez – but confirm impressive strength and presence, qualities which are rather muffled on the trio set with guitarist Kawasaki.

The trio with McBee and Foster immediately gains from a sympathetic hand at the controls. The sound is lovely, with lots of definition on both bass and percussion. Foster is perhaps a little straight-ahead for this type of thing, but McBee (who gets a thank-you later with 'Can This McBee?') is absolutely solid and sings along under the piano vamp on 'Manha De Carnaval'. The larger group misfires, replacing subtlety with sheer strength. Instead of keeping in line, Marsalis and Blanchard jostle and barrack out front, and the ensembles are disappointingly uncoordinated.

*****(*) Live At Maybeck Recital Hall, Volume 1**

Concord CCD 4409 *Brackeen solo.* 6/89.

It's refreshing at last to turn to Brackeen as a solo performer. Her Maybeck recital turns out to be a significant moment, kicking off a series that has become almost definitive in its coverage of contemporary jazz piano. Brackeen seems to have been responsible for getting Concord boss Carl Jefferson to record in the little Berkeley hall in the first place, a telephone conversation memorialized in 'Calling Carl'. She certainly didn't let him down. From the opening bars of 'Thou Swell' to a jovial and ironic 'Strike Up The Band' at the finish, she sounds completely in command. 'Dr Chu Chow', 'African Aztec' and 'Curved Space' demonstrate her capacity for unfamiliar tonalities and rhythmic patterns, while 'Yesterdays' sheds almost all its romantic ballast to re-emerge as a big, bold statement of intent.

***** Breath Of Brazil**

Concord CCD 4479 *Brackeen; Eddie Gomez (b); Duduka Fonseca (d); Waltinho Anastacio (perc).* 4/91.

Breath Of Brazil is a rather reserved and thoughtful set underneath all the noise and bustle, sign perhaps of a change of direction (already partly signalled by the Maybeck set) towards a more lyrical approach.

*****(*) Turnaround**

Evidence 22123 *Brackeen; Donald Harrison (as); Cecil McBee (b); Marvin 'Smitty' Smith (d).* 2/92.

Taped at Sweet Basil in New York, Brackeen's group kicks into top gear straightaway, with a finely judged version of 'There Is No Greater Love'. The set is dominated, though, by the original 'Picasso' (no discernible relation to the famous Coleman Hawkins solo) and by Ornette Coleman's 'Turnaround', which is played very straight and confounds any notion that Brackeen avoids playing in orthodox blues formats. Harrison is hesitant here and there, forming his solos with unusual care, perhaps thrown off slightly by the pianist's use of unconventional supplementary harmonies. Smith and McBee are a dream combination and the whole set is very well recorded, if a little toppy in places.

*****(*) Take A Chance**

Concord CCD 4602 *As above.* 6/93.

*****(*) Power Talk**

Turnipseed Music TMCD 08 *Brackeen; Ira Coleman (b); Tony Reedus (d).* 4/94.

The concert documented on *Power Talk* takes the wheel on an extra turn. Opening with a magnificent stop-action reading of 'There Is No Greater Love', she powers through a mostly standards trio, repeating 'Picasso' and 'Cosmic Ties And Mud Pies' from *Where Legends Dwell* and giving both the big treatment. Her young colleagues don't show her undue deference, forging ahead a couple of times as she pauses to elaborate points and then defiantly accelerating again as she changes pace to catch up. It must have been an exhilarating night. Incidentally, Turnipseed Music operates out of Metairie, Louisiana. So now you know.

****** Pink Elephant Magic**

Arkadia 70371 *Brackeen; Nicholas Payton (t); Dave Liebman (ss); Chris Potter (ss, ts); John Patitucci (b); Horacio El Negro Hernanadez (d); Jamey Haddad (perc); Kurt Elling (v).* 3/99.

This sounds like a template for about five very different albums and a proving ground for as many unpredictable and creative bands. As a soloist Brackeen is not as prominent as on her trio recordings, but she is emphatically in charge of the music and the set showcases half a dozen wildly original new numbers. 'Beethoven Meets The Millennium In Spain' is a clever meeting of musical languages, the title-piece is sheer playfulness and wit, and 'What's Your Choice, Rolls Royce?' (which seems to contain references to Mary Lou Williams) provides Kurt Elling with a wacky feature. His is not the only guest voice on the album. The ever-inventive Liebman is supreme on two numbers. Perhaps the centrepiece of the album is an unaccompanied variation on Dave Brubeck's 'Strange Meadowlark', a meditative but by no means sombre excursion that transforms the old ballad into something quite mysterious and fugitive.

Don Braden (born 1964)

TENOR SAXOPHONE

Braden is a swinging mainstream player with a sophisticated harmonic sense and a good deal of taste. He proved his worth as an accompanist on Betty Carter's Grammy winner, Look What I Got, and he won another with Jeanie Bryson. He often plays with a light, slightly feminine tone, contrasting with powerful pedal notes in a much lower register.

***** The Time Is Now**

Criss Cross Criss 1051 *Braden; Tom Harrell (t, flhn); Benny Green (p); Christian McBride (b); Carl Allen (d).* 1/91.

*****(*) Wish List**

Criss Cross 1069 *As above, except add Steve Turre (tb).* 12/91.

Braden's debut album, *The Time Is Now*, was widely praised, but it wasn't a patch on *Wish List*, an elegant set of standards and refreshingly straightforward originals. Instead of overloading themes with harmonic changes, Braden builds in bridge sections which shift the tempo from fours to threes. He's an intelligent arranger, too. Turre and Harrell wouldn't on the face of it be everyone's notion of a *simpatico* brass-line, but Braden has them working in easy tandem without diluting what each does best. Harrell is unwontedly fiery on 'Just The Facts', a schematic minor blues with a gentle twist in its tail. It's the title-track, appropriately closing the record, that confirms Braden's enormous potential, a dreamy, almost wistful song that steadily uncovers its hidden riches. Braden has already played with the best – Carter, Tony Williams, Wynton Marsalis – so this record isn't a 'wish list' date in that sense. Braden palpably doesn't need the support of star names, just the company of like-minded and equally dedicated players.

****** After Dark**

Criss Cross 1081 *Braden; Scott Wendholt (t, flhn); Noah Bless (tb); Steve Wilson (as); Darrell Grant (p); Christian McBride (b); Carl Allen (d).* 5/93.

Braden's third Criss Cross record marks a sudden and dramatic maturing of his style. Not only is he playing as well as before; suddenly his writing and arranging skills seem to have made a quantum step forward. There is a nocturnal programme to the record which gives it a darker and more sombre emphasis. Originals like the uneasy 'R.E.M.' and the gently upbeat 'Dawn' are interspersed with 'You And The Night And The Music', 'Monk's Dream' and Stevie Wonder's 'Creepin''. The group plays well, and trombonist Bless must have staked a claim with producer Gerry Teekens for a solo outing of his own.

*** Organic

Columbia 481258 *Braden; Tom Harrell (t, flhn); David Newman (ts); Jack McDuff, Larry Goldings (org); Russell Malone (g); Cecil Brooks III, Winard Harper (d); Leon Parker (perc).* 9–12/94.

Braden's bow for a major label is entertainingly delivered, but it scarcely measures up to the innate promise of the Criss Cross discs. The opening duet with Malone on 'Moonglow' is lovely, and some of the other pieces hit a productive groove in the organ/soul-jazz mode. Otherwise this feels disappointingly close to a man in mid-career casting around for a fresh idea. If Braden still gets off some strong solos, the real star here is Malone, whose guitar adds grit as well as polish when he takes a solo.

***(*) The Open Road

Double Time DTRCD 114 *Braden; Tim Hagans (t); Kenny Werner (p); Larry Grenadier (b); Billy Hart (d).* 7/96.

It is remarkable how quickly Braden has developed an identifiable creative personality. From the opening moments of the title-track, which opens the album, there can be no doubt who is playing. Yes, there are influences on view – and there is no point rehearsing them here – but the voice is assured, individual and one of a kind. Even when he tackles well-signposted themes like 'Maiden Voyage' or 'Someday My Prince Will Come', which has Miles's pawprint all over it, he manages to find things of his own to say. The group contributes more than its share to the success of the session. Werner is still an unsung hero of the current scene, an adaptable player who never submerges his own ideas in the ensemble but keeps the interests of the two afloat and side by side. Grenadier and Hart work in easy combination. The closing 'Lush Life' is the most mature work we've heard from Braden yet and, if the album as a whole lacks a touch of focus, it's still moving in interesting directions.

***(*) The Voice Of The Saxophone

RCA 09026 68797 *Braden; Randy Brecker (t, flhn); Frank Lacy (tb); Vincent Herring (as); Hamiet Bluiett (bs, cl, cbcl); George Colligan, Darrell Grant (p); Dwayne Burno (b); Cecil Brooks III (d); Bill Cosby, Jimmy Delgado (perc).* 2 & 3/97.

An intriguing idea, octet arrangements of songs associated with saxophone players. Co-produced by Benny Golson and under the tutelage of Bill Cosby, who turns in a nifty cowbell and timbals performance on 'Monk's Hat', the theme from *Cosby*, the set goes in too many directions to be entirely coherent. Sam Rivers's 'Point Of Many Returns' sits a little awkwardly in the same set as Hank Mobley's 'Soul Station', but the fact that Braden feels no strain means that none comes across in the playing. The version of Shorter's 'Speak No Evil' is one of the best we have heard, and 'After The Rain', often these days thought of as a pianistic epic, is handled magnificently by the saxophones. Bluiett should have done more sets like these; he's a fantastic player, with a tone that seems to come out of the earth, and alongside Braden's quite muscular sound they occupy the whole sound-space. The set closes with Jimmy Heath's 'The Voice Of The Saxophone', a nice nod to the underrated gifts of the Artist Formerly Known as Little Bird, but now revealed as another of Braden's artistic forebears.

***(*) The Fire Within

RCA Victor 09026 63297 2 *Braden; Darrell Grant, Julian Joseph (p); Dwayne Burno, Orlando LaFleming, Christian McBride (b); Cecil Brooks III, Mark Mondesir, Jeff Tain Watts (d).* 6–11/98.

Very much back to normal business with what looks like a relay team of rhythm sections to keep pace with a saxophonist suddenly possessed with an urgent message to pass on. The title-track is the most convincing Braden composition yet, performed with a brisk ferocity that doesn't let passion get entirely in the way of accuracy. Like half the album, it's the responsibility of the Grant–Burno–Brooks axis which, rightly or wrongly, feels like the working band here. The trio with McBride and Watts yields three very fine covers, of Miles's 'Solar', of Freddie Hubbard's 'Thermo' and of Dexter Gordon's 'Fried Bananas'. Lively and engaging improvisation from all three and edgier than the other tracks in the absence of a piano player; but this was probably a unit that needed more time and perhaps a full album to get its point across. The only disappointment is the performance of British star, Julian Joseph. His own 'Doctone' is a great tune, but he sounds unnaturally ebullient and insistent on both of his featured tracks. Braden is not yet forty and doubtless has his best years ahead of him. This is an impressive showing and offers further promise of future excitement.

Bobby Bradford (born 1934)

TRUMPET, CORNET

Played with Ornette Coleman in Los Angeles in the '50s, and eventually replaced Don Cherry in the quartet in 1961; then closely associated with John Carter, as both a duo and in group contexts. Now mostly teaches in LA.

** Lost In LA

Soul Note 121068 *Bradford; James Kousakis (as); Roberto Miguel Miranda, Mark Dresser (b); Sherman Ferguson (d).* 6/83.

** One Night Stand

Soul Note 121168 *Bradford; Frank Sullivan (p); Scott Walton (b); Billy Bowker (d).* 11/86.

Bradford's best work with Ornette is supposed to have gone the way of desert flowers, and the recordings made under his own name are curiously unsatisfactory, full of good things (like his superbly constructed solos) but ultimately underachieved. There isn't much in the catalogue at present, anyway. *Lost In LA* has precious few striking moments and the single-horn format of *One Night Stand* prompts some more of his bravura and his most thoughtful solos; but these are largely indifferent works. An important and adventurous player, Bradford has yet to recapture the brilliance of the 1973 *Secrets* with Carter; even the live sets seem to lose something of their burnish at the mixing desk.

Ruby Braff (born 1927)

CORNET, TRUMPET

Reuben – 'Ruby' – Braff left his native Boston at the start of the 1950s and began to record in New York with the likes of Vic Dickenson and Urbie Green. His powerful, melodic cornet is one of the most distinctive sounds in mainstream jazz, backed by a seemingly limitless flow of ideas. After a brief eclipse in his career – which some would put down to a volatile temperament – Braff has continued to make fine records into his seventh and eighth decade.

(*) **Hustlin' And Bustlin'

Black Lion BLCD 760908 *Braff; Vic Dickenson (tb, v); Dick LeFave (cl, ts); Edmond Hall (cl); Kenneth Kersey, Sam Margolis (ts); George Wein (p); John Field, Milt Hinton (b); Bobby Donaldson, Jo Jones (d).* 51–6/54.

*** **Hi-Fi Salute To Bunny**

RCA 2118250 *Braff; Benny Morton (tb); Pee Wee Russell (cl); Dick Hafer (ts); Nat Pierce (p); Steve Jordan (g); Walter Page (b); Buzzy Drootin (d).* 3 & 4/57.

***(*) **Easy Now**

RCA 211852 *Braff; Emmett Berry, Roy Eldridge (t); Bob Wilber (cl, ts); Hank Jones (p); Mundell Lowe (g); Leonard Gaskin (b); Don Lamond (d).* 8/58.

Not the most personable or accommodating figure to do business with (the 'Mr Hyde and Mr Hyde' joke has been heard in his vicinity more than once), Braff is a hugely entertaining performer whose cornet style seems to have arrived a generation too late; it has an almost vocal agility that balances delicacy of detail with a strong underlying pulse and harmonic richness. Like Roy Eldridge, who joins him on some of the *Easy Now* tracks, he is a player who bridges the gap between early jazz and swing, and then between swing and (hard as it may be to square this with his conservative/mainstream niching) bebop. Listen, though, to the phrasing on the tribute to Bunny Berigan, and it is possible to hear strong intimations of Fats Navarro and even that other style-switcher, Charlie Shavers.

The early material on Black Lion is more conservatively angled. The opening 'Hustlin' And Bustlin'' is associated with Louis Armstrong and binds Braff to the mainstream that went underground with the advent of Dizzy Gillespie and Clifford Brown. 'Shoe Shine Boy' has a bright polish and the self-written 'Flaky' an intriguingly ironic edge. And it's perhaps in that irony, that nod to the audience that he knows he is dealing in archaisms, that Braff's great strength lies. The two RCAs see him develop into a different player, and in embryo the protean stylist he was to remain until the 1990s. Comparing these lushly mastered sessions with a recent Concord does the RCA technical department no favours, but it also confirms that Braff's mature style was in place almost from the beginning rather than coming along later in a bid to keep pace with the youngsters. One further indication of his bridge-building capacity is that old-school players like Morton and Russell manage to sound comfortable alongside the bustly Hafer.

***(*) **Hear Me Talkin'**

Black Lion BLCD 760161 *Braff; Alex Welsh (t); Roy Williams (tb); Al Gay (ts); Johnny Barnes (bs); Jim Douglas (g); Fred Hunt (p); Ron Rae (b); Lennie Hastings (d).* 11/67.

Recorded in London at the tail-end of a mouth-watering 'Jazz Expo' package which introduced British players to some of their American idols. The Welsh band had been playing with Wild Bill Davison at the 100 Club before these sessions were recorded, and something of Davison's brisk attack creeps into the brass chase that ends 'No One Else But You'. Though Welsh mostly defers to Braff as far as solo space is concerned (can you picture an argument between the two?), the real star of the set is trombonist Roy Williams, who plays a marvellous solo on 'Ruby Got Rhythm' and even more outstandingly on 'Smart Alex Blues', two originals worked up by the American for the gig. Braff's own finest moment is on the long 'Between The Devil And The Deep Blue Sea', where he plays in his distinctive lower register. The Welsh band was probably the finest mainstream unit of its day, with no reason to defer to transatlantic visitors. It had recently proved its worth at Antibes, and Newport was beckoning for 1968. It offered Braff congenial and often challenging company, and he responds with a sparky, disciplined performance, a little tighter rhythmically than he would normally prefer, but on the money throughout, while in Williams and Welsh he had frontline partners well up to his mettle.

(*) **Ruby Braff–Buddy Tate With The Newport All Stars

Black Lion BLCD 760138 *Braff; Buddy Tate (ts); George Wein (p); Jack Lesberg (b); Don Lamond (d).* 10/67.

A little soft-centred by Braff's usual standard, this was a session recorded in London, presumably in the gaps left by a touring schedule. Braff slips into Pops mode, punching out the notes with more intensity than usual but without much finesse. There are alternative takes of much of the music included – 'Mean To Me', 'Take The "A" Train' and 'The Sheik Of Araby' – but they don't reveal much more than the slightly programmed quality of Braff's music at this time. Tate plays very well indeed, but it's his fluffs that lead to calls for further versions of these songs.

*** **Grand Reunion**

Chiaroscuro 117 *Braff; Ellis Larkins (p).* 72.

This was the first reunion of a duo that had got together in 1955 and was to repeat the experiment 20 years on again. The pace is mostly gentle, partly to suit Larkins, who is a fine ballad player, but also to highlight a more reflective side to Braff. Ruby invests even his most languid solos with a hint of fires beneath, and when occasion demands he simply doubles up the tempo and raises the ante that way. There are a couple of extra tracks not on the original LP, but the best of the session is still to be found in 'Love Walked In' and a lively but philosophical version of 'Ain't Misbehavin''.

***(*) **Live At the New School**

Chiaroscuro CRD 126 *Braff; George Barnes, Wayne Wright (g); Michael Moore (b).* 4/74.

***** Plays Gershwin**

Concord CCD 6005 *As above.* 7/74.

****(*) Plays Rodgers & Hart**

Concord CCD 6007 *As above.* 7/74.

In the end, despite the amiably waspish chat on the first of these, they couldn't get along together, but while they were playing rather than squabbling Braff and Barnes produced some of the best small-group jazz of the day. Needless to say, the critics were looking in the other direction at the time. The Chiaroscuro documents an entire concert at the prestigious New School for Social Research, a recording made by the audio engineering class. It was actually the last gig in an influential series known as Jazz Ramble, and it seems appropriate that it should have been a group touching so many stylistic bases that rang down the curtain. Braff's sponsorship of the young wasn't limited to having students in the booth. The inclusion of young Michael Moore in the quartet was a master-stroke, bringing forward one of the best mainstream-modern bassists of his generation and taxing him to the limit. You can almost *hear* Moore learning on some of the less familiar material, things like 'With Time For Love' and Don Redman's 'Nobody Else But You', just two of ten tracks that were not included on the original release. A doubly valuable document, then, of a short-lived group that continued for only a few months more, basically long enough to make the Concords and to work with Tony Bennett.

The first of the pair for Carl Jefferson's recently established label isn't just another 'Goishwin' route-march but a genuine attempt to get inside the tunes and unpick their still far too little understood progressions. Unfortunately, if Braff is on his usual plateau of excellence, there is something slightly unresolved about Wayne Wright's rhythm guitar and Moore's bass. The mix is perhaps better on the Rodgers & Hart set. 'Spring Is Here' is completely masterly and Barnes seems happier with this material than with the Gershwin. On a toss-up, though, Gershwin's writing breaks the deadlock.

***** Pipe Organ Recital Plus One**

Concord CCD 43003 *Braff; Dick Hyman (org).* 4/82.

Brass and organ has been a winning combination for 400 years, and this is no exception. The slightly emphysemic organ pretends to be older and poorer-winded than it is, and Hyman turns in lovely, flowing lines. Braff is responsive and alert, but also deeply evocative.

***** Mr Braff To You**

Phontastic CD 7568 *Braff; Scott Hamilton (ts); John Bunch (p); Chris Flory (g); Phil Flanigan (b).* 12/83.

The title offers an insight into Braff's – shall we say robust? – personality, but it also shows him capable of sending himself up. This early encounter with Hamilton is one of their best. There's an almost folksy quality to Braff's theme statements, and it's this that Hamilton picks up on, leaning back into relaxed, saloon-bar solos on 'Ida, Sweet As Apple Cider', 'Poor Butterfly' and 'Miss Brown To You' with complete relaxation. Bunch is a tower of strength throughout, to the extent that Flory and Flanigan are almost superfluous.

***** A First**

Concord CCD 4274 *As above, except add Chuck Riggs (d).* 2/85.

***** A Sailboat In The Moonlight**

Concord CCD 4296 *As above.* 2/85.

A generation younger, Scott Hamilton is a co-religionist in his refusal to accept the orthodoxy of bop and his insistence that there is a good deal of creative mileage in the mainstream. He and Braff blend as effectively as any reed player he has partnered over the years, and the two albums move with an unstinted eloquence, punctuated by moments of real fire.

*****(*) Me, Myself And I**

Concord CCD 4381 *Braff; Howard Alden (g); Jack Lesberg (b).* 6/88.

*****(*) Bravura Eloquence**

Concord CCD 4423 *As above.* 6/88.

Ten years back, at the age of sixty, Braff suddenly went through some kind of creative rejuvenation which has not left him since. His imagination has never been more fleet and expansive and his tone is as ringingly strong as ever. He has a mastery of melodic form which allows him to move seamlessly from 'Smile' to 'Who'll Buy My Violets?', and in the long, superb 'Judy [Garland] Medley' he takes some extraordinary harmonic liberties not just with the inevitable 'Rainbow' but also with 'If I Only Had A Brain'. On *Me, Myself And I* he even takes a shot at the big number from *Swan Lake*, and makes a convincing job of it into the bargain. Lesberg and Alden provide sterling support, by no means mere journeymen but time-served collaborators.

***** Music From My Fair Lady**

Concord CCD 4393 *Braff; Dick Hyman (p).* 7/89.

***** Younger Than Swingtime**

Concord CCD 4445 *As above.* 6/90.

America The Beautiful, a duo Braff made with Hyman on organ, has now disappeared from the catalogue, but these show-tune records are an acceptable alternative for the moment. The music is familiar to the point of banality but that seems to inspire Braff to ever greater feats of invention. Last time round, we were inclined to think he was doing little more than pushing the tempos or else decelerating them until the tune lost its cohesion, either way an easy enough strategy. Repeated hearings suggest that what he is doing is much subtler and more effective. Though 'With A Little Bit Of Luck' is the most characteristic performance, it's worth hanging around for 'I've Grown Accustomed To Her Face', a wonderful grudging and unbending performance.

The *South Pacific* material is more accessibly lyrical and is confronted in a much more conventional way, with fewer of the quirks and asides that Braff uses to propel the earlier session. Here it's Hyman who takes a lot of the responsibility, and he acknowledges the fact with 'There Is Nothing Like A Dame', on which there is nothing like a cornet, a splendid solo excursion. 'Bali Ha'i' frames the session nicely. For choice, the first record is more interesting, but the second may be more immediately winning. As they say on TV, the choice is yours.

*****(*) And His New England Songhounds: Volume 1**
Concord CCD 4478 *Braff; Scott Hamilton (ts); Dave McKenna (p); Frank Tate (b); Alan Dawson (d).* 4/91.

***** And His New England Songhounds: Volume 2**
Concord CCD 4504 *As above.* 4/91.

Fans misted over at the thought of this group in the studio. Braff and McKenna last did a studio session together in 1956, when the cornetist cut the fine *Braff!* for Epic. The chemistry still works. The hand-picked band offers the leader a warmly swinging background for one of the best performances of recent years. The original 'Sho-Time' is dedicated to Scott Hamilton's son, a relatively rare writing credit for Braff, but further evidence of his skill as a melodist. Stand-out tracks have to be 'My Shining Hour', Billie's 'Tell Me More' and the brief closing 'Every Time We Say Goodbye'. Mainstream jazz at its best.

Volume 2 was always going to be worth the wait and it delivers royally, though we're increasingly persuaded that the best of the music is contained in the original record. Braff's clipped, brusque delivery on 'Indian Summer' tempers the sugariness that always threatens to come through, and that's what's happening throughout the record. Oddly, Hamilton sounded better on the first volume but the Songhounds have clicked into gear, and one hopes there will be more soon.

*****(*) Cornet Chop Suey**
Concord CCD 4606 *Braff; Ken Peplowski (cl); Howard Alden (g); Frank Tate (b); Ronald Zito (d).* 3/91.

This is essentially a trio record, with Peplowski and Zito guesting on just five of the dozen tracks. Given the obvious *simpatico* of the well-established Braff–Alden–Tate trio, it might have been as well to hold them in reserve for another session altogether. These are remarkable performances. Lead lines are swapped and played back reharmonized on the spot; Tate and Alden seem to enjoy a rapport that provides Braff with the sort of ambiguous context he thrives on. To give one clear example: Louis Armstrong's 'Cornet Chop Suey' is taken at a furious pace, far brisker than Pops ever intended and with a variant in the melody which, as Braff himself suggests, aligns it to Charlie Parker and bebop. It wouldn't do to overstate this line of argument, but it makes better sense of this highly inventive and thoughtful player than does the received view of him as a curmudgeonly reactionary who stopped listening to anything recorded after the Hot Fives.

***** As Time Goes By**
Candid 79741 *Braff; Howard Alden (g); Frank Tate (b).* 5/91.

Recorded live in London, with a thoroughly sympathetic group and an intriguing programme of songs. Braff is in excellent form, trying out variants on familiar harmonies and sometimes wholly recasting old songs. Mary Lou Williams's wonderful 'Lonely Moments' is too rarely covered and following 'Shoe Shine Boy' as it does gets the album off to a stunningly good start which isn't quite sustained. Not a bad track in the bunch, though.

*****(*) Live At The Regattabar**
Arbors ARCD 9131 *Braff; Gray Sargent (p); Jon Wheatley (g); Marshall Wood (b).* 11/93.

***** Controlled Nonchalance**
Arbors ARCD 9134 *As above, except add Scott Hamilton (ts), Dave McKenna (p), Chuck Riggs (d); omit Wheatley.* 11/93.

The earlier of these – by just a few days – was recorded on the 30th anniversary of President John F. Kennedy's assassination and in the heart of Kennedy country: the Regattabar is in the Charles Hotel, Cambridge, Massachusetts. Though there is no mention of the date's significance on the record, can it be that it contributed something to the quiet centredness of the session, which conveys a mood closer to melancholy than to nonchalance? Control, though, definitely. Braff's activities had been curtailed somewhat in the previous couple of years by attacks of the wind player's curse, emphysema; but he is fit enough to take charge of both these groups, leading them through two superbly crafted programmes of standard material. 'No One Else But You' is revived and gives Jon Wheatley his most effective feature, and here Braff's increasingly obvious interest in playing saxophone lines on cornet (Ben Webster is his avowed model) is given full rein. Gray Sargent has a more plangent, blues-influenced style, which is effectively deployed on 'Give My Regards To Broadway' and on the brand-new 'Orange', a departure in the Braff canon in that the composer introduces it on piano. That warms the instrument up nicely for big Dave McKenna, four nights later with the augmented group. Qualitatively there really isn't much to choose between these groups, but one misses the stillness and precision of the drummerless quartet and the slight sense that, except for 'Struttin' With Some Barbecue' (played with a Latin spin) and 'Sunday', both of which are triumphant, Braff is slightly eclipsed by the others.

***** Ruby Braff And Dick Hyman Play Nice Tunes**
Arbors ARCD 19141 *Braff; Dick Hyman (p).* 94.

Indeed they do – but, for some reason, perhaps because Braff sounds short-winded and weary, they don't get much firmer than that. This is a curiously drab album, with a flat and uninvolving sound, and, while both men play with great competence, there is nothing that lifts it up out of the ordinary.

****** Calling Berlin: Volume 1**
Arbors ARCD 19139 *Braff; Ellis Larkins (p); Bucky Pizzarelli (g).* 6 & 7/94.

***** Calling Berlin: Volume 2**
Arbors ARCD 19140 *As above, except omit Pizzarelli.* 6 & 7/94.

The cover has them huddled round a kitchen table, with a short-wave receiver, cans and a mic, except that the Berlin they're calling on isn't the German capital but the great composer. This is the kind of intimate setting and this is the sort of material that suits Braff to a 't', and he plays superbly. 'Blue Skies' and 'Alexander's Ragtime Band' on the first volume are impossible to fault, and 'How Deep Is The Ocean?' has a wise and almost philosophical quality that is utterly engaging. Working with Ella Fitzgerald turned Larkins into a front-row accompanist. He is never less than interesting; even when he and Braff seem to start in different keys, the pianist makes something of a virtue of their displacement. Pizzarelli doesn't appear on the second volume at all, a pity because he adds light and shade to 'It's A Lovely Day Today' and 'Russian Lullaby', and it would have been good to get more of him.

****** Inside & Out**

Concord CCD 4691 *Braff; Roger Kellaway (p).* 9/95.

Songful, bright and shady, above all *detailed* and full of invention, this is a beautiful set that makes a virtue of simplicity. Kellaway's accompaniment on 'Between The Devil And The Deep Blue Sea' is masterful, following Braff's radical reinvention every step of the way. 'I Got Rhythm' receives the attention and respect it deserves; but it is on 'Yesterdays' – far and away the most striking single item on the set – that the chemistry begins to fizzle. It doesn't come a lot better than this.

***** Concord Jazz Heritage Series**

Concord Jazz 4833 *As for above Concord releases.* 74–95.

As with so many of these estimable records, the real value will be for those who either don't know Ruby's work or can't afford to amass the original discs. All the things you'd expect to find are here, along with a couple of wild cards like the original 'Here's Carl', a dedication to the label's president. Inevitably, it lacks the logic and shading of an official release but, track for track, it's a jewel.

*****(*) Being With You**

Arbors ARCD 19163 *Braff; Joe Wilder (flhn); Jon-Erik Kellso (c); Dan Barrett (tb); Scott Robinson (bs, cl); Jerry Jerome (ts); Bucky Pizzarelli (g); Johnny Varro (p); Bob Haggart (b); Jim Gwin (d).* 4/96.

Pops was always the single greatest influence on Braff's playing, and this nicely crafted tribute shows some of the ways. The group is a mixture of the great-and-good (Wilder, Barrett, Pizzarelli) and relative unknowns, but the playing is of the highest quality and, though fellow-cornetist Joe is around for only a single track, the long 'Royal Garden Blues', he brings such colour and vibrancy to it as to colour the whole album. The opening take on 'I Never Knew (Where Roses Grew)' sets the tone for a richly varied session that ends on the theme tune ('When It's Sleepy Time Down South') and on a point of rest. There isn't anyone else around who could have invested this material with such conviction and grace.

****** First Set**

Zephyr ZECD 15 *Braff; Warren Vaché (flhn); Roy Williams (tb); Brian Lemon (p); Howard Alden (g); Dave Green (b); Allan Ganley (d).* 9/96.

*****(*) The Second Set**

ZECD 16 *As above.* 9/96.

Not, as it probably sounds, a live album but an exquisitely crafted studio session that sees Braff tackling a batch of unusual and rarely visited standards and bringing to them all a now familiar but no less startling creative verve. His ability to climb inside the harmonic structure of the tune and to reinvent it wholesale is endlessly satisfying, and on this occasion he is joined by three players – Vaché, the estimable Williams and Zephyr's leading light, Lemon – to create two hours of vibrant and intelligent jazz. The first set includes a long version of 'Take The "A" Train' and 'The Very Thought Of You', while the second majors on an extended reading of the Sweets and Basie jumper, 'Jive At Five'. Williams is supreme, poised and unflustered by the fastest and sometimes not the most secure change of pace and key; and the rhythm section, who have been tested almost to destruction over the years, deliver a rich, elastic beat that is the perfect platform for Braff. Two excellent records that should gladden the hearts of every mainstream fan on the planet.

***** You Can Depend On Me**

Arbors 19165 *Braff; Johnny Varro (p); Bucky Pizzarelli (g); Bob Haggart (b); Jim Gwin (d).* 9/98.

Rising seventy, Ruby is sly and subtle, turning familiar material like 'The Man I Love' into rich exercises in harmony and melody. The group is supportive but slightly anonymous, with the exception of the wonderful Pizzarelli, who bounces from tune to tune, agile and unflappable. Ruby's solos on 'S'posin'' and 'Big Butter And Egg Man' are among his best in recent years.

***** Born To Play**

Arbors 19203 *Braff; Kenny Davern (cl); Howard Alden, Bucky Pizzarelli, Jon Wheatley (g); Michael Moore, Marshall Wood (b); Jim Gwin (d).* 4/99.

This is not a collective personnel but the actual line-up for a most unusual band, Braff as ever experimenting and trying out new combinations of sound. The combination of three guitars is excellent, filling out a rich harmonic backdrop for the two horns. Davern is in quiet and thoughtful form, but Ruby goes for broke with big solos on Charlie Chaplin's 'Smile' and on the opening 'Avalon'. He decides to sing on the final number, 'Born To Lose', but the performance is so weighted with irony that one is inclined to grant him the small self-indulgence in return for so imaginative and unexpected a set.

***** Ruby Braff And Strings**

Arbors 2732 *Braff; Brian Lemon (p); Bucky Pizzarelli (g); strings.* 99.

Stop press. An elegant and mostly very good strings album, marked by solid and unspectacular solos. Lemon is masterly and Bucky Pizzarelli lopes along with amiable inattention, often sounding as if he's listening to some other set on headphones. For a more measured appraisal, we'll get back to you.

Anthony Braxton (born 1945)

ALTO SAXOPHONE, ALL OTHER SAXOPHONES AND CLARINETS, FLUTE, ELECTRONICS, PERCUSSION

Few modern musicians, in any genre, can have been so extensively documented as the Chicago-born multi-instrumentalist, and yet the very density of the documentation serves only to heighten the enigma that is Anthony Braxton. His cultural background is very much the experimental ethos of the AACM and its devotion to new sound-sources and an abandonment of old hierarchies. But Braxton is a rather special kind of radical. He claims the close harmony of Frankie Lymon and the Teenagers as an influence; having worked, somewhat improbably, in one of Dave Brubeck's groups, he adduces the cool, white sound of Paul Desmond and Warne Marsh as being important to his development as a saxophonist. Braxton's enormous composition list combines relatively straightforward pulse-driven themes, akin to jazz composition, with quasi-conceptual work for unconventional instrumentation (including amplified shovels) and with grand music-theatre projects with a strong ritual component. He has also projected future work for performance on orbiting space stations, which makes Stockhausen's 'Helicopter Quartet' seem rather tame. It will obviously be many years before such projects are realizable, which is perhaps the point. A line of André Gide's applies admirably to Braxton: 'Please do not understand me too quickly.'

***** Three Compositions Of New Jazz**
Delmark DS 423 *Braxton; Leo Smith (t, perc); Leroy Jenkins (vn, vla, perc); Muhal Richard Abrams (p, clo, cl).* 68.

It would be a brave man indeed who would now claim a more than passing familiarity with the whole of the Anthony Braxton discography. The simple statistic is that there is now more material bearing Braxton's name in the public domain, than there is by John Coltrane and Ornette Coleman *put together*. Whether or not this reflects his real importance to the American music of today is scarcely the point. It is a fact, and it means that assessing his body of recorded work is enormously and increasingly difficult. The number of imprints featuring his work increases by the month, and the appearance of his own imprint, Braxton House, in the 1990s almost seals the issue. In what follows, we have attempted to do little more than register the main recordings and their relative merits. There will, inevitably, be omissions, but we hope they occur only in the more ephemeral and elusive corners of the picture. The question of what Braxton's music *is*, generically speaking, is one that should no longer worry anyone. Whatever the prevailing definition of jazz, Braxton's music conforms majestically: rhythmic, virtuosic, powerfully emotive, constantly reinventing itself. He has been able to translate his solo concept (in the late 1960s he pioneered unaccompanied saxophone performance) to the largest orchestral scale.

The dateline on *Three Compositions Of New Jazz* is significant. Braxton's first major statement – indeed, his recording debut as leader – came in the year of revolutions (or at least of revolutionary thinking throughout America and Europe) and openly declares itself as standing at the end of a played-out cultural tradition. Though he can expect to rake over the ashes of that tradition for some time, this is the critical historical moment which Braxton's music addresses. The disc contains three compositions of decreasing length, two by Braxton, one by Smith. As John Litweiler suggests in a useful biographical liner-note, the middle piece is the one in which the new language that Braxton, Smith and Abrams are articulating can most readily be accessed. The saxophonist still sounds hot and fierce, the disciple of Parker and Dolphy rather than of the cooler, whiter voices (Desmond, Marsh) he turned to in the '80s. All the same, these graduation exercises by the 1968 AACM show class. The loose, drummerless concept works well for all three, and the music, though still slightly raw, stands up well after 30-plus years.

*****(*) Silence / Time Zones**
Black Lion BLCD 760221 *Braxton; Leo Smith (t, perc); Leroy Jenkins (vn, perc); Richard Teitelbaum (syn).* 7/69–9/76.

Richard Teitelbaum has pointed out that Braxton's interest in the white avant-garde (and Stockhausen most obviously) was no different from, and no less valid than, his own in the black. This is a hugely welcome reissue, not just for opening up another facet of the saxophonist's association with the former Musica Elettronica Viva man, but also for the further light it sheds on his work with AACM and some of its associated players. The trios with Smith and Jenkins are very much of their time, but they are also undeniably powerful. Interestingly, there are no Braxton compositions on the album, and one feels that even joint credit with Teitelbaum is undue, and certainly doing no favours to Smith and Jenkins, who appear on and write the first two numbers. Braxton plays his usual range of horns, concentrating on sopranino and alto saxophones and contrabass clarinet on the long 1976 duos. The earlier of these is dedicated to Roscoe Mitchell and might almost be a Mitchell gig, were it not for the distinctive timbre of Braxton's reed, hard but not unbluesy, cool but not emotionless.

****(*) In The Tradition**
Steeplechase 31015 *Braxton; Tete Montoliu (p); Niels-Henning Orsted Pedersen (b); Albert 'Tootie' Heath (d).* 5/74.

*****(*) In The Tradition**
Steeplechase 31045 *As above.*

In The Tradition was Braxton's first sustained essay in revisionism, his first attempt to show that underneath the hard edge there was a jazz spirit. It's an awkward and in some respects unappealing session, largely because the piano player, the blind Catalan, Tete Montoliu, was so patently at odds with his intentions. Braxton's lyrical lines – on shibboleths like 'Ornithology' and 'Goodbye Pork Pie Hat' – are so clearly drawn as to render the chords and Montoliu's embellishments almost redundant. The bass and drums by contrast are almost ideally adapted to Braxton's needs, a particular tribute to NHOP's resilience and catholicity of taste. A quarter of a century on, these records sound almost antiquated and grievously lacking in subtlety. However adaptable Braxton's chops at the time, he was to prove himself in later years a much finer and more responsive performer of jazz material. Never a player of powerful emotion, more of ideas, he doesn't quite have the rhetoric yet to convince.

***** First Duo Concert**
Emanem 4006 *Braxton; Derek Bailey (g).* 6/74.

We were present at this much-heralded and thoroughly extraordinary encounter, and what a revelation it turned out to be. Braxton and Bailey, representing (as became increasingly clear) two very different approaches to improvisation, met and rehearsed the day before the concert and swapped notes. It was made clear that Braxton did not want to improvise freely, while Bailey, who came from precisely that idiom, did not want to play predetermined structures. The ensuing concert represented a compromise in which each piece – or 'area' – was about certain types and categories of sound: staccato, sustained, and so on. Two pieces were set aside as solos. Braxton's 'Area 9' is one of his unaccompanied alto solos, very much in line with what he had been doing in that direction for some time: quite straightforward, jazz-based and emotionally unemphatic. By contrast, Bailey seems much more anarchic and ironic, and the conclusion, now as then, is that this was a mismatch of creative personalities which nevertheless managed to yield some fascinating music.

***** Composition No. 94 For Three Instrumentalists (1980)**
Leo/Golden Years of New Jazz GY 3 *Braxton; Ray Anderson (tb); James Emery (g, elec).* 4/80.

Braxton's association with Ray Anderson was one of the happiest and most fruitful of his career, albeit brief. It offered him a range of singing tonalities not available from other instruments, and whenever the two worked together Braxton's own playing seemed to open out with ever greater generosity of spirit. Recorded live in Bologna, just a few months before that city was tragically changed for ever, the three sections of 'Composition No. 94' are played forwards and then, risible as it may sound, played backwards. This is apparently the only recording of the trio, which mitigates its poor quality somewhat, though only somewhat. Graham Lock points out in his informed and illuminating liner-note that Braxton was increasingly thinking in terms of visual parallels at this time, and much of the piece seems to be concerned with the movement of water or cloud, or with the shifting patterns of fabric. It's a good analogy for a composer who is often, unfairly, thought to be abstract and dryly cerebral.

*****(*) Composition No. 96**

Leo CD LR 169 *Braxton (cond); Dave Scott, James Knapp (t); Julian Priester, Scott Reeves (tb); Richard Reed (frhn); Rick Byrnes (tba); Nancy Hargerud, Rebecca Morgan, Denise Pool (f); Aileen Munger, Laurri Uhlig (ob); Bob Davis (eng hn); Marlene Weaver (bsn); Paul Pearse, Bill Smith (cl); Ray Downey (bcl); Denny Goodhew (as); Julian Smedley, Mathew Pederson, Jeannine Davis, Libby Poole, Jeroen Van Tyn, Sandra Guy, Becky Liverzey, Mary Jacobson (vn); Betty Agent, Jean Word, Sam Williams, Beatrice Dolf (vla); Page Smith-Weaver, Scott Threlkold, Marjorie Parbington (clo); Scott Weaver, Deborah De Loria (b); Motter Dean (hp); Ed Hartman, Matt Kocmieroski (perc).* 5/81.

Dating from the end of the 1970s, *Composition No. 96* is a large-scale composition dedicated to Karlheinz Stockhausen and reflecting Braxton's interest in the relationship between 'dynamic symbolism' (the Jungian archetypes, close enough) and planetary change. The symbols are realized as photographic slides of actual physical phenomena, which are then projected as part of a strict parallelism between perceptual systems. Braxton's earlier experiments with large-scale orchestral 'composition' – difficult to hear any of it as uniformly scored – were not particularly happy. It's ironic that while one of the routine criticisms levelled at his small-group work is that it is too rigidly formalized, his orchestral works can sound unproductively chaotic. *Composition No. 96*, which comes from a particularly fruitful phase in Braxton's career, is a huge, apocalyptic thing that might serve as a soundtrack for some post-creationist epic of the Next Frontier.

Graham Lock's immensely detailed liner-note explains the genesis and structure of the music, but essentially *Composition No. 96* consists of 16 separate elements and their numerological product, seven distinct parts, which move from the vibrant collisions of the opening through slower and faster sections, punctuated by *fermata* or pauses like those that signal the beginning of cadenzas in classical concertos. Braxton's large-scale works were a logical extension of what he had been doing throughout the 1970s, but they were also part of his effort to raise Afro-American music out of the 'jazz' ghetto. Even at the level of pure sound, with no reference to its complex structural synchronization, *Composition No. 96* is an impressive achievement. The Composers and Improvisers Orchestra has a rather *ad hoc* feel, and some of the transitions sound fudged and incomplete. The only recognizable jazz name in the ensemble is trombonist Julian Priester, and one wonders how sympathetic some of the players actually were to Braxton's conception. There are places when the playing is more exact and 'legitimate' than the context seems to demand; but such perceptions may be the result of residual expectations of what jazz musicians are 'supposed' to sound like, and for that reason alone should be resisted.

***** Four Compositions (Quartet) 1984**

Black Saint 120086 *Braxton; Marilyn Crispell (p); John Lindberg (b); Gerry Hemingway (d).* 9/84.

*****(*) Quartet (London) 1985**

Leo CD LR 200/201 2CD *As above, except Mark Dresser (b) replaces Lindberg.* 11/85.

*****(*) Quartet (Birmingham) 1985**

Leo CD LR 202/3 2CD *As above.* 11/85.

****** Quartet (Coventry) 1985**

Leo CD LR 204/205 2CD *As above.* 11/85.

****(*) Five Compositions (Quartet) 1986**

Black Saint 120106 *As above, except David Rosenboom (p) replaces Crispell.* 7/86.

For all his compositions for amplified shovels, 100 tubas and galactically dispersed orchestras, the core of Braxton's conception remains the recognizably four-square jazz quartet. This is where he was heard to best advantage in the 1980s. The minimally varied album-titles are increasingly confusing; for instance, *Four Compositions (Quartet) 1983* with George Lewis has now disappeared, leaving the near-identical-sounding set above. Fortunately, there is a straightforward rule of thumb: if Marilyn Crispell is on it, buy it. The Braxton Quartet of 1984–5 was of remarkable vintage and Crispell's Cecil Taylor-inspired but increasingly individual piano-playing was one of its outstanding features. There are unauthorized recordings of this band in circulation, but the Leo sets are absolutely legitimate, and pretty nearly exhaustive; the CDs offer good-quality transfers of the original boxed set, six sides of quite remarkable music that, in conjunction with the other quartet sessions, confirm Braxton's often stated but outwardly improbable interest in the Lennie Tristano school, and in particular the superb harmonic improvisation of Warne Marsh. Those who followed the 1985 British tour may argue about the respective merits of different nights and locations, but there really isn't much to separate the London, Coventry and Birmingham sets for the non-specialist. For reference, the material performed on each pair of discs is as follows: London – Compositions 122 (+ 108A), 40(O), 52, 86 (+ 32 + 96), 115, 105A, piano solo from 96, 40F, 121, 116; Birmingham – 110A (+ 96 + 108B), 69M (+ 10 + 33 + 96), 60 (+ 96 + 108C), 85 (+ 30 + 108D), 105B (+ 5 + 32 + 96), 87 (+ 108C), 23J, 69H (+ 31 + 96), 40(O); Coventry – 124 (+ 30 + 96), 88 (+ 108C + 30 + 96), piano solo from 30, 23G (+ 30 + 96), 40N, 69C (+ 32 + 96), percussion solo from 96, 69F, 69B, bass solo from 96, 6A. It will be noted how often compositions in the above list are 'collaged' with 'Composition No. 96', the 'multiple-line' orchestral piece listed above. It serves as a reference point, most obviously in the Coventry concert. This also includes an intriguing conversation interview with Braxton, conducted by Graham Lock and covering such subjects as Frankie Lymon, John Coltrane, Warne Marsh, chess, the blues, and the nature of music itself.

Though the Birmingham set reaches a hectic climax with an encore performance of 'Kelvin 40(O)' that does further damage to Braxton's undeserved reputation as a po-faced number-cruncher, the extra half-star has to go to Coventry, first for the interview material, but also for the most sheerly beautiful performance in Braxton's entire recorded output, the peaceful clarinet music on 'Composition No. 40(N)' that ends the first set. Nothing else on the remaining five discs quite reaches that peak of perfection. Rosenboom is a poor substitute for Crispell on the 1986 set, but the rhythm section of Dresser or Lindberg and Hemingway was beginning to sound custom-made by this stage, perfectly attuned to the music.

*** Duets 1987

Music & Arts CD 1026 *Braxton; Gino Robair (perc).* 10/87.

Braxton concentrated heavily on duo performance during this period, and this was one of the happiest of his associations. Robair is an enormously talented percussionist, with a thoroughgoing musicality and an instinct for the unexpected. The set consists of three spontaneously improvised pieces, including the delightful 'Ballad For The Children', two compositions by Robair and three by Braxton, including 'No. 136', which is one of the most visual and dramatic in the workbook. The instrumentation isn't specified on the record, but after a few moments this seems quite irrelevant, so consistent is the sound Braxton gets. Not the most spectacular of the records, but warmly recommended.

*** Duets Vancouver 1989

Music & Arts 611 *Braxton; Marilyn Crispell (p).* 6/89.

Duetting with Braxton must be a daunting gig. His London appearances in the 1970s with Derek Bailey (*mutatis mutandis*) were frankly disappointing, largely again because Braxton's idiom is still jazz and Bailey's is something else; the saxophonist's 1976 partnership with Muhal Richard Abrams, a living conduit of the black musical tradition, makes for telling comparison. In that regard Crispell more than holds her own, with a sympathetic awareness that contrasts sharply with the arrogant insouciance one heard from the likes of George Lewis. The Vancouver duets are as warmly approachable as anything Braxton has done. There is no soft-pedalling from Crispell, and she may even be the more compelling voice. There are some signs – minor here – that Braxton is settling into an uneasy alternation between a relatively fixed style and sudden, nihilistic eruptions.

**** Six Monk's Compositions (1987)

Black Saint 120 116 *Braxton; Mal Waldron (p); Buell Neidlinger (b); Bill Osborne (d).* 7/87.

Braxton more than most had eventually to prove himself as a performer of standards. Even before *In The Tradition* it was clear that he was deeply rooted and by no means the scorched-earth revolutionary sceptics liked to think him. The Monk sessions are a triumph. Far from the usual pastiche, these are reinvented versions of a half-dozen obscurer items from the monastic *œuvre*. Pianist Mal Waldron is there to confirm the apostolic succession, but Braxton's readings are thoroughly apostate, furiously paced and unapologetically maximal.

** 19 (Solo) Compositions 1988

New Albion Records NA023 *As above.* 4/88.

In 1968 Braxton set the jazz world back on its heels with an album of solo saxophone improvisations entitled *For Alto*. There was nothing fundamentally new about unaccompanied saxophone – Coleman Hawkins had done it years before with the intriguingly abstract 'Picasso' – but *For Alto* was stingingly powerful, abstract and daring. It was, perhaps, Braxton's finest hour. Twenty years on from that, *19 (Solo) Compositions* is thin stuff indeed, almost as if that remarkable technique has become a polished manner which can be taken on and off at will. 'Compositions' they may be; pointlessly enigmatic they certainly are.

***(*) 2 Compositions (Järvenpää) 1988

Leo CD LR 233 *Braxton; Mircea Stan (tb); Seppo Baron Paakkunainen (ts, bs, f); Pentti Lahti (as, ss, f); Pepa Päivinen (ts, ss, bcl, f); Mikko-Ville Luolajan-Mikkola (vn); Teppo Hauta-aho (b, clo); Jukka Wasama (d).* 11/88.

**** Eugene (1989)

Black Saint 120137 *Braxton; Rob Blakeslee, Ernie Carbajal, Jorn Jensen (t); Mike Heffley, Tom Hill, Ed Kammerer (tb); Thom Bergeron, Jeff Homan, Carl Woideck (reeds); Mike Vannice (reeds, p); Toddy Barton (syn); Joe Robinson (g); Forrest Moyer (b); Charles Dowd (vib, perc); Tom Kelly (perc).* 1/89.

In the autumn of 1988, Braxton toured Finland with an *ad hoc* group called Ensemble Braxtonia. It is to their credit – considerable collective experience notwithstanding – that they coped so well with numbers 144 and 145, and the ease with which these were communicated to a highly enthusiastic audience at the Tampere Jazz Happening (Järvenpää is Sibelius's home and a point of pilgrimage for Finnish musicians) gives some sense of the movement of Braxton's work from the far periphery to something near the hub of contemporary creative music. There is nothing here that would frighten the horses, just intense, very focused music of a high order. Only the recording lets it down.

Eugene is one of Braxton's finest discs, and certainly the most accessible of the larger-group recordings; this features eight compositions dating from 1975 to the present day, and was recorded in Eugene, Oregon, during a 'creative orchestra' tour of the Pacific North-West. Much of the credit for the project has to go to trombonist Mike Heffley, who originally proposed and subsequently organized the tour. The earliest of the pieces, 'Composition No. 45', was written for a free-jazz festival in Baden-Baden and is defined by Braxton in his *Composition Notes C* as 'an extended platform for the challenge of post-Coltrane/Ayler functionalism'. A march, it anticipates the more complex 'Composition No. 58' (not included here) but demonstrates how creatively Braxton has been able to use the large-scale 'outdoor' structures he draws from Henry Brant, Sun Ra and traditional marching music, to open up unsuspected areas of improvisatory freedom; the link with Ayler's apocalyptic 'Truth Is Marching In' is immediately obvious. 'Composition No. 91' is a delicately pointillistic piece with a much more abstract configuration. Less propulsive than 'No. 45' or the more conventional ensemble-and-soloists outline of 'No. 71', it underlines the composer's brilliant grasp of instrumental colour; synthesizer and electric guitar provide some unfamiliar tonalities in the context of Braxton's work and, perhaps in reaction, he limits his own playing to alto saxophone. Braxton's work has taken on an increasingly ritualistic quality, as in the processional opening and steady two-beat pulse of the most recent piece, 'Composition No. 134'. As such, it stands beside the work of Stockhausen and the composers mentioned above. If its underlying philosophy is millennial, its significance is commensurate with that.

*** Eight Duets – Hamburg 1991

Music & Arts CD 710 *Braxton; Peter Niklas Wilson (b). 2/91.*

The duets with Wilson are a bit of a throwback, recalling a set recorded with John Lindberg in the 1980s and released on Cecma. Braxton, who was working in Hamburg on 'Composition No. 151' (see above), often sounds as if he is simply filling in time, though when he does fire, as in 'Composition No. 153' when his alto burns fiercely, the music is very impressive indeed. Braxton uses four instruments twice in all; in addition to alto, he plays flute (brilliantly on the well-established '40(A)'), contrabass clarinet (on which he often recalls Dolphy's duets with Richard Davis) and soprano saxophone, which pairs only rather uneasily with Wilson's refreshingly fleet bass playing.

*** Duo (Amsterdam) 1991

Okkadisk OD 12018 *Braxton; Georg Gräwe (p). 10/91.*

To the best of our understanding, these two long, one short pieces were spontaneously improvised, with no predetermined logic or direction for the music. Even so, there are continual hints and reminders of Braxton's current compositional interests, palindromic shapes and stretching pulses, which suggest the extent to which he used public performance of this sort as a laboratory for ideas which would take on a more detailed form later. Braxton's flute and clarinet playing is extremely impressive, the former especially.

**** Four (Ensemble) Compositions

Black Saint 120124 *Braxton; Robert Rumboltz (t); Roland Dahinden, John Rapson (tb); Don Byron (cl, bcl); Marty Ehrlich (f, picc, cl, as, ts); J.D Parran (f, cl, bcl, acl, bamboo f); Randy McKean (cl, as, bcl); Ted Reichman, Guy Klucevesek (acc); Amina Claudine Myers (org, v); Jay Hoggard (vib, mar); Lynden Achee, Warren Smith (perc). 92.*

***(*) Composition No. 165

New Albion NA 050 *Braxton; University of Illinois Creative Music Orchestra: Thomas Tait, Jeff Helgesen, Judd G Danby (t); Erik Lund, Douglas Farwell, Keith Moore (tb); Jesse Seifert-Gram (tba); Paul Martin Zonn (as, cl, slide sax); Graham Kessler (as, cl); Andrew Mitroff (ts, f); Kevin Engel (ts, bsn, cl); Mark Barone (bs, bcl); Tom Paynter (p); Mark Zanter (g); Drew Krause (syn); Adam Davis (b); Justin Kramer, Tom Sherwood (perc). 2/92.*

The material on *Four (Ensemble) Compositions* is a combination of brand-new compositions – numbers 163 and 164 – with a fascinating performance of the pivotal 'Composition No. 96'. This time, the orchestra includes time-served jazz players and improvisers, and the piece takes on a limber, relaxed charm that it can't altogether claim on the Leo recording. 'Composition No. 165', on the New Albion, is surprisingly direct and unfussy, but it lacks the element of sheer shock that Braxton used to bring, and there are moments when it is drifts perilously close to cosy classicism. Once again, one wonders to what extent these players understand where Braxton is coming from. The wonderful thing about the ensemble on the Black Saint is that they've all been there too. These sessions, like some of their predecessors, pose one intriguing question about Braxton's future work. Will he come to see himself more and more as a composer/conductor, less and less as an improvising instrumentalist; or does he believe that he can sustain both strands? For the sake of improvised music, one hopes so.

*** Duets (1993)

Music & Arts CD 786 *Braxton; Mario Pavone (b). 1/93.*

Pavone has still not made the impact one would have expected, either as a leader (see below under his name) or as a sideman. His response to 'Composition No. 6(O)', which has become standard Braxton fare, is highly individual and even idiosyncratic, preserving the unmistakable contours of one of the saxophonist's most expressive conceptions but also steering it in a new and unexpected direction, where pure melody becomes an issue again. Braxton has played better, and now and again he lapses into a pointless *sotto voce* which tends to lose the thread. A more than acceptable session, though, and dedicated collectors will certainly not be disappointed.

***(*) 9 Standards (Quartet) 1993

Leo CD LR 237/238 2CD *Braxton; Fred Simmons (p); Paul Brown (b); Leroy Williams (d). 2/93.*

An intriguing view of Braxton working, not with a regular ensemble, but with what is effectively a pick-up group, albeit a highly experienced one. Simmons is known to have worked with Dewey Redman, while Brown and Williams were a useful hard-bop partnership in the 1970s. As a working unit, they sound seamless and instinctive. With the exception of Simmons's opening 'In Motion', all the tunes are standards or blowing themes. The set includes Braxton's first documented version of 'On Green Dolphin Street', though we must correct Art Lange's suggestion that Braxton hasn't tackled Coltrane's 'Impressions' more than once before. There are two or three versions currently available, none more straightforwardly in the tradition of the classic quartet than this, though.

Performing 'What's New' on flute is an interesting oddity. This is now one of Braxton's least-used instruments, and it's fascinating to hear him negotiate the changes at some speed (in vertical terms, if not in actual enunciation). 'Cherokee' is not much more than a settler, to follow the Simmons tune and give the band some familiar material to stretch out on. Heard unannounced, Braxton sounds resolutely mainstream, suggesting one of the white saxophonists of the 1950s, curbing any hint of whoop or holler. A fascinating double set, but two more CDs for the Braxtonophile to negotiate.

**** Duo (London) 1993

Leo CD LR 193 *Braxton; Evan Parker (ts). 5/93.*

**** Trio (London) 1993

Leo CD LR 197 *As above, except add Paul Rutherford (tb). 5/93.*

Braxton has been quoted as saying that these recordings gave him more solace in times of doubt and uncertainty than anything he had played for many years. Contrary to expectation, both men sound cool and thoughtful. The understanding with Parker is almost telepathic as intricate, bleached lines spiral upwards at ever higher levels of organization. Parker in particular sounds as though he has awakened ancestral ghosts, at a couple of points sounding disconcertingly like one of Braxton's masters, Warne Marsh, and hovering on the verge of harmonic improvisation throughout the set. In strict harmonic terms, he may even be ahead of his partner in this sort of project. He seems to be able to hear harmonics two places above the ostensible playing position and to bring them into play quite seamlessly and unforcedly.

He is doing the same thing on the trio set, recorded at the same London festival. Rutherford's contribution is to make the music more abstract. Any intention on Braxton's part to restore elements of jazz language is confounded and, as so often in a European environment, he is pushed out into unfamiliar and very challenging territory, where he is obliged to examine his procedures note by note. These are exhilarating performances, among his most radical small-group works.

*****(*) The Braxton Quartet Plays Twelve Braxton Compositions**

Music & Arts CD 835 2CD *Braxton; Marilyn Crispell (p); Mark Dresser (b); Gerry Hemingway (d, mar).* 7/93.

How wonderful to hear the 'classic quartet' recorded again. Everyone who heard the group during their residencies in Santa Cruz and at Yoshi's nightclub in Oakland (near his old stamping ground of Mills College) concedes that it was playing at its peak, while these recordings are probably the best and most generously balanced this line-up had enjoyed to date, which undoubtedly helps the complex, richly textured music to make its maximum impact. Braxton dips back into his composition books to revive some early ideas like '23C' and '40(O)', one of the early Kelvin series, but he also includes some of the more recent, theatre-based works, such as 'Composition 173', later documented with a full orchestral ensemble and released on Black Saint. The choice of material is slightly less varied on the Yoshi's discs which were released on hat ART and are currently deleted, and the playing is rather compressed in places. However, Crispell (who is the only other member of the group photographed on the cover) is in exceptional form and plays with unqualified brilliance from start to finish, demonstrating how far she has travelled since. In this version it sounds inevitably much closer to jazz roots, and the two performances make for a fascinating comparison. For most listeners, though, the best route here is simply to allow these long performances to impinge slowly over time. Whether one recognizes compositional strategies, let alone numbers, is ultimately irrelevant.

*****(*) Braxton At The Leipzig Gewandhaus**

Music & Arts CD 848 *Braxton; Ted Reichman (acc, p).* 8/93.

Like the later duos with Brett Larner, this is fascinating for the way it exposes Braxton to a new and unexpected sound-world. Reichman seems instinctively sympathetic to the five, mostly recent, Braxton compositions, and he brings an intense focus and intelligence to these concert performances. The sound could be better, especially when Reichman switches to piano, but there is no mistaking the quality of the playing throughout.

(***) Composition No. 174

Leo CD LR 217 *Arizona State University Percussion Ensemble.* 2/94.

Though we stand by our assertion that Braxton's music is readily accommodatable on CD, one wonders about this piece, which is written for percussion ensemble and constructed environment and which seems to concern a party of mountaineers and an expedition that is a cross between *The Ascent of F6* and a virtual reality primer to Braxton's compositional method. There are oddities in the registration of the instruments – a broad-ranging percussion ensemble – which demand an answer to the question as to whether the music is played accurately or whether hitches and uncertainties have persisted in this première performance. Unless you are Anthony Braxton, impossible to judge.

*****(*) Duet: Live At Merkin Hall**

Music & Arts CD 949 *Braxton; Richard Teitelbaum (syn).* 4/94.

A hint of irony on the front and back covers. On the front, the old pals face off underneath a poster advertising the Tyson–Spinks face-off. Inside, the two pugilists glower dangerously at one another. As it turns out, this April 1994 recital is much less of an anticlimax than the boxing bout was. Braxton and Teitelbaum are hardly prizefighters and their performing relationship is after this amount of time and shared experience a great deal more Zen-like and undialectical. Indeed, it's hard to hear any element of contention in these two massive pieces at all. In more than an hour, Braxton plays nothing that resembles a set-piece lick or phrase and Teitelbaum resolutely resists anything that sounds like simple accompaniment. Concentrating (in so far as is possible) on one musician rather than the other, it's clear that there is a certain trading of material, but often after many minutes of speculative thought, reintroducing an idea rather than simply throwing it back. Perhaps the best recorded of their encounters, it lacks some of the excitement and bite of earlier records; fascinating music none the less.

***** Knitting Factory (Piano / Quartet): Volume 1**

Leo CD LR 222/223 2CD *Braxton; Marty Ehrlich (as, ss, cl); Joe Fonda (b); Pheeroan akLaff (d).* 94.

***** Piano Quartet, Yoshi's, 1994**

Music & Arts CD 849 4CD *As above, except omit akLaff; add Arthur Fuller (d, perc).* 6/94.

It was no surprise to anyone who has heard him play keyboard that Braxton should want to release something of this sort; he is also an accomplished drummer, and we can't rule out a future percussion project. What is astonishing is that he should have permitted the release of *six* CDs, with the explicit promise of more – volumes two, three? more? – on Leo. These are exclusively jazz repertoire sessions, a detailed and highly respectful examination of composers who have affected Braxton and his music. The range of material is astonishing: Mingus, Brubeck, Monk, Golson, Noble, Miles, Dolphy, Gryce and (on the Leo) Shorter, Mingus and Monk again, Ellington, Tristano. It is difficult to gauge how we might assess these performances if the pianist were anyone but Braxton. In a sense, he does not sound 'like himself'. The switch of register, the harmonic resource, the relative unfamiliarity, all make a profound difference, and yet it is clear that he is directing operations in a quite interventionist way. Ehrlich is a strong player but not a particularly passionate structuralist, and he seems to follow where Braxton leads, allowing his pitching and coloration to be determined quite explicitly by the chords and by a deep-level 'pulse' in the music.

***** Duo (Wesleyan) 1994**

Leo CDLR 228/229 2CD *Braxton; Abraham Adzinyah (perc).* 94.

The percussionist's name is listed first on the cover, seemingly at Braxton's insistence. From a less generous and open-spirited man, one might almost suspect that this selflessness camouflages a recognition that this is less than a central Braxton recording. Overlong at 100 minutes of continuous music spread over two CDs, verbose in the extreme and curiously difficult to relate to Braxton's current projects.

***(*) Small Ensemble Music (Wesleyan) 1994

Splasc(h) 2034 *Braxton; Roland Dahinden (tb); Jeanne Choe (p); other personnel.* 94.

An unexpected artist to launch the usually bop-orientated Italian label's international series, but a chance to revisit one of Braxton's classic compositions. 'Composition No. 107' was originally performed by Garret List and Marianne Schroeder, and it returns here with a pleasurable shock of familiarity. Braxton's duo and trio appearances are also attractively accessible and only the mostly new sextet work packs any kind of alien punch. An unexpected release, but a very welcome one.

(***) Composition No. 173

Black Saint 120166 *Braxton; Melinda Newman (ob); Brandon Evans (sno, bcl); Jennifer Hill (cl); Bo Bell (bsn); Nickie Braxton, Danielle Langston (vn); Brett W Larner (koto); Kevin O'Neil (g); Sandra Miller, Jacob Rosen (clo); Dirck Westervelt, Joe Fonda (b); Josh Rosenblatt (perc); actors.* 12/94.

'"I hear an influence coming in from the CKA areas," cried Miss Tishingham' is about the most illuminating commentary on this one. Another of Braxton's multi-media pieces, it transfers to disc no more incompletely and insecurely than its successor (which was recorded first). Like 'No. 174', it has moments of real musical beauty, especially here when the woodwinds are soloing; but to what extent the 'score' can be separated from the *mise en scène* and the stage apparatus is beyond our competence. It may still be jazz music, but not as we know it, Jim.

***(*) Seven Standards 1995

Knitting Factory KFW 168 *Braxton; Dave Douglas (t); Thomas Chapin (as, picc, f); Mario Pavone (b); Pheeroan akLaff (d).* 1/95.

The sort of line-up you jot down on the back of an envelope late at night with no expectation that it will ever happen. For us, this harks back to the group with Kenny Wheeler and Chick Corea, with Braxton this time in Chick's role, playing the entire set at the piano. Dave Holland was the bassist in that early group and the nominal co-leader here, Mario Pavone is, if anything, even more emphatic. In the midst of a fabulously productive time for Braxton, he sounds delighted by the company of Douglas and the late Tom Chapin, playing unhurried and completely idiomatic versions of Charlie Parker's 'Dewey Square' and Monk's 'Eronel'. Not by any means the most virtuosic pianist on the planet, nevertheless he more than holds his own, though the record is perhaps more interesting for what it contains of the trumpeter and of a saxophonist whose career was tragically foreshortened.

**** 11 Compositions (Duo) 1995

Leo CDLR 244 *Braxton; Brett Larner (koto).* 3/95.

Braxton acknowledges the prior example of Tony Scott, Joe Harriott and Don Cherry in introducing the multi-stringed *koto* to this kind of improvisational environment. His own intentions are no less supra-national, even cosmic, and with Larner he creates a web of sounds of great complexity and gentleness, hard to locate culturally but equally and typically hard to tie to 'storylines' other than those which determine areas of sound and time. 'Composition 72H' is said to be 'solemn and grave and without forgiveness' and, later, like a 'slow freight train', one of those Mid-West monsters which despite its movement gives an impression of eternity. In 'Composition 72F', another of the series, the voices murmur up and down, one slowly ceding to the other, one quietly dominating. A near-perfect album of duo improvisation, unexpected in sonority, rich in association, played magnificently.

**** Four Compositions (Quartet) 1995

Braxton House 5 *Braxton; Ted Reichman (acc); Joe Fonda (b); Kevin Norton (d, vib, perc).* 8/95.

Finely detailed and refreshingly clear-sighted performances of four closely related compositions – numbers 181 to 184 – which very clearly establish the lineage of the recent Ghost Trance Musics back to the improvisational structures of past years. If there is an obvious point of comparison for this record, it is early recordings with Chick Corea, Dave Holland and Barry Altschul. The dynamics and the relaxed, almost meditative drive are the same. The soundscape is very different, of course, but identifying the similarities once again focuses attention on how consistent Braxton's course has been. Brightly recorded in performance at Wesleyan University, the music communicates well on CD.

**** Sextet (Istanbul) 1995

Braxton House 1 2CD *Braxton; Roland Dahinden (tb); Jason Hwang (vn); Ted Reichman (acc); Joe Fonda (b); Kevin Norton (d, vib, mar, perc).* 10/95.

This is perhaps the clearest and most coherent invocation of Braxton's newest line of development, what he refers to as the Ghost Trance Musics. These long, powerful improvisations, recorded at a jazz festival in Turkey, attempt to put players and listeners close to the heightened consciousness experienced in Native-American and Eastern ritual, prolonged improvisation of an unmannered, ego-less sort that for the first time seems closer to the long-form, process-dominated music of AMM and other British ensembles than to the jazz tradition (though, of course, Braxton continues to espouse this line as well, in both musical language and instrumentation). 'Composition No. 186' is titanic, almost exactly an hour in length and reminiscent in its focus and intensity of some of the late Coltrane sessions when standard material was shredded, reconstituted and finally re-created as something new and transcendent. Though not based on any recognizable melodic material, Braxton's usual dependency on simple motifs and cells is less evident here because in sheer durational terms the development is much further from the statement. It would be a mistake, though, to suggest that this is dramatically different or apart from the continuum of his work. Like Miles Davis, Braxton seems consumed with a need to change, but in change he always remains consistent with his own ongoing concerns.

**** Ensemble (New York) 1995

Braxton House 7 *Braxton; J.D Parran (cl, bsx); Lily White (as); Aaron Stewart (ts); Libby Van Cleve (eng hn); Melinda Newman (ob); Jacquie Carrasco, Gwen Laster (vn); Nioka Workman (clo); Joe Fonda (b); Kevin Norton (d, vib, perc).* 11/95.

****** Octet (New York) 1995**

Braxton House 6 *Braxton; Roland Dahinden (tb); Brandon Evans (f, wood f, bcl, ss, ts); Andre Vida (f, ss, as, ts, bs); Jason Hwang (vn); Ted Reichman (acc); Joe Fonda (b); Kevin Norton (d, vib, perc).* 11/95.

The group of the moment caught live at a special Braxton event held at the Knitting Factory in New York City. Having surrounded himself with like-minded multi-reed persons, Braxton himself carries less of the sheer weight of the music than he once did. Now that there are second-generation players around who understand his premisses as well as his intentions, he has been able to devolve at least some of the responsibilities of leadership. The period of Ghost Trance Musics is pretty well established by now. If some of this and other records are reminiscent of Minimalism, that is not accidental. Braxton has not been entirely forthcoming about stylistic antecedents for this phase of his career, perhaps because in the past he has been able to espouse unfashionable sources. Here he runs the risk of *appearing* to jump on a bandwagon that has already begun to lose momentum. There were, of course, Minimalist elements in his work before now – less Glass and Reich than Young and Riley – and these have been more or less widely acknowledged. It is surprising to find them occupying the foreground at this juncture, but there is no mistaking the vitality and the rigour with which Braxton has invested them.

Both records contain just one long composition. *Ensemble*, with its expanded sound-palette (and some striking compositional echoes of Ornette Coleman's early experiments with legitimate formations), is devoted to 'Composition No. 187'. This is one of the best representations of his 'Tri-Centric' philosophy, the three-in-one of structure, ideas and ritual; architecture, philosophy and ritual; symbolic function, structured space and mutable logic. The balance of voices is clearly still very important, but more so is the need to read off very different parameters in the music, functioning all at once. 'Composition No. 188', which occupies the second of the two records from the event, is a more straightforward piece in some respects, but also more abrasively rhythmic and propulsive. Both are absolutely compelling and should be sought out by anyone interested in the future direction of American music.

***** Solo Piano (Standards) 1995**

No More Records No. 2 2CD *Braxton (p solo).* 12/95.

Stories abound of Braxton playing piano and even drums behind young musicians in informal settings and at masterclasses. It was presumably only a matter of time before a solo piano album came along – and it would have been worth taking odds that it would be a double set. Strictly speaking, this isn't a standards set at all, but a collection of jazz compositions. Coltrane's 'Central Park West', one of the few tunes on which he didn't solo, is an interesting choice, with McCoy Tyner's flowing solo replicated in more angular and abrasive form; 'Straight Street' is less familiar and less satisfactory. A couple of takes of 'Pannonica' and one of 'Skippy' establish Braxton's relationship to Monk. There are a couple of Mingus compositions and material by Wayne Shorter, Mal Waldron (two versions of 'Dee's Dilemma') and Benny Golson. The first of the two discs is perhaps the stronger, and there is every reason to think that an edited single would have been quite adequate in this case. Braxton's debt to Dave Brubeck, with whom he once recorded, is pretty clear, but he is as much his own man on piano as on reeds. An accomplished, thoroughly enjoyable record.

***** Composition 192**

Leo Records CDLR 251 *Braxton; Lauren Newton (v).* 6/96.

This piece for two musicians in a constructed environment consisting of a fairground Wheel of Fortune and a video projection of the environs of New York City through a car windshield is said to be the first of Braxton's new cycle of 'Ghost Trance Musics'. This is what Braxton has described as a 'new image logic', seemingly a way of converting ordinary, even domestic environments into cosmic spaces by endless, weaving melodies, here played on saxophones and clarinets, while Lauren Newton recites the letters of the alphabet. This was the first encounter between Braxton and Newton, curiously enough. Whatever she thought and however much she understood of the music's premisses, she enters into it with great enthusiasm and with a wry humour.

*****(*) Tentet (New York) 1996**

Braxton House 4 *Braxton; Roland Dahinden (tb); J.D Parran (acl, picc); Brandon Evans (ss, as, ts, bcl, f); Andre Vida (ss, as, ts, bs); Jacquie Carrasco, Gwen Laster (vn); Ted Reichman (acc); Joe Fonda (b); Kevin Norton (d, vib, perc).* 6/96.

A large, saxophone-dominated ensemble for 'Composition No. 193' and a very fine performance from all concerned. Reichman is profoundly clued in to Braxton's music, and the two fiddlers both contribute substantially to the very textured and modulated sound Braxton has tried to achieve with this recent work. Generically, it seems to sit somewhere between his pulse-driven and jazz-derived works and his more obviously theatrical output. The interweaving of the horns suggests some of Stan Kenton's more spacious endeavours, and there are phrases here and there towards the end which recall Bob Graettinger arrangements, so perhaps Braxton has added yet another arrow to his quiver of stylistic derivations.

***** Composition No. 102**

Braxton House 3 *Braxton; Sam Hoyt, Steve Laronga, Zach See (t); Taylor Bynum (flhn); Daniel Young (c); John Speck (tb); Stewart Gillmor (euph); Niko Higgins, David Kasher, Matthew Lee, Allen Livermore (as); Jackson Moore (as, cl); April Monroe, Christine Whitledge (f); Rafael Cohel (ob); Sung Kim (hca); Michael Buescher, Ronaldo Garces, Eric Ronick, Michael Thompson, Kevin Uehinger (p); Edmond Cho, Nathaniel Delafield, Thom Loubet, Kevin O'Neil (g); Nickie Braxton (vn); Vivian Lee, Anil Seth (clo); Brett Larner (koto); Dave Gilbert (g); Michael Lenore (b); Rene Muslin, Josh Rosenblatt (perc).* 96.

Originally written in 1982 and premièred in Houston, Texas, 'Composition No. 102' is scored for orchestra and puppet theatre and cuts across European, American and African folklores to create an environment of calm mystery. Like much of Braxton's work, so forbiddingly complex on the surface, it is made up of relatively simple materials, rising and falling figures, shifts of dynamics and attack, and rhythmic variation right across the field of the orchestra. Like many of the composer's recent works, it probably makes less than complete sense as a purely aural experience and it would be wonderful to see a video version of a complete performance. This – or some more sophisticated audio-visual technology – seems an inevitable next step for Braxton. Much as we admire the music here, it is difficult to be excited about it. The Wesleyan orchestra is well-drilled and seemingly very precise, though how much of its occasional stiffness is intended (perhaps to suggest or reflect puppet movements) again remains hard to assess.

Joshua Breakstone (born 1955)

GUITAR

Studied at Berklee and then followed a neoclassic path, playing open-toned electric guitar in a conventional bop format.

***** Evening Star**

Contemporary CCD-14040-2 *Breakstone; Jimmy Knepper (tb); Tommy Flanagan (p); Dave Shapiro (b); Keith Copeland (d).* 89.

***** 9 By 3**

Contemporary CCD-14062-2 *Breakstone; Dennis Irwin (b); Kenny Washington (d).* 90.

***** Sittin' On the Thing With Ming**

Capri 74042-2 *Breakstone; Kenny Barron (p); Ray Drummond (b); Keith Copeland (d).* 1/93.

*****(*) Let's Call This Monk!**

Double-Time DTRCD-121 *Breakstone; Dennis Irwin (b); Mickey Roker (d).* 12/96.

***** This Just In ...**

Double-Time DTRCD-149 *Breakstone; Sid Simmons (p); Dennis Irwin (b); Kenny Washington (d).* 2/99.

Breakstone loves the sound of traditional jazz guitar, as in cool, clear, single-note lines delivered with a soft articulation and a tone that insinuates rather than jumping out of his amplifier. He can peel melodies off the frets with little effort, but sometimes his manner is so relaxed that his improvisations go to sleep; with impeccable but deferential rhythm sections on most of these records, that's a small but significant problem. *Evening Star* has Jimmy Knepper to add some spice to the line-up, but more typical are the several sessions with Barron at the piano. *9 By 3* was cut straight after a tour in which Breakstone had no pianist on hand, and the session is slightly looser as a result – though not necessarily better.

Sittin' On The Thing With Ming goes off at a busy pace with the title-tune and shifts through the expected cadences of such a session without much surprise. All but one of the tunes are originals, which is something of a departure for the guitarist, but his writing is scholarly rather than exciting. Barron, Drummond and Copeland add the extra notch with their unimpeachable class.

The surprise record in the batch is the recent *Let's Call This Monk!*. Breakstone and Monk may not have much in common, but the lean aspects of the guitarist's style sit very comfortably with the ten Monk tunes on display here. Breakstone picks some of the toughest and least tractable tunes from the book – 'Work', 'Let's Call This', 'Brilliant Corners' – and plays them with a kind of deadpan bite that makes one hear the material afresh. Irwin and Roker make an immaculate team, and their unfussy and tersely swinging style suits the occasion perfectly.

This Just In ... is a perfectly plausible continuation but, with so much else going on with the guitar in jazz at present, Breakstone may need to do something startling to gain the attention of new listeners. This is another pacific set of bop material (he even starts with 'Bebop' itself), played skilfully and painlessly.

Michael Brecker (born 1949)

TENOR SAXOPHONE, EWI

One of the most admired and emulated saxophonists in contemporary jazz. He began playing in rock and soul bands in the late 1960s, worked with Horace Silver and Billy Cobham in the '70s and put together the very successful Steps Ahead group in 1979. His tenure as a session-man has polished his style into something superbly confident and muscular, a Coltrane without the questing inner turmoil. After many years as a superleague sideman, he finally began making discs under his own name in 1987, and has only infrequently chosen to continue that regimen.

***** Michael Brecker**

GRP 050113-2 *Brecker; Kenny Kirkland (ky); Pat Metheny (g); Charlie Haden (b); Jack DeJohnette (d).* 87.

****(*) Don't Try This At Home**

GRP 42229 *Brecker; Don Grolnick, Herbie Hancock, Joey Calderazzo (p); Mark O'Connor (vn); Mike Stern (g); Charlie Haden, Jeff Andrews (b); Jack DeJohnette, Adam Nussbaum, Peter Erskine (d).* 88.

The sax-playing one of the Brecker brothers has appeared on some 500 record dates but has still made only a handful of discs as sole leader. His steely, brilliant sense of structure ensures that almost every solo he plays is impressive; whether he is emotionally involving may depend on the listener's willingness to believe.

Michael Brecker, his 1987 debut, suggested that he had been unreasonably shy about recording as a leader: his own compositions, 'Sea Glass' and 'Syzygy', are attractive if not exactly haunting, while producer Don Grolnick's tunes elicit some suitably herculean solos. The interplay with DeJohnette inevitably recalls something of the Coltrane–Elvin Jones partnership, while Kirkland, Haden and the unusually restrained Metheny combine to create a super-session of genuine commitment. But *Don't Try This At Home* seemed like a too casual follow-up, with several of the pieces sounding like left-overs from the first session and Brecker cruising through the record in his session-man identity rather than imposing a leader's presence.

***** Now You See It ... (Now You Don't)**

GRP 9622 *Brecker; Jim Beard, Joey Calderazzo (ky); Jon Herington (g); Victor Bailey, Jay Anderson (b); Adam Nussbaum, Omar Hakim (d); Don Alias, Steve Berrios, Milton Cardona (perc).* 90.

Brecker's third record as a leader is a mixed success. Too few of the eight themes are truly memorable or demanding on anything other than a technical level, and some of the synthesizer orchestration is a distraction rather than a benefit. The best jazz comes in the tracks where the saxophonist gets a clear run at the listener: on 'Peep', which turns into a kind of abstract funk, and 'The Meaning Of The Blues', which is unadorned tenor-plus-rhythm. The slow intensification of the saxophonist's improvisation on 'Minsk' is the one moment when Brecker best displays his mastery: it's staggeringly well played. Don Grolnick's production is snappy and clean without being as glaring as many fusion records.

***** Tales From The Hudson**

Impulse! 051191-2 *Brecker; Joey Calderazzo, McCoy Tyner (p); Pat Metheny (g); Dave Holland (b); Jack DeJohnette (d); Don Alias (perc).* 96.

***** Two Blocks From The Edge**

Impulse! 051261-2 *Brecker; Joey Calderazzo (p); James Genus (b); Jeff Tain Watts (d); Don Alias (perc).* 98.

Brecker continues to be sparing with his own records. These two are rewarding on their own terms without throwing out a masterpiece. The leader contributes several themes to *Tales From The Hudson* but only three to *Two Blocks From The Edge*, and he seems little interested in composing. There's the expected quota of hard-nosed tenor playing on each disc, and he varies his methods from solo to solo: 'African Skies' on the first is an explosive display of licks, while gentler tempos elicit a longer line. Ballads, though, still seem carved out of an impersonal block, and his reluctance to characterize remains a source of frustration. There's another all-star feel to *Hudson*, with Tyner sitting in on two tracks, but the smaller and less imposing group on *Two Blocks* is really a better situation for Brecker: he can play powerfully without seeming to compete. Enough moments of excitement on both to satisfy his followers, of whom there are many.

*****(*) Time Is Of The Essence**

Verve 547844-2 *Brecker; Larry Goldings (org); Pat Metheny (g); Elvin Jones, Jeff Tain Watts, Bill Stewart (d). n.d.*

Brecker has fronted some fine bands before, and the three different quartets on this disc – each distinguished by a different drummer – are at least as strong as any of them. He chose Larry Goldings as Larry Goldings, rather than as an organ-player for the date, and with Metheny digging into his funky rather than impressionist bag, the results are only occasionally like the world's highest-paid bar band. As a mix of personalities, it's a blend worth sampling, but the main effect may be on Brecker himself. At fifty, he's currently relaxing perhaps as much as he'll ever let himself relax. Chord-sequences are harvested for notes as intensively as ever, but one feels that Brecker wants to throttle back now at moments when he might have gone for broke before. The warm undertow of Goldings's chords and pedal bass and the lyricism of Metheny (however harsh he might want to be, Pat is always going to sound fundamentally lyrical) add up to a disc which, for all its muscle-flexing, a sympathetic listener can almost cosy up to.

Randy Brecker (born 1945)

TRUMPET

The older Brecker sibling left college to go on the road, stayed in Europe for a time, and then returned home to join R&B giants, Blood, Sweat And Tears. Unlike Michael, who has devoted himself to a post-Coltrane idiom, Randy still likes to dabble in fusion. He has recorded surprisingly little under his own name.

***** Into The Sun**

Concord Vista CCD 3591 *Brecker; Dave Bargeron (tb); David Taylor (btb, tba); David Sanborn (as); Bob Mintzer (bcl); Keith Underwood (af, bf); Lawrence Feldman (bf); Gil Goldstein (ky); Adam Rogers (g); Bakithi Kumalo (b); Jonathan Joseph (d); Café (perc); Maúcha Adnét (v); Richard Sussman (syn prog).* 97.

Brecker has always been most successful when working his own version of jazz-rock. It surfaces again on the recent *Into The Sun*. Unlike most other trumpeters in the field, Brecker has never remotely sounded like a Miles clone. If anything, his tonality comes from Dizzy and Freddie Hubbard, and both influences are still in place today, even though he has developed a strongly individual voice along the way. 'The Sleaze Factor' and 'Just Between Us' are the strongest tracks on the Concord, relying on a careful integration of parts and on strong, concise soloing. One quality Brecker does share with Miles is an ability to make single notes and tiny phrases stand out and represent much. The album depends largely on subtle colorations from an unusual array of horns, mostly favouring lower pitches.

The Brecker Brothers

GROUP

Michael and Randy Brecker began working as co-bandleaders in 1975 and scored some very successful albums before they chose to disband the group in 1982. They re-formed as an occasional recording and touring collaboration in the '90s.

***** The Brecker Brothers**

Arista 74321 22103-2 *Randy Brecker (t, flhn); Michael Brecker (ss, ts); David Sanborn (as); Don Grolnick (ky); Bob Mann (g); Will Lee (b); Harvey Mason (d); Ralph MacDonald (perc).* 1/75.

***** Detente**

Arista 74321 31313-2 *As above, except add Steve Khan, Hiram Bullock (g), Steve Gadd (d); omit Sanborn, Mann, Mason.* 77.

***** Heavy Metal Be-Bop**

Arista 74321 19257-2 *Randy Brecker (t, ky); Michael Brecker (ss, ts); Barry Finnerty (g); Neil Jason (b); Terry Bozzio (d); Sammy Figueroa, Rafael Cruz (perc).* 78.

***** Straphangin'**

Arista 74321 31312-2 *Randy Brecker (t, flhn); Michael Brecker (ss, ts); Mary Gray (ky); Barry Finnerty (g); Marcus Miller (b); Richie Morales (d); Sammy Figueroa, Manolo Badrena (perc).* 81.

***** The Brecker Brothers Collection Vol. 1**
RCA ND 90442 *As above Arista discs.* 75–81.

***** The Brecker Brothers Collection Vol. 2**
RCA ND 83076 *As above.* 75–81.

*****(*) Priceless Jazz Collection**
GRP 059948-2 *Randy Brecker (t, flhn); Michael Brecker (ss, ts); David Sanborn (as); Robbie Kilgore, George Whitty, Dean Brown, Mike Stern (g); James Genus, Will Lee, Armand Sabal-Leco (b); Steve Jordan, Max Risenhoover, Dennis Chambers (d); Steve Thornton, Don Alias (perc). n.d.*

***** Return Of The Brecker Brothers**
GRP 059684-2 *Similar to above. n.d.*

***** Out Of The Loop**
GRP 059784-2 *Similar to above. n.d.*

The most popular fusion band of their era: where Weather Report were Zawinul's electro-impressionists, the Breckers were a playing band, overloaded with chops but often creating music of drilled excitement. Michael Brecker, the foremost technician of his era, was a soloist of ferocious power, and the essentially more lyrical Randy made a sometimes piquant contrast to his brother, although that comes through more effectively on their GRP albums. The Arista material will be nostalgic for many who return to it in the CD era: dog-eared copies of the original vinyl must still sit on the dustier shelves of former followers of the style. These records are usually dated by their wah-wah guitars and rhythm sections, which sometimes sound as if they're trying to play a sort of muscle-bound disco music. But a lot of the original excitement remains. Some of the freshness went out of their albums as they neared the end of the band's original life, but the insuperable skills of the players persist, and both the Breckers were seeking a genuine musical result, rather than the confections of smooth jazz. We're grading all the albums the same because, despite any differences in style, they really do all emerge in much the same way. Either of the two RCA collections is a good bet for the curious.

After individual success during the '80s, the Breckers decided to get together again for occasional recording projects. The 1992 *Return* traded slightly more on atmosphere than on punch and made deeper use of studio resources; but most will recognize it all as business as usual, continued on *Out Of The Loop*. But the mid-price *Priceless Jazz Collection*, which is effectively a cheap best-of covering the two GRP discs, is the best single way to put the BBs on your shelf.

Buddy Bregman

COMPOSER, ARRANGER

Bregman worked in Hollywood in the '50s, mostly accompanying and arranging for singers such as Bing Crosby, but he made several records in a contemporary big-band idiom for Verve.

*****(*) Swinging Kicks**
Verve 559514-2 *Conte Candoli, Maynard Ferguson, Ray Linn, Pete Candoli, Conrad Gozzo (t); Milt Bernhart, George Roberts, Frank Rosolino, Lloyd Ulyate (tb); Herb Geller, Bud Shank (as); Georgie Auld, Bob Cooper, Ben Webster, Stan Getz (ts); Jimmy Giuffre (bs); André Previn, Paul Smith (p); Al Hendrickson (g); Joe Mondragon (b); Stan Levey, Alvin Stoller (d).* 12/56.

Bregman is a kibitzer in jazz history, but his few Verve dates as a leader are great fun and this one has kept its sparkle. Seventeen tracks, many of them not even broaching the two-minute barrier, offer tiny episodes of West Coast jazz at its wittiest. The group is split into big-band, quartet, quintet, sextet and septet formations, and the record ends on a duet for Ben Webster and André Previn! 'Mulliganville' is a clever take on the saxophonist's œuvre, 'Terror Ride' seems petty mild, and elsewhere there are good opportunities for Conte Candoli, Shank and Rosolino to have their say. Getz makes one imperious appearance on 'Honey Chile'. Remastered with superb crispness, and the period cover shot is intact.

Dave Brennan

BANJO, GUITAR

A veteran of northern trad, Brennan has led his Jubilee Jazz Band for more than 30 years.

****(*) Take Me To The Mardi Gras**
Lake LACD 20 *Brennan; Pat O'Brien (t, v); Dale Vickers (tb); Frank Brooker (cl, as, ts); Mick Kennedy (b); Terry Kennedy (d).* 4/90–2/91.

Dave Brennan's anniversary set is scarcely a milestone in British trad, but it sums up both the pros and cons of the genre. The material is determinedly unhackneyed and includes Henry Allen's 'Ride Red Ride', 'Rip 'Em Up Joe', 'Eccentric Rag' and 'Dauphine Street Blues'; the playing ranges from rumbustious energy to a surprisingly delicate touch on the filigree treatment of 'Mood Indigo'; the echoes of George Lewis and Bunk Johnson are integrated into a home-grown spirit which is by now just as 'authentic'; and the best of the individual contributions, particularly Dale Vickers's trombone solos, are impressive. On the other side of the coin are the vocals (always the least appealing aspect of British trad); the frequently flat dynamics; and a sense of *ennui* which the restrictive practices of the genre encourage rather than exonerate. But it would be churlish to deny the best of this music. The recording is truthful and lifelike.

John Wolf Brennan

PIANO, KEYBOARDS, ELECTRONICS, COMPOSER

An Irishman who has been based on the continent for many years, Brennan has an utterly distinctive touch at the keyboard and is the composer of complex but intensely beautiful themes which are almost impossible to locate stylistically.

****(*) Mountain Hymn**
L + R 45002 *Brennan; Urs Leimgruber (ts, ss, bsx, bamboo f, etc.).* 9/85.

He has gratifyingly taken to heart our previous characterization of him as combining the romanticism of his Irish roots and the watchmaker precision of his Swiss home. In company with

Leimgruber he perhaps demonstrates more of the second, constructing secure but never entirely comfortable harmonic contexts for the reedman's wilder excursions. The sheer diversity of sound here is both the greatest plus and the most serious failing. It is an album without much consistency of direction and, if this is the overall weakness and failing of Brennan's output – a sequence of brilliant miniatures without much in the way of solid architecture – that has certainly been addressed and answered in more recent years.

**** Entupadas**

CreativeWorks CD 1013 *Brennan; Corinna Curschellas (v, dulcimer, kalimba, acc, f, police siren, perc).* 11/85.

***** An Chara**

L + R 45007 *As above.* 1/86.

We have often found Curschellas to be a rather overpowering singer. This may simply be male anxiety about a strong female artist; if so, the lowly grading for *Entupadas* is only really because it seems a less-than-successful Brennan record; he is pretty much sidelined. *An Chara* is a much more generous and accurate representation, and the sound for both is more fluently directed.

***** Henceforward**

Core COCD 900871 *Brennan; Christy Doran (g, effects).* 5/88.

**** Polyphyllum**

L + R 45013 *As above.* 5/89.

***** MAP (Music For Another Planet)**

L + R 45021 *As above, except add Norma Winstone (v).* 8/88, 5/89.

Doran is unmistakably a soulmate, a musician who is as much at ease with the intricacies of form as with a lachrymose ballad, as devoted to the mechanics of music as to its emotional tugs and rip-tides. Of these albums, only *Polyphyllum* fails to deliver that hard-to-master combination, and again mainly because Brennan seems rather incidental to parts of it, unable to stamp his considerable personality on the music. His piano playing has a flowing grace and elegance, but it lacks the rugged left-hand substructure one normally expects from a 'jazz' musician, and this may be why Brennan appeals only slowly to jazz fans, and then only to those who like their music to levitate and break free of the chords and the basic time-signatures.

The addition of Winstone on the ethereal *MAP* (which may be a reference to the soprano part at the end of Schoenberg's Second String Quartet, with its reference to 'airs from other planets') was a master-stroke. A more sensitive and responsive singer than Curschellas, she is also far more deeply rooted in jazz, and she helps to restore just some of the foundations we feel the lack of elsewhere in JWB's otherwise sterling work.

***** The Beauty Of Fractals**

Creative Works CW 10171 *Brennan (ky solo).* 12/88.

****(*) Iritations**

Creative Works CW 1021 *As above, except add Martin Spahler (sound objects).* 4/90.

***** Ten Zentences**

L + R CDLR 45066 *Brennan; Daniele Patumi (b).* 5/91.

The title of *Iritations*, which is characterized as a 'nonsolopiano' project, may well be intended as a reference to Erik Satie. Certainly there is something of the playful insouciance of the half-Scot, half-Frenchman's *Vexations* embedded in these intriguing performances, which draw their additional resonance from Spahler's acoustic environments. *Fractals* is closer to his more familiar improvisational language, an elegantly crafted record with a deftly sequenced programme of pieces drawn from both live and studio tapes. As a guide to what Brennan is about, there is probably nowhere better to start. The duos with Patumi anticipate some of their interplay with Pago Libre. Patumi is highly sensitive to the creative potential of space and silence, and he exploits both to the full on these intriguing miniatures. Brennan himself is more expansive than one would expect and more linear in development. He sounds wonderful, though.

***** Text, Context, Co-Text, Co-Co-Text**

Creative Works CW 1025 *Brennan (p solo).* 94.

A broodingly thoughtful album containing music as thoughtfully self-referential as the title might suggest. Almost every piece seems to be a meditation on its own origins, tightly wrapped into one or two basically simple ideas. There is one piece for prepared piano, deployed intelligently and with great feeling. It comes a little unexpectedly in the middle of the session, which one finds oneself listening to almost in a trance. Delightful music for the mind and the heart.

*****(*) Shooting Stars And Traffic Lights**

Bellaphon CDLR 45090 *Brennan; John Voirol (ts, ss); Tscho Theissing (vn); Daniele Patumi (b); Alex Cline (d, perc).* 95.

The other members of Pago Libre might not thank us for including this here rather than separately, but it does seem very much to be Brennan's group. He is not always the dominant instrumental voice, but he is certainly the driving force in the music, shaping, texturing and stirring the forms. Theissing and Patumi interact with him magnificently, and one can almost imagine a 'string' trio without horn or percussion working almost as well. A leaven of humour does no harm at all.

***** Moskau-Petuschki / Felix-Szenen**

Leo Lab CD 034 *Brennan; Lars Lindvall (t, flhn); Martin Mayes (hn, v); Marion Namestnik, Tscho Theissing (vn); Daniele Patumi (b); Oscar Bingisser, Liana Schwanja (v).* 7/94, 6/95.

Two superb theatre-pieces inspired by the work of Wenedikt Jerofejew and Robert Walser respectively, *Moskau-Petuschki* and the *Felix-Szenen* take Brennan a further step along the road. Jerofejew was an alcoholic who wrote only incidentally, and yet his work has a dreamed magnificence one would simply not find in a writer more literary and aware. Brennan's 'micromonotonal' poem is broodingly beautiful, not so much intense as highly focused, with the heightened perception one might associate with drunkenness (the poet's, not the composer's!).

We find the Walser material less immediately compelling, a somewhat different sound-world despite the similarity of instrumentation – violin, trumpet, piano and bass, as against violin, horn, piano and bass for the Jerofejew piece – and a more openly expressive setting that lacks the prismatic exactness of the earlier piece.

****** ... through the Ear of a Raindrop**

Leo CD LR 254 *Brennan; Paul Rutherford (tb); Evan Parker (ts, ss); Peter Whyman (bcl); Chris Cutler (d, perc); Julie Tippetts (v).* 7/97.

And, at last, the record we always knew he would make: a rich and vividly textured marriage of poetry – Shakespeare, Poe, Heaney, Paulin and Paula Meehan, together with a poem by Julie Tippetts – and instruments. The three horns blend together wonderfully and unexpectedly, with Parker working in the quieter and less abrasive style that he occasionally brings to vocal accompaniments. Rutherford is a poet himself and is constantly responsive to the cadence and fall of words. Here he surpasses himself. Someone somewhere down the line should consider prising Julie away from home and a long-standing duo with the old man and getting her to record a duo set with Brennan. He seems the ideal foil, the perfect yin–yang partner for her own wonderful synthesis of the everyday and the magical. On every track here they have things to communicate to one another, and the lilt and flow of Brennan's piano playing is endlessly attractive.

*****(*) Wake Up Call: Live In Italy**

Leo CD LR 272 *Brennan; Tscho Theissing (vn, v); Arkady Shilkloper(frhn, flhn); Daniele Patumi (b).* 9/97.

Remarkably, Pago Libre has been functioning as a unit for more than a decade; since most of that time it has gone undocumented at festivals and concerts, it is appropriate that this should be a live release, recorded to two-track at the Sol-Fest open-air festival, Sicily. Theissing's title-piece gets the set under way with a gentle urgency. Brennan is featured on his own 'Toccattacca', a brilliant sequence that includes Fibonacci series, palindromic inversions and a kind of sun-kissed serialism. Shilkloper switches to flugelhorn for both his own 'Folk Song' and Brennan's 'Kabak', the latter an unexpectedly funky theme that provides the record's main climax. Long may Pago Libre continue and thrive.

*****(*) Momentum**

Leo CD LR 274 *Brennan; Gene Coleman (bcl, melodica); Christian Wolfarth (perc).* 10/98.

Live duos and trios from a wonderfully confected group. Brennan's prepared-piano sounds are very different from those deployed by, say, Keith Tippett; their strangeness is more unsettling. In conjunction with percussion and then with bass clarinet on the opening 'Robots Don't Cough' and 'Poco Loco' with Wolfarth and Coleman respectively, Brennan takes you into a realm which is almost beyond human music; if the record has a running theme, it is the disjunctions between the human and the machine, even a machine as familiar as the piano and as humanely vocalized as the melodica. Wonderful stuff again from the Irishman.

Patrick Brennan (born 1954)

ALTO SAXOPHONE

Detroit-born Brennan won Cadence and Coda accolades with his very first recording, back in 1982, but hasn't broken through to the big time. Roscoe Mitchell and Ornette Coleman are the only obvious influences on saxophone.

***** Saunters, Walks, Ambles**

CIMP 187 *Brennan; Lisle Ellis (b).* 9/98.

A rather misleadingly laid-back title for an album of such focus and intensity, unless perhaps Brennan is aware that it was no less an authority than Henry David Thoreau who declared that sauntering and ambling were the key disciplines for an American philosopher. Duos of this kind are always demanding, but Brennan has attempted to lend a bit of familiarity to his slightly esoteric approach by including two Monk tunes, the opening 'Crepuscule With Nellie' and two versions of 'Misterioso'.

'Nellie' is by far the longest thing on the set, and it serves as an introduction and warm-up number. It's only when Brennan and Ellis really get into the meat of their encounter on the four-part 'saunter, walk, amble' that things heat up. Brennan has a rather clenched and inconsistent tone, but Ellis is wise to every harmonic waver and shift and he stays with the line, whatever is going on. The key track is Roscoe Mitchell's composition, 'Nonaah', which brings out the best in both men. 'Bucket-A-Blood' is for unaccompanied saxophone and suggests that Brennan might yet do interesting things in that direction.

Willem Breuker (born 1944)

SAXOPHONES, CLARINETS, RECORDER

There has been a hint of Year Zero in modern Dutch music, a response to the (in some cases) near total destruction of the cultural infrastructure – buildings, people, Willem Pijper's entire MSS – during the war. Breuker has thrived in its blasted spaces, creating not just a musical 'style' but a new approach to music out of the ashes and remnants. Compounded of jazz, special effects, classical forms, jingles and church tunes, there is nothing else quite like it.

*****(*) Baal Brecht Breuker Handke**

BVHAAST CD 9006 *Breuker; Cees Klaver (t); Bernard Hunnekink (tb); Jan Wolff (hn); Donald Blakeslee (tba); Bob Driessen (as); Herman De Wit (ts); Louis Andriessen (p, org, hpd); Maarten van Regteren Altena (b); Han Bennink (d, tap dance).* 10/73–10/74.

***** Bertolt Brecht / Herman Heijermans**

BVHAAST CD 9003 *Breuker; Al Klink, Jos Kieft (t); Bernard Hunnekink (tb); Leonore Pameijer (f, picc); Rob Bouwmeester (ob); Leon Bosch (cl); Wim Jonas (bsn, cbsn); Henk De Jonge (p, acc); Jan Erik van Regteren Altena, Lorre Trytten (vn); Eduard van Regteren Altena (clo); Ernst Glerum (b); Rob Verdurmen (perc).* 9/73.

****** De Onderste Steen**

Entr'acte CD 2 *Breuker; Andy Altenfelder, Cees Klaver, Boy Raaymakers (t); Iman Soetemann, Jan Wolff (frhn); Bernard Hunnekink (tb, tba); Gregg Moore (tb); Willem Van Manen (tb, v); Dil Engelhardt (f); André Goudbeek (as); Peter Barkema (ts, bs); Emil Keijzer, Reinbert De Leeuw, Bert Van Dijk (p); Leo Cuypers (p, hca); Henk De Jonge (p, acc, ky); Louis Andriessen (p, org, hpd); Johnny Meyer (acc); Michael Waisvisz (syn); Sytze Smit (vn); Maarten van Regteren Altena, Arjen Gorter (b); Han Bennink, Martin Van Duynhoven, Rob Verdurmen (perc); Frits*

Lambrechts, Olga Zuiderhoek (gamelan); Mondriaan Strings; Ernö Ola String Quartet; Daniël Otten String Group. 74–91.

***** Twice A Woman / Twee Vroumen**

BVHAAST CD 9708 *Breuker; Al Klink, Wim Van der Vliet (t); Hans Van Balen, Bernard Hunnekink (tb); Eddie Van Dijke (frhn); Rieke Van der Heide (ob); Werner Herbers, Jan Kouwenhoven, Nico Schaafsma (eng hn); Henk De Wit (bsn); Hens Otter, Wiebe Schuurmans, Rob Van Stiphout (as); Iwan Bossini, Rami Koch, Ernö Ola (vn); Leo Vleeschouwer (vla); Hans Bonsel (clo); Kees Olthuis, Henk De Jonge (p, syn, acc); Arjen Gorter, Tonny De Gruyter (b); Rob Verdurmen (d).* 9/78, 1/79.

***** De Illusionist, Kkkomediant**

BVHAAST CD 920 *Breuker; Jos Kieft, Al Klink, Jelle Schouten, Carlo De Wild (t); Bernard Hunnekink, Chris Abelen, Hans Van Balen (tb); Roel Koster (frhn); Loes Kerstens, Leonore Pameijer (f, picc); Fred Man (Pan f); Evert Weidner (ob); Rob Bouwmeester (eng hn); André Kerver (cl); Guus Dral, Jos De Lange, Wim Jonas (bsn); Hens Otter (tarogato); Henk De Jonge (p, ky, acc); Julian B Coco, Jan De Hont (g); Ernestine Stoop (hp); Jan Vermeulen, Thom De Ligt (b); Rob Verdurmen, Martin Van Duynhoven (perc); Rami Koch, Stanislaw Lukowski (vn); Michel Samson (vla); Henk Lambooij (clo); B Borden, Ananda Goud, Hans Pootjes, Richard Zook, Hans Vermeulen, Jody Pijper (v).* 3/83–2/85.

*****(*) To Remain**

BVHAAST CD 8904 *Breuker; Andreas Altenfelder, Boy Raaymakers (t); Chris Abelen, Bernard Hunnekink, Garrett List, Gregg Moore (tb); André Goudbeek (as); Peter Barkema, Maarten Van Norden (ts); Henk De Jonge (p, ky); Arjen Gorter (b); Rob Verdurmen (d, perc).* 9/83–4/89.

****** Bob's Gallery**

BVHAAST CD 8801 *Breuker; Boy Raaymakers (t); Chris Abelen (tb); Bernard Hunnekink (tb, tba); André Goudbeek (as); Peter Barkema (ts); Henk De Jonge (p, syn); Arjen Gorter (b); Rob Verdurmen (perc, xyl); Peter Kuit Jr (tapdance).* 12/87.

***** Metropolis**

BVHAAST CD 8903 *Breuker; Andreas Altenfelder, Boy Raaymakers (t, v); Gregg Moore (tb, v); Bernard Hunnekink (tb, tba, v); André Goudbeek (as, v); Peter Barkema (as, ts, bs); Henk De Jonge (p, cel, syn); Arjen Gorter (b); Rob Verdurmen (perc); Toby Rix (Toeterix, hca); Mondriaan Strings: Jan Erik van Regteren Altena, Erik Kromhout, Alison Wallace (vn); Aimée Versloot, Jan Schoonenberg (vla); Wieke Meyer, Eduard van Regteren Altena (clo).* 11/87–4/89.

*****(*) Parade**

BVHAAST CD 9101 *As for Metropolis, except omit Rix; add Alex Coke (ts, f).* 12/90.

****** Heibel**

BVHAAST CD 9102 *As for Parade, except omit Coke; add Greetje Bijma (v); Lorre Trytten (vn).* 12/90, 5/91.

***** Meets Djazzex**

BVHAAST 9513 *As above, except omit Bijma, Trytten.* 5/92.

****** Deze Kant Op, Dames / This Way, Ladies**

BVHAAST CD 9301 *As for Parade, except omit Mondriaan Strings; replace Verdurmen with Arend Niks (perc); Loes Luca (v).* 12/92.

***** Sensemaya**

BVHAAST CD 9509 *Breuker; Andy Altenfelder, Boy Raaymakers (t); Nico Nijholt (tb); Bernard Hunnekink (tb, tba); Alex Coke (ts, f); Peter Barkema (as, ts); Han De Vries (ob); Henk De Jonge (p, syn); Arjen Gorter (b); Rob Verdurmen (d); Greetje Kauffeld (v); strings.* 6/95.

****** The Parrot**

BVHAAST CD 9601 *Drawn from listing above.* 80–95.

If the Dutch soccer side of the 1970s played 'total football', then this is 'total jazz'. Joachim Berendt likens Breuker's use of Dutch and Low German folk music to Roland Kirk's un-ironic and loving use of the less elevated music of the black tradition. Eclecticism of this sort has been a feature of post-war Dutch music. Composers like Louis Andriessen (who appears on *De Onderste Steen*) and Misha Mengelberg have made extensive use of jazz and rock forms as a way of breaking down the tyranny of serialism and of rigid formal structures. Like the late Frank Zappa, whom Breuker in some respects resembles and whose strange critical marginality he shares, the Dutchman was turned on to classical music by hearing Varèse, whose enthusiastic embrace of chaos is very much a part of what Breuker and Mengelberg are about; but Breuker has made a point of guying the more pompous aspects of all the musics he has a hand in. In structural terms, he does so by simple juxtaposition, placing popular melodies alongside quasi-classical themes. In terms of instrumental colour, he relies on the populist associations of saxophones, tubas; on *Baal*, ukuleles and mandolins, elsewhere invented (non)instruments like Toby Rix's. Clearly, a good deal of this music fits only rather uncomfortably into a 'jazz' category. Breuker's Kollektief is a performance band in the fullest sense. Whether the music transfers successfully to record will depend largely on personal taste and on a level of sympathy with what Breuker is about. However, it is necessary to point out that most of the performances listed, even the concert recordings by the Kollektief, depend to some extent on visual components which the listener at home has no access to.

Breuker has also frequently been likened to Kurt Weill (he includes 'Pirate Jenny's Song' from *Die Dreigroschenoper* on *Driesburgen-Zeist*) and is as likely to use harmonic devices, structural principles, and occasionally straight quotes from concert music ('Prokof' on *In Holland* is a good example) as from popular sources; he is also a fundamentally theatrical composer, and several of these records are of music written for dramatic performance or for films, as in the case of *De Illusionist, Kkkomediant*, which represents the soundtracks to two movies by Freek de Jonge, whose work is never going to trouble Orson Welles, even on a good day.

Twice A Woman/Twee Vrouwen was written for movies by George Sluizer and René van Nie. The orchestrations and arrangements are typically imaginative but there is something slightly drab and functional about the music.

Another obvious parallel is with Brecht and Weill, whose experiments in total theatre have been absorbed into the mainstream only rather slowly. A melody from Weill's *Lady In The Dark* opens *Metropolis*, but the most extended examinations are the music for Brecht's *Baal*, and for his parable of fascism, *The Resistible Rise Of Arturo Ui*, which is paired with music for a television documentary on the novelist and playwright, Herman Heijermans. The *Baal* disc also contains a score for the Austrian novelist Peter Handke's hallucinatory drama, known in English as *The Ride Over Lake Constance*. In all of these, the music is ironic, referential, collaging a bizarre variety of materials, such as 'White Cliffs Of Dover' on *Baal*, tags from hymns and national anthems on *Parade*. This is the most formal of the records in some respects, developing material by Satie and Weill ('Aggie's Sewing Machine Song' from *Johnny Johnson*) alongside music written more specifically for the Kollektief. The title-piece on *Metropolis* is a realization of a piece by Ferde Grofé, whose *Grand Canyon Suite* is a concert favourite. The remainder of the programme consists of a typically diverse (not to say perverse) array of materials, including Haydn's 1796 'Trumpet Concerto', in which the soloist's part is taken by former singing cowboy, Toby Rix, with his patented Toeterix, an instrument constructed out of chromatically tuned car-horns. It reappears on the closing 'I Want To Be Happy'; Rix also plays harmonica on two traditional songs arranged by Breuker.

It's unfortunate that a number of the saxophonist's more improvisational records are not currently on release. Of the Kollektief albums, by far the best known (and probably the best initial bet) is the FMP/BVHAAST co-release, *Live In Berlin*, which is still worth looking out for and which will doubtless reappear soon. The obvious model is Ellington; Breuker uses his soloists in the same individualistic but still disciplined way (one wonders how 'anarchic' these bands *really* are). Recorded versions of 'Creole Love Call' and other straight repertoire like the Gershwin arrangements on a currently unavailable 1987–8 tribute are played remarkably straight – though such is the imaginative tension the Kollektief generates that one finds oneself listening more intently than usual, in constant expectation of a sudden chorus of raspberries or a dramatic swerve of tone. It's possible that critics and even Breuker have overplayed the comic hand; *To Remain*'s 11 movements suggest that his reputation as a *farceur* is (like Roland Kirk's) emphasized at the expense of understanding his remarkable technical and structural abilities.

Though it has probably now been overtaken by a vigorous new CD programme, *De Onderste Steen* is still an indispensable sampling of Breuker's improvised and compositional work over a decade and a half. The opening piece is a traditional Indian melody; the next is the magnificent threnody for Duke Ellington, marked by an emotional growl solo by Raaymakers (who has obviously absorbed Rex Stewart and Cootie Williams) over a throbbing, dead-march *ostinato*. There are two tangos, a gamelan, some cod Vivaldi, and a bizarre swing blues called 'My Baby Has Gone To The Schouwburg', which eventually collapses in harmonic(a) chaos, a Satie-influenced composition for Reinbert de Leeuw (a distinguished interpreter of Satie piano pieces) and two theatre pieces. Musically, it's the best available profile of Breuker's work over nearly 20 years, but availability may very well be a moot point.

It should be easier to find Breuker's own sampling of his work on *The Parrot*. This really covers the early 1980s, with just a single track, 'Potsdamer Stomp', from 1995, offering a perspective that would be slightly skewed were the Kollektief not so absolutely consistent in their unpredictability. It does seem that just about any point of entry makes no less sense than any other, so it is often a good idea just to jump in.

Even so, the next best choices for the newcomer are undoubtedly *To Remain* and *Bob's Gallery*. On the latter, the wonderfully skew-whiff title-track, which is inspired by a Gary Larson cartoon, features magnificent solos by Goudbeek, Raaymakers and Breuker. 'Morribreuk', with Altenfelder and Raaymakers processing from the back of the hall to the stage, is a dedication to Ennio Morricone. There is also a dedication to the offbeat jazz pianist and composer (has Breuker ever done 'Yellow Waltz'?) Richard Twardzik, and a selection of pieces from the theatre work, *Thanks, Your Majesty*, making this one of the jazzier Kollektief records. That's a factor which may appeal to those who find his media-mixing a turn-off. However, the two '90s recordings are also extremely attractive. *This Way, Ladies* is a musical, co-written with Ischa Meijer. It concerns the silver anniversary celebrations of Louise (played by Loes Luca) and the Count Guillaume de Breuckelaere (a figure who presents a disconcerting resemblance to our hero, the saxophonist and composer). Much of the action takes place in his concussed brain as a notably democratic celebration carries on around him. The dreamlike action and several of the themes, notably 'Dirge For An Insignificant Musician', suggest that Breuker may have been drinking at the same well as Carla Bley: shades of her *Genuine Tong Funeral* and *Escalator Over The Hill*. However, the pace and the wry dynamics of the thing are Breuker's own and, for once, the absence of the theatrical element doesn't seem to matter unduly.

The curiously packaged *Heibel* (it comes in a cheese box) combines a concert recording by the Kollektief with superb solo contributions from Raaymakers on the Ellington threnody, 'Duke Edward/Misère', and from the redoubtable Verdurmen. The second half of the set consists of another mini-opera, this time for the astonishing voice of Greetje Bijma, a solo singer of great presence and range. It's a slighter – if rather more sober – piece than *This Way, Ladies* and depends more on the soloists (Lorre Trytten has a prominent part) than on the usual Breuker mayhem.

***(*) Kurt Weill

BVHAAST CD 9808 *As for records above, except add Andy Altenfelder, Boy Raaymakers (t); Bernard Hunnekink, Nico Nijholt (tb); Alex (picc, f); Peter Barkema (as); Henk De Jonge (p); Rena Scholtens, Lorre Lynn Trittel (vn); Aimée Versloot (vla); Arjen Gorter (b); Rob Verdurman (perc); Loes Luca (v).* 83–97.

A nicely compiled anthology of earlier Weill-inspired recordings, with new interpretations of the 1928 *Ol Musik* which feature the dynamic, theatrical voice of chanteuse Loes Luca. There is also a wonderful 1997 performance of 'My Ship' from *Lady In The Dark*, which highlights the skills of saxophonist and flautist Alex Coke, a relatively recent addition to the Breuker stable. Again, some of the arrangements were made for film and television purposes, but this time they also sound like performance works rather than utility music.

***(*) Pakkepapèn

BVHAAST CD 9807 *Breuker; Andy Altenfelder, Boy Raaymakers (t); Bernard Hunnekink (tb, tba); Nico Nijholt (tb); Alex (ts, picc); Henk De Jonge (p, perc); Lorre Trytten (vn); Arjen Gorter (b); Rob Verdurmen (d).* 9/97.

**** Psalm 122

BVHAAST CD 9803 *Breuker; Andy Altenfelder, Boy Raaymakers (t); Nico Nijholt (tb); Bernard Hunnekink (tb, tba); Peter Barkema (as); Alex Coke (ts, f, bf); Henk De Jonge (p, syn);*

Arjen Gorter (b); Rob Verdurmen (d); Trytten Strings; Koor Nieuwe Muziek. 2/98.

The recent batch of Breukeriana includes a now familiar mix of fierce playing, wry satire, genuine emotion and a gift for imaginative packaging. *Pakkepapèn* comes in a textured, semi-transparent slipcase featuring abstract images of instruments. The group interplay is strongly reminiscent of early pre-theatrical Breuker albums. Breuker is scarcely featured, leaving the solo space to some familiar names from the past – Gorter and Raaymakers memorably on 'Pakkepapèn 6' – and relative newcomer Alex Coke, who narrates 'Hello, My Name Is Joe' before turning in a superb tenor solo on 'Worksong Part 2'. This is one of the best Breuker albums for years.

The real stunner is Breuker's meditation on Psalm 122, with its joyous apotheosis of Jerusalem as the refuge and triumph of the scattered tribes. One feels that much of what Breuker has been about down the years is concentrated and focused here. It is very much a piece about arrival.

Something of John Zorn's interrogation of the Judaic tradition with Masada can be heard here and there, but Breuker's approach is actually much more rigorous and daring. Barrel-organ renditions and a wonderfully executed *a cappella* performance of the psalm – more properly, song of degree – punctuate a long and complex suite. The ending is quite breathtaking: another barrel-organ turn gives way to the blessing of 'Peace be within thy walls', with Coke on bass flute and tenor saxophone; and then, breathtakingly, Lorre Lynn Trytten and Breuker on soprano bring the whole work to a climax. Even if you have not previously heard Breuker's music, this should be a priority. Rich, deeply cadenced music.

Dee Dee Bridgewater

VOCALS

Hailed as a natural successor to Ella Fitzgerald, Dee Dee has the same unfailing swing and instinct for complex harmony. A commanding presence on the stand, she communicates equally well in the studio. Her ex-husband is the respected trumpet player, Cecil Bridgewater.

***(*) Keeping Tradition

Verve 519607-2 *Bridgewater; Thierry Eliez (p); Hein Van de Geyn (b); André Ceccarelli (d).* 92.

**** Love And Peace: A Tribute To Horace Silver

Verve 527470-2 *As above, except add Stéphane Belmondo (t), Lionel Belmondo (ts), Horace Silver (p).* 94.

***(*) Dear Ella

Verve 527896-2 *Bridgewater; Cecil Bridgewater, Byron Stripling (t); Bob Flowers (tb); Antonio Hart (as); Lou Levy (p); Milt Jackson (vib); Kenny Burrell (g); Ray Brown (b); Grady Tate (d).* 1 & 2/97.

*** Dee Dee Bridgewater

Atlantic 76567 80 760-2 *Bridgewater; Barry Beckett, Tom Hensley, Joe Sample, Harold Wheeler (ky); Pete Carr, Jerry Friedman, Jimmy Johnson, Chris Morris, Ray Parker Jr, Dean Parks, Melvin Ragin, David T Walker (g); Herb Bushler, Wilton Felder, David Hood (b); Henry Davis, Ed Green, Roger Hawkins, Alan Schwartzberg (d); Gary Coleman, Bobby Hall (perc); Vivian Cherry, Gwendolyn Guthrie, Arlene Martell, Linda November (v).* 76.

The title of the first album is a strong clue to Dee Dee's musical instincts. Her cool, limber swing works brilliantly on 'Fascinating Rhythm', 'Just One Of Those Things' and a superb medley of 'I'm A Fool To Want You' and 'I Fall In Love Too Easily'. If her debt to Ella weren't obvious from this, it's heavily underscored on the 1997 tribute album, which was recorded with a star-laden band over four nights in New York and Chicago. She starts with a light, buoyant reading of 'A Tisket A Tasket', establishing her voice before reaching for something more in the ballads. Bridgewater's ability to convey the drama of 'How High The Moon' and 'Stairway To The Stars' while exploring their complex harmonic potential – echoes of bebop in her interchanges with Brown, the former Mr Fitzgerald – is endlessly impressive.

Like the eponymous Atlantic, *Love And Peace* is a funkier conception, as befits its dedication to the music of Mr Funk himself. Surprisingly, Horace Silver's tunes lend themselves very well to vocal performance, and Dee Dee is quite content to swap tags and allusions with the composer, who has always been a one-man dictionary of musical quotations. Good to hear him playing with such obvious enjoyment. The guitar- and keyboard-heavy Atlantic reissue frankly isn't much to our taste and comes across like a bid to relocate Bridgewater in a rock-tinged mainstream. The material featuring Crusaders Sample and Felder is top drawer but the album as a whole smacks of commercial compromise.

Arthur Briggs (*c.* 1899–1991)

TRUMPET

Born in Charleston, Briggs played in army bands and the Southern Syncopated Orchestra, 1919–21, then travelled through Europe, often leading his own bands through the '30s. Interned during the war, then returned to France and taught.

*** Hot Trumpet In Europe

Jazz Archives 158472 *Briggs; George Hirst, Bobby Jones, Theodore Brock (t); Jean Naudin, F Monetti, Isidore Bassard, Billy Burns (tb); Georges Jacquemont-Brown (cl, as, ts); Peter Duconge, Franz Feith, Billy Barton (cl, as); Carlos Vidal (cl, bs); Mario Scanavino (cl, ts, bs); Alcide Castellanos (as); Francis Giulieri (ts, bs); U Irrlicht, Marek Weber, Eugen Bermann, Armin Lieberman (vn); Egide Van Gils, Georg Haentzchel, Stephane Mougin, Freddy Johnson (p); Frank 'Big Boy' Goudie (cl, ts); C.B Hilliom (bs, bsx); Al Bowlly (g, v); Sterling Conaway (g); Harold M Kirchstein, Mike Danzi, Maceo Jefferson (bj); Hans Holdt, Arthur Brosche (tba); Juan Fernandez (b); Eugene Obendorfer, Dick Stauff, Jean Taylor, Billy Taylor (d); Spencer Williams, Louis Cole (v).* 3/27–7/33.

When Briggs enlisted with Will Marion Cook's orchestra and came to Europe in 1919, he seldom went back. His records are obscure compared with those of Jabbo Smith or Henry Allen, but he could claim to be as convincing an Armstrong disciple as they and he worked in relative jazz isolation in Europe through the 1920s and '30s. This disc brings together the sides made by his

Savoy Syncopators in 1927, an otherwise all-European band that handled themselves capably enough, although it's only on his solos that the records sit up. The trumpet on 'Ain't She Sweet?' is an interesting blend of styles, and the music works best in the hot-dance vein; when they get to a 'genuine' jazz piece such as King Oliver's 'Snag It', the results are comparatively disappointing. Eight tracks from 1933, rare items, give Briggs his best opportunities, and two duets with pianist Freddy Johnson are a glimpse of what he could really do. He sounds a little too urbane for the blues on 'Grabbin' Blues' since there's a certain sweetness in his manner, but a cultivated, elegant stylist he undoubtedly was. A few of the earlier tracks are a bit rough, but the remastering is mostly strong and clear.

Bright Moments

GROUP

A reunion band which collects several leading lights of more than one generation of the Chicagoan avant-garde.

**(*) Return Of The Lost Tribe

Delmark DE-507 *Kalaparusha Maurice McIntyre (ts); Joseph Jarman (as, f, v); Adegoke Steve Colson (p); Malachi Favors (b); Kahil El'Zabar (d).* 12/97.

The promise of the personnel and the notion to reunite some of the most distinguished spirits in Chicagoan music is sadly unfulfilled. El'Zabar, whose initiative this was, tries his best to direct and fan the flames, but McIntyre sounds woefully rusty, Jarman is merely indifferent and the rhythm section are left to press the buttons themselves. The seven tracks all seem too long and lack any specificity.

Nick Brignola (born 1936)

BARITONE, SOPRANO, TENOR AND ALTO SAXOPHONES, CLARINET, ALTO CLARINET, BASS CLARINET, FLUTE, PICCOLO

A reed specialist of wide-ranging abilities, Brignola is first and foremost a baritone man. Originally from New York State, he worked in different settings and different parts of the US, trying a fusion band in the early 1970s and returning to hard bop in the '80s. He favours the big side of the big horn, playing a hard-bop vocabulary with great power and command.

*** A Tribute To Gerry Mulligan

Stash STCD 574 *Brignola; Randy Brecker (t); Paul Johnson (vib); Don Friedman (p); Sal Salvador (g); Gary Mazzaroppi (b); Butch Miles (d).* 11/82–11/84.

Brignola has been a familiar name on the baritone for many years, but currently his nominal discography starts here, a reissue of two albums originally put out under Sal Salvador's name, now with Brignola co-credited – appropriately, since he is easily the outstanding player. Salvador's own playing tends towards glibness, padding solos out with irritating quotes, and Brecker's turns show little interest. In contrast, Brignola plays with a dependable aggression that doesn't disavow the good humour of Mulligan's tunes, and he also makes the most of 'Blue Monk'. Five tracks without him elicit a quick, trim sound from the group, and here Salvador seems more at ease.

*** Raincheck

Reservoir RSR CD 108 *Brignola; Kenny Barron (p); George Mraz (b); Billy Hart (d).* 9/88.

**** On A Different Level

Reservoir RSR CD 112 *Brignola; Kenny Barron (p); Dave Holland (b); Jack DeJohnette (d).* 9/89.

*** What It Takes

Reservoir RSR CD 117 *Brignola; Randy Brecker (t); Kenny Barron (p); Rufus Reid (b); Dick Berk (d).* 10/90.

Brignola has now had a long sojourn with the independent label Reservoir and they have served him wonderfully well, with a sequence of albums that any saxophonist would envy. Brignola's facility goes hand in hand with a consistently imposing sound – as fluently as he plays, he always makes the baritone sound like the big horn that it is – and the flat-out burners are as tonally effective as the big-bodied ballads which are dotted through these sessions. *Raincheck* is a trifle diffuse, since Brignola turns to clarinet and soprano every so often, and *What It Takes* brings on Randy Brecker for a little variation in the front line, which is bought at the expense of the music's more personal feel (and the leader again doubles on the other reeds). *On A Different Level*, though, is suitably head-and-shoulders above the others. Brignola sticks to baritone as his sole horn here, and the solos on 'Tears Inside', 'Hot House' and 'Duke Ellington's Sound Of Love' are sustained with fantastic strength, mirrored in the playing of the rhythm section, which is the kind of team that makes any horn player sound good. Brignola's shrewd choice of tunes here encapsulates a pocket history of jazz baritone – from Carney on 'Sophisticated Lady' to Adams on the Mingus tune – but he puts it all under his own flag, with DeJohnette and Holland marking superb time behind him. A great modern baritone set.

*** It's Time

Reservoir RSR CD 123 *Brignola; Kenny Barron (p); Dave Holland (b).* 2/91.

A singular feat of overdubbing – Brignola brings out not only the baritone but also all of his clarinets, flutes, other saxes and a piccolo. Mike Holober's arrangements create intelligent variations on the standard reed section and introduce all sorts of counterpoint and texture. But producer Mark Feldman doesn't secure a convincing enough mix: there's too much artifice here, as naturally and enthusiastically as Brignola approaches the project. 'Dusk' and 'Renewal' are pleasing scores, and there are a couple of straighter blows on 'Speak Low' and a clarinet treatment of 'I Thought About You'. Holland, as usual, is marvellous, especially on 'Dusk'.

*** Live At Sweet Basil, First Set

Reservoir RSR CD 125 *Brignola; Mike Holober (p); Rich Syracuse (b); Dick Berk (d).* 8/92.

Given that he deliberately avoided having a drummer on the previous date, there's some irony about this one: all the real dialogue goes on between Brignola and drummer Dick Berk, whose hefty, momentous style is a fine foil for the burliness of the leader's baritone. The soprano comes out on 'Mahjong' and the alto for part of 'Sister Sadie', but otherwise it's all baritone, on a clear-eyed 'Everything Happens To Me', a nicely paced 'I Hear A Rhapsody' and a grandly articulated 'East Of The Sun'. Occasional club-date longueurs, but otherwise this is a fine continuation of possibly the best sequence of baritone records of recent times.

*****(*) Like Old Times**

Reservoir RSR CD 133 *Brignola; Claudio Roditi (t, flhn); John Hicks (p); George Mraz (b); Dick Berk (d).* 5/94.

*****(*) The Flight Of The Eagle**

Reservoir RSR CD 145 *Brignola; Kenny Barron (p); Rufus Reid (b); Victor Lewis (d).* 6/96.

The tenets of the blowing date are followed without any suspicion of routine on *Like Old Times*. The two long blow-outs on 'When Lights Are Low' and 'The Night Has A Thousand Eyes' are marked by perfectly controlled dynamics, with no loss of excitement as one solo passes into another. Roditi is in rare form and Hicks supplies all the right leads, but the saxophonist surrenders nothing to either of them, with a pointed clarinet meditation on 'More Than You Know' and his terrific solo on 'Thousand Eyes' as particular highlights. Rudy Van Gelder still doesn't put enough air round the horns, and this cuts back on the music's impact to a degree.

No problems with the sound on the impeccably registered *The Flight Of The Eagle*. Brignola returns to a simple quartet setting and sticks to the baritone for eight pieces, measured out with the utmost finesse by all four hands. Barron, Reid and Lewis don't seem to know how to put a foot wrong, and the leader is at his most civilized. 'Gerrylike' is a nod of farewell to Mulligan, the gentlest guying of the older man's methods, while the complex changes of the title-tune are wholly absorbing. There is also a near-perfect ballad in 'My Foolish Heart', where Lewis steps aside. The only quibble might be that the music is at times almost bloodless in its excellence, but it seems folly to carp.

***** Spring Is Here**

Koch 3-6905-2 *Brignola; Netherlands Metropole Orchestra.* 94–97.

A dream date for a horn player, this matching with the Netherlands Metropole Orchestra brings out Brignola's sunniest side. He almost gambols through 'Gerrylike' and is just as perky with 'Baubles, Bangles And Beads'. Some of the lushness of 'When You Wish Upon A Star' is a bit lost on such a hearty executant, and the arrangements are rather weeping-waterfall on the ballads. Brignola fans will still want this.

***** Poinciana**

Reservoir RSR CD 151 *Brignola; Phil Markowitz (ky); Steve LaSpina (b); Billy Hart (d); Café (perc).* 4/97.

This one's a bit disappointing. Nick sounds a little sleepless on a couple of the tunes and for once the band doesn't seem to really respond to him. There are still some pieces worth savouring, such as the musing 'What'll I Do', but this isn't among the best of his Reservoirs.

Gordon Brisker

TENOR SAXOPHONE

A West Coaster and an ex-Woody Hermanite, Brisker has been around that scene since the 1960s, and his occasional records showcase an orthodox but fluent modern saxophonist.

***** The Gift**

Naxos 86001-2 *Brisker; Tim Hagans (t, flhn); Marc Copland (p); Jay Anderson (b); Jeff Hirshfield (d).* 1/96.

Brisker has been absent since our first edition, but he makes a decent job of leading this enjoyable if generic hard-bop date. Perhaps inevitably, the star turns come mainly from the splendid Hagans, who shares with Tom Harrell the ability to turn up, scan the charts and deliver effortless and quite beautiful solos. Brisker is more closely associated with the West rather than the East Coast, and his playing has the slightly sun-baked quality of the Californian reedman: propulsive but laconic. The tunes are a thinker's set of originals and, although nothing really stands out, it's an hour of quality time.

Alan Broadbent (born 1947)

PIANO

Born in New Zealand, he went to Berklee in 1966 and then joined Woody Herman as pianist-arranger. He's been in demand since in both capacities and is the pianist in the Charlie Haden Quartet West.

****** Live At Maybeck Recital Hall Vol. 14**

Concord CCD 4488 *Broadbent (p solo).* 5/91.

****** Alan Broadbent / Gary Foster Duo Series Vol. 4**

Concord CCD 4562 *Broadbent; Gary Foster (as, ts).* 3/93.

There's a great clarity of thought about Alan Broadbent's playing: his interpretations of jazz and show standards seem thought through and entire and, while that may suggest a lack of spontaneity, he also manages to make the music sound fresh. These are very satisfying records. The pianist takes his first cues from Parker and Powell, yet one seldom thinks of bop while listening to him: there is much interplay between the hands, a sly but considerate cunning and a striking concern to develop melodies which are entirely faithful to the material. Good as his earlier trio albums are, it's the Maybeck Hall setting which brought out the best in the pianist: Broadbent's internal rhythms are springy enough to keep even his ballads on a simmering heat, and the neatly tucked readings of such as 'Oleo' (most of the pieces run out to only three or four minutes) or the cleverly shaded 'Sweet And Lovely' are genuinely fascinating. The sound is as fine as is customary for this series. In conversation with the similarly undervalued Foster, Broadbent shines just as convincingly. Foster's languorous sound and silky phrasing disguise an acute musical mind, and when the two start spinning out contrapuntal lines on bebop themes it's at least as telepathic as a Konitz–Tristano encounter. Hoagy Carmichael's lovely 'One Morning In May' is one end of the seam,

Parker's 'Relaxin' At Camarillo' the other, and there's not a wasted moment in any of the improvising. Excellent location sound.

*****(*) Pacific Standard Time**

Concord CCD 4664 *Broadbent; Putter Smith (b); Frank Gibson Jr (d).* 1/95.

The only drawback here is the choice of material: some of the themes are just a shade too familiar and, since Broadbent's way is to personalize by small, well-chosen gestures, the trio don't quite characterize each piece as strongly as they might. That said, this is still a very fine record. Broadbent's touch is so lucid and refined that he makes one hear every note as a specific choice, and his sense of swing is good enough to lift slow tempos and mediate fast ones. Smith and Gibson are unadventurous but completely in sympathy with him. 'Summer Night', 'Django' and 'Easy To Love' are about as close to perfect as they can be.

****** Personal Standards**

Concord CCD 4757-2 *Broadbent; Putter Smith (b); Joe LaBarbera (d).* 10/96.

Words like 'civilized' and 'cultured' are as likely to be disparaging as complimentary when discussing jazz, yet there's simply no avoiding them when considering Broadbent's music. This superlative record continues one of the great sequences of recent times. Here he tackles eight of his own originals, plus one he wishes he'd written himself, Putter Smith's 'North'. As before, the playing is so impeccable, the interplay so refined – surely LaBarbera has never played better than this – and the insights so profound that one is left at a loss for words. Broadbent deserves the highest acclaim. Our only grumble is that he doesn't seem to have recorded anything new since our last edition!

Bosse Broberg

TRUMPET

Veteran Swedish modernist whose rare records as a leader only commenced when his career was fully mature.

***** East Of The Sun**

Dragon DRCD 235 *Broberg; Joakim Milder (ts); Gösta Rundqvist (p); Red Mitchell (b); Martin Löfgren (d).* 2/92.

****(*) A Swede In Copenhagen**

Music Mecca 2033-2 *Broberg; Ole Stolle (t); Soren Kristiansen (p); Ole Skipper Mosgaard (b); Leif Johansson (d).* 6/95.

***** Regni**

Phono Suecia PSCD 93 *Broberg; Peter Asplund, Magnus Broo, Hans (t, flhn); Jan Allan (t); Thomas Driving (flhn); Olle Holmquist (tb, tba, euph); Nils Landgren, Bertl Lovgren (tb); Sven Larsson (btb, tba, didjeridu); Krister Andersson (as, ts, cl); Lennart Aberg (as, ts); Dave Wilczewski (ss, ts); Jon Högman (bs); Gösta Rundqvist (p); Dan Berglund (b); Martin Löfgren (d).* 12/95.

It took many years for Broberg to get his name up front on a record marquee, and even then the Dragon album is nominally shared with Red Mitchell, on one of his last sessions before returning to the USA. It's a thoughtful set of post-bop, conservatively styled – even with Milder in the group – but effective for all that. Broberg's Milesian affinities come to the fore when he has the mute in, but he can sometimes go off on wailing, swing-style blasts when he feels he needs to wake himself up. The duet with Mitchell on 'I Cover The Waterfront' is especially fine, but some of the other tunes ramble a bit. *A Swede In Copenhagen* catches Bosse sitting in with a local group, and he is sometimes nearly outplayed by the excellent Stolle, who gets no features to himself but turns in some sturdy solos. Here and there Broberg seems fallible, and some of his forays into very long phrases followed by short ones all but coin a cliché. The set offers seven pretty obvious standards and could perhaps have used more preparation.

No such complaint against the orchestral music on *Regni*. Some of it is so intensely written – nothing more so than the labyrinthine 'Monkey Serenade' – that one applauds the chops of the players for just getting through it. This kind of jazz suggests that Broberg has been storing up his composing for, if anything, too long: it feels overworked. But some of the scores, such as the intriguing 'Portrait Of Uriah' with its astonishing feature for Lennart Aberg's tenor, and the brief reduction of 'Sir Gil Ahead' with a typically shining solo from Jan Allan, hold the attention decisively. The band is first class, too.

Bob Brookmeyer (born 1929)

VALVE TROMBONE, PIANO

The Missourian is the first brass player since Juan Tizol to favour the valve trombone over the slide instrument. He began his career as a pianist and continued to play keyboard for many hears, but it was his emergence as Chet Baker's replacement in the Mulligan pianoless quartet that really established his name. Brookmeyer spent many years as a studio musician and in the Jones–Lewis big band, and the experience has strongly coloured his own arranging and composition.

*****(*) The Dual Role Of Bob Brookmeyer**

Original Jazz Classics OJC 1729 *Brookmeyer; Jimmy Raney (g); Teddy Charles (vib); Teddy Kotick (b); Mel Lewis, Ed Shaughnessy (d); Nancy Overton (v).* 1/54, 6/55.

***** Quintets**

Vogue 2111503 *Brookmeyer; Henri Renaud (p); Jimmy Gourley (g); Red Mitchell (b); Frank Isola (d).* 6/54.

Almost the first sounds to be heard on the classic *Jazz on a Summer's Day* soundtrack are the mellow tones of Bob Brookmeyer's valve trombone interweaving with Jimmy Giuffre's clarinet on 'The Train And The River'. It's a curiously formal sound, almost academic, and initially difficult to place. Valve trombone has a more clipped, drier sound than the slide variety, and Brookmeyer is probably its leading exponent, though Maynard Ferguson, Stu Williamson and Bob Enevoldsen have all made effective use of it.

Brookmeyer has always been keen to share piano duties and is a very considerable keyboard player, as he proves on *The Dual Role*. 'Rocky Scotch' and 'Under The Lilacs' are both readily categorized as 'cool' jazz, but there is a surprising degree of variation in Brookmeyer's tone that anticipates the more inflected and expressive playing of later years.

Quintets is shared with Lee Konitz, but the trombonist's four tracks are extremely vivid, and one wonders if there are alternative takes in the vaults; there are *seven* Konitz rejects on the disc, three of 'I'll Remember April' alone.

*** Brookmeyer

RCA Victor 74321 59152 2 *Brookmeyer; Al Derisi, Joe Ferrante, Bernie Glow, Louis Oles, Nick Travis (t); Joe Singer (frhn); Don Butterfield (tba); Gene Quill (as); Al Cohn (as, ts, cl); Al Epstein, Eddie Wasserman (ts); Sol Schlinger (bs); Hank Jones (p); Milt Hinton, Buddy Jones (b); Osie Johnson (d).* 9 & 10/56.

This was an attempt to showcase Brookmeyer in three rather different contexts, from large band down to octet. The big-band arrangements, like the opening 'Oh, Jane Snavely', are interestingly pared down, almost folkish in conception, but arranged in the most interesting way with four trumpets, three tenors, baritone and rhythm providing the background for the solitary trombone. The next session was very different, with a pair of trumpets, french horn and tuba, but just two reeds, alto doubling clarinet, and, once again supporting a roomy bottom end, Sol Schlinger's baritone. The results are no less spare and undramatic, but the subtlety and control are equally striking, and these are more compelling performances than the two octets, 'Confusion Blues' and 'Zing Went The Strings Of My Heart', which seem to have been taped a further week later. These sessions represented quite a substantial investment in Brookmeyer's growing reputation. Even given the tastes of the time, which embraced everything from Kentonish swing to the stirrings of the Third Stream, they must have been quite difficult records to sell. Like a lot of material of the same vintage, though, they come up to date very impressively.

***(*) Traditionalism Revisited

Blue Note 94847 *Brookmeyer; Jimmy Giuffre (ts, bs, cl); Jim Hall (g); Joe Benjamin, Ralph Pena (b); Dave Bailey (d).* 7/57.

Late-1950s recordings, like *Traditionalism Revisited*, saw Brookmeyer exploring classic material with an augmented version of Giuffre's Newport trio and in an idiom the clarinettist was to christen 'folk jazz'. The aim here was something that almost became the legitimacy in the '90s, playing classic jazz tunes and standards with due respect to the tradition, but with markedly modern harmonies. The effect is most noticeable on 'Sheik Of Araby' and 'Louisiana', which bracket the set, but the entire session is handled with a great consistency of vision, as much to the credit of Jimmy Giuffre as to Brookmeyer. On 'Honeysuckle Rose' there are some choruses on which Bob accompanies himself on piano without double-tracking, a rather extreme example of the 'dual role' he has adopted throughout his performing career.

*** Oslo

Concord CCD 4312 *Brookmeyer; Alan Broadbent (p, ky); Eric Von Essen (b); Michael Stephans (d).* 86.

In legato passages (inevitably harder to execute on a valve instrument) he can sound almost like an alto saxophonist – Lee Konitz, say – at the lower end of his range, but Brookmeyer mingles this with sly growls and purrs (as on 'With The Wind And The Rain In Your Hair') and austere, almost toneless equations that sound more like a formula for music than a realized performance. He is also capable of quite broad humour and isn't above adding the odd Dicky Wells effect to an otherwise straightforward solo. Perhaps the biggest criticism and irony of Brookmeyer's *later* work is that it has become humourless as his tone has relaxed and broadened.

**(*) Dreams

Dragon DRCD 169 *Brookmeyer; Gustavo Bargalli, Jan Kohlin, Lars Lindgren, Fredrik Norén, Stig Persson (t, flhn); Mats Hermansson, Mikael Raberg, Bertil Strandberg (tb); Sven Larsson (btb); Dave Castle (as, ss, cl); Hakan Broström (as, ss, f); Johan Alenius, Ulf Andersson (ts, ss, cl); Hans Arktoft (bs, bcl); Anders Widmark (p, ky); Jan Adefeldt (b); Johan Diedelmans (d).* 8/88.

In the later '80s Brookmeyer seemed to be coming to the fore again, both as a player and more particularly as a composer and bandleader. Given what was to come later, *Dreams* is not a particularly inspiring example. It's a dull piece, lifted by one or two passages on 'Cats' and 'Missing Monk', but lacking the coherence and warmth which had become a signature element of his work once the initial cool period was tempered.

*** Electricity

Act 892 192 *Brookmeyer; John Abercrombie (g); Rainer Bruninghaus, Frank Chastenier (ky); Dieter Ilg (b); Danny Gottlieb (d); WDR Big Band.* 3/91.

Based in Europe, Brookmeyer found more opportunities for large-scale sessions than he ever had back home. *Electricity* isn't, to be frank, a particularly wonderful set, but it is immaculately arranged and recorded and, of the soloists, Brookmeyer and Abercrombie are capable of something special, even when the material doesn't appear to be promising. Bob's tone has lightened a touch over the years (unless it is simply modern microphones) and he often now puts more notes into a phrase than he did before.

*** Paris Suite

Challenge 70026 *Brookmeyer; Kris Goessens (p); Riccardo Del Frà (b); Dre Pallemaerts (d).* 10/93, 1/94.

With the exception of Berg's 'Chaconne', played in a delicately swinging way, this is entirely dominated by originals. Pianist Goessens is responsible for three of them, including the *déjà-vu* 'Gospel Song', while Brookmeyer contributes 'Chanson' (the longest track) , 'Airport Song' and 'Erik Satie', which may draw its inspiration from one of the *Gnossiennes*. The group interaction is consistently interesting and Goessens's solos are far from negligible.

***(*) Old Friends

Storyville STCD 8292 *Brookmeyer; Thomas Clausen (p); Mads Vinding (b); Alex Riel (d).* 11/94.

Brookmeyer's gifts as an arranger have occasionally deflected attention from his skills as a live performer. This was recorded in the Jazzhus, Copenhagen: five long numbers packed with invention, if a little hampered by Brookmeyer's cool, slightly expressionless delivery. Perhaps oddly at this juncture, his phrasing on 'Polka Dots And Moonbeams' recalls no one more than Jimmy

Giuffre, though elsewhere on the set he is brassier and more impacted. The closing 'All Blues' is the only track that doesn't quite work – though for reasons which are never entirely clear – and perhaps only because the rhythm section seem to have gone to sleep a bit. Not a great album, but an immensely attractive one.

****** New Works / Celebration**

Challenge CHR 70066 *Brookmeyer; Thorsten Beckenstein, Jorg Engels, Ralf Hesse, Torsten Mass, Sebastian Strempel (t); Christian Jakso, Ludwig Nuss, Ansgar Striepens (tb); Edward Partyka (btb); Marko Lackner, Stefan Pfeifer (as); Nils Van Haften, Paul Heller (ts); Marcus Bartelt, Scott Robinson (bs); Kris Goessens (p); Jurgen Grimm (ky); Ingmar Heller (b); John Hollenbeck (d); Christopher Dell (perc).* 7/97.

The earlier music on this delightful set was written for a festival in Lubeck in 1994, with Gerry Mulligan as guest soloist. Posthumously documented on record, it features the multi-talented Scott Robinson in the solo role, turning the folk- and dance-based material into something at once familiar and strange. Robinson is a formidable soloist and he brings a genuine individuality to the part. Of the other tracks, 'Cameo' is essentially a solo spot for Brookmeyer, while 'Duets', built on one of Bob's minimalist themes, is a great basis for improvisation and includes some inventive drumming from John Hollenbeck. The closing item, 'Boom Boom', is derived from the earlier 'Danish Suite' and provides a light-toned and joyous closer. Brookmeyer has rarely written or played better.

****(*) Out Of This World**

Koch International 6913 *Brookmeyer; Ruud Breuls, Henk Keijink, Jan Hollander (t); Paul Woesthuis (tb); Cor Bakker, Hans Vroomans (p, syn); Peter Tiehuis (g); Jan Hollestelle (b); Eddy Koopman, Cees Kranenburg (d, perc); woodwinds; strings.* 98.

Very much a solo showcase for Brookmeyer, to the detriment sometimes of charts that are intelligently prepared – by Rob Pronk, Lex Jasper, Henl Meutgeert and others – but which need a touch of improvisational tension or at very least some other voices to lend them focus. Brookmeyer has been doing unconventional readings of standard material for years and one might have expected something spikier and more illuminating than these bland settings. Some of the responsibility lies with the arrangers and some with the orchestra, who fail to generate much excitement. Perhaps the session was put together at speed. It seems odd that an arranger of Brookmeyer's gifts should not be represented other than as a player.

Roy Brooks (born 1938)

DRUMS, PERCUSSION, SAW

Born in Detroit and strongly influenced by Elvin Jones, Brooks has largely subordinated performance to educational work down the years and is under-represented on record. He was a member of the Horace Silver band, later taken over by Blue Mitchell; later he joined Max Roach's percussion orchestra, M'Boom.

*****(*) Duet In Detroit**

Enja 7067 2 *Brooks; Woody Shaw (t); Geri Allen, Don Pullen, Randy Weston (p).* 8/83, 5/84.

Roy's first major recording session was Mitchell's *Blue's Moods*, a gritty, uncomplicated session that still stands up well. Since then, he's worked as a jobbing drummer, mostly in New York, but attracting modest fame during Charles Mingus's stormy 1972 European tour, when Brooks charmed the pants off French audiences with his musical saw. He brings it out here to add some colours to a spirited duet with Don Pullen, the most immediately effective of these head-to-head encounters, two tracks each. The others take a little more work, but Brooks quickly establishes a strong empathy, particularly with Shaw on the long 'Elegy For Eddie Jefferson'. Though a generation younger and not obviously in sympathy with all of Brooks's New Thing mannerisms, Allen has no difficulty keeping up, and their opening 'Samba Del Sol' is a delight.

As well as membership of M'Boom, Brooks runs his own 17-piece drum ensemble, called the Aboriginal Percussion Choir, and a group called the Artistic Truth. There are a couple of other records – for Jazz Workshop and Muse – in the back-catalogue and some hope that the latter at least may soon reappear.

Bobby Broom

GUITAR

A New Yorker, Broom learned his guitar craft in the 1960s and '70s, playing with Al Haig and Sonny Rollins while still a teenager, then with a wide range of leaders. He decamped for Chicago in the '80s.

*****(*) No Hype Blues**

Criss Cross 1109 *Broom; Ron Perillo (p); Peter Washington (b); Lewis Nash (d).* 6/95.

***** Waitin' And Waitin'**

Criss Cross 1135 *Broom; Ron Blake (ts); Dennis Carrol (b); George Fludas (d).* 12/96.

Broom starts *No Hype Blues* with a Wes Montgomery tune, and his warm tone and fat sound immediately put him in the Wes lineage. He is a very experienced sideman, and there's a pleasing take-my-time feel to these confident but not excessively ambitious records. The two discs are a straight split between Chicago and New York: Perillo is in Broom's regular Chicago group, and so are Carrol and Fludas on the second date. Perillo is an interesting member of the quartet: noisy and unpredictable, he gets a heavy, bluesy sound out of the piano. 'Father' and Perillo's 'Mirthy' are both harmonically interesting ballads, making a neat balance to the standards and a not-too-fast 'Pent-Up House'.

Waitin' And Waitin' is similarly relaxed and, with no keyboard, Broom seems even more expansive in his use of time and space. If anything, Blake is a distraction, even though he's on only four tracks and blows with pointed intensity. Next to the empathy achieved by the core trio, he's an intruder.

Håkan Bröstrom (born 1955)

SOPRANO, ALTO AND TENOR SAXOPHONES

Born in Hotala, Sweden, Bröstrom began playing tenor in blues bands, before switching to alto and going into post-bop. Works on the Stockholm contemporary scene.

*** Dark Light

Dragon DRCD 190 *Bröstrom; Bobo Stenson (p); Max Schultz (g); Christian Spering (b); Anders Kjellberg (d).* 12/90.

*** Celestial Nights

Dragon DRCD 257 *As above, except omit Schultz.* 2/94.

*** Still Dreaming

Dragon DRCD 297 *Bröstrom; Tim Hagans (t); Marc Copland (p); Christian Spering (b); Jeff Hirshfield (d).* 11/95.

Bröstrom's manner sheds a pale (though not pallid) Swedish light on the post-bop vocabulary. He is a fluent and ambitious improviser on all three horns, although the tenor comes out only on the first record, and he isn't shy about his composing since every theme was written by him. Some of the music is merely meandering, and little really compels the attention – yet that isn't really Bröstrom's style anyway: he likes to set up long, drifting pieces which let the players communicate without undue stress. 'Dark Light' and 'Till Cornelis' on the first disc, 'Spring' on the second and the haunting 'Carmilla' on the third are fine examples of the kind of thing he's trying to achieve. The first two discs benefit from Stenson's typically idiosyncratic playing, quick and intelligent yet quirkily shaped. Spering is splendid on all three discs, but there is a change of pace on the third with the arrival of the American players. 'Three-Year-Old Cowboy' suggests a slightly difficult rapprochement between Europe and the USA but, after that one, Bröstrom seems to inveigle the visitors into playing it his way. All three records should appeal to Europhiles of a certain temperament.

Brotherhood Of Breath

GROUP

Formed in 1970 by SA expatriate Chris McGregor in London. Active mostly in the early '70s, but '80s reunions until McGregor's death kept the name alive.

***(*) Live At Willisau

Ogun OGCD 001 *Chris McGregor (p, leader); Harry Beckett, Marc Charig, Mongezi Feza (t); Nick Evans, Radu Malfatti (tb); Dudu Pukwana (as); Evan Parker, Gary Windo (ts); Harry Miller (b); Louis Moholo (d).* 1/73.

The trick was to keep breathing, because Death was always near by. Chris McGregor's passing and Dudu Pukwana's, and before them Johnny Mbizo Dyani's, Harry Miller's and Mongezi Feza's, confirmed that there was a shadow across this music, as if the life that was breathed into it had to be paid for in some way that had nothing to do with technical exactness or acoustic precision. From the opening moments of 'Do It', with its searing Evan Parker solo, to the relative ease of the closing 'Funky Boots', this is affirmative music of a rare sort, bringing together African *kwela*, post-Ellington swing, free jazz, and even touches of classicism in a boiling mix that grips the heart throughout. Pukwana, Charig and Feza are perhaps the dominant soloists, but the two trombone players have their moment in the sun on 'Kongi's Theme' (a McGregor original for Malfatti) and 'Andromeda'. The only player under-represented on this particular occasion is the survivor, Moholo, who carries on the Blue Notes/Brotherhood tradition into the new, post-apartheid age.

Peter Brötzmann (born 1941)

ALL SAXOPHONES AND CLARINETS, TAROGATO

Studied art in Wuppertal, then played trad jazz as a teenager before moving into free playing in the early '60s, one of the first European saxophonists to do so. Led a trio with Han Bennink and Fred van Hove from 1968. While most renowned at home and in Europe during the '70s, in the '80s he began acquiring an American status and has since become a godfather-figure to more than one generation of free-jazz explorers.

♛ **** Machine Gun

FMP CD 24 *Brötzmann; Willem Breuker, Evan Parker (ts); Fred Van Hove (p); Buschi Niebergall, Peter Kowald (b); Han Bennink, Sven Ake Johansson (d).* 5/68.

Brötzmann's influence over the European free-music scene is enormous, and many of his pioneering achievements have only recently been acknowledged in the wider domain. He was playing free jazz in the early 1960s and by the time of this astounding album – originally pressed and distributed by the saxophonist himself – was a stylist whose intensity and sureness of focus were already established. The huge, screaming sound he makes is among the most exhilarating things in the music and, while he has often been typecast as a kind of sonic terrorist, that does insufficient justice to his mastery of the entire reed family. The only precedents for his early work are to be found in the contemporary records of Albert Ayler, but Brötzmann arrived at his methods independently of the American. His first trio record (currently out of print) is of a similar cast to, say, Ayler's *Spiritual Unity*, a raw, ferocious three-way assault, yet it is surpassed by *Machine Gun*, one of the most significant documents of the European free-jazz underground. The three saxophonists fire off a ceaseless round of blasting, overblown noise, built on the continuous crescendo managed by Bennink and Johansson, and, as chaotic as it sounds, the music is informed by an iron purpose and control. Although the recording is crude, the grainy timbre is a fitting medium for the music. In 1990, *Machine Gun* was reissued on CD with two alternative takes which match the original versions in their fearsome power.

*** The Berlin Concert

FMP CD 34/35 2CD *Brötzmann; Albert Mangelsdorff (tb); Fred Van Hove (p); Han Bennink (cl, d, perc).* 8/71.

The Berlin Concert, originally released as three separate albums, was culled from two days of performance at the Berlin Free Music Market, where the (long-standing) trio was augmented by trombonist Albert Mangelsdorff, whose experience in many other areas of jazz left him unintimidated by the demands of this group. Sound is again only average, but the vigour and earthy bravado of the quartet sustain the listener through the unglamorous circumstances of the music-making. There's little to choose among the various improvisations, but there is a long, compelling feature for Mangelsdorff in 'Alberts', and 'Couscouss De La Mauresque' includes some finely detailed playing by van Hove, even though his piano is often obscured.

***** Reserve**

FMP CD 17 *Brötzmann; Barre Phillips (b); Gunter Sommer (d).* 11/88.

A big jump forward from 1971, since the deletion of FMP's catalogue on vinyl has decimated this period of the Brötzmann discography, at least for the time being. Here, on relatively conventional turf, with the more gently inclined Phillips at the bass, Brötzmann digs through three long improvisations. Even on CD, sound is still only reasonable in fidelity, but the music has some attractive empathy, particularly between the leader and Phillips.

***** Wie Das Leben So Spielt**

FMP CD 22 *Brötzmann; Werner Ludi (as).* 9/89.

Ludi has drifted in and out of free playing for many years, but he sounds enthusiastic enough about being added to Brötzmann's pack of sparring partners on record. Playing only alto, while Brötz runs through his whole arsenal of reeds, Ludi concocts a stuttery romanticism (of sorts) to set against his companion's fields of fire. Highly invigorating, as usual.

*****(*) No Nothing**

FMP CD 34 *Brötzmann.* 8/90.

The saxophonist still has plenty of new things to say on his third solo album, perhaps the most quiescent of the three, yet often exploding into a logical catharsis. He changes between various saxes and clarinets during the 14-track programme and manages to sustain close to 75 minutes of music, all of it faithfully recorded by Jost Gebers.

*****(*) Dare Devil**

DIW 857 *Brötzmann; Haruhiko Gotsu (g); Tetsu Yahauchi (b); Shoji Hano (d).* 10/91.

Yet another sensational – and sensationally effective – blow-out. Recorded live in Tokyo with what sounds like some kind of Japanese hardcore band, Brötzmann sounds completely at home and enjoying every second of the challenge. Hano, who produced the record, beats out minimal but brazenly effective tattoos and Gotsu is a modest master at making riffs into feasible compositions. Brötzmann just goes at it head first.

***** The Marz Combo**

FMP CD 47 *Brötzmann; Toshinori Kondo (t); Paul Rutherford, Hannes Bauer (tb); Werner Ludi, Larry Stabbins (saxes); Nicky Skopelitis, Caspar Brötzmann (g); William Parker (b); Anton Fier (d).* 2/92.

Not, perhaps, one of the great Brötzmann sessions: the saxophonists are scarcely a match for the leader, or a useful contrast; while Rutherford is as magnificent as ever, few of the others really rise to the challenge of sharing time with Peter himself. Yet there are still moments of incandescence during the 74 minutes of music and the energy level rarely drops below invigorating.

***** Songlines**

FMP CD 53 *Brötzmann; Fred Hopkins (b); Rashied Ali (d).* 10/91.

*****(*) Die Like A Dog**

FMP CD 64 *Brötzmann; Toshinori Kondo (t, elec); William Parker (b); Hamid Drake (d).* 8/93.

***** Sacred Scrape**

Rastascan BRD-015 *Brötzmann; William Parker (b); Gregg Bendian (d).* 92.

As an elder statesman of free playing, Brötzmann is working steadily but not carelessly: his records are still soaked in the intensity which he's been pursuing for 30 years and, like Bailey or Parker, he alights on new situations and turns them to fit some part of an entrenched but flexible aesthetic. *Die Like A Dog* is the starkest, most Gothic of these three discs, a harrowing meditation on the life and work of Albert Ayler, whose earliest work mirrored Brötzmann's own. This is fuming and at times almost intractable stuff, but its spiritual measure is palpable, and the quartet play with stunning commitment. *Songlines* is more a 'traditional' free trio, the American team of Ali and Hopkins playing with a flair and (indeed!) swing which Brötzmann uses for shape and context with his own severe kind of lyricism. *Sacred Scrape* sets him alongside another generation of American improvisers, and this is a more scattershot battle of wits, Bendian's broken mass of rhythm and noise cracking around the reedman's grand oratory. Parker, a veteran of many a Cecil Taylor scrap, calmly finds his own space in the music. Three good ones.

***** Nothing To Say**

FMP CD 73 *Brötzmann (saxes, cl, tarogato solo).* 11/94.

Solo number four is in dedication to Oscar Wilde and is the calmest record of Brötzmann's career. He picks up the tenor only once, is rumbustious on the bass sax for the title-track but delivers an almost sorrowful lament on the same instrument for 'A Heavy Creeping Shade'. The tarogato and the alto sax bring out his most experimental and piercing solos. There is some stasis here and there; for once, a Brötzmann record seems a shade too long.

****** The Dried Rat-Dog**

Okkadisk 12004 *Brötzmann; Hamid Drake (d).* 5/94.

***** The 'WELS' Concert**

Okkadisk 12013 *As above, except add Mahmoud Gania (guembri, v).* 11/96.

Drake is a particularly perceptive and persuasive partner for Brötzmann. The great advantage of *The Dried Rat-Dog* is Bradley Parker-Sparrow's excellent sound, which lets one hear the nuances in both men's playing. Drake's rhythms have a steadier, more momentous pulse than most free-jazz drumming, and his use of frame drums and tablas adds a global touch that sits quite comfortably next to the saxophonist's characteristic energy. There are six pieces, brimful of eloquent interplay, and on 'Trees Have Roots In The Earth' and 'Dark Wings Carry Off The Sky', Brötz uncorks some of his most vivid tenor playing for a long time.

The live record is less impressive, perhaps since Gania's powerful role tends to undercut Brötzmann a little. Much of the dialogue in three long pieces is between Gania and Drake, with the former's shamanic vocals and thunderous vamps lending a Middle-Eastern flavour that Brötzmann tends to decorate rather than find a way into. Still a worthwhile event, though.

*** Sprawl

Trost 070 *Brötzmann; Alex Buess (reeds, elec); Stephan Wittwer (g); William Parker (b); Michael Wertmüller (d).* 8/96.

This is the group, Sprawl – possibly a one-off for this recording, so we are listing it under Brötzmann's name. Some of the time he's buried underneath a typhoon of electronics – whether engendered by Wittwer or Buess isn't entirely clear – and it's a bit of a sonic mudbath. The spookier textures of 'Martyrdom Und Genuss' are more absorbing. And there is also Parker to listen to – now not only a major individual voice, but a superb exponent of *arco* bass playing. A mysterious recording.

***(*) Evolving Blush Or Driving Original Sin

PSFD-79 *Brötzmann; Haino Keiji (v).* 4/96.

It's rare indeed for Brötzmann to be upstaged, yet Haino's vocals – a spectrum of sighs and whispers at one end and unearthly screams at the other – are, if anything, the more striking element here. The Japanese is better known as a guitarist, but he uses his throat exclusively on this extraordinary hour of music. Documented with starkly beautiful clarity, this is spacious, outward-going music, with tracts of silence surrounding the two voices and few hints of mere madness.

**** The Chicago Octet / Tentet

Okkadisk OD12022 3CD *Brötzmann; Joe McPhee (c, vtb, ss); Jeb Bishop (tb); Mars Williams (ts, as, cl); Ken Vandermark (ts, cl, bcl); Mats Gustafsson (bs, fluteophone); Fred Lonberg-Holm (clo); Kent Kessler (b); Michael Zerang, Hamid Drake (d).* 1–9/97.

Should be fairly described as a landmark recording on several levels: a major documentation of Brötzmann on an American label, a rare instance of his large-group music, and a definitive meeting of himself with some of the many American masters – from McPhee to Vandermark – who've been influenced by him. (We should also remark that the simple elegance of the design and artwork, also by Brötzmann, makes a mockery of the elaborate and preposterous packaging which major labels such as Verve seem to be investing so much effort in.) There are one and a half discs each of live and studio material, with three compositions appearing in each incarnation. In fact, Brötz himself contributes only two pieces, 'Burning Spirit' and 'Foolish Infinity'; the others come from Bishop, Gustafsson, Zerang, Drake and Lonberg-Holm, so it can fairly be said to be a co-operative effort, even if the saxophonist's name features on the marquee. Of course he plays a huge role as a performer, but so do the other reed players, besides the other participants. The sheer exhilaration of hearing Brötzmann, Williams, Vandermark and Gustafsson piledriving along as a reed section is about as awesome as you'd expect, but there's much else here to surprise and captivate: the worldly groove of 'Makapoor', the sombre granite-block textures of 'Other Brothers' which explode into a fast shuffle. An affecting tribute to the great man and his influence on a world of improvising which is still evolving and expanding – but the players were clearly having too much of a good time to get all weepy and emotional about it. Rah! Rah! Rah!

*** The Wild Man's Band

Ninth World Music 013 *Brötzmann; Johannes Bauer (tb); Peter Friis Nielsen (b); Peter Ole Jørgensen (d).* 97.

A rare encounter between Brötzmann and Bauer which is, in the end, somewhat disappointing. The clarinet comes out more often than the tenor, and Bauer settles for an expressionism which sometimes deteriorates into space-filling, even on a CD which only brushes the 40-minute mark.

**** Litle Birds Have Fast Hearts No. 1

FMP CD 97 *Brötzmann; Toshinori Kondo (t, elec); William Parker (b); Hamid Drake (d).* 11/97.

**** Little Birds Have Fast Hearts No. 2

FMP CD 101 *As above.* 11/97.

A return visit to the 'Die Like A Dog Quartet'. Parker and Drake are the best 'rhythm section' (if they can admit to that limited description) that Brötzmann has had for years. Kondo, one of the most unfettered and genie-like spirits in free playing, is far too seldom encountered in this kind of situation now, and his madcap sounds are the heat-haze high-altitude counter to Peter's massive, earth-rooted oratory. Recorded over three nights at the 1997 Total Music Meeting, these are all of a piece, and without any demerits. We're hoping that there's still enough left for a third volume.

***(*) Live At The Empty Bottle

Okkadisk 10005 *Brötzmann; Kent Kessler (b); Hamid Drake (d).* 7/98.

Kessler may not be William Parker's equal but he does pretty well, and Brötz sounds both passionate and cheery on this set of performances from Chicago. Drake isn't a muscleman drummer, but the leader has had so many of those behind him over the years that Hamid's more tractable, polymorphous sound is a source of refreshment: there's nothing wanting. An hour of top music.

***(*) Noise Of Wings

Slask SLACD 019 *Brötzmann; Peter Friis Nielsen (b); Peeter Uuskyla (d).* 3/99.

Have horn, will travel. Here he is in Kungälv, Sweden, for another bout. Nielsen is the surprise card, playing a juicy electric bass that keeps on bubbling up through the sound of wings beating. Uuskyla keeps hammering on his snare as if he has a Sisyphean requirement to stop it rolling back over him. The saxophonist sets up and goes, and gives it his all.

Ari Brown (born 1943)

TENOR, ALTO AND SOPRANO SAXOPHONES, FLUTE, PIANO

A veteran of Chicago's AACM, Brown has stayed as a local player and can be spotted with bandleaders such as as Kahlil El'Zabar and Malachi Thompson, as well as leading his own group.

***** Ultimate Frontier**

Delmark DE 486 *Brown; Kirk Brown (p); Yosef Ben Israel (b); Ayreeayl Ra (d); Dr Cuz, Enoch (perc).* 1/95.

Brown has been associated with many players in the AACM but he's fundamentally a conservative: the best things on this record come when he delivers a big, beefy ballad performance as on 'One For Luba' and 'Sincerity'. Much of the rest is an unmistakable Chicagoan stew of churning post-bop, 'Big V' and the crashing 'Motherless Child' sending the saxophonist to blaze away over a busy if rather faceless rhythm-section. For all his impetus, Brown is a rather galumphing horn-player, his phrases falling squarely on or around the beat. Taken a piece at a time, this is quite exciting but listeners may find themselves rather weatherbeaten by the end of it.

***** Venus**

Delmark DE 504 *Brown; Kirk Brown (p); Josef Ben Israel, Thaddeus Expose (b); Avreeayl Ra (d); Art Burton, Enoch (perc).* 3/98.

Brown has been steadily working on his Chicago turf, including a weekly gig at Fred Anderson's place, and making the occasional appearance on record to remind us that he's still out there. What's more or less the same band as last time finds him musing on some old spirits: Willie Pickens, Roscoe Mitchell, and several unspoken nods towards Coltrane. 'Rahsaan In The Serengeti' has him doing the Kirk thing by playing soprano and alto simultaneously. But it's still the more inward playing that suits him best: his duet with Kirk Brown on 'Oh What A World' is secular gospel of an individual order.

Clifford Brown (1930–56)

TRUMPET

Relative to the length of his career, Clifford Brown perhaps had a greater impact on the music than any comparable instrumentalist. A whole generation of jazz trumpeters were affected by his combination of fast attack and broad, lyrical tone, which sounded like a hybrid of Fats Navarro and Miles Davis. Brownie's early death was a genuine tragedy for the music, its reverberations still felt two generations later.

*****(*) The Beginning And The End**

Columbia 477737 *Brown; Vance Wilson (as, ts); Ziggy Vines, Billy Root (ts); Sam Dockery, Duke Wells (p); Eddie Lambert (g); James Johnson, Ace Tisone (b); Osie Johnson, Ellis Tolin (d); Chris Powell (v, perc).* 3/52–6/56.

****** The Complete Blue Note And Pacific Jazz Recordings**

Blue Note CDP 8 34195 4CD *Brown; J.J Johnson (tb); Stu Williamson (vtb); Gigi Gryce (as, f); Lou Donaldson (as); Charlie Rouse, Zoot Sims (ts); Jimmy Heath (ts, bs); Bob Gordon (bs); Russ Freeman, Elmo Hope, John Lewis, Horace Silver (p); Percy Heath, Joe Mondragon, Curley Russell, Carson Smith (b); Art Blakey, Kenny Clarke, Philly Joe Jones, Shelly Manne (d).* 6/53–8/54.

***** Clifford Brown Memorial**

Original Jazz Classics OJC 017 *Brown; Art Farmer, Idrees Sulieman (t); Herb Mullins, Ake Persson (tb); Arne Domnérus, Gigi Gryce (as); Benny Golson (ts); Oscar Estell, Lars Gullin (bs); Tadd Dameron, Bengt Hallberg (p); Percy Heath, Gunnar Johnson (b); Philly Joe Jones, Jack Noren (d); collective personnel.* 6–9/53.

*****(*) Clifford Brown Quartet In Paris**

Original Jazz Classics OJC 357 *Brown; Henri Renaud (p); Pierre Michelot (b); Benny Bennett (d).* 10/53.

*****(*) Clifford Brown Sextet In Paris**

Original Jazz Classics OJC 358 *Brown; Gigi Gryce (as); Henri Renaud (p); Jimmy Gourley (g); Pierre Michelot (b); Jean-Louis Viale (d).* 10/53.

*****(*) The Complete Paris Sessions: Volume 1**

Vogue 114561 *Brown; Gigi Gryce (as); Henri Renaud (p); Jimmy Gourley (g); Pierre Michelot (b); Jean-Louis Viale (d).* 10/53.

*****(*) The Complete Paris Sessions: Volume 2**

Vogue 114562 *As above, except add Art Farmer, Walter Williams, Quincy Jones (t), Jimmy Cleveland (tb), Anthony Ortega (as), André Dabonneville, Clifford Solomon (ts), William Boucaya (bs).* 10/53.

***** The Complete Paris Sessions: Volume 3**

Vogue 114872 *As above.* 10/53.

In the days after Clifford Brown died – Richie Powell with him – and as the news filtered through to clubs and studios up and down the country, hardened jazz musicians put away their horns and quietly went home to grieve. Only twenty-six, Brown was almost universally liked and admired. Free of the self-destructive 'personal problems' that haunted jazz at the time, he had seemed destined for ever greater things when his car skidded off the turnpike.

To this day, his influence on trumpeters is immense, less audibly than Miles Davis's, perhaps, because more pervasive. Though most of his technical devices – long, burnished phrases, enormous melodic and harmonic compression within a chorus, internal divisions of the metre – were introduced by Dizzy Gillespie and Fats Navarro, his two most significant models, it was Brownie who melded them into a distinctive and coherent personal style of great expressive power. Almost every trumpeter who followed, including present-day figures like Wynton Marsalis, has drawn heavily on his example; few though have managed to reproduce the powerful singing grace he took from the ill-starred Navarro.

After a first, near-fatal car accident, Brown gigged in R&B bands (the tail-end of that period is documented on the Columbia) and then worked briefly with Tadd Dameron, before touring Europe with Lionel Hampton towards the end of 1953, on which he enjoyed a good-natured and stage-managed rivalry with Art Farmer, and recorded the excellent quartet, sextet and big-band sides now reissued on OJC and sampled on *Blue And Brown*. By this time, he had already recorded the session on the confusingly titled *Memorial* (OJC) and *Memorial Album* (Blue Note). The former combined European and American sessions and isn't the most compelling of his recordings, though Dameron's arrangements are as challenging as always, and there are some fine moments from the Scandinavians on the September date.

The four-CD compilation of all the Blue Note and Capitol recordings is as elegantly remastered and packaged as anyone could possibly wish. Two of these sessions were recorded under the leadership or co-leadership of J.J. Johnson, Art Blakey and Lou Donaldson. The live Birdland sessions of February 1954 are splendidly extended and afford the best possible glimpse of the young genius on the brink of his breakthrough. The rest of the material simply teems with promise and it is almost inconceivable – indeed heartbreaking – listening to the first three discs, to think that none of it would ever come to proper fruition. The sheer fecundity of Brown's musical imagination never fails to amaze.

The Complete Paris Sessions volumes are full of interesting material, but nowhere does the trumpeter really knock sparks off any of the themes, and he seems hampered by busy or hesitant arrangements. Perhaps the best of the tracks are the two sextet takes of 'All The Things You Are' and the three quartet versions, each subtly different, of 'I Can Dream, Can't I?'. *Blue And Brown* doesn't offer either, but it might seem an attractive alternative, if only for the fact that its selection of tracks from the 1953 Paris sessions is so determinedly perverse. There have to be some doubts about the French rhythm section, experienced as it was, but it shapes up pretty well in comparison to the Scandinavian players on *Memorial*.

****** Brownie**

Emarcy 838 306-16 10CD *Brown; Maynard Ferguson, Clark Terry (t); Herbie Mann (f); Danny Bank (f, bs); Herb Geller, Joe Maini (as); Walter Benton, Harold Land, Paul Quinichette, Sonny Rollins (ts); Kenny Drew, Jimmy Jones, Junior Mance, Richie Powell (p); Barry Galbraith (g); Joe Benjamin, Keter Betts, Curtis Counce, Milt Hinton, George Morrow (b); Oscar Pettiford (b, clo); Bobby Donaldson, Roy Haynes, Osie Johnson, Max Roach (d); Helen Merrill, Dinah Washington, Sarah Vaughan (v); strings arranged and conducted by Neal Hefti; collective personnels.* 8/54–2/56.

****** Jazz Masters: Clifford Brown**

Emarcy 842933 *Brown; as above.* 2/54–2/56.

****** Alone Together**

Verve 526373-2 *Brown; Harold Land, Hank Mobley, Paul Quinichette, Sonny Rollins (ts); Danny Bank (bs); Herbie Mann (f); Ray Bryant, Jimmy Jones, Richie Powell (p); Barry Galbraith (g); Joe Benjamin, Milt Hinton, George Morrow (b); Roy Haynes, Osie Johnson, Max Roach (d); Helen Merrill, Sarah Vaughan (v); strings.* 8/54–1/56.

***** Study In Brown**

Emarcy 814 646 2 *Brown; Harold Land (ts); Richie Powell (p); George Morrow (b); Max Roach (d).* 55.

***** More Study In Brown**

Emarcy 814 637 2 *As above, except add Sonny Rollins (ts).* 56.

Brownie gathers together all the material Brown recorded for Emarcy between 2 August 1954 and 16 February 1956. It includes no fewer than nine previously unreleased takes, together with a number of alternative takes that have appeared in other contexts. The research was done by the indefatigable Kiyoshi Koyama and the recordings remastered digitally from the originals held at the Polygram Tape Facility at Edison, New Jersey. The liner-notes are by Dan Morgenstern and are impeccably detailed.

Inevitably, the best of the music is in the Roach–Brown sessions. The drummer's generosity in making the younger man co-leader is instantly and awesomely repaid. On the earliest of the sessions (Discs 1 and 2, originally released as *Brown And Roach Incorporated*), there is a brilliantly impressionistic arrangement of Bud Powell's 'Parisian Thoroughfare' (whose onomatopoeic effects are echoed on a 'Take The "A" Train' from February 1955, Disc 9), a superb 'Jordu', and an offcut of Brown soloing on 'Sweet Clifford', a reworking of the 'Sweet Georgia Brown' changes. Whether cup-muted or open, he sounds relaxed and completely confident. Land plays a more than supportive role and is generously featured on 'Darn That Dream'.

The next session (Discs 3 and 4) was a studio jam recorded a week or so later, with Herb Geller, the un-chancy Joe Maini and Walter Benton all on saxophones, and Kenny Drew, Curtis Counce and Roach filling out the band. There are three takes (the first incomplete) of a blues called 'Coronado' (Disc 3), then extended versions of 'You Go To My Head', 'Caravan' – and a fragmentary variant, 'Boss Man' – and 'Autumn In New York'. Posthumously released as *Best Coast Jazz* and *Clifford Brown All Stars*, they contain some of the trumpeter's weakest and most diffuse playing. Always eminently disciplined, his solos lost much of their shape in this context. However, it's worth it for Maini's contribution.

The 14 August jam with Dinah Washingon (Discs 5 and 6) includes over-long versions of 'What Is This Thing Called Love', 'Move' and 'I'll Remember April', but there are two fine medleys and Brown is superb on 'It Might As Well Be Spring', which extends his accompanist's role. He has less space round Sarah Vaughan (Disc 7), but he compresses his responses to the vocal line into beautifully polished choruses and half-choruses; Paul Quinichette is magnificent. Brown also accompanies Helen Merrill (Disc 8) on her debut recording; this is slighter, even prettified, and Quincy Jones's arrangements are definitely overcooked, but the trumpeter's contributions are gently effective.

The first quintet sessions for six months (Disc 9) find the group in rattling form. *Study In Brown* marks the trumpeter's emergence as an individual star of formidable magnitude. He takes 'Cherokee' at a dangerous pace and doesn't fudge a single note (there are bootleg recordings of him doggedly alternating and inverting practice phrases). Throughout the album, his entries have real *presence* and his delivery floats over the rhythm section without ever losing contact with Roach's compelling metres. 'Jacqui' is relatively unusual fare, and it may be significant that Land, with his West Coast roots, handles it most comfortably. This was the saxophonist's last studio date with the band. His replacement, Sonny Rollins, has at this point in his career a slightly crude approach. He is nevertheless bursting with ideas that push the group's capabilities to the utmost and his first statement on 'Gertrude's Bounce' may suggest recourse to the review button, so daring is it in conception and execution. Brown himself sounds as though he must be reading off prearranged sequences, firing out eight-, four- and two-bar statements that seem to contain more and more musical information the shorter they get. This is the material released as *At Basin Street*.

Koyama has dug out previously unsuspected masters of 'Love Is A Many Splendored Thing' (taken at a distinctly unslushy pace) and 'Flossie Lou' (which reworks 'Jeepers Creepers'). A rehearsal fragment of the latter is included on a 3-inch bonus CD single, like the cherry on top of the cake. *Brownie* is a bulky and, inevitably, expensive work of documentation. The trumpeter has scarcely a bad moment, but there is a lot of material to digest, and newcomers might prefer to begin with the excellent

Jazz Masters compilation, which draws from all but the unfeasibly long jam-sessions and consists of 'The Blues Walk', 'I Get A Kick Out Of You', 'Jordu', 'Parisian Thoroughfare', 'Daahoud', 'It's Crazy', 'Stardust', 'I'll Remember April', 'I've Got You Under My Skin', 'Yesterdays' and the original release of 'Flossie Lou'. For accessibility and sheer value it could hardly be bettered. At least some of those who invest will want to move on to the Complete Works. Brown's qualities ring out on every bar.

Alone Together, it should be made clear, consists of one CD of Brownie material (much of it with Roach) and one CD of somewhat later Roach recordings; these latter are discussed in the appropriate place. As a package it makes a very attractive introduction to both artists. Of Brownie, there is the magnificent 'Joy Spring' from August 1954, the February 1955 'Cherokee' from *A Study In Brown*, 'Gertrude's Bounce' from January 1956 with 11 other tracks from the Emarcy sessions. No surprises, but elegantly packaged and very desirable.

Study In Brown and *More* contain material already covered elsewhere but they are also attractive individually. Brown's 'Cherokee' is still one of the most arresting performances in modern jazz and his solo on 'Take The "A" Train' is a masterpiece of organization, holding a typically long line in suspension over many bars.

****** The Ultimate Clifford Brown**

Verve 539776-2 *Brown; as for Verve recordings above.* 54–56.

Another in Verve's excellent series of artist-selected compilations. This time, it's new man Nicholas Payton who chooses the tracks, including doubtless a few that had a direct impact on his own playing style. Nearly all standards and covers, in the event, and with perhaps too diplomatic an emphasis on Brownie's work as accompanist to Helen Merrill, Sassie and Dinah Washington, but irreproachable apart from that. Anyone who encounters the opening 'Gertrude's Bounce' and catches the Brown–Roach–Rollins–Richie Powell–Morrow band for the first time is likely to be hooked for the duration.

*****(*) Clifford Brown With Strings**

Emarcy 558 078 *Brown; Richie Powell (p); Barry Galbraith (g); George Morrow (b); Max Roach (d); strings.* 1/55.

Beautifully repackaged and presented, the January 1955 sessions are, in retrospect, most remarkable for Neal Hefti's delicately nuanced arrangements which always seem to deliver up surprises. The 12 tracks are almost perfectly uniform in length and delivery, and it's all the more remarkable that they remain fresh and inventive. Brown sounds as bright as a new pin in this digitally remastered version, but he isn't artificially foregrounded in front of the strings; they receive their due share as well.

Jeri Brown

VOCAL

A modern standards singer with an approach somewhere between classic and experimentalist.

*****(*) Mirage**

Justin Time JUST 38 *Brown; Fred Hersch (p); Daniel Lessard (b).* 2 & 3/91.

The big difference between Broadway and opera singers, or between musicals and opera, is that the former always does (or always should) sound conversational. The lovely Jeri Brown has the ability to make every song sound as if spoken directly and without artifice. Even her scatting sounds like a kind of thinking aloud, unhistrionic and much subtler than might at first appear.

The first of these records is certainly the most conventional, and *Mirage* is almost hijacked by Fred Hersch's wonderfully subtle accompaniments. He is credited with the title-tune and with 'A Child's Song', and is co-writer on the ambitious 'Ten Twenty', which may have been kept to last deliberately but seems rather thrown away in that lowly position. Brown is not a confident bopper – 'Good Bait' is not going to catch anything – but she positively glows on the less rhythmic, more through-composed pieces. Very definitely an album that grows.

****** 'Unfolding' The Peacocks**

Justin Time JUST 45 *Brown; Michael Dubeau (ss, shakuhachi); Peter Leitch (g); Kirk Lightsey (p); Rufus Reid (b); Wali Muhammad (d); Suzanne Doucet, Shawn Smith (v).* 2/92.

****** A Timeless Place**

Justin Time JUST 70 *Brown; Jimmy Rowles (p, v); Eric Von Essen (b).* 5/94.

The long-underrated Jimmy Rowles has been a big influence on Ms Brown's work. He is the guiding spirit of *'Unfolding' The Peacocks*, and he appears on the later record, playing and singing. Ms Brown effectively deconstructs Rowles's classic 'The Peacocks', turning it into a rich vocalization somewhat in the manner of Norma Winstone (who provides the lyrics to 'A Timeless Place' on the later record). The mournful yelp of the male peafowl is suggested by Michael Dubeau's shakuhachi part; his only other contribution to the record is a soprano line on 'Jean', but both are clinchers. Lightsey and Reid develop atmospheric, sepia-tinted backdrops, but the attention is constantly on the singer. 'Orange Coloured Sky' is wholly delightful, and Bob Dorough's 'Wouldn't You' sounds freshly minted. The two backing singers appear on the eerie 'Tuang Guru', a Saharan chorale by Abdullah Ibrahim, further evidence of Ms Brown's adventurousness.

The vocal duet with Rowles on 'Don't Quite Know' is glorious, and Jimmy's playing throughout the album has a quietly magisterial quality. He co-wrote 'Morning Star' with the great Johnny Mercer and delivers it many years later as if it had only just risen in his mind.

*****(*) Fresh Start**

Justin Time JUST 78 *Brown; Greg Carter (ss); Cyrus Chestnut (p); Avery Sharpe (b); Wali Muhammad (d).* 5/95.

***** April In Paris**

Justin Time JUST 92 *Brown; Alain Jean-Marie (p); Pierre Michelot (b); John Betsch (d).* 4/96.

Was a fresh start needed? Or did Jeri Brown merely want to explore other dimensions of her vocal talents? Certainly there was nothing to suggest that she wasn't working a fertile and long-lasting seam, but the new record sees her working in a much lower register than before, not always with absolute assurance. The opening 'Come, Come And Play With Me', co-written with Greg Carter, is unexpectedly oblique and seemingly influenced by stuff Cassandra Wilson was doing back in M-BASE days. Brown's scat is dark-toned and angular, pitched just in front of a superb solo from Avery Sharpe, who is the most prominent band member. (Carter is featured on just one track, and it might have been good to have heard a little more from him.) She works approximately the same territory on a wordless version of Oscar Pettiford's 'Harlem After Dark', followed later by Tadd Dameron's expansively boppish 'You're A Joy'. Cyrus Chestnut has backed Betty Carter, and she seems another feasible source for at least some of the material. 'Orange Sky' is mentioned again, obviously a strong personal resonance, and there is a rather unexpected version of 'Shall We Gather By The River', before the title-piece is reprised. A nicely shaped album, but not one that really plays to her strengths.

The death of Jimmy Rowles meant that there were to be no more duets. *April In Paris* includes 'Morning Lovely', a Rowles tune which seems to sit outside either her normal or even her more recent range, but it works beautifully nevertheless. Again, the band is very good. Jean-Marie has more than a hint of Bill Evans about him and John Betsch is exactly the sort of delicate, tuneful drummer singers revel in. It's Michelot, though, who provides most of the drama, light and shade aplenty and seemingly endless invention throughout a rather odd roster of songs: 'Once Upon A Summertime', 'The Twelfth Of Never', 'Summertime', 'Greensleeves' and 'The Windmills Of Your Mind'. Co-written with Kenny Wheeler, 'Gentle Piece' is thrown away in the opening slot; 'When April Comes Again' would have been a better call, both musically and thematically. Dare we say ... a slightly disappointing record. Established Jeri Brown fans will find much to treasure on it, but anyone who hasn't yet been converted should perhaps begin elsewhere.

*****(*) Zaius**

Justin Time JUST 117-2 *Brown; Don Braden, David Murray (ts); John Hicks (p); Curtis Lundy, Avery Sharpe (b); Sangoma Everett (d).* 98.

****** I've Got Your Number**

Justin Time JUST 122-2 *As above, except add Wali Muhammad (d); Leon Thomas (v).* 1 & 11/98.

'I've Got Your Number' is not just an excellent vocal performance. It's also a reference to Jeri's bulging contacts book. The best measure of her growing confidence and reputation is her ability to call together a band like this. For some reason, the chemistry doesn't quite come off on the first of the pair. Hicks and bassists Lundy and Sharpe (who share duties) are superb vocal accompanists, underpinning the spooky drama of 'You Must Believe In Spring' and always leaving lots of space round the singer. They all must have done 'Softly, As In A Morning Sunrise' a thousand times before, but it still comes across as fresh as the new day.

David Murray's interest in song has been more emphatically stated than acted upon. His role on 'Midnight Sun' and on Gerry Niewood's 'Joy' is a revelation. Don Braden makes more of an impact on *Zaius* and only re-emerges for 'As Long As You're Living' on the second record which is well sequenced and comfortably paced. It seems only the day before yesterday that Jeri Brown was a new face and one to watch. Looking at that face has never been arduous, but it's maybe distracted us from the sheer quality, and now the amount, of her recorded output.

Marion Brown (born 1935)

ALTO SAXOPHONE

Studied music in his native Atlanta, then was caught up in New York's free jazz of the '60s. After some years in Europe, returned to the USA, and has since worked mainly in education, specializing in African musical and linguistic traditions.

*****(*) Three For Shepp**

Impulse! IMPCD 12692 *Brown; Grachan Moncur III (tb); Dave Burrell, Stanley Cowell (p); Norris Jones (b); Bobby Capp, Beaver Harris (d).* 12/66.

****** Porto Novo**

Black Lion BLCD 760200 *Brown; Leo Smith (t); Maarten Altena (b); Han Bennink (d).* 12/67, 12/70.

***** Afternoon Of A Georgia Faun**

ECM 527710-2 *Brown; Anthony Braxton (as, ss, cl, cbcl, Chinese musette, f, perc); Bennie Maupin (ts, af, acorn, bells, wood f, perc); Chick Corea (p, bells, gong, perc); Larry Curtis (p); Jack Gregg (b, perc); Billy Malone (d); Andrew Cyrille (perc); William Green (Top O'Lin, perc); Jeanne Lee (v, perc); Gayle Palmore (v, p, perc).* 8/70.

****** Recollections – Ballads And Blues For Saxophone**

Creative Works CW 1001 *Brown (as solo).* 87.

Possessed of a sweet, slightly fragile tone and a seemingly limitless melodic resource, Brown is nevertheless one of the most undervalued of contemporary saxophonists. There is a certain poignant irony in the fact that his finest recorded work should be solo saxophone, for he is a dedicated educator with a long-standing commitment to collective – and often untrained or amateur – music-making. Brown's one and only recording for ECM, *Afternoon Of A Georgia Faun*, came out of that ethos, performed by six instrumentalists and three assistants on 'little instruments' like Brown's invented Top O'Lin (pot lids fixed to a board and bowed like a fiddle). All the performers permutate their instruments at work-stations in fulfilment of Brown's ideal of 'interchangeable discourse'. The results, predictably, are very uneven and slightly unkempt, but there is some very affecting music on the album. Chick Corea's solo on the title-piece is near perfect, and both Braxton and Maupin produce passages of great beauty.

Archie Shepp famously may or may not have appeared uncredited in the closing moments of John Coltrane's momentous *A Love Supreme*. One certainly expects to hear him on *Three For Shepp*, not least because he glowers out at the listener from the cover, a pose in sharp contrast to Brown's intent and slightly cautious stare. The session consists of three Brown compositions and three – 'Spooks', 'West India' and 'Delicado' – by Shepp. The two had worked together for Impulse! when the alto man played on Shepp's *Fire Music* and the musical sympathy established there is unmistakable. Brown's 'Fortunato' suggests a direct influence, albeit without Archie's fierce ideological muscle. The contrast between the two rhythm sections is interesting and instructive. Sirone plays on both, but the partnership of Dave Burrell and Bobby Capp works ideally for the leader's own themes, while the more emphatic and blues-influenced Shepp tunes call for players of Cowell's and Harris's authority. The front-row combination of alto and trombone still sounds faintly alien, but Moncur is such an expressive player that the slight mismatch of register – still evident on CD – doesn't jar more than incidentally.

Porto Novo offers the irresistible attraction of hearing Brown and Smith together, a meeting between two musical eccentrics neither of whom hears pitch in quite the same way as anyone else. 'Sound Structure' is immensely powerful, fuelled by Bennink's offbeat swing and Altena's fruity bass chords. A surprise and a delight. Good to have it back in circulation.

Recollections shouldn't be overlooked at any price. A near-perfect set of standards, ranging from 'Angel Eyes' and 'Black And Tan Fantasy' to 'Blue Monk' and 'After The Rain', it poignantly exposes Brown in reverie. His blues are technically watertight and, though the tempo is varied only minimally, the whole set communicates a wide range of emotions. Very warmly recommended indeed.

Ray Brown (born 1926)

DOUBLE BASS, CELLO

The most frequently cited artist in our first and subsequent editions was bassist Ray Brown, whose career has spanned the bebop era and a myriad sessions as sideman and leader since then. Brown was born in Pittsburgh, witnessed the birth-pangs of bebop, acted as music director for his wife, Ella Fitzgerald, played with Dizzy Gillespie and as a result was involved in the formation of what became the Modern Jazz Quartet. He also worked with Oscar Peterson and was a founder member of the LA4, whose brand of soft Latin jazz was a perfect vehicle for Brown's uncluttered rhythm and tasteful melodic sense.

*****(*) Much In Common**

Verve 533259-2 2CD *Brown; Nat Adderley (c); Joe Newman, Ernie Royal, Clark Terry, Snooky Young (t); Jimmy Cleveland, Paul Faulise, Urbie Green, Melba Liston, Tom McIntosh, Tony Studd, Britt Woodman (tb); Ray Alonge (frhn); Bob Ashton, Danny Bank, Jimmy Heath, Romeo Penque, Phil Woods (reeds); Cannonball Adderley, Earl Warren (as); Seldon Powell (ts); Jerome Richardson (bs, f); Milt Jackson (vib); Tommy Flanagan, Hank Jones (p); Wild Bill Davis (org); Kenny Burrell (g); Sam Jones (b); Albert 'Tootie' Heath, Osie Johnson, Grady Tate (d); Marion Williams (v).* 1/62–1/65.

A valuable compendium of three of Brown's albums for Verve, co-starring with vibist Milt Jackson (his companion on the small-group *Much In Common* from 1964 and the eponymous co-fronted session from the following January) and also Cannonball Adderley, who is the featured soloist on the earliest of the three sessions. This date, credited to Brown's All-Star Big Band, also affords a chance to hear Brown the cellist on three numbers, and the reissue includes valuable alternatives of 'Work Song' and his own 'Cannon Bilt'. The sides with Jackson are the best on the record, though, inventive to the highest degree and brimming with ideas at every turn. Three versions of 'Stella By Starlight' is probably pushing it a bit, but there is more than enough strong music to fill an attractive double CD, and fans of any of the three principals (or indeed of arrangers Ernie Wilkins, Oliver Nelson and Jimmy Heath) will find much to enjoy. Modern sound cleans up the textures considerably and the bassist is properly audible on *Much In Common* at last.

***** Brown's Bag**

Concord CCD 6019 *Brown; Blue Mitchell (t); Richie Kamuca (ts); Dave Grusin, Art Hillery (p); John Collins (g); John Guerin, Jimmie Smith (d).* 12/75.

***** Something For Lester**

Original Jazz Classics OJC 412 *Brown; Cedar Walton (p); Elvin Jones (d).* 6/77.

Bassists seem to job quite promiscuously, and bassists of Brown's calibre are hard to find. As with Paul Chambers and Ron Carter, the Brown discography is enormous. Unlike the other two, however, his output as a leader is proportionately and qualitatively substantial. He is almost certainly best heard in any of the trios featuring pianist Gene Harris, his most sympathetic collaborator, but the relaxed session on *Brown's Bag* features some fine moments from the still-undervalued Kamuca and the lamented Blue Mitchell. The sound is a shade flat, but the music is well up to Brown's impressive standard. The OJC is an old Contemporary release, with that label's openness of sound. Jones isn't perhaps the ideal drummer and he gets in the way on 'Georgia On My Mind', but all in all this is a very enjoyable session and Brown's introductory statements on 'Love Walked In' are pure class.

*****(*) As Good As It Gets**

Concord CCD 4066 *Brown; Jimmy Rowles (p).* 12/77.

***** Tasty!**

Concord CCD 4122 *As above.* 10/79.

Some musical partnerships add weight to the hypothesis that a deity – not necessarily omniscient or omnipresent, but definitely swinging – oversees human affairs. *As Good As It Gets* is an accompanists' master class. Rowles used to work for Billie Holiday and others; Brown was Ella Fitzgerald's husband. Together, they play quietly and lyrically, tracing out a programme of favourite tunes – 'Alone Together', 'Sophisticated Lady', 'Like Someone In Love' – with consummate professionalism.

Recorded a couple of years later, *Tasty!* is something of a retread, but exquisitely done, and in some respects the material selected is even better suited to the two players. The set opens with 'A Sleeping Bee', includes 'My Ideal', 'Come Sunday' and 'Nancy (With The Laughing Face)' and ends with Charlie Chaplin's deathless 'Smile', which is exactly what this lovely set will make you do.

**** Live At The Concord Jazz Festival**

Concord CCD 4102 *Brown; Monty Alexander (p); Jeff Hamilton (d); Ernestine Anderson (v).* 79.

With his foot off the gas, Brown can be as ordinary as the next guy. Most of the running here seems to come from the interplay between Alexander and the impressive Hamilton, but that impression may be unfairly compounded by an uneasy sound-mix. Ernestine Anderson is an acquired taste which not everyone may have the patience to acquire. She shares something of the great Al Hibbler's surrealist diction but little of his latterly wacky charm. The stars are mostly for Hamilton.

*****(*) Soular Energy**

Concord CCD 4268 *Brown; Red Holloway (ts); Gene Harris (p); Emily Remler (g); Gerryck King (d).* 8/84.

A really fine album which only needs Jeff Hamilton in his usual slot behind the drums to lift it into minor-classic status. King is a fine drummer but lacks sparkle and is inclined to hurry the pulse unnecessarily. Perhaps in retaliation, Brown takes the '"A" Train' at a pace which suggests privatization may be around the corner. Slowed down to an almost terminal grind, it uncovers all manner of harmonic quirks which Brown and the attentive Harris exploit with great imagination. Red Holloway and – rather more anonymously – the late Emily Remler sign up for a shortish and slightly inconsequential 'Mistreated But Undefeated Blues'. Brown's counter-melody figures on 'Cry Me A River' and, especially, the closing 'Sweet Georgia Brown' could almost be taped as his calling-card. Exemplary.

**** Don't Forget The Blues**

Concord CCD 4293 *Brown; Al Grey (tb); Ron Eschete (g); Gene Harris (p); Grady Tate (d).* 5/85.

***** The Red Hot**

Concord CCD 4315 *Brown; Gene Harris (p); Mickey Roker (d).* 11 & 12/85.

The first is a cheery 'all-star' – so why Eschete? – session that never really amounts to much. Tate is another in a line of first-class drummers to have recorded under Brown's leadership. In some regards he is the most conventional, though Roker is no revolutionary either, and there is a slightly stilted quality to some of the medium-tempo tracks. Just when things were looking bleak for 1985, Brown turns in *Red Hot*, a strong, gamey trio with one of his most effective partners, the highly adaptable Harris. 'Love Me Tender' is a bit of fluff, but 'Have You Met Miss Jones?' and 'Street Of Dreams' are both substantial performances.

*****(*) Bam Bam Bam**

Concord CCD 4375 *Brown; Gene Harris (p); Jeff Hamilton (d).* 7/88.

***** Summer Wind**

Concord CCD 4426 *As above.* 12/88.

Two superb live sets from an excellent working trio who interweave seamlessly and earn their solo spaces many times over. Brown's writing and arranging have been much more confident of late. The version of 'A Night In Tunisia' on *Bam Bam Bam* is quite remarkable, featuring hand percussion from Hamilton, and the tributes on both albums to Sonny Rollins ('T.S.R.'), Victor Feldman ('Rio') and Art Blakey ('Buhaina Buhaina') are intelligent reinventions of some unexpected stylistic associations. Brown's blues stylings get more assured with each passing year. Originals like 'The Real Blues', the eponymous 'Bam Bam Bam' and Milt Jackson's oblique, bebop-flavoured 'Bluesology' all repay careful attention. 'If I Loved You', 'Summertime' and 'Days Of Wine And Roses' all comfortably fit the former Mr Ella Fitzgerald, while 'It Don't Mean A Thing', 'Mona Lisa' and 'Put Your Little Foot Right Out' uncover quite different aspects of Brown's increasingly complex musical persona.

*****(*) 3 Dimensional**

Concord CCD 4520 *Brown; Gene Harris (p); Jeff Hamilton (d).* 5/89, 2/91.

*****(*) Moore Makes 4**

Concord CCD 4477 *As above, except add Ralph Moore (ts).* 91.

Vintage stuff from the very best of Brown's groups. This line-up has the easy cohesion of Oscar Peterson's trios, and Brown's busy lines often suggest Peterson's approach to a melody. Following on from an Ellington medley, Coltrane's 'Equinox' on *3 Dimensional* is a rare stab at the post-bop repertoire, and the group handle it comfortably. There are signs, though, that Brown is over-eager to diversify, and the album's a bit shapeless.

Does Moore make more? On balance, yes. The cover depicts a saxophone standing in as fourth leg of a tea-table. The Brown trio has stood up on its own for years now and scarcely needs the help. On the other hand, Moore's forceful tenor adds such an effective element to 'My Romance' and the superb 'Stars Fell On Alabama' that one wonders what filled those spaces before. Brown's bass lines are still among the best in the business, and the desk-slide was pushed well up to catch them.

*****(*) Bassface**

Telarc CD 83340 *Brown; Benny Green (p); Jeff Hamilton (d).* 93.

***** Don't Get Sassy**

Telarc CD 83368 *As above.* 94.

The shift to Telarc was a positive one for Brown, and to date it has yielded more albums than he had been able to release on Concord. The working trio of the time was to be one of the best he ever assembled, and these two albums are testimony to the understanding that grew between them. There's not much to say about either critically, beyond the obvious point that the sound-quality is the equal of the Concord sessions, but that Brown himself doesn't seem to be stretching and he remains content to leave the spadework to his two younger cohorts.

***** Some Of My Best Friends Are ... The Piano Players**

Telarc CD 83373 *Brown; Benny Green, Ahmad Jamal, Geoff Keezer, Dado Moroni, Oscar Peterson (p).* 94.

*****(*) Some Of My Best Friends Are ... The Sax Players**

Telarc CD 83388 *Brown; Benny Carter, Jesse Davis (as); Joe Lovano, Ralph Moore, Joshua Redman, Stanley Turrentine (ts); Benny Green (p); Gregory Hutchinson (d).* 11/95.

It's axiomatic that Brown adapts to almost any musical company. These two sessions set out to nail the point for ever. The choice of piano players was scarcely controversial, though Moroni perhaps sticks out as the least celebrated of the bunch. Jamal is predictably smooth and over-prepared, and it's Peterson who approaches the session with the most open mind, pitching into his cameos with cheerful good grace.

It's the saxophone album, no less appealing in concept or execution, which stands out; if you wanted to provide someone with a sampler which helped explain how rhythm sections shift their premisses and adapt to a new voice, then this would be the logical primer. Everyone is absolutely in character. Jesse Davis does his now-accomplished Parker impression on 'Moose The Mooche' and a quieter, Hodges-tinged take on 'These Foolish Things'. Carter is featured on 'Love Walked In' and 'Fly Me To The Moon', proving once again that he is indestructible. Redman and Moore are inevitably less assured and they have less experience with standards, and in the event the laurels go to the veteran Turrentine and the younger Lovano, who kicks off with 'How High The Moon' and continues with 'Easy Living', while big Stan contributes the Illinois Jacquet theme, 'Port Of Rico', and 'God Bless The Child'. Programmed into the CD are brief conversation tracks with each guest, which can be cued to play just before the relevant number. After a couple of goes, most listeners will dispense with them, but they're nice to have.

***** Seven Steps To Heaven**

Telarc CD 83384 *Brown; Benny Green (p); Ulf Wakenius (g); Gregory Hutchinson (d).* 95.

Wakenius has been making waves in recent years and has proved himself to be a guitarist of genuine initiative and talent. Even so, he's a surprising guest on this trio set, and he melds only rather uneasily with a settled line-up. Green and Hutchinson are both in rather muted form, and much of the emphasis this time out falls to Brown himself.

***** SuperBass**

Telarc CD 83393 *Brown; Benny Green (p); John Clayton Jr, Christian McBride (b); Gregory Hutchinson (d).* 10/96.

Recorded live at Sculler's nightclub in Boston, this fascinating encounter is a feast for bassophiles. Brown and former Basie stalwart Clayton stand for the older generation, but McBride, hip as he is, is well clued up on the history of his instrument, and most certainly he isn't left standing. After stating the 'SuperBass' theme, the three stringfellows launch into a riveting interpretation of 'Blue Monk'. After very little time, it's easy to separate the voices and determine who's playing what. Brown tends to favour the fast, upper register lines, Clayton the low, gentle throb, and McBride the intermediate harmonic region, never overawed or diffident, but certainly paying his elders due respect. 'Bye Bye Blackbird' has him duetting with the boss, as Clayton does on 'Lullaby Of Birdland'. There are just two tracks from Brown's regular trio of Green and Hutchinson, who sound excellent on both 'Who Cares?' and the specially composed 'Sculler Blues'. Hutchinson appears elsewhere, but Green seems a little underused in the circumstances. McBride's 'Brown Funk' is the closer, a new theme that sounds as if it has been around for generations.

***** Some Of My Best Friends Are ... Singers**

Telarc 83441 *Brown; Antonio Hart (as); Ralph Moore (ts); Russell Malone (g); Geoff Keezer (p); Gregory Hutchinson (d); Dee Dee Brigewater, Etta Jones, Nancy King, Kevin Mahogany, Marlena Shaw, Diana Krall (v).* 12/97, 4/98.

Ray's years with Ella must have sensitized him to the needs of singers, and he is all taste and unobtrusive support on these dozen songs featuring the talents of half that number of talented and even idiosyncratic modern vocalists. Rising star Diana Krall is strongly featured in the top half of the record on 'I Thought About You' and 'Little Boy', performances deeply (which is to say not superficially) influenced by Ella's extraordinary musicianship and sense of rhythm. The two tracks with Etta Jones are equally good and 'There Is No Greater Love', with Russell Malone on guitar, is a revelation. The pairing of guest instrumentalists and singers is very subtle, but the key to the whole elegant package is the now seasoned trio.

Reuben Brown (born 1939)

PIANO

Brown has rarely ventured much further than the local scene afforded by his native Washington, DC, although as a young man he tried a spell in New York and he's occasionally been sighted in touring groups. He learned to play stride as a teenager but is stylistically otherwise in the bop-and-after mainstream.

****** Ice Scape**

Steeplechase SCCD 31423 *Brown; Rufus Reid (b); Billy Hart (d).* 1/94.

*****(*) Blue And Brown**

Steeplechase SCCD 31445 *Brown (p solo).* 1/94.

Nils Winther has a knack for finding pianists with an unemphatic but quietly individual touch, and Brown is right in that pocket. *Ice Scape* would earn four stars just for the outstanding version of 'Mack The Knife': played in a very slow three, full of space and low light, it is a brilliant personalization of a very unlikely vehicle. But Brown also comes up with strikingly nuanced treatments of 'A Night In Tunisia' and 'Lush Life', and his own writing reveals a deep thinker: the title-piece is a curious ballet worthy of, say, Ran Blake. Reid and Hart – the latter a high-school pal of Brown's – do sterling work on an unhackneyed and exemplary record.

Sadly, Brown suffered a stroke before the record was released and he is apparently not yet able to play again. *Blue And Brown*, recorded as a solo set at the same sessions, is therefore no more than a postscript to the other disc. Although many of the 15 themes are familiar, Brown goes to great lengths to treat them differently, both from each other and from previous interpretations. He might drop in a staccato right-hand figure, in the manner of Paul Bley, to surprise an otherwise placid momentum, or he may find a unique tempo on a tune that otherwise follows a different drum. Listeners fed up at the prospect of yet another 'Round Midnight' will be startled at how fresh Brown makes this one sound. Just here and there he takes things a shade too slowly, and we might have liked to hear more of his tunes in the programme; only 'Look Away' and the title-piece are Brown's. But this is otherwise a pair of discs that deserve a much wider attention than they've received so far.

Rob Brown (born 1962)

ALTO SAXOPHONE

Brown began making his mark in the 1980s, a free-form altoman whose willingness to go a long way out is tempered by a penchant for lyricism.

***** Breath Rhyme**

Silkheart SHCD-122 *Brown; William Parker (b); Dennis Charles (d).* 4/89.

***** Youniverse**

Riti CD3 *Brown; Joe Morris (g); Whit Dickey (d).* 6/92.

Breath Rhyme offers a powerful reminder of the kind of skirling declamations that first-wave free players would deploy against a rhythm section which works in rhythmic waves. Brown's own playing is a litany of overblown wails and long, anguished cries, although he is more temperate on the slower pieces. The sense of disorder is deceptive, for closer listening reveals subtle differentiations between pieces and a shrewd sense of detail – but that doesn't prevent some of the longer pieces from becoming monotonous. Slower, briefer episodes such as 'Stillness' may be more convincing for some. Parker is immensely interesting, but unfortunately the sound-balance does him few favours.

The most telling difference with *Youniverse* is the presence of Joe Morris, whose playing abjures obvious influences and displaces jazz, rock and other guitar traditions. Dickey, a pupil of Milford Graves, is right in the free tradition. The result is a clearer, more songful music that retains its intensity.

***** Blink Of An Eye**

No More 3 *Brown; Matthew Shipp (p).* 10/96.

Two exhaustively long duets, the second just breasting the half-hour mark, form the body of this disc and, for all their intensities and ingenuities, the players struggle to sustain interest across this length and with this bare instrumentation. Shipp and Brown specifically avoid the obvious Taylor–Lyons comparisons, but they have insufficient material at their fingertips to justify a format which calls for the highest levels of improvisational finesse – at least, on this evening. The brief third piece, which acts as a coda to the first two, is so much more focused and persuasive that one feels all the more disappointed at the longueurs of the first two.

*****(*) Scratching The Surface**

CIMP 161 *Brown; Assif Tsahar (ts); Chris Lightcap (b); Lou Grassi (d).* 10/97.

Bob Rusch's sleeve-note seems to hint at a disappointment that this band is playing in a fundamentally conservative style as far as free music is concerned. Brown does, indeed, even hint at a Konitz influence in the broken ballad, 'Stray Arrow', and Tsahar is a lot more effective in this temperate setting than he is on some of his all-out sessions. Lightcap and Grassi are as happy to play a slow four like 'A Hatful' as they are to be the time-and-motion men of 'Clean Sweep'. The result is surely the best record Brown's put his name on.

Sandy Brown (1929–1975)

CLARINET, VOCAL

Born in India, Brown grew up in Edinburgh and was playing clarinet there in rhythm clubs as a teenager. Formed a band with childhood friend Al Fairweather and came to London. Moved from simple trad beginnings to a mainstream style which became increasingly sophisticated, although he recorded little. Also worked as an architect, building sound studios, and was a gifted writer, but illness curtailed his activities and he died young in 1975.

****(*) The Historic Usher Hall Concert 1952**

Lake LACD94 *Brown; Al Fairweather (t); Bob Craig (tb); Stan Greig (p, d); Norrie Anderson (b); Dizzy Jackson (b); Jim 'Farrie' Forsyth (d).* 1/52.

****** McJazz And Friends**

Lake LACD58 *Brown; Al Fairweather (t); Jeremy French (tb); Dick Heckstall-Smith (ss); Ian Armit, Dill Jones, Dave Stephens, Harry Smith (p); Diz Dizley (g, bj); Cedric West, Bill Bramwell (g); Tim Mahn, Major Holley, Brian Brocklehurst, Arthur Watts (b); Graham Burbidge, Stan Greig, Don Lawson, Eddie Taylor (d).* 5/56–11/58.

*****(*) In The Evening**

Hep 2017 *Brown; Ray Crane (t); John Picard (tb); Bruce Turner (ss, as, ts); Tony Coe (ts); Brian Lemon (p); Tony Archer, Dave Green (b); Bobby Orr (d).* 6/70–5/71.

Brown has assumed almost legendary status among British musicians and fans of a certain age, although the memories are starting to fade and there is precious little left to remember him by in terms of recordings. The 1952 recording (of fair amateur quality) catches the Brown–Fairweather axis before it moved to London and, while the leaders are already players of some character, the rest of the band aren't. Much stronger is the later Lake disc, which reissues the Nixa LP *McJazz* and adds tracks from various EPs and compilations, four of them under Heckstall-Smith's leadership. Both Brown and Fairweather play beautifully on the *McJazz* tracks, with Brown's interest in high-life music adding a unique tang to many of the ensembles: the result is a worldly British mainstream which still sounds impressively individual. Brown's clarinet had shed most of an early Johnny Dodds influence and had become strikingly his own: fluent, but with a carefully controlled gaspipe edge to it that let him stand out in any ensemble. The original LP is the important material here, but the makeweight tracks all have lots of interest: 'Portrait Of Miles' is a classic quartet performance. An indispensable reissue for anyone interested in this period.

Brown's playing never declined, even if his health ultimately did. His final quartet record, from 1971 and originally issued on Doug Dobell's 77 label, is on the Hep CD, plus a few tracks with a larger group, cut a year earlier. The tone is a little more mellifluous but still takes on a tart edge when he wants to make some point, and the lines he plays still seem completely original, even on a blues or a familiar standard. A one-off.

Dave Brubeck (born 1920)

PIANO

Born in Concord, Massachusetts, Brubeck was educated on the West Coast, where he studied composition under Milhaud, a period of study interrupted by a spell in a services band. Brubeck's first trio was augmented to a quartet with the addition of altoist Paul Desmond, whose peerless sound became definitive of Brubeck's music; Desmond was also the composer of the group's best-known theme, 'Take Five'. The pianist's blocky chordal compositions and smooth melodic runs were apt to be dismissed as college or cocktail jazz, but he has continued in the same vein for more than half a century and was still making fine records in his seventies.

***(*) **The Dave Brubeck Octet**

Original Jazz Classics OJC 101 *Brubeck; Dick Collins (t); Bob Collins (tb); Paul Desmond (as); Dave Van Kriedt (ts); Bill Smith (cl, bs); Ron Crotty (b); Cal Tjader (d).* 48–49.

*** **The Dave Brubeck Trio**

Fantasy CDJZD 005 2CD *Brubeck; Ron Crotty (b); Cal Tjader (d, vib, perc).* 48–50.

***(*) **Dave Brubeck–Paul Desmond**

Fantasy F 24727 *Brubeck; Paul Desmond (as); Ron Crotty, Wyatt Ruther (b); Herb Barman, Lloyd Davis, Joe Dodge (d).* 52, 53, 54.

*** **Stardust**

Fantasy F 24728 *As above, except add Norman Bates, Fred Dutton (b).* 52–54.

Often derided as a white, middle-class formalist with a rather buttoned-down image and an unhealthy obsession with classical parallels and clever-clever time-signatures, Brubeck is actually one of the most significant composer-leaders in modern jazz. Tunes like 'Blue Rondo A La Turk', 'Kathy's Waltz' and Paul Desmond's 'Take Five' (which Brubeck made an enormous hit) insinuated their way into the unconscious of a whole generation of American college students. Though he has contributed very little to the 'standards' gene-pool ('In Your Own Sweet Way' is probably the only Brubeck original that is regularly covered), he has created a remarkable body of jazz and formal music, including orchestral pieces, oratorios and ballet scores. The Brubecks constitute something of a musical dynasty. His elder brother, Howard, is a 'straight' composer in a rather old-fashioned Francophile vein, while his sons, bassist and trombonist Chris, drummer Danny and keyboard player Darius, have all played with him.

It used to be conventional wisdom that the only Brubeck records which mattered were those that featured the liquid alto of Paul Desmond. Such was the closeness – and, one might say, jealousy – of the relationship that it was stated in Desmond's contract that his own recordings had to be pianoless. What no one seemed to notice was that Desmond's best playing was almost always with the Brubeck group. Brubeck himself was not a particularly accomplished soloist, with a rather heavy touch and an unfailing attachment to block chords, but his sense of what could be accomplished within the bounds of a conventional jazz quartet allowed him to create an impressive and often startling body of music that demands urgent reassessment.

The early Octet catches Brubeck at the height of his interest in an advanced harmonic language (which he would have learnt from Darius Milhaud, his teacher at Mills College); there are also rhythmic transpositions of a sort that popped up in classic jazz and were subsequently taken as read by the 1960s avant-garde, but which in the 1950s had been explored thoroughly only by Max Roach. Relative to Gerry Mulligan, Brubeck has been not been widely regarded as a writer-arranger for larger groups, but the better material on this rather indifferently recorded set underlines how confidently he approached the synthesis of jazz with other forms. Tracks like 'Serenades Suite' and 'Schizophrenic Scherzo' are a great deal more swinging than most products of the Third Stream, a movement one doesn't automatically associate with Brubeck's name. The trios are bubbly and smoothly competent but lack the luminous quality that Desmond brought. Brubeck disbanded the trio after injuring his back in a swimming accident. The lay-off was a significant one and led indirectly to his most creative association. Desmond joined the reconvened group in 1951 (Tjader had gone off to do other things) and immediately transformed it. His duos with Brubeck on the later Fantasy are a measure of their immediate mutual understanding; 'Over The Rainbow' is one of the loveliest improvisations of the period, caught in a whispery close-up. Tjader is still an interestingly varied player at this period, far from the bland stylist he was to become later.

The quartets with Crotty (he succeeded Norman Bates; no, not that one) and Davis aren't considered to be the classic Brubeck groups; that was the later line-up with Wright and Morello, but they were excellent on their own less ambitious terms. *Brubeck–Desmond* compiles two earlier Fantasy LPs, *Jazz At The Black Hawk* and *Jazz At Storyville*. There's an intriguing rehearsal version of the 'Trolley Song' that suggests something of what went into this music. *Stardust* is more of a grab-bag and is perhaps the dullest compilation from this early period; there are, though, fine Desmond performances throughout, and Brubeck fans will want to have some less familiar material collected there.

**** **Jazz At Oberlin**

Original Jazz Classics OJC 046 *Brubeck; Paul Desmond (as); Ron Crotty (b); Lloyd Davis (d).* 3/53.

*** **Jazz At The College Of The Pacific**

Original Jazz Classics OJC 047 *As above.* 12/53.

*** **In Concert**

Fantasy 60-013 *Brubeck; Paul Desmond (as); Ron Crotty (b); Joe Dodge (d).* 53.

Jazz At Oberlin was an enormous success on its first release and is still durable nearly 50 years later, with some of Brubeck's and Desmond's finest interaction; one of the pianist's innovations was in getting two musicians to improvise at the same time, and there are good examples of that on the Oberlin College set. It's all standard material, and there are excellent performances of 'Perdido', 'Stardust' and 'How High The Moon' which adumbrate Brubeck's later interest in unconventional time-signatures. The other 1953 set was another of Brubeck's celebrated college gigs, a shrewd promotional move that opened up his music and jazz more generally to a young, well-educated audience. Desmond has a slightly quieter night than usual in Stockton, but Brubeck, back at his alma mater, is in exceptional form, playing well within himself but showing all his class and sophistication.

In Concert is a slightly pointless compression of the two live records. Given that both are still available, there seems little reason for a sampler, though a budget double-CD would be welcome. The repetition of 'Stardust' and 'All The Things You Are' confounds the notion that this was a 'reading' band, too stiff to improvise. The sound is a bit remote and Crotty isn't always clearly audible.

***(*) **Brubeck Time**

Columbia CK 65724 *Brubeck; Paul Desmond (as); Bob Bates (b); Joe Dodge (d).* 10/54.

This was recorded round a film shoot by the celebrated Gjon Mili and George Avakian's brother Aram (who went on to film *Jazz on a Summer's Day*). A purist to his suede shoes, Mili had taken a good deal of convincing that Brubeck was a worthy subject but had relented. There is a story that Mili's dismissiveness spurred Brubeck to angry heights not normally associated with him. Certainly, 'Stompin' For Mili' sounds as if he might have meant the preposition to read 'On'. There is some fabulous music on the disc. Desmond's solo on 'Why Do I Love You' is brilliantly subtle, and 'Audrey' (a soft minor blues intended to counterbalance the thudding Mili piece) is delicate to the point of fragility. This really was Brubeck time. He appeared on the cover of *Time* magazine, and was pushing jazz's demographics into territory no one had anticipated. The music stands up pretty well, too.

*****(*) Brubeck Plays Brubeck**
Columbia Legacy CK 65722 *Brubeck (p solo).* 56.

***** Dave Brubeck Plays And Plays And Plays ...**
Original Jazz Classics OJC 716 *Brubeck (p solo).* 2/57.

After these, Brubeck more or less gave up solo performance for the next few decades. *Brubeck Plays Brubeck* is distinguished by his most famous composition, 'In Your Own Sweet Way', a gloriously understated performance. 'The Duke' is rarely covered, but it is another of Dave's great conceptions, moving cleverly and logically through the twelve keys. *Plays And Plays ...* is less sparkling but no less packed with ideas.

***** Reunion**
Original Jazz Classics OJC 150 *Brubeck; Paul Desmond (as); Dave Van Kriedt (ts); Norman Bates (b); Joe Morello (d).* 2/57.

***** Brubeck A La Mode**
Original Jazz Classics OJC 200 *Brubeck; Bill Smith (cl); Eugene Wright (b); Joe Morello (d).* 5 & 6/60.

***** Near-Myth**
Original Jazz Classics OJC 236 *As above.* 5/60.

From the end of his association with Fantasy (he'd signed for Columbia in 1954) *Reunion* brings back the full-voiced van Kriedt and Bates from the early bands. There's a greater preponderance of 'classical' tags – 'Pieta', 'Prelude', 'Divertimento', 'Chorale' – most of them interpreted rather loosely. *A La Mode* introduced another regular associate, fellow-Californian Smith, who has a lumpier touch than Desmond and a far less sophisticated improvisational sense. Interesting writing on *Near-Myth*, but both the playing and the reproduction are a shade muted. None of these should be considered essential, though van Kriedt is worth checking out.

*****(*) The Great Concerts**
Columbia 462403 *Brubeck; Paul Desmond (as); Eugene Wright (b); Joe Morello (d).* 3/58, 2/63.

This pulls together the double-LP, *At Carnegie Hall*, with *Brubeck In Amsterdam*. 'Great' is pushing it a bit for the earlier of the two, but the Dutch gig is quite special, and the recordings are miles better than the amateurish Moons. Morello's easy swing on 'Wonderful Copenhagen' (from 1958) sets the pace and the standard for most of the disc, which is more than usually even in tempo and might have benefited from a more judicious trawl through the material. Good value for money, though.

****** Time Out**
Columbia CK 65122 *Brubeck; Paul Desmond (as); Eugene Wright (b); Joe Morello (d).* 6–8/59.

Catalogued as a 'Historic Reissue' (industry-speak for a golden egg), this is the music everyone associates with Brubeck. So familiar is it that no one actually hears what's going on any more. As the title suggests, Brubeck wanted to explore ways of playing jazz that went a step beyond the basic 4/4 that had remained the norm long after jazz threw off the relentless predictability of B flat. The opening 'Blue Rondo A La Turk' (with its Mozart echoes) opens in an oddly distributed 9/8, with the count rearranged as 2-2-2-3. It's a relatively conventional classical *rondo* but with an almost raucous blues interior. 'Take Five' is in the most awkward of all key signatures, but what is remarkable about this almost iconic slice of modern jazz is the extent to which it constantly escapes the 5/4 count and swings. Morello's drum solo is perhaps his best work on record (though his brief 'Everybody's Jumpin'' solo is also excellent) and Brubeck's heavy vamp has tremendous force. Though it's almost always identified as a Brubeck tune, 'Take Five' was actually written by Desmond.

Most of the other material is in waltz and double-waltz time. Max Roach had explored the idea thoroughly on *Jazz In 3/4 Time*, but not even Roach had attempted anything as daring and sophisticated as the alternations of beat on 'Three To Get Ready' and 'Kathy's Waltz', which is perhaps the finest single thing on the album. Desmond tends to normalize the count in his solo line, and it's easy to miss what is going on in the rhythm section if one concentrates too exclusively on the saxophone. The Desmond cult may be fading slightly and as it does it may be possible to re-establish the Brubeck Quartet's claim *as a unit* to be considered among the most innovative and adventurous of modern-jazz groups.

***** Take Five**
Vipers Nest VN 160 *Brubeck; Paul Desmond (as); Joe Dodge, Eugene Wright (b); Joe Morello, Norman Bates (d).*

No firm date or location for these live sets from the later 1950s. A nice blend of familiar and less familiar material, with 'Take Five' taking its rightful place towards the end in the midst of 'New Material In New Tempi'. The biggest single statement is Brubeck's 'Two Part Contention', as clever a piece of part-writing as he ever conceived. There are two takes of '"A" Train' and a lovely performance of 'Gone With The Wind', the first track on the album to feature Morello rather than Bates, and what a difference it makes!

***** Brubeck & Rushing**
Columbia Legacy CK 65727 *As above, except add Jimmy Rushing (v).* 60.

Mr 5/4 meets Mr 5-by-5. One of the unlikelier encounters in modern jazz, but also one of the happiest as Brubeck gets down to some serious blues comping in support of the former Basie vocalist whose compact frame and big voice are a constant delight. 'Ain't Misbehavin'' finds them both on familiar ground and the chemistry is remarkable, confounding any abiding impression of Brubeck as a buttoned-down college boy. As with most of these reissues, there is just one additional track, an engaging if slight version of 'Shine On, Harvest Moon'.

***** Time Further Out**
Columbia Legacy CK 64668 *As above, except omit Rushing.* 61, 63.

There weren't many groups of the time or since that included the time-signature of each number beside the title, but so central to Brubeck's idiom had metre become that it was almost expected. The lead-off track here, in a sequence of tunes which constitute a suite dedicated to painter Joan Miró, is 'It's Raggy Waltz', laid in a relatively conventional time. What makes it particularly interesting is the inclusion of a live version, recorded at Carnegie Hall two years later, which suggests how comfortable the group was with non-standard times. 'Unsquare Dance', 'Bru's Boogie Woogie' and 'Blue Shadows In The Street' are all effective ideas, executed with classical authority. Desmond is in sparkling form, rawer and more blues-based than usual.

***** Brandenburg Gate: Revisited**

Columbia Legacy CK 65725 *Brubeck; Paul Desmond (as); Eugene Wright (b); Joe Morello (d); orchestra.* 61.

The title-piece was written for the *Jazz Impressions Of Eurasia* date, and Brubeck reworks it here as a set of 11 orchestral variations in which a string ritornelle provides the 'rhythm section' for small-group improvisation. This includes some impressive work, not just from the leader and Paul Desmond, but also from bassist Wright, who has a firm tone and an impressive array of blues lines at his disposal. Brother Howard Brubeck's arrangements of 'Kathy's Waltz' and 'In Your Own Sweet Way' keep respectfully close to the original performances, augmenting them and rethinking their improvisational course. Howard acknowledges that the interplay between sympathetic soloists – and Dave and Paul Desmond were almost telepathically close – is more sensitive than anything an arranger can pull off, but he has attempted to give the settings the same light, responsive feel, and *Brandenburg Gate: Revisited* is a model for jazz recording with strings.

***** Bravo! Brubeck!**

Columbia Legacy CK 65723 *As above, except add Benjamin Chamnin Correa (g); Salvador Rabito Agueros (perc).* 5/67.

***** Buried Treasures**

Columbia Legacy CK 65777 *As above, except omit Correa, Agueros.* 5/67.

Brubeck's sold-out tour to Mexico in 1967 opened up to him yet another new range of musical impulses, and they are prominently displayed in this excellent live record. Apart from 'Poinciana', 'Besame Mucho' and his own 'Nostalgia De Mexico', all the songs are drawn from traditional material arranged for the quartet by Brubeck. The anchor of the group is Wright, who seems to revel in this idiom. Desmond is less forthright and expressive than usual and his solos are far short of their usual expressive brilliance. A fine album nevertheless, and interesting to hear the classic group augmented with two local players.

The material on *Buried Treasures* wasn't heard on an official release until 1998. It isn't by any means as compelling as the earlier record, but the central sequence of 'Sweet Georgia Brown', 'Forty Days' and 'You Go To My Head' contains the essence of a Brubeck concert of the time. The sound is also very good, presumably the result of an official recording rather than a mere concert documentation.

*****(*) Greatest Hits**

Columbia 32046 *Brubeck; Paul Desmond (as); Eugene Wright (b); Joe Morello (d).*

Fairly predictable packaging of standard fare. For the record: the single-album set includes 'Take Five', 'It's A Raggy Waltz', 'Camptown Races', 'Unsquare Dance', 'Mister Broadway', 'I'm In A Dancing Mood', 'The Trolley Song', 'In Your Own Sweet Way' and 'Blue Rondo A La Turk'.

***** This Is Jazz: Dave Brubeck Plays Standards**

Columbia Legacy CK 65450 *Brubeck; Paul Desmond (as); Gerry Mulligan (bs); Bob Bates, Jack Six, Eugene Wright (b); Alan Dawson, Joe Dodge, Joe Morello (d).* 7/55–10/68.

A widely scattered trawl of tunes from Brubeck's Columbia catalogue. It was Desmond who insisted that the group write its own material (or hire someone to do so) and it is surprising that nowadays no one thinks of Brubeck as first and foremost a standards performer. These eight tracks give the lie to that, with long live performances of 'St Louis Blues', 'Like Someone In Love' and 'Sometimes I'm Happy', culled from the *Great Concerts* disc (the first two) and *Interchanges* (the Caesar/Youmans tunes). All of this material is available elsewhere, but as a sample of what Dave could do with familiar themes it's a very good introduction, cleanly transferred and with informative sleeve-notes.

****** Live At The Berlin Philharmonie**

Columbia 481415 2CD *Brubeck; Gerry Mulligan (bs); Jack Six (b); Alan Dawson (d).* 11/70.

Considerably augmented with two previously unissued tracks, including the opening 'Out Of Nowhere' and no fewer than six tracks not previously issued in the USA, this double-CD set restores one of the legendary concerts of the period. It catches both Brubeck and Mulligan on top form, playing with great spontaneity and charm. Their exchanges on 'St Louis Blues', 'Limehouse Blues' and 'Basin Street Blues', the middle segment of the second disc and (except for the first) previously unheard in the States, casts a new light on both men's musical background, while on more deliberate material like 'Blessed Are The Poor' and 'Out Of The Way Of The People' Mulligan shows himself to be equal to Brubeck's more reflective side. The trio is competent without being unduly inspired, for this was an evening for the front men and only modest duties were expected from anyone else.

***** The Last Set At Newport**

Atlantic 81382 *As above.* 7/71.

***** We're All Together Again For The First Time**

Atlantic 81390 *As above, except add Paul Desmond (as).* 10/72, 11/72.

Brubeck and Desmond teamed up again for one-shot tours all through the early '70s, and they played to huge crowds. Something of the magic had gone, though. Desmond's playing still provokes a thrill, especially when he weaves round Mulligan on 'Rotterdam Blues' on the *All Together Again* European tour compilation. Mulligan fitted perfectly into Brubeck's conception, swinging hard in uneven measures when there was a call for it, caressing a ballad the next moment. The Newport session is mostly upbeat, a show-stopping bravura performance that lacks subtlety but confirms Brubeck's remarkable ability to work a crowd. Desmond, one suspects, was happier in more intimate settings. He often sounds slightly frail on the European dates.

***** All The Things We Are**

Atlantic 81399 *Brubeck; Lee Konitz, Anthony Braxton (as); Jack Six (b); Alan Dawson, Roy Haynes (d).* 7/73, 10/74.

The eye-popping presence of avant-gardist Anthony Braxton in the line-up is not a misprint. This perhaps helps put into context his much-discussed affection for the cool, 'white' saxophone sound of Paul Desmond and Warne Marsh. On 'In Your Own Sweet Way' he sounds very much like a younger, more accommodating version of himself. Paired with Konitz on 'All The Things You Are', he's more conventionally boppish, and the combination is pleasantly awkward. Haynes adds a bit of beef to the engine room, sounding very much like old swingers like Krupa and Dave Tough. There's actually only one track from the July '73 session, a trio medley of Jimmy van Heusen songs; pleasant, but hardly startling.

***** Paper Moon**

Concord CCD 4178 *Brubeck; Jerry Bergonzi (ts, b); Chris Brubeck (b, btb); Randy Jones (d).* 9/81.

****(*) Concord On A Summer Night**

Concord CCD 4198 *Brubeck; Bill Smith (cl); Chris Brubeck (b, tb); Randy Jones (d).* 8/82.

****(*) For Iola**

Concord CCD 4259 *As above.* 8/84.

***** Reflections**

Concord CCD 4299 *As above.* 12/85.

****(*) Blue Rondo**

Concord CCD 4317 *As above.* 11/86.

***** Moscow Night**

Concord CCD 4353 *As above.* 3/87.

***** New Wine**

Musicmasters 5051-2 *As above.* 7/87.

The Concord years suggest that whatever Brubeck once had has now been thoroughly run to ground. Only the most dedicated fans will find much to get excited about on these albums, though there are lovely things on *Paper Moon* which hark back to the old days. 'We Will All Remember Paul' on *Reflections* is a heartfelt tribute to Desmond (who died in 1977) and the surrounding material seems to be lifted by it. *Moscow Night* also seems to be up a gear and the versions there of 'Three To Get Ready', 'Unsquare Dance' and 'St Louis Blues' are the best for years. Otherwise non-essential. Brubeck *fils* and Jones are curiously stiff and unswinging, and Smith's initial promise seems (temporarily at least) to have evaporated; he is probably a less sophisticated player now than he was in 1960. Jerry Bergonzi was one of a number of young radicals introduced to Dave by Chris and Danny. It's still clear whose record it is, but there are signs that Brubeck was able to take on board new ideas, often far removed from his primary concerns.

****(*) Trio Brubeck**

Musicmasters 844 337 *Brubeck; Chris Brubeck (b, btb); Danny Brubeck (d).* 88.

Musically, the third brother was hardly missed (Darius lives in South Africa), but this still needs something to give it a bit of substance. The two Brubeck sons are competent players, with odd sparks of fire here and there; but the only thing that keeps the music from being entirely static is Dave's remarkable energy. He carries the whole thing.

***** Quiet As The Moon**

Musicmasters 65057-2 *Brubeck; Bob Militello (as, ts, f); Jack Six (b); Chris Brubeck (b, btb); Matthew Brubeck (clo); Danny Brubeck, Randy Jones (d).* 9/88, 12/89, 5/91.

****** Once When I Was Very Young**

Musicmasters 65083-2 *Brubeck; Bill Smith (cl); Jack Six (b); Randy Jones (d).* 5/91.

Despite some health problems, Brubeck entered the 1990s like so many musicians of his generation, artistically rejuvenated and enjoying renewed attention and critical respect. *Quiet* cobbles together material from a 30-month period and is inevitably patchy. The reunion with Six prompts some of the happiest music, though Militello is never much more than Desmond-and-water. Smith, despite the reservations above, emerges as very much his own man. *Very Young* is one of Brubeck's most centred and coherent performances since the 1950s, one of those records that seem to exist as an entity, almost irrespective of the distribution of tracks and personnel. Smith's rich *chalumeau* can sound very like Desmond, but he lacks the saxophonist's other side, the 'dry martini' chill that could be a little forbidding. A very welcome return to form.

****** Time Signatures: A Career Retrospective**

Columbia/Legacy 472776-2 4CD *Brubeck; Dick Collins (t); Bob Collins (tb); Paul Desmond (as); Bobby Militello (as, f); Dave Van Kriedt, Jerry Bergonzi (ts); Gerry Mulligan (bs); Bill Smith, Perry Robinson (cl); Darius Brubeck, Billy Kyle (p); Bob Bates, Norman Bates, Joe Benjamin, Chris Brubeck, Ron Crotty, Charles Mingus, Jack Weeks, Dave Powell, Wyatt Ruther, Jack Six, Eugene Wright (b); Herb Barman, Danny Brubeck, Lloyd Davis, Alan Dawson, Joe Dodge, Randy Jones, Joe Morello (d); Cal Tjader (vib, d, perc); Salvatore Agueros, Howard Brubeck, Teo Macero, John Lee (perc); Louis Armstrong, Carmen McRae, Jimmy Rushing, Lambert, Hendricks and Ross (v); New York Philharmonic Orchestra conducted by Leonard Bernstein.* 46–91.

This is *the* stocking-filler for a Brubeck fan, a magnificently packaged four-CD box with immaculately reproduced liner photographs and a detailed booklet breaking down each and every track. There is also a long biographical essay by Juul Anthonissen. The recordings (items marked with a † not recently available) are drawn from the 1946 *Old Sounds From San Francisco*†, *Trio Featuring Cal Tjader, Octet, Brubeck–Desmond, Jazz At Storyville*†, *Jazz At Oberlin, Jazz Goes To College*†, *Brubeck Time, Jazz: Red, Hot And Cool*†, *Brubeck Plays Brubeck, And Jay And Kai At Newport*†, *Jazz Impressions Of The USA*†, the underrated *Dave Digs Disney, In Europe, Newport 58, Jazz Impressions Of Eurasia, Gone With The Wind, Time Out* (of course!), *Southern Scene*† (a companion to *Gone*), *The Riddle*†, *Brubeck And Rushing, Bernstein Plays Brubeck Plays Bernstein, Tonight Only!*†, the inevitable follow-ups *Time Further Out, Time Changes*† and *Time In, Countdown Time In Outer Space*†, *Brandenburg Gate:*

Revisited, The Real Ambassadors† (with Louis Armstrong), *Summit Sessions*†, *Bossa Nova USA*†, *At Carnegie Hall, Jazz Impressions Of Japan*†, and of *New York*†, *Angel Eyes*†, *Anything Goes!*†, *Bravo! Brubeck!, The Last Time We Saw Paris*†, *Compadres*† and *In Berlin*† (with Mulligan), *Brother, The Great Spirit Made Us All*† (with the sons and unexpected Brubeckians, Perry Robinson and Jerry Bergonzi), and the recent *Quiet As The Moon* and *Once When I Was Very Young*. There is also a previously unreleased live session from Moscow, recorded in the spring of 1987. From the collector's point of view, it's a shame that there isn't far more unreleased material; but the point is, as this astonishing list shows, that Brubeck has been unusually well documented over the years. There has undoubtedly been stuff left on the editing-room floor and in the vaults, but there has also been an unusually severe quality-control process.

There are wonderful oddities in the playlist: the duo with Mingus on 'Sectarian Blues', the 12-tone rumba from *Jazz Impressions Of New York*, the vocal items with Pops, Carmen and Jimmy Rushing, the odd 'Lost Waltz' from 1965's *Time In*. What they reveal is not so much an 'experimental' or an unexpected Brubeck as a man propelled by what John Aldridge called 'the energy of new success' into the centre of the musical culture and allowed to pick and choose, and to initiate, the projects which interested him. *Time Signatures* has been selected with the music, not the matrix numbers, in mind, and it offers an ideal introduction to one of the music's most popular and enduring figures.

*** Late Night

Telarc 83345 *Brubeck; Bobby Militello (as, ts, f); Jack Six (b); Randy Jones (d).* 10/93.

*** Nightshift

Telarc 33351 *As above, except add Chris Brubeck (btb), Bill Smith (cl).* 10/93.

This was a good spell for Brubeck. *Late Night* was recorded at the Blue Note and is a model for anyone wanting to make a live jazz recording, with every instrument realistically located in the mix and every note and nuance exactly registered. The music isn't as inspiring as the sonics, unfortunately, though Dave's relaxed and quite possibly unrehearsed procession through the Ellington songbook is one of his best performances of the great man's work, so similar and yet so radically different from his own.

Though *Nightshift* is essentially a trio album with guest appearances by the horns, it is the augmented tracks that remain in the ear. Smith is in cracking from on 'You Go To My Head', dizzy and sober at the same time. Militello captures attention almost every time he is featured. His under-employed tenor is very fine on 'Travelin' Blues' and is almost reminiscent of Booker Ervin, while his alto feature on 'Yesterdays' once again had critics and most listeners reaching for comparisons with Paul Desmond.

*** In Their Own Sweet Way

Telarc 83355 *Brubeck; Darius Brubeck (p); Matthew Brubeck (clo); Chris Brubeck (b, btb); Dan Brubeck (d).* 1/94.

The great snowstorm of January 1994 in New York had a few unintended musical consequences, not least an opportunity for the Brubeck family to make this rare quintet record. Matthew is the obvious outsider, but his cello gives an extra weight to the middle register. Most of the real action takes place between Dave and Darius and their self-titled duet is by far the best thing on the record. Brubeck's only really established standard, of which the album title is an obvious variant, gets the disc off to a good start, but it also confirms just how solidly this is the old man's record. Every tune, except the closing 'Sweet Georgia Brown', is his. As a one-off encounter, *In Their Own Sweet Way* is entertaining enough, but it's by no means a classic.

*** Just You, Just Me

Telarc 33363 *Brubeck (p solo).* 94.

Remarkably, Dave hadn't recorded solo for nearly 40 years when this was released. He's instantly identifiable from the very first bars but, without a group, the ideas run a little thin. Brubeck's mastery of a certain idiom – chordal, melodic – is unchallengeable, but it is also unchallenged and it would be more interesting to hear him pushed into new situations rather than be allowed to muse like this.

*** Young Lions & Old Tigers

Telarc CD 83349 *Brubeck; Roy Hargrove (t); Ronnie Butacavolli (flhn); Michael Brecker, Joe Lovano, James Moody, Joshua Redman (ts); Gerry Mulligan (bs); George Shearing (p); Chris Brubeck, Christian McBride, Jack Six (b); Randy Jones (d); Jon Hendricks (v).* 95.

It wasn't a bad idea to pair Brubeck with old and new friends but, as with so many projects of this type, no single relationship is given enough time to establish basic ground-rules, let alone develop into something more substantial. Joe Lovano's conservatism has led him into more than one project of this sort and on the tango specially written for him he sounds respectful and slightly constrained. There are also named dedications to Chris McBride, Roy Hargrove, James Moody, Gerry Mulligan and Michael Brecker, all of them redolent of a relaxed, jamming atmosphere. It might have been more effective if Brubeck had elected to do what he did with George Shearing and play an established tune (in this case his own established repertory piece, 'In Your Own Sweet Way') with whatever wrinkles and variations the youngsters chose to work on it. As things stand, it is quite hard to gauge how securely they are all engaged with his work. A thoroughly enjoyable album up to a point, but something of a wasted opportunity, given the range of talent on offer.

***(*) Triple Play

Telarc 83449 3CD *As for Late Night, Just You, Just Me, Young Lions & Old Tigers.* 93, 94, 95.

A good-value compilation of three albums from the early to mid-'90s. There is no additional material to reel in specialist collectors, so this may well appeal to those who don't have the original issues.

*** A Dave Brubeck Christmas

Telarc 83410 *Brubeck (p solo).* 6/96.

Bah, humbug, and, yes, God bless us every one also. Santa Brubeck offers more than a few thought-provoking moments on this mostly generic Yuletide record. His own 'To Us Is Given' and 'Run, Run, Run To Bethlehem' are delightful, and his approach to the traditional themes – including 'Silent Night', 'Away In A Manger' and 'Jingle Bells' – is as accomplished as you would expect, mining previously unheard subtleties from the old tunes. But tell us, when do you all listen to Christmas albums? Only when there's snow on the ground? Or with heavy irony in July?

*****(*) So What's New?**

Telarc CD 83434 *Brubeck; Bobby Militello (sax, f); Jack Six (b); Randy Jones (d).* 97.

Issued to coincide with the fortieth anniversary of Brubeck's first visit to Britain in 1958. The writing is as vivid and stretching as ever: 'Fourth Of July' shifts in just that interval with a summery, affirmative sound; 'Her Name Is Nancy' is a dazzlingly clever set of changes and 'Chorale' is another Bach tribute.

Even past his 75th birthday, Brubeck continued to compose with unabated enthusiasm, and this record boldly consisted of brand-new material, seemingly devised to counter any impression that the old man had settled back into sepia-tinted ballad playing. 'It's Déjà Vu All Over Again' is a clever exercise in nostalgia-that-isn't, recapturing the classic group sound, but finding new and challenging things to say in the old block chord style. Three additional tunes stand out: 'Marian McPartland' was written for that lady and featured in a duet version with her in the same spring as this was recorded; 'Thing You Never Remember' is another antidote to the life lived backwards; 'Waltzing' is simply and sheerly beautiful, an instant standard. The 'new' quartet pushes no boundaries but sticks very much to the idiom of its predecessors. Militello has a quiet session, perhaps because in this studio session and with such challenging new compositions he was happier to leave the spotlight to the boss; Bobby's moment was to come on the road.

*****(*) 40th Anniversary Tour Of The UK**

Telarc 83440 *Brubeck; Bobby Militello (as); Alec Dankworth (b); Randy Jones (d).* 11/98.

Anticipation was heightened by rumours that Dave's health was once again causing concern and that he might not be able to fulfil engagements. In the event, the 1998 tour was packed with good material, though most of the exciting playing was from saxophonist Militello, who has established himself as the new Paul Desmond. Alec Dankworth also sounds as if he had listened to a good few early Brubeck records in his mum and dad's collection. What was particularly interesting was how readily Brubeck experimented with the set-list, including unexpected things like his own 'Salmon Strike', the tango-based 'Time Of Our Madness' and 'Oh, You Can Run (But You Can't Hide)', in which the famous Joe Louis line might seem to be an ironic comment on the need to keep down to business: making the date and playing the blues, which Brubeck does with notable darkness and vigour. The closing number is a solo tribute to the departed Gerry Mulligan, 'Goodbye Old Friend'.

Jimmy Bruno

GUITAR

Philadelphia-based guitarist who has played that scene for many years with few concessions to a worldlier jazz résumé. His style is a throwback, but timeless with it.

****(*) Sleight Of Hand**

Concord CCD 4532 *Bruno; Pete Colangelo (b); Bruce Klauber (d); Edgardo Cintron Orchestra.* 4–5/91.

***** Burnin'**

Concord CCD 4612 *Bruno; Craig Thomas (b); Craig Holloway (d).* 2/94.

Bruno is a Philadelphia homebody whose playing sits squarely in the big-toned electric tradition. He's more fond of chords, octave playing and parallel lines than of single-string solos, and it gives his improvisations a meaty texture that fleshes out his simple tunes. That said, the first record is impressively skilful but not very exciting. The 'orchestra' is a Latin rhythm section that sits in on two tracks for a useful change of pace, but otherwise Bruno has to carry everything himself, since Colangelo and Klauber offer anonymous support. *Burnin'* goes up a notch since Thomas and Holloway bring some muscle of their own to the date. Two deft solos by Bruno include a thoughtful revision of Coltrane's 'Central Park West' that's quietly effective.

***** Like That**

Concord CCD 4698 *Bruno; Joey DeFrancesco (org, t); Craig Thomas (b); Steve Holloway (d).* 95.

***** Live At Birdland**

Concord CCD 4768 *Bruno; Bobby Watson (as); Craig Thomas (b); Vince Ector (d).* 12/96.

*****(*) Live At Birdland II**

Concord CCD 4810 *As above, except Scott Hamilton (ts) replaces Watson.* 12/96.

Like That is an agreeable balance. DeFrancesco impresses as much on trumpet as he does on organ – the duet between guitar and horn on 'Stars Fell On Alabama' is a nice surprise – and Bruno finds plenty of ways of varying his own pace, 'Razer's Edge' in particular going some way outside. He has also built up a fruitful relationship with Thomas, who impresses again on the first *Birdland* record. This is more like heartland bebop; if Bruno doesn't quite catch the excitement that Ron Affif found in a similar situation, he plays a theme like 'Move' with a sort of refined fire. Watson joins in for the second half of the programme and turns up the heat on the likes of 'Au Privave'.

The return visit (actually a second helping from the same season) might be Bruno's best calling-card, since the first half has some of his most appealing playing on the likes of 'Poinciana', and the second benefits from the presence of guest Scott Hamilton. Temperamentally, these two are a good match, and something as juicily rhapsodic as 'Lover Man' makes one forget how many times this tune's been done before.

Ray Bryant (born 1931)

PIANO

A Philadelphia man, Bryant is a major and often undersung player of bebop piano, with blues and gospel subtexts never far away. A frequent leader and record-maker for 40-plus years.

***** Ray Bryant Trio**
Original Jazz Classics OJC 793 *Bryant; Ike Isaacs (b); Specs Wright (d).* 4/57.

*****(*) Alone With The Blues**
Original Jazz Classics OJC 249 *Bryant (p solo).* 12/58.

Bryant is not an orthodox bopper in the way Hampton Hawes once was, and his solo performances are even further away from the predominant Bud Powell model of bop piano. Noted for an imaginative and influential alteration of the basic 12-bar-blues sequence on his 'Blues Changes', Bryant is a distinctive pianist who resembles Hawes superficially but who, unlike the older man, has often been content to record solo. The two early OJCs (originally done for Prestige and New Jazz) are both welcome revivals, the solo set in particular a thoroughgoing investigation of Bryant's favourite form.

Original blues compositions are interwoven with an affecting 'Lover Man' and a delicious, gospelly 'Rockin' Chair'. Bryant's coming out as a solo performer could hardly have been more gracefully handled.

***** Cold Turkey**
Collectables Records COL 5749 *Bryant; other personnel unidentified.* 63.

****(*) Groove House**
Collectables Records COL 5753 *Bryant; Wally Richardson (g); Tom Bryant (b); Bobby Donaldson, Panama Francis (d).* 63.

****(*) Soul**
Collectables Records COL 5754 *Bryant; Tom Bryant (b); Sonny Brown, Walter Perkins (d).*

*****(*) Live At Basin Street East**
Collectables Records COL 5755 *Bryant; probably as above.*

These are valuable reissues for Bryant fans, though we might wish for a little more information on their provenance. Some of the sessions at least were made for Sue Records and, while we have no reason to think these CDs are anything but aboveboard, the presentation is decidedly slipshod.

The most desirable of the bunch is the live set, which opens with a superb 'What Is This Thing Called Love' and swings in every measure from there to the close. *Cold Turkey* is a more acerbic set, but with some strong points. *Soul* is a disappointment and *Groove House* could do with some variation of pace. A feast for confirmed Bryant fans, but nothing of any real moment for casual listeners.

***** Hot Turkey**
Black and Blue BLE 233089 *Bryant; Major Holley (b); Panama Francis (d).* 10/75.

***** Montreux 77**
Original Jazz Classics OJC 371 *Bryant (p solo).* 12/76.

*****(*) Here's Ray Bryant**
Original Jazz Classics OJC 826 *Bryant; George Duvivier (b); Grady Tate (d).* 1/76.

***** Solo Flight**
Original Jazz Classis OJC 885 *Bryant (p solo).* 12/76.

***** All Blues**
Original Jazz Classics OJC 778 *Bryant; Sam Jones (b); Grady Tate (d).* 4/78.

***** Potpourri**
Original Jazz Classics OJC 936 *Bryant; Jimmy Rowser (b); Mickey Roker (d).* 5/80.

The solo and trio material on *Hot Turkey* is worth checking out, though there's still a slight feeling of uncertainty, as if Bryant wasn't yet sure what direction his revived career was going to take. That was to become much clearer over the next few years, with a signing to Pablo; since our last edition, most of these albums have returned via the OJC series. They're a strong, idiomatic sequence of blues-to-bop piano and there's little to choose between them, although our pick if pressed would be the impeccably programmed *Here's Ray Bryant.*

****** Tribute To His Jazz Piano Friends**
JVC 9031-2 *Bryant; Ray Drummond (b); Winard Harper (d).* 6/97.

Ray has always been unnecessarily self-effacing when asked to locate himself in the jazz piano tradition. This intriguing visitors' book of an album has him playing out of his skin as he tackles 11 tracks by admired contemporaries and predecessors, the former as far apart as Randy Weston, Vince Guaraldi and Joe Zawinul, the latter more predictably led off by Duke, Bobby Timmons and Monk.

Bryant has the chops to give 'Cast Your Fate To The Wind' a fresh and even muscular presence, and he works a special magic with the overworked 'Birdland', but it is when he turns to Horace Silver's 'Doodlin'' and Bobby Timmons's 'Moaning' that he really lets rip. These two tunes bracket the core of a splendid record on which Bryant is ably assisted by namesake Drummond and the resourceful Harper.

Jeanie Bryson

VOCALS

American vocalist mixing classic and contemporary material.

*****(*) I Love Being Here With You**
Telarc CD 83336 *Bryson; Wallace Roney (t); Don Braden (ts); Kenny Barron, Ted Brancato (p); Steve Nelson (vib); Vic Juris (g); Bob Crane, Ray Drummond (b); Ron Davis (d); Rudy Bird (perc).* 1/93.

***** Tonight I Need You So**
Telarc CD 83348 *As above, except omit Roney, Barron, Drummond; add Claudio Roditi (t), Jay Ashby (tb), Paquito D'Rivera (as), Danilo Perez (p), Christian McBride (b), Ignacao Berroa (d).* 94.

Bryson's excellent debut record was somewhat overshadowed by her unfortunately timed claim that she was the child of Dizzy Gillespie. Like its successor, the first album benefited hugely from the presence of top-flight players. Barron is exemplary, and Braden and Roney provide tough *yang* counterbalances to her unexpected fragility. 'Bittersweet' and 'A Sleeping Bee' – ironically the two tracks on which Brancato replaces Barron – are exceptional performances, but there is scarcely a false note throughout the session; a word also has to go to Ray Drummond for his lush, full-bodied accompaniment, filling in a part of the vocal spectrum where Bryson is apt to sound uncertain.

On *Tonight* he is replaced by the now equally ubiquitous McBride, who also brought along his electric bass for a couple of soul numbers: Stevie Wonder's 'Too Shy To Say' and Luther Vandross's 'What Can A Miracle Do?'. It would have been fascinating to have heard a simple voice–bass duet – perhaps 'Alone Together'? – to highlight what sounds like a very fruitful relationship. Roditi is a very different kind of player from Roney, but his warm, reservedly passionate sound is perfect for a session of this sort, and he holds in check the busier and more assertive D'Rivera and Braden.

The Buck Clayton Legacy

GROUP

A mainstream repertory group dedicated to the music of Buck Clayton.

*****(*) All The Cats Join In**

Nagel-Heyer 006 *Randy Sandke (t); Jerry Tilitz (tb); Antti Sarpila (cl, ss, ts); Harry Allen, Danny Moss (ts); Brian Dee (p); Len Skeat (b); Oliver Jackson (d).* 11/93.

***** Encore Live**

Nagel-Heyer 018 *As above, except add Scott Robinson (bs), Butch Miles (d); omit Jackson.* 11/94.

One of the principal ways in which jazz repertory is enduring is through projects like this. Clayton became a great eminence as composer/bandleader after he had to give up playing, and Sandke's enthusiasm for that legacy has engendered this band, which mixes old-time Clayton staples like 'Buckin' the Blues' with some of his less familiar charts. The first album is studio, the second live; since there are twin versions of nine of the tunes, maybe only a committed fan needs both. Or maybe not: this is awfully good swing-styled jazz. Some of the themes have been done to decrepitude over the years, and still the group summons a freshness about 'Jumpin' At the Woodside' (a quite classic treatment on the studio disc, a trifle winded on the live one), 'Robbins Nest' and some of the others. The studio set edges ahead on the basis of the stricter ensembles, a thrilling two-tenor workout for Allen and Moss on 'Lester Leaps In' and three previously unknown Clayton scores. But the live set has plenty of atmosphere and Robinson and Sarpila (on only three of the studio tracks) to beef up the front line. Jackson's drumming abets the earlier disc: since he died not long afterwards, Miles takes over for the concert and, if he's hardly a master of subtlety, the extra weight does kick the band along.

The Buddy Rich Big Band

GROUP

A tribute band formed to make this pair of albums.

***** Burning For Buddy**

Atlantic 82699-2 *Dave Stahl, Ross Konikoff, Greg Gisbert, Scott Wendholt, John Millikan, Craig Johnson, Dan Collette, Mike Ponella, Joe Magnarelli, Tony Kadleck (t); John Mosca, Rick Trager, George Gesslein (tb); Steve Marcus, Andy Fusco, Dave D'Angelo, Walt Weiskopf, Jack Stuckey, Gary Keller (reeds); Jon Werking (p); John Hart, Chuck Loeb, Bill Beaudoin (g); Chuck Bergeron (b); Kenny Aronoff, Bill Burford, Billy Cobham, Steve Ferrone, Steve Gadd, Omar Hakim, Manu Katché, Mino Cinelu, Joe Morello, Rod Morganstein, Neil Peart, Simon Phillips, Max Roach, Ed Shaughnessy, Marvin 'Smitty' Smith, Steve Smith, Matt Sorum, Dave Weckl (d).* 5/94.

***** Burning For Buddy Vol. II**

Atlantic 83010-2 *As above, except add Buddy Rich, Gregg Bissonette, David Garibaldi (d), Cathy Rich, Annie Ross, Domenick Allen, Annette Sanders (v); omit Cobham, Ferrone, Hakim, Katché, Cinelua, Morganstein, Roach, Shaughnessy, Sorum.* 5/94.

The rock drummer Neil Peart put these tribute albums together, featuring a host of ex-Rich sidemen in the orchestra and a guest drummer on every track. Though recorded simultaneously, the records were released a distance apart: the first concentrates on the rockier (or at least the more 'contemporary') pieces in the band's repertoire, the second on more direct jazz charts. It was a productive idea: the music scores quite often on sheer chutzpah, and even if there's a certain twanging tightness about the overall sound (which Rich would probably have applauded) it all swings in its slightly frightening way. There are predictable chances for drummers like Weckl and Gadd to show off, although nobody's embarrassing and nobody steals the show. Roach, rather demurely, doesn't work with the band on the first disc but garners a couple of tiny solo interludes to himself. Smitty Smith is arguably the greatest groovemaster on the second disc with his work on 'Standing Up In A Hammock', but we enjoyed the blowout versions of 'Mercy, Mercy, Mercy' and 'Love For Sale' on the first disc just as much. The second set ends on 'Channel One Suite', where the band plays over an old Rich drum-track and the vocalists sing a fulsome lyric in homage.

John Bunch (born 1921)

PIANO

Worked on the West Coast in the 1950s in big bands and small groups, then often with Benny Goodman during the '60s and '70s, and MD for Tony Bennett. Gradually achieved a wide recognition, but his reputation is largely confined to mainstream musicians' circles.

*****(*) John Bunch Plays Kurt Weill**

Chiaroscuro CD(D) 144 *Bunch (p solo).* 5/75–1/91.

***** The Best Thing For You**

Concord CCD 4328 *Bunch; Phil Flanigan (b); Chuck Riggs (d).* 6/87.

***** Struttin'**

Arbors ARCD 19157 *Bunch; Phil Flanigan (b).* 11/95.

***** Arbors Piano Series At Mike's Place Vol. 1**

Arbors ARCD 19184 *Bunch (p solo).* 11/96.

Despite his seniority, John Bunch was a little-known sideman, accompanist and orchestra pianist until he was in his fifties. In the 1970s and '80s he secured wider attention as a member of the mainstream clan championed by Concord. There's nothing demonstrative about his style, which is in the aristocratic swing tradition of Teddy Wilson, but he can play with power when he wants, as well as with fingertip delicacy.

The *Kurt Weill* album is a rare and strikingly imaginative project: only a handful of Weill's tunes have entered the jazz repertoire, and Bunch's thoughtful settings – some at ballad tempo, others with a flavour of stride, some delivered with Monk-like rhythms – make all of them sound like plausible vehicles. The original (1975) sessions have been extended with six tracks cut in 1991, and there's amazingly little to choose between them in terms of both sound and interpretation.

Bunch's other discs have a less decisive quality about them, as if he was prepared to settle for a sort of routine excellence – nice, but nothing really to make one want to return to the music very often. The Concord album is good if rather so-so, in the unemphatic manner of the company. *Struttin'*, a series of duets with the solid Flanigan, points up how bebop touched Bunch's style: he does 'Crazeology' and Oscar Pettiford's 'Laverne Walk' among some standards, but it's bebop down a couple of gears. The later solo session offers 18 pleasant interpretations, with just a bare handful of surprises in the set-list, and, though the pianist's even-handed approach and respect for the melodies is warmly agreeable, it's a bit stately.

Jane Bunnett

SOPRANO SAXOPHONE, FLUTE

Bunnett owed much of her early prominence to the wise tutelage of Don Pullen, with whom she recorded. The young Canadian has specialized in the treacherously pitched soprano saxophone, creating a voice which is as light and fleet as her flute-playing, but with a surprisingly hard edge. Partner Larry Cramer's trumpet helps soften it when they play together. In recent years, Bunnett has concentrated very largely on Cuban music.

*** New York Duets

Music & Arts CD 629 *Bunnett; Don Pullen (p).* 89.

Like Steve Lacy, her acknowledged model on soprano saxophone, Canadian Jane Bunnett has led a band almost wholly dedicated to Monk themes. Don Pullen, who clearly recognized talent when he heard it, gives her the quirky harmonies and off-centre count that she hears in them. On the duets, he coaxes and provokes, encouraging Bunnett's unstuffy progressions; together, they make an interesting job of 'Bye Ya' and 'Little Rootie Tootie'. Bunnett's chill soprano is better suited to the more abstract duet settings than to a relatively straightforward blowing session. She concentrates largely on textures, leaving the piece to plod its own way home.

***(*) The Water Is Wide

Evidence 22091 *Bunnett; Larry Cramer (t); Don Pullen (p); Kieran Overs (b); Billy Hart (d); Sheila Jordan, Jeanne Lee (v).* 8/93.

Augmented – indeed, graced – by vocalists Sheila Jordan and Jeanne Lee, the band tackles an ambitiously eclectic set of tunes. Bunnett kicks off with three originals, of which 'Real Truth' is the most distinctive. She then switches to flute for Roland Kirk's idiosyncratic 'Serenade To A Cuckoo', which is just quirky enough. Sheila's feature is a magnificent 'You Must Believe In Spring' which simply underlines her fantastic musicianship. Much of the remaining material is by Cramer, though two Monk tunes, 'Pannonica' and 'Brake's Sake', allow Jane to show off her Steve Lacy influence once more. The two vocalists are united on the closing 'Water Is Wide', the old spiritual taking on an almost unearthly quality as the differences between the two voices and the two horns are exploited to the full.

**(*) Rendez-Vous Brazil / Cuba

Justin Time JUST 74 *Bunnett; Larry Cramer (t, flhn); Sabine Boyer (af); Hilario Durán Torres (p); Filo Machado (g, v, perc); Carlitos Del Puerto (b); Celso Machado (perc).* 6/95.

The *Brazil/Cuba* project is dominated by Filo Machado compositions, and he is clearly the effective co-leader of a session that almost puts Bunnett's solo skills at a discount in favour of a highly rhythmic and dance-orientated group sound. It's all doubtless very authentic, and Cramer could find work in wedding bands any day of the week, growing a lot more comfortable with this type of material every time he goes out, but one wonders whether it's the most effective direction for the young Canadian.

**(*) Chamalongo

Blue Note 23684 *Bunnett; Larry Cramer (t); Hilario Durán, Frank Emilio (p); Tata Guines, Pancho Quinto (perc); Amado J Dedeu, Gregorio Hernandez, Pedro Martinez, Merceditás Valdes (v).* 3/98.

A Blue Note contract is supposed to be nothing but good. Unfortunately, on this occasion it seems to have blunted Jane's peerless tone and stilted her phrasing. There is also a heavy emphasis on vocals and, while some of the tracks are fascinating in and of themselves – we specially liked the unusual 'Descarga à la Hindemith' – the overall impact is rather lightweight.

Albert Burbank (1902–76)

CLARINET

Played in New Orleans during the 1920s and '30s; after war service, was with Herb Morand, Paul Barbarin and Kid Ory. Rarely sighted away from his hometown and was a regular with Preservation Hall groups until his death.

*** Albert Burbank With Kid Ory And His Creole Jazzband

Storyville STCD 6010 *Burbank; Alvin Alcorn (t); Kid Ory (tb); Don Ewell (p); Ed Garland (b); Minor Hall (d).* 5–7/54.

Burbank scarcely ever left New Orleans, and it's an irony that the only disc currently under his own name should have been recorded elsewhere (he toured briefly with Ory's band and returned home the same year). These tracks, culled from six different 1954 concerts at San Francisco's Club Hangover, were made under Ory's leadership, and it's rather a matter of paying respects that they appear under Burbank's name; Ory and Alcorn have just as major a role in the music. But the clarinettist has much to say, too. He was a dramatic player, switching between long and short phrases and possessing an odd, shrimpy vibrato which gives his high notes a peculiarly affecting quality. There are fine solos on 'Fidgety Feet' and the rest of a frankly ordinary set of material, but the epic 'Blues For Jimmie Noone', which runs for 11 minutes, has a funereal grandeur that is only finally undercut by Garland's disastrous *arco* passage. Alcorn is, as ever, in rousing form, too. Fair recording, given the source material.

John Burgess

TENOR SAXOPHONE, BASS CLARINET, FLUTE

Scots saxophonist, part of a new wave of players based around Edinburgh.

***** The Beautiful Never**
Urge 2 Burge [no number] *Burgess; Theo Saunders (p); Henry Franklin (b); Willie Jones III (d).* 1/97.

***** The Urge To Burge**
Caber 012 *Burgess; Kevin MacKenzie (g); Mario Caribé (b, perc); John Rae (d).* 4/99.

The Edinburgh-based reed man is possessed of a lovely sound and an impressive stock of ideas. The debut disc was made in California with a skilful American group. Saunders and Jones are at the heart of things at all times, freeing Burgess to make his slightly querulous but heartfelt declarations. The more atmospheric numbers go straight on the personal playlist, mostly for late-nite use; the tougher swingers are as challenging as one might hope.

The follow-up is very much a consolidation. Burgess stays well within himself and relaxes enough to create some genuinely beautiful and moving solos, notably on the opening 'Once Upon A Long Ago', which sets out his trademark Webster-influenced saxophone. As before, his bass clarinet work is moody and atmospheric. An oddly sequenced album, *The Urge To Burge* doesn't come to life until the fourth track, 'The North Beach Hi-Life', which ironically is a flute feature. It's also the only shared credit, a co-composition with bassist Caribé, who provides a steady foundation throughout. As often when a guitarist is preferred to a piano player, the harmonic language is much more ambiguous. MacKenzie probably ought to spend a couple of years in New York to polish up his basic chops, but you can't fault his taste and timing, and his acoustic accompaniment on 'Nine Lives' is impeccable.

Burgess is locked into a mainstream ballad approach that will certainly win him admirers but doesn't challenge him enough. What he needs at this stage is just one raw and rough-edged session of blues and bebop material. He'd come back all the stronger.

Raymond Burke (1904–86)

CLARINET

Began playing home-made instruments as a teenager, then graduated to sax and clarinet. Played in New Orleans for most of his life, through revivalism and beyond, and was closely associated with Preservation Hall from 1960, and with Kid Thomas Valentine.

(***) Raymond Burke's Speakeasy Boys 1937–1949
American Music AMCD-47 *Burke; Wooden Joe Nicholas, Vincent Cass (t); Joe Avery (tb); Louis Gallaud, Woodrow Rousell (p); Johnny St Cyr (g); Austin Young (b); Bob Matthews (d).* 37–5/49.

Burke's clarinet playing stands squarely in the line of the New Orleans masters: he had the sweet-toned delivery of Willie Humphrey but could be as elaborate and blues-inflected as Johnny Dodds when he wished. Some of this can be gleaned from a very rough CD in the American Music series. Most of the tracks come from 1949 acetates by a band from which Burke stands out: Nicholas sounds terribly weak and shaky when he struggles to the front, and Avery's trombone is inept enough to make one wince (even the sleeve-notes describe him as 'ratty'). The loudest person in the band is St Cyr! Despite all that, Burke still weaves some lovely solos out of the situation. The other tracks are even more obscure: a 1937 'Solitude' with George Hartman's (unknown) band, a couple of duets with Woodrow Rousell, and four dusty tracks with Vincent Cass's (unknown) band. Sound-quality ranges from dire to moderately decent (two final acetates were turned up in a New Orleans flea market in 1993). For New Orleans scholars only.

*****(*) Raymond Burke And Cie Frazier With Butch Thompson In New Orleans**
504 CDS27 *Burke; Butch Thompson (p); Cie Frazier (d).* 8/79.

This is more like the way Raymond Burke should be remembered. Though already late in life, he was still playing very well in 1979, his understated delivery the mark of a man whose unassuming approach to his art has helped it endure. In itself, the music is nothing much: a battery of tunes, played at more or less the same tempo, with Frazier marking out a steady pulse and Thompson comping and taking easy-going solos. But scarcely any of the 15 tunes are too familiar – there are New Orleans rarities like A.J. Piron's 'I Want Somebody To Love', 'Gypsy Love Song' and 'Oh Daddy' – and each is played with genuine pleasure by the three men. Thompson never pushes too hard, and Burke's musing solos have an eloquence all their own. On a hot day, with a jug of iced tea to hand, this can sound like the very heart of jazz.

Chris Burn

PIANO, PERCUSSION, TRUMPET

British improviser, basically working from the piano, with a big-scale idea of setting free playing alongside detailed compositional references.

****** Music For Three Rivers**
Victo CD 050 *Burn (p, perc).* 95–97.

****** Navigations**
Acta 12 *Burn; Axel Dorner (t); John Butcher (ts, ss); Jim Denley (f); John Russell (g); Rhodri Davis (hp); Phil Durrant (vn); Stevie*

Wishart (vn, hurdy gurdy); Marcio Mattos (clo, b); Mark Wastell (clo); Matthew Hutchinson (syn, elec). 9/97.

Poised on the teetering edge of some giant, funky blues, 'Storyfall' and the long title-track that follows are masterpieces of improvised pianism, large-scale works of awesome technical and imaginative range. Questions of 'how' sounds are produced may be interesting, but are ultimately redundant. This is concentrated performance which demands the evenly suspended attention Freud considered to be the crux of all aesthetic appreciation. Time was, we would have been satisfied with these two pieces as opposite sides of a single LP (there are classic Cecil Taylor records of shorter duration). As it is, the later, shorter tracks are interesting and adept, but add very little to the majestic sweep of the opening two tracks. An extraordinary record, rich in ideas and unstinting in its creativity.

Navigations is no less difficult to locate within a 'jazz' or improvised sound-language. Much of it sits closer to new music in an advanced idiom. There are few genuinely soloistic passages, and Burn's own playing (doubling on trumpet for a single track) is steady, thoughtful and exploratory, cementing a group which consistently performs outside the expected range and sonority of its constituent instruments. There is, needless to say, no conventional 'rhythm section'; if anyone, it's Russell, Mattos and Hutchinson (and, to a degree, Burn himself) who provide the rhythmic reference-points and the key points of transition. (Burn has also recorded 21 piano pieces by the maverick Henry Cowell for the same label; though it falls outside the scope of this book, it's a fascinating project that helps cast light on some overlaps between jazz and the twentieth-century avant-garde. As with both these records, it's anything but forbidding.)

Ralph Burns (born 1922)

PIANO, ARRANGER

Burns arrived in New York in 1942 and contributed major pieces to the Charlie Barnet and Woody Herman band books, particularly the latter, with whom he worked until the 1950s. He then did various studio arrangements and by the 1970s was working mostly in film and theatre scoring.

*** Bijou

Original Jazz Classics OJC 1917 *Burns; Tal Farlow (g); Clyde Lombardi (b); Osie Johnson (d).* 55.

Burns's contribution to jazz is as an arranger and composer; his piano playing is capable but unremarkable. The main point of this set is to hear some of his most renowned pieces – 'Spring Sequence', 'Bijou', Autobahn Blues' – in a quartet setting. He points up how the harmonies work and, with Farlow taking a back-seat role, it's good dinner music. 'Perpetual Motion' might be the most interesting piece, since he overdubs a second piano part and the results have a Tristanoesque feel. His other albums for Decca, which featured larger groups, are somewhat more interesting but have yet to be reissued.

Dave Burrell (born 1944)

PIANO, KEYBOARDS

Grew up in Hawaii and studied at Berklee, before joining the New York free-jazz movement in the late '60s. Most frequently encountered of late as a David Murray sideman.

*** High Won – High Two

Black Lion BLCD 760206 *Burrell; Sirone (b); Bobby Kapp, Sunny Murray (d); Pharoah Sanders (perc).* 2 & 9/68.

Burrell has never fallen easily into any stylistic categories. He has worked with Marion Brown, Giuseppi Logan, Archie Shepp and Sonny Sharrock, among many others. In the late 1960s, as these associations suggest, he was much involved with the avant-garde while retaining an affection for standards jazz and for non-jazz styles such as ragtime, calypso and, at more of a sceptical distance, elements of the so-called 'Third Stream'. It is only really possible to say that Burrell himself represents a fourth or umpteenth stream. On *High Won – High Two*, his medley, 'Theme Stream', touches on many of these components, reworking five of the other tracks on the record into a single, consecutive piece. Among those it absorbs are 'Dave Blue', 'Bittersweet Reminiscence' and 'Margie Pargie', a cross between a rag and a morning *raga*. The long 'East Side Colors' replaces Kapp (this whole group was part of Noah Howard's rhythm section) with the more fluent but no less fierce Murray. Sanders, for those who are confused by the instrumentation, only plays tambourine.

*** Daybreak

Gazell GJCD 4002 *Burrell; David Murray (ts).* 3/89.

*** Brother To Brother

Gazell GJCD 4010 *As above.*

**** In Concert

Victo CD016 *As above.* 10/91.

A now well-established duo partnership with the prolific David Murray now represents the bulk of Burrell's released output. It is very much an even-handed relationship. Compositional duties are shared out and very often the piano is placed in the foreground, with Murray playing ostinato figures in accompaniment. The 1991 Victoriaville duo and its rather stilted predecessor on Gazell were widely and perhaps inevitably received as two more David Murray albums. While both are collective performances, there's some justification in claiming them for Burrell, whose discography as leader is thinner than ever with the disappearance of his large-scale *In:Sanity*, not yet transferred to Black Saint's CD list.

The pianist contributes all but one of the compositions on *Daybreak* and three out of five on *In Concert*. Of these, 'Punaluu Peter' and 'Teardrops For Jimmy', a threnody to Coltrane's bassist, Jimmy Garrison, are both on *Windward Passages* and have become important repertory pieces for Burrell, who reworks both themes tirelessly.

It's clear that Murray's revisionist approach to the black music tradition has been much influenced by the man who plays on many of his best records. The stride accompaniments on 'Punaluu Peter' suddenly erupt into volcanic outbursts of sound that suggest something of the pressure that always comes up from below in Burrell's work. Murray's well-worked 'Hope Scope' almost becomes a feature for the pianist, but on 'Ballad For The Black Man' that is reversed, with Burrell patiently comping for Murray's calm statement of his own theme and then sustaining a harmonic base for some incredibly sustained upper-register whistles. 'Intuitively' and 'Teardrops For Jimmy' bring the performance to a moving and effective close. The sound is excellent for a live recording, with no distortion or drop-out at either end of the dynamic scale. Strongly recommended as an introduction to either man.

There's nothing with quite that level of intensity on *Daybreak*, but the long 'Blue Hour' has a hypnotic quality, and the bass clarinet duo on Murray's own vestigial 'Sketch No. 1' is one of his best things on the big horn.

***** Esquisses For A Walk**

NTCD 319 *Burrell; Daniel Huck (as, v); Carl Schlosser (ts, f); Ricky Ford (sax); Chris Henderson (d); Laurence Allison (v).* 98.

Jointly led by saxophonist Huck, this rather strange session takes Burrell a step further into his exploration of jazz styles. There is a wonderful reading of 'Honeysuckle Rose', which manages to touch base with Waller and Tatum but nevertheless bears Burrell's signature in every bar. A new approach to 'Trade Winds' isn't quite as successful, but shows how much mileage there is in the material. 'Lush Life' has a kind of defiant melancholy which suits the song, but you won't have heard it performed quite like this before.

Don't be put off by the rather pretentious and enigmatic title. This is a strong, intriguing album with some fine contributions from Ford and the other saxophonists. Not in the front rank of Burrell's output, but well worth hearing and probably a grower.

Kenny Burrell (born 1931)

GUITAR

Born in Detroit, Burrell had already played with Dizzy Gillespie and Oscar Peterson before moving to New York in 1956. Ever since, he has been the most dependable of sidemen and the most quietly inspiring of leaders, mixing both blues and bebop into a style which remains conservative but genuine and unemphatically direct. He has been closely associated with Jimmy Smith's small groups over the years, and has a penchant for Duke Ellington's music: in both cases, the admiration was mutual.

***** All Night Long**

Original Jazz Classics OJC 427 *Burrell; Donald Byrd (t); Hank Mobley (ts); Jerome Richardson (ts, f); Mal Waldron (p); Doug Watkins (b); Art Taylor (d).* 12/56.

***** All Day Long**

Original Jazz Classics OJC 456 *Burrell; Donald Byrd (t); Frank Foster (ts); Tommy Flanagan (p); Doug Watkins (b); Art Taylor (d).* 1/57.

***** Blue Moods**

Original Jazz Classics OJC 019 *Burrell; Cecil Payne (bs); Tommy Flanagan (p); Doug Watkins (b); Elvin Jones (d).* 2/57.

***** The Cats**

Original Jazz Classics OJC 079 *Burrell; Idrees Sulieman (t); John Coltrane (ts); Tommy Flanagan (p); Doug Watkins (b); Louis Hayes (d).* 4/57.

***** Kenny Burrell & John Coltrane**

Original Jazz Classics OJC 300 *Burrell; John Coltrane (ts); Tommy Flanagan (p); Paul Chambers (b); Jimmy Cobb (d).* 3/58.

Burrell is one of the great enduring lights in the music. He's the most gentlemanly of musicians, never losing his grip on a playing situation and in command of a seemingly inexhaustible supply of interesting licks. He has a tone as lulling as that of Joe Pass, but he shies away from that player's rococo extravagances. It's difficult to pick out the best of Burrell, for his earliest sessions are as maturely formed as his later ones, and while he's played with a vast number of musicians he manages to fit seamlessly into whatever the context happens to be. In the 1950s he was a popular man to have on blowing dates, and his early work for Prestige is mostly in that mould. The sessions that were designated as all-day and all-night don't actually go on that long, but some of the solos seem to, and there's little to especially recommend them beyond a few livelier moments. *Blue Moods* is a reflective canter through a typical programme of blues and standards, with a feature for Jones on 'Drum Boogie'. OJC 300 finds Coltrane in his restless early period, but Burrell seems to be a calming influence, and they have a beautifully shaded duet on 'Why Was I Born?'. *The Cats* benefits from Flanagan's leadership, and the pianist's shapely contributions add further lustre to the music, all of it very well engineered.

*****(*) Blue Lights**

Blue Note 57184-2 2CD *Burrell; Louis Smith (t); Tina Brooks, Junior Cook (ts); Duke Jordan, Bobby Timmons (p); Sam Jones (b); Art Blakey (d).* 5/58.

Two blowing dates that have the edge on the Prestige sessions – just that bit sharper and more swinging and, with Smith, Cook and the star-crossed Brooks in attendance, the horns are that bit more interesting too. Blakey lets nobody coast and, even though the material is routine, it doesn't much matter. Originally split across two albums, they're restored to CD with a long look at 'I Never Knew' as the bonus.

****** Bluesy Burrell**

Original Jazz Classics OJC 926 *Burrell; Leo Wright (as); Coleman Hawkins (ts); Tommy Flanagan, Gildo Mahones (p); Major Holley, George Tucker (b); Eddie Locke, Jimmie Smith (d); Ray Barretto (perc).* 9/62–8/63.

What a marvellous session this was. Burrell sounds at his most seductive on 'I Thought About You', at his most suavely blue on 'Montono Blues'; but it's his interplay with the imperious Hawkins, in one of his last great periods, that makes the record special. 'Tres Palabras' is a classic performance, given further weight by Flanagan's wonderfully economical solo, and here and on his three other appearances Hawkins carries all before him. One bonus track from a session made the following year, with Wright and Mahones, is nothing special, and the remastering seems laden with tape-hiss, but the music comes over with plenty of presence.

*****(*) Midnight Blue**

Blue Note 95335-2 *Burrell; Stanley Turrentine (ts); Major Holley (b); Bill English (d); Ray Barretto (perc).* 1/63.

Many a copy of this was worn smooth on vinyl, and the two new-to-CD tracks, 'Kenny's Sound' and 'K Twist', are a welcome bonus, especially in the handsome sound of the RVG Edition. Somewhat atypically low-flame for a Blue Note date, even if Burrell had already visited these climes on the *Night Lights* sessions, they take the soul-food licks of 'Chitlins Con Carne' some way towards ferocity, but the implacable beat refuses to get too nasty, and the following 'Mule' is more typical. Beautifully paced and as elegant a record as the label ever released, this is still an ideal choice for the time and mood of the title.

*****(*) Blue Bash!**

Verve 557453-2 *Burrell; Jimmy Smith (org); George Duvivier, Milt Hinton (b); Bill English, Mel Lewis (d).* 7/63.

Three days of spare studio time while Smith was at work on a big-band date led to this hugely enjoyable blowing date, meat and potatoes for the two principals. Their interplay on the title-track sums up their whole musical relationship: punchy, bluesy, but soaked in the good humour of playing for kicks. Seven extra takes might have spoiled the balance of the record, but for once the extra music means extra enjoyment.

***** Soul Call**

Original Jazz Classics OJC 846-2 *Burrell; Will Davis (p); Martin Rivera (b); Bill English (d); Ray Barretto (perc).* 4/64.

Burrell's reluctance to assert any special kind of leadership tells against him on a date like this, when the supporting players have little to say by themselves. The title-piece and 'Mark One' are solid slow blues, and all the licks are smoothly executed. Otherwise, little to remember.

*****(*) Guitar Forms**

Verve 521403-2 *Burrell; Johnny Coles, Louis Mucci (t); Jimmy Cleveland, Jimmy Knepper (tb); Andy Fitzgerald, George Marge (cor, f); Ray Alonge, Julius Watkins (frhn); Steve Lacy (ss); Ray Beckenstein (as, f); Lee Konitz (as); Richie Kamuca (ts, ob); Bob Tricarico (bsn, f); Roger Kellaway (p); Bill Barber (tba); Ron Carter, Joe Benjamin (b); Elvin Jones, Charli Persip, Grady Tate (d); Willie Rodriguez (perc).* 12/64–4/65.

This is arguably the closest Burrell has come to a singular achievement, even if it is more by association with Gil Evans, who arranged it. Burrell's sanguine approach might make him a less characterful soloist than those who've handled other of Evans's concerto set-pieces, but in some ways that works to the music's advantage: without misleading emotional resonances of the kind associated with, say, Miles Davis cracking notes, the purity of Evans's veils of sound emerges the more clearly in the likes of 'Lotus Land'. The new Master Edition issue includes a great many extra and alternative takes which frankly are best programmed out except when one is in an especially scholarly mood.

***** Kenny Burrell: Jazz Masters 45**

Verve 527652-2 *As above, except add Jimmy Nottingham, Thad Jones, Ernie Royal, Marvin Stamm, Joe Shepley (t), Wayne Andre, Urbie Green, Tony Studd (tb), Jerome Richardson (woodwinds), Harvey Philips (tba), Phil Woods (as), Richard Wyands, Herbie Hancock (p), Jimmy Smith (org), Vince Gambella (g), Ron Carter (b), Mel Lewis, Donald McDonald (d), Johnny Pacheco (perc).* 64–69.

This creams off some of *Guitar Forms* along with tracks from *A Generation Ago Today, Blues: The Common Ground, For Charlie Christian And Benny Goodman, Asphalt Canyon Suite* and *Night Song*, so there's a fair amount of otherwise-unavailable Burrell here. That said, several of those discs weren't among his finest hours, and he sounds as happy here on a single track with Jimmy Smith as he does on his own-name projects. *Guitar Forms* is a better bet as a single disc, but collectors will certainly want this one too.

****(*) Ode To 52nd Street**

Chess 051824-2 *Burrell; orchestra and strings arranged by Richard Evans.* 4/66–9/67.

Now back on its own, after previously being coupled with a different Chess album, *Ode To 52nd Street* is nothing special. The arranged pieces are more like snooze music and certainly nothing like *Guitar Forms*. Burrell's class brings a mild edge to the situation.

****** Ellington Is Forever Vol. 1**

Fantasy FCD-79005-2 *Burrell; Jon Faddis, Snooky Young (t); Thad Jones (c, flhn); Jerome Richardson (ss, ts); Joe Henderson (ts); Jimmy Jones (p); Jimmy Smith (org); Jimmie Smith (d); Mel Lewis, Richie Goldberg (perc); Ernie Andrews (v).* 2/75.

Burrell's greatest album looks unpromising from a distance, after countless tribute records have become such a catch-all theme in the past 25 years. But this salute to Ellington remains one of the great examples of the genre. Cut at a couple of loose-knit sessions over two days, the cast is a shifting one, from 12 men on a hard-hitting 'Caravan' to a Burrell solo on 'Jump For Joy' and Jimmy Jones's moving soliloquy on 'Take The "A" Train'. 'C Jam Blues' sets Faddis and Thad Jones against the rhythm section, a blues medley allows a rare sighting of Snooky Young as a soloist, and Henderson is splendid on 'I Didn't Know About You'. Most affecting of all is the absolutely definitive treatment of 'My Little Brown Book' by Ernie Andrews and Jimmy Jones. Burrell may be just a bystander at times, but he presided over a magnificent session.

***** Ellington Is Forever Vol. 2**

Fantasy 79008-2 *As above, except add Nat Adderley (c), Quentin Jackson (tb), Gary Bartz (cl, as), Sir Roland Hanna (p), Stanley Gilbert, George Mraz, Monk Montgomery (b), Philly Joe Jones (d); omit Jimmie Smith, Lewis, Goldberg.* 11–12/75.

The return match was a disappointment, even though there are delightful moments: Smith's lovely glide through 'Solitude', and Thad Jones and Young together on 'Come Sunday'. Too many of the other pieces sound routine or merely very good.

***** Tin Tin Deo**

Concord CCD 4045 *Burrell; Reggie Johnson (b); Carl Burnett (d).* 3/77.

***** When Lights Are Low**

Concord CCD 4083 *As above, except Larry Gates (b) replaces Johnson.* 9/78.

(*) **Moon And Sand
Concord CCD 4121 *Burrell; John Heard (b); Roy McCurdy (d); Kenneth Nash (perc).* 12/79.

One could complain that Burrell's unflappability and Concord's smooth, welcoming presentation tend to anaesthetize rather than stimulate, and there's little to make one sit up and take notice on these discs. But Burrell was in his prime as an improviser and, if the format doesn't encourage innovation, the solos on, say, 'Tin Tin Deo' or 'It Shouldn't Happen To A Dream' are evidence of his mettle. The two trio albums are from a fine vintage and still afford much understated pleasure. *Moon And Sand* is a shade more disappointing in that the rhythm section seem less happy and Burrell sounds less involved.

***(*) **At The Village Vanguard**
RCA Camden 74321 610842 2CD *Burrell; Larry Gales, Rufus Reid (b); Sherman Ferguson (d).*

By themselves these are somewhat rote Burrell dates, but as a budget-priced package they go up a notch for sheer good value. It gathers the three Muse albums *Live At The Village Vanguard, Live In New York* and *Ellington A La Carte* into a single two-disc set. Gales and Ferguson give plenty of shove in the engine-room on the first two, but the third is a more pensive set of treatments of Kenny's beloved Ellington material, with only Reid for company (and since this one was cut at the Village Gate, it slightly spoils the title).

(*) **Guiding Spirit
Contemporary 14065 *Burrell; Jay Hoggard (vib); Marcus McLaurine (b); Yoron Israel (d).* 8/89.

Burrell continued to work through the 1970s and '80s in his patient, unhurried way. So here he is in 1989: still pretty, still bebop, still no trouble, still fine; not that great, unless one needs a late-night painkiller.

***(*) **Sunup To Sundown**
Contemporary CCD-14065-2 *Burrell; Cedar Walton (p); Rufus Reid (b); Lewis Nash (d); Ray Mantilla (perc).* 6/91.

A good one. 'Out There' hits a fine groove from the outset, and it's quickly apparent that Walton, Reid and Nash are bringing the best out of the nominal leader, whose solos find an extra pinch of energy and grit without surrendering any of his smoothest moves.

***(*) **Lotus Blossom**
Concord CCD 4668 *Burrell; Ray Drummond (b); Yoron Israel (d).* 6/95.

*** **Live At The Blue Note**
Concord CCD 4731 *Burrell; Jimmy Owens (t, flhn); Steve Turre, Benny Powell (tb); Jerome Richardson (ts, f); Sir Roland Hanna (p); Ray Drummond, Marcus McLaurine (b); Sherman Ferguson, Horace Arnold (d); Vanessa Rubin, Jeanie Bryson (v).* 7/96.

Lotus Blossom is a patient reminder of Burrell's beguiling excellence. As with his original Concords of almost 20 years earlier, he does little more than tackle a good set of jazz and standard tunes, assign a sensible rhythm section to follow him, and spin thoughtful lines out of them that whisper of the blues and bebop without speaking them out loud. This would be neoclassicism in other hands; with Burrell, it's the real thing.

The Blue Note date is a slight but enjoyable set with some old-stagers working over some familiar fare. Burrell's well-meaning vocal on his own 'Dear Ella' wasn't a great idea, but having Jeanie Bryson do 'I've Got A Crush On You' certainly was.

*** **The Best Of Kenny Burrell**
Blue Note 830493-2 *As Blue Note albums above, except add Grover Washington (ss), Frank Foster, Hank Mobley (ts), Seldon Powell (f), Tommy Flanagan, Horace Silver, Herbie Hancock, Hank Jones (p), Bobby Broom, Rodney Jones (g), Ben Tucker, Dave Jackson, Reggie Workman, Doug Watkins, Milt Hinton, Oscar Pettiford (b), Shadow Wilson, Louis Hayes, Osie Johnson, Jack DeJohnette, Kenny Washington (d), Ray Barretto (perc).* 3/56–10/86.

Thirty years (on and off) of Burrell on Blue Note. A couple of rarities – a single release of 'Loie' and a quartet track with Hancock – plus some familiar fodder from the early days, along with tracks from the so-so *Togethering* and *Generation* albums.

*** **Kenny Burrell And The Jazz Giants**
Prestige 60-028 *As OJC albums listed above.*

A solid if rather bitty compoilation from Burrell's many appearances on Prestige, and the roll-call – from Coleman Hawkins to Stanley Turrentine – is the expected who's who for this nonpareil sideman.

Abraham Burton (born 1972)

ALTO SAXOPHONE

Young post-bopper playing New York metropolitan jazz.

***(*) **Closest To The Sun**
Enja ENH 8074 *Burton; Marc Cary (p); Billy Johnson (b); Eric McPherson (d).* 3/94.

***(*) **The Magician**
Enja ENJ 9037 *As above.* 3/95.

It took Abraham Burton some time to realize that he didn't have to burn up the stand every number. That's probably why the second and better of these albums begins with a slow, measured interpretation of 'I Can't Get Started' on which the young altoist leans heavily on the melody, embellishing it only colouristically. *The Magician* was recorded live to two-track at Visiones in Greenwich Village (whose talent-booker was Gust William Tsilis, co-producer of the debut CD). The sound isn't pristine, but it sounds immediate and, as before, very intense. A raw, unvarnished reading of Jackie McLean's slippery 'Little Melonae' is outstanding, and Cary's long original 'An Addition To The Family' is the other high point, but there is also a powerful arrangement of Satie's 'Gnossienne No. 1' on which McPherson – who in many respects is the key to this band – excels himself, producing a dark, heavy sound which oddly recalls Rashied Ali at his most brooding. The Coltrane quartet is one obvious source for what Burton is doing. The main influence on his alto playing is Jackie McLean, whose 'Minor Mach' kicks off the first album.

What's impressive, though, is the instinctive understanding between the group members. Though much was made of the fact that they hadn't gigged more than once or twice before recording *Closest To The Sun*, those first concerts were said to be electrifying; Burton, Cary and Johnson had in any case struck up an understanding while working with Arthur Taylor's Wailers, while Burton and McPherson were high school pals who spent hours busking duets. Just past forty, Johnson is the oldest, but the whole unit sounds seasoned and mature. Spare a brief, envious thought for those who get to hear this band live on a regular basis, and then settle down to the next best thing.

Gary Burton (born 1943)

VIBRAPHONE

Unusually for a player and musician of his stature, Burton has mostly preferred to play the compositions of others, notably Carla Bley. A distinguished educator, his groups have long been a proving ground for young talent, while his four-mallet approach and distinctive approach to arrangement create an instantly recognizable sound.

***** Tennessee Firebird**

Bear Family 14458 *Burton; Chet Atkins, Jim Colvard, Ray Edenton (g); Buddy Emmons (steel g); Charlie McCoy (hca, b); Bobby Osborne (mandola); Sonny Osborne (bj); Norman Spicher (vn); Henry Strzelecki, Steve Swallow (b); Grady Martin (b, g); Kenneth A Buttrey, Roy Haynes (d).* 9/66.

***** Duster**

Koch Jazz 7846 *Burton; Larry Coryell (g); Steve Swallow (b); Roy Haynes (d).* 4/67.

***** Lofty Fake Anagram**

One Way 34489 *As above, except omit Haynes; add Bob Moses (d).* 8/67.

*****(*) A Genuine Tong Funeral**

RCA Victor 07863 66748 2 *Burton; Michael Mantler (t); Jimmy Knepper (tb, btb); Howard Johnson (tba, bs); Steve Lacy (ss); Gato Barbieri (ts); Carla Bley (p, org); Larry Coryell (g); Steve Swallow (b); Lonesome Dragon, Bob Moses (d).* 67, 68.

*****(*) Country Roads And Other Places**

Koch Jazz 7854 *Burton; Jerry Hahn (g); Steve Swallow (b); Roy Haynes (d).* 9/68.

Burton's early recordings were driven by an ambition to synthesize jazz, rock and country music with some elements of classical form. The very early *Tennessee Firebird* is almost a country set, as the personnel must suggest, though Burton's own playing points in other directions. The mix of up-tempo tunes like 'Panhandle Rag' with gentler-paced ballads (notably 'Black Is The Color Of My True Love's Hair') prevents the album, which is rather brief, from settling into a monotonous groove. Perhaps too Nashville for some tastes, but think what Bill Frisell was doing to great critical acclaim three decades later, and most jazz purists will swallow their disdain for a record featuring Chet Atkins and Charlie McCoy.

By contrast, *Duster* was one of the very first jazz-rock records and, though it seems rather tame compared to later work by the Mahavishnu Orchestra, Return To Forever, Lifetime and, of course, Weather Report, it undoubtedly had an impact on at least some of those outfits, even if only as permission to mix rock beats and distorted guitar into a jazz performance. Michael Gibbs's 'Sweet Rain' is the outstanding track, a modern classic, but Carla Bley's 'Sing Me Softly Of The Blues' runs it a very close second. One of his most striking recordings, though, was a performance of Carla Bley's 'dark opera without words', *A Genuine Tong Funeral*. This was intended for full staging with costumes and lights but is really known only as a recorded piece. Bley intended no connection whatsoever with actual Chinese music, and the basic provenance of the album is that same synthesis of modern styles which Burton himself was pursuing at the time. The work has a brooding, processional quality, using suspended harmonies and minor variants to create an atmosphere of loss and, on occasion, inexplicable dread. 'Mother Of The Dead Man' is perhaps the best-known single component, largely because Mike Gibbs included it in concert programmes, but it's the centrepiece, 'Silent Spring', originally written for Steve Swallow but now dominated by Gato Barbieri, Larry Coryell and Burton, which stands out. Burton's playing is more open and abstract than at any other point in his career. The CD reissue is augmented by a few tracks from *Lofty Fake Anagram* (which you can work out for yourselves). This 1968 disc has also long been out of circulation and, while it lacks the energy and grace of *Country Roads*, it's a valuable comeback and a tremendous showcase for Coryell.

Country Roads is still a joy after more than 30 years, and plaudits to Koch for bringing it back. The playing is as fresh and unfettered as it ever seemed, and themes like 'Family Joy', 'And On The Third Day' and 'Country Roads', which may be better known from composer Mike Gibbs's versions, occupy a vivid corner in the folk-memory of anyone who grew up with jazz at this time. The album marked the debut of guitarist Hahn, who keeps his occasional excesses well under control and plays smoothly legato lines with a lot on rhythmic pace. Burton is in excellent form, dancing on the bars, and then suddenly changing pace to accommodate the gracious sweep of 'My Foolish Heart' and 'Wichita Breakdown'. There is even a small Ravel arrangement, handled in a way reminiscent of guitarist Larry Coryell's approach to classical themes.

****** Gary Burton And Keith Jarrett**

Rhino 8122 71594 *Burton; Keith Jarrett (p, ss); Sam Brown, Jerry Hahn (g); Richard Greene (vn); Steve Swallow (b); Bill Goodwin (d).* 6/69, 7/70.

****(*) Good Vibes**

Koch Jazz 8515 *Burton; Richard Tee (p); Eric Gale, Jerry Hahn (g); Chuck Rainey, Steve Swallow (b); Bill Lavorgna (d, perc).* 9/69.

***** Paris Encounter**

Atlantic 112783 *Burton; Stéphane Grappelli (vn); Steve Swallow (b); Bill Goodwin (d).* 11/69.

Ever since the late 1960s, and the band that established his name and mature style, Burton has shown a marked preference for the quartet format, and for working with guitarists. The 1967 band included Larry Coryell, Steve Swallow and Bob Moses, and it remains perhaps his most consistently inventive unit. Swallow has been a steady presence and provides a consistent but imaginative bottom line for Burton's occasionally fly-away approach.

In 1969 and 1970 Burton co-led a group with Keith Jarrett and recorded the magnificent *Throb*, also included on the Rhino compilation and still – for us at least – one of the most evocative records produced at the time. Michael Gibbs's title-track is a *Zeitgeist* moment, a wry, innocent thing with an almost European depth of focus.

Good Vibes is an almost forgotten Atlantic release, now rescued from oblivion by the obliging Koch. There is no avoiding the impression of a musician – and a label – trying to rise to the challenge presented by rock. There is too much guitar and too much heavy backbeat, and Burton's own playing dissolves into shapelessness, even on his own material. 'Vibrafinger', 'Boston Marathon' and 'Leroy The Magician' are originals.

The 35-year age gap did nothing to dim Burton's meeting with Hot Club veteran Grappelli. *Paris Encounter* is a delicious set, opening with Django's 'Daphne' and including Mike Gibbs's 'Sweet Rain' (a dedication to Burton) and Steve Swallow's much-covered 'Eiderdown'. Grappelli seems to enjoy the pitch and pace of the vibes and the rhythm section, of which Burton himself is of course a part, laying out bright, buoyant chords even as he develops a melody line. One of the happiest records of his career.

***** Alone At Last**

32 Jazz 32115 *Burton (vib, p, org). 6–9/71.*

Lennie Tristano did it, Bill Evans did it, and Burton does it too on this subtly overdubbed solo session, which also includes material from the Montreux Jazz Festival. Live and undubbed, Burton shows what a formidable player he could be, and the additional studio version of 'Chega De Saudade (No More Blues)' is a *tour de force.* The overdubbing, which makes use of acoustic and electric piano and organ, yields a very textured and multi-dimensional sound, though it's difficult to see why some of these tracks couldn't have been performed with something like Burton's regular quartet. All in all, a very likeable and successful record, and another rescued from oblivion by a sympathetic reissue label.

***** The New Quartet**

ECM 835002-2 *Burton; Mick Goodrick (g); Abraham Laboriel (b); Harry Blazer (d). 3/73.*

The New Quartet was a more or less self-conscious attempt to synthesize the earlier band; the newcomers are by no means faceless epigoni, and the resulting album is robustly conceived and performed, and is marked by some of the best writing Burton had to work with. There are pieces by Carla Bley, Gordon Beck and Michael Gibbs; 'Olhos De Gato' and Beck's 'Mallet Man' are masterly.

***** Ring**

ECM 829191-2 *Burton; Mick Goodrick, Pat Metheny (g); Steve Swallow (b); Bob Moses (d). 74.*

****(*) Dreams So Real**

ECM 833329-2 *As above, except add Eberhard Weber (b). 75.*

***** Passengers**

ECM 835016-2 *Burton; Pat Metheny (g); Steve Swallow, Eberhard Weber (b); Dan Gottlieb (d). 11/76.*

Burton's mid-1970s albums with rising star Metheny and the distinctive Weber now sound a little tarnished, but their blend of country softness and Weber's slightly eldritch melody-lines still make for interesting listening, even if the group never sounds quite as enterprising as it did live. The three ECMs are pretty much of a piece, but *Passengers*, actually co-credited to Weber, is probably the one to go for initially.

Burton makes a considerable virtue out of what might have become an awful clutter of strings and percussion. The themes are open and clearly stated, even when they are relatively complex, as on 'The Whopper', and Weber's forceful, wailing sound is strongly contrasted to those of the two guitarists; Swallow as usual plays bass guitar with a pick, getting a clean, exact sound whose coloration is totally different from Metheny's rock-influenced sustains. Weber's own composition, 'Yellow Fields', undergoes an attractive variation.

***** Matchbook**

ECM 835014-2 *Burton; Ralph Towner (g). 7/74.*

****** Hotel Hello**

ECM 835586-2 *Burton; Steve Swallow (b). 5/74.*

****(*) Duet**

ECM 829941-2 *Burton; Chick Corea (p). 10/78.*

At first blush, the Burton/Corea partnership looked like a marriage made in heaven, and they toured extensively. In practice, and at least on record, the collaboration fell foul of the inevitable similarity between piano and vibraphone and of the performers' out-of-synch musical personalities. The earlier *Crystal Silence* is more properly credited to Corea, since he is the chief writer. On *Duet*, the pianist never seems far from whimsicality, and it is interesting to see how much more positively and forcefully Burton responds to Towner's light but well-anchored style. *Matchbook* is surprisingly disciplined and coherent for all its lacy textures and delicate, almost directionless transitions; *Slide Show* (ECM 1306) reversed the performers' names on the cover and so – by our ruthlessly alphabetical rubric – stops for T. Disappointing, though.

Hotel Hello is by far the most impressive of Burton's two-handers and an ideal opportunity to examine the vibist in close-up. The overture and vamp to 'Hotel Hello' are worthy of Carla Bley and the detailed interplay between the co-leaders is often revelatory. This is one of the high points of ECM's distinguished catalogue.

***** Works**

ECM 823267-2 *Burton; Chick Corea (p); Mick Goodrick, Pat Metheny, Ralph Towner (g); Abe Laboriel, Steve Swallow, Eberhard Weber (b); Harry Blazer (d); Bob Moses (perc); orchestra. 72–80.*

Works is one of the better balanced of ECM's 15th-anniversary artist samplers, with a good range of material from what some would consider his vintage years. Virtually all the material is readily available elsewhere, though.

***** Real Life Hits**

ECM 825235-2 *Burton; Makoto Ozone (p); Steve Swallow (b); Mike Hyman (d). 1/82, 11/84.*

Real Life Hits is understated and rather inward looking, but renewed acquaintance reveals a record of unsuspected depth and dimension. As so often, the compositions are from other hands – Carla Bley, John Scofield, Ozone, Swallow, Duke Ellington – but Burton has the gift of transforming them into his own creative idiolect. The interpretation of Duke's 'Fleurette Africaine' is exquisite, and Carla's 'Syndrome' and 'Real Life Hits' give the band something to chew on. We are as guilty as anyone, but an easily underestimated record.

****(*) Whiz Kids**

ECM 831110-2 *Burton; Tommy Smith (ts); Makoto Ozone (p); Steve Swallow (b); Martin Richards (d).* 6/86.

Though Ozone (who has a fine CBS album to his credit) resurfaced to great effect on *Whiz Kids*, all the buzz was about the Scottish *Wunderkind* Smith, another pupil of Burton's at Berklee, and just at this time beginning to receive serious critical attention on the other side of the Atlantic. The results (perhaps inevitably, given all the hype) are a shade disappointing. Burton has never been easy with saxophone players (see his two tracks with Michael Brecker on *Times Like These*), and the lead voices clutter and compete furiously, without any logic or drama. Ozone keeps things more or less tidy, but it is an uncomfortable set and definitely missable.

***** Reunion**

GRP 95982 *Burton; Pat Metheny (g); Mitch Forman (p, ky); Will Lee (b); Peter Erskine (d).* 5/89.

Burton's association with Pat Metheny continued to yield reciprocal benefits, and *Reunion* is rather good. The introduction of Forman is slightly mystifying. His unctuous and rather overripe tonality isn't what's needed on this set and he is inclined to indulge large chromatic fantasies where simple statement of themes and background chords is all that is required of him.

****(*) Six Pack**

GRP 059685-2 *Burton; Bob Berg (ts); Jim Hall, Mulgrew Miller (p); Kevin Eubanks, B.B King, Kurt Rosenwinkel, John Scofield, Ralph Towner (g); Paul Shaffer (p, org); Larry Goldings (ky, org); Steve Swallow (b); Jack DeJohnette (d).* 10/91–4/92.

Burton's continuing love affair with the guitar goes public with this rather odd line-'em-up. The title-track and 'Double Guatemala' with B.B. King are a joke, Rosenwinkel is pretty anonymous, and only Sco and Hall really seem to know what they're about. Burton's own playing has gone to pot, in the sense that he seems content to string together bits and pieces from old solos. There are, of course, moments of interest, but for the most part this is a rummage sale.

***** Departure**

Concord CCD 4749 *Burton; Fred Hersch (p); John Scofield (g); John Patitucci (b); Peter Erskine (d).* 96.

Despite a line-up to die for, this set never manages to ignite and remains stalled in its own good taste and elegance. Burton's playing has reached a level where he no longer thinks instrumentally but musically, using the vibes merely as a way station. Because Hersch is more deliberate and ironic and Scofield more pressingly emphatic, the expected revelation never quite happens and, though 'Chick's Japanese Waltz' is lovely and 'Poinciana' serves as a reminder of how good a repertory player Burton can be, neither track is able to lift the set as a whole.

***** Astor Piazzolla Reunion: A Tango Excursion**

Concord CCD 4793 2 *Burton; Daniel Binelli, Marcello Nisinman, Astor Piazzolla (bandoneon); Nicholas Ledesma, Makoto Ozone, Pablo Ziegler (p); Horacio Malvicino (g); Fernando Suarez-Paz (vn); Hector Console (b).*

Gary's association with Piazzolla started in 1985 and continued in mutual admiration and respect for the remainder of the brilliant bandoneonist's life. At the end of the record, and probably best consigned to afterthought, a 'virtual' duet between the vibist and the late Piazzolla, recorded playing 'Mi Refugio'. It's affecting enough, but there are far more convincing performances elsewhere on the disc that steer away from necrology and pastiche. Burton's arrangements are deft and in keeping with the spirit of the original. 'Soledad' and 'Lunfarno' cover much of the emotional spectrum, dark, intense and throbbing with complex internal rhythms. Daniel Binelli and Marcello Nisinman stand in place of the great man on a number of tracks but, for the most part, Piazzolla's presence is in the music, and any hint of pastiche is avoided.

*****(*) Like Minds**

Concord 4803 *Burton; Chick Corea (p); Pat Metheny (g); Dave Holland (b); Roy Haynes (d).* 11/98.

The degrees of propinquity are too complicated to work out, but suffice it to say that, while the paths of these five musicians have crossed many times over the years, they have never worked together in the same group. Burton is very much the lead voice, and although both Corea and Metheny, who had not (to our knowledge) worked together before, are accorded plenty of solo space, they indulge it sparingly. The choice of tunes could hardly have been happier, with Metheny getting the lion's share of credits, outstandingly on 'Tears Of Rain'. Chick's 'Windows' is a well-established modern classic and receives a wonderful interpretation from the group. Gary's own solos on 'Country Roads' and 'Like Minds' are models of structure and form. Supergroup albums are very hit-and-miss. This, though, is one that can be heartily recommended. The individual elements cohere splendidly round a rhythm section to die for, and one hopes this band might some day hit the road. Unlikely, but an enticing thought.

John Butcher

TENOR, SOPRANO AND BARITONE SAXOPHONES

A London-based improviser, Butcher's main instruments are soprano and tenor saxophones, although he is also interested in altering their sound via electronics or studio techniques.

****** Thirteen Friendly Numbers**

Acta 6 *Butcher (ss, ts, bs solo).* 3–12/91.

A British improviser whose playing is highly accomplished and strikingly individual, Butcher's recital is unlike any other solo-saxophone record. Nine of the 13 tracks are real-time solos on either tenor or soprano, while the other four create some unprecedented sounds and textures through overdubbing: 'Bells And Clappers', for instance, piles up four tenors into a brittle choir of humming overtones that has a chilling, sheet-metal sound, while the amplification introduced into the very brief 'Mackle Music' is peculiarly disturbing. On the more conventional solo tracks, Butcher's mastery of the instrument creates a vocabulary which can accommodate pieces as disparate as 'Notelet', which is like a single flow of melody, and the explorations of single aspects of performing technique, as on 'Humours And Vapours' and 'Buccinator's Outing'. Assisted by a very clear and suitably neutral recording, this is a masterful record which should be investigated by anyone interested in free playing.

***(*) **Concert Moves**

Random Acoustics RA 011 *Butcher; Phil Durrant (vn); John Russell (g).* 11/91–9/92.

Butcher's sparse discography up to this point is to be regretted since he is obviously in his prime; a typical Braxton documentation would have had this as at least a three-disc set, and the group is great enough to stand it. Lyrical when you expect frenzy, light and airy when darkness seems about to fall, the trio don't confound expectations so much as create freshness from moment to moment. Russell almost always plays quietly; Durrant prefers a vocabulary of small, scratchy gestures; so it's left to Butcher to use the largest range of device, songful high motifs, circular riffs, blatted notes, slap-tongue devices, all sorts of everything. It is as fine a set of free playing as one could encounter in recent times, with a piece such as 'Playfair's Axiom' almost a model of what-can-be-done, though it probably won't convert anyone to this aesthetic. Docked a fraction for the sound-mix: Russell is further away than even he would surely prefer.

***(*) **London And Cologne**

Rastascan BRD 026 *Butcher (ss, ts solo).* 10/94–4/96.

Perhaps less secure technically than some of his solo-sax peers, Butcher's soliloquizing has a palpable humanity about it. One can almost feel the grain of his playing as he essays it, and this gathering of live solos is suitably involving. He gets a vocalized sound out of the tenor which is nevertheless under quite a stringent control: there's little 'abandon' in his playing, and the rather explosive soprano piece, 'Our Man In Acton' (a place in West London), is a surprise after the different rigours of the tenor solos. If this is slightly less absorbing a disc than the earlier *Thirteen Friendly Numbers*, there's still the one studio piece, 'Shrinkdown', a quite amazing treatment for four sopranos which opens another new sound-world.

*** **Secret Measures**

Wobbly Rail WOB 006 *Butcher; Phil Durrant (elecs).* 11/97.

***(*) **The Scenic Route**

Emanem 4029 *Butcher; Phil Durrant (vn); John Russell (g).* 3–5/98.

***(*) **Music On Seven Occasions**

Meniscus MNSCS 004 *Butcher; Jeb Bishop (tb); Veryan Weston (p); Thomas Lehn (syn); John Corbett (g); Terri Kapsalis (vn); Fred Lonberg-Holm (clo); Alexander Frangenheim (b); Gino Robair, Michael Zerang (perc).* 6/96–2/98.

***(*) **Light's View**

Nuscope 1004 *Butcher; Georg Gräwe (p).* 4/98.

Butcher is beginning to get on record in a big way, though each of these releases will be found with varying degrees of difficulty, depending on where you are. *Secret Measures* is the least appealing for us, since it consists entirely of Butcher's playing undergoing real-time electronic treatment by Durrant, and the results are more like randomized electronic music than free improvisation. Interesting, but for rarefied tastes.

Not that *The Scenic Route* is any less hard-core, a repeat match for the trio of *Concert Moves* which finds them in the same resilient form at two concerts a week apart in London and Paris. The opening 'Heavy Merge', 20 minutes of severely attractive interplay, arguably says everything they have to on the disc, but there are a further 47 minutes of music anyway.

Music On Seven Occasions is a good way to sample Butcher's music. It gathers together 14 duets and four solos from various (mostly brief) encounters in England and America, and stretches from the melodious three minutes with Bishop to the frosty shape-making with Lehn.

Light's View is a surprise encounter with new-music polymath Gräwe. With no residual jazz thinking traceable in the work of either man, the playing has a sometimes chilly rigour about it, but Butcher isn't averse to mining at least a melodic motif, and in its rather glacial way the music has plenty of purpose to it.

Jaki Byard (1922–99)

PIANO, TENOR SAXOPHONE, VIBRAPHONE, DRUMS

Born in Worcester, Massachusetts, Jaki started out as a brass player and continued to practise multi-instrumentalism for much of his career, though doubling on saxophone rather than trumpet or trombone. He worked with Earl Bostic, with Maynard Ferguson and, later, with Charles Mingus, a career pattern that usefully hints at his forceful, rootsy approach. Blessed with a powerful left hand and a free approach to harmony, Jaki was able to work in almost any context, from gospelly blues to the avant-garde.

**** **Out Front!**

Original Jazz Classics OJCCD 1842 *Byard; Richard Williams (t); Booker Ervin (ts); Ron Carter, Bob Cranshaw, Walter Perkins (b); Roy Haynes (d).*

***(*) **Blues For Smoke**

Candid CCD 79018 *Byard (p solo).* 12/60.

***(*) **Here's Jaki**

Original Jazz Classics OJCCD 1874 *Byard; Ron Carter (b); Roy Haynes (d).* 61.

***(*) **Hi-Fly**

Original Jazz Classics OJCCD 1879 *Byard; Ron Carter (b); Pete LaRoca (d).*

*** **Live! At Lennie's On The Turnpike**

Prestige PCD 24121 *Byard; Joe Farrell (ts, ss, f); George Tucker (b); Alan Dawson (d, vib).* 4/65.

Byard's enormous power and versatility are grounded on a thorough knowledge of brass, reeds, drums and guitar, as well as piano, and there are passages in solos which suggest some attempt to replicate the phrasing of a horn rather than a keyboard instrument. On a straight comparison between two solo sets two decades apart, it seems that Byard does now play more pianistically, though the distinctive left- and right-hand articulation of themes – based on a highly personal synthesis of ragtime and stride, bop and free jazz – is still strongly evident in 1981.

The early Prestige and New Jazz sets reissued on OJC are uniformly excellent. *Out Front!* remains our favourite, largely because it shows off Byard's infallible instinct for horn voicings relative to the piano. Tracks like 'European Episode' and a melting 'Lush Life' are well worth studying in some detail. The idiom is much the same, though obviously simplified, on the trio albums, two thoroughly original selections which challenge many of the existing clichés imposed by precedent on this type of group. Byard allows melody lines to swing round the band, exploiting Carter's tremendous fingering on 'Giant Steps' (*Here's Jaki*) and 'Round Midnight' from *Hi-Fly*, which also includes the fascinating 'Excerpts' from *Yamecraw*. LaRoca is a much undervalued drummer, only recently returned to the recording studio; like Haynes, he has a delicate, pattering touch that always makes the beat sound mobile rather than fixed.

Blues For Smoke is a minor classic, with the wonderful 'Aluminium Baby', originally written for trumpeter/bandleader Herb Pomeroy, and 'Diane's Melody'. Recommended, as is the live quartet from 1965, which highlights the seriously underrated Farrell in one of his most attractive and sympathetic settings. The charts are rather sketchy and a couple of them sound like run-throughs; it's the musicianship rather than anything in the writing that makes them work.

*** On The Spot!

Original Jazz Classics OJCCD 1031 2 *Byard; Jimmy Owens (t, flhn, perc); Paul Chambers, George Tucker (b); Alan Dawson, Billy Higgins (d).* 4/65, 2/67.

The most distinctive track on this rather brief session, augmented for CD only by 'Snow Flakes', is the live version of 'Spanish Tinge', which adds Morton to Tatum and Powell amid Jaki's personal pantheon. The chemistry with trumpeter Owens, long undersung and overlooked, is riveting on most of the tracks, and the other members of the studio rhythm section, Chambers and Higgins, are in absolutely crackling form. Jaki's two forays on alto saxophone won't have scared any ghosts, but they're effective enough. Nicely remastered, and a welcome addition to the man's discography.

*** Freedom Together!

Original Jazz Classics OJCCD 1898-2 *Byard; Richard Davis (b); Alan Dawson (d); Junior Parker (v).* 1/66.

Byard's eclectic virtuosity is strongly in evidence here. In addition to piano, he plays tenor saxophone, vibes and drums. 'Ode To Prez' is a homage to his great idol and underlines how instinctive an understanding Jaki has of pre-bebop styles. The trio with Davis and Dawson was seasoned and road-hardened, but limited by its own broad remit. A more concentrated programme might have offered a better representation of what all three are about. The closing 'Young At Heart' is a throwaway, amusing enough but out of place. Parker's feature, 'Getting To Know You', has its strengths, but again it doesn't seem entirely in keeping with the rest of the album. A qualified success, this one is an acquired taste.

***(*) The Jaki Byard Experience

Original Jazz Classics OJCCD 1913-2 *Byard; Roland Kirk (sax, cl); Richard Davis (b); Alan Dawson (d).* 9/68.

Jaki knew Roland Kirk from the Mingus band and had always found much in common with him, musically and temperamentally. However quirky the two men were, they shared a deep and insightful awareness of the music's history, and Jaki's playing here is a primer of jazz piano styles from the dawn of jazz to the bop revolution. Kirk adds distinctive clarinet, on which he sounds a generation older than his chronological or stylistic age, and Davis and Dawson add their usual intelligent contributions. Too quirky and casual to be entirely satisfactory, this is nevertheless a fascinating jazz record.

**(*) To Them, To Us

Soul Note 121025 *Byard (p solo).* 5/81.

*** Phantasies

Soul Note 121075 *Byard; The Apollo Stompers: Roger Parrett, Al Bryant, John Eckert, Jim White (t); Steve Wienberg, Steve Swell, Carl Reinlib, Bob Norden (tb); Stephen Calia (btb); Bob Torrence, Manny Boyd (as); Jed Levy, Alan Givens (ts); Preston Trombly (bs); Dan Licht (g); Ralph Hamperian (b); Richard Allen (d); Denyce Byard, Diane Byard (perc, v).* 9/84.

*** Foolin' Myself

Soul Note 121125 *Byard; Ralph Hamperian (b); Richard Allen (d).* 8/88.

***(*) Phantasies II

Soul Note 121175 *Byard; The Apollo Stompers: as above, but omit Eckert, Wienberg, Norden, Boyd, Givens, Trombly, Licht, Denyce Byard; replace with Graham Haynes (t), Rick Davies (tb), Susan Terry (as), Bud Revels (ts), Don Slatoff (bs), Peter Leitch (g), Vincent Lewis (v).* 8/88.

***(*) At Maybeck: Maybeck Recital Hall Series, Volume 17

Concord CCD 4511 *Byard (p solo).* 9/91.

Byard's solo performances are perhaps his best and most characteristic. The Concord set is one of the 'out'-est of a high-quality but generally mainstream series. Byard's 'Tribute To The Ticklers', 'European Episode' and 'Family Suite' are characteristically expansive, and the Monk collage is judged to perfection. More romantic material like 'My One And Only Love' is gruffly unsentimental. The (deleted) Muse from 1972 is more uncompromising and marked by some of Byard's most unchecked blues playing. Of the solo sets, it's probably the closest to the sound he cultivated around Mingus, and that may appeal to some listeners.

Byard is inclined to swamp sidemen with weather-changes of idiom or mood. No such problems with *Foolin' Myself*. Hamperian and Allen have grown into Byard's music and become confident interpreters. The set's full of oblique harmonies and wonderfully off-centre themes; the CD offers a big sound with a lot of warmth, typical of Giovanni Bonandrini's in-house production at Soul Note.

Working with Maynard Ferguson and then Mingus gave Byard some insight into how to steer at high speed. Without any doubt, his excellence as a section player fed into his solo and small-group playing as well. *Phantasies* is an uncomfortable big-band excursion with vocals from Byard's Denyce and Diane (she of the melody – see above); though well produced and more than adequately executed, the album runs pastiche a little too close for comfort and lands somewhere between at least three stylistic stools. That said, it contains some great ensemble work on the Ellington material, and some of the modernist things – 'Lonely Woman', 'Impressions' – are excitingly done. A change of heart since the first edition, prompted by the emergence of *Phantasies II*, an altogether better-structured and more together exercise in nostalgia. Byard's skills as a comping pianist and bandleader are seen nowhere better than on 'Concerto Grosso', a playful look at a Baroque form within the context of a jazz band. Vincent Lewis does a convincing job as an Apollo crooner, with a rich baritone that owes something to Eckstine. Musically, though, the most interesting thing is 'II IV I', a title which refers to the cadence minor/dominant/major which dominates the piece. It takes Byard back to the great days of the Harlem stride pianists.

Don Byas (1912–72)

TENOR SAXOPHONE

Born in Muskogee, Oklahoma, Byas served his apprenticeship in a variety of big bands. Often considered to be a bridge between the swing and bebop generations, he often anticipates Charlie Parker's solo development, stringing together whole series of tiny melodic ideas into a coherent line with a challenging harmonic profile. In later life he was a fine ballad player, though his critical standing was much eclipsed by younger players.

***** Midnight At Minton's**

High Note HCD 7044 *Byas; Joe Guy (t); Thelonious Monk (p); Kenny Clarke (d); Helen Humes (v); other personnel unknown.* 41.

***** Don Byas, 1944–1945**

Classics 882 *Byas; Charlie Shavers, Joe Thomas (t); Rudy Williams (as); Johnny Guarnieri, Kenny Watts (p); Clyde Hart (p, cel); John Levy, Slam Stewart, Billy Taylor (b); Cozy Cole, Slick Jones, Jack The Bear Parker (d); Big Bill Broonzy (v).* 7/44–3/45.

***** Don Byas 1945**

Classics 910 *Byas; Buck Clayton, Dizzy Gillespie (t); Gene Sedric (cl); Jimmy Powell (as); Hal Singer (ts); Johnny Guarnieri, Sammy Price (p); Leonard Ware (g); Al Hall, Eddie Safranski, Oscar Smith (b); Denzil Best, Big Sid Catlett, J.C Heard, Harold Doc West (d); Rubel Blakey, Albinia Jones (v); other personnel unknown.* 4–9/45.

***** Don Byas, 1945: Volume 2**

Classics 959 *Byas; Emmett Berry, Benny Harris, Dick Vance (t); Errol Garner, Johnny Guarnieri, Cyril Haynes, Jimmy Jones, Dave Rivera (p); Al Casey, Milt Hinton, John Levy, Eddie Safranski, Slam Stewart (b); J.C Heard, Fred Radcliffe, Harold Doc West (d).* 8/44–11/45.

*****(*) Original 1945 Recordings**

Tax S-8 *As Classics 910, except omit Gillespie, Sedric, Price, Ware, Smith.* 1–11/45.

A respectful pause for those figures condemned to the limbo of the 'transitional'. Don Byas dominates the strip of turf midway between Coleman Hawkins and Charlie Parker, combining the old man's vibrato and grouchy tone with Bird's limber solo style and fresh, open diction. Hard these days to recognize just how highly regarded Byas once was, until one actually hears him.

The earliest of these recordings was made by a young student at Columbia University, Jerry Newman, who trawled the clubs and taped hours of music for his own satisfaction. These cuts were originally released on Onyx Records in the early 1970s, but no one seems able to cast light on who was playing. Monk is already pretty unmistakable on four of the tracks, including a magnificent 'Stardust' and 'Exactly Like You', but the remaining personnels are lost to history. Inevitably, the sound is less than professional, but Byas's tenor cuts through the fog and Malcolm Addey's remastering sharpens the focus considerably.

Byas left the Basie band in 1943 and became one of the unsung heroes of early bebop, matched – for sheer class and undue neglect – only by Lucky Thompson. To a degree, Byas rode his luck for (like one of those actresses said to be 'loved' by the camera) he was always hugely flattered by the microphones of the time. The early material for Savoy, documented on the earlier Classics compilation, captures a polished stylist who is already in command of a vibrant tone and a thoroughly coherent solo approach. Shavers is as abrupt and pugnacious as ever, a wonderful mismatch of temperaments that works to perfection. The July tracks are better than the later session, largely because they are simpler and concentrate on straight major-key exchanges between the two horns.

In January 1945 Byas cut four sides for Jamboree, disappointing because they seem to slip back half a generation to the jump and swing styles that were disappearing, to be replaced by bop. 'Jamboree Jump' is also known as 'Byas-A-Drink', a neat feature for saxophone and Joe Thomas's Eldridge-like trumpet. Later material for Hub is dominated by Big Bill Broonzy vocals and officially credited to Little Sam and Orchestra, which was probably a good idea, given how pedestrian this material now sounds. Later in 1945 Byas recorded for National (backing singer Albinia Jones in a session which included Dizzy Gillespie), Jamboree again (with Buck Clayton), Super Disc with the marvellous group that numbered Garner, Stewart and West, American and Hub, the last an oddly plaintive session with singer Rubel Blakey and an instrumental version of 'Poor Butterfly' with Powell and Singer. Pianist Guarnieri is a much-underrated performer and an ideal accompanist for Byas on three of these dates, matching the saxophonist's smooth transitions between keys with an effortless charm. The September 1945 encounter with Stewart and Heard, which included lovely versions of 'Laura' and 'Stardust', is vintage Byas. The second Classics volume for 1945 also includes some material recorded under the leadership of Emmett Berry and Cyril Haynes, but there is some wonderful material from Don's quartet and quintet, including the variation on 'How High The Moon' that would shortly be transformed by Benny Harris into 'Ornithology'. These are the birth pangs of bebop.

As the dates will suggest, the Tax compilation straddles the two Classics compilations chronologically, misses the autumn 1945 date with Singer and Jimmy Powell (thus omitting 'Gypsy', 'Nancy' and 'Poor Butterfly') but includes two dates the French label hasn't reached yet in its chronological (or 'chronogical', as Classics have always preferred) trawl down the years. Of these, the better is from 1 November with Errol Garner, Slam Stewart and Doc West, a re-run of the August session for Super Disc. The sound on Tax is probably a little clearer and less muffled and, unless you are looking for a complete run of Byas, it's the one to go for.

***** Don Byas, 1946**

Classics 1009 *Byas; Peanuts Holland (t, v); Tyree Glenn (tb); Hubert Rostaing (cl); Beryl Booker, Humphrey Brannon, Sanford Gold, Billy Taylor (p); Leonard Gaskin, John Simmons, Frank Skeete, Ted Sturgis (b); Buford Oliver, Fred Radcliffe, Max Roach (d).* 5–12/46.

***** Don Byas, 1947**

Classics 1073 *Byas; Peanuts Holland (t); Tyree Glenn (tb); Hubert Rostaing (as); Jacques Diéval, Gene Schroeder, Billy Taylor (p); Tony Gottuso, Jean-Jacques Tilché (g); Jean Bouchety, Slim Dunham, Lucien Simoens (b); Johnny Blowers, Armand Molinetti, Buford Oliver (d).* 45–6/47.

In 1946, Byas joined the Don Redman orchestra for a European tour and, though he returned during the course of the year and recorded sessions for Gotham and Savoy, he was soon to move his base and live away from America for the rest of his life. Some of the 1946 material is less than pristine, but Don's solos are always immaculately judged. The May 1946 session is merely a set of accompaniments for the saxophonist, mostly in ballad form. 'London Donnie' is a curious misreading of 'The Londonderry Air' and Don's solo is flat and unimaginative; but the rest of the set, notably 'Cherokee', points to the bebop revolution that was fomenting elsewhere. The August date is distinguished by a more balanced and responsive band who are required to do more than simply touch in backgrounds. The following month saw him recording for Gotham with Beryl Booker on piano, and then at the end of the year Don was in Paris recording under his own, Peanuts Holland's and Tyree Glenn's leadership.

The 1947 recordings were all made in Paris, and mostly for Blue Star. The key track, almost worth the price of the disc on its own, is a magnificent version of 'Laura', which marks an exception to the concentration on bebop. The groups Don was working with were for the most part competent and highly professional, but they lack the bounce of the Redman alumni who came to France with him. The latest Classics volume is rounded out with a version of 'Annie Laurie', made in New York in 1945 and previously overlooked.

***** Featuring Mary Lou Williams Trio and Beryl Booker Trio**

BMG 74321 61021 2 *Byas; Beryl Booker, Maurice Vander, Mary Lou Williams (p); Sadi (vib); Alvin Banks, Pierre Michelot, Bonnie Wetzel (b); Benny Bennett, Elaine Leighton, Roger Paraboschi, Gérard Pochonet (d).* 12/53–5/55.

Compiled from the Vogue LPs, *Don Carlos Meets Mary Lou* and *A Paris*, these sides find Byas at his cool, confident best. Williams's effortless hybridization of swing and the new language of bebop offered him a thoroughly sympathetic background, but it is the pianist who seems to be in charge. 'Mary's Waltz' is a treasure. The tracks with Beryl Booker and her all-female group are more flattering to the saxophonist, though he finds himself less stretched harmonically. Beryl's vocal on 'I Should Care' is a reminder of what a clever all-round musician she was. Rounding out the album are four tracks Byas cut with Maurice Vander, Sadi, Michelot, and either Benny Bennett or Roger Paraboschi.

****(*) A Night In Tunisia**

Black Lion BLCD 760136 *Byas; Bent Axen (p); Niels-Henning Orsted Pedersen (b); William Schiopffe (d).* 1/63.

****(*) Walkin'**

Black Lion BLCD 760167 *As above.* 1/63.

The two Black Lions are pretty pedestrian. One senses the rhythm section would like to up the pace, but Byas is constantly holding back, coasting through the set. 'A Night In Tunisia' serves as a reminder of what he was capable of when the spirit took hold, and 'Billie's Bounce' and 'All The Things You Are' (on which he appears to quote a Paul Gonsalves figure) are both played appealingly. Something has gone, though. The broad, chocolatey tone has a sour edge and there is a tiredness in the playing which will disappoint anyone who retains an affection for the 1940s material.

***** Autumn Leaves**

Ronnie Scott's Jazz House JHAS 613 *Byas; Stan Tracey (p); Rick Laird (b); Tony Crombie (d).*

Recorded at Ronnie Scott's club with the house rhythm-section (Laird subsequently gave up playing for photography) and running down a weel-kent programme of standards and jazz tunes. Byas's deceptively but harmonically exact tone is spot-on for 'Autumn Leaves' itself, a taut and wise reading of one of his favourite standbys. 'I Remember Clifford' and 'All The Things You Are' are sharper and more boppish, full of oblique references to other tunes and unpredictable harmonic shifts, many of them driven by Tracey's percussive attack and lateral imagination. Recording quality isn't of the very best, straight to a machine in the club, but it communicates a lot of presence and the quiet intensity of Byas's well-worked routine.

Charlie Byrd (1925–2000)

GUITAR

Uneventful career until he settled in Washington in the '50s, where he cemented a reputation that eventually led to the hugely successful bossa nova albums with Stan Getz. A gently effective if unremarkable stylist whose methods may have had some influence on the rise of soft, fusion-lite music.

***** Mr Guitar**

Original Jazz Classics OJC 998 *Byrd; Keter Betts (b); Bertil Knox (d).* 59.

***** The Guitar Artistry Of Charlie Byrd**

Original Jazz Classics OJC 945 *Byrd; Keter Betts (b); Buddy Deppenschmidt (d).* 60.

***** Byrd At The Village Vanguard**

Original Jazz Classics OJC 669 *As above.* 1/61.

***** Bossa Nova Pelos Pássaros**

Original Jazz Classics OJC 107 *Byrd; Keter Betts (b); Bill Reichenbach (d).* 4/62.

****(*) Byrd At The Gate**

Original Jazz Classics OJC 262 *As above, except add Clark Terry (t), Seldon Powell (ts).* 5/63.

The release in 1962 of the evergreen *Jazz Samba* with Stan Getz, and the legal kerfuffle that followed, put Charlie Byrd firmly on the map. Like all hugely successful products, there was an element of *ersatz* about it, and Byrd's Latin stylings have never sounded entirely authentic and are often quite rheumaticky in articulation. Here, though, is a historically valuable selection of albums, the Village Vanguard set in particular full of that characteristically American syndrome that John Aldridge called 'the energy of new success' and which comes just before what the French call the *crise de quarante*. Byrd sounds full-toned and quick-fingered, and the themes still have a bloom they were to lose all too quickly in the years that followed. There's very little to choose between what is now a pretty comprehensive run of Byrd's early Riverside albums. Betts and the various drummers keep tabs on the leader, who's always musical but only rarely doing something to really make one listen beyond the pleasant drift of what's coming out of the speakers. The horns add very little to the Gate set except extra noise. The problem with Byrd was that, even at the Village Vanguard, he always sounded as if he was preparing for Carnegie Hall.

***** Tambu**

Fantasy FCD 9453 *Byrd; Cal Tjader (vib); Mike Wolff (p); John Heard (b); Joe Byrd (b); Michael Stephans, Dick Berk (d, perc); Mayoto Correa (perc).* 9/73.

Like a lot of jazz records from around this time, *Tambu* is constrained not by indifferent playing but by certain giveaway tics in the sound. Wolff's electric piano and Joe Byrd's duh-duh-duh bass guitar conspire with an overlit and glaringly contrastive mix to bleach all the character out of Byrd's playing. Tjader was the co-leader on this date, and the vibes, too, are all over the place, jingling like a bead-curtain and then improbably tolling down at the bass end. It all mars some very good playing, from virtually all concerned.

***** Three Guitars**

Concord 6004 *Byrd; Barney Kessel, Herb Ellis (g); Joe Byrd (b); Johnny Rae (d).* 7/74.

Promoters and A&R men have always recognized that there's an audience for guitar specials like this. Put together any three saxophonists of similar stature, and the take on the door or through the record-shop tills will be significantly smaller. Musically, it's polished and shiny and ever so polite. Kessel and Ellis play a duo, Byrd plays with his own trio, rents it out to the other pair for 'Slow Burn', and then they all get together for 'Undecided', 'Topsy' and 'Benny's Bugle'. Honours just about even.

****(*) Blue Byrd**

Concord CCD 4082 *Byrd; Joe Byrd (b, v); Wayne Phillips (d).* 8/78.

**** Sugarloaf Suite**

Concord CCD 4114 *As above.* 8/78.

**** Isn't It Romantic**

Concord CCD 4252 *As above, except replace Phillips with Chuck Riggs (d).* 8/79.

Byrd had a dull time for much of the 1970s. These discs find him less becalmed than usual and, on *Blue Byrd*, just occasionally inspired. He handles mainstream standards well, surprising now and again with a figure completely out of left field; but the trio format leaves him much too exposed for comfort, and the up-close recording almost parades his stiffness.

****(*) Brazilville**

Concord CCD 4173 *Byrd; Bud Shank (as); Joe Byrd (b); Chuck Redd (d).* 5/81.

****(*) It's A Wonderful World**

Concord CCD 4374 *Byrd; Scott Hamilton (ts); John Goldsby (b); Chuck Redd (d).* 8/88.

Byrd's quality in a horn-led band suggests that he was done only economic favours by having greatness thrust upon him so suddenly, 30 years ago. With both Shank and Hamilton he plays elegantly and with considerable taste. Both albums show a marked centring of Byrd's stylistic range; by no means everything is automatically Latinized and on *Wonderful World* in particular he displays an improvisational confidence that seemed to have deserted him in the 1970s. Nobody looks to Byrd for fire and brimstone, but there's an edgy, slightly restless quality to both of these that belies their bland packaging and suggests a genuinely improvisatory spirit at work. The Ellington and Arlen pieces are particularly fine.

***** Byrd & Brass**

Concord CCD 4304 *Byrd; Joe Byrd (b); Chuck Redd (d); Annapolis Brass Quintet.* 4/86.

A surprisingly sharp and swinging set from an offbeat and unpromising line-up. Byrd pushes things along with unwonted enthusiasm; the brass is generously voiced and the rhythm work tighter than Byrd normally favours. Well recorded, too.

***(*) The Charlie Byrd Christmas Album**

Concord CCD 42004 *Byrd (g solo).* 6/82.

This is fine for those who like this sort of thing, as Jean Brodie might say. Almost everyone else will hate it with a passion.

***** The Bossa Nova Years**

Concord CCD 4468 *Byrd; Ken Peplowski (ts, cl); Dennis Irwin (b); Chuck Redd (d); Michael Spiro (perc).* 4/91.

One of the astonishing things about Byrd's career is his relentless conservatism in the choice of material. One would hardly expect an artist of his inclinations or stature to desert an established audience by adopting Jimi Hendrix songs, but one might reasonably expect him to challenge that audience a little more often than he does. *The Bossa Nova Years* contains precisely the roster of soft-centred Jobim/Gilberto themes you probably began whistling as you read the title. What makes it more galling is that they're all played superbly, in the sense that there isn't a hair out of place on any of them. Peplowski can usually be relied on for a bit more than he offers here. As a performance, this is brushed and pomaded to the point of anonymity. A shame, really.

***** Charlie Byrd / The Washington Guitar Quintet**

Concord CCD 42014 *Byrd; Carlos Barbosa-Lima, Howard Alden, Washington Guitar Quintet: John Marlow, Jeffrey Meyerriecks, Myrna Sislen, Larry Snitzler (g); Joe Byrd (b); Chuck Redd (d).* 4/92.

What's disappointing about this brilliantly arranged and very beautiful record is how numbingly obvious the programme turns out to be: 'Nuages', 'Django', *Concierto De Aranjuez* segued with Chick Corea's 'Spain', Stanley Myers's 'Cavatina' from *The Deer-hunter*, another Reinhardt tune, Jobim, Almeida. With a little more imagination this could have been a masterpiece. Instead, it all too swiftly runs aground. Only when Alden's electric guitar is introduced for three numbers before the end – Cole Porter's 'Easy To Love' and Kurt Weill's 'I'm A Stranger Here Myself' and 'Speak Low' – is there much in the way of dramatic variation. The other members of the Washington Guitar Quintet (Byrd himself makes up the five) try to invest the earlier tunes with a bit of percussive spice, but again the material draws them down.

**** Aquarelle**

Concord CCD 42016 *Byrd; Ken Peplowski (cl); Carlos Barbosa-Lima, Jeffrey Meyerriecks, Myrna Sislen, Larry Snitzler (g).* 8/93.

This collaboration with members of the Washington Guitar Quintet is pastelly and insipid, soft-focus washes of colour overlaid on some notably bland and sentimental melodies. The analogy with wallpaper won't stay in its basket.

***** Moments Like This**

Concord CCD 4627 *Byrd; Ken Peplowski (cl); Bill Douglass (b); Chuck Redd (d, vib).* 94.

Immediately and wholly better. The blend of guitar, bass, clarinet and (mostly) vibraphone is very appealing, and Byrd exploits the possibilities to the maximum. His chording on 'Rose Of The Rio Grande' is highly distinctive, often moving outside the natural sequence, and Douglass is a willing assistant in keeping many of the pieces from becoming predictable. A fine record by a musician whose career has taken some odd turns over the years.

*****(*) Du Hot Club De Concord**

Concord CCD 4674 *Byrd; Johnny Frigo (vn); Hendrik Meurkens (hca); Frank Vignola (g); Michael Moore (b).* 6/95.

Better than it might have been, and largely because the Hot Club parallel isn't pushed too far or too long. The sound is very much more Latin, less straightforwardly swinging and melodically more varied. Byrd himself seems to enjoy this line-up and plays with great ease on 'Besame Mucho', 'Old New Orleans Blues' and 'Cottontail', to pick just three outstanding tracks. Delightful in every way.

***** For Louis**

Concord CCD 4879-2 *Byrd; Joe Wilder (t); Steve Wilson (ss, as); Robert Redd (p); Dennis Irwin (b); Chuck Redd (d).* 9/99.

Recorded at the end of Byrd's life, this doesn't, though, have any kind of valedictory feel about it. The tracks (except the bizarre choice of 'Petite Fleur', actually a Bechet staple) are all Armstrong associations. Wilder and Wilson drop in and out of the picture, but it remains Byrd's album, and he sounds in pretty good fettle on the improbable likes of 'Struttin' With Some Barbecue' and 'Indian Summer', even if Pops and bossa nova feel sometimes go awkwardly together.

Donald Byrd (born 1932)

TRUMPET, FLUGELHORN

Born in Detroit, Byrd joined the Jazz Messengers early on and by the end of the 1950s had already worked with a wide range of leaders and had recorded prolifically. His tenure with Blue Note continued in this vein, and he became one of the most recorded of the hard-bop trumpeters, although he subsequently became much more heavily involved in teaching. His crossover period of the early '70s yielded the hit album, Blackbyrd, although this amounted to selling off the bebop family silver. Later years were spent studying law and in more teaching, although he did some recording in the '80s and '90s.

**** First Flight**

Delmark 407 *Byrd; Yusef Lateef (ts); Barry Harris (p); Bernard McKinney (euph); Alvin Jackson (b); Frank Gant (d).* 8/55.

First Flight is the first album under Byrd's own name, recorded at a concert in Detroit, and, while it gave a smart indication of his own promise, it's Lateef's more commanding solos that take the attention. Harris, perhaps the quintessential Detroit pianist, is also imposing, although he has to contend with a poor piano, and the location sound is disappointingly muddy.

****(*) Fuego**

Blue Note 46534 *Byrd; Jackie McLean (as); Duke Pearson (p); Sam Jones (b); Lex Humphries (d).* 10/59.

***** At The Half Note Café, Vols 1 & 2**

Blue Note 57187-2 2CD *Byrd; Pepper Adams (bs); Duke Pearson (p); Laymon Jackson (b); Lex Humphries (d).* 11/60.

***** Free Form**

Blue Note 84118 *Byrd; Wayne Shorter (ts); Herbie Hancock (p); Butch Warren (b); Billy Higgins (d).* 12/61.

By the time he signed a deal with Blue Note in 1958, Byrd had already made more records than any of the other up-and-coming trumpeters of the day. It was his easy-going proficiency which made him sought-after: like Freddie Hubbard, who was to the early 1960s what Byrd had been to the previous five years, he could sound good under any contemporary leader without entirely dominating the situation. His solos were valuable but not disconcertingly personal, dependably elegant but not strikingly memorable. His records as a leader emerged in much the same way: refined and crisp hard bop which seems to look neither forward nor backwards. Choosing from the above selection – all of them available only as US releases at present – is more a matter of which of the accompanying musicians is most appealing, since Byrd's own performances are regularly polished – almost to the point of tedium, some might say. *Fuego* has some good McLean, but the tunes are dull. The live sessions at New York's Half Note are impeccably played and atmospherically recorded, but they tend to show the best and worst of Byrd: on the first number on Volume 1, 'My Girl Shirl', he peels off chorus after chorus of manicured licks, and this process gets repeated throughout. One is impressed but dissatisfied, and Humphries's less than outstanding drumming is another problem, although Adams is again splendid. The latest edition of this set includes some bonus material and is now generously spread across two discs. *Free Form* puts Byrd among altogether more difficult company, and there's an unflattering contrast between his prim solo on the gospel cadences of 'Pentecostal Feeling' and Shorter's bluff intensity. But he plays very prettily on Herbie Hancock's 'Night Flower' (which sounds like 'I Left My Heart In San Francisco'), and the more severe leanings of the title-track suit Byrd's punctilious manner well.

***(*) Groovin' For Nat

Black Lion BL 760132 *Byrd; Johnny Coles (t); Duke Pearson (p); Bob Cranshaw (b); Walter Perkins (d).* 1/62.

** A New Perspective

Blue Note 99006 *Byrd; Hank Mobley (ts); Herbie Hancock (p); Donald Best (vib); Kenny Burrell (g); Butch Warren (b); Lex Humphries (d); choir.* 12/63.

*** Mustang

Blue Note 59963-2 *Byrd; Sonny Red (as); Jimmy Heath, Hank Mobley (ts); McCoy Tyner (p); Walter Booker (b); Freddie Waits, Joe Chambers (d).* 11/64–6/66.

*** Blackjack

Blue Note 21286-2 *Byrd; Sonny Red (as); Hank Mobley, Jimmy Heath (ts); Cedar Walton, Herbie Hancock (p); Walter Booker, Eddie Khan (b); Billy Higgins, Albert 'Tootie' Heath (d).* 5/63–1/67.

After dozens of straightforward hard-bop dates, Byrd branched out with mixed success. *Groovin' For Nat* is measure for measure one of his most enjoyable records: Coles, a splashier but characterful player, spars with him through a dozen duets, and the unusual combination of two trumpets and rhythm proves to be a joyous rather than a one-dimensional setting. Nevertheless it's Coles who steals the record with a very expressive turn through 'Friday's Child'. The Black Lion CD includes three previously unavailable alternative takes, and the sound is very persuasive.

A New Perspective has remained popular and contains the seeds of Byrd's wider success in the 1970s: his own playing is set against large-scale scoring and the use of a choir and, while there was talk at the time of gospel-inspired fusions, it seems clear that the music aimed for an easy-listening crevice somewhere between soul-jazz and mood music. Set against the stricter tenets of the records which came before it, it's dispensable. *Mustang* and *Blackjack* return him to more familiar Blue Note blow-outs. Made up from four sessions over three years, the two discs contain a lot of engaging hard bop in the label's almost ritualized manner and, if Byrd himself does no more than play graciously, there are worthy statements from each of the other horns at various points – and look at the roll-call of pianists.

*** Kofi

Blue Note 31875-2 *Byrd; William Campbell (tb); Lew Tabackin (ts, f); Frank Foster (ts); Duke Pearson (p); Ron Carter, Bob Cranshaw (b); Mickey Roker (d); Airto Moreira, Dom Um Romao (perc).* 12/69–12/70.

**(*) Electric Byrd

Blue Note 36195-2 *Byrd; Bill Campbell (tb); Jerry Dodgion (as, ss, f); Frank Foster (ts, cl); Lew Tabackin (ts, f); Pepper Adams (bs, cl); Duke Pearson (p); Wally Richardson (g); Ron Carter (b); Mickey Roker (d); Airto Moreira (perc).* 5/70.

*** Blackbyrd

Blue Note 84466 *Byrd; Alan Barnes (ts, ob, f); Kevin Toney (p); Barney Perry (g); Joe Hill (b); Keith Kilgo (d); Perk Jacobs (perc).* 74.

**(*) Street Lady

Blue Note 53923-2 *Byrd; Roger Glenn (f); Fonce Mizell (ky, t); Jerry Peters, Fred Perren (ky); Chuck Rainey (b); Harvey Mason (d); Stephane Spruill, King Erricson (perc).* 73.

** Places And Spaces

Blue Note 54326-2 *Byrd; Raymond Brown (t); George Bohannon (tb); Tyree Glenn Jr (ts); Larry Mizell, Skip Scarborough (p); Fonce Mizell (ky, t); Craig McMullen, John Rowin (g); Chuck Rainey (b); Harvey Mason (d); Mayoto Correa, King Erricson (perc); James Carter (whistler).* 8/75.

*** The Best Of Donald Byrd

Blue Note 798638-2 *Byrd; various line-ups.* 69–76.

The previously unreleased *Kofi* fares better than some of Byrd's other music from the period, cut at two sessions a year apart but with basically the same band on each occasion. Byrd's four pieces are vague stabs at a modal/African impressionism, but it's the pragmatic Tabackin and Foster who come off best: sounds as if Byrd had been listening to Miles more than the musicologists he mentions in the self-serving comments on the sleeve, though to no terrific effect. Somehow the innate bustle of these tracks led towards the shinier, mediated soul-grooves of *Blackbyrd* – modishly arranged round a concept that struck a resonantly harmonious note at the time. It sold past the million mark and outdid all of Blue Note's previous releases. Twenty years on, it sounds much the same: simple, lightweight crossover, with Byrd masking his declining powers as an improviser with a busy group. To paraphrase Swamp Dogg, he wasn't selling out, he was buying in.

And he kept on buying. The process had actually begun rather earlier, as the several recently restored albums now demonstrate. It's interesting to speculate on the connection between these albums and the similarly inclined progress of Miles Davis at the same moment. Certainly *Electric Byrd* takes off from *In A Silent Way*, with echoplexed sounds reverberating around a basically timeless pulse; but it's simplistic stuff next to what Davis was setting down. When they get to the groove tune, 'The Dude', it seems as if Byrd is breathing a sigh of relief that he can drop the arty stuff and get on with something he feels comfortable with. *Blackbyrd* was perhaps the logical thinning-out of this sound, and suddenly Byrd found himself a hit-maker.

It was a hard act to follow. *Street Lady* has its moments, but not too many, and, by trading off top-of-the-line jazzmen for skilful funk players, Byrd was to some extent playing swings and roundabouts. There's certainly even less worth keeping on the soupy *Places And Spaces*, soaked in strings and bounced off the supple but strict rhythms of Rainey and Mason. Besides, Byrd's own tootling isn't even a match for Freddie Hubbard on his sappiest outings. The curious might be satisfied with *The Best Of Donald Byrd*, which goes for his later phase rather than the hard-bop material.

**(*) Landmarks

32 Jazz 32080 *Byrd; Kenny Garrett (as); Joe Henderson (ts); Donald Brown (p); Peter Washington (b); Al Foster (d).* 10/89.

***** Attitude**

RCA Camden 74321 610852 2CD *As above, except add Mulgrew Miller (p), Bobby Hutcherson (vib), Rufus Reid (b), Marvin 'Smitty' Smith, Carl Allen (d).* 9/87–1/91.

Byrd's return to straight-ahead in the 1980s was far from auspicious. His chops sound weak and the ideas are thin. Surrounded by such top-drawer players, he sometimes holds his own but is more often a cause for embarrassment. The stars are for everyone else, even though none of them are actually breaking much of a sweat. These are both drawn from the Muse albums, *Harlem Blues, Getting Down To Business* and *A City Called Heaven*, but the Camden offers all the music in a bargain two-disc package.

Don Byron

CLARINET, BASS CLARINET, BARITONE SAXOPHONE

A passionate, articulate and politically engaged artist, Byron has also been associated with a revival of interest in jazz clarinet. At times self-defeatingly eclectic and sometimes wearing his education at the New England Conservatory a little too ostentatiously, he has nevertheless been one of the most potent catalysts to experiment in jazz.

*****(*) Tuskegee Experiments**

Elektra Nonesuch 79280 *Byron; Bill Frisell (g); Joe Berkovitz, Edsel Gomez (p); Kenny Davis, Lonnie Plaxico, Reggie Workman (b); Richie Schwarz (mar); Pheeroan akLaff, Ralph Petersen Jr (d); Sadiq (v).* 11/90, 7/91.

Don Byron's emergence was almost as great a sensation as that of his poetic namesake. The sight of a young black man in dreadlocks playing Duke Ellington tunes on clarinet of all instruments was, even in 1990, astonishing enough; to then find Byron fronting a klezmer band was a little like discovering that fellow-clarinettist Woody Allen had joined the Art Ensemble of Chicago.

Byron's debut was a robustly eclectic showcase that in hindsight was hoist by its own teeming ambitions. Listening to it six or seven years on is a slightly unsatisfactory experience. Though the title-piece, which refers to a cynical 'medical' programme in 1930s Alabama in which black syphilitics were denied treatment, is undeniably powerful, dark and threatening, it sits uneasily alongside a straight reading of Robert Schumann's *Auf einer Burg* and the romantic 'Waltz For Ellen', both solos. What Byron is doing, obviously, is showing off his range, and without doubt it's impressive. On 'Diego Rivera' (not often one finds a name-check of the great Mexican muralist on a jazz record) and 'In Memoriam: Uncle Dan' he shows what a fine bass clarinettist he is, closer to Harry Carney than to Dolphy. Ellington's 'Mainstem' cements the association.

The sound isn't altogether satisfactory, a little too bottom-heavy and one-dimensional, but again obviously aimed at foregrounding the young star. What followed was bound to be interesting ...

***** Plays The Music Of Mickey Katz**

Elektra Nonesuch 79313 *Byron; Dave Douglas (t, v); Josh Roseman (tb, v); J.D Parran (cl, bcl, ss, f); Mark Feldman (vn, v).*

The ink was scarcely dry on the reviews for *Tuskegee Experiments* before the backlash hove into view. Perhaps fortunately for his future credibility, Byron was already shapeshifting. The composer John Adams likes to alternate serious and 'trickster' pieces, and Byron seems to have set himself the same course. Even so, nothing quite prepared anyone who didn't know his interests for *The Music Of Mickey Katz*. Byron had played for some time with a klezmer band and, in interview, had been as apt to name-check Katz as George Russell, Ellington or Dolphy. Katz's *schtick* was to yiddishize popular tunes like 'Home On The Range' ('Heim Afen Range') and 'Sabre' – *seder* – 'Dance'. What Byron adds is a virtuosic intelligence that refuses to categorize music hierarchically into 'serious', 'classical', 'popular' or whatever.

The unbending, composerly title of *Music For Six Musicians* (currently unavailable) was a clear attempt to re-establish credentials. Where a temperamentally different musician might have recorded a bebop album or a set of standards, Byron offered up a new version of himself: Byron the writer, dry, terse, *engagé*, not without humour but certainly not the entertainer of the klezmer record. This is a jazz disc, with the emphasis on structure rather than blowing. Byron himself sounds tight, clipped and emphatic. Graham Haynes is the ideal partner, trading on an abrasive sound and an impatient, bustling development. Bill Frisell does his usual thing with aplomb, and the only serious quibble is with a rhythm section which manages to be both understated and over-recorded; no mean feat.

These ill-matched sequels established a pattern Byron seemed likely to repeat ...

*****(*) No-Vibe Zone**

Knitting Factory Works KFW 191 *Byron; Uri Caine (p); David Gilmore (g); Kenny Davis (b); Marvin 'Smitty' Smith (d).* 1/96.

****(*) Bug Music**

Nonesuch 7559 79438 *Byron; Steve Bernstein, Charles Lewis, James Zollar (t); Craig Harris (tb); Steve Wilson (as); Bob DeBellis (ts); Uri Caine (p, v); David Gilmore (g); Paul Meyers (bj); Kenny Davis (b); Pheeroan akLaff, Joey Baron, Billy Hart (d); Dean Bowman (v).*

As the '90s advanced, Byron quickly established himself as a valuable specialist sideman, much as Marty Ehrlich and Bill Frisell had done. The difference was that the clarinettist's own career seemed stalled in self-consciousness, the intelligence of his aims and ideas never quite borne out by the resulting records.

The premise of *Bug Music* is unimpeachable, the practice not quite so hot. The title comes from an episode of the Flintstones in which the citizenry of Bedrock are assailed by the Stone Age equivalent of the Beatles (Bug Music, Beatles, get it?). Byron sees the cartoon as a small parable of the way music is categorized and marginalized. Having a direct line to the Creator is a handy critical device. 'It matters very little to God', Byron asserts, 'whether or not a piece of music is Jazz, only that it is a compositional act. This is the only universal truth in music and the entirety of musical art.'

God smiles, then, even on such overlooked or kitsch figures as John Kirby, whose chamber jazz is now somewhat overlooked, and Raymond Scott, who enjoys a certain ironic 'downtown' cachet, despite the obvious fact that both are deeply influenced by Duke Ellington's early work. All three are celebrated on the album, 16 tracks which range from jazz repertoire like 'St Louis

Blues', 'Royal Garden Blues' and the Ellingtonian 'Cotton Club Stomp', for which Harry Carney and Johnny Hodges claim a co-credit, to exotica like Scott's 'War Dance For Wooden Indians' and 'Tobacco Auctioneer'.

'Compositional acts' may be one thing; musical performance is another. We're sufficiently at peace with God ourselves to be able to say that Byron's raw and lumpy attempt to recapture the smooth grace of Kirby's underrated band or the sheer physicality of the Ellington orchestra is *not* currently featuring on the heavenly jukebox, or indeed on the Almighty's personal stereo. Like the Katz project, the album is interesting as an idea and makes for an interesting diversion. It certainly does not stand up at this length. We've found that only the promotional edits of the klezmer record have ever made their way back into the machine. That may be the fate of *Bug Music*, too, and if that simply proves Byron's pessimistic point, so much the worse.

He can, fortunately, be heard at his staccato, pungent best on *No-Vibe Zone*, a live set at the Knitting Factory, recorded during the spectacular blizzard of January 1996 and in front of an audience (members of the NY Inuit community, presumably) who braved the snow. It sounds like a single-figure crowd. Those who stayed at home missed a fine set. The record kicks off with Ornette's 'WRU', not so very often covered and here given a tough, uncompromising workout. The two main originals – 'Sex/Work', 'Next Love/The Allure Of Entanglement' – sound a little hung up on glorifying the compositional act again, though Caine and Smith seem disinclined to allow the boss to over-indulge in composerly gestures. By the time it comes to a reworking of 'Tuskegee Strutter's Ball' from the debut CD, the band is cooking nicely. Byron restricts himself to clarinet, a Buffet horn with a surprisingly 'proper' timbre and very clean articulation. Again, no mistaking the strength of Byron's talent. Six months solid gigging with a band like this will take him further than half a dozen well-intentioned projects like the Katz and *Bug Music*. The jury, which had started out with every sign of unanimity, is deadlocked again.

*** Nu Blaxploitation

Blue Note CDP 4 93711 *Byron; James Zollar (t); Curtis Fowlkes (tb); Uri Caine (p, org, ky, v); David Gilmore (g); Reggie Washington (b, v); Rodney Holmes, Ben Wittman (d); Johnny Almendra (perc); The Diabolical Biz Markie, Monique Curnen, Sadiq (v).* 12/97–1/98.

Byron is not so much in search of an identity as saddled with several of his own invention. Anyone who dedicates an album to Arnold Schoenberg, The Artist Formerly Known As Prince, Thomas Dolby and Chris Rock is either genuinely confused or else protesting too much. These are characteristically urgent telegrams from the America of Rodney King and O.J., nameless drive-bys and, above all, for Byron, the 'evasion of civil, focused discussion of racial issues'. Unfortunately, this doesn't always make for compelling music and there is much sign here that, unlike *Tuskegee Experiments*, Byron has been tripped by his own admirable right-mindedness.

Poet Sadiq returns from the first album and now seems to be the other key creative input into Existential Dred. Byron's writing, on 'Domino Theories' (inspired by *Two Nations* sociologist Andrew Hacker), and his playing, on the long 'Schizo Jam', are as pungent as ever, but he is actually too thoughtful, too rational a man to be entirely at ease even on the fringes of a hip-hop sensibility. The purely musical components are as well crafted as one would expect. Caine is masterful in an eclectic range of situations, and there are well-judged guest slots for Zollar, Jazz Passenger Fowlkes and one-time M-Base homey Gilmore. *Nu Blaxploitation* landed on the mat only just before we went to press with the last edition. Even hindsight finds it wanting.

*** Romance With The Unseen

Blue Note 4 99545 2 *Byron; Bill Frisell (g); Drew Gress (b); Jack DeJohnette (d).* 1–3/99.

Difficult to hear this as anything other than a reflexive reaction to the aggressive category-busting of *Nu Blaxploitation*. Byron is the weakest link in the chain. His slightly sharp, very linear clarinet playing (and he sticks with clarinet throughout) rarely catches the attention in the way that his colleagues almost routinely do. Frisell's subtle comping and solo statements are as arresting as ever; DeJohnette creates a swirly but unflagging pulse and even Gress, not previously thought of as a virtuosic soloist, has some fine moments. The opening meditation on Duke's 'Mural From Two Perspectives' is significant, because it catches Byron out so comprehensively; a lame fragmentary solo, studded with tags from bebop themes and even 'Coming Through The Rye'.

The more impressionistic themes, like Byron's own 'Sad Twilight' and 'Basquiat' (a tribute to the talented, self-destructive artist who grew up in Warhol's shadow), are more effective but still sound like special pleading. 'Bernhard Goetz, James Ramseur And Me' has the usual touch of the soapbox; but then, with typical perversity, Byron throws in a reading of the Beatles' 'Here Comes The Sun' which catches the breath and lifts the heart.

The album ends with 'Closer To Home', another touch of beauty, though here again it's hard to judge how much of the credit goes to Bill Frisell. The talent is undoubted, the commitment unquestionable, but where Byron goes now is hard to predict.

George Cables (born 1944)

PIANO

Gained small-group experience with Art Blakey and Max Roach in the '60s, then backed horn players, notably Freddie Hubbard and Art Pepper. Something of a journeyman, but his stature has been enhanced by the fine solo and trio albums of the '80s and '90s.

*** Circles

Contemporary C 14015 *Cables; Joe Farrell (f); Ernie Watts (ts); Tony Dumas, Rufus Reid (b); Peter Erskine, Eddie Gladden (d).* 3/79.

*** Cables Vision

Original Jazz Classics OJCCD 725 *Cables; Freddie Hubbard (t, flhn); Ernie Watts (ts, ss); Bobby Hutcherson (vib); Tony Dumas (b); Peter Erskine (d); Vince Charles (perc).* 12/79.

Cables is a great accompanist, an essentially modest man who has never been an aggressive soloist but who prefers always, always to service the song. He's still probably best known for his duo performances with the late Art Pepper on the marvellous Galaxy, *Goin' Home*. Cables has a slightly sharp touch that adds an unexpected measure of tension. He plays an electric instrument with great taste and economy throughout *Cables Vision* with the exception of a single acoustic duo with Bobby Hutcherson called 'The Stroll', a wonderful, conversational performance which sounds exactly like a companionable wander by old friends.

Circles is very fine, a richly textured and often very sophisticated set to which Farrell's rapid, light-winged flute and Watts's mature, unemphatic tenor contribute strongly. These are somewhat different from later sets in that Cables is not the only – or even the main – focus of attention, but a member of an ensemble or, rather, two very good ensembles. Only later did he emerge as a clearly defined piano stylist.

****** Phantom Of The City**

Contemporary C 14014 *Cables; John Heard (b); Tony Williams (d). 5/85.*

A beautifully balanced piano-trio record, and one of the very best recorded appearances by Tony Williams in the 1980s. It's the drummer who gives the set much of its character, and on the Cables composition, 'Dark Side, Light Side', a tune that would reappear in years to come, he brings a jaw-dropping musical intelligence, playing the melody as if working on a tuned instrument. Heard benefited hugely from the transfer to CD some years back; he never lets the pace drop, even nudging at Williams on occasion when the drummer seems content to let the tempo ease in the middle choruses.

Cables is completely in command, opposing long, rippling melody-lines with a firm chordal pattern and working a whole spectrum of harmonic variations on the basic shape of the tune. His touch is still lighter than one would expect from a self-confident front-man, but it is hugely attractive and this is an unmissable record.

*****(*) By George**

Contemporary C 14030 *Cables; John Heard (b); Ralph Penland (d). 2/87.*

*****(*) Cables Fables**

Steeplechase SCCD 31287 *Cables; Peter Washington (b); Kenny Washington (d). 3/91.*

****** Night And Day**

DIW 606 *Cables; Cecil McBee (b); Billy Hart (d). 5/91.*

We rather weakly failed to reach a verdict on these splendid trio sets last time out. The 1987 Gershwin set – a tribute from one George to another – is richly sophisticated, and the solo performances of 'Embraceable You' and 'Someone To Watch Over Me' are excellent examples of his innate rhythmic sense. *Cables Fables* is a tribute to the intuitive understanding that exists between the (unrelated) Washingtons, but retrospect suggests that this is a less confident set than those on either side of it.

Initially, we found the sound on the Japanese-produced *Night And Day* rather hard and unresonant, but it grows with every hearing. The selection of material is more imaginative than usual, mixing well-worn standards like 'Night And Day' (given a little twist in the middle chorus), 'I Love You' and 'I Thought About You' with more enterprising numbers like Rollins's 'Doxy', Bill Evans's 'Very Early' (another possible source for Cables's pianism) and Jaco Pastorius's *misterioso* 'Three Views Of A Secret'. An able composer, Cables has tended to keep this side under wraps, but 'Ebony Moonbeams' suggests his book of songs is well worth checking out.

*****(*) Beyond Forever**

Steeplechase SCCD 31305 *Cables; Joe Locke (vib); Santi Debriano (b); Victor Lewis (d). 12/91.*

This was the first time on record that Cables had tried this kind of instrumentation since the gig with Hutcherson in 1979. The absence of horns is the key difference, allowing the two keyboard/percussion instruments to interact and interweave in long, winding, horn-like passages. 'I Fall In Love Too Easily' is moving and intense, and 'Little B's Poem', written by Hutcherson and featuring Locke, obviously enough, is flawlessly executed, packed with those ladder scales the older vibist bequeathed to his successors.

***** I Mean You**

Steeplechase SCCD 31334 *Cables; Jay Anderson (b); Adam Nussbaum (d). 4/93.*

Not the best of the more recent crop, either under-rehearsed or else lacking the instinctive communication that a trio of this type needs. The title-tune, by Monk, is very flat indeed, played literally and without much spin, and, while the rest sounds accurate and often very tuneful, the disc fatally lacks character.

*****(*) Maybeck Recital Hall Series: Volume 35**

Concord CCD 4630 *Cables (p solo). 1/94.*

Cables unaccompanied is immediately and gratifyingly more intense and more driven than Cables in a group setting. The light, responsive acoustic of the little concert hall in Berkeley suits him to a 't' and he turns in one of the most unfussily expressive performances of his career. 'Someone To Watch Over Me' is prominent again, and there is a deeply moving rendition of 'Bess, You Is My Woman Now' in which he balances the vocal and the pianistic in near-perfect measure, dramatic and abstract music.

*****(*) Quiet Fire**

Steeplechase SCCD 31357 *Cables; Ron McClure (b); Billy Hart (d). 4/94.*

'Quiet fire' would do very nicely as a characterization of Cables's qualities as a player. This is a fine record, building on an inventive roster of tunes: John Hicks's 'Naima's Love Song' and Freddie Hubbard's seldom-covered 'The Decrepit Fox'. These come at the end of a session which hasn't lacked either pace or expressive variety from the off. McClure and Hart both know the set-up well and respond with performances that are as focused as they are relaxed.

****** Person To Person**

Steeplechase SCCD 31369 *Cables (p solo). 4/95.*

A seemingly unimaginative programme of material – starts with 'My Funny Valentine', ends with 'Body And Soul' – but an immaculate solo performance that has melody at a premium and never for a moment drifts off into chordal side-roads. The only weak link is the original 'Sweet Rita Suite', a very slight idea that significantly outstays its welcome. The piano sounds great and

George is in expansive but disciplined form. 'I Remember Clifford' is the outstanding track.

*** **Skylark**

SCCD 31381 *Cables; Jay Anderson (b); Albert 'Tootie' Heath (d).* 4/95.

***(*) **Dark Side, Light Side**

Steeplechase SCCD 31405 *Cables; Jay Anderson (b); Billy Hart (d).* 10/96.

Skylark seems to have been an attempt to find a new, Latin-influenced groove. It's an appealing enough record, but it lacks the sheer grace of the 1996 trio, offering bravado rather than imagination. With Hart at the helm, Cables obviously feels he can do anything, and his playing on 'In A Sentimental Mood' is stretched out to ten minutes, and on the closing tribute to George Adams, Don Pullen's 'Ah, George, We Hardly Knew You', is as close to piano heaven as you're entitled to expect. The later session opens on a version of Herbie Hancock's 'Dolphin Dance' that should be transcribed and passed on to all young piano players. The original 'Dark Side, Light Side' is exquisitely idiomatic, and thereafter the mix of Herbie, Monk and Duke (with Pullen to come) suggests how carefully Cables is looking back into the jazz piano tradition. A remarkable, endlessly attractive record.

Mimmo Cafiero

DRUMS

Italian drummer of the new school, an unassuming but enthusiastic leader.

*** **Domani E Domenica**

Splasc(h) 425-2 *Cafiero; Salvatore Bonafede (p); Paolino Dalla Porta (b).* 2/94.

*** **Triangles**

Splasc(h) 604-2 *Cafiero; Stefano D'Anna (ss, ts); Diederik Wissels (p); Pietro Condorelli (g); Dario Deidda (b).* 9/96.

Cafiero doesn't set out to dominate these records, but he's a big physical presence and he gives plenty of lift to two engaging if unexceptional sessions. The trio on the earlier disc tackle a conservative programme of standards and three originals, and it's made valid by the obliging mastery of the playing. Bonafede has all kinds of lyricism under his fingers and Dalla Porta (reliable as usual) and Cafiero give him every support, with the long, thoughtful treatment of the title-track a particular pleasure. The quintet date benefits from a few surprises. Though the programme is basically straightahead, Deidda's popping electric bass lines lend an almost funky edge to the music at times and, with Cafiero occasionally overdubbing a conga line on to his kit parts and D'Anna alternately reserved and bristling, this is a clever variation on the standard formula – and Cafiero's all-original programme deserves applause.

Michael Cain (born 1966)

PIANO

Contemporary American pianist, prominent as a Jack DeJohnette sideman and with these solos to his credit.

(*) **Strange Omen

Candid CCD 79505 *Cain; Bruce Saunders (g); Glen Velez (perc).* 11/90.

*** **What Means This?**

Candid CCD 79529 *Cain; Anthony Cox (b); Marvin 'Smitty' Smith (d); Paul Hannah (perc).* 3/91.

**** **Circa**

ECM 1622 *Cain; Ralph Alessi (t, flhn); Peter Epstein (ss, ts).* 8/96.

If we had opened a stud book in 1990, it would have suggested that Mike Cain be picked up by ECM. From the very start, he sounded like a latter-day version of Chick Corea, not a copyist, but someone who was developing a concept very like Chick's thoughtful swing-as-philosophy/philosophy-as-swing. The album with Saunders and Velez is interesting enough, though it's the guitarist who provides the two most interesting pieces. Cain's 'Piano Sketch' sequence is quintessentially Corean.

The 1991 set with Cox and Smith was obviously an attempt to create a more mainstream jazz sound. The problem is that – again – Cain is upstaged by his playing partners. The piano often seems to be addding an accompaniment to what is going on with the bass and drums. It's still all very imprecise and indefinite, though; why invite trouble by calling a piece 'Meander'?

Circa came as a hugely refreshing change. Cain conceives of the piece as a rite of passage, inspired by the landscapes of Nevada and the curious cultural environment of Las Vegas, where he spent part of his childhood. One almost thinks of the Desert d'Or Norman Mailer conjures up in *The Deer Park*, a place compounded of showbiz huckstering and an almost apocalyptic beauty. Cain's own writing is superb, with 'Red Rock Rain', 'And Their White Tigers' and 'Top O' The Dunes', which come in the latter part of a notably coherent set, standing out. The instrumentation is as effective as it is unusual. Lacking a rhythm player and someone to anchor the chords means that the pianist has to work very differently. Cain almost plays as if he is accompanying singers, shadowing a line, shading in its contours, ironizing and reinforcing by turns. Superb.

Uri Caine

PIANO

In straight jazz terms, he has more in common with Herbie Hancock than with anyone else, but Caine's musical interests lie much further afield than that, and much of his surviving body of recorded work – the early JMT albums are no longer available – consists of bold reworkings of classical material.

***(*) Urlicht / Primal Light

Winter & Winter 910 004 *Caine; Dave Douglas (t); Josh Roseman (tb); Dave Binney (ss); Don Byron (cl); Danny Blume (g, elec); Mark Feldman (vn); Larry Gold (clo); Michael Formanek (b); Joey Baron (d); DJ Olive (turntables); Aaron Bensoussan (v, perc); Dean Bowman, Arto Lindsay (v).* 6/96.

*** Wagner in Venezia / Wagner In Venice

Winter & Winter 910 013 *Caine; Mark Feldman (vn); Erik Friedlander (clo); Drew Gress (b); Dominic Cortese (acc).* 96.

**** Gustav Mahler in Toblach: I Went Out This Morning Over The Countryside

Winter & Winter 910 046 2 *Caine; Ralph Alessi (t); David Binney (as); Mark Feldman (vn); Aaron Bensoussan (oud, v); Michael Formanek (b); Jim Black (d); DJ Olive (elec, turntables).* 7/98.

Chosen to kick off Winter & Winter's 'New Edition' imprint, *Urlicht* is an extraordinary feat of imaginative projection, and it almost succeeds. The basic concept for the label is clearly modelled on ECM's swing towards new music, though perhaps Stefan Winter is more interested in fusion and crossover experimentation than is Manfred Eicher. The notion that Mahler's music, for much of the last two decades (and certainly before the popular advent of Górecki, Pärt, *et al.*) the only classical composer to appeal to a rock generation, might be adaptable to a jazz aesthetic, is a pretty startling one. For the most part, the studio album works very well. Caine takes themes from the first and second symphonies (including the 'primal light' theme from the *Resurrection Symphony*), as well as songs from *Kindertotenlieder* and *Des Knaben Wunderhorn*, and turns them into open-ended, loose-woven melodic shapes that invite not so much harmonic improvisation as retexturing. This is what Caine does best; it is also the limiting factor on both these records: after a couple of hearings, there is surprisingly little left to chew on.

The live recording of the same material is a revelation, however, and we are irresistibly reminded of how much more successful Mike Westbrook's live recording of his Rossini makeover was than the studio version. From the tightly reined-in piano introduction to the funeral march from the Fifth Symphony, with its wry Beethoven reference and high harmonics from Feldman and the DJ, to the sweeping romanticism of 'The Farewell' from *Das Lied*, the audience is taken along on a journey that has little to do with musicological orthodoxy, but everything to do with thoughtful deconstruction. Caine intuits how much of Mahler's music comes from folk sources and he hands over these famously sonorous themes to a wailing village band. The strange swoops of live electronics are a convincingly alien presence, hinting at birdcalls, spirit-possession, or merely creaking wheels and axles. We are not so very far from Joe Zawinul's 'His Last Journey'.

The two selections from *Kindertotenlieder* are exquisitely done. '*Oft denk Ich, Sie sind nur ausgegangen*' is recast as a mournful duet for violin and trumpet, ever more distant and desolated; taped calls of children also recall Zawinul, whose kids patter and call briefly in the background on Weather Report's *Mysterious Traveller*. There are fresh interpretations of 'Urlicht', the Adagietto from the Fifth Symphony and songs from *Des Knaben Wunderhorn* and *Lieder eines fahrenden Gesellen*. A remarkable conception, now matched by a completely satisfying performance.

We are not fans of the Wagner project (which was recorded live in the Piazza San Marco), not so much because of any ideological scruples, but because these immensely sophisticated themes, with their indistinct architecture, really do not lend themselves to this sort of manipulation. Ironically, a harder-edged approach, with guitars and electronics very much to the fore, might have worked better.

There are, of course, things to admire but they are episodic, and Caine has not managed to carry over his intuitive understanding of Mahler's small- and large-scale structures into this superficially similar project. There are also some concerns about the recording itself, which is very hard and dry for a live taping.

*** The Sidewalks Of New York / Tin Pan Alley

Winter & Winter 910 038 2 *Caine; Ralph Alessi, Dave Douglas (t); Josh Roseman (tb); Bob Stewart (tba); Don Byron (cl); Bob DeBellis (f); Dominic Cortese (acc, v); Eddy Davis (bj); Mark Feldman (vn); James Genus (b); Ben Perowsky (d); Nancy Anderson, Sadiq Bey, Fay Galperin, Saul Galperin, Susan Haefner, Philip Hernandez, Brian D'Arcy Jones, Renae Morway-Baker, Nancy Opel, Stuart Zagnit (v).* 2/99.

A dramatic shift of tone. *Sidewalks* is a bold attempt to create a montage of songs and tunes that evoke turn-of-the-century New York. Songs like 'Has Anyone Here Seen Kelly' (sung with character by Nancy Opel) sit alongside George Cohan's 'Life's A Very Funny Proposition After All' (recited with grim definition by Stuart Zagnit) and a raft of material from Berlin, Joplin, Edward Bert Madden, Ben Shields, Shelton Brooks and others. The best clue to the inspiration for this is the presence of Don Byron in the ensemble and a set of parody lyrics – '*Ver Shlepste Mir Tsu Dem Ball Game*' – to Jack Northworth and Albert von Tilzer's classic. We're very close to Byron's tribute to the klezmer of Mickey Katz, except that Caine is concerned more with atmosphere and very much less with bringing his chosen material up to date. The most personal clue is the dedication to his late grandfather, who presumably grew up in these streets. It's exquisitely done, often very touching.

***(*) Blue Wail

Winter & Winter 910 034-2 *Caine; James Genus (b); Ralph Peterson Jr (d).* 2/98.

Bookended by unexpected, jaggy interpretations of 'Honeysuckle Rose', Caine's return to jazz has more continuities with previous projects than might appear. His own writing is very much in an American song tradition, which in turn drew heavily on European classicism. 'Bones Don't Cry' and the title-track are closest to the feel of the blues, but in 'Digature Of The Line' and 'The Face Of Space', Uri explores tonalities which don't normally play much part in jazz. The trio opens out on 'Blue Wail' and 'Sweet Potato', giving room to Genus and the increasingly impressive Peterson to express themselves, but most of the tracks are terse, tightly structured and sound almost fully written out. Winter & Winter are juggling jazz with other styles and genres, so far successfully. Caine may yet prove to be the label's signature artist.

Cab Calloway (1907–94)

VOCAL

One of the most enduring jazz entertainers, Calloway began playing drums in Chicago but switched to singing and being frontman when he took over The Missourians in 1931. A regular gig at the Cotton Club brought them to prominence and they were among the leading American bands during the rest of the 1930s and early '40s. Disbanding in 1948, Calloway worked with a small group but thereafter focused largely on theatre work and general show-biz appearances. He was still performing and appearing when in his late eighties.

*** Cab Calloway 1930–1931

Classics 516 *Calloway; R.Q Dickerson, Lamar Wright, Ruben Reeves, Wendell Culley (t); De Priest Wheeler (tb); Thornton Blue, Arville Harris (cl, as); Andrew Brown (bcl, ts); Walter Thomas (as, ts, bs, f); Earres Prince, Benny Payne (p); Morris White (bj); Jimmy Smith (bb, b); Leroy Maxey (d).* 7/30–6/31.

***(*) Cab Calloway 1931–1932

Classics 526 *As above, except add Edwin Swayzee, Doc Cheatham (t), Harry White (tb), Eddie Barefield (cl, as, bs), Al Morgan (b); omit Dickerson, Culley, Prince and Blue.* 7/31–6/32.

***(*) Cab Calloway 1932

Classics 537 *As above, except add Roy Smeck (g), Chick Bullock (v); omit Reeves and Smith.* 6/32–12/32.

*** Cab Calloway 1932–1934

Classics 544 *As above, except omit Smeck and Bullock.* 12/32–9/34.

The rough, almost violent playing of The Missourians, a black dance band recording in New York but drawing most of its talent from the Mid-West, was as impassioned as that of any band of the day. Their dozen records are currently unrepresented on CD, but they were then taken over by a flamboyant vocalist and leader, Cab Calloway. At his very first session – in July 1930, with an astonishingly virtuosic vocal on 'St Louis Blues' – he served notice that a major jazz singer was ready to challenge Armstrong with an entirely different style.

It didn't take long for Calloway to sharpen up the band, even though he did it with comparatively few changes in personnel. Unlike the already-tested format of a vocal feature within an instrumental record, Calloway's arrangers varied detail from record to record, Cab appearing throughout some discs, briefly on others, and usually finding space for a fine team of soloists. Some of the discs are eventful to an extraordinary extent: listen, for instance, to the 1935 'I Ain't Got Nobody' or the dazzling 1930 'Some Of These Days' to hear how enthusiastically the band tackled its charts. The lexicon of reefers, Minnie the Moocher and Smokey Joe, kicking gongs around and – of course – the fabulous language of hi-de-ho would soon have become tiresome if it hadn't been for the leader's boundless energy and ingenious invention: his vast range, from a convincing bass to a shrieking falsetto, has remained unsurpassed by any male jazz singer, and he transforms material that isn't so much trite as empty without the investment of his personality. This was a very popular band, long resident at the Cotton Club, and the stability of the personnel says much about the good pay and working conditions. The prodigious number of records they made both during and after the Depression was matched by scarcely any other bandleader, and it has taken the Classics operation no fewer than ten well-filled CDs to cover them all. Unfortunately, reproduction is rather a mixed bag. The earlier sides were made for Banner and other budget labels and suffer from some booming recording; but there is a fair amount of surface noise, too. However, there's nothing unlistenable here and, since Calloway's music is at its freshest, casual listeners may choose one of these earlier discs as representative.

(***) Cab Calloway 1934–1937

Classics 554 *As above, except add Shad Collins, Irving Randolph (t), Claude Jones, Keg Johnson (tb), Garvin Bushell, Thornton Blue (cl, as), Ben Webster (ts), Milt Hinton (b).* 9/34–3/37.

***(*) Cab Calloway 1937–1938

Classics 568 *As above, except add Chu Berry (ts), Chauncey Haughton (cl, as), Danny Barker (g); omit Swayzee, Culley, Cheatham and Morgan.* 3/37–3/38.

*** Cab Calloway 1938–1939

Classics 576 *As above, except add June Richmond (v), Cozy Cole (d); omit Webster and White.* 3/38–2/39.

***(*) Cab Calloway 1939–1940

Classics 595 *As above, except add Dizzy Gillespie, Mario Bauza (t), Tyree Glenn (tb, vib), Quentin Jackson (tb), Jerry Blake (cl, as); omit Maxey, Bushell and Richmond.* 3/39–3/40.

*** Cab Calloway 1940

Classics 614 *As above, except omit Collins, Randolph, Jones and Blue.* 3–8/40.

*** Cab Calloway 1940–1941

Classics 625 *As above, except add Jonah Jones (t).* 3/40–7/41.

Calloway progressed through the 1930s with unquenchable enthusiasm. He took fewer risks on his vocals and chose to set down some more straightforward ballad interpretations on several of the later sides, but the singing is still exceptional, and there are new points of interest among the soloists: Ben Webster appears on several tracks on the 1934–7 disc, and Chu Berry follows him in as a regular soloist, while Gillespie, Jackson and Jefferson also emerge. The 1940 disc features some arrangements by Benny Carter and the bizarre 'Cupid's Nightmare' score by Don Redman, a mystifying mood-piece. Jonah Jones, the last great soloist to arrive in this era, sparks several of the 1941 tracks. Reproduction is mostly clean if sometimes lacking in sparkle on the later discs, but the 1934–7 disc is marred by preposterously heavy surface-noise on the opening tracks and we must issue a caveat in this regard.

*** Cab Calloway 1942-1947

Classics 996 *Calloway; Russell Smith, Shad Collins, Jonah Jones, Lamar Wright, Paul Webster, Shad Collins, Roger Jones, Johnny Letman (t); Tyree Glenn (tb, vib); Quentin Jackson, Keg Johnson, Fred Robinson, John Haughton, Earl Hardy, James Buxton (tb); Jerry Blake (cl, as); Hilton Jefferson, Al Gibson (as); Rudy Powell, Andrew Brown (as, bs); Ted McRae, Walter 'Foots' Thomas, Skinny Brown, Ike Quebec, Bob Dorsey, Sam Taylor (ts); Greely Walton (bs); Bennie Payne, Dave Rivera (p); Danny Barker, John*

Smith (g); Milt Hinton (b); Cozy Cole, Panama Francis, J.C Heard, Buford Oliver (d); Dotty Salters (v). 2/42–12/47.

Calloway kept an excellent band together through the '40s, as a look through the personnel suggests, but the records don't give them too many chances to step out and the material had by now fallen into a rut. Even so, Calloway himself was largely undaunted, though some of the time he sounds like he's trying to compete with Louis Jordan: on the last session, both 'The Calloway Boogie' and 'Everybody Eats When They Come To My House' ('Pass me a pancake, Mandrake') could have come off Jordan's set-list. These are mostly Columbia sessions, though there are also three V-Disc titles. Some of the transfers sound dusty, but they clean up towards the end.

*****(*) Cruisin' With Cab**

Topaz TPZ 1010 *As above discs.* 12/30–43.

RCA have put their Calloway holdings aside for the moment, so the Topaz compilation is about the only general cross-section of his music in the racks – a sturdy and well-chosen set.

Gary Campbell

TENOR AND SOPRANO SAXOPHONES

A journeyman reed specialist, renowned as teacher and theorist, Campbell bases himself in southern Florida and has taken a special interest in finding a fresh slant on Latin/jazz fusion.

***** Intersection**

Milestone MCD-9236-2 *Campbell; Mike Orta (p); Nicky Orta (b); Ignacio Berroa (d); Rafael Solano (perc).* 12/93.

It's idiosyncratic enough that this small-group date sounds quite unlike the accustomed crossover: instead of vamps and overheated solos, Campbell looks for subtle pulses that can trigger different kinds of improvisation. 'Lago Turvo' and 'Hair Of The Dog' open and close the disc in lively fashion, but more typical are the pensive 'Almost Lost', the odd mix of pep and sobriety in 'J.A.' (dedicated to John Abercrombie) and the stern tranquillity of 'Tango'. If anything, the music seems a little too studied in its attempts to get away from cliché, and it doesn't help that Campbell has a stone-faced quality to his playing that disengages the power of some otherwise interesting solos.

John Campbell

PIANO

Mainstream-modernist pianist with his own take on a bebop language.

***** After Hours**

Contemporary 14053 *Campbell; Todd Coolman (b); Gerry Gibbs (d).* 89.

****(*) Turning Point**

Contemporary 14061 *Campbell; Clark Terry (t); Jay Anderson (p); Joel Spencer (d).* 90.

*****(*) John Campbell At Maybeck: Maybeck Recital Hall Series, Volume 29**

Concord CCD 4581 *Campbell (p solo).* 5/93.

Campbell is a fresh-faced mid-Westerner whose farmboy demeanour may arouse musical expectations closer to his namesake Glen than to the reality of his tough but sophisticated bop playing. The Maybeck disc, as so often, is the best place to sample him. Like many of his predecessors in the series, he uses the occasion as an opportunity to show off a couple of test-pieces (like the opening interpretation of 'Just Friends' with its odd turnarounds and harmonic nervousness) or simply to enjoy old favourites (like 'You And The Night And The Music', to which again he gives an unusual twist). 'Emily' is more straightforwardly romantic, though not without its reserves of guile.

The trios with Coolman and Gibbs are uniformly good, especially the partially deconstructed 'Donna Lee'. Its successor, unfortunately, is pretty feeble. Terry probably thinks it's all a bit high-falutin' and, in a strange way, it is.

Roy Campbell (born 1952)

TRUMPET, FLUGELHORN, CORNET, POCKET-TRUMPET

A New Yorker, Campbell studied with Yusef Lateef in the early '70s and has explored jazz in a world-music context. Founder member of Other Dimensions In Music, and as likely to play free as anything boppish. Divides his time between Holland and the USA and collects horror films.

*****(*) New Kingdom**

Delmark DE-456 *Campbell; Zane Massey (ts); Ricardo Strobert (as, f); Bryan Carrott (vib); William Parker (b); Zen Matsuura (d).* 10/91.

***** La Tierra Del Fuego**

Delmark DE-469 *Campbell; Alex Lodico (tb); Ricardo Strobert (as, f); Zane Massey (ts); Klaas Hekman (bs); Rahn Burton (p); Hideji Taninaka (b); Reggie Nicholson (d); Talik Abdullah (perc).* 12/93.

***** Communion**

Silkheart SHCD 139 *Campbell; William Parker (b); Reggie Nicholson (d).* 9/94.

Campbell plays like the offspring of Lee Morgan (who was actually his teacher) but imbued with a hankering to go much further outside than Morgan ever would have. He loves lyrical playing and, on Parker's piece dedicated to Cecil Taylor, 'For C.T.', he counters the inspiration by playing some of his sweetest horn. But the idea of *New Kingdom* is to create music that salutes the tradition and still pays heed to the avant-garde. The three trio pieces for Campbell, Parker and Matsuura are an expertly constructed bridge, and beautifully played by all three men. Massey and Strobert are sound, if relatively unremarkable saxophonists, but Carrott is a fine participant, moving smoothly between roles as colourist, ensemble man and fleet improviser.

La Tierra Del Fuego is an intermittently exciting stew of traditions and new ideas, with nods to Booker Little and various threads of Afro-Cuban jazz and the hottest modal bands of the 1960s. Campbell assembles a rather ragtag cast for this one, with the surprising Hekman a wild card, and as a result it comes off hit and miss. He empties out the studio for *Communion*, which spotlights his freest playing, and this time evokes – perhaps all too obviously – some of Don Cherry's small-group recordings. Probably ten or fifteen minutes too much here, since the record palls a little over the full stretch; inventively though Parker and Nicholson play, one hears graft and perspiration rather than flair. But Campbell remains a gratifying and lyrical performer, even at his furthest out.

Tony Campise

TENOR, ALTO AND SOPRANO SAXOPHONES, FLUTE, BASS FLUTE

Texas-born saxophonist whose post-bop style has been documented so far mainly by the independent Heart label.

****(*) First Takes**

Heart 021 *Campise; Rick Jackson (p); Erich Avinger (g); Bill Miller (b); Steve Allison (d).* 90.

****(*) Once In A Blue Moon**

Heart 04 *As above, except Joe Locascio (p) replaces Jackson and Avinger.* 12/90.

***** Ballads Blues Bebop And Beyond**

Heart 006 *Campise; Dennis Dotson (t); John Milles (ts, bs); Joe Locascio, Sandy Allen, Doug Hall (p); Mitch Watkins, Erich Avinger (g); Evan Arredondo, Chris Marsh, Dave Morgan (b); Steve Summer, A.D Mannion (d).* 94.

Campise's bluff, open-hearted approach to the sax – his primary horn seems to be the tenor, but there is alto and soprano as well as flute on these discs – is cheering in small doses but a little unconvincing over the long haul. He piles into his solos as if worried that he won't have the time to say all he wants, and the results can be predictably exhausting, something between Trane-like intensity and the swaggering line of the great Texas tenors (Campise is from Houston). The first two albums are rough-and-ready mixtures of standards, blues and the occasional original line, and on both of them the weight falls on Campise, with mixed results. *Ballads Blues Bebop And Beyond* is the best by a narrow margin: Watkins, excellent as usual, adds tonal contrast to the five tracks he appears on, Dotson is useful on 'Teo' and (a brave stab at this one) Mingus's 'Haitian Fight Song', and there is a hell-for-leather blow-out on 'Impressions' which is genuinely exciting.

Canal Street Ragtimers

GROUP

Veteran British trad group of long ago, in their sole featured album.

****(*) Canal Street Ragtimers**

GHB BCD-4 *Roy Bower, Tony Smith (t); Chris Brown (tb); Martin Rodger (cl); John G Featherstone (p); Derek Gracie (bj); Colin Knight (b); Derek Hamer, Mo Green (d).* 10/61–1/62.

Some irony in that it took a Louisiana-based label to record this pick-up band of Manchester trad stalwarts back in the early '60s. For those with memories of the scene, it's a nice souvenir, but on its own terms the record doesn't deliver that much. The nine tunes ('Old Rugged Cross' appears twice) were well-worn even then, and if the Ragtimers give them an enthusiastic ragging it's not much more than an echo now. Dusty sound affects the drums in particular.

Conte Candoli (born 1927)

TRUMPET

Born in Mishawaka, Indiana, Candoli toured with several big bands from the late 1940s onwards and he moved to California in 1954, becoming a fixture on the West Coast scene there. He has basically worked there since, having long associations with Shorty Rogers groups, the Doc Severinsen Orchestra, Supersax and with a small group he co-leads with his brother Pete (born 1923), also a trumpeter.

***** The Five**

RCA Victor ND 74397 *Candoli; Bill Perkins (ts); Pete Jolly (p); Buddy Clark (b); Mel Lewis (d).* 55.

****(*) Double Or Nothin'**

Fresh Sounds FSR-CD197 *Candoli; Lee Morgan (t); Frank Rosolino (tb); Benny Golson, Bob Cooper (ts); Dick Shreve, Wynton Kelly (p); Red Mitchell, Wilfred Middlebrooks (b); Stan Levey, Charli Persip (d).* 2/57.

***** Sweet Simon**

Best Recordings BR 92101-2 *Candoli; Pete Christlieb (ts); Frank Strazzeri (p); Monty Budwig (b); Ralph Penland, Roy McCurdy (d).* 92.

Conte Candoli is one of the great West Coast brassmen. Often as content to be a foot-soldier as a leader, he's seldom helmed his own dates, and these discs (the second and third at least a generation apart) suggest an unassumingly likeable style. *The Five* offers a dozen Shorty Rogers arrangements for a prototypical Californian quintet of the era. Candoli and Perkins stroll through the situation almost nervelessly at times, but the playing has the customary élan that these groups lived by. *Double Or Nothin'* is a Howard Rumsey date co-credited to Conte and Lee Morgan, but neither man really has much space to shine: Morgan's youthful swashbuckling is penned in by the charts and, though Golson contributes three good tunes, the material is delivered flatly. Golson and Morgan take some good choruses on 'Blues After Dark', but the two-trumpet tracks are disappointingly tame, and this is hardly Candoli's show. Still awaited on CD from this period are his 1954 quartet date for Bethlehem and Atlantic's cracking *West Coast Wailers* with Lou Levy and Bill Holman.

Sweet Simon is a veteran bopper's notebook. He graciously covers two tunes by his old friend, Frank Rosolino, adds a couple of Frank Strazzeri originals and two of his own, picks out a neat Al Cohn piece called 'Travisimo' and turns it all into an hour of good-humoured blowing. 'Lush Life' doesn't really suit the trumpeter, and he probably cedes too much space to the others, especially bluff tenorman Christlieb; but the pleasure he takes in his own playing shows how much Conte enjoys his work. Impeccable studio sound.

*****(*) Portrait Of A Count**
Fresh Sound FSR 5015 *Candoli; Jan Lundgren (p); Chuck Berghofer (b); Joe LaBarbera (d). 9/96.*

Some of the best of Conte's early sets are still out of circulation, but no matter when the man is still in good heart and making records as enjoyable as this. Lundgren is making a speciality of this kind of date and he gives the trumpeter unselfish support, while bass and drums have pedigrees far longer than their arms. The leader's phrasing is a drop more deliberate and hefty than before, but what a gorgeously clear sound he gets, nicely caught by Dick Bank and engineer Jim Mooney. Eleven good standards and a blues.

Frank Capp (born 1931)

DRUMS

Working in Los Angeles from 1953, Capp spent much of the time in small groups, backing singers and doing TV work. In 1975 he founded the Capp–Pierce Juggernaut, a big band co-led with Nat Pierce, and it still prevails as an old-fashioned swing-to-mainstream orchestra.

****(*) Juggernaut**
Concord CCD 4040 *Capp; Blue Mitchell, Gary Grant, Bobby Shew (t); Buster Cooper, Britt Woodman, Alan Kaplan (tb); Bill Green, Marshal Royal (as); Richie Kamuca, Plas Johnson (ts); Quin Davis (bs); Nat Pierce (p); Al Hendrickson (g); Chuck Berghofer (b); Ernie Andrews (v). 79.*

***** Live At Century Plaza**
Concord CCD 4072 *Capp; Al Aarons, Bobby Shew, Frank Szabo, Bill Berry (t); Garnett Brown, Buster Cooper, Alan Kaplan, Britt Woodman (tb); Bob Cooper, Bill Green, Lanny Morgan, Herman Riley, Marshal Royal (reeds); Nat Pierce (p); Ray Pohlman (g); Chuck Berghofer (b); Joe Williams (v).*

***** Juggernaut Strikes Again!**
Concord CCD 4183 *Capp; Bill Berry, Snooky Young, Johnny Audino, Frank Szabo, Al Aarons, Warren Luening (t); Alan Kaplan, Buster Cooper, George Bohannon, Mel Wanzo (tb); Marshal Royal, Joe Roccisano, Jackie Kelso (as); Pete Christlieb, Bob Cooper, Bob Efford (ts); Bill Green (ss, bs); Nat Pierce (p); Bob Maize (b); Ernie Andrews (v). 10–11/81.*

****(*) Live At The Alley Cat**
Concord CCD 4336 *Capp; Bill Berry, Snooky Young, Frank Szabo, Conte Candoli (t); Charles Loper, Garnett Brown, Buster Cooper (tb); Dave Edwards, Joe Romano (as); Red Holloway, Bob Cooper (ts); Bill Green (bs); Nat Pierce (p); Ken Pohlman (g); Chuck Berghofer (b); Ernestine Anderson (v). 6/87.*

***** In A Hefti Bag**
Concord CCD 4655 *As above, except add Bob Summers (t), Andy Martin, Thurman Green, Alan Kaplan (tb), Marshal Royal, Lanny Morgan, Danny House, Rickey Woodard, Pete Christlieb, Jack Nimitz (reeds), Gerry Wiggins (p), Dennis Budimir, John Pisano (g); omit Loper, Brown, Cooper, Edwards, Romano, Holloway, Cooper, Pierce, Pohlman, Anderson. 11/94–3/95.*

Co-led by Capp, a drummer loaded with big-band experience, and Pierce, *Juggernaut* is essentially a troupe of sessionmen out for a good time on the stand. Because they're such proficient players, there's nothing casual about the music; but that also means that it never becomes quite as freewheeling as the musicians might imagine. Too many of the arrangements rely on stock devices pulled from the Basie and Herman books, while the section playing is sometimes overwound, especially on *Strikes Again!*. Nevertheless, so many good players are on hand that the results are seldom less than enjoyable, and when somebody cuts loose – as, say, Buster Cooper does on 'Things Ain't What They Used To Be', on CCD 4183 – it's as thrilling as they intend. The first live record features the majestic Williams, the second Anderson, and she is in fair voice, and never as fulsome as Andrews is on the other two discs. *In A Hefti Bag* finds Capp's men piling through 'authentic' Basie charts; as a polished piece of repertory – with the sax section now stronger than the band has ever shown, too – it's an impressive show, with choice moments for Young, Woodard and Candoli, and a farewell blow from Marshal Royal.

***** Frank Capp Presents Rickey Woodard**
Concord CCD 4469 *Capp; Rickey Woodard (as, ts); Tom Ranier (p); Chuck Berghofer (b, v). 91.*

***** Quality Time**
Concord CCD 4677 *As above except add Nolan Smith (t). 10/93–1/94.*

Capp lends his name to a date (*Presents*) that's really a showcase for the splendid Woodard, a stylist whose dedication to swing is as strong as his allegiance to bebop. The material is straightforward stuff, but Woodard characterizes it all with full-blooded enthusiasm. *Quality Time* is a harmless repeat, with Nolan Smith adding a little brass bite to two tracks.

***** Play It Again Sam**
Concord CCD 4747-2 *Capp; Frank Szabo, Carl Saunders, Bob Summers, Bill Berry, Conte Candoli (t); Andy Martin, Thurman Green, Dana Hughes, Wendell Kelly, Alan Kaplan, George Bohannon (tb); Jackie Kelso, Steve Wilkerson (as); Rickey Woodard, Pete Christlieb (ts); Bob Efford (bs); Gerry Wiggins (p); John Pisano, Barry Zweig (g); Chuck Berghofer, Dave Carpenter (b). 9–10/96.*

'Sam' is Sammy Nestico, who contributes the dozen charts on offer here, and what we get is basically a good facsimile of the Basie band as it stood in the last couple of decades of its (original) life. It must be a good show in person, but on record one has to question the point of the exercise. That said, there are the expected rousing moments when Capp stokes them up, and the whole band get four bars each on '88 Basie Street'.

Arrigo Cappelletti

PIANO

Contemporary Italian pianist with a broad range of sympathies, his modern bent tempered by romantic leanings.

****** Samadhi**
Splasc(h) 111-2 *Cappelletti; Roberto Ottaviano (ss, as); Piero Leveratto (b); Massimo Pintori (d).* 4/86.

***** Pianure**
Splasc(h) 308-2 *Cappelletti; Giulio Visibelli (ss); Maurizio Deho (vn); Gianni Coscia (acc); Hami Hammerli, Luca Garlaschelli (b).* 3–5/90.

*****(*) Singolari Equilibri**
Splasc(h) 390-2 *Cappelletti; Hami Hammerli (b); Billy Elgart (d).* 4/92.

Cappelletti is scarcely an original voice – his underlying romanticism is tempered by a linear approach to improvised melody which, especially on *Singolari Equilibri*, can make him closely akin to Paul Bley – but he's a skilful and unusually clear thinker at the keyboard. There's little waste in his compositions, which are unfailingly lyrical, and his harmonies are sparsely voiced, as if he's anxious not to obscure the sonority of individual notes. He asks for highly developed interplay from companions, and the quartet and trio sessions are both memorably characterful. Ottaviano has seldom sounded better than he does on *Samadhi*, which includes two good tunes of his own as well as a thoughtful treatment of John Taylor's 'Windfall' and Cappelletti at his composing best in 'Neve' and 'Incipit'. The trio record is over-full at 77 minutes but there is much ingenuity from all three men, with Elgart's improvisations as interesting as those of the others. *Pianure* is a modest departure, with Cappelletti looking to try his hand at the tango music of Astor Piazzolla: there are many fine moments, but it feels relatively polite and tame next to the passions which Piazzolla himself could generate and the other players can't match the leader in the quality of their solos.

***** Todos Los Nombres Del Agua**
Splasc(h) 433-2 *Cappelletti; Gianni Coscia (acc); Gioconda Cilio (v).* 11/94.

*****(*) Ananda**
Splasc(h) 485-2 *Cappelletti (p solo).* 6/96.

Todos Los Nombres Del Agua sets poetry by Octavio Paz to music, as well as some lyrics by Cilio, and the results tend to go the way of such things: sparse, meditative, the music pressed to match the evocations of the words and sometimes getting there. Cilio, Coscia and Cappelletti each bring something interesting to the situation, but this is one for firmly acquired tastes.

The solo record carries great conviction. Cappelletti's debt to Paul Bley comes out in 'Bleyniana' and there is a dedication to Bartók, as well as Ellington and Monk covers. Performed slowly and gracefully and with very little in the way of pretension, this is more enjoyable than many higher-profile piano records.

Claudio Capurro

ALTO AND SOPRANO SAXOPHONES, CLARINET

Experienced as a big-band section player, Capurro has often worked with singer Paolo Conte and also as a classical player. His jazz work places him as a mainstream modernist.

***** Algonchina**
DDQ 128011-2 *Capurro; Paolo Silvestri, Franco D'Andrea (p); Aldo Zunino (b); Alfred Kramer (d, vib).* 9–10/93.

Capurro plays this colourful set of a dozen originals with fine flair and gusto, taking a flavoursome Eurobop vocabulary and embellishing it with solos that lack nothing in style and conviction. There are tunes that sound steeped in Italian harmony, the certain Mediterranean feel which has been Italy's gift to the modern-jazz spectrum; but perhaps it would have been useful to centre the music with a couple of standards of some kind: 12 quickly dispatched themes fail to reveal any notable peaks. D'Andrea sits in for Silvestri on two duets with the leader, and the clarinet–piano feature, 'Jadis', is a charmer. The slightly grainy studio sound may not be to all tastes.

Thomas 'Mutt' Carey (1891–1948)

TRUMPET

Carey played in the teens of the century with Joe Oliver and others, but his main association was with Kid Ory, with whom he worked in California from 1919. He was bypassed in the '30s but became a revivalist star when returning to work with Ory in the '40s.

***** Mutt Carey And Lee Collins**
American Music AMCD-72 *Carey; Lee Collins (t); Hociel Thomas (p, v); Lovie Austin, J.H Shayne (p); Johnny Lindsay (b); Baby Dodds (d); Bertha 'Chippie' Hill (v).* 2–8/46.

Carey was an early giant of New Orleans trumpet, but his representation on record is relatively slight, certainly in terms of being in the limelight. His contribution to the one CD under his name consists of six accompaniments to the piano and vocals of classic blues singer Thomas, still in good voice even though she'd been living in obscurity for many years at that point. This isn't some of Carey's best work, though. He sounds surprisingly uncomfortable at several points and much of the playing seems hesitant, butthere's some superb interplay on 'Go Down Sunshine', and Thomas herself does very well. Collins, another frequently unsung trumpeter, sounds rather better on his eight tracks, where he plays behind another veteran, Chippie Hill. This is all rough music and it gets close to the core. Good restoration from the original Circle masters.

Rüdiger Carl (born 1944)

CLARINET, TENOR SAXOPHONE, PIANO, CONCERTINA, ACCORDION, PERCUSSION

Carl became involved in free playing in the late 1960s as a saxophonist, but from the late '70s onwards he has increasingly turned his attention to the accordion and, when he plays a reed instrument, the clarinet. He has frequently worked with Irène Schweizer and Hans Reichel in duo and group situations and, in the '80s, formed the COWWS Quintet.

*****(*) Buben Plus**
FMP CD 78 *Carl; Hans Reichel (vn, daxophone).* 5/78–2/94.

*****(*) Solo**

FMP CD 86 *Carl (acc, cl solo).* 1/93–7/95.

***** Grooves 'N' Loops**

FMP CD 59 *Carl; Irène Schweizer (p, perc); Phil Wachsmann (vn, vla, elec); Stephan Wittwer (g); Jay Oliver (b).* 1/93.

****** Book / Virtual COWWS**

FMP OWN-90007/9 3CD *As above, except add Maarten Altena (c), Lol Coxhill (ss, v), Hans Reichel (vn), Alex von Schlippenbach (p), Mayo Thompson (g, v), Lars Rudolph, Joe Sachse (g), Matthias Bauer, Johnny Dyani, Arjen Gorter (b), Louis Moholo, Paul Lovens, Gunter Sömmer, Sven-Ake Johansson, Han Bennink (d), Andrew Unruh (tubing), Lupa Herz (v).* 10/77–11/96.

Carl's early appearances were as a typically fraught and scattershot saxman in the FMP roll-call, but he has subsequently spent at least as much time with the concertina and accordion. These are what he uses exclusively on the splendidly bizarre *Buben Plus*, which reissues the 1978 FMP LP, *Buben*, with a dozen further duets from 1994. On the latter pieces Carl switches from concertina to accordion and Reichel drops his violin in favour of the daxophone, which is something like a more 'vocalized' violin in timbre. The improvisations bridge wheezing and scraping with lovely singing tones and minimalist counterpoint. The feel of both sessions is enduringly spontaneous. Excellent liner-notes by Steve Beresford.

The *Solo* album might be deemed to be for specialist tastes – though Carl's music is never exactly driven by playing to any crowd. There is a 1995 live performance at Frankfurt's Adler-Werke, an enormous, abandoned factory space, and a set of 18 'miniatures' for solo accordion from some two years earlier. At work in the huge acoustic of the place, Carl finds a blend of intimacy and vastness. His clarinet on 'Hungen 609' sounds like a ship's foghorn. A strange record, but if you are attuned to Carl's music you'll find it a fine, absorbing listen.

The COWWS Quintet, to which the next one and one-third albums should properly be credited, seems to be Carl's band in leadership terms, and its instrumentation and temper suggest a chamber ensemble. There are surprisingly conventional notes in the directions taken by the group, but a subtext of a sort of civilized anarchy: maybe it's best exemplified by 'Gunst I', a guitar solo by Wittwer which starts as a string of funk clichés and ends in sonic mayhem. Pieced together from two evenings of live playing, it's hit and miss.

If Carl has been somewhat neglected by recordings in recent years, the enormous *Book/Virtual COWWS* makes up for it with what amounts to a scrapbook of his progress over 20 years of playing. Jump-cutting between group and solo recordings, live and studio, extracts from *Buben* and *Tuned Boots*, private and concert and rehearsal tracks, this is the autobiography of a charming extremist. The patchwork nature of it can seem pointlessly eccentric at times, particularly as so many of the pieces are fragments from larger works, but it is never boring: nothing else in this book sets Thelonious Monk's 'Misterioso' to a commentary on a chess game (spoken by Mayo Thompson, who does follow the melody).

The COWWS disc (number three of the set) is entirely different from what the quintet had attempted earlier. Carl says that he has seen the group as something 'combining improvised music with a "cool" head and a certain feeling of distance'. For this recording, he went to rather extraordinary lengths to crystallize that aim. A system of notation was devised out of a mix of numerical and diagrammatic series, and the musicians were obliged to play parts which amounted to a series of linear blocks or segments, each with a manner of playing described in no more than three words ('icy', 'very heavy movement', and so on). Each musician worked alone in the studio for some two hours, acting on the notation, Carl himself giving the beginning and end signals with the use of a stopwatch. Six pieces were then made out of these overlaid parts, with a seventh constructed out of loops and edits. The results are, in effect, a series of virtual group improvisations, hence the title. As music, it is certainly fascinating, not least for how often it seems that the players are responding to one another – when they are, in fact, never doing anything of the kind.

Mike Carr (born 1937)

ORGAN

Born in South Shields, Carr was playing jazz in the Newcastle area from 1960. He moved to London and led several trios, eventually backing Ronnie Scott in the early '70s, and still plays in many small-group situations. A renowned expert on the subject of Hammond organs.

***** Bebop From The East Coast 1960/1962**

Birdland MC596 *Carr; Ian Carr (t); Gary Cox (ts); John McLaughlin (g); Midge Pike, John O'Carroll, Spike Heatley (b); Johnny Butts, Ronnie Stephenson, Jackie Denton (d).* 60–62.

A faded but lively memento of a particular part of modern British jazz, the scene around Newcastle in the early '60s. This is monochrome hard bop of surprisingly vivid integrity, Cox's tenor the outstanding voice in a number of quartets/quintets which keyboardist Carr organized, often with his brother Ian on trumpet. The notes suggest a comparison with the Brown–Roach group, which isn't so far-fetched. They must have been even better live – although a few live tracks (one stray one from 1967 with young man McLaughlin on guitar) are actually no stronger than the studio ones.

***** Good Times And The Blues**

Cargogold CGCD 191 *Carr; Dick Morrissey (ts); Jim Mullen (g); Mark Taylor (d).* 3/93.

Three British venerables (Mark Taylor isn't quite as senior) having fun on blues and bop lines and getting a good record out of it. While the writing is merely functional, the solos work up a rare head of steam, with Morrissey and Mullen eschewing the politely funky licks of their jazz-funk past and digging in. Carr likes to put the Hammond on a rasping, trebly setting and it gives some of his lightning runs an agreeably spine-tingling quality. An outside producer might have served them better, though, and given Taylor a superior drum sound.

Baikida Carroll (born 1947)

TRUMPET

Based in St Louis, Carroll became a major figure in the Black Artists Group in the '70s but has only rarely been sighted on record, and he has remained something of a 'local' figure, while still a skilful and adventurous brass player.

****** Shadows And Reflections**

Soul Note 121023 *Carroll; Julius Hemphill (as, ts); Anthony Davis (p); Dave Holland (b); Pheeroan akLaff (d).* 1/82.

*****(*) Door Of The Cage**

Soul Note 121123 *Carroll; Erica Lindsay (ts); Steve Adegoke Colson (p); Santi Debriano (b); Pheeroan akLaff (d).* 3/94.

These are high ratings for a musician who is not generally very well known. He grew up in St Louis and became a leading force in the Black Artists Group (BAG), sacrificing a good deal in professional terms to commit himself to radical community music-making when his bright chops and fertile ideas would surely have won him considerable prominence as a leader. As it was, Carroll didn't record on his own account until the late 1970s when he cut *Shadows And Reflections*, like so many of his advanced contemporaries, for the Italian IREC group, the umbrella organization for Soul Note and Black Saint. 'This project was born out of sheer dedication.' It has repaid handsomely: Carroll assembled a superb group of musicians for the date. Hemphill was returning the favour of an important solo part on his *Dogon A.D.*, but it is Holland who emerges as the key player, rooting the music in something dark and tremulously substantial, great shadowy bass-lines that seem to push the two horns ever higher on 'Jahi Sundance Lake' and the long Pharoah Sanders-like 'Pyramids'.

It's more than a decade before Carroll emerges as a leader again. *Door Of The Cage* is almost inevitably a slight disappointment after the sheer excellence of its predecessor, but it is still an enormously impressive record. Astonishing that Lindsay hasn't recorded more; it's a rich, warm-toned sound with a hard edge when called for. It's called for less on this second record. In keeping with the times, Carroll favours a more line-driven, melodic approach and a softer, more plangent tone. There is still a brassy bite on numbers like 'King' and 'At Roi', which was originally written for Hemphill (whose chosen name was Roi Boye) in friendly revenge for some of the charts he gave the young trumpeter to play.

Paolo Carrus

PIANO

A Sardinian, Carrus plays post-bop piano but seeks to put it into the context of his local, native music.

***** Sardegna Oltre Il Mare**

Splasc(h) 373-2 *Carrus; Paolo Fresu (t, flhn); Giorgio Baggiani (flhn); Pietro Tonolo (ss); Massimo Carboni (ts); Andrea Pinna (launeddas); Salvatore Majore (b); Billy Secchi (d).* 7/90–1/92.

***** Odras**

Splasc(h) 622-2 *Carrus; Paolo Fresu, Giovanni Sanna Passino (t, flhn); Giorgio Baggiani (t); Maurizio Ligas (tb); Gavino Mele (frhn); Giampiero Carta (cl); Dante Casu (as); Massimo Carboni (ts); Giovanni Agostinbo Frassetto (f); Piero Di Rienzo (b); Billy Sechi (d).* 1–4/97.

Carrus is making a spirited attempt at placing what he feels are his local roots into a broader jazz perspective. On the earlier disc the results are mixed, and perhaps it's unfair to say that the record works best when it's at its least obviously Sardinian. The main intrusion is the sound of the launeddas, the triple clarinet that makes a skirling, bagpipe-like addition to five of the ten tracks. It's a memorable noise but, since the talented Pinna is never actually allowed to fit in as part of the ensemble – he mostly plays march-like statements at some point in the tune when the other horns drop out – it can seem a little peculiar; the solo piece, 'Ballo In Minore', is certainly his most vivid appearance. Elsewhere, though, there is some beautifully sensitive post-bop, with Fresu in characteristically Milesian mode on the ballad, 'No', and Tonolo appearing on one tune, 'Apri'. Carrus has taken care to let native melodies colour his writing, and if that hardly makes the record stand out the players still have plenty to say.

Odras is more conventionally directed, with the Sardegna Oltre il Mare (Sardinia beyond the Sea) Ensemble working through seven originals by Carrus and one by drummer Sechi. There's a new version of 'Passo' from the previous disc. Thoughtfully prepared, the music seems effortful, as if Carrus was trying to cram in too much, and it's difficult for the rhythm section to lift charts that are too complex to fly. That said, guest Fresu is his usual impeccable self on his solos, and some of the pieces muster the slightly awkward prettiness which Carrus seems to be after.

Ernie Carson

CORNET, VOCAL

Born in Portland, Oregon, Carson is a brassman who's played in West Coast revivalist circles for many years. He took over the Castle Jazz Band in 1983, but has led many sessions of his own.

****** Southern Comfort**

GHB BCD-162 *Carson; Charlie Bornemann, Steve Yokum (tb); John Otto, Tom Fischer (cl); Steve Pistorius (p); Bill Rutan (bj, v); Debbie Shreyer (bj); Hal 'Shorty' Johnson, Tom Saunders (tba); Hal Smith, Ken Hall (d).* 1/83–5/93.

***** At The Hookers' Ball**

GHB BCD-125 *Carson; Charlie Bornemann (tb); Herman Foretich, Kim Cusack, Tom Fischer (cl); Steve Pistorius (p); Bill Rutan (bj); Mike Moore, Hal 'Shorty' Johnson (tba); Chuck Chamison, Don Hooker, Hal Smith (d).* 83–99.

*****(*) Ernie Carson And The Social Polecats**

GHB BCD-307 *Carson; Tom Bartlett (tb); Kim Cusack (cl); Wally Rose (p); Bill Rutan (bj, v); Debbie Shreyer (bj); Mike Walbridge (tba); Wayne Jones (d).* 5/91.

*****(*) One Beer**

GHB BCD-297 *Carson; Charlie Bornemann (tb); Rick Fay (cl, ss); Butch Thompson (p); Bill Rutan (bj, v); Hal 'Shorty' Johnson (tba); Debbie Schreyer (d, bj).* 93.

****** Every Man A King**

GHB BCD-327 *Carson; Tom Bartlett (tb); Kim Cusack (cl); Pete Clute (p); Debbie Schreyer (bj); Mike Wallbridge (tba); Wayne Jones (d).* 3/93.

****** If I Had A Talking Picture Of You**

GHB BCD-385 *Carson; Steve Yokum (tb); Tom Fischer (cl); Steve Pistorius (p); Debbie Schreyer (bj); Tom Saunders (bsx); Ken Hall (d).* 6/93.

***** Wher'm I Gonna Live?**

Stomp Off 1277 *Carson; Tom Bartlett (tb); Kim Cusack (cl); Pete Clute (p); Bob Leary (bj); Bill Carroll (tba); Wayne Jones (d).* 3/94.

After going through so many earnest and deadly serious records in the course of our survey, it's something of a relief to unwrap the collected works of Ernie Carson, cornetist, singer (more or less) and custodian of much that would otherwise be forgotten in the annals of old-time hot music and jazz. Carson began as a teenage brassman with his old mentor, Monte Ballou of the Castle Jazz Band. In his prime, which might as well be around the time of these sessions, he plays tough-as-nails cornet, recalling the spit and fire of the great Chicagoans more than any revivalist hornman, and he masterminds groups that swing ferociously over such ancient ground as (to pick one from each CD) 'I'm Skipping Rope With A Rainbow', 'You Can Tell Her Anything Under The Sun', 'That Ragtime Minstrel Band', 'Powder Your Face With Sunshine', 'When A Peach From Georgia Weds A Rose From Alabam', 'Melon Time In Dixieland' and 'Honey, I Could Fall In Love'. Each has its share of almost outrageous arcana, going even further than Marty Grosz would. *One Beer* goes back to the English music hall with a knockabout version of Mark Sheridan's 'You Can Do A Lot Of Things', but it also has a fine trio version of 'Maple Leaf Rag' and a ludicrous novelty in 'The Farm Yard Cabaret'. *Every Man A King* is a flawless display of what Carson's gang (many of them borrowed from the Salty Dogs) can do, and it gets the nod in front of the others. Nobody will ever top Sheila Steafel's 'Popsy Wopsy', but Carson's crew get close.

Southern Comfort, dedicated to songs from the South, is pure carnival (beefed up with three extra tracks from 1993). *At The Hookers' Ball* has a rather glaring sound on its earlier tracks which takes some of the gilt off the music, though the music is as bumptious as ever. *Social Polecats* has comparatively restrained material but the band are playing with top gusto. *If I Had A Talking Picture Of You* has a great studio sound, Saunders contributes some fine bass sax, and the best tracks sound like they're going on rocket fuel. *Wher'm I Gonna Live?* is comparatively disappointing. Maybe it was a bit too cute doing tunes by Billy Ray Cyrus and David Nye, since country music doesn't need wits such as Carson to make it seem ridiculous. The sound of the Stomp Off album is also a shade too nice: this kind of thing needs to be driven right into your face, which is how the GHB records are.

Benny Carter (born 1907)

ALTO SAXOPHONE, TRUMPET, CLARINET, VOCALS

By 1928 Carter was already arranging for various New York bands, and he led his own group on and off from then until 1936, when he went to London as staff arranger for the BBC Dance Orchestra. Back in the USA, he led his own big band, 1939–41, but had to cut back to a sextet before moving to Hollywood in 1945. Wrote extensively for film and TV thereafter, but also for jazz record dates and singers' albums, while also making records featuring his own playing. In 2000, he was enjoying semi-retirement but still talking about musical projects. The most dapper of saxophonists, an excellent trumpeter, and an arranger with few peers, he is a link to a jazz age now long gone.

*****(*) Benny Carter 1929–1933**

Classics 522 *Carter; Louis Bacon, Shad Collins, Leonard Davis, Bill Dillard, Frank Newton, Howard Scott, Bobby Stark, Rex Stewart (t); J.C Higginbotham, Wilbur De Paris, George Washington, Dicky Wells (tb); Jimmy Harrison (tb, v); Howard Johnson (as); Don Redman (as, v); Wayman Carver (as, f); Chu Berry, Coleman Hawkins (ts); Horace Henderson, Red Rodriguez, Luis Russell, Fats Waller, Teddy Wilson (p); Benny Jackson, Lawrence Lucie (g); Richard Fulbright, Ernest Hill (b); John Kirby (b, bb); Cyrus St Clair (bb); Big Sid Catlett (d, vib); Kaiser Marshall, George Stafford (d); other personnel unidentified.* 9/29–5/33.

*****(*) Benny Carter 1933–1936**

Classics 530 *Carter; Henry 'Red' Allen (t, v); Dick Clark, Leonard Davis, Bill Dillard, Max Goldberg, Otis Johnson, Max Kaminsky, Eddie Mallory, Tommy McQuater, Irving Randolph, Howard Scott, Russell Smith, Duncan Whyte (t); Ted Heath, Keg Johnson, Benny Morton, Bill Mulraney, Floyd O'Brien, Wilbur De Paris, Fred Robinson, George Washington, Dicky Wells (tb); Howard Johnson, Andy McDevitt (cl, as); Wayman Carver (cl, as, f); Glyn Pacque, E.O Pogson, Russell Procope, Ben Smith (as); Coleman Hawkins (cl, ts); Chu Berry, Buddy Featherstonehaugh, Johnny Russell, Ben Webster (ts); Pat Dodd, Red Rodriguez, Teddy Wilson (p); George Elliott, Clarence Holiday, Lawrence Lucie (g); Al Burke, Ernest Hill, Elmer James (b); Big Sid Catlett, Ronnie Gubertini, Walter Johnson (d); Charles Holland (v).* 5/33–4/36.

*****(*) Benny Carter 1936**

Classics 541 *Carter; Max Goldberg, Tommy McQuater, Duncan Whyte (t); Leslie Thompson (t, tb); Lew Davis, Ted Heath, Bill Mulraney (tb); Freddie Gardner, Andy McDevitt (cl, as); E.O Pogson (as); Buddy Featherstonehaugh (ts); Pat Dodd, Billy Munn, Gene Rodgers (p); George Elliott, Albert Harris, Ivor Mairants (g); Al Burke, Wally Morris (b); George Elrick, Ronnie Gubertini (d).* 4–10/36.

*****(*) Benny Carter 1937–1939**

Classics 552 *Carter; Jack Bulterman, Sam Dasberg, Rolf Goldstein, Tommy McQuater, Lincoln Mills, Joe Thomas, Leslie Thompson, George Van Helvoirt, George Woodlen, Cliff Woodridge (t); Jimmy Archey, Lew Davis, George Chisholm, Vic Dickenson, Bill Mulraney, Harry Van Oven, Marcel Thielemans (tb); Tyree Glenn (tb, vib); Freddy Gardner, Andy McDevitt,*

Andre Van der Ouderaa, Wim Poppink, Jimmy Williams (cl, as); Fletcher Allen, Carl Frye, James Powell, Louis Stephenson (as); Alix Combelle, Sal Doof, George Evans, Buddy Featherstonehaugh, Coleman Hawkins, Bertie King, Castor McCord, Ernie Powell, Jimmy Williams (ts); Eddie Heywood Jr, Freddy Johnson, Eddie Macaulay, Nich De Roy, York De Souza (p); Albert Harris, Ulysses Livingston, Django Reinhardt, Ray Webb (g); Len Harrison, Alvis Hayes, Wally Morris, Jack Pet (b); Al Craig, Kees Kranenburg, Robert Montmarche, Henry Morrison (d). 1/37–6/39.

*****(*) The Various Facets Of A Genius**

Black & Blue BLE 59.230 *Carter; Henry 'Red' Allen, Bill Coleman, Shad Collins, Sam Dasberg, Bill Dillard, Harry James, Max Kaminsky, Joe Smith, Russell Smith, Otis Johnson, Lincoln Mills, Irving Randolph, Sidney De Paris, Leonard Davis, Bobby Stark, Joe Thomas, Cliff Woodridge, Rolf Goldstein, George Woodlen (t); Jimmy Archey, George Chisholm, Vic Dickenson, Harry Van Oven, Jimmy Harrison, Benny Morton, Keg Johnson, Floyd O'Brien, Claude Jones, Gene Simon, Dicky Wells, Wilbur De Paris, George Washington, Sandy Williams, Milton Robinson (tb); Tyree Glenn (tb, vib); Wayman Carver, Howard Johnson, Don Redman (cl, as); André Ekyan, George Dorsey, Jimmy Powell, Carl Frye, Dave Matthews, Ben Smith, Russell Procope, Louis Stephenson (as); Chu Berry, Alix Combelle, Herschel Evans, Coleman Hawkins, Bertie King, Ernie Powell, Jimmy Williams, Ted McCord, Babe Russin, Stafford Simon, Sammy Davis, Ben Webster (ts); Stéphane Grappelli, Horace Henderson, Eddie Heywood, Freddy Johnson, Billy Kyle, Luis Russell, Sonny White, Teddy Wilson (p); Fats Waller (p, cel); Lionel Hampton (vib); Clarence Holiday, Ray Webb, Ulysses Livingston, Lawrence Lucie, Django Reinhardt (g); Benny Jackson, Dave Wilborn (bj); John Kirby (tba, b); Hayes Alvis, Len Harrison, Eugene D'Hellemes, Ernest Hill, Elmer James, Billy Taylor (b); Tommy Benford, Big Sid Catlett, Cozy Cole, Walter Johnson, Kaiser Marshall, Mezz Mezzrow, Robert Montmarche, Keg Purnell (d); Nan Wynn (v).* 11/29–5/40.

****** Benny Carter 1940–1941**

Classics 631 *Carter; Emmett Berry, Doc Cheatham, Bill Coleman, Roy Eldridge, Jonah Jones, Lincoln Mills, Sidney De Paris, Rostelle Reese, Russell Smith, Nathaniel Williams (t); Jimmy Archey, Joe Britton, Vic Dickenson, John McConnell, Benny Morton, Milton Robinson, Madison Vaughan (tb); Eddie Barefield, George Dorsey, Chauncey Haughton, Ernie Purce, Bill White (as); George James (as, bs); Georgie Auld, Alfred Gibson, Coleman Hawkins, George Irish, Fred Mitchell, Ernie Powell, Stafford Simon, Fred Williams (ts); Sonny White (p); Bernard Addison, Everett Barksdale, William Lewis, Ulysses Livingston, Herb Thomas (g); Hayes Alvis, Charles Drayton, John Kirby, Wilson Myers, Ted Sturgis (b); Big Sid Catlett, J.C Heard, Yank Porter, Keg Purnell, Berisford Shepherd, Al Taylor (d); Roy Felton, Maxine Sullivan, Joe Turner, The Mills Brothers (v).* 5/40–10/41.

By 1930, Carter was being widely recognized as a gifted young arranger and multi-instrumentalist. Carter's charts, like his playing, are characteristically open-textured and softly bouncing, but seldom lightweight; though he had a particular feel for the saxophone section, as is often noted, and he pioneered a more modern approach to big-band reeds, his gifts extend throughout the orchestra. As a soloist, he developed in a direction rather different from that of Johnny Hodges, who explored a darker register and a less buoyant sensibility. Carter's earliest recordings with the Chocolate Dandies (the band included Coleman Hawkins) and with McKinney's Cotton Pickers put considerable emphasis on his multi-instrumentalism. Set against trombonist Quentin Jackson's surprisingly effective vocals, he sounds poised and elegant – the essential Carter qualities – whatever his horn; and two takes each of 'Do You Believe In Love At First Sight' and 'Wrap Your Troubles In Dreams' demonstrate how beautifully crafted and custom-made his choruses habitually were.

None of these performances is included on the Classics format which is, on the face of it, rather surprising, since the first two sets include sides Carter recorded with Spike Hughes's Negro Orchestra. In the early 1930s Carter's band had been increasingly identified as a proving ground for young talent, and the number of subsequently eminent names appearing in Carter sections increases as the decade advances. In 1936 the urbane young American took up a post as staff arranger for the BBC Dance Orchestra, then under Henry Hall. The London period saw some excellent recording with the local talent, including 'Swingin' At Maida Vale', and there are two separate Vocalion sessions with Elisabeth Welch, the first yielding the classic 'When Lights Are Low', the later and better superb arrangements of 'Poor Butterfly' and 'The Man I Love'.

Later sets with Kai Ewans's orchestra and a variety of European bands are less striking, perhaps because after five well-filled discs Carter's particular mastery does, unjustifiably, begin to pall. There is little tension in a Carter solo, which is presented bright and fresh like a polished apple, and his seemingly effortless approach is rather hard to square with a new construction of jazz improvisation which came in with bebop. However, these sides and those following on in the early 1940s are significant because, for much of the next 25 years, Carter concentrated on lucrative film music and small groups.

The personnels to the Black and Blue compilation may have a rather redundant, usual-suspects air, but this is actually a very valuable anthology of material that would suit anyone who didn't want a completist shelf-load of Carter. Nothing, oddly, from 1936, but there is a Coleman Hawkins Jam Band session from Paris in the following year, with the Hot Club stars present, and dates under Hamp's and Teddy Wilson's leadership, recorded the following year. A track each from the Cotton Pickers and Carter's Chocolate Dandies, one from Spike Hughes's Negro Orchestra, and so on, right through to the Gentlemen of Jazz package in 1940. Good value for money.

***** When Lights Are Low**

Conifer/Happy Days CDHD 131 *Carter; Max Goldberg, Tommy McQuater, Duncan Whyte (t); Leslie Thompson (t, tb); Lew Davis, Ted Heath, Bill Mulraney (tb); Freddie Gardner, Andy McDevitt (cl, as); E.O Pogson (as); Buddy Featherstonehaugh (ts); Pat Dodd, Billy Munn, Gene Rodgers (p); George Elliott, Albert Harris, Ivor Mairants (g); Al Burke, Wally Morris (b); George Elrick, Ronnie Gubertini (d).* 4–10/36.

A useful abstract of the London sessions Carter made for Vocalion. Conifer have even managed to unearth one track – a rejected take of 'Gin And Jive' – not covered by Classics' completism. Oddly, though, they skip two better tracks, 'Scandal In A Flat' and 'Accent On Swing', from the same session. Carter returned to 'Gin

And Jive' in January 1937 and cut a vastly superior version with essentially the same band. Swings and roundabouts again, but the Conifer reissue will appeal to anyone who has a particular interest in the development of hot music in Britain in the 1930s.

***(*) Benny Carter, 1943–1946

Classics 923 *Carter; Felix Barboza, John Carroll, Paul Cohen, Claude Dunson, Emmett Berry, Lewis Botton, Neal Hefti, Idrees Sulieman, Karl George, Louis Gray, Wallace Jones, William Johnson, Joe Newman, Shorty Rogers, Irving Lewis, Fred Trainer, Talib Dawud, Edwin Davis, Milton Fletcher, Jake Porter, Ted Buckner, Loyal Walker, Freddy Webster, Gerald Wilson (t); Alton Moore, J.J Johnson, Charlie Johnson, Al Grey, John Morris, Henry Coker, Shorty Haughton, Bart Varsalona, George Washington, Dicky Wells, Andy Williams, Trummy Young (tb); Joe Epps, Jewell Grant, Porter Kilbert, Russell Procope (as); Willard Brown (as, bs); Tony Scott (as, cl); Don Byas, Harold Clark, Dexter Gordon, Eugene Porter, Bumps Myers, Flip Phillips (ts); Humphrey Bannon, Rufus Webster, Sonny White, Gerald Wiggins (p); James Cannady, Al Casey, W.J Edwards, Freddie Green, Ulysses Livingston, Herman Mitchell (g); Charles Drayton, Thomas Moultrie, Curley Russell, John Simmons (b); Oscar Bradley, Percy Brice, J.C Heard, Max Roach (d); Savannah Churchill, Dick Gracy, Bixie Harris, Timmie Rogers, Maxine Sullivan (v).* 10/43–1/46.

A good vintage for the Carter orchestra, as witness all the stars in the making buried away in its ranks. The session of 21 May 1944 marked the recording debut of eighteen-year-old Max Roach, but it is also special for a superb Carter alto solo on 'I Can't Get Started', switching to trumpet for 'I Surrender Dear'. A couple of 1945 dates are under the nominal leadership of singers Savannah Churchill and Timmie Rogers, but they are very much in the line of Carter's own style of the time, and the vocals are not much more than a pleasant distraction. In 1945, Carter moved to California but he continued to work and record on the East Coast. A session for Capitol in December yielded 'Prelude To A Kiss' and 'Just You, Just Me', again on alto and trumpet respectively, with some strong soloing from the underrated Bumps Myers. Neal Hefti joined as arranger, with no sign that he made a significant difference to the way the band sounded, and the early 1946 material for De Luxe is a refinement of what Carter had been doing for a decade and more, with just a tiny acknowledgement here and there that bebop was happening. The disc closes with a couple of tracks featuring Maxine Sullivan, still in very good voice. The transfers are patchy throughout the disc, and some listeners may prefer to pick up the better material in other forms.

*** Groovin' High In LA, 1946

Hep CD 15 *Carter; Miles Davis, Fred Trainer (?), Calvin Strickland (?), Walter Williams (?), Ira Pettiford (?) (t); Al Grey, Charlie Johnson, Johnny Morris, Candy Ross (tb); Willard Brown, Joe Epps (as); Harold Clark, Bumps Myers (ts); Bob Graettinger (bs); Sonny White (g); James Cannady, Thomas Moultrie (b); Percy Brice (d).* 7/46.

Carter returned to the United States in 1938, by which time the big-band era was well under way. His sterling talents seem to have appealed more to other musicians than to the public at large and, as the war progressed, he switched coasts. *Metronome* concluded around this time that Carter's bands died so slowly that *rigor mortis* had no chance to set in. From the point of view of the dance floor, he offered little enough, but his arrangements have more than survived transfer to unforgiving CD, and there is some astonishing musicianship. Miles Davis appears on the Hep compilation of Armed Forces Radio Service Jubilee transcriptions, a disc shared with the West Coast bands of Wilbert Branco, Gerald Wilson and Jimmy Mundy. Perhaps of greater historical than musical interest, these capture a very specific moment in jazz, the final flowering of the big swing bands before economic constraints began to bite and before bop took over the running.

**** 3, 4, 5: The Verve Small Group Sessions

Verve 849395 *Carter; Don Abney, Oscar Peterson, Teddy Wilson (p); Herb Ellis (g); Ray Brown, George Duvivier (b); Louie Bellson, Jo Jones, Bobby White (d).*

***(*) Cosmopolite: The Oscar Peterson Sessions

Verve 521673 *Carter; Bill Harris (tb); Oscar Peterson (p); Herb Ellis, Barney Kessel (g); Ray Brown (b); J.C Heard, Buddy Rich, Bobby White (d).* 9/52–11/54.

Irritatingly, no exact dates are provided for the sterling *3, 4, 5* sessions for Norman Granz's label. The trio sides with Teddy Wilson and Jo Jones are seeing the light of day only after 40 years in the vaults; mysteriously, because a similar session with Art Tatum and Louie Bellson *was* released. Far from wondering at the absence of a bass player (and Wilson wasn't one of the big left-hand men), one might almost wish that the under-recorded Jones had been left out altogether, so bright is the interplay between alto and piano. Wilson is supreme on 'June In January' and the Parker/Sanicola/Sinatra 'This Love Of Mine', a perfect vehicle for Carter's sinuous para-bop phrasing. An 'audio disclaimer' pointing out 22 seconds of 'slight wow and warbling' on 'Moonglow' has to be considered somewhat diversionary, for the music on the middle quartet section really isn't up to the rest of the album. Originally released as *Moonglow: Love Songs By Benny Carter And His Orchestra (sic)*, the material is a bit lame, however beautifully played. The final three tracks, also unreleased, come from a super-session with rising star Oscar Peterson. Again, the drummer – added for the date – makes very little mark on the music, which includes the intriguing 'Don't You Think', written by Stuff Smith. Despite some reservations about the middle tracks, this makes a superb introduction to Carter the player (there's not a single writing credit) at a fine stage in his distinguished career.

Cosmopolite brings together material from the LPs *Benny Carter Plays Pretty, Alto Saxes* and *New Jazz Sounds*, as well as the one whose title has been recycled. They are by no means as compelling as the earlier reissue, but there are, inevitably, some precious moments, as on 'The Song Is You' with trombonist Harris, Ellis, Brown and Rich, a lovely, centred performance with not a hint of strain. Together these records cover an important period and association in Carter's career. Only the first is obviously essential, but Carter fans will be satisfied only with both.

***(*) New Jazz Sounds: The Urbane Sessions

Verve 531637 2CD *Carter; Roy Eldridge (t, flhn); Bill Harris (tb); Bruce McDonald, Oscar Peterson (p); Herb Ellis, Barney Kessel (g); Ray Brown, John Simmons (b); Buddy Rich, Alvin Stoller (d); horns; strings.* 52–55.

This double set complements the material on 3, 4, 5 and *Cosmopolite* and rounds out Carter's work for Norgran. The first disc is heavily padded with alternative takes and may contain material that is surplus to all but specialist requirements. The strings also cloy a little, recorded with the fulsome presence they always had on Granz's labels. The real delight is the disc of small-group sessions. The ballad medley on 'I Remember You', 'Chelsea Bridge' and 'I've Got The World On A String' is classic Carter, executed with a gracious ease that doesn't exclude emotion. Perhaps ironically, the really startling tracks do not include Carter at all but consist of a sequence of trumpet and drum duets featuring Eldridge (ever the experimenter) and drummer Alvin Stoller. Eldridge is also double-tracked on piano on his own 'Wailing'. Roy always tinkered with the fringes of the acceptable and was to be an important bridge to the modernist movement. To that degree he is very different philosophically from the more traditionalist Carter, but when they come together on the 1955 material that yielded *The Urbane Jazz of Roy Eldridge And Benny Carter* they sound completely of a mind. On 'Just One Of Those Things' and 'The Marriage Blues' with Dizzy, Bill Harris and Oscar Peterson, another voice takes over, playful, slightly eccentric, a foil to the smoother, more accommodating Carter. The second disc is rounded out with an alternative of Alfred Newman's 'Street Scene', a quintet with Peterson, Kessel, Brown and Heard, noisily recovered from a disc, but riveting all the same. This is very much a bin-end set, but it contains enough good music for most tastes.

****** Jazz Giant**

Original Jazz Classics OJC 167 *Carter; Frank Rosolino (tb); Ben Webster (ts); André Previn, Jimmy Rowles (p); Barney Kessel (g); Leroy Vinnegar (b); Shelly Manne (d).* 6/57–4/58.

***** Swingin' The Twenties**

Original Jazz Classics OJC 339 *Carter; Earl Hines (p); Leroy Vinnegar (b); Shelly Manne (d).* 11/58.

Carter's trumpet playing was still sounding remarkably adept at this stage; it tailed off a bit in later years, though he was still able to maintain what is always thought of as the most difficult instrumental 'double' right into the 1990s. The material on *Swingin'* is generally pretty bland, though 'A Monday Date' and 'Laugh, Clown, Laugh' uncover some interesting harmonic wrinkles. The rhythm section was one of the best money could buy at the time, nicely balancing old and new. *Jazz Giant* is one of Carter's best small-group records, full of imagination and invention, and the interchanges with Webster are classic. Originally released on Contemporary, it's very much in line with that label's philosophy of easy swing. The CD of *Swingin'* includes some interesting alternative takes.

****** Further Definitions**

Impulse! 051229-2 *Carter; Bud Shank, Phil Woods (as); Buddy Collette, Teddy Edwards, Coleman Hawkins, Bill Perkins, Charlie Rouse (ts); Bill Hood (bs); John Collins, Barney Kessel, Mundell Lowe (g); Dick Katz (p); Ray Brown, Jimmy Garrison (b); Jo Jones, Alvin Stoller (d).* 11/61–3/66.

This is the best-known of all Carter's albums, now filled out with material recorded five years after the original sessions, with another mid-size band. Economics may have enjoined this type of ensemble, but Carter's feel for reed voicing is such that loss is turned to gain. The added profit is a spacious but intimate sound. Carter and Hawkins had recorded together in Paris before the war in exactly the same configuration as these sides: four saxophones, piano, bass, drums and guitar (a part that was taken by Django Reinhardt first time around). Johnny Collins isn't quite up to that standard, but he has a sure, subtle touch which is both effective and unobtrusive. All the saxophones solo on 'Cotton Tail', with Benny leading off and Bean bringing things to a magisterial, slyly witty close. 'Crazy Rhythm' is an echo of the first meeting and both the senior men quote from each other's past solo, a nice touch of self-reference. 'Blue Star' is intriguing: a complex, deceptive theme with another effective saxophone interchange.

The later session came after a two-year hiatus in Carter's jazz activities, during which he had concentrated almost entirely on film and television work; the only jazz session he had played in the interim had not been released. The intention was obviously to reduplicate the sound and the success of *Further Definitions*. To a degree, it's a success. Mundell Lowe and Barney Kessel are in a different league from Collins, and the guitar part has a prominence far beyond the earlier date. Shank and Edwards are both in strong, individual form, and Bill Perkins is splendidly Hawksian on a remake of 'Doozy'. This material was originally released as *Additions To Further Definitions*, one of the lamest album-titles ever, and one which belies a crisp, more contemporary-sounding recording. Having them together now is a huge plus. The 20-bit transfers are impeccable and, at more than 70 minutes, it's a good-value purchase.

*****(*) The King**

Pablo 2310768 *Carter; Milt Jackson (vib); Joe Pass (g); Tommy Flanagan (p); John B Williams (b); Jake Hanna (d).* 2/76.

Jackson was another brilliant improviser whose mellifluous approach has led detractors to suspect him of giving short weight. Here again, he underlines his genius with a dozen blues choruses of immense sophistication. The closing D-flat blues opens up the kind of harmonic territory on which Carter and Flanagan both thrive, and the set ends with a ringing affirmation. Williams is rather anonymous and Pass seems to miscue slightly on a couple of faster ensembles. Otherwise hard to fault.

***** Carter Gillespie Inc**

Original Jazz Classics OJC 682 *Carter; Dizzy Gillespie (t); Joe Pass (g); Tommy Flanagan (p); Al McKibbon (b); Mickey Roker (d).* 4/76.

*****(*) Wonderland**

Pablo 2310922 *Carter; Harry 'Sweets' Edison (t); Eddie 'Lockjaw' Davis (ts); Ray Bryant (p); Milt Hinton (b); Grady Tate (d).* 11/76.

Remarkable to think that as long ago as 1976 Carter was approaching his seventieth birthday. There's a slightly ponderous, aldermanic quality to the AGM with Diz, much polite deference, some cheerful banter but not a great deal of classic music. He sounds in better form on the relaxed *Wonderland*, ably accompanied by Edison (Carter let others handle the brass duties by this stage) and an uncharacteristically cool Lockjaw Davis. 'Misty' was to remain a favourite, played with curious emphases and a wry unsentimentality.

***** BBB & Co**

Original Jazz Classics OJC 758 *Carter; Shorty Sherock (t); Ben Webster (ts); Barney Bigard (cl); Jimmy Rowles (p); Dave Barbour, Leroy Vinnegar (b); Mel Lewis (d).*

A mainstream supergroup with lots of miles on the clock and not a terrific amount to say for itself. The combination of Carter, Webster and Bigard may sound inviting, but it turns into a dry and unforthcoming jam during which everyone defers to everyone else and the fires don't start until the later choruses of 'When The Sun Goes Down Blues'. Carter plays well within himself, elegant as ever but almost diffident in his approach to solos. Interesting for the personnel, but not a wonderful record.

*****(*) Montreux '77**

Original Jazz Classics OJC 374 *Carter; Ray Bryant (p); Niels-Henning Orsted Pedersen (b); Jimmie Smith (d).* 7/77.

*****(*) Live And Well In Japan**

Original Jazz Classics OJC 736 *Carter; Cat Anderson, Joe Newman (t); Britt Woodman (tb); Budd Johnson (ts); Cecil Payne (bs); Nat Pierce (p); Mundell Lowe (g); George Duvivier (b); Harold Jones (d).* 77.

1977 was a monster year at Montreux, and a good deal of the music performed over the main weekend has been preserved on live Pablo releases (and subsequently on OJC). The Carter set is one of the best of them. Though his soloing here doesn't quite match up to some choruses on a Count Basie jam from the following day, 'Three Little Words', 'Body And Soul' and 'On Green Dolphin Street' are absolutely sterling. The band swings comfortably and NHOP plays delightful counter-melodies on 'In A Mellow Tone'.

Turning seventy, Carter seemed eager to dismiss biblical estimates of an average lifespan by playing like a man half his age. In an all-star line-up in Japan (a country he has come to love and where he is treated like a minor deity) he trades superbly crafted licks with all and sundry. The sound is rather cavernous but there's great atmosphere, and the playing makes up for all other deficiencies.

***** Summer Serenade**

Storyville STCD 4047 *Carter; Kenny Drew (p); Jesper Lundgaard (b); Ed Thigpen (d); Richard Boone (v).* 8/80.

Carter's small-group encounters, like this Scandinavian session, were a well-polished act; but it takes a certain genius to make the umpteenth version of quite banal tunes like 'Back Home In Indiana' and 'When Lights Are Low' sound quite as freshly minted as Carter does here. The rhythm section is admirably professional and Boone holds his wheesht for all but one track, which is all to the good.

****(*) The Best Of Benny Carter**

Pablo PACD 2405 *Carter; Cat Anderson, Harry 'Sweets' Edison, Joe Newman (t); Britt Woodman (tb); Eddie 'Lockjaw' Davis, Budd Johnson (ts); Cecil Payne (bs); Ray Bryant (p); Mundell Lowe (g); George Duvivier, Milt Hinton, Niels-Henning Orsted Pedersen (b); Harold Jones, Jimmie Smith, Grady Tate (d).*

Odd and uninspired choice of material. Better to stick to the original Pablos.

***** Skyline Drive And Towards**

Phontastic PHONTCD 9305 *Carter; Jan Allan (t); Arne Domnérus (as); Plas Johnson (ts); Jerome Richardson (ts, ss); Putte Wickman (cl); Bengt Hallberg (p); Rune Gustafsson (g); Georg Riedel (b); Magnus Persson (d); other personnel.* 29–39, 82.

This is essentially a Swedamerican All Stars record with eight early tracks pasted on to make up a reasonably proportioned CD. The 1982 material is smoothly professional and as good as Carter is solo to solo. The archive stuff, which includes 'I'd Love It' by McKinney's Cotton Pickers and 'I'm In The Mood For Swing' under Hamp's leadership, may prove useful for anyone who hasn't already got some early Carter. Others may feel that this isn't distributed quite right and decide to pass.

*****(*) A Gentleman And His Music**

Concord CCD 4285 *Carter; Joe Wilder (t, flhn); Scott Hamilton (ts); Ed Bickert (g); Gene Harris (p); John Clayton Jr (b); Jimmie Smith (d).* 8/85.

A wonderfully urbane set which puts Carter in the company of the young traditionalist, Scott Hamilton, whose tone and relaxed inventiveness are perfectly in keeping with Carter's own. No real surprises; just a generously proportioned album of first-rate jazz music, professionally performed and recorded.

***** Meets Oscar Peterson**

Pablo 2310926 *Carter; Oscar Peterson (p); Joe Pass (g); Dave Young (b); Martin Drew (d). 86*

How much more interesting this might have been as a duo. Even allowing for some melodic breaks from Pass, the rhythm backings are bland and undynamic enough to seem superfluous. 'Baubles, Bangles And Beads' moves at the gentle lope both men seem to prefer nowadays, and Peterson's statement of the theme is about as straightforward as he's ever been.

*****(*) In The Mood For Swing**

Musicmasters 65001-2 *Carter; Dizzy Gillespie (t); Sir Roland Hanna (p); Howard Alden (g); George Mraz (b); Louie Bellson (d).* 11/87.

A pally but still communicative set of gently paced tunes, designed to let the four main soloists – Carter, Gillespie, Alden and Hanna – stretch out at their leisure. There's nothing self-indulgent about it. Carter's as crisp as ever, though Diz goes a bit OTT on 'South Side Samba'. Good, warm sound.

***** My Kind Of Trouble**

Pablo 2310935 *Carter; Art Hillery (p); Joe Pass (g); Andy Simpkins (b); Ronnie Bedford (d).* 88.

Disappointing only because the band is. The rhythms never quite cohere and on 'Berkeley Bounce' and 'Gee, Baby, Ain't I Good To You', Carter appears to be leading the count rather than playing on top of it. Nevertheless, he is in finer voice than seems decent for a man entering his eighties and well past his fiftieth year of climbing on and off bandstands.

***** Cooking At Carlos I**

Musicmasters 65033-2 *Carter; Richard Wyands (p); Lisle Atkinson (b); Al Harewood (d).* 10/88.

Record-shop staff are well used to punters coming in with queries along the lines of: 'I really liked *Live/Blues/Round Midnight/Whatever At Carlos I*. Can you tell me if volume two is out yet?' Carlos 1 was actually a much-loved New York City jazz club, one of the few beacons of the music during the '80s. Lest *Cookin'* suggests something like boiling intensity, it might be more accurate to characterize Carter's visit as a slow simmer. His playing on 'All The Things You Are' and 'Key Largo' is almost statesmanly, and the excellent rhythm-section pay him considerable respect throughout, relaxing the tempo, almost always easing back on the throttle after Wyands, bursting with ideas as always, has taken a solo spot. Carter gets out his trumpet for the final 'Time For The Blues'.

*** My Man Benny, My Man Phil

Musicmasters 65036-2 *Carter; Phil Woods (as, cl); Chris Neville (p); George Mraz (b); Kenny Washington (d).* 11/89.

Not quite the mutual admiration society that the two title-pieces might suggest. Carter's lyric tribute has to be heard to be believed, though: 'Adolphe Sax / Before he made that horn / Knew some day, somewhere, / A Phil Woods would be born', and so on. Musically, there's some great stuff. Carter dusts off his trumpet again, Woods his woefully underexposed clarinet, for 'We Were In Love', and Carter sticks with brass for his own 'People Time'. Two takes of 'Just A Mood' give a sense of how *happy* a session this obviously was.

***(*) All That Jazz – Live At Princeton

Musicmasters 65059-2 *Carter; Clark Terry (t, flhn, v); Kenny Barron (p); Rufus Reid (b); Kenny Washington (d); Billy Hill (v).* 11/90.

Carter first played at Princeton University in 1928, as a member of the Fletcher Henderson Orchestra. In the late 1970s, he became a visiting professor and was awarded an honorary doctorate. This 1990 concert was treated as a triumphant homecoming. Thelonious Monk's 'Hackensack' was played cold, after Clark Terry hummed the melody to Carter as they walked onstage. The band get in behind and off they all go. 'I'm Beginning To See The Light' and 'Misty' were more familiar themes to the saxophonist, but he gives the Garner/Burke tune a curious off-balance feel that is unexpectedly witty. 'Now's The Time' is renowned as a Parker tune, though the theme is known to be much older. Carter delves down into its roots and comes up with something that seems to unite swing and bop approaches. Terry growls round him like a friendly dog pretending to be tough. Most Carter enthusiasts would have willingly dispensed with the services of Billy Hill, who comes on for the last four tunes. The title-track has some vocals from the two horn men, but the charm is strictly limited.

***(*) Harlem Renaissance

Musicmasters 65080-2 2CD *Carter; John Eckert, Richard Grant, Virgil Jones, Michael Mossman (t); Eddie Bert, Curtis Hasselbring, Benny Powell, Dennis Wilson (tb); Frank Wess, Ralph Bowen (as, f); Loren Schoenberg, Jeff Rupert (ts); Danny Bank (bs, f); Chris Neville (p); Remo Palmier (g); Lisle Atkinson (b); Kenny Washington (d); Rutgers University Orchestra.* 2/92.

Picture-in-the-attic time now, surely? Carter's level of energy is, for a man in his ninth decade, quite astonishing. This double-CD is a recording of a major concert he gave at the invitation of the Rutgers Institute of Jazz Studies. To celebrate the 85th birthday, Carter was commissioned to write a new piece. Suggesting a combination of jazz big-band and chamber orchestra, he actually set about *two* pieces with the twin themes of Japan and Harlem.

The 'Tales Of The Rising Sun Suite' is conventionally pictorial and slightly wan in colour, with a few interesting shapes breaking through on 'Samurai Song' and 'Chow Chow', the last two pieces. The 'Harlem Renaissance Suite' is more interesting. Harking back to the burgeoning black culture of the 1920s, it takes up the challenge of Paul Whiteman's long-discredited 'symphonic jazz' (James P. Johnson worked in a similar vein) and the Carnegie Hall concerts of James Reece Europe's celebrated band. To his credit, Carter has done something more than simply drape a few solos over coathanger themes. The suite has a good deal of inner consistency. What it probably lacks is the bustle and frenetic activity one associates with the period he is celebrating. Here, undoubtedly, the orchestra hold him back a bit, defeating even his peerless arranging skills. Though the strings and woodwinds are integrated into the main fabric of the piece (rather than serving merely as a backdrop, as in most 'with strings' projects), the execution is rather lifeless. Carter himself solos with a good deal of pep, and most fans will prefer the first disc, which has him in front of the big band, grazing down a menu of attractive originals (his own 'Vine Street Rumble', 'Sao Paolo' and the beautiful 'Evening Star', which prompts the most coherent solo of the disc), with a couple of standards thrown in for good measure. A set of two halves, as the football commentators say.

***(*) Elegy In Blue

Musicmasters 65115 *Carter; Harry 'Sweets' Edison (t); Cedar Walton (p); Mundell Lowe (g); Ray Brown (b); Jeff Hamilton (d).* 5/94.

This is a man who has been making fine music for a biblical lifespan, here still playing gloriously lyrical jazz. On this record, he's keeping the sort of company that almost guarantees quality. There was still a fiery dynamism to Sweets' trumpeting, and the rhythm section is not inclined to defer to age and let things slip. Hamilton has a deceptively easy but insistent swing, and Lowe is a very underrated musician who has spent large periods of time away from jazz proper but who always comes back fired up with ideas. BC remains the focus, though, quoting Hodges on 'Good Queen Bess' and 'Prelude To A Kiss', sounding dogged and unflustered on 'Blue Monk' and touchingly unsentimental on the closing title-piece. A beautiful record that would grace any jazz collection.

Betty Carter (1930–98)

VOCALS

Known as 'Betty Bebop' when she sang with Lionel Hampton in the '40s, Carter broke off from performing to raise a family, but on her return in 1969 became the most demanding and virtuosic of jazz singers. Her touring groups were little academies for young players, like a miniature Jazz Messengers, and until her unexpected death she maintained a ferocious appetite for performing both in clubs and on bigger stages.

***** Meet Betty Carter And Ray Bryant**

Columbia COL 485099 *Carter; Conte Candoli, Joe Ferrante, Bernie Glow, Nick Travis (t); Jimmy Cleveland, Urbie Green (tb); Danny Bank, Al Cohn, Sam Markowitz, Seldon Powell (reeds); Jerome Richardson (f); Ray Bryant, Hank Jones (p); Milt Hinton, Wendell Marshall (b); Osie Johnson, Philly Joe Jones (d); Gigi Gryce (cond).* 5 & 6/55, 4/56.

***** Finally**

Roulette Jazz 53332 *Carter; Norman Simmons (p); Lisle Atkinson (b); Al Harewood (d).* 12/69.

Billie Holiday once said that she didn't feel like she was singin', she felt like she was playin' a horn. So, too, with Betty Carter, who transcended the 'bop vocalist' tag and created a style that combined the fluent, improvisational grace of an alto saxophone with an uncanny accuracy of diction. Even when her weighting of a lyric is almost surreal, its significance is utterly explicit and often sarcastically subversive. The latter quality has allowed her to skate on the thin ice of quite banal standard material, much of which has acquired a veneer of 'seriousness' from nowadays being heard only as instrumentals; 'Body And Soul' is the obvious example, medleyed with 'Heart And Soul' on the 1969 live album, taped at New York's Judson Hall.

The Columbia makes available again the record that brought Carter to the attention of the jazz public. It's included here, along with half-a-dozen trio tracks by Bryant and four on which Carter fronts a big band conducted and arranged by Gigi Gryce, and on which she still sounds very much like an orthodox band-singer. Most of the material has been available before on the Carter compilation, *Social Call*, but it hasn't been seen for some time and, as far as we are aware, this is its first appearance on CD. Some of the pieces on *Finally* are left deliberately raw. 'Girl Talk' talk is wild, but what is she thinking about as she sings 'The Sun Died' or 'You're A Sweetheart'? With Carter the charge of emotion isn't always obvious and often requires a certain shift of perspective in the listener. What these sides consistently demonstrate – and this was to remain a stock-in-trade – is the ability to take and reshape a song so radically that it becomes something quite new, a 180° reorientation of something familiar which retains only a few subtle reminders of its original. A process similar, in other words, to the contrafacts on standard material made by the bebop pioneers, but with the added complication of words which also overturn expectations of what female jazz singers might be concerned about or required to say.

♛ ** The Audience With Betty Carter**

Verve 835684 2CD *Carter; John Hicks (p); Curtis Lundy (b); Kenny Washington (d).* 79.

Carter could sound becalmed in a studio. Because she needs a crowd to bounce off just as much as she needs rhythmically and harmonically subtle accompanists (and she recruits only the best), the title of *The Audience With Betty Carter* is a multiple pun. She works the room with consummate skill, sliding from the slightly squeaky *faux-naïf* mannerisms that prompted Lionel Hampton to call her 'Betty Bebop' (a less condescending and more accurate nickname than she liked to acknowledge) to soaring climbs up off the bottom that wouldn't disgrace Sarah Vaughan. It's a long album and one that requires a bit of time spent with it. The opening piece 'Sounds (Movin' On)' is a staggering 25 minutes in length. 'The Trolley Song' is an orthodox swinger, but who else would have thought of handling Carlos Garnett's 'Caribbean Sun' in this way, and who else is capable of giving 'Everything I Have Is Yours' a drench of irony? The pace changes on disc two, and the first instinct might be that Carter has run out of steam. Emphatically not so. 'Can't We Talk It Over' medleyed with 'Either It's Love Or It Isn't' and later 'Spring Can Really Hang You Up The Most' are remarkable (re)inventions, subtle and deeply coded. Eyebrows were raised when we awarded *The Audience* a crown (when Billie Holiday doesn't have one, it was often pointed out); sample it and hear why.

***** I'm Yours, You're Mine**

Verve 533182 *Carter; Andre Hayward (tb); Mark Shim (ts); Xavier Davis (p); Matt Hughes, Curtis Lundy (b); Gregory Hutchinson (d).* 96.

For all her eminence, Carter was commercially unsuccessful as a recording artist, even in jazz terms: most of her Verve albums have lately disappeared from print, which is a tacit hint that, for all her greatness as a performer, she only rarely managed to translate that to a studio situation. Officially a Verve/Bet-Car co-release, *I'm Yours, You're Mine* is frankly a disappointment. But for the title-track and a long performance of 'September Song', and but for another first-rate band, this would be ignorable. Carter's ability to invest a song with multiple meanings has for some reason been set aside. The springy rhythm has turned staccato and the humour seems strained. Lundy and Hutchinson perform brilliantly, and there is genuine pleasure in hearing Carter negotiate her course through the accompaniment, but there's not much on *I'm Yours* for the enthusiast.

James Carter (born 1969)

ALTO SAXOPHONE, TENOR SAXOPHONE, BARITONE SAXOPHONE, BASS CLARINET

From Detroit, Carter has made a great impact with his name records for DIW and Atlantic, blending traditionalism and a near-avant-garde sensibility with self-conscious but charismatic assertion.

*****(*) JC On The Set**

Columbia 476983-2 *Carter; Craig Taborn (p); Jaribu Shahid (b); Tani Tabbal (d).* 4/93.

***** Jurassic Classics**

Columbia 478612-2 *As above.* 94.

When you arrive on the scene wearing messianic initials, much is expected; not miracles perhaps, but certainly something special. Carter emerged from a faintly preposterous ensemble known as the Tough Young Tenors, the only one of the bunch who sounded anything like as tough and streetwise as he looked. The basic sound was hard-edged and earthy, but with some of the deconstructive trappings of the avant-garde, and Carter was said to have a practice room at home stuffed full of old horns, the better to explore the untouched registers of his voice. He had worked with the ever under-remarked Frank Lowe, and that was probably as close as anyone was going to get to find a valid comparison. Certainly a very different player from Josh Redman, whose skills were being loudly bruited at the same time.

Carter sounds like a Detroit player through and through: metallic, brisk, and not above a quiver of sentiment. The debut album delivered in trumps. Not least, it delved into unexpected corners of the repertoire: Sun Ra's 'Hour Of Parting', the somewhat obscure Texan John Hardee's 'Lunatic', alongside Duke's 'Caravan' and 'Sophisticated Lady'. And Carter demonstrated that he had things of his own to say, whether down in baritone range or squealing and testifying as he did on the original 'Blues For A Nomadic Princess'. Choosing a Don Byas tune, 'Worried And Blue', pointed to a more than fashionable interest in classic jazz and its forgotten warriors. The phrasing is immaculate, the tone youthfully wayward here and there but still authentic.

Jurassic Classics probably came too soon, certainly too soon on top of what had been a tough and busy year. Suddenly the burnish wasn't quite bright enough to blot out some of the weaknesses: a tendency to barge through a tune, shake it painfully by the hand in a mistaken outflow of respect, fail to do it justice. The second album put him ever more clearly in touch with the jazz mainstream, but it found him flailing a bit, not so much out of his depth, but with an inelegant stroke.

**** The Real Quietstorm

Atlantic 782742 *As above, except add Dave Holland (b); Leon Parker (d).* 10–11/94.

Signing for Atlantic was a positive move. It seemed to impose a certain corporate discipline and 'house style', death to the spirit for some artists but salutary for someone like Carter, who seemed to be going in umpteen directions at once. To some extent, it's a showcase, a chance to try out paces on six different horns, including bass flute on the extraordinary 'Ballad For A Doll', which also features Holland. But it's also an album that demonstrates that Carter is not just a flash multi-instrumentalist but a musician who chooses his persona carefully. The tenor monologue, 'The Stevedore's Serenade', is still one of the most startling saxophone performances of the 1990s, and though the title is dismal, 'Intimacy Of My Woman's Beautiful Eyes' is alto playing that invites comparison with Dolphy's on 'Tenderly'. It's the two baritone duets, with Taborn on 'Round Midnight' and Shahid on 'Eventide', that stand out, and it may be that in years to come Carter will settle on alto and baritone, similarly pitched if not equally weighted, as his two main instruments.

**** Conversin' With The Elders

Atlantic 7567 82908 *As above, except omit Holland and Parker; add Lester Bowie, Harry 'Sweets' Edison (t); Larry (as); Buddy Tate (ts); Hamiet Bluiett (bs).* 10/95–2/96.

An inspired idea: to throw Carter up against the very ancestral voices that haunt and propel him. Both guests and material come from out of a past not always so very distant, but certainly very different from the scene the young man inherited. Carter's loyalty to Shahid, Tabal and Taborn is exemplary, and they form a unified background for the guest spots.

The most venerable, chronologically speaking, are Edison and Tate, and 'Lester Leaps In' and 'Centrepiece' with Sweets and 'Moten Swing' and 'Blue Creek', the latter with Buddy on clarinet, are convincingly, supremely authentic. The paired altos on 'Parker's Mood' almost cancel each other out, so rigorously do they observe the master's cadence, and Smith – heard, as all the guests are, through the left channel – doesn't seem to want to bust loose. The set kicks off, wonderfully but rather deceptively, with Bowie's 'Freereggaehibop', on which his entire armoury of rips, snorts, smears, and impossibly low-register vocalizations are used. Appropriately, he comes back to round off the album with 'Atitled Valse', but by then the honours have already been secured by Bluiett and by two fantastic baritone duets, on Coltrane's 'Naima' and, more boldly, on Anthony Braxton's 'Composition 40Q', one of the more approachable themes in the Braxton canon, but still a startling piece to cover.

Carter is playing with dazzling confidence and restrained power. His early tendency to overblow and over-emphasize the attack has now given way to a breathy, almost intimate sound which can be scaled up or down in keeping with the material.

***(*) In Carterian Fashion

Atlantic 83082-2 *Carter; Dwight Adams (t); Cassius Richmond (as); Henry Butler, Cyrus Chestnut, Craig Taborn (org); Kevin Carter (g); Steve Kirby, Jaribu Shahid (b); Alvester Garnett, Leonard King, Tani Tabbal (d).* 98.

Carter faces up to the end of his twenties with a swirling, raucous album, centred on the blues and marked by a choppy, rhythmically agitated organ sound. Oddly, despite featuring three such different players as Taborn, Chestnut and Butler on the Hammond, the sound is rather uniform. The young saxophonist is still conversing with elder spirits, including two arrangements of traditional material, 'Down To The River' and 'Trouble In The World', the latter emerging out of free-form chaos and into one of the most orderly and plain-spoken things on any of the records. 'Skull Grabbin'' is restless and fractured, an uneasy piece that sounds too much like a grab for shock value. Carter's bass clarinet work on 'Odyssey' weaves an illuminating counterpoint with trumpet and alto over a softer than usual Hammond track. 'Frisco Follies' is the somewhat token workout on the other horns, baritone and soprano. Increasingly, though, Carter sounds like a genuine tenor man. The tribute to Lockjaw Davis builds an idiosyncratic solo round two almost subliminal Jaws licks. Yves Beauvais's production is crisp and deliberately unresonant, leaving the horns floating in free space.

John Carter (1928–91)

CLARINET, ALTO AND TENOR SAXOPHONES, FLUTE

Born in Fort Worth, where he played with Ornette Coleman in the '40s, he moved west in 1961 and formed a regular partnership with Bobby Bradford four years later. A dedicated teacher, he brought his own studies of clarinet and Afro-American lore together in a rich and detailed jazz which was very much his own.

*** Tandem 1

Emanem 4011 *Carter; Bobby Bradford (c).* 4/82.

*** Tandem 2

Emanem 4012 *As above.* 4/82.

In 1964, Carter founded the New Art Jazz Ensemble with Bobby Bradford, one of a number of quietly influential groups that give the lie to received notions about 'West Coast' jazz. *Seeking* is credited to the Ensemble, the group's debut on disc, and, if it precedes the best work the two men were to do in the studio, the extraordinary *Secrets*, made for Revelation in 1971 and 1972, it is still a powerful record (alas, both discs are currently unavailable). On *Secrets*, Carter and Bradford anticipated what is arguably the most radical phase of their career, technically speaking, by playing the first section as an unaccompanied duo for clarinet and cornet. 'Circle', the track in question, resurfaces as a live performance on the first volume of *Tandem*, and it underlines as well as anything how close and intuitive the two men's working relationship was. Carter is often the normalizing element, bringing the music back to a more logical and discursive position, tempering Bradford's fieriness and then blowing the whole thing open himself. The tandem principle applies throughout, though. Once one man is in motion, the other is bound to follow.

It should be said that the sound on these recordings is pretty deplorable. The April 1982 concert from Worcester, Massachusetts, which is heard in order on Volume One with the final couple of numbers carried over to the sequel, is marred by print-through, a disconcerting pre-echo (the trick is to store music tape tail-out) and also traffic noise, while the remaining pieces, recorded three years earlier in Los Angeles, were on cassette. 'Tandem' kicks off both sessions, a warm-up piece with enough unselfconscious showmanship to win round the flintiest sceptic. There are solos on both discs: Bradford's forcefully romantic 'Woman' on *Tandem 2* and 'Portrait Of JBG' on the first disc, Carter's 'Angles' (Emanem 4011), two versions of 'Echoes From Rudolph's' (one on each) and the startling 'Les Masses Jigaboo' on the second volume, which anticipates his ambitious Afro-suite of coming years. All credit to Martin Davidson for deciding that this music was significant enough to overturn doubts about its technical quality.

***** Dauwhe**

Black Saint 120057 *Carter; Bobby Bradford (c); Charles Owens (ss, cl, ob); James Newton (f); Red Callender (tba); Roberto Miguel Miranda (b); William Jeffrey (d); Luis Peralta (perc).* 2 & 3/82.

****** Castles Of Ghana**

Gramavision 8603 *Carter; Bobby Bradford (c); Baikida Carroll (t, v); Benny Powell (tb); Marty Ehrlich (bcl, perc); Terry Jenoure (vn, v); Richard Davis (b); Andrew Cyrille (d).* 11/85.

In the decade before his death, Carter worked at a multi-part sequence of suites called *Roots And Folklore: Episodes In The Development Of American Folk Music*. Unfortunately, not all the episodes have remained in print, but two have: *Dauwhe*, which traces the African origins, and *Castles Of Ghana*, which finds African culture held in suspension before its forcible exportation (the castles in question were, effectively, trans-shipment pens for slaves). Other sections included *Dance Of The Love Ghosts* (also with an African setting) and *Fields* and *Shadows On A Wall*, which dramatized the black experience in America, north and south. Of the surviving pair, *Dauwhe* is strongly articulate and is marked out by some excellent playing, from Newton in particular; but *Castles* is by far the most profound: deeply felt, stressed music of great richness, performed by a masterfully constructed group. Carter's unaccompanied 'Capture' is one of his strongest clarinet statements, but the sense of loss and the comradeship that imbues 'Conversations' and the profound melancholy and spirituality of 'Evening Prayer' lift this music into the top ranks of modern American music. Whether it can still be described as jazz is almost a redundant issue.

Kent Carter (born 1939)

DOUBLE BASS

The multi-talented Carter, who also plays violin, cello and keyboards, was born in New Hampshire and has often seemed to gravitate to quieter locations; nevertheless he was part of the free revolution in jazz, worked with Paul Bley, Steve Lacy and the Jazz Composers Orchestra. His strong sense of rhythm is matched by an interest in abstraction.

***** The Juillaguet Collection**

Emanem 4033 *Carter; Albrecht Maurer (vn).* 8/96.

There may be some curious musical destiny in names to explain why the Parkers have so taken to the saxophone and why there are so many Carters in jazz, including one other master of the bass. These days, Kent lives somewhat out of the way, in a tiny village in the south of France where he and his partner run a music, arts and dance studio (MAD). This quiet and thoughtful string collaboration was recorded there. Maurer is the bassist's junior by two decades, but their musical understanding is complete and the ten full-length performances and final fragment are each and all worthy of prolonged attention. This is a record that needs some time and application, but it unmistakably comes from within a modern jazz sensibility.

Regina Carter

VIOLIN

Previously spotted with String Trio of New York, Carter has made major-label debuts at both Atlantic and Verve.

***** Rhythms Of The Heart**

Verve 547177-2 *Carter; Kenny Barron, Werner Gerig (p); Rodney Jones, Romero Lubambo (g); Richard Bona (g, b, perc, v); Peter Washington (b); Lewis Nash (d); (v); Mayra Casales (perc).* 11 & 12/98.

Some jazz fiddlers never forget getting laughed at on the way home from music lessons and spend a whole career acting out all those fantasies about whipping open the case and producing a Thompson – or these days an Uzi – rather than a Strad. Carter is refreshingly *un*embarrassed about carrying her violin on the block. Her idol is Stuff Smith, unmistakably so on the evidence of the opening 'Lady Be Good'. Like Smith, she cocks a snook at the instrument's canonical status while demonstrating an enviable technical facility.

A natural swinger, she tackles Tadd Dameron's 'Our Delight' with the exuberance of a whole horn section. The only shortcoming in this debut recording is a rather flat and unexpressive approach to ballads. 'Spring Can Really Hang You Up The Most' is way too downbeat and Carter's phrasing goes out of idiom. Verve's habit of propping up new talent with star names works well here, but it also underlines a hint of inexperience. Cassandra

Wilson and guitarist Rodney Jones hijack 'Papa Was A Rolling Stone'; an inspired choice of material but perversely handed over to the guests. Kenny Barron checks in with two originals and stamps his authority over 'Spring ...' as well. The descending four-note figure that repeats throughout 'Cook's Bay' is made for the string instrument, but it is Barron's own statement that commands attention. Similarly, Richard Bona dominates his own 'Mandingo Street'. It might have been preferable to offer Carter a bit of tough love and let her grow up a bit more exposed. She is capable of much more than what's on show here.

Ron Carter (born 1937)

DOUBLE BASS, CELLO, PICCOLO BASS

Joined Chico Hamilton in 1962, then with Miles Davis, 1963–8. Recognized since as a musicians' musician, and in demand as sessionman and teacher, although his own records have often been mixed successes: flirtations with jazz-rock, chamber-music forms and more conventional straight-ahead playing have yielded little in the way of a masterpiece.

***** Where?**

Original Jazz Classics OJC 432 *Carter; Eric Dolphy (as, bcl, f); Mal Waldron (p); George Duvivier (b); Charli Persip (d).* 6/61.

Doubts that a young black boy could possibly play convincing cello led to the pre-teen Carter switching to bass, and launching a remarkable career. Perhaps only Ray Brown has recorded more on the instrument, but whereas Brown's solo career was rather late in starting, Carter has such innate musicality that he has always been able to sustain progress as a leader in his own right. With *Where?* he is unfortunate in that the record will always be seen as an item in the Eric Dolphy discography, rather than Carter's own. It's dominated by a brilliant bass/clarinet duo of the sort Dolphy created many times with Charles Mingus, and by a fine, unsentimental reading of 'Softly, As In A Morning Sunrise'. Carter plays cello on 'Really' and 'Saucer Eyes' as he had on Dolphy's second album, *Out There*, also originally released on New Jazz. Waldron and (on the two cello tracks) Duvivier give firm support, and Persip once again displays the skills that should have guaranteed him a higher rating than he currently receives in histories of the music.

**** Pastels**

Original Jazz Classics OJCCD 665 *Carter; Kenny Barron (p); Hugh McCracken (g, hca); Harvey Mason (d); strings.* 10/76.

There is nothing inherently wrong with wanting to play with strings, but in this case Carter has done no more than take a competent and uninspired jazz record and pour syrup over it. If the basic tracks were more uplifting, this would scarcely matter, but they're not and the arrangements do nothing to help.

***** Peg Leg**

Original Jazz Classics OJCCD 621 *Carter; Jerry Dodgion, Walter Kane, George Marge (reeds); Jay Berliner (g); Kenny Barron (p); Buster Williams (b); Ben Riley (d).* 11/77.

With almost all of Carter's Blue Note work unavailable in the West, it is quite hard to identify his best recordings on CD. *Peg Leg* is very good indeed, with a first-rate version of Monk's 'Epistrophy', featuring the light, fast sound of his piccolo bass. There remain some doubts about the sound, which even on CD is floaty and indistinct in character. The band is interesting rather than involving or strong-voiced. Dodgion is in good form and has some strong ideas to air, but he never quite gets on top of challenging themes and arrangements, and too often seems to go for obvious ideas and quirky sound, rather than a well-constructed statement.

****** Third Plane**

Original Jazz Classics OJCCD 754 *Carter; Herbie Hancock (p); Tony Williams (d).* 78.

A killer band, and easily Carter's most impressive showing under his own name. There is a good deal of solo bass material, as one would expect, but all of it makes sense in context and is so well constructed and executed that it never palls. Commercial pressures being what they were, it wasn't easy for players of Hancock's and Williams's generation to make an acoustic piano record in 1978. Williams doesn't quite get the point and he thrashes about at inopportune moments, but Carter's big gloopy fills on 'Stella By Starlight' and Hancock's 'Dolphin Dance' are absolutely perfect for the job.

***** Uptown Conversation**

Embryo/Rhino 7567 81955 *Carter; Hubert Laws (f); Herbie Hancock (p); Sam Brown (g); Billy Cobham, Grady Tate (d).* 10/69.

A rather odd record, alternating cheesy jazz funk with some brilliant solo bass interludes (indexed but not listed or titled). Laws seems more in place here, and on the long 'Half A Row' and 'Little Waltz' the components of Carter's curiously stretched sound-world start to make sense at last. Produced by Herbie Mann, which may explain why the flute sound is so good, the record has a bright, spacious quality that one didn't often get from Carter. The reissue has been filled out with alternative takes which add little or nothing to the original release.

***** New York Slick**

Original Jazz Classics OJC 916 *Carter; Art Farmer (flhn); J.J Johnson (tb); Hubert Laws (f); Kenny Barron (p); Jay Berliner (g); Billy Cobham (d); Ralph McDonald (perc).* 12/79.

***** Patrao**

Original Jazz Classics OJCCD 778 *Carter; Chet Baker (t); Amaury Tristao (g); Aloisio Aguiar, Kenny Barron (p); Jack DeJohnette, Edison Machado (d); Nana Vasconcelos (perc).* 5/80.

Smooth, sweet, but not cloying, and not really all that 'slick', either: the 1979 session doesn't exactly have the constituents breaking sweat, but the pleasure of having such a line-up is something that Carter clearly delighted in, and if the results are still on the predictable side it's a handsome effort.

Three tracks featuring just Baker, Carter, Kenny Barron and Jack DeJohnette stand out head and shoulders from the rest on the slightly wet and uninspired *Patrao.* None of the *norteamericanos* (Barron here and there excepted) sounds at ease with the basic idiom and a good deal of the scene-setting is discursive and flat. The trumpeter was playing well around this time, whatever else was going on in his life, and he turns in a couple of beautifully weighted and crafted solos. Barron is rock steady and never less than convincing, but he has been mixed very oddly, with what sounds like a lot of compression, which isn't the case with the other musicians.

***** Heart And Soul**
Timeless SJP 158 *Carter; Cedar Walton (p).* 12/81.

Like Barron, Cedar Walton is a fine composer/pianist who understands how to impart swing to quite complex rhythmic ideas. This is a delightfully intimate session that doesn't seem quite right for public consumption, almost as if it has been eavesdropped. Walton's long melodic lines allow Carter to play with greater freedom than usual and there are many moments when the two men seem equally inspired by the other's presence, generating ideas at a remarkable rate.

***** Live At Village West**
Concord CCD 4245 *Carter; Jim Hall (g).* 11/82.

****** Telephone**
Concord CCD 4270 *As above.* 8/84.

Carter's bass is unmistakably a string instrument. He made that clear on his fruitful collaboration with the Kronos Quartet, and he does again on these two fine duos with guitarist Hall. The sound on the live disc leaves something to be desired, but there are excellent performances of 'All The Things You Are', 'Embraceable You', 'Bags' Groove', 'Baubles, Bangles And Beads' and Sonny Rollins's calypso, 'St Thomas'. *Telephone* is a delicious record: a pristine mix, entirely in keeping with pristine performances. No surprise to learn that the key track is that old duo standard, 'Alone Together'.

Carter has lately made a couple of sets for Somethin' Else, the Japanese imprint which has Blue Note distribution in the USA, but these have been available only fitfully and are unlikely to be easy to find.

Dick Cary (1916–94)

PIANO, TRUMPET

Worked in New York from the early '40s, including stints with Louis Armstrong's All Stars, Jimmy Dorsey, Eddie Condon and Bobby Hackett. Moved to Los Angeles in 1959 and freelanced, with much involvement in rehearsal and with big bands for which he had a vast book of arrangements.

***** Dick Cary And His Tuesday Night Friends**
Arbors ARCD *Cary; Dick Forrest, Betty O'Hara, Bob Summers (t); Dick Hamilton, Barrett O'Hara, Ernie Tack (tb); Lee Callett, Fred Cooper, Terry Harrington, Abe Most, Tommy Newsom (reeds); Dave Koonse (g); Herb Mickman (b); Gene Estes, Jerry McKenzie (d).* 5–8/93.

A charming discovery. Dick Cary is best remembered as a Condonite and member of Armstrong's All Stars, but he wrote a vast number of arrangements for numerous bands, and his house in Sunland, California, was in his final years a favourite haunt of this rehearsal band. Some of their informal sessions are set down here. There are 14 of Cary's arrangements – dedicated to friends, dogs and streets, they're a wryly ingenious lot, not so much quirky as full of unexpected turns, shafts of light, unexpected chords. The band is full of professionals who obviously loved the music and, though every one is a first take and not meant for posterity, there are very few fluffs or wrong steps. This sound is home-made too, but that doesn't stop the beauty of 'Bud', 'Henry' or 'Vallen's Waltz' coming through. Think of a very gentle West Coast outfit spirited from the '50s to the '90s and you're some of the way there.

Marc Cary (born 1967)

PIANO

Post-bop pianist with plenty of sideman and these leadership dates to his name.

***** Cary One**
Enja ENJ 9023 *Cary; Roy Hargrove (t); Ron Blake (ts); Yarborough Charles Laws (f); Dwayne Burno (b); Dion Parson (d); Charlene Fitzpatrick (v).* 1/94.

*****(*) Listen**
Arabesque AJ0125 *As above, except omit Hargrove, Burno and Fitzpatrick; add Terell Stafford (t), Billy Johnson (b), Daniel Moreno (perc).* 8/96.

The debut disc was impressively grounded in jazz history, with Sonny Clark's 'Melody In C' picked out of the ashpit, and a couple of strong originals that linked Cary back to his own Native-American ancestry and his own lineage in the music; it turns out that his grandfather was a cousin of Cootie Williams, which puts him in the jazz aristocracy, if only by collateral descent. The second album is even more obviously bred in the bone. Stafford is a more secure presence than Hargrove, and Laws has a key role in an unfolding suite that culminates in a trio of deeply personal originals, 'Leaving Home', 'New Blues' and 'Mr Lucky', a sequence which back in LP days would have amounted to most of an album. That's perhaps the only quibble here. The best is very good indeed, but both records have too much filler.

Casa Loma Orchestra

GROUP

Formed by saxophonist Glen Gray, they played in New York from 1929 and recorded extensively in 1931–7. Gray fronted the band from 1940 and, although touring ceased around 1950, he continued to lead versions of the group on record.

****(*) Casa Loma Stomp**
Hep 1010 *Bobby Jones, Dub Shoffner, Joe Hostetter, Frankie Martinez (t); Pee Wee Hunt (tb, v); Billy Rauch (tb); Glen Gray (as); Pat Davis (as, ts); Les Arquette (cl, ts); Ray Eberle (as, cl); Howard Hall (p); Mel Jenssen (vn); Gene Gifford (g, bj); Stanley Dennis (b, tba); Tony Briglia (d); Jack Richmond (v).* 10/29–12/30.

***** Maniac's Ball**
Hep 1051 *As above, except add Grady Watts, Sonny Dunham, Frank Zullo (t), Fritz Hummel (tb), Art Ralston (as, ob, bsn),*

Clarence Hutchenrider (cl, as), Kenny Sargent (as, v), Jack Blanchette (g); omit Martinez, Arquette. 3/31–2/37.

Glen Gray led this band, originally formed from a group called the Orange Blossoms, and they have a rather odd place in the music's history. The early records sound like no more than competent dance-band fare, although something peculiar happens halfway through a very stodgy 'Happy Days Are Here Again' (the third title on disc one) when it suddenly bursts into a hot performance fired up by Hunt's trombone. Most of the tracks on *Casa Loma Stomp* are pretty uneventful, but there are some exceptions: 'San Sue Strut' seems to be twice as fast as anything else here, and the signature-title tune is at least a fair display of early white swing. But it's the second disc, *Maniac's Ball*, which has all the famous Casa Loma music: Gene Gifford's charts for 'White Jazz', 'Black Jazz' and 'Maniac's Ball' design the orchestra as a precision-driven locomotive, riffs piling one over another, the tempos mercurial yet uncomfortably stiff. If it was Gifford's idea of jazz, it seemed an awkward transition between old-style hot music, the functional dance bands and the swing orchestras that were about to emerge. Aside from Hunt, a genuine personality, the soloists lacked much individuality and the reed players seem especially unremarkable. There's something exhilarating about their assault on 'Put On Your Old Grey Bonnet', but by the time of their second version of 'Royal Garden Blues' the band sounds anonymous. Larry Clinton took over from Gifford and his 'A Study In Brown' is the farewell track here: it led nowhere. Scholars should welcome these Hep compilations, handsomely prepared and mastered, but the story is not a fascinating one.

Geoff Castle (born 1949)

KEYBOARDS

Experienced British midstream-modernist, drifting between fusion and post-bop settings.

****(*) Expanded**

Turret Records FORT 1 *Castle; Gerard Presencer (t, flhn); Steve Waterman (t); Mark Nightingale (tb); Paul Cantel (as, ss); Tim Garland (ts, ss); Brendan Power (hca); Teena Lyle (vib, perc); Rufus Philpot (b); Steve Taylor (d).* 94.

Pub jazz of an engaging and undemanding sort from a player who's been around long enough to know this sort of thing won't wash for long on CD. Castle features himself on all but two of the ten tracks; he also produces and engineers and must be suspected of having lost perspective on things. There are, inevitably, good solo spots from Presencer, Nightingale, Garland and, more unexpectedly, from Power, but as a whole *Expanded* is just that, a series of small ideas pumped full of air.

Castle Jazz Band

GROUP

West Coast revivalists of long standing, the original band dating back to the early 1950s, later line-ups under the direction of Ernie Carson.

**** The Famous Castle Jazz Band**

Good Time Jazz GTCD 10030-2 *Don Kinch (t); George Bruns (tb); Bob Gilbert (cl); Freddie Crews (p); Monte Ballou (bj, v); Bob Short (tba); Homer Welch (d).* 8/57.

**** Plays The Five Pennies**

Good Time Jazz GTCD 10037-2 *As above.*

Stragglers from the Lu Watters-inspired revival of the 1940s, these traditionalists re-formed for the purposes of these dates. It might have appeased their original fans, but the music sounds like second-hand revivalism today, and the players perform with a rather gauche humour in their delivery. There is one rarity on the first album in 'I've Been Floating Down The Old Green River', but everything else has been done better elsewhere, both before and since. Covering the Five Pennies, the Red Nichols band which by then was covering itself anyway, was a singularly unpromising idea.

Philip Catherine (born 1942)

GUITAR, ELECTRIC GUITAR, GUITAR SYNTHESIZER

Catherine is of mixed English/Belgian parentage. His first guitar influence, apart from the unavoidable Django Reinhardt, was the brilliant Belgian René Thomas (who died prematurely in 1975), but he was quick to respond to the jazz-rock techniques of both John McLaughlin and Larry Coryell. He has a limpid but by no means languid style, still with strong tinges of Django's easy swing.

***** Transparence**

Inak 8701 *Catherine; Michael Herr (ky); Diederik Wissels (p); Hein Van Der Geyn (b); Aldo Romano (d).* 11/86.

***** September Sky**

September 5106 *As above, except omit Herr and Wissels.* 9/88.

'René Thomas' repays an early debt, and *Transparence* (originally released as Timeless SJP 242) is an album of often moving *hommages*. 'Father Christmas' is dedicated to Charles Mingus and 'Galeries St Hubert' to the ghost of Django Reinhardt; there is also an unexpected tribute to the British multi-instrumentalist, Victor Feldman, which opens up another putative line of descent for the guitarist. *September Sky* is an album of (mainly) standards; but what is immediately obvious in both these backward-looking sets is how confidently in possession of his own voice and interpretative skill Catherine now is. On the earlier album, 'L'Eternel Désir' may bear a more than striking thematic resemblance to Ralph Towner's 'Silence Of A Candle', but it is far more deeply suffused with the blues than Towner has ever been, and far more dramatically modulated. Of the standards, 'Body And Soul', 'Stella By Starlight' and 'All Blues' stand out.

*****(*) I Remember You**

Criss Cross Criss 1048 *Catherine; Tom Harrell (flhn); Hein Van Der Geyn (b).* 10/90.

*****(*) Moods: Volume 1**

Criss Cross Criss 1060 *As above, except add Michael Herr (ky).* 5/92.

***** Moods: Volume 2**

Criss Cross Criss 1061 *As for Volume 1.* 5/92.

Recorded as a tribute to the late Chet Baker, *I Remember You* reunites the line-up that made *Chet's Choice* for Criss Cross in 1985, with Tom Harrell's floating melancholic flugelhorn steering dangerously close to Baker's weary, self-denying diction. Harrell contributes two fine originals – the softly swinging 'From This Time, From That Time' and 'Songflower' – Van Der Geyn one and Catherine two. The opening 'Nardis' serves as an unintended farewell to Miles. Hank Mobley's 'Funk In Deep Freeze' and the closing 'Blues For G.T.' are slightly unexpected in this context but, drummerless, take on the same slightly enervated quality that is raised only by Catherine's astonishingly accurate rhythm guitar. 'My Funny Valentine'? Well, yes, of course; they could hardly have got away without it. Harrell's statement and subsequent solo are pretty much in the Baker vein, and again it's the guitarist who lifts the performance a notch, using his pedals imaginatively. A beautiful album.

Attractive as they are in many regards, one wonders whether the *Moods* sessions really yielded enough for two full-length discs. As the title doubtless unconsciously hints, there is a just a crickle of suspicion that Catherine is drifting towards an elegantly jazzy mood-music. The three interesting tracks on *Volume 2*, significantly, are the Tom Harrell compositions whose rather deprecating titles, 'The Waltz' and 'Twenty Bar Tune', disguise a considerable expenditure of imaginative effort.

***** Art Of The Duo**

Enja ENJ 8016 *Catherine; Niels-Henning Orsted Pedersen (b).* 2/91.

Class meets class. Two players of quietly understated brilliance, recorded in a Swiss jazz club. Therein lies the problem. The whole session is so gracefully undemonstrative and unassertive that it is difficult to sustain the appropriate level of attention throughout a substantial set. Appropriate, because these are both improvisers who get right inside a tune, not just the chord structure but also the melody, and courteously reinvent it. 'All The Things You Are', 'My Foolish Heart' and 'Stella By Starlight' are each subjected to subtly complex variations, none of which sound predetermined but seem utterly spontaneous and, if not vivid, never less than intelligent. For refined tastes only.

***** Live**

Dreyfus 36587 *Catherine; Bert Van Den Brink (p, ky); Hein Van de Geyn (b); Hans Van Oosterhoud (d).* 3/96.

A long and delightfully uncomplicated set from the guitarist and his Dutch quartet, *Live* almost feels like a career summation, with superb versions of 'René Thomas', 'Mingus In The Sky', Hermeto Pascoal's 'Nem Um Talvez', Miles's blues, 'Freddie Freeloader', and 'Stella By Starlight'. Catherine's guitar-sound has changed very little over the years, but outside the studio it inevitably has a more spiny and percussive quality, and it suits him very well. His solos are immaculately shaped and always expressive. Our own reservation concerns the group. Van de Geyn is a hugely gifted player and brings very much the qualities Catherine found in NHOP. The other three, though, sound slightly plodding in comparison.

***** Guitar Groove**

Dreyfus 36599 *Catherine; Alphonso Johnson (b); Rodney Holmes (d).* 99.

This is an unusually straightahead trio for Catherine, and it's mostly very convincing. Apart from 'Stardust', all the compositions are by Catherine, some of them evident reworkings of past themes and ideas, many of them written in a deliberately upbeat (that is, both upbeat and deliberate) style. 'Merci Afrique' and 'Guitar Groove' itself will be a revelation to anyone who thinks they have Catherine taped (that is, stereotyped) as a dreamy impressionist. Holmes and Johnson offer solid if unspectacular support, but the light falls squarely on the guitarist throughout.

Sid Catlett (1910–51)

DRUMS

Born in Evansville, Indiana, Catlett became a great New York drummer. He worked with Henderson, Goodman, Redman and Armstrong, and eventually joined Armstrong's All Stars in 1947. He took bebop rhythm in his stride. Much loved by other musicians, he became ill at the end of the '40s and died after collapsing at a concert in Chicago.

*****(*) Sid Catlett 1944–1946**

Classics 974 *Catlett; Charlie Shavers, Joe Guy, Gerald Wilson (t); Barney Bigard, Edmond Hall (cl); Bull Moose Jackson, Willie Smith (as); Eddie 'Lockjaw' Davis, Illinois Jacquet, Frank Socolow, Ben Webster (ts); Art Tatum, Marlowe Morris, Eddie Heywood, Horace Henderson, Pete Johnson (p); Bill Gooden (org); Al Casey, Jimmy Shirley (g); Oscar Pettiford, John Simmons, Gene Ramey (b).* 1/44–46.

Catlett's reputation has increased in recent years with the re-evaluation of many of the swing-era giants, and he will be remembered as one of the great jazz drummers. Dead of a heart attack at 41, his legacy is comparatively small, but he was a complete master of drums and cymbals whose virtuoso technique was unflashy and skilful. He seldom drew attention to himself yet played with fabulous panache and dominated his groups without seeming to overwhelm them. This hotchpotch of small-band dates – for V-Disc, Commodore, Session, Delta, Regis, Capitol and Manor – is fascinating. Most of them were under his nominal leadership. The opening 'Rose Room' is from a V-Disc jam session and is virtually a duet with Barney Bigard, an extraordinary display that brings out the best in each man. Six quartet tracks with Ben Webster and Marlowe Morris are similarly electric, and five more with horns including Shavers, Hall and Socolow, though indifferently recorded, include some splendid moments. The next five sessions are a mixed lot and have rather less interest, but for its first half the CD is close to indispensable. Catlett's mercurial style, with cymbal playing that glistens even through the unsatisfactory recording, unexpected rimshot fusillades and the most detailed snare rhythms, was one of the few swing-based methods that didn't sound passé in the bebop era.

André Ceccarelli

DRUMS

French drummer in a post-bop mould, a regular member of the Dee Dee Bridgewater group.

***** From The Heart**

Verve 529851 *Ceccarelli; Denis Leloup (tb); Sylvain Beuf (ts, ss); Bernard Arcadio, Jean Michel Pilc (p); Thomas Bramerie, Remy Vignolo (b); Louis-César Ewande (djembe); Dee Dee Bridgewater, Oumou Kouyate, Margan Diabate (v).* 9/95.

Remarkable how many French sidemen who, after years spent making themselves unobtrusively useful, pop up and turn in work of genuine originality. *From The Heart* is quietly but insistently idiosyncratic, fuelled by Ceccarelli's relaxed but insistent pulse and Jean Michel Pilc's engagingly dissonant single-note outbursts and raw comping, which sounds as though Bud Powell had come alive again and taken up citizenship papers.

Ceccarelli carries the beat mostly on the cymbals, with tom-toms and bass drum used almost exclusively for embellishment and accent; Kenny Clarke might be the obvious ancestor, and the Frenchman uses the same extra-long sticks with exactly the same precision and delicacy. Beuf is not widely known. He has a slightly rasping, plangent tone that some may not take to immediately, but it is spot-on for this music. The two add-on tracks are an Afro-tinged thing with djembe and vocals, and a song feature for Dee Dee Bridgewater, that underlines how good an accompanist Ceccarelli has been; they've worked together before and it's fascinating to hear how the relationship shifts when he's calling the shots.

Oscar 'Papa' Celestin (1884–1954)

CORNET, VOCAL

Celestin was in all the early major New Orleans bands, eventually leading the Tuxedo Brass Band in the 1910s. He led some of the few New Orleans recording dates in the '20s but more or less retired in the '30s, coming back to great success in the revival of the late '40s.

♛ ** Papa Celestin & Sam Morgan**

Azure AZ-CD-12 *Celestin; Kid Shots Madison, Ricard Alexis, George McCullum, Guy Kelly (c); Williams Ridgley, August Rousseau, William Matthews, Ernest Kelly (tb); Willard Thoumy, Paul Barnes, Earl Pierson, Sid Carriere, Clarence Hall, Oliver Alcorn (reeds); Manual Manetta, Jeanette Salvant (p); John Marrero, Narvin Kimball (bj); Simon Marrero (b, bb); Abby Foster, Joziah Frazier (d); Charles Gills, Ferdinand Joseph (v).* 1/25–12/28.

Little enough music was actually recorded in New Orleans in the 1920s to make any surviving tracks valuable. But the sessions led by Celestin and Morgan (the latter dealt with under his own entry) would be remarkable anyway. Despite the importing of devices from dance-band trends elsewhere, particularly in the later tracks, they really sound like no other jazz of the period. The first three tracks are by the Original Tuxedo Jazz Orchestra, with Madison and Celestin as the front line, and the deliriously exciting 'Original Tuxedo Rag' is a blazing fusion of ragtime, jazz and dance music that makes one ache to hear the band as it might have sounded live. The 13 subsequent titles from 1926–8 are less frantic and are occasionally troubled by the mannerisms of the day, weak vocals in particular. But the reed sections manage their curious blend of sentimentality and shrewd, hot playing – a New Orleans characteristic – with surprising finesse; the ensembles are consistently driving, and the two-cornet leads are frequently as subtle and well ordered as those of King Oliver's band. Celestin himself, a great veteran of the city's music even then, has been undervalued as a soloist: he plays very well on 'My Josephine' and the superb slow piece, 'It's Jam Up'. Taken together with the equally fine Sam Morgan tracks, we rate this as a five-star record, especially given the outstandingly clear and powerful remastering.

***** The 1950s Radio Broadcasts**

Arhoolie CD 7024 *Celestin; Bill Mathews (tb); Alphonse Picou (cl); Octave Crosby (p, v); Ricard Alexis (b, v); Christopher 'Black Happy' Goldston (d).* 7/50–6/51.

These are valuable reminders that Celestin continued to be a force in New Orleans jazz many years after the seminal tracks listed above. Although a car accident and spells of ill-health made his appearances erratic in the 1940s, Papa was leading this band regularly on radio in the early '50s, and these surviving airshots show how spirited and uplifting their take on the tradition was. The most surprising thing is how vigorous and hard-knuckled the rhythm section are, especially when one is used to the fairly genteel pulse adopted by most NO revivalists. Mathews is boisterous in the Ory tradition, Picou has some nice moments and Celestin himself obviously enjoys his Indian summer. The sound is boxy and flat, as one might expect from the source material, but collectors will know what to expect.

Andrea Centazzo

DRUMS AND PERCUSSION

An Italian drummer-percussionist heavily involved in the free-music scene of the '70s, documenting much music via his Ictus LP label.

***** Trio Live**

New Tone 5027-2 *Centazzo; Steve Lacy (ss); Kent Carter (b).* 12/76.

***** Drops**

New Tone 5037-2 *Centazzo; Derek Bailey (g).* 4/77.

***** Real Time**

New Tone 5029-2 *Centazzo; Evan Parker (ss, ts); Alvin Curran (p, t, syn).* 12/77.

***** Environment For Sextet**

New Tone 5026-2 *Centazzo; Toshinori Kondo (t); John Zorn (reeds); Tom Cora (clo); Polly Bradfield (vn); Eugene Chadbourne (g).* 11/78.

***** USA Concerts West**

New Tone 5028-2 *Centazzo; Vinny Golia (reeds); John Carter (cl); Greg Goodman (p).* 12/78–7/79.

***** The Bay**

New Tone 5037-2 *Centazzo; Bruce Ackley (ss, cl); Jon Raskin (as, cl); Andrew Voigt (ss, as, f); Larry Ochs (ts, as).* 12/78.

These reissues will be a nostalgic reminder for many collectors of the improvised music scene of the 1970s. Documented on tiny labels, it was a frail but hardy outcropping which survived in the smallest margin of the industry. Ictus was a label owned and run by percussionist Andrea Centazzo and he managed to get out a small string of releases in the late '70s which all feature him in various instrumental combinations. Centazzo himself has largely disappeared from recording, but these CDs resuscitate his original efforts. None of them is exactly outstanding from a purely musical point of view, but they're as relevant to their scene as any bunch of Blue Notes or Riversides. Centazzo persuaded many a leading light from the free-playing pantheon to perform with him, and the results chart an episodic adventure in the form. *Trio Live* is a decent Lacy gig from the period – three chunks of his favourite 'The Way', plus a particularly thorny treatment of 'Ducks' – at which Centazzo seems a bit of a bystander. *Drops* has him duelling with Bailey in his most snapping form, although the guitarist seems to go his own way for the most part. *Real Time* is a surprising triologue with Parker and Curran, in which the participants cover some scratchy sonic ground, analogue synthesizer, saxes and percussion in a sometimes exhilarating muddle. *Environment For Sextet* brings together six free spirits in another rather cloudy situation, emphasizing that the principal difficulty with most of these records is the poor fidelity: Centazzo seems to have favoured a very high top end and little bass, which gives his own drums a hissing, glassy quality and undercuts many of the textures. This is still a valuable if sometimes naïve glimpse of Zorn, Chadbourne and Co. in their early days, although – then as now – it's Kondo who sounds the most liberated and radical voice. *The Bay* performs a similar function for ROVA, whose other early discs have yet to make it to CD. Centazzo himself still sounds like a kibitzer on his own date, though.

Arguably the most interesting of the six discs is the one offering previously unreleased material, *USA Concerts*. The lengthy duet with Goodman is a disappointing mess, but the piece with Golia and Carter is wonderful: the clarinettist dominates a beautiful improvisation, including a long solo clarinet passage, and the three musicians find a genuine empathy. Centazzo himself does little on any of the discs to suggest that he was any kind of major voice: perhaps he is more of an Eddie Condon type, a great organizer but a comparatively insignificant contributor in purely instrumental terms.

Henri Chaix (born 1925)

PIANO

A leading member of the Swiss jazz movement in post-war years, Chaix is a dedicated mainstream pianist whose homegrown recordings have rarely reached a wider audience. He occasionally plays trombone.

***** Jumpin' Punkins**

Sackville SKCD2-2020 *Chaix; Alain Du Bois (b); Romano Cavicchiolo (d).* 10/90.

***** Jive At Five**

Sackville SKCD2-2035 *As above.* 8/93.

'A listener could close his eyes and never believe that this is a Swiss playing in Geneva' – thus did Rex Stewart commend Henri Chaix's playing in 1967. Chaix became Switzerland's mainstream leader in the 1940s, and he backed many American visitors. But his own circumstances have seldom taken him to international audiences. *Jumpin' Punkins* finds him in vigorous form, touching few intensities but taking a satisfyingly personal route through jazz-piano tradition. His favourite manner is a medium-tempo stride, a variation which is faithful to James P. Johnson's methods, and he makes 'Yesterdays' and 'All God's Chillun Got Rhythm' into believable stride vehicles. Yet his unassumingly romantic treatment of 'Ruby My Dear' suggests that more demanding jazz material holds few terrors for him. Du Bois and Cavicchiolo stay out of his way, and the recording pays handsome regard to the Bösendorfer piano.

Jive At Five is no more and no less than a second helping, three years on. The material is more mainstreamed than ever, and one could wish that Chaix would look around for one or two more interesting tunes. But this is his style and he's right at home in it.

Serge Chaloff (1923–57)

BARITONE SAXOPHONE

Worked with several big bands before an important spell with Woody Herman, 1947–9. Based himself in his home town of Boston in the '50s, but contracted spinal paralysis which eventually killed him. One of the few baritone men to make a go of bop, his few own-name records are marginalized classics.

*****(*) We The People Bop: Serge Chaloff Memorial**

Cool & Blue C&B CD 102 *Chaloff; Sonny Berman, Miles Davis, Gait Preddy, Red Rodney (t); Ernie Royal (t, v); Mert Goodspeed, Bennie Green, Bill Harris, Earl Swope (tb); Woody Herman (cl, v); Charlie Mariano (as); Al Cohn, Allen Eager, Flip Phillips, Sonny Stitt (ts); Al Haig, Ralph Burns, Barbara Carroll, Lou Levy, Bud Powell, George Wallington (p); Terry Gibbs (vib); Artie Bernstein, Chubby Jackson, Oscar Pettiford, Curley Russell, Frank Vaccaro, Chuck Wayne (b); Denzil Best, Tiny Khan, Don Lamond, Max Roach, Pete DeRosa (d).* 9/46–12/49.

*****(*) The Fable Of Mabel**

Black Lion BLCD 760923 *Chaloff; Capazutto, Herb Pomeroy (t); Gene DiStachio (tb); Charlie Mariano, Boots Mussulli (as); Varty Haritounian (ts); Russ Freeman, Dick Twardzik (p); Ray Oliver, Jimmy Woode (b); Buzzy Drootin, Jimmy Zitano (d).* 6–9/54.

****** Blue Serge**

Capitol 94505 *Chaloff; Sonny Clark (p); Leroy Vinnegar (b); Philly Joe Jones (d).* 3/56.

Hugely talented, but the career was riven by 'personal problems' and the end was dreadful. Chaloff's approach to the unwieldy baritone was restrained rather than virtuosic (the result of an extended apprenticeship with Jimmy Dorsey, Georgie Auld and Woody Herman) and concentrated on the distinctive timbre of the instrument rather than on outpacing all opposition. Nevertheless, he was an agile improviser who could suddenly transform a sleepy-sounding phrase with a single overblown note. Very little of Chaloff's work has ever been easy to find. *Boston Blow Up!* is still in limbo. Two takes of his famous 'Blue Serge' itself are included on the memorial record, which contains a good selection of Chaloff in the studio and on stage, over some of his most productive years. Some effort has been made to ferret out tracks that feature him strongly, such as 'Serge's Urge' with Red Rodney, and one comes away with a surprisingly clear sense of his stormy musical personality.

Recorded before the onset of a final decline which was interrupted only by the brilliance of *Blue Serge*, *The Fable Of Mabel* reflects the blocked intensity of his playing. A Chaloff solo, as on the three takes of 'The Fable Of Mabel', two of 'Eenie Meenie Minor Mode', always seems about to tear its own smooth fabric and erupt into something quite violent; 'Blue Serge' was, oddly, an exception. Harmonically and rhythmically subtle, they also seem to represent a triumph of self-control. The later All Stars sessions, from which these tracks come, are in every way superior to the quintet tracks recorded in June, which are rather bland. Though his phrasing is quite conventional, Mariano's alto sound is wild and penetrating and Dick Twardzik's crabby piano is perfect for the setting. With the exception of Pomeroy, the rest of the band are virtually unknown.

At last we can welcome back *Blue Serge* itself. Chaloff's masterpiece is both vigorous and moving, not for the knowledge that he was so near to his own death but for the unsentimental rigour of the playing. 'Thanks For The Memory' is overpoweringly beautiful as Chaloff creates a series of melodic variations which match the improviser's ideal of fashioning an entirely new song. 'Stairway To the Stars' is almost as fine, and the thoughtful 'The Goof And I' and 'Susie's Blues' show that Chaloff still had plenty of ideas about what could be done with a bebopper's basic materials. This classic session has retained all its power.

Joe Chambers (born 1942)

DRUMS, VIBRAPHONE

Studied and played in Washington, DC, in the early '60s, then moved to New York and played – and wrote – on a wide range of Blue Note and post-bop sessions. Though less often visible now, he's still occasionally sighted on record.

***(*) Phantom Of the City

Candid CCD 79517 *Chambers; Philip Harper (t); Bob Berg (ts); George Cables (p); Santi Debriano (b).* 3/91.

Joe Chambers has featured in post-bop jazz mostly as a drummer, but he is a gifted composer as well, and several of his earlier themes – particularly the four he wrote for Bobby Hutcherson's *Components* (Blue Note) – deserve to be better known than they are. He numbers Jimmy Giuffre as a crucial influence, and there's certainly a parallel between the thinking of both men regarding free and formal structures. That said, only two of the themes on this recent date are Chambers compositions: 'For Miles Davis', a serene yet vaguely ominous *in memoriam*, and the brighter 'Nuevo Mundo'. Chambers the drummer has become a thoughtful, interactive performer, seldom taking a driving-seat initiative and preferring a careful balancing of tonal weights and measures. He has a near-perfect band for his needs here: Berg's tenor is habitually analytical, Cables is a romantic with a terse streak of intelligence, and Harper's Berigan-like low notes and dryly spun lyricism – featured on an extended reading of 'You've Changed' – add further spice. The live recording, from New York's Birdland, is clear and full-bodied.

***(*) Mirrors

Blue Note 96685-2 *Chambers; Eddie Henderson (t); Vincent Herring (as, ts, ss); Mulgrew Miller (p); Ira Coleman (b).* 7/98.

Invited to do a one-off album for Blue Note's anniversary, this rather marginalized but intriguing figure came up with a project which seems to have its most obvious roots in his work with Bobby Hutcherson. Nowhere is this more evident than in 'Circles', which has him multi-tracking himself on drums and vibes to create a shimmering rhythmic and harmonic swirl that is the record's clear highlight. 'Tu-Way-Pock-E-Way' brings New Orleans to New York and 'Caravanserai' does the same thing for unspecified eastern modes. Henderson and Herring give the impression of being less well-travelled and here and there one could have wished for more worldly horn players, but this is a pleasing entry for Chambers the composer and leader. His drumming remains exemplary.

Paul Chambers (1935–1969)

BASS

Raised in Detroit, he began working as a prominent small-group sideman in 1954, and next year joined Miles Davis, staying until the end of 1962. Then with Wynton Kelly, and sundry other gigs. Narcotics and other health problems led to his early death, at only 33. A pioneer of individuality in bass after bebop, Chambers was one of the first to assert a soloist's position on the instrument, as well as introducing arco playing and fashioning an ensemble role which was suitably oblique and modern for the new music.

*** Whims Of Chambers

Blue Note 37647-2 *Chambers; Donald Byrd (t); John Coltrane (ts); Horace Silver (p); Kenny Burrell (g); Philly Joe Jones (d).* 9/56.

Chambers led only a handful of record dates. These were early days to feature the bass in a spotlight role, and the session feels artificially showcased around his solo work: the *arco* passages may have been groundbreaking, but the tone still grates at times. That aside, it's a solid and sometimes sparky hard-bop date, and rather a forgotten item in the Coltrane discography at least – Trane charges at both 'Nita' and 'We Six' in his best 1956 form. But the star soloist overall is probably Burrell.

Thomas Chapin (1958–98)

ALTO SAXOPHONE, FLUTE, SOPRANO SAXOPHONE, MEZZO-SOPRANO SAXOPHONE, SOPRANINO SAXOPHONE

Thomas Chapin died of leukaemia aged just forty, but leaving behind a remarkably compressed and expressive body of music that now seems definitive of the New York downtown scene of the 1990s. In his final couple of years, Chapin moved towards a more mainstream sound but, dabbling in unfamiliar tonalities like the mezzo-soprano saxophone, he always sounded fresh and radical.

*****(*) Radius**

Mu MUCD 1005 *Chapin; Ronnie Mathews (p); Ara Dinkjian (oud); Ray Drummond (b); John Betsch (d); Sam Turner (perc).* 90.

Chapin's eclecticism may be judged from previous employment with both Lionel Hampton and Chico Hamilton, both of them leaders famous for bringing on adventurous sidemen. Tom's flute playing on *Radius* recalls another Hamilton graduate, Eric Dolphy, while both 'Forgotten Game' and the following 'Jitterbug Waltz' (played on the awkwardly pitched mezzo, which plays in F) sound like a cross between Dolphy and Cannonball Adderley. The addition of an *oud* to 'Forgotten Game' recalls the world music interests that quietly matured over the next few years and would emerge again at the end of his life.

***** Third Force**

Knitting Factory KFWCD 103 *Chapin; Mario Pavone (b); Steve Johns (d).* 11/90, 1/91.

***** Anima**

Knitting Factory KFWCD 121 *As above, except add Michael Sarin (d etc.).* 12/91.

Third Force is gruffer and in some respects less adventurous, adhering to a narrower groove, often trading on rather limited ideas. 'Ahab's Leg' is the strongest individual item, but the set as a whole works well cumulatively; the combination of Pavone and Johns boded well for future projects and, with the involvement of Michael Sarin, established the axis of what was to be Chapin's working group, polished and intuitive when they made a first visit to Europe in 1995.

Anima provides further live performances and offers three unwontedly stretched-out tracks on which the saxophonist solos at length, though with a minimum of actual development, ceding the foreground to the rhythm section for much of the time. Chapin's sound is ever more refined, and certainly by no means as blunt as formerly; but the Dolphy influence is still in place on both versions of 'Lift Off' and has allowed him to explore the limits of harmonic organization, while staying inside essentially jazz structures.

*****(*) Insomnia**

Knitting Factory KFWCD 132 *As above, except add Al Bryant, Frank London (t), Curtis Fowlkes, Peter McEachern (tb), Marcus Roja, Ray Stewart (tba).* 12/92.

***** I've Got Your Number**

Arabesque AJ 0110 *Chapin; Ronnie Mathews (p); Ray Drummond (b); Steve Johns (d); Louis Bauzo (perc).* 1/93.

*****(*) You Don't Know Me**

Arabesque AJ 0115 *Chapin; Tom Harrell (t, flhn); Peter Madsen (p); Kyoto Fujiwara (b); Reggie Nicholson (d).* 8/94.

Chapin isn't usually as smoothly accommodating as on *I've Got Your Number*, and it makes one wonder whether he wouldn't have received wider recognition if he had stuck to mainstream agenda. He sounds superficially like Richie Cole, but on Bud Powell's 'Time Waits' he reverts to a version of his Jackie McLean delivery. It's a most effective record, with a generally able band (though Ray Drummond must have had round shoulders by the end of the afternoon, having carried them throughout). It comes a bare month after the live project documented on *Insomnia*, where Chapin experiments with a larger group for the first time on disc. It's a jolly good record by any standard but, relative to the saxophonist's output, a rather important one, suggesting that he may yet develop into a significant mainstream/modern composer and arranger, full as it is of arresting ideas.

In a very real sense, *You Don't Know Me* is its logical sequel, a beautifully crafted set which finds Chapin at his most expressive and open-hearted. Interesting to hear him working outside the comfort zone of the Pavone/Johns/Sarin axis, and with a piano player. Far from impeding him, it seems to have broadened his harmonic range considerably. Harrell is masterful, of course, and adapts surprisingly quickly to the opening sequence of numbers identified as 'Safari Notebook', on which Chapin moves into Sonny Fortune territory. The most sympathetic of the records to date though, as we have suggested, not necessarily the most representative or revealing.

*****(*) Menagerie Dreams**

Knitting Factory KFWCD 167 *Chapin; John Zorn (as); Vernon Frazer (g); Mario Pavone (b); Michael Sarin (d).* 94.

****** Haywire**

Knitting Factory KFWCD 176 *Chapin; Mark Feldman (vn); Mario Pavone (b); Michael Sarin (d).* 96.

Chapin was already suffering indifferent health when the second of these two fine albums was recorded at the Knitting Factory. The trio was by this stage functioning like a unit and Chapin himself was relaxed enough to play as straight or free as circumstances and instinct dictated. Much of the time, perhaps drawing inspiration from the work for Arabesque, he sticks to an inside groove and relatively straightforward harmonics, leaving some of the more extravagant embellishment to Pavone. Every now and then, though, he gives notice of not having left behind his leftfield side and, with the like-minded Zorn on hand, *Menagerie Dreams* is one of his most searching records.

****** Sky Piece**

Knitting Factory KFR 208 *Chapin; Mario Pavone (b); Michael Sarin (d).* 7/96.

Doubtless there are other live recordings (and perhaps unreleased studio sessions) still lying in the vaults, but for the moment this exquisite album has to be Thomas Chapin's sign-off and epitaph. Its dominant sounds aren't, curiously, his ever widening array of saxophones and flutes (he adds sopranino saxophone, bass flute and the wooden pinkullo this time), but the sounds of nature and the more sinister cadence of an alarm clock, ticking quietly on 'Just Now', ringing vociferously on 'Alphaville'. It may be that Chapin didn't know or intuit at this point how little time was actually left to him, and he seems to have included the clock (and the Godard title) in a bid to explore ideas of expanded or – as in Dali – melted time. His explorations in nature yield the title-piece, inspired by a trip to Namibia in 1993 and introducing the sombre sound of Chapin's bass flute, perfectly attuned to Pavone's bass figurings; then there is 'Essaouira', evoking the Moroccan coastal town with an almost shawm-like tone; and also 'Night Bird Song', the longest piece, which documents some of the sounds heard on a nature trek in Connecticut. Somewhat unusually, Chapin also includes a repertory tune, Monk's 'Ask Me Now', the second time on the album that the all-important present tense is mentioned in a title.

****** Night Bird Song**

Knitting Factory Works KFR CD 240 *Chapin; Mario Pavone (b); Michael Sarin (d). 8–9/92.*

We include this out of chronological sequence because it is a posthumous release and because it was Thomas's decision to release it as the follow-up to *Sky Piece*. Listening to it now is to return whole to a point in Chapin's career when the future seemed open-ended and full of potential, with few clouds on the horizon. He had put the session aside, waiting for an ideal moment, and had even picked the cover art, a fragment of *mola* cloth from the Blas islands in Panama which he found while touring with Lionel Hampton. The album is as tightly woven as a piece of cloth, a suite of segued themes that is as satisfyingly coherent as anything he ever recorded. Three of the tunes – 'Alphaville', the title-track, and 'Changes Two Tires' – appeared on *Sky Piece*. The former pair are welded together on a dark, almost chordal tone on saxophone, which is picked up by Pavone on bass. 'Cliff Island' is played on sopranino, as is the cartoony 'Tweeter's Last Adventure'. Constantly experimenting with new timbres, he plays (blows? sings?) a reedless alto on 'The Roaring S', a brilliant example of how much Thomas was influenced by natural environments and places.

For those who cherish his work, though, the most deeply moving piece is the flute track, 'Aeolus', which half a decade later was to be the last piece Thomas played in public before his final sickness. Soaring, anchored, paradoxical, it's essentially a duet with Pavone, who emerges more and more clearly as the secret sharer in Chapin's brief, brilliant, foreshortened career. Wonderful stuff; even if it isn't the final word, it has the magisterial confidence of a major statement.

Bill Charlap

PIANO

The son of a songwriter, Moose Charlap, and a singer, Sandy Stewart, Charlap is a young New Yorker with a fundamentally mainstream approach.

***** Along With Me**

Chiaroscuro CR(D) 326 *Charlap; Sean Smith, Andy Eulau (b); Ron Vincent (d). 6/91–8/93.*

***** Souvenir**

Criss Cross 1108 *Charlap; Scott Colley (b); Dennis Mackrel (d). 6/95.*

***** The Gerry Mulligan Songbook**

Chiaroscuro CRD 349 *Charlap; Ted Rosenthal (p); Dean Johnson (b); Ron Vincent (d). 6/96.*

****(*) Distant Star**

Criss Cross 1131 *Charlap; Sean Smith (b); Bill Stewart (d). 12/96.*

A pupil of Jack Reilly, Charlap has worked under many leaders; his own records are a confident display of his powers. *Along With Me* is sweetly handled, from Sean Smith's pretty ballad, 'Has This Song Been Written For You Before?', to an almost rhapsodic treatment of Parker's 'Donna Lee', but the record is so even-tempered that it could use a little excitement. *Souvenir* is certainly the pick of the four. The two opening blues, Coleman's 'Roundabout' and Reilly's 'Half Step', are ingenious variations which the pianist relishes, and he plays them with tremendous panache. Colley and Mackrel make a convincing team and, although there are a couple of makeweights – the extended 'Alone Together' is overdone, and Jim Hall's 'Waltz New' is undercooked – it's a good record.

The duets with Rosenthal on Gerry Mulligan material (both men served time under Jeru) are capably done and will appeal to those interested in what remains something of a novelty form in jazz. Something's a little amiss on *Distant Star*, though. The more quiescent material becalms the group, and somehow the spirit which ignited the first Criss Cross date can't get started here.

Teddy Charles (born 1928)

VIBES, PIANO

A vibesman with several big bands at the end of the swing era, Charles turned to composition in the 1950s and recorded several albums in a modestly experimental style, forming associations with Miles Davis and Charles Mingus along the way.

*****(*) Collaboration: West**

Original Jazz Classics OJC 122 *Charles; Shorty Rogers (t); Jimmy Giuffre (ts, bs); Curtis Counce (b); Shelly Manne (d). 8/53.*

***** Evolution**

Original Jazz Classics OJC 1731 *As above, plus J.R Monterose (ts); Charles Mingus (b); Jerry Segal (d). 8/53–1/55.*

***** Coolin'**

Original Jazz Classics OJC 1866 *Charles; Idrees Sulieman (t); John Jenkins (as); Mal Waldron (p); Addison Farmer (b); Jerry Segal (d). 4/57.*

Charles's few available sessions as a leader have never progressed beyond a collectors' reputation. He is usually respected as a harbinger of Coleman's free music: the first two records aim for an independence of bebop structure which still sounds remarkably fresh. The two 1953 sessions, spread across the two discs, explore contrapuntal textures in a way which only Lennie Tristano had already tried, and there is a wonderful sense of interplay with Rogers and Manne especially. 'Variations On A Theme By Bud' from *Collaboration: West* is a small classic of anticipatory freedom, the music played around key centres rather than a framework of chords. But Charles's interest in harmony and arrangement required larger groups than these, and the quartet session with Mingus, Monterose and Segal is less impressive. *Coolin'* features a surprising line-up of rarely encountered horns in a programme of evenly divided originals. Charles takes a relatively back-seat role, contributing only one tune and taking his turn in the round-robin of solos. This is a more conventional hard-bop session, but the tunes have some piquant interest: Waldron's off-centre 'Staggers' and 'Reiteration', a typical piece of minor-key brooding, are worth reviving. Jenkins plays with splendid intensity, but Sulieman's solos are mere bop convention, quotes and all.

**** Live At The Verona Jazz Festival 1988**
Soul Note 121183 *Charles; Harold Danko (p); Ray Drummond (b); Tony Reedus (d).* 6/88.

An indifferent comeback by Charles, who had effectively retired from music for many years. He plays well with an imposing rhythm section, but, as noted above, this kind of casual blowing session is hardly his forte, and the live recording isn't distinguished.

Charleston Chasers

GROUP

Britishers playing their contemporary version of old hot dance music.

***** Pleasure Mad**
Stomp Off CD 1287 *Ian Hintersley, Sean Colan (c, t); Bob Hunt (tb, c); Claire Murphy (cl, as, cmel, ts, bs); Nik Payton (cl, as, Cmel, bs, v); Zoltan Sagi (cl, as, ts, bs); Raina Reid (p, v); Tom Langham (bj, g, v); Malcolm Sked (sou); Debbie Arthurs (d, v).* 8–9/94.

***** Steaming South**
Stomp Off CD 1314 *As above, except Mike Henry (t), Tony Carter (cl, as, ts), Steve Shaw (tb), Graham Roberts (bj, g) replace Hintersley, Hunt, Murphy, Langham.* 4/96.

English – *very* English, once you hear the vocals – hot dance music, based around Gloucestershire but recorded in Stratford and Maidstone. Their repertoire is virtually all from the bandbooks of the likes of Jean Goldkette, Ted Weems and various pillars of New York society, but they sometimes drop in some Ellington or Beiderbecke, and all of it is performed with much panache and evident pleasure. Payton sounds like the outstanding soloist, although none of them is a slouch; and Raina Reid's arrangements have as much flair as the original charts. That said, there is little reason to listen to their 'Since My Best Girl Turned Me Down' when one can hear the Beiderbecke version, and some of it falls into the metronomic category. It is, though, in good sound – and it might tempt ears unused to the ancient timbres of original hot dance.

The Chartbusters

GROUP

All-star group formed to record hits of the jazz past.

***** Mating Call**
Prestige PRCD-11002-2 *Randy Brecker (t); Donald Harrison (as); Craig Handy (ss, ts); Lonnie Smith (org); David Fiuczynski (g); Idris Muhammad (d).* 10/95.

An *ad hoc* group of famous names have at some evergreens from the Prestige catalogue: beside Tadd Dameron's title-track there is Dolphy's '245', McLean's 'Minor March' and three Sonny Rollins tunes, as well as dedications to Gene Ammons and Mose Allison. The horns drift in and out of the tracks and Fiuczynski turns up only on the fierce 'Oleo', but Smith and Muhammad are there throughout. The major player is Handy, who brings gravitas and elegance alike to his solos and turns in an especially fine soprano statement on '245'. Harrison does well, without startling anyone, and Brecker is merely the seasoned pro. Not bad.

Allan Chase

ALTO AND SOPRANO SAXOPHONES

Contemporary American saxophonist in a broad-based bop-and-beyond idiom.

***** Silver Linin**
Accurate AC 5013 *Chase; Ron Horton (t, flhn); Tony Scherr (b); Matt Wilson (d, perc).*

Chase seems inclined to reject the more obvious parallel with the classic Ornette Coleman quartet, suggesting that the main inspirations here are the Sonny Rollins and Gerry Mulligan groups of the same period. Certainly, the music is not 'outside', in the manner of Ornette, but sticks pretty much to the changes, though even a standard like 'East Of The Sun' receives an unfamiliar twist. Opening with a Sun Ra tune – 'Dark Clouds With Silver Linings' gives the session its name – is a bold stroke, but Chase pulls it off with considerable aplomb, and the two Bud Powell tunes which follow later – 'Comin' Up' and 'Borderick' – are executed with grace and confidence. An excellent record, which has created an appetite for more from the same source. We look forward to it.

Doc Cheatham (1905–97)

TRUMPET, VOCALS

Adolphus Cheatham was born in Nashville and started out in burlesque bands, where he backed Bessie Smith among others. He went on to have one of the longest careers in jazz history, with McKinney's Cotton Pickers, Cab Calloway and, in the '50s following a spell away from the music, with many Latin-American bands. In his eighties and nineties he was a revered old master, still playing a weekly gig in Greenwich Village.

***(*) **Duets And Solos**
Sackville SKCD-5002 2CD *Cheatham; Sam Price (p).* 11/76–11/79.

***(*) **The Fabulous Doc Cheatham**
Parkwood PW 104 *Cheatham; Dick Wellstood (p); Bill Pemberton (b); Jackie Williams (d).* 10/83.

Adolphus 'Doc' Cheatham became one of the most enduring jazz musicians of his time – and his time seemed to span much of the history of the music. He was effectively rediscovered in the 1970s after many years of society band work, having been among the most esteemed of lead trumpeters in the big-band era. He was recording in the late 1920s and his studio work of some 60 years later shows amazingly little deterioration in the quality of his technique, while the ideas and appetite for playing remained wholly unaffected by the passage of time. It's not so much that one feels a sentimental attachment to such a veteran, but that Cheatham's sound represents an art which literally died out of modern jazz: the sweet, lyrically hot style of a swing-era man. Prior to his records in the 1980s, Cheatham's main work was with Cab Calloway in the 1930s, Eddie Heywood in the '40s (often backing Billie Holiday), and in various settings in the 1950s and '60s; but it wasn't until these albums that he was heard at length as a leader.

Duets And Solos is arguably Cheatham's most valuable recording, since it both recalls the earlier age which he seems so much a part of – the trumpet/piano format recalls Armstrong and Hines, and the material mixes rags, stomps, blues and whiskery pop – and sits comfortably in modern sound and with a knowing air of sagacity. Price (whose session of 12 solos fills up spare space on the two-disc set) is fine, and often better than he is on his own featured recordings, although his solo showpieces are less impressive as rather mechanical blues and light boogie. The Parkwood album is good, too. Here Cheatham's solos have a classical economy and a courageous spring to them, and the tiny shakes and inflexions in his sound only help to make it uniquely his own, with a songful high register and choruses which, after 60 years of playing, he knows exactly how to pace. The session benefits a little from Wellstood's attacking piano, and Cheatham's dapper, delicate vocals on several tracks only add to the fun.

*** **At The Bern Festival**
Sackville 2-3045 *Cheatham; Roy Williams (tb); Jim Galloway (ss); Ian Bargh (p); Neil Swainson (b); Terry Clarke (d).* 4/83–1/85.

This live session finds Cheatham unfazed by a hard-swinging and quite modern-sounding band, with Roy Williams sitting in on the first six tracks – he has a delightful feature on 'Polka Dots And Moonbeams' – and Galloway's soprano measuring the distance between Sidney Bechet and Steve Lacy. Three later tracks were taped on more local ground in Toronto. If the rhythm section sometimes crashes rather more than it might for Cheatham's taste, he still sounds invigorated by the setting, and his hand-muted playing on 'Creole Love Call' or the firm, silvery solos on 'Cherry' and 'Love Is Just Around The Corner' are commanding examples of his best work.

(*) **Live!
Natasha NI-4023 *Cheatham; Glenn Zottola (t); Joey Cavaseno (cl, as); Phil Bodner (cl); Loren Schoenberg, George Kelly (ts); Richard Wyands, Marty Napoleon (p); Victor Gaskin, Major Holley (b); Ronnie Cole, Ray Mosca (d).* 2–12/85.

*** **Live At Sweet Basil**
Jazzology JCD-283 *Cheatham; Jerry Zigmont (tb); Sammy Rimington (cl, as ts); Jon Marks (p); Arvell Shaw (b); John Russell (d).* 4/92.

Much of Doc's latter-day legacy will exist in the form of live albums. These two are seldom less than enjoyable while never quite hitting a top gear. *Live!* collects material from two Highlights In Jazz concerts with two different bands. The groups are somewhat ratty and occasionally brash, and Doc sounds like the most cultured man on the stage by far. Better is the Jazzology disc. It often has the feel of a Louis Armstrong date, what with old-time All Stars bassist Shaw in the line-up and several tunes associated with Pops, so it's interesting to hear Cheatham's style on his old rival's material, as well as the versatile Rimington partnering the maestro. The rest of the group are a bit ordinary but there's a pleasing feel of New-Orleans-in-New-York about it all.

*** **The Eighty-Seven Years Of Doc Cheatham**
Columbia 474047-2 *Cheatham; Chuck Folds (p); Bucky Calabrese (b); Jackie Williams (d).* 9/92.

With his regular band, the group he played with every week in New York, Doc continued to defy Father Time. He is fading a little on some of the tracks, although one notices it more in his singing than in his trumpet playing, which retains so much of his cultivated delivery that he still turns back the clock to an earlier age. The detailed, dynamic treatment of Benny Carter's 'Blues In My Heart' proves that he is more than just a history act. The regular team provide faithful support, and Phil Schaap's clean production is perfectly apposite.

*** **Swinging Down In New Orleans**
Jazzology JCD-233 *Cheatham; Brian O'Connell (cl); Butch Thompson (p); Les Muscutt (g, bj); Bill Huntington (g, b); Peter Badie (b); Ernest Elly (d).* 92.

(*) **You're A Sweetheart
Sackville SKCD2-2038 *Cheatham; Sarah McElcheran (t); Jim Galloway (ss, vbs); Jane Fair (cl, ts); Norman Amadio (p); Rosemary Galloway (b, v); Don Vickery (d).* 3–11/92.

Doc seems neither more nor less than his usual self on both of these, so it comes down to the settings as to which is preferable: no real contest. Jazzology's seasoned team of veteran modern traditionalists (if that doesn't sound too absurd) provide a springy, amiable and perfectly appropriate background for the trumpeter's lean, sometimes puffy solos and singing, with Thompson a model of deftness. They play plenty of tunes from the old town and make them all sound as if they're worth the attention. The Canadian sessions captured on the Sackville disc are more routine and, though there's a very sweet ballad in 'Under The Moonlight Starlight Blue', most of this is rather too ordinary.

*****(*) Doc Cheatham And Nicholas Payton**
Verve 537062-2 *Cheatham; Nicholas Payton (t); Tom Ebbert (tb); Jack Maheu (cl); Butch Thompson (p); Les Muscutt (g); Bill Huntington (b); Ernie Elly (d).* 9/96.

What a wonderful farewell for the old master. Paired with precocious young firebrand Payton, who's so in love with Doc's playing that he doesn't dare do anything but elevate his senior partner, Doc ambles through some of his favourites for a final time. The match with Payton brings on so many felicitous moments that one scarcely notices the frailties in Cheatham's own playing. This is perhaps as much about his singing as the trumpet-playing, with some of his most ruminative and affecting turns with the voice: listen to the half-spoken 'Save It Pretty Mama', and Nicholas's beautiful underscoring of the words. Payton has a few shots to himself – a terrific bounce through 'Dinah', for instance – and when the two horns ride out 'I Gotta Right To Sing The Blues' the years roll back. Abetted by a crack team of New Orleans pros, this will be the Cheatham disc that most will play most often.

Jeannie Cheatham

PIANO, VOCAL and

Jimmy Cheatham

BASS TROMBONE, VOCAL

Husband-and-wife team who take a genial, often gentle route through R&B flavoured by jazz horns and swing rhythms.

***** Sweet Baby Blues**
Concord CCD 4258 *Jimmy Cheatham; Jeannie Cheatham; Snooky Young (t, v); Jimmie Noone (ss, cl); Charles McPherson (as); Curtis Peagler (as, ts); Red Callender (b, tba); John 'Ironman' Harris (d); Danice Tracey, Chris Long (v).* 9/84.

***** Midnight Mama**
Concord CCD 4297 *As above, except add Dinky Morris (ss, ts, bs), Eddie Lockjaw Davis (ts); omit McPherson, Tracey and Long.* 11/85.

***** Homeward Bound**
Concord CCD 4321 *As above, except add Eddie Vinson (as, v).* 1/87.

***** Back To The Neighbourhood**
Concord CCD 4373 *Jimmy Cheatham; Jeannie Cheatham; Clora Bryant (t, flhn); Curtis Peagler (as, ts); Jimmie Noone (ss, ts, cl); Herman Riley (ss, ts); Dinky Morris (bs); Papa John Creach (vn); Red Callender (b); John 'Ironman' Harris (d).* 11/88.

***** Luv In The Afternoon**
Concord CCD 4429 *As above, except add Nolan Smith (t, flhn); omit Bryant, Riley and Creach.* 5/90.

***** Basket Full Of Blues**
Concord CCD 4501 *As above, except add Rickey Woodard (as, ts, cl), Frank Wess (ts, f); omit Noone.* 11/91.

***** Blues And Boogie Masters**
Concord CCD 4579 *As above, except add Snooky Young (t), Charles Owens, Hank Crawford (as), Richard Reid (b); omit Wess, Peagler, Callender.* 7/93.

***** Gud Nuz Blues**
Concord CCD 4690 *Jimmy Cheatham; Jeannie Cheatham; Snooky Young (t); Nolan Smith (t, flhn); Louis Taylor (ss, as); Rickey Woodard (ss, ts); Plas Johnson (ts); Charles Owen (bs, bcl); Richard Reid (b); John 'Ironman' Harris (d).* 95.

Like many of their somewhat younger counterparts on Concord, the Cheathams have now been doing this kind of record for the label long enough to create their own little genre. Some may find Concord's spotless recording not much in keeping with the rougher spirits of what is a variation on jump-band blues, but the horns are perfectly cast and the material is smartly chosen to get the most out of the formula. Jeannie Cheatham's singing is a nice blend of girlishness and acting tough, and husband Jimmy plays Butterbeans to her Susie. Very little to choose among the records. The first two or three are, inevitably, the freshest, but it's a formula that's yet to go stale and the later discs benefit in particular from the presence of Woodard, an inspired addition to the group. Their eighth and latest, *Gud Nuz Blues*, has a guest saxophonist in Plas Johnson and is as assured and unhackneyed as the others.

Chris Cheek

TENOR SAXOPHONE

Inside-to-out saxophonist, currently busy in the New York scene.

***** I Wish I Knew**
Fresh Sound FSNT 022 *Cheek; Kurt Rosenwinkel (g); Chris Higgins (b); Jorge Rossy (d).* 10/96–1/97.

****** A Girl Named Joe**
Fresh Sound FSNT 032 *Cheek; Mark Turner (ts); Ben Monder (g); Marc Johnson (b); Jorge Rossy, Dan Rieser (d).* 5/97.

A self-effacing debut from the American saxophonist who's done some accomplished foot-soldiering elsewhere. A solitary original hides in the middle of a programme of standards, quietly thought out at ballad tempos, and although firmly articulated by all hands the music has a melancholy air which seems to crystallize in the tenorman's injured timbre. Rosenwinkel plays limpid lines in counterpoint to Cheek, and they score a kind of reluctant success.

Two tenors, guitar, bass and two drummers: Cheek's hardly chosen a conventional set-up for his second Fresh Sound set. This one is very much about the composing: contrapuntal lines, parallel melodies, close-cropped harmony. He could hardly have a more responsive or tuned-in group to perform a subtle and vivid set of music: Johnson, a supreme hired gun at this point, is the perfect bassman for the job, melodious but inquiring; Monder is an unassuming master; Turner is one of the keenest sax voices of the moment. And Cheek himself stands as tall as anyone on the date. Another exceptional set from the Fresh Sound New Talent imprint.

Don Cherry (1936–95)

POCKET TRUMPET, WOODEN FLUTES, DOUSSN'GOUNI, PIANO, KEYBOARDS, MISCELLANEOUS INSTRUMENTS, VOICE

Born in Oklahoma, Cherry played R&B before meeting Ornette Coleman in 1956. Worked in his quartet, then with John Coltrane and the New York Contemporary Five. Visited Europe and thereafter retained a base there as well as in America. An inveterate traveller, he listened to seemingly all the world's musics and, besides doing his own extravagantly multi-cultural records, gigs and events, played Coleman's music again (in Old & New Dreams and with his former leader) and turned up in guest situations, though his playing was affected by lip trouble; he succumbed to liver failure in Spain in 1995.

***(*) The Sonet Recordings

Verve 533049 2CD *Cherry; Irfan Sumer (ts, perc); Bernt Rosengren (tarogato); Christer Bothen (p); Selcuk Sun (b); Okay Temiz (d, perc); Bengt Berger, Agneta Ernstrom (perc).* 11/69–5/73.

The death of Don Cherry in 1995 imposed a more profound silence than most such passings. In a very real sense, Cherry's recorded output is beside the point. He was a musical gypsy, a kind of planetary *griot*, as someone once put it, who defined his musical art as that of people 'listening and travelling'. He himself never stopped doing either – or, of course, playing. The last time one of the authors met him was at the Jazz Jamboree in Warsaw in 1993. He was as likely to turn up in India, Korea or Latin America; for some time he lived in Scandinavia, and the Sonet compilation brings together two albums, one made in the studio in Stockholm in 1973 and one recorded live in Ankara four years earlier. There is no *typical* Don Cherry album. Though he adds an unforgettable voice to things like the classic Ornette Coleman Atlantics, he is not primarily an instrumentalist and certainly not a trumpet innovator. The first thing to be registered about these recordings is that Cherry plays no trumpet at all on *Eternal Now*, the Swedish session, but ranges across a bizarre variety of percussion and stringed instruments, piano and harmonium. Aficionados of the Scandinavian scene will cherish a track featuring the great tenorist Bernt Rosengren on *tarogato*, a folksy cousin to the soprano saxophone made of rosewood. 'Love Train' is perhaps the most jazz-based piece on the session. The remaining tracks are squarely in the world-music idiom that Cherry was to make his own in years to come. *Live Ankara* is closer to the work with Ornette: tight, compressed lines on the cheap little Pakistani pocket trumpet Cherry favoured, and two Ornette themes just to cement the connection. Typically, though, much of the material is folk-inspired, arrangements of Turkish tunes by Maffy Falay. Cherry does, though, include two or three of his own pieces and these, 'St John And The Dragon' and 'Man On The Moon' especially, sound more securely within his comfort zone.

*** El Corazon

ECM 829199-2 *Cherry; Ed Blackwell (d).* 2/82.

Like fellow-trumpeter Leo Smith, Cherry had a rather intermittent association with ECM, returning to the label just before the end of his life for the very mixed *Dona Nostra*. Apart from the records with Codona, his ECM output was limited to the 1993 disc and these duos with Blackwell who, after Ornette and Collin Walcott, was probably his closest associate from the jazz end of the spectrum. Cherry and Blackwell recorded as a duo in 1969, a set known as *Mu*, originally issued on BYG and transferred to CD by Affinity. The later encounter lacks the rawness of performance one responds to on *Mu* but gains infinitely in sheer clarity of sound. It also includes what by this stage in his career had become a rare standard item, Thelonious Monk and Denzil Best's 'Bemsha Swing'. Blackwell is immense, as ever, relishing the space and music which is freed from the vertical hierarchies of harmonic jazz. Those who heard the duo workshopping and gigging report that *El Corazon* is only a muted version of what they were capable of. It's a solid but in the end rather uneventful record.

***(*) Art Deco

A & M 395258-2 *Cherry; James Clay (ts); Charlie Haden (b); Billy Higgins (d).* 8/88.

Signs in the later 1980s that Cherry, or those who were signing him up, wanted to mainstream his work, lead him back towards jazz and away from the centrifugal spin of world music. There are moments when this might almost be a later *Ornette On Tenor*; Clay has had a quiet career since the 1950s, but he comes from the same Texas soil and brings a refreshingly down-home touch to Coleman tunes like 'The Blessing' and 'Compute'. Again, there are a couple of standards, 'When Will The Blues Leave', 'Body And Soul' (which is really Clay's feature) and a further, indifferent version of 'Bemsha Swing'. Cherry plays mostly muted and seemed to have reverted to a cross between his old, rather tentative self and mid-period Miles Davis, softer and more accommodating than one might like to hear. Along with the Ornette tribute band, Old And New Dreams, this is probably as good as it got until CherryCo enterprises actually got back together again in the early 1990s.

***(*) Multi Kulti

A & M 395323 *Cherry; Bill Ortiz (t, v); James Harvey (tb); Jeff Cressman (tb, v); Bob Stewart (tba); Carlos Ward (as); Jessica Jones, Jony Jones (ts); Peter Apfelbaum (ts, ky, perc); Peck Allmond (bs); Will Bernard, Stan Franks (g); David Cherry, Frank Serafine (syn); Karl Berger (mar); Bo Freeman, Mark Loudon Sims (b); Ed Blackwell, Deszon X Claiborne (d); Joshua Jones V (d, perc, v); John L Price (d programmes); Frank Ekeh, Robert Buddha Huffman, Nana Vasconcelos (perc); Anthony Hamilton, Ingrid Sertso (v); collective personnel.* 12/88–2/90.

This is the closest Cherry ever came and was ever likely to come to a big crossover hit. Adding a sophisticated studio gloss to his polystylism didn't blunt it in any way, though there are moments when one wants to hear a live equivalent, something a little blunter and more ragged. The horns are consistently excellent, with Ward providing a voice not unlike Ornette's to stir those ancestral memories. The presence of Peter Apfelbaum, who went on to found the Cherry-influenced Hieroglyphic Ensemble, is an indication of his growing impact on a younger generation of players who were kicking against the restrictions of formula bebop and looking for other inputs. Difficult to judge how much Cherry himself was drawing at the time from stepdaughter Neneh Cherry, who had graduated from the James Brown-meets-bop Rip, Rig & Panic and was striking out on her own with a jazzy hybrid of hip-hop and rap styles.

***** Dona Nostra**
ECM 521727-2 *Cherry; Lennart Aberg (sax, f); Bobo Stenson (p); Anders Jormin (b); Anders Kjellberg (d); Okay Temiz (perc).* 3/93.

There are sparks of brilliance here, but they are lost in ashpits of compromise. The wind that stirs the coals, significantly, is Ornette Coleman, two of whose pieces are included. The old pairing was to go on the road later the same year, and Cherry seems keen to pack his strong-voiced solos with tags and phrases remembered from years, even decades, before. Restricting himself to trumpet, he eases through 'Race Face' with less fury than the composer brings to it; for 'Fort Cherry' and 'Prayer' (still the outstanding cut), he injects a warmer-than-usual tone, prompting the question whether he has switched to a more conventional horn. The sound is magnificent, and Stenson demonstrates once again what a superbly responsive player he is, and Aberg (still not widely known outside Scandinavia) amply justifies his shared credit. It is not, overall, much of a showing for such a considerable musician, but Cherry never seemed like a man much concerned with his place in posterity, and his elusiveness on record is in some ways appropriate. Blue Note released his early *Complete Communion* as a limited edition early in 2000, and that is certainly worth acquiring if any copies remain by the time this edition sees print.

Andrew Cheshire

GUITAR

Contemporary American post-bop guitarist, recording for his own Joule label and for CIMP.

***** Water Street Revival**
Joule 03 *Cheshire; James Weidman (p); Bryan Carrott (vib); Lonnie Plaxico, Marcus McLaurine, Tyler Mitchell (b); Yoron Israel, Marvin 'Smitty' Smith, Greg Bandy (d).* 6/90–2/92.

*****(*) Another View**
Joule 02 *Cheshire; Kurt Weiss (t); Rich Perry (ts); Ron McClure (b); Jeff Hirshfield (d).* 5/97.

***** Relax, Keep The Tension, Please**
CIMP 165 *Cheshire; Dominic Duval (b); Jay Rosen (d).* 1/98.

Cheshire's a conservative, keeping to a clean, warm, open tone and unspooling lines that seek nothing illogical or unsteadying in their make-up; but these records are a very satisfying listen. He writes themes that seem thick with interesting harmonies yet which float very sweetly over whatever pulse the rhythm players are delivering in the engine-room. An accurate, quick-witted improviser, he never tries for anything too outlandish, but he can sustain very long lines with such ease that they seem to come naturally to his fingers. The best of these three is probably *Another View*, which sets him up in an excellent quintet where nobody outshines the leader. Although not released until 1998, *Water Street Revival* is a mixed bag of halfway-house sessions from the early '90s: four pieces with Carrott, Weidman, Plaxico and Smith are outstandingly fine and make one wish that they'd made a whole album. Although the other tracks are more ordinary, there's still a lot of exemplary guitar-playing. The CIMP session, with its characteristically no-make-up-allowed timbre, suffers slightly at times from the heavy weather which Duval and Rosen make of swinging a simple line, but again Cheshire's own playing makes a virtue of his unflashy but particular ideas.

Cyrus Chestnut

PIANO

Chestnut grew up, musically speaking, in church, playing gospel music for choirs in his native Baltimore. He studied there and in Boston before working with George Adams, Jon Hendricks and in the Betty Carter group.

*****(*) Nut**
Evidence 22152-2 2CD *Chestnut; Christian McBride (b); Carl Allen (d).* 1/92.

***** Another Direction**
Evidence 22135-2 *As above.* 4/93.

***** Revelations**
Atlantic 82518-2 *Chestnut; Christopher J Thomas (b); Clarence Penn (d).* 6/93.

Chestnut seems set fair to be a major part of the next wave of the jazz mainstream. These albums (the Evidence sets are reissues of records originally released in Japan) are already old enough to be classed as juvenilia, but they're very enjoyable in their own right. *Nut* and *Another Direction* burst with good humour and inventiveness, the pianist assisted by superb backup from McBride and Allen, and, although the material is relatively familiar (Ellington, standards and the occasional gospel piece) and the treatments unstartling, the joy in the music is unmistakable.

Chestnut, Thomas and Penn were the members of one of Betty Carter's recent rhythm sections, and the deftness of the *Revelations* trio certainly bespeaks mutual familiarity. The opening 'Blues For Nita' is a beautifully controlled workout in which Chestnut controls the dynamics as sagaciously as any keyboard veteran. Instead of coming from the post-bop piano masters, he looks back to those who bridged swing and bop, in particular Oscar Peterson: 'Little Ditty' features a trademark show of virtuosity, while the gospel inflexions of 'Lord, Lord, Lord' might have come from Ray Bryant. The down-side of this direction is a certain sameness and predictability about some of his solos, as if he'd already fallen into patterns of playing. But the quiet gravity of his solo ballad, 'Sweet Hour Of Prayer', suggests that he has other sides to develop, too.

*****(*) Dark Before The Dawn**
Atlantic 82719-2 *As above, except Steve Kirby (b) replaces Thomas.* 8/94.

One of the interesting things about Chestnut is his take on gospel roots. So few modern jazz pianists have tackled the issue of gospel melody and harmony within a post-bop context – beyond the customary 'soulful' clichés – that Chestnut's meditative approach is something of a rarity. Here, on 'It Is Well (Within My Soul)', he plays a beautifully modulated treatment of a traditional hymn, but more important is the way he integrates gospel materials into his overall approach. It lends a distinctive touch to most of the pianism on show here and plays a notable part in his choice of dynamics: he can play remarkably delicately, but – and he's physically a very big man – he can really thump the keyboard when he wants to. That range is splendidly exploited by the variety of the themes on display, and Kirby and Penn offer exemplary support. Still, there are contrivances here and there, even if this strong record will do for now.

*****(*) Blessed Quietness**
Atlantic 82948-2 *Chestnut (p solo).* 4/96.

Chestnut goes all the way with an album of hymns, spirituals and carols – 'What you hear is simply my heart'. Rather than playing any of them 'straight', he creates a gently persuasive form for such commonplace pieces as 'We Three Kings', 'Amazing Grace' and 'Silent Night', delineating melodies with absolute clarity yet fashioning his own framework for each piece. That lends both surprise and familiar warmth to, say, 'The First Noel', a well-worn tune given a delicate new grace. Unbelievers may find a whole disc of this something of a stretch, but the pianism is marvellous. Perhaps Chestnut can do this only once in his career. If so, he's made a near-perfect job of it with this disc.

*****(*) Cyrus Chestnut**
Atlantic 83140-2 *Chestnut; James Carter (as); Joe Lovano (ts); Ron Carter (b); Billy Higgins, Lewis Nash (d); Anita Baker (v).* 98.

Back on the solid ground of post-bop, Chestnut handles this unfrilly session with implacable assurance. Carter sticks to alto and is, for him, on surprisingly bubbly form, leaving some of his importance at home for the date. His extravagant sound on 'The Journey' is infectiously high-spirited. Lovano strolls in for two tracks and trades jabs with Carter on the closing 'Sharp'. Cyrus enjoys being in charge of this set, and he confers a light touch on the whole session. Even the two guest vocals by Anita Baker, who sings 'Summertime' softly and 'My Favourite Things' delicately, don't sit uncomfortably with the other tracks.

Chicago Underground Duo/Trio

GROUP

New music from Chicagoan experimenters.

***** 12 Degrees Of Freedom**
Thrill Jockey 060 *Robert Mazurek (c, p, f); Jeff Parker (g); Chad Taylor (perc, vib).* 1–6/97.

*****(*) Possible Cube**
Delmark DE-511 *Robert Mazurek (c, elec, vib, mar, org); Jeff Parker (g, org); Noel Kupersmith (b, vib); Chad Taylor (d, vib).* 5/98.

Mazurek (who has more conventional records listed under his own name), Taylor and Kupersmith are the CUT, with Parker seemingly an honorary member. The music is a low-key mix of post-bop and music (or sound) that has drifted in from many other points. Several of the pieces on *Possible Cube* are more or less conventional sequences for cornet, bass and drums, but they're interspersed with percussion episodes, wandering improvisations in free time, and electronics. 'Othello', the first track, starts in familiar territory but dissolves into what's almost a dream serquence for synthesizers. Very brief tracks intermingle with pieces like the marathon 'Into Another You', underpinned by the bleating organ-lines that Parker contributes. The Thrill Jockey record is cooler and more abstract and even has one piece ('Waiting For You Is Like Watching Stillness Grow Into Enormous Wings') that sounds like a self-contained piece of minimalist composition. But both are interesting proposals to blend genuine jazz material with what's coming out of Chicago's avant-garde rock community. Underground, but maybe not for long.

Billy Childs

PIANO

A post-bop pianist based on the West Coast, Childs has been recording occasionally as leader since 1988.

***** The Child Inside**
Shanachie 5023 *Childs; Terence Blanchard (t); Luis Bonilla (tb); Steve Wilson (ss, as); Ravi Coltrane (ts); Dave Holland (b); Jeff Tain Watts (d).* 1/96.

Two earlier albums for Windham Hill found Childs in convincing form; this one is a touch less distinctive, forcefully though everyone plays. The nucleus is Childs, Holland and Watts, with Blanchard on several tracks, Wilson on three and Bonilla and Coltrane on one. The leader seems to save his best ideas for his own originals: 'Lover Man' and 'Alone Together' are played obstreperously fast and lose their point, although Jerry Goldsmith's 'Theme From Chinatown' is made into a rather good ballad. 'Just Another Day', an intense piece with a lyrical core, is excellent. But despite the top-flight personnel, the music feels realized a bit hastily, and the studio sound is naggingly unsatisfactory: Holland and Watts sound improbably thin and unfocused.

George Chisholm (1915–97)

TROMBONE

Born in Glasgow, Chisholm came to London in 1935 and quickly established himself on the dance-band/jazz scene. He played with Fats Waller three years later and was arranging for The Squadronaires during the war years. In the '50s he became a favourite on radio and subsequently on TV, in commercials and on variety shows, but his credentials as a trad-to-mainstream trombonist were unimpaired, as his occasional recordings showed. In the '80s and '90s he remained a favourite at clubs and in festivals, and his career only faded following the death of his wife in 1995.

***** In A Mellow Tone**
Lake LACD108 *Chisholm; Kenny Baker (t); Tony Coe (cl, as, bs); Tommy Whittle (ts, f); Alan Branscombe (p, vib); Brian Lemon (p); Lennie Bush, Kenny Baldock (b); Bobby Orr, John Richardson (d).* 8/72–5/73.

Chisholm was a marvellous part of British jazz for decades and the slightness of his legacy on record is to be regretted. Lake have salvaged this obscure mainstream date for Rediffusion in 1973 which shows the old warrior still in impeccable form, alongside Baker, Coe, Whittle and the rest. 'Walk Right Up Folks', taken at a fearsome tempo, shows what he could do in a hot mainstream situation and the subsequent 'Star Dust' (the sleeve listings have transposed this title with 'The Boy Next Door') shows off his finely groomed tone. A couple of live tracks with rhythm section alone are the makeweights. Unpretentious music which should make British readers experience a nostalgic warmth.

Herman Chittison (1909–67)

PIANO, VOCALS

Nicknamed 'Ivory', this gifted pianist from Flemingsburg, Kentucky, had a tendency to perfectionism which may have hampered his career as a recording artist. He worked in Europe and in Egypt until the start of the war, when he returned to America to launch a radio career as Ernie the Blue Note Pianist.

****(*) Herman Chittison, 1933–1941**

Classics 690 *Chittison; Ikey Robinson (g, v); Arita Day (v).* 33–41.

***** Herman Chittison, 1944–1945**

Classics 1024 *Chittison; Carl Lynch, Jimmy Shirley (g); Calton Powell, Cedric Wallace (d); Thelma Carpenter (v).* 5/34–5/45.

Chittison's great mistake was to take on Tatum and Waller at their own game, trying to accelerate his ragtime and stride approach to such an extent that he was able to play very fast but only rather vapidly. And yet he was capable of playing with astonishing beauty, as on 'Where Or When', from the second Classics volume. He was also greatly drawn to classical material, and 'Schubert's Serenade' is one of the highlights of the January 1944 session for World Transcriptions.

The earlier volume contains some valuable sides, the bulk of them recorded in France. The solo 'Honeysuckle Rose' is unashamedly Walleresque, and it very nearly works. The solo stuff is almost always better, and the album might receive a slightly higher rating if it weren't for the dreary material with Robinson and the two tracks with Day, who shouldn't be confused with Anita O'Day (and wouldn't be if you could hear her sing).

The later trio underlines Chit's preference for playing solo with the most minimal accompaniment. Jimmy Shirley and both Cedric Wallace and Calton Powell are accomplished players but rarely come to the fore. Almost all of this material was recorded back in New York City, the sole exception being a single track, 'You Gave Me Everything But Love', recorded for Brunswick in Paris a decade earlier, and included here to fill out an earlier chapter in an extraordinary and still unappreciated career.

Ellen Christi

VOCAL

Although Chicago-born, Christi is based in Italy, working loosely in an improvising-vocalist idiom.

**** Dreamers**

Splasc(h) H 311 *Christi; Claudio Lodati (g).* 4/90.

***** A Piece Of The Rock**

Splasc(h) H 393-3 *Christi; Masahiko Kono (tb); Carlo Actis Dato (ts, bs, bcl); Enrico Fazio (f); Fiorenzo Sordini (d).* 1/91.

Christi's manner suggests a position somewhere between Jeanne Lee and Urszula Dudziak, and she hovers between words and sounds in a confident but sometimes unappealing manner: neither a committed improviser like Maggie Nicols nor a convincing bop-scat singer, she doesn't always characterize her material with enough certainty to persuade a listener that she really knows what she's doing. The duet session with Lodati sounds dated, relying on overdubs and cooing textures that suggest a throwback to some of the improvising experiments of the 1970s. But *A Piece Of The Rock* is far superior. Christi has worked with Dato before, on the vinyl-only *Senza Parole*, and both of them are part of a convincing bop-to-free group that gets extra weight from Kono's sombre trombone and the crisp rhythms of Fazio and Sordini (who is credited as co-leader). Christi's vocabulary of groans may still turn some listeners off, but the music holds some power.

Charlie Christian (1916–42)

GUITAR

Played in touring groups in the early '30s, and was playing an electric guitar by 1937. Heard by Benny Goodman, he joined the Goodman orchestra and small group and was otherwise found jamming at New York's Minton's Club, an early crucible of bebop. Hospitalized for TB in 1941, he died the next year after contracting pneumonia.

****** The Genius Of The Electric Guitar**

Columbia 460612-2 *Christian; Alec Fila, Irving Goodman, Cootie Williams (t); Cutty Cutshall, Lou McGarity (tb); Gus Bivona, Skippy Martin (as); Georgie Auld, Pete Mandello (ts); Bob Snyder (bs); Lionel Hampton (vib); Count Basie, Dudley Brooks, Johnny Guarnieri, Fletcher Henderson (p); Artie Bernstein (b); Nick Fatool, Harry Jaeger, Jo Jones, Dave Tough (d).* 39–41.

****** Solo Flight**

Topaz TPZ 1017 *As above, except add Henry 'Red' Allen, Ziggy Elman, Dizzy Gillespie, Johnny Martell, Jimmy Maxwell (t), Red Ballard, Vernon Brown, J.C Higginbotham, Ted Vesley (tb), Edmond Hall (cl), Earl Bostic, Benny Carter, Buff Estes, Skippy Martin, Toots Mondello, Hymie Schertzer (as), Bus Basey, Coleman Hawkins, Jerry Jerome, Ben Webster (ts), Clyde Hart, Ken Kersey (p), Meade Lux Lewis (cel), Israel Crosby, Milt Hinton (b), Big Sid Catlett, Cozy Cole (d).* 39–41.

Who actually invented bebop? Parker and Gillespie seemed to arrive at near-identical solutions to the blind alley of jazz harmony. Thelonious Monk was never an orthodox bopper, but he had his two cents' worth. And then there was Charlie Christian, who in some accounts was the first to develop the long lines and ambitious harmonic progressions of bop. Christian's appetite for booze and girls was only ever overtaken by his thirst for music. He once improvised 'Rose Room' for nearly an hour and a half, a feat which prompted Benny Goodman to hire him. Though Christian's greatest contributions, in terms of musical history, were the historic jams at Minton's in New York out of which bebop emerged, his role in the Goodman and Lionel Hampton bands, documented rather well on *Solo Flight*, represent the bulk of what is left to us. There are versions around of the Minton's material, but they enjoy a slightly uncertain existence. Christian's first commercial outings were the September 1939 sides with Hampton. A single track from it ('One Sweet Letter From You') and one from a month later ('Haven't Named It Yet') give a sense of the excitement the bandleader obviously felt at this freshly discovered young voice.

Christian was arguably the first guitarist to make completely convincing use of an electric instrument and, though his style blended Texas blues riffing with Lester Young's long-limbed strolls, he was able to steer a path away from the usual saxophone-dominated idiom and towards something that established guitar as an improvising instrument in its own right. Goodman clearly recognized that and gave him considerable solo space in his sextet. Amplification meant that the guitar could be heard clearly, and Christian's solos on 'Rose Room' and 'Star Dust' remain models for the instrument.

There is considerable overlap between the two records, but the absence of 'Air Mail Special' on the Topaz might just swing things in favour of the Columbia ... except that it includes another excellent Goodman big-band number, 'Honeysuckle Rose', and – a fascinating sidelight on a short career – Christian's contribution to a February 1941 session by clarinettist Edmond Hall, on which no less than Meade Lux Lewis plays celeste; 'Profoundly Blue' is a one-off, but it is a very lovely singleton. As one might expect, there is some pretty routine passage-work on both records – 'I Surrender Dear' from April 1940 is the first time Christian sounds prepared to recycle his own ideas – but the best of it (and we might add the tersely swinging 'Seven Come Eleven' from November 1939 to that list) requires a place in any properly representative collection of modern jazz.

Jodie Christian (born 1932)

PIANO

A veteran of the local Chicago jazz scene, Christian, despite his considerable experience, didn't start recording as a leader until 1992. While broadly based in a hard-bop idiom, he has also worked with Roscoe Mitchell.

***(*) Experience

Delmark DD-454 *Christian; Larry Gray (b); Vincent Davis (d).* 5/91–2/92.

*** Rain Or Shine

Delmark DE-467 *As above, except add Paul McKee (tb), Roscoe Mitchell (ss, as, ob), Art Porter (as), Ernie Adams (d), George Hughes (d), Francine Griffin (v).* 5/91–12/93.

Christian opens the first record with a Byzantine exploration of the blues on 'Bluesing Around', and it gives the impression that he couldn't wait to get stuck into his first date as a leader, on the cusp of his sixtieth birthday. A local Chicagoan through and through, he can play for anybody, yet, unlike all too many such sidemen, he has a distinction of his own. More than half of the CD is solo piano, with a very slow 'Mood Indigo' and a lovely original called 'Faith' as particular standouts; and Christian's decisive touch and complex but clear voicings bespeak a talent that has absorbed everything it needs from the jazz tradition. Gray and Davis help out assiduously on the four trio tracks.

The follow-up is by comparison a bit disappointing. 'Let's Try' is a fine opener with sterling work by McKee and Porter – who sounds quite different from his Verve Forecast self – and the ballad medley works well, with an especially impressive turn by the trombonist on 'Polka Dots And Moonbeams'. But the tracks with Roscoe Mitchell, who sounds notably sour and argumentative, just don't fit in, no matter how nobly Christian tries to bring them round. Griffin sings on two tracks and Jodie himself croons one number.

*** Soul Fountain

Delmark DE 498 *Christian; Odies Williams (t); Roscoe Mitchell (as, f); Art Porter (as); John Whitfield (b); Ernie Adams (d).* 8/94.

*** Front Line

Delmark DE 490 *Christian; Sonny Cohn (t); Norris Turney (as); Eddie Johnson (ts); John Whitfield (b); Ernie Adams, Gerryck King (d); Francine Griffin (v).* 1/96.

Soul Fountain at least integrates Mitchell rather more successfully into Christian's format, odd though it is to hear him blowing on 'Now's The Time', even if the long 'Consequences' doesn't really work, and again there's the feeling that this is a record where too many styles are being jostled together. The piano solos, 'Everlasting Life' and 'Blessings', are further evidence of Christian's gifts, and the lovely duet with Porter on 'My One And Only Love' makes a touching farewell to the since-departed altoman.

Front Line assembles a nice group of old-timers for a set of old-time tunes – Ellington, Basie, standards. Turney still has his Hodges and Willie Smith sound beautifully together, but Sonny Cohn sounds a bit shaky, cleverly though he disguises it, and Johnson is merely big and bluff. Christian acts as referee here and gets the best he can out of the team; it's good fun.

Denny Christianson

TRUMPET

Canadian trumpeter whose records usually find him in his big-band format.

*** Suite Mingus

Justin Time JUST 15 *Christianson; Pepper Adams (bs); Roger Walls, Danile Doyon, Ron Di Lauro, Jocelyn Laponte (t); Patrice*

Dufour, Muhammad Abdul Al-Khabyyr, André Verreault (tb); Bob Ellis (btb); Joe Christie Jr (as, f, cl, ss, picc); Pat Vetter (as, cl, f); Richard Beaudet (ts, f, cl); Jean Lebrun (ts, f, ss, picc); Jean Frechette (bs, bcl); Kenny Alexander (p); Richard Ring (g); Vic Angelillo (b); Pierre Pilon (d). 8/86.

*****(*) Shark Bait**

Justin Time JUST 60 *Christianson; Roger Walls, Jocelyn Couture, Richard Gagnon, Robert Piette (t, flhn); André Verreault, Muhammad Abdul Al-Khabyyr, Kelsley Grant (tb); Colin Murray (btb); Jean-Pierre Zanella (as, ss, f, cl); François D'Amour (as, ss, f); Richard Beaudet (ts, f); Jacques Lelievre (ts, f, cl); Colin Biggin (bs, bcl); Jan Jarczyk (p); Richard Ring (g); Vic Angelillo, Sylvain Gagnon (b); Jim Hillman (d). 11–12/93.*

Christianson is an accomplished Canadian trumpeter with a tone startlingly close to that of compatriot Kenny Wheeler, but with a more straightahead approach to improvisation. In the earlier of the pair, he expertly fronts his well-schooled big band in a showcase for baritonist Pepper Adams, a former Mingus sideman. The main event is a suite by Curt Berg called 'Three Hats', which largely consists of three original Mingus compositions – 'Slop', 'Fables Of Faubus' and '1 × Love' – with a linking theme. Adams's bronchial tone stands out rather too starkly from Christianson's smooth arrangements. It works beautifully on an arrangement of 'My Funny Valentine' – in the non-Mingus part of the programme – but palls a little over the long haul. Christianson himself solos with authority on 'Faubus' and two of the Alf Clausen themes that open the set, but he is relatively modest in his claim on solo space.

His main contributions to the later record are a moving flugelhorn solo on his own composition, 'Monk-ing', and a crisper duet with Walls on 'Back To The Office'. For the most part, he is happy to leave the spotlight to others, and there are excellent band contributions: Al-Khabyyr's on 'Blenda Lee' and 'Geezers On Parade' (another Berg composition), Zanella's Sonny Fortune-like alto on 'C'est Quoi?'. The band is nicely balanced and very professionally recorded with a natural, 'acoustic' sound that gives the music a lot of presence.

Ian Christie (born 1927)

CLARINET and

Keith Christie (1931-1980)

TROMBONE

The Christie brothers were a sometimes explosive combination in the combustible years of British trad. Ian retired to the sidelines and worked as a TV critic, returning to occasional playing in the 1980s, but Keith took a nomadic path through British jazz, moving from trad to Ted Heath to Tubby Hayes and studio and theatre work. He died in 1980, his last years troubled by alcoholism.

*****(*) Christie Brothers Stompers**

Cadillac SGC/MEL CD 201 *Ian Christie; Keith Christie; Ken Colyer (c); Dickie Hawdon (t); Pat Hawes, Charlie Smith (p); Nevil Skrimshire (g); Ben Marshall (bj); Mickey Ashman, Denny Coffee (b); George Hopkinson, Bernard Saward, Pete Appleby (d); Bill Colyer (wbd); Neva Raphaello (v). 6/51–8/52.*

This captures the sometimes crazed intensity of original British trad better than any of the more renowned Colyer, Lyttelton or Barber reissues. The Christies originally put together the group with players from the Lyttelton and Crane River bands, and the CD collects tracks from various sessions for Melodisc, along with four live tracks from a previously unknown acetate. Though the first few numbers suffer from poor sound, they belt along with bewildering power. Colyer's lead is less self-consciously 'authentic' than he would later become, and Keith Christie delivers some hair-raising solos. The later sessions with Dickie Hawdon in for Colyer are comparatively steady, but the fierce rhythm-sections, Ian Christie's gargling but supple solos and the queer blend of high spirits and grim determination that seems to typify this music keep everything fresh. Remastering has been done very capably from some less than ideal sources. The CD is also beautifully packaged and annotated.

Pete Christlieb (born 1945)

TENOR SAXOPHONE

A Los Angeles resident, Christlieb has been an unassuming but valuable figure in West Coast jazz for decades, through countless studio dates and accompanist roles. He has a strong kinship with muscular, versatile players such as Zoot Sims and Lew Tabackin.

***** Conversations With Warne Vol. 1**

Criss Cross 1043 *Christlieb; Warne Marsh (ts); Jim Hughart (b); Nick Ceroli (d). 9/78.*

***** Live**

Capri 74026-2 *Christlieb; Bob Cooper (ts); Mike Wofford (p); Chuck Berghofer (b); Donald Bailey (d). 2/90.*

Christlieb's proficiency as sessionman and section-player with numerous West Coast big bands has let his status as soloist drift over the years. These two dates, each with another tenorman, present him as the energy source on both occasions, even though Cooper and Marsh come over as far more individual. Next to Marsh's serpentine, querulous solos, Christlieb's improvisations sound almost simple, but the senior man plays with much more attack and a rather less pinched tone than usual. Whether this dissipates any of the characteristic Marsh qualities is a moot point, but the playing – on a series of sequences devised by Christlieb and Hughart – has a prodigious intensity.

Next to that, the club recording with Cooper is easy-going music. They both burn through 'Shaw 'Nuff', but Cooper's solo turns on 'Come Sunday' and the mid-tempo 'Touch Of Your Lips' are more typical. The location recording is rather muted.

Gunter Christmann (born 1942)

TROMBONE, CELLO

An improviser with a long-standing involvement in European free music, Christmann began recording for FMP in the early 1970s. Primarily a trombonist, he now plays cello almost as often.

His evolving project, Vario, established in 1979, is the name given to the differing improvising groups that he puts together; it has reached Vario 34 at least. He also works extensively in film and has explored the connections between improvised music and film-making.

*****(*) Alla Prima**

Concepts Of Doing 001 *Christmann; Alexander Frangenheim (b).* 1/97.

****** Here Now**

Concepts Of Doing 003 *Christmann; Evan Parker (ss, ts).* 1–4/98.

***** Water Writes Always In Plural**

Concepts Of Doing 004 *Christmann; Mats Gustafsson (ss); Thomas Lehn (syn); Christian Munthe (g); Alexander Frangenheim (b); Paul Lovens (d).* 7/98.

Welcome back to this maverick spirit, who hasn't been particularly well-served by CD to date. These albums on Concepts Of Doing supplement the issues on Edition Explico, Christmann's own tiny label which issues records in minuscule runs. He is one of the great individualists of the trombone: a vocabulary of gasps, smears, wheezes, etc., etc., but a sensibility that seems to think in long-form as well as in the moment-to-moment strangeness which his music runs by. The duets with Frangenheim will evoke memories of his old FMP albums with Detlef Schonenberg, but this is better recorded and more fully achieved. Though both men work very quietly for much of the way, Christmann's playing in particular is as spontaneous and unpredictable as ever: his trombone will suddenly bark out a note that shocks the listener. With Parker, there's an almost sing-song quality to their interplay. A perfectly rounded disc which starts with two long soprano solos by Parker in his most magisterial style, continues with three duets ('Here Now 2', for tenor and trombone, is especially fine), and finishes with Christmann at his nuttiest in three unfathomable solos.

Water Always Writes In Plural is by Vario 34, a recent incarnation of Christmann's ongoing group music. Considering the players involved, it's a surprisingly low-key event, scissored into nine pieces in which the players appear to be circling rather respectfully round one another.

*****(*) One To (Two)**

Okkadisk 10002 *Christmann; Mats Gustafsson (ss, ts, bs).* 8/97.

A rare American record for Christmann, even if it was recorded in Hanover. Gustafsson is a more incendiary performer than the trombonist (or should we now call him cellist? He plays the string instrument on 12 of the 18 tracks), but he inevitably bows to Gunter's more insidious aesthetic. These pecked-off miniatures are taut, concentrated, eccentric, and often very funny, as well as disquieting: one of those records when you're never sure what will happen next.

June Christy (1926–90)

VOCAL

Followed Anita O'Day as Stan Kenton's singer in 1945, and sang with him regularly for years while also having her own recording career, mostly with Capitol in the '50s and '60s. When her career waned she basically retired, although she recorded a couple of sessions in the '70s. Married to Bob Cooper.

*****(*) Day Dreams**

Capitol 832083-2 *Christy; Stan Kenton (p); orchestras directed by Frank DeVol, Bob Cooper, Pete Rugolo, Shorty Rogers.* 3/47–5/55.

****** Something Cool**

Capitol 96329-2 *Christy; Pete Rugolo Orchestra.* 53–55.

***** Duet**

Capitol 89285-2 *Christy; Stan Kenton (p).* 55.

****** The Misty Miss Christy**

Capitol 98452-2 *Christy; Pete Rugolo Orchestra.* 56.

*****(*) Fair And Warmer & Gone For The Day**

Capitol 95448-2 *Christy; orchestra.* 57.

****** The Song Is June**

Capitol 55455-2 *Christy; Pete Rugolo Orchestra.* 7/58–8/60.

*****(*) Ballads For Night People & The Intimate Miss Christy**

Capitol 96728-2 *Christy; Bud Legge (f); Al Viola (g); Don Bagley (b); orchestra arranged by Bob Cooper.* 60–63.

*****(*) Big Band Specials**

Capitol 498319-2 *Christy; Conte Candoli, Lee Katzman, Al Porcino, Ray Triscari (t); Vern Friley, Lew McCreary, Frank Rosolino, John Haliburton, Ken Shroyer, Dick Nash (tb); Bob Cooper, Joe Maini, Jack Nimitz, Bill Perkins, Bud Legge, Charlie Kennedy (saxes); Jimmie Rowles (p); Joe Mondragon (b); Mel Lewis (d).* 10–11/62.

****** The Best Of The Jazz Sessions**

Capitol 53922-2 *Christy; various groups as above.* 9/49–8/68.

June Christy might be the great lost jazz singer of her era. She is not forgotten: her years with Stan Kenton and several solo hits have sustained her legend. But jazz-vocal followers have seemed reluctant to place her in the same league as Ella or Billie or Sarah. We beg to differ. Christy's wholesome but peculiarly sensuous voice is both creative and emotive. Her long, controlled lines and the shading of a fine vibrato suggest both a professional's attention to detail and a tender, solicitous feel for the heart of a song, something which makes the often dark material of her later years the more affecting. Her greatest moments are as close to creating definitive interpretations as any singer can come.

She was already, when barely into her twenties, a confident and stylish singer, a swing-era canary with a feel for the cooler, more knowing pulse of the years ahead. *Day Dreams* collects various singles and a few unreleased pieces from 1947–50, including a rare scat vehicle on 'The Way You Look Tonight' (just the sort of thing Christy wasn't supposed to be good at, though she handles it superbly), a gorgeous treatment of Gershwin's 'Do It Again', Bob Graettinger's bizarre chart for 'Everything Happens To Me' and a couple of fine Ellington treatments. Two duet tracks with Stan Kenton from 1955 are leftovers from their *Duet* session.

Her best work was done with arranger Pete Rugolo (although numerous charts by her husband, Bob Cooper, shouldn't be forgotten). The masterpieces are certainly *Something Cool* and *The Misty Miss Christy*. The original LPs were perfectly programmed and meticulously tailored to Christy's persona. 'Something Cool' itself is a story that bears endless retelling, but 'Midnight Sun', 'I Should Care' and several others seem like definitive interpretations, a marvel for Christy's technique – perfect breath control and vibrato – as well as for her emotional colouring. The original *Something Cool* programme has no fewer than 13 tracks added to it for the CD version, some of them less than marvellous, but there's nothing that can spoil the record. *The Misty Miss Christy* is its equal: her version of 'Round Midnight' ought to go down as one of the great treatments of that much-covered song. Rugolo's inventiveness is unstinting throughout, handling the orchestra in surprising ways but doing nothing to unsettle or take the attention away from the singer. *Fair And Warmer* is doubled up with *Gone For The Day*, two further 1957 sessions with Rugolo, and these breezy songs still have a tang of melancholy about them which singer and arranger seem to encourage in each other.

The *Duet* album with her longtime boss, Kenton, is the oddity among her sessions: Kenton clunks away and Christy, exposed as never before, for once seems to falter in her own technique. Though there's a bittersweetness in all of her records, here she sounds fatalistic.

The Song Is June, which couples that album with the later *Off Beat*, is unmissable. While there are some swingers here, including delightful versions of 'A Sleepin' Bee', 'The One I Love (Belongs To Somebody Else)' and 'The Song Is You', the nocturnal brooding of 'Saturday's Children', 'Nobody's Heart' and 'You Say You Care' is more typical. Rugolo never did a better chart than his astonishing one for 'Remind Me', and Christy's mature style blends the sweetness of her youth with a serene melancholy that can be deeply affecting. These have never been famous records; they should be.

The British end of Capitol has issued a double-up of *Ballads For Night People* (arranged by Bob Cooper and featuring his own tenor in a particularly fine 'My Ship', although 'Kissing Bug' and an achingly slow 'Bewitched' are also very fine) and *The Intimate Miss Christy*, where June has only a Julie Londonish accompaniment behind her. It's a moot point as to whether her version of 'Ev'ry Time' outdoes Chris Connor's: a close thing. *Big Band Specials* offers her a dozen hits from the swing era, some rarely sung, such as 'Skyliner', 'Swingin' On Nothin'' and 'Until'. Must have been a nostalgic exercise for her in 1962, and charts by Cooper, Bill Holman and Shorty Rogers make the grade. All in all, it's a pleasure to see so many of her Capitol albums back in circulation, though their availability will vary depending on where you are.

Best Of The Jazz Sessions is an astute compilation that goes as far as a small-group session of 1968. One can complain about some of the omissions, but there is more than enough great Christy here to make it essential for those who might prefer to sample some of her work.

***** A Friendly Session Vol. 1**

Jasmine JASCD 341 *Christy; Johnny Guarnieri (p); others unknown.* 50.

****(*) A Lovely Way To Spend An Evening**

Jasmine JASMCD 2528 *Christy; Stu Williamson (t); Herb Geller (as); Russ Freeman (p); Monte Budwig (b); Shelly Manne (d);*. 57–59.

These are shoddy but nevertheless useful survivals. The earlier disc finds Christy on a set of radio transcriptions with a Johnny Guarnieri small group: 20 songs, including at least one tantalizing rarity, 'The Sky Without The Stars'. Sound is one-dimensional but listenable. The sound is thin and weakly spread on the later Jasmine disc, too; but the performances find the singer in inventive and bright form, and both the tracks with Manne's group and with the Jerry Gray band are hip and swinging affairs.

Antonio Ciacca (born 1969)

PIANO

Taught by Barry Harris and Jaki Byard, the young Italian has already worked with Larry Smith, Steve Lacy, Johnny Griffin and Craig Bailey.

****(*) Hollis Avenue**

yvp 3075 *Ciacca; Brian Hoberon, Markus Trikland (ts); Azhi Osada, Brandon Owen (b); Marcus Baylor, Tommaso Cappellatto (d).* 1/99.

Recorded in New York with two different quartets, on the same day, Ciacca's second album (his first, *Driemotyr* (C-Jam), has not come our way) is a sound if middleweight modern session. One group features student players, the others are hopeful young Turks, and Ciacca himself is confident but in need of a distinctive route. When he plays Monk ('Ask Me Now') he sounds slavishly like the master, and his Ellington and Strayhorn treatments are agreeable but uneventful. Hoberon and Trikland do nothing wrong and leave little trace. Awaiting further development.

Circle

GROUP

A short-lived quartet featuring the four principals, which came together when Braxton joined the already-working trio of Corea, Holland and Altschul.

***** Paris-Concert**

ECM 843163-2 2CD *Anthony Braxton (reeds, perc); Chick Corea (p); Dave Holland (b); Barry Altschul (d).* 2/71.

Something of a historical document at this point, although unsatisfactory in many respects. This was recorded on the group's one European tour, and it was a quartet that wouldn't last long, mainly because of tensions building up between Braxton and Corea. This concert souvenir is full of hustle and bustle, but it doesn't seem to go anywhere in particular. There's a yearning for freedom by all hands, but Corea isn't really interested in following Braxton's approach any more than Braxton is interested in playing 'Nefertiti' and 'There Is No Greater Love', which start and finish the album. Their playful 'Duet', though, is an unexpected highlight. Holland and Altschul play a lot of music, but they are very poorly served by the sound, which is atypically thin and clattery for an ECM session. Scholars of the period have found it fascinating, though.

Clarinet Summit

GROUP

The dominance of the saxophone in jazz had so largely eclipsed the clarinet that to play the older horn seemed quite radical and appealed most to players of an experimental bent, as in this intriguing meeting of generations.

***** In Concert At The Public Theater**

India Navigation IN 1062 *Alvin Batiste, John Carter, Jimmy Hamilton (cl); David Murray (bcl).* 82, 83.

*****(*) Southern Bells**

Black Saint 120107 *As above.* 3/87.

This is one of those one-off projects – the concert documented on the India Navigation disc – that proved so durable that the group reconvened as often as individual commitments permitted. What made the line-up fascinating was the appearance side by side of two mainstream-traditionalists (Batiste, Hamilton) alongside two modernists of markedly individual temperament. Murray's voice is, inevitably, the easiest to pick out of the throng, but the three B-flat clarinets are woven so closely together that it is only when a trademark device emerges, like Hamilton's softly decelerating phrases towards the end of a chorus, that it is possible to identify who is playing. 'Jeep's Blues' acknowledges Hamilton's swing loyalties, but the most enticing single performance is 'Groovin' High', in which Carter takes a prominent lead. 'Sweet Lovely' gives Murray a chance to show off his more lyrical side and features some great ensemble playing as well. There is more emphasis on individual expression on the follow-up, but with the same mix of styles: 'Mbizo' alongside 'Perdido', 'I Want To Talk About You' before 'Beat Box'. These are beguiling juxtapositions and this is a much better-recorded disc, which means that the very different textures of the four horns are much more evident. Either one will delight.

Clarion Fracture Zone

GROUP

Australian contemporary outfit mixing modal bop with a lick of fusion.

***** Blue Shift**

Rufus RF 040 *Sandy Evans (ts, ss); Tony Gorman (as, ts, cl, perc); Alister Spence (p, syn); Steve Elphick (b); Andrew Dickeson (d).* 3/90.

***** Zones On Parade**

Rufus Records RF 001 *Sandy Evans (ts, ss); Tony Gorman (as, ts, cl, perc); Alister Spence (p, syn); Steve Elphick (b, tba); Louis Burdett, Tony Buck, Lucien Boiteaux (d).* 3 & 4/92.

*****(*) What This Love Can Do**

Rufus RF 010 *Sandy Evans (ts, ss); Tony Gorman (as, cl, perc); Alister Spence (p, syn); Lloyd Swanton (b); Toby Hall (d); Greg Sheehan (perc).* 11/93.

***** Less Stable Elements**

Rufus Records RF 020 *As above, except add Darryl Pratt (perc).* 6/95.

Strong, slightly moody contemporary sounds from a Scottish/Australian group who have become a solid live act. The husband-and-wife front line exchange featured roles with seemly even-handedness, though Sandy Evans, composer of the suite, *What This Love Can Do*, has emerged as the stronger voice. Initially a good deal of responsibility was devolved to Spence; on the debut album he shows a relaxed touch that tempers the slight fussiness of some of the arrangements. The sound on *Zones On Parade* is immediately better, with a business-like, road-tested feel, abetted by a more professional mix. Further changes to the rhythm section for record number three, and it's here that things are quite clearly not 100 per cent. CFZ have yet to present a convincing drum-sound, and there isn't enough propulsion from the back. Ironically, the *What This Love* suite might have worked better with a drummerless concept and with a couple of guest spots for brass. Gorman wisely sticks to alto and gives his clarinets more prominence; a better texture up front. Spence, as always, is unflustered and competently expressive. Plaudits to Evans, though, for an impressive composition. The most recent disc throws the compositional weight back on to Spence and Gorman, with just one track credited to Evans. It's a more straightforward record, though not any less subtle in inflexion for that. The playing gets better every time, though on this occasion the writing has perhaps taken a back seat. The long opening tracks probably sound better live, but they're energetic enough even in a studio setting, and Gorman's closing number, 'Nomads', sounds as if it might yield an extravagant jam if given time and scope, though at 13 minutes it's already generously proportioned.

Sonny Clark (1931–63)

PIANO

Recorded on the West Coast from 1953, on the East from 1957, and recorded constantly for the next six years, though alcohol and heroin ruined him.

*****(*) Sonny Clark Trio**

Blue Note 51238-2 *Clark; Paul Chambers (b); Philly Joe Jones (d).* 1/57.

****** Cool Struttin'**

Blue Note 95327-2 *As above, except add Art Farmer (t); Jackie McLean (as).* 1/58.

***** Standards**

Blue Note 21283-2 *Clark; Paul Chambers, Jymie Merritt (b); Wes Landers (d).* 11–12/58.

Clark approached music with a joyous abandon. As long as there was a piano in the corner, a bottle opened and some business to attend to in a back room, he seems to have been content. Perhaps because the darkness of his private life – a pendulum back and forth between alcohol and narcotics – never seems to have impinged on his ability to play, he enjoyed a steady if short-lived tenure as Blue Note's house pianist. Note perfect, rhythmically bouncy and always ready with a quirky idea, he was an ideal group-player, rather less convincing in the context of a hornless group like the eponymous 1957 date. Chambers, then approaching his heyday, has a greater than usual share of the spotlight, perhaps because Sonny's capacity for solos was never substantial.

Cool Struttin', now reissued in Blue Note's Rudy Van Gelder series, is an immaculately tasteful jazz album. The title-piece is a long-form blues, with room for the horns to stretch out. Sonny's own finest moment is his solo on 'Blue Minor', another original. His three-note trills are almost Monkian and the percussive, spacious attack is reminiscent of the bebop giant at his most capacious. Though Clark rarely strays far from the blues, one can hear Farmer itching to break through into other dimensions. The reissue contains two extra tracks unreleased on LP: his own 'Royal Flush' and a wayward interpretation of Rodgers and Hart's 'Lover'. Easy to see why it was excluded.

The standards album lacks character. Clark's great strength, like Monk's and Powell's, lay in imposing his own personality on algebraically simple materials. Here he is required to play melodically and he sounds merely workmanlike. Landers is a very pedestrian drummer by the standards set by Philly Joe. Two superb Blue Notes – *Sonny's Crib* and *Leapin' And Lopin'* – are currently unavailable in most territories. Until they are reissued, it will be hard to frame a definitive assessment of Clark's real strengths, which lay mostly in his writing. For the moment, he remains something of a musicians' musician.

Kenny Clarke (1914–85)

DRUMS, XYLOPHONE

Born in Pittsburgh, Clarke came from a musical family and had an early facility on a wide range of instruments, a level of musicianship that suffused everything he did. He is one of the prime movers of the bebop movement but remained in a more swing-orientated idiom than either Art Blakey or Max Roach. Clarke spent his later years in France and was something of a hero in his adoptive country.

***(*) Pieces Of Time

Soul Note 121078 *Clarke; Andrew Cyrille, Milford Graves, Famoudou Don Moye (d, perc).* 9/83.

'Klook', so called because of the distinctive 'klook-mop' sound of his favourite cadence, is one of the most influential drummers of all time. There are those who allow him a hand in the invention of bebop, and certainly in recent times the focus of the bebop revolution has shifted away from the horn-men and towards the rhythm section that gave bop its ferocious energy and drive. While working with Dizzy Gillespie in the early 1940s, having made his recording debut at 24 in Sweden with the dire James Anderson on vocals, Clarke began to depart from normal practice by marking the count on his top cymbal and using his bass drum only for accents. With his left hand he rattled out the counter-rhythms that weave their way through all his records. It became the distinctive sound of bebop, imitated and adapted by Blakey and Roach, who came to the music with rather different presuppositions about it, and it remains essential background work for drummers even today. Clarke had a strong but also quite delicate sound. The cover of *Plays André Hodeir* (now deleted, more's the pity) shows him wielding extra-long sticks, as he did from time to time throughout his career; they enabled him to get around his kit and to pick out a highly nuanced sound that lesser drummers could never duplicate.

Unfortunately, his Savoys are now again awaiting reissue, and there's only this unrepresentative later disc in the catalogue. Though the record was hailed on release as a much-needed reminder that Milford Graves was still alive and functioning, Klook was the elder statesman at this astonishing confrontation, and he more or less steals the show with a seemingly effortless display that has the younger guys diving into their bags for ever more exotic wrinkles on the same basic sound. Not to all tastes, perhaps, but an intriguing and historic record nevertheless.

Clarke–Boland Big Band

GROUP

Co-led by the Belgian pianist and the American drummer, this all-star band ran intermittently but often with a stable personnel over the period 1961–72.

*** All Blues / Sax No End

MPS 523525-2 *Kenny Clarke (d); Francy Boland (p); Benny Bailey, Jimmy Deuchar, Tony Fisher, Dusko Goykovich, Shake Keane, Idrees Sulieman (t); Erik Van Lier, Nat Peck, Ake Persson, Jiggs Whigham (tb); Derek Humble (as); Carl Drewo, Johnny Griffin, Eddie 'Lockjaw' Davis, Ronnie Scott (ts); Tony Coe (ts, cl); Sahib Shihab (bs, ss, f); Jean Warland, Jimmy Woode (b); Fats Sadi (perc).* 67–68.

*** Three Latin Adventures

MPS 529095-2 *Kenny Clarke (d); Francy Boland (p); Benny Bailey, Idrees Sulieman, Milo Pavlovich, Jimmy Deuchar, Dusko Goykovich (t); Ake Persson, Nat Peck, Erik Van Lier (tb); Derek Humble, Phil Woods, Johnny Griffin, Ronnie Scott, Tony Coe, Sahib Shihab (reeds); Jimmy Woode, Jean Warland (b); Shake Keane, Albert 'Tootie' Heath, Tony Inzalaco, Sabu Martinez (perc).* 8–12/68.

One of the most exciting big bands of the post-war years. Joint leadership did them nothing but good. Boland steered the harmonies, Clarke piled on the coal and steamed. It was a near-perfect combination of strengths and it lasted them for many years. These are welcome reissues, missing for many years. Studio sound is roomy and generous, with plenty of space round bass and drums. The sections are filled with players of a calibre – in terms of both playing excellence and box-office draw – which it would surely be impossible to replicate now; yet the albums have languished in comparative obscurity for far too long. Perhaps Boland's charts could sometimes edge towards pretentiousness, or the playing in the studio didn't quite catch the flash and ebullience of their best gigs, but this was a marvellous institution and it is worth remembering through these two sets, which bring together four original albums in total.

Paul Clarvis (born 1963)

PERCUSSION

British drummer-percussionist at home in a variety of settings.

***** For All The Saints**
Village Life MRFD 97132 VL *Clarvis; Stan Sulzmann (sax, f); Tony Hymas (p, syn). 7/96.*

A strong debut recording from the British percussionist who has made a name for himself as a classical player, not least in a controversial piece by Harrison Birtwistle, commissioned for the last night of the London Proms. This disc is based very largely on traditional or 'folk' themes from Britain and further afield. Some work more convincingly than others, though there is no mistaking the strong musicality all three players bring to the session. Hymas is the least assertive, but he brings a very definite slant to the material, and Clarvis responds with alacrity, playing joyously and with evident enthusiasm.

The Classic Jazz Quartet

GROUP

A quartet of knowing old dogs in the classic-mainstream idiom. Their existence was effectively terminated by Wellstood's death.

****** The Complete Recordings**
Jazzology JCD-138/139 2CD *Dick Sudhalter (c); Joe Muranyi (cl, ss); Dick Wellstood (p); Marty Grosz (g, v). 11/84–3/86.*

The Classic Jazz Quartet – they preferred their original name, The Bourgeois Scum – were one of the pioneer outfits who helped create the renewed taste for old(er) jazz repertory in the 1980s and '90s. This package is a comprehensive set of their work – two studio LPs, plus about an LP's worth of previously unreleased, live-without-an-audience music – set down before Wellstood's untimely death ended the group. They resuscitate much-neglected material from the 1920s and '30s, fill in with the odd chestnut and sneak by a few originals. The range of arrangement and dynamic which a quartet can touch on is surprising at this length, and the band always surprises, though the Germanic treatment of 'Mississippi Mud' will be tiresome to some. Grosz's wit has become relatively familiar in the last ten years, but the feel of this music has a freshness about it that some subsequent revivalism has missed; Sudhalter does a fine line in neo-Bix, the undervalued Muranyi is consistently strong; and 'the engine, the generator, driving the whole contraption', Wellstood shows why the band went down when he did. The notes in the booklet are rather exhaustingly clever, and the remastered sound is very fine.

Thomas Clausen (born 1949)

PIANO

Studied at the Copenhagen Academy before forging a name in the Danish jazz scene of the '70s, accompanying Dexter Gordon, working with his own trio, and building an international reputation through the '80s and '90s.

****** Psalm**
Storyville STCD 4185 *Clausen; Mads Vinding (b); Alex Riel (d). 6/94.*

This exemplary trio date – we listed a fine solo session in a previous edition – affirms Clausen's imaginative powers. It was an audacious idea to open the disc with the slow, dynamically surprising title-piece, and there are more surprises as the session proceeds: 'Dancing In The Dark' hardly refers to its melody at all, and the bare spaces of 'Soft' are beautifully handled. Clausen is at ease at any tempo and refuses to offer too many notes, while Vinding is as much a melodist as a timekeeper. Riel has seldom played better: he is very upfront in the mix, but engineer Hans Nielsen gives him a wonderful sound and his playing on, say, 'Skygger' gives terrific impetus to what otherwise would have been a mere mood piece.

*****(*) Turn Out The Stars**
Storyville STCD 4215 *Clausen; Severi Pyysalo (vib). 6/97.*

For sheer beauty of sound this pairing makes waves, and the musical interaction is pretty fine, too. Pyysalo plays with enough aggression and point to defer suggestions of excess prettiness, and his improvising (such as the astringent solo on Coleman's 'The Turnaround') is similarly tough-minded. But the players don't shy away from making the music sound harmoniously beautiful too. Clausen brought three themes to the session and 'Green Eyes' lingers in the mind.

James Clay (born 1935)

TENOR SAXOPHONE

A Texan saxophonist with only a handful of records to account for a big reputation, based on his playing on the local circuit in the late 1950s. A brief comeback on record in the 1980s seems to have led nowhere.

***** The Sound Of The Wide Open Spaces**
Original Jazz Classics OJC 257 *Clay; David Newman (ts); Wynton Kelly (p); Sam Jones (b); Art Taylor (d). 4/60.*

***** A Double Dose Of Soul**
Original Jazz Classics OJC 1790 *Clay; Nat Adderley (c); Victor Feldman (vib); Gene Harris (p); Sam Jones (b); Louis Hayes (d). 10/60.*

Clay is a semi-legendary figure whose reported influence on Ornette Coleman is interesting but scarcely borne out by these early records. *The Sound* gets into the brawling spirit typical of such two-tenor encounters but offers only a glimpse of Clay as a distinctive force. *A Double Dose* is only marginally more interesting, given that the date is organized as little more than a rote hard-bop affair, but Feldman's vibes are an unusual foil on three tunes, and 'Linda Serene' and 'Lost Tears' are mildly interesting originals.

Buck Clayton (1911–91)

TRUMPET

Though Buck was leading his own big band as early as 1934, it was his time with Basie which established him as a soloist of distinction, a player with a warm, brassy tone and a softness of delivery that was well suited to ballad playing and to accompanying singers. His recording career was long and fruitful, and only towards the end did Buck's standards slip.

***** Buck Clayton 1945–1947**

Classics 968 *Clayton; Dicky Wells, Trummy Young (tb); George Johnson (as); Scoville Browne (as, cl); Ed Hall (cl); Flip Phillips (ts); Lucky Thompson (ts); Sammy Benskin, Johnny Guarnieri, Billy Taylor, Teddy Wilson (p); Brick Fleagle, Freddie Green, Tiny Grimes (g); Al Hall, Milt Hinton, Al McKibbon, Slam Stewart (b); Danny Alvin, Jimmy Crawford, J.C Heard, Sid Weiss, Shadow Wilson (d); Canada Lee, Sylvia Sims, Kenneth Spencer (v).* 5/45–11/47.

***** The Classic Swing Of Buck Clayton**

Original Jazz Classics OJC 1709 *Clayton; Dicky Wells, Trummy Young (tb); Buster Bailey, Scoville Brown (cl); George Johnson (as); Jimmy Jones, Billy Taylor (p); Brick Fleagle, Tiny Grimes (g); John Levy, Al McKibbon, Sid Weiss (b); Cozy Cole, Jimmy Crawford (d).* 46.

Clayton is one of the great players of mainstream jazz. Responsible for no particular stylistic innovation, he managed to synthesize much of the history of jazz trumpet up to his time with a bright, brassy tone and an apparently limitless facility for melodic improvisation, which made him ideal for the open-ended jams he recorded for Columbia and, latterly, Chiaroscuro. He played with Basie until 1946, the year of the fine *Classic Swing* sessions, and after a stint in the army struck off on his own again, forming a productive association with shouter Jimmy Rushing which survived long enough for the European tour featured on the Steeplechase set below. The OJC set has much to enjoy: 'Harlem Cradle Song', with Young and Wells, has a lovely, easy swing, and there is a fine instrumental version of 'I Want A Little Girl', normally a Jimmy Rushing feature. The record is, however, now basically a duplication of the Classics set, which has other material too.

Most of Classics 968 was recorded under his own name, though the earliest date, from the day the bomb was dropped on Hiroshima, is under Freddie Green's name, and there is a later session for Keynote led by drummer J.C. Heard. Enough of the *echt* Clayton comes through on the sides for HRS which were recorded in 1946, including classics like 'Harlem Cradle Song' and 'Dawn Dance', tunes which bespeak a gentle artistry and an absolute musical integrity. There is some excellent stuff from Teddy Wilson (originally billed as Theodocius) and from all the reedmen, but the disc could have done without the educational 'Jazz Band', narrated by Canada Lee and sung by Kenneth Spencer, an oddity with a single B-take part for Buck. Clayton was a superb vocal accompanist, and his fills and subtle responses are always tasteful, but he's heard to better effect on the instrumental All Stars tracks from the same occasion, tackling 'Moonglow' with consummate artistry and taste.

****(*) Copenhagen Concert**

Steeplechase SCCD 36006/7 2CD *Clayton; Emmett Berry (t); Dicky Wells (tb); Earl Warren (as, cl); Buddy Tate (ts); Al Williams (p); Gene Ramey (b); Herbie Lovelle (d); Jimmy Rushing (v).* 9/59.

Plenty of old friends in this band, from the lubricious Wells to the galvanic Rushing, and Clayton sheriffs the ensemble with his expected panache. Eighty-five minutes of music is rather generously spread over two CDs and since it isn't all deathless stuff, it might have been better reduced to a single disc of the real highlights. But the real problem is the sound, and nobody suffers worse than Buck himself, who is way off mike for many of his solos.

*****(*) Buck & Buddy**

Original Jazz Classics OJCCD 757 *Clayton; Buddy Tate (ts); Sir Charles Thompson (p); Gene Ramey (b); Mousie Alexander (d).* 12/60.

***** Buck & Buddy Blow The Blues**

Original Jazz Classics OJCCD 850 *As above.* 9/61.

These document a happy association. Buddy Tate was a player of similar lineage, and all their recordings together have a warmth of genuine understanding. Much of the music on *Buck & Buddy* was formerly on the Prestige double-LP, *Kansas City Nights*. Originally recorded for Swingville, it gives a near-perfect sense of where Buck was at the end of his last really productive decade before the trumpeter's curse, persistent lip problems, began to curtail his activity. There's certainly no sign of difficulty here. He trades figures with Tate on 'Birdland Betty' and more romantic shapes on 'When A Woman Loves A Man'.

Blow The Blues is pretty much more of the same, but the heat is off and, with the sterling exception of 'Don't Mind If I Do', the individual numbers fail to catch fire.

****(*) Buck Clayton All-Stars, 1961**

Storyville STCD 8231 *Clayton; Emmett Berry (t); Dicky Wells (tb); Earl Warren (as); Buddy Tate (ts); Sir Charles Thompson (p); Gene Ramey (b); Oliver Jackson (d).* 4/61.

***** Basel, 1961**

TCB 2072 *As above.* 5/61.

Over in Europe, Buck's brand of swing didn't seem old-fashioned in 1961 and this touring octet was applauded to the rafters right across the continent. Part of TCB's Swiss Radio Days Jazz Series, the album is a typically well-mastered broadcast session. At rising fifty, Buck sounds absolutely in command of tone and articulation, and he phrases effectively from the original 'Swinging At The Copper Rail' onwards. 'Robbin's Nest' and 'Night Train' both receive long readings with the horns trading lonely figures on the Jimmy Forrest classic. State-of-the-art swing from a band of past masters, anxious to demonstrate that, away from America at least, they weren't past it. Recorded just a few weeks earlier, the Storyvillle set comes from a Paris show. A very similar set and the band are in equally good heart, but the sound is nothing like as good, Jackson hugely loud, Sir Charles peeking through the cymbals, and the horns sometimes here, sometimes there.

***** Buck Clayton Meets Big Joe Turner**
Black Lion BLCD 760170 *Clayton; Bosko Petrovic (vib); Davor Kajfes (p); Kresimir Remeta (b); Silvije Glojnaric (d); Big Joe Turner (v).* 6/65.

Joe Turner appears rather more briefly than the title would suggest, and it seems a little cynical to have billed the set this way. Essentially, it's Buck with vibist Petrovic's well-drilled group, recorded in Zagreb. The Yugoslavs play with the faintly hysterical concentration of men who know they're not going to believe this in the morning; but they don't let the guest down, even if they crowd him a little here and there. On 'I Can't Get Started' he simply ignores the beat and lets his solo find its own route and pace.

***** Baden, Switzerland, 1966**
Sackville 2028 *Clayton; Michel Pilet (ts); Henri Chaix (p); Isla Eckinger (b); Wallace Bishop (d).* 2/66.

By the mid-'60s, Clayton was an international star and, like many jazz musicians of his generation, he found Europe a happier hunting-ground than back home in the States. The Swiss air was obviously good for him and on this amiable set he cuts loose on an array of standards, notably 'Stompin' At The Savoy' and 'One O'Clock Jump', with coltish enthusiasm. These weren't the occasions for softer and more expressive performance, but Buck does also perform well on the slower numbers and he gets sterling assistance from an experienced Swiss band.

***** Ben And Buck**
Sackville SKCD 22037 *Clayton; Ben Webster (ts); Henri Chaix (p); Alain Du Bois (g); Isla Eckinger (b); Romano Cavicchiolo (d).* 67.

***** A Buck Clayton Jam Session**
Chiaroscuro CRD 132 *Clayton; Doc Cheatham, Joe Newman (t); Urbie Green (tb); Earl Warren (as); Budd Johnson, Zoot Sims (ts); Joe Temperley (bs); Earl Hines (p); Milt Hinton (b); Gus Johnson (d).* 74.

***** A Buck Clayton Jam Session 1975**
Chiaroscuro CRD 143 *Clayton; Joe Newman, Money Johnson (t); Vic Dickenson, George Masso (tb); Lee Konitz, Earl Warren (as); Budd Johnson, Sal Nistico, Buddy Tate (ts); Tommy Flanagan (p); Milt Hinton (b); Mel Lewis (d).* 6/75.

***** A Swingin' Dream**
Stash STCD 16 *Clayton; Spanky Davis, Paul Cohen, Johnny Letman (t); Dan Barrett, Bobby Pring (tb); Chuck Wilson (as, cl); Kenny Hing, Doug Lawrence (ts); Joe Temperley (bs); Mark Shane (p); Chris Flory (g); Ed Jones (b); Mel Lewis (d).* 10/88.

Buck wasn't playing at all towards the end. He suffered a serious collapse immediately after the *Ben and Buck* concert and after that was never up to soloing with any sort of attack or pressure. Clayton doesn't play at all on the Chiaroscuro jams, but conducts an all-star band in a selection of originals. His various jam-session dates for Columbia were great successes in their day, but they're all out of print for now (Mosaic have collected them in one of their boxed editions). The first date was something of a late revival of the form. The band is close to matchless as far as swing-to-mainstream line-ups are concerned and, while nothing much happens that deserves immortality, the session gets by on sheer charisma.

The 1975 set is doubly valuable for the inclusion of two rehearsal takes of 'The Duke We Knew' and 'Glassboro Blues', two of the best things he did in later years. On *A Swingin' Dream*, just a couple of years away from the end, he conducts a small big band (same size as Chick Webb's at its peak) in a selection of mostly new or recent compositions. Only 'Avenue C' is an oldie, though almost any of the numbers – the ballad 'Smoothie', for instance – might have come from the old days with Basie. For non-specialist collectors, the limiting factor here is Buck's position as leader and conductor rather than soloist, but big-band fans will be well satisfied and will echo Earl Warren's enraptured shout of 'All right! All right!' at the close of the blues, 'Margaux'.

***** The Buck Clayton Swing Band Live From Greenwich Village, NYC**
Nagel Heyer CD 030 *Clayton; John Eckert, Jordan Sandke, Byron Stripling, Warren Vaché (t); Matt Finders, Bobby Pring, Harvey Tibbs (tb); Jerry Dodgion (as); Doug Lawrence, Frank Wess (ts); Scott Robinson, Joe Temperley (bs); James Chirillo, Dick Katz (g); Lynn Seaton (b); Dennis Mackrel (d).* 2/90.

From the moment he laid down his horn, Clayton concentrated on writing and arranging charts with a startling energy and commitment. Though one immediately misses that full-throated voice and the ease with which it negotiated tricky changes and tough expressive transitions, the band is utterly idiomatic and unmistakably the work of Wilbur Clayton. Even as close to the end as this, there isn't a speck of tarnish on the sound, as if Buck had been able to pass on an apostolic blessing. Either oddly or significantly, depending on how you view it, the brasses are played down in the distribution of solos. Guitarist Katz is ludicrously over-featured, and there is more than enough from the one-dimensional Dodgion (though he is very good on 'B.C. Special' and 'Black Sheep Blues'). Vaché comes into his own on 'Cadillac Taxi', a little too late to make his mark on the session as a whole. The real interest, though, lies in the charts, which are as briskly and confidently executed as ever. A fitting memorial to a remarkable survivor.

Jay Clayton

VOCALS

Billie Holiday used to say that she wasn't singing, she was playing a horn. That's true of Jay Clayton as well, a singer who improvises like an instrumentalist, less convincing as an interpreter of emotive libretti than as a weaver of harmonic spells.

***** The Jazz Alley Tapes**
Hep CD 2046 *Clayton; Jay Thomas (t, as); Jeff Hay (tb); Don Lanphere (ts); Marc Seales (p, ky); Chuck Deardorf (b); Dean Hodges (d).* 9/88.

Clayton is a vividly gifted vocal improviser whose feel for a lyric is perhaps less convincing than her ability to mimic horn lines. Though rooted in bebop, she's also capable of tackling more demanding harmony, like the variations of Coltrane's 'Mr P.C.' on *Tapes*. Oddly, she sounds too close to Don Lanphere's saxophone for that now well-established relationship to work as well as they seem to feel it does. They obviously play comfortably together (Clayton is also featured on his *Go … Again*), but there's something rather too bland and pat about it.

****** Beautiful Love**
Sunnyside SSC 1066 *Clayton; Fred Hersch (p).* 96.

Exquisitely beautiful. Hersch is one of the genuinely great vocal accompanists and his playing here is impossible to fault. With delicious perversity, he sticks close to the original song, while Clayton ranges out into unexpected harmonic territory. Wayne Shorter's 'Footprints' and that understated classic, 'Blame It On My Youth', are handled with consummate grace and skill. The sound is blushingly intimate and Clayton throws herself into her various parts with utter abandon.

*****(*) Circle Dancing**
Sunnyside SSC 1076 *Clayton; Jim Knapp (p); Briggan Krauss (as); Randy Halberstadt (p); Phil Sparks (b); Aaron Alexander (d).* 97.

This one comes with a sharp insistence that all the sounds heard are made in real time and unsweetened. Clayton manipulates digital delay with virtuosic skill and her bluesy, intense delivery, melded with two horns, is as compelling as ever. The material is largely original and is all thoroughly assimilated and personalized. Catch Jay's first entry on the title-tune and her floating, nippy phrasing on 'Sappho' and 'Ditto'. A fine record from a genuine vocal star.

Clayton–Hamilton Jazz Orchestra
GROUP

A midstream big band co-led by ex-Basieite John Clayton and the sessionman drummer, Jeff Hamilton.

***** Groove Shop**
Capri 74021 *Bobby Bryant, Snooky Young, Oscar Brashear, Clay Jenkins (t, flhn); George Bohannon, Ira Nepus, Thurman Green (tb); Maurice Spears (btb); Jeff Clayton (ss, as, ts, ob, f); Bill Green (as, cl, f); Rickey Woodard (ts, cl); Charles Owens (ts, cl); Lee Callett (bs, bcl); Bill Cunliffe (p); Doug MacDonald (g); John Clayton (b); Jeff Hamilton (d).* 4/89.

***** Heart And Soul**
Capri 74028 *As above, except Jim Hershman (g) replaces MacDonald.* 2/91.

***** Absolutely!**
Lake Street LSR 52002 *As above, except add Chuck Findley (t), Dave Bjur (b).* 94.

It's the arranging, by John Clayton, which gives this blithe orchestra its character: there are some good soloists here, especially Snooky Young and Rickey Woodard, but the integration and polish of the sections are what make the music come alive. Clayton seeks little more than grooving rhythms and call-and-response measures, and they all figure dutifully enough in the arrangements, though occasionally – as on the very slow and piecemeal variation on 'Take The "A" Train' on *Heart And Soul* – the band have something more out-of-the-ordinary to play. Detailed and full-blooded recording lets one hear how all the wheels go round. The most recent album, *Absolutely!*, continues this serene sequence. The opening Basie-like 'Blues For Stephanie' is a grand manifesto which some of the later tracks don't quite carry off – 'Prelude To A Kiss' and 'A Beautiful Friendship' are rather ordinary – but the enthusiasm of the band seems undiminished, and the straightforward arrangements are a modest tonic at a time when big-band charts seem to be growing more like obstacle courses.

Gilles Clement
GUITAR

French guitarist whose affectionate debt to Wes Montgomery is obvious from this session.

****(*) Wes Side Stories**
Musidisc 500492 *Clement; Alain Jean-Marie (p); Yves Torchinsky (b); Eric Dervieu (d).* 5/93.

Attractively unpretentious guitar jazz, broadly in the style of the master, with a few unexpected wrinkles thrown in by Jean-Marie, who has seen service with Abbey Lincoln, Teddy Edwards and, out in left field, Charles Tolliver. The mix of originals and Montgomery compositions is varied by a Thelonious Monk composition ('Hackensack') and by 'Close Your Eyes', which the pianist may have brought in from Abbey's book. Unfortunately, it is isn't quite varied enough, and it's a slightly worrying situation when you sit up and take notice of bass solos rather than the front man.

Dave Cliff (born 1944)
GUITAR

Born in Northumberland, Cliff began as a rock player before studying at Leeds College and switching his sympathies to jazz. He has worked widely with both British and American musicians, mostly in a broad-based mainstream idiom.

***** Sippin' At Bells**
Spotlite SPJ-CD 553 *Cliff; Geoff Simkins (as); Simon Woolf (b); Mark Taylor (d).* 94.

***** Play The Music Of Tadd Dameron**
Spotlite SPJ-CD 560 *Cliff; Geoff Simkins (as); Roy Hilton (p); Simon Woolf (b); Steve Brown, Ron Parry (d).* 3/96.

***** When Lights Are Low**
Zephyr ZECD 18 *Cliff; Howard Alden (g); Dave Green (b); Allan Ganley (d).* 11/96–5/97.

Cliff's unassuming style might be read by some as British diffidence. He is a thinking guitar player whose cool tone and bebop diction make up a voice of experience and, when paired with the similarly minded Simkins, the irresistible comparison is Billy Bauer with Lee Konitz – particularly when they play some duets on the first Spotlite record. The second is all Dameronia (there is an interesting old interview with Dameron and Benny Golson stuck on the end of the disc) and very persuasively done. The Zephyr album is an off-the-cuff meeting with the on-tour Howard Alden, over thistledown rhythms from Green and Ganley. Nothing to find fault with anywhere, yet the very palpable *politesse* of the music may prove enervating to some.

Alex Cline (born 1956)

DRUMS, PERCUSSION

A California-based drummer with an interest in percussive exotica and a freely focused manner that lets him move between post-bop, free playing and a rockier kind of world music.

***** The Lamp And The Star**

ECM 1372 *Cline; Aina Kemanis, Nels Cline (v); Jeff Gauthier (vn, vla, v); Hank Roberts (clo, v); Wayne Peet (p, org); Eric Von Essen (b); Susan Rawcliffe (didjeridu).* 9/87.

***** Montsalvat**

Nine Winds NWCD 0174 *As above, except omit Nels Cline, Roberts and Rawcliffe.* 5/92.

***** Right Of Violet**

Nine Winds NWCD 0184 *Cline; Jeff Gauthier (vn); G.E Stinson (g etc.).* 4/95.

While his brother Nels has sometimes sought out rockier climes, Alex has pursued a music based around lush textures and thick, harmonic swirls – an unusual course for a percussionist, perhaps, although his vast kit of drums, cymbals, bells and percussive devices is as appropriate to melodic needs as much as to rhythmical ones (there is a double-LP of solo percussion in vinyl history). Both *The Lamp And The Star* and *Montsalvat* have a non-specifically devotional programme, characterized by Cline's imagistic titles – 'A Blue Robe In The Distance', 'Emerald Light', 'The Kiss Of Peace' – but there is nothing mushy or New Age-ish about the music, which has a strong and very individual resonance. Kemanis's wordless singing is neither too wispy nor too overpowering but a logical part of the flow. The later disc is preferred, if only because the long pieces such as 'He Hears The Cry' and 'In The Shadow Of The Mountain' come closest to the kind of transcendence Cline is after.

Right Of Violet has ten collective improvisations by the trio and, while this is tougher music, it still moves off the shimmering base which Cline uses as his touchstone. The opening 'An Elegy Of Waves' says it all, Gauthier's lines spiralling off Stinson's battery of effects, and the formula is set here: the violinist carries most of the melodic parts while Stinson and Cline fashion the atmospherics. The record is rather exhaustingly long but when they get to a piece as eerily beautiful as 'Sophia' there's a proper sense of timelessness.

Nels Cline (born 1956)

GUITAR

Brother of Alex, Cline is a thinking-man's fusion kind of guitar player.

***** Angelica**

Enja ENJ 6063 *Cline; Stacey Rowles (t, flhn); Tim Berne (as); Eric Von Essen (b); Alex Cline (d).* 8/87.

Like almost every guitar player of his generation, Cline trades off rock, but he does so with sufficient sophistication and originality so that it's possible to think he's made the whole thing up. He makes full use of the electric guitar's expanded repertoire of sounds, distortion, fuzz, bent notes and an aggressive, almost percussive attack. After a decade, *Angelica* still sounds fresh. There are moments when it sounds almost like an ECM session from the previous decade, Cline picking lines that are reminiscent of Sam Brown, Tim Berne wailing like a shawm, and brother Alex slipping into a groove that is strongly reminiscent of Paul Motian. The trumpeter is Jimmy Rowles's daughter and it would be surprising if she were not confidently lyrical throughout this brightly registered set of dedications.

*****(*) Silencer**

Enja ENJ 6098 *Cline; Mark Loudon Sims (b); Michael Preussner (d).* 12/90.

***** Chest**

Little Brother 006 *Cline; Bob Mair (b); Michael Preussner (d).* 6/93.

***** Ground**

Krown Pocket 0002 *As above.* 7/94.

The stripped-down dynamics suit Cline well. All three records strike a balance between power and subtlety. While superficially reminiscent of Terje Rypdal's trio, the group is more exactingly detailed, and successive albums have opened up more and more areas of interest, not least in Cline's own writing. *Silencer* is notable for a vivid opening, Gil Evans's 'Las Vegas Tango', and sustains a high level of invention thereafter. *Chest* is tightly organized, almost like a suite, and *Ground* occupies a dark space Cline hasn't previously explored, an ebb-and-flow of consistently interesting, if rather one-dimensional, ideas.

Rosemary Clooney (born 1928)

VOCAL

She made her name as a Hollywood actress and a musicals star, but her 1956 Duke Ellington album suggested Clooney's aptitude for jazz, and her many albums for Concord since the mid-'70s have confirmed her talent for the idiom.

****** Blue Rose**

Columbia CK-65506 *Clooney; Willie Cook, Ray Nance, Clark Terry, Cat Anderson (t); Gordon Jackson, Britt Woodman, John Sanders (tb); Johnny Hodges (as); Russell Procope (as, cl); Jimmy Hamilton (cl, ts); Paul Gonsalves (ts); Harry Carney (bs); Duke Ellington (p); Jimmy Woode (b); Sam Woodyard (d).* 1–2/56.

Ellington's collaborations with singers were few, and the pairing with Rosemary Clooney was, on the face of it, surprising. In fact, she overdubbed her parts on to already-recorded Ellington tracks. Yet it works very well: as a pop stylist who recognized rather than courted jazz-singing principles, she handles Ellington's often difficult (for a singer) songs with attentive finesse, and it culminates in one of the most gracious and thought-through versions of 'Sophisticated Lady' on record. The whole project was very carefully overseen by Billy Strayhorn, whose advice to Clooney – 'Just pretend you're a girl getting ready for a date, you hear Duke Ellington on the radio, almost subconsciously you start humming along with the band' – sets up exactly the kind of (in Will Friedwald's phrase) 'muted emotion' which is the hallmark of Ellington's urbane passion. This excellent new edition gives the Ellington men a very big sound and there are two extra tracks missed from the original LP.

***** Everything's Coming Up Rosie**
Concord CCD 4047 *Clooney; Bill Berry (t); Scott Hamilton (ts); Nat Pierce (p); Monty Budwig (b); Jake Hanna (d).* 77.

***** Rosie Sings Bing**
Concord CCD 4060 *As above, except omit Berry; add Cal Collins (g).* 78.

***** Here's To My Lady**
Concord CCD 4081 *As above, except add Warren Vaché (c); omit Collins.* 79.

*****(*) Sings The Lyrics Of Ira Gershwin**
Concord CCD 4112 *Clooney; Warren Vaché (c, flhn); Scott Hamilton (ts); Roger Glenn (f); Nat Pierce (p); Cal Collins (g); Chris Amberger (b); Jeff Hamilton (d).* 10/79.

***** With Love**
Concord CCD 4144 *Clooney; Warren Vaché (c, flhn); Scott Hamilton (ts); Nat Pierce (p); Cal Tjader (vib); Cal Collins (g); Bob Maize (b); Jake Hanna (d).* 11/80.

***** Sings The Music Of Cole Porter**
Concord CCD 4185 *As above, except add David Ladd (f).* 1/82.

*****(*) Sings The Music Of Harold Arlen**
Concord CCD 4210 *Clooney; Warren Vaché (c); Scott Hamilton (ts); Dave McKenna (p); Ed Bickert (g); Steve Wallace (b); Jake Hanna (d).* 1/83.

Clooney virtually quit music in the 1960s and went through some difficult personal times, but her re-emergence with Concord in the 1970s and '80s has been one of the most gratifying returns of recent years. She has become one of the most prolific artists on the label, and the best of them, even in a very consistent run, set a very high standard. If she is not, at her own insistence, a jazz singer, she responds to the in-house team with warm informality and the breadth of her voice smooths over any difficulties with some of the more intractable songs. Her voice has a more matronly and less flexible timbre than before, but pacing things suits her style, and good choices of tempo are one of the hallmarks of this series. The 'Songbook' sequence is one of the best of its kind: the Arlen and Gershwin records are particularly fine. *With Love* has some indifferent 'contemporary' tunes from the likes of Billy Joel, but the rest of it more than matches up. Countless cameos from Hamilton, Vaché and the others lend further class.

***** My Buddy**
Concord CCD 4226 *Clooney; Scott Wagstaff, Mark Lewis, Paul Mazzio, Bill Byrne, Dan Fornero (t, flhn); Gene Smith, John Fedchock (tb); Randy Hawes (btb); Woody Herman (cl, as); Frank Tiberi (ts); Mark Vinci, Jim Carroll (ts, f); Nick Brignola (bs); John Oddo (p); John Chiodini (g); John Adams (b); Jeff Hamilton (d).* 8/83.

***** Sings The Music Of Irving Berlin**
Concord CCD 4255 *Clooney; Warren Vaché (c, flhn); Scott Hamilton (ts); John Oddo (p); Ed Bickert, Chris Flory (g); Phil Flanigan (b); Gus Johnson (d).* 6/84.

*****(*) Rosemary Clooney Sings Ballads**
Concord CCD 4282 *As above, except Chuck Israels (b), Jake Hanna (d) replace Flory, Flanigan and Johnson.* 4/85.

***** Sings The Music Of Jimmy Van Heusen**
Concord CCD 4308 *As above, except Michael Moore (b), Joe Cocuzzo (d) replace Israels and Hanna; add Emily Remler (g).* 8/86.

****** Sings The Lyrics Of Johnny Mercer**
Concord CCD 4333 *As above, except Dan Barrett (tb) replaces Remler.* 8/87.

*****(*) Show Tunes**
Concord CCD 4364 *Clooney; Warren Vaché (c); Scott Hamilton (ts); John Oddo (p); John Clayton (b); Jeff Hamilton (d).* 8–11/88.

***** Sings Rodgers, Hart And Hammerstein**
Concord CCD 4405 *Clooney; Jack Sheldon (t, v); Chauncey Welsh (tb); Scott Hamilton (ts); John Oddo (p); John Clayton (b); Joe LaBarbera (d); The L.A. Jazz Choir (v).* 10/89.

John Oddo began working regularly with Clooney with the Woody Herman album and has been MD of most of the records since. But the steady, articulate feel of the records is a continuation of what came before. The Johnny Mercer is perhaps the single best record Clooney has ever done: the choice of songs is peerless, and she has the measure of every one. *Show Tunes*, though something of a mixture, is another very good one, and the *Ballads* and Jimmy Van Heusen discs are full of top-rank songs. Very little to choose between any of these sets, though the Mercer would be our first choice for anyone who wants just a taste of what Rosie can do.

****(*) For The Duration**
Concord CCD 4444 *Clooney; Warren Vaché (c); Scott Hamilton (ts); John Oddo (p); Chuck Berghofer, Jim Hughart (b); Jake Hanna (d); strings.* 10/90.

***** Girl Singer**
Concord CCD 4496 *Clooney; Warren Luening, George Graham, Larry Hall, Bob Summers (t, flhn); Chauncey Welsh, Bill Booth, Bill Elton, George Roberts (tb); Brad Warnaar (frhn); Dan Higgins (c, as, ts, f); Joe Soldo (cl, as, f); Gary Foster (as, af, f); Pete Christlieb (cl, ts, f); Bob Cooper (ts, f); Bob Tricarico (bs, bcl, f); John Oddo (ky); Tim May (g); Tom Warrington (b); Joe LaBarbera (d); Joe Porcaro (perc); Monica Mancini, Ann White, Mitchel Moore, Earl Brown, Mitch Gordon (v).* 11–12/91.

If anything, these are slightly disappointing. *For The Duration* is a set of wartime songs similar to one attempted by Mel Torme and George Shearing, and Clooney belabours what is occasionally trite (or at least over-exposed) material. *Girl Singer* features an orchestra which has one thinking about the small group of the earlier records: if that formula had perhaps been used to the point of diminishing returns, this one is a top-heavy alternative which suits Clooney's voice less well. Still, Oddo's arrangements leave room for some solos from the horns, and the singer moves from Dave Frishberg to Duke Ellington to Cy Coleman songs with her customary resilience.

*****(*) Do You Miss New York?**
Concord CCD 4537 *Clooney; Warren Vaché (c); Scott Hamilton (ts); John Oddo (p); John Pizzarelli (g, v); Bucky Pizzarelli (g); David Finck (b); Joe Cocuzzo (d).* 9/92.

***** Still On The Road**
Concord CCD 4590 *Clooney; Warren Luening, Rick Baptist, George Graham, Larry Hall, Larry McGuire (t, flhn); Chauncey Welsh, Bill Elton, Charley Loper, Phil Teele, Lew McCreary (tb); Gary Foster, Nino Tempo, Joe Soldo, Tommy Newsom, Bob Tricarico, Dan Higgins, Don Ashworth (reeds); John Oddo (ky); Tim May, Steve Lukather (g); Chuck Berghofer (b); Jeff Hamilton (d); Joe Porcaro, Dan Greco (perc); Earl Brown, Jack Sheldon (v).* 11/93.

Turning 65, Rosie still sounds in very good form, although some of Concord's production decisions seem designed to push her towards kitsch rather than great singing situations. *Do You Miss New York?* is an album of Big Apple memories and her best since *Show Tunes* – excellent material, the Concord house-team in strong form and the singer notably relaxed and amiable. 'As Long As I Live' and a duet with John Pizzarelli on 'It's Only A Paper Moon' work out very well. *Still On The Road* is one of those travelogue albums (Rosie did a similar one years ago with Bing Crosby) and benefits from some high-stepping, big-band charts, but Willie Nelson and Paul Simon are composers she shouldn't bother with, and guest spots by Earl Brown and Jack Sheldon were misguided ideas.

***** Demi-Centennial**
Concord CCD 4633 *As above, except add Wayne Bergeron (t), Fred Simmons (tb), Ron Jannelli, Vince Trombetta (reeds), Thomas Warrington (b), Steve Houghton (d); omit Hall, McCrearey, Tempo, Newsom, Tricarico, Lukather, Hamilton, Greco, Brown, Sheldon.* 10–11/94.

***** Dedicated To Nelson**
Concord CCD 4685 *As above, except add George Roberts (tb), Gene Cipriano (reeds), Dennis (g), Gregg Field (d); omit Simmons, Jannelli, Warrington, Houghton, Teele, Higgins, Ashworth, May, Porcaro.* 9/95.

Demi-Centennial celebrates Clooney's fiftieth anniversary as a performer, and all the songs have personal ties. Some of the record comes close to drowning in American schmaltz, but it's hard not to find some of the songs affecting, and the sincerity of the singing is a given. Both this and the subsequent *Dedicated To Nelson* are so sumptuously recorded that it's possible just to enjoy the production values by themselves. For the latter, Clooney goes back to some transcriptions of arrangements which Nelson Riddle did for an old TV series: stretched to recordable length, they're brought to life by Oddo's crack team of studio pros. Very well done, and the singer enjoys herself, though her voice has lost some of the bloom of her earlier Concords.

****(*) Mothers And Daughters**
Concord CCD 4754-2 *Clooney; Warren Luening (t, flhn); Gary Foster (reeds); Vince Trombetta (ts); John Oddo (p); Dennis Budimir (g); Chuck Berghofer (b); Joe LaBarbera (d); Keith Carradine, Betty Clooney (v).* 54–10/96.

Unless one is infatuated with a newborn, this set of songs about, well, mothers and daughters will seem particularly glutinous. Concept albums are hurting jazz: discuss. For undiscriminating fans only.

***** At Long Last**
Concord CCD 4795-2 *Clooney; Michael Williams, Scotty Barnhart, Shawn Edmonds, Bob Ojeda (t); David Keim, Clarence Banks, Alvin Walker II (tb); William Hughes (btb); John Kelson (as, f); Brad Leali (as); Doug Miller (ts, cl, f); Kenny Hing (ts, cl); Gary Foster (ts); John Williams (bs, bcl); Terence Conley, John Oddo (p); Will Matthews (g); James Leary (b); Butch Miles (d); Barry Manilow (v); Grover Mitchell (cond).* 11/97–6/98.

Back on form with the Basie band, Rosie steers assuredly through this one. John Oddo's charts are shared with three each by Allyn Ferguson and Peter Matz and the programme is all evergreens. Barry Manilow does his credibility some good with a duet on 'How About You' and, though the soloists don't add much, the band is the purring Basie machine for sure. The singer's great records are probably behind her now, but only a churl would dislike this.

Clusone 3

GROUP

What began as a one-off group for the 1980 Clusone Festival, and originally as a quartet with pianist and composer Guus Janssen, turned into one of the unlikeliest but most successful ménages à trois on the scene.

***** Clusone 3**
Ramboy 02 *Michael Moore (cl, bcl, as, hca, cel); Ernst Reijseger (clo); Han Bennink (d, perc).* 90.

*****(*) I Am An Indian**
Ramboy/Gramavision GCD 79505 *As above.* 6–12/93.

****** Soft Lights And Sweet Music**
hat ART CD 6153 *As above.* 11/93.

*****(*) Love Henry**
Gramavision GCD 79517 *As above.* 7/96.

*****(*) Rara Avis**
hatOLOGY 513 *As above.* 96.

This is a group that knows how to enjoy itself, even poker-faced. There are moments when the clarinettist and cellist – good, solid conservatory instruments, both – look as if they might have been detailed to keep a watch on the drummer, whose notion of 'playing the room' is sometimes literally just that; Bennink does a celebrated party-piece where he pushes a janitor's broom round the floor to a shuffle rhythm that would do Dave Tough proud. As in the best such dramas, you look and listen again and realize that both Moore and Reijseger have a funny look in their eye, and that behind those proper sounds – the clarinet's melancholy wail and the cello's philosophizing – there are some extremely offbeat ideas at play and it's Bennink who's keeping it all in check. That's never been more obvious than on the recent live album, a set of four extended medleys taking in compositions by the group members as well as Kurt Weill, Lee Konitz, Misha Mengelberg and, as ever, Irving Berlin.

Both the second and third records were largely dominated by Berlin, the latter almost exclusively, and the range of other material is consistent with an approach to jazz (broadly similar to hat ART labelmate Franz Koglmann's) that looks to the fringes, the repressed: on *I Am An Indian*, a Berlin title itself, there is Herbie Nichols's 'The Gig' and Dewey Redman's fierce and rarely covered 'Qow'. The approach is quirky but also very direct, almost naïve, and in some cases disarmingly literal. 'Let's Face The Music And Dance' on *Soft Lights* ... is probably the best version of the song ever put on disc. Like all of hat ART's 6000 series, this is now technically deleted, but sufficient copies should be in circulation, and there is every chance of a digipack reissue under the hatOLOGY imprint on which the swansong, *Rara Avis*, appears. If it is the last word from the group, it's a faintly disappointing one. Much of the cohesion that made the trio so powerful in the past is absent and the individual components sound as if they would probably be better addressed on the members' solo projects. Even so, it's a fine album by anyone's standard and well worth having.

The live CD is the best record of their freewheeling, associative concert approach. However settled the set-list, their gigs always give the impression of happening spontaneously. Reijseger's squally bass figures and big guitar-like strums have never been more effective, and Moore's nervy, quizzical lines make their own sense. Some performing chemistry is quite simply very special, and the Clusone 3 make an addictive compound. Sample, but don't say we didn't warn you.

Arnett Cobb (1918–89)

TENOR SAXOPHONE

Cobb went into Lionel Hampton's band as a replacement for Illinois Jacquet but later made a name as a hard-blowing leader whose Texan honks and wails were tempered with a genuinely feeling touch on the occasional ballad. Having undergone spinal surgery when he was thirty, Cobb was seriously injured and disabled less than a decade later. His subsequent career is testament to his great strength of will and unfailing appetite for jazz.

****(*) The Wild Man Of The Tenor Sax, 1943–1947**

EPM Musique JA 159422 *Cobb; Cat Anderson, Wendell Curley, Duke Garrette, Joe Morris, Jimmy Nottingham, David Page, Leo Shepherd, Joe Wilder, Lamar Wright, Snooky Young (t); Fred Beckett, Sonny Craven, Allan Durham, Al Hayes, Al King, Andrew Penn, Vernon Porter, Booty Wood, Jimmy Wormick (tb); Earl Bostic, George Dorsey, Gus Evans, Ben Kynard, Bobby Plater (as); Johnny Griffin, Al Sears, Fred Simon (ts); Charlie Fowlkes (bs); Herbie Fields, Rudy Rutherford (cl); Dardanelle Breckenridge, Milt Buckner, George Rhodes (p); Lionel Hampton (p, vib); Billy Mackel, Eric Miller (g); Walter Buchanan, Joe Comfort, Charlie Harris, Vernon King, Ted Sinclair (b); Fats Heard, George Jenkins, George Jones, Fred Radcliffe (d); Wynonie Harris, Milton Larkins, Dinah Washington (v).* 43–47.

****(*) Arnett Cobb, 1946–1947**

Classics 1071 *Cobb; Wendell Culley, Joe Morris, David Page (t); Al King, Booty Wood (tb); Herbie Fields (ts); Charlie Fowlkes (bs); Milt Buckner, George Rhodes (p); Billy Mackel (g); Walter Buchanan, Charles Harris (b); George Jenkins, George Jones (d); Milton Larkins (v).* 46–8/47.

***** Arnett Blows For 1300**

Delmark 471 *As above, except omit Culley, Fields, Fowlkes, Buckner, Mackel, Harris, Jenkins.* 47.

The most significant recent addition to the Arnett Cobb discography are these compilations of his early work for Apollo and – in the case of the Classics set – for Hamp-Tone, too. While Ellingtonians frequently recorded side-projects, it was relatively rare for members of Hamp's band to record apart from the leader. The EPM compilation basically gathers together solos from the early years under Hampton, Wynonie Harris and Dinah Washington, and then takes the story up to the saxophonist's post-war foray into leadership. The quotient of actual Cobb material is rather low, but for anyone interested in exploring his roots and influences it's invaluable.

Unusually for Classics, the first item included was actually made under Milt Buckner's leadership, but all the rest of the material is by Arnett's first groups after striking out on his own. Old associations die hard, though, and two tracks on the May 1947 date are intended to recall happy days with Hamp. Both 'Still Flyin'' and 'Top Flight' recall Cobb's featured solos on 'Flyin' Home'. Thereafter, Arnett seemed more inclined to strike out on his own and, while some of his compositions are no more than generic themes for blowing, he seems to have found a niche for the early group. The sound is immediately better with Apollo, rich and unmuffled, and generous to the saxophone.

An even longer-standing debt is paid when vocalist Milton Larkins, one of Cobb's first employers, steps up to take three songs as part of the August 1947 recording. It was the session that included the definitive performance of 'Arnett Blows For 1300' which gives the Delmark issue its title. This basically reprises all the tracks the saxophonist made for Apollo. The transfers are crisp and clear.

***** Blow, Arnett, Blow**

Original Jazz Classics OJC 794 *Cobb; Strethen Davis (p); George Duvivier (b); Arthur Edgehill (d).* 59.

****(*) Party Time**

Original Jazz Classics OJC 219 *Cobb; Ray Bryant (p); Wendell Marshall (b); Arthur Taylor (d).* 5/59.

***** More Party Time**

Original Jazz Classics OJCCD 979 *Cobb; Tommy Flanagan, Bobby Timmons (p); Sam Jones (b); Art Taylor (d); Danny Barrajanos, Buick Clarke (perc).* 2/60.

***** Smooth Sailing**

Original Jazz Classics OJC 323 *Cobb; Buster Cooper (tb); Austin Mitchell (as); George Duvivier (b); Osie Johnson (d).* 60.

***** Blue And Sentimental**

Prestige PRCD 24122 *Cobb; Red Garland (p, cel); George Duvivier, George Tucker (b); J.C Heard (d).* 11/60.

Cobb overcame serious illness and a crippling motor accident (several covers picture him propped on his crutches as he plays) to keep his career afloat in the 1960s and after. A powerful saxophonist in the so-called 'Texas tenor' tradition, he was an ideal big-band player – with Lionel Hampton mainly – who never scaled down quite enough for small-group work. On *Blow, Arnett, Blow* and the following *Party Time*, he is clearly still suffering the after-effects of the accident, playing awkwardly and doing not much more than going through the motions, however much sheer energy and drive he managed to muster.

As the personnel details confirm, *More Party Time* wasn't further material or out-takes from the May 1959 session but a completely separate recording. Flanagan doesn't seem quite the right piano player for Arnett at this stage in his career, but the chemistry is pretty good. Bobby Timmons was on hand the following day and 'Down By The Riverside' has the soulful, revivalist energy one expects of him. A thoroughly entertaining record.

The earlier records for Prestige, now available on OJC, are far from sophisticated but there is a delicacy to Cobb's playing which becomes obvious only over time, and we have previously noted an unexpected similarity between some of his slower tunes and Coltrane's early ballad performances, a similarity that points at similar sources rather than any direct influence or crossover.

*** **Arnett Cobb Is Back**

Progressive PCD 7037 *Cobb; Derek Smith (p); George Mraz (b); Billy Hart (d).* 6/78.

(*) **Live

Timeless SJP 174 *Cobb; Rein De Graaff (p); Jacques Schols (b); John Engels (d).* 11/82.

*** **Show Time**

Fantasy F 9659 *Cobb; Dizzy Gillespie (t); Clayton Dyess (g); Paul English (p, org); Kenny Andrews, Sammy Price (p); Derrick Lewis (b); Malcolm Pinson, Mike Lefebvre (d).* 8/87.

Going Dutch suits Cobb pretty well. De Graaff is a fine, responsive accompanist who will go to his grave with a bent back from having carried so many visiting 'singles' over the years. Cobb plays well, if a little fruitily, and the sound is mostly adequate. The material on Fantasy is pretty late and frail. Cobb shares the Houston stage and the disc with Dizzy Gillespie and the singer, Jewel Brown. Two years before his death the tone is still intact, but there really isn't much to say any more and there's a queasy sense of going through the motions once too often. Newcomers might like to start with either of the 1973 discs.

(*) **Texas Sax

Aim 1302 *Cobb; Willie Cook (t); Joe Gallardo (tb, p); Clarence Hollimon (g); Don Jones (b); Carl Lott, Malcolm Pinson (d); Henrique Martinez (perc).*

Later in life, Arnett had the chance to play with musicians who'd grown up worshipping his brand of Texas tenor. Though he sounds tired and off the pace, the band are prepared to go through hoops for him and there's enough on this mid-price reissue to satisfy most fans of the saxophonist.

***(*) **Tenor Tribute**

Soul Note 121184 *Cobb; Jimmy Heath (ts, ss, f); Joe Henderson (ts); Benny Green (p); Walter Schmocker (b); Doug Hammond (d).* 4/88.

(*) **Tenor Tribute, Volume 2

Soul Note 121194 *As above.* 4/88.

Though this was always conceived as a collective project with a three-saxophone front line, Cobb gets the nod on grounds of alphabetical priority, seniority, and not least because this Nuremberg concert came in the last full year of the Texan's life. Like most similar things, this is full of exciting and entertaining episodes but won't hang together as a whole. Cobb sounds pretty good, considering. His choruses on 'Smooth Sailing' and during a lengthy ballad medley (all on Volume One) are nicely weighted and well – perhaps too well – thought out. However, he's comprehensively blown away by the two youngsters, who both sound full of vim and ideas. He does better on 'Cottontail', which opens Volume Two, but there isn't enough top-flight stuff to support a second disc, and it palls very quickly; even 'Flying Home' at curtain time lacks sparkle. Heath's lighter tone and occasional forays into soprano and flute broaden the range a bit, for this is otherwise pretty heavy fare. Green does his best to push it along, but there's not much manoeuvrability in a band like this, and he has to rein in quite sharply more than once. Avid collectors only.

Junie Cobb (1896–1970)

CLARINET, SOPRANO AND TENOR SAXOPHONES, VIOLIN, PIANO, VOCAL

A multi-instrumentalist who worked in the Chicago scene of the 1920s, Cobb was recorded as a reed player and leader, but he also played banjo and later in life took to the piano. His music is typical of the small-group barrelhouse style of the day which, by the 1960s – when he recorded again – was softer but no less energetic.

***(*) **The Junie Cobb Collection, 1926–29**

Collector's Classics COCD-14 *Cobb; Jimmy Cobb (c, t); Cicero Thomas (t); Arnett Nelson (cl, ts); Angelo Fernandez, Johnny Dodds, Darnell Howard (cl); Ernie Smith (bs, bsx); George James (as, bs); Tiny Parham, Jimmy Blythe, Frank Melrose, Alex Hill, Earl Frazier (p); Tampa Red (g); Eustern Woodfork (bj); Walter Wright (tba); Bill Johnson (b); Jimmy Bertrand (d, xy, slide-whistle); Clifford Jones (d, kz); Tommy Taylor, Harry Dial (d); W.E Burton, Georgia Tom Dorsey (v).* 6/26–10/29.

This is classic Chicago jazz of its period. Cobb's groups – The Hometown Band, The Grains Of Corn and the Kansas City Tin Roof Stompers are three of those here – bounce along in a rough-and-ready barrelhouse manner, never touching the sophistications of Armstrong or Dodds (who turns up as sparring partner for Cobb on two early tracks) but creating their own peculiar exhilaration. Cobb's saxophone style, an idiosyncratic mix of slap-tonguing and the more progressive manner of Hawkins, gets a wild momentum going on some tracks; and reliable stompers such as Blythe, Melrose and Hill keep the music hot in the rhythm section, as does Woodfork's banjo. Jimmy Cobb plays most of the trumpet parts, often surprisingly effectively. There are also (among a generous 24 tracks) three cuts from a hitherto lost 1929 session for Vocalion. The transfers show variable levels of surface noise, but the remastering is lively and vivid throughout.

****(*) Chicago The Living Legends: Junie C. Cobb And His New Hometown Band**

Original Jazz Classics OJC 1825-2 *Cobb; Fip Ricard (t); Harlan Floyd (tb); Leon Washington (cl, ts); Ikey Robinson (bj); Walter Hill (b); Red Saunders (d); Annabelle Calhoun (v).* 9/61.

Rediscovered in 1961, Cobb had given up clarinet in favour of piano. The pick-up band assembled for this session is mostly younger hands rather than old-timers (Robinson and Saunders are the exceptions) and some of the music sounds like tourist trad. But Cobb's enthusiasm carries much of the music, even if Washington is a comparatively ordinary substitute as reedsman.

Billy Cobham (born 1944)

DRUMS, PERCUSSION, ELECTRONICS, PIANO

Born in Panama and raised in New York, Cobham was early in the jazz-rock field with Miles Davis and with his own group, Dreams, before forming the Mahavishnu Orchestra with John McLaughlin. The power and complexity of his playing merits comparison with Elvin Jones and Tony Williams, and yet Cobham seems to have been content on occasion to play unimaginative fusion in which mere fireworks overcame his natural gifts.

*****(*) Spectrum**

Atlantic 781428 *Cobham; Jimmy Owens (t, flhn); Joe Farrell (as, ss, f); Jan Hammer (p, ky); Tommy Bolin, John Tropea (g); Ron Carter, Lee Sklar (b); Ray Barretto (perc).* 5/73.

***** Shabazz**

Atlantic/Wounded Bird 8139 *Cobham; Randy Brecker (t); Glenn Ferris (tb); Michael Brecker (ts); Milcho Leviev (ky); John Abercrombie, John Scofield (g); Alex Blake (b).* 7/74.

***** Total Eclipse**

Atlantic/Wounded Bird 8121 *Cobham; Randy Brecker (t, flhn); Glenn Ferris (tb, btb); Michael Brecker (ts, f); Milcho Leviev (p, ky); Sue Evans (mar); Cornell Dupree (g); Alex Blake (b).* 74.

***** Crosswinds**

Atlantic/Wounded Bird 7300 *Cobham; Randy Brecker (t); Garnett Brown (tb); Michael Brecker (ts); George Duke (ky); John Abercrombie (g); John Williams (b); Lee Pastora (perc).* 74.

Billy Cobham could almost qualify these days as the forgotten giant of the fusion era, but for the steady return of some of his earliest solo work and a burgeoning recording schedule in the 1990s. A superb technician and clearly a man of great musical intelligence and resource, he has nevertheless committed some awful clunkers to record. Whereas *Spectrum*, his debut as leader, was one of the finest records of the jazz-rock era, a record to set alongside *Birds Of Fire*, *Head Hunters* and the earlier Return To Forever discs, much of what has followed has been remarkably hazy, and a stint with GRP in the mid- to late 1980s was decidedly ill-advised. Luckily for his rep, the Atlantic is a survivor and one of the few Cobham albums that still hang around the racks. The cliché about Cobham – that he is all fire and fury and 20-minute drum solos – has never stood up to scrutiny. In actuality, he is a somewhat introspective drummer whose compositions are often blurry and unmemorable. Enjoy *Spectrum* for its bravado and some fine contributions from the various hands – not least the drummer himself.

Recorded live in Europe, *Shabazz* reprised a couple of the tunes from *Spectrum* and turned all the dials up to 11. 'Taurian Matador' and 'Red Baron' stand up to the punishment pretty well, and there are also a couple of new tracks, 'Tenth Pin' and the title-piece which were road-tested on Billy's tour. The recording is classic '70s 'in concert' fare, cavernous and booming, with the drums mixed well up. Twenty-five years on, it stands up better than it has any right to.

Crosswinds isn't quite as fresh in retrospect. Billy's solo feature on 'Storm' is the centrepiece of what is virtually a concept album, mood music and tone poems cranked up high. Duke is a key element of the band right from the off, prefiguring the Billy–George encounters of the later '70s. Here, though, the big man has a surprising deftness of touch.

Total Eclipse was the third solo release on Atlantic and, in some respects, the most ambitious and enigmatic. Again somewhat themed round the moon landings and the space programme generally, it begins with 'Solarization', a suite of pieces distinguished by a remarkable solo from Leviev. Billy's own big feature comes at the end of the album and is easily programmed out; five and a half minutes of solo percussion at this intensity constitutes cruel and unusual punishment. He does a Jack DeJohnette on 'The Moon Ain't Made Of Green Cheese', coming out from behind the kit to play piano behind Brecker's gorgeous flugelhorn. Abercrombie's ability to switch from limpid purity to pumped-up aerobatics is consistently impressive, and his solo on 'Moon Germs' is one of the best things he recorded in the '70s. The long 'Sea Of Tranquility' is a loose, band jam and a more fitting end to the record than Billy's clattering 'Last Frontier'.

***** A Funky Thide Of Sings**

Atlantic 2894 /Koch International 8527 *Cobham; Walt Fowler (t); Randy Brecker (t, flhn); Bones Malone (tb); Michael Brecker (ts, f); Larry Schneider (sax); Milcho Leviev (p, ky); John Scofield (g); Alex Blake (b).* 75.

This is the record that marks the transition from Cobham's largely successful post-Mahavishnu recordings to a period of drab, slugging funk. The line-up was pretty well established by now, but the addition of Scofield gives the group a harder-edged blues quality which wasn't always in evidence before. Oddly, the most appealing thing on the album is the drum solo, 'A Funky Kind Of Thing', which immediately precedes the long closing 'Moody Modes' by Leviev. An otherwise rather dull record ends on the most unexpected of highs.

**** On Tour In Europe**

Atlantic 113797 *Cobham; George Duke (ky, v); John Scofield (g, g syn); Alphonso Johnson (b).* 76.

Oh, dear; oh, Lord. This is what we used to groove to in the 1970s and it hasn't aged at all well. Billy and fellow frontman George Duke obviously had a ball with this project, and there are some mildly entertaining moments: Scofield's 'Ivory Tattoo' is very good indeed, but it is valuable mainly as a foretaste of his maturer work; Duke's 'Do Whatcha Wanna' is as embarrassing as a shameless decade ever got. Billy can still generate excitement, as he does on 'Frankenstein Goes To The Disco', but why Atlantic have seen fit to reissue this in preference to far finer material in their back-catalogue is something of a mystery ... unless of course there's a huge Cobham–Duke fanbase we don't know about.

***** The Best Of Billy Cobham**

Atlantic 781588 *Cobham; Glenn Ferris (tb, btb); Randy Brecker (t); Michael Brecker (sax); John Abercrombie, Tommy Bolin, Cornell Dupree, John Scofield (g); Jan Hammer (p, ky); Milcho Leviev (ky); George Duke (ky, v); Alex Blake, Alphonso Johnson, Lee Sklar (b).*

A rarity: a best-of that really lives up to its catch-all title. This brings together material from the 1970s, including such favourite tracks as 'Snoopy's Search', 'Red Baron' and 'Quadrant', all of which, coincidentally, highlight the band that featured Jan Hammer and the late, lamented Tommy Bolin. Entirely idiomatic within the context of its era – flash, smoke and brawn – and an entertaining potpourri.

***** Flight Time**

Inakustik 1723 *Cobham; Don Grolnick (p, ky); Barry Finnerty (g); Tim Landers (b).* 6/80.

***** Stratus**

Inakustik 813 *Cobham; Gil Goldstein (p, ky); Mike Stern (g); Michal Urbaniak (ts, vn, violone, lyricon, v); Tim Landers (b).* 3/81.

These are among the rarer items in Cobham's catalogue, which seems a pity because in the much-missed Don Grolnick and guitarist Barry Finnerty he seems to have found a sympathetic and inventive group, while the later band offers the intriguing prospect of Cobham in conjunction with the young Mike Stern, who is already highly individual. Finnerty's only composition on *Flight Time*, 'Jackhammer', is also the only questionable lapse into crudity. The rest, and in particular Grolnick's 'Six Persimmons', is finely modulated and thoughtful. Cobham still pounds his kit at higher tempos, but the sophistication of his phrasing is peerless and makes this a record that should be sought out by all fans of the drummer.

Stratus has many more *longueurs* and a good deal less showboating at the kit by Billy, but it has definite strengths. Michal Urbaniak makes a vivid difference, and so on occasion does the one-off brilliance of Gil Goldstein. Odd that none of the tunes, all of which merit some space, are developed beyond three or four minutes, almost as if Billy had wearied of those very performance skills which had made his name in the first place. The Glass Menagerie – as the groups of this period were known – was sounding rather fragile.

**** Warning**

Cleopatra 510 *Cobham; Onaje Allan Gumbs (p, ky); Gerry Etkins (ky); Dean Brown (g); Sa Davis (perc).* 85.

****(*) Power Play**

Cleopatra 508 *As above.* 86.

Testosterone levels were getting dangerously high on Billy's records of the mid-'80s, originally made for GRP and now reissued on his own imprint. The best measure of the change is a remake of 'Stratus' on the well-named *Warning*, a drably supercharged interpretation of one of the most durable fusion compositions of the time. There's more to enjoy on the slightly later disc; less weight on the keyboards and some fine, imaginative work from Billy on the suite, 'Summit Afrique'.

***** Picture This**

Cleopatra 507 *Cobham; Randy Brecker (flhn); Grover Washington Jr (ss, ts); Tom Scott (lyricon); Michael Abene (p, ky); Gerry Etkins (ky); Abe Laboriel (b); Sa Davis (perc).* 87.

This was an unexpected return to form. Billy built a modest supergroup round his own working band of the period and, with Randy Brecker guesting on 'Taurian Matador' (another fine '70s composition), he pulls one out of the hat. Grover Washington is elegance itself on his featured tracks, and the inclusion of Prince's 'Sign O' The Times' was a cheeky masterstroke. Good to hear Tom Scott, the butt of jazz purists for a decade and a half, making a lyricon sound more expressive than most orthodox saxophone players could manage with an original Adolphe Sax instrument.

****(*) By Design**

Cleopatra 505 *Cobham; Ernie Watts (ts); Joe Chindamo (p); Brian Bromberg (b).* 91.

Billy's return to a more jazz-influenced sound was no great surprise, given shifting market trends at the start of the '90s. The basic conception is still strongly tinged with his fusion work, but Cobham has simplified his drumming to a degree and has overcome his apparent suspicion of common or regular time-signatures. The tunes could come from almost any period in his career. 'Permanent Jet Lag' and 'Mirror's Image', which is reprised as a solo feature, are very much the Cobham of yore, though there are also signs that Billy is interested in a more modulated and song-like approach; 'Slidin' By' and 'Panama' are delightful.

***** Incoming**

Cleopatra 472 *Cobham; Rita Marcoltulli (p); Peter Wolpl (g); Ira Coleman (b); Nippy Noya (perc).* 92.

****(*) The Traveler**

Cleopatra 509 *As above, except omit Marcotulli; add Joe Chindamo (ky), Mike Mondesir (b), Gary Husband (d, ky), Carole Rowley (v).* 11/93.

***** Focused**

Cleopatra 482 *Cobham; Randy Brecker (t, flhn); Gary Husband (ky, perc); Carl Orr (g).* 2/99.

Overlooked on their release, these revealed a new and much gentler side to Cobham. *Incoming* now seems like a turning point in the drummer's career, and it is ironic that all the critics (ourselves included on occasions) who complained about his febrile power drumming, which Billy and Gary Husband spoof on *The Traveler*, should have failed to respond to a more measured approach. The group on *Focused* couldn't be better tailored, and young Carl Orr emerges as a potentially significant player whose composition, 'Nothing Can Hurt Her Now', is one of the high spots of the record, not least for the solo it inspires from Brecker, who seems to respond to working in Billy's groups.

***** Nordic**

Cleopatra 506 *Cobham; Tore Brunborg (ts); Bugge Wesseltoft (p); Terje Gewelt (b).* 96.

The Scandinavian line-up isn't in Billy's usual line of things, but the group finds a great deal of common ground to explore, and there is imaginative writing from everyone concerned, Cobham himself taking something of a back seat with just four compositions out of ten. He also moderates his dynamics and attack to accommodate some quite complex ideas going on between Wesseltoft and Gewelt: slight, almost folkish themes woven together into much larger structures. The saxophonist is perhaps the wild card; Brunborg is a very talented player but a guitarist might, as ever in Billy's bands, have offered a more consistent and idiomatic sound.

Michael Cochrane

PIANO

Post-bop pianist who started working in New York from 1974. An experienced teacher and sideman.

*****(*) Elements**

Soul Note SN 121151-2 *Cochrane; Tom Harrell (t); Bob Malach (ts); Dennis Irwin (b); James Madison (d).* 9/85.

The ensembles are keenly pointed, the solos have great contextual power, and Cochrane's tunes are all just slightly out of the ordinary; in sum, this is a very interesting post-bop record by a leader looking hard for new ground. 'Tone Row Piece No. 2' is the most surprising theme, the melody organized with strict adherence to 12-tone technique, and, although it's a little less fluid than the other pieces, one can't fault Cochrane's ambitions. Or his own playing: he has a terse, improvisational flair, tempered by a romantic streak. Harrell and the fine and underrated Malach sound in very good shape, and the contrast between the boisterous 'Reunion' and the steadily darkening 'Waltz No. 1' shows the extent of the range on offer here.

***** Song Of Change**

Soul Note 121251-2 *Cochrane; Marcus McLaurine (b); Alan Nelson (d).* 11/92.

Not exactly a retreat, but Cochrane's session pulls back on his ambitions to some degree, as the sleeve-notes seem to aver ('no agenda, no ideology, no big ideas'). He still sounds convincing without the cover of horns, and the trio work up some impressive interplay within the ensembles, even in such lightweight material as 'Once I Loved'. But the five standards receive comparatively straightforward piano-trio treatment, and Cochrane's four originals are a shade less compelling than some of his previous writing. It goes out on a very swinging 'Bemsha Swing' indeed.

***** Cutting Edge**

Steeplechase SCCD 31430 *Cochrane; David Gross (as); Ron McClure (b); Yoron Israel (d).* 9/97.

***** Gesture Of Faith**

Steeplechase SCCD 31459 *Cochrane; Eddie Gomez (b); Alan Nelson (d).* 4/98.

Cutting Edge is a solid entry from a gifted musician. There's something almost Tristano-like about his 'Lines Of Reason', and the record finds a good balance between the originals, four standards and pieces by Corea and Powell. Gross is a fluent if somewhat anonymous altoist.

He's back to a trio for *Gesture Of Faith*. Gomez and Nelson are a glittering team, as their fours on 'Baby Steps' make clear, and they give the pianist all he could want in terms of energy and interactivity. But the date still feels a little prosaic in comparison with some of Cochrane's earlier music.

Codona

GROUP

Short-lived but memorable, Codona reinforced what Walcott's other group, Oregon, was doing. This is what might be called 'world jazz', a cosmopolitan free style that, even after 20 years, still sounds fresh and alert.

*****(*) Codona**

ECM 829371-2 *Don Cherry (t, f, doussn'gouni, v); Collin Walcott (sitar, tabla, hammered dulcimer, sanza, v); Nana Vasconcelos (berimbau, perc, v).* 9/78.

***** Codona 2**

ECM 833332-2 *As above.* 5/80.

***** Codona 3**

ECM 827420-2 *As above.* 9/82.

In 1978, at Collin Walcott's behest, three musicians gathered in Tonstudio Bauer, Ludwigsburg, and recorded one of the iconic episodes in so-called (but never better called) 'world music'. Any tendency to regard Codona's music, or Walcott's compositions, as floating impressionism is sheer prejudice, for all these performances are deeply rooted in modern jazz (Coltrane's harmonies and rhythms, Ornette Coleman's melodic and rhythmic primitivism) and in another great and related improvisational tradition from Brazil. Nothing done subsequently quite matches the impact of the original *Codona*. It featured three long Walcott pieces (most notably the closing 'New Light'), the collectively composed title-track, and a brief, witty medley of Ornette Coleman tunes and Stevie Wonder's 'Sir Duke'. The permutations of instrumental sound are astonishing, but rooted in a basic jazz-trio format of horn, harmony and percussion. All three men contribute string accompaniment: Walcott on his sitar, Vasconcelos on the 'bow-and-arrow' berimbau, Cherry on the Malian *doussn'gouni*. The interplay is precise and often intense. The members' developing interests and careers created a centrifugal spin on the later albums, which are by no means as coherent or satisfying. At their best, though, which is usually when Walcott's writing is at its best, they are still compelling. 'Walking On Eggs' on *Codona 3* is one of his and their best performances.

Chris Cody

PIANO

Australian contemporary pianist.

***** Oasis**

Naxos Jazz 860188-2 *Cody; James Greening (tb, pkt-t); Jon Pease (g); Lloyd Swanton (b); John Bertram (d); Fabian Hevia (perc).* 4/98.

If Australasia is the new melting pot, Chris Cody's band Coalition is a fair representation of its creative diversity. The set opens with 'El Bahdja', the Arabic word for Algeria, a slow, rocking theme for pocket trumpet and staccato piano phrases, evoking a culture rich in imports but proudly self-sufficient. Naxos's developing love-affair with the trombone writes another chapter in the title-track, a lively and joyous blowing theme which sits just right for Greening's brisk delivery. He features again on 'Flooze Blooze', in an arrangement that would be ruined by a conventional, saxophone-driven sound.

Cody is by no stretch of the imagination a virtuosic soloist. His strength is in shaping a group sound, creating atmospheres. On 'Shadows Across The Land' and 'After The Storm', the latter another radiant feature for Greening's pocket trumpet, he patiently colours in backgrounds, content to stay out of the limelight. Only on 'Shadows' does he cut loose and show glimpses of what he might achieve in years to come.

Tony Coe (born 1934)

TENOR SAXOPHONE, CLARINET, SOPRANO SAXOPHONE

Possessed of an instantly recognizable sound, whether on tenor or his old rosewood clarinet, Coe had his first major professional stint with Humphrey Lyttelton, before striking out on his own. Canterbury-born, he always has a hint of both folksong and church music in his solo work.

**** Some Other Autumn

Hep CD 2037 *Coe; Brian Lemon (p); Dave Green (b); Phil Seamen (d).* 1/71.

Tony Coe guaranteed his small – albeit rarely credited – corner of music heaven when he played the lead saxophone part in later versions of Henry Mancini's *Pink Panther* theme; apparently Plas Johnson played on the original. The other oft-told story about him is that he turned down a place in the Count Basie Orchestra – though, given that he was past thirty and already a leader and a writer of some standing, it's perhaps less surprising.

He went on to record the material on *Some Other Autumn* in company that will have aficionados of the British scene of the 1960s blinking with nostalgia. A superb personnel and some inspired playing from Coe. If 'Body And Soul' is the tenor saxophonist's Everest – and we're still inclined to insist that it is – then Coe negotiates it without breathlessness and with a grand sweep that is entirely reciprocated by Lemon and Green. Seamen is called upon less here than on other tracks, but throughout the set he shows his extraordinary quality. He was house drummer at Ronnie Scott's at the time and was playing in exceptional company. His wilder touches are kept in check here, though he does some interesting stuff on 'Perdido'.

The three tracks that follow are the real pay-off: a superb 'When Your Lover Has Gone', with Coe leaning into the melody, importunate and mournful, then 'In A Mellow Tone' and the closer, 'Upper Manhattan Medical Group', which is the kind of performance you simply want to re-cue again and again. A superb record and certainly the place to begin. Sadly, the wonderful hat ART album, *Nutty on Willisau*, is now out of print, thus denying a glimpse of Coe in rather more avant-garde mode.

*** Tournée du Chat

Nato 777 709 *Coe; Alan Hacker (cl); Robert Cornford (p); Chris Laurence, John Lindberg (b); Nic Williams (d); Violetta Ferrer (v).* 5 & 9/81, 4/82.

The warm chalumeau of Coe's rosewood clarinet is one of the most sheerly beautiful sounds you'll encounter anywhere in this volume. Paired with that of Alan Hacker, as it is on the opening 'The Jolly Corner', it's getting close to clarinet heaven. This album hasn't been around for some years, and it's a very welcome reissue. 'The Jolly Corner' is the only group track. Based on the Henry James story, it's constructed round a ghostly motif which is played by Coe on a C clarinet and Hacker on a wry-sounding A instrument.

The remainder are either duos with Lindberg (and notably the superb 'Iberiana'), a solo ('Chantenay') and a piece based on Lorca's poem 'Debussy', which is recited by Violetta Ferrer. The only tenor track is one of the duos with the bassist, 'Makoko', and in a funny way it spoils the consistency of an otherwise near-flawless record.

**** Mainly Mancini

Nato 530 262 *Coe; Tony Hymas (p); Chris Laurence (b).* 8/85.

Mancini's critical reputation seems to grow with the passing years. Inevitably, and appropriately, this starts with 'The Pink Panther', but it's 'Crazy World' from *Victor Victoria* which grabs the attention. 'Hank Neuf' is a Coe original, as is 'Mancinissimo', which is subtitled 'How I Learned To Stop Worrying And Love Giant Steps'; two glorious performances, absolutely in the spirit of not one but two masters. Coe's Coltrane influence surfaces only somewhat rarely in audible form, but it is there.

The closing track – 'Charade' – is an overdubbed duo, Coe on both tenor and piano. Were it not for 'Days Of Wine And Roses', it would be the most memorable thing on the record, but the great ballad wins hands down.

***(*) Canterbury Song

Hot House HHCD 1005 *Coe; Benny Bailey (t); Horace Parlan (p); Jimmy Woode (b); Idris Muhammad (d).* 88.

Coe had no need to worry about his ability to stand up in company like this. He had encountered some of them in the Clarke–Boland Band (whose invitation he *did* accept) and they knew what he was about. Parlan is a responsive partner. Allegedly restricted as a soloist by a bout of polio, he nevertheless lays out exquisitely shaped chordal frames for Coe's soprano solo on 'Re: Person I Knew', and he gives 'Blue And Green' an open-ended, roomy feel that's just right for this group. Two fine originals in 'Lagos' and 'Canterbury Song' itself, and in the closing 'Morning Vehicle' there's a superb vehicle for that distinctive clarinet.

***(*) Les Sources Bleues

Nato 53002.2 *Coe; Tony Hymas (p); Chris Laurence (b).* 88, 4/92.

A delightful drummerless record that once again underlines the disappearance of *Nutty On Willisau*, which featured an altogether more combustible playing partner in the shape of Tony Oxley. This is most gentle and melodic, but there are mordant touches to Coe's own playing. The opening 'Tangellen' has a hidden bite and both 'Jardin de Sable' and a lovely version of 'Canterbury Song' suggest an artist using an amiable and sympathetic setting to let loose some darker instincts as well.

Hymas is a musician who deserves more attention. A great enabler, he has the ability to make those around him play better, anyone from Coe to the old lion of the avant-garde, Sam Rivers. Here he is bright-toned and articulate on his solo statements as well as being an exemplary accompanist. About Chris Laurence there is little more to say save to repeat that he is a master of the art.

*****(*) Captain Coe's Famous Racearound**

Storyville STCD 4206 *Coe; Palle Bolvig, Jan Kohlin, Henrik Bolberg Pedersen, Benny Rosenfeld, Lars Togeby (t, flhn); Steen Hansen, Kjeld Ipsen, Vincent Nilsson (tb); Giordano Bellinicampi, Axel Windfeld (btb); Bob Brookmeyer (vtb, cond); Michael Hove, Jan Zum Vorde (as, reeds); Uffe Markussen, Bob Rockwell (ts, reeds); Flemming Madsen (bs, reeds); Nikolaj Bentzon, David Hazeltine (p); Anders Lindvall, Thomas Ovesen (g); Steve Arguëlles, Jonas Johansen (d); Ethan Weisgard (perc).* 3/95.

In 1995, Tony Coe was awarded the prestigious Jazzpar Prize, no small but certainly belated recognition of his gifts. Would that he were as highly regarded back home in Britain. Part of the award is a new composition and performance with the Danish Radio Jazz Orchestra. The title-piece makes a strong and lyrical climax to an album that combines big-band charts and a superb small combo consisting of Pedersen, the mellifluous Brookmeyer, Hazeltine, Ovesen and Arguëlles; the drummer provides two of the compositions, 'Toy Box' and 'Antonia'. There are two further compositions by Brookmeyer and Maria Schneider, 'Nasty Dance' and 'My Lament' respectively, the latter a wonderful orchestral conception.

Unusual for a Jazzpar winner to be so reticent about his own work, but Coe was awarded primarily as a player, one suspects, and it would be a waste if he weren't to play standards. 'Fools Rush In' and 'How Long Has This Been Going On?' (the latter for full orchestra) are both superb. Coe's tone is, as ever, as pure as spring water, with none of the quavering 'oboe' sound that he reacts so badly against, while accepting that it suited Coltrane's purposes perfectly. Brookmeyer has an unerring sense of orchestral dynamics and he conjures some inch-perfect ensembles out of the Danes. A splendid record.

*****(*) Blue Jersey**

AB CD 4 *Coe; Dave Horler (vtb); John Horler (p); Malcolm Creese (b); Allan Ganley (d).* 4/95.

****** In Concert**

AB CD 6 *Coe; John Horler (p); Malcolm Creese (b).* 3/97.

Two exceptional live albums. The earlier was made at the Jersey Jazz Festival, with the Brookmeyer-influenced Dave Horler on valve trombone. He contributes to an unusual arrangement of 'I Got Rhythm', but it's Coe's clarinet solo that blows the whole thing apart, a truly remarkable performance that gets the set off to a great start. To be frank, nothing that follows quite matches up, though 'You Stepped Out Of A Dream' and an unexpectedly paced 'What Is This Thing Called Love?' run it close, with the trombonist playing magnificently again on the latter. The other Horler shows his skills as a composer on two tunes: 'Solid Silver' is inspired by Horace of that ilk, but it ranges far and wide for ideas, with even a hint of Debussy in the middle section; the closing 'Royal Blues' works some unusual wrinkles on a fairly basic idea.

If we've been slightly niggardly with the stars on *Blue Jersey*, that's simply because as a Tony Coe album it sits a little behind the splendid live set recorded a couple of years later at St George's, Brandon Hill, in Bristol. Drummerless, and with no second horn, it's an ideal showcase for Coe, and he responds with near-perfect versions of 'Body And Soul' and 'Re: Person I Knew' which even casual readers will recognize as shibboleths, and a lovely 'You Stepped Out Of A Dream'. St George's has a warm, churchy acoustic and the piano is in excellent shape. Creese (who produced these CDs) is sounding more communicative every time one hears him, and he brings a robust presence both to ballads and to up-tempo songs. If you haven't sampled Tony Coe before, either of these will provide a crash course; the latter is our strong recommendation.

****** Days Of Wine And Roses**

Zephyr ZECD 22 *Coe; Alan Barnes (as, bs, ss, cl, bcl); Brian Lemon (p); Dave Cliff (g); Dave Green (b); Allan Ganley (d).* 1 & 2/97.

This is simply exquisite. The pairing of Coe's tenor and Barnes's alto on the closing choruses of 'My Old Flame' is a high point in recent British jazz. Coe's woody clarinet is featured on the title-track, a virtuosic scatter of notes as the melody is reinvented, re-examined and, finally, heart-stoppingly stated with magnificent simplicity.

The rhythm section could hardly be improved upon, and there is a wonderful tenor/guitar duet on 'Flamingo' which once again highlights Dave Cliff's special talents. *Days* could hardly be bettered, the jewel in Zephyr's already sparkling crown. Coe has also co-starred on other Zephyr recordings, but these we have covered under cornetist Warren Vaché's entry.

*****(*) Ruby**

Zah Zah ZZCD 9802 *Coe; Brian Dee (p); Matt Miles (b); Steve Arguëlles (d).* 98.

Typical of Coe to create a standards album that surprises more than it lulls. The title-piece is an interesting choice, a film tune which has been covered – to our knowledge – only by Ray Charles. The reason for its inclusion becomes clear when Tony plays an additional figure of his own, inspired by the initials of his first granddaughter, Ruby Elizabeth Delaney (Coe), with *Re* generating the first element in the phrase D-E-D-C.

It's just one of a series of tasteful reinventions on the disc. 'My Shining Hour' nods in the direction of John Coltrane but has its own statement to make, and the clarinet and piano conversation of 'More Than You Know' almost remakes the tune. The original 'Backward Tracings', which gives the album much of its character, is a reworking of familiar chords, presumably 'Yesterdays' but possibly combined with another motif.

Of the band, Arguëlles stands out strongly and is given due prominence in the mix. Another exile to France, he has absorbed a great deal of music in the last five years and now sounds entirely in command of his own voice. His solo on 'Love Walked In' is a model, using a bebop diction to suggest the kind of swinging work one might have heard from Dave Tough in the old days. A splendid record from a small but enterprising label.

Avishai Cohen

DOUBLE BASS, PIANO, PERCUSSION

Young virtuoso bassist, a Chick Corea sideman and now recording for Corea's own imprint.

*****(*) Adama**
Stretch Records SCD 9015-2 *Cohen; Steve Davis (tb); Steve Wilson (ss); Chick Corea, Jason Lindner, Brad Mehldau, Danilo Perez (p); Amos Hoffman (g, oud); Jeff Ballard, Jordy Rossi (d); Don Alias (perc); Claudio Acuna (v).* 97.

***** Devotion**
Stretch SCD 9021-2 *Cohen; Steve Davis (tb); Jimmy Greene (ss, ts, f); Jason Lindner (p); Amos Hoffman (g, oud); Jeff Ballard (d).* 98.

This young associate of Chick Corea always looked likely to carve his own path. Cohen wasn't so much a virtuoso bassist as a thoroughly musicianly member of Chick's group, the kind of player who does the job at hand with consummate professionalism but who manages to leave you with the feeling that he will need to be checked out subsequently.

His debut is all the more impressive for the skill of the writing. Everything except 'Besame Mucho' is by Cohen. The tunes range from bright swingers like 'Ora' to a pair of items lifted from a 'Bass Suite'. The first is played just by trombone, soprano saxophone and broodingly eloquent bass, an unexpected instrumentation that is more than merely quirky. What emerges might well be a stripped-down section of a big-band piece and it would be no surprise if this was where Cohen's career heads in years to come. Middle Eastern influences are in evidence here and there, not just in the use of an *oud*, but also in the writing, which favours non-Western scales. Label-boss Chick Corea pops up to give his blessing on 'Gadu', playing Fender Rhodes alongside Danilo Perez on acoustic piano and sounding as if he might have been called away from something more important. Chick is also the dedicatee of 'The Gift' on the second album; if only he had been around to perform as well.

Trombonist Davis returns for the second album, which is pretty much more of the same. There are two more fragments of 'Bass Suite', though this increasingly looks like a flag of convenience for otherwise untitled material. The stand-out track is 'Ot Kain', inspired by a poem of Shay Yemini, which in turn takes its inspiration from Akhenaten's hymn to the sun.

Two elegantly crafted albums, perhaps not quite differentiated enough to be really special, but far from ordinary nevertheless.

Greg Cohen

BASS

Mainstream-to-modern-to-out bassist who seems happy in most situations and divides his time between East and West Coasts.

*****(*) Way Low**
DIW 918 *Cohen; Dave Douglas (t); Joel Hellany (tb); Scott Robinson (cl, ts, bsx, f); Ted Rosenthal (p); Romero Lubambo (g); Tony Denicola (d); Kenny Wolleson (perc).* 12/96.

***** Moment To Moment**
DIW 928 *Cohen; Teddy Edwards (ts); Gerry Wiggins (p); Donald Bailey (d).* 9/96.

Cohen might be best known for some of his work in John Zorn's Masada group. Here he's in some surprising company. The band on *Way Low* is an intriguing mix of personalities and Cohen gets them to work beautifully as a unit. The title-piece and 'Creole Rhapsody' are vintage chunks of Ellingtonia, realized with perfect freshness, and they sit comfortably beside a group of originals that mix blues, bebop and mainstream-modern lines without a hint of strain. Douglas, Robinson and Hellany are willing players entirely up to the eclecticism of it all.

Moment To Moment was recorded a few weeks earlier on the West Coast. The main features are the luscious studio sound and the splendid playing by the rhythm section on three originals and seven interesting standards. Edwards, though, is beginning to sound a little tired. Principal honours go to Bailey, still a master of the drums, and Cohen himself, clearly delighted by the company.

Tom Cohen

DRUMS

Contemporary drummer speaking a mainstream post-bop language.

***** Tom Cohen Trio**
Cadence CJR 1067 *Cohen; Ron Thomas (p); Mike Richmond, Bill Zinno (b).* 2/95–6/96.

Cohen doesn't give himself a lot of solos but he definitely leads from the front. The tracks which bookend the record, 'Things You Were' and 'Motion Potion', are as trenchant as you like, and elsewhere he and Richmond (Zinno comes in for only one track) set up a powerful undertow for Thomas's piano. The music is a scrupulous and swinging essay on the piano-trio style. There are three Bill Evans compositions, but it's the hard-hitting side of Evans's music that they take off from; the other material – mostly originals by Thomas, though 'Things You Were' is a thin disguise for 'All The Things You Are' – is effective if not terribly vivid. John Anthony's studio mix pushes everything to the front, which can make it a little tiring to listen to.

Al Cohn (1925–88)

TENOR SAXOPHONE

Cohn was the consummate jazz professional. His arrangements were foursquare and unpretentious and his saxophone-playing a model of order and accuracy. He was perhaps never more completely himself than as one of the Four Brothers, the legendary Woody Herman saxophone section. Later in life, though, his soloing took on a philosophical authority, unexciting but deeply satisfying.

***** Broadway**

Original Jazz Classics OJC 1812 *Cohn; Hal Stein (as); Harvey Leonard (p); Red Mitchell (b); Christy Febbo (d).* 7/54.

****** Al And Zoot**

Chess GRP 18272 *Cohn; Zoot Sims (ts, cl); Mose Allison (p); Teddy Kotick (b); Nick Stabulas (d).* 3/57.

***** Either Way**

Evidence ECD 22007 *Cohn; Zoot Sims (ts); Mose Allison (p); Bill Crow (b); Gus Johnson (d); Cecil Collier (v).* 2/61.

***** From A To Z**

RCA 47790 *Cohn; Dick Sherman (t); Zoot Sims (ts); Hank Jones, Dave McKenna (p); Milt Hinton (b); Osie Johnson (d).* 62.

Virtually all one needs to know about Al and Zoot's long-standing association can be found on the sober-sounding 'Improvisation For Two Unaccompanied Saxophones' on the less than sober-sounding *Hot Tracks For Cool Cats*, which is not currently in circulation. All the virtues – elegant interplay, silk-smooth textures – and all the vices – inconsequentiality and Sims's tendency to blandness – are firmly in place. A and Z were apt to cover the whole expressive gamut from A to B, as Dorothy Parker once memorably said about Miss Hepburn.

The Evidence set is sparky enough, if only because Allison is such an enlivening presence. Still wholly underrated as a pianist and misplaced in the history of the music – filed under 'vocal', or 'easy listening' in one major store of our acquaintance – Allison brings a touch of acidity to the slightly sweet harmonies Sims for one seems to prefer. Cohn was always a more adventurous player, and he responds well to the pianist's sly, stealthy cues. With the whole Xanadu catalogue currently *hors de combat* and awaiting CD transfer, this session and the quartet/quintet material packaged half and half on *Tones* and *Progressive* become all the more valuable and all the harder to distinguish qualitatively.

The *Broadway* disc is exceedingly well behaved, even dull, until Cohn launches into a ballad medley that simply takes one's breath away. Stein is virtually unknown; he's recorded with Teddy Charles and fellow-altoist Phil Woods, and on the basis of this performance might have expected to make more of a splash on his own account. The rest of the band do their jobs like men on an hourly rate.

The Chess disc was issued to mark the tenth anniversary of Al's death. The two kings dominate it pretty completely, but Allison is once again good value and the rhythm section work together comfortably, often making slightly lumpy charts sound highly sophisticated; Stabulas is an underrated performer in situations like this. 'Two Funky People' sees the two horns swapped for clarinets, two strong solos and a glorious 'flutter' behind Kotick's excellent bass solo. A vivid document of a special creative partnership, *Al And Zoot* breathes friendly rivalry and shared humour.

The RCA compilation is only recently back in catalogue. It's pretty standard Al and Zoot material, though above-average production and mastering and a nicely presented package. A handful of extra takes – including 'Tenor For Two, Please, Jack' and 'More Bread' – fill out the picture and will be an additional draw for fans of this long-standing pairing.

***** Body And Soul**

32 Jazz 32017 *Cohn; Zoot Sims (ts); Jaki Byard (p); George Duvivier (b); Mel Lewis (d).* 3/73.

Al recorded virtually nothing under his own name during the mid- and late-'60s, working instead as a studio composer and arranger. *Body And Soul* was originally recorded for Muse and it finds both saxophonists in good form, blending together much as they did in the old days but with an edge to some of the performances as well. The long 'Brazilian Medley' is an object lesson in space and texture, with the horns perfectly distinct and individual. Zoot takes the Rod McKuen song, 'Jean', on soprano and, as ever, gives the smaller horn a full voice and a good deal of bottom end. Cohn and Byard have some intriguingly cross-grained moments on the tenor classic, 'Body And Soul'. A fine record and a welcome return from Al.

***** Nonpareil**

Concord CCD 4155 *Cohn; Lou Levy (p); Monty Budwig (b); Jake Hanna (d).* 4/81.

****(*) Tour De Force**

Concord CCD 4172 *Cohn; Scott Hamilton, Buddy Tate (ts); Cal Collins (g); Dave McKenna (p); Bob Maize (b); Jake Hanna (d).* 8/81.

***** Overtones**

Concord CCD 4194 *Cohn; Joe Cohn (g); Hank Jones (p); George Duvivier (b); Akira Tana (d).* 4/82.

***** Standards Of Excellence**

Concord CCD 4241 *Cohn; Herb Ellis (g); Monty Budwig (b); Jimmie Smith (d).* 11/83.

A brilliant arranger, Cohn wasn't always the most convincing soloist, leaving his own most compelling ideas rather hanging in the air. This latter-day set has him in fine voice and with a tougher, more segmented delivery than previously. The bossa nova stylings bear comparison with the rather muffled versions recorded with Zoot Sims. Ellis is a less satisfactory foil than Levy, and he overcooks some of the simpler transitions. Generally, though, standards of excellence are well up to form, and Cohn sounds deliciously relaxed on 'Embraceable You', a wonderful tune with a consistency somewhere between marshmallow and quicksand that has lured and lost many a soloist.

Overtones is again workmanlike rather than spectacular. The saxophonist's four compositions are thoughtful and well argued but somewhat lacking in emotional resonance. The backing of Cohn Jr and Jones should have allowed him to cut loose a little more freely and confidently, but Al sounds reserved, almost cautious. 'Woody's Lament', 'Pensive' and the standard 'I Don't Want Anybody At All' (the latter featuring some lovely work from Jones) are the key to the album.

Tour De Force is something of a throwback to the multi-tenor sessions Cohn made with Zoot, Brew Moore, Allen Eager and Stan Getz back in 1949; it's engaging enough stuff, but surely not sufficiently compelling to merit the critical raves it received on its appearance in 1981. Nineteen years on, it definitely sounds a bit thin.

***** Skylark**

EJ 606 2CD *Cohn; Dan Wall (p); Neal Starkey (b); Brian Childers (d).* 83.

One of the last sets recorded at the enterprising Atlanta club E.J.'s, where someone had the foresight to record some of the best moments. As ever, there's not much in the way of selection or editing down; the music is presented, one assumes, pretty much as it happened. The local rhythm-section is basically very good, though they do little more than provide an accommodating environment for the big man. Cohn sticks pretty much to standard material, but he has also dropped in a couple of originals, 'Woody's Lament' and 'Danielled', and he improvises a couple of tunes with Wall. Al's solo on 'Lover Man' is the pick of the set, long, thoughtful and full of resonant emotion, his tone as accurate and unflustered as ever.

***** Keeper Of The Flame**

Jazz House JHCD 022 *Cohn; Dick Pearce (t, flhn); Pete Beachill (tb, vtb); Andy Mackintosh (as); Dave Hartley (p); Chris Laurence (b); Quinny Laurence (d).* 5/87.

*****(*) Rifftide**

Timeless SJP 259 *Cohn; Rein De Graaff (p); Koos Serierse (b); Eric Ineke (d).* 6/87.

Rifftide is an absolutely marvellous set, with Cohn's brooding tone working an unhurried magic over 'Speak Low', 'Blue Monk' and 'Hot House', as surprising and moving a group of tunes as he's ever recorded. Three other tracks are less familiar but, if anything, better played, with 'We'll Be Together Again' and the title-tune underlining how subtle an accompanist de Graaff can be. Further proof, if any were needed, of Cohn's creative stamina.

The London recording was made in a studio rather than in concert, but it has the easy flow of a sympathetic gig. The Jazz Seven play 'Keeper Of The Flame' in tribute and Cohn takes a couple of tracks with rhythm only. These are the most effective of all – which is no surprise. He sounds calm, untroubled and completely on top of things. Less than a year later, he was gone.

Joe Cohn

GUITAR

The son of the eminent saxophonist is a guitarist who has by now gathered a broad range of experience in most modern jazz styles.

***** Two Funky People**

Double-Time DTRCD-126 *Cohn; Doug Raney (g); Dennis Irwin (b); Barry Ries (d).* 11/96.

A belated leadership record for Joe Cohn, who's done plenty of sterling work across a wide range of settings in the last ten years. Paired with Raney, not quite a doppelgänger but scarcely a glaring contrast, he helms a smoothly enjoyable set here. Material by both Al Cohn and Jimmy Raney makes it an affectionate family-affair. Raney can be identified by his ever-so-slightly cloudier tone, but the two men are in absolute accord and when they sweep through a piece like 'Motion' one simply basks in the impeccable musicianship. Satisfying without stirring the blood, and best directed to classic jazz-guitar followers.

Steve Cohn

PIANO, SHAKUHACHI, SHOFAR, PERCUSSION

Cohn's theories about infinite tonalism are a mixture of George Russell, Harry Partch and Eastern idiom. Moving between piano and wind instruments allows him to deploy single-note lines against drones and glissandi from other instruments, much as in the temple music of Japan and Korea.

***** Bridge Over The X-Stream**

Leo CDLR 288 *Cohn; Tom Varner (frhn); Jason Hwang (vn); Reggie Workman (b).* 1/99.

Though Cohn's own main instrument is programmed to play single notes and differentiated chords, he achieves astonishing levels of overtone harmonics. Horn tones and double-stopped patterns on violin and bass create a shifting background of sometimes boggling complexity. Workman and Hwang between them create orchestral textures which are reminiscent of Webern's fuller scores, while Varner ranges between blaring, trombone tones and softer, almost ethereal harmonics. An impressive and consistently involving record from a musician who will make a substantial impact.

George 'Kid Sheik' Cola (born 1908)

TRUMPET, PIANO, VOCAL

This New Orleans brassman was fronting bands by the age of seventeen, and he rambled around the city's music and as an ambassador overseas into the 1980s, working in small groups as leader and in the city's most renowned brass bands, the Olympia and the Eureka.

**** Kid Sheik With Charlie Love And His Cado Jazz Band – 1960**

504 CDS 21 *Cola; Charlie Love (t); Albert Warner (tb); Emile Barnes (cl); Louis Gallaud (p); Emanuel Sayles (bj); Albert Jiles (d).* 8/60.

**** Kid Sheik's Swingsters 1961**

American Music AMCD-91 *Cola; Eddie Sommers (tb); Harold Dejan (as); John Smith (p); Alcide Slow Drag Pavageau (b); Alex Bigard (d).* 2/61.

**** In Boston And Cleveland**

American Music AMCD-69 *Cola; Louis Nelson, Albert Warner (tb); John Handy (cl, as); James Sing Miller, Louis Gallaud (p); Fred Minor (bj); Chester Zardis, John Joseph (b); Alex Bigard, Cie Frazier (d).* 61–69.

***** First European Tour**

GHB BCD-187 *Cola; Jack Weddell (tb); Sammy Rimington (cl); Paul Sealy (bj); Barry Richardson (b); Barry Martyn (d).* 6/63.

***(*) Kid Sheik & Brother Cornbread In Copenhagen**

Jazz Crusade JCCD-3002 *Cola; Peter Goetz (tb); Joe 'Brother Cornbread' Thomas (cl); Peter Nissen (bj); Niels Henrik Ross-Petersen (b); Keith Minter (d).* 11/74.

Kid Sheik Cola was much loved in the ranks of New Orleans brassmen, and the notes to several of these discs detail the affection he inspired on his travels. CD listeners will find his music hard going, though. He plays in the mould of the short-breathed frontman and packs a punch only occasionally: solos tend to be self-effacing, and he usually lets someone else drive things along. This mixed bag of records doesn't fare too well. The 504 date offers a band which sounds almost enfeebled at times, even as weathered New Orleans music goes. Charlie Love is the bandleader, and Kid Sheik sits out on six tracks – but even when he's there the music flickers into real life only occasionally, as on a rickety but spirited 'Down In Honky Tonk Town'. *Swingsters 1961* was recorded by Barry Martyn and features Cola's regular band of the day, but Martyn's notes reveal all sorts of alarums and excursions before the session was done, and it sounds like a shambles for much of the time. Cola plays a couple of ramshackle blues at the piano for a change of pace. *In Boston And Cleveland* includes two knockabout sessions which are largely dominated by Handy: sound-quality is indifferent and there's some awful singing, but it's listenable. The pick is surely *First European Tour*, in which Kid Sheik was chaperoned by Martyn and Rimington through a spirited session that still sounds good. Recorded at Egham Cricket Club.

The notes to the Jazz Crusade set remember the occasion of the recording with much nostalgia, which makes the fairly awful music a terrible disappointment. The main culprit is Brother Cornbread's clarinet, which flies out of tune at every opportunity, though nobody seems to care much. Obviously a happy night, but you definitely had to be there.

Freddy Cole (born 1931)

PIANO, VOCAL

The youngest of the Cole brothers, it took Freddy until the 1990s to get himself noticed and on record in a significant way. His piano work is much more modest than Nat's, but his voice certainly makes the most of the family resemblance.

****(*) I'm Not My Brother, I'm Me**

Sunnyside SSC 1054 *Cole; Ed Zad (g); Eddie Edwards (b). 4/90.*

***** Always**

Fantasy FCD-9670-2 *Cole; Byron Stripling (flhn); Robin Eubanks (tb); Jeff Scott (frhn); Frank Perowsky (ss, ts, f); Grover Washington (ss); William Kerr (as, f); Antonio Hart (as, ts); Javon Jackson (ts); Roger Rosenberg (bs); Mel Martin (af); Cyrus Chestnut (p); Lionel Cole (ky); Joe Locke (vib); Tom Hubbard, George Mraz (b); Yoron Israel, Russ Kunkel (d); Steve Berrios (perc); strings. 12/94.*

***** Live At Vartan Jazz**

Vartan 005 *Cole; Jerry Byrd (g); Tom Hubbard (b). 10/94.*

***** I Want A Smile For Christmas**

Fantasy FCD-9672-2 *Cole; Joe Ford (ss); Larry Willis (p); Joe Locke (vib); Jerry Byrd (g); Tom Hubbard (b); Steve Berrios (d). 7/94.*

*****(*) A Circle Of Love**

Fantasy FCD-9674-2 *As above, except add Danny Moore (t), Don Braden (ss), Mel Martin (f), Cyrus Chestnut (p), George Mraz (b). 9/93–12/95.*

*****(*) To The Ends Of The Earth**

Fantasy FCD-9675-2 *As above, except add Byron Stripling (t), Robin Eubanks (tb), Antonio Hart (as), Javon Jackson (ts), Frank Perowsky (cl), William Kerr (as, f), Roger Rosenburg (bcl), Yoron Israel (b); omit Willis, Byrd, Moore, Braden. 1/97.*

Though he is *still* best known as Nat's brother, Freddy Cole's fine sequence of Fantasy albums has helped set him up as an artist of some stature in his own right. Freddy seemed to be falling over to invite comparisons on the first album, what with 'He Was The King' and a Nat medley among the titles, and the trio format is a not-disagreeable update on his brother's pioneering work. But there seems little enough to make one want to return. The Fantasy records, though, make a convincing sequence, prepared with great care and thoughtfulness by producer Todd Barkan. The glittering line-up of names on the first disc sets the precedent, with a programme of meticulously arranged standards: nobody really has any space to cut loose, but the splendid Chestnut is magisterial at the piano, Washington (especially fine on 'You Must Believe In Spring') and Hart take apposite cameos, and the result is a laid-back but not soporific entry. Cole stays away from the piano and sticks to husking through the lyrics. There are a couple of clinkers – 'The Rose' seems to have strayed in from another project altogether. The Christmas collection is, surprisingly, almost as good, centred round the small group listed in the personnel. Willis plays with quiet dignity and Ford, a surprise choice for sole horn, traces filigree lines over the sometimes unpromising Yuletide material. It's to Cole's credit that when they get to 'The Christmas Song' he sings it in a way that's nothing like Nat.

A Circle Of Love mixes a session done for the Alfa label, dating back to 1993, with three newer tracks, one of them a quite immaculate take on an unlikely Paul Williams song, 'You're Nice To be Around'. This and the subsequent *To The Ends Of The Earth* proceed with and polish a formula which Cole seems completely at home with: older standards mixed with newer pop tunes, the blend brought into focus by the carefully chosen tempos and instrumentation. A slow and thoughtful 'Manha de Carnaval' and a fine 'If I Had You' highlight the first disc, while a shimmering duet with Locke on 'Once You've Been In Love' and a handsome treatment of Abbey Lincoln's 'Should Have Been' stand out on the second. Barkan has assembled what is by now a repertory cast of players and they work with perfect sensitivity to the way Cole sings. *Live At Vartan Jazz* is a good-natured souvenir of one of Freddy's stage shows, a little more one-note than the studio albums but very enjoyable, with a couple of his set-pieces captured for posterity.

***** Le Grand Freddy**

Fantasy 9863-2 *Cole; Lew Soloff (t); Lou Marini (ts, f); Grover Washington (ts); Cedar Walton, Cyrus Chestnut, Mike Renzi (p); Joe Locke (vib); George Mraz, David Williams (b); Kenny Washington, Grady Tate, Yoron Israel, Ben Riley (d). 12/94–2/99.*

Ouch! An awful pun for the title of this collection in which Freddy sings Michel Legrand. While much of this is new, some tracks were lifted off Cole's earlier Fantasy sets. There are surprising successes, such as 'Windmils Of Your Mind', and some songs which definitely don't suit him, like a far too blasé 'Once Upon A Summertime'.

Nat Cole (1917–65)

PIANO, VOCAL

Born in Montgomery, Alabama, Cole was equally adept at playing the piano and singing, although it was his voice that brought him stardom. He began leading a piano–guitar–bass trio in 1939, and his keyboard style – much influenced by Earl Hines and Teddy Wilson – suggested a transition between swing and what would become the bebop vocabulary. The trio was so successful that it set the main precedent for piano small groups. Cole became enormously popular as a singer, though, and gradually left the keyboard behind, rarely playing in a jazz setting after 1950. A chain-smoker from morning till night, he died from cancer in 1965. His daughter Natalie and brother Freddy carry on his performing tradition.

***** Nat King Cole 1936–1940**
Classics 757 *Cole; Kenneth Roane (t); Tommy Thompson (as); Bill Wright (ts); Oscar Moore (g); Wesley Prince, Eddie Cole (b); Jimmy Adams, Lee Young (d); Bonnie Lake, Juanelda Carter (v).* 7/36–2/40.

***** Nat King Cole 1941–1943**
Classics 786 *Cole; Lester Young (ts); Oscar Moore (g); Wesley Prince, Red Callender, Johnny Miller (b).* 7/41–11/43.

***** Nat King Cole 1943–1944**
Classics 804 *Cole; Shad Collins (t); Illinois Jacquet (ts); Oscar Moore (g); Johnny Miller, Gene Englund (b); J.C Heard (d).* 11/43–3/44.

*****(*) Sweet Lorraine**
Vintage Jazz Classics VJC 1026-29 4CD *Cole; Oscar Moore (g); Wesley Prince (b).* 10/38–2/41.

Cole began with deceptively lightweight, jiving music (sample titles: 'Scotchin' With The Soda', 'Ode To A Wild Clam') which masked the intensity of his piano style to a large extent. Smooth, glittering, skating over melodies, Cole's right-hand lines were breaking free of his original Earl Hines influence and looking towards a dashing improvisational freedom which other players – Powell, Haig, Marmarosa – would turn into the language of bebop. Cole was less inclined towards that jagged-edge approach and preferred the hip constrictions of songs and good-natured jive. With pulsing interjections from Moore and Prince (subsequently replaced by Miller), this was a surprisingly compelling music. Classics start their usual chronological survey with four obscure 1936 titles by a group led by Eddie Cole. The trio proper begins in 1939 with 12 titles cut in a single day and moves on through a session with Lester Young and Red Callender (Classics 786) and a single quintet date with horns (Classics 804). The latter disc is probably the best single representation of Cole's early music, with hits such as 'Straighten Up And Fly Right' and some deft interpretations of standards. Transfers, from unlisted sources, seem good.

Sweet Lorraine is a superb collection of transcriptions, some four-and-a-half hours of music on four CDs. The surprising thing is that, even taken at a long stretch, listener-fatigue doesn't set in. The hipness of the sound, the playing and the singing makes even the most trifling songs endure.

***** The Jazzman**
Topaz TPZ 1012 *As above, except add Wesley Prince (b); omit vocalists.* 40–44.

***** The McGregor Years 1941–1945**
Music & Arts CD 911 4CD *Cole; Oscar Moore (g); Wesley Prince, Johnny Miller (b); Anita O'Day, Ida James, The Barry Sisters, Anita Boyer (v).* 2/41–5/45.

*****(*) Nat King Cole 1944–1945**
Classics 861 *Cole; Bill Coleman (t); Buster Bailey (cl); Benny Carter (as); Coleman Hawkins (ts); Oscar Moore (g); John Kirby, Johnny Miller (b); Max Roach (d); Kay Starr (v).* 11/44–5/45.

*****(*) Nat King Cole 1945**
Classics 893 *Cole; Charlie Shavers (t); Herbie Haymer (ts); Oscar Moore (g); Johnny Miller, John Simmons (b); Buddy Rich (d).* 5–12/45.

*****(*) Nat King Cole 1946**
Classics 938 *Cole; Willie Smith (as); Oscar Moore (g); Johnny Miller, Red Callender (b); Jackie Mills (d).* 2–6/46.

*****(*) Nat King Cole 1946–1947**
Classics 1005 *As above, except omit Smith, Callender, Mills; add Jack Parker (d), strings.* 8/46–7/47.

*****(*) Nat King Cole 1947**
Classics 1031 *As above, except omit Parker, strings.* 7/47.

*****(*) Nat King Cole 1947 Vol. 2**
Classics 1062 *As above, except add Johnny Mercer (v), strings.* 8/47.

*****(*) The Vocal Classics 1942–1946**
Capitol 833571-2 *Cole; Oscar Moore (g); Johnny Miller, (b).* 42–46.

*****(*) The Best Of The Trio (Instrumental)**
Capitol 798288-2 *As above, except add Irving Ashby (g), Joe Comfort (b), Jack Costanza (perc).* 43–49.

***** Straighten Up And Fly Right!**
Vintage Jazz Classics VJC-1044 *Cole; Oscar Moore (g, v); Johnny Miller (b, v); Frank Sinatra (v).* 12/42–1/48.

*****(*) Live At The Circle Room**
Capitol 521859-2 *Cole; Oscar Moore (g); Johnny Miller (b).* 9/46.

*****(*) Jazz Encounters**
Capitol 796693-2 *Cole; Dizzy Gillespie, Bill Coleman, Ernie Royal, Ray Linn (t); Bill Harris (tb); Buddy DeFranco, Buster Bailey (cl); Coleman Hawkins, Charlie Barnet, Flip Phillips, Herbie Haymer (ts); Benny Carter (as); Heinie Beau, Fred Stulce, Harry Schuman (reeds); Billy Bauer, Irving Ashby, Oscar Moore, Dave Barbour (g); Eddie Safranski, Johnny Miller, Joe Comfort, Art Shapiro, John Kirby (b); Buddy Rich, Max Roach, Nick Fatool, Earl Hyde (d); Woody Herman, Jo Stafford, Nellie Lutcher, Johnny Mercer, Kay Starr (v); Stan Kenton Orchestra.* 12/47–1/50.

Cole made a tremendous number of recordings with his trio; Mosaic once issued a comprehensive survey which ran to 18 CDs (currently out of print). Classics's ongoing survey is up to 1947 and offers a sensible way of collecting these tracks. The *1944–1945* set includes one date for V-Disc and has a session by the Capitol International Jazzmen. Carter and Hawkins have starring roles but the highlights of the session are the two vocals by the young Kay Starr, who handles 'If I Could Be With You' and 'Stormy Weather' quite beautifully. *1945* offers a date where Cole played with the Herbie Haymer Quintet, the saxophonist shining on four engaging titles; the rest is solid Cole trio music. *1946* starts with a Keynote session where Cole sat in with Willie Smith and rhythm section; the rest is nearly all Capitol material and includes his hit, 'Route 66'. All the trio sessions maintain an enviable standard and there are very few duds among all the tracks; only occasionally does a song offer too little for Cole and cohorts to work with. The pianist's luxuriant swing and dextrous touch and his intelligently varied arrangements for the Trio and their wonderfully responsive following of his leads all seem inexhaustible. Moore is, indeed, almost Cole's equal on an executive level, and their best playing often runs in dazzling, parallel lines.

The VJC collection pulls together a collection of airchecks which act as a counterweight to the studio material. The 'Route 66' here pre-dates the Capitol studio version by a matter of days, and Sinatra turns up to sing on 'I've Found A New Baby' (not really him) and 'Exactly Like You' (a shade more appropriate).

Classics 1005, covering 1946–7, has a discouraging preponderance of so-so ballads, but the boppish 'That's What' and a flying 'Honeysuckle Rose' pick matters up towards the end. Not one of the best in this series, though. Classics 1031 shows how hard Cole was working: he cut 19 of these titles in a single week. Song-quality is up here and, with only the three trio members involved, it's a good single-disc representation of their music. Classics 1062 calls in Johnny Mercer to sit in on four hip titles, including 'My Baby Likes To Be-Bop', but matters deteriorate from there, with a strings session (including Nat's first 'Nature Boy'), a couple of nursery rhyme novelties and some more forgotten songs, although 'Lament In Chords' is an attractive mood-piece with fine work by Moore.

Music & Arts have expanded their previous set of broadcast transcriptions into a huge, four-disc edition. There are a lot of vocals by Anita Boyer, Anita O'Day and the baby-voiced Ida James and together with the occasional roughness in the transfers this adds up to a package aimed more at completists than at the general collector; plenty of good jazz, all the same. The Topaz disc covers tracks from Capitol, Decca and seven airchecks and is a capable selection, though the field is starting to get crowded for this material. Capitol's own set of *Vocal Classics* includes all the obvious jive tunes and will please most looking for a single disc of Cole the singer-pianist – as opposed to the other way around, which is catered for by the instrumental disc. Oddly enough, here one keeps waiting for Nat to start singing! Capitol have also recently uncovered a live date from the Circle Room, nothing very different from what Nat was doing in the studio or on the radio, but solid KC Trio fare.

Capitol's *Jazz Encounters* disc is a remarkable demonstration of Cole's versatility, bringing together seven dates in which he acted in the main as a sideman yet still usually dominated the tracks. Two pieces with the Metronome All Stars – including Gillespie and Harris – are followed by one with Kenton and the session with the swing-styled Capitol International Jazzmen. A beautiful set of Jo Stafford songs, a couple of jive routines with Woody Herman and a date with Capitol boss Johnny Mercer make the record essential for Cole's admirers.

*** Anatomy Of A Jam Session

Black Lion BLCD 760137 *Cole; Charlie Shavers (t); Herbie Haymer (ts); John Simmons (b); Buddy Rich (d). 6/45.*

Not a great deal of music here – 38 minutes, and that includes six alternative takes – but it's a swinging interlude in the normal run of Cole's records of the time, with Haymer and Shavers in knock-about form and Rich at his most brusque. Cole himself is unperturbed by the surrounding racket and makes cool, elegant space for himself. The sound is mostly good, with only some surface noise present.

**(*) The King Cole Trios Live: 1947–48

Vintage Jazz Classics VJC-1011-2 *Cole; Duke Ellington (p); Oscar Moore, Irving Ashby (g); Johnny Miller (b); Clark Dennis, The Dinning Sisters, Pearl Bailey, Woody Herman (v). 3/47–3/48.*

Taken from *King Cole Time* broadcasts, the routine here is that each guest on the show chats with Nat, 'chooses' songs, and does one number with the Trio. Main interest, inevitably, is on Ellington, who sounds under-rehearsed but does a neat solo on 'Mood Indigo', while the other singers offer slighter stuff. The rest is neither more nor less than Cole and the Trio on their regular form, though several of the tunes are dispatched very quickly. Sound-quality varies from fairly terrible on the Pearl Bailey and Dinning Sisters shows to quite good with Herman and Ellington. For dedicated Cole fans only.

***(*) Big Band Cole

Capitol 796259-2 *Cole; Count Basie, Stan Kenton orchestras. 50–58.*

A compilation of sessions with Basie's band (minus Basie) and two tracks with the Kenton orchestra, plus two other songs with a top-flight studio band. Cole should have made more big-band jazz records than he did – for all the beauty and warmth of his 'straight' records – and this compilation shows the missed opportunity. Cole doesn't swing noticeably harder here than he does normally, but set-pieces such as 'The Blues Don't Care' and 'Wee Baby Blues' establish a very different mood from his normal regimen, and he sounds as comfortable and good-humoured as he ever did elsewhere. Beautifully remastered, this is highly recommended.

***(*) After Midnight

Capitol 520087-2 *Cole; Harry Edison (t); Juan Tizol (vtb); Willie Smith (as); Stuff Smith (vn); John Collins (g); Charlie Harris (b); Lee Young (d); Jack Costanzo (perc). 8–9/56.*

Cole's one latter-day jazz date has a huge reputation, but there are disappointing aspects to it: Cole didn't seem to want to stretch out in the music, and the tracks are all rather short. Tizol was a strange choice as one of the horn soloists, and Edison, while effective enough, tends to stroll through it all, as was often his wont. But the music is still an unblemished and beautifully groomed example of small-group swing, and Cole proves that his piano-playing was undiminished by his career switchover. There are several tracks that were left off the original LP and an alternative take.

Nat's later Capitol albums are without exception dedicated to his singing and, although we have opted not to list them here, they are uniformly recommended as examples of great vocal records.

Richie Cole (born 1948)

ALTO AND TENOR SAXOPHONES

A New Jersey native, Cole studied alto with Phil Woods and made a string of albums in the 1970s and early '80s, also touring a bebop group called Alto Madness. He has had more of a low profile in the '90s.

****(*) Richie & Phil & Richie**

32 Jazz 32065 *Cole; Phil Woods (as); Eddie Davis (ts); John Hicks (p); Walter Booker (b); Jimmy Cobb (d).* 7/80.

***** Pure Imagination**

Concord CCD 4314 *Cole; Vic Juris (g); Ed Howard (b); Victor Jones (d); Ray Mantilla (perc).* 11/86.

***(*) Popbop**

Milestone 9152 *Cole; Dick Hindman (p); Vic Juris (g); Marshall Hawkins, Eddie Howard (b); Victor Jones (d); Kenneth Nash, Tim Hauser (perc).* 87.

**** Signature**

Milestone 9162 *Cole; Ben Sidran (ky); Tee Carson (p); Vic Juris (g); Keith Jones, Marshall Hawkins (b); Mel Brown (d); Andy Narell, Babatunde Olatunji (perc).* 88.

****(*) Bossa Nova International**

Milestone 9180 *Cole; Hank Crawford (as); Emily Remler (g); Marshall Hawkins (b); Victor Jones (d).* 6/87.

****(*) Profile**

Heads Up HUCD 3022 *Cole; Dick Hindman (p); Rich Kuhns (ky); Henry Johnson (g); Seward McCain, Frank Passantino (b); Scott Morris (d).* 4/93.

There was a time when Richie Cole seemed on the verge of some kind of international jazz stardom, but his impact has waned dramatically since the late 1970s and early '80s, when most of his better recordings were made. A former student of Phil Woods, at his best he sounds like a good version of Woods, which – when the original has so many records available – tends to raise the question as to whether it's worth listening to a good copy. A little unfair, perhaps, but none of these records has the kind of sustained interest that makes one want to return to them very often. He plays alongside his mentor on *Richie & Phil & Richie*, tracks from a concert in Denver with Lockjaw Davis sitting in on 'Save Your Love For Me'. It's all right but, as jamming goes, there are many more worthwhile records and Cole's other albums for Muse are an excitable but finally unconvincing lot. A subsequent move to Milestone didn't reap any greater artistic rewards – *Popbop* is as disastrous as its title suggests, and *Signature* forsakes bebop heat for damp soul-jazz – but *Bossa Nova International* benefits from the felicitous presence of Emily Remler, whose comping binds the music together.

Some personal problems have kept Cole out of the limelight in recent years, but the Heads Up album is his cautious return to active duty. His alto playing has much of the old bounce, though tempered with time, and on a tune like 'One For Monterey' he seems to have reconciled pace with elegance more effectively than before. Even 'Volare' sounds rather nice, and Tom Waits's 'A Foreign Affair' was a good choice for a ballad. But there is some gloop, too – 'Sarah' is a feeble tribute to Sarah Vaughan, and the sidemen make no impression.

Bill Coleman (1904–81)

TRUMPET, FLUGELHORN

Born in Kentucky, he switched to trumpet from clarinet after hearing Louis Armstrong. Played in New York bands, 1927–35, and then moved to Paris, where he became a celebrity. Returned to New York, 1940, but was summoned back to Paris in 1948 and this time remained in Paris, occasionally travelling but mostly playing in France.

*****(*) Hangin' Around**

Topaz TPZ 1040 *Coleman; Henry 'Red' Allen, John Butler, Shad Collins, Bill Dillard (t); Billy Burns, J.C Higginbotham, Dicky Wells (tb); George Johnson, Albert Nicholas (cl, as); Andy Fitzgerald, Joe Marsala (cl); Edgar Courance, Frank Goudie (cl, ts); Pete Brown, Willie Lewis, Joe Hayman (as); Charlie Holmes (as, ss); Coleman Hawkins, Teddy Hill (ts); Herman Chittison, Garnet Clark, John Ferrier, Ellis Larkins, Luis Russell (p); Stéphane Grappelli (vn, p); Oscar Aleman (g); Will Johnson (bj, g); Al Casey, Carmen Mastren, John Mitchell, Django Reinhardt, Joseph Reinhardt (g); June Cole, Eugene D'Hellemes, Pops Foster, Richard Fulbright, Wilson Myers, Oscar Pettiford, Gene Traxler (b); Paul Barbarin, Bill Beason, Tommy Benford, William Diemer, Ted Fields, Shelly Manne (d).* 9/29–12/43.

***** Bill Coleman, 1936–1938**

Classics 764 *Coleman; Christian Wagner (cl, as); Eddie Brunner, Edgar Courance, Frank Goudie (cl, ts); Alix Combelle, Noel Chiboust (ts); Herman Chittison, John Ferrier, Emile Stern (p); Stéphane Grappelli (vn, p); Oscar Aleman, John Mitchell, Django Reinhardt, Joseph Reinhardt (g); Roger Grasset, Eugene D'Hellemes, Wilson Myers, Lucien Simoens (b); Tommy Benford, William Diemer, Ted Fields, Jerry Mengo (d).* 1/36–9/38.

***** Bill Coleman Meets Guy Lafitte**

Black Lion BLCD 760182 *Coleman; Guy Lafitte (ts); Marc Hemmeler (p); Jack Sewing (b); Daniel Humair (d).* 7/73.

Many people encounter this fine trumpeter only in the context of sessions with the great Django Reinhardt. Having worked with Don Redman and Luis Russell, he first went to Paris in 1933, and he finally settled there three years after the war. The Topaz includes one early track, recorded under Russell's leadership in 1929. Though his contribution is brief and outclassed by Allen's, it is enough to mark him down as a player to be followed. The next tracks jump on to the Paris sojourns, activity with Garnet Clark's Hot Clubs Four and a duo with Herman Chittison on 'I'm In The Mood For Love', one of the things that overlap with the Classics volume. There is obviously a good deal of overlap between these, though the Classics set kicks off with only a slightly earlier (a week, to be exact) encounter between the pair, with bassist Eugene D'Hellemes in support on 'What's The Reason' and 'After You've Gone'.

Classics omit the material recorded under the leadership of Dicky Wells and Willie Lewis but for some reason (the quality of the solos presumably) do include five tracks made with clarinettist and tenorman Eddie Brunner, and of course the Topaz extends forward in time to the war years. Of the years in common, the only big loss is a storming version of 'I Got Rhythm' for Dicky Wells, with Django powering the band along. If his is the dominant voice on the instrument in this time period, the Argentinian, Oscar Aleman, suggests a range of alternatives and an arresting solo style on the same January 1936 session as the Chittison/D'Hellemes cuts.

Coleman has a bright, uncomplicated tone and delivery, and a nice singing voice. He probably reached his peak in the mid- to late 1930s, but he had the sort of chops that can go on pretty much for ever, unpressured, distinct and slightly discursive. The later material with Guy Lafitte, recorded when this American-in-Paris was rising seventy, is pretty lightweight festival stuff, but there is no doubt who is playing, even in the opening choruses of 'Blue Lou', which he reharmonizes slightly. Using the same Montreux rhythm-section as Stéphane Grappelli, he swings lightly and rather politely, but there is no mistaking that he is still swinging.

****(*) Au Caveau De La Huchette**

Caveau De La Huchette 5980026 *Coleman; Rolf Buhrer (vtb); Danny Doriz (vib); Patrice Authier (p); Henry Tischitz (b); Michel Denis (d).* 79.

Elegant to the end, Coleman was still in good spirits and enjoying himself with this local band, 30 years after he settled in Paris for good. The music's bonhomie is undeniable, but the band is scarcely full of great talent and Coleman himself – on flugelhorn as well as trumpet – is rather wayward with his phrasing, even if his tone remains bright and clear.

George Coleman (born 1935)

TENOR, ALTO AND SOPRANO SAXOPHONES

Greatly admired by other players, and once recruited by that peerless talent-spotter, Miles Davis, the Memphis-born saxophonist has rarely enjoyed commensurate public success. His complex harmonic awareness occasionally pushes outside orthodoxy entirely but, even when playing the changes, Coleman is a challenging improviser.

***** Amsterdam After Dark**

Timeless SJP 129 *Coleman; Hilton Ruiz (p); Sam Jones (b); Billy Higgins (d).* 12/78.

****(*) Manhattan Panorama**

Evidence ECD 22019 *Coleman; Harold Mabern (p); Jamil Nasser (b); Idris Muhammad (d).* 82 or 83.

*****(*) At Yoshi's**

Evidence ECD 22021 *Coleman; Harold Mabern (p); Ray Drummond (b); Alvin Queen (d).* 8/87.

Like his near-namesake of the boxing ring, George Coleman plays a little weight-bound but gets in the odd spectacular punch. The records are few and far between only because Coleman looks on record producers the way some prize-fighters look on Don King: with the justifiable suspicion that they don't have his interests entirely at heart. Consequently, the few records that have appeared have tended to be self-produced, and they are always reliably packed with the muscular soloing that has influenced some of the younger generation of British tenor players who heard him at Ronnie Scott's in 1978 on the same European stint as Timeless SJP 129.

Given the long and sometimes rough ride the city's given him, it's hard to tell how sincere Coleman's love affair with the Big Apple really is. Woody Allen turned the same skyline into a wry, Gershwin-drenched poem. Coleman, with an eye on 'El Barrio' and the 'New York Housing Blues', is by no means so dewy-eyed; the inevitable 'Manhattan' and 'I Love New York' are both in place, but there's also a vocal tribute to 'Mayor Koch' that suggests a much tougher perspective, and there's a chill wind blowing through 'Autumn In New York' on the Timeless album. The Mabern–Muhammad rhythm axis fuels some fine solos from Coleman, who also plays his alto on this date with a fleet diction that belies any charges of ponderousness.

The Dutch cityscape is even finer, with an absolutely superb rhythm section and a beautiful registration that picks up all the tiny, grainy resonances Coleman gets across his reed. Ruiz and Higgins play with perfect understanding, and Sam Jones must be one of the best slow-tempo players on the scene.

Yoshi's is a small club in Oakland, California, which puts the emphasis on music rather than mark-up at the bar. Coleman feels comfortable playing there, and it shows on the Evidence set. Again, the band has the hand-picked feel and telepathic understanding of good cornermen, and Coleman's playing is full of instinctive invention, as when he knocks off the oddly metred 'Laig Gobblin' Blues' standing up. There are three long tracks that feature most of the group: 'They Say It's Wonderful', Freddie Hubbard's 'Up Jumped Spring' and Mal Waldron's 'Soul Eyes' which brings the set to an entirely satisfactory end. It isn't the sort of album that makes reputations, but it confirms that big George is still very much a contender.

**** Meditation**

Timeless SJP 110 *Coleman; Tete Montoliu (p).* 4/77.

A not entirely successful collaboration. Coleman's meditative mode is still a little tense and, without the backing of a section, he seems uncertain about metres. Montoliu is a much less linear player, and there are moments when the two seem to be occupying different musical spaces. Coleman fans will find it intriguing, though.

***** Playing Changes**

Ronnie Scott's Jazz House JHCD 002 *Coleman; Hilton Ruiz (p); Ray Drummond (b); Billy Higgins (d).* 4/79.

For anyone who has worn smooth their copy of the old Pye LP, *Ronnie Scott Presents George Coleman 'Live'*, mentioned above, this could be a fair substitute. Recorded during the same 1979 residency at Frith Street, *Playing Changes* consists of just three – two *long*, one shorter – takes. Coleman's attack is typically robust and veined with unexpected harmonic ore. However, anyone whose copy of the original LP survives may feel that they already have the best of the deal. The long 'Laura' is, at 23 minutes plus, a tad *too* long, and slightly overgenerous to both Ruiz and the still-inexperienced Drummond; by contrast, 'Stella By Starlight', which occupies a whole side of the Pye, is a much more coherent performance. The best of the saxophonist's work occurs when he moves sideways of the given changes and into his inventive high harmonic mode. There are either misfingerings or symptoms of a weary reed in the closing ensembles of the end-of-set 'Moment's Notice' which detract a little from an intriguing variation on the Coltrane original. On balance, it might have been better to put together a stronger 65-minute CD integrating the best of the two sessions. Scratches aside, most listeners will be returning to the Pye a lot more often than to this.

*****(*) Blues Inside Out**

Ronnie Scott's Jazz House 46 *Coleman; Peter King (as); Julian Joseph (p); Dave Green (b); Mark Taylor (d).* 97.

Back at Ronnie's with a later version of the house band and a swinging set of standard and repertory tunes. Only the title-track and 'Venus Flytrap' are originals, the latter a tricksy and sinuous theme that brings out the very best in the gifted Joseph. Long versions of 'Never Let Me Go', 'Tune Up' and 'Oleo' are more routine blowing numbers, but 'Nancy (With The Laughing Face)' is a reminder of how expressive George can be playing ballads. The recording, presumably done on the club's own desk, is rather boxy and there are a few moments of unnecessary distortion, but this is another worthwhile set from a location where Coleman is always an honoured and much-liked visitor.

***** I Could Write A Book: The Music Of Richard Rodgers**

Telarc 83439 *Coleman; Harold Mabern (p); Jamil Nasser (b); Billy Higgins (d).* 5/98.

The initial inspiration for this record seems to have been a guest spot in a Carnegie Hall Jazz Band concert devoted to the music of Rodgers. The material selected is hardly unexpected, but George finds new things to do with 'Lover' and 'My Funny Valentine', roughening up the changes and investing 'Valentine' with a dark sobriety that banishes any hint of winsomeness. The band includes two old friends from Memphis, Mabern and Nasser, and the presence of Higgins at the kit guarantees a pungent swing. 'Thou Swell' is a duet for saxophone and drums alone, and 'People Will Say We're In Love' is just by the rhythm section. There are echoes here and there of Sonny Rollins, John Coltrane and Joe Henderson, but George never quite stamps his authority on standard material as imaginatively as that great trio did and do.

Ornette Coleman (born 1930)

ALTO SAXOPHONE, TENOR SAXOPHONE, TRUMPET, VIOLIN

Born in Fort Worth, Texas, Coleman began working in R&B bands, frequently attracting derision, before finding players for his own group, including Don Cherry and Charlie Haden. Worked with Paul Bley in Los Angeles and made his recording debut there. Sensational New York debut of his quartet in 1959, and a string of ground-breaking albums for Atlantic followed. In the '60s he learned trumpet and violin, made trio and small-group records for Blue Note, RCA and Columbia, performed orchestral music, and generally went his own way. Developed a theory of 'harmolodics' and played in electric groups in the '70s and '80s, recording only occasionally. In the '90s, signed a new association with Verve, but the records have again been infrequent. The principal godfather of free jazz, Coleman's music is an endlessly reshaped fantasy spun from his mild-mannered, enigmatic self.

***** Something Else!**

Original Jazz Classics OJCCD 163 *Coleman; Don Cherry (t); Walter Norris (p); Don Payne (b); Billy Higgins (d).* 2/58.

***** Tomorrow Is The Question**

Original Jazz Classics OJCCD 342 *Coleman; Don Cherry (t); Percy Heath, Red Mitchell (b); Shelly Manne (d).* 1, 2 & 3/59.

No jazz musician – possibly ever – has so comprehensively and irremediably divided opinion. To some (and the supporters included Gunther Schuller) he is a visionary genius who has changed the shape of modern music; to others he is a fraud, innocent or otherwise, whose grasp of musical theory is at best shaky and for the greater part unbearably pretentious. Long before anyone had heard of 'harmolodics' – and don't search below for a quotable definition – it was thought that Coleman represented the third spur of the modernist revolution, a shift in approach to melody and rhythm to match Coltrane's skyscraping harmonics and Cecil Taylor's introduction of atonality.

Though the 1958 Hillcrest Club residency with Paul Bley represents something of a crux in Coleman's development, it is still startling to hear him with a pianist, and it was to be thirty years before he was inclined to repeat the experiment. Coleman got the first of these sessions at Red Mitchell's behest, and it suffers all the drawbacks of haste; problems that were largely ironed out on the more thoughtful *Tomorrow Is The Question*, a set which includes 'Tears Inside', perhaps the most beautiful single item in the whole Coleman canon. *Tomorrow* is also notable for Shelly Manne's impeccably hip contribution; an unlikely recruitment on the face of it, even given his tenure at Contemporary, but absolutely bang up to the moment.

Forty years have dented the sheer alienating swipe of these discs, but they certainly confound the received view of Coleman as a raucous tent-show turn. The tone is as wayward and raw as could be, but with an intense loneliness at the heart.

****** The Shape Of Jazz To Come**

Atlantic 8122 72398-2 *Coleman; Don Cherry (pkt-t); Charlie Haden (b); Billy Higgins (d).* 10/59, 7/60.

****** Change Of The Century**

Atlantic 781341 *As above.* 10/59.

*****(*) This Is Our Music**

Atlantic 7567 80767-2 *As above.* 7/60.

*****(*) Art Of The Improvisers**

Atlantic 90978 *As above, except add Jimmy Garrison, Scott LaFaro (b).* 59–60.

****** Free Jazz**

Atlantic 8122 72397-2 *Coleman; Don Cherry (pkt-t); Freddie Hubbard (t); Eric Dolphy (bcl); Charlie Haden, Scott LaFaro (b); Ed Blackwell, Billy Higgins (d).* 12/60.

*****(*) Ornette On Tenor**

Atlantic 781394 *Coleman; Don Cherry (pkt-t); Jimmy Garrison (b); Ed Blackwell (d).* 3/61.

***** Art Of The Improvisers**

Atlantic 781572 *Coleman; Don Cherry (pkt-t); Jimmy Garrison, Charlie Haden, Scott LaFaro (b); Ed Blackwell, Billy Higgins (d).* 59–61.

♛ ** Beauty Is A Rare Thing**

Rhino/Atlantic R2 71410 6CD *As above, except add Robert DiDomenica (f); Bill Evans (p); Eddie Costa (vib); Jim Hall (g); George Duvivier (b); Sticks Evans (d); The Contemporary String Quartet.* 5/59–3/61.

Difficult – perhaps impossible – to reconstruct the impact these records had when they first appeared or the frustration that some of the players understandably evinced in trying to get to grips with Coleman's ideas. Bassist Jimmy Garrison is said to have lost his temper on the stand one night, baffled by playing off-notes rather than chords, increasingly convinced that the whole thing was a scam.

These, though, are the classic Coleman albums, even if one retains a degree of scepticism. CD transfer has brought forward the other members of the group, underlining Cherry's role and bringing Haden out of the shadows. Brash as the titles are, the music is surprisingly introspective and thoughtful. The first two in the group were actually released out of chronological sequence, which was major sucks to all the critics who talked – and still do – about 'development' and 'progress'.

Most of the essential Coleman pieces are to be found here, though interestingly only one of them – 'Lonely Woman' – has ever come close to repertory status. Bubbling under are 'Una Muy Bonita' from *Change*, 'Congeniality' and 'Focus On Sanity' on *Shape*, and things like the alphabetical themes from *Ornette!* (not seemingly available separately at the moment, but included in its entirety on the wonderful, indispensable *Beauty Is A Rare Thing*). Another of the missing CDs, *This Is Our Music*, includes the single standard of this vintage, 'Embraceable You', which takes the theme as far beyond Charlie Parker as Bird was beyond the Gershwin original.

Of the major statement of jazz modernism, *Free Jazz* and Coltrane's *Ascension* are key documents, sharing some personnel. Jimmy Garrison's onstage tantrum had led to his departure from the Coleman group and a switch to Trane's quartet. The difference is exactly what the young bassist identified. No chords here, just gestural splashes of sound which make sense of the Jackson Pollock cover and the Abstract Expressionist aesthetic embodied by the Double Quartet. Oddly, the music was still locked into theme-and-solos conventions (as was *Ascension*, to be fair) and doesn't break free of personality. What redeems it is the sheer variety of sound-colours the group conjures up in its paired soloists: Dolphy's fruity, fraught bass clarinet, contrasted to Ornette's thin tone; Hubbard and Cherry sounding like non-zygotic twins; LaFaro's alchemical transformations sitting still while Haden lopes around like Wilbur Ware in jogging pants. Separating Higgins and Blackwell *is* possible, but largely redundant.

Like Bird's one session on tenor, *Ornette On Tenor* has attained a status out of all proportion to its actual merits. It hooks Ornette back into the raw R&B of his Texas roots, but it never sounds like anything other than himself in a lower register and somewhat diminished in pace. It takes its place without undue trouble in the magnificent compilation set which brings together 57 separate tracks, six of which have not been released before, most of them from the July 1960 session which fed into *This Is Our Music*, the most unemphatic of the Atlantics. *Beauty* (and the title comes from a track on the same disc) brings together extra material that has already appeared on compilations like *Twins*, *Art Of The Improvisers* and the Japan-only and ungrammatical *To Whom Who Keeps A Record*. Of the new material, 'Revolving Doors' from July 1960 and the long 'Proof Readers' from January 1961 with Scott LaFaro are perhaps the most interesting. A pity that no one thought to include or to keep interview material with Ornette for this issue and, of course, we'll all never stop regretting the fire that destroyed so much of the material from this period.

***** Chappaqua Suite**

Columbia 480584 2CD *Coleman; Pharoah Sanders (ts); David Izenzon (b); Charles Moffett (d); other personnel unidentified; Joseph Tekula (cond).* 6/65.

This is emphatically not an official Coleman release. It was written and performed as a soundtrack score for a film by avant-garde director Conrad Rooks, who seemed to win over the hesitant Ornette with an unwontedly respectable cash deal. When the music was finished, though, Rooks declined to use it, on the flimsy ground that it was too strong and self-contained for the film (equivalent to telling a woman that she's too beautiful, intelligent and good to marry the likes of you), and then commissioned Ravi Shankar to perform an alternative soundtrack. Whether Rooks seriously meant all this, whether he feared his film would be overpowered, or whether, like many before and after him, he simply hadn't a clue what the hell was going on isn't clear, but with exquisite perversity Columbia, or at least the French and Japanese arms of a company that had been deeply sceptical of Ornette's work, rushed out the one record he didn't want heard.

It's an odd piece, strident boppish figures rising like *T. rex* out of swampy orchestral textures. Ornette's keening sound is as evocative as ever, but there's no context for it. Sanders is credited but pretty anonymous, and the sound is distant and spatially uncertain. The unusual circumstances of its creation, its slightly shadowy, almost bootleg, emergence, and some wonderful cover photography have conspired to give *Chappaqua Suite* a cachet out of all proportion to its real merits. It remains a curiosity, almost paradigmatic of Coleman's wayward progress.

****** At The Golden Circle, Stockholm: Volume 1**

Blue Note 84224 *Coleman; David Izenzon (b); Charles Moffett (d).* 65.

****** At The Golden Circle, Stockholm: Volume 2**

Blue Note 84225 *As above.* 65.

Blue Note's purchase on the modernist movement was uncomfortably peripheral: a single Coltrane release, a brief skirmish with Cecil Taylor's fierce atonality, and a tentative, but in the event patiently sustained, engagement with Ornette. These sessions from Sweden catch the trio at its peak: densely textured, dark-toned and fierce. Much has been made of Ornette's lack of reliance on pianos, but it's obvious from these sessions that Izenzon fulfils that function. The leader may not lean on chords and progressions, may even 'hear' the changes differently, but, as with Dewey Redman later, he needs an anchor.

Coleman plays superbly throughout. Guess-the-next-note pieces like 'European Echoes' work less well than 'Morning Song' and 'The Riddle', and the obligatory fiddle-and-trumpet feature, 'Snowflakes And Sunshine', is unusually bland. 'Faces And Places' is typical of the way Ornette built a theme out of seemingly unrelated melodic cells, a honeycomb of sound without undue sweetness and without conventional symmetry. The sound is good for a club recording, faithful to the bass and to Moffett's restless overdrive. CD transfer did, however, put a hard digital edge on the leader's alto; those who hung on to decent, playable vinyl can be reassured that they're getting the real thing.

*** New York Is Now

Blue Note 84287 *Coleman; Dewey Redman (ts); Jimmy Garrison (b); Elvin Jones (d).* 4–5/68.

*** Love Call

Blue Note 84356 *As above.*

Coltrane was dead a little under a year. As there was to be in American poetry on the death of Robert Frost, there was a palpable unease in jazz as to who was the titular head of the pack. Teaming Ornette with Trane's old rhythm section was something of a misalliance, not least given Jimmy Garrison's stated misgivings. Perhaps because they're on hand, Coleman relies on some unwonted vertical improvisation, building on chords that are never quite explicit. Redman, like Izenzon before him, does the foundation work. As he was to do on the magnificent live *Crisis*, he offers capacious pedal-points and comfortably contoured lower-register figures. Whatever else they do, these reduce the dynamism of Coleman's solos, turning them into long, spun-out noodles.

The two opening tracks ('The Garden Of Souls' on *NY Is Now* and 'Airborne' on *Love Call*) might have made a respectable single album. Much of the rest is makeweight. An alternative take of the already tedious R&B 'Broad Way Blues' constitutes an ambiguous 'bonus' and 'We Now Interrupt For A Commercial' (pointlessly stripped of a small morsel of satirical actuality for the CD version) is plain silly, though it may well have inspired Redman's later 'Funcitydues'.

A pity that Coleman's association with this label and its resources could not have developed further.

***(*) Friends And Neighbours: Live At Prince Street

RCA Victor 47795 *Coleman; Dewey Redman (ts); Charlie Haden (b); Ed Blackwell (d).* 2/70.

Recorded almost a year after the apocalyptic set at New York University's Loeb Center, a set which yielded the still-deleted *Crisis* album, this catches Ornette in his NY loft. The audience does community singing on the opening 'Friends And Neighbours' which finds Ornette sawing joyously on fiddle. An instrumental version of the same track follows, before he switches to alto for the beautiful, subtly crafted 'Long Time No See'. There is a single trumpet track, 'Let's Play', before the set ends with 'Forgotten Songs', which seems to be related to some of the *Skies Of America* themes, and the long 'Tomorrow', which includes the most substantial Ornette solo of the record.

Friends And Neighbours seems to have been an unofficial release, unauthorized at the time, even though Bob Thiele is listed as co-producer. It catches Ornette in particularly laid-back form, sounding relaxed even in the squalls of violin on the title-track and creating blues progressions of astonishing originality on the alto tracks. Whatever its standing, it's a more than worthwhile addition to the catalogue.

**** Body Meta

Verve/Harmolodic 531916 *Coleman; Charles Ellerbee, Bern Nix (g); Jamaaladeen Tacuma (b); Ronald Shannon Jackson (d).* 12/75.

*** Dancing In Your Head

A&M 396 999 *As above, except add Robert Palmer (cl);.* 1/73, 12/75.

It was a shock to the system in 1975, hearing Coleman with what initially sounded like a rock band and then continued to sound like a rock band, except that repeated exposure reveals how many layers and subtleties this music camouflages. Purists were appalled by the relentlessly thudding rhythm of the two long 'variations' on 'Theme From A Symphony' from *Dancing*; but even they can't pretend that the music doesn't have dimensions that by-the-yard orchestral writing lacks. The harmolodic method, which applied a radical democracy to every parameter of the music – rhythm, melody, harmony – was by no means new at this point. Theoretically, everything was already in place on the Town Hall gig; the means of expression were still old-fashioned, though.

Ornette's alto playing is fiercely linear but jumps up and down the levels like some pixilated hero in an arcade game. The 'rock' influence is largely superficial, since the rhythmic approach is the opposite to rock's relentless emphasis on strong beats. The Grateful Dead (with whose guitarist, Jerry Garcia, Ornette was to record towards the end of the 1980s) were doing something like this in their long-form jams, but with a blissed-out insouciance which is the opposite of Ornette's drivenness and urgency. Rhythmically, almost everything is there: march cadences, rags, swing, stop-time, hints of reggae and long passages in the bass.

There is another track from 1973, with Coleman in the company of the Master Musicians of Joujouka, who had been 'discovered' by Brian Jones of the Rolling Stones. Herbally enhanced harmolodics, anyone? This was recorded in 1973. *Pace* the liner-note, the main session was taped in 1975, not 1976, and this is confirmed by John Litweiler's book, *The Harmolodic Life.* The session also included the material released as *Body Meta* on Ornette's own label, Artist's House. Its reappearance on Harmolodic (Ornette's imprint within the Polygram empire) is hugely welcome.

The five tracks include a reworking of 'European Echoes' (already heard on the Gyllenecirkelt records). Its performance here underlines once again the continuity of Coleman's enterprise at this time; what had seemed satirical first time around, this time is played rather straighter. The presence of guitars, and the fibrillating groove set up by the former Rudy McDaniel (Tacuma), is the only real difference, but it's largely a superficial one, and we still maintain that it was Izenzon who – consciously or not – pushed Ornette ever further in this direction.

Chronologically earlier in the sessionography, *Body Meta* is the better record, more concentrated and intense, less rambling. It was also the first time Ornette had been allowed decent rehearsal time before a recording. The ballad, 'Fou Amour', is magnificent, and 'Macho Woman' is wincingly powerful, with Shannon Jackson in some sort of overdrive. A key moment in Coleman's progress.

****** Soapsuds Soapsuds**
Verve/Harmolodic 531917 *Coleman; Charlie Haden (b).* 1/77.

Some writers have suggested that *Ornette On Tenor* was the man's only outing on the bigger horn, a detail which would keep him in line with Charlie Parker. The difference this time out is the sound he gets: a light, alto-range tone which irresistibly recalls Lester Young, and which sits perfectly alongside Haden's bass. This is an unexpectedly lyrical record, the one in the OC canon which will always catch out (figuratively) blindfolded testees. 'Sex Spy' is a romp with a surprise ending; Haden's own 'Human Being' has an edgy grace; and 'Some Day', the trumpet feature, brings the album to a weirdly peaceful conclusion. Not considered to be an A-list record, but we're carrying a torch for it.

***** In All Languages**
Verve/Harmolodic 531915 *Coleman; Don Cherry (pkt-t); Charles Ellerbee, Bern Nix (g); Charlie Haden, Al MacDowell, Jamaaladeen Tacuma (b); Denardo Coleman, Billy Higgins, Calvin Weston (d).* 87.

As we've noted elsewhere, John Coltrane's recording career was packed into a single decade, from 1957 to 1967. Ornette started out at the same time, enjoyed slimmer pickings along the way, but was still around to celebrate the thirtieth anniversary of his debut. How differently it all might have gone.

In All Languages is a breathless showcase for the front man. Reuniting the original band was a fantastic idea at this juncture, but, to be honest, Cherry, Haden and Blackwell scarcely get a look in, providing a lighter and less supercharged background for Ornette's increasingly uninflected solo playing. It's possible to imagine almost any of these solos being grafted on to almost any track, so careless is he of tempo as well as of harmonics. No violin this time, and no trumpet with the 1950s line-up, though he does bring in his tenor for a couple of spots. And when we say breathless ... there are 10 tracks from the original quartet and 13 from the by-now-long-established Prime Time band, only one of the total over four minutes in length. To his credit, Ornette doesn't dip into the back-catalogue, though of course everyone wanted to hear the early apostles doing stuff like 'Beauty Is A Rare Thing' and 'Lonely Woman'. In market terms, this probably sent some listeners who had only climbed on board during the harmolodic years scurrying back to the classic Atlantics, which is well and good. Crisply produced (by Denardo) and elegantly packaged – but, even on its own terms, a scant offering.

***** Virgin Beauty**
Columbia RK 44301 *Coleman; Charles Ellerbee, Jerry Garcia, Bern Nix (g); Al MacDowell, Chris Walker (b); Denardo Coleman (ky, d, perc); Calvin Weston (d).* 87–88.

Famous for the inclusion of Grateful Dead guitarist Jerry Garcia, this one set off a whole new spasm of 'sell-out' complaints. In fact, it's an absolutely four-square Coleman album, lighter in texture and more accessible than most, but certainly not untypical.

Ornette asked Garcia to take part, having gone to a Dead concert with Cecil Taylor and been as much impressed with the devotion of the Deadheads as with the music. Garcia's involvement is actually quite small and probably largely symbolic. Otherwise the music is standard Prime Time. 'Bourgeois Boogie' is pastiche Motown and 'Happy Hour' sounds very much like a latter-day version of 'Doughnut'. Ornette shows every willingness to play, as on the unaccompanied introduction to 'Unknown Artist', which might well have been conceived as some sort of autobiographical statement.

***** Tone Dialing**
Verve/Harmolodic 527483 *Coleman; Dave Bryant (ky); Chris Rosenberg, Ken Wessell (g); Bradley Jones, Al MacDowell (b); Denardo Coleman (d); Badal Roy (perc).* 95.

This was the first fruit of Ornette's new contract with Polygram: an imprint of his own, with A&R responsibilities and a chance to reissue some of the back-catalogue material discussed above. As had happened with *Virgin Beauty*, critical reaction to this one was hijacked by incidentals, in this case Ornette's decision to work with a keyboard player for the first time in years. There had, of course, been hints of it on *Virgin Beauty*, where Denardo threw a few shapes, but Bryant doesn't register much. A piano introduction to 'Search For Life' has the ears pricked for something different, but it's hustled off stage pretty quickly and inconsequentially.

For the most part, *Tone Dialing* is just another Prime Time record. 'Kathelin Gray' reappears from the currently deleted *Song X*, a collaboration with Pat Metheny, another Bryant introduction to vary the softly arpeggiated guitars. With the exception of Denardo, who's grown in stature (literally) since his debut, the players are worrisomely anonymous, as undifferentiated as the personnel in one of Glenn Branca's guitar 'symphonies'. As before, most of the tracks are short, but this time one or two, like 'Search For Life' and 'Miguel's Fortune', stretch out a bit.

***** Sound Museum: Three Women**
Verve/Harmolodic 531657 *Coleman; Geri Allen (p); Charnett Moffett (b); Denardo Coleman (d); Lauren Kinhan, Chris Walker (v).* 96.

***** Sound Museum: Hidden Man**
Verve/Harmolodic 531914 *As above, except omit Kinhan and Walker.* 96.

A curious, indeed typically perverse undertaking: two albums of almost identical material, performed back to back by the same band. The only real difference in sequence is that *Three Women* includes a song performed by Kinhan and Walker, while *Hidden Man* has a variation on 'What A Friend We Have In Jesus' and a slightly altered running order. Ornette's insistence on an absolute democracy of listening and response is carried to extraordinary lengths here; it is often difficult to gauge how these performances actually vary, and to what extent the two albums are supposed to have a consistent identity. To take just the most familiar item, 'European Echoes' is no more than incidentally reworked, while 'Mob Job' and 'Macho Woman' are much of a muchness, tempo changes notwithstanding.

Allen's role is broadly similar to what the guitarists were doing on earlier records. Her M-Base background hasn't been so thoroughly sloughed that she isn't responsive to this kind of thing; that whole project drew much of its inspiration, consciously or otherwise, from Ornette, and she (more than most) responded to the historical antecedents. Denardo's skill as a producer becomes more evident with almost every release. The sound here is immaculate, with lots of space round the piano and drums.

****** Colors**

Verve/Harmolodic 537789 *Coleman; Joachim Kühn (p).* 8/96.

On the face of it an unlikely combination, but one which yielded Ornette's most evocative album of recent years. Interesting to compare it with another, almost contemporary Verve release, the *1 + 1* duo by Herbie Hancock and Wayne Shorter. It's pipe and slippers compared to this restless, searching set, recorded live in Germany, at the Leipzig Opera. The worst thing about it is a slightly cavernous sound. The performances are extraordinary.

Kühn has recorded in a duo context before, with CMP in-house genius Walter Quintus, and with guitarist (and former front man with Focus) Jan Akkerman. Both times he has demonstrated a responsive intelligence that thrives on harmonic ambiguity and on a suspension of conventional harmonic resolutions. All the pieces, quite short by live-performance standards, were written specially for the date. 'Refills', 'Story Writing' and 'Night Plans' are the most substantial pieces, though most of the detail comes from Kühn rather than Ornette. A wholly unexpected meeting of minds, and one of the happiest dates Ornette has put on record in years.

Steve Coleman (born 1956)

ALTO SAXOPHONE, SOPRANO SAXOPHONE, VOCALS

Steve Coleman's approach to jazz is thoroughly mystical, believing that music is a symbolic language that probes deeper than rational ideas and expresses both the order and the chaos of the universe. Given that dual status, his arrangements are either whirlingly chaotic or disconcertingly four-square, an ambiguity that he exploits much as Sun Ra did. Coleman's saxophone lines are long and discursive, a long way removed from classic bebop.

*****(*) Phase Space**

DIW 865 *Coleman; Dave Holland (b).* 1/91.

Typically, Coleman uses a range of black rhythms as a basis for complex melodies that ride, sometimes precariously, atop often unvarying patterns. The duo album with Dave Holland confirms the enduring value of an earlier relationship. The saxophonist plays with great assurance, and also more freely, in the sense that he appears confident enough with his partner not to stick to one settled groove. There's a suspicion, though, that the disc should more properly be credited to the bassist, so dominant is he.

***** The Sign And The Seal**

RCA 7432 140727 *Coleman; Ralph Alessi (t); Yosvany Terry Cabrera, Ravi Coltrane (ts); Andy Milne (p); Anthony Tidd (b); Oliver Gene Lake (d); Francisco Cespedes, Francisco Zamora Chinino, Kokayi, Rosangela Silvestre, Sara Gomes Villamil (v); percussion; chorus.* 2/96.

Coleman's subtitles are no more illuminating than ever. This one is underwritten 'Transmission of the metaphysics of a culture'; but which culture is it, and who is transmitting to whom? From the USA to Cuba, the Caribbean to Brooklyn? From past to future? Or is it the future trying to get in touch with tradition? Recorded in Havana with an array of local guests, *The Sign And The Seal* is billed as a Mystic Rhythm Society record. Ravi Coltrane's presence is perhaps more important to Coleman than his playing, and the young man isn't allowed to do anything that will expose him unduly or unfairly. Alessi is much more important to the sound, and Milne's keyboards do much of the rest. Too much voodoo singing for our taste, and a bewildering array of guest vocalists and percussionists to muddy the sound. The problem is not with either the Sign (the Americans) or the Seal (the Cubans), but with a deep lack of understanding between them. More than ever, *they* seem divided by the common language of jazz.

***** Sonic Language Of Myth: Believing, Learning, Knowing**

RCA Victor 64123 *Coleman; Ralph Alessi, Shane Endsley (t); Tim Albright (tb); Ravi Coltrane, Craig Handy (ts); Vijay Lyer, Robert Mitchell, Jason Moran (p); Stefon Harris (vib); Sara Parkins, Todd Reynolds, Mary Rowell (vn); Dave Gold (vla); Dorothy Lawson (clo); Reggie Washington, Anthony Tidd (b); Sean Rickman (d); Miguel Diaz (perc); Earl Charlston, Karen McVoy, Eugene Palmore, Jeanne Ricks, Rosangela Silvestre (v).* 5/99.

The twin poles of Coleman's musical language are evident here, with stately, almost swing-based arrangements giving way to some of the most hectic group improvisation since Coltrane's *Ascension*. The use of strings is imaginative and unexpected, featuring players who obviously understand the language of this difficult music. The leader's voice is ever more emphatic and discursive, but just occasionally Coleman drifts off line and into long footnotes and digressions. Generally, though, he treats this as a collective endeavour and leaves considerable room for band members to bear witness of their own. The set consists of five long compositions and two brief interludes. 'Precession' is highly involved and bewilderingly structured, but it stands as overture to the album as a whole and establishes a mood of dark wisdom; Handy is superb on it. One of the most intriguing passages is 'The Gate', with Ravi Coltrane and Albright joining the leader for a mysterious transition that is over almost before one quite understands what is going on. Coleman's pantonality and his ability to have several voices working simultaneously is evident on the final two sections – 'Ausar (Reincarnation)' and 'Heru (Redemption)' – which represent the climax and dénouement of the whole ritual. This is the kind of music Anthony Braxton has long striven to create. It may be that Coleman, coming from his direction, has created a body of work every bit as thoughtful and philosophically entire as the great man's.

Johnny Coles (1926–97)

TRUMPET

Coles's talents have featured in a bewildering array of bands and in the service of an astonishingly eclectic spectrum of styles, from the avant-garde to Laurence Welk. He worked beside John Coltrane in Eddie Vinson's group and recorded with Count Basie, Ray Charles, Duke, Herbie Hancock, Charles Mingus, James Moody and many others. Perhaps inevitably, he made few records of his own, but all are marked by a firm grasp of form, an easy swing and a bright, mellow tone.

***** The Warm Sound Of Johnny Coles**

Koch Jazz 7804 *Coles; Kenny Drew, Randy Weston (p); Peck Morrison (b); Charli Persip (d).* 4/61.

Any addition to the Coles discography is welcome and the reappearance of *The Warm Sound* is doubly so, given how fine a recording it is. Originally for Epic, it teams the trumpeter with a well-balanced band and affords a rare chance to hear Randy Weston as a sideman; there is an additional take of his classic 'Hi-Fly' on this CD reissue. Coles is recorded very warmly, and close enough to hear odd valve clicks and breath noises, but the intimacy of 'If I Should Lose You' and the poignant immediacy of another Weston tune, 'Babe's Blues', more than makes up for the naïve production.

****** New Morning**

Criss Cross Criss 1005 *Coles; Horace Parlan (p); Reggie Johnson (b); Billy Hart (d).* 12/82.

There is a long gap, indeed almost 20 years, before there is anything else under Coles's name, and it seems appropriate that it should be for the label that is being dubbed the Blue Note of its day. *New Morning* catches him well played in, visiting Europe with the posthumous Mingus Dynasty. Coles has a round, slithery tone which sounds great on the blues but which drops down well for ballads. Opening with Charles Davis's 'Super 80', an unusual but effective curtain-raiser, they tackle the rarely played Wayne Shorter theme, 'United', Mingus's 'Sound Of Love' (a brisk, unsentimental interpretation) and three Coles originals, of which the title-track is the most substantial in thematic terms. The closing 'I Don't Know Yet' is improvised from scratch, a performance possible only with a rhythm section of this pedigree. Parlan seems to be behind the leader every step of the session, coaxing, teasing with incomplete chords and out-of-tempo passages. Coles is more fiery than of yore and with a new punch and attack at the start of his phrases.

John Colianni (born 1963)

PIANO

Played in Washington, DC, bars and clubs, then worked with Lionel Hampton and has made occasional leadership dates.

***** John Colianni**

Concord CCD 4309 *Colianni; Joe Wilder (t); Emily Remler (g); Bob Field (b); Connie Kay (d).* 8/86.

****(*) Blues-O-Matic**

Concord CCD 4367 *Colianni; Lew Tabackin (ts, f); Lynn Seaton (b); Mel Lewis (d).* 8/88.

***** Maybeck Recital Hall Vol. 37**

Concord CCD 4643 *Colianni (p solo).* 94.

The most impressive thing about this youthful mainstreamer is his rock-steady rhythm: that confidence means he can take a slow-to-mid-tempo tune such as Ray Brown's engaging 'Soft Shoe', on *John Colianni*, and make it swing. The first record is divided into solo, trio and quartet tracks, with Wilder sitting in for one tune, and it's all bright and affectionate music. The second session is a fraction less appealing, since Tabackin seems a vaguely distracted participant, and the pianist is a tad less decisive. His Maybeck session is about par for the course and, though Colianni plays as well as he ever has on record, there's not a great deal of special distinction about it.

Collective Quartet

GROUP

International alliance of improvisers and explorers.

*****(*) The Ropedancer**

Leo Lab CD 021 *Jeff Hoyer (tb); Mark Hennen (p); William Parker (b, tba); Heinz Geisser (d).* 11/94.

****** Orca**

Leo Lab CD 031 *As above.* 10/96.

***** Live At Crescent**

Leo Lab CD 043 *As above.* 5/97.

Abstract Expressionism is much misunderstood. Wooed by the idea of 'action' painting, too many viewers see mere gesture, form without substance. This is more relevant than it might seem in this context, because those who write about the Collective Quartet (or 4tet, as they seem to prefer) almost invariably draw their analogies from fine art. Nothing wrong with that, provided no one is misled into thinking that this is shapelessly abstract music. It is packed with melodic figures that rise out of the ensemble sound in much the way intelligible shapes emerge out of Jackson Pollock's shimmering surfaces.

The group's catalyst is the Zurich-based Heinz Geisser, a self-taught percussionist whose first instrument is classical guitar. Much of the melodic activity emerges in the interplay between pianist Mark Hennen and bassist William Parker, who is one of the key players of the contemporary movement. Like Hennen, trombonist Jeff Hoyer has worked with Bill Dixon, and something of Dixon's angular structure and delicate sonics has crept into Hoyer's playing. His opening to 'Invocation', the first piece on *Orca*, is completely *sui generis*, owing nothing to Albert Mangelsdorff or Roswell Rudd, or any other modern trombone player. His duet with Hennen on 'Boa' is exquisite, and a good example of how naturally this group divides down its instrumental axes.

It is probably on the long pieces, 'Invocation' and 'Orca' and 'The Ropedancer' on the earliest record, that the Collective 4tet achieve the near-telepathic unity which sets them apart. But it is often when the scale is much smaller and the detail more intimate that the language of the group becomes obvious. Both studio records are immaculately recorded, but it is the ringingly bright sound that engineer Jon Rosenberg gets on *Orca* which earns it the nod, with Parker particularly favoured.

The live set was taped at the Crescent Arts Centre in Belfast during a short British tour. By contrast with the previous night's concert in London, which was taped by the BBC, Parker sounds tired and unengaged, and it is Hoyer and Hennen who hold the floor. The set falls into two long improvisations, each more than 30 minutes long, with Hoyer switching to piano for a brief encore. It is still obvious that this is a group without a long performing history as a unit, but that is almost certainly the Collective 4tet's great strength, an exploratory dialectic with no imposed premisses. Even when direct communication seems to fail, as during the latter half of 'Sonic Flowers', individual paths are still compelling enough to sustain interest.

Buddy Collette (born 1921)

REEDS AND WOODWINDS

Born in Los Angeles, Collette worked with Charles Mingus in 1946, but made his mark as a prominent member of the LA session fraternity in the '50s. With Chico Hamilton, 1955–6, but otherwise led his own bands and freelanced, later doing much teaching, and organizing big bands for the Monterey Festival.

****(*) Man Of Many Parts**

Original Jazz Classics OJC 239 *Collette; Gerald Wilson (t); Dave Wells (tb); Bill Green (as); Jewell Grant (bs); Gerald Wiggins, Ernie Freeman (p); Barney Kessel (g); Gene Wright, Red Callender, Joe Comfort (b); Max Alright, Bill Richmond, Larry Bunker (d).* 2–4/56.

***** Nice Day With Buddy Collette**

Original Jazz Classics OJC 747 *Collette; Don Friedman, Dick Shreve, Calvin Jackson (p); John Goodman, Leroy Vinnegar (b); Bill Dolney, Shelly Manne (d).* 11/56–2/57.

****(*) Jazz Loves Paris**

Original Jazz Classics OJC 1764 *Collette; Frank Rosolino (tb); Howard Roberts (g); Red Mitchell (b); Red Callender (tba); Bill Douglass (d).* 1/58.

Buddy Collette had the misfortune to be a pioneer on an instrument whose jazz credentials remain in doubt: though he was a capable performer on alto, tenor and clarinet, he became renowned as a flautist and consequently got stuck in the role of novelty sessionman in the West Coast scene of the mid-1950s. On his own dates, at least, he got to handle the rest of the instruments from his music room. *Man Of Many Parts*, originally issued on Contemporary, is gimcracked around his multi-instrumentalism and is mildly enjoyable without catching much fire. A shade better is the entertaining *Nice Day*: his prime instrument here is clarinet, his woodsy sound isn't so far from Jimmy Giuffre's, and it makes an interesting gambit on the minor blues, 'Minor Deviation' (on which the little-known Shreve plays an outstanding solo), and the queer arrangement of 'Moten Swing'. The record is let down a little by switching between three different rhythm sections, but it ends usefully on the tenor feature, 'Buddy Boo'. Excellent remastering. The players can't do very much with *Jazz Loves Paris*, a pretty thin concept, based round songs about, er, Paris. Callender's tuba introduces a novelty element and all the tracks are too short to let the players breathe, but there are still a few nice moments: Roberts on 'La Vie En Rose', the hopped-up reading of 'The Last Time I Saw Paris' and any of Rosolino's brief turns out front. Four alternative takes beef up the CD reissue.

***** Flute Talk**

Soul Note 121165 *Collette; James Newton (f); Geri Allen (p); Jaribu Shahid (b); Gianpiero Prina (d).* 7/88.

Collette's return to the studios, recorded on an Italian tour, is hurried but agreeable enough, and this is probably the best group he's ever led on record. The meeting with Newton is more respectful than combative, and Allen is her usual unpredictable self, alert in places, asleep in others. The recording could be sharper.

Max Collie (born 1931)

TROMBONE, VOCALS

Born in Melbourne, Collie arrived in London in 1962 and four years later formed his own Dixieland outfit. Character and determination saw the band build up a big audience, even when that music was completely out of public favour. He's still out there playing.

***** Frontline**

Timeless TTD 504 *Collie; Denny Ilett (c); Phil Mason (t); Jack Gilbert (cl); Jim McIntosh (bj); Trefor Williams (b); Ron McKay (d).* 12/82.

****(*) Backline**

Timeless TTD 508 *As above.* 12/82.

****(*) Sensation**

Timeless TTD 530 *As above, except replace Gilbert with Paul Harrison (cl), McKay with Peter Cotterill (d); add J Johnson (p, v).* 7/86.

****(*) Latest And Greatest**

Reality RCD 113 *As above, except replace Harrison with Steve Mellor (cl), McIntosh with Chris Marney (bj), Johnson with Lord Arsenal (p); add Pauline Pearce, Marilyn Middleton Pollock (v).* 9/93.

This sort of music doesn't really sound right on a CD and, if there is such an entity as the 'CD generation', they probably don't buy it anyway. Collie works at the blue-collar, Transit van end of the Bilk–Ball–Barber spectrum, a rough-diamond revivalist with a big strong tone, notably tight and well-schooled bands and an entertainment potential that goes off the scale. These albums do little more than provide tasters of the live act. Far from awarding himself a sabbatical on reaching his fifties, Collie has been working harder than ever. Perversely, he was better documented on record 15 years ago. The first 1982 recording is one of his best, cheerfully unfashionable and utterly untroubled by any recent rethink of traditionalism in jazz. There are no fiery solos, no fancy arrangements. Songs are simply counted off and played. Full stop. The '86 band has a rather more 'authentic' feel (whatever that means) than its immediate predecessor, whose output is now only to be found on second-hand vinyl; replacing Denny Ilett's sharp, brassy cornet with Mason's more polished sound did the group no particular favours. Fine performances, though, better material and a clearer pick-up on the rhythm section.

Interestingly, the rationale behind *Latest And Greatest* was to provide a representative CD sampling of Collie material for fans who had just bought a player. Simple enough formula: just turn up and play lots of the old stuff. The inclusion of Pearce and Middleton Pollock was doubtless intended as a plus but, unlike Ottilie Paterson's contribution to Chris Barber records, it doesn't work out quite like that. 'Dippermouth Blues', 'Fidgety Feet', 'When You And I Were Young, Maggie', 'Shimmee Sha Wabble', and so on, and so forth. Wholly undisturbing fun.

Graham Collier (born 1937)

COMPOSER, DOUBLE BASS

Collier's 1960s groups were consistently fascinating, but in later years, even as a retired bass player whose interests had moved towards composition and education, he has continued to make interesting and compelling music.

*** Songs For My Father

DNA CD 001 *Collier; Harry Beckett (t, flhn); Derek Wadsworth (tb); Tony Roberts, Alan Skidmore, Brian Smith, Alan Wakeman, Bob Sydor (ts); Geoff Castle, John Taylor (p); Philip Lee (g); Chick Webb (d).* 70.

Collier's early records were of surpassing thoughtfulness – which is perhaps why they won fulsome critical plaudits and then disappeared. This welcome reissue, a first release from DNA, is the most accessible. The seven 'songs' are identified only by time-signature or other marking – 7/4, ballad, 9/8, a waltz in 4/4, rubato, dirge and 4/4 figured – but they are much more expressive than that suggests.

Collier has always had a gift for writing charts which are both demandingly complex and open-ended enough to give soloists space to express themselves. Harry Beckett is the main soloist on the album, though Skidmore and the rather more anonymous Wakeman each receive generous space. Tenorist Bob Sydor was a regular in Collier groups, but then he seemed to drift out of the limelight; a pity, since he has an engaging presence.

Beckett has the true bluesman's gift of combining hard times and melancholy with absolute unfettered joy, and he touches both ends of the spectrum on *Songs For My Father*. His phrasing on 'Song Four', that 4/4 waltz, is immaculate and his ability to play expressively and at speed in unusual time-signatures is a mark of his talent. Two additional tracks were recorded live (glorious mono!) in Brighton in May 1970. (Incidentally, the Chick Webb credited here is *not* the Chick Webb of the swing era. Just in case you wondered.)

*** Charles River Fragments

Boathouse BHR 004 *Collier; Henry Lowther, Steve Waterman, Patrick White (t); Hugh Fraser (tb); Bill Mee (btb); Andy Grappy (tba); Art Themen (ts, ss, bsx); Mark Lockheart (ts, ss); Geoff Warren (as, af); Chris Biscoe (bs, acl); Pete Saberton (p); Ed Speight (g); Dudley Phillips (b); John Marshall (d).* 95.

Fifteen years ago Collier organized a jazz orchestra called Hoarded Dreams which was responsible for some of the most vividly creative music ever performed in the British Isles under the umbrella of 'jazz'.

The main piece on this CD was commissioned by the BBC for performance at the London Jazz Festival. Dedicated to Herb Pomeroy, with whom Collier had studied at Berklee College, and to Charles Mingus, it's a large, sprawling work for improvising ensemble which relies heavily on the gifts of the players. Fraser, Lowther, Themen and Lockheart are the most important front-line players. The ideas are, as ever, expansive, and the balance between big shapes and small details is maintained with great consistency.

The only other item on the set is the (relatively) short 'The Hackney Five', on which Waterman is prominently featured. It's a mere prelude, though, to the longer work. Some of Collier's earlier, small-group records are tabled for reissue, but at time of writing are still not available. When they do reappear, they may well prompt a serious reassessment of this important British artist, out of whom much of the most inventive latter-day British jazz, including that anarchic collective Loose Tubes, has emerged.

***(*) The Third Colour

ASC CD 28 *Collier; Simon Finch, Steve Waterman (t); Ed Sarath (flhn); Mat Colman, Hugh Fraser (tb); Oren Marshall (tba); Steve Main, Karlheinz Miklin, Art Themen, Geoff Warren (sax); Roger Dean (ky); Ed Speight (g); Andy Cleyndert (b); John Marshall (d).* 11/97.

One of the marks of Collier's great strength as a composer is that he regards music as a medium in which performers express themselves, not one in which the composer attempts to make a mark. Hence 'Three Simple Pieces', hence 'Shapes, Colours, Energies', 'The Third Colour' and 'The Miró Tile', all performed at Collier's sixtieth birthday celebration. It was one of a sequence of special events in 1997. 'Three Simple Pieces' was written for a birthday concert at the Guildhall, where he teaches, and is a generous invitation to solo elaboration. The band is somewhat lacking in punch, but Themen and John Marshall bring real power to the third of the sequence.

The drummer's tubist namesake is strongly featured on 'Energy Squared', part of 'Shapes …' and he shows up again on the opening 'Groove' of 'The Third Colour', testimony to Collier's interest in writing for low horns. The title-piece takes its inspiration from art theorist Clement Greenberg's suggestion that line is the 'third colour', a reflection of Collier's interest in the space between composition and improvisation.

Made with a slightly low-key recording, resonant enough but with little real sense of occasion, *The Third Colour* asks a lot of first-time listeners. An hour or two in the library with some of Graham's early records (and more reissues are promised) might make things a lot clearer.

George Colligan (born 1970)

PIANO, ORGAN, SYNTHESIZER, TRUMPET, DRUMS

Born in Maryland, Colligan is one of the leading younger pianists in New York. He leads his own groups and has frequently worked as accompanist to Vanessa Rubin and with Gary Thomas.

*** Activism

Steeplechase SCCD 31382 *Colligan; Dwayne Burno (b); Ralph Peterson (d).* 11/95.

***(*) The Newcomer

Steeplechase SCCD 31414 *Colligan; Ingrid Jensen (t, flhn); Mark Turner (ts); Dwayne Burno (b); Billy Drummond (d).* 4/97.

Colligan is exciting to hear, even if the records don't always impress as complete entities; give him time. The trio session has some head-turning playing from all hands. Colligan contributes only one original, the title-piece, and for the rest chooses tunes by Monk, Silver, Shorter, Pearson and others. Some of his playing is brilliant enough to find the results a bit oversmart, even cruel: his take on Waller's 'Jitterbug Waltz' seems almost sarcastic. There's a lot to enjoy here, but several tracks go on too long, as often happens on Steeplechase sessions; Burno, not a terribly interesting soloist, is given too much space; and Peterson, enjoyably overplaying as usual, might not be the ideal drummer for the situation. On a relatively restrained piece such as 'Estate' the pianist comes into his own.

The Newcomer suggests that Colligan feels comfortable in a band situation, and maybe this will always be his best context. It certainly puts improvisations like that on Shorter's 'The Big Push' into useful perspective: mercurial blocks, trills, bebop lines, locked-hands, Colligan can find a use for every device in jazz piano. He brought three interesting themes to the date and the band is excellent, with Jensen and Turner both surpassingly thoughtful in their improvisations.

*****(*) Stomping Ground**

Steeplechase SCCD 31441 *Colligan; Drew Gress (b); Billy Hart (d).* 9/97.

*****(*) Constant Source**

Steeplechase SCCD 31462 *Colligan; Jon Gordon (as, ss); Mark Turner (ts); Ed Howard (b); Howard Curtis (d).* 4/98.

*****(*) Small Room**

Steeplechase SCCD 31470 *Colligan (p solo).* 9/98.

The trio record is a clear advance on Colligan's first Steeplechase in this format. He had only rarely played with Gress and Hart and there was little preparation, so the results are formidably well-shaped and the playing on a very high level. Colligan restricts himself to a single original and his tune choices are a fan's notes on modern jazz: Billy Harper's 'Priestess', Kenny Wheeler's 'For Jan', Charles Tolliver's 'Right Now'. Here and there Colligan overcooks a tune: 'What Are You Doing The Rest Of Your Life' meanders into a remote and not terribly interesting place. Mostly, though, his vigour and salty aggression, tempered by an innately fine touch, bring these pieces vividly to life, abetted by top work from the other two men.

There is one standard, a fairly drastic revision of 'I'm Getting Sentimental Over You', but otherwise the quintet record, *Constant Source*, concentrates on Colligan's own material. 'Void' is a somewhat amazing bridge between emptiness and form. 'Pitchrider' has a remote connection with blues changes but goes somewhere quite different and was inspired by Gary Thomas's music. Considering that he leads from the piano, Colligan shows a surprising penchant for evading tone centres and encouraging his horn players to take a journey into clear space. He harmonizes them in sometimes discomforting ways, as in the title-track, which seems ready to spiral off into abstract Konitz–Marsh counterpoint before it falls into place. Lucky to have Gordon and Turner, who can extemporize their way out of whatever trouble he's plotted. Brimful of ideas.

The solo record is no premature indulgence. If anything, it's a rather sober effort after the previous two. Some of the material, such as Gary Thomas's 'Exile's Gate', is used to investigate what he can wring out of a specific formula, in that case the piling of structure on to an unchanging left hand. 'Elves' is Chick Corea impressionism without the whimsicality. 'When Your Lover Has Gone' is a ballad treatment in which the melody (of both verse and chorus) is ingeniously recast and it should be compared with 'Some Other Time', which banishes memories of the Bill Evans version. A tough and decidedly idiosyncratic effort.

***** Unresolved**

Fresh Sound FSNT 054 *Colligan; Jon Gordon (as); Mark Turner (ss, ts); Kurt Rosenwinkel (g); Drew Gress (b); Howard Curtis (d).* 98.

*****(*) Desire**

Fresh Sound FSNT 071 *Colligan; Perico Sambeat (as, ss, f); Mario Rossy (b); Marc Miralta (d).* 2/99.

Unresolved is Colligan's most multifarious and ambitious record so far. Besides piano, he plays organ, synth, trumpet and even drums on one track. Turner is present throughout, Gordon and Rosenwinkel appear twice each. If anything, there's a sense that Colligan may be trying a shade too hard with this one. The electric keyboards cloud the picture more than they introduce useful colour, and the opportunity to use Gordon and Turner together consistently, as he did on *Constant Source*, is rejected. 'Evil Ambition' feels over-written; 'Unresolved' is as inconclusive as its title. But there are still enough ideas in the best of it to compel the attention: 'Modeidi's Modalities' is a menacing development out of 'Donna Lee', 'Nebulosity' gets a great performance out of Turner, and when he gives himself some open space Colligan injects some inspirational touches.

Desire focuses on a quartet once again. Colligan pleads for this to be heard as something other than a blowing session: having seen the chart for the opening 'Battle Cry', we doubt if the musicians would have entertained that thought for a moment. Fine as Sambeat is, he doesn't overturn memories of Gordon and Turner on the earlier records, and Rossy and Miralta are similarly not quite as powerful as some of their predecessors. As considerable as Colligan's composing and playing is, it can at times seem a shade cryptic unless it has interpreters who can really open it up, and to that extent we prefer the Steeplechase records. But even here there are memorable things: the pianist's compact, ingenious solo on the title-track, the askew balladry of 'Last November'.

Jay Collins (born 1968)

TENOR SAXOPHONE, FLUTES

Works in and around Portland, Oregon, in a variety of playing situations from straight-ahead to acid jazz.

***** Uncommon Threads**

Reservoir RSR CD 135 *Collins; Kenny Barron (p); Joe Locke (vib); Rufus Reid (b); Ben Riley (d).* 6/92.

**** Reality Tonic**

Reservoir RSR CD 142 *Collins; Frank Lacy (tb); James Hurt (p); Santi Debriano (b); Michael Mazor (d).* 10/95.

The saxophonist holds his own in distinguished company on his leadership debut. He plays with the acid-jazz combo, TUBA, and was a sometime break-dancer – none of which squares with the big, almost classical sound of his tenor playing, steeped in the tradition. Three nice originals, a version of 'Dearly Beloved' that spins off a funky bass vamp and a rare Monk tune, 'Played Twice', are the prime elements in an interesting programme. Collins shines in some of his solos but sounds a little rote in others: he never characterizes 'You've Changed', done as a duet with Barron, with enough guts, and some of the tempos encourage a noodling rather than a purposeful feel. The others sound fine, and Locke is his usual challenging self. Nobody is that well served by the listless studio mix, though.

Reality Tonic is less effective all round. The group play with faceless chops and Collins chooses to involve folk elements via some flute features that lack much charm.

Alice Coltrane (born 1937)

PIANO, HARP

Also known as Turiya and Sagittananda, Alice McLeod grew up in Detroit, studied classical music and took piano lessons with Bud Powell. Her highly distinctive style is based on long, rippling arpeggios, very much in keeping with husband John's advanced harmonics, though debate still continues sporadically as to how much she contributed to his thinking in later years. Prayerful and intense, Alice Coltrane's albums are not for the cynically disposed.

***** A Monastic Trio**

Impulse! IMP 12023 *Coltrane; Pharoah Sanders (ts); Jimmy Garrison (b); Rashied Ali, Ben Riley (d).* 68.

***** Ptah, The El Daoud**

Impulse! IMP 12210 *Coltrane; Joe Henderson, Pharoah Sanders (ts, af); Ron Carter (b); Ben Riley (d).* 1/70.

***** Journey In Satchidananda**

Impulse! IMP 12410 *Coltrane; Pharoah Sanders (ss, perc); Vishnu Wood (oud); Charlie Haden, Cecil McBee (b); Tulsi (tamboura); Rashied Ali (d); Majid Shabazz (perc).* 11/70.

***** Astral Meditations**

Impulse! IMP12422 *Coltrane; Frank Lowe (ts); Reggie Workman (b); Ben Riley (d); Elaine (timp); strings.*

***** Alice Coltrane: Priceless Jazz**

GRP/Universal GRT 1345 *As for A Monastic Trio, Ptah, The El Daoud, Journey In Satchidananda, except add Jimmy Garrison (b), Rashied Ali, Clifford Jarvis, Jack DeJohnette (d), Tuksi (perc); strings inc. John Blair, Leroy Jenkins (vn).* 68–72.

Alice McLeod was introduced to John Coltrane by, of all people, Terry Gibbs, with whom she had recorded *Jewish Melodies In Jazztime*. Increasingly after Trane's death in 1967, his widow was drawn into quite another religious tradition – or, rather, an eclectic synthesis of Egyptian, Indian and Oriental systems. Her first solo record is a pretty straightforward tribute to her late husband, and very much bound up with the music they were making together over the last couple of years. It also establishes Pharoah Sanders as her most responsive and sympathetic playing companion, at this stage a shriller and more acerbic performer than Coltrane but occasionally capable, as on 'Ohnedaruth' and 'The Sun', of reaching the heights Trane aspired to. The American edition of the CD has two extra tracks, but it isn't for our money as good a mastering. Opt for the slightly shorter Japanese version if you get the chance.

Ptah is the highest avatar of God in Egyptian religion, and the title-piece is a rippling essay in transcendence, the paired horns coming from quite different directions (though one questions whether Mrs Coltrane's suggestion that Henderson is 'intellectual' and Sanders 'abstract, more transcendental' quite hits the mark). Their doubling on alto flute on 'Blue Nile' is magnificent, a perfect complement to piano and harp. By the time this record was made, Alice Coltrane had already recorded for Impulse! without horns. 'Turiya & Ramakrishna' retreads that sound, a simple three-note cell expanded into a huge meditation that is the triple-distilled spirit of lightness. Carter is a hugely important component at this stage, though one does wonder whether Ben Riley was the right drummer for the gig.

Unfortunately, the second of Alice Coltrane's 1970 recordings (also made at the home studio at Dix Hills, New York) is a rather lumpy affair, the spirit of sinking. 'Something About John Coltrane' is a drab workshop version of a D minor idea that had recurred throughout Trane's later work. 'Isis And Osiris', which follows and ends the album, is a good illustration of Mrs Coltrane's growing interest in non-European scales (represented by the North African oud), just as elsewhere the tamboura evokes drones that have – or had then – no accepted part in Western music. Sanders limits himself to soprano – not his natural horn and a not entirely comfortable sound. McBee, Haden and Ali are more obviously attuned to this music, but somehow the chemistry obstinately fails to work. It might be thought that preferring the more conventional of these two sets is itself a failure to understand and accept Alice Coltrane's more radical experiments. The ideas are clearly more sophisticated on *Journey* ...; the execution falls some way short.

Astral Meditations finds Alice in the company of another Trane disciple, Frank Lowe, a strong and in some ways more challenging voice than Pharoah Sanders. Lowe is interested in things which Alice tends to pass over, melody most obviously, and the encounter is a fruitful one. Touring again towards the end of the '90s, Alice Coltrane sounded strong and individual and still capable of surprise.

The Priceless compilation includes material from two other Impulse! records which have not been reissued: *Hunting Ashram Monastery* and *Universal Consciousness*. The latter is pretty way out but includes some strong jazz-based material, and the string arrangements are by Ornette Coleman, of all people.

John Coltrane (1926–67)

TENOR SAXOPHONE, SOPRANO SAXOPHONE, ALTO SAXOPHONE, FLUTE

Arguably the most influential musician in modern jazz, both technically and spiritually, Coltrane had a relatively conventional and unspectacular apprenticeship in R&B, working with the likes of King Kolax, Earl Bostic and Eddie Cleanhead Vinson. By 1949, though, he had become involved in bebop and recorded for the first time with Dizzy Gillespie, before signalling a shift towards a more open-ended experimentalism with membership of Miles Davis's remarkable quintet which introduced modalism to his work. A brief period with Thelonious Monk effectively signalled the start of Coltrane's career as leader; over the next ten years (and particularly in the company of McCoy Tyner, Jimmy Garrison and

Elvin Jones (later Rashied Ali)) his quartet brought about a seismic shift in jazz harmony. The group's ever longer improvisations seemed bent on packing in every conceivable variation and inversion of an often conventional pop theme, and they made use of ever greater tonal distortion and timbral effects. In 1960, inspired by Sidney Bechet and Steve Lacy, Coltrane added soprano saxophone to his repertoire. Problems with narcotic and then alcohol addiction were left behind when Coltrane began to espouse an intense, somewhat personalized version of Judaeo-Christianity, with a few elements of African animism and Eastern mysticism thrown in. It sustained him through the latter phase of his foreshortened career. Coltrane died of liver cancer at the age of forty.

****(*) Dakar**

Original Jazz Classics OJCCD 393 *Coltrane; Pepper Adams, Cecil Payne (bs); Mal Waldron (p); Doug Watkins (b); Art Taylor (d).* 4/57.

***** Coltrane**

Original Jazz Classics OJCCD 020 *Coltrane; Johnny Splawn (t); Sahib Shihab (bs); Mal Waldron (p); Paul Chambers (b); Albert 'Tootie' Heath (d).* 5/57.

If this was, as is often claimed, the most influential player in modern jazz, then his turbulent achievement was all the more remarkable in being packed into a single decade of music-making. Almost exactly ten years separate the first records as leader and the dark, sometimes anguished curtain-call of *Expression*, made weeks before Trane's death in 1967.

If Coltrane's career had ended with the closure of his Prestige contract, how would we understand and rate him now? As a major innovator? Probably not, though there are signs from the very beginning that Trane was pushing for something beyond the existing conventions of hard bop. As a distinctive saxophone stylist? Yes, to a degree. The biting tone had been burnished in numerous big bands, and more than a year in Miles Davis's group (whose apotheosis was to come in March and April 1959 with *Kind Of Blue*) had promoted a restless, tumbling solo style. In fairness, though, it is hard to hear any of these early albums as anything other than way-stations to greatness. *Dakar* was supervised by vibraharpist Teddy Charles, who included three of his own tunes in the session and presumably negotiated the unusual tenor-and-two-baritones front line. Transfer to CD helped the sound enormously, ungluing some of the ensembles and putting a little needed space between Coltrane and the other two reeds. Adams's relatively simple 'Mary's Blues' and the Mal Waldron tune, 'Velvet Scene', are probably the best tracks, as simple and direct as the minor feel allows. Charles's own 'Dakar' and 'Cat Walk' are too fanciful and sound under-rehearsed. *Coltrane* redeems the bottom-heaviness of the earlier session by building in Johnny Splawn, who always sounds as if he's just rushed in with a telegram. Chambers is on excellent form, dancing lightly through the changes. Trane himself sounds a good deal more assured than even a month before.

**** Tenor Conclave**

Original Jazz Classics OJCCD 127 *Coltrane; Al Cohn, Hank Mobley, Paul Quinichette, Zoot Sims (ts); Red Garland (p); Paul Chambers (b); Art Taylor (d).* 9/56.

***** Cattin' With Coltrane And Quinichette**

Original Jazz Classics OJCCD 460 *Coltrane; Paul Quinichette (ts); Mal Waldron (p); Julian Euell (b); Ed Thigpen (d).* 5/57.

****(*) Wheelin' And Dealin'**

Original Jazz Classics OJCCD 672 *Coltrane; Paul Quinichette, Frank Wess (ts); Mal Waldron (p); Doug Watkins (b); Art Taylor (d).* 57.

This was a time when American recording executives tended to regard the tenor saxophone in much the same way as the post-Korea military regarded atomic bombs and missiles. One awesomely powerful weapon of destruction and control: good. Lots of ditto: very good. Listening to these records, though, is a little closer to how Beethoven must have felt during the French bombardment of Vienna, intimidated, a little deafened, and desperate for a waltz to break up the lockstep of 4/4s. One difference: the French cannon were state-of-the-art; these tenorists simply sound old-fashioned. Inevitably, Coltrane stands out. No one else, then or since, has ever sounded like that, and a combination of law-of-averages and the competitive ethos that was part of such multi-horn sessions guarantees some excellent moments. The pairing with Quinichette is the most relaxed. *Cattin'* is an underrated album with a light, almost joyous feel, two guys of markedly different temperament discovering a companionable middle ground.

***** Lush Life**

Original Jazz Classics OJCCD 131 *Coltrane; Donald Byrd (t); Red Garland (p); Earl May (b); Louis Hayes, Albert 'Tootie' Heath, Art Taylor (d).* 5/57–1/58.

An album of oddments, really, garnered from three distinct sessions over a six-month period. This was the time when Sonny Rollins was experimenting at the Village Vanguard with a pianoless trio. Coltrane's more tentative step in the same direction – which was to be repeated only sporadically in years to come – was actually enforced when Garland failed to show for the date. May is too anonymous a player to go the extra yard required for this exacting discipline. There are unexpected inconsistencies of register and articulation in Coltrane's own performances, perhaps suggesting reed, mouthpiece or (even at this stage) dental problems. The title-piece has the rugged grandeur of many of Trane's ballad meditations, but the often remarked resemblance to Stan Getz is already fading fast.

***** Bahia**

Original Jazz Classics OJCCD 415 *Coltrane; Freddie Hubbard (t); Wilbur Harden (flhn); Paul Quinichette (ts); Red Garland, Mal Waldron (p); Paul Chambers (b); Jimmy Cobb, Art Taylor (d).* 57, 58.

More oddments from the Prestige years. Trane and Quinichette were something of a mismatch and their jammed piece doesn't sit all that well with the other material, which jumps forward to Trane's last recording for the label. This does include the incendiary Hubbard on a magnificent version of 'Then I'll Be Tired Of You', but by this stage it's Trane who sounds tired.

*****(*) Traneing In**

Original Jazz Classics OJCCD 189 *Coltrane; Red Garland (b); Art Taylor (d).* 8/57.

This is much more like the thing, Coltrane and rhythm, and the first group that sounds as if it might contain the germ of the later classic quartets. And not just any old off-the-peg rhythm section either, but Miles Davis's current line-up. The title-piece is one of the first of the saxophonist's open-form blowing themes, a progression of chords which doesn't so much propel the scant melody as catapult it across the changes. Trane's solo is fiery and committed to the hilt, the sound of a virile pretender not yet rising to the majesty of later years. He also shows a remarkably delicate touch with a ballad; 'You Leave Me Breathless' is also a key moment, and a valuable reference point when one compares it with *Soultrane*, recorded with the same group six months later.

*****(*) Blue Train**

Blue Note 7460952 *Coltrane; Lee Morgan (t); Curtis Fuller (tb); Kenny Drew (p); Paul Chambers (b); Philly Joe Jones (d).* 9/57.

*****(*) The Ultimate Blue Train**

Blue Note 53428 *As above; includes CD-ROM material.*

A perfect example of the Blue Note effect, an over-valued record which bathes in the cachet of what turned out to be a fleeting association with the most glamorous label of its time. Michael Cuscuna has explained that, during the winter of 1956–7, it seems Coltrane visited the Blue Note offices because he wanted to get hold of some Sidney Bechet records, though apparently not yet to study soprano saxophone technique. Alfred Lion was present and mooted the possibility of the saxophonist recording for the label. It was Lion's partner, Francis Wolff, who handled contracts and, though some money seems to have changed hands, Wolff was not in the office on the day concerned and the agreement to record for Blue Note was settled on a handshake. It was almost a year later that Coltrane remembered the commitment and the good-faith payment and insisted on honouring it. That there was to be no follow-up is a shame, one of the most intriguing might-have-beens and what-ifs of recent musical history.

That aside, the unavoidable conclusion is that *Blue Train* is not an unalloyed masterpiece. It certainly wasn't recorded on the fly. Part of the Blue Note ethos was paid rehearsal, and there seems to have been ample studio time. The band fulfil their responsibilities perfectly well, but this was far from an ideal line-up for Coltrane. The rhythm section had already recorded together for Blue Note under Chambers's leadership, and Chambers and Jones were already familiar to Coltrane from Miles's band. Though Drew sounds out of sympathy with the charts, the real question marks are against the names of Morgan and Fuller, both gifted players, but both locked on stylistic trolley-lines. Morgan seems content with a subsidiary role, but Fuller blusters and registers a positive presence only on 'Locomotion'. The opening is still where it all happens; the title-tune is a starkly powerful blues which propels Coltrane into his first unquestionably major recorded solo. Once heard, it's a sound that is not easily forgotten, at once plaintive and urgent, hard-edged but also vulnerable. The rest of the album falls away. 'Moment's Notice' was to become a staple in years to come; here, it is repertory hard bop. 'Lazy Bird' is based on a Tadd Dameron theme and is quite effective; 'I'm Old Fashioned' is a slightly formulaic ballad which would have been very much more appropriate as a quartet item, just tenor and rhythm.

Coltrane is said to have spoken of *Blue Train* as his own favourite among his records. Needless to say, Blue Note have a stake in reinforcing the point. It has long been wondered whether anything further was taped and preserved at the session of 15 September 1957. Forty years later – and also to mark the thirtieth anniversary of Coltrane's death – Capitol released an 'enhanced' CD-ROM of the session, including two alternative takes, an extra 17 minutes of music in all, as well as documentary footage and interviews. Interestingly, controversy broke out within the ranks. Rudy van Gelder, who had engineered the session, referred to release of some of the material as a 'desecration', objecting to the issue of an earlier, unsatisfactory take of 'Blue Train'. What Blue Note had initially done was to issue take number nine of that famous opening track, but to issue it with the better piano solo from take eight spliced in. On *The Ultimate Blue Train* take eight can be heard for the first time entire, and with the same piano solo restored to its original position. The rights and wrongs of this would occupy much of this section; most listeners who know 'Blue Train' well will be fascinated and probably reassured to know that, whatever chemistry takes place between takes, the definitive version is the one they already know (Coltrane was to have problems along these same lines later in his career, with 'Ascension'). Neither the alternative of 'Lazy Bird' nor, indeed, the CD-ROM material on the final track adds very much, though the outer packaging of *The Ultimate* features a much better crop of Francis Wolff's famous cover portrait of Trane. Perhaps only diehard purists will insist on sticking to the original version.

**** The Bethlehem Years**

Bethlehem BET 804 2CD Coltrane; various personnel 10 & 12/57.

A complete con: there were no Bethlehem years, just a couple of sessions for other leaders, recorded only a matter of weeks apart. The Winner's Circle octet was a collective project but, by and large, this is a sideman album and only for dedicated completists.

***** The Believer**

Original Jazz Classics OJCCD 876 *Coltrane; Donald Byrd, Freddie Hubbard (t); Ray Draper (tba); Gil Coggins, Red Garland (p); Spanky DeBrest, Paul Chambers (b); Louis Hayes, Larry Ritchie, Art Taylor (d).* 12/57–12/58.

A fascinating compilation for early sight and sound of young talent. McCoy Tyner is composer of the title-piece, two years before he joined Coltrane's group. Hubbard, who solos to startling effect on 'Do I Love You Because You're Beautiful?', is already a monster. Two tracks are under the joint leadership of tubist Draper, a figure always destined to be marginal but capable of some fine and emotive playing on a cumbersome horn.

*****(*) Soultrane**

Original Jazz Classics OJCCD 021 *Coltrane; Red Garland (p); Paul Chambers (b); Art Taylor (d).* 2/58.

***** Settin' The Pace**

Original Jazz Classics OJCCD 078 *As above.* 3/58.

What a difference it must have been turning back to Prestige, scant rehearsal time and a consequent need to stick with familiar material. One senses that this is the point in Coltrane's career when he should be opening up and exploring his own ideas. Of course, in a sense he was. Even now, some enthusiastic supporters mislocate the much-cited 'sheets of sound' period, assuming that the phrase refers to the teeming wails and seemingly endless solos of later years. In fact, it relates to the work Trane was doing through the extended public woodshed that was 1958. *Soultrane*, to be fair, is an excellent record. One can very quickly hear how much further the saxophonist was able to push the harmonic language than he had been doing with the same group in August 1957. 'I Want To Talk About You' was to become another of Coltrane's favourite standards, and this is a hugely thoughtful and technically adroit reading, ranging without strain across two and a half octaves. *Settin' The Pace* is much less venturesome and might easily be mistaken for a second-string selection from the same date, except that it was recorded a month later. The outstanding track is the Jackie McLean composition, 'Little Melonae', which the rhythm section seems to know inside out.

***** The Last Trane**
Original Jazz Classics OJCCD 394 *Coltrane; Donald Byrd (t); Red Garland (p); Paul Chambers, Earl May (b); Louis Hayes, Art Taylor (d).* 8/57, 3/58.

'Last' not quite in the barrel-scraping sense, for the out-takes from the Garland, Chambers and Taylor date are actually very good indeed and, for anyone who finds this period of Coltrane's career more appealing than later work, 'Come Rain Or Come Shine' is likely to be a welcome addition to the collection.

**** Black Pearls**
Original Jazz Classics OJCCD 352. *As for the above, except add Donald Byrd (t).* 5/58.

For our money, one of the drabbest sessions in the whole Coltrane canon. Even Homer nods, but the problem here is that no one seems prepared to nod out, opting to grind away pretty remorselessly. Byrd can be an engaging player, but this certainly wasn't his natural gig.

***** Plays The Blues**
Prestige 11005 *Coltrane; Donald Byrd (t); Gene Ammons, Paul Quinichette (ts); Pepper Adams (bs); Jerome Richardson (f); Tommy Flanagan, Red Garland, Mal Waldron (p); Kenny Burrell (g); Paul Chambers, George Joyner, Earl May, Jamil Nasser (b); Jimmy Cobb, Art Taylor (d).* 57–58.

Further salami-slicing from the Prestige and issued as part of a roots series in which major artists concentrate on the blues. No more surprising than announcing 'Lawrence Welk Plays Polkas', and much better sampled on the original releases.

***** Like Sonny**
Capitol 93901 *Coltrane; Ray Draper (tba); John Maher, McCoy Tyner (p); Steve Davis, Spanky DeBrest (b); Billy Higgins, Larry Ritchie (d).* 58, 60.

Valuable for that first glimpse of Coltrane in the company of McCoy Tyner, the pianist whose instinctive grasp of modal principles was to be a key factor in the saxophonist's spectacular progress over the next few years. This basically puts together two quite different sessions, one of them featuring the tubist Ray Draper and his anonymous rhythm section. It includes some interesting material, including Draper's own 'Essii's Dance', but it's the nascent quartet with Steve Davis and Billy Higgins which really points the way forward.

***** The Standard Coltrane**
Original Jazz Classics OJCCD 246 *Coltrane; Wilbur Harden (t, flhn); Red Garland (p); Paul Chambers (b); Jimmy Cobb (d).* 7/58.

***** Bahia**
Original Jazz Classics OJCCD 415 *As above, except add Art Taylor (d).* 7 & 12/58.

***** The Stardust Session**
Prestige 24056 *As above.* 7 & 12/58.

It takes a certain wishful attitude to think of these as 'transitional' records, except in the rather general sense that everything Coltrane did was in transit to some other spiritual or musical reality. It's easy enough to untangle these three late releases from the Prestige period. *The Standard* pretty much explains itself, a low-intensity operation with the emphasis on ballads. Two tracks from the same session, 'My Ideal', 'Something I Dreamed Last Night' and 'I'm A Dreamer (Aren't We All)' are included on *Bahia*, though the liner details inconsistently imply that the middle item was taped on the December date, which seems unlikely. Harden's warm, unemphatic trumpet-playing is perfectly appropriate to the setting and it rarely attempts anything that will scare the horses. He and the leader seem to have worked out the approach only rather notionally, and each of their improvisations has an informal, loose-limbed quality that is attractive but hardly dynamic. *The Stardust Session* is a Prestige compilation including all of *The Standard Coltrane* and a couple of items from *Bahia*, reasonable value if you can find it.

*****(*) The Prestige Recordings**
Prestige 25104 6CD *As above.* 11/56–7/58.

**** Jazz Showcase**
Original Jazz Classics 6015 *As for Prestige recordings above.* 11/56–7/58.

The boxed set offers the most comprehensive and, for most listeners, exhaustive documentation of Trane's time with the label, which as always in these matters was shorter than it seems in retrospect. It reveals the saxophonist still in larval stage and not yet the compellingly beautiful imago of the Atlantic years. The single CD sampler is unsatisfactory in almost every respect.

***** Coltrane Time**
Blue Note 7 84461 *Coltrane; Cecil Taylor (p); Chuck Israels (b); Louis Hayes (d).* 10/58.

No inconsistency: *Blue Train* was indeed Trane's only session for Blue Note. *Coltrane Time* – or *Coltranetime*, cover and spine differ – was a United Artists release, reissued by Capitol much later. Chanced upon, and especially when Coltrane is not soloing, the session sounds rather anonymous. Its importance – like the mid-1957 dates under Thelonious Monk's leadership – is the unique opportunity to hear two of the great modernist pioneers together. Unfortunately, they seem to cancel one another out. Both are playing rather circumspectly, perhaps in deference to the other, and the real star of the session, his contribution greatly enhanced by CD, turns out to be Israels, composer of the excellent final tune, 'Double Clutching', which mirrors Dorham's opening 'Shifting Down'. Neither of the two leaders contributes any writing. If part of the intention was to widen Taylor's appeal (and this seems to have been the aim), it is done at the expense of his most distinctive characteristics. Coltrane comes out of it rather better, but equally constrained by the two standards, 'Just Friends' and 'Like Someone In Love', which allow him to do little more than hang out a few more sheets of sound before stepping back to allow Taylor some solo space of his own, which he seems disinclined to indulge.

**** Giant Steps

Atlantic 781337 *Coltrane; Tommy Flanagan, Wynton Kelly, Cedar Walton (p); Paul Chambers (b); Jimmy Cobb, Lex Humphries, Art Taylor (d).* 3, 5 & 12/59.

Moving from Prestige to Atlantic had the same effect on Coltrane as a more extended association with Blue Note might have done. The first album is the product of time and preparation, and it cements its status as Trane's first genuinely iconic record, with no fewer than seven original compositions, most of them now squarely established in the repertory. The big stylistic shift is the move away from chordal jazz, and a seemingly obsessive need to cross-hatch every feasible subdivision before moving on to the next in the sequence. In its place, a faster-moving, scalar approach that was to achieve its (in the event) brief apotheosis in the title-track. That this was a technically exacting theme is underlined by the false starts and alternative takes included on *The Heavyweight Champion* set (below), but there is a chance to sample an earlier version of the tune on this CD reissue, performed a month and a half before the issued recording (which featured Flanagan, Chambers and Taylor) with another group. Cedar Walton just about goes through the motions at the 26 March session. He finds the beautiful ballad 'Naima' a more approachable proposition, though this time the released version was actually from a later session still, with Wynton Kelly and Jimmy Cobb. It remains one of Trane's best-loved themes, a million miles away from the pitiless drive of many of his solos. Dedicated to the bassist, 'Mr P.C.' is a delightful original blues which has become part of most contemporary horn players' repertoire. 'Syeeda's Song Flute' is a long, spun-out melody for Trane's daughter. The remaining tracks are 'Spiral', 'Countdown' and the funky, homely 'Cousin Mary'. *Giant Steps* was released on the cusp of a new decade, in January 1960. It threw down a quiet, unaggressive challenge. Once again, it is difficult to see it as anything other than a transitional record. Flanagan doesn't sound much more confident with the new idiom than Walton had been on the dry run, though he is a more intuitively lyrical player.

**** Coltrane Jazz

Atlantic 781344 *Coltrane; Wynton Kelly, McCoy Tyner (p); Paul Chambers, Steve Davis (b); Jimmy Cobb, Elvin Jones (d).* 11 & 12/59, 10/60.

Again, sessions overlap. Much of this comes from the date that yielded the issued 'Naima', but there is also a later track, 'Village Blues', which features Tyner and Jones, meaning that the classic quartet is just around the corner. At this point, four years after picking up those Bechet records from Alfred Lion (but seemingly inspired by having heard straight horn specialist Steve Lacy), Trane was deliberating on what was to be his only significant 'double', the querulously pitched soprano saxophone. Even when he is playing tenor, though, there are signs that he is looking for new pitch relationships, and he can be heard exploring split tones on 'Harmonique'. With the exception of Johnny Mercer's 'My Shining Hour', all the material is original, a consolidation and in some regards a slight retreat from the innovations of *Giant Steps*. However, by this point 'Coltrane jazz' does begin to sound like a distinct stylistic subspecies.

*** The Avant-Garde

Atlantic 8122 79892-2 *Coltrane; Don Cherry (t); Charlie Haden, Percy Heath (b); Ed Blackwell (d).* 6 & 7/60.

A needlessly, perhaps off-puttingly self-conscious title for an album which was intended to square the circle by putting Coltrane in contact with the third of the modernist triumvirate, Ornette Coleman, or at least his group and his music. Three of the numbers played are Ornette's 'The Blessing', 'Focus On Sanity' and 'The Invisible'; 'Cherryco' is the trumpeter's; and 'Bemsha Swing' is by Monk and Denzil Best. Except on the last – and presumably most familiar – of these, Trane sounds untypically awkward. His soprano playing is not yet either idiomatic or nimble, and on 'The Blessing' he makes even Ornette's eccentric pitching sound dead centre. A curiosity rather than a major recording.

**** My Favorite Things

Atlantic 8122 75350-2 *Coltrane; McCoy Tyner (p); Steve Davis (b); Elvin Jones (d).* 10/60.

**** Coltrane's Sound

Rhino/Atlantic R2 75588 *As above.* 10/60.

**** Coltrane Plays The Blues

Atlantic 7567 81351-2 *As above.* 10/60.

The Avant-Garde didn't appear until rather later, and Coltrane's real coming out as a soprano player was disguised behind the unthreatening banner of a Rodgers and Hammerstein tune. Yet who could have anticipated the sheer strangeness of his take on 'My Favorite Things'? Call it what you will, a radical subversion of American popular song, the quintessence of the scalar approach, a new synthesis of western and eastern idioms (and all of these have been advanced and substantiated), it is a remarkable, unsettling performance. In later years, 'My Favorite Things' was to become a regular feature of Coltrane's live sets, often spun out to several times the length of this relatively controlled, 13-minute version. Here, it has all the freshness and innocence of the original song and, though Tyner follows his boss in largely ignoring its chord structure, he still manages to retain the familiar contours.

A year and a half after *Kind Of Blue*, Trane still sounds as if he is hearing versions of the Miles Davis group in his head. 'Summertime', 'Every Time We Say Goodbye' and 'But Not For Me' are all marked by Miles's cool modality. The two Gershwin songs are taken on tenor, and 'Summertime' points forward to some of the things Coltrane was to be doing on the larger horn over the next couple of years, with basically this group. (Davis was shortly to be replaced.)

The all-standards programme was a marketing strategy as much as anything, for there was to be a good deal of very mixed material, including some originals, in the extended session that ran from 20 to 26 October. *Colrane's Sound* was programmed to deliver a much darker sound and was issued in a sleeve on which Coltrane's calm face was reduced to smears of paint; he is reported to have been distressed by it. The album starts as dramatically as anything since *Blue Train* with a roiling interpretation of 'The Night Has A Thousand Eyes' which is both in the spirit of and dramatically different from his treatment of 'My Favorite Things'. Coltrane merely states the theme of 'Central Park West' on his soprano; otherwise it is a feature for Tyner. The leader is back with a vengeance on 'Liberia', as blackly intense as anything he was to do in the Atlantic period. Nothing else on the album (that is, nothing on the original second LP-side) quite matches up. Trane's Afro-excursion on that tenor player's rite of passage, 'Body And Soul', sounds rather predictable in the context, though, given that the saxophonist was redefining the parameters almost session by session, that's a highly relative judgement.

The blues album, made over the same long session as most of the *Coltrane's Sound* tracks, is often overlooked or reviewed as if it were a separate and distinct project. Much of the interest lies in Tyner's withdrawal from some of the numbers, a first experiment with a pianoless trio since Prestige days. Here once again simplicity of statement and sophistication of harmonic structure lie in fertile balance. Worth dusting off.

*** Ole Coltrane

Atlantic 8122 75351-2 *Coltrane; Freddie Hubbard (t); Eric Dolphy (as, f); McCoy Tyner (p); Art Davis, Reggie Workman (b); Elvin Jones (d).* 5/61.

The end of Coltrane's time with Atlantic and already overlapping with the *Africa/Brass* project, which was to be his first Impulse! recording. There has always been debate about Trane's influences and associations: how much he learnt from Monk, how much he understood or appreciated what Cecil Taylor and Ornette Coleman were doing, and to what extent he was influenced by Eric Dolphy, or Dolphy by him. The difference was that he enjoyed a warm personal association with the younger man, who was to bring his own distinctive touch to some of Coltrane's greatest compositions and contrafacts when they toured Europe later in 1961, following the Village Vanguard residency. It seems increasingly clear that Dolphy's role in 'arranging' *Africa/Brass* was less central than once thought. His part in *Ole Coltrane* was also supportive rather than central. Dolphy was even obliged for contractual reasons to appear as 'George Lane'. His flute shadows Coltrane's soprano on the title-track, switching to alto for 'Dahomey Dance' and for McCoy Tyner's prescient 'Aisha'. These are the only three tracks on the original release, though an inititally untitled ballad, known as 'To Her Ladyship' and credited to Billy Frazier, was also recorded. The presence of Hubbard also helped expand the timbral range, pointing to the new, more orchestrated sound Coltrane was interested in developing at the time. Interesting as it is episodically, *Ole* never quite holds the attention.

**** The Heavyweight Champion

Atlantic/Rhino 8122 71984 7CD *Personnel as for Atlantic recordings above.* 1/59–5/61.

We have not previously felt moved to demote a coronetted item, though in this case we did make threatening noises on the grounds that this capacious box and the artist it celebrates deserved a more appropriate title. Given that all the Atlantic records are available singly, and that some of the more important alternatives and rejected material have been released on two still widely available compilations, *The Coltrane Legacy* and *Alternate Takes*, only the most dedicated and well-heeled of fans will feel the need to have this set.

There will always be disagreement between those who want to understand the archaeology of a classic session – in this case, *Giant Steps* – and to be able to track back through umpteen false starts and breakdowns, and those who simply want to have the pristine performances. There are no fewer than ten alternatives of 'Giant Steps' itself, most of them grouped on the last CD of the set, a collection of out-takes packaged in a mock-up of an old tape-box. The evolution of the definitive performance, and of a piece that Coltrane was not to perform in concert or to re-record, is of course part of the history of the music, and we are privileged to have access to it; the studio banter is relaxed and funny, underlining most musicians' recollection of Coltrane as a gentle, easy-going man who was only obdurate when it came to writing playable themes. For anyone who has none of the Atlantics, this is a worthwhile buy, though we'd still recommend them in their issued form.

**** The Very Best Of John Coltrane

Rhino 79778 *As for Atlantic/Rhino releases, above.* 59–61.

We are not great lovers of compilations and best-of collections, but should a young nephew or niece ever betray complete ignorance of Coltrane and his work, this would be the ideal introduction, to the middle, gentler phase of his career at least. It begins boldly with 'Giant Steps' and includes 'Cousin Mary', 'Naima', 'My Favorite Things', 'Central Park West' and Summertime', along with a couple of blues and standards. And when they say, 'Uncle, this has changed my life,' you can reminisce about how it changed yours as well.

**(*) The Last Giant: The John Coltrane Anthology

Rhino 71255 *As for Atlantic/Rhino releases, above; additional personnel.* 46–67.

There are probably people out there who think 'anthology' means something different from 'best of' or 'compilation'; but not even the prospect of having a glimpse of Trane playing bebop in 1946, doing a radio session with Dizzy Gillespie, or accompanying Gay Crosse's 'Good Humor Six' in 1952 will be enough to persuade hardened collectors to part with their cash for this retread of the formula. All the obvious Altantic benchmarks are there, as they'd have to be, and there are two hours plus of music; but as an introduction, it's a poorer bet than others.

**** The Complete Africa / Brass Sessions

Impulse! 21682 2CD *Coltrane; Freddie Hubbard, Booker Little (t); Britt Woodman (tb); Carl Bowman, Charles Greenlee, Julian Priester (euph); Jimmy Buffington, Donald Corrado, Bob Northern, Robert Swisshelm, Julius Watkins (frhn); Bill Barber (tba); Eric Dolphy (as, f, bcl); Garvin Bushell (picc, reeds); Pat Patrick (bs); McCoy Tyner (p); Paul Chambers, Art Davis, Reggie Workman (b); Elvin Jones (d).* 5 & 6/61.

Coltrane's debut for Impulse! was to have, like some of the masterworks that followed, a slightly muddled history. Only with the release of this properly annotated double-CD is it possible to gain an accurate understanding of what was going on. Still with some effort, unfortunately, for even after two CD generations there are still inaccuracies. The first and obvious point to make about the music is that, while Trane clearly was becoming interested in large-scale ensemble playing and in a bigger, more collective sound, this is essentially a quartet album with a fairly minimal – though undeniably powerful – orchestration done by Coltrane, Tyner, Dolphy (who has previously had too much of the credit) and, on one track, the initially rejected 'The Damned Don't Cry', Romulus Franceschini.

As before, chord structures are left implicit at best and time-signatures are never as clear-cut as they might appear. Even the waltz-time – or 6/8 – feel Coltrane had begun to favour for long-form soprano improvisations is breaking up into constituent subdivisions. The impact of African music on the title-piece is difficult to pin down or quantify, but it is unmistakably there and it was to mark a new departure for Coltrane. The original *Africa/Brass* CD consisted of just three tracks: 'Africa' itself, a huge conception generated by the simplest of two-note bass figures; 'Greensleeves', another soprano deconstruction of a familiar tune; and 'Blues Minor' (the notes here suggest that it consisted of 'Greensleeves' and two takes of 'Africa': nonsense). In the mid-1970s, Impulse! released *Africa/Brass Sessions – Volume 2* which consisted of 'Song Of The Underground Railroad' and alternatives of 'Greensleeves' and 'Africa', while a further version of the title-piece and a Cal Massey composition called 'The Damned Don't Cry' emerged on the double-LP compilation, *Trane's Modes*. This is still garbled and there are still some question marks over the exact composition of the orchestra (a previous CD release claims Jimmy Garrison was involved, in advance of his signing as the Coltrane Quartet's regular bassist) but the above is our best effort.

The music is extraordinary. Coltrane sounds exalted on 'Africa' and turns in performances of markedly different emotional temperature on each of the three available versions. For students of his soprano work, the two versions of 'Greensleeves' are equally a revelation. A bright, swinging idea, 'Blues Minor' is in some respects a throwback to the Atlantic years, but 'Song Of The Underground Railroad' looks defiantly forward, indeed is perhaps the most prescient thing on the entire set, anticipating the saxophone/drums axis of work with Elvin Jones and, still more, Rashied Ali.

****** The Complete 1961 Village Vanguard Recordings**

Impulse! IMPCD 054232-2 4CD *Coltrane; Eric Dolphy (bcl); Garvin Bushell (ob, cbsn); McCoy Tyner (p); Jimmy Garrison, Reggie Workman (b); Ahmed Abdul-Malik (oud); Elvin Jones, Roy Haynes (d).* 11/61.

It was seemingly Coltrane's decision to record material in a club setting where a measure of direct communication with the audience was possible. For the better part of four decades, these performances at one of New York's premier jazz spots were available in scattered form and with uncertain identification of personnel. The situation seemed to be eased considerably when reissue producer Michael Cuscuna played the surviving tapes to Reggie Workman, who was able to nail the question of who played on which track.

The original *Live At The Village Vanguard* included 'Spiritual', a half-remembered song from long before, taped on the night of 3 November and featuring an extraordinary vocalized bass clarinet solo from Dolphy; after it, 'Softly As In A Morning Sunrise' without Dolphy and also taped the night before and coming with an almost physical shock, the torrential tenor outpouring of 'Chasin' The Trane', a trio piece which Tyner sits out but which, like a couple of other tracks, includes Dolphy in the final cadence. There had been nothing quite like this in jazz; no one had dared to create a solo as freely stressed, polytonal and downright ugly since the days of the early blues men, except that Coltrane was sustaining this level of invention for more than a quarter of an hour. It was an approach that sparked off instant controversy. It is now confirmed that Garrison was the bassist on 'Chasin' The Trane' and, with all the benefit of hindsight, it does have a more urgent and percussive sound than Workman's.

Other material from the November 1961 residency first appeared on *Impressions*, which was released two years later and included the mysterious 'India', on which Trane's soprano floated over twinned basses; it could almost be shawm and drones, were it not so hard-edged. The solo on 'Impressions', which was recorded on the same night as 'India' and 'Spiritual', is one of the most important in Coltrane's whole career, a staggering edifice which looks disorderly only from a certain aesthetic distance. Internally, it is as rigidly watertight and non-impressionistic as it is possible to imagine.

The 1963 release was augmented with two studio tracks recorded that year, 'Up Against The Wall' and the intensely beautiful 'After The Rain'. Thereafter, material from the 1961 Vanguard stint was to appear on compilation discs: six tracks, including another 'Greensleeves', another 'India' and 'Spiritual' from Sunday, 5 November (with guest musicians Bushell and Abdul-Malik), a version of 'Chasin' The Trane' with Dolphy in tow, and 'Brasilia', which had previously been known as 'Untitled Original', were released on a 1977 compilation, *The Other Village Vanguard Tapes*. There was more material on the previously mentioned *Trane's Modes* (including yet another 'Chasin' The Trane' on which Tyner *does* briefly appear but on which Jones is replaced by Roy Haynes) and two further items, variants on 'India' and 'Spiritual', were released on *From The Original Master Tapes* (now deleted).

It is now clear that only numbers that were thought likely to be worthy of release were actually taped at the Vanguard, so the remaining material is not as wearisomely exhaustive as might have been feared. Even so, *The Complete 1961 Village Vanguard Recordings* is a formidable document, a body of work which, like Miles's Plugged Nickel sessions, allows the devoted listener to graph changes in emphasis, temper, pitching and approach, night on night. A measure of devotion is certainly required. The set amounts to four and a half hours of concentrated music. David A. Wild's archiving work and commentary are as useful a path through it as one could wish for. One of the points he is at pains to make is how integral Dolphy was to this group, a prominence that seemed to be minimized in the original releases. This doesn't seem to have arisen from any hostility or suspicion regarding the younger man's work, simply a desire to foreground and enhance an Impulse! artist instead. Whether the quartet 'Chasin' The Trane' is better or not, it certainly is less securely Coltrane's. Just to muddy the water further, there is also 'Chasin' Another Trane' with Dolphy and (very briefly) Tyner as well. It has now surfaced on *Newport '63* (below).

In the event, there are only three previously unissued items, which may sway the final decision whether to purchase or not. All three, interestingly, feature Dolphy on bass clarinet. Wild suggests that it was Dolphy who wrote 'Miles's Mode', which is back-titled as such after its appearance on *Coltrane* the next year, but which is referred to in the Vanguard tapes as 'The Red Planet'. 'Naima' is always to be treasured, and again Dolphy almost steals the show with his solo.

****** Live At The Village Vanguard: The Master Takes**
Impulse! IMP 12512 *Coltrane; Eric Dolphy (bcl); McCoy Tyner (p); Jimmy Garrison, Reggie Workman (b); Elvin Jones (d).* 11/61.

The budget option for those who can't or won't shell out for the whole schtick. This reunites 'Spiritual', 'Softly As In A Morning Sunrise' and 'Chasin' The Trane' from the original *Live*, with 'India' and 'Impressions' from the later *Impressions*. We can't argue with the music, but we do wonder how many more ways GRP will find to slice this particular salami.

*****(*) Coltrane**
Impulse! 051215-2 *Coltrane; McCoy Tyner (p); Jimmy Garrison (b); Elvin Jones (d).* 4 & 6/62.

This is the classic quartet's first manifestation in the studio, and it is a slightly odd, even rather formulaic, record. The requisite show-tune feature for soprano this time falls to 'The Inch Worm', a rather irritating Frank Loesser song from the film, *Hans Christian Andersen*. 'Miles's Mode' (a.k.a. 'The Red Planet') is dealt with rather briskly, and 'Tunji' is one of the more forgettable items in Trane's book. Ultimately, the album stands or falls on a truly dramatic reading of the Arlen/Mercer song, 'Out Of This World'. It's an inspired if unexpected first item; it's then followed by Mal Waldron's 'Soul Eyes', a tune of grace and elegant emotion. The album's worth having for those two alone.

***** The European Tour**
Pablo Live 2208222 *Coltrane; McCoy Tyner (p); Jimmy Garrison (b); Elvin Jones (d).* 62.

*****(*) Bye Bye Blackbird**
Original Jazz Classics OJCCD 681 *As above.* 62.

***** The Paris Concert**
Original Jazz Classics OJCCD 781 *As above.* 62.

***** Ev'ry Time We Say Goodbye**
Natasha NI-4003 *As above.* 11/62.

A year after the visit with Dolphy, Trane and the quartet were back in Europe and pulling down extraordinary reviews. There are, in addition to these records, several more of questionable or indeterminate provenance, including a complete recording of the Graz concert which yields the Natasha disc. *Bye Bye Blackbird* is probably the best of the bunch, consisting of just two mammoth performances, the title-track and another 'Traneing In'. There is some valuable material on the Pablo disc, and one rarity, 'The Promise'. The Paris date has also appeared in other forms and with very mixed sound-quality; the blues, 'Mr P.C.', is terrific, the rest less so. The Charly issue of the Graz concert offers a rather better sound-quality.

*****(*) Ballads**
Impulse! 051156-2 *Coltrane; McCoy Tyner (p); Jimmy Garrison (b); Elvin Jones (d).* 9–11/62.

***** John Coltrane And Johnny Hartman**
Impulse! 051157-2 *As above, except add Johnny Hartman (v).* 3/63.

America in 1962 was no place to be black and angry. LeRoi Jones's play *Dutchman* is susceptible of a good many readings, but among other things it is about white America's ambivalent willingness to let black anger discharge itself, in order to destroy and negate it. In John Coltrane, there was a constant war between rage and beauty. Compounded by personal pain and not yet redeemed by the great spiritual awakening celebrated on *A Love Supreme*, it often saw him zig-zag between celebration and an almost nihilistic ferocity. In the second half of 1962 Coltrane had been experiencing further dental problems and was having difficulty with his articulation. Partly to work around that limitation, partly no doubt to generate some market-friendly product, Bob Thiele suggested the *Ballads* project, and also the session with singer Johnny Hartman; he had also managed to arrange the historic encounter with Duke Ellington. Coltrane had always been an exquisite ballad-player and the material he chose for the date was guaranteed to please: 'Too Young To Go Steady', 'I Fall In Love Too Easily' and a brief, flawless 'Nancy (With The Laughing Face)'. The CD bonus is 'Vilia'.

The slightly frustrating thing about the session with Hartman is that, with the exception of 'Lush Life', there isn't a vocal performance of one of the standard songs Trane had made his own. How interesting it would have been to hear Hartman singing 'I Want To Talk About You' ('My Favorite Things' sounds less probable). Ironically, too, Trane's tone seems to have hardened up again by the spring of 1963 and is obviously being kept in check, whereas on the *Ballads* date he is not quite coasting but is certainly holding back a little, ceding a lot of the foreground to Tyner, who fills the air with rolling chords and delicate right-hand fills. Garrison also seems to relish the pace and the space, producing cello-line tones that are reminiscent of Oscar Pettiford or, closer at hand, Paul Chambers. These are now available as part of the Impulse! Reissue Series, with enhanced audio, 20-bit super-mapping, gatefold design (we're quoting now, you understand), rare photos and original liner-notes. The sound *is* good, but probably not good enough to make you want to throw away your old copy.

***** Live At Birdland And The Half Note**
Cool & Blue C&B CD 101 *Coltrane; McCoy Tyner (p); Jimmy Garrison (b); Elvin Jones (d).* 5/62–5/65.

*****(*) Coltrane Live At Birdland**
Impulse! 051198-2 *As above.* 10–11/63.

Despite his hostility towards more or less everything that happened after bebop, Philip Larkin rather liked *Live At Birdland*. He did, however, suggest that Coltrane spent too much time 'rocking backwards and forwards as if in pain between two chords'. By the end of 1962, it would have taken a well-schooled musician to identify those chords reliably, but in a sense Larkin is right. LeRoi Jones's typically hyped-up liner-note to the same record points once again to the anomaly of so much beauty existing amidst so much pain. The early 1960s were a strange time for black Americans. The club tracks on the album – and, despite the title, there are a couple of studio items as well – were recorded a month before JFK's assassination, with the country poised between hope and violence. The end of 'Afro-Blue' is an intense cry of pain and blame, commingled with defiance; and 'The Promise', the soprano feature heard on the European tour the autumn before, has a more ironic sound in an American setting. By this stage

Trane was able to play the more familiar standard tunes in his bag with a trance-like freedom. 'I Want To Talk About You', which appears in different versions on both discs, is a million miles from the Billy Eckstine song; on the Impulse! version, it ends with a fiercely intense, unaccompanied coda. Jones perceptively describes the way Coltrane's music of this period seems to break through an impenetrable fog of sound with a sudden, almost miraculous directness of statement. The two studio tracks are powerful examples; 'Alabama' was, as is well known, inspired by the death of schoolchildren in a bomb outrage in Birmingham, and 'Your Lady' was a love poem to Alice McLeod, shortly to be his wife; a less celebrated theme than 'Naima', but no less beautiful.

The Cool & Blue disc brings together performances from quite a long span of time – and then includes them out of chronological sequence. 'My Favorite Things' and 'Body And Soul' come from June 1962, and it is surely not fanciful to note the dramatic darkening of intent between these performances and the album's closing 'Song Of Praise' from May 1965. Along with the Eckstine tune, the other item from 1963 is 'One Up And One Down', a tune which somehow seems made for Eric Dolphy, who was off at the time making his own next – and, as it turned out, next-to-last – jump forward.

***(*) Newport '63

Impulse! GRP 11282 *Coltrane; Eric Dolphy (as); McCoy Tyner (p); Jimmy Garrison, Reggie Workman (b); Roy Haynes (d).* 11/61, 7/63.

Not to be confused with *New Thing At Newport*, which was recorded at the Festival two years later and is shared with Archie Shepp. All the tracks from 1963 had been available before, on the Impulse! albums, *Selflessness* and *To The Beat Of A Different Drummer*. The different drummer in this case was Haynes, who was standing in for the increasingly erratic Jones, a heroin user. Haynes has a lighter, springier sound and consequently these three very familiar themes – 'I Want To Talk About You', 'My Favorite Things' and 'Impressions' – are rather differently channelled. Coltrane seems to shadow-box with the drummer, placing his notes differently. Tyner and Garrison aren't well served by the recording, but they're audible and both seem to be playing well.

The anomaly of a 1961 reference and the unquoted presence of Dolphy and Workman is explained by the makeweight track, 'Chasin' Another Trane', a reworking of the big blowing theme from the Village Vanguard residency. It has previously been issued on *Trane's Modes* and also now on the Vanguard *Complete* set. Just to confirm that we are awake, McCoy Tyner is not listed in the track credits on this CD. He *is* there, but just for two choruses; then he makes his excuses and leaves.

**** Afro-Blue Impressions

Pablo Live 2620101 2CD *Coltrane; McCoy Tyner (p); Jimmy Garrison (b); Elvin Jones (d).* 63.

It may seem strange to describe a Coltrane record as 'professional', but this is one of the most polished performances in the canon. No real screaming highs, no dark inscapes, but rugged, straightforward versions of 'Naima', 'Impressions' and, not much represented in the live discography, 'Cousin Mary' from *Giant Steps*. There is also a foretaste of 'Lonnie's Lament', which was to be included on *Crescent* the following spring. The 1963 European tour has always been regarded as something of an anti-climax after the remarkable tours of '61 and '62. Not so, we find.

***(*) Crescent

Impulse! 051200-2 *Coltrane; McCoy Tyner (p); Jimmy Garrison (b); Elvin Jones (d).* 4 & 6/64.

Of all the new-generation CDs, this is the one which seems to have gained most from 20-bit super-mapping, yielding a brighter sound and opening up a silver lining in what has always seemed to be Coltrane's most melancholy record. *Crescent* is often seen as the dark hour that comes just before the spiritual dawning of *A Love Supreme*. 'Wise One' and 'Lonnie's Lament' are certainly among the least effusive of his tunes, drawn once again from memories of field calls, spirituals and spontaneous blues; but 'Bessie's Blues' emerges ever more vividly, a flash of light like a morning star. We are not sure what the exact circumstances were, but *Crescent* seems to have had a troubled birth. The band recorded versions of all five numbers on the album – and a head arrangement of 'Song Of Praise' – at a session on 27 April 1964. Two of those masters no longer exist, 'Crescent' and 'Bessie's Blues' being replaced with shorter versions on the LP. Unless purely technical concerns intervened, it's possible that Jones was the factor. He seems wildly inconsistent on the record, out of focus and removed one minute, but also claiming his first significant written feature on 'The Drum Thing'. Either way, a very significant record.

♛ **** A Love Supreme

Impulse! 051155-2 *Coltrane; McCoy Tyner (p); Jimmy Garrison (b); Elvin Jones (d).* 12/64.

The first records in Coltrane's career as a leader were the work of a man who had submerged himself in heroin and alcohol and who had mortgaged his physical health as a result. If, as superstition and a measure of biological science suggest, people are transformed every seven years, then Coltrane is something like proof positive. Few spiritual breakthroughs have been so hard won, but he had also reinvented himself technically in that time, creating a body of music in which simplicity of materials generates an almost absurd complexity of harmonic and expressive detail. This is quintessentially true of *A Love Supreme*. Its foundations seem almost childishly slight, and yet what one hears is a majestic outpouring of sound, couched in a language that is often brutally violent, replete with split notes, multiphonics and toneless breath noises.

It is not a piece that can be separated from the creator's intentions and programme. Coltrane explicitly stated that the final movement, 'Psalm', should be understood as an instrumental expression of the text that was printed on the sleeve. The rest has the pace of a liturgical act of the kind that might have been encountered in a field mission. 'Acknowledgement' begins with a sweeping fanfare that will return at the close. A sonorous 8-bar theme creates the background to the four simple notes – 'A love su-preme' – which have become some of the most familiar in modern jazz. Stated by Garrison, they are re-worked and varied through the scale by Coltrane, whose solo defies categorization. The chant is husky, strangely moving, and seems to occupy a different space and imprint from the hectic movement of the rhythm section. If this was to be Garrison's finest hour with the group, it is probably Jones's as well. He plays figures of great complexity that seem to change shape and direction every time one listens to the record.

They are slightly simpler on 'Resolution', but only in the interest of piling up the emotional pressure still more. Coltrane's entry has an almost violent impact, and in LP days it was difficult to find the resolve to flip the disc over and essay the other side, even though it is clear that the music is left hanging, still bereft of the other sort of resolution. 'Pursuance' takes us into the dark wood, a troubled, mid-life moment. From now until the very end, the rhythms are anxious, fractured, unsure. Horn and piano stagger like pilgrims from one brief point of rest to another. The closing 'Psalm' has an almost symphonic richness, culminating in a final 'Amen', a two-note figure in which a second saxophone (said to be Archie Shepp's) joins Coltrane. A partial restatement of the opening fanfare provides a reminder of the road travelled and also of the circularity of all such journeys.

Even extreme familiarity fails to tarnish *A Love Supreme*. It is without precedent and parallel, and though it must also be one of the best-known jazz records of all time, it somehow remains remote from critical pigeonholing. At the same time one yearns to hear more from these sessions and simultaneously that their mystery will be preserved. We have suggested before that the record documents a group at that moment of maximum energy before it sunders. Certainly, Tyner no longer seems at ease, and Jones is almost too forceful, too over-determining. The original release credited Coltrane alone and mentioned Tyner, Garrison and Jones only by their first names, reinforcing the idea that *A Love Supreme* was a great personal testament rather than a group effort. That's no longer seen to be the case. If all great art is the product of grace under pressure, then here the music seems to emerge out of several atmospheres, heavy, almost choking, but immensely concentrated and rich.

***(*) The John Coltrane Quartet Plays

Impulse! 051214-2 *Coltrane; McCoy Tyner (p); Art Davis, Jimmy Garrison (b); Elvin Jones (d).* 2 & 5/65.

A bare two months after completing *A Love Supreme*, Coltrane was back in the studio. Not surprisingly, the intention seems to have been to record another standards package. There was to be something of a hiatus before the set was completed, and in the event it included the original theme, 'Brasilia' (spelt with a 'z' in this version), from the Village Vanguard days, and also a complete version of 'Song Of Praise' which had been tabled and recorded as a head on the *Crescent* date. What problems Coltrane was experiencing or degree of emotional and creative burn-out he might have felt after *A Love Supreme*, we don't know. It's clear that, as ever, his mind is searching in new directions. The first session on *Plays* yielded a version of 'Nature Boy' with two bass players. The following day, a master version was cut, along with the Bricusse/Newley 'Feelin' Good', on which Davis also appears. It wasn't until 17 May that the remaining tracks were recorded, though in the meantime Coltrane and the quartet (without Davis) had included 'Nature Boy' in a set at the Village Gate. All three versions are now included on the CD, along with 'Feelin' Good', which was rejected. The obligatory show-tune this time out is the odious 'Chim Chim Cheree', another soprano essay, but this time inexplicably truncated, the shortest thing on the album; it may be that Coltrane decided to narrow his parameters slightly or it may simply be that he was now tiring of this long-standing formula. *Plays* is a fine record and the interaction of the group, both standard and augmented, is faultless. It is, however, a difficult item to place personally and artistically.

***(*) The Gentle Side Of John Coltrane

Impulse! 051107-2 *Coltrane; Duke Ellington, McCoy Tyner (p); Aaron Bell, Jimmy Garrison (b); Roy Haynes, Elvin Jones, Sam Woodyard (d); Johnny Hartman (v).* 62–65.

The Gentle Side is one of those records which – like *Mellow Miles* – seems to miss the point. It is, however, eminently approachable, even by those who are unpersuaded by Trane's more incendiary side, and it offers a pleasant, late-night option for those who've found *Ascension* to be a little abrasive for dinner parties. In addition to material from *Ballads* and the Hartman date, and the eternal 'Soul Eyes', there is 'After The Rain' from *Impressions*, 'Wise One' from *Crescent*, and 'Dear Lord' from *Transition*. Good value.

♛ **** Ascension

Impulse! 543413-2 *Coltrane; Freddie Hubbard, Dewey Johnson (t); Marion Brown, John Tchicai (as); Pharoah Sanders, Archie Shepp (ts); Donald Garrett (bcl, b); Joe Brazil (b, perc); McCoy Tyner (p); Art Davis, Jimmy Garrison (b); Frank Butler, Elvin Jones (d); Juno Lewis (perc, v).* 6/65, 10/65.

There is nothing else like *Ascension* in Coltrane's work; indeed, there is nothing quite like *Ascension* in the history of jazz. Ornette Coleman's *Free Jazz* experiment is almost mannerly and formal by comparison. By the middle of 1965, Coltrane had done as much with the quartet, technically speaking, as he seemed likely to. Even so, no one could have foreseen what was to emerge from the session of 28 June. If ever Eric Dolphy was missed, it must have been on this occasion, but Dolphy had died in Berlin the previous year and the one player who might have wholly understood what Coltrane was about was no more.

In the simplest way, *Ascension* continues what Coltrane had been doing on *A Love Supreme*. The pattern of notes which begins the piece is a clear reference to the fanfare to 'Acknowledgement', but the vast collective improvisation which follows is almost antithetical to the highly personal, almost confessional quality of the earlier piece. The group was similarly constituted to the 'double quartet' which recorded *Free Jazz*, though much less schematic. Coltrane devised a situation in which signals – from Hubbard and Tyner, in the main – could be given to switch modes, introducing new scalar and harmonic patterns. Soloists had a measure of freedom, and distinct ideas do seem to emerge within a broken field of gestural sounds. Everything is determined by the first few bars; nothing is determined entirely. It is a work that synthesizes the rules of classic jazz with the freedoms of the New Thing. Its success is difficult to gauge; its impact is total, overwhelming.

As with much of Coltrane's association with Impulse!, the circumstances of release are now hopelessly confused. It seems that Coltrane had originally authorized the release of the first version recorded, and this was issued in late 1965 as Impulse! AS-95. Then the saxophonist decided that the 'wrong' master had been used, and the second take was substituted, leaving 'Ascension – Edition I' as a piece of jazz apocrypha. Hearing them on this compilation, it is difficult to argue with Marion Brown's support of Coltrane's position. The second take is more cohesive and more expressive.

The involvement of players like Brown and Tchicai – and Shepp and Sanders in particular – afforded a first chance to hear the 'school of Coltrane' in action. Predictably, no one sounds anything like the master, but the overall impact of the piece does suggest that warriors were gathering round the standard.

Individual performances serve a very different purpose here than on previous records and on other large-scale projects of the time like Coleman's. On *Free Jazz*, solos emerge out of the ensemble and impose a rather normative structure. Here, they provide an internal commentary that does not even threaten to disrupt the integrity of the piece. The main obvious difference between the two versions is the order of play. On the revised release (Edition II) the solos run: Coltrane, Johnson, Sanders, Hubbard, Brown, Shepp, Tchicai, Tyner and a bass duet (try to imagine the impact of *that*), while on Edition I Shepp and Tchicai are in front of Brown, and Elvin Jones solos near the end. Coltrane must have had reasons for his preference (though even he seems to have been uncertain), but there is not so very much separating the two versions qualitatively. After a time, they resemble a rock formation seen from a subtly different angle, but still unchangeably the same outcrop.

If Coltrane had not reached his fortieth birthday, if his already diminishing lifespan had gone no further than the end of 1965, he would still have been guaranteed greatness on the strength of *A Love Supreme* and *Ascension* alone. There is no doubt which of the two is more approachable. Probably ten times more people own *A Love Supreme* than have even heard of the later masterpiece. That is one measure. The sheer scale and range of Coltrane's vision and ambition is another, no less important.

(Formerly coupled with *Kulu Se Mama* in a bigger edition, *Ascension* was restored to its unenhanced state as we went to press. *Kulu Se Mama* will be relisted next time.)

*** New Thing At Newport

Impulse! 543414-2 *Coltrane; McCoy Tyner (p); Jimmy Garrison (b); Elvin Jones (d); other material by the Archie Shepp Quartet.* 7/65.

Ascension was recorded on 28 June. Less than a week later, the quartet appeared on stage at Newport. Introduced by Fr Norman O'Connor, who seems to think that Elvin Jones is a 'newcomer' to jazz, they kick into 'One Down, One Up', the same theme as 'One Up And One Down' on the Cool & Blue Birdland disc, and not so very different from the reading there. The piece that reveals the proximity of *Ascension* is a barbed version of 'My Favorite Things', which was originally released on the *Mastery Of John Coltrane* compilation and was added to this two-header only when it was transferred to CD. Just the two tracks by Coltrane; the remainder of the material is by Archie Shepp, whose discipleship was already paying rich dividends.

**** Sun Ship

Impulse! 051167-2 *Coltrane; McCoy Tyner (p); Jimmy Garrison (b); Elvin Jones (d).* 8/65.

This remains one of the least known of Coltrane's albums, recorded in between *Ascension* and the 'Om' and 'Kulu Se Mama' sessions. There is a short nugget of conversation before 'Dearly Beloved', a minor-key ballad which sees Coltrane working on top of a gently unfolding, continuous rhythm. The angle of attack is much sharper on the title-piece, and it is tempting to wonder (not just because of the title) whether Trane was once again listening to his lost creative twin, John Gilmore. Certainly the resemblance here is quite overt. The solo, pitched very high in the *altissimo* range, is based on a four-note figure that might suggest any number of genealogies. 'Attaining' is quieter, a freely pulsed minor blues which, as the sterling David Wild suggests, is generically related to several other of Coltrane's folk-tradition pieces. Its climax is extraordinary. A fourth star may seem extravagant, but it's high time this fine record was better known.

***(*) Live In Seattle

Impulse! 21462 2CD *Coltrane; Pharoah Sanders (ts); Donald Garrett (bcl); McCoy Tyner (p); Jimmy Garrison (b); Elvin Jones (d).* 9/65.

It is tempting to suggest that the whole grunge movement, fomented by those who reached their majority in the mid-1980s, represented the genetic fall-out of Coltrane's visit to Washington State 20 years earlier. From now to the end of his life, Coltrane's live performances were to be at times agonizingly protracted. 'Evolution' lasts more than half an hour and is oddly uninvolving for much of its length, save for a wonderful moment when the three horns demonstrate the kind of interweaving line and block texture that was attempted on *Ascension*. Garrett is not Dolphy, but he has certainly learned something of Dolphy's idiom. Sanders is not quite flat out yet, perhaps saving himself for the Vanguard and Japanese dates of the following year. By this stage, Tyner is lost. He plays manfully both in Seattle and in the subsequent studio set (which is included in *The Major Works*), but this is no longer his music. Even Jones, once so ubiquitously evident, has dropped into the shadows.

**** First Meditations

Impulse! GRP 11182 *Coltrane; McCoy Tyner (p); Jimmy Garrison (b); Elvin Jones (d).* 2/65.

***(*) Meditations

Impulse! 051199-2 *As above, except add Pharoah Sanders (ts), Rashied Ali (d).* 11/65.

These two related sessions, which cover essentially the same material, bridge the end of the classic quartet and the opening phase of the new, augmented group with Sanders and Ali. This is music that emerges directly out of *A Love Supreme*, tiny, motivic ideas, often stated by Garrison, generating huge, sprawling improvisations, scalar segments proliferating into enormous harmonic fissions. In February 1965 (which, remember, is the same month as the preliminary sessions for *Plays*) Coltrane and the quartet recorded a version of a new five-part suite consisting of 'Love', 'Compassion', 'Joy', 'Consequences' and 'Serenity'. When he returned to the studio in November, the saxophonist substituted the unbelievably turbulent 'The Father And The Son And The Holy Ghost' for the original opening movement, and moved 'Love' to what was the start of the continuous second side of the released LP.

The most important difference, apart from the addition of a second horn (an initiative that almost began on *A Love Supreme*) and of Ali's almost unpulsed, pure-sound drumming, is that the movements are run together almost seamlessly, whereas on *First Meditations* the breaks are quite distinct even though the sections are played without pause. On grounds of simple beauty and perhaps out of sentimental attachment to the group that was breaking up, the early version is to be preferred, though it clearly no longer represented what Coltrane wanted to do.

The CD of the February session includes an alternative version of 'Joy', the piece that sets in motion the final, multi-part movement. It's obvious that Coltrane is already trying to escape the sticky webs which Jones had woven for him. Had the old and new drummers been able to play together, 'Father/Son/Holy Ghost' suggests that something quite out of the ordinary might have occurred. As it is, *Meditations* and its Ur-text represent the final – and this time absolute – split between Coltrane and the rhythm of bebop.

****** Live At The Village Vanguard Again!**

Impulse! 051213-2 *Coltrane; Pharoah Sanders (ts); Alice Coltrane (p); Jimmy Garrison (b); Rashied Ali (d); Emmanuel Rahid (perc).* 5/66.

That arch-conservative critic of jazz, Philip Larkin, was disposed to like elements of *Live At Birdland*; he considered this set, taped five years after the exhaustive 1961 sessions, to represent in triple-distilled form the 'blended insolence and ugliness' of the New Wave. Ugliness is debatable; there is not a scrap of insolence about it, unless it be to play such a passionate and beautiful poem to one wife while another is playing piano behind you. Much has been said about what the one-time Alice McLeod brought to the group. Like her harp and organ playing, she tends to work in blocks of sound-colour rather than linear developments. That is partially evident on 'Naima', but it comes out most strikingly on a huge deconstruction of what had been *the* Coltrane standard. This 'My Favorite Things' is almost the *reductio ad absurdum*. The version in Japan (see below) is almost the equivalent, if this isn't too unfortunate an analogy, of bombing Nagasaki just days after laying waste to Hiroshima. The point has been made, even if Jimmy Garrison's long, rambling introduction threatens never to clear the floor. Ali is already a key element, though here he has a percussionist as foil. It is easy to make the mistake of thinking that this is from the earlier Vanguard sessions – easy, that is, if one doesn't check personnel or listen to any of the music. It is drastically, diametrically different. There is no forward motion, no predetermined resolution; there is only music, always and eternally at the ear. Its insistence is both its triumph and, at those few moments when concentration lapses, yes, its hint of insolence.

***** Living Space**

Impulse! 051246-2 *Coltrane; McCoy Tyner (p); Jimmy Garrison (b); Elvin Jones (d).* 65.

The last word from the classic quartet, and not much more than a selection of largely untitled and generic oddments. Easy to romanticize a piece called 'The Last Blues' when there was in fact still a mile or two left on the extraordinary journey of John Coltrane, but it brings an intriguing and often very beautiful album to a satisfying end. Once again, the label have tried and failed to capture the quality of the original Impulse! covers.

****** The Classic Quartet: The Complete Impulse! Studio Recordings**

GRP 280 8CD *Coltrane; McCoy Tyner (p); Jimmy Garrison (b); Elvin Jones (p); plus Art Davis (b); Roy Haynes (d).* 61–65.

Important to register that this is *not* the compleat Coltrane on Impulse!. The 66 cuts do include alternatives and some other unissued material, but only of the quartet itself and not of those augmented sessions when other players were recruited, so look in vain for *Ascension*, and for the sets with Duke Ellington and Johnny Hartman. The only exceptions are when Roy Haynes was standing in for the troubled Jones and some extra bass from Art Davis. The sessions are organized chronologically and almost symbolically from the residual prettiness of 'Greensleeves' to the fractured intensity of 'Living Space', and there is obviously considerable merit in hearing the music develop (and occasionally regress) rather than in the issued form, which often jumped out of or mixed the actual sequence of recording. However, the original releases are so much a part of the mind-set of a whole musical generation that it is hard to forget them, and most committed Coltrane fans will probably quickly return to the individual LPs. That said, this is a magnificently packaged and organized document and it stands as a memorial to one of the truly great groups in the history of jazz.

*****(*) Priceless Jazz**

GRP 9874 *As above.* 61–65.

***** More Priceless Jazz**

GRP 059915-2 *As above.* 61–65.

The first of these is another good introductory record, though it does seem to concentrate on the darker and more brooding side of Coltrane's output for Impulse!, which was an interesting production decision. 'Naima' is included alongside the first movement of *A Love Supreme*, 'Alabama', 'Big Nick', 'Dear Lord', 'Bessie's Blues' and 'After The Rain'. By contrast, the second volume is more anonymous and almost entirely devoted to standards, 'Up 'Gainst The Wall' being the perverse exception.

****** Interstellar Space**

Impulse! 543414-2 *Coltrane; Rashied Ali (d, perc).* 2/67.

The final masterpiece. Only long after his death did Andrew Cyrille start to explore in detail the rhythmic implications of some of Coltrane's late work. It had been axiomatic that he had taken bebop harmony as far as humanly possible, and then some. The records after *Africa/Brass* are very largely devoted to a search for the time beyond time, an uncountable pulse which would represent a pure musical experience not chopped into bars and choruses. Only with the induction of the unconventionally tutored Rashied Ali did such a thing become practically possible. With Coltrane on tenor and Ali running a gamut of percussion, this is the purest sound-experience of all the records. 'Mars', the first of the planetary sequence, is characterized as the 'battlefield of the cosmic giants', and that is exactly how it sounds, with huge, clashing brass tones and a dense clangour from the drum kit. 'Venus' is appropriately quieter, amorous and almost delicate, with Ali barely scuffing his cymbals with wire brushes. 'Jupiter (Variation)' was known to Coltrane fans even when *Interstellar Space* was out of catalogue, being included on one of the *Mastery Of John Coltrane* compilations of out-takes and ephemera. The release version is the shortest item on the set, a stately expression of 'supreme wisdom', coming immediately before the climactic evocation of joy that is 'Saturn'. 'Leo' is known in a live version from the Tokyo concerts but wasn't on the original album.

***** Expression**

Impulse! 11312 *Coltrane; Pharoah Sanders (ts, picc, perc); Alice Coltrane (p); Jimmy Garrison (b); Rashied Ali (d).* 2 & 3/67.

****(*) Stellar Regions**

Impulse! 051169-2 *As above.*

It would be wonderful if the final studio sessions really had represented the final wisdom of the greatest saxophonist since Parker, but *Expression* and the additional material issued as *Stellar Regions* (like the track titles, named long afterwards by Alice Coltrane) is a murky, often undistinguished work. There's some interest in hearing Coltrane on flute ('To Be', this from a man born in Hamlet, North Carolina) and there are a couple more instrumental quiddities, but what little of the music really convinces occurs on 'Offering' and 'Expression' itself, both of which are notably becalmed, almost resigned. 'Number One' is a new addition on CD. The suspicious thing about *Stellar Regions* is that the best track is 'Offering' again, not an alternative but the identical version which appears on *Expression*. This isn't so much sharp practice (God knows, GRP must have enough stuff salted away) as desperation, an attempt to rescue an otherwise dud album which even falls down on the typography of a pastiche cover. The talking point is 'Tranesonic', which appears in two takes. Though credited with tenor only (and there are no further flute tracks), the sound seems smaller, fatter, more tightly focused and, though most of the pitching is comfortably within tenor range, the positioning suggests a different horn, presumably an alto. This was confirmed on BBC Radio 3 by Evan Parker, though at least one correspondent vehemently denies it, as if alto playing were an unforgivable offence. Oddly, and quite unlike much of the Impulse! catalogue, *Expression* manages to sound worse on CD than on the notoriously muddy LP. *Stellar Regions* is an improvement, though back-to-back auditions of 'Offering' suggest that the difference is too slight even to be cosmetic. An achievement as great as this somehow calls for a better conclusion, but life and art both conform to an inexorable logic of decline. Coltrane might still have been playing in the '70s, '80s, '90s; might, even as you read, be shuffling out to play 'My Favorite Things' for the hundred-and-umpteenth time. The fact is that he isn't; but what he did during that extraordinary, packed decade cannot be changed or gainsaid or diluted by slow, inevitable compromise.

Ken Colyer (1928–88)

CORNET, TRUMPET, GUITAR, VOCAL

The purist's purist, Colyer was born in Great Yarmouth and taught himself the cornet. He co-founded the Crane River Jazz Band, before joining the merchant navy and deserting in New Orleans, where he met idols like George Lewis. In 1953 he began bandleading in Britain with Chris Barber and subsequently led numerous bands based around the New Orleans sound. For a time in the '50s he also played guitar in a skiffle offshoot. His Studio 51 Club was an important traditional venue. Ill-health dogged his later years, but he stuck to his musical principles, always.

***** In The Beginning**

Lake LACD 014 *Colyer; Chris Barber, Ed O'Donnell (tb); Acker Bilk, Monty Sunshine (cl); Lonnie Donegan, Diz Disley (bj); Jim Bray, Dick Smith (b); Stan Greig, Ron Bowden (d).* 9/53–9/54.

***** The Unknown New Orleans Sessions**

504 CD 23 *Colyer; Albert Artigues (t); Jack Delaney (tb); Raymond Burke (cl); Stanley Mendelson (p); Edmond Souchon (g, v); Bill Huntington, Lawrence Marrero (bj); Dick Allen (tba); Alcide Slow Drag Pavageau (b); Harold 'Katz' Maestri, Charles Merriweather, Abbie Brunies (d).* 12/52–2/53.

(***) The Complete 1953 Recordings

504 CD 53 *Colyer; Jarrison Brazlee (tb); Emile Barnes (cl); Bill Huntington (bj); Albert Glenny, George Fortier (b); Albert Jiles (d).* 2/53.

Colyer has a unique place in British jazz. Nobody has ever been more revered than he in local circles, and few were so righteously dogmatic about their music. At a time when the trad boom of the 1950s was just getting under way, he abjured such 'modern' role models as Armstrong and Morton and insisted on the earlier New Orleans methods of George Lewis and Bunk Johnson. Colyer's records from the period emerge as an intriguing muddle of stiff British orthodoxy and something that finds a genuine accord with the music that obsessed him. The 504 sessions were made on Colyer's fabled visit to New Orleans – where he even spent time in the local jail for breaking immigration laws – and find the young cornetist sitting in with various local players. The tracks on *Unknown New Orleans Sessions* were lost for years and this is the first appearance for most of them: there's a real vitality and a bluff panache about the playing, with Colyer's deliberately primitive lead firmed up by the sheer force of his obsessions. Listeners should be warned, though, that the sound is inevitably pretty dingy. It's even worse on *The Complete 1953 Recordings*, which has all the music from two evenings spent at Emile Barnes's house on La Harpe Street. Colyer plays well with some of his spiritual forebears but it's hard to hear what's going on for much of the time. *In The Beginning* stands as an important document for British jazz if only for the musicians involved – Barber, whose subsequent disagreements with the trumpeter led him to assume command of a different edition of the band; Bilk, whose erratic clarinet had yet to acquire the distinctive glow of his later records; Sunshine, who stayed with Barber and has since enjoyed an immortal reputation with European trad audiences; and Donegan, who became the major name in skiffle. If the music is comparatively stilted, its formal strictness pays off in the music's terseness.

**** The Decca Skiffle Sessions**

Lake LACD 07 *Colyer; Bob Kelly (p); Alexis Korner (g, mand); Johnny Bastable (g, bj); Mickey Ashman, Ron Ward (b); Bill Colyer, Colin Bowden (wbd).* 6/54–11/57.

***** Sensation!**

Lake LACD 1 *Colyer; Mac Duncan (tb); Ian Wheeler (cl); Ray Foxley (p); Johnny Bastable (bj); Dick Smith, Ron Ward (b); Stan Greig, Colin Bowden (d).* 4/55–5/59.

***** Marching Back To New Orleans**

Lake LACD 21 *As above, except add Bob Wallis, Sunny Murray (t), Mick Clift (tb), Dave Keir (as), Derek Easton (ts), Maurice Benn (tba), Neil Millet, Stan Greig (d).* 4/55–9/57.

***** Up Jumped The Devil**

Upbeat URCD114 *Colyer; Mac Duncan (tb); Ian Wheeler (cl); Ray Foxley (p); Johnny Bastable (bj); Ron Ward (b); Colin Bowden (d).* 57–58.

***** The Famous Manchester Free Trade Hall Concert 1957**

504 CD51/2 *As above, except add George Lewis (cl).* 4/57.

*****(*) Studio 51 Revisited**

Lake LACD 25 *As above, except omit Lewis.* 58.

***** Serenading Auntie**

Upbeat URCD 111 *As above, except add Graham Stewart (tb), Sammy Rimington (cl), Dick Smith (b), Bill Colyer (wbd).* 6/55–8/60.

Colyer worked hard at his subject and, as the 1950s progressed, his music became a genre unto itself. The most useful reissues are *Lonesome Road, Marching Back To New Orleans* and *Sensation!*, effectively an alternative live version of the unavailable *Colyer Plays Standards*, although much of the material – 'Underneath The Bamboo Tree' and 'Bluebells Goodbye', to name two – would hardly be classed as standards in most band books. *Marching Back To New Orleans* opens with seven tracks from the session which produced *Sensation!* – including an uproarious 'Red Wing' – and then includes the entire date by the Omega Brass Band, where Colyer tried his hand at an 'authentic' New Orleans parade band: shambling, stentorian, it's a bizarre sound, and actually surprisingly close to the genuine article. Typically, Colyer refused to pick obvious tunes, and chose instead 'Isle Of Capri', 'Tiger Rag' and 'Gettysburg March', which occasionally rise in an almost hysterical crescendo. *Sensation!* collects various single and EP tracks, including all four from the sought-after *They All Played Ragtime* EP, which is in some ways Colyer's most distinctive achievement: it includes such rarities as 'Kinklets' (recorded by Bunk Johnson at his final session), 'Fig Leaf Rag' and what might be the first jazz version of 'The Entertainer', many years before Joshua Rifkin and *The Sting*. This is an ensemble music: Colyer was a reluctant soloist, and although Wheeler and Duncan are lively they struggle a bit when left on their own. Foxley is actually the most impressive improviser on the basis of *Lonesome Road*, reissued on LP some years ago but still to reach CD. Colyer's steady, unflashy lead, and the four-square but oddly hypnotic beat of the rhythm section (using a banjo to the end), still manage to add their own character. The one avoidable disc is *Skiffle Sessions*, which enshrines Colyer's heartfelt if bizarre interest in that movement. His own guitar playing goes on like a machine, and though Korner, who at least knew how to play feasible blues, is also on hand, this is for the curious only.

Up Jumped The Devil documents various live sessions at Studio 51. This was one of the best Colyer bands and, though the sound is rather muffled, their hard-won vitality breaks through to surprising effect. They manage to sustain 'Milneburg Joys' for chorus after chorus and, as sometimes happens in this kind of jazz, the sheer determination of the music becomes almost hypnotic. Much the same thing happens on *Studio 51 Revisited*, the echoes of a single night at the club in 1958. The sound is surprisingly good, considering it was captured by one microphone slung from the ceiling, and again the music is all of a piece – tough, committed, rather unsmiling but rewarding on its own terms. The concert tour with George Lewis was another legendary moment, and 504's documentation of their Manchester show, spread across two CDs, reeks of authenticity. The enthusiasm of the audience is infectious, and Lewis himself responds with his best form, even on chestnuts he'd played countless times. The sound is sometimes distant but mostly quite clear and clean.

Serenading Auntie splices together material from five different Colyer dates for the BBC (radio and even one TV session) over a five-year period. Some of the music seems a bit thin, as if they were cutting some of the tunes short, but on the ragtime material particularly the spirit abides, and there is one of Colyer's most wistful vocals on 'In The Evening'. One of the sessions sounds like it's on a radio that's drifting on- and off-station, but the rest are all right.

****(*) When I Leave The World Behind**

Lake LACD 19 *Colyer; Geoff Cole (tb); Sammy Rimington (cl); Johnny Bastable (bj); Ron Ward (b); Pete Ridge (d).* 3/63.

*****(*) Colyer's Pleasure**

Lake LACD 34 *As above.* 62–63.

***** On Tour**

GHB BCD-16 *As above, except Bill Cole (b), Brian Hetherington (d) replace Ward and Ridge.* 65.

If everything on *When I Leave The World Behind* was as good as a terrifically swinging account of J.C. Higginbotham's 'Give Me Your Telephone Number', this would be a classic record. As it is, it's an interesting memento of Colyer's 1960s band, playing a broad range of rags, King Oliver tunes, and other odds and ends. Rimington weaves interesting lines all through the music, Cole is a strong, hard-bitten trombonist; only the rhythm section, bothered by the pedestrian Ridge, is weaker. The recording, salvaged by Paul Adams from some private tapes, is variable and rather boomy, but it's listenable enough.

Much better is *Colyer's Pleasure* – indeed, this has claims to be Colyer's best available CD. The band never sounded better in a studio (actually a pub back room), with Colyer and Rimington loud and clear, and the excellent set-list gets a varied and inventive treatment: 'Dardanella' is a classic performance. The original LP (once issued on the old budget label, Society) is augmented by five previously unissued acetates by the same band.

On Tour finds them in Malmö, Sweden, before a small but keen audience. It's a particularly interesting programme – 'Minstrel Man', 'Hilarity Rag', 'Swipsey Cakewalk', 'Ghost Soldier' – and the band sound in fine shape, although Hetherington's drums are on the brash side. Another surviving amateur tape: Colyer's archivists have always been a diligent crowd.

***** Out Of Nowhere**

Lake LACD101 *Colyer; Geoff Cole (tb); Sammy Rimington (cl); Richard Simmons (p); John Bastable (bj); Bill Cole (b); Bryan Hetherington (d).* 4/66.

A solid Colyer date with six extra tracks from the original session which never saw release. The horns are in good temper, Rimington especially, but the rhythm section fare less well and Simmons's playing is little short of shambolic (admittedly it's a dreadful piano).

**** One For My Baby**

Joy JOY-CD-1 *Colyer; Geoff Cole (tb); Tony Pyke (cl); John Bastable (bj); Bill Cole (b); Malcolm Murphy (d).* 1–2/69.

****(*) Live At The Dancing Slipper**
Azure AZ-CD-25 *As above.* 69.

**** Spirituals Vol. 1**
Joy JOY-CD-5 *As above, except Ken Ames (b) replaces Cole.* 69.

**** Spirituals Vol. 2**
Joy JOY-CD-6 *As above.* 69.

**** Watch That Dirty Tone Of Yours – There Are Ladies Present**
Joy JOY-CD-3 *As above.* 5/70.

**** At The Thames Hotel**
Joy JOY-CD-4 *As above.* 5/70.

****(*) Ragtime Revisited**
Joy JOY-CD-2 *As above, except add Ray Smith (p).* 70.

These are solid examples of Colyer at work and there's little here to detain any but the fanatic: the 1950s music is fresher, and the band with Rimington had a superior front line. Colyer was already suffering from poor health and he sometimes lacks the stamina to sustain an album's worth of material. Still, there are better moments on most of the records. The first *Spirituals* has a firmer grip, the *Thames Hotel* live set has a neat set-list, and the *Ragtime Revisited* disc continues Colyer's grappling with the rag form to create a viable bridge between styles. The sound is much as it was on the original LPs and, for those who were there, the two live sets (*Thames Hotel* and *One For My Baby*) will rekindle the atmosphere. So will *Live At The Dancing Slipper*, a favourite Colyer haunt in Nottingham, and, although there's an awful version of 'The Peanut Vendor', things go quite well. Colyer's original sleeve-note also captures the nature of the man better than anything.

****(*) More Of Ken Colyer And His Handpicked Jazzmen**
Ken Colyer Trust KCT3CD *Colyer; Mike Sherbourne (tb); Jack Gilbert (cl); Jim McIntosh (bj); Ray Holland (b); Tony Scriven (d).* 1/72.

***** Boston Church Service**
GHB BCD-351 *Colyer; Barry Palser (tb); Sammy Rimington (cl); Ray Smith (p); Pete Morcom (bj); Alan Jones (b); Colin Bowden (d).* 6/72.

**** Very Very Live At The 100 Club**
Upbeat URCD 130 *Colyer; Keith Avison (tb); Sammy Rimington (cl); Ron Weatherburn (p); John Griffith (bj); Annie Hawkins (b); Colin Bowden (d).* 6/72.

***** Won't You Come Along With Me**
Ken Colyer Trust KCT5CD *Colyer; Dale Vickers (tb); Chris Blount (cl); Pete Trevor (p); John Bly, Dave Brennan (bj); Harry Slater (b); Mike Ellis (d).* 10/73–12/77.

***** Ken Colyer In Holland**
Music Mecca 1032-2 *Colyer; Cor Fabrie (tb); Butch Thompson (cl); Jos Koster (bj); Ad Van Beerendonk (b); Emiel Leybaert (d).* 11/76.

****(*) Urgent Request**
GHB BCD-184 *Colyer; Dale Vickers (tb); Chris Blount (cl); Ray Smith (p); Dave Brennan (bj); Harry Slater (b); Mick Ellis (d).* 11/78.

***(*) Painting The Clouds With Sunshine**
Black Lion 760501 *Colyer; Mike Sherbourne (tb); Bruce Bakewell (cl); Ray Smith (p); Bill Stotesbury (bj); Alyn Shipton (b); Colin Bowden (d).* 10/79.

**** Darkness On The Delta**
Black Lion BLCD 60518 *As above, except add Tony Pyke (cl), Bill Cole (b), Paul Rosenberg (d); omit Bakewell, Shipton, Bowden.* 7/79.

Colyer disbanded his regular group in 1971, partly due to illness, and these are mementoes of the motley situations he found himself in after that. *Boston Church Service* is one of his most interesting latter-day discs. The church was actually an enormous gothic-looking pile in Lincolnshire; the band play mostly sacred tunes and they are blessed by an unexpectedly fine concert sound: a good one. The earlier KCT disc comes in clean sound and the band sound very enthusiastic, but this is a ragbag affair which could use a little finesse. Colyer played with Chris Blount's pro-am group many times in the early to mid-'70s and *Won't You Come Along With Me* is a collection of scraps from various surviving live tapes. Much of the playing is pretty shambolic but there are some queerly affecting moments, such as the wistful singing by Colyer on 'Basin Street Blues' and the atmosphere of the East Midlands in the 1970s which seems to permeate tracks that were cut in pubs in Derby, Ilkeston and Fadler Gate. *Very Very Live At The 100 Club* has plenty of atmosphere and Colyer and Rimington play soundly, but Avison's grotesque trombone doesn't help and the sound is pretty scruffy. *Urgent Request* is from a date in Derby where Ken sat in with Chris Blount's band and, if the music goes off well enough, there's little to remember. *In Holland* finds Ken joining the long-established Storyville Jazzband, who sound rather better than he does: much of his trumpet work from this period seems to get by on irascibility alone. A solid programme, in listenable sound. *Painting The Clouds With Sunshine* is nothing like as good. The rhythm section provides Colyer's favoured chugging momentum, but the horns are frankly unmemorable. *Darkness On The Delta* is from a set at the North Sea Jazz Festival, and it has its moments, but the band seem tired and some of the music limps along.

***** Blame It On The Blues**
Azure AZ-CD-33 *Colyer; Jean-François Bonnel (cl); Paul Sealey (bj, g); Ken Ames (b).* 1/85.

***** Wrap Your Troubles In Dreams**
Azure AZ-CD-34 *As above.* 1/85.

**** Too Busy**
CMJ 008 *Colyer; Les Hanscombe (tb); Dave Bailey (cl); Tim Phillips (bj); Keith Donald (b); John Petters (d).* 2/85.

****(*) Together Again**
Lake LACD 53 *Colyer; Les Hanscombe (tb); Acker Bilk (cl); Pat Hawes (p); Brian Mitchell (bj); Julian Davies (b); Pete Lay (d).* 7/85.

Colyer's illness cut him down in the end, and his later recordings are a mix of sad decline and a reflective, almost introspective approach as he adapted his circumstances to his music. There's no better example than *Blame It On The Blues*, which features a gentle, airy quartet working patiently through ten favourites at London's Pizza Express. Bonnel is a deferential partner and the sound is lovely. *Wrap Your Troubles In Dreams* is a second helping from the same occasion, and really is just as good: Colyer's playing on the closing 'Trouble In Mind' is more specifically emotive than he usually allowed himself to be, and it makes a rather poignant valediction. *Too Busy* is missable: Colyer guests with the John Petters group, and he is clearly taking things very gingerly. The band plays decent, fat-free trad, but the trumpeter's own contribution is unexceptional. He is, alas, also the weak link on *Together Again*, a surprise reunion with Bilk, again at the Pizza Express. Hawes has a bad time with the awful 'old' PE piano and Colyer's lead sounds very shaky; the stars are for Acker, returning to some heartland repertoire and again proving himself one of our best jazzmen.

Company

FLEXIBLE IMPROVISING ENSEMBLE

First organized by Derek Bailey as a week of 1977 concerts in London, where a pool of improvisers played together over the course of an evening in a series of more or less ad hoc groupings. It grew into a sequence of such events stretching over many years, until Bailey called a halt in the '90s. Probably most of them were recorded, but only a small number have actually emerged in CD form; several vinyl-only records are long since gone.

****** Company 6 & 7**

Incus CD07 *Derek Bailey (g); Leo Smith (t, f); Anthony Braxton (as, ss, f, cl); Evan Parker (ts, ss); Lol Coxhill, Steve Lacy (ss); Steve Beresford (p, g); Tristan Honsinger (clo); Maarten van Regteren Altena (b).* 5/77.

****** Once**

Incus CD04 *Derek Bailey (g); Lee Konitz (as, ss); Richard Teitelbaum (ky); Carlos Zingaro (vn); Tristan Honsinger (clo); Barre Phillips (b); Steve Noble (perc, bugle).* 5/87.

****** Company 91**

Incus CD16 *Yves Robert (tb); John Zorn (as); Derek Bailey, Buckethead (g); Alexander Balanescu (vn); Paul Rogers (b); Paul Lovens (perc); Pat Thomas (elec, ky); Vanessa Mackness (v).* 91.

****** Company 91**

Incus CD17 *As above.* 91.

*****(*) Company 91**

Incus CD18 *As above.* 91.

Incus, the label Derek Bailey co-founded in 1970 with saxophonist Evan Parker and drummer Tony Oxley, has dedicated part of its catalogue to the documentation of the occasions when Bailey brought together groups of British and international improvisers, some with a free-jazz background, some coming more from a classical environment, for a weekend or week of unstructured improvisation. Company was founded in 1977 and became the most important locus of free improvisation in Britain during its existence. It is, of course, moot whether existential performances which admit of no gap between conception and execution and which are completely conditioned by intuition really belong on record. What is remarkable about the above records (and the vanished LPs recorded at other events) is the extent to which they remain compellingly listenable long after the occasion of their performance is past; newcomers are directed particularly to *Once* and *6 & 7* which seem to encapsulate the challenges and beauties of Company in equal measure.

The music is extremely difficult to quantify or categorize. It was clear from the earlier encounters that it was necessary to negotiate a divide between free music which owned to no generic ties and a deep structure drawn from jazz. The first Company Week proper was in 1977, and it is fondly remembered for the then rare chance to see important overseas players like Braxton, Smith and Lacy playing with the Europeans. However, the visiting Americans (notably Braxton) appeared to find the radical and collective freedom on which Bailey quietly insisted rather unsettling; against that, both Steve Lacy and, much more surprisingly, former Tristano disciple Lee Konitz (who took part in the 1987 Company documented on *Once*) have managed to assimilate their notably dry approach to Bailey's. It's very instructive to compare what Parker does with Braxton here and on their 1993 London duo released on Leo (for which, see under Braxton's entry). As so often, it's the smaller combinations that stick in the mind. Tristan Honsinger's duo with Leo Smith on the same record is a tiny masterpiece.

Perhaps because Company Weeks are no longer annual events, the 1991 gathering is remembered with special clarity and affection and amply merits such full documentation. As always, the line-up included players not usually associated with the free-music scene, and the set begins, appropriately, with a duo by the classically trained Vanessa Mackness and classical violinist Alex Balanescu who, having got the remaining starch out of his instrument, simply goes for it. His duo with Bailey on Volume 2 is almost equally good. One of the oddities of 1991 was the inclusion of the heavy metal guitarist, Buckethead, who performs in mask and costume. The trio on Volume 2 which features him with Zorn and the young British improviser, Pat Thomas, was one of the high points of the week, though the chemistry didn't work quite so well when the guitarist joined Rogers and Balanescu (a duo would have been good) at the end of that same disc. The final part documents the Friday and Saturday. Historically, musical relationships are expected to develop as the week advances. There were signs in 1991, though, that some were unravelling. The performances on Volume 3 are by no means so well calibrated, and there are signs of weariness in the American ranks. That said, this disc is dominated by Zorn, first in duo with Robert (a quirky and unpredictable performer) and then with various larger combinations. The set ends with a noisy exchange between Bailey and Buckethead to which the audience makes an equally noisy contribution.

Concord All Stars

GROUP

Less a genuine band, more a flag of convenience for a group of musicians associated with the Concord label and performing together in various live situations.

***** Tour De Force**

Concord CCD 4172 *Al Cohn, Scott Hamilton, Buddy Tate (ts); Dave McKenna (p); Cal Collins (g); Bob Mate (b); Jake Hanna (d).* 8/81.

***** Take 8**

Concord CCD 4347 *Warren Vaché (c); Dan Barrett (tb); Red Holloway (as); Scott Hamilton (ts); Dave McKenna (p); Steve Wallace (b); Jimmie Smith (d).* 11/87.

***** Ow!**

Concord CCD 4348 *As above, except add Ed Bickert (g), Ernestine Anderson (v).* 11/87.

****(*) On Cape Cod**

Concord CCD 4530 *Scott Hamilton (ts); Dave McKenna (p); Gray Sargent (g); Marshall Wood (b); Chuck Riggs (d); Carol Sloane (v).* 5/92.

Casually organized but informed by the innate discipline of some of the best-focused players in the mainstream, these civilized jam sessions may lack the brawling excitement of Jazz at the Philharmonic, but they also expunge the excessive solos and ragged ensembles in that kind of jazz. *Tour De Force* concentrates on the three tenors, and Hamilton holds his own with Cohn and Tate without problems: 'Tickle Toe', 'Broadway' and 'Rifftide' are classic tenors-all-out features, but the slower moments let them wear hearts on sleeves too. The other session is basically the Vaché–Hamilton band with Holloway as an extra front-line guest, and this unit's suave manner with standards and swing staples is effortlessly maintained. Anderson joins in for three tracks on *Ow!*, finishing on 'Down Home Blues'. After a five-year vacation, the name was revived for a hotel engagement by the latest edition of the All Stars. Everyone plays comfortably on a familiar-looking programme, Carol Sloane strolls in for the last three songs, it's all nicely done, and one is tempted to ask, so what?

Eddie Condon (1905–73)

GUITAR

Born in Indiana, Condon became the quintessential Chicago jazzman, though he actually spent relatively little of his career there. A ringleader of the gang of young white players in Chicago in the '20s, he arrived in New York in 1928 and hustled his way to prominence, making famous associations with the Commodore record label, Nick's club and eventually his own place, on West Third Street. He was much on radio and later on TV. He toured extensively in the 1950s and '60s but was finally slowed up by illness. As a rhythm guitarist, he was often barely audible, but he was unassumingly talented.

****** Eddie Condon 1927–1938**

Classics 742 *Condon; Jimmy McPartland, Bobby Hackett (c); Max Kaminsky, Leonard Davis (t); George Brunies, Floyd O'Brien, Jack Teagarden (tb); Mezz Mezzrow, Frank Teschemacher, Pee Wee Russell (cl); Bud Freeman, Happy Caldwell (ts); Joe Sullivan, Alex Hill, Jess Stacy, Joe Sullivan (p); Art Miller, Jim Lannigan, Artie Bernstein, Artie Shapiro, Art Miller (b); George Wettling, Gene Krupa, Johnny Powell, George Stafford, Big Sid Catlett (d).* 12/27–4/38.

****** Eddie Condon 1938–1940**

Classics 759 *As above, except add Muggsy Spanier (c), Marty Marsala (t), Miff Mole, Vernon Brown (tb), Brad Gowans (vtb), Joe Bushkin, Fats Waller (p), Clyde Newcombe (b), Lionel Hampton, Dave Tough (d); omit McPartland, Davis, O'Brien, Mezzrow, Teschemacher, Caldwell, Hill, Lannigan, Bernstein, Miller, Krupa, Powell, Stafford, Catlett.* 4/38–11/40.

*****(*) Eddie Condon 1942–1943**

Classics 772 *As above, except add Yank Lawson (t), Benny Morton (tb), Gene Schroeder (p), Al Morgan, Bob Casey (b), Tony Sbarbaro (d); omit Spanier, Marsala, Mole, Brown, Waller, Newcombe, Hackett, Hampton, Tough, Teagarden.* 1/42–12/43.

***** Chicago Style**

ASV AJA 5192 *As above discs.* 27–40.

***** Windy City Jazz**

Topaz TPZ 1026 *As above.* 27–42.

***** The Definitive Eddie Condon And His Jazz Concert All Stars: Volume 1**

Stash ST-CD-530 *Condon; Bobby Hackett, Muggsy Spanier (c); Billy Butterfield, Max Kaminsky (t); Hot Lips Page (t, v); Lou McGarity, Benny Morton (tb); Ernie Caceres (cl, bs); Edmond Hall, Pee Wee Russell (cl); Gene Schroeder, Jess Stacy (p); Bob Haggart (b); Joe Grauso, George Wettling (d); Liza Morrow, Lee Wiley (v).* 6 & 10/44.

*****(*) Eddie Condon 1944–1946**

Classics 1033 *Condon; Bobby Hackett, Wild Bill Davison (c); Hot Lips Page (t, v); Sterling Bose, Billy Butterfield, Max Kaminsky, Yank Lawson (t); Lou McGarity, Miff Mole, Jack Teagarden, Fred Ohms (tb); Brad Gowans (vtb); Pee Wee Russell, Edmond Hall, Tony Parenti (cl); Joe Dixon (cl, bs); Bud Freeman (ts); Ernie Caceres (bs); Gene Schroeder, Joe Bushkin, Jess Stacy, James P Johnson (p); Bob Casey, Bob Haggart, Sid Weiss, Jack Lesberg (b); Dave Tough, Joe Grauso, George Wettling, Johnny Blowers (d); Lee Wiley, Bubbles Sublett (v).* 3/44–7/46.

*****(*) Eddie Condon In Japan**

Chiaroscuro GRD 154 *Condon; Buck Clayton (t); Vic Dickenson (tb); Bud Freeman (ts); Pee Wee Russell (cl); Dick Cary (p, ahn); Jack Lesberg (b); Cliff Leeman (d); Jimmy Rushing (v).*

Condon was the focus of Chicago jazz from the 1920s to the 1940s, garnering a personal reputation that far exceeds his actual musical significance. Condon is now best seen as a catalyst, a man who made things happen and in the process significantly heightened the profile of Dixieland jazz in America. He was rarely anything more than a straightforward rhythm guitarist, generally avoiding solos, but he had a very clear sense of what his role ought to be and frequently 'laid out' to give the piano player more room. His chords have a rather melancholy ring, but are always played dead centre.

The Classics discs offer a chronological overview of a career that didn't really get seriously under way on record until the 1940s. The five sessions from the '20s are key staging-posts in the evolution of Chicago jazz, starting with the four classic titles cut by the McKenzie–Condon Chicagoans in 1927, in which McPartland and the ill-fated Teschemacher made up a superbly vibrant front line. Two 1929 sessions feature some top-notch early Teagarden, and the 1933 band date includes the original versions of Freeman's famous turn on 'The Eel'. But it then goes quiet until the first sessions for Commodore in 1938. These take up most of the remaining two discs: relaxed but smart, graceful and hot at the same moment, Condon's various bands made eloquent jazz out of what were already becoming Dixieland warhorses. The four-part version of 'A Good Man Is Hard To Find' from 1940 is a little masterpiece, but almost anything from these sessions has its memorable moments, and players like Kaminsky, Brunies and Bushkin never found a better context to work in. All these discs are recommended, but transfers (from unlisted sources) are, as usual, a mixed bunch – though Commodore's own recording could vary from session to session. The Topaz and ASV compilations are each a good bet for anyone wanting a single disc from the period: ASV cover most of the early dates and add some titles by Billy Banks, Joe Marsala and Bud Freeman, while Topaz offer the earliest sessions and some of the Commodore tracks.

The MCA compilation of studio sessions from the early 1940s has been dumped, so follow the story on Classics 772 and 1033. Here are most of the Condon stalwarts playing to three-minute, 78-r.p.m. length, tucking small, gem-like solos into otherwise powerhouse ensembles – the rhythm sections were always good – and making all the choruses count. They may have had dubious reputations off the bandstand, but Condon's men were disciplined about their kind of jazz. Classics 1033 features three V-Disc titles (Lips Page sings 'Uncle Sam's Blues' on one of them) but the sessions otherwise originate from Decca. The mysterious Bubbles Sublett sings on 'Atlanta Blues' (which is misnumbered on the sleeve.

The 1944 transcriptions on Stash are straightforward Condon fare, played with considerable professionalism and marked by some fine solos from Russell, Page, Morton (with his vintage-style trills on 'Royal Garden Blues') and the lyrical Hackett, but with a slight chill about them, too. There are some first takes and breakdowns, but three of the latter amount to less than five seconds apiece and really don't merit inclusion in a compilation of this type.

Condon enjoyed a long and very successful association with Columbia, who released a substantial body of work in the 1950s. But there is nothing in the catalogue at present (it has been reissued as a Mosaic complete edition). As a compensation, there's the live set from Japan, rather poorly balanced and a little make-shift but still worthwhile for Condonites.

*****(*) The Town Hall Concerts Vol. 1**

Jazzology JCD 1001/2 2CD *Collective personnel for this and following ten discs: Condon; Muggsy Spanier, Dick Cary (c); Billy Butterfield, Sterling Bose, Bobby Hackett, Jonah Jones, Hot Lips Page, Max Kaminsky, Wingy Manone, Yank Lawson (t); Jack Teagarden, Bill Harris, Benny Morton, Miff Mole, Lou McGarity, Tommy Dorsey, Vernon Brown (tb); Pee Wee Russell, Joe Marsala, Edmond Hall, Jimmy Dorsey, Hank D'Amico (cl); Sidney Bechet (ss); Ernie Caceres (bs, cl); Gene Schroeder, James P Johnson, Willie 'The Lion' Smith, Norma Teagarden, Jess Stacy, Cliff Jackson, Dave Bowman (p); Carl Kress (g); Bob Haggart, Bob Casey, Jack Lesberg, Johnny Williams, Sid Weiss (b); George Wettling, Joe Grauso, Cozy Cole, Gene Krupa, Rolo Layon, Johnny Blowers, Danny Alvin, Big Sid Catlett (d); Lee Wiley, Red McKenzie, Harry The Hipster Gibson (v).* 6/44.

*****(*) The Town Hall Concerts Vol. 2**

Jazzology JCD 1003/4 2CD *As above.* 6/44.

****** The Town Hall Concerts Vol. 3**

Jazzology JCD 1005/6 2CD *As above.* 7/44.

*****(*) The Town Hall Concerts Vol. 4**

Jazzology JCD 1007/8 2CD *As above.* 8/44.

*****(*) The Town Hall Concerts Vol. 5**

Jazzology JCD 1009/1010 2CD *As above.* 9/44.

***** The Town Hall Concerts Vol. 6**

Jazzology JCD 1011/2 2CD *As above.* 10/44.

****** The Town Hall Concerts Vol. 7**

Jazzology JCD 1013/4 2CD *As above.* 11/44.

***** The Town Hall Concerts Vol. 8**

Jazzology JCD 1015/6 2CD *As above.* 12/44.

*****(*) The Town Hall Concerts Vol. 9**

Jazzology JCD 1017/8 2CD *As above.* 1/45.

*****(*) The Town Hall Concerts Vol. 10**

Jazzology JCD 1019/20 2CD *As above.* 2–3/45.

*****(*) The Town Hall Concerts Vol. 11**

Jazzology JCD 1021/2/3 3CD *As above.* 3–4/45.

*****(*) Live At Town Hall**

Jass J-CD-634 *Condon; Billy Butterfield, Hot Lips Page, Max Kaminsky (t); Miff Mole (tb); Pee Wee Russell, Edmond Hall (cl); Joe Bushkin, Cliff Jackson (p); Bob Casey, Pops Foster (b); George Wettling, Kansas Fields (d).* 3/44.

Condon's Town Hall concerts became an institution on radio during 1944–5, and Jazzology's superb edition has put together all 46 of them. The Jass disc slightly predates them, one of the best-sounding of these sessions and a curtain-raiser to the long series of double-CD sets which Jazzology have issued. Each of these packages contains four half-hour shows, compèred with a mixture of genial bonhomie and irascibility by Condon himself. He credits every player, sets the beat up for every number, kids around at the expense of most of the others (but especially the benighted Pee Wee Russell) and makes sure that proper standards of Dixieland are maintained at all times. Choosing among the discs is a little invidious since all of them are patchy, all are occasionally troubled by the sound (which is, though, usually quite listenable) and each falls back on routine instead of inspiration at some point. But the general standard of music is surprisingly high, given the showbiz feel of some of the situations. The second volume has a tribute to Fats Waller, the third a tribute to Bix Beiderbecke. If Russell is consistently the star player, there are often precious glimpses of men who would seldom make much more music in the studios: Spanier, Mole, Marsala, Manone. *Volume 7*, which features Jack and Norma Teagarden as guest stars, is a very good one, and perhaps the best to sample. *Volume 10* brings in regular guest Sidney Bechet, who usually gets a feature or two to himself, and has the coup of getting both Dorsey brothers into one of the bands. *Volume 11* has completed the series, and is extended to a third disc, also including two try-out shows for a Chesterfield sponsorshop which ultimately never happened. All of them have period feel and excellent music in great measure, a lasting tribute to Condon's bluff expertise, and an incomparably valuable document of a particular moment in the music's course.

***** Dr Jazz Vol. 1: Eddie Condon With Johnny Windhurst, No. 1**

Storyville STCD 6041 *Johnny Windhurst (t); Cutty Cutshall (tb); Edmond Hall (cl); Gene Schroeder (p); Bob Casey, Bill*

Goodall (b); Cliff Leeman, Buzzy Drootin, Monk Herbert (d). 1–6/52.

***** Dr Jazz Vol. 8: Eddie Condon With Johnny Windhurst No. 2**

Storyville STCD 6048 *As above, except add Condon; omit Goodall, Herbert.* 1–5/52.

***** Dr Jazz Vol. 5: Eddie Condon With Wild Bill Davison**

Storyville STCD 6045 *As above, except add Wild Bill Davison (c), Ralph Sutton (p), Bill Goodall (b), Don Lamond, George Wettling (d); omit Windhurst.* 12/51–3/52.

Radio broadcasts from Eddie's club, dating from the early '50s. Sound is occasionally scruffy but decent enough. The main point of the first two discs is to hear the seldom-recorded Windhurst whose blend of Armstrong and Hackett gave his playing a lovely dancing quality that still manages to power a front line. Obvious material, but worth a listen; as is the disc with Davison – though, given his ubiquitous discography, this scarcely goes down as essential. Condon doesn't play on the first disc, but he turns up here and there on the other two. There should be more latter-day Condon in the catalogue: this handful of titles is a very inadequate showing.

Chris Connor (born 1929)

VOCAL

Born in Kansas, she started out with Claude Thornhill, then joined Stan Kenton in 1952. Thereafter she worked as a solo, recording many albums for Bethlehem and Atlantic. Only occasional records in the '60s and '70s, but she was more visible in the '80s.

*****(*) Chris Connor**

Atlantic 7567-80769-2 *Connor; Nick Travis (t); Sam Marowitz, Ray Beckenstein (as); Zoot Sims (ts); Danny Bank (bs); John Lewis, Moe Wechsler (p); Barry Galbraith (g); Oscar Pettiford, Milt Hinton (b); Connie Kay, Osie Johnson (d).* 1–2/56.

****** Sings The George Gershwin Almanac Of Song**

Atlantic 2-601 2CD *Connor; Joe Newman, Doc Severinsen (t); Eddie Bert, Jimmy Cleveland, Jim Thompson, Warren Covington (tb); Sam Most, Peanuts Hucko (cl); Herbie Mann (f); Eddie Wasserman, Al Cohn (ts); Danny Bank (bs); Ralph Sharon, Stan Free, Hank Jones (p); Barry Galbraith, Joe Puma, Mundell Lowe (g); Milt Jackson (vib); Wendell Marshall, Milt Hinton, Oscar Pettiford, Vinnie Burke (b); Osie Johnson, Ed Shaughnessy, Ronnie Free (d); Johnny Rodriguez (perc).*

****** Warm Cool – The Atlantic Years**

32 Jazz 32108 2CD *Connor; as discs above, plus other orchestras, strings.* 1/56–4/62.

The cool vocalist *par excellence*. Her records for Bethlehem and Atlantic showcased the ex-Kenton singer in a way that led to some definitive interpretations: her versions of 'Ev'ry Time', 'It's All Right With Me', 'I Wonder What Became Of Me' and several more are unlikely to be bettered. She has remained something of a cult figure, but in her prime she sold records to a wide audience and several of her Atlantics were considerable hits in their way. The debut, *Chris Connor*, is a welcome revival in Atlantic's fiftieth anniversary programme. Four tracks with the quartet of Lewis, Galbraith, Pettiford and Kay – a band that should have made its own record – are a marvel, and so is 'When The Wind Was Green'. Her open-vowel sounds have an oddly yearning quality which is heightened by the way she can sing low notes very softly, yet make them emphatic.

Connor's Gershwin collection is almost as comprehensive as Fitzgerald's, in the company of seven different instrumental groups. Trifles such as 'Bla Bla Bla' or 'I Can't Be Bothered Now' are graced with thoughtful readings, the swingers dispatched unhurriedly, the ballads lingered over; despite the size of the project, there's no sense of routine. A much-neglected 'song-book' project.

At present, the catalogue is frustratingly empty of Connor's other Atlantic originals: *Chris Craft, A Portrait Of Chris* and *He Loves Me, He Loves Me Not* are three favourites which should surely return at some point. It's taken 32 Jazz to do a decent compilation of this material, probably at the behest of longtime fan Will Friedwald, who does the excellent sleeve-notes. *Warm Cool* offers 40 songs on two discs and, while we would carp at a couple of omissions, it's hard to argue with the choice of what is here.

***** Two's Company**

Roulette 37201-2 *Connor; Maynard Ferguson, Chet Ferretti, Rolf Ericson, Bill Berry (t); Ray Winslow, Kenny Rupp (tb); Lanny Morgan (as, f); Joe Farrell (ts, ss, cl); Willie Maiden (ts); Frank Hittner (bs); Jaki Byard (p); John Neves (b); Rufus Jones (d).* 61.

One of two albums Connor made with the Maynard Ferguson orchestra. There are haunting versions of Alec Wilder's 'Where Do You Go' and 'The Wind', but some of the swingers go off the scale in the Ferguson manner, and 'Guess Who I Saw Today' belongs to Nancy Wilson.

*****(*) Lover Come Back To Me**

Evidence 22110 *Connor; Fred Hersch (p); Steve LaSpina (b); Tony Tedesco (d).* 9/81.

A New York club show. Chris still sounds in her prime. Hersch's team accompany with a completely *simpatico* outlook and a choice set of standards comes up just fine. It closes on her concert set-piece of 'My Heart Stood Still', but all the songs are well chosen.

*****(*) Classic**

Contemporary C-14023 *Connor; Claudio Roditi (t, flhn); Paquito D'Rivera (as); Michael Abene, Richard Rodney Bennett (ky); Rufus Reid (b); Akira Tana (d).* 8/86.

A fine return to the studios for Connor. Although some of the accompaniments are a shade too bright, the material is a refined choice of standards, and the vocalist shows few signs of advancing years. She revisits 'Blame It On My Youth' with poignant sincerity and elsewhere handles the pulse of Bennett's arrangements with undiminished skill.

****(*) New Again**

Contemporary C-14038 *Connor; Claudio Roditi (t, flhn); Bill Kirschner (ss, as, ts, f, cl); Dave Valentin (f); Michael Abene, Richard Rodney Bennett (ky); Michael Moore (b); Buddy Williams (d); Sammy Figueroa (perc).* 8/87.

Something of a let-down after the sublime *Classic*. The band is a little too pushy and loud for the singer to come through clearly, and some of the songs are inappropriate choices for a vocalist whose strengths lie in more traditional interpretation. But a handful of tunes, especially 'I Wish I'd Met You', approach Connor's best form.

*****(*) As Time Goes By**
Enja 7061-2 *Connor; Hank Jones (p); George Mraz (b); Keith Copeland (d). 4/91.*

Connor has never before made such a straightahead jazz album and, with blue-chip accompaniment from the incomparable Jones, this session swings even at slow tempos. Yet the singer's concentrated readings of 'As Time Goes By', 'Gone With The Wind' and 'Goodbye' are on the level of her classic recordings.

Bill Connors (born 1949)

GUITAR

Second-generation fusion guitarist with a sequence of moody records from the '70s and mid-'80s.

***** Theme To The Guardian**
ECM 829387-2 *Connors (g solo). 11/74.*

***** Of Mist And Melting**
ECM 847324-2 *Connors; Jan Garbarek (ts, ss); Gary Peacock (b); Jack DeJohnette (d). 12/77.*

***** Swimming With A Hole In My Body**
ECM 849078-2 *Connors (g solo). 8/79.*

****(*) Step It**
Evidence ECD 22080 *Connors; Steve Khan (g); Tom Kennedy (b); Dave Weckl (d). 6–10/84.*

****(*) Double Up**
Evidence ECD 22081 *Connors; Tom Kennedy (b); Kim Plainfield (d). 85.*

Once Chick Corea's guitarist in Return To Forever, Connors shares his old boss's galling tendency to short-change exceptional technical ability with rather bland and self-indulgent ideas. The later trios have a certain energy and immediacy, but they're crude in comparison to the Corea-influenced solo projects. Connors's acoustic work is finely detailed and there are some interesting things on *Swimming*, albeit worked out in a shut-off, self-absorbed way that, like a lot of Alan Holdsworth's work, may appeal to guitar technicians but which can be curiously off-putting for everyone else. *Theme*, long in the tooth now, was probably the most satisfactory of the bunch until *Of Mist And Melting* reappeared on CD; the presence of Garbarek and of a rhythm section that cooks along in a dark strain adds quantifiably to the range, yielding more of his typically tense atmospheric pieces.

Contraband

GROUP

Organized and led by trombonist Willem van Manen, this Dutch big band follows a line somewhere between the Willem Breuker Kollektief and the more strait-laced jazz orchestras of middle Europe.

*****(*) Live At The Bimhuis**
Bvhaast 8906 *Toon De Gouw, Louis Lanzing, Ad Gruter (t); Willem Van Manen, Hans Sparla, Hans Visser (tb); Theo Jorgensmann, Paul Van Kamenade, Rutger Van Otterloo, Maarten Van Norden, Eckard Koltermann (reeds); Ron Van Rossum (p); Hein Offermans (b); Martin Van Duynhoven (d). 11/88.*

*****(*) De Ruyter Suite**
Bvhaast 9104 *As above, except Chris Abelen (tb), Jeroen Van Vliet (p), Eric Van der Westen (b) replace Sparla, van Rossum and Offermans. 4/91.*

***** Boy Edgar Suite**
VPRO EW 9412 *As above, except Frans Vermeersen (reeds), Charles Huffstadt (d) replace van Norden and van Duynhoven. 5/94.*

Contraband is Willem van Manen's 'occasional' big band. The trombonist and veteran of Holland's post-bop and free-music scene is a skilled and dynamic composer-arranger, and the first two records – the first live, the second studio, and both written almost entirely by van Manen – are packed with incident. The group delivers all the power and finesse of the great big bands, and it glories in soloists who crackle their way out of complex charts. But sometimes there are hints of strain or of over-familiar effects – clustering muted trumpets or high reeds, for instance, or fast cutting from passages of rigid orthodoxy to all-out freedom – which suggest that it's a best of both worlds which the band can't quite grasp. It would be churlish, though, to deny the vividness, sweep and panache of a band which ought to be far better known than it is. 'Contra-Suit' from the live record, and the three-part title-piece of *De Ruyter Suite*, dedicated to Dutch critic Michiel de Ruyter, are grand yet wholly coherent big-scale structures, and the soloists – especially Jorgensmann on clarinet and van Kamenade on alto – refuse to dilute the intensity of the whole band.

Boy Edgar Suite may disappoint some in that van Manen's two pieces are presented rather soberly, one a tribute to the Dutch jazz eminence, Boy Edgar, the other a threnody for Miles Davis. The other composition, Eckard Koltermann's two-part 'Constant Pictures', is rather more boisterous and has a particularly fine solo from Chris Abelen. All that said, Contraband 94 (as they are billed) are in fine shape, with the brass sections colouring van Manen's scores with characteristic aplomb; and the composer's own improvisation in Part Three of the 'Edgar Suite' is especially gripping.

*****(*) Hitit**
Bvhaast 9802 *Toon De Gouw, Louis Lanzing, Willem Schoenmaker (t); Willem Van Manen, Chris Abelen, Hans Visser (tb); Theo Jorgensmann, Paul Van Kamenade, Rutger Van*

Otterloo, Frans Vermeersen, Eckard Koltermann (reeds); Stevko Busch (p); Arnold Dooyeweerd (b); Charles Huffstadt (d). 12/97.

Contraband have grown into a complex entity. Willem van Manen seems to have an awkward relationship with the prevailing mummery of big-band music: he likes to make things swing, and he leaves necessary space for jazz solos in all his pieces, but his scores have the intricacy and flavour of different composing traditions, and sometimes one can hear him wrestling with his various angels. His four pieces here (there is a fifth by Chris Abelen) refer to jazz rather than revelling in it, and it's a progression which can be traced from *Live At The Bimhuis* to here. There is also little in the way of theatre, satire or some of the other staples which this school is supposed to dwell on. In its undemonstrative way, this is the kind of ensemble which is pointing a way out of the impasse of the big-band tradition.

Henry Cook

SOPRANO AND ALTO SAXOPHONES, FLUTE

A Boston-based performer-teacher, long associated with the Billy Skinner Double Quartet.

***** Dimensional Odyssey**

Accurate AC 5012 *Cook; Cecil Brooks (t); Jacques Chanier (p); Brian McCree (b); Bobby Ward (d).* 11/94.

A bebop instrumentation, but no bebop licks. Cook and his group play an airy kind of free bop, propulsive but with lots of space – almost as if the players were set far apart and were calling to one another. That gives a pleasing lilt to cookers like 'Echoes Of Nichols' or 'Dimensional O.D.C.', and the collective free-for-all, 'Mind's Eye', is similarly lacking in clutter. There are interesting contributions from everybody, with the leader playing almost as much flute as saxophone, and Ward giving everybody a terrific groove, but if there's a weak link it's Brooks, whose solos tend to sputter out before they've found a result. Cut live at a gig in Massachusetts: not many people, but they sound like they enjoyed it.

Junior Cook (1934–92)

TENOR SAXOPHONE

Joined Horace Silver in 1958 and stayed with front-line partner Blue Mitchell until 1969. Taught and led small groups through the 1980s.

****(*) Senior Cookin'**

32 Jazz 32095 *Cook; Bill Hardman (t, flhn); Slide Hampton (tb); Mario Rivera (bs); Albert Dailey, Cedar Walton (p); Walter Booker, Buster Williams (b); Leroy Williams, Billy Higgins (d).* 6/79–6/81.

***** The Place To Be**

Steeplechase CCD 31240 *Cook; Mickey Tucker (p); Wayne Dockery (b); Leroy Williams (d).* 11/88.

***** On A Misty Night**

Steeplechase SCCD 31266 *As above, except Walter Booker (b) replaces Dockery.* 6/89.

***** You Leave Me Breathless**

Steeplechase SCCD 31304 *Cook; Valery Ponomarev (t); Mickey Tucker (p); John Webber (b); Joe Farnsworth (d).* 12/91.

Junior Cook's work with Horace Silver and a few other leaders revealed a tenorman of staunch loyalty to the hard-bop language and, though he never quite broke through to the front rank, he left many inventive solos on record. As a leader, he was rather less successful. The Muse albums, *Good Cookin'* and *Somethin's Cookin'*, are coupled on the 32 Jazz reissue. His old friend Bill Hardman helped settle the front line on the earlier date, which has Rivera's baritone as a sometimes dead weight; but the quartet date with Walton which rounds out the disc is probably a better example of Junior's playing. Still, nothing on either disc really grips the listener, and Junior sounds oddly unsure of himself for much of the way – listen to the way his solo on 'Fiesta Espanol' peters out, as if he just couldn't think of anything much to play.

He came into his own again during the final decade of his oddly underachieving career. Steeplechase has been a profitable home for many a journeyman hard-bopper, with the label's comfortable house-sound and familiar menus making plenty of otherwise disenfranchised musicians feel at home. Cook's records for the company worked out rather well, but none of them can claim classic status. If the saxophonist's dependability was his strongest suit, he nevertheless manages to find enough in the way of ear-catching ideas to give his up-tempo workouts an edge of involvement which grants even something as simple as 'Cedar's Blues' on *The Place To Be* a tough credibility. His powers were also in decline to some extent, but that tends to lend such a professional player a further challenge: how does he deal with it? Cook's answer seems to be to shy away from over-familiar material and to turn to more timbral variation than he would have bothered with as a younger man. *On A Misty Night* is marked by a considered choice of material – 'By Myself', 'Make The Girl Love Me', 'My Sweet Pumpkin' – and the leader's thoughts on the title-tune, once associated with Coltrane, stake his place in the grand tenor lineage. *You Leave Me Breathless* was his last date, made a few months before his death, and although there is some rambling – a few solos have one chorus too many, for instance – Cook's playing has a candid, clear-eyed quality which is quite affecting. Ponomarev is rather ordinary; but all three records are greatly assisted by the presence of Tucker, sympathetic, and driving when he has to be.

India Cooke

VIOLIN

A contemporarty violinist, classically trained but with a wide experience of jazz in and around San Francisco, where she has been based since the early 1980s.

***** RedHanded**

Music & Arts 51 *Cooke; George Lewis (tb); Larry Ochs (sno, ts); Lisle Ellis (b); Donald Robinson (d); Lee (sic) (perc).* 96.

Cooke is from North Carolina, but her base is in the Bay Area jazz scene, and she was also in a late edition of Sun Ra's Arkestra: 'Ra Storm' is presumably a nod to him here. This is a combustible unit which she leads with aplomb, playing as full-blooded a role as any of the horns in the uproar of 'Cut To Break' and setting the tone for the spiralling 'Ala's Wing', not the only piece with a hint of shamanism about it. The playing by Lewis and Ochs is dependably imaginative and the journey is from free bop to free, but Cooke herself seems to fall back on certain sawing figures, a repetitive streak which to some degree infects the music as a whole: after halfway, one feels there is little more to hear, although the closing 'Jerry Head ... I've Got Your Number' is perhaps the most ambitious of the six pieces.

Al Cooper (1911–81)

CLARINET, ALTO AND BARITONE SAXOPHONES and

Bob Cooper (1925–93)

TENOR SAXOPHONE, OBOE

One of the major West Coast saxophonists of the 1950s, Cooper's utter professionalism and consistency suggest a kinship with like-minded players such as Zoot Sims, although his light tone and unemphatic phrasing were in close harmony with the Californian playing of the period. A former sideman with Stan Kenton (he was also married to Kenton vocalist June Christy), he worked extensively with Shorty Rogers and Howard Rumsey, as a partnership with Bud Shank, in various big bands and in the prolific studio-session work of the 1960s. He remained a versatile and swinging player up until his death from a heart attack in 1993.

***** Coop! The Music Of Bob Cooper**

Original Jazz Classics OJC 161 *Cooper; Conte Candoli, Pete Candoli, Don Fagerquist (t); Frank Rosolino, John Halliburton (tb); Lou Levy (p); Victor Feldman (vib); Max Bennett (b); Mel Lewis (d). 8/57.*

Because he chose to spend much of his career away from any leadership role, Cooper's light has been a little dim next to many of the West Coast players of the 1950s, especially since he often worked as an accompanist to his wife, vocalist June Christy. His flute-and-oboe sessions with Bud Shank are out of print, but this sole feature album, recorded for Contemporary, displays a light, appealing tenor style and arrangements which match rather than surpass the West Coast conventions of the day. The drily effective recording is typical of the studios of the period.

***** Milano Blues**

Fresh Sound FSR-CD 179 *Cooper; Hans Hammerschmid, Pim Jacobs (p); Rudolf Hansen, Ruud Jacobs (b); Victor Plasil, Wessel Ilcken (d). 3–4/57.*

Two sessions from a European visit, both with local rhythm sections, a studio date in Milan and a live show in Holland. Cooper sounds a little over-relaxed on the Italian date, but the livelier 'Cappuccino Time' is sinuously done, and the live tracks feature a fine tenor blow on 'Indiana'. A couple of oboe features don't assert a great jazz role for the instrument. Goodish sound throughout, though the drums are a bit thin on the studio date.

***** For All We Know**

Fresh Sound FSR-CD 167 *Cooper; Lou Levy (p); Monty Budwig (b); Ralph Penland (d). 8/90.*

***** The Bob Cooper–Conte Candoli Quintet**

VSOP 93 *Cooper; Conte Candoli (t); Ross Tompkins (p); John Leitham (b); Paul Kreibich (d). 6/93.*

Cooper made rather sporadic returns to the studios in the 1980s and '90s but he remained a guileful player, his tone deceptively languid: when the tempo picks up, the mastery of the horn asserts itself, and he gets the same kind of even-handed swing which the more demonstrative Zoot Sims or Al Cohn could muster. The wistful *For All We Know* stands as an honest studio farewell: typically thoughtful preparation by Cooper and Levy, on good and unhackneyed standards and with quartet arrangements that make the most of the various combinations of players. But Coop worked until he died, and the VSOP live album was done just weeks before his passing. Recorded at the Hyatt Newporter on Newport Beach, this is a vigorous set of old pro's bebop, longish solos for all hands, but good humour and skill prevail. Cooper's ballad feature on 'We'll Be Together Again' says his goodbyes.

Jim Cooper (born 1950)

VIBES

Chicago-based vibesman who works in a straightforward hard-bop setting.

****(*) Tough Town**

Delmark DD-446 *Cooper; Ira Sullivan (ts); Bob Dogan (p); Dan DeLorenzo (b); Charlie Braugham (d); Alejo Poveda (perc). 91.*

***** Nutville**

Delmark DD-457 *As above, except Sullivan also plays t and ss. 11/91.*

Cooper's fluency and drive on the vibes lend piquancy to his music, but these records are too diffuse to make any significant impact. The original compositions are musicianly rather than melodically compelling, while bebop updates such as 'Cheryl' and 'Bemsha Swing' aren't strong enough to transcend mere repertory playing. The best moments come in Dogan's contributions to the second record, notably the complex but hard-swinging 'Sui Fumi' and 'Cabbie Patch'. Sullivan is his usual chameleonic self, although he sticks to tenor for the first record; and occasionally one feels that a more decisive horn would be a better partner for Cooper, who sometimes drifts into clouds of notes. The music isn't well served by a flat production on both discs, but *Nutville* is worth trying for vibes lovers.

Keith Copeland (born 1947)

DRUMS

Son of trumpeter Ray Copeland, Keith is a drummer who has played professionally since the age of fifteen and is equally active as an educator, holding professorships in Germany and other posts in both the USA and Ireland.

***** The Irish Connection**
Steeplechase SCCD 31469 *Copeland; Tommy Halferty (g); Ronan Guilfoyle (b).* 95.

***** Round Trip**
Steeplechase SCCD 31425 *As above.* 9/96–2/97.

***** Postcard From Vancouver**
Jazz Focus JFCD 023 *Copeland; Miles Black (p); Rick Kilburn (b).* 97.

***** Live In Limerick**
Steeplechase SCCD 31469. *As Steeplechase albums.* 2/98.

Halferty's thick tone and juicy blend of bebop lines and fat, resonant chords tend to dominate the first two records, though Copeland and Guilfoyle are no slouches and the resultant trio music has plenty of grip. Highlights would be a somewhat Latinized 'You Don't Know What Love Is' and a very gritty blues called 'Minor Infringement', both on the second record. A rare example of Steeplechase recording in Ireland!

The Canadian date is with players from another local scene, not much known of outside Vancouver, although Kilburn in particular has done a great deal of sideman work. This is another spirited date, pushed hard by the drummer, with a good set of bop and hard-bop covers in the programme. Black is gifted with a good piano sound (he plays electric sometimes too) and his variations on three different Monk tunes are particularly incisive.

Back to Ireland for the third record by that trio. They repeat their arrangement of 'You Don't Know What Love Is', among others, and these versions are looser and funkier, though soundwise a whit less focused than they were in the studio. John Scofield's 'Chariots' is a neat sublimation of the master's style by Halferty.

Marc Copland

PIANO, KEYBOARDS

Copland arrived in New York in the early 1970s, spent a period in the Chico Hamilton group, and has since been a regular presence in the area, although his records as a leader have been only intermittent.

***** Never At All**
Future Music FMR CD05 28193 *Copland; Stan Sulzmann (as, ss, f).* 2/92.

*****(*) Stompin' With Savoy**
Denon/Savoy CY-75853 *Copland; Randy Brecker (t); Bob Berg (ts); James Genus (b); Dennis Chambers (d).* 3/93.

****** Second Look**
Savoy XCY018001 *Copland; John Abercrombie (g); Drew Gress (b); Billy Hart (d).* 4/96.

*****(*) Softly...**
Savoy CY-18076 *Copland; Tim Hagans (t); Joe Lovano, Michael Brecker (ts); Gary Peacock (b); Bill Stewart (d).* 9/97.

Copland isn't well-known as a leader, but he's been around the block, and these various sessions are strong enough to stand pretty tall in a competitive environment. The session with Sulzmann was an 'old pals' encounter and the pieces were put down more or less spontaneously. Predictably, Copland's use of synthesizers is both individual and tasteful. The highlight perhaps is the flute chase on 'Phobos And Demos', though Copland's 'Guinevere', which closes the album, is lovely, too.

The three albums for Savoy – known for its illustrious past, but the label name is still being used for some contemporary projects, mainly via Japanese investment – are cultured, cultivated and eloquent contemporary jazz, with picked teams of players and Copland's own themes as the touchstone. Not on *Stompin' With Savoy*, though: this is a revisionist look at ten venerable pieces of the hard-bop repertoire. The beautifully polished treatment of 'I Loves You, Porgy', with Brecker doing his best Miles impersonation, is typical, and the record is shaded with sufficient individuality to make it seem considerably more than a genre exercise. 'Footprints' has never sounded stealthier, and even the ironclad Berg softens up here and there. It's a band of heavyweights, but it's Copland's guileful hand which stops them sounding musclebound.

Copland and Abercrombie go a long way back – they were bandmates together with Chico Hamilton – and *Second Look* is a superbly effective reunion. Bar a single standard, they split compositional credits between them, and the record unfolds with an impeccable lyricism which here and there borders on the ecstatic, most particularly in the gorgeous duet treatment of Abercrombie's old classic, 'Timeless': if anything, this surpasses his ECM original. Gress and Hart are worthy cohorts in a quite wonderful record.

An extraordinary line-up was assembled for *Softly ...*, which is carefully deployed by the pianist for maximum effect: there is a single quintet track, and Hagans, Lovano and Brecker are elsewhere rationed for the horn roles, with the emphasis otherwise squarely on the rhythm section. Copland allows himself three of his own tunes, and the others include a brittle reworking of 'Softly As In A Morning Sunrise', Joni Mitchell's 'Blue' and Marvin Gaye's 'What's Going On'. As with the other discs, Copland impresses not so much by his own improvising – unemphatic, and as interesting in accompaniment as in solo space – but by the poised, temperate feel he imposes on his surroundings. These may not be easy records to find, but they should be sought out.

Jon Corbett

TRUMPET, VALVE TROMBONE

Corbett is a British improviser whose long experience on the British free scene has resulted in comparatively few recordings, although his experience dates back to 'roots in the blues with Alexis Korner and Joe Harriott'. He can also be found on some of the LJCO albums with Barry Guy.

****** Another Fine Mess**
Slam 217 *Corbett; Steve Done (g).* 12/94.

Properly credited to both Corbett and Done, these nine improvised duets establish a further unique corner in improvised music. Persistently quiet, the playing on occasion dips almost to subliminal levels, and it is particularly rewarding when played fairly softly, in order to concentrate the ears on the minutiae of the music. Corbett's phrasing is an unbroken line of broken pieces: he hardly ever plays a sustained note, and instead shapes what might in other situations be jazz phrases into an oratory of Byzantine detail. Done's guitar parts are similar in their restraint, with the electric instrument no 'louder' or more effect-driven than the acoustic one. He also seems to draw on jazz and rock vocabularies from moment to moment without ever falling into recognized paths. The resulting music is calmly fascinating. Sometimes, as on 'Waltz For Debris', they begin a piece with a very clear contrapuntalism and step further and further away from each other without once losing touch. Corbett picks up the valve trombone for 'Square Midnight' for a little variety, although there is enough differentiation in all the playing to sustain a long record.

Chick Corea (born 1941)

PIANO, KEYBOARDS, COMPOSER

Over the years, Chick Corea has created a body of music that has embraced Latin funk, a strong Bartók influence, free jazz, extended rock and, more recently, classical forms as well. A consummately expressive player with a complex intellectual stance, he has not been afraid to flirt with banality, a sure sign of creative greatness.

****** Tones For Joan's Bones**

Atlantic 75352 *Corea; Stuart Blumberg, Woody Shaw (t); Joe Farrell (ts, f); Steve Swallow (b); Joe Chambers (d).* 11–12/66.

***** Early Days**

Laserlight 17082 *Corea; Woody Shaw (t); Bennie Maupin (ts); Hubert Laws (f, picc); Dave Holland (b); Horace Arnold, Jack DeJohnette (d).* 69.

Corea is a pianist and composer of remarkable range and energy, combining a free-ish jazz idiom with a heavy Latin component and an interest in more formal structures. The obvious parallel is with his ECM stable-mate, Keith Jarrett, an even more prolific keyboard improviser with a similar facility for melodic invention within relatively conventional popular forms or in more loosely conceived improvisatory settings; they also share a certain ambivalence about audiences. Corea's stated ambition is to assimilate the 'dancing' qualities of jazz and folk musics to the more disciplined structures of classical music. He has written a half-dozen classic melodies, notably the much-covered 'La Fiesta', 'Return To Forever' and 'Tones For Joan's Bones'.

Given that he had already been playing for 20 years, there is no reason to regard either *Tones* or *Early Days* as the work of a prodigy. Chick has said in interview that he felt under no particular pressure to record as a leader and approached the first session, which was produced by Herbie Mann, with a very relaxed attitude. That is evident in every track. The title-piece is a jazz classic and the opening 'Litha' deserves to be better known. Corea's classical interests are evident in the brief 'Trio For Flute, Bassoon And Piano', which is very different from the extended hard-bop idiom of the rest of the set, but well worth hearing all the same. Chick already sounds very much his own man and in possession of every resource that he was to exploit in future years. The writing is crisp and assured, with a gutsy swing. Tunes like 'Sundance', 'Converge' and 'The Brain' are embryonic Corea, but far from undeveloped. The band is brilliantly coloured, deep blues and shouting reds, and the remainder of the rhythm section as effective as any on the scene.

*****(*) Piano Improvisations Vols 1 & 2**

ECM 811979-2 & 829190-2 *Corea (p solo); Ida Kavafian (vn); Fred Sherry (clo).* 4/71.

****(*) Children's Songs**

ECM 815680-2 *As above.* 7/83.

Valid as the comparison with Jarrett is, there is a world of difference between the miniatures on *Piano Improvisations* and Jarrett's hugely rambling excursions. Corea is superficially less demanding, but he still repays detailed attention. If his taste was to lapse in the following years, he was surely never more decorously apt than in these 1971 sessions, which after 20 years are still wearing well. *Children's Songs* is a much less compelling set.

****** Now He Sings, Now He Sobs**

Blue Note 90055 *Corea; Miroslav Vitous (b); Roy Haynes (d).* 3/68.

****** The Song Of Singing**

Blue Note 84353 *Corea; Dave Holland (b); Barry Altschul (d).* 4/70.

***** A.R.C.**

ECM 833678-2 *Corea; Dave Holland (b); Barry Altschul (d).* 1/71.

****(*) The Beginning**

Delta 17083 *As above.*

***** Trio Music**

ECM 827702-2 2CD *Corea; Miroslav Vitous (b); Roy Haynes (d).* 11/81.

****(*) Trio Music, Live In Europe**

ECM 827769-2 *As above.* 9/84.

The trios offer the best internal evidence of Corea's musical and philosophical trajectory. *Sings/Sobs* is a fine, solid jazz set with some intelligently handled standard material, but at this point Chick was dabbling in free music and much of the material sounds collectively improvised. We're not entirely sure about the material on *The Beginning*, a sour recording of some wonderfully inventive improvisations. Hi-fi enthusiasts will baulk but there is enough substance to justify the disc's inclusion in a serious Corea collection.

A bare three years later, Corea, falling under the influence of the Scientology movement, was playing altogether more experimentally, with a searching, restless quality that he lost in later years. *The Song Of Singing*, which is probably the best of the trio records, is marked by fine melodic invention and some remarkably sophisticated group interplay which demands that the record be heard as a trio performance, not just as Corea plus rhythm. The two 'Ballads', numbered I and III, are credited to the three musicians and are presumably improvised over predetermined structures; one wonders how many were left on the editing-room floor. Corea's two compositions, 'Rhymes' and

'Flesh', are slightly vapid but sharpen up on familiarity. 'Nefertiti' is a modern jazz classic and this bare version should be compared with the Circle version.

A.R.C. isn't entirely successful, but the quality of Holland and Altschul renders it a credible essay that Corea was never fully to develop. He left the demanding Circle (whose single record contained versions of Holland's 'Toy Room' and Wayne Shorter's 'Nefertiti', both covered on *The Song Of Singing*) later in 1971, convinced that the music was losing touch with its audience. This is the beginning of the pianist's awkward populism, which was to lead him to a commercially successful but artistically null flirtation with fusion music of various sorts.

The reconvened Vitous/Haynes trio perfectly illustrates Corea's change in attitude. Vitous and Haynes are both superbly gifted players, but they take no discernible chances, sticking close to a conception laden with Corea's increasingly vapid philosophizing. By 1984, there isn't much left on Old Mother Hubbard's shelves.

****** Return To Forever**

ECM 811978-2 *Corea; Joe Farrell (ss, f); Stanley Clarke (b); Airto Moreira (d, perc); Flora Purim (v, perc).* 2/72.

****** Light As A Feather**

Verve 557115-2 2CD *As above.* 10/72.

Lightweight it may be in some regards, but *Light As A Feather* is a perennial favourite. Repackaged with extra tracks from the sessions, including several versions of 'What Games Shall We Play?', it is one of Chick's most engaging and approachable records. The leaders bounces joyously and unselfconsciously throughout, transforming relatively simple themes like '500 Miles High', 'Captain Marvel' and the ubiquitous 'Children's Song' into grand dancing processions. The earlier record is in some respects better still, more improvisational in cast but still constructed around song forms. Purim's voice was never better, and Clarke keeps his lead guitarist ambitions to himself for the present. Moreira is rarely heard on a regular drum kit, and he offers an unconventional pulse that gives both sets a distinctive tilt. He plays a particularly strong role on 'Return To Forever' and on the long, buoyant 'Sometime Ago/La Fiesta'.

***** Hymn Of The Seventh Galaxy**

Polydor 825 336 *Corea; Bill Connors (g); Stanley Clarke (b); Lenny White (d, perc).* 8/73.

****(*) Where Have I Known You Before**

Polydor 825206 *Corea; Al DiMeola (g); Stanley Clarke (b); Lenny White (d, perc).* 7–8/74.

*****(*) Return To The Seventh Galaxy**

Verve 533108-2 2CD *As for Light As A Feather, Hymn Of The Seventh Galaxy, Where Have I Known You Before, except add Steve Gadd (d), Mingo Lewis (perc).* 10/72–3/75.

***** The Best of Return To Forever**

Columbia CK 36359 *As for the above, except add Jim Pugh (tb), Gayle Moran (v).* 72–75.

The following year, Corea formed an electric group called Return to Forever. Not to be confused with the group that made the ECM record; only Clarke remains. There's something very '70s about *Hymn Of The Seventh Galaxy* and *Where Have I Known You Before.* Compared to the Mahavishnu Orchestra, which was very cheeseclothy and intense, Return to Forever was rather closer to a dance group, and the very buoyancy of the music often glossed over its subtleties. Though both records are painfully dated, certainly in technical terms and even despite careful remastering, they do retain some of the freshness and energy of the earlier, acoustic band, and it's perfectly possible to shut one's eyes to Corea's quasi-mystical titles.

The best of the group's material, plus some tapes from Chick's personal archive, are included on the two-CD Verve set, which is a more than adequate memorial to the group. 'Hymn Of The Seventh Galaxy', 'Captain Senor Mouse' and 'Theme To The Mothership' are all there, as well as '500 Miles High', 'Captain Marvel' and 'Light As A Feather' from the earlier group. The bonus is three tracks from a live radio broadcast from Quiet Village, Long Island, a long version of 'Spain' and two Stanley Clarke numbers, 'After The Cosmic Rain' and 'Bass Folk Song'.

The material on disc two, which includes two tracks from the 1975 *No Mystery*, documents the decline and end of what was undeniably a highly inventive band. In this form, the material is very welcome, though most listeners will find themselves returning to the first set very much more often.

The Columbia 'best of' isn't strictly that but a rock-orientated survey of some of the band's most full-on playing. It may yet bring in new listeners to Corea's music, but most initiates will find this selection one-dimensional.

****(*) The Leprechaun**

Polydor/Verve 519798-2 *Corea; Danny Cahn, John Gatchell, Bob Millikan (t); Wayne Andre, Bill Watrous (tb); Joe Farrell (reeds); Annie Kavafian, Ida Kavafian (vn); Louise Shulman (vla); Fred Sherry (clo); Eddie Gomez, Anthony Jackson (b); Steve Gadd (d); Gayle Moran (v).* 75.

**** My Spanish Heart**

Polydor 2669034 2CD *Corea; 17-piece band, including strings; Jean-Luc Ponty (vn); one track of Corea; Stanley Clarke (b); Narada Michael Walden (perc).* 10/76.

****(*) The Mad Hatter**

Verve 519799-2 *Corea; John Thomas, Stuart Blumberg, John Rosenberg (t); Ron Moss (tb); Charles Veal, Kenneth Yerke (vn); Denyse Buffum, Michael Nowack (vla); Dennis Karmazyn (clo); Herbie Hancock (ky); Joe Farrell (ts, f, picc); Eddie Gomez, Jamie Faunt (b); Steve Gadd, Harvey Mason (d); Gayle Moran (v).*

***** Friends**

Polydor 849 071 *Corea; Joe Farrell (ts, ss, f); Eddie Gomez (b); Steve Gadd (d).* 78.

Things went a little awry thereafter. *The Leprechaun* was so intent on being charming that it ended up deeply charmless. It marked some sort of a return to acoustic jazz, though Corea himself lined up a bank of then state-of-the-art keyboards, most of which now sound no more contemporary than a clavichord might. He added horns and a few strings and tied himself up in a drab fantasy realm that muffled even the sub-Bartókian melodies which had emerged from time to time in Corea's work and had their apotheosis in the *Children's Songs* (above, and – numbers five and fifteen – on *Friends*). *The Mad Hatter* was in the same dismal vein, with horns and strings clogging up some of the most promising material. The one bright spot is Joe Farrell's part on 'Humpty Dumpty', a typically elegant and feeling tenor break.

Friends was the one with the embarrassing Smurfs cover which must have put off hundreds of potential buyers. Perversely, it's better than the two previous items. The long 'Smaba Song' and the title-track are close to his best for this vintage, and Farrell and Gomez give the session a considerable boost. Corea was still publicly thanking L. Ron Hubbard for his 'continual inspiration', but it was never clear how exactly the fantasy realm into which these works dipped was the product of a clear – or Clear – vision that went beyond verbalized or abstract concepts and to what extent they were a sign of creative exhaustion.

My Spanish Heart was a rare instance of Corea working with a large band. It gives every impression of having been got up for the tourists. It's a rather ersatz Latin concoction that never seems to earn its climaxes or justify the band's rather strained enthusiasm.

****** Jazz Masters 3**
Verve 5198202-2 *As above.* 72–78.

A cracking anthology, ideal as a portable or automobile backup. Includes 'Spain', 'Light As A Feather', 'My Spanish Heart', 'Captain Marvel' and more. Next time someone says, 'Chick Corea? Never heard of him,' this is your natural recourse.

**** Corea Hancock**
Polydor 835360 *Corea; Herbie Hancock (p).* 2/78.

***** Crystal Silence**
ECM 831331-2 *Corea; Gary Burton (vib).* 10/79.

****(*) In Concert, Zurich, October 28, 1979**
ECM 821415-2 2CD *As above.*

****(*) Lyric Suite For Sextet**
ECM 815274-2 *As above, except add string quartet.* 9/82.

Interesting duo performances of 'La Fiesta' and 'Maiden Voyage' on *Corea Hancock* (a compositional credit apiece), but by no means a compelling album, with some of Hancock's notions baffling in the extreme. *Crystal Silence* is a lot more substantial than it initially sounds and the music holds up well on the subsequent concert performance, which for a time was a worthwhile substitute, though CD has given the sound a cleaner and more distinctive edge. 'Senor Mouse' and 'Crystal Silence' reappear from the studio disc and there is a fine eponymous Bud Powell tribute that is well worth the admission price.

The *Lyric Suite* recalls Ravel more readily than Alban Berg, which is no bad thing. It's delicate, attractive music, sensibly limited in scope, firmly and, as always, beautifully executed. Less baroquely ambitious than Jarrett's classical compositions, it comes across as something of a by-blow.

***** Tap Step**
Stretch GRS 00092 *Corea; Alan Vizutti (t, flhn); Joe Henderson (ts); Joe Farrell (ts, ss); Hubert Laws (f, picc); Bunny Brunel, Stanley Clarke, Jamie Faunt (b); Tommy Brechtlein (d); Don Alias, Airto Moreira, Laudir Oliveira (perc); Nani Vila Brunel, Shelby Flint, Flora Purim, Gayle Moran (v).* 12/79, 1/80.

The Stretch Collector series was planned as a way of releasing previously unheard or unavailable Corea material, partly (as in the case of the item below) to offset bootleg issues, partly, one suspects, as a reaction to the pianist's rather difficult relationship with the recording industry.

The stuff on *Tap Step* is pretty much of a muchness; a heavy emphasis on electric piano, synth and clavinet, a fondness for rock settings, Latin percussion and, here and there, voices. Only on 'Grandpa Blues' with Bunny Brunel on fretless bass and Stanley Clarke on his piccolo bass is there anything that really grabs the attention. The few glimpses of Joe Farrell are welcome as always, and Joe Henderson, who in these years was quite close to Corea (see below), contributes a typically unstuffy and intelligent part to 'Flamenco', which belongs in the *Light As A Feather* league. Other than these two tracks, little of distinction to report.

*****(*) Live In Montreux**
Stretch GRS 00122 *Corea; Joe Henderson (ts); Gary Peacock (b); Roy Haynes (d).* 81.

Chick wore a T-shirt emblazoned with the legend 'EAT CARROTS'. Haynes played throughout as if on a diet of raw steak. Henderson and Peacock just snacked away happily. This is a further dip into the Corea archive for Stretch, a supergroup encounter introduced with due sense of occasion by Montreux organizer Claude Nobs, who just about gets off-stage quick enough before the fireworks begin. Though things like 'Folk Song' and 'Psalm' are not in themselves demanding, the standard of musicianship required to last in this company is awesome. On 'Hairy Canary' (which may be an oblique reference to Charlie Parker's music), the four jostle a bit and generally check one another out. The main weight of the session falls to the two tracks already mentioned and an extended improvisation on 'Trinkle Tinkle', a version of Chick's 'Quintet No. 2' and Peacock's 'Up, Up, And ...' Even though the horn sound is often rather uncertain and indistinct, Henderson remains the key to the whole proceedings, an improviser of undimmed resource and patience, required to work in a notably floaty and uncertain harmonic landscape. Not a great recording, but a splendid record all the same.

***** Works**
ECM 825426-2 *Corea (p solo and with various bands).* 71–83.

A well-selected sample of the pianist's decade-plus with ECM. Not many surprises, though it's interesting how thin the short piano improvisations from ECM 1014 and 1020 sound when heard out of context.

**** Voyage**
ECM 823468-2 *Corea; Steve Kujala (f).* 7/84.

**** Septet**
ECM 827258-2 *As above, except add strings and french horn.* 7/84, 10/84.

Voyage is a flimsy confection that is very difficult to take entirely seriously. Part of the problem is that the two players take it very seriously indeed, when what it cries out for is a little lightness of touch. *Septet* is no more pulse-quickening, but it has the benefit of a certain variation of register and timbre that is episodically quite interesting.

***** Akoustic Band**
GRP 059 582 2 *Corea; John Patitucci (b); Dave Weckl (d).*

****(*) Alive**
GRP 059 627 2 *As above.*

From the very first notes of 'My One And Only Love' and 'Bessie's Blues' on the first of these, Corea is unmistakable. For better or worse, he still has perhaps the most distinctive stylistic signature in contemporary jazz piano, a rippling fullness of sound that cloys very quickly. Here, then, the promised Akoustic Band and a mainly standards set. Compared to what Keith Jarrett has done with similar repertoire, the thinness of Corea's conception becomes clearer. *Akoustic Band* has its moments, mostly on original material, and *Alive* is an uncomplicated, entertaining set; the pianos both sound first rate and the production is spot-on.

***** Three Quartets**
Stretch GRS 00032 *Corea; Michael Brecker (ts); Eddie Gomez (b); Steve Gadd (d).* 1 & 2/81.

Stretch is Corea's own imprint, licensed through GRP and devoted not just to archive material like the Montreux concert (above) but to new recording as well. The *Three Quartets* were structured jazz compositions with a wide range of classical influences, and they see Corea exploring some of the territory Bill Evans (who had died prematurely the year before) left uncolonized. 'Quartet No. 2' is the only one broken down into parts – dedications, respectively, to Duke Ellington and John Coltrane – and it is harmonically the most varied. The other two are unmistakable Corea, mixing funky lines with a floating, very classical sound which the Bösendorfer Grand richly accentuates.

After the main session ended, the band filled in studio time with a few untried originals and an off-the-cuff run-through of Charlie Parker's 'Confirmation'. Though they don't quite fit in with the three main items for the original LP, they contain (perversely enough) some of the leader's best playing on the record. Michael Brecker was still developing what has since become the most ubiquitous contemporary tenor sound after John Coltrane and Jan Garbarek, and he still sounds adventurous and forceful.

****(*) The Chick Corea Elektric Band**
GRP 059 535 2 *Corea; Scott Henderson, Carlos Rios (g); John Patitucci (b); Dave Weckl (d, perc).*

***** Inside Out**
GRP 059 6012 *As above, except omit Henderson, Rios; add Eric Marienthal (sax), Frank Gambale (g).*

****(*) Beneath The Mask**
GRP 059 649 2 *As above.*

****(*) Eye Of The Beholder**
GRP 059 564 2 *Corea; Eric Marienthal (sax); John Novello (syn); Frank Gambale (g); John Patitucci (b); Dave Weckl (d).*

****(*) Paint The World**
GRP 059 741 2 *Corea; Eric Marienthal (sax); Mike Miller (g); Jimmy Earl (b); Gary Novak (d).*

***** Priceless Jazz**
GRP 059 878 2 *As for the above.* 86–93.

We've never been convinced by the Elektric Band but, given Chick's almost incurable inventiveness, there is always something to ponder and enjoy. The first album is disconcertingly crude, but with the introduction of Marienthal the textures are softened and there are several moments even sceptical visitors would be happy to revisit. *Paint The World* was credited to Elektric Band II; the formula is very much the same. The compilation disc is a very decent compromise, though we'd quibble with the specific choice of tracks.

****(*) Touchstone**
Stretch 00042 *Corea; Alan Vizutti (t); Lee Konitz (as); Steve Kujala (ts, f); Al DiMeola, Paco De Lucia (g); Carlos Benavent, Stanley Clarke, Bob Magnusson (b); Lenny White (d); Carol Shrive (vn); Greg Gottlieb (vla); Alex Acuña, Don Alias, Laudir Oliveira (perc); Gayle Moran (v).*

Prefaced by a nutty fable about the Singing Woman and Rivera, 'Touchstone' itself has the same soapy unreality as Hollywood fantasies like *Legend*. Scored for keys, guitar, voice, bass and percussion, it is no more than a couple of slight themes, lent a papier-mâché superstructure and then vaguely jazzed up. There are more interesting things on the record. Lee Konitz's contribution to 'Duende' is a reminder of Getz's *Sweet Rain*, and 'Compadres' reunites Return to Forever for an overlong but attractive blow. The main problem with *Touchstone* is its bittiness. There is more musical substance than on *The Mad Hatter*, but as a disc it's all over the place and can really be seen only as a haphazard sampler.

*****(*) Expressions**
GRP 900732 *Corea (p solo).* 93.

Significant on two counts: the first solo record for some time, and a very welcome return to standards. Corea includes only two of his own compositions (a wonderful reading of 'Armando's Rhumba'), but he scans the history of modern piano jazz with a typically eclectic range of vision. The second original is a 'Blues For Art' and the whole session is dedicated to Tatum. There are tunes by Strayhorn, Monk and Bud Powell, but in each case it's the Tatum strand that is most evident. It's beautifully recorded (Corea is listed as both producer and 'recordist') with a full, old-fashioned sound, pleasantly different from GRP's usual glitter.

*****(*) Time Warp**
Stretch GRS 00152 *Corea; Bob Berg (ts, ss); John Patitucci (b); Gary Novak (d).* 4/95.

A quasi-narrative suite with a sci-fi storyline, bog-standard stuff: purplish glows, names with too few vowels, unbidden transitions from place to place, a little philosophy and dogma ... and yet, one of the best and straightest Corea albums for some time. There is little obvious musical connection between the numbers, nor needs there to be, but Corea has woven the whole package into a suite with interpolated cadenzas from saxophone – bridging 'The Wish' and 'Terrain', his own intro to 'New Life', by far the most important track on the disc – and Patitucci's switch to Garrison mode to set 'Discovery' in motion.

'New Life' is as boldly optimistic and as quietly chastened as anything since *Song Of Singing* on Blue Note. It was a trio, and in some ways this record has the feel of a trio performance with Berg superadded, mostly effectively as here, but sometimes more jarringly where it seems clear that he is working his own agenda. The mystery – other than what exactly is going on in the story of Arndok – is why Corea should have felt drawn to a drummer as leaden and hostile as Novak. But for him, and a few raw edges elsewhere, this would be up with Corea's very best, rather than teetering problematically on the fringes.

*****(*) Remembering Bud Powell**

Stretch SCD 9012 *Corea; Wallace Roney (t); Kenny Garrett (as); Joshua Redman (ts); Christian McBride (b); Roy Haynes (d).* 96.

Bud in his last days was as troubled as Chick has been Clear, and on the face of it this seems an unlikely permutation. It also seems surprising that Corea should have put together such a substantial line-up for a tribute to Powell, when a basic piano trio might have seemed the better and more likely option. In the event, *Remembering* is a small triumph, an understated and affectionate album that gives a clear impression of its subject – as understood by a follower – but without succumbing to sycophancy. Apart from a specially written tribute, all the tracks are credited to Powell. There is a superb quintet version of the brooding, problematic 'Glass Enclosure', a brisk, almost antagonistic version of 'Oblivion', and more thoughtful renditions of 'Tempus Fugit' (didn't it just?) and 'I'll Keep Loving You'. Corea's touch is exquisite and one has the sense that he has steeped himself in the literature before tackling the session. As ever, Redman is flash without much profundity, and Garrett occasionally covers up his more profound responses with a meretricious gloss, while remaining faithful to the source material and his own slowly evolving talent. It's left to Haynes to establish a direct line to the original and, as always, the wee man is right on the ball.

****** Music Forever And Beyond: The Selected Works Of Chick Corea – 1964–1996**

GRP GRD 5 9819 5CD *Selected from the above.*

A sumptuously packaged, sensibly chronicled and themed set that will keep any Corea fan happy for weeks. The first three discs are chronological, followed by two which cover standards (with Berg, Patitucci and Novak), solos, duets and 'surprises'. Of these last, the most appealing is a 1949 78-r.p.m. recording made by indulgent parents of the boy wonder playing 'I Don't See Me In Your Eyes Anymore'. There are also unreleased tracks from a Montreux concert in 1982 with John McLaughlin, and a specially recorded version of 'Round Midnight' with string quartet, made for this release. It may feel that some of the material on offer has been round the track once too often, most particularly the stuff on disc two, but there is more than enough new material to keep the fussiest collector happy, though bootleggers may have beaten GRP to the punch on some of the live tracks. Hard to fault on any count.

*****(*) Native Sense: The New Duets**

Stretch SCD 9014 *Corea; Gary Burton (vib).* 97.

An old partnership, to be sure, but one which never sounded as if it had exhausted all the ideas. This latter-day set is more robustly recorded than previous encounters, with a plain, unadorned sound that does neither man any harm. It's quite a long record and, aside from a couple of brief 'Bagatelles' and a short, delightful 'Armando's Rhumba', the tracks are played out at length, with plenty of time and space to exchange ideas. The two outstanding performances are 'No Mystery' (which of course contains at least one, a harmonic puzzle) and the more free-floating 'Rhumbata', which is a joyous dance theme.

****** Origin: Live At The Blue Note**

Stretch 9018 *Corea; Steve Davis (tb); Steve Wilson (ss, as, f, cl); Bob Sheppard (ss, ts, bcl, f); Avishai Cohen (b); Adam Cruz (d).* 1/98.

*****(*) A Week At The Blue Note**

Stretch 9020 6CD *As above.* 1/98.

Anything Miles and Keith Jarrett can do, Chick can do every bit as well. To deal with business matters first, the material on these CDs was all recorded during a residency at the Blue Note club in New York. The single album is not a sampler or taster; none of the tracks is reduplicated on the complete set, which is inevitably going to have a limited shelf-life. Taped over three nights at the very start of the year, the sets have pretty much the same configuration. The joy is in hearing how Chick and the horns approach them differently set to set.

The single disc showcased what was obviously an important new band for Corea, one that offered him a chance to experiment with complex voicings but also still swing like crazy. The closing version of the Van Heusen classic, 'It Could Happen To You', is magnificent and far ahead of the single version on the boxed set, and there are stunning versions of originals like 'Dreamless', 'Molecules' and 'Soul Mates'. We can't but conclude that the very best material was selected for the original release and that the rest was expected to gain in force by sheer bulk and repetition. To be clear, there are three versions of 'Bewitched, Bothered And Bewildered', two of 'Molecules' and 'Sifu', three of the blues, 'Matrix', and five of the brief 'Say It Again', which comes in two parts. *A Week* also includes three Monk tunes and Charlie Parker's 'Bird Feathers'. Completism is almost always excessive and only serious students of Chick's pianism will find themselves working through the box more than once. Some of the themes are quite ragged and 'Molecules' in particular doesn't quite come off, though it does point to a growing Ellington influence on Chick's thinking. We say plump for the single album and, if you're lucky enough to find the Japanese release, you should find an extra version of 'Sifu', run down at home with just the trio, which should have you purring all the louder.

*****(*) Change**

Stretch 9023 *As above, except replace Cruz with Jeff Ballard (d).* 98.

Having debuted Origin on the Blue Note sets, Chick took the slightly altered line-up into the studio for a relaxed, swinging set that seems to restore the Latin emphasis. 'Little Flamenco' is a joyous thing, with fine flute work from Wilson and authentic handclaps from the drummer. 'Early Afternoon Blues' might almost be Horace Silver, and there are a couple of moments when Chick seems to namecheck Dr Funk. 'Armando's Tango' is now almost a repertory piece, but it has rarely sounded as fresh and alert, and 'Awakening' which closes the set is as near as you'll get to a career summation in six and a quarter elegant minutes. The only surprise of the set, apart from Cohen's lovely original 'Lylah', is Chick's recorded debut on marimba on 'Wigwam'. He plays with mallets like he plays with his fingers, but the extra percussive edge is delightful and sets the tone for a fresh, inventive record that really does mark a change of direction as well as consolidation of 40 years on the job.

Rich Corpolongo

ALTO AND SOPRANO SAXOPHONES, CLARINET

One of the Chicagoan cognoscenti occasionally recorded by Delmark, Corpolongo is a homebody saxophonist who has seldom played outside the city.

***** Just Found Joy**

Delmark De-489 *Corpolongo; Larry Luchowski (p); Jeff Czech (vn); Erich Hochberg (b); Mike Raynor (d); Paul Wertico (perc).* 7/95.

He played bebop with Herbie Hancock in college, but since then Rich Corpolongo has been no more than a local hero in various Chicagoan circles. He studied with Joe Daley, and there is certainly something of Daley's exuberant free bop in this music; also a little of Eric Dolphy, whose 'Straight Up And Down' is recalled by the rhythmical staggers of the title-tune here. Corpolongo is a mercurial player, almost over-reaching himself in the speed circles of 'Time Impulse', but he likes the clarinet a lot and he gets out some intriguing solos on that horn on some of these tracks. The music is a rather rough-and-ready brew of various free-thinking styles, and the occasional raggedness is perhaps typical of how a relatively closed local scene develops in its own careless way. His quartet (Czech and Wertico play only on the final track) offer enthusiastic support, but Corpolongo himself is the only one to really compel the ear, and in his belated leadership debut he's made a rough, likeable testament.

Larry Coryell (born 1943)

GUITAR

Coryell was born and raised in Galveston, Texas. He played in pianist Mike Mandel's group before joining Chico Hamilton and Gary Burton, where his rock-tinged sound came to wide notice. In later years, he formed the group Eleventh House which, along with Return To Forever and the Mahavishnu Orchestra, was definitive of the jazz-rock boom of the early '70s. In more recent years, Coryell has moved between pure bop, fusion and Latin styles. His limpid delivery and almost classically accurate lines conceal real power, most evident in his early, Hendrix-influenced days, but still evident in the later, Latin-inspired work.

***** Lady Coryell**

Vanguard VCD 6509 *Coryell; Jimmy Garrison, Miroslav Vitous (b); Elvin Jones, Bob Moses (d).* 69.

***** Spaces**

Vanguard 79345 *Coryell; Michael Lawrence (t); Chick Corea (p, ky); John McLaughlin (g); Miroslav Vitous (b); Billy Cobham (d).* 7/70.

***** Introducing Larry Coryell And The Eleventh House**

Vanguard 79342 *Coryell; Randy Brecker, Michael Lawrence (t); Chick Corea, Mike Mandel (p, ky); Melvin Bronson, Danny Trifan (b); Billy Cobham, Harry Wilkinson (d).* 72.

***** At Montreux**

Vanguard 79410 *Coryell; Michael Lawrence (t); Mike Mandel (ky); Danny Trifan (b); Alphonse Mouzon (d, perc).* 7/74.

***** Planet End**

Vanguard VCD 79367 *Coryell; Michael Lawrence (t); Chick Corea, Mike Mandel (p, ky); Steve Khan, John McLaughlin (g); Will Lee, Danny Trifan, Miroslav Vitous (b); Billy Cobham, Alphonse Mouzon (d).* 75.

***** The Essential Larry Coryell**

Vanguard VCD 79575/6 2CD *Coryell; Randy Brecker (t); Steve Marcus (ss); Mike Mandel (p, syn); John McLaughlin (g); Melvin Bronson, Chuck Rainey, Albert Stinson, Danny Trifan, Miroslav Vitous (b); Billy Cobham, Elvin Jones, Bob Moses, Alphonse Mouzon, Bernard Pretty Purdie, Harry Wilkinson (d); Julie Coryell (v).* 68–75.

*****(*) Improvisations: The Best Of The Vanguard Years**

Vanguard VCD 79614/5 2CD *As above, except add Michael Lawrence (t), Darius Brubeck (p), Steve Khan (g), Chris Brubeck, Ron Carter, Jimmy Garrison (b), Danny Brubeck (d), Ray Mantilla (perc).* 68–75.

'Schizophrenic' is a wildly misused critical adjective, but if there was ever a split musical personality, it is Coryell. The guitarist never seemed able to make up his mind whether he wanted to be Chet Atkins, Jimi Hendrix or Segovia; and there were always doubts about his chops as an improviser. The idea of simultaneous evolution is better attested in natural history than in human culture and yet it seems that parallel developments do occur without direct 'influence' from one artist to another. Though Coryell does sound superficially similar to Miles Davis on 'Yin' (actually a Wolfgang Dauner tune) and touches on similar territory to the Mahavishnu Orchestra with John McLaughlin on 'Spaces (Infinite)', the real story is of shared discovery rather than tutelage. Coryell is the unsung hero of the fusion movement, and a fine compilation like this helps to redress the balance.

Perhaps better to go back to the original albums, of which *Spaces* is the most celebrated, a floaty, meditative disc with a solid core of invention and some formidable interaction between the two very different guitarists. McLaughlin so often worked best in dialogue with another guitar player, whether Coryell, Santana or Pace De Lucia and Al DiMeola in later years, and on *Spaces* he is thoughtful and intense. The stereo separation is a bit drastic by later standards, but it contributes to the nostalgic appeal of the record. The inclusion of Scott LaFaro's 'Gloria's Step' and René Thomas's 'René's Theme' was an obvious signal that this was not another rock group but an outfit schooled in the modern jazz tradition.

Lady Coryell was more obviously influenced by rock. The title-track, dedicated to Julie, is a fusion classic and has rather eclipsed the rest of a fine and thoughtful album, which saw the aesthetic of the John Coltrane Quartet and of the MC5 (who always claimed to have been influenced by Trane) brought full circle. 'You Don't Know What Love Is' sounds like a token standard.

Planet End was Larry's last album for Vanguard and is little more than a series of loose and rather sloppy jams. The Eleventh House formula was well established by this stage but one can almost hear the guitarist coasting towards the end of a contract, and the only track which combines the excitement and elegance of earlier days is Larry Young's 'Tyrone'.

The two samplers in their different ways pretty much cover the waterfront in terms of the Vanguard years. *Improvisations* is longer and much more detailed and has probably superseded the sketchier sampling on *Essential*. The two-CD set includes all the obvious things: 'Lady Coryell', 'René's Theme', 'Spaces (Infinite)' with McLaughlin, the fiery 'Jam With Albert', 'Low-Lee-Tah' and the enigmatic 'Scotland 1', which was inspired by Larry's visit to the Buddhist community at Eskdalemuir. All in all, a fitting summation of a highly creative period that wouldn't be matched for sheer energy until the mid-'80s.

*** Twin House

Act 9202 *Coryell: Philip Catherine (g); Joachim Kühn (p).* 76, 77.

Indifferently recorded in London and Hamburg, these are mainly guitar duets, with just one opening for Kühn. Coryell leads off a great version of 'The Train And The River', and there's a companionable 'Nuages'; but for the most part the material is original and very fresh. The two guitars are rather crudely separated and could do with narrowing a bit, but there are passages where it's impossible to judge who's playing what, though generally Catherine plays with a fuller, less rhythmic intonation.

*** Bolero

Evidence ECD 22046 *Coryell; Brian Keane (g).* 4/81.

Coryell's classical interests are to the fore here, with versions of *Le tombeau de Couperin* and an improvisation on Ravel's famous 'Bolero' dominating the first half of an album that consists of ten solos and four duets with Keane, who also plays a solo 'Piece For Larry'. Coryell's entire range is on view here, except for the headlong fusion stuff, and with a strong emphasis on acoustic playing. As such, it makes a decent introduction to his guitar style.

**(*) A Quiet Day In Spring

Steeplechase SCCD 31187 *Coryell; Michal Urbaniak (vn); Jesper Lundgaard (b).* 11/83.

This was an interesting pairing. The Polish-born fusion violinist has had a fairly up-and-down career and can sound rather sentimental in a more intimate setting like this. However, Coryell gets him going on tunes like his own 'Polish Reggae' and two lovely waltzes on which he combines delicate open-string passages with rich, triple-stopped chords that conjure up the Polish Romantic composers. Coryell takes a back seat where necessary, as on the violinist's feature, 'Stuff's Stuff', but is at his expressive best on 'Rue Gregoire Du Tour', picking out soft, sustained variations on the melody.

***(*) Major Jazz Minor Blues

32 Jazz 32058 *Coryell; Kenny Barron, Stanley Cowell, Albert Dailey (p); George Mraz, Buster Williams (b); Beaver Harris, Billy Hart, Marvin 'Smitty' Smith (d); Julie Coryell (v).* 2/84–10/89.

Coryell's spell with Muse was a fruitful one, albeit one of the less obviously eclectic and experimental phases of his career. The three records represented on this excellent compilation – in chronological order *Comin' Home, Toku Do* and *Shining Hour* – are firmly anchored in bebop, as the titles and the personnels probably suggest. Even 'Toku Do' itself is not the item of exotica the title might suggest but a fine blues theme by Buster Williams. The more lyrical approach of Albert Dailey and George Mraz suits Coryell better than the percussive attack of Stanley Cowell. The third of the pianists, Kenny Barron, is tersely lyrical and his comping on 'My Shining Hour' opens up new dimensions even on the most familiar changes and melodies. For those who find Coryell too whimsically eclectic, this is the record that will win them round to the idea of Larry the Jazzer.

*** Together

Concord CJ 4289 *Coryell; Emily Remler (g).* 8/85.

Emily Remler's death from a heart attack, aged only 32, robbed America of one of its foremost instrumental voices and a jazz musician of considerable stature. *Together* delivers handsomely, a warm, approachable album which does not lack for subtleties. Recommended.

*** Dragon Gate

Shanachie 97005 *Coryell; Stefan Grossman (g).* 89.

Coryell credits Ellis Marsalis with the revelation that allowed him to play Coltrane's 'Giant Steps' as a solo guitar piece: recast the piece in waltz time and slow it right down, and the changes would make sense ... and so they do. Throughout the album, Coryell pays tribute to the masters who made him want to be a musician, and his version of Wes Montgomery's 'West Coast Blues' has to be heard in that light. Coryell plays alone, overdubbed, and in duet with Grossman. *Dragon Gate* is beautifully textured, well paced, but perhaps a little too technical for the casual listener.

*** Twelve Frets To One Octave

Shanachie 97015 *Coryell (g solo).* 91.

Covering everything from raw, rootsy blues to the sober, classical shapes of 'Bartok Eleven' to the lovely lilt of 'Transparence' (not to be confused with the Philip Catherine tune of the same name). Technically, Coryell has it all taped. His single-note runs are fleet and dexterous, his chording has harmonic mass and bulk, and his rhythms and counter-rhythms frequently create the impression that more than one musician must be involved. We have re-examined at least half-a-dozen spots on this album, persuaded that some sort of overdubbing was used, but apparently and convincingly not.

*** Sketches Of Coryell

Shanachie 5024 *Coryell; Alex Sipiagin (t); Dave Mann (ss, ts); Bob Berg (ts); Julian Coryell, Peter Moffitt, Mark Sherman (ky); Rodney Jones (g, ky); Kennan Keating (b, ky); Kenwood Dennard (d); Jonathan Abrams, Emedin Rivera (perc).* 96.

This mixed and patchy album includes compositions by Moffitt, Sherman and Keating, as well as Stevie Wonder's 'I Am Singing' and an arrangement of the Miles-endorsed 'Concierto De Aranjuez'. Coryell's playing long since reached a peak of confidence, but one misses the energy and freshness of his early fusion work and his first dabbling in classical repertoire. These days, he seems more bent on affirming his eclecticism and range.

*** Spaces Revisited

Shanachie 5033 *Coryell; Bireli Lagrene (g); Richard Bona (b); Billy Cobham (d).* 2/97.

It had been rumoured for some time that the group which made *Spaces* at the turn of the '70s, one of the finest fusion records of all time, might reconvene for a recording. In the event, Lagrene is an interesting replacement for John McLaughlin and Cameroonian Richard Bona makes a very different sound from Miroslav Vitous. Coryell's 'Variations On Pork Pie Hat' and his introduction to an interpretation of 'Ruby My Dear' are of the highest calibre. This is not so much a nostalgic re-creation of the original group as an entirely new working of a sound that might otherwise be rather dated and time-warped. Bona's funky bass sits just as well with Cobham's percussion, but it also has a percussive edge its predecessor lacked. A remarkable record in its own right.

***(*) Monk, Trane, Miles & Me

High Note HCD 7028 *Coryell; Willie Williams (ts); John Hicks (p); Santi Debriano (b); Yoron Israel (d).* 5/98.

For all his interest in classical, Latin and fusion music, Coryell has remained very much devoted to straight, bop-based jazz, and this tough, funky album is a testament to his ongoing engagement with modern jazz and its great masters. Larry kicks off with two brisk standards, 'Star Eyes' and 'Alone Together', and starts to engage with his ancestors in an interpretation of Monk's 'Trinkle Tinkle'. Coltrane is represented by 'Naima', which is obvious fare for the guitarist, but also the more aggressive 'Up Against The Wall'. Miles is limited to a rather dull version of 'All Blues', while 'me' is represented in two originals, 'Fairfield County Blues', generic and rather bland, and the closing 'Almost A Waltz'. Oddly, the most effective composition and performance of the set is down to bassist Santi Debriano; 'Patience' is a moody waltz and Larry admits that he had to go back to the Van Gelder studio to re-record his part and master the strange, slashing chords the bassist had written for him.

*** Cause & Effect

Tone Center 40022 *Coryell; Tom Coster (org, ky); Victor Wooten (b); Steve Smith (d).* 8/98.

Given the revival of interest in '70s fusion towards the end of the century, it wasn't so very surprising to hear Coryell return to the idiom. Coster and Smith are veterans of Carlos Santana's jazz-orientated rock band. The session consisted largely of open-ended jams, created with a freshness that couldn't have been guaranteed had Coryell insisted on recording old tunes from the Eleventh House days. Coryell's 'Bubba' is as greasy and funky as anything he has ever done and the finale, 'Wes And Jimi', a heart-felt tribute to two profound influences. The obvious source for all this is Tony Williams's Lifetime, but we were also reminded of the trio reconvened in the '90s by former Lifetime man, Jack Bruce, with saxophonist Dick Heckstall-Smith and drummer John Stevens. Terrific stuff. Pure nostalgia for those who remember the first generation; a treat even for those who don't.

*** Private Concert

Acoustic Music 1159 *Coryell (g solo).* 4/99.

Smoothly elegant and thoughtful jazz but the 'private' side of it is perhaps overstated. Always given to introspection, even in his more furious moments, Coryell sounds as though he is playing for his own entertainment rather than ours.

*** Coryells

Chesky 192 *Coryell; Julian Coryell (g); Murali Coryell (g, v); Brian Torff (b); Alphonse Mouzon (perc).* 99.

Larry and Julie were long-time collaborators, but this disc features a new generation of Coryells, the first time that fellow-guitarists Julian and Murali have joined dad on record. It's a project that includes material like 'Low-Lee-Tah', which was written before they were born. The best interaction between the three comes on Larry's classic 'Transparence' and on Julian's composition, 'Sink Or Swim', which suggests that in future years he will also be an impressive writer. Murali additionally sings on a couple of cuts and Julian has a couple of numbers to himself, accompanied only by bassist Brian Torff, whose touch is impeccable. Mouzon sticks to hand drums throughout, occasionally recalling his role in Larry's fusion band, Eleventh House, but also suggesting just how inventive a musician he has always been in his own right.

***(*) New High

High Note 7052 *Coryell (g solo).* 99.

Effortlessly swinging, packed with ideas and very much in a jazz idiom, *New High* saw Coryell enter a new decade and a new age with supreme confidence. His solo on 'Bags' Groove' is almost arrogantly straightforward and unfussy, and the dying falls of 'Old Folks' are tempered by a wise and sanguine major key theme. Cracking stuff.

Louis Cottrell (1911–78)

CLARINET

A student of Lorenzo Tio and Barney Bigard, Cottrell was working with the Young Tuxedo Band while still a teenager, and he toured and recorded with Don Albert in the 1930s. He played the old-fashioned French Albert system clarinet.

*** The Louis Cottrell Trio

Original Jazz Classics OJC 1836-2 *Cottrell; Emanuel Sayles (g); McNeal Breaux, Alcide Slow Drag Pavageau (b).* 1/61.

One of the least-known albums in Riverside's *New Orleans: The Living Legends* series featured this charming trio music by a clarinettist far less remembered than most of the city's favourite sons on this horn. Cottrell's style has none of the harshness of the George Lewis manner: he preferred the soft tone and modest vibrato that typified the old-fashioned elegance of the Lorenzo Tio style. He never had a better showcase than this one, with the spirited strum of Sayles and the no-frills line of Breaux alongside (Pavageau appears on only one brief track). On some songs he seems careless about his phrasing and falters here and there, but on others – 'Rose Room' is a good instance – the purling variations on the tune secure a surprising intensity. Two tracks, previously available only on an anthology LP, have been added to the original programme for the CD reissue.

Curtis Counce (1926–63)

DOUBLE BASS

Counce moved from Kansas City, where he had won some experience with one of the last territory bands, to join the best of the West Coast boppers in Los Angeles. Reminiscent of other West Coasters like Red Mitchell and Monty Budwig, he had a big, swinging delivery which suited solo exposure.

***** You Get More Bounce**

Original Jazz Classics OJC 159 *Counce; Jack Sheldon, Gerald Wilson (t); Harold Land (ts); Carl Perkins (p); Frank Butler (d).* 10/56.

*****(*) Landslide**

Original Jazz Classics OJC 606 *As above.* 4/57.

***** Carl's Blues**

Original Jazz Classics OJC 423 *As above.* 8/57.

***** Sonority**

Contemporary C 7655 *As above.* 1/58.

*****(*) Exploring The Future**

Boplicity CD 7 *Counce; Rolf Ericson (t); Harold Land (ts); Elmo Hope (p); Frank Butler (d).* 4/58.

'More bounce' promised, more bounce delivered. Elasticity aplenty in Counce's late-1950s quintet, one of the better and more resilient bands working the West Coast scene at the time. Perhaps the best of the albums is *Exploring The Future*, but *Landslide* is a fine one too, showcasing Land's beefy tenor and Sheldon's very underrated soloing. Perkins, remembered best for his weird, crab-wise technique, was probably on better form with this band than anywhere else on record, but the real star – a point recognized by the drum solo 'The Butler Did It' on *Carl's Blues* and 'A Drum Conversation' on the bin-end *Sonority* – was Frank Butler, a powerful technician who shared Counce's own instinctive swing. He is also the dedicatee of 'A Fifth For Frank' (do they mean the interval or the measure of whisky?) on *Landslide*. Most of the material stems from the same half-dozen sessions but is none the worse for that, given the quality of the material. *Sonority* initially sounded like the makeweight, but repeated hearings suggest it's a stronger statement than we originally thought. Counce's own contribution to 'A Night In Tunisia' and 'How Long Has This Been Going On' is worthy of anyone's notice.

Though he lived for another few years and certainly recorded again, this is his last record as leader. The original Dootone release of *Exploring The Future* is now a considerable rarity and it's good to have the music back in circulation. This is hard bop without the strut and the sneer, just laid-back, swinging music, played to challenging charts and arrangements (largely) by Elmo Hope. The pianist's 'Race For Space' and 'Countdown' are both quite advanced and the titles suggest how much these guys wanted to be seen as part of something new rather than a music that was beginning to sound dated. The transfers are very good, with Counce settled into the middle of the ensemble. Ericson and Land are sometimes a touch off-mic, but not to any troubling extent.

Stanley Cowell (born 1941)

PIANO

Cowell's vocation was decided when at the age of six he saw Art Tatum. College-educated, his real apprenticeship was with Roland Kirk; but it was the association with Charles Tolliver, with whom he founded the Strata East label, that really shaped his dark, complex style which draws on Bud Powell and Monk as well as Tatum.

***** Travellin' Man**

Black Lion BLCD 760178 *Cowell; Steve Novosel (b); Jimmy Hopps (d).* 6/69.

*****(*) Brilliant Circles**

Black Lion BLCD 760204 *Cowell; Woody Shaw (t, perc); Tyrone Washington (ts, f, cl, perc); Bobby Hutcherson (vib); Reggie Workman (b); Joe Chambers (d).* 9/69.

Cowell is a supremely gifted player who has managed to bridge the pianism of bebop (and Bud Powell especially) with the free movement of the 1960s. For far too long his recorded output was restricted to work as a jobbing sideman on the Galaxy label – his own 1978 Galaxy LP, *Equipoise*, is long out of print – backing Art Pepper, John Klemmer and Johnny Griffin, among others.

Recorded in London by the enterprising Alan Bates, *Travellin' Man* offers a good synopsis of what Cowell was doing at the end of his first full decade as a professional, a period when he gigged with Marion Brown and Max Roach. 'You Took Advantage Of Me' is a tribute to Art Tatum, who apparently visited the Cowell home in Toledo, Ohio, and hammered the family piano into submission. Cowell's own gentler side would take some time to settle; too often early in his career he sounds merely sentimental, though 'Travellin' Man', like 'Blues For The Viet Cong', is taken on electric piano, for which he has had a long-standing affection and on which he always finds interesting clusters and colours. The two long tracks, 'The Shuttle' and the oddly titled 'Photon In A Paper World', are both quite densely structured, with internal reverses and subtly varied repeats. Novosel and Hopps battle gamely but give no real sense of understanding what's expected of them. The sound is about scratch for the period, a touch brusque here and there, but perfectly listenable.

The other Black Lion was recorded in New York with a much more venturesome group. Cowell had worked with Hutcherson in Harold Land's group and the rapport is immediate and powerful. Bobby's low metallic chimes on the title-tune are the perfect complement to Cowell's percussive attack; this reissue includes a second take of the Monk-inspired piece, as well as 'Musical Prayers', a slightly lumpen composition by the little-known Tyrone Washington, whose multi-instrumentalism is an interesting element of the record. He is also credited with 'Earthly Heavens', a much more effective invention. Cowell's big solo statements on 'Brilliant Circles' are matched by sterling work from the rest of the band. Workman is in stunningly good form, clear-voiced and articulate as ever, and Chambers makes the kit work like a whole section. Congenial as the company is, this isn't one of Woody Shaw's better recordings of the period. He sounds short-winded and rather distracted, even on his own 'Boo Ann's Grand', though the tone is as rich and caramelly as ever. 'Bobby's

Tune' was apparently brought in by Hutcherson at the last minute and run down without a rehearsal, underlining just how responsive a group this was. Not perhaps a crucial Cowell album – there are more obviously personalized projects from before and since – but a very fine modern-jazz record.

***(*) We Three

DIW 807 *Cowell; Buster Williams (b); Frederick Waits (d).* 12/87.

As the title suggests, this was issued as a collaborative trio rather than as a Cowell session. Waits and the fecund Williams contribute half the charts between them and the high points tend to come on Williams pieces: 'Air Dancing' and 'Deceptacon' are good enough to be in anyone's book. Cowell's own main statement comes on 'Sienna', an ongoing compositional essay that recurs in his work of these years. This is a particularly fine rendition of it, though the composer's solo on the Steeplechase trio below just edges it into second place.

Waits died less than a year after the session, an unsung hero. He plays with the lyrical touch Cowell seemed to value after his stint with Max Roach. Waits's 'My Little Sharif' has a touching charm that does not pall with repeated listenings, though we don't recall it having been recorded by anyone else.

**** Sienna

Steeplechase SCCD 31253 *Cowell; Ron McClure (b); Keith Copeland (d).* 7/89.

This may very well be Cowell's finest moment on record, a tightly marshalled, endlessly inventive trio session that comes at the beginning of a period of intense creativity. The two opening tracks, 'Cal Massey' and the gentle ballad, 'I Think It's Time To Say Goodbye', take the measure of Cowell's extraordinarily expressive range. Copeland seems a little out of place on slower tracks, which might well have been done as duos with the excellent McClure, but the drummer's abrupt unison accents on 'Evidence' are startlingly effective. This is quite the best version of Monk's tune since the master's own and it represents a peak from which the album can only decline. A long 'I Concentrate On You' adds nothing to the hundreds that have gone before, waffling round the chords in an almost detached way. It's only with the title-track, just one of a cycle of 'Sienna'-related compositions, and with the closing 'Dis Place' that Cowell lets loose his remarkable harmonic and rhythmic intelligence. An excellent album, recorded in an odd, rather claustrophobic acoustic.

*** Back In The Beautiful

Concord CCD 4398 *Cowell; Steve Coleman (as, ss); Santi Debriano (b); Joe Chambers (d).* 7/89.

A curious record and one that breaks the run of vintage performances that stretches over these few years. Coleman seems an unlikely collaborator, and there are a couple of occasions when he almost deliberately breaks the mood. He most certainly isn't in tune with the piano, either harmonically or creatively, and roars through 'But Beautiful' and 'A Nightingale Sang In Berkeley Square'. The trio functions pretty well, with one or two reservations about Debriano's time-feel, which is often perverse. 'Prayer For Peace' is the strongest statement on the set, with the best balance of elements. Otherwise, a mish-mash.

***(*) Live At Maybeck Recital Hall

Concord CCD 4431 *Cowell (p solo).* 6/90.

Cowell was early in the frame in this remarkable series, and he provides one of the most revelatory of the sessions. He features himself only sparingly as a composer: 'I Am Waiting', 'Little Sunny' and the concluding 'Cal Massey', which had also been included on *Sienna*. Typically, though, Cowell doesn't approach the standard material without a twist. 'Softly As In A Morning Sunrise' opens in the uncontroversially pianistic key of C minor, but then undergoes an astonishing *twelve* changes; the effect is astonishing, with more sheer invention packed into its length than most players would achieve in a dozen tracks. The effect might be gimmicky rather than virtuosic were it not for the sheer invention Cowell packs in. 'Stella By Starlight' and 'I'll Remember April', 'Out Of This World', 'Autumn Leaves' and 'Django' also receive subtly off-centre readings, not deconstructions but crafty recentrings of melody. Wayne Shorter's 'Nefertiti' is a *tour de force*, rarely attempted without horns; Charlie Parker's 'Big Foot' (aka 'Air Conditioning') is a finger-breaker. If the Maybeck series was intended as a showcase of piano artistry, then Cowell probably comes out of it more significantly enhanced than anyone. He manages to combine thoughtfulness with sheer excitement, originality and a resolute attachment to the tradition.

**** Close To You Alone

DIW 603 *Cowell; Cecil McBee (b); Ronnie Burrage (d).* 8/90.

This comes from the high summer of Cowell's purple patch, just a couple of months after the Maybeck gig. It begins on dramatic bass accents from McBee on his own '"D" Bass-ic Blues'. Cowell's entry is reminiscent of 1950s Cecil Taylor but ripples off in his characteristic Bud Powell vein. There are strong signs that the pianist had been listening to Bud again during this period – either that or experiencing some creative return of the repressed; it's Bud's phrasing and chord shapes that one keeps hearing, though rarely a Powell composition.

McBee and Burrage maintain a steady flow of invention and between them are responsible for four of the seven tracks, reinforcing the impression that, as with *We Three*, this is a collaborative trio. Given that another of the tracks is a standard, a rather less secure version of 'Stella By Starlight' than at Maybeck, it does seem as if Cowell has some resistance at this point to foregrounding his own material. 'Equipoise', though, makes a welcome reappearance, its curiously balanced, rather static initial theme sounding almost as if it is built out of some five-note Chinese scale (and Cowell's stiff-fingered 'Chopsticks' attack increases the effect) but then breaking out into a good-natured funk roll. Few current pianists are more interesting to listen to; Cowell seems quite genuinely to be expanding the improvising vocabulary within the confines of standards and blues-based jazz. High marks for McBee and Burrage, too, though the drummer's compositional skills aren't yet up to his playing.

***(*) Departure No. 2

Steeplechase SCCD 31275 *Cowell; Walter Booker (b); Billy Higgins (d).* 10/90.

*** Games

Steeplechase SCCD 31293 *Cowell; Cheyney Thomas (b); Wardell Thomas (d).* 8/91.

*** Bright Passion

Steeplechase SCCD 31328 *As above.* 4/93.

Turning fifty, Cowell had acquired a new creative momentum. Recorded in Denmark and marking a new and very fruitful association with Steeplechase, *Departure* is his most jagged and pugnacious recording for some time. 'Photon In The Paper World' (or is it *A Paper World*?) reappears from 1969 and 'Splintered Ice' has the same harmonic virtuosity as 'Softly' on the Maybeck disc. In both cases, though, Cowell manages to combine technical mastery with genuine expressiveness. 'Four Harmonizations Of The Blues' is almost as mechanical as it sounds. There has always been a strain of sheer cleverness in Cowell's playing, games with false symmetries and weird harmonic regresses; when it breaks through as obviously as this, it's decidedly tiresome.

The later dates are hampered by an inexperienced and below-par rhythm section, and one has to ask what the motivation was. Cowell transcends it triumphantly on *Games*, playing with huge authority and often without seeming reference to his colleagues. There are some majestic episodes on 'From The Rivers Of Our Father', but they fail to add up to anything larger. 'Sienna: Welcome To The New World' is perfunctory and bland, and the new material fails to get things moving. The trio is a lot tighter and more responsive on the later set, but Cowell is muted and workaday, and there's an odd, perfunctory air to the date. After the triumphs of the last couple of years, we can readily spare him an off-day. These last two are for resolute collectors only.

***(*) Live

Steeplechase SCCD 31359 *Cowell; Cheyney Thomas (b); Wardell Thomas (d).* 4/93.

As purple patches go, this was of the deepest mauve, Cowell and his young trio at the Copenhagen Jazz House. The piano certainly isn't of studio quality and there are a couple of notes that sound dead here and there (on early tracks, so perhaps we aren't hearing them in real-time order), but it has enough presence to lift the set. Cowell sticks mainly to standards and jazz tunes, opening with 'Anthropology' and closing with 'In Walked Bud', but mostly staying away from bebop in between. The three originals, 'Bright Passion', 'Brilliant Circles' and a long 'Prayer For Peace', are easily the most interesting things on the record, and perhaps it was merely in deference to the rhythm section that Cowell didn't include more of his own compositions. Nils Winther produces with a sure touch, delivering a set that is both atmospheric and (but for that piano) technically spot-on.

**** Angel Eyes

Steeplechase SCCD 31339 *Cowell (p solo).* 4/93.

How very different he sounds without the constraint (as it often seems) of a group. *Angel Eyes* offers a solid hour of flawless piano jazz. From the opening, Coltrane-tinged 'The Night Has A Thousand Eyes' to the small group of more demanding originals at the close – 'Akua', 'The Ladder', 'Abscretion' – Cowell grips the attention. Following his harmonic logic is beyond most listeners and certainly most of his fellow-players, but it's none the less impressive. The house piano at Steeplechase sounds rather light in this solo context, certainly not one of those great woofing concert things, nor with the purring, woody resonance of the piano at Maybeck; but it's responsive enough for Cowell to weave a subtly inflected spell. Even John Lennon's 'Imagine', a fairly unpromising theme, is woven into something of genuine grandeur.

***(*) Setup

Steeplechase SCCD 31349 *Cowell; Eddie Henderson (t); Dick Griffin (tb); Rick Margitza (ts); Peter Washington (b); Billy Hart (d).* 10/93.

Cowell has never seemed an excessively brooding player, but this is joyously upbeat by any standard. It had been some considerable time since he released a group record with horns and it does the old heart good. The key track is 'Sendai Sendoff', featured in solo form on *Angel Eyes* but here arranged for an excellent and thoroughly sympathetic band. Henderson is in sterling form, always at his best when relieved of the responsibilities of leadership. A word, too, for the unsung Griffin, who gives the ensemble passages a rich, caramelly texture. The saxophonist is less well adapted to Cowell's idiom, and there are a few moments of uncertainty there. The Steeplechase sound is flawless and Nils Winther has managed to create a *simpatico* environment in which the musicians are encouraged to play as they feel, rather than keeping their eye on the clock and an ominously clicking metre. Cowell has rarely sounded more relaxed than over these past few years and, even allowing for a philosophical change of pace that comes with age, the label set-up has to take much of the credit.

***(*) Mandara Blossoms

Steeplechase SCCD 331386 *Cowell; Bill Pierce (ts); Jeff Halsey (b); Ralph Petersen (d); Karen Francis (v).* 11/95.

A wholly unexpected departure. Debby Randolph's lyric to 'Equipoise' sounds as if it was always intended to be there, and Karen Francis's rich, well-trained voice lifts the song up out of the ordinary. With the strongly vocalized Pierce on the session, this has a rich, choral feel that is quite startling and it is certainly not readily identified as a Cowell set. He writes his own lyrics for 'This Life' (the best of the bunch) and the title-track. Randolph and John Scott are responsible for the remaining words. 'Mandara Blossoms' is the briefest thing on the set, a haunting watercolour built on a falling figure, and intended to suggest a moment of philosophical calm. Difficult to say why and where the elements don't quite cohere, but we have some misgivings. The sound isn't always balanced very persuasively and it's occasionally difficult to hear what Cowell himself is doing. The best (and longest) track of all is Billy Strayhorn's 'Daydream', complete with extra verse, and it succeeds largely because it does pitch Karen and Stanley against each other, with saxophone coming in at exactly the right juncture.

***(*) Hear Me One

Steeplechase SCCD 31407 *Cowell; Bruce Williams (as); Dwayne Burno (b); Keith Copeland (d).* 10/96.

The unexpected inclusions here are Monk's 'Ruby My Dear' and that bebop groaner, 'Anthropology'. Neither is within Cowell's normal spectrum. He is by no means a devoted Monkian, and so handles this one with more respect and fidelity than one would expect. He tells the story of having met Monk and telling him that he had written some tunes in his style. 'How can you write tunes in my style when all my songs are different?' Fair point, and that more than anything Cowell has taken on board. There is no Cowell 'style'. Each song is the 'cry of its occasion', as the poet said.

'Banana Pudding' is an Eastern-sounding idea, constructed round a non-jazz scale. 'Tinged' is new, and apparently intended to be played with some electronic and vocal elements. As a straight group piece, it lacks for nothing. 'Photon In A Paper World' (and it does seem to be *A*, not *The*) is revived, one of his durable originals. A dramatic reworking of 'Anthropology' is successful up to a point, though Williams's Parkerisms are unconvincing; the saxophonist contributes one original, the closing track, 'Ferrell', and he sounds like a promising writer. Cowell's recording career now spans more than 30 years. There have, inevitably, been highs and lows; there has also been an impressive consistency of purpose and the highest level of musical thought.

Lol Coxhill (born 1932)

SOPRANO SAXOPHONE, TENOR SAXOPHONE, SOPRANINO SAXOPHONE

Deeply rooted in jazz, but ranging over free music, instrumental chanson and an idiosyncratic quasi-folk, Lol is a vastly talented soprano specialist with an utterly individual tone; it ranges from aching sweetness to hard-edged multiphonics. Lol on record isn't quite the point, but there is now at least a representative selection on offer.

****(*) Ear Of Beholder**

See For Miles SEECD 414 *Coxhill; Burton Greene, Jasper Van't Hof (p); Pierre Courbois (d); David Bedford (p, v); various walk-ons, environments.* 7/70, 1/71.

***** Toverbal Sweet ... Plus**

See For Miles SEECD 480 *Coxhill; Jasper Van't Hof (p); Pierre Courbois (d).* 72.

There is no one quite like Lol Coxhill, which may be why he has been neglected, relegated to the role of festival MC and resident clown of the British free scene. The only musician one might feasibly liken him to, however improbable it may sound, is Lee Konitz. Coxhill has carved a path from straight standards playing to abstract improvisation, taking in rock groups (like Kevin Ayers's proto-slacker Whole World outfit) along the way. If that is the point at which he deviates from jazz loyalist Konitz, the resemblance is reinforced again by Lol's fragile, endlessly lyrical soprano tone.

It has been said that he is not so much an improviser as an instant composer. This is only half true, for his grasp of vertical harmony is impeccable, as can be heard on 'Lover Man', included on *Ear*. However, his great strength is the busker's ability to turn out simple, effective tunes, seemingly by the yard. *Ear Of Beholder* was recorded for BBC DJ John Peel's Dandelion label. It consists of a few studio tracks, some festival material, like the tenor 'Deviation Dance', on which the sound is pushed through a Gibson Maestro, and some tunes busked out on London streets, like the opening 'Hungerford', recorded where Lol used to have a regular pitch on the pedestrian bridge outside Charing Cross railway station. A double LP has been compressed on to a single CD with the omission of just one track. It could have been cropped and edited further. The long 'Rasa Moods' with Van't Hof, Courbois and Greene was recorded in Utrecht; the sound is grim but the playing is fascinating, with some effective use of the Maestro again. A whimsical grab-bag (there's even a track of kids singing 'I Am The Walrus'), very much in the spirit of Peel's own wayward enthusiasms, it doesn't wear particularly well and will be of most interest to those who've lost their (now very tradeable) vinyl and want to recapture something of those faraway years.

The trio material on *Toverbal Sweet* is more consistent. A club recording, it is more evenly proportioned, representing the mid-ground between jazz and free music all three were exploring in their different ways at the time. Van't Hof uses both electric and acoustic piano, but much of the action comes from Courbois's expanded kit. Very much a group effort, harder-edged than Lol's work with the Johnny Rondo Duo and the Melody Four.

****** Coxhill On Ogun**

Ogun OGCD 008 *Coxhill; Michael Garrick (el p); Veryan Weston (p); Ken Shaw, Richard Wright (g); Dave Green, Paul Mitchell-Davidson (b); Colin Wood (clo); John Mitchell (perc).* 77–78.

Glorious. Bringing together two of Lol's best records, *The Joy Of Paranoia* and *Diverse*, from the later 1970s, this is the place to start if you've never encountered him before. *Joy* began with a live group improvisation recorded in Yorkshire; 'The Wakefield Capers' is the perfect illustration of Lol's ability to play free forms with all the sweetness of a Johnny Hodges and little of fellow-soprano specialist Steve Lacy's acidulous attack. Accompanied by the three guitars of Paws for Thought – Mitchell-Davidson on a wibbly bass – he weaves two long, thoughtful solos full of long, bent notes, sliding intervals and little melodic ideas which seem to rise up out of nowhere. 'The Cluck Variations' is a collaboration with pianist Weston, quite formally cast but full of anarchic invention. 'The Joy Of Paranoia Waltz' should be played at all wedding receptions just at the moment when new in-laws start to eye one another across the dance floor; it uses inventive over-dubs on a simple riff. The clinching joy of the 1978 album for us, though, was the pair of standards, 'Lover Man' and 'Perdido', played as duets with Michael Garrick on electric piano. These offer further strong evidence of Lol's gifts as a standards player. The Tizol tune is a revelation, reinvented wholesale.

Diverse is not so immediately appealing, but it is a very strong and inventive set consisting of one solo piece and a quartet. 'Diver' is more strictly a duet with a loose floorboard at Seven Dials in London; the quartet consists of cello, bass and percussion. Played entirely free, these pieces come from a jaggier end of the idiom than 'Wakefield Capers'.

****** The Dunois Solos**

Nato 95 *Coxhill (ss solo).* 81.

Direct, almost song-like improvisations that constantly dip in and out of jazz idiom. These two long pieces have the intimacy of conversation and the self-absorption of monologue in equal measure; this has to be considered one of his very best recorded performances, if not *the* very best. The tone is light and pliable, as if he is playing an aluminium horn, and there is a sparkly exuberance as well as a faint touch of melancholy. The recording is of very good quality, faithful to the presence of the man – breaths, clicks, sighs – as well as to the detail of the music.

*****(*) Three Blokes**
FMP CD 63 *Coxhill; Steve Lacy, Evan Parker (ss).* 94.

Stylistically Coxhill is very different from either fellow-Briton Evan Parker or Steve Lacy, the other main soprano specialists. His first influence seems to have been Charlie Parker, though he had a solo apprenticeship in R&B groups as well. He plays a curious part in these sessions. The concept was a mixture of solos, duos and trios, and Lol finds himself playing something like the Dewey Redman role in the Ornette Coleman band of the 1970s, rationalizing, normalizing, finding a middle ground and occasionally injecting a moment of gruff humour into some fairly dry and dour proceedings. No reason to say that this is his record rather than theirs, except that his is by some way the smallest extant discography of the three, and he does seem to occupy an important middle ground that makes him the fulcrum and the catalyst.

***** Solos East / West**
Slam CD 308 *Coxhill; George Haslam (bs).* 90, 95.

Unfortunately, Lol and George don't play together at any point; the title is strictly accurate. Interesting to compare the two approaches. Haslam comes to free jazz from an interest in West Coast cool and, though he has never sounded like a Mulligan acolyte (Chaloff is perhaps more his speed), he shares something of Gerry's awareness of large-scale modal structure. Lol is much more of a vertical improviser, albeit one who is highly sensitive to melody as well as harmonics. His solos are a cross between advanced changes-playing and spontaneous composition. Occasionally here, one senses the imminence of a familiar standards idea, but these rarely announce themselves unambiguously. The rating is based solely on Coxhill's contribution and doesn't reflect on a high-quality album.

*****(*) Halim**
Nato DK 018.53031 *Coxhill; Pat Thomas (p, elec).* 92, 93.

***** One Night In Glasgow**
Scatter 03 *As above.* 7/94.

In the early '70s, Coxhill visited the Edinburgh Festival fringe to play some duos with guitarist Gerry Fitzgerald. Opening one set, he announced that Alan Jackson (the poet, not the drummer) had complained that much of Lol's playing was self-indulgent and meandering; Lol announced that he was going to play 'Alan Jackson's Meandering Blues', and then ripped off a tightly disciplined, harmonically dense reading of 'I Can't Get Started', in which not a single note was wasted. He does it again here on *Halim*, a brilliant performance of a Coxhill staple.

The other disc was recorded on the other side of Scotland, at the 1994 Glasgow Jazz Festival. It catches both men on a good night, and only a much better sound-quality (and that glorious standard) pushes the Nato disc out ahead. The long pieces on *One Night* are excellent, sustained and controlled improvisations, with equal weight given to Thomas's keyboards and Lol's (on this occasion) rather breezy tone.

He has never sought the obvious routes to recognition, and so it has come only very slowly. One of the best-liked figures around, he is only now being properly acknowledged for the vividness and imagination of his music-making as well.

*****(*) Boundless**
Emanem 4021 *Coxhill; Veryan Weston (p).* 1/98.

They recorded before, in 1978, with a superb performance on Lol's *The Joy Of Paranoia*. Like Lol, Weston is a brilliant miniaturist, and the combination of the two is exquisite. Not that many of these 15 tracks are particularly short. The longest are over six minutes and are developed in the saxophonist's familiar, jazz-based style. Weston is no less lateral a thinker, but his sources are very different, and part of the joy of the session is the combination of two seemingly unlike personalities who find huge areas of common enthusiasm, almost against the odds. Though Coxhill concentrates almost entirely on soprano these days, it might have been preferable to vary the colours a little bit. It's a long record – almost exactly 70 minutes of music – and the tonality remains light and sharp throughout, an impression reinforced by a rather severe digital recording. Great stuff, though, and further reminder of Coxhill's improvisational skills.

***** Alone And Together**
Emanem 4034 *Coxhill; Stevie Wishart (vn, hurdy-gurdy); Marcio Mattos (clo, elec).* 10/91–5/99.

Emanem's Martin Davidson is still sourcing an extraordinary range of overlooked tape material documenting Britain's free scene. This disc brackets almost a decade of material, but though the settings are very different the basic rules of engagement remain Lol's own. The big difference here is that for the first four tracks he doubles on sopranino, a tough horn to discipline and a rather piercing sound when heard at any length. 'A Rare Sopranino Solo' confirms that it holds no terrors, but it's not the easiest of listens. Three of the four are duets with Wishart, who brings along her hurdy-gurdy as well, creating a witch's kettle of bagpipe drones; very effective. The duet with Mattos is characteristically thoughtful and again constructed over a drone background, this time using live and gently responsive electronics. The remainder of the set, not so comfortably recorded, consists of a solo soprano recital at the Queen Elizabeth Hall (and presumably in the lobby). A continuous 20-minute improvisation, with a tiny encore tacked on the end, it's just one of a thousand such gigs Lol must have played over the years, but no less valuable for that.

Hank Crawford (born 1934)

ALTO AND BARITONE SAXOPHONES

Like David Newman, Crawford had long experience in the Ray Charles touring band and, also like Newman, he made a string of bluesy soul-jazz dates for Atlantic in the 1960s. Born in Memphis, he started on baritone but took up the alto in 1959. Spells in commercial music took him away from jazz but Milestone's albums have reasserted his roots in R&B and small-combo jazz.

***** Midnight Ramble**
Milestone MCD-9112-2 *Crawford; Waymon Reed, Charlie Miller (t); Dick Griffin (tb); David 'Fathead' Newman (ts); Howard Johnson (bs); Dr John (ky); Calvin Newborn (g); Charles Greene (b); Bernard Purdie (d).* 11/82.

****(*) Indigo Blue**
Milestone MCD-9119-2 *Crawford; Martin Banks, Danny Moore (t); David 'Fathead' Newman (ts); Howard Johnson (bs);*

Melvin Sparks (g); Wilbur Bascomb (b); Bernard Purdie (d). 8/83.

**** Mr Chips**

Milestone MCD-9149-2 *Crawford; Randy Brecker, Alan Rubin (t); David 'Fathead' Newman (ts); Howard Johnson (bs); Richard Tee (ky); Cornell Dupree (g); Wilbur Bascomb (b); Bernard Purdie (d). 11/86.*

***** Night Beat**

Milestone MCD-9168-2 *Crawford; Lew Soloff, Alan Rubin (t); David 'Fathead' Newman (ts, f); Howard Johnson (bs); Dr John (ky); Melvin Sparks (g); Wilbur Bascomb (b); Bernard Purdie (d). 9–10/88.*

***** Groove Master**

Milestone MCD-9182-2 *Lou Marini (ts) replaces Newman; add Gloria Coleman (org); others as above. 2–3/90.*

Hank Crawford says that he tries 'to keep the melody so far in front that you can almost sing along', and that irresistibly vocal style lends his simple approach to the alto a deep-rooted conviction. His best records are swinging parties built on the blues, southern R&B – Crawford apprenticed in the bands of Ike and Tina Turner and Ray Charles – and enough bebop to keep a more hardened jazz listener involved. He recorded 12 albums for Atlantic in the 1960s, but you need to go to the *Heart And Soul* collection below to find any CD representation. His renewed career has been thanks to the initiative of Milestone, who began by providing him with consistently sympathetic settings. There's little to choose among the albums listed above, all of them smartly organized around Crawford's libidinous wail: *Mr Chips* gets lower marks for a mundane choice of material, while *Midnight Ramble*, *Night Beat* and *Groove Master* are enlivened by the inspiring presence of Dr John on piano and organ. Typical of Crawford's mature command is the way he empowers Whitney Houston's 'Saving All My Love For You' on *Groove Master* with a real authority.

***** Soul Survivors**

Milestone MCD-9142-2 *Crawford; Jimmy McGriff (ky); George Benson, Jim Pittsburg (g); Mel Lewis, Bernard Purdie (d). 1/86.*

****(*) Steppin' Up**

Milestone MCD-9153-2 *Crawford; Jimmy McGriff (ky); Billy Preston (p); Jimmy Ponder (g); Vance James (d). 6/87.*

****(*) On The Blue Side**

Milestone MCD-9177-2 *As above. 7/89.*

Crawford shares leadership duties with McGriff on these small-group albums, and between them they try to update the sound of the 1960s organ combo without surrendering the juice and fire of the original music. *Soul Survivors* is the best of the three because the renewed partnership is at its freshest, and Benson is for once employed in a worthwhile jazz context; but, taken a few tracks at a time, all three discs are enjoyable if lightweight.

****(*) Portrait**

Milestone MCD-9192-2 *Crawford; David 'Fathead' Newman (ts); Johnny Hammond (org); Jimmy Ponder (g); Vance James (d). 90.*

***** South-Central**

Milestone MCD-9201-2 *Crawford; Stan Hope, Dr John (p); Gloria Coleman (org); Melvin Sparks (g); Peter Martin Weiss, Wilbur Bascomb (b); Grady Tate, Bernard Purdie (d). 2/90–8/92.*

**** Tight**

Milestone MCD-9529-2 *Crawford; Earl Gardner, David Rubin (t); David 'Fathead' Newman (ts, f); Howard Johnson (bs); Danny Mixon (p, org); Melvin Sparks (g); Stanley Banks (b); Idris Muhammad (d). 4–5/96.*

Crawford's more recent records are basically disappointing. *South-Central* has its moments, especially on a rollicking 'Splanky'; but elsewhere Crawford sounds like he's starting to take it easy, and perhaps one can't altogether blame him. *Tight*, though, does no credit to anyone. 'Breezin'' sounds thin and hapless in this incarnation and, while the band is full of old pros, they sound like they're staggering through this date. Bob Porter's production also hides Hank somewhere in the back row: what happened to that sound?

*****(*) Heart And Soul**

Rhino/Atlantic R2 71673 2CD *As above Milestone albums, plus: Marcus Belgrave, Lee Harper, Phil Guilbeau, John Hunt, Fielder Floyd, Joe Newman, Ernie Royal, Bernie Glow, Snooky Young (t); Jimmy Cleveland, Benny Powell, Tom Malone (tb); Frank Wess (as); Seldon Powell, James Clay, Harvey Thompson, Abdul Baari, Wendell Harrison (ts); Leroy Cooper, Howard Johnson, Pepper Adams, Alonzo Shaw, Ronnie Cuber, Jim Horn (bs); Ray Charles, Richard Tee, Clayton Ivey (p); Lucky Peterson (org); Frankie Crawford (ky); B.B King (g, v); Steve Cropper, Will McFarlane, Sonny Forrest, Eric Gale, Hugh McCracken (g); Edgar Willis, Charlie Green, Ron Carter, Gary King, Willie Weeks (b); Richie Goldberg, Milt Turner, Bruno Carr, Bernard Purdie, Roger Hawkins (d); Etta James (v). 7/58–5/92.*

Another handsome package in the Rhino/Atlantic series gives us something close to the definitive Hank Crawford retrospective. It starts, fittingly, with the Ray Charles band at Newport, but the key early tracks on disc one are those from the *More Soul*, *Soul Clinic* and *From The Heart* albums (otherwise unavailable on CD). Here is the fulsome, slow, blues-drenched Crawford sound on 'Angel Eyes' and 'Misty', plus the peppery grooves of 'The Peeper' and 'Read 'Em And Weep'. Crucially, the arrangments are horn-based and use no keyboards, so the charts take on a declamatory, gospelized strain that underlines the soul only in the alto solos. It's a grand formula, but a formula none the less, and it palls a little over two long CDs. So the second disc, after a few Creed Taylor rhapsodies from the 1970s, turns to the Milestone albums for the rest of the compilation. Tracks with B.B. King and Etta James restore to Crawford his righteous role as a signifying sideman and pretty much close the circle on this middleweight's gratifying career. Remastering is exemplary throughout, with the Atlantic tracks sounding as good as new.

****(*) Road Tested**

Milestone MCD-9274-2 *Crawford; Jimmy McGriff (org); Wayne Boyd (g); Bernard Purdie (d). 7/97.*

(*) **After Dark

Milestone MCD-9279-2 *Crawford; Danny Mixon (p, org); Melvin Sparks (g); Stanley Banks, Wilbur Bascomb (b); Bernard Purdie (d).* 2/98.

*** **Crunch Time**

Milestone MCD-9287-2 *Crawford; Jimmy McGriff (org); Melvin Sparks, Cornell Dupree (g); Bernard Purdie (d).* 11/98.

The old firm of Crawford and McGriff share the billing on the first and third of these. If you have any of their earlier collaborations, it's hard to see why you'd want these to go with them, since there's nothing new, and nothing much worth revisiting on either of them. These are seasoned pros who can turn out these records to order and, while there's nothing amiss, what is there to remember? Wayne Boyd is a very busy guitarist on the first date, which also has an overly reverberant sound, as if they were trying to make the band sound bigger. Bob Porter tightens that up on *Crunch Time*, and this makes the band sound leaner and fitter so it's a marginally better record. Bernard Purdie is not the world's subtlest drummer, but that's what they want.

Hard to see the point of the interim *After Dark*. It's meant to show off Hank's worldliness as a bluesman, but tunes such as 'My Babe' and 'Git It!' are the kinds of thing he's been playing all his life anyway. Bernard Purdie is not the world's bluesiest drummer, either; but he's still giving them what they want.

Marilyn Crispell (born 1947)

PIANO

Famously, Crispell was turned on to modern jazz when she heard a John Coltrane record. Her classical training and very exact, flowing style were uniquely well suited to a transition to polytonal jazz. Crispell's improvisations are always densely detailed and powerfully emoted. Her association with Anthony Braxton in another classic quartet was yet another key relationship.

*** **Live In Berlin**

Black Saint 120069 *Crispell; Billy Bang (vn); Peter Kowald (b); John Betsch (d).* 11/82.

Crispell was, in retrospect, probably overdocumented for a number of years; more recently, things have gone rather quieter on the disc front, but she has been one of the most significant piano improvisers of the last two decades. When all is said and done, the Coltrane and Cecil Taylor influences weighed much less heavily on her earliest recordings than was routinely thought and, though she has regularly returned to Coltrane in particular as a kind of guiding spirit (see below), she is certainly not a slavish imitator. She holds up strongly in some pretty rugged company in this early set from the Total Music Meeting. The shift to CD has lifted the piano considerably and effects a bit of separation and space in the background. The set is dominated by a huge piece, 'ABC', dedicated to her next most important influence, Anthony Braxton, with whom she has worked very profitably for many years. Her background in classical, particularly Baroque, music is still clearly audible as she negotiates oblique contrapuntal passages and wild, seamless fugues. The two string-players seem worlds apart and don't interact very effectively. Kowald replaced guitarist Wes Brown, who had appeared on an earlier Cadence LP called *Spirit Music* and seemed much more in tune with Crispell's conception.

**** **For Coltrane**

Leo CDLR 195 *Crispell (p solo).* 7/87.

***(*) **Live In San Francisco**

Music & Arts 633 *As above.* 10/89.

Solo performances by Crispell are dramatic, harmonically tense and wholly absorbing. Though the excellent *Rhythms Hung In Undrawn Sky* has disappeared from the Leo catalogue, along with *And Your Ivory Voice Sings*, a duo with percussionist Doug James, they have been replaced by a recording of a remarkable concert given in London in the summer of 1987, when Crispell supported Alice Coltrane and the two Coltrane boys, Ravi and Omar, with a solo set dedicated to Alice's late husband. Opening with a torrid 'Dear Lord' and closing with the billowing 'After The Rain', she improvised a series of 'collages' in memory of the great saxophonist. She also performed a piece called 'Coltrane Time', a title of convenience for a sequence of rhythmic cells on which the saxophonist had been experimenting in the period immediately before his death. A beautiful record, *For Coltrane* is a companion-piece to the deleted *Labyrinths* on Victo and is more immediately appealing than the San Francisco session. Recorded shortly after the Californian earthquake of 1989, the latter alternates the subdued aftershocks and beatific restorations of her own 'Tromos' and Coltrane's 'Dear Lord' with some unexpectedly light and romantic touches. 'When I Fall In Love' has a hesitant shyness that makes the theme statement all the more moving; the same applies to the humour of Monk's 'Ruby, My Dear', which underlines Crispell's impressive rhythmic awareness. (Interestingly, the CD also contains two 'sampler' tracks from other Music & Arts titles featuring Crispell: the long 'Composition 136' with Anthony Braxton from the Vancouver duets record mentioned above (CD 611) and a shorter group track with another senior collaborator, Reggie Workman, and his highly inventive ensemble (CD 634).)

*** **The Kitchen Concert**

Leo LR 178 *Crispell; Mark Dresser (b); Gerry Hemingway (d).* 2/89.

This marks a slight but significant change of direction for Crispell. In place of free or structured improvisation, *The Kitchen Concert* documents a first, rather tentative confrontation with written forms of her own. Her own recorded misgivings are reflected to some degree in the music itself, which exposes areas of hesitancy rarely encountered in her improvised performances. The tonalities are a little forced, in sharp contrast to her normal instinctive 'centring' of a piece. By her own remarkable standards a less than wholly successful album, it still merits close attention, not least for the contributions of Dresser and of Hemingway, whose insistent (if rather similar) solos on 'Ahmadu/Sierra Leone' and the Tristano-dedicated 'For L.T.' lend the music a much-needed impulse.

**** **Gaia**

Leo Records LR 152 *Crispell; Reggie Workman (b); Doug James (d, perc).* 3/87.

***** Live In Zurich**

Leo Records LR CDLR 122 *As above, except omit James; add Paul Motian (d, perc).* 4/89.

Gaia is one of the finest composition/improvisation records of the 1980s, a hymn to the planet that is neither mawkish nor sentimental, but tough-minded, coherent and entire. Spared conventional rhythm-section duties, Workman and James combine extremely well, producing both a dense *ripieno* for Crispell's dramatic *concertante* effects and a powerful drama of their own. *Live In Zurich* finds her working against a much more conventional rhythm (though Motian shares James's delicacy of touch). Though it consists of individual pieces (including the obligatory Coltrane, 'Dear Lord'), the Zurich set comes to resemble a single suite, opening with some haunting North African vocalese (an equally obligatory nod in Taylor's direction) and developing strongly into one of her finest recorded piano performances.

****** Overlapping Hands: Eight Segments**

FMP CD30 *Crispell; Irène Schweizer (p).* 90.

*****(*) Piano Duets**

Leo CD LR 206/207 2CD *Crispell; Georg Gräwe (p).* 10 & 12/91.

Like much of Crispell's best work, *Overlapping Hands* is a concert performance, and a duo at that. There are moments when it might almost be one person playing, so close is the understanding between the two women, but for the fact that they do sound very different. Schweizer's sound is sharper and more Europeanized; Crispell's draws deeper on an American tradition and constantly refers to tonal centres that her collaborator wants to push away to the very boundaries of the music. The recording is near perfect, and a tremendous advance on some of FMP's more Heath Robinsonish concert efforts; the music is a joy.

The duos with Gräwe are fascinating, largely for the second disc, on which they play detuned pianos. Pitched a quarter-tone apart in the middle register, with upper and lower strings sharped and flattened respectively in accordance with Thomas Henke's 'diagonal tuning' system, they sound alien and unfamiliar. The improvisations are understandably more textural than usual, obviating the minor culture clash of the performances with Schweizer. Unfortunately, the recording levels are too fierce to register all the finer detail and, though there are substantial individual contributions from both players (who are not difficult to distinguish), it's a pity that Crispell hasn't had an opportunity to explore this line of inquiry more fully and in a purely solo context. The duets provide an information overload.

***** Duo**

Knitting Factory KFWCD 117 *Crispell; Gerry Hemingway (perc).* 92.

*****(*) Marilyn Crispell Trio: Highlights From The 1992 American Tour**

Music & Arts CD758 *Crispell; Reggie Workman (b); Gerry Hemingway (d).* Summer 92.

The 1990s saw a change in Crispell's work and a gradual movement towards more structured composition. The main substance of the music is, however, still generated by improvisation, and that is particularly noticeable on the first two items. The trio with Reggie Workman is marked by slow harmonic transformations that largely develop in the bass register, accented by piano right hand and percussion. Though several of the pieces remain 'open', there is a developing emphasis on determinant form, as in the 'Suite For Trio' and the quite brief 'Mouvements Changeables' which appears (perhaps accidentally) to quote from the Dutch composer Ton de Leeuw's *Mouvements rétrogrades*. Hemingway is the common factor in the group. A strong but by no means aggressive player, he concentrates on the spaces in the music, stippling them with detail. On the duo, it becomes almost too self-conscious a mannerism. It works wonderfully well in the combination with Workman, for which Hemingway (true to his surname) strips down to essentials.

***** Inference**

Music & Arts CD 851 *Crispell; Tim Berne (as).* 6/92.

As a sidebar to an extraordinary year of music-making, this is not a great astonishment, nor is it as good as it might be. Berne's curious bluster often overpowers what otherwise seems impressively vivid and reciprocal music-making. The opening 'For Alto And Piano II' has A. Braxton written all over it, a Crispell composition in name only, one suspects. The rest is divided between the two, with the pianist's 'Sorrow' and Berne's 'Bass Voodoo' the outstanding tracks. Recorded at the Downtown Jazz Festival in Toronto, the sound-quality is a touch cavernous and not always entirely fair on either player, though it's Berne who probably has more cause for complaint, sometimes coming across rather distantly, as if he has drifted off-mike.

(****) Stellar Pulsations / Three Composers

Leo CD LR 194 *Crispell; Don Byron (cl); Ellen Polansky (p); Gerry Hemingway (d); WDR Radio Orchestra, David de Villiers (cond).* 7/92.

A further step away from the immediate concerns of this *Guide*, the marvellous *Stellar Pulsations* represents the work of three composers who are exploring the borderlines of improvisation and formally scored music. Manfred Niehaus's *Concerto For Marilyn* has a wholly scored and fixed orchestral part, with partial notation for the piano player in the first movement. This part is called 'Concerto For Chico'; movements three and four also refer to the Marx Brothers. The second movement is a swaying 'unhoused tango' in which piano and orchestra conjoin in open-ended tempo. 'Concerto For Harpo' is a piano/harp duet. A timpanist joins in for 'Concerto To Provoke Groucho', leading to a final cadenza for Crispell.

Pozzi Eschot's *Mirabilis II* draws on music by Mother Hildegard (a figure much admired by both Crispell and Anthony Braxton) to create a framework for trio improvisation. As before, Crispell and Hemingway seem to be in complete communication, but Don Byron's part is a little less sure-footed and often sounds as if he's merely reading off. The balance of composition and improvisation is clearer in Robert Cogan's *Costellar Pulsations*, which starts the disc. Here Crispell improvises over Ellen Polansky's notated (but not immutable) score, from which the performer can select and re-order elements. Echoing the language and ideas of *Overlapping Hands* (above), Crispell allows the piece to divide naturally into expressive segments, some of which strongly suggest tonality, others the orderly but indefinable progress of natural (or cosmic) events. Though less likely to appeal to straight jazz fans, this is another beautiful record and, in its way, another important stage in Crispell's development as an artist.

***(*) Hyperion

Music & Arts CD 852 *Crispell; Peter Brötzmann (sax, cl, tarogato); Hamid Drake (d, hand d).* 6/92.

*** Cascades

Music & Arts CD 853 *Crispell; Barry Guy (b); Gerry Hemingway (d, vib, gamelan).* 6/93.

Two contrasting trios documenting Crispell's growing stature as darling of the festival circuit. Both were recorded in Canada but at different locations. *Cascades* reunites her with Hemingway, who increasingly sees himself not just as a drummer but also as a tuned percussionist, contributing vibes and gamelan to the mix; Guy is also a highly structured and often tuneful player, and the combination is sometimes too cluttered, though the bassist also understands better than the two Americans how to leave light and shade, space and air, in this music. The trio with Peter Brötzmann and Hamid Drake is, predictably, more intense and frenetic, though the saxophonist does also have his delicately lyrical side, and he defers at moments during 'Hyperion I' to Crispell's desire to take the music down a more expressive path. Which is not to say he has to defer to her 'feminine' side. She sets off like an express train as usual and, as often in the past, it's difficult to gauge how responsive, how much of a listening player she now is. Solo performance (see below) may still be her forte.

**** Santuerio

Leo CD LR 191 *Crispell; Mark Feldman (vn); Hank Roberts (clo); Gerry Hemingway (d).* 5/93.

Santuerio marks Crispell's full emergence as a composer. Again, much of the music is improvised, but it is linked by elemental structures – pieces include 'Air/Fire', 'Water', 'Burning Air/Wood', 'Red Shift', 'Repercussions Of Air And Light' – and a visionary spirit. The opening 'Entrances Of Light', inspired by a Nathaniel Mackey poem, would fit comfortably into a programme of contemporary composition. Introduced by a rapturous Mark Feldman solo, it develops slowly and quietly, anticipating the underlying drama of the 13-minute title-track which lies at the centre of the disc. Here the central action is between Crispell and Hemingway. The drummer's solo is stunning, but what follows is even more impressive: a long, restless tussle between percussion and piano. Cello and violin break in with heavy *ostinato* shapes, and Feldman briefly rises out of the mêlée with an echo of his opening phrases. Like *Gaia*, *Santuerio* tackles huge themes, but there is nothing grandiose or overblown about it. The music is beautifully controlled and specific. Crispell's finest hour.

**** Spring Tour 1994

Alice ALCD 13 *Crispell; Anders Jormin (b); Raymond Strid (d).* 94.

Well, the season seems completely apposite for music as fresh and affirmative as this. There used to be – probably still is – an awful test-piece for pianists by Christian Sinding called 'Rustle Of Spring'. No one need ever perform or listen to it again ... Where often Crispell can sound slightly dense and introspective, here she dares to play somewhat more simply and directly. She is undoubtedly encouraged by her two colleagues. Strid has a brisk, beery exuberance (and does a famous line in homebrew, incidentally) which doesn't invite tortured, existential dramatics, while the bassist is quite simply one of the most beautiful stylists currently working on the instrument. Heady, uplifting stuff, perhaps more immediately winning than the excellent things below.

**** Band On The Wall

Matchless MRCD 25 *Crispell; Eddie Prévost (d, perc).* 5/94.

***(*) Destiny

Okkadisk OD 12003 *Crispell: Fred Anderson (ts); Hamid Drake (d, perc).* 8/94.

Recorded live during the 'Women of New Music' festival in Chicago, the Okkadisk set is marred – Crispell-wise – only by having the piano mixed down too low and occasionally swamped by saxophone and percussion. Otherwise it finds her in thoroughly sympathetic company. Anderson's diction is Coltrane-influenced but generously varied and thoroughly personalized. As with Braxton and Prévost (below), this seems like a relationship written in the stars, and it allows them to build up whole areas of interaction in which the exchange of ideas is almost too fast to follow. Drake provides sterling accompaniment and, like Prévost, often takes the initiative in breaking up Crispell's long, suspended lines into shorter, more discursive sections.

The Matchless disc was also recorded live, at the Manchester venue called Band on the Wall. It's a fiery, sometimes almost violent performance in which ideas are run together with a challenging insouciance. Extravagant as she often is, Crispell has rarely sounded so thoroughly unfettered; oddly, perhaps, because Prévost is a highly disciplined drummer and certainly one of the most swinging in a free idiom. One slight oddity of the set is the inclusion of the Denny Zeitlin composition, 'Quiet Now', towards the end. How many repertory pieces has this pairing explored?

***(*) Live at Mills College, 1995

Music & Arts CD 899 *Crispell (p solo).* 1/95.

Very much a showcase performance, back on a campus which in many respects helped define the type of music Crispell plays. 'As Our Tongues Lap Up The Burning Air' reappears from the session with Prévost, in an even more incendiary version, despite the appearance of restraint. There is a further nod to the Coltrane heritage with a wonderful medleyed version of 'The Night Has 1,000 Eyes', and a slightly congested Monk cover, 'Reflections'. 'Song For Abdullah' is a relatively long-standing original, having been written for the Leo set, *Rhythms Hung In Undrawn Sky*, more than a decade ago. Neither the hall acoustic nor the piano sounds quite right for a recital hall at a major music college, but it's possible that the poor thing is going out of tune as she plays. It has been known.

***(*) The Woodstock Concert

Music & Arts CD 929 *Crispell (p solo).* 4/95.

**** Contrasts: Live At Yoshi's

Music & Arts CD 930 *As above.* 6/95.

The solo performance at the Kleinert/James Arts Center in Woodstock, New York, was something of a homecoming for the globetrotting Crispell, who has made her home in the area for the better part of 20 years but has rarely had the chance to play there.

This set contains the best of her solo work for many moons, and also some pointers to what is now problematic about her work. The opening 'Await' is thoughtfully tentative, carefully developed and superbly logical. The closing 'Empty Sirens' is just that, vacuous pianism of almost aggressive banality. In between – mercifully – Crispell shows how completely in command she is, executing a long, wonderful suite of pieces, negotiating Bill Evans's 'Time Remembered' and creating some exquisite harmonic and rhythmic devices on 'In Lingering Air'. Any doubts about her quality are easily dispelled, but there are warning signs here and there which might usefully be taken into consideration.

The Yoshi's gig from the club in Oakland is interesting in being more obviously jazz-based than anything she has released in recent years. That Bill Evans remains a constant presence, perhaps more important to her now than either Coltrane or Braxton were in past years, seems obvious. That she has assimilated his work and taken it on a step is equally clear. What is intriguing about numbers like 'Flutter' and 'Ruthie's Song' is how straightforward and full-hearted they seem. Gone for the time being at least are the dense, dark washes and the battering-ram tonality. Crispell has found the courage to be simple, and it becomes her wonderfully well.

****** Nothing Ever Was, Anyway**

ECM 537222-2 2CD *Crispell; Gary Peacock (b); Paul Motian (d).* 96.

Crispell included Annette Peacock's 'Gesture Without Plot' on each of the two sets documented above, and this exquisitely recorded tribute marks a more extended engagement with the finest female jazz composer of recent times, Carla notwithstanding. The choice of material scarcely matters, because the album becomes a type of mini-opera without words, an extended portrait of one fine artist's engagement with another. There are moments when the Peacock/Motian partnership is almost too strong-voiced and runs some risk of overpowering the piano, which occupies a now familiar spectrum of dynamics. Crispell has seldom (if ever) played as elegantly and with such control. Perhaps the discipline of staying within the bounds set by another composer – and one with a much more melodic approach than Coltrane, say – allowed her to free up one hitherto suppressed aspect of her musical personality. Suffice it to say that we consider this a contemporary masterpiece. To miss it would be to overlook a piano trio the equal of anything since the late Bill Evans.

Sonny Criss (1927-77)

ALTO SAXOPHONE, SOPRANO SAXOPHONE

Born in Memphis, he played in R&B bands before recording as a bebop leader. Latterly worked in rehabilitating young offenders but became afflicted by depression and took his own life.

***** California Boppin'**

Fresh Sound FSR CD 156 *Criss; Al Killian, Howard McGhee (t); Teddy Edwards, Wardell Gray (ts); Charlie Fox, Russ Freeman, Hampton Hawes, Dodo Marmarosa (p); Barney Kessel (g); Harry Babasin, Red Callender, Addison Farmer (b); Tim Kennedy, Jackie Mills, Roy Porter (d).* 4, 6, 7 & 10/47.

*****(*) Memorial Album**

DIW 302 *Criss; Al Killian, Clark Terry (t); Dexter Gordon, Wardell Gray (ts); Gil Barrios, Jimmy Bunn, Charles Fox, Hampton Hawes (p); Dave Bryant, Billy Hadnott, Shifty Henry, Clarence Johnson (b); Frank Butler, Tim Kennedy, Billy Snyder, Chuck Thompson (d); Damita Jo (v).* 10/47, 8/50, 9/52, 6/65.

*****(*) Sonny Criss Quartet, 1949–1957**

Fresh Sound FSRCD 64 *Criss; Hampton Hawes (p); Iggy Shevack, Buddy Woodson (b); Chuck Thompson (d).* 9/49, 11/57.

Criss was perhaps a little too tightly wrapped for the destiny that seemed to await him. Though it was the altogether more robust Sonny Stitt – with whom Criss is occasionally confused – to whom Charlie Parker promised 'the keys of the Kingdom', it was Criss out on the West Coast who inherited most of the ambiguities of Parker's legacy.

California wasn't a happy place for Bird, by and large, and there's something hectic, almost desperate, in Criss's super-fast runs and soaring, high-register figures. The earliest of the material is rather derivative but provides several excellent opportunities to hear Criss's pure, urgent tone and delivery; he comes in behind Wardell Gray on 'Groovin' High' almost impatiently, with a little flurry of notes, before stretching out and shaping those distinctive wailing passages and held notes. The June 1947 material, with the rhythm section that backed Parker at the Hi-De-Ho in Los Angeles earlier that year (Hawes, Farmer, Porter), is probably the best on the disc, with a particularly fine version of 'The Man I Love' that also features Teddy Edwards and Howard McGhee. Two long jam-sessions have lots of episodic interest but are marred by Al Killian's dreary high-note work.

The DIW memorial is an excellent buy, offering a bitty but reasonably comprehensive survey of the whole career with the exception of Criss's brief Indian summer of the mid-'70s. Unfortunately, there's an overlap with *California Boppin'*, and quite a substantial one; doubly unfortunately, it's the October 1947 Portland jam with Killian and Wardell Gray. However, the record's worth having for the 1965 material with Hampton Hawes (see below), and a one-off track from 1950 ('I Can't Give You Anything But Love') with Clark Terry and Dexter Gordon, on which Criss more than holds his own. Hawes spurs him.

He's on hand for both the sessions on the other Fresh Sound, playing a little neatly on the 1949 tracks, which have a brittle politeness suggestive of buried tensions in the studio, but opening out majestically on the two standards which start the November 1957 session. On 'Willow Weep For Me', Criss delivers a gently sorrowful solo, spoken with manly regret and without a wasted gesture. Hawes matches him, and bassist Woodson – an unremarked player – comes in with a fluent statement of his own. In this still small discography, this has to be considered a significant release.

*****(*) Intermission Riff**

Original Jazz Classics OJCCD 961-2 *Criss; Joe Newman (t); Bennie Green (tb); Eddie Davis (ts); Bobby Tucker (p); Tommy Potter (b); Kenny Clarke (d).* 10/51.

These tapes were hidden away from 1951 until 1987. Criss's talent had been spotted early on and, when he was still in his teens, he was asked to join Norman Granz's Jazz at the Philharmonic collective on a nationwide tour. This was a return fixture and any hint of diffidence or uncertainty has long since evaporated. Still flaunting his Parker influence with superb insouciance, Criss creates some breathtaking solos, notably on 'Peridido', which rubberstamps his bebop visa, but also on a lovely version of 'Body And Soul', on which he doffs his cap to Benny Carter and Johnny Hodges as well.

Davis and the underrated Green play a full part and they and the splendid rhythm section come through superbly on an overdue CD transfer that plugs a significant gap in the Criss discography.

***(*) This Is Criss!

Original Jazz Classics OJCCD 430-2 *Criss; Walter Davis (p); Paul Chambers (b); Alan Dawson (d).* 66.

**** Portrait Of Sonny Criss

Original Jazz Classics OJCCD 655-2 *As above.* 67.

These are probably the two best Criss albums currently available. His ability to invest banal tunes with real feeling (see *I'll Catch The Sun!*, below, for real alchemy) is evident on 'Sunrise, Sunset', a tune from *Fiddler On The Roof* given a brief but intense reading on *This Is Criss!*. Criss does something similar, though at greater length, to 'Days Of Wine And Roses', adjusting his timbre subtly throughout the opening choruses.

'Wee' on *Portrait* takes him back to bop days, an astonishing performance that manages to skate over a lack of solid ideas with sheer virtuosity. 'Smile' bears comparison with Jackie McLean's readings, but the real stand-out tracks are 'On A Clear Day', which is hugely emotional, and 'God Bless The Child'. The CD also offers a bonus 'Love For Sale', which probably deserved to be left out first time round. The band is good and Davis (who wrote 'Greasy' on *This Is Criss!* and 'A Million Or More Times' on *Portrait*) is the mainstay.

**** Sonny's Dream

Original Jazz Classics OJCCD 707-2 *Criss; Conte Candoli (t); Dick Nash (tb); Ray Draper (tba); David Sherr (as); Teddy Edwards (ts); Peter Christlieb (bs); Tommy Flanagan (p); Al McKibbon (b); Everett Brown Jr (d).* 68.

This is a most welcome CD reissue of a project subtitled 'Birth Of The New Cool' and featuring six Horace Tapscott compositions and arrangements. Though he has only recently begun to receive wider recognition, Tapscott's influence on the West Coast has been enormous, and this was a rare chance for Criss to play in front of a carefully orchestrated mid-size band.

'Sonny's Dream' is an astonishing opener, with luminous solos from both Criss and Tommy Flanagan. Criss switches to soprano for the brief 'Ballad For Samuel', dedicated to a respected teacher, but profoundly marked by Coltrane (who had recently died). Tapscott's inventiveness and political sensibilities are equally engaged on 'Daughter Of Cochise' (an unusually relaxed solo from Criss) and 'Black Apostles', originally dedicated to Arthur Blythe (another Angeleno saxophonist who made a personal accommodation with Bird's idiom) but transformed into a brooding and ferocious lament for the three martyrs of the black liberationist movement.

A remarkable album that lapses only to the extent that the band is sometimes reduced to providing highly coloured backdrops for Tapscott's American history lessons and Criss's soloing (which bears comparison with Parker's on the 'With Strings' sessions).

*** Up, Up And Away

Original Jazz Classics OJCCD 982-2 *Criss; Cedar Walton (p); Tal Farlow (g); Bob Cranshaw (b); Lenny McBrowne (d).*

*** Rockin' In Rhythm

Original Jazz Classics OJCCD 1022-2 *Criss; Walter Davis, Eddie Green (p); Paul Chambers, Bob Cranshaw (b); Alan Dawson (d).*

Like many jazz players of the time, Criss felt he had to respond to the challenge of pop. 'Up, Up And Away' was a gift for his soaring, risky, joyous tone, and the partnership with Farlow gives the material a taut, swinging excitement. Cedar Walton is disappointing by his own high standard and seems to do little more than mark time when he's not actually soloing. 'Scrapple From The Apple' plights Sonny's troth with bebop afresh, though by this point in the story it's clear that he's aware the chapter is over. There's a touch of pastiche in his solo choruses.

Rockin' In Rhythm returns to pop rather more circumspectly. 'Misty Roses' is delightful and 'Eleanor Rigby' preserves much of that song's melancholy poetry. The real bonus on this CD reissue, though, is a previously unissued 'All The Things You Are', with Walter Davis in exceptional form. Two lovely, undemanding records.

***(*) I'll Catch The Sun!

Prestige PR 7628 *Criss; Hampton Hawes (p); Monty Budwig (b); Shelly Manne (d).* 1/69.

Something of a comeback for Criss, and perhaps the most amenable and sympathetic band he ever had, reuniting him with Hawes. The material is vile, but players like these made a living out of turning sows' ears into silken purses, and both 'California Dreaming' and 'Cry Me A River' have a genuine depth of focus. Criss sounds composed and confident in this company, and solos with impressive logic and considerable emotion.

*** Out Of Nowhere

32 Records 32028 *Criss; Dolo Coker (p); Larry Gales (b); Jimmie Smith (d).*

*** Crisscraft

32 Records 32049 *As above, except add Ray Crawford (g).*

Even in the lumpiest and most uninflected of contexts, Criss still shines through. This not a classic band by any stretch of the imagination, but Sonny's playing is taut and precise and never lacks interest. The first of the pair is dominated by standards – 'All The Things You Are', 'My Ideal', 'Brother, Can You Spare A Dime' and the magnificent title-track – but with Criss's personality etched on every phrase and solo.

The other album is more idiosyncratic, but tunes like 'Crisscraft' and 'The Isle Of Celia' also betray a moving tremor of uncertainty which adds to the drama. Somehow, having to play in the most unpromising of circumstances always spurred him on to something extra. These are better than bin-ends and, just as wonderful things sometimes turn up in unexpected places in the cellar, there are some vintage Criss moments buried amid the dust.

John Crocker

CLARINET, ALTO AND TENOR SAXOPHONES, VOCAL

A long-standing sideman in the Chris Barber Band and a trad-to-swing exponent.

****(*) Easy Living**

Timeless TTD 561 *Crocker; Roger Munns (p); Vic Pitt (b); Jimmy Tagford (d).* 6/89.

****(*) All Of Me**

Timeless TTD 585 *As above.* 4/93.

A stalwart of Chris Barber's groups, Crocker's style hews closely to a dated rather than a neo-classic idea of what swing-style clarinet should sound like – exaggerated phrasing, plush tone but a glibness standing in for fluency. On tenor, when he tries to do a Websterish treatment of 'I Can't Get Started', it sounds all wrong, and the alto treatment of 'I Hadn't Anyone Till You' isn't much more appealing. But Goodman staples like 'Avalon' and 'Rose Room' turn out better: Crocker knows this stuff well, and he plays it well. The rhythm section play cheerfully behind him. *All Of Me* follows a similar line, and does it that bit better. Docked a notch for the vocals, though.

Bob Crosby (1913–93)

VOCAL, LEADER

Bing's brother was a decent light vocalist and something of a figurehead for his band. When he left the Tommy Dorsey group in 1935, he became frontman for an orchestra that was a rarity: a big band that preferred Dixieland to the smoother side of swing. It was very successful until its disbandment in 1942. Crosby kept his solo career going and presided over many reunions of his old colleagues.

***** You Can Call It Swing**

Halcyon DHDL121 *Crosby; Yank Lawson, Phil Hart, Zeke Zarchy, Andy Ferretti (t); Ward Silloway, Art Foster, Warren Smith, Mark Bennett (tb); Gil Rodin, Matty Matlock (cl, as); Noni Bernardi (as); Eddie Miller (cl, ts); Dean Kincaide (ts); Bob Zurke, Gil Bowers, Joe Sullivan (p); Nappy Lamare (g); Bob Haggart (b); Ray Bauduc (d); Judy Garland, Connie Boswell (v).* 4/36–2/37.

***** A Strange New Rhythm In My Heart**

Halcyon DHDL122 *As above, except add Billy Butterfield (t), Bill DePew, Joe Kearns (as), Kay Weber (v); omit Hart, Foster, Bowers, Sullivan, Garland and Boswell.* 2–11/37.

***** You're Driving Me Crazy**

Halcyon DHDL123 *As above, except add Charlie Spivak (t), Connie Boswell (v); omit Ferretti, Bennett, Bernardi, Kincaide.* 11/37–2/38.

***** How Can You Forget?**

Halcyon DHDL125 *As above, except add Irving Fazola (cl); omit Boswell.* 2–3/38.

*****(*) Bob Crosby**

Zeta/Jazz Archives ZET 766 *Crosby; Yank Lawson, Charlie Spivak, Billy Butterfield, Zeke Zarchy, Sterling Bose, Andy Ferretti (t); Ward Silloway, Mark Bennett, Warren Smith (tb); Irving Fazola (cl); Matty Matlock (cl, as); Noni Bernardi, Joe Kearns (as); Eddie Miller (cl, ts); Gil Rodin, Dean Kincaide (ts); Bob Zurke (p); Nappy Lamare (g); Bob Haggart, Haig Stephens (b); Ray Bauduc (d).* 36–38.

***** The Big Noise**

Halcyon DHDL 126 *As above, except add Bing Crosby (v); omit Ferretti, Bennett, Stephens, Bose, Bernardi.* 3–10/38.

***** Strange Enchantment**

Halcyon DHDL 127 *As above, except add Sterling Bose, Bill Graham (t), Jimmy Emmert (tb), Bill Stegmeyer (cl, as), Marion Mann, Andrews Sisters (v); omit Spivak, Silloway, Kincaide, Lawson, Bing Crosby.* 10/38–3/39.

***** Them There Eyes**

Halcyon DHDL 128 *As above, except add Shorty Sherock (t), Ray Conniff (tb), Joe Sullivan, Floyd Bean (p), Teddy Grace (v); omit Bose, Graham, Matlock.* 3–11/39.

***** High Society**

Halcyon DHDL 130 *As above, except add Max Herman (t), George Koenig (as), Jess Stacy (p), Helen Ward (v); omit Bean, Emmert, Mann, Zurke.* 7–10/39.

***** Reminiscing Time**

Halcyon DHDL 131 *As above, except add Eddie Wade (t), Marion (v); omit Sullivan.* 10/39–2/40.

*****(*) Bob Crosby's Bob Cats Vol. One 1937–1938**

Swaggie CD 501 *Crosby; Yank Lawson, Billy Butterfield, Sterling Bose (t); Warren Smith (tb); Matty Matlock, Irving Fazola (cl); Eddie Miller (cl, ts); Bob Zurke (p); Nappy Lamare (g, v); Bob Haggart (b); Ray Bauduc (d); Connie Boswell, Marion Mann (v).* 11/37–10/38.

***** Bob Crosby's Bob Cats Vol. Two 1939**

Swaggie CD 502 *As appropriate records above.* 11/37–9/39.

***** Bob Crosby's Bob Cats Vol. Three 1940**

Swaggie CD 503 *Crosby; Billy Butterfield, Max Herman (t); Muggsy Spanier (c); Warren Smith, Floyd O'Brien (tb); Irving Fazola, Hank D'Amico (cl); Eddie Miller (ts); Jess Stacy (p); Nappy Lamare (g, v); Bob Haggart (b); Ray Bauduc (d); Marion Mann, Bing Crosby, The Merry Macks (v).* 2–12/40.

***** Bob Crosby's Bob Cats Vol. Four 1941–1942**

Swaggie CD 504 *Crosby; Bob Goodrich, Yank Lawson (t); Floyd O'Brien (tb); Hank D'Amico, Matty Matlock (cl); Eddie Miller (ts); Jess Stacy (p); Nappy Lamare (g, v); Bob Haggart (b); Ray Bauduc (d); Mary Lee, Bing Crosby (v).* 3/41–6/42.

***** I Remember You**

Vintage Jazz Classics VJC-1046 *Crosby; Yank Lawson, Max Herman, Lyman Vunk (t); Floyd O'Brien, Elmer Smithers, Buddy Morrow, Bruce Squires, Pete Carpenter (tb); Matty Matlock (cl); Art Mendelsohn, Arthur Rando, Ted Klein (as); Eddie Miller (ts, cl); Gil Rodin (ts); Jess Stacy (p); Nappy Lamare (g); Bob Haggart (b); Ray Bauduc (d); Liz Tilton, Gloria DeHaven, Muriel Lane, Lee & Lyn Wilde, David Street (v).* 41–42.

Crosby's band – fronted by the handsome crooner himself, brother of Bing and a charming vocalist, if hardly a jazz singer – worked an unusual furrow among the swing-era bands. Their small-group sides, under the name the Bob Cats, were cast in a tempestuous Dixieland style, the music a throwback to the best hot music of a decade before, and many of the full band's best sides – 'South Rampart Street Parade', 'Royal Garden Blues', 'Wolverine Blues' – were made from the same mould. The fuming trumpet of Yank Lawson, Eddie Miller's fluently hot tenor, the New Orleans-styled clarinets of Irving Fazola and Matty Matlock, all created an authenticity which, say, Tommy Dorsey's Clambake Seven could only hint at. The Crosby orchestra was almost unique among its contemporaries in that it carried the small-group Dixieland style into the bigger format. Haggart's adept arrangements, the timbre of the soloists – even when filling in eight or sixteen bars relatively straight, they sounded tough – and the rhythm section's genuine swing all made the big band surprisingly hot when given their head. Yet, as usual, so many of the full orchestra's records were tainted by schmaltz and novelty that the integrity of the best music is always compromised in any chronological survey. Crosby was game enough to give his men their share of solo space, on the lesser tracks as well as the jazz-directed ones, which means that all is seldom lost. But in the end even the Bob Cats were playing the miserable likes of 'Adios Americano', 'Oh Mistress Mine' and 'You Oughta Hang Your Heart In Shame'.

The Halcyon discs are a complete ongoing survey in chronological order, but that means that the best sides are mixed with the mediocre, and the shoddy packaging and sometimes dull remastering are often discouraging.The earlier material tends to be the more interesting but the remastering is sounding better as it has gone on. Swaggie have collected all the Bob Cats tracks on their four discs (some tracks by the full 1937 band are included on the second volume as a makeweight) and the remastering is very fine. Even though the group was unhappy with the material they were being given by Decca, they still managed (on the January 1942 session from *Volume Four*) to turn in an exemplary show of small-group Dixieland that stands with the best of their work. *Volume One* includes the tremendous debut session by the small group, and the first six tracks almost garner four stars on their own, but the rest is let down by the likes of 'Big Bass Viol'. The Zeta collection is a solid cross-section of tracks from the band's best period. *I Remember You* features rare material by the wartime band – some material of the 'We're Riding For Uncle Sammy Now' ilk – but the band can still boil water when it wants.

****(*) So Far So Good**

Halcyon DHDL 132 *Crosby; Eddie Wade, Max Herman, Billy Butterfield, Bob Peck (t); Warren Smith, Ray Coniff (tb); Irving Fazola (cl); George Koenig, Bill Stegmeyer (as); Eddie Miller (cl, ts); Gil Rodin (ts); Jess Stacy (p); Nappy Lamare (g); Bob Haggart (b); Ray Bauduc (d); Marion Mann (v).* 2–3/40.

**** From Another World**

Halcyon DHDL 133 *As above, except add Muggsy Spanier (c), Al King (t), Floyd O'Brien (tb), Hank D'Amico (cl), Doc Rando, Matty Matlock (cl, as), Bonnie King, The Bob-O-Links (v); omit Wade.* 3–9/40.

**** Gone, But Not Forgotten**

Halcyon DHDL 135 *As above, except add Elmer Smithers (tb), Bing Crosby, Connie Boswell, The Merry Macs (v); omit Butterfield, Peck, Smith, Koenig, Stegmeyer, Mann.* 9–12/40.

****(*) Far Away Music**

Halcyon DHDL 136 *As above, except add Bob Goodrich (t), Bonnie King, Liz Tilton (v); omit Bing Crosby, Boswell, The Merry Macs.* 1–6/41.

***** Something New**

Halcyon DHDL 137 *As above, except add Yank Lawson, Lyman Vunk (t), Buddy Morrow (tb), Art Mendelsohn (as); omit Goodrich, D'Amico, Spanier, King.* 5/41–1/42.

The Crosby story continued apace – this band made a huge number of records and, with the Halcyon series close to its conclusion, they take up a lot of shelf space. But this was a dreary period for the band on record. Despite the arrival of Spanier (who's mostly wasted, although he gets the occasional few bars) the orchestra's records were flabby with bad songs, routine charts and a marked absence of the Dixie-to-swing feel which made them popular in the first place. There's also the usual quota of vocals to get through. Very little worth keeping on four of the above discs, but matters perked up with the return of Yank Lawson in 1941, and *Something New* goes out on a session where the band was back with its original hot material. Remastering is clean enough throughout, although it doesn't seem to have much sparkle.

Connie Crothers

PIANO

A former student of Lennie Tristano, Crothers is a leading figure in a group of improvisers who are keeping the Tristanoite tradition alive and are building on his compositions and methods as repertory.

****(*) Perception**

Steeplechase SCCD 31022 *Crothers; Joe Solomon (b); Roger Mancuso (d).* 74.

***** Swish**

New Artists NA1001 *Crothers; Max Roach (d).*

***** Concert At Cooper Union**

New Artists NA1002 *Crothers (p solo).* 1/84.

***** Duo Dimension**

New Artists NA1003 *Crothers; Richard Tabnik (as).* 85.

Crothers is immersed in the language and lore of Lennie Tristano, intensely enough to generate a feeling – at least among her early records – that she is merely following in his footsteps (intimidating though that might be). But just as the best of the young hard-boppers found new wrinkles in that currency, Crothers has much of her own to say and, given the still-unexplored expanse of Tristano's methods, it still sounds fresh, even as repertory music. The Steeplechase album, recently reissued on CD, finds her taking tentative steps towards her own style, with a preponderance of literal translations of themes such as 'Perception'. Solomon and Mancuso are a functional assist. But the start of a sequence of records for the New Artists label marks a much more interesting documentation. The meeting with Roach finds the pianist far from overwhelmed by her illustrious partner on six improvised duets; the solo record is an open-handed display of thoughtful virtuosity; and the duets with the (inevitably) Konitz-like Tabnik run along probing paths. Crothers plays with the familiar evenness and uses the long, steady, deliberate lines of the style, but her dynamics offer unexpected contrasts of touch and her chordings can build to massive weight and intensity.

***(*) **Love Energy**
New Artists NA1005 *Crothers; Lenny Popkin (ts); Cameron Brown (b); Carol Tristano (d).* 4/88.

***(*) **New York Night**
New Artists NA1008 *As above.* 12/89.

*** **In Motion**
New Artists NA1013 *As above.* 11/89.

***(*) **Jazz Spring**
New Artists NA1017 *As above.* 3/93.

The formation of this excellent quartet, little-known though it is, has been a valuable means of exploring Tristano's music as repertory. Lenny Popkin builds on Warne Marsh's grey, scratchy tone with fretful cadences of his own, Carol Tristano secures a quietly propulsive swing, and Brown's unobtrusively forceful lines eliminate any sense that the music could grow static, either rhythmically or harmonically. Crothers plays for the band yet manages to make her best improvisations distinctive and freely developed, while still minding the essential logic of the form. This is tough, serious jazz, a little self-regarding in its selflessness, but none the worse for that. If Popkin is – so far – never quite the individual voice that he might be, he's still a determined improviser. *In Motion* gets a fractionally lower score for the foreshortened delivery of most of the pieces; but any of the discs offers a fine portrait of the group.

*** **Deep Into The Center**
New Artists NA1020 *Crothers; Roger Mancuso (d).* 12/93–12/94.

*** **Music From Everyday Life**
New Artists NA1025 *Crothers (p solo).* 3/93–6/96.

The duets with Mancuso, taken from 'informal sessions' over a period of a year, are hard work – all but two are severe improvisations, and 'I'll Remember April' is left as something of a corpse. The performers tend to run in parallel rather than interact, with Mancuso particularly oblique in his responses, and the monochrome sound may leave some listeners discouraged. But such deliberately unglamorous jazz has its rewards, and others will find the concentration in the playing absorbing enough. So too with *Music From Everyday Life*. 'Good Morning Heartache' is spare and intense, 'Star Eyes' cut entirely adrift from its body. The improvisation on a Bartók folk dance is a charmer, though, and the miniature 'Be' which starts the disc is a near-perfect improvised composition. It's a patchwork of sessions over three years, and suits eavesdroppers.

***(*) **Session**
New Artists NA1027 *Crothers; Lenny Popkin (ts); Rich Califano (b); Carol Tristano (d).* 96.

Califano is a new recruit, but otherwise it's music as usual from this remarkable quartet. Eight fastidiously shaped tracks, with the melodies of 'I Remember You' and 'Easy Living' dismissed from view, the unfathomably long line of 'Starline' a breathing test for Popkin, and the eternal, selfless pulse set down by bass and drums. In one sense, a pointless music, delivered as a seamless, smooth, yet unpredictable line.

The Crusaders

GROUP

The group's personnel came together out of a group of players working together at a high school in Houston. They made many albums for Pacific Jazz in the 1960s, polishing a soulful variation on the small-group West Coast jazz of the time, before making a long sequence of successful soul-funk-jazz albums in the '70s.

*** **Live At The Lighthouse '66**
Pacific Jazz 37988 *Wayne Henderson (tb); Wilton Felder (ts); Joe Sample (ky); Stix Hooper (d).* 1/66.

*** **Scratch**
GRP 050115-2 *As above, except add Larry Carlton (g), Max Bennett (b).* 74.

***(*) **Those Southern Knights**
GRP 050117-2 *As above, except omit Bennett.* 76.

*** **Street Life**
MCA 101815-2 *As above, except add Robert O Bryant (t), Garnett Brown (tb), Maurice Spears (btb), Jerome Richardson (as), Oscar Brashear, Robert Bryant Jr (ts), Bill Green (bs), Arthur Adams, Billy Rogers, Roland Bautista, Barry Finnerty, Paul Jackson, David T Walker (g), Alphonso Johnson, James Jamerson (b), Randy Crawford (v); omit Henderson and Carlton.* 79.

*** **Live In Japan**
GRP 059746-2 *Wilton Felder (ts); Joe Sample (ky); Barry Finnerty, Roland Bautista (g); Alphonso Johnson (b); Stix Hooper (d); Rafael Cruz (perc).* 81.

Dropping the word 'jazz' from the name was, of course, a form of critical suicide; it happened in 1971, and since then the Crusaders have for some been a byword for commercial compromise. Despite which, the group has maintained a consistency and occasionally a perverse integrity of purpose since first emerging in 1961 out of a Houston high-school band. The basic line-up – Felder, Hooper, Sample, Henderson – has been in place from the start, despite individual projects and excursions, fallings-out and Star Chamber reshuffles. The Crusaders offer a solidly funky combo music which might almost have been programmed by a computer; it hinges on Sample's bar-room piano, Felder's and Henderson's uncomplicated horn lines, and Hooper's accurate but curiously undynamic drumming. No less, and seldom any more; but the group has made some very good records along the way and the chaotic state of its discography is a pity.

The live date from Hermosa Beach in 1966 offers what is presumably a pretty faithful version of what the band sounded like in concert around this time: slick, capable and unshakeably jazz-centred, doing versions of 'Round Midnight', Trane's 'Some

Other Blues', 'Milestones' and 'You Don't Know What Love Is', alongside the originals. These include Sample's 'Blues Up Tight', Felder's 'Miss It', Henderson's 'Scratch' and Vinnegar's rootsier 'Doin' That Thing'. Sixteen minutes are added to the original LP release.

The addition of outside players (guitarists and bassists most obviously) seldom disrupted the basic formula; Larry Carlton was the *de facto* 'fifth Crusader' for many years. But the group's progress is impossible to follow on the basis of the currently available records. There are an incredible 14 other albums on Pacific Jazz, made between 1961 and 1969, that have yet to reach CD. Even more damaging to their standing is the absence of most of the music made for MCA's Blue Thumb imprint in the early '70s, including *Crusaders 1, Second Crusade, Chain Reaction, Southern Comfort* and *Unsung Heroes*, all of which are worth seeking out on increasingly in-demand vinyl.The two surviving dates, *Scratch*, which is live, and *Those Southern Knights*, which is studio, are fine – the latter in particular showing how a pop-funk-jazz album could still be committed and based around creative playing.

Street Life, spotlit by Randy Crawford's vocal, was their commercial breakthrough but largely their undoing as a close-knit ensemble. The big-band arrangement and the drafting in of a raft of guitarists to replace Carlton gnawed through the group's hard-won independence, and their music increasingly drifted towards a lite-soul feel. The Japanese live album shows some sparks still flying, all the same.

Recent years have seen the band's legend tarnished by all manner of litigious uproar. Some of the members are still working together, but Sample, for so long their compositional backbone, is not involved. A couple of '90s albums are too sad to list here.

Ronnie Cuber (born 1941)

BARITONE, ALTO AND TENOR SAXOPHONES, FLUTE

Born in Brooklyn, Cuber started on baritone in 1959 at the behest of Marshall Brown, and it became his main horn. He worked with Maynard Ferguson and Woody Herman, as well as with numerous Latin groups and in support of soul artists. He is an in-demand clinician all over the USA.

***** Cubism**

Fresh Sound FSRCD 188 *Cuber; Joe Locke (vib, ky); Bobby Broom (g); Michael Formanek (b); Ben Perowsky (d); Carlos Patato Valdes (perc).* 12/91.

***** Airplay**

Steeplechase SCCD 31309 *Cuber; Geoff Keezer (p); Chip Jackson (b); Ben Perowsky (d).* 4/92.

*****(*) The Scene Is Clean**

Milestone 9218 *Cuber; Lawrence Feldman (f); Geoff Keezer (ky); Joey DeFrancesco (org); George Wadenius (g); Tom Barney, Reggie Washington (b); Victor Jones (d); Manolo Badrena, Milton Cardona (perc).* 12/93.

***** NY Cats**

Steeplechase SCCD 31394 *Cuber; Ryan Kisor (t); Michael Weiss (p); Andy McKee (b); Tony Reedus (d).* 3/96.

***** Love For Sale**

Koch 6914-2 *Cuber; Netherlands Metropole Orchestra.* 93.

Cuber has played on many, many sessions as a section-man, but his records as leader are down to a handful. He gets a light, limber feel out of the baritone when he wants to, though he will make it sound gruff and monstrous if he has to, and his odd adaptability to Latin rhythms means that his own discs usually have more than a few traces of Brazilian bop about them. The feel on *Cubism* is directed towards a lite kind of jazz-funk, but Locke's typically shrewd playing and a few worthwhile licks from the valuable Broom lift it out of the rut that Cuber was in on some of his earlier releases. *Airplay*, despite the somewhat ironic title, puts Cuber back into hard bop with Keezer's fine work as his line to earth. Most of the tunes work a rather old-fashioned groove, as if this were a tribute to the great days of Blue Note and Prestige, but the baritone work is as forthright and full-bodied as Cuber has ever sounded. *The Scene Is Clean* is another blend of styles: the Dameron title-tune, the modal jazz theme, 'Song For Pharoah' and the winsome 'Flamingo' are more traditionally sewn, but the bristling Latin tunes again carry an infectious spirit and it's obvious that the leader feels right at home here. Cuber picks up tenor and alto here and there, but the big horn is what holds his soul and he sounds appreciative on this date.

NY Cats is something of a misfire, despite the promising line-up and some pleasing tunes: George Benson's 'Mimosa' is an engaging piece, 'Do Nothin' Till You Hear From Me' is a smart baritone vehicle, and there's some tremendous blowing on the closing 'Better Git It In Your Soul'. But the band sound untogether, Reedus especially all over the place, and for once the Steeplechase sound is unpleasing, with Cuber given an unfortunately flat timbre. Remaining honours go to Kisor.

The gig with the Netherlands Metropole Orchestra has been something of a dream date for several saxophonists now, and Cuber sounds as pleased as any of them to have the chance. The arrangements are luxury-class rather than especially challenging, but Cuber doesn't hold anything back in his playing: his solos are packed with notes, the delivery on the ballads quite terse and scratchy.

Bill Cunliffe

PIANO

Bop-derived contemporary American pianist.

***** Bill Plays Bud**

Naxos 86024 2 *Cunliffe; Ralph Moore (ts); Dave Carpenter (b); Joe LaBarbera (d); Papo Rodriguez (perc).* 10/96.

Previous sightings of Cunliffe with the Clayton–Hamilton Orchestra and with the Minnesotan trumpeter Bruce Paulson suggested a competent, unspectacular player. As leader, he is much more emphatic and he brings an authentic flavour to these more- and less-familiar Bud Powell themes. His phrasing on 'Comin' Up' can't be faulted: terse, slightly off-centre and robustly percussive. Familiar material is reworked, including a substantial rethink of '52nd Street Theme' and 'Un Poco Loco'. He also digs out a couple of rarities, 'Willowgrove', an effusive bop blues theme, and the strange 'Dusk At Saudi', which seems to be a version of 'Midnight Sun'. The set is nicely framed by Cunliffe's own composition, 'Melancolia', and a closing essay on 'Glass Enclosure'.

Moore's contribution is restricted to 'Polka Dots And Moonbeams' and '52nd Street' but, as ever, he finds things to say in that still-hard-to-place economical delivery. Like Cunliffe, Moore sounds as if he has skipped the Coltrane–Tyner generation entirely. It's very much the leader's set, though, a showcase for a fine talent who will be worth following in albums to come.

Ted Curson (born 1935)

TRUMPET, POCKET TRUMPET

He moved from Philadelphia to New York in the '50s and had an important spell with Charles Mingus, 1959–60. Co-led a small group with Bill Barron, before moving to Europe in the late '60s; he has since divided his time between Europe and the USA. A prominent educator and a rare example of an American who has pushed European jazz back home, Curson moves easily between hard bop and more free areas in his own playing.

***** Plays Fire Down Below**

Original Jazz Classics OJC 1744 *Curson; Gildo Mahones (p); George Tucker (b); Roy Haynes (d); Montego Joe (perc).* 12/62.

*****(*) Tears For Dolphy**

Black Lion BLCD 760190 *Curson; Bill Barron (ts, cl); Herb Bushler (b); Dick Berk (d).* 8/64.

****** The New Thing & The Blue Thing**

Koch CD 8531 *Curson; Bill Barron (ts); George Arvanitas (p); Herb Bushler (b); Dick Berk (d).* 65.

Thin representation for a highly significant innovator who came to prominence with Mingus, wrote the beautiful 'Tears For Dolphy' and then spent much of his time in Europe. A radical with a strong interest in classic jazz, Curson's work on piccolo trumpet often resembles Rex Stewart's, though he's closer to Fats Navarro on the concert horn. *Fire Down Below* is a reasonable representation of his pungent, unsentimental style. Mahones laces a basically conventional approach with figures reminiscent of Carl Perkins. Tucker and Haynes might explain a resemblance to Eric Dolphy's debut album on New Jazz, on which they played, and they're equally impressive here. The drummer is quietly forceful on the two quartet tracks, 'The Very Young' and 'Only Forever', but he sounds slightly cramped by the addition of congas on the remainder.

Tears For Dolphy was recorded a month or so after the death of its dedicatee, and there is a raw sorrow in the title-tune that was less evident in later versions. Barron provides solid support and chips in with four strong charts, including the Dolphyish '7/4 Funny Time' and 'Desolation'. The rhythm section is also very solid, but it is Curson's high, slightly old-fashioned sound on the small trumpet that commands attention. 'Searchin' For The Blues' is the other highlight.

Koch's rescue programme has had few worthier objects than Curson's 1965 Atlantic, *The New Thing & The Blue Thing*, which is not two albums stuck together but a reference to the stylistic poles of Curson's work. It teams him with the like-minded Barron, who plays brightly on 'Straight Ice' and 'Elephant Walk', two Curson originals, but wanders off course a bit elsewhere. Arvanitas is a fascinating player, with a robustly lyrical touch, tracking Curson's maverick line on 'Star Eyes' with real imagination. Ted sticks to concert trumpet throughout, or so it sounds, but even here he manages to squeeze out tight, high tones that suggest a piccolo instrument. His phraseology on 'Reava's Waltz', an early appearance of what was to become a long-standing favourite, is very precise and expressive. Arvanitas sits this one out.

***** Sugar'N'Spice**

Level Green 2208 *Curson; Michael Cochrane (p); Lenny Argese (g); Calvin Hill (b); Bruce Cox (d).* 4/99.

Recorded, mixed and mastered in a day, and it sounds pretty much like it. This is a relaxed, uncomplicated set of mostly mid-tempo tunes. Ted sounds laid-back and reflective and seems to have conceived the set as a stroll through his working life. He uses the occasion to remind us that it was he, not Clifford Brown, who was the first trumpeter to play Duke Jordan's 'Jordu'. The title-tune was recorded for Atlantic but was only ever released in Japan, and it's a fair reflection of Ted's skills as a composer. So is the opening 'Playhouse March', which the liner-note claims was written for a gig at '*Mitten*'s Playhouse' in Harlem – you know the place. This march doesn't sound as if it could be played wearing gloves; its formal pace is deceptive. In addition to setting the record straight on a few points, Ted also pays tribute to a few of his musical influences, Dizzy ('Tin Tin Deo') and Miles ('Dig' and 'Milestones') foremost among them. We'd still recommend the earlier material, but *Sugar'N'Spice* is an agreeable mainstream disc, with enough stylistic individuality to keep the listener guessing.

Enthusiasts for Curson need to get hold of *Blue Piccolo And Fireball* from 1976 and *The Ted Curson Trio* from 1979 (both currently deleted); there is also a fine tribute to Mingus and a rare 1962 live set from La Tête de l'Art in Toronto, originally released on Trans World and briefly reissued on Can-Am.

Leo Cuypers (born 1947)

PIANO

Expelled from Maastricht Conservatory 'due to his views on art and life', Cuypers came to attention at the 1969 Loosdrecht jazz competition and later joined the Willem Breuker Kollektief, staying until 1980. His 1995 album marked a return after some years away from music.

***** Zeeland Suite & Johnny Rep Suite**

Bvhaast 9307 *Cuypers; Willem Van Manen (tb); Bob Driessen (ss, as, bs); Willem Breuker (ss, as, ts, bcl); Piet Noordijk (as); Hans Dulfer (ts); Harry Miller, Arjen Gorter (b); Martin Van Duynhoven, Rob Verdurmen (d).* 9/74–9/77.

Cuypers is known internationally only as one of Willem Breuker's cronies, but these two vintage sessions from the Bvhaast catalogue, usefully reissued on a single CD, give him some modest limelight as a leader. That said, the 'Zeeland Suite' in particular is much like a Breuker cross-section of riffs and ideas and is more impressive as a framework for the players – Gorter and Miller on

'Two Bass Shit', Breuker and Driessen on 'Bach II And Bach' – than as any thematic sequence. The 'Johnny Rep Suite' is again dominated by Breuker himself, delivering 'Kirk' as a roaring tribute to the eponymous Roland; but at least Cuypers gets a couple of pieces more or less to himself at the end. The original recording is rather rough and a little unkind to the piano.

***** 'Songbook'**

Bvhaast 9502 *Cuypers (p solo).* 8/95.

A comeback after a number of years of retreat. Cuypers prepared a studio album, but on hearing the tape of this informal recital preferred this off-the-cuff session. There are 17 original tunes, some little more than embellished vamps but others showing the most acute and inventive harmonic thinking. A handful seem like flawless gems, such as the haunting 'Joplin' or 'Bouquet Mélancholique'; others have a nearly throwaway air about them. Cuypers seems rusty at some moments, virtuosic at others; one follows the record through, wondering what will emerge next.

Andrew Cyrille (born 1939)

DRUMS

Born in Brooklyn, Cyrille played with leaders from Nellie Lutcher to Roland Kirk, before starring in Cecil Taylor's mid-'60s trio, staying until 1975. His own groups push a colourful and lively blend of post-bop with other musical vernaculars, fuelled by his own virtuosic playing.

*****(*) Metamusicians' Stomp**

Black Saint 120 025 *Cyrille; Ted Daniel (t, flhn, wood f); David S Ware (ts, f); Nick DiGeronimo (b).* 9/78.

****** Nuba**

Black Saint 120 030 *Cyrille; Jimmy Lyons (as); Jeanne Lee (v).* 6/79.

****** The Navigator**

Soul Note 121 062 *Cyrille; Ted Daniel (t, flhn); Sonelius Smith (p); Nick DiGeronimo (b).* 9/82.

Twenty years ago, Cyrille took part in a series of concerts entitled 'Dialogue Of The Drums'. Somewhat behind the great wave of the avant-garde – or the 'New Thing' – he, Milford Graves and Rashied Ali demonstrated what they had brought to it. What was immediately evident was that though he seemed a quieter and more accommodating player, less addicted to the free-form thrash, Cyrille was the most instinctively musical of the trio. The only other name that ought to have been there was Sunny Murray, whom Cyrille replaced in the Cecil Taylor Trio in 1964, staying with the pianist for just over a decade and playing on the apocalyptic *Unit Structures*.

Something of Taylor's turbulent language creeps into *Nuba*, which also features Taylor's loyal saxophonist, Jimmy Lyons. Including a setting from Jeanne Lee's *The Valley Of Astonishment And Bewilderment*, this highly lyrical album is almost a miniature opera, developing the ideas on Cyrille's astonishing solo record, *What About?*, which finds him vocalizing – albeit without words – the pain and frustration of the black experience in America. Lyons's calm and stoical approach is the perfect conduit for this music, and both men seem to be working at the opposite extreme from the fierce abstractions of the Taylor group.

Metamusicians' Stomp and *The Navigator* feature the group Cyrille called Maono, and they signal his increasing interest in an Africanized language for jazz. On the latter record, each of the players introduces a section, adding bearings and compass points to a collective navigation back to the source. As with many of Cyrille's records, it asserts the jazz tradition by seeming to shed it, layer by layer. What this and the earlier *Metamusicians' Stomp* seem to suggest is that, the further jazz goes back towards its point of ancestral departure, the more completely it is itself.

***** Galaxies**

Music & Arts CD 672 *Cyrille; Vladimir Tarasov (d, perc, elec).* 6/90.

Tarasov was the most securely jazz-based of the Ganelin Trio, and in America this aspect of his musical personality became ever more evident. Music & Arts have been adept at putting together this kind of partnership – and this is one of the best, as well as the most unexpected. From Cyrille's point of view, the key track is 'One Up, One Down', the result of his long study of John Coltrane's later rhythmic ideas, an important perspective on a musician whose contribution has long been thought to be predominantly – and indeed exhaustively – harmonic.

Tarasov's own compositions are fascinating, not least for the subtle use of electronics; but it is Cyrille who commands attention, not just for the Coltrane piece, but also for 'No. 11', which reaffirms his devotion to jazz rhythms.

***** My Friend Louis**

DIW 858 *Cyrille; Hannibal (t); Oliver Lake (as, ss); Adegoke Steve Colson (p); Reggie Workman (b).* 11/91.

The 1990s saw a resurgence in Cyrille's fortunes. Transfer to CD began to clarify just how much he and fellow-drummers and -bassists had contributed to the revolution of the 1960s. *My Friend Louis* is dedicated to the South African, Louis Moholo, and explores a shared pool of atavistic dialects, free jazz confronting the most basic communicative rhythms. The only criticism of the record is that Lake, who dominates proceedings, is perhaps too sophisticated a stylist, and that the sound of the saxophone is alien to what Hannibal and the underrecorded Colson are doing. Workman is his usual cavernous self, and the recording is as full and intense as anyone might wish.

*****(*) The X-Man**

Soul Note 121 262 *Cyrille; James Newton (f); Alex Tit Pascal (g); Anthony Cox (b).* 5/93.

****** Good To Go, With A Tribute To Bu**

Soul Note 121 292 *Cyrille; James Newton (f); Lisle Atkinson (b).* 10/95.

Flute and guitar add a new spectrum to *X-Man*, one that seems closer to Cyrille's basic understanding of melody. Newton's 'E-Squat' is a strong, clearly stated idea from a player who seems to understand Cyrille's intentions from the bottom up, and the drummer responds with some of his simplest and least cluttered playing on record. 'Simple Melody' is extraordinary, something out of a far-off place that yet seems as familiar and immediate as the most overworked standard.

Atkinson had alternated with Nick DiGeronimo in Maono and he's a welcome addition to the later trio. The set is bracketed by two takes of Cyrille's brilliant impersonation of Art Blakey *in excelsis*. They and the other title-piece are essays in freedom and responsiveness. The surprises on this album are a version of John Carter's 'Enter From The East' (how one thirsts for a chance to hear the composer's clarinet cutting into this), a reading of Andrew Hill's 'Nicodemus', with Atkinson touching in the chords, John B. Gordon's 'Aftermath', and, more surprising yet, a standard, 'The Inch Worm', done as if another JC hadn't thought of it yet. If you have yet to sample Cyrille's work on record, meet a master in his pomp.

Carsten Dahl

PIANO, ORGAN

Danish pianist, putting a contemporary spin on bebop piano.

***** Will You Make My Soup Hot And Silver**
Storyville STCD 4203 *Dahl; Lennart Ginman (b); Frands Rifbjerg (d).* 12/96.

***** Message From Bud**
Storyville STCD4232 *As above.* 12/98.

From the brisk momentum of 'Autumn Leaves' onwards on the first disc, it's clear that Dahl is minded to take an unhackneyed path through this set of often very familiar materials: 'Giant Steps', 'Take Five', 'Caravan', and others. He does several pieces associated with Miles Davis and not one of them is quite what you'd expect. 'Freddie The Freeloader' is done over a choppy, bustling rhythm, 'I Thought About You' is unrecognizably slow and distant. He frequently has his rhythm players set up a groove of some sort while he lays elliptical comments over the top; melodies are left alone or reharmonized. It keeps you listening in a whatever-next way, although sometimes the approach seems almost deliberately and unconvincingly cute. His only originals are a blues and a bluesy vamp tune.

He says that the title-piece of *Message From Bud* came to him in a dream in which he was drinking with Bud Powell. It sounds like a clever Powell copy, for sure. This second disc is slightly less arch than the first one, and there's a Garneresque twist to the two-fisted way he swings some of the standards. 'Blue In Green' is effective because he doesn't sound much like Bill Evans, preferring a heavier, more deliberate touch.

Del Dako (born 1955)

BARITONE AND ALTO SAXOPHONES

Canadian saxophonist rarely sighted outside his local scene and specializing in baritone.

****(*) Balancing Act**
Sackville SKCD2-2021 *Dako; Richard Whiteman (p); Dick Felix (b); Mike McClelland (d).* 3–11/90.

Dako waited until he was 35 before making his debut album. Although he plays alto in places, notably on the thoughtful original 'Steve The Weave' which opens the record, Dako's primary horn is the baritone, which he employs with a gruff, bull-headed swing: he loves the grouchiness of baritone timbre, and his solo on 'Just Don't Slip With That Axe' is a memorable string of complaints. But the music is rhythmically less assured, Dako not quite authoritative enough to command the best from a so-so rhythm section, and it results in a bit of a potboiler.

Meredith D'Ambrosio

VOCAL, PIANO

A Bostonian, D'Ambrosio has been recording since 1978, often in the company of her husband, pianist Eddie Higgins. A speciality is her melding of a standard with a newly composed variation of both the words and the melody.

***** Lost In His Arms**
Sunnyside SSC 1081D *D'Ambrosio; Ray Santisi (p); Norman Coles (g); Chris Rathbun (b).* 7–10/78.

***** Another Time**
Sunnyside SSC 1017D *D'Ambrosio.* 2/81.

*****(*) Little Jazz Bird**
Sunnyside SSC 1040D *D'Ambrosio; Phil Woods (cl, as); Hank Jones (p); Gene Orloff, Fred Buldrini (vn); Julian Barber (vla); Fred Slatkin (clo); Steve Gilmore (b); Bill Goodwin (d).* 3/82.

****** It's Your Dance**
Sunnyside SSC 1011 *D'Ambrosio; Harold Danko (p); Kevin Eubanks (g).* 3/85.

****(*) The Cove**
Sunnyside SSC 1028D *D'Ambrosio; Lee Konitz (as); Fred Hersch (p); Michael Formanek (b); Keith Copeland (d).*

*****(*) South To A Warmer Place**
Sunnyside SSC 1039D *D'Ambrosio; Lou Colombo (t); Eddie Higgins (p); Don Coffman (b); Danny Berger (d).* 2/89.

*****(*) Love Is Not A Game**
Sunnyside SSC 1051D *D'Ambrosio; Eddie Higgins (p); Rufus Reid (b); Keith Copeland (d).* 12/90.

***** Shadowland**
Sunnyside SSC 1060D *D'Ambrosio; Ron Kozak (f, bcl); Blair Tindall (cor, ob); Eddie Higgins (p); Johnny Frigo (vn); Erik Friedlander (clo); Jay Leonhart (b); Ben Riley (d).* 7/92.

****(*) Sleep Warm**
Sunnyside SSC 1063D *D'Ambrosio (p, v).* 2/91.

A vocalist whose approach is so soft and unemphatic that sometimes she barely seems to be present at all. But her choice of songs is so creative and the treatments so consistently refined that the records are unexpectedly absorbing. *Another Time* is a reissue of a privately produced session, and its bare-bones approach is perhaps a little too austere, but it's still an impressive recital of 18 songs. Another reappearance is the 1978 session, *Lost In His Arms*, which unfolds at the steady, thoughtful pace of all of her music. *Little Jazz Bird*, despite an eccentric studio production by Rudy van Gelder, is ingeniously programmed to accommodate Woods and the string quartet, and the songs encompass Dave Frishberg, Gene Lees, Loonis McGloohan and two exceptional pieces by

Deborah Henson-Conant, 'How Is Your Wife' and 'When The End Comes'. *It's Your Dance* is arguably D'Ambrosio's most fully realized record: with only Danko and Eubanks (who's never played better) in support, D'Ambrosio maintains a supernal glow throughout the record. Almost all the songs are unusual, from her own lyrics to 'Giant Steps' and Dave Brubeck's 'Strange Meadowlark' to Al Cohn's 'The Underdog', the title-track's reworking of John Carisi's 'Israel' and the lovely Burke–Van Heusen rarity, 'Humpty Dumpty Heart'. The vocalist's choice of material and the hip understatement of her singing create the core of her work. Her voice is too small and unambitious to make any play for jazz virtuosity, but she achieves a different authenticity through economies of scale.

That said, it goes a little wrong on *The Cove*, which is too composed and sleepy, the playing sounding fatigued rather than laid-back. But *South To A Warmer Place* restores her run: Colombo plays a Bobby Hackett-like role and, since many of the songs are relatively familiar, this may be the best place to start hearing D'Ambrosio's enchanting work. *Love Is Not A Game* has some more memorable treatments: 'Autumn Serenade', J.J. Johnson's 'Lament', Denny Zeitlin's 'Quiet Now'. On 'Oh Look At Me Now', she extends the song into a coda which has her composing new lyrics for a variation on the tune, and that approach is carried over into 5 of the 12 tunes on *Shadowland*, perhaps with mixed success. She still sounds at her best on the introspective, soliloquy-like material, such as Burton Lane's 'A Rainy Afternoon', and Noël Coward's 'Zigeuner' is another surprising and successful choice. Eddie Higgins, her husband, provides sympathetic piano throughout, although her own playing isn't negligible. *Sleep Warm* is for more specialized tastes, perhaps, since it is mainly a set of modern and old-fashioned lullabies for a child.

***** Because Of Spring**
Sunnyside SSC 1069D *D'Ambrosio; Eddie Higgins (p); George Mraz (b); Jeff Hirshfield (d). 9/94.*

***** Silent Passion**
Sunnyside SSC 1075D *D'Ambrosio; Gene Bertoncini (g). 1/96.*

***** Echo Of A Kiss**
Sunnyside SSC 1078 *D'Ambrosio; Mike Renzi (p); Jay Leonhart (b); Terry Clarke (d). 8/97.*

D'Ambrosio extends her placid progress with more albums. *Because Of Spring* continues her songs-out-of-other-songs method on four tracks, and her strong suit continues to be her song selection: 'Moon Dreams' and 'Through A Long And Sleepless Night' were two good ideas, but, as so often with her records, it often teeters into a quiet, quiet margin that makes no impression. Although *Silent Passion* reduces the cast to two – and Meredith handles the piano duties – it's a degree more intense and an ounce more involving, with Bertoncini making elegant work out of his dialogue and the singer a shade more assertive. *Echo Of A Kiss* tries her out with a new line-up, although she's settled so deeply into her meditative groove that there's now a danger that she's going to make the same record each time with slowly diminishing returns. 'April Fooled Me' and 'Snowfall' are the rediscoveries, to go with her own originals.

Tadd Dameron (1917–65)

COMPOSER, BANDLEADER, PIANO

Born in Cleveland, Dameron was writing arrangements from the mid-'30s and worked for Harlan Leonard in New York from 1939. Soon got caught up in bebop and wrote for the Gillespie band, before leading his own small groups in the late '40s with Fats Navarro and Miles Davis. Drug problems slowed him down in the '50s and he was imprisoned for three years from 1957. Returned for a few further projects but died from cancer at a time when jazz had basically left him behind.

***** Cool Boppin'**
Fresh Sound FSCD 1008 *Dameron; Miles Davis (t); Kai Winding (tb); Sahib Shihab (as); Benjamin Lundy (ts); Cecil Payne (bs); John Collins (g); Curley Russell (b); Kenny Clarke (d); Carlos Vidal (perc). 2/49.*

*****(*) Fontainebleau**
Original Jazz Classics OJC 055 *Dameron; Kenny Dorham (t); Henry Coker (tb); Sahib Shihab (as); Joe Alexander (ts); Cecil Payne (bs); John Simmons (b); Shadow Wilson (d). 3/56.*

***** Mating Call**
Original Jazz Classics OJC 212 *Dameron; John Coltrane (ts); John Simmons (b); Philly Joe Jones (d). 11/56.*

****(*) The Magic Touch**
Original Jazz Classics OJC 143 *Dameron; Ernie Royal, Charlie Shavers, Clark Terry, Joe Wilder (t); Jimmy Cleveland, Britt Woodman (tb); Julius Watkins (frhn); Jerry Dodgion, Leo Wright (as, f); Jerome Richardson (ts, f); Johnny Griffin (ts); Tate Houston (bs); Bill Evans (p); Ron Carter (b); Philly Joe Jones (d); Barbara Winfield (v). 2–4/62.*

It's Dameron's fate to be remembered now largely for a handful of compositions – 'Hot House' and 'Lady Bird' pre-eminently – which became standards. As such, Dameron is a much-underrated performer who stands at the fulcrum of modern jazz, midway between swing and bebop. Combining the broad-brush arrangements of the big band and the advanced harmonic language of bop, his own recordings are difficult to date blind. The title of one of the most renowned tunes, 'On A Misty Night', catches the sense of evanescence which seems to surround both the man and the music.

Fats Navarro played as well with Dameron as he did with anyone; the Blue Note sets issued as *The Fabulous Fats Navarro* should strictly be credited to the Tadd Dameron Sextet/Septet and to Bud Powell's Modernists, but became known as a posthumous tribute to the brilliant young trumpeter who died in 1950. Navarro's big, ringing brass-tone is superb on a second take of 'Anthropology' (Dameron features on the first), two takes of 'Good Bait' and a witty 'Oh! Lady Be Good'.

Another young genius took a significant stride forward under Dameron's wing. John Coltrane's solo on 'Soultrane' and the ballad construction on 'On A Misty Night' are among the best things in his early career. Though *Mating Call* is often discussed as if it were a Coltrane album, it's the pianist who's firmly in the driving seat, directing an ensemble sound subtly different from anything else that was coming out of bebop. Though dedicated to the memory of another ill-fated trumpet genius, Clifford Brown's *Memorial* set (listed under his name) is also valuable for insights into Dameron's methods. 'Theme Of No Repeat', 'Dial "B" For Beauty' and 'Philly J.J.' are relatively little known compared to 'Lady Bird' and 'Good Bait', but they evidence a consummate grasp of instrumental voicing; the last of the three also stands up well on the Dameronia recording reviewed below. Also shared is *Cool Boppin'*, which fuels debate about the real parentage of Cool School jazz by pairing Dameron's Royal Roost session of February 1949 with Miles Davis's residency there the previous autumn and winter; Miles also plays with Dameron's group. 'Good Bait' isn't a vintage performance, but the treatments of 'April In Paris' and 'Webb's Delight' point in interesting directions that help refocus appreciation of Dameron's art.

Fontainebleau originates from Dameron's last full year of freedom before the term of imprisonment that more or less ended his career. It's a fine set, with no clutter in the horns. The title-piece is wholly written out, with no scope for improvising, but there is plenty of individual work elsewhere, notably from Dorham. Never a virtuoso soloist, Dameron prefers to work within the very distinct chord-progressions of his tunes, big, lush confections that are too sharp-edged ever to cloy. The final record, *The Magic Touch*, was a great disappointment at the time. It revisits signature pieces such as 'On A Misty Night' and even 'Fontainebleau', but in foreshortened and even glib versions which, while not without interest, suggest that Dameron himself had perhaps lost interest in his own music.

Dameronia

GROUP

A tribute band to Tadd Dameron's legacy which produced this one-off live record and an earlier (and unavailable) studio set.

***(*) Live At The Théâtre Boulogne-Billancourt, Paris

Soul Note 121202 *Don Sickler, Virgil Jones (t); Benny Powell (tb); Frank Wess (as, f); Clifford Jordan (ts); Cecil Payne (bs); Walter Davis Jr (p); Larry Ridley (b); Kenny Washington (d).* 5/89.

The original idea for Dameronia came from drummer Philly Joe Jones, who wanted to see Tadd Dameron's achievement properly recognized. The work of transcription and re-orchestration from records (the original MSS had gone missing years before) was done by Don Sickler, who conducts on this concert performance, and by pianist John Oddo. They did a strikingly good job. The group's first LP was issued on the small Uptown label, but it was live appearances in New York that attracted all the critical attention. By the time the group got together again in 1989, Philly Joe was dead, so these sessions serve a further memorial function. Like Mingus Dynasty and Big Band Charlie Mingus, the intention is to represent the composer's music accurately, but with the same level of freedom for soloists to express themselves. Clearly neither Sickler nor Virgil Jones has the passionate ring of a Fats Navarro who interpreted the blues 'Good Bait' and 'The Squirrel' in the late 1940s, but their performances are more than routine on both. The star turn on 'The Squirrel' is Cecil Payne, who represents the last remaining line of succession. His barrel-chested tone had been heard on *Fontainebleau* in 1956. The 1989 version of Dameron's little suite is beautifully orchestrated and balanced, with a delicate touch from everybody concerned.

Paolo Damiani

BASS, CELLO, VOCAL

Italian bassist and bandleader trying different post-bop directions.

*** Poor Memory

Splasc(h) HP 07 *Damiani; Paolo Fresu (t, flhn); Gianluigi Trovesi (ss, as, bcl); Claude Barthelemy (g); Aldo Romano (d).* 7/87.

*** Eso

Splasc(h) H 404-2 *As above, except Danilo Rea (p), Antonio Iasevoli (g), Roberto Gatto (d), Raffaela Siniscalchi, Sabina Macculi (v) replace Barthelemy and Romano.* 93.

Poor Memory is a fine concert recording, featuring several of the brightest contemporary talents in Italian jazz. Fresu continues to impress as a lyrical voice, but Trovesi's hard-hitting reed solos and Barthelemy's harsh, rock-directed guitar provide piquant contrast. Damiani's compositions find a suitable middle ground between hard bop and freer modes, and the live recording is agreeably rough-edged and human-sounding.

Eso has a few unexpected vocal contributions, including those by the leader, although Siniscalchi is the one with the outstanding voice. In the main, this is the mix as before, with Fresu and Trovesi both in excellent voice.

***(*) Song Tong

Splasc(h) H 460-2 *Damiani; Kenny Wheeler (flhn, t); Gianluigi Trovesi (as, acl); Maurizio Giammarco (ss, ts); Stefano Battaglia (p); Jean Marc Montera (g); Joel Allouche (d); Fulvio Maras (perc); Maria Pia De Vito, Tiziana Simona Vigni (v).* 8/91.

Actually recorded before *Eso* but getting a rather belated CD release, this must be Damiani's best work. A terrific group make vivid work out of a rather fanciful set of charts: the title-tune moves from lament to percussion fantasia to neo-African vamp. Each musician has an important part without anyone dominating, and the way Damiani makes the most of Wheeler's vulnerable tone and Trovesi's and Giammarco's contrasting styles is superbly effective. Just occasionally the music sounds a trifle arch but it's sustained in the most accomplished way.

*** Mediana

EGEA SCA 067 *Damiani; Carlo Marianni (launeddas); Sandro Satta (as); Carlo Rizzo, Michele Rabbia (perc).* 1/99.

Damiani and cohorts try their hand at a style previously investigated by Paolo Carrus, the Sardinian folk music played on such instruments as the *launeddas*. It's joyful music and far from the untempered, unsophisticated feel one might expect: Damiani brings the skirl of the pipes and the 'local' percussion into a brimmingly modern improvisational context. Satta's quicksilver alto works well in this situation. The record isn't really sustained to the end, and there's still an inescapable feeling of worldly novelty, but it will please adventurous tastes.

Franco D'Andrea (born 1941)

PIANO, KEYBOARDS

Worked on radio in Rome in the early '60s and spent much of that decade in free forms – with Gato Barbieri, the Modern Art Trio and the jazz-rock Perigeo. Later turned to more conservative post-bop forms, but he remains a restless stylist and has roamed far and wide in his recording activities.

***** Kick Off**

Red 123225-2 *D'Andrea; Giovanni Tommaso (b); Roberto Gatto (d).* 4/88.

***** Earthcake**

Label Bleu LBLC 6539 *D'Andrea; Enrico Rava (t, bugle); Miroslav Vitous (b); Daniel Humair (d).* 1/91.

***(*) Enrosadira**

Red 123243-2 *D'Andrea; Luis Agudo (perc).* 91.

****** Airegin**

Red 123252-2 *D'Andrea; Giovanni Tommaso (b); Roberto Gatto (d).* 4/91.

***** Flavours**

Penta Flowers CDPIA 024 *D'Andrea; Glenn Ferris (tb); Tino Tracanna (ts); Saverio Tasca (vib); Attilio Zanchi (b); Gianni Cazzola (d); Naco (perc).* 5/92.

***** Current Changes**

Penta Flowers CDPIA 035 *D'Andrea; David Boato (t); Naco (perc).* 12/93.

***** Live In Perugia**

Penta Flowers CDPIA 41 *D'Andrea (p solo).* 7/94.

D'Andrea is a senior figure among Italy's post-bop musicians; his playing has a scholar's penchant for irony and dramatic construction and, while there's plenty of Mediterranean fire in his music, he's just as partial to a meditative frame of expression. Either of the two trio sessions for Red, with two of his favourite partners, will make a good place to start hearing D'Andrea's jazz. *Kick Off* offers comparatively short measure with only five tunes, and the sound-balance isn't too kind to the piano, but the trio demonstrate a very refined empathy, the balance of initiative shifting almost from measure to measure. *Airegin*, though, is even better. There are some superb reworkings of the jazz repertoire on 'Epistrophy', 'Doxy', 'Airegin' and 'Blue In Green', as well as some fine originals, with Tommaso's 'My Dear One' and D'Andrea's own 'Things Called'. The pianist takes a lot of trouble to reharmonize or otherwise vary the delivery of the familiar pieces without making it seem effortful.

The Label Bleu disc is something of an all-star session and, while nothing extraordinary happens, it's a significantly democratic affair, with compositions from each man and the title-piece standing as a highly articulate and detailed improvisation. *Enrosadira*, though, is eminently avoidable, a muddle of electronic keyboards pitched against Agudo's splashy percussion: good therapy for D'Andrea, perhaps, but tedious to listen to. *Flavours* is a recording by the quintet that D'Andrea led for several years, with Tracanna, Zanchi and Cazzola, embellished by contributions from Ferris and Naco. The music is pitched somewhere between D'Andrea's personalized hard bop and a touch of Afro-jazz on five long tunes and one coda. Some of the pieces trail rather aimlessly on, but the pianist plays an authoritative role in pulling them round with an incisive solo or fragment of arrangement. Well worth hearing.

The previous brush with electronics on *Enrosadira* was so discouraging that one views *Current Changes* with alarm – D'Andrea returns to the Clavinova keyboard synthesizer for this trio outing. But Boato's refreshingly bright playing and Naco's gently propulsive percussion set up an amiable atmosphere and D'Andrea uses the keyboard with restraint. Not without appeal. His first solo set for some time, *Live In Perugia*, is better, though: two themes common to both discs sound firmer and more characterful on the acoustic piano. Rhythmically, D'Andrea isn't always the most ingenious of players, and some of these pieces have to rely on harmonic substance to sustain what can be rather stolid performances. But his reduction of a Mahler *adagietto* is charming.

****** Chromatic Phrygian**

YVP 3057 *D'Andrea; Stephan Schertler (b); Billy Elgart (d).* 10/89.

A belated release, but what a great one! The trio format always seems to bring out the best in this fundamentally reluctant player who would rather defer to his *politesse* in a solo situation. Schertler and Elgart are having none of that. Elgart's way of swinging the music is a marvel: he fills up every space without getting in anybody's way and has all kinds of business to offer without seeming to overplay. It's a pity, in a way, that the programme is mostly originals from either D'Andrea or Schertler (and there is one item which is seemingly improvised by all three men), since they do so well with the opening take on 'This Can't Be Love', full of shadows and sudden lights, that one wishes that the programme was all made up of familiar standards, to be suddenly invigorated. But this is still a quite splendid record.

***** 3 Lines**

Philology 77-2 *D'Andrea (p solo).* 3/96.

****(*) Jobim**

Philology 125-2 *D'Andrea; Andrea Ayace Ayassot (as); Aldo Mella (b); Alex Rolle (d).* 1/97.

***** Ballads And Rituals**

Philology 127-2 *As above.* 5/97.

3 Lines is an exercise in overdubbing meant to evoke the Bill Evans of *Conversations With Myself*. It feels like an album out of its time: Evans made his enlightened experiment in a pre-digital age, and D'Andrea's constructions say little that he might not have said with a single piano track. That said, the best tracks have a judicious and sometimes clever deployment of resources that makes, say, 'Tango In Three Colours' rather fetching. The homage, if such it is, to Jobim is fair enough, but the butterfly delicacy of the composer's best melodies is rather taken to the cleaners by this group and D'Andrea seems to be presiding over an ill-conceived event.

The same group reconvenes for *Ballads And Rituals*. Mella and Rolle get into all sorts of interesting rhythms from the start, with the clumping stomp of 'Dancing Colors' suggesting a kind of dub-like atmosphere. Ayassot is a difficult player to warm to, sounding at times as if he'd rather be heading into the eye of some freely formed hurricane, and his tart playing is a sometimes grating contrast to D'Andrea's romantic bent – something he can't entirely leave behind, no matter how far afield he looks. But the pianist gets in some fine moments when nobody seems to be looking, as in the lovely piano intro to 'Shifting Melody'. We are happy to find him alive and well!

Putney Dandridge (1902–46)

PIANO, VOCALS

A vaudeville singer and pianist, Dandridge led a string of sessions over two years which included some fine players behind him; a brief but interesting career on record.

**(*) Putney Dandridge 1935–1936

Classics 846 *Dandridge; Henry 'Red' Allen, Richard Clarke, Shirley Clay (t); Buster Bailey (cl, as); Tom Mace, Gene Sedric (cl, ts); Chu Berry, Kenneth Hollon, Johnny Russell (ts); Harry Grey, Teddy Wilson (p); Arnold Adams, Dave Barbour, Clarence Holiday, Nappy Lamare (g); Artie Bernstein, Ernest Hill, John Kirby, Grachan Moncur (b); Bill Beason, Cozy Cole, Walter Johnson, Manzie Johnson (d).* 3/35–3/36.

*** Putney Dandridge 1936

Classics 869 *Dandridge; Henry 'Red' Allen, Doc Cheatham, Wallace Jones, Bobby Stark (t); Tom Mace (cl); Joe Marsala (cl, as); Charles Frazier, Teddy McRae (ts); Clyde Hart, Ram Ramirez, James Sherman, Teddy Wilson (p); Arnold Adams, Eddie Condon, Allan Reuss, John Trueheart (g); Ernest Bass Hill, John Kirby, Wilson Myers, Mack Walker (b); Big Sid Catlett, Cozy Cole, Slick Jones (d).* 6–12/36.

Fame is notoriously fickle, but she seems to have treated Putney Dandridge with more than her typical disdain. There can be few recording careers so abruptly foreshortened. Dandridge cut his first sides for Vocalion in March 1935 and stopped recording for good with the last of these sessions, taped with Doc Cheatham, Teddy Wilson and Sid Catlett on 10 December 1936. Not quite a mainstream jazz singer, he should have been able to dicker a natural vaudevillean's facility with a lyric into a sustainable career. There was certainly no shortage of able players on the few records he did make. His piano playing would never have set the room on fire, and for all but the first two tracks on the earlier volume he was able to rely on Teddy Wilson's calm professionalism. The earliest track is 'You're A Heavenly Thing', which is enlivened by a chorus or two on celeste; nothing is known about the other musicians involved but theories abound as to who they might be. Three months later, an impeccably pedigreed group backed him on a totally hokey 'Nagasaki' (complete with pre-war stage Japanese), 'Chasing Shadows' (a lovely break from Berry) and 'When I Grow Too Old To Dream'. After that, or maybe after 'I'm In The Mood For Love' with Red Allen (a.k.a. 'Gabriel') and Buster Bailey, all but the most resilient fans will have drifted off.

The 1936 sessions drift ever further into novelty singing. 'Mary Had A Little Lamb' and 'Here Comes Your Pappy (With The Wrong Kind Of Load)' are a waste of Allen, Marsala and Cole, though the drummer gets off an excellent break on 'If We Never Meet Again'. A month earlier, Dandridge had defied all reasonable expectation with back-to-back readings of 'These Foolish Things' and 'Cross Patch' which touch something deeper. The smooth arrangements are marred by some ropy solo work. Allen and Doc Cheatham are, needless to say, consistently good, but Bobby Stark surely wasn't up to a professional date in this company. The curtain falls with 'Gee! But You're Swell' in December 1936.

Peter Danemo

DRUMS

Swedish drummer working in the post-bop mainstream.

*** Baraban

Dragon DRCD 206 *Danemo; Inge Petersson (ts); Esbjorn Svensson (ky); Klavs Hovman (b).* 5/91.

A session very much in the house style of the company: drifting, modal jazz with a hard centre, expertly recorded. Danemo wrote most of the 11 themes here and, while they start with simple materials, the quartet transmute them into frequently intense explorations of a motif or a mood. The opening 'Below The Surface', for instance, is built into an impressively intense ensemble piece. Solos tend to emerge as part of the overall fabric: Petersson, another in the line of fine Swedish tenors, plays a co-operative rather than a front-line role, and Svensson, who contributes two charming compositions, is a thoughtful source of support.

Eddie Daniels (born 1941)

CLARINET, TENOR SAXOPHONE, ALTO FLUTE

Daniels studied at Brooklyn College, joined the Thad Jones–Mel Lewis Orchestra, staying for six years, then freelanced and led his own record dates as a leader. He is a rare example of a post-bop musician specializing on clarinet.

**(*) First Prize!

Original Jazz Classics OJC 771 *Daniels; Roland Hanna (p); Richard Davis (b); Mel Lewis (d).* 9/66.

Daniels was allegedly once told by Tony Scott to stick to the tenor saxophone, advice he subsequently ignored, as his many clarinet records bear witness to. Even on tenor, though, he wasn't terribly exciting. Five tracks on sax, three on clarinet, and the scarcity of the original album suggests that Daniels wouldn't have been all that missed on either instrument in the long run. Competent but uninvolving playing.

**(*) Beautiful Love

Shanachie 5029 *Daniels; Ron Odrich (bcl); Lawrence Feldman (af); Bob James (p); Chuck Loeb (g); David Finck, Tim LeFebvre (b); Wolfgang Haffner (d); David Charles (perc).* 10/96.

Daniels's move from GRP has depleted his catalogue. This recent entry from Shanachie suggests no dramatic new departures. The arrangements of Bach, Satie and Rachmaninov are about as innovative as one would expect, and the presence of mood-jazz supremo James underlines the conception. Very pretty, and about as substantial as marshmallow.

Lars Danielsson (born 1958)

BASS, KEYBOARDS

He came to prominence as a sideman on the Swedish scene in the early 1980s and worked with many American players before leading small groups of his own.

***(*) New Hands

Dragon DRCD 125 *Danielsson; David Liebman (ss); Bobo Stenson (p); Goran Klinghagen (g, ky); Jon Christensen (d).* 12/85.

**** Poems

Dragon DRCD 209 *As above, except omit Klinghagen.* 4/91.

This is a very fine group, and *New Hands* is certainly the equal of any of Liebman's records with Quest. The bassist's six compositions range from a mysterious electronic lament on 'Chrass' to the memorable ballads of 'It's Your Choice' and 'Johan', the former featuring a bass solo of astonishing virtuosity. Stenson and Christensen live up to their reputation as two of the most outstanding Europeans on their respective instruments, and Liebman's work is typically broad in its sympathies, from gnarled volleys of notes to long-breathed lines of high lyrical beauty.

Poems, recorded after a brief 'reunion' tour by the band, is a degree finer even than *New Hands*. Liebman contributes the funky, brittle 'Little Peanut' and two other tunes, while the bassist turns in some of his best writing for the haunting 'Crystalline' and 'Suite'; but it's the interaction of four master-musicians which engenders the magic here: there really are no joins to be seen and, with Christensen at his most robustly inventive, the rhythmic layers are as songful as those created by Liebman and Stenson. Richly recorded and highly recommended.

***(*) Fresh Enough

L + R CDLR 45051 *Danielsson; David Liebman (ss); Bill Evans (ts); Niels Lan Doky (p); John Scofield, Ulf Wakenius (g); Jack DeJohnette (d).* 1/91.

The first two tracks on album three suggest that Danielsson has traded his elusiveness for Big Apple muscle, a power trio with Scofield and DeJohnette and another slugfest with Evans and Doky joining in too. But after those knockabouts comes a typically serene ballad called 'Far North', and Liebman and Wakenius displace the uptown brawn of the other music. Liebman turns 'Autumn Leaves' into one of the challenging revisions that he has become a master of when it comes to standards, and there are two other thoughtful originals apiece by Danielsson and Doky. More top-flight playing that wears its virtuosity lightly.

*** European Voices

Dragon DRCD 268 2CD *Danielsson; Niels-Petter Molvaer (t); Nils Lindgren (tb); Sven Fridolfsson (as); Joakim Milder (saxes); Michael Riessler (cl, bcl, sno); Lars Jansson (p); Tobias Sjogren, Eivind Aarset (g); Marilyn Mazur (d).* 12/93.

*** ... Continuation

L + R CDLR 45085 *Danielsson; John Abercrombie (g); Adam (d).* 1/94.

European Voices is two discs of various groupings, improvisations and compositions, boiled down from seven hours of material. Perhaps surprisingly, the range of moods is actually more limited than on some of Danielsson's other discs – the tone stretches from pastel calm to craggy, restless discord, but rhythmically it's rather flat and unmoving. There are some beautiful passages, such as the carefully wrought 'Eden' or the vigorous 'Falling Down'; but overall this feels like a project that's of more importance to its maker than to his audience. A couple of the same tunes turn up on ... *Continuation*, but this is a lighter, brisker date, centred round the interplay among the three men and inevitably rather dominated by Abercrombie and his vocabulary of guitar sounds. Danielsson's own playing here is as good as he's ever given, though one misses some of the freshness of the first records.

*** Live At Visiones

Dragon DRCD 309 *Danielsson; David Liebman (ss); Bobo Stenson (p); Jon Christensen (d).* 3/96.

The quartet's live album is a pleasing souvenir of one gig, though it doesn't stand the closest comparison with their studio efforts. Five tunes from their book get an expanded treatment, not always to advantage: the ramblings which open and close 'Folk Song', for instance, detract from the gripping middle section. But this is such a talented group that there are many felicities to enjoy, with Liebman very fine on 'Little Peanut' and Stenson affirming his mastery in virtually every phrase.

Palle Danielsson (born 1946)

DOUBLE BASS

One of Europe's most eminent modern bassists, Danielsson came to prominence via his sideman recordings for ECM in the 1970s and has accrued a considerable reputation since.

*** Contra Post

Caprice CAP 21440 *Danielsson; Joakim Milder (ts, ss); Rita Marcotulli (p); Goran Klinghagen (g); Anders Kjellberg (d).* 94.

Danielsson has an enormous CV and a huge range of session credits, including some of the finest Jan Garbarek recordings of earlier years. This, though, is his first record as leader. Some of the material – including an unaccompanied solo – is recorded at home near Stockholm, but the rest was taped at the renowned Rainbow Studio in Oslo, where Jan-Erik Kongshaug has established an unbeatable technical standard. Not all the material lives up to that standard. Rita Marcotulli's minimalist '7 Notes, 7 Days, 7 Planets' has an attractively mysterious quality, and Milder is similar enough in basic tonality to Garbarek to reinforce the 'ECM feel' on some tracks. The best of the material, though, recording-quality notwithstanding, is home-produced, notably a fine duo, 'Monk's Mood', with Klinghagen.

Harold Danko (born 1947)

PIANO

One of Danko's most successful playing associations has been with Lee Konitz, and he shares the saxophonist's idiosyncratic mix of cool and intense emotion. There is an almost classical correctness to his pianism, which borrows somewhat from Ellington.

***** Mirth Song**

Sunnyside SSC 1001 *Danko; Rufus Reid (b).* 4/82.

These days he bears an uncanny physical resemblance to American composer Morton Feldman, and there is a touch of Morty's unexpected mixture of dense abstraction and low-down swing in Danko's playing. It comes across immediately in this intimate, thoughtful duo with Reid, a record that kicked off the Sunnyside imprint. Opening with 'In Walked Bud' was obviously intended as some kind of statement of intent. The rate of delivery hardly falters thereafter, but without for a moment sacrificing intelligence to speed or to the self-conscious noodling that sometimes arises in settings like this. There is a sterling version of Jackie McLean's 'Omega', also Bird's rarely covered 'Red Cross' and Wayne Shorter's 'Penelope', a piece whose phrasing and offbeat harmonic structure appeal strongly to the pianist's sensibility. Sits surprisingly well for the piano, too.

***** Alone But Not Forgotten**

Sunnyside SSC 1033 *Danko; Marc Johnson, Michael Moore (b); Joe LaBarbera (d); Bob Dorough (v); strings arranged by John LaBarbera.* 11/85–5/86.

This is a softly romantic session with a good deal more musical substance than might be expected, given the lush string settings. Danko's interest in Brazilian music – Jobim, the percussionist Edison Machado and singer Ellis Regina – is reflected in the title-piece and in Edu Lobo's 'O Circo Mistico', his European roots in the lovely ballad, 'Marina'. His admiration for Bill Evans is reflected in almost every note, but more specifically in a vocal version of 'Laurie', while the opening 'Wayne Shorter' confirms the connection. The string arrangements – by the drummer's brother – are a model of their kind and should be studied by all producers who want to orchestrate ballad albums.

***** The First Love Song**

Jazz City 660 53 011 *Danko; Tom Harrell (t, flhn); Rufus Reid (b); Mel Lewis (d).*

This should have been better than it is. Harrell is one of the best harmonic improvisers in the music today, and the under-appreciated Mel Lewis has the ability to build a rhythmic scaffolding that could support anything from a cohort to a legion. Here, Harrell sounds rather flat and uninflected and Lewis lets things drift unconscionably, almost undisciplined in places. The in-escapable truth is that this is a solo session with bit-parts for the others. Danko wanders off on his own, paying very little mind to what the group does. One suspects there was little time to prepare for the date, and once or twice he has to scurry to cover up for what sound like uneasy transitions. Not the best.

***** Next Age**

Steeplechase SCCD 31350 *Danko; Rich Perry (ts); Scott Colley (b); Jeff Hirshfield (d).* 10/93.

A first recorded glimpse of what was to become a fairly regular line-up. The move to Steeplechase has been nothing but positive for Danko. Producer Nils Winther has an intuitive feel for piano players and he gives Harold a well-rounded, spacious sound that enhances his increasingly positive and resonant playing. A pity in some ways that this wasn't a trio set, but the circumstances of the recording were that it was a return fixture for a group who had recorded under saxophonist Perry's leadership some weeks before. 'Next Age' is optimistically dedicated to Bill Clinton, and the saxophone part is wet and undefined enough to have been performed by the Pres himself. Perry, to be fair, is a fine player, soft and yielding as the original President, but less thoughtful. He sounds perfectly in keeping on 'For Bud', but he seems (to our ears) less appropriate on the more adventurous contrafacts like 'Gregarious Solitude' and 'Silk Lady'. There is another tribute to Edison Machado in 'Subindo' – rising, ascending – which is paired with another, originally 'straight' concert-piece called 'Luz Caverna'. Characteristically intelligent, and straightly beguiling.

****** After The Rain**

Steeplechase SCCD 31356 *Danko (p solo).* 8/94.

The obvious point of comparison here is another record of Coltrane tributes by Tommy Flanagan (who did actually play with the great man, and on one of his most significant dates). Where Flanagan treats the date as an occasion for fulsomely abstract meditations on the basic material, Danko approaches them both more modestly and more radically. He tackles no fewer than 14 Coltrane compositions, ranging from 'After The Rain' (the most obviously pianistic), 'Lonnie's Lament' and 'Syeeda's Song Flute', but moving on to less obvious material like 'Dahomey Dance', 'Mr Day' and 'Straight Street'. What is remarkable is that Danko makes these tunes sound ideally suited to the piano, and also utterly his own. Though clearly intended as a homage, there is no obstacle to wholesale reinvention, and Danko recasts songs like 'Mr Sims', a deep blues, and 'Wise One', a brooding meditation on the tradition, with a free hand. The sound is entirely suited to the material, open and spacious without being cavernous, exact without the close-miked over-definition that some labels favour for sets of this kind.

***** New Autumn**

Steeplechase SCCD 31377 *Danko; Rich Perry (ts); Scott Colley (b); Jeff Hirshfield (d).* 4/95.

****** Tidal Breeze**

Steeplechase SCCD 31411 *As above.* 4/95, 10/96.

*****(*) The Feeling Of Jazz**

Steeplechase SCCD 31392 *As above.* 3/96.

They stride towards the camera on the cover of *Tidal Breeze* like the cast of some benign adaptation of *Reservoir Dogs*: Mr Blues, Mr Blues, Mr Blues and Mr White. Perry's bleached and colourless tone works only episodically, and it isn't always clear why Danko considers him such an important component of this group. He sounds best on the Ellington and Strayhorn tribute, *The Feeling Of Jazz*, though this is the record on which Danko cedes more of the foreground to his colleagues, aiming for a more rounded group sound.

The originals on *New Autumn* and *Tidal Breeze*, both of them all-Danko sets, are more and more idiosyncratic. Just one track from April 1995 turns up on the later record, but it ('Personal Cornucopia') is so good that one can't quite understand why it wasn't included in the original set. Danko writes with a dark and sometimes impenetrable authority. On the most recent album he reprises 'Wayne Shorter' and follows it with 'McCoy's Passion', two numbers which underscore two of the most obvious (make that the least and then the most obvious) influences on his playing and writing style. 'Pastoral Landing' on the same record is a fascinatingly extended workout, and one minor quibble regarding this body of work as a whole is that Danko seldom takes the option to stretch out and really develop ideas.

That is what he allows himself to do on the Ellington album, just seven numbers which (to be strictly accurate) consist of compositions of Ellington, Strayhorn and one ('Big Nick') by John Coltrane. These are the same tunes and in the same sequence as on Duke's 1962 encounter with the saxophonist for Impulse!. It may be that Danko has exhausted this particular line and may have to revert on future discs to solo or trio formats. For the moment, though, this is the combination which seems to engage his talents most fully. Strong statements, immaculately performed.

*****(*) This Isn't Maybe**
Steeplechase SCCD 31471 *Danko (p solo).* 7/98.

It's typical of Danko that he should have conceived this tribute to Chet Baker without the inclusion of 'My Funny Valentine'. There isn't an obvious or conventional gesture on the whole album, which breathes with the trumpeter's spirit, but in dialogue with an admirer who clearly learnt much from it. Most of the tracks are quite short and melodic and, apart from 'These Foolish Things' and 'The Touch Of Your Lips', aren't obvious choices. Jimmy Heath's 'D's Dilemma', two Dameron tunes and Phil Urso's 'Way To Go' give an idea of how carefully Harold has thought out his approach to Chet, his influences, associations and legacy.

Jacqui Dankworth

VOCALS

Vocalist from the famous Dankworth family, here in a contemporary small-group setting.

***** First Cry**
EFZ 1010 *Dankworth; Anthony Kerr (vib); Stan Sulzmann (f); Paul Clarvis (d); Bosco De Oliveira (perc).* 93–94.

No disrespect to Ms Dankworth, but this is notable mainly for some elegantly lyrical vibes from Kerr, who in a few short years has turned into an able, sympathetic accompanist for singers, and a soloist of some substance. Dankworth herself has a full but somehow not very resonant voice, which may have something to do with the studio and desk on this record, because her live performances sound very different. Kerr contributes most of the musical material, Dankworth the words, a successful chemistry that yields nicely balanced and unforced songs which might have been around for years, always a promising sign. Sulzmann's flute is always a welcome guest, but what the record actually needs is a touch of one of his saxophones; it's a little too light and delicate.

Alec and John Dankworth Generation Band

GROUP

An occasional project featuring the father-and-son team which is a central dynasty in British modern jazz.

***** Nebuchadnezzar**
Jazz House JHCD 029 *Guy Barker, Gerard Presencer, John Barclay (t, flhn); Mark Nightingale (tb); Keith Riby (frhn); John Dankworth (ss, as, Cmel, f); Andy Panayi (as, f); Tim Garland (ss, ts, f); Jimmy Hastings (bs, cl, f); Robin Aspland (p); John Parricelli (g); Christian Garrick (vn); Dave Powell (tba); Alec Dankworth (b); Ralph Salmins (d).* 10/93.

***** Rhythm Changes**
Jazz House JHCD 043 *As above, except add Noel Langley (t, flhn), Dave Laurence (frhn), Stuart Hall (vn, g); omit Barclay, Riby, Garrick.* 7/95.

The family firm in fine fettle. John Dankworth's representation on CD is disappointingly thin at present, considering his stature in post-war British jazz, but at least these two absorbing discs of big-band music – where he shares leadership duties with son Alec – are readily available. *Nebuchadnezzar*, recorded in a single day at the Ronnie Scott Club (though not in front of an audience), packs a dozen scores by various hands into its duration. The results are somewhat mixed, but the successes – Alec's take on 'Ida Lupino', Andy Panayi's treatment of 'Black Narcissus' and John's waltz-time blues, 'Nebuchadnezzar' – are performed with great panache and attention to dynamics: the band is often at its best when playing on the softest tones. *Rhythm Changes* was cut during a 'proper' set at the club (and a fine sound engineer Chris Lewis secured, too), and is inevitably more shouting – but better played all round. 'I Got Rheumatics' is a flag-waver in which the obvious prototype gets a glittering respray; 'Around The Track' is another refined show of dynamics; and throughout, as with the earlier disc, one is struck by the band's notably adept use of the sonorities of the brass section, with the tuba parts a crucial note of individuality. The soloists are a stellar lot in British terms, but the band's the thing.

Stefano D'Anna (born 1959)

TENOR SAXOPHONE

Contemporary Italian saxophonist in a 'classic' post-bop idiom.

****** Leapin' In**
Splasc(h) H 374-2 *D'Anna; Enzo Pietropaoli (b); Fabrizio Sferra (d).* 12/91.

D'Anna says that he admires the 'sculpture-like clarity' of Sonny Rollins's improvising, and his own playing strives to secure the same lucidity. If he is in Rollins's debt, though, he also goes to exceptional lengths to evade modern saxophone cliché. Rhythmically he eschews easy double-time passages or tonal distortions: there's an evenness to his line which gives his solos an irresistible flow, and a steely clarity to his tone that doesn't detract from his lyricism. His seven compositions here all differ from one another, and three standards are scrupulously remodelled: 'I've Grown Accustomed To Her Face' is strikingly different from the classic Rollins reading, 'Be-Bop' is fantastically fast and biting, and 'Body And Soul', done as a duo for tenor and uncredited soprano, refers to the melody hardly at all and reminds us of a Konitz–Marsh collaboration. A stunning recital all round. A new set (at last!) from D'Anna was due as we went to press.

Giovanni D'Argenzio

SOPRANO AND TENOR SAXOPHONES

Milan-based post-bop saxophonist.

**(*) Domestic Standards

Splasc(h) H 358-2 *D'Argenzio; Aldo Farias (g); Angelo Farias (b); Umberto Guarino (d).* 2–4/91.

A pleasing set of Italian pop tunes (with Lehár's 'You Are My Heart's Delight' apparently also qualifying), prettily played by this quartet of jazzmen from Campania. On a few occasions the rhythm section settle for a rock beat, which doesn't turn out so well, but D'Argenzio's tenor strikes a few impassioned sparks out of the unlikely material, and his soprano has a wiry elegance. Lightweight, but not without charm.

David Darling (born 1941)

CELLO, PERCUSSION

Classically trained cello improviser, coming at it from an 'impressionistic' side.

**(*) Journal October

ECM 827410-2 *Darling (clo solo).* 10/79.

** Cycles

ECM 843172-2 *Darling; Jan Garbarek (ts, ss); Steve Kuhn (p); Oscar Castro-Nueves (g); Arild Andersen (b); Collin Walcott (perc, sitar, tabla).* 11/81.

*** Darkwood

ECM 523750-2 *Darling (clo solo).* 85.

***(*) Cello

ECM 511982-2 *Darling (clo solo).* 11/91–1/92.

At first blush, there isn't much more to David Darling's music than rather haphazard scratchings that border on self-absorption if not self-abuse. Repeated hearings confirm that, far from abusing his enormous technical talent, Darling is striving for a music commensurate with it.There is, of course, already a substantial body of jazz cello: Oscar Pettiford, Ron Carter, Dollar Brand, Dave Holland, Tristan Honsinger. Perhaps inevitably, Darling's basic conception, particularly when he uses his 8-string, solid-bodied, amplified instrument, is closest to that of ECM stablemate Eberhard Weber, who has considerably extended the timbral and tonal range of amplified bass playing. Darling's music is less dynamic and more textural; it is certainly more 'classical' in structure and may prove a little too evanescent for tastes conditioned by jazz rhythms and structures.

Though *Cycles* is probably the closest thing one could find to an identikit ECM record – shapelessly impressionistic themes and poster-print ethnic soundscapes, redeemed only by Jan Garbarek's unmistakable voice – *Cello* really is very good indeed, a more shapely and coherent album than *Darkwood*, which always seems to be striving for effect. *Cello* is the record one would like to have heard first, suggesting a learning curve that wasn't in evidence on the earlier records. Where *Journal October* sounded like eavesdropped musical jottings, the most recent has an almost cinematic precision of focus. Interestingly, ECM producer and film-maker Manfred Eicher is listed as co-composer on a couple of tracks, one of them a dedication to movie director, Jean-Luc Godard. Darling doesn't seem to record very often, but his most recent ECM entry is to be found under Ketil Bjørnstad's listing.

Carlo Actis Dato

REEDS

Co-founder of the pioneer Italian post-bop band, Art Studio, Dato has been active since the early '70s and is involved with several groups, of which his Quartet is the principal focus.

***(*) Ankara Twist

Splasc(h) H 302 *Dato; Piero Ponzo (cl, bcl, as, bs, f); Enrico Fazio (b); Fiorenzo Sordini (d).* 10/89.

Though Dato plays some tenor, he is most at home on baritone and bass clarinet, and he's a volatile and unpredictable player with a compensating brilliance of timing: just when one thinks he's gone too far in a solo, he pulls it around and returns to the structure. As a composer, he writes themes that suggest some bridging-point between jazz and Balkan folk music, and the bucolic air of, say, 'Moonlight In Budapest' on *Oltremare* (currently still on LP only and in need of CD transfer) is counterpointed by the very next tune on the record, 'Portorico Smog'. The tracks on this quartet album are rather brief and have a programmatic feel to them, but they're played with great verve and enthusiasm by the group: Ponzo is a useful foil to the leader, Fazio is authoritative, Sordini full of bustle.

***(*) Dune

Splasc(h) H 354-2 *Dato; Laura Culver (ss, clo, berim); Alex Rolle (xy, perc); Massimo Barbiero (d, mar).* 2/91.

Rolle and Barbiero join in the fun and the quartet take some aspects of 'world music' to the cleaners: march and tango rhythms are mischievously undercut by Carlo's tendency to jump into bawling improvisations – he lets off another almost brutal baritone assault on 'Ketchup' – and by Laura's deadpan drones and vamps on the cello. The two percussionists are pressed into subsidiary roles, leavening the sometimes sparse arrangements, and sometimes the action seems a little too contrived on a very long (74 minutes) CD: 'Mar Del Plata' is delivered rather stiffly. But the crackerjack liveliness of the best playing is a delight.

***** Tree**

Penta Flowers CDPEL 0139 *Dato; Laura Culver (ss, clo); Alex Rolle (d).* 6/93.

Another hour of tangos, blues, jazz and so forth from Dato and his gang. This time, though, it's delivered not quite so irrepressibly. The solo spots tend to expose Culver's limitations as an improviser, Rolle offers minimalist percussion, and even Dato himself sounds contained. The best music still has flair and invention, but fans of the earlier discs may be a little disappointed.

***** Urartu**

Leo 220 *Dato (bs, bcl, ts solo).* 3/94.

Dato's first solo set is a typically mercurial and imaginative effort. He caricatures his reeds and loves to make excessive, elaborate noise with them, using circular breathing, slap-tonguing and whatever else he can think of and, though he plays a couple of standards, they come out rather cold. Most of the pieces seem like lightning sketches and, once he's finished with the idea, it's done. Maybe not an important Dato record but another very enjoyable one.

*****(*) Blue Cairo**

Splasc(h) 454-2 *Dato; Piero Ponzo (as, cl, bcl); Enrico Fazio (b); Fiorenzo Sordini (d).* 7/95.

Back with his original quartet, Dato picks up where he left off and draws out a personal synthesis of musics which are looking eastwards again – this time to Katmandu (where an element of 'A Night In Nepal' was recorded), Egypt, and maybe some points unspecified which the market-place overtones and snake-charmer solos on offer in many of the tracks seem to celebrate. This is funny, sentimental music that can suddenly shock you with a heartbreaking melody or a burst of anger; for all its globalism it's quite one-dimensionally simple in feel, dependent often on a tune curling up like smoke from the horns, but it's vibrantly alive. Ponzo, Fazio and Sordini know the moves and have them covered.

*****(*) Pasodoble**

Splasc(h) 642 *Dato; Enzo Rocco (g).* 6/97.

May they have this dance? Dato shows off some jazz roots here – he might make you think of classic hard-bop tenor on the likes of 'Ordinary Bus' – and Rocco can be Jim Hall or Billy Bauer when he wants to be. Yet they both throw in dissonance, timbral contrasts, odd mixed matches of style and tempo – it's a typically extravagant Dato date, even if there's only two of them playing the music. And with 19 tracks dispatched inside the hour, boredom thresholds are never once flirted with.

***** Son Para El Che**

Splasc(h) 675 *Dato; Massimo Rossi (ss, as); Antonio Fontana (g); Frederico Marchesano (b); Dario Bruna (d).* 10/97.

A new band for Dato, but the agenda's a familiar one for him: if this is a dedication to Che Guevara, it goes to the Argentine via the most convoluted of routes. Fontana is probably the key man and frankly he often overdoes it, taking his effects pedals to the cleaners on the final 'Last Blow' and generally trying to push his way to the front. The genre-hopping, for once in Dato's music, at times seems exaggerated beyond its effectiveness. But some of the leader's own solos break through and grip.

****** Delhi Mambo**

yvp 3065 *Dato; Piero Ponzo (as, ncl, cl, picc); Enrico Fazio (b); Fiorenzo Sordini (d).* 2/98.

On holiday from Splasc(h) for a moment, Dato calls back the quartet and they dash off their best record. 'Et Voilà' introduces the band one at a time, before their footsteps are heard beating a hasty retreat. But they come back for another hour or so of music. As ever, the tunes are full of Eastern promise, but the travelogue elements have fused into the collective spirit of the band so solidly that there's no sense of distances flippantly travelled. They're at home wherever they are, and whatever they're playing, be it bossa, bop or something they heard at the local café. A great one.

Wolfgang Dauner (born 1935)

PIANO, KEYBOARDS

Born in Stuttgart, Dauner was taught piano by his aunt and began as a professional in 1957. Worked in the '60s with Eberhard Weber and Fred Braceful and committed various avant-garde outrages on unsuspecting audiences. Became more involved in teaching and formal composition, then founded the United Jazz & Rock Ensemble in 1975. His Mood label has been the principal focus for his recording activity in recent years.

*****(*) Get Up And Dauner**

MPS 533548-2 *Dauner; Robert Demmer, Friedrich Hujer, Conny Jackel, Herbert Joos, Ernst Lamprecht, Robert Politzer, Kenny Wheeler (t, flhn); Roy Deuvall, Albert Mangelsdorff, Garney Hicks, Eric Kleinschuster (tb); Rudolf Josel (btb); Gerd Dudek (ts); Hans Koller (sno, ss, ts); Zbigniew Seifert (v, as); Jean-Luc Ponty (vn); Jasper Van't Hof (ky); Pierre Cavalli (g); Siegfried Schwab (g, sitar, v); Eberhard Weber (b, clo, v); Gotz Wendland, Jurgen Karg, Niels-Henning Orsted Pedersen, Adelhard Roidinger, John Lee, Gunter Lenz (b); Janusz Stefanski, Alphonse Mouzon, Fred Braceful, Daniel Humair, Roland Wittich (d); Kurt Bong, Mani Neumeier (perc).* 62–10/75.

This hugely entertaining anthology goes some way to filling a considerable gap, covering some of the many bases which Dauner touched on in his earlier years on record. Two early (1962) tracks show him an adept practitioner of the piano trio, though Bong's bongos hint at a wider rhythmic interest, and by the time of 'Disguise' (1967) Dauner is exploring a much broader palette, with Dudek and Ponty in challenging mode. There is some old hippie fun on 'Take Off Your Clothes And Feel The Setting Sun' and a ludicrous version of 'A Day In The Life', before the extraordinary 'Kunstkopfindianer', recorded under Koller's leadership but dominated by Dauner's playing. 'Tango Teclado' is an amusing update of the tango idiom to '70s jazz-rock, before the gargantuan blowout of 'Yin', where all the brassmen listed above spar with Dauner's keyboards and rhythm section at a 1975 Vienna concert. Drawn from a wide range of MPS albums, this is a valuable pathfinder for those interested in some often-forgotten areas of European jazz. Remastering is good, though unwary ears might be surprised at the idiosyncratic quality of some of the original mixes.

**** Changes**

Mood 33.613 *Dauner (ky solo).* 3–9/78.

****(*) Solo Piano**

Mood 33.600 *Dauner (p solo).* 82.

***** Two Is Company**

Mood 33.614 *Dauner; Albert Mangelsdorff (tb).* 12/82.

****(*) Meditation On A Landscape – Tagore**

Mood 33.622 *Dauner; Charlie Mariano (as, f); Ernst Stroer (perc). n.d.*

*****(*) One Night In '88**

Mood 33.623 *As above, except Dino Saluzzi (acc) replaces Stroer.* 4/88.

****** Pas De Trois**

Mood 33.630 *As above. n.d.*

****(*) Zeitlaufe**

Mood 007 *Dauner (ky solo).* 8/88.

Dauner's back-catalogue on Mood has been making its way on to CD, though it makes him seem much more hermetic than he was on the MPS albums. The 1978 solo album is not the happiest of places to start, the music sounding akin to the meanderings of the decade's art rock with synthesizer sounds that now seem antiquated. The multi-tracked pianos of *Solo Piano* are more interesting, although this too sounds academically inclined: much exercise, little development. His stentorian manner makes a nice foil for Mangelsdorff, though, on the live *Two Is Company*. Dauner ladles out bluff, staccato passages while the trombonist writhes on top, sometimes noodling to himself but always making an intriguing noise. Less-than-perfect live sound doesn't matter too much.

The three albums with Charlie Mariano suggest that Dauner has found a soulmate of a kind. *Meditation On A Landscape* is a bit solemn and slow, the music done for a film on the life of Rabindranath Tagore, and only when Stroer adds some livelier percussion does the sound get much beyond a drone. But the two albums with Saluzzi are superb stuff. *One Night In '88* has a loose, largely improvisatory feel, the music structured round four longish and free-flowing triologues; but the more firmly centred *Pas De Trois* is beautifully modulated and balanced among the three voices: Mariano's achingly lovely 'Randy' is the clearest highlight, but all this music is almost ecstatically rich and songful. Dauner is often no more than anchor, but his playing honours the situation, and Mariano returns to the alto for most of both discs, his most searching horn by far. A more recent survival is a third solo disc, *Zeitlaufe*, which consists of 12 miniatures, some for solo piano, some for mixed keyboards. Not much jazz comes out of it – 'Besinnung' sounds like a chunk of Rachmaninov – but it's not without charm.

Kenny Davern (born 1935)

CLARINET

Born on Long Island, Davern began playing in New York's traditional jazz circles in the 1950s. He was known as a sideman until the '70s, when his association with Soprano Summit, with Bob Wilber, brought him wider recognition. Has investigated the avant-garde, but he plays mostly in a swing-mainstream idiom, and these days sticks exclusively to clarinet.

*****(*) Stretchin' Out**

Jazzology JCD-187 *Davern; Dick Wellstood (p); Chuck Riggs (d).* 12/83.

*****(*) Never In A Million Years**

Challenge CHR 70019 *As above, except omit Riggs.* 1/84.

*****(*) Playing For Kicks**

Jazzology JCD-197 *Davern; Martin Litton (p); John Petters (d).* 11/85.

***** One Hour Tonight**

Musicmasters 5003-2 *Davern; Howard Alden (g); Phil Flanigan (b); Giampaolo Biagi (d).* 1/88.

***** I'll See You In My Dreams**

Musicmasters 5020-2 *As above.* 1/88.

***** My Inspiration**

Musicmasters 65077-2 *Davern; Howard Alden (g); Bob Haggart (b); Bobby Rosengarden (d); strings.* 9/91.

***** East Side, West Side**

Arbors ARCD 19137 *Davern; Dan Barrett (c, tb); Joel Helleny (tb); Bucky Pizzarelli (g); Bob Haggart (b); Tony DeNicola (d).* 6/94.

***** Kenny Davern & The Rhythm Men**

Arbors ARCD 19147 *As above, except omit Barrett and Helleny; add John Bunch (p).* 6/95.

****** Breezin' Along**

Arbors ARCD 19170 *Davern; Bucky Pizzarelli, Howard Alden (g); Greg Cohen (b); Tony DeNicola (d).* 6/96.

In his sixties, Kenny Davern has claims to being the major clarinettist in jazz, having now forsaken the soprano sax ('I play soprano once a year and it takes only a few moments to confirm that I made the right decision'). He had little in the catalogue under his own name until the 1980s, but recent years have seen him setting down several fine records. There's little waste in his execution, garrulous though his phrasing often is, and he succeeds in playing in what is essentially a swing-based clarinet style while suggesting that he's also perfectly aware of every jazz development that has taken place since (he once recorded with Steve Lacy, Steve Swallow and Paul Motian on *Unexpected*, Kharma PK-7, still not on CD).

Stretchin' Out is one of the best showcases for his own playing, starting with a mellifluous and perfectly paced 'The Man I Love' and proceeding through five more standards with unflagging inventiveness. Wellstood is a superb partner, harrying and supporting him in equal measure, but the drawback is the presence of Riggs, who's not only too loud in the mix but superfluous to what should have been a duo session. The recently issued *Never In A Million Years* finds Davern and Wellstood alone together at New York's Vineyard Theatre and, though the bare format is a little dry across CD length, there is some marvellous sparring between the two men. *Playing For Kicks* goes back to the trio and, while Litton isn't remotely up to Wellstood's standard, it's another great clarinet set, with the ancient ('Willie The Weeper') and the comparatively modern ('Lullaby Of The Leaves') on the agenda. Much the same happens on both *One Hour Tonight* and *I'll See You In My Dreams*, though with Alden on hand rather than a pianist the music has a lighter, more fluid feel to it, and the treatment of some of the older pieces – especially 'Riverboat Shuffle' – strikes up something of the chamber-jazz feel of a Venuti–Lang group. Again, Davern himself is irreproachable. *My Inspiration* features string arrangements by Bob Haggart, dreamily played, with Davern relishing his opportunity and submitting his most graceful and romantic horn; yet the production isn't quite right, Rosengarden's drums oddly miked, and the balance tips into schmaltz just fractionally enough to waylay some of the tunes. *East Side, West Side* and *Rhythm Men* are two recent Davern sessions for Arbors. Barrett is a valuable front-line partner, playing cornet for the most part, though he picks up his slide for a very ripe duet with Helleny on 'Sidewalks Of New York'. Davern seems in good spirits on both sessions, and the rhythm section fits like a comfortable shoe. In the end, though, both dates sound a little hindered by their lack of preparation – expert playing, fine solos, but nothing to lift them a notch above what is now a bulging bracket of mainstream records.

If that seems a bit harsh, we have stopped sitting on the fence and given an unqualified fourth star to *Breezin' Along*. The band is a peach: Pizzarelli and Alden are a great team, driving the fast numbers along and softly suggesting all the harmonic detail in the slower ones, while Cohen and DeNicola are strong without seeming obtrusive. Davern himself measures the material with an almost insouciant virtuosity: two Beiderbecke chestnuts, 'Since My Best Girl Turned Me Down' and 'Jazz Me Blues', are super, but we'd single out the gorgeous variations on 'Baby Won't You Please Come Home' as Davern at his peak.

*****(*) Spanish Eyes**

Chiaroscuro CD(D) 344 *Davern; Phil Woods (as); Flip Phillips (ts); Derek Smith (p); Howard Alden (g); Milt Hinton (b); Joe Ascione (d).* 11/95.

Whatever else was played at the 1995 Floating Jazz Festival, it can't have outswung or otherwise smoked this set. Davern seems to be at the top of his game from the off – his 'Elsa's Dream' solo is both far out and inside – and Flip, as ever, defies Father Time. The rhythm section are completely in the groove – Smith risks some things which a more stoic pianist wouldn't have thought about, and Alden is as ever a man for all seasons – and, to cap it all, Phil Woods strolls in for a final 'Lover Come Back To Me'. There are one or two vagaries in the sound, but nothing too serious.

***** Smiles**

Arbors ARCD 19207 *Davern; Howard Alden, Bucky Pizzarelli (g); Greg Cohen (b); Tony DeNicola(d).* 98.

In Ira Gitler's words, 'easy listening jazz from the Irish-Jewish soul of a story-telling reedsman'. This re-run of *Breezin' Along* isn't as consistently fine as its predecessor. The choice of tunes is less interesting, and Davern sounds a whit less involved. But this is still mainstream jazz of tremendous calibre, and Alden and Pizzarelli are again a marvellous team.

Anthony Davis (born 1951)

PIANO, KEYBOARDS, COMPOSER

Born in New Jersey, but associated with the new jazz in Chicago in the '70s, Davis was of a more scholarly bent than many and went on to teach regularly at Yale and to compose in operatic and classical forms. He has seemingly dropped out of sight in the last ten years.

***** Hidden Voices**

India Navigation IN 1041 *Davis; George Lewis (tb); James Newton (f); Rick Rozie (b); Pheeroan akLaff (d).*

****(*) Lady Of The Mirrors**

India Navigation IN 1047 *Davis (p solo).* 80.

Davis often seems like one of the most scholarly and introspective of the Chicagoans who emerged on to a wider scene in the 1970s and '80s. He has made some more recent albums for Gramavision which seem to drift in and out of circulation, but has recorded little in the '90s. Inclined to be slightly abstract and structure-bound in his solo performances (a legacy of his work with the new-music outfit, Episteme), Davis loosens up considerably in freer company. Newton's Dolphyish flute contrasts very sharply with Davis's mannerly runs and long, discursive progressions in and out of harmony. In the quintet with Lewis, the music has a slightly arch quality – perhaps born out of a relatively dry and unfamiliar instrumentation – but there is a spare intensity that emerges out of the criss-crossing lines.

Lady Of The Mirrors is a similarly ascetic and rhythmically quiescent solo album which hasn't worn all that well. Davis has done better work and he deserves the opportunity to let us hear what he's been doing of late.

Eddie 'Lockjaw' Davis (1922–86)

TENOR SAXOPHONE

Born in New York, Davis made his name with Cootie Williams, before joining Count Basie in 1952; he stayed, on and off, until 1960. Frequently paired with Shirley Scott or Johnny Griffin in the '60s, he spent seven further years with Basie before working as a solo through the late '70s and '80s; died unexpectedly in Las Vegas.

*****(*) Eddie 'Lockjaw' Davis 1946–1947**

Classics 1012 *Davis; Fats Navarro (t); Sadik Hakim, Al Haig, John Acea (p); Bill De Arabngo, John Collins, Huey Long (g); Gene Ramey (b); Denzil Best, Butch Ballard (d).* 5/46–4/47.

This is almost pre-history for the Davis most familiar to LP collectors. The most important tracks are the eight sides for Savoy, with Fats Navarro, by Eddie Davis And His Be Boppers. Davis straddles bop and swing in his phrasing; if anything, with his swallowed notes, sandpapery tone and sudden shrieks, he's already a genre unto himself. Navarro is not quite the budding genius he would shortly become, but he's budding nevertheless, and this is exciting music. The rest of the disc is made up of sessions for Haven, Apollo, Lenox and three tracks which later turned up on a Plymouth LP. Some of the material is obscure enough to have an unidentified personnel, and recording quality is, as with many indie labels of the '40s, often indifferent; but Davis barrels through all these dates with the boldness that would characterize his career. A very enjoyable set.

***(*) **The Cookbook Vol. 1**

Original Jazz Classics OJC 652 *Davis; Jerome Richardson (ts, f); Shirley Scott (org); George Duvivier (b); Arthur Edgehill (d).* 6/58.

*** **Jaws With Shirley Scott**

Original Jazz Classics OJC 218 *As above, except omit Richardson.* 9/58.

*** **Smokin'**

Original Jazz Classics OJC 705 *As above, except Richardson returns.* 9–12/58.

*** **The Cookbook Vol. 2**

Original Jazz Classics OJC 653 *As above.* 12/58.

*** **The Cookbook Vol. 3**

Original Jazz Classics OJC 756 *As above.* 12/58.

*** **Jaws In Orbit**

Original Jazz Classics 322 *As above, except add Steve Pulliam (tb); omit Richardson.* 5/59.

*** **Gentle Jaws**

Prestige PRCD-24160-2 *As above, except add Red Garland (p), Sam Jones (b), Arthur Taylor (d).* 60.

By the time he got to the LP era, Davis had become one of the most honest, no-nonsense soloists in the music. He hardly changed his methods from one date to another. Whatever else is going on around him, he gives it his best shot. His apprenticeship in New York big bands in the 1940s led him towards rhythm-and-blues rather than bebop, but it was as either a section soloist with Basie or a jazz combo leader that Jaws functioned best. His sound was, on reflection, a surprisingly complex matter. Unlike many of the players working in the organ-combo format, where Jaws made his biggest impact, his phrasing had an elongated quality that he broke up only with his matter-of-fact brusqueness: as if he was masking emotion with a temperament that told him to get on with it.

He spent the late 1950s leading the group which made the OJC reissues listed above. The records are formulaic – blustering solos over bluesy organ riffs – but endowed with a spirit that makes the discs highly enjoyable, taken one at a time. All three *Cookbook* albums are entertaining displays of good-natured fisticuffs, with the food theme followed through in all the titles ('The Chef', 'Skillet', 'In The Kitchen' and so on) and Jaws taking the roof off on 'Have Horn, Will Blow', which garners an extra notch for the first disc. Richardson's flute is a needless cooling-off device on most of the tracks, but these are fun records. *Gentle Jaws*, if that title doesn't sound like a contradiction, puts together a couple of small-hours sessions where the man huffs and hustles his way through a selection of top-notch ballads, sentiment without slop.

**** **Very Saxy**

Original Jazz Classics OJC 458 *Davis; Coleman Hawkins, Arnett Cobb, Buddy Tate (ts); Shirley Scott (org); George Duvivier (b); Arthur Edgehill (d).* 4/59.

Prestige called in three other tenormen on their books to sit in with the Davis–Scott combo, and the results were barnstorming. The programme is all simple blues, but the flat-out exuberance of the playing is so exhilarating that it would be churlish to give it anything less than top marks, particularly in the excellent remastered sound. As competitive as it might appear, nobody is bested, and the clout of Davis and Cobb is matched by the suaver Tate and the grandiloquent Hawkins. Their 'Lester Leaps In' is a peerless display of saxophone sound.

(*) **Afro-Jaws

Original Jazz Classics OJC 403 *Davis; Clark Terry, Ernie Royal, Phil Sunkel, John Bello (t); Lloyd Mayers (p); Larry Gales (b); Ben Riley (d); Ray Barretto (perc).*

***(*) **Trane Whistle**

Original Jazz Classics OJC 429 *Davis; Clark Terry, Richard Williams, Bob Bryant (t); Melba Liston, Jimmy Cleveland (tb); Jerome Richardson, Oliver Nelson, Eric Dolphy, George Barrow, Bob Ashton (reeds); Richard Wyands (p); Wendell Marshall (b); Roy Haynes (d).* 9/60.

*** **Streetlights**

Prestige PRCD 24150-2 *Davis; Don Patterson (org); George Duvivier (b); Paul Weedon, Billy James (d).* 11/62.

Afro-Jaws puts the saxophonist in front of brass and percussion to no very telling effect. But *Trane Whistle*, a set of Oliver Nelson arrangements for a cracking big band, puts him in his element and, though the charts are perhaps too functional to make the record a classic, the knock-out power of Davis's blowing is thrilling. An Ernie Wilkins arrangement of 'You Are Too Beautiful' shows off his skills with a ballad, too. *Streetlights* puts him back in the organ-combo setting with the slightly more 'modern' style of Patterson. Nobody puts himself out particularly, and the tunes are mostly obvious, but the playing is hard to fault.

**** **The Tenor Scene**

Original Jazz Classics OJC 940 *Davis; Johnny Griffin (ts); Junior Mance (p); Larry Gales (b); Ben Riley (d).* 1/61.

They were a famous team, and rightly so. The important thing was that neither man approached their collaboration as a mere blowing situation: Davis remembers that they rehearsed regularly and never let the set-list atrophy. This set from Minton's in 1961 has nothing fancy about it in terms of the tunes, but the playing has whipcrack impact, the rhythm section are right on top of it, and the light work made of a difficult tune such as 'Straight No Chaser' shows how masterful these tenormen were. A classic jazz record.

***(*) **Straight Blues**

Prestige 11014-2 *As OJC albums listed above, plus Harry Edison (t), Count Basie (p), John Heard (b), Jimmie Smith (d).* 12/58–5/76.

An enjoyable compilation of some of Jaws's bluesiest moments from his Prestige years, with the 'Untitled Blues' from a Harry Edison Pablo date tacked on for extra measure. Not a second wasted.

***(*) **Eddie 'Lockjaw' Davis With Michel Attenoux**
Storyville STCD 5009 *Davis; Patrick Artero (t); Claude Gousset (tb); Michel Attenoux (as); Gabriel Garvanoff (p); Jean-Pierre Mulot (b); Teddy Martin (d). 7/75.*

***(*) **Leapin' On Lenox**
Black & Blue 926.2 *Davis; Eddie Vinson (as); Milt Buckner (p); Bill Doggett (org); Jimmy Leary, Milt Hinton (b); Gus Johnson, J.C Heard (d). 7/74–7/78.*

(*) **Swingin' Till The Girls Come Home
Steeplechase SCCD 31058 *Davis; Thomas Clausen (p); Bo Stief (b); Alex Riel (d). 3/76.*

*** **Straight Ahead**
Original Jazz Classics OJC 629-2 *Davis; Tommy Flanagan (p); Keter Betts (b); Bobby Durham (d). 5/76.*

*** **Montreux '77**
Original Jazz Classics OJC 384 *Davis; Oscar Peterson (p); Ray Brown (b); Jimmie Smith (d). 7/77.*

Davis went the journeyman route of wandering freelance through the 1970s and '80s. The Black & Blue disc is a superior repackaging of two sessions, one with Buckner, and a second (though only three tracks long) with Vinson and Doggett. The first is more like straight-ahead, the second has something of a soul-jazz feel, with Vinson wailing in on 'Double Eddie', but they make a fine match and it's a pleasure to hear Buckner in particular get some individual space. The real stars of the Montreux concert recording are Peterson and Brown, whose hard clarity creates a formidable platform for the nominal leader; but Davis himself sounds somewhat below par, his solos overwrought, and the music is exciting only inconsistently.

The pick of the rest is certainly the Storyville session with a team of French mainstreamers. Impromptu as the session was – Davis simply harmonized his parts with Attenoux on the scores – it's played with enormous gusto by all seven men, the horns matching Jaws in their surly attack, and rollicking events like Neal Hefti's 'Midnite Blue' get a good thrashing. Yet there are three terrific ballad solos by the tenorman on 'Moonlight In Vermont', 'What's New?' and 'Lush Life'. Excellent sound. The Steeplechase set seems much more ordinary, and even the OJC disc with Flanagan rarely gets much above professional expertise.

*** **Eddie Lockjaw Davis**
Enja 3097 *Davis; Horace Parlan (p); Reggie Johnson (b); Oliver Queen (d). 2/81.*

*** **All Of Me**
Steeplechase SCCD 31181 *Davis; Kenny Drew (p); Jesper Lundgaard (b); Svend-Erik Norregaard (d). 8/83.*

Davis was still a commanding player up until his unexpected death in 1986. His recording regimen was a casual one, and his later discs have a pot-luck quality, but the leader himself secures an unusual level of commitment: all his records manage to be recommendable for his own tenor playing. The Enja date matches him with a fine trio and is excellently recorded; the Steeplechase date is similarly acomplished and genial. He was always good value.

Jesse Davis (born 1965)

ALTO SAXOPHONE

A New Orleans man, Davis studied with Ellis Marsalis and then in New Jersey and New York. Basically a hard-bop player, with traces of what came before and after sifted in.

*** **Horn Of Passion**
Concord CCD 4465 *Davis; Antoine Roney (t); Mulgrew Miller (p); Tyler Mitchell, Rufus Reid (b); Jimmy Cobb, Eric McPherson (d). 1/91.*

Concord's founder, the late Carl Jefferson, spoke of Davis with profound affection and clearly regarded him, after Scott Hamilton, as one of his own most prescient signings. Since 1991, the albums have come just about once a year and they bespeak a steadily maturing player.

The debut is more promising than exceptional. A callowness which never seemed to affect Davis in live performance mars what is otherwise a competent and enjoyable record. Roney (the less well-known brother) is an effective presence on the quintet tracks, and Davis's own Bird- and Cannonball-influenced alto steadily acquires authority. Miller, Reid and Cobb add a finishing gloss.

(*) **As We Speak
Concord CCD 4512 *Davis; Robet Trowers (tb); Jacky Terrasson (p); Peter Bernstein (g); Dwayne Burno (b); Leon Parker (d). 2/92.*

*** **Young At Art**
Concord CCD 4565 *Davis; Ted Klum (as); Brad Mehldau (p); Peter Bernstein (g); Dwayne Burno (b); Leon Parker (d). 3/93.*

The next two albums were in some respects a step back, not in the sense that Davis's own playing retrenches, but rather that the idiom seems dated, almost retro, conjuring up rather anonymous Blue Note sessions from around 1965. Trowers has never quite made the impact he deserves and is not entirely well served by the engineer here. Terrasson is as over-the-top as ever, and Bernstein lapses into a Grant Green sound-alike pose which quickly palls.

Young At Art is stronger and more clearly personalized, despite the inconspicuous addition of Klum; Ted Who? shouts the crowd until the two altoists peel off 'One For Cannon'. Mehldau is as revelatory as he always is, and Burno and Parker make a very decent fist of the old-fashioned sound Davis was looking for on the earlier record.

***(*) **High Standards**
Concord CCD 4624 *Davis; Nicholas Payton (t); Robert Trowers (tb); Dado Moroni (p); Peter Washington (b); Lewis Nash (d). 6/94.*

The nice thing about this record is the choice of material. Wayne Shorter's 'The Big Push', Junior Mance's 'Jubilation' and an original from the trombonist, who has been restored to the front line alongside Davis and Payton, all contribute to a record that sounds confident, unfussy and, for the first time, completely individual.

This is how contemporary jazz is supposed to sound: balanced, wry and aware.

***(*) **From Within**

CCD 4727 *Davis; Nicholas Payton (t); Hank Jones (p); Ron Carter (b); Lewis Nash (d).* 4/96.

Whatever happened in 1995, the lay-off did Davis some good. He has assembled some excellent tunes for this date. The opening trio of 'Journey To Epiphany', 'Tai's Tune' and 'Portrait Of Desiree' suggest a young man who has broadened his listening considerably. The ballad, 'From Within', suggests a deeper understanding not just of the chords but of life as a whole, a poised, mature performance. The minor feel of 'Tai's Tune' evokes the bittersweet experiences of fatherhood, while 'Introspection' has the aura of a chance idea yielding wisdoms its perpetrators don't entirely understand.

Nash, Carter and Jones anchor proceedings, and though the pianist's contributions are resolutely predictable one can't deny their beauty. This is the most heavyweight set so far, sold very largely on the strength of Davis's appearance in the Robert Altman movie, *Kansas City*, but nearer and nearer the money for all that.

Miles Davis (1926–91)

TRUMPET, FLUGELHORN, ORGAN

One of the pivotal artists of the twentieth century, Miles was a shapeshifting imp of the perverse, capable of extraordinary beauty and a kind of self-negating ugliness almost by turns. He grew up in comfortable circumstances in Alton, Ilinois, and never once, even at the zenith of the Black Power movement, affected any plantation or ghetto poses. He went to New York to study and to follow in the footsteps of Charlie Parker, with whom he worked, not entirely at ease with the rapid, declamatory language of bebop. After the war, he began to experiment with Gerry Mulligan and others, using cooler modalities and larger groups. This eventually brought him within the orbit of one of the two men who were to exert the greatest influence on his recording career. Gil Evans worked with Miles in workshop sessions and later arranged some of his greatest big-band recordings. In the mid-'50s the trumpeter formed a quintet and recorded classic discs for Prestige, culminating in Kind Of Blue. He also dabbled in film music, an experience which led him in a new direction and a new, more floating approach to harmony and structure. This became most evident in the fierce, loosely organized jams which producer Teo Macero, his other éminence grise, transformed into releasable albums. Ill-health, disenchantment and scrapes with the law and corporate politics led Miles to withdraw from music-making for some time, emerging only to play organ on some of the darkest and most troublous music he or any artist ever recorded. Late years brought a measure of renewed and belated superstardom and, though he showed signs of returning to blues-based jazz, he was required to play pop-derived hits to festival audiences who worshipped him as a natural rebel and an icon of style.

(*) **Bopping The Blues

Black Lion BLCD 760102 *Davis; Gene Ammons (ts); Connie Wainwright (g); Linton Garner (p); Tommy Potter (b); Art Blakey (d); Earl Coleman, Ann Hathaway (v).* 10/46.

If one were to pick two figures to encapsulate the diversity, continuity within change, and the sheer artistic grace of jazz, then one could only point to Duke Ellington and to a figure who in some ways is Duke's dark opposite, in other ways his equal, but who grew to distrust the very name 'jazz' as a white commercial construct. In his lifetime, Miles Davis experienced a curious combination of adulation and disdain; endlessly changing yet never sounding like anyone other than himself, endlessly experimenting yet innately hostile to the self-conscious experimentalism of the avant-garde; an enigma wrapped up in a conundrum, yet expressed by a voice of fragile purity. And never was the epithet 'vocal' better applied to a horn player, for even after he had scoured his own voice down to the famous husky growl of later years (against medical insistence, he shouted at an agent following throat surgery), his trumpet playing was pristine.

It should be understood from the start that Miles Davis was not a virtuoso trumpeter. There were plenty of other slim black men (and some heftier ones, like Dizzy) around at the end of the war who could blow him offstage without effort. Miles's great gift was musical rather than technical. He could place a note with the precision and accuracy of the painters he admired, and he was a total musician in that everything that happened within his orbit somehow came to sound like part of his own conception.

Miles made the first recordings under his own name in August 1947 with a tenor-wielding Charlie Parker returning a favour to his young trumpeter. This Black Lion set is too obscure even to be specified in Ian Carr's meticulous discography, and only devoted completists will be at all anxious to have the disc. There are some attractive moments. Miles and Jug sound not quite in sympathy but still capable of some warm interchanges. The two singers are pretty much off the peg, but not unappealing by the standards of the time.

**** **Birth Of The Cool**

Capitol CDP 792862 *Davis; Kai Winding, J.J Johnson (tb); Junior Collins, Gunther Schuller, Sandy Siegelstein (frhn); John Barber (tba); Lee Konitz (as); Gerry Mulligan (bs); Al Haig, John Lewis (p); Nelson Boyd, Al McKibbon, Joe Shulman (b); Kenny Clarke, Max Roach (d); Kenny Hagood (v).* 1/49–3/50.

***(*) **Cool Boppin'**

Fresh Sound FSCD 1008 *As above, except add Mike Zwerin (tb), Sahib Shihab (as), Benjamin Lundy (ts), Cecil Payne (bs), Tadd Dameron (p), John Collins (g), Carlos Vidal (perc).* 9/48–2/49.

**** **The Complete Birth Of The Cool**

Blue Note 94550 *As above.* 9/48–3/50.

... and then suddenly we are in the presence of a major innovator. But who? Since Miles's death, Gerry Mulligan has gone on record, without rancour but with unmistakable emphasis, to claim a much larger hand in these astonishing performances than the attribution of *Birth Of The Cool* to Miles alone has ever allowed. It had been clear, even from his tenure with Charlie Parker, that Miles was not a natural bebopper, favouring a much cooler, less abrasive sound. As the released tracks all demonstrate, Miles and his collaborators were more interested in texture and structure than in stratospheric soloing and cutting contests. Whoever was the main creative force, Miles was certainly the enabler, bringing together like-minded players in New York City, and, though the results (recorded at three sessions over the span of a year) were a commercial failure at the time, these pioneering efforts by arrangers Mulligan, Gil Evans and John Carisi are allusive, magical scores that channelled the irresistible energy of bebop into suprising textures and piquant settings for improvisation.

Davis and Konitz play as if in sight of some new musical world. One can almost share in their delight and surprise as unexpected harmonic fragrances waft off the landscape in front of them. Airshot material by a different line-up has been available as *The Real Birth Of The Cool* on Bandstand. This was taped before the now-classic studio sessions and shows the same music – 'Jeru', 'Budo', 'Godchild' – in evolution rather than finished and definitive. Nine of the same tracks appear on *Cool Boppin'*, which is valuable for some great early solos by the leader. The sound, recorded at the Royal Roost club, is no better than average for this kind of material, but there is sufficient of interest in the performances to make it a worthwhile buy, and there is some fine material under Tadd Dameron's leadership on the same disc, including some glorious moments when Davis lifts Dameron's wonky lyricism to new heights. The *Complete* brings together all the available material from this historic experiment, beautifully remastered and nicely packaged.

***** Quintet With Lee Konitz; Sextet With Jackie McLean**

Fresh Sound FSCD 1000 *Davis; Don Elliott (mel, vib); Lee Konitz, Jackie McLean (as); Gil Coggins, John Lewis (p); Connie Henry, Curley Russell (b); Connie Kay, Max Roach (d); Kenny Hagood (v). 9/48–5/52.*

Things were moving rather slowly for Miles on the recording front, but these sessions, which straddle the *Birth Of The Cool* period, are a useful guide to what he was doing round the scene. The 1948 session finds him in company with Konitz on four titles, most of them unwontedly upbeat and ebullient. The only change of pace is for 'You Go To My Head', which is kept to a lugubrious meander for the benefit of Kenny Hagood. Rare to hear Miles going for high notes with quite this enthusiasm, though absolutely no mistaking, even at this early date, the sinuous grace of Konitz's improvising; and in retrospect what an influence – sometimes literal, sometimes negative – it was to have on Miles's own approach.

The sextet date is rather disappointing, cluttered and somewhat regressive in idiom. Certainly much less sign of the Davis of the future; more of the querulous bopper he was leaving behind. Also airshot recordings, these share the technical limitations of the quintet date, but more damagingly, since it's much harder to pick out the detail. Miles is soloing confidently. His own 'Out Of The Blue' is confident, clean-limbed and strong, and McLean is beginning to sound like a star in the making.

****(*) Miles Davis With Horns**

Original Jazz Classics OJCCD 053 *Davis; Bennie Green, Sonny Truitt (tb); Al Cohn, Sonny Rollins, Zoot Sims (ts); John Lewis (p); Leonard Gaskin, Percy Heath (b); Kenny Clarke, Roy Haynes (d). 1/51–2/53.*

***** Dig**

Original Jazz Classics OJCCD 005 *Davis; Jackie McLean (as); Sonny Rollins (ts); Walter Bishop Jr (p); Tommy Potter (b); Art Blakey (d). 10/51.*

It would be some while before Miles repaid Prestige's confidence in him with a completely authoritative and satisfying record. Had one done an end-of-year audit in December 1951, would he have seemed a likely contender? The earlier set is almost dreary and ill-defined and, though Miles solos with great confidence on 'My Old Flame' and 'Blueing', there isn't much else to write home about. *Dig* is most obviously questionable on technical grounds. Whatever has happened to players as forceful as Potter and Blakey, lost in a disagreeable mix? 'Conception' reappears in a less challenging form, and there is a positively banal approach to 'It's Only A Paper Moon'. If the story hadn't gone a great deal further than this, Miles might have been a footnote. *Birth Of The Cool* notwithstanding, he had still to produce a work of real individuality.

***** Conception**

Original Jazz Classics OJCCD 1726 2 *Davis; J.J Johnson, Kai Winding (tb); Charlie Kennedy, Lee Konitz, Jackie McLean (as); Stan Getz, Sonny Rollins, Zoot Sims (ts); Gerry Mulligan (bs); Tony Aless, Walter Bishop Jr, Al Haig, Sal Mosca (p); Billy Bauer (g); Arnold Fishkind, Chubby Jackson, Tommy Potter, Gene Ramey (b); Art Blakey, Roy Haynes, Don Lamond, Stan Levey, Max Roach (d). 3/51.*

A largely forgotten and overlooked album, featuring Miles in the company of Stan Getz and Lee Konitz, three graceful exponents of cool improvisation together at the threshold of the '50s and each destined to make a very different impact on the music of the next two decades. The arrangements are somewhat too big and fussy to suit the soloists, but there is no mistaking how professional they are. Most of the tracks are very short indeed, but 'My Old Flame' offers an opportunity to stretch out a touch more generously. This was intended as a limited-edition reissue, but copies have been widely available.

*****(*) Miles Davis: Volume 1**

Blue Note 7815012 *Davis; J.J Johnson (tb); Jackie McLean (as); Jimmy Heath (ts); Gil Coggins, Horace Silver (p); Percy Heath, Oscar Pettiford (b); Art Blakey, Kenny Clarke (d). 5/52–3/54.*

*****(*) Miles Davis: Volume 2**

Blue Note 7815022 *As above.*

***** The Best Of Miles Davis**

Blue Note 7982872 *As above and Capitol sessions, except add Cannonball Adderley (as), Hank Jones (p), Sam Jones (b). 1/49–3/58.*

Time, strength, cash and patience; Herman Melville said these were the key to an artistic career. When Blue Note picked up Miles, he was an artist who needed all four, temperamentally and creatively. These are inconsistent records, but they are also the first tokens of a genuinely personal vision and a solo style that could never be mistaken for anyone else. Although still addicted to heroin when the first two sessions were made, and with his professional life in some disarray, Davis was beginning to move beyond the confines of small-group bebop and explore the more expansive musical language he had sketched in with the *Birth Of*

The Cool ensemble. Nothing quite as ambitious here; but definite signs, even in these rather brief and pithy tracks, that he has changed gear. The music is intense yet restrained, cool yet plangent. The first date seems comparatively hurried, but the second, with fine compositions from Johnson, Heath and Bud Powell, is indispensable, the first Davis record since *Birth* that *must* be in your collection. The third features Davis with rhythm, and as sole horn it properly includes some very strong playing, with fast, eventful solos on 'Take Off' and 'The Leap', as well as an idiosyncratic reading of Monk's 'Well, You Needn't'.

The jumbled sequencing of the original LPs has been corrected on CD; the first and third sessions are complete on the first volume and the second is on Volume 2. Remastering has perked up the rhythm section no end, but otherwise there is no appreciable gain. *The Best Of* collection covers the Blue Note albums, *Birth Of The Cool* and twenty minutes of material from Cannonball Adderley's 1958 *Somethin' Else*. A pleasant enough introduction, but nothing here that could replace the original records.

***** Collectors' Items**

Original Jazz Classics OJCCD 071 *Davis; Charlie Parker, Sonny Rollins (ts); Walter Bishop Jr, Tommy Flanagan (p); Paul Chambers, Percy Heath (b); Philly Joe Jones, Art Taylor (d).* 1/53–3/56.

***(*) At Last! Miles Davis And the Lighthouse All Stars**

Original Jazz Classics OJCCD 480 *Davis; Chet Baker, Rolf Ericson (t); Bud Shank (as); Bob Cooper (ts); Russ Freeman, Lorraine Geller (p); Howard Rumsey (b); Max Roach (d).* 9/53.

The 1953 session with Parker on tenor is a curio and it makes an odd makeweight for the accompanying later quintet with Rollins, which includes a skilful solo by the saxophonist on 'Vierd Blues' and a fine investigation of Brubeck's 'In Your Own Sweet Way' by Davis. The session, along with *Blue Moods* (for which, see below), may also still be available as the double-LP, *Collectors' Items*, on Prestige. The live jam session recorded at the Lighthouse is best forgotten by admirers of the trumpeter whose desultory playing was hardly worth preserving on ponderous versions of 'Infinity Promenade' and 'Round Midnight'. Interesting to hear him in company with 'the white Miles Davis', and we must concede that the sound-quality is very good for a club date.

***** Blue Haze**

Original Jazz Classics OJCCD 093 *Davis; Dave Schildkraut (as); John Lewis, Charles Mingus, Horace Silver (p); Percy Heath (b); Art Blakey, Kenny Clarke, Max Roach (d).* 5/53–4/54.

****** Walkin'**

Original Jazz Classics OJCCD 213 *Davis; J.J Johnson (tb); Dave Schildkraut (as); Lucky Thompson (ts); Horace Silver (p); Percy Heath (b); Kenny Clarke (d).* 4/54.

*****(*) Bags' Groove**

Original Jazz Classics OJCCD 245 *Davis; Sonny Rollins (ts); Milt Jackson (vib); Thelonious Monk, Horace Silver (p); Percy Heath (b); Kenny Clarke (d).* 6/54, 12/54.

****** Miles Davis And The Modern Jazz Giants**

Original Jazz Classics OJC 347 *Davis; John Coltrane (ts); Milt Jackson (vib); Red Garland, Thelonious Monk (p); Paul Chambers, Percy Heath (b); Kenny Clarke, Philly Joe Jones (d).* 12/54–10/56.

Things are beginning to take shape. Though none of these dates is by itself a classic, an impression is beginning to consolidate of a formidable artist with the capacity to reinvent his language wholesale, while remaining demonstrably within a tradition. The *Blue Haze* set is split between a merely good quartet date from 1953 and three altogether excellent tracks from the following March, by the same quartet that cut the final date for Blue Note. Few will even know Dave Schildkraut's name, but he makes a positive contribution to a single track from the April 1954 session, which is more fully covered on *Walkin'*.

Here and on *Bags' Groove* Davis hits stride at last. The earlier session includes two clear-cut masterpieces in the title-track and 'Blue'N'Boogie'; the solos are diamond-sharp, absolutely without fat or verbiage, and elegantly executed. Most of *Bags' Groove* features a quintet with Rollins, a group which produced fine if slightly less than exalted music. It's marked out as the first occasion – and 'Oleo' the first track – on which he used the Harmon mute which was to define his sound in future years. Two compelling takes of the title-track round out a solid performance; these actually come from a Christmas Eve 1954 date which is otherwise contained in *Meets The Modern Jazz Giants* and documents the only official encounter between Davis, Monk and Jackson. The clash between the vibrapharpist's typically fleet lines and the different kinds of astringency represented by Monk and Davis made for a tense and compelling situation. This disc is, in turn, completed by a very fine 'Round Midnight' by the quintet with John Coltrane.

****(*) The Musings Of Miles**

Original Jazz Classics OJCCD 004 *Davis; Red Garland (p); Oscar Pettiford (b); Philly Joe Jones (d).* 6/55.

***** Blue Moods**

Original Jazz Classics OJCCD 043 *Davis; Britt Woodman (tb); Teddy Charles (vib); Charles Mingus (b); Elvin Jones (d).* 7/55.

*****(*) Quintet / Sextet**

Original Jazz Classics OJCCD 012 *Davis; Jackie McLean (as); Milt Jackson (vib); Ray Bryant (p); Percy Heath (b); Art Taylor (d).* 8/55.

Davis's final quartet session prior to the formation of his famous quartet is surprisingly lacklustre. Jones and Pettiford were allegedly exhausted, though this has in other contexts been a euphemism for other problems, and it does seem that Pettiford was drunk. He certainly sounds less than on the case, and Davis is left to hold the music together, playing rather grimly.

The brief *Blue Moods* session, though poor value on a single disc, is interesting for using an instrumentation he was never to experiment with again. The outstanding track, and one of the best things he did in these years, is a deeply melancholy version of 'Nature Boy' that points forward to the lorn poetry of future years. 'Alone Together', 'There's No You' and 'Easy Living' complete a very attractive session. Given how much padding has gone on elsewhere, it's strange that nothing could have been found to add a bit of value to this one, though we're not wedded to the practice of padding for padding's sake.

The August 1955 session is something of a farewell to Davis's most carefree music, with four pacey and involving workouts on mainly blues material – though, at little over half an hour, this is also particularly poor value for a single CD. McLean plays on 'Dr

Jackle' and 'Minor March', and these are all the better for his brash, blustery presence.

****(*) Hi-Hat All Stars**

Fresh Sound FSRCD 13 *Davis; Jay Migliori (ts); Bob Freeman, Al Walcott (p); Jimmy Woode (b); Johnny Zitano (d).* 55.

Eavesdroppings from the bootleg capital of America. By the time this was recorded, Miles had moved far beyond an idiom his colleagues at the Hi-Hat were only just learning to cope with. They give him no help whatsoever and, though it fills in a tiny corner of the story, it's of little more than specialist documentary detail. As might be expected, the sound doesn't gladden the ear.

***** Miles**

Original Jazz Classics OJCCD 006 *Davis; John Coltrane (ts); Red Garland (p); Paul Chambers (b); Philly Joe Jones (d).* 11/55.

****** Relaxin'**

Original Jazz Classics OJC 190 *As above.* 5/56–10/56.

*****(*) Workin'**

Original Jazz Classics OJCCD 296 2 *As above.* 5/56–10/56.

****** Steamin'**

Original Jazz Classics OJCCD 391 2 *As above.* 5/56–10/56.

****** Cookin'**

Original Jazz Classics OJCCD 128 2 *As above.* 11/55, 10/56.

****** The Complete Prestige Recordings (1951–1956)**

Prestige 8PCD 012 2 8CD *As for Prestige recordings above.* 51–56.

Great music is sometimes made in inauspicious circumstances. Another 'Quintet of the Year' two years earlier showed a marked disinclination to tear themselves away from sport on television and play a concert, and yet Bird, Dizzy, Bud Powell, Mingus and Max Roach turned in one of the great performances of all time. Miles's 1956 quintet cut these records to round out a contract before moving on to Columbia, and yet they represent a purple patch in his output. As far as the jazz of the time is concerned, they are time-capsule material, though gallingly it is impossible to pick out a single outstanding disc. They are uneven in inspiration, but at their greatest they bespeak an extraordinary sense of spontaneity, a brilliant assemblage of players in creative flux. The greatest contrast, much discussed, is between Davis – spare, introverted, guileful – and the leonine, blistering Coltrane, who was still at a somewhat chaotic stage in his development. But equally telling are the members of the rhythm section, who contrive to create a different climate behind each soloist and sustain the logical flow of the tunes. Recorded at just a handful of marathon sessions, each record has its special rewards: a slow, pierced 'My Funny Valentine', on *Cookin'*, the supple swing of 'I Could Write A Book' and revitalized bebop of 'Woody'N'You' from *Relaxin'*, a haunted version of 'It Never Entered My Mind' on *Workin'*. It would be possible to throw up another half-dozen contenders, and everyone will have particular favourites. One further unlikely contender is 'Surrey With The Fringe On Top' and the following track, the bebop classic, 'Salt Peanuts', on *Steamin'*, details of which, and for *Workin'*, mysteriously disappeared from our last edition.

The message remains the same: these records should be in every serious jazz collection. Whether or not one wants to plump for the exhaustive Prestige box containing them all will depend on bank balance and individual appetite for such all-in-one packages. As will be seen, the box preserves material from much earlier in the trumpeter's association with Prestige, but there is much to be said for sampling all these records in something close to their original form. Rudy van Gelder's splendid engineering and Bob Weinstock's production have ensured that the music has survived in excellent condition, and the CD reissues sound well enough, if a little compressed. The English company Ace has released *Cookin'* and *Relaxin'* on a single CD, which is superb value and may well still be available.

*****(*) Round About Midnight**

Columbia CK 40610 *As above.* 10/55–9/56.

Released on the new label but recorded for the old, this inevitably sounds like a footnote. The material is fine but somehow fails to cast quite the consistent spell which the Prestige sessions do.

****** Miles Ahead**

Columbia CK 65121 *Davis; John Carisi, Bernie Glow, Taft Jordan, Louis Mucci, Ernie Royal (t); Joe Bennett, Jimmy Cleveland, Frank Rehak (tb); Tom Mitchell (btb); Tony Miranda, Willie Ruff (frhn); Lee Konitz (as); Sid Cooper, Romeo Penque (woodwinds); Danny Bank (bcl); Paul Chambers (b); Art Taylor (d); Gil Evans (cond).* 5/57.

Miles had worked with Gil Evans before, of course, but this first full-length collaboration highlighted their like-mindedness and an illuminating reciprocity of vision. Curiously, given the reputation that these records have garnered, they aren't always well played (excepting the soloist, of course), with fluffs aplenty and shaky ensembles, though this first outing is pristine compared to the shaky passage-work on *Porgy And Bess*, later. *Miles Ahead* was rightly identified as a concerto for Miles, a work of classical ambitions, and though some thought that condemned it to some Pale beyond jazz, it is absolutely central to what Miles and Gil were about. Recorded over four sessions in May 1957, it has great internal consistency. It no longer makes much sense to talk about 'tracks', for the internal subdivisions here are effectively moments in a long, continuous work. Even so, certain things do stand out: 'The Maids Of Cadiz', 'My Ship', the title-track and a lovely version of Ahmad Jamal's 'New Rhumba'. Frailties of performance apart, Evans gave the music a great depth of focus, doubling up bass lines and creating distance and tension between upper and lower lines in a way that was to affect Miles for the rest of his career, even after he had given up using unamplified orchestrations. Though it is far from being expressively one-dimensional – there are moments of playful humour – the pervading tone is a melancholy lyricism. This was the first time Miles was to record with flugelhorn, an experiment which added an instrumental 'double' to just about every horn player's bag but which the initiator was to repeat only very briefly. The flugelhorn's sound isn't so very different from his trumpet soloing, though palpably softer-edged. Though he plays open all the time, as he was to do again on *Milestones*, some of the burnish seems to be lost. A quiet masterpiece, all the same, and one with a guaranteed place in the top flight of Miles albums.

****** L'Ascenseur pour l'échafaud**

Fontana 836305 *Davis; Barney Wilen (ts); René Urtreger (p); Pierre Michelot (b); Kenny Clarke (d).* 12/57.

One of the most discussed items in the entire canon, strangely enough, given that it was written as soundtrack music. It did, though, provide Miles with his first real compositional challenge, something more than blowing themes, and it helped steer him in the direction of the abstract, themeless experiments of the following decade. Interesting as it is on record, the music makes complete sense only when combined with the images of Louis Malle's bleak thriller, ostensibly a murder story, but actually about the claustrophobic impact of social technology. Most of the fragments – and the requirements of the medium also steered Miles towards a more open-ended and unresolved approach – are slow and moody, though inevitably there is a motorway number. So successful was Miles's scoring that he effectively redraws the movie's inner landscape, accentuating its psychological elements and the philosophical reserve of its somewhat fugitive subtext. The other players contribute a good deal to the whole, with the late Barney Wilen particularly prominent. This unsung hero of European jazz died shortly before our last edition was published. Would that more of his atmospheric playing were available to include in this one.

****** Milestones**

Columbia CK 40837 *Davis; Cannonball Adderley (as); John Coltrane (ts); Red Garland (p); Paul Chambers (b); Philly Joe Jones (d).* 4/58.

Sometimes sidelined as a 'transitional' record, a pause at the portals before entering into the magnificence of *Kind Of Blue* a year later. Retrospect suggests that the distance between them isn't so very great, either musically or qualitatively. In April 1958, Miles hadn't recorded a small-group date for more than a year. A lot of thinking, woodshedding, a lot of hard conceptual work had been done in the interim. On *Milestones* the trumpeter is certainly still working out ideas that were adumbrated on *L'Ascenseur*, but there is no sense whatever that this is anything other than a completely achieved performance, and a highly accomplished one. There are no standards, and all the material is harmonically and rhythmically challenging, sometimes simply by suspending conventional harmony and by constraining complex ideas within a deceptively simple 4/4. One of the profound differences between Miles and the saxophonists is that, while they tend to play on the beat, he is almost always across it. Adderley isn't always right for the music, and he sounds awkward and shuffling on 'Sid's Ahead', one of the album's truly great tracks. Standing alongside two of the greatest soloists in the music, then and ever, one understands his slight discomfiture. He is much more to the fore on 'Straight, No Chaser', but again it is Miles's solo which commands attention, actually quoting 'When The Saints Go Marching In' without obvious irony, a gesture that confounds all those who accused him of being a scorched-earth modernist with no interest in the past. If 'Sid's Ahead' is brooding and mournful, then 'Milestones' itself, on which he returns briefly to flugelhorn, is sharply ambiguous in its dancing exuberance, a truly startling performance. This is one of the very great modern-jazz albums.

*****(*) Miles And Coltrane**

Columbia 460824 *Davis; John Coltrane (ts); Cannonball Adderley (as); Bill Evans, Red Garland (p); Paul Chambers (b); Jimmy Cobb, Philly Joe Jones (d).* 10/55–7/58.

*****(*) '58 Miles**

Columbia CK 47835 *As above, except omit Garland, Jones.* 58.

*****(*) Mostly Miles**

Phontastic NCD 8813 *As above, except add Louis Smith (t), Lee Konitz (as), Junior Cook (ts), Horace Silver (p), Henry Grimes, Gene Taylor (b), Louis Hayes, Ed Levinson (d).* 7/58.

****** Miles Davis & Thelonious Monk: Live At Newport 1958 & 1963**

Columbia/Legacy C2K 53585 2CD *As for '58 Miles, except add Charlie Rouse (ts), Pee Wee Russell (cl), Thelonious Monk (p), Butch Warren (b), Frankie Dunlop (d).* 7/58, 7/63.

The historic Newport Festival appearance of July 1958 has been available in rather scattered form for some time, and it is very good to have it complete on the double-CD Legacy set, albeit rather awkwardly paired with a much later Monk set. Any impression that the two giants are playing together should be quickly corrected. The only connection here is Newport. Miles and Coltrane are playing brilliantly throughout, with the saxophonist firing on all cylinders, and sounding lighter-hearted than he often does, on 'Ah-Leu-Cha' and 'Bye Bye Blackbird'. Once again, the contrast with Miles's spare and angular approach is very striking. The 1958 compilation brings together material that was formerly issued on *Black Giants* and *Jazz At The Plaza* (of which, a little more below). 'Oleo' and 'My Funny Valentine' were the best things on that fine set, which is now restored to catalogue. *Miles And Coltrane* is filled out by two much earlier items, 'Little Melonae' and 'Budo', from 1955. We can but recommend the budget-priced Davis/Monk double. Fans of either will find this an agreeable bit of repackaging.

****** Porgy And Bess**

Columbia CK 65141 *Davis; John Coles, Bernie Glow, Louis Mucci, Ernie Royal (t); Joseph Bennett, Jimmy Cleveland, Richard Hixon, Frank Rehak (tb); Willie Ruff, Gunther Schuller, Julius Watkins (frhn); Bill Barber (tba); Cannonball Adderley, Danny Bank (as); Phil Bodner, Romeo Penque, Jerome Richardson (f); Paul Chambers (b); Jimmy Cobb, Philly Joe Jones (d).* 7–8/58.

In his biography of Miles, Ian Carr very accurately attributes the difference between this album and the similarly constituted *Miles Ahead* to Miles's own role as preacher, engaged in a call-and-response dialogue with the congregation/ensemble. While 'Summertime' and 'It Ain't Necessarily So' are straightforward solo features, albeit very remarkable ones, 'Prayer' is an astounding *tour de force*, harmonically suspended, and with Miles's most extraordinary recorded solo to date punctuated by agonized screams and shouts, whether of affirmation or suffering it isn't always easy to judge. Miles was not in good physical condition during the making of the record, which perhaps explains the twisting intensity, the bent notes and slurs which seem to express some inner pain. It is less easy in the circumstances to explain the simple grandeur of 'The Buzzard Song' or indeed of the two solos mentioned above; 'Summertime' has an aura of calm that was seldom again to enter into his playing. We have already pointed to shortcomings in the playing of the ensemble. These frankly are as nothing compared to the sheer quality of the music performed.

*** Jazz At The Plaza Vol. 1

Columbia 471510 *Davis; Cannonball Adderley (as); John Coltrane (ts); Bill Evans (p); Paul Chambers (b); Philly Joe Jones (d).* 9/58.

Out of circulation for quite a long time, this one has struggled to maintain profile among the superb sessions that surround it. Probably the stand-out track recorded at the New York City hotel is 'My Funny Valentine', which features just Miles and rhythm. Adderley sits out 'If I Were A Bell'; but this isn't one of Trane's better nights, and the interplay between the two giants isn't as earth-shaking as one by now (selfishly) feels it ought to be. Unlike some of the official live sessions, this doesn't have an in-built aura of history, but it comes across as rather more than just another date. Perhaps this band was incapable of 'just another date'. With what was to come within the year, though, it inevitably palls into relative insignificance.

♛ **** Kind Of Blue

Columbia CK 64935 *Davis; Cannonball Adderley (as); John Coltrane (ts); Bill Evans, Wynton Kelly (p); Paul Chambers (b); Jimmy Cobb (d).* 3–4/59.

In the summer of 1997 Jimmy Cobb described this celebrated album, one of the most famous of all time, as 'just another date for us'. So history is made, unnoticed and perhaps unappreciated by the participants. There is no other record with quite the general appeal of *Kind Of Blue*, and modern sampling has now delivered up what must be considered the definitive version of it. The key presence may be that of Evans (Wynton Kelly plays only on the blues, 'Freddie Freeloader') and it is his allusive, almost impressionistic accompaniments which provide the ideal platform for the spacious solos created by the horns. This was the first widely acknowledged 'modal jazz' date, and it is interesting how thoroughly it has now been absorbed into mainstream language. Presumably it once sounded a good deal less familiar. Tension is consistently established within the ensembles, only for Davis and Coltrane especially to resolve it in songful, declamatory solos. The steady mid-tempos and the now familiar plaintive voicings on 'So What' and 'All Blues' reinforce the weightless, haunting qualities Miles was bringing to his music. If you have anything approximating to a jazz collection, you will already have this record, on some format and with one or other of the issued numbers. Even if you do, you may want to consider investing in this impeccable version.

***(*) Sketches Of Spain

Columbia CK 65142 *Davis; John Coles, Bernie Glow, Taft Jordan, Louis Mucci, Ernie Royal (t); Dick Hixon, Frank Rehak (tb); John Barrows, Jimmy Buffington, Earl Chapin, Tony Miranda, Joe Singer (frhn); Bill Barber (tba); Albert Block, Eddie Caine, Harold Feldman, Romeo Penque (woodwinds); Jack Knitzer (bsn); Danny Bank (bcl); Janet Putnam (hp); Paul Chambers (b); Jimmy Cobb, Elvin Jones (d).* 11/59–3/60.

Similarly improved by CD transfer and enhanced sampling, but still in our view overrated. Though it has moments of luminous beauty, it's hard to escape the feeling that this is a record which has acquired a mystique over and above its musical virtues. Despite – or perhaps because of – far more time in the studios than on the earlier collaborations with Gil Evans, the whole is poorly focused, with the ambitious 'Concierto de Aranjuez' sometimes (heresy!) sounding like inflated light music, with only Miles's occasional intensities driving energy into the whole.

The dialogue between trumpet and ensemble on 'Solea' is the best sequence on the session, raising the improvisational stakes more than a little. Although the trumpeter is giving of his best throughout, the sometimes haphazard percussion tracks and muzzy ensembles suggest a harbinger of some of the trance music Miles would later delve into in the 1970s. Curiously, extra time in the studio failed to deliver good sound, and the CD transfer is very dry.

***(*) Miles Davis In Stockholm Complete

Dragon DRCD 228 4CD *Davis; John Coltrane (ts); Sonny Stitt (as, ts); Wynton Kelly (p); Paul Chambers (b); Jimmy Cobb (d).* 3 & 10/60.

A number of live recordings exist from this period, away from Miles's officially sanctioned releases, and the material on Dragon – excellently recorded by Swedish Radio – affords valuable glimpses of two European sojourns in 1960. The concert with Coltrane (which includes a six-minute interview with the saxophonist) suggests a battle of giants: Trane piles in with all his most abandoned lines, while Davis remains – especially in a nearly anguished 'All Blues' – almost aloof. The rhythm section play with impervious jauntiness, and it adds up to a tremendous concert recording. The concert with Stitt is only slightly less effective. Stitt, admittedly, wrestles with no dark demons, but his plangency and itch to play are scarcely less powerful than Coltrane's, and his switching between alto and tenor offers more light and shade. Davis is again bitingly inventive, even on material which by this stage he must have played many, many times.

*** Live In Zurich 1960

Jazz Unlimited JUCD 2031 *Davis; John Coltrane (ts); Wynton Kelly (p); Paul Chambers (b); Jimmy Cobb (d).* 4/60.

Stuff that has been available before, but done quite professionally here and showing the band at relaxed medium pace, neither stretching unduly nor merely coasting. 'If I Were A Bell' is the most impressive of the four numbers. 'So What' sounds a little shrugged off, and Miles and Trane seem to get their wires crossed once or twice.

*** Some Day My Prince Will Come

Columbia 466312 *Davis; John Coltrane, Hank Mobley (ts); Wynton Kelly (p); Paul Chambers (b); Jimmy Cobb, Philly Joe Jones (d).* 3/61.

***(*) Friday Night At The Blackhawk: Volume 1

Columbia 463334 *As above, except omit Coltrane, Jones.* 4/61.

***(*) Saturday Night At The Blackhawk: Volume 2

Columbia 465191 *As above.* 4/61.

Although a fine, individual, tenor player, Hank Mobley never sounded right in the Davis band – at least not after Coltrane, whose 'guest' appearance on the somewhat lethargic *Some Day My Prince Will Come* is astonishing; he plays two solos, on the title-track and on 'Teo', which put everything else in the shade. The sessions from The Blackhawk were Davis's first attempts at an official live album and, although Mobley plays well – he negotiates the tempo of a rocketing 'Walkin'' without any bother – he sounds at some remove from the rest of the group, and is edited out of a couple of cuts. The group was sparking under the leader at this time. Miles's solos, both muted and open, mix a spitting intensity with thoughtful, circling phrases at both fast and medium tempos. 'Oleo' again stands out, but there are robust investigations of 'If I Were A Bell', 'Prancing' and 'On Green Dolphin Street'. Miles's renewed interest in standard fare is balanced by his development of his own thematic ideas; 'Teo' reappears here as 'Neo', the change of name reflecting a subtle shift in the structure and Miles's own angle of attack. By no means as exhaustive and comprehensive as the Plugged Nickel dates four years later, but fascinating stuff; a portrait of an artist on the brink of further change.

**** The Complete Columbia Recordings: Miles Davis With John Coltrane, 1955–1961

Sony 65833 8CD *As for Round About Midnight, Milestones, Kind Of Blue, Some Day My Prince Will Come.* 55–61.

Miles's rate of progress from the cautious modal idiom of *Round About Midnight* to the majestic credo of *Kind Of Blue* is one of the great transitions in the whole of jazz. It doesn't represent any great epiphany, analogous to those which were supposed to herald the coming of bebop, nor does it correspond to any great spiritual reawakening. It is, much more impressively, the result of steady and concentrated application to the transformation of American song.

What makes this set valuable to collectors is the inclusion of 18 unreleased alternatives from the period. As ever, though, our recommendation is that you experience these albums in their released forms, certainly before closing with the complexities of issued and rejected takes. The albums are here intact in any case, with the exception of *Someday My Prince Will Come* and the original order is easy enough to programme. An essential purchase for the Miles completist and a fantastic gift for anyone falling in love with his work of this period, but a pricey and perhaps overglamorous piece of product that fails to disguise the fact that the real action is already out there.

***(*) Miles Davis At Carnegie Hall 1961

Columbia CK 65027 2CD *Davis; Johnny Coles, Bernie Glow, Louis Mucci, Ernie Royal (t); Dick Hixon, Jimmy Knepper, Frank Rehak (tb); Paul Ingraham, Bob Swisshelm, Julius Watkins (frhn); Bill Barber (tba); Hank Mobley (ts); Danny Bank, Eddie Caine, Romeo Penque, Jerome Richardson, Bob Tricarico (reeds, woodwinds); Wynton Kelly (p); Paul Chambers (b); Janet Putnam (hp); Bobby Rosengarden (perc).* 5/61.

Davis's Carnegie Hall concert of 1961 set the seal on his emergence as a jazz superstar over the preceding five years. Split between music by the quintet and Gil Evans's arrangements of some of the material from their albums together, the night was distinguished by the leader's own playing, executed with more incisiveness on the Evans material than on the studio versions. 'Teo' and 'No Blues' include compelling solos, as alert and packed with attitude as anything he was to do throughout his career. On the down side, Mobley is still no match for the departed Coltrane, and 'Concierto de Aranjuez' is not dignified by the setting. Time was when this material was rather scattered. One quickly gets used to having it properly marshalled, and it is difficult to get past the sheer grandeur of the conception. Even in 1961, at what must be considered the peak of his career, no jazz musician could possibly have expected a setting as sumptuous as Gil gives him. When our last edition appeared, the complete CBS box was still in the making; it rounded out the picture on the Miles and Gil association. Few places sum it up better than this, though.

**(*) Quiet Nights

Columbia CK 65293 *Davis; Johnny Coles, Bernie Glow, Louis Mucci, Ernie Royal (t); Dick Hixon, Jimmy Knepper, Frank Rehak (tb); John Barrows, Paul Ingraham, Robert Swisshelm (frhn); Bill Barber (tba); Steve Lacy (ss); Bob Banks, Eddie Caine, Romeo Penque, Jerome Richardson, Bob Tricarico (reeds); George Coleman (ts); Janet Putnam (hp); Victor Feldman (p); Ron Carter, Paul Chambers (b); Frank Butler, Jimmy Cobb, Elvin Jones (d); Bobby Rosengarden (perc).* 7, 8 & 11/62.

Miles was furious when this record was released, accusing Teo Macero of working behind his back. It is pretty thin stuff, anonymous, big-band arrangements with just one small-group track, 'Summer Night', recorded in Los Angeles with the *Seven Steps To Heaven* sextet. Some of the tunes, 'Corcovado' and 'Slow Samba' in particular, are very beautiful, but it's hard to get the notion of easy listening out of one's head.

*** Seven Steps To Heaven

Columbia 466970 *Davis; George Coleman (ts); Victor Feldman, Herbie Hancock (p); Ron Carter (b); Frank Butler, Tony Williams (d).* 4 & 5/63.

Two oddities on this: Miles playing with a West Coast band and including such classic jazz pieces as 'Basin Street Blues' and 'Baby, Won't You Please Come Home'. The later session unveiled his new group, with Herbie Hancock and the very young Tony Williams. They sound relatively sure-footed on 'Seven Steps' and Hancock certainly understands the need for subtler harmonic – or, rather, chromatic – shading in the music. As so predictably often with Miles, it's possible to hear in this record the seeds of change, but it's an album that is much more illuminating retrospectively, once Miles's later and more revolutionary work has been absorbed.

**** Miles In Antibes

Columbia 462960 *Davis; George Coleman (ts); Herbie Hancock (p); Ron Carter, Richard Davis (b); Tony Williams (d).* 6/63, 5/66.

***(*) My Funny Valentine

Columbia 471276 *As above, except omit Richard Davis.* 2/64.

**** The Complete Concert, 1964

Columbia 471246 2CD *As above.* 2/64.

Coleman is the unsung hero of the Davis discography. Indeed, for our money he is one of the unsung heroes of modern jazz. His scouring, muscular style is very different from that of Coltrane: less intense, more straightforward and yet not without subtlety. *In Antibes* is a very fine concert set, recorded just weeks after this band had been formed. 'Autumn Leaves' is the kind of jazz performance that gets the music a good name: sleek, tough and unsentimental, but not unfeeling, and powered by the young prodigy at the drum-kit. All of the music is unpredictable and exciting, unpredictable largely because familiar material is shone through a prism that mixes abstraction with a genuine delight in melody.

Recorded at the Philharmonic Hall in Lincoln Center, *My Funny Valentine* has a moody and elegiac quality which Miles attributed to President Kennedy's death the previous November. The group plays with almost ritual stateliness, and there is a plangent, wounded quality to the trumpet sound that was to emerge less frequently thereafter. The double-CD set brings together *My Funny Valentine* with *Four & More*. Excellent value.

*****(*) Miles In Berlin**
Columbia CD 62976 *As above, except Wayne Shorter (ts) replaces Coleman.* 9/64.

Wayne Shorter's arrival stabilized the new group, since Shorter was a major composer as well as soloist. Although the set in Berlin is the standard one of 'So What' and so on, the pungency of Davis's solos is matched by a new depth of interplay with the rhythm section, as well as by Shorter's phenomenally harsh-sounding parts. The highlight is a superbly intense reading of 'Autumn Leaves'. There is a huge amount of bootleg material from this period – not as much as for the 1980s band, but still in distracting quantities. We have long since given up noting even the better of these issues. This is how the group should be heard: unmistakably live and present, but professionally recorded and mastered.

****** E.S.P.**
Columbia 467899 *As above.* 1/65.

****** Miles Smiles**
Columbia CK 65683 *As above.* 10/66.

*****(*) Sorcerer**
Columbia CK 65680 *As above.* 5/67.

*****(*) Nefertiti**
Columbia CK 65681 *As above.* 6–7/67.

***** Miles In The Sky**
Columbia CK 65684 *As above, except add George Benson (g).* 1 & 5/68.

***** Filles De Kilimanjaro**
Columbia CK 46116 *As above, except omit Benson; add Chick Corea (ky), Dave Holland (b).* 6–9/68.

This has always been an enigmatic period in Miles's career, a band and a set of relationships which didn't so much develop as go through a looping sequence of self-discoveries and estrangements. The leader himself often sounds almost disengaged from the music, perhaps even alienated from it, though one always senses him there, listening. *Miles Smiles* opens up areas that were to be his main performing territory for the next few years, arguably for the rest of his career. The synthesis of complete abstraction with more or less straightforward blues-playing (Shorter's 'Footprints' is the obvious example of that) was to sustain him right through the darkness of the 1970s bands to the later period when 'New Blues' became a staple of his programmes. After *Smiles*, *E.S.P.* is probably the best album, with seven excellent original themes and the players building a huge creative tension between Shorter's oblique, churning solos and the leader's private musings, and within a rhythm section that is bursting to fly free while still playing time. Miles returns to his old tactic with Coltrane of paring away steadily, often sitting out for long periods or not soloing at all. It is simply that with Shorter he has a saxophonist who is capable of matching that enigmatic stance, rather than rushing off on his own. He does not solo on 'Nefertiti', one of the great compositions from this time, on which the horns simply pace away over Williams's boiling rhythm. The album which bears its name is cool and strong, again largely due to the writing. As on its predecessor, Miles cedes compositional duties to Shorter and only starts writing again with *Miles In The Sky*, which is ironically the weakest of the bunch. It is also unmistakably a transitional work, and the arrival of Corea and Holland for two tracks on *Filles De Kilimanjaro* points forward to the next phase in this extraordinary story. As always, though, Miles is looking back as well as forward. The standard treatments on the live albums, things like an exhaustive 'Stella By Starlight' and (what almost counts as a standard) 'All Blues', are occasionally rambling but always have something of importance to register, no matter when and in what mood one hears them.

♛ ** The Complete Live At The Plugged Nickel**
Columbia CXK 66955 7CD *Davis; Wayne Shorter (ts); Herbie Hancock (p); Ron Carter (b); Tony Williams (d).* 12/65.

*****(*) Highlights From The Plugged Nickel**
Columbia 481434 *As above.* 12/65.

The Rosetta Stone of modern jazz: a monumental document written in five subtly and sometimes starkly different dialects but within which much of the music of the post-bop period has been defined and demarcated. When future histories of the music are written – and it would be possible to write a convincing version of the story from 1945 to 1990 merely by reference to Miles's part in it – these sessions will be adduced as a turning point. Arguably Miles's best ever group – dispute it if you will – working its way out of one phase and into another in which time and harmony, melody and dynamics were radically rethought. The improvisations here would have been inconceivable a mere couple of years earlier; they don't so much float on the chords as react against them like phosphorus. Three years later, they fed directly into Miles's electric revolution and the beginning of what was to be the long dramatic coda.

To set the time and place, these were recorded (officially, by Columbia engineers) at the Plugged Nickel Club in Chicago. Though the Blackhawk sessions are better than most, the registration here is superb, not much different from what one would hope for in a studio. At first glance, and with an eye to the predictably high price, one might wonder whether so repetitive a documentation would be worth either the cash or the patience (or the time and strength, just to complete Herman Melville's sequence). The short answer is an emphatic yes and unambiguously so, because here it is possible to observe at the closest quarters Miles and his musicians working through their ideas set by set in ways that make the named material, the songs, more or less irrelevant. Even when it is clear he is working from 'Stella By Starlight' or 'My Funny Valentine', Miles is moving out into areas of harmonic/melodic invention and performance dynamics which were unprecedented in the music, and doing so within the concentrated span of two nights at the club.

Unlike the two original LPs, on which Columbia had forgivably presumed to deliver up the 'best' of the sessions, it is now possible to hear Carter clearly. His role is absolutely crucial and there are times when one can almost visualize Miles flicking from one solid outcrop to another like a caddis fly. Hancock occasionally sounds diffident and detached, and he is the only one of the group who resorts to repeated licks as the sets progress. He may have been tired, but he may also, as McCoy Tyner was to do at almost exactly the same time, have realized that he was to some extent external to the real drama of this extraordinary music.

The sampler album is a perfectly decent representation of the whole, but in most cases it will do no more than whet an appetite for the complete box. These are genuinely historic recordings. It would be better to go without a dozen – make that two dozen – run-of-the-mill jazz records to finance this glorious package.

***** Circle In The Round**

Columbia 467898 2CD *Davis; Cannonball Adderley (as); John Coltrane, Hank Mobley, Wayne Shorter (ts); Chick Corea, Bill Evans, Red Garland, Herbie Hancock, Wynton Kelly, Joe Zawinul (p); Joe Beck, George Benson (g); Ron Carter, Paul Chambers, Dave Holland (b); Jimmy Cobb, Philly Joe Jones, Tony Williams (d).* 10/55–1/70.

An interesting (if seldom very involving) compilation of out-takes from Davis's Columbia albums over a 25-year period. The long title-track is an attempt at a mesmerizing mood-piece which works for some of the time, but fades in and out of focus. Earlier pieces with the great quintet are more vital and include a marvellous 'Love For Sale' from 1958. The CD omits some of the music from the original double-LP.

♛ ** Miles Davis And Gil Evans: The Complete Columbia Studio Sessions**

Columbia CXK 67397 6CD *As for Columbia recordings above, except add Dick Leith (btb), Bill Hinshaw, Art Maebe, Richard Perissi (frhn), Buddy Collette, Paul Horn (f), Gene Cipriano (ob), Fred Dutton (bsn), Herbie Hancock (p), Ron Carter (b), Tony Williams (d).* 57–68.

Utterly, sandbaggingly wonderful – and, alas, expensive as well. This is the kind of set into which one can disappear for weeks at a time. Most of the material has been around for a long time, but there is a mass of studio interaction, alternative takes and two previously unreleased suites, *The Time Of The Barracudas* and *Falling Water*, both retrospectively titled, but from 1963 and 1968 respectively. The figures speak for themselves; six hours of music on 116 selections, all of them remixed from the original masters using super bit sampling. How much more, and how much more pristine, could anyone possibly want?

****** In A Silent Way**

Columbia 450982 *Davis; Wayne Shorter (ts); Chick Corea (p); Joe Zawinul (p, org); John McLaughlin (g); Dave Holland (b); Tony Williams (d).* 2/69.

One feels a touch self-conscious describing yet another Miles Davis record as 'transitional'. As an artefact, *In A Silent Way* is already a long way even from the increasingly abstract work of the previous couple of years. It was in every sense a collage using 'found objects', put together with a view to the minimum detail and coloration required to make an impact. Two of the 'objects' were John McLaughlin, recruited on the nod and apparently unheard by the trumpeter, and Joe Zawinul, whose 'In A Silent Way' became a centrepiece of the album. Three electric instruments give the band a sound completely unlike the previous incarnation, though it is clear that there are very significant continuities between this record and *Miles Smiles* or *E.S.P.*, and these should not be overlooked. In order to bring the performances up to LP length, Teo Macero stitched repeats of certain passages back into the fabric of the music, giving it continuity and a certain hypnotic circularity. Once again, a practical contingency (Miles was apparently happy with the short chunks that had been recorded) resulted in a new creative development, no less significant than Charles Mingus's overdubbing on *The Black Saint And The Sinner Lady*. Even if one had no inkling of what had gone before, *In A Silent Way* is a very beautiful album, touching and centred. The title-piece and 'Shhh/Peaceful' are among the most atmospheric recordings in modern jazz.

****** Sketches Of Spain / Kind Of Blue / In A Silent Way**

Sony 65604 *As for the original albums.* 59–69.

Easy for us to be slightly cynical about repackaging like this, but try to imagine you are a seventeen-year-old who has never heard of Miles Davis and receiving the gift of this wonderfully priced budget set of three of his greatest records. What an incomparable thrill to hear 'Concierto de Aranjuez' and 'Freddie Freeloader' and 'In A Silent Way' for the very first time.

****** Bitches Brew**

Columbia 460602 2CD *Davis; Wayne Shorter (ts); Bennie Maupin (bcl); Chick Corea, Larry Young, Joe Zawinul (p); John McLaughlin (g); Harvey Brooks, Dave Holland (b); Charles Alias, Jack DeJohnette, Lenny White (d); Jim Riley (perc).* 8/69.

***** The Complete Bitches Brew Sessions**

Columbia C4K 65570 4CD *As above.* 8/69.

Much less beautiful than *In A Silent Way* and far more unremittingly abstract, this is one of the most remarkable creative statements of the last half-century, in any artistic form. It is also profoundly flawed, a gigantic torso of burstingly noisy music that absolutely refuses to resolve itself under any recognized guise. There are stories (authenticated by Teo Macero) that the recordings were made under the cloud of an enormous dust-up between producer and star. Certainly Miles plays with a dour aggression but also, on 'Sanctuary' (apparently the first item to be recorded), with an odd vulnerability which surfaced only occasionally during his later career. Though there had been experiments before with tape editing, *Bitches Brew* was made in an unprecedented way. Basically, the tapes were set to roll and the musicians improvised in the studio, creating a huge body of music which would later be assembled by Miles and Macero. There being no question of alternative or rejected 'takes', the complete sessions contain a huge body of music not used and unrelated to anything on the now repackaged and remastered release edition.

Listening to the complete sessions underlines what an intuitive genius Macero was. Far from augmenting the reputation of the album, the full picture tends to deplete it. Individually, there are some lovely themes, like the Latin 'Yaphet' and 'Corrado' on disc two, but most of the unused material, like 'Trevere' on the next disc, is extremely tentative and lacks focus and engagement. Valuable as it doubtless is to gain some insight into how this extraordinary album was made, it is evident that attention wavers after the first disc, not because attention spans are getting shorter, but quite simply because the quality of the music is not up to scratch. The most significant change in personnel from previous bands was the replacement of Williams and his very linear approach with the more sculptural DeJohnette. The rhythms are immediately more shifting and uncertain, matching the complete polytonality of much of the music. It is rarely possible to decide what key the pieces are in, once they are under way, and there is never much consistency between the key of a 'solo', if such they are, and what the rest of the band is about. The electric keyboards (with Young drafted in to play his distinctive clusters) create a shimmer out of which Miles stabs out some of his most maximal trumpet playing on record, hordes of ideas packed together into a relatively small space on 'Miles Runs The Voodoo Down' and 'Bitches Brew'. Zawinul and McLaughlin don't play on every track, but the naming of a piece after the guitarist suggests how important he became to this sound. Again, the whole package is less of a performance in the old-fashioned sense than an artefact, the details of which are secondary to the overall effect. And that – for all the sheer awkwardness of some passages and the internal inconsistency of the music – is shattering.

***(*) Big Fun

Columbia CK 63973 2CD *Davis; Carlos Garnett, Steve Grossman, Wayne Shorter (ss); Bennie Maupin (bcl); Chick Corea, Herbie Hancock, Lonnie Smith (p); Joe Zawinul (p, org); John McLaughlin (g); Khalil Balakrishna, Bihari Sharma (sitar, tambura); Harvey Brooks, Ron Carter, Michael Henderson, Dave Holland (b); Billy Cobham, Jack DeJohnette, Al Foster (d); Airto Moreira (perc).* 11/69–6/72.

Recorded during what was perhaps the most intensely productive period of his life, this wasn't released until four years after the earliest of the sessions, by which time Miles had declared himself bored with the music, stating with unmistakable emphasis that he was already somewhere else. The period after *Bitches Brew* wasn't so much a time of consolidation as one of further exploration and redefinition. The elements of the music are firmly in place, and if this is a less powerful set than its predecessor that is merely because it lacks the sudden, alienating wallop, already seems almost familiar. The key elements of the sound are in place: a distorted, almost pain-racked trumpet, the dissonant bleat of soprano saxophone, electric keyboards, thumping, funk-laden bass and a great slew of percussion. The medley of 'Great Expectations'/'Muhler Laranja' is titanic, a huge slab of electric sound. 'Go Ahead John' is again focused on the British guitarist who landed on Miles's world and found himself at home there. 'Ife' is an African tapestry, brightly coloured but also dark and dangerous. This may very well be the least-known item in the whole Miles Davis discography. It certainly isn't the best thing he ever did, but it is absolutely of its moment, and hard to overlook.

**** Jack Johnson

Columbia 471003 *Davis; Steve Grossman (ss); Herbie Hancock (ky); John McLaughlin (g); Michael Henderson (b); Billy Cobham (d).* 1 & 11/70.

A hugely underrated item in the canon, to a large extent it resolves some of the unfinished business of *Bitches Brew*. Made for a movie soundtrack, like *L'Ascenseur pour l'échafaud* before it, *Jack Johnson* offers a perfect example of Miles's imagination being channelled and focused by a project. The opening track, 'Yesternow' (one side of the original LP), has a boiling intensity that perfectly matches the clubbing power and cat-like grace Johnson showed in the boxing ring. Miles was, of course, greatly interested in the fight game and he appreciated the social and cultural dimension of Johnson's life story as well. The later session, recorded in the autumn, is more spacious and delicate, an almost perfect balance to the first half. It may well be that, in time to come, this will be regarded as one of the trumpeter's finest statements (he is playing fantastically well, with a huge, confident tone) and *Bitches Brew* consigned to the ambiguous ranks of failed masterpieces.

**** Live–Evil

Columbia C2K 65135 2CD *Davis; Gary Bartz (as, ss); Steve Grossman (ss); John McLaughlin (g); Chick Corea, Herbie Hancock, Joe Zawinul (p); Keith Jarrett (p, org); Ron Carter, Michael Henderson, Dave Holland (b); Khalil Balakrishna (sitar); Billy Cobham, Jack DeJohnette (d); Airto Moreira (perc); Hermeto Pascoal (p, v); Conrad Roberts (v).* 2, 6 & 12/70.

There was the slim, centred aesthete called Miles Davis, and there was the dark monster from the id called Selim Sivad, presiding deity of this boilingly intense, unremitting record. 'What I Say', which dominates the latter part of the first disc, is perhaps the most extreme performance Miles was ever to record, one of four tracks on this double set recorded at the Cellar Door in Washington, DC. Some have suggested that the presence of John McLaughlin, not at this time part of the regular gigging group, had a negative impact. Certainly the studio tracks without the Englishman's presence have a very different feel, a quieter and more centred sound on 'Selim' and 'Nem Um Talvez' (albeit both very brief) which makes one wonder if this is the case. Davis looks for a dense, almost sculptural sound in which layers of keyboard clusters generate a shifting, swampy undertow, difficult to penetrate, hard to resist. Abdul Mati's disturbing, surreal cover art contributes more than a little to the impact of this record, its juxtaposition of affirmative beauty and perverse ugliness. Not many records of the time remain so compulsively disturbing, and so unexpectedly beautiful.

***(*) Black Beauty

C2K 65138 2CD *Davis; Steve Grossman (ss); Chick Corea (p); Dave Holland (b); Jack DeJohnette (d); Airto Moreira (perc).* 4/70.

***(*) At Fillmore

C2K 65139 2CD *As above, except add Keith Jarrett (org).* 6/70.

Miles found himself – and jazz – a new audience in 1969 and 1970, appearing on stages more familiarly graced by Jefferson Airplane and the Grateful Dead. These two sets, from the Fillmores West and East respectively, extended the *Bitches Brew* formula: churning rhythm, staccato trumpet stabs, swirling harmonic colours and splashes. The material is repetitive, the treatments constantly shifting. 'Bitches Brew', 'Sanctuary', 'It's About That Time' and, less expectedly, the standard 'I Fall In Love Too Easily' appear several times across both albums. The big difference is the recruitment of Jarrett as an organist between April and June, a richness of texture that enhances the music enormously, though in every other respect the West Coast date is better.

***(*) Get Up With It

Columbia C2K 63970 2CD *Davis; Sonny Fortune (as, f); Carlos Garnett, John Stubblefield (as); Steve Grossman (ss); David Liebman (f); Wally Chambers (hca); Cedric Lawson (p, org);*

Herbie Hancock, Keith Jarrett (ky); Pete Cosey, Cornell Dupree, Dominique Gaumont, Reggie Lucas, John McLaughlin (g); Khalil Balakrishna (sitar); Michael Henderson (b); Billy Cobham, Al Foster, Bernard Purdie (d); Airto Moreira, Mutume, Badal Roy (perc); additional brass and rhythm arrangements by Wade Jarcus and Billy Jackson. 70–74.

Miles's first attempt to make Ellington dance with Stockhausen. Dedicated to the recently deceased Duke and dominated by a huge, mournful tribute, *Get Up With It* is more coherent than its immediate predecessors and very much more challenging than its marginal reputation would suggest. Recorded over a period of four years, and put together very much after the fact, it traces Miles's growing interest in a whole range of apparently irreconcilable musics. In his ghosted autobiography, he explains his attachment to Sly Stone's technologized Afro-funk on the one hand and Stockhausen's brooding music-as-process on the other. What united the two, beyond an obvious conclusion that pieces no longer needed to end or be resolved, was the idea that instrumental sound could be transformed or mutated almost infinitely and that the interest of a performance could be relocated from harmonic 'changes' and settled on the manipulation of sound textures over a moving carpet of rhythm. Since *Bitches Brew*, and very noticeably on an album like *Jack Johnson*, Miles had been willing to consider the studio and the editing suite a further instrumental resource. With *Get Up With It* and the two live albums that follow, Miles went a step further, putting together bands that create similar phases and process-dominated 'improvisations' in real time.

There is a conventional wisdom that Miles's trumpet-playing was at a low ebb during this period: health problems are adduced to shore up the myth of a tortured genius robbed of his truest talent, clutching at even the most minimal musical opportunities. Even those who *had* heard the mid-1970s albums, which acquired an added mystique by being the last before Miles's five-year 'retirement', were apt to say that he 'no longer played trumpet'. Though distorted by wah-wah pedals and constantly treading water in its own echo, Miles's horn was still doing precisely what the music required of it; the same applied to his resort to organ ('Rated X') and piano ('Calypso Frelimo'). The poorer tracks ('Maishya' and 'Red China Blues' start off very late-nite) give only a misleading representation of how finely balanced Miles's radical populism actually was; a live version of 'Maishya' from the infamous Osaka gig is altogether tougher. The essence of the 'new' Miles is to be found on the Duke composition, 'He Loved Him Madly', a swarthy theme that sounds spontaneously developed, only gradually establishing a common pulse and tone-centre but replete with semi-conscious, almost dreamed references to Ellington's work. 'Honky Tonk', by contrast, is an actual throwback to the style and personnel of *Jack Johnson*. Though put together piecemeal and with Miles apparently willing to let Teo Macero edit greater or lesser chunks out of extended performances, *Get Up With It* is of considerable historical importance, looking forward not just to the apocalyptic live performances of 1975 but to the more polished and ironic pop-jazz of the comeback years.

**(*) On The Corner

Columbia CK 63980 *Davis; Teo Macero (as); David Liebman, Carlos Garnett (ts); Chick Corea, Herbie Hancock, Harold I Williams (ky); David Creamer, John McLaughlin (g); Collin Walcott (sitar); Michael Henderson (b); Badal Roy (tabla); Jack DeJohnette (d); William W Hart (d, perc); Don Alias, Mtume (perc).* 72.

The notorious Corky McCoy cover, featuring Miles's new constituency of latter-day zoot-suiters, Afros, gays, steatopygous chicks in hot-pants, and Willie The Pimp look-alikes. The trumpet has a flex and plug. The wah-wah pedal remains firmly depressed throughout. The critics hated it. Mostly they were right. *On The Corner* is pretty unrelieved, chugging funk, and one has to dig a little bit for the experimental subtleties that lie in Miles's most unpromising records. Where electronics gave him a sinister, underground sound at the apocalyptic Osaka concert documented on *Agharta* and *Pangaea*, here the sound is tinny and unfocused. The supporting cast is also questionable. Garnett was to have something of a solo career on the back of his association with the great man, but he never convinces in this company.

***(*) Dark Magus

Columbia C2K 65137 2CD *Davis; David Liebman (ts, ss); Azar Lawrence (ts); Peter Cosey, Dominique Gaumont, Reggie Lucas (g); Michael Henderson (b); Al Foster (d); Mtume (perc).* 3/74.

Recorded in Carnegie Hall – but, oh, how very different from 13 years earlier. This was a further variation. *Out* the electric sitar, *in* a third guitarist, *out* every last vestige of the cool poet who had recorded *In A Silent Way*, and *in* the dark abstractionist who was to turn in *Agharta* and *Pangaea*, both recorded and released in Japan a year later. *Dark Magus* is divided into four parts, thematically non-identical but so closely related that they sound, and should sound, like aspects of some great granitic slab. Nothing to separate 'Moja', 'Wili', 'Tatu' and 'Nne' but shadings and striations of sound and, as one gets to know these recordings better, one becomes almost fixated on the tiniest inflexions. Which is where Miles enthusiasts will find meat and drink in this.

***(*) Agharta

Columbia 467897 2CD *Davis; Sonny Fortune (as, ss, f); Pete Cosey (g, syn, perc); Reggie Lucas (g); Michael Henderson (b); Al Foster (d); Mtume (perc).* 2/75.

**** Pangaea

Columbia 467087 2CD *As above.*

It bears repeating: Miles's trumpet-playing on these bruising, unconscionable records is of the highest and most adventurous order, not the desperate posturing of a sick and cynical man. The use of a wah-wah pedal – routinely interpreted as a sign of creative failure – is often fantastically subtle, creating surges and ebbs in a harmonically static line, allowing Miles to build huge melismatic variations on a single note. The truth is that the band, Fortune apart, aren't fully understanding of the leader's conception; Henderson ought to be on the case by this stage but he tends to plod, and the two guitarists are apt to get off on long, spotlit solos that are almost laughably tame and blustery when set alongside Miles's knife-fighter reserve and reticence.

A re-run 'Maishya' and a long edit from the *Jack Johnson* theme (miscredited on the original release of *Agharta*) underline the importance of two underestimated earlier albums, *Live–Evil* and *Get Up With It*. The idiom scarcely touches any longer on

European norms, adding Stockhausen's conception of a 'world music' that moves like creeping tectonic plates ('Pangaea' and 'Gondwana', the other great slab of sound, are the names palaeogeographers give to the primeval super-continents) to Afro-American popular forms, though it should be pretty clear that Sly Stone has by this stage been left as far behind as bebop. 'Gondwana' is the most coherent performance on either album. It opens on Fortune's suprisingly delicate flute and proceeds trance-like, with Miles's central trumpet episode bracketed by shimmering organ outlines and sullen, percussive stabs. It is difficult music to cut into slices and wrap. Key centres are only notional and deceptive; most of the rhythmic activity – unlike Ornette's Prime Time bands, which were revving up around this time – takes place along a single axis, but with considerable variation in the intensity and coloration of the pulse; the solos – like Weather Report's – are constant but also inseparable from the main thrust of the music. There is a growing appreciation of these admittedly problematic recordings (which were originally considered worthy of release only in Japan) but time will tell how significant they are in the overall trajectory of Miles's music.

****(*) The Man With The Horn**

Columbia 468701 *Davis; Bill Evans (ss); Barry Finnerty (g); Rod Hill (g, v, ky); Robert Irving III (p, ky); Felton Crews, Marcus Miller (b); Al Foster, Vince Mendoza (d); Sammy Figueroa (perc).* 81.

***** We Want Miles**

Columbia 469402 *Davis; Bill Evans (ss); Mike Stern (g); Marcus Miller (b); Al Foster (d); Mino Cinelu (perc).* 6 & 7/81.

***** Star People**

Columbia 25395 *As above, except add John Scofield (g), Tom Barney (b).* 83.

This is perhaps the period in Miles's career that most urgently requires reassessment. Yes, he had been ill and out of circulation. No, these are not classic records. In retrospect, though, they sound much closer in spirit to the Miles of 1960 than to the Miles of 1970. Selim Sivad has been exorcized and, though at moments his remnant sounds like a mere husk, there is a lot going on musically even in Miles's foreshortened, almost minimal statements. 'Back Street Betty' sounds as if it might have been around for more than a decade, and the cheeky 'Jean-Pierre' which accompanies it on *The Man With The Horn* was to become a concert staple in these years, reappearing on the live *We Want Miles*. There's a bravura pastiche on a theme from *Aida*, apparently a remnant of a plan to make a full-scale operatic record on the lines of the great suites with Gil. In addition, and rarely for this period, a standard, too, a feeling interpretation of 'My Man's Gone Now' which gives the lie to the notion that the trumpeter had lost his jazz chops along the way.

Star People has long been a favourite of ours. Though never a big critical or commercial success, it stands out in this period as one of the first unambiguous signs that Miles was trying to reinscribe himself in a jazz tradition. Punctuated by pre-recorded organ interludes, it mixes swing-era choruses over Motown riffs, dark blues shapes and passages that seem to hark all the way back to Buddy Bolden. An astonishing performance, marred by cluttered arrangements and a fuzzy mix.

****(*) Decoy**

Columbia 468702 *Davis; Branford Marsalis (ss); John Scofield (g); Darryl Jones (b); Robert Irving III (syn); Al Foster (d); Mino Cinelu (perc).* 84.

Something of a dud. *Decoy* was recorded up in Canada, where Davis had sensationally snubbed the trumpet star of the new generation, Wynton Marsalis. Miles's curiously ambivalent attitude to saxophonists (perhaps less curious from a man who had played with Charlie Parker and John Coltrane) is underlined by the insulting underuse of the elder Marsalis brother. The sound is hard, brittle and unlovely, and there are passages when almost anyone might be playing, or even no one, so programmed and pre-set is the sound. One has to listen long and hard for brief glimpses of what had made Miles great, and when they come they are lost in a drab electronic landscape as featureless as a neon arcade.

*****(*) You're Under Arrest**

Columbia 468703 *Davis; Bob Berg (ss); Robert Irving III (ky); John McLaughlin, John Scofield (g); Darryl Jones (b); Al Foster (d); Steve Thornton (perc); Marek Olko, Sting (v).* 85.

The final studio release with Columbia (issued with a preposterous cover shot of a sick-looking Miles posing grouchily with what looks like a toy long-stock pistol) has acquired classic status on the strength of his loveliest latter-day transformations of pop material. His version of Cyndi Lauper's 'Time After Time', a medium-tempo waltz, is straightforwardly lovely, etched in melting top notes and passionate sours; but the finest performance on the record is the version of Michael Jackson's 'Human Nature'. The title-track is set up with some engaging 'read him his rights' / 'you got one phone call' nonsense from the guest vocalists and there's some steaming funk on 'Katia'. McLaughlin and Scofield vie for attention, but the dominant sound is the solid whoomph of Darryl 'The Munch' Jones's thumb-slap bass. Not jazz as we know it, Jim, but a hugely entertaining record and a happier end to the long, tempestuous association with Columbia than *Decoy* would have been.

****** Aura**

Columbia 463351 *Davis; Palle Bolvig, Perry Knudsen, Palle Mikkelborg, Benny Rosenfeld, Idrees Sulieman, Jens Winther (t, flhn); Jens Engel, Ture Larsen, Vincent Nilsson (tb); Ole Kurt Jensen (btb); Axel Windfeld (tba, btb); Niels Eje (ob, eng hn); Per Carsten, Bent Jaedig, Uffe Karskov, Flemming Madsen, Jesper Thilo (reeds); Thomas Clausen, Ole Koch-Hansen, Kenneth Knudsen (ky); John McLaughlin, Bjarne Rouype (g); Lillian Tbernqvist (hp); Niels-Henning Orsted Pedersen, Bo Stief (b); Lennart Grustvedt, Vince Wilburn (d); Marilyn Mazur, Ethan Weisgard (perc); Eva Thaysen (v).* 85.

Miles's first big-band record since the Gil Evans projects of the later 1950s. In 1984 he had been awarded the prestigious Sonning Prize by the Danish government, an accolade normally accorded only to 'straight' composers. In recognition, and as a personal tribute to the influence of Miles's music, Palle Mikkelborg composed 'Aura' and persuaded the trumpeter to appear as soloist. CBS promptly sat on it for three years, further evidence of their cavalier treatment of one of the unquestionably great artists of the twentieth century. A suite of eight 'colour poems' with an introduction and wonderful variation on 'Red', the piece is built up out of a slightly bizarre ten-tone scale – stated by John McLaughlin in a brief 'Intro' – derived from the letters of Miles's name. This in turn yields a chord and a basic theme, which is then transformed by all the usual processes of serial composition, inversion, retrograde inversion and so on, and also by Miles's familiar colouristic alchemy. Miles's inclusion clearly lent the music a considerable fillip and some much-needed critical cachet, and Mikkelborg (a gifted trumpeter with a particular expertise in electronic shadings and transformations) might just as readily have taken the lead role himself. It is, though, marvellous to have Miles ranged against a large group again, and Mikkelborg's arrangements (particularly on 'Green', which is an explicit attempt to recapture his classic sound) are clearly influenced by Gil Evans's grouping of instruments and interest in pitching top and bottom lines against one another in unusual sonorities.

Miles's duet with NHOP on 'Green' is one of the finest moments on the record, spacious and delicately executed. He's almost as good on 'Orange', which makes specific references to the *Bitches Brew* period, and on the two versions of 'Red'/'Electric Red', where he tries out the theme a second time, muted, and moves outside the structure entirely to lay bright watercolour washes over the insistent riff. Mikkelborg's intention seems to have been to inscribe Davis yet more firmly into the history of American music. The solitary musings of 'White' are repeated with Mikkelborg's carefully stacked horns on 'Yellow' (which also restates the M.I.L.E.S D.A.V.I.S row) drawing the trumpeter into the musical community that he helped to create. There are more or less explicit references to such touchstones as *Kind Of Blue* and *Sketches Of Spain*. There are also plenty of generic references: hints of bebop harmony, subtle modes and, on 'Blue', reggae. The closing 'Violet' is a blues, an idiom to which Miles returned more and more frequently in his last years. It's also, though, a tribute to two former Sonning winners, Igor Stravinsky and Olivier Messiaen (whose colour mysticism seems to have made an impact on Mikkelborg). In referring to them, and to Charles Ives on the pivotal 'Green', the Dane also allows Miles to take his place in a broader musical continuum, not just in the condescending by-way that came to be known (though not by Miles) as jazz. Unique among the later records, and all the more precious for it, *Aura* has an unexpected power to move.

*** Tutu

Warner Brothers 925 490 *Davis; George Duke, (p, ky); Adam Holzman, Bernard Wright (ky); Michal Urbaniak (vn); Marcus Miller (b, ky); Omar Hakim (d, perc); Paulinho Da Costa, Steve Reid (perc).* 86.

***(*) Amandla

Warner Brothers 925 873 *Davis; Kenny Garrett (as); Rick Margitza (ts); Jean-Paul Bourelly, Michael Landau, Foley McCreary, Billy Spaceman Watson (g); Joe Sample (p); Joey DeFrancesco, George Duke (ky); Marcus Miller (ky, b, etc.); Al Foster, Omar Hakim, Ricky Wellman (d); Don Alias, John Bigham, Mino Cinelu, Paulinho Da Costa, Bashiri Johnson (perc).* 89.

You know the feeling when some favourite movie or TV series is reincarnated as an animated cartoon: somehow something quite essential isn't there. Nothing to do with Warner Brothers, who probably couldn't quite believe their luck, picking up Miles at this point in his career, but there is something of that about these records. The first post-CBS records were an uneasy blend of exquisite trumpet miniaturism and drab cop-show funk, put together with a high production gloss that camouflaged a lack of real musical substance. Though he was acutely sensitive to any perceived put-down by middle-class whites, little was known about Miles's specific political beliefs at this or any previous time. The Jack Johnson tribute – written for someone else's project – was as close as he came to an explicit statement of solidarity. Talking to a French interviewer, he said that naming albums for Bishop Desmond Tutu and after the African National Congress rallying cry – 'Amandla' – was the only contribution he felt he could make to the liberation struggle in South Africa; Miles also namechecks Mandela on 'Full Nelson', though this is also a reference to his own earlier 'Half Nelson' and simultaneously signals a reawakening interest in blues and bop harmonies which was to occupy him for much of the rest of his life.

The horn sounds as deceptively fragile as ever, but it's made to dance in front of shifting sonic backdrops, put together in a cut-and-paste way that succeeds very much better on *Amandla* than on the earlier set. 'Big Time' and 'Jilli' have a hectic, thudding energy, while at the other end of the spectrum Miles's dedication to the late 'Mr Pastorius' catches him in convincingly lyrical form. There's no mistaking the ultimate provenance of Marcus Miller's vivid techno-arranging. In particular, his use of synthesized percussion on 'Hannibal' recalls 'La Nevada' on Gil Evans's *Out Of The Cool*, an influence that became explicit to the point of pastiche later.

*** Music From Siesta

Warner Brothers 925 655 *Davis; Marcus Miller (ky, b, etc.).*

The film, based on a novel by Patrice Chaplin, has long been forgotten (though it isn't anything like as bad as was suggested at the time) but the music survives and stands up very convincingly on its own. By this time, Miller had taken over writing and arranging duties almost completely and Miles was beginning to take on an unaccustomed Grand Old Man demeanour and series of guest appearances. The trumpeter's free-hand Spanish sketches inevitably conjure up an earlier attempt to evoke that 'tinge'. In many respects, this is a tighter, more focused and more imaginatively marshalled project than *Sketches Of Spain*, though one obviously misses the blood-orange richness of Evans's orchestrations. Appealingly abstract, if a little undemanding; we think better of this one every time we hear it.

**(*) Ballads

Columbia 461099 *Personnels as for Quiet Nights, Seven Steps To Heaven, In Person, Friday Night At The Blackhawk.* 61–63.

The 'European menu' album for those 'who don't like anything too spicy'. The music is lovely, of course, but one immediately misses the lights and shades, the change of pace and mood that was so much a part of the story.

***(*) Mellow Miles

Columbia 469440 *Personnels as for Columbia.*

When Norman Mailer – a big Miles fan and another would-be boxer – was asked if he thought he was getting mellower with age, he replied, 'Well, I guess I'm about as mellow as old camembert.' There's still a sharp whiff of risk and enterprise coming up off this outwardly bland, life-style packaging of late-night Miles hits, but it's unlikely in itself to send anyone hitherto unfamiliar with the trumpeter's work scuttling out to buy a copy of *Milestones* or *Agharta*. There is, needless to say, nothing from the later work included here, but it does kick off with 'Miles' (aka 'Milestones') and runs a reasonably predictable course from there: 'So What' and 'Freddie Freeloader' from *Kind Of Blue*, 'Summertime' and 'It Ain't Necessarily So' from *Porgy And Bess*, the title-tune of *Miles Ahead*, 'Round Midnight' and 'Bye Bye Blackbird' from *Someday My Prince Will Come* and, jumping a whole generation, 'Human Nature' and the exquisite 'Time After Time' from *You're Under Arrest*. Reasonable value, but most true believers will still prefer their own mental compilation of 'Hostile Miles'.

*** Dingo

Warner Brothers 7599 26438 *Davis; Chuck Findley, Oscar Brashear, Ray Brown, George Graham (t); George Bohannon, Thurman Green, Jimmy Cleveland, Lew McGreary, Dick Nash (tb); David Duke, Marnie Johnson, Vince De Rosa, Richard Todd (frhn); Buddy Collette, Kenny Garrett, Bill Green, Jackie Kelso, Marty Krystall, Charles Owens, John Stephens (reeds); Kei Akagi, Michel Legrand, Alan Oldfield (ky); Mark Rivett (g); Foley McCreary, Abraham Laboriel, Benny Rietveld (b); John Bigham, Harvey Mason, Alphonse Mouzon, Ricky Wellman (d, perc).* 91.

Though Rolf de Heer's movie will undoubtedly draw a little extra resonance from the casting of Miles as trumpeter/shaman 'Billy Cross', the music may again be a little more vital than the images it was written to accompany, as with *Siesta*. Michel Legrand's scores and orchestrations are predictably slick and rather empty, but there are some nice touches and a couple of sly echoes (presumably intentional) of Miles's work for Louis Malle's *L'Ascenseur pour l'échafaud*. Lest anyone be alarmed at what has happened to Miles's lip on the opening 'Kimberley Trumpet', solo duties are shared with Chuck Findley in the role of 'Dingo Anderson'. Attractive, but a slightly sad memorial of a dying man. This was Miles's last year on the planet, and it seems a pity to begin it so far from home, at the opposite side of the world from Alton, Illinois.

*** Doo-Bop

Warner Brothers 7599 26938 *Davis; Easy Mo Bee, J.R, A. B Money (v); other personnel unspecified.* 91.

Almost the end. Perhaps inevitably, it isn't of earth-shaking significance but, equally predictably, it finds Miles taking another ostensibly rejuvenating stylistic turn. Unfortunately, Easy Mo Bee's doo-wop/rap stylings are so soft-centred and so lyrically banal as to deny 'The Doo-Bop' and almost anything else on the record any real credibility: 'Let's kick a verse for man called Miles / Seems to me his music's gonna be around for a long while / 'Cuz he's a multi-talented and gifted musician / Who can play any position'. Right.

Neither 'Blow' nor the 'posthumous' 'Fantasy', compiled after Miles's death, offer much in the way of succour. It seems that Miles brought in material recorded in the late 1980s and known as the RubberBand session, so this final set might be likened to the grab-bag approach of *Get Up With It*, or indeed to the *ex post facto* constructions of Teo Macero, except that in this case no discernible musical nous is in evidence, no real creative energy expended. Miles plays well and with surprising aggression in places, but the backgrounds are uniformly trite and the samples (from Kool & The Gang, James Brown, Donald Byrd's 'Street Lady', Gene Ammons's 'Jungle Strut', among others) are used with an almost perverse lack of imagination. As a farewell to the studio, it's a severe disappointment.

*** Miles Davis & Quincy Jones Live At Montreux

Warner Brothers 45221 *Davis; Miles Evans, Lew Soloff (t); Benny Bailey, John D'Earth, Wallace Roney, Ack Van Rooyen, Marvin Stamm, Jack Walrath (t, flhn); Roland Dahinden, Conrad Herwig, Tom Malone (tb); David Bargeron, Earl McIntyre (tb, euph); Dave Taylor (btb); Alex Brofsky, John Clark, Claudio Pontiggia, Tom Varner (frhn); Howard Johnson (tba, bs); Sal Giorgianni (as); Bob Malach (ts, f, cl); Larry Schneider (ts, ob, f, cl); Jerry Bergonzi (ts); Alex Weber (cl); Christian Gavillet, Roger Rosenberg (bcl, bs); Xavier Duss, Judith Wenziker (ob); Reiner Erb, Christian Rabe (bsn); Xenia Schindler (hp); George Gruntz, Dave Seghezzo, Tilman Zahn (p); Delmar Brown, Gil Goldstein (ky); Carlos Benavent, Mike Richmond (b); Kenwood Dennard, Grady Tate (d).* 7/91.

His last bow. Miles and Quincy had never worked together. For years the trumpeter had refused to retread his great material. Presto! The ultimate wish-list booking for a 25th anniversary event, something that would galvanize Montreux like nothing else. It was clear that Miles was ailing at the time, and his solos often find him out of breath (though not of ideas) and lacking in any real physical or creative stamina. The arrangements are grandly overdone, but there's no mistaking the rapturous nature of the reception from the Montreux crowd. It was a career retrospective up to *Sketches Of Spain*. After 'Boplicity' from *Birth Of The Cool*, the band launches into medleys from *Miles Ahead* and *Porgy And Bess*. It doesn't take long to recognize that Quincy Jones is no Gil Evans, and it's a pity that the smaller Evans group (a ghost band by this stage, alas) couldn't have been entrusted with the music instead of the huge George Gruntz Concert Jazz Band (*and* guests), who play with typical precision but with the sort of dead-centredness one expects of studio house-bands. Jones hails Miles Davis as a 'great painter' and that is exactly what he was. He left some masterpieces, some puzzling abstracts, and a pile of fascinating sketches. The Leonardo of our time.

**** Panthalassa: The Music Of Miles Davis, 1969–74

Columbia CK 67909 *Personnels as for Columbia albums, 1969–74; assembled by Bill Laswell.* 97.

*** Panthalassa: The Remixes

Columbia 69897 *As above; remixes by various hands.* 98–99.

There was every good reason to fear the heresies of the epigoni, and yet in the event this is a classic Miles Davis album, created not as pastiche but out of the material he left behind, and according to methods that he and Teo Macero had pioneered. Laswell was given access to the original masters – and who knows what must have gone on in smoky rooms before the final signature was given? – and assembled a magnificent collage out of the work of the electric period. 'In A Silent Way' begins mysteriously and majestically, only slowly coming into focus as the theme one remembers and loves. There are huge, stretched passages which bear only tangential relation to the original, but they are unmistakable for all that. The material from *Agharta*, transformed into a vast chthonic dub, is magnificent and must have had Miles smiling in whatever heaven he currently occupies. Similarly, 'He Loved Him Madly', the trumpeter's tribute to the only other jazz musician who rivals him for sheer grace and inventiveness, Duke Ellington, is definitively reconstructed. Some were sceptical and suggested that this was a catchpenny gimmick, designed to wring a few more dollars out of Columbia's holding. In fact, it is a record that Miles would have been proud to make. For a score of reasons, and not least because there is a technical coolness about it which no amount of reverberant production will mitigate, it will never win the affection that the source material attracts. It is, however, absolutely central to the story, and no Miles Davis fan should be without it.

Given the music culture of the time, and the kind of aesthetic Miles himself was gravitating towards in his last years, and given further the origin of many of his works as studio artefacts, it's not surprising to see Miles accorded the remix treatment. We are not on the strongest ground here, but most of these makeovers are firmly in the spirit of the original. The work of Doc Scott and Jamie Myerson on some of Miles's darkest electric musings does little more than underscore their intensity. DJ Cam should be horsewhipped for what he does to 'In A Silent Way' but, by and large, taste and good sense prevail and, this being very much a vinyl culture, there is an LP edition, with extra tracks.

Nathan Davis (born 1937)

TENOR AND SOPRANO SAXOPHONES

Born in Kansas, Davis went to Europe during army service in the '60s and stayed there, playing and recording, until 1969. Occasional sightings since in such company as The Paris Reunion Band, but he remains an elusive figure.

***(*) Two Originals

MPS 539082-2 *Davis; Carmell Jones, Woody Shaw (t); Francy Boland, Larry Young (p); Jimmy Woode (b); Billy Brooks, Kenny Clarke (d).* 1–9/65.

*** London By Night

DIW 813 *Davis; Dusko Goykovich (t, flhn); Jean Toussaint, Stan Robinson (ts); Kenny Drew (p); Jimmy Woode (b); Al Levitt (d).* 8/87.

Nathan Davis once commented that where he grew up in Kansas City, it wasn't hip to smoke grass or carry a knife, it was hip to be well-read and intelligent. Something of that has worn off, for Davis is one of the most thoughtful players you'll encounter round the place. He signed up with Jay McShann when still a teenager, and then went on to the University of Kansas where playing jazz was considered to be sacrilegious and was banned. Davis's self-education in the devil's music went on hold. The two albums compiled on the MPS set were recorded in Europe, where Davis sojourned in the 1960s, working with Eric Dolphy at the end of his life and generally working the scene. Two albums resulted: *Happy Girl* and *The Hip Walk*. The first of these is remarkable for the inclusion of Woody Shaw (who wrote 'Theme From Zoltan') and also Larry Young, who at this stage was still playing piano. Most of the material is written by Davis himself, who doubles on woodwind for 'The Flute In The Blues', and devises his own long, winding line on 'Happy Girl' and 'Evolution'. The later session with Carmell Jones and Francy Boland is not nearly so successful, but Davis's own character peeps through again and again, not least on the nostalgic 'That Kaycee Thing'.

It's something of a jump to the DIW set almost a quarter of a century later. The same session yielded Dusko Goykovich's own *Celebration*, and it's the quality of the largely Europe-based rhythm section that really makes the difference. The two quartet performances – 'I Thought About You' and 'But Beautiful' – are relaxed and free-swinging, with Drew's extended and almost unbarred right-hand lines rightly forward in the mix. 'Shades', arranged for three saxophones and rhythm, is far less successful, but the quintet tracks could almost be from an undiscovered Jazz Messengers tape. Goykovich's flugelhorn has a fat, luxuriant quality that blends well with Davis, and there are fine, controlled solos all round, notably on 'Dr Bu', where the Blakey/Messengers debt is most openly acknowledged.

Richard Davis (born 1930)

BASS

Played in Chicago classical orchestras as well as with Ahmad Jamal, before touring and then freelancing in New York from 1960. He had associations with artists as diverse as Eric Dolphy and Van Morrison before a long stint with the Jones–Lewis band, followed by teaching, which has only occasionally been interrupted with new recordings.

***(*) Persia My Dear

DIW 805 *Davis; Sir Roland Hanna (p); Frederick Waits (d).* 8/87.

***(*) One For Frederick

Hep CD 2047 *Davis; Cecil Bridgewater (t); Ricky Ford (ts); Sir Roland Hanna (p); Frederick Waits (d).* 7/89.

Stravinsky's favourite bass player, Davis draws heavily on the example of fellow-Chicagoan Wilbur Ware, bringing considerable rhythmic virtuosity and a tremendous range of pitches and timbres to solo performances. Whatever the merits of his pizzicato work (and there are those who find him much too mannered, relative to Ray Brown and Ron Carter), there is no one to touch him as a soloist with the bow. His *arco* statements on 'Manhattan Safari', the opening track of the excellent studio *Persia My Dear*, rather take the sting out of Hanna's funky lines, but Hanna too shares an ability to mix dark-toned swing with a sort of classical propriety, as he shows on three compositions. On the later set, recorded live at Sweet Basil, bass and piano combine particularly well for 'Misako', a Monk-influenced Davis original which also appears on the excellent *Four Play*, with Clifford Jordan, James Williams, Ronnie Burrage and Davis. The same influence is even more explicit on 'De Javu Monk', which offers probably the best representation on record of Davis's unaccompanied style, all weird intervals and changes of metre. As on the closing 'Strange Vibes' (a Horace Silver tune), Hanna comes in to balance the bassist's tendency to abstraction. The Hep album is dedicated to drummer Waits, who died four months after the recording. His introduction to 'City Bound' (and to the album) is very strong, and he turns in a fine, accelerated solo on 'Brownie Speaks', one of the stronger tracks on *Persia My Dear*.

Steve Davis

DRUMS

Contemporary American drummer with wide sideman experience in the post-bop field.

***** Explorations And Impressions**

Double-Time DTRCD-123 *Davis; Richie Beirach (p); François Moutin (b). 9/96.*

An off-the-cuff session: they literally went in, sat down, and played. It was Davis's studio and his idea, but it's Beirach who calls many of the shots, and some indication of the spontaneity is where you can hear him calling out the changes of 'Elm' to the unprepared Moutin. Fresh and enjoyable music, which sidesteps any difficulty with the circumstances. The closing medley of 'Stella By Starlight' and 'Solar' runs almost 30 minutes and is perhaps the only real indulgence.

Wild Bill Davis (1918–1995)

ORGAN, PIANO

Davis studied music in Texas and joined the Louis Jordan band in 1945, before switching to the electric organ and doing some freelance arranging. He was one of the first of the R&B school of organ players and worked as a soloist until his death.

****(*) In The Groove!**

Fresh Sound FSR-CD 308 *Davis; George Clarke (ts); Bill Jennings (g); Grady Tate (d). 59–60.*

****(*) In the Mellow Tone**

Fresh Sound FSR-CD 309 *As above. 59–60.*

Fair representations of the kind of music Davis was making at the time, small-combo tracks which are more like instrumental pop than anything with much jazz in it – they give themselves the occasional solo, but mostly these are simple renditions of familiar tunes from 'Satin Doll' on down. Despite the titles of this pair, which are drawn from the same sessions, each is a mixture of up-tempo and ballad set-pieces. Davis's most worthwhile records remain the albums he cut with Johnny Hodges in the 1960s, but these remain out of favour so far as reissues are concerned.

Walter Davis Jr (1932–90)

PIANO

In and out of the music (he even spent some time out working as a tailor), Davis never really built on his remarkable start with Charlie Parker and Max Roach. He recorded later with Archie Shepp and Sonny Rollins, but only rarely as a leader.

***** In Walked Thelonious**

Mapleshade 56312 *Davis (p solo). 87.*

*****(*) Scorpio Rising**

Steeplechase SCCD 31255 *Davis; Santi Debriano (b); Ralph Peterson (d).*

At fifty-five, Davis doesn't sound as if he has a point to prove. His long apprenticeship was coloured by the almost mystical belief that Monk and Bud Powell visited him in spirit and coloured his playing. Tinged it may be, but what is striking about his solo performances of stalwarts like 'Ruby, My Dear' and 'Crepuscule With Nellie' is that they are more thoroughly personalized than most pianists dare to suggest. 'Round Midnight' is played twice, with subtle structural changes and none of the late-nite fuzz the tune has collected over the years. A decent album by an almost forgotten player.

The trio record is interesting for the insight it offers into Davis the composer. Obviously defined by bop, he stretches the harmonic language back and forward, touching base with swing as well as pushing on – most notably on 'Four Hundred Years Ago, Tomorrow' and the title-track – into new territory. His ability to articulate complex phrases as if they were raw blues themes is as engaging as ever, but what is new and exciting about *Scorpio Rising* is how Davis unpicks and then elaborates simple structures and exposes them to an almost symphonic development.

With a broader discographical context, both albums might make greater sense and be easier to place. Davis remains a lost hero of the music in its great days; good luck to anyone who tries to hunt him up more thoroughly on record.

Wild Bill Davison (1906–90)

CORNET

Davison worked in Ohio and Chicago in the 1920s and was in Milwaukee for most of the '30s, before arriving in New York in 1941. He was quickly associated with the Condon circle and made strings albums in the '50s. From 1960 he freelanced, touring and recording relentlessly almost until his death.

*****(*) The Commodore Master Takes**

Commodore CMD 14052 *Davison; George Brunies, Lou McGarity, Vernon Brown, George Lugg (tb); Pee Wee Russell, Ed Hall, Joe Marsala, Albert Nicholas (cl); Bill Miles (bs); Gene Schroder, Dick Cary, Joe Sullivan (p); Eddie Condon (g); Bob Casey, Jack Lesberg (b); Danny Alvin, George Wettling, Dave Tough (d). 11/43–1/46.*

***** This Is Jazz**

Jazzology JCD-42 *Davison; Jimmy Archey (tb); Albert Nicholas, Edmond Hall (cl); Ralph Sutton, James P Johnson (p); Danny Barker (g); Pops Foster (b); Baby Dodds (d). 47.*

***** Showcase**

Jazzology JCD-83 *Davison; Jiri Pechar (t); Jimmy Archey, Miloslav Havranek (tb); Garvin Bushell (cl, bsn); Josef Reiman (as, cl); Karel Mezera (ts); Ivor Kratky (bs); Ralph Sutton, Pavel Klikar (p); Miroslav Klimes (g, bj); Zdenek Fibrish (tba); Sid Weiss (b); Morey Feld, Ales Sladek (d). 12/47–10/76.*

Born in Defiance, Ohio, Wild Bill Davison looks to have slung the town sign round his neck as a badge of identity. His Commodore sessions – all 24 titles neatly gathered on the recent CD – show that he was both at home and slightly uncomfortable as a Condonite. These are typically strong, no-frills Dixieland dates with notably fine work from the undersung Brunies and Wettling, among the many sidemen, and Davison's punchy lead fits well; but you can tell, at times, that he'd rather be going his own way than acting as a purely nominal leader of a gang that really belonged to Eddie Condon.

There's more early stuff on JCD-42 and JCD-83, typical This Is Jazz fare, with a good if workmanlike band (Sutton is the outstanding player) and a frowsy Davison vocal on 'Ghost Of A Chance'. Clean sound on both releases; the second is shared with a curious 1976 session, made in a Czech castle with a local team who aren't up to the challenge, even if Davison sounds in good spirits.

*****(*) Wild Bill Davison & His Jazzologists**
Jazzology JCD-2 *Davison; Lou McGarity (tb); Tony Parenti (cl); Hank Duncan (p); Pops Foster (b); Zutty Singleton (d).*

****(*) Rompin' And Stompin'**
Jazzology JCD-14 *Davison; Bruce Gerletti (tb); John McDonald (cl, ts); Bob Butler (p); Eddie Collins (g); Jim Joseph (tba); Frank Foguth (d).* 10/64.

***** Surfside Jazz**
Jazzology JCD-25 *Davison; Tom Saunders (c); Guy Roth (tb); Jim Wyse (cl); George Melczek (p); Frank Harrison (b); Gene Flood (d).* 8/65.

***** After Hours**
Jazzology JCD-22 *Davison; Kenny Davern (cl); Charlie Queener (p); George Wettling (d).* 66.

****(*) Jazz On A Saturday Afternoon Vol. 1**
Jazzology JCD-37 *Davison; Wray Thomas (tb); Herman Foretich (cl); Ernie Carson, Eustis Tompkins (p); Jerry Rousseau (b); Mike Hein (d).* 6/70.

****(*) Jazz On A Saturday Afternoon Vol. 2**
Jazzology JCD-38 *As above.* 6/70.

**** Just A Gig**
Jazzology JCD-191 *Davison; Slide Harris (tb, v); Tom Gwaltney (cl); John Eaton (p); Van Perry (b); Tom Martin (d); Johnson McRee (kz, v).* 11/73.

*****(*) 'S Wonderful**
Jazzology JCD-181 *As above, except add Vic Dickenson (tb), Buster Bailey (cl), Dick Wellstood (p), Willie Wayman (b), Cliff Leeman (d).*

***** Lady Of The Evening**
Jazzology JCD-143 Davison; various groups as above, 65–81.

***** Solo Flight**
Jazzology JCD-114 *Davison; Paul Sealey, Denny Wright (g); Harvey Weston (b).* 10/81.

Davison took every chance he had to make records, it seems, and the big run of Jazzology records contains a rather mixed bag of work. McGarity and Parenti are admirable and underrated players, and they make up a very good front line with Bill on the Jazzologists date: as righteous Dixieland goes, this is arguably the best record of the bunch. The Surf Side Six were a local band working in Detroit when Davison muscled in on their gig (a habitual occurrence) and shook the rafters on a few tunes. Nothing fancy, but some nice music. Much the same scenario with the *After Hours* date, where Bill drove by a gig where George Wettling was in charge, sat in, taped it, and counted his royalties. The footwork with Davern is rather good. *Rompin' And Stompin'* is another of his hired-gun sessions with a crew of local (as in Detroit) Dixielanders of little distinction. This one is definitely for Davison completists.

The two *Saturday Afternoon* gigs aren't very exciting either, an Atlanta group providing the backdrop for the Davison horn, and the following *Just A Gig* is just as it says, this time hailing from downtown Manassas, Virginia. Some very shaky sidemen on this one (and we don't just mean their vibrato). A couple of leftovers turn up on *'S Wonderful*, which is by a much superior group: Davison and Dickenson are a dream front line, the snarling bite of the one with the droll, loping gait of the other; if neither is quite at his best, it's a tonic after some of the other playing on these CDs. *Lady Of The Evening* is a hotchpotch collection of one session with rhythm section from 1971 and several out-takes from some of the prior dates: some strong, bruising horn on the main date, though.

Solo Flight finds him in London in 1981. Wright, Sealey and Weston make so much reverberant noise that at times even Davison has to struggle to make himself heard. It's worth the effort, though, since, despite some fluffs, he battles on with the kind of fierce licks that, rasp by rasp, made up an unrepeatable jazz persona.

***** Swinging Wild**
Jazzology JCD-219 *Davison; Bert Murray (tb); Bruce Turner (cl, as); Ronnie Gleves (p, vib); Dave Murphy (b); Tony Allen (d). circa.* 66.

*****(*) With Freddy Randall**
Jazology JCD-160 *As above, except add Freddy Randall (t), George Chisholm (tb), Lennie Felix (p), Dave Markee (b); omit Murray and Murphy. circa.* 66.

Davison enjoyed British company, and these dates (from roughly the same period) are a congenial setting for him. *Swinging Wild* was cut live at the Nottingham Dancing Slipper and the sound is dusty, but the playing has plenty of vinegar in it. Better, though, is the meeting with Randall's band. Interesting to hear Freddy alongside one of his great influences and, although he defers to Bill most of the way, they have a great scrap over 'Royal Garden Blues'. Chisholm, in excellent fettle, is a further bonus. The final four tracks are from an unidentified gig by a similar line-up.

***** Jazz Ultimate**
Jazzology JCD-241 *Davison; Lou McGarity (tb); Joe Muranyi (cl); Chuck Folds (p); Jack Lesberg (b); Cliff Leeman (d).* 12/70.

***** Wild Bill In New Orleans**
Jazzology JCD-170 *Davison; George Masso (tb); Noel Kalet (ss, cl); David Paquette (p); Ed Garland (b); Bob Bequillard (d).* 4/75.

****(*) Live At The Memphis Jazz Festival**
Jazzology JCD-133 *Davison; George 'Doc' Ryan (c); Jim Beebee (tb); Chuck Hedges (cl); Joe Johnson (p); Milt Hinton (b); Barrett Deems (d); Sherri Connor (v).* 6/82.

Still more Wild Bill from Jazzology. *Jazz Ultimate* is a good-natured, ambling set from a club in Connecticut with a band co-led by Lou McGarity. *In New Orleans* includes the reliable Masso and has explosive soprano from the little-known Kalet, which resulted in Davison ordering him to get back to the clarinet, since he didn't like the horn! The set from Memphis isn't very well balanced in terms of sound, the microphones apparently right next to the drum set, and Sherri Connor is more like Mae West than Bessie Smith, but Davison comes blasting through regardless. Although these are all good in their way, Davison wasn't a great one for varying his material, and all but the most intent followers of the man may feel that these are each several notches below essential.

****(*) With Fessor's Big City Jazz Band**
Storyville STCD 5525 *Davison; Otto Hansen, Verner Nielsen (t); Ole Fessor Lindgreen (tb); Elith Nykjaer (cl, as); Steen Vig (ss, ts); Jesper Thilo (ts); Ralph Sutton, Torben Petersen, Hans Kjaerby (p); Lars Blach (g); Preben Lindhart, Hugo Rasmussen, Ole Mosgaard (b); Thorkild Moller, Svend Erik Norregaard (d).* 12/73–12/78.

***** But Beautiful**
Storyville STCD 8233 *Davison; Per Carsten Petersen (as); Jesper Thilo (ts, cl); Uffe Karskov, Steen Vig (ts); Flemming Madsen (bs); Niels Jorgen Steen, Torben Munk (g); Hugo Rasmussen (b); Ove Rex (d).* 2/74.

***** Wild Bill In Denmark Vol. 1**
Storyville STCD 5523 *Davison; Ole Stolle (t); Arne Bue Jensen (tb); Jorgen Svare (cl); Bent Jaedig (ts); Jorn Jensen (p); Lars Blach (g); Jens Solund (b); Knud Ryskov Madsen (d).* 2/74–1/77.

***** Wild Bill In Denmark Vol. 2**
Storyville STCD 5524 *As above, except omit Stolle.* 2/74–7/75.

***** Wild Bill Davison With Papa Bue**
Storyville STCD 5526 *Davison; Ole Stolle (t); Arne Bue Jensen (tb); Jorgen Svare (cl, ts); Jorn Jensen (p); Lars Blach (g); Jens Solund (b); Knud Ryskov Madsen (d).* 5/75–1/77.

***** Sweet And Lovely**
Storyville STCD 4060 *Davison; strings.* 8/76.

****(*) Together Again!**
Storyville STCD 8216 *Davison; Ole Fessor Lindgreen (tb); Jesper Thilo (cl, ss, ts); Ralph Sutton (p); Lars Blach (g); Hugo Rasmussen (b); Svend Erik Norregaard (d).* 5/77.

****(*) All-Stars**
Timeless TTD 545 *Davison; Tom Saunders (t, v); Bill Allred (tb); Chuck Hedges (cl); Danny Moss (ts); Johnny Varro (p); Isla Eckinger (b); Butch Miles (d); Banu Gibson (v).* 10/86.

Storyville have been trawling through their archives for some more Davison. The first four listed above all date from a similar period in Copenhagen, where he was a frequent visitor, and there's actually little to choose between them. The tracks with Fessor Lindgreen are rather more ordinary, despite the presence of Sutton (and an uncredited harmonica player), and this merits a slightly lower rating. All three discs with Papa Bue cover several sessions and there are some excellent things in 'When It's Sleepy Time Down South', 'You Are Too Beautiful' and 'Driftin' Down The River', Bill sounding much more at home here than he did with many home-grown Dixielanders. The rhythm section in particular is good enough to keep everyone on the straight and narrow. *But Beautiful* features a similar crew and the reed team shine in particular. Davison's patented rasp and fat-free phrasing have become a little blurred by time but he seems unbothered by that issue. With the *All-Stars* album, Davison marked his arrival in the CD era. At eighty, and with an unforgiving playback, his articulation was roughening further, and the line-up and repertoire were not entirely in his usual line. His energy and raw humour are nevertheless undiminished. The singing is very so-so indeed. The inimitable snarl is present and sounds intermittently correct on the album with strings, a blissful carpet of violins that Davison, well, spits on. This, indeed, is jazz.

Which leaves the Storyville reunion with Ralph Sutton – pity, though, that this wasn't a great moment for either man. Bill sounds a bit out of sorts, the material is a little too sloppy for his tastes, and Sutton is poorly recorded. Still a few good blasts in the locker, and four alternative takes as a bonus.

Rein De Graaff (born 1942)

PIANO, KEYBOARDS

Born in Groningen, De Graaff started as a swing-mainstreamer, but his long-standing quartet with saxophonist Dick Vennik and frequent duties as an accompanist have found him as more of a hard-bopper.

***** Be-Bop, Ballads & Blues**
Timeless CD SJP 354 *De Graaff; Charlie Rouse (ts); Henk Haverhoek, Koos Serierse (b); John Engels, Eric Ineke, Leroy Williams (d).* 10/76–5/85.

***** New York Jazz**
Timeless CD SJP 130 *De Graaff; Tom Harrell (t, flhn); Ronnie Cuber (bs); Sam Jones (b); Louis Hayes (d).* 2/79.

****(*) Jubilee**
Timeless CD SJP 294 *De Graaff; Jarmo Hoogedijk (t); Bart Van Lier (tb); Dick Vennik (ts); Koos Serierse (b); Eric Ineke (d).* 2/89.

***** Nostalgia**
Timeless CD SJP 429 *De Graaff; Gary Foster, Marco Kegel (as); Barry Harris (p); Koos Serierse (b); Eric Ineke (d); The Metropole Orchestra.* 3/91–9/94.

***** Baritone Explosion!**
Timeless CD SJP 431 *De Graaff; Ronnie Cuber, Nick Brignola (bs); Koos Serierse (b); Eric Ineke (d).* 3/94.

A superb accompanist, with a real flair for the contours of a vocal line or a saxophone solo, De Graaff has rarely sounded as convincing on his own account. His chops are beyond scrutiny, but often he seems to lack a convincing plot. *Be-Bop, Ballads & Blues* is an attractive compilation of different personnels over a near-decade span, and the quintet with Harrell is gorgeous whether at an accelerated tempo ('Au Privave') or on one of the slower tracks, coaxing De Graaff into one of his spun-out, lyrical notions. *Jubilee* is a bit overpowered by co-leader Vennik's unremarkable saxophone, but even here there are good things to be found. *Nostalgia* is an entertaining mixed bag: five tunes for trio-plus-orchestra, two bouncing duets with Barry Harris and four chunks of Tristano-ism with Foster and Kegel standing in for Marsh and Konitz. The tracks with the Metropole Orchestra go straight down the middle of the road, but those with the altomen are great fun. So, in its way, is the tear-up for the two baritonists, cut at a 1994 concert in Laren. De Graaff tends to referee the event rather than trying any punches for himself, and maybe 40 rather than 64 minutes is enough of this sort of thing, but it's hard not to enjoy.

Laurent De Wilde (born 1960)

PIANO

Born in Washington, DC, to French parents, de Wilde studied piano with Mulgrew Miller and Kirk Lightsey and returned to Europe to play and record.

*****(*) The Back Burner**

Columbia 480784 *de Wilde; Eddie Henderson (t); Antonio Hart (as); Ira Coleman (b); Billy Drummond (d).* 4 & 5/95.

***** Spoon-A-Rhythm**

Columbia 487235 *de Wilde; Ira Coleman (b); Dion Parson (d); Bobby Thomas (perc).* 11/96.

These are not de Wilde's first records, but they are the only ones that may still be available outside France. A swinging, technically assured player with an imaginatively eclectic approach to the repertoire, he can be faulted only for a seeming unwillingness to let a theme alone. On *The Back Burner* he dives into 'Yesterdays' with altered chords – D flat suspended to the fore – and a superb bass introduction from Coleman, who detunes his E string to give a rumbling resonance. As befits a former philosophy student, de Wilde favours thoughtfulness and touch over speed. 'Late Bloomer' is a medium-paced original which opens up all sorts of possibilities but doesn't hector. Wayne Shorter's 'Lost' is a spacey waltz which seems to arrive in some mid-Atlantic dialect. The band is consistently excellent, with Coleman the key figure. Hart and Henderson are such individual voices that they always add a dimension to a set. Here, they are simply glorious.

Spoon-A-Rhythm somewhat lacks a horn voice, but it does throw more emphasis on de Wilde's steadily developing solo style. 'Spoon-A-Rhythm' itself is very much in the Monk manner, and more than just successful pastiche. Interestingly, almost all the tracks this time out are originals, which was perhaps over-ambitious and creates a slightly airless quality. One looks for something more familiar than 'Relaxin' At Camarillo' (which doesn't sit all that comfortably for piano, even in this arrangement) and the creaking 'Round Midnight' to apply a little light and shade.

Elton Dean (born 1945)

ALTO SAXOPHONE, SAXELLO

Began with blues bands and then with Soft Machine, 1968–72, since when he has led various bands of his own and had particular associations with pianists Keith Tippett and Howard Riley. A great inside-to-outside player with a passionate sound, at ease in most jazz situations.

***** Unlimited Saxophone Company**

Ogun OGCD 002 *Dean; Trevor Watts (as); Paul Dunmall, Simon Picard (ts); Paul Rogers (b); Tony Levin (d).* 89.

*****(*) The Vortex Tapes**

Slam CD 203 *Dean; Nick Evans (tb); Simon Picard, Jerry Underwood, Trevor Watts (sax); Howard Riley, Keith Tippett (p); Marcio Mattos, Paul Rogers (b); Tony Levin, Louis Moholo, Nigel Moris, Mark Sanders (d).* 9/90.

He gifted his name to Elton John (honestly!) and took his inspiration from the saxophone heavyweights like Trane and Joe Henderson. Along the way, assisted by a now 75-year-old King saxello, a sort of curvy soprano, he has created a sound all his own, tight-toned and highly expressive. All through his career, perhaps beginning with Ninesense in the 1970s, Dean has attempted to put together larger-scale groups. The USC is a recent incarnation, a big reed front line with tremendous depth of focus and lots of light and shade.

The Vortex sessions are inevitably more varied. They come from a short season of improvisational encounters at the north London club and they're distinguished for bringing together younger and less well-documented players with veterans like Tippett, Moholo, Rogers and Riley. They are the real stars, not to diminish the achievement of the less-experienced men. Some may feel that the language used is anachronistic rather than forward-looking but, with players of such quality, almost everything played is of interest.

*****(*) Two's And Three's**

Voiceprint VP167 *Dean; Paul Dunmall (ts); Keith Tippett (p); John Etheridge, Mark Hewins (g); Fred Thelonious Baker, Marcio Mattos, Paul Rogers (b); Tony Levin (d).* 94.

***** If Dubois Only Knew**

Voiceprint VP 194 *Dean; Paul Dunmall (ts, ss, Cmel).* 2/95.

The title isn't exactly grammatical but it gets the point across: five duos, two trios and, as it turns out, one quartet track, the only time on the disc that a second horn and a drum-kit are heard. For the most part, then, it's Dean plus strings or piano. For sheer density and idiosyncrasy of sound, the pairing with Rogers (and with Dean on the saxello) is the most impressive, but there's an innate musicality to the duet with Mattos, a deconstructed bebop idea called 'Riolity'. For some reason, bassist Fred Thelonious Baker, listed on the front, isn't credited on 'Uprising' with John Etheridge; perhaps significantly, Freddie Baker is one of the most underrated and underused figures on the British scene. The quartet track is 'The Duke', another of Dean's song-form pieces and one which reflects his long-standing engagement with Ellington. He combines wonderfully with the big-chested, throaty roar of Dunmall's tenor and the intricate patterning of Mujician men Rogers and Levin, an association that was to be very important for him in the mid-'90s. It bade fair for the duo album with Dunmall, a tougher and more concentrated listen but an excellent set; of the three long numbers, only 'The Tale Of Two Horns' sounds spontaneous. All the rest reflect the two saxophonists' abiding interest in song and structure.

*****(*) Silent Knowledge**

Cuneiform RUNE 93 *Dean; Paul Dunmall (ts); Sophia Domancich (p); Paul Rogers (b); Tony Levin (d).*

This is, in effect, an augmented Mujician, with the lyrical Domancich in for Keith Tippett. Mujician had already recorded for the Maryland-based label, who seemed to contract a considerable enthusiasm for these British improvisers – timely, given the lack of effort British promoters have shown. Dunmall wisely sticks to tenor throughout, while Dean scribbles furiously in the air. The only reservation is that the two horns tend to dominate, acoustically at least. The very fine Domancich (who isn't British, but French) isn't well served. She's a less percussive player than Tippett can be and she seems on occasion to be fighting to be heard. The key track is the long opening 'Gualchos', more than half an hour of intense improvisation. Nothing that follows quite reaches that standard, and there is a faint air of predictability hanging over the last few minutes.

****** Rumours Of An Incident**
Slam SLAMCD 223 *Dean; Roswell Rudd (tb); Alex Maguire (p); Marcio Mattos (b); Mark Sanders (d).* 10/96.

***** Bladik**
Cuneiform RUNE 92 *Dean; Roswell Rudd (tb); Paul Dunmall (ts); Keith Tippett (p); Paul Rogers (b); Tony Levin (d).* 10/96.

Not the least of Dean's achievements in recent years has been to provide a new platform for one of the great outsiders of modern jazz, trombonist Roswell Rudd. They had met almost 20 years before in Carla Bley's touring band and had maintained some contact since, even though Rudd was no longer working very regularly. These encounters were recorded, two days apart, during Rudd's trip to London in the autumn of 1996. Two very different-sounding bands, and if we give the nod to the live Slam session, it's simply because the less familiar rhythm-section has a fascination and a quality all its own. Maguire and Mattos establish an immediate rapport, and drummer Sanders, who has yet to receive proper recognition, is in magnificent form. The disc documents the beginning of the first set (nothing tentative, straight into the action) and the end of the last, by which time things are beginning to unravel a little, though the intensity is still there.

Dean positively revels and it's a shame that he sounds so much less assured two days later for the studio session. The middle track of three, of dramatically increasing length, is called 'Too Suchmuchness', and it's tempting to say that this is the problem, a faint sense of time being marked and ideas being reprocessed to fill out the session. Rudd certainly sounds less engaged than at the Vortex club two nights before and on a radio session broadcast after the trip, and the constituent elements don't cohere as one would expect, given the personnel.

****** Newsense**
Slam CD 229 *Dean; Jim Dvorak (t); Roswell Rudd, Paul Rutherford, Annie Whitehead (tb); Alex Maguire (p); Marcio Mattos (clo); Roberto Bellatalla (b); Mark Sanders (d).* 11/97.

The title is a pun, of course, but it also refers back to Dean's superb Ninesense, six paired horns and rhythm, which gigged and recorded for Ogun in the late 1970s. The new outfit is further fruit of Dean's association with Roswell Rudd. This is a superb band. The brass are excellent, with American-born Dvorak more than holding his own against the trombones. The paired bass and cello is very effective with Mattos's wailing, almost mystical sound pushed well to the fore. He and Dean are the two most provocative and moving voices in the ensemble. Dean has rarely sounded as exuberant and joyous, and the improvised 'Snap, Crackle And Pop' with Rudd and Whitehead is a delight from start to finish.

Santi Debriano

DOUBLE BASS

Debriano is a vividly melodic bass player who doesn't neglect his engine-room duties. Intelligent and thoughtful, he is reminiscent of Oscar Pettiford and of Ron Carter's more lyrical moments.

***** Circlechant**
High Note HCD 7016 *Debriano; Miri Ben-Ari (vn); Helio Alves (p); Horacio El Negro Hernandez (d); Waltinho Anastacio (perc).*

A beautifully conceived record, combining bright, sensitive originals with an eclectic programme of jazz pieces (Duke's 'Isfahan'), pop songs (T.A.F.K.A. Prince's 'Kiss'), and Astor Piazzolla's delightfully sombre 'Prelude To A Cyclical Night'. Debriano is paired in the mix with violinist Ben-Ari and set over against a busy percussion section. Alves holds the band together harmonically without bringing much of an improvisational nature, but Debriano himself is interesting enough to sustain attention. Well worth a listen.

December Jazz Trio

GROUP

Contemporary Italian trio of piano, bass and drums.

***** The Street One Year After**
Splasc(h) H 329-2 *Giorgio Occhipinti (p); Giuseppe Guarrella (b); Francesco Branciamore (d).* 8/90.

***** Concert For Ibla**
Splasc(h) H 359-2 *As above, except add Pino Minafra (t, flhn).* 1/91.

It's appropriate that the trio is democratically named, for this is genuine group-music, a highly accomplished and detailed mixture of form and improvisation, touching on jazz and avant-garde elements alike. The key player is, in many ways, Branciamore whose propulsive and momentous playing suggests an orchestral concept and who never lets the music settle into random doodling. Occhipinti varies his contributions from locked-hands passages to long, meandering lines, but seldom seems at a loss for an idea, even over some very long tracks on both records; and Guarrella plays with unassuming virtuosity. Minafra's guest role on the live recording is sometimes recorded a little remotely, and the overall sound on the studio disc is significantly superior, but both feature a great deal of interesting music.

The Dedication Orchestra

GROUP

An orchestra put together in tribute to the spirit of the original Blue Notes from South Africa.

*****(*) Spirits Rejoice**

Ogun OGCD 101 *Guy Barker, Harry Beckett, Kenny Wheeler (t); Claude Deppa (t, v); Dave Amis, Malcolm Griffiths, Radu Malfatti, Paul Rutherford (tb); Dave Powell (tba); Django Bates (eng hn); Neil Metcalfe (f); Lol Coxhill (ss, ts); Ray Warleigh (as, f); Elton Dean (as); Evan Parker, Alan Skidmore (ts); Chris Biscoe (bs); Keith Tippett (p); Paul Rogers (b); Louis Moholo (d, v).* 1/92.

*****(*) Ixesha (Time)**

Ogun OGCCD 102/103 2CD *Harry Beckett, Claude Deppa, Ian Hamer, Pat Higgs, Henry Lowther, Kenny Wheeler (t); Jim Dvorak (t, v); Marc Charig (c, thn); Dave Amis, Roland Bates, Malcolm Griffiths, Paul Rutherford (tb); Andy Grappy, Dave Powell (tba); Neil Metcalfe (f); Lol Coxhill (ss, ts); Elton Dean, Mike Williams (as); Evan Parker (ts); Sean Bergin (ts, as); Chris Biscoe (bs); Keith Tippett (p); Paul Rogers (b); Louis Moholo (d, v).* 1/94.

On New Year's Day, 1992, the less hung-over of London's jazz fans piled into the 100 Club in Oxford Street to hear a gig by a stellar band that encompassed two generations of British improvisers. The intention was to commemorate lost comrades: saxophonist Dudu Pukwana, trumpeter Mongezi Feza, composer Chris McGregor and bassists Johnny Mbizo Dyani and Harry Miller; and also to launch the Spirits Rejoice Trust, a fund to help support and develop young talent in their native South Africa. Others were being remembered, too, but it was the music of these men (with a final piece by drummer Louis Moholo, now the last surviving member of the legendary Blue Notes) that went to the making of *Spirits Rejoice*. Two days after the 100 Club gig, the orchestra reconvened in a London studio and recorded a set every bit as scorching and beautiful as the concert versions. Arrangements were by Keith Tippett (who makes a beautiful job of Miller's 'Dancing Demon'), Kenny Wheeler (ditto for the gentle 'B My Dear', one of Pukwana's most affecting themes), Eddie Parker, John Warren, Jim Dvorak, Django Bates, Radu Malfatti and John Warren. Outstanding among the soloists are Harry Beckett on Pukwana's 'Hug Pine', Jim Dvorak on his own arrangement of Feza's 'Sonia' and Evan Parker and Keith Tippett on McGregor's 'Andromeda'. A throwback to days when conglomerations like this were still economically viable, *Spirits Rejoice* has a pleasingly old-fashioned sound (albeit crisply produced by Steve Beresford with Evan Parker) and will awaken nostalgic memories of great days in British jazz.

Ixesha was recorded two years on, with a slightly different orchestra but in the same format. If anything, the compositions and arrangements are even better, nothing quite on a par with 'B My Dear', but Johnny Dyani's 'Wish You Sunshine' and McGregor's 'The Serpent's Kindly Eye' (arranged by Alex Maguire and John Warren respectively) are excellent. The only slight quibble this time relates to the playing. There's more of a Buggins's turn feel, and some tracks are overcrowded with solo spots. The best are still very fine, inevitably, but this is a long record and it might have been tackled in a more relaxed way. Both sets, though, should be considered priority purchases for anyone interested in the legacy of the five great South Africans.

Joey DeFrancesco (born 1971)

ORGAN, PIANO, SYNTHESIZER, TRUMPET, VOCAL

Himself the son of a Hammond B3 player, DeFrancesco grew up in Philadelphia and came to wider attention following the 1987 Thelonious Monk Contest. He signed to Columbia after that, but five albums for the label are already out of the catalogue. He has since worked in a John McLaughlin group and has recorded for smaller labels.

****(*) The Street Of Dreams**

Big Mo 20252 *DeFrancesco; Bruce Gates, Rick Sigler (t); Rick Lillard, Doug Elliott (tb); Dudley Hinote (btb); Pete Berrenbregge (ts); Paul Bollenback (g); Keter Betts (b); Byron 'Wookie' Landham (d).* n.d.

**** All In The Family**

High Note HCD 7021 *DeFrancesco; Bootsie Barnes, Houston Person (ts); Papa John DeFrancesco (org); Melvin Sparks (g); Byron Landham (d).* 8/97.

***** Goodfellas**

Concord CCD-4845-2 *DeFrancesco; Frank Vignola (g); Joe Ascione (d).* 3/98.

***** The Champ**

High Note HCD 7032 *DeFrancesco; Randy Johnston (g); Billy Hart (d).* 5/98.

DeFrancesco, now pushing thirty, is still a young man, but already he seems like a veteran of the scene, having numerous albums and associations already behind him. He plays respectable trumpet and handles piano with equal facility, but it's his organ-playing (he actually uses a modified C-3) which is his calling-card. His albums tend to be cheery, excitable affairs which are an entertaining listen but rarely call for regular returns to the CD system, and his tenure with Columbia doesn't seem to have led him anywhere special.

The Street Of Dreams includes a horn section to some tracks and there's a notably tough and focused version of Wayne Shorter's 'Black Nile'. What will make or break the disc for most listeners, though, are the four vocals by the leader. A departure to be sure: Messrs Smith, McGriff, Patton, McDuff, etc., never felt this particular need.

On the evidence of his recent albums, DeFrancesco is searching for context. The meeting with his dad has its moments, but the record is sonically unkempt (a surprisingly poor Rudy Van Gelder engineering job) and pretty shabby as an album. *The Champ* benefits from Johnston's supercharged solos (he sounds a sight livelier than Kenny Burrell ever did in this role) and Joey works up the appropriate heads of steam on a straightforward homage to Jimmy Smith. But there's an air of pointlessness about it all.

The most characterful of these is *Goodfellas*, from its great cover photo inwards. It celebrates Italian-American pop with such pasta-sauce-stirrers as 'Volare', 'All The Way' and 'Fly Me To

The Moon' (as well as, peculiarly, Monk's 'Evidence'!) done by a trio of popular Italian-Americans. This is a good little band and DeFrancesco, clearly enjoying the rapport, plays with a nice mix of boisterousness and sensitivity.

Buddy DeFranco (born 1923)

CLARINET

With several swing bands in the '40s, on alto and clarinet, he then worked with small groups through the 1950s. In California from the early '60s, leading a Glenn Miller ghost band from 1966 and later teaching extensively. Returned to more active recording and performing duties in the '80s. The master technician of the clarinet, but his best work is out of print and he is in much need of reputation-restoration.

***** Free Fall**

Candid CHCD 71008 *DeFranco; Victor Feldman (p); John Chiodini (g); Victor Sproles (b); Joe Cocuzzo (d).* 7/74.

***** Gone With The Wind**

Storyville STCD 8220 *DeFranco; Willie Pickens (p); Todd Coolman (b); Jerry Coleman (d).* 77.

***** The Buenos Aires Concerts**

Hep CD 2014 *DeFranco; Jorge Navarro (p); Richard Lew (g); Jorge López-Ruiz (b); Osvaldo López (d).* 11/80.

***** Mr Lucky**

Original Jazz Classics OJC 938 *DeFranco; Albert Dailey (p); Joe Cohn (g); George Duvivier (b); Ronnie Bedford (d).* 82.

(***) Mr Lucky

JLR 103.610 2CD *DeFranco; Dan Wall (p); Neil Starkey (b); Brian Childers (d).* 2/82.

***** Hark**

Original Jazz Classics OJC 867 *DeFranco; Oscar Peterson (p); Joe Pass (g); Niels-Henning Orsted Pedersen (b); Martin Drew (d).* 4/85.

***** Holiday For Swing**

Contemporary 14047 *DeFranco; Terry Gibbs (vib); John Campbell (p); Todd Coolman (b); Gerry Gibbs (d).* 8/88.

*****(*) Like Someone In Love**

Progressive PCD-7014 *DeFranco; Derek Smith (p); Tal Farlow (g); George Duvivier (b); Ronnie Bedford (d).* 3/89.

***** Five Notes Of Blues**

Musidisc 500302 *DeFranco; Alain Jean-Marie (p); Michel Gaudry (b); Philippe Cobelle (d).* 12/91.

Nobody has seriously challenged DeFranco's status as the greatest post-swing clarinettist, although the instrument's desertion by reed players has tended to disenfranchise its few exponents (and Tony Scott might have a say in the argument too). DeFranco's incredibly smooth phrasing and seemingly effortless command are unfailingly impressive on all his records. But the challenge of translating this virtuosity into a relevant post-bop environment hasn't been easy, and he has relatively few records to account for literally decades of fine work. He's also had to contend with the usual dismissals of coldness, lack of feeling etc.

His early records with Sonny Clark remain in limbo and should surely see wider release before much longer, although we are starting to have our doubts on that: a whole raft of excellent Verve material, amounting to some 15 albums, seems to be permanently out of favour with that label. Until it returns, DeFranco seems destined to be a marginalized figure. He issued little in the 1960s and '70s while teaching and bandleading, but the recent reappearance of *Free Fall* offers a glimpse of him in 1974. Nice to be reminded of Feldman's pianism, and there is a great workout on the title-track, but hints elsewhere of a modish tinge date the music. *Gone With The Wind* catches him on the hoof in Chicago with a local rhythm section, and it has its moments, but this is obviously just another gig. Pablo took DeFranco on board for a while in the '80s. *Hark* and *Mr Lucky*, both now back in the OJC programme, are spit-polished recitals which earn their stars just for the calibre of the clarinettist's impeccable delivery and musical rigour, although neither is exactly exciting. The association with the exuberant Terry Gibbs has given him a better focus and, although there are better things listed under Gibbs's own name, *Holiday For Swing* bounces through a well-chosen programme in which DeFranco creates some febrile improvisations.

Like Someone In Love is, by a squeak, perhaps the best of the more recent studio dates. The rhythm section is guided in the main by the effortless Duvivier and, with Farlow at his most beguiling in a guest role, DeFranco sounds perfectly relaxed and on top of the programme. The fast pieces show the expected flair, but it's the almost honeyed interpretations of the title-tune and 'How Long Has This Been Going On?' which impress the most.

The live concerts caught on the Hep and Musidisc releases offer lively music, and DeFranco tends to take more chances in this situation: he really takes apart 'Billie's Bounce' in Buenos Aires and responds vigorously to a pushy rhythm-section. In Paris, with the local rhythm-section, he plays a more quiescent set which includes a finely caressed 'Early Autumn'. Neither disc is ideally recorded, though, and the Argentinian players probably get more space than is comfortable.

The JLR *Mr Lucky* finds DeFranco working with the house rhythm-section at E.J.'s in Atlanta, with Wall (these days rather better known as an organist) getting plenty of space. There are some splendid examples of the clarinettist in full drive, with 'Scrapple From The Apple', to take one example, something of a copybook lesson in taking the bebop vocabulary to the clarinet. But the sound-balance nearly spoils everything, with DeFranco the least audible of the four players, and we have to offer a warning on that score.

***** Chip Off The Old Bop**

Concord CCD 4527 *DeFranco; Larry Novak (p); Joe Cohn (g); Keter Betts (b); Jimmy Cobb (d).* 7/92.

*****(*) You Must Believe In Swing**

Concord CCD 4756 *DeFranco; Dave McKenna (p).* 10/96.

*****(*) Do Nothing Till You Hear From Us!**

Concord CCD 4851 *As above, except add Joe Cohn (g).* 7/98.

Concord threw a line to players of DeFranco's sensibilities. *Chip Off The Old Bop* gets a little sting out of the presence of Cohn, who adds a flavour that was missing on the Pablo records, and DeFranco is clearly enjoying himself. The one to get, though, is the magisterial encounter with Dave McKenna, still as fiercely full-blooded as ever at the keyboard, and musician enough to have DeFranco working at his top level. 'Poor Butterfly', 'The Song Is You' and 'Invitation' are worth the admission price, and there are seven others.

There's a return match on the newest Concord, with Joe Cohn sitting in again. At 76, DeFranco is sounding immortal: there's no lessening in the technique, and he even brought a couple of originals to the date. Cohn is a respectful bystander, but his chording adds an extra layer of rhythmic propulsion which adds to the swing.

Bob Degen

PIANO

Degen had the same piano teacher as Herbie Hancock and Steve Kuhn. He has, though, gone his own way, creating melodic, horn-derived lines that are genuinely individual.

*** Catability

Enja ENJ 9332-2 *Degen; Michael Formanek (b); Bill Stewart (d).* 4/97.

Degen's Enja debut in 1976, *Sequoia Spring*, won him a cult following, most obviously in Japan, where quirky, changes-based jazz of this sort is still a quasi-religion. The present line-up is the strongest group Degen has put together since the mid-'60s, when he had a shifting trio with bassists Mark Levinson and Gary Peacock and drummer Paul Motian, an association that sadly went unrecorded. It mixes material by Ornette Coleman and Kenny Wheeler with original material and originals like 'My Old Flame'. A strong piano-trio album that bears comparison with Paul Bley's influential '60s sessions.

Jack DeJohnette (born 1942)

DRUMS, PIANO, KEYBOARDS, MELODICA

Studied piano in Chicago and kept pace with that on drums too. Joined Charles Lloyd in 1966 and was with Miles Davis, 1969–71; since then has basically freelanced at the highest levels, including Jarrett Standards Trio, and led his own diverse groups, touching on fusion and worldly music but mostly in a driven personalization of post-bop language.

*** The DeJohnette Complex

Original Jazz Classics OJCCD 617 *DeJohnette; Bennie Maupin (ts); Stanley Cowell (p); Eddie Gomez, Miroslav Vitous (b); Roy Haynes (d).* 12/68.

In past editions, bassists Ray Brown and Milt Hinton and drummer Billy Higgins have seemed to be the most frequently recorded jazz performers of all time. Every evidence is that Jack DeJohnette, still the right side of sixty, is going to overtake them in the outside lane and with time and room to spare. What sets this extraordinary musician apart, though, isn't the sheer bulk of his output but its vivid musicality. Everything he does is marked with intelligence, controlled fire and an enviable instinct for both texture and form.

This early album was recorded a mere month after his first studio date with Miles Davis, for whom he played on *Bitches Brew*, having played with Coltrane and Jackie McLean. It's a fine band he's assembled, fairly conventional in emphasis, but with Cowell and Vitous the maverick component. DeJohnette reverted to piano, on which he'd started out, playing rock'n'roll, for the first day's session. On the second, he reverts to the kit, showing a cymbal technique that owes something to Tony Williams, but much more to earlier masters like Philly Joe. Not a classic album, but an impressive start to the discography and certainly a pointer to what was to come later.

*** Sorcery

Original Jazz Classics OJCCD 1838-2 *DeJohnette; Bennie Maupin (ts, bcl); John Abercrombie, Mick Goodrick (g); Michael Fellerman, Dave Holland (b).*

Dominated by DeJohnette's 'Reverend King Suite', this is an awkwardly paced album that never quite makes sense as a totality. Whatever the circumstances of its creation, it smacks of hesitancy. Even the passionate tribute to Black America's martyr-saint fails to lift it above the ordinary. That said, Maupin and Holland are both superb, and the title-piece – part of a sequence – and 'Four Levels Of Joy' offer useful pointers to where DeJohnette wanted to go with his music.

*** Pictures

ECM 519284-2 *DeJohnette; John Abercrombie (g).* 2/76.

With typical prescience, Manfred Eicher signed DeJohnette up for ECM, recognizing the kind of totalizing musical imagination he is always drawn to. Abercrombie was a highly effective partner, and the duos are more satisfying than the solo performances with piano, organ and drums. The guitarist is typically light, fleet and subtle, spinning off lines that are both lyrical and tightly woven, even when moving with deliberation. DeJohnette himself was clearly wrestling at this time with the tension between his own sterling musicianship and the need to be a good group player, a more obviously functional sideman. Whether he has ever entirely solved this knotty equation remains unclear, but on this record he shows both sides of his creative personality very clearly.

*** New Directions

ECM 829374-2 *DeJohnette; Lester Bowie (t); John Abercrombie (g, mand g); Eddie Gomez (b).* 6/78.

Caught live on a record now deleted, this group demonstrates what an extraordinary and exciting player DeJohnette can be. He has never sounded as convincing in the studio – or at least never under his own name. The thinnish air of Willisau hasn't cut his wind, or Bowie's, though Abercrombie sounds oddly out of condition. Apart from the final, improvised 'Multi Spiliagio', where he stutters out a nervous cross-beat to DeJohnette's hissing cymbal and free-ish tom-tom accents, he remains pretty much in the background. His solos are caught a lot more cleanly in the studio, and some may well prefer the subtler sound-mix. DeJohnette himself is well recorded on the earlier record, clean and detailed but lacking the rich musicality of the live date.

***(*) Special Edition

ECM 827694-2 *DeJohnette; David Murray (ts, bcl); Arthur Blythe (as); Peter Warren (b, clo).* 3/79.

*****(*) Tin Can Alley**

ECM 517754-2 *DeJohnette; Chico Freeman (ts, f, bcl); John Purcell (as, bs, f); Peter Warren (b, clo).*

***** Album Album**

ECM 823467-2 *DeJohnette; David Murray (ts); John Purcell (as, ss); Howard Johnson (tba); Rufus Reid (b).* 84.

DeJohnette didn't so much suffer an identity crisis in these years as an ongoing difficulty in establishing a clear market identity for his music. Band and album names (and there was even one called *Untitled*) were almost deliberately flat and uninflected, all the odder when DeJohnette was trying to create a new and different group approach, marked by an interest in quite extreme instrumental sonorities – tuba, bass, piccolo, alto clarinet – and relatively complex charts. He was also able to call on some highly inventive players. Murray, who sounds wonderful on the original *Special Edition*, was just coming into his own, and Arthur Blythe, who spent the next few years in a creative trough, is still at this point playing out of his skin. 'One For Eric' is a richly inventive tribute to Dolphy, but it might have been better for a little brass; it's certainly our strong feeling that these groups – like New Directions before them – were better for the addition of a horn player, and Carroll's blunt, pugnacious approach is just right.

Purcell's multi-instrumentalism, kept in check on the two late recordings, works well in the context of the more experimental *Inflation Blues* (not available at present), softening Carroll's attack and complementing Freeman's rather linear approach. One of the least known of DeJohnette's albums, *Tin Can Alley* is certainly one of the very best, with an increasingly rock- and funk-coloured approach balancing Purcell's rather more abstract styling and Warren's imaginative, off-line patterns and rich timbre. DeJohnette's solo spot – a peril of drummer-led albums – is the vivid 'Gri Gri Man'.

*****(*) Dancing With Nature Spirits**

ECM 1558 *DeJohnette; Steve Gorn (ss, cl, f); Michael Cain (p, ky).* 5/95.

So much potential for misty mysticism here, elegantly avoided by DeJohnette's beautifully modulated new trio. Judicious use of keyboards and Gorn's horns (including the rich tone of a Bansuri flute) gives the group a generous range of sounds, and all three contribute compositional materials. Gorn's main input is 'Anatolia', the most self-consciously 'ethnic' piece in the set; Cain's 'Emanations' is, as it sounds, more abstract, but the main bulk of the record is taken up with two long, largely improvised pieces. The title-track is richly textured and surprisingly logical in its development, not at all impressionistic; 'Healing Song For Mother Earth' is a little longer, and feels more so, tailing off into reworked ideas. Again, DeJohnette concentrates on percussion, and the music gains immeasurably.

****** Oneness**

ECM 537343-2 *DeJohnette; Jerome Harris (g); Michael Cain (p); Don Alias (perc).* 1/97.

An unexpected sound-world for DeJohnette, partly a return to the early ECM days but also striking out into new territory. Cain seems an increasingly significant component, and on the two collectively composed tracks, 'Free Above Sea' and 'From The Heart', he becomes the dominant voice. DeJohnette and Alias share the opening 'Welcome Blessing', a brief, delightful introduction to an album that manages to plug into something profound and stay with it from start to finish. The closing track is almost half an hour long, seguing from a collective improvisation into DeJohnette's 'C.M.A.' and rounding out the set with a flash of passion and fire sometimes missing from his music. Our only hesitation concerns the atmospheric 'Priestesses Of The Mist', who outstay their welcome by a few minutes.

Barbara Dennerlein (born 1964)

ORGAN, KEYBOARDS

Born in Munich, Dennerlein began playing organ at eleven and was already working in clubs at sixteen. She is very well known in her home country, frequently appearing on the broadcast media, and since signing to Verve has begun to build an international audience.

***** Orgelspiele**

Bebab 003 *Dennerlein; Jorg Widmoser (vn); Peter Wolpl (g); Harald Ruschenbaum (d).* 5/84.

***** Bebab**

Bebab 250964 *Dennerlein; Hermann Breuer (tb); Allan Praskin (as); Jurgen Seefelder (ts); Joe Nay (d).* 7/85.

**** 'Live' On Tour!**

Bebab 250965 *Dennerlein; Oscar Klein (t, cl, g); Charly Antolini (d).* 1/89.

Her first releases marked Dennerlein out as a compelling, surprising performer. It's still rare enough to find anyone taking up the organ as their main keyboard – and she doesn't even sound like any of the acknowledged masters of the Hammond – but her interest in different settings is just as unusual. *Orgelspiele* has its novelty elements, including rather kitschy versions of Chopin's Prelude No. 4 and Bach's 'Jesu, Joy Of Man's Desiring', but the unusually thoughtful reading of Chick Corea's 'Spain' is intriguing, and Wolpl and Widmoser have plenty of their own to say. *Bebab* offers more conventional organ-band hard bop, chirpily performed with infectious enthusiasm. The live session with Klein and Antolini, two veterans of the German scene, is a rather odd meeting, since Dennerlein's bristling energy on the likes of 'Au Privave' sounds in a different world from that of her companions' more mainstream thinking.

*****(*) Straight Ahead!**

Enja 5077 *Dennerlein; Ray Anderson (tb); Mitch Watkins (g); Ronnie Burrage (d).* 7/88.

*****(*) Hot Stuff**

Enja 6050 *Dennerlein; Andy Sheppard (ts); Mitch Watkins (g); Mark Mondesir (d).* 6/90.

Straight Ahead! belies its title with some unexpectedly adventurous music: the blues accounts for three of the compositions, but they're blues blown open by Anderson's yawning trombone expressionism, Watkins's post-modernist funk and Burrage's wide range of rhythms. Dennerlein sounds happiest on the uptempo numbers, such as the heroically delivered title-piece, but her use of organ colour maximizes the potential of a cumbrous instrument.

Hot Stuff is in some ways more conventional, with Sheppard a less wayward spirit than Anderson, but the band cooks harder than before and the compositions – especially 'Wow!', 'Birthday Blues' and 'Polar Lights' – take organ-band clichés and turn them on their head. Mondesir's excitable drumming adds to the intensity.

***** That's Me**

Enja 7043-2 *Dennerlein; Ray Anderson (tb); Bob Berg (ts); Mitch Watkins (g); Dennis Chambers (d).* 3/92.

With some of the cast of *Straight Ahead!* coming back into the frame, this is a good but non-committal album from Dennerlein. The presence of Berg and Chambers tends to up the testosterone count at the expense of some of the freewheeling exuberance which marks the organist's best music: they beef up the tempos and the sonic weight without adding anything else of much moment. Anderson grows ever more outlandish – his 'One For Miss D' is over the top, even for him – and a finale like 'Downtown N.Y.' hints that Dennerlein might be looking towards cop-show themes as her next forte. But there is still much gutsy, entertaining playing here.

***** Take Off!**

Verve 527664-2 *Dennerlein; Roy Hargrove (t, flhn); Ray Anderson (tb); Mike Sim (ss, as, ts, bs); Mitch Watkins (g); Joe Locke (vib); Lonnie Plaxico (b); Dennis Chambers (d); Don Alias (perc).* 3/95.

With another illustrious band, Dennerlein makes her major-label move. It's to her credit that she remains the centre of the music and the main force behind it: as prodigious as her colleagues here are, nobody outplays her. On the other hand, there are times, on some of the longer, up-tempo themes, where one wishes that someone would step forward and dominate what are otherwise cheerful workouts. The most vivid piece is 'Purple', in which Dennerlein's sense of line and texture elevates an otherwise conventional ballad.

***** Junkanoo**

Verve 537122-2 *Dennerlein; Randy Brecker (t, flhn); Frank Lacy (tb); David Murray (ts, bcl); David Sanchez (ts, ss); Thomas Chapin (f); Howard Johnson (bs, tba); Joe Locke (vib); Mitch Watkins (g); Lonnie Plaxico (b); Dennis Chambers (d); Don Alias (perc).* 10/96.

Another entertaining and colourful record in which Dennerlein assembles an even more formidable line-up for nine original charts. The expected cameos by the likes of Murray and Sanchez again don't overpower the leader's own quick-witted playing; and again the music is rarely more than the sum of its parts, bubbling along but never quite finding the ignition which fired some of her earlier music.

*****(*) Outhipped**

Verve 547503-2 *Dennerlein; Darren Barrett (t); Alex Sipiagin (flhn); Ray Anderson (tb); Antonio Hart (ss); Craig Handy (ts, bs); Steve Slagle (f, af, picc-f); Steve Nelson (vib, marim); Mitch Watkins (g); James Genus (b); Jeff Tain Watts (d); Don Alias (perc); Ada Dyer, André Smith (v).* 99.

Kudos to Dennerlein for varying the sound and style of her records. This sounds like the best of her Verve entries – good tunes, apposite charts, another terrific line-up, and some witty transformations, such as 'Satisfaction' turned into a New Orleans shuffle. Out of the gang, it's her old chums Anderson and Watkins who turn in the best solos.

Karl Denson

SOPRANO, ALTO AND TENOR SAXOPHONES, FLUTE

American post-bop saxophonist, sometimes associated with the Wesley–Parker funk school but here playing in determined straight-ahead style.

****(*) Blackened Red Snapper**

Minor Music MM801024 *Denson; Ron Stout (t); Deron Johnson, Reginald Webb (p); Jeff Littleton, John Patitucci, Jesse Murphy (b); Don Littleton (d); Munyungo, Milton Commeaux (perc).* 92.

***** Herbal Turkey Breast**

Minor Music MM801032 *As above, except Nedra Wheeler (b), Tom White (d) and Bruce Cox (d) replace Webb, Jeff Littleton, Patitucci, Murphy, Don Littleton and Munyungo.* 5/93.

*****(*) Chunky Pecan Pie**

Minor Music MM801041 *Denson; Pee Wee Ellis (ts); Gust William Tsilis (mar); Dave Holland (b); Jack DeJohnette (d).* 1/94.

Denson has played with Fred Wesley's band and stands somewhere between funk and hard bop on the balance of these discs. The first two offer a boppish mix that shades from competent to good across the two albums: none of his companions is especially outstanding and, with Denson himself lacking the last ounce of inventiveness, the music never takes on a convincing enough cast. Stout copes well enough and the second record closes on a brief, piercing 'Goodbye Porkpie Hat'. This hardly prepares one for the sudden upswing of *Chunky Pecan Pie*, though. Most of the session is tenor–bass–drums in the tradition of the Rollins Vanguard sessions and, while Denson is hardly up to that model, he's plenty more inspired than before: 'Waltz For Leslie' has real assertion in every part of its 3/4 make-up, 'Heart Of The Wanderer' is a wrenching slow tune (even if it does sound like 'A Whiter Shade Of Pale') and the duel with guest star Ellis on 'Blue-Eyed Peas' is a likeable dose of tenor madness. What lifts things is the superlative playing of Holland and DeJohnette, who each play out of their skins, even if this is a sessionman ticket for both of them. DeJohnette in particular takes the roof off on 'Is It A Bell?'. Presumably coffee and *petits fours* will come next on the menu.

***** Baby Food**

Minor Music MM801048 *Denson; Ron Stout (t); Bob Cunliff (p); Nedra Wheeler (b); Tom White (d).* 6/94.

Well, not exactly. But there's nothing on this live-in-Cologne set that wouldn't slip down just as easily. Denson's regular band perform with great enthusiasm, and Stout in particular shines more brightly than he does on the studio dates. The opening number is Wayne Shorter's 'Armageddon', originally one of its composer's darkest themes, and the jaunty treatment it gets here is slightly bemusing. That seems to typify Denson's approach: he's a man of good spirits, not one to wait for the end of the world, and where others have passion he has a kind of gutsy, grand humour which is undeniably enlivening.

Ted Des Plantes

PIANO, VOCAL

Des Plantes and his Washboard Wizards are a studio band formed to play the classic jazz of the 1920s in modern sound and with a soupçon of modern style.

****** Midnight Stomp**

Stomp Off CD 1231 *Des Plantes; Leon Oakley (c); Jim Snyder (tb, v); Larry Wright (cl, as, ts, ocarina, v); John Otto (cl, as, v); Frank Powers (cl, as); Mike Bezin (tba, v); Jack Meilahn (bj); Hal Smith (wbd, d).* 3–4/91.

Never a dull moment with this superb traditional outfit, barrelling through a connoisseur's choice of classic material in Ohio. They have the measure of all 18 tracks, and even at over 70 minutes the record never runs out of puff. Individually, each man has the right blend of chops and enthusiasm: nobody pretends to outright virtuosity, but there are no painful mistakes either. Oakley is a properly salty cornet lead, Snyder is a ripe 'bone man, but it's Wright and Otto, their styles harking back to the oldest Chicago masters as if bebop had never happened, who lend a rare authenticity. Smith's washboard (the group is actually called The Washboard Wizards, though Des Plantes is the affable leader) lends a rare crispness to the rhythms, and even the singing is more than passable. Des Plantes chooses real obscurities from the oldest days of the music, including tunes from the books of Bennie Moten, Perry Bradford, Doc Cook, Alex Hill and The Pods of Pepper, and everything sounds fresh-minted in outstanding studio sound.

***** Ain't Cha Got Music?**

Jazzology JCD-225 *Des Plantes; Chris Tyle (t, v); David Sager (tb); Tom Fischer (cl, as, ts); Barry Wratten (cl); John Gill (bj); Tom Saunders (b, tba); Hal Smith (d, wbd, v).* 5/92.

The time-frame moves forward about eight years to the early swing-era styles here, with Des Plantes' Louisiana Swingers recreating the manner of that day on another 17 songs. If this one seems more ordinary, it's because the material is sometimes more familiar and the approach already mined: Marty Grosz does this kind of thing with perhaps an ounce more character and, while the New Orleans-based group have the measure of Henry Allen's 'Algiers Stomp' and James P. Johnson's title-track, they don't do so well by 'The Touch Of Your Lips'. That aside, the playing is still pleasantly hot and swinging.

*****(*) Ohio River Blues**

Stomp Off CD 1290 *Des Plantes; Leon Oakley (c); John Otto (cl, as); Larry Wright (cl, as, ts); Ken Keeler (g, bj); Ray Cadd (tba); Hal Smith (d, wbd).* 10/94.

Des Plantes strikes again with a fresh team and another set of archaeological discoveries: King Oliver's repertoire gets a shake-down (though none of the obvious titles), and there's even a nod to our own Fred Elizalde in 'Stomp Your Feet'. Back at home in the 1920s, Ted's team sound in great nick, and the only disappointment is that there isn't more of his ridiculous singing.

*****(*) Shim Sham Shimmy Dance**

Stomp Off CD 1325 *As above, except John Gill (bj, v) replaces Keeler.* 8/97.

Ted has another go at the Clarence Williams songbook this time, something of a homecoming since this was the material The Washboard Wizards were first formed to play. The 19 tunes are dispatched with the band's familiar geniality; we especially liked the ensemble singing and Larry Wright's ocarina solo on 'Pile Of Logs And Stones (Called Home)', but it's idle to single out any one track in a consistently enjoyable set. Ted has taken us to task in his sleeve-note for calling his singing 'ridiculous'. All right, then; how about 'warm-hearted'?

Paul Desmond (1924–77)

ALTO SAXOPHONE

Desmond's warm, glowing tone and melodic ease are almost definitive of the cool saxophone, and he has had a large if unexpected impact on modernists like Anthony Braxton. Such was the Californian's importance to pianist Dave Brubeck, for whom Desmond wrote the classic 'Take Five', that there was a contract stipulation insisting Desmond never recorded on his own account with another piano player. Premature death denied him and us what would surely have been a maturing and ever wiser performer.

***** Quintet / Quartet Featuring Don Elliott**

Original Jazz Classics OJC 712 *Desmond; Don Elliott (t, mellophone); Dave Van Kriedt (ts); Jack Weeks, Barney Kessel (g); Norman Bates, Bob Bates (b); Joe Chevrolet, Joe Dodge (d); Bill Bates Singers.* 2/56, 57.

***** East Of The Sun**

Discovery DSCD 840 *Desmond; Jim Hall (g); Percy Heath (b); Connie Kay (d).* 59.

It's still fashionable among the more categorical sort of jazz enthusiast to anathematize anything committed to record by Dave Brubeck *unless* it also features Paul Desmond. In addition to downplaying Brubeck's considerable significance, this rather overplays Desmond's occasionally self-conscious style and rather begs the question why most of his better performances tended to be with Brubeck in any case. Desmond did, however, strike up a fruitful association with the members of the MJQ and made some excellent recordings with them, of which some good samples remain. Desmond's own-name outings were, by verbal agreement with Brubeck, always made without piano. There are hints on both *East Of The Sun* and the earlier sessions with Don Elliott of Gerry Mulligan's pianoless quartets. There was also the added plus of Jim Hall, who perfectly fitted Desmond's legato approach and interest in top harmonics (an approach that improbably influenced Anthony Braxton).

****** The Complete RCA Victor Recordings: 1961–65**
RCA Victor 7432 142530 7CD; consists of:

***** Desmond Blue**
RCA Victor 7432 137751 *Desmond; Tony Miranda, Albert Richman (frhn); Phil Bodner, Robert Doty, George Marge, Romeo Penque, Stan Webb (reeds); Jim Hall (g); Gloria Agostini, Gene Bianco (hp); Gene Cherico, Milt Hinton (b); Connie Kay, Osie Johnson, Bobby Thomas (d); strings.* 9 & 10/61, 3/62.

*****(*) Glad To Be Unhappy**
RCA Victor 7432 131311 *Desmond; Jim Hall (g); Gene Cherico, Gene Wright (b); Connie Kay (d).* 6/63–9/64.

****** Two Of A Mind**
RCA Victor 7432 125764 *Desmond; Gerry Mulligan (bs); John Beal, John Benjamin, Wendell Marshall (b); Connie Kay, Mel Lewis (d).* 6–8/62.

***** Take Ten**
RCA Victor 7432 125760 *Desmond; Jim Hall (g); Gene Cherico, Gene Wright (b); Connie Kay (d).* 6/63.

****** Easy Living**
RCA Victor 7432 131393 *As above, except add Percy Heath (b).* 6/63–6/65.

***** Bossa Antigua**
RCA Victor 7432 122110 *As above, except omit Cherico, Heath.* 7–9/64.

**** All Across The City**
RCA Victor 7432 132726 *As above.* 9/64.

*****(*) Polka Dots And Moonbeams**
Bluebird ND 90637 *As above.* 63–64.

*****(*) The Best Of The Complete Paul Desmond**
RCA Victor 63634 *As above.* 61–65.

Desmond's recordings for RCA Victor are the pinnacle of his career and anyone seriously interested in his work will need to invest in this lavish, French-issue boxed set. A good deal of the material may well still be available on single CDs, which is why we have listed the titles separately. If contractual promises meant he was unable to record with a piano player, Desmond found the perfect alternative in Hall and, as will be seen, managed to maintain a consistent line-up for nearly all of his time with the label. He also sustained an extraordinary consistency of performance. It is difficult in all conscience to make distinctions between these sessions. Desmond's tone and quiet, lyrical delivery almost never vary from date to date. Occasionally, he will throw in a discordant interval or roughen up his timbre to add a measure of drama. It is astonishing, listening to this music in bulk, to discover how modern, even avant-garde, it is in impact. For all Anthony Braxton's insistence on Desmond as a primary influence, no one has ever quite taken the point at face value. These extraordinary sides point up how immensely thoughtful Desmond was, less cerebral than Braxton's other bellwether, Warne Marsh, but brimming with harmonic intelligence.

Though there are seven CDs in the set, the final one, *All Across The City*, is no more than a bonus single containing just two tracks, 'By The River Saint Marie' and the title-piece. This disc isn't available separately. Now that sales of the box have probably fallen away substantially, RCA are offering a single-CD distillation of the set. How this sits with other 'best of' compilations isn't quite clear, but it is a sensitively selected album with 'Body And Soul', 'When Joanna Loved Me', 'The Night Has A Thousand Eyes', 'My Funny Valentine', 'Take Ten' and five others.

***** Late Lament**
RCA 5778 *As above.* 9/61–3/62.

A garnering of tracks from the *Desmond Blue* sessions and very much part of RCA's salami-slicing reissue programme. 'Autumn Leaves' and the aching 'Then I'll Be Tired Of You' stand out, but there isn't a dud in the set.

*****(*) Greatest Hits**
RCA 52061 *As above.* 61–65.

***** Falling In Love With Paul Desmond**
RCA 63620 *As above.* 61–65.

The *Greatest Hits* is a generous, 12-track sampling of Desmond's RCA years. No surprises, no unissued bonuses, just a simple and effective distillation of a wonderfully melodic body of work. Might we suggest, though, that *Falling In Love To Paul Desmond* might be a better title for this and others in RCA's budget romance series – though no one we have spoken to so far could claim any direct experience of a budget romance. Eleven melting ballads from 'When Joanna Loved Me' to 'Then I'll Be Tired Of You'. A little unrelieved, tempo-wise, but not unrepresentative of the unhurried pace of those years.

***** From The Hot Afternoon**
A&M 75021 0824 2 *Desmond; Irwin Markowitz, Marvin Stamm (t, flhn); Paul Faulise (btb); Jimmy Buffington (frhn); Phil Bodner, George Marge (as, cl, ob); Don Hammond, Hubert Laws (f, af); Stan Webb (f, af, perc); Pat Rebillot (ky); Dorio Ferreira, Edú Lobo (g); Ron Carter (b); Airto Moreira (d, perc); Jack Jennings (perc); Wanda De Sah (v); strings.* 6–8/69.

One of the few occasions when Desmond seemed in some peril of bowing to market pressure and making a pop album. At first hearing, this is somewhat similar to the bouncy Latin style that Charles Lloyd was making a commercial success of at around the same time. The obvious difference is Paul himself. Not by any means a natural Latin player – even a soft bossa doesn't quite sit right for his phrasing – he is more thoughtful than rhythmic, and the short tracks don't really allow him to develop ideas fully. A beautiful record, though, sensitively arranged and immaculately produced and engineered. By no means merely a 'summer of '69' curiosity.

***** Skylark**
CTI ZK 65133 *Desmond; Gene Bertoncini, Gabor Szabo (g); Bob James (p); George Ricci (clo); Ron Carter (b); Jack DeJohnette (d); Ralph MacDonald (perc).* 12/73.

***** Like Someone In Love**
Telarc 83319 *Desmond; Ed Bickert (g); Don Thompson (b); Jerry Fuller (d).* 3/75.

The 1970s were a period of retrenchment rather than decline for Desmond. His health was already suspect by the turn of the decade, and those who dealt with him at close hand seem to have been aware that not all was well. Qualitatively, there is not much to choose between these records, though the settings are very different and the technical quality ranges from pristine to documentary roughness. The Telarc session was recorded live in Toronto and pitches the saxophonist up against a sympathetic but rather passive group who do everything they can to back him but conspicuously fail to challenge or beguile him.

Skylark puts him in company with younger players who have swallowed the rock and roll potion. Carter and DeJohnette remain true believers but, even at this stage, both were experimenting with rock grooves. The long 'Romance De Amor' is pretty free of any such posturing, and a retake of the title-track suggests how much Desmond himself was resisting the drift. The setting is not conducive to his best work, though, and of all his records, and for all the fine playing on it, this is the one which seems most seriously time-locked.

***** Pure Desmond**
Sony ZK40806 *Desmond; Ed Bickert (g); Ron Carter (b); Connie Kay (d).* 9/74.

Desmond's time with Columbia/CTI was productive without being especially adventurous. Lush Creed Taylor production allowed the saxophonist to coast gently through the sort of material that suited his tone and delivery but which wouldn't stretch him too much. This ranges here from the inevitable 'Nuages' to the soft pop of 'Suicide Is Painless (Theme from *M*A*S*H*)'. Bickert's guitar work is exemplary, less mettlesome and questioning than Jim Hall's but absolutely where it should be at every turn. A less reliable player might have pushed Desmond a little harder, but there could hardly be a more smooth-running and professional group than this.

***** The Best Of Paul Desmond**
Sony ZK48454 *Desmond; Chet Baker, Randy Brecker, Alan Rubin, Joe Shepley (t); Wayne Andre, Garnett Brown, Warren Covington (tb); Paul Faulise, Alan Raph (btb); James Buffington, Earl Chapin, Peter Gordon (frhn); Phil Bodner, Jerry Dodgion (f); Sir Roland Hanna, Don Sebesky (p); Bob James (p, ky); Ed Bickert, Gene Bertoncini, Jim Hall, Gabor Szabo (g); Milt Jackson (vib); Ron Carter (b); Billy Cobham, Jack DeJohnette, Connie Kay (d); Phil Kraus, Ralph MacDonald (perc); Jackie Cain, Roy Kral (v); strings.* 72–75.

This compilation of a relatively short period of work for CTI excludes any work Desmond did for Dave Brubeck, but it does include his appearances under the leadership of Jim Hall, Chet Baker and a couple of others, including Don Sebesky's rather good 'Giant Box'. Obliged to work with guitarists in fulfilment of his promise to Brubeck, Paul finds sympathetic collaborators in Gabor Szabo (notably on 'Take Ten') and the ever thoughtful Ed Bickert, who is a revelation here. Desmond was never a revolutionary and in these years he seemed content to lie back and spin out his long melodic solos at an easy and untroubled pace. There is certainly better and more representative work available, but this is an amiable compilation and one or two tracks – 'Song To A Seagull', 'You'd Be So Nice To Come Home To' and 'Autumn Leaves' – are very much in the front rank of Desmond solos.

It may be that Desmond's reputation can never quite be wrested clear of the work he did with Dave Brubeck. If not, one of the great stylists of modern jazz, in his way the equal of Johnny Hodges, will languish out of the mainstream. That would be an injustice.

Furio Di Castri (born 1955)

BASS, PIANO

A prolific contributor to the modern Italian movement, Di Castri has worked frequently as both leader and sideman.

***** What Colour For A Tale**
Splasc(h) H 351-2 *Di Castri; Stefano Cantini (ss, perc); Ramberto Ciammarughi (ky); Manhu Roche (d).* 4/91.

***** Urlo**
YVP 3035 *Di Castri; Paolo Fresu (t, flhn, elec).* 1–2/93.

*****(*) Mythscapes**
Soul Note 121257-2 *As above, except add Jon Balke (p), Pierre Favre (d).* 1/95.

The bassist is an inquisitive stalwart of the contemporary Italian scene. Across the very long *What Colour For A Tale*, Di Castri displays a fine ear for nuance and interplay in a quartet that features the most delicate electronic additions from the mainly acoustic Ciammarughi and pert, fiery soprano from Cantini. One standard, Jimmy Van Heusen's 'Nancy', turns up in the middle, but otherwise the tunes are mostly penned by the leader.

He has frequently worked with Paolo Fresu, and the duo record, *Urlo*, is an absorbing account of their partnership, sketched across 27 miniatures (some no more than a few seconds long), embellished by occasional electronics and the merest touch of overdubbing. Perhaps inevitably, this comes out as piecemeal: they develop an immaculate interplay on longer pieces such as 'Blind Streets', but at other times the tunes seem like props for the two players to show off the exquisite sound they get. Not that that's unpleasant.

The quartet record, *Mythscapes*, is democratically credited, though the two Italians take the lion's share of the composing credits. Di Castri's strong ear for melody breaks through on his tunes, especially the very fetching 'Suenos', which sounds like a sketch straight from Spain. Fresu, naturally, does his Miles impersonation here and there, though Balke's incisive piano parts and Favre's ingenious drums avert any idea of pastiche. Formless here and there, but all beautifully done.

*****(*) Wooden You**
Splasc(h) 694-2 *Di Castri; Mauro Negri (cl, bcl); Andrea Dulbecco (mar); Billy Elgart (d).* 3/99.

Di Castri's idea was to have a group of 'wooden' instruments playing Monk's music, though by the time of the record only two tunes by the master remained and the rest was original. The nimble Negri and the thoughtful Dulbecco make a satisfyingly full-textured sound, with Di Castri's tunes a strong platform. There's an occasional tendency towards lugubriousness, but we may be mistaking that for Italian romanticism.

Guido Di Leone (born 1964)

GUITAR

Contemporary guitarist, at work in the Milanese jazz community.

***** All For Hall**

Splasc(h) H 323-2 *Di Leone; Paolo Fresu (t); Attilio Zanchi (b); Ettore Fioravanti (d).* 7/90.

***** Scherzo**

Penta CDPIA 031 *As above, except add Claudio Fasoli (ss, ts), Saverio Tasca (vib); omit Fresu.* 10/92.

Lovingly crafted guitar music, with the bonus of Fresu's muted horn on five tracks. The title is a giveaway that Di Leone is a Jim Hall disciple and, while he prefers Hall's gentility over his incisiveness, the music has substance as well as tranquillity. Zanchi and Fioravanti are always looking to play more than a simple bottom line: hear, for instance, the drummer's dramatic work on 'Auschwitz'.

Scherzo is a somewhat tougher continuation. The players appear in various combinations, and the three quintet tracks are teeming with lines, working up a real wildness on 'Rafting'. Tasca's vibes have a rather thin and chilly sound, yet they're oddly effectve on the ghostly ballad, 'Saudade A Salice'. Not a masterpiece but a satisfying hour of music.

Robert Dick

FLUTES

Dick is an avant-garde concert flautist who has also found a niche in improvisation and the outer reaches of jazz. He is also a member of eclectic trio New Winds. A superb performer on all the flutes (he can even make the F contrabass instrument sound feasible), he has a huge tonal and timbral range which he uses to maximum effect on these records.

*****(*) The Other Flute**

GM Recordings GM 2013 *Dick (f solo).* 86.

***** Venturi Shadows**

O.O Records 7 *Dick; Mary K Fink (f); Ned Rothenberg (shakuhachi); Steve Gorn (bansuri); Neil B Rolnick (elec).* 91.

***** Tambastics**

Music & Arts CD 704 *Dick; Denman Maroney (p); Mark Dresser (b); Gerry Hemingway (d).* 1/92.

***** Steel And Bamboo**

O.O Records 12 *Dick; Steve Gorn (bamboo f).* 92.

*****(*) Third Stone From The Sun**

New World 80435 *Dick; Marty Ehrlich (bcl); Jerome Harris (b, g); Jim Black (d); Shelley Hirsch (v); Soldier String Quartet: Laura Seaton, Dave Soldier (vn); Ron Lawrence (vla); Mary Wooten (clo).* 1/93.

****** Worlds Of If**

Leo CDLR 224 *Dick; Ned Rothenberg (as).* 2/94.

Dick is a latter day Gazzeloni, the flautist who inspired Eric Dolphy and who lies behind one of Eric's best-loved improvisations. It is featured on *The Other Flute*, an album dominated by Edgard Varèse's 'Density 21.5', one of the real classics of the modern flute repertoire. Its presence alongside Paganini's 'Caprice in E Minor, Op. 1' might suggest that this is essentially a classical project and inappropriate to this book. And yet everything Dick tackles has a tense, improvisational edge. His jazz-based activities are best sampled on the Music & Arts disc featuring Tambastics (those who already know the work of Dresser and Hemingway will be able to gauge the approximate territory), and he is also a member of the ADD Trio with drummer Steve Arguëlles and guitarist Christy Doran. He is also a member of New Winds.

The material on *Venturi Shadows* is closer to his 'straight' repertoire. Rolnick's sampling locates 'A Black Lake With A Blue Coat In It' in the midst of a huge sonic landscape. By contrast, 'Further Down' and 'Heart Of Light' are unaccompanied solo pieces on flute and piccolo respectively. Dick duets with Steve Gorn on 'Bassbamboo', with Mary K. Fink on 'Recombinant Landscapes', and with Rothenberg on 'Daytime'. The final track is a mish-mash of overdubbed sounds, disconcertingly undisciplined from a player of Dick's taste and precision.

The duets with *bansuri* master Gorn on *Steel And Bamboo* are interesting rather than involving. The contrast in timbre palls rather quickly and there are passages when the two participants seem be thinking and working in entirely opposite directions. Students of flute will undoubtedly be fascinated and should be aware that all of Dick's scores and transcriptions are available from his publishing house, Multiple Breath.

There have been many jazz-centred Hendrix tributes over the last few years, but *Third Stone From The Sun* is one of the most unexpected and imaginative. Dick and arranger Dave Soldier give 'Pali Gap', 'Purple Haze' and 'Voodoo Chile' workouts that are obviously influenced by the Kronos Quartet's tongue-in-cheek approach but which are far more inventive musically. Producer Marty Ehrlich and Shelley Hirsch play on the title-track only, giving it an extra dimension the whole album could do with. Not to be missed, though.

For sheer, astonishing impact, *Worlds Of If* is the Dick record to start with. It begins with percussive, hollow sounds on the F bass flute (it might almost be some sort of marimba), stalking a range a full octave beyond a conventional bass instrument. 'Sea Of Stories', dedicated to novelist Salman Rushdie, shows how far Dick has come with the concept of overdubbing. Here, he weaves a mysterious carpet of sound in which threads of melody pop up in unexpected places, like characters returning from some distant enchantment. 'Eleven In Use' is a duo with Ned Rothenberg, the man Dick describes as the 'Jules Verne of the saxophone'; whatever it means, great music comes of it. There are other literary inspirations, as well, ideas from science-fiction writers Philip K. Dick and Ron Goulart (*Worlds of If* was the name of an influential SF magazine), but there is no mistaking the absolute musicality of Dick's approach. He makes a palimpsest of Edgard Varèse's 'Density 21.5', playing it straight but multi-tracking additional interpretations, written as if Varèse himself had lived long enough to hear (and doubtless appreciate) Hendrix. That influence, with substantial input from Ornette Coleman, comes out on 'Lapis Blues', scored for 'harmolodic flute ensemble'. To borrow a tag from some other SF comics, *Astounding, Amazing* and *Fantastic*!

***** Irrefragable Dreams**

Random Acoustics RA 018 *Dick; Mari Kimura (vn).* 96.

A taut and remarkably disciplined set of improvised duets with a Japanese violinist who shares the same eclectic background in jazz and new music. Some of these pieces sound fully written out, most obviously when Dick plays his concert flute, but as ever the bulk of the set explores extreme sonorities and unconventional technique, and there is an obvious responsiveness in the exchanges which suggests that the dozen tracks really are spontaneously created. Kimura has a lovely tone, balanced and carefully inflected, and Dick as recorded is right close up, punctuated with breaths and occasional mouth noises. Very authentic.

**** Instinct

Bellaphon CDLR 45104 *Dick; Christy Doran (g, elec); Steve Arguëlles (d).* 96.

Along with New Winds, the ADD Trio is Dick's most effective and durable group. As ever, he samples a bewildering range of flute sonics, including the contrabass and piccolo instruments; with the addition of buzzing membranes, which gives him a timbre remarkably similar to the saxophone, Dick's phrasing has never sounded closer to Dolphy's saxophone and bass clarinet work. Arguëlles is an utterly musical player and Doran's familiar array of effects is used with unusual discretion but undoubted power; there are occasions when the group is reminiscent of nothing more than Cecil Taylor's bass-less trio of the '60s.

***(*) Aurealis

Victo CD 052 *Dick; John Wolf Brennan (p, prepared p); Daniele Patumi (b).* 97.

Strictly speaking, this is credited to Trio Aurealis, which joins the AAD Trio and New Winds in Dick's roster of associations; but, unlike the last of these at least, it sounds very much like his own group. Brennan is himself a gifted and enormously expressive performer and a brilliant composer, but this is a context which induces him to set aside some of his characteristic mix of complexity and lyricism in order to improvise in a more linear way. Dick's familiar quiver of flutes has rarely been deployed so sensitively. The sequence of astronomical pieces grouped as 'Stellar Nursery' is particularly effective.

***(*) Jazz Standards On Mars

Enja ENJ 9327-2 *Dick; Regina Carter (vn); Dave Soldier (vn, metal vn); Judith Insell (vla); Dawn Buckholz (clo); Richard Bona, Mark Dresser, Kermit Driscoll (b); , Ben Perowsky (d); Valerie Naranjo (perc, v).* 98.

Perhaps the most immediately accessible Dick album to date, featuring arrangements of material by John Coltrane ('India'), Eric Dolphy again ('Gazzelloni' and 'Something Sweet, Something Tender'), Jimi Hendrix ('Machine Gun') and Wayne Shorter ('Water Babies'). Arranged for the Soldier String Quartet and rhythm section by violinist Dave Soldier, it's a record that straddles Dick's interest in jazz and new music. The pace is necessarily slower than one might expect from some of the material, but Carter is an impressive front-line player and Dresser, playing upright bass rather than electric, gives the group a taut, propulsive rhythm. Some of the tracks sound a touch over-arranged and 'Machine Gun' is probably too close to Kronos's now clichéd approach to Hendrix for comfort. All the same, a very good, very listenable record that will win Dick new listeners.

Vic Dickenson (1906–84)

TROMBONE

Raised in Ohio, Dickenson started out with territory bands before working with Bennie Moten and Claude Hopkins. He worked in and around Boston in the 1940s and '50s and later played with the revivalist swing outfit, Saints And Sinners, in New York, as well as with his great friend, Bobby Hackett, in many groups. A much-liked and admired figure among fellow musicians, Dickenson was also an accomplished songwriter, although comparatively few of his songs were ever puiblished.

**** Breaks, Blues And Boogie

Topaz TPZ 1065 *Dickenson; Louis Armstrong (t, v); Sidney De Paris, Emmett Berry, Doc Cheatham, Lincoln Mills, Courtney Williams, Dick Vance, Howard McGhee, Hot Lips Page (t); Jimmy Archey, Joe Britton (tb); Barney Bigard, Edmond Hall (cl); Benny Carter (as, ts); Willie Smith, Lem Davis, Ernie Purce, Eddie Barefield (as); Ben Webster, Lester Young, Red Williams, Ernie Powell, Don Byas, Coleman Hawkins (ts); Sonny White, Albert Ammons, Eddie Heywood, Mary Lou Williams, James P Johnson, Sir Charles Thompson, Wesley Jones, Dodo Marmarosa, Charlie Beal, Sanford Gold (p); Herb Thomas, Al Casey, Allan Reuss (g); Charles Drayton, Al Lucas, Red Callender, Oscar Pettiford, Curtis Counce, John Simmons, Israel Crosby, Billy Taylor (b); Al Taylor, Tucker Green, Denzil Best, Johnny Otis, Zutty Singleton, Big Sid Catlett, Jack Parker (d).* 4/41–9/46.

**** Gentleman Of The Trombone

Storyville STCD 5008 *Dickenson; Johnny Guarnieri (p); Bill Pemberton (b); Oliver Jackson (d).* 7/75.

*** Ding Dong

Storyville STCD 8229 *Dickenson; Buddy Tate (ts, bs); Red Richards (p); George Duvivier (b); Oliver Jackson (d).* 4/76.

Much of the contemporary trombone vocabulary comes from the playing of Vic Dickenson. His bravura range of sounds on the horn laid the groundwork for everything that players such as Ray Anderson and Craig Harris do. He spent his early years hidden away in trombone sections, but the Topaz compilation presents a valuable cross-section of music from his coming-out years. A glance through the personnels gives some idea of the heavy company Dickenson was keeping, and he sounds at home in all of the settings. The stand-out tracks are arguably the session by James P. Johnson's Blue Note Jazzmen, a scintillating group with superb work from De Paris, Dickenson and Webster in the front line. A couple of blues with Edmond Hall eke out some typically wry solos, while Vic's contribution to Coleman Hawkins's otherwise rhapsodic 'I'm Through With Love' is an outrageous agglomeration of oddball licks and smears on the horn. Finally, four tracks with Louis Armstrong show that Dickenson found the company of Pops quite as congenial as that of modernists like McGhee and Marmarosa. Good transfers on an unusual and absorbing range of material.

It's a big jump from there to the Storyville dates. On *Gentleman Of The Trombone*, the tunes are nearly all standards or blues, but Dickenson liked a wide repertoire and, even when one of the tunes might seem a dull choice, he makes it new: there are few versions of 'Bye Bye Blackbird' that can stand next to this one.

The peppery delivery, unpredictable accents, huffing low notes and barking high ones, even his charmingly doleful singing: all are essential parts of a great jazzman who always gave his best. For all the humour in his work, there's an underlying feeling for blues that deepens all his solos, and his own composing is represented by the typically wistful 'Just Too Late'. Guarnieri's rococo touches get a bit much at times, but the record is all about Dickenson.

Ding Dong has all the expected good spirits, but the music is rather lumbered by the presence of Tate, who isn't having an especially good day. Vic and the rhythm section by themselves offer the best value, as in a lusciously blathery 'Blue And Brokenhearted'.

Walt Dickerson (born 1931)

VIBRAPHONE

Philadelphia-born, he worked on both coasts in the late '50s and early '60s, gaining much attention as a new voice on vibes; but he faded from view until a long sequence of records for Steeplechase in the '70s. A deep thinker on the instrument, with a style that steps aside from the inherent prettiness of the vibes.

***** This Is Walt Dickerson**
Original Jazz Classics OJC 1817 *Dickerson; Austin Crowe (p); Bob Lewis (b); Andrew Cyrille (d). 3/61.*

****(*) A Sense Of Direction**
Original Jazz Classics OJC 1794 *Dickerson; Austin Crowe (p); Edgar Bateman (b); Ernest Guillemet (d). 5/61.*

*****(*) Relativity**
Original Jazz Classics OJCCD 1867 *Dickerson; Austin Crowe (p); Ahmed Abdul-Malik (b); Andrew Cyrille (d). 1/62.*

****** To My Queen**
Orginal Jazz Classics OJCCD 1880 *Dickerson; Andrew Hill (p); George Tucker (b); Andrew Cyrille (d). 9/62.*

Despite a recent revival of enthusiasm for his vividly original vibes approach, Walt Dickerson has never enjoyed the kind of critical praise heaped on Bobby Hutcherson's head. While Hutcherson is unquestionably the more innovative player, with a direction that diverges sharply from the orthodoxy laid down in the late 1940s and early '50s by Milt Jackson, Dickerson is arguably the more interesting player, with a style that combines something of Jackson's piano-based approach with Lionel Hampton's exuberantly percussive sound and an ear for tunes that head off in unexpected directions like the wonderful 'Time' and 'Death And Taxes' on *This Is*.

To My Queen is his best record, not least for the pairing of Hill and Cyrille, and for the beautiful title track, dedicated to the vibist's wife Elizabeth. A duet with Tucker on 'God Bless The Child' bespeaks a close understanding that is also evident on the title piece. We resolutely refuse to be put off fine records by the absence of additional material, but this weighs in at just a fraction over half an hour, and with the best will in the world it's hard not to want more.

Cyrille was a stalwart of Dickerson groups until he went off to join Cecil Taylor. On *Relativity*, alongside Abdul-Malik and the little-known Crowe he gets his teeth into a this time mostly standards programme, sounding less immediately identifiable than in future years, but certainly not a formula player. Seven tracks give an illusion of greater duration, though this disc is also under 35 minutes.

***** Serendipity**
Steeplechase SCCD 31070 *Dickerson; Rudy McDaniels (b); Edgar Bateman (d). 8/76.*

*****(*) Peace**
Steeplechase SCCD 31042 *Dickerson; Lisle Atkinson (b); Andrew Cyrille (d). 11/76.*

****(*) To My Queen Revisited**
Steeplechase SCCD 31112 *Dickerson; Albert Dailey (p); Andy McKee (b); Jimmy Johnson (d). 7/78.*

***** To My Son**
Steeplechase SCCD 31130 *As above, except omit Dailey. 9/78.*

On the best of the Steeplechases, *Peace*, Cyrille drives things along with great generosity of spirit. The addition of Albert Dailey, a pianist of comparatively limited conceptual range, to an already successful trio was a tactical error. Vibes and piano are apt to cancel each other out; when they don't on *To My Queen Revisited*, they merely sound mismatched.

To My Son has recently reappeared on CD. Working without a piano, Dickerson sounds both edgier and more uncomplicatedly expressive. This is a throwback to the work of the '60s, and a much more convincing version of that style than the previous item. The sound has been greatly enhanced as well.

***** Divine Gemini**
Steeplechase SCCD 31089 *Dickerson; Richard Davis (b). 2/77.*

***** Tenderness**
Steeplechase SCCD 31213 *As above. 2/77.*

*****(*) Dialogue**
Steeplechase SCCD 31345 2CD *As for Divine Gemini and Tenderness. 2/77.*

****(*) Visions**
Steeplechase SCCD 31126 *Dickerson; Sun Ra (p). 7/78.*

***** I Hear You John**
Steeplechase SCCD 31146 *Dickerson; Jimmy Johnson (d). 10/78.*

The duo was probably Dickerson's ideal performing context. A busy player, he nevertheless revelled in space (and not always the kind of space that a collaboration with Sun Ra implies). For all its cosmic subtexts, *Visions* is remarkably restrained, with Ra playing some of his most intimate and earthbound piano. Once considered a minor classic (and certainly Dickerson's most playlisted recording), it has lost a lot of its original sheen.

Richard Davis is a well-practised duo improviser – most notably with Eric Dolphy – and he falls in at once with Dickerson's conception, giving the whole session a rich, almost symphonic depth of tone and breadth of development. The two albums have been compiled as *Dialogue*, though for the time being they may be found separately. *I Hear You John* is rather prosaic, though there is no mistaking the amount of emotion that has gone into it. As an attempt to make a record with another percussionist, it is fascinating.

The Dickerson discography is in better shape now than at any time since our first edition. He remains a somewhat peripheral figure, but now there is no excuse to overlook him.

Whit Dickey (born 1954)

DRUMS

Working loosely within a circle of improvisers on the American East Coast, Dickey initially studied with Milford Graves, and he plays in a 'classic' free-form style.

***(*) Transonic

AUM Fidelity 005-2 *Dickey; Rob Brown (as); Chris Lightcap (b).* 1/98.

Dickey and Brown are frequent workmates, and Lightcap does a sound job in finding a way between them: this is flaring and exciting trio free-jazz, much of it played at full tilt, yet never so chaotically noisy that you feel the players are blowing just for the hell of it. Dickey notes, interestingly, that several of the eight themes were inspired by a couple of Monk tunes, 'Off Minor' and 'Criss Cross', and that grounding in a central jazz language suggests how they keep sight of a solid form behind the spontaneities. Virile and volatile.

Neville Dickie (born 1937)

PIANO

Born in County Durham, Dickie was playing professionally in his teens. He has a huge knowledge of pre-swing piano styles and is particularly devoted to Fats Waller and the stride masters.

***(*) Shout For Joy

Southland SCD-31 *Dickie; Dick Morrisey (ts); Al Casey (g); Mickey Ashman (b); Terry Jenkins (d).* 5/89.

This is a lot of fun, and up to this point Dickie had never had a better sound on a record – cut at The Bull's Head in Barnes, the very close-up sound gives the group a real physicality which, when they dig in on the stompers, is enormously effective. Fifteen favourites from various books – Albert Ammons, Freddie Shayne, Leroy Carr, plus various standards – give Britain's answer to Don Ewell and Ralph Sutton the chance to execute some of the steadiest of his steady-rolling blues-to-boogie lines. Al Casey is on hand to add a smiling authenticity, but the real surprise is the presence of Morrisey, spreading around his best R&B licks at a period when he was doing the soft-funk of Morrisey Mullen. When they pile into 'Swanee River', it's sheer joyful abandon.

*** The Piano Has It

Stomp Off CD1269 *Dickie; Mickey Ashman (b); John Petters (d).* 4–9/93.

Dickie gets one of his most sympathetic outings here, though the concept is a mite dusty: 21 treatments of piano-roll solos, all played in faithful approximation to the originals, often solo but sometimes with the support of Ashman and Petters. This is a scholar's record and it stands up well on that count, with Dickie obviously enjoying himself and the best of the pieces – James P. Johnson's 'Modernistic', for instance – securing a strong virtuosity. It *is* all rather samey, though, and, capable though he is, Dickie doesn't quite have the bullish impact of his heroes. This kind of piano needs a soupçon of bluster to make it come fully alive.

*** Oh! Play That Thing

Stomp Off CD1309 *Dickie; Mickey Ashman (b); Norman Emberson (d).* 8–9/95.

As before, really, although this time Dickie goes for the most sacred institution of revivalists, the King Oliver Creole Jazz Band. Nearly all of these pieces are out of Oliver's 1923 repertoire, and this time Dickie has some more provocative points to make. His version of 'Snake Rag', for instance, points up the crossover between early jazz and ragtime with startling clarity, as well as underlining how ragtime *had* to turn itself into jazz. The few later pieces, such as a terrific version of 'Wa Wa Wa' (from the Dixie Syncopators' repertoire), are a valuable addendum to the basic list, and Ashman and Emberson embellish (to no special advantage) on eight tracks; but once again the record runs aground on its sameness, for all the energy and dedication on show.

***(*) Charleston Mad

Stomp Off CD1324 *Dickie (p); Martin Wheatley(bj, g).* 6–7/96.

***(*) Don't Forget To Mess Around

Stomp Off CD1341 *Dickie; Alex Revell (cl); Martin Wheatley (bj).* 8/98–1/99.

Dickie and producer Bob Erdos have been shrewd in varying the settings for his sometimes steamrollering style. It's hard to imagine anyone wanting all of his records, but each of them has bountiful rewards, and this latest pair might be his best – although the usual Stomp Off generosity (these two are 77:00 and 77:52 respectively!) can be a bit exhausting. *Charleston Mad* arose out of the idea to do numbers by the classic (female) blues singers of the vaudeville era, and there are some terrific obscurities along with more familiar tunes. Dickie essays his customary striding for much of the disc, but he tempers the momentum with barrelhousing of a less pugilistic sort, and there is the excellent Wheatley, who underscores (and solos) with banjo or guitar on ten tracks.

Don't Forget To Mess Around re-creates the Armstrong repertoire of the 1920s. Dickie is obviously at home on fast, stomping tunes like 'Struttin' With Some Barbecue' but the record is cleverly paced, with Revell and Wheatley adding piquancy in their several walk-on roles. Dickie will never tap into any kind of delicacy, but on a tune such as 'I'm Goin' Huntin'' at least he tricks a certain daintiness out of his right-hand figures. It's merry music.

Danny D'Imperio (born 1945)

DRUMS

Veteran New York-area drummer, dedicated to hardcore hard bop and leading groups, whose style is unflinching and straight to the point. Much big-band experience, culminating in a tour with the Buddy Rich band after the leader's death.

***** Danny D'Imperio Sextet**
VSOP 71 *D'Imperio; Steve Lampert (t); Andy Fusco (as); Ralph Lalama (ts); Mike Pellera (p); Chuck Bergeron (b).* 5/88.

****** Blues For Philly Joe**
VSOP 81 *D'Imperio; Greg Gisbert (t); Gary Pribek (as); Ralph Lalama (ts); Hod O'Brien (p); Steve Brown (g); Dave Shapiro (b).* 9/91.

*****(*) Hip To It**
VSOP 86 *As above, except add Jimmy Johns (tb), Andy Fusco (as); omit Pribek.* 10/92.

*****(*) Glass Enclosure**
VSOP 96 *D'Imperio; Andy Gravish (t); Gary Pribek (as); Ralph Lalama (ts); Hod O'Brien (p); Steve Brown (g); Dave Shapiro (b).* 9/91.

*****(*) The Outlaw**
Sackville SKCD2-3060 *D'Imperio; Greg Gisbert, Andy Gravish (t); Chris Persad (flhn); Gary Pribek (as); Ralph Lalama, John Rohde (ts); Joe Carello (bs); Hod O'Brien (p); Dave Shapiro (b); Steve Brown (perc).* 8/94–8/96.

Superbly accomplished hard bop without frills, bluster or wasted space, despite the repertorial tunes and long running-times. D'Imperio originally called the band the Metropolitan Bopera House but got into a famous spat with the Met itself and had to stand down. The bruising quality of the music suggests that he couldn't have given up without a fight. Each set-list admits no originals, just classic or neglected set-pieces from the golden years of hard bop, and the band, in whichever incarnation, plays the hell out of them. The individual soloists have their standout moments, although Gisbert, then virtually unknown, makes a remarkable appearance on *Blues For Philly Joe* and Lalama is consistently fine across all five records. Away from any leadership or compositional duties, the horns seem entirely relaxed while still able to burn, and perhaps the most notable element is how crisp the ensemble work is: unison lines have the crisp intensity of great big-band section playing. With everything coming democratically from the past, the formula also lets obscurer pieces stand as tall as obvious chestnuts like 'Nica's Tempo'. D'Imperio himself is commanding without trying to take over: he keeps himself to fills and breaks and, if he seems entirely in thrall to Art Blakey (listen to how he drives the band on the Wayne Shorter arrangement of 'One By One' from *The Outlaw*), so be it. With no agenda beyond playing the music, the band actually sound more in keeping with this tradition than many a more self-consciously respectful unit.

Maybe the first record is a trifle routine, but by the time of the second the group sounds almost imperious. *Blues For Philly Joe* remains our favourite – for Gisbert, and for the beautiful studio sound – and we award it a token extra point; but the next three are almost as fine, and Gravish is a very exciting import on the most recent records.

Gene DiNovi (born 1928)

PIANO

Played on 52nd Street through the '40s, worked as an accompanist in the '50s and wrote for film and TV in the '60s. Latterly settled in Canada.

*****(*) Renaissance Of A Jazz Master**
Candid CACD 79708 *DiNovi; Dave Young (b); Terry Clarke (d).* 3/93.

It might be easier to list the great players Gene DiNovi *hasn't* worked with. He made his debut with Joe Marsala while still in his teens, trading on a precocious, cocksure talent that quickly brought him to the attention of Boyd Raeburn, Buddy DeFranco, Artie Shaw and Lester Young. His only other reference in this volume is as pianist on the Benny Goodman recording of 'Stealin' Apples', with the ill-starred Fats Navarro and Wardell Gray. Though drawn into Charlie Parker's sometimes fatal orbit, DiNovi survived both personally and professionally, becoming a successful composer/arranger in Hollywood and New York. In the 1970s he emigrated to Canada and gradually began to reconstruct his stalled career as an improvising player. *Renaissance* is a beautifully balanced set, with the emphasis on upbeat, forward-looking themes. Opening with 'A Cockeyed Optimist', the late John Carisi's 'Springsville', 'Till The Clouds Roll By' and 'Right As The Rain' suggests a pretty sanguine stance and somehow belies the Bud Powell inflexions that hover round the perimeter of solos. 'Elegy' shouldn't be confused with the Powell tune; it's one of three DiNovi originals ('Have A Heart' is co-credited to Johnny Mercer, no less) and the difference in emotional temper is instructive. DiNovi is above all an elegant player who loves songs and never lets the melody disappear behind mere harmonic artifice. His colleagues have a wealth of experience, not least Young's stints with Oscar Peterson, and the rhythm lines are both accurate and relaxed.

Joe Diorio (born 1936)

GUITAR

A veteran modernist in jazz guitar, Diorio is a noted teacher and theorist who didn't get on record under his own name in a serious way until the '90s.

***** Double Take**
RAM RMCD 4502 *Diorio; Riccardo Del Frà (b).* 4/92.

*****(*) We Will Meet Again**
RAM RMCD 4501 *Diorio (g solo).* 5/92.

***** The Breeze And I**
RAM RMCD 4508 *Diorio; Ira Sullivan (f, af, ss, as, perc).* 6/93.

*****(*) More Than Friends**
RAM RMCD 514 *Diorio; Steve LaSpina (b); Steve Bagby (d).* 6/93.

He knows all the tunes, obviously loves them immoderately, but still manages always to impart a little personal spin and variation to even the most hackneyed warhorse standard. These are all supremely elegant, affectionate and mainly thoughtful, and it is immensely difficult to draw qualitative distinctions between subtly different sessions. In our judgement, the duos with Mick Goodrick (listed under Goodrick's name) are less appetizing than the trio discs or the pairing with Sullivan, a player who trades up a limited stock of ideas by the sheer variety of sounds he can command on his horns. The other duo session, with del Frà, is alternately exquisite and drab (two takes of 'Summertime' isn't quite gilding the lily). Like it, most of the sessions consist of standards, but graced with so much intelligence that almost all sound as if they have just been written. And then there are the unexpected coups, like 'The Summer Knows' on *The Breeze And I*, which jolt the whole thing into a new dimension. Diorio keeps going in and out of focus as a solo artist. This recent batch is a pretty good sample of the vintage, an artist who has a very personal take on harmonic improvisation (see his book, *Intervallic Designs*) and who has managed to reconcile it comfortably with straight chordal accompaniment, polyphonic ideas and some carefully selected aspects of free improvisation.

Bruce Ditmas

DRUMS

New York post-bop drummer, here on a rare outing as leader.

**** What If

Postcards POST 1007 *Ditmas; Sam Rivers (ss, ts); Paul Bley (p); John Abercrombie (g); Dominic Richards (b).* 12/94.

An unobtrusive sideman in all sorts of previous playing situations, Ditmas's sole entry as leader is enormously impressive. As usual with releases on the Postcards imprint, the band assembled is a dream ticket that manages to live up to the billing. On the astounding title-track Ditmas pilots a course that suggests a spontaneous improvisation among the quintet which still musters the structure and refinement of a finished composition. Compare this with the closing track, a mystery song with speckles of rhythm and droplets of melody, an ECM-like watercolour. Yet elsewhere Ditmas has inveigled the recently reserved Abercrombie into his most dynamic and explosive form since the original *Gateway* albums of 20 years before; he has Bley playing in an atypically outgoing and attacking frame of mind; and he bridges old and new in the oddball tribute to New Orleans encapsulated in the three-part '3348 Big Easy'. Rivers plays an almost deferential role on most of his appearances, but check the harsh timbres of 'Power Surge'. Swinging, yet uncompromisingly contemporary, this is a very fine disc.

Bill Dixon (born 1925)

TRUMPET, FLUGELHORN, PIANO

Half a lifetime ago, which is also almost half the lifetime of recorded jazz, Bill Dixon presented what he described as the 'October Revolution' in modern jazz, a key moment in the avant-garde. When it comes time to write the definitive history of jazz, Dixon's name will stand out more prominently than it does now. As a player, he combines long, elaborate lines with a whole array of extended techniques: smears, microtones, pure noise. A key figure, deserving of the closest attention.

***(*) Bill Dixon In Italy: Volume 1

Soul Note 121008 *Dixon; Arthur Brooks, Stephen Haynes (t); Stephen Horenstein (ts, bs); Alan Silva (b); Freddie Waits (d).* 6/80.

**** November 1981

Soul Note 121038 *Dixon; Mario Pavone, Alan Silva (b); Laurence Cook (d).* 11/81.

** Thoughts

Soul Note 121111 *Dixon; Marco Eneidi (as); John Buckingham (tba); Peter Kowald, William Parker, Mario Pavone (b); Laurence Cook (d).* 5/85.

*** Son Of Sisyphus

Soul Note 121138 *As above, except omit Eneidi, Kowald and Parker.* 6/88.

Having made a substantial mark with Cecil Taylor – notably on *Conquistador* – Dixon's own work seemed to languish somewhat during the 1970s and it was only the enthusiasm of Giovanni Bonandrini (blessings rain on him for many mercies) that gave the trumpeter an outlet commensurate with his gifts. Even so, the discography is still rather patchy and incomplete.

The 1980 disc – a studio recording, despite what the title may imply – is very much in the Taylor line, and the closing suite ('Anacrusis'/'Conversation'/'New Slow Dance') is dedicated to the pianist. Dixon typically doesn't feature himself all that prominently, spreading much of the higher voicing across the three-trumpet front line. Horenstein has an unenviable job keeping up and is much more effective on his baritone. Silva and Waits generate a maelstrom underneath.

November 1981 may well be Dixon's masterpiece, patiently conceived and executed, and generously proportioned. Dixon likes to build his statuesque ideas on rich drones and has often worked with two bass players. Silva is a very considerable artist in his own right, adhering to a style of bass playing (Richard Davis is the best example) that is clearly premissed on orchestral requirements. As ever, the trumpet is used quite sparingly, often doing little more than sustaining quasi-pedal points against which the bassists move restlessly. Music as concentrated as 'Penthesilea' or the 'Llaattiinnoo Suite' requires certain adjustments of musical expectation; but they are consistently satisfying, and Bonandrini provides a generous, albeit intimate, sound which suits Dixon very well indeed.

Pavone and Cook survive from the earlier grouping, but *Thoughts* lacks the impact of the earlier disc and drifts off into inconsequential and even slightly pretentious ramblings (for which, see 'For Nelson And Winnie: A Suite In Four Parts'). Here again, Dixon's own playing is at a discount and is often lost in a disconcertingly scrunched-up mix that for once blurs a lot of detail. No obvious reason for this: hurry? budgetary squeeze?

Son Of Sisyphus (the title refers to an earlier large-scale composition) is superior in almost every regard. It opens with a brooding duo for bass and Dixon on piano. 'Silences For Jack Moore' is a threnody for a dancer friend, cast in the familiar bass range Dixon favours. The sonorities are even darker on the long title-track, where Buckingham's tuba fills the role accorded a trio of string bassists on *Thoughts*, but the overriding impression is of tremendous space and movement, and there's a sense in which Dixon's melancholically graceful soloing conforms to Cecil Taylor's much-quoted assertion that his own improvisations imitate the leaps that a dancer makes in space. It also has much in common with the trumpeter's other great passion; Dixon's paintings are featured on the covers of more than one of his records, richly gestural abstracts based on an intelligently restricted palette.

*****(*) Vade Mecum**

Soul Note 121208 *Dixon; Barry Guy, William Parker (b); Tony Oxley (d).* 8/93.

*****(*) Vade Mecum 2**

Soul Note 121286 *As above.* 8/93.

Behind almost all of Dixon's small-group performances there is a sort of dark, inner pressure, like the imprint of a much larger conception that has been denied expression. That is profoundly evident again on the *Vade Mecum* sessions, in which he is joined by Britons Guy and Oxley. This is not easy music to categorize. Like Anthony Braxton, Dixon works within a compositional philosophy which makes complete sense when taken entire and on its own terms but which tends to fall apart when subjected to analysis or when interpreters question its premisses.

It might be argued that Guy and Oxley in particular are too 'strong' (in Harold Bloom's sense of the word) to conform easily to Dixon's exceptionally disciplined approach. However sympathetic they may be, both – and Parker, too – are too individual and self-determining to be part of a project which requires a certain suspension of personal agenda. These are highly effective records, nevertheless, even if on occasion they seem to be moving in too many directions at once.

****** Papyrus: Volume 1**

Soul Note 121308-2 *Dixon; Tony Oxley (d, perc).* 6/98.

The rhetoric here is slightly odd. Dixon is credited with the 'linear configuration' while the 'background sound ambience' is credited to Oxley, a division of responsibility that may suggest a certain challenge for authorship. Eleven out of twelve tracks are credited to Dixon, while one – 'The Statesman' – is described as 'the result of a combined effort by Bill Dixon and Tony Oxley', which seems slightly overstated, given the collaborative nature of most music of this sort, except ... except there is so little music truly of this sort.

Dixon is certainly in command. His lines have become ever more elaborate and detailed, and are now very far away indeed from the conventional rhetoric even of modern jazz. Many of the pieces are very short and highly concentrated, but 'Palimpsest', perhaps the best example of Oxley as an ambient engineer, has the majestic architecture of a classical work, relatively untouched by jazz idiom. 'Cinnamon' is – either deliberately or unconsciously – closer to the language and tradition of Louis Armstrong and Baby Dodds. The use of Italian titles or markings – 'Indirizzo', 'Ritratto', 'Quadro' – suggests that Dixon may well want these remarkable tracks to be regarded as quasi-generic, not canonical in the normal sense, but conforming to something beyond the taut and rather fraught atmosphere of the studio.

Make no mistake, none of this implies any criticism of a truly remarkable modern record. Whatever its origins, whatever the division of credits, it is a collaboration in the fullest sense, the work of two brilliant individualists who, whatever the rhetoric, have subordinated self-expression to the demands of a highly demanding music. Deeply powerful and endlessly thought-provoking.

Baby Dodds (1898–1959)

DRUMS, VOCAL

Johnny's brother was playing drums at sixteen and developing great showmanship. With King Oliver in 1922, then in Chicago for 20 years, before playing in New York with Bunk Johnson. Exemplifying the New Orleans style while remaining at a tangent from it, Dodds finally slowed down in the 1950s after suffering a series of strokes.

(****) Baby Dodds

American Music AMCD-17 *Dodds; Bunk Johnson, Kid Shots Madison, Wooden Joe Nicholas (t); Jim Robinson, Joe Petit (tb); George Lewis, Albert Burbank (cl); Adolphe Alexander Jr (bhn); Isidore Barbarin (ahn); Lawrence Marrero (bj); Red Clark, Sidney Brown (tba); Alcide Slow Drag Pavageau (b).* 44–45.

One of the best examples of living history in the catalogue, *Baby Dodds* features the leading drummer of New Orleans jazz talking at some length about his traps, his cymbals, his style and how it all comes together – for jazz bands, marching bands, funeral parades and whatever else a drummer had to play for. Most of the music is actually lifted from other records, notably Bunk Johnson's American Music CDs, but this is the place to hear Baby's history lesson. Some of it is horse sense that still holds good – 'Tiger Rag is played too fast,' he grumbles, and then we hear the tempo he liked to play for it – and when he talks us through a lesson in technique, the good-natured generosity of the man comes alive again, four decades after his death. Re-mastering of all the speech/drum tracks is excellent, and though the music comes in mainly for illustration the compilers have chosen some fine slices of New Orleans to go with the talk.

Johnny Dodds (1892–1940)

CLARINET, ALTO SAXOPHONE

Dodds and his brother Baby grew up in New Orleans and took the archetypal route north to Chicago, where jazz flourished in its new environment. Though he did take some lessons with Lorenzo Tio Jr, the clarinettist was mainly self-taught and this may account for some idiosyncrasies of technique, matters of articulation and pitching which, though not strictly correct, contributed very considerably to Dodds's distinctive sound on a blues. He was one of the great early soloists of jazz.

****** Johnny Dodds, 1926**

Classics 589 *Dodds; Freddie Keppard, George Mitchell (c); Kid Ory, Eddie Vincent (tb); Junie Cobb (cl); Joe Clark (as); Lockwood Lewis (as, v); Lil Hardin Armstrong, Jimmy Blythe,*

Arthur Campbell, Tiny Parham (p); Curtis Hayes, Cal Smith, Freddy Smith (bj); Eustern Woodfork, Johnny St Cyr (bj, v); Clifford Hayes (vn); W.E Burton (wbd, v); Earl McDonald (jug, v); Jimmy Bertrand, Jasper Taylor (d, perc); Papa Charlie Jackson, Trixie Smith (v). 5–12/26.

**** **Johnny Dodds 1927**

Classics 603 *Dodds; Freddie Keppard (c); Eddie Ellis (tb); Lil Hardin Armstrong, Jimmy Blythe, Tiny Parham (p); Jasper Taylor (d); Baby Dodds (wbd).* 1–10/27.

**** **Johnny Dodds 1927–8**

Classics 617 *Dodds; Natty Dominique, George Mitchell (c); R.Q Dickerson (t); Honoré Dutrey, Kid Ory, John Thomas (tb); Charlie Alexander, Jimmy Blythe (p); Bud Scott (bj); Bill Johnson (b); Baby Dodds (d); W.E Burton (wbd, v); Julia Davis (v).* 10/27–7/28.

*** **Johnny Dodds 1928–40**

Classics 635 *Dodds; Natty Dominique, Herb Morand (c); Charlie Shavers (t); Honoré Dutrey, Preston Jackson (tb); Charlie Alexander, Lil Hardin Armstrong, Jimmy Blythe, Richard M Jones, Frank Melrose (p); Teddy Bunn, Lonnie Johnson (g); Junie Cobb (g, v); Bill Johnson, John Kirby, John Lindsay (b); O'Neil Spencer (d, wbd, v); Baby Dodds (d, wbd).* 7/28–5/40.

**** **Johnny Dodds & Jimmy Blythe, 1926–1928**

Timeless CBC 015 *Dodds; Louis Armstrong, Natty Dominique, Freddie Keppard (t); Punch Miller (c); Roy Palmer (tb); Jimmy Blythe (p); Bud Scott (bj); Jimmy Bertrand (wbd); W.E Burton (wbd, v); Jasper Taylor (d, wbd); Trixie Smith (v).* 5/26–3/28.

***(*) **King Of The New Orleans Clarinet, 1926–1938**

Black & Blue 59.235 *Dodds; Natty Dominique, George Mitchell, Herb Morand, Charlie Shavers (t); John Thomas, Honoré Dutrey, Kid Ory (tb); Joe Clark (as); Charlie Alexander, Lil Hardin Armstrong, Frank Melrose (p); Teddy Bunn, Johnny St Cyr (bj); Bud Scott (g); Bill Johnson, John Kirby (b); Baby Dodds (d, wbd); O'Neil Spencer (d, wbd, v).* 7/26–1/38.

Johnny Dodds was the model professional musician. He rehearsed his men, frowned on alcohol and drugs, and watched the cents. In 1922 he was a member of King Oliver's Creole Jazz Band at Lincoln's Garden in Chicago, the band that included Louis Armstrong, Lil Hardin Armstrong, trombonist Honoré Dutrey, and Dodd's wayward younger brother, Warren 'Baby' Dodds. The clarinettist left in 1924, after a quarrel about money, and set out on a highly successful recording career of his own that faltered only with the beginnings of the swing boom. Dodds died in 1940 and was promptly canonized by the revivalists.

His tone was intense and sometimes fierce, rather removed from the soft introspections of Jimmie Noone or George Lewis's folksy wobble. Like Jimmy Giuffre two generations later, Dodds favoured the lower – *chalumeau* – register of the instrument in preference to the piercing *coloratura*. He doubles briefly on alto saxophone on July 1926 cuts (Timeless CD above) with Jimmy Blythe. The switch may have been an attempt to get some change out of Paramount's insensitive microphones for, unlike Sidney Bechet, Dodds never seriously considered a full turn to the saxophones.

Though much of his most renowned work was with Louis Armstrong's Hot Five and Seven, the Classics compilations are the essential Dodds documents. They contain work for Brunswick, Columbia, Gennet, the ropey Paramount, Victor and Vocalion. The real classics are the cuts made for Columbia with the New Orleans Wanderers/Bootblacks, a line-up that included George Mitchell, Kid Ory, Joe Clark, Johnny St Cyr and Lil Hardin Armstrong. There are fine clarinet duets with Junie Cobb (and without brass) from 26 August 1926 which have been rather overlooked in the rush of enthusiasm for the Wanderers/Bootblacks performances of the previous month. Inevitably, very little matches up to these classics, but Dodds's reconciliation with King Oliver in September for a single track ('Someday Sweetheart') underlines the great might-have-been of their interrupted association. Dodds by this time was making too much regular money in Burt Kelly's Stables, a South Side club much frequented by Italian businessmen (if you follow), to pursue or accept a longer recruitment. A pity, because there's a definite falling-off after 1926. The duets with Tiny Parham are interesting, and there are excellent things on the Vocalion trios of April 1927; too many pick-up bands, though, and on a lot of the material Dodds is overpowered by other voices, notably Louis Armstrong (in for a Black Bottom Stompers session that also included Barney Bigard and Earl Hines) and Jelly Roll Morton. The Classics format omits the two Morton tracks but does reinstate a number, 'Cootie Stomp', from the State Street Ramblers session of August 1927 and includes a rare June 1928 session with the vocalist Julia Davis (allegedly half her entire recorded output) and trumpeter R.Q. Dickerson. The 1927–8 disc does, though, include some of the material excerpted on the *Blue Clarinet Stomp*, below. The final Classics volume ends with a bit of a rush and there really isn't much in it that even those who love Dodds's music will greatly treasure, beyond a trio 'Indigo Stomp' with Lil Hardin Armstrong and Bill Johnson from February 1929 – although the 1938 session with the young Shavers includes one quite beautiful piece in '29th And Dearborn'.

The Black & Blue and Timeless compilations cover the same ground in different permutations. Both are quite decently done and neither will disappoint anyone who isn't interested in following the Classics sequence right through to its heartbreaking banal end with the feeble 1940 session. The personnel and dates attached to each disc are the best guide to possible overlaps, but the Timeless is particularly good on alternative takes.

*** **Paramount Recordings**

Black Swan BSCD 32 *Dodds; Natty Dominique, Freddie Keppard, Tommy Ladnier (c); Kid Ory, Eddie Vincent (tb); Lovie Austin, Jimmy Blythe, Arthur Campbell, Tiny Parham (p); Blind Blake (g); Eustern Woodfork (bj); Jasper Taylor (perc); Jasper Taylor (wbd); Buddy Burton (wbd, v); W.E Burton (d); Baby Dodds (d, wbd); Viola Bartlette, Edmonia Henderson, Charlie Jackson, Elzadie Robinson, Trixie Smith, Henry Williams (v).* 10/24–12/27.

A collection of oddments from the Paramount label, almost all of them recorded under other leaders, often singers. The earliest of them is a session with Edmonia Henderson, back in October 1924. Sometimes this was exactly what brought out the best in the clarinettist, as in his dazzling solo behind Lovie Austin on the August 1926 session, when he turns 'Chicago Mess Around' into a miniature epic. Three tracks recorded the next year feature Dodds in a happy-sounding duo with Tiny Parham; '19th Street Blues' and 'Loveless Love' are well worth savouring. Many of the personnels listed are best guesses, since Paramount's ledgers were all destroyed during the Depression, but for the most part these sound accurate and are consistent with known activity. Not much more than a footnote on the Dodds story, but a valuable purchase for collectors of early Chicago jazz.

*****(*) Blue Clarinet Stomp**
Frog DGF 3 *Dodds; Natty Dominique (c); Honoré Dutrey (tb); Charlie Alexander, Lil Hardin Armstrong (p); Bill Johnson (b); Baby Dodds (d, wbd).* 7/28–2/29.

There are several things which make the Frog desirable: having the Victor sessions together, having them relatively untinkered with, having the (seemingly) correct discographical story of 'Pencil Papa' for which dates and sessions seem to have been transposed. All to the good. Collectors will be satisfied; newcomers can feel they have a reasonable sampling of the classic material; and the remastering is top-notch. Dodds is one of those jazzmen who may be in danger of slipping into history, and a reissue as meticulous as this does play its part in keeping a crucial memory of early jazz alive.

Christian Minh Doky

BASS

The bass-playing half of the Doky brothers has had less of an individual impact than his sibling, but he is a strong performer of modal-to-fusion contemporary jazz.

***** Appreciation**
Storyville STCD 4169 *Doky; Thomas Schneider (ts); Thomas Clausen (ky); Larry Petrowsky (d).* 1/89.

***** The Sequel**
Storyville STCD 4175 *Doky; Ulf Wakenius (t); Bill Evans (sax); Niels Lan Doky (p, ky); Adam Nussbaum (d).* 90.

*****(*) Letters**
Storyville STCD 4177 *Doky; Randy Brecker (t, ky); Niels Lan Doky (p, ky); Hans Oxmond (g); Adam Nussbaum (d).* 2–4/91.

Brother of and frequent collaborator with the brilliant young piano player, Niels Lan Doky, Minh Doky has a firm, controlled tone on the bass and the kind of popping smoothness in faster runs that is derived from the better bass guitarists. Like his fellow-Dane, the great NHOP, Minh Doky favours the lower register of his instrument and moves down the bridge only for occasional dramatic accents. The opening album is polished but not particularly inspired and the later, Shorter-tinged writing hasn't yet made much impact. In fact the best things on *Appreciation* are a lilting but unsentimental version of 'When You Wish Upon A Star' and an original version of the bassist's warhorse, 'Alone Together'. The second album is a disappointment but is also clearly transitional, placing greater emphasis on collective skills. In mood and structure it is fleetingly reminiscent of similar projects by Ron McClure.

With *Letters*, Minh Doky really comes into his own. Brecker's spare lines are used effectively on the opening title-track and thereafter, and the bassist's brother plays crisply and with his now familiar ability to work quite abstractly within the confines of a melody. Oxmond provides Scofield-derived guitar touches on two tracks, and the closing traditional 'Lullaby' is a bass solo with just washes of synthesizer for accompaniment. The finest track, however, is the gentle ballad, 'Please, Don't Leave Me', on which Minh Doky develops a minimal idea at length over a shifting, steadily changing background. As producer, he has given himself a resonant acoustic, with a strong touch of echo, which suits his tone very well indeed.

Niels Lan Doky (born 1963)

PIANO

Of Danish-Vietnamese parentage, Doky started on guitar and switched to piano at twelve. Went to the USA and Berklee in 1978 and settled in New York afterwards. Has recorded for Storyville, Milestone and Blue Note, and is now signed to Verve. Also produces a wide range of other jazz artists.

*****(*) Here Or There**
Storyville STCD 4117 *Doky; Niels-Henning Orsted Pedersen (b); Alvin Queen (d).* 1/86.

***** The Target**
Storyville STCD 4140 *Doky; Niels-Henning Orsted Pedersen (b); Jack DeJohnette (d).* 11/86.

****(*) The Truth**
Storyville STCD 4144 *Doky; Bob Berg (ts); Bo Stief (b); Terri Lyne Carrington (d).* 6/87.

***** Daybreak**
Storyville STCD 4160 *Doky; John Scofield (g); Niels-Henning Orsted Pedersen (b); Teri Lyne Carrington (d).* 9/88.

*****(*) Close Encounter**
Storyville STCD 4173 *Doky; Gary Peacock (b); Alex Riel (d).* 7/89.

Doky's early records might have created more of a stir than they did and, looking back at them even now, this already seems like his best and most undervalued work. He plays with dazzling fluency, has a biting, percussive touch, relishes fast tempos and has a decisive, linear manner. He writes terrific riff tunes, too. Storyville's five albums are all strong examples of what he can do, brusquely recorded to show off his sound. While there's little to choose among the three trio dates, all of which are made up of originals plus a favourite standard or two, we've given the edge to the debut record for the sheer excitement that seems to energize every minute of the music. *The Truth*, a live session, loses some immediacy over the course of four long pieces, but it's an accomplished quartet, even if Berg's occasionally faceless tenor isn't an ideal match. *Daybreak* adds Scofield's dependably handsome guitar to the proceedings and 'Jet Lag' and 'Natural' find Doky's writing at its wittiest.

***** Dreams**
Milestone MCD-9178-2 C *Doky; Randy Brecker (t); Bob Berg (ts); John Scofield (g); Christian Minh Doky (b); Adam Nussbaum (d).* 8/89.

*****(*) Friendship**
Milestone MCD-9183-2 *Doky; Randy Brecker (t); Bill Evans (ss); Rick Margitza (ts); John Abercrombie, Ulf Wakenius (g);*

Christian Minh Doky, Niels-Henning Orsted Pedersen (b); Adam Nussbaum, Alex Riel (d). 8–9/90.

Doky had already graduated from Berklee in 1984 and moved to New York, so his first 'American' albums are scarcely a departure from his earlier work. *Dreams* has two of his catchiest themes in 'That's It' and 'Faxed', and the writing is generally good enough to overcome any hint of *ennui* which the star sidemen might have introduced. But *Friendship* is even better, split between sessions in Copenhagen and New York, with Doky's native crew outdoing the New Yorkers for bravura and unity, and the album produced (by Doky himself) in stunningly upfront sound.

***** Paris By Night**

Soul Note 121206-2 *Doky; Randy Brecker (t); Christian Minh Doky (b); Daniel Humair (d).* 2/92.

Something of a holding operation, this on-the-hoof live date from Paris is nothing more or less than an accomplished blow on some jazz standards, with Brecker in firm voice and the brothers displaying their usual seamless drive.

***** Doky Brothers**

Blue Note 836909-2 *Doky; Randy Brecker (t); Michael Brecker (ts); Frank Stangerup (ky); Ulf Wakenius (g); Christian Minh Doky (b); Alex Riel, Terri Lyne Carrington, Klaus Suonsaari, Anders Mogenson (d); Deborah Brown, Curtis Stigers (v).* 8–9/95.

****(*) Doky Brothers 2**

Blue Note 856458-2 *As above, except add Paul Mazzio (t), Bill Evans (ss), David Sanborn (as), Joyce Imbesi, Randy Cannon, Mitch Forman (ky), Louis Winsberg, John Scofield, Chris Parks (g), Toots Thielemans (hca), Jeff Tain Watts, Trilok Gurtu, Jeff Boudreaux (d), Darryl Munyungo Jackson, Xavier-Desandre Navarre (perc), Gino Vanelli (v, ky), Dianne Reeves, Al Jarreau, Susanne Salomonsen, Sharon Fuller (v); omit Michael Brecker, Suonsaari, Stangerup, Stigers, Brown.* 9/96–1/97.

Credited jointly to the brothers, these albums are a specific attempt at bridging at least some parts of contemporary jazz and pop. While jazz has the upper hand on the first record, the truce grows a little uneasy on the second. Niels does more composing, but he often leaves Christian to take the lead melodic role, and some of the music on the first album is a successful blend of the pop hook with tough-minded improvisation. The two guest vocals work well enough, and the Breckers have solid if unremarkable guest spots. But the record suffers from its miscellaneous feel, changing awkwardly from track to track, and the feature for Wakenius, 'Hope', sounds as if it's ready to turn into a Wishbone Ash anthem.

That trend continues, and arguably worsens, on the second Blue Note album. Two dreary features for Jarreau and Salomonsen and a not much better version of 'Waiting In Vain' with Dianne Reeves shipwreck the project, and it earns its stars for the originals, 'Silent Prayer', 'Waiting On You' and 'Reminiscence', the last a lovely feature for Toots Thielemans. Here the brothers play to their strengths with Niels leading a strong rhythm section, and the raft of guest stars elsewhere are forgotten. It seems churlish to berate a project which tries to make a go of this kind of 'fusion', but the point is that the record just isn't good enough.

***** Niels Lan Doky**

Verve 559087-2 *Doky; Louis Winberg (g); Lars Danielsson (b, clo); Jeff Boudreaux, Terri Lyne Carrington (d); Xavier-Desandre Navarre (perc); Viktoria Tolstoy (v).* 98.

***** Asian Sessions**

Emarcy 546656-2 *Doky; Nguyen Quoc Trung (ky); Nguyen Ngan Ha (dan tranh); Phan Nhut Dung (dan xen); Luong Ngoc Huynh (dau bau, sao truc); Song Fei (erhu); Wu Yuxia (pipa); Lars Danielsson (b); Jeff Boudreaux, Paul Wertico (d); Xavier-Desandre Navarre (perc); Thanh Lam, Caecilie Norby (v); China National Traditional Orchestra.* 99.

Doky's Verve debut is an interesting mix of originals with pop standards of varying vintage, such as R. Kelly's 'I Believe I Can Fly', Prince's 'Kiss' and Peter Gabriel's 'Sledgehammer'. Tolstoy sings on one piece, the soupy ballad 'More To Come'. These are handled with conviction, Doky often handing the melody line over to Danielsson while he tinkers with the harmonies; but, if anything, he's too respectful with the tunes, and it seems like a recital – hipper than a smooth-jazz treatment, but still shying away from the more thoroughgoing transformations which Brad Mehldau has essayed. The originals are rather more interesting.

He goes back to his roots on *Asian Sessions*, a whirlwind trip through Vietnamese, Chinese and other musics – we think we hear a Caribbean groove in there somewhere – as well as a nod back to the previous project with a version of Phil Collins's 'Against All Odds'. More a feat of logistics than anything, with the various traditional players and the Chinese orchestra integrated into his own group sound, the record seems too much like a travelogue, and the cultures clash more than they sing together. Thanh Lam's vocals, though, are wonderful.

Klaus Doldinger (born 1936)

TENOR AND SOPRANO SAXOPHONES

A Berliner, Doldinger was something of a star at home in the '60s and formed the jazz-rock outfit, Passport, in 1971. Since the late '70s he's mostly been concerned with film and TV writing.

*****(*) Doldinger's Best**

ACT 9224 *Doldinger; Benny Bailey, Donald Byrd, Jon Eardley, Dusko Goykovich, Johnny Renard, Idrees Sulieman (t); Albert Mangelsdorff, Nat Peck, Ake Persson, Eje Thelin (tb); Steffan Von Dobrcinsky, Johnny Scott (as); David Newman (ss); Johnny Griffin, Olaf Kubler, Rolf Kühn (ts); Sahib Shihab (bs); Herbie Mann (f); Ingfried Hoffmann (p, org); Kristian Schulze (ky); Richard Tee (p); Philip Catherine, Pierre Cavalli, Volker Kriegel, Brian Ray, Sigi Schwab, Attila Zoller (g); Jeff Berlin, Helmut Kandlberger, Lothar Maid, Niels-Henning Orsted Pedersen, Wolfgang Schmid, Peter Trunk, Klaus Voorman (b); Curt Cress, Egil Johansen, Steve Jordan, Gibson Kemp, Wolfgang Pap, Cees See, Klaus Weiss, Pete York (d); Tony Inzalaco (d, perc); Charles Campbell, Fats Sadie, Claudio Szenkar (perc); Etta James, Les McCann (v).* 1/63–7/77.

Doldinger grew up at a time when American jazz and R&B were the musics of the moment. Like a number of his countrymen, he responded instinctively and idiosyncratically to the music and played it with his own unmistakable style. Working largely with pianist and organist Ingfried Hoffmann and with a group known as Passport, Doldinger negotiated something of a reputation in the USA, but was a hero back home. This valuable set brings together a huge range of material, from 'Blues For George', recorded in Hamburg in 1963, to an Etta James performance at Montreux, almost 15 years later. Passport is represented by a single track, 'Compared To What', on which visiting Americans Johnny Griffin (a Doldinger supporter) and Les McCann perform. Perhaps the best single track is a 1969 version of Cream's 'I Feel Free', but anywhere from there to the roots of Dixie was Doldinger's territory. A fine writer and a formidable saxophone voice, he is well worth catching up with, and this is certainly the place to make his acquaintance.

Eric Dolphy (1928–64)

ALTO SAXOPHONE, BASS CLARINET, FLUTE, CLARINET

Born in Los Angeles, Dolphy made his first recordings with the bebop-based Roy Porter band as early as 1949. His own recording career, though, was packed into just four hectic years. A definitive multi-instrumentalist, Dolphy pioneered use of the bass clarinet as a solo improvising instrument. His Parker-derived alto saxophone was strongly identified with advances in post-bop harmony, but Dolphy was also involved in the jazz/classical synthesis of the Third Stream. Much of his best work as performer and arranger was in the company of John Coltrane and Charles Mingus, and there was clearly a reciprocal influence in both cases. Unable to find sufficient challenging work in the United States, and anxious to prove himself before his forthcoming marriage, Dolphy travelled Europe as a 'single' but died of undiagnosed diabetes in Berlin. Though much loved, he remains a classic outsider whose real impact is only slowly being assimilated.

*** Outward Bound

Original Jazz Classics OJCCD 022 *Dolphy; Freddie Hubbard (t); Jaki Byard (p); George Tucker (b); Roy Haynes (d).* 4/60.

Since his tragically premature death, Eric Dolphy has acquired an almost saintly reputation. His generosity of spirit is well attested by almost everyone who ever worked with him, and in his short performing and recording career he worked with Charles Mingus and John Coltrane, as well as with Oliver Nelson, Ron Carter and Ken McIntyre.

Dolphy's mastery of alto saxophone is undoubted, a sound and idiom that marked a definite step forward from the prevailing Charlie Parker style, but combining elements of Ornette Coleman's radicalism as well. What makes him unique, though, is the ability to improvise with equal ease on the seemingly unwieldy bass clarinet, the first player to give it a convincing solo voice, and to a somewhat lesser extent on flute. His debut as leader also found him playing straight clarinet as well.

It was to be more than a decade after his studio debut with Roy Porter before Dolphy made a record of his own. *Outward Bound* was taped on April Fool's Day, 1960. Dolphy had been working in the band of another drummer, Chico Hamilton, and it's thought that bassist George Tucker arranged the session which led to this disc. By later standards it's a fairly cautious initiative and, if Dolphy had never made anything else, it seems unlikely that he would have been regarded as anything other than a footnote to bebop, and perhaps a bystander in the revolution of the early 1960s. However, there are enough points of interest to suggest that something interesting was happening.

'G.W.' is dedicated to the Californian bandleader, Gerald Wilson, who had taught Dolphy something about arranging. It's in an unorthodox, slightly top-heavy form. '245', apparently the number of Dolphy's house, is an equally heterodox blues, while 'Les', named for trombonist Lester Robinson, is a 14-bar theme which establishes an unsettling harmonic tension between melody-line and accompaniment. Dolphy's bass clarinet is heard on 'Miss Toni' and 'On Green Dolphin Street', and his flute on 'Glad To Be Unhappy' and, while all three are confident, even original, there's not yet the alienating originality that was to come later.

Hubbard's role is interesting, not least because he was to appear much later on Dolphy's epoch-making *Out To Lunch!*, but there are signs already that the band don't quite understand what the leader is about.

**(*) Other Aspects

Blue Note CDP 7 48041 *Dolphy; Ron Carter (b); Gina Lalli (tabla); Roger Mason (tamboura); other musicians unidentified.* 7/60–62.

The tapes represented here were kept for almost 20 years by Dolphy's close friends, Juanita and Hale Smith, when he left for Europe to work with Charles Mingus. After his death in Berlin, they remained in Hale Smith's care, and it was only after a memorial concert in 1985 that they were unearthed and considered for release.

It remains unclear whether Dolphy himself ever saw these five performances, of which he named only two, 'Jim Crow' and 'Improvisations And Tukras', as being suitable for commercial release. They were, however, studio performances and the sound is certainly more than adequate. The most substantial piece is the 15-minute 'Jim Crow', on which Dolphy plays all three of his horns over a backing of piano, bass, percussion and a strangely affecting female vocal, obviously intended to recall a mournful spiritual, but with the same Indian cast as the flute 'Improvisations And Tukras'. Two pieces now known as 'Inner Flight #1 & 2' are also for flute, albeit much less convincingly voiced, and 'Dolphy-N' is a duet with Carter. Whoever the bassist is on the November 1960 session, it certainly *isn't* Carter and, though some circumstances and some aspects of the sound point to its being George Duvivier, there is no way of confirming this.

In a sense, the provenance doesn't matter. These are candid snapshots of a master musician caught at the point of creative take-off in his career. Even if they are less than wholly satisfying, they add to a disconcertingly small and compressed discography, and one can see why Blue Note, who were responsible for Dolphy's one acknowledged masterpiece, wanted to release them.

***(*) Out There

Original Jazz Classics OJCCD 023 *Dolphy; Ron Carter (clo); George Duvivier (b); Roy Haynes (d).* 8/60.

This is where the promise begins to pay dividends. Since recording *Outward Bound*, Dolphy had appeared on five albums under the leadership of Charles Mingus, Oliver Nelson and Ken

McIntyre, and he was to work with John Lewis, Eddie 'Lockjaw' Davis, Mingus again, Abbey Lincoln, Gunther Schuller, his stylistic nemesis Ornette Coleman and even the Latin Jazz Quintet before the year was over. Of them all, it was to be Mingus and Coleman who exerted the greatest influence, though Dolphy also had an important role in Schuller's 'Third Stream' experiments.

It's Mingus who lurks in the background of *Out There.* Dolphy's decision to dispense with piano and rcplace it with Ron Carter's cello might well have been inspired by Nathan Gershman in the Chico Hamilton group, but the language is much closer to what Mingus was doing at the time, the tonal centre pitched low. 'Eclipse' was one of the very first Mingus compositions to be picked up by another bandleader, and it affords a rare glimpse of Dolphy playing a regular, concert-pitched clarinet. The E-flat blues, 'Serene', is outwardly about as conventional as anything he ever did, but already Dolphy is hearing new and unexpected dimensions to chords and is experimenting with unconventionally subdivided structures, as on the title-track and the modified 12-bar blues, '7 West'.

As with its predecessor, *Out There* was issued with a drably surreal cover obviously intended to suggest that Dolphy and his music were pretty wacky. One suspects that most potential purchasers who hadn't heard of his reputation wouldn't have been buying on the strength of the cover.

**** Caribe**

Original Jazz Classics OJCCD 819 *Dolphy; Gene Casey (p); Charlie Simons (vib); Bill Ellington (b); Manny Ramos (d, perc); Juan Amalbert (perc).* 8/60.

It's come to something when even the record company makes apologies about the music inside. The Latin Jazz Quintet was a south-of-the-border, poor man's MJQ. Though hardly in John Lewis's league, Casey was a pretty decent bop pianist and the session is confident if scarcely effortful or particularly involving. One wonders why, other than the chance of a paying gig, Dolphy was drawn to it. The only other explanation is some ancestral loyalty to Caribbean music; Dolphy's father was intensely proud of his Panamanian origins.

As might be expected, Dolphy Jr devotes himself mainly to alto and flute, with the bass clarinet featuring only briefly on 'First Bass Line', and there it has a rather functional role. The two flute numbers, 'Sunday Go Meetin'' and 'Spring Is Here', are quite delicately shaded, and there are flashes of invention on 'Blues In 6/8' and the title-track. Otherwise, this is a fallow episode. Confusingly, Dolphy recorded with another, entirely different group known as the Latin Jazz Quintet less than a year later, a mostly standards set which was released on United Artists, but which has never (as far as we are aware) appeared on CD.

****** Far Cry**

Original Jazz Classics OJCCD 400 *Dolphy; Booker Little (t); Jaki Byard (p); Ron Carter (b); Roy Haynes (d).* 12/60.

The week before Christmas 1960 was a quite astonishing one in Dolphy's career. On Tuesday, 20 December, he took part in Gunther Schuller's *Jazz Abstractions* project, taping two Third Stream pieces in the company of Ornette Coleman, Scott LaFaro, Bill Evans and Jim Hall. The following day he played in Ornette's ambitious double quartet, the sessions that were to yield one of the definitive statements of the jazz avant-garde, *Free Jazz.* The very same day, he went over the river to Hackensack, New Jersey, and recorded *Far Cry*, his one studio recording with the brilliant and ill-fated Booker Little.

Interestingly – and it's not clear whether he simply wanted to rework them or that he simply needed a couple of more familiar themes – he decided to re-record two items from *Out There.* The title-piece of the August album becomes the title-piece of this, tougher and boppish in style, while 'Serene' remains essentially the same, which is perhaps why it was dropped from the original release. Byard brought in two pieces which helped turn side one of the LP into an extended tribute to Dolphy's most obvious creative forerunner: 'Mrs Parker Of K.C. (Bird's Mother)' and 'Ode To Charlie Parker'.

The record is most remarkable for the first recorded appearance of what was to be Dolphy's most celebrated composition, 'Miss Ann', a delightful 14-bar theme that he was to play until the very end of his life. Little drops out for 'It's Magic', one of the first times one feels Dolphy is doing something really special on bass clarinet, and the whole band sits out 'Tenderly', leaving Dolphy to carve an astonishing, unaccompanied alto solo, a piece of work that bridges Coleman Hawkins's pioneering 'Picasso' and Dolphy's own later solo bass clarinet excursions on 'God Bless The Child', except that here the tune is still very much in evidence. Some have suggested that he was influenced by Sonny Rollins's unaccompanied 'Body And Soul', recorded just two years earlier. Doubtless he knew it, but whether the influence is direct and deliberate, coincidental or semi-conscious is difficult to tell.

Whatever the circumstances, and despite the unavoidable conclusion that here is a young man still open to influence, *Far Cry* is an astonishingly accomplished performance.

****** At The Five Spot: Volume 1**

Original Jazz Classics OJCCD 133 *Dolphy; Booker Little (t); Mal Waldron (p); Richard Davis (b); Ed Blackwell (d).* 7/61.

*****(*) At The Five Spot: Volume 2**

Original Jazz Classics OJCCD 247 *As above.* 7/61.

****** Memorial Album**

Original Jazz Classics OJCCD 353 *As above.* 7/61.

Dolphy's working association with Little was to be tragically short-lived. The two-week residency at the Five Spot in New York was the group's major point of exposure, and it's immensely frustrating that only one night, 16 July 1961, was documented. It's often been suggested that this was a group in rapid transition, and it would be of immense value to document that happening, night on night.

Even so, the music that was recorded is exceptional. Interesting how often Dolphy albums are defined by unaccompanied performances, and the Five Spot dates include a first recorded outing for 'God Bless The Child', which was to become Dolphy's bass clarinet feature, a sinuous, untranscribable harmonic exercise that leaves the source material miles behind. Dolphy had recently recorded *The Quest* under Waldron's leadership and the pianist's two compositions, 'Fire Waltz' and 'Status Seeking'. Here Dolphy takes the initiative, roughening the texture of both pieces and suggesting a more joyous take on Waldron's typically dark writing. Little contributes 'Aggression', 'Booker's Waltz' and the splendid 'Bee Vamp', a tough, off-centre theme that was to fall only rather uncomfortably under the horn-player's fingers.

Perhaps the finest thing of all is Dolphy's own 'The Prophet', which was directed to Richard Jennings, who had designed those slightly half-baked covers for *Outward Bound* and *Out There.* It's also quite clearly an autobiographical piece, an insight into Dolphy's own quicksilver personality and forward-looking intelligence. No flute, incidentally, on these cuts, perhaps because Dolphy was becoming aware that the bass clarinet – and most particularly its unfettered soliloquy on 'God Bless The Child' – had become a voice of equal weight.

A mere matter of weeks after the Five Spot residency ended, Booker Little was dead, felled by uraemia. Speculation about what might have been is as fascinating as it is futile, but the thought that this group might have gone on and grown is hugely beguiling.

***** Berlin Concerts**

Enja ENJ 3007 2CD *Dolphy; Benny Bailey (t); Pepsi Auer (p); Jamil Nasser (b); Buster Smith (d).* 8/61.

Less than three years after these (seemingly televised) performances from the Deutschlandshalle in Berlin, Dolphy was dead. They're poignant as a first sign of Dolphy 'going single', working the more open European scene with pick-up bands. This one was better than most, not just because Bailey's tense, boppish sound occasionally recalls Little, but also because Auer and Smith lean hard on the beat and push things along briskly. 'G.W.' is remarkably similar to the version on *Outward Bound,* Bailey tends to dominate on 'Hot House' (not surprisingly) and 'I'll Remember April', on which he is unsentimentally lyrical. He sits out 'When Lights Are Low' by namesake Benny Carter, and Dolphy thrives on the extra space. Even so, he sounds constrained on these tracks, not even opening up on the now obligatory 'God Bless The Child'. A curiosity, and a significant one in the foreshortened Dolphy canon, but certainly not one for casual buyers.

*****(*) In Europe: Volume 1**

Original Jazz Classics OJCCD 413 *Dolphy; Bent Axen (p); Chuck Israels, Erik Moseholm (b); Jorn Elniff (d).* 9/61.

***** In Europe: Volume 2**

Original Jazz Classics OJCCD 414 *As above.*

***** In Europe: Volume 3**

Original Jazz Classics OJCCD 416 *As above.*

***** Stockholm Sessions**

Enja ENJ 3055 *Dolphy; Idrees Sulieman (t); Knud Jorgensen, Rune Ofwerman (p); Jimmy Woode (b); Sture Kalin (d).* 9/61.

The *In Europe* dates were recorded in Copenhagen two days apart in September 1961. We were probably too negative about these in previous editions. The Danish players are certainly not even close to Dolphy's standard, and clearly they don't understand his more advanced ideas, but they are all decent, time-served players and, while some of their accompaniments are callow in the extreme, they don't really seem to affect the blissfully tolerant Dolphy all that much. Two versions of 'Don't Blame Me' are taped on 6 September. Moseholm bungles his bass solo and Dolphy simply says, 'Let's try it again.' It's the drummer who makes a mess of 'When Lights Are Low', but there are no retakes, and Dolphy opts for the revised bridge popularized by Miles Davis, rather than Carter's original.

The second date, recorded in a more generous acoustic at the Studenterforeningens Foredragssal, a lecture theatre rather than a concert hall, is altogether better. 'Les' is played again, though for some reason it was mistitled 'Miss Ann' when the discs were first released. Dolphy seems content to settle back into the bebop idiom that the Danish players are comfortable with. 'Laura' is a tremendous alto performance, laced with Parker quotes; 'Oleo' is one of the most effective bass clarinet outings documented to this point, and this must be considered the definitive recording of 'God Bless The Child', Dolphy's innate creativity suddenly freed from the constraints of playing down and breaking loose in an extraordinary outpouring of ideas.

The other intriguing item from Copenhagen is a duet version of 'Hi Fly', recorded on flute and bass; Chuck Israels was in Scandinavia with the Jerome Robbins dance company and obviously came and sat in. The *Stockholm Sessions* were released much later. The Swedes are arguably more adventurous but technically less adept, and here and there Dolphy seems to be having problems with reed, mouthpiece or articulation. Perhaps he was simply tired. 'Miss Ann' is lacklustre, and even 'God Bless The Child' lacks the emotional clout he was bringing to it earlier in the month. These were the last recordings that Dolphy was to make for Prestige. It had been an important experience for him, though the circumstances of the final year suggest that he wasn't entirely at ease.

***** Here And There**

Original Jazz Classics OJCCD 673 *Dolphy; Booker Little (t); Jaki Byard, Mal Waldron (p); Richard Davis, Erik Moseholm, George Tucker (b); Ed Blackwell, Jorn Elniff, Roy Haynes (d).* 1/60–8/61.

A rag-bag of oddments from the Prestige years. Most interesting is 'April Fool' from the session which yielded *Outward Bound,* a quartet track without Hubbard. 'Status Seeking' and 'Don't Blame Me' are also out-takes, and there is a version (almost inevitably) of 'God Bless The Child'. The total discography is thin enough to make any survivals interesting and worth having, but the appearance of the complete Prestige sessions renders this compilation pretty redundant.

****** The Complete Prestige Recordings**

Prestige 9PRCD 418 9CD *Dolphy; other personnel as for the above, plus Bobby Bryant, Clark Terry, Richard Williams (t); Jimmy Cleveland, Melba Liston (tb); Oliver Nelson (as); Ken McIntyre (as, f); Bob Ashton, Eddie 'Lockjaw' Davis, Jerome Richardson (ts); George Barrow (bs); Walter Bishop Jr, Richard Wyands (p); Joe Benjamin, Sam Jones, Wendell Marshall (b); Charli Persip, Arthur Taylor (d).* 4/60–9/61.

Dolphy's association with Prestige spanned the period 1 April 1960 to 8 September 1961, when he recorded the second of the Copenhagen sessions. During his contract, he made records under the leadership of Oliver Nelson, Ron Carter, Mal Waldron and, often forgotten, Eddie 'Lockjaw' Davis; the record with the Latin Jazz Quintet was also, strictly speaking, a sideman gig.

Screamin' The Blues was his first recording with Nelson, made in late May 1960. Dolphy played bass clarinet on the title-track but otherwise stuck to alto. Nelson plays tenor, except on 'Alto-itis', which is the best point of comparison for their work on the E-flat horn. This is fairly basic bebop material. On

23 February, Dolphy joined Nelson again to play on *Blues And The Abstract Truth* for another label, Impulse!. He had the call again for what was to be Nelson's *Straight Ahead*, made on 1 March for Prestige. Dolphy cut three tracks on alto, three on bass clarinet, including the extraordinary 'Ralph's New Blues', easily his best solo of the session.

In late June, Dolphy played on sessions for Ron Carter's *Where?* and Mal Waldron's *The Quest*. On the latter, Dolphy encountered the notably abrasive Booker Ervin, a pairing that resulted in some tough and pliant solos. Harmonically and rhythmically, this was a challenging set. For the first time on record since *Outward Bound*, Dolphy plays only alto and clarinet. Waldron was in some respects the ideal foil at this point in Dolphy's career. Earlier, in June 1960, multi-instrumentalist Ken McIntyre had offered him a chance to play with a top-flight rhythm section and with a degree of freedom he would have been hard pressed to find elsewhere. The result, originally released on *Looking Ahead*, is more interesting than genuinely involving, and the session with Lockjaw Davis is more of a curiosity than anything, a set released as *Trane Whistle* on which Dolphy does not solo.

Having this material in a single-box set, chronologically organized, properly documented and complete with alternatives, adds something to the Dolphy story. Expensive as it is, most genuine fans will find it revealing and full of unexpected insights.

**(*) Candid Dolphy

Candid 9033 *Dolphy; Benny Bailey, Ted Curson, Kenny Dorham, Roy Eldridge, Lonnie Hillyer, Booker Little (t); Jimmy Knepper, Julian Priester (tb); Charles McPherson (as); Walter Benton, Coleman Hawkins (ts); Nico Bunink, Tommy Flanagan, Don Friedman, Mal Waldron (p); Ron Carter, Art Davis, Charles Mingus, Peck Morrison (b); Jo Jones, Dannie Richmond, Max Roach (d); Roger Sanders, Robert Whitley (perc); Abbey Lincoln (v).* 10/60–4/61.

Though Dolphy worked exclusively for Prestige as a leader, he did work for other labels during 1960 and 1961. His involvement with Charles Mingus was one of the most intense creative relationships of his life; by comparison, his work with Coltrane is off-centre, creating an impression of two men on parallel but quite separate courses. The first take of 'Stormy Weather' with Mingus is extraordinary. Other tracks catch him with Little, under the trumpeter's leadership in March 1961, and with Abbey Lincoln, under the auspices of the Jazz Artists' Guild. A compilation of this sort is inevitably patchy. Without context, it probably won't mean much to anyone.

**(*) Vintage Dolphy

Enja ENJ 505 *Dolphy; Edward Amour, Don , Nick Travis (t); Jimmy Knepper (tb); Phil Woods (as); Benny Golson (ts); Lalo Schifrin (p); Barry Galbraith, Jim Hall (g); Warren Chiasson (vib); Art Davis, Richard Davis, Chuck Israels, Barre Phillips (b); Gloria Agostini (hp); Sticks Evans, J.C Moses, Charli Persip (d); string quartet.* 3/62–4/63.

Almost worth it for Charles Stewart's sleeve photograph alone: Dolphy in profile, beard jutting, lips pursed, his bass clarinet looped over his shoulder and neck like a serpent. Musically, it's not such a big deal, a slightly uneasy combination of jazz and Third Stream material. 'Iron Man' is fine, but there isn't much else that suggests an urgent reassessment and, as with the Candid compilation, it never quite tots up to more than the sum of its parts.

***(*) The Illinois Concert

Blue Note 4 99826 2 *Dolphy; Cecil Bridgewater (t, frhn); Larry Franklin, Joe Kennon, Dick Montz, Roman Popowycz, Bruce Scafe (t); Bob Barthelmy, Bob Edmondson, Jon English, Dick Sporny (tb); Carol Holden, Ralph Woodward (frhn); Aaron Johnson (tba); Nick Henson, Bob Huffington, Vince Johnson, Kim Richmond, Ron Scalise (reeds); Herbie Hancock (p); Eddie Khan (b); J.C Moses (d).* 3/63.

So tiny is the official discography that every addition is welcome. This live recording from the last full year of Dolphy's life isn't an attic discovery. It has been known about for years, played on radio by Brian Saunders, and available in low-quality bootlegs, but only in 1996 was it brought to the direct attention of discographer Alan Saul and to Dolphy's aunt, Luzmilda Thomas, who authorized its issue through the services of Michael Cuscuna.

Dolphy attended a seminar/workshop on improvisation at the University of Illinois in March 1963 as part of the 11th Festival of Contemporary Arts. He performed an evening concert with his working quartet, and with a brass ensemble drawn from the studentship. The recording quality is far from pristine, particularly on the flute feature, 'South Street Exit', a tune also recorded on *Last Date*, but this belated release is a key step in building a more complete picture of Dolphy's foreshortened development.

The great delight of this recording is, of course, the chance to hear two of the great composer/performers of modern jazz working together. Hancock was already beginning to make his own way in 1963, but this is clearly Dolphy's project. The set opens with 'Softly, As In A Morning Sunrise', with the leader on bass clarinet. The interplay between horn and piano is hypnotic and extraordinarily extended, and really the meat of the session is in this first track. The pianist resists the temptation to go outside conventional tonality altogether but, by his present and later standard, this is an 'outside' performance which dispenses with direct melodic statement until the final measures.

What follows is a brief statement of a theme, 'Something Sweet, Something Tender', which was to figure strongly on Dolphy's culminating Blue Note album, *Out To Lunch!*. Almost as soon as it is has been registered, it gives way to Dolphy's trademark meditation on 'God Bless The Child', again and as ever played on bass clarinet. There is probably a musicology Ph.D. waiting for someone with the analytical nous to compare the half-dozen existing versions. Our feeling is that this was a slightly constrained performance, with a hint of bitterness that isn't typical of Dolphy. Those present in March 1963 say that Dolphy was upset by some rather offhand treatment by academics and academic composers at the symposium component of the arts festival; perhaps something of that affront spilled over into his playing.

'South Street Exit' is marred by technical shortcomings, as mentioned above, but it is a vigorous and astute performance on what was always Dolphy's least assured horn. He switches to alto for 'Iron Man', which was to be recorded in studio later in the year. A review at the time seems to have referred to this piece as 'Bombs', which is just one of a couple of titular puzzles. For the second half of the recital, he stays on alto but now in the company of an *ad hoc* brass ensemble including then student Cecil Bridgewater and with the university big band. The final track is a reworked arrangement of *Outward Bound*'s 'G.W.' (which presumably had always been intended for a large group), but the really interesting one is 'Red Planet', a composition essentially identical to 'Miles's Mode', which has always been attributed to John Coltrane. Given the closeness of the two saxophonists, the piece may well have been co-composed, but it seems pretty likely that Dolphy at least had a hand in it.

'G.W.' recalls the large-scale brass arrangements Dolphy had done for Coltrane on *Africa/Brass*. The Illinois recital shows how close his thinking still was to Trane's, even though he seemed to be moving in other directions. By our calculation, the entire known Dolphy catalogue is only about 10 per cent of the total known discography of John Coltrane; given such a quantification, almost anything that survives is going to seem of disproportionate value, but *The Illinois Concert*, officially sanctioned, professionally mastered and elegantly produced, is a real find. There are stories that more material from the same period will shortly be forthcoming. We look forward to hearing it.

*** Iron Man

Charly CHCD 1094 *Dolphy; Woody Shaw (t); Clifford Jordan (ss); Sonny Simmons (as); Prince Lasha (f); Bobby Hutcherson (vib); Richard Davis, Eddie Khan (b); Charles Moffett, J.C Moses (d).* 6/63.

***(*) Conversations

Celluloid CELD 5014 *As above.* 6/63.

Producer Alan Douglas had almost barometric intuitions about what was happening in jazz and new music. He supervised five consecutive nights of recordings with Dolphy in the spring of 1963. Unattractively packaged and of less than pristine sound-quality, they have often been overlooked or treated as subsidiary items in the Dolphy canon. They are, however, key works, paving the way towards his great late masterpiece and important in setting him in some larger-than-usual ensembles.

'Iron Man' is a strong, muscular theme, and Dolphy's alto-playing is replete with wild overtone surges and unexpected harmonic outbreaks. Fats Waller's 'Jitterbug Waltz' (on *Conversations*) is a lively flute feature, arguably his most effective performance on the instrument to date. Woody Shaw is perfect on 'Burning Spear' (*Iron Man*), perhaps a more appropriate brass sound than Hubbard had been and was to be again. Jordan (misidentified as 'Clifford Jarvis' on some early releases) sounds unfamiliar on soprano, but is tightly marshalled on his solo spot. Jaki Byard's 'Ode To C.P.' is a version of the piece Dolphy first recorded back in 1960, but here, one of three duets with Richard Davis (the other two on bass clarinet), it has a wry, haunted character. 'Love Me' (*Conversations*) is the first unaccompanied alto solo since 'Tenderly' for Prestige, a poignant, tender ballad.

The subsidiary players are uniformly impressive. Sonny Simmons is one of the unsung heroes of the avant-garde, and Prince Lasha – pronounced 'le-shay' – is Dolphy's musical twin on flute. The key addition, though, is Hutcherson on vibraphone, soon to be a mainstay of the *Out To Lunch!* band, offering a very different, percussive sound to the ensembles.

Tantalizingly, it is thought that more material exists from these sessions – not surprisingly, given that they took place over several nights – but so far none of it has surfaced. It is a great pity that the sound is not more generous, but Dolphy himself is usually quite well served, and the quality of the music sustains both records.

♛ **** Out To Lunch!

Blue Note CDP 746522 *Dolphy; Freddie Hubbard (t); Bobby Hutcherson (vib); Richard Davis (b); Tony (d).* 2/64.

This was the third time Dolphy had used the word 'out' in an album title. Oddly, perhaps even paradoxically, *Out To Lunch!* now seems both more outside and more mainstream than his earlier work. It also stands in a slightly curious relation to what is already a quite small and concentrated recording output. When the readers of a British music magazine voted it the finest jazz of all time, how many of them would have been familiar with *Outward Bound* or with the *Iron Man/Conversations* sessions? How much of their response was conditioned by the commonplace tragedy of Dolphy's imminent death (not in a car wreck, a shooting or by an overdose, but simply from an untreated riot of sugar in the blood), by Reid Miles's brilliant cover imagery, and indeed by the enormous cachet of Blue Note.

This was a unique association, Dolphy's own other release for the label the posthumous *Other Aspects*, though a month later he was to have a major role in Andrew Hill's *Point Of Departure*. How high does *Out To Lunch!* stand? If it is a masterpiece, then it is not so much a flawed as a slightly tentative masterpiece. Since the spring 1963 sessions for Alan Douglas, Dolphy had quite audibly been working towards a new compositional sophistication. The session of 25 February 1964 was engineered by Rudy Van Gelder. The sound is strong and very centred, and the new band (with Tony Williams in for J.C. Moses and the incendiary Freddie Hubbard in for the rather more measured Woody Shaw) was better suited to Dolphy's increasingly dissonant and fractured conception. Even so, however wayward these five tunes look and occasionally sound, every one of them is anchored in tradition, to some degree, and there is a shifting equipoise – track by track – between harmonic, rhythmic and timbral elements.

The solitary flute track is inspired by the great modernist, Severiano Gazelloni, and might be expected to be a quasi-concert piece reminiscent of Varèse's 'Density 21.5', which Dolphy had played. Not so. In fact, 'Gazelloni' is a relatively conventional bop theme, but one distinguished by Dolphy's virtuosic articulation and biting attack. In the same way, 'Straight Up And Down' and 'Out To Lunch' itself, the two alto pieces, are bordering on complete harmonic freedom, but again anchored in a rhythmic groove that could support heavy rail transport. Transfer to CD was good for bass players generally, but in this case it particularly underlined the role of Richard Davis (a fine orchestral player, of course, indeed Stravinsky's favourite) in touching in harmonies that would otherwise be unstated or tacit. Hutcherson doesn't function much like a piano player, but unleashes percussive and often polytonal lines that allow Dolphy maximum freedom of invention.

Long exposure suggests that the real, radical core of *Out To Lunch!* lies in the two opening numbers. 'Hat And Beard', a tribute to Monk, and 'Something Sweet, Something Tender' are both taken on bass clarinet, and the sheer physicality and dynamic cohesion of Dolphy's entry on the first tune is the key moment in his entire output. It is 'angular', as the cliché runs, but it is also profoundly lyrical and unmistakably thoughtful. The later tracks are by no means a falling away, but they certainly represent a consolidation rather than an advance on what Dolphy does in those opening moments. The irony of *Out To Lunch!* is that there was to be no sequel and that, precisely as Dolphy found his voice, he was prepared to submerge it (to a degree) in a responsive ensemble. This is not yet a great group record, but the lineaments were there.

*** Last Date

Emarcy 5101242 *Dolphy; Misha Mengelberg (p); Jacques Schols (b); Han Bennink (d). 6/64.*

Following *Out To Lunch!*, Dolphy recorded with Andrew Hill, then he rejoined the Charles Mingus Jazz Workshop for an eventful Town Hall concert and then a European tour, which was to be the most densely documented period of his career, a slew of live recordings (some of them unauthorized) issued under Mingus's name. The late spring found Dolphy on his own in Paris and the Netherlands, going single as he had three years earlier. In the last week of June he was in Berlin, to play at a new club called The Tangent, but he was unwell and managed only one or two sets. On the 29th he died in the Achenbach Hospital, having suffered a cardiac and circulatory collapse brought on by diabetes.

An unfortunate aura of glamour surrounds the last words of the great. Because there will be nothing more, they have a certain finality and definitiveness. *Last Date*, recorded in Hilversum on 2 June, is certainly not the last time Dolphy played. There are bits and pieces from later on in the month, and there are inevitable rumours of other tapes. However, this is the last formal recording available, made in front of record executives and guests, who supply the 'live' applause. The performances are very good indeed and Misha Mengelberg's trio are sympathetic and responsive foils. Dolphy opens with Monk's 'Epistrophy', an interesting kick-off point after the Monk-inspired opening of *Out To Lunch!*. Inevitably, this is milder, but the bass clarinet sound is as urgent and alien as ever. 'Hypochrismutreefuzz' is a Mengelberg original, very much in the bebop idiom, which dominates the session and is somewhat old-fashioned sounding. 'The Madrig Speaks, The Panther Walks' is actually a reworking of 'Mandrake' from the Douglas sessions, and a slightly conventional containment of it. The real delights on this disc are the two flute themes, 'South Street Exit', in which Dolphy conjures up a light, joyous sound, and a 'conference of the birds' theme. The key performance, unusually at this stage, is the standard, 'You Don't Know What Love Is', a masterpiece of construction and expression which prompts an audible sigh of delight from one of the audience (said to be actor Hans Veerman) at the end of its 11-minute span.

Which leaves just 'Miss Ann', a plain and unfussy alto theme which was probably as close as possible to triple-distilled Dolphy, the affectionate, generous spirit everyone who came close to him remembers. A certain mythology surrounds this track, which ends the album. The Philips release – and this Emarcy reissue – appended Dolphy's own voice, a statement that has become his curtain-call: 'When you hear music, after it's over, it's gone in the air. You can never recapture it again.' This wasn't said at the recording, but during an interview with jazz historian Michiel de Ruyter, some time earlier in the spring of 1964. There is much of Dolphy that can never be recaptured, which is what makes that which survives so precious. Even as he experimented, even as he overthrew the rules, he managed to maintain a solidity of presence, a foothold in the tradition, which meant that his music, however fleeting, would never be gone in the air.

Sophia Domancich

PIANO

French pianist who has sometimes worked with fusion and art-rock groups, occasionally making music in more of a free-bop style.

*** L'Année Des Treize Lunes

Seventh A XV *Domancich; Paul Rogers (b); Tony Levin (d).* 12/94.

The music might not fit Rainer Werner Fassbinder's film, but it's a fine essay on the piano trio form. Domancich seems eager to involve her superb rhythm section as much as possible, and they give ideal support to her propulsive and clear-headed improvising. Rogers, arguably, does the most impressive things here: 'Parrots', which starts out like a stately Charlie Haden kind of melody, is rousted by his explosive bass solo and evolves into a gripping three-way conversation. He also has one entire piece to himself ('Min'). But sometimes, as on the very long centrepiece 'Annie, Pierre Et Les Enfants', the music settles into a kind of beautiful lassitude, interesting from moment to moment but not quite convincing in the long run. Excellent studio sound provided by Gérard Lhomme.

Natty Dominique (1896–1982)

TRUMPET

Anatole Dominique was born in New Orleans but went to Chicago in 1913 and did most of his playing there. He recorded often with Johnny Dodds in the '20s, but his later appearances on record were very few.

**(*) Natty Dominique's Creole Dance Band

American Music AMCD-18 *Dominique; Preston Jackson (tb); Darnell Howard (cl); Ralph Tervalon (p); Sam Casimir (g); Bill Settles (b); Baby Dodds, Bob Mathews (d).* 9/53.

Recorded at a hotel gig in 1953, this is an interesting discovery of some obscure Chicago jazz of its day. Dominique recorded little after the 1920s and his trademark – a vibrato shake that makes his horn sound like it's constantly trembling – is hardly ideal stuff to lead a band with. But it's not a bad group: Howard plays some sly solos, Jackson is good, and Baby Dodds, whose beat Dominique always thought unsurpassable, keeps the band honest. Natty reminisces about his glory days on a couple of tracks.

Arne Domnérus (born 1924)

ALTO SAXOPHONE, CLARINET, BARITONE SAXOPHONE

The 25-year-old Domnérus's appearance at the Paris Jazz Fair wakened an interest in Swedish jazz. He honed his technique as a member of the Swedish Radio Big Band, but it was Dompan's small-group playing, influenced by bop but also by Scandinavian folk forms, which established a reputation that has lasted for almost half a century. On saxophone and clarinet, he is crisp, light-toned and nimble.

***(*) Portrait

Phontastic PHONT CD 9313 *Domnérus; other personnel includes Clifford Brown, Rolf Ericson, Art Farmer, Clark Terry (t), Putte Wickman (cl), Benny Carter (as), Rolf Blomquist, Jerome Richardson (ts, f), Lars Gullin (bs), Bengt Hallberg (p, org), Lars Estrand (vib), Sture Akerberg, George Mraz, Georg Reidel (b), Rune Carlsson, Oliver Jackson, Johan Lofcrantz (d).* 46–93.

'Jazz is Melody, Swing and Vitality.' That is the legend and the promise that surrounds the photograph of Dompan. One of the finest Scandinavian jazz musicians of his generation, Domnérus oversaw a shift away from the heavily bop-influenced Scandinavian idiom of the early 1950s towards something more straightforwardly romantic and impressionistic. The early sessions are not presently available, but they reveal Domnérus sounding closer to Benny Carter than to Parker in his phrasing, with a wan, meditative quality that frequently refers to diatonic folk themes and hymn tunes. (It may be Domnérus whom the ageing bopper is thinking about in the great jazz movie, *Sven Klangs Kvintett* (purportedly a fictionalized biography of Lars Gullin), when he says that the only places you could hear jazz in Scandinavia in the 1970s were churches. For a time at least, Domnérus performed in 'sacred concerts' that combined jazz and liturgical materials.)

Portrait, as it suggests, is a career profile, 18 tracks covering the period from the end of the war (a single cut from a Sonora disc called *Ben's Music*, 1946) right up to *Sugar Fingers*. There's a quite extraordinary performance of Strayhorn's 'Blood Count', played as a duet with long-term associate Hallberg at the organ of the Stockholm Konserthus, and there is a single track from their New York trip, *Downtown Meeting*, where they recorded with Clark Terry, George Mraz and Oliver Jackson. There's return traffic on the Quincy Jones-conducted Swedish All-Stars session of 1953, an Art Farmer vehicle also featuring Clifford Brown and the great Swede, Lars Gullin. There's also a Swedamerican summit from 1982 with the veteran, Benny Carter, originally released as *Skyline Drive And Towards*.

Useful as *Portrait* is for a career summary, it makes for unsatisfactory listening as a continuous whole. It's a slightly ramshackle sampling, put together more with an eye to coverage than to the creation of a well-balanced CD; an aircheck from the Salle Pleyel in Paris, May 1949, makes it in only as a historical oddity and, second track in, it's a touch off-putting. These misgivings apart, it's still the best Domnérus album, or we should say *surviving* album. The best of all is the 1977 duo with Hallberg, *Hypertoni*. Enthusiasts can have fun looking for that.

*** Antiphone Blues

Proprius PRCD 7744 *Domnérus; Gustaf Sjovkvist (org).* 8/74.

Inspired by Duke Ellington's sacred concerts, and recorded in Spaanga Church, these moving duets draw heavily on Ellington compositions, alongside spirituals, Russian and Swedish vespers, Schumann's 'Träumerei', and an arrangement of a Vivaldi largo. The Ellington themes – 'Almighty God', 'Come Sunday' and 'Heaven' – are deeply moving, but the real measure of Domnérus's brilliance is the improvisation, 'Antiphone Blues', a thoughtful and beautifully constructed piece that lends a shape to the whole, otherwise logically constructed, record.

*** In Concert

Phontastic PHONT CD 9303 *Domnérus; Rolf Ericson (t); Claes Rosendahl (f, ts); Bengt Hallberg (p); Rune Gustafsson (g); Georg Riedel (b); Egil Johansen (d).* 8/78.

Dompan's solo on 'Isfahan' isn't quite out of the book, but it's close enough and sits well in a section of the concert played 'with Duke in mind'. The folklore side is accounted for in Bengt Hallberg's 'Visa fran Utanmyra', a piano solo. There are also three guest spots for trumpeter Ericson, back visiting his ancestral homeland; he sat in on Monk's 'Well You Needn't', followed by 'You've Changed' and the closing 'Stony Lonesome', lifting the proceedings a notch. This was a period of consolidation for the saxophonist. One of the authors saw him perform in Norway, six months after this record was made, and Domnérus was suffering serious articulation problems, and there are hints of that here and there. No problems with melody, but swing and vitality are both in surprisingly short measure.

**** Swedish Rhapsody

Phontastic PHONT CD 9316 *Domnérus; Jan Allan (t); Putte Wickman (cl); Claes Rosendahl (ts, cl); Bengt Hallberg (p); Rune Gustafsson (g); Georg Riedel (b); Egil Johansen, Magnus Persson (d).* 5/80–7/82.

Originally named *Blue & Yellow* after the Toots Thielemans piece which kicks off the concert, this was another gala performance at the Swedish Academy of Music. (There are four tracks from another Phontastic LP, *AD 1980*, as well.) The new title is taken from another of Domnérus's classical arrangements, this time after Hugo Alfvén. It sits comfortably in an eclectic programme that includes Quincy Jones's 'Stockholm Sweet'nin'' and three wonderful Billy Strayhorn tunes: 'Chelsea Bridge', 'Johnny Come Lately' and 'Blood Count'.

Domnérus has rarely played better, and the supportive presence of Wickman and Hallberg as always spurs him on to ever more adventurous harmonic explorations. He rarely sounds as relaxed as this in a studio, and it's good to hear him given the space to stretch out and really develop ideas. There are some flaws in the recorded sound, including a couple of moments when tape slowing may have occurred, perhaps during the mastering process. These are subliminal, though, and will not put anyone off. First-rate record.

(***) Blåtoner Fra Troldhaugen

FXCD 65 *Domnérus; Rune Gustafsson (g); Bengt Hallberg (p); Georg Riedel (b).* 9/86.

In *Blåtoner*, Domnérus tackled a figure almost as sacrosanct in Scandinavia as the liturgical themes he was examining at the end of the 1970s. This beautiful chamber session, recorded without a drummer, is based entirely on compositions by Edvard Grieg, mostly the *Lyric Pieces*, the *Nordic Dances*, the inevitable *Peer Gynt Suite* (which yields the lovely 'Solveig's Song') and *Norwegian Folk Tunes*. It's light and delicate, with only a rather attenuated jazz content, and most of Domnérus's improvisations are along the lines of conventional Romantic variations, with little vertical-harmonic inventiveness. Worth trying, though it gives only a rather poor account of the Swede's skills as a jazzman.

***** Dompan At The Savoy**

Phontastic PHONT CD 8806 *Domnérus; Ulf Johansson (p, tb, v); Sture Akerberg (b); Aage Tanggaard (d).* 9/90.

****(*) Sugar Fingers**

Phontastic PHONT CD 8831 *Domnérus; Jan Lundgren (p); Lars Estrand (vib); Sture Akerberg (b); Johan Lofcrantz (d).* 7/93.

His typical sound, even on the alto and clarinet, is low, soft and somewhat undynamic. In later life, this has become even more pronounced – though, like Lee Konitz, Domnérus is occasionally able to surprise with brief episodes of dissonance. *Sugar Fingers*, recorded at the Swedish Academy of Music rather than in church, has a politely respectful, elder-statesman feel, and the band hover round him like courtiers. Pianist Lundgren's title-track sounds almost tailor-made for the leader but, ironically, it's the one number he sits out.

Dompan At The Savoy is unusual in that Hallberg is absent. In his place is Ulf Johansson, who came in to jam and show off his multi-instrumentalism by contributing trombone solos to 'Honeysuckle Rose' and 'Solitude'. It's a relaxed, affectionate session ('Dompan' is the saxophonist's nickname in Sweden) that doesn't purport to offer much more than easy, mid-paced swing. No sign at all of Domnérus's more acerbic, Konitz-influenced side, and as such not a particularly representative or flattering point of contact.

***** Reflections Of Songs / Suite For BBB**

Musik i Blekinge MiBCD 98041 *Domnérus; Joakim Andersson, Anders Gustafsson, Staffan Jonsson, Mats Landesman, Roy Wall, Joakim Wickstrom (t); Olle Lind (tb, f); Ulf Akesson, Jimmy Ludwigsson, Ingvar Sandstrom, Haakan Thunér (tb); Bjorn Hangsel (btb); Karl-Martin Almqvist, Per-Magnus Ekstrom, Slevert Forsberg, Karl Petermann, Inge Pettersson, Ronny Stensson, Per Thornberg (reeds); Jan Lundgren (p); Rune Gustafsson (g); Gunnar Nilsson (b); Rasmus Kihlberg (d).* 11/90–3/91.

Two long works for the Blekinge Big Band, the first of which features Domnérus in the company of guitarist Rune Gustafsson, performing a folkloric suite of dance themes written by Bengt-Arne Wallin. It's all very slick and polished and without much to chew on, though Arne's solo spots are as elegant as ever.

*****(*) Happy Together**

Ladybird LBCD 0019 *Domnérus; Putte Wickman (cl); Rune Gustafsson (g); Jan Lundgren (p); Jesper Lundgaard (b); Aage Tanggaard (d).* 12/95.

Recorded, you'll not be surprised to learn, at the Royal Academy of Music in Stockholm, over two nights, this contains no real surprises. Both Wickman and Domnérus had been awarded the Swedish Gold Medal Illis Quorum the previous year for their services to music, and much of the music that followed had a faintly ritual, almost honorific quality, roughened up here and there by association with younger players, as on these sessions. Lundgaard is the main culprit, pushing the pace along faster than the two veterans might like and then holding back maddeningly on the slower tunes. It's all very good-natured jockeying and the frontmen are absolutely in control of the situation. Dompan's tone has broadened a little with the passing years. The resemblance to Benny Carter is more pronounced, though occasionally nods to Johnny Hodges still flicker through. The choice of material is as eclectic as ever: two Ellington tunes, Thad Jones's 'Three And One', Roger Kellaway's seldom covered 'I Have The Feeling I've Been Here Before', Bobby Timmons's 'Moanin'' and a misspelt Horace 'Parland''s tune, a surprise package for the very end of a hugely enjoyable if a little formal performance.

*****(*) In Concert: Live '96**

Caprice CAP 21526 *Domnérus; Bosse Broberg (t); Lennart Aberg (ts, f); Bengt Hallberg (p); Rune Gustafsson (g); Georg Riedel (b); Egil Johansen (d).* 10/96.

A typically eclectic and well-paced septet date which ranges from original, blues-based material by Riedel and Hallberg to folkloric explorations arranged by Jan Johansson and others. Domnérus was quick to spot the potential of traditional Scandinavian musics in a jazz context, and what is striking here is that the 'trad' format conceals a powerful measure of experiment. The leader is less emphatic than in years gone by, his tone blurry and ill-defined, but the flow of ideas is unstaunchable. Aberg and Hallberg are inventive partners, and the rhythm section has a springy, buoyant quality that lifts what might have been a rather ponderous date.

****** Face To Face**

Dragon DRCD 344 *Domnérus; Bernt Rosengren (ts, f); Jan Lundgren (p); Hans Backenroth (b); Aage Tanggaard (d).* 99.

Two great masters of European jazz playing a set of relaxed standards with an expert and unobtrusive rhythm section. There is more to the story than that, not least Arne and Bernt's clever referencing of jazz history, notably moments from the recorded collaborations of Lee Konitz and Warne Marsh. Kicking off with Warne's curtain-piece, 'Out Of Nowhere', was just a gentle warm-up, and in the event the horns leave much of the passage-work to the piano player. The really interesting stuff begins with 'Body And Soul', which is taken on clarinet and flute, overturning expectations and giving the old groaner a new and quietly vivid life. 'That Tired Old Routine Called Love' is a feature for the trio, 'St Louis Blues' and 'Just One Of Those Things' are spots for Rosengren out on his own, while Arne takes the spotlight on 'Stardust' and, back on clarinet, 'What Kind Of Fool Am I?', a duet with Lundgren. This is a wonderful jazz record, clearly thought out and articulated, packed with relaxed invention and some genuinely moving moments. Thoroughly recommended.

Miles Donahue

TRUMPET, TENOR SAXOPHONE

Father played trumpet, but Charlie Mariano inspired Donahue to take up sax. Played in soul bands, then piano, then returned to saxophone and trumpet with a side embouchure. Based in Boston/New Hampshire area.

****(*) Double Dribble**
Timeless SJP 392 *Donahue; Kenny Werner (p); Bruce Gertz (b); George Schuller (d). 4/92.*

***** The Good Listener**
RAM RMCD4510 *As above, except Adam Nussbaum (d) replaces Schuller; add Jerry Bergonzi (ts). 6/93.*

Donahue may still be an unfamiliar name, but he's been around and is now in his fifties. Both discs were recorded at New Hampshire college gigs a year apart, and each has a lot of enjoyable contemporary blowing, without touching any special highs or lows. Like most who double on brass and reeds, Donahue sounds stronger on the saxophone, and he plays that horn for most of the earlier session: a tough 'Inner Urge' and the surprisingly cantankerous treatment of 'When I Fall In Love' which closes the show are the picks, but some of the tracks bog down in rhetoric and Werner plays so many notes that it seems he's trying to take over. The quintet date is stronger, though Bergonzi tends to outplay the leader: 'Tab' is a nicely bruising mêlée for the two horns. Yet Donahue's solo tenor turn on 'I'm Old Fashioned' has a furry beauty to it, and his more generous allocation of trumpet sits well with Bergonzi's tendency to collar the situation. Better recording on the second disc, too.

John Donaldson

PIANO

The Briton has a fresh, unaffected approach and some very interesting ideas, using diatonic melody up against rich and evocative harmony.

***** Meeting In Brooklyn**
Babel BDV 9405 *Donaldson; Iain Ballamy (ts, ss); Ray Drummond (b); Victor Lewis (d). 9/93.*

En route to California, Donaldson and Ballamy stopped off to cut this refreshingly spontaneous and unfussy session with two excellent American players who've rubbed shoulders with the best. The sheerest mark of their quality is the total simplicity and unaffectedness of approach, Drummond patiently chording behind Ballamy's delightful arrangement of 'Scarborough Fair', before handing over to Lewis to whip through the double-time second section. Donaldson's solo doesn't depart very far from the melody, but then he is primarily a melodist, as his two compositions on *Meeting In Brooklyn* demonstrate. Quite where he is coming from as a melodist isn't absolutely clear. There are hints of Django Bates's approach in 'Big Loss In Lewisham' and 'Medjugorje' (a pilgrim destination in the former Yugoslavia), but Donaldson likes to play it pretty straight and shows little of Bates's appetite for pure sound. He plays elegantly and with feeling on Cole Porter's 'All Of You', but even here one has to conclude that he has been thoroughly upstaged by his colleagues.

Lou Donaldson (born 1926)

ALTO SAXOPHONE

Arrived in NYC in the early '50s and worked with Monk, Blakey and Mingus, as well as leading his own groups. An unreconstituted bebopper, he played enough blues and gospel licks in his solos to forge the path towards soul-jazz in the '60s. Still performing in Europe and the USA.

****(*) Blues Walk**
Blue Note 46525-2 *Donaldson; Herman Foster (p); Peck Morrison (b); Dave Bailey (d); Ray Barretto (perc). 7/58.*

***** Good Gracious!**
Blue Note 54325-2 *Donaldson; John Patton (org); Grant Green (g); Ben Dixon (d). 1/63.*

****(*) Alligator Boogaloo**
Blue Note 84263-2 *Donaldson; Melvin Lastie Sr (c); Lonnie Liston Smith (org); George Benson (g); Leo Morris (d). 4/67.*

***** Everything I Play Is Funky**
Blue Note 31248-2 *Donaldson; Eddie Williams, Blue Mitchell (t); Charles Earland, Lonnie Liston Smith (org); Melvin Sparks (g); Jimmy Lewis (b); Idris Muhammad (d). 8/69–1/70.*

Lou Donaldson has remained among the most diligent of Charlie Parker's disciples. His playing hardly altered course in 40 years of work: the fierce tone and familiar blues colourings remain constant through the 1950s and '60s and, if he's as unadventurous as he is assured, at least his records guarantee a solid level of well-executed improvising. He replaces Parker's acidity with a certain sweetness which can make his work pall over extended listening and, considering his reputation, his albums seem to add up to a disappointing lot.

Donaldson's stack of Blue Note albums have drifted in and out of circulation. *Blues Walk*, true to its title, is Donaldson at his bluesiest, and Bailey and Barretto make a propulsive combination; the material, though, is rather dull. *Good Gracious!* looks like another rote Blue Note affair, but with Patton and Green present and in rattling good spirits, both of them outplaying the leader, it comes off as one of his best. *Alligator Boogaloo* comes from the period when the saxophonist was trying to make the best of the soul-jazz trend, without much success on this occasion – routine playing on lightweight back-beat music, though the album was a hit in its day and has remained popular. *Everything I Play Is Funky* lives out the title convincingly enough, the record drawn from a brace of sessions a few months apart (Mitchell and Smith sub for Williams and Earland on the second). No masterwork, but the funky side of soul-jazz hadn't yet lost its edge and it grooves along.

****(*) Play The Right Thing**
Milestone MCD 9190 *Donaldson; Lonnie Liston Smith (org); Peter Bernstein (g); Bernard Purdie (d); Ralph Dorsey (perc). 90.*

**** Birdseed**
Milestone MCD 9198-2 *Donaldson; David Braham (org); Peter Bernstein (g); Fukushi Tainaka (d); Ralph Dorsey (perc). 4/92.*

****(*) Caracas**
Milestone MCD 9217-2 *Donaldson; Lonnie Liston Smith (org); Peter Bernstein (g); Kenny Washington (d); Ralph Dorsey (perc).*

Lou's flame burns a little more brightly here, but he's still sounding a bit worn out after 40 years of bebop: most of his old attack has gone, the articulation furred over. Smith is a feeble prop and Bernstein plays many of the best licks on *Play The Right Thing*, although the organist sounds in better form on *Caracas*. Everyone sounds all-in on *Birdseed*, which is something Parker wouldn't have tolerated; but matters perk up a degree on *Caracas*. There's no shape to the albums, though, just casual blowing. Donaldson is still at work in the jazz clubs of the world, but he's done no new records of late.

Michel Doneda

SOPRANO AND SOPRANINO SAXOPHONES

French improviser, specializing in the highest saxophone frequencies and investigating multi-national partnerships.

***** Open Paper Tree**
FMP CD 68 *Doneda; Paul Rogers (b); Le Quan Ninh (perc).* 5/94.

This must have been a remarkable set – performed at Berlin's Free Music Workshop in 1994 – but, as so often with great improvisations, something's been lost in the translation. For once, Jost Gebers doesn't seem to have secured a very faithful sound, and the grand range of Le Quan's percussion parts has been withheld. Rogers also suffers. The surviving document still has a raw, wound-up quality, which makes for unsettling listening over a long disc. Doneda's soprano begs no great virtuosity and he makes an awkward voice with the others, yet this makes the music the more intense and hard-won. There's little obvious textural interest, more a drawn-out struggle among three rather disparate voices, or entities. Tough work, and absorbing stuff for those who like a challenge.

***** Ce N'est Pourtant ...**
L'Empreinte Digitale 13056 *Doneda; Benat Achiary (v, perc).* 4/95.

*****(*) M'Uoaz**
Scissors 002 *Doneda; Tetsu Saitoh (b); Alain Joule (d); Antonella Talamonti (v).* 11/95.

The magical moments on *Ce N'est Pourtant* ... come when the duettists are recorded in the open air, and the chime of bells and birdsong intersperse their improvisations. Achiary is something between noise-maker and lieder virtuoso and between them they create some spellbinding moments, lusty bawling underpinned by the hectoring saxophone. But it's a tough act to sustain over 70 minutes, and the three long pieces get tired before they're done.

M'Uoaz includes another singer, although she appears only on the second of four long pieces. The only musician common to all four tracks is Saitoh, since there are two duets, a trio and a quartet improvisation. It's fitting, since much of the music overall seeks an unspecified but clear Japanese feel, Joule's percussion sounding like the backdrop for a kabuki theatre-band and Talamonti singing almost in a ritual tongue. 'T'Zane', the trio piece, which runs for close to half an hour, is full of sparkle and colour.

****(*) Anatomie Des Clefs**
Potlatch 598 *Doneda (ss solo).* 98.

The solo album, a nettle which Doneda grasps to only intermittent reward. 'Intermittent' is one way of describing the music, too, since much of it (especially the half-hour opening track) seems to have as much silence as sound in it. Elsewhere he recalls some of Roscoe Mitchell's more therapeutic pieces for saxophone players, mustering every outlandish technique he can think of to get a result out of the fish horn. This needs a lot of tolerance.

**** Not**
Victo 068 *Doneda; Jean-Marc Montera (g, elec); Erik M (turntables, records etc.).* 5/99.

Doneda has his name on some interesting records, but he rarely seems to be the outstanding player. Montera and Erik M set the agenda for this live record, while the saxophonist is left to squeak and squiggle over the top. This kind of situation often seems to devolve into random electronic music, and frankly this is tiresome to listen to, oddly humourless for much of its dank duration.

Dorothy Donegan (1922–98)

PIANO, VOCAL

Born in Chicago, Donegan was playing in church at eleven. Performed in clubs and studied informally with Art Tatum. Despite a formidable technique, she was more of an entertainer, and appeared regularly in films and shows from the '40s and at clubs and festivals in her later years, singing and doing impersonations as well as playing piano.

***** Makin' Whoopee**
Black & Blue 59146-2 *Donegan (p solo).* 3/79.

***** Live In Copenhagen 1980**
Storyville STCD 8262 *Donegan; Mads Vinding (b); Ed Thigpen (d).* 5/80.

**** The Explosive Dorothy Donegan**
Audiophile ACD-209 *Donegan; Jerome Hunter (b); Ray Mosca (d).* 3/80.

**** I Just Want To Sing**
Audiophile ACD-281 *As above.* 3/80.

****(*) Live At The 1990 Floating Jazz Festival**
Chiaroscuro CD(D) 312 *Donegan; Jon Burr (b); Ray Mosca (d).* 10–11/90.

****(*) Live At The 1991 Floating Jazz Festival**
Chiaroscuro CR(D) 318 *As above, except add Dizzy Gillespie (t).* 10/91.

***** Live At the Floating Jazz Festival 1992**
Chiaroscuro CR(D) 323 *As above, except Clark Terry (t) replaces Gillespie.* 10/92.

A veteran whose greatest fame came very late in her career, Donegan was a pianist whose exuberance and sometimes hysterical virtuosity make her difficult to assess. *Makin' Whoopee* is the most temperate of these recordings and, while it explores the range of her talent – taking in Tatum, Garner, stride, cocktail-lounge playing and an extravagant sense of humour – the scaled-down approach makes it perhaps the most approachable of these discs. Her version of 'Yesterday', for instance, manages a unique take on the song without destroying its lyricism. But the recently issued Storyville set from a gig in Copenhagen is another good one, with excellent support from Vinding and Thigpen, the latter proving himself to be Donegan's most swinging drummer. 'The Best Things In Life Are Free' and 'Take The "A" Train' are attacking set-pieces which turn out particularly well. The two Audiophiles, both taken from one session, are much less successful, gathering together a muddle of standards and medleys in unattractive sound on a day when Donegan's least sensitive instincts were in charge.

Her show-stopping appearances on Hank O'Neal's Floating Jazz cruises brought her some useful notoriety in the 1990s. The 1990 session includes her celebrated impersonations of Lena Horne, Pearl Bailey, Eartha Kitt and (dead on) Billie Holiday, which are worth hearing once. But there's also some strong piano, and this rhythm section knows her well enough to make the music swing and stay together. Gillespie makes only the most desultory appearance on the 1991 date, which also has a very engaging 'Tea For Two'. Terry is more generously featured on his guest role the following year, and this is probably the one to get out of the three, although her spoken reminiscences at the end of the previous two discs make an interesting postscript. She is a phenomenon, whatever one thinks about the music, and a sensible best-of culled from all these recordings would be something to hear.

Christy Doran (born 1949)

GUITARS, EFFECTS

Guitarist-improviser whose technique and range of interests let him wander, with mixed results, through most areas of contemporary music.

*** Henceforward

Leo Lab CD 015 *Doran; John Wolf Brennan (p, prepared strings).* 5/88.

A superb technician with considerable imaginative range, Doran has, like his Irish compatriot and fellow exile, John Wolf Brennan, come uncomfortably close on occasion to an awkward New Ageism. There are moments on *Henceforward*, notably the opening bars of 'Waltz For Erik Satie', when he appears to be bent on nothing more than ersatz 'Gymnopédies' for the 1990s. But Doran is too uncompromising an improviser for lassitude and complacency. He has a fierce and occasionally biting tone which complements Brennan's complex arpeggiations (the opening track is nothing but) and is unembarrassed about placing plain, folksy strums in open tunings among all the effects.

*** Musik Für Zwei Kontrabasse, Elektrische Gitarre Und Schlagzeug

ECM 847941-2 *Doran; Bobby Burri, Oliver Magnenat (b); Fredy Studer (d).* 5/90.

Doran's second ECM album is an uncomfortable and ultimately unsatisfactory affair which veers between hard, almost industrial sound and a nervous, algebraic discourse. The formal 'new music' title isn't really reflected in the eight tracks (one of which is by Burri and only two of which, 'Chemistries I/II', are related – by name only). Doran's sound is as pumped up as usual, and it's tempting to speculate whether the music would have had greater impact had the *zwei Kontrabasse* been stood down for the afternoon. Recording twin basses is an engineer's nightmare; but for a rather crude channel separation, they are virtually indistinguishable. Production is credited to the band; one wonders how ECM chief Manfred Eicher might have handled it.

**** Race The Time

MGB CD 973 *Doran; Jamaaladeen Tacuma (b); Fredy Studer (d).* 5/97.

It would be stretching a point to suggest that here is a trio which interacts with the subtlety and sophistication of Bill Evans's classic Village Vanguard group. Not far off, but not quite there. Doran's elegant chordal approach and delay-laden melody lines are the next step on, but this is a sound that also draws on the Jimi Hendrix Experience and Cream, the rock power trio pacified enough to accommodate the guitarist's elemental sound. Apart from the title-track and 'New Outline', all the tunes are by Doran and they re-affirm his gift for sweet, untroubled themes that open out on to vast landscapes of sound. The opening 'Circumstances' is deceptively brief, and it's only with the middle sequence of 'Race The Time', 'No Matter Where You Roam' and 'Incognito' that the real flavour of the set comes through. Doran has rarely played better and never (so far) had playing partners who so completely echo his intentions.

Pierre Dørge (born 1946)

GUITAR

A Danish guitarist whose conventional start in modal bop and fusion settings didn't prepare one for his sometimes outlandish adventures in his New Jungle Orchestra.

*** Landscape With Open Door

Steeplechase SCCD 31115 *Dørge; Walt Dickerson (vib).* 8/78.

*** Ballad Round The Left Corner

Steeplechase SCCD 31132 *Dørge; John Tchicai (ss, as); Niels-Henning Orsted Pedersen (b); Billy Hart (d).* 10/79.

The Dane is an experienced performer in jazz-rock and free settings, although his guitar tone is bright and clear, almost in a mainstream jazz tradition. But these small-group settings don't suit him very well. The duo session with Dickerson blends counterpoint almost too cleanly and tends to pall rather quickly, while the quartet date, despite the promising line-up – Tchicai has been a frequent collaborator with the guitarist – is depressingly low in vitality, the compositions given only a perfunctory treatment.

*** **Brikama**

Steeplechase SCCD 31188 *Dørge; Michael Marre (t, euph); Kenneth Agerholm, Niels Neergaard (tb); John Tchicai (ts, bcl); Jesper Zeuthen (as); Morten Carlsen (ts, bcl, bsx, ney, tarogato); Doudou Gouirand (as, ss); Bent Clausen (vib, perc); Irene Becker (ky); Johnny Dyani (perc, v); Hugo Rasmussen (b); Thomas Akuru Dyani (perc); Marilyn Mazur (d, perc).* 3/84.

***(*) **Very Hot – Even The Moon Is Dancing**

Steeplechase SCCD 31208 *Dørge; Harry Beckett (t, flhn); Kenneth Agerholm, Niels Neergaard (tb); Soren Eriksen, Doudou Gouirand (ss, as); Jesper Zeuthen (as); John Tchicai (ts, v); Morten Carlsen (ts, bsx, f, tara, cl, zurna); Irene Becker (ky, perc, v); Bent Clausen (vib, perc); Johnny Dyani (b, p, v); Hugo Rasmussen (b); Marilyn Mazur (d); Ahmadu Jarr (perc).* 7/85.

***(*) **Johnny Lives**

Steeplechase SCCD 31228 *As above, except omit Neergaard, Eriksen, Gouirand, Dyani and Jarr; add Hamid Drake (d), Thomas Dyani (perc).* 4/87.

These albums are by New Jungle Orchestra, the nearly-big band under Dørge's leadership, which was among the most enterprising and unpredictable outfits of its kind in the late '80s. Dørge explores the idea of a global jazz village by pushing what is basically a post-bop orchestra into African, European and any other climes he can assimilate: roistering horn parts might emerge from a lush percussive undergrowth, or heartbreaking ballads may be brightened by Dørge's own sparkling high-life guitar solos. Inevitably there are moments on the records that sound misconceived or cluttered, but these are surprisingly few: what one remembers is the joyful swing of the ensembles, the swirling tone-colours and rhythmic pep. There are fine soloists too in Tchicai, Carlsen and Beckett. *Brikama* is absolutely stunning, with vivid voicings and a bewildering range of instrumental characters. *Very Hot* is slightly fresher, with a winning reworking of Ellington's 'The Mooche' and two very long yet convincing pan-global jams; but it would be unwise to pass up *Johnny Lives*, dedicated to the late Johnny Dyani, which has some beautiful writing and playing in such as 'Lilli Goes To Town' and 'Mbizo Mbizo'. The CD issues of both records include extra material, and each is expansively recorded, while retaining a lively feel.

(*) **Live In Denmark

Olufsen DOC 5077 *Dørge; Jan Kaspersen (p, picc).* 9/87.

A surprisingly sober and careful meeting between two of the more madcap spirits in Danish jazz. They work as a kind of chamber duo on a selection of self-composed and standard material, with three variations on Satie's 'Gnossiennes' typical of the sort of feel of the programme. The best things are a reflective piece by Kaspersen called 'Snail Trail' and a bittersweet reading of 'Blue Monk', though the oddball duets on altohorn and piccolo at the end of the record bring the most applause! The sound is a little chilly and recessed.

*** **Music From The Danish Jungle**

Dacapo DCCD 9423 *Dørge; Kenneth Agerholm (tb, African t); Mads Hyhne (tb, Tibetan t); Jesper Zeuthen (as, bcl); Morten Carlsen (ts, tarogato, cymbals); Irene Becker (p, ky, v); Hugo Rasmussen (b, perc); Bent Clausen (d); Ayi Solomon (perc); Aviaja Lumholt (v).* 11–12/95.

Dørge's later work has gone almost full circle, back into the studiously primitive sound of the Ellington Jungle Orchestras. 'Fullmoon For A Rhino' is the most obvious derivative; elsewhere Dørge develops soundscapes which graft elements of pure, elemental sound on to sophisticated horn-and-rhythm charts. 'Give Me A Break' has a rock influence and reflects raised energy levels throughout the record. The vocals are generally competent but rather dull. Dørge remains in search of the one album which will establish him as the star he undoubtedly is.

Kenny Dorham (1924–72)

TRUMPET, VOCALS

His given name was McKinley, which is why it's sometimes given as 'Kinny' Dorham. Born in Fairfield, Texas, and a veteran of local bands, he seemed to pop up at the all major points of change in modern jazz, with Billy Eckstine's band, with Dizzy Gillespie, with Charlie Parker, and as founding trumpeter of the Jazz Messengers. Later in his career he spent considerable time in Europe, where his classically tinged modernist ideas gained a more sympathetic hearing. Dorham was also an effective singer.

***(*) **Kenny Dorham Quintet**

Original Jazz Classics OJC 113 *Dorham; Jimmy Heath (as, bs); Walter Bishop Jr (p); Percy Heath (b); Kenny Clarke (d).* 12/53.

*** **Afro-Cuban**

Blue Note 7468152 *Dorham; J.J Johnson (tb); Hank Mobley (ts); Cecil Payne (bs); Horace Silver (p); Oscar Pettiford (b); Art Blakey (d); Carlos Patato Valdes (congas).* 1/55, 3/55.

Dorham never sounded more like Dizzy Gillespie than on *Afro-Cuban*, punching out single-note statements across the rhythm. The marvellous 1953 quintet features gulping blues passages that manage to thrive on the thinnest harmonic oxygen; never a mere showman, it is Dorham's mental stamina that impresses, a concentration and attention to detail that make him one of the most coherent and structurally aware of the bebop players. He is also one of the better composers, a fact – 'Blue Bossa' apart – which is generally overlooked.

***(*) **Kenny Dorham And The Jazz Prophets: Volume 1**

Chess GRP 18202 *Dorham; J.R Monterose (ts); Dick Katz (p); Sam Jones (b); Arthur Edgehill (d).* 4/56.

At the turn of 1956, Dorham left the Messengers to form his own group, which in a less than coincidental echo of his former employ he called the Prophets. The minor-key theme-piece, 'The Prophet', makes for an arresting opening, with Dorham and an in-form Monterose swapping tiny phrases. 'Blues Elegante' opens with Katz and Jones, followed by Dorham playing muted and coming as close as he ever did to the Miles Davis sound, which he flirts with again on the Billie Holiday ballad, 'Don't Explain'. The transfers are far from perfect, with occasional distortions and some noise which is presumably explained by tape wear. However, these are valuable enough sides to overcome any technical quibbles. Fans of Dorham's now underrated and certainly understated approach will welcome this reissue.

***(*) **'Round About Midnight at the Café Bohemia Vol. 2**
Blue Note 46542 *Dorham; J.R Monterose (ts); Kenny Burrell (g); Bobby Timmons (p); Sam Jones (b); Arthur Edgehill (d).* 5/56.

... and at around midnight a sequence of minor keys would seem to be in order. Whatever else, Dorham always had a predilection for a unified mood, and this session, combining the Monk tune, 'Autumn In New York', and 'A Night In Tunisia' with three originals (more fuel to our conviction that he is a neglected writer), manages to sustain a slightly brooding, intensely thoughtful atmosphere. As a foil, Monterose was an excellent recruitment. Burrell swings with the usual horn-like attack and Timmons vamps righteously, though without ever really showing his mettle. Dorham's own solos are models of grace and tact, always giving an impression of careful construction and development, and an unfailing sense of texture. Francis Wolff's subtly doctored cover shot offers an intriguing impression of the man, showing Dorham in a bright check jacket, but with a faraway look in his eyes as he clutches the microphone; above him, a ghostly image of an American townscape, vivid but also fleeting.

*** **Jazz Contrasts**
Original Jazz Classics OJC 028 *Dorham; Sonny Rollins (ts); Hank Jones (p); Oscar Pettiford (b); Max Roach (d); Betty Glamann (hp).* 5/57.

*** **Two Horns / Two Rhythm**
Original Jazz Classics OJC 463 *Dorham; Ernie Henry (as); Wilbur Ware (b); Granville T Hogan (d).* 11/57–12/57.

The pianoless horn-and-rhythm experiment posed interesting problems for Dorham. Ware's big bass almost fills in the gap; but what is interesting about the set as a whole is how Dorham adjusts his delivery, counting rests much more carefully, filling in with a broader intonation on ensemble passages. Henry and Hogan are by no means passengers, but the real drama of the recording is played out across the three octaves that divide trumpet and bass on some of the bridging passages. Rollins wasn't at first glance the ideal partner for Dorham, but he began to steer him in the direction of an altogether different approach to thematic variation which really became evident only towards the end of the decade. *Horns/Rhythm* gains a star for boldness; *Jazz Contrast* drops back one for the wishy-washy sound.

*** **This Is The Moment**
Original Jazz Classics OJC 812 *Dorham; Curtis Fuller (tb); Cedar Walton (p); Sam Jones (b); G.T Hogan, Charli Persip (d).* 7 & 8/58.

Like Chet Baker, Dorham always considered his singing to be an integral part of what he was and did as a musician. He had sung with Dizzy's band in the 1940s but had made the decision to concentrate on his horn. Even here, it's his 15 July 1958 playing that counts and, while it's tempting to reverse the emphasis and say that it's as lyrical as his singing is improvisatory and horn-like, almost the reverse is the case. Dorham doesn't sing like a horn man but he gives the lyric almost deliberate weight and emphasis, closer to speech rhythms than to top-line jazz. Unlike many hyphenate players, he makes a hard and fast distinction between the two 'voices'. 'From This Moment On' is done as an instrumental but 'I Remember Clifford' is adorned with the Jon Hendricks lyric, when it might have been more interesting the other way round. Both horns are muted throughout, lending the whole a soft, staccato bounce that is no less attractive for being determinedly understated. Historically, the album is significant for being Cedar Walton's first recording. He's not yet the presence he was to be in future years, a sapling rather than the solidly rooted sideman-for-all-seasons that he was to become. Nevertheless his soloing is adroit and uncliché'd and his accompaniment firm without being domineering. A telling debut.

*** **Blue Spring**
Original Jazz Classics OJC 134 *Dorham; David Amram (frhn); Cannonball Adderley (as); Cecil Payne (bs); Cedar Walton (p); Paul Chambers (b); Jimmy Cobb, Philly Joe Jones (d).* 1–2/59.

***(*) **Quiet Kenny**
Original Jazz Classics OJC 250 *Dorham; Tommy Flanagan (p); Paul Chambers (b); Art Taylor (d).* 11/59.

*** **The Arrival Of Kenny Dorham**
Fresh Sound FSRCD 200 *Dorham; Charles Davis (bs); Tommy Flanagan (p); Butch Warren (b); Buddy Enlow (d).* 1/60.

(*) **West 42nd Street
Black Lion BLCD 760119 *Dorham; Rocky Boyd (ts); Walter Bishop Jr (p); Ron Carter (b); Pete LaRoca (d).* 3/61.

*** **Osmosis**
Black Lion BLCD 760146 *Dorham; Curtis Fuller (tb); Frank Haynes (ts); Tommy Flanagan (p); Ben Tucker (b); Dave Bailey (d).* 10/61.

Dorham enjoyed a brief resurgence towards the end of the 1950s, and any of the above would serve as a reasonable introduction to his more deliberate, Miles-influenced approach of that period. *Quiet Kenny* is a minor masterpiece. The blues-playing is still as emotional as ever but there is a more relaxed approach to the basic metres, and Tommy Flanagan in particular invites a quieter and more sustained articulation of themes. *Arrival* sees him in good voice, tooting through a light but demanding programme that includes Rollins's favourite 'I'm An Old Cowhand' and 'Stella By Starlight' with the most open tone he'd produced. *West 42nd Street*, good as it is, isn't a Dorham album. It was recorded and originally released on Jazztime under the leadership of tenor player, Rocky Boyd, which rather explains the order and emphasis of the solos. The two takes each of 'Stella By Starlight' and 'Why Not?' soon dispel a faint aroma of marketing cynicism.

Osmosis is rather better, if a little more padded out. Partnered this time by the callow but developing Curtis Fuller and the all-but-unknown Frank Haynes (whose obscurity seems, on this showing, entirely understandable), Dorham plays with a good deal of fire, often more or less stealing the limelight from his colleagues and at least twice copping an extra couple of choruses, to Flanagan's evident surprise. No one could blame him; the group aren't exactly stiff, but they aren't wildly exciting either; as for Dorham, he was having a good night.

*****(*) Matador / Inta Somethin'**
Blue Note 84460 *Dorham; Jackie McLean (as); Walter Bishop, Bobby Timmons (p); Teddy Smith, Leroy Vinnegar (b); J.C Moses, Art Taylor (d).* 1/61, 4/62.

**** Short Story**
Steeplechase SCCD 36010 *Dorham; Allan Botschinsky (flhn); Tete Montoliu (p); Niels-Henning Orsted Pedersen (b); Alex Riel (d).* 12/63.

**** Scandia Skies**
Steeplechase SCCD 6011 *As above, except Rolf Ericson (t, flhn) replaces Botschinsky.* 12/63.

***** Scandia Story**
Steeplechase SCCD 37047/48 2CD *As for Short Story, Scandia Skies.* 12/63.

Despite the sustained energy of *Una Mas* (recently available only as a limited edition) and of *Trompeta Toccata* (both of which paired the trumpeter's brightly burnished tone with the muscular tenor of Joe Henderson), Dorham seemed to be running out of steam in 1963; 'one more time' was beginning to sound like once too often. The Steeplechases are essentially footnote albums to a remarkable career which still had nearly a decade to run, in purely chronological terms at least. Artistically, Dorham was already recycling desperately. Both albums are perfectly respectable and eminently listenable but lack the profound emotional urgency that was Dorham's trademark, whether he was playing fast, high-register runs or sustained blues cadences. The writing is good but increasingly precise, and Dorham's occasional 'classical' experiments, the beautifully cadenced 'Trompeta Toccata' and, on the Latin-influenced *Matador*, a Villa-Lobos prelude for Dorham and the unsuitable Timmons, don't quite effect the kind of syntheses he managed in Henderson's company. Produced in the wake of a South American tour, *Matador* (originally released on United Artists) is touched by Brazilian rather than Afro-Cuban rhythms. McLean plays beautifully, especially an anguished introduction to 'Lover Man' that recalls Parker's disastrous Dial recording of the tune.

For some reason, Steeplechase still list the composite *Scandia Story* and the two single albums which comprise it. Given that the label's recent doublings have been on a mid-price imprint, it makes sense to go for the twofer.

***** The Art Of The Ballad**
Prestige 11013 *Dorham; David Amram (frhn); Cannonball Adderley, Ernie Henry (as); Harold Land, Oliver Nelson, Sonny Rollins (ts); Jimmy Heath (ts, bs); Cecil Payne (bs); Walter Bishop, Ray Bryant, Kenny Drew, Tommy Flanagan, Amos Trice, Cedar Walton (p); Betty Glamann (hp); Paul Chambers, Percy Heath, Clarence Jones, Wendell Marshall, Eddie Mathias, Oscar Pettiford, Wilbur Ware (b); Kenny Clarke, Jimmy Cobb, G.T Hogan, Max Roach, Art Taylor (d).* 53–59.

Good to see Kenny represented alongside more obvious players in this budget series. The trumpeter was a finely sensitive interpreter of ballads. And yet the album represents somewhat thin pickings for anyone eager to hear Kenny highlighted at length. Rightly, in our view, Prestige have gone for great performances rather than for tunes which highlight Dorham to the exclusion of others. Many of the tracks were made for other leaders, Ernie Henry, Harold Land and Oliver Nelson, and with Cannonball Adderley as co-leader. And yet it's the very quietness and almost reticence of Kenny's solo on 'Passion Flower' for Nelson that steals the record. That, and Cannonball Adderley's glorious, blues-drenched choruses on 'It Might As Well Be Spring'. An attractive package, and one that may well send newcomers in search of Dorham's original LPs.

Jimmy Dorsey (1904–57)

ALTO AND BARITONE SAXOPHONES, CLARINET, TRUMPET

The elder, reed-playing Dorsey brother worked with his sibling on the New York session-scene of the '20s before co-leading a band which he eventually took over after a quarrel with Tommy. A superb technician on his horns, admired by Charlie Parker and others, Dorsey's music matched his basically mild-mannered demeanour. He was reconciled with his brother, and their final venture as co-leaders ended with Tommy's death, followed by Jimmy's passing only months later.

****(*) Pennies From Heaven**
ASV AJA 5052 *Dorsey; George Thow, Toots Camarata, Joe Meyer (t); Don Mattison (tb, v); Bobby Byrne, Joe Yukl, Bruce Squires (tb); Fud Livingston (as, ts); Jack Stacey, Len Whitney (as); Skeets Hurfurt, Charles Frazier (ts); Bobby Van Eps, Freddy Slack (p); Roc Hillman (g, v); Slim Taft, Jack Ryan (b); Ray McKinley (d, v); Bob Eberle, Frances Langford (v).* 3/36–6/37.

***** Amapola**
ASV AJA 5287 *As above, except add W.C Clark, Shorty Sherock, Ralph Muzillo, Nate Kazabier, Johnny Napton, Shorty Solomon, Jimmy Campbell, Ray Anthony, Paul McCoy, Bob Alexy, Ray Linn, Marky Markowitz, Phil Napoleon (t), Sonny Lee, Jerry Rosa, Al Jordan, Phil Washburne, Andy Russo, Nick Di Maio (tb); Noni Bernard, Dave Matthews, Sam Rubinowich, Milt Yaner, Frank Langone, Bill Covey (as), Leonard Whitner, Herbie Haymer, Don Hammond, Babe Russin (ts); Chuck Gentry, Bob Lawson (bs); Freddy Slack, Joe Lippman, Johnny Guarnieri, Dave Mann (p), Guy Smith, Allan Reuss, Tommy Kay (g), Jack Ryan, Bill Miller (b), Buddy Schutz (d), Bing Crosby, The Andrews Sisters, Helen O'Connell, Kitty Kallen (v).* 7/36–10/43.

****(*) At The 400 Restaurant 1946**
Hep CD 41 *Dorsey; Bob Avery, Claude Bowen, Ray Linn, Tonny Picciotto, Nathan Solomon, Seymour Baker, Irving Goodman, Louis Mucci (t); Simon Zentner, Thomas Lee, Nick Di Maio, Anthony Russo, Fred Mancusi, Don Mattison, Bob Alexander (tb); Jack Aiken, Frank Langone, Bill Covey, Cliff Jackson (as); Bobby Dukoff, Charles Frazier, Charles Travis, Gill Koerner (ts); Bob Lawson, Johnny Dee (bs); Marvin Wright, Lou Carter (p); Herb Ellis, Teddy Walters (g); Jimmy Middleton, Norman Bates (b); Adolf Shutz, Karl Kiffe (d); Dee Parker, Paul Chapman (v).* 1/46.

The elder Dorsey brother was a saxophonist of the highest technical accomplishment, though it tended to lead him to merely show off on many of the records he made as a sessionman in the 1920s. The band he formed in 1935 after splitting up with his brother was a commercial dance unit rather than any kind of jazz orchestra, but the group could swing when Dorsey wanted it to, and there was some impeccable section-playing, particularly from the trombones. The ASV disc pulls together 18 tracks from this period, a mixture of vocal features for Eberle, Langford and McKinley and more jazz-orientated titles. 'Dorsey Dervish' harks back to the leader's technical exercises of the decade before, but 'Stompin' At The Savoy' is creditable enough, and Bobby Byrne's beautiful lead trombone on 'In A Sentimental Mood' (contrary to the sleeve-notes, Byrne doesn't sing on this tune) outdoes even Tommy Dorsey for mellifluousness. It's a pity, though, that titles such as 'Swamp Fire', 'Major And Minor Stomp' and 'Cherokee' are omitted. The remastering is rather lifeless.

Amapola collects 24 of the biggest hits by Dorsey's band over a seven-year period. The emphasis here is on the ballad and vocal-feature side of Dorsey's discography, and if this is what you want, it's an ideal record – from the title-track, Helen O'Connell's signature rendition of 'Green Eyes' and Kitty Kallen's 'Besame Mucho' to the somewhat more swinging 'I Fall In Love With You Every Day' and the novelty 'Six Lessons From Madame La Zonga', these are the memories which Dorsey's amen corner will probably remember best. The odd soloist pops up here and there to remind us that it was basically a good band. Better transfers than on the earlier ASV CD.

The Hep CD is a lot more modernistic: among the opening four tracks, which date from 1944, is a Dizzy Gillespie arrangement of 'Grand Central Getaway'. The remainder are airshots taken from a New York engagement two years later and, while the band has nothing very outstanding about it, there are one or two worthwhile solos from Bob Avery and the leader whose attractive score, 'Contrasts', hints at directions which he never really followed. Generally, though, there is rather more jazz-inflected material here than on the earlier CD, and remastering makes the best of the broadcast recording.

Tommy Dorsey (1905–56)

TROMBONE, TRUMPET

A ubiquitous figure on the New York dance-band circuit of the 1920s, Dorsey went on to lead one of the most successful swing-era big bands, although the jazz content of the records was often in doubt. The 'Sentimental Gentleman' of swing was a martinet of a leader, but he kept his band going through the ups and downs of the post-swing era, eventually reuniting with his brother Jimmy in their final orchestra. His perfect legato trombone style and singing high tone were his signature, something which heavily influenced his band singer, Frank Sinatra. In 1956, he choked to death in his sleep.

***** Tommy Dorsey 1928–1935**

Classics 833 *Dorsey; Manny Klein, Andy Ferretti, Sterling Bose, Bill Graham (t); Joe Ortolano, Ben Pickering, Dave Jacobs (tb); Jimmy Dorsey, Sid Stoneburn (cl, as); Noni Bernardi (as); Clyde Rounds (as, ts); Johnny Van Eps (ts); Paul Mitchell, Fulton McGrath, Frank Signorelli (p); Arthur Schutt (harmonium); Eddie Lang, Mac Cheikes (g); Gene Traxler, Jimmy Williams (b); Sam Rosen, Sam Weiss, Stan King (d); Edythe Wright, Eleanor Powell (v).* 11/28–11/35.

Classics' opening disc takes in Dorsey's great 1928–9 dates where he plays trumpet – a bit shaky, but tremendously fierce, with terrific Eddie Lang support. These sound very clean and bright, which is why the rotten quality of the 1935 orchestra dates is so disappointing. These can't have been direct transfers. Either way, Dorsey got off to a modest start with five fairly nondescript sessions – though the fourth released his hit theme, 'I'm Getting Sentimental Over You'.

****(*) Tommy Dorsey 1935–1936**

Classics 854 *Dorsey; Sterling Bose, Andy Ferretti, Joe Bauer, Max Kaminsky, Sam Skolnick (t); Ben Pickering, Joe Ortolano, Walter Mercurio (tb); Joe Dixon (cl, as, v); Sid Stoneburn (cl, as); Fred Stulce, Noni Bernardi (as); Clyde Rounds (as, ts); Sid Block, Johnny Van Eps (ts); Dick Jones (p); Bill Schaffer (g); Gene Traxler, Dave Tough, Sam Weiss (d); Edythe Wright, Buddy Gately, Jack Leonard (v).* 12/35–3/36.

***** Tommy Dorsey 1936**

Classics 878 *As above, except add Steve Lipkins (t), Red Bone, Les Jenkins (tb), Bud Freeman (ts), Carmen Mastren (g), The Three Esquires (v); omit Bose, Ferretti, Ortolano, Stoneburn, Bernardi, Block, Van Eps, Weiss, Gately.* 4–10/36.

***** Tommy Dorsey 1936–1937**

Classics 916 *As above, except add Bunny Berigan, Bob Cusumano, Andy Ferretti, Jimmy Welch (t), Artie Foster (tb), Slats Long (cl, ts); omit Skolnick, Pickering, Schaffer.* 11/36–2/37.

***** Tommy Dorsey 1937**

Classics 955 *As above, except add Pee Wee Erwin (t), Mike Doty, Johnny Mince (cl, as), Howard Smith (p); omit Berigan, Lipkins, Cusumano, Foster, Three Esquires.* 2–5/37.

Like all the great swing orchestras, Dorsey's band was as much about dance music as it was about jazz, and listening through these tracks may disappoint some expectations. Relatively few of the songs can be called survivors of the era since there is a lot of forgettable chaff among the material. Many of the arrangements are more functional than challenging, solos are usually kept to a minimum, and the feel of the orchestra harks back to Dorsey's earlier days as often as it looks ahead. All that said, the trombonist could claim several virtues. While he was the principal soloist, he could call on several fine jazzmen: Freeman, Dixon, Mince and – above all – Berigan, whose tantalizing first stint with the band (a mere five sessions) resulted in 'Song Of India', 'Marie', 'Mr Ghost Goes To Town' and 'The Goona Goo', to cite four memorable solos (all on Classics 916). Dorsey also had one of the best band singers of the era, Edythe Wright, as well as his Clambake Seven small group (discussed below). Sometimes an unpromising title will turn out surprisingly well, and on a piece like 'Keepin' Out Of Mischief Now' (Classics 916) the whole band shows what it could do. There is also the splendid swing drumming of Dave Tough to listen to.

Of these four discs, the first gets lower marks for a low ration of worthwhile tracks and some very sloppy remastering, the quality of which seems to vary from track to track. The standard improves on the next three, although a listen to the Retrieval CD listed below against the Clambake Seven tracks on Classics 955 shows how much better a job can be done with a little care and some mint originals. Classics 916 is probably the pick for the tracks with Berigan.

***** Tommy Dorsey 1937 Vol. 2**

Classics 995 *Dorsey; Pee Wee Erwin, Joe Bauer, Andy Ferretti (t); Les Jenkins, Red Bone (tb); Johnny Mince, Mike Doty (cl, as); Fred Stulce, Skeets Herfurt (as); Bud Freeman, Tony Antonelli (ts); Howard Smith (p); Carmen Mastren (g); Gene Traxler (b); Dave Tough (d); Edythe Wright, Jack Leonard (v).* 5–7/37.

***** Tommy Dorsey 1937 Vol. 3**

Classics 1035 *As above, except Walter Mercurio (tb) replaces Bone; omit Antonelli and Doty; add Lee Castle (t).* 7–9/37.

***** Tommy Dorsey 1937–1938**

Classics 1078 *As above, except add Earle Hagen (tb), Maurice Purtill (d); omit Bauer, Mercurio.* 10/37–3/38.

Dorsey was making records at an incredible pace: he cut 22 sessions in 1937 alone, proof of the band's popularity. As usual, though, the results are the swing-era mix of worthwhile music and softcore ballads and schmaltz. When the vocalist sits out and Dorsey gives the soloists some space, the full band delivers something fine, such as 'Canadian Capers' (Classics 1035), but for the most part the jazz content is left to the Clambake Seven sessions, where Dorsey, Freeman and the underrated Mince especially put some real heat into the proceedings. But there are also other compensations: Edythe Wright's singing is always a pleasure, and the mellifluous sound of the leader is frequently parlayed into similarly graceful playing by the whole band. There is the quota of jazzed classics, from such unlikely sources as Dvořák and Rimsky-Korsakov, on Classics 995; and Classics 1078 has his big hit, 'The Dipsy Doodle', arranged by Larry Clinton, although the second half of the disc is let down by some particularly bland material. Transfers aren't startling, but the music comes through cleanly enough.

***** The Song Is You**

Bluebird 66353-2 5CD *Dorsey; Bunny Berigan, Jimmy Blake, Ray Linn, Clyde Hurley, Ziggy Elman, Chuck Peterson, Al Stearns, Manny Klein, Jimmy Zito, Roger Ellick, Mickey Mangano, Dale Pierce, George Seaberg, Charlie Shavers, Gerald Goff (t); Dave Jacobs, Elmer Smithers, Ward Silloway, Lowell Martin, George Arus, Les Jenkins, Walter Mercurio, James Skiles, Walt Benson, Nelson Riddle, Tex Satterwhite, Karle De Karske, William Haller, Richard Noel (tb); Johnny Mince, Fred Stulce, Skeets Herfurt, Dean Kincaide, Babe Russin, Hymie Schertzer, Paul Mason, Don Lodice, Heinie Beau, Manny Gershman, Bruce Snyder, Harry Schuchman, Buddy DeFranco, Sid Cooper, Gale Curtis, Al Klink, Bruce Branson, Babe Fresk, Dave Harris, Gus Bivona, Vido Musso, Bill Shine (saxes); Howard Smith, Joe Bushkin, Milt Raskin, Milt Golden, John Potoker (p); Carmen Mastren, Clark Yocum, Bob Bain, Sam Herman (g); Joe Park (tba); Gene Traxler, Sid Weiss, Phil Stevens, Sid Block (b); Cliff Leeman, Buddy Rich (d); Frank Sinatra (v).* 2/40–7/42.

***** Tommy Dorsey & His Orchestra With Frank Sinatra**

RCA Tribune 15518-2 2CD *Similar to above.* 40–42.

The Song Is You is of relatively peripheral interest, since it puts together a complete edition of all Frank Sinatra's vocals with Dorsey. Inevitably, jazz takes a back seat to the band's smoochier style but, if it's Sinatra you want to hear, this is as good a set as one could hope for, and the painstaking remastering should please all but those who have access to a set of mint originals. The Tribune set boils it down to a couple of discs' worth.

*****(*) The Best Of Tommy Dorsey And His Clambake Seven 1936–1938**

Retrieval RTR 79012 *Dorsey; Max Kaminsky, Pee Wee Irwin (t); Joe Dixon, Johnny Mince (cl); Bud Freeman (ts); Dick Jones (p); Bill Schaffer, Carmen Mastren (g); Gene Traxler (b); Dave Tough, Maurice Purtill, (d); Edythe Wright (v).* 12/35–2/47.

***** The Panic Is On!**

Vipers Nest VN-154 *Dorsey; Max Kaminsky (t); Joe Dixon (cl); Sid Block (ts); Dick Jones (p); Bill Schaffer (g); Gene Traxler (b); Dave Tough (d); Edythe Wright (v).* 3–4/36.

Dorsey's small group was an initiative he began almost as soon as the bigger band became successful, and he ran it on and off alongside the main orchestra for the rest of his career. As with the big band, though, the group's material is often thin and prone to the occasional novelty tune which spoils what should have been a definitive small-group swing outfit. Retrieval's 21-track selection mystifyingly leaves out some very good Sevens (including our favourite, 'Rhythm Saved The World', which at least is on Classics 854) but otherwise offers a vivid portrait of some of Dorsey's best playing – his own solos a marriage of urbanity and heat – and excellent spots for Freeman, Erwin and Dixon. The best thing, though, is the superlative remastering by John R.T. Davies, which lets one hear what Carmen Mastren and Dave Tough were doing for the first time in any reissue and makes one aware of what a swinging rhythm section this was.

The Panic Is On! offers airshots from the same period. Some of these have some fine moments for Dorsey and Kaminsky, and 'I'll Bet You Tell That To All The Girls' is untypically hot and swinging. Some of the material is pretty awful, but it's a worthwhile glimpse of the Clambake Seven in serious action. Sound is faded but not too dusty.

****(*) Palladium 1940 & Raleigh Show 1943**

Jazz Hour JH-1035 *Personnel unlisted.* 40–43.

****(*) 1942 War Bond Broadcast**

Jazz Hour JH-1013 *Personnel unlisted.* 7–10/42.

Both these discs of airshots are for hardcore followers only. The earlier set has some good if rusty 1940 material with Sinatra and, though the 1943 show is in surprisingly bright and clear hi-fi, the band sounds jolted and there's a lot of irrelevant speech-making. The 1942 disc starts off in poor sound, which gets increasingly worse until halfway through, when the October programme cleans up and works off a couple of nice if familiar Sy Oliver arrangements.

***** The Carnegie Hall V-Disc Session April 1944**

Hep CD 40 *Dorsey; Pete Candoli, George Seaberg, Sal La Perche, Dale Pearce, Bob Price, Ralph Santangelo, Mickey Mangano (t); Walter Benson, Tommy Pederson, Tex Satterwhite, Nelson Riddle (tb); Buddy DeFranco, Hank D'Amico (cl, as); Sid Cooper, Leonard Kaye (as); Gail Curtis, Al Klink, Don Lodice, Mickey Sabol (ts); Bruce Branson, Manny Gershman (bs); Dodo Marmarosa, Milt Raskin (p); Dennis Sandole, Bob Bain (g); Joe Park (tba); Sid Block (b); Gene Krupa, Maurice Purtill, Buddy Rich (d); Bing Crosby, Frances Langford, Georgia Gibbs, Bob Allen, The Sentimentalists, Bonnie Lou Williams (v); plus string section.* 10/43–9/44.

****(*) The All Time Hit Parade Rehearsals**

Hep CD 39 *As above, except omit Candoli, Price, Santangelo, D'Amico, Kaye, Klink, Gershman, Raskin, Sandole, Krupa and Purtill, Crosby and Gibbs; add Judy Garland, Frank Sinatra (v).* 6–9/44.

Although there isn't a great deal of jazz on these records, they give a clearer idea of the sound of Dorsey's band since John R.T. Davies's superb remastering puts many reissues to shame. *All Time Hit Parade* is drawn from acetate transcriptions of rehearsals for a radio show of that name and, while they tend to display the sweeter side of Dorsey's band, the smooth power of the sections is put across smartly by the sound. Sinatra has a couple of fine features in 'I'll Walk Alone' and 'If You Are But A Dream', and there's a showcase for Marmarosa on 'Boogie Woogie'. The V-Disc material, again in splendid restoration, is rather more exciting, with a number of spots for La Perche, DeFranco and Klink. Crosby and Langford deliver a couple of messages to the troops as a bonus.

**** Tommy Dorsey Plays Sweet And Hot**

Tax CD 3705-2 *Dorsey; Zeke Zarchey, Lee Castaldo, Jimmy Blake (t); Ward Silloway, Lowell Martin (tb); Johnny Mince (cl, as); Fred Stulce, Les Robinson (as); Babe Russin, Paul Mason (ts); Bob Kitsis (p); Bob Heller (g); Gene Traxler (b); Buddy Rich (d); Frank Sinatra, Jo Stafford, The Pied Pipers (v).* 2/40.

*****(*) Well, Git It!**

Jass J-CD-14 *Dorsey; Pete Candoli, Bob Price, George Seaberg, Sal La Perche, Vito Mangano, Dale Pierce, Gerald Goff, Charlie Shavers, Paul McCoy, Mickey Mangano, Cy Baker, Chuck Genduso (t); Walter Benson, Tommy Pedersen, Tex Satterwhite, Nelson Riddle, Richard Noel, Karle De Karske, Al Esposito, Bill Siegel, Bill Schallen, Sam Levine (tb); Hank D'Amico, Buddy DeFranco, Gus Bivona (cl, as); Sid Cooper, Leonard Kaye (as); Bruce Branson (ts, as, bs); Hank Lodice, Gail Curtis, Mickey Sabol, Al Klink, Babe Fresk, Boomie Richman (ts); Manny Gershman (bs); Milt Raskin, Jess Stacy, Dodo Marmarosa, John Potoker (p); Sam Herman, Danny Sandoli (g); Sid Block, Joe Park (b); Alvin Stoller, Buddy Rich, Gene Krupa (d); Skip Nelson, Stuart Foster, Bonnie Lou Williams, The Sentimentalists (v).* 43–46.

There could hardly be a more striking contrast than there is between these two discs of airshots. The Tax CD offers a complete show from the Meadowbrook Ballroom in New Jersey from February 1940, and it's all sweet and not very hot: there are corny arrangements of college songs, novelty tunes and a few worthwhile ballads – with Sinatra and Jo Stafford perhaps the main points of interest in the broadcast. There isn't much jazz, but the sound of the band is caught very clearly by Jack Towers's fine remastering of the material. The Jass collection is a little rougher, but it's infinitely more exciting, opening on a wildly over-the-top 'Well, Git It!' featuring guest Gene Krupa (Buddy Rich has his own turn on another version at the end of the disc). In between are new versions of many of Dorsey's better hits, a few of the superior sweet items, and solo turns for DeFranco, Shavers, Candoli and more. A first-class compilation of its kind.

***** Live In Hi-Fi At Casino Gardens**

Jazz Hour JH-1018 *Personnel unlisted.* 6–8/46.

The first show here is OK but nothing special, with Charlie Shavers's feature on 'At The Fat Man' the only standout; but the second, with extended workouts on six good charts by Bill Finegan and others, is much more like it. There's a lot of badinage between Tom and the announcer, which will either charm or repel, but the music's strong and the sound, if not exactly 'hi-fi', is quite listenable.

****(*) At The Fat Man's 1946–1948**

Hep CD 43 *Dorsey; Jack Dougherty, Mickey Mangano, George Seaburg, Ziggy Elman, Charlie Shavers, Claude Bowen, Vern Arslan, Chuck Peterson (t); Larry Hall, Tex Satterwhite, Greg Philips, John Youngman, Charles La Rue, Red Benson, Nick Di Maio, Dick Noel (tb); Buddy DeFranco, Billy Ainsworth, Marshall Hawk, Louis Prisby (cl, as); Sid Cooper, Bruce Branson (as); Boomie Richman, Don Lodice, Babe Fresk, Corky Corcoran, Marty Berman (ts); Joe Koch (bs); John Potoker, Rocky Coluccio, Paul Smith (p); Sam Herman, Tony Rizzi (g); Sid Block, Sam Cheifetz, Norman Seelig (b); Alvin Stoller, Louie Bellson (d); Stuart Foster, Denny Dennis, Lucy Ann Polk, Gordon Polk, The Sentimentalists (v).* 5/46–12/48.

*****(*) The Post-War Era**

Bluebird 66156-2 *Similar to above, except add Charlie Shavers, Paul McCoy, Cy Baker, Irving Goodman, Johnny Martel, Bernie Glow, Hal Ableser, Chris Griffin, Stan Stout, Doc Severinsen, Ray Wetzel, Billy Butterfield, Art Depew, Johnny Amoroso (t), Bill Siegel, Sam Levine, Bill Schallen, Larry Hall, Sol Train, Al Mastren, Buddy Morrow, Dean Kincaide, Will Bradley, Bill Pritchard, Ange Callea (tb), Abe Most, John Rotella, Billy Ainsworth, George Kennon, Walt Levinsky, Hugo Lowenstein, Sol Schlinger, Danny Bank, Jerry Winner (reeds), Gene Kutch, Lou Levy (p), Ward Erwin, Bob Baldwin (b), Buddy Rich (d).* 1/46–6/50.

Dorsey's later records deserve a wider hearing than they've been given by posterity. He had no more hits on the scale of 'Marie' or 'Song Of India', but he remained – as then-new arranger Bill Finegan, responsible for the best arrangements on the Bluebird CD, asserts in the sleeve-note – a keen-eared musician and less conservative than many of his contemporaries. *The Post-War Era* is a splendid cross-section of the pick of Dorsey in the 1940s, with smart scores such as 'Hollywood Hat', with its amazing brass figures, or 'Tom Foolery' sounding as good as anything in his earlier work. There are some previously unissued tracks among the 22 on offer, and the sound, though dry, is clean and sharp. The Hep compilation suffers from some very variable sound-sources and, though these airchecks feature some fine alternative versions of some of the scores on the Bluebird disc (as well as a couple of delicious vocals by Lucy Ann Polk), it stands very much in the shadow of the studio disc.

Dorsey Brothers Orchestra

GROUP

As bandleaders, the brothers put aside their many differences for a while at least. While their early bands were studio-only outfits, they formed a 'real' Dorsey Brothers Orchestra in 1934, but it lasted only a year before Jimmy took it over after a quarrel with his sibling. Their last co-led band ran from 1953 until Tommy's death.

***** The Dorsey Brothers' Orchestra Vol. 1**

Jazz Oracle BDW 8004 *Leo McConville, Fuzzy Farrar, Mickey Bloom, Nat Natoli, Mannie Klein (t); Tommy Dorsey (t, tb); Jack Teagarden, Carl Loffler, Glenn Miller (tb); Jimmy Dorsey (cl, as); Arnold Brilhart (cl, as, f); Frank Teschemacher (cl, ts); Herbert Spencer, Bill Green (ts); Adrian Rollini (bsx); Frank Signorelli, Arthur Schutt (p); Charles Dondron (vib); Carl Kress (g, bj); Eddie Lang (g); Tony Colucci (bj); Jimmy Williams (b); Joe Tarto, Hank Stern, Jack Hansen (tba); Stan King, Chauncey Morehouse (d); Smith Ballew, Hal Kemp, Nye Mayhew, Saxie Dowell, Skinny Ennis, Irving Kaufman (v).* 2–11/28.

***** The Dorsey Brothers' Orchestra Vol. 2**

Jazz Oracle BDW 8005 *Similar to above, except add Phil Napoleon, Muggsy Spanier, Frank Guarente (t), Joe Yukl (tb), Ollie Boyd (cl), Max Farley (as, f), Alfie Evans, Larry Abbott (as), Lucien Smith (ts, v), Jim Crossan, Paul Mason (ts), Phil Raines (bsn), Irving Brodsky (p), Al Duffy, Leo Kroucrick, Murray Kellner, Sam Rates, Nat Brusiloff, Sam Freed (vn), Emil Stark (clo), Jimmy Mullen (b), Ray Bauduc (d); Bing Crosby (v).* 1/29–1/30.

***** The Dorsey Brothers' Orchestra Vol. 3**

Jazz Oracle BDW 8006 *Similar to above, except add Bunny Berigan, Bill Moore, Louis Gracia, Charles Margulis (t), Foster Morehouse, Larry Binyon, Bud Freeman (ts), Fulton McGrath (p), Tony Sacco (g, bj, v), Dick McDonough (g), Artie Bernstein (b), Scrappy Lambert, Wes Vaughan, Elmer Feldkamp (v).* 11/30–4/33.

***** Harlem Lullaby**

Hep CD 1006 *Manny Klein, Sterling Bose, Bunny Berigan (t); Tommy Dorsey (tb); Larry Binyon (cl, as, ts); Jimmy Dorsey (cl, as); Joe Venuti, Harry Hoffman, Walter Edelstein, Lou Kosloff (vn); Joe Meresco, Fulton McGrath (p); Dick McDonough (g); Artie Bernstein (b); Stan King, Chauncey Morehouse, Larry Gomar (d); Bing Crosby, Mae West, Ethel Waters, Mildred Bailey, Lee Wiley (v).* 2–7/33.

The Dorseys could call on their best pals for their many studio dates, even before the 'official' formation of their orchestra in 1934. A string of sessions for OKeh (and a couple for other labels) are comprehensively covered by the nicely presented Jazz Oracle CDs, which include numerous alternative takes, a few rare tests and the various 'solo' sessions which the brothers undertook in the period. Considering how often they threw in 8 or 16 hot bars into the many conventional dance records they played on, it's a bit surprising that their own bands were not much more jazz-orientated than their bread-and-butter dates. The pickings on both of the first two discs are regrettably slim. The January 1929 date has some fine vocals by Bing Crosby, but too many of the tracks are troubled by feeble singing and only a few brief glimpses of a soloist (despite the often stellar line-ups, it's only Tommy and Jimmy who do the real improvising). A track such as 'Breakaway' on the second volume is a comparative corker. But the solo sessions that were features for each Dorsey separately are still fondly remembered by collectors, and they're presented in admirable sound here: Jimmy's clarinet feature on 'Prayin' The Blues' still sounds terrific, and it reminds one of why Charlie Parker and Dexter Gordon both held him in high esteem.

The third volume is arguably the best, since Berigan shows up and has some excellent solo spots of his own, along with those of the brothers: sample the rollicking 'Parkin' In The Moonlight' as a choice example. The disc closes five more feature-sessions for the Dorseys as individual soloists. Tommy's turn on 'Maybe' doesn't have much jazz in it, but this rare pair of test-takes shows just why he was the greatest smooth-man of his day. First-rate transfers, although the January 1930 date for Cameo has taxed even John R.T. Davies to the limit as far as getting something out of the shellac goes.

Hep's compilation offers the chance to hear the brothers and their men backing four vocalists of the day. Mae West's pair of titles are little more than a not especially tuneful extension of her man-eating persona, and Wiley's session shows the singer still in raw shape, but the four tracks with Crosby show how much the singer had learnt from jazz players, and the eight featuring Mildred Bailey are delightful, her light and limber voice gliding over the music with little effort. There are brief solos for the Dorseys and Berigan here and there, but the record belongs mainly to the singers. First-class remastering throughout.

****(*) The Dorsey Brothers Orchestra – 1935**

Circle CCD-20 *George Thow, Jerry Neary, Charlie Spivak (t); Tommy Dorsey, Joe Yukl, Don Matteson (tb); Jimmy Dorsey (cl, as); Jack Stacey (as); Skeets Herfurt (ts); Bobby Van Eps (p); Roc Hillman (g); Delmar Kaplan (b); Ray McKinley (d); Bob Crosby (v).* 1/35.

Thirteen transcriptions for WBC, with the orchestra in fine fettle. Crosby is restricted to four vocals and the emphasis is on the band, but the charts tend towards the sweet rather than the hot, and when they do tackle a fast one – as with 'Sugar Foot Stomp' or 'Eccentric' – the ensemble sound and a certain rhythmic squareness suggest that the Dorseys hadn't yet got their feet out of the 1920s. The sound is clean if a little muffled. The rest of the CD is given over to 12 tracks by Arnold Johnson's orchestra.

***** Casino Gardens Ballroom 1946**

Hep 59 *Bob Alexy, Ray Linn, Irving Goodman, Tony Picciotto, Shorty Solomon, Cy Baker, Tony Faso, George Seaburg, Mickey Mangano, John Dougherty, Ziggy Elman, Charlie Shavers, Claude Bowen, Harold Ableser (t); Tommy Dorsey, Mickey Iannone, Sonny Lee, Andy Russo, Nick Di Maio, Bob Alexander, Don Matteson, Fred Mancusi, Chauncey Welsh, Larry Hall, Tex Satterwhite, Greg Philips, John Youngman, Charles La Rue, Walt Benson (tb); Jimmy Dorsey, Jack Aiken, Frank Langone, Tino Isgrow, Buddy Williams, Bob Lawson, Norman Stern, Cliff Jackson, Gilbert Koerner, Vince Francis, Serge Chaloff, Buddy De Franco, Sid Cooper, Don Lodice, Babe Fresk, Boomie Richman, Abe Most, Bob Dawes, Louis Prisby, Bruce Branson, Marty Berman, Corky Corcoran, Joe Koch (reeds); Marvin Wright, Rocky Coluccio, Joe Potoker, Lou Carter (p); Herb Ellis, Tony Rizzi, Bob Bain (g); Joe Stutz, Sid Block, Sam Chiefitz, John Frigo (b); Buddy Schutz, Karl Kiffe, Alvin Stoller, Louie Bellson (d); Dee Parker, Stuart Foster, Bob Carroll (v).* 1/45–7/47.

Strictly speaking, not the brothers together at all, but their respective orchestras featured together in a number of 'battles of the bands' broadcasts. The music is the typical late-swing mix of flag-wavers and crooner ballads. Not much to get excited about, but both bands are as well-heeled as you'd expect, and there are nice glimpses of Herb Ellis and Serge Chaloff with Jimmy's band on a genial treatment of 'Perdido'.

**** 'Live' In The Big Apple 1954/5**

Magic DAWE44 *Charlie Shavers (t); Tommy Dorsey, Jimmy Henderson (tb); Jimmy Dorsey (cl, as); Buddy Rich (d); Johnny Amoroso, Billy Raymond, Dick Haymes, Kitty Kallen, Lynn Roberts (v); rest unknown.* 1/54–10/55.

The brothers had long since patched up their differences by the 1950s, although the orchestra here was principally Tommy's. Neither man was long for this world, and the jazz content here is low: a swinging 'Puddlewump' and 'Skirts And Sweaters' have to fight for space with some feeble vocals (aside from Dick Haymes's beautiful 'Our Love Is Here To Stay') and dining and dancing music. Most of the band is appropriately anonymous. Culled from various radio broadcasts, the sound is lo-fi but listenable.

Dave Douglas (born 1963)

TRUMPET

In less than a decade, Douglas has established himself as a key figure in modern jazz, an individualistic stylist whose grasp of history is apparent mainly in elision and omission rather than homage. A seasoned and responsive performer on other leaders' records, he now has a substantial body of work under his own name.

*****(*) Parallel Worlds**

Soul Note 121226 *Douglas; Mark Feldman (vn); Erik Friedlander (clo); Mark Dresser (b); Michael Sarin (d).* 93.

None other than Gunther Schuller turns up in the sleeve-notes to drop names like Stravinsky, Bartók, Berg and Lutoslawski, as well as Don Ellis, Bob Graettinger and Leo Smith, and to say how much 'I like the Webernesque textures'. Unlike, say, Paul Smoker or Franz Koglmann, two other trumpeters who have attempted some confluence between free jazz and twentieth-century classical forms (and both to be stablemates of Douglas on hat ART), the now ubiquitous Douglas actually includes some canonical material in this quietly ambitious programme. There can't be many more startling openings to a 'jazz' record than 'Sehr Bewegt', an arrangement of the third of Webern's Op. 5, *Five Movements For String Quartet.*

Elsewhere on the album, alongside half a dozen highly idiosyncratic originals, Douglas includes a 'Grand Choral' by Stravinsky (part of *L'Histoire du Soldat*) as well as Weill's 'Ballad In Which MacHeath Asks Everyone To Forgive Him', and Ellington's 'Loco Madi'. This, plus an unconventional instrumentation in jazz terms, makes for an interesting prospect. By the turn of the 1990s, Douglas was being touted as the coming thing – like Bill Frisell a stylist sufficiently unimprisoned by style to make a significant intervention on almost anyone's disc. Membership of John Zorn's ridiculously prolific Masada group cemented perceptions of him as a strong, dry, essentially melodic player whose sound fell somewhere between Booker Little, Miles and Don Ellis. The release of *Parallel Worlds* suggested strongly that Douglas wasn't going to be imprisoned by generalities, either. It's a generously eclectic set, very much within a jazz idiom. The long title-piece and 'For Every Action' are beautifully structured, with crisp, responsive writing for the strings, loaded bass-lines and acres of free space for (mostly) mid-paced improvisation.

As was to become obvious on later records, not least in songs about Bosnian children on the *The Tiny Bell Trio*, Douglas often seems as much inspired by humanitarian and political concerns as by purely musical ones, and there is no mistaking the passion and the commitment he brings to his evocation of 'Parallel Worlds', lives lived under conditions that fall far short of ideal. However academic his influences might sound – and it is Schuller, rather than Douglas, who does that – he is far from uncommunicative, far from unemotional.

*****(*) The Tiny Bell Trio**

Songlines SGL 1504 *Douglas; Brad Schoeppach (g); Jim Black (d).* 12/93.

***** Tiny Bell Trio**

Arabesque Jazz AJ 0126 *As above.* 96.

With the formation of the Tiny Bell Trio, Douglas cemented his interest in European song form. The first of these two extraordinary records includes arrangements of pieces by Joseph Kosma ('La Belle Saison' and 'Fille d'Acier'), Weill again ('Drowned Girl'), a piece by Germaine Tailleferre, the only female member of Les Six, and a traditional Hungarian *csárdás* (all on the Songlines disc). The very good *Constellations* on hat ART included compositions by Schumann, George Brassens and Herbie Nichols, as well as a dedication to Scriabin, but, like all the label's innovative 6000 series, it has been deleted.

A setting like this would be too exacting for a less than supremely confident player. Douglas floats almost unconcernedly over Schoeppach's guitar chords, often in a key which is relative to the implied location of the piece. His attack seems a little brighter and sharper than on the Soul Note, but this may be a function of better recording.

The live set on Arabesque is a touch disappointing, and certainly not up to some of the performances the group turned in over this period. Interestingly, Douglas seems to lean more heavily on chord structures in a setting like this, but there is ample evidence of his left-field approach, and committed enthusiasts will be delighted with further evidence of his talents.

****** In Our Lifetime**

New World/Countercurrents 80471 *Douglas; Josh Roseman (tb); Chris Speed (cl, ts); Marty Ehrlich (bcl); Uri Caine (p); James Genus (b); Joey Baron (d).* 12/94.

****** Five**

Soul Note 121276 *As for Parallel Worlds, except Drew Gress (b) replaces Dresser.* 8/95.

Reconvening the band which made *Parallel Worlds* was an interesting initiative in the context of the progress Douglas seemed to have made with *In Our Lifetime.* The second of the pair has a broader, more orchestral sound, the supplementary horns deployed for depth of focus rather than for surface detail, and that is perhaps the big change in the string group. Feldman, Friedlander and Gress are treated much less as solo strings than as members of an ensemble (admittedly more autonomous than one might usually expect).

The presence of a piano on the earlier disc appears to restrict Douglas somewhat, though Caine is hardly unaware of the musical language being explored. The diversions into atonality seem less doctrinaire and there are signs that Douglas is taking a more mainstream tack on jazz harmonies. Both albums are heavily tinged with a Booker Little influence; 'Strength And Sanity' (on *In Our Lifetime*) is a Little composition, rapidly followed by four miniatures in the spirit of his playing. On the later disc, Woody Shaw, composer of 'Actualities', is an additional influence, and immediately one hears a new and significant facet of what Douglas is about.

***(*) Sanctuary

Avant AVAN 066 2CD *Douglas; Cuong Vu (t); Chris Speed (ts, cl); Mark Dresser, Hilliard Greene (b); Dougie Bowne (d); Anthony Coleman, Yuka Honda (samples). 8/96.*

A hefty slice of slightly retro free jazz, written in the spirit of Coltrane's *Ascension*, Ornette's abstract expressionist canvas for double quartet, *Free Jazz*, and Boulez's percussive masterpiece, *Le Marteau sans maître*. Douglas's most ambitious musical structure to date is inspired by the building of Santa Maria del Fiore Cathedral in Florence, which took more than a century and a half to complete. How this relates to Douglas's music isn't always entirely clear, except that there is an architectural solidity to the writing which one hasn't heard before and an even more patient exposition, even when the subject material is quite perverse.

The pairing of instruments doesn't quite work technically, mainly because the symmetry is too slavishly observed in some respects but not always reflected in the sound. Cuong Vu, barking through the right channel, often seems to be far away from Douglas, while the electronic components are frequently at odds. Dresser is as compelling as ever, though, and Douglas Bowne makes an impressive fist of a percussion role that might be thought to be surplus but which steadily gains in authority.

***(*) Tiny Bell Trio Live In Europe

Arabesque AJ 0126 *Douglas; Brad Schoeppach (g); Jim Black (d, perc). 10/96.*

The best of the earlier Tiny Bell records, the now-deleted *Constellations*, was recorded off-road but mid-tour. It and this suggest that it's a unit which needs sustained activity and an accretion of musical understanding to work well.

Douglas seems confident in his partners, allowing Black in particular to stretch out and express himself. As accordionist Guy Klucevesek was to do in later groups, Schoeppach throws deliciously complex harmonic shapes, a crushed-velvet foil to the trumpeter's bright lines. As before, '*Csárdás*' is something of an encore piece, but the real glory of the set is an almost-12-minute 'Zeno', which opens a central section of compelling modern jazz that is bookended by Douglas's trademark Schumann arrangement. There is some makeweight material, but Douglas fans will find much to ponder in the shorter pieces as well.

*** Stargazer

Arabesque AJ 0132 *Douglas; Joshua Roseman (tb); Uri Caine (p); Joey Baron (d). 12/96.*

At first blush the most conventional set Douglas has yet recorded, this is still sufficiently original to command attention. The leader leans more heavily than usual on chords and a straightforward count, albeit dressed up in Baron's usual skittery style. Strong, confident, but, by the standard of Douglas's recent output, somewhat pedestrian.

*** Magic Triangle

Arabesque AJ 0139 *Douglas; Chris Potter (ts); James Genus (b); Ben Perowsky (d). 5/97.*

Apparently, this is Douglas's biggest-selling album to date, which is rather disappointing, because again it's a rather conventional and only occasionally teasing set. The leader's tone is limpid and softly burnished, and Potter gives further notice of a broad musical capacity. The compositions are all original and the real interest of the album lies in the writing, which shows what a brilliant touch Douglas has with rather more straightforward jazz heads and themes: 'Padded Cell', 'Odalisque' and 'The Ghost' suggest a kinship with an unexpected array of mostly keyboard-based composers, Herbie Nichols, Herbie Hancock, Horace Tapscott.

The absence of a harmony instrument is the most radical departure from Douglas's usual practice and sharply distinguishes this record from what was to follow, but Genus covers the ground admirably and provides enough rhythmic punch to allow Perowsky the kind of expressive freedom Jim Black claimed in the Tiny Bell Trio.

**** Charms Of The Night Sky

Winter & Winter 910 015-2 *Douglas; Guy Klucevesek (acc); Mark Feldman (vn); Greg Cohen (d). 9/97.*

A line-up calculated to combine musical complexity with the purest aesthetic grace. The language is very similar to that of the Tiny Bell Trio but, with Klucevesek and Feldman in the group and no drummer, the pace is slower and more deliberate, a musingly graceful album that never subordinates musicality to mere effect.

'Dance In Thy Soul' is a long tribute to Charlie Haden, conceived somewhere between a classical sonata and one of Haden's beloved torch songs of the 1940s. Klucevesek's touch with shorter, song-like forms can be heard in a sequence of three 'Mug Shots', tiny sketches that would gladden the heart of any lyricist and possibly drive him to despair at the same time.

For a change, there is a jazz standard, Herbie Hancock's 'Little One', and a version of Francesco Cilea's 'Poveri Fiori', a performance that squares perfectly with Winter & Winter's intriguing hybrid of jazz, folk and classical idioms. Where the label catalogue keeps them apart and compartmentalized, Douglas likes to hear them cross-pollinate. This is a record beyond category, full of jazz but something else as well, the kind of record which points forward to new directions for the music's second century.

***(*) Moving Portraits

DIW 934 *Douglas; Bill Carrothers (p); James Genus (b); Billy Hart (d). 12/97.*

Once again an intriguing blend of idiomatic jazz-writing and some unexpected borrowed material, like the two Joni Mitchell songs which begin the album's final section. The closing track, 'Romero', is one of Douglas's most substantial jazz performances, and 'Moving Portrait' is the best evidence yet of how thoroughly he has absorbed modern classical procedures, rather than just importing *ad hoc* themes and ideas.

The presence of Hart is interesting. Jabali has been a constant source of inspiration over the years and he plays here with a calm, swinging authority, all the while responsive to the demands of Douglas's music. Carrothers is not the sort of player to set the heather on fire, but he has a nice touch, sounds as if he might have played the odd bit of Schumann in his youth, and clearly enjoys the challenge of these inventive compositions.

****** Convergence**
Soul Note 121316-2 *Douglas; Mark Feldman (vn); Erik Friedlander (clo); Drew Gress (b); Michael Sarin (d).* 1/98.

This, of course, is the same band that made *Parallel Worlds* and *Five*, with the single change of Drew Gress for Mark Dresser. The latter album was so named because the leader didn't want the project to be thought of as Douglas-and-strings. Five years on, it's a well-proven point. The quintet plays like a unit and puts down roots, throws out shoots all over the place.

No surprise by this stage in the game to find Douglas programming 'Desseins Eternels' from Olivier Messiaen's organ work, *La Nativité du Seigneur*, and following it with Weill's 'Bilbao Song'. The trumpeter claims he first heard the Messiaen piece in a blindfold test set by a friend, and thought it was 'Joe Zawinul, early Weather Report', which attests not to musical illiteracy but to a grasp of the basic seamlessness of musical styles, for the French composer's strong bass pedals are very similar to Zawinul's signature procedure.

The two key tracks here are a farewell to drummer Tony Williams, a perfect illustration of Douglas's ability to invest long form with real significance, and 'Meeting At Infinity', which indirectly gives the album its title and underlines how Douglas likes to have separate musical lines converge only virtually, leaving them to their own instrumental logic. Anyone who has those early records and nothing else will feel on familiar ground and will sense that there's been a fair amount of musical progress along the way. Anyone who's kept pace with the Dave Douglas story will be well satisfied with the synthesis he makes.

*****(*) Songs For Wandering Souls**
Winter & Winter 910 042-2 *Douglas; Brad Shepik (g); Jim Black (d, perc).* 12/98.

The guitarist has either changed his name or is the victim of an egregious typo. He certainly hasn't changed his approach, though on occasion there is something slightly blunter and more guttural in his attack. Along with the obligatory Schumann 'standard' and a group of new compositions, Douglas unexpectedly includes Roland Kirk's 'Breath-A-Thon', which was originally a solo piece on Rahsaan's *Natural Black Inventions: Roots Strata*. By this stage, though, stage expectations of Douglas are pretty open-ended anyway.

The sound is very good, engineered by Joe Perla, with the educated ears of Stefan Winter guaranteeing the quality control. Not the most compelling item in the Douglas canon, but a marvellous representation of his gifts, all the same.

Down Home Jazz Band

GROUP

A West Coast revivalist institution, run for many years by brassman Chris Tyle.

***** Dawn Club Joys**
Stomp Off CD1241 *Bob Schulz (c, v); Chris Tyle (c); Tom Bartlett (tb, v); Bob Helm (cl, v); Ray Skjelbred (p); Jack Meilahn (bj); Mike Bezin (tba); Hal Smith (d).* 7/91.

***** Back To Bodega**
Stomp Off CD1273 *Chris Tyle (t, v); Bob Mielke (tb); Bob Helm (cl, ss, bcl, v); Wally Rose (p); Carl Lunsford (bj, v); Mike Walbridge (tba); Hal Smith (d); Barbara Dane (v).* 8/93.

***** Dancing The Jelly Roll**
Stomp Off CD1316 *Chris Tyle (c, v); John Gill (tb, v); Frank Powers (cl); Steve Pistorius (p, v); Leah Bezin (bj); Mike Walbridge (tba); Hal Smith (d).* 10/96.

Chris Tyle's group has been a fixture in West Coast traditional circles for many years, though there was a ten-year disbandment in the 1970s. The first two discs pay tribute to the Lu Watters Yerba Buena sound, which had a huge impact on revivalists in the USA. There are a few oddities – such as 'When Ragtime Rufus Rags The Humoresque' on *Back To Bodega*! – but much of the material is from a relatively familiar pocket. The distinction comes in the tight syncopation of the ensembles, the particular jig-jog rhythm and the blend of knowingness and genuine enthusiasm which American trad relies on. It helps that original Yerba Buena man Helm is on hand for an extra drop of authenticity. *Dancing The Jelly Roll* is all ragtime – of sorts – even though the Down Home style of rag is less formally 'right' and more in the Turk Murphy style. They go far enough forward to dip into the Bennie Moten repertoire for items like 'Goofy Dust' and generally make a valid case for all 21 pieces.

Mark Dresser (born 1952)

DOUBLE BASS

Dresser is often assumed to be a lifelong New Yorker, but he actually cut his musical teeth in his native Los Angeles, where he studied with Bertram Turetzky and worked with an array of figures on the West Coast free scene, including David Murray and Arthur Blythe. His membership of the Anthony Braxton Quartet was important in steering him towards leadership.

***** The Cabinet Of Dr Caligari**
Knitting Factory Works KFWCD 155 *Dresser; Dave Douglas (t); Denman Moroney (prepared p).* 93.

****** Force Green**
Soul Note 121273 *As above, except add Phil Haynes (d), Theo Bleckmann (v).* 9/94.

***** Invocation**
Knitting Factory 173 *As above, except add Gerry Hemingway (d, perc).* 95.

Though Dresser uses the bow rather sparingly, there is something very proper and legitimate about his plucked lines, even when they are free form. He uses such lines to create a mood on the first of these, written as live accompaniment to the cult silent film. Prepared piano gives a dry, alienating sound that is ideally suited to the bleak expressionism of *Caligari*, and the ubiquitous Douglas conveys an urgency and sense of menace, allied perhaps to his own passionate response to recent war and violence.

On 'Bosnia', one of the tracks on *Force Green*, he utters despairing, pain-racked cries over Dresser's harmonic squeaks and rumbles, an intense evocation of both men's (Dresser is the composer) humanitarian reaction; Bleckmann, who is used as a second horn rather than a lyric vocalist, comes in with muezzin cries and wails that reinforce the Balkan/Middle Eastern tonality. The previous track, 'Ediface', is a more obviously jazz-based structure and allows Douglas to stretch out, counterpointed by Bleckmann's slightly nasal scats. The long 'Castles For Carter' is an elaborate fantasy for the late clarinettist, John Carter, and a passing reference to his *Castles Of Ghana* album. Tightly organized round a series of pan-tonal themes, it never sounds like a blowing piece, nor as if it is wholly written out; and it's here for the first time on the set that the young Moroney and Haynes come into their own. Up to that point it could almost have been another trio. Douglas blows a thoughtful remembrance of his great predecessor on 'For Miles', with a sly quote from a famous solo, before Bleckmann reverts to falsetto for a gorgeous dialogue that consigns Dresser to the background for a few minutes. Moroney experiments with preparation again, creating a strange, sitar-like tone. This is otherwise very much the bassist's record, but only in the proper sense that he steers the music. Co-producer Tim Berne keeps him properly located in the mix – even the unaccompanied intro to 'Castles' is naturally balanced – and the total effect is of an ensemble rather than a loose coalition of individuals, which is what this music requires.

Dominating *Invocation* is the extraordinary 'Polystop For Multiple Solo Bass', a virtuosic piece of performance and production which recalls, not for the first or last time in his recording career, the kind of work Mark must have done with Turetzky. It's a dazzling display, and worthy of the closest attention. The 'Threnody For Charles Mingus' is co-written with Gerry Hemingway. Closer in feel to jazz, it's affecting and powerfully structured music.

***** Banquet**

Tzadik 7027 *Dresser; Mathias Ziegler (f, cl); Marcus Roja (tba); string quartet.* 11/97.

Dominated by a passionate mourning song for the victims of TWA Flight 800, *Banquet* is one of Dresser's most beautiful and unusual projects to date. 'Loss Of The Innocents' is scored for cello, tuba and clarinet, while the remainder of the album is a species of mini double concerto for flute and bass with string quartet, a piece which allows Dresser to explore extremes of sonority and pitch with great sophistication. A most unusual record, but a highly effective one that embraces expressiveness and formal control.

***** Eye'll Be Seeing You**

Knitting Factory 211 *Dresser; Chris Speed (ts, cl); Anthony Coleman (p, org).* 97.

If you've seen the notorious Buñuel/Dalí short, *Un Chien andalou*, you'll know how bad a pun the title of this album is. If not, settle for another imaginative set of silent-movie-inspired improvisations. Dresser's ability to create a mood is second to none and, in collaboration with Anthony Coleman (who is credited as composer of all the second-half material, for *Propos de Nice*), he has made an album that is satisfying in and of itself and quite apart from any external reference. These records now represent a substantial meditation on one of the classic arts of the twentieth century, and they more than bear comparison with the work of more celebrated composers, Philip Glass and Carl Davis, who have also written music for the silents.

***** Sonomondo**

Cryptogramophone 104 *Dresser; Frances-Marie Uitti (clo).* 99.

Uitti is best known as an exponent of extended cello technique and an interpreter of challenging contemporary composition, such as the work of Giacinto Scelsi. In this (presumably improvised) setting, she is no less impressive, coaxing everything from great motorcycle revs to bat-squeak harmonics from her instrument. Dresser may well have experimented with settings like this during his time with Bert Turetzky. The results are variable as a listening experience, and we found our enjoyment waning after 'Sonomondo' and 'Grati'. What follows is sketchier and less achieved, but this is still a very intriguing and worthwhile album, and string players of all complexions will find it an endless source of ideas.

Kenny Drew (1928–93)

PIANO

Drew's first influences were Art Tatum and Fats Waller, and these were so deeply inscribed that later contact with Bud Powell and Thelonious Monk didn't have quite the overwhelming impact it had on some players of that generation. The gracious New Yorker spent many years in Europe, first in Paris, and later in Copenhagen in a long lasting and well-documented residency with Niels-Henning Orsted Pedersen at the Jazzhus Montmartre. Drew's expressive talent has been passed on to his son, Kenny Jr.

****(*) The Kenny Drew Trio**

Original Jazz Classics OJCCD 065 *Drew; Paul Chambers (b); Philly Joe Jones (d).* 9/56.

Kenny Drew's death still seems untimely, though it wasn't a career that lacked fulfilment. He began recording in 1949 with Howard McGhee's orchestra, in which he was, by all accounts, a rock of reliability. The first of the Riversides is no better or worse than many another piano-trio date of the day: light, bluesy variations on a flock of standards. Chambers and Jones are typically strong in support, but the material is under-characterized. 'Ruby My Dear' never quite makes it to the starting line and the better tracks are lighter-weight material like 'It's Only A Paper Moon' and 'Caravan', where Drew's elegant, deceptive swing has an opportunity to unfold without pressure.

****(*) This Is New**
Original Jazz Classics OJC 483 *Drew; Donald Byrd (t); Hank Mobley (ts); Wilbur Ware (b); G.T Hogan (d).* 3–4/57.

***** Pal Joey**
Original Jazz Classics OJC 1809 *Drew; Wilbur Ware (b); Philly Joe Jones (d).* 10/57.

***** Trio / Quartet / Quintet**
Original Jazz Classics OJC 6007 *As above.* 57.

Nothing very new here, despite both the title and the period; this sort of hard-bop fare was already becoming a standard repast in 1957. It may say something for the principals involved that the most interesting presence appears to be Ware, who is constantly inventive. The recording is somewhat reticent in dealing with the horns. *Pal Joey* is a typical jazz-goes-to-Broadway album of the day: it earns an extra notch, though, for Ware's hungry, probing lines and the crisper lines that this trio secures.

Trio/Quartet/Quintet is a compilation of tracks from this early Riverside contract. It's probably the best representation of the period, missing out most of the chaff and including a good smattering of the better tracks.

***** Plays The Music Of Harry Warren And Harold Arlen**
Milestone 47070 *Drew; Wilbur Ware (b).*

An evocative and elegant compilation of tunes by two of America's finest songwriters. Supported by the broad-toned and responsive Ware, Drew plays most of these themes pretty straight. Items like 'The Boulevard Of Broken Dreams' are more or less melodic transcriptions; elsewhere he probes a little deeper into the chords, attempting to realign rather than rewrite. Little real jazz action, but an unfailingly attractive record with a full, unmuddied sound.

***** Solo–Duo**
Storyville STCD 8274 *Drew; Niels-Henning Orsted Pedersen, Bo Stief (b).* 66, 12/78, 9/83.

Two blocks of duo material, recorded a decade and a half apart, with a solo set from 1978 wedged in between. The four unaccompanied tracks are brief and relatively uninspired. Drew seems to draw sustenance from the two bassists, and on the live tracks with Stief from 1983 he hits a wonderful groove. 'There Is No Greater Love' is the most finished performance of the set, though the opening 'Everything I Love' with NHOP has an emphatic presence as well, a clear studio sound which renders every tiny detail audible.

***** Duo**
Steeplechase SCCD 31002 *Drew; Ole Molin (g); Niels-Henning Orsted Pedersen (b).* 4/73.

***** Duo 2**
Steeplechase SCCD 31010 *As above, except omit Molin.* 2/74.

***** Duo Live In Concert**
Steeplechase SCCD 31031 *As above.* 6/74.

****(*) Everything I Love**
Steeplechase SCCD 31007 *Drew (p solo).* 10–12/73.

Drew left America for Europe in 1961 and worked and recorded there until his death. His numerous records for Steeplechase are modest successes, but the pianist's very consistency is perhaps his undoing: it's frequently hard to tell one disc – or even one performance – from another. The three duo sessions with NHOP are the best, if only because there is a fine clarity of interplay and the bassist doesn't settle for Drew's plainer modes of expression. The solo date is rather too quiescent.

***** If You Could See Me Now**
Steeplechase SCCD 31034 *Drew; Niels-Henning Orsted Pedersen (b); Albert 'Tootie' Heath (d).* 5/74.

***** Dark Beauty**
Steeplechase SCCD 31016 *As above.*

*****(*) Dark And Beautiful**
Steeplechase SCCD 37011/12 2CD *As above.*

Drew went to Copenhagen in 1966 and became a stalwart of the jazz scene there, playing a long residency at the legendary Jazzhus Montmartre with NHOP, Tootie Heath and whatever guests were in town. We've previously accused these discs of blandness, but of course there are subtleties as well, and perhaps the best place to start, and to take a measure of Drew's pianism, is the two-CD set, *Dark And Beautiful*. Here, stretched out over a generous playing time, Drew's patient exposition and almost conversational phrasing.

Dark Beauty is distinguished by a more than usually varied array of song-writing credits, as if Drew were deliberately casting his net wide and then moulding each song – from his old favourite Harry Warren's 'Summernight' to Thomas Clausen's 'Silk Bossa' – to the particular character of this group. He also programmes Miles's 'All Blues' and Brubeck's 'In Your Own Sweet Way', and he closes with a version of 'Stranger In Paradise' which suggests he knows his Borodin as well as he knows his Broadway songbook.

***** Morning**
Steeplechase SCCD 31048 *Drew; Philip Catherine (g); Niels-Henning Orsted Pedersen (b).* 9/75.

***** Lite Flite**
Steeplechase SCCD 31077 *Drew; Thad Jones (c); Bob Berg (ts); George Mraz (b); Jimmy Cobb (d).* 2/77.

***** In Concert**
Steeplechase SCCD 31106 *Drew; Philip Catherine (g); Niels-Henning Orsted Pedersen (b).* 2/77.

***** Ruby My Dear**
Steeplechase SCCD 31129 *Drew; David Friesen (b); Clifford Jarvis (d).* 8/77.

A further group of Steeplechases in rather more varied company. The obvious comparison is between the NHOP trio and the one on *Ruby My Dear*. Friesen is a similarly cultivated bass-player with a very large and handsome tone. On the title-track, one of Drew's relatively infrequent nods to Monk, he sounds amazingly like Wilbur Ware. Jarvis's sound is perhaps the closest Drew has found to the drummers of the classic swing era and the set skates along on his unfailing beat. There are three originals, a version of Austin Wells's rarely covered 'Sunspots' and, more surprisingly, a version of Jobim's 'Gentle Rain'.

Lite Flite doesn't have the most probable of line-ups, but it works. Berg is in good form, obviously straining every sinew to make the grade in this company. He certainly sounds less relaxed than his seniors. The gracious Thad Jones glides through his solos as if he were sitting in an armchair, and he even allows himself a couple of subtly corrected fluffs – though it's pity none of Thad's tunes were included on the list. Mraz and Cobb are very much the kind of rhythm section Drew has always relied on, big-toned and very straightforward.

Morning and *In Concert* are an intriguing extension of the familiar Montmartre partnership. Catherine is perhaps over-indulged on the live album with his own 'Twice A Week', which seems too frequent or, rather, too long. For the rest, it's a mild-mannered run-through of material that would have been familiar to all three: John Lewis's 'Django', 'Here's That Rainy Day', Pettiford's 'Blues In The Closet' and a breezy closing 'On Green Dolphin Street'. Certainly worth a listen but, like *Morning*, perhaps a little too mild and unemphatic for many tastes.

***** Your Soft Eyes**

Soul Note 121040 *Drew; Mads Vinding (b); Ed Thigpen (d).* 11/81.

Vinding and Thigpen are swinging enough, but there is not much substance to this record. Good to have it on CD, which improves the sound no end, but nothing to get excited about.

****(*) And Far Away**

Soul Note 121081 *Drew; Philip Catherine (g); Niels-Henning Orsted Pedersen (b); Barry Altschul (d).* 2/83.

Drew made several records for the Japanese Baystate company in the early 1980s, as well as this session for Soul Note: his compositions continue to work a slight, pretty seam to rather soporific ends, but the record benefits from the presence of Altschul, whose ear for texture helps to create a more integrated and purposeful sound to such Drew originals as 'Rianne'.

***** Recollections**

Timeless SJP 333 *Drew; Niels-Henning Orsted Pedersen (b); Alvin Queen (d).* 5/89.

It might be thanks to digital sound of tremendous impact, but this set sounds like a revitalization of Drew's music. Whether tackling standards or originals, he digs in with a verve and a decisive attack that will surprise anyone familiar with the earlier trio dates. NHOP and Queen respond with appropriate vigour of their own. This was a flurry of unexpected drama towards the end of a long and dignified career. It always looked as if Kenny Drew could go on for ever playing music of this quality and it was a genuine surprise when one day that calm voice was silenced for ever.

Kenny Drew Jr

PIANO

There are few signs of son-of-a-famous-father syndrome round Kenny Drew Jr. His dad graced the jazz world quietly and without arrogance and he seems to have cast no overpowering shadow. Kenny Jr's development has been very individual, drawing on musics outside jazz and following its own determined logic.

***** Rainbow Connection**

Bellaphon 66053010 *Drew; Charnett Moffett (b); Codaryl Moffett (d).* 88.

*****(*) At Maybeck: Volume 39**

Concord CCD 4653 *Drew (p solo).* 8/94.

Kenny Jr never really sounded like his dad, who would never have owned up to allowing 'a little Schoenberg or Messiaen' into his playing. Classically trained, though, young Kenny uses non-blues intervals to a far greater extent and has a less percussive attack. His presence on record has so far been rather intermittent; but recent years have seen a new flush of recordings, and the early trio with the Moffett boys, also second-generation jazz men, is now available again, though you may find yourself swithering over a pricey import copy.

Pianists seemed to approach Maybeck gigs in one of two rather different ways: they either took leave to experiment or they stuck very squarely to the tradition. Kenny takes the latter tack, and very convincingly too, leaving his own growing body of compositions for other occasions. The player who once included a meditation on the name of Haydn (on a deleted Antilles record) sounds refreshingly unacademic; not a hint of a classical *étude* in sight. His closing 'Autumn Leaves' is flawlessly conventional, and the two Monk tunes, 'Ugly Beauty' and 'Straight, No Chaser', would have pleased the master himself – and appealed to Kenny Sr as well, a sometimes hesitant Monkian. It's a very controlled set, rather too proper and unengaged, but consistently impressive.

***** Portraits Of Mingus And Monk**

Claves 50 1194 *Drew; Lynn Seaton (b); Marvin 'Smitty' Smith (d).* 94.

****** Secrets**

TCB 98502 *As above.* 95.

This was a wonderful working group, packed with dynamism and full of ideas. Kenny does 'Light Blue' and 'Weird Nightmare' as solo pieces on the *Portraits* album, both of them subtly modulated and multi-dimensional. But it's really the trios that catch the ear. Kenny includes his own arrangement of a piece by Mompou which is subtle and swinging and irresistibly recalls Chick Corea. His playing more and more resembles Chick's as well, an outpouring of lyricism that seems to have no limit, and it's fascinating to compare the two versions of 'Serial Blues' and hear how comprehensively he revises his approach from one take to another.

There is only one Corea composition on *Secrets*, the highly concentrated and structurally challenging 'Mirror Mirror', but his distinctive voicings seem to invest the album from start to finish. Also in the programme, Steve Swallow's 'Falling Grace' with its rippling, rhapsodic feel, two tunes by Kenny Sr, both lovingly executed, and an arrangement of Vince Guaraldi's 'Great Pumpkin Waltz'.

The earlier album, also astutely produced by Aleardo G. Buzzi, is less to our taste but is still a fine jazz album. A touch too busy in places, as if Smitty is eager to get off to his next gig, but the full sound has enough space around it not to sound crowded.

*****(*) This One's For Bill**

TCB 99352 *Drew (p solo).* 11/95.

Kenny recorded 'This One's For Bill', almost a decade ago on his Antilles album, but it obviously has a place again here in this meditation on Evans and his influence. The piece kicks off this thoughtful and expressive set, which touches on some forgotten corners of the Evans canon, pieces like 'Remembering The Rain' and 'The Two Lonely People' with its long, elaborate form. Kenny also plays a stretched-out version of Miles's 'Nardis', one of the trumpeter's most pianistic ideas, and the Johnny Mandel theme for *M*A*S*H*, 'Suicide Is Painless'. The recording was made in a Masonic Hall on West 25th Street in New York City, a woody, responsive space which brings out the very best in the big Hamburg Steinway Kenny opted to play for the gig. Its tone is just right for him, and the set flows sweetly from the very first bars.

***** Crystal River**

TCB 98202 *Drew; Michael Philip Mossman (t, flhn); Ravi Coltrane (ss, ts); Steve Nelson (vib); Lynn Seaton (b); Tony Reedus (d).* 97.

Conceived on a larger-than-usual scale, but somehow less than the sum of its parts. Drew's sextet is almost like a scaled-down big band and the sound is very full, very generously arranged. Mossman and Coltrane Jr are slightly anonymous as soloists, but the pianist carries the day. Of all Drew's albums, this is the least kindly recorded. The piano is very forward and the other trio members with him, and their prominence isn't properly balanced by a strong enough register from horns and vibes. Disappointing.

*****(*) Passionata**

Arkadia 70561 *Drew; Peter Washington (b); Lewis Nash (d); strings.* 98.

Sensitive and moving, this is Kenny's tribute to his late father, titled after the unfinished song which he completes and records here for the first time. The set also includes Drew Sr material like 'Dark Beauty', one of the old man's finest compositions, and standards that he must have played a thousand times. Young Kenny's gift is to take them on a stage again, and his interpretation of 'Summertime' has a classical feel that distances it a little from the average jazz reading. This is certainly the most accommodating and inventive trio Kenny has worked with since the days of Lynn Seaton and Smitty Smith. Washington has an enormous range and a capacity for free, fulsome melody that doesn't get in the way of a strong, sure beat, leaving Nash to embellish and elaborate more freely than usual in such a context. The strings are arranged by Bob Belden, unobtrusive, idiomatic and very cleanly registered.

***** Follow The Spirit**

Sirocco FJL 1004 *Drew; Steve Wilson (ss, as); Lynn Seaton (b); Tony Jefferson (d).* 98.

*****(*) Winter Flower**

Milestone MCD 9289-2 *As above, except omit Wilson.* 6/98.

Two delightful albums from a now fully mature talent, a musician with his own distinctive vision. It's no longer possible to tease apart the influences that go to make Kenny Drew Jr. Increasingly, he sounds like himself. The session with Wilson is rather flatly recorded, which means that the horn parts are more prominent than they ought to be and the all-important rhythm work of Seaton is rather dull and recessed. However, the band does wonderful things on tunes like 'Serial Blues' (now an established item in Drew's repertoire), 'Soldier In The Rain' and a delightful standard, 'Wrap Your Troubles In Dreams'.

The Milestone disc is certainly to be preferred. Jefferson has established a place in Drew's employ and sounds more confident with his role every time out. This time, Kenny nods to Chopin in a lilting A minor waltz, to Ellington in 'Isfahan', which is not just a horn player's song, and to the great Astor Piazzolla in 'Argentine Rhapsody', which opens up the group's rhythmic language considerably. Nicely recorded and packaged; a significant further step in the pianist's career.

Paquito D'Rivera (born 1948)

ALTO, SOPRANO AND TENOR SAXOPHONES, CLARINET

A prodigy in Havana, playing in his father's band at six, D'Rivera was a founder (with Chucho Valdes and Arturo Sandoval) of Irakere. He defected to the USA in 1980. Since then he's been involved in bop and Cuban music in about equal measure.

***** Tico! Tico!**

Chesky 034 *D'Rivera; Danilo Perez (p); Fareed Haque, Romero Lobambo, Tibero Nascimiento (g); David Finck, Nilsson Matta (b); Portinho, Mark Walker (d).* 7–8/89.

D'Rivera was the first of the recent wave of Cuban musicians to defect to the USA, and his intensely hot, infectiously runaway style on alto has enlivened quite a number of sessions. He has the same difficulty which besets his compadre, Arturo Sandoval: finding a consistently productive context for a talent which is liable to blow away on the winds of its own virtuosity. D'Rivera is never short of a string of firecracker phrases, but they can often be as enervating to a listener as the most laid-back of jazz easy-listening dates. His Columbia albums tended to end up as Latinized hard bop, no better or worse than a typical neo-classical session, if a little more sparky than most. But this Chesky album suggests ways that D'Rivera can make a more convincing kind of fusion. The bolero, waltz and bossa nova rhythms are integrated into a setting which sifts bebop into an authentic South American stew, and the leader turns to the clarinet as well as the alto (and a little tenor) to decorate the pulse. Chesky's brilliant sound only heightens the sunny qualities of Paquito's music.

***** Havana Café**

Chesky JD 80 *D'Rivera; Danilo Perez (p); Fareed Haque, Ed Cherry (g); David Finck (b); Jorge Rossy (d); Sammy Figueroa (perc).*

More of the same, really. But the very quick tempos tend to underline D'Rivera's difficulty in finding a context: he can handle these rapid-fire speeds, but other members of the band – Perez and Haque in particular – find it difficult both to sustain the pace and to have anything interesting to say. Two classical pieces, 'Improvisation' and 'Contradanza', offer a little more variety, and this time D'Rivera brings out his soprano rather than his tenor.

***** Who's Smoking?**

Candid CCD79523 *D'Rivera; Claudio Roditi (t, flhn); Mark Morganelli (flhn); James Moody (ts); Danilo Perez, Pedriot Lopez (p); Harvie Swartz (b); Al Foster (d).* 5/91.

Lots more gilt-edged hard bop, heavy on smoke, glitter and flash but short on anything beyond the showmanship. D'Rivera and Roditi strike sparks off each other until they're practically smouldering, and there is a rather good 'Giant Steps' which emerges out of it all. Taken moment by moment, fair game.

*****(*) Live At Manchester Craftsmen's Guild**

Blue Jackel MCG 1003 *D'Rivera; Diego Urcola, Mike Ponella (t); Conrad Herwig (tb); William Cepeda (tb, conch); Scott Robinson (as); Andres Boiarsky (ts, ss); Marshall McDonald (bs, ts); Dario Eskenazi (p); Fareed Haque (g); Oscar Stagnaro (b); Mark Walker (d).* 2/97.

That's Manchester, Pennsylvania, British readers should note. The band is the United Nation Orchestra, as founded by Dizzy Gillespie and now passed on to D'Rivera, and the rhythmic subtexts come not only from Brazil and Cuba but also from Uruguay, Puerto Rico and Argentina. Dishevelled and seemingly under-rehearsed, the band's jostling, rather fractious delivery proves more effective than that of many a better-drilled and more confident outfit. Several of the tunes have the teeming, shouting quality which one feels this music should aspire to, and for once D'Rivera's solos have to simply take their place in a rich, tempestuous fabric. His duet with bassist Stagnaro, D'Rivera on clarinet, is a real surprise, almost melancholy in timbre even as the virtuosity abides. A fine live souvenir.

***** 100 Years Of Latin Love Songs**

Inak 30452 *D'Rivera; Dario Eskenazi (p); Roberto Perera (hp); Aquiles Baez (g, cuatro); Fareed Haque, David Oquendo (g); Oscar Stagnaro (b); Mark Walker (d); Luis Conte (perc); strings.* 9/98.

***** Tropicana Nights**

Chesky JD 186 *D'Rivera; Mike Ponella, Diego Urcola, Gustavo Bergalli, Adalberto Lara, Alejandro Odio (t); Noah Bless, Luis Bonilla, Jimmy Bosch, William Cepeda (tb); Manuel Valera (as); Andres Boiarsky, Ocar Feldman (ts); Marshall McDonald (bs); Oriente Lopez, Daniel Eskenazi (p); David Oquendo (g); Joe Santiago (b); Mark Walker (d); Ralph Irizarry, Joe Gonzalez, Mailton Cardona (perc); Brenda Feliciano, Lucrecia (v).* 99.

D'Rivera is looking for contexts and these showbiz situations suit him as well as anything. *100 Years Of Latin Love Songs* takes us decade by decade through a century of South American music, although frankly it's all treated in much the same way by Paquito's band and Bob Belden's sweet-natured string charts. Charming light music, shaken into wakefulness now and then by D'Rivera's solos. *Tropicana Nights* puts him in front of another show band, too big to attain any great jazz mobility or personality, but loaded with fine players out for a good time. Plenty of Latin kitsch, with some more pointed improvising from the leader.

Billy Drummond

DRUMS

Born in Virginia, he followed his father's footsteps in becoming a drummer, arriving in New York in 1988. Joined the OTB band and has since freelanced with many groups, leading occasional dates of his own.

***** Native Colours**

Criss Cross CRISS 1057 *Drummond; Steve Wilson (as, ss); Steve Nelson (vib); Renee Rosnes (p); Ray Drummond (b).* 3/91.

*****(*) The Gift**

Criss Cross CRISS 1083 *Drummond; Seamus Blake (ts, ss); Renee Rosnes (p); Peter Washington (b).* 12/93.

****** Dubai**

Criss Cross CRISS 1120 *Drummond; Chris Potter (ts, ss, bcl); Walt Weiskopf (ts); Peter Washington (b).* 12/95.

There can't be many busier players around at the moment. Drummond's relaxed facility and knack of piling on the pace as and when required have made him a first-call player in recent years. Much of the action takes place on the cymbals, a light, fast, highly tuneful sound punctuated with sudden dramatic accents and edgy metallic chimes.

Drummond has now recorded three times for Criss Cross and has sounded steadily more confident and self-possessed. The debut is rather muddled, with vibes and piano getting in each other's way and Wilson fighting a rather congested sound. Blake is better on *The Gift* because he has the power and determination to make his presence felt. Rosnes, who is also Mrs Drummond, is never quite as assured as on her own dates, but she contributes to a well-balanced programme which includes Harold Land's 'Ode To Angela' and Charles Lloyd's unexpected and very beautiful 'Apex'.

Dubai dispenses with a harmony instrument altogether, and the result is quite startling. Drummond's closeness to Max Roach suddenly becomes evident, and the originals – his own 'Dubai', Potter's 'Bananfish' and Weiskopf's 'Invisible Sun' and 'Drumhead' – take on a stark but intensely melodic quality. As well as his original compositions, Weiskopf is strongly featured on Strayhorn's gruffly romantic 'Daydream'. Potter shines particularly on Pat Metheny's 'The Bat', another number where Drummond leaves his traps alone and concentrates entirely on cymbals, a most effective trademark. He also figures strongly on the closing 'Mushi Mushi', a Dewey Redman theme which should be heard more often.

Ray Drummond (born 1946)

BASS

Studied in business school, 1974–7, but returned to bass playing, his first vocation, and then worked extensively on the New York scene from the 1980s.

***** Camera In A Bag**
Criss Cross Jazz 1040 *Drummond; David Newman (ts, f); Kenny Barron (p); Steve Nelson (vib); Marvin 'Smitty' Smith (d).* 12/89.

***** Excursion**
Arabesque AJ0106 *Drummond; Craig Handy (ss, as, ts, f); Joe Lovano (ss, ts, f); Danilo Perez (p); Marvin 'Smitty' Smith (d); Mor Thiam (perc).* 6/92.

Drummond has appeared on numerous sessions as sideman, but his outings as a leader are rarer. The Criss Cross session works out very well, although nothing exactly arrives with a bang. Newman plays as much flute as tenor and sounds full and funky on both instruments, while Nelson functions peripherally; the strongest music, though, comes from the rhythm section, which develops a tremendously assured momentum across the nine compositions, four of them by Drummond. *Excursion* is a complete contrast. The polished post-bop of the earlier date is traded for a looser, noisier ensemble sound in which Mor Thiam's percussion sets the tone. Handy's wild solos are a polar opposite to Lovano's considered improvising, and Perez contributes his carefully heated piano manner to what is a thick, percussive ensemble sound. But Drummond's writing doesn't quite have a handle on the situation: it's enjoyable from moment to moment, yet the music sounds confused as often as it is exhilarating.

*****(*) Continuum**
Arabesque AJO11 *Drummond; Randy Brecker (t); Thomas Chapin (f); John Scofield (g); Kenny Barron (p); Steve Nelson (vib); Marvin 'Smitty' Smith (d); Mor Thiam (perc).* 1/94.

Drummond's best record works on grounds of both simplicity and detail. The continuum is the blues, which provides the source for most of these pieces, be they a simple melodic line such as the leader's own 'Blues From The Sketchpad' or the Japanese chords of 'Sakura'. There is great blowing by a band stuffed with masters, but Drummond was smart enough to vary the textures by keeping Chapin on flutes rather than alto and bringing the chime of Nelson's vibes into the picture. Here and there, as in the fine turbulence of Strayhorn's 'Intimacy Of The Blues', the music moves far beyond boppish origins into a thickly textured stew. The only reservation might be the sometimes unspecific sound-mix which the leader favours as producer.

*****(*) Vignette**
Arabesque AJ0122 *Drummond; Gary Bartz (as, ss); Chris Potter, John Richmond, Joe Lovano (ts); Renee Rosnes (p); Billy Hart (d).* 95.

Another exceptional band, with Richmond and Lovano sitting in on the handsomely voiced treatment of 'Eleanor Rigby'. The rhythm section are more than the core of the group, with Rosnes and Hart meshing with the leader's lines and ideas at a very high level and, as finely as Bartz and Potter play, one finds the ears constantly being drawn to what piano, bass and drums are doing. In his writing and sense of group organization, the leader seems regularly drawn to a closely argued kind of freedom – unusually so for a musician so valued by others for his timekeeping and ability to keep everything within the frame. This is a sequence of records worth following.

The Dry Throat Fellows

GROUP

Swiss jazz jokers quite capable of playing it serious and straight.

***** Do Something**
Stomp Off CD 1226 *René Hagmann (c, tb, cl, as, bsx); Jacques Ducrot (cl, ss, as, v); Bertrand Neyroud (cl, ts, gfs, v); Pierre-Alain Maret (g, bj); Michel Rudaz (tba); Raymond Graisier (wbd, perc, v).* 11–12/90.

Since trad has long since colonized Europe, it should come as no surprise that this wry troupe of Swiss players should be as adept as they are. If this is the humorous side of traditional playing, though, how come their version of Clarence Williams's 'Red River Blues' cuts anyone else's? Secret weapon René Hagmann, who does most of the arranging, is equally at home with brass or reeds; Bertrand Neyroud plays the most vibrant clarinet this side of Don Byron; and new recruit Jacques Ducrot (there are two earlier LPs on Stomp Off) sounds right at home with an alto style that seems to have heard of nothing after 1932. He also puts a ridiculous vocal on 'Sweet Sue (Just You)'. Sounds daft on a CD player, but sounds pretty good anywhere else.

Goff Dubber

CLARINET, SOPRANO AND TENOR SAXOPHONES

Veteran British clarinettist/saxman working in trad circles.

****(*) Clarinet Marmalade**
Lake LACD78 *Dubber; Neville Dickie (p); Mickey Ashman (b); Norman Emberson (d).* 12/96–1/97.

A stalwart clarinettist in British trad, Dubber plays it rather self-consciously safe on this long set of tunes. Plenty of familiar benchmarks and Dickie's characteristic strong touch is a help, but there's too much music – more than 70 minutes of this sort of thing has the CD wearing out its welcome – and too much the same. He picks up the tenor for two tracks, which makes one think that maybe the change of tone wasn't a good idea. Dubber isn't really helped by the sound, either, which never seems to put him in the foreground.

Marc Ducret (born 1957)

GUITAR, GUITAR-SYNTHESIZER

A Parisian, Ducret came to international notice via his stint in the Orchestre National Du Jazz. Later associated with Louis Sclavis and more recently with Tim Berne.

***** La Théorie Du Pilier**
Label Bleu LBL 6508 *Ducret; Michel Benita (b); Aaron Scott (d).* 87.

*****(*) Le Kodo**
Label Bleu LBL 6519 *Ducret; Larry Schneider (ss, ts); Michel Benita (b); Adam Nussbaum (d).* 12/88.

***** Gris**
Label Bleu LBL 6531 *Ducret; Enrico Rava (t); Yves Robert (tb); François Jeanneau (ss); Andy Emler (p); Michel Benita, Renaud Garcia Fons (b); Joel Allouche (d).* 5/90.

Ducret has been making waves in a wider context since, but his early albums for Label Bleu are worth returning to. He may someday be cited as a pioneer in the fusion of jazz, blues and rock accents into their current polystylistic state. *La Théorie Du Pilier* is a temperate trio record, concentrating on the interplay of the group, with Ducret sticking mainly to a clean, traditional guitar tone; but *Le Kodo* is a far tougher and more exciting session, the underrated Schneider piling through his solos and Ducret upping the ante on his own playing by several notches. Nussbaum plays with all the requisite energy, but sometimes one wishes for a drummer with a little more finesse. *Gris* varies the pace again: 'Elephanta' is a guitar–drums duet, Rava, Emler, Jeanneau and Robert drift in and out of the other tracks, and both bassists appear on 'Danser'. All three records have their share of good tunes as well as intelligent solos: Ducret pens a pleasing melody.

***** (detail)**
Winter & Winter 910003-2 *Ducret (g solo).* 1/96.

***** Un Certain Malaise**
Screwgun 70005 *Ducret (g solo).* 6–7/97.

Performed with chiming clarity and precision, *(detail)* features Ducret alone on acoustic six- and twelve-string guitars. *Un Certain Malaise* is a live album where the guitarist is again by himself, though this time on electric. His virtuosity, inventiveness of thought from moment to moment and skilful blending of genres are never in question. Neither disc, though, entirely escapes from a certain *ennui*. The scrawling treatment of 'What Did I Forget?/Old Brown Shoe' which opens *Un Certain Malaise* is an impressive show of chopsmanship, but it's not so different from listening to Edward van Halen and, deprived of anything but his own context, Ducret seems landlocked. *(detail)* sometimes sounds like mere strumming, for all his refinements.

***** In The Grass**
Enja 9343-2 *Ducret; Bobby Previte (d, ky).* 9/96.

Two knowing practitioners stir together an hour or so of sparring on guitars, drums and keyboards. Plenty of interesting bits and pieces which add up to the usual mixed result.

Ted Dunbar (1937–98)

GUITAR

From Texas, Dunbar arrived in New York in the '60s and worked in big bands, small groups and jazz-rock ensembles, although he subsequently returned to open-toned, classic stylings.

****(*) Gentle Time Along**
Steeplechase SCCD 31298 *Dunbar; Mickey Tucker (p); Ray Drummond (b); David Jones (d).* 12/91.

Dunbar's restrained and even dynamic, coupled with his soft-toned picking style, made him a jazz guitarist somewhat at odds with the current school. He and Tucker work well together – perhaps a little too well: it's the sort of empathy that sends the music to sleep rather than making fresh points. Superior sound opens out the subtlety of the guitarist's ideas, though, and the rhythm section keep a watchful eye on the back line.

Paul Dunmall

SAXOPHONES, CLARINET

Bebop, free jazz, folk forms and increasingly large-scale composition all play a part in Dunmall's thinking. He is a charter member of free group, Mujician, but increasingly follows his own demanding star.

*****(*) Soliloquy**
Matchless MRCD 15 *Dunmall (solo).* 10 & 12/86.

The only obvious comparison – in terms of instrumentation, sound and basic conception – is John Surman, who has similarly experimented with solo performance and with multi-tracking. However, a more valid comparison might be Evan Parker's tense, complex improvisations, though Dunmall has a folk-influenced side which is far removed from Parker's usual territory. The most remarkable piece on this excellent set is 'Voyage', solo soprano playing which finds a route and a niche midway between those fellow-Brits and fellow-reedmen. 'Human Atmospheres' is a more extreme performance, exploring the limits of pitch, while 'Holocaust', which opens with huge 'unison' siren effects, becomes a sober, extended meditation on destructiveness and loss. Intimately and often viscerally recorded, this isn't music to put on and walk away from. Some will find it a tough listen, but Dunmall's music pays big aesthetic dividends.

***** Folks**
Slam CD 212 *Dunmall; Paul Rogers (b); Polly Bolton (v).* 12/89, 9/93.

***** Essential Expressions**
Cadence Jazz Records CJR 1079 *Dunmall; Tony Levin (d).* 1/96.

Rogers was – and still occasionally plays as – a member of Mujician, a superb improvising ensemble comprising Dunmall, Keith Tippett and Tony Levin, who partners Paul on *Essential Expressions*. Hearing the group's bassist and reed player in isolation helps unpack one – albeit secondary – element of Mujician's distinctive language, which is a folky melodism, traditionless and quite abstract, almost like the bare skeleton of a tune, thrown up as if in X-ray.

Rogers's fierce, almost competitive style is down a notch in this more intimate setting and there is less of his percussive strumming than usual. Alternating four- and five-string basses, though, he still produces a powerful sound, providing an effective bed for Dunmall's full range of clarinets and saxophones. The presence of Polly Bolton on a single track suggests there may be some future mileage in a vocal disc, an area of interest which has been increasingly important to Slam over the last few years. (Something has gone awry with the track listing on the record, which doesn't match up with the instruments heard, but we have seen a printed correction slip which makes the situation clearer.)

The duos with Levin sound more spontaneous and less deliberate. Levin is a treasure. Like Eddie Prévost, he combines freedom with unmistakable swing and, on the evidence of the title-track, it would be hard to distinguish him from some of the American masters whose idiom he has absorbed and colonized. The admixture of jazz is less obvious here, though the soprano feature ('I Found An Angel') touches on a couple of standard themes. Dunmall otherwise sticks to a blunt tenor sound that is frequently reminiscent of session producer Evan Parker. Technically, *Essential Expressions* is more impressive, but most listeners will find *Folks* the more approachable of the pair.

***(*) Quartet And Sextet / Babu

Slam CD 207 2CD *Dunmall; John Corbett (c); Simon Picard (ts); John Adams (g); Paul Rogers (b); Tony Levin (d).* 9/93.

Mujician has functioned as a trio without Rogers; Babu is a trio without Keith Tippett. Inevitably, it is less harmonically rich and on occasions sounds rather stark, an effect heightened by a rather unresponsive acoustic. However, the two larger groups seem to occupy a bigger space and Dunmall's voice is proportionately stronger and more obviously sensitized to its surroundings. The one sextet track, 'Apocalypse Now And Then', is the only one to feature a harmony instrument, and Dunmall responds fulsomely, broadening his tone and attacking the line with vigour. The quartet with Picard, bass and drums is very intense and yields some of Dunmall's best music on record.

**** Ghostly Thoughts

hatOLOGY 503 *Dunmall; John Adams (g); Mark Sanders (d).* 7/96.

A tremendous record, pay-off for years of effort. As an example of small-group playing, the closing 'Up And Down The Back', with its internal symmetry and straightforward logic, is hard to beat; after a percussion introduction, Adams joins Sanders for a while before Dunmall, who concentrates on tenor and baritone this time out, sweeps in to gather the music up into a great peak before letting it settle again. As on the longest item, 'Abit Of Rice, Nice', the pace is more thoughtful than frenetic. 'Human Machines' is the big baritone feature, dark and ruggedly textured. Sanders is heroic throughout the session, playing with great concentration and – if this doesn't sound like hyperbole – recalling not so much fellow-Briton Eddie Prévost as Prévost's great precursors, Max Roach and Ed Blackwell. Adams is less well known but he, too, contributes his full.

*** Desire And Liberation

Slam SLAMCD 225 *Dunmall; Gethin Liddington (t); Chris Bridges, Annie Whitehead (tb); Simon Picard (ts); Keith Tippett (p); Paul Rogers (b); Tony Levin (d).* 11/96.

Early fruit of Dunmall's growing interest in large-scale composition for improvising groups. Inspired by the thinking of Shri Ramakrishna, *Desire And Liberation* is a free-flowing suite compounded of Dunmall's now familiarly folkish themes and some fine jazz blowing. Though essentially continuous, each of the sections is dominated by one instrument or, in one case, by a duet for trombones. The obvious model is Coltrane's *Ascension*. The basic material is more complex, the responses less frenetic, but the set-up is much the same. Dunmall leads off with great authority, followed by bass, the trombones, Picard, Levin, Liddington (the least known of the group but making a strong showing) and finally Tippett in less than expansive form, keeping things much tighter than usual. The BBC live recording is good, though the clarity of the horns is compromised a little here and there.

**** Bebop Starburst

Cuneiform RUNE 112 *As above.* 6/97.

An even more assured performance by the Octet and by Dunmall the composer, digging back into the music which first got him involved in jazz. *Bebop Starburst* is a five-part suite which sounds both thoroughly written out and also free. There are occasional hints here and there of 'I Got Rhythm' and 'How High The Moon'; but this isn't a memorial quilt of contrafacts and standards, but an effort to write in the spirit of the originators. Once again, Liddington is in strong form, showing that he can 'do' Dizzy *and* Howard McGhee. Annie Whitehead is as expressive as ever, and the two saxophonists, neither of them Bird clones, blend very effectively indeed. The Octet's anchor is, of course, the now almost telepathically responsive Mujician. Tippett's sense of structure is second to none and Rogers and Levin are always right on the case. This is music that deserves the widest exposure, the kind of thing that the Founding Fathers of bop would love to have done but lacked either the wherewithal or the final jump of imagination. Excellent modern music, with ties to the past.

***(*) Totally Fried Up

Slam CD 235 *Dunmall; John Adams (g); Mark Sanders (d).* 3/98.

The second outing from Dunmall's free-bop trio doesn't have quite the slapping impact of its predecessor, but it's still a powerful record. The defining sound is Adams's hard-scrabble guitar, which is also capable of great delicacy, as at the end of 'Samskaras'. Perhaps in deference to label boss George Haslam, himself a distinguished baritonist, Dunmall leaves the big horn at home. A pity; what these five tracks could do with is just a touch of timbral and harmonic variation. Sanders is as compelling a drummer as ever, with a limitless rhythmic facility and a fine judgement for the placing of more abstract accents. Good stuff all round.

Phil Durrant

VIOLIN, ELECTRONICS

A Londoner who has worked extensively in the home-grown improvisation scene, Durrant has moved from mainly group work to the solo environments suggested by the first record, which explore the violin's possibilities as an amorphous sound-source via electronic treatments.

*** Sowari

Acta 10 *Durrant (vn, elec solo).* 11/96–2/97.

As fiercely demanding a disc as one could expect in improvised music, this solo effort compiles Durrant's various adventures with acoustic and electronically altered violin. The four untreated pieces are pretty hard work, often seeming like plays on the barest of structural themes, while the electronic episodes give rise to the occasional doubt, as in the funny, alarming 'Chew 3': is he actually in control of all the squelch and zap that's coming out of the speakers? Detailed exposure is more reassuring: this isn't trance music or any kind of minimalism, rather a refined exploration of a very particular playing medium.

***** Further Lock**
Concepts Of Doing 002 *Durrant; Alexander Frangenheim (b).* 3/97.

Durrant sticks to an unamplified and otherwise untreated instrument here, with Frangenheim doing the same, and the results are sometimes dry to the point of desiccation: this is dour, unexciting music, but it is played with a severe concentration which in its way is compelling. Because both men tend to deny any sweetness in the playing, it feels like hard work, but the best of these 14 mostly quite brief duets stand up to the closest scrutiny.

Dominic Duval

BASS

Duval has been at work on the edges of jazz since the 1960s, although he has got on to record only recently. He has been closely connected with the Cadence/CIMP nexus of players, and it wouldn't be unreasonable to see him as an East Coast 'undergrounder' of his day, which is roughly right now.

***** Nightbird Inventions**
Cadence CJR 1072 *Duval (b solo).* 12/96–1/97.

***** The Wedding Band**
CIMP 137 *Duval; Jay Rosen (d).* 1/97.

Duval is a prodigiously skilled player who likes working on the broadest canvas. His solo album finds his bass doctored in numerous ways – with long echo, stereo panning, chorusing and more – for 13 pieces; and for once the comparative brevity of the individual tracks is a slight disadvantage: fewer, longer expositions might have effected a more convincing whole. But his inventiveness is undeniable, his use of his effects board subtle and persuasive, and here and there he comes up with a sonically ravishing idea, such as the closing 'Final Thoughts – Look Through Windows In Rain'.

The duets with Rosen feature the bass unadorned, and with the drummer playing with restraint on a modest kit the music has an evenly modulated flow – effective in small doses yet, as so often, monotonal over almost 70 minutes of music. Recorded at an astonishingly low level, this is a disc to sample as a series of brief encounters, which is how it works best.

****(*) The Navigator**
Leo LR 257 *Duval; Jason Hwang (vn); Ron Lawrence (vla); Tomas Ulrich (clo). n.d.*

***** Equinox**
Leo LR 267 *As above, except Michael Jefry Stevens (p, perc) replaces Hwang and Lawrence.* 8/97.

***** State Of The Art**
CIMP 141 *Duval; Mark Whitecage (ss, as, cl); Jason Hwang (vn); Tomas Ulrich (clo).* 2/97.

***** Live In Concert**
Cadence CJR 1097 *As above, except add Joe McPhee (t, ts).* 8/98.

Variously credited to The C.T. String Quartet, The Equinox Trio and Duval's String Ensemble, these quite difficult records extend the approach of the earlier discs in different ways: they're heavier, gloomier, louder, more complex, and ultimately quite exhausting to get through. *The Navigator* is so elephantine in feel – the resonant sound is no help at all – that the interesting textures are hard work to decipher, never mind appreciate. Much of this is closer to formal chamber music than to any kind of jazz, and the improvisations, if such they be, are set to what seem to be specifically controlled energy levels. *Equinox* is a good deal easier to follow and Stevens is a good alternative to the other two, but this is still rather mysteriously cryptic music-making.

State Of The Art benefits enormously from CIMP's famously dry and naturalistic recording. You can hear every microtone and string-squeak, and the busy interaction recalls Incus's famous *Company 1* LP. But Duval's interest in very low, groaning *arco* chords does tend to bog the music down just when it seems like an improvisation should be flying. The concert recording was done at New York's Knitting Factory, in decent enough sound, although again the ensembles tend to congeal a bit. McPhee walks into this situation with his usual fearlessness, and his saxophone parts, alternately sonorous and barkingly aggressive, are powerful enough, although he tends to sit on top of the group rather than work within it. For hardy souls!

Jim Dvorak

TRUMPET, POCKET TRUMPET, VOCAL

A powerful, impassioned improviser, Dvorak is a member of the Bardo State Orchestra, in which the musical language is intensely spiritual. His other work has a rawer, less reflective edge that resembles the pioneering trumpeters of bebop and later exponents like Leo Smith.

****(*) This Isn't Sex**
Slam CD 504 *Dvorak; Eric Mingus (b, v).* 1/99.

Reminiscent of the Beat poetry performances of the 1960s, this strange duo record essentially consists of recitations by Eric Mingus with trumpet obbligatos from Dvorak. Apart from a few pre-recorded beats on a couple of tracks, that is all there is to it. Dvorak's high, flittering sound is the most consistently interesting aspect of an album that it is unlikely anyone will want to listen to very often, so one-dimensional is it. The session was recorded in Dill Katz's kitchen but, had it been done in a full-scale studio with access to more sophisticated technology, there might have been an opportunity to create some vivid soundscapes round Mingus's oddly Puritanical lyrics, a tendency he may have inherited from his dad. There is a strange and intriguing version of The Who's 'Baba O'Riley'. Otherwise, all the material is by the duo.

Johnny Mbizo Dyani (1945–86)

BASS

Joined Chris McGregor's Blue Notes in 1962 and came to London with them in 1965. Settled there for five years before eventually moving to Denmark and playing with John Tchicai, Don Cherry, the trio, Detail, and others.

***(*) Witchdoctor's Son

Steeplechase SCCD 31098 *Dyani; John Tchicai (as, ss); Dudu Pukwana (as, ts); Alfredo Do Nascimento (g); Luiz Carlos De Sequeira (d); Mohamed Al-Jabry (perc).* 3/78.

*** Song For Biko

Steeplechase SCCD 31109 *Dyani; Dudu Pukwana (as); Don Cherry (c); Makaya Ntoshko (d).* 7/78.

*** Mbizo

Steeplechase SCCD 31163 *Dyani; Dudu Pukwana (as, ss); Ed Epstein (as, bs); Churchill Jolobe (d).* 2/81.

The late Johnny Dyani was calmly visionary, with a deep swelling of anger and irony underneath; technically robust; stylistically various. More than any of the South African exiles, Dyani absorbed and assimilated a wide variety of styles and procedures. He spent much of his active life in Scandinavia, where he forged close artistic relationships with John Tchicai, Don Cherry and with Dollar Brand (Abdullah Ibrahim) with whom he shared a particular vision of Africa. The music is strongly politicized but never programmatic. *Witchdoctor's Son* and *Song For Biko* come from Dyani's most consistently inventive period. Some of the early 1980s material is a little more diffuse and, though Pukwana – another who has since re-entered Azania beyond life – is a powerfully compelling solo voice, he always seemed to mute Dyani's more inventive progressions as if there could only be one strong voice at a time.

The self-named *Mbizo* hasn't been in circulation for some little while, and it's a welcome reissue on CD. It is certainly the starkest and darkest of Dyani's records, with Pukwana wailing and shouting on both his horns and Epstein filling in behind with full-chested baritone and a more measured alto sound which is reminiscent of Tchicai. It's an unsettling record, unmistakably personal and stressed, glowing with dark anger.

*** Afrika

Steeplechase SCCD 31186 *Dyani; Ed Epstein (as, bs); Charles Davis (as); Thomas Ostergren (b); Gilbert Matthews (d); Rudy Smith (steel d); Thomas Akuru Dyani (congas).* 10/83.

*** Born Under The Heat

Dragon DRCD 288 *Dyani; Mosa Gwangwa (tb); Charles Davis (as); Ulf Adaker (t); Krister Andersson, Ed Epstein, Peter Shimi Radise (ts); Pierre Dørge (g); Thomas Ostergren (b); Gilbert Matthews (d).* 11/83–5/85.

***(*) Angolian Cry

Steeplechase SCCD 31209 *Dyani; Harry Beckett (t, flhn); John Tchicai (ts, bcl); Billy Hart (d).* 7/85.

Afrika is probably the weakest of Dyani's records, marred by an ill-matched rhythm-section and out-of-character horns. Dyani never found another drummer with Ntoshko's instincts and empathy, but he came briefly close with Churchill Jolobe and then again towards the end of his life with Billy Hart. *Angolian Cry* is a strong record, brimming with the pathos and joy that marked *Song For Biko*. Beckett is an uncut national treasure and it's interesting to hear Tchicai on the less familiar tenor. *Born Under The Heat* reappears with two new live tracks, quartet performances recorded at the Lund Museum of Art with Epstein, Dørge and Matthews, a glimpse of Mbizo in the last year of his life. Not all the horns play together on the other tracks. Gwangwa appears only on 'The Boys From Somafco' and 'Song For The Workers', two of the more obviously political compositions. Johnny plays piano on 'Wish You Sunshine', 'Portrait Of Tete Mbambisa' and 'Song Of The Workers' and, as ever, one wonders what he might have done on a solo piano disc. The absence of a harmony instrument elsewhere isn't a problem, but it occasionally leaves the sound unanchored and hard to get a purchase on. Dyani's short life was packed with music, but listening back to these discs forces the inevitable conclusion that his best work never made it on to record. Almost always, the atmosphere of the studio and the lack of an audience to warm the air leaves one of the most distinctive bass players since Charles Mingus uninspired by comparison with his own extraordinary standard.

The Eagle Brass Band

GROUP

A 'modern' group led by drummer Barry Martyn, created to uphold the disappearing tradition of old-style New Orleans brass bands.

*** The Last Of The Line

GHB BCD-170 *Leo Dejan, Herbert Permillion, Andrew Blakeney, Emery Thompson, Milton Batiste, Dan Pawson (t); John Ewing, Alex Iles, Wendell Eugene, Mike Owen (tb); Al Carson (bs horn); Joe Darensbourg, Chris Burke (cl); Floyd Turnham, Harold Dejan (as); Sam Lee, Fred Kemp (ts); Teddy Edwards, Emile Martin, Barry Martyn (d).* 1/83–5/89.

Barry Martyn's notes espouse a kind of New Orleans fundamentalism which the music echoes as a mix of battle-cry and last hurrah. Martyn formed his Eagle Brass Band as a final rallying point of the old brass-band tradition of the city, and these late recordings – one session was actually cut in Los Angeles in 1983, but the second was made in New Orleans – are a defiant staring-down of pretenders like The Dirty Dozen Brass Band. Whether old pros or young believers, the players in the two bands which Martyn assembled, six years apart, seem to have the authentic style in their bones, and they can crack notes and wobble their vibratos on the tattered likes of 'Just A Little While To Stay Here', 'Eureka March' and 'Bourbon Street Parade' without a shred of self-consciousness. The raw, fragile music is certainly unlike virtually anything else in jazz, while seemingly central to the music's existence. That said, many will find a CD's worth of this group a very long haul.

Larry Eanet (born 1931)

PIANO

A local man in Washington, DC, Eanet worked as a dermatologist until finally retiring to concentrate on music in 1996. A club, party and restaurant pianist for the most part, he has also done the usual accompanist's stint to many visiting jazz luminaries.

***** Piano Solos Vol. 1**
Jump JCD12-20 *Eanet (p solo).* 11/97.

***** Piano Solos Vol. 2**
Jump JCD12-21 *Eanet (p solo).* 11/97.

***** Sunset Stomp**
Arbors ARCD 19220 *Eanet; Ron Hockett (cl, ss, ts); Tommy Cecil (b); Harold Sumney Jr (d).* 7/98.

'Relaxed, warm, laid back, not a moment of bad taste ...' Thus one reviewer, to which the unsympathetic might add 'boring'. That's not being fair to Eanet, but years of playing in situations in which it's his job to be undemanding have left him with a polished and equitable style that will have many listeners drifting off over CD length. He plays the music graciously, but a little more in the way of dynamic variation wouldn't hurt. The solo albums are all of a piece and they dwell too much in the realms of a modest mid-tempo. It's a pity that Eanet doesn't feel the need to impose more of himself on the music, because the programmes are full of surprising and even inspired choices: Pete Rugolo's 'Interlude', Porter's 'Goodbye, Little Dream, Goodbye', Strayhorn's 'Multicoloured Blue'... he has a very impressive book of tunes.

The quartet session for Arbors runs to the same temperament – this is Eanet's regular group for local gigs. Hockett is a smoothly adaptable player, though largely a conformist. More good tune-selection, though, going as far back as the old Bix & His Gang favourite, 'Rhythm King'.

Charles Earland (1941–2000)

ORGAN

Organ combo leader from Philadelphia, who actually began as a saxophonist and played with the Jack McDuff group. He switched to organ in 1963. Black Talk!, his definitive album, was a considerable hit in its day, though he never recaptured the same measure of success.

*****(*) Black Talk!**
Original Jazz Classics OJC 335 *Earland; Virgil Jones (t); Houston Person (ts); Melvin Sparks (g); Idris Muhammad (d); Buddy Caldwell (perc).* 12/69.

***** Leaving This Planet**
Prestige PRCD-66002-2 *Earland; Freddie Hubbard (t, flhn); Eddie Henderson (t); Joe Henderson (ts); Dave Hubbard (ss, ts, af); Patrick Gleeson (ky); Eddie Arkin, Greg Crockett (g); Brian Brake, Harvey Mason (d); Larry Killian (perc); Rudy Copeland (v).* 12/73–1/74.

The recent revival of interest in 'traditional' jazz organ rekindled Earland's career. He made a key album, *Black Talk!*, at the very end of the 1960s. Earland updated the heavier style of players such as Jack McDuff and Jimmy Smith, chose more pop-orientated material and delivered it with a percussive attack. Jones and Person are useful props, but Earland drives the music – even an unpromising piece like 'Aquarius' becomes a convincing, bluesy groove piece. *Leaving This Planet*, though it comes with some of the excess baggage of the era – dopey space effects, wah-wah guitars and the like – isn't far behind, and summons a first-rate cast to hammer through what's really a blowing session with some space-age debris. Hubbard's own set-piece, 'Red Clay', also features.

***** Front Burner**
Milestone M 9165 *Earland; Virgil Jones (t); Bill Easley (ts); Bobby Broom (g); Rudy Williams (d); Frank Colon (perc).* 6/88.

****(*) Third Degree Burn**
Milestone MCD-9174-2 *Earland; Lew Soloff (t); David Newman, Grover Washington (ss, ts); Bobby Broom (g); Buddy Williams (d); Ralph Dorsey (perc).* 5/89.

****(*) Blowing The Blues Away**
High Note HCD 70109 *Earland; James Rotundi (t); Eric Alexander (ts); Bob De Vos (g); Greg Rockingham (d).* 2/97.

***** Slammin' And Jammin'**
Savant SCD 2008 *Earland; Carlos Garnett (ts); Melvin Sparks (g); Eric Sealls (b); Bernard Purdie (d); Gary Fritz (perc).* 5/97.

The second wave of Earland's career was largely respectable rather than eventful so far as records were concerned. The Milestone albums have a degree of freshness which a couple of subsequent efforts for Muse missed altogether. *Blowing The Blues Away* is a smidgeon sharper and livelier, with Rotundi and Alexander playing the faithful horn disciples, and *Slammin' And Jammin'*, though not much more subtle than its title (and its cover art), has a straightahead simplicity and power that works nicely a couple of tracks at a time. Maybe 'The Mighty Burner', who died at the start of the new century, found little new in a genre which has probably reached the end of its creative journey; but he played good repertory.

Earthbound

GROUP

Tentative and all too earthbound, this eclectic line-up plays modern-to-free without conviction.

**** Unity**
Leo CD LR 189 *Alexandros (p); Alex Foster (ss); Andy McKee (b); Victor Jones (d); Cosa Ross (perc).* 4/92.

Possibly the most disappointing record ever to be issued by this normally enterprising label. It has a rehearsal/workshop feel and a dismal low-fi sound that will prove off-putting to many. Foster is an interesting player moment to moment, and Jones has some very worthwhile ideas. One suspects that leader Alexandros – no forename – might be more unfettered playing on his own, without the need to create dialogues.

Bill Easley (born 1943)

REEDS

Studied at Juilliard; with George Benson 1968–70, then a variety of gigs through the '70s. In the '80s played in theatre orchestras, then a sideman with Jimmy Smith and many others. By his own admission, a reluctant leader.

****(*) Wind Inventions**
Sunnyside SSC 1022 *Easley; Mulgrew Miller (p); Victor Gaskin (b); Tony Reedus (d).* 9/86.

This talented multi-instrumentalist is a proven asset as a sideman, but this debut as a leader was often colourless. He performs most of this programme on clarinet and, while it's a welcome change from hearing yet another prodigious saxophonist, his improvisations are facile rather than compelling. The sleeve-note compares the date to Buddy DeFranco's '50s records, but Easley doesn't approach DeFranco's piercing insight, and his swing-into-bop manner sounds bland across the length of an album. The soft-edged sound doesn't assist him.

***** First Call**
Milestone MCD-9186-2 *Easley; Bill Mobley (t); George Caldwell (ky); Roland Hanna, James Williams (p); J.J Wiggins, Dave Jackson (b); Grady Tate (d).* 10/90.

The lavish tenor treatment of 'It's All In The Game' gets the record off to a fine start, and Easley is enjoying himself here in the company of two different quintets, Hanna and Williams changing places at the piano. Standard material and the easy-going fluency of both pianists give the date a lighter, more knowing air than the debut and, while there's still nothing remarkable here, it's persuasive music.

*****(*) Easley Done**
Evidence ECD 22183-2 *Easley; Bill Mobley (t, flhn); George Coleman (ts); Donald Brown (p); Ron Carter (b); Billy Higgins (d).* 9/94.

It's quite a band, and Easley has them playing close to their best: 'Gypsy', Ron Carter's tune, blends singular and collective improvising to a rare degree, and in a clever set of tunes (including two by Frank Strozier) the leader's customary multi-instrumentalism is the point of variety in what might have been a set of professional licks.

Eastern Rebellion

GROUP

Originally a collective band of hard boppers, it came to be directed largely by Cedar Walton and made records from 1975 into the mid-'90s.

****** Eastern Rebellion**
Timeless SJP 101 *Cedar Walton (p); George Coleman (ts); Sam Jones (b); Billy Higgins (d).* 12/75.

*****(*) Eastern Rebellion 2**
Timeless CD SJP 106 *As above, except Bob Berg (ts) replaces Coleman.*

*****(*) Mosaic**
Musicmasters 65073-2 *Cedar Walton (p); Ralph Moore (ts); David Williams (b); Billy Higgins (d).* 12/90.

*****(*) Simple Pleasure**
Musicmasters 518 014 *As above.* 6/92.

****** Just One Of Those ... Nights At The Village Vanguard**
MusicMasters 65116-2 *As above.* 95.

Led by pianist Walton, Eastern Rebellion is a more collective enterprise than his solo records, though he is still the main composer. The group's essentially a piano trio but, in line with the earlier Walton band of which Clifford Jordan became an integral part, there has always been a place for a hornman. Higgins has been a stalwart from the start and is probably the main point of continuity with Walton's other records. The original *Eastern Rebellion* is still arguably the finest record Walton has put his hand to; the version of 'Naima', with Coleman sounding magisterial as he cuts through the harmonies, compares more than favourably with that on the excellent *Bluesville Time* (see under Walton), where Dale Barlow takes the lead.

The addition of British-born Ralph Moore brings a fresh, vocalized tone, first heard to effect on 'John's Blues' on *Mosaic*, a track that also shows off Higgins's formidable talents. There are fewer highs and lows on *Simple Pleasures*, a more straightforward blowing date, but the musicianship is consistently high and the empathy between the three senior members is as close as ever. By the time of the Village Vanguard sessions, it sounds unquestionably like a well-established group. Moore is wholly integrated and often very impressive indeed, and there are signs that he is stamping his personality on the music as well as following his elders. Again, much of the material is Walton's, but there are expansive versions of Thad Jones's 'A Child Is Born' and John Lewis's 'Django', and the long, long 'Seven Minds', a Sam Jones piece, is as full of drama, light and shade as one could wish.

Peter Ecklund (born 1945)

TRUMPET, CORNET, BUGLE

Formerly a Boston schoolteacher, Ecklund turned pro in the '70s and began playing in pop and American folk-jazz settings. Later studio work led to a reputation for his repertory skills, and he is in demand in that situation; he has also published studies of Armstrong and Beiderbecke.

*****(*) Ecklund At Elkhart**
Jazzology JCD-246 *Ecklund; Dan Barrett (tb); Bobby Gordon (cl); Mark Shane (p); Marty Grosz (g, v); Greg Cohen (b); Hal Smith (d).* 7/94.

*****(*) Strings Attached**
Arbors ARCD 19149 *Ecklund; Scott Robinson (cl, ss, as, bs); Jay Ungar (vn); Lenny Pickett (cl, srspn); Kenny Kosek (mand); Chris*

Flory, Frank Vignola, Marty Grosz, Molly Mason (g); Cynthia Sayer (bj); Greg Cohen, Murray Wall (b); Richard Crooks (d). 4/92–3/95.

Ecklund is beginning to come into his own after some years of excellent foot-soldiering. Though under his nominal leadership, *Ecklund At Elkhart* is really nothing more or less than another of the ineffably hot and good-humoured jazz parties which always seem to take place when Marty Grosz and his pals are on hand. Another 15 chestnuts from 1918 to 1939, some of which only the Grosz gang would dare go near these days, especially the once-frightful 'Trees', here given a peppery rendition. Barrett and Gordon have plenty of good solos and Shane is a model of light-fingered swing, but Ecklund does take marginal honours with cornet playing of finesse and pukka good cheer.

Pieced together from six sessions over three years, *Strings Attached* ranges from duos to septets and is often awfully good: try 'Try A Little Tenderness', completely shorn of its Otis Redding bathos and turned into a lilting lament, or a tune we've waited to hear in jazz for a long time, the lovable novelty, 'Wedding Of The Painted Doll'. There are winning vignettes from Robinson and Ungar and, when Ecklund simply plays a classic standard such as 'Too Marvelous For Words', it's just marvelous (*sic*). But titles like 'All-Purpose Cowboy Melody' give away the one weakness: there's an in-joke feel that lays the dead hand of kitsch on some of this stuff.

***** Gigs – Reminiscing In Music**
Arbors ARCD 19230 *Ecklund; Dan Block (cl, as, bs); Bobby Gordon (cl); Joel Martin, Warren Bernhardt (p); Keith Ingham (cel); Jay Ungar (vn); Peter Davis (g, bj, cl); Steve Cardenas, Madeleine Peyroux, Molly Mason, Frank Vignola (g); Guy Fischetti (pedal steel); Cynthia Sayer (bj); Howard Johnson (tba); Greg Cohen, Pete Toigo, Marty Grosz, Murray Wall, Kelly Friesen, Harry Aceto (b); Richard Crooks (d).* 1/98–1/99.

Tunes and musicians who remind Ecklund of places he's played and jobs he's worked. He can hardly escape the charge of self-indulgence with an agenda like that but, good-natured fellow that he is, he makes this a charming set of performances. A lot of it has the feel of folk music – from barn dances or back porches – but the players are anything but Saturday-night amateurs. If they were, they might have summoned a bit of useful hamfistedness here and there – for the most part, the music's so polite it's almost perfumed. But that's the price of being a pro. Highlight: Leroy Carr's 'Midnight Hour Blues'.

Billy Eckstine (1914–93)

VOCAL, TRUMPET, VALVE TROMBONE

Though a competent brass player, it was Eckstine's voice that was his fortune. When he arrived in Chicago in 1938, he found success as vocalist with the Earl Hines band, and he subsequently ran his own big band during 1944–7, giving employment to many of the sharpest young talents in the nascent bebop scene. He turned to small-group work from 1947 and spent the rest of his career as a soloist, finding much MOR success but always with a jazz flavour somewhere.

***** Billy Eckstine 1944–1946**
Classics 914 *Eckstine; Dizzy Gillespie, Freddy Webster, Shorty McConnell, Al Killian, Gail Brockman, Boonie Hazel, Fats Navarro, Raymond Orr (t); Trummy Young, Howard Scott, Claude Jones, Jerry Valentine, Taswell Baird, Chippy Outcalt, Walter Knox (tb); Budd Johnson, Jimmy Powell, John Jackson, Bill Frazier, Sonny Stitt, John Cobbs (as); Gene Ammons, Dexter Gordon, Wardell Gray, Thomas Crump, Arthur Sammons (ts); Rudy Rutherford, Leo Parker, Teddy Cypron (bs); John Malachi, Clyde Hart, Richard Ellington (p); Connie Wainwright (g); Oscar Pettiford, Tommy Potter (b); Shadow Wilson, Art Blakey (d); Sarah Vaughan (v).* 4/44–10/45.

Eckstine's orchestra was a legendary incubator for young bebop talent, as a glance at the personnel shows, and it's a pity that the band's surviving performances are mostly of ballads and features for the leader. Not that one should decry anything that Eckstine himself does: his massive, smooth, sumptuous voice has its own virtues, and on the rare occasion when he handles an up-tempo piece – 'I Love The Rhythm In A Riff' – he is just as adept. There are glimmers of Gordon, Ammons, Gillespie and Navarro here (as well as Vaughan's debut on 'I'll Wait And Pray') but it's the power of the band as a whole, the lift given by the young Art Blakey and the rapt power of Eckstine's balladeering which are the merits of these tracks. Docked a point for the sound – never good off the original masters for De Luxe and National, but they probably ought to sound better than this.

*****(*) Together**
Spotlite SPJ-CD 200 *Eckstine; Gail Brockman, Boonie Hazel, Shorty McConnell, Fats Navarro (t); Taswell Baird, Chippy Outcalt, Howard Scott, Jerry Valentine (tb); John Jackson, Bill Frazier (as); Gene Ammons, Budd Johnson (ts); Leo Parker (bs); John Malachi (p); Connie Wainwright (g); Tommy Potter (b); Art Blakey (d); Lena Horne, Sarah Vaughan (v).* 2–3/45.

These Jubilee broadcast transcriptions, in mostly excellent sound, offer arguably the best evidence of the calibre of the Eckstine orchestra. Johnson, already a veteran at 35, is one of the most impressive soloists, but there are precious glimpses of Navarro, features for Horne and Vaughan, and the power of the sections – especially the trumpets – comes bursting through. Great hipster announcements too by MC Bubbles Whitman!

***** Billy Eckstine 1946–1947**
Classics 1022 *Eckstine; Boonie Hazel, Shorty McConnell, Raymond Orr, Kenny Dorham, Fats Navarro, Miles Davis, Hobart Dotson, Leonard Hawkins, King Kolax, Ray Linn (t); Chippy Outcalt, Robert Scott, Jerry Valentine, Walter Knox (tb); Norris Turney, Junior Williams, Sonny Stitt, John Cobbs, Sonny Criss (as); Gene Ammons, Arthur Sammons, Josh Jackson, Wardell Gray (ts); Tate Houston, Leo Parker, Cecil Payne (bs); Richard Ellington, Jimmy Golden, Linton Garner, Warren Bracken (p); Connie Wainwright (g); Bill McMahon, Tommy Potter, Shifty Henry (b); Art Blakey, Tim Kennedy (d); strings.* 1/46–4/47.

These six sessions for National are again dominated by ballads and the incomparable Eckstine voice, but a glance through the personnels show what an abundance of jazz talent there was on hand: Blakey is always booting the band along, Navarro breaks through here and there, and the final date is a small-group session which offers Wardell Gray soloing on 'She's Got The Blues For Sale'. The original sound is still poor, although the later sessions show National improving their microphones to some extent.

*****(*) Billy's Best!**

Verve 526440-2 *Eckstine; orchestras of Hal Mooney, Bobby Tucker.* 8/57–9/58.

***** Imagination**

Emarcy 848162-2 *Eckstine; Pete Rugolo Orchestra.* 58.

***** At Basin Street East**

Emarcy 832592 *Eckstine; Benny Bailey, Clark Terry, Ernie Royal (t); Curtis Fuller (tb); Julius Watkins (frhn); Phil Woods (as); Jerome Richardson, Eric Dixon (ts, f); Sahib Shihab (bs); Patti Bown (p); Don Elliott (vib); Don Arnone (g); Stu Martin (d).* 61.

****** Everything I Have Is Yours**

Verve 819442-2 2CD *Eckstine; various groups.* 47–57.

*****(*) Verve Jazz Masters: Billy Eckstine**

Verve 519693-2 *Eckstine; various groups.* 49–58.

It was the ripest, most luxuriant voice in black music and, though his later records suggest a man who was fundamentally a conservative, one shouldn't forget how radical a role it was for a black singer to adopt such a romantic persona in the 1940s. Eckstine's many records for Mercury from the 1950s and '60s have been neglected until recently. Of the surviving 'original' albums, *At Basin Street East* is a rousing encounter with Quincy Jones's big band. The contrast here is between Eckstine's opulent, take-my-time delivery and the scintillating punch of what was a fierce, slick, note-perfect organization. *Imagination* is more in the slicked-down ballad mode, and some of these tunes have never oozed quite so much; Rugolo provides limousine-class charts. *Billy's Best* is a beauty which we have petitioned for reissue in the past, so it is a special pleasure to welcome it in such splendid remastering. 'When The Sun Comes Out' shows how Eckstine could handle a high-stepping arrangement without seeming to require any exertion of his own, and the following 'I Got Lost In Her Arms' presents ardour as the most gentlemanly of emotions. The arrangements walk a line between vigour and schmooze, and there are six bonus tracks added to the original LP programme.

First choice here, though, must go to the two-disc set, *Everything I Have Is Yours*, which charts Eckstine's course with all his hits and a few plum rarities of the order of 'Mister You've Gone And Got The Blues'. The *Jazz Masters* disc boils it down to 16 tracks and throws in a previously unissued obscurity to tempt diehard collectors, 'I Lost My Sugar In Salt Lake City'.

****** No Cover No Minimum**

Roulette 98583-2 *Eckstine; Charlie Walp (t); Bucky Manieri (tb); Charlie McLean, Buddy Balboa (saxes); Bobby Tucker (p); Buddy Grievey (d).* 8/60.

A superlative example of Eckstine's art, and surely still his best record in print. Recorded at a Las Vegas lounge, the 21 tracks (12 of them previously unissued) luxuriate in Bobby Tucker's simple arrangements and bask in the grandeur of Eckstine's voice and phrasing. 'Moonlight In Vermont' has never sounded more richly expansive, 'Lush Life' is a proper ode to barfly poetry, and the swingers are delivered with an insouciance and a perfect mastery of metre that creates shivers of delight. The remastering is very full and vivid on what is an indispensable issue.

Harry 'Sweets' Edison (1915–99)

TRUMPET

Born in Columbus, Ohio, Edison worked in territory groups before joining Count Basie in 1938, staying until 1950. After that there were countless studio dates (with Sinatra and many other singers), all-star sessions and the like; Sweets became the most revered of elder statesmen and was playing right up until his death in 1999.

***** Jawbreakers**

Original Jazz Classics OJC 487 *Edison; Eddie 'Lockjaw' Davis (ts); Hugh Lawson (p); Ike Isaacs (g); Clarence Johnston (d).* 4/62.

***** Edison's Lights**

Original Jazz Classics OJC 804 *Edison; Eddie 'Lockjaw' Davis (ts); Count Basie, Dolo Coker (p); John Heard (b); Jimmie Smith (d).* 5/76.

****(*) Simply Sweets**

Original Jazz Classics OJC 903 *Edison; Eddie 'Lockjaw' Davis (ts); Dolo Coker (p); Harvey Newmark (b); Jimmie Smith (d).* 9/77.

Ubiquitous as an accompanist/soloist, Edison made surprisingly few records of his own, given the length of his career. Like many players of his type, he often sounds better on other people's sessions, though the presence of Basie on *Edison's Lights* audibly inspires him (compare the rather lacklustre tracks made on the same day with Coker). The 1970s association with Lockjaw Davis produced some of the best of his work, a bright, bursting sound which can also be quite reserved and contemplative; *Jawbreakers* comes highly recommended, a big, raw session that springs a romantic version of 'A Gal In Calico' which contrasts well with the tough funk of 'Oo-ee!'. The Pablo OJCs have a good, full sound.

*****(*) For My Pals**

Pablo 2310934 *Edison; Buster Cooper (tb); Curtis Peagler (as, ts); Art Hillery (p, org); Andrew Simpkins (b); Albert 'Tootie' Heath (d).* 12/88.

***** Swing Summit**

Candid CCD 79050 *Edison; Buddy Tate (cl, ts); Frank Wess (ts, f); Hugh Lawson (p); Ray Drummond (b); Bobby Durham (d).* 4/90.

***** Live At Ambassador Auditorium**

Concord CCD 4610 *Edison; Ken Peplowski (cl, ts); Howard Alden (g); Ben Aronov (p); Murray Wall (b); Tom Melito (d).* 2/94.

Edison's artistic longevity was remarkable; his ability and willingness continually to develop was nothing short of miraculous. *For My Pals*, with a larger than usual group, marked a welcome return to form; 'Lover Man' and 'There Is No Greater Love' are both top-notch performances and the sound is immaculate. *Swing Summit* contains less interesting material, but is brightly and faithfully recorded, and excellent value. His drop-in with the Ken Peplowski group at the Ambassador Auditorium in Pasadena is masterfully timed and judged. Like all great statesmen, he says nothing of substance but gives even vacancy a kind of grandeur.

Marc Edwards

DRUMS

Previously known as a Cecil Taylor sideman from the 1970s, Edwards reappears as an energy-music group leader and drummer.

***** Red Sprites And Blue Jets**

CIMP 128 *Edwards; Sabir Mateen (ts); Hill Greene (b).* 10/96.

Blending full-on energy music with slow, stately lamentation, Edwards's trio are in a noble tradition of free playing, and the drummer's previous appearances with Cecil Taylor are a clue to the kind of jazz this is. Mateen has the sort of grand, slightly worn sound that's ideal for the situation, and the leader is a tireless powerhouse. Greene, though, may have wondered on the playbacks why he is virtually inaudible in all but the quiet passages – but that is the recording style of CIMP.

Teddy Edwards (born 1924)

TENOR SAXOPHONE, CLARINET

Arrived in Los Angeles in 1944 after working in territory bands, and has basically remained there since, active through the '50s and '60s and then making guest appearances in the '80s and '90s. A blend of Southwestern blues and West Coast cool informs his sound.

*****(*) Steady With Teddy**

Cool N' Blue C & B CD 115 *Edwards; Benny Bailey, Howard McGhee (t); Iggy Shevack (tb); Dexter Gordon (ts); Duke Brooks, Hampton Hawes, Dodo Marmarosa, Jimmy Rowles (p); Arvin Garrison (g); Red Callender, Addison Farmer, Bob Kesterson (b); Roy Porter (d).* 10/46–8/48.

These are the earliest glimpses of Edwards on record, with boppers who put a lyrical spin on the familiar changes. Tracks like 'Dilated Pupils' from the 1946 session (a McGhee composition, significantly) suggest the sort of background he was working against. Though he has had his ups and downs, Edwards's relaxed, imperturbable manner has sustained him well; 'steady with Teddy' has been the watchword.

*****(*) Teddy's Ready**

Original Jazz Classics OJC 1785 *Edwards; Joe Castro (p); Leroy Vinnegar (b); Billy Higgins (d).* 8/60.

***** Back To Avalon**

Contemporary CCD 14074 *Edwards; Nathaniel Meeks (t); Lester Robertson (tb); Jimmy Woods (as); Modesto Brisenio (bs); Danny Horton (p); Roger Alderson (b); Lawrence Marable (d).* 12/60.

Recorded in 1960, *Back To Avalon* was an interesting attempt at arrangement for a mid-size band. The problem is that the Octet doesn't generate quite the head of steam the blandness of these charts requires in compensation, and there isn't enough going on on the solo front, including a rather subdued and preoccupied Edwards. Even the workhorse, 'Good Gravy', fails to raise a cheer. Lester Koenig's recording can't shoulder any significant blame, and the remix for CD restores a lot of detail. Nothing quite compares, then, to the session with McGhee listed below, though *Teddy's Ready* (originally on Contemporary) has a timeless vigour that makes it endlessly repeatable. It followed a period of ill-health – unrelated, it should be said, to the usual perils of a jazzman's life in those days – and one can hear the relief and delight in the slightly too hasty attack on 'Scrapple From The Apple' and 'Take The "A" Train'. In later years, Edwards was reliably to be found *behind* the beat. Not a great deal is known nowadays about Arizonan Castro and he tends to be thought of as an accomplished accompanist (Anita O'Day and June Christy) who never quite made it as a straight jazz player. On this showing he's more than worthy, and the support of his two colleagues here goes without saying.

****** Together Again!**

Original Jazz Classics OJC 424 *Edwards; Howard McGhee (t); Phineas Newborn Jr (p); Ray Brown (b); Ed Thigpen (d).* 5/61.

*****(*) Good Gravy**

Original Jazz Classics OJC 661 *Edwards; Danny Horton, Phineas Newborn Jr (p); Leroy Vinnegar (b); Milton Turner (d).* 8/61.

Edwards's reunion with a cleaned-up Howard McGhee in 1962 led to one of the best mainstream albums of its day. *Together Again!* is beautifully and almost effortlessly crafted. The ultra-straight 'Misty' showcases Edwards's moody ballad approach and there is a fine 'You Stepped Out Of A Dream'. Three months later, and without a second horn, Edwards waffles and digresses engagingly but doesn't quite get into the frame. Horton depped for Newborn for much of the three-day session; he's a bright enough lad, but lacks horsepower and swing. Vinnegar is as sure-fire as ever.

***** Heart And Soul**

Original Jazz Classics OJC 177 *Edwards; Gerry Wiggins (org); Leroy Vinnegar (b); Milton Turner (d).* 62.

***** Nothin' But The Truth**

Original Jazz Classics OJC 813 *Edwards; Walter Davis Jr (p); Phil Orlando (g); Paul Chambers (b); Billy Higgins (d); Montego Joe (perc).* 12/66.

***** Out Of This World**

Steeplechase SCCD 1147 *Edwards; Kenny Drew (p); Jesper Lundgaard (b); Billy Hart (d).* 12/80.

****(*) Good Gravy**

Timeless SJP 139 *Edwards; Rein De Graaff (p); Henk Haverhoek (b); John Engels (d).* 12/81.

Heart And Soul is warm enough, but there's a hint that Teddy would like some company in the front line and, for all the guileful support he gets from Wig and the others, it's a bit routine in parts. The rather later *Nothin' But The Truth* is well-mannered but, with the exception of 'But Beautiful' and the title-track (to but no more buts than that), it's a rather average set. Even with a rhythm section of this quality, Edwards doesn't sound inclined to hurry or be infused with anything more dynamic than his usual step-up-and-play approach. The 1980s material is pretty much of a piece, but Edwards isn't on form for the confusingly titled *Good Gravy*. He also lacks a convincing bass player. Spoilt by Leroy Vinnegar, Edwards never again found someone who could put so much relaxed spring into his solo gait. Haverhoek copes manfully but hasn't the lyricism to match the firmly accented pulse.

***** Midnight Creeper**

High Note Records HCD 7011 *Edwards; Virgil Jones (t); Richard Wyands (p); Buster Williams (b); Chip White (d).* 3/97.

A new label for Edwards – his several Verve albums of the '90s have all been axed – and for former Muse-man Houston Person, who produces with his usual skill, letting the music work rather than trying to sweeten it artificially. If Edwards's recording activities have been less in evidence in recent years, despite the renaissance with Polygram, there's certainly nothing wrong with either his technique or his enthusiasm. The album opens with the eponymous nocturnal wanderer, a thing of shadows with a ghostly wail. There are two other originals, 'Walkin' In The Rain', which sounds as if it might have been written for a larger group, and the medium ballad, 'Sensitive'. Jones plays only on these three and 'Sunday', and the remainder of the set consists of standards, which is perhaps a pity, though the quality of playing on 'Tenderly', the longest track, and the closing 'Almost Like Being In Love' makes up for everything. Williams is in cracking form throughout the album and along with Wyands and White creates the kind of relaxed but positive vibe on which Edwards thrives. Not a classic album, but a damn fine one from the oldster.

Marty Ehrlich (born 1955)

REEDS, FLUTES

Studied in Boston in the '70s, with Ran Blake and others, then moved to New York in 1978, and has been at the centre of the jazz and new music scene since.

****** Pliant Plaint**

Enja 5065 *Ehrlich; Stan Strickland (ss, ts, f); Anthony Cox (b); Bobby Previte (d).* 4/87.

*****(*) The Traveller's Tale**

Enja 6024 *As above, except Lindsey Horner (b) replaces Cox.* 5–6/89.

Ehrlich's Enja albums provide entertaining samplers for the breadth of contemporary jazz. His compositions are eclectic in the best way, drawing on different rhythmic and formal backgrounds but impressed with his own spirited playing. Strickland, a gutsy and agile tenor player, is an excellent foil for the leader and both rhythm sections are fine, though Cox is marginally more responsive than Horner. We prefer *Pliant Plaint* for its sense of variety: there's an impeccable composed piece, 'After After All', played by Ehrlich alone in a series of overdubs, and an enchanting flute duet on 'What I Know Now', along with more familiar thematic improvising on the other pieces. *The Traveller's Tale* is nearly as good, though, with Ehrlich sounding strong on four different reeds.

*****(*) Side By Side**

Enja 5065-2 *Ehrlich; Frank Lacy (tb); Wayne Horvitz (p); Anthony Cox (b); Andrew Cyrille (d).* 1/91.

Side By Side continues an exceptionally rewarding sequence of records. Ehrlich's instinct for good tunes accompanies ensemble playing and direction which go about as far out from hard-bop orthodoxy as they can: it's highly melodic and rhythmically liberated free playing, with enough arranged detail to keep a composer's sensibility happy. Lacy and Ehrlich are all over their horns, and the rhythm section play just as strongly.

***** Emergency Peace**

New World NW 80409 *Ehrlich; Muhal Richard Abrams (p); Abdul Wadud (clo); Lindsey Horner (b).* 12/90.

Ehrlich sets himself another difficult programme here, with the contrasting resonances of Wadud and Horner making an intriguing bottom-line (Abrams plays piano on only two of the nine tracks). Ehrlich can't help but recall Julius Hemphill in duo with Wadud, and when they actually do a Hemphill tune ('The Painter') the comparison doesn't really favour him. Ehrlich calls this group the 'Dark Woods Ensemble', a useful image, and when the three of them (Ehrlich on bass clarinet) execute the grave dance of 'Unison' they make a real identity out of it. But some of it either merely meanders or runs on too long.

*****(*) Can You Hear A Motion?**

Enja 8052-2 *Ehrlich; Stan Strickland (ts, f); Michael Formanek (b); Bobby Previte (d).* 9/93.

***** Just Before The Dawn**

New World/CounterCurrents 80474 *Erhrlich; Vincent Chancey (frhn); Erik Friedlander (clo); Mark Helias (b); Don Alias (perc).* 94.

Ehrlich invites many comparisons in his playing, but the spirit which is starting to seem closest to his is Anthony Braxton's. While the opening clarinet tune on *Can You Hear A Motion?* is a dedication to John Carter, it's Braxtonian tone and logic one hears. Ehrlich humanizes the approach: he gets bite and swing out of this woodsy-sounding quartet and inculcates a rural feel into a team which includes such urbanites as Formanek and Previte. 'The Welcome' pivots on a township-like melody, while 'Ode To Charlie Parker' is a chamber-piece for clarinet, flute and bass, and a lovely one too. This probably counts as Ehrlich's best disc since *Pliant Plaint*. The next Dark Woods Ensemble record, *Just Before The Dawn*, is as highly coloured but a shade less vivacious in the playing: sometimes the group gets a little hung up on its own sounds and shadings, perhaps.

****** New York Child**

Enja 9025-2 *Ehrlich; Stan Strickland (ts); Michael Cain (p); Michael Formanek (b); Bill Stewart (d).* 2/95.

Assured, vibrant and intensely beautiful for much of its duration, this is surely Ehrlich's finest hour to date. His sound goes so well with Strickland's that they invite comparisons with Konitz and Marsh: each has a pliable, unshowy tone, ideal for the plaiting of timbres which the unisons seek to achieve. Cain has seldom played better than here – his improvised duet with Ehrlich on 'Prelude' and the luminous solo on Julius Hemphill's 'Georgia Blue' are quite gorgeously done – and Stewart and Formanek are entirely admirable. Ehrlich's writing follows a patient course: 'I always find it easier to play within the context of a melody, and I always look for what is specific about the language of a given piece.' That peaceable logic gives Ehrlich's outside-isms complete conviction.

*****(*) Light At The Crossroads**
Songlines SGL 1511-2 *Ehrlich; Ben Goldberg (cl, bcl); Trevor Dunn (b); Kenny Wolleson (d).* 1/96.

The pleasures here are in the jousting between Ehrlich and Goldberg and the subtle, almost sneakily swinging rhythms set down by Dunn and Wolleson. On a clever piece like Wayne Horvitz's Monk inversion, 'Ask Me Later', they find a humorous counterpoint which touches a comic aspect in their reeds without resorting to pastiche or clowning. Elsewhere they're irreproachably sober. Light, and dark.

*****(*) Live Wood**
Music & Arts CD-986 2CD *Ehrlich; Erik Friedlander (clo); Mark Helias (b).* 3–4/96.

Generously spread across two discs, this souvenir of a Dark Woods tour of Europe is an absorbing set even when the music gets occasionally dour – perhaps unavoidable, given the instrumentation. Ehrlich's bass clarinet still sounds like his most eminent horn and on themes such as 'Eliahu' the sonorities of the group are enough to mesmerize. The fierce clarinet solo on 'Time And The Wild Words' show how the even dynamic of the trio can still give rise to urgency, and the cello's key role as both texturalist and front-line voice is handled with fine skill by Friedlander. Best sampled a few tracks at a time.

*****(*) Relativity**
Enja 9341-2 *Ehrlich; Michael Formanek (b); Peter Erskine (d).* 2/98.

Ehrlich's name comes first, but this is really a co-operative trio and, if there's a dominant personality, it's Erskine whose constant creativity within free and time playing is a wonderful resource for any group. As Ehrlich says: 'the harmony moves through the drums, the melody spins a long line from the bass, and I can feel free to make my horn into a ride cymbal'. Ten compositions are shared round the group, with a nice reminder of Don Grolnick (whose band Ehrlich and Erskine played in together) with his 'Taglioni'. Spontaneous but cultured and cultivated playing by all three sets of hands.

Thore Ehrling (born 1912)

TRUMPET, VOCAL

Born in Stockholm, Ehrling played in Frank Vernon's dance band from 1930, then formed his own small group in 1938 and developed it into a successful big band, which endured until 1957. He also worked extensively in music publishing.

***** Jazz Highlights**
Dragon DRCD 236 *Ehrling; Gosta Redlig, Gosta Pettersson, Gosta Torner, Rune Ander, Yngve Nilsson, Olle Jacobson, Arnold Johansson, Putte Bjorn, John Linder, Nisse Skoog (t); George Vernon, Sverre Oredsson, Sven Hedberg, Andreas Skjold (tb); Ove Ronn, Curt Blomqvist, Erik Andersson, John Bjorling, Carl-Henrik Noren, Casper Hjukstrom, Stig Gabrielsson, Gunnar Lunden-Velden, Arne Domnérus, Harry Arnold, Fritz Fust, Rolf Londell, Georg Bjorklund, Mats Borgstrom (reeds); Stig Holm, Mats Olsson (p); Folke Eriksberg, Sven Stiberg (g); Thore Jederby, Hasse Tellemar (b); Anders Solden, Gosta Heden, Uffe Baadh, Henry Wallin, Bertil Frylmark (d).* 1/39–12/55.

****(*) Swedish Swing 1945–1947**
Ancha ANC 9503-2 *Similar to above.* 3/45–7/47.

A sizeable slice of Swedish jazz history is packed on to this 26-track Dragon CD, decently remastered from some rare originals. Ehrling had already worked in dance bands for many years before forming his first orchestra in 1938 – he had been a Benny Carter sideman two years earlier – and, although his band made as many concessions to popular taste as did Basie and Ellington, they made enough good jazz-directed records to grant this retrospective more than a passing interest. Among the early tracks, a very swinging 'Roses Of Picardy' and a Dorsey-like 'Meditation' are impressive. Carl-Henrik Noren's arrival brought his interesting tunes to the book, including the Ellingtonian 'Mississippi Mood'; but the later tracks suggest that Ehrling never got much further than the solidly competitive swing style that was established by the early 1940s. Soloists are more functional than inspiring, although Ove Ronn's Hodges-like alto is always worth catching, as is Noren, and Domnérus appears on one track. A pleasing tribute to a great name in Swedish jazz.

The Ancha disc is for more dedicated tastes, since it covers a couple of broadcasts from the mid-1940s. The first is all-Ellington, done with a surprising amount of panache, though the arrangements seem like slavish copies. The second is by a nonet, with Bjorling's clarinet taking a significant role and a couple of kitsch items betraying the music's dance-hall origins. The second set is a bit crackly, but sound is otherwise clear enough.

8 Bold Souls

GROUP

An octet led and organized by Chicagoan saxophonist Edward Wilkerson, performing his post-AACM compositions.

*****(*) Sideshow**
Arabesque AJO103 *Robert Griffin (t, flhn); Isaiah Jackson (tb); Edward Wilkerson (as, ts, bs, cl); Mwata Bowden (ts, bs, cl); Aaron Dodd (tba); Naomi Millender (clo); Harrison Bankhead (b); Dushun Mosley (d).* 11/91.

*****(*) Antfarm**
Arabesque AJO114 *As above.* 7–8/94.

By emphasizing the unusual timbres of the instrumentation, Chicagoan Edward Wilkerson's band creates a singular ensemble sound that is finally more interesting than the often impassioned solos. The use of low brass (Dodd is a key player) and the ponderous tempos were more interesting than the sometimes incoherent faster pieces in their early music, but that problem had seemingly been dealt with by the time of *Sideshow*. Wilkerson takes his time – there are only five pieces on a record running well over an hour – and the opening 'Black Herman' is an ominous masterpiece, grown from a simple riff into a fascinating series of contrasting groupings, with the leader's severe tenor solo as the icing on a rich cake. It's slightly disappointing that he grants himself only one further improvisation on the record, and the very long rendition of Coleman's 'Lonely Woman' is a shade unconvincing in its explosive central section; but the contributions from Griffin, Bowden, Dodd and Millender are vivid compensation, and the stealthy, deliberate pace of the record is finally hypnotic.

Antfarm is a fine continuation. Again, Wilkerson refuses to hurry himself, with the title-piece running at 16 minutes and the shortest of the others reaching 8 minutes 27 seconds. His debt to Henry Threadgill's early work is perhaps even more clear, with his own tenor solo on 'Half Life' re-creating the atmosphere of a classic Air performance, and the rumbustious ensembles and bizarre contrasts walk in Henry's footsteps. But the group has its own democratic character: Jackson, Bowden and Griffin impress as individual voices, growing in stature, and the leader's writing always seems to have a surprise up its sleeve.

****** Last Option**

Thrill Jockey 071 *As above, except Gerald Powell (tba) replaces Dodd.* 8/99.

It took him five years, but Wilkerson has at last brought us a new 8 Bold Souls record, courtesy of Chicago's adventurous new-music label, Thrill Jockey. The personnel remains stable, with only a single change, and the ensemble's music is taking on an increasingly lived-in and confident feel, irregular as its reports are. With Henry Threadghill's groups seemingly in abeyance at present, there's little else being made and played in this style. Among the soloists, Griffin and Bowden are this time outstanding, and Wilkerson restricts himself to only two appearances in that capacity. Once again, though, the ensemble's the thing. The fugitive shapes of 'Last Option' or the rumbustious parade music of 'Third One Smiles' aren't in and of themselves blaringly new ideas, but it takes a tremendously accomplished group and a singular leader to sustain these pieces and interlink them across an hour-long CD. A marvellous feast of new jazz.

Bruce Eisenbeil (born 1963)

GUITAR

A subtle young Chicagoan, Eisenbeil is a rather 'pure' technician in the Derek Bailey mould. He sounds more like a cross between Sonny Sharrock and David Moss, though.

***** Nine Wings**

CIMP 144 *Eisenbeil; Rob Brown (as); Lou Grassi (d).* 3/97.

*****(*) Mural**

CIMP 194 *Eisenbeil; J Brunka (b); Ryan Sawyer (d).* 2/99.

Eisenbeil sounds like a wild man in spite of himself. He plays unadorned electric guitar, without effects or accoutrements, in a simple open tone that's bent into service as an avant-garde instrument. With the peripatetic Brown, something of a free-playing veteran by now, and the tinkering Grassi, he leads the trio through eight compositions (and one brief improv) that break down structure into bloody three-way confrontations. 'Hermitage Of Xzeng Xzu' and 'Mercury' are especially all out. Brown's experience comes to the fore and he makes light of his exposed position, but Eisenbeil is arguably the more interesting performer since he tries to reconcile his melodicism with playing out.

The CIMP no-tricks sound isn't much help on this occasion, but it has certainly been tweaked for the second album, which is an arresting panel of soundscapes, shaped round two long tracks, 'Caesar' and 'Woman With A Handful Of Rain'. Sawyer's fast-decay cymbal sound is a key element, but Eisenbeil himself has broadened his range of articulations, and he creates a new vocabulary of 'natural' effects which broadens and deepens the musical discourse considerably.

Either/Orchestra

GROUP

Led and organized by Russ Gershon and based in and around Massachusetts, this big contemporary ensemble now has a 15-year history behind it, playing material from jazz, rock and other modern-music sources.

***** Dial E**

Accurate AC-2222 *Tom Halter, Dave Ballou, Bob Sealy, Dan Drexter (t); Russell Jewell, Josh Roseman (tb); Rob Rawlings, Bob Sinfonia (as); Russ Gershon (ts); Steve Norton (bs); Kenny Freundlich (ky); John Dirac (g); Mike Rivard (b); Jerome Deupree (d).* 7/86.

*****(*) Radium**

Accurate AC-3232 *Tom Halter, John Carlson (t, flhn); Russell Jewell, Curtis Hasselbring (tb); Rob Rawlings (as); Russ Gershon (ss, ts); Charlie Kohlhase (bs); Kenny Freundlich (ky); John Dirac (g); Mike Rivard (b); Jerome Deupree (d).* 8/87–1/88.

*****(*) The Half-Life Of Desire**

Accurate AC-3242 *As above, except add Douglas Yates (ss, as), Dave Finucane (bcl), John Medeski (ky), Mark Sandman (g, v).* 89.

****** The Calculus Of Pleasure**

Accurate AC-3252 *As above, except add Bob Nieske (b), Matt Wilson (d); omit Freundlich, Dirac, Rivard, Deupree, Finucane, Sandman.* 4–6/90.

****** The Brunt**

Accurate AC-3262 *As above, except add Dan Fox (tb), Andrew D'Angelo (as, bcl, cl), Chris Taylor (ky), John Turner (b); omit Hasselbring, Yates, Medeski, Nieske.* 5/93.

A modest-sized big band full of outsize talents, Either/Orchestra have made scarcely any international impact. Leader Russ Gershon has squeezed these CDs out of the impossible restrictions that modern budgets have set for this kind of band if it wants to work and make records: it's a heroic accomplishment that the group is as swinging, exciting and cheerfully cutting-edge as it is. All the first three records are a rag-bag of favourite cover versions, bristling originals and complexities which only the most skilful and hungry players could go for broke with. *Dial E*, their debut, has made it to CD only recently: comparatively rough-and-ready compared with the finesse of the later discs, it's still an exciting and unpredictable record. Rollins's 'Doxy' is turned into an outlandish shuffle, they have the chutzpah to take apart 'Brilliant Corners', and the extravagantly extended '17 December' is an early manifesto of what the band could do. *Radium* is all live and runs the gamut from a tragedian's version of 'Willow Weep For Me' to a madcap distillation of 'Nutty' and 'Ode To Billie Joe', with Roscoe Mitchell's 'Odwallah' as a bonus. *The Half-Life Of Desire* expands the palette a little by dint of Medeski's arrival: this brilliant keyboardist has a sure grasp of which electronics will and which won't work in a neo-trad context, and on Gershon's 'Strange Meridian' he blends acoustic and electric parts with perfect aplomb. Rock and 'world' musics get only a modest look-in on this group's work: their materials come largely from within jazz language itself, which sets them a little apart from such groups as Peter Apfelbaum's ensemble. Yet they still manage to cover the King Crimson metal blow-out, 'Red', and tamper with Miles Davis's 'Circle In The Round' on the same record.

The Calculus Of Pleasure, part live and part studio in origin, is arguably their best to date. There is an astonishing arrangement of Horace Silver's 'Ecaroh', previously a piano-trio tune, and a sour, lavish update of Benny Golson's 'Whisper Not' which is an object lesson in renewing stale jazz repertory. Julius Hemphill's 'The Hard Blues' also comes in for a grandly decadent interpretation, brass and reeds fattening up the harmonies as never before – which leaves five originals from within the band's own ranks. Mention should also be made of soloists such as Medeski, Hasselbring, Yates and Kohlhase, foot-soldiers and front-liners alike.

There is no falling off in quality with *The Brunt*. Though both Hasselbring and Medeski have departed, the team remains terrifically strong as a playing unit: the complexities of 'Notes On A Cliff' and the swaggering 'Permit Blues' are shrugged off, and the title-piece, a bequest by Hasselbring, is a feast of overlapping ideas. One of their most dramatic repertory adventures takes place in Mal Waldron's 'Hard Talk', and only the Ellington piece, 'Blues For New Orleans', disappoints – but that is classic Ellington. The charming retread of Bob Dylan's 'Lay Lady Lay' is a fitting finale and reminds that the band's secret may lie in acting good-humoured rather than merely being humorous. This is also their best-recorded CD.

***(*) Across The Omniverse

Accurate AC-3272 2CD *As above discs. 7/86–9/95.*

Two packed discs of out-takes from their first five albums. Some good Ellington/Hodges, some Sonny Simmons, and the usual slew of maverick originals. If there's an air of second choice about some of it, the E/O spirit abides and it would take a churl not to enjoy it – and the sleeve-note stories, such as the wedding gig they played where the bride asked for something by Philip Glass. A new studio record by the E/O was due as we went to press.

Mats Eklöf

BARITONE SAXOPHONE, CLARINET

Contemporary Swedish saxophonist with a satirical bent, formerly in Position Alpha.

*** Get Stupid

Dragon DRCD 317 *Eklöf; Staffan Svensson (t); Niclas Rydh (tb); Thomas Jäderlund (ss, as, bcl); Thomas Gustafson (ts, ss); Jonny Axelsson (vib, mar, perc); Johannes Lundberg (b); Goran Kron (d). 5/97.*

Anything but stupid. Eklöf's sleeve-note betrays a peculiar sense of humour, and this extravagant record, which sews together 15 compositions in a virtually unbroken whole, is deadpan-funny in a way that only Swedish jazz can be (one might wish to consult the penultimate track, 'The Swedish Way', for further discussion on that note). Impenetrable harmonies, solos that bounce between brooding and hilarious, off-colour carnival melodies and the strange use of Axelsson's vibes as a sort of narrative-thread make this as individual as anything in this *Guide*. Eklöf sounds ready to stake his place in a great tradition of European mavericks, but the record will strike many as a particularly acquired taste.

Roy Eldridge (1911–88)

TRUMPET, VOCAL, PIANO

Roy Eldridge is the bridge between swing trumpet and the bebop revolution, and it's no accident that his theme, 'I Remember Harlem', should also have appeared on one of Ornette Coleman's breakthrough performances. The archetypal high-note artist, Little Jazz became an all too enthusiastic participant in cutting contests, sometimes neglecting expression in favour of excitement and competition. And yet he remains perhaps the greatest brass player of the generation after Louis Armstrong, putting an indelible stamp on modern jazz.

***(*) The Big Sound Of Little Jazz

Topaz TPZ 1021 *Eldridge; Al Beck, Bill Coleman, Torg Halten, Mickey Mangano, Norman Murphy, Joe Thomas, Dick Vance, Graham Young (t); Fernando Arbello, Joe Conigliaro, Ed Cuffee, John Grassi, Jay Kelliher, Babe Wagner, Dicky Wells (tb); Buster Bailey, Benny Goodman, Cecil Scott (cl); Omer Simeon (cl, as, bs); Russell Procope (cl, as); Sam Musiker (cl, ts); Scoops Carey, Benny Carter, Joe Eldridge, Ben Feman, Andrew Gardner, Hilton Jefferson, Howard Johnson, Rex Kittig, Jimmy Migliore, Clint Neagley, Mascagni Ruffo (as); Tom Archia, Walter Bates, Chu Berry, Don Brassfield, Coleman Hawkins, Teddy Hill, Ike Quebec, Ben Webster, Elmer Williams, Dave Young (ts); Sam Allen, Teddy Cole, Rozelle Gayle, Clyde Hart, Horace Henderson, Bob Kitsis, Joe Springer, Jess Stacy, Teddy Wilson (p); Bernard Addison, Danny Barker, Ray Biondi, John Collins, Bob Lessey, Lawrence Lucie, Allan Reuss, John Smith (g); Biddy Bastien, Israel Crosby, Richard Fullbright, John Kirby, Ed Mihelich, Truck Parham, Artie Shapiro, Ted Sturgis (b); Bill Beason, Big Sid*

Catlett, Cozy Cole, Gene Krupa, Zutty Singleton, Harold Doc West (d). 2/35–11/43.

*** Roy Eldridge, 1935–1940

Classics 766 *Similar to above.*

***(*) After You've Gone

GRP Decca 16052 *Eldridge; Gus Aiken, Henry Clay, Paul Cohen, Sidney De Paris, Andy Ferretti, Bill Graham, Tom Grider, John Bugs Hamilton, Marion Hazel, Elton Hill, Yank Lawson, Sylvester Lewis, Robert Mason, Jimmy Maxwell, Dave Page, Pinky Savitt, Jim Thomas, Clarence Wheeler, Elmon Wright (t); Nat Atkins, Will Bradley, Wilbur De Paris, Vic Dickenson, Richard Dunlap, Charles Greenlee, Ted Kelly, John McConnell, Hal Matthews, Fred Ohms, Albert Riding, Fred Robinson, George Robinson, Ward Silloway, George Stevenson, Sandy Watson, Sandy Williams, Gerald Wilson (tb); Buster Bailey (c); Curby Alexander, Mike Doty, Ray Eckstrand, Joe Eldridge, Andrew Gardner, Edmond Gregory (Sahib Shihab), Chris Johnson, Porter Kilbert, Sam Lee (as); Tom Archia, Chu Berry, Charles Bowen, Al Green, Franz Jackson, George Lawson, Walt Lockhart, Don Purvance, Ike Quebec, Mike Ross, Hal Singer, Harold Webster (ts); Ernie Caceres, Dave McRae, Cecil Payne, Al Townsend (bs); Dave Bowman, Ted Brannon, Tony D'Amore, Teddy Cole, Rozelle Gayle, Buster Harding, Duke Jordan (p); Sam Allen, Mike Bryan, John Collins, Luke Fowler (g); Louis Carrington, John Kirby, Carl Pruitt, Rodney Richardson, Ted Sturgis, Billy Taylor, Carl Wilson (b); Lee Abrams, Big Sid Catlett, Cozy Cole, Les Erskine, Earl Phillips, Mel Saunders, Harold Doc West (d).* 2/36–9/46.

**** Heckler's Hop

Hep CD 1030 *Similar to above, except add Prince Robinson, Franz Jackson (ts), Panama Francis (d), Helen Ward, Gladys Palmer, Laurel Watson (v).* 36–39.

Roy Eldridge has been widely acknowledged as the bridge between swing and bebop trumpet. Listening to Dizzy Gillespie at the (in)famous Massey Hall concert with Charlie Parker, Charles Mingus, Bud Powell and Max Roach, there is very little doubt about the ancestry of the trumpeter's high-register accents. However, Eldridge can't just be seen as Moses who led his people out of the desert of late swing and up to the borders of bop's promised land. Eldridge did his thing longer and more consistently than the modernists' version of the story would have you believe.

Eldridge moved to New York in 1934 and was quickly recognized as a new star. The introductory bars of '(Lookie, Lookie, Lookie) Here Comes Cookie', first item on the valuable Topaz compilation, offer a glimpse of the excitement the youngster must have caused. His ability to displace accents and play questionable intervals with perfect confidence and logic is immediately evident. More than just a high-note man, Eldridge combined remarkable rhythmic intuition with an ability to play intensely exciting music in the middle and lower register, often the acid test that separates the musicians from the instrumentalists. His solo on 'Blue Lou', recorded with the Fletcher Henderson band in March 1936 (see *After You've Gone*) is a perfect case in point. He does the same kind of thing with the Teddy Wilson band on 'Blues In C Sharp Minor', fitting his improvisation perfectly to the moody key; Chu Berry's follow-up and Israel Crosby's tensely throbbing bass complete a masterful performance. At the other end of the emotional spectrum, there are the starburst top Cs (and beyond) of 'Heckler's Hop', high point of an excellent set as leader with a band anchored on Zutty Singleton's tight drumming. The vocal tracks with Mildred Bailey are often quite appealing and show how responsive an accompanist Eldridge was, again able to play quietly and in contralto range when called upon. A solitary Billie Holiday track – 'Falling In Love Again' – gives a flavour only of that association, which is more fully documented under her name.

After You've Gone (disappearing fast, so be quick) is a valuable compilation of 'Little Jazz''s American Decca recordings of the late war years, with one brief glimpse back at the sessions with clarinettist Buster Bailey and tenor saxophonist Chu Berry, two years before the more familiar Little Jazz Ensemble dates on Commodore Classics' valuable Chu Berry compilation, *A Giant Of The Tenor Sax*. The set includes some material never before released commercially, like a 'St Louis Blues' used on a 1965 Decca promotional for *Life* magazine (doubtless pitched in *Life*'s inimitably condescending way). The transfers are done on the Sonic Solutions' NoNoise system, which leaves the masters clean but a little bleached-out in some areas. Eldridge occupies most of the foreground, whacking out top notes like Satchmo had never been heard of; the opening of (an unissued) 'I Surrender, Dear' is almost absurdly skyscraping. Unfortunately, Eldridge has been saddled with the reputation of being a high-note man. His muted 'stroll' opening to his own composition, 'The Gasser', is equally typical, giving way to a fine soulful solo from Ike Quebec, and then Eldridge again in more familiar mode on open horn.

The sound is less crystalline on the Topaz (and decidedly muddy in places on the weirdly inconsistent Classics), but both of these cover pretty much the same material. As the massed personnels will again suggest, it selects from the broadest range of bands and sessions, starting with Teddy Hill, taking in Krupa, Henderson, the Little Jazz Ensemble with Chu, the Chocolate Dandies with Carter, and the other Teddy, the urbane Wilson. In just over an hour it offers a pretty straightforward and representative account of the first decade of activity.

Long before he became known as a JATP stalwart and itinerant sitter-in, Eldridge had sounded comfortable in front of big bands, where his reaching tone and simple phrasing sounded less forced than they can in smaller groups. There is a lovely 'Body And Soul' (compare the version with Berry, above) and a fine 'I Can't Get Started' with the October 1944 line-up that yields the teasing, stop-start 'After You've Gone' (it's the only piece with an alternative take, though there are a couple of incompletes). 'Embraceable You' from the following year is equally fine; but the quality thins badly around this point in the compilation. None of the later tracks matches up to the astonishing ripping intensity of his tone on 'Stardust' with the 1943 group, which counts as one of his finest performances ever, studded in the middle chorus with a single high note.

There is much to recommend the Hep selection, not least a high-quality transfer that renders such notes with absolute clarity and minimum distortion. Though it covers a shorter chronological span and puts undue emphasis on less than startling singers, its immediacy and presence (check out the end of 'After You've Gone', a classic Eldridge moment) make it the item of choice for us.

Given the dominance of Dizzy and the alternative direction opened up by Miles, Eldridge's work has been at something of a premium in recent years. These, though, are essential – and usefully complementary – documents of modern jazz and they offer a salutary lesson for anyone who still tends to think of the music as a sequence of upper-case historical styles.

***(*) Roy Eldridge, 1943–1944

Classics 920 *Eldridge; Thomas Aiken, Emmett Berry, Bugs Hamilton, Cookie Mason, Joe Thomas, Clarence Wheeler (t); Ted Kelly, Jack Teagarden, Andrew Williams, George Wilson (tb); Barney Bigard (cl); Joe Eldridge, Andrew Gardner, Sam Lee (as); Tom Archia, Franz Jackson, Ike Quebec, Hal Singer (ts); Dave McRae (bs); Ted Brannon, Rozelle Gayle, Johnny Guarnieri, Art Tatum (p); Napoleon Allen, Al Casey (g); Lionel Hampton (vib); Israel Crosby, Oscar Pettiford, Ted Sturgis, Billy Taylor (b); Big Sid Catlett, Cozy Cole, Harold Doc West (d).* 11/43–10/44.

After leaving Gene Krupa, Eldridge recorded some sides for Brunswick in the late autumn of 1943, before finding himself pitched into the free-for-all atmosphere of the jam sessions for V-Disc which prefigured the Jazz at the Philharmonic summits of later years. An *Esquire* jam at the Metropolitan Opera House yielded 'Tea For Two' with Jack Teagarden, Barney Bigard, Hamp and Oscar Pettiford, the beginning of a sequence of loose jams which pressurized Eldridge into stratospheric high-note playing at the expense of the delicacy he amply demonstrates on the earlier 'Stardust'. Early 1944 saw the Little Jazz Trumpet Ensemble with Thomas and Berry recording four sides for Keynote, of which 'I Want To Be Happy' and 'St Louis Blues' illustrate much the same tendency. Eldridge's harmonic brilliance and absolutely assured technique do mean that these, like later discs, are of the highest quality; but one does wonder whether his talents were best deployed in this very limited way. A later session for Decca has him giving a vocal rendition of 'St Louis Blues' at the front of a big, well-drilled orchestra. By the end of the war, Little Jazz had cornered the market in a certain style of trumpet playing. If Dizzy Gillespie was more fashionable and seemingly more in touch with cutting-edge developments, Eldridge remained vital and persuasive, maintaining an edge which was to last until the end of his life.

*** Roy Eldridge, 1945-1947

Classics 983 *Eldridge; Henry Clay, Andy Ferretti, Bill Graham, Thomas Sleepy Grider, Marion Hazel, Elton Hill, Yank Lawson, Sylvester Lewis, Jimmy Maxwell, Dave Page, Jim Thomas, Elmon Wright (t); Nat Atkins, Will Bradley, Mort Bulman, Richard Dunlap, Charlie Greenlea, John McConnell, Hal Matthews, Fred Ohms, Al Riding, Fred Robinson, George Robinson, Ward Silloway, Sandy Watson (tb); Ray Ekstrand, Mike Doty, Joe Eldridge, Chris Johnson, Porter Kilbert, Sahib Shihab (as); Ernie Caceres (cl); Tom Archia, Charles Bowen, Nick Caiazza, Al Green, George Lawson, Walt Lockhart, Flip Phillips, Harold Webster (ts); Cecil Payne, Don Purvance, Hank Ross, Al Townsend (bs); Dave Bowman, Mike Coluchio, Buster Harding, Duke Jordan, Billy Roland (p); Napoleon Allen, Mike Bryan, Al Casey, Luke Fowler, Allan Hanlon (g); Trigger Alpert, Louis Carrington, Carl Pruitt, Rodney Richardson, Eddie Safranski, Ted Sturgis (b); Lee Abrams, Cozy Cole, Earl Phillips, Specs Powell, Melvin Saunders (d).* 3/45–5/47.

Roy had worked with Artie Shaw for a time in the last two years of the war, before going out with his own small groups again. The third Classics volume brings together the big-band sides he made for Decca, Coral and Vox, but with the addition of three fascinating V-Discs cut just after the end of the war, the first of them 'Roy Meets Horn', remembered for its spoken introduction by Eddie 'Rochester' Anderson. The two early Deccas catch him at opposite extremes, buoyantly walking the high wire on 'Little Jazz Boogie' and doing tough'n'tender on 'Embraceable You', both of them superb arrangements by Buster Harding. The 1946 dates are evenly spaced through the year and find Roy on a high, punching out terse, evocative choruses with a minimum of fuss. His playing on these sides is almost always more satisfying than any of his JATP spots. The vocals are kept to a minimum but they're engaging enough. Of the later tracks 'Lover Come To Me' from September is an excellent example of how Eldridge's control of dynamics were his most powerful tool. 'Tippin' Out' and 'Yard Dog' from the May session are marred by an odd imbalance between soloist and ensemble, the latter sounding very distant. The WNEW Saturday Night Swing Session with fellow JATP stalwart Flip Phillips includes two tracks on which Eldridge clearly doesn't play, unusual practice for Classics. There is still too much distortion at the top end on these reissues. With some artists, that isn't too serious a problem, but Eldridge's rips and smears are too often reduced to noise.

**** Little Jazz: The Best Of The Verve Years

Verve 523338-2 *Eldridge; Joe Ferrante, Bernie Glow, Ernie Royal, Nick Travis (t); Jimmy Cleveland, J.J Johnson, Fred Ohms, Kai Winding, Benny Morton, Vic Dickenson (tb); Eddie Barefield (cl); Sam Marowitz, Hal McKusick, Benny Carter, Johnny Hodges, Sonny Stitt (as); Aaron Sachs, Eddie Shu, Coleman Hawkins, Ben Webster (ts); Danny Bank (bs); Oscar Peterson (p, org); Dave McKenna, Dick Wellstood, Billy Strayhorn, Bruce Macdonald, Hank Jones, Ronnie Ball (p); Barney Kessel, Barry Galbraith, Herb Ellis (g); Ray Brown, John Drew, Walter Page, John Simmons, Jimmy Woode, Bennie Moten, George Duvivier (b); Jo Jones, J.C Heard, Gene Krupa, Alvin Stoller, Buddy Rich, Sam Woodyard, Eddie Locke, Mickey Sheen (d); Anita O'Day (v); Russell Garcia Orchestra, George Williams Orchestra.* 12/51–6/60.

Say what you like about Norman Granz, he gets the best people to his parties. The Verve years were happy and productive for Little Jazz. There is hardly a dull track on this excellent compilation. Only the opening number, Roy's classic 'I Remember Harlem', is disappointing, not because the trumpeter is less than superb but because the George Williams Orchestra is less than ideally registered. The live cut with Stitt, Peterson and Ellis at the 1957 Newport Festival is good enough to have merited more than a single representation from that triumphant day, and the same goes for the March 1955 stuff with Benny Carter, who induces Eldridge to play more quietly and thoughtfully. Peterson proves to have been the most sympathetic accompanist, whether on piano or organ (the latter, memorably, on 'Blue Moon'), but the late group with Ronnie Ball does some wonderful things with 'Dreamy' and 'When I Grow Too Old To Dream'. He never did.

***(*) Roy And Diz

Verve 521647-2 *Eldridge; Dizzy Gillespie (t, v); Oscar Peterson (p); Herb Ellis (g); Ray Brown (b); Louie Bellson (d).* 10/54.

They enjoyed this. A little friendly sparring, with just enough edge to get the juices on the move. Alongside the man who influenced his style more than any other, Dizzy sounds comfortable and in good humour. On 'Pretty Eyed Baby' they take turns at accompanying the other's scat chorus, but the gloves are off for 'Limehouse Blues', where they try to cut one another like a pair of teenagers. Though thoroughly bested, Gillespie gets off a sarky quote from Eldridge's 'Heckler's Hop', only to find it taken up, turned around and thrown back with interest. Despite the obvious kinship, it's interesting to compare their styles. Gillespie gets cornered on the long blues only because he's taken some chances with the sequence. Eldridge, by contrast, stays as close as possible to the original melody, embroidering it and turning it around, but not veering off into quite distant keys as the bop-nurtured Diz does almost as a matter of course. Peterson gives both hornmen a solid leg-up from time to time, but it's clear that his sympathies are mainly with Little Jazz. An old-fashioned, unpretentious session, and a good one.

***** Roy Eldridge And His Little Jazz: Volume 1**
BMG International 51141 *Eldridge; Benny Vasseur (tb); Don Byas, Albert Ferreri (ts); William Boucaya (bs); Claude Bolling, Raymond Fol (p); Barney Spieler (b); Armand Molinetti (d).* 50.

***** Roy Eldridge And His Little Jazz, Volume 2**
BMG International 55952 *As above.* 50.

Eldridge was an instant hit in Paris, where he had originally gone with the Benny Goodman Orchestra. He was, to all intents and purposes, an artistic defector, and being lionized did him no harm at all. Much of his best work of the time was made in the company of Claude Bolling, with whom he reprised the famous Armstrong–Hines duet, 'Fireworks'. It can be found on Volume Two, which is actually the better of the pair, also including the classic 'I Remember Harlem' and suffering only slightly from a preponderance of generic high-register features for the trumpeter. The French band have a whale of a time and, while the introduction of Don Byas keeps the quality up, Ferreri, Boucaya and Vasseur are well up to the challenge of trading choruses with 'Tit Jazz.

***** Just You, Just Me – Live In '59**
Stash 531 *Eldridge; Coleman Hawkins (ts); Don Wilson (p); Bob Decker (b); Buddy Dean (d).* 59.

****** The Nifty Cat**
New World 80349 *Eldridge; Benny Morton (tb); Budd Johnson (ts, ss); Nat Pierce (p); Tommy Bryant (b); Oliver Jackson (d).* 11/70.

*****(*) Montreux '77**
Original Jazz Classics OJC 373 *Eldridge; Oscar Peterson (p); Niels-Henning Orsted Pedersen (b); Bobby Durham (d).* 7/77.

***** Happy Time**
Original Jazz Classics OJC 628 *Eldridge; Oscar Peterson (p); Joe Pass (g); Ray Brown (b); Eddie Locke (d).*

***** What It's All About**
Original Jazz Classics OJC 853 *Eldridge; Budd Johnson, Norris Turney (sax); Milt Jackson (vib); Norman Simmons (p); Ted Sturgis (b); Eddie Locke (d).*

***** Jazz Maturity ... Where It's Coming From**
Pablo 2310928 *Eldridge; Dizzy Gillespie (t); Oscar Peterson (p); Ray Brown (b); Mickey Roker (d).*

***** Roy Eldridge & Vic Dickenson**
Storyville STCD 8239 *Eldridge; Vic Dickenson (tb); Budd Johnson (ts); Tommy Flanagan (p); Major Holley (b); Eddie Locke (d).* 5/78.

Much of Eldridge's recorded output was for a time tucked away on trumpet compilations and festival albums. The major compilations above have done much to improve the situation; perhaps only the Benny Carter discography has been so comprehensively turned around in the same period. Even so, there is quite a lot of valuable Eldridge to be found on one-off sessions from later years. The Pablo with Diz and Peterson is pretty much a reworking of studio associations, but there were occasions in later years when the trumpeter found himself not so much reliving his old amities as reinventing them. The connection with Budd Johnson was a good case in point. The 1978 concert in St Peter's Church on Storyville is very relaxed and mild, but there are moments on the New World disc (an unexpected place to find Eldridge material) which are quite startling in their harmonic language, a further sign that Roy was always prepared to try new angles. Johnson doesn't hustle and bluster as Hawkins tended to do at this period, so there is every encouragement for the wee guy to proceed with some interestingly wayward stuff.

What It's All About is disappointing in that Eldridge seems content to do little more than punch out high notes and then swoop down to swoony ballad territory, then up, then down. By this stage in his career it had all got too easy and predictable, though one or two articulation problems seem to have crept in and were certainly affecting his attack on material like 'The Heat's On', which needs to be pretty exact if it isn't to sound banal.

Along with the New World, perhaps the best of the later stuff is the Montreux set, part of a good series documenting what was considered to be a vintage year. The trumpeter appears to have regained some of his fire and sparkle and doesn't seem to require much notice for the upper-register stabs. The 1978 concert from St Peter's Church in New York is as laid-back and comradely as could be, with some wise musicianship but not much excitement. A decade from the end of his life, Roy had won all the bouts he cared about; merely playing seemed to be reward enough.

Eliane Elias (born 1960)

PIANO

Born in São Paolo, Brazil, she worked in big bands before moving to New York in 1981. Briefly with Steps Ahead and Randy Brecker (to whom she was married) and since then she worked as a leader and recorded in a light but effective fusion of Brazilian and post-bop forms.

****(*) Plays Jobim**
Blue Note 793089-2 *Elias; Eddie Gomez (b); Jack DeJohnette (d); Nana Vasconcelos (perc).* 12/89.

***** Fantasia**

Blue Note 796146-2 *Elias; Eddie Gomez, Marc Johnson (b); Jack DeJohnette, Peter Erskine (d); Nana Vasconcelos (perc); Ivan Lins, Amanda Elias Brecker (v).* 91.

***** Paulistana**

Blue Note 789544-2 *As above, except add Jim Beard (syn), Cafe, Portinho (perc), Malcolm Pollack (v).* 92.

*****(*) Solos And Duets**

Blue Note 832073-2 *Elias; Herbie Hancock (p).* 11–12/94.

Elias's sequence of Blue Note albums make up an unashamedly enjoyable and increasingly personal synthesis of Latin and American jazz. If the *Plays Jobim* album seemed a mere confection, the subsequent records suggested that Elias was creating a good-natured but well-crafted interpretation of the best of her native Brazilian music which is more subtle and impressive than at first hearing. On each record she uses top-notch support in the bass and drums department, with the Gomez/DeJohnette and Johnson/Erskine teams grooving through multiple variations of bossa nova, samba and 4/4 jazz rhythms, while she chooses the most princely compositions by Jobim, Nascimento, Bonfa, Barroso and others alongside an occasional original of her own. The surprising revisions of 'The Girl From Ipanema' and 'No More Blues' on *Fantasia* and 'Black Orpheus' on *Paulistana* show a pleasing attempt to sidestep the clichés those tunes have built round themselves, and her discreet use of synthesizer and her own voice add further variety.

Solos And Duets is perhaps even stronger. Although Hancock sits in for six entertaining duets, her own solo pieces are at least as impressive, with the spirited 'Autumn Leaves' and lush harmonies of 'Asa Branca' particularly appealing. The most 'American' of her records, but still attractively tinged with a Brazilian lilt.

*****(*) The Three Americas**

Blue Note 53328-2 *Elias; Dave Valentin (f); Gil Goldstein (acc); Mark Feldman (vn); Oscar Castro-Nueves (g); Marc Johnson (b, v); Satoshi Takeishi (d); Cafe (perc, v); Manolo Badrena (perc); Amanda Elias Brecker (v).* 96.

*****(*) Sings Jobim**

Blue Note 95236-2 *Elias; Michael Brecker (ts); Oscar Castro-Nueves (g); Marc Johnson (b); Paulo Braga (d); Cafe (perc).* 97.

In her quiet and uncomplicated way, Elias has created a more genuine and affecting synthesis of American music than many a more self-consciously pioneering type. *The Three Americas* seeks to align North, South and Central American rhythms, harmonies and melodies in a seamless whole, and with the chamberish instrumentation, folkish tunes and soft, settled textures she makes the fusion a plausible and generous creation that's beautifully sustained across themes like 'Chorango', 'Caipora' and 'Jungle Journey'. There are just a few dips into mere light-music pleasantry, but this is mostly a convincing entry.

Sings Jobim might have been crashingly obvious, yet Elias manages to take an unpredictable course through most of the tunes. Even with tenor and rhythm on hand, she makes 'Desafinado' sound nothing like the Getz–Gilberto version. 'So Danco Samba' is quirkily crisp and precise. 'Samba De Uma Nota So' is as gentle as featherfall. Her voice would win no prizes at jazz singing school, but neither would Astrud Gilberto's. Johnson, as always, is a little giant in these situations and he's an indispensable presence on both discs.

*****(*) Everything I Love**

Blue Note 520827-2 *Elias; Rodney Jones (g); Marc Johnson, Christian McBride (b); Jack DeJohnette, Carl Allen (d).* 99.

This time the focus is squarely on bebop material and its encumbrances: can anything new be wrought out of 'Woody 'N You', 'Nostalgia In Times Square' and a string of standards that would have been regulation fare on 52nd Street bandstands? What she does is look for the sweetness and the lyricism in the tunes, without sacrificing improvisational finesse. It helps that she's become a characterful singer, a small voice but not an unsteady or shy one. The accompaniments are as high-grade as the names suggest, and this is altogether as pleasing a 'repertory' record as one could envisage in this field.

The Elite Syncopators

GROUP

Group dedicated to performing original ragtime repertory in ensemble form.

***** Ragtime Special**

Stomp Off CD1286 *Terry Parrish (p); James Marshall (bj); Steve Ley (tba); Mike Schwimmer (wbd, v).* 4–5/94.

Ragtime piano as a singleton enterprise is specialized enough, but placing it in the context of a repertory group is quite something in the 1990s. Of the 26 tracks here, all but three are original rags, two-steps or cakewalks of differing vintages, and it's some tribute to the expertise of the quartet – and that of the composers – that the music doesn't go stale across the duration of a long CD. The sometimes unvarying jollity of ragtime is tempered by intelligent programming – an occasional vocal, or the juxtaposition of reflectively melodic as opposed to pop-tune rags – and the graceful syncopation of the playing. Parrish's liner-notes offer useful background on all the tunes for hardcore scholars and, though this is a lot to take in at one sitting, determined cakewalkers will find it an indispensable primer.

Art Ellefson (born 1932)

TENOR AND SOPRANO SAXOPHONES

Ellefson played on the British scene during the 1950s and '60s and can be heard on numerous big-band and orchestral records of that period. He subsequently left for Canada, where he has played since.

***** As If To Say**

Sackville SKCD2-2030 *Ellefson; Lee Ellefson (g); Russell Botten (b); Buff Allen (d).* 2/92.

Hidden away in British Columbia, Ellefsen, who lived and played in the UK through most of the 1950s and '60s, is an accomplished hybrid of swing player and bopper. He has a way of phrasing a line that is almost nerveless in its placid inevitability, but there's a darker side to his tone that can make an improvisation turn sour at the edges. In this pianoless quartet, with his son Lee on guitar, the music has an air of abstraction which undercuts the songful melodies without defeating them. It's a little too unambitious and workmanlike, and Botten and Allen are content to play within themselves, but the music is absorbing enough, and the 11 original themes are shot through with interesting touches.

Kurt Elling (born 1967)

VOCALS

A Chicagoan, Elling sent a demo tape to Blue Note and won a deal. He's a sophisticated beat vocalist for the '90s.

*****(*) Close Your Eyes**

Blue Note 30645 2 *Elling; Von Freeman, Edward Peterson (ts); Laurence Hobgood (p); Dave Onderdonk (g); Rob Amster, Erich Hochberg (b); Paul Wertico (d, perc).* 2–11/94.

****** The Messenger**

Blue Note 52727 2 *As above, except omit Freeman; add Orbert Davis (t, flhn); Eddie Johnson (ts); Jim Widlowski (perc); Cassandra Wilson (v).* 7–12/96.

*****(*) This Time It's Love**

Blue Note 93543 2 *Elling; Brad Wheeler (ss); Eddie Johnson (ts); Laurence Hobgood (p); Dave Onderdonk (g); Johnny Frigo (vn); Rob Amster (b); Michael Raynor, Paul Wertico (d, perc).* 12/97–1/98.

It's easy to see Elling as a younger, more contemporary version of Mark Murphy, but the death of Frank Sinatra and subsequent reassessment of Frank's extraordinary output suggests that he was a powerful influence as well. Elling shares Murphy's poetic understanding, and *Close Your Eyes* includes two poems by Rainer Maria Rilke, including 'Now It Is Time That Gods Came Walking Out', in which he manages to hint at the Charlie Parker title as well. Elling is one of the last great exponents of vocalese, setting specially written words to recorded jazz solos, though it is now clear that many of his most demanding vocalese pieces have still to be recorded. It's perhaps a style which has yet to be fully rediscovered. The other Rilke text is 'How The Thimble Came To Be God', which is part of a vocalese reading of Paul Desmond's solo on Brubeck's 'Balcony Rock'. He also provides a vocal introduction and coda to 'Dolores' Dream', based on Wayne Shorter's solo intro on the 1977 VSOP version. The other poet, the American anarchist Kenneth Rexroth, is represented by 'Married Blues'.

One of the great joys of vocalese has always been the ability to tell a story, and Elling blends a narrative by Jim Heynen into 'Storyteller Experiencing Total Confusion'. He makes Fran Landesman's 'Ballad Of The Sad Young Men' sound as fresh as the day it was written. The guest spots, by Von Freeman on the punning '(Hide The) Salome' and Edward Peterson on 'Storyteller' and Herbie Hancock's 'Hurricane', are nicely judged and the basic band, who provide most of the musical arrangements, are impossible to fault. They sound much less like a working band than the line-up on *The Messenger*, which is a studio album but divided into two 'sets' that one can imagine the group doing in a club setting. It briefly brings together the two finest jazz singers of the 1990s. An unexpected choice of repertoire, but Rod Argent's 'Time Of The Season' teams Kurt Elling and Cassandra Wilson, an exquisite blending of voices that combine an absolutely authentic jazz sensibility with the power and inflexion of rock and soul singers. Elling opens with a glorious version of 'Nature Boy' that brings it back from the abstractions of John Coltrane and restores some of the fragile melancholy of the Nat Cole hit. 'April In Paris' is a little routine, but the suite that follows – 'The Beauty Of All Things', 'The Dance' and 'Prayer For Mr Davis' – is superb, three strong Hobgood/Elling compositions that top anything on the first album. 'Gingerbread Boy' and a melting 'Prelude To A Kiss' set up a virtuosic climax, 'Time Of The Season', and then the long 'The Messenger', a composition by Edward Peterson into which Elling builds a spontaneous narrative on the death of his brother. Subtle and deeply moving.

The highlight of *This Time It's Love* is a superb vocalese based on Lester Young's solo on 'She's Funny That Way', but it's almost topped by 'Freddie's Yen For Jen', which takes its inspiration from Freddie Hubbard and is one of the most compelling vocal performances of recent times. Irving Berlin's 'The Best Things Happen When You're Dancing' receives a notably straight and melodic reading, but 'Every Time We Say Goodbye' is slyly recast with altered chords. Frigo's violin and Onderdonk's acoustic strumming add an old-fashioned swing and shimmer to 'I Feel So Smoochie'. A bittier album than its predecessors, it works triumphantly in individual episodes but may perhaps disappoint as a whole.

Duke Ellington (1899–1974)

PIANO

Born in Washington, DC, to a middle-class family, Ellington learned piano as a child, became interested in the local ragtime players, and started leading his own groups from around 1918. Duke Ellington & His Washingtonians worked in New York from 1924, and his residency at the Cotton Club from 1927 sealed his breakthrough. Long tours also followed, with trips to Europe in the 1930s, and an almost continuous presence in the recording studios. In the '40s, he played a series of annual Carnegie Hall concerts, wrote for the stage and briefly dispersed the big band, but reassembled it in 1949 with 18 players. Although the '50s saw a decline in his fortunes at home, his Newport appearance in 1956 reasserted his eminence. He also wrote for film and TV, and in the '60s he continued to tour relentlessly, in every part of the world. His final illness slowed him down, but he was working up until his hospitalization for cancer early in 1974. Besides his major works, his individual compositions – with and without his frequent collaborator, Billy Strayhorn – number in the thousands, and his recorded legacy is surely the largest and grandest that jazz will ever be able to boast. He recorded for every major American label during a 50-year career on record, and there are in addition almost countless broadcast and concert recordings of his music.

***** Duke Ellington 1924–1927**

Classics 542 *Ellington; Bubber Miley, Pike Davis, Harry Cooper, Leroy Rutledge, Louis Metcalf, June Clark (t); Jimmy Harrison (tb, v); Charlie Irvis, Joe 'Tricky Sam' Nanton (tb); Don Redman (cl, as); Otto Hardwick (Cmel, as, ss, bs); George*

Thomas (as, v); Edgar Sampson (as); Prince Robinson, Rudy Jackson (ts, cl); Harry Carney (cl, ts, bs); George Francis, Fred Guy (bj); Mack Shaw, Henry 'Bass' Edwards (bb); Sonny Greer (d, v); Alberta Jones, Irving Mills, Adelaide Hall (v). 11/24–11/26.

Ellington continues to bestride the history of jazz on record, a quarter-century after his passing. The sheer volume of recorded works – authorized and otherwise – continues to enrich our understanding of the music, while offering many frustrations and disappointments to go with the numberless masterworks. After the enormous and comprehensive LP reissues of the 1970s – specifically the multiple-disc sets issued by French RCA and CBS, as well as numerous and lengthy sequences of broadcast material from private labels – the industry has made plenty of headway in reissuing all this material on CD. With the copyright lapsed on all the pre-1947 records, smaller labels have taken up the challenge of chronological reissues. The Classics sequence, meanwhile, currently stands at over 30 discs, and goes as far as 1947; more will doubtless be available by the time we are in print.

Classics are content to stick to the band sides leading up to the Victor version of 'Black And Tan Fantasy' in 1927; they have omitted a handful of obscure early accompaniments to singers. However, the very early material will be of interest only to scholars and the merely curious. Poor recording – the mastering of several tracks is rough and, in the absence of hearing high-quality originals ourselves, we're unsure as to how good a job has been done on some of the items – and a primitive, clumsy ensemble will be almost shocking to any who've never been acquainted with the earliest Ellington. Certainly the stiff rhythms and feeble attempts at solos on all the pre-1926 records are sometimes painful to hear and, if it weren't for Bubber Miley, the man who made Ellington 'forget all about the sweet music', there'd be nothing to detain anyone here. Yet Miley is already distinctive and powerful on his solo on The Washingtonians' 'Choo Choo' from November 1924. With 'East St Louis Toodle-oo', from the first important Ellington session, the music demands the attention. Any comprehensive edition will include much duplication, since Ellington spread himself around many different record labels: he recorded for Broadway, Vocalion, Gennett, Columbia, Harmony, Pathé, Brunswick, OKeh and Victor in the space of a little over three years. It also includes the debut versions of 'Black And Tan Fantasy', Ellington's first masterpiece, and Adelaide Hall's vocal on 'Creole Love Call'. Remastering is occasionally indifferent.

*****(*) Duke Ellington 1927–1928**

Classics 542 *Ellington; Bubber Miley, Jabbo Smith, Louis Metcalf, Arthur Whetsol (t); Joe 'Tricky Sam' Nanton (tb); Otto Hardwick (ss, as, bs, bsx); Rudy Jackson, Barney Bigard (cl, ts); Harry Carney (bs, as, ss, cl); Fred Guy (bj); Wellman Braud (b); Sonny Greer (d); Adelaide Hall (v).* 10/27–3/28.

*****(*) Duke Ellington 1928**

Classics 550 *As above, except add Lonnie Johnson (g), Baby Cox, The Palmer Brothers (v); omit Jackson, Smith.* 3–10/28.

***** Duke Ellington 1928–29**

Classics 559 *As above, except add Freddy Jenkins (t), Johnny Hodges (cl, ss, as), Ozie Ware, Irving Mills (v); omit Metcalf, Cox and the Palmers.* 10/28–3/29.

Ellington progressed quickly from routine hot-dance records to sophisticated and complex three-minute works which showed a rare grasp of the possibilities of the 78-r.p.m. disc, a trait which he developed and exemplified better than anyone else in jazz from then until the 1950s. Yet during these years both Ellington and his band were still seeking a style that would turn them into a genuinely distinctive group. Having set down one or two individual pieces such as 'Black And Tan Fantasy' didn't mean that Duke was fully on his way. The 1926–8 records are still dominated to a high degree by the playing of Bubber Miley, and on a track such as 'Flaming Youth' (Classics 559), which was made as late as 1929, it is only Miley's superb work that makes the record of much interest. Arthur Whetsol made an intriguing contrast to Miley, his style being far more wistful and fragile: the way he plays 'The Mooche' on the 1928 Victor version is in striking contrast to Miley's delivery (all versions are on Classics 550), and his treatment of the theme to 'Black Beauty' (also on Classics 550) is similarly poignant. Joe Nanton was a shouting trombonist with a limited stock of phrases, but he was already starting to work on the muted technique which would make him into one of Duke's most indispensable players. It was already a great brass team. But the reeds were weaker, with Carney taking a low-key role (not always literally: he played as much alto and clarinet as baritone in this era), and until Bigard's arrival in 1928 it lacked a distinctive soloist. Hodges also didn't arrive until October 1928. When the Ellington band went into the Cotton Club at the end of 1927, the theatricality which had begun asserting itself with 'Black And Tan Fantasy' became a more important asset, and though most of the 'Jungle' scores were to emerge on record around 1929–30, 'The Mooche' and 'East St Louis Toodle-oo' show how set-piece effects were becoming important to Ellington. The best and most 'Ellingtonian' records of the period would include 'Blue Bubbles' (Classics 542), 'Take It Easy' and 'Jubilee Stomp' (1928 versions, on Classics 550), and 'Misty Mornin'' and 'Doin' The Voom Voom' (both Classics 559), but even on the lesser tunes or those tracks where Ellington seems to be doing little more than copying Fletcher Henderson, there are usually fine moments from Miley or one of the others. The Classics CDs offer admirable coverage, with a fairly consistent standard of remastering, and, though they ignore alternative takes, Ellington's promiscuous attitude towards the various record companies means that there are often several versions of a single theme on one disc (Classics 542, for instance, has three versions of 'Take It Easy').

*****(*) Duke Ellington 1929**

Classics 569 *Ellington; Cootie Williams (t, v); Arthur Whetsol, Freddy Jenkins (t); Joe 'Tricky Sam' Nanton (tb); Barney Bigard (cl, ts); Johnny Hodges (ss, as, cl); Harry Carney (bs, cl, as); Fred Guy (bj); Wellman Braud (b); Sonny Greer (d, v); Ozie Ware (v).* 3–7/29.

***** Duke Ellington 1929–1930**

Classics 577 *As above, except add Juan Tizol (vtb), Teddy Bunn (g), Bruce Johnson (wbd), Harold Randolph, Irving Mills (v); omit Ware.* 8/29–1/30.

***** Duke Ellington 1930**

Classics 586 *As above, except add Cornell Smelser (acc), Dick Robertson (v); omit Bunn, Johnson and Randolph.* 1–6/30.

***** Duke Ellington 1930 Vol. 2**

Classics 596 *As above, except add Charlie Barnet (chimes), Sid Garry, Jimmy Miller, Emanuel Paul (v); omit Smelser.* 6–11/30.

***** Duke Ellington 1930–1931**
Classics 605 *As above, except add Benny Paine (v, p), Chick Bullock, Frank Marvin, Smith Ballew (v); omit Barnet, Robertson, Miller and Paul.* 11/30–1/31.

The replacement of Bubber Miley by Cootie Williams was the key personnel change in this period: Williams was a leaner, less outwardly expressive version of Miley, but equally fiery; his scat singing was a fast development of Armstrong's vocal style, and he gave the brass section a new bite and brightness, even if he lacked Miley's ability to growl quite so intently. Hodges and Carney, too, were coming into their own and, along with the increasing mastery of Ellington's handling of his players, the band was now growing in assurance almost from session to session. The Victor date of 7 March 1929 (Classics 569) exemplifies many of the new powers of the orchestra. 'Hot Feet' includes a superb Hodges solo, Williams singing and playing with great authority, and the band moving out of the older hot style without sacrificing any drive. It was the now extraordinarily powerful swing of the rhythm section that was responsible for much of this advance: the same session is a fine instance of what they could do, from Braud's subtly propulsive drive on the excellently scored 'The Dicty Glide' to his outright stomping line on 'Hot Feet', with Greer taking a showman's role on his cymbals and traps and the remarkable Guy strumming a quick-witted counterpoint that made the banjo seem far from outdated (he would, though, soon switch to guitar). The two important Victor sessions on this disc (a third, two parts of a Cotton Club medley, is less substantial) make this a valuable issue, and there are two fascinatingly different versions of the small-group blues, 'Saratoga Swing', as well as little-known Ellington attempts at 'I Must Have That Man' and an accompaniment to singer Ozie Ware.

Ellington was recording at a prodigious pace – surprisingly so, given the state of the industry at that time – and there are some three CDs' worth of material from 1930. Classics 586 includes some tunes that reek of Cotton Club set-pieces – 'Jungle Nights In Harlem', 'Jungle Blues' – and some thin novelty tunes, but new versions of 'The Mooche' and 'East St Louis Toodle-oo' and new originals like 'Shout 'Em Aunt Tillie', 'Hot And Bothered' and 'Cotton Club Stomp' are more substantial. Classics 596 has three different versions of 'Ring Dem Bells', each with outstanding solos by Williams, three of 'Old Man Blues', and a first try at 'Mood Indigo'. Classics 605 has three versions of 'Rockin' In Rhythm', each showing a slight advance on the one before, the tempo brightening and the reeds becoming smarter, and a slightly ironic reading of 'Twelfth Street Rag' which hints at Duke's later treatment of other people's jazz standards. But the record closes with his first lengthy work, the two-part 'Creole Rhapsody', where for perhaps the first time the soloists have to take a firm second place to the arrangement (this is the 10-inch 78 version; the subsequent 12-inch version is on the next disc in the Classics sequence). Remastering is mainly good and full-bodied: some of the records from more obscure companies sound a little rougher, there are some tracks in which bass boom overcomes mid-range brightness, and frequent hints that these are not first-hand dubbings. Still, only more demanding ears may be particularly troubled by the mixed transfer quality.

***** Duke Ellington 1931–1932**
Classics 616 *Ellington; Arthur Whetsol, Freddy Jenkins, Cootie Williams (t); Joe 'Tricky Sam' Nanton, Lawrence Brown (tb); Juan Tizol (vtb); Johnny Hodges (as, ss, cl); Barney Bigard (cl, ts); Harry Carney (bs, cl); Fred Guy (bj, g); Wellman Braud (b); Sonny Greer (d); Frank Marvin, Ivie Anderson, Bing Crosby (v).* 1/31–2/32.

***** The Brunswick Sessions 1932–1935 Vol. 1**
Jazz Information CAH 3001 *As above, except add Otto Hardwick (as, bsx); omit Marvin.* 2–5/32.

***** Duke Ellington 1932–1933**
Classics 626 *As above, except add Ray Mitchell, Adelaide Hall, The Mills Brothers, Ethel Waters (v); omit Crosby.* 5/32–1/33.

***** The Brunswick Sessions 1932–1935 Vol. 2**
Jazz Information CAH 3002 *As above, except add Joe Garland (ts); omit Mitchell, Hall, Mills Bros, Waters.* 5/32–5/33.

****** The Brunswick Sessions 1932–1935 Vol. 3**
Jazz Information CAH 3003 *As above, except add Rex Stewart, Charles Allen (t), Billy Taylor Sr (b, bb), Hayes Alvis (b).* 5/33–3/35.

*****(*) Duke Ellington 1933**
Classics 637 *Similar to above.* 2–8/33.

*****(*) Duke Ellington 1933–1935**
Classics 646 *Similar to above.* 9/33–3/35.

The second 'Creole Rhapsody' opens Classics 616, a longer and better-played though still imperfect version, but the rest of the disc is more conventional Ellington, with 'It Don't Mean A Thing' and 'Lazy Rhapsody' the highlights in a programme which is mainly made up of other writers' songs. The arrival of both Lawrence Brown and Ivie Anderson is more important: Brown gave the brass section a new mellifluousness, and Anderson was probably the best regular singer Duke ever employed. Classics 626 has 10 Ellington themes out of 23 tracks and loses impetus at the end with sundry accompaniments to singers, but there are four substantial pieces in 'Slippery Horn', 'Blue Harlem', 'Ducky Wucky' and especially 'Lightnin'', though the orchestra often sounds sloppy here.

The three Jazz Information albums, with fine remastering from original 78s and excellent sleeve-notes, cover all of Duke's work for Brunswick (he was still also recording for Columbia and Victor in the same period, though to a lesser extent) up to 1935. Most of the first two discs are also on the final two Classics discs, but remastering here is rather better. The third volume, though, is essential. Two Ellington standards make their debut here – 'Sophisticated Lady' and 'Solitude' – and there are at least four more major pieces in 'Bundle Of Blues', 'Harlem Speaks', 'Saddest Tale' and 'Sump'n 'Bout Rhythm'. Stewart and Allen arrive in time for four tracks and Stewart already makes a mark on the brass sound of the orchestra on 'Margie'. Classics 637 and 646 divide this material between them, and 646 covers a number of important Victor sessions as well: 'Stompy Jones', the locomotive classic, 'Daybreak Express', 'Blue Feeling'.

***** Jazz Cocktail**
ASV AJA 5024 *As appropriate discs above.* 10/28–9/32.

****(*) Rockin' In Rhythm**
ASV AJA 5057 *As appropriate discs above.* 3/27–7/36.

***** The Duke Plays Ellington Vol. 1**

Topaz TPZ 1020 *As above.* 3/27–6/38.

****** Great Original Performances 1927–1934**

Jazz Classics In Digital Stereo RPCD 624 *As appropriate discs above.* 27–34.

****** Swing 1930 To 1938**

Jazz Classics In Digital Stereo RPCD 625 *As appropriate discs above, except add Wallace Jones, Harold Shorty Baker (t), Ben Webster (ts).* 11/30–1/38.

*****(*) The Music He Recorded Only Once**

Verve 531696-2 *As appropriate discs above.* 11/26–10/30.

****** Early Ellington**

GRP 053640-2 3CD *As appropriate discs above.* 3/27–5/32.

The various compilations of early Ellington offer a considerable choice. The two ASV discs aren't really competitive since the remastering is rather grey and undefined, especially on ASV AJA 5057. Topaz do a decent job with their 19-track set, with the obvious favourites and a couple of idiosyncratic choices. Robert Parker's two Jazz Classics compilations use the finest original 78s for remastering and, while we must include the usual reminder that Parker's use of a very slight reverberation to simulate concert-hall conditions may be unpleasing to some ears, these are exceptionally fine, clear and full-bodied transfers, among his finest efforts to date. The tracks are a well-chosen selection from a dozen years of Ellingtonia. The French Verve disc, from the collection of Daniel Filipacchi, has the clever idea of isolating 20 tunes that Ellington set down only a single time in the studios – everything from obscurities like 'The Creeper' and 'Goin' To Town' to surprisingly well-known pieces like 'Jungle Nights In Harlem' and 'Stevedore Stomp'. The remastering is well done from particularly fine originals. GRP's three-disc set covers all of Ellington's Brunswick material up to 1932 and makes a particularly enjoyable and welcome package.

*****(*) Duke Ellington 1935–1936**

Classics 659 *Ellington; Charlie Allen, Cootie Williams, Arthur Whetsol (t); Rex Stewart (c); Joe 'Tricky Sam' Nanton, Lawrence Brown (tb); Juan Tizol (vtb); Johnny Hodges (cl, ss, as); Harry Carney (cl, as, bs); Otto Hardwick (as); Barney Bigard (cl, ts); Ben Webster (ts); Fred Guy (g); Hayes Alvis, Billy Taylor (b); Fred Avendorf, Sonny Greer (d); Ivie Anderson (v).* 4/35–2/36.

*****(*) Duke Ellington 1936–1937**

Classics 666 *As above, except add Pete Clark (as), Brick Fleagle (g); omit Allen, Avendorf.* 2/36–3/37.

*****(*) Duke Ellington 1937**

Classics 675 *As above, except add Wallace Jones (t), Sandy Williams (tb), Bernard Addison (g), Chick Webb (d); omit Whetsol, Clark and Fleagle.* 3–5/37.

****** Duke Ellington 1937 Vol. 2**

Classics 687 *As above, except add Freddy Jenkins (t), Jack Maisel (d); omit Sandy Williams, Webb.* 5–10/37.

****** Duke Ellington 1938**

Classics 700 *As above, except add Harold Shorty Baker (t), Mary McHugh, Jerry Kruger (v); omit Jenkins and Maisel.* 1–4/38.

****** Duke Ellington 1938 Vol. 2**

Classics 717 *As above, except add Scat Powell (v).* 4–8/38.

*****(*) Duke Ellington 1938 Vol. 3**

Classics 726 *As above, except omit Anderson, Kruger, McHugh and Powell.* 8–12/38.

Ellington's mid- and late-1930s output is a blend of commerce and art, as in most of his work; but it's astonishing how seldom he lets a duff track slip through. Even the most trifling pieces usually have something to commend them. Classics 635 is important for the four-part original recording of 'Reminiscing In Tempo', a dedication to Ellington's mother that was one of the first of his extended works; but it also has the joyful 'Truckin'', and two early 'concerto' pieces in 'Clarinet Lament' for Bigard and 'Echoes Of Harlem' for Cootie Williams. Classics 666 starts with some unpromising material magically illuminated: Rex Stewart's filigree touches on 'Kissin' My Baby Goodnight', the lovely scoring on 'Maybe Someday'. Several tracks here are small-group crossovers with the Columbia discs (see below), but there are top-drawer records by the full group, including 'In A Jam', 'Uptown Downbeat', the rollicking 'Scattin' At The Kit Cat' and an example of Ellington's revisionism in 'The New East St Louis Toodle-oo'. One of the best in this sequence.

In contrast, Classics 675 is a bit thin so far as the full-band tracks are concerned, though two versions of 'Azure' shouldn't be missed. Much stronger is Classics 687, which peaks on the still remarkable first recording of 'Diminuendo And Crescendo In Blue' but which also has the tremendous 'Harmony In Harlem', 'Chatterbox' and 'Jubilesta', as well as several of the small-group sessions. Classics 700 includes a lot of distinctive Ellingtonia that has been obscured by some of his obvious hits: 'Braggin' In Brass', 'The Gal From Joe's', the new version of 'Black And Tan Fantasy', superbly played by the band which transforms itself from dance orchestra to complex jazz ensemble – and back again. Though seldom commented on, the rhythm section of Guy, Taylor or Alvis and Greer is unobtrusively fine. There are more neglected winners on Classics 717, including 'I'm Slappin' Seventh Avenue' (which Cecil Taylor always admired), 'Dinah's In A Jam', the lovely treatment of 'Rose Of The Rio Grande' and the very fine 'The Stevedore's Serenade'. The next disc might be a little behind in class, but there are more fine small-group sides led by Hodges (see below) and further lesser-known Ellington originals. The remastering in this series is inconsistent but, for the most part, very listenable; as a sequence of records, it's of a very high calibre.

****** The Duke's Men: Small Groups Vol. I**

Columbia C2K 46995 2CD *Ellington; Cootie Williams, Freddy Jenkins (t); Rex Stewart (c, v); Lawrence Brown, Joe 'Tricky Sam' Nanton, Sandy Williams, George Stevenson (tb); Juan Tizol (vtb); Johnny Hodges (ss, as); Rudy Powell (cl, as); Otto Hardwick (as); Barney Bigard, Bingie Madison (cl, ts); Harry Carney (bs); Roger 'Ram' Ramirez, Tommy Fulford (p); Fred Guy, Bernard Addison, Brick Fleagle, Ceele Burke (g); Billy Taylor Sr, Hayes Alvis, Wellman Braud (b); Sonny Greer, Chick Webb, Jack Maisel (d); Charlie Barnet (perc); Sue Mitchell (v).* 12/34–1/38.

****** The Duke's Men: Small Groups Vol. II**

Columbia C2K 48835 2CD *Basically as above.* 3/38–3/39.

Ellington's sidemen recorded a number of small-group dates under the nominal leadership of one or other of them during the late 1930s, and these superb compilations bring many of these dates together. Some of the thunder of these sets has been stolen by the Classics compilations listed above, but the presentation here is impressive. There are a few undistinguished arrangements of pop tunes, but for the most part this is inventive and skilful small-group jazz of the period. Duke is at the piano as often as not and there are a number of scarce Ellington tunes here; but many of the sides are features for Stewart, Bigard or Williams, who are the three main leaders (Hodges is credited with only two tracks, but most of his great work comes later, for Victor). 'Caravan', 'Stompy Jones', 'Back Room Romp', 'Tea And Trumpets', 'Love In My Heart' and 'Echoes Of Harlem' are all essential slices of Ellingtonia, but all 45 tracks have at least something of interest. Columbia have made one of their better efforts at remastering, and there is an excellent accompanying essay by Helen Oakley Dance, who was involved in producing many of the records.

The second volume maintains the high standard of the first. The Hodges session of March 1938 has 'Jeep's Blues' and 'I Let A Song Go Out Of My Heart', but that for August of the same year is even better: six little classics. Most of the other tracks are under the stewardship of Cootie Williams, but the second disc wraps up with a pleasing date under Rex Stewart as leader. A shade behind the earlier set in track-for-track quality, but still excellent stuff, in good sound. (We have left these two sets in for now, although they may no longer be available in many territories.)

*****(*) Duke Ellington 1938–1939**

Classics 747 *Ellington; Wallace Jones, Cootie Williams, Louis Bacon (t); Rex Stewart (c); Lawrence Brown, Joe 'Tricky Sam' Nanton (tb); Juan Tizol (vtb); Barney Bigard (cl, ts); Johnny Hodges (ss, as, cl); Otto Hardwick (as); Harry Carney (bs, as, cl); Fred Guy, Brick Fleagle (g); Billy Taylor Sr (b); Sonny Greer (d); Jean Eldridge (v).* 12/38–3/39.

*****(*) Duke Ellington 1939**

Classics 765 *As above, except add Billy Strayhorn (p); omit Bacon, Fleagle and Eldridge.* 3–6/39.

*****(*) Duke Ellington 1939 Vol. 2**

Classics 780 *As above.* 6–10/39.

****** Duke Ellington 1939–1940**

Classics 790 *As above, except add Ben Webster (ts), Jimmy Blanton (b); Ivie Anderson (v).* 10/39–2/40.

****** Duke Ellington 1940**

Classics 805 *As above.* 2–8/40.

****** Duke Ellington 1940 Vol. 2**

Classics 820 *As above, except add Herb Jeffries (v).* 9–11/40.

****** Duke Ellington 1940–1941**

Classics 837 *As above, except Ray Nance (t) replaces Williams.* 11/40–7/41.

****** Duke Ellington 1941**

Classics 851 *As above, except add Junior Raglin (b).* 7–12/41.

****** The Blanton–Webster Band**

RCA Bluebird 74321 13181 2 3CD *Ellington; Wallace Jones, Cootie Williams, Ray Nance (t); Rex Stewart (c); Joe 'Tricky Sam' Nanton, Lawrence Brown (tb); Juan Tizol (vtb); Barney Bigard, Chauncey Haughton (cl); Johnny Hodges (ss, as, cl); Harry Carney (bs, cl, as); Otto Hardwick (as, bsx); Ben Webster (ts); Billy Strayhorn (p); Fred Guy (g); Jimmy Blanton, Junior Raglin (b); Sonny Greer (d); Ivie Anderson, Herb Jeffries (v).* 3/40–7/42.

With all of the late-1930s Ellington now back in print, it's easier to see that he had been working towards this exceptional period for the band for a long time. Ellington had been building a matchless team of soloists, his own composing was taking on a finer degree of personal creativity and sophistication and, with the arrival of bassist Jimmy Blanton, who gave the rhythm section an unparalleled eloquence in the way it swung, the final piece fell into place. The 6 May 1940 session, which opens *The Blanton–Webster Band*, is one of the great occasions in jazz history, when Ellington recorded both 'Jack The Bear' (a feature for Blanton) and the unqualified masterpiece, 'Ko Ko'. From there, literally dozens of classics tumbled out of the band, from originals such as 'Harlem Air Shaft' and 'Main Stem' and 'Take The "A" Train' to brilliant Ellingtonizations of standard material such as 'The Sidewalks Of New York' and 'Clementine'. The arrival of Billy Strayhorn, Ellington's closest collaborator until Strayhorn's death in 1967, is another important element in the music's success.

With the Classics sequence of discs now stretching through this period as well, the RCA collections have some serious competition. The four discs covering 1939 include many of the small-group dates led by Bigard, Hodges and Williams, and those who have the Columbia sets may not want to duplicate this material (however, followers of Duke's piano solos will want Classics 747, which includes a couple of little-known 1939 items, 'Just Good Fun' and 'Informal Blues'). Classics 790 includes some important stuff: the Ducal solo 'Blues' and the duets with Blanton, 'Blues' and 'Plucked Again'. Thereafter, the 1940–41 discs cover much the same ground as the three-disc Bluebird set. All this is four-star material and, for those who would prefer to have it a disc at a time, this isn't a bad way forward. Transfers are all right, though no improvement on Bluebird's, and sources are as usual unlisted.

Bluebird's set collects 66 tracks over a two-year period, which many hold as Ellington's greatest on record, and it's certainly the summation of his work within the three-minute confines of the 78-r.p.m. record. There are one or two minor errors in the set, and the remastering is showing its age. We understand that the tracks remastered for RCA's complete collection will be made separately available to replace this and the *Black, Brown & Beige* set, so our advice is to wait for those editions, which were not yet announced at the time of going to press with this edition. For this reason we are (temporarily!) withdrawing our crown recommendation.

****** Fargo, ND 11/7/40**

Vintage Jazz Classics VJC-1019/20 2CD *As above, except omit Haughton, Strayhorn and Raglin.* 11/40.

****** Fargo 1940 Vol. 1**

Tax CD 3720-2 *As above.* 11/40.

****** Fargo 1940 Vol. 2**

Tax CD 3721-2 *As above.* 11/40.

Of the many surviving location recordings of the Ellington band, this is one of the best, catching over two hours of material from a single dance date in North Dakota, part of it broadcast but most of it simply taken down by some amateur enthusiasts. The sound has been extensively cleaned up by both VJC and Tax and there is little to choose between the two editions, though the VJC version is available only as a double set. Here is the Ellington orchestra on a typical night, with many of the best numbers in the band's book and the most rousing version of 'St Louis Blues' to climax the evening. The sound is inevitably well below the quality of the studio sessions, but it's a very fine supplement to them, and an almost definitive glimpse into the working diary of one of the great swing orchestras.

*****(*) Take The 'A' Train**

Vintage Jazz Classics VJC-1003-2 *As above, except omit Williams; add Junior Raglin (b).* 1–12/41.

A fascinating set of studio transcriptions. There are eight tunes which Duke never recorded in the studio again, including 'Madame Will Drop Her Shawl' and Strayhorn's 'Love Like This Can't Last', a pretty feature for Webster on 'Until Tonight' and unexpected things like a boisterous 'Frenesi', a Rex Stewart feature called 'Easy Street' and debut recordings of 'West Indian Stomp', 'Moon Mist' and 'Stomp Caprice'. The sound is mostly clear and fine, if a fraction below first-class.

*****(*) Duke Ellington 1942–1944**

Classics 867 *Ellington; Wallace Jones, Shorty Baker, Dizzy Gillespie, Scad Hemphill, Taft Jordan, Cootie Williams (t); Ray Nance (t, vn); Rex Stewart (c); Joe 'Tricky Sam' Nanton, Lawrence Brown, Claude Jones, Juan Tizol (tb); Barney Bigard, Chauncey Haughton, Jimmy Hamilton (cl); Johnny Hodges (as); Otto Hardwick (as, bsx); Ben Webster, Skippy Williams, Al Sears (ts); Harry Carney (cl, bs); Billy Strayhorn (p); Fred Guy (g); Junior Raglin, Jimmy Blanton, Wilson Myers (b); Sonny Greer (d); Ivie Anderson, Herb Jeffries, Al Hibbler (v).* 11/39–5/44.

****** Duke Ellington 1944–1945**

Classics 881 *As above, except add Cat Anderson (t), Duke Brooks (p), Red Callender (b), Hilliard Brown (d), Joya Sherrill, Kay Davis (v); omit Jones, Baker, Gillespie, Cootie Williams, Stewart, Webster, Skippy Williams, Blanton, Jeffries, Anderson.* 12/44–4/45.

***** Duke Ellington 1945**

Classics 915 *As above, except add Bob Haggart (b), Marie Ellington (v), Tommy Dorsey (tb) and his orchestra.* 4–5/45.

****** Duke Ellington 1945 Vol. 2**

Classics 951 *As above, except omit Haggart, Marie Ellington and Dorsey and orchestra.* 5–7/45.

Classics brings together a mix of studio dates and V-Discs for these releases. Classics 867 starts with the final Victor sessions before the recording ban, and there are masterpieces of the order of 'What Am I Here For?' and 'Main Stem' before four sessions for V-Disc from 1943–4: some excellent Hodges, and there's an extended 'Boy Meets Horn' for Rex Stewart. Peculiarly, they fill up the disc with two 1939 V-Disc tracks that were missed off an earlier disc. Classics 881 returns to Victor for four pop tunes before the studio version of 'Black, Brown And Beige', a Capitol small-group date led by Sonny Greer which has Jordan and Bigard in top form, and the delightful V-Disc debut of 'Perfume Suite', including Duke's dapper piano treatment of 'Dancers In Love'. A splendid issue. Classics 915 looks promising but is let down by very poor sound on a V-Disc version of 'Black, Brown And Beige' (a subsequent 'Harlem Air Shaft' sounds much better). Some of the Victor material is relatively lightweight, although the disc does include the famous occasion when the Duke sat in with the Tommy Dorsey band and the trombonist returned the favour by sitting in with the Ellington band on the following day. Classics 951 includes ten further titles from V-Disc and there are some beauties among them, including excellent takes on 'Hollywood Hangover' (actually a Buck Clayton composition) and 'Ring Dem Bells', and a masterly treatment of 'New World A-Comin''. For the rest, more Victor sessions, including the studio version of 'Perfume Suite' (which mystifyingly omits 'Dancers In Love') and the debut of 'Diminuendo And Crescendo In Blue'.

*****(*) Duke Ellington & His Orchestra Vols 1–5**

Circle CCD-101/2/3/4/5 (5CD, only available separately) Basically as above discs in this period, 43–45.

Since the American recording ban was in full swing, Ellington's studio work was limited to material like this, transcriptions in the World Broadcast Series. Circle have included what seems to be every available fragment from these sessions, which means multiple takes and many false starts. If this detracts from a general recommendation, it ought to be remembered that this was the greatest Ellington orchestra in top form, and there are countless things to marvel at in the likes of (to pick a few of our personal favourites) 'Air Conditioned Jungle', 'Let The Zoomers Drool', 'Blues On The Double', 'In A Jam', 'Blue Cellophane', 'Three Cent Stomp' and many more. Besides, the many breaks allow an intriguing insight into Duke's way of working. Excellent notes and impressive remastering.

****** Black, Brown And Beige**

RCA Bluebird 86641 3CD *Ellington; Taft Jordan, Cat Anderson, Shelton Hemphill, Ray Nance, Rex Stewart, Francis Williams, Harold Shorty Baker (t); Claude Jones, Lawrence Brown, Joe 'Tricky Sam' Nanton, Tommy Dorsey, Wilbur De Paris (tb); Jimmy Hamilton (cl, ts); Otto Hardwick (as); Johnny Hodges (as); Al Sears (ts); Russell Procope (cl, ts); Harry Carney (bs); Fred Guy (g); Junior Raglin, Sid Weiss, Oscar Pettiford, Al Lucas, Bob Haggart (b); Sonny Greer, Big Sid Catlett (d); Al Hibbler, Joya Sherrill, Kay Davis, Marie Ellington, Marian Cox (v).* 12/44–9/46.

While this ultimately stands a notch below the music on *The Blanton–Webster Band*, it is still an essential Ellington collection. Besides numerous further examples of the composer's mastery of the three-minute form, there are the first of his suites to make it to the studios, including most of 'Black, Brown And Beige' – which was never finally recorded in its entirety in the studio – and 'The Perfume Suite'. New Ellingtonians include Cat Anderson and Taft Jordan – two brilliantly individual members of the brass section – as well as the lyrical Shorty Baker, Al Sears and Russell Procope. Ellington's confidence may have been sagging a little from the loss of major soloists – Webster, Williams – and the indifference to some of his higher ambitions as a composer, but the orchestra itself is still inimitable. Remastering is kind enough, even if not always wholly respectful of the music, but most will find it acceptable. However, please see our remarks concerning *The Blanton–Webster Band* set, above.

*****(*) The Duke Ellington Carnegie Hall Concerts January 1943**

Prestige 34004 2CD *Ellington; Rex Stewart, Harold Shorty Baker, Wallace Jones (t); Ray Nance (t, vn); Joe 'Tricky Sam'*

Nanton, Lawrence Brown (tb); Juan Tizol (vtb); Johnny Hodges, Ben Webster, Harry Carney, Otto Hardwick, Chauncey Haughton (reeds); Fred Guy (g); Junior Raglin (b); Sonny Greer (d); Betty Roche (v). 1/43.

*****(*) The Duke Ellington Carnegie Hall Concerts December 1944**

Prestige 24073 2CD *As above, except add Shelton Hemphill, Taft Jordan, Cat Anderson (t), Claude Jones (tb), Al Sears, Jimmy Hamilton (reeds), Hilliard Brown (d), Kay Davis, Marie Ellington, Al Hibbler (v); omit Baker, Jones, Webster, Haughton, Greer, Roche.* 12/44.

*****(*) The Duke Ellington Carnegie Hall Concerts January 1946**

Prestige 24074 2CD *As above, except add Francis Williams (t), Wilbur De Paris (tb), Al Lucas (g), Oscar Pettiford (b), Sonny Greer (d), Joya Sherrill (v); omit Stewart, Nanton, Guy, Raglin, Brown, Marie Ellington.* 1/46.

*****(*) The Duke Ellington Carnegie Hall Concerts December 1947**

Prestige 24075 2CD *As above, except add Harold Shorty Baker, Al Killian (t), Tyree Glenn (tb, vib), Russell Procope (reeds), Fred Guy (g), Junior Raglin (b); omit Jordan, Anderson, De Paris, Hamilton, Lucas, Sherrill.* 12/47.

*****(*) Carnegie Hall November 1948**

Vintage Jazz Classics VJC-1024/25 2CD *As above, except add Quentin Jackson (tb), Ben Webster (ts); omit Jones.* 11/48.

Ellington's Carnegie Hall appearances began in 1943 and continued on an annual basis. The only surviving recordings are mainly in indifferent condition and none of the Prestige CDs can really be called hi-fi, despite extensive remastering work. Nevertheless, Ellington scholars will find them essential, and even casual listeners should find much to enjoy. The 1943 concert premiered 'Black, Brown And Beige' and its lukewarm reception became a notorious snub that decimated Ellington's confidence in the work. These surviving extracts are fascinating but inconclusive. The rest of the programme includes many greatest hits and one or two scarcer pieces. The 1944 concert includes many less-familiar tunes – 'Blutopia', 'Suddenly It Jumped', 'Blue Cellophane' – plus more 'Black, Brown And Beige' and the debut of 'The Perfume Suite', as well as a glorious finale showcase for Nanton on 'Frankie And Johnny'. Notable in the next concert were a reworking of 'Diminuendo And Crescendo In Blue' and some fine miniatures, including 'Magenta Haze', Joya Sherrill's fine interpretation of 'The Blues' and a euphoric treatment of 'Solid Old Man'. The 'Liberian Suite' is one of the principal items of the 1947 set, but the Ray Nance feature in 'Bakiff', Duke's own spot on 'The Clothed Woman' and Carney on 'Mella Brava' are of equal interest. While all the concerts have their weak spots, each has enough fine Ellington to make it more than worthwhile. The recently released 1948 concert features a guest return by Ben Webster and a rare recording of 'Lush Life'; sound-quality is again imperfect but listenable.

***** The Great Chicago Concerts**

Musicmasters 65110-2 2CD *Ellington; Shelton Hemphill, Taft Jordan, Cat Anderson, Harold Shorty Baker, Ray Nance, Francis Williams, Bernard Flood (t); Lawrence Brown, Claude Jones, Wilbur De Paris (tb); Otto Hardwick, Johnny Hodges, Jimmy Hamilton, Harry Carney, Al Sears (reeds); Django Reinhardt, Fred Guy (g); Oscar Pettiford (b); Sonny Greer (d).* 1–11/46.

A couple of Chicago dates in unusually good sound for the period, though there are the usual anomalies in balancing the sections. The January date is a shade ordinary, but the November concert has a strongly played version of 'The Deep South Suite' and features guest Django Reinhardt sitting in on four tunes. Worthwhile.

*****(*) Duke Ellington 1946**

Classics 1015 *Ellington; Ray Nance (t, vn, v); Taft Jordan, Shelton Hemphill, Cat Anderson, Francis Williams, Harold Shorty Baker (t); Lawrence Brown, Claude Jones, Wilbur De Paris (tb); Jimmy Hamilton (cl, ts); Johnny Hodges (as); Russell Procope (as, cl); Al Sears (ts); Harry Carney (bs, cl); Fred Guy (g); Oscar Pettiford (b); Sonny Greer (d); Marion Cox, Kay Davis (v).* 8–11/46.

A mixed bag: the final sessions for Victor, two tracks that were issued only in France on the Swing label, the first of several dates for Musicraft and six V-Discs drawn from the November Carnegie Hall Concert, including the four-part 'Deep South Suite'. Sound on the latter isn't so good, but the other transfers are fine. The Victor material includes some of Ellington's ingenious transformations of other material, such as 'Beale Street Blues' and 'My Honey's Lovin' Arms', and 'Magenta Haze' is a typically gorgeous Hodges feature.

*****(*) Duke Ellington 1946–1947**

Classics 1051 *As above, except add Dud Bascomb (t), Tyree Glenn (tb), Al Hibbler, Chester Crumpler (v); omit Cox.* 11/46–9/47.

Thirteen more titles for Musicraft, a V-Disc session and seven titles celebrating Duke's return to the Columbia label. The Musicrafts have been in and out of the catalogue, and this edition seems to be about as good as any other in terms of the sound. Memorable moments include the raucous 'Happy-Go-Lucky Local', Al Sears buzzing through 'Hiawatha (The Beautiful Indians)', the four-horn concerto, 'Jam-A-Ditty', and a vintage Ellington pastel in 'Lady Of The Lavender Mist'.

***** Duke Ellington 1947**

Classics 1086 *As above, except add Harold Shorty Baker (t), Billy Strayhorn (p), Woody Herman, Delores Parker (v); omit Anderson, De Paris and Crumpler.* 9–11/47.

All these were Columbia sessions, though several tracks were not heard until the LP era. There is some commercial flab here, including versions of 'Singin' In The Rain', 'Cowboy Rhumba' (with guest vocalist Woody Herman!), 'Put Yourself In My Place' and 'I Fell And Broke My Heart'. The only really characteristic Ellington date is from November 1947, with 'Stomp, Look And Listen', 'Air Conditioned Jungle' and 'Three Cent Stomp'.

****** The Complete Duke Ellington & His World Famous Orchestra**

Hindsight HBCD501 3CD *Ellington; Shelton Hemphill, Francis Williams, Harold Shorty Baker, Ray Nance, Dud Bascomb, Bernard Flood, Cat Anderson (t); Lawrence Brown, Claude Jones, Tyree Glenn, Joe 'Tricky Sam' Nanton (tb); Russell Procope, Johnny Hodges, Jimmy Hamilton, Al Sears, Harry*

Carney, Otto Hardwick (reeds); Billy Strayhorn (p); Fred Guy (g); Oscar Pettiford, Wilson Myers (b); Sonny Greer (d). 3/46–6/47.

These transcriptions have drifted in and out of circulation over many years, but this fine three-disc set brings them all together in mostly clean and quite lively sound. There are a host of rarities – 'Violet Blue', 'Park At 106th', Ray Nance doing 'St Louis Blues', Al Sears tearing up 'The Suburbanite', Harry Carney's 'Jennie' ... and so on. Quite a feast, and a fine addendum to the studio tracks of the period.

*** The Seattle Concert 1952

RCA 66531-2 *Ellington; Clark Terry, Cat Anderson, Willie Cook (t); Ray Nance (t, vn); Quentin Jackson, Britt Woodman (tb); Juan Tizol (vtb); Jimmy Hamilton (cl, ts); Willie Smith, Russell Procope (as); Paul Gonsalves (ts); Harry Carney (bs); Wendell Marshall (b); Louie Bellson (d).* 3/52.

The first-ever legitimate release of an Ellington concert when it originally appeared, this hasn't worn quite as well as others of the period (or later). The main point is 'Harlem Suite', which still stands up as one of the best of Duke's longer pieces, but filler material like 'Skin Deep', 'The Hawk Talks' and the medley of hits lets the rest down. Sound is rather cloudy for the period.

**(*) Live At Birdland 1952

Jazz Unlimited JUCD 2036 *Ellington; Clark Terry, Willie Cook, Ray Nance, Cat Anderson (t); Quentin Jackson, Britt Woodman (tb); Juan Tizol (vtb); Hilton Jefferson, Jimmy Hamilton, Russell Procope, Harry Carney (reeds); Wendell Marshall (b); Louie Bellson (d); Betty Roche, Billy Grissom (v).* 11/52.

A complete Birdland broadcast, marred by very intrusive announcements (it was a programme in honour of Duke's 25th anniversary, and they never let us forget it) and repetitive material. But 'Monologue' and 'The Tattooed Bride' seldom turn up in live recordings. Clear sound for the period.

***(*) Piano Reflections

Capitol 92863-2 *Ellington; Wendell Marshall (b); Butch Ballard, Dave Black (d); Ralph Colier (perc).* 4–12/53.

Ellington's apparent reluctance to document himself extensively as a pianist must be a source of regret, but these 1953 sessions find him pondering on 14 of his own tunes (and Mercer's 'Things Ain't What They Used To Be'). Most of them are too short to show any great development from the original themes, and Duke's habitual cat-and-mouse with the listener takes some of the pith out of the session; but it shows how distinctive his touch had become, how mannerism could become even more inimitable than Basie's minimalism, and how Ellington could fashion moving little episodes out of mere fragments.

*** Duke Ellington In Hamilton 1954

Music & Arts 1051 2CD *Ellington; Clark Terry, Willie Cook, Cat Anderson (t); Ray Nance (t, vn); Britt Woodman, George Jean, Quentin Jackson (tb); Jimmy Hamilton (cl, ts); Russell Procope (cl, as); Rick Henderson (as); Paul Gonsalves (ts); Harry Carney (bs, bcl, cl); Wendell Marshall (b); Dave Black (d).* 2/54.

A characteristic concert of the period, recorded in Ontario and spread over two CDs. Although there are the staple hits, Ellington scholars will welcome 'Serious Serenade', 'Theme For Trambean', the 'Pretty And The Wolf' monologue and 'Blue Jean Beguine'. Sound is not bad, if subject to the vagaries of location recording.

*** Ellington '55

Capitol 520135-2 *Ellington; Clark Terry, Cat Anderson, Willie Cook (t); Ray Nance (t, vn, v); Quentin Jackson, Britt Woodman, Alfred Cobbs, George Jean, John Sanders (tb); Russell Procope (as, cl); Rick Henderson (as); Paul Gonsalves (ts); Jimmy Hamilton (cl, ts); Harry Carney (bs, bcl); Billy Strayhorn (cel); Wendell Marshall, Jimmy Woode (b); Dave Black (d).* 12/53.

Ellington's first twelve-inch album, but not his most auspicious. The bland mix of old favourites and standards like 'Body And Soul' suggests the impasse the band was in prior to its Newport comeback. Gonsalves gets a blow on 'Body And Soul' and there is a marathon 'It Don't Mean A Thing', previously unissued.

**** Ellington At Newport 1956 (Complete)

Columbia C2K 64932 2CD *Ellington; Cat Anderson, Willie Cook, Ray Nance, Clark Terry (t); Quentin Jackson, John Sanders, Britt Woodman (tb); Johnny Hodges, Russell Procope (as); Paul Gonsalves, Jimmy Hamilton (ts); Harry Carney (bs); Jimmy Woode (b); Sam Woodyard (d).* 7/56.

*** Duke And Friends, Connecticut Jazz Festival 1956

IAJRC 1005 *As above, except add Buck Clayton (t), Willie 'The Lion' Smith, Hank Jones (p), Jimmy Grissom (v).* 7/56.

The 1956 Newport Festival marked a significant upswing in Duke's critical and commercial fortunes. In large part, the triumph can be laid to Paul Gonsalves's extraordinary 27 blues choruses on 'Diminuendo And Crescendo In Blue', which CBS producer George Avakian placed out of sequence at the end of what was to be Ellington's best-selling record. Gonsalves's unprecedented improvisation (which opened up possibilities and set standards for later tenor saxophonists from John Coltrane to David Murray) was clearly spontaneous, yet in a way it dogged him for the rest of his life, and Ellington continued to introduce him, years later, as 'the star of Newport'.

Gonsalves himself suggested that a particularly competitive edge to the band that night was the real reason for his playing. Johnny Hodges had just returned to the fold after a brief stint as an independent bandleader. His beautiful, almost stately solo on 'Jeep's Blues' was intended to be the climax to the concert, but Hodges found himself upstaged in the subsequent notices, and the concert firmly established Gonsalves as one of the leading soloists in jazz. Unfortunately, much of the solo was played badly off-mike (of which more later) and in the past it was slightly difficult to get a complete sense of its extraordinary impact. It does, nevertheless, dominate the album, overshadowing Hodges and, more significantly, the three-part 'Festival Suite' – heard in its original live form for the first time here – which Ellington and Strayhorn had put together for the occasion. The first part, 'Festival Junction', is more or less a blowing theme for a parade of soloists, including a first excursion by Gonsalves, who gives notice of what's to come with some blistering choruses (though not 27) on the third part, 'Newport Up'.

Columbia's new edition of the music puts an entirely fresh slant on the occasion. The circumstances of how a 'virtual' stereo production are too complex to detail here (go to Phil Schaap's notes in the booklet for that), but essentially Columbia's mono tape was combined with a *second* mono recording of the music, made by Voice Of America. It was their microphone which Gonsalves was mistakenly playing into, thereby making him seem remote in the original Columbia mono mix! Instead, VOA's recording (rediscovered at the Library of Congress in the 1990s) is on one channel and Columbia's on the other, meticulously synchronized.

The result is certainly an astonishing advance on previous versions of this famous event. The attempted 're-creations' of the live event on the following Monday, such as the repeat of 'I Got It Bad And That Ain't Good' with two notes repaired and canned applause added, are here, as is the studio 'Newport Jazz Festival Suite' with Norman O'Connor's remarks from the live event spliced in. There are no fewer than ten new tracks too, mostly from the concert itself. The overall sound is excellent and fully conveys the near-pandemonium of the occasion! Absolutely essential Ellington.

The Connecticut set was played 22 days later. Ellington's 'Newport Jazz Festival Suite' gets another airing, but the rest is a bit of a mess, with throwaway versions of some of the hits and some blues, plus a fairly uproarious Nance feature of 'Her Cherie'. Of some interest are extra tracks with Clayton fronting a small Ellington group and three numbers by The Lion. Good concert sound.

****** Such Sweet Thunder**

Columbia CK 655684 *Ellington; Cat Anderson, Willie Cook, Ray Nance, Clark Terry (t); Quentin Jackson, John Sanders, Britt Woodman (tb); Johnny Hodges, Russell Procope (as); Paul Gonsalves, Jimmy Hamilton (ts); Harry Carney (bs); Jimmy Woode (b); Sam Woodyard (d).* 8/56–5/57.

The wit and sagacity of his nod to Will Shakespeare makes for one of the most delightful of all Ellington records. Hard to choose between the pleasures of hearing Clark Terry cough out the words (or so it seems) 'Lord, what fools these mortals be' through his horn at the end of 'Up And Down'; or Britt Woodman's remarkable solo on 'Sonnet To Hank Cinq'; or Hodges's heartbreaking delineation of 'Star-Crossed Lovers'. Sweet, swinging, perfect Ellingtonia. This new edition sounds terrific, with the music all in stereo for the first time, and there are an extra ten tracks of alternative takes, a few associated pieces from nearby sessions, and the huge (nine-minute) first version of 'Star-Crossed Lovers'.

****(*) Ellington Indigos**

Columbia CK 44444 *As above, except add Shorty Baker (t), Rick Henderson (as), Ozzie Bailey (v).* 10/57.

This sounds like a chore for the company. Ten smoochy ballads, only three of them by Duke, with the band set on snooze. The players play themselves rather than playing, so to speak. But Shorty Baker is still a marvel on 'Willow Weep For Me'.

***** A Drum Is A Woman**

Columbia CK 65567 *As above, except add Betty Glamann (hp), Candido Camero, Terry Snyder (perc), Margaret Tynes, Joya Sherrill (v).* 57.

Ellington's 'history of jazz' is a sly oratorio with virtuoso singing by Tynes and Sherrill, as well as an amusing commentary on jazz history by Duke as narrator and composer. Somewhat dated, perhaps, though not a bad antidote to the earnest history-mongering of the 1990s from one of the music's sharpest intellects.

*****(*) Live At The 1957 Stratford Festival**

Music & Arts 616 *Ellington; Cat Anderson, Willie Cook, Clark Terry (t); Ray Nance, (t, vn); Quentin Jackson, Britt Woodman (tb); John Sanders (tb, vtb); Russell Procope (as, cl); Johnny Hodges (as); Jimmy Hamilton (ts, cl); Paul Gonsalves (ts); Harry Carney (bs, bcl); Jimmy Woode (b); Sam Woodyard (d).* 57.

Unusual and highly inventive material, beautifully remastered for CD with a bright, clear mono sound that puts space round individual voices in the ensembles and gives the rhythm section a better-than-average profile. A slightly larger band than its immediate predecessor, it produces a denser sound, with a lot more resolution in the bass and a shade more colour in the horns. Tracks include 'Harlem Air Shaft' and 'La Virgin De La Macarena'.

****** Black, Brown & Beige**

Columbia CK 65566 *Ellington; Cat Anderson, Harold Shorty Baker, Clark Terry (t); Ray Nance (t, vn); Quentin Jackson, John Sanders, Britt Woodman (tb); Jimmy Hamilton (cl); Bill Graham (as); Russell Procope (cl, as); Paul Gonsalves (ts); Harry Carney (bs); Jimmy Woode (b); Sam Woodyard (d); Mahalia Jackson (v).* 2/58.

This is one of the worthiest of Columbia's Ellington centenary reissues. Duke was hurt by the indifferent reception that his great work received on its debut, and this truncated version was his only full-scale studio treatment of it. Even this was coolly received, but it sounds like vintage and often glorious Ellington now. Mahalia Jackson's magisterial presence adds to what now seems like the first sacred concert. There is what amounts to an entire alternative take of the suite via a number of extra tracks, and all of it is in beautifully remastered sound, with great notes. Bravo!

*****(*) Live At Newport 1958**

Columbia C2K53584 2CD *Ellington; Harold Shorty Baker, Clark Terry, Cat Anderson (t); Ray Nance (t, v); Quentin Jackson, John Sanders, Britt Woodman (tb); Harry Carney, Paul Gonsalves, Jimmy Hamilton, Johnny Hodges, Russell Procope, Gerry Mulligan (reeds); Mildred Falls (p); Jimmy Woode (b); Sam Woodyard (d); Lil Greenwood, Mahalia Jackson, Ozzie Bailey (v).* 7/58.

The original *Newport 1958* LP was actually a studio re-creation, cut a few weeks later. This set restores the original performances and covers plenty of extra ground. Some useful rarities such as 'Princess Blue', the Clark Terry feature, 'Juniflip', and a track where the guesting Mulligan spars with Harry Carney, 'Prima Bara Dubla'. Mahalia Jackson is another unlikely drop-in and she belts out an impressive 'Come Sunday'. There are plenty of loose ends, as with most Festival shows, but this is a good one to have restored.

****** Back To Back**

Verve 521404-2 *Ellington; Johnny Hodges (as); Harry 'Sweets' Edison (t); Les Spann (g); Al Hall, Sam Jones (b); Jo Jones (d).* 2/59.

****** Side By Side**

Verve 521405-2 *As above, except add Roy Eldridge (t), Lawrence Brown (tb), Ben Webster (ts), Billy Strayhorn (p), Wendell Marshall (b).* 58–59.

Back To Back is a small-group (and small-hours) classic, now given a new remastering in Verve's Master Edition series. The opening 'Wabash Blues' sets an attractive 32-bar theme over an initially disconcerting Latin rhythm that goes all the way back to W.C. Handy's experiments with tango measures in a blues context. Hodges and Edison take contrasting approaches on their solos, with the trumpeter working the changes in fairly orthodox fashion, Hodges sticking very much closer to the melody. 'Basin Street Blues' features Spann in a slightly wavering but completely authentic solo, after which Hodges comes in with two delightfully varied choruses. Ellington's own solo is a curious affair, with a slightly wistful quality but also marked by repeated references to his own youthful style, in particular the descending arpeggios that became something of a tic.

The varied 12-bar form of 'St Louis Blues' is further developed in Ellington's fast, accurate introduction. The two horns do a call-and-response routine that further underlines their different approaches. Duke is the featured soloist again on 'Loveless Love' ('Careless Love'), a traditional tune with some kinship to the blues, but not a strict blues at all. Fittingly, though, the set ends with 'Royal Garden Blues', an orthodox 12-bar structure given a deliberately basic (Basie-like?) treatment.

The companion piece, *Side By Side*, brings Strayhorn in for Ellington at the piano and enlists Webster, Eldridge and Brown. Hodges dominates again, though his friends all have some pertinent remarks, and although the material is jam-session stuff as usual, it falls open to the expertise on show here. Three tracks from the session with Duke, including a classic 'Stompy Jones', are carried over to this one.

**** The Duke D.J. Special**

Fresh Sound 141 *Ellington; Cat Anderson, Harold Shorty Baker, Clark Terry (t); Ray Nance (t, vn); Quentin Jackson, John Sanders, Britt Woodman (tb); Jimmy Hamilton (cl,ts); Russell Procope (cl, as); Johnny Hodges (as); Paul Gonsalves (ts); Harry Carney (bs); Jimmy Woode (b); Jimmy Johnson (d).* 3/59.

***** Live At The Newport Jazz Festival '59**

Emarcy 842071-2 *Ellington; Cat Anderson, Harold Shorty Baker, Fats Ford, Clark Terry (t); Ray Nance (t, vn); Quentin Jackson, John Sanders, Britt Woodman (tb); Jimmy Hamilton (cl, ts); Russell Procope (cl, as); Johnny Hodges (as); Paul Gonsalves (ts); Harry Carney (bs); Jimmy Woode (b); Sam Woodyard (d).* 7/59.

*****(*) Live At The Blue Note**

Roulette 828637-2 2CD *As above, except add Billy Strayhorn (p), Johnny Pate (b), Jimmy Johnson (d).* 8/59.

The Emarcy is a lively concert performance with the trumpets in particularly good throat. Juan Tizol's 'Perdido' makes a welcome return to the band-book. The CD transfers are good, with very little dirt. The slightly earlier *Special* has a near-identical band in lower gear and with an occasionally slipping clutch. While it's comforting to know that Homer nods, there's no compelling need to have him doing it on your stereo.

The session at Chicago's Blue Note is drawn from three sets on a single night. Overhead mikes caught the performances, which consequently have a live but slightly askew feel, as if we're listening from the gods. Four tunes from the *Anatomy Of A Murder* score get a welcome outing, Strayhorn comes on to do a duet, Stan Kenton and June Christy drop by to say hello ... a typical night's work for the master. Best moment: the perennially underrated Shorty Baker blowing as sweet as he could on 'Almost Cried'.

*****(*) Blues In Orbit**

Columbia CK 44051 *Ellington; Cat Anderson, Harold Shorty Baker, Clark Terry (t); Ray Nance (t, vn); Quentin Jackson, John Sanders, Britt Woodman, Booty Wood (tb); Matthew Gee (bhn); Harry Carney, Paul Gonsalves, Bill Graham, Jimmy Hamilton, Johnny Hodges, Russell Procope (reeds); Billy Strayhorn (p); Jimmy Woode (b); Jimmy Johnson, Sam Woodyard (d).* 2/58, 2/59.

If 'Blues In Orbit' was some sort of Ducal welcome to the age of Sputnik, the previously unreleased 'Track 360' is an elegant train-ride, Pullman-class and with a nod in the direction of Honegger's popular concert-opener, 'Pacific 231', swaying over a track laid down by Sam Woodyard; the drummer fell ill shortly afterwards and isn't heard on the rest of the album.

There are two more tracks which weren't on the original release. 'Brown Penny' is a state-of-the-art Hodges solo, played in imitation of Kay Davis's earlier vocal version and sounding as if it is being poured out of a bottle. The other also features Hodges, on a slightly too syrupy reading of 'Sentimental Lady' (aka 'I Didn't Know About You'). Hodges rather dominates the album, even being featured on 'Smada', which was usually a Hamilton spot. Hamilton himself has mixed fortunes, sounding anonymous on tenor on his own 'Three J's Blues' and 'Pie Eye's Blues', a rackety 12-bar that compares badly with the subsequent 'C Jam Blues', where he goes back to clarinet, rounding off a sequence of solos that includes excellent work by Gonsalves, the little-known Matthew Gee and Booty Wood. A very fine album, with just enough new compositional input – 'Blues In Blueprint' and 'The Swinger's Jump' – to vary a slightly predictable profile.

***** Anatomy Of A Murder**

Columbia CK 65569 *As above, except add Gerald Wilson (t); omit Gee and Woodyard.* 5–6/59.

Ellington's score for Otto Preminger's film strikes a moderate number of sparks. The main-title theme shows he could write thriller material as strong as anything Pete Rugolo and Shorty Rogers were turning out for Hollywood, but the more impressionistic music tends to sound like middleweight Ellington. Columbia's fresh edition adds a lot of odd bits and pieces – the single version of the title-piece, an interview with Ellington, and so forth – interesting stuff, but really for scholars only.

*****(*) Live At Monterey 1960**

Status DSTS 1008

***** Live At Monterey 1960 Part Two**

Status DSTS 1009 *Ellington; Willie Cook, Andres Meringuito, Eddie Mullins (t); Ray Nance (t, v); Quentin Jackson, Booty Wood, Britt Woodman (tb); Juan Tizol (vtb); Jimmy Hamilton, Russell Procope (cl, as); Johnny Hodges (as); Paul Gonsalves (ts);*

Harry Carney (bs, cl); Aaron Bell (b); Sam Woodyard (d); Lil Greenwood, Jimmy Rushing (v). 9/60.

In fine concert sound, here's some previously unheard Ellington from 1960. Volume One has several seldom-encountered tunes; the second disc is slighter stuff, with Rushing doing three amiable turns and a run across 'Red Carpet' (the rest of the disc features the Cannonball Adderley group). Wally Heider did the original recording and, though some of the soloists drift off, the clout of the band comes over very well.

***** The Ellington Suites**

Original Jazz Classics OJC 446 *Ellington; Cat Anderson, Harold Shorty Baker, Mercer Ellington, Money Johnson, Eddie Preston, Clark Terry (t); Ray Nance (t, vn); Quentin Jackson, Vince Prudente, John Sanders, Malcolm Taylor, Booty Wood, Britt Woodman (tb); Johnny Hodges, Harold Minerve, Norris Turney (as); Russell Procope (as, cl); Jimmy Hamilton (ts, cl); Russ Andrews, Harold Ashby, Paul Gonsalves (ts); Harry Carney (bs, bcl); Joe Benjamin, Wulf Freedman, Jimmy Woode (b); Jimmy Johnson, Rufus Jones (d).* 2/59–10/72.

An interesting collection of extended and medley pieces from the 1959 'Queen's Suite' to the late and indifferent 'Uwis Suite'. Significantly or not, the most arresting track on the whole album, which has good sound-quality throughout, is 'The Single Petal Of A Rose', a duo for Ellington and bassist Jimmy Woode.

***** Hot Summer Dance**

Red Baron AK 48631 *Ellington; Willie Cook, Fats Ford, Eddie Mullens (t); Ray Nance (c, v); Lawrence Brown, Booty Wood, Britt Woodman (tb); Russell Procope (as, cl); Johnny Hodges (as); Jimmy Hamilton (ts, cl); Paul Gonsalves (ts); Harry Carney (bs, bcl); Aaron Bell (b); Sam Woodyard (d).* 7/60.

Recorded at the Mather Air Force Base in California, this is very immediate stuff, with an entirely convincing live feel. After the obligatory '"A"' Train', Ellington tries out a new 'Paris Blues', a couple of arrangements from *The Nutcracker Suite*, 'Such Sweet Thunder' and, for a climax, Paul Gonsalves's party piece, which on this occasion gets a slightly strained reading. Being a dance gig, most of the tracks are taken at a brisk clip and the band squeeze in 16 tunes (or 15 and a medley) in just over an hour. The tapes have been decently handled and the soloists all come across strongly, with Jimmy Hamilton in particularly strong form on 'Tenderly'.

***** First Time!**

Columbia CK 65571 *Ellington; Cat Anderson, Thad Jones, Willie Cook, Sonny Cohn (t); Ray Nance (c, vn); Quentin Jackson, Louis Blackburn, Lawrence Brown (tb); Frank Foster, Paul Gonsalves, Harry Carney, Frank Wess, Johnny Hodges, Jimmy Hamilton (reeds); Count Basie (p); Freddie Green (g); Eddie Jones, Aaron Bell (b); Sam Woodyard, Sonny Payne (d).* 7/61.

Never highly regarded, but if one approaches this meeting of the Basie and Ellington bands in a spirit of undemanding fun, that's what comes out. There is a share of over-the-top blitzkrieg, as in the preposterous 'Battle Royal', but several nimble little touches – the sonorous trombone backdrop for Jackson on 'To You', the extended Basie blues, 'Segue In C', which offers chances for both pianists, and the jovial 'BDB' by Strayhorn – keep the scale of the occasion under control, and a feeling of grand good humour prevails. The new edition comes in handsome sound and adds six alternative takes or rehearsals.

****** The Duke**

Columbia C3K 65841 3CD *Ellington with various groups;* 27–62.

This is the place to consider Columbia's Centenary compilation from their Ellington holdings. It starts with 1927's 'Hot And Bothered' and ends on the titanic 'Battle Royal' bust-up with Basie. There are plenty of interesting and unobvious choices, particularly on disc two, which covers the period 1947–52 and is otherwise largely missed by Columbia's other reissues. A detailed booklet is a pleasng extra, with many photographs, and the remastering is up to the new standards which the majors have lately been setting. An excellent buy.

****(*) The Feeling Of Jazz**

Black Lion BLCD 760123 *Ellington; Cat Anderson, Harold Shorty Baker, Bill Berry, Roy Burrowes, Ray Nance (t); Lawrence Brown, Chuck Connors, Leon Cox (tb); Jimmy Hamilton (cl, ts); Johnny Hodges, Russell Procope (as); Paul Gonsalves (ts); Harry Carney (bs); Aaron Bell (b); Sam Woodyard (d).* 2–7/62.

A very unexceptional mixed programme of old and newer material. Even at third or fourth hearing, it seems indistinguishable from half a dozen early-1960s concert recordings, and even the solos come straight off the peg. Serious collectors only.

***** Featuring Paul Gonsalves**

Original Jazz Classics OJC 623 *Ellington; Cat Anderson, Bill Berry, Roy Burrowes, Ray Nance (t); Lawrence Brown, Chuck Connors, Leon Cox (tb); Russell Procope (cl, as); Johnny Hodges (as); Paul Gonsalves (ts); Jimmy Hamilton (cl, ts); Harry Carney (bs); Aaron Bell (b); Sam Woodyard (d).* 5/62.

A deserved album feature for a saxophonist who contributed enormously to the Ellington sound and who has made a considerable impact on contemporary players like David Murray, but whose reputation has been somewhat eclipsed by that of Johnny Hodges. The tenorist's solo material is typically extended and supremely logical, and his tone, sometimes a little muffled and lacking in individuality, is razor-sharp here. Whether the 'name' ranking was planned beforehand or was awarded in recognition of particularly inspired playing isn't clear, but this is a significant set by one of the unsung geniuses of the saxophone, who joins Warne Marsh and Richie Kamuca in the ranks of those who have been passed over in favour of noisier talents.

***** Duke Ellington Meets Coleman Hawkins**

Impulse 051162-2 *Ellington; Ray Nance (c, vn); Lawrence Brown (tb); Johnny Hodges (as); Coleman Hawkins (ts); Harry Carney (bs, bcl); Aaron Bell (b); Sam Woodyard (d).* 8/62.

The sketchy nature of this meeting of giants finally tells against it. The good-natured fun of 'Limbo Jazz' is the tonic note of the date and, while there is much entertaining playing by the small band on hand, one wishes for some of the gravitas which at least got into the date with Coltrane (see below). 'Solitude' is added to the original LP programme.

***(*) Duke Ellington And John Coltrane

Impulse! 051166-2 *Ellington; John Coltrane (ts, ss); Aaron Bell, Jimmy Garrison (b); Elvin Jones, Sam Woodyard (d).* 9/62.

It's known that Coltrane was going through a difficult transitional phase when this remarkable opportunity was presented to him. Six months before, he had recorded the simply titled *Coltrane* with what was to be the classic quartet. He was, though, stretching for something beyond its surprisingly relaxed lyricism and had managed to wreck his mouthpiece (no minor loss for a saxophonist) trying to improve its lay. His work around this time is, in retrospect, quite conventional, certainly in relation to what was to follow, and it's often Ellington, as so often in the past, who sounds the 'younger' and more adventurous player. It is, for all that, a slightly disappointing record which peaks early with a brilliant reading of 'In A Sentimental Mood' but never reaches such heights again.

***(*) Money Jungle

Blue Note 46398 *Ellington; Charles Mingus (b); Max Roach (d).* 9/62.

Set up by United Artists, this was intended to put Duke in the company of two modernists of the next generation, both of whom (Mingus especially) had drawn particular sustenance from his example. It was the first trio recording the bassist had done since the 1957 Jubilee sessions with Hampton Hawes and Dannie Richmond and, despite his apparent misgivings before and during the session, he completely steals the show, playing complicated countermelodies and dizzying, out-of-tempo runs in every register. Much of the material seems to have been put together at speed and inevitably relies quite heavily on the blues. 'Money Jungle' itself and 'Very Special' are both reasonably orthodox 12-bars and both sound improvised. 'La Fleurette Africaine' is clearly developed from a very simple melodic conception, stated at the beginning by the piano. Long-standing Ellington staples, 'Warm Valley' and 'Caravan', are rather less successful and it isn't clear on the former whether a rather agitated Mingus is unfamiliar with the changes or whether he is suffering one of the minor huffs Ellington recounted later.

*** Recollections Of The Big Band Era

Atlantic 790043-2 *Ellington; Cat Anderson, Bill Berry, Roy Burrowes, Eddie Preston, Cootie Williams (t); Ray Nance (t, vn); Lawrence Brown, Chuck Connors, Buster Cooper (tb); Russell Procope (cl, as); Jimmy Hamilton (cl, ts); Johnny Hodges (as); Paul Gonsalves (ts); Harry Carney (bs, cl, bcl); Ernie Shepard (b); Sam Woodyard (d).* 11/62.

Something of a novelty set, bringing together some of the most famous theme- and signature-tunes of the pre- and immediately post-war bands. Billy Strayhorn's arrangement of Don Redman's 'The Chant Of The Weed' and piano part on the Harry James-associated 'Ciribiribin' are noteworthy, but there are also name-checks for Woody Herman ('The Woodchopper's Ball'), Erskine Hawkins ('Tuxedo Junction'), Louis Armstrong ('When It's Sleepy Time Down South'), Paul Whiteman (Gershwin's 'Rhapsody In Blue') and, inevitably, Basie's 'One O'Clock Jump' and Cab Calloway's 'Minnie The Moocher'. Thoroughly enjoyable, and something more than just a nostalgic wallow. Some of Ellington's own arrangements are strikingly original, virtually re-conceiving the material.

***(*) The Great Paris Concert

Atlantic SD 2-304 *Ellington; Cat Anderson, Roy Burrowes, Cootie Williams (t); Ray Nance (c, v); Lawrence Brown, Chuck Connors, Buster Cooper (tb); Johnny Hodges (as); Russell Procope (cl, as); Jimmy Hamilton (cl, ts); Paul Gonsalves (ts); Harry Carney (bs, cl); Ernie Shepard (b); Sam Woodyard (d).* 2/63.

Great? Very nearly. Oddly, perhaps, the quality of this set doesn't lie so much in the solos as in the ensembles, which are rousing to an almost unprecedented degree. 'Suite Thursday' is an unexpected gem for anyone who hasn't encountered it before, and there are lovely settings of 'Rose Of The Rio Grande' and the *Asphalt Jungle* theme. The sound is big and resonant, as it presumably was in the hall, and, more than almost any of the live recordings of the time, it conveys something of the excitement of a concert performance.

*** The Great London Concerts

Musicmasters 518446-2 *As above, except add Rolf Ericson, Herbie Jones (t), Milt Grayson (v).* 1/63–2/64.

A re-run at the same temperature, but with somewhat less interesting material: the only tunes outside the Ellington hits canon are 'Harlem' and 'Single Petal Of A Rose'. But the playing has rare enthusiasm (Duke liked London) and the sound is very lively.

*** My People

Columbia/Red Baron AK 52759 *Billy Berry, Ray Nance, Ziggy Harrell, Nat Woodward (t); Britt Woodman, John Sanders, Booty Wood (tb); Russell Procope, Rudy Powell, Bob Freedman, Harold Ashby, Pete Clark (reeds); Billy Strayhorn (cel); Jimmy Jones (p); Joe Benjamin (b); Louie Bellson (d); Juan Amalbert (perc); Jimmy Grissom, Lil Greenwood, Jimmy McPhail, Bunny Briggs, Joya Sherrill, Irving Burton Singers (v).* 63.

One of Ellington's extended vocal/orchestral works, with the composer participating only as narrator. Some more background on the piece would have been helpful (there is a rambling note by Stanley Crouch instead) and Ellington's sometimes doubtful choice of vocalists militates against some of the pieces having the impact they might; as do parts of the libretto. The reworkings of 'Come Sunday' and 'The Blues Ain't' have grandeur and fire, though; even as sketches for a longer and more ambitious work, it should be heard by serious Ellington followers.

*** Harlem

Pablo 2308-245 *Ellington; Cat Anderson, Rolf Ericson, Herbie Jones, Cootie Williams (t); Lawrence Brown, Buster Cooper, Chuck Connors (tb); Russell Procope (as, cl); Johnny Hodges (as); Jimmy Hamilton (cl, ts); Paul Gonsalves (ts); Harry Carney (bs, bcl, cl); Major Holley, Jimmy Woode (b); Sam Woodyard (d).* 64.

In 1964 Ellington made a triumphal return to Carnegie Hall, scene of the famous wartime concerts. The title-piece remains one of Duke's most effective big-scale works, and the rest is a useful mix of standard hits and well-turned features for the band's good guys.

***(*) In The Uncommon Market

Pablo 2308-247 *Ellington; Cat Anderson, Roy Burrowes, Cootie Williams (t); Ray Nance (t, vn); Lawrence Brown, Chuck Connors, Buster Cooper (tb); Johnny Hodges (as); Russell*

Procope (as, cl); Jimmy Hamilton (ts, cl); Paul Gonsalves (ts); Harry Carney (bs); Ernie Shepard (b); Sam Woodyard (d).

Undated, but this probably comes from the same period as the above. Challengingly unfamiliar scores – 'Bula', 'E.S.P.', 'Silk Lace' – and trio performances of two concepts of 'The Shepherd' make this a valuable session. The soloing is not so much below par as clearly subordinated to collective values, and the ensembles repay the closest attention.

*****(*) The Symphonic Ellington**

Discovery 71003 *As above, except add symphonic orchestras of Paris, Hamburg, Stockholm, Milan. n.d.*

An on-the-road musician and composer all his life, Ellington must have wondered what it was like to have stayed home and written for symphony orchestras. These are little more than fragments from his vast output, shaped for the occasion into vehicles for the band plus various symphonic institutions (it was recorded in Paris, Hamburg, Stockholm and Milan). There was little departure from his accustomed methods: in Milan, he found he had two hours with the La Scala Orchestra at five, and he started writing at ten that morning. The beguiling 'La Scala, She Too Pretty To be Blue' is the result. Besides this, there are old pieces from 1955 ('Night Creature') and 1949 ('Non-Violent Integration') plus an extended variation on 'Harlem Air Shaft', all reworked for the various occasions in Ellington's typical nothing-goes-to-waste style. If little here strikes one as a forgotten masterpiece, the four pieces are a lively and sometimes sensuously attractive adjunct to the body of Ellington's writing and, though most of it must have been rehearsed and recorded in haste, all the forces involved do well: the uncredited oboe player from Hamburg even gets off an extraordinary Dolphyesque solo on 'Non-Violent Integration'.

***** New York Concert**

Musicmasters 65122-2 *Ellington; Willie 'The Lion' Smith, Billy Strayhorn (p); Peck Morrison (b); Sam Woodyard (d).* 5/64.

A rare example of Ellington the pianist in the spotlight. Much of this is infected by the way he chose to distract attention from his individual instrumental skills – he just doesn't take anything very seriously. The Lion and Strayhorn turn up to do a couple of party pieces, but it's not until the final few numbers – 'Melancholia/Reflections In D', 'Bird Of Paradise' and 'The Single Petal Of A Rose' – that the piano player sets himself any genuine interpretative challenges. Inessential and perhaps revealing of how little Ellington was prepared to reveal.

*****(*) En Concert Avec Europe 1**

RTE 1503-2 2CD *Ellington; Cat Anderson, Herbie Jones, Cootie Williams, Mercer Ellington, Ray Nance (t); Lawrence Brown, Chuck Connors, Buster Cooper (tb); Russell Procope (as, cl); Johnny Hodges (as); Jimmy Hamilton (ts, cl); Paul Gonsalves (ts); Harry Carney (bs); John Lamb (b); Sam Woodyard (d).* 1/65.

****(*) Yale Concert**

Original Jazz Classics OJC 664 *As above, except Jeff Castleman (b) replaces Lamb; omit Nance.* 4/65.

The French recording, from the Théâtre Des Champs Elysées, is particularly well recorded and the band play with top-level enthusiasm – a fine example of an Ellington show from this period. *Yale Concert* has its moments but suffers from the surfeit of available Duke-in-concert: apart from 'A Chromatic Love Affair' and a beautiful Hodges medley, there's nothing worth cutting classes for.

*****(*) Berlin '65 Paris '67**

Pablo 5304-2 *As above, except add Ray Nance, Money Johnson (t), John Lamb (b), Rufus Jones (d); omit Castleman.* 65–67.

Echoes from a couple of European stopovers, although smartly chosen and with numerous highlights. The great set-piece of 'Ad Lib On Nippon' features Ellington playing cat-and-mouse with John Lamb; but it's the features for Gonsalves and Hodges, each at their most magnetic and songful, that raise the enjoyment level to the maximum. A pleasing new discovery.

*****(*) Soul Call**

Verve 539785-2 *As above, except omit Nance and Johnson.* 7/66.

The vast amount of music on Verve's eight-disc box, *Complete Côte d'Azur Concerts*, includes a lot of Ellington, but we are discussing it under Ella Fitzgerald's name. This Verve LP originally appeared as a stand-alone disc, and it's been extended to CD length with music from four different festival sets at Juan-Les-Pins. The important pieces are a vivacious reading of 'La Plus Belle Africaine', deliciously lit up by Woodyard's skittering rhythms and Carney's stately solo, the bubbling near-calypso, 'West Indian Pancake', and a couple of *Such Sweet Thunder* excerpts. Loaded with atmosphere.

***** A Concert Of Sacred Music**

Status DSTS 1015 *As above, except add Louie Bellson (d), Bunny Briggs (tap), Tony Watkins, Jon Hendricks, Jimmy McPhail, Esther Merrill, Herman McCoy Choir (v); omit Rufus Jones, Woodyard.* 66.

Although not all of this is new material as such – it includes both 'New World A-Comin'' and 'Come Sunday' – this live set from Grace Cathedral in Los Angeles is effectively the first Sacred Concert. The band is often peripheral to the various singers and choirs engaged for the concert: Hendricks has four showcases, the effulgent Tony Watkins and Esther Merrill have three, Bunny Briggs taps his way through 'David Danced Before The Lord' and the Herman McCoy Choir handle three pieces in the spirit. Ellington's own principal involvement comes in his piano solo version of 'New World A-Comin'', an impressive treatment. If this is more a collection of interesting bits and pieces, it's an inconclusive part of the composer's rather awkward sacred canon. Salvaged from damaged tapes, and in really quite respectable sound.

***** The Popular Duke Ellington**

RCA 68705-2 *As above, except Sam Woodyard (d) replaces Bellson; omit vocalists.* 66.

Dave Hassinger secured a big, almost voluptuous sound for the band at RCA's Music Center Of The World studio, and it served them well on this session of remakes, 11 venerable nuggets from the book plus a new blues called 'The Twitch'. The performances are in some ways nothing special, but somehow the band summoned considerable heart on tunes they must have done thousands of times. Hodges is almost lubricious on 'I Got It Bad And

That Ain't Good' and Williams is sublime in 'The Mooche' and 'Creole Love Call'.

****(*) Live At The Greek Theatre**

Status DSTS 10143 *As above, except add Jimmy Jones (p), Jim Hughart, John Lamb (b), Ed Thigpen (d), Ella Fitzgerald (v).* 9/66.

Duke's spoken intros sound like he's broadcasting from Mars, but the band sound all right, and they do a typical tour of service for the period. Ella sings a short set with her trio and does 'Cotton Tail' with the band. Hardly a deathless discovery.

****(*) Masters Of Jazz – Volume 6**

Storyville STCD 4106 *Ellington; Cat Anderson, Harold Shorty Baker, Bill Berry, Eddie Mullens, Ray Nance (t); Lawrence Brown, Chuck Connors, Leon Cox (tb); Jimmy Hamilton (cl, ts); Russell Procope (as, cl); Johnny Hodges (as); Paul Gonsalves (ts); Harry Carney (bs, cl, bcl); Aaron Bell (b); Sam Woodyard (d).* 62–66.

The performances here are pretty much *comme il faut*, but again it's Ellington's solo medley, recorded somewhat later than the rest, which really catches the ear. The complexity of his delivery is quite astonishing, even when it is clearly calculated to beguile. Not a great album, but enthusiasts will want the solo spot.

****** The Far East Suite – Special Mix**

Bluebird 66551-2 *Ellington; Cat Anderson, Mercer Ellington, Herbie Jones, Cootie Williams (t); Lawrence Brown, Chuck Connors, Buster Cooper (tb); Harry Carney, Paul Gonsalves, Jimmy Hamilton, Johnny Hodges, Russell Procope (reeds); John Lamb (b); Rufus Jones (d).* 12/66.

It should really have been *The Near East Suite*. In 1963, the State Department sent the Ellington band on a tour that took in Ceylon, India and Pakistan, most of the Middle East, and Persia. The tour was eventually interrupted by the assassination of JFK, but Duke and co-writer Strayhorn slowly absorbed the sights and tone-colours of those weeks, and nearly three years later went into the studio to record the suite. Typical of Ellington's interpretation of the genre, it is really little more than a well-balanced programme of individual songs but with a greater-than-usual degree of overall coherence, summed up at the end by 'Amad'. 'The Tourist Point Of View' serves as overture and reminder of the Duke's characteristic sound, and introduces two of the most important solo voices, Anderson and Gonsalves. 'Bluebird Of Delhi' relates to a mynah that mocked Billy Strayhorn with a beautiful song (played by Jimmy Hamilton) and then brought him down with the resounding raspberry one hears at the end of the piece.

What follows is arguably the most beautiful single item in Ellington's and Strayhorn's entire output. Hodges's solo on 'Isfahan' is like attar of roses, almost (but not quite) *too* sweet and, once smelt, impossible to forget. Critical attention has almost always focused on Hodges, but it's important to be aware of the role of the backing arrangements, a line for the saxophones that seems as monumental as the place it celebrates. The other unquestionable masterpiece of the set is 'Mount Harissa', a soft, almost spiritual opening from Ellington, building up into a sinuous Gonsalves solo over a compulsive drum-and-cymbal pattern and huge orchestral interjections. An evocation of Agra, location of the Taj Mahal, is quite properly assigned to Harry Carney, in superb voice.

Ellington's ability to communicate points of contact and conflict between cultures, assimilating the blues to Eastern modes in tracks like 'Blue Pepper (Far East Of The Blues)', never sounds editorialized or excessively self-conscious. This remains one of the peaks of post-war Ellington. The 'special mix' tag derives from the discovery of original session tapes, which are free of the tonal distortion on previous LP and CD issues, and which also include four alternative takes.

***** Collages**

MPS 547199-2 *Ellington; Ron Collier Orchestra.* 7/67.

A curiosity, recorded in Toronto, with Ellington guesting alongside the Ron Collier Orchestra. 'Nameless Hour' is with strings, 'Aurora Borealis' with strings and orchestra, and four other pieces are with orchestra only, although Ellington himself plays piano throughout. It tends to prove how important his own orchestra was in realizing his music, but these are interesting enough rarities.

*****(*) The Intimacy Of The Blues**

Original Jazz Classics OJC 624 *Ellington; Cat Anderson, Willie Cook (t); Lawrence Brown (tb); Norris Turney (f); Johnny Hodges (as); Harold Ashby, Paul Gonsalves (ts); Harry Carney (bs); Wild Bill Davis (org); Joe Benjamin, Victor Gaskin, Paul Kondziela, John Lamb (b); Rufus Jones (d).* 3/67–6/70.

Delightful small-group settings, of which the 1967 'Combo Suite' (incorporating the title-piece, 'Out South', 'Near North' and 'Soul Country') is far and away the best. Even in restricted settings like this, Ellington still manages to get a tremendous depth of sound, and the disposition of horns is such that Carney's line often suggests that a whole section is at work. The tenor is contrastingly quieter and less forceful, which has the same effect.

****** ... And His Mother Called Him Bill**

Bluebird ND 86287 *Ellington; Cat Anderson, Mercer Ellington, Herbie Jones, Cootie Williams (t); Clark Terry (flhn); Lawrence Brown, Chuck Connors, Buster Cooper, John Sanders (tb); Harry Carney, Johnny Hodges, Paul Gonsalves, Jimmy Hamilton, Russell Procope (reeds); Aaron Bell, Jeff Castleman (b); Steve Little, Sam Woodyard (d).* 8–11/67.

This is Ellington's tribute to Billy Strayhorn, who died in May 1967. The mood is primarily one of loss and yearning, and Strayhorn titles like 'U.M.M.G.', standing for 'Upper Manhattan Medical Group', and 'Blood Count' bear poignant witness to his prolonged final illness. Hodges's solo on the latter is almost unbearable and it is surpassed in creative terms only by the later 'Day-Dream'. 'U.M.M.G.' has an urgent, ambulance-ride quality, largely conveyed by Ellington's clattering piano that sets it in sharp opposition to the easy swing of the opening 'Boo-Dah'.

The CD has four previously unreleased tracks, including 'Smada', 'My Little Brown Book' and (another Hodges feature) 'Lotus Blossom'; but the main interest focuses on the tracks mentioned above and on the astonishing 'All Day Long', which counts as one of Duke's most devastating orchestral conceptions, as daring as anything in the modern movement.

****(*) The Intimate Ellington**
Original Jazz Classics OJC 730 *Ellington; various line-ups.* 69–71.

Definitions of intimacy must vary. This isn't an obvious choice for last thing at night with a glass of malt and the dimmer turned down. Apart from the feeble 'Moon Maiden', on which Ellington plays celeste, it's an averagely appealing album with some assured big-band playing and a useful sample of Ellington's still-underrated trio performances (which may yet come to seem more significant than essays on the scale of 'Symphonette'). The sound wobbles a bit from track to track, an almost inevitable problem on compilations for quite various forces, and there is a problem with the bass register.

***** Second Sacred Concert**
Prestige P 24045 *Ellington; Cat Anderson, Mercer Ellington, Cootie Williams (t); Lawrence Brown, Buster Cooper (tb); Harry Carney, Paul Gonsalves, Johnny Hodges, Russell Procope (reeds); Jeff Castleman (b); Sam Woodyard (d); voices.* 68.

Ellington's last few years were often spent writing liturgical music. The first of the sacred concerts has now appeared on Status (listed above). The second is a blend of jazz, classical and black gospel materials, profoundly influenced by the large-scale Masses and praises of Mary Lou Williams, Ellington's only serious rival in jazz composition on the large scale. Despite the dimensions of the piece and the joyous, ringing concords, it is a surprisingly dark work, with a tragic sub-theme that constantly threatens to break through. Non-believers will still appreciate the extraordinary part-writing; for Christians of whatever persuasion, it remains an overwhelming musical experience.

*****(*) Latin American Suite**
Original Jazz Classics OJC 469 *Ellington; Lawrence Brown, Buster Cooper (tb); Johnny Hodges (as); Paul Gonsalves (ts); Harry Carney (bs); only soloists identified.*

Typically, this late suite is not an attempt to reduplicate the sounds and rhythms Ellington and his band heard on their first trans-equatorial trip in 1968 (surprisingly late in his career, on the face of it). Rather, it records the very personal impressions the southern half of the Americas made on a mind so fine that it was never violated by anything as vulgar as a new influence, and never so closed-off as to reject any new stimulus. Where most composer/bandleaders would have packed the rhythm section with congas, shakers and timbales, as Stanley Dance points out, Ellington conveys a strong Latin feel with his regular rhythm section. On the short 'Tina', an impression of Argentina, he uses a small rhythm group with two bassists and works a bluesy variation on the tango. The bass is again important on the jovial 'Latin American Sunshine', paired with Ellington on a rather untypical theme statement. The opening 'Oclupaca', a title that follows the jazz cliché of reversing names, is a bright, danceable theme that recalls the Latin-influenced big bands of the 1930s and '40s. And that is the overall impression of the set. Perhaps fittingly, there is a nostalgic feel underneath its typically adventurous arrangements and voicings. There's a wistful quality to 'The Sleeping Lady And The Giant Who Watches Over Her', ostensibly the two mountains overlooking Mexico City; but one wonders if Ellington wasn't thinking about Latin America and the neo-colonial United States, with its cultural dominance and magpie eclecticism, and expressing a tinge of regret that he hadn't plunged into the music of the southern continent earlier in his career.

****(*) Up In Duke's Workshop**
Original Jazz Classics OJC 633 *Ellington; Johnny Coles, Willie Cook, Mercer Ellington, Money Johnson, Jimmy Owens, Eddie Preston, Alan Rubin, Fred Stone, Cootie Williams (t); Tyree Glenn, Bennie Green, Benny Powell, Julian Priester, Vince Prudente, Malcolm Taylor, Booty Wood (tb); Russell Procope (as, cl); Johnny Hodges, Harold Minerve, Buddy Pearson, Norris Turney (as); Harold Ashby, Paul Gonsalves (ts); Harry Carney (bs); Joe Benjamin, Victor Gaskin, Paul Kondziela (b); Rufus Jones (d).* 4/69–12/72.

The line-ups don't actually vary very much, but there are a number of relatively unfamiliar names, notably those trying to fill Johnny Hodges's shoes, for which they should have been assigned rabbit's feet. As the title implies, these are working sessions – and slightly tentative ones at that. The early 'Black Butterfly' and the interesting 'Neo-Creole' are significant pieces, but in only eight cuts there's a fair bit of slack.

Duke Ellington: The Private Collection

10 CDs as follows:

****** Volume 1: Studio Sessions, Chicago 1956**
Saja 791041/Kaz 501 *Ellington; Cat Anderson, Willie Cook, Ray Nance, Clark Terry (t); Quentin Jackson, John Sanders, Britt Woodman (tb); Johnny Hodges (as); Russell Procope (cl, as); Jimmy Hamilton (cl, ts); Paul Gonsalves (ts); Harry Carney (bs, cl); Jimmy Woode (b); Sam Woodyard (d).* 3–12/56.

***** Volume 2: Dance Concerts, California, 1958**
Saja 791042/Kaz 509

***** Volume 6: Dance Dates, California, 1958**
Saja 791230/Kaz 510 *Ellington; Harold Shorty Baker, Clark Terry (t); Ray Nance (t, v, vn); Quentin Jackson, John Sanders, Britt Woodman (tb); Russell Procope (as, cl); Bill Graham (as); Paul Gonsalves (ts); Jimmy Hamilton (ts, cl); Harry Carney (bs, cl, bcl); Jimmy Woode (b); Sam Woodyard (d); Ozzie Bailey (v).* 3/58.

***** Volume 3: Studio Sessions, New York, 1962**
Saja 791043/Kaz 503 *Ellington; Cat Anderson, Bill Berry, Roy Burrowes, Ray Nance, Cootie Williams (t); Lawrence Brown, Chuck Connors, Buster Cooper, Britt Woodman (tb); Johnny Hodges, Russell Procope (as); Paul Gonsalves (ts); Jimmy Hamilton (ts, cl); Harry Carney (bs); Aaron Bell (b); Sam Woodyard (d); Milt Grayson (v).* 7–9/62.

***** Volume 4: Studio Sessions, New York, 1963**
Saja 791044/Kaz 504 *Ellington; Ray Nance (c); Cat Anderson, Rolf Ericson, Eddie Preston, Cootie Williams (t); Lawrence Brown, Chuck Connors, Buster Cooper (tb); Johnny Hodges, Russell Procope (as); Jimmy Hamilton (cl, ts); Paul Gonsalves (ts); Harry Carney (bs); Ernie Shepard (b); Sam Woodyard (d).* 4–7/63.

*****(*) Volume 5: The Suites, New York, 1968 & 1970**
Saja 791045/Kaz 507 *Ellington; Cat Anderson, Dave Burns, Willie Cook, Mercer Ellington, Al Rubin, Fred Stone, Cootie*

Williams (t); Chuck Connors, Cliff Heathers, Julian Priester, Booty Wood (tb); Johnny Hodges (as); Russell Procope (as, cl); Norris Turney (as, f); Harold Ashby, Paul Gonsalves (ts); Harry Carney (bs); Joe Benjamin, Jeff Castleman (b); Rufus Jones (d); Dave Fitz, Elayne Jones, Walter Rosenberg (perc). 11/68–6/70.

*** **Volume 7: Studio Sessions, 1957 & 1962**

Saja 791231/Kaz 502 *Ellington; Cat Anderson, Bill Berry, Roy Burrowes, Willie Cook, Ray Nance, Clark Terry (t); Lawrence Brown, Chuck Connors, Leon Cox, Quentin Jackson, John Sanders, Britt Woodman (tb); Harold Ashby, Harry Carney, Paul Gonsalves, Jimmy Hamilton, Johnny Hodges, Russell Procope (reeds); Billy Strayhorn (p); Aaron Bell, Jimmy Woode (b); Sonny Greer, Sam Woodyard (d); Milt Grayson (v).* 1/57–6/62.

*** **Volume 8: Studio Sessions, 1957, 1965–7, San Francisco, Chicago, New York**

Saja 791232/Kaz 505 *Ellington; Nat Adderley, Cat Anderson, Willie Cook, Mercer Ellington, Herbie Jones, Howard McGhee, Ray Nance, Clark Terry, Cootie Williams (t); Lawrence Brown, Chuck Connors, Buster Cooper, Quentin Jackson, John Sanders, Britt Woodman (tb); Harry Carney, Paul Gonsalves, Jimmy Hamilton, Johnny Hodges, Russell Procope (reeds); John Lamb, Jimmy Woode (b); Louie Bellson, Chris Columbus, Rufus Jones, Steve Little, Sam Woodyard (d).* 1/57–7/67.

***(*) **Volume 9: Studio Sessions, New York, 1968**

Saja 791233/Kaz 506 *Ellington; Cat Anderson, Willie Cook, Money Johnson, Cootie Williams (t); Lawrence Brown, Chuck Connors, Buster Cooper (tb); Harold Ashby, Harry Carney, Paul Gonsalves, Johnny Hodges, Russell Procope (reeds); Jeff Castleman (b); Rufus Jones (d); Trish Turner (v).* 11–12/68.

*** **Volume 10: Studio Sessions, New York & Chicago, 1965, 1966 & 1971**

Saja 791234/Kaz 508 *Ellington; Cat Anderson, Mercer Ellington, Money Johnson, Herbie Jones, Eddie Preston, Paul Serrano, Cootie Williams, Richard Williams (t); Ray Nance (c, v); Lawrence Brown, Chuck Connors, Buster Cooper, Malcolm Taylor, Booty Wood (tb); Harold Ashby, Harry Carney, Jimmy Hamilton, Johnny Hodges, Buddy Pearson, Russell Procope, Norris Turney (reeds); Joe Benjamin, John Lamb (b); Rufus Jones, Sam Woodyard (d); Tony Watkins (v).* 3/65–5/71.

Duke Ellington was one of the first composers – in any field – to recognize the aesthetic implications of recording. His own forays into the industry were not marked with unqualified success; his investment in both Musicraft and Sunrise (a gamble prompted by the post-war recording ban) was largely lost, and the later Mercer label, administered by his son, was a flop. It did, though, become Ellington's practice to document his work on tape, and this remarkable ten-CD set represents at least part of the Duke's personal archive of compositions and arrangements. Given its bulk and the availability elsewhere of most of the compositions covered, it's chiefly for serious Ellington scholars. However, discs can be purchased individually, and the best of them have sufficient intrinsic merit to be attractive to more casual listeners. British readers now also have the option of acquiring the discs at budget price on the Kaz label, though the packaging isn't as handsome.

Best of all, perhaps, is Volume 1, devoted to a vintage year for the Ellington band. Johnny Hodges had just returned to the band after his solo foray, and Newport in the summer was to be the scene of Ellington's greatest triumph. At the festival, Paul Gonsalves played one of the historic solos of modern jazz, a staggering 27 choruses on 'Diminuendo And Crescendo In Blue'. Appropriately, it's Gonsalves, rather than the returned prodigal, Hodges, who dominates the Chicago *Studio Sessions*. He is brilliant on 'Satin Doll' and 'In A Sentimental Mood' and takes over from Ray Nance on Mercer's 'Moon Mist', a theme originally composed for Ben Webster but which became inextricably associated with the fiddle-playing trumpeter. Hodges stakes his claim with a beautiful chorus on 'Prelude To A Kiss'.

Hodges and Cat Anderson don't appear on the 1958 dance concerts, which are spread across Volumes 2 and 6, the latter disc covering a second night at the Travis Air Force Base in California. Both are jolly, rather shambolic affairs, beautifully recorded by Wally Heider but somewhat lacking in substance. On the first of the pair, Nance sings a second version of 'Take The "A" Train' and there's a wild, impromptu arrangement of 'Oh! Lady Be Good'. Perhaps the best track, ironically, is an arrangement of Basie's 'One O'Clock Jump' theme, with Ellington taking off his friendly rival in the opening statement and the ensembles rocking along in good Kansas City fashion. Baker's solo on 'Willow Weep For Me' looks like being the high point of Volume 6 until Ray Nance steps in with a perfectly crafted solo on 'Caravan'. The version of 'Blues In Orbit' is longer and more open-textured than the issued version, above, and Ellington's piano work is supreme.

'E.S.P.' was written as a feature for Gonsalves, who tries it out on Volume 3 with characteristic self-confidence and speed of thought. In the same way, Johnny Hodges's reading of the classic 'Isfahan' on the 1963 New York sessions (Volume 4) is a try-out for the magnificent *Far East Suite*. The great satisfaction of these recordings is in being able to hear Duke work out new and challenging arrangements. 'Take It Slow', again from New York in 1962, is scored for three trombones, three saxophones and rhythm, and it steers a wistful course under Gonsalves's fine solo. 'Cordon Bleu' is interesting in that Ellington and Strayhorn alternate at the piano and duet briefly when Duke arrives back from a spot of conducting. Cootie Williams had just returned to the fold and was welcomed back with a 'New Concerto' and with a ranking solo on 'September 12th Blues'.

'The Degas Suite' on Volume 5 was written for the soundtrack of a film about the French Impressionist painter. When the project ran out of money, Ellington was given back the score in recompense. It's a brightly lit work, scored for a much smaller band than usual, with a lot of humour and dabbed with detail that close up or on a score would make no sense, but which contributes perfectly to the overall impact. Volume 5 is completed with a run-down of an original danced score, *The River*, commissioned for the American Ballet Theater. It's a meditative, rather inward work, bubbling up from the 'The Spring', a solo piece by the piano player, and then flowing down towards Carney's deep, dark solo on 'Her Majesty The Sea', taking in obvious geographical features on the way, but also touching human settlements like 'The Neo-Hip-Hot Kiddies Communities' and the contrasting 'Village Of The Virgins' along the way. It's hard to judge which community Duke would have felt most at home in.

Like Volume 6, the last four discs jump back in time somewhat, taking in a decade's worth of studio material, leading up to the death of Billy Strayhorn in 1967. Some of the tapes have deteriorated rather badly and the sound is somewhat unreliable, but they give a fascinating glimpse of Ellington in a workshop setting and represent a valuable checklist of his compositional output throughout his career. Highlights? Hodges's 'Sophisticated Lady' with just rhythm on Volume 9 and his rather inward 'Something Sexual' on 7; Anderson's blood'n'sand 'El Viti' on 8; and the sections from *Black, Brown And Beige* on the final volume.

No one had ever or has since done more with the jazz orchestra, and these recordings (some of them merely torsos, some of commercially unacceptable sound-quality) are a fitting monument to Ellington's genius. They are also something more important: a living laboratory for musicians, composers and arrangers, which was Ellington's other purpose. The 'stockpile', as he called it, was expected to pay dividends of one sort or another.

****** New Orleans Suite**

Atlantic 1580-2 *Ellington; Cootie Williams, Money Johnson, Al Rubin, Fred Stone (t); Booty Wood, Julian Priester, Chuck Connors (tb); Dave Taylor (btb); Johnny Hodges, Russell Procope, Norris Turney, Harry Carney, Paul Gonsalves (reeds); Wild Bill Davis (org); Joe Benjamin (b); Rufus Jones (d).* 4–5/70.

This remains our favourite among the later big-scale works. Ellington looked to create another of his quasi-historical overviews here, but there was no commentary, just a sequence of intensely beautiful vignettes. The rollicking 'Blues For New Orleans' which opens the set features Davis in a very effective cameo, but the wellspring of this album is the sound of the orchestra rather than individual soloists: the reed section is truly on song for the last time (Hodges died during the making of the album and is absent from the final tracks). Gonsalves and Carney abide, though, and the scoring for 'Second Line', 'Bourbon Street Jingling Jollies' and 'Portrait Of Mahalia Jackson' is sadly beautiful, exceptionally expressive. 'Portrait Of Wellman Braud' is also a fascinating rhythmic exercise.

****** The Afro-Eurasian Eclipse**

Original Jazz Classics OJC 645 *Ellington; Mercer Ellington, Money Johnson, Eddie Preston, Cootie Williams (t); Chuck Connors, Malcolm Taylor, Booty Wood (tb); Russell Procope (cl, as); Norris Turney (as); Harold Ashby, Paul Gonsalves (ts); Harry Carney (bs); Joe Benjamin (b); Rufus Jones (d).* 71.

'World music' of a very high order. Ellington's understanding of non-Western forms was often limited to a grasp of unusual tone-colours, but here, on 'Chinoiserie', 'Didjeridoo' and 'Afrique', he produces something that sounds genuinely alien. The original Fantasy release sounded veiled and mysterious, but the CD reissue is quite bright, perhaps too much so for music of this sort. However, sharper resolution does confirm a strong impression that, far from being a by-blow, these pieces are essential items in the Ellington canon.

***** Togo Brava Suite**

Blue Note 30082-2 *Ellington; Cootie Williams, Johnny Coles, Mercer Ellington, Eddie Preston, Harold Johnson (t); Chuck Connors, Malcolm Taylor, Booty Wood (tb); Russell Procope (as, cl); Harold Minerve (as); Norris Turney (as, f); Paul Gonsalves, Harold Ashby (ts); Harry Carney (bs); Joe Benjamin (b); Rufus Jones (d); Nell Brookshire (v).* 10/71.

Recorded on tour in England, this finds the band starting to slip into its final phase, with Hodges, Brown and Anderson all gone and Ellington's own health in decline. This is nevertheless a spirited and often absorbing set: 'Togo Brava Suite' and 'La Plus Belle Africaine' don't have the feel of major Ellingtonia, but they're delivered with great brio, and there are good turns elsewhere for Turney (whose introduction of flute was new to Duke's palette), Gonsalves and the ageless Carney.

***** Never-Before-Released Recordings, 1965–1972**

Musicmasters 65041-2 *As discs listed above, 65–72.*

A very enjoyable pot-pourri of oddments from the workshop. There are two preliminary tries at three of the 'New Orleans Suite' pieces, as well as surprisingly effective features for Wild Bill Davis.

****(*) Live At The Witney**

Impulse! 11732 *Ellington; Joe Benjamin (b); Rufus Jones (d).* 4/72.

Another rare concert featuring the piano player – entirely by himself on many of the tunes. Nine rambling minutes of 'New World A-Comin'' and a tune called 'A Mural From Two Perspectives', which is so clumsily played that it seems even Duke doesn't know it, are rather discouraging. There is much kidding around with the audience on the up-tempo pieces and the hits, and he even chucks in a minute or so of 'Soda Fountain Rag', his first composition. The piano-sound is bass-heavy and there is an audible hum during quiet passages.

***** This One's For Blanton**

Original Jazz Classics OJC 810 *Ellington; Ray Brown (b).* 12/72.

An inventive idea of Norman Granz, to pay tribute to Blanton via his boss and a later disciple. It's no great masterwork, though, since Ellington seems to have gone at it with the usual throwaway elegance that he invested all of his spotlight piano work with; but the interesting piece is the 'Fragmented Suite For Piano And Bass'. Probably the best of the later albums starring Duke's piano, all the same.

****(*) Duke's Big 4**

Pablo 2310703 *Ellington; Joe Pass (g); Ray Brown (b); Louie Bellson (d).* 73.

A joshing sort of set that put little demand on the improvisational instincts of any of the participants. This was the kind of stuff they could all do blindfold at festivals and, apart from some of Duke's chording, which is typically unpredictable, there's not much to listen to.

***** Digital Duke**

GRP 059548-2 *Mercer Ellington (cond); Kamau Adilifu, Barry Lee Hall, Lew Soloff, Clark Terry, Ron Tooley (t, flhn); Al Grey, Britt Woodman (tb); Chuck Connors (btb); Norris Turney (as); Jerry Dodgion (as, cl); Branford Marsalis (ts); Eddie Daniels, Herman Riley (ts, cl); Charles Owens (bs, cl, bcl); Roland Hanna, Gerald Wiggins (p); Bucky Pizzarelli (g); J.J Wiggins (b); Louie Bellson, Rocky White (d).* 87.

***** Music Is My Mistress**

Musicmasters 65013-2 *Barry Lee Hall, John Longo, Tony Barrero, Tony Garruso, Kamau Adilifu (t); Ed Neumeister, Muhammad Abdul Al-Khabyyr, Britt Woodman, Raymond*

Harris (tb); Chuck Connors (btb); Sayyd Abdul Al-Khabyyr, Kenny Garrett, Victor Powell, Harold Minerve, Patience Higgins, Herman Riley, Bill Easley, Danny Bank, Joe Temperley (reeds); Sir Roland Hanna, Mulgrew Miller (p); Thomas James (ky); Kenny Burrell (g); Gerald Wiggins (b); Quentin White (d); Rudolph Bird, Ken Philmore (perc). 89.

Like most of the big bands that are great, the Ellington orchestra continued to perform after the leader's death. Frank Foster carried on the Basie band with great success, but Ellington had a literal heir among his musicians. Mercer Ellington took up the most daunting mantle in jazz with great professionalism. *Digital Duke* is perhaps the finest tribute to his work and, though some potential (or even actual) purchasers may feel let down when they realize the eponymous Duke is no longer present in the flesh, these latter-day performances of absolutely standard Ellington fare are not to be sneezed at.

Roland Hanna clearly isn't Ellington, but he mimics enough of the master's approach to the opening bars of 'Satin Doll' to more than pass muster. Elsewhere, he shares the solo space with Gerald Wiggins. Soloff makes a convincing high-note man ('Cottontail'), but Clark Terry is the real thing on '22 Cent Stomp' (the US postage stamp of that denomination, celebrating Ellington, is on the cover) and 'Perdido'. Turney is another who had worked with the Duke in life, and he sounds poised and reflective in the Hodges role. Herman Riley and Branford Marsalis stand in for Gonsalves. Michael Abene's 32-track production is cracklingly precise, sometimes a little too up-front, ironically exposing just a hint of one-dimensionality in the arrangements, which completely lack Duke's mysterious ambiguities and daringly voiced chords. But it's a perfectly valid set.

As an encore, *Music Is My Mistress* is more ambitious but a shade less persuasive. Mercer finally tip-toes into the spotlight with three charts, including the extended title-piece, but one of these is a revision of his father's 'Azure', and the big work is a somewhat mixed success. But the band play with great gusto, the recording does well by the textures – a fine 'Jack The Bear' is a convincing interpretation of a classic Ellington sound – and this is certainly more impressive than the work Frank Foster has done with the ghost Basie band.

****(*) Only God Can Make A Tree**

Musicmasters 65117-2 *Barry Lee Hall, Tony Barrero, John Longo, Anthony Garruso, Ron Tooley, James Zollar (t); Muhammad Abdul Al-Khabyyr, Raymond Harris, Art Barron, Brad Shigeta, Gregory Paul (tb); Charlie Young, Mark Gross, Sayyd Abdul Al-Khabyyr (as); Shelly Paul, Zane Zachoroff (ts); Jay Brandford (bs); Thomas James, Shuzuko Yokoyama (p); Steve Fox (g); Hassan Abdul Ash-Shakur, Peter Wiggins (b); Quentin White, Max Roach (d).* 95.

Though titled as if it were another sacred concert, this mix of the spiritual and the profane is Mercer's farewell, since he died in January 1996. It doesn't much sound like any Ellington band one remembers and, though there are some intriguing choices of Ducal material – 'Ballet Of The Flying Saucers', 'Calyph', 'Matumbe' – this sequence of pieces associated with specific places is a colourful and enthusiastically played set. Not a very distinctive one, though. 'Caravan' and 'Trees' add the extra weight of the Brooklyn Philharmonic; Steve Fox's pieces are quite anonymous. The weakness lies in the rhythmic element: drawing beats out of rock, Latin and other pulses may be a modern necessity, but it's scarcely a progressive one, and it tends to make the band sound like any capable college outfit.

****** The Complete RCA Victor Recordings (1927–1973)**

RCA 09026-63386-2 24CD Ellington; various groups as above, 27–73.

Officially a limited edition, this monument will probably have disappeared from most outlets by the time this edition is in print, but it would be remiss of us not at least to mention its existence. RCA went to extraordinary lengths with their 78-era masters in particular, and the sound of these eclipses all earlier reissues of the same material. The tracks by the Blanton–Webster band especially are wonderfully alive. Some of the LP-era material sounds less impressive, but for the most part this is a set no one will regret acquiring, even if soon enough it may be on collectors' auction lists. RCA apparently intend to reissue the earlier material in individual editions, a move which we shall greatly welcome!

Don Ellis (1934–78)

TRUMPET

Though born in Los Angeles, Ellis studied in Boston and worked in New York big bands in the late '50s. Played with George Russell in 1961 and cut three 'experimental' albums of his own before forming a big band that won festival and crossover popularity, despite the music's complexity. Film-score work took up the early '70s, but a heart attack in 1975 slowed him and he died three years later.

***** ... How Time Passes ...**

Candid 9004 *Ellis; Jaki Byard (p, as); Ron Carter (b); Charli Persip (d).* 10/60.

***** Out Of Nowhere**

Candid 9032 *Ellis; Paul Bley (p); Steve Swallow (b).* 4/61.

***** New Ideas**

Original Jazz Classics OJC 431 *Ellis; Al Francis (vib); Jaki Byard (p); Ron Carter (b); Charli Persip (d).* 6/61.

*****(*) 'Live' At Monterey**

Pacific Jazz 94766-2 *Ellis; Bob Harmon, Paul Lopez, Glenn Stuart, Ed Warren, Alan Weight (t); Ron Meyers, Dave Wells (tb); Terry Woodson (btb); Reuben Leon (ss, as, f); Tom Scott (as, saxello, f); Ira Schulman (as, ts, cl); Ron Starr (ts, cl); John Magruder (bs, cl); Dave Mackay (p, org); Chuck Domanico, Ray Neapolitan, Frank De La Rosa (b); Steve Bohannon, Alan Estes (d); Chino Valdes (perc).* 9 & 10/66.

****** Electric Bath**

Columbia CK 65522 *Ellis; Bob Harmon, Glenn Stuart, Ed Warren, Alan Weight (t); Ron Meyers, Dave Sanchez, Terry Woodson (tb); Reuben Leon, Joe Roccisano (as, ss, f); Ira Schulman (ts, f, picc, cl); Ron Starr (ts, f, cl); John Magruder (bs, f, bcl); Mike Lang (p, ky); Ray Neapolitan (b, sitar); Frank De La Rosa (b); Dave Parlato (b); Steve Bohannon (d); Alan Estes, Mark Stevens, Chino Valdes (perc).* 9/67.

'I believe in making use of as wide a range of expressive techniques as possible.' Ellis never lost sight of his own artistic credo, making some of the most challenging music of recent times. Draw a line from Jimmy Giuffre to Maynard Ferguson, and somewhere around its imaginary mid-point you might find Don Ellis; he has been alternately praised and decried as a latter-day Kenton, but he actually belongs to a much older and more jazz-centred tradition. *How Time Passes* was made before the Third Stream finally ran dry. Half the album is devoted to 'Improvisational Suite No. 1', in which the soloists are asked to extemporize, not on chord progressions or standard melodies, but on a relatively orthodox 12-tone row, distributed among the instruments and out of which chords can be built. The material is less reminiscent of Arnold Schoenberg, who'd spent his last years in Ellis's native California, than of Ernst Krenek, another European exile to the West Coast. Miraculously, it still swings.

The title-track is loosely inspired by Stockhausen's views on musical duration. The extraordinary accelerations and decelerations of tempo are initially almost laughable; but it's a highly significant piece, and Ellis's own solo (with Byard following less convincingly on his alto saxophone 'double') is superbly structured. The ballad 'Sallie' has a more straightforward modal theme.

Out Of Nowhere is much more conventional and standards-based, but Ellis plays lines and melodic inversions of considerable inventiveness, always striking out for the microtonal terrain he was to colonize later in the 1960s when he began to work on a four-valve quarter-tone trumpet. 'All The Things You Are' – a fifth take, incidentally – is quite extraordinary, running from free abstract patterns round the subdominant to fast, almost Delta-ish runs in quadruple time. The two versions of 'I Love You' show how he miscues occasionally here – but always in pursuit of metrical accents no one else was attempting at the time. Bley plays superbly, though unfortunately Swallow is a bit recessed in the mix.

On *New Ideas* Ellis moves effortlessly between the D flat blues of 'Uh Huh', the atonal 'Tragedy', the strict canon of 'Imitation' and the stark, improvisational approach of 'Despair To Hope' and a piece for unaccompanied trumpet. Even with a more conventional jazz context, the opening 'Natural H' and 'Cock And Bull' are strikingly original, with Ellis demonstrating an ability to assimilate advanced harmonic ideas to jazz. Challenging, provocative music, sympathetically recorded by Rudy Van Gelder. The band are on the case from start to finish, with a particular word of praise for Francis, who has a demanding role. Ellis's own liner-notes are very informative about his methods.

He helpfully pops up with a breakdown of the 19-beat figure at the start of his big band's legendary 1966 Monterey appearance: '33 222 1 222 … of course, that's just the area code!' Everything about Ellis's band was distinctive. He fielded three basses and three percussionists, he played a four-valve, quarter-tone trumpet, and he played programmed jazz tunes with names like 'Passacaglia And Fugue' and 'Concerto For Trumpet'. All of which could seem like mere gimmickry, except that Ellis's solo on the opening track and his statements throughout the album sound absolutely like the real thing. Monterey MC Jimmy Lyons compares the impact of the band to the Stan Kenton Orchestra. That to some ears might sound two-edged but, like Kenton, Ellis manages to combine intellectual sophistication and visceral impact. Hank Levy's 'Passacaglia And Fugue' is a perfect example. Tom Scott's funky solo never once diverts from classical forms but still manages to swing its butt off.

The original album also included the 'Concerto', which was recorded a month later at the Pacific Jazz Festival; apparently the Monterey version of the same piece did not satisfy Ellis. His playing on the issued version isn't flawless, but it has great power. The reissue includes three previously unissued cuts: a short thing called 'Crete Idea', which features trombonist Ron Meyers, the swing pastiche of 'Beat Me Daddy, Seven To The Bar' and another rhythmic exercise called – and in – '27/16'. To put this last into context, Ellis mildly notes on the album sleeve that the longest metre he had attempted to date was 85, though he modestly defers to folk forms where the count is well into three figures!

In 1966, the world of music seemed a much bigger place. The Beatles were still reinventing the popular song, John Coltrane, Ornette Coleman and Cecil Taylor were rethinking harmony and melody, and Ravi Shankar was teaching the West that Western music was just one among many. Don Ellis had already staked his place in that great experiment; but with *Electric Bath*, recorded at the high-water mark of the rock revolution, he showed that jazz – albeit unorthodox – could still generate the level of excitement youngsters had come to expect as of right. To hear it from another perspective, *Electric Bath* was recorded in the same year as John Coltrane's death and doesn't for a moment cede priority to Trane's harmonic and rhythmic innovations.

As with earlier work, what immediately strikes the listener is a whole slew of unexpected time-signatures but, by this stage in his career, Ellis had no difficulty in combining metrical complexity with hot blowing. His own solos on 'Indian Lady' and 'Turkish Bath' are endlessly fascinating. Even seasoned brass players, perhaps forgetting that four-valve horn, still wonder how some of the phrases were articulated. The orchestra isn't quite up to speed all the time. Asking a working band to play and swing in 17/4 is asking a lot, and yet the lineaments of the music are as clear today as they must have seemed baffling 30 years ago. The new issue is superbly remastered, with a ripe, fruity bass. Rounding out an entrancing album are the single versions of both the compositions mentioned above. What happened when 'Turkish Bath' or 'Indian Lady' came on the jukebox or the car radio? How many listeners stopped dancing or wondered if they were on the brink of a Roswell moment? No one else sounded like this. Tough as it sometimes is, Ellis's music is never less than exhilarating.

Herb Ellis (born 1921)

GUITAR

Studied at North Texas State and played with Jimmy Dorsey in the 1940s. Major association was with the Oscar Peterson Trio, 1953–8, and as a singers' accompanist. Much studio work and subsequent club dates as a senior swing-to-bop stylist.

**** Nothin' But The Blues

Verve 521674-2 *Ellis; Roy Eldridge, Dizzy Gillespie (t); Stan Getz, Coleman Hawkins (ts); Oscar Peterson (p); Ray Brown (b); Stan Levey, Gus Johnson (d).* 10/57–5/58.

This is the classic Ellis album, cut in 1957 with a small group of Eldridge, Getz, Brown and Levey in tow. Despite the magisterial presence of the horns – Eldridge is absolutely commanding, peeling off some scalding open-horn choruses and a lovely, stealthy one with the mute on 'Tin Roof Blues', and Getz does his stomping-tenorman bit as well as the lyrical one – it's the guitarist who sets the tone: soft-spoken but swinging, artfully pushing the music forward, colouring the harmonies and opening up the pianoless group's sound, Ellis leads from behind and takes some of his best solos too. There are eight terrific tracks like this, with four makeweights from a session for some film music in which Gillespie and Hawkins also have brief cameos. In beautiful remastered sound.

***** Jazz / Concord**
Concord CCD 6001 *Ellis; Joe Pass (g); Ray Brown (b); Jake Hanna (d).* 72.

****(*) Seven Come Eleven**
Concord CCD 6002 *As above.* 7/73.

***** Soft Shoe**
Concord CCD 6003 *Ellis; Harry 'Sweets' Edison (t); George Duke (p); Ray Brown (b); Jake Hanna (d).* 74.

**** Rhythm Willie**
Concord CCD 6010 *Ellis; Ross Tompkins (p); Freddie Green (g); Ray Brown (b); Jake Hanna (d).* 75.

***** Hot Tracks**
Concord CCD 6012 *Ellis; Harry 'Sweets' Edison (t); Plas Johnson (ts); Mike Melvoin (ky); Ray Brown (b); Jake Hanna (d).* 76.

****(*) Soft And Mellow**
Concord CCD 4077 *Ellis; Ross Tompkins (p); Monty Budwig (b); Jake Hanna (d).* 8/78.

***** Doggin' Around**
Concord CCD 4372 *Ellis; Red Mitchell (b, v).* 3/88.

***** Roll Call**
Justice JR 1001-2 *Ellis; Jay Thomas (flhn, ts); John Frigo (vn); Mel Rhyne (org); Jake Hanna (d).* 91.

Ellis was one of the early members of the Concord stable and his first discs for the label set something of the house style: tempos at an easy jog, standard programmes with one or two eccentric choices ('Inka Dinka Doo' on *Soft Shoe*, 'Squatty Roo' on *Hot Tracks*), and bands that are like an assembly of old rogues joshing one another about old glories. The two albums with Edison and Brown are probably the best, with Ellis digging in a little harder than usual, the trumpeter turning in some of his wryest solos, and Brown insuperably masterful as always. The discs with Pass and Green tend to go the way of all such encounters, the pleasantness of the sound cancelling out most of the musical challenges, and the disc with Green is almost somnambulistic in parts. *Soft And Mellow* is another one that tends to live up to its title. But *Doggin' Around*, made after Ellis had been away from the label for some time, is probably the most engaging album of the lot. Red Mitchell thrived in this kind of open and relaxed situation, which gives him the chance to unearth some of his ripest licks, and Ellis sounds keen-witted in a way that he perhaps disguises on the earlier records. His playing at its best is as swinging and hard-hitting as that of more modern guitarists such as Farlow and Raney, but he can send himself to sleep at times. Still, any of these sessions will go down well as a late-night palliative after a hard day. The Justice record pulls together an unlikely personnel for a good-natured set that bounces between blues, hoedown (courtesy of Frigo) and small-hours swing. There's even a touch of gospel at the end with 'Amazing Grace', though that might not have been such a good idea.

***** An Evening With Herb Ellis**
Jazz Focus JFCD019 *Ellis; Bill MacDonough (p); Chuck Israels (b); John Nolan (d).* 2/95.

Not a bad way to spend an evening. The Ellis trademarks – a gutsy, physical style of playing, with his south-western twanging delivery, independence of single-string lines and bluesy chording – are intact and well to the fore. But it does seem like a simple pick-up date, with the rhythm section doing little more than their duty.

L. S. (Lisle) Ellis

BASS

American bassist, traversing post-bop, free and contemporary-composition sympathies.

***** Children In Peril**
Music & Arts 1016 *Ellis; Joe McPhee (t, saxes); Marco Eneidi (as); Peter Apfelbaum (saxes, perc); Dana Reason (p). n.d.*

Ellis's major recent work is with the trio, What We Live, but he also has this group record under his name. *Children In Peril* is effectively a single suite of sometimes very Colemanesque free playing. It's a little difficult to determine who plays what and when, and the musicians seem to drift in and out of focus (and earshot) in a sort of montage that changes with interesting restlessness. Some moments of fine lyricism, but also a fair amount of aimless ambling.

Ziggy Elman (1914–68)

TRUMPET

Joined Benny Goodman in 1936, then was with Tommy Dorsey, 1940–47, before leading own (unsuccessful) big band. After that, worked mostly in TV and radio, though alcohol troubled his later years. His 1938–9 sessions were feature dates with a studio band.

***** Ziggy Elman 1938–39**
Classics 900 *Elman; Noni Bernardi, Toots Mondello, Hymie Schertzer (as); Jerry Jerome, Arthur Rollini, Babe Russin (ts); Milt Raskin, Jess Stacy (p); Ben Heller (g); Artie Bernstein, Harry Goodman, Joe Schwartzman (b); Nick Fatool, Al Kendis (d).* 12/38–12/39.

***** Ziggy Elman And His Orchestra, 1947**
Circle CCD 70 *Elman; Harry DeVito (tb); Clint Garvin (cl); Johnny Hayes (ts); Virginia Maxey, Bob Manning (v); other personnel unidentified.* 3–4/47.

The man born Harry Finkelman played trumpet with enormous power, but he has somehow been dismissed in recent years as a *Schmaltzmeister* with no real jazz feel. Ziggy's image was set in stone by his appearance as himself in *The Benny Goodman Story*, though by then he was too ill to play his own solos, and his parts had to be dubbed in by Mannie Klein. Goodman had hired him in 1936, impressed by his adaptablity and tone (and not put off by the weird embouchure; Ziggy played, literally, out of the side of his mouth). The post-war material is better known, but it is never much more than routine. Johnny Hayes is a similarly underrated player, but he was to do more interesting things elsewhere, and DeVito always had fascinating ideas to share. What made the pre-war band interesting was the unusual front-line of single trumpet and saxophone section. 'Fralich In Swing' is a Jewish wedding-dance tune which Goodman had turned into a hit song, 'And The Angels Sing'. It loses none of its freshness with Elman blaring away in front. The remaining material for Bluebird sticks to the basic formula and relies on essentially the same pool of Goodman-trained players, which may account for the tightness of the section work. The absence of Goodman may account for the joyous, just-let-out-of-jail quality of some of the playing. Noni Bernardi is exceptional, immediately distinguishable from his fellow-altoists, and Jess Stacy and Milt Raskin hold down the chords with calm precision. The sound-quality on the whole is good, though there is some distortion on the December 1938 session, which may be an artefact on the transfers or, more likely, a result of engineers unused to Elman's bravura style.

Elsie Jo

GROUP

An opportunist recording of a sextet drawn in part from the ranks of the London Jazz Composers Orchestra.

***** Elsie Jo Live**

Maya MCD 9201 *Conrad Bauer (tb); Evan Parker (ts, ss); Irène Schweizer (p); Barry Guy, Barre Phillips (b); Paul Lytton (d).* 3/91.

She sounds as if she ought to be wearing rhinestones and a big hat, and singing about men who done her wrong. Elsie Jo really deserves an entry to her/itself, even though she's bassist Barry Guy's secret love-child and has long been a ward of the London Jazz Composers Orchestra. The title came from a simple but incurable metathesis of LJCO by Alex von Schlippenbach, with whom Guy's outfit had been collaborating. The music on the CD represents part of a free concert given by the sextet during a brief tour which followed Irène Schweizer's fiftieth birthday. What resulted is an almost definitive example of contemporary Anglo-European improvisation. Grounded on the twin basses and Schweizer's flawless pianism, the group improvises with the vivid abstraction of a painting by Albert Irvin, a friend of Guy and May Homburger, whose work has graced a number of the label's covers. Parker is in splendidly good form, sounding relaxed and unpressured, and he and Schweizer produce some of the best music of the whole set on the duo 'Ta'ay (Now)'. It's Bauer, though, who emerges as the real star. An exuberant player at the best of times, he conjures light and shade almost with every breath, and interacts sympathetically with the two basses, with whom he apparently played a trio piece elsewhere in the same concert.

Kahil El'Zabar

DRUMS, PERCUSSION, FLUTE

A prime mover in contemporary Chicago jazz, and a leading light among the spirits who emerged from the 1970s period of the AACM, El'Zabar is a drummer-percussionist who uses individual hand drums as often as the regular kit, and whose small-scale groups – such as the Ethnic Heritage Ensemble and the Ritual Trio – seek big-scale results in terms of creating new Afro-American fusions.

****(*) The Ritual**

sound aspects sas 011 *El'Zabar; Lester Bowie (t); Malachi Favors (b).* 11/85.

***** Sacred Love**

sound aspects sas 021 *As above, except add Raphael Garrett (cl, perc).* 11/85.

***** Another Kind Of Groove**

sound aspects sas 016 *El'Zabar; Billy Bang (vn, bells); Malachi Favors (b, perc).* 5/86.

***** Ancestral Song**

Silkheart SH 108 *El'Zabar; Joseph Bowie (tb, mar, perc); Edward Wilkerson (ts, cl, perc).* 5/87.

****** Dance With The Ancestors**

Chameleon 8808 *As above.* 91.

***** Big Cliff**

Delmark DE-477 *El'Zabar; Ari Brown (ts, p); Billy Bang (vn); Malachi Favors (b).* 9/94.

El'Zabar is a percussionist with a knack for creating exciting musical situations out of elemental materials. He often refers to his groups as the Ethnic Heritage Ensemble, and the Silkheart and Chameleon releases listed above go under that name (unfortunately, the debut album by the group, the splendid *Three Gentlemen From Chicago* on Moers 01076, is still not on CD). *The Ritual* rambles on rather too much, consisting of a single 42-minute improvisation, with the usual quota of dead spots as well as some more telling interplay. When he is joined by Garrett, in a session recorded on the same occasion, the music becomes more expressive, more sonorously powerful, with the coda of 'There Is No Greater Love' sounding oddly poetic. *Another Kind Of Groove* adds another maverick voice, that of Billy Bang, to El'Zabar's mix: his tersely swinging violin parts sit well with the rhythm team, though an extra horn might have alleviated the occasional dryness in the trio's sound.

The three releases by the trio of El'Zabar, Bowie and Wilkerson suggest a group that has grown in stature with each release. *Ancestral Song* was a somewhat modest start, with Bowie's lines offering only cautious counterpoint to Wilkerson's intensities. *Dance With The Ancestors*, though, makes clear the relationships within the group: Bowie acts more as a bassman than as second horn, with most of the themes pivoting round him, while El'Zabar's percussion parts lend colour and melodic variations as well as rhythm. Wilkerson, in mighty form on tenor, commands the real attention in improvising terms. Whether marching through 'Take The "A" Train' or one of their own, somewhat enigmatic, free pieces, the group suggests fresh avenues for Chicago jazz to turn down next.

Big Cliff gets its biggest kicks out of the title-piece, in which Bang and Brown take boiling solos, and the funky fun of 'Another Kind Of Groove', where the sawing violin over the bomp rhythms starts to get a hypnotic happening under way. Though the music is dedicated to El'Zabar's late father, this is celebratory music and, if scarcely a new take either on what he's done before or on Chicago jazz itself, it's a very satisfying record.

*****(*) 21st Century Union March**
Silkheart SHCD 142 *El'Zabar; Joseph Bowie (tb, perc); Edward Wilkerson (ts, acl, perc).* 6/95.

***** Jitterbug Junction**
CIMP 150 *El'Zabar; Ari Brown (ts, ss); Malachi Favors (b).* 6/97.

The Ethnic Heritage team return to an almost chamberish feel on *21st Century Union March*. This time Bowie takes a more prominent soloist's role, Wilkerson seems the more reserved, and the music has a gentle way of unfolding, even when El'Zabar works up some thunder at his various drums. There is some merely filled-in time, but the best of it has all their qualities on show and they remain a unique group.

The Ritual Trio are responsible for the CIMP session, which is generally more volatile and loudly spoken. Brown isn't as strong a player as Wilkerson, and the attempted masterwork in 'The Sweet Nectar Of Cacophony' is finally unconvincing, but the dedication to Coltrane miniaturizes the quartet's passions rather effectively and the trio play with great enthusiasm.

*****(*) Papa's Bounce**
CIMP 167 *El'Zabar; Joseph Bowie (tb, perc); Ernest Dawkins (as, ts); Atu Harold Murray (perc, f).* 2/98.

****** Freedom Jazz Dance**
Delmark DE-517 *As above, except Fareed Haque (g, perc) replaces Murray.* 3/99.

CIMP's dry, 'real' sound suits the EHE just fine, and they've seldom made a record as lucid and spontaneous-sounding as *Papa's Bounce*. Dawkins is an excellent recruit, the whole tradition of Chicago saxophone running through his greasy, gritty yet perversely romantic sound, and Bowie's range of trombone effects seems to have been extended further of late. When El'Zabar hits on a multi-kulti groove like 'Blue Rwanda', he gets as close as anyone has to blending the different deltas of Afro-American sound with an ancestral tinge.

The addition of Haque gives the band yet another sound, even while still working off the simple formula of two horns and a drum. The title-piece nods towards El'Zabar's Chicagoan mentor, Eddie Harris, and allows Dawkins to uncork one of his most sweeping solos, starting out in bebop and pulsing in and out of the tradition from there. Haque doesn't get in the way of the horns, here or elsewhere, but he provides a new, lean textural ground for them to work from in addition to the leader's colourful beats. That gives an extra pinch of harmonic spice to tracks such as 'Katon' and 'So Low But Not Alone'. And Bowie seems to progress with every record. The result is arguably the best EHE album to date.

**** Conversations**
Delmark DE-514 *El'Zabar; Archie Shepp (ts); Ari Brown (ts, p); Malachi Favors (b).* 1/99.

Oh dear – no, no, and again we say, no. Not a bad idea of El'Zabar to harness some fine old spirits of the vintage Chicago avant-garde, but he made the forgivable – though disastrous – mistake of asking Archie Shepp to be one of them. Shepp's ludicrous, fumbling playing is all wrong, and when poor Ari Brown (who has to settle for the piano stool for much of the date) is allowed to get his saxophone out, the results should have made Shepp pack up and go home. El'Zabar and Favors still manage to get some grooves going, so two stars for them anyway.

Jorgen Emborg (born 1953)

PIANO

Born in Frederiksberg, Emborg is a pianist with a broad range of experience in the Danish mainstream of the last 20 years.

*****(*) Over The Rainbow**
Storyville STCD 4183 *Emborg; Fredrik Lundin (ss, ts); Steve Swallow (b); Alex Riel (d); Lisbeth Diers (perc).* 3/92.

This disc was commissioned as part of the annual JAZZPAR awards, made by Skandinavisk Tobakskompagni and the Danish Jazz Centre, Emborg inviting Swallow to work with him. The result is an airy, graceful, modern set of wonderful lyricism. Emborg's cultivated touch and flowing line pay their dues to the Evans school and, with a translucent version of 'Peace Piece' in the programme, that debt is almost too obvious. But rhythmically he's his own man, and the balance of the group is beautifully poised, the ensembles spacious but with plenty of inner life. Swallow and Riel are something of a dream team at the back, with the bassist doubling guitar-like runs with solid formations and Riel scampering around the time. Lundin is a shade less interesting, though the closing five tracks, each a duet for sax and piano, are a purposeful meditation. Strongly recommended.

James Emery (born 1951)

GUITAR

An innovative and imaginative guitarist who took his cue from Charlie Parker, Emery quickly made his own synthesis of modern jazz styles and, even if his recorded output is still skimpy, he is utterly distinctive.

****** Standing On A Whale Fishing For Minnows**
Enja ENJ 9312-2 *Emery; Marty Ehrlich (as, cl, f); Michael Formanek (b); Gerry Hemingway (d, mar, vib).* 9–10/96.

****** Spectral Domains**
Enja ENJ 9344-2 *Emery; Marty Ehrlich (ss, as, f); Chris Speed (ts, cl); Kevin Norton (vib, mar, perc); Mark Feldman (vn); Michael Formanek (b); Gerry Hemingway (d).* 9/97.

Emery had recorded once or twice before, but even if this isn't a CD debut, *Standing* ... is a cracking achievement for a player who hadn't yet made much impact as a leader. The group is perfectly poised and balanced and, with Ehrlich's usual range of horns and voices and Hemingway's superb touch on marimbas and vibes as well as the kit, the range of sound is quite startling.

The title-track is a turbulent, angular thing, with Hemingway strongly featured. Ehrlich understandably takes the lead voice on most tracks, though it's often what Emery himself is doing underneath which merits attention, and his deployment of guitar and soprano guitar, and the hard-to-pin-down sounds on the down-home 'Texas Koto Blues' are continuously interesting. Just one standard, a throwaway 'Crepuscule With Nellie'; otherwise all the songs are Emery's own, combining power and wit, a straight-ahead feel and subtle inflexions from outside jazz altogether. Great name, great record.

Monk features again on the second record, where one of the key tracks is a crisp version of 'Trinkle Tinkle'. Equally briefly, Emery attacks Ornette's 'Kathelin Gray' and comes up with a version that knocks the composer's into a cocked hat. His own interest in the interface between jazz and modern compositon is most obvious on 'Chromosphere' and the long – perhaps over-long – 'Sound Action Seven', where he manages to balance open-form improvisation with subtle writing. A version of 'Standing on a Whale ...' suggests how far he has stretched even in a year. Hemingway and Formanek are magnificent and the horns and violin fill out a hugely expansive sound.

Giuseppe Emmanuele

PIANO

Catanian pianist, with a Bill Evans character, but exploring the wider reaches of the jazz tradition too.

***** A Waltz For Debby**

Splasc(h) H 200 *Emmanuele; Paolo Fresu (t, flhn); Pietro Tonolo (ss, ts); Nello Toscano (b); Pucci Nicosia (d).* 1/90.

***** Reflections In Jazz**

Splasc(h) H 389-2 *As above, except Orazio Maugeri (as), Paolo Mappa (d) replace Fresu and Nicosia.* 12/91.

A Waltz For Debby is a lovely record. Emmanuele is a Bill Evans admirer, and the quintet's version of the title-song pays suitable homage to its composer; but the four originals by the pianist show a light but clear watermark of his own, and he plays with strength as well as delicacy: the solo on an unusually sunny reading of Lennie Tristano's 'Wow' even suggests some of the energy of the young Tristano himself. Fresu and Tonolo, though, are probably the most accomplished players here and both have plenty of chances to shine. *Reflections In Jazz* is perhaps a degree less involving: Maugeri is a bustling player, but Fresu's elegance is missed and, though there is a limpid version of Ellington's 'On A Turquoise Cloud' to commence with, Emmanuele's music seems a fraction less beguiling this time. Tonolo, though, continues to impress.

***** Into The Tradition**

Splasc(h) H 458-2 *Emmanuele; Giovanni La Ferlita, Maurizio Agosta, Giuseppe Privitera, Enzo Gulizia, Vito Giordano (t); Camillo Pavone, Antonio Caldarella, Filippo Nascone Pistone, Matteo Miraglia (tb); Salvo Famiani, Ercole Tringale, Carlo Cattano, Umberto Di Pietro, Salvo Arena, Giancarlo Cutuli, Larry Smith (reeds); Claudio Cusmano (g); Nello Toscano (b); Pucci Nicosia (d); Maria Patti (v).* 3/95.

Emmanuele arranges ten pieces, most of them standards, for the City Brass Orkestra. The occasional wobble in the section-work wouldn't be tolerated in American big bands but there's a compensating sense of Mediterranean sun in the melodic fabric and Emmanuele likes to keep them busy in his charts – there's always something interesting to listen to, even if the soloists aren't especially arresting. Guest Larry Smith does the most ear-grabbing things on alto.

***** From USA To Mediterraneo**

Splasc(h) 486-2 *Emmanuele; Alberto Amato (b); Pucci Nicosia (d).* 5/96.

*****(*) Reflection No. 2**

Splasc(h) 673-2 *As above, except add Vito Giordano (t, flhn), Pietro Tonolo (ss, ts); strings.* 7/96–7/98.

The trio record is nicely titled: it starts with three American tunes and, for the rest, relies on Emmanuele himself and other Italians for the compositions. On this showing, though, America's ahead. Bix Beiderbecke's 'In A Mist' is an audacious choice, and it's handsomely transformed into a modern vehicle; 'All the Things You Are' and Ellington's 'Reflection In D' are just as good. But the unfamiliar pieces are less strongly characterized and the playing is gracious but not always inolving.

The quintet date is stronger, with a new version of 'Fine Stagione' from the previous record, and flavoursome treatments of 'Time Remembered' and 'Israel'. The use of strings adds a further element; though they were recorded two years after the quintet set down their music, Emmanuele has cleverly integrated the scoring and they're used to darken rather than sweeten the situation.

Sidsel Endresen

VOCALS

Norwegian vocalist starting in folk parameters and moving towards a free expression.

***** So I Write**

ECM 841776-2 *Endresen; Nils Petter Molvaer (t, flhn, perc); Django Bates (p); Jon Christensen (d).* 6/90.

*****(*) Exile**

ECM 521721-2 *As above, except add Bugge Wesseltoft (ky); David Darling (clo).* 8/93.

***** Nightsong**

ACT 9004-2 *Endresen; Bugge Wesseltoft (p, syn).* 94.

*****(*) Duplex Ride**

ACT 9000-2 *As above, except add Jon Bang (v).* 97–98.

Working rather obliquely outwards from a jazz/folk/improvised idiom, Endresen sings with a deceptive range that pushes her up into the lyric-soprano register and down into contralto accents on the more sombre songs. Jon Balke's settings on the first record, to 'So I Write', 'This Is The Movie' and 'Dreamland', perfectly suit her slightly prosaic lyrics. There are no up-tempo tracks but, whether singing exactly on the beat or drawing out the words without any pretext of verse-metre, Endresen seems completely confident, and the accompanying group is superb though often minimal in gesture. Bates – who's credited with the two weakest compositions – plays beautifully: no electronics, no horn, no additional percussion, just beautifully modulated stylings which accord with the accompanist's duty to point up the words without swamping them.

The second record has a much richer instrumental palette. Bates takes along his tenor horn. Endresen's singing is stronger and more pointedly articulated, so there is no risk of her being overpowered. The songs are interspersed with instrumental variations in which Darling plays a big part, and the overall impact is of a much more musicianly product, carefully thought out and immaculately performed.

Endresen's relationship with Wesseltoft has yielded some classic live performances. The later album is a better measure of what they have done together. It combines some entirely improvised pieces with repertory material like the classic Paul Simon song, 'Fifty Ways To Leave Your Lover', which Endresen turns into a slow, bleached lament. Following it is 'And Later, The Rain', a quiet narrative of loss accompanied by soft, aggrieved percussion. 'Duplex Ride' itself combines recitative with abstract vocal sounds, synth patterns and an uneasy journey across London. 'Six Minutes Or So' is a scarifying inscape, anxious, stressed, moving and completely musical.

Nightsong is more conventional, not because it contains standard material like 'The Lady Is A Tramp' and 'I Think It's Gonna Rain Today', but because the relation between vocal line and accompaniment is so much less challenging. Even so, both of these albums are fascinating extensions of what Endresen has done before. Her talent finds ever more challenging contexts.

Enten Eller

GROUP

Piedmontese bop-to-fusion band, formed in the late '80s.

***** Antigone**

Splasc(h) H 352-2 *Mario Simeoni (ts, f); Carlo Actis Dato (ts, bs, bcl); Ugo Boscain (p); Giovanni Maier (b); Massimo Barbiero (d); Alex Rolle, Andrea Stracuzzi (perc).* 1/91.

****(*) Trait D'Union**

Splasc(h) 623 *Alberto Mandarini (t, flhn); Maurizio Brunod (g); Giovanni Maier (b); Massimo Barbiero (d, mar).* 4/97.

***** Melquiades**

Splasc(h) 805 *As above, except add Tim Berne (as).* 5/99.

This band is from Piedmont, which has spawned several of the best new Italian groups (Enrico Fazio, Claudio Lodati, Carlo Actis Dato). *Antigone* is their second album and is, if anything, even more brawling than their rough-and-ready earlier set, with the opening tracks, 'Il Mago' and 'Pragma', blown open by Actis Dato and Simeoni; but a lengthy set also includes ballads, and the basic quintet know each other's moves to make this blend of modal, bop and fusion leanings into an entertaining whole.

Trait D'Union picks up the thread a full six years on, with a very different line-up. Brunod's guitar tends to set the tone, which leans towards out-and-out fusion, although Mandarini makes sure that some bop vernacular survives. For all its frequent energy, this is rather bland stuff.

Melquiades brings in Tim Berne as surprise guest star. As if under threat, Brunod doubles his assault and introduces more loops, effects and whatever else he can think of to keep the attention; even so, there are still moments of quiet such as 'Per Emmanuela'. Berne seems content to be a band member but still gets in some imposing remarks.

Rolf Ericson (1922–97)

TRUMPET

Born in Stockholm, he learned trumpet as a child and, after playing with local groups, went to the USA in 1947. Acquired experience with a wide range of leaders, from Charlie Barnet and Woody Herman to Charles Mingus, eventually joining Ellington in 1963. Also returned home to tour, lead his own Swedish big band and take a sojourn in Berlin. One of the Europeans who made most international impact in the '40s and '50s.

***** Rolf Ericson & The American Stars 1956**

Dragon DRCD 255 *Ericson; Lars Gullin, Cecil Payne (bs); Duke Jordan, Freddie Redd (p); Tommy Potter, John Simmons (b); Joe Harris, Art Taylor (d); Ernestine Anderson (v).* 6 & 7/56.

***** Stockholm Sweetnin'**

Dragon DRCD 256 *Ericson; Nisse Sandstrom (ts, p); Claes Crona (p); Goran Lindberg (b); Mel Lewis (d).* 8/84–7/85.

***** Ellington & Strayhorn**

Sittel SITCD 9223 *Ericson; Lennart Aberg (ss, ts, f); Bobo Stenson (p); Goran Klinghagen, Max Schultz (g); Dan Berglund (b); Egil Johansen (d); Rose-Marie Aberg (v).* 1/95.

****** I Love You So ...**

Amigo AMCD 879 *Ericson; Bernt Rosengren (ts); Lars Sjøsten (p); Bjorn Alke (b); Fredrik Norén (d).* 97.

The gifted and likeable Ericson left a very fine legacy on record, though comparatively little is under his own name. A totally reliable section-player – Lew Soloff or Jack Walrath would be obvious current parallels – he tended to hide away a gentler and more lyrical side, and it's this which comes out on *I Love You So* ... which reached us, bizarrely, the day Ericson's death was announced.

The 1956 recordings date from a tour when Rolf was asked to front a band of Americans for a Swedish visit. The first tour was wrecked by the narcotic problems of two of the visitors, and only four tracks by this sextet survive. The bulk of this disc has Ericson and Gullin in the front line, with Redd, Potter and Harris in the rhythm section. Despite the problems, the tour was instrumental in bringing a wave of hard bop to Sweden, previously drawn more to American cool. Ericson and Gullin are in brimming form, though the live recording isn't ideal. Anderson sings on six tracks.

Ericson was still in fine fettle on the 1984 date for Dragon: a good, juicy selection of jazz tunes and standards by an accomplished band, with Sandstrom's Lestorian tenor a fine foil for the trumpet; there are four previously unreleased trumpet–piano duets as a bonus on the CD. Ericson takes things a little more gingerly on the set of Ellington and Strayhorn tunes for Sittel, but it's an even better band – Aberg's solemn tenor, Stenson's unfailingly intelligent piano, the light, deep rhythm section. One or two too-obvious choices, but a couple of nice rarities – and the studio sound is gorgeous: try Rolf's muted work on 'Star-Crossed Lovers'.

The title-piece on *I Love You So* ... is the only Ericson composition on a set of surpassing elegance and sophistication, the leader's own gifts more than matched by the peerless Rosengren and by a hugely experienced rhythm section. 'I Had The Craziest Dream' is the most substantial single piece, a long exploration of those slightly wayward chords and offbeat melody line. Harold Ashby's 'Ashes' is an intriguing choice, not often covered, but Ericson saves his most pungent statement for 'Brownie Speaks', written by the superb Clifford B. but rarely heard to better effect than here. Ericson's clean, unfussy delivery works well in just about every mood from flat-out blowing to the most delicate and Chet Baker-like of ballads. *I Love You So* ... was intended to celebrate Ericson's return to Sweden from a long stay in Germany. Sadly, but appropriately, it has turned into his memorial.

Peter Erskine (born 1954)

DRUMS

Starting out with Stan Kenton, Erskine has become one of the most sought-after drummers in American jazz, also taking the occasional rock gig for fun. Stints with Weather Report and John Abercrombie were crucial to his developing outlook, and he has also created a considerable body of work as a composer.

*** Peter Erskine

Original Jazz Classics OJC 610 *Erskine; Randy Brecker (t, flhn); Michael Brecker (ts); Bob Mintzer (ts, bcl); Don Grolnick, Kenny Kirkland (p); Mike Mainieri (vib); Eddie Gomez (b); Don Alias (perc).* 6/82.

Erskine is (justifiably) among the most admired drummers of the contemporary American circuit: besides his formidable technique, he's gregarious enough to handle virtually any musical situation and is a thoughtful composer to boot. His first record as a leader found him in charge of a relatively straightforward post-bop session; but, with such a heavyweight gathering of studio craftsmen all on their toes, the results are impressive if a little too brawny here and there.

**(*) Big Theatre

Ah Um 004 *Erskine; Vince Mendoza (t, flhn); Peter Gordon, Jerry Peel (frhn); Don Grolnick (ky); Will Lee (b, v); Paulinho Da Costa (perc).* 86–89.

Erskine has been commissioned to do a number of theatre scores, and this is the music from three different Shakespeare plays. Harmless, pretty putterings from the workshop, with sweet synthesizer dances and other fragments, most of them no more than a moment or two long; only Will Lee's vocal on 'O Mistress Mine' (no Elizabethan, he!) is unpalatable. But it's hardly much more than a distraction, or light background music.

*** You Never Know

ECM 1497 *Erskine; John Taylor (p); Palle Danielsson (b).* 7/92.

***(*) Time Being

ECM 1532 *As above.* 11/93.

This has become a trio of considerable stature. *You Never Know* seemed disappointing, perhaps, in that Erskine himself deferred so much to Taylor: there is but a single composition by the leader, with four by Taylor and three (very good) by Vince Mendoza; this is really a piano album in which Erskine does conscientious time and duty. But though it does seem a less fully-realized record than the later discs, it's still a strong set, although it relies on Taylor's lean pastoralisms, which are always interesting, seldom compelling. *Time Being* follows the same path but is more involving. One reason is a greater sense of group identity, with the three men finding a teetering balance between their parts; another is the wider variation in material, with Staffan Linton's 'Liten Visa Till Karin' a particularly delightful choice; another is Danielsson's increasing involvement, his bass parts securing an eminent voice inside the trio. Impeccable.

***(*) As It Is

ECM 1594 *As above.* 9/95.

Ever more impeccable. Where DeJohnette never quite gives up on a drummer's muscle, even in the midst of a set of the balmiest, sweetest tunes, Erskine is prepared to lie back and stroke the gentlest rhythms out of the kit. Since Taylor and Danielsson are the kind of players who glove their intensities anyway, pieces like 'Glebe Ascending' and 'For Ruth' emerge as a distinctive blend of rural impressionism and sophisticated strength. Here also is another version of 'Touch Her Soft Lips And Part', memorably recorded on the drummer's 1991 date for Novus: maybe Erskine can't get the tune out of his mind; when the results are as gorgeous as this, who can blame him?

***(*) Juni

ECM 539726-2 *As above.* 7/97.

Diminishing returns may set in at some point, but not yet. None of these eight themes really stands out in the mind, but they're treated as vehicles for group chemistry and are arguably best heard as a single interconnected piece. Erskine continues to do a tremendous amount at the kit without once sounding intrusive or overbearing; Taylor and Danielsson pace thoughtfully around him. This kind of trio music won't be to all tastes, but it's tremendously well done.

***(*) Behind Closed Doors Vol. 1

Fuzzy Music PEPCD 005 *Erskine; Randy Brecker (t); Bob Mintzer, Joe Lovano (ts); Alan Pasqua, Kenny Werner (p); Mike Mainieri (vib); Anand Bennet (vn); John Scofield (g); Marc Johnson, Dante Pascuzzo (b); Alex Acuna, Zakir Hussain (perc); WDR Big Band.* 3/91–3/96.

Released on Erskine's own label, this is an absorbing collection of outtakes and leftovers from a number of sessions, apparently dating as far back as the date which produced his *Sweet Soul* set for BMG. Some of this is outstanding: Kenny Werner's 'Herbie Nichols', with Erskine, Lovano and Johnson, is strong enough to make one want to hear the whole date, and the worldly 'A To Z' is an offbeat but intriguing meeting with Bennet, Hussain,

Pascuzzo and Acuna. There's a couple of less impressive outings with the WDR Big Band and a typically self-effacing solo (if a drum solo can ever be self-effacing) from Peter himself.

Lars Erstrand (born 1936)

VIBRAPHONE

Born in Uppsala, Erstrand tried piano, tuba and trombone before taking up vibes after hearing Lionel Hampton. He worked with Ove Lind in the '60s, played with Benny Goodman in 1972 and has been a sideman and leader in numerous situations since.

***** Two Sides Of Lars Erstrand**

Opus 3 8302 *Erstrand; Roland Jivelid (ts); Knud Jorgenson (p); Bertil Fernqvist (g); Arne Wilhelmsson (b); Pelle Hulten (d).* 5–6/83.

***** Lars Erstrand And Four Brothers**

Opus 3 8402 *As above.* 6/84.

***** Tribute To Benny Goodman Quartet**

Opus 3 8603 *Erstrand; Ove Lind (cl); Rolf Larsson (p); Pelle Hulten (b).* 12/86.

****(*) Dream Dancing**

Opus 3 9101 *Erstrand; Kjell Ohman (org); Tommy Johnson (b); Gus Dhalberg (d).* 2/91.

***** Beautiful Friendship – The First Set**

Sittel SITCD 9204 *As above, except add Ken Peplowski (cl, ts), Frank Vignola (g).* 6/92.

***** Beautiful Friendship – The Second Set**

Sittel SITCD 9205 *As above.* 6/92.

*****(*) International All Stars – Live At Uttersberg '98**

Gemini GMCD 98 *Erstrand; Roy Williams (tb); Jan Lundgren (p); Hans Backenroth (b); Joe Ascione (d).* 8/98.

Erstrand's enduring admiration for the Lionel Hampton style – as best evidenced in their meeting on *Two Generations*, Phontastic 8807 – disguises a rather broader range of interests. *Two Sides* also touches on bebop in 'Sweet And Hot Mop' and even traces of European echoes of the MJQ in such as the Bach 'Invention In C Major'. This and the *Four Brothers* disc feature an entertaining band – Jivelid's nicely Lestorian tenor floats agreeably over the rhythm players, and Jorgenson unobtrusively steals the show on several tracks with some quick-witted improvisations. The Goodman tribute is an accurate-sounding evocation, with Lind's wonderfully supple lines twining round the vibes apparently effortlessly. The organ band with Ohman puts the pots on, at least compared with the other discs, and it encourages the vibesman to dig in more wholeheartedly than he does on some of the other records. *Dream Dancing* suffers from a few more laid-back and almost sleepwalking ballads, but the two live albums on Sittel have some genuine fire in the belly on the up-tempo tunes: 'Jim Dawgs' is almost over the top in its energies and 'Lady Be Good' personifies the swinging small combo. Peplowski is an unlikely man for a grooving organ/tenor band, but he puts his romantic hat on for the ballads and 'I Thought About You' on the first disc is a charmer. Second guest Vignola prefers strumming over single notes. But both discs have a sound-problem: the organ sounds either tinny or buzzy at different moments, and the overall mix seems rougher than it should have been. Erstrand enjoys it all, though.

The 1998 concert set from Uttersberg is a notch ahead of the other discs because everyone's on his mettle and the band is an intriguing mix of personalities. Young lions such as Lundgren and Backenroth blow alongside an enthusiastic Erstrand and the admirable Williams, who often ends up in soporific mainstream situations but here is asked a few questions and comes up swinging mightily. A great session.

Booker Ervin (1930–70)

TENOR SAXOPHONE

Originally a trombone player, Ervin taught himself saxophone while in the services and instinctively veered towards the kind of blunt, blues-soaked sound of fellow-Texans like Arnett Cobb and Illinois Jacquet. He had his big break with Mingus, who liked his raw, unaffected approach. The career was painfully short, but Booker packed a lot in. He's still missed.

*****(*) That's It**

Candid CCD 79014 *Ervin; Horace Parlan (p); George Tucker (b); Al Harewood (d).* 1/61.

Texan tenor of a rather special sort. Booker started out on trombone and carried over some of the brass instrument's broad portamento effects into his reed work. He made his name with the Charles Mingus group and has only rather slowly established a reputation as a solo recording star, despite an impressive range of records. On the Candid album, Ervin is in full, fierce voice, blending elements of Don Byas and John Coltrane into a typical Texan shout. 'Uranus' is his finest ballad performance. George Tucker's deliberate introduction to 'Booker's Blues' takes the music down into some South-western storm cellar, where it spins out its unhurried message. To avoid contractual problems, Parlan was originally credited (with rather arcane literary humour) as 'Felix Krull', but there is nothing fraudulent about his playing on the album.

***** Exultation**

Original Jazz Classics OJCCD 835 *Ervin; Frank Strozier (as); Horace Parlan (p); Butch Warren (b); Walter Perkins (d).* 6/63.

*****(*) The Song Book**

Original Jazz Classics OJC 779 *Ervin; Tommy Flanagan (p); Richard Davis (b); Alan Dawson (d).* 2/64.

*****(*) The Blues Book**

Original Jazz Classics OJC 780 *Ervin; Carmell Jones (t); Gildo Mahones (p); Richard Davis (b); Alan Dawson (d).* 6/64.

***** Groovin' High**

Original Jazz Classics OJCCD 919 *As above.* 12/63–10/64.

****** The Freedom Book**

Original Jazz Classics OJC 891 *As above, except omit Mahones, Jones; add Jaki Byard (p).* 12/63.

*****(*) The Space Book**

Original Jazz Classics OJCCD 896 *As above.* 10/64.

***** Groovin' High**

Original Jazz Classics OJCCD 919-2 *As above.* 63–64.

With the inclusion of *Groovin' High*, a further round-up of material from the prolific 'Book' sessions, most of Ervin's recordings for Prestige are available again. These are consistently excellent discs, marking the core of Ervin's output as a solo artist. Davis and Dawson are strong rhythm players of the kind the saxophonist needed, and their ability to play gently on the ballad album is as impressive as their driving beat on 'No Booze Blooze'. *The Freedom Book*, with its wider remit, is probably the best of the lot, with Byard a more robustly percussive and blues-aware pianist. *The Space Book* serves as reminder of just how concentrated these sessions were and how ideas from one take and tune inevitably spilled over into the next. Reading the 'books' in sequence is an instructive exercise, the kind of in-depth coverage a label like Prestige and producer Bob Weinstock were able to give a developing artist in those days. We can only suggest that you try the experiment yourselves or, if in doubt about the investment, plump for *The Freedom Book* first, that way avoiding some of the more formulaic bop. *Exultation* was more of a loose jam, a rather uncentred and shapeless record that never seemed like good value for money and which isn't much improved by the addition of extra tracks.

*****(*) Settin' The Pace**

Prestige PRCD 24123 *Ervin; Dexter Gordon (ts); Jaki Byard (p); Reggie Workman (b); Alan Dawson (d).* 10/65.

***** The Trance**

Original Jazz Classics OJCCD 943-2 *As above, except omit Gordon.* 10/65.

***** Heavy!!!**

Original Jazz Classics OJCCD 981-2 *As above, except add Jimmy Owens (t), Garnett Brown (tb).* 66.

The conjunction of Ervin and the not-too-dissimilar Dexter Gordon on *Settin' The Pace* makes for interesting listening, though it's Dexter who establishes the ground-rules and sets the pace for most of the tunes. 'The Trance' is included, and there is a bouncing, fiery workout on 'Dexter's Deck', the kind of theme he drank by the gallon and played by the hour.

The Trance was recorded at the same session in Munich. It's a lean and straightforward jazz album, not without its subtleties. 'Groovin' At The Jamboree' is a blowing blues, nothing fancy but powerfully argued. 'Speak Low' is handled with a gruff grace, but the real emotional weight of the album is concentrated in the title-track, a memorial to the bassist George Tucker. Appropriate that a player who would not so very long after attract such a moving tribute himself should have written such an effective threnody to a fellow-player.

Heavy!!! is an odd record. Including some of Ervin's most exploratory playing, it is also one of his most unvarnished performances. The material is decidedly left-field, opening with 'Bachafillen', including 'Bei Mir Bist Du Schön' and Byard's weirdly wonderful 'Aluminum Baby' and closing with 'Ode To Charlie Parker'. The three-horn front line is reminiscent of Coltrane's *Blue Train* session, with a similar mis-match of voices and styles, but on the whole it works.

****** Booker'N'Brass**

Pacific Jazz 7243 4 94509 2 *Ervin; Martin Banks, Johnny Coles, Ray Copland, Freddie Hubbard, Charles Tolliver, Richard Williams (t); Garnett Brown, Bennie Green (tb); Benny Powell (btb); Kenny Barron (p); Reggie Johnson (b); Lenny McBrowne (d).* 9/67.

Teddy Edwards arranged and conducted this often-overlooked large-ensemble record on which Ervin is plonked in front of a superbly crafted horn section and plays his heart out. The tracks were recorded over three days at Webster Hall in New York City. For a time a shoddy bootleg purporting to document additional material from the same session went the rounds; listening carefully to Bob Belden's remastered issue, we're convinced that this was at very best a rehearsal tape. There are still flaws here and there on the issued version, not least a clinker towards the end of his solo on 'I Left My Heart In San Francisco', but it's a set that works when it's relaxed and expressive. Alternative takes of 'LA After Dark' suggest how assiduously Teddy worked to get the band to sound loose and unfussy while hitting the beats and pitches square on.

Ervin pays tribute to Duke Ellington on 'East Dallas Special', which is rich enough to prompt a feeling that he might have gone on to become a brilliant big-band composer and performer. 'Do You Know What It Means To Miss New Orleans' and 'St Louis Blues' are unexpected inclusions, but Ervin brings a contemporary flavour to both. Good to see this Pacific release back in the catalogue. It's an ideal showcase for Ervin's still-underrated talents.

*****(*) Lament For Booker Ervin**

Enja ENJ 2054 *Ervin; Kenny Drew, Horace Parlan (p); Niels-Henning Orsted Pedersen (b); Alan Dawson (d).* 10/65, 5/75.

Parlan was always Ervin's most sympathetic sideman, and it was Parlan who spun out the 'Lament' for Ervin on the Enja, adding a sad, posthumous afterthought to a 1965 European session that rounds out the story with teasing intimations of what might have been. Towards the end of his effective life as a recording artist (there was a Blue Note session called *The In Between* a couple of years later), he sounded more and more like a musician of a previous generation guesting with younger players. There is a tremendous gravitas and wisdom to his soloing on *Lament*, and the band respond fulsomely to the challenge. It now seems a small tragedy that the record should have been released only as a memorial.

Christian Escoudé

GUITAR

Belgian guitarist with a clear line to the Reinhardt manner, although he brings a more contemporary edge to his most provocative work.

***** Gypsy Waltz**

Emarcy 838772 *Escoudé; Paul Challain, Jimmy Gourley, Frédéric Sylvestre (g); Marcel Azzola (acc); Vincent Courtois (clo); Alby Cullaz (b); Philippe Combelle (d).* 5/89.

***** Three Of A Kind**

JMS 186622 *Escoudé; Boulou Ferret, Babik Reinhardt (g).*

***** Gypsy Morning**

JMS 186 542 *Escoudé; Olivier Hutman (g); Nicholas Fiszman (b); Gene-My Truong (d); Reuben Dankas (perc).*

In the Reinhardt tradition, but sounding nothing like the master, Escoudé favours a more smoothly picked line and, on occasion and to our regret, veers close to easy listening. Tough listeners will make up their own minds. When Escoudé does attempt to swing, the results can be impressive. Since Universal have deleted several of his best records, the showing is unfortunately rather depleted at present. Much of the available material trades on 'gypsy' atmospherics, with very little jazz content and very little sense of improvisational edge. At best, the JMS albums are colourful evocations of an old style, but Escoudé doesn't seem to have grasped that behind the gracefully swept chords and light bounce there was always something much more jagged and pointed. It's the sense of risk and danger that one misses.

Dave Eshelman

TROMBONE

West Coast sessionman leading his own mainstream-modern big band.

*****(*) Deep Voices**

Sea Breeze SB 2039 *Eshelman; Rich Theurer, Bill Resch, Dave Bendigkeit, Steve Campos (t, flhn); John Russell, Mike Humphrey, Chris Braymen, Phil Zahorsky (tb); Mary Park (as, f); Rory Snyder (as, f, cl); Daniel Zinn (ts, f); Glenn Richardson (ts, f, cl, picc); Joe Henderson (ts); Bob Farrington (bs, f, cl, bcl); Smith Dobson (p); Bruce Forman (g); Seward McCain (b); Russ Tincher (d).* 10/88.

***** When Dreams Come True**

Sea Breeze SB 2045 *Eshelman; Marvin McFadden, Bill Resch, Steve Campos, Dan Buegelsen (t, flhn); John Russell, Dave Martell, Chip Tingle, Dave Gregoric (tb); Phil Zahorsky (btb); Larry Osborne (frhn); Mary Fettig, Rory Snyder, Paul Contos, Dan Zinn, Bob Farrington, Bennett Friedman, Dominic Teresi, Steve Parker (reeds); Susan Muscarella, Smith Dobson (p); Tom Volpicella (g); Dennis Cooper (vib); Seward McCain (b); Russ Tincher (d); Michael Spiro (perc).* 12/91–1/92.

Southern California has been a spawning ground for a number of interesting bands in the past 25 years, with such West Coast hold-outs as Gerald Wilson maintaining a West Coast tradition which groups like Eshelman's Jazz Garden Big Band – a San Francisco fixture through the late 1970s and '80s – amplified still further. These are unflashy, thoughtful sessions that are beautifully performed without resorting to mere slickness. A trombonist himself, Eshelman gets a fine, singing timbre out of his 'bone section, and he pitches it to scintillating effect against the trumpets and woodwinds: sample the fascinating arrangement of 'Softly As In A Morning Sunrise' on *Deep Voices*. This album takes the lead for a couple of guest spots by Joe Henderson and Bruce Forman, whose guitar solo on 'To Catch A Rainbow' is a thrilling beat-the-clock feat. Even the title-work on *Deep Voices*, which tackles the favourite Californian topic of whale-song, sidesteps bathos. If the more recent *When Dreams Come True* is a shade behind, it's only because the soloists in it make a more functional mark than their illustrious predecessors on the earlier disc. Eshelman's own writing continues to put his personal stamp on what is often a glib, overslick genre: the beautiful reshaping of 'Invitation' and 'Old Folks' is as accomplished as his amusing Latin pastiche, 'Tumbao Nuevo'.

Ellery Eskelin (born 1959)

TENOR SAXOPHONE

Raised in Baltimore, where his mother played the Hammond B-3, Eskelin has moved on to be an experienced figure in New York's new jazz of the '90s and beyond. His principal group is a current trio with Jim Black and Andrea Parkins.

****** Figure Of Speech**

Soul Note 121232-2 *Eskelin; Joe Daley (tba); Arto Tuncboyaciyan (perc).* 7/91.

*****(*) Premonition**

Prime Source 2010 *Eskelin (ts solo).* 7/92.

***** Jazz Trash**

Songlines SGL 1506-2 *Eskelin; Andrea Parkins (acc, sampler); Jim Black (d).* 10/94.

Eskelin is a tenor player who stands some way apart from the throng. The saxophonist has a querulous tone and likes to stretch phrases into elongated shapes that push against what are otherwise fairly conventional parameters: he chooses standards or simple thematic constructions to play on, and he sounds to be good at moving in and out of familiar tonalities. There are a couple of unavailable earlier records, but *Figure Of Speech* was the real breakthrough. Eskelin's purposeful avoidance of the obvious routes of improvisation – specifically, theme-and-variation structures – brings a rare sense of something new to this project in particular. Daley's tuba and Tuncboyaciyan's quiet, pattering percussion are important voices, but their essentially simple figures throw the detail and complexity of Eskelin's own playing into very sharp relief. The tunes revolve round carefully coded motifs or structural ideas without depending on them: the improvisations usually form separate entities of their own, contrasting with (rather than commenting on) the written material. This is a rare kind of freedom, negotiated with superb assurance by all three men.

The solo album, *Premonition*, might be for more rarefied tastes, but there's no doubting Eskelin's mastery of the horn or his ingenuity in dealing with the chosen material here. While there are three improvisations that deal with timbral extremes, wide intervals and rhythmic variations, the three further solos based on standard tunes are even more remarkable, culminating in a bizarre demolition of 'Besame Mucho'. Much is reminiscent here of an early David Murray solo album, particularly Eskelin's big tone and busker's vibrato, but this is less obviously experimental, more achieved.

Jazz Trash has 'interesting' writ large, but goes little further. Eskelin skirmishes with Parkins and Black rather than creating any tangible interplay and, while there are numerous intriguing moments – 'Rain' is a nicely abstruse essay on ballad form, for instance – there's a certain paucity to the textures which makes it hard to sustain over the 70-odd minutes.

***** The Sun Died**
Soul Note 121282-2 *Eskelin; Marc Ribot (g); Kenny Wolleson (d).* 2/96.

Recorded in New York but steeped in Chicago, which is where John Corbett's entertaining travelogue/sleeve-note takes us, this is some kind of tribute from a man who grew up in Baltimore. The tunes are all bar-b-q specials from the greasy cookbooks of Gene Ammons, Harold Vick, Jack McDuff – but especially Ammons, whose homage comes specifically in Eskelin's gruff, grizzled tone and buzzsaw licks. It takes two or three tracks to acclimatize, but the trio kick this material good-naturedly around until one feels at home in a distorted language. Problematically, though, the record seems to run short of steam by the end, and Ribot sounds a tad too self-conscious about it all to support Eskelin to the best. Wolleson, though, is great: how did he get those sounds on 'The People's Choice'?

***** Green Bermudas**
Eremite MTE02 *Eskelin; Andrea Parkins (sampler).* 6/96.

****** One Great Day**
hatOLOGY 502 *As above, except add Jim Black (d).* 9/96.

Green Bermudas is his most abstract disc, in which the saxophonist decorates Parkins's oddball array of sampled sounds (bland singalong pop, varispeed drums, even chunks of Eskelin himself from *Premonition*) with some of his sparsest playing. A lot of it feels like experimental bits and bites of music, at least until the two long tracks which close the record, each a testing dialogue between the two performers. *One Great Day*, though, feels like a huge advance over the trio's previous *Jazz Trash*. This time there's a palpable interplay between the trio and the duos which emerge when somebody sits out. Black's compendium of jazz, rock and free rhythms is spontaneously exciting, just as Parkins conjures unpredictable shapes out of her instrument. Eskelin himself has never sounded stronger or more figurative about the physicality of the sax: he often seems to be grabbing and twisting the sounds as they emerge.

***** Dissonant Characters**
hatOLOGY 534 *Eskelin; Han Bennink (d).* 12/98.

More or less positioned by jazz time, these friendly and generous duets are entertaining if somewhat dashed-off in feel. Bennink enjoys Eskelin's evasiveness – 'Just when you think you've got him, he gets away' – and the two of them gambit and counter-gambit with each other. Sometimes the playfulness can be a bit irritating to us bystanders, and you wish they'd settle into something; but that's hardly the point of what's a fun exercise. A bonus is the excellent sound which Peter Pfister creates for them.

*****(*) Kulak 29 & 30**
hatOLOGY 521 *Eskelin; Andrea Parkins (acc, sampler); Jim Black (d).* 10/97.

*****(*) Five Other Pieces (+2)**
hatOLOGY 533 *As above.* 10/98.

Two and a quarter hours of non-stop invention. Eskelin takes a very considered approach to the music of his trio, both in his originals (*Kulak 29 & 30*) and in the pieces he chooses to cover (*Five Other Pieces (+2)*). Parkins, who might be the key individual in the group, continues to use her sampler to, most frequently, sound like a somewhat more gothic Hammond, which might be taking Eskelin back to his salad days; either way, the music here is less self-consciously eclectic than in some of their earlier collaborations. There's a droll side to pieces such as 'Fifty Nine' and 'Visionary Of The Week' and it lightens what might otherwise be an occasionally dour palette. Courtesy of Black's lurching rhythms, the music sways rather than swings. When they tackle a piece such as the old Mahavishnu Orchestra chestnut, 'The Dance Of Maya', the result is blackly comic, without giving the impression that they're playing it for laughs. Eskelin himself refuses to settle into familiar free licks and sounds: some of his solos are huge slices of saxophone oratory, scaled down to fit the dimensions of what remains an intimate group, focusing on details. One has the impression that their records may never quite measure up to what they can communicate in a live performance. But that's an old saw anyway.

John Etheridge (born 1948)

GUITAR

A self-taught guitarist, in the '70s he became one of the most noted and technically adept British jazz-rock players with Soft Machine. Has since worked for himself and a variety of leaders, in situations ranging from duos to Nigel Kennedy's fusion orchestra.

***** Sweet Chorus: A Tribute To Stéphane Grappelli**
Dyad DY001 *Etheridge; Christian Garrick (vn); Dave Kelbie (g); Malcolm Creese (b).* 6–7/98.

The obvious point of comparison here is fellow-guitarist Martin Taylor's now well-established Spirit of Django project. Both men had the privilege of working with the late Stéphane Grappelli, but seem to have learnt rather different things. Whereas Taylor is above all a melodist, Etheridge has a more analytical, sometimes a more schematic approach to the material. Not all of it is directly associated with Grappelli, though the performances are in the right spirit and don't lack for authenticity.

It takes something special now to invest 'Nuages' with any degree of originality and conviction, but the group sounds so completely sensitized to the Hot Club aesthetic that even this tired old warhorse sounds completely fresh. The same is true of Jobim's 'How Insensitive' and the Reinhardt/Grappelli title-tune. Young Christian Garrick is a chip off the old block, though it's hard to tell where the bloodlines are strongest: his dad Michael's intense harmonic awareness or Stéphane Grappelli's transformation of the fiddle into a singing, expressive jazz voice. Malcolm Creese can do this stuff standing on his head, and his contribution is very significant on things like 'Rhythm Futur' and 'Shine', two of the strongest tracks. Others break down the basic group into trios, duos and Etheridge solos. The last of these lack something. Not technique, not expressiveness, but perhaps a basic confidence. The guitarist has, after all, worked a roundabout path from the shoe-gazing English avant-rock of Soft Machine to the much cleaner sound of this record. He pulls it off without strain, but still sounds like a man who expects to break loose at any second and crank up some feedback or smash a guitar. He's always sounded fine without stadium histrionics, and these cuts are a welcome re-introduction to his manifold talents.

Robin Eubanks (born 1959)

TROMBONE, BASS TROMBONE, KEYBOARDS

The Eubanks family is the Philadelphia equivalent of the Marsalises. Robin is a versatile, expressive player, with a distinctively flowing line which lends itself to straight jazz settings, while brother Kevin has always flirted with jazz-rock. Busy as a sideman, Eubanks has nevertheless been able to record fairly regularly on his own account, although most of it is currently deleted.

*****(*) Wake Up Call**

Sirocco SJL 1001 *Eubanks; Duane Eubanks (t); Antonio Hart (as); Eric Lewis (p); Lonnie Plaxico (b); Gene Jackson (d).* 2/97.

Wake Up Call is the first release on John Priestley's Sirocco label. It's a quiet, thoughtful record, mixing standard material – the Rodgers and Hart standard, 'You Are Too Beautiful', Lee Morgan's 'Ceora' and Bird's bebop classic 'Scrapple From The Apple' – with a group of well-crafted originals. 'Soliloquy' is the best, a gently rocking ballad which immediately sounds familiar. There are two Wayne Shorter tunes, pointing to one of Eubanks's less obvious influences. A shame that he simply fades out on 'Oriental Love Long', which somehow deserves a more considered ending. However, it does give way to the brisk and breezy title-track, which restores a measure of shape and urgency.

Eureka Brass Band

GROUP

Augmented by George Lewis for the day, this is the Eureka BB as it stood in 1951, one of the city's leading parade bands of the day.

(****) New Orleans Funeral And Parade

American Music AMCD-70 *Percy Humphrey, Willie Pajeaud, Edie Richardson (t); Albert Warner, Sunny Henry (tb); George Lewis (cl); Ruben Roddy (as); Emanuel Paul (ts); Joseph 'Red' Clark (sou); Arthur Ogle, Robert 'Son' Lewis (d).* 8/51.

Probably the most authentic example of old New Orleans music in its original environment, even if this recording of traditional funeral and parade music was recorded in a French Quarter alleyway rather than actually on the job. The regulars of the Brass Band, as they then were, were augmented by Lewis for the day, although he plays flat, and the brass are similarly wayward in their intonation. The recording is musty, the tempos ragged, the extra takes of four of the numbers come as an anticlimax and some of the dirges threaten to dissolve altogether. But many will find this a moving, rather magnificent recording – seldom has the old music sounded so affecting, the workmanlike attitude of the players lending something like nobility to it all. The remastering has actually been done very well, considering the source material, and the superb documentation – by Alden Ashforth, the then-teenage enthusiast who recorded the session – adds to the undeniable mystique.

European Music Orchestra

GROUP

A featured setting for Kenny Wheeler, surrounded by a crack team of contemporary Italians.

***** Featuring Kenny Wheeler**

Soul Note 121299 *Kenny Wheeler, Andrea Bellotti, Gianluca Carallo, Yllich Fenzi, Maurizio Scamparin (t, flhn); Alessandro Azzolini, Toni Constantini, Stefano Giuliani (tb); Moreno Milanetto (btb); Guido Bombardieri (as, ss); Rosarita Crisafi (as); Claudio Fasoli (ts, ss); Marco Strano, Nicholas Camardi (ts); Gianluca Carollo (vib); Paolo Birro, Sergio Pietruschi (p); Ermanno M Signorelli (g); Stefano Liudello (b); Enzo Carpentieri, Aldo Romano (d); Luca Palmarin (perc).* 1/94.

Though the soloist is kept in fairly constant focus throughout this absorbing set, the section work by some of Italy's finest contemporary players is equally satisfying and provides Wheeler with the perfect setting for his floating, ethereal lines. There isn't as much straightforward drive and energy as one might look for in an American band, but on its own terms the EMO (note no reference to jazz, which may be telling) is spot-on, and the version of Wheeler's favourite 'W.W.' could hardly be bettered.

Bill Evans (1929–80)

PIANO

Evans's first notable gig was with the Tony Scott group, in 1956, and his most important early liaison was with Miles Davis, with whom he recorded the Kind Of Blue album. Thereafter he worked more or less continuously in the trio format for the rest of his life, although there are solo sessions, records with singers and a few with horns or orchestral arrangements. Prolific in the studio and in being recorded in concert, Evans's enormous influence may have happened in two ways: his records were widely disseminated and listened to by musicians, and their attractive surface also appealed to an audience seeking sophisticated but easy-going new jazz. He suggested to more than one generation of pianists a way of dealing with modality, and his harmonic thinking showed a subtle way out of the dead-end of bebop changes. A difficult personal life was exacerbated by his dependence on various drugs, which ultimately ruined his health and led to an early death.

***** New Jazz Conceptions**

Original Jazz Classics OJC 035 *Evans; Teddy Kotick (b); Paul Motian (d).* 9/56.

Evans's discography is extensive anyway, but he is in such demand by fans and collectors that almost everything he did is now available on CD again: the kind of accolade very few of the major artists in this book can claim. Taken altogether, it is an incredible body of work, flawed and even repetitive though much of it may be, and it is particularly rewarding to work through it chronologically. Evans began modestly enough with a fine, comfortable set of boppish trio performances which created little stir at the time (the record sold some 800 copies over the course of one year).

Orrin Keepnews, the producer, was convinced he should record Evans by hearing a demo tape played over the telephone, and the pianist's distinctive touch and lovely tone are already apparent: he makes bop material such as Tadd Dameron's 'Our Delight' into comprehensive structures, and the three tiny solos – including the very first 'Waltz For Debby', his most renowned original – hint at what was to come. But it's clearly a talent in its early stages.

****** Everybody Digs Bill Evans**

Original Jazz Classics OJC 068 *Evans; Sam Jones (b); Philly Joe Jones (d).* 12/58.

Perennially reluctant, busy with the Miles Davis group, Evans didn't record as a leader for another two years. This superb record was worth the wait, though. Jones and Jones back him with enough spirit to bring out his most energetic delivery, and the assertiveness he'd found with Davis lent Evans an assurance that makes 'Night And Day' and 'Oleo' into driving performances. But 'Peace Piece', a translucent reshaping of the opening phrases of 'Some Other Time', which Evans came up with in the studio, is one of his most affecting soliloquies, and the ballad reading of 'Young And Foolish' makes an almost astonishing contrast to the up-tempo pieces. 'Some Other Time', which was omitted from the original LP, is present on the CD version of the reissue.

****** Portrait In Jazz**

Original Jazz Classics OJC 088 *Evans; Scott LaFaro (b); Paul Motian (d).* 12/59.

****** Explorations**

Original Jazz Classics OJC 037 *As above.* 2/61.

♛ ** Sunday At The Village Vanguard**

Original Jazz Classics OJC 140 *As above.* 6/61.

♛ ** Waltz For Debby**

Original Jazz Classics OJC 210 *As above.* 6/61.

****** At The Village Vanguard**

Riverside 60-017 *As above.* 6/61.

Evans was having trouble finding good bassists, but LaFaro's arrival precipitated the advent of one of the finest piano trios jazz has ever documented. The bassist's melodic sensitivity and insinuating sound flowed between Evans and Motian like water and, while notions of group empathy have sometimes been exaggerated in discussion of this music – it was still very much directed by Evans himself – the playing of the three men is so sympathetic that it set a universal standard for the piano–bass–drums set-up which has persisted to this day. Both *Portrait In Jazz* and *Explorations* have their small imperfections: there's an occasional brittleness in the latter, possibly a result of the quarrel which LaFaro and Evans had had just before the session, and the recording of both does less justice to LaFaro's tone and delivery than it might. But 'Autumn Leaves', 'Blue In Green', 'Beautiful Love' and the transformation of John Carisi's 'Israel' to the trio format are as sublimely integrated and inspiring as this kind of jazz can be. Yet the two records culled from a day's work at the Village Vanguard are even finer. Evans's own playing is elevated by the immediacy of the occasion: his contributions seem all of a piece, lines spreading through and across the melodies and harmonies of the tune, pointing the way towards modality yet retaining the singing, rapturous qualities which the pianist heard in his material (Evans retained a relatively small repertoire of favourite pieces throughout his career). All the Vanguard music is informed by an extra sense of discovery, as if the musicians were suddenly aware of what they were on to and were celebrating the achievement. They didn't have much time: LaFaro was killed in a car accident ten days later. There are extra tracks and alternative takes on the CD editions of all the above and, because the trio finally left very little music behind them, they are indispensable. *At The Village Vanguard* offers nothing new, simply ten tracks culled from the other two records – a nice single-disc representation, but the others must be heard in their entirety. This is music which, more than most in the jazz literature, continues to provoke marvel and endless study by listeners and musicians alike.

*****(*) Moon Beams**

Original Jazz Classics OJC 434 *Evans; Chuck Israels (b); Paul Motian (d).* 5–6/62.

****** How My Heart Sings!**

Original Jazz Classics OJC 369 *As above.* 5–6/62.

Chuck Israels replaced LaFaro, although Evans was at first so upset by the bassist's death that he stopped playing for a while. After some months of work, the pianist felt they were ready to record, and Keepnews, who'd wanted to get an all-ballad album out of Evans, cut both the above discs at the same sessions, alternating slow and up-tempo pieces and saving the ballads for *Moon Beams*. There are five Evans originals – 'Very Early' and 'Re: Person I Knew' on *Moon Beams*, 'Walking Up', 'Show-Type Tune' and '34 Skidoo' on *How My Heart Sings!* – and the slightly unfocused readings by the trio can be accounted for by the fact that the pianist revealed them to the others only at the dates. But this was otherwise a superb continuation of Evans's work. Israels plays pushy, hard-bitten lines and meshes very capably with Motian, and it spurs Evans into a sometimes pugnacious mood: 'Summertime' numbers among the more dramatic revisions of this standard, and 'In Your Own Sweet Way', present on the CD of *How My Heart Sings!* in two different takes, negotiates Brubeck's theme with a hint of asperity. Not that the ballads are wispy: 'Stairway To The Stars', for instance, is a model of firm melodic variation.

****** Undercurrent**

Blue Note 790538-2 *Evans; Jim Hall (g).* 4–5/62.

***** Interplay**

Original Jazz Classics OJC 308 *Evans; Freddie Hubbard (t); Jim Hall (g); Percy Heath (b); Philly Joe Jones (d).* 7/62.

Temperamentally, Evans and Hall hit it off perfectly in the studios. Their duet album is a masterpiece of quiet shadings, drifting melancholy and – perhaps surprisingly – hard swinging, the latter quality emerging on a particularly full-blooded 'I'm Getting Sentimental Over You'. But it's the nearly hallucinatory ballads, 'Dream Gypsy' and 'Romain', which stick in the mind, where harp-like tones and gently fingered refrains establish a rare climate of introspection. The *Interplay* session, organized by Keepnews to keep Evans in funds, is comparatively desultory, but Hubbard plays rather well, and 'When You Wish Upon A Star' retains its powdery charm.

*****(*) At Shelly's Manne Hole**
Original Jazz Classics OJC 263 *Evans; Chuck Israels (b); Larry Bunker (d).* 5/63.

An understated yet tremendously intense 'Round Midnight' is among the highlights of this considerable club recording. Bunker and Israels were again given sight of some of the material only on the night of the recording, and their concentration adds to the tense lyricism which Evans was spinning out at the piano. A couple of rare excursions into the major blues, 'Swedish Pastry' and 'Blues in F/Five', complete a very strong programme, and the recording is particularly fine and well balanced.

****** The Solo Sessions Vol. 1**
Milestone M 9170 *Evans.* 1/63.

*****(*) The Solo Sessions Vol. 2**
Milestone M 9195 *Evans.* 1/63.

These solo records were both made on the same evening, as part of a contract-fulfilling exercise, and they lay unreleased for over 20 years. The music finds Evans at his most exposed (the tunes include 'Why Was I Born?' and 'What Kind Of Fool Am I?'), and there's an underlying tone of aggressive disquiet – which has to be set against some deliriously lyrical passages. Two medleys, of 'My Favourite Things/Easy To Love/Baubles, Bangles And Beads' and 'Love Theme From Spartacus/Nardis', are particularly revealing (both are on *Volume 1*) and there's a reading of 'Ornithology' on the second disc which sounds as vital and energized as anything that Evans recorded for Riverside.

****** The Complete Riverside Recordings**
Riverside 018 12CD *Personnel collected from all above-listed OJC records.* 56–63.

This huge collection is certainly a breathtaking monument to Evans's art, and it would merit coronation if the individual albums weren't so easily available. It includes all the music listed on the OJC albums above, as well as the two solo discs on Milestone, which originally made their first appearance in this boxed set.

*****(*) Empathy / A Simple Matter Of Conviction**
Verve 837757-2 *Evans; Monty Budwig, Eddie Gomez (b); Shelly Manne (d).* 8/62–10/66.

Although Budwig is excellent and Gomez, making his debut with Evans, is superb, it's the partnership with Manne which is the most interesting thing about these records. Evans seldom responded to a hard-driving drummer – a meeting with Tony Oxley in the 1970s was fairly disastrous – but Manne's canny momentum creates sparks of interplay without disturbing the pianist's equilibrium. That said, the high spontaneity of these sessions sometimes misses the clarity of thought which is at the core of Evans's music, and although there's a flashing ingenuity in their playing on, say, 'With A Song In My Heart' with its mischievous coda, the more considered strengths of the pianist's regular trios are finally more satisfying. But Evans fans mustn't miss it.

*****(*) Conversations With Myself**
Verve 521409-2 *Evans (p solo).* 1–2/63.

*****(*) Trio '64**
Verve 539058-2 *Evans; Gary Peacock (b); Paul Motian (d).* 12/63.

These discs show how much music Evans was coming up with in this period: an entire album of overdubbed three-way piano, something only Tristano had tried before, and another new trio taking on a striking set of fresh material. *Conversations* has aroused sometimes fierce views both for and against its approach, but in an age where overdubbing is more or less the norm in record-making, its musicality is more important. Carefully graded, each line sifted against the others, this is occasionally too studied a record, and the follow-up *Further Conversations With Myself* is arguably more graciously realized; but 'Theme From Spartacus' and a fine-grained 'Round Midnight' are pieces where Evans seems to gaze at his own work and find it compelling. The trio record features Peacock's only official appearance with Evans, and the empathy is stunningly adventurous: on 'Little Lulu', for instance, the reach of the bassist's lines and his almost flamenco-like rhythms score brilliant points against the pianist's own energetic choruses. Motian, for once, seems subdued. Both of these are now available in Verve's Master Edition series, and *Trio '64* has been expanded to include seven alternatives and one 'new' piece, 'My Heart Stood Still'.

***** Trio '65**
Verve 519808-2 *Evans; Chuck Israels (b); Larry Bunker (d).* 2/65.

***** Bill Evans Trio With Symphony Orchestra**
Verve 821983-2 *Evans; Chuck Israels (b); Larry Bunker, Grady Tate (d); strings, directed by Claus Ogerman.* 9–12/65.

Trio '65 documents a good rather than a great edition of the trio on a middling day in the studios, although it still sounds better than most piano-trio dates. The tempos sound rather brusque – this is a good one to play to people who still think Evans was pure marshmallow – and some of the tracks seem to be curtly dismissed, but there is still a good 'Round Midnight' and a fine 'If You Could See Me Now'. The album with arrangements by Claus Ogerman is very pretty, if hardly a milestone in jazz meets the symphony. Ogerman's charts are sweetly romantic rather than overbearing, and this gives the trio some space to work in; if the confections which the arranger makes out of Bach, Chopin, Fauré and Granados are scarcely challenging, he manages to make it sound a plausible backdrop to the pianist's musings, and 'Time Remembered' and 'My Bells' sound fine, too.

*****(*) At Town Hall**
Verve 831271-2 *Evans; Chuck Israels (b); Arnold Wise (d).* 2/66.

*****(*) Intermodulation**
Verve 833771-2 *Evans; Jim Hall (g).* 66.

*****(*) Further Conversations With Myself**
Verve 559832-2 *Evans (p solo).* 8/67.

*****(*) At The Montreux Jazz Festival**
Verve 827844-2 *Evans; Eddie Gomez (b); Jack DeJohnette (d).* 6/68.

***** Alone**
Verve 833801-2 *Evans (p solo).* 9–10/68.

***** The Best Of Bill Evans On Verve**
Verve 527906-2 *As above Verve discs.* 5/63–12/69.

Evans's period with Verve went on to produce two further in-concert albums and his first officially released solo record, aside from the multi-tracked albums. *At Town Hall* includes some exquisite playing on his favourite standards, together with the long 'Solo – In Memory Of His Father', a requiem that includes 'Turn Out The Stars'. Wise makes his only appearance in the Evans canon and keeps out of the way. The Montreux disc was a Grammy winner in its day and is another one-time-only appearance for DeJohnette – hardly the ideal man for the position – but, along with fellow recruit Gomez, he pushes Evans into his most tigerish form. 'Nardis' and 'A Sleepin' Bee' sound particularly strong. Much of the solo album's music sounds low-voltage, even for Evans, but the very long (over 14 minutes) exploration of 'Never Let Me Go' investigates what would become Keith Jarrett territory, with both prowess and resource to spare. The CD includes alternative takes of three of the pieces. *Intermodulation* is maybe not quite as perfect as was *Undercurrent*, their earlier disc; the choice of material encourages a slightly less ethereal feel. But this is still Evans and Hall together, which ought to be commendation enough.

Further Conversations With Myself repeats the trick of his earlier overdubbed solo set and, though this one is far less well known, we prefer it for its more complete picture of Evans as a soloist, talking to himself. 'Emily' is played almost friskily; 'The Shadow Of Your Smile' is meticulously prepared from its simple beginnings. Sometimes he takes a wrong turning, but it remains a rather endearing kind of record. The sound, though, is still not very kind, even in this Verve Master Edition.

The Best Of Bill Evans On Verve is a taster for the complete edition of 18 CDs listed below. This picks a dozen tracks from 12 albums to make a very playable sampler. If one returns to his Riverside albums as the best of Evans, the Verve sequence has plenty of treasure, usefully dipped into here.

*****(*) The Complete Bill Evans On Verve**
Verve 527953-2 18CD *Evans; Don Elliott (mel, vib, perc); Phil Woods (cl); Stan Getz (ts); Jeremy Steig (f); Sam Brown, Jim Hall (g); Monty Budwig, Eddie Gomez, Chuck Israels, Ron Carter, Richard Davis, Gary Peacock, Ernie Furtado (b); Shelly Manne, Ed Shaughnessy, Elvin Jones, Philly Joe Jones, Larry Bunker, Grady Tate, Arnold Wise, Jack DeJohnette, Marty Morell, Al Beldini (d); Monica Zetterlund (v); strings and brass.* 7/57–3/70.

The size and packaging of this set, one of the biggest single-artist reissues of all time, has excited much comment (it comes in a slowly oxidizing metal container, which one has to get used to, since it's no straightfoward matter getting the CDs out). What, though, of the music? It collects all of Evans's sessions for Verve, with a lot of previously unheard material included, starting with an obscure set from the 1957 Newport Festival with Don Elliott (dispensable) and going as far as Mickey Leonard's arrangements for strings and Evans's electric piano (uneventful). In between are all the Verve discs discussed above, and much else.

The most significant prize is surely the full collection of tracks by Evans with Gomez and Philly Joe Jones from the Village Vanguard in August 1967. The original double-LP of 14 tracks is expanded to an astonishing 46 tunes on three discs. Evans liked to play with Jones, whom he had worked with in the Miles Davis band years before, and the drummer's prodding, restless manner brought out a rare kind of intensity in the pianist. Instead of his collected self, there's a more improvisatory – almost daredevil – manner at certain moments which few other performers seemed to find in him. For these items alone the set is valuable.

The session with Monica Zetterlund is a favourite of ours, although one has to have a certain sympathy with this idiosyncratic singer, and as graciously as Evans plays he could hardly have seen this as an essential part of his work. Most of the remaining material is discussed above, although it's good to have also *Further Conversations With Myself*, his second overdubbed-solo album, and the often-forgotten album with Gary McFarland arrangements from 1963. Several sessions have extra takes and the final couple of discs offer various offcuts, including a complete deconstruction of the MGM album, *From Left To Right*, with numerous alternatives. Aside from the material with Jones, which will surely be released separately in the fullness of time, there's actually little here to truly excite any re-evaluation, although the remastered sound seems very well handled throughout. The accompanying booklet (more like a book) includes all documentation and several interviews. It is a tempting package – although, good as the best of it is, there is enough middling material to warrant our withholding a top recommendation. Evans scholars will want it anyway; the rest of us may be more inclined to pull the individual discs off the shelf.

***** From Left To Right**
Verve 557451-2 *Evans; Sam Brown (g); Eddie Gomez (b); Marty Morell (d); orchestra.* 69–70.

Originally released on MGM, this is one of Evans's most obscure records (though it also appears in the set listed above). Evans plays acoustic and electric pianos, there are some not especially edifying arrangements by Mickey Leonard, and there's a hint of Creed Taylor in the overall feel. For completists only.

***** You're Gonna Hear From Me**
Milestone 9164 *Evans; Eddie Gomez (b); Marty Morell (d).* 11/69.

***** Montreux II**
Columbia 481264-2 *As above.* 6/70.

****(*) The Bill Evans Album**
Columbia CK 30855/480989-2 *As above.* 5/71.

***** The Tokyo Concert**
Original Jazz Classics OJC 345 *As above.* 1/73.

***** Live In Tokyo**
Columbia 481265-2 *As above.* 1/73.

****(*) Live In Europe Vol. I**
EPM FDC 5712 *As above.* 74.

****(*) Live In Europe Vol. II**
EPM FDC 5713 *As above.* 74.

Some of the steam had gone out of Evans's career on record at this point, after the astonishing consistency of his first ten years in the studio. Gomez, a great technician, has an immediately identifiable 'soulful' sound which tends to colour his lines a mite too highly: his interplay with the leader assumes a routine excellence which Morell, a fine if self-effacing drummer, tends to play alongside rather than inside; and bass and piano take more conspicuously solo turns rather than seeking out the three-way interplay of the earlier trios. On their own terms, the individual albums are still usually very good and highly enjoyable. *You're Gonna Hear From Me*, cut live at Copenhagen's Montmartre, is a lively date, with 'Waltz For Debby' taken at possibly its fastest-ever tempo, a surprisingly light-hearted 'Round Midnight' and an excellent 'Nardis' in a generally bountiful session. Evans dabbles with a little electric piano on *Album*, but both Japanese concerts are straight-ahead and flow with ideas: 'Up With The Lark' on the OJC is a marvellous piece, and the Columbia version is almost as good. The problem with the two EPM discs seems to be an erratic speed level: many of the tracks sound as if they're playing back too fast. *The Bill Evans Album* was always a weak note in the Evans discography and the latest edition sounds no better. *Montreux II* is fine on its own terms, but this is a very familiar programme and nothing especially stands out.

***** The Secret Sessions**

Milestone 4421-2 8CD *Evans; Teddy Kotick, Eddie Gomez (b); Arnie Wise, Philly Joe Jones, Jack DeJohnette, John Dentz, Marty Morell, Eliot Zigmund (d).* 3/66–1/75.

Evans was the kind of musician to create disciples in listeners as well as musicians, and there was none more diligent than Mike Harris, who lugged in a semi-portable tape-machine to the Village Vanguard over a period of ten years to catch Evans at work. The tapes have been cleaned up by Milestone and feature various incarnations of the trio over a decade of jazz. Aside from the earliest date, where Teddy Kotick does a good job, it's Eddie Gomez all the way, with six different drummers. The sessions with Philly Joe Jones are especially interesting, although Verve's big box elicits much similar material in better sound. It's the fidelity which is the real problem with these eight discs. Perhaps it's better than most amateur recordings, but not much: the bass booms (and always seems over-prominent), the crowd chatters, and finely though Evans often plays, he's never done justice by the equipment and one feels that only the most hungry of admirers won't be disappointed. Still, besides the obvious linchpins of the Evans repertoire, there are a number of tunes he seldom looked at and, for all the dustiness of the sound, Milestone have clearly done their best to create a singular document – which this is.

***** Symbiosis**

MPS 523381-2 *Evans; orchestra directed by Claus Ogerman.* 2/74.

Another jazz-meets-the-classics project, even if the parties involved would demur at the tag. Ogerman's two-movement orchestration creates a backdrop that is shakily kaleidoscopic: it's not as if this is a display of range, more a ragbag of many elements. Evans seems interested enough, though he plays a particularly reverberant electric piano for much of the piece, which tends to date the whole enterprise. An interesting diversion, but a footnote in the Evans discography.

***** Since We Met**

Original Jazz Classics OJC 622 *Evans; Eddie Gomez (b); Marty Morell (d).* 1/74.

***** Re: Person I Knew**

Original Jazz Classics OJC 749 *As above.* 1/74.

***** Jazzhouse**

Milestone M 9151 *As above.* 74.

***** Blue In Green**

Milestone M 9185 *As above.* 74.

***** Intuition**

Original Jazz Classics OJC 470 *As above, except omit Morell.* 11/74.

***** Montreux III**

Original Jazz Classics OJC 644 *As above.* 7/75.

Evans signed to Fantasy (the source of the OJC material listed above) and with his assiduous producer, Helen Keane, created a big body of work that lasted through the 1970s. *Since We Met* and *Re: Person I Knew* both come from a single Village Vanguard engagement and, though Gomez and Morell don't erode memories of LaFaro and Motian, the music speaks with as much eloquence as this trio could muster. *Jazzhouse* and *Blue In Green* are more recent 'discoveries' of Evans concerts, which tell us nothing new about him and must be considered for collectors only, even if the playing is mostly impeccable. Consistency had become Evans's long suit, and he seemed content to tinker endlessly with his favourite pieces, disclosing little beyond the beauty of his touch, which by now was one of the most admired and imitated methods in piano jazz. The two albums with Gomez as sole partner explore a wider range of material – *Montreux III* is a particularly well-turned concert set – but one still misses the extra impetus of a drummer.

*****(*) Alone (Again)**

Original Jazz Classics OJC 795 *Evans (p solo).* 12/75.

***** Crosscurrents**

Original Jazz Classics OJC 718 *Evans; Lee Konitz (as); Warne Marsh (ts); Eddie Gomez (b); Eliot Zigmund (d).* 2–3/77.

****(*) Quintessence**

Original Jazz Classics OJC 698 *Evans; Harold Land (ts); Kenny Burrell (g); Ray Brown (b); Philly Joe Jones (d).* 5/76.

***** I Will Say Goodbye**

Original Jazz Classics OJC 761 *Evans; Eddie Gomez (b); Eliot Zigmund (d).* 5/79.

***** Eloquence**

Original Jazz Classics OJC 814 *Evans; Eddie Gomez (b).* 11/73–12/75.

***** The Complete Fantasy Recordings**

Fantasy 1012 9CD *As all Fantasy/OJC sessions listed above.* 73–79.

The Fantasy material isn't on a par with the magnificent complete Riverside set, but it has many rewards and includes two bonuses: an interview with Marian McPartland from her *Piano Jazz* radio series, and a 1976 date in Paris. A few recent reissues have brought some other Fantasy sessions back into general circulation. *Crosscurrents* is another interesting if ultimately unremarkable meeting with two great horn players; *I Will Say Goodbye* finds the trio tackling some relatively unfamiliar material in 'A House Is Not A Home', 'Quiet Light' and 'Seascape'. But it's good to have the neglected *Alone (Again)* as a separate release. This features some very fine Evans on five favourite standards, with a long and wide-ranging exploration of 'People' as the highlight. *Quintessence* provided some answer as to what Evans would have done if he'd recorded more frequently with a bigger group in his later years: he would have made an amiable and not especially interesting Evans-plus-horns date. *Eloquence* is a mixture of solos and duets with Eddie Gomez, some studio, some live. Losing the drummer doesn't do anything special for the situation, but two ballads, 'In A Sentimental Mood' and 'But Beautiful', are notably effective.

****** The Tony Bennett / Bill Evans Album**

Original Jazz Classics OJC 439 *Evans; Tony Bennett (v).* 6/75.

Pairing Evans with Tony Bennett was an inspired idea that pays off in a session which has an illustrious kind of after-hours feel to it. Bennett, as big-hearted as always, lives out the helpless-Romeo lyrics of such as 'When In Rome', and sounds filled with wonder when working through a gorgeous 'The Touch Of Your Lips'. He also sings what's surely the definitive vocal version of 'Waltz For Debby', where the corn of Gene Lees's lyric suddenly sounds entirely right. Evans plays deferentially but creates some lovely accompaniments and seems to read every mood with complete accuracy.

***** New Conversations**

Warner Bros 7559-27505-2 *Evans (p solo).* 1–2/78.

***** Affinity**

Warner Bros 7599-27387-2 *Evans; Larry Schneider (ss, ts, f); Toots Thielemans (hca); Marc Johnson (b); Eliot Zigmund (d).* 10–11/78.

***** We Will Meet Again**

Warner Bros 7599-27504-2 *Evans; Tom Harrell (t); Larry Schneider (ts, ss, f); Marc Johnson (b); Joe LaBarbera (d).* 8/79.

*****(*) The Paris Concert Edition One**

Warner Bros 7559-60311-2 *As above, except omit Harrell and Schneider.* 11/79.

*****(*) The Paris Concert Edition Two**

Warner Bros 7599-60311-2 *As above.* 11/79.

Evans's Warners albums are comparatively neglected and little talked-of. *Affinity*, co-credited with Toots Thielemans, was the first album to feature his final bassist, Marc Johnson, and some of the music is heartbreakingly lovely – although Thielemans, when tuned in to the typical Evans wavelength, can often sound helplessly doleful on his horn. There are some tunes which Evans was trying out as new elements of his set, such as Paul Simon's 'I Do It For Your Love', and even Schneider contributes 'Tomato Kiss'. Somehow it feels a bit stiff and produced, though, and 'The Other Side Of Midnight' and one or two others come out sounding like mere mood music. *We Will Meet Again*, in dedication to Bill's late brother, Harry Evans, brings in Harrell and LaBarbera. Once one gets past the idea that a two-horns-plus-rhythm quintet is simply not Evans's natural environment at this point, the playing seems fine but, despite some more new tunes and Harrell's flowing solos, the music lacks focus – or particularity, even – which is rather discouraging.

New Conversations restores the multiple-overdubbing technique which Evans had tackled during his Verve years. He uses acoustic and electric pianos for some extra tonal variation, and the results are very pleasing rather than compelling. 'Remembering The Rain', for instance, is characteristically beautiful in the pianistic touch, but more of a pretty-pastel piece than anything.

The live albums are both from the same Paris concert. Though the trio was still quite new, it was already forging new momentum out of the pianist's favourite pieces, and there are some very fine things here: 'Re: Person I Knew', 'Laurie' and 'Quiet Now' are good enough to stand with the best of his many versions of these, and he has another go at 'I did It For Your Love' on the first record. Sound is mostly good, though Johnson's bass – less 'pneumatic' than Gomez – isn't quite focused in the mix.

***** Half Moon Bay**

Milestone 9282-2 *Evans; Eddie Gomez (b); Mary Morell (d).* 11/73.

***** Homecoming**

Milestone 9291-2 *Evans; Marc Johnson (b); Joe LaBarbera (d).* 11/79.

In the search for fresh and unheard Evans, Milestone have uncovered these two dates. *Half Moon Bay* was done at a favourite little beach-house club in California and finds the 1973 trio in rare form, the usual set but played with particular intensity. *Homecoming* is from the days of the final trio and was done at Bill's old alma mater in Hammond, Louisiana – hence the title. Again, the music is played with considerable gutsiness – hear the almost thunderous ending to 'But Beautiful' – and is personalized by the pianist's many spoken introductions, a rarity in the Evans discography. We award only moderate ratings, though, since each is an amateur recording and well short of the accustomed standard: admirers will certainly want to hear them, but casual followers may be disappointed.

***** Letter To Evan**

Dreyfus 191064-2 *Evans; Marc Johnson (b); Joe LaBarbera (d).* 7/80.

*****(*) The Brilliant**

Timeless CDSJP 329 *As above.* 8–9/80.

*****(*) Consecration 1**

Timeless SJP 331 *As above.* 8–9/80.

*****(*) Consecration 2**

Timeless SJP 332 *As above.* 8–9/80.

Evans was still being almost obsessively documented by concert microphones. Several months with Philly Joe Jones at the drums seem to have gone undocumented, but Johnson and LaBarbera eventually proved to be a challenging team which propelled the pianist through a remarkable burst of creativity. He compared this group to his original band with LaFaro and Motian, and there's certainly a sense of an evolving music, with the three men playing as a close-knit ensemble and Evans stretching out in improvisations which were roaming much more freely than before. Even long solos had hitherto kept a relatively tight hold of the thematic material underpinning them but, in all the concerts which these discs cover, Evans sounds unencumbered by frameworks, and such pieces as 'Letter To Evan' (*The Brilliant*) are as close to clear freedom as he ever came. The Timeless records all come from an engagement at San Francisco's Keystone Korner and chart a very high level of playing, with Johnson especially challenging memories of the many great bassmen who had worked with Evans. Fine recording. They have now also been combined as a three-disc box (Timeless SJP 009). *Letter To Evan* is marred by confused sound, but there's still some very committed and powerful music here.

*****(*) Turn Out The Stars**

Warner Bros 45925-2 6CD *Evans; Marc Johnson (b); Joe LaBarbera (d).* 6/80.

Released at last, here is the final Evans group in an extended series of performances, again from a Village Vanguard residency. It is in many ways a great set of performances. Evans was clearly prepared to try new things with this group, and although one sometimes feels the music is struggling rather aimlessly with form, as if reluctant to seek a freedom that would ultimately be more confining, the group feels vital in a way that Evans's trios hadn't touched on in some time. There are the expected tunes, present and correct, and in the best of them – 'Nardis', for instance – Evans, Johnson and LaBarbera find genuine new ground in repertoire that the pianist might otherwise have done to death.

The only drawback may be a sense of loss which long-time Evans admirers might feel is palpable in the music. The seraphic glow in Evans's early and middle-period is sometimes glimpsed here, but seldom; for all the ingenuities on show, some of the songlike beauty which enlightens his most affecting music has vanished. In its place is a certain heaviness of hand and probably heart. Johnson and LaBarbera, team players of a different disposition, in some ways seem more at home in these expanded settings than Evans does. Either way, devotees will want to decide for themselves.

Bill Evans (born 1958)

TENOR AND SOPRANO SAXOPHONES

Studied in North Texas and New Jersey, then with Dave Liebman, who recommended him to Miles Davis. With Davis, 1980–84, then worked with his own groups and in various fusion-orientated situations.

****(*) Petite Blonde**

Lipstick 89012-2 *Evans; Mitch Forman (ky); Chuck Loeb (g); Victor Bailey (b); Dennis Chambers (d).* 7/92.

****(*) Push**

Lipstick 89022-2 *Evans; Chris Botti, Dave Stahl (t); Mike Davis, Keith O'Quinn, Conrad Herwig (tb); Gary Smulyan (bs); Clifford Carter, Philippe Saisse (ky); Bruce Hornsby (p); Chuck Loeb, Jeff Glub, Nick Moroch (g); Christian Minh Doky, Marcus Miller (b); Billy Ward, Max Risenhoover (d); voices.* 93.

****(*) Live In Europe**

Lipstick 89029-2 *Evans; Charles Blenzig, Jon Werking (ky); Gary Poulson, Adam Rogers (g); Ron Jenkins (b); Scooter Warner (d); K.C Flight, Marc Allison (v).* 94.

***** Escape**

Escapade ESC 03650-2 *Evans; Wallace Roney (t); Jim Beard (ky); Lee Ritenour, Jon Herington, Gary Poulson, Nick Moroch (g); Victor Bailey, Marcus Miller, Mark Egan, Ron Jenkins (b); Billy Kilson, Steve Ferrone (d); Manolo Badrena (perc); MC 900 Ft Jesus, Mark Ledford, Ahmed Best (v).* 12/95–1/96.

Evans got off to a high-profile start with his work in the Miles Davis band of the early 1980s. His star has remained reasonably bright since then, although a stint with Blue Note led him nowhere in particular and his group records for Jazz City and Lipstick have been mixed successes. He seems to enjoy the fusion-blowing context while wishing to keep at least one foot in a bop-pish environment. *Petite Blonde* is a typically hard-hitting concert set. For sheer beef the opening 'Two Price Hit' takes some beating and, with the redoubtable Chambers on board, it's obvious that the session is going to turn into a slugging match. Nothing else on the record packs quite such a wallop, but even at cruising speed the band sound hard. Effective, but only for those who like a lot of testosterone. Evans's touring band, Push, are responsible for the next two, though *Push*, the studio set, is more a collection of studio exercises – shots of impressionism such as 'Nightwing' and 'Road To Run' come off well, but the more self-consciously funky music is less impressive. Much the same applies to the tour record, which comes unstuck when K.C. Flight starts rapping and Evans is reduced to the role of accompanist. This backs off from the sheer wallop of *Petite Blonde*, but there isn't that much in its place.

Jim Beard's artful production enhances *Escape*, which is typical of the new breed of art-jazz that's starting to come out of what used to be straightahead fusion dates. Beard adds lots of touches to the mix, cocooning Evans and the other soloists in glittering keyboard and percussion surrounds. A piece such as 'Coravilas' is pure studio dreamtime, and Evans decorates the environment very prettily. That said, it's difficult to hear this as either deep or enduring.

***** Modern Days And Nights**

Double-Time DTRCD-120 *Evans; Andy LaVerne (p); John Patitucci (b); Steve Davis (d).* 11/96.

***** Starfish And The Moon**

Escapade 03654-2 *Evans; Jim Beard, Henry Hey (ky); Adam Rogers (g, mand); Jon Herington (g, b); James Genus (b); Vinnie Colaiuta (d); Arto Tuncboyaciyan (perc, v); David Blamires, Caroline Leonhart (v).* 97.

Modern Days And Nights, a slow-burning set of Cole Porter pieces, is by a co-operative group where LaVerne seems to have taken most of the arranging decisions. Some of the tunes are clever in the slightly exasperating way that LaVerne often enjoys, melodies reharmonized and rhythms destabilized as if to make sure that players of this accomplishment aren't just going over standards they know backwards. The environment suits Evans, who finds his most plaintive tone for 'Everytime We Say Goodbye' in particular, but the record has an air of calculation that undercuts its appeal. *Starfish And The Moon* continues with the feel of *Escape*, Beard handling the textural elements again, and Evans certainly seems as much at home here as in unadorned fusion camp. The two sides of the story are told by 'It's Only History', close to an electronic pastorale, and 'Red Dog', a trim, forceful blow.

Gil Evans (1912–88)

PIANO, ARRANGER, COMPOSER

His name – famously – is an anagram of Svengali and Gil spent much of his career shaping the sounds and musical philosophies of younger musicians. His association with Miles Davis was definitive of one strain of modern jazz, but Gil went on to rewrite the musical legacy of Jimi Hendrix as well. Born in Canada, and serving a hard-knocks apprenticeship in Claude Thornhill's band (which also had a big impact on Miles), Gil drew heavily on Duke Ellington as both composer and arranger. His peerless voicing for brasses and horns is instantly recognizable.

***** Gil Evans And Ten**

Original Jazz Classics OJC 346 *Evans; John Carisi, Jack Loven, Louis Mucci (t); Jimmy Cleveland, Bart Varsalona (tb); Willie Ruff (hn); Lee Konitz (as); Steve Lacy (ss); Dave Kurtzer (bsn); Paul Chambers (b); Jo Jones, Nick Stabulas (d).*

****** Out Of The Cool**

Impulse! 11862 *Evans; Johnny Coles, Phil Sunkel (t); Keg Johnson, Jimmy Knepper (tb); Tony Studd (btb); Bill Barber (tba); Ray Beckenstein, Eddie Cane (as, f, picc); Budd Johnson (ts, ss); Bob Tricarico (f, picc, bsn); Ray Crawford (g); Ron Carter (b); Elvin Jones, Charli Persip (d).* 12/60.

*****(*) The Individualism Of Gil Evans**

Verve 833804-2 *Evans; Ernie Royal, Johnny Coles, Bernie Glow, Louis Mucci (t); Jimmy Cleveland, Tony Studd (tb); Ray Alonge, Jimmy Buffington, Gil Cohen, Don Corado, Robert Northern, Julius Watkins (frhn); Bill Barber (tba); Al Block, Garvin Bushell, Eric Dolphy, Andy Fitzgerald, Steve Lacy, George Marge, Jerome Richardson, Wayne Shorter, Bob Tricarico (reeds); Kenny Burrell, Barry Galbraith (g); Bob Maxwell, Margaret Ross (hp); Paul Chambers, Richard Davis, Milt Hinton, Gary Peacock, Ben Tucker (b); Osie Johnson, Elvin Jones (d).* 9/63, 4 & 7/64.

***** Verve Jazz Masters 23: Gil Evans**

Verve 516728-2 *Similar to above.*

The sessions on *Gil Evans And Ten*, recorded four months after his epochal arrangements for *Miles Ahead*, are oblique, intelligent modern jazz, with Carisi's trumpet prominent, Lee Konitz and Steve Lacy lending the reed parts the floating feel typical of an Evans chart.

Out Of The Cool is Evans's masterpiece under his own name (some might want to claim the accolade for some of his work with Miles) and one of the best examples of jazz orchestration since the early Ellington bands. It's the soloists – Coles on the eerie 'Sunken Treasure', a lonely-sounding Knepper on 'Where Flamingoes Fly' – that most immediately catch the ear, but repeated hearings reveal the relaxed sophistication of Evans's settings, which give a hefty band the immediacy and elasticity of a quintet. Evans's time-sense allows Coles to double the metre on George Russell's 'Stratusphunk', which ends palindromically, with a clever inversion of the opening measures. 'La Nevada' is one of his best and most neglected scores, typically built up out of quite simple materials. The sound, already good, has been enhanced by digital transfer, revealing yet more timbral detail.

Individualism is a looser album, made with a pool of overlapping ensembles, perfectly tailored to the compositions and all securely grounded in the bass. The solos are now mainly improvised rather than written, and stray more freely from the original composition, in anticipation of the 1980s bands. 'Hotel Me' is an extraordinary performance, basically very simple but marked by throaty shouts from the brass that set up Evans's own churchy solo. 'El Toreador' again features Coles, less certain-sounding than on *Out Of The Cool*, but still a soloist of considerable imagination. Remarkable as the music is, there's an oddly unfinished feel to the record, as if it had been put together out of previously rejected bits and pieces. It isn't just a CD round-up, though. The Jazz Masters doesn't pretend to be anything else, but it's actually a well-paced and wholly convincing survey, ideal for anyone coming at Gil's music with no previous acquaintance or no stock of old vinyl.

**** Blues In Orbit**

Enja 3069 *Evans; Johnny Coles, Mike Lawrence, Ernie Royal, Snooky Young (t); Garnett Brown, Jimmy Cleveland, Jimmy Knepper (tb); Ray Alonge, Julius Watkins (hn); Howard Johnson (bs, tba); Hubert Laws (f); George Marge (f, ss); Billy Harper (f, ts); Joe Beck (g); Gene Bianco (hp); Herb Bushler (b); Elvin Jones, Alphonse Mouzon (d); Sue Evans, Donald McDonald (perc); collective personnel.* 69, 71.

Highly regarded, but now wearing rather badly. Evans's instincts seem for once to have deserted him. The arrangements are a touch ragged and the solos have a centrifugal energy that leaves the ensembles firmly earthbound. A rather bright register kills a lot of interesting activity down in the bass.

*****(*) Svengali**

ACT 9207 *Evans; Tex Allan, Hannibal Marvin Peterson, Richard Williams (t); Joseph Daley (tb, tba); Sharon Freeman, Peter Levin (frhn); David Sanborn (as); Billy Harper (ts, f); Trevor Koehler (ss, bs, f); Howard Johnson (bs, tba, flhn); David Horowitz (syn); Ted Dunbar (g); Herb Bushler (b); Bruce Ditmas (d); Sue Evans (perc).* 73.

'Zee Zee' reappears on *Svengali* as a feature for the incendiary Peterson, who turns it into a prolonged cry of anger, exhilaration and commanding abstraction, surprisingly different from his usual run of things. The other big number is Harper's own 'Cry Of Hunger', a companion piece on this concert recording, prominently featuring the composer and apparently reassembled at the production stage by Evans, who thus becomes an *ex post facto* composer in the way that he and Teo Macero often were on Miles projects. The sound is very good, given the live provenance, and the horns all come through with striking clarity. Not so some aspects of the extended rhythm section, which often sounds distant and out of focus.

*****(*) Play The Music Of Jimi Hendrix**

Bluebird ND 88409 *Evans; Hannibal Marvin Peterson, Lew Soloff (t, flhn); Tom Malone (tb, btb, f, syn); Peter Gordon (frhn); Pete Levin (frhn, syn); Howard Johnson (tba, bcl, b); David Sanborn (ss, as, f); Billy Harper (ts, f); Trevor Koehler (as, ts, f); David Horovitz (p, syn); Paul Metzke (syn, b); Joe Gallivan (syn, perc); John Abercrombie, Ryo Kawasaki, Keith Loving (g);*

Warren Smith (vib, mar); Don Pate, Michael Moore (b); Bruce Ditmas (d); Sue Evans (perc). 6/74, 4/75.

A title like that probably did raise eyebrows in 1974. Evans's championing of Hendrix's compositions – 'Little Wing' most immortally – was a controversial but ultimately career-stoking decision. It's a little difficult to tell, while listening to these powerful tracks, whether the quality of the music is testimony to Hendrix's genius as a composer or Evans's as an arranger, or to some strange posthumous communication between the two. Some of the tunes are inevitably moved a long way from source; '1983 A Merman I Should Turn To Be' takes on a new character, as does 'Up From The Skies', two takes of which are included. 'Little Wing' remains the touchstone, though, and the recording, from the following spring, is superb.

***** There Comes A Time**
RCA 5783 *Evans; Marvin Hannibal Peterson (t, perc, koto, v); Ernie Royal, Lew Soloff (t, flhn); Tom Bones Malone (tb); Joseph Daley (tb, tba); Howard Johnson (tb, tba, bs, bcl); John Clark, Peter Gordon (frhn); Bob Stewart (tba); David Sanborn (ss, as, f); George Adams, Billy Harper (ts, f); David Horowitz (p, org, syn); Pete Levin (org, syn, frhn); Joe Gallivan (syn, g, perc); Ryo Kawasaki (g); Paul Metzke (g, syn, b); David Bushler (b); Tony Williams (d); Sue Evans (mar, cel, perc); Warren Smith (vib, mar, perc).* 3–6/75.

This wasn't simply a reissue of the original LP of the name, but effectively a new compilation. Some Hendrix material – notably 'Little Wing' – had gone to the making of the compilation above, making way for three previously unissued tracks, of which Brownie's 'Joyspring' is the most remarkable. Remixed by Evans, the album begins with a bang, David Sanborn momentarily inhabited by the spirit of Cannonball Adderley on 'King Porter Stomp', and continues with a rousing version of 'Meaning Of The Blues' on which Gil's two signature tenors, Adams and Harper, are supreme. The final two items, 'There Comes A Time' and 'Anita's Dance', are less compelling, but they fill out a tremendous record which – reorganized and reworked – was perhaps Gil's most accomplished hybridization of old-fashioned big-band jazz with the hard edge of an electric rock band.

***** Little Wing**
DIW 329 *Evans; Lew Soloff (t, picc t); Terumasa Hino (t); Gerry Niewood (as, ss, f); George Adams (ts, f, perc); Bob Stewart (tba); Pete Levin (syn); Don Pate (b); Bob Crowder (d).* 10/78.

Evans's wish to record with Hendrix was thwarted by the guitarist's death. His interest in the music continued, and by the late 1970s 'Stone Free' and 'Little Wing' became staple items in his concert performances. There have been a good many bootleg or, at best, questionable issues of material from the 1976 tour, but we are no longer listing these, even at the price of a rather smaller entry for Evans. The rather later DIW is recommendably kosher in provenance and the performances are both highly professional and modestly adventurous; Adams is in full, not to say vociferous, voice throughout.

****(*) Live At The Public Theater Volume 1**
Storyville STCD 5003 *Evans; Jon Faddis, Hannibal Marvin Peterson, Lew Soloff (t); George Lewis (tb); Dave Bargeron (tb, tba); Arthur Blythe (as, ss); Hamiet Bluiett (bs, a f); John Clark (hn); Masabumi Kikuchi, Pete Levin (syn); Tim Landers (b); Billy Cobham (d).* 2/80.

****(*) Live At The Public Theater Volume 2**
Storyville STCD 5005 *As above.* 2/80.

A transitional band in most regards, with all the lags and hesitancies that implies. Individual performances are generally good, but there's a lack of excitement about the music and a greater abstraction than in preceding and later line-ups. Hendrix sits very comfortably alongside Evans's favourite Mingus, 'Orange Was The Color Of Her Dress ...'

***** Farewell**
Evidence ECD 22031 2 *Evans; Miles Evans, Shunzu Ohno, Lew Soloff (t); Johnny Coles (flhn); Dave Bargeron, Dave Tucker (tb, btb); John Clark (frhn); Chris Hunter (ss, as, f); Bill Evans (ss, ts, f); Hamiet Bluiett (bs, cl, bcl); Gil Goldstein, Pete Levin (syn); Hiram Bullock (g); Mark Egan (b); Danny Gottlieb (d).* 12/86.

***** Bud And Bird**
Evidence ECD 22003 2 *As above.* 12/86.

The Monday Night Orchestra was the most exciting big band of its day, with a massive spectrum of sound at its disposal. Caught here at Sweet Basil around the time of Gil's 75th birthday, the band does its level best to lift the roof for the old man. Like the Mingus big band which was to steal Evans's laurel in the '90s, the orchestra combined a sprawling anarchy with tremendous discipline and control and was, as ever, a launch pad for some inspired soloing.

The best of *Farewell* comes in its second half, with Gil's long 'Waltz' and a new, slightly rearranged version of 'Little Wing'. John Clark, already one of the orchestra's best soloists, contributes a fine composition, 'Your Number', which bids fair for any future ensemble projects of his own. The other album is more diffuse and lacks the climactic power of *Farewell*'s last half-hour. And yet it has its own very distinctive strengths. Johnny Coles guests on 'Half Man, Half Cookie' and delivers a rich-toned and sensitive solo which departs substantially from Gil's chart. Bassist Mark Egan is also encouraged forward to showcase his 'Gates-Illumination', another example of Evans alumni being eased on to the next phase in their careers. 'Bud And Bird' is the keynote composition, and an object demonstration in how far Evans had taken the language and harmony of bebop and blended it back into a wider musical continuum.

***** A Tribute To Gil**
Soul Note 121209 *Miles Evans (t, perc); Lew Soloff (t); Dave Bargeron, Tom Bones Malone (tb, tba); Chris Hunter (as, f); Alex Foster (ts); Gil Goldstein (ky); Bireli Lagrene (g); Michal Urbaniak (vn); Mark Egan (b); Danny Gottlieb (d); Urszula Dudziak (v, elec).* 7/88.

Gil's death came along with the band's festival diary pretty full and, not surprisingly, the decision was taken to fulfil as many engagements as possible, with Gil Goldstein as concertmaster. These performances were recorded in Italy during July 1988. The two main items selected are long versions of 'Orgone' and 'London' with, by comparison, very short, almost schematic readings of 'Moonstruck One' and 'Eleven', neither of which goes over the two-minute mark. It's to be wondered why and how these selections were made, for they don't seem to answer any obvious logic. Urszula Dudziak is characteristically dramatic in her feature, 'Duet', and the horn, violin and synth solos are all sharp, emphatic and to the point. Even so, we are left to wonder what else was recorded on the tour and why we haven't heard more of it.

Don Ewell (1916–83)

PIANO

Born in Baltimore, Ewell was working in the city from the mid-'30s onwards, playing in a style that harked back to the New Orleans fashion of Morton, from a decade earlier. He later often played with New Orleans musicians such as Bunk Johnson and George Lewis, and he worked with Jack Teagarden from 1956 to 1962, returning to New Orleans after that. He later toured Europe in the years leading up to his death, but he suffered, first through his daughter's illness and then his own, dying at 66.

***** Music To Listen To Don Ewell By**

Good Time Jazz 12021-2 *Ewell; Darnell Howard (cl); Minor Hall (d).* 3/56.

***** Man Here Plays Fine Piano!**

Good Time Jazz 10043-2 *Ewell; Pops Foster (b); Minor Hall (d).* 2/57.

The much-recorded Ewell hasn't been well served by CD so far, but the recent GTJ reissues restore some of his eminence. A structured, disciplined practitioner of stride piano, Ewell took his cues from New Orleans musicians – his early sessions in the 1940s were with Bunk Johnson and George Lewis – without succumbing to any raggedly 'authentic' mannerisms. One hears an almost prim sense of detail in his playing, the tempos unerringly consistent, the left hand a meticulous counterpoint to the right, the variations as refined and logical as in ragtime. The pair of GTJ reissues find him with the great New Orleans drummer, Minor Hall, and between them they offer a seasoned kind of classic jazz piano, without the music ever losing its balance.

***** Live At The 100 Club**

Solo Art SACD-89 *Ewell (p solo).* 2/71.

**** Don Ewell With The Yarra Yarra Band – Nicholas Hall Concert**

GHB BCD-378/9 2CD *Ewell; Maurie Garbutt (t); Roger Janes (tb); Paul Martin (cl, ts); Paul Finerty (g, bj); Don Heap (b); Peter Clowsey (d).* 10/75.

The solo format was arguably not Ewell's natural métier, and the Solo Art session is solid but oddly wearisome over CD duration. His treatment of Fats Waller was somewhere between fanciful and respectful: 'Keepin' Out Of Mischief Now' is almost rococo in some of its designs, while the following 'Handful Of Keys' is very fast, and seems to pirouette on tiptoe.

Nicholas Hall Concert finds him on tour in Australia. The Yarra Yarra Band are doughty but not exactly outstanding local players, and this is a pretty average chunk of trad on the road. Docked an extra notch for being released as an expensive double-CD: the best of this could easily have been boiled down to a single disc, with no loss to posterity.

Excelsior Brass Band

GROUP

One of the most long-standing of New Orleans brass bands, the EBB trace their roots back to the nineteenth century and maintain a venerable tradition.

*****(*) Jolly Reeds And Steamin' Horns**

GHB BCD-290 *Teddy Riley, James May (t); Gregory Stafford (c); Fred Lonzo, Clement Tervalon (tb); Michael White (cl); Oscar Rouzan (as); David Grillier (ts); Walter Payton (bb); Freddie Kohlman, Calvin Spears, Stanley Stephens (d).* 10/83.

The rich yet carefully 'restricted' tradition of New Orleans brass bands is slowly getting through to CD, and this disc by perhaps the oldest institution in the genre – the EBB was originally formed in 1880 – is a very fine example of the tradition as it stands in contemporary times (or at least in 1983). The digital sound allows one to hear all the detail which scrappy old recordings eliminated, and the ineffable bounce of the drummers (two on snare, one on bass), the old-fashioned tremble of the reeds and the sheer brassiness of the brass create some sense of a living tradition on material which is profoundly historical ('Just A Closer Walk With Thee', 'Amazing Grace', 'Down In Honky Tonk Town', 'Just A Little While To Stay Here' and so on). At the same time, the primitivism of the band can only be affected: players such as White, Lonzo and Riley could probably go bebop if they wanted to, which one could never say about original brass-band stalwarts. Whether that matters may depend on the ear of the behearer. It still makes for a very spirited and enjoyable session.

Jon Faddis (born 1953)

TRUMPET, FLUGELHORN

Often rather dismissively pigeon-holed as a Dizzy Gillespie clone, the Californian has developed into a more individualistic player than that suggests. Having recorded under his own name while still quite young, Faddis has since seemed to prefer the anonymity of studio work and larger ensembles. Apprenticeship with Lionel Hampton and Thad Jones–Mel Lewis has refined a delicately nuanced approach to arrangement.

***** Legacy**

Concord CCD 291 *Faddis; Harold Land (ts); Kenny Barron (p); Ray Brown (b); Mel Lewis (d).* 8/85.

*****(*) Remembrances**

Chesky JD 166 *Faddis; Jim Pugh (tb, euph); John Clark, Stewart Rose (frhn); George Young (as, f); Lawrence Feldman, Dale Kleps (as, f); Paquito D'Rivera (ss, ts, cl); Bill Easley (ts, cl); Blair Tindall (ob, eng hn); Ken Hitchcock, Roger Rosenberg (bs, bsn); David Hazeltine (p); Peter Washington (b); Clarence Penn (d).* 10/97.

Faddis recorded as leader (or co-leader with Billy Harper) when he was just 21 (it's deleted). On *Legacy* 'A Night In Tunisia' contains a couple of barely disguised allusions to Gillespie's solo at the famous Massey Hall concert with Parker, Bud Powell and

Charles Mingus, but otherwise the record is estimably fresh and individual. The more recent *Remembrances* is all elegance and grace, pitching Faddis into a gentler and somewhat smoother context. The arrangements by Carlos Franzetti are far from bland, and the set features some inspired playing from the trumpeter (notably the solo on his own 'Johnny Bug') as well as limber big-band tunes. The best of the record comes in the middle section, a sequence that begins with Herbie Hancock's 'Speak Like A Child', continues with Wayne Shorter's 'Footprints' and Trane's love ballad, 'Naima', and ends with 'Johnny Bug'. Nothing else on the set quite matches up and, at 67 minutes, it's probably over-length. Franzetti has his stamp all over Guastavino's 'La Rosa y el Sauce', which is almost filmic in its mournful romanticism and sounds as if it has floated in from another session entirely. Generally, though, a fine showcase for Faddis and a record without a single ugly moment.

Peter Fairclough

DRUMS, PERCUSSION

British drummer and composer, playing contemporary jazz with a touch of English pastoral.

***** Shepherd Wheel**

ASC CD 1 *Fairclough; Paul Dunmall (ts, ss, Cmel); Peter Whyman (as, ss, cl); Pete Saberton (p); Rick Bolton (g); Tim Harries, Tim Holmes (b); Richard Newby (d, perc); Christine Tobin (v).* 1/95.

***** Wild Silk**

ASC CD 8 *Fairclough; Keith Tippett (p, perc, zither).* 12/95.

*****(*) Permission**

ASC CD 18 *Fairclough; Tim Whitehead (ts); Mike Walker (g); Dudley Phillips (b).* 3/97.

The great strength of a musician like Peter Fairclough is that he never sounds as though he's hitting anything, even when he is playing forcefully. Keith Tippett is, in this regard, a perfect partner and foil. How many times have reviewers attempted to describe his piano playing as 'percussive but lyrical', or words to that effect? Often, on *Wild Silk*, Fairclough sounds to be playing a melody line to one of Tippett's flowing, multi-layered accompaniments. In addition to keyboard, Tippett also leans deep into the piano interior, using his favoured woodblocks and pebbles on the strings, always sounding fresh and spontaneous, never 'prepared'. The two long tracks, 'The Emerald Tree' and 'In The Glade Of The Woodstone Bird' (titles courtesy of Mrs Tippett), call on a huge array of sounds which need not be identified and sourced to enjoy this music. Indeed, it's probably better that they aren't. As with Ovary Lodge, in which the Tippetts were joined by Harry Miller and Frank Perry, it is positively beneficial to forget who might be playing what.

Unfortunately, that isn't the case with *Shepherd Wheel*, a sincere but rather forced attempt to forge a synthesis between English folk forms and jazz improvisation. The main interest here lies with the solo material, and in particular the contrasting performances of Whyman and Dunmall, both of whom are highly idiosyncratic players. Fairclough's long indenture to the Mike Westbrook group has paid dividends in terms of structure, voicing and pace, but the record as a whole doesn't quite satisfy and comes out a little less than the sum of its parts.

Permission is a relaxed, thoroughly competent contemporary-jazz record, thoughtful rather than powerfully engaged, and marked by attention to basics rather than more ambitious ends. Fairclough's writing has acquired a Latinate feel, almost as if influenced by Chick Corea's *Light As A Feather* period. The opening 'Relic' and 'Misnomer' are heavily marked by Phillips's Stanley Clarke-inspired electric bass lines, less prominent – or perhaps merely easier to overlook – later on the record. There are a couple of collectively written or improvised pieces, of which 'Sandscribe' is the more interesting, and a couple credited to Fairclough and guitarist Walker, who turns in his usual eclectic performance. Of these, 'Wildlife' is the most arresting: big, squally chords laid over a multi-layered percussion figure. Whitehead hasn't the most attractive tone, but it somehow suits this repertoire perfectly, its slight sharpness holding it just ahead of Walker's rather prosaic chords and runs. Fairclough himself plays very quietly and with a lot of space. A good record, easy to overlook.

Al Fairweather (1927–93)

TRUMPET

Born in Edinburgh, Fairweather co-led groups with his frequent partner, Sandy Brown, from the early 1950s and helped pioneer the development of the British mainstream sound. He worked with Acker Bilk in the '60s, but thereafter became a full-time teacher and played less often.

*****(*) Fairweather Friends Made To Measure**

Lake LACD75 *Fairweather; Kenny Ball (t); Tony Milliner (tb, btb); John Picard, Chris Barber (tb); Sandy Brown (cl); Bruce Turner, Tony Coe (as); Red Price, Dick Heckstall-Smith (ts); Ian Armit, Stan Greig (p); Bill Bramwell (bj); Tim Mahn (b); Graham Burbidge, Allan Ganley (d).* 11/57–11/61.

This will be nostalgic for readers who were around when the British mainstream was just coming into being, as trad gave way to a more settled idea of small-group swing. *Fairweather Friends* was made for Pye, and the extremely rare *Made To Measure*, issued originally as a limited edition of 100 copies, came out on Ristic. The latter set has the surprise of Kenny Ball sharing front-line duties with Fairweather's big sound, remaining under the Armstrong spell but starting to lean, as was Humphrey Lyttelton, in the direction of Buck Clayton. Solid, but more inventive, is the excellent *Fairweather Friends*, which has the 22-year-old Coe playing handsome alto and the trumpeter turning in some of his best performances. There is a peculiar bonus in the shape of a B-side by the Laurie Johnson Orchestra with Fairweather, Barber and Brown playing 'Doin' The Racoon', an old '20s hot dance number.

Digby Fairweather (born 1946)

TRUMPET, CORNET, MELLOPHONE, VOCALS

Not to be confused with the Scottish cornetist Al Fairweather, Digby turned professional in the 1970s – though he continues to write and broadcast – and played with a variety of traditional groups. He has an accurate and expressive tone and solos strongly. We're also happy to report that he is co-author of a jazz reference book almost as distinguished as this one.

***** A Portrait Of Digby Fairweather**

Black Lion BLCD 760505 *Fairweather; Stan Barker, Brian Lemon (p); Ike Isaacs, Denny Wright (g); Ted Taylor (ky, syn); Len Skeat (b); Stan Bourke (d); Chris Ellis (v).* 7 & 12/79, 84.

***** Songs For Sandy**

Hep CD 2016 *Fairweather; Roy Crane, Al Fairweather (t); John Picard (tb); Tony Coe (ts); John Barnes (as, cl, bcl); Alan Cooper (bcl); Brian Lemon (p); Dave Green (b); Tony Allen, Bobby Orr (d).* 70, 82.

***** With Nat In Mind**

Jazzology JCD 247 *Fairweather; Pete Strange (tb); John Barnes (cl, as, bs); Pat Smuts (ts); Dave Lee (p); Paul Sealey (g); Jack Fallon (b); John Armatage (d); Wild Bill Davison, Lisa Lincoln (v).* 94.

*****(*) Squeezin' The Blues Away**

Spirit Of Jazz SOJ CD 10 *Fairweather; Tony Compton (acc, d machine); Lisa Lincoln (v).*

Digby Fairweather's embouchure has been baffling fans and trumpet students for years. Like Ziggy Elman's, it appears to project from just under his right ear. However odd the angle, though, it hasn't adversely affected Fairweather's sound, which is richly toned and curiously delicate, especially at slower tempos.

There are still some who think that it was Digby, not Al Fairweather, who was the great Sandy Brown's playing partner. Dig stands in very comfortably for his namesake on the 1982 *Songs*, a superb convocation of British talent and songs which culminates in a remastering of the great man himself with Brians Lemon and Prudence and Terry Cox, recorded privately. A fitting end to a heartfelt tribute. The bulk of the record, though, is Digby's suite of songs, which tell Brown's life in music. 'Singing Away The Cold In Edinburgh' is a legendary anecdote of Sandy and Al still making music even when their horns have been hocked. The other material is equally intense and idiomatic.

The Black Lion *Portrait* brings together two sessions from what must be considered the beginning and end of Fairweather's golden period. He became a full-time musician only in the late '70s, but by 1984 he was already losing his initial momentum. The partnership with Barker was a regular gig, resulting in the fine *Let's Duet* LP, and it's perhaps these tracks that should be sampled first, if for no other reason than to get the full flavour of the leader's cornet-playing. The sextets and quartets contain few surprises, though there are phrases on 'Cherokee' which suggest that, given a different set of circumstances, Fairweather might have gravitated towards a more contemporary idiom.

His tribute to the veteran Nat Gonella is eloquent, nicely paced and includes some of his most characteristic playing. The guest stars span the generations, establishing a link back to Nat's Georgians and their origins in the Lew Stone orchestra. Nat's theme, 'Georgia On My Mind', is given a fulsome airing, with Wild Bill taking the vocal. 'I Must See Annie Tonight' carries references of the old master's association with American greats like Benny Carter, and it's treated with due respect. There are less-expected things as well: 'I'm Feelin' Like A Million' is arranged from Nat's original solo, and 'September Song', which he never actually recorded but which here offers him an opportunity to express his satisfaction with the proceedings.

The duos with Compton take a moment or two to get used to, but they are consistently fascinating thereafter. Fairweather plays with a breezy, unfussy clarity, and the accordion wheezes and chugs after its manner, an undersubscribed sound in jazz but one with plenty of untapped potential. Lisa Lincoln, also featured on the Nat tribute, contributes two lovely vocals. (We could, frankly, have done without the drum machine.)

***** Something To Remember Us By**

Jazzology JCD 288/289 2CD *Fairweather; Stan Barker (p).* 84.

****(*) The Mick Potts Tribute Concert**

Flat Five GBHCD02 *Fairweather; Roy Williams (tb); Dave Shepherd (cl); Kathy Stobart (ts); Brian Lemon (p); Norman Fisk (b); Brian Rogerson (d).* 11/93.

Memories of two lost friends and colleagues. Digby worked with pianist and educator Stan Barker many times and recorded an LP, *Let's Duet*, with him. This is included here, along with a dozen tracks recorded at an arts centre bar in Southport. The live cuts are pretty decently registered, but the studio sound is very flat and unresponsive and there's probably no more than one good CD spread over the time. It does, though, celebrate an association and the interplay of instruments on 'Lover Man' (two versions), and 'Something To Remember Us By' is definitive of the best of British traditional jazz.

Potts was a fine trumpeter in much the same mould as Digby. Founder of Britain's Greatest Jazz Band, he died unseasonally young, leaving a hole in British jazz. A measure of the affection in which he was held is this BBC-recorded live session from Carlisle. Highlights of a brisk and celebratory evening include Kathy Stobart's feature on 'Emily' and the Fairweather/Lemon duet on 'I Can't Give You Anything But Love'.

***** Recorded Delivery**

Loose Tie Records LOTCD 4310 *Fairweather; Roy Williams (tb, v); Dave Shepherd (cl); Al Gay (ts, cl); Brian Lemon (p); Jim Douglas (g); Len Skeat (b); Allan Ganley (d).* 10/97.

Sponsored by the Post Office, so no surprise to find 'Airmail Special', 'Penny Black Blues', 'I'm Gonna Sit Right Down And Write Myself A Letter' and, of course, 'My Funny Valentine' in this bright, attractive session by some of Britain's senior traditionalists. Fairweather's arrangements are as taut and amiable as ever, and his playing and singing are full of bonhomie.

Dalia Faitelson

GUITAR, VOICE

Danish guitarist of mild fusion temperament.

***** Common Ground**

Storyville STCD 4196 *Faitelson; Susi Hyldgaard (ky, acc); Johannes Lundberg (b); Niels Werner Larsen (d); Marilyn Mazur (perc).* 4–5/94.

It would be a pity to pass by this thoughtful, measured record on account of its unfamiliar names. Faitelson's pitch is a kind of impressionist fusion and, while there are a couple of misplaced attempts at rocking out, most of the music is quiet and intelligent. The leader is shy about putting herself out front, and there is at least as much improvising space for the effective Hyldgaard and the agile Lundberg, who closes the record with a fine solo over Faitelson's calm strumming. The production is somewhat flat, though that may be in keeping with the players' intentions.

Maffy Falay (born 1930)

TRUMPET

A Turk who made his home in Sweden many years ago, Falay became a modest pioneer of world-jazz when he introduced some of his native dialects to the European modernism of his day. The albums by his early-'70s group Sveda are currently out of print but would be welcome on CD.

***** Hank's Tune**

Liphone 3157 *Falay; Elvan Araci (tb); Bernt Rosengren (ts); Ake Johansson (p); Per-Ola Gadd (b); Ronnie Gardiner (d).* 3/93.

Maffy Falay came from Ankara to Sweden in 1960 and has been a resident for over 30 years. He and Rosengren are great cronies, and they take more or less equal billing on this hearty set of hard-bop tunes. The two hornmen have a good ballad apiece, and Araci chips in here and there, mostly to thicken the sound of the front line. One wishes, actually, that there was more writing for the horns since the tracks otherwise resolve into the usual strings of solos, well turned though they are. Falay has a mellow sound that makes him seem like a natural for the flugelhorn, even if he sticks to trumpet here.

Charles Fambrough (born 1950)

BASS

When the Philadelphia-born bassist first recorded under his own name, he was already 41. By then, though, he had a substantial CV, including stints with the Messengers and with McCoy Tyner's band.

*****(*) The Proper Angle**

CTI R2 79476 *Fambrough; Roy Hargrove, Wynton Marsalis (t); Roy Ford, Branford Marsalis (ts, ss); Kenny Kirkland (p); Jeff Tain Watts (d); Jerry Gonzalez, Steve Berrios (perc).* 5/91.

****(*) The Charmer**

CTI 1010 *Fambrough; Roy Hargrove (t); Kenny Garrett (as); Grover Washington Jr (ss); Abdullah Ibrahim, Stephen Scott (p); Bill O'Connell (p, ky); Billy Drummond, Yoron Israel, Jeff Tain Watts (d); Doc Gibbs, Bashiri Johnson (perc).* 9/92.

***** Blues At Bradley's**

CTI 10113 *Fambrough; Steve Turre (tb, shells); Donald Harrison (as); Joe Ford (ss); Bill O'Connell (p); Bobby Broom (g); Ricky Sebastian (d); Steve Berrios (perc).* 2/93.

****(*) Keeper Of The Spirit**

Audioquest AQ 1033 *Fambrough; John Swana (t, EWI); Grover Washington (ss); Ralph Bowen (ts, ss, f); Art Webb (f); Joel Levine (recs); Edward Simon (p); Adam Holzman, Jason Shatill (ky); Lenny White (d); Marlon Simon (d, perc); Joe Gonzalez (perc).* 12/94.

The Proper Angle is a smooth and sophisticated session, and Fambrough's ability to call on a stellar array of guest players gives the disc plenty of local interest. Wynton Marsalis's solo on 'The Dreamer' is a high spot; he features on another six tracks, including the respectful 'Our Father Who Art Blakey', an old boys' reunion. The quartet tracks with just Ford, Kirkland and Watts offer the best opportunity to hear Fambrough working in space. He favours a solid, lower-register sound that sometimes recalls Paul Chambers, sometimes Mingus; and there's certainly a hint of Mingus in the Latin-tinged themes. Arranging credits are shared, and there are one or two queston marks here, with some tracks faded down rather than ending satisfactorily.

This becomes more of an issue on *The Charmer*, which lives up to its title rather too assiduously. Despite another impressive line-up, the music has become disconcertingly bland. Washington solos with his usual facility, and you'd be forgiven for thinking you'd stumbled across one of the saxophonist's own records. Even Abdullah Ibrahim, guesting on his own 'Beautiful Love', can't inject any sense of urgency. Garrett roughens things up a little with his latter-day Sonny Stitt phrasing and tone, but he gets going properly only on the long closing 'Sparks', by which time *The Charmer* has probably been consigned to the late-nite pile.

If one thing was significantly lacking, it was the chance to hear Fambrough and his music stretched out in a live setting. On the evidence of *Blues at Bradley's*, he's more than capable of sustaining interest over the long haul. The opening items weigh in at 15 and 13 minutes respectively and are as full of meat as double-yolked eggs. Bradley's in New York City is the present-day home of Paul Desmond's much-loved piano (and O'Connell twice appears to quote from 'Polka Dots And Moon Beams', unless the old chap still haunts the room and dictates that his signature be heard), and its wooden walls afford a warm, resonant acoustic for Fambrough's rebuilt but three-centuries-old bass. Steve Turre contributes the concluding blues and is as evocative as ever in his solo.

Keeper Of The Spirit embraces some unlikely sounds, including tenor recorder on 'Save That Time' and the ever-irritating wheeze-and-squeak of EWI throughout. In some respects this is a more ambitious album than its predecessors, but it lacks the straightforwardness and precision that make the others such compelling listening. Washington, a much underrated soloist, provides the leaven, but there is also a drabness and lack of vitality which is depressing after earlier highs.

Tal Farlow (1921–98)

GUITAR

Self-taught, Farlow got his first break by working with the Red Norvo Trio in 1949. Norvo's dexterity inspired Farlow to accelerate his own technique. It was a very popular group and, after he left it, Farlow worked as a leader in his own right, although after his marriage in 1958 he went into a kind of semi-retirement and spent much of his time as a sign painter. He was seen more frequently in the 1980s and '90s, his technique intact.

****** The Swinging Guitar Of Tal Farlow**

Verve 559515-2 *Farlow; Eddie Costa (p); Vinnie Burke (b).* 56.

****** Tal Farlow: Jazz Masters 41**

Verve 527365-2 *Farlow; Bob Enevoldsen (vtb); Bill Perkins (ts); Bob Gordon (bs); Claude Williamson, Eddie Costa, Gerry Wiggins (p); Red Mitchell, Ray Brown, Monty Budwig, Oscar Pettiford, Vinnie Burke, Bill Tackus, Knobby Totah (b); Stan Levey, Chico Hamilton, Joe Morello, Jimmy Campbell (d).* 1/55–3/58.

*****(*) The Return Of Tal Farlow**

Original Jazz Classics OJC 356 *Farlow; John Scully (p); Jack Six (b); Alan Dawson (d).* 9/69.

One could hardly tell from the catalogue that Farlow is one of the major jazz guitarists, since most of his records – as both leader and sideman – are currently out of print. His reticence as a performer belied his breathtaking speed, melodic inventiveness and pleasingly gentle touch as a bop-orientated improviser. His tenure at Verve included some marvellous sessions and at least *The Swinging Guitar Of Tal Farlow* has returned – there are plenty more that could be reinstated in the catalogue. Farlow's virtuosity and the quality of his thinking, even at top speed, have remained marvels to more than one generation of guitarists and, given the instrument's current popularity in jazz, his neglect is mystifying.

The Jazz Masters compilation remains an excellent introduction to his work, creaming off the pick of seven albums at Verve. Trios with Eddie Costa and Vinnie Burke are especially fine, but so is the date with Gerry Wiggins, Ray Brown and Chico Hamilton, which features one of the fastest treatments of 'Cherokee' ever recorded. Unassumingly though he plays, one never feels intimidated by Farlow's virtuosity, even when he takes the trouble to reharmonize a sequence entirely or to blitz a melody with single-note flourishes. An indispensable compilation. *The Return* is hardly less fine, and Farlow plays just as quickly, with comparable insight: try the lovely variations on 'My Romance'.

***** A Sign Of The Times**

Concord CCD 4026 *Farlow; Hank Jones (p); Ray Brown (b).* 77.

***** On Stage**

Concord CCD 4143 *As above, except add Red Norvo (vib), Jake Hanna (d).* 8/76.

*****(*) Chromatic Palette**

Concord CCD 4154 *Farlow; Tommy Flanagan (p); Gary Mazzaroppi (b).* 1/81.

***** Standards Recital**

FD Music 151932 *Farlow; Philippe Petit (g).* 11/91.

On *A Sign Of The Times* the music's delivered with pristine accuracy and brightness by these infallible pros, but somehow there's a spark missing. Even though they've gone to the trouble of arranging a dark, contrapuntal framework for 'You Don't Know What Love Is', for instance, or treating 'Stompin' At The Savoy' in a unique way, one misses the sizzle of Farlow's older work. Sumptuously recorded and balanced among the three players, though, and hard not to enjoy. *On Stage* was cut the year before, and the presence of Norvo and Hanna, as well as the concert setting, puts a bit more zip into the situation, but again this isn't more than the sum of its parts: the onstage mix is somewhat wayward (Norvo's vibes sound prissy) and the music tends towards strings of solos, graceful though they are.

Chromatic Palette is just a shade better than the first two. Flanagan digs in a little harder than he often does, and Farlow's own playing has a majestic breadth to it on some of the tunes, all of which are dispatched quickly and with few frills. Mazzaroppi sounds somewhat like a more youthful Red Mitchell on the bass. Try the hard-bitten 'Nuages' as a sample.

Farlow seldom encountered other guitarists (on record, at least) and his gentlemanly encounter with Petit is graceful and suffused with bonhomie. Like most such records, it's a little too polite to sustain a long programme unless one is hung up on harmonic subtleties, but there's no denying the empathy of the players. Farlow gets a three-tune medley to himself at the end and sounds, amusingly, like two players.

Art Farmer (1928–99)

FLUGELHORN, TRUMPET

Born in Iowa and raised in Phoenix, Arizona, Farmer had a long and distinguished career. He settled in Los Angeles in the late 1940s and did not make the inevitable move to New York until the mid-'50s. Associations with Gigi Gryce, Horace Silver and Gerry Mulligan followed, and he co-led The Jazztet with Benny Golson from 1959. He worked extensively in Europe through the '60s and '70s, and by the '80s was an admired elder statesman of bebop trumpet, though his soft and persuasive style found him playing flugelhorn or the hybrid 'flumpet' more often than not. His twin brother, Addison (1928–63), was a bassist.

***** Art Farmer Septet**

Original Jazz Classics OJC 054 *Farmer; Jimmy Cleveland (tb); Clifford Solomon, Charlie Rouse (ts); Oscar Estell, Danny Bank (bs); Quincy Jones, Horace Silver (p); Monk Montgomery, Percy Heath (b); Art Taylor, Sonny Johnson (d).* 7/53–6/54.

*****(*) When Farmer Met Gryce**

Original Jazz Classics OJC 072 *Farmer; Gigi Gryce (as); Freddie Redd, Horace Silver (p); Addison Farmer, Percy Heath (b); Kenny Clarke, Art Taylor (d).* 5/54–5/55.

****** The Art Farmer Quintet**

Original Jazz Classics OJC 241 *Farmer; Gigi Gryce (as); Duke Jordan (p); Addison Farmer (b); Philly Joe Jones (d).* 10/55.

****(*) Two Trumpets**

Original Jazz Classics OJC 018 *Farmer; Donald Byrd (t); Jackie McLean (as); Barry Harris (p); Doug Watkins (b); Art Taylor (d).* 8/56.

***** Farmer's Market**

Original Jazz Classics OJC 398 *Farmer; Hank Mobley (ts); Kenny Drew (p); Addison Farmer (b); Elvin Jones (d).* 11/56.

Art Farmer began his recording career with the ten-inch album, *Work Of Art*, the contents of which are on OJC 018. Although pitched around Farmer's trumpet solos, the music is as much in debt to the composing and arranging of Jones and Gryce, and witty originals such as 'Elephant Walk', 'The Little Band Master' and 'Wildwood' make up the programme. Yet Farmer's skilful contributions elevate the scores and it's clear that his style was already firmly in place: a pensive restraint on ballads, a fleet yet soberly controlled attack on up-tempo tunes, and a concern for tonal manipulation within a small range of inflexions. If he was comparatively unadventurous, then as later, it didn't stop him from developing an individual style.

This begins to come clear in the small-group work of the mid-1950s. The group he led with Gigi Gryce has been forgotten somewhat in recent years, but the two OJC reissues are both impeccable examples of a more considered approach to hard-bop forms. While *When Farmer Met Gryce* is the better known, it's slightly the lesser of the two: *Art Farmer Quintet* has some of Gryce's best writing in the unusual structures of 'Evening In Casablanca' and 'Satellite', while 'Nica's Tempo', constructed more from key centres than from chords, might be his masterpiece; in the sequence of long solos, Farmer turns in an improvisation good enough to stand with the best of Miles Davis from the same period. The rhythm section, too, is the most sympathetic of the three involved.

The two-trumpet meeting with Byrd is capable but routine, a typical Prestige blowing session of the period, while *Farmer's Market* suffers slightly from unexpectedly heavy tempos and an erratic performance from Mobley, although Kenny Drew takes some crisp solos. The remastering of all these reissues is cleanly done.

****** Portrait Of Art**

Original Jazz Classics OJC 166 *Farmer; Hank Jones (p); Addison Farmer (b); Roy Haynes (d).* 4–5/58.

Though as unassumingly handled as everything in Farmer's discography, this one has long been signposted as a classic. The rhythm section is beautifully balanced and offers exemplary support to the leader, whose playing summons elegance, fire and craftsmansip in almost perfect accord, with his ballad-playing particularly refined. Never as fêted as any comparable session by Miles Davis, this is still jazz trumpet playing on an exalted level and should be acknowledged as such.

****** Modern Art**

Blue Note 84459-2 *Farmer; Benny Golson (ts); Bill Evans (p); Addison Farmer (b); Dave Bailey (d).* 9/58.

The Blue Note album, originally on United Artists and finely remastered, is one of Farmer's most successful records of the period. Golson contributes one excellent theme, 'Fair Weather', but most of the others involve subtle reworkings of familiar standards: a surprisingly jaunty 'The Touch Of Your Lips', a beguilingly smooth reading of Junior Mance's 'Jubilation', a stately 'Like Someone In Love'. The presence of Evans makes a telling difference: his solos are so finely thought out that it makes one wish he'd become the regular man in the Jazztet.

*****(*) Blues On Down**

Chess GRP 18022 *Farmer; Tom McIntosh (tb); Benny Golson (ts); Cedar Walton (p); Tommy Williams (b); Albert 'Tootie' Heath (d).* 9/60–5/61.

The balance of two albums by The Jazztet, *Big City Sounds* and *The Jazztet At Birdhouse.* If Golson was the prime mover as far as arranging and material were concerned, Farmer's soft, insinuating lines and long-form view of a solo remain the most absorbing elements in the group's sound, and they balance Golson's more obviously powerful delivery. McIntosh is a somewhat subservient third voice but he does nothing wrong, and the rhythm section is fine – hear the often-forgotten Williams especially, with his superb playing on 'Five Spot After Dark'. These were excellent small-group albums, as good in their way as anything by The Messengers in the same era.

****** Out Of The Past**

Chess GRP 18092 *Farmer; Tommy Flanagan, Harold Mabern (p); Tommy Williams (b); Roy McCurdy, Albert 'Tootie' Heath (d).* 9/60–10/61.

Another peerless example of Farmer plus rhythm section, this draws together most of two Argo LPs, *Art* and *Perception* (for an unexplained reason, producer Orrin Keepnews has left off one track from each disc, despite there being room enough on the CD). The earlier date with Flanagan is close to perfect, a measured, unflashy but deeply felt reading of seven tunes that peaks on 'Goodbye, Old Girl' and 'I'm A Fool To Want You'. The second date, with Mabern, was done on flugelhorn and is only a whit behind. Quite essential.

*****(*) Live At The Half Note**

Atlantic 90666 *Farmer; Jim Hall (g); Steve Swallow (b); Walter Perkins (d).* 12/63.

Not much of Farmer's work as a leader in the 1960s remains easy to find. The empathy between Farmer and Jim Hall makes the live Half Note session a compelling occasion: long and unflagging renditions of 'I Want To Be Happy' and 'Stompin' At The Savoy' feature both men in vibrant improvisations, and each has an engaging ballad feature. Discographies list a sheaf of unissued tracks from these sessions: when will we hear them?

*****(*) To Sweden With Love**

Koch KOC CD 8510 *Farmer; Jim Hall (g); Steve Swallow (b); Pete LaRoca (d).* 4/64.

Recorded in Stockholm during a Swedish tour, the only record by this quartet features improvisations based around six traditional Swedish folk tunes. Though some of the playing is a little cautious, possibly due to the unfamiliarity of the material, Farmer and Hall are again sparkling in their solos and interplay, and Swallow and LaRoca support so well that one regrets there was nothing further from this band. Some 32 minutes makes the running-time miserly.

*****(*) Sing Me Softly Of The Blues**

Atlantic 7567-80773-2 *Farmer; Steve Kuhn (p); Steve Swallow (b); Pete LaRoca (d).* 3/65.

Kuhn displaces Hall and, though one immediately misses the deftness and subtlety of the master guitarist, the pianist is far from an unworthy substitute. Basically ballad-directed, with Farmer keeping to the flugelhorn, the playing is immaculate and slow-burning as only Farmer's records can be.

***** On The Road**

Original Jazz Classics OJC 478 *Farmer; Art Pepper (as); Hampton Hawes (p); Ray Brown (b); Shelly Manne, Steve Ellington (d).* 7–8/76.

An exceptional band, although the music is not quite as good as one might have hoped. The sole outstanding group performance is 'Namely You', where Farmer and Pepper both turn in superb solos, while 'Will You Still Be Mine?' and 'What Am I Here For?' are merely very good. Pepper, entering his Indian summer in the studios, was still a little unfocused, and Hawes is not quite at his best. But Farmer is as consistently fine as ever, by now using the flugelhorn almost exclusively, and the recording captures much of the quality of his tone.

*****(*) Manhattan**

Soul Note 121026-2 *Farmer; Sahib Shihab (ss, bs); Kenny Drew (p); Mads Vinding (b); Ed Thigpen (d).* 11/81.

*****(*) Mirage**

Soul Note 121046-2 *Farmer; Clifford Jordan (ts); Fred Hersch (p); Ray Drummond (b); Akira Tana (d).* 9/82.

***** Warm Valley**

Concord CCD 4212 *As above, except omit Jordan.* 9/82.

Farmer spent the early part of the 1980s recording, like so many of his colleagues, for European rather than American companies. *Manhattan* blends excellent original material from Drew, Horace Parlan and Bennie Wallace with a jaunty reading of Parker's 'Passport', and Shihab is an unexpected but rumbustious partner in the front line; *Mirage* is perhaps a shade better, with Jordan at his most fluent, Hersch numbering among Farmer's most sympathetic accompanists and another Parker tune, 'Barbados', taken at an ideal tempo. Drummond and Tana are also splendid. The Concord date misses only the stimulation of another front-line horn to set off against Farmer's most introspective playing, although Hersch's finely wrought ballad, 'And Now There's You', is the kind of track that makes any record worth keeping for that alone. All three discs are recorded with great presence and very sharp clarity.

****(*) In Concert**

Enja 4088-2 *Farmer; Slide Hampton (tb); Jim McNeely (p); Ron McClure (b); Adam Nussbaum (d).* 8/84.

***** You Make Me Smile**

Soul Note 121076-2 *Farmer; Clifford Jordan (ts); Fred Hersch (p); Rufus Reid (b); Akira Tana (d).* 12/84.

The Enja concert recording is inauspicious, a less than scintillating day in the players' lifetimes, although Farmer turns on his ballad mode for 'Darn That Dream' to agreeable effect. The music on *You Make Me Smile* is a mite disappointing after the exemplary earlier Soul Notes – but only by those standards, since Farmer and Jordan are basically their usual pedigree selves.

***** The Jazztet: Moment To Moment**

Soul Note 121066-2 *Farmer; Curtis Fuller (tb); Benny Golson (ts); Mickey Tucker (p); Ray Drummond (b); Albert 'Tootie' Heath (d).* 5/83.

*****(*) Real Time**

Contemporary 14034-2 *As above, except Marvin 'Smitty' Smith (d) replaces Heath.* 2/86.

*****(*) Back To The City**

Original Jazz Classics OJC 842 *As above.* 2/86.

The occasionally re-formed Jazztet is rather more of a showcase for Golson – as both composer and performer – than it is for Farmer. Their Soul Note session is a somewhat perfunctory return, with the six themes passing in prescribed fashion; but the Contemporary album, recorded live at a single residency at New York's Sweet Basil, gives a vivid idea of the group's continued spirit. *Real Time* offers lengthy readings of Golson staples such as 'Whisper Not' and 'Are You Real'. There's also an expansive treatment of 'Autumn Leaves' which finds all the soloists at their best. Coltrane's influence on Golson is arguably never more clear than in this music; Farmer is keenly incisive with the muted horn, romantically ebullient with it open; and Tucker emerges as a considerable soloist and accompanist: his solo on 'Autumn Leaves' is sweepingly inventive. Smith, the most audacious drummer of his generation, is the ideal occupant of the drum stool. *Back To The City* is now back on CD and features some lesser-known items from the band's book – including a rare outing for Farmer as composer, 'Write Soon'.

****(*) Azure**

Soul Note 121126-2 *Farmer; Fritz Pauer (p).* 9/87.

Although Farmer clearly enjoys the company of Pauer, these nine duets are not very compelling listening. One can't avoid the feeling that Farmer relaxes more in the company of a full rhythm section and, adept as Pauer is at filling the rhythmic and harmonic backdrops, the results seem a little stiff here and there, despite showcasing Farmer's flugelhorn tone at its most beguiling.

****** Something To Live For**

Contemporary CCD-14029-2 *Farmer; Clifford Jordan (ts); James Williams (p); Rufus Reid (b); Marvin 'Smitty' Smith (d).* 1/87.

♛ ** Blame It On My Youth**

Contemporary CCD-14042-2 *As above, except Victor Lewis (d) replaces Smith.* 2/88.

****** Ph. D**

Contemporary CCD-14055-2 *As above, except Marvin 'Smitty' Smith (d) replaces Lewis; add Kenny Burrell (g).* 4/89.

As he entered his sixties, Art Farmer was playing better than ever. The three albums by this wonderful group speak as eloquently as any record can on behalf of the generation of players who followed the first boppers (Farmer, Jordan) yet can still make modern music with a contemporary rhythm section (Williams, Reid, Lewis, Smith). The first record, dedicated to Billy Strayhorn's music, is a little doleful on the ballads but is otherwise perfectly pitched. *Blame It On My Youth*, though, is a discreet masterpiece. Art's reading of the title-track is one of his very finest ballad interpretations, even by his standards; Jordan plays with outstanding subtlety and guarded power throughout and has a memorable feature of his own on 'I'll Be Around'; Williams leads the rhythm section with consummate craft and decisiveness. But it's Lewis who, like Smith, shows amazing versatility and who really makes the music fall together, finding an extra ounce of power and crispness in every rhythm he has to mark out. *Ph. D* doesn't quite maintain this exalted level but, with Burrell guesting in jovial mood, it's as good-humoured and fluent as the others. Outstanding production work from Helen Keane.

***** Central Avenue Reunion**

Contemporary CCD-14057-2 *Farmer; Frank Morgan (as); Lou Levy (p); Eric Von Essen (b); Albert 'Tootie' Heath (d).* 5/89.

The reunion is between Farmer and Morgan, friends from the Los Angeles scene of the early 1950s, yet never together on record before. The music, from a live engagement at Kimball's East in California, is finally disappointing: Morgan's keening and late-flowering interest in what extremes he can reach on his horn isn't a very apposite partner for Farmer's unflappable flugelhorn, and the rhythm section have few ambitions beyond comping. Some fine moments amid a generally routine record.

***** Soul Eyes**

Enja 7047-2 *Farmer; Geoff Keezer (p); Kenneth Davis (b); Lewis Nash (d).* 5/91.

Beguiling, graceful, this is Farmer cruising amiably through the autumn of his career. The tempos are on the stately side, and the man with the horn feels no need to rush a tune like 'Soul Eyes' or 'Isfahan', one of several interesting choices – but the closing 'Straight No Chaser' is rather warmer. Keezer continues to impress, Nash is one of today's great drummers. Recorded live at one of Japan's Blue Note clubs.

***** The Company I Keep**

Arabesque AJ0112 *Farmer; Tom Harrell (t, flhn); Ron Blake (ss, ts); Geoff Keezer (p); Kenny Davis (b); Carl Allen (d).* 1/94.

The title is appropriate in a slightly discomfiting way. Farmer sounds like the senior citizen of this party, and virtually all the best strokes are pulled by his much younger companions. Harrell takes most of the brass honours, Blake is fleet and incisive, Keezer is masterful: his harmonically intriguing 'Song Of The Canopy' is certainly the best original here. Art takes measured, dark solos, but he sounds more like a patron than a leader.

***** Art In Wroclaw**

Emarcy 536632-2 *Farmer; Piotr Baron (ts); Kuba Stankiewicz (p); Harvie Swartz (b); Adam Czerwinski (d).* 96.

A souvenir of a Polish tour. Art sounds in benign form, and Swartz internationalizes the rhythm section to some purpose, though he might be a little too heavily featured here and there. The local team are keen to please, and they do well. Unremarkable, perhaps, but it clearly meant a lot to this jazz community, and there is a lovely sleeve-note by Jan Mazur.

***** Live At Stanford Jazz Workshop**

Monarch MR1013 *Farmer; Harold Land (ts); Bill Bell (p); Rufus Reid (b); Albert 'Tootie' Heath (d).* 8/96.

A seasoned team of five old pros offers a more settled and perhaps more congenial home for Farmer here. Three Monk tunes are on offer, and Art gets the flumpet to work on 'If You Could See Me Now' to cockle-warming effect. Land's similarly unfancy approach sits smilingly alongside.

*****(*) Silk Road**

Arabesque AJ0130 *Farmer; Ron Blake, Don Braden (ss, ts); Geoff Keezer (p); Kenny Davis (b); Carl Allen (d).* 6/96.

If this proves to be Farmer's last studio date, it's a splendid farewell: he sounds stronger and more involved than he did on *The Company I Keep*, and the band is terrific, Keezer acting more or less as MD and coming up with a cracking chart for Ray Bryant's 'Tonk' to start the disc. Keezer's own two tunes are very effective, there is a rare glimpse of Farmer's own writing in 'Flashback', and the two saxophonists are a piquant contrast to each other and to the brassman. A version of 'Stardust' which is thoughtful but steely is Art's parting nod to the ballad form he put so much trust in.

Allen Farnham (born 1961)

PIANO

Pianist and composer flitting between mainstream and post-bop idioms; he often does A&R work for Concord Records.

****(*) 5th House**

Concord CCD 4413 *Farnham; Tom Harrell (t, flhn); Joe Lovano (ss, ts); Drew Gress (b); Jamey Haddad (d).* 10/89.

***** Play-cation**

Concord CCD 4521 *As above, except add Dick Oatts (ss, as, ts), Rufus Reid (b); omit Lovano and Harrell.* 5/92.

***** The Common Thread**

Concord CCD 4632 *Farnham; Joe Lovano (ts); Jamey Haddad (b); Drew Gress (d).* 1/86–7/94.

***** At Maybeck Recital Hall Vol. 41**

Concord CCD 4686 *Farnham (p solo).* 6/94.

Farnham's dexterity masks a certain indecisiveness about what he wants to do, at least on the first record. An eclectic muddle of tunes stretches from Shorter and Coltrane to a Farnham original called 'Despair', with Lovano and Harrell putting in desultory appearances. For Concord, though, this is really left-field stuff, and the subsequent *Play-cation* is much more confident and unified. Gress and Haddad make a lively rhythm section (though bass chores are partly entrusted to Reid on the second set) and the talented, slippery playing of Oatts sits very compatibly on the music, distinguished this time by some sharper writing: the title-piece especially is an inventive one. *The Common Thread* is a set of leftovers of varying vintages: six tracks come from a 1986 session with Lovano, two more date from *Play-cation* and two makeweight solos were cut in 1994. This is a darker, at times almost lugubrious session: lots of minor keys, ginger tempos and nocturnal sonorities, the one exception coming in an almost explosive solo treatment of Jobim's 'No More Blues'. Lovano has a terrific outing on the title-piece and there are interesting trio versions of tunes by Ralph Towner and Steve Swallow, but the record's doleful theme is a bit oppressive. Farnham's turn in the Maybeck spotlight displays a chameleonic bent: on Evans, Brubeck and McPartland tunes he sounds like he's following the composers without imposing too much of himself. A blues and two original sketches show an adept if fundamentally derivative tack. A solid entry in the series, but hardly one of the essential ones.

*****(*) Allen Farnham Meets The RIAS Big Band**

Concord CCD 4789-2 *Farnham; Greg Bowen, Till Bronner, Jordan Kapitanov, Christian Grabandt (t); Dan Gottshall, John Marshall, Thomas Loup (tb); Andy Grossman (btb); Klaus Marmulla (cl, as); Gregoire Peters (as, bcl); Walter Gauchel (ts, f); Chris Potter (ts); Rolf Von Nordenskjold (bs, bcl); Hendrik Meurkens (hca); Chris Berger (b); Tim Horner (d); Jiggs Whigham (cond, tb).* 11/96.

Well met. Farnham's best, although it's a bit of a back-handed compliment since a lot of the time he's a bystander on his own record. The RIAS Big Band are a skilful team, if not noticeably different from any of many capable European orchestras; but the idea of having the quintet of Potter, Meurkens, Farnham, Berger and Horner as the centrepiece of the scoring works well and there's some typically eloquent playing from both the soloists. Farnham came up with a particularly attractive score in 'Rias-Ticity', 'Work Song' is handsomely reshaped and 'My Foolish Heart' is a winning set-piece for Potter and the RIAS brass.

Joe Farrell (1937–86)

TENOR AND SOPRANO SAXOPHONES, FLUTE

Arrived in New York from Chicago in 1960 and worked with many of the leading outfits there – Mingus, Byard, Russell – in that decade. Founder member of the Jones–Lewis Orchestra and later with Chick Corea in the original Return To Forever. Turned mostly to West Coast session-work in the '70s, before returning to touring in his final years.

*****(*) Sonic Text**

Original Jazz Classics OJC 777 *Farrell; Freddie Hubbard (t, flhn); George Cables (p); Tony Dumas (b); Peter Erskine (d).* 11/79.

Farrell's best album, *Sonic Text*, originally on Contemporary, has appeared only belatedly on CD. It captures perfectly his adventurous modal approach and his interest in pure sound. His flute part on Cables's 'Sweet Rita Suite' is both effective and unusual. He was perhaps a better flautist than saxophonist, but his soprano work always had what one-time colleague Flora Purim describes as a 'singing' quality that eliminates the horn's often rather shrill character. Hubbard may be too assertive a player for Farrell's music – the trumpeter's own 'Jazz Crunch' is slightly out of character for the set as a whole – but when he switches to flugelhorn for 'When You're Awake' and the slightly melancholy 'If I Knew Where You're At', which might almost be by Chick Corea, he sounds spot on. The closing 'Malibu', reminiscent of some of the things with Corea, is Farrell's best testament. Trawl the index for other appearances by this undervalued player.

Claudio Fasoli

TENOR AND SOPRANO SAXOPHONE

Italian post-bop saxophonist, frequent sideman, occasional leader.

***** Cities**

Ram RMCD4503 *Fasoli; Mick Goodrick (g); Paolino Dalla Porta (b); Billy Elgart (d).* 93.

***** Ten Tributes**

Ram RMCD4517 *As above, except add Kenny Wheeler (t, flhn), Henri Texier (b); omit Dalla Porta.* 4/94.

***** Mirror**

RAM RMCD4522 *Fasoli; Stefano Battaglia (p); Jay Clayton (v, elec).* 5/94–5/95.

Fasoli's various discs under his own leadership have dipped a toe into the water of differing jazz styles without sounding especially at ease in any one of them. When he tries to go outside familiar parameters, as on the edgy 'Surfaces' on *Cities*, his broken phrasing can sound contrived. But otherwise this is an interesting session, made up of dedications to different metropolises. Goodrick's versatile range is a more authoritative force than the leader's playing, binding the parts together and taking liquid, affably lyrical solos in his own time. Dalla Porta and Elgart play restlessly, unwilling to settle into any simple groove; yet when the four of them find the same pulse – '20121' is a good example – the results are very pleasing. *Ten Tributes* is slow and thoughtful and just a bit heavy-going: Fasoli blends five standards and five originals and takes the trouble to slightly alter the fabric of each of the familiar tunes. It's interesting – 'Yesterdays' adds a bar of silence to each eight measures, like a regular pause for thought – but some may find it a degree too painstaking to enjoy.

One feels, again, that Clayton's stream-of-larynx style of singing isn't especially congenial for either Fasoli or Battaglia. Yet despite some merely meandering passages, the best of *Mirror* is very good indeed. The writing is shared among the three of them and there is a dry and – in the context – quite fetching demeanour to the title-piece and 'Within', both by the saxophonist. The most charming moment comes, though, when he steps aside and lets singer and pianist uncover the most unlikely lyricism in Kermit the Frog's 'Bein' Green'.

Riccardo Fassi (born 1955)

KEYBOARDS

Italian keyboard player, adept in small-group and orchestral settings as both composer and performer.

****(*) Notte**
Splasc(h) H 345-2 *Fassi; Claudio Corvini, Aldo Bassi, Flavio Boltro (t); Roberto Rossi (tb, shells); Mario Corvini (tb); Michel Audisso (ss); Sandro Satta (as); Torquato Sdrucia (bs); Antonello Salis (acc); Fabio Zeppetella (g); Luca Pirozzi, Francesco Puglisi (b); Massimo D'Agostino, Alberto D'Anna, John Arnold (d); Alfredo Minotti (perc, v).* 2/91.

****(*) Toast Man**
Splasc(h) H 307 *Fassi; Flavio Boltro (t, flhn); Dario La Penna (g); Massimo Moriconi (b); Alberto D'Anna (d); Massimo Rocci, Alfredo Minotti (perc).* 2–4/90.

***** One For Leonardo**
Splasc(h) H 379-2 *Fassi; Flavio Boltro (t, flhn); Riccardo Luppi (ss, ts, f, af); Sandro Cerino (bcl, cbcl); Massimo Moriconi, Paolino Dalla Porta (b); Alberto D'Anna (d); Alfredo Minotti (perc).* 4/92.

Fassi works both in small-group settings and with his big Tankio Band, which is responsible for *Notte*. His orchestral scores are colourful and fluent if not always individual and, as so often, it's the soloists who make *Notte* catch fire, even if only here and there. British readers will be reminded of Kenny Wheeler with John Taylor when they hear 'Octopus' and 'La Foresta' on *Toast Man*. Some of the other tracks here, though, aim for a studious kind of fusion, Fassi turning to synthesizer over piano, and his lyrical bent is obscured by those settings, although Boltro is attractively elegant throughout. The trumpeter gets even more space on *One For Leonardo*, which is probably Fassi's best work with the big group. There is only a dash of electronics this time and the soundscape is widened by the bass reeds of Cerino; not all the sonic effects are convincingly integrated into Fassi's arrangements, and he seems short on real melodic invention, but Boltro and the useful Luppi play with great purpose on the date.

***** New York Trio**
YVP 3036 *Fassi; Rufus Reid (b); Marvin 'Smitty' Smith (d).* 12/92.

***** Plays The Music Of Frank Zappa**
Splasc(h) 428 *Fassi; Claudio Corvini, Mike Applebaum, Giancarlo Ciminelli, Flavio Boltro (t); Massimo Pirone (tb, tba); Mario Corvini (tb); Sandro Satta, Michel Audisso, Torquato Sdrucia, Francesco Marini, Riccardo Luppi (reeds); Fabio Zeppetella (g); Francesco Lo Cascio (vib, mar); Antonello Salis (acc); Luca Pirozzi (b); Alberto D'Anna (d).* 5/94.

The New York album is unexpectedly straight-ahead, lean, immediate: Fassi brought a portfolio of strong themes to the studio, and Reid and Smith play up to their best form in support. The Zappa tribute-album returns Fassi to the Tankio Band format. He chooses a group of Zappa favourites – all from the 1960s output, though – and sets them up as something between blowing vehicles and smartly arranged pastiches. As homage, it's probably too respectful, but it does get a lot of good jazz out of the likes of 'Twenty Small Cigars'.

*****(*) Walkabout**
Splasc(h) DH 475-2 *Fassi; Paolino Dalla Porta (b); Billy Elgart (d).* 1/96.

Fassi's latest trio session is another strong effort, less direct than the New York record, more elusive and at times – especially Dalla Porta's mysterious 'Game 1' – openly free. Yet there is still plenty of bebop in 'Di Coccio' and 'What Cosa?', and Fassi and his team sit very comfortably in both milieus. Elgart is crucially effective, constantly busy without seeming intrusive, and Dalla Porta offers some lovely countermelodies: his 'Message From The Earth' is one of the prettiest things on any of Fassi's records.

*****(*) L'Amico Immaginario**
Splasc(h) 630.2 *Fassi; Gary Smulyan (bs); Massimo Moriconi (b); Giampaolo Ascolese (d).* 3–12/94.

Much of this is a straightforward duet with Smulyan, on the shelf for six years before release, but surely among Fassi's most successful recordings. The lovely harmonies of 'Why Buddha' are given a thoroughgoing exploration which is nevertheless simply and benignly affecting. Free from any heavyweight agenda, both men play in their breeziest and most generous manner. There are two trio tracks without Smulyan and only a single quartet piece, the brisk 'Near The River'.

Nick Fatool (born 1915)

DRUMS

A great veteran of swing-era drumming, Fatool went the route of several dedicated craftsmen and ended up playing good Dixieland when good swing bands faded away. Early work with Goodman, Shaw and others is listed elsewhere in the book. He later enjoyed many Dixieland associations, especially around the Lawson–Haggart circle.

***** Nick Fatool's Jazz Band**
Jazzology JCD-158 *Fatool; Ernie Carson (c); Johnny Mince (cl); Eddie Miller, Bud Freeman (ts); Lou Stein, Ray Sherman (p); Bill Rutan (g, v); Howard Alden (g); Bob Haggart, Phil Stevens (b).* 1/82–3/87.

This rare outing as a leader for the grand old swing drummer is very good fun. The band are all veteran campaigners and though some of the playing isn't exactly light on its feet they get up a good head of steam on 'Shine', 'Hotter Than That' and similar chestnuts. Carson provides the fireworks while Miller, Mince and Stein take joshing solos. Fatool gives himself some breaks but otherwise lets the others take the limelight. Lively and full-blooded sound, which is somewhat diminished on two 1982 tracks with Freeman and Alden, cut live at a club engagement, which fill out the disc.

Dan Faulk (born 1969)

TENOR AND SOPRANO SAXOPHONES

From Philadelphia, Faulk is a post-bopper with a few strong sideman credits to his name and these confident leadership sets.

*****(*) Focusing In**
Criss Cross 1076 *Faulk; Barry Harris (p); Rufus Reid (b); Carl Allen (d).* 12/92.

Benny Golson contributes an appreciative liner-note, and at first hearing Faulk might well be a player of Golson's generation and experience. He has a big, slightly old-fashioned tone to go with his racy delivery of new and standard material. His own 'Quintagon' quickly demonstrates his ability to push bebop chords a step further. Faulk frequently departs from the basic harmonic structure but in ways that give even 'wrong' notes an aura of relatedness. Harris is, of course, an ideal collaborator in this, and the partnership comes into its own on two Monk tunes, 'Nutty' and 'Epistrophy'; 'Barry's Tune' is offered by way of thanks. Though the liner details list only tenor, Faulk shifts to the straight horn for one of the oddest takes on 'I Love Paris' ever committed to disc. Allen is at his best here and on 'Lover', laying off threes against fours, speeding up, then softening the count. If, as Golson suggests, ballads offer the most accurate index of a young player's chops, then Faulk is definitely on the up, with a long and flawless version of Horace Silver's 'Peace' that constantly finds new things to do with the tune. This is an excellent album. The only quibble with it is that the sound is a little too condensed and central, an arrangement that masks Reid's contribution and frequently finds Harris and the leader right on top of each other.

*** Spirits In The Night

Fresh Sound New Talent FSNT 024 *Faulk; Myron Walden (as); Joe Martin (b); Jorge Rossy (d).* 10/96.

Jordi Pujol's New Talent imprint is offering valuable studio time to developing players and Faulk has created a strong and individual statement here. His Coltrane influence is most in evidence on 'The Night Has A Thousand Eyes', the opening cut, and it emerges here and there in the originals which follow, not least 'Three Cheers For Paul Chambers', which is less breathless than it sounds. The basic trio is competent if unspectacular, and Walden, who is special guest on five tracks, has some interesting things to say on 'The Heath Blues', his own 'Stop'N'Go' and the Chambers song. The session could have done with a sprinkle of producerly magic dust; competent but lacking an extra dimension.

Pierre Favre (born 1937)

DRUMS, PERCUSSION

Favre's career has embraced almost every style from Dixieland (while still in his teens he had gigs with Albert Nicholas and Lil Armstrong) to bebop and the avant-garde. An instrument-maker as well as a percussionist, he is interested in how sound functions and the relationship between sound and substance.

**(*) Singing Drums

ECM 823639-2 *Favre; Paul Motian (d, gongs, crotales, calabashes, rodbrushes); Fredy Studer (d, gongs, log d, cym); Nana Vasconcelos (berimbau, tim, congas, water pot, shakers, bells, voice).* 5/84.

*** Window Steps

ECM 529348-2 *Favre; Kenny Wheeler (t, flhn); Roberto Ottaviano (ss); David Darling (clo); Steve Swallow (b).* 6/95.

Singing Drums rapidly degenerates into an acoustically pristine sampling of effects and devices with no sense of centre and very little coherent development. Ironically, on such a crowded canvas, the music seems to call out for horns or strings to draw the various strands together and there is a slight feeling that the participants are working from very different cultural and technical premisses, which don't quite manage to communicate as they should. If the first of this pair appeals only to rather specialist tastes, the second is accessible to all. The presence of Wheeler and the much-admired Ottaviano guarantees music of interest, and this session has to be considered one of Darling's most focused and aware. Favre himself is seldom out of focus, but he is never intrusive and he holds the long 'Lea' together with great intelligence.

*** Portrait

Unit UTR 5004 *Favre (perc solo).* 97.

Portrait is a fairly chewy listen, but a rewarding one, given a degree of patience. Percussionists will doubtless have a field day trying to identify the sources of the sounds, which are admirably varied and unclichéd, but for most listeners it will be a case of cautious sampling a track or two at a time. The basic pulse is almost impossible to track without recourse to quite complex mathematical procedures. Whether unconsciously or deliberately, Favre seems to like experimenting with prime numbers – 1, 2, 3, 5, 7, 11 – and with the Fibonacci sequence – 0, 1, 1, 2, 3, 5, 8 – as he builds patterns within patterns. The recording is of very high quality, sounding 'live' without compromising on detail.

**** Soufflés

Intakt CD 049 *Favre; Michel Godard (tba, serpent); Roberto Ottaviano (ss); Lucas Niggli (perc).* 6/97.

The dynamism of this fascinating group takes a moment or two to sink in. As often as not, what is happening is that the two horns fulfil an accompanying role to the two percussionists. Aside from that, the whole ethos of the group is rhythmic, interlocking patterns, phased metres and that same dark pulse. Niggli comes from Cameroun and currently lives in Uster, near to Favre's base in Zurich. He is the Swiss's dark twin, a robust performer with his own ideas, but with a sound which is familiar to anyone who has followed Favre's work. In conjunction, they create a music of some complexity, not always easy to absorb at a single hearing, as on the deceptive 'Felix Dancing In Own Space', but always yielding up new dimensions each time it is heard ... and this is a record that should be listened to often. Favre at his very best.

Wally Fawkes (born 1924)

CLARINET, SOPRANO SAXOPHONE

A British trad veteran – though born in Vancouver – Fawkes is still best known for his long association with Humphrey Lyttelton. Strongly influenced by Sidney Bechet and some of the New Orleans masters, his big tone and aggressive phrasing are a contrast to his self-deprecating approach to his jazz career. Daily Mail readers know him better as the artist of the long-running Flook comic strip, under the name Trog.

*** **Fidgety Feet**

Stomp Off CD1248 *Fawkes; Tony Davis (t, v); Alan Bradley (tb); Roy Hubbard (cl, v); Ken Freeman (p); Brian Mellor (bj); Phil Matthews (tba); Brian Lawrence (b); Derek Bennett (d).* 1–2/92.

'Trog' has seldom taken leadership duties in the recording studios, but he gets top billing here as guest with the Zenith Hot Stompers. The band don't exactly break into a muck sweat, but there's plenty of vim on the upbeat numbers and Fawkes forms a neat partnership with Hubbard on several of the tunes. The clarinettist gargles the odd note, but for the most part he is still in great nick and this 'Trog's Blues' is probably as good as any he's given of late. Recorded in dry but lively sound at the Bull's Head by the redoubtable Dave Bennett.

Rick Fay (1927–99)

TENOR, ALTO AND SOPRANO SAXOPHONES, CLARINET, VOCAL

A modest trooper in various big-band and mainstream-swing settings, Fay got on record in a big way when Mat Domber of Arbors began a record label specifically to document his playing.

(*) **Live At Lone Pine

Arbors 19101 *Fay; David Jones (c); George Palmer (tb); Bob Leary (g, bj, v); Lee Richardson (sou); Pat Doyle (d).* 9/89.

*** **Hello Horn**

Arbors 19102 *Fay; Ernie Carson (c, v); Charlie Bornemann (tb, v); Tom Baldwin (p); Paul Scarvarda (bj, g); Lee Richardson (sou); Pat Doyle (d).* 4/90.

*** **Memories Of You**

Arbors 19103 *Fay; Ernie Carson (c); Dan Barrett (tb); Johnny Mince (cl); Tom Baldwin (p); Bob Leary (g, bj, v); Lee Richardson (sou); Pat Doyle (d).* 1/91.

(*) **Glendena Forever

Arbors 19104 *Fay; Jackie Coon (flhn, v); Charlie Bornemann (tb); Bob Phillips (p); Eddie Erickson (g, bj, v); Lee Richardson (sou, b); Eddie Graham (d).* 5/91.

*** **This Is Where I Came In**

Arbors 19106 *Fay; Jon-Erik Kellso, Peter Ecklund (c); Dan Barrett (tb); Bobby Gordon (cl); Keith Ingham (p); Marty Grosz (g, v); Greg Cohen (b); Hal Smith (d).* 6/91.

*** **Rollin' On**

Arbors 19108 *Fay; Jon-Erik Kellso (t); Dan Barrett (tb); Chuck Hodges (cl); Dick Cary (p, ahn); Paul Scarvarda, Howard Alden (g, bj); Lou Mauro (b); Joe Ascione (d).* 12/91.

*** **Live At The State**

Arbors 19112 *As above, except Chuck Folds (p), Bob Haggart (b), Eddie Graham (d) replace Cary, Scarvarda, Alden, Mauro and Ascione.* 4/92.

(***) **Sax-O-Poem Poetry With Jazz**

Arbors 19113 *Fay; Johnny Varro (p); Doug Mattocks (g); David Stone (b); Gene Estes (d).* 9/92.

(*) **With A Song In My Heart

Arbors ARCD 19205 *Fay; John Katalenic (p); Bob Leary (g); Rick Shaw (b); Ed Metz Jr (d); strings.* 6/98.

Rick Fay's unassuming brand of Dixie-into-swing was extensively documented by the Arbors label, and there's some amusing and good-hearted music on all these discs. The first three lean more towards revivalism, with Fay's Hot Five handling the Lone Pine date in good spirits, though without a deal of finesse. Carson's energetic and rasping manner is a useful fillip on *Hello Horn* and *Memories Of You*, and the latter benefits further from the arrival of the catalytic Barrett to bring the group up to an octet (Fay's Big Eight). *Glendena Forever* is marred by too many vocals, shared among Fay, Coon and Erickson, and some of the material here is a bit shop-worn; but the next three albums are more particular. *This Is Where I Came In* features the strongest band Fay has organized (credited this time as his Summa Orchestra) and the subsequent *Rollin' On* follows up with somewhat rarer material and a singularly smart arrangement of Beiderbecke's 'In The Dark'. The live date returns to more familiar Dixieland terrain, but Kellso and Hodges sound in notably fine fettle.

Fay himself stands in the swing tenor tradition of the likes of Eddie Miller and Boomie Richman, a big sound but a light and fluent way with it. When he picks up soprano, he worships Sidney Bechet. *Sax-O-Poem* shows off his poetry: he starts each track with a reading, with the music fading up from underneath, and though his declamations are a bit flat, the end result is not without charm. An acquired taste, and much the same can be said about his singing, which some of the tracks on several of these discs can probably do without.

With A Song In My Heart, his final album, saw him fulfil every saxman's dream by making a strings record. It's done smilingly and, although by now not in the best of health, Fay plays with surprising energy, especially on the brighter tunes. But his singing remains something that only family and friends are likely to take much pleasure in.

Enrico Fazio

BASS

A frequent sideman, but also an ambitious composer-arranger – especially for large groups – Fazio is characteristic of the broad sweep of the Italian modern-mainstream.

***(*) **Euphoria!**

Splasc(h) H 327-2 *Fazio; Alberto Mandarini (t); Lauro Rossi (tb); Francesco Vigone (ss, as); Carlo Actis Dato (ts, bs, bcl); Fiorenzo Sordini (d, vib, mar); Franca Silveri (v).* 7/89.

*** **Favola**

CMC 9921-2 *Fazio; Alberto Mandarini (t); Floriano Rosini (tb); Sergei Letov (ss); Francesco Vigone (ss, as); Piero Ponzo (as, bs, cl, bcl); Andrea Chenna (ob); Eleonora Nervi (tba); Giuliano Palmieri (elec); Fiorenzo Sordini (d); Vittorio Bestoso (v).* 11/90.

*** **Gracias!**

CMC 9951-2 *Fazio; Alberto Mandarini (t, flhn); Gianpiero Malfatto (tb, tba); Francesco Vigone, Pablo Ledesma (ss, as); Carlo Actis Dato (ts, bs, bcl); Luis Nacht (f, ss); Fiorenzo Sordini (d); Pini Levalle, Marcelo Garcia, Pablo Rodriguez (perc).* 3/91–7/95.

Fazio loves an exciting, kinetic band, full of carnival colours and offbeat energies. While the longest section of *Euphoria!* is a tribute to Charles Mingus which incorporates four Mingus themes, it doesn't sound much like a Mingus band: trombone, bassoon and oboe make only fleeting appearances, but the central unit of three horns, bass and drums swarms all over Fazio's pleasing melodies enough to convince that there's a bigger band at work here than the numbers suggest. Mandarini is very different from the cool trumpeters who set today's brass norm: notes seem to topple out of his horn, and long, barely controlled lines spiral crazily over the ensemble. Actis Dato's typically zesty ripostes and Vigone's brusque, pinchy alto lines fill in the rest. *Favola* is a festival commission, a 12-part suite with vocal commentary by Bestoso and some more strong writing by the leader. Ponzo and Letov are worthy substitutes for Actis Dato, but the music is a little more constrained and less freewheeling this time. *Gracias!* has a very long title-track, a short piece dedicated to Raymond Burr and Dmitri Shostakovich, an even shorter studio coda and two live tracks that go back to a 1991 Buenos Aires concert. The live items, for which the group goes up to ten pieces, feel like fillers, and it's the other music which works. Fazio still gets his men to give their all and, despite the occasional wrong turning, it remains head-turning music.

Leonard Feather (1914–94)

PIANO, CELESTE

One of the great voices to speak up for jazz for many decades, Feather was a Londoner in love with the music who went to America in the mid-'30s and continued to be fiercely involved for the rest of his long life. Though he worked extensively as a producer, often as a composer, and occasionally as a performer, it's as a commentator on the music and a distinguished historian-critic that he will be best remembered.

*** Leonard Feather 1937–1945

Classics 901 *Feather; Bobby Hackett (c, g); Dave Wilkins (t, v); Buck Clayton, Archie Craig (t); Benny Carter (t, as); Edmond Hall, Andy McDevitt (cl); Pete Brown (as); Joe Marsala (cl, ts); Buddy Featherstonehaugh, Bertie King, Coleman Hawkins (ts); Joe Bushkin (p, cel); Dan Burley, Eddie Macaulay, Billy Kyle (p); Alan Ferguson, Eddie Freeman, Remo Palmieri, Tiny Grimes (g); Wally Morris, Len Harrison, Artie Shapiro, Hayes Alvis, Carl Powell, Oscar Pettiford, Jack Lesberg (b); Al Craig, George Wettling, Hymie Schneider, Cozy Cole, Specs Powell, Morey Feld (d); Leo Watson (v).* 5/37–1/45.

Pleasing to have a CD available under the nominal leadership of this great proselytizer, journalist and general man-about-jazz. Although Feather went to the USA as a young man and remained there most of his life, there are two London sessions here by some of his British friends under the name Ye Olde English Swynge Band. On such wholly unpromising material as 'Colonel Bogey' they actually sound pretty good, given that they basically dispense with the melodies as quickly as possible. More substantial are three All-Star Jam Band dates which Feather organized, including such luminaries as Hackett, Carter, Clayton and Hawkins. Nobody really excels, but there is some fine small-band swing and Hawk gets a feature to himself on the 1944 date, 'Thanks For The Memory'. The disc closes on the rare session when Leonard and fellow-scribe Dan Burley sat at two pianos alongside Tiny Grimes, Jack Lesberg and Morey Feld for some blues and boogie fun. Transfers are from clean originals, but there is some turntable rumble and other flaws that a little care could have eradicated.

John Fedchock

TROMBONE

Fedchock's strong experience in modern big bands, which included a long stint with Woody Herman as his MD, stands him in the very best stead for these albums of modern big-band music.

**** New York Big Band

Reservoir RSRCD 138 *Fedchock; Tony Kadleck, Greg Gisbert, Barry Ries, Tim Hagans (t, flhn); Keith O'Quinn, Clark Gayton, George Flynn (tb); Jon Gordon (ss, as); Mark Vinci (as); Rich Perry, Rick Margitza (ts); Scott Robinson (bs); Joel Weiskopf (p); Lynn Seaton (b); Dave Ratajczak (d); Jerry Gonzalez (perc).* 9/92.

***(*) On The Edge

Reservoir RSR CD 153 *As above, except add Scott Wendholt (t, flhn), Charles Pillow (ss, as, cl), David Taylor (btb), Allan Farnham (p), Bobby Sanabria, Emedin Rivera (perc).* 10/97.

A glance through the personnel shows immediately that this is far from being another anonymous studio big band: Fedchock has creamed off some of the sharpest of New York's contemporary players and created a meticulous and skilful, yet passionate orchestra. The leader spent seven years with Woody Herman and knows his trade: he has a sonorous if not especially distinctive style as a soloist, which gives the featured treatment of 'Ruby, My Dear' a glistening quality, but he leaves the showstopping moments to players such as Perry, Robinson, Hagans, Margitza and Gisbert. 'Limehouse Blues' is a brilliant flag-waver, tempestuous but perfectly controlled; 'La Parguera' is melodically lovely, far more than the typical Latin potboiler; and when they end on the dreaded *Flintstones* theme, Fedchock takes the trouble to reharmonize it and actually takes the parodic element out. Glittering digital recording lends extra attack.

We grade the follow-up, *On The Edge*, a notch lower, although it's still a splendid record. Fedchock mixes his own writing with another expert choice of jazz themes – Oliver Nelson's '111-44', Pastorius's 'Teen Town' and more – and the orchestra, present as before but with even a few extra names, still sounds Rolls-Royce. Maybe the sheer freshness of the debut has been dissipated but, on a flagwaver such as Thad Jones's 'Ain't Nothin' Nu', this still sounds like one of the great orchestras in jazz.

James Fei

REEDS

A brilliant, demanding technician, whose work straddles jazz-based improvisation and new classical music.

***** Solo Works**

Leo Lab CD 059 *Fei (solo reeds).* 4 & 6/98.

Instantly and unavoidably reminiscent of solo woodwind performances by Anthony Braxton, except that Fei is never going to be confused with anyone but himself. The instrumentalism – here embracing soprano, alto and bass saxophones and bass clarinet – is equally expansive and virtuosic, but Fei has created his own logic and his own philosophy of performance, and these nine pieces are full of abstract drama. No point in pretending that *Solo Works* doesn't sit at the fringes of our concerns in this *Guide*, but anyone interested in creative music should sample these sounds.

Mark Feldman (born 1955)

VIOLIN

Feldman learned violin in his native Chicago and was playing the bar circuit as a teenager, before moving to Nashville in 1980 and playing on hundreds of country-music sessions. He later moved to New York and became heavily involved in the downtown scene.

***** Music For Violin Alone**

Tzadik TZ 7006 *Feldman (vn solo).* 4/94.

His sideman work has been so consistently provocative and exciting that in some ways Feldman's solo record is a shade disappointing. In part, it's because this is more a record of violin music than a jazz or an improviser's set. Several of the 11 pieces demonstrate his brimming virtuosity and catholic range, but the symmetry and neatness of much of it means that the electric excitement he brings to his group playing is diminished. Only on the very last piece, '4 Spiker', does one hear the kind of free-flowing invention which dominated Leroy Jenkins's solo violin record (still awaited on CD). That said, the sheer mastery which Feldman displays throughout will delight any who admire the instrument, in a jazz context or any other.

Victor Feldman (1934–87)

PIANO, VIBRAPHONE, DRUMS

Originally a drummer, the Londoner switched to vibes and piano just before the first of these records was recorded, a time when he was working with Ronnie Scott. His career took off in America and he was guaranteed his moment in jazz Valhalla when Miles Davis recorded 'Seven Steps To Heaven'. In later years, Feldman dabbled in rock and with electric keyboards. His acoustic style was far more distinctive.

*****(*) Suite Sixteen**

Original Jazz Classics OJC 1768 *Feldman; Jimmy Deuchar, Dizzy Reece, Jimmy Watson (t); Ken Wray (t, bt); John Burden (frhn); Jim Powell (tba); Derek Humble (as); Tubby Hayes, Ronnie Scott (ts); Harry Klein (bs); Tommy Pollard, Norman Stenfalt (p); Lennie Bush, Eric Peter (b); Tony Crombie (d, p); Phil Seamen (d).* 8 & 9/55.

*****(*) With Mallets A Fore Thought**

VSOP 13 *Feldman; Frank Rosolino (tb); Harold Land (ts); Carl Perkins (p); Leroy Vinnegar (b); Stan Levey (d).* 9/57.

****** The Arrival Of Victor Feldman**

Original Jazz Classics OJCCD 268 *Feldman; Scott LaFaro (b); Stan Levey (d).* 1/58.

It was probably inevitable that Feldman would move to America, but there's enough fine musicianship on *Suite Sixteen* to suggest that he might equally easily have stayed and played at home had London just offered enough adventurous paying gigs. Divided into big-band, septet and quartet tracks, *Suite Sixteen* was cut just prior to his first American trip. It isn't a classic like *Arrival*, which is also remembered as a precious addition to the brief Scott LaFaro discography, but it's a fine record all the same. As a cross-section of the local talent – Deuchar, Scott, Hayes, Crombie, Seamen, Reece – it's a remarkable document. Musically, it doesn't come up to some of the later, American sessions, but it features four excellent Feldman originals (the ambitious title-piece was actually written by Tony Crombie), Allan Ganley's 'Duffle Coat', Dizzy Reece's exuberant 'Maenya', which makes a fine closer, and Kenny Clarke's and Gerald Wiggins's 'Sonar'.

Feldman plays all three of his instruments but concentrates on vibes, with excellent solos on his own brief 'Elegy', where he follows the fiercely melancholic Deuchar, and on 'Maenya'. It's an interesting aspect of his solo work that its quality always seems to be in inverse proportion to its length. Feldman was a master of compression who often lost his way beyond a couple of choruses. The septet and quartet tracks are less buoyant, though 'Brawl For All', which features the leader's only piano contribution, is excellent. The sound is good but needs to be adjusted according to personnel.

Mallets (as bad a pun as you get) is reissued from a long-gone Interlude LP. Feldman concentrates on vibes, and the mesh with pianist Perkins, possessor of that famous crablike technique, is very good indeed. Rosolino and Land are featured on only half the tracks, but they bring to the session a breezy bounce that is engaging and endlessly refreshing. As always, Vinnegar and Levey generate a brisk, propulsive context for the band.

Arrival is a marvellous record, completed just after Victor had settled in Los Angeles. LaFaro's role in extending the vocabulary of the piano trio is well documented in his association with Bill Evans but, given how tragically foreshortened his career was, it's surprising that these sides haven't received more attention. As ever, the young bassist is firm-toned, melodic and endlessly inventive, and the interplay with the piano is stunning: long, highly wrought lines round a basic bop figuration. Levey's accents are quietly insistent and the whole recording seems to have been miked very close, as was the practice at the time. 'Serpent's Tooth', 'Satin Doll' and 'There Is No Greater Love' are the outstanding tracks. This should certainly be in the collection of anyone interested in the evolution of the piano trio in jazz, and it's good to see it in CD format at last.

***** Merry Olde Soul**

Original Jazz Classics OJC 402 *Feldman; Hank Jones (p); Sam Jones, Andy Simpkins (b); Louis Hayes (d).* 60, 61.

Altogether more predictable than *Arrival* – and perhaps an indication of the toll exacted by Feldman's time as an in-demand session player. 'Bloke's Blues' contains flashes of originality (though Hank Jones didn't seem to know what it was all about) and there's a wonderful shimmering quality to the vibes on 'Serenity'. Otherwise, it's rather bland standards fare.

***** His Own Sweet Way**

Ronnie Scott's Jazz House JHAS 605 *Feldman; Rick Laird (b); Ronnie Stephenson (d).* 2/65.

Caught live at Ronnie Scott's old premises in London's Gerrard Street, this was a happy homecoming for the exiled Feldman, a residency with real warmth and class. Feldman plays piano on all but three tracks, and the only pity is that there isn't rather more of his glittering vibraphone playing. The recording quality is only so-so and doesn't help numbers like a long and rambling version of Liszt's 'Liebestraum' or the Brubeck-written title-piece. Laird and Stephenson show their class as accompanists from the very start and, on originals like 'Azul Serape' and 'Too Blue', show how responsive they were to what clearly were not familiar themes. Much of London's jazz fraternity turned out to see these gigs and the bonhomie and warm rivalry are palpable, even on disc.

****(*) The Artful Dodger**

Concord CCD 4038 *Feldman; Jack Sheldon (t, v); Monty Budwig, Chuck Domanico (b); Colin Bailey (d).* 1/77.

As with Hampton Hawes, the switch to electric piano at the end of the 1960s did Feldman no favours, robbing him of that characteristically percussive touch and blurring the edges of his lines. This is an agreeable and sometimes surprising set but, apart from a very direct 'Limehouse Blues' and the title-piece, it errs on the fussy side and isn't helped by a soft-focus mix which is very much of its time.

***** Rio Nights**

Hindsight 615 *Feldman; Hubert Laws (f); Fred Tackett (g); Chuck Domanico, John Patitucci (b); Trevor Feldman, Harvey Mason Sr (d); Eddie Karam (perc).* 12/77–5/83.

A mixed bag of electric and acoustic material, recorded some distance apart. Some of the material has been available on a LP called *In My Pocket*, which is one of the more forgettable items in the already scant Feldman canon. There is some doubt about the date given for the trio sessions with Patitucci and Trevor Feldman, which the album suggests comes just two days before Victor's death. We are assuming that these items are offcuts from the session which yielded the 1983 album, *To Chopin With Love*. The combination of track and styles isn't a very happy one and this is probably an item for serious collectors only.

Simon H. Fell (born 1959)

BASS, KEYBOARDS, ELECTRONICS

Working out of Haverhill, Suffolk, Fell proposes a mature and fully thought-out synthesis of improvisation and composition in his work. While many of his small-group recordings are of uncompromised free music, he is also very interested in large-scale composition, and how its processes can be applied to the improvising group.

*****(*) Bogey's**

Bruce's Fingers BF 31 *Fell; Alan Wilkinson (ss, as, bs); Paul Hession (d).* 6/91.

****** Foom! Foom!**

Bruce's Fingers BF5 *As above.* 2/92.

*****(*) The Horrors Of Darmstadt**

Shock SX025 *As above.* 6/93.

***** Music For 10(0)**

Leo Lab 013 *Fell; Guy Llewellyn (frhn); Charles Wharf, Pete Minns, Mick Beck, Alan Wilkinson (reeds); Mary Schwarz (vla); Paul Buckton (g); John McMillan (b); Paul Hession (d); Ben Watson (v).* 11/93.

The best precedent for this music is the old Brötzmann trio with van Hove and Bennink: exploding, tumultuous, improvised sound. There is little point in cold analysis of Wilkinson's saxophones (primarily baritone, for which he is creating a valuable new outlook) as they roar over the top of Fell's bass and Hession's drums, or the amazing internal dialogues which the trio manage to create even as they break the sound barrier. It's a welcome, cold-shower experience at a time when acoustic free-jazz has dropped many of its confrontational aspects: these men revivify the intensities of Ayler, Brötzmann and others in the small but noble tradition of great noise. A CD is a poor substitute for a live performance, but *Foom! Foom!* (six pieces, from the lengthy 'Ballad Of Otis Twelvepersons' to the almost snapshot-like 'The Alphabet Poised Like Twenty-Six Frozen Ducklings') is a fine place to start, and the live *The Horrors Of Darmstadt* (recorded at the legendary Leeds Termite Club) is the essential in-concert aftermath, opening on the 32-minute mayhem of the title-track. Recording on the live CD is indifferent, but both are splendid records. *Bogey's* is a recent revival of a 1991 set at the Huddersfield club celebrated in the title: sound is again less than ideal, but anything the group was doing in this period is worth keeping.

Music For 10(0) celebrates a decade of achievement at the Termite Club with a symphony for ten improvisers and one poet. Though close listening reveals much scrupulous organization by Fell, the music writhes in ways that sound utterly spontaneous, and many of the textures and juxtapositions are as dramatic and undiscovered as anything free music can throw out. Though the full-scale version of the work runs for about 90 minutes, this one works perfectly well at some 75 minutes. The libretto is provided (and shouted) by Ben Watson, a sequence of love letters to or tirades about the various record shops which exist in the city. Watson's bellowing may discourage repeat plays, but it's all pretty hilarious and great and ludicrous in roughly equal measure.

*****(*) Frankenstein**

Bruce's Fingers BF 25 *Fell; Charles Wharf (ss, ts, cl, bcl, ky).* 3/92–10/96.

If there's one thing Fell enjoys, it's density. This is a long-standing duo (there are some previous records now in vinyl heaven) and their music is a great boiling soup of sound, treated and mistreated either in real time or by the studio. Fell also takes to keyboards and electronics for these eight multi-part pieces, recorded over six sessions across four years. A flowchart usefully explains how the music was put together, although a basic grasp of atomic physics may be of some use in deciphering it. Bach and 'Here's That Rainy Day' put in guest appearances and there are several versions of Fell's underground hit, 'Crammed With Distressing Brain'. It is also, *en passant*, a concept album based around James Whale's *Frankenstein*.

*** Registered Firm

Incus CD33 *Fell; Alan Wilkinson (as, bs); Joe Morris (g); Paul Hession (d).* 6/96.

Joe Morris walks into the lion's den with eyes open and plectrum at the ready. Recorded at yet another Leeds celebrity hangout, The Blizzard Condition, this is an amiable blow, but it's hard to avoid the feeling that Morris is either kibitzing from the sidelines or holding the others back. That said, 'Bows And Buttons' is as juicily violent as it should be.

*** 9 Points In Ascent

Bruce's Fingers BF 24 *Fell; Graham Halliwell (as).* 7/97.

Fifty-two minutes of improvising by Fell and altoman Halliwell. The saxophonist is an anti-virtuoso, the bassist a virtuoso who makes light of that skill. Awkward, edgy, full of sudden squalls, or very occasional shafts of light.

**** Composition No. 30: Compilation III

Bruce's Fingers BF 27 2CD *Fell; Gary Farr, Tom Rees-Roberts, Joanne Baker (t); Paul Wright, Carol Jarvis, Matthew Harrison (tb); David Tollington, Tim Page (frhn); Becky Smith (cl); John Butcher (ss, ts); Carl Raven (ss, cl); Simon Willescroft (as); Hayley Cornick (as, f); Mick Beck, Katy Hird (ts); Jo Luckhurst (bs, bcl); Alan Wilkinson (bs); Nikki Dyer (f, picc); Charles Wharf (cbcl); Sam Koczy (ob); Jeremy Webster (bsn); Jon Halton (contrabass bsn); James Cuthill (p); Fardijah Freedman (hpd); Orphy Robinson (vib); Thanea Stevens (dulcichord); Justin Quinn, Stefan Jaworzyn, Colin Medlock, Damien Bowskill, Andrew Stewart (g); Mark Wastell, Matthew Wilkes, Kate Hurst (clo); Rhodri Davies (hp); John Preston (b); Paul Hession, Mark Sanders (d).* 1–4/98.

'As a piece based almost entirely on the principles of total serialisation, *Compilation III* has an unnecessarily complex, ornate and mathematical basis to every aspect of its existence' – this composer pulls no punches. For further enlightenment, ask for a copy of Fell's 136-page score. Recorded at numerous sessions involving the RNCM Big Band, the Anglia X Ensemble and sundry (and many familiar) improvisers, the result is a mighty two-disc work which, despite its rigorous structural undertow, nevertheless seems like a phantasmagoric improvisation from end to end, where the performers arrive and depart in predestined but spontaneous ways. Many of the 'constructs' which exist within the piece are clearly organized to the last letter, but only if you want to hear them that way. We prefer to hear it as the lifetime masterpiece by a major contemporary musician – except, of course, Fell is hopefully going to be delivering much more music to us yet.

We would also recommend to adventurous ears the excellent *Pure Water Construction* (Discus 11), an electroacoustic suite masterminded by Fell and another maverick composer-organizer, Martin Archer. Just outside this book's parameters, but it will appeal to any who enjoy the above discs.

Eric Felten

TROMBONE

Post-bop trombonist with a debut recording from the early '90s.

***(*) T-Bop

Soul Note 121196 *Felten; Jimmy Knepper, Tom Everett, Evan Dobbins (tb); Joshua Redman (ts); Jonny King (p); Paul LaDuca, Paul Henry (b); Jorge Rossy (d).* 4/91.

Felten has the stinging, brassy tone that went out of fashion for a while after J.J. Johnson devised a new, rapid-action delivery that was chiefly inspired by the saxophone. Felten's solos are notably spare and unfussy and, if he lacks his senior partner's glorious facility, he has other virtues on which to trade: strength, evenness and very exact pitching. It's clear from the opening track (on which Knepper quite properly leads off) that they're working in a very different vein from Jay and Kai, weaving together subtly voiced lines rather than alternating harmonized unisons and cutting-session chases. Knepper doesn't so much keep to the background as avoid crowding the younger man. When they solo on the same track, as on 'T-Bop' and 'Ontology', there's not much between them technically, but it's perfectly clear who has the greater poise and experience. Perhaps their most effective partnership comes on an absolutely lovely 'Stella By Starlight' on which the two other brasses briefly feature. Felten has a couple of tracks all to himself with just bass for company, the original 'Love Muffin' and 'I Guess I'll Hang My Tears Out To Dry'.

Maynard Ferguson (born 1928)

TRUMPET, FLUGELHORN, VALVE TROMBONE, BARITONE HORN, BANDLEADER

Born in Verdun, Canada, and an alumnus of the big bands of Boyd Raeburn and Charlie Barnet, Ferguson combined a fiery tone and fast articulation with a structure influenced by Count Basie and Stan Kenton. MF has always been receptive to new repertoire and many of his most distinctive themes are derived from recent pop music.

***(*) Jazz Masters 52: Maynard Ferguson

Verve 529905-2 *Ferguson; Buddy Childers, Don Palladino, Ray Linn, Pete Candoli, Tom Slaney, John Bello, Joe Burnett (t); Milt Bernhart, Bobby Burgess, Jimmy Cleveland, Herbie Harper (tb); Jimmy Ford, Anthony Ortega (as, ts); Bud Shank (as, f); Benny Carter, Herb Geller (as); Bob Cooper (ts, ob); Georgie Auld, Bill Holman, Ben Webster, Al Cohn, Ernie Wilkins, Willie Maiden, Nino Tempo, Willie Maiden (ts); Bob Gordon (bs, bcl); Tate Houston (bs); Russ Freeman, Lorraine Geller, Bobby Timmons, Gerry Wiggins (p); Howard Roberts (g); Ray Brown, Curtis Counce, Richard Evans, John Kirby, Red Mitchell, Joe Mondragon (b); Gary Frommer, George Jenkins, Shelly Manne, Alvin Stoller (d); Larry Bunker (d, vib); Irene Kral (v).* 12/51–8/57.

***** Live At Peacock Lane, Hollywood**

Jazz Hour JH 1030 *Ferguson; personnel includes Herb Geller (as); Richie Kamuca (ts); Mel Lewis (d); others not indicated.* 1/57.

There are few sights more impressive in animal physiology than the muscles in Maynard Ferguson's upper thorax straining for a top C. Unfortunately, on record there are no such distractions; putting a Ferguson disc on the turntable evokes sensations ranging from walking into a high wind to being run down by a truck. The Verve compilation fills in what until recently had been a missing part of the story, the early stuff for Emarcy on *Dimensions*, *Round The Horn* and *Boy With Lots Of Brass*. The earliest item of all is actually from a Ben Webster session arranged by Benny Carter, in whose august company Ferguson sounds a touch too brassy and brash. There is also a track, 'Can't We Talk It Over?', from a Mercury album by arranger Pete Rugolo. The rest, though, is pure double-smelted Ferguson.

The material on Jazz Hour gives a fairly reliable account of what the MF Orchestra sounded like (to change the metaphor yet again) at its hormonal peak: brash, brazen, curiously likeable even when it is slapping the listener jovially round the mouth. There is as little point commenting analytically on these tracks – say, for example, 'Stand Up And Preach' – as analysing a rainstorm or the tide: it's just there, and you have to deal with it or not. What may be slower to register is the sheer grace and elegance of some of the leader's gentler features, like 'My Funny Valentine'.

***** The New Sounds Of Maynard Ferguson And His Orchestra**

Fresh Sound FSRCD 2010 *Ferguson; Rick Kiefer, Dusko Goykovich, Harry Hall, Nat Pavone (t); Don Roane, Kenny Rupp (tb); Lanny Morgan (f, as); Willie Maiden, Frank Vicari (ts); Ronnie Cuber (bs); Mike Abene, Roger Kellaway (p); Linc Milliman (b); Tony Inzalaco, Rufus Jones (d); Willie Rodriguez (perc); other percussionists unidentified.* 64.

This was a smaller, rather subtler and more coherently inflected Ferguson outfit than many before or since. Benefiting from arrangements by Don Sebesky, Oliver Nelson, Bill Holman and others, and sticking to short, pungent durations (rather than the blowsier format of the live act), it packs 20 tracks into a generous 75 minutes that will delight converts and leave the uninitiated still a little winded. It's the usual blend of contemporary material (Hancock's 'Watermelon Man' and Alex North's 'Anthony and Cleopatra Theme') with jazz staples like Golson's 'Whisper Not' and Basie's 'One O'Clock Jump', together with non-mainstream items like 'The Londonderry Air'.

***** Maynard Ferguson Sextet 1967**

Just A Memory 9503 *Ferguson; John Christie (as); Brian Barley (ts); Jean Lebrun (bs); Art Maiste (p); Tony Romandini (g); bass, drums unidentified.* 67.

****(*) Maynard Ferguson Orchestra 1967**

Just A Memory 9504 *As above; additional personnel unidentified.* 67.

In 1967, Ferguson was invited to appear as a keynote artist at the Canadian pavilion for the Montreal Expo. What seems a worthy accolade is rendered slightly surprising because it came in what was a measurable dip in MF's critical and commercial fortunes. The band he took with him was not a regular working unit and contained fewer strong musical personalities than usual. The sextet performances were recorded during his stay in Montreal. Ferguson seems in unusually thoughtful mood and includes three delightful ballads in the set; 'I Can't Get Started' was always a favourite, but here he surpasses himself, rising above a very plodding accompaniment. 'Summertime "Revisited"' is a variant on the Gershwin theme, played at an unexpected pace. Only on 'Polecat' does the rest of the band come into focus, with tenor man Barley asserting himself as a independent-minded soloist. The big-band tracks are somewhat pedestrian and are unlikely to appeal to any but devoted Ferguson fans.

***** Live At The Great American Music Hall**

Status DSTS 1004 *Ferguson; Lyn Biviano, Wayne Naus, John DeFlon, Bob Summers (t); Billy Graham (tb, vtb); Eddie Byrne (vtb, btb); Andy Mackintosh (as); Tony Buchanan (ts); Bruce Johnstone (bs); Pete Jackson (ky); Joel Di Bartolo (b); Randy Jones (d).* 3/73.

***** Live At The Great American Music Hall: Volume 2**

Status DSTS 1007 *As above.* 3/73.

This was the period when it was virtually *de rigueur* to cover pop hits, so 'MacArthur Park' (a big hit for Ferguson) and 'Hey Jude' take their place alongside 'Take The "A" Train'. The energy level is as high as always on this closely but accurately recorded live record which is high on atmosphere, if occasionally wanting in respect of subtle improvisational activity. Interestingly, even at this point a good deal of the solo space is devolved to other players, notably the ecclesiastically named but decidedly unpriestly Billy Graham and Brubeck's one-time standby, drummer Randy Jones.

****(*) Chameleon**

Columbia Legacy 46112 *Ferguson; Bob Summers (t, flhn, perc); Stan Mark, Lynn Nicholson, Dennis Noday (t, flhn); Jerry Johnson, Randy Purcell (tb); Andy Mackintosh (ss, as, f, perc); Brian Smith (ts, f, perc); Bruce Johnston (bs, f, perc); Allan Zavod (p); Rick Petrone (b); Danny D'Imperio (d).* 4/74.

An odd mix of jazz classics and pop tunes, *Chameleon* was one of MF's less successful bids for crossover appeal. His version of Herbie Hancock's 'Chameleon' is full of charm and he makes a wonderful job of Chick Corea's 'Fiesta', bringing a joyous, bright-toned bounce to both. But Wings's 'Jet' and Stevie Wonder's 'Living For The City' are pretty drab. A short interpretation of 'I Can't Get Started' sounds like a sop to more mainstream jazz fans, and the only surprise of the set is the trumpet/baritone duet on 'Superbone Meets The Bad Man', a theme written for the session by arranger Jay Chattaway. Should anyone ever tell you that Teo Macero never produced a dodgy record, this is the one to pull out.

***** Conquistador**

Columbia 34457 *Ferguson; James Bossy, Randy Brecker, Jon Faddis, Bernie Glow, Giuseppe, Stan Mark, Irvin Markowitz, Dennis Noday, Alan Rubin, Marvin Stamm, Ron Tooley (t); Wayne Andre, Roger Homefield, Julian Priester, Randy Purcell, David Taylor (tb); Donald Corrado, Brooks Tillotson (frhn); Mark Colby (ss, as, ts); Mike Migliore (ss, as); George Young (as); Joe Farrell (ts); Bobby Militello (bs, f); Bob James (p, ky); Kenny*

Ascher, Biff Hannon (ky); George Benson, Eric Gale, Jeff Layton, Lance Quinn (g); Gordon Johnson, Gary King, Will Lee (b); Peter Erskine, Phil Kraus, Harvey Mason Sr, Alan Schwatzberg (d); Ralph MacDonald (perc); Patti Austin, Richard Berg, Ellen Bernfield, Ernie Bernfield, Vivian Cherry, Lani Groves, Gwen Guthrie, Martin Nelson, Linda November (v); strings. 77.

Dominated by the themes from *Rocky* (which had some chart success) and from *Star Trek*, this is an easy album to overlook so long after its release, but it was a second turning-point in the trumpeter's career, propelling him into new prominence. The bands he put together in those days were a notable mix of brilliant instrumentalists and poppy sessionmen. The vocal component on 'Mister Mellow' is likely to prompt second thoughts from anyone who was captured by the sheer bravura of 'Gonna Fly Now', Bill Conti's theme-song for *Rocky*, but there is enough strong playing right across the board to win over the most sceptical of listeners. A typically over-egged production – by Jay Chattaway – significantly dates the sound, but *Conquistador* was a strong indication of how determined Maynard was to win new audiences and to keep the mettle of his playing well up to the mark. His playing would get stronger still in the following decade, but as a band record this one is still hard to beat.

***** This Is Jazz: Volume 16**

Columbia CK 649790 *As for Columbia records above; additional personnel.*

Very much a chart-dominated compilation, with 'Birdland', 'Gonna Fly Now' and, of course, 'McArthur Park' taking up most of the space. Not much for Ferguson specialists, but presumably intended as a user-friendly introduction to the trumpeter's work.

***** Live From San Francisco**

Rhino 71704 *Ferguson; Hoby Freeman, Hugh Ragin, Alan Wise (t); Chris Braymen, Steve Wiest (tb); Tim Ries (ss, as); Daniel Jordon (ts); Denis DiBlasio (bs, v); Ron Pedley (p, ky); Gregg Bissonette (b, d).* 8/83.

Recorded at the Great American Music Hall in San Francisco, the set is centred on the allusive and cleverly structured 'Bebop Buffet', which does exactly what the title suggests, sampling the tastiest bop themes. Trombonist Steve Wiest's 'South 21 Street Shuffle' is generic bop, but the mix of originals and standards keeps the texture nicely varied. MF is in unusually moody form on 'Lush Life'; though he doesn't seem likely to settle back into a moody, ballad-playing old age, he can turn on the schmaltz with the best of them. Interesting, too, to see the name of Hugh Ragin, usually very much a modernist, in this line-up.

****(*) Body And Soul**

Jazz Alliance 10027 *Ferguson; Wayne Bergeron, Alan Wise (t, flhn); Alexander Iles (btb, ts); Rick Margitza (ss, ts); Tim Ries (ss, as, ts, f); Denis DiBlasio (f); Todd Carlon (ky); Dave Carpenter (b); Dave Miller (d); Chad Wackerman (d prog); Steve Fisher (perc).* 1/86.

Sauced with cheesy electronics and lethally overproduced by Jim Exon and Chad Wackerman, this is far from vintage Ferguson. The high note work is as impressive as ever and Bergeron, Margitza and Ries are strong in support. 'Body And Soul' is a striking performance; more usually associated with the tenor saxophone, it responds to the brass treatment very well indeed. Matt Harris's themes and arrangements are spot-on for the group, if a little formulaic.

***** Maynard Ferguson – Footpath Café**

Hot Shot HSR 8312 *Ferguson; Roger Ingram, Jon Owens, Brian Thompson (t); Dante Luciani (tb); John Kricker (btb); Scaglione (as); Chip McNeil (ts, ss); Matt Wallace (as, ts); Glen Kostur (bs); Doug Bickel (p, ky); Dennis Marks (b); Jim White (d).* 7/92.

Attention all shipping in sea areas Dogger, Wight and Portland: Hurricane Maynard blowing in from Heist-op-den-Berg in Belgium. The Big Bop Nouveau Band contains the changes and improvements of recent years. Ferguson switches to flugelhorn more than of yore and gets a rich, squeezed sound out of it, like hot taffy being spun out of a sugar boiler. The pace is still ferocious, but there are a few signs of elder statesmanly reserve creeping in.

***** These Cats Can Swing**

Concord CCD 4669 *Ferguson; Carl Fischer, Jon Owens, Joey Tartell (t); Tom Garling (tb); Chip McNeill (ss, ts); Matt Wallace (ss, ts); Ron Oswanski (p, org, ky); Chris Berger (b); Jason Harnell (d); Lorenzo Martinez, Sandea (perc).* 94.

***** One More Trip To Birdland**

Concord CCD 4729 *Ferguson; Scott Englebright, Carl Fischer, Larry Foyen (t); Tom Garling (tb, g); Christopher Farr (ss, as, ts); Matt Wallace (as, ts, v); Dan Zank (p, ky); Paul Palombi (b); Marko Marcinko (d, perc).* 6/96.

Pumped up and fiery, Maynard puts together latter-day bebop, much of it composed by the resourceful Tom Garling and by arrangers Denis DiBlasio and Alan Baylock with a more measured and harmonically subtle approach. As a live outfit Big Bop Nouveau were one of the most exciting around in the mid-'90s and, though some of it can be dismissed as mere excitement, overheated and overloud, there is more lyricism on *These Cats* than on earlier projects. 'Caravan' is wonderful, and so too is the long 'Sweet Baba Suite (Bai Rav)', which underlines how good MF can be when he stretches out over a long line rather than shorter bebop phrases. Here and on *One More Trip* the weight of the arrangements still falls pretty heavily on the trumpets, but Matt Wallace more than holds his own on alto and could be one of the finds of the last few years. A cover of Joe Zawinul's 'Birdland' manages to avoid most of the hackneyed mannerisms.

***** Brass Attitude**

Concord CCD 4848 *Ferguson; Wayne Bergeron, Carl Fischer, Frank Greene (t); Tom Garling (tb); Sal Giorgianni, Matt Wallace (as, ts); Denis DiBlasio (bs, v); Paul Thompson (b); Dave Throckmorton (d).* 10/98.

More restrained and lyrical than in years gone by, MF is still capable of risky high-wire acrobatics and the odd touch of experimentalism, as on the Indian 'Misra-Dhenuka'. Here as elsewhere, Maynard seems torn between styles and traditions, and the strain is perhaps greater than the synthesis. Nicely recorded, the album suggests that the old fellow hasn't yet finished growing.

Dale Fielder

SOPRANO AND TENOR SAXOPHONES

Free-bop saxophonist, here leading a big ensemble through a big work.

***** Ocean Of Love And Mercy**

Cadence CJR 1071 *Fielder; Brian Swartz (t, flhn); George Bohannon (tb, euph); Dan Weinstein (tb); Daniel Jackson (ts); Jane Getz (p); Bill Markus (b); Thomas White (d); Taumbu (perc).* 12/96.

An extended 'Passion Suite' led by saxophonist Fielder, this concert recording is a big, sprawling affair which isn't as intimidating as the titles might seem. The musicians work a basically conservative kind of free bop and the unambitious work of the soloists is well in keeping with Fielder's hearty melodies and consonant ensembles. Swartz, Jackson and Fielder himself perhaps emerge best, although the leader's soprano is a little sour, and the rhythm section suffer a bit in the mix, as happens so often in concert situations (it was recorded at a Lutheran church in Glendale).

Scott Fields

GUITAR

Fields is a veteran of the Chicago free-jazz scene of the 1960s who quit in 1975 and has returned to active duty (from a new base in Madison, Wisconsin) only in the '90s.

****(*) 48 Motives**

Cadence CJR 1064 *Fields; Joseph Jarman (as); Marilyn Crispell (p); Matt Turner (clo); John Padden, Hans Sturm (b); Vincent Davis, Geoff Brady (perc); Stephen Dembski (cond).* 1/96.

***** Disaster At Sea**

Music & Arts CD-961 *Fields; Matt Turner (clo); Vincent Davis (d).* 5/96.

***** Five Frozen Eggs**

Music & Arts CD-987 *Fields; Marilyn Crispell (p); Hans Sturm (b); Hamid Drake (d).* 10/96.

***** Sonotropism**

Music & Arts CD-1007 *Fields; Larry Ochs (sno, ts); Marilyn Crispell (p); Matt Turner (clo).* 10/96.

These albums mark the re-emergence of an interesting talent. Each disc has its moments, although none strikes us as indispensable and they do give the impression of a man with a lot to say, trying to get it all out as fast as possible. *48 Motives* and *Sonotropism* both experiment specifically with long-form ideas. The Cadence disc sets the ensemble a structure of 48 eight-bar melodic fragments, subdivided and shared among the ensemble with various rhythmic motives stirred in. The result is a continuous piece lasting almost an hour, the sound ebbing and flowing among the players. Somehow the music sounds far less structured than one expects, often resolving into a kind of drone, and, although everyone is clearly giving their all, the piece is troubled by a muzzy sound-mix which badly affects the overall impression. Dembski is cast here in a Butch Morris-like role, and he steps further into the limelight on *Sonotropism*, which is a 50-minute composition-improvisation which he notated and directed. The feel here is of an exquisite piece of chamber jazz just sufficiently dirtied to keep it lively. Crispell, who's done so much of this kind of playing with Anthony Braxton, is perfect for the job, and Ochs is equally capable. Three brief improvisations by the quartet fill out the playing time.

Fields himself is content to be a busy ensemble player on those two, but he is more forward on *Disaster At Sea*, which he describes as an *opera seria*, based around a seafaring tragedy. The trio hit an extraordinary level of intensity on 'Sputter', which seems like a vivid evocation of panic, and the subsequent pieces carry the story through: yet there is a sameness about the dynamics which fails to sustain the attention through what is ultimately a rather dry piece of music-making. Turner, insufficiently recognized as a master of his instrument, is at least as strong as Fields in this music.

Five Frozen Eggs – the sleeve-notes explain the title – strikes something of a balance among the various styles Fields is investigating, loosening the chamberish qualities of some of the pieces without surrendering the rather formal, almost courtly kind of free organization he seems to be interested in. His own playing here eschews much in the way of effects (employed more extensively on *Disaster At Sea*) and there is a sense of contrapuntalism among the four musicians which makes this record perhaps the best place to sample Fields's music – energetic, occasionally volatile, but fundamentally about form and its effect on content.

Sigi Finkel (born 1960)

ALTO AND TENOR SAXOPHONES

A Bavarian, Finkel has become a significant player in the contemporary Austrian scene, though he is scarcely known outside that milieu.

*****(*) Sweet Sue**

Alex Merck Music AMM JL 11143/EFA 01163 *Finkel; Enrico Rava (t); John Abercrombie (g); Ed Schuller (b); Wolfgang Reisinger (d).* 6/93.

***** Dervish Dances**

ORF CD 155 *Finkel; Tim Richards (p).* 12/96.

Finkel settled in Vienna at the start of the '80s and has become an important figure on the Austrian scene. He has recorded before with Abercrombie and with Tomasz Stanko (co-fronting a band called Caoma with the Polish trumpeter). These, however, are the only currently available albums we have been able to find. The band on *Sweet Sue* is called Special Station after an earlier record. Abercrombie is a key dimension in the sound, adding a depth of focus to Finkel's superficial (a word we intend neutrally rather than judgementally) approach, much as Richards does on the collection of duos. 'Almost A Reggae' and 'Tobasco' are strong, upbeat tunes, while 'Domino Blue' suggests that Finkel has gifts as a ballad composer and performer, a dark-toned, meditative piece whose low wattage camouflages a good deal of careful thought. Rava sounds as laid-back and unaggressive as ever, but capable of adapting himself to every change in the leader's mercurial personality, and on 'Sweet Sue' (an original and not the standard tune) the two horns balance one another almost perfectly.

Dervish Dances is a much more mainstream jazz record, not least because Richards is so deeply and intelligently steeped in the blues. The guys contribute six numbers apiece, with 'Somewhere Over The Rainbow' included as an encore. Compare Finkel's 'Dervish' with Richards's freshly contemporary, but still traditional 'Back Street Blues' for the best indication of the differences in their musical personalities. There's something not quite right about the sound, though Austrian Radio is normally noted for attention to detail and for impressive production values. That apart, an attractive, well-balanced record.

Firehouse Five Plus Two

GROUP

Formed by trombonist Ward Kimball, this semi-pro revivalist band of the '50s and '60s was originally drawn from the staff at Walt Disney Studios. They proved to be unexpectedly popular and made many records.

**** The Firehouse Five Plus Two Story**

Good Time Jazz 2GTJCD-22055-2 2CD *Johnny Lucas, Danny Alguire (t); Ward Kimball (tb); Clark Mallory, Tom Sharpsteen, George Probert (cl); Ed Penner (bs, tba); Frank Thomas (p); Dick Roberts (g, bj); Harper Goff (bj); Jim McDonald, Monte Mountjoy, Jerry Hamm (d).* 5/49–3/54.

****(*) Goes South!**

Good Time Jazz GTJCD-12018-2 *As above, except omit Mallory, Sharpsteen and Hamm.* 1/54–10/56.

****(*) Dixieland Favourites**

Good Time Jazz GTJCD-10040-2 *As above, except Ralph Ball, George Bruns, Don Kinch (tba, b) replace Penner; Eddie Forrest (d) replaces McDonald.* 9/59–3/60.

**** Goes To Sea**

Good Time Jazz GTJCD-100282 *As above.* 2–11/57.

**** At Disneyland**

Good Time Jazz GTJCD-10049-2 *As above.* 7/62.

**** Twenty Years Later**

Good Time Jazz GTJCD-10054-2 *As above, except K.O Ecklund (p) replaces Thomas; Bill Newman (uke) replaces Roberts; add George Bruns (tba).* 10/69.

It's difficult to offer a serious criticism of this group who played their good-time jazz mainly for the fun of it yet became mystifyingly popular. The music seldom varies from record to record, even from track to track – it's Dixieland done with vigorous enthusiasm rather than panache, and it's as formulaic as anything done by British trad groups. Yet there's a certain degree of authenticity which the group conferred on itself, largely through sheer persistence. The earlier versions of the band play with clockwork momentum, and there is an almost Spike Jones-like feel to their music, occasionally underlined by Kimball's use of sirens and washboards to point up what was already a kitsch act. The personnel which settled down in the later 1950s, though, made some rather more personal and quite successful records, notably the *Dixieland Favourites* set and *Goes South!*. The brass players were often rather reticent about taking solos and it was left mainly to Probert to be the chief improviser: his playing is often sour and he can't sustain solos for very long, but there's an interestingly quirky edge to his best moments, and that tends to go for the band as a whole, too.

First House

GROUP

A late-'80s British group featuring Django Bates and saxophonist Ken Stubbs.

****(*) Erendira**

ECM 827521-2 *Ken Stubbs (as, ss); Django Bates (p, thn); Mick Hutton (b); Martin France (d).* 7/85.

***** Cantilena**

ECM 839619-2 *As above.* 3/89.

First House were always a very different proposition from Human Chain, Bates's other extracurricular sortie from the surprisingly demanding keyboard and writing/arranging desk at Loose Tubes. It's a more thoughtful band, relying less on sheer energy and more on Bates's intelligent structures. But little really happens of any consequence. Stubbs is by no means a charismatic player, and the results are forgettable. The later *Cantilena* is more thoroughly achieved and lacks some of the pretentiousness and rough edges of *Erendira* and of Bates's subsequent recording and concert band, Powder Room Collapse.

Clare Fischer (born 1928)

PIANO, KEYBOARDS

After studying in his home state of Michigan, Fischer moved to Los Angeles in 1957, worked with vocal groups and big bands as arranger and MD, and generally made himself prolific in almost every kind of musical situation – in the '80s he was arranging for Madonna and Prince. His piano style remains a thoughtful and warmer extension of the Tristano style. He also has a special interest in Brazilian music, having lived there for a time.

***** Latin Patterns**

MPS/Motor 557424-2 *Fischer; Gary Foster (as, f, rec); David Acuna (f); Rick Zunigar, John Chiodini (g); David Troncoso, Brent Fischer, Andy Simpkins, Oscar Meza (b); Peter Riso, Andre Fischer, Larry Bunker (d); Alex Acuna, Ildefonso Sanchez, Hector Andrade, Aaron Ballesteros, Luis Conte (perc); Foreign Exchange (v group).* 1/78–9/80.

**** Lembrancas**

Concord CCD 4404 *Fischer; Dick Mitchell (reeds); Brent Fischer (b); Tris Imboden (d); Michito Sanchez, Luis Conte (perc).* 6/89.

***** Just Me**

Concord CCD 4679 *Fischer (p solo).* 3–4/95.

Fischer remains neglected by CD. There are some fine and important records for Revelation, all of them languishing in the vinyl wasteland. Fischer's interest in Latin rhythms has been important in his career, bringing many arranging assignments for a bewildering variety of artists, but it's also encouraged a populist streak which has resulted in some more recent records being as fluffy and inconsequential as his earlier ones were lean and intense. *Lembrancas* is like that: Fischer plays only synthesizer, and the music is a pretty concoction of light Latin fusion styles, pleasant and forgettable. But the *Latin Patterns* set, a compilation from four original MPS albums, is, if seldom very profound, a frothily enjoyable set of tracks. Fischer plays either electric piano or an ex-42 combo organ throughout, there is always a busy team of percussionists on hand, and the group Foreign Exchange – who are rather like Singers Unlimited, who also recorded for MPS – add zippy harmony vocals to four tracks. Fischer's playing has its share of subtleties, too, even in this situation.

His several solo discs for Revelation are ruminative classics, and at least he's made one recent record in this vein. Perhaps *Just Me* isn't one of his very best. The meditative mood dries out some of these interpretations, and the even dynamics becalm several pieces. At a slightler faster tempo, as with the beguiling treatment of 'I'm Getting Sentimental Over You', Fischer's clever way with the tune is both charming and insightful.

Ella Fitzgerald (1917–96)

VOCAL

Came to New York as a child and, after several attempts at singing work, won a Harlem talent contest and began working with Chick Webb, with much success. Took over his band after his death, then worked as a solo in the 1940s. Managed by Norman Granz, she became America's favourite jazz singer, and her Verve albums in the mid-'50s established both the label and her eminence as a songbook interpreter. Toured throughout the '60s and '70s, recording latterly for Granz's Pablo label; but spells of poor health slowed her down in the '80s and her final years were spent in seclusion.

(***) Ella Fitzgerald
ASV AJD 055 2CD *Fitzgerald; Taft Jordan, Mario Bauza, Bobby Stark, Gordon Griffin, Zeke Zarchey, Ziggy Elman (t); Sandy Williams, Nat Story, Claude Jones, Murray McEachern, Red Ballard (tb); Benny Goodman (cl); Teddy McRae, Louis Jordan, Pete Clark, Edgar Sampson, Elmer Williams, Wayman Carver, Garvin Bushell, Chauncey Haughton, Hymie Schertzer, Bill DePew, Arthur Rollini, Vido Musso (reeds); Tommy Fulford, Joe Steele, Jess Stacy (p); John Trueheart, Allan Reuss, Bobby Johnson (g); Beverley Peer, Bill Thomas, Harry Goodman (b); Chick Webb, Gene Krupa (d).* 10/35–12/37.

***** The Early Years Part 1**
GRP 052618-2 2CD *As above.* 35–37.

****(*) Ella Fitzgerald 1935–1937**
Classics 500 *As above, plus Frankie Newton (t), Benny Morton (tb), Chu Berry (ts), Teddy Wilson (p), Leemie Stanfield (b), Cozy Cole (d).* 6/35–1/37.

****(*) Ella Fitzgerald 1937–1938**
Classics 506 *As above, except omit Griffin, Zarchey, Elman, McEachern, Ballard, Goodman, Schertzer, DePew, Rollini, Musso, Stacy, Reuss, Goodman, Newton, Morton, Berry, Wilson, Stanfield and Cole; add George Matthews (tb), The Mills Brothers (v).* 1/37–5/38.

***** Ella Fitzgerald 1938–1939**
Classics 518 *As above, except add Dick Vance (t), Hilton Jefferson (as); omit The Mills Brothers.* 5/38–2/39.

**** Ella Fitzgerald 1939**
Classics 525 *As above, except add Bill Beason (d).* 2–6/39.

***** Ella Fitzgerald 1939–1940**
Classics 566 *As above, except add Irving Randolph (t), John Haughton, Jimmy Archey, Floyd Brady, John McConnell (tb), Sam Simmons (ts), Roger Ramirez (p); omit Webb.* 8/39–5/40.

***** Ella Fitzgerald 1940–1941**
Classics 644 *Similar to above, except add John McConnell, Earl Hardy (tb), George Dorsey (as), Elmer Williams (ts), Ulysses Livingston (g), Jesse Price (d); omit Sandy Williams and Ramirez.* 5/40–7/41.

***** The Early Years Part 2**
GRP 052623-2 2CD *As appropriate discs above.* 39–41.

**** Live From The Roseland Ballroom New York 1940**
Jazz Anthology 550032 *Fitzgerald; Dick Vance, Taft Jordan, Bobby Stark (t); George Matthews, Nat Story, Sandy Williams (tb); Garvin Bushell (cl, ss); Hilton Jefferson (as); Wayman Carver (as, ts, f); Teddy McRae (ts, bs); Tommy Fulford (p); John Trueheart (g); Beverley Peer (b); Bill Beason (d).* 40.

Fitzgerald's fabled break came when she won an Apollo Theatre talent contest in 1934, still aged only seventeen, and by the following year she was singing for Chick Webb's band. When Webb died in 1939, the singer inherited leadership of his band; by this time she was its undoubted star. But her recordings of the period are often hard to take because the material is sometimes insufferably trite: after Ella had a major hit with the nursery-rhyme tune, 'A Tisket A Tasket', she was doomed – at least, until the break-up of the band – to seek out similar songs. The Classics CDs offer a chronological survey of her work up to 1941 and, while the calibre of her singing is consistent enough – the voice at its freshest, her phrasing straightforward but sincerely dedicated to making the most of the melody – the tracks seem to spell the decline of what was, in the mid-1930s, one of the most swinging of big bands. The arrangements are often blandly supportive of the singer rather than creating any kind of partnership, and when the material is of the standard of 'Swinging On The Reservation' it's difficult to summon up much enthusiasm. Still, there are perhaps many minor successes. The 1937–8 CD includes the session which produced Webb's only 12-inch 78, 'I Want To Be Happy' and 'Halleleujah', arranged by Turk Van Lake, and 'Rock It For Me' and 'Bei Mir Bist Du Schön' look forward to the authority which Fitzgerald would bestow on her later records. The 1939–40 disc, although it sports 'My Wubba Dolly', has a number of swinging features such as 'After I Say I'm Sorry', 'I'm Not Complainin'' and a fine 'Baby, Won't You Please Come Home?'. Fitzgerald tends to treat all the songs the same – there's little of Billie Holiday's creative approach to the beat – but the lightness of her voice lets her float a lyric without losing her grip on it.

The remastering of all these discs is very mixed. The earlier discs vary almost from track to track, some laden with hiss, some foggy, others crisp. 'A Tisket A Tasket', on the 1937–8 volume, is dreadfully brassy. Only the 1939–40 set has consistently clear transfers. The ASV two-disc set offers a cross-section from Ella's earliest sessions, but the remastering is bass-heavy and listening isn't much fun. The best bets are the two GRP anthologies, which come in reasonably consistent sound at least. With all this material out of copyright, there are other sets on the market, too: a double-set on Memoria, *Savoy Ambassadors*, and a single-disc ASV release called *Rhythm And Romance*. Collectors can choose at their leisure, but we commend the GRP set for completists. We also issue a warning that there are numerous cheap multi-disc sets which mix out-of-copyright studio dates of this period with indifferent broadcast material, often packaged to suggest the Ella of later years. Buyers beware. The Jazz Anthology set captures a 1940 airshot which mixes superior material – 'Royal Garden Blues', 'Sugar Blues' – with tunes of the order of 'Chewin' Gum', but it's not without period charm, though the sound is indifferent.

***** Ella Fitzgerald 1941–1944**

Classics 840 *Fitzgerald; John McGhee (t); Eddie Barefield (as); Teddy McRae (ts); Tommy Fulford, Bill Furness, Bill Doggett (p); Ulysses Livingston, Slim Furness, Bernie Mackey (g); Peck Furness, Beverley Peer, Bob Haggart (b); Bill Beason, Kenny Clarke, Ernie Hatfield, Johnny Blowers (d); The Ink Spots (v).* 10/41–11/44.

The beginning of Ella's 'solo' career, away from the Chick Webb band. It starts with a lovely version of 'Jim', and the first three sessions have some excellent material, but the 1942 dates with The Four Keys are more novelty-orientated, and two sessions with The Ink Spots are missable. The 1944 tracks see her with an orchestra again. Transfers are from unlisted sources and are good enough.

***** Ella Fitzgerald 1945-1947**

Classics 998 *Fitzgerald; Louis Armstrong (t, v); Charlie Shavers (t); Lou McGarity (tb); Peanuts Hucko (cl); Al Sears (ts); Buddy Weed, Renee Knight, Billy Kyle, Nick Tagg, Eddie Heywood (p); Joe Mooney (acc); Jimmy Shirley, Remo Palmieri, Hy White (g); Trigger Alpert, Junior Raglin, Billy Taylor, Haig Stephens, Lemont Moten (b); Buddy Rich (d, v); George Wettling, Big Sid Catlett, Sylvester Paine, Keg Purnell, Eddie Bourne (d); The Ink Spots (v); plus groups led by Randy Brooks, Vic Schoen, Louis Jordan & His Tympany Five, Bob Haggart.* 2/45–3/47.

***** Ella Fitzgerald 1947-1948**

Classics 1049 *Fitzgerald; Idrees Sulieman (t); Illinois Jacquet (ts); Sir Charles Thompson (org); Hank Jones (p); Hy White (g); Ray Brown, John Simmons (b); J.C Heard (d); plus group led by Bob Haggart.* 3/47–11/48.

All but a few of these tracks are from sessions for Decca, the exceptions being a handful of titles on Classics 998 made for V-Disc (including an entertaining dust-up with Buddy Rich on 'Blue Skies'). Ella was still getting some very thin material – her exuberant scat showcase on the 1945 'Flying Home' was followed by a ludicrous 'Stone Cold Dead In De Market' with Louis Jordan – but the voice was starting to bloom into its full maturity and there are some lovely things scattered amidst the lesser pieces: 'I'm Just A Lucky So And So', 'A Sunday Kind Of Love', 'That Old Feeling' and a hip and convincingly boppish 'How High The Moon'.

***** 75th Birthday Celebration**

MCA GRP 26192 2CD *Fitzgerald; small groups featuring Louis Armstrong (t, v); Taft Jordan, Aaron Izenhall, Leonard Graham (t); Sandy Williams (tb); Louis Jordan (as, v); Josh Jackson, Hilton Jefferson, Teddy McRae (reeds); Bill Doggett (p, org); Billy Kyle, Bill Davis, Ellis Larkins, Don Abney, René Knight, Hank Jones, John Lewis (p); Carl Hogan, John Trueheart, Bill Jennings, Hy White, Bernie Mackay, Jimmy Shirley (g); Arnold Fishkind, Jesse Simpkins, Ray Brown, Haig Stephens, Bob Bushnell, Joe Mondragon, Beverley Peer, Bob Haggart, Junior Raglin (b); Larry Bunker, Sylvester Payne, George Wettling, Chick Webb, Johnny Blowers, Eddie Byrd, Joe Harris, Rudy Taylor (d); Dick Jacobs, Harry Dial, Vic Lourie (perc); The Ink Spots (v); plus orchestras of Bob Haggart, Chick Webb, Vic Schoen, Sy Oliver, Gordon Jenkins, Benny Carter and Toots Camarata.* 5/38–8/55.

***** The War Years 1941–1947**

GRP 052268-2 2CD *Similar to above.* 41–47.

***** The Last Decca Years 1949-1954**

Decca/GRP 050668-2 *Fitzgerald; Sy Oliver Orchestra; Louis Armstrong (v, t).* 49–54.

****** Pure Ella**

GRP 051636-2 *Fitzgerald; Ellis Larkins (p).* 9/50–3/54.

Universal's Ella holdings are now vast, since they bring together both the Decca and the Verve material. The birthday collection (although packaged more like a wedding album, and now a bit dated since she's passed on) is an intermittently convincing cross-section of her best for Decca over some 17 years. The early tracks are given short shrift since there are only two tracks with Webb and, accurate though it may be as a portrait of her Decca period, there's too much pap chosen from the 1940s – rubbish with The Song Spinners and The Ink Spots, and thinly spread jive with Louis Jordan. Premium scat on 'Lady Be Good' and a gorgeous duet with Pops on 'Dream A Little Dream Of Me' salvage the day, and the '50s stuff is better, with a full session of Benny Carter charts and one track from the collaboration with Larkins. *The War Years* covers her uncertain early period at Decca more comprehensively, while *The Last Decca Years 1949–1954* is devoted mostly to Sy Oliver arrangements and is a sometimes frustrating mixed bag. Some of Oliver's charts are mysteriously banal – he makes 'I've Got The World On A String', to choose one promising piece, almost vaudevillian – and 'Goody Goody' wasn't the sort of song to bring Ella any grown-up appeal. But her singing is approaching its great period, and she does some wonderful things with 'You'll Have To Swing It (Mr Paganini)', 'In The Evening' and 'Angel Eyes', among others.

Pure Ella is a masterpiece, her first great album (*Ella Sings Gershwin*) coupled with *Songs In A Mellow Mood*, all of it with Larkins's gentle, persuasive accompaniments. Her voice bridges the girlish timbre of her early days with the grander delivery she moved on to for her Verve albums; and on this almost ideal programme of standards nothing is out of place. Fine remastering and an essential Fitzgerald item.

****** The Cole Porter Songbook**
Verve 537257-2 2CD *Fitzgerald; Buddy Bregman Orchestra.* 2/56.

****** The Rodgers And Hart Songbook**
Verve 537258-2 2CD *Fitzgerald; Buddy Bregman Orchestra.* 8/56.

****** Sings The Duke Ellington Songbook**
Verve 559248-2 3CD *Fitzgerald; Cat Anderson, Willie Cook, Clark Terry, Harold Baker (t); Quentin Jackson, Britt Woodman, John Sanders (tb); Jimmy Hamilton (cl, ts); Johnny Hodges (as); Russell Procope (cl, as); Ben Webster, Paul Gonsalves, Frank Foster (ts); Harry Carney (bs, bcl, cl); Duke Ellington, Paul Smith, Oscar Peterson (p); Stuff Smith (vn); Barney Kessel, Herb Ellis (g); Jimmy Woode, Joe Mondragon, Ray Brown (b); Alvin Stoller, Sam Woodyard (d).* 9/56–10/57.

*****(*) The Irving Berlin Songbook Vol. 1**
Verve 829534-2 *Fitzgerald; Paul Weston Orchestra.* 3/58.

*****(*) The Irving Berlin Songbook Vol. 2**
Verve 829535-2 *Fitzgerald; Paul Weston Orchestra.* 3/58.

****** The George & Ira Gershwin Songbook**
Verve 539759-2 4CD *Fitzgerald; Nelson Riddle Orchestra.* 1–3/59.

****** Ella Sings Arlen Vol. 1**
Verve 817527-2 *Fitzgerald; Billy May Orchestra.* 8/60–1/61.

****** Ella Sings Arlen Vol. 2**
Verve 817528-2 *Fitzgerald; Billy May Orchestra.* 8/60–1/61.

***** The Jerome Kern Songbook**
Verve 821669-2 *Fitzgerald; Nelson Riddle Orchestra.* 63.

***** The Johnny Mercer Songbook**
Verve 539057-2 *Fitzgerald; Nelson Riddle Orchestra.* 10/64.

***** The Songbooks**
Verve 823445-2 *As above discs.* 56–64.

****** Best Of The Songbooks**
Verve 519804-2 *As above discs.* 56–64.

*****(*) Best Of The Songbooks – The Ballads**
Verve 521867-2 *As above discs.* 56–64.

***** Day Dream: Best Of The Duke Ellington Songbook**
Verve 527223-2 *As Ellington set, above.* 9/56–10/57.

***** Oh, Lady Be Good! Best Of The Gershwin Songbook**
Verve 529581-2 *As Gershwin set, above.* 3/59.

****** The Complete Songbooks**
Verve 519832-2 16CD *As above discs.* 56–64.

In January 1956, Fitzgerald began recording for Norman Granz's Verve label, and the first release, *The Cole Porter Songbook*, became the commercial rock on which Verve was built. It was so successful that Granz set Ella to work on all the great American songwriters, and her series of 'songbook' albums are an unrivalled sequence of their kind. The records work consistently well for a number of reasons. Fitzgerald herself was at a vocal peak, strong yet flexible, and her position as a lyric interpreter was perfectly in tune with records dense with lyrical detail; each disc carefully programmes familiar with lesser-known material; the arrangers all work to their strengths, Bregman and May delivering hard-hitting big-band sounds, Riddle the suavest of grown-up orchestrations; and the quality of the studio recordings was and remains outstandingly lifelike and wide-ranging on most of the discs. The new Master Editions of the Porter, Rodgers and Hart, Gershwin and Mercer albums sound more handsome than ever.

Arguably the greatest achievement is the Gershwin set, once a five-LP box, now a resplendent four-CD set, which works patiently through 53 songs without any suspicion of going through the motions. The delight in listening to these discs one after another lies in hearing some almost forgotten tunes – 'The Half Of It, Dearie, Blues', 'You've Got What Gets Me', even 'Just Another Rhumba' – alongside the premier Gershwin melodies, and Fitzgerald's concentration is such that a formidable standard is maintained. Verve's new Master Edition adds a fourth disc to the original three and includes the only surviving alternative takes (Ella complains on take eight of 'Oh, Lady be Good' that she may never get it – she does) as well as ten songs in their mono mixes – quite a revelation, since the voice actually comes through more clearly on these tracks, and it makes one wish to hear the whole set that way on CD as well. Listening through this great archive, one notices here and there how even Ella was discomfited by some of Ira's more pernickety lyrics but, pro that she is, it doesn't dismay the singer.

We have listened again to the other discs, some in the light of their new Master Edition formats. It now seems clear that our reservations about the Rodgers and Hart set were largely unfair. Ella is so supremely effective on the best tracks that one forgives the occasional blandness in handling Lorenz Hart's wit. The Harold Arlen and Cole Porter sets remain singular masterpieces, too. Arlen's songs are among a jazz singer's most challenging material, though, and Fitzgerald is ebulliently partnered by Billy May, who sounds more pertinent here than he did on some of the sessions he did with Sinatra. The Mercer record is slightly disappointing after the previous Gershwin triumph with Riddle, and the Kern collection, though fine enough, is also a secondary choice. The two discs dedicated to Berlin are a bit patchy, but the first volume starts off with a quite unsurpassable reading of 'Let's Face The Music And Dance', in which Ella negotiates all the changes in backdrop without the slightest hint of discomfort and goes on to wonderfully tender versions of 'Russian Lullaby' and 'How Deep Is The Ocean'. The second disc works further miracles with 'Isn't This A Lovely Day' and 'Heat Wave'.

The collection made with Duke Ellington is a somewhat different matter, with the composer himself working with the singer. It's been an undervalued record in the past, with charges of under-rehearsal flying about, and there's certainly a major difference between these sessions and the others: Riddle would surely never have tolerated the looseness of some of the playing, or Sam Woodyard in any circumstances. Yet the best of the disc finds Ellington inspired, with such as 'Caravan' evoking entirely new treatments and swingers like 'Drop Me Off In Harlem' fusing Ella's imperturbable time with the rough-and-ready movement of the band in full cry. Some of the tracks feature her with a small group, and there is an 'I Got It Bad And That Ain't Good' which finds Ben Webster almost oozing out of the speakers. Highly recommended, although we are a little disappointed with the new remastering, which makes the Ellington band sound improbably fierce at times.

The best-of pick on *The Songbooks* isn't bad, with 19 tracks and a little over an hour of music, but it emphasizes how little fat there is in the original albums. The more recent *Best Of The Songbooks* is a neat pocket-edition, with some lesser-known tracks alongside the obvious winners. There are also the subsequent *The Ballads* and single-disc editions filleted from the Ellington and Gershwin sets. But the addictive qualities of these albums often leave one hankering for more, and the solution to that problem is the 16-CD set which collects the whole lot.

***** One O'Clock Jump**
Verve 359806-2 *Fitzgerald; Count Basie Orchestra; Joe Williams (v).* 1/56–4/57.

***** At Newport**
Verve 559809-2 *Fitzgerald; Don Abney, Mal Waldron, Junior Mance, Ray Bryant (p); Wendell Marshall, Joe Benjamin, Ike Isaacs (b); Jo Jones, Jimmy Cobb, Specs Wright (d); Carmen McRae (v, p); Billie Holiday (v).* 7/57.

***** Get Happy!**
Verve 523321-2 *Fitzgerald; orchestras led by Frank DeVol, Russell Garcia, Marty Paich, Nelson Riddle, Paul Weston.* 7/57–10/59.

Three new additions to the catalogue which in the main are rounding up what there is left of Ella that still hasn't been reissued. She gets top billing on *One O'Clock Jump*, which is an outrage since she sings only on the first of 13 tracks, and even that is a duet with Joe Williams! The rest of the disc is a middleweight Basie date of the period, somewhat R&B in feel, with Williams showcased extensively. The Newport album brings together the sets sung at the 1957 Festival by Ella, Billie and Carmen, and is at times close to a shambles. Fitzgerald has a difficult time with her trio and is fighting them over the tempos of more than one song, although 'Air Mail Special' is a stunning scat showcase. Holiday is in awful shape and struggles through her set. McRae gets off to a dreadful start, since half of her group didn't show up until three numbers in (she sounds like she's cheering when they do arrive) and she gets barely any time onstage anyway. Fascinating documentary record, but whether listeners would want to return to it very often is debatable.

Get Happy! is an unhappy set of songs – 'Beat Me Daddy Eight To The Bar', 'Like Young', 'Cheerful Little Earful' – strung together from five different sessions under five different leaders. In the circumstances, consummate pro that she is, Ella still turns in some fine work.

****** Like Someone In Love**
Verve 511524-2 *Fitzgerald; Ted Nash (as); Stan Getz (ts); Frank DeVol Orchestra.* 10/57.

***** At The Opera House**
Verve 831269-2 *Fitzgerald; Roy Eldridge (t); J.J Johnson (tb); Sonny Stitt (as); Coleman Hawkins, Stan Getz, Flip Phillips (ts); Oscar Peterson (p); Herb Ellis (g); Ray Brown (b); Connie Kay (d).* 9–10/57.

****** Ella Swings Lightly**
Verve 517535-2 *Fitzgerald; Don Fagerquist, Al Porcino (t); Bob Enevoldsen (vtb); Bud Shank (as); Bill Holman (ts); Lou Levy (p); Mel Lewis (d).* 58.

***** Ella In Rome (The Birthday Concert)**
Verve 835454-2 *Fitzgerald; Oscar Peterson, Lou Levy (p); Herb Ellis (g); Ray Brown, Max Bennett (b); Gus Johnson (d).* 4/58.

*****(*) The Intimate Ella**
Verve 829838-2 *Fitzgerald; Paul Smith (p).* 60.

***** Mack The Knife (Ella In Berlin)**
Verve 519564-2 *Fitzgerald; Paul Smith (p); Jim Hall (g); Wilfred Middlebrooks (b); Gus Johnson (d).* 2/60.

***** Ella Returns To Berlin**
Verve 837758-2 *Fitzgerald; Lou Levy, Oscar Peterson (p); Herb Ellis (g); Wilfred Middlebrooks, Ray Brown (b); Gus Johnson, Ed Thigpen (d).* 2/61.

*****(*) Ella Wishes You A Swinging Christmas**
Verve 827150-2 *Fitzgerald; Frank DeVol Orchestra.* 60.

***** Clap Hands, Here Comes Charlie!**
Verve 835646-2 *Fitzgerald; Lou Levy (p); Herb Ellis (g); Joe Mondragon, Wilfred Middlebrooks (b); Stan Levey, Gus Johnson (d).* 1–6/61.

*****(*) Ella Swings Brightly With Nelson**
Verve 519347-2 *Fitzgerald; Nelson Riddle Orchestra.* 59–61.

***** Ella Swings Gently With Nelson**
Verve 519348-2 *Fitzgerald; Nelson Riddle Orchestra.* 61–62.

***** Rhythm Is Our Business**
Verve 559513-2 *Fitzgerald; Bill Doggett Orchestra.* 1/62.

*****(*) Ella And Basie**
Verve 539059-2 *Fitzgerald; Joe Newman, Al Aarons, Sonny Cohn, Don Rader, Fip Ricard (t); Henry Coker, Grover Mitchell, Benny Powell, Urbie Green (tb); Marshal Royal (as, cl); Eric Dixon (ts, f); Frank Wess (ts, as, f); Frank Foster (ts); Charlie Fowlkes (bs); Freddie Green (g); Buddy Catlett (b); Sonny Payne (d).* 7/63.

***** These Are The Blues**
Verve 829536-2 *Fitzgerald; Roy Eldridge (t); Wild Bill Davis (org); Herb Ellis (g); Ray Brown (b); Gus Johnson (d).* 10/63.

*****(*) Verve Jazz Masters: Ella Fitzgerald**
Verve 519822-2 *Fitzgerald; various groups.* 55–62.

The 'songbook' albums may be Fitzgerald's best-remembered at Verve, but there were many more good ones, and a fair number of them are still in print. Essential: *Like Someone In Love*, a very fine programme of major standards and rarities, with Getz taking solos on four tracks; *Ella Swings Lightly*, arranged by Marty Paich with his West Coast band handling the backings; the meeting with Basie, which is a little more fun than her encounters with Ellington, brash and exciting but tempered by the invulnerable machine that was Basie's band; *The Intimate Ella*, a one-on-one meeting with underrated pianist Paul Smith, and a good instance of the big voice being shaded down; and the Christmas album, the least affected and most swinging seasonal jazz album ever made. Good ones: *At The Opera House*, which is a bit of a typical JATP rave-up but has its moments; *Clap Hands, Here Comes Charlie!*, a swinging small-group encounter, and something of a rarity in her record dates from this period; and the recently issued *Returns To Berlin*, which comes in excellent sound. The original *Berlin* set has been beefed up with some extra tracks in its latest incarnation and includes the famous version of 'Mack The Knife'.

Disappointing, but still worth hearing, are *These Are The Blues*, which tends to prove that Ella is no great queen of the idiom, despite the nicely simmering back-ups from Davis and Eldridge, and the Rome concert. *Rhythm Is Our Business* seems like a shot at some kind of youth market, with Doggett's R&B-flavoured scores and material like 'Hallelujah I Love Him So'. Ella sings gamely enough, but this isn't really her thing. The *Swings Brightly/Swings Gently* albums with Riddle are welcome appearances on CD: the *Brightly* set is the superior one, if only for the irresistible treatment of 'Don't Be That Way'; but the ballads disc is fine, too. The Verve Jazz Masters disc picks its way past some of the other Ella compilations and delivers an interesting summary for those who don't want to trawl through the whole Verve catalogue. Her albums with Louis Armstrong are listed under his name.

***** Ella At Duke's Place**

Verve 529700-2 *Fitzgerald; Cat Anderson, Herbie Jones, Cootie Williams (t); Lawrence Brown, Buster Cooper, Chuck Connors (tb); Jimmy Hamilton (cl, ts); Russell Procope (cl, as); Johnny Hodges (as); Paul Gonsalves (ts); Harry Carney (bs); Duke Ellington (p); John Lamb (b); Sam Woodyard (d).* 10/65.

If only the whole album had been as good as the opening, a wonderful reading of 'Something To Live For'. The other ballads in the first half are nearly as good. But the up-tempo pieces show both singer and band at something less than their best, Ellington's notorious weakness for inappropriate speeds getting the better of him and Ella not quite on top of the situation, even if the good things were worth salvaging.

***** Ella And Duke At The Côte D'Azur**

Verve 539030-2 2CD *As above, except add Dud Bascomb, Mercer Ellington (t), Ben Webster (ts), Jimmy Jones (p), Jim Hughart (b), Grady Tate (d).* 7/66.

*****(*) Côte D'Azur Concerts**

Verve 539033-2 8CD *As above.* 7/66.

This is the original double-LP set with just a few extra tracks, whetting the appetite for the *eight*-disc set that covers all the concerts from this occasion by Fitzgerald and Ellington. In what is effectively a truncated form, this seems like little more than a patchwork of some pieces by Ellington and some by Ella with her trio (Jones, Hughart and Tate). Since neither situation finds the artists at their greatest heights, this goes down as an enjoyable but familiar sampling of festival routine. Highlight: Ella's serenely effective 'The More I See You'.

The big set is more about Ellington than Ella, and it includes on the final disc a full-scale rehearsal of three pieces which will intrigue Ducal scholars. Our grading may be on the generous side: there's much to enjoy on each of the discs, but presenting what is effectively four days of work, with all the various repetitions and routines of the artists exposed, is a demystification which many will not particularly welcome, and it's symptomatic of the size-matters philosophy which the CD era and reissue programmes have almost obsessively encouraged in recent years.

*****(*) Something To Live For**

Verve 547800-2 2CD *Fitzgerald; various accompanists, most listed above.* 35–66.

In the overcrowded marketplace of Fitzgerald compilations, at least this one breaks new ground, covering both her Decca and Verve material in one package and two CDs. Excellent sound throughout and fine documentation will make this a worthwhile choice for many, but the track listing seems to have been closely tied in with a PBS documentary and in consequence feels compromised – any Ella admirer will be disappointed at some of the omissions.

****(*) In Budapest**

Pablo 5308-2 *Fitzgerald; Tommy Flanagan (p); Frank De La Rosa (b); Ed Thigpen (d).* 5/70.

A rare sighting of Ella in Eastern Europe, from a period when she wasn't making many records. The concert set has many of the usual pieces, and she has a go at 'Spinning Wheel', one of the worst songs of the era (and she says as much). There's a lovely Cole Porter medley, and she manages to make the most of 'Raindrops Keep Falling On My Head' and even 'I'll Never Fall In Love Again'. For completists.

***** Take Love Easy**

Pablo 2310-702 *Fitzgerald; Joe Pass (g).* 73.

****(*) Fine And Mellow**

Pablo 2310-829 *Fitzgerald; Clark Terry (t, flhn); Harry 'Sweets' Edison (t); Eddie 'Lockjaw' Davis, Zoot Sims (ts); Tommy Flanagan (p); Joe Pass (g); Ray Brown (b); Louie Bellson (d).* 1/74.

*****(*) Ella In London**

Pablo 2310-711 *Fitzgerald; Tommy Flanagan (p); Joe Pass (g); Keter Betts (b); Bobby Durham (d).* 4/74.

***** Montreux 1975**

Pablo 2310-751 *As above, except omit Pass.* 7/75.

*****(*) Ella And Oscar**

Pablo 2310-759 *Fitzgerald; Oscar Peterson (p); Ray Brown (b).* 5/75.

***** Fitzgerald And Pass ... Again**

Pablo 2310-772 *Fitzgerald; Joe Pass (g).* 1–2/76.

**** Dream Dancing**

Pablo 2310-814 *Fitzgerald; Nelson Riddle Orchestra.* 6/72–2/78.

****(*) Lady Time**

Pablo 2310-825 D *Fitzgerald; Jackie Davis (org); Louie Bellson (d).* 6/78.

***** A Perfect Match**

Pablo 231-2110 *Fitzgerald; Pete Minger, Sonny Cohn, Paul Cohen, Raymond Brown (t); Booty Wood, Bill Hughes, Mel Wanzo, Dennis Wilson (tb); Kenny Hing, Danny Turner (ts); Eric Dixon, Bobby Plater (as); Charlie Fowlkes (bs); Count Basie (p); Freddie Green (g); Keter Betts (b); Mickey Roker (d).* 7/79.

***** A Classy Pair**

Pablo 2310 132 *As above, except add Nolan Smith (t), John Clayton (b), Butch Miles (d); omit Cohen, Betts and Roker.* 2/79.

***** Digital III At Montreux**

Original Jazz Classics OJC 996 *Similar to above, except add Paul Smith (p), Joe Pass (g), Niels-Henning Orsted Pedersen(b).* 7/79.

Back with Norman Granz again, Ella recorded steadily through the 1970s, but there was little to suggest she would either repeat or surpass the best of her earlier music. If encroaching age is supposed to impart a greater wisdom to a singer of songs, and hence into the interpretation of those songs, it's a more complex matter with Fitzgerald. While her respectful delivery of lyrics honours the wordsmithing, she brought little of the personal gravitas to the American songbook which was Sinatra's trademark. Her scatting grew less fluent and more exaggerated, if no less creative in its construction; her manipulation of time and melody became more obvious because she had to push herself harder to make it happen. There are still many good records here, but no really great ones, and all of them miss a little of the grace and instinctive improvisation which float off all her older records.

Granz recorded her in several settings. With Joe Pass, the bare-strings accompaniment is initially intimate but finally dull: Pass can't devise enough variation to make the music stay awake, and Fitzgerald isn't always sure how strongly she's able to come on. Their duet albums are nice enough, but one is enough. *Fine And Mellow* is a rather noisy and brash session, but the title-track is a very good version of the Holiday favourite, which sounds just as good in Ella's hands. The Montreux and Nice live sets are merely OK, and much better is the London date from 1974: probably the final chance to hear Ella in a club setting, and it's a racy and sometimes virtuosic display by the singer, a fine souvenir of what was a memorable visit. The 1979 Montreux set is unexciting: most of it is average Basie or Pass, and Ella does only one ballad and a lumber through 'Flying Home'. Of the big-band dates, *Dream Dancing* features Nelson Riddle at his sententious worst and is missable, while the two sets with Basie are boisterous if comparatively uneventful. *Lady Time* is an unusual setting which tries Ella out as a kind of club-class blueswoman; she makes a game go of it. The other must-hear record, though, is the duet (almost – Ray Brown offers discreet support) with Oscar Peterson, *Ella And Oscar*. The pianist plays as hard as usual, but instrumentalist and vocalist bring out the best in each other, and there are at least three near-classics in 'Mean To Me', 'How Long Has This Been Going On?' and 'Midnight Sun'.

****(*) Ella Abraça Jobim**

Pablo 2630-201 *Fitzgerald; Clark Terry (t); Zoot Sims (ts); Toots Thielemans (hca); Mike Lang, Clarence McDonald, Terry Trotter (ky); Joe Pass, Oscar Castro-Nueves, Paul Jackson, Mitch Holder, Roland Bautista (g); Abe Laboriel (b); Alex Acuna (d); Paulinho Da Costa (perc).* 9/80.

****(*) The Best Is Yet To Come**

Original Jazz Classics 889 *Fitzgerald; Al Aarons (t); Bill Watrous (tb); Marshal Royal (as); Bob Cooper (ts); Jimmy Rowles (p); Art Hillery (org); Joe Pass, Tony Tedesco (g); Jim Hughart (b); Shelly Manne (d); strings and woodwinds.* 2/82.

****(*) Nice Work If You Can Get It**

Pablo 2312-140 *Fitzgerald; André Previn (p).* 5/83.

***** Speak Love**

Pablo 2310-888 *Fitzgerald; Joe Pass (g).* 3/83.

***** Easy Living**

Pablo 2310-921 *As above.*

**** All That Jazz**

Pablo 2310-938 *Fitzgerald; Clark Terry, Harry 'Sweets' Edison (t); Al Grey (tb); Benny Carter (as); Mike Wofford, Kenny Barron (p); Ray Brown (b); Bobby Durham (d).* 3/89.

***** The Best Of Ella Fitzgerald**

Pablo 2405-421 *As various Pablo discs above.*

***** Bluella: Ella Fitzgerald Sings The Blues**

Pablo 2310-960 *As various Pablo discs above.*

The 1980s saw Fitzgerald slackening off her workload as illness and perhaps sheer tiredness intervened. The Jobim collection came too late, since every other singer had already had their shot at this kind of thing; *The Best* was another tiresome set of Nelson Riddle arrangements; and the duo album with Previn was a pointless bit of star-matching. Which left two more albums with Pass and what proved to be a farewell set in the strained and unconvincing *All That Jazz*. At least the best-of is a good selection from the pick of the above. *Bluella* tackles the thorny issue of Fitzgerald in her most vulnerable idiom by settling for pseudo-blues items such as 'C-Jam Blues' 'Duke's Place' and 'Smooth Sailing'. Not bad.

*****(*) The Concert Years**

Pablo 4414-2 4CD *Basically as Pablo albums above.* 53–83.

Distilled from Fizgerald's live appearances as a headliner and with JATP, this is a very strong four-disc set which should be the first stopping-point for those who want to hear Ella the improviser and jazz musician. Starting with JATP material from the 1950s, it takes in three different shows with Ellington, the 1974 set at Ronnie Scott's club, three Montreux appearances from the 1970s, and a final (1983) show in Tokyo. If there are occasional lapses in judgement, where her scatting or phrasing can become almost parodic, the quality of her musicianship wins through. Cameos from many famous names add to the interest.

Paul Flaherty

ALTO AND TENOR SAXOPHONES

Based in and around Connecticut, Flaherty is the nominal leader of a gang of unreconstituted free-jazzers, most of whom appear on these records.

*****(*) Fat Onions**

Cadence CJR 1054 *Flaherty; James 'Chumly' Hunt (t, pkt-t); Stephen Scholz (vn); Mike Murray (g); Richard Downs (b); Randall Colbourne (d).* 11/93.

***** Visitants**

Zaabway 2001 *As above, except omit Hunt and Scholz.* 3/94.

Flaherty is an irascible-sounding saxophonist who takes his cues from the unadorned energy playing of the 1960s and early '70s. He co-leads these groups with drummer Colbourne, and together they marshal a music which forms around dense, braying collectives, sometimes recalling the heterophony of the Ayler ensemble, sometimes a golden-age FMP session, and sometimes creating something peculiarly their own. It's an exhilarating experience – and an exhausting one, handled over CD length; but endemic to this kind of listening is a sense of shared work-experience with the players. Hence the slightly superior rating for *Fat Onions*, with its bigger ensemble and heavier, cloudier music, because it's harder work. There are moments of lyricism and quiet, though these are annihilated soon enough, and the group breaks into a kind of hymnal mode when it wants to sound celebratory. For the committed only, perhaps, but it's pleasing to know that this kind of jazz is still being explored and created. Recording is all right, if on the dry side on both sessions.

***** Third Rail**

Zaabway 2002 *Flaherty; Richard Downs (b, sou); Randall Colbourne (d, v).* 9/95.

*****(*) Ringtaw**

Zaabway 2004 *As above, except add James 'Chumly' Hunt (t, perc); Matt Moran (vib, perc); Mike Murray (g).* 9/96.

***** Resonance**

Zaabway 2005 *Flaherty; Raphe Malik (t, p); Daniel Carter (t, cl, as, ts, f, p); Sabir Mateen (as, ts, cl, f, p, v); Randall Colbourne (d, p).* 5/97.

Flaherty and Colbourne soldier on, from the 'hotbed of free jazz', Connecticut. *Third Rail* is the axis at its most pure: Flaherty simply roars on and on, with the other two scuttling about below, though Downs gets off a bit of a surprise when he starts parping on a sousaphone on 'Rosebud Ricochet'. *Ringtaw* is surely their finest hour so far, three long but dourly beautiful improvisations in which the sextet achieve a genuinely conspiratorial music at the same moment as each one is blowing his head off. Or so it seems. 'Part 1' is a modest triumph, though some unexpected lyricism blossoms in 'Part 2'. They could use a better studio-sound, though – Colbourne especially gets short-changed with the mix on offer.

Resonance is a souvenir of a let's-walk-on-and-see-what-happens kind of concert, where Connecticut's finest met with Malik, Mateen and Carter, apparently shouldering an Art Ensemble's worth of instruments among them. Exhilarating as usual and a nice mix of voices, though again the rough live sound hinders appreciation at times.

*****(*) Anahad**

Cadence CJR 1107 *Flaherty; James 'Chumly' Hunt (t, flhn, pkt-t); Mike Murray (g); Richard Downs (b); Randall Colbourne (d).* 11/98.

The team return for another freewheeling, free-ranging and freely formed set of free jazz (only the record is not free – you'll have to pay for it). As usual, they open with a tremendous blow on 'Smokeshop', almost 29 minutes long, and follow it with three more which are more or less more of the same, only different. The sound is never going to get crystal-clear, but it works. As ever, hugely enjoyable if you like this kind of music; if you don't, you'll relate to the 26 put-downs which Flaherty cheerfully lists in the sleeve-note, the kind of thing these guys and many like them must have heard their whole playing lives. Our favourite is 'My wife said to get your record outta the house'.

Tommy Flanagan (born 1930)

PIANO

One of the piano masters of Detroit, he played on many major recordings in the late '50s but thereafter sought an accompanist's security behind Ella Fitzgerald and Tony Bennett. Emerged as an undimmed creative spirit in the '70s and '80s, a bebopper of gentlemanly distinction.

***** The Cats**

Original Jazz Classics OJC 079 *Flanagan; Idrees Sulieman (t); John Coltrane (ts); Kenny Burrell (g); Doug Watkins (b); Louis Hayes (d).* 4/57.

***** The Complete 'Overseas'**

DIW 305 *Flanagan; Wilbur Little (b); Elvin Jones (d).* 8/57.

***** Jazz ... It's Magic**

Savoy SV 0153 *Flanagan; Curtis Fuller (tb); Sonny Red (as); George Tucker (b); Louis Hayes (d).* 9/57.

If it's difficult to make fine qualitative distinctions within Tommy Flanagan's discography, it isn't difficult to distinguish his output from the average piano trio of the last 30 years. The earlier albums date from a period before he became known as one of the finest accompanists in the business, backing Tony Bennett and, more memorably, Ella Fitzgerald in her great late-1960s resurgence. *The Cats* is officially a Prestige All Stars session, but it is Flanagan's stewardship of the house rhythm section that makes the gig his own, and there is a wonderful 'How Long Has This Been Going On' for trio which clinches the deal. He is always at the heart of the action, helping out the hornmen when they lose their way, once or twice cutting through the verbiage to get back to the song. There is also material from this period and from similar line-ups on other discs.

Flanagan's touch at this point lacks the fabled delicacy it acquired later, but he has a fine, boppish attack that is complemented by Jones on the excellent European sessions, and by the adaptable Hayes. Fuller adds an interesting dimension to the Savoy session, riding the rails with Flanagan on 'Club Car' with the kind of precarious ease both seem to specialize in. Unfortunately the saxophonist is pretty dreary (though he seems to have been drinking from the same spring as the young Coltrane) and the trio tracks on the same disc are well below par for Flanagan.

***** The Tommy Flanagan Trio**

Original Jazz Classics OJC 182 *Flanagan; Tommy Potter (b); Roy Haynes (d).* 5/60.

This plain-label session is as blunt and straightforward as the title suggests and helps plug a longish gap in the available documentation. Flanagan rolls his sleeves up and wades straight into a nicely judged programme of standards with an emphasis on medium-paced ballads. He's at his best on 'In The Blue Of The Evening' and 'In A Sentimental Mood', the opening and closing numbers, while 'You Go To My Head' underlines his determination to stay in sight of the lyric at all times.

****(*) The Tokyo Recital**

Original Jazz Classics OJC 737 *Flanagan; Keter Betts (b); Bobby Durham (d).* 2/75.

****(*) Montreux '77**

Original Jazz Classics OJC 372 *As above.* 7/77.

***** The Best Of Tommy Flanagan**

Pablo PACD 2405 410 *As above.* 2/75 & 7/77.

****(*) Something Borrowed, Something Blue**
Original Jazz Classics OJC 473 *As above, except Jimmie Smith (d) replaces Durham.* 1/78.

***** Eclipso**
Enja 2088 *Flanagan; George Mraz (b); Elvin Jones (d).* 2/77.

****(*) Confirmation**
Enja 4014 *As above.* 2/77 & 11/78.

*****(*) Our Delights**
Original Jazz Classics OJC 752 *Flanagan; Hank Jones (p).* 1/78.

***** Ballads And Blues**
Enja 3031 *Flanagan; George Mraz (b, duo).* 11/78.

****(*) Plays The Music Of Harold Arlen**
DIW 328 *Flanagan; George Mraz (b); Connie Kay (d); Helen Merrill (v). n.d.*

*****(*) Super Session**
Enja 3059 *Flanagan; Red Mitchell (b); Elvin Jones (d).* 2/80.

***** You're Me**
Phontastic CD 7528 *As above, except omit Jones.* 2/80.

****** Giant Steps: In Memory Of John Coltrane**
Enja 4022 *Flanagan; George Mraz (b); Al Foster (d).* 2/82.

****(*) Thelonica**
Enja 4052 *Flanagan; George Mraz (b); Art Taylor (d).* 12/82.

Throughout the 1970s and early '80s, Flanagan explored aspects of harmony most closely associated with the late John Coltrane, often stretching his solos very far from the tonal centre but without lapsing into the tuneless abstractions that were such a depressing aspect of Coltrane's legacy.

Elvin Jones's presence and multidirectional approach are always a plus on Flanagan dates. *Eclipso* (and *Confirmation*, which uses up some unreleased masters from the February 1977 session) develops the relationship further; *Super Session* brings it to a peak; recorded three weeks later, *You're Me* manages to hang on to some of the same energy. Increasingly, though, it is the partnership of Flanagan and bassist Mraz which dominates and Jones who tends to follow. *Ballads And Blues* is a piano–bass duo, and pithy in the extreme. *Our Delights* has all the signs of a real meeting of minds. As usual, not a particularly adventurous roster of tunes: 'Our Delight', 'Jordu', 'Lady Bird', two takes of 'Robbins Nest', 'Autumn Leaves' – but beautifully crafted all the same.

The Best Of ..., which brings together much of the preceding Pablo with the live session from Montreux '77, might more usefully have been labelled a Strayhorn tribute, since he is the main composer represented. Flanagan sounds bright and airy but also a little empty of ideas, and some of his colleagues' work is decidedly pedestrian and uninspired.

It's often forgotten that it was Flanagan who accompanied John Coltrane on (most of) the original *Giant Steps*. The quartet sessions with Harden occasionally recall those days, but not particularly memorably; the homage to Coltrane, though, is a marvellous set. Flanagan repeats several of the tracks from *Giant Steps*, adds 'Central Park West', and tackles 'Naima', which Coltrane had entrusted to Wynton Kelly on a later session. Flanagan's reinterpretations are emotive, often harmonically clearer, and very beautiful. As is the most recent of these records: featuring Mraz again and the brightly swinging Kenny Washington. Flanagan's a wonderfully lyrical performer, with the widest imaginable range of diction and association. There is not a dull or fudged set in the bunch, but it's hard to go past *Giant Steps* or *Jazz Poet*, below.

****** Jazz Poet**
Timeless SJP 301 *Flanagan; George Mraz (b); Kenny Washington (d).* 1/89.

'Jazz poet' would be a fair passport entry for what Flanagan does. A beautifully judged and perfectly performed record you'll find yourself playing often. Though a studio session, it has the relaxed but subtly challenging feel of one of Flanagan's club dates. Outstanding tracks include the opening 'Raincheck', 'Caravan', and an unexpected performance of 'St Louis Blues'. Mraz is at the top of his powers and Washington doesn't attempt to muscle in but keeps to his business patiently and accurately. Lovely.

*****(*) Beyond The Bluebird**
Timeless SJP 350 *Flanagan; Kenny Burrell (g); George Mraz (b); Lewis Nash (d).* 4/90.

After concert and recorded tributes to Ellington and Coltrane, Flanagan turns back to bebop and the spirit of Charlie Parker. The pianist, though, has always been conscious that music is very precisely mediated by time and place, specific contexts. The Bluebird Inn in Detroit was a significant bop locus; Flanagan and Elvin Jones both played in the house band there, as did Barry Harris, whose 'Nascimento' anchors the second half of the disc. The first half of the set is dedicated to it and the music played there: two (relatively unfamiliar) Parker compositions, 'Bluebird' and 'Barbados', a long 'Yesterdays' featuring Burrell at his most contemplative, Benny Carter's 'Blues In My Heart' and '50-21' (the Bluebird's address) by trumpeter/bandleader Thad Jones, like his brother a stalwart of the club.

The second half of the set is, in the words of Flanagan's title-piece, 'Beyond The Bluebird', dispelling any imputation of mere nostalgia, and further bracketed by Burrell's closing 'Bluebird After Dark'. 'Something Borrowed, Something Blue' reappears from the old Galaxy session reissued on OJC 473, above, a fine reinvention. Typical of Flanagan's eclectic approach is the inclusion of Dizzy Reece's rarely played 'The Con Man', whose unusual blues tonality provides a vivid setting for remarkable solos by Flanagan and George Mraz.

*****(*) Let's**
Enja ENJ 8040 *Flanagan; Jesper Lundgaard (b); Lewis Nash (d).* 4/93.

Thad Jones's music, most famously 'A Child Is Born', has been well covered by big bands and by horn groups, but never before by a piano trio. (Mal Waldron has covered Jones tunes on club dates, but never with this degree of concentration.) Flanagan knew Thad years ago when they were both starting out. One suspects that they were temperamentally similar, and these treatments bespeak a warm sympathy. It's a generous programme; as well as the title-piece and 'Child', there are performances of 'Mean What You Say', 'To You', 'Bird Song' and 'Scratch' (Nash standing out prominently on these), 'Thadrack', 'Three In One', 'Quietude', 'Zec' and, finally, 'Elusive', which closes the record on a high. The disc was made as part of the 1993 Jazzpar project in Denmark.

Flipside

GROUP

Intercontinental group, based in New York.

***** Flipside**

Naxos 86013-2 *Jérome Sabbagh (sax); Greg Toohey (g); Matt (b); Darren Beckett (d).* 12/97.

Two New Zealanders, a deft Irish drummer and a French saxophonist, all based in New York City: testimony to the quality and range of musical talent currently available in the Big Apple. The material is all original and refreshingly free of cliché, favouring open harmonies and crisp rhythm. Saxophonist Sabbagh and guitarist Toohey sound like players to watch. A few more road miles and Flipside could well be a band to reckon with.

Bob Florence (born 1932)

PIANO, ARRANGER

Active since the late '50s as an arranger in the Los Angeles area, Florence has provided scores and playing situations for many Californian groups, and his own big-band records are unambiguously complex and modernistic playing situations for the best musicians he can find.

***** Name Band – 1959**

Fresh Sound FSCD 2008 *Florence; Johnny Audino, Tony Terran, Jules Chaikin, Irv Bush (t); Bob Edmondson, Bobby Pring, Don Nelligan, Herbie Harper (tb); Bob Enevoldsen (vtb); Herb Geller, Bernie Fleischer (as); Bob Hardaway (ts); Don Shelton (ts, cl); Dennis Budimir (g); Mel Pollan (b); Jack Davenport (d).* 11/58.

*****(*) Funupmanship**

Mama MMF 1006 *Florence; Larry Ford, Warren Luening, Steve Huffsteter, Wayne Bergeron, Charlie Davis, (t, flhn); Rick Culver, Don Waldrop, Alex Iles (tb); Bob Efford, John Lowe, Dick Mitchell, Lanny Morgan, Kim Richmond, Lee Callett (reeds); Tom Warrington (b); Steve Houghton (d).* 92.

***** With All The Bells And Whistles**

Mama MMF 1011 *As above, except add Carl Saunders (t, flhn), Bob McChesney (tb), Terry Harrington, Bob Carr (woodwinds), Brian Kilgore (perc); omit Ford, Culver.* 2/95.

****** Earth**

Mama MMF 1016 *As above, except add George Graham (t, flhn), Charlie Loper (tb), Trey Henry (b), Gregg Field (d); omit Lowe, Morgan, Callet, Warrington, Houghton, Kilgore.* 4/96.

*****(*) Serendipity 18**

Mama MMF 1025 *As above, except add Rick Baptist, Ron Stout (t), Jeff Driskill (ts, cl, f), Dick Weller (d); omit Davis, Mitchell, Carr, Field.* 8/98.

Florence has done sterling work as a big-band arranger, leader and performer over 40 years. His bread has been buttered in Los Angeles studio work, but none of these records sounds compromised by that background: he likes big, swinging, powerful bands, and his charts are stuffed with activity. Soloists seldom get by without counterpoint or some other sort of support, and – unusually for the Californian orchestral tradition – he's as interested in long-form writing as he is in punchy three- and four-minute numbers. His bands are usually staffed by the best executants, with two or three knockout soloists as a bonus, and the Fresh Sound reissue shows that that's been the case from the start. There are marvellous turns by Herb Geller and Bob Enevoldsen here, but the section-work, though filled with unfamiliar names, lacks nothing in polish and attack. The disc is stuffed with alternative takes, but there's plenty of interest throughout.

Florence resumed his recording in the late '70s with seven albums for Discovery, but they all seem to be missing in action for now. His albums for Mama bring the story up to date. *Funupmanship* gains an extra ounce of energy from the live recording, and here Florence really puts the band on its mettle: 'Slimehouse' comes out of the stalls ferociously, and 'Come Rain Or Come Shine' is smart enough to have would-be arrangers scratching their heads. Among the soloists, Kim Richmond plays a key role: a modernist with sufficient tradition in him to uphold and transcend his surroundings. After that, *With All The Bells And Whistles* seems like a pressure drop, and 'Teach Me Tonight' is too arch to convince. Compensations include the rough-housing by the two saxes of Mitchell and Harrington on 'Tenors, Anyone?', which just about makes up for its title. *Earth*, though, finds Florence and team back to top form. These are some of his most challenging and head-turning charts, with 'Straight No Chaser' an extraordinary example of a transformation of a jazz standard. As ever, the soloists seem compelled to give of their best – too many excitements in this department to catalogue here – and if Florence perhaps doesn't quite edge out the peerless Bill Holman on creative terms, he's one of the few arrangers fit to walk in Holman's steps.

No real drop in intensity on *Serendipity 18*, which undergoes a few changes in personnel (Weller is a powerhouse addition to the rhythm section) and finds Florence at his most feisty: 'I haven't simplified anything.' As ever his scores are extravagant with detail and complexity, at times to the point of super-abundance, but the impact of the band in delivering these scores is little short of awesome and, on a more mediated piece such as 'Tres Palabras', the wit of the scoring comes through more clearly. A tremendous sequence of big-band records.

Chris Flory

GUITAR

A knowledgeable young mainstreamer when he joined Benny Goodman in 1979, Flory stayed with him for six years and thereafter has worked in numerous groupings within the idiom.

***** For All We Know**

Concord CCD 4403 *Flory; Mike LeDonne (p, org); Phil Flanigan (b); Chuck Riggs (d).* 1/88.

***** City Life**

Concord CCD 4589 *Flory; John Bunch (p); John Webber (b); Chuck Riggs (d).* 3/93.

*****(*) Word On The Street**

Double-Time DTRCD-119 *Flory; Mike LeDonne (org); Mark Taylor (d).* 9/96.

With three records in ten years, Flory has appeared only sparingly as a leader. He began as a member of the Concord repertory of young mainstreamers, sounding quite at home on both records: the first has a touch of variety lent by LeDonne playing both piano and organ, the second has a more interesting programme of originals and standards (his swinging treatment of 'Besame Mucho' is particularly engaging). But there was little in either disc that made one take notice of anything beyond the merely very good playing. *Word On The Street* isn't a record to grab the attention either, yet the calibre of the playing is such that it finally transcends the clichés of the organ–guitar combo setting. With Taylor virtually an unobtrusive bystander, this is really a dialogue between Flory and LeDonne. The leader's soft touch and nimble phrasing are unlike what one might expect from a guitarist in this situation, and LeDonne too plays a rather light and athletic role. With material by Ellington and Basie and some choice standards, the set-list gets away from the usual blues, and 'I'm A Fool To Want You' is as sombre as a requiem.

Fonda–Stevens Group

GROUP

A regular group of free-boppers working under the nominal leadership of Messrs Fonda and Stevens.

***** The Wish**

Music & Arts CD 916 *Herb Robertson (t, flhn); Mark Whitecage (as, ss); Michael Jefry Stevens (p); Joe Fonda (b); Harvey Sorgen (d); Laura Arbuckle (v).* 6/93–8/95.

***** Parallel Lines**

Music & Arts CD 979 *As above, except omit Arbuckle.* 96.

***** Live From Brugge**

Dwerf 010 *As above.* 4/97.

A group of largely 'unfashionable' improvisers explore the parameters of free bop on this likeable set of records. Robertson and Whitecage are both conservative radicals whose most splenetic moments wouldn't cause an earthquake disturbance. It's their solos and dialogues with different members of the rhythm section that tend to direct the music, even though the writing is all by Fonda and Stevens. The compositions tend to be either open-ended sketches or Coleman-like melodies counterpointed between the instruments, and if the latter carry less conviction it's because the playing seems to run ragged when it should be pointed. Whitecage in particular is a wayward voice who's at his best when least fettered by his surroundings. *The Wish* is the least focused of the three, *Parallel Lines* the most specific, *Live from Brugge* the liveliest (and the one that admits of a collective sense of humour, as in 'The Money Thing' and 'Down On The Delta'). But there is so little to choose qualitatively between the three that it seems unwise to make a clear distinction.

Ricky Ford (born 1954)

TENOR SAXOPHONE

Began recording in the '70s and had spells with Mercer Ellington, Charles Mingus and Dannie Richmond, before leading his own dates. A considerable technician and hearty player, yet to achieve much wider recognition.

***** Loxodonta Africana**

New World 80204 *Ford; Oliver Beener, Charles Sullivan (t); Janice Robinson (tb); James Spaulding (as); Bob Neloms (p); Jonathan Dorn (tba); Richard Davis (b); Dannie Richmond (d).* 77.

***** Manhattan Blues**

Candid CCD 79036 *Ford; Jaki Byard (p); Milt Hinton (b); Ben Riley (d).* 3/89.

*****(*) Ebony Rhapsody**

Candid CCD 79053 *As above.* 6/90.

An erratic but occasionally brilliant player, Ford is best known for his work with Mingus and Abdullah Ibrahim. His own records are ambitious in extent, covering a range of idioms from bop, modal-to-free harmony, and back to a broad swing style. The New World album is a recent CD appearance of an interesting early session. The instrumentation varies between quartet and nonet and the playing, though a bit raw, has some illuminating moments, even if the mix of players is a little awkward. On the 1989 *Manhattan Blues* Ford's breadth of reference is instantaneously answered by the eclectic Byard and by the bassist and drummer; Ford's soloing is thoughtful but still curiously uninvolving. *Ebony Rhapsody*, with the same line-up, irons out the occasional awkwardnesses and finds Ford with a band that seems increasingly responsive to his changes of direction; 'Mirror Man', a duet with Milt 'The Judge' Hinton, has an authority worthy of Coleman Hawkins, and the other originals bespeak a growing compositional talent.

*****(*) Hot Brass**

Candid CCD 79518 *Ford; Lew Soloff, Claudio Roditi (t); Steve Turre (tb); Danilo Perez (p); Christian McBride (b); Carl Allen (d).* 4/91.

The arrangements here are sharp and pungent. 'Banging, Bashing, Bowing and Blowing' is a superb band workout, and '11/15/91' is a chromatic lament for Martin Luther King Jr, written at the time of the Gulf War, while 'Carbon 14' draws its inspiration from Ford's interest in Afro-Americana and the theory that black Africans may have discovered America long before Columbus. Digging ever deeper into those roots, the resulting music is mightily impressive.

Michael Formanek (born 1958)

DOUBLE BASS

Solo bass performance is one of the toughest of all musical disciplines within the embrace of jazz. Formanek is one of the few around – one thinks also of Barre Phillips and Mark Dresser –

who is capable of sustaining interest at length. Most of his recording under his own name has been with sympathetic small groups, but Formanek has also been able to go out alone.

*****(*) Wide Open Spaces**
Enja ENJ 6032 *Formanek; Greg Osby (as, ss); Wayne Krantz (g); Mark Feldman (vn); Jeff Hirshfield (d).* 1/90.

***** Extended Animation**
Enja ENJ 7041 *As above, except Tim Berne (as, bs) replaces Osby.* 11/91.

***** Loose Cannon**
Soul Note 121261 *As above, except omit Krantz and Feldman.* 10/92.

More than an adaptable sideman, Formanek is a musician of considerable intelligence and range, with ideas that probably need more extended exposure. Mingus is probably the main source, though Formanek rarely leads from the front, preferring a more unassuming role (*Low Profile*, title of a later disc, gets it about right). What makes all his records distinctive in their surprisingly different ways is his approach to texture and space, and his ability to give individual voicings a thoroughly idiomatic cast. His use of Krantz and Feldman on the first two records is quite fascinating, and one initially misses their absence on *Loose Cannon*, except that it is quite clearly an exercise in freedom and in a more linear approach. Perhaps fortunately, because the Soul Note sound is not as full and resonant. We are not aware what occasioned the switch of label, but it seems to have been a temporary shift.

Berne is a sourer and more acerbic player than Osby and occasionally he seems pushed too far forward in the mix. What he brings, though, is a solid, blocky presence around which Formanek's own natural lyricism flows like water round a splintery rock. Berne also contributes much of the writing to *Loose Cannon* and, while it's easy to see where the bassist sees fruitful common ground, it would have been good to hear more of his own ideas.

****** Low Profile**
Enja ENJ 8050 *Formanek; Dave Douglas (t); Kuumba Frank Lacy (tb); Tim Berne (as, bs); Marty Ehrlich (as, ss, cl, bcl); Salvatore Bonafede (p); Marvin 'Smitty' Smith (d).* 10/93.

****** Nature Of The Beast**
Enja ENJ9308 *Formanek; Dave Douglas (t); Steve Swell (tb); Tim Berne (as); Tony Malaby (ts); Chris Speed (cl); Jim Black (d).* 3/96.

These are urgent, compelling modern-jazz records, created by a formidable repertory band. It is now almost axiomatic that Douglas's presence is guarantee of something exceptional, but he fits into this concept with particular ease, and on 'Paradise Revisited' he and the estimable Lacy manage to sound like a whole brass section. It is unusual to hear a piano player on a Formanek record; Bonafede, though, has a sufficiently distinctive attack to sustain interest, and on 'Great Plains' he tees up some interesting ideas for the leader's own most ambitious solo feature on disc. Berne blusters and barks, making what was soon to be a regular appearance on baritone. Ehrlich is, of coure, a one-man effects studio, and often his contribution is textural rather than structural, as if Formanek is still looking for some of the unfamiliar tonalities he got from Krantz and Feldman.

Interestingly, reeds are quite deliberately downplayed on the 1996 record, restricted to just four of the eight tracks. In addition, all the recording credits are Formanek's, a long suite of compositions with a very definite, if unprogrammatic, consistency. The long 'Grand Bizarre' pits Douglas against Swell in a cleverly structured theme which exploits the two horns' differences in articulation and pitch. Less of a presence than Lacy, he nevertheless suits this music very well indeed. Malaby is relatively unknown, but he sounds like a prospect. Formanek has not previously looked to a tenor player but for the long closing diptych, 'Thick Skin/Dangerous Crustaceans' (which is Speed's only appearance), he needs a big reed sound.

***** Am I Bothering You?**
Screwgun SCRU U 70006 *Formanek (b solo).* 12/97.

In our last edition we suggested that it would be good to find Formanek a commission for big band or orchestra. It speaks volumes about our prescience – and about the realities of jazz performance – that the next disc should be in that chewiest of all improvising forms: solo bass. Michael's Lowinsky bass sings through the whole session. Whether playing pizzicato or with bow, as he does at the start of 'Overhead Justice', he brings a terrific momentum and charge to what might otherwise be bleakly abstract music. Ending with a flourish on Muddy Waters's 'Rollin' Stone' was a masterstroke.

Jimmy Forrest (1920–80)

TENOR SAXOPHONE

Forrest will always be associated with the mournful swinger, 'Night Train', which was inspired by Duke Ellington. The saxophonist worked with Jay McShann (alongside Charlie Parker) and Andy Kirk, before establishing himself as a leader. Though by no means an innovator, he had a thoroughly individual voice on tenor, raw and tender by turns.

*****(*) Night Train**
Delmark DD 435 *Forrest; Chauncey Locke (t); Bart Dabney (tb); Charles Fox, Bunky Parker (p); Herschel Harris, John Mixon (b); Oscar Oldham (d); Percy James, Bob Reagan (perc).* 11/51–9/53.

***** All The Gin Is Gone**
Delmark 404 *Forrest; Harold Mabern (p); Grant Green (g); Gene Ramey (b); Elvin Jones (d).* 12/59.

***** Black Forrest**
Delmark 427 *As above.* 12/59.

Forrest is the mid-point, stylistically if not quite geographically, between Charlie Parker and Ornette Coleman. His early R&B experience invested his work with a strong, funky sound, which evolved into something richer and more complex, but always straight down the line rhythmically. After leaving the Ellington orchestra, he scored a big hit with 'Night Train', an R&B classic based on Duke's 'Happy Go Lucky Local'. It's the leading item on the eponymous Delmark, an album packed with short, funky themes that really ought to be heard on a jukebox rather than a home hi-fi. It's still a hugely engaging session and confirms that, even in his pop days, Forrest was never merely a honker and wailer but a fine melodist.

Just as later sessions are treasure for glimpses of cult heroes like Joe Zawinul and Larry Young, so the presence of Grant Green on these early sessions has both attracted notice and deflected it away from Jimmy's own melodic hard-bop approach. *All The Gin Is Gone* predates the better-known sessions for New Jazz and Prestige, but it has great strengths and the version of 'Caravan' is masterly. Here, too, the documentation is now complete with the release of *Black Forrest*, a 1972 release drawn from the same sessions as *All The Gin Is Gone*. The date saw the saxophonist lined up with the massive Mabern and precocious youngster Green on a beefy set of blues and ballads. Typically tough and direct playing from all hands.

***** Forrest Fire**
Original Jazz Classics OJC 199 *Forrest; Larry Young (org); Thornel Schwartz (g); Jimmie Smith (d).* 8/60.

***** Out Of The Forrest**
Original Jazz Classics OJC 097 *Forrest; Joe Zawinul (p); Tommy Potter (b); Clarence Johnston (d).* 4/61.

***** Sit Down And Relax With Jimmy Forrest**
Original Jazz Classics OJC 895 *Forrest; Hugh Lawson (p); Calvin Newborn (g); Tommy Potter (b); Clarence Johnston (d).* 9/61.

***** Most Much!**
Original Jazz Classics OJC 350 *As above, except omit Newborn; add Ray Barretto (perc).* 10/61.

***** Soul Street**
Original Jazz Classics 987 *As above, plus Art Farmer, Idries Sulieman (t), Jimmy Cleveland, George Cooper (tb), Jerome Richardson (as, f), George Barrow, King Curtis, Oliver Nelson, Seldon Powell (ts), Pepper Adams (bs), Ray Bryant, Gene Casey, Chris Woods (p), Tiny Grimes, Mundell Lowe (g), George Duvivier, Wendell Marshall (b), Roy Haynes, Osie Johnson, Ed Shaughnessy (d).* 61.

Understandably, much of the interest of these centres on a pre-Weather Report Zawinul and the late, great Larry Young, but Forrest is an intriguing performer in his own right. For reasons never satisfactorily explained, there weren't that many tenor saxophonists in the bebop revolutions. Like Big Nick Nicholas and Lucky Thompson, Forrest was something of a players' player, with only a rather marginal following now. That's a pity for, as these sets amply demonstrate, his playing was full of character, a little rough-hewn in places but capable of greater subtlety than his big hit, 'Night Train', might suggest.

Forrest Fire pits him against the brimstone stomp of Young's Hammond; between them, they roll up the floor. It's the biggest possible contrast to the lighter and more detailed sound of *Out Of The Forrest*, but in most respects this is the right context for the saxophonist, who had no desire to play delicately detailed changes. *Sit Down And Relax* sounds like a ballad date but there is the expected ration of slowly burning groovers, and the Detroit pianist, Hugh Lawson, arrives to underline the soulful side of the group.

Most Much! is a fine set, restoring two tracks from the same session previously released only as part of *Soul Street* on New Jazz. It has now been restored to the catalogue, which means that all of Forrest's work for Prestige and New Jazz is in catalogue. The new CD includes material by an Oliver Nelson-led octet, but it also features Nelson and King Curtis on the superb 'Soul Street', which may be the definitive Forrest cut after 'Night Train', ear candy for tenor enthusiasts. A slightly bitty compilation, it's still greater than the sum of the parts. *Most Much!* demonstrates what a developed time-feel Forrest had. The first three tracks could hardly be more different in emphasis. 'Matilda' is a traditional calypso, given a forceful reading, with the saxophonist closely backed by the unsung Lawson. 'Annie Laurie' is similarly upbeat but seldom departs from the melody. 'Autumn Leaves' is full of glassy harmonies and a first taste of the curious rhythmic displacements and imaginative harmonic inflexions that make him such a significant way-station between bop and the New Thing. The closing 'Most Much' is a tough rocker, with strong upper-register effects. The recording isn't really up to standard but, as usual, it's 'only' Tommy Potter who suffers unduly.

Sonny Fortune (born 1939)

ALTO SAXOPHONE, SOPRANO SAXOPHONE, FLUTE

Fortune has never been a prolific composer, and he is in some respects a very straightforward saxophone stylist, retaining elements of the R&B style, in which he originally worked. Employment with Elvin Jones, McCoy Tyner, Miles Davis and Buddy Rich broadened his horizons and in the 1990s he entered a second, very effective period as a leader in his own right.

*****(*) Laying It Down**
Konnex KCD 5030 *Fortune; Kenny Barron (p); Cecil McBee (b); Billy Hart (d).* 89.

***** It Ain't What It Was**
Konnex KCD 5033 *Fortune; Mulgrew Miller (p); Santi Debriano (b); Billy Hart (d).* 91.

***** Monk's Mood**
Konnex KCD 5048 *Fortune; Kirk Lightsey (p); David Williams (b); Joe Chambers (d).* 1/93.

Fortune was in the 1975 Miles Davis group that made the darkly exotic *Agharta*. Miles's illness curtailed the group's activities, but that same year Fortune recorded a fine solo album, *Awakening*, for A&M which suggested that, like Gary Bartz before him, he was destined for great things. In the event, things have proceeded more quietly. An in-demand sideman who specializes in a sharp, keening tone that recalls Asian or African music – he'd previously recorded with McCoy Tyner, notably on *Sahara* – Fortune seemed to have fallen through the net until he popped up with these suprisingly straight-ahead sessions. It may well be that they were intended to demonstrate his competence as a jazz player rather than merely as an exotic colourist.

The earlier rhythm section suits him rather better. McBee favours drone-like effects that work well underneath Fortune's quarter-tones and indefinite slides, and Barron has always (recent appearances aside) favoured Afro-Asian contexts. Fortune has guested with Santi Debriano's group; the bassist is a limber, fast-moving player but he lacks McBee's subtlety, and Miller (if you'll forgive the pun) is too light. The two familiar repertoire pieces on *It Ain't*, 'Lush Life' and Coltrane's 'Straight

Street', are both competently played without suggesting that Fortune's rating as a improviser needs to be altered significantly.

Monk's Mood benefits immeasurably from Lightsey's presence; he's springily rhythmic on the title-track, softly romantic elsewhere, and his solo statements are always spot-on. Fortune himself allows the pace to lag a bit and once or twice gets sidetracked into rather unpromising digressions. Generally, though, well up to scratch.

*****(*) In The Spirit Of John Coltrane**

Shanachie 5063 *Fortune; John Hicks (p); Reggie Workman (b); Rashied Ali, Steve Berrios, Ronnie Burrage, Julio Collazo (d).* 99.

Past contact with both McCoy Tyner and Elvin Jones may have given Fortune a clearer than usual insight into the legacy of John Coltrane. Interestingly, despite superficial similarities of timbre and attack, and coming from the same home-town, he has never sounded like a Trane disciple. Significantly, too, this tribute record consists largely of originals. The only Coltrane tunes are 'Olé' and 'Africa', not by any means obvious choices. Two more former associates of Trane's – Reggie Workman and Rashied Ali – turn up on this dark-hued and mostly reflective disc, which has an old-fashioned sound and might well be some lost session from the '60s. Sonny's three main horns are all heard, and there is a nice variation of approach, though almost every track makes some reference to the great man (or to 'Mr Jones'). Ali is in fine form on his appearance, but Ronnie Burrage is the revelation, quoting figures from the classic Quartet records, often against the metre of the song. Fortune's phrasing has become more exact over the years, and there is a stiffness about his delivery on 'Hangin' Out With JC Again' which is at odds with its relaxed, comradely feel. An attractive record, rather than a great one, but certainly different from the usual run of Trane memorials.

Frank Foster (born 1928)

TENOR SAXOPHONE, SOPRANO SAXOPHONE

Like Jimmy Heath, Cincinnati-born Foster turned to the tenor saxophone largely to free himself of the all-pervasive influence of Charlie Parker. He has remained profoundly influenced by bop, even when experimenting with large-scale composition, and even as leader of the Basie band, a responsibility he took on in the mid-1980s and which he handled with great skill for a decade.

***** Fearless**

Original Jazz Classics OJCCD 923 *Foster; Virgil Jones (t); Albert Dailey (p); Bob Cunningham (b); Alan Dawson (d).* 1/65.

*****(*) Soul Outing!**

Original Jazz Classics OJCCD 984 *Foster; Virgil Jones (t); Pat Rebillot (p); Billy Butler (g); Richard Davis (b); Bob Cunningham (b, d); Alan Dawson (d, perc).* 66.

Although Frank Foster made his name with Basie in the 1950s – and a less bop-orientated band one couldn't wish to find – he had assimilated enough of the music of Charlie Parker into his playing to make him stand out as a particularly vivid soloist in that tightly integrated unit. The pun in *No Count* points to the heightened boppishness of the Savoy material, though there's nothing no-'ccount about the music within. The septet format affords him plenty of opportunity for broad-brush arrangement, but the real interest of these sessions is the interplay of the individual horns. The relationship with Wess was already a firm one, but Powell is also a responsive partner.

Fearless is one of a couple of dates he made for Prestige in the mid-1960s, and it's a solid, if formulaic, example of what the label managed to eke out of its various signings during the period. Foster opts for five originals and a long, joyous version of 'Jitterbug Waltz'. There are signs that he has been listening to John Coltrane, though the disciplined bop of the early records is still the dominant impression. The group sounds rigorously prepared but not so note-perfect that the playing loses freshness, and Jones and Dailey in particular respond with great alacrity to the challenge of the new material.

Soul Outing! was the second release as leader after leaving the Basic camp, and it's a step on in terms of style and conception. This time, Foster keeps it very tight and disciplined, and he modulates his own new material with two songs from the Adams/Strouse musical, *Golden Boy*, neither of them songs that have otherwise had much place in jazz repertory. His own 'Chiquito Loco' is an engaging swinger and 'Skanaroony' a look back to bebop. The contributions of guitarist Butler are kept to a minimum and are all the more effective for that.

***** The House That Love Built**

Steeplechase SCCD 31170 *Foster; Horace Parlan (p); Jesper Lundgaard (b); Aage Tanggaard (d).* 9/82.

The early-1980s sessions are entertaining examples of Foster's mighty swing and full-blooded improvising, yet the settings somehow don't demand enough of him to make him give of his absolute best. Despite comprising mainly original material, the Steeplechase quartet date emerges as much like any other modern tenor-plus-rhythm session, although 'I Remember Sonny Stitt' is an imposing tribute to the then recently departed saxophonist.

***** Two For The Blues**

Original Jazz Classics OJCCD 788 *Foster; Frank Wess (as, ts, f); Kenny Barron (p); Rufus Reid (b); Marvin 'Smitty' Smith (d).* 10/83.

****(*) Frankly Speaking**

Concord CCD 4276 *As above.* 12/84.

These meetings with Frank Wess, another Basie colleague to whom Foster seems wedded through all eternity, are rather carefully conceived, as if the players were trying too hard to avoid the blowing clichés which sometimes dominate such records. Wess is a subtler and more varied player, but Foster is a crafty character and often has the last word.

The first album includes three Wess originals and just one composition by Foster, but the real surprises come in the opening ten minutes. The brisk, bright title-track, with some nice harmonic reworkings by both hornmen, is followed by a galloping 'Send In The Clowns', a most surprising rendition of the Sondheim classic and probably the high point of the album, though the paired readings of 'Nancy (With The Laughing Face)' and 'Spring Can Really Hang You Up The Most' are delightful too.

The Concord set reunites the same line-up, but with a more brittle and percussive sound which is presumably down to production rather than performance. Neal Hefti's 'Two Franks' is the showboat piece.

***** Swing**
Challenge 70051 *Foster; Mickey Tucker (p); Earl May (b); Billy Hart (d).*

Caught live, Foster's quartet delivers an hour of tough, sensitive jazz. Frank signs off with Coltrane's 'Giant Steps', just to show that he can play those hallowed changes every bit as well as the younger guys, and do it at a stroll. There's a fine version of 'Chiquito Loco' and a long 'Shiny Stockings', which he's been doing since God was a small boy. Not the most elegant of albums, but an accurate representation of the man at work and sounding full of life.

*****(*) Leo Rising**
Arabesque 0124 *Foster; Derrick Gardner (t); Stephen Scott (p); Christian McBride (b); Lewis Nash (d).* 8/96.

Having shrugged off the responsibility of the Basie band, Foster concentrated on an Indian summer as a soloist and small-group leader. His soprano work has never been more individual than on 'Leo Rising' itself, which is a hard track to identity, heard out of context. Now approaching seventy, Foster sounds poised and mature, and the group is full of wise heads on young shoulders. Scott and McBride trade quips and quotations while keeping a weather eye on the oldtimer. He knows they're at it but never wavers for a moment. The years have been kind to Foster in that his kind of tenor playing is a virtual orthodoxy, and yet he always manages to pack a lot of history into his solos, not by quotation, as the younger men do, but rather in sheer range of expression. Trumpeter Gardner joins in for a single track, enough to register a presence and suggest that he, too, may be a voice to listen up for in years to come.

Lem Fowler

PIANO, VOCAL

A Chicagoan pianist working in the local studios during the early and middle 1920s.

****(*) Complete Recorded Works 1923–1927**
RST JPCD-1520-2 *Fowler; Sidney De Paris, Seymour Trick, Clarence Wheeler (t); Ernest Elliott (ss, cl); Percy Glascoe (cl, as); Charlie Holmes (as); Stanley Harding, Al Brunson (wbd); Helen Baxter, Mae Scott, George Williams, Helen McDonald (v).* 5/23–7/27.

Lemuel Fowler is a shadowy figure about whom almost nothing is known, but he made a fair number of records as accompanist and bandleader, and all of the earlier sides are here. A capable writer – there are three versions of his hit 'You've Got Ev'ry Thing A Sweet Mama Needs But Me' included here – he had a confident and somewhat Mortonesque manner at the piano: interesting to hear a version of 'Jelly Roll Blues' among the band sides. The accompaniments number ten and are the usual somewhat dour lot for the period, but the tracks by Lem's Washboard Wonders have a lot more go in them. A pity, though, that the sidemen – especially Wheeler, Trick and the clownish Glascoe – are an awful lot. Only on the last few tracks, where De Paris and a larger band come in (there are several unknowns among the personnel), is everyone playing properly and together. Knockabout stuff, not without appeal, although the transfers are a rum effort: one of the early couplings, from an OKeh original, has a bad speed wobble.

Donal Fox (born 1952)

PIANO

A Bostonian intererested in various styles of long-form composition, here bridging jazz with more chamber-directed music.

*****(*) Gone City**
New World NW 80515 *Fox; Oliver Lake (as); Eric Thomas (cl); John Lockwood (b); William Brown, Quincy Troupe (v).* 11/91–5/94.

Fox is of mixed race, the son of a Panamanian mother and a European Jewish father. It might be argued that a similar combination also runs in his musical veins, since much of the work on this record is through-written. Only 'T-Cell Countdown', though, is entirely without an improvisational component; it's a passionate response to the AIDS crisis, articulated by tenor William Brown and with John Lockwood joining the pianist on double bass. The song picks up the anguished sounds heard on the opening 'River Town Packin' House Blues', which is somewhat reminiscent of Frederic Rzewski's take on the blues. The central piece is a concert version of the ballet score which gives the CD its title, a three-part meditation for clarinet, piano and double bass. It's the most recent composition of those represented, which (as will be seen) were recorded over a lengthy span of time. The earliest is 'Jazz Sets With T.T.', a duet with Lake, with whom Fox has recorded in a more obviously jazz-based context, though here the saxophonist is afforded unfettered use of his whole repertoire of sound effects and extended techniques. Two items feature the poet/performer Quincy Troupe, who ghosted Miles Davis's autobiography and who for us has always been more convincing on paper than in performance. An engaging, fascinating disc, at the fringes of what we're mainly concerned with, but worth an hour of anyone's time.

Tomas Franck (born 1958)

TENOR SAXOPHONE

Swedish saxophonist who studied at Malmö, now living in Copenhagen. Greatly influenced by Dexter Gordon in particular.

***** Bewitched**
Stunt STUCD 18905 *Franck; Thomas Clausen (p); Jesper Lundgaard (b); Leroy Lowe (d).* 11/88.

***** Tomas Franck In New York**
Criss Cross Jazz Criss 1052 *Franck; Mulgrew Miller (p); Kenny Washington (b); Billy Drummond (d).* 12/90.

***** Crystal Ball**
Stunt STUCD 19408 *Franck; Jorgen Emborg (p); Lennart Ginman (b); Jonas Johansen (d).* 9/94.

A stalwart of the Danish Radio Big Band, Franck sounds much like many another hard-bop tenorman, heavily in hock to Coltrane, Gordon and so forth. But it must be admitted that he has the style down as well as most, and these three discs are an expansive fund of music from an enthusiastic performer. *Bewitched* was his debut and, though the seven originals are nothing special, the playing has weight and guts to it, with Clausen in typically inventive accompaniment and the musing version of the title-piece particularly effective. The studio sound is a bit glassy, though. The prospect of recording a quartet date on a first trip to New York seems to have held no terrors for Franck at all. Miller is his usual courteous and thoughtful self, and Washington and Drummond keep good time. The writing is again unremarkable, but Franck knows how to get the best out of himself as an improviser: the long solo on the opening 'Triton' shows no lack of ideas. *Crystal Ball* is the pick of the three. Back on home turf (almost – Franck may be based in Copenhagen, but he's actually a Swede), the saxophonist plays some of his most intense music. The extended improvisation on 'Fahrenheit 451' is a prodigious display of how commanding he can be on the horn and, if it touches no startling new ground, the authority is impressive by itself.

Hugh Fraser

PIANO, TROMBONE

Contemporary Canadian post-bopper with wide experience of leading his own groups.

***** Red & Blue**
Boathouse BHR–CD002 *Fraser; Campbell Ryga (as, ss); Ross Taggart (ts, p); Ken Lister, Rick Kilburn (b); Blaine Wikjord (d).* 6/93–4/94.

****(*) Back To Back**
Jazz Focus JFCD025 *Fraser; Jean Toussaint (ts); Arnie Somogyi (b); Keith Copeland (d).* 9/96.

****(*) In The Mean Time**
Jazz Focus JFCD020 *Fraser; Campbell Ryga (ss, as); Ross Taggart (ts, p); Ken Lister (b); Blaine Wijkord (d).* 12/96.

Fraser is a contemporary eminence in Canadian jazz and a rather extraordinary example of the musician who doubles: he plays piano and trombone, and his records suggest that he likes to divide his time equally between the two instruments. On the two albums by his Canadian group, he solves any instrumentation problems by having a tenorman who also doubles on piano. None of these, though, really gives the best evidence of Fraser's talents. The set for Boathouse is the best of them, ten originals and an Egberto Gismonti tune each given a thoughtful treatment, often at quite a slow pace. But as a record it feels shapeless and never quite traps the listener's attention for long, with a rather flat sound-mix not assisting.

Sound is also a problem with he two Jazz Focus sets, both recorded live. *In The Mean Time* is by his regular band, and they play another version of the ludicrously fast 'Herbildoodlyu' off the previous record. It's a so-so affair with probably too many long solos and club-set routines. *Back To Back* catches Fraser in London with Jean Toussaint, and again this seems like no more than just a record of a gig, a souvenir if you were there but hardly pressing enough to demand a place in the collection. Fraser has done better work in the past and he's perhaps unfairly represented by these three.

Free Jazz Quartet

GROUP

Veteran British improvisers in a 'classic' quartet situation.

****** Premonitions**
Matchless MR18 *Paul Rutherford (tb); Harrison Smith (ts, ss, bcl); Tony Moore (clo); Eddie Prévost (d).* 7/89.

If the group's title is a wry reference to the Modern Jazz Quartet (see also Prévost's punning Supersession), it takes in Ornette Coleman's seminal *Free Jazz* as well. The terminology is used advisedly, for this superb recording is more obviously rooted in one of the dialects of post-bop than, say, the process-dominated free improvisation of AMM. The underlying motif of *Premonitions* is warning: 'Red Flags', 'Roman Geese', 'Gathering Clouds', 'Cry Wolf', 'Tocsin' and even 'Old Moore's' (an oblique reference to the trombonist's *Old Moore's Almanack* album). The music is tense and often powerfully dramatic, strung along highly attenuated motivic threads. Prévost's drumming is as good as he has ever been on record and Rutherford is, as always, good enough to listen to on his own. Just as Prévost and his circle have tended to reject the bland triumphalism of the doctrinaire left politically, so musically he clearly rejects the anything-goes attitude that gives free improvisation a bad name. This is intense and concentrated music. A warning: please do not 'understand' it too quickly.

Bud Freeman (1906–91)

TENOR SAXOPHONE, CLARINET

One of the legendary Austin High School Gang, the elegant Chicagoan was the first significant tenor saxophonist, a lighter but certainly not pallid Coleman Hawkins. It was a long career, and Freeman continued to sound like no one but himself right to the end. 'The Eel' was a classic performance, almost a novelty tune, but at the same time bespeaking a brilliant improvisational talent.

****** Great Original Performances, 1927–1940**
Jazz Classics in Digital Stereo RPCD 604 *Freeman; Jimmy McPartland (c); Joe Bauer, Andy Ferretti, Bunny Berigan, Pee Wee Erwin, Charlie Spivak, Max Kaminsky, Johnny Mendel (t); Glenn Miller, Will Bradley, Tommy Dorsey, Red Bone, Les Jenkins, Floyd O'Brien (tb); Jack Teagarden (tb, v); Brad Gowans (vtb); Benny Goodman, Bud Jacobson, Pee Wee Russell, Frank Teschemacher (cl); Johnny Mince, Jim Cannon, Fred Stulce, Mike Doty, Milt Yaner (cl, as); Dave Matthews (as); Adrian Rollini (bsx); Dave North, Dave Bowman, Jose Sullivan, Howard Smith, Jess Stacy, Claude Thornhill (p); George Van Eps, Dick McDonough, Carmen Mastren (g); Eddie Condon (g, bj); Norman Foster (bj); Joe Venuti (vn); Jim Lannigan, Artie Bernstein, John Mueller, Grachan Moncur, Clyde Newcomb,*

Delmer Caplan, Artie Shapiro, Mort Stuhlmaker, Gene Traxler (b); Danny Alvin, Cozy Cole, Big Sid Catlett, Gene Krupa, Neil Marshall, Morey Feld, Dave Tough (d). 12/27–7/40.

***** Bud Freeman, 1928–1938**

Classics 781 *Freeman; Bobby Hackett (c); Bunny Berigan, Johnny Mendel (t); Joe Bushkin (t, p); Floyd O'Brien (tb); Bud Jacobson, Pee Wee Russell (cl); Dave Matthews (as); Dave North, Jess Stacy, Claude Thornhill (p); Eddie Condon (g); Norman Foster (bj); Grachan Moncur, John Mueller, Artie Shapiro (b); Cozy Cole, Gene Krupa, Marty Marsala, Dave Tough, George Wettling (d); Red McKenzie, Minerva Pious (v).* 12/28–11/38.

***** Bud Freeman, 1939–1940**

Classics 811 *Freeman; Max Kaminsky (t); Jack Teagarden (tb, v); Brad Gowans (vtb); Pee Wee Russell (cl); Dave Bowman (p); Eddie Condon (g); Clyde Newcomb, Pete Peterson, Mort Stuhlmaker (b); Danny Alvin, Morey Feld, Al Sidell, Dave Tough (d).* 7/39–7/40.

*****(*) Swingin' With 'The Eel'**

ASV AJA 5280 *As above, except add Muggsy Spanier (c), Joe Bauer, Pee Wee Erwin, Andy Ferretti (t), Les Jenkins, Earle Hagen, Walter Mercurio (tb), Peanuts Hucko (cl), Skeets Hurfurt, Fred Stulce (as, cl), Johnny Mince (ts), Howard Smith (p), Carmen Mastren, Hy White (g), Trigger Alpert, Gene Traxler (b), George Wettling (d).* 10/33–7/39.

Freeman was perhaps the first truly significant white tenor player. If he looked, and chose to behave, like the secretary of some golf club in the Home Counties – episode one of his autobiography was called 'You don't look like a musician' – his saxophone walked all over the carpets in spikes, a rawer sound than Lester Young's (to which it is often likened) and with a tougher articulation.

Freeman developed late, worked in some unpromising contexts, and ended up one of the most distinctive tenorists of all time (and any colour). Until recently the available discography was pretty thin. The situation improved with the appearance of Robert Parker's superbly remastered Jazz Classics in Digital Stereo compilation. This is the essential Freeman record for the CD collector. It contains all his best work of the period, including the November 1933 'The Eel' and a marvellous tune called 'The Buzzard', recorded with Bunny Berigan. There is inevitably a large overlap of material on the Classics imprint, though these will be preferred (sound-quality notwithstanding) by collectors who want a more complete and idiosyncratic selection, or who are dismayed by Parker's bonging reverb. Where Parker goes for excellent performances, even under other leaders like Joe Venuti and Eddie Condon, Classics tend to stick to just those sessions where Freeman was leading his Windy City Five, his Gang, or his later Summa Cum Laude orchestra (who reprised 'The Eel' in 1939).

Classics (*1928–1938*) include one astonishing oddity, a piece of ham acting by Freeman and the bizarrely named Minerva Pious; no verbal description will quite suffice ... The 1938 trio with Stacy and Wettling is excellent evidence for Freeman's gifts as a highly focused improviser. His harmonic shifts and deceptively easy chromatic transitions on 'I Got Rhythm' (January of that year and an astonishing performance) and 'Three Little Words' (a later session, in November) have a cut-out-and-keep quality that will endear them to all saxophone players.

The 1939 recording of 'The Eel' is the final track on the ASV compilation which, unlike Classics, includes work done for other leaders: Eddie Condon, Tommy Dorsey and Muggsy Spanier. The real collectables are Bud's own cuts, though, and the November 1938 trios with Stacy and Wettling are among the best of his small-group statements, stripped down, muscular but still urbane. The sound is very much better than on the French label which further recommends this sampling of half a decade's material.

***** Bud Freeman, 1945–1946**

Classics 942 *Freeman; Yank Lawson (t); Lou McGarity, Bill Mustarde (tb); Edmond Hall, Peanuts Hucko (cl); Gene Schroeder, Buddy Weed (p); Carmen Mastren (g); Herman Alpert, Bob Haggart (b); Ray McKinley (d); Five De Marco Sisters (v); other personnel unidentified.* 8/45–46.

****(*) Bud Freeman, 1946**

Classics 975 *Freeman; Wild Bill Davison (c); Billy Butterfield, Charlie Shavers (t); Will Bradley, Vernon Brown (tb); Ernie Caceres, Edmond Hall, Peanuts Hucko (cl); Bill Dohler (as); Bus Davis, Jack Gardner, Gene Schroeder, Paul Jordan, Tut Soper, Joe Sullivan (p); Carl Kress, Carmen Mastren (g); Bob Casey, Bob Haggart, Al Hall, Jim Lanigan, Mike Rubin, John Simmons, Sid Weiss (b); Jim Barnes, Frank Rullo, George Wettling (d); Marilyn Hall, Five De Marco Sisters (v).* 11 & 12/45, 9/46.

Following Freeman's release from the army, he signed up for the Majestic, though he made some additional recordings for V-Disc in October 1945. Unlike Lester Young, he didn't re-enter civilian life bearing a sackful of woe, but he was certainly not as sharp as he had been in pre-war days. Versions of 'I'm Just Wild Abut Harry' and 'I Got Rhythm', cut in September, have some of the old grace and agility, but almost everything else on the set seems stuffy by comparison. The V-Disc material is sourly ironic; 'For Musicians Only (A Musical Treatise On Jazz)' fails to convince, even as satire, and the later tracks, recorded with an unknown band, are oddly drab. The only other curiosity on this set is 'The Atomic Era', a duet with drummer McKinley.

The follow-up is unusual in being largely from 1945 rather than the given date. The quality material is the set of cuts made for Emarcy and Keynote in December, with Peanuts Hucko, Wild Bill Davison, and the rapidly developing Charlie Shavers all in attendance The three-point front line on 'You Took Advantage Of Me', 'Sentimental Baby' and 'You're My Everything' is just about all anyone needs from this disc, which is padded out with some pretty feeble vocal material and a few tracks under pianist Paul Jordan's nominal leadership.

*****(*) Chicago / Austin High School Jazz In Hi-Fi**

RCA 13031 *Freeman; Jimmy McPartland (c); Billy Butterfield (t); Tyree Glenn (tb); Jack Teagarden (tb, v); Peanuts Hucko, Pee Wee Russell (cl); Dick Cary, Gene Schroeder (p); Al Casamenti (g); Leonard Gaskin, Al Hall, Milt Hinton (b); George Wettling (d).* 3, 4 & 7/57.

***** Something To Remember You By**

Black Lion BLCD 760153 *Freeman; Dave Frishberg (p); Bob Haggart (b); Don Lamond (d).* 1/62.

Almost as welcome as the restoration of the early material is the reappearance of the 1957 'Austin High School Gang' dates, featuring Freeman's Summa Cum Laude orchestra. These sides included some of his most unrestrained and relaxed solos. Pieces like LaRoca's 'At The Jazz Band Ball', something of an anthem for the Chicago players, is absolutely on the money, with Teagarden playing at his best and Peanuts Hucko diving around the two slower-moving men at the front. The cuts with Russell are almost equally good, but there's no version of 'The Eel', a Freeman favourite which became a bit of a millstone round his neck. The Black Lion is fine as far as it goes, but a rash of alternative takes includes nothing of any devastating novelty and the set is rather pinched by Frishberg, an entertaining player at the best of times, playing at top form here.

***** Superbud**

Jazzology 185 *Freeman; Keith Ingham (p); Pete Chapman (b); Johnny Armitage (d).* 74, 92.

Originally released on the British 77 label, this has now been enhanced by half a dozen rare Freeman compositions, performed solo by pianist Ingham. The group material from the original record is greatly entertaining, with Bud in strong and confident voice, and his improvisations on ''S Wonderful' and 'Tea For Two' (the latter long a favourite) are both excellent. Decent sound, and the 1992 tracks are an unexpected bonus.

***** California Session**

Jazzology 277 *Freeman; Dick Cathcart (t); Betty O'Hara (tb, euph); Bob Reitmeier (cl); Ray Sherman (p); Howard Alden (g); Phil Stephens (b); Nick Fatool (d).* 82.

Unreleased until 1997, this remarkable session was supposed to have been a cameo walk-on by the 75-year-old Freeman. But, when he turned up at an LA concert put on by the Poor Angel Hot Jazz Society, he decided that it would be entertaining to sit for the whole set. He sounds a little unprepared and there are awkwardnesses along the way, even on the surprisingly brisk version of 'Body And Soul', but Bud sounds in excellent spirits and form, tackling familiar material like 'Just A Closer Walk With Thee' and 'Tea For Two'. Howard Alden was new on the scene, but he immediately establishes himself as a deft and clever soloist, spinning alert counter-melodies and showing no sign of being intimidated by appearing – unexpectedly in the event – on the same stage as the great man.

***** The Real Bud Freeman**

Principally Jazz 01 *Freeman; Stuart Katz (p); Bob Roberts (g); John Bany (b); Barrett Deems (d).* 12/83.

Bud's recorded swansong was made on his return to Chicago after a long stint in Britain. The home band roll out the carpet for him, and guitarist Roberts is a particularly responsive partner, trading some lovely ideas with the leader on 'I Cover The Waterfront'. Deems is one of the best mainstream drummers located in the Windy City and it's he as much as anyone who gives the set its perky swing, certainly belying the saxophonist's advanced age. There are couple of fluffs and a few moments when Bud doesn't seem to know quite where he's going with a solo, as on 'My Romance', where he drifts off in another melodic direction entirely, thinks better of it, and then doesn't quite get back in the groove. Otherwise, though, a wholly attractive set and a decent farewell to the studio. The CD includes a bonus three tracks that weren't on the original release.

Chico Freeman (born 1949)

TENOR AND SOPRANO SAXOPHONE, BASS CLARINET, CLARINET, FLUTE

Von Freeman's son and occasional collaborator audibly belongs to a different jazz generation. And yet, behind the Coltrane-influenced harmonics and advanced techniques like circular breathing, Chico has remained loyal to the basic principles of Chicago blues and jazz. Over the years, he has flirted with free jazz and with funk and fusion in his Brainstorm group. He is at his best, though, in front of a small group with a programme of challenging modern themes.

***** Beyond The Rain**

Original Jazz Classics OJCCD 479 *Freeman; Hilton Ruiz (p); Juni Booth (b); Elvin Jones (d).* 6/77.

Freeman was one of the first to demonstrate the indisputable but not always obvious point that radicalism and an awareness of tradition were not incompatible. His playing always sounds entirely of the moment, technically adroit, rooted in the past but always searching for something beyond. What may seem an ill-matched personnel actually delivers a very responsive ensemble. Freeman himself is hard-edged but lyrical, highly focused but also relaxed and unforced. Jones and Booth sound rather old-fashioned in this context, and one wonders whether Ruiz was the right piano player; but in the last analysis it is the product that counts and one can't argue with the quality of this early record.

*****(*) Chico**

India Navigation IN 1031 *Freeman; Muhal Richard Abrams (p); Cecil McBee (b); Steve McCall (d); Tito Sampa (perc).* 77.

****** Chico Freeman Quartet**

India Navigation IN 1042 *Freeman; John Hicks (p); Cecil McBee (b); Jack DeJohnette (d).* 78.

The titles just about say it all. While the first of these, fine as it is, now seems like a rather self-indulgent exercise in self-discovery, a first real foray into the avant-garde, the second is an absolutely cracking group-record. In it, Freeman finds a way of using the intense and compacted technique which was rapidly coming under his command to create some first-rate modern jazz, cutting-edge stuff which doesn't advertise its own cleverness. We're still greatly drawn to the earlier disc, not least because McBee and McCall sound so good on CD. This was a key period for Chico, a time of consolidation and advance. This pair of discs perfectly demonstrates the sources he was working through, some of them unfashionable at the time, like Paul Gonsalves, and the distinct personality he was beginning to stamp on them.

*****(*) The Outside Within**

India Navigation IN 1042 *As above.* 78.

Restored to the catalogue in 1992, this is pretty much in the same line: a confident, tough-minded set of three Freeman originals and one, 'Undercurrent', by McBee. The leader's bass-clarinet playing seems particularly vivid on this occasion for some reason, strong angular ideas with a lot of detail thrown in on 'The Search', which is also a high point for McBee, playing with his bow, and for Hicks, who lifts it and turns it into something philosophical, full of blues grandeur. 'Luna' is very different, an almost Oriental scale which doesn't go the way one expects it to, but which fuels a truly extraordinary solo from the leader, who is consistently up to form, albeit in darker mood than on some of the albums.

***** Spirit Sensitive**
India Navigation IN 1070 *Freeman; John Hicks (p); Jay Hoggard (vib); Cecil McBee (b); Billy Hart, Famoudou Don Moye (d).* 78.

*****(*) Still Sensitive**
India Navigation IN 1071 *Freeman; John Hicks (p); Cecil McBee (b); Winard Harper (d).*

*****(*) No Time Left**
Black Saint 120036 *Freeman; Jay Hoggard (vib); Rick Rozie (b); Famoudou Don Moye (d).* 6/79.

Take our greybeard word for it, this was a surprise when *Spirit Sensitive* came out: players of Freeman's radical disposition were not expected to make records of standards. In a roundabout way this release did more to encourage the Young Turks to look back into the tradition, to get out their Ellington and Strayhorn charts, than anything else going on at the time. This is the direct ancestor of David Murray's repertoire projects and as such is a very important document. Passing time has, we feel bound to report, blunted its listenability more than somewhat. The performances are a little raggedy here and there and the addition of Hoggard to the line-up does nothing to clean up the ensembles, but nor does it add a measure of fruitful ambiguity either. Why have a player as richly gifted as Hicks on hand and then muddy what he's best at? These are quibbles, and pretty meaningless at this distance, but they may explain a less sanguine rating.

We are honestly not clear about the dating of *Still Sensitive*. The disc is undated, but it is billed as a 'sequel' and it bears a consecutive release number, though it re-emerged on CD only in 1995. We must work on the assumption that it is roughly contemporary, an assumption made with some resistance, it has to be said, because in many respects this feels like a later, maturer recording. Again standards-based, it has a more obviously romantic slant and in some ways is less subtle, less tempered with occasional moments of irony. When Chico plays 'Nature Boy' and 'Someone To Watch Over Me', you get the strong feeling that he isn't playing games but is telling it from the heart. Not the most obvious of ballad players, he has done something very special here.

The first of the Black Saint albums is actually little known compared to its predecessor. It immediately makes sense of Hoggard's involvement. Without a piano player, the sound is much more open, more scurrying and complex and also, at this stage, when Chico seemed to be concerned with speeding his delivery on up-tempo numbers, much more responsive. Otherwise, it's a tight and accurate little group, and the Italian label's sound-quality is more than a match for anything Chico got at India Navigation.

***** Freeman & Freeman**
India Navigation IN 1069 *Freeman; Von Freeman (ts); Muhal Richard Abrams, Kenny Barron (p); Cecil McBee (b); Jack DeJohnette (d).* 4/81.

The family firm. The Freemans play well together, with Von's sliding tonalities closing the gap between his more mainstream approach and Chico's pure-toned modernism. Their gruff partnership on 'The Shadow Of Your Smile' invests a hokey tune with considerable dignity, and 'I Can't Get Started' is an excellent performance from both. A fascinating band, familiar enough in this context by now and held together by DeJohnette's endlessly interesting figures and powerful surges; the two keyboard men undertake a concise exercise in comparative pianistics, Chicago *v.* Philly, with Barron coming out fractionally ahead on points.

****** Destiny's Dance**
Original Jazz Classics OJCCD 799 *Freeman; Wynton Marsalis (t); Bobby Hutcherson (vib); Dennis Moorman (p); Cecil McBee (b); Ronnie Burrage (d); Paulinho Da Costa (perc).* 10/81.

One of the great jazz records of the 1980s, it has remained in our premier league ever since its release, and it shows no signs of dating or tarnishing. The presence of Hutcherson, the premier vibraharpist of the day and a giant of an improviser, is a huge part of it, and Wynton is playing straightforwardly and with all his fire. Once again – and apologies if this is becoming a rant – it seems odd to pitch Hutcherson up against a piano player, and one of limited if perfectly serviceable talent, except that Moorman respects his space and the sound is so smoothly crafted that there is a lot of room around both, good separation and none of the muddiness that ruins such encounters. The material is all original and all strongly idiomatic, allowing Freeman to air his growing repertoire of circular breathing, extended harmonics and overblown notes; again, though, as on *Chico Freeman Quartet*, technique never takes the place of musicality. A marvellous record that has given us consistent pleasure for nearly 20 years, and of how many can that be said?

****(*) You'll Know When You Get There**
Black Saint 120128 *Freeman; Eddie E.J Allen (t, flhn); Von Freeman (ts, p); Geri Allen (p, ky); Don Pate (b); Victor Jones (d); Norman Hedman (perc); Joel Brandon (whistling).* 8/88.

The only real disappointment in the catalogue, though still more than worthy of a listen. It's a curiously muted record with no real centre of gravity and none of the character of its predecessors. Freeman was already involved in the fusion project known as Brainstorm, and this seemed to send him off in a new, electrically supercharged direction which didn't always allow him as much creative freedom as he seemed to think. Hearing him perform with Dad again was well worthwhile but Geri Allen seems rather wasted, and the ancillary players don't bring a lot of genuine interest.

*****(*) Luminous**
Jazz House JHCD 010 *Freeman; Arthur Blythe (as); John Hicks (p, ky); Donald Pate (b); Victor Jones (d); Norman Hedman (perc).* 2/89.

*****(*) The Unspoken Word**
Jazz House JHCD 017 *Freeman; Arthur Blythe (as); Julian Joseph (p); Curtis Lundy (b); Idris Muhammad (d).* 9 & 10/93.

Freeman's association with the erratic and frustratingly inconsistent Blythe has been a fruitful one for both, and Freeman's occasional sojourns at Ronnie Scott's Club in London have always been the cue for some of his fieriest and most committedly engaged music. Monk's 'Rhythm-A-Ning' is common to both discs, as is Cecil McBee's 'Peacemaker' and an original 'Playpen'.

More than four years separate the sessions, and the second features a very different group, anchored by the young British pianist, but the quality is consistent and consistently high. Freeman still indulges his now quite seamless circular breathing and there are moments when he seems to be indulging technical facility for its own sake; but for the most part these are highly musical performances, with some great ensemble playing and an almost routine delivery of virtuosic solos from both frontmen. Hard to separate them, but with a gun at our temple we'd grudgingly plump for the earlier of the two.

***** Up And Down**

Black Saint 120136 *Freeman; Mal Waldron (p); Rocky Knauer (b); Tiziana Ghiglioni (v).* 7/89.

The interplay between Freeman and Waldron, who is one of the great jazz colourists, is consistently fascinating and would have made a fine duo album. The other two participants in this drummerless session are more questionable. Knauer never stamps his personality on the music, and Ghiglioni (an excellent vocalist on her own turf) is completely wrong for this relatively straight context. Something of an oddity in the Freeman catalogue, it hasn't been seen or heard much of since its release.

*****(*) Focus**

Contemporary CCD 14073 *Freeman; Arthur Blythe (as); George Cables (p); Santi Debriano (b); Yoron Israel (d).* 5/94.

Another shift of label, and a more mainstream sound. There is an almost magisterial calm to some of the playing of this vintage. It is certainly hard to fault his articulation and his shaping of a solo, and at least part of the excitement of this highly accomplished record is hearing how Freeman, even with a very gifted harmonic improviser at his back in the person of George Cables, is able to bring himself back to some point of rest at the end of a solo. But he always does, and it is exhilarating to take to the air with him.

***** The Emissary**

Clarity 1015 *Freeman; Andrienne Wilson (f, v); Stan Franks (g, v); Geoff Brennan (b); John Jones (d, perc); Norman Hedman, Babou Sagna (perc); Scheherazade Stone (v).* 11 & 12/95.

For the first 20 minutes or so, this is excellent. The opening section, from 'Spirit Catcher' to 'Murcia' is almost a mini-suite. Thereafter, the record degenerates into routine pop covers and lite-jazz vamping, with only 'Seven Steps To Heaven' standing out in the second half, albeit wrongly credited to Miles Davis. Freeman's saxophone playing loses none of its strength of tone or authority of gesture in contexts like this, but one does wonder what he finds satisfying in retreading a style that Herbie Hancock virtually cornered with the Headhunters. The band is mostly anonymous, though Franks has always been an interesting player in the Hiram Bullock mould.

Von Freeman (born 1922)

TENOR SAXOPHONE

Von has had an oddly shaped career. For a long time he was very much in the shadow of his son, Chico, and he spent a lot of time away from jazz altogether. In his fifties, though, he returned to the fold and since then has created a body of eccentrically clustered but virile swing.

***** Serenade And Blues**

Chief CD 3 *Freeman; John Young (p); David Shipp (b); Wilbur Campbell (d).* 6/75.

***** Walkin' Tuff**

Southport S-SSD 0010 *Freeman; Jon Logan, Kenny Prince (p); Carroll Crouch, Dennis Carroll (b); Wilbur Campbell, Mike Raynor (d).* 89.

***** Fire With Von Freeman**

Southport S-SSD 0014 *As above.* 91.

*****(*) Never Let Me Go**

Steeplechase SCCD 31310 *Freeman; Jodie Christian (p); Eddie De Haas (b); Wilbur Campbell (d).* 5/92.

*****(*) Lester Leaps In**

Steeplechase SCCD 31320 *As above.* 5/92.

***** Dedicated To You**

Steeplechase SCCD 31351 *As above.* 5/92.

Opening with Glenn Miller quotes may be, as the fashion advisers say, 'very ageing', but Von Freeman has never been impressed by trends. While his son and fellow-tenorist, Chico, has explored sometimes baffling extremes of free jazz and neo-funk, Von Freeman has stuck with a curious down-home style that occasionally makes his saxophone sound as if it is held together with rubber bands and sealing wax. Stylistically it is closer to Ornette Coleman (or Roland Kirk) than to Lester Young and it fitted quite seamlessly into Chico's band in the 1980s, but in the sense that Ornette is himself a maverick traditionalist.

Serenade And Blues is a relaxed and wholly untroubled set of standards, cut with a friendly rhythm section; the session was originally released, shorn of a track, on the parent Nessa as *Have No Fear*. It's also 15 years old; the decision to stay back in Chicago did nothing for Freeman's recording schedule. 'Von Freeman's Blues' and the strong closing 'I'll Close My Eyes' were, for long enough, the closest thing on record to a Freeman set at the Enterprise Lounge. Since then, though, two additions to the list. The studio selections on the two Southports are obviously meant to sound as in-yer-face and immediate as a club date. Logan/Crouch/Campbell are the first-string linebackers: punchy, upfront and slightly cavalier about the rule book. When the pace slows a bit, and the *dee*-fence are called on, Messrs Prince, Carroll and Raynor take the field. They claim an assist on both 'Nature Boy' and 'But Beautiful', but get a bit waylaid on 'Blues For Sunnyland'. Halfway through, the saxophonist goes on a long solo run, playing 'How Deep Is The Ocean' completely unaccompanied. Very effective, too.

Any fears that Freeman was going to be John Lee Hookered, turned into an overnite sensation just in time for his bus-pass, failed to materialize. His more recent career has been a self-confident demonstration that a recording contract is a spoonful of jam, but not necessarily bread and butter to a jazz musician. However, for his seventieth birthday, the old boy treated himself to a Paris trip, on which *Never Let Me Go* and *Lester Leaps In* were recorded. Both discs have a resolutely old-fashioned air and might easily have been recorded in 1975. This has something to do with the sound of Christian's electric piano, but also the very foursquare beat that Campbell favours. The Rollins accents that Freeman brings to 'The End Of A Love Affair' and 'I'll Remember April' on *Never*, and still more noticeably to 'A Nightingale Sang In Berkeley Square' on *Lester Leaps In*, haven't been so much in evidence before. The delicacy that used to be dusted only sparsely over ballads is now a major component of the sound, and there are touches of near-genius on the chestnut, 'Alone Together', and the heart-on-sleeve Cole Porter 'I Love You' which alone make this a vintage performance. The latest of the Steeplechases is a bit lacking in punch, a further example of the label's tendency to squeeze every last drop out of a recording session.

*****(*) 75th Birthday Celebration**

Half Note Records 4903 2 *Freeman; Chico Freeman (ts); Willie Pickens (p); Brian Sandstrom (b); Robert Shy (d); Dianne Reeves (v).* 7/98.

*****(*) Von & Ed**

Delmark 508 *As above, except add Ed Petersen (ts); omit C. Freeman, Reeves.* 98.

As the date suggests, the 75th birthday album was actually a year late, but the idea was sparked by an appearance by Von and Chico and Von's guitarist brother George at the Chicago Jazz Festival the year before; drummer Bruz Freeman, another brother, stayed home in Hawaii, but remarkably Von's mother, almost 100, is there in spirit, listening to the show go out on radio.

Having honoured the old man back home, Chico's idea was to give him a further party in New York and at the Blue Note, and the record is a document of two spring nights with Chico's group there. The material is pretty much out of the book: 'Softly As In A Morning Sunrise', 'There Is No Greater Love' and 'Lover Man', but they also do Chico's delightful 'To Hear A Teardrop In The Rain'. It's great to hear the Freemans playing together, as it always is, the lad all fabulous technique and gleaming speed, the dad content with pedal power and guile, but still getting there ahead as often as not. Dianne Reeves does a pretty guest spot on 'Comes Love', but since it's placed early in the set, it doesn't really change its character, which is thoughtful, driving saxophone improvisation, culminating in Newk's 'Tenor Madness'.

A very different second horn on the set with Petersen. The only piece in common in a rather boppish set is 'Lover Man', and this more than anything exposes differences in the respective rhythm sections. Ed and Von have much in common, not least the kind of sweetness that boils dangerously, like overheated caramel. There are touches of that on the opening 'Mr P.C.', which brings a rootsy but exploratory quality to Trane's blues theme. Miles's 'Four' is more straightforwardly interpreted, though Von, coming through the left channel and from left-field, to a large degree ignores the modes. The rest of the set is a dip back into the bop bag, with 'Lover Man' followed by 'A Night In Tunisia' and a long, closing version of 'Lover', which lets the two horns loose on the Rodgers theme in a real explosion of ideas. Studio-recorded, Von sometimes sounds a bit ropey, but Riverside in Chicago is on the back doorstep and Von obviously has a rapport with engineer Paul Serrano and supervising producer Robert Koester, and he treats the gig pretty much as if it were a club set. Not quite as compelling as the birthday party, but possibly of more interest to hardcore Vonskians.

Paolo Fresu (born 1961)

TRUMPET, FLUGELHORN, CORNET

Grew up in Sardinia and played as a teenager in the town band. Moved towards jazz and began recording in the '80s; he has since become one of the highest-profile new-school Italian players. Heavily involved in education, theatre music and some contemporary composition.

***** Ostinato**

Splasc(h) H 106-2 *Fresu; Tino Tracanna (ss, ts); Roberto Cipelli (p); Attilo Zanchi (b); Ettore Fioravanti (d).* 1/85.

***** Inner Voices**

Splasc(h) H 110-2 *As above, plus David Liebman (ss, f).* 4/86.

*****(*) Mamut: Music For A Mime**

Splasc(h) H 127-2 *As above, except omit Liebman; add Mimmo Cafiero (perc).* 11/85–5/86.

***** Quatro**

Splasc(h) H 160-2 *As above, except omit Cafiero.* 4–6/88.

***** Live In Montpellier**

Splasc(h) H 301-2 *As above.* 7/88.

An outstanding exponent of the new Italian jazz, Fresu is in much demand as a sideman, but his records as a leader offer some of the best views of his music. Fresu's early quintet included the agile Tracanna and the expert bassist Zanchi, and together they follow an energetic yet introspective kind of jazz that suggests a remote modern echo of an early Miles Davis group – the trumpeter does, indeed, sound like the Davis of the mid-1950s often enough to bother some ears. Most of the time the resulting music is engaging rather than compelling: the soloists have more to say than the compositions and, although the group works together very sympathetically, the records never quite take off. Liebman is soon at home on the session he guests on; the live record from Montpellier is scrappy yet often more exciting than the others; and *Quatro* has some bright originals. *Mamut*, though, is the best of these records: although the programme is a collection of fragments for the theatre, the miniatures include some of Fresu's most vivid writing, and the title-piece and 'Pa' are themes which hang in the memory. Fresu even finds something new to say on a solo reading of 'Round Midnight'.

*****(*) Ensalada Mistica**

Splasc(h) 415 *Fresu; Gianluigi Trovesi (as, cl, bcl); Tino Tracanna (ss, ts); Roberto Cipelli (p); Attilo Zanchi (b); Ettore Fioravanti (d).* 5/94.

A decade of work has made this into a very confident, imposing group. Fresu is generous about sharing space, but his is still the most impressive single voice: luxurious brass sound, firm delivery, staunchless flow of ideas. Still, Trovesi and Tracanna make a formidable front line, and the rhythm section continue to grow. This is elegant and eloquent post-bop which speaks in any language, and this is a group that can stand on any world stage.

***** Wanderlust**

BMG 74321 46435-2 *As above, except Erwin Vann (ts) replaces Trovesi.* 5/96.

Somewhat of a disappointment, though it's hard to say exactly why. There are some typically elegant originals and the closing 'Touch Her Soft Lips And Part' suits the leader so well that it might have been written for him. A drooping spirit seems to hang over some of the music, though, as if the band were actually tired (it was recorded on a single day on a tour stop-off) and, while one doesn't expect bebop fireworks from this band, the preponderance of slow tempos lends a rather lachrymose feel.

*****(*) Metamorfosi**

RCA Victor 74321 65202-2 *Fresu; Nguyen Lê (g); Antonello Salis (fisarmonica, whistle, v); Furio Di Castri (b); Roberto Gatto (d).* 12/98.

For sheer songful beauty, Fresu's writing is hard to over-value and, although he's generous in also allowing his sidemen composing space, it's his own writing – 'Elogio Del Discount', 'Nightly' and 'Nymphéas' in particular – which hangs in the mind. His Angel Quartet are full of seraphic souls and Lê is brilliantly appropriate for the leader, modernist enough to bring in all his effects pedals but sensitive to his surroundings and reluctant to overpower the unadorned jazz language which the leader is so adept with (even if he, too, adds a smidgen of electronics to his own tone here and there). Di Castri and Gatto, veterans of this scene by now, play bruisingly fast at times, as in Gatto's own 'Giravolta', but they can create what's needed for subtle acoustic music as well. Against expectations, this also owes very little to any Miles Davis music – even if they do end on 1 minute 11 seconds of Davis's ancient bebop script, 'Little Willie Leaps'.

Erik Friedlander

CELLO

A regular on many a New York new-music session, Friedlander uses the cello as a stand-alone instrument, equally happy as soloist or ensemble player, and he seems unbothered by its few jazz credentials.

***** Topaz**

Siam SMD-50003 *Friedlander; Andy Laster (as); Stomu Takeishi (b); Satoshi Takeishi (perc).* 12/97.

Friedlander's tunes are abetted in this programme by two Eric Dolphy numbers and Miles Davis's 'Tout De Suite', all three of which receive quiet transformations into what is essentially a chamber-music language. Laster's melodious playing, the incisive but not overbearing thrum of Stomu Takeishi's electric bass and the spare patterns of Satoshi Takeishi's percussion instruments are intermingled with a simple generosity. Since each man is seemingly reluctant to step out, the music comes across as all of a piece, although one occasionally wishes for an outburst to enliven what some might find a rather monochromatic palette (a title like 'Three Desperate Men' doesn't live up to its billing). But the improvising has the polish of experience and high craft.

Dave Friedman (born 1944)

VIBRAPHONE, MARIMBA, PERCUSSION

Studied percussion at Juilliard and worked in New York classical circles before moving into jazz with Wayne Shorter and other leaders. Formed a duo with Dave Samuels in the '70s; later led his own small groups.

***** Of The Wind's Eye**

Enja 3089 *Friedman; Jane Ira Bloom (ss); Harvie Swartz (b); Daniel Humair (d).* 7/81.

****(*) Shades Of Change**

Enja 5017 *Friedman; Geri Allen (p); Anthony Cox (b); Ronnie Burrage (d).* 4/86.

Friedman's methods are unusual among vibes players in that he seems at least as interested in the percussive and rhythmic qualities of the instrument as he is in harmony and melody. He also uses the marimba as often as he does the vibraphone. It adds up to a purposeful style that deglamorizes the often shallow prettiness which the vibes can settle into, although Friedman's own romantic streak can allow his playing to meander to nowhere in particular. His work as a leader in the 1970s and '80s – he also co-led the group Double Image with Dave Samuels – is interesting rather than especially memorable. The best album, *Of The Wind's Eye*, is now on CD: the quartet respond well to the programme, with Humair outstandingly vivid on 'A Swiss Celebration' and Bloom in piquant form. Allen, Cox and Burrage are a close-knit trio, and Friedman sounds as if he's decorating their lines rather than integrating with them: tonally this is a rather bland group, although the Enja recording is as resonant as usual.

***** Other Worlds**

Intuition 3210-2 *Friedman; Jean-Louis Matinier (p acc); Anthony Cox (b); François Verly (perc).* 97.

The most singular voice here is Matinier, who makes light of the accordion's café connotations. Friedman plays a rather subdued role, working more closely with Cox than in the front line, and the music that results has an ethereal feel which doesn't quite evade the blandness that often troubles the leader's work. The Jobim tune, 'O Grande Amor', is typical of the tuneful if slender repast on offer.

Don Friedman (born 1935)

PIANO

Studied classical piano before working in and around San Francisco, 1950s–'60s; played with Jimmy Giuffre, Herbie Mann, Ornette Coleman and Charles Lloyd, then slipped from view until a recent revival with the Steeplechase label.

***** A Day In The City**

Original Jazz Classics OJCCD 1775 *Friedman; Chuck Israels (b); Joe Hunt (d).* 6/61.

*****(*) Circle Waltz**

Original Jazz Classics OJCCD 1885 *Friedman; Chuck Israels (b); Pete LaRoca (d).* 5/62.

***** Flashback**

Original Jazz Classics OJCCD 1903 *Friedman; Dick Kniss (b); Dick Berk (d).* 63.

Friedman's experimentalism is of a relaxed, Californian sort. He started out as a relatively orthodox West Coaster, bringing aspects of the Bill Evans style to work with Shorty Rogers, Jimmy Giuffre and others, but increasingly he has incorporated elements of classical composition and twelve-tone technique, as well as abstraction, to his playing. The *leitmotif* that governs *A Day In The City* is actually kept well disguised. Subtitled 'Six Variations On A Theme' and devoted to the hours from dawn through rush hour to the mildly threatening hush of the night, it isn't so much a theme-with-variations as a piece that never quite declares its central subject but toys with several possibilities. Elegantly and atmospherically played, it could almost be a Bill Evans session; certainly the nocturne has that feel.

Flashback also courted the inevitable comparison with Evans but was sufficiently original to survive and thrive. Friedman's bebop skills were evident from the opening 'Alone Together' and the brisk 'News Blues', but the real substance of the sessions, which featured a little-known rhythm section, was on 'Ochre' (subdivided theme–solo–duet–theme), the original 'Ballade in C Sharp Minor' and the elegant title-track which ends the set. Perhaps too many stylistic influences jockeying for position, but a fine record all the same.

Circle Waltz introduces LaRoca, a more beguiling presence than Hunt, and it is probably his brisk, tuneful cymbal work which makes the difference between the two sets. Typically, Friedman sticks largely to familiar material, a superb rendition of 'I Hear A Rhapsody' which almost conjures up the lyric, so expressive is it, and a forceful, unsentimental intepretation of Dave Brubeck's 'In Your Own Sweet Way'. A splendid record.

*****(*) Dreams And Explorations**

Original Jazz Classics OJC 1907 *Friedman; Attila Zoller (g); Dick Kniss (b); Dick Berk (d).* 64.

*****(*) Metamorphosis**

Original Jazz Classics OJC 1914 *Friedman; Attila Zoller (g); Richard Davis (b); Joe Chambers (d).* 2/66.

Credit to Fantasy for bringing back so much of the work of an unfashionable and, in the end, rather obscure figure. These two sets are notable for the introduction into the group of Zoller, who takes some of the pressure off Friedman as far as being the main improvisational voice is concerned and who establishes a surprising and progressive dialogue with the pianist as well as with the rest of the group. Although there are a couple of standards on the first disc, most of the music is based around originals by both Friedman and Zoller (the latter even gets three to the pianist's two pieces on the second set). Between them, and with the sympathetic if slightly distanced rhythm-sections, they create a jazz which flirts with freedom, often runs on contrapuntal or even confrontational lines, and recollects something of the Tristanoite doctrine, even if the results seem much hotter and less inward-looking than any Tristano record. After four intense, unsparing originals on *Dreams And Explorations*, it comes almost as a relief when they tackle the melody of John Carisi's 'Israel', which would be the most demanding piece on many a record. The later *Metamorphosis* seems to be pitched as the masterpiece; although there are some fascinating pieces – Giuffre's 'Drive' and Zoller's 'Troubadours Groovedour' in particular – there's a certain fussiness which holds the group back (Berk is, curiously enough, a better drummer for the group than the outwardly more adventurous Chambers). These obscure and all-but-forgotten records are well worth a revival, but don't expect an unjustly neglected masterwork.

***** Hot Pepper And Knepper**

Progressive PCD 7036 *Friedman; Jimmy Knepper (tb); Pepper Adams (bs); George Mraz (b); Billy Hart (d).* 6/78.

This is not entirely characteristic and has to be co-credited to the hornmen name-checked. Adams brings the original 'Hellure', there is a cover of Rollins's 'Audubon' (plus a very good alternative take) and a long medley that strings together 'Alfie', 'Laura', 'Prelude To A Kiss' (another Friedman enthusiasm) and 'I Got It Bad (And that Ain't Good)'. In addition, two takes of 'I'm Getting Sentimental Over You' and 'Beautiful Love', both of which show how restless an improviser Friedman can be, and how fettered he patently is by the conventional round of themes and solos. Halfway through the longer first take of 'Beautiful Love' he sounds as if he is going to take the whole thing off in an entirely new direction, but the inertia of the band holds him back, and the B-minor tonality reasserts itself.

*****(*) At Maybeck: Volume 33**

Concord CCD 4608 *Friedman (p solo).* 93.

As with many contemporary pianists, it was a Maybeck recital that gave him renewed prominence. It's clear that he enjoys the sweet-tempered piano and the quiet, respectful atmosphere of the hall. His own 'Memory For Scotty' is a classically conceived piece replete with echoes and allusions to the great Evans/LaFaro exchanges on the Riverside sessions. His choice of standards is predictably romantic – 'I Concentrate On You', 'How Deep Is The Ocean' and a Friedman favourite, 'I Hear A Rhapsody' – and there is a surpassingly elegant interpretation of Duke's 'Prelude To A Kiss', which has an almost operatic emotional range.

*****(*) Almost Everything**

Steeplechase SCCD 31468 *Friedman; Ron McClure (b); Matt Wilson (d).* 4/95.

At sixty, Friedman seemed disinclined to ease up on the pace. This is one of his most upbeat and joyful sessions ever, a resilient demonstration of his multifarious skills. Even 'On Green Dolphin Street', which sometimes seems to have yielded up all its secrets, receives a fresh intepretation. There is a brief group of originals, most impressively 'Before The Rain', which presumably name-checks the Coltrane tune beloved of pianists, and 'Waltz For Marilyn', the longest thing on the set. McClure is sterling in support and the little-known Wilson goes about his business with assurance.

****** My Romance**

Steeplechase SCCD 31403 *Friedman (p solo).* 11/96.

Sounding like a man with nothing to prove, Friedman works through some of his favourite songs. Beginning with 'How Deep

Is The Ocean', he nails the usual Evans analogy from the off. Yes, it is and no, it isn't. The harmonic understanding is the same, but underneath there is a tense, rhythmic restlessness which was not part of Bill's bag at all. He continues with 'These Foolish Things', 'My Foolish Heart' (is he trying to make a point here?), 'I Can't Get Started', 'My Romance', 'My Funny Valentine', 'Angel Eyes', 'Sophisticated Lady' and 'Darn That Dream', as self-deprecating a roster of songs as you could assemble and yet united by the same ironic intelligence Friedman brings to everything he does. Piano jazz of a high order, and probably now our album of choice.

The Fringe

GROUP

A long-standing trio of free-boppers, with at least ten years of service behind them.

*****(*) It's Time For The Fringe**

Soul Note 121205 *George Garzone (sax); John Lockwood (b); Bob Gullotti (d); Nick Racheotes (v).* 4/92.

***** Live**

A.V. Arts ADJ CD 004 *As above, except omit Racheotes.* 3/93.

The Fringe play a pleasantly old-fashioned variety of free bop that is rather reminiscent of 1960s British bands like Trevor Watts's Amalgam trio. Garzone is probably a more diverse player in the sense that he gravitates much less to fixed tonalities. The caveman poses on the cover of *It's Time For* are doubly ironic, since this is such civilized improvisation, polite even when Garzone is screeching up in the false register. (The cover shot is, incidentally, a reference to 'Neanderthal Man', on which guest performer Racheotes delivers an, ahem, recitation.) It isn't clear why the live record is attributed to the George Garzone Trio, since the personnels are identical and The Fringe is still functioning as a unit. Taped at Catania, it offers the group's sunnier side; it also offers a standard, 'My One And Only Love', interpreted with just enough eccentricity to save it from tedium.

Bill Frisell (born 1951)

GUITAR, ELECTRIC GUITAR, BANJO, GUITAR SYNTHESIZER, EFFECTS

Raised in Denver, studied at Berklee and began recording at the beginning of the '80s. Associated with downtown New York jazz of that period, but he has since touched numerous other bases and has a vast discography. One of the first jazz-based guitarists to build an aesthetic around an electronic-effects system.

***** In Line**

ECM 837019-2 *Frisell; Arild Andersen (b).* 8/82.

A man of engaging modesty, even shyness, Frisell is the first-call guitar man of the contemporary scene, a player who, within a few short years of his emergence as a countrified Hendrix with robust jazz chops, became one of the most widely recorded guitarists of his generation. A simplifier rather than an embellisher, he builds ideas out of the simplest materials, though often very basic and stripped-down ideas disguise harmonic experiments of great sophistication.

In Line was effectively a solo album, with some quiet and unassertive bass-line support from the redoubtable Andersen. The basic ideas could be jotted down on a couple of sides of stave paper, and yet one feels Frisell could have spun ideas out of this material all day and most of the following night. The best track, 'Throughout', so appealed to the British composer Gavin Bryars that he turned it into an atmospheric concert piece, 'Sub Rosa'. For the most part, though, Frisell's free modal themes are geared to open-ended improvisation.

***** Smash And Scatteration**

Minor Music 005 *Frisell; Vernon Reid (g, syn).* 12/84.

The joke here, of course, is that the quiet guy in the specs is the crazy one while Reid, who betrays – let's face it – a more convincing physical resemblance to Hendrix, is the one who holds the whole schtick together with his big but surprisingly accommodating chords. Some of the tracks are solo vehicles for both men, and here the Living Color guitarist reveals his slight limitations. It's Frisell who pushes the whole thing into overdrive.

***** Rambler**

ECM 825234-2 *Frisell; Kenny Wheeler (t, c, flhn); Bob Stewart (tba); Jerome Harris (b); Paul Motian (d).* 8/84.

*****(*) Lookout For Hope**

ECM 833495-2 *Frisell; Hank Roberts (clo, v); Kermit Driscoll (b); Joey Baron (d).* 3/87.

Frisell's emergence as a convincing leader was, not unexpectedly, slow in coming. Both of these albums suffer from a certain waywardness of focus and a lack of real drive and centre, though *Lookout For Hope* is certainly one of the very strongest things he has done. For that, much of the credit has to go to the combination of Driscoll and Baron, a dream team for a player of Frisell's sensibilities. *Rambler* certainly doesn't succeed at every level and lacks a real acoustic punch, but it is a beautifully structured record with a fascinating instrumental blend, and it was to establish a pattern of ambitious instrumentation which Frisell was to sustain over the next few years.

On *Lookout* he samples a wide variety of styles, including an interest in country that was to become dominant in later years. Some of it recalls work by Larry Coryell at a similar stage in his career; whereas Coryell was a quick-change artiste rather than a genuine synthesizer, Frisell does seem bent on creating something new and unprecedented out of disparate resources.

***** Before We Were Born**

Elektra Musician 960843 *Frisell; Billy Drewes, Julius Hemphill (as); Doug Wieselman (bs); Arto Lindsay (g, v); Peter Scherer (ky); Hank Roberts (clo, v); Kermit Driscoll (b); Joey Baron (d, perc); Cyro Baptista (perc).*

Frisell's Elektra debut trades almost too self-consciously on his eclecticism and on the seeming divide between his gentle, country-boy personality and occasional bad-boy grandstanding. The supporting cast are well distributed and each is allowed to make his mark, though it's a rare session that has Hemphill sounding as anodyne as he does here. The Driscoll/Baron axis comes up trumps yet again, though, and Roberts and Lindsay are their usual idiosyncratic selves.

***** Is That You?**
Elektra Musician 960596 *Frisell; Dave Hofstra (t, tba); Wayne Horvitz (ky, b); Joey Baron (d).* 8/89.

****(*) Where In The World?**
Elektra Nonesuch 7559 61181 *As above.* 91.

Is That You? was a rather self-conscious dive down into the guitarist's roots, taking its country trashing, big generous sweeps of abstract sound, jazz and a touch of free-form improv. By contrast, the follow-up sounds curiously self-absorbed and anything but interactive. All the usual infusion of country and folk themes (though these are turned head over heels on 'Rob Roy'), bludgeoning blues and abstractionist devices, but there's a polymorphous New Age quality to much of the music that from a player of Frisell's gifts seems downright perverse.

*****(*) This Land**
Elektra Nonesuch 79316 *Frisell; Curtis Fowlkes (tb); Don Byron (cl, bcl); Billy Drewes (as); Kermit Driscoll (b); Joey Baron (d).* 10/92.

****** Have A Little Faith**
Elektra Nonesuch 79301 *As above, except omit Fowlkes, Drewes; add Guy Klucevesek (acc).* 3/93.

On *This Land*, Frisell experiments further with stylistic hybrids, putting together elements of jazz and country music, abstract shapes and tuneful miniatures that have the resonant familiarity of the melodies in Aaron Copland's *Appalachian Spring* and *Billy the Kid*. Sonically, it's a fascinating combination, with Fowlkes and Byron often combining to provide elegant dissonances (as on 'Jimmy Carter, Part 1') that are taken over by accordion master Klucevesek on *Have A Little Faith*.

Frisell's marvellous examination of Americana takes in Stephen Foster, Sousa, Ives, Copland, Sonny Rollins, Bob Dylan and, most controversially, Madonna. There's no attempt to debunk or satirize, and even Madonna's 'Live To Tell', despite a heavily distorted cadenza with all Frisell's switches and pedals on, sticks pretty close to the original. As was noted on their tour of Britain, Byron's role was rather marginal, and it's Klucevesek and Baron whom one particularly remembers, both enjoying themselves mightily.

Perhaps the only reservation about its predecessor is a slight sententiousness that seems at odds with most of Frisell's compositions. The repertoire and pop pieces on *Faith* encourage a more playful approach and make for a less coherent but far more varied record.

***** American Blood / Safety In Numbers**
veraBra vBr 2064 *Frisell; Brian Ales (elec); Victor Bruce Godsey (v).* 94.

'All sounds on this recording are made by the guitar or the human voice.' *Safety In Numbers* is the result of Ales's sampling and manipulation of a 27-minute guitar solo by Frisell, who seems then to have played a live guitar part over the resultant tape. *American Blood* sets lyrics by Godsey with somewhat less totalizing manipulation from Ales. The results are two dense collage pieces, very much in keeping with Frisell's other work as far back as *Smash And Scatteration*, but also subtly differentiated by the input of his two collaborators. Interesting, rather than compelling.

*****(*) Go West: Music For The Films Of Buster Keaton**
Elektra Nonesuch 79350 *Frisell; Kermit Driscoll (b); Joey Baron (d).* 95.

***** The High Sign / One Week: Music For The Films Of Buster Keaton**
Elektra Nonesuch 79351 *As above.* 95.

Like Don Byron, Frisell has become increasingly interested in the preterite corners of American popular music, the inaudible backwash of the demotic. Nowhere is that better *seen* than in the movies of Buster Keaton, who makes Chaplin seem like a superficial sentimentalist. Unfortunately, much of the music Frisell has to work with is pretty tatty, and though the trio play superbly from start to finish (with Driscoll better favoured in the mix than on *Live*) there is not much to chew on here beyond a bittersweet kitsch. Frisell sounds wonderful, of course, but only in short bursts.

****(*) Nashville**
Elektra Nonesuch 79415 *Frisell; Pat Bergeson (hca); Jerry Douglas (dobro); Ron Block (bjo, g); Adam Steffey (mandolin); Viktor Krauss (b); Robin Holcomb (v).* 9/95, 10 & 11/96.

A weak and watery collage of country themes. The instrumentation is not quite as Nashville in effect as it looks on the page, and Robin Holcomb's vocal presence on two tracks serves as pretty irrefutable evidence that this isn't an entirely straight project. Interesting to compare this, though, with some of the things Pat Metheny has done in similar vein. Frisell now sounds more *faux-naïf* than genuinely innocent, and one spends much of *Nashville* waiting for a joke to be sprung which simply isn't there.

On the positive side, it's played freshly enough and there are sufficient ideas floating around to keep the mind engaged. Even so, it is perhaps the most one-dimensional record Frisell has ever made.

****** Quartet**
Elektra Nonesuch 79401 *Frisell; Ron Miles (t, picc t); Curtis Fowlkes (tb); Eyvind Kang (vn, tba).* 96.

A stunningly beautiful album featuring the most enterprising instrumentation Frisell has deployed since the earlier ECMs. Some of the material again derives from a Keaton film, this time *Convict 13*, but the bulk of the themes were written for a Gary '*Far Side*' Larson television special, and they have that sweetly illogical, uncomplicatedly lyrical slant that Larson himself always brings.

The combination of guitar with two – and sometimes three – brass is irresistible, and the pairing of guitar and violin against trumpet and trombone is hard to argue with. Frisell is playing quite simply but at a high level of invention, and in Miles he has a player of markedly similar temperament: quiet, unassertive, but capable of caustic blasts and sudden dark turns.

The cover reproduces American regionalist Thomas Hart Benton's 'The Boy', a slightly sentimental but unalloyed image of a farm kid heading off, leaving the homestead for the city or some other unknown future. Hard not to think of this as Frisell himself, and hard not to feel that he shares the ambiguity. This is the album Frisell was born to make.

*****(*) Gone, Just Like A Train**
Elektra Nonesuch 79479 *Frisell; Viktor Krauss (b); Jim Keltner (d). 97.*

Surreal power trio pop-jazz from the new trio, with the experienced Keltner offering a great deal more than the solid backbeat that runs through the record. He is a musician of great subtlety, and this is a record that, while somewhat disconcerting at first, repays careful listening.

We are less sanguine about Krauss, certainly as a replacement for the wonderful Driscoll; but on most of these tracks he makes his presence felt and creates rich counter-lines to the guitar. Odd, but nudging its way up towards the front rank.

*****(*) Good Dog, Happy Man**
Elektra Nonesuch 79536 *Frisell; Ry Cooder, Greg Leisz (g); Wayne Horvitz (ky); Victor Krauss (b); Jim Keltner (d). 99.*

Flawlessly executed and almost ridiculously beautiful, this takes Frisell nowhere musically, but must surely have won him new fans. The presence of Cooder on the traditional 'Shenandoah', reshaped much like Madonna's 'Live To Tell' on *Have A Little Faith*, will intrigue many who have no interest in 'jazz guitar'. Those who do will have long concluded that Frisell now has little to do with conventional jazz picking and rhythm play and has moved into a new and self-defining realm which reintegrates jazz with a whole slew of other popular forms.

Keltner has made his greatest impact on the rock and blues scene, but here he shows himself to be a responsive and often subtle player, blending a steady backbeat with a more sophisticated time feel. His work on 'Cadillac 1959' initially sounds at odds with Frisell's concept, but it soon becomes clear that he is the anchorman.

It would probably be refreshing at this juncture to hear Bill either shelve some of the technology or else push it to the maximum. Recent albums have done everything except surprise.

David Frishberg (born 1933)

PIANO, VOCAL

Originally a journalist, he worked as an intermission pianist in the 1950s, then began working in small groups with Bud Freeman and Gene Krupa. His songwriting, witty and literate, has been more successful than his playing career. But he is a clever, accomplished player, a fine no-voice singer and a good MD of small groups.

*****(*) You're A Lucky Guy**
Concord CCD 4074-2 *Frishberg; Bob Brookmeyer (vtb); Al Cohn (ts); Jim Hughart (b); Nik Ceroli (d). 78.*

****** Classics**
Concord CCD 4462 *Frishberg; Steve Gilmore (b); Bill Goodwin (d). 12/82–3/83.*

*****(*) Live At Vine Street**
Original Jazz Classics OJC 832 *Frishberg (p, v solo). 10/84.*

***** Can't Take You Nowhere**
Fantasy FCD 9651 *Frishberg (p solo). 87.*

***** Let's Eat Home**
Concord CCD 4402 *Frishberg; Snooky Young (t); Rob McConnell (vtb); Jim Hughart (b); Jeff Hamilton (d). 1/89.*

***** Where You At?**
Bloomdido BL 010 *Frishberg; Glenn Ferris (tb); Turk Mauro (bs); Michel Gaudry (b). 3/91.*

***** Double Play**
Arbors ARCD 19118 *Frishberg; Jim Goodwin (c). 10/92.*

Although Frishberg himself notes that a supply sergeant once told him that 'Jazz is OK, but it ain't got no words', he has done his best to deliver hip songwriting in a form that fits with his individual brand of mainstream piano. If he's become best known as a cabaret recitalist, Frishberg nevertheless has a strong, swinging keyboard style that borrows from the swing masters without making him seem like a slavish copyist. He has worked extensively as a sideman – check, for instance, his discs with Rebecca Kilgore – and seems most suited to swing-styled groups with enough space for him to let loose his favourite rolling, two-fisted solos. Of those recordings under his own name currently in print, *Classics* is the best, since it gathers all his best-known songs together on a single CD (which is a reissue of two LPs made for Omnisound). Sparsely but crisply presented by the trio, here are the prototype versions of such Frishberg favourites as 'My Attorney Bernie', 'Dodger Blue' and 'Do You Miss New York?', bittersweet odes which he is very good at investing with both warmth and wryness. The sound has been dried out by CD remastering but isn't disagreeable.

The return of his Concord debut pushes that one very close, though. Nicely balanced between songs and jazz, the music gets a huge fillip from the presence of in-form horns Cohn and Brookmeyer, Frishberg himself purveys a kind of delicate jauntiness on his solo, 'That Old Feeling', and as a record it's beautifully programmed. A fine live set for Fantasy has made it to CD in the OJC series. It's a useful souvenir of an evening with Frishberg: some of his smartest songs, a Johnny Hodges medley where he gets to show off his pianism, and the corncrake voice put to work on his wryest lyrics. A special favourite of ours is the opener, 'You Would Rather Have The Blues', but any of his nine songs here sounds good. *Can't Take You Nowhere* is a few more pages from Frishberg's notebooks of Americana, as is the recent Concord set, although the horns are more of a distraction than a bonus. Actually, the three other participants on the Bloomdido session add some useful seasoning. This time there are medleys dedicated to Ellington and (a nice touch) Ivie Anderson.

Double Play is one where he keeps his voice down and plays alongside the salty cornet of Jim Goodwin. They make a good fist of a fine clutch of old songs ('One, Two, Button My Shoe' was an inspired choice) and Goodwin's thick, rasping tone is unfailingly entertaining, but, for once, Frishberg's piano parts are a bit samey from track to track.

Frisque Concordance

GROUP

One of Georg Gräwe's group projects, featuring himself with British improviser Butcher.

***(*) **Spellings**

Random Acoustics RA 001 *John Butcher (ts, ss); Georg Gräwe (p); Hans Schneider (b); Martin Blume (d). 10/92.*

Founded by the classically inclined Gräwe, this free-music group hinges on the relationship between the pianist and the young British saxophonist who has become one of the most roundedly accomplished European players in this idiom. The fact that Gräwe runs the label (this item is issued in a plain, grey card cover) in no way compromises quality control. All five lettered 'Spellings', of steadily increasing length, seem to combine the title's promise of linguistic straightforwardness and magic combined. There is a certain amount of Morse and background traffic on 'A' and 'B' but, once the pace has picked up – and we are assuming that the music is tracked in the order recorded – there is a whirling intensity and mystery which owners of Butcher's *Thirteen Friendly Numbers* will recognize. Our only slight reservations relate to the bassist and drummer, who sometimes seem to drift away from the main action.

Tony Fruscella (1927–69)

TRUMPET

Grew up in an orphanage and after military service played a sideman role with Lester Young, Stan Getz and others. Made a modest impact on the late bop scene, but drink and narcotics ruined him, and his last years featured no music.

*** **The Complete Recordings**

Jazz Factory JFCD 22808/9 4CD *Fruscella; Chauncey Welsch (tb); Phil Woods, Chick Maures, Herb Geller (as); Phil Urso, Allen Eager, Stan Getz (ts); Gene Allen, Danny Bank (bs); Bill Truglia, Hank Jones, Johnny Williams (p); Bill Keck (g); Red Mitchell, Teddy Kotick, Wendell Marshall, Bill Anthony, Paul Chambers (b); Art Madigan, Shadow Wilson, Frank Isola, Howie Mann, Junior Bradley, Roy Hall (d). 12/48–8/59.*

***(*) **Tony Fruscella**

Atlantic 8122-75354-2 *Fruscella; Chauncey Welsch (tb); Allen Eager (ts); Danny Bank (bs); Bill Triglia (p); Bill Anthony (b); Junior Bradley (d). 3–4/55.*

Despite a formidable reputation among some collectors, Fruscella has remained an obscure figure. Jazz Factory's set collects absolutely everything that he did: surviving airshots, live tapes and studio sessions. Much of it is desperate. Most of the live music (in mainly indifferent sound) has very little going for it, including a set from New York's Open Door Club (previously on a Spotlite LP) where the players wind up drunk, and a high school concert with Phil Woods effortlessly outplaying the trumpeter. The studio session with Chick Maures (previously on Spotlite SPJ 126) is a bit better: pale, interesting bebop with a glance towards Tristano, and the two horns play carefully spun improvisations that at least take a different tack from bop convention.

Fruscella's great moment was his 1955 date for Atlantic, and this is easily the best music on offer. All his idiosyncrasies – the undemonstrative tone, laid-back dynamics, penchant for the low register and thin but insistent melodicism – came almost accidentally together into an apologetic whole. It's a very interesting record. But the entire session has now finally been reissued by Atlantic themselves, and this is the one to get as his best legacy.

Wolfgang Fuchs

SOPRANINO SAXOPHONE, CLARINET, BASS CLARINET, CONTRABASS CLARINET

German multi-instrumentalist and reed specialist, playing in the further reaches of improvisation.

(*) **FinkFarker

FMP CD 26 *Fuchs; Georg Katzer (elec). 6/89.*

***(*) **Binaurality**

FMP CD 49 *Fuchs; Gunter Christmann, Radu Malfatti (tb); Peter Van Bergen (ts, bcl, cbcl); Luc Houtkamp (as, ts, cl); Phil Wachsmann (vn, elec); Melvyn Poore (tba); Torsten Muller (b); Paul Lytton (d, elec); Georg Katzer (elec, computer). 6/92.*

*** **Bits & Pieces**

FMP OWN-90004 *Fuchs; Evan Parker (ss); Jean-Marc Montera (g). 9/95.*

Fuchs is an improviser who's especially interested – as his choice of instruments suggests – in timbral extremes. He extracts a cruel vocabulary of sounds out of the sopranino and the bass clarinet, phrases diced into the smallest fragments, and, while one can construe lines out of the sonic splinters, deconstruction is Fuchs's speciality. *FinkFarker* operates across wide soundscapes, the reed player combating Katzer's electronics in pieces entitled 'Vicious', 'Confrontation' and so on. Interesting but rarefied.

Binaurality is by Fuchs's larger group, King Ubu Orchestra. Big though the ensemble is, Fuchs has clearly thought very carefully about the balance of instruments and the differing nature of the players, and the result is a free group of unusually specific empathies. The cloudy nature of the brass instruments contrasts with the filigree, pecking lines of the reed players, with Wachsmann's elegance and the surprise elements of Lytton and Katzer adding to the flavour without distorting any lines of communication. As always with this kind of music, there are dead ends and disappointments as well as achievements: 'Translation No. 4', for instance, loses its way at the halfway mark after an utterly riveting development – it peters out into typical free-jazz crescendo and diminuendo. Yet there are so many fascinating passages here that the record deserves a full hearing.

Half of *Bits & Pieces* is solo, with Fuchs putting his reed family through their most extreme paces. John Corbett's suggestion that Fuchs gets a sound akin to an analogue synthesizer out of the contrabass clarinet is about right, and setting these primeval rumbles next to the sharp, splintery chips of the sopranino is an interesting exercise in contrasts. Whether listeners will feel enjoined to follow what seems like a technical inquiry is another matter. No such issue arises, though, with the duets with Parker and Montera which make up the rest of the disc. The two saxophonists strike explosive sparks, while Montera's unpredictable soundboard makes for a satisfying confrontation.

Full Monte

GROUP

A band of familiar British improvisers and post-bop stylists.

***** Spark In The Dark**

Slam CD 209 *Chris Biscoe (as, ss, acl); Brian Godding (g, g syn); Marcio Mattos (b); Tony Marsh (d, perc).* 11/90–12/93.

Biscoe and Godding were regular playing partners in the Mike Westbrook Orchestra; Mattos and Marsh are mainstays of British free jazz. As a unit, they cover a lot of bases. The great beauty of the sound is its textural variety. Godding and Mattos take a great deal of credit for that, but not all of it, for Marsh is an atmospheric drummer and Biscoe makes full use of his horns (including the increasingly popular alto clarinet) to give each track a distinctive character. Formed in 1988, the group has the old shoe feel you get only from settled combinations. All but two of the tracks have been in the can for some time (dating from the time of Slam's *Saxophone Phenomenon* compilation) but the longer of the two recent cuts (the other, 'Wind Dance', is only two minutes long) suggests that they've continued to get to know one another over the intervening time. 'Spiritual Cleavage II' is testimony to the members' spiritual empathy.

Curtis Fuller (born 1934)

TROMBONE

Detroit-born Fuller owes much to Kai Winding's modernization of trombone technique (he later worked with the Dane in a version of the Jay & Kai format) and he also owes much to J.J.'s demonstration of the instrument's solo potential. However, it was the harmonic language of John Coltrane and Miles Davis that marked him most profoundly.

***** New Trombone**

Original Jazz Classics OJCCD 077 *Fuller; Sonny Red (as); Hank Jones (p); Doug Watkins (b); Louis Hayes (d).* 5/57.

*****(*) With Red Garland**

Original Jazz Classics OJCCD 1862 *As above, except omit Jones, Watkins; add Red Garland (p), Paul Chambers (b).* 5/57.

Curtis Fuller made his mark on one of the most memorable intros in modern jazz, the opening bars of Coltrane's 'Blue Train'; and for many the story stops there – ironically, since the Blue Note session with Trane was hardly representative of what this mellifluous trombonist was about. Possessed of an excellent technique, slightly derivative of J.J. Johnson, he occasionally found it difficult to develop ideas at speed and tended to lapse, as he had on 'Blue Train', into either repetition or sequences of bitten-off phrases that sounded either diffident or aggressive, depending on the context. The saxophone-influenced delivery, mixed in with rich bell-notes and a trademark enharmonic slide, helped create an ambiguity not accessible to valved or keyed horn players.

There was some excitement about Fuller in 1957, and these two sessions for Prestige, supervised by the redoubtable Teddy Charles, promised much. Sonny Red was the working name of one Sylvester Kyner, a slightly raw player who isn't the obvious choice to work opposite Fuller but who acquits himself on both sets with enthusiasm and some ruggedly straightforward ideas. He's better on the later set, kicking off Garland's cleaner-cut blues chords. The rhythm section is much stronger on the latter disc. Chambers comes through powerfully and the mix of material, with a big saxophone feature on 'Slenderella' and a gorgeous original from Fuller, 'Cashmere', gives Mr PC all the space he could want to develop his own solid, singing lines.

****(*) Four On The Outside**

Timeless SJP 124 *Fuller; Pepper Adams (bs); James Williams (p); Dennis Irwin (b); John Yarling (d).* 9/78.

****(*) Meets Roma Jazz Trio**

timeless SJP 204 *Fuller; Danilo Rea (p); Enzo Pietropaoli (b); Roberto Gatto (d).* 12/82.

Fuller's career drifted after the mid-1960s and took some time to recover. The first Timeless record is really quite dull, and only the presence of Pepper Adams, gruffing away at the chords, lifts it. Though the later band is unexceptionable, exactly the sort of unflamboyantly professional but still creative outfit one finds in Italy, *Meets Roma Jazz Trio* is uncommunicative and Fuller's normally reliable medium blues phrasing sounds off.

*****(*) Blues-ette II**

Savoy SV 75624 *Fuller; Benny Golson (ts); Tommy Flanagan (p); Ray Drummond (b); Al Harewood (d).* 1/93.

Half a biblical lifespan on and the old gang reconvenes, minus Garrison, for a run-through of some familiar charts. There isn't the pep and bounce of the original session, but Fuller still has that lovely wuffly tone, as if the horn is wrapped in velvet, and Flanagan has become so urbane in the intervening years that the session has an almost ambassadorial gravity and solidity. Golson's part is sterling as always, though he is a little too forthright on 'Bluesette 93' for the balance of the piece.

Stephane Furic

BASS

Bassist following a fusion of composed and improvised forms which interlock with specific precision.

***** Kishinev**

Soul Note 121215 *Furic; Chris Cheek (ts, ss); Patrick Goraguer (p); Jim Black (d).* 7/90.

*****(*) The Twitter-Machine**

Soul Note 121225 *As above.* 5/92.

Furic likes to describe what he does as 'suburban music', an art of common people leading ordinary lives, but also art on the edges, at the outer range of all the big comfortable generalizations. The debut Soul Note juxtaposes compositions by Ornette Coleman, Wayne Shorter and Lil Hardin Armstrong, and cues some impressive early work by Cheek. The follow-up (named after a Paul Klee design for a mechanical bird) pushes the collectivist philosophy a step further, four voices conjoined with the logic and beauty of an engine. Furic takes a wry, very European stance on the jazz tradition, pulling in influences that range from Miles Davis and John Coltrane to the cool angularity of Warne Marsh (and one can almost imagine Marsh acolyte Anthony Braxton enjoying a sojourn in this group).

Andy Fusco

ALTO SAXOPHONE

Fusco wavered between music and pro-football: the sax eventually won. He's a tough, accomplished hard-bop altoman.

***** Out Of The Dark**

Criss Cross 1171 *Fusco; Joe Magnarelli (t); Joel Weiskopf (p); Peter Washington (b); Billy Drummond (d).* 12/98.

Slightly more ragged and flaring than the typical Criss Cross date, this has some exciting music, although the mollifying ballad, 'Epitaph For Sal Amico', and Walt Weiskopf's chart for 'Lament' lack nothing in finesse. But it's probably the pianoless 'It's You Or No One', on a direct current from Charlie Parker, that sums up Fusco's hearty, amiably aggressive playing. Everyone plays to their strengths and it's a satisfying hour of music.

Slim Gaillard (1916–90)

PIANO, GUITAR, VOCALS

In latter years, Gaillard was the perennial guest MC and hipster-about-town, but his impact on the bop'n'beat generation of the 1940s and early '50s is hard to exaggerate. The inventor of 'Vout' – a hipster slang generated by adding '-oroonie' to every significant word – was born in Detroit and spent many of his later years in London. Larger than life, he comes across on record only in diluted form.

***** Slim Gaillard, 1937–1938**

Classics 705 *Gaillard; Kenneth Hollon (ts); Sam Allen (p); Slam Stewart (b); Pompey Dobson (d).* 37–38.

****(*) Original 1938 Recordings: Volume 1**

Tax S1 *As above.* 2–11/38.

****(*) Original 1938–39 Recordings: Volume 2**

Tax S2 *As above, except add Al Killian, Cyril Newman (t), Herman Flintall (as), Loumell Morgan (p), William Smith (b), Herbert Pettaway (d).* 11/38–4/40.

He always looked gorgeous: an ice-cream suit, shoes that looked as if you could get into them and drive away, a big slob cap tipped over one delightedly un-ironic eye, and the coolest pepper-and-salt beard ever, out of which came a constant stream of song, anecdote and – above all – the hip, nonsensical patois known as 'Vout'. Hard as it may be to recognize this now, Slim was a key personality in the bebop movement. His presence on the Savoy Parkers underlines that. As such, he is a valuable corrective to the notion that bop was hard, serious and antagonistic; above all it was about play and playfulness, and a title like 'Klactoveeseedstene' was not so very far from the kind of semantic juggling Slim loved to indulge in. A long involvement with Slam Stewart, trading as Slim'n'Slam, remains his most memorable, but Gaillard was around for long enough and was personable enough to have worked with most of the greats in some capacity. It's hard to maintain equanimity in the face of something like 'Laughing In Rhythm', which is just that.

*****(*) Slim Gaillard, 1939–40**

Classics 724 *Gaillard; Henry Goodwin, Al Killian, Cyril Newman (t); Garvin Bushell (cl); Herman Flintall (as); Kenneth Hollon (ts); Loumell Morgan (p); William Smith (b); Herbert Pettaway (d).* 9/39–8/40.

***** Slim Gaillard, 1940–42**

Classics 787 *Similar to above.* 40–42.

****(*) Original 1940–42 Recordings: Volume 3**

Tax S3 *As above.* 40–42.

Not everyone is a fan of the Classics approach, and almost everyone has some misgivings about transfer quality. However, the French label is certainly the place to turn to if you are a devoted collector of Gaillard, not because it covers the same material better (there is surprisingly little overlap) but because it has better stuff to offer. The basic material is all there, is mostly pristine (by the standards of the label at least), and all, all of it is hugely entertaining. You either buy into this man's sound or you don't. If you don't, no one will ever explain it to you. If you do, aim for both sets of releases and enjoy in good health.

***** Slim Gaillard, 1945**

Classics 864 *Gaillard; Karl George, Howard McGhee (t); Vic Dickenson (tb); Teddy Edwards, Wild Bill Moore, Lucky Thompson (ts); Dodo Marmarosa, Fletcher Smith (p); Bam Brown (b); Zutty Singleton, Leo Watson (d).* 45.

*****(*) Slim Gaillard, 1945: Volume 2**

Classics 911 *Gaillard; Dizzy Gillespie (t); Charlie Parker (as); Jack McVea (ts); Dodo Marmarosa (p); Bam Brown (b, v); Zutty Singleton (d).* 12/45.

Slim spent the early part of America's war in the forces. He wouldn't have been doing much recording anyway, since there was a ban in operation; but it's clear that, once he was out of uniform and ensconced in Los Angeles, he started recording for as many of the new labels springing up on the Coast as would have him; all the items in Volume Two were made within a single winter month. Just to keep up the pace, Slim also appeared in the manic jive movie, *Hellzapoppin*, which makes tiring viewing even 50 years on.

The first of the 1945 groups was the Boogiereeners, with Howard McGhee, Teddy Edwards and Wild Bill Mooore all among the horns, and Lucky Thompson taking the bulk of the solos, notably on 'Slim Gaillard's Boogie' and 'Harlem Hunch', both from September. Later still in the year, he would record with Charlie Parker, a session just after Christmas which yielded the immortal 'Flat Foot Floogie'. That same session also included Diz, Dodo Marmarosa and Zutty Singleton. Some of the earlier stuff has him doubling on harpsichord and novachord, constantly on the look-out for a new and unexpected sound, but it is always the lyrics that catch the attention, especially when they are as surreally arresting as those of 'Atomic Cocktail', made for the label of that name. The trio stuff puts his voice at centre, with not much more than accompaniment, but there should be no mistaking the quality of Slim's musicality. If he was a novelty act, he was a very good one.

***** Slim Gaillard, 1946**

Classics 962 *Gaillard; Howard McGhee(t); Marshall Royal(cl); Lucky Thompson (ts); Bill Early, Dodo Marmarosa (p); Wini Beatty (p, v); Bam Brown (b, v); Oscar Bradley, Scatman Crothers, Zutty Singleton (d); Leo Watson(d, v).* 1–5/46.

Including the deathless 'Opera In Vout' and some of the V-Discs Slim made at the end of the war, this is an extremely attractive package. The January material for Bel-Tone, recorded in Los Angeles, stands up well after more than half a century and, with the likes of Howard McGhee, Marshall Royal, Lucky Thomson, Dodo Marmarosa and Zutty Singleton on the strength, the cuts are musically interesting as well as entertaining. Dodo is the probable pianist as well on an uncertainly dated session for Savoy towards the end of the year which includes the unusual sound of Slim on piano, playing the line of 'Oxydol Highball'. Good stuff, and a must for the Gaillard collector.

*****(*) Laughing In Rhythm: The Best of the Verve Years**

Verve 521651-2 *Gaillard; Taft Jordan (t); Bennie Green (tb); Buddy Tate, Ben Webster (ts); Bam Brown, Cyril Haynes, Maceo Williams (p); Ray Brown, Clyde Lombardi (b); Milt Jackson, Charlie Smith (d); Jim Hawthorne (v).* 4/46–1/54.

The Verve sessions are a little more contrived, but there is still some astonishing musicianship buried in these hectic sessions. The long 'Opera in Vout (Groove Juice Symphony)' is a *tour de force* and 'Genius' has Gaillard out-Sidneying Bechet with a one-man overdub of truly manic proportions. The 1951 sessions, which are about the last of the really good ones, included various Ellingtonians on things like 'Chicken Rhythm', while the oddly named Shintoists group provided a platform for some wonderfully mellow and poised solos from Ben Webster. An excellent compilation, but of an artist who had already gone some way past the fresh spontaneity of early years.

***** The Legendary McVouty**

Hep CD 6 *Gaillard; Jay Thomas (t); Digby Fairweather (c); Buddy Tate, Jay Thomas (ts); Jay McShann (p); Peter Ind (b); Allan Ganley (d).* 10/82.

The 1982 sessions reintroduced Gaillard, who had become a festival favourite, to a new audience of young and hip fans who were turning on to a new generation of young British players. Gaillard had eventually settled in London, and this is a mainly British line-up, drawn from established players. The man's energy is unflagging and his inventiveness unstinting; though by this stage listening to Gaillard on record seemed almost redundant when he might very likely turn up at your club on a Friday night, he always makes for an entertaining listen.

Richard Galliano

ACCORDION, PIANO, KEYBOARDS, TROMBONE

Galliano is a compelling improviser with a wonderfully expressive sound and a subtle swing, mostly in three-quarter time and tango rhythms. In smaller ensembles he uses the harmonic richness of the accordion to create an almost orchestral effect, but he is also content to create sparse single-note melodies with minimum harmonization when surrounded by like-minded players.

*****(*) Spleen**

Dreyfus Jazz Line FDM 36513 *Galliano; Eric Giausserand (flhn); Denis Leloup (tb); Franck Stibon (p, syn, v); Jean-Marc Jafet (b); Luiz Augusto (d, perc).* 6/85.

***** Coloriage**

Quadrivium SCA 031 *Galliano; Gabriele Mirabassi (cl).* 7/92.

***** Viagio**

Dreyfus Jazz Line FDM 36562 *Galliano; Bireli Lagrene (g); Pierre Michelot (b); Charles Bellonzi (d).* 6/93.

****** Laurita**

Dreyfus Jazz Line FDM 36572 *Galliano; Michel Portal (bcl); Didier Lockwood (vn); Toots Thielemans (hca); Palle Danielsson (b); Joey Baron (d).* 11/94.

*****(*) Blow Up**

Dreyfus Jazz Line FDM 36589 *Galliano; Michel Portal (bcl, cl, ss, bandoneon, jazzophone).* 5/96.

Astor Piazzolla and, more recently, Dino Saluzzi are the presiding geniuses of modern accordion and bandoneon playing. Galliano is by no means in thrall to either but, like any accordion player, he draws heavily on Piazzolla themes, notably 'Libertango' on the wonderful *Laurita*. This is the only Galliano album you really need to have – though, if you love it as much as we do, the set of duos with the multi-faceted Portal will surely follow. Original material like 'Spleen' and 'Il Viaggio' is already well trodden, and the very pared-down instrumentation on the Quadrivium disc is a good place (if you can find it) to sample both these pieces and to get a measure on Galliano's style. The early album is something of a collage, pieced together in a ramshackle way that has distinct charm but lacks an element of finish. The group with Lagrene, on the contrary, is a blowing gig, with plenty of solo space for all concerned.

What we like about *Laurita* and *Blow Up* is that they combine spontaneity with polish and a wonderfully rich sound-spectrum. Portal's brooding sound lifts both records immeasurably; Toots Thielemans is mistily beautiful on 'Laurita', and then Lockwood has his moment in the spotlight with 'Decisione', whirling it away like a cross between Grappelli and a New Orleans clarinet player. On *Blow Up*, there are once again a couple of Hermeto Pascoal numbers, a retread of 'Libertango' and a number of originals by Galliano and Portal, including the excellent 'Little Tango' and the tiny closing-piece, both of them credited to the saxophonist but both absolutely suited to this pairing.

Joe Gallivan

DRUMS, PERCUSSION

A spirited journeyman whose career has been a litany of ambitious projects, many of which he has fulfilled, from early efforts at fusion to large-scale free playing and more. Records with long-time partner Charles Austin are being scheduled for reissue.

*****(*) Innocence**

Cadence CJT 1051 *Gallivan; Guy Barker, Claude Deppa, Gerard Presencer (t); Paul Rutherford (tb); Ashley Slater (btb); Neil Metcalfe (f); Elton Dean (as, saxello); Evan Parker (ts, ss); Marcio Mattos (b).* 8/91.

Joe Gallivan – who does not merit an entry in the *Grove Dictionary of Jazz* or *The Rough Guide to Jazz* – is one of the forgotten pioneers of the music. Now based in Hawaii (although as we went to press he was preparing to decamp for New York once again), he was a member of the fabled Love Cry Want, successors to Lifetime and the Miles Davis group in the search for a viable fusion of jazz and rock; and he later went on to invent a viable drum synthesizer. For much of his playing career, like Tony Oxley, he has moved eclectically inside and outside a countable beat, and he has used both acoustic and amplified percussion.

Innocence is cast in cycles of form, freedom and surrender and is concerned thematically with the innocence of creative music-making in an essentially pragmatic culture. Though the basic structures are scored and are typically sophisticated, they are open-ended enough to allow the soloists to explore their own natures and their own stance on the basic dilemmas of accommodation or resistance. If it all sounds grandiose, it works. Gallivan has assembled a band of old friends from his years in London, with the addition of younger players like Barker, Deppa and Presencer (where else could three players of this quality be found?) and a last-minute recruit, flautist Neil Metcalfe, who brings an air of thoughtful simplicity to the opening 'Materialism'. On 'Voices Of Ancient Children', Evan Parker combines darkly with Elton Dean, establishing the sonority that will dominate the session, very British, but here heard in an unexpected framework. It's to Gallivan's credit that he has stamped so much of his own personal authority on players as experienced as these, without turning this into an exercise in auteurism.

****** The Origin Of Man**

No Budget Records NB 102 *Gallivan; Elton Dean (as, saxello); Brian Cuomo (p, ky).*

The result of several sessions improvising in a studio in Maui, Hawaii, and pared down from there. Dean and Gallivan have worked together many times, and the big drummer bunked with him in London for a while. It's a close, highly instinctive relationship and, on pieces like the opening 'Origin Of Man' and the two long tracks, 'The Opening Of The Heart' and 'Piece Of Resistance', it's clear that they are absolutely of one mind. Cuomo is nothing like as well known, but he's a player to watch, with a good feel for the dynamics of the music and a strong improvisational instinct, though one suspects that he might be happier playing straight jazz than the other two.

*****(*) Orchestral Meditations**

New Jazz NJC 002 *Gallivan; Charles Austin (ts, ss, f, bf, ob, eng hn); John McMinn (syn, ts); Tim Richards (perc); Billy Johnson (v).*

Austin and Gallivan have worked together a good deal over the years. While they come from very different places musically, there is enough common ground for a genuine creative interchange. Joe always sounds loosest and most comfortable in Austin's company, and the man with the horns clearly feels much the same way. A genuine multi-instrumentalist who doesn't use a horn unless he has something to say on it, Austin is a closet romantic; this sweeping programme, built up over the talented McMinn's inventive but improvised synth figures, suits him to a 't'. Though it's anything but a straight jazz date, they do a trio of standards – 'Body And Soul', 'Prelude To A Kiss' and 'Stella By Starlight' – and a couple of classical themes by Fauré and Granados, in addition to two Austin originals. It might more properly be credited to the saxophonist, except that it is once again Gallivan who has made this possible. Time he was recognized.

Hal Galper (born 1938)

PIANO, KEYBOARDS

One of the most responsive piano players on the scene, Galper received a classical training and established himself early as a persuasive and sophisticated soloist, having worked with a range of leaders from Herb Pomeroy and Chet Baker to Cannonball Adderley and Anita O'Day. His solo work is inclined to the florid, but with a solid foundation of blues harmony, even if he rarely plays a straight blues.

*****(*) Reach Out**

Steeplechase CCD 31067 *Galper; Randy Brecker (t); Michael Brecker (ts, f); Wayne Dockery (b); Billy Hart (d).* 11/76.

***** Now Hear This**

Enja 2090 *Galper; Terumasa Hino (t, flhn); Cecil McBee (b); Tony Williams (d).* 2/77.

*****(*) Children Of The Night**

DoubleTime Records DTRCD *Galper; Randy Brecker (t); Michael Brecker (ts); Wayne Dockery (b); Bob Moses (d).* 2/78.

*****(*) Redux '78**

Concord CCD 4483 *As above.* 2/78.

Galper's wide, sweeping keyboard style needs bass and drums to temper occasional sugariness. *Reach Out* is a vivid, hard-hitting set. The Brecker brothers have seldom combined so effectively under anyone else's leadership, and the arrangements are razor-fine. The later *Speak With A Single Voice* has now been reissued as *Children Of The Night*. Hearing it again after an absence of some years, it is a stronger and more coherent performance than we originally thought. Twenty years on, it sounds as if it was ahead of its time, combining a Coltrane-like intensity (guaranteed by Mike Brecker's presence) with the richness of Galper's Tyner-influenced piano. Recorded live, the sound was all over the place on vinyl, but it sounds much better on these careful transfers. The reissue takes its title from a long, previously un-issued track, probably from early in the session at Rosy's in New Orleans. Neither of the horns sounds convincingly played in. A welcome addition to the catalogue, though. *Redux '78* is drawn from the same live sessions. Perhaps not quite as strong a set, it consists of three long tracks, 'Triple Play', 'Shadow Waltz' and 'This Is The Thing', all Galper originals, and four shorter tracks that never quite occupy enough time to catch fire. Galper and producer Carl Jefferson give the band its quintessential sound, though, and the balance between horns and piano is impeccable. A couple of tiny edits might have been done more cleanly; otherwise, no complaints.

Now Hear This lacks a front-line voice of real authority. Hino is a limited soloist with a narrow improvisational range, and it is only the presence of McBee and Williams that lifts the record. Even Galper sounds lacklustre, as if struggling with a less than perfectly tuned piano

****(*) Ivory Forest**
Enja 3053 *Galper; John Scofield (g); Wayne Dockery (b); Adam Nussbaum (d).* 10–11/79.

The star of the fine *Ivory Forest* is Scofield, who plays a brilliant, unaccompanied 'Monk's Mood' that cuts through the thicket with almost brutal efficiency. Galper plays a duo with the guitarist ('Continuity') and with Dockery ('Yellow Days'), and there are three strong quartet tracks.

****(*) Dreamsville**
Enja 5029 *Galper; Steve Gilmore (b); Bill Goodwin (d).* 3/86.

****** Portrait**
Concord CCD 4383 *Galper; Ray Drummond (b); Billy Hart (d).* 2/89.

Of the trios, *Portrait* stands out, for a wonderfully profound 'Giant Steps' that rivals Tommy Flanagan's. The 1986 line-up is, predictably, less than wholly convincing by comparison, and though there are some fine things on the record it is marred as a whole by an awful earnestness, as if a serious point is being drilled home on every track. The Concord sound was to suit Galper very much better. Not too closely miked, with a nice, warm acoustic and good separation of parts, it's a model of how to record a trio of this sort.

****(*) Live At Maybeck Recital Hall**
Concord CCD 4438 *Galper (p solo).* 7/90.

*****(*) Invitation To A Concert**
Concord CCD 4455 *Galper; Todd Coolman (b); Steve Ellington (d).* 11/90.

***** Live At Port Townsend '91**
Double Time 105 *As above.* 91.

***** Tippin'**
Concord CCD 4540 *As above, except Wayne Dockery (b) replaces Coolman.* 11/92.

The solo Maybeck Hall set is unusually self-sufficient and quite free of Galper's lapses into saccharin. His touch is exact; the ideas come unimpeded but rarely glibly. There is, though, a lack of any real drama, and the set doesn't repay repeated hearings, largely because it lacks any sense of adventure.

The post-Maybeck Concords (AM and PM have become important historical benchmarks for piano players) are both very smooth, but without the florid chromatic embellishment that Galper might once have resorted to. He's still an immensely elegant player, but a growing understanding of ancestors like Monk has straightened out his conception very considerably, and much to his benefit.

The Port Townsend set is an unexpected mix, with Trane's 'Giant Steps' and the rarely covered Brubeck/Desmond theme, 'Balcony Rock', prominent. The key track, though, is a wonderfully imaginative version of 'I'll Remember April'. Top-flight piano jazz.

*****(*) Just Us**
Enja ENJ 8058 *Galper; Jerry Bergonzi (ts); Pat O'Leary (b); Steve Ellington (d).* 9/93.

This is a pretty straightforward session, but not without subtleties and elegance. At first blush, Bergonzi doesn't sound quite the right kind of horn player for Galper's conception, but he fits in from the off and contributes very considerably to a relaxed and very swinging set. The high point is unquestionably the leader's solo on 'Lover Man', a tissue of pianistic references that confirms his familiarity with the literature. As always, it is Galper's intelligence and taste that we applaud. Fireworks can be exhilarating, but these are more lasting satisfactions.

*****(*) Rebop**
Enja ENJ 9029 *Galper; Jerry Bergonzi (ts); Jeff Johnson (b); Steve Ellington (d).* 8/94.

Signs from the start that Galper was looking here for something closer to the sound he got with the Breckers back in the 1970s, and indeed it could have done with an additional horn. They kick off with 'All The Things You Aren't', a much-removed contrafact on the standard with a couple of wry nods in the direction of Charles Mingus along the way. Unusually, it's the one and only 'original' on the disc, which sticks mainly to standards. Monk's 'Jackie-Ing' is played with bustling enthusiasm and Duke's 'Take The Coltrane' reveals Galper in unusually terse mood at the end of the set. Bergonzi is no Michael Brecker, but he is a player with more character than at first appears, and his soloing is brisk, bright and flawlessly structured.

***** At Café des Copains**
Philology 35 *Galper (p solo).* 12/94.

Another imaginative live set which runs through an almost bewilderingly fast rotation of standard and repertory themes, from Golson's 'Whisper Not' to 'Polka Dots And Moonbeams' and 'Willow Weep For Me' to the rarely covered Sammy Cahn masterpiece, 'Teach Me Tonight'. Galper is more pungent and percussive than on his group recordings, and he does seem to be contending with a less than ideal piano, but this is a more than worthwhile session.

*****(*) Fugue State**
Blue Chip Jazz 74005 *Galper; Jeff Johnson (b); Steve Ellington (d).* 2/97.

Released on a relatively obscure label and recorded in the slightly unlikely setting of Manchester's Craftsmen's Guild, this is nevertheless a fine record, with a more than usually imaginative take on the basic piano trio. Unusually, there are no original compositions, but Galper seems determined to push tunes like 'End Of A Love Affair', 'Fascinatin' Rhythm' and 'If You Are But A Dream' to the limits. The trio is consistently supportive and Johnson makes an impression with his crisp stopping on 'Small Feats' and 'Cottontail', ending an impressive session on a personal high. Good luck finding it, and don't be afraid to ask.

***** Maybeck Duets**
Philology 139 *Galper; Jeff Johnson (b).* 6/99.

We have some slight anxieties about the provenance and official standing of this release, but it is a fine record. Almost a decade after his solo Maybeck appearance, Hal seems to be glad to renew contact with that fine piano. The recording isn't anything like as full and resonant as it should be, but the character of the instrument comes through at once on Strayhorn's 'Isfahan' and Miles's 'Blue In Green'. Johnson isn't particularly well known, but his playing relationship with Galper is firmly established and there is good understanding between the pair.

Vyacheslav (Slava) Ganelin (born 1944)

PIANO, SYNTHESIZERS

Known best as the pianist in the Ganelin Trio, he has since exiled himself to Israel and been generally less visible on record of late.

***** Opuses**

Leo CD LR 171 *Ganelin; Viktor Fonarev (clo, b, gamelan); Mika Markovich (d, perc, gamelan); Uri Abramovich (v).* 12/89.

*****(*) On Stage ... Backstage**

Leo CD LR 216 *Ganelin (ky, syn solo).* 4/92, 7/93.

***** Trio Alliance**

Leo Lab CD 042 *Ganelin; Petras Vysniauskias (sax); Arkadi Gotesman (d, perc).* 10/95.

It is over a decade since Slava Ganelin went into exile in Israel, effectively disbanding the pioneering – indeed, epoch-making – Ganelin Trio in the process. Opinions vary as to the effect of the move on his work. The more sanguine saw it as a development; sceptics saw it as a softening and dilution; a more measured historical view accepted that he wasn't a figure whose work could be accurately judged without reference to political and historical events. For a time, as on *Opuses* and its predecessor, *Jerusalem February Cantabile*, which has not been transferred to CD, he continued to use the name Ganelin Trio. This was a mistake, for there was no continuity between the two. Even with the addition of other sounds – cello, gamelan, and a guest appearance from Abramovich – this is a more conventional configuration: piano, bass, drums. The music from this period is in marked contrast to the predominantly tragic and highly theatrical performances of the original Trio. It is austere, sometimes to the point of frostiness, a development that is perhaps reflected in Ganelin's acquisition of a synthesizer, which he utilizes at this stage with notable restraint and to largely abstract effect, though more recent projects like *On Stage ... Backstage* have seen him take it a huge step forward. The singing tones of 'Cantabile' and 'Cantus', number three of the *Opuses*, seem less alien than any of the Russian-period pieces, and a certain tension has gone out of the music, perhaps because it is being made in a 'free' environment. On its own terms, and they are ambitious ones, this is a fine record, with moments that equal anything in the earlier catalogue.

It is only with the remarkable *On Stage ... Backstage* that one begins to get a fix on what Ganelin might yet do. There was a faintly Heath Robinson/Rube Goldberg quality to the early work of the Trio but, if anything, it tended to camouflage just how ambitious a musician Ganelin was. The first fruits of his belated encounter with electronics were surprisingly tentative, but with the advance of the 1990s he began to push off into areas of experiment that recalled nothing more strongly than Russian composer Aleksander Skryabin's desire to create a super-instrument which would in turn create a new musical language. Skryabin never lived to see the 'Mysterium' made, but Ganelin has been able to work with a remarkable 'backstage' set-up, comprising digital sound-modules, synths and multi-track recorders, that affords him similar dramatic potential. The dense, complex sound he achieves 'onstage' with piano, synth and drums (a long and a short piece recorded in Munich in 1992) is as nothing compared to the 'orchestral improvisations' he creates with his integrated electronics. The ability to synthesize instrumental combinations – string quartet and percussion, viola and wind quartet, flugelhorn, tuba and drums, orchestra and chorus – and to have each permutation 'perform' at a level far beyond human capacity creates a musical language of immense potential ... and some risk. At moments, the 'backstage' portions resemble nothing more than Frank Zappa's Synclavier epics on *Jazz From Hell* and are no less brittle and forbidding.

It's clear that, even with this at his disposal, Ganelin still hankers after some version of the old acoustic group with its intermediate technology. *Trio Alliance* was recorded on tour in Lithuania, and it's very difficult to see this music as much other than a nostalgic attempt to recolonize an old style. Vysniauskias is a powerful player and a more natural free improviser than his leader, who has always required structures, even ironic and vestigial ones. Gotesman does on occasion sound very similar to Tarasov, but he is working in a very different idiom and climate, and it doesn't blend at all well with Ganelin's cool detachment. A disappointing record, and one that is difficult to square even with Slava's own recent history.

Ganelin Trio

GROUP

The Soviet threesome who created a great stir in the West in the early 1980s, following the release of records made from smuggled tapes and their subsequent appearances in Berlin, Italy and London. Disbanded in 1987 when Ganelin left the USSR for Israel.

***** Poco A Poco**

Leo CD LR 101 *Vyacheslav Ganelin (p, basset, g, perc); Vladimir Chekasin (as, ts, basset cl, cl, ob, v, perc); Vladimir Tarasov (d, perc). n.d.*

****** Catalogue: Live In East Germany**

Leo CD LR 102 *As above.* 4/79.

*****(*) Encores**

Leo CD LR 106 *As above.* 6/78–11/81.

♛ ** Ancora Da Capo**

Leo CD LR 108 *As above.* 10–11/80.

*****(*) ... Old Bottles**

Leo CD LR 112 *As above.* 6/82–3/83.

*****(*) Con Affetto**

Leo Records Golden Years GY 2 *As above.* 11/83.

***** San Francisco Holidays**

Leo CD LR 208/209 *As above, except add Larry Ochs (ts); Bruce Ackley (ss); Jon Raskin (bs); Andrew Voigt (as).* 6/86.

History has moved, and moved in unexpected ways, since our first edition. By far the most significant single event has been the collapse of the Soviet Union, never more than a vast, improbable federation, punctured and leaking at almost every point, but enormously powerful even if only as an idea. Inevitably, its demise has prompted serious questioning of almost every aspect of its politics and culture.

The Ganelin Trio can now perhaps be seen as an expression of that culture's final phase. Theirs was a *fin de siècle* music, a mysterious, provocative collage that drew on jazz, on twentieth-century composition, on primitive technologies and, to a degree, on the ironic theatrics of the *yurodivy*, the Holy Fool. To what extent their music was genuinely subversive, to what extent a kind of licensed jestering remains as difficult to untangle as the question of what Shostakovich 'really' intended to say in the Fifth Symphony. The music remains, and it remains one of the most significant bodies of work of the last 20 years.

For this edition, we have separated the work of the original Trio with work done under the leadership of Slava Ganelin in the West, even when he has chosen to give these groups the same name. Nor are we going to comment more generally on the group's complex aesthetic, or on the extraordinary circumstances of its arrival and release in the West. For that, we'd ask you to look at previous editions. The question remains: how relevant is the Trio's work in a dramatically changed climate?

To stumble over the conclusion, *Catalogue: Live In East Germany* still seems an immensely powerful record, not simply because of its associations, but because of the music itself. It stands up as strongly now as ever before. We have, however, revised our valuation of the record in the light of one significant recent development. Confusion has remained about the titling of the group's large-scale suites, though Leo Feigin has done sterling work in sorting out the problem. Since our last edition, though, Leo has brought out a CD of *Ancora Da Capo* which brings together a recording of Part One, made in Leningrad at the famous Autumn Rhythms Festival, of which the Trio were the only home stars, with a recording of Part Two, made a few weeks earlier in Berlin.

This was a breakthrough occasion for the Ganelin Trio. Their work was publicly hailed by the German critic, Joachim Ernst Berendt, and their reputation in the West was established. Two years later they were to appear at the extraordinary event in London we have described in previous editions. Though Leo Feigin was present at the Berlin event, not until recently did he have a tape of it. The first release of this music was two LPs documenting successive nights at the Leningrad event. Feigin has now replaced the second of these with the Berlin performance of Part Two, and we are now persuaded that this is the Ganelin Trio's definitive performance. Even though somewhat separated by geography and time, and by significant changes in acoustic, this two-part suite has a monolithic intensity which condenses everything the group was about at its best: a shining expressiveness, dense, passionate playing, humour and, underlying it all, an ironclad discipline. It is, quite simply, a masterpiece, and we strongly recommend it to your attention.

This is not in any way to denigrate or downgrade *Catalogue*. It is a continuous cycle, alternating quiet, formal sections with occasional explosions of improvisational frenzy in which Chekasin's saxophone is the main voice. Like much of the Trio's work, the mood is predominantly dark and tragic, but with a redemptive quality, perhaps more deeply buried here than in *Non Troppo* and *Ancora Da Capo*. If the idiom seems very far removed from the usual theme-and-variations, harmonic approach of jazz, it does play an important role, albeit in reverse, with melodic and sometimes standard material serving as the culmination rather than the starting point, as in *Non Troppo*, where 'Too Close For Comfort' is the source (or destination).

One of the definitive characteristics of the Trio's sound is a dry, unpropulsive rhythm, an aspect that can make their work seem remote to listeners schooled on jazz. It's an issue that has also arisen in the context of Anthony Braxton's work – 'Who Is Afraid Of Anthony Braxton?' they ask rhetorically on *Encores* – the same unexpected dependence on white jazz musicians like Dave Brubeck, Lennie Tristano and Warne Marsh. Tarasov deliberately avoids any settled groove in favour of a light, springy metre that can move in almost any direction or in none. There is no conventional bass, though Ganelin makes distinctive use of the basset. (This mustn't be confused with the basset horn or with the basset clarinet which Chekasin plays; it is in fact a small keyboard instrument which mimics the sound of a string bass, but in a flat and uninflected way, giving the Trio its distinctively unswinging metre.)

We make no apology for grouping all these records together, confusing as it may seem. The only reasonable approach to this music is to work through the records patiently, learning how the suites interrelate and learning to identify what elements belong to each. Liner-notes by Leo Feigin, Efim Barban (on *Catalogue*) and Alexander Kan (on *Ancora Da Capo*) help sort out the story, which is a complex and intertextual one. A piece from the London concert, entitled 'Old Bottles', and related to the work known as 'New Wine', but included on the CD *Old Bottles* (hope that makes sense) can be found on the limited-issue boxed set, *Document: New Music From Russia – the 80s*. If you are very lucky indeed, some copies of this exceptional record may still be around.

Feigin's achievement in bringing the group to Western ears cannot be overestimated, even if the relationship has not always been an easy or a wholly comprehending one. After 1980 the Ganelin Trio were able to perform on a world stage; whether what they did was to be accounted jazz or not, jazz musicians were required to take notice, as Rova did in 1986 when a notably relaxed Trio played with them in San Francisco. That occasion may now seem the beginning of the end. Much of the tension has gone out of the music, and Ganelin in particular sounds discursive. There is a long, lifeless version of *New Wine* and a very long piece called 'Ritardando', which is too persistently evasive and reticent to sustain interest over its 45-minute span. There should be no surprise hearing them do a standard, 'Mack The Knife' (there is more standards-playing on *Encores*), but the qualities that made earlier references to the tradition so powerful have gone, and it almost sounds kitsch.

The Kurt Weill song reappears on *Con Affetto*, a previously unreleased Moscow performance of 'Semplice', recorded in Moscow in 1983 and brought to the West by television producer Olivia Lichtenstein. It's the first of three encores that follow a moving performance of one of the Trio's most straightforwardly expressive suites. 'Con Affetto' makes for surprising listening now, not because it reproduces the shock we all felt on seeing and hearing Ganelin for the first time, but because it seems to anticipate so much of the slow, stressed, classically inspired music that became a kind of orthodoxy in the later 1980s.

The Ganelin Trio belongs to a particular phase in modern music. It failed to outlive that phase as a group and, though the members continue to experiment, they inevitably do so apart. A reunion seems unthinkable and, given how much water has passed under the bridges of the Neva, the Dnieper and the Don, is probably undesirable as well.

Jan Garbarek (born 1947)

TENOR AND SOPRANO SAXOPHONES, BASS SAXOPHONE, FLUTES, KEYBOARD, PERCUSSION

Turned to jazz after hearing John Coltrane records in his native Norway. Studied with George Russell in the late '60s and began recording as a post-bop leader in 1971 for ECM, his label ever since. Has gone deeper into native Norwegian music since 1980's Eventyr, and has increasingly turned to material and settings remote from jazz; popular and successful despite the esoteric nature of his music.

*****(*) Afric Pepperbird**

ECM 843475-2 *Garbarek; Terje Rypdal (g, bugle); Arild Andersen (b); Jon Christensen (d).* 9/70.

***** Sart**

ECM 839305-2 *As above, except add Bobo Stenson (p).* 4/71.

In 1997 Jan Garbarek celebrated his fiftieth birthday as one of the best-known, and certainly one of the most easily identified improvising musicians anywhere in the world. His high, keening saxophone, with the cathedral echo ECM have habitually given it, is one of the most readily universalized instrumental sounds in contemporary music. If you know it is Garbarek, it will evoke Nordic landscapes; if not, it suggests nothing more than somewhere far off, desert rather than tundra, the wastes of Africa rather than the northern lands. Few artists of his stature have stayed loyal to a single record label throughout their careers, so much so that it is difficult to tell whether ECM shaped Garbarek or whether he gave definitive voice to that much-discussed chimera, the 'ECM sound'. With the release of *Officium* in the mid-1990s, a non-jazz work made in collaboration with the Hilliard Ensemble, Garbarek followed another ECM artist, Keith Jarrett, into immense crossover appeal. Critical response to *Officium* has already been enormous and it has turned into one of ECM's most lucrative releases, but we do take leave to wonder what this artist might have done in a more promiscuous career, and with more concentration on jazz playing, for he has extraordinary gifts here as well, not just as a colourizing instrumentalist.

Afric Pepperbird was an astonishing debut, and it certainly makes the point that the reflex response to Garbarek's playing would, at this stage at least, have been 'cool', 'impressionistic', 'unmistakably Nordic'. This is by far his most 'out' recording, influenced by Coltrane, but also by Ayler's multiphonic intensity and with strong elements of Dexter Gordon's phrasing. Garbarek's flute, not much heard in later years, has a thin, folksy timbre that is particularly effective when overblown. The rhythm partnership of Andersen and Christensen was hard to beat at the time (though Eberhard Weber and Palle Danielsson became the bassists of choice in future) and Rypdal's abstract, unmetrical chording is more or less perfect for the gig.

Sart is a typical second album, trying to reduplicate the first and show how much the leader has 'developed' at the same time. Though Stenson is a wonderful player and we won't hear a word said against him, this is one of his least impressive showings ever. Garbarek again uses flute and, this time out, bass saxophone, though not yet the Wayne Shorter-influenced soprano that was to be such a trademark in years to come.

*****(*) Triptykon**

ECM 847321-2 *Garbarek; Arild Andersen (b); Edward Vesala (d, perc).* 11/72.

In an admittedly unfair and skewed blindfold test conducted during the preparation of our last edition, three avowed Garbarek fans failed to recognize their hero on this. Certainly, anyone who climbed on board with or after *Dis* would have difficulty recognizing the hard tone and the free-form language. There are signs that both saxophonist and drummer are dissatisfied with free music, and Andersen is hesitant, breaking up his rhythm shapes with the deliberateness of a man swearing in a foreign language. This is also the last real appearance of Garbarek the multi-instrumentalist, doubling on soprano, baritone (a hint of Lars Gullin there, perhaps) and flute. In the final analysis, it's the Finn who wins the day, playing brilliantly from start to finish. From the point of view of future projects, *Triptykon* says more about him than about Garbarek.

*****(*) Witchi-Tai-To**

ECM 833330-2 *Garbarek; Bobo Stenson (p); Palle Danielsson (b); Jon Christensen (d).* 11/73.

***** Dansere**

ECM 829193-2 *As above.* 11/75.

Things were beginning to come together for Garbarek at this point, both critically and commercially, and *Witchi-Tai-To* was probably the first of his records about which it was possible to say that it was both characteristic and surprising, both impressionistic and funky, European and jazz-based. The saxophone tone is more relaxed, indeed more relaxed than it would be very often again, with a less pressurized embouchure and more sense of playing in distinct breath-groups or verses. The folk element was not so much a departure as a logical extension of what he'd been doing up to this point. The title-piece is a version of Jim Pepper's surprise hit, a delightful performance that is as fresh now as ever.

Dansere was a quieter session for the saxophonist, but it plays now almost as a co-led session with the steadily developing Stenson, who commands much of the attention and who might have been worthy of a couple of trio tracks. Indeed, had this session been taped in the 1990s, that is probably what ECM would have done.

****** Dis**

ECM 827408-2 *Garbarek; Ralph Towner (g, 12-string g); wind harp; brass sextet.* 12/76.

****** Places**

ECM 829195-2 *Garbarek; Bill Connors (g); John Taylor (org); Jack DeJohnette (d).* 12/77.

*** Photo With Blue Sky

ECM 843168-2 *Garbarek; Bill Connors (g); Eberhard Weber (b); Jon Christensen (d).* 12/78.

Few modern jazz records have been as thoroughly plundered for atmospheric cameos as *Dis*. From wildlife movies about the snowy owl, to more threatening jeremiads on the effects of Chernobyl on Sami reindeer herds, it has been the soundtrack. The copyright kickbacks notwithstanding, it's a beautiful album, quintessential Garbarek pitched against a windharp and the softly articulated sound of brass ensemble. It established a style which the saxophonist was to return to many times in years ahead, spells and riddles on soprano saxophone (and wood flute) and a deep, mourning tone that floats and drifts over the rhythm.

The end of the 1970s saw a pattern established whereby Garbarek went into the studio at each year's end to consolidate and capture what had been learnt in performance and to send out new feelers for the year ahead. It is what a village bard might have done in winter quarters, spin tales about the year past and boast about what would come when the sun returned. *Dis* was also the first of a group of records with a guitarist, on which Garbarek experimented with more open and ambiguous harmonies and textures. *Places* has never been as highly regarded as *Dis*, but it is a small masterpiece, dominated by one long track, a pattern that repeats itself throughout Garbarek's output. 'Passing' begins with misterioso organ from Taylor, tense drum rips from DeJohnette, and an unresolved, questioning figure on the guitar. Garbarek's entry picks it up without variation; for much of the record, similar or identical ideas are distributed round the band. There is no real linear argument to a Garbarek solo by this stage. Ideas are static, unpropulsive and almost sculptural in impact. It is a style that served him well but also proved to be something of a straitjacket.

** Aftenland

ECM 839304-2 *Garbarek; Kjell Johnsen (org).* 12/79.

On a checklist of ECM and Garbarek clichés, this scores highly: 'Nordic', 'moody', 'atmospheric', and resolutely unfunky. Reminiscent of some of Keith Jarrett's experiments of the same time, but lacking Jarrett's insouciant arrogance, it proves to be a very difficult record to listen to and like. Some of the material might well have been interesting in a concert setting, but as a commercial release this is the closest the estimably disciplined Norwegian has ever come to self-indulgence.

*** Eventyr

ECM 829384-2 *Garbarek; John Abercrombie (g, 12-string g, mand); Nana Vasconcelos (talking d, perc, v).* 12/80.

*** Paths, Prints

ECM 829377-2 *Garbarek; Bill Frisell (g); Eberhard Weber (b); Jon Christensen (d).* 12/81.

*** Wayfarer

ECM 811968-2 *As above, except omit Christensen; add Michael DiPasqua (d, perc).* 3/83.

This is the only stage in Garbarek's career when he seems to be marking time. These are formulaic records, clearly intended to capitalize on the success of *Dis*, but rarely rising to its splendours. Each of the three has its merits, and Abercrombie and Frisell are more appropriate players for the context than the unpredictable Connors who can be great or unutterably bland. Vasconcelos is probably too much of a one-man band to fit into anyone else's concept, but he is a great entertainer and records featuring him are never dull. A word for DiPasqua as well, a big heart and the chops to give *Wayfarer* the sort of swing and thrust it deserves.

*** It's OK To Listen To The Gray Voice

ECM 825406-2 *Garbarek; David Torn (g); Eberhard Weber (b); Michael DiPasqua (d).* 84.

The title reference is to a poem by Tomas Tranströmer, one of the great voices of modern European literature. It's refreshing to hear Garbarek tackling something new, and this is certainly a departure for him. How the poetry of Tranströmer relates to the music Garbarek is playing is never made entirely explicit and sometimes isn't an entirely convincing source of inspiration, but what one hears is tough and strong, and without a shred of self-indulgence.

** All Those Born With Wings

ECM 831394-2 *Garbarek (sax solo).* 8/86.

This is a disappointment, albeit a not unexpected exercise at this stage in his career. Garbarek was working through a number of personal and stylistic changes, and was bound to miscue on occasion. We've never found this to be anything other than dully introspective and unemphatic.

*** Legend Of The Seven Dreams

ECM 837344-2 *Garbarek; Rainer Bruninghaus (ky); Eberhard Weber (b); Manu Katché (d); Nana Vasconcelos (perc, v).* 7/88.

*** Rosensfole

ECM 839293-2 *Garbarek; Agnes Buen Garnås (v).* 88.

*** I Took Up The Runes

ECM 843850-2 *As for Legend Of The Seven Dreams, except add Bugge Wesseltoft (syn); Annte Ailu Gaup (v).* 8/90.

Towards the end of the 1980s, Garbarek began to explore Nordic folk musics and myth in a more structured way, thus turning the casually unsubstantiated generalizations about his Nordic style back on themselves. *Rosensfole* is really Garnås's album and is none the worse for that, Garbarek limited in the main to providing a shifting, minimal stage for her dramatic singing. The opening 'He Comes From The North' on *Legend* is based on a Lappish *joik*, converted into state-of-the-art 'world music' by Vasconcelos's unplaceable percussion and vocal. There are also three brief, unaccompanied tracks, two on soprano saxophone, one on flute, to demonstrate how Garbarek has pared down his playing once again to the barest bones of melody.

Runes is in the same vein, but the experiment of adding a rock drummer and synthesizer player to the core trio was an inspired one, and the long central track is one of Garberek's most ambitious works. The energy of the live performance doesn't quite come across on record, but there is more than enough of interest to bridge occasional lapses of pace.

***(*) Star

ECM 849649-2 *Garbarek; Miroslav Vitous (b); Peter Erskine (d).* 1/91.

This was widely thought to be Garbarek's return to straight jazz playing, but any such expectation is confounded at the first fence, a rather woolly number which is the saxophonist's only composition of the set. What the piece does is lay out an array of tone colours that are imaginatively deployed by the trio throughout the album, which has a stripped down and business-like feel. Garbarek's tone is still his unique selling point and he manages to infuse his tenor playing with a brittle-edged fragility one would normally associate with the soprano horn. There is still a tendency to place long notes like personal monograms, but the signature is in a new, bolder sans-serif which reads as freshly as *Triptykon* did 20 years ago.

Vitous is purposive and surely grounded; the clouds are in the mountains now, not vice versa. Erskine doesn't seem the obvious choice, but the obvious alternative – Christensen – hasn't the simplicity and directness the session seems to call for. The improvised 'Snowman' is indicative of how far Garbarek has progressed during his folksy sabbatical from blowing jazz, and it may even be a satirical response to all the editorial blah about his cool and stiffness. In Wallace Stevens's words, it takes a 'mind of winter' to make music like this; that doesn't mean it lacks passion.

*** Ragas And Sagas

ECM 511263-2 *Garbarek; Manu Katché (d); Ustad Shaukat Hussain (tabla); Ustad Nazim Ali Khan (sarangi); Ustad Fateh Ali Khan, Deepika Thathaal (v).* 5/90.

*** Madar

ECM 519075-2 *Garbarek; Anouar Brahem (oud); Ustad Shaukat Hussain (tabla).* 8/92.

These two records are 'world music' in the most positive sense. They demonstrate the essential irreducibility of what Garbarek is about. Karnatic ideas had cropped up in his work before and there are certain *raga*-like sequences even in the early albums, harmonically static, rhythmically mobile but not conventionally swinging. *Ragas And Sagas* was a perfectly logical step. It succeeds for the most part a good deal better than the collaboration with oud player Brahem (on whose own records Garbarek has also recorded), but only because Garbarek himself is in better voice. Though the combination of Norwegian and non-European styles is every bit as seamless on both, Garbarek simply plays better with Hussain and his colleagues.

**** Twelve Moons

ECM 519500-2 *Garbarek; Rainer Bruninghaus (ky); Eberhard Weber (b); Manu Katché (d); Marilyn Mazur (perc); Mari Boine, Agnes Buen Garnås (v).* 9/93.

Appropriately, it was Garbarek who was chosen to front ECM's 500th release with this magnificently packaged offering. It finds him at an interesting point of development, still exploring folklore but also easing his way back into a more jazz-orientated programme. There's a very heavy emphasis on soprano saxophone, perhaps to blend better with the voices, but even here the tone is stronger and heavier than of yore, and on occasions almost sounding full enough to be an alto.

Katché is essentially a rock drummer, with a crude but immensely vibrant delivery. One thinks occasionally of Ginger Baker, but among previous associates he is closer to Edward Vesala than to Jon Christensen. This time around, in addition to Sami *joiks*, Garbarek includes an arrangement of national composer Edvard Grieg's gentle 'Arietta', and a new version of the late Jim Pepper's 'Witchi-Tai-To', which has been a staple piece much of his career. A beautiful record, by far the best of the later releases.

(***) Officium

ECM New Series 445369-2 *Garbarek; Hilliard Ensemble (v).* 9/93.

So much critical copy has been directed at this, and so many copies sold, that it seems redundant to add to the chorus. An anthology of fourteenth- and fifteenth-century church music, arranged for vocal ensemble and saxophone, it has hooked into a vast appetite for 'faith minimalism' and for music of spiritual uplift. Immaculately recorded and featuring some exquisite saxophone playing, it makes no pretence to being jazz or even some close cognate. Listening to it now, in the context of the later (and, in our view, very much more accomplished) *Mnemosyne*, it is clear how Garbarek and his colleagues are feeling their way towards a shared musical language that will take account of both written and improvised elements. The problem for us is that the composed elements are too literally interpreted, while the improvisations drift free of any sure anchor.

*** Visible World

ECM 529086-2 *Garbarek; Rainer Bruninghaus (p, ky); Eberhard Weber (b); Marilyn Mazur (d, perc); Manu Katché (d); Trilok Gurtu (perc); Mari Boine (v).* 6/95.

Officium was always going to be a tough act to follow, and Garbarek wisely chose to go with what was effectively his working group of the moment. The majority of these tracks are for trio, with either Bruninghaus or Weber and Katché or Mazur. There are also some searching duos, including the 'The Creek' with Katché, in which Garbarek seems to be experimenting in a quiet way with new rhythmic ideas. The longest track, 'Aftenlandet', was originally written as a music–video collaboration; featuring Boine and Mazur, it has a delicately mysterious quality. Garbarek briefly plays clarinet on this disc, suggesting that he may also be interested in hearing new colours and sounds. No sign yet of those occupying the foreground, but lots of possibilities sketched into this essentially consolidating record.

*** Rites

ECM 559006-2 2CD *Garbarek; Bugge Wesseltoft (syn, acc, elec); Rainer Bruninghaus (p, ky); Eberhard Weber (b); Marilyn Mazur (d, perc); Jansug Kakhidze (v); Tbilisi Symphony Orchestra; Sølvguttene Boys' Choir.* 3/98.

To his credit, and ECM's, Garbarek has so far resisted the temptation to release baggy, multi-disc sets. Almost all of the albums, whether ultimately successful or not, have stressed economy of content over completeness. Presumably a substantial archive of unreleased material waits in the vaults. Here, for the first time, Garbarek has released a set which doesn't justify its length.

It is, of course, a very beautiful work, but it has longueurs and if it is pitched at an audience who may be turning to jazz from ambient music and contemporary styles like trip-hop, then it falls short of their hypnotic grip. *Rites* is at once over-extended and too busy. It is also curiously programmed. The title-track might almost be an out-take by pop band Enigma, who combine dance beats with Gregorian chant. Wesseltoft is very adept at this kind of synthesis, and it's interesting as an extension of the work

Garbarek has been doing with the Hilliard Ensemble. Generally, though, the tracks are the familiar mixture of acoustic jazz and folk themes. Bruninghaus is a secure technician but one who doesn't alter his approach when he plays electronic keyboards, even analogue types, and so he manages to lose his passage-work on 'Vast Plain, Clouds' between idioms. He is closer to the mark on an interesting version of 'It's OK To Listen To The Grey Voice', an unexpected but welcome reappearance of a Garbarek composition that always seemed to have more mileage than it got on the album of that name.

The second disc is a mirror of the first. Wesseltoft's electronics establish the mood for 'It's High Time', and contributes some effective and moving accordion to a version of Don Cherry's 'Malinye'. Elsewhere, though, it's the interplay of Weber and Mazur which creates the dramatic interest. 'Pan' is solo Garbarek. What follows is both intriguing and slightly enigmatic. First, the saxophonist is joined by a boys' choir in 'We Are The Stars', and then, for no very solid reason, he includes a recording of the 62-year-old Georgian singer and composer performing his own 'The Moon Over Mtatsminda'. Garbarek has no hand whatever in the composition.

The album peters out with two further electronics-driven pieces, 'Evenly They Danced' and 'Last Rite'. The second is obviously intended to give the set as a whole some symmetry and a sense of ending, but most listeners will have flagged and switched off by then. As so often, a fine single CD has been lost in an excess of uncompelling material.

*****(*) Mnemosyne**
ECM 465122-2 2CD *Garbarek; Hilliard Ensemble.* 4/98.

Garbarek and the Hilliards returned to the monastery of St Gerold five years on with a considerable body of shared experience. Many performances of *Officium* had opened up a rich palette of musical connections. Inspired by a poem of Friedrich Hölderlin which is about chaos and loss and the reach towards the abyss, it is a more turbulent but also more accepting conception than *Officium*.

Drawing on church music – by Tallis, the Abbess of the Paraclete, Orthodox psalm- and hymn-composer William Billings – as well as Native-American themes, a Scottish love song, and a second-century Greek invocation of the sun, it becomes a complex tapestry of musical associations, woven together by some mercurial improvisation and the Hilliards' trademark note-perfect ensembles. The cover imagery is drawn from Ingmar Bergman's film, *The Seventh Seal*, but anyone dismayed at the prospect of Baltic gloom can be reassured that *Mnemosyne* is a much more joyous and open-hearted work than the art-work might suggest. It has light and shade, a genuine sense of drama and a warmth that has been harder to find in Garbarek's recent work.

Ronnie Gardiner

DRUMS

An American who decamped for Sweden many years ago, Gardiner is a solid middleweight drummer who seems quite at home in any mainstream-to-modern situation.

***** Click!**
Sittel SITCD 9242 *Gardiner; Marten Lundgren (t, flhn); Anders Norell (tb); Claes Brodda (ts); Mathias Algotsson (p); Claes Askelof (g); Hasse Larsson (b); Rene Martinez (perc).* 3/97.

Gardiner has been a fixture in the Swedish jazz scene for many years. He gets the chance to lead a good group of local talent on this engaging if lightweight set of swing material. The six familiar tunes are actually the least interesting things here – fairly ordinary covers of 'Take The "A" Train', 'Willow Weep For Me' and so forth – since there are ten charming originals from various hands in the band. Lundgren's neat turns of phrase, Norell's louche trombone and Brodda's suave tenor make for a productive front line, and Gardiner sounds as if he's beaming with pleasure from the back.

Jeff Gardner (born 1953)

PIANO

Born in New York, Gardner studied with Jaki Byard and John Lewis and has played in the usual broad range of jazz situations, with a particular interest in Brazilian music.

***** Second Home**
Musidisc 500722 *Gardner; Rick Margitza (ss, ts); Nelson Varas (g); Riccardo Del Frà (b); Simon Goubert (d). 8/94*

Co-led by Gardner and Margitza, this doesn't quite have the impact of some of the saxophonist's own dates. 'Paths' is a tremendously propulsive opener, underlining the strengths of Del Frà and Goubert, and the circling 'Gypsies' is a peculiarly compelling Margitza original, sustained for more than nine minutes. But some of the other pieces are merely so-so, and Gardner himself is a capable rather than an inspiring soloist. They end, though, on a beautiful rumination on the Villa-Lobos melody, 'Pobre Cega'.

*****(*) The Music Of Chance**
Axolotl Jazz Y 225 079 *Gardner; Ingrid Jensen (t); Rick Margitza (ts); Drew Gress (b); Tony Jefferson (d).* 6/99.

A set of themes inspired by the writings of Paul Auster. Gardner seems to have looked long and hard at his approach to the occasion, since the music has a beautifully shaped feel to it, charts, interplay and solos very precisely balanced with each other. In style, it's reminiscent of Don Grolnick's small-group writing, which in our book is considerable praise. Sometimes it's a shade too worked-through, perhaps. But the starting-points are certainly provocative enough to push both Jensen and Margitza into their best form – even the blues is surprisingly inventive. And smaller pieces such as 'Ghosts' and 'City Of Glass' have a suitably *noir*ish feel.

Red Garland (1923–84)

PIANO

Born in Dallas, Garland was a minor figure in the first phase of bebop, but he became eminent through his association with the great Miles Davis group of the mid-'50s – the leader was very taken with his light but hip style. He made a long sequence of records for Prestige but gradually faded from prominence, eventually returning to Dallas.

***** A Garland Of Red**
Original Jazz Classics OJC 126 *Garland; Paul Chambers (b); Art Taylor (d).* 8/56.

***** Groovy**
Original Jazz Classics OJC 061 *As above.* 12/56–8/57.

***** Red Garland's Piano**
Original Jazz Classics OJC 073 *As above.* 3/57.

***** The P.C. Blues**
Original Jazz Classics OJC 898 *As above, except add Philly Joe Jones (d).* 3/56–8/57.

*****(*) Red Garland Revisited!**
Original Jazz Classics OJC 985 *As above, except add Kenny Burrell (g); omit Jones.* 5/57.

***** It's A Blue World**
Original Jazz Classics OJC 1028 *As above, except omit Burrell.* 2/58.

***** Manteca**
Original Jazz Classics OJC 428 *As above, plus Ray Barretto (perc).* 4/58.

***** Rediscovered Masters Vol. 1**
Original Jazz Classics OJC 768 *As above.* 6/58.

***** Can't See For Lookin'**
Original Jazz Classics OJC 918 *As above, except omit Barretto.* 6/58.

***** All Kinds Of Weather**
Original Jazz Classics OJC 193 *As above.* 11/58.

***** Red In Bluesville**
Original Jazz Classics OJC 295 *As above, except Sam Jones (b) replaces Chambers.* 4/59.

***** Rojo**
Original Jazz Classics OJC 772 *Garland; George Joyner (b); Charli Persip (d); Ray Barretto (perc).* 8/58.

***** At The Prelude Vol. 1**
Prestige 24132 *Garland; Jimmy Rowser (b); Specs Wright (d).* 10/59.

Graceful yet unaffectedly bluesy, Red Garland's manner was flexible enough to accommodate the contrasting styles of both Miles Davis and John Coltrane in the Davis quintet of the mid-1950s. His many records as a leader, beginning at about the same period, display exactly the same qualities. His confessed influences of Tatum, Powell and Nat Cole seem less obvious than his debts to Erroll Garner and Ahmad Jamal, whose hit recording of 'Billy Boy' from the early 1950s seems to sum up everything that Garland would later go on to explore.

All of the listed trio sessions feature the same virtues: deftly fingered left-hand runs over bouncy rhythms coupled with block-chord phrasing which coloured melodies in such a way that Garland saw no need to depart from them. Medium–up-tempo treatments alternate with stately ballads, and Chambers and Taylor are unfailingly swinging, if often constrained, partners. The later sessions feature a slightly greater empathy, but we find it very hard to choose a favourite among these records. The choice may depend on the tunes on each record, some of which are presented thematically (*All Kinds Of Weather*, for instance, is made up of 'Rain', 'Summertime', and so on). The guest role for Barretto on *Manteca* is a mostly peripheral one – he plays a quiet second line of percussion – although he's given a couple of lively features with Taylor on the title-tune and 'Lady Be Good'. The remastering is clean, although Chambers, while conspicuously present, is seldom awarded anything better than a dull bass sound. *At The Prelude* is a snapshot of Garland at work in a New York club, though he doesn't sound appreciably different away from the studios.

Of the newest arrivals on CD, *Can't See For Lookin'* is a solid workout with a particularly pleasing treatment of the Gershwin standard, 'Soon', and *It's A Blue World*, though it features an interminable *arco* solo by Chambers on 'This Can't Be Love', is much brighter than its title suggests, with a lightning canter through 'Crazy Rhythm'. *The P.C. Blues*, originally conceived as a tribute to Chambers, starts with the Miles Davis-session 'Ahmad's Blues' and goes through two exemplary ballads before reaching the absurd – though impeccably handled – 'Tweedle Dee Dee'. Line for line, this is one of our favourite Garlands. *Revisited!*, though, is our first choice for any who want a single Garland set fom the period. His own version of 'Billy Boy' is here, there are two classic slow-burners in 'Everybody's Somebody's Fool' and 'The Masquerade is Over', and Burrell shows up to spar on 'Four' and 'Walkin''.

***** All Mornin' Long**
Original Jazz Classics OJC 293 *Garland; Donald Byrd (t); John Coltrane (ts); George Joyner (b); Art Taylor (d).* 11/57.

*****(*) Soul Junction**
Original Jazz Classics OJC 481 *As above.* 11/57.

*****(*) High Pressure**
Original Jazz Classics OJC 349 *As above.* 11–12/57.

****(*) Dig It!**
Original Jazz Classics OJC 392 *As above, plus Paul Chambers (b).* 3/57–2/58.

Garland's recordings with Coltrane are typical of the long, relaxed blowing sessions which Prestige were recording at the time, and some of the tracks are very long indeed: 'All Mornin' Long' runs for 20 minutes, 'Soul Junction' and 'Lazy Mae' from *Dig It!* for 16 apiece. There are inevitable *longueurs* in this approach, and Byrd, though accomplished, lacks the greater authority which he would bring to his later, Blue Note albums. But there are some solos of immense power from the tenor saxophonist, and the playing on *Soul Junction* and *High Pressure* especially is as purposeful as the format allows (all the recordings from November 1957 were made on the same day). *Dig It!*, patched together from three sessions and including a fairly routine trio version of 'Crazy Rhythm', is slightly inferior.

*****(*) Rediscovered Masters Vol. 2**
Original Jazz Classics OJC 769 *Garland; Richard Williams (t); Oliver Nelson (as, ts); Doug Watkins, Peck Morrison (b); Specs Wright, Charli Persip (d).* 8/59–3/61.

***** Soul Burnin'**

Original Jazz Classics OJC 921 *As above, except add Sam Jones (b), Art Taylor (d).* 8/59–3/61.

***** Red Garland Trio With Eddie 'Lockjaw' Davis Vol. 1**

Original Jazz Classics OJC 360 *Garland; Eddie 'Lockjaw' Davis (ts); Sam Jones (b); Art Taylor (d).* 12/59.

***** The Nearness Of You**

Original Jazz Classics OJC 1003 *Garland; Larry Ridley (b); Frank Grant (d).* 12/61.

****(*) Solar**

Original Jazz Classics OJC 755 *Garland; Les Spann (g, f); Sam Jones (b); Frank Grant (d).* 1/62.

***** When There Are Grey Skies**

Original Jazz Classics OJC 704 *Garland; Wendell Marshall (b); Charli Persip (d).* 9/62.

Davis appears on only three tracks of OJC 360, but it's enough to enliven an otherwise somnolent disc of ballads, originally issued in Prestige's Moodsville series; a stentorian reading of 'When Your Lover Has Gone' works especially well. The second volume of *Rediscovered Masters* couples a very good session by Red's favourite trio, with Watkins and Wright, strolling through a quickfire 'Blues In The Closet' and a long, languorous 'Mr Wonderful', with a scarce quintet date featuring Williams and Nelson in the front line: nothing extraordinary, since both men sometimes sound as if they've strolled into the date by accident, but Nelson's sombre tenor makes a pleasing foil to Williams's more elegant horn. Two more tracks from this date are on *Soul Burnin'*, including a particularly pretty 'If You Could See Me Now', and four characteristic trio tracks round out an enjoyable disc. *Solar* returns Garland to a rhythm format, although Les Spann's presence isn't very useful; *The Nearness Of You* is another enjoyable stroll through eight standards; and *When There Are Grey Skies* was to be Red's last album for nearly ten years. He delivers one of his most considered interpretations here in the almost painstaking exploration of 'Nobody Knows The Trouble I've Seen', beautifully sustained over some 12 minutes.

***** Crossings**

Original Jazz Classics OJC 472 *Garland; Ron Carter (b); Philly Joe Jones (d).* 12/77.

****(*) Red Alert**

Original Jazz Classics OJC 647 *Garland; Nat Adderley (c); Harold Land, Ira Sullivan (ts); Ron Carter (b); Frank Butler (d).* 12/77.

****(*) Feelin' Red**

32 Jazz 32091 *Garland; Sam Jones (b); Al Foster (d).* 5/78.

****(*) I Left My Heart ...**

32 Jazz 32107 *Garland; Leo Wright (as); Chris Amberger (b); Eddie Moore (d).* 5/78.

**** Misty Red**

Timeless SJP 179 *Garland; Jamil Nasser (b); Frank Grant (d).* 4/82.

Garland continued to make records in the 1970s and '80s, and those that remain show his style unchanged, although some of the litheness went out of his touch. *Red Alert* is a decent if impersonal attempt at recapturing one of Red's old Prestige blowing dates: nice enough cameos by the horns, but the prettiest music is when they sit out and let the pianist play 'It's Impossible'. *Crossings* features such fine support from the rhythm section that the music gathers its own momentum, but the two Muse albums, reissued on 32 Jazz, are both routine. *I Left My Heart* ... was cut at the Keystone Korner and Wright appears on three tracks, but it's nothing special. The Timeless album is also rather dull.

Erroll Garner (1926–77)

PIANO, HARPSICHORD

Moved from Pittsburgh to New York in 1944 and was quickly established as a nightclub pianist, working for the rest of his career as a soloist or in trios. After the huge success of the Concert By The Sea album for Columbia, he became an enduring international star. A unique stylist, somewhat like a mix of Earl Hines, the stride players and the boppers, his self-taught mastery – he never learned to read and other pianists were sometimes engaged to teach him songs – only seemed to increase his likeability with his many admirers.

**** Erroll Garner 1944**

Classics 802 *Garner (p solo).* 11–12/44.

****(*) Erroll Garner 1944 Vol. 2**

Classics 818 *Garner (p); John Simmons (b); Harold Doc West (d).* 12/44.

**** Erroll Garner 1944 Vol. 3**

Classics 850 *Garner; Inez Cavanaugh (v).* 12/44.

*****(*) Errol Garner 1944–1945**

Classics 873 *Garner; Charlie Shavers (t); Vic Dickenson (tb); Hank D'Amico (cl); Lem Davis (as); Slam Stewart, Eddie Brown (b); Cliff Leeman, Harold Doc West (d).* 12/44–3/45.

***** Erroll Garner 1945–1946**

Classics 924 *Garner; John Levy Jr (b); George DeHart (d).* 9/45–2/46.

***** Erroll Garner 1946-1947**

Classics 1004 *Garner; Red Callender (b); Nick Fatool, Lou Singer, Harold Doc West (d).* 4/46–6/47.

***** Long Ago And Far Away**

Columbia 460614-2 *Garner; John Simmons (b); Shadow Wilson (d).* 6–10/50.

***** Body And Soul**

Columbia 467916-2 *As above.* 1/51–1/52.

Erroll Garner was one of a kind. He was as *outré* as the great beboppers, yet bop was alien to him, even though he recorded with Charlie Parker. He swung mightily, yet he stood outside the swing tradition; he played orchestrally, and his style was swooningly romantic, yet he could be as merciless on a tune as Fats Waller. He never read music, but he could play a piece in any key, and delighted in deceiving his rhythm sections from night to night. His tumbling, percussive, humorous style was entirely his own.

Garner's earliest recordings were done semi-privately and, though issued on Blue Note in the 1950s, they're in often atrocious sound, and one has to be either scholar or devoted fan to get much out of them. Most of his style is in place, even though these are often rambling and discursive pieces compared with what came later, and one can hear his debt to Tatum already. The first three Classics discs include what there is of these survivals, and it's a difficult listen.

Classics include one Savoy date on Classics 924, but otherwise the next two discs in their sequence are rather more interesting. *1944–1945* puts together a session which has been a collector's piece for many years: a jam with Shavers, Dickenson, D'Amico and Davis which includes extended versions of 'Gaslight' and some impromptu blues: lovely stuff, with the principals all in good fettle, and a very rare glimpse of Garner with horns. A trio date with Brown and West (for Black And White) and a solo session for Signature fill up the disc. *1945–1946* includes a scruffy-sounding solo date for Disc before a pithy if unmomentous string of solos done for Mercury in 1945. Two solos for V-Disc round things off, but the spoken intro by Bob Hope sounds like he was auditioning for The Chipmunks and there's clearly a speed problem here. Classics 1004 includes two trio dates for Mercury and one for Dial, then four solos for Victor and an eight-title solo date for Dial. The Victor coupling of 'Erroll's Bounce' and 'Erroll's Blues' is one of his most characteristic pieces up to this point in the discography, and it sounds good in this transfer; some of the other titles are rather foggy, but even the originals aren't so good.

The two Columbia albums round up his earliest sessions for the company, with the compatible team of Simmons and Wilson: still pinned to three-minute lengths, but the improved studio sound grants a better look at his early style.

***** Erroll Garner Collection Vol. 3: Too Marvellous For Words**

Emarcy 824419-2 *Garner; Wyatt Ruther (b); Eugene 'Fats' Heard (d).* 5/54.

*****(*) Contrasts**

Verve 558077-2 *As above.* 7/54.

By this period Garner had settled into his format as well as his style – swashbuckling trios which plundered standards with cavalier abandon. Bass and drums have only to keep up with Garner, but they provide a deceptively important anchor, for otherwise his treatments might simply wander off. The drummer's role is particularly important: as percussive as the pianist is, he leaves many accents to the man with the traps, and Heard has to concentrate hard to keep up. Garner's heartiness, his fondness for extravagantly arpeggiated ballads and knockabout transformations of standards can grow wearisome over the length of an album, and his favourite mannerisms become irritating. But there are undervalued aspects to these records, too. He is a quirky but resonant blues player; he keeps the melody sacrosanct, even at his most mischievous; he always swings. *The Original Misty* has now been supplanted by a Master Edition version of its original album, *Contrasts*, in better sound and with the famous track effectively cleaned up. The *Collection* albums are all of previously unreleased material.

****** The Erroll Garner Collection Volumes 4 & 5: Solo Time!**

Emarcy 511821-2 2CD *Garner (p solo).* 7/54.

*****(*) Solitaire**

Mercury 518279-2 *Garner (p solo).* 3/55.

***** Soliloquy / At The Piano**

Columbia 465631-2 *Garner (p solo).* 2/52–2/57.

Garner made few solo records, but these sessions are among his finest. The *Solo Time!* collection was set down in a single afternoon of one-take performances at a Detroit radio station. Garner indulges himself in long, immoderate performances that show his imagination at its most free-spirited and abundant. The treatment of 'It Might As Well Be Spring' is archetypal: over eight and a quarter minutes he changes keys, builds huge orchestral crescendos, throws in a waltz-time passage, mocks and cherishes the melody, and finishes with an edifice that stands alone. Most of the tracks are variations on that manner, to a greater or lesser degree, and even when he falls back on Garnerisms the energy and spontaneity are something to marvel at. Only a shade behind is the 'proper' studio session which produced *Solitaire*: here are 10 minutes of 'Over The Rainbow', and perhaps the only jazz treatment of 'When A Gypsy Makes His Violin Cry'. Excellent remastering in both cases, the piano sounding a shade harder on *Solitaire*. The Columbia album doubles up a couple of solo dates five years apart, both characteristically mercurial, if slightly less lavish.

*****(*) Concert By The Sea**

Columbia 451042-2 *Garner; Eddie Calhoun (b); Denzil Best (d).* 9/55.

Garner's most famous album, and one of the biggest-selling jazz records ever made, *Concert By The Sea* is essentially neither more nor less than a characteristic set by the trio in an amenable setting. Moments such as the teasing introduction to 'I'll Remember April', the flippant blues of 'Red Top' and the pell-mell 'Where Or When' find Garner at his most buoyant; but rather more interesting is his well-shaped treatment of 'How Could You Do A Thing Like That To Me'. The recording was never outstanding but the reissue serves it well enough.

***** Paris Impressions**

Columbia 475624-2 *Garner; Eddie Calhoun (b); Kelly Martin (d).* 3–5/58.

A souvenir of Garner's visit to Paris a few months earlier, even if it was recorded in New York. The tunes have suitable connections – 'The French Touch', 'La Vie En Rose', 'Left Bank Swing' and so on – and Garner must have enjoyed his trip, since it sounds particularly affectionate.

***** Close Up In Swing / A New Kind Of Love**

Telarc CD-83383 *Garner; Eddie Calhoun (b); Kelly Martin (d); strings, brass, woodwinds; Leith Stevens (cond).* 7/61–7/63.

***** Dreamstreet / One World Concert**

Telarc CD-83350 *Garner; Eddie Calhoun (b); Kelly Martin (d).* 59–8/63.

***** That's My Kick / Gemini**

Telarc CD-83332 *Garner; Arthur Ryerson, Wally Richardson (g); Ernest McCarty, Milt Hinton (b); George Jenkins, Herbie Lovelle, Jimmie Smith (d); Johnny Pacheco, Jose Mangual (perc).* 66–72.

Telarc have pulled these out of the lengthy list of Garner albums lying in the back-catalogue; as two-for-one deals on CD, they're decent value. That said, most of these sessions are unlikely to stir much excitement except among hardcore devotees. *Dreamstreet* is nice, the *One World* show notably lively, *That's My Kick* has a slightly augmented band with guitar and percussion, and *Gemini* found Erroll taking a turn at the harpsichord. Garner remains interesting from moment to moment, but over CD length his style's limitations tend to show up on ordinary albums, which is basically what these are.

The exception is *Close Up In Swing/A New Kind Of Love*. The first album is another regulation trio date, but the second is a film score for which Garner, despite his illiteracy, put together the music via block arrangements that were subsequently scored and left open for him to improvise the piano parts. The results say little that's profound about his music, but it's an interesting diversion to hear him magnified via a full orchestra.

*****(*) Erroll Garner Collection Vol. 1: Easy To Love**
Emarcy 832994-2 *Garner; Eddie Calhoun (b); Kelly Martin (d).*

***** Erroll Garner Collection Vol. 2: Dancing On The Ceiling**
Emarcy 834935-2 *As above.* 6/61–8/65.

With much of Erroll's work still out of print, the appearance of previously unreleased material may seem like a luxury; but this is quality Garner. Both discs round up nuggets from various early-'60s sessions, and there are some fine things on both, such as the dizzying opening to 'It Had To Be You' or the prime after-hours Garner of 'Like Home'.

***** Plays Gershwin & Kern**
Mercury 826224-2 *Garner; Eddie Calhoun, Ike Isaacs (b); Kelly Martin, Jimmie Smith (d).* 8/64–2/68.

***** Jazz Around Midnight – Erroll Garner**
Verve 846191-2 *Garner; Red Callender, John Simmons, Leonard Gaskin, Wyatt Ruther (b); Lou Singer, Harold Doc West, Charlie Smith, Eugene 'Fats' Heard (d).* 12/45–3/55.

***** Erroll Garner: Jazz Masters 7**
Verve 518197-2 *Garner; Wyatt Ruther (b); Eugene 'Fats' Heard (d); Candido Camero (perc).* 54–55.

*****(*) This Is Jazz**
Columbia CK 64968 *Garner; John Simmons, Wyatt Ruther, Al Hall (b); Shadow Wilson, Specs Powell, Eugene 'Fats' Heard (d).* 6/50–2/57.

Many of Garner's albums from the late 1950s and '60s have been lost from the catalogue, and the Gershwin and Kern set is no more than typical of the period. But Garner is well served by the *Around Midnight* compilation, which closes with the very long and unpredictable 'Over The Rainbow' from *Solitaire*; and the *Jazz Masters* disc is sound value, a smart choice of solo and trio pieces from the Mercury sessions. Columbia's *This Is Jazz* is a pleasing set drawn from their various holdings: 'Moonglow' is a particularly fine treatment.

Carlos Garnett (born 1938)

TENOR, ALTO, SOPRANO AND BARITONE SAXOPHONES

Born in Panama, Garnett is a self-taught saxophonist. He arrived in New York in 1962 and worked with various leaders in the '60s, culminating in a spell with the Miles Davis electric group. In the '70s he made a string of albums which fused Panamanian music, jazz and soul, a style he called Universal Black Force.

****(*) Fire**
32 Jazz 32043 *Garnett; Cyril Greene, Angel Fernandez, Preston Holas, Wayne Cobham, Roy Campbell, Charles Sullivan, Quentin Lowther, Abdul Malik, Olu Dara, Terumasa Hino (t); Kiane Zawadi, Clifton Anderson, Andrew Washington, James Stowe (tb); Charles Dougherty, Al Brown, Robert Wright (as); Randy Gilmore, Zane Massey, Akum Ra Amen-Ra, Yah Ya (ts); Carlos Chambers (bs, uke); Mauricio Smith (f); Hubert Eaves, Joe Bonner (ky); Kenny Kirkland, Onaje Allan Gumbs (p); Junior McCleary, Reggie Lucas (g); Anthony Jackson (g, b); (Fish), Alex Blake, John Lee (b); Howard King, Billy Hart, Norman Connors, Alphonse Mouzon (d); Charles Pulliam, Neil Clarke, Mtume, Guilherme Franco, Timan (perc); Ayodele Jenkins, Prema (v).* 9/74–5/77.

***** Fuego En Mi Alma**
High Note HCD 7001 *Garnett; Carlton Holmes (p); Brad Jones (b); Shingo Okudaira (d); Neil Clarke (perc).* 9/96.

*****(*) Under Nubian Skies**
High Note HCD 7023 *As above, except add Russell Gunn (t); omit Clarke.* 9/97.

Garnett's Muse albums have a bit of a cult following among the so-called Acid Jazz movement, but they may disappoint many who hear them now on the basis of that reputation; the best-of which 32 Jazz has released, *Fire*, shows mostly that Garnett didn't know how to make his grand fusion work in the studios. The big band on 'Saxy' (seven trumpets, eight reeds!) is all over the place, and several of the other tracks are lost in a stew of percussion. The interminable 'Taurus Woman' is just far too long. But here and there Garnett's ambitious conception pays some charismatic dividends, not least in his own vigorous playing.

His return to active duty in the late '90s is very welcome, if the excellent *Under Nubian Skies* in particular is anything to go by. 'I feel I'm doing better soloing than I did back in my earlier days,' Garnett says, and he's right, sticking to the tenor and thinning out the verbiage of the old music. *Fuego En Mi Alma* could have used a little more contrast (supplied by Gunn on the later date), and here and there he sounds just a tad rusty, but it's spirited and generous music, which the deferential rhythm section is particulary well suited to. Garnett is coming straight out of classic-period Coltrane for much of *Under Nubian Skies* and, since again the rhythm section are supportive rather than combative, it throws his sound into a sharper relief. Gunn is happy to be a good-natured foil and there are some useful, boppish originals for them to work out on. An enjoyable surprise.

Kenny Garrett (born 1960)

ALTO SAXOPHONE, FLUTE, OTHER INSTRUMENTS

Arrived in New York in 1980, and his stint as a sideman with Miles Davis lifted his reputation; has since worked prolifically as both leader and sideman, close to hard-bop foundation but with an awareness of funk and everything else.

***** Introducing Kenny Garrett**

Criss Cross CRISS 1014 *Garrett; Woody Shaw (t, flhn); Mulgrew Miller (p); Nat Reeves (b); Tony Reedus (d).* 11/84.

Garrett's old boss Miles Davis once accused him of wearing 'Sonny Stitt's dirty drawers', which is a typically acute if slightly bitchy way of characterizing the youngster's plangent, blues-soaked style. Garrett was one of the more successful of Miles's later generations of saxophone players and he has gone on to carve a distinctive and successful career for himself as leader.

The debut on Criss Cross – and Gerry Teekens has proved to be almost as prescient as Miles himself at spotting talent – is a more than decent effort. The inclusion of Woody Shaw was a powerful stroke. Woody is a far more sympathetic partner than the bustling, somewhat aggressive Roney on a subsequently deleted Paddle Wheel disc although, four years on, Garrett sounds more than ready to cope with the extra octane. Roney is of course the closest thing around to Miles in his prime; Shaw is a very different stylist, superficially closer to the great man's softly enunciated tone but utterly different in phrasing and in his approach to solos.

Garrett tackles all the material with a freshness and lack of prejudice that is instantly appealing. His bluesy phrasing is very exact, for all its relaxed delivery, and his habit of lingering on low tones just a fraction longer than you expect gives his solos a very solid, anchored presence, which has allowed him to work on occasion without a harmony instrument; it is always clear that he *hears* the bottom line very clearly, and it may even have been that facility which recommended him to Miles.

***** Prisoner Of Love**

Atlantic 82046 *Garrett; Miles Davis, Barry Lee Hall Jr (t); Muhammad Abdul Al-Khabyyr (tb); Sayydah Garrett (cl); Foley McCreary, Darryl Jones, Marcus Miller (b); Ricky Wellman (d); Rudy Bird, Mino Cinelu (perc); vocal choir.* 89.

Graced by an appearance from Miles Davis, and featuring much of the great man's working band of the time, this was Garrett's testimonial for good service. It's a well-crafted and somewhat ambitious record. Taking his cue from Marcus Miller, who plays everything going, Garrett plays all the instruments on three tracks, including an affecting and rather powerful version of 'Lift Ev'ry Voice And Sing'. Otherwise, it's pretty squarely in late Miles mode and, but for the prominence of the saxophone, many will guess that they're listening to out-takes from some otherwise undocumented session. This isn't to decry Garrett's contribution, but there is a faint sense that he is swamped by more dominant partners, guests who've hijacked his party.

***** African Exchange Student**

Atlantic 82156 *Garrett; Mulgrew Miller (p); Ron Carter, Charnett Moffett (b); Elvin Jones, Tony Reedus (d); Rudy Bird, Tito Ocasio, Steve Thornton (perc).* 90.

*****(*) Black Hope**

Warner Bros 9362 45017 *Garrett; Joe Henderson (ts); Kenny Kirkland (p, syn); Donald Brown (syn); Charnett Moffett (b); Brian Blade, Ricky Wellman (d); Don Alias (perc).* 92.

Straddling a change of label, and also something of a shift in Garrett's approach to things, these are both convincing statements by a young man still coming to terms with his artistic inheritance. The difference between them is that on *Black Hope* he is no longer processing 'influences' but responding to predecessors as an equal. He certainly isn't put off by the presence of Henderson on 'Transit Dance' and 'Bye Bye Blackbird' on the later disc. Joe's solo construction is so magisterial that any partner runs the risk of sounding banal, but Garrett more than holds his own, and the lessons absorbed pay huge dividends on future projects. Kirkland is a more naturally lyrical player than Mulgrew Miller and provides a wider and more vivid range of colours.

As before, Garrett shows himself capable of working without a harmony instrument, and *African Exchange Student* includes a pianoless trio with Carter and Jones, good enough to make one wish for a whole album of it. Pure greed, for it's an excellent enough album as it stands, marked down only a notch for lacking overall shape and construction, too much like a hotch-potch of sessions, not enough like a coherent project.

****** Trilogy**

Warner Bros 9 45731 *Garrett; Kiyoshi Kitagawa, Charnett Moffett (b); Brian Blade (d).* 95.

This is a very special record, made with Garrett's working trio (and with a couple of tracks featuring old pal Moffett). Garrett is still content to play standards and repertoire pieces, and he brings fresh angles to Brubeck's 'In Your Own Sweet Way' and the old warhorse, 'Giant Steps', which he plays with a respectful insouciance as if it really doesn't matter if he stumbles. His major encounter with Coltrane was still to come, but it is clear that Trane's music and presence are increasingly important to him at this time.

There's refreshingly little ego on any of these discs, and *Trilogy* above all suggests the work of a young master musician who clearly recognizes the way he has to go relative to the towering achievement that has gone before him. The dedication to Henderson and Rollins is perhaps a sign of where his thinking now lies; *pace* 'Giant Steps', Garrett doesn't sound like a Coltrane disciple, but does obviously recognize that until he confronts this giant in his lair, he cannot quite claim to have won his sword.

****** Pursuance**

Warner Bros 9 46209 *Garrett; Pat Metheny (g); Rodney Whitaker (b); Brian Blade (d).* 96.

Perhaps as he worked his way through the tortuous chords of 'Giant Steps' on *Trilogy*, Kenny Garrett recognized this album would have to be made sooner or later. Coltrane tributes were ten a penny over a couple of years surrounding the thirtieth anniversary of his death, but this is one of the very best. Having a guitarist on board, and a guitarist of Metheny's undersold gifts, opened up the structure of almost all the songs included, and Garrett's ability to second-guess harmonic progressions and a straight chordal accompaniment make this a very free interpretation indeed.

They kick off with 'Countdown' and 'Equinox', continue with 'Liberia' and 'Dear Lord', and really hit pace with a terse and wonderful version of 'After The Rain'. The title-piece begins a gigantic coda which includes a very brief, almost throwaway version of 'Giant Steps' again. The other Trane compositions included are 'Lonnie's Lament', 'Like Sonny', 'Alabama' and 'Latifa', each of them intelligently rethought and reworked.

*****(*) Songbook**

Warner Bros 9 4651 *Garrett; Kenny Kirkland (p); Nat Reeves (b); Jeff Tain Watts (d).* 97.

Almost inevitably, Garrett followed up the Coltrane project with a set entirely of originals. The big statements, 'Brother Hubbard', 'November 15' and 'She Waits For The New Sun', all sound as if they have been gestating for some time, and are brilliantly worked by the band. Garrett at this stage could easily have gone for an augmented unit with extra horns, but it's refreshing hearing him with just rhythm again, and Kirkland responds to what was presumably new and unfamiliar material with a great deal of imagination.

The sound is very immediate, and though there are a couple of edits here and there which don't sound quite right, as if the pitch has shifted a little from one take to the next, the finished product is about as good as it could be.

*****(*) Simply Said**

Warner Bros 9 8759 *Garrett; Sheldrick Mitchell (p, org); Mulgrew Miller (p, v); Pat Metheny (g); Marcus Miller, Nat Reeves (b, v); Chris Dave, Jeff Tain Watts (d, v); Bashiri Johnson (d); Raymond Harris (v).* 98.

The absent guest here is Kenny Kirkland, who died shortly before and whose loss perhaps adds to rather than explains a rather melancholic sound to the album as a whole. Even upbeat, Garrett sounds thoughtful and even guarded. Always a player who takes time to process the lessons of the recent past, he can sound repetitive. Here, though, he cheerfully recaps and compresses solos from *Trilogy* and *Songbook*, without seeming to play musical leftovers.

Garrett's new band is fresh and unaffected. Mitchell is an interesting organ player and a decent writer as well, claiming a single but valuable credit with 'Words Can't Express'. The only question mark hangs over Dave's unvarying count. Metheny is in for only two tunes and Marcus Miller for three. Big Mulgrew has a guest spot alongside Jeff Watts, helping to keep the sound varied and subtly weighted. Pointless to expect a dramatic step forward from this patient and hard-working artist. By now, though, reasonable to expect an effective and professional statement, which is exactly what *Simply Said* is.

Michael Garrick (born 1933)

PIANO

Best known for his Jazz Praises project, Enfield-born Garrick has taken Duke's 'sacred' music on a step, using jazz as the basis for a body of liturgical music which swings with the gift of tongues. An able and dexterous soloist, he is one of the finest jazz pianists to come out of Britain since the war.

****** A Lady In Waiting**

Jazz Academy JAZA 1 *Garrick; Dave Green (b); Alan Jackson (d).* 93.

When the Big Audit is completed, Britain will find itself in trouble for not having disclosed a national asset on the scale of Michael Garrick, or for not having found an appropriate outlet for his talents. Even though his extra-curricular activities as teacher, writer and administrator have occasionally intruded, Garrick's fleet, uncomplacent keyboard style and elegant compositional touch have not been fully appreciated. Though perhaps best understood as a big-band composer in the tradition of Ellington, Garrick is also a formidable small-group player, and this seasoned trio plays scaled-down versions of pieces originally conceived for orchestra. The most accurate measure of the leader's skills is his approach to repertory material like Hancock's 'Dolphin's Dance' and John Lewis's wonderfully pianistic 'Two Degrees East, Three Degrees West'. The group is recorded clearly and uncomplicatedly, and the album as a whole is both exhilarating and moving.

*****(*) Meteors Close At Hand**

Jazz Academy JAZA 2 *Garrick; Andy Bush, Mike Diprose, Ollie Preece, Martin Shaw, Steve Waterman, Ian Wood (t, flhn); Brian Archer, Matt Coleman, Pat Hartley, Bill Mee, Mark D'Silva (tb); Scott Garland, Jimmy Hastings, Mike Hall, Martin Hathaway, Bob McKay, Mike Page, Jim Tomlinson, Matt Wates (sax); Phil Lee, Colin Oxley (g); Paul Moylan (b); Alan Jackson (d).* 6 & 7/94.

A generous studio sampling of material from Garrick's *Royal Box* (a reaction of tabloid mayhem) and from his Thomas Hardy, J. R. R. Tolkien and jazz character suites. Just to establish continuity with the small-group album, there is a lovely version of 'A Lady In Waiting', with solos from Bill Mee and Pat Hartley on trombones (each differently voiced), Martin Hathaway and Steve Waterman. The *Hardy Country* tunes include some of Garrick's best writing. Waterman is the star turn again on 'Middle Piddlecombe', though Garrick himself turns in a relatively rare solo on the lovely 'Blues As An Autumn Mist', which could hardly be more Ellingtonian if it tried. Portraits of Dizzy Gillespie, Arturo Sandoval and Lester Young exercise a gifted and beautifully balanced band, and the Tolkien obsession which has yielded up some of Garrick's quirkiest and most memorable writing emerges in 'River Running', a delicately phrased theme for bass clarinet, tenor saxophone and the leader's piano. Old-stagers like Jimmy Hastings and younger guys like Matt Wates and Scott Garland fill out a superb reed section. The horns aren't quite so compelling, but the arrangements are so good that the absence of fiery front-line playing isn't missed. Some quibbles about the recording, but a genial and thoroughly entertaining album.

***** Parting Is Such**

Jazz Academy JAZA 3 *Garrick; Don Rendell (ts); Chris Garrick (vn); Dave Green (b); Alan Jackson (d).* 95.

The addition of Christian Garrick and the urbane Rendell lifts an otherwise rather one-dimensional record. In addition to nine originals, the trio tackles the famous Canteloube 'Baïlero', Lennon/McCartney's 'Here, There And Everywhere' and 'My Funny Valentine'. Garrick is on excellent and relaxed form, phrasing less formally than usual but with great expressiveness.

****** For Love Of Duke ... And Ronnie**

Jazz Academy JAZA 4 *Garrick; Gabriel Garrick, Ollie Preece, Steve Waterman, Ian Wood (t); Brian Archer, Bill Mee, Mark D'Silva (tb); Mike Hall, Martin Hathaway, Bob McKay, Jim Tomlinson, Matt Wates (sax); Colin Oxley (g); Paul Moylan (b); Alan Jackson (d); Jacqui Dankworth (v).* 95, 96.

*****(*) Down On Your Knees**

Jazz Academy JAZA 5 *Garrick; Mark Armstrong, Gabriel Garrick, Paul Jayasinha, Martin Shaw, Steve Waterman (t); Brian Archer, Matt Coleman, Dave Holt, Bill Mee, Mark Nightingale, Malcolm Earl Smith (tb); Paul Booth, Ben Castle, Mike Hall, Bob McKay, Jim Tomlinson, Matt Wates (sax); Dominic Ashworth (g); Paul Moylan (b); Alan Jackson (d); Anita Wardell (v).* 99.

Garrick is gradually assembling a full documentation of his output as a big-band composer. It seems on the face of it perverse that works like 'Jazz Praises' should be recorded piecemeal – another two pieces are recorded on *For Love Of ...* – except that they fit perfectly well into the broader context of his work. Equally, more of the *Hardy Country* material – 'The Storm (Was Its Lover)' – juxtaposes nicely with tunes dedicated to Ellington and written in memory of altoist Joe Harriott, whose free-form writing and playing had such a huge impact on the British scene. The final dedication is, of course, to the late Ronnie Scott, with whom Garrick worked only very rarely but for whom he shares a widespread affection and debt.

The use of Jacqui Dankworth to fill in what would have been a whole choir on the original score is underlined once again in Anita Wardell's work on the recent *Down On Your Knees*. Anita's ability to inflect songs with apposite and accurate emotion represents an important dramatic resource to Garrick, who can concentrate on leading a band of undoubted technical sophistication and iron-clad swing. The live version of 'Take The "A" Train', recorded at the Vortex club in London, is a joyous curtain-piece, but the mood overall is more thoughtful, even when the pace is intense. As ever, Garrick is mining material that goes back to the Rendell–Carr quintet of the 1960s and its reaction to the advanced harmonics of the John Coltrane Quartet, while 'Torrent' is lifted from a 1970 Garrick LP, *The Heart Is A Lotus*. The title-track plays around with topical memories of Ms Monica Lewinsky, whose embouchure can't have been any better than soloist Mark Armstrong's.

Both albums are recorded quite plainly but with lots of instrumental colour and, taken together with *Meteors*, should help relocate Garrick as a major catalytic force in British jazz, a lighter-voiced but in some respects more compelling figure than the more obviously combustible Stan Tracey.

George Garzone

TENOR AND SOPRANO SAXOPHONES

Garzone is one of the most articulate and passionate educators in jazz, and his Coltrane-influenced approach is always fascinating, though scantily represented on record.

***** Fours And Twos**

NYC 6024-2 *Garzone; Joe Lovano (ts); Joey Calderazzo (p); John Lockwood (b); Bill Stewart (d).* 96.

*****(*) Moodiology**

NYC 6031 2 *Garzone; Douglas Yates (as, bcl); Claire Daly (bs); Kenny Werner (p); Mike Maineri (vib); John Lockwood (b); Bob Gullotti (d).* 98.

Garzone plays with a notably hard edge and with an unfailingly logical solo development. His great strength is the articulation and unravelling of fast-paced melody lines with a very open-ended chord-structure. Any feeling that he is trapped at the same evolutionary point as the Coltrane of the classic Atlantic sessions is easily confounded, but those albums are the best point of comparison.

Fours And Twos is the kind of thing that ends up being called a 'connoisseur's record'. Garzone may be less renowned than front-line partner Lovano but he plays with as much authority and heft, and hearing the two tenors carve up some of these pieces – even in the oblique way that they do – is a fine example of nonconformist exhilaration. The tenor solos tend to be split up by contributions from the rhythm section so there's no sense of a cutting contest, anyway. Because there's no conscious effort at variety in the make-up of the record, it stands on the quality of thinking and execution and, abetted by a terrific trio, the saxophonists deliver royally on that count. The originals are good enough, the standards (a powerhouse 'Have You Met Miss Jones' and a sax duo on 'In A Sentimental Mood') beguiling, and they're further blessed by a vivid sound in the studio.

Moodiology is very much a tribute to friends and influences. The prelude is a dark, Trane-influenced blues, and the great man's influence is also reflected in 'Naima', though for some mysterious reason that wonderful love poem is credited as a Garzone composition. George's fragile soprano statement certainly isn't enough to wrest it from the real creator. The other repertory pieces, 'I'll Remember April', 'Summertime' and 'Soul Eyes', are handled with grace and real authority.

Geoff Gascoyne

BASS

British bassist with a wide range of stylistic experience, occasional leader and currently in the Guy Barker group.

*****(*) Voices Of Spring**

Jazzizit JITCD 9605 *Gascoyne; Gerard Presencer (flhn); Andy Panayi (ts, f); Tim Garland, Mark Lockheart (ts); Gareth Williams (p); Jim Mullen (g); Jeremy Stacey (d); Claire Martin, Ian Shaw (v).* 9/95.

***** Winter Wonderland**

Jazzizit JITCD 9710 *Gascoyne; Andy Panayi (ss, af); Pete Churchill (p); Adam Glasser (hca).* 3–7/97.

Voices Of Spring showcases both Gascoyne's elegant playing and writing and the smart, unfussy methods of a stalwart group of British performers: the four horns each have excellent cameos, with the saxophonists in particular showing strong individual colours, and Martin and Shaw have a distinctive song apiece. Old salt Mullen lends some nonchalant fire and the leader has the wit to feature himself only sparingly. The excellent studio sound ices the cake.

Winter Wonderland is a Christmas album and among the prettiest of its genre, mostly duets between Churchill and Gascoyne, with the melodies surviving a modest element of improvisation.

Giorgio Gaslini (born 1929)

PIANO, KEYBOARDS

Studied composition in Milan, and composed and conducted into the early '60s, before forming a jazz quartet, which he performed with in factories and hospitals in an effort to bring jazz to a new audience. Has written operas and large-scale works, along with striking revisions of familiar composers. One of the most distinguished players in the Italian jazz lineage.

**** Gaslini Plays Monk

Soul Note 121020 *Gaslini (p solo).* 5/81.

*** Schumann Reflections

Soul Note 121120 *Gaslini; Piero Leveratto (b); Paolo Pellegatti (d).* 7/84.

Only a performer and composer whose stated aim is 'total music', a grand unified synthesis of jazz, serialism, pop, classical forms and electro-acoustic procedures, could possibly relate with equal ease to Thelonious Monk, Robert Schumann and Albert Ayler. This, though, is what the remarkable Milanese has done. Playing and writing since his early teens, he has combined jazz with orchestral music, and he is an experienced conductor. As the Monk album clearly demonstrates, his sense of form is rock solid, and what may be surprising about these tracks is how little he attempts to subvert the basic outlines. He remains faithful to the outlines of the piece from first to last but is obviously intrigued by internal consistencies, rhymes and chimes, and he blends individual songs into an elegantly crafted suite which ought to be listened to as a whole if possible.

The Schumann material is less obviously tractable to this kind of performance, and there are moments when one will have the impression of listening to a Bill Evans record put through some strange diffraction grid. The harmonic richness of the original leaves an improviser with less to do than when dealing with the bone and sinew of a Monk tune, but at the same time with an infinity of possibilities that may trip up even a subtle improviser. The trio setting doesn't seem quite right for this material, and Pellegatti is a rather lumpish player for jazz.

*** Multiple

Soul Note 121220 *Gaslini; Roberto Ottaviano (as, ss, sno, bcl); Claudio Fasoli (ts, ss); Bruno Tommaso (b); Giampiero Prina (d).* 10/87.

This is an interesting group. Ottaviano is more than just a utility player, but he has certainly traded in soloistic virtuosity in favour of an ability to create a spectrum of sound-textures. Fasoli is more obviously straightahead and, as the spearhead of the group with Gaslini, he makes for a convincing frontman. The rhythm section sounds terribly European, not because it doesn't swing but because the swing is so terribly exact and unvaried. A little bend and stretch here and there would improve this session immeasurably, and yet it's a record one goes back to, more out of curiosity than affection, but often enough to suggest that it has its virtues.

***(*) Ayler's Wings

Soul Note 121270 *Gaslini (p solo).* 7/90.

An extraordinary undertaking. Transcribing Albert Ayler, seemingly the most anti-pianistic of improvisers, would appear to be an almost absurdly quixotic task. So much of what Ayler was about fell between the conventional pitches that it would seem impossible to render it on a piano, and yet Gaslini converts that fierce microtonality into ripples and arpeggios that are as provocative as they are unexpectedly appealing. There is not as much darkness and passion as one would expect to hear, given the source material, but in its place there is a sort of grandeur that Albert never quite achieved. Superimposing 'Omega Is The Alpha' over 'Bells' is an oddity that works against the odds, and the versions of 'Ghosts' and 'Truth Is Marching In' have a Bachian simplicity. A genuine homage, profoundly felt and wholly successful. Some question marks about the recording; none about the music therein.

**** Lampi

Soul Note 121290 *Gaslini; Daniele Di Gregorio (vib, mar, perc); Roberto Bonati (b); Giampiero Prina (d).* 1/94.

One of Gaslini's most characteristic devices is a sudden dead halt over a heavy drum-beat. On *Lampi* it stands for the shocked pause that comes between a bolt of lightning (which is what the word means) and the rumble of thunder. In that flashbulb silence, nothing but the sound of the heart, and Gaslini plays strange tricks with the pulse rate on this remarkable record, pushing and stretching the beat, setting one instrument against the others, bending time. Never before has he made such imaginative use of percussion; Di Gregorio is a more than able second lead, a player with ideas of his own and a technique that recalls Bobby Hutcherson. Bonati and Prina fulfil their roles more modestly, but neither sounds out of sympathy with this demanding music.

***(*) Jelly's Back In Town

DDQ 128020 *Gaslini; Paolo Fresu, Umberto Marcandalli, Sergio Orlandi (t); Luca Begonia, Pierluigi Salvi (tb); Oscar Gelmi (hn); Tino Tracanna (ts, ss); Gianluigi Trovesi (as, bcl); Guido Bombardieri, Maurizio Moraschini (as, cl); Alberto Nacci (ts); Roger Rota (bs); Maurizio Beltrami (f, picc); Ugo Gelmi (bsn); Adelio Leoni (g); Fabrizio Garofoli (p); Sandro Massazza (b); Vittorio Marinoni (d); Stefano Bertoli (perc); Silvia Infascelli (v).* 2/96.

Monk, Schumann, Ayler ... and now Jelly Roll Morton. Gaslini's arrangements are embedded into a suite which in the pale, bleached light of the city at dawn – 'La citta all'alba' – allows Morton to move freely between past and present, between the roots of jazz and its uncertain future. After 'Billy Goat Stomp', there are three Creole and French songs from Louisiana, tiny and exquisitely played. After that, 'Spanish Swat', 'Wolverine Blues' and 'Freakish', and then a real shock, the 'Miserere' from *Trovatore*, a shock because it serves as a further reminder of the sheer diversity of Morton's sources. The remainder of the set is less compelling, though Gaslini's original material is superb. The Ensemble Mobile was convened for the festival at Bergamo, and the three guest soloists – Fresu, Tracanna (a revelation) and Trovesi – provide an appealing diversity of approach.

*****(*) Mister O**

Soul Note 121300 *Gaslini; Livio Simone Ramasso (c); Luca Calabrese, Sergio Casesi, Alberto Mandarini (t); Gianpiero Malfatto, Lauro Rossi (tb); Erik Zavaroni (tba); Giulio Visibelli (f); Gianluigi Trovesi (as, ss); Maurizio Moraschini, Guido Bombardieri (as, cl); Riccardo Luppi (ts, ss); Carlo Actis Dato (bs, bcl); Michelangelo Cagnetta, Vitaliano De Rossi (vn); Stefano Montaldo (vla); Andrea Anzalone (clo); Vittorio Rabagliati (p); Daniele Di Gregorio (vib, xyl, perc); Roberto Bonati (b); Giampiero Prina (d); Arturo Testa, Paolo Lorenzi, Bernardo Lanzetti, Maurizio Sciuto, Laura Conti, Marco Radaelli, Cristiano Pecchio, Piero Lucarelli, Luca La Penna, Lucia Minetti, Rosella Liberti, Daniela Panetta (v).* 7/96.

Mister O is the Moor Othello, transposed and transformed in this ambitious jazz-opera. Gaslini has experimented with theatrical and staged performances for many years, including an early attempt at an operatic event based on the life of Malcolm X, but this is the most ambitious thing he has written to date. To a large extent, it falls outside the strict remit of this *Guide*, but there is enough of a jazz element, and it is close enough to past work – notably the 'Miserere' on the last record – for it to be of interest to anyone who has kept pace this far. Arturo Testa is superb as Mister O, and Paolo Lorenzi is convincingly frail as 'Des' (Desdemona), but the key performance is, as it should be, Bernardo Lanzetti's as Jago. He is some distance from Verdi's villain, a more moderate and humane creation with a defence of forgivable weakness on his side. Also in the mix, three rappers and young people of the New Village, who bring a contemporary slant to the story. Vittorio Franchini has been a collaborator with Gaslini for some time; he excels himself here. The jazz orchestra performs magnificently. With solo space at a premium, individual voicings become ever more important. Every instrument is registered cleanly and vividly; every bar and phrase is made to count.

Bruce Gates Jazz Consortium Big Band

GROUP

Gates leads this occasional big band of studio pros through a couple of letting-the-hair-down blowing dates.

***** Forced Air Heat**

Sea Breeze SB-2060 *Bruce Gates, Chris Walker, Bill Moore, Rick Sigler (t, flhn); Rick Lillard, Don Elliott, Dan Haverstock, Ben Hall, Dudley Hinote (tb); Joe Eckert, Andy Axelrod (as); Saul Miller, Scott Silbert (ts); Leigh Pilzer (bs); Wade Beach (p); Rick Whitehead (g); Paul Henry (b); C.E Askew (d).* 7–8/94.

***** Joyous Reunion**

Sea Breeze SB-2086 *As above.* 6–8/96.

Front-line pros from the Washington, DC, area cutting loose on 19 (across the two discs) standards of sorts. There are some nice touches in the choosing – Lee Morgan's 'Ceora' and 'Speedball', Harold Danko's 'Tidal Breeze', Jimmy Smith's 'Off The Top'. There's lots of the usual grandstanding, but the music's played for fun and the feel comes through fetchingly enough. Saul Miller's tenor has perhaps the best solo honours, but the two-trombone tear-up by Elliott and Lillard on 'Ceora' (*Forced Air Heat*) is splendid. Cut and recorded with the usual Sea Breeze finesse.

Gateway

GROUP

Convened for a single ECM date in 1975, the group subsequently reconvened for a second set in 1977 and then for a belated revisitation in 1994.

***** Gateway**

ECM 829192-2 *John Abercrombie (g); Dave Holland (b); Jack DeJohnette (d).* 3/75.

***** Gateway 2**

ECM 847323-2 *As above.* 7/77.

*****(*) Homecoming**

ECM 527637-2 *As above.* 12/94.

*****(*) In The Moment**

ECM 529346-2 *As above.* 12/94.

It's part of the mythology of American culture that there are no second acts and that you can't go home again. The appearance in 1995 of a new Gateway record confounded all that. An almost two-decade gap had cemented the instinctive understanding of three players who, one way and another, had pegged out much of the territory of modern jazz. Abercrombie's gently arpeggiated and almost countrified picking had been one of the definitive sounds of ECM's early years. Holland and DeJohnette came with more baggage than it seemed possible to carry and, predictably, the first album didn't quite gel. The bassist sounds almost pedestrian in places, seemingly not fired by Abercrombie's writing, and it's interesting that, when the group reconvenes in 1994, the title-piece of *Homecoming* is a long Holland composition that addresses exactly the shortcomings of the first disc. *Gateway 2* was an engaging enough follow-up, but it has all the hallmarks of an obligatory sequel. Still, the group's early-'90s live appearances were revelatory and sent fans scurrying back to the original records; whatever their shortcomings, they retained a freshness that is as engaging as it is unexpected. *In The Moment* is supergroup playing of a high order, three hugely experienced musicians interacting without anxiety and with dazzling ease. The long 'Shrubberies' is probably the best single item in the Gateway catalogue, and if anyone has yet to sample the group, this is the place to start.

Jacques Gauthé

CLARINET, SOPRANO SAXOPHONE

Gauthé is a Frenchman who heard Bechet in Paris in the 1950s and has been trying to follow in those footsteps ever since. His Creole Rice Yerba Buena Jazz Band also draws inspiration from the Lu Watters–Monte Ballou style of Californian revivalism.

*****(*) Someday, Sweetheart**

GHB BCD-299 *Gauthé; Scott Black, Chris Tyle (c, v); Tom Ebbert (tb); John Royen (p); Amy Sharpe (bj); Tom Saunders (tba, v); Trevor Richards (d).* 7/89.

***** Paris Blues**

Stomp Off 1216 *Gauthé; Daniel Barda (tb); Alain Marquet (cl); Louis Mazetier (p); Enzo Mucci (bj, g); Michel Marcheteau (sou).* 2/90.

*****(*) Creole Jazz**

Stomp Off 1256 *Gauthé; Chris Tyle (t); Duke Heitger (c); John Gill (tb, ky, d, v); Tom Ebbert (tb); Steve Pistorius (p); Amy Sharpe (bj); Tom Saunders (tba); Hal Smith (d).* 7/92.

***** Echoes Of Sidney Bechet**

Good Time Jazz 15006 *Gauthé; Duke Heitger (t); Mike Owen (tb); Steve Pistorius (p); Lars Edegran (g); Tom Saunders (b); Chris Tyle (d).* 1/97.

Gauthé has been leading the Creole Rice Jazz Band in New Orleans for many years. His passionate dedication to Sidney Bechet gets full rein on the Good Time Jazz disc, which sounds like the old master has walked into the '90s without blinking and set down his favourite pieces in modern sound. Gauthé walks a slightly awkward line between homage and pure re-creation here, playing soprano almost throughout, but the sheer intensity of his mission is rather inspiring – after all, in a world full of Coltrane disciples, Bechet's followers aren't exactly swarming all over the bandstands. The band tend to play second fiddle here, and that is a further authenticity.

On the other discs, Gauthé grants more space all round. *Paris Blues*, cut on a return visit home to France, is meant as a two-clarinet showcase with Marquet, yet the quickfire Mazetier and the barking Barda get in plenty of shots of their own. Gauthé sticks to clarinet on both this and *Creole Jazz*, finding as much Dodds as Bechet on this horn.

We would pick *Creole Jazz* as the best of these, since the material is a cheerful set of crusty antiques such as 'Auntie Skinner's Chicken Dinner', revivalist set-pieces like the Claude Luter tunes and silvery memories of Armstrong, Morton and Oliver. But the earlier *Someday, Sweetheart* is only a whisker behind – lots of Oliver and Armstrong done modestly but with no little skill and warmth.

***** Bechet Summit**

GHB BCD-397 *Gauthé; Claude Luter (cl, ss); Bob Wilber (cl); Steve Pistorius (p); Lars Edegran (g); Tom Saunders (b); Chris Tyle (d).* 5/97.

Gauthé, Luter and Wilber have all been playing long enough to assert themselves over Bechet's looming influence, and if this is mostly material associated with the master, they play it as themselves. Wilber is present on only the first two tracks, and thereafter Gauthé and Luter play it as a gentlemanly joust, with the rhythm team in jolly support. Undemanding fun.

Jeff Gauthier

VIOLIN

A member of the Californian avant-garde regularly documented by labels such as Nine Winds, Gauthier brings a classical sensibility to an impressionistic jazz-rock situation.

***** Internal Memo**

Nine Winds NWCD 0164 *Gauthier; David Witham (ky); Eric Von Essen (b, hca); Alex Cline (d).* 9/93.

Gauthier's favoured ground is at the sweet end of jazz violin: his tone and delivery are amiable enough to sit soundly in a QHCF situation. But this is a Nine Winds date and, though it doesn't always suit him, he seems more interested in a long, tough, abstract piece like the closing 'Olivier's Nightmare'. The dedication to Richard Grossman, 'Seriously Twisted Blues', is a successful narrowing of range: when Witham drops out and the trio dig in, the music finds a real intensity. Elsewhere, on the charming pastorale of 'Astor' and the gracious 'Refuge', the group concoct a brainy sort of mood music. An appealing if inconsistent mixed bag.

***** The Present**

Nine Winds NWCD 0196 *Gauthier; David Witham (ky); Joel Hamilton (b); Alex Cline (d).* 5/96.

Same again, really, although some three years later the players sound that bit more accomplished in the way they make this mood-y sort of jazz work. While the solos by Gauthier and Witham have their degree of substance, it's the textures and the various ensemble contrasts that give the music its character. Country and tango influences aren't so much paraded as absorbed into a plausible fabric that probably has as much world-music as jazz in it.

Charles Gayle (born 1939)

TENOR SAXOPHONE

Born in Buffalo, Gayle has a shadowy jazz presence prior to the late 1980s, when he was suddenly lionized as a master of unadorned free playing in a style after Albert Ayler. Often playing as a street musician, and sometimes allegedly homeless or without material possessions, he is a mix of folkloric savant and nurtured star-performer.

****(*) Always Born**

Silkheart 115 *Gayle; John Tchicai (as, ts); Sirone (b); Reggie Nicholson (d).* 4/88.

***** Homeless**

Silkheart 116 *Gayle; Sirone (b); Dave Pleasant (d).* 4/88.

*****(*) Spirits Before**

Silkheart 117 *As above.* 4/88.

Gayle's early music seems like mere sketchwork for what was to come. He lived the life of a street musician in Manhattan for some years, and these three records were all recorded in the same week on what was effectively a field trip by Silkheart. Gayle is like a folk musician in other ways, too: he harks back to unreconstructed energy music of the 1960s, blowing wild, themeless lines with an abandon that sometimes sounds neurotic, sometimes pleading, occasionally euphoric. He seems oblivious to all 'fashions' in jazz, keeps faith with only a few players – drummer Pleasant, whose fractured and weirdly illogical time is a prime feature of the two records he appears on, and bassist Sirone appear to be two of them – and questions the status quo with unblinking certainty. *Always Born* is a well-meaning failure through Tchicai's efforts: Gayle wasn't really meant to play with another saxophonist, even a venerable veteran of the wave which he harks back to. *Homeless* and, especially, *Spirits Before* are the real, hard stuff, with 'Give' a particularly knotty and troubling performance.

♛ **** **Touchin' On Trane**
FMP CD 48 *Gayle; William Parker (b); Rashied Ali (d).* 10–11/91.

**** **Repent**
Knitting Factory Works KFWCD 122 *Gayle; Vattel Cherry, Hilliard Greene (b); David Pleasant (d).* 1–3/92.

**** **More Live**
Knitting Factory Works KFWCD 137 2CD *As above, except add William Parker (b, cel, vn), Michael Wimberley, Marc Edwards (d); omit Greene and Pleasant.* 1–2/93.

**** **Consecration**
Black Saint 120138-2 *As above, except omit Edwards.* 4/93.

***(*) **Translations**
Silkheart SHCD 134 *As above.* 1/93.

***(*) **Raining Fire**
Silkheart SHCD 137 *As above.* 1/93.

*** **Kingdom Come**
Knitting Factory Works KFW157 *Gayle; William Parker (b); Sunny Murray (d). n.d.*

***(*) **Unto I Am**
Victo CD032 *Gayle (ts, p, bcl, d solo).* 9/94.

These records still seem like an astonishing outburst, even in the aftermath of so many kinds of free-jazz outrage. Perhaps it is Gayle's very starkness and simplicity which are so disturbing. He has clearly developed the iron chops that go with playing in the open for hours on end, but the conception and realization of these records is monumental. His holy, holy delivery inevitably makes one think of both Coltrane and Ayler in their most consciously spiritual guise, and a performance like 'Jesus Christ And Scripture' (*Repent*) has all the biblical intensity that one might imagine; but there is also Gayle's own superbly harsh lyricism to go with that. He is unusually adept at both the highest register of the tenor and control of the most outlandish overblowing. Solos are not so much fashioned as drawn straight from the moment: all that seems to be created in advance is an instantaneous planning of a performance that might run on seemingly without end. The rhythm players on the Knitting Factory and Black Saint records are all little known, apart from the admirable Parker, who is as central to events as he is with Cecil Taylor; but they are wonderfully behind Gayle all the way. The opening of 'Deliverance' (*More Live*) suggests that they would be quite an ensemble even without him.

The outright masterpiece is the FMP album, which seems likely to be a central document in the free music of the decade: the three men touch on Coltrane from moment to moment (and Ali renews his old relationship in triumph) but this is new, brilliant, eloquent free playing. The two records cut live at New York's Knitting Factory are exhausting manifestos (particularly the double-disc set) which struggle towards ecstasy or chaos, depending on one's own tolerance. A piece such as 'Sanctification' (*More Live*) certainly goes further in building on Ayler's legacy than even Brötzmann ever has. *Consecration* catches them in the studio and shows only the slightest scaling-down, with 'Justified' another *tour de force*.

It might seem as if Gayle is suddenly being too widely documented, and it's true that his records tend to follow similar patterns. But so far they are still unlike one another. The two newer Silkheart releases document more by his working quartet and, though two discs without much relief is probably too much even for Gayle addicts, it can't be denied that there's some awesomely powerful interaction here. The only weak spot is Gayle's taste for instruments which don't really suit him: he fiddles away on a viola for some of the time, and it's no more enlightening than Ornette Coleman's violin playing.

Kingdom Come gets its power from three serene, muscular encounters with Murray and Parker. The drummer doesn't seem to be quite the force of old but he does well enough, and Gayle marches almost obliviously on. Two piano solos and a trio are less inspiring. The all-solo Victo release has a dispensable drum solo and a middling work-out on piano again; but the two tenor solos and the bass-clarinet item are astoundingly heavyweight pieces. Gayle has never sounded as close-up and direct as he does here, the saxophone terrorizing the microphone. And the quality of his thinking is remarkable, even as he appears to lose himself in the music.

*** **Berlin Movement From Future Years**
FMP CD 90 *Gayle; Vattel Cherry (b); Michael Wimberley (d).* 8/93.

*** **Abiding Variations**
FMP CD 100 *As above.* 8/93.

***(*) **Testaments**
Knitting Factory 174 *Gayle; Wilber Morris (b); Michael Wimberley (d).* 7/95.

*** **Delivered**
2.13.61 21324-2 *Gayle; James Jones (p); Gerald Benson (b); Kalil Madi (d). n.d.*

**** **Solo In Japan**
PSF PSFD-94 *Gayle (ss, ts, p solo).* 7/97.

Recent Gayle records have been somewhat mixed in their impact, even diffuse at times. The *Berlin* date on FMP is disappointingly cloudy and, for all its strength-sapping length, this is a merely middling performance from the trio, otherwise heard to better effect on some of the discs listed above. *Abiding Variations* offers a second helping from the same period. The album on Henry Rollins's 2.13.61 label, *Delivered*, is similarly under-achieved: Jones, Benson and Madi are an unremarkable crew who don't do enough to take the ear but won't stay entirely out of Gayle's way. Only a fierce medley of spirituals makes an impression. *Testaments* is much more severe and reaches its apogee in the monolith of 'Faith Evermore', a tenor saxophone outburst that can stand with any of Gayle's great moments. He still defuses the overall impact with bass clarinet and piano, though.

Gayle's second all-solo album is an unrelieved masterpiece, the sound tattooed on the air, each phrase carved and sculpted with the cruel intensity of an artist utterly driven. Unglamorous but truthful, the studio sound catches a musician with his guard down but with his delivery unflinching. Gayle still insists on picking up the soprano or turning to the piano, yet when alone with the tenor he creates some of the most disturbingly powerful music jazz has yet borne witness to.

***** Ancient Of Days**

Knitting Factory KFW 263 *Gayle; Hank Johnson (p); Juni Booth (b); Michael Wimberley (d).* 9/99.

With a stack of albums behind him in a short space of time, suddenly Gayle almost seems like an artist with his own repertory, his own 'expected' record. So he does some surprising things here: enlist a pianist, and keep himself within a relatively tractable orbit, not so much a diminishing of the great sound but a rationalizing of it ('Draw Me Nearer' is still close to overpowering, nevertheless). By the standards of other Gayle records, he sounds almost tamed. It's still a considerable passion.

Gianni Gebbia

SOPRANO SAXOPHONE, ALTO SAXOPHONE, BARITONE SAXOPHONE

Italian saxophonist who is a determined exponent of free improvisation in extremis.

***** Cappuccini Klang**

Splasc(h) CDH 383 *Gebbia; Peter Kowald (b); Gunter Baby Sommer (d).* 3/92.

The Italian improvisation scene is one which remains all too little known in the rest of Europe. A somewhat abstract performer, Gebbia has won the respect and the unflagging support of players of Peter Kowald's stature. This tireless promoter of new talent, ably abetted by Sommer, gives the young man exactly the platform he needs for a fierce, undogmatic programme of improvisations. It might be argued that he errs on the side of abstraction, especially on soprano, where he exploits the treacherous pitching to the full, and there are moments on the Splasc(h) when one hankers after a measure of straightforward lyricism. The 'Cappuccini Suite', though, is exemplary, with some wry pseudo-classical gestures that recall his fellow-countryman, Giorgio Gaslini.

*****(*) Body Limits**

Splasc(h) CDH 462 *Gebbia (as solo).* 95.

The spirit of Braxton's pioneering *For Alto* shouldn't be far away from this, and yet Gebbia seems to come from an entirely different sound-world, one in which Lee Konitz and Ornette Coleman battle without much conviction for his soul. There are 17 tracks, most of them not unexpectedly very short, and Gebbia gets a sound from his 1961 Selmer Mark VI (so we are told) which is both classical and utterly contemporary, idiosyncratic and squarely in the tradition.

***** Il Libro Degli Eroi**

Victo CD 051 *Gebbia; Vittorio Villa (d, perc, didgeridoo, v); Miriam Palma (v, perc).* 5/97.

The combination of saxophone (including the eldritch sopranino on this occasion), percussion and voice gives this live set from the Musique Actuelle Festival at Victoriaville an unexpected power and presence. As the title suggests, Gebbia is dealing with strong psychic presences, and his playing suggests exorcism as well as straightforward expressiveness. There are ugly aspects to this record, not just technically but also in the music itself. Not everyone will be convinced, and our advice is to start with the solo saxophone pieces and then perhaps forage a little further afield.

Jonathan Gee

PIANO

Young British pianist working in the homegrown post-bop environment.

***** Closer To**

ASC CD14 *Gee; Steve Rose (b); Winston Clifford (d).* 7/95–9/96.

***** Your Shining Heart**

ASC CD21 *As above.* 9/97.

Gee is a strong and imaginative pianist whose progress has been a pleasure to observe for British gig-goers over recent years. These outings as a trio-leader aren't so much premature as slightly compromised by the homebrew limitations of record-making in local jazz. Patched together from three sessions, *Closer To* has an unglamorous sound which doesn't do the players any favours and detracts from some interesting writing and a couple of shrewd covers: 'Bye Bye Blackbird' has an almost Tristano-ish feel, and Kenny Wheeler's 'Everybody's Song But My Own' is tersely lyrical. *Your Shining Heart* is much stronger – better recorded (though still less than ideal), better played and, with eight originals by Gee, an intelligent showcase for his composing. Listen to the ingenious climax of 'The Frevo Dreaming' or the pellucid feel of the melodies he draws out of the title-piece. Besides his own playing, the record is a fine opportunity to hear Winston Clifford, another national treasure, and a brilliant exponent of kit playing that draws the ear without unsettling the group. They will make better records yet, but this one's worth auditioning.

Matthew Gee (1925–79)

TROMBONE

Born in Houston, Gee played with Dizzy Gillespie, Illinois Jacquet and Count Basie in the 1950s, but his most important association was with Duke Ellington, 1959–63. He slipped away from view after that, though he continued to perform in clubs.

***** Jazz By Gee**

Original Jazz Classics OJC 1884 *Gee; Kenny Dorham (t); Ernie Henry (as); Frank Foster (ts); Cecil Payne (bs); Joe Knight (p); John Simmons, Wilbur Ware (b); Art Taylor (d).* 7–8/56.

The notes contain a verdict that Gee was one of the best bop-influenced trombonists, but he seems ill-suited to leadership duties on this pair of serviceable but sloppy sessions. He shares front line with Henry on one and with Dorham, Foster and Payne on the other, and the record seems rowdy and ill-judged. Gee's solos veer between a barking delivery and a much more subtle, almost inward-looking manner: listen to his solo on, of all things, 'Sweet Georgia Brown'. There's a rare chance to hear Henry on the quintet titles, but he doesn't seem at his most interesting. The septet titles are better, more organized, and if nobody exactly covers themselves with glory, at least the music has a curious vividness to it: it sounds more interesting than some of the more efficient records of the period.

Herb Geller (born 1928)

ALTO SAXOPHONE, SOPRANO SAXOPHONE, FLUTE, VOCALS

Geller has told his own musical life-story of late (see below), but the bare bones of it are encompassed by an early sojourn in New York, where he met his wife, pianist Lorraine Walsh, and a long stint on the West Coast with the likes of Shorty Rogers and Maynard Ferguson. Herb and Lorraine co-led their own small group, and after her untimely death he has continued to work mostly with young and adventurous bands.

****** That Geller Feller**

Fresh Sound FSR CD 91 *Geller; Kenny Dorham (t); Harold Land (ts); Lou Levy (p); Ray Brown (b); Lawrence Marable (d).* 3/57.

**** A Jazz Songbook Meeting**

Enja 6006 *Geller; Walter Norris (p); John Schroeder (g); Mike Richmond (b); Adam Nussbaum (d).* 7/88.

*****(*) Birdland Stomp**

Fresh Sound FSRCD 174 *Geller; Kenny Drew (p); Niels-Henning Orsted Pedersen (b); Mark Taylor (d).* 5/90.

****** The Herb Geller Quartet**

VSOP 89 *Geller; Tom Ranier, Jimmy Rowles (p); John Leitham (b); Louie Bellson (d).* 8/93.

Relatively untroubled by fashion, Geller set out as an orthodox, Parker-influenced bopper – *rara avis* on the West Coast in those days – before turning towards a more broadly based and decidedly cooler style which incorporated elements of Paul Desmond, Johnny Hodges and even Benny Goodman, with whom he worked in the later 1950s. Until recent years, he's been hard to spot, buried in a German radio big band and other groups. He is, though, a brilliant songwriter in the tradition of Berlin, Gershwin and Porter, and he has also written musicals.

That Geller Feller is the best of the available sets. The originals – 'S'Pacific View', 'Marable Eyes', 'An Air For The Heir' and 'Melrose And Sam' – are tightly organized and demand considerable inventiveness from a group that frequently sounds much bigger than a sextet. Dorham plays a lovely, crackling solo on the opening track but is otherwise rather anonymous when out on his own. Geller's own introduction to 'Jitterbug Waltz' is wonderfully delicate, with more than a hint of Benny Carter in the tone and phrasing. He also does a fine version of the Arlen–Gershwin rarity, 'Here's What I'm Here For', which John Williams picked up on later in 1957 on the excellent *Plays The Music Of Harold Arlen*. The quintet sessions on *Songbook* are slightly disappointing, largely because Geller's soloing is just off-line.

Confusingly titled, given the existence of an Enja record of the same name, *Birdland Stomp* is way ahead on quality. At 62, Geller has a beautiful tone and the Ellington–Strayhorn medley with which the Spanish-recorded session ends suggests he has renewed his debt to Hodges. His articulation on Parker's 'Cheryl' isn't all it might be, and even the capable Drew sounds a bit sticky, but both are magnificent on the title-tune and 'Autum Nocturne'. Recorded with a heavy emphasis on NHOP's bass, this is nevertheless one of Geller's best latter-day recordings, topped only by the VSOP.

Ruby Braff calls one recent CD *Controlled Nonchalance*. It's a title that would double very happily for the recent Geller release. At 65 he sounds utterly relaxed and in command of his craft. Of the originals, 'Chromatic Cry' and 'Stand-Up Comic' stand out. The first, an exquisite ballad, sounds like something that may have popped into his head during a solo or else in the rehearsal room; the second is a wry look at another group of improvising entertainers – 'Comedy is not the same / social critic is the game' – a vocal tribute topped by a piquant soprano solo. Geller's forte these days is the evocative ballad. 'Isfahan' is totally restructured in the middle section, otherwise played *à la* Hodges. Jimmy Rowles guests on his own evergreen, 'The Peacocks', with its softly eldritch cries and brooding mystery. A wonderful record by a seldom acknowledged master who charted his own course out of orthodox bebop.

*****(*) Plays The Al Cohn Songbook**

Hep CD 2066 *Geller; Tom Ranier (ts, cl, bcl, p); John Leitham (b); Paul Kreibich (d); Ruth Price (v).* 7/94.

Blessed by Flo Cohn, this is an imaginative sample of Al's capacious catalogue of tunes. The addition of multi-instrumentalist Ranier adds a whole range of colours and allows a reprise of Cohn's writing for Zoot Sims. 'Halley's Comet' is the best of these (Zoot's real name was John Haley), though interestingly it's played on alto and clarinet. Ranier's bass clarinet is deployed to superb effect on ''T Ain't No Use', a low, mournful sound that conveys a wealth of emotion. Herb transforms the sinuous line of 'Infinity', and plays a remarkable unaccompanied chorus that underlines how thoughtful an improviser he remains. His late wife Lorraine had once told him that jazz was neither an Olympic sport nor a fashion show, and this solo is entirely true to that principle, relying on basic musicality rather than technique and on felt experience rather than stylistic vogue. A fine record, and a fitting tribute to a great jazz composer.

***** Playing Jazz: The Musical Autobiography Of Herb Geller**

Fresh Sound FSR 5011 *Geller; Tom Ranier (p); John Leitham (b); Paul Kreibich (d); Lothar Atwell, Mike Campbell, Rich Crystal, Stephanie Haynes, Chuck Niles, Polly Podewell (v).* 1/95.

This is a most extraordinary record. Essentially it is a stage musical without images, a journey through Herb's life from the day he gets his first saxophone, to playing opposite Lenny Bruce with Lorraine, to her death and his subsequent attempt to 'Pick Up The Pieces'. His own younger self is portrayed by Lothar Atwell, Lorraine by Stephanie Haynes, with the other singers taking the other roles, held together with a narration by Chuck Niles. Like all musicals, it is an uneasy mix of rather prosaic recitative (Herb's jazz lecture is a particularly embarrassing example) and some glorious songs and playing. His solo on 'My Favorite Songs', a tribute to the great songwriters who are just about to be assailed by rock'n'roll, is as good as he has recorded in years, and Tom Ranier's following chorus is all simplicity and grace. Sometimes it's unconsciously funny, sometimes more effectively so, as when his first teacher, Max Flack, tells Pop Geller: 'One day, listen to Max / A *President* will play the sax'. Indeed. 'Playing jazz is telling your life story' has always been Herb's motto and this one-off record makes that explicit. Not the easiest of listens and unlikely to find its way back to your CD player very often, but an intriguing idea beautifully executed.

*****(*) I'll Be Back**
HEP CD 2074 *Geller; Edward Harris (g); Thomas Biller (b); Heinrich Koebberling (d).* 8/96.

***** You're Looking At Me**
Fresh Sound FSR 5018 *Geller; Jan Lundgren (p); Dave Carpenter (b); Joe LaBarbera (d).* 2/97

The line-up on *I'll Be Back* was the working group of the mid-'90s, and Herb's communication with his young players is consistently impressive. Unusually, he favours guitar over piano in this line-up, and the more open harmonies suit Herb's strongly melodic approach. Most of the original material comes from a musical he wrote about the great Josephine Baker, *La Bakair*. 'A Bitter Dream' and 'Too Little Time' are darkly mature compositions; sandwiching Hoagy Carmichael's 'One Morning In May', they bring the album to a wholly satisfying climax. It begins with Porter's 'Dream Dancing', and one can hear how subtly Geller programmes this and, indeed, all his records, modulating keys, rhythms and emotional pitch, constructing a musical drama rather than a procession of song. Three of the Baker tunes appear on *You're Looking At Me* and the contrast is very striking. It's a long album, perhaps overlong, and very much more conventional in outlook. As he has done consistently over the last decade, Geller uses it as an opportunity to revisit his own musical education and growth – the album even features a photograph of himself at ten, playing his first alto – and to air some favourite melodies, like Strayhorn's 'Orson' and Earle Warren's '9:20 Special'. Herb's tone is tighter and more staccato than usual and his pitching on soprano isn't entirely secure.

The Georgia Melodians

GROUP

Early example of the 'territory' band, although their records were made in New York in the 1920s.

**** Georgia Melodians 1924–1926**
Timeless Historical CBC 1-031 *Ernie Intlehouse, Red Nichols (c); Herb Winfield, Abe Lincoln (tb); Merrit Kenworthy (cl, as, bsx); Clarence Hutchins (cl, ts, bs); Oscar Young (p); Elmer Merry (bj, g); Carl Gerrold (d); Vernon Dlahart (v).* 7/24–4/26.

They came from Savannah, Georgia, to New York City, where the Edison Company recorded them on numerous occasions – although Joe Moore's notes reveal that the band broke up at the end of 1924, they continued to record until 1926, and the personnel listed is somewhat uncertain. Players like Intlehouse, Kenworthy and Hutchins are about as obscure as jazz history can provide, and listening to the music reveals why. This is hot dance music with a generous ration of solos (Edison's vertical-cut discs allowed for much longer playing time than normal 78s) and an honourable intention to swing, but it's poker-stiff at times and disheartening to hear how little the band improved over two years (the very earliest tracks, once available on a Retrieval LP, are missing from this otherwise complete edition, which adds three previously unissued cuts). Staple numbers such as 'Spanish Shawl' and 'Everybody Loves My Baby' can be heard better elsewhere, although they do a respectable job on 'San'. Beautifully clean transfers, though.

The Georgians

GROUP

Early small group of white jazzmen, drawn from the Paul Specht band and led by trumpeter Frank Guarente.

***** The Georgians 1922–23**
Retrieval RTR 79003 *Frank Guarente (t); Ray Stilwell, Russ Morgan, Archie Jones (tb); Johnny O'Donnell, Frank Smith, Dick Johnson, Harold 'Red' Sailier (reeds); Arthur Schutt (p); Russell Deppe (bj); Joe Tarto (tba); Chauncey Morehouse (d).* 11/22–11/23.

A long-overdue CD release for a significant early jazz band. They were originally a contingent from Paul Specht's more straight-laced dance orchestra, working at New York's Hotel Alamac, and, with the excellent Guarente leading the group, they stood at a point somewhere between the simple ensemble style of the Original Memphis Five and the looser, more inventive methods of the early black Chicago bands: Guarente, a white Italian-American, even took some lessons from Joe Oliver in New Orleans. He was the only improviser of any special merit in the band, but Arthur Schutt, hitherto largely ignored by jazz history, contributed an increasingly sophisticated book of arrange-ments. The later tracks here, especially the likes of 'Land Of Cotton Blues' and 'Old Fashioned Love', show real finesse coupled with a proper sense of swing. Most of the tunes have something to commend them, and even novelty pieces like 'Barney Google' are sustained by Guarente's work, although here and there (as in the plodding treatment of 'Farewell Blues') the group fails to make much out of the music. These are the first 24 tracks they recorded, and there is more to come. Top-of-the-line transfers from excellent originals and splendid notes by Mark Berresford.

German Jazz Orchestra

GROUP

A band assembled to demonstrate young jazz talent in Germany.

***** First Take**

Mons 6458 *Thomas Vogel, Thorsten Benkenstein, Claus Reichstaller, Torsten Maas, Stephan Zimmermann, Herman Marstatt (t); Ludwig Nuss, Peter Feil, Bjoern Strangmann, Georg Maus (tb); Klaus Graf, Jens Neufang, Andreas Maile, Mathias Erlewein, Steffen Schorn, Wolfgang Bleibel, Peter Weniger (reeds); Hubert Nuss (p); Henning Sieverts (b); Holger Nell (d); Roland Peil (perc); Jiggs Whigham (cond).* 6/94.

The impersonal name masks a big band fashioned to showcase a new generation of German players and composers. There are nine pieces here by eight hands and, while there's nothing spectacularly attention-grabbing, the music yields plenty of felicities on the way. Thorsten Wollmann's 'Concerto For Soprano Saxophone', with Weniger the very skilful soloist, is the obvious standout, although Frank Reinshagen's 'In The Best Tradition' runs it close, thanks to Steffen Schorn's fine feature role on, of all things, bass saxophone. Avuncular presence: Jiggs Whigham, who conducts.

Bruce Gertz

BASS

Based in Boston, the bassist leads a regular group across close to a decade's worth of work.

****(*) Blueprint**

Freelance FRL CD 017 *Gertz; Jerry Bergonzi (ts); John Abercrombie (g); Adam Nussbaum (d).* 2–3/91.

***** Third Eye**

RAM RMCD 4509 *As above, except add Joey Calderazzo (p).* 10/92.

*****(*) Red Handed**

Double Time DTRCD-155 *As above, except Bruce Barth (p) replaces Calderazzo.* 10/98.

Unlike, say, Ed Schuller, another young bassist-leader, Gertz lacks a roundness of musical personality on the evidence of *Blueprint*. The writing is actually quite interesting, but almost every track on the first record leaves the listener with an uncomfortable yearning to hear exactly the same tune played by a totally different group. Abercrombie carries the whole thing along on his shoulders, with occasional effective interjections by Bergonzi. The two live dates on the RAM disc are more effective. Abercrombie is not quite so dominant; the group sounds seasoned and collaborative, and the two standards, 'Alone Together' and 'In Your Own Sweet Way', are sufficiently different from the usual run to suggest that there may yet be more of interest from this source.

Red Handed is the work of a by-now-settled and substantial group, even if they do rarely get out of their Boston stamping ground. Gertz has thought carefully about his materials, his players and his sources, and has come up with a detailed and absorbing set which is rather like an essay on what a skilful and chops-heavy band like this can do in 1998. 'Giant Steps' is refreshingly cast as a reflective bass-and-drums duet. 'Sun Flash' is tough and assertive and full of appropriate heat. The title-track looks south towards New Orleans, and 'Big Heart' is an open modal sketch which men like Bergonzi and Abercrombie were made to fill in and out. A fine piece of work which surpasses the early stuff by a long way.

Stan Getz (1927–91)

TENOR, SOPRANO AND BARITONE SAXOPHONES

After various big-band engagements, Getz made his name with the Woody Herman orchestra (1947–9). A group leader himself thereafter, he recorded for Roost and Verve in the '50s, though often working in Europe. Won enormous popular acclaim with his albums of bossa nova material, 1962–4, then returned to his own small groups. Financial success allowed him to work as and when he pleased in the '70s and '80s. Toyed with fusion but quickly returned to straight-ahead playing. Though troubled by terminal cancer, he continued to play into the final year of his life. A peerless sound on the saxophone, total fluency of phrasing and a lovely way with every melody he played made him perhaps the most widely admired saxophonist of those who followed in Lester Young's footsteps.

***** Early Stan**

Original Jazz Classics OJC 654 *Getz; Shorty Rogers (t); Earl Swope (tb); George Wallington, Hall Overton (p); Jimmy Raney (g); Curley Russell, Red Mitchell (b); Shadow Wilson, Frank Isola (d).* 3/49–4/53.

****(*) The Brothers**

Original Jazz Classics OJC 008 *Getz; Zoot Sims, Al Cohn, Allen Eager, Brew Moore (ts); Walter Bishop Jr (p); Gene Ramey (b); Charlie Perry (d).* 4/49.

***** Prezervation**

Original Jazz Classics OJC 706 *Getz; Kai Winding (tb); Al Haig (p); Gene Ramey, Tommy Potter (b); Roy Haynes, Stan Levey (d); Junior Parker, Blossom Dearie, Jimmy Raney (v).* 6/49–2/50.

***** Stan Getz Quartets**

Original Jazz Classics OJC 121 *Getz; Al Haig, Tony Aless (p); Gene Ramey, Tommy Potter, Percy Heath (b); Stan Levey, Roy Haynes, Don Lamond (d).* 6/49–4/50.

After starring as one of Woody Herman's 'Four Brothers' sax section, and delivering a luminous ballad solo on the 1948 'Early Autumn', Getz went out on his own and at first seemed much like the rest of the Lester Young-influenced tenormen: a fast, cool stylist with a sleek tone and a delivery that soothed nerves jangled by bebop. The 'Brothers' idea was pursued in the session on OJC 008 (the rest of the disc is devoted to a Zoot Sims–Al Cohn date): the five tenors trade punches with panache and it's a fun session, if hardly an important one (the CD includes three alternative takes not on the LP issue). *Early Stan* finds Getz as a sideman with a septet led by Terry Gibbs and a quartet under Jimmy Raney's direction. Bright, appealing cool-bop on the Gibbs date, but the

Raney session, from 1953, is more substantial, the quartet whisking through four stretching exercises, including 'Round Midnight'.

Prezervation rounds up some odds and ends, including an improbable alliance with Junior Parker on two tracks and a Haig sextet date with Winding and two vocal duets by Jimmy Raney and Blossom Dearie! Not very important. But the *Quartets* set is an attractive dry run for the upcoming four-piece sessions for Roost, and it features the tenorman in very lithe form. The sound on most of these issues was fairly indifferent to start with, and these latest editions emerge well enough.

♛ ** The Complete Roost Recordings**

Roost 859622-2 3CD *Getz; Sanford Gold, Duke Jordan, Horace Silver, Al Haig (p); Jimmy Raney, Johnny Smith (g); Eddie Safranski, Teddy Kotick, Bill Crow, Leonard Gaskin, Bob Carter (b); Frank Isola, Tiny Kahn, Roy Haynes, Don Lamond, Morey Feld (d); Count Basie Orchestra on three tracks.* 5/50–12/54.

So much attention has fallen on Getz's later work that these magnificent sessions are sometimes overlooked. No longer any need for that, now that the complete works have been gathered across three generously filled CDs, with three 'new' tracks. The earliest tracks, from a session in May 1950, catch a young man with his head full of bebop and his heart heavy with swing-era romanticism. Those contrary strains sometimes come together, such as in the headily beautiful 'Yesterdays', in a marriage of intellect and emotion that is rare not only in Getz's work but in jazz itself. These two early dates, one with Al Haig, one with Horace Silver, are little short of electrifying. By 1951, he already sounds like the more settled, invincible Getz, but the short track-lengths (a relic of the 78 era) give the music considerable point and direction. The live session from Boston's Storyville Club with Jimmy Raney has long been a prized classic, both musicians unreeling one great solo after another. Two studio dates with a similar band are at a lower voltage but are scarcely less impressive. Eight tracks with Johnny Smith, including the achingly lovely 'Moonlight In Vermont', offer Getz the lyricist in fullest flow, while the three with Basie at Birdland are like a fun bonus. There is so much top-flight jazz in this set that it's quite indispensable and, brought together in one place and remastered to a consistent standard, it's breathtaking.

(***) At Carnegie Hall

Fresh Sound FSCD 1003 *Getz; Kai Winding (tb); Al Haig, Duke Jordan (p); Jimmy Raney (g); Bill Crow, Tommy Potter (b); Frank Isola, Roy Haynes (d).* 12/49–11/52.

(***) Birdland Sessions

Fresh Sound FSR-CD 149 *Getz; Horace Silver, Duke Jordan (p); Jimmy Raney (g); Nelson Boyd, Charles Mingus, Gene Ramey (b); Phil Brown, Connie Kay (d).* 4–8/52.

There's some excellent Getz on both these discs – but we have to withhold a firm recommendation because of the sound-quality. He sounds in prime form at both of the two Carnegie Hall concerts on FSCD 1003, but the sound deteriorates (frustratingly, after a good start) to complete muddiness by the end of the 1952 show. Jordan tends to toss out clichés, but the interplay with Raney is as subtle as usual. The Birdland recordings have been available on various pirate LPs over the years, and this edition is about as listenable as the others. For Getz addicts only.

***** Together For The First Time**

Fresh Sound FSCD-1022 *Getz; Chet Baker (t); Russ Freeman, Don Trenner (p); Carson Smith, Joe Mondragon, Gene Englund (b); Larry Bunker, Shelly Manne, Jimmy Pratt (d).* 9/52–12/53.

An interesting discovery: the Mulligan quartet at the Haig with Getz subbing for the leader. He sounds perfectly at home with Baker, Smith and Bunker, and there are some forthright variations on six tunes, including 'Half Nelson' and 'Yardbird Suite'. A subsequent quintet version of 'All The Things You Are' is a lot more dispirited, and there are four quartet airshots from 1952 to fill up the disc, which is in surprisingly good sound for the most part, the Haig titles having been apparently recorded by Richard Bock.

*****(*) Stan Getz Plays**

Verve 833535-2 *Getz; Jimmy Rowles, Duke Jordan (p); Jimmy Raney (g); Bob Whitlock, Bill Crow (b); Frank Isola, Max Roach (d).* 12/52–1/54.

****** At The Shrine**

Verve 513753-2 *Getz; Bob Brookmeyer (vtb); John Williams (p); Bill Anthony (b); Art Madigan, Frank Isola (d).* 11/54.

Getz's long association with Norman Granz and Verve starts here. *Plays* features some of the best recording he was given in the period, and much of the playing is as fine as it is on the Roost dates, with the 1954 quartet session with Rowles particularly pretty. But it's the live sessions from The Shrine in Los Angeles, long a collector's-item album, which stand out. Getz plays with unstinting invention throughout, Brookmeyer is a witty and unfailingly apposite partner, and the remastered sound is fine.

****** The West Coast Sessions**

Verve 531935-2 3CD *Getz; Conte Candoli (t); Lou Levy (p); Leroy Vinnegar (b); Stan Levey, Shelly Manne (d).* 8/55–8/57.

****** West Coast Jazz**

Verve 557549-2 *As above, except omit Levey.* 8/55.

****** The Steamer**

Verve 547771-2 *As above, except add Stan Levey (d); omit Candoli and Manne.* 11/56.

*****(*) Award Winner**

Verve 543320-2 *As above.* 8/57.

What a great period for tenor saxophone playing this was, with Rollins laying down his masterpieces on one coast and Getz on the other. Given that Getz is scarcely the prototypical West Coast player, there's a certain irony in the situation. With this distinctively Californian group, though, he set down a quite classic series of sessions, once issued as three LPs, now expanded to three discs with a number of alternative takes. Candoli, present on the original *West Coast Jazz* date, plays handsomely and is an excellent foil, but it's Getz and the rhythm sections who unfurl the most gorgeous colours: stomping on 'Shine', profoundly inventive on the blues in 'Blues For Mary Jane', winsomely beautiful in ballads like 'You're Blasé'. Relatively unprepared, and programmed around tunes they all knew, the records are, like Art Pepper's rather different sessions for Contemporary, sax–rhythm dates of intuitive greatness. For those who'd prefer a pocket edition of highlights, Verve also have *Best Of The West Coast Sessions* (537084-2). They have also brought back the three original albums in their Master Edition series, which makes a handsome alternative since each has the various alternative takes added to the programmes. Our favourite remains *The Steamer*, but all three offer a string of great rewards.

***** Stan Meets Chet**

Verve 837436-2 *Getz; Chet Baker (t); Jodie Christian (p); Victor Sproles (b); Marshall Thompson (d).* 2/57.

***** Stan Getz And The Oscar Peterson Trio**

Verve 827826-2 *Getz; Oscar Peterson (p); Herb Ellis (g); Ray Brown (b).* 10/57.

***** At The Opera House**

Verve 831272-2 *Getz; J.J Johnson (tb); Oscar Peterson (p); Herb Ellis (g); Ray Brown (b); Connie Kay (d).* 10/57.

***** Getz Meets Mulligan In Hi-Fi**

Verve 849392-2 *Getz; Gerry Mulligan (bs, ts); Lou Levy (p); Ray Brown (b); Stan Levey (d).* 10/57.

***** Stan Getz & Dizzy Gillespie: Jazz Masters 25**

Verve 521852-2 *Getz; Dizzy Gillespie (t); J.J Johnson (tb); Paul Gonsalves, Coleman Hawkins (ts); John Lewis, Lalo Schifrin, Wynton Kelly (p); Herb Ellis (g); Ray Brown, Art Davis, Wendell Marshall (b); Max Roach, Stan Levey, Chuck Lampkin, J.C Heard (d); Candido Camero (perc).* 12/53–11/60.

Getz's 1950s tracks are still incomplete as far as current CD representation is concerned, but they're getting there. As a body of records, curiously few stand out: there's certainly nothing here on a par with the West Coast dates listed above. The meeting with Baker was done in Chicago with a local rhythm section and it feels like an on-the-hoof event: they simply blow together. Next to Getz's meetings with Dizzy Gillespie, this is pale stuff. The session with Peterson is as ebullient as expected, and the Opera House concert with J.J. Johnson includes some extrovert playing from everyone, especially on a snorting romp through Bud Powell's 'Blues In The Closet'. Listening to this kind of playing makes one wonder at Getz's reputation for being a featherlight stylist (he preferred 'stomping tenorman'). The session with Mulligan is beautifully dovetailed: although, somewhat notoriously, they chose to swap instruments for part of the session, the sound of the two horns speaks of a tonal fraternity which sounds rare and entrancing. The *Jazz Masters* disc picks four tracks from two studio dates with Gillespie, plus a JATP piece and a jovial meeting with Gonsalves and Hawkins in 1957.

*****(*) In Sweden 1958–60**

Dragon DRCD 263 2CD *Getz; Benny Bailey (t); Ake Persson (tb); Erik Norström, Bjarne Nerem (ts); Lars Gullin (bs); Jan Johansson, Bengt Hallberg (p); Gunnar Johnson, Ray Brown, Torbjørn Hultcrantz, Georg Riedel (b); William Schiopffe, Sune Spangberg, Joe Harris (d).* 8–9/58.

A spell in Stockholm led to some recording with Swedish musicians and these admirable sessions were the result, a Swedish variation on the cool manner with Getz sounding perfectly comfortable in Hallberg's and Johansson's charts. Gullin and Hallberg himself shine too – and so does the remarkable Johansson, whose status as the lost master of Swedish jazz is further enhanced by his playing here. The previous edition of this music has now been beefed up with some concert and radio material from 1960 and it's a close-to-indispensable package.

***** Stan Getz With Cal Tjader**

Original Jazz Classics OJC 275 *Getz; Cal Tjader (vib); Vince Guaraldi (p); Eddie Duran (g); Scott LaFaro (b); Billy Higgins (d).* 2/58.

A one-off session with Cal Tjader which looks forward with some prescience to the bossa nova records that were to come: certainly the coolly pleasant backings of Tjader's rhythm section make up a cordial meeting-ground for tenor and vibes to play lightly appealing solos, and the charming version of 'I've Grown Accustomed To Her Face' is a winner.

*****(*) Stan Getz At Large Plus! Vol. 1**

Jazz Unlimited JUCD 2001 *Getz; Jan Johanssen (p); Daniel Jordan (b); William Schiopffe (d).* 1/60.

*****(*) Stan Getz At Large Plus! Vol. 2**

Jazz Unlimited JUCD 2002 *As above.* 1/60.

Two very rare Getz albums, recorded in Copenhagen with a local team, and he sounds in wonderful form throughout. The opening 'Night And Day' on the first disc is delivered with heavenly grace and is sustained over chorus after chorus at a perfect tempo. There are some interesting choices of material – by Johnny Mandel, Al Cohn, Harold Land – and though both albums are weighted towards slow to mid-tempos, Getz stays concentrated and inspired throughout. The rhythm section are capable rather than challenging, and the sound is slightly less than ideal, but the music is terrific.

***** Cool Velvet / Voices**

Verve 527773-2 *Getz; Herbie Hancock, Hank Jones (p); Dave Hildinger (vib); Jim Hall (g); Blanchie Birdsong (hp); Freddy Dutton, Ron Carter (b); Sperie Karas, Grady Tate (d); Artie Butler, Bobby Rosengarden, Bill Horwath (perc); strings, voices.* 3/60–12/66.

It was inevitable that Getz would do a full-blown encounter with strings, and Russ Garcia's arrangements for the *Cool Velvet* album are workmanlike settings for the lovely sound. *Voices* was arranged by Claus Ogerman, and in the brief frameworks he devises Getz sounds professionally involved though not much more. Pleasant music, but hardly a competitor to the indispensable *Focus*.

*****(*) Jazz Samba**

Verve 521413-2 *Getz; Charlie Byrd (g); Keter Betts (b); Gene Byrd (g, b); Buddy Deppenschmidt, Bill Reichenbach (d).* 2/62.

***** Big Band Bossa Nova**

Verve 825771-2 *Getz; Doc Severinsen, Bernie Glow, Joe Ferrante, Clark Terry (t); Tony Studd, Bob Brookmeyer, Willie Dennis (tb); Ray Alonge (frhn); Jerry Sanfino, Ray Beckenstein (f); Eddie Caine (af); Babe Clark, Walt Levinsky (cl); Romeo Penque (bcl); Hank Jones (p); Jim Hall (g); Tommy Williams (b); Johnny Rae (d); Jose Paulo, Carmen Cossa (perc).* 8/62.

*****(*) Jazz Samba Encore**

Verve 823613-2 *Getz; Antonio Carlos Jobim (g, p); Luiz Bonfa (g); George Duvivier, Tommy Williams, Don Payne (b); Paulo Ferreira, Jose Carlos, Dave Bailey (d); Maria Toledo (v).* 2/63.

****** Getz / Gilberto**

Verve 521414-2 *Getz; Antonio Carlos Jobim (p); Joao Gilberto (g, v); Tommy Williams (b); Milton Banana (d); Astrud Gilberto (v).* 3/63.

***** Getz Au Go Go**

Verve 821725-2 *Getz; Gary Burton (vib); Kenny Burrell (g); Gene Cherico (b); Joe Hunt, Helcio Milito (d); Astrud Gilberto (v).* 64.

*****(*) The Girl From Ipanema**

Verve 823611-2 4CD *As above discs, except add Steve Kuhn (p), Laurindo Almeida (g), Edison Machado, Jose Soorez, Luiz Parga (perc).* 62–64.

*****(*) Round Midnight: Stan Getz**

Verve 841445 *As above.* 62–64.

Getz's big commercial break. However much he protested that he played other stuff besides the bossa nova in later years, his most lucrative records – and some of his best playing – were triggered by the hit versions of first 'Desafinado' from the first album and then 'The Girl From Ipanema' with Gilberto, the tune that a thousand wine-bar bands have had to play nightly ever since. The original albums still hold up very well. Getz actually plays with as much pungency and alertness as anywhere else and, even though the backings sometimes threaten to slip into a sleepwalk, there's always an interesting tickle from the guitar or the bass to keep the music alive; and the melodies, by Bonfa, Gilberto and Jobim, have proved their quality by how well they've endured. *Jazz Samba* and *Jazz Samba Encore* are excellent, but the famous *Getz/Gilberto*, which has hummed seductively round cafés, wine-bars and bedrooms for over 30 years, remains peerless. Both the latter and *Jazz Samba* have been remastered in Verve's Master Edition series.

The big-band set has some clever arrangements by Gary McFarland, but sundering the intimacy of these whispery settings seems a fairly pointless exercise. And *Getz Au Go Go*, which had the vocals by Gilberto dubbed in subsequently, sounds just a mite too forceful, as though Getz were hurrying to push on to something else. Astrud Gilberto's singing isn't so much an acquired taste as a languid, ghostly sound on the breeze; many will prefer Maria Toledo on the third record listed. *The Girl From Ipanema* collects all the music plus the session for *Stan Getz/ Laurindo Almeida*. The *Round Midnight* disc is a functional one-volume sampler with all the hits.

****** Nobody Else But Me**

Verve 521660-2 *Getz; Gary Burton (vib); Gene Cherico (b); Joe Hunt (d).* 3/64.

Unreleased for 30 years, this one's a marvel. Supposedly put on the shelf so as not to cause any distraction from Getz's bossa nova hit-making, the music here – amazingly, the only studio recording by a group that was a popular concert attraction – is lush and romantic, with the backbone of a master improviser's intelligence. Burton contributes '6-Nix-Pix-Flix' and opens up the harmonic base just enough to give Stan clear, lucid space for his solos. 'Summertime' is a classic, 'Waltz For A Lovely Wife' is rapture, but there's nothing less than great here.

***** Stan Getz & Bill Evans**

Verve 833802-2 *Getz; Bill Evans (p); Richard Davis (b); Elvin Jones (d).* 5/64.

A curiously unsatisfying match. If one expected feathery ballads and lavishly romantic music, the results were the complete opposite: the only real ballad is 'But Beautiful'; the rest go from mid-tempo to stomp, and Davis and Jones break up the beat and harry the two nominal leaders. Both can handle it, but it's disappointing that something on the level of the almost telepathic Evans–Jim Hall records wasn't secured. The CD has several alternative and unissued takes.

****** Focus**

Verve 521419-2 *Getz; Eddie Sauter Orchestra.* 4–6/65.

Nobody ever arranged for Getz as well as this, and Sauter's luminous and shimmering scores continue to bewitch. This isn't art-jazz scoring: Sauter had little of Gil Evans's *misterioso* power, and he was shameless about tugging at heartstrings. But within those parameters – and Getz, the most pragmatic of soloists, was only too happy to work within them – he made up the most emotive of frameworks. It doesn't make much sense as a suite, or a concerto; just as a series of episodes with the tenor gliding over and across them. In 'Her', the tune dedicated to Getz's mother, the soloist describes a pattern which is resolved in the most heart-stopping of codas. This was surely Getz's finest hour. The latest version is in Verve's Master Edition series, and the previously spotty CD edition has been significantly improved, though there's still a degree of tape hiss if you're listening for it.

*****(*) Sweet Rain**

Verve 815054-2 *Getz; Chick Corea (p); Ron Carter (b); Grady Tate (d).* 3/67.

This was an excellent group, and the youthful Corea proved to be a sympathetic and encouraging partner for the cantankerous leader. Maybe the pianist is too sweet and noodling at times, but 'O Grande Amor' and 'Windows' blend the brightness of Getz's bossa nova years with a spare, precise lyricism, and Carter and Tate have the measure of the situation.

***** What The World Needs Now**

Verve 557450-2 *Getz; Chick Corea, Herbie Hancock (p); Jim Hall, Phil Upchurch (g); Walter Booker, Ron Carter (b); Roy Haynes, Curtis Prince, Grady Tate (d); Bill Horwath (cymbalom); Artie Butler, Bobby Rosengarden (perc); strings, brass, choir.* 12/66–1/68.

An album of Burt Bacharach tunes, arranged by Richard Evans, which Getz strolls through, sometimes all but overpowered by the surrounding players (the remastering does nothing to diminish their role, either). As if to compensate, he plays more fiercely than usual in places, and there are some surprising stretches of tonal distortion. 'The Look Of Love' finds his sound magnified by studio reverb. A period piece, worth reviving, but hardly a Getzian milestone.

*****(*) Dynasty**

Verve 839117-2 2CD *Getz; Eddie Louiss (org); René Thomas (g); Bernard Lubat (d).* 1–3/71.

Recorded at a live engagement in London, Getz was in happy and swinging form here, and the quartet stretch out as far as they want on the material. Louiss is far more flexible and discreet than most jazz organists and Getz is untroubled by anything the instrument produces, while the reliable Thomas takes some excellent solos.

*****(*) The Best Of The Verve Years Vol. 2**
Verve 517330-2 2CD *Getz; various groups as above.* 52–71.

*****(*) Verve Jazz Masters: Stan Getz**
Verve 519823-2 *Getz; various groups, as above.*

The double-CD compilation goes for a wide-ranging, packed retrospective, from the earliest Verve material up to *Dynasty*; the VJM disc is more modest but includes 'Her', 'Desafinado', 'Shine' and 'Ipanema'. Each would be a fine introduction to this big period of Getz's music.

****(*) Captain Marvel**
Columbia 468412-2 *Getz; Chick Corea (p); Stanley Clarke (b); Tony Williams (d); Airto Moreira (perc).* 3/72.

**** Best Of Two Worlds**
Columbia CK 33703 *Getz; Albert Dailey (p); Joao Gilberto (g. perc, v); Oscar Castro-Nueves (g); Clint Houston, Steve Swallow (b); Billy Hart, Grady Tate (d); Airto Moreira, Ruben Bassini, Ray Armando, Sonny Carr (perc); Heloisa Buarque De Hollanda (v).* 5/75.

***** The Master**
Columbia 467138-2 *Getz; Albert Dailey (p); Clint Houston (b); Billy Hart (d).* 10/75.

***** Live At Montmartre**
Steeplechase SCS 1073 2CD *Getz; JoAnne Brackeen (p); Niels-Henning Orsted Pedersen (b); Billy Hart (d).* 1/77.

***** The Essential Stan Getz**
Columbia 460819-2 *As above discs.*

***** The Lyrical Stan Getz**
Columbia 471512-2 *As above discs.*

This wasn't a vintage period for Getz. The Columbia albums range from perfunctory to mildly engaging: nothing very wrong with the settings (aside from *Best Of Two Worlds*, which is a very pallid re-run of the bossa nova years), but Getz's own playing has taken on a wayward, purposeless quality, and the licks he sometimes fell back on when bored recur frequently enough to be troublesome. *Captain Marvel* was meant to be an energetic new beginning, but the noise created by Moreira drowns out even Williams at times, and Getz never sounds at ease, despite some of his old gumption breaking through. The Montmartre set suffers from a rhythm section that don't really work with him. *The Master*, though, is a better record; it doesn't shake the earth but it finds the leader very comfortable on the bed of rich chords which Albert Dailey lays down.

Columbia have at least two anthologies available and each is a quite attractive selection from this somewhat spotty period. *The Lyrical* would just get the nod since it concentrates on what the title suggests.

*****(*) Billy Highstreet Samba**
Emarcy 838771-2 *Getz; Mitch Forman (ky); Chuck Loeb (g); Mark Egan (b); Victor Lewis (d); Bobby Thomas (perc).*

*****(*) The Dolphin**
Concord CCD 4158 *Getz; Lou Levy (p); Monty Budwig (b); Victor Lewis (d).* 5/81.

*****(*) Spring Is Here**
Concord CCD 4500 *As above.* 5/81.

****** Pure Getz**
Concord CCD 4188 *Getz; Jim McNeely (p); Marc Johnson (b); Victor Lewis (d).* 1/82.

****** Blue Skies**
Concord CCD 4676 *As above.* 1/82.

*****(*) Live In Paris**
Dreyfus FDM 36577-9 *As above.* 82.

Not so much a miraculous return to form as an artist reasserting his artistry. Getz passed fusion leanings by and moved back to his greatest strength, tenor and rhythm section, of which the Concord albums are triumphant illustrations. *The Dolphin* and its recently issued companion, *Spring Is Here*, offer live sessions with a first-class band: Getz is at his most expansive here, reeling off very long but consistently expressive and well-argued solos, his tone a shade harder but still with a misty elegance that softens phrases at key moments. *Pure Getz*, recorded in the studio, is perhaps even better: there is a celebrated version of Billy Strayhorn's 'Blood Count', which alternates between harsh cries and soft murmurings and which became a staple part of Getz's live set at the time; but the variations on 'Come Rain Or Come Shine' and a terse 'Sippin' At Bells' are probably even more masterful. But *Billy Highstreet Samba* is by no means a second-rate Getz album: here, for once, he adapted well to what could have been a fusion-led project. The material (by Loeb and Forman) is unusually perspicacious, and Getz responds with bright and committed playing against a group more concerned with playing music than licks. There is also a strong 'Body And Soul' and a couple of rare outings for Getz on soprano.

Blue Skies is a new discovery, dating from the same sessions as *Pure Getz*, and though we might have given it a fractionally lower rating there is still some transcendent playing, especially on the slower pieces: Getz's gravitas on a ballad was never more perfectly revealed than in the likes of 'How Long Has This Been Going On?'. The live date is a valuable pendant to the studio sessions, and this was clearly a band in top gear: the only slight drawback is some extra reverb added to the remix, with McNeely's piano also sounding imperfect.

***** The Stockholm Concerts**
Verve 537555-2 3CD *Getz; Chet Baker (t, v); Jim McNeely (p); George Mraz (b); Victor Lewis (d).* 2/83.

*****(*) Quintessence Vol. 1**
Concord CD 4807-2 *As above.* 2/83.

Stan meets Chet, again – but in very unhappy circumstances. The saxophonist at times almost bullies Baker offstage during these concerts, and the trumpeter often responds by literally quaking through his parts. The Verve set is an unhappy encounter, not helped by McNeely playing almost on autopilot (he had got off a plane from Australia only hours before!). And yet ... Getz himself plays some magnificent things, such as the first show's quite wonderful 'We'll Be Together Again' and 'How Long Has This Been Going On?'. The original pair of Sonet LPs has been expanded to a full three-CD set and, while the blemishes will trouble some, for Getz's playing alone many will prioritize this one. The Concord album sees the group travelling to Norway for the next stop on the tour. Maybe they had settled down a bit; either way, Baker sounds considerably happier and in stronger voice, and even Stan thaws a bit. Excellent concert sound.

****** Anniversary**
Emarcy 838769-2 *Getz; Kenny Barron (p); Rufus Reid (b); Victor Lewis (d).* 7/87.

****** Serenity**
Emarcy 838770-2 *As above.* 7/87.

Pristine examples of his art. Sometimes it seems as if there is nothing there but his sound, the 'incredibly lovely sound', as he once murmured to himself, and it's possible to find a strange, inward-looking emptiness at the heart of this music. Certainly he had no pretence to playing anything but long, self-regarding lines that had little to do with anything going on around him: impeccably though both of these rhythm sections play, their function is purely to sketch in as painless a backdrop as possible for the unfurling of Getz's sound. But it is such a breathtaking beauty he creates that these might be the most sheerly pretty jazz albums of their day. The two Emarcy sets are splendidly recorded and let the listener bathe in the rapturous sound of the tenor.

*****(*) Yours And Mine**
Concord CCD 4740 *Getz; Kenny Barron (p); Ray Drummond (b); Ben Riley (d).* 6/89.

*****(*) Soul Eyes**
Concord CCD 4783 *As above, except add Yasuito Mori (b).* 6–7/89.

What a trouper. Here's the old man in never-say-die fettle on some of his favourite standards, plus a nice Kenny Barron tune and Thad Jones's title-song. Caught live at Glasgow's Jazz Festival, the sound isn't ideally close, but you can catch most of the nuances and hear enough to tell that Getz was still the man. The rest of the concert appears on *Soul Eyes*, together with three tracks from a Copenhagen show a week later, with Mori in for Drummond. Getz sounds a bit sour on 'Slow Boat To China', but the following 'Warm Valley' is divine. Two excellent additions to the canon.

***** Apasionado**
A&M 395297-2 *Getz; orchestra.* 89.

Though already troubled by his terminal illness, Getz still plays handsomely on this superior example of mood music. His earlier records with strings wait to be reissued, so this one – with keyboards substituting for the string parts and a mélange of soft rhythms and whispering brass in support – will serve to illustrate this most soothing side of his art.

*****(*) People Time**
Emarcy 510134-2 2CD *Getz; Kenny Barron (p).* 3/91.

Cut not long before his death, Getz has his moments of struggle on this imposing, double-length series of duets with Kenny Barron, his last keyboard partner. Some of the butter has run out of his tone, and unlike many valedictory recordings there isn't a compensating ardour of delivery to go with it: he sounds as if he's just trying to be the same old Getz. But knowledge of his impending death still, inevitably, lends a poignancy to this music which even those previously unmoved by the saxophonist's work may find themselves responding to. Nor should Barron be relegated to the role of mere accompanist: he is a full-fledged partner in these pieces and he turns in some of the best improvising.

***** A Life In Jazz: A Musical Biography**
Verve 535119-2 *Getz; various Verve sessions as listed above.* 1/52–3/91.

Released to tie in with a Getz biography, this is an interesting hotchpotch rather than a definitive sampler. It rescues a few rarities – 'Hymn To The Orient' from *Plays*, a solo with Ella Fitzgerald from her *Like Someone In Love* album, and the sultry backing to Abbey Lincoln on 'I'm In Love' from her *You Gotta Pay The Band*. For someone who doesn't have too much Stan, this is a nice variation on the normal hits selection.

Terje Gewelt

BASS

Has done sterling service as a sideman with the likes of Tommy Smith, and this is a somewhat belated leadership bow for the experienced Norwegian.

*****(*) Hide And Seek**
Resonant RM2-2 *Gewelt; Jason Rebello (p); Jon Eberson, Staffan William-Olsson (g); Päl Thowsen, Billy Cobham (d).* 11/98.

Fresh, lively but considered music from a group which Gewelt leads from the front, while suggesting that he has the sense to know that bassist-leaders can also be crashing bores. There's no boring modal blowing, nothing pushed past its useful lifespan – only four of the ten tracks even break the five-minute barrier. Some of it is memorably beautiful. 'End Off ...' is a Metheny-like ballad with unemphatic but gorgeous chord-changes that Rebello and Eberson shape to beguiling effect. But the record works through a broad stylistic range without making it seem like a shopping-list. There's free playing, nostalgically old-fashioned fusion ('Hide And Seek' itself, which has guest Billy Cobham sitting in), even a coolly mediated blues in Carla Bley's 'Sing Me Softly Of The Blues', which is followed by an almost countrified track featuring William-Olsson. It's a sampler of what Gewelt can do and what kind of things he's interested in and, though that recipe often turns into self-indulgence and waste, here it's refreshing.

Tiziana Ghiglioni (born 1956)

VOCAL

Based in Milan, Ghiglioni is an Italian whose dedication to jazz singing begins with the classic style yet goes far further, taking in the songs of Steve Lacy, Monk and Giorgio Gaslini.

****(*) Streams**

Splasc(h) H 104 *Ghiglioni; Luca Bonvini (tb); Maurizio Caldura Nunez (ss, ts); Luca Flores (p); Franco Nesti (b); Alessandro Fabbri (d).* 12/84.

***** Onde**

Splasc(h) H 133 *Ghiglioni; Carlo Actis Dato (ts, bs, bcl); Claudio Lodati (g); Enrico Fazio (b); Fiorenzo Sordini (d, perc, mar).* 6/87.

***** Yet Time**

Splasc(h) H 150 *Ghiglioni; Roberto Ottaviano (ss); Stefano Battaglia (p); Paolino Dalla Porta (b); Tiziano Tononi (d).* 3/88.

***** Lyrics**

Splasc(h) H 348 *Ghiglioni; Paul Bley (p).* 3/91.

***** Something Old, Something New, Something Borrowed, Something Blue**

Splasc(h) H 370 *Ghiglioni; Enrico Rava (t); Giancarlo Schiaffini (tb); Steve Lacy (ss); Umberto Petrin (p); Attilo Zanchi (b); Tiziano Tononi (d, perc).* 4 & 5/92.

Since she seems to appear in a quite different setting almost from record to record, it's a little difficult to focus on the merits of Tiziana Ghiglioni's singing. Her albums for Splasc(h) find her both fronting groups and working as an integral element within them: she is almost peripheral to *Onde*, where she guests with Actis Dato's Art Studio band, yet her singing on 'Rosso Di Sera' and 'Voci' is a striking wordless invention. *Streams* and *Yet Time* find her taking a Norma Winstone-like role of alternating pastoral scat with cool readings of lyrics. She has a big, rangy voice which she's reluctant to use in a big way, so many of her vocal improvisations sound restrained; fluency doesn't come easy to her, either. Yet the improvisation on Ornette Coleman's 'Round Trip' on *Yet Time* is sustained with great skill, and her meeting with Schiaffini, which includes bare-bones readings of 'When I Fall In Love' and 'All Blues' as well as more *outré* material, shows her unfazed by working alone with an improvising trombonist. Her enunciation always makes one aware that she's not singing in her native language, and her self-written lyrics are awkward, but she's a charismatic performer.

***** Somebody Special**

Soul Note 121156-2 *Ghiglioni; Steve Lacy (ss); Franco D'Andrea (p); Jean-Jacques Avenel (b); Oliver Johnson (d).* 4/86.

***** I'll Be Around**

Soul Note 121256-2 *Ghiglioni; Enrico Rava (t); Mal Waldron (p).* 7–8/89.

Ghiglioni's albums for Soul Note seek out a more conservative context, with mixed results. Steve Lacy's iron presence is the dominant feature of *Somebody Special* and, while Ghiglioni is a better singer than Irene Aebi, and the quartet are in excellent form, the vocalist doesn't make a strong case for besting Lacy's sometimes intractable forms. *I'll Be Around* is dedicated to Billie Holiday, an inspiration rather than an influence, and in this collection of deathly slow ballads the singer does surprisingly well with Waldron and Rava, the latter especially at his most hauntingly poignant.

***** Sings Gaslini**

Soul Note 121297-2 *Ghiglioni; Renato Geremia (vn); Roberto Bonati (b); Giampiero Prina (d); string ensemble.* 1–2/95.

The songs, lyrics and arrangements are all by Giorgio Gaslini, and they elicit Ghiglioni's most measured, thoughtful work. Sometimes one wishes that she'd let go a little, in the manner of some of her less formal records: the singing is beautifully done, and the arrangements are impeccable, but this is a very temperate climate, and across a CD's length it's a little becalmed. The most *outré* moments are actually provided by the eccentric violin of Geremia.

***** My Essential Duke**

Philology W122.2 *Ghiglioni; Tony Scott (cl, p); Maurizio Caldura (as, ts); Lee Konitz (as); Giovanni Ceccarelli, Gianluca Tagliazucchi, Roberto Cipelli (p); Attilio Zanchi (b); Gianni Cazzola (d); Cristiano Pecchio, Lena Aboo, Camilla Battaglia (v).* 2–7/95.

Certainly an untypical Ellington tribute, with Ghiglioni's vocals varying between irreverence, sulkiness and pure bop-scat. She earns the stars through sheer *chutzpah*, really: the eccentricities never stop, with Scott mumbling an Italian monologue on one track (and playing pretty strange clarinet), Tiziana tootling on a toy sax on another and having her seven-year-old daughter sing on another. Konitz ambles on for two bemused appearances. Main playing honours go to Caldura and Cipelli, but it's the singer's show.

****(*) Spellbound**

YVP 3058 *Ghiglioni; Gianluigi Trovesi (ss, as, picc-cl, bcl); Guido Di Leone (g); Attilio Zanchi (b); Gianni Cazzola (d).* 2/96.

A typically uncompromised project from the singer, with originals primarily by Zanchi and words by the vocalist. Trovesi acts as her front-line partner. There are several fine pieces, with the curious reworking of 'Cheek To Cheek' particularly good; yet there's a somewhat bizarre tendency for Ghiglioni to try to adopt a hipsterish persona which doesn't really suit her at all.

Maurizio Giammarco (born 1952)

TENOR SAXOPHONE

Italian saxophonist steeped in his local hard-bop tradition.

*****(*) Inside**

Soul Note 121254 *Giammarco; Mauro Grossi (p, ky); Piero Leveratto (b); Andrea Melani (d).* 7/93.

Like his late, much-lamented countryman, Massimo Urbani, Giammarco brings something quite fresh and unexpected to the saxophone, a quality of intonation or *accent* one would simply not hear from an American player. Giammarco attracted attention with a symphonic arrangement of pieces by Enrico Rava, and he has also led a notably vibrant electric group called Lingomania. His free-tonal compositions and improvisations alternate unfamiliar-sounding progressions with chromatic blues that often recall Joe Lovano's more way-out pieces. *Inside* features the group he calls his Heart Quartet, a band centred on Leveratto's rattly, plucked bass and Melani's Motian-influenced cymbals. The opening 'Urgency' establishes the pace and idiom without wasting a gesture, setting up for a more relaxed and swinging mood in the remaining nine tracks. Grossi sounds like a dozen European keyboard players but he never puts a foot wrong in the context of this particular music, and his solo on 'Inside News' is a model of spareness and logic. Giammarco himself favours a nasal, vocalized tone on both tenor and soprano. It sounds perfect on things like Carlo Alberto Rossi's 'E Se Domani', which closes the set, but it isn't quite limber enough for the faster items.

Michael Gibbs (born 1937)

TROMBONE, PIANO, BANDLEADER

Born in Rhodesia, Gibbs studied at Berklee and Lenox in the USA and came to London in 1965, where he worked as a leader and a studio musician. Went back to teach at Berklee in 1974 but returned to London in 1985. Long list of credits with many orchestras and ensembles around the jazz world, and one of the most noted composer-arrangers of his era, which continues.

****** Michael Gibbs**

Deram 844 907-2 *Gibbs; John Wilbraham (picc t); Nigel Carter, Ian Hamer, Maurice Miller, Derek Watkins, Kenny Wheeler (t, flhn); Cliff Hardie, David Horler, Bobby Lambe, Chris Pyne (tb); Maurice Gee, Ken Goldy, Ray Premru (btb); Jim Buck Jr, Nicholas Busch, Alan Civil, Valerie Smith (frhn); Martin Fry, Dick Hart (tba); Duncan Lamont, Mike Osborne, Tony Roberts, Alan Skidmore, John Surman, Barbara Thompson, Ray Warleigh (reeds); Bob Cornford, Mike Pyne (ky); Ray Russell, Chris Spedding (g); Fred Alexander, Alan Ford (clo); Jack Bruce, Brian Odges (b); John Marshall, Tony Oxley (d).* 70.

*****(*) Tanglewood 63**

Deram 844 906-2 *Gibbs; Harry Beckett, Nigel Carter, Henry Lowther, Kenny Wheeler (t, flhn); Malcolm Griffiths, David Horler, Chris (tb); Dick Hart, Alf Reece (tba); Tony Roberts, Alan Skidmore, Brian Smith, Stan Sulzmann, John Surman (reeds); Gordon Beck, Mike Pyne, John Taylor (ky); Chris Spedding (g); Bill Armon, Hugh Bean, George French, Tony Gilbert, Raymond Moseley, Michael Rennie, George Wakefield (vn); Fred Alexander, Allen Ford (clo); Roy Babbington, Jeff Clyne (b); John Marshall, Clive Thacker (d, perc); Frank Ricotti (perc, vib).* 11 & 12/70.

Few recording careers have got off to such a glorious start as Mike Gibbs's. The opening moments of 'Family Joy, Oh Boy!' on the eponymous debut could split clouds and ripen grain. Gibbs had come to Britain from his native Rhodesia via a spell at Berklee. A very few gigs later he was being talked about as the most vibrant new talent on the scene. Gibbs has the gift that all great leaders of big bands seem to require: that of making complex and daring ideas seem natural and inevitable. In these early records he fused advanced harmonic ideas with a groove that drew on Ellington, Gil and Miles, and rock. As he demonstrated on *Tanglewood 63*, he could move from sun-kissed delight to moonstruck melancholy in a moment. Something about the voicing of the horns – and Gibbs was and is a reluctant trombonist – marked him down as an individualist. He rarely asks for stratospheric playing, concentrating on the middle register. 'Sojourn', which follows 'Tanglewood 63' and the appended 'functional' fanfare, is a lonely stroll through a musical landscape whose topography is rich in associations.

The first album pays some dues – to Stan Getz, John Dankworth, Bob Moses and Gary Burton – but it is utterly individual in conception and execution. Gibbs's charts look challenging, but he has the gift of making difficult passage-work sound coherent and expressive. 'Sweet Rain', 'Throb' and 'And On The Third Day' are classics of British jazz. Surman, Warleigh and Skidmore solo on the first and last, joined on 'Third Day' by Mike Osborne and trombonist Chris Pyne for an exuberant finale that brings a wonderful album to a climax.

The end of *Tanglewood 63* is no less joyous, a long feature for guitarist Spedding over a richly textured rhythm, held together by Roy Babbington's bass guitar, a near-perfect marriage of rock and jazz that was to be Gibbs's staple for years to come, even when the idea of fusion was in retreat. A whole generation of British jazz fans cut their teeth on these records. It's wonderful to have them back.

*****(*) The Only Chrome Waterfall Orchestra**

Ah Um 009 *Gibbs; Derek Watkins, Ian Hamer, Kenny Wheeler, Henry Lowther (t); Chris Pyne (tb); Ray Warleigh, Stan Sulzmann (as); Charlie Mariano (as, nagaswaram); Tony Coe (ts, bcl); Alan Skidmore (ts); Philip Catherine (g); Steve Swallow (b); Bob Moses (d).* 75.

****** Big Music**

ACT 9231 *Gibbs; Ian Carr, Earl Gardner, Alan Rubin, Lew Soloff (t); John Clark (frhn); Dave Bargeron (tb); David Taylor (btb); Julian Arguëlles (ss); Jim Odgren (as); Chris Hunter (as, ss, ts, f); Lou Marini (ts, ss, f); Bob Mintzer (ts, f, bcl); Dave Tofani (f, af, picc); Dave Bristow, Brad Hatfield (ky); Django Bates (p); Kevin Eubanks, David Fiuczynski, Bill Frisell, Duke Levine, John Scofield (g); Kai Eckhardt (b); Bob Moses (d, d prog); Bad Bill Martin, Ben Wittman (d prog, perc).* 88, 9/90.

Gibbs was and remains a pioneer of a 'pure' kind of fusion: rock instruments and rhythms used to extend rather than diminish the scope of the improvisations. He always makes one feel the breadth and power of a big band, though, insisting on its weight and sonic force rather than breaking it down or using simple solo/accompaniment strategies.

Only Chrome Waterfall Orchestra is his most Gil Evans-like work. As with Gil, the secret is a combination of quality soloists and finely constructed compositions. Tony Coe's solo on 'Antique' is a perfect case in point, and elsewhere Mariano's Indian horn and Catherine's tasteful chromatic shapes are played over backgrounds that demand careful attention. There is a version of one of Gibbs's 'Lady Mac' pieces and the superb 'Unfinished Sympathy', which is one of his most ambitious creations.

Big Music was assembled in a latter-day Teo Macero style, building up heads, solos, intros and overdubs in the studio to produce the rich and multidimensional style which Gibbs's work demands. It is due to the efforts of John L. Walters that the project happened at all, and it took eight years to get it on to CD. Walters explains that he was looking for 'a missing link between *Out Of The Cool* and *Bitches Brew*; between Charles Ives and Salif Keita' and he points to Bob Moses's band, Mozamba, as a key moment in determining the actual sound. Moses is certainly the crucial element. His rhythmic brilliance makes 'Wall To Wall' the ideal opening track, a madly brilliant dance-floor jam with Jim Odgren's solo an additional bonus. The most obvious nod in the direction of the old Svengali – Gil Evans – is 'Mopsus', which includes overdubbed solos by Bill Frisell and Dave Bargeron. Gil's spirit is also on hand in 'Almost Ev'ry Day', a feature for Chris Hunter's strong, bluesy alto and a piece that might have been around for ever, so strong a hold does it take on first hearing. 'Pride Aside' is the coda, with an immaculate, Miles-influenced solo from Ian Carr. 'Waterfront' is a bonus track featuring Julian Arguëlles on soprano and Django Bates on piano, recorded some time after the main sessions and not originally available for the record. This is a glorious album which entirely merits its place at the start of ACT's 'World's Greatest Jazz Orchestras' series.

*****(*) By The Way ...**

Ah Um 016 *John Barclay, Kenny Wheeler, Richard Iles, Steve Sidwell (t); Pete Beachill (tb); Dave Stewart (btb); John Rooke, Cormac OhAhodain, Andrew Clark (frhn); Julian Arguëlles, Iain Dixon, Iain Ballamy, Evan Parker, Charlie Mariano (reeds); John Taylor, Nikki Iles (p); Mike Walker, John Parricelli (g); Oren Marshall (tba); Steve Swallow (b); Bob Moses, John Marshall (d).* 4–5/93.

By The Way ... was a rare new recording from an artist whose work seemed to be consigned to the back catalogue and to the virtual space defined by his fans' memories of past glories. Gibbs has devoted much time in more recent years to film and other projects, arranging and orchestrating in the main. It was only with his involvement with the Creative Jazz Orchestra and a reawakening awareness in Britain of his gifts that he began to be prominent in jazz circles again.

This large-scale piece is ample testimony to his powers. There are fine moments for Mariano again, for Wheeler and Parker and, although the predominantly British orchestra sometimes plays with characteristic reserve, this is mostly vivid and exciting music, and a hint that Gibbs's earlier music deserves a CD comeback.

*****(*) Europeana**

ACT 9220 *Gibbs; Markus Stockhausen (t); Albert Mangelsdorff (tb); Django Bates (thn); Douglas Boyd (ob); Christof Lauer (ts, ss); Klaus Doldinger (ss); Joachim Kühn (p); Richard Galliano (acc); Jean-François Jenny-Clark (b); Jon Christensen (d); Radio Philharmonie Hannover NDR.* 95.

Gibbs has been characteristically modest about his part in this moody, beautifully evoked 'Jazzphony', which is intended to express European unity by drawing material from the constitutent nations of the EU. The folky material is much simpler, less layered and dense than most of Gibbs's work, and this may explain his faint unease with the results (which are unabashedly beautiful, by the way).

Kühn is the chief soloist, providing a coherence that might otherwise have been impossible to sustain. 'Black Is The Colour' is a feature for the peerless oboe work of Douglas Boyd, paired with Django Bates on tenor horn. 'Stevtone', a Norwegian psalm, is a feature for Markus Stockhausen, who also leads on piccolo trumpet on 'Lo Ceu n'a Creat'. Klaus Doldinger's soprano saxophone turns 'She Moved Through The Fair' into a brooding lament, and Ireland, like France, has a second bite with a moving version of the 'Londonderry Air', with concertmaster Volker Worlitzsch providing the violin solo. A strange, very beautiful record, somewhat difficult to place in the overall schema of Gibbs's work, but bearing his stamp at every turn. Not for every taste, but impeccably tasteful.

Terry Gibbs (born 1924)

VIBRAPHONE, DRUMS

Born in Brooklyn, Gibbs had a relatively uneventful time of it in late swing bands before settling in Los Angeles in 1957 and running a part-time big band of studio pros, as well as recording for Mercury. Worked extensively in TV in the '60s and '70s, but was still touring and performing in the '80s and '90s.

***** Dream Band**

Contemporary CCD 7647 *Gibbs; Conte Candoli, Al Porcino, Ray Triscari, Stu Williamson (t); Bob Enevoldsen (vtb); Vernon Friley (tb); Joe Cadena, Med Flory, Bill Holman (ts); Joe Maini, Charlie Kennedy (as); Jack Schwartz (bs); Pete Jolly (p); Max Bennett (b); Mel Lewis (d).* 3–11/59.

***** The Sundown Sessions**

Contemporary CCD 7562 *As above, except add Johnny Audino (t), Bob Burgess (tb).* 11/59.

***** Flying Home**

Contemporary CCD 7654 *As above, except add Frank Higgins (t), Lou Levy (p), Buddy Clark (b).* 3–11/59.

The Gibbs bands combined the high-energy swing of Lionel Hampton with the sophistication of the Thad Jones/Mel Lewis outfits (Mel Lewis straddled the drum stool during Gibbs's most productive period). The arrangements, by Marty Paich, Lennie Niehaus and others, are all good, but with a sometimes uneasy emphasis on the higher horns. Gibbs's playing is closer to Hampton's percussive bounce than to any of the competing influences, and he solos with considerable verve; unfortunately the excellent *Main Stem*, arguably the best of this sequence, is currently out of print. It's a style that draws a great deal from bop and it's no less well adapted to the small-group performances which he has been focusing on more recently. We could do with some representation of the several sets which Gibbs cut for Mercury around the same period.

***** Chicago Fire**

Contemporary 14036 *Gibbs; Buddy DeFranco (cl); John Campbell II (p); Todd Coolman (b); Gerry Gibbs (d).* 7/87.

***** Air Mail Special**

Contemporary 14056 *Gibbs; Buddy DeFranco (cl); Frank Collett (p); Andy Simpkins (b); Jimmie Smith (d).* 10/81.

*****(*) Memories Of You**

Contemporary 14066 *Gibbs; Buddy DeFranco (cl); Herb Ellis (g); Larry Novak (p); Milt Hinton (b); Butch Miles (d).* 4/91.

***** Kings Of Swing**

Contemporary CCD 14067 *As above.* 4/91.

Lively latter-day sets from a player who must be taking multi-vitamins. All of these feature him in the company of fellow New Jerseyan DeFranco in a series of friendly but competitive sets, which were also repeated with the clarinettist as (strictly nominal) leader, but what's a credit among friends? *Memories Of You* is perhaps the best all-round set, with an excellent reading of 'Flying Home' and a romantic but un-schmaltzy 'Poor Butterfly'. *Kings Of Swing* is the poorer half of the same sessions. Of the remainder, *Air Mail Special* ('Love For Sale', 'Blues For Brody', 'Body And Soul') is particularly recommended, with *Chicago Fire* (unexpected versions of 'Giant Steps' and the '52nd Street Theme'). The big-band stuff is the most wholly authentic, but Gibbs's small groups are perhaps more in tune with prevailing tastes.

John Gill

BANJO, TROMBONE, VOCAL

Californian revivalist with multi-thread credentials as trombonist, banjo strummer, bandleader and arranger. Sometimes he sings too.

****(*) Smile, Darn Ya, Smile**

Stomp Off CD 1227 *Gill; Charles Fardella (t); David Sager (tb, v); Lynn Zimmer (ss, ts, cl); Tom Fischer (as, cl); Steve Pistorius (p, v); Debbie Markow, Elliot Markow (vn); Tom Saunders (tba); Hal Smith (d).* 12/90.

***** Headin' For Better Times**

Stomp Off CD 1270 *As above, except add Dan Levinson (ts, cl).* 7/91–12/92.

Shading between revivalism and a straight and strict re-creation of hot dance music, Gill's outfit errs on the side of the latter, which will tend to switch off all but the more dedicated archivists. There are two or three tunes on both discs that build up a bigger head of steam, and both ride out on a hot one: 'Here Comes The Hot Tamale Man', which Freddie Keppard once blew on, was a good idea for the second record. For the rest, though, it's often re-created schmaltz. Which still sounds like schmaltz, however much ironic salt and pepper gets milled over the melodies.

****** Looking For A Little Bluebird**

Stomp Off CD 1295 *Gill; Chris Tyle, Duke Heitger (t); Frank Powers (cl, v); Steve Pistorius (p); Eddy Davis (bj, v); Vince Giordano (tba); Hal Smith (d).* 12/94.

*****(*) Take Me To The Midnight Cakewalk Ball**

Stomp Off CD 1304 *As above.* 8/95.

*****(*) Listen To That Dixie Band**

Stomp Off CD 1321 *As above, except add Lavay Smith (v).* 5/97.

Gill plays trombone rather than banjo here, calls the group The Dixieland Serenaders, and has them play the stuffing out of a repertoire brimful of Oliver, Morton, Dodds – and the Lu Watters/Turk Murphy axis of revivalism. Except that this group actually sounds better than the old-timers of San Franciscan jazz usually did. The two-trumpet front line blows over the rest of the band like a particularly cussed zephyr, and Giordano and Smith give the group a terrific lift even when they're playing a simple two-beat. The result is a shakedown of a lot of mothballed tunes that puts a new lease on almost all of them. We fractionally prefer *Looking For A Little Bluebird* for its maniacal 'Alligator Hop' and the beautiful extended treatment of 'Farewell To Storyville', and for Richard Bird's sound, which shoves the band right in your face while still giving them a full and clear balance. The subsequent *Take Me To The Midnight Cakewalk Ball* is barely a step behind, though, with notable treatments of 'Wa Wa Wa' and 'Grandpa's Spells' ... and 16 more.

The fun continues on *Listen To That Dixie Band*. Quite a ration of blues this time, with four Bessie Smith numbers sung by guest Lavay Smith (on vacation from the Red Hot Skillet Lickers) and the band still sounding in their most flavoursome form. All highly recommended!

Dizzy Gillespie (1917–93)

TRUMPET, PERCUSSION, PIANO, VOCAL

Born in Cheraw, South Carolina, Gillespie started on trumpet at thirteen. Moved to Philadelphia in 1935 and joined Teddy Hill in 1937, then Cab Calloway in 1939. Formed coterie of after-hours players with Parker, Monk and Kenny Clarke in the early '40s, then began leading his own small groups from 1945, playing the new music of bebop. Led his own big band, 1946–50, and during that time pioneered the fusion of jazz with Latin and Afro-Cuban music. Then returned to small-group work, though he toured with big bands for the State Department, 1956–8. A small group featuring James Moody was his main vehicle in the early '60s, but occasional big-band work and a campaign to run for the presidency also intervened (he failed to be elected). In the '70s and '80s, he assumed the role of elder statesman of modern jazz and was the focal point for the re-evaluation of bop during that time. Celebrated his 75th birthday with a season of New York concerts, but was diagnosed with cancer shortly afterwards. The guiding theoretician behind bop, the supreme virtuoso of jazz trumpet in the '40s and '50s, a profound teacher, a visionary with regard to jazz and its capacity to fraternize with other musics, and the great entertainer of his era, which lasted 50 years.

***** Dizzy Gillespie 1945**

Classics 888 *Gillespie; Trummy Young (tb, v); Tony Scott (cl); Charlie Parker, Johnny Bothwell (as); Dexter Gordon, Don Byas (ts); Clyde Hart, Jimmy Jones, Frank Paparelli (p); Mike Bryan, Remo Palmieri (g); Oscar Pettiford, Gene Ramey, Slam Stewart, Al Hall, Murray Shipinski (b); Specs Powell, Ed Nicholson, Cozy Cole, Irv Kluger, Shelly Manne (d); Rubberlegs Williams, Sarah Vaughan (v).* 1–2/45.

*****(*) Dizzy Gillespie 1945–1946**

Classics 935 *Gillespie; Howard McGhee, Karl George, Snooky Young (t); Vic Dickenson, George Washington, Ralph Bledsoe, Henry Coker (tb); Charlie Parker, Willie Smith, Marvin Johnson (as); Don Byas, Lucky Thompson, Fred Simon (ts); Gene Porter (bs); Al Haig, George Handy, Wilbert Baranco (p); Bill De Arango, Buddy Harper (g); Curley Russell, Charles Mingus, Ray Brown, Al McKibbon (b); Big Sid Catlett, Earl Watkins, Stan Levey, J.C Heard, Roy Haynes (d); The Three Angels, Sarah Vaughan (v).* 5/45–4/46.

♛ **** **The Complete RCA Victor Recordings**

Bluebird 66528-2 2CD *As above, except add Bill Dillard, Shad Collins, Lamar Wright, Willie Cook, Benny Harris, Miles Davis, Fats Navarro (t), Dicky Wells, Ted Kelly, J.J Johnson, Kai Winding (tb), Buddy DeFranco (cl), Benny Carter, Russell Procope, Ernie Henry (as), Yusef Lateef, Coleman Hawkins, Ben Webster, Charlie Ventura, Don Byas, Robert Carroll, Teddy Hill (ts), Al Gibson, Ernie Caceres (bs), Lionel Hampton (vib), Lennie Tristano, Sam Allen, James Foreman (p), Charlie Christian, Billy Bauer (g), Milt Hinton, Richard Fulbright, Al McKibbon, Eddie Safranski (b), Bill Beason, Teddy Stewart (d), Vince Guerra, Sabu Martinez, Chano Pozo (perc), Johnny Hartman (v).* 5/37–1/49.

John Birks Gillespie had already been recording for almost a decade when he made the earliest of these tracks, and in the Cab Calloway and Teddy Hill bands he cut the outline of a promising Roy Eldridge disciple. His associations with Thelonious Monk and Charlie Parker, though, took him into hitherto uncharted realms. While he continued to credit Parker as the real inspirational force behind bebop, Gillespie was the movement's scholar, straw boss, sartorial figurehead and organizer: his love of big-band sound led him into attempts to orchestrate the new music that resulted in some of the most towering jazz records, particularly (among those here) 'Things To Come' and 'Cubano Be-Cubano Bop'. But his own playing is at least as powerful a reason to listen to these tracks. Gillespie brought a new virtuosity to jazz trumpet just as Parker created a matchless vocabulary for the alto sax. It scarcely seems possible that the music could have moved on from Louis Armstrong's 'Cornet Chop Suey' to Gillespie's astonishing flight on 'Dizzy Atmosphere' in only 20 years. A dazzling tone, solo construction that was as logical as it was unremittingly daring, and a harmonic grasp which was built out of countless nights of study and experimentation: Gillespie showed the way for every trumpeter in post-war jazz. His Guild and Musicraft recordings include a single sextet track with Dexter Gordon ('Blue 'N' Boogie'), seven with Parker, four with Sonny Stitt and Milt Jackson, and the balance with his big band.

The RCA set sweeps the board as the cream of Gillespie's studio work in the period. The big-band tracks are complete and in good sound, all the Victor small-group sessions are here, there are prehistory tracks with Teddy Hill and Lionel Hampton as a taster of things to come, and four tracks with the Metronome All-Star bebop group, where Dizzy lines up with Miles, Bird, Fats and J.J. Absolutely indispensable and some of the most exciting jazz of the era.

Classics have rounded up some useful obscurities in their survey. Classics 888 mixes bebop's earliest sounds – a January 1945 date with the first versions of 'Good Bait' and 'Be-Bop' itself – along with dates under the leadership of either Clyde Hart or Trummy Young (who somehow manages to get himself on five of the seven sessions here!). Three dates are almost ruined by the vocals, including the bizarre and inebriated warblings of Rubberlegs Williams; but Gillespie, Byas and Parker (a little restrained) salvage something out of it. Three tracks with Tony Scott and Ben Webster are interesting. Classics 935 includes the first seven titles for Dial (with Parker absent on the second date), adds the first small-band date for Victor, offers four very cloudy and speed-wobbled tracks with a Johnny Richards orchestra and four all-star big-band tracks led by Wilbert Baranco: 'Night And Day' is a great one, even though Gillespie (masquerading as 'John Burk') doesn't solo. This is a scrappy way to hear this music, but diehard Gillespie collectors will want these discs.

***(*) **Pleyel 48**

Vogue 74321 134152 *Gillespie; Dave Burns, Benny Bailey, Lamar Wright, Elmon Wright (t); Ted Kelly, Bill Shepherd (tb); Howard Johnson, John Brown (as); George Gales, Big Nick Nicholas (ts); Cecil Payne (bs); John Lewis (p); Al McKibbon (b); Kenny Clarke (d); Chano Pozo (perc); Kenny Hagood (v).* 2/48.

***(*) **Dizzy Gillespie & His Big Band In Concert**

GNP Crescendo GNPD 23 *As above, except add Willie Cook (t), Cindy Duryea, Jesse Tarrant (tb), Ernie Henry, James Moody (reeds), James Foreman (p); Nelson Boyd (b), Teddy Stewart (d); omit Bailey, Lamar Wright, Kelly, Johnson, Nicholas, Lewis, McKibbon, Clarke, Hagood.* 48.

Although the big band made only a small number of studio records, it was caught on the wing at a number of concerts, even if seldom in hi-fi conditions. These, though, are two splendid gigs, and only the exasperatingly imperfect sound holds them back from top ratings. Although much of the material is duplicated across the two concerts, some of it is strikingly different: the Pasadena (GNP) concert has a three-minute 'Round Midnight' while the one from Paris runs to almost nine minutes. Gillespie's interest in Latin rhythms brought semi-legendary percussionist Pozo (killed not long after these concerts) into the fold, and there is typically exciting stuff on 'Manteca'. If the orchestra never moves with the neurotic immediacy of small-group bebop, it's still a remarkable sound.

*** **Pleyel Concert 1953**

Vogue 74321 154662 *Gillespie; Bill Graham (bs); Wade Legge (p); Lou Hackney (b); Al Jones (d); Joe Carroll (v).* 2/53.

*** **Ooh-Shoo-Be-Doo!**

Natasha NI-4018 *As above.* 3–4/53.

When economics required Gillespie to dissolve the big band, he carried on with small groups. Operating at something of a tangent to bop – he still performed with Parker on a few occasions, and there is a superb session for Verve with Monk and Bird, as well as the famous Massey Hall concert of 1953 – his playing began to take on a grandeur that sounded even more ravishing than Parker's alto did when confronted with strings. At the same time he continued to delight in on-stage horseplay, and this record of a French concert includes plenty of interplay with Joe Carroll on the likes of 'Ooh-Shoo-Be-Doo-Be'. What's missing is anyone to challenge him in the way Parker or Powell could. The Natasha album collects tracks from Birdland broadcasts of the same period: there are four versions of 'Ooh-Shoo-Be-Doo-Be', which is probably three too many, and flashes of great trumpet amid a lot of enjoyable nonsense. How well one responds is a matter of how Gillespified one wants to be.

*** **Diz And Getz**

Verve 833559-2 *Gillespie; Stan Getz (ts); Oscar Peterson (p); Herb Ellis (g); Ray Brown (b); Max Roach (d).* 12/53.

(*) **For Musicians Only

Verve 837435-2 *As above, except add Sonny Stitt (as), John Lewis (p), Stan Levey (d); omit Peterson and Roach.* 10/56.

*** Sonny Side Up

Verve 521426-2 *Gillespie; Sonny Stitt, Sonny Rollins (ts); Ray Bryant (p); Tommy Potter (b); Charli Persip (d).* 12/57.

These all-star encounters have perhaps been overrated. It's interesting to hear Gillespie on what was effectively mainstream material on *Diz And Getz* – two Ellington tunes, three standards and a single Latin theme – but the group strike a surprisingly shambolic note in places, seldom managing to play together, and the superfast blues, 'Impromptu', is a virtual disaster. Worth salvaging are a lovely trumpet treatment of 'It's The Talk Of The Town', some moments from the otherwise audibly ruffled Getz, and a version of 'It Don't Mean A Thing' in which the tempo is actually matched by the intensity of the playing. The music has never sounded like a great feat of engineering, and the latest CD transfer improves little on previous editions. *For Musicians Only* is even more of a blow-out, with 'Be-Bop' and 'Dark Eyes' running over 12 minutes each and Stitt treating it as a carving session: the tempos are almost uniformly hell-for-leather. Exhilarating in small doses, but it's hardly as significant a date as it might have been with a little preparation. *Sonny Side Up* is pretty desultory stuff, too, but with Rollins in his greatest period and Stitt as combative as usual, the two long blues tracks strike some sparks, and Rollins's solo on the brief 'I Know That You Know' is prime cut. Dizzy referees with aplomb.

**** Birks Works

Verve 527900-2 2CD *Gillespie; Joe Gordon, Quincy Jones, E.V Perry, Carl Warwick, Talib Daawud, Lee Morgan (t); Melba Liston, Frank Rehak (tb); Rod Levitt, Ray Connor (btb); Jimmy Powell, Phil Woods, Ernie Henry (as); Billy Mitchell, Benny Golson, Ernie Wilkins (ts); Marty Flax, Billy Root, Pee Wee Moore (bs); Walter Davis Jr, Wynton Kelly (p); Paul West, Nelson Boyd (b); Charli Persip (d); Austin Comer (v).* 6/56–7/57.

Long awaited in a comprehensive edition, these tracks cover the work of a band that Gillespie toured with as a cultural ambassador, though this is all studio work. Studded with great players, the orchestra also benefits from some of the most perceptive scoring of the day – by Liston, Wilkins, Jones, Golson and other hands – and, with Gillespie in stratospheric form as soloist, the band could hardly have failed. Yet the three original albums remain comparatively forgotten, or at least neglected, which makes the reissue even more welcome.

*** At Newport

Verve 513754-2 *Gillespie; Lee Morgan, Ermit Perry, Carl Warwick, Talib Daawud (t); Melba Liston, Al Grey, Chuck Connors (tb); Ernie Henry, Jimmy Powell (as); Billy Mitchell, Benny Golson (ts); Pee Wee Moore (bs); Wynton Kelly, Mary Lou Williams (p); Paul West (b); Charli Persip (d).* 7/57.

**** Gillespiana / Carnegie Hall Concert

Verve 519809-2 *Gillespie; John Frosk, Clark Terry, Nick Travis, Carl Warwick, Ernie Royal, Joe Wilder (t); Urbie Green, Frank Rehak, Britt Woodman, George Matthews, Arnette Sparrow, Paul Faulise (tb); Jimmy Buffington, Al Richman, Gunther Schuller, Julius Watkins, John Barrows, Richard Berg (frhn); Leo Wright (f, as); Lalo Schifrin (p); Don Butterfield (tba); Art Davis (b); Chuck Lampkin (d); Candido Camero, Willie Rodriguez, Ray Barretto, Julio Collazo, Jose Mangual (perc); Joe Carroll (v).* 11/60–3/61.

***(*) Ultimate Dizzy Gillespie

Verve 557535-2 *Gillespie; various groups.* 6/54–11/64.

Gillespie's Verve contract was arguably a little disappointing in that it produced no single indispensable record. The big- and small-band dates were pot-pourris of dazzling breaks and solos that never quite gelled into the long-playing masterpiece Gillespie surely had in him at this time. Having already outlived many of his key contemporaries in bebop, he was beginning to be a player in search of a context. The best single disc is certainly the one that couples *Gillespiana* – a marvellous assemblage of orchestral charts by Lalo Schifrin, some of his finest work on record, to which Gillespie rises superbly – and the subsequent *Carnegie Hall Concert* of a few months later, not quite so memorable, though this 'Manteca' and the extravagant 'Tunisian Fantasy' are exhilarating. The Newport set from 1957 has some great moments – a fine 'I Remember Clifford', the chunks from Mary Lou Williams's 'Zodiac Suite' with the composer sitting in – and some concert schtick. Roy Hargrove's choice for *Ultimate* focuses on the small-group Gillespie, from 'Bloomdido' with Monk and Bird onwards.

***(*) Dizzy Gillespie And The Double Six Of Paris

Philips 830224-2 *Gillespie; James Moody (as); Kenny Barron, Bud Powell (p); Chris White, Pierre Michelot (b); Kenny Clarke, Rudy Collins (d); The Double Six Of Paris (v).* 7–9/63.

This almost-forgotten record doesn't deserve its obscurity. The tracks are small-group bop, with the Double Six group dubbing in supremely athletic vocals later – normally a recipe for aesthetic disaster, but it's done with such stunning virtuosity that it blends credibly with the music, and the interweaving is done with some restraint. Gillespie himself takes some superb solos – the tracks are compressed into a very short duration, harking back to original bop constraints, and it seems to focus all the energies – and even Powell, in his twilight, sounds respectable on the ten tracks he plays on.

*** Dizzy For President

Knit Classics KCR-3001 *Gillespie; James Moody (ts, as, f); Sleepy Matsumoto (ts); Kenny Barron (p); Chris White (b); Rudy Collins (d); Jon Hendricks (v).* 63.

*** Something Old – Something New

Verve 558079-2 *As above, except omit Matsumoto and Hendricks.* 63.

*** Jamboo Caribe

Verve 557492-2 *As above, except add Kansas Fields (perc), Ann Henry (v).* 64.

*** The Cool World / Dizzy Goes Hollywood

Verve 531230-2 *Gillespie; James Moody (ts, as, f); Kenny Barron (p); Chris White (b); Rudy Collins (d); strings.* 9/63–4/64.

Gillespie's quintet of the early 1960s has been largely forgotten. It's not so much a miscarriage of justice as a fact of documented jazz life: they didn't do much recording, and what there is is relatively unremarkable. Moody was a splendid presence, garrulous foil or straight man as the occasion required, and with the young Kenny Barron in the rhythm section the group had unusual strength in depth. Yet they never did much of great consequence on record. *Dizzy For President* is a recent discovery of their Monterey Jazz Festival set from 1963. Surviving great moments have to compete with a lot of horseplay (the routine prior to 'Morning Of The Carnival' is priceless), including Dizzy's presidential campaign-song which a guesting Jon Hendricks delivers. Excellent live sound catches the occasion very well, but it may not stand up to many repeat plays. *Something Old – Something New* revisits nuggets such as 'Bebop' and 'Good Bait', along with newer pieces such as 'November Afternoon', but the temperature seems low and the playing inexplicably cautious. *Jamboo Caribe* is described as a 'sensuous calypso adventure', but this was one area of world music which Dizzy never conquered, and a lot of it is trivial. Even so, he gets a beautifully considered solo into 'And Then She Stopped', and the closing 'Trinidad, Goodbye' is a fast, attacking piece that Gillespie and Moody plunder very effectively.

The Cool World, Mal Waldron's score for Shirley Clarke's film, is coupled with the set of movie themes on *Dizzy Goes Hollywood* – some vivid and exciting playing by all hands, but the tracks seem deliberately short and predigested, and the music-making feels contained.

*****(*) The Monterey Festival Jazz Orchestra**
Blue Note 80370-2 *Gillespie; Harry 'Sweets' Edison, Melvin Moore, Fred Hill, Johnny Audino (t); Lester Robinson, Francis Fitzpatrick, Jim Amlotte (tb); Herman Lebow, Sam Cassano, David Burke, Alan Robinson (frhn); Buddy Collette, Gabe Baltazar, Bill Green, Carrington Visor Jr, Jack Nimitz (reeds); Phil Moore (p); Bobby Hutcherson (vib); Dennis Budimir (g); Jimmy Bond (b); Earl Palmer (d).* 65.

Gil Fuller's charts for this band miss some of the freewheeling excitement he gave to the first Gillespie big band in the 1940s, but there's real glitter and polish in the playing that the trumpeter responds to with some acrid, pinpoint improvising. It's over too soon.

***** Swing Low, Sweet Cadillac**
Impulse! 051178-2 *Gillespie; James Moody (ts, as, f); Mike Longo (p); Frank Schifano (b); Otis Finch (d).* 67.

After his Verve and Limelight records, Impulse! had a go at getting a record out of Dizzy. It has its moments, for both Gillespie and Moody, but as before there's a sense that the leader simply wasn't much interested in making records and wanted to get on to the next gig.

***** Live At The Village Vanguard**
Blue Note 80507-2 2CD *Gillespie; Garnett Brown (tb); Pepper Adams (bs); Chick Corea (p); Ray Nance (vn); Richard Davis (b); Mel Lewis, Elvin Jones (d).* 10/67.

One of the oddest line-ups Gillespie ever figured in – Nance and Brown swap places, Jones sits in on two tunes, but otherwise the band is as listed. These are club jams rather than thought-out situations, and there are the usual dead spots; but Gillespie takes some magisterial solos – his thoughts on the blues in 'Blues For Max' are worth a close listen – and Adams in particular is in tough, no-nonsense form.

*****(*) Dizzy Gillespie's Big 4**
Original Jazz Classics OJC 443 *Gillespie; Joe Pass (g); Ray Brown (b); Mickey Roker (d).* 9/74.

****(*) The Trumpet Kings Meet Joe Turner**
Original Jazz Classics OJC 497 *Gillespie; Roy Eldridge, Clark Terry, Harry 'Sweets' Edison (t); Connie Crayton (g); Jimmy Robbins (b); Washington Rucker (d); Joe Turner (v).* 9/74.

**** The Trumpet Kings At Montreux '75**
Original Jazz Classics OJC 445 *Gillespie; Roy Eldridge, Clark Terry (t); Oscar Peterson (p); Niels-Henning Orsted Pedersen (b); Louie Bellson (d).* 7/75.

***** At The Montreux Jazz Festival 1975**
Original Jazz Classics OJC 739 *Gillespie; Eddie 'Lockjaw' Davis, Johnny Griffin (ts); Milt Jackson (vib); Tommy Flanagan (p); Niels-Henning Orsted Pedersen (b); Mickey Roker (d).* 7/75.

***** Bahiana**
Pablo 2625-708 *Gillespie; Roger Glenn (f, bf, vib); Al Gafa, Michael Howell (vib); Earl May (b); Mickey Roker (d); Paulinho Da Costa (perc).* 11/75.

**** Dizzy's Party**
Original Jazz Classics OJC 823 *Gillespie; Rodney Jones (g); Benjamin Franklin Brown (b); Mickey Roker (d); Paulinho Da Costa (perc).* 9/76.

****(*) Montreux '77**
Original Jazz Classics OJC 381 *Gillespie; Jon Faddis (t); Milt Jackson (vib); Monty Alexander (p); Ray Brown (b); Jimmie Smith (d).* 7/77.

***(*) Free Ride**
Original Jazz Classics OJC 740 *Gillespie; band arranged by Lalo Schifrin.* 2/77.

****(*) The Trumpet Summit Meets The Oscar Peterson Big 4**
Original Jazz Classics OJC 603 *Gillespie; Freddie Hubbard, Clark Terry (t); Oscar Peterson (p); Joe Pass (g); Ray Brown (b); Bobby Durham (d).* 3/80.

***** The Alternate Blues**
Original Jazz Classics OJC 744 *As above.* 3/80.

****(*) Digital At Montreux 1980**
Original Jazz Classics 882 *Gillespie; Toots Thielemans (hca); Bernard Purdie (d).* 7/80.

***** Musician Composer Raconteur**
Pablo 2620-116 2CD *Gillespie; James Moody (ts, as, f); Milt Jackson (vib); Ed Cherry (g); Michael Howell (b); George Hughes (d).* 7/81.

**** The Best Of Dizzy Gillespie**
Pablo 2405-411

Gillespie's Pablo period marked a return to regular recording after some years of neglect in the studios. The *Big 4* album was the first session he did, and it remains perhaps the best. There is a superb display of trumpet chops in 'Be Bop', a very good ballad in 'Hurry Home' and an intriguing revision of 'Jitterbug Waltz' in which Pass and Gillespie push each other into their best form. *Bahiana* rambles on a bit and the supporting group are unworthy, but Gillespie plays with fire and decision and he elevates his surroundings with some distinction. The other records seem to betray Norman Granz's indecision as to how best to employ Dizzy's talents. The four Trumpet Kings/Summit encounters are typical of their kind: brilliant flashes of virtuosity interspersed with rhetoric and mere showing-off. The best is probably the Joe Turner meeting, where the great R&B singer puts everyone through their paces. *Montreux '77* is Gillespie featuring his young protégé, Jon Faddis, who xeroxes the young Gillespie style but comes up with a remark or two of his own. The earlier set, from 1975, includes some righteous jousting with Davis and Griffin, though it tends to go the way of all such festival showdowns. The best-of set is weak, picking some tracks off records that have thankfully disappeared. *Free Ride* is a hopeless collaboration with Lalo Schifrin that comes as a nasty shock after the great *Gillespiana* from 25 years earlier. *Dizzy's Party* is another one where there's no need to weep over a lost invite. *Musician Composer Raconteur* is a further Montreux appearance and, although Jackson and Moody are made into somewhat hapless guest stars, the grand good humour of the occasion will please those who remember Gillespie's latter-day concerts, and he plays some fine trumpet at various points. *Digital At Montreux 1980* is even more of a one-man show, Thielemans and Purdie excepting. There is something to enjoy on all these records, but they stretch Gillespie's legend very thin at times.

***** Dizzy Gillespie Meets Phil Woods Quintet**

Timeless SJP 250 *Gillespie; Tom Harrell (t); Phil Woods (as); Hal Galper (p); Steve Gilmore (b); Bill Goodwin (d).* 12/86.

****(*) Live At the Royal Festival Hall**

Enja 6044 *Gillespie; Arturo Sandoval, Claudio Roditi (t); Slide Hampton (tb); Steve Turre (tb, conch); Paquito D'Rivera (as, cl); James Moody (ts, f, as); Mario Rivera (ss, ts, perc); Danilo Perez (p); Ed Cherry (g); John Lee (b); Ignacio Berroa (d); Airto Moreira, Giovanni Hidalgo (perc); Flora Purim (v).* 6/89.

The haphazard nature of Gillespie's recording regimen in the 1980s brings home how much the industry wasted the opportunity to provide a meaningful context for such a creative musician. Perpetually on the road, perhaps Dizzy simply wasn't so interested in making records; but the point remains that his legacy of genuinely great records is disappointingly small and is mainly concentrated at the other end of his career. His guest appearance with the Phil Woods band is respectable fare as such things go: there is yet another 'Round Midnight' of little interest, and Tom Harrell (uncredited) takes all the really strong trumpet parts, but it's a goodish Woods album with Dizzy making a few remarks. The Festival Hall concert catches something of the exuberance which continues to attend this kind of global-summit band and, though it's best approached as a souvenir for anyone who heard the group in concert, there are felicitous moments from a band very eager to please their boss.

*****(*) Max + Dizzy, Paris 1989**

A&M 6404 2CD *Gillespie; Max Roach (d).* 3/89.

A unique, moving, exciting experience. Bop's most eminent surviving champions reflect on close to 50 years of their music in an encounter which is as free as either man will ever play. Across some 90 minutes of music (the final section features the two of them talking it over), Roach sometimes pushes Dizzy a shade uncaringly, for the trumpeter's powers aren't what they were; but most of the horn playing is astonishingly clean and unmarked for a man in his seventies. As a kind of living history lesson, or a record of two of jazz's great personalities having a final exchange of ideas, it's a singular and generously entertaining occasion. Excellent sound.

****(*) To Bird With Love**

Telarc CD-83316 *Gillespie; Paquito D'Rivera (as, cl); Jackie McLean, Antonio Hart (as); Clifford Jordan, David Sanchez, Benny Golson (ts); Danilo Perez (p); George Mraz (b); Lewis Nash (d); Bobby McFerrin (v).* 1/92.

****(*) Bird Songs**

Telarc CD-83421 *As above, except add Kenny Washington (d).* 1/92.

***** To Diz With Love**

Telarc CD-83307 *Gillespie; Wynton Marsalis, Charlie Sepulveda, Claudio Roditi, Red Rodney, Wallace Roney, Jon Faddis, Doc Cheatham, Lew Soloff (t); Junior Mance (p); Peter Washington (b); Kenny Washington (d).* 1–2/92.

From the concerts which were meant to inaugurate a year of celebration for Dizzy's 75th birthday and which instead turned out to be his final appearances. The trumpet feast on the third disc has the edge, with a hint of a cutting contest in the air, whereas some of the sax players burn each other out on the first two records. Diz sounds frail but unprepared to admit it.

Ginger Pig New Orleans Band

GROUP

British band of would-be authentic traditionalists.

***** The Ginger Pig New Orleans Band Featuring Sammy Remington**

[sic] GHB BCD-232 *Jim Holmes (t); Dale Vickers (tb); Sammy Rimington (cl, as); John Hale (cl); John Richardson (p); John Coles (bj); Annie Hawkins (b); Colin Richardson (d).* 12/87.

Another group of Brits masquerading as New Orleans players, the Ginger Pig combo play an august sort of trad, with guest Rimington lending some authentic flavour. On a more 'modern' piece such as 'Mahogany Hall Stomp' they lack the necessary finesse, but a slow piece such as 'Till Then' is done quite convincingly, and the sound of the record – it was made at Northampton's Black Bottom Club! – is a good counterfeit of a proper Louisiana setting.

Vince Giordano

TUBA, BASS SAXOPHONE, BASS

A specialist in brass-bass, string bass and the bass saxophone, Giordano has done many sessions and performed in numerous bands covering the hot-dance and 'society' end of '20s jazz.

***** Bill Challis' The Goldkette Project**

Circle CCD-118 *Giordano; Peter Ecklund (t, c); Spanky Davis, Dave Gale, Randy Rinehart (t); Stew Pletcher (c); Dan Barrett, Herb Gardner, Spiegel Wilcox (tb); Marc Lopeman, Ted Nash, Jack Stuckey (cl, as, bs); Bob Wilber (ts, cl); Dick Wellstood (p); Stan Kurtis (vn); James Chirillo, Frank Vignola (bj, g); Arnie Kinsella (d).* 88.

*****(*) Quality Shout!**

Stomp Off CD1260 *Giordano; Peter Ecklund, Jon-Erik Kellso (c); Herb Gardner (tb); Jack Stuckey, Scott Robinson, Dan Block (reeds); Jeremy Kahn (p); John Gill, Matt Trimboli (bj, g); Arnie Kinsella (d).* 9/92–3/93.

A band that names their record, made in the '90s, after a track by Paul Howard's Quality Serenaders should be of interest to all inquiring jazz listeners. As the first-call man on bass instruments for any revivalist project in the New York area, Giordano has cornered the market in bass sax and tuba specialities. His band, The Nighthawks (name borrowed from the Coon–Sanders outfit), take a line in revivalism that would be fanatical but for their good humour and magically light touch. All 22 tracks on *Quality Shout!* are based on original records, all cited in the sleeve-notes, and archivists will be astonished at finding transcriptions of the likes of Cliff Jackson's 'The Terror', Sam Wooding's 'Bull Foot Stomp' and Alex Hill's 'Southbound'. In some cases they even follow the transcribed solos, as with the California Ramblers' Edison version of 'Zulu Wail'. As a repertory record, it's beautifully done – Ecklund and Kellso are a sparkily brilliant front line, the reeds have their original vibratos down pat, and the rhythm feels poised between something clockwork and something a little looser, which feels just right for the period. Recommended to ears of any vintage.

The Goldkette album is a more specific homage, recorded under the eye of Goldkette's arranger, Bill Challis, and with the coup of having original Goldkette sideman Wilcox in the band. They get a beautiful sound in the studio, old-fashioned and immediate at the same time; but anyone who knows the original Goldkette records might find some of these re-creations tame: they miss the terrific rush of 'My Pretty Girl', probably Goldkette's best record, and some of the individual parts falter – Stan Kurtis, for instance, sounds no match for Joe Venuti on 'I'd Rather Be The Girl In Your Arms'. But it's a charming and enjoyable tribute.

George Girard (1930–57)

TRUMPET, VOCAL

New Orleans trumpeter who emerged at the tail-end of the '40s revival and whose brief career was terminated by cancer.

***** George Girard**

Storyville STCD 6013 *Girard; Santo Pecora, Bob Havens (tb); Raymond Burke, Harry Shields (cl); Lester Bouchon (ts); Jeff Riddick (p, v); Bob Discon (p); Emil Christian, Chink Martin (b); Monk Hazel, Paul Edwards (d).* 9/54–7/56.

Girard, who died young after contracting cancer, was a very fine trumpeter. He made his name in the Basin Street Six with Pete Fountain, but these recordings – one session made at the Municipal Auditorium in 1954, the other at the Parisian Room in 1956, only a few months before his death – offer formidable evidence of a great, idiosyncratic New Orleans hornman, somewhat in the manner (if not the style) of Henry Allen. Girard's firm lead is countered by his unpredictable solos which may suddenly flare up into wild high notes or stay in a sober middle range: he's hard to second-guess, even on warhorse material such as the tunes played at the 1956 session, which also has excellent work from Havens and Shields. The earlier date is marred by the recording, which is poorly balanced and muffled, and by the feeble tenor work of Bouchon; but Girard and Pecora are both very good: the trumpeter's brilliant solo on 'A Good Man Is Hard To Find' is a small masterpiece of controlled tension. The 1956 recordings are more than adequate, and it's hard to believe that Girard's playing is the work of a man who was already very ill.

Greg Gisbert (born 1966)

TRUMPET, FLUGELHORN

Gisbert spent some years playing lead trumpet with Buddy Rich and Woody Herman, and in the '90s he freelanced in the New York area.

***** Harcology**

Criss Cross Criss 1084 *Gisbert; Chris Potter (ts, ss); John Campbell (p); Dwayne Burno (b); Gregory Hutchinson (d).* 12/92.

***** The Court Jester**

Criss Cross 1161 *Gisbert; Conrad Herwig (tb); Jon Gordon (ss, as); Tim Ries (ss, ts, f); Janice Friedman (p); Jay Anderson (b); Gregory Hutchinson (d).* 12/96.

The Criss Cross debut is a bright, unfussy date, strongly marked by the example of Clark Terry, Thad Jones and Tom Harrell, the most obvious influences on Gisbert's trumpet style. He plays clean, uncomplicated lines in a frankly old-fashioned style. Over almost exactly an hour there is nothing that will frighten the horses, and nothing that is not resolutely tasteful and coherent. His big solos are on the title-piece (a solitary Gisbert original), Campbell's 'Turning Point' and the standard, 'Autumn In New York'. For much of the remainder he is happy to sit back and let colleagues take front stage. *The Court Jester* is a trifle more ambitious, with the neatly orchestrated 'Robyn Song' getting it off to a coolly impressive start. Friedman is a strong presence, contributing a couple of originals, and the ensemble play is pretty much step-perfect, although again it's a set marked more by consistency than daring. Gisbert comes into his own on a clear-eyed treatment of 'My Ideal'.

Jimmy Giuffre (born 1921)

CLARINET, TENOR SAXOPHONE, SOPRANO SAXOPHONE, FLUTE, BASS FLUTE

Born in Dallas, Giuffre studied in his home State, played in an army band and then worked with a series of big bands, before working with Howard Rumsey and Shorty Rogers. Later, Giuffre formed the first of two extraordinary trios which were to transform one branch of jazz. Originally with Jim Hall and Ralph Pena, then with Bob Brookmeyer, and then with Paul Bley and Steve Swallow, Jimmy moved from a kind of organic folk jazz to something approaching free jazz. Later years saw Giuffre concentrate on arranging and teaching, but in the late '80s his playing career was revived just as his early recordings were revived and reassessed.

*****(*) The Jimmy Giuffre 3**

Atlantic 90981 *Giuffre; Jim Hall (g); Jim Atlas, Ralph Pena (b).* 12/56.

*****(*) Hollywood & Newport, 1957–1958**

Fresh Sound FSCD 1026 *Giuffre; Bob Brookmeyer (vtb); Jim Hall (g); Ralph Pena (b).* 1/57–10/58.

Cultivating a brown *chalumeau* register on his clarinet and defending the aesthetic benefits of simple quietness, Giuffre created what he liked to call 'folk jazz'. *The Jimmy Giuffre Clarinet* and *Music Man*, recorded for Atlantic in the 1950s, evoked a middle America which had hitherto played little part in jazz. Giuffre's soft meditations and homely foot-tapping on the earlier album suggested a man playing out on his front porch, sufficiently solitary and unselfconscious to forget the rules and try out unfamiliar tonalities.

The Jimmy Giuffre 3 contains some of the essential early material, notably a fine version of 'The Train And The River', on which Giuffre moves between baritone and tenor saxophones and clarinet, and the long 'Crawdad Suite', which intelligently combines blues and folk materials. Giuffre's out-of-tempo playing recalls the great jazz singers. Jim Hall was his longest-standing and most sympathetic cohort; they were partnered either by trombonist Bob Brookmeyer or a bassist, most successfully Ralph Pena or Buddy Clark (Jim Atlas plays on only two bonus tracks on the Atlantic CD).

The Giuffre–Brookmeyer–Hall trio appears behind the credits on the great movie, *Jazz on a Summer's Day* (the top of Hall's head is just about visible), playing 'The Train And The River'. The Fresh Sound captures that whole set, together with earlier and later material from the West Coast, where this kind of jazz seemed to have a more natural home. Brookmeyer's slightly lazy, wall-eyed delivery was an ideal foil for Giuffre. He kept to the same end of the tonal spectrum and shared a love of easy tempos.

****** 1961**

ECM 849644-2 2CD *Giuffre; Paul Bley (p); Steve Swallow (b).* 3 & 8/61.

♛ ** Free Fall**

Columbia CK 65446 *As above.* 62.

Giuffre's subsequent drummerless trios and cool, almost abstract tonality created nearly as much stir as Gerry Mulligan's pianoless quintets and encountered considerable critical resistance at the end of the 1950s. Nothing that had come along before quite prepares us for the astonishing work that Giuffre created with Paul Bley and Steve Swallow in two 1961 albums called *Fusion* (a term which hadn't yet taken on its 1970s associations) and *Thesis* (which seemed equally unpromising as the title of a jazz album). Paired and remastered as *1961*, they constitute ECM's first ever reissue; it's interesting, first, how modern the music sounds after 40 years (compare it with the Owl sets, below) and then how closely it seems to conform to ECM's familiar aesthetics of great formal precision and limpid sound. Herb Snitzer's session photographs have often been commented on. In deeply shadowed and evocatively focused black and white, they say something about the music. It's arguable that Giuffre's playing is equally monochrome and its basic orientation uncomfortably abstract; but again one notices its sometimes urgent but always compelling swing. The slightly earlier *Fusion* is perhaps the more daring of the two sets, balancing starkly simple ideas, as on 'Jesus Maria' and 'Scootin' About', with some complex harmonic conceptions (to which all three contribute). *Thesis*, though, is tighter and more fully realized, and tunes like 'Ictus' and 'Carla' (the former written by the dedicatee of the latter, Bley's then wife, Carla) have been an inexhaustible element of the pianist's concert improvisations ever since. By contrast, the music on *Fusion* seems fixed in and of its moment.

Free Fall, by contrast, is a trickier and more insidious sound altogether. A mixture of Giuffre solos (including some of his most piercing and antagonistic recorded statements) with duos and trios, it catches the group late on in its brief initial history. Remarkable to think of Columbia taking on a project like this in 1962 but, whatever the exact intention of the title, it was clear that the studiousness and philosophical calm which overlaid the previous discs was no longer to be expected. What you're hearing is something that has almost run its course in practical terms but which creatively is far from exhausted. Swallow's fiery scrabbles and sharply plucked single-note runs lend the music a new momentum and the sort of energy to be found in free jazz. Bley may be the most least comfortable of the three by this stage, but he has always been a restless experimenter and by 1962 his eye was probably on the next step. Giuffre often sounds as if he is in a world of his own, intensely focused, totally aware, but communicating ideas for which there was no ready-made language or critical rhetoric.

These – and *Free Fall* especially – are essential documents in the development of a broader jazz idiom that refused to see bop as the only recourse. Giuffre's pioneering has only slowly been recognized and it's valuable to jump straight from these sessions to *Diary Of A Trio*, below. Almost nothing has changed, except that Giuffre's tone has lost its slightly discursive quality, an effect underlined by his use of soprano saxophone, and Steve Swallow has renounced upright bass, on which he creates throbbing lines and interjections (these are, perhaps, the most dramatic sounds on *1961*), in favour of bass guitar.

*****(*) The Train And The River**

Candid Choice CHCD 1011 *Giuffre; Kiyoshi Tokunaga (b); Randy Kaye (perc).* 4/75.

A long quote from Herman Hesse's *Siddhartha* on the inner sleeve might stir a few warning doubts, which are in the end not necessary at all. Giuffre throws himself 'lovingly' into the 'river' of this music, but does so with an absolute lack of self-consciousness. The very fact that he should be willing to kick off with 'The Train And The River' after so many years is an indication that he hasn't overthrown his folk-jazz loyalties. However, tunes like 'Elephant', 'Tibetan Sun', 'The Listening' and 'Om' which follow do suggest an extra dimension in his work. Increased use of flute and bass flute invests some of these tunes with a fugitive, misterioso quality. Tokunaga and Kaye have interesting playing backgrounds, ranging from the Paul Winter Consort and Howard McGhee in the bassist's case, and Roswell Rudd to Jimi Hendrix in the drummer's. Here and there, such eclecticism becomes too obvious a dimension of their playing, but for the most part they are solid, responsive partners, completely in tune with what Giuffre is doing.

***** Quasar**
Soul Note 121108 *Giuffre; Pete Levin (ky); Bob Nieske (b); Randy Kaye (d).* 5/85.

***** Liquid Dancers**
Soul Note 121158 *As above.* 4/89.

For much of the later 1960s and '70s, the most intuitive improviser of his generation was obliged to teach improvisation to college students, gigging only in relative obscurity. Randy Kaye was a loyal and dependable supporter in those days, and he adds just the right kind of softly enunciated percussion to Giuffre's 1980s quartet albums (a third Soul Note, *Dragonfly*, is currently unavailable). Bob Nieske's 'The Teacher', on *Liquid Dancers*, pays no less a tribute. Scored for Giuffre's bass flute, it has a crepuscular, meditative quality that isn't altogether typical of a lively and almost self-consciously ('Move With The Times') contemporary set. Levin's keyboard stylings are perhaps a little too blandly atmospheric, but they open up the texture for Giuffre's familiar chalumeau clarinet and a surprisingly agile soprano saxophone. The earlier *Quasar* is equally fine and the writing may even be a little better.

*****(*) Eiffel**
CELP C6 *Giuffre; André Jaume (bcl, sax).* 11/87.

***** Momentum: Willisau, 1988**
hatOLOGY 508 *As above.* 88.

The best of these thoughtful, often delicate duos recall the best of Giuffre's work with Brookmeyer. Jaume has the same intensity and dry wit, and the register of his bass clarinet is not so far from that of the trombone. Recorded in concert, *Eiffel* consists of scored and improvised duets, none longer than five minutes, most around three. Jaume's saxophone on 'Stand Point' tends to break the mood a little but the studied, contemplative tone otherwise remains intact, and Giuffre's articulation and tone have seldom been more compelling. The Willisau set is gently floating, thoughtful and in some respects a little dull, unless you're prepared to give it the attention it deserves. Jaume is happy to play second fiddle, even as Giuffre defers and hesitates, and the best of the set is when the two voices are interwoven.

****** Diary Of A Trio: Saturday**
Owl 059 *Giuffre; Paul Bley (p); Steve Swallow (b).* 12/89.

****** Diary Of A Trio: Sunday**
Owl 060 *As above.* 12/89.

*****(*) Fly Away, Little Bird**
Owl 068 *As above.* 4/92.

When Jimmy Giuffre went back into the studio with Paul Bley and Steve Swallow in December 1989, the first notes he improvised were identical to a figure he had played on their last meeting, nearly 30 years before. Whether conscious or not, the gesture helps underline not just the intervening period of (for Giuffre) relative neglect but also the tremendous understanding that developed in the trio that produced *Free Fall*, *Fusion* and *Thesis*.

Diary Of A Trio is an astonishing achievement, whatever the chronology. A series of solos, duos and trio pieces, it has considerable spontaneity and freedom. There are, of course, significant changes from the early records. Swallow is now wholly converted to electric bass and is perhaps the leading bass guitarist in improvised music; Bley, though, has passed through his romance with electronics and now concentrates almost exclusively on acoustic piano. Giuffre, who was always a formidable tenor player as well as clarinettist, has added soprano saxophone, relishing both its directness and its untameable 'wildness' of pitch. Not least of the differences is a willingness to play standards, which they do with a characteristically oblique touch. Most highly recommended.

Owl's attempt to repeat the experiment in 1992 comes off only partially. Giuffre sounded tired, as he did throughout the European tour of that year, and much of the emphasis falls on exchanges between Bley and Swallow, with mere elaborations from saxophone and clarinet. They included some standards to keep the purists quiet. 'All The Things You Are', 'Sweet And Lovely', 'Lover Man' and 'I Can't Get Started': if only they'd thought to do that in 1961, Giuffre's CV and discography might well have read very differently!

*****(*) River Station**
CELP C 26 *Giuffre; Joe McPhee (tb); André Jaume (ts, bcl).* 9/91.

Repeating the triumphs of 30 years before, Giuffre found himself an honoured elder in Europe. With the exception of Bley and Swallow, it was nearly always Frenchmen who wanted to perform with him. This session has an air of relaxed preparedness. Some of the duos recall the Giuffre/Konitz encounter of 1978 (see above) and the walk-on contribution of Joe McPhee with his trombone on 'Three Way Split' sounds like a long after-echo of the classic Brookmeyer trio. Giuffre's wife had been writing a good deal of music before this time, and she contributes the outstanding 'When Things Go Wrong'. The only thing that has gone wrong with the recording is that both players seem to be placed at opposite ends of the studio. A little 'false mono' might actually have helped.

Frode Gjerstad

ALTO AND TENOR SAXOPHONES

Norwegian improviser who came to some prominence with a John Stevens group in the '80s and has since worked variously across two continents, with a burst of recent recording.

*****(*) Seeing New York From The Ear**
Cadence CJR 1069 *Gjerstad; William Parker (b); Rashid Bakr (d).* 3/96.

***** Ikosa Mura**
Cadence CJR 1089 *Gjerstad; Bobby Bradford (t); Borah Bergman (p); Pheeroan AkLaff (d).* 9/97.

***** Through The Woods**
CIMP 159 *Gjerstad; Bobby Bradford (t); Wilber Morris (b); Newman Baker (d).* 9/97.

***** Ultima**
Cadence CJR 1108 *Gjerstad; William Parker (b); Hamid Drake (d).* 10/97.

***** Borealis**

Cadence CJR 1091 *Gjerstad; Didrik Ingvaldesen (t); Oyvind Torvund (g); Oyvind Storesund, John Lilja (b); Endre Landsnes, Paal Nilssen-Love (d).* 2/98.

*****(*) Invisible Touch**

Cadence CJR 1099 *Gjerstad; Peter Brötzmann (ts, cl, tarogato).* 7/98.

Gjerstad will be remembered by British audiences for his work in the band, Detail, with John Stevens and John Dyani, in the mid-'80s. He's been less frequently heard from since then but has rather suddenly become much more ubiquitous with a flurry of releases on the Cadence and CIMP labels. Spending what seem to be equal amounts of time on alto and tenor, he's a blustery, energy-filled improviser whose playing rarely makes a profound impact but whose ideas thrive on sheer momentum and intensity; he's carried exultantly along by a thunderous groove or a dense stew of voices. *Seeing New York From The Ear* is much like a vintage Jimmy Lyons performance, Gjerstad's alto borne aloft on Bakr's splendid tumult, with Parker's ferocious lines binding it together. It may be music in a familiar mould, but the playing has staunch self-belief and inventiveness.

The two quartet records with Bobby Bradford are something of a reunion, since the trumpeter had previously played with Detail. *Ikosa Mura* is at times so dense and clotted with sound that the music all but congeals. If there's a culprit, it's the fulsome Bergman, who rarely does anything other than overplay; even so, the group often fuses into an exhilarating and rumbustious collective roar. *Through The Woods*, cut in the no-frills surroundings of the CIMP studio, seems very different. Faced with the noisy situation of the previous record, Bradford falls back on a kind of pattern-playing, but on this lighter stage his songful bent emerges. Morris and Baker create a softer, more scuffling rhythmic base. Lyrical moments such as the opening section of 'Frodiodi' are worth waiting for, but there's plenty of little consequence and Gjerstad is often the least impressive player.

Ultima is a single festival set which runs just under an hour. Drake doesn't make such a strong impression as Bakr did on the earlier trio date; for that reason this comes in as an also-ran, though the playing still has its momentous passages. *Borealis* is by Gjerstad's Norwegian crew, the Circulasione Totale Orchestra. Though a studio recording, it seems rather thin and stringy in sonic terms, which mitigates the sense of 'the wind blowing from the North', and the squalls are diminished more than they might be. Nevertheless, a welcome change of pace from the other records, with Torvund's electric whine howling through the core of the band's sound.

The meeting with Brötzmann is from a club gig in Stavanger. Gjerstad is far from overawed by his great contemporary, and if anything is the more ferocious competitor, sticking to alto on this occasion. The final movements are rather peaceable, resolute and collaborative while still in the raw.

Ole Amund Gjersvik

BASS

Norwegian bassist-composer, playing impressionistic small-group post-bop.

***** Milonga Triste**

Acoustic ACR 9808 *Gjersvik; Jan Kåre Hystad (saxes, f); Morten Faerestrand (g); Stein Inge Braekhus (d); Tone Lise Moberg (v).* 98.

We listed some earlier sets by Gjersvik for Acoustic in our second and third editions. He's popped up again with a fifth record for the label. 'The Gentle Rain', with a guest vocal by Moberg, sums up the style of this one: sweet, melancholy music, no special spark but graciously done, much of it delivered to a Europeanized Latin lilt.

Globe Unity Orchestra

GROUP

Formed in 1966 by Alex von Schlippenbach to perform his 'Globe Unity' composition, the Orchestra is a pan-European band of improvisers whose occasional appearances over some 35 years have been rare, but worth waiting for.

*****(*) Rumbling**

FMP CD 40 *Kenny Wheeler (t); Paul Rutherford, Albert Mangelsdorff (tb); Evan Parker (ss, ts); Steve Lacy (ss); Gerd Dudek (bs, bcl, f); Alex Von Schlippenbach (p); Peter Kowald (b); Paul Lovens (d).* 3/75.

****** 20th Anniversary**

FMP CD 45 *Manfred Schoof, Kenny Wheeler (t); Gunter Christmann, Paul Rutherford (tb); Peter Brötzmann, Rüdiger Carl, Gerd Dudek, Evan Parker, Michel Pilz (reeds); Alex von Schlippenbach (p); Derek Bailey (g); Peter Kowald (b, tba); Han Bennink (d, perc, cl); Paul Lovens (d).* 11/86.

Only two discs to show for an incomparable free-music institution. Formed in 1966, the Globe Unity Orchestra has had to sustain itself with rare concerts and even rarer records, an unworthy fate for arguably the finest group to attempt to reconcile big-band forms with free improvisation. Although there has been a revolving cast of players throughout the group's existence, a few hardy spirits (notably Alex Schlippenbach, the original organizer) act as a point of reference. The *Rumbling* CD is by what is more like a contingent from the orchestra. There is Monk's title-tune, a march by Misha Mengelberg and a tune by Lacy, while 'Into The Valley' is a nearly continuous 38-minute piece. The latter is the best demonstration of the group's powers, moving through solo and duet passages between the horns to thunderous all-in tussles. Problematically, the original LP editions of this music sounded grey and boxy, but the sound is much bigger and more convincing here.

To celebrate their twentieth anniversary, the Orchestra held a Berlin concert at which the 66-minute work on FMP CD 45 was played. While a shade below their 1977 masterpiece, *Pearls*, this is still a vivid, bristling assemblage of ideas and individual spontaneities: Schlippenbach's hand is on the tiller, but each man asserts his individual mastery in his personal way. A very good way of making acquaintance with many of the great modernists of the past 30 years. But will we ever hear more from them? This recording is now 14 years old, and the GUO seems to belong to the past.

Ben Goldberg

CLARINET, BASS CLARINET

New York-based improviser, aligning his work around the clarinet family.

****(*) Junk Genius**
Knitting Factory Works KFW 160 *Goldberg; John Schott (g); Trevor Dunn (b); Kenny Wolleson (d).* 2–3/94.

***** Here By Now**
Music & Arts 1004 *Goldberg; Trevor Dunn (b); Elliot Humberto Kavee (d).* 3/96.

*****(*) Eight Phrases For Jefferson Rubin**
Victo 057 *Goldberg; Larry Ochs (sno, ts); John Schott (g); Trevor Dunn, Lisle Ellis (b); Michael Sarin (d).* 11/96.

***** Ghost Of Electricity**
Songlines SGL 1525-2 *Goldberg; John Schott (g); Trevor Dunn (b); Kenny Wollesen (d).* 2/99.

Goldberg is an experienced voice in and out of jazz; one of his groups was called the New Klezmer Trio. He plays somewhat proper clarinet, unwilling to make much out of tonal adventures, and that makes *Junk Genius* a less than suitable platform for him. It's a rather scruffy, madcap exploration of old bebop tunes in which the instrumentalists fall over and around the melody lines with flair and clumsiness alike. All right, but a little of it goes a long way. *Here By Now* is almost a recital of nine pieces by Goldberg in which the trio more or less play the tunes with the minimum of elaboration, improvisation or fuss. Goldberg's phrasing may strike some as prim and his tone takes on a neutral quality in this situation; the music's more about playing a piece as an entire, already-completed structure, with the jazz element residing in feel alone. If that appeals, then the trio's collective gravitas will impress.

Eight Phrases For Jefferson Rubin, in dedication to a childhood friend who had recently been killed in an accident, is his most personal and effective record. Some of the 'phrases' are rather ponderously long, such as 'Plain Of Jars', but the intriguing instrumentation and pensive, slightly ominous feel of the music are surprisingly powerful, often recalling the feel of Dave Holland's great *Conference Of The Birds* album. Goldberg frequently defers to his fellow players, and the result is a democratic but quite powerfully realized group record of some moment.

Ghost Of Electricity reconvenes the group from the debut record, with five years of growth in between. Strains of old, lost musics – 'hymns, stomps, hollers, anarchic strum-alongs' – are what the record seems to be after. With Schott taking the Frisell route of conjuring every kind of Americana out of the electric guitar's resources, he tends to dominate the soundscaping here, leaving Goldberg to take a rather lonely course over the top. Dunn and Wollesen play what they think will work. The results are often striking – and, just as often, almost arbitrary.

Larry Goldings

ORGAN, PIANO, MELODICA

Born in Massachusetts, Goldings became a principal on the New York scene in the early '90s, specializing in Hammond organ and adaptable to many kinds of playing situation. Spent a period with John Scofield and he has also featured on piano on one of his own dates.

***** Intimacy Of The Blues**
Minor Music 801017 *Goldings; David 'Fathead' Newman (ts); Peter Bernstein (g); Bill Stewart (d).* 91.

***** Light Blue**
Minor Music 801026 *As above, except omit Newman.* 92.

The virtue of Goldings's approach to the Hammond B-3 is its easeful simplicity. Both albums are thoughtfully titled, given the plain, small-hours moods which Goldings prefers to evoke instead of all-stops-out virtuosity. The subtly shaded solo treatment of 'Here, There And Everywhere' on *Light Blue* is typical. Bernstein plays the Grant Green role with loose-limbed skill, and Stewart is guileful at the drums, while Newman makes three cameo appearances on the first record. All that said, there's very little here that hasn't been done on a McGriff or Smith record: only the big-screen digital sound is a novelty, when most of the classic organ-jazz records date from the 1960s.

***** Caminhos Cruzados**
Novus 01241 63184-2 *Goldings; Joshua Redman (ts); Peter Bernstein (g); Bill Stewart (d); Guilherme Franco (perc).* 12/93.

*****(*) Whatever It Takes**
Warner Bros 945996-2 *As above, except add Fred Wesley (tb), David Sanborn, Maceo Parker (as), Richard Patterson (b); omit Franco.* 95.

The Novus album is more of the same as the Minor Music records, though more healthily energetic: 'So Danco Samba', normally taken at a tempo that would slow most dancers to a crawl, skips along. Redman appears on three tracks and blows some hearty solos. *Whatever It Takes*, though, is more cannily presented. The material is biased towards funky pop – Stevie Wonder, Sly Stone, Ray Charles – and the spots by Sanborn, Parker, Wesley and Redman (again) add a touch of class without sounding too much like here-comes-the-guest-star. But it's not done at the expense of Goldings's cool blue side, since 'Slo-Boat' and 'Willow Weep For Me' handle that very effectively. Excellent, full-blooded studio sound seals the deal.

***** Big Stuff**
Warners 946271-2 *Goldings; John McKenna (ts); Peter Bernstein, Kurt Rosenwinkel (g); Bill Stewart, Idris Muhammad (d); Bashiri Johnson, Guilherme Franco (perc).* 3/96.

***** Awareness**
Warners 946621-2 *Goldings; Larry Grenadier (b); Paul Motian (d).* 12/96.

Goldings is clearly a gifted and ambitious player, and these discs are a sound continuation of an interesting if not quite arresting body of work. Goldings loves the organ, but he probably realizes its limitations: some clever choices of material on *Big Stuff*, such as Carla Bley's 'Ida Lupino' and Ellington's 'Purple Gazelle', receive thoughtful treatments, and even though there's a tenor player and a couple of guitarists involved, it sounds nothing much like an organ–tenor–guitar–drums record. But the material still seems insufficiently characterized. If Goldings wants to do something new and personal in this area, this essentially reserved approach isn't enough.

Awareness sidesteps the issue altogether by presenting him exclusively on piano. Much of the record is rather self-consciously individual: 'Embraceable You' is almost indecipherably oblique, and the original themes are a likeably fanciful collection. His delivery has a Monk-like tinge which goes rather well with Paul Motian's drum parts. But little about it suggests the stature of a great record, more an episode in an evolving œuvre – he must hope he gets the chance to expand it further.

Per Goldschmidt

BARITONE SAXOPHONE

Danish saxophonist specializing in baritone, with international experience.

***** Cage Rage**
Olufsen DOCD 5095 *Goldschmidt; Erling Kroner (tb); Nikolaj Bentzon (p); Klavs Hovman (b); Preben Petersen (d).* 11/88.

***** Another Night, Another Day**
Olufsen DOCD 5129 *As above.* 11/88.

***** The Frame**
Timeless SJP 290 *Goldschmidt; Niels Lan Doky (p); Lonnie Plaxico (b); Jack DeJohnette (d).* 2/87.

***** Frankly**
Milestone MCD-9224-2 *As above, except add Tom Harrell (t, flhn), Niels-Henning Orsted Pedersen (b), Alvin Queen (d); omit Plaxico, DeJohnette.* 12/93.

Goldschmidt is no romantic fool on the baritone. He loves its weight and impact and he powers along with few concessions to its size: even on ballads he prefers to take a terser line than Mulligan or Chaloff ever would have done. Structurally, he's a hard-bopper who can't abide the clichés of the genre. Some of the tunes on the Olufsen albums are mere sketches to blow on, but he never takes the easy line, chopping his phrasing, bouncing off the drive of the rhythm section, wrestling with himself to make it turn out new. Not that any one of these is a masterpiece. The Olufsens were recorded back-to-back in one marathon session – the second ends with an alternative take of track one on the first – and their sheer rough-and-tumble merits applause. Bentzon is wildly excitable at the piano, playing with Pullen-like intensity, and Petersen hammers and rolls through the rhythms. Kroner is sober, almost deadpan, and that sits usefully with Goldschmidt's sometimes blustering improvising. The horns are weakened by the indifferent mix and the records never peak, but they're an exhilarating pair.

The Timeless album assembles a classier band. Goldschmidt plays with fine energy and purpose and the band are behind him, but the music misses decisiveness, and that sometimes results in rambling: the ironic bossa nova of 'Loneliness', for instance, merely turns hollow. Nor is Doky's production very agreeable. He also produces the Milestone session, which sounds terrific, and there are some marvellous moments here: 'Theme For Eve', for baritone, bass and drums only, is exquisitely modulated, and Goldschmidt plays with extra swagger and resilience on the up-tempo tracks. But the concept, playing songs associated with Frank Sinatra, seems intended to tame the leader's most adventurous side, and Harrell, if dependable, seems a notch below his best.

Vinny Golia

CLARINETS, FLUTES, SAXOPHONES, SHAKUHACHI, ETC.

Based in the Los Angeles area, Golia and his Nine Winds label are at the heart of the Californian free-playing community. He came to attention in the 1970s as a multi-instrumentalist and has led numerous sessions, from solo to big-ensemble performance. His arsenal of wind instruments is vast and he delights in exploring every timbral register.

***** Worldwide And Portable**
Nine Winds NWCD 0143 *Golia; Wayne Peet (p); Ken Filiano (b).* 2/86.

****** Regards From Norma Desmond**
Fresh Sound FSNT 008 *Golia; John Fumo (t); Wayne Peet (p); Ken Filiano (b); Alex Cline (d).* 10/86.

***** Haunting The Spirits Inside Them ...**
Music & Arts CD-893 *Golia; Joelle Léandre, Ken Filiano (b).* 4/92.

*****(*) Against The Grain**
Nine Winds NWCD 0159 *Golia; Rob Blakeslee (t); Nels Cline (g); Ken Filiano (b); Billy Mintz (d).* 10/93.

Vinny Golia has been a central figure in the West Coast avant-garde for many years, and with his Nine Winds label he's been undertaking virtually a one-man documentation of the improvising underground of California – far less 'fashionable' than anything out of New York, but no less significant in the grain of American free jazz. By himself, in the small-group context, Golia reveals an obsession with doubling on numerous instruments: he plays 11 different woodwinds on *Worldwide And Portable*, changing the weave with each different reed. He calls this group The Chamber Trio, and the mood is assuredly sober, the ambitions of the group seemingly based around texture rather than individual lines. The most swinging piece, peculiarly enough, is a dedication to Kafka! But Golia, Peet and Filiano know each other's work very well, and there is much subtlety of interaction. *Against The Grain* is another admirable outing for his quintet: Golia's fascination with long form comes out in the 24-minute 'Presents To Savages/Alternation', and there is some superb contrapuntalism in 'SBB-CFF'. He sticks to sopranino and soprano saxes and two clarinets here; on the meeting with Filiano and Léandre, a chance session following a concert, he plays only flutes, clarinets, piccolo, ocarina, shakuhachi and sheng. This is a whispery, introverted music, the two basses somewhat distant in the sound-mix and Golia laying out as often as pitching in, with sometimes mixed results.

It might seem perverse to pick out a rare record for another label as one of Golia's best. But the recently issued 1986 session for Fresh Sound is a corker. Golia sticks to baritone sax throughout *Regards From Norma Desmond*, and with one of his favourite line-ups they blaze through 50 minutes of free bop that's gripping from first to last, with the outstanding threnody for Booker Little, 'The Cry', particularly fine.

*****(*) Razor**
Nine Winds 0169 *Golia; Michael Vlatkovich (tb); Nels Cline (g); Joel Hamilton (b); Billy Mintz (d).* 4/95.

*****(*) Dante No Longer Repents**
Music & Arts C-992 *Golia; Rob Blakeslee (c, t, flhn); Tad Weed (p); Michael Bisio (b); Billy Mintz (d).* 4/96.

*****(*) Nation Of Laws**
Nine Winds NWCD 0189 *Golia; Rob Blakeslee (c, t, flhn); Nels Cline (g); Joel Hamilton (b); Alex Cline (d).* 7/96.

Three different editions of Golia's quintet. Because Golia himself is partial to such a wide range of horns, the textural possibilities of his groups seem limitless but, just to make sure, there are crucial changes in line-up across the three discs. Vlatkovich uses plenty of variation by himself, mutes and open tones constantly under review, and with Cline changing his own set-up and Mintz and Hamilton booting the group along, this is a restless occasion, provocatively delivered. *Dante No Longer Repents* has some striking contributions from Weed: if Wayne Peet is a more frequent confederate, Weed still summons some beautiful commentaries on the rest of the music, and his harmonic balancing stops the music going too wayward at a few critical moments. Golia is at his most spontaneously inventive on some of these tracks, picking up the piccolo at one point for a startling solo, and although a few pieces outstay their welcome – one often feels that Golia and his various bands love to play so much that it's hard to get them to stop – it's a fine record. *Nation Of Laws* carries on the sequence in good style. The Cline brothers bring their own strengths, and in some ways Nels is the star of the date: listen to his contrasting solos on 'Not Very Pleasance' (crazily mercurial) and 'Perfect In the Pocket' (quickfire post-bop). Golia and Blakeslee push their way forward with a constant exploratory air, as if trying out their front-line sounds and changing their tone and dynamic just to see what new wrinkles they can negotiate. All three, even with their occasional blind turnings, objectify the ways this kind of freeish but already-formulated language can be kept fresh.

***** The Art Of Negotiation**
CIMP 111 *Golia; Ken Filiano (b).* 3/96.

Golia isn't one to parade his technique, but for once – playing clarinet, bass clarinet and sopranino – he takes a stance of aggressive virtuosity, which Filiano sometimes follows (and sometimes not). Though some of these duos run dry before their chops do, there's plenty to listen to.

***** Halloween '96**
CIMP 129 *Golia; Paul Smoker (t); Ken Filiano (b); Phil Haynes (d).* 10/96.

Cut as a long, loud blow, this kind of date isn't really Smoker's ideal situation, his lines dispersing into a buzz, and with Golia sticking to baritone sax the music's rather grainy and unrelievedly dark (maybe the season played its part). That said, the quartet give their all to the situation, and on the less intense moments some of Smoker's patient lyricism gleams through.

****(*) 11 Reasons To Begin**
Music & Arts CD-966 *Golia; Bertram Turetzky (b).* 3/96.

***** Prataksis**
Nine Winds NWCD 0199 *As above, except add Leo Smith (t).* 4/97.

A previous collaboration between Golia and Turetzky is listed under the bassist's name. For *11 Reasons*, Golia brings out his most worldly instruments – sheng, cor anglais, double clay flute, Ghanaian and Chinese flutes, nagaswaram, moxena, Mexican clay ocarina and bon-di – and the results are a curious blend of the exotic and the ascetic. Turetzky's skills as an improviser remain somewhat in doubt, but the best of these duets are as vividly strange as they aspire to be.

When Smith joins in for *Prataksis*, the music becomes altogether more declamatory without exactly raising its voice. The trumpeter's signature gravitas lends an authority to the occasion which raises the music-making to a higher level, although the uncommitted will probably find this something of a meander. Golia himself has a more decorative role: he never quite has a counter for Smith's stoic melody lines.

***** Duets**
Nine Winds NWCD 0204 *Golia; Susan Allen (hp).* 5/98.

*****(*) Lineage**
Nine Winds NWCD 0214 *Golia; Bobby Bradford (t); Ken Filiano (b); Alex Cline (d).* 8/98.

The duo record with harpist Susan Allen is a good example of Golia's instrumental range: he goes from piccolo to contrabassoon, with seven other instruments in between. Allen is a new-music and classical performer and, while she's played with many jazz musicians, her own methods tend towards a sympathetic formality: her responses to Golia depend primarily on her harmonic imagination. It's a record best sampled two or three duets at a time, since over the long haul it tends to follow a repetitious pattern.

Lineage is an encounter with that distinguished West Coast eminence, Bobby Bradford. He may not have been on any of Golia's previous Nine Winds records, but they know each other's playing well and, with Filiano and Cline veterans of this music too, the record is a generous conversation among old friends. The cadences of the playing have a well-worn and settled quality: it's a music not of surprise but of supportive empathy. The pleasures come in the skill and grace which these experts use as they go into free space – something not unlike a band of veteran beboppers sifting a chord sequence for a fresh result.

*****(*) Pilgrimage To Obscurity**
Nine Winds NWCD 0130 *Golia; John Fumo, Ralf Rickert, Sal Cracchiolo (t, flhn); Michael Vlatkovich, Doug Wintz, John Rapson (tb); David Stout (btb); Mike Acosta, Steve Fowler, Wynell Montgomery, David Ocker (reeds); David Johnson (vib, mar); Eric Messerschmidt (tba); Ken Filiano, Roberto Miranda (b); Billy Mintz (d); Alex Cline (perc).* 12/85.

*****(*) Decennium Dans Axlan**

Nine Winds NWCD 0140 *Golia; Mark Underwood, John Fumo, Rob Blakeslee (t, flhn); Bruce Fowler, George McMullen (tb); Phil Teele (btb); Emily Hay, Steve Fowler, Bill Plake, David Ocker (reeds); Wayne Peet (ky); Jeff Gauthier (vn); Jonathan Golove, Dion Sorell (clo); Ken Filiano, Joel Hamilton (b); Alex Cline (d); Brad Dutz (perc).* 4/92.

*****(*) Commemoration**

Nine Winds NWCD 0150/0160 2CD *As above, except add Marissa Benedict (t), Michael Vlatkovich (tb), Kim Richmond (reeds), Harry Scorzo (vn), Greg Adamson, Matt Cooker (clo), William Roper (tba), David Johnson (perc).* 91–92.

***** Tutto Contare**

Nine Winds NWCD 0170 *As above, except add Eric Jorgensen, Joey Sellars (tb), Charles Fernandez (bsn), Steve Adams (reeds), Michael Jacobsen (clo); omit Bruce Fowler, Hay, Gauthier, Benedict, Golove, Adamson, Sorell.* 11/95.

*****(*) Portland 1996**

Nine Winds NWCD 0180 *As above, except add Sal Cracchiolo (t, flhn), Robie Hioki (btb), Kim Richmond (reeds), Jeff Gauthier (vn), Jonathan Golove, Peggy Lee (clo); omit Jorgensen, Sellars, Jacobsen, Ocker.* 2/96.

Golia's Large Ensemble stands apart from his small-group work. The records are fragments from ten years of work with this vast orchestra which Golia apparently keeps going out of his own pocket; with several CDs now available, however, their grand, purposely monumental repertoire is starting to get a fair showing. The group moves like some sea-going leviathan: ponderous, sluggish at times, but suddenly raising itself and achieving grace and beauty. Golia always insists on the weight and thick sonority of the orchestra: sections call and respond to one another somewhat in the big-band tradition, but there is little that one can call swinging, more the contrast of great blocks of sound, the emergence of a soloist to say his piece, the chattering of brass or lowering of a bass reed section. *Pilgrimage To Obscurity* – self-effacing to be sure – alternates between rousing all-hands-on pieces and thinned-out, dirge-like textures. *Decennium Dans Axlan* starts even more slowly, with the gradually accumulating power of 'Tapestry Of Things Before', and ends on the similarly inclined 'Man In A Bottle'; in between, there are some beautiful solos by Rob Blakeslee, Bruce Fowler and Steve Fowler from the round-robin of improvisers. *Commemoration*, though a more recent release, was in part recorded prior to *Decennium Dans Axlan*. Again, Golia marshals his forces around key points, waving in some instruments, keeping others under wraps, and only rarely going for the big climax – though when he does, as on the towering 'Tumulus Or Griffin', it's mightily impressive. *Tutto Contare* is for some reason just slightly less involving: 'Chromazoid', with a superb solo by Rob Blakeslee, is exceptional, but the other pieces are neither more nor less than interesting pieces from the repertory of an imposing orchestra. Their set from Portland finds them back to form immediately in the beautiful 'Surrounded By Assassins', which has some ingenious textural points to make even before the gripping solos by Fernandez (bassoon) and Gauthier (violin). This leads into the mighty sprawl of 'Blue Hawk', a discrete homage to Hawkins, Young and Webster. Golia has long since been using the Ensemble to explore a world that lies somewhere between jazz, improvisation and formal composition: in some of this music especially, he seems close to alighting on a unique world. But the problem which troubles the earlier discs seems just as intrusive on these later ones: the recording quality simply isn't good enough; in a group with two bassists and three percussionists, playing scores of this much complexity, it has to be a lot closer to standard to make the music come fully to life on record.

*****(*) The Other Bridge (Oakland 1999)**

Nine Winds NWCD 0210/0220 2CD *Golia; John Fumo, Jeff Kaiser, Rob Blakeslee (t); Mike Vlatkovich, Danny Hemwall, Scott Ray (tb); Kim Richmond, Paul Sherman, Bill Plake, Eric Barber, Steve Adams, Alan Lechusza, Tara Speiser, Sarah Shoenbeck (woodwinds); Wayne Peet (ky); Harry Scorzo, Jeff Gauthier (vn); Jonathan Golove, Guenevere Measham, Colin Pearson (clo); Bill Roper (tba); Ken Filiano (b); David Johnson, Brad Dutz, Alex Cline (perc); Stephanie Henry (cond).* 8/99.

Golia thinks big for his large-scale recordings, and here's another two and a half hours of music for the Large Ensemble. He may have written and scored all the music, but it's scarcely a setting for personal grandstanding: he gives himself just one solo across the entire two discs. The bustling, ebullient 'Thread For Fred' should silence any who feel that jazz is only a modest part of the Large Ensemble's direction, and the soloists – out of the stellar cast, Kim Richmond, Jeff Kaiser and John Fumo merit a particular huzzah – honour the composer's intentions. We feel there is little to add, though, to our judgement on the Ensemble's earlier records. It still sounds like a decent amateur recording rather than the kind of document the Ensemble deserves, but the quality of the music manages to overcome the presentation shortcomings.

Benny Golson (born 1929)

TENOR SAXOPHONE

A Philadelphian, Golson went from jazz and R&B combos in the early 1950s to arranging for Dizzy Gillespie in 1956; then a stint with Art Blakey, and the formation of The Jazztet with Art Farmer in 1959. In the '60s and '70s his main work was as a composer for film and TV, but in the '80s he returned to regular jazz gigs and has recorded frequently since. His book of jazz compositions is one of the most enduring of its kind, with several pieces among the most-played hard-bop compositions.

***** Benny Golson's New York Scene**

Original Jazz Classics OJC 164 *Golson; Art Farmer (t); Jimmy Cleveland (tb); Julius Watkins (frhn); Gigi Gryce (as); Sahib Shihab (bs); Wynton Kelly (p); Paul Chambers (b); Charli Persip (d).* 10/57.

***** The Modern Touch**

Original Jazz Classics OJC 1797 *Golson; Kenny Dorham (t); J.J Johnson (tb); Wynton Kelly (p); Paul Chambers (b); Max Roach (d).* 12/57.

***** Benny Golson And The Philadelphians**

Blue Note 494104-2 *Golson; Lee Morgan, Roger Guerin (t); Ray Bryant, Bobby Timmons (p); Percy Heath, Pierre Michelot (b); Philly Joe Jones, Christian Garros (d).* 11–12/58.

*****(*) Gone With Golson**

Original Jazz Classics OJC 1850 *Golson; Curtis Fuller (tb); Ray Bryant (p); Tom Bryant (b); Al Harewood (d).* 6/59.

****** Groovin' With Golson**

Original Jazz Classics OJC 226 *Golson; Curtis Fuller (tb); Ray Bryant (p); Paul Chambers (b); Art Blakey (d).* 8/59.

***** Gettin' With It**

Original Jazz Classics OJC 1873 *Golson; Curtis Fuller (tb); Tommy Flanagan (p); Doug Watkins (b); Art Taylor (d).* 12/59.

***** The Other Side Of Benny Golson**

Original Jazz Classics OJC 1750 *Golson; Curtis Fuller (tb); Barry Harris (p); Jymie Merritt (b); Philly Joe Jones (d).* 11/58.

***** Stockholm Sojourn**

Original Jazz Classics OJC 1894 *Golson; Benny Bailey, Bo Broberg, Bengt-Arne Wallin (t); Grachan Moncur III, Eje Thelin (tb); Cecil Payne (bs); Roman Dylong (b); others. n.d.*

Golson will always be considered, primarily, as a composer/ arranger of such standards as 'I Remember Clifford', 'Whisper Not' and 'Stablemates'. His powers as a saxophonist have tended to be overshadowed, although his still-growing discography has reasserted the stature of his own playing. Despite contributing several of the staple pieces in the hard-bop repertoire, his own playing style originally owed rather more to such swing masters as Hawkins and Lucky Thompson: a big, crusty tone and a fierce momentum sustain his solos, and they can take surprising and exciting turns, even if the unpredictability sometimes leads to a loss of focus. The earlier of the two 1957 sessions concentrates on the more reflective side of his work, with three tracks by a nonet, three by a quintet with Farmer, and a ballad interpretation of 'You're Mine You' with the rhythm section alone: all well played but comparatively reserved. *The Modern Touch* is impeccably tailored hard bop, bedecked with good writing by the leader and suave playing by the sextet, but it's uneventful rather than exciting.

The later discs contain the seeds of the group which would, when joined full time by Farmer, become the Jazztet. The best is *Groovin'*, titled appropriately since the band hit a splendid pace from the start, and Golson and Fuller turn in inspired solos. *Gone With Golson* is only a notch behind: Golson fashions a catchy arrangement of Bryant's 'Staccato Swing', takes an impassioned course through 'Autumn Leaves' and turns in a fine 'Blues After Dark'. *Gettin' With It* is rather too casual here and there, starting with a 'Baubles, Bangles And Beads' which is so relaxed it scarcely comes off the starting blocks. There's consolation in 'Tippin' On Thru' and a very slow and consummately controlled 'April In Paris'. *The Other Side* is also at a lower temperature but is still very worthwhile. *Stockholm Sojourn* is more about Golson the arranger than the player, and features a Swedish ensemble with various expatriate guests. The scores seem a little restricted by LP playing-time but there are some interesting touches, and Benny Bailey makes a moving statement out of this version of 'I Remember Clifford'.

A recent arrival is *Benny Golson And The Philadelphians*, which is now a Blue Note CD but was originally a United Artists LP. The original album is a fine and characteristic set of hard bop, with 'Thursday's Theme' one of the best of Golson's less-remembered tunes: he and Morgan hit it off as well as they ever did. Four tracks made in France with a local group a few weeks later are less involving and water down the programme somewhat, though Golson's playing is as committed as always.

*****(*) Three Little Words**

Jazz House JHAS 609 *Golson; Stan Tracey (p); Rick Laird (b); Ronnie Stephenson, Billy Hart (d).* 11/65.

A fascinating discovery and a very rare example of Golson captured live in his prime, on a residency at the Ronnie Scott Club. Seven long pieces chronicle an evening's work and even though the CD runs a whisker under 80 minutes it's consistently gripping. The intensities which Golson finds in his favourite 'Stablemates' or in a marathon 'Stella By Starlight' are almost shocking: when the former is followed by a caressing treatment of the melody of 'My Foolish Heart' it's a disturbing change of mood. Golson always insists that Coltrane never really influenced his methods and it's intriguing to hear how he is both like and unlike his illustrious contemporary. This is tenor playing of controlled but formidable power and it makes a strong case for reconsidering Golson the saxophonist. The disc also affords a chance to hear Tracey at length, and splendid he is too (Hart replaces Stephenson on the final three numbers). One has to make allowances for the scruffy recording, which is why we have to take off a point.

**** Tune In, Turn On**

Verve 559793-2 *Golson; Art Farmer (t, flhn); Richard Tee (p); Eric Gale (g); James Tyrell (b); Bernard Purdie (d); Warren Smith (perc).* 4/67.

It's not Golson's fault that rubbish like this has returned to the racks: some record companies will stop at nothing to make the most of their back pages. This set of 'the hippest commercials of the '60s' is suitably cheesy: oboes, harpsichords and dub-dub-dah-dah singers vying for attention on jingle-based pieces such as 'Music To Think By'(!). The miracle is that Golson himself still manages to inject a few soulful solos into this situation. The whole is probably not really kitsch enough for some tastes.

***** California Message**

Timeless SJP 177 *Golson; Oscar Brashear (t); Curtis Fuller, Thurman Green (tb); Bill Mays (p); Bob Magnusson (b); Roy McCurdy (d).* 10/80.

***** Time Speaks**

Timeless SJP 187 *Golson; Freddie Hubbard, Woody Shaw (t); Kenny Barron (p); Cecil McBee (b); Ben Riley (d).* 12/84.

****(*) This Is For You, John**

Timeless SJP 235 *Golson; Pharoah Sanders (ts); Cedar Walton (p); Ron Carter (b); Jack DeJohnette (d).* 12/83.

Back in a playing milieu after many years in studio work, Golson cuts an interesting figure. Though his tone has weakened and taken on a querulous edge, his playing hasn't so much declined in stature as changed its impact. He had traded his swing influences for Coltrane 20 years earlier and, by the 1980s – after a sabbatical in film and TV scoring – it had resulted in the kind of introspective passion which marks out some of Coltrane's music, even if Golson chose a more conservative set of aims. These three Timeless albums include some top-drawer sidemen, but Golson is invariably the most interesting presence on each session. *California Message* is a sound if rather routine date; *Time Speaks* is better, with the stellar line-up clearly enjoying itself. Golson's solo on the opening 'I'll Remember April' is a textbook example of how he adapted Coltrane's methods to his own ends. Unfortunately the interplay between Hubbard and Shaw is rather splashy, and the piano is too remote in the mix (a characteristic Rudy Van Gelder trait). *This Is For You, John* should have been a classic meeting with Sanders, with Golson confronting Coltrane's influence to the full, yet the session too often degenerates into rambling solos to maintain real interest.

***** Up Jumped Benny**

Arkadia 70741 *Golson; Kevin Hays (p); Dwayne Burno (b); Carl Allen (d).* 5/86.

*****(*) Live**

Dreyfus 191057-2 *Golson; Mulgrew Miller (p); Peter Washington (b); Tony Reedus (d).* 2/89.

*****(*) Domingo**

Dreyfus 191132-2 *Golson; Jean-Loup Longnon (t); Curtis Fuller (tb); Kevin Hays (p); James Genus (b); Tony Reedus (d).* 11/91.

Golson sounds in wonderful voice on *Live*, captured on a European stopover in Porto Maggiore. There's a feathery, rippling treatment of 'I Remember Clifford' which makes it clear that, although there have been countless versions of this ballad, the composer himself still has fresh things to say about it. 'Jam The Avenue' is the kind of blow-out that has to have everyone's chops in good order, and Golson has no trouble there. 'Sweet And Lovely' shows that he is still learning from Coltrane, too. The studio date features an impressive quintet (Longnon turns up only for 'Blues March') and continues the long and intriguing partnership between Golson and Fuller, a dialogue seldom remarked on but as productive as any in the post-bop era. The title-track was originally arranged for Lee Morgan in the 1950s and has hardly been heard since, but Golson comes up with a fine new arrangement, and it's a pity that he otherwise contributes only one new piece, 'Thinking Mode'; the rest are staples from his book, as well as Fuller's spirited 'A La Mode' and Brubeck's 'In Your Own Sweet Way'.

Up Jumped Benny is an appearance with a young rhythm section, recently issued, in which Golson again makes the running on some of his favourites, along with the nice touch of including Clifford Brown's 'Tiny Capers'. The Swiss audience tends to be a bit noisy, but Golson again impresses with his no-nonsense approach to the material.

***** I Remember Miles**

Evidence ECD 22141-2 *Golson; Eddie Henderson (t); Curtis Fuller (tb); Mulgrew Miller (p); Ray Drummond (b); Tony Reedus (d).* 10/92.

Rather an obvious premiss, with Golson leading a seasoned troupe through six Davis staples and a couple of originals, and with Henderson putting in his mute and donning the mantle; by the time they get to 'So What' one wonders at the point of it all. But this is such a great band that it's hard not to enjoy the motions they're going through.

*****(*) Tenor Legacy**

Arkadia Jazz 0742 *Golson; Branford Marsalis, James Carter, Harold Ashby (ts); Geoff Keezer (p); Dwayne Burno (b); Joe Farnsworth (d).* 1/96.

What at first seems like a mismatch blossoms into a compelling, cross-generational recital that blends old spirits like Golson and Ashby with young firebrands such as Carter and the rhythm section. Each track is in dedication to a tenorman of yore (bar Sonny Rollins, still with us) and the treatments are apposite and surprising too. 'Cry Me A River', for instance, catches much of Dexter Gordon's lonesome wit, but is updated by Carter's lightning insights. Ashby sounds a bit frail on his five appearances, but there's no denying his character, and it's a strong counter to Carter's explosive cameos on his feature tracks. Branford arrives only to share 'Body And Soul' with Benny, a cryptic, fascinating version. Golson's thick, foggy sound fittingly wraps things up with a poignant 'In Memory Of', dedicated to his first great influence, Don Byas. Not without its flaws, but a deep and memorable record.

***** Remembering Clifford**

Milestone 9728-2 *Golson; John Swana (t); Ron Blake (ts); Mike LeDonne (p); Peter Washington (b); Joe Farnsworth (d); Tito Puente, Carlos Patato Valdes (perc).* 2/97.

Golson leads a team of youngish boppers through some new originals, a couple of old favourites and a surprising take on 'Lullaby Of Birdland'. Pushing seventy, the maestro still sounds in great nick: compared to Ron Blake, he has a chestier and less mobile sound, but he surrenders nothing in expressiveness on the ballad, 'You're The First To Know'. The pick of the others, perhaps surprisingly, is LeDonne, whose fills and solos have a jaunty and quick-witted edge that makes plenty of appeal.

Eddie Gomez (born 1944)

BASS

Born in Puerto Rico, Gomez built his career in New York and became a member of the classic Bill Evans trio after an apprenticeship in an array of modern and avant-garde outfits. His fast, inventive style is an asset in almost every conceivable context.

****(*) Next Future**

Stretch GRS 00062 *Gomez: Rick Margitza (ts, ss); Jeremy Steig (f); James Williams (p); Chick Corea (p, syn); Lenny White (d).* 93.

***** Dedication**

Evidence ECD 2208 *Gomez; Stefan Karlsson (p); Jimmy Cobb (d).* 4/98.

Gomez hasn't been extensively recorded as leader. *Next Future* is pretty drab, a bland studio set redeemed only by the two Chick Corea tunes, 'Lost Tango', a lament for Astor Piazzolla, and 'Basic Trane-ing'. Margitza is an uninspiring choice for this set-up, but Williams plays rhythmically and well in a modified version of Corea's own piano idiom.

Dedication consists largely of tunes that Eddie would have played in his decade-plus with Bill Evans, though a dazzling arrangement of Wayne Shorter's 'Footprints', promising pianist Karlsson's 'Spider Song' and the title-track, which closes the record, open it up to a more recent repertoire. Eddie's bass playing is at its most fluent and expressive and his *arco* melody line on 'Spartacus Love Theme' is grace incarnate. Jimmy Cobb is as magisterial on 'Nardis' and 'Autumn Leaves' as you might expect. Albums by Gomez as leader are rare, so this one is to be cherished.

Nat Gonella (1908–98)

TRUMPET, VOCALS

Began playing in minor dance bands before joining Billy Cotton in 1929. In the '30s, with his Georgians, he became a star performer, broadcaster and recording artist. Tried bop briefly after the war, then worked in music hall and variety, with a career revival in 1959, subsequently eclipsed by rock. An honoured elder statesman, he was still singing in the last year of his life.

***** Nat Gonella And His Georgians**
Flapper PAST CD 9750 *Gonella; Bruts Gonella, Johnny Morrison, Chas Oughton, Jack Wallace (t); Miff King (tb); Jack Bonser, Jock Middleton, Joe Moore, Ernest Morris, Mickey Seidman, Albert Torrance (cl, as, bs); Pat Smuts, Don Barigo (ts); Harold Hood, Monia Liter, Norman Stenfalt (p); Roy Dexter, Jimmy Mesene (g); Will Hemmings (b); Bob Dryden, Johnny Roland (d).* 1/35–10/40.

Nat's Georgians – in which brother Bruts played Joe Oliver to his Pops – was one of the most successful British hot bands of the pre-war years. There have been various 'Georgian' revivals (the title was taken from his big hit, 'Georgia On My Mind') since that time and in the 1980s Nat was still singing, though no longer playing his horn. The Armstrong influence is so overt as to be unarguable, and yet Gonella brought something of his own as well, a wry, philosophical shrug as he threw off neat aphoristic solos with the biting tone and earthy humour his fans loved. The Flapper disc is a very good selection of early material. Nat spent a little time in America at the end of the decade, and its influence can be heard in the bluesier and more relaxedly rhythmic swing of the later cuts. The New Georgians stuff from 1940 is – heretical though it may be – superior to the original band's output. There's a novelty edge to many of the tracks, but Nat's vocal on 'The Flat Foot Floogie' and even 'Ol' Man River' is never less than musical and in the latter case quite moving. A bit of an institution, who will be fondly remembered by anyone over the age of sixty and who may prove mystifying to anyone under.

Paul Gonsalves (1920–74)

TENOR SAXOPHONE

'Mex' was a Bostonian who started with Basie but joined Ellington in 1950 and stayed for the rest of his life. Drink and narcotics troubled his career, but Ellington stood by him and coaxed out countless great performances: Newport 1956 was his apotheosis.

***** Ellingtonia Moods And Blues**
RCA Victor 7432 147793-2 *Gonsalves; Ray Nance (t); Mitchell Booty Wood (tb); Johnny Hodges (as); Jimmy Jones (p); Al Hall (b); Oliver Jackson (d).* 2/60.

****** Gettin' Together**
Original Jazz Classics OJC 203 *Gonsalves; Nat Adderley (t); Wynton Kelly (p); Sam Jones (p); Jimmy Cobb (d).* 12/60.

*****(*) Tell It The Way It Is**
Impulse! 547 960-2 *Gonsalves; Rolf Ericson (t); Ray Nance (c, vn); Johnny Hodges (as); Walter Bishop Jr (p); Dick Hyman (org); Kenny Burrell (g); George Duvivier (b); Ernie Shepard (b, v); Roy Haynes, Osie Johnson (d); Manny Albam (bell tree).* 5 & 9/63.

***** Jazz Till Midnight**
Storyville STCD 4123 *Gonsalves; Jan Johansson (p, org); Bob Cranshaw (b); Albert 'Tootie' Heath (d).* 1/67.

***** Just A-Sittin' And A-Rockin'**
Black Lion BLCD 760148 *Gonsalves; Ray Nance (t, vn, v); Norris Turney (as, cl); Raymond Fol, Hank Jones (p); Al Hall (b); Oliver Jackson (d).* 8/70.

***** Meets Earl Hines**
Black Lion BLCD 760177 *Gonsalves; Earl Hines (p); Al Hall (b); Jo Jones (d).* 12/70, 11/72.

****(*) Mexican Bandit Meets Pittsburg Pirate**
Original Jazz Classics OJC 751 *Gonsalves; Roy Eldridge (t, v); Cliff Smalls (p); Sam Jones (b); Eddie Locke (d).* 8/73.

A quarter-century after his premature death, it's probably past time for a reassessment of Gonsalves's work. We were privileged to have a glimpse of the mouthpiece he used over the last few years of his life, a gnarled, snaggly thing, almost bitten through, testimony to a foreshortened lifetime of intense improvisation and an unflinching technique. Gonsalves stands in a direct line with earlier masters like Chu Berry and Don Byas, and with young Turks like Frank Lowe and David Murray. It would be absurd to compare his influence with Coltrane's, but it's now clear that he was experimenting with tonalities remarkably similar to Coltrane's famous 'sheets of sound' long before Coltrane; it's also unarguably true that more people heard Gonsalves (albeit in his more straight-ahead role as an Ellington stalwart). His fabled 27 choruses on 'Diminuendo And Crescendo In Blue' at the Newport Jazz Festival in 1956 can be considered the first important extended saxophone solo in modern jazz.

The 1960s Ellingtonia session is – unfortunately for Gonsalves – hijacked by Hodges, who claims composer or co-composer credits on four of the tracks, including the closing 'D A Blues'. The tenor man is listed as author of 'Chocataw' and 'The Line-Up', but his main feature is 'Daydreams', a solo statement worthy of Coleman Hawkins, but also anticipating something of Sonny Rollins's later melodic style. The scaled-down orchestral sound smacks a little of Ellington-and-water, but that was the price Duke exacted of all his sidemen's groups. Had he been present, instead of the workmanlike but pedestrian Jones, a rather ordinary session might have been raised a notch, but Ducal spin-offs without the great man were somehow always contrived to sound like second-division affairs.

Hodges again tends to dominate on *Tell It The Way It Is*, which is now repackaged with the slightly earlier *Cleopatra – Feelin'*

Jazzy, a slightly odd concept album inspired by Elizabeth Taylor's pyramidal epic. Hodges's arrangements on *Tell It* are more subtly crafted than any he ever recorded on his own account, and Bob Thiele's production gives the individual horns generous space while allowing the sound to meld and blend. A valuable reissue.

Gettin' Together is a remarkable album, beautifully played and recorded. Wynton Kelly's piano playing on 'Walkin'' and 'I Cover The Waterfront' (a Gonsalves favourite) is of the highest quality, and Adderley's slightly fragile, over-confident tone fits in perfectly. Most strongly recommended.

Hines delivers more reliably than the saxophonist at their 1970 encounter (there's actually just one brief track from '72). Gonsalves saves his best shot for 'Moten Swing', where he plays three choruses of pure invention, before Hines tugs the whole tune away in a new direction. 'Over The Rainbow' is whispery and delicate, just one run through the tune with a minimum of embellishment, but at a pace in which every note is made to count.

'I Cover The Waterfront' is again the stand-out track on Black Lion's relaxed, old-pals reunion. Nance is a less dramatic soloist than Gonsalves's more familiar foil, Cat Anderson, and his singing and fiddle-playing are less than compelling, but he blends beautifully in the ensembles and is imaginative enough to essay out-of-tempo sequences and slurred sounds around the saxophonists. Turney, a not quite time-served Ellington employee, plays exceedingly well.

The last of the group makes sad listening after the earlier sessions or any of the great Ellington occasions. Gonsalves at this point had less than a year to live and, while a meeting with the incendiary trumpeter might have been marvellous 15 years earlier, the tenor-playing sounds fractious and tired. Eldridge has a few characteristic squalls to deliver, but seam out the other discs first.

Dennis Gonzalez (born 1954)

TRUMPET, POCKET TRUMPET, FLUGELHORN, OTHER INSTRUMENTS

Learned trumpet as a teenager and arrived in Dallas in 1977, where he started the Daagnim label, broadcast, and acted as a focus for the somewhat embattled new-music community of the area.

****** Stefan**

Silkheart SHCD 101 *Gonzalez; John Purcell (bcl, bf, eng hn, syn, v); Henry Franklin (b, v); W.A Richardson (d).* 4/86.

*****(*) Namesake**

Silkheart SHCD 106 *Gonzalez; Ahmed Abdullah (t, flhn, balafon); Charles Brackeen (ts, perc); Douglas Ewart (bcl, as, f); Malachi Favors (b); Alvin Fielder (d).* 2/87.

*****(*) Catechism**

Music & Arts CD 913 *Gonzalez; Rob Blakeslee (t); Kim Corbet (tb); Elton Dean (as, saxello); Keith Tippett (p); Marcio Mattos (b); Louis Moholo (d).* 7/87.

****** Debenge, Debenge**

Silkheart SHCD 112 *Gonzalez; Marlon Jordan (t); Charles Brackeen (ts); Kidd Jordan (sno, as, bcl); Malachi Favors, Henry Franklin (b); Alvin Fielder, W.A Richardson (d).* 2/88.

*****(*) The Desert Wind**

Silkheart SHCD 124 *Gonzalez; Kim Corbet (tb); Charles Brackeen (ts, ss); Michael Session (ss, ts, as); Michael Kruge (clo); Henry Franklin (b); Alvin Fielder (d).* 4/89.

Gonzalez's recordings for the Silkheart label are part of a determined effort to wrest initiative back from New York and the West Coast and to restore the South's, and particularly the Delta's, slightly marginal standing in the new jazz. The band assembled for *Debenge, Debenge* goes under the uncomfortably agglutinative name New Dallasorleanssippi, that for *Desert Wind* New Dallasangeles, formulae which give no sense at all of their coherence and directness of statement. Gonzalez's other great achievement is to have tempted the great tenor player, Charles Brackeen, out of a self-imposed semi-retirement.

Stefan is probably the trumpeter's masterpiece. The opening 'Enrico', dedicated to the Italian trumpeter, Enrico Rava, opens a path for magnificent flugelhorn figurations over a bass/bass-clarinet accompaniment. 'Fortuity' is calm and enigmatic, like the title-track (a dedication to Gonzalez's son) a simple theme on open chords, but with a strange, dramatic interlude for voices. 'Hymn For Don Cherry' is based on 'At The Cross' and reflects two more of Gonzalez's influences. 'Boi Fuba', the briefest and least successful track, explores Brazilian materials, while John Purcell's closing 'Deacon John Ray' features his Dolphyish alto, and the trumpeter is superbly instinctive on the borders of total harmonic abstraction. A masterful record.

Namesake only suffers by comparison, but it shouldn't be missed. The long title-piece is a complex 7/4 figure that manages to sound completely coherent and also as if it were being played by a very much larger band, as if Gonzalez had been listening to Mingus's appropriations of Ellington on *The Black Saint And The Sinner Lady*. 'Separation Of Stones' is tranced and dreamy, and the solos are softly enunciated, with Gonzalez muted and the Armstrong-influenced Abdullah on flugelhorn. A percussion overture sets up a mood of combined grief and triumph in anticipation of 'Hymn For Mbizo', a threnody for South African bassist Johnny Dyani, but is interrupted by the lightweight 'Four Pigs And A Bird's Nest', on which Gonzalez plays his Cherry-patented pocket trumpet, muted on this occasion.

Debenge, Debenge, along with Brackeen's own *Banaar* and *Worshippers Come Nigh* (Silkheart 105 & 111), quickly consolidated the label's quality and confirmed Gonzalez's considerable musical intelligence. The multi-talented Kidd Jordan builds a bridge between Gonzalez's ringing, sometimes slightly sharp-toned trumpet and Brackeen's powerful tenor; his son, Marlon Jordan, is a fresh new voice and the Art Ensemble of Chicago veteran, Favors, shows more of his formidable technique than for some time. A superb record, beautifully engineered and produced.

The most recent of the Silkhearts, *Desert Wind*, opens with a mournful 'Hymn For Julius Hemphill'. Kruge's cello establishes the mood, before Brackeen, then Gonzalez, come in with turbulent solos. They're joined by Session, the other main soloist, again on 'Aamriq'aa' and 'The Desert Wind'. For the latter, Brackeen shifts to soprano and a keening, Middle Eastern tonality. The record tails off a bit after that, and Fielder's drum solo on 'Max-Well' is a bit of a bore.

The earlier *Catechism*, recorded in London, is rawer and the British free-scene players dictate a greater emphasis on collective improvisation. Dean and Tippett are the most prominent as soloists. The writing (two *kwelas* dedicated to the trumpeter's wife, Gerard Bendiks's delightfully titled 'The Sunny Murray–Cecil Taylor Dancing Lesson', and 'Catechism', written for the Creative Opportunity Orchestra in Austin, Texas) is of consistently high quality, and only a rather flat sound and the likelihood of limited availability keeps this one down to three and a half stars.

*****(*) Hymn For The Perfect Heart Of A Pearl**
Konnex KCD 5026 *Gonzalez; Carlos Ward (as, f); Tim Green (ts); Paul Plimley (p); Paul Rogers (b); Louis Moholo (d).* 4/90.

A shift both of label and of emphasis for Gonzalez, this sees him re-enter the free-jazz idiom hinted at on *Catechism*, but mostly kept at arm's length there. 'Angels Of The Bop Apocalypse' is a group improvisation, with the European-based Rogers and Moholo prominent (as they are throughout the set) and Plimley guesting in Cecil Taylor mode. The long suite of the title has an Ellingtonian surge and diversity of detail, with sections apparently tailor-made for individual soloists. Curiously, perhaps, Ward and Green seem to have greater prominence than the leader, who tends to restrict himself to taut, almost antagonistic perorations. Rogers follows him on both the title-piece and the second movement, 'Astonishing Emptiness', a piece which evokes the same parched beauty of the Silkheart bands, but with a much more abstract edge. There is a 'Hymn For Louis Moholo', on which the horns ride precariously over the drummer's wonderfully splintery and unpredictable lines. Plimley reappears for his own 'Parachute', sounding disconcertingly like another Brit, Keith Tippett (also on *Catechism*), and then the final movement is an all-in New Orleans stomp with emphatic gestures from the whole group, which Gonzalez has called his Band of Sorcerers.

****** The Earth And The Heart**
Konnex KCD 5028/Music & Arts 960 *Gonzalez; Nels Cline, Mark Hewins (g); Ken Filiano (b); Alex Cline (d, syn); Andrew Cyrille (d).* 7 & 12/89.

*****(*) Welcome To Us**
GOWI CDG 10 *Gonzalez; Nils Petter Molvaer (t); Bugge Wesseltoft (p, syn); Terje Gewelt (b, tabla); Pal Thowsen (d, perc); Sidsel Endresen (v).* 3/93.

The mystical strain in Gonzalez's imagination becomes ever more evident. *The Earth And The Heart* consists largely of a suite written to celebrate the tenth birthday of the Creative Opportunity Orchestra. The pervasive theme of tension between earth and heaven – or between material and spiritual natures – is one that seems to haunt the trumpeter and which is ideally suited to his intense, bugling tone. More than ever before, he seems the heir of Don Cherry on these records. His gift for putting together unexpected bands in whatever locale circumstance finds him echoes Cherry's gypsy temperament. The spontaneity and freshness of the solos on *The Earth And The Heart* is breathtaking. Cyrille performs magnificently, as do the Cline brothers, and the lesser-known Hewins plays with taste and quiet sophistication on the opening movement and on Cyrille's 'Simple Melody'. The LA sessions with the Clines are rather more polished and lack something of the immediacy of the New York date. Even so, this is a beautifully balanced album, and Gonzalez finds the right sound for each of the participants.

The Nordic Wizards band is issued on a Polish label and includes elements of another suite, 'Warszawa'. Another stylistic parallel immediately springs to mind, that of Tomasz Stanko. Gonzalez is more oblique and softer-toned than usual, and the overall accent of the record is one of muted gentleness. Molvaer does much of the straight trumpet playing, but they might almost be creative twins. There are perhaps too many texts, but Endresen's voice is consistently interesting, as in her own recordings, and the additional material – Asian percussion, a choir of refugee Afghani children – is not intrusive. A lovely, if slightly untypical record. Disappointingly, nothing new from Gonzalez for several years, after a memorable burst of creativity.

Jerry Gonzalez (born 1949)

TRUMPET, FLUGELHORN, PERCUSSION

Though he often turns up as a big-band percussionist (he teaches percussion in New York), Gonzalez is best as an ebullient leader of Afro-Cuban bands where his trumpet playing can get some space.

***** The River Is Deep**
Enja 4040 *Gonzalez; Steve Turre (tb, btb); Papo Vasquez (tb); Wilfredo Velez (as); Jorge Dalto (p); Edgardo Miranda (g); Andy Gonzalez (b, v); Steve Berrios (d, v); Gene Golden, Hector 'Flaco' Hernandez, Nicky Marrero, Frankie Rodriguez (perc).* 11/82.

***** Obalata**
Enja 5095 *Gonzalez; John Stubblefield (ts); Larry Willis (p); Edgardo Miranda (g); Andy Gonzalez (b); Steve Berrios (d); Nicky Marrero, Milton Cardona, Angel 'Papa' Vacquez (perc).* 11/88.

Jerry Gonzalez has been surpassed in popularity by Arturo Sandoval but he is a trumpeter and front-man of comparable gifts, whose efforts at blending jazz and Latin genres have all the necessary ingredients: zesty, explosive rhythm sections, pellucid brass breaks, sunny melodies and an element of kitsch: one of his records included a version of the *I Love Lucy* theme. But Gonzalez likes to interpret Thelonious Monk and Wayne Shorter and, though he sometimes turns their compositions into unsuitably happy-go-lucky vehicles, there's a sensitive streak in his treatment of 'Footsteps' (*Obalata*). The earlier record is the more energetic, while *Obalata* benefits from the considerable presence of Stubblefield and the thoughtful Willis in a slightly smaller band.

***** Rumba Para Monk**
Sunnyside SSC 1036 *Gonzalez; Carter Jefferson (ts); Larry Willis (p); Andy Gonzalez (b); Steve Berrios (d).* 88.

*****(*) Earthdance**
Sunnyside SSC 1050 *As above, except add Joe Ford (ss, as).* 10/90.

*****(*) Moliendo Café: To Wisdom The Prize**
Sunnyside SSC 1061 *As above.* 9/91.

Gonzalez has stabilized the personnel of this band and it's shown real growth on record, though it hardly matches the excitement it can generate live. The earliest of the bunch is an attempt to filter back out some of the Latin influences on Monk's rhythmic conception. 'Monk's Mood', 'Bye-Ya', 'Ugly Beauty' and 'Little Rootie Tootie' are transformed into south-of-the-border flag-wavers without sustaining any damage or bowing to compromise. There is a slight feeling that, having established his premiss, Gonzalez doesn't quite know how to go any further with it, and some of his own soloing is very limited in scope. However, the sheer *joie de vivre* of the session gets it through a lot. Jefferson and Ford make a canny front line, reminiscent of the horn sections McCoy Tyner worked with in his 1970s bands, and while neither man seems especially individual it suits the democratic blend of the group. Willis is the cooling ingredient in a rhythm section that's always ready to stoke the polyrhythmic fires, and Gonzalez himself plays eloquent or fiery horn as the occasion demands. There are more glances towards Monk and Shorter (a very fine 'El Toro' on *Moliendo Café*), and the later album also includes 'Summertime' and 'Corcovado' – kitsch choices that the band very nearly pull off. The earlier disc is slightly stronger, but either one has a lot of joyful music.

****** Crossroads**

Milestone MCD 9225 *As above, except replace Jefferson with John Stubblefield (ts).* 4 & 5/94.

***** Pensativo**

Milestone MCD 9242 *As above.* 95.

*****(*) Fire Dance**

Milestone MCD 9258 *As above.* 2/96.

The arrival of John Stubblefield toughened up the sound quite a bit, but also brought a new expressive dimension which has enhanced the Fort Apache Band more than a little. On the two parts of 'Rumba Columbia', the best track on *Crossroads*, he is a revelation, roaring away happily in the sourest and most piquant tonality imaginable, a sound that is absolutely complementary to Gonzalez's own. He is at home with the Monk material which seems to have become a regular component of Gonzalez's bandbook, with 'Ruby, My Dear' on the quieter, almost ruminant *Pensativo*, 'Ugly Beauty' on the most recent record. Gonzalez also plays homage to Billy Strayhorn on the earlier disc with a wonderful interpretation of 'A Flower Is A Lovesome Thing'. There is some fine interplay between the horns which suggests that they have worked out a productive relationship. Ford is the most passive and accommodating of the three, but still capable of some sly interjections, and on *Fire Dance* he moves out into the spotlight rather more on soprano. A vintage crop of material from Gonzalez.

Benny Goodman (1909–86)

CLARINET

Studied clarinet from age of eleven, began working two years later, and joined the Ben Pollack band in Chicago. Studio work in New York followed until he began bandleading in 1934. Indifferent results until a sensational gig in Los Angeles, then he built the band to become one of the most popular in America, hiring Harry James, Lionel Hampton, Teddy Wilson and Gene Krupa. Survived the big-band decline and toyed with bebop, though with little commitment, as well as occasionally playing the classical repertoire. Continued to tour with big bands (occasionally) and small groups (more frequently) into the '70s and '80s. Despite his martinet reputation, Goodman remained a hugely successful leader. The early hot style matured into an impeccable if calmer manner, and his approach to his own instrumentalism was of unflinching dedication.

***** Benny Goodman 1928–1931**

Classics 693 *Goodman; Wingy Manone (t); Jimmy McPartland (c); Tommy Dorsey, Glenn Miller (tb); Fud Livingston, Larry Binyon (cl, ts); Sid Stoneburn (cl, as); Bud Freeman (ts); Vic Breidis, Joe Sullivan, Mel Stitzel (p); Eddie Lang, Dick Morgan (g); Herman Foster (bj); Harry Goodman (b); Bob Conselman, Gene Krupa (d); Harold Arlen, Grace Johnston, Scrappy Lambert, Paul Small (v).* 1/28–2/31.

***** Benny Goodman 1931–1933**

Classics 719 *Goodman; Charlie Teagarden, Manny Klein, Shirley Clay, Bunny Berigan (t); Jack Teagarden, Tommy Dorsey, Glenn Miller (tb); Sid Stoneburn (cl, as); Larry Binyon (cl, ts, f); Art Karle (ts); Irving Brodsky, Joe Sullivan (p); Eddie Lang, Dick McDonough (g); Artie Bernstein (b); Gene Krupa, Ray Bauduc, Johnny Williams (d); Billie Holiday, Smith Ballew, Paul Small, Dick Robertson (v).* 3/31–12/33.

Goodman's earliest dates as a leader are rough-and-ready New York jazz, with McPartland's gruff lead adding to the grit, and with Benny doubling on alto and baritone. The notorious 'Shirt Tail Stomp', in which the group lampooned the jazz clichés of the time, became a minor hit. His two solos, 'That's A Plenty' and 'Clarinetitis', are virtuoso stuff, and a subsequent date in Chicago yielded two more gutsy small-group titles with Manone and Freeman. After that, though, his New York sessions, which take up the rest of Classics 693 and all of 719, are polite, inconsequential dance music. Elements of swing start to creep in as time goes on, but the often stellar personnel have trouble getting any jazz into the records, and the most notable thing is the arrival of young Billie Holiday on two of the final tracks. Sound is mixed – very rough and scratchy on some of the transfers, particularly on the latter sessions on Classics 693.

****(*) Benny Goodman 1934–1935**

Classics 744 *Goodman; Manny Klein, Charles Margulis, Charlie Teagarden, George Thow, Russ Case, Jerry Neary, Sam Shapiro, Pee Wee Irwin, Art Sylvester, Ralph Muzillo (t); Sonny Lee, Jack Teagarden, Red Ballard, Jack Lacey (tb); Hymie Schertzer, Ben Kantor, Toots Mondello (as); Coleman Hawkins, Hank Ross, Arthur Rollini, Dick Clark (ts); Claude Thornhill, Arthur Schutt, Frank Froeba, Teddy Wilson (p); Dick McDonough, George Van Eps, Benny Martel (g); Artie Bernstein, Harry Goodman, Hank Wayland (b); Ray McKinley, Sammy Weiss, Gene Krupa (d); Mildred Bailey, Ann Graham, Helen Ward, Buddy Clark (v).* 2/34–1/35.

***** Benny Goodman 1935**

Classics 769 *Goodman; Jerry Neary, Pee Wee Irwin, Bunny Berigan, Nate Kazebier, Ralph Muzillo (t); Red Ballard, Jack Lacey, Jack Teagarden, Joe Harris (tb); Toots Mondello, Hymie*

Schertzer (as); Arthur Rollini, Dick Clark (ts); Frank Froeba (p); Allan Reuss, George Van Eps (g); Harry Goodman (b); Gene Krupa (d); Helen Ward, Ray Hendricks, Buddy Clark (v). 1–7/35.

***** Benny Goodman 1935–1936**

Classics 789 *As above, except add Harry Geller (t), Bill De Pew (as), Teddy Wilson, Jess Stacy (p); omit Neary, Lacey, Teagarden, Van Eps, Hendricks, Clark.* 7/35–4/36.

***** Benny Goodman 1936**

Classics 817 *As above, except add Chris Griffin, Manny Klein (t), Murray McEachern (tb); omit Mondello, Froeba.* 4–8/36.

*****(*) Benny Goodman 1936 Vol. 2**

Classics 836 *As above, except add Sterling Bose, Zeke Zarchy, Ziggy Elman (t), Vido Musso (ts), Lionel Hampton (vib); omit Klein, Geller.* 8–11/36.

*****(*) Benny Goodman 1936–1937**

Classics 858 *As above, except add Irv Goodman, Harry James (t), George Koenig (as), Margaret McCrae, Jimmy Rushing, Frances Hunt (v); omit Bose, Zarchy.* 12/36–7/37.

***** Benny Goodman 1935 Vol. 1**

Tax CD 3708-2 *Goodman; George Erwin, Nathan Kazebier, Jerry Neary (t); Red Ballard, Jack Lacey (tb); Toots Mondello, Hymie Schertzer (as); Arthur Rollini, Dick Clark (ts); Frank Froeba (p); Allan Reuss (g); Harry Goodman (b); Gene Krupa (d).* 6/35.

***** Benny Goodman 1935 Vol. 2**

Tax CD 3709-2 *As above.* 6/35.

***** The Birth Of Swing (1935–1936)**

RCA Bluebird ND90601 3CD *Goodman; Bunny Berigan, Pee Wee Erwin, Ralph Muzillo, Jerry Neary, Nathan Kazebier, Harry Geller, Chris Griffin, Manny Klein, Sterling Bose, Ziggy Elman, Zeke Zarchy (t); Red Ballard, Jack Lacey, Jack Teagarden, Murray McEachern (tb); Toots Mondello, Bill De Pew, Hymie Schertzer (as); Arthur Rollini, Dick Clark, Vido Musso (ts); Frank Froeba, Jess Stacy (p); George Van Eps, Allan Reuss (g); Harry Goodman (b); Gene Krupa (d); Helen Ward, Ella Fitzgerald, Joe Harris, Buddy Clark (v).* 4/35–11/36.

Goodman was struggling as a bandleader until the mystical night of 21 August 1935 when the swing era apparently began, following his broadcast from Los Angeles. He already had a good band: the reed section was skilful, the trumpets – boosted by the arrival of Bunny Berigan, who had a terrific impact on Goodman himself – strong, and the book was bulging with material. The two Tax CDs, of transcriptions for radio, contain 50 numbers yet were recorded in a single day's work. There were Fletcher Henderson arrangements which would help to make Goodman's fortune – 'Blue Skies', 'King Porter Stomp', 'Basin Street Blues' – and Jimmy Mundy and Edgar Sampson charts of a similar calibre. There was Gene Krupa at the drums and Goodman, perhaps the first great virtuoso of the swing era, himself.

It may surprise some, at this distance, to hear how Goodman actually played more of an ensemble role than that of a star leader – at least in terms of the sound of his clarinet and its place on the records. Solos are usually quite short and pithy and, though he takes the lion's share, that was only right and proper – he was far and away the best improviser (Berigan aside, who didn't last very long) in his own band. What one notes about the records is their smooth, almost ineluctable power and fleetness: Krupa's drumming energized the orchestra, but its brass and reed sections were such fine executants (only Lunceford's band could have matched them) that they generated their own kind of inner swing. Henderson, Mundy and Sampson all supplied arrangements which, in a gesture that has dominated big-band writing to this day, pointed up those strengths without looking for fancy textures or subtleties.

The Classics series, moving chronologically through the Columbia and Victor sessions, offers a comprehensive overview. Classics 744 finds the band still in an awkward, transitory phase, which is more or less resolved by the end of Classics 769 – here are the first Henderson arrangements, the classic reading of 'King Porter Stomp' and the big hit, 'Blue Skies'. The sound of the band, comparatively muffled on the Columbia sessions (though the erratic Classics' remastering doesn't help), is smoother, bigger and more sophisticated by the time the Victor dates were properly under way. Classics 789 also includes the first tracks by the BG trio, and though this disc also marks Berigan's departure – leaving Goodman short of a major trumpeter until the arrival of Harry James – one can hear the orchestra growing in stature. Classics 817 and 836 see Jimmy Mundy coming on board as arranger; Ziggy Elman's arrival in the trumpet section in October 1936 adds some extra firepower to the brass. Classics 858 sees Harry James coming into the band, and the record ends on the studio version of 'Sing, Sing, Sing', one of the most familiar set-pieces of the whole swing era. There is the occasional clinker in terms of material, but for the most part Goodman was able to record songs and charts of a consistently high quality and, even where Helen Ward's vocals dominate a record, the band's eminence is obvious. Transfers of the Victor material are usually strong and without much surface noise.

The Tax CDs (broadcast transcriptions) are in excellent sound and, though there are plenty of second-rate tunes and occasional dead passages, the standard stays surprisingly high, with Goodman in good to inspirational form. The Bluebird three-CD set should be the definitive document of the start of the swing era, but it's let down badly by inconsistent remastering: a handful of tracks (including 'Blue Skies') sound as if they were recorded under water, and the general standard, though listenable enough, varies almost from track to track. That said, it's of consistent musical interest, and Loren Schoenberg's excellent notes add to the impact of the set.

*****(*) The Harry James Years Vol. 1**

Bluebird 07863 66155 2 *Goodman; Harry James, Ziggy Elman, Gordon Griffin (t); Red Ballard, Murray McEachern, Vernon Brown (tb); Hymie Schertzer, Bill De Pew, George Koenig (as); Babe Russin, Arthur Rollini, Vido Musso (ts); Jess Stacy (p); Allan Reuss (g); Harry Goodman (b); Gene Krupa (d).* 1/37–2/38.

****** The Harry James Years Vol. 2**

Bluebird 07863 66549 2 *As above, except add Irv Goodman, Corky Cornelius (t), Bruce Squires (tb), Noni Bernardi, Dave Matthews, Milt Yaner (as), Lester Young, Jerry Jerome, Bud Freeman (ts), Freddie Green, Ben Heller (g), Walter Page (b), Dave Tough, Buddy Shutz (d), Martha Tilton (v); omit McEachern, Koenig.* 3/38–5/39.

*****(*) Benny Goodman 1937**

Classics 879 *Similar to above.* 7–11/37.

*****(*) Benny Goodman 1937–1938**
Classics 899 *Similar to above.* 11/37–3/38.

***** Benny Goodman 1938**
Classics 925 *Similar to above.* 3–8/38.

***** Benny Goodman 1938 Vol. 2**
Classics 961 *Similar to above.* 11/38.

The Bluebird discs offer two good slices of the band in its prime. The arrangements are by Henderson, Mundy, James, Sampson, Basie and even Mary Lou Williams – Goodman took them from many hands. Much better sound than on many earlier Bluebird discs. Volume 2 starts with a session where various Basieites sat in, takes in the arrival of Bud Freeman and Dave Tough, and includes two rare takes of otherwise familiar items. As samplers of Goodman's output in the 1930s, these two are hard to beat, though the Hep discs, below, also have a strong claim.

Classics, meanwhile, carry on with their chronological survey. Since these also mix in the trio and quartet sessions, they're in some ways a more truthful look at Goodman's progress. The drawback is that the refusal to cherrypick means that Goodman's more routine material is here too. Still, the quality level on both Classics 879 and 899 is consistently high; the two 1938 CDs just slip back a notch in terms of the material. Transfers, from unlisted sources, seem fair.

****** At Carnegie Hall 1938 – Complete**
Columbia C2K 65143 2CD *Goodman; Ziggy Elman, Buck Clayton, Harry James, Gordon Griffin (t); Bobby Hackett (c); Red Ballard, Vernon Brown (tb); Hymie Schertzer, George Koenig, Johnny Hodges (as); Arthur Rollini, Lester Young, Babe Russin (ts); Harry Carney (bs); Jess Stacy, Teddy Wilson, Count Basie (p); Lionel Hampton (vib); Allan Reuss, Freddie Green (g); Harry Goodman, Walter Page (b); Gene Krupa (d).* 1/38.

A very famous occasion indeed, and the music still stands up extraordinarily well. This was one of those events – like Ellington at Newport nearly two decades later – when jazz history is spontaneously changed, even if Goodman had clearly planned the whole thing as a crowning manoeuvre. Unmissable points: Krupa's fantastically energetic drumming throughout, leading to the roof coming off on 'Sing, Sing, Sing', an Ellington tribute and a jam on 'Honeysuckle Rose' with various guests from other bands (George Simon called it 'ineffectual', but it's very exciting), Ziggy Elman powering through 'Swingtime In The Rockies' and the original quartet going through their best paces. But the whole affair is atmospheric with the sense of a man and a band taking hold of their moment.

Columbia's new edition of this music is a model effort, masterminded by Phil Schaap, whose indomitable detective work finally tracked down the original acetates and gave us the music in the best sound we'll ever get. Most of the previously unheard material is limited to introductions and the like, but there is some new music, and the ambience of the occasion is powerful, even thrilling.

*****(*) Benny Goodman 1938–1939**
Classics 990 *Goodman; Harry James, Ziggy Elman, Gordon Griffin, Charlie Spivak, Bunny Berigan, Sonny Dunham, Irving Goodman (t); Red Ballard, Vernon Brown, Jack Teagarden, Tommy Dorsey (tb); Dave Matthews, Noni Bernardi, Hymie Schertzer (as); Arthur Rollini, Jerry Jerome, Eddie Miller (ts); Jess Stacy, Teddy Wilson, Bob Zurke (p); Lionel Hampton (vib, d); Ben Heller, Carmen Mastren (g); John Kirby, Bob Haggart, Harry Goodman (b); Buddy Schutz, {f}; Ray Bauduc (d); Martha Tilton, Johnny Mercer (v).* 12/38–4/49.

*****(*) Benny Goodman 1939**
Classics 1025 *As above, except add Corky Cornelius, Jimmy Maxwell, Johnny Martell (t), Bruce Squires, Ted Vesely (tb), Toots Mondello, Buff Estes (as), Bus Bassey (ts), Fletcher Henderson (p), Arnold Covey, Charlie Christian (g), Artie Bernstein (b), Nick Fatool (d), Louis Tobin (v); omit James, Spivak, Dunham, Irving Goodman, Teagarden, Dorsey, Miller, Wilson, Zurke, Hampton, Mastren, Kirby, Haggart, Bauduc.* 4–9/39.

*****(*) Benny Goodman 1939 Vol. 2**
Classics 1064 *As above, except add Johnny Guarnieri (p), Lionel Hampton (vib), Mildred Bailey (v); omit Cornelius, Griffin, Rollini, Stacey, Cover, Tilton, Mercer.* 9–12/39.

The band sounds invincibly handsome and powerful in these sessions, in spite of some personnel fluctuations: James departs halfway through Classics 990, as does Jess Stacy, with Fletcher Henderson taking over at the piano and adding several more arrangements to the band's book. Christian's arrival is also a matter of celebration. Goodman had his share of indifferent material, but he seemed to get less ephemera than, say, the Dorseys had to handle, and every session has at least one good opportunity for band and soloist. Among the highlights are 'Blue Lou' and 'The Blues', made by an all-star Victor entourage at a one-off session (Classics 990); 'The Kingdom Of Swing' and 'Jumpin' At The Woodside' (Classics 1025, the latter title from Goodman's first session for Columbia); Christian's first small-group date, and Goodman's theme, 'Let's Dance' (Classics 1064). The Victor tracks are in excellent sound but the Columbia sessions are less predictable in transfer quality.

****** Plays Fletcher Henderson**
Hep 1038 *As appropriate discs above.* 4/35–4/39.

****** Plays Jimmy Mundy**
Hep 1039 *As appropriate discs above.* 9/35–11/37.

These two excellently remastered discs offer a good way of exploring the key points of Benny's music in the 1930s. It was Henderson's arrangements, still rooted in his favourite call-and-response patterns, that gave Goodman's band their first real identity, and the best of them are collected here. Mundy's charts follow on from Henderson's and are scarcely more subtle: his favourite riff devices occur again and again, and only in some of his saxophone writing is there any genuine freshness; but the band's superb craftsmanship makes the arrangements fit snugly into what Goodman wanted. None of this music challenges the best of Ellington, Basie or Lunceford, but the particular crispness of Goodman's band is undeniable.

***** The Complete Madhattan Room Broadcasts Vols 1–6**
Viper's Nest VN 171/2/3/4/5/6 *Goodman; Harry James, Ziggy Elman, Chris Griffin (t); Red Ballard, Vernon Brown (tb); Hymie Schertzer, George Koenig (as); Arthur Rollini, Vido Musso (ts); Jess Stacy, Teddy Wilson (p); Lionel Hampton (vib); Allan Reuss (g); Harry Goodman (b); Gene Krupa (d); Martha Tilton (v).* 10–11/37.

***** More Camel Caravans**
Phontastic PHONTCD 8841/2 2CD *As above, except add Murray McEachern (tb); omit Brown.* 8/37.

***** More Camel Caravans**
Phontastic PHONTCD 8843/4 2CD *As above, except Brown returns, add Will Bradley (tb), Dave Matthews, Noni Bernardi (as), Ben Heller (g), Dave Tough (d); omit Schertzer, Koenig, McEachern.* 11/37–9/38.

***** More Camel Caravans**
Phontastic PHONTCD 8845/6 2CD *As above, except add Corky Cornelius (t), Bruce Squires (tb), Toots Mondello, Buff Estes (as), Bus Bassey, Jerry Jerome, Bud Freeman (ts), Fletcher Henderson (p), Arnold Coivey (g), Artie Bernstein (b), Nick Fatool (d), Louise Tobin (v); omit Bradley, Musso, Reuss, Tilton.* 9/38–9/39.

***** Camel Caravan Broadcasts Vol. 1**
Phontastic 8817 *As above, except add Cy Baker (t), Jack Teagarden (tb, v), Joseph Szigeti (vn), Johnny Mercer, Billie Holiday, Leo Watson (v).* 1/39.

***** Camel Caravan Broadcasts Vol. 2**
Phontastic 8818 *As above, except omit Baker, Teagarden, Szigeti, Mercer, Holiday and Watson.* 2–3/39.

***** Camel Caravan Broadcasts Vol. 3**
Phontastic 8819 *Similar to above.* 3–4/39.

Airshots have survived in copious quantities as far as the Goodman band is concerned, and these hefty reissues ought to satisfy the most diligent devotee. They are taken from broadcasts sponsored by Camel on the three Phontastic CDs. The sound on the Phontastic discs is clean, if rather fusty. These call for a lot of patience since there are frequent interruptions from the sponsor, dialogue and other distractions; that aside, the group play handsomely, though there's the usual quota of feeble titles. Phontastic have recently dug up three more two-disc sets which cover the earlier years of this Camel-sponsored show and, though there are numerous exhortations to smoke, the music more or less wins through. Better, though, are the looser and usually more swinging 'Madhattan Room' broadcasts, available on six separate discs from Viper's Nest. Each disc has a share of charts and songs which Goodman otherwise never recorded, and the sound is marginally better than the Phontastic discs can offer. The VJC discs listed below are still the best airshots around, but those listed above will interest the dedicated.

****** The Complete Small Group Sessions**
RCA Victor 68764 3CD *Goodman; Lionel Hampton (vib); Teddy Wilson, Jess Stacy (p); John Kirby (b); Buddy Schutz, Dave Tough, Gene Krupa (d).* 7/35–4/39.

Goodman's small groups set a new standard for 'chamber jazz', the kind of thing Red Nichols had tried in the 1920s, but informed with a more disciplined – and blacker – sensibility. That said, Goodman's own playing, for all its fineness of line and tonal elegance, could be blisteringly hot, and he is by far the strongest personality on all their records, the presence of domineering figures like Hampton and Krupa notwithstanding. This comprehensive edition is a timely addition to the Goodman discography: these tracks have been out many times over the years, but this is a notably handsome and genuine presentation of them, all in one place. Perhaps the Trio sessions, made before Hampton's arrival, are the most satisfying, since the brilliant empathy between Goodman and Wilson – one of the great unspoken jazz partnerships – is allowed its clearest expression. Certainly the likes of 'After You've Gone' and 'Body And Soul' express a smooth yet spontaneously refined kind of improvisation. Hampton made the music 'swing' a little more obtrusively, yet he often plays a rather quiet and contained ensemble role, the vibes shimmering alongside Wilson's playing, and it created a fascinating platform for Goodman's lithest playing. While this quickly became formulaic jazz, it was a very good formula.

****** Solo Flight**
Vintage Jazz Classics VJC-1021-2 *Goodman; Cootie Williams (t); Georgie Auld (ts); Lionel Hampton (vib); Fletcher Henderson, Johnny Guarnieri, Count Basie (p); Charlie Christian, Freddie Green (g); Artie Bernstein, Walter Page (b); Jo Jones, Gene Krupa, Nick Fatool (d).* 8/39–6/41.

****** Roll 'Em!**
Vintage Jazz Classics VJC 1032-2 *Goodman; Jimmy Maxwell, Billy Butterfield, Cootie Williams, Slim Davis (t); Lou McGarity, Cutty Cutshall (tb); Gene Kinsey, Clint Neagley (as); George Berg, Vido Musso, Pete Mondello (ts); Skip Martin, Chuck Gentry (bs); Mel Powell (p); Tommy Morganelli (g); Walter Looss, John Simmons, Marty Blitz (b); Big Sid Catlett (d).* 7–10/41.

Two fabulous collections of airshots and V-Discs. Various breakdowns and alternative takes sunder the flow on *Roll 'Em!* to some extent, but the band sound absolutely mercurial, careering through a sensational 'Henderson Stomp' and coming through loud and clear in excellent remastering. It's also a rare opportunity to hear one of the great drummers in jazz, Sidney Catlett, swinging the Goodman band as few ever did. The collection with Christian features the guitarist in wonderful extended solos, but Goodman himself matches him blow for blow and, though the sound is dustier, it's perfectly listenable. Essential supplements to a Goodman collection.

****** Sextet Featuring Charlie Christian**
Columbia 465679-2 *Goodman; Cootie Williams (t); Georgie Auld (ts); Fletcher Henderson, Johnny Guarnieri, Count Basie (p); Lionel Hampton (vib); Charlie Christian (g); Artie Bernstein (b); Nick Fatool, Jo Jones, Dave Tough (d).* 39–41.

***** The Rehearsal Sessions 1940–1941**
Jazz Unlimited JUCD 2013 *As above, except add Ken Kersey (p), Harry Jaeger (d); omit Henderson, Guarnieri, Hampton, Fatool, Tough.* 11/40–1/41.

***** Small Groups 1941–1945**
Columbia 463341-2 *Goodman; Lou McGarity, Cutty Cutshall (tb); Red Norvo (vib); Teddy Wilson, Mel Powell (p); Tom Morgan, Mike Bryan (g); Slam Stewart, Sid Weiss (b); Morey Feld, Ralph Collier (d); Peggy Lee (v).* 10/41–2/45.

Christian was a once-in-a-lifetime collaborator with Goodman, who had bad luck with some of his best sidemen (Christian, Berigan, Hasselgård – all of whom came to untimely ends). The first *Sextet* compilation is full of finely pointed small-group jazz, hinting every now and then at bop, but not so much as to give anyone any trouble. Equally interesting is the mixture of personalities – Williams, Goodman, Auld, Basie – which gives the sextet performances a blend of coolness and resilience that seems to be a direct extension of the leader's own ambitions. Goodman had led a nearly perfect double-life with the small groups and the big band, balancing dance material and 'listening' jazz and making both commercially and artistically successful; and part of that freshness which the small groups created may be due to the fact that several participants – Wilson, Hampton, Christian – weren't regular members of the big band. But after a reorganization in 1941 he started using regular band-members, who turn up on the *Small Groups 1941–5* compilation. While this is a less impressive set than the earlier small-band discs, with Cutshall and McGarity standing as curious choices and the timbre of most of the tracks sounding like a slightly paler echo of what had gone before, Goodman still plays very well. Respectable remastering on both discs. The *Rehearsal Sessions* brings together multiple takes on four tunes plus a remarkable 27-minute track that details the sextet working towards a finished version of 'Benny's Bugle' (where Cootie Williams eventually has to play the intro 23 times). For Goodman scholars rather than the general collector, but intriguing stuff.

*****(*) Plays Mel Powell**
Hep 1055 *Goodman; Alec Fila, Jimmy Maxwell, Cootie Williams, Irving Goodman, Laurence Stearns, Tony Faso, Vince Badale, Al Cuozzo, Frank LePinto, Chris Griffin, John Best, Conrad Gozzo, Bernie Privin, Billy Butterfield, Nate Kazebier, Jimmy Blake (t); Lou McGarity, Cutty Cutshall, Charlie Castaldo, Trummy Young, Chauncey Welsh, Eddie Aulinoi, Kai Winding, Dick LeFave (tb); Skip Martin, Gus Bivona, Bob Snyder, Clint Neagley, Hymie Schertzer, Aaron Sachs, Bill Shine, Jerry Sanfino, Jimmy Horvath, Gene Kinsey, Les Robinson, John Prager (as); Georgie Auld, Jack Henderson, George Berg, Vido Musso, John Walton, Leonard Sims, Al Epstein, Stan Getz, Peanuts Hucko, Pete Mondello, Gish Gilberston, Cliff Strickland (ts); Danny Bank, Bob Poland, Chuck Gentry, Art Ralston (bs); Mel Powell, Count Basie, Johnny Guarnieri, Teddy Wilson, Charlie Queener (p); Johnny White (vib); Mike Bryan, Dave Barbour (g); Artie Bernstein, Cliff Hill, Barney Spieler, Clyde Lombardi, Walter Looss (b); Morey Feld, Louie Bellson, Buddy Rich, Dave Tough, Big Sid Catlett, Ralph Ciollier, Jo Jones, Howard Davies (d).* 1/41–5/46.

Not quite the twilight years, even if Goodman eventually disbanded his orchestra in December 1946. This is a strong and thoughtfully chosen set of tracks from a relatively unconsidered period in the Goodman discography. Besides Mel Powell's arrangements, there are charts by Jimmy Mundy (an excellent feature for Cootie Williams on 'Fiesta In Blue'), Edgar Sampson, Margie Gibson, Skip Martin and Buster Harding, although Powell's scores are arguably the most interesting: 'Jersey Bounce', 'Mission To Moscow', 'Clarinade' and, above all, his early pieces, 'The Count' and 'The Earl'. Besides Williams, there are one or two surprise soloists – including Stan Getz on 'Lucky'. A useful issue.

*****(*) Goodman – The Different Version Vol. 1**
Phontastic NCD 8821 2CD *As discs above.* 39–40.

*****(*) Goodman – The Different Version Vol. 2**
Phontastic NCD 8822 2CD *As above.* 41.

*****(*) Goodman – The Different Version Vol. 3**
Phontastic NCD 8823 2CD *As above.* 41–42.

*****(*) Goodman – The Different Version Vol. 4**
Phontastic NCD 8824 2CD *As above.* 42–45.

*****(*) Goodman – The Different Version Vol. 5**
Phontastic NCD 8825 2CD *As above.* 45–47.

***** The Permanent Goodman Vol. 1**
Phontastic CD 7659 *As above.* 26–38.

*****(*) The Permanent Goodman Vol. 2**
Phontastic 7660 *As above.* 39–45.

There is some irony in that, while no comprehensive edition of Goodman's proper studio releases exists quite yet (though Classics will be there soon), enterprises like this have appeared instead. The five-volume Phontastic set covers ten CDs of alternative takes to the more familiar studio sides – virtually all of it from legitimate, V-Disc or transcription sessions, so the sound-quality is consistently good, if not quite as lively as some reissue projects. The documentation is detailed and superbly organized and, although the alternative takes themselves seldom tell anything strikingly new about Goodman's work – changes amount to matters of precise detail, rather than glaring contrasts – it makes a very impressive series of programmes. So, too, are the alternatives offered up on the other two *Permanent Goodman* discs, which follow a similar course but go back to 1926 (some of the early Ben Pollack sessions) and somehow avoid any duplication with these other sets. A remarkable undertaking, previously released as a long series of LPs but welcome in the new format.

*****(*) 'Way Down Yonder**
Vintage Jazz Classics VJC-1001-2 *Goodman; Lee Castle, Frank Muzzillo, Charlie Frankhauser, Johnny Dee, Frank Berardi, Mickey Mangano (t); Bill Harris, H Collins, Al Mastren (tb); Heinie Beau, Eddie Rosa, Hymie Schertzer, Leonard Kaye (as); Al Klink, Zoot Sims (ts); Ernie Caceres, Eddie Beau (bs); Jess Stacy, Mel Powell, Teddy Wilson (p); Red Norvo (vib); Sid Weiss (b); Morey Feld, Gene Krupa, Johnny DeSoto (d); Lorraine Elliott (v).* 12/43–1/46.

More broadcast material. Goodman hadn't lost the keys to the kingdom but his popularity was past its peak and the big bands were starting to enter their steep decline. Nevertheless this collection of V-Discs includes some very impressive and hard-hitting performances, and some new faces – Zoot Sims, for one – add further interest. Very good transfers, considering the source of the material.

***** Benny's Bop**
Hep CD 36 *Goodman; Howard Reich, Doug Mettome, Al Stewart, Nick Travis (t); Milt Bernhart, Eddie Bert, George Monte (tb); Stan Ake Hasselgård (cl); Mitch Goldberg, Angelo Cicalese (as); Wardell Gray, Eddie Wasserman (ts); Larry Molinelli (bs); Mary Lou Williams, Buddy Greco, Barbara Carroll (p); Billy Bauer, Francis Beecher (g); Clyde Lombardi (b); Mel Zelnick, Sonny Igoe (d); Louis Martinez (perc); Jackie Searle, Terry Swope (v).* 7/48–3/49.

Goodman was interested by the new music but he never felt very comfortable with it, and Hasselgård, present on three tracks here, was much more at home in bop's surroundings. There isn't anything here that would have troubled Parker and Gillespie. More involving is some superb playing from Wardell Gray. This is V-Disc and broadcast material, conscientiously remastered, and the leader (aside from one clinker) plays imperturbably well.

****** Undercurrent Blues**

Capitol 832086-2 *As above, except add Nate Kazebier, Manny Klein, Zeke Zarchy, Joe Triscari, Irv Goodman, Ziggy Schatz, John Wilson, Fats Navarro (t), Tommy Pederson, Lou McGarity, Ed Kusby, Bill Byers, Mario Daone (tb), Gus Bivona, Heinie Beau (as), Babe Russin, Jack Chaney (ts), Chuck Gentry, Bob Dawes, Joe Casalaro (bs), Jess Stacy (p), Allan Reuss, Mundell Lowe (g), Larry Breen, Bob Carter (b), Sammy Weiss (d).* 1/47–10/49.

Loren Schoenberg's notes make an eloquent case for reconsidering Goodman's allegedly miserable relationship with bebop, and the music on the disc makes an even better one. Two arrangements by Mary Lou Williams offer him a superb showcase in 'Lonely Moments', the sextet swinger 'Shirley Steps Out' is a near-classic, but the version of 'Stealing Apples', where he jousts with Navarro and Gray, is a real ear-opener for those who haven't heard it before. The remaining material includes some more fine small-group stuff and some excellent Chico O'Farrill arrangements. If Goodman left bop alone again at this point, it wasn't exactly because he couldn't play it. The remastering has been done superbly, with the music sounding vibrant and clear.

****** B.G. In Hi-Fi**

Capitol 92684-2 *Goodman; Ruby Braff, Charlie Shavers, Chris Griffin, Carl Poole, Bernie Privin (t); Will Bradley, Vernon Brown, Cutty Cutshall (tb); Al Klink, Paul Ricci, Boomie Richman, Hymie Schertzer, Sol Schlinger (saxes); Mel Powell (p); Steve Jordan (g); George Duvivier (b); Bobby Donaldson, Jo Jones (d).* 11/54.

Goodman left the big-band era with his finances and his technique intact and, although this was a more or less anachronistic programme of trio, quintet and big-band sides in 1954, the playing is so good that it's a resounding success. A few Goodman staples are mixed with Basie material such as 'Jumpin' At The Woodside', and Benny's readings are by no means outdone by the originals. Shavers, Braff, Richman and Powell all have fine moments, but Goodman himself is peerless. The sound is a trifle dry but otherwise excellent, and the CD reissue adds four tracks – including a beautiful trio version of 'Rose Room' – to the original LP.

****** The Complete Capitol Trios**

Capitol 521225-2 *Goodman; Teddy Wilson, Jimmy Rowles, Mel Powell (p); Jimmy Crawford, Tom Romersa, Eddie Grady, Bobby Donaldson (d).* 11/47–11/54.

Ten tracks from 1947, with Wilson and Crawford, then ten more from 1954, four with Rowles and six with Powell. No evidence that Goodman saw the LP format as an excuse to stretch out: only two of the later pieces break the three-and-a-half-minute barrier. Throughout all these sessions, he plays marvellous things, often in ways he wasn't supposed to be so good at: try the blues solo on 'After Hours'. Wilson, Rowles and Powell are all excellent in their different ways, Powell arguably taking the honours. Indispensable Goodman.

***** Yale Archives Vols 9 & 10**

Jazz Heritage 523983 2CD *Goodman; Charlie Shavers (t); Mel Powell, Teddy Wilson (p); Steve Jordan (g); Lionel Hampton (vib); Israel Crosby (b); Gene Krupa, Morey Feld (d).* 54–63.

A live set from 1954 with Shavers, Powell, Jordan, Crosby and Feld; a quartet reunion from 1963, with a set of previously unheard studio tracks. The teaming of Goodman and Shavers always seems irresistibly odd, the more so since the trumpeter makes a fist of the occasion, and this is a long, detailed set of interpretations. Goodman feels like he's coasting some of the time, but it's capable. The quartet tracks, like other reunions by the group, seem uneventful, as if they were waiting to pick up a pay cheque.

***** Yale Archives Vol. 2: Live At Basin Street**

Musicmasters 5006-2 *Goodman; Ruby Braff (t); Urbie Green (tb); Paul Quinichette (ts); Teddy Wilson (p); Perry Lopez (g); Milt Hinton (b); Bobby Donaldson (d).* 3/55.

This recording, from Goodman's personal collection now in Yale University, catches a characteristic club engagement by a typical Goodman band, only eight in number but big enough to suggest the swing of the leader's orchestras. The material is old-hat, even for Goodman, but the unusual gathering of names lends a fresh twist, and Braff and Green sound in particularly good shape. Well recorded and remastered.

*****(*) The Benny Goodman Story**

Capitol 833569-2 *Goodman; Chris Griffin, Billy Butterfield, Doc Severinsen, Jimmy Maxwell, Carl Poole, Harry James, Bernie Glow, Jon Durante, Bernie Privin, Ruby Braff (t); Urbie Green, Will Bradley, Lou McGarity (tb); Hymie Schertzer, Phil Bodner, Milt Yaner (as); Al Klink, Peanuts Hucko, Boomie Richman (ts); Dick Hyman, Morris Wechsler, Mel Powell (p); Lionel Hampton (vib); Tony Mottola, Al Caiola (g); George Duvivier, Milt Hinton (b); Bobby Donaldson, Don Lamond (d); Martha Tilton (v).* 12/55.

Occasioned by his film life-story, this remodelling of some old favourites was well done. 'Sing Sing Sing' was a necessary chore, 'And The Angels Sing' didn't improve with time, and there is some other so-so music; but the sound of the orchestra was handsomely caught by the Capitol engineers, and the small-group tracks at the end are handled with stinging aplomb. Excellent remastering.

***** Happy Session**

Columbia 476523-2 *Goodman; John Frosk, Allan Smith, Ermit Perry, Benny Ventura (t); Rex Peer, Hale Rood, Buster Cooper (tb); Herb Geller, James Sands, Bob Wilber, Babe Clark, Pepper Adams (reeds); André Previn, Russ Freeman (p); Barney Kessel, Turk Van Lake (g); George Duvivier, Milt Hinton, Leroy Vinnegar (b); Shelly Manne (d).*

Happy but not ecstatic. This sounds like Goodman meets the West Coast: Californian brass and reed sounds styled around the King's somewhat isolated clarinet. Plenty to hear, but hardly a great Goodman record.

****(*) Bangkok 1956**

TCB 43042 *Goodman; Mel Davis, John Frosk, Billy Hodges (t); Peanuts Hucko, Al Bock (as); Budd Johnson, Bill Slapin (ts);*

Hank Jones (p); Steve Jordan (g); Israel Crosby (b); Mousie Alexander (d). 12/56.

*****(*) Basel 1959**

TCB 43032 *Goodman; Jack Sheldon (t); Bill Harris (tb); Jerry Dodgion (as, f); Flip Phillips (ts); Red Norvo (vib); Russ Freeman (p); Jimmy Wyble (g); Red Wootten (b); John Marksham (d).* 10/59.

European souvenirs. The 1956 band was a good rather than a great Goodman outfit and, what with playing two numbers by the King of Thailand, the Bangkok date has the flavour of a group on its best behaviour rather than a fired-up ensemble. The Basel date is another matter. Goodman is clearly in good heart here, with a pellucid clarinet treatment of 'Memories Of You' one of several highlights, and, with favoured sideman Sheldon and the inimitable Harris both in top fettle, this set gener-ates some real heat. The sound is a bit fusty in parts, but not too bad.

***** Yale Archives Vol. 3**

Musicmasters 65007-2 *Goodman; Billy Hodges, Taft Jordan, John Frosk, Ermit Perry (t); Vernon Brown, Willie Dennis, Rex Peer (tb); Al Block, Ernie Mauro (as); Zoot Sims, Seldon Powell (ts); Gene Allen (bs); Roland Hanna (p); Billy Bauer (g); Arvell Shaw (b); Roy Burns (d); Ethel Ennis, Jimmy Rushing (v).* 5/58.

The band is a bit of a ragtag troupe, lacking the kind of punctilious precision one expects of a Goodman ensemble, and they can't finesse their way through some of the more risky moments in the scores. But it's still an interesting orchestra and, on what are familiar Goodman programmes, the leader summons enough spirit of his own to see them through.

****(*) Yale Archives Vol. 4: Big Band Recordings**

Musicmasters 65017-2 *Goodman; John Frosk, Allan Smith, E.V Perry, Benny Ventura, Jimmy Maxwell, Mel Davis, Al Mairoca, Fern Caron, Joe Wilder, Joe Newman, Tony Terran, Ray Triscari, Jimmy Zito, Taft Jordan, Billy Butterfield, Buck Clayton (t); Rex Peer, Harry DeViuto, Vern Friley, Bob Edmondson, Jimmy Knepper, Willie Dennis, Wayne Andrew, Hale Rood, Buster Cooper, Vernon Brown, Eddie Bert (tb); Herb Geller, Jimmy Santucci, Bob Wilber, Babe Clark, Pepper Adams, Gene Allen, Walt Levinsky, Al Block, Budd Johnson, Bill Slapin, Phil Woods, Jerry Dodgion, Zoot Sims, Tommy Newsom, Skeets Furfurt, Herbie Steward, Teddy Edwards, Bob Hardaway (reeds); Pete Jolly, Russ Freeman, Roland Hanna, Hank Jones, John Bunch (p); Kenny Burrell, Turk Van Lake, Benny Garcia, Steve Jordan (g); Milt Hinton, Henry Grimes, Irv Manning, Bill Crow, Monty Budwig (b); Mousie Alexander, Shelly Manne, Roy Burns, Mel Lewis, Colin Bailey (d); Martha Tilton, Mitzi Cottle (v).* 11/58–6/64.

There's some dreary stuff – including a terrible version of 'People' – on this hotchpotch of leftovers from bands that Goodman led in the late 1950s and early '60s. Many major players are involved here, and some of them take the odd solo, but Goodman is at centre stage and the main interest remains on his own solos. For Goodman collectors only, who'll have to salvage bits and pieces.

***** In Stockholm 1959**

Phontastic NCD 8801 *Goodman; Jack Sheldon (t); Bill Harris (tb); Jerry Dodgion (as, f); Flip Phillips (ts); Red Norvo (vib); Russ Freeman (p); Jimmy Wyble (g); Red Wootten (b); John Markham, John Poole (d); Anita O'Day (v).* 10/59.

Although the leader plays very well on this memento of a European tour which Goodman scholars credit as a peak period in his later work, the rather desultory presentation of the music – too many offhand introductions by Benny, and the inclusion of crowd-pleasing pieces like 'Sing Sing Sing' and the hits medley – take some of the fizz out of the record. The band aren't granted too much individual space – which is frustrating, since Sheldon, Norvo and Freeman all sound excellent – and Goodman's habit of whistling through other people's solos is caught by the mostly very clear recording, which suffers from only occasional drop-outs.

*****(*) Yale University Archives Vol. 5**

Musicmasters 65040-2 2CD *Goodman; Jack Sheldon, Bobby Hackett (t); Bill Harris, Urbie Green (tb); Jerry Dodgion (as, f); Flip Phillips (ts); Modesto Bresano (ts, f); Red Norvo (vib); Gene DiNovi, John Bunch (p); Jimmy Wyble (g); Steve Swallow, Red Wootten, Jimmy Rowser (b); John Markham, Ray Mosca (d).* 11/59–6/63.

***** Yale University Archives Vol. 7**

Musicmasters 65058-2 *Goodman; Bill Harris (tb); Flip Phillips (ts); Martin Harris (p); Leo Robinson (g); Al Simi (b); Bob Binnix (d).* 8/59.

*****(*) Yale University Archives Vol. 8**

Musicmasters 65093-2 *Goodman; Bernie Privin, Manny Klein, Conrad Gozzo, Irv Goodman, Don Fagerquist (t); Joe Howard, Murray McEachern, Milt Bernhart, Lou McGarity (tb); Toots Mondello, Herb Geller, Bud Shank (as); Zoot Sims, Buddy Collette, Dave Pell (ts); Chuck Gentry (bs); André Previn, Hank Rowland, Mel Powell, Russ Freeman (p); Eddie Costa (vib); Tony Mottola, Al Hendrickson, Barney Kessel (g); Leroy Vinnegar, George Duvivier (b); Frank Capp, Roy Burnes, Morey Feld (d); Martha Tilton (v).* 9/58–2/61.

More from Goodman's own archive. There is some happy and spirited playing by these sometimes improbably constituted small groups. The first band on *Volume 5* features Phillips, Norvo and Sheldon, and generates some agreeable swing re-creations, but the second is graced by the lovely trumpet-playing of Bobby Hackett and merits an extra notch on the ratings. The line-up on *Volume 7* is a little more routine, but the group play very capably. *Volume 8* includes a session of Hawaiian tunes from 1961 (improbable but rather good), a small group with Previn (flat), and two exquisitely shaped medleys with Mel Powell. Plus one big-band shot, a blossoming 'Bei Mir Bist Du Schön', with Martha Tilton back as vocalist. A good one.

***** Benny Goodman Swings Again**

Columbia 475625-2 *Goodman; Jack Sheldon (t); Murray McEachern (tb); Jerry Dodgion (as); Flip Phillips (ts); Russ Freeman (p); Red Norvo (vib); Jimmy Wyble (g); Red Wootten (b); John Markham (d); Maria Marshall (v).* 60.

Nine tunes, most of them old-timers from the Goodman book, played live with plenty of pep by this curious-looking line-up. Goodman's strange penchant for including rowdy players such as McEachern, as if to offset his own impeccably cultivated playing, will strike some as odd, but Sheldon, whose company

Goodman always enjoyed, is in good heart and Phillips is fine. Norvo's vibes make a lot of curious noise on 'Gotta Be This Or That', at the conclusion of which somebody shouts out, 'Go, man go!'

***** Together Again**

RCA Victor 68593-2 *Goodman; Lionel Hampton (vib); Teddy Wilson (p); Gene Krupa (d). 2–8/63.*

Although they were together again, most of the tunes they played didn't come from the original book of the Quartet. The result is rather placid and amiable, lacking nothing in finesse but considerably short on the kind of cumulative power which the original sessions touched on.

***** Yale University Archives Vol. 6**

Musicmasters 65047-2 *Goodman; Joe Newman, Doc Cheatham (t); Zoot Sims (ts); Bernie Leighton, Herbie Hancock (p); Les Spann, Attila Zoller (g); George Duvivier, Al Hall (b); Morey Feld, Joe Marshall (d); Annette Sanders (v). 6/66–6/67.*

Two very strange line-ups for these live dates from the Rainbow Grill: one has Herbie Hancock and Doc Cheatham together on the stand. That both of them are plausible Goodman bands says something, perhaps, about the leader's inflexible will. He allows no stretching out – only three tracks run over the five-minute mark – and little adventure. But the playing conforms to the usual stern standard.

***** Jazz Masters 33**

Verve 844410-2 *Goodman; Warren Vaché (t); George Young (as); Scott Hamilton, Zoot Sims, Buddy Tate, Frank Wess (ts); Mary Lou Williams (p); Lionel Hampton (vib); Percy Heath (b); Connie Kay (d). 70–78.*

***** 40th Anniversary Concert – Live At Carnegie Hall**

London 820349-2 2CD *Goodman; Victor Paz, Warren Vaché, Jack Sheldon (t); Wayne Andre, George Masso, John Messner (tb); George Young, Mel Rodnon (as); Buddy Tate, Frank Wess (ts); Sol Schlinger (bs); Mary Lou Williams, Jimmy Rowles, John Bunch (p); Lionel Hampton (vib); Cal Collins, Wayne Wright (g); Michael Moore (b); Connie Kay (d); Martha Tilton, Debi Craig (v). 1/78.*

Goodman's enduring facility as a clarinettist is the most absorbing thing about these sessions, on both sets. The Jazz Masters disc collates material from various appearances during the 1970s, including a number of different generations involved, and makes a worthwhile sampler of Goodman's final period. At Carnegie Hall the band played a functional rather than challenging role, the job being to replicate standard scores as flawlessly as the leader wished and, although there are many fine players involved, Goodman's iron hand stifles anything free-wheeling which might have emerged. But he drives himself as hard as the others: the clarinet still sounds august, refined, imperious.

*****(*) Yale Archives Vol. 1**

Musicmasters 65000-2 *Goodman; Ermit Perry, Taft Jordan, Buzz King, John Frosk, Joe Newman, Ruby Braff, Allan Smith, Benny Ventura, Jack Sheldon, Joe Mosello, Randy Sandke, John Eckert (t); Vernon Brown, Eddie Bert, Harry DeVito, Urbie Green, Bill Harris, Buster Cooper, Rex Peer, Hale Rood, Matt Finders, Dan Barrett (tb); Ernie Mauro, Skippy Colluchio, Jerry Dodgion, Herb Geller, Jimmy Sands, Jack Stuckey, Chuck Wilson (as); Zoot Sims, Buddy Tate, Dick Hafer, Flip Phillips, Bob Wilber, Babe Clark, Paul Quinichette, Ken Peplowski, Ted Nash (ts); Gene Allen, Pepper Adams (bs); Bernie Leighton, Roland Hanna, Dave McKenna, Martin Harris, Gene DiNovi, Russ Freeman, Teddy Wilson, Ben Aronov (p); Red Norvo (vib); Attila Zoller, Chuck Wayne, Steve Jordan, Leo Robinson, Jimmy Wyble, Turk Van Lake, Perry Lopez, Billy Bauer, James Chirillo (g); George Duvivier, Henry Grimes, Tommy Potter, Al Simi, Red Wootten, Milt Hinton, Arvell Shaw, Murray Wall (b); Joe Marshall, Roy Burns, Bobby Donaldson, Bob Binnix, John Markham, Shelly Manne, Don Lamond, Louie Bellson (d). 9/55–1/86.*

What was the first collection from Goodman's personal archive is a fascinating cross-section of work, most of it from the 1950s, but with two tracks by a 1967 septet featuring Joe Newman and Zoot Sims and one by the 1986 big band that must be among his final testaments. That his playing on that final session is as impeccable as ever says much for Goodman's tireless devotion both to the clarinet and to the rigorous, swinging music which he believed was his métier. Small groups of five, seven and eight predominate in this selection and, although there's little that can be called surprising, the themes chosen – including 'Macedonia Lullaby', 'Marching And Swinging' and 'Diga Diga Doo' – are at least unfamiliar Goodman fare. A delightful 'Broadway' with Bill Harris and Flip Phillips is one highlight, and shrewd programming makes the CD consistently interesting, with all the recordings, despite their differing vintage, sounding well.

Andy Goodrich

ALTO SAXOPHONE

A distinguished 'local' man in the Chicago area, Goodrich has had almost no exposure on record, being an imprtant figure in education.

***** Motherless Child**

Delmark DE 495 *Goodrich; Eddie Henderson (t); Harold Mabern, James Williams (p); Buster Williams (b); Billy Hart (d). 1/96.*

Like vibist Carl Leukaufe (also on Delmark), the affable Goodrich is making his recording debut relatively late in life. To say that he was teacher to Booker Little, Charles Lloyd and Harold Mabern, who anchors this bright, uncomplicated session, is a measure of his contribution to the jazz scene in Michigan. Along with Robert Harris, he founded the first black music programme at the State University evening college, an important point of focus for young players in and around the Windy City. The album is dedicated to the memory of his mother, who died shortly before Andy received his own master's degree there. It closes with a feeling version of the old spiritual, arranged with great sensitivity by Brenton Banks, who worked with Andy and with W.O. (Bill) Smith during his Nashville years. Banks is also responsible for a fine version of Gigi Gryce's 'Reminiscing', which lifts a slow starter on to a new plane after four tracks. Andy's bluesy tone is superficially reminiscent of Eddie Cleanhead Vinson, but with a strong infusion of Charlie Parker, whose 'Quasimodo' is the most overt nod in the direction of bebop. The key tracks are a long, long version of 'Stranger In Paradise', on which Mabern also excels (James Williams is restricted to just three tracks), and 'Serenade In Blue', which coaxes some lovely work from Henderson, who's in an unexpectedly upbeat mood elsewhere on the disc. Buster Williams and Billy Hart are worth the cover price in themselves; even on slower numbers the pace never lags for a moment. Tautly played and faithfully recorded, it's a delightful introduction to a man hitherto known only by reputation and from the warm acknowledgements of those who have benefited from his wisdom.

Mick Goodrick (born 1945)

GUITAR

Taught at Berklee before joining Gary Burton in 1973. Has been associated with several major groups since, but is more renowned as a teacher and patrician influence; his own records are comparatively rare.

***** In Passing**

ECM 847327-2 *Goodrick; John Surman (ss, bs, bcl); Eddie Gomez (b); Jack DeJohnette (d).* 11/78.

*****(*) Biorhythms**

CMP CD 46 *Goodrick; Harvie Swartz (b); Gary Chaffee (d).* 10/90.

***** Rare Birds**

RAM RMCD 4505 *Goodrick; Joe Diorio (g).* 4/93.

Goodrick's brand of electric-guitar impressionism has been slow to make an impact, at least in comparison to that of such peers as Frisell and Metheny (Goodrick worked with Metheny in Gary Burton's mid-1970s band). He seems to have fewer ambitions as a leader, but these records reveal an intelligent grasp of form and a shrewd management of resources. The 1978 session is a little diffuse: Surman is a more dominant voice than Goodrick, and the music aspires to the pastel tones of a typical ECM session. *Biorhythms* is a follow-up that took a long time to emerge, but it's a feast of guitar playing, with excellent support from Swartz and Chaffee, who can play jazz or funk time with equal aplomb. Goodrick's themes range from the peppy groove of the title-tune and 'Groove Test' through to a reflective sequence for Emily Remler, 'Bl'ize Medley', and the lavish farewell of '(I'll) Never Forget'. Restrained use of overdubs and crystal-clear sound by engineer Walter Quintus ensure that the music holds the interest even across generous CD length. The pairing with Joe Diorio on *Rare Birds* is a meeting of minds which are seemingly a little too alike: with each man using long, liquid sustain and a rippling melodic flow, the six standards and half-dozen improvisations have a seamless but soporific beauty about them. Here and there, as on a particularly lovely 'Blue In Green', the music intensifies just a fraction.

Bobby Gordon (born 1941)

CLARINET

Studied with Joe Marsala, then was a regular at Eddie Condon's in the late '70s, followed by a variety of mainstream work. Now based in San Diego and leading his own group there.

***** Don't Let It End**

Arbors ARCD 19112 *Gordon; Adele Girard Marsala (hp); Ray Sherman (p); Morty Corb (b); Gene Estes (d).* 7/92.

***** Bobby Gordon Plays Bing**

Arbors ARCD 19172 *Gordon; Peter Ecklund, Randy Reinhart (c, t); Dan Barrett (tb); Scott Robinson (ts, bs, bsx); Keith Ingham (p, cel); Marty Grosz (g); Greg Cohen (b); Hal Smith (d).* 6/96.

***** Clarinet Blue**

Arbors ARCD 19223 *Gordon; Dave McKenna (p); Frank Tate (b); Joe Ascione (d).* 5/99.

Mellow fruitfulness is the sound of Gordon's clarinet. A veteran mainstreamer, he was once a pupil of Joe Marsala, so it was a nice idea to have him record the charming *Don't Let It End* with Adele Girard Marsala. Quiet tempos and gentle embellishments characterize the date. The tunes are all museum-pieces of the order of 'Love Nest' and 'Emaline'. It's done with enough grace to make it work: in its mannerly way, it's a little unique.

The Bing tribute offers a stack of Crosby tunes from the earlier part of the singer's career, going as far back as 'There Ain't No Sweet Man Worth The Salt Of My Tears', which he did with Whiteman and Beiderbecke. A gang of the usual suspects is on best behaviour here, sticking closely, and tenderly, to Keith Ingham's arrangements. Gordon comes out as a bit of a bystander. If not exactly stiff, it's hardly the liveliest record these players have ever delivered.

Gordon often sounds like a calmer, less brazen version of Pee Wee Russell on *Clarinet Blue*. McKenna downsizes his own methods to accommodate him, and the music is genteel but not without its rewards. Gordon's homey sound grows on you. Highlight: an almost suave 'I Wish I Could Shimmy Like My Sister Kate'.

Dexter Gordon (1923–89)

TENOR AND SOPRANO SAXOPHONES

Dexter's own life achieved mythical proportions when he appeared in Bernard Tavernier's Round Midnight, playing a hybrid of himself and Bud Powell. Originally influenced by Lester Young, Gordon favoured easy, behind-the-beat phrasing which could be turned to more confrontational use when required. In 1962, having gone through all too familiar difficulties with narcotics, he moved his base to Europe and stayed for the next decade and a half. In later years, having become a star under Tavernier, he started returning to the USA.

***** Dexter Gordon 1943–1947**

Classics 999 *Gordon; Harry 'Sweets' Edison, Leonard Hawkins (t); Melba Liston (tb); Wardell Gray (ts); Bud Powell, Jimmy Rowles, Argonne Thornton (p); Jimmy Bunn (g); Red Callender,*

Gene Ramey (b); Johnny Miller, Ed Nicholson, Roy Porter, Chuck Thompson (d). 43–47.

One of the giants (literally) of modern jazz, Gordon made an impact on players as dissimilar as Sonny Rollins and John Coltrane, but himself remained comparatively unrecognized until a comeback in the 1960s (Gordon had lived and worked in Scandinavia in the early half of the decade), by which time many of the post-Lester Young stylistic devices he had introduced were firmly in place under others' patents. Classics now have a firm foot in the bebop era as well, and this first Gordon volume picks up the story while he is working with Fletcher Henderson and just beginning to strike out on his own account. Most of the later material is available in other – and mostly better-quality – configurations, but for early material like 'I've Found A New Baby' and 'Rosetta', which were recorded when the saxophonist was just twenty, it's a useful insight. To a degree, Gordon had outgrown his strength; his solo spots sound strained and overblown, and the microphones don't capture much of the breathy resonance that was to be a feature of his mature style. The other personnel are, of course, fascinating, but many of these associations can be picked up again later in the story; despite the issue number, this needn't be considered a priority purchase.

****** Dexter Gordon On Dial: The Complete Sessions**

Spotlite SPJ CD 130 *Gordon; Melba Liston (tb); Teddy Edwards, Wardell Gray (ts); Jimmy Bunn, Charles Fox, Jimmy Rowles (p); Red Callender (b); Roy Porter, Chuck Thompson (d).* 6/47.

Gordon's on-off partnership with fellow-tenorist Wardell Gray was consistently productive, pairing him for much of the late 1940s with another Lester Young disciple who had taken on board most of the modernist idiom without abandoning Young's mellifluously extended solo style. The Dial sessions – with Gray and, at Christmas 1947, Teddy Edwards – are pretty definitive of what was going on on the West Coast at the time. The Spotlite brings together all the material, including a track with just Edwards up front. 'The Chase' was a studio version of the saxophone contests that Dexter and Gray had been conducting night after night in LA's Little Harlem. The earliest of the sessions features Melba Liston, who was presumably recruited for her skill as an arranger. The charts to 'Mischievous Lady' and 'Lullaby In Rhythm' sound tight and well organized, more coherent than the ultimately rather tiresome 'Chase'. On the same day, Gordon also laid down three tracks with just rhythm, of which 'Chromatic Aberration' is perhaps the most interesting vis-à-vis the development of bebop, but 'It's The Talk Of The Town' is the occasion for one of his most expressive ballad solos of these years. The final Dial session, with Rowles at the piano, was made just before the AFM recording ban began the brief eclipse which skews our perception of what was going on stylistically at this point.

***** The Bethlehem Years**

Fresh Sound FSR 154 *Gordon; Conte Candoli (t); Frank Rosolino (tb); Kenny Drew (p); Leroy Vinnegar (b); Lawrence Marable (d).* 9/55.

***** Daddy Plays The Horn**

Bethlehem BET 6005 *As above.* 9/55.

Not normally thought of as a West Coast man in the stylistic sense, Gordon enjoyed his sojourn back in California during 1955. Charlie Parker's death in March created a vacuum at the head of the saxophone rankings and Gordon looked like an ideal contender. *The Bethlehem Years* compilation is good value for money. Neither Candoli nor Rosolino is a charismatic soloist but they spur Gordon on and lend 'Ruby My Dear' a beefy resonance. Drew and Vinnegar play exceptionally well, and the CD transfer is generally good. In 1955 Gordon had already cemented the style he was to utilize virtually to the end of his career. Its easy, but never shallow, expressiveness and light, springy time-feel were directly related to Lester Young. He was, though, playing in the interim between two drug-related prison sentences that more or less wound up the 1950s, which should have been his decade.

****(*) The Resurgence Of Dexter Gordon**

Original Jazz Classics OJC 929 *Gordon; Martin Banks (t); Richard Boone (tb); Dolo Coker (p); Charles Green (b); Lawrence Marable (d).* 10/60.

Sometimes known as *Pulsation*, this is a little-known Jazzland date which didn't quite live up to its title: that would happen with the Blue Note sequence which comes next. Gordon seems more like a sideman here than anything, with a cool and no more than proficient team of Angelenos supporting him, and its obscurity is probably deserved.

****** Doin' Alright**

Blue Note 784077 *Gordon; Freddie Hubbard (t); Horace Parlan (p); George Tucker (b); Al Harewood (d).* 5/61.

Back in the world and doing all right. Gordon's first recording after a long and painful break is one of his best. Critics divide on whether Gordon was influenced by Coltrane at this period or whether it was simply a case of the original being obscured by his followers. Gordon's phrasing on *Doin' Alright* certainly suggests a connection of some sort, but the opening statement of 'I Was Doin' Alright' is completely individual and quite distinct, and Gordon's solo development is nothing like the younger man's. This is one of Gordon's best records and should on no account be missed.

***** Dexter Calling**

Blue Note 46544 *Gordon; Kenny Drew (p); Paul Chambers (b); Philly Joe Jones (d).* 5/61.

Recorded three days later and reflecting the same virtues. With a better-drilled but slightly more conventional band, Gordon is pushed a little wider on the solos, ranging much further away from the stated key (as on a memorable mid-chorus break on 'Ernie's Tune') and varying his timbre much more than he used to. As indicators of how his harmonic language and distinctive accent were to develop, the two 1961 Blue Notes are particularly valuable. The sound is a little better on the later record.

***** Go!**

Blue Note 98794 *Gordon; Sonny Clark (p); Butch Warren (b); Billy Higgins (d).* 8/62.

***** A Swingin' Affair**

Blue Note 784133 *As above.* 8/62.

Typically good husbandry on the part of Blue Note to get two albums from this not altogether riveting date, one of the first since his return to normal circulation. *Swingin' Affair* stands and falls on a lovely version of 'You Stepped Out Of A Dream'. *Go!*, now available in a crisp new edition, includes Gordon's simplest and finest reading of 'Where Are You', a relatively little-used standard with interesting changes and a strong turn in the middle. The hipsters' motto (pinched from novelist John Clellon Holmes) was meant to suggest relentless improvisatory progress. Gordon was to play better, but rarely with such directness, and it's not entirely idle to ask whether he felt himself hampered by a rhythm section that was not always responsive. 'I Guess I'll Hang My Tears Out To Dry' has him soaring away on his own, almost out of touch with the rest of the band.

**** Cry Me A River**

Steeplechase SCCD 36004 *Gordon; Atli Bjorn (p); Benny Nielsen, Marcel Rigot (b); Finn Frederiksen, William Schiopffe (d).* 11/62, 6/64.

A pretty dismal album by any standard, much of it is given over to Bjorn's own trio. The title-track receives a predictably fulsome and emotive reading, but Bjorn seems to be all over his keyboard in contrast to Gordon's discipline and reserve. Not an album for the A-list.

****** Our Man In Paris**

Blue Note 746394 *Gordon; Bud Powell (p); Pierre Michelot (b); Kenny Clarke (d).* 5/63.

Gordon's 'purest' bebop album since the early 1950s, *Our Man* also shows how much he had continued to absorb of the pre-bop sound of Lester Young and Johnny Hodges. There are hints of both in his ballad playing and in the winding, almost incantatory solo on 'Night In Tunisia', which is one of his finest performances on record. A classic.

***** One Flight Up**

Blue Note 84176 *Gordon; Donald Byrd (t); Kenny Drew (p); Niels-Henning Orsted Pedersen (b); Art Taylor (d).* 6/64.

Three extended performances, dominated by 'Darn That Dream' (see also *Ballads*, below) and the turned-sideways 'Coppin' The Haven' theme. Byrd was still an impressive player at this period, though he's rarely as adventurous as Hubbard, and Drew is a brilliant accompanist. It's easy to see, particularly on 'Darn', how Gordon continued to influence John Coltrane's harmonic development.

*****(*) Gettin' Around**

Blue Note 46681 *Gordon; Bobby Hutcherson (vib); Barry Harris (p); Bob Cranshaw (b); Billy Higgins (d).* 5/65.

One of the most engaging of Gordon's Blue Note recordings, *Gettin' Around* is also a showcase for the burgeoning talent of Bobby Hutcherson. Though the charts are relatively scant and unchallenging, the standard of performance is very high; Bobby's starburst patterns, executed round Harris's quiet and definite comping, are full of detail and excitement. The material is fairly basic and familiar, with just three Gordon compositions – not much more than blowing themes – tucked away at the end of the album. 'Manhã de Carnaval' gets the record off to a breezy start, and the ensembles here are worthy of study; clean-lined, joyous and absolutely exact, yet with the spontaneity of a first take. Frank Foster's 'Shiny Stockings' was a favourite of the time with tenor players, and Dexter milks it enthusiastically.

***** The Complete Blue Note Sessions**

Blue Note 834200 6CD *Gordon; Freddie Hubbard, Donald Byrd (t); Bobby Hutcherson (vib); Barry Harris, Kenny Drew, Horace Parlan, Sonny Clark, Bud Powell (p); Bob Cranshaw, Butch Warren, George Tucker, Paul Chambers, Pierre Michelot, Niels-Henning Orsted Pedersen (b); Philly Joe Jones, Al Harewood, Kenny Clarke, Art Taylor, Billy Higgins (d).* 61–65.

Gordon's Blue Notes make a worthy entry in the boxed-set constituency, although exposure at length does tend to show up his vulnerabilities at least as much as his strengths, so our rating is relatively stingy. The woozy relationship with the beat is one problem, and his liking for well-trodden phrases and quotes does tend to pall over the long haul. Collectors will welcome the inclusion of scarcer sessions such as *Clubhouse*, otherwise unavailable; though our favourite remains the excellent *Doin' Alright*, there is much else here for Blue Note followers to enjoy.

****(*) Cheese Cake**

Steeplechase SCCD 36008 *Gordon; Tete Montoliu (p); Benny Nielsen, Niels-Henning Orsted Pedersen (b); Alex Riel (d).* 6/64.

***** King Neptune**

Steeplechase SCCD 36012 *As above.* 6/64.

***** I Want More**

Steeplechase SCCD 36015 *As above.* 7/64.

***** Love For Sale**

Steeplechase SCCD 36018 *As above.* 7/64.

****(*) It's You Or No One**

Steeplechase SCCD 36022 *As above.* 8/64.

****(*) Billie's Bounce**

Steeplechase SCCD 36028 *As above.* 8/64.

***** Stable Mable**

Steeplechase SCCD 31040 *Gordon; Tete Montoliu, Horace Parlan (p); Benny Nielsen, Niels-Henning Orsted Pedersen (b); Alex Riel, Tony Inzalaco (d).* 11/74.

***** Bouncin' With Dex**

Steeplechase SCCD 31060 *Gordon; Tete Montoliu (p); Benny Nielsen, Niels-Henning Orsted Pedersen (b); Alex Riel, Billy Higgins (d).* 3/75–9/75.

***** Something Different**

Steeplechase SCCD 31136 *Gordon; Philip Catherine (g); Niels-Henning Orsted Pedersen (b); Billy Higgins (d).* 9/75.

Newly settled in Scandinavia, Gordon turns the tap on full. There's still the emotional equivalent of an airlock, slightly spluttering hesitations alternating with sudden, scalding flows, but it all starts to fit together as this fascinating if very spotty sequence of albums progresses. A more comprehensive pianist, Parlan or Flanagan, might have varied the structures a little, but Montoliu is sympathetic and very lyrical.

The touchstone 'Body And Soul' is beautifully enunciated on *King Neptune* and the band gels in the ensemble passages with little of the slightly mechanistic pulse that afflicted the earlier *Cheese Cake* session. *I Want More* and *Love For Sale* are the best of this group. Gordon's understanding with the players seems increasingly telepathic and his approach to themes correspondingly inventive. *It's You Or No One* and *Billie's Bounce* suffer from longueurs which this somewhat obsessive documentation is wont to fall prey to.

Bouncin' With Dex takes essentially the same band forward a decade. By the time of *Swiss Nights* (below), the act is consummately polished. Montoliu sounds relaxed and confident and plays with considerable authority. The addition of guitarist Catherine adds a new band of the spectrum on *Something Different*. From the opening 'Freddie Freeloader' till it closes with 'Polka Dots And Moonbeams' and 'Yesterday's Mood', it exudes bonhomie and relaxed invention.

***** Both Sides Of Midnight**

Black Lion BLCD 760103 *Gordon; Kenny Drew (p); Niels-Henning Orsted Pedersen (b); Albert 'Tootie' Heath (d).* 7/67.

*****(*) Body And Soul**

Black Lion BLCD 760118 *As above.* 7/67.

***** Take The 'A' Train**

Black Lion BLCD 760133 *As above.* 7/67.

These are vintage albums from a two-shift session in July 1967. Two releases would probably have been sufficient, but Dexter is playing so well and with such a responsive and sympathetic band that both nights are worth hearing in their entirety. *'A' Train* uses up some of the alternative takes ('For All We Know' from the former, and 'Blues Walk' from the second) and is a little dilute as a consequence. And yet there is nothing here that won't delight any fan of Dexter's. Even a few slight intonation problems and what sounds like a failing reed at one point are turned to advantage as he slithers down the familiar chromatic escape lane. Drew is a more rhythmic pianist than Montoliu, and the metre of Gordon's solos tends to stretch, fragment, re-integrate at great speed when in his company. A nice piece of documentation, generously presented.

***** Live at The Amsterdam Paradiso**

Le Jazz 28 *Gordon; Cees Slinger (p); Jacques Schols (b); Han Bennink (d).* 2/69.

These guys had no reason to feel any tiepidation at the prospect of playing with Dex. Enough distinguished Americans – and not least Eric Dolphy, five years before – had passed through to permit a degree of confidence in their powers. Dexter responds in kind and delivers one of his most relaxed and happy sets of the period. Dex had a nice feel for the shape of a club date, opening with his own 'Fried Bananas' and building to an early climax with Dameron's 'Good Bait' and Monk's 'Rhythm-A-Ning', before slowing the pace with 'Willow, Weep For Me' and ending on a killer punch with Bird's 'Scrapple From The Apple'. It's easy to see why Han Bennink became such a key figure on the European avant-garde, his amiable eccentricity masking a formidable technique. A fine record; good to have it back in circulation.

***** The Tower Of Power!**

Original Jazz Classics OJCCD 299 *Gordon; James Moody (ts); Barry Harris (p); Buster Williams (b); Albert 'Tootie' Heath (d).* 4/69.

****(*) More Power**

Original Jazz Classics OJCCD 815 *As above.* 4/69.

Dexter was beginning to visit the USA slightly more frequently again, and this was made on one of his trips. He still sounds tentative on American soil, and not even the presence of James Moody on 'Montmartre' sets things alight, partly because the two tenors manage to cancel one another out. Beware the use of exclamation marks in jazz album titles. It usually indicates that the contents are less exciting than the label would have you believe. As if to prove the point, the sequel turns out to be more interesting than the original release, with a strong version of 'Lady Bird' (which again features Moody) and a brisk dispatch of Dexter's own 'Fried Bananas', part of his staple diet at this period. From the perspective of 30 years later, these sound like diplomatic soundings, preparatory to Gordon's triumphal return; but in themselves they are far from essential additions to a Gordon collection.

***** Tenor Titans**

Storyville 8288 *Gordon; Palle Mikkelborg, Lars Togeby (t); Kjeld Ipsen (tb); Jesper Nehammer, Ben Webster (ts); Thomas Clausen, Kenny Drew (p); Bo Steif (b); Alex Riel, Bjarne Rostvold, Kasper Winding (d).* 69, 72.

A confrontation across the generations and, though unexpected, a more logical conjunction than perhaps it appears. Dexter is heard with his quartet and orchestra from a live concert in 1972; Webster is on the same bill, but the two tenor tracks are from a rather earlier set, when they share the lead on three Ellington tunes (if 'Perdido' can be so attributed). Dexter actually takes the initiative on all three and is certainly not minded to defer to the old master.

***** Blue Dex**

Prestige 11003 *Gordon; various line-ups as above OJC albums.* 69–72.

A playable compilation of Gordon blowing on the blues from his various Prestige albums. The main point of interest to Dexter specialists will be the inclusion of alternative takes of 'Sticky Wicket' and 'The Jumpin' Blues'.

***** The Art Of The Ballad**

Prestige 11009 *Gordon; Thad Jones (t); Tommy Flanagan, Barry Harris, Hampton Hawes, Hank Jones, Wynton Kelly, Junior Mance, Cedar Walton (p); Stanley Clarke, Bob Cranshaw, Sam Jones, Larry Ridley, Martin Rivera, Buster Williams (b); Roy Brooks, Kenny Clarke, Alan Dawson, Louis Hayes, Albert 'Tootie' Heath, Billy Higgins, Oliver Jackson (d).* 4/69–7/73.

One doesn't automatically think of Dexter as a ballad performer, but this compilation, part of a Fantasy series, finds him in brilliant form on a wide range of material from 'Days Of Wine And Roses', 'Sophisticated Lady' and the old tenor saxophone groaner, 'Body And Soul', to unexpectedly folkish material. Mary Hopkin's 'Those Were The Days' and 'The First Time Ever I Saw Your Face' are exquisite and worth the price on their own.

***** At Montreux**

Prestige PCD 7861 2 *Gordon; Junior Mance (p); Martin Rivera (b); Oliver Jackson (d).* 7/70.

*****(*) The Panther!**

Original Jazz Classics OJCCD 770 *Gordon; Tommy Flanagan (p); Larry Ridley (b); Alan Dawson (d).* 7/70.

*** Jumpin' Blues

Original Jazz Classics OJCCD 899 *Gordon; Wynton Kelly (p); Sam Jones (b); Roy Brooks (d). 8/70.*

Dexter's visit to the USA in 1970 confirmed his growing critical stature. He played at Newport, an appearance documented on *At Montreux*, and managed to sound accommodating and almost deferential. For once, a guest player might have lent the proceedings some edge and bite, but as it stands Dexter doesn't sound willing to rock the boat.

Following the modest success of *The Tower Of Power!*, Dex recorded *The Panther!* and, a little later, *Jumpin' Blues* in the USA. It is generally thought that one of the panther's most effective characteristics is its silence, which makes the exclamation mark slightly redundant. In point of fact, the 1970 record marks a stage in Gordon's development in which he was able and willing to play more quietly, using fewer notes, a greater dynamic range and a willingness to dwell on effective phrases rather than rush them past like trolleybuses. 'Body And Soul' is, almost inevitably, the touchstone here again, a delicate, almost kaleidoscopic reading, with Flanagan's immaculate accompaniment using altered chords. 'Mrs Miniver' is an original and is one of the saxophonist's most interesting and little-known tunes; medium tempo and song-like, it has a brilliantly simple bridge and coda that confirms the strength of Gordon's conception at this point in his career.

The August session is notable for one of the last recorded performances by Wynton Kelly, who gives the session a solid blues foundation to originals 'Evergreenish' and the title-track, as well as a group of standard and bebop themes. Dexter is in fine form and plays exquisitely on 'For Sentimental Reasons'. A worthy group of records, though only serious collectors will find room for all three on the shelf.

*** The Jumpin' Blues

Original Jazz Classics OJC 899 *Gordon; Wynton Kelly (p); Sam Jones (b); Roy Brooks (d). 8/70.*

*** Generation

Original Jazz Classics OJC 836 *Gordon; Freddie Hubbard (t); Cedar Walton (p); Buster Williams (b); Billy Higgins (d). 7/72.*

Cut for Prestige on two of Gordon's occasional visits home, these were more like reminders to the jazz audience that the old lion was still out there rather than meaningful statements. Both bands are studded with formidable talents, but the obvious lack of specific preparation makes both seem like mere pick-up dates, capable though the playing often is.

** The Shadow Of Your Smile

Steeplechase SCCD 31206 *Gordon; Lars Sjøsten (p); Sture Nordin (b); Fredrik Norén (d). 4/71.*

**(*) After Hours

Steeplechase SCCD 31226 *As above, except add Rolf Ericson (t). 4/71.*

These are weak performances. 'Polka Dots And Moonbeams' on *Shadow* suffers some difficulties in the first dozen measures, mostly down to the Danish rhythm-section. Not usually lacking in proportion, Gordon sounds merely grandstanding on 'Secret Love' and never quite gets hold of 'Shadow Of Your Smile'. Ericson has a bold, swinging tone, but it cuts across Gordon's development on 'All The Things You Are' quite disconcertingly. Two to miss with a clear conscience.

***(*) Ça'Purange

Original Jazz Classics OJCCD 1005 *Gordon; Thad Jones (c, t); James Moody (ts); Barry Harris (p); Stanley Clarke, Buster Williams (b); Louis Hayes, Albert 'Tootie' Heath (d). 6/72.*

We had forgotten how good this almost-forgotten Prestige LP was until OJC revived it. The partnership with Thad Jones was a gift from the gods, and it is slightly surprising that none of Thad's compositions made it to the record. It is a rare jazz disc that includes a Ewan MacColl song, but 'The First Time Ever I Saw Your Face' is exquisitely shaped and Dexter's solo is intense and formally perfect. Always a brief album, it has been boosted by a second take of Sonny Rollins's 'Airegin', but we are disinclined to dismiss it for short measure; anyone who has fallen under Dexter's gruff spell will be captivated; anyone who has yet to be convinced can scarcely resist.

*** Generation

Original Jazz Classics OJCCD 836 *Gordon; Freddie Hubbard (t); Cedar Walton (p); Buster Williams (b); Billy Higgins (d). 7/72.*

*** Tangerine

Original Jazz Classics OJCCD 1041 *Gordon; Thad Jones (t, flhn); Hank Jones, Cedar Walton (p); Stanley Clarke, Buster Williams (b); Louis Hayes, Billy Higgins (d). 72.*

Two records originally recorded for Prestige, *Generation* keeps up the quality of the early-'70s albums. Hubbard imparts an urgency and snap to the session and he cheekily ups the ante on 'Milestones' with a brisk and rhythmic statement that is as different as possible from the composer's sanctified version. The CD reissue includes an alternative take of the same tune with, if anything, a better Hubbard feature, though Dexter's solo is flat and off-balance. Monk's 'We See' was a favourite of Dexter's and is sensitively handled; but the surprise hit of the album is André Previn's 'Scared To Be Alone', a tune that sits perfectly for the saxophone.

Tangerine marks an interesting change of pace, a faster delivery and a more pungent attack. Fuelled by two very different rhythm-sections, Dexter declines to veer very far from his usual delivery, but it's interesting to hear how differently he phrases in front of Walton and the more lyrical but less challenging Jones.

***(*) Round Midnight

Steeplechase SCCD 31290 *Gordon; Benny Bailey (t); Lars Sjøsten (p); Torbjørn Hultcrantz (b); Jual Curtis (d). 74.*

Bailey was a terrific partner: tight, energetic and unfailingly lyrical. To a large extent they ignore the well-intentioned accompaniment of the Swedish trio (Sjøsten is an able player, the others not) and head off on a companionable jaunt round a set of themes that fall easily under their respective approaches. Gordon is completely at home on 'Round About Midnight' and 'Stella By Starlight'; Bailey takes the initiative on 'Blue 'N' Boogie' and 'What's New', and fans of the little trumpeter (one wonders what they must have looked like, side by side on the stand) will find this one of the most profitable of his live recordings.

****** More Than You Know**

Steeplechase SCCD 31030 *Gordon; Palle Mikkelborg, Allan Botschinsky, Benny Rosenfeld, Idrees Sulieman (t, flhn); Richard Boone, Vincent Nilsson (tb); Axel Windfeld (btb); Ole Molin (g); Thomas Clausen (p, electric p); Kenneth Knudsen (syn); Niels-Henning Orsted Pedersen (b); Alex Riel, Ed Thigpen (d); Klaus Nordsoe (perc); chamber winds and strings.* 2–3/75.

**** Strings And Things**

Steeplechase SCCD 31145 *Gordon; Allan Botschinsky, Markku Johansson (t); Eero Koivistoinen, Pekka Poyry (reeds); George Wadenius, Ole Molin (g); Niels-Henning Orsted Pedersen (b); unknown ensemble.* 2/65, 5/76.

***** Something Different**

Steeplechase SCCD 31136 *Gordon; Philip Catherine (g); Niels-Henning Orsted Pedersen (b); Billy Hart (d).* 9/75.

****(*) Sophisticated Giant**

Columbia CK 65295 *Gordon; Benny Bailey, Woody Shaw (t, flhn); Wayne Andre, Slide Hampton (tb); Frank Wess (f, as, picc); Howard Johnson (tba, bs); Bobby Hutcherson (vib); George Cables (p); Rufus Reid (b); Victor Lewis (d).* 6/77.

Beautifully arranged and orchestrated (by Mikkelborg), *More Than You Know* sets Gordon in the middle (as it sounds) of a rich ensemble of textures which are every bit as creatively unresolved and undogmatic as his solo approach. 'Naima' rarely works with a large band, but this is near perfect and Gordon responds with considerable emotion and inventiveness.

Gordon rarely played with a guitarist, but Catherine was an inspired choice for the September 1975 session, alternating warm, flowing lines with more staccato, accented figures towards the top of his range. NHOP responds with firmly plucked and strummed figures and Gordon rides on top in a relatively un-familiar programme for him – Miles's 'Freddie Freeloader', 'When Sunny Gets Blue', 'Polka Dots And Moonbeams'.

Sophisticated Giant is an energetic but occasionally oblique album that shows off more of Gordon's Coltrane mannerisms. The arrangements (by Slide Hampton) and the overmixed Columbia sound mask some of the subtlety of Gordon's soloing and the true sound of his soprano. The trumpets are a trifle brittle, and this might be considered a later gap-filler rather than an essential buy.

Strings And Things is a diffident, rather shapeless compilation of material with none of the bite of Mikkelborg's usually intelligent orchestration.

**** The Apartment**

Steeplechase SCCD 31025 *Gordon; Kenny Drew (p); Niels-Henning Orsted Pedersen (b); Alex Riel (d).* 8/75.

***** Swiss Nights – Volume 1**

Steeplechase SCCD 31050 *As above.* 8/75.

***** Swiss Nights – Volume 2**

Steeplechase SCCD 31090 *As above.* 8/75.

****(*) Swiss Nights – Volume 3**

Steeplechase SCCD 31110 *As above.* 8/75.

****(*) Lullaby For A Monster**

Steeplechase SCCD 31156 *As above, except omit Drew.* 6/76.

The Apartment isn't one of Gordon's best records; it sounds curiously timebound now, far more than anything else he did, and there's a flatness to some of the solo work. Whatever the reason, the three volumes of *Swiss Nights* sound vigorous, pumped-up and highly coherent. There probably wasn't enough material for three albums, though the last is just about justified by 'Sophisticated Lady'. Together, they make a good summation of what this quartet was about.

Lullaby, a pianoless trio and thus unusual for Gordon, sees him trying rather unsuccessfully to bridge the gaps that Drew's absence leaves. It contains some of his freest solos, notably 'On Green Dolphin Street', but there's an element of constancy lacking.

****(*) Swedish Nights**

Steeplechase SCCD 37017/18 2CD *Gordon; Lars Sjøsten (p); Sture Nordin (b); Per Hulten (d).*

Mid-price; but more than mid-career and in only middling form, Dexter waffles and meanders far more than usual on seven stretched-out themes and never gets to the knock-out. Miles's 'Prancin'' is desperately verbose and lacks punch. The best of the playing comes early on, with versions of 'All The Things You Are' and 'Darn That Dream'; the second half limps desperately and, cheap as it is, this really doesn't merit the double-CD format.

*****(*) Biting The Apple**

Steeplechase SCCD 31080 *Gordon; Barry Harris (p); Sam Jones (b); Al Foster (d).* 11/76.

****(*) Featuring Joe Newman**

Monad 806 *Gordon; Joe Newman (t); Jodie Christian (p); Sam Jones (b); Wilbur Campbell (d).* 11/76.

Prodigal comes home. In 1976, Gordon made a rare return visit to the States. The response was so overwhelmingly positive that he decided to end his exile permanently. 'Apple Jump' is a joyous homecoming and 'I'll Remember April' one of his loveliest performances. Harris, Jones and Foster fit in comfortably, and the sound is good.

The record with Joe Newman is almost as interesting for the trumpeter's contributions as it is for Dexter's. Unfortunately, the quality of the source tape is so poor that only incomplete performances are available, which means that this remains a fascinating, collectable rarity, but not by any means an essential Gordon album.

***** Live At Carnegie Hall: Complete**

Sony CK 65312 *Gordon; Johnny Griffin (ts); George Cables (p); Rufus Reid (b); Eddie Gladden (d).*

A prestigious venue, but a drab blowing session that has Dex and Griff vying for the limelight. The material is a mixture of the old-fashioned themes – 'Blues Up And Down' – and pop tunes, and Dexter makes sure that he is the leading voice on all tracks, though Griffin, playing as fast and furious as he had a decade earlier, holds his own. We've found this a pretty unsatisfying set, diffuse and unfocused, but Gordon fanatics will treasure some elongated solos and able sparring with a fellow tenorman.

Joe Gordon (1928–63)

TRUMPET

With impeccable credentials from the New England Conservatory and an extended apprenticeship with Georgie Auld, Lionel Hampton and Charlie Parker, Gordon was a considerable trumpeter. He was a Jazz Messenger for a short time and appeared in the film, The Proper Time, with Shelly Manne. Like Woody Shaw, he mismanaged – or failed to manage – his solo career and his life; at the age of 35 he burned to death in a rooming-house fire that was apparently started by a cigarette on his mattress.

***** West Coast Days**

Fresh Sound FSCD 1030 *Gordon; Richie Kamuca (ts); Russ Freeman (p); Monty Budwig (b); Shelly Manne (d).* 7/58.

A slightly brittle tone, always pitched a little sharp, but affectingly vocalized and never less than expressive: Gordon was an individualist. The recorded legacy is thin but impressive. Unfortunately, the OJC *Lookin' Good* has disappeared for now, which leaves only the scrappy Fresh Sound (which is in any case shared with Scott LaFaro material). Here Gordon takes second place to Kamuca and Freeman and never quite settles to the task. The recordings are average for the time (1958) and place (the legendary Lighthouse), though 'Poinciana' finds him several hundred yards off-mike. There is better sound and music, if a little smoothed out, on the OJC.

Jon Gordon

ALTO SAXOPHONE, SOPRANO SAXOPHONE

Bobby Watson has publicly wondered why Gordon hasn't been pounced on and head-hunted by one of the majors. On the strength of these, it is surprising, but Jon has continued to forge his own determined path. Unlike many players of his type, he communicates brilliantly on record and uses the studio with great imagination.

***** The Jon Gordon Quartet**

Chiaroscuro CR (D) 316 *Gordon; Phil Woods (as); Kevin Hays (p); Scott Holley (b); Bill Stewart (d).* 3/92.

***** Spark**

Chiaroscuro CR (D) 330 *Gordon; Benny Carter, Phil Woods (as); Bill Charlap (p); Sean Smith (b); Tim Horner (d).* 4/94.

When Benny Carter and Phil Woods are lining up to play on your record and Joe Lovano's on hand to write an enthusiastic liner-note, it's pretty clear that something is happening. Gordon is young, bright and effortlessly accomplished, with none of the brashness and over-confidence that often come with 'effortless' talent (which of course it ain't). He handles tricky material with a naturalness born of considerable application, as when he negotiates the curves of Lovano's 'Land Of Ephysus' on the first record.

Predictably, the two Chiaroscuros were sold largely on the strength of the guest artists; but, excellent as Woods and (on the second disc) Carter are, they never quite steal the show from Gordon himself. If, as is now often suggested, the label he was soon to join, Criss Cross, is the Blue Note of the 1990s, who does he most resemble? Woods is the main inspiration, but one might also be tempted to point to Jackie McLean; not the obvious parallel in terms of sound, but for sheer joyous involvement in the music, as both performer and writer, it's close. 'Spark' clinches it, a strong, simple idea that is both robust enough for the road and delicate enough to lay claims to real beauty.

*****(*) Ask Me Now**

Criss Cross Criss 1099 *Gordon; Tim Hagans (t); Bill Charlap (p); Larry Grenadier (b); Billy Drummond (d).* 12/94.

*****(*) Witness**

Criss Cross Criss 1121 *Gordon; Tim Hagans (t); Mark Turner (ts); Bill Charlap (p); Sean Smith (b); Tim Horner (d).* 12/95.

The move to Criss Cross was good for Gordon, putting him in the way of a growing pool of young, relatively like-minded musicians who are not constrained by fashion, or indeed by retro ideologies, but who are simply dedicated to mainstream jazz. Gordon makes an early statement of intent with an effortless (that weasel word again!) ride through the scarifying changes of 'Giant Steps' and a showing for his own (presumably Lovano-inspired) 'Joe Said So', as well as the Monk tune that gives *Ask Me Now* its title. The follow-up record is, if anything, less settled, more ambitious. 'Individuation' is an exercise in group counterpoint that slightly outstays its welcome, though it does establish the parameters of the group. 'Interlude' and 'Waking Dream' are a linked pair, the latter a study in complex harmonic organization. 'House Of Mirrors' is by the bassist and features Smith in a solo outing that plucks some of its ideas straight out of Gordon's soprano improvisation, in itself a strong reminder that he has this second voice in reserve.

****** Along The Way**

Criss Cross Criss 1138 *Gordon; Mark Turner (ts); Kevin Hays (p); Joe Martin (b); Billy Drummond (d).* 6/97.

*****(*) Currents**

Double Time DTRCD 136 *Gordon; Ed Simon (p); Ben Monder (g); Larry Grenadier (b); Bill Stewart (d); Adam Cruz (perc).* 2/98.

Gordon continues to consolidate. The final Criss Cross album – for the time being at any rate – is a delightfully confident combination of original material and standards. As a winner of the Thelonious Monk Competition, Gordon has every right to tackle 'Friday The 13th' with the insouciant confidence he brings to the jagged theme. He also understands the internal rhythms of a tune like Joe Henderson's 'Inner Urge' and he has incorporated much of that thinking into his own writing. A richly textured 'Body And Soul' sounds like an attempt to write himself into a long saxophone tradition.

On *Currents*, Jon is more concerned to let his own voice come through as a writer. Apart from a couple of repertory pieces, all the compositions are by the saxophonist and they suggest an artist on the brink of great things, though not yet with the maturity to execute his ideas convincingly. 'Twilight Soul' is profoundly influenced by Wayne Shorter, while 'Intention' draws in elements of reggae and ska as well as jazz. The real eye-opener, though, is 'Shape Up', a dense and complex piece which requires many hearings to unravel, and even then resists analysis. Though the band doesn't quite pull it off, Jon is absolutely assured and convincing.

A player still going places, and perhaps it's time now for one of those majors to throw some money his way.

Liz Gorrill

PIANO, VOCAL

Based in upstate New York, Gorrill is part of the small but dedicated enclave of disciples of the Lennie Tristano manner.

***** Phantasmagoria**
New Artists NA1004 *Gorrill; Andy Fite (g, v).* 3/88.

***** A Jazz Duet**
New Artists NA1007 *Gorrill; Charley Krachy (ts).* 10/89.

***** Cosmic Comedy**
New Artists NA1012 *Gorrill; Andy Fite (g).* 3/90.

***** Dreamflight**
New Artists NA1010 *Gorrill (p solo).* 5/90.

Unlike Connie Crothers, who seems to follow directly in the master's footsteps, Gorrill is a pianist who casts her range more widely. Her left-hand parts can be thunderously heavy and dark, and such favourite standards of this circle as 'You'd Be So Nice To Come Home To' – which appears in two utterly different versions in this sequence, one on *A Jazz Duet* and another on *Dreamflight* – aren't so much restructured as demolished by the weight of their new identity. Her approach to rhythm can be pedantic in its dogged avoidance of traditional swing: 'It Could Happen To You', also on *Dreamflight*, is a shipwreck rather than any floating of a new idea. But at least her methods eschew simple clichés, without surrendering an often graceful pianism.

The solo album is perhaps the best of these records, but both the duet sessions with Fite are well worth hearing: *Phantasmagoria* is a blend of standards and brief, almost staccato originals, while the concert recording of *Cosmic Comedy* lets them stretch out on nine seemingly improvised pieces. Some of the interplay sounds static, even repetitive, but they can also lock into a glowering kind of groove that is exhilarating, too. The slightly eerie vocals on two tracks of the earlier album may be a bonus for some listeners. With Krachy, who resembles a gruff and somewhat shopworn edition of Warne Marsh, Gorrill is the dominant partner, though the best of their duets are again fiercely original. Three of the discs were recorded at New York's Greenwich House, in sometimes less-than-perfect sound: the session with Krachy in particular suffers from top-end distortion.

***** For The Beauty Of The Earth**
New Artists NA 1030 *Gorrill (p solo, v).* 5/97–1/98.

Gorrill's first for a while is based around texts by the poets, Jalal-ud-Din Rumi and Colette Aboulkar-Muscat. There are two standards, 'How Deep Is The Ocean', which she also sings (without following the original melody-line) and a barely recognizable 'Stella By Starlight'; the other pieces are often brief, at times haiku-like. She remains a dedicated stylist of her strange, somewhat shapeless, but often quite compelling music.

Simon Goubert

DRUMS, PIANO

Reminiscent of compatriot Daniel Humair and his easy swing, but also seemingly influenced by Joe Morello and American percussionists of that generation. Goubert's leadership is propulsive but discreet and unobtrusive.

****** Haïti**
Seventh SRA 7 *Goubert; Jean-Michel Couchet (as); Steve Grossman (ts, ss); Laurent Fickelson (p); Stéphane Persiani (b).* 2/91.

****(*) Encierro**
Seventh SRA 18 *Goubert; David Sauzay (ts, ss); Jean-Michel Couchet (as, ss); Arrigo Lorenzi (ss); Michel Graillier (p); Stéphane Persiani (b).* 8/95.

***** Le Phare Des Pierres Noires**
Seventh SRA 25 *Goubert; Jean-Michel Couchet (ss, as); David Sauzay (ss, ts); Laurent Fickelson (p); Stéphane Persiani (b).* 8/98.

Goubert is a regular member of Steve Grossman's trio and he has played a significant role in re-energizing the saxophonist's career. On *Haïti* the favours are reversed. Grossman isn't over-used and spends much of his time lazily doodling round Couchet's relaxed but forceful alto. They combine well on the long title-track (a Goubert composition), but the real star-turns are covers of Coltrane's ballad, 'Naima', and a breathtaking version of Paul Desmond's 'Take Five', which gives a rather unfashionable MOR favourite more than a degree of cred.

It looked for a time as if *Haïti* was a one-off. The follow-up is a flat disappointment, competent hard bop with over-mixed drums, predictable, guess-the-next-note solos and – except on the long 'Sunrise' by guest Lorenzi – little of the breezy grace of the earlier record. *Le Phare Des Pierres Noires* – the Black Rock Lighthouse – returns to the two-saxophone-and-rhythm formula and does so with much greater pizzazz and conviction. Goubert doubles on Fender Rhodes for two of the more mysterious tracks, 'Organum' and 'Campanella', but otherwise provides his useful deft touch and impetus.

Frank Goudie (1899–1964)

CLARINET, VOCAL

Goudie started on trumpet and worked in New Orleans in the 1910s and early '20s, before spending 15 years in Europe with many bandleaders. Worked in France and Berlin after the war and returned to San Francisco in the late '50s.

****(*) Frank 'Big Boy' Goudie With Amos White**
American Music AMCD-50 *Goudie; Amos White (t); J.D Banton (ts); Jimmy Simpson, Burt Bales (p, v); Al Levy (g); Al Conger (b); James Carter (d).* 9/60–3/61.

Goudie is an obscure figure, even among New Orleans musicians, but he was much admired by Albert Nicholas, and these somewhat grimy recordings reveal an idiosyncratic, vigorous clarinettist (his previous spell in the limelight came with a date in Paris in 1937 with Bill Coleman and Django Reinhardt which produced 'Big Boy Blues'). Five tracks with White, Banton, Simpson, Levy and Carter are unexceptional New Orleans dance-hall music (though recorded, like all the tracks, in San Francisco) but the four duets and three trios with Bales and Conger are more substantial. Goudie chews over the melody lines rather than elaborating on them, and there's a folkish lilt to some of his ideas. Recommended, though to New Orleans specialists only.

Dusko Goykovich (born 1931)

TRUMPET, FLUGELHORN

The Yugoslav trumpeter is a disciple of Miles Davis, but the infusion of folk forms adds an extra dimension to his music, which is characteristically swinging, though often with an unexpected balance to outwardly familiar metres.

***(*) Swinging Macedonia

Enja 4048 *Goykovich; Eddie Busnello (as); Nathan Davis (ts, ss, f); Mal Waldron (p); Peter Trunk (b); Cees See (d).* 8/66.

One of the most convincing attempts to synthesize jazz and the curious scalar progressions of Balkan folk music. Born in the former Yugoslavia, Goykovich studied at Berklee and saw action with Maynard Ferguson, Woody Herman and with the Clarke–Boland Big Band. His most characteristic work, though, has been with smaller groups. He is a bright, rhythmic player, with a full, rather folksy sound that draws somewhat selectively on the bop trumpet tradition. *Swinging Macedonia* was a bold stroke, with an impact akin to that of Ivo Papasov's much-hyped Bulgarian Wedding Band. Goykovich, though, is more purely a jazz player, and a more adventurous improviser. He's ably supported by an international line-up that hinges on the two American exiles. Waldron deals splendidly with some unfamiliar chord changes, Davis sounds authentically Slavonic (indeed, much like Papasov) and the little-known Busnello makes three or four very effective interventions. More than just an oddity, this deserves to be known more widely.

***(*) Celebration

DIW 806 *Goykovich; Kenny Drew (p); Jimmy Woode (b); Al Levitt (d).* 8/87.

**** Soul Street

Enja ENJ 8044 *Goykovich; Jimmy Heath (ts); Tommy Flanagan (p); Eddie Gomez (b); Mickey Roker (d).* 93.

**** Bebop City

Enja ENJ 9015 *Goykovich; Abraham Burton (as); Ralph Moore (ts); Kenny Barron (p); Ray Drummond (b); Alvin Queen (d).* 95.

There weren't many better mainstream-to-modern rhythm sections doing the rounds in the late 1980s than Drew, Woode and Levitt. Behind Goykovich, they are seamless and sympathetically responsive to his still occasionally surprising harmonic shifts. This, though, is his most Western album (one can't strictly say 'American'), with hints of everything from the Ellington small groups to the Jazz Messengers. Goykovich negotiates 'Blues In The Closet' and 'The Touch Of Your Lips' with admirable self-confidence. The originals have a clean bop edge, with just a hint of that indefinable Adriatic tinge that isn't quite Middle Eastern, but certainly isn't 'European' either. That is even more in evidence on the excellent *Soul Street*, which is probably Goykovich's best record. It has the sterling advantage of an absolutely top-class rhythm section and a guest appearance by Jimmy Heath, who sounds relaxed and assured. The record is intended as a tribute to Miles Davis, who had died not long before. Unlike many who laid flowers at the great trumpeter's grave, Goykovich doesn't attempt to emulate him. His approach still seems to stem from an earlier age, but the 'Ballad For Miles' includes one or two of the very slyest quotes and a tiny moment where Goykovich slips a semitone exactly in the great man's accent.

The '95 record is equally elegant and unfussy. This is the best band Goykovich has been able to put together, a rhythm section of surpassing quality and hungry young hornmen who divide up duties. The darkness is more evident this time around, a throb at the centre of the music that bespeaks something more than just blues and bebop changes. These must have been difficult years for Goykovich as his old country tore itself apart.

*** Balkan Blue

Enja 9320 2CD *Goykovich; Gianni Basso (ts); Bora Rokovic (p); Bruno Castellucci (d); Wolfgang Schluter (perc).* 96.

What looks and occasionally sounds like a conventional hard-bop unit is turned to much more adventurous purpose in this long and heartfelt sequence of pieces inspired by Goykovich's native corner of the planet. It is in a sense a musical autobiography, with influences – swing, bebop – acknowledged on the way. Some of the music is merely colouristic and slightly bland in conception, and two CDs-worth is asking a lot of the uncommitted or unconvinced listener. And yet at moments, as in the long 'Bosnia Calling' and 'Macedonia', the blend of folk melodies with jazz harmony and the obvious intensity of expression is very effective indeed. Basso is one of a generation of terse, adventurous Italian saxophonists, little known outside his own country but utterly individual in every note.

Paul Grabowsky

PIANO, SYNTHESIZER

Australian pianist and post-bopper, lately moving into soundtrack composition.

*** Tee Vee

VeraBra vBr 2050 *Grabowsky; Simon Kent (tb); Ian Chaplin (as, ss); Dale Barlow (ts); Ed Schuller (b); Niko Schauble (d).* 92.

**(*) Viva Viva

East West 994167 *Grabowsky; Scott Tinkler, Bobby Venier (t); Stephen Grant (c); Simon Kent (tb); Ian Chaplin (as, ss); Timothy Hopkins (ts); Ren Walters (g); Doug DeVries (dobro); Gary Costello, Ed Schuller (b); Andrew Gander, Niko Schauble (d).* 93.

Grabowsky is an able Australian who writes good tunes but hasn't quite got the band to deliver them with sufficient panache. Our hope that Grabowsky might be 'mainstreamed' by a major jazz label hasn't quite happened. The East West record is immaculately produced, with a sharp edge, but it takes him a further step away from jazz. As the portraits of Elvis on the front cover suggest, *Viva Viva* draws on other sources of inspiration, equally valid, but taking him further and further away from what we judge to be his forte. Schuller is still a major asset, and the horns are cleverly varied; Grabowsky seems to have a particular affection for the way a trombone lies relative to piano, and it would be good to hear him develop this further in a straight blowing context, except that we suspect this isn't the way his ambitions lie. Of late he has been doing much writing for film, which will probably push him even further away from jazz.

Bob Graf (1927–81)

TENOR SAXOPHONE

Chicagoan saxman of the '50s, much in thrall to Lester Young.

****(*) At Westminster**

Delmark DD-401 *Graf; Ron Ruff (ts, f); Jimmy Williams (p); Bob Maisel (b); Al St James (d).* 1/58.

A faded but entertaining memento of the modern scene in St Louis in the late 1950s. Both Graf and Ruff were Lester Young disciples, though the nominal leader had a slightly more boppish feel to his delivery, and their light-toned, slithery lines decorate the plain-speaking work of the rhythm section with plenty of inventive intensity. There are too many slips and wrong turnings in the solos, but it's sometimes a relief after listening to a lot of the rote hard-bop of the day. The recording, though, is only about as good as that on an average bootleg. It comes from a concert that should have featured trumpeter Bill Buxton and the group's original themes, but Buxton was ill and they played standards. We'll never know what the group might have sounded like, because they never recorded again.

Grand Dominion Jazz Band

GROUP

Together since the early 1980s, the GDJB's members are based in the Pacific North-West and include British emigrants and Americans, playing in a George Lewis–Ken Colyer style.

***** Half And Half**

Stomp Off CD3989 *Bob Jackson (t); Jim Armstrong (tb, v); Gerry Green (cl, as); Bob Pelland (p); Mike Cox (bj, v); Mike Duffy (b); Stephen Joseph (d).* 3/86–6/88.

***** San Jacinto Stomp**

Stomp Off CD1268 *As above, except Mike McCombe (d) replaces Joseph.* 1/93.

***** The Spiritual Album**

Stomp Off CD1291 *As above.* 10/94.

***** Smiles**

Stomp Off CD1330 *As above, except Jim Marsh (bj) replaces Cox.* 8/97.

***** Daddy's Little Girl**

Stomp Off CD1337 *As above.* 8/97.

Somewhat in the style of Ken Colyer's revivalism, this is a sturdy and impressive group of (mainly) trad veterans. Two of their earlier LPs were reissued on *Half And Half*: a bit livelier and more, er, virile than their later CDs, this has an interestingly catholic choice of material, with music-hall tunes such as Joe O'Gorman's 'Bedelia' rubbing shoulders with Wally Fawkes's 'Trog's Blues' and Joe Oliver's 'Snag It'. *San Jacinto Stomp* brought them into the CD era. With most of the tracks rolling expansively past the six- and seven-minute mark, they generate a steadily building momentum that's very effective on the likes of 'Bugle Boy March' and Adrian Rollini's 'Old Fashioned Swing'. Jackson is a rather wiry, short-breathed soloist, but Green's wide-bodied alto is nice and the rhythm section play with great heart.

The Spiritual Album is played with respect rather than any deep feeling and will appeal most to dedicated fans. *Smiles* brings in newcomer Jim Marsh on banjo (he has more hair than the others, but it's just as grey) and it wobbles between the sacred ('Oh Lord, Is It I ?') and the secular (Ma Rainey's 'Oh My Babe Blues'), though there's nothing that could qualify as the profane. This is the point at which to mention that their vocals are in the trad-band disaster area.

Daddy's Little Girl keeps up the old tradition. 'Spanish Shawl' is a favourite that will never go stale. 'Shout 'Em Aunt Tillie' has a lot more life in it (her?) than when Marcus Roberts played it. They end with Joe Jordan and his 'Teasin' Rag'. The singing is, alas, as before, but there is, hooray, not too much of it. Good show!

Jerry Granelli .

DRUMS

Experienced drummer with a knack for assembling surprising line-ups and forging some fresh fusions of jazz with other styles of improvisation.

***** Koputai**

ITM Pacific 970058 *Granelli; Julian Priester (tb); Denny Goodhew (as); Robben Ford (g); Ralph Towner (syn); Charlie Haden (b); Jay Clayton (v).* 11/88.

**** Forces Of Flight**

ITM Pacific 970061 *Granelli; Glenn Moore (b); Annabel Wilson (v).* 90.

***** A Song I Thought I Heard Buddy Sing**

ITM Pacific 970066 *Granelli; Julian Priester (tb); Denny Goodhew (ss); Kenny Garrett (as); Bill Frisell (g, bj); Robben Ford (g); Anthony Cox, J. Anthony Granelli (b).* 1 & 2/92.

*****(*) Another Place**

veraBra vBr 2130 *Granelli; Julian Priester (tb); Jane Ira Bloom (ss); David Friedman (vib, mar); Anthony Cox (b).* 92.

****** Broken Circle**

Songline/Tonefield INT 3501 *Granelli; Kai Bruckner, Christian Kogel (g); Andreas Walter (b).* 96.

Granelli's most obvious influence would seem to be Paul Motian, a delicate but never lightweight approach that caught the attention of guitarist/pianist Ralph Towner, who recruited him and at one point (or so it is rumoured) considered him to replace Collin Walcott in Oregon. Towner appears on the first of these records, playing synth unfortunately, and bassist Glenn Moore turns up on the second of the ITMs, a disappointing piece of nonsense that wouldn't get any of them a gig anywhere. One of the big pluses of these records is the appearance of Priester, an under-recorded trombonist with a markedly modernist style who was briefly sponsored by ECM but who has recorded only rather sporadically in recent years. He makes a substantial difference to *A Song ...*, tucking into a slightly busy front line with great economy and a wonderfully full, uncomplicated tone. The veraBra finds him in a sparser setting, and it suits him admirably. Bloom solos with great conviction, and Friedman's tuneful percussion is a perfect complement to the leader's.

The most intriguing recording of the group is *Broken Circle*, an original suite called 'Song Of A Good Name' inspired by the history of Native Americans, together with an imaginative trawl of jazz and popular material, including Prince's 'Sign O' The Times', Peter Gabriel's 'Washing Of The Water', Mingus's 'Boogie Stop Shuffle' and Coltrane's 'Lonnie's Lament'. The two-guitar sound is occasionally reminiscent of Prime Time, more often of Pat Metheny's pastel-and-wash collaborations with Lyle Mays, particularly when Bruckner and Kogel are required to add slide, 'textural' or 'atmospheric' guitar. The Native American suite is very powerful, touching here and there on the folksy sound of Jim Pepper, but by and large more straightforward acoustically than the earlier tracks. A very beautiful record that deserves to be much better known.

*****(*) Enter, A Dragon**
Songlines SGL 1521-2 *Granelli; Curtis Hasselbring (tb); Peter Epstein (ss, as); Briggan Kraus (as); Chris Speed (cl, ts); Jamie Saft (ky, acc, g); J. Anthony Granelli (b).* 9/97.

*****(*) Crowd Theory**
Songlines SGL 1526-2 *As above.* 9/98.

The titles on *Enter, A Dragon*, as well as the longer pieces being interspersed by six so-called 'Haikus', suggest an Eastern concept, but the only real line to that is in Granelli's own exotica of bells, cymbals and chimes. It's otherwise an ensemble of New Yorkers creating a sound that seeks to be hard-hitting but sensuous, big on texture – from the swells of percussion to accordion, fat electric bass and scratchy slide guitar – over which the horns march in and out of earshot. It's often rather pretty, pictorial music from which episodes like the disjointed funk of 'Sting Thing' emerge as strange surprise packages. A very entertaining show. *Crowd Theory* is, suitably enough, thicker and with a heftier ensemble sound. A broader range of material brings in such as Wayne Horvitz's 'The Front', but Granelli's own themes, including the raddled terpsichorea of 'Tango', still have much to captivate.

Stéphane Grappelli (1908–97)

VIOLIN

A more complex and enigmatic figure than first appears, Grappelli's apparent affability and lightness of touch seemed to mask a boiling personality, full of contradictions. It makes little sense to think of him simply as the temperamental opposite of his great partner in the Quintet du Hot Club de France, Django Reinhardt. Grappelli was born in Paris and was largely self-taught, which is perhaps why his approach to jazz violin (and along with Stuff Smith and Joe Venuti he more or less invented its use as a jazz instrument) is so idiomatic. A typical Grappelli line is fast, fleet and accurate, but with grace notes and embellishments which suggest a darker tonality as well.

****** Grappelli Story**
Verve 515807-2 2CD *Grappelli; Django Reinhardt, Philip Catherine, Larry Coryell, Pierre Cavalli, Diz Disley, Leo Petit, Roger Chaput, René Duchaussoir, Joe Deniz, Dave Wilkins, Alan Hodgkiss, Ike Isaacs, Eugène Vées, Jack Llewellyn, Sid Jacobson, Chappie D'Amato (g); Stan Andrews (t, vn); Bill Shakespeare (t); Frank Weir (cl); Dennis Moonan (cl, ts, vla); Stanley Andrews (vn); Harry Chapman (hp); Reg Conroy, Roy Marsh, Michel Hausser (vib); Frank Baron, Raymond Fol, Charlie Pude, George Shearing, Yorke De Sousa, Marc Hemmeler, Maurice Vander (p); George Gibbs, Hank Hobson, Joe Nussbaum, George Senior, Louis Vola, Benoît Quersin, Guy Pedersen, Lennie Bush, Coleridge Goode, Pierre Michelot, Isla Eckinger, Niels-Henning Orsted Pedersen, Eberhard Weber (b); Arthur Young (novachord); Tony Spurgin, Dave Fullerton, Kenny Clarke, Rusty Jones, Alan Levitt, Jack Jacobson, Daniel Humair, Jean-Baptiste Reilles, Jean-Louis Viale, John Spooner (d); Beryl Davis (v); orchestra conducted by Michel Legrand.* 1/38–5/92.

***** Stéphane Grappelli, 1935–1940**
Classics 708 *Similar to above.*

*****(*) Stéphane Grappelli, 1941–1943**
Classics 779 *Similar to above.*

*****(*) Special Stéphane Grappelli, 1947–1961**
Jazz Time 794481 *Grappelli; Joseph Reinhardt, Roger Chaput, Henri Crolla, Jimmy Gourley, Georges Megalos (g); Jack Dieval (p); Pierre Spiers (hp); Pierre Michelot, Benoît Quersin, Emmanuel Soudieux (b); Armand Molinetti, Baptiste Reilles (d).* 10/47–3/61.

*****(*) Jazz Masters 11: Stéphane Grappelli**
Verve 516758-2 *As above, except add Alex Riel (d).* 9/66–5/92.

*****(*) Anniversaire**
Musidisc 500412 *Grappelli; Baden Powell, Philip Catherine, Roger Chaput, Eugène Vées, Ernie Cranenburgh, Gérard Niobey, Lennie Bush, Pierre Ferret, Jimmy Gourley, Georges Megalos, Joseph Reinhardt (g); Bill Coleman (t); Marc Hemmeler, Alan Clare, Oscar Peterson (p); Eddie Louiss, Maurice Vander (org); François Jeanneau (syn); Pierre Spiers (hp); Jean-Luc Ponty (vn); Tony Bonfils, Niels-Henning Orsted Pedersen, Louis Vola, Pierre Michelot, Guy Pedersen (b); Armand Molinetti, André Ceccarelli, Kenny Clarke, Pierre-Alain Dahan, Michel Delaporte, Daniel Humair, Louis Vola, Jorge G Rezende, Clément De Waleyne (d).* 5/36–10/77.

***** Special**
Jazztime 251286 *Grappelli; Roger Chaput, Henri Crolla, Jimmy Gourley, Georges Megalos, Joseph Reinhardt (g); Jack Dieval (p); Pierre Spiers; (hp); Pierre Michelot, Benoît Quersin, Emmanuel Soudieux (b); Armand Molinetti, Baptiste Reilles (d).* 47–61.

Grappelli's association with Django Reinhardt and the Quintet du Hot Club de France is one of the legendary stories of jazz. It was Grappelli's pleasure and burden equally to carry that legend forward into one decade after another, a player of enormous range and facility linked by a mystical band to another artist who, by all accounts, made his life extremely difficult. Grappelli's limber, graceful style is so familiar that it hardly needs to be described. Because jazz fiddlers are relatively thin on the ground, he may be the most instantly recognizable jazz musician in the world – an astonishing situation if true. The Classics volumes do their usual good job of dotting 'i's and crossing 't's without worrying too much about the quality of recording or transfer, and there can be no better way of familiarizing oneself with that legacy than the Verve double-CD set which covers everything from the pre-war years to a high-budget recording session with Michel Legrand in 1992, Grappelli's 85th year. It's almost pointless to rehearse the treasures within: 'Nuages', 'Body And Soul', 'Fascinating Rhythm', the 'Nocturne' with Django. There is nothing that will disappoint.

The Jazz Masters compilation is a quicker fix, but again a perfectly acceptable one, with the label's usual scrupulous detailing of sessions and previous releases. The Jazztime *Special* is an excellent and well-transferred sampler of non-Django material, covering the period from their post-war reunion to the great guitarist's death in 1953 and beyond. Grappelli once said somewhat wearily that he would rather play with lesser musicians than ever again have to suffer Django's 'monkey business'. There's enough evidence here to confirm both the violinist's independent stature as an improviser and the plentiful supply of like-minded players. Half a dozen tracks locate Grappelli in harpist Spiers's fine, standards-based quartet. Earlier – 1954 – sets find him alongside the excellent pianist Dieval, yielding a lovely 'The World Is Waiting For The Sunrise', and the guitarist Henri Crolla, who plays in an idiom intriguingly removed from Django's. A single track from the immediately post-war Hot Four, which included Hot Club veterans Chaput and Django's brother, Joseph Reinhardt, marks it unmistakably as Grappelli's band, with a less ambitious improvisatory focus than the great original. 'Tea For Two' is a charmingly slight piano solo from Grappelli.

Anniversaire is a useful complement to the Verve set, containing a number of interesting sessions not included there. One, with Jean-Luc Ponty, points forward to a new style of jazz violin playing that was to develop out of Grappelli's example. Though there are only a couple of early tracks and some largish gaps in the selection, the pieces included are so consistently interesting and pleasurable that one stops worrying about the completeness or otherwise of the trawl.

***(*) Violins No End

Original Jazz Classics OJCCD 890 *Grappelli; Stuff Smith (vn); Oscar Peterson (p); Herb Ellis (g); Ray Brown (b); Jo Jones (d).* 5/57.

How different they sound, these two masters of an instrument that is still problematic in jazz, still not quite *echt*. Grappelli is all stratocirrus and clear skies; Smith always carries within his line a hint of storms to come. They don't break out on this occasion, but the hint of friendly threat and the insouciance that greets it from the other side of the stage is what makes this such an appealing record. Peterson gets less than his usual due of the limelight and seems happy to do accompanying duties, firing off fewer notes than usual and digging into his memories of stride and blues playing here and there with a procession of mischievous quotes that piano fans can have fun identifying.

*** Meets Barney Kessel

Black Lion BLCD 760150 *Grappelli; Barney Kessel (g); Nino Rosso (g); Michel Gaudry (b); Jean-Louis Viale (d).* 6/69.

**(*) Limehouse Blues

Black Lion BLCD 760158 *As above.*

It might have been better had they restricted both of these to a duo. The second guitar, though it follows a sanctified precedent, really adds nothing to the overall sound (which??) and Grappelli scarcely needs a drummer as prosy as Viale to keep him to the mark. Kessel, who is a disciple of Charlie Christian rather than a practising Djangologist, sounds bluesier than most of Grappelli's usual cohorts, but the combination works surprisingly well on a roster of unexceptionable standards.

Limehouse Blues scrapes together more material from the same Paris studio sessions. There are previously unreleased readings of Kessel's 'Copa Cola' and 'Blues For Georges', 'I Got Rhythm', and a fine 'Perdido', together with an alternative take of 'Honeysuckle Rose'.

***(*) To Django

Accord 401202 *Grappelli; Alan Clare, Marc Hemmeler (p); Ernie Cranenburgh, Lennie Bush (b); Chris Karan (d).* 6/72.

*** Joue George Gershwin Et Cole Porter

Accord 402052 *Grappelli; Marc Hemmeler, Maurice Vander (p); Eddie Louiss (org); Jimmy Gourley, Ike Isaacs (g); Guy Pedersen, Luigi Trussardi (b); Daniel Humair (d).*

The Gershwin/Porter material is fairly predictable and played with either jaunty insouciance or syrupy romanticism, neither of which does much credit to Grappelli or the composers he is honouring. Despite sounding as if it were recorded in a cathedral, *To Django* is much preferable. The opening version of 'Djangology' is one of the best available, and there are lovely versions of 'Manoir De Mes Rêves' and 'Nuages' (featuring Hemmeler and Clare respectively on electric piano). There's a warmth and richness to Grappelli's tone that suggest viola rather than orthodox fiddle. That's particularly noticeable on the longest track, an extended 'Blues' co-written with Django before the war, as was 'Minor Swing', which receives a particularly sensitive reading.

*** Stéphane Grappelli / Jean-Luc Ponty

Accord 556552 *Grappelli; Jean-Luc Ponty (vn); Marc Hemmeler, Maurice Vander (p); Eddie Louiss (org); Philip Catherine, Jimmy Gourley (g); Tony Bonfils, Guy Pedersen (b); André Ceccarelli, Kenny Clarke (d).* 11/72, 12/73.

This is not quite the 'Violin Summit' one of the tracks proclaims. Half the material is by Grappelli's own group, recorded a year earlier than the session with his most obvious heir, who in those days was touting a brand of jazz-rock that never quite shook off the Hot Club mannerisms. The 'Summit' itself is a showpiece. Better things lie in 'Golden Green' and 'Memorial Jam For Stuff Smith', which has the two fiddlers exchanging ideas at a furious pace. Both men also briefly switch to baritone violin, an unusually attractive sound that seems pitched somewhere in the viola-to-cello range. A novelty effect, perhaps, but not so much so that it dilutes Grappelli's musical personality.

***** Stardust**

Black Lion 760117 *Grappelli; Alan Clare (p, cel).* 3/73.

There aren't too many 'alternate takes' of Grappelli performances available. The *Stardust* CD affords a valuable opportunity to study how the violinist thinks and rethinks his way through a theme, subtly roughening textures and sharpening the basic metre on a second take of 'Tournesol' (the original is also sampled on a good label compilation, *Artistry In Jazz* – BLCD 760100) and rescuing two rather schmaltzy 'Greensleeves' with firm bow-work.

***** Just One Of Those Things**

Black Lion BLCD 760180 *Grappelli; Marc Hemmeler (p); Jack Sewing (b); Daniel Humair (d).* 7/73.

A great favourite at Montreux, Grappelli always rises to the occasion, as on this 65th birthday bash. Just when most men are looking forward to retirement, he is gearing up for another two decades of extremely active music-making. This wasn't the best band he had around this time (the group on *Parisian Thoroughfare*, below, is heaps better), but Hemmeler knows when to step in and when to lift his foot off the gas, and that's virtually all that's required of him. 'Misty' and 'All God's Chillun' are the highlights of a set that runs the emotional gamut from A to about D.

***** Sweet Georgia Brown**

Black Lion BLCD 7602 *Grappelli; Alan Clare (p, cel); Roland Hanna (p); Diz Disley, Denny Wright (g); George Mraz, Len Skeat (b); Mel Lewis (d).* 9 & 11/73.

*****(*) Parisian Thoroughfare**

Black Lion 760132 *Grappelli; Roland Hanna (p, electric p); George Mraz (b); Mel Lewis (d).* 9/73.

A further counter to the persistent *canard* that Grappelli is an MOR entertainer with no real jazz credibility. Working with a first-class mainstream rhythm section, he sounds fantastically assured but also probingly sceptical about the broader and better-trodden melodic thoroughfares. Hanna's electric piano is a little over-bright and loses some of the firmness he invests in left-hand chords, but Mraz and Lewis combine superbly. *Sweet Georgia Brown* contains more from the same session, and from a concert by the Hot Club of London in the Queen Elizabeth Hall. A certified Djangologist, Disley plays the parts with great expressiveness, though the medleys are a touch contrived.

***** Live In London**

Black Lion BLCD 760139 *Grappelli; Diz Disley, Denny Wright (g); Len Skeat (b).* 11/73.

'Not jazz', the promoters muttered; and Grappelli's ultimately successful 1972 British tour made a round of folk clubs and small theatres, thereby reinforcing a growing popular appeal (certainly much more effectively than if he had remained on the jazz circuit). The performances on *Live In London* aren't quite vintage, but they represent a more than useful documentation of the sensibly weighted nostalgia of the Hot Club of London. There's a fine 'Nuages', which Grappelli appears to have rationed since, and a lovely 'Manoir De Mes Rêves'.

*****(*) La Grande Réunion**

Musidisc 557322 *Grappelli; Baden Powell (g); Guy Pedersen (b); Pierre-Alain Dahan (d); Jorge G Rezende, Clément De Waleyne (perc); orchestra conducted by Christian Chevallier.* 74.

Grappelli and guitarist Powell were old jamming partners. They slide into this session, as old friends should, without missing a beat. It's standard-issue Latin jazz and bossa nova, with Grappelli fronting a string orchestra for half a dozen (mostly Beatles) tunes at the end of the set. There are more exciting Grappelli albums around, but few with quite this measure of laid-back enjoyment.

***** Stéphane Grappelli Meets Earl Hines**

Black Lion BLCD 760168 *Grappelli; Earl Hines (p).* 7/74.

If only Livingstone and Stanley had been jazz musicians. Black Lion have flogged the 'meets' formula to the brink of cruel and unusual punishment. Every now and then, though, it throws up something quite special. This is one of them. Temperamentally, Grappelli and Hines are just unalike enough for the chemistry to be right. They know each other's history well enough to have fun with it, Hines rolling off little Django flourishes with the left hand, Grappelli quoting Louis Armstrong fills in the upper register. Great fun.

*****(*) Young Django**

MPS 815672 *Grappelli; Philip Catherine, Larry Coryell (g); Niels-Henning Orsted Pedersen (b).* 1/79.

This is such a gift of a pairing that it's almost a surprise it works so well. Coryell is mannered and rather pretentious in places, but Catherine has this repertoire in his bloodstream and responds to the situation with alacrity, purring beautiful streams of notes and soft, chiming chords. The recording is very good indeed, but it might have been better expended on a slightly more adventurous programme of material. This one suffers slightly from obviousness.

****** Tivoli Gardens, Copenhagen, Denmark**

Original Jazz Classics OJC 441 *Grappelli; Joe Pass (g); Niels-Henning Orsted Pedersen (b).* 7/79.

A superb set, marred only slightly by variable sound. Grappelli's interpretations of 'Paper Moon', 'I Can't Get Started', 'I'll Remember April', 'Crazy Rhythm', 'How Deep Is The Ocean?', 'Let's Fall In Love', 'I Get A Kick Out Of You' reaffirm his genius as an improviser and also his ability to counter slightly saccharine themes with the right hint of tartness. Pass, who occasionally errs on the side of sweetness, plays beautifully, and NHOP is, as always, both monumental and delicate.

***** Satin Doll**

Musidisc 440162 *Grappelli; Eddie Louiss (org); Marc Hemmeler (p); Jimmy Gourley (g); Guy Pedersen (b); Kenny Clarke (d).*

This is so Gallic in conception you can almost taste the *aioli*. Louiss's playing will be a revelation to anyone who hasn't encountered it before, darkly sauced and salty, accented by Clarke and the greatly underrated Pedersen (what genetic trick makes such fine bass players of this clan?). There is, predictably, little innovation to report, but that will not perturb Grappelli fans at this stage in the story.

***** At The Winery**
Concord CCD 4139 *Grappelli; John Etheridge, Martin Taylor (g); Jack Sewing (b).* 9/80.

***** Vintage 1981**
Concord CCD 4169 *Grappelli; Mike Gari, Martin Taylor (g); Jack Sewing (b).* 7/81.

Taylor has been Grappelli's most sympathetic latter-day collaborator, and they complement each other near-perfectly on the live set, recorded in 1981. Taylor's amplified sound adds a little sting to Grappelli's playing, which is always more robust live than in an acoustically 'dead' and feedback-free studio situation. Better known as a jazz-rock player in one of the many later versions of the protean Soft Machine, Etheridge nevertheless fits in well with Grappelli's conception on *At The Winery*. Hard to choose between the two sets, though enthusiasts will want both.

***** Stephanova**
Concord CCD 4225 *Grappelli; Marc Fosset (g).* 6/83.

The relatively unfamiliar material suggests either momentary impatience with his usual regimen of personalized standards or else a genuine desire to branch out into new areas. Fosset is a more interesting player in this more sharply focused context than in a group setting (see below), and the two trade a range of interesting and occasionally adventurous ideas.

***** One On One**
Milestone M 9181 *Grappelli; McCoy Tyner (p).* 4/90.

The outwardly improbable duo with McCoy Tyner works astonishingly well, including Coltrane's 'Mr P.C.' and the Coltrane-associated 'I Want To Talk About You', alongside more familiar repertoire like 'I Got Rhythm' and 'St Louis Blues'. Ever the romantic stylist, Tyner plays with impeccable taste, never losing contact with the basic structure of a tune. Recommended.

*****(*) Stéphane Grappelli: 1992 Live**
Birdology 517392 *Grappelli; Philip Catherine, Marc Fosset (g); Niels-Henning Orsted Pedersen (b).* 3/92.

And so it went on, seemingly unstoppable. Grappelli's association with Catherine became, remarkably, of longer standing than that with Reinhardt and, as one might expect, their understanding is considerable. This is a joyous disc, recorded in concert at Colombes. 'Oh, Lady Be Good' has the light bounce and unaffected grace that you'd expect, but there are unprecedented depths to 'Blues For Django And Stéphane', which Catherine brought forward for the session. For a live recording, the sound is very good indeed, though there are moments when Grappelli almost sounds detuned: a tape problem? heat?

****** Reunion**
Linn AKH 022 *Grappelli; Martin Taylor (g).* 1/93.

One of the happiest new partnerships of more recent years was with the brilliant young British guitarist Taylor, whose solo career was taking off at the time of this utterly enjoyable record. It has the relaxed feel of something put down between lunch and dinner, but there is a steely precision behind the guitarist's relaxed mien and Grappelli is, of course, no pushover. 'Drop Me Off At Harlem' and 'La Dame Du Lac' are the most taxing workouts, but 'Paper Moon' takes the biscuit for sheer charm, if charm is indeed awarded with biscuits.

****** Flamingo**
Dreyfus FDM 36580 *Grappelli; Michel Petrucciani (p); George Mraz (b); Roy Haynes (d).* 6/95.

Who would ever have expected to hear Grappelli in company like this? If at first glance it seems a startling engagement, it is immediately clear that these are players ideally suited to his light, swinging approach. Haynes has the most delicate touch of all the bebop drummers and in recent years has shown how much he responds to song-settings. Mraz almost defines modern swing bass accompaniment, adding his own counterlines under Petrucciani, who seems to be enjoying himself hugely. Rightly, for the most part they stick to standard material. 'Misty' is the closest it all comes to hokiness, but it is done with such open-hearted delight and lack of self-consciousness that it runs no very serious risks. 'I Can't Get Started' and 'I Got Rhythm' between them demonstrate a good change of pace, with Haynes and Petrucciani seeming to dictate the rhythmic course within each track, so that the former has an almost symphonic logic and structure. Very impressive indeed.

*****(*) Celebrating Grappelli**
Linn AKD 094 *Grappelli; Gerard Presencer (t, flhn); Jack Emblow (acc); John Goldie, Martin Taylor (g); Terry Gregory (b); Claire Martin (v).* 93, 96.

A posthumous tribute drawn from *Reunion* and from Martin Taylor's Spirit of Django record, *Years Apart*. As a souvenir of the guitarist's long and happy association with Grappelli, it's hard to beat: a relaxed, swinging 50 minutes that manage to seem very much shorter. Anyone who has the original albums won't find it very useful, but it's a nicely judged selection of the best of both. Grappelli's technique stands out all the more for the miracle that it was in younger company like this. There is even a moment on 'Jive At Five', not noticed by us before, when he makes a mistake and instantly turns it to advantage, an improvised mend that he converts into an embellishment. The celebration closes with 'Manoir De Mes Rêves', which seems entirely appropriate.

Georg Gräwe

PIANO, BANDLEADER, COMPOSER

Pianist-composer much in the new tradition of classical study mixed with free improvisation, and seemingly equally content in both idioms.

*****(*) The View From Points West**
Music & Arts CD 820 *Gräwe; Ernst Reijseger (clo); Gerry Hemingway (d, perc).* 6/91.

*****(*) Flex 27**
Random Acoustics RA 007 *As above.* 12/93.

****** Saturn Cycle**
Music & Arts CD 958 *As above.* 11/94.

In addition to a duo with the drummer, Willi Kellers, Gräwe has worked regularly with two very different improvising trios: well-received work with tubist Melvyn Poore and GrubenKlang-Orchester member Phil Wachsmann (see below), and the trio captured in striking form on these discs. These are three players of markedly different temperaments, united by a resistance to the fixed resolutions of both 'jazz' and 'New Music'. They play undogmatically and with great exactness, as if they have been rehearsing these pieces for years. Like Eddie Prévost, Hemingway manages to swing even when playing completely free, and his range of articulation is quite extraordinary. Gräwe, one of the most enterprising of the post-Schlippenbach pianists, is apt to dissolve his own most acute observations in a flood of repetitions and curious evasions, but the ideas are strong enough to resist corrosion. Reijseger, by contrast, knows how to enjoy an idea and when to dispense with it. The Random Acoustics set is immensely detailed, full of exactitudes and tiny, outwardly meaningless gestures that seem to propel things forward to the next crux. The festival performances documented on *The View From Points West* are more relaxed and strung out and do tend to fall back on settled licks and patterns more often, especially on the long 'Lighthouse', nearly half an hour of concentrated music delivered without a hint of strain.

Saturn Cycle also benefits from its live context, a performance at the LOFT in Cologne. Here the emphasis is once again, as on the last Music & Arts release, a mixture of abstraction and a loose swing. 'Fortyfications' is a Germanic equivalent of a second-line funeral band, transforming a mournful dirge into a bright, loose-woven swing march. There are two versions of 'La Bonne Vitesse', which all three members would insist represents a further shift beyond European forms into the collective, percussion-based ensembles of African and Asian musics. 'Future References', though, brings it all back home again, a shower of acoustic shards hurled forward into unknown space and over hard-to-determine stretches of time. Gräwe gives the piece the shape it has, but it is shape as process rather than shape as form. This is the most radical, the most far-reaching and, oddly, the most amenable of the group's records to date. Strongly recommended.

***** Chamber Works**

Random Acoustics 003 *Gräwe; Horst Grabosch (t); Melvyn Poore (tba); Michael Moore (cl, bcl); Philip Wachsmann (vn); Ernst Reijseger (clo); Anne LeBaron, Hans Schneider (hp); Gerry Hemingway (d); Phil Minton (v).* 91–92.

Random Acoustics, Gräwe's own label, now has a rather impressive list of new music. This is the boss's day in court, a run-down of some of his more adventurous projects at the turn of the decade. The trio is represented again, but so, too, are some of Gräwe's more formal pieces and the celebrated trio with Poore and Wachsmann in which nothing sounds as one would expect it to and there is no obvious heading or trajectory for the music, just a concentrated sense of immediacy and presence as the players feed off one another.

****** Melodie Und Rhythmus**

Okkadisk OD 12016 *Gräwe; Frank Gratkowski (as, cl); Kent Kessler (b); Hamid Drake (d, perc).* 96.

Just melody and rhythm, and a carefully bracketed emphasis on these dimensions. It may be that Gräwe has been thinking about Ornette Coleman's groups. Certainly he avoids much emphasis on vertical improvisation, driving the group along the flat with a punchy, one-idea-at-a-time impetus. Drake is a very different kind of player from Hemingway, coming from a different percussion school and lacking either the rock-pumped force or the ability to drift out of time altogether. Kessler is now almost as ubiquitous as William Parker and he has much of Parker's generous intelligence and ability to seed himself at the centre of big, busy structures and still maintain his function, a skill bequeathed to jazz by the great Charles Mingus. Listeners who have previously found that Gräwe is lacking in jazz content may enjoy better fortunes with this one.

Wardell Gray (1921–55)

TENOR SAXOPHONE

Gray was born in Oklahoma but grew up in Detroit, where he played in a variety of local groups. His professional breathrough was with Earl Hines, but he is best remembered for an exhilarating two-tenor project with Dexter Gordon, The Chase. Like Lester Young and Don Byas, Gray maintained a foot in a pre-bop idiom and favoured a loose, eloquent style with few jagged edges. He died young, some believe at the hands of drug dealers to whom he was in debt. This is now questioned.

****(*) One For Prez**

Black Lion BLCD 760106 *Gray; Dodo Marmarosa (p); Red Callender (b); Chuck Thompson, Harold Doc West (d).* 11/46.

****(*) Way Out Wardell**

Boplicity CDBOP 014 *Gray; Ernie Royal, Howard McGhee (t); Vic Dickenson (tb); Vido Musso (ts); Erroll Garner, Arnold Ross (p); Red Callender, Harry Babasin (b); Irving Ashby, Barney Kessel (g); Jackie Mills, Don Lamond (d).* 48.

****** Memorial: Volume 1**

Original Jazz Classics OJC 050 *Gray; Frank Morgan (as); Sonny Clark, Al Haig, Phil Hill (p); Teddy Charles (vib); Dick Nivison, Tommy Potter, Johnny Richardson (b); Roy Haynes, Lawrence Marable, Art Mardigan (d).* 11/49, 4/50, 2/53.

****** Memorial: Volume 2**

Original Jazz Classics OJC 051 *Gray; Art Farmer, Clark Terry (t); Sonny Criss (as); Dexter Gordon (ts); Jimmy Bunn, Hampton Hawes (p); Harper Crosby, Billy Hadnott (b); Lawrence Marable, Chuck Thompson (d); Robert Collier (perc).* 8/50, 1/52.

Like his friend and collaborator, Dexter Gordon, Wardell Gray often had to look to Europe for recognition. His first recordings, made just after the war, were not released in the United States. There were not to be very many more, for Gray died in rather mysterious circumstances in 1955, three months after Charlie Parker. The shadow cast by Bird's passing largely shrouded Gray's no less untimely departure. Unlike Gordon, Gray was less than wholly convinced by orthodox bebop, and he continued to explore the swing style of bop's immediate ancestor, Lester Young. *One For Prez* is, as it sounds, an extended tribute to Young. Heavy on alternative takes, but sufficiently inventive to merit the inclusion of all but a few. Gray is in firm voice and Marmarosa, who has since vanished from sight, plays brilliantly.

The jams on *Way Out Wardell* were originally issued as a Crown LP. They're interesting but scarcely overwhelming. Gray is obviously in difficulties here and there, though the reason for this isn't clear. Several of his solo choruses resort to exactly identical ideas and/or mechanical inversions of them. He was capable of very much more.

The two-volume *Memorial* remains the best representation of his gifts. The earliest of the sessions is a quartet consisting of Haig, Potter and Haynes, and it includes 'Twisted', a wry blues since covered and vocalized by Annie Ross and, much later, by Joni Mitchell. Ross's version has tended to overshadow the original, which is a perfect place to gauge Gray's Prez-influenced style and his softly angular approach to the basic changes. The CDs include some alternative takes that are frankly pretty redundant both interpretatively and acoustically. Too often Gray tries to reduplicate what he feels are successful ideas rather than wiping the slate clean and trying again from scratch. The best of the rest is a 1952 session with Hawes and Farmer, who do interesting things with 'Farmer's Market' and that Parker shibboleth, 'Lover Man'. The second volume is also notable for the first recorded performances by Frank Morgan, who copied not just Bird's articulation but also some of his offstage habits and found himself in San Quentin for his pains. It's still a thin haul for a player of Gray's class, but these should be considered the essential purchases.

***** Live At The Haig 1952**

Fresh Sound FSR CD 157 *Gray; Art Farmer (t); Hampton Hawes, Amos Trice (p); Howard Roberts (g); Joe Mondragon (b); Shelly Manne (d). 9/52.*

He was no less fortunate in having the gloriously expressive Hampton Hawes on all but one track of this fine 1952 date (one Amos Trice, better known for his work with Harold Land, plays on 'Lady Bird'). Gray had been working with Count Basie before these sessions and his conception is significantly pared down, even from the uncluttered approach of *One For Prez*. There is, though, a creeping weariness and inwardness in the voice, sadly reminiscent of Young's own rather paranoid decline, and it's left to Hawes and a pre-flugelhorn Art Farmer to keep spirits up. The mix of styles is just about right and the sound perfectly respectable for material nearly five decades old.

Great Circle Saxophone Quartet

GROUP

A well-rounded saxophone group.

****(*) Child King Dictator Fool**

New World 80516-2 *Chris Jonas (ss); Randy McKean (as, cl); Dan Plonsey (ts, cl); Steve Norton (ss, bs, bcl). 6/93–2/94.*

These four non-stars of the saxophone make a good case for their quartet music, but in the end there's little to set it aside from what's now a familiar lexicon and not quite enough spit and polish to invigorate the reiteration of the language. They don't make much of a play of their melodies and their improvisations are strong but unlikely to remain impressed in the memory. Split between tiny cameos and full-on epics, the CD passes entertainingly enough without validating the existence of another saxophone quartet.

Bennie Green (1923–77)

TROMBONE

A Chicagoan, Green worked with Earl Hines in the '40s and '50s, then led hard-bop groups in the '50s and early '60s. His final years were spent in hotel bands.

***** Blows His Horn**

Original Jazz Classics OJC 1728 *Green; Charlie Rouse (ts); Cliff Smalls (p); Paul Chambers (b); Osie Johnson (d); Candido (perc). 6–9/55.*

****(*) Walking Down**

Original Jazz Classics OJC 1752 *Green; Eric Dixon (ts); Lloyd Mayers (p); Sonny Wellesley (b); Bill English (d). 6/56.*

***** Bennie Green With Art Farmer**

Original Jazz Classics OJC 1800-2 *Green; Art Farmer (t); Cliff Smalls (p); Addison Farmer (b); Philly Joe Jones (d). 4/56.*

***** Glidin' Along**

Original Jazz Classics OJC 1869-2 *Green; Johnny Griffin (ts); Junior Mance (p); Paul Chambers (b); Larry Gales, Ben Riley (d). 3/61.*

While these are good records, they rate some way below the excellent discs Green made for Blue Note in 1958–9 (*Soul Stirrin'* has been available briefly as a Blue Note Connoisseur edition: 859381-2). Albums for Time, Bethlehem and Jazzland, all from the early 1960s, would also be welcome in reissue form, though *Glidin' Along* has now reappeared: a good-natured blow with Griffin, with a set of scrappy originals betraying the lack of preparation. Although he was one of the first trombonists to fraternize with bop – as a teenager, he was in the Earl Hines orchestra that included Parker and Gillespie – Green's personal allegiance remained with a less demanding approach. The 1955 session highlights his singing tone and straightforward phrasing on attractive versions of 'Travellin' Light' and 'Body And Soul'. The band is a congenial one and Rouse's solos are an ounce more interesting than the leader's. *Walking Down* features a less impressive group and as a result is slightly less interesting, though Green is again in swinging form. Best of the four is the edition of the Prestige session which matched Green with Art Farmer, whose affable and calmly intense playing is a piquant complement to the somewhat more boisterous leader: compare their solos on Farmer's 'Skycoach', the trombonist a louche performer.

Benny Green (born 1965)

PIANO

Early experience with Betty Carter set this skilful pianist on his way. Though only in his mid-thirties, he is something of a young veteran of the contemporary scene, having cut a raft of albums for Blue Note in particular. His style is relatively conservative – he professes to want to entertain audiences with the most swinging music he can – and he comes from a school that counts Horace Silver, Wynton Kelly and other midstream boppers among its influences.

***** Prelude**

Criss Cross 1036 *Green; Terence Blanchard (t); Javon Jackson (ts); Peter Washington (b); Tony Reedus (d). 2/88*

***** In This Direction**

Criss Cross 1038 *Green; Buster Williams (b); Lewis Nash (d).* 12/88–1/89.

Green came to prominence as pianist with Betty Carter's group, and his mastery of bebop piano – particularly the chunky rhythms of Horace Silver – was leavened by an apparent interest in swing styles as well: Green hits the keyboard hard on up-tempo tunes, and his preference for beefy chords and straight-ahead swing can make him sound like a more 'modern' Dave McKenna. These albums for Criss Cross feature a lot of piano, but there's nothing particularly outstanding about them: the quintet date sounds too much like a mere blowing session for any of the players to make a distinctive mark, and the trio set seems hastily prepared, although the rhythm section lend impressive support.

*****(*) Kaleidoscope**

Blue Note 852037-2 *Green; Stanley Turrentine (ts); Antonio Hart (as); Russell Malone (g); Ron Carter (b); Lewis Nash (d).* 6/96.

*****(*) These Are Soulful Days**

Blue Note 499527-2 *Green; Russell Malone (g); Christian McBride (b).* 1/99.

With a lot of records behind him, some might be tempted to take Green for granted, and his departure from Blue Note (and their culling of much of his back-catalogue) seems a pity since his two final albums are surely his best to date. *Kaleidoscope* features eight Green originals and there's not a duff one among them. 'Patience' and 'You're My Melody' are charming ballads, transparently beautiful and played with great feeling, while 'My Girl Bill' and 'The Sexy Mexy' take a new look at Green's penchant for funky piano; underlined by Malone's attentive guitar and shrewdly covered by the rhythm section, these are insidious rather than bumptious. Since Nash sits out on three tracks, Green is placed under a softer light at crucial moments, and it suits him. His improvisations throughout are some of his best work. The only slight letdown lies in the contributions of Hart and Turrentine: their various appearances are uneventful enough to make one wonder why they were booked.

These Are Soulful Days is as ferociously swinging as ever, but without a drummer and, with the snapping rhythms of both Malone and McBride wiring the forward momentum, Green sounds at his most carefree and daring. The three men are caught up in a whirl of multi-levelled lines on tracks such as 'Virgo', but the cooling-off that takes place on Elmo Hope's 'Bellarosa' (a beautiful choice) and Cal Massey's title-piece is just as absorbing. The eight tunes are all connoisseur-choices from the Blue Note book of tunes, and the only regret must be that there wasn't room for one of Benny's own hits – he's come up with some great, catchy themes, after all, which is right in the BN tradition. Green has since signed to Telarc and his first album was due for release before the end of 2000.

Grant Green (1931–79)

GUITAR

Deeply rooted in the blues, St Louis-born Green brought a devastating simplicity to the basic guitar–organ trio. He spent much of his career, and still is in hindsight, in the shadow of Wes Montgomery, but he is an altogether different player; less subtle harmonically, he had the ability to drive a melody line and shape a solo as if he were telling a quietly urgent solo. His legacy is complex and arguably more far-reaching than Wes's.

****(*) Grant's First Stand**

Blue Note 21959 *Green; Baby Face Willette (org); Ben Dixon (d).* 1/61.

****(*) Reaching Out**

Black Lion BLCD 760129 *Green; Frank Haynes (ts); Billy Gardner (org); Ben Tucker (b); Dave Bailey (d).* 3/61.

****(*) Sunday Mornin'**

Blue Note 52434 *Green; Kenny Drew (p); Ben Tucker (b); Ben Dixon (d).* 7/61.

He began, as he was to end in the post-detox 1970s, chugging out a bland hybrid of funk and jazz. Yet Green was to be an influential figure, helping to pioneer what was soon to be the familiar guitar, organ, drums sound that later would excite the acid-jazz generation. His has been an impressive posthumous comeback. At the end of his life, and for a time thereafter, Green was consigned to that ironic fate which awaits certain kinds of poet: the 'anthology artist'. It was perfectly possible to assemble a reasonable amount of his work on CD, but only if you were prepared to fork out for an array of themed compilations, usually with some permutation of *Cool*, *Blue* and *Funk* in the title. There was an obvious pun on Green's name, of course, and it usefully conveyed how fresh-voiced he could sound, with his linear approach (derived from saxophone players) and his almost total disregard for chromatic harmony, qualities and choices which in the right company could make a Green tune seem as new and uncomplicated as a spring shoot. The first Blue Note has been a considerable rarity but is now available on CD. Kicking off with 'Miss Ann's Tempo', an original composition, Grant impresses as a bright, uncomplicated player who has delved deeply into the tradition without being in thrall to any one voice. The blues dominate throughout.

The Black Lion catches him at the threshold of his maturity and on the brink of what was to be his most creative connection. It's a less than satisfactory record, with a drab band, and Green himself is not playing with his usual fluidity and freedom. Also long out of print was *Sunday Mornin'*, which unusually had Green working with a piano player. As ever, the guitarist favours clean-picked single-note runs, fleet and expressive but somehow missing a dimension which, fortunately, Drew is on hand to supply. 'God Bless The Child' and 'So What' are exceptional performances that would have an influence on a whole generation of soul-jazz and later acid-jazz performers.

*****(*) Standards**

Blue Note 21284 *Green; Wilbur Ware (b); Al Harewood (d).* 8/61.

Not technically perfect – there is a curious phrasing on Harewood's cymbals on a couple of tracks – but a most valuable release, helping to bring up to date some more Green material not previously available in the Occident. By the standards of the time, these are complex readings of familiar material. 'I'll Remember April' is a typical call-and-response solo, but entirely unpredictable in cast. Green had on occasion expressed a special preference for the uncluttered sound of a guitar, bass, drums trio, rather than one with organ, and one sees what he means here. The pace is light, fast and dancing, and Ware's solos are models of invention. A pity about anomalies in the sound, which seem to have arisen when the tapes were remastered in 1980. Save for the most fastidious of listeners, these won't diminish the pleasure.

*** Grantstand

Blue Note 46430 *Green; Yusef Lateef (ts, f); Jack McDuff (org); Al Harewood (d).* 8/61.

**** Born To Be Blue

Blue Note 84432 *Green; Ike Quebec (ts); Sonny Clark (p); Sam Jones (b); Louis Hayes (d).* 12/61, 3/62.

Grantstand established the sound and the approach that was to make Green – and Blue Note – a good deal of money over the next few years, to the dubious benefit of the former, who had narcotic problems for some time as a result of both fame and career pressure. The combination of Green's smooth lines, Lateef's simple but inventive tenor and delicate flute tone, and McDuff's swirling lines and choked-off probings is very effective indeed, even if the balance is sometimes off, even on CD. 'Old Folks' and 'My Funny Valentine' give the horn-man lots to do, and he responds with some of the best recorded playing from this stage in his career.

We've always liked *Born To Be Blue* best of all the Blue Notes, along with the splendid *Idle Moments* and *Street Of Dreams*. Quebec, who was the label's musical director at the time, is still not widely admired, but he's on cracking form here, and his pitch and phrasing on 'Someday My Prince Will Come' should be a lesson to all young jazz players. Green has, for us, his finest hour, rippling through 'My One And Only Love' and 'If I Should Love You' with a ruggedness of emotion that goes hand in hand with the simplicity of diction. Not a single note is wasted. 'Count Every Star' actually comes from an earlier session, but it too is judged to perfection, toned down just as it threatens to get schmaltzy. Sonny Clark, another Blue Note signing who has only recently been rediscovered and reassessed, is also in sparkling form, with just enough light and shade to temper his colleagues' bluff romanticism.

**** The Complete Quartets With Sonny Clark

Blue Note 571924 2CD *Green; Sonny Clark (p); Sam Jones (b); Art Blakey, Louis Hayes (d).* 12/61, 1/62.

The first five items on disc one were available for a time as *Nigeria*, a re-reversal of the Sonny Rollins staple, 'Airegin', which kicked off the set. Everything else on this valuable reintroduction has been issued previously only in Japan. Blue Note completists will know the material from *Gooden's Corner* and *Oleo*. There are alternative takes of both Rollins tunes (the rejected 'Oleo' had already been heard on a 1989 Mosaic box), a superb pre-Coltrane interpretation of 'My Favorite Things', an exquisite 'Moon River', and an equally beautiful 'Nancy (With The Laughing Face)'. If all this suggests sessions heavy on lyricism rather than swinging pace, this is partly true. The presence of the long-neglected, now canonized Clark guarantees that the tempo never slackens, even on the gentlest ballads, and that the harmonic configuration is always adventurous. Hayes is the drummer on all the 1962 cuts, though Blakey's work on *Nigeria* is inventive first to last. The key performance of the set is a ten-minute workout on 'It Ain't Necessarily So', which is completely reworked melodically and marked out by Green's long winding phrases which cut across Blakey's 12/8 pattern. A remarkable performance, and a highly valuable addition to the Green canon.

*** The Latin Bit

Blue Note 37645 *Green; Ike Quebec (ts); Johnny Acea (p); Wendell Marshall (b); Willie Bobo (d); Carlos Patato Valdes (perc); Garvin Maseaux (shekere).* 4 & 9/62.

Once Blue Note recognized that they were dealing with a marketable talent, there was increasing pressure on Green to make themed records. This is the 'south of the border' session. Quebec is featured only on the two tracks recorded in September 1962, both of them pretty dispensable, as unfortunately is most of the record. Despite Green's fleet invention, there is a plodding obviousness to much of the setting. Acea was probably fine as a straight Latin player, but he understands too little of the subtler side of Green to be a genuinely creative partner.

***(*) Feelin' The Spirit

Blue Note 84682 *Green; Herbie Hancock (p); Butch Warren (b); Billy Higgins (d); Garvin Maseaux (tamb).* 12/62.

Blue Note A&R thought it would be a good idea to have Green record an album of gospel tunes. Nobody else at this juncture would have thought it a winning idea, but what emerges is a superbly balanced and movingly performed set that never troubles to up or change the pace, but just keeps on bearing soulful witness. 'Just A Closer Walk With Thee' sounds momentarily as if it might break into a closer jogtrot, and 'Go Down Moses' – or 'Go *Down!* Moses' – pushes the ecstatic button a little too firmly. However, these are excellent performances and Herbie seems to be enjoying himself, sounding a little like a mischievous choirboy with flattened-down hair who's going to add some rolls and scats to every hymn.

**** Idle Moments

Blue Note 99003 *Green; Joe Henderson (ts); Bobby Hutcherson (vib); Duke Pearson (p); Bob Cranshaw (b); Al Harewood (d).* 11/63.

Strange how much happened in America in November 1963. This vies with *Born To Be Blue* as Green's finest session. Perhaps the former is more securely *his* date. This one featured three other men – Henderson, Hutcherson and Pearson – who were also trying to make a mark of one sort or another at Blue Note, and Green is sometimes eclipsed by the vibist. He holds his own on John Lewis's 'Django' and turns the song around with a lovely, uncomplicated solo. Henderson is rather remote in the mix, and one can see why Rudy van Gelder might have wanted him held back a notch. A lighter-voiced reed player would have been better sonically, but Joe's intelligence and grave humour would have been missed.

***** Matador**

Blue Note 78444 *Green; McCoy Tyner (p); Bob Cranshaw (b); Elvin Jones (d).* 5/64.

***** Solid**

Blue Note 33580 *As above, except add James Spaulding (ss, as), Joe Henderson (ts).* 5/64.

The Blue Note sessions were coming thick and fast by this stage, and Green seemed inclined to experiment. So counter to both market trend and his own recent output was *Solid* that it wasn't allowed to see the light of day for another 15 years. It's certainly one of the boldest of the guitarist's albums, and the presence of Joe Henderson ups the improvisational ante quite considerably. 'Ezz-Thetic' and 'The Kicker' occupy the opposite musical poles here, but both are hauled into shape by a very strong group.

It was a bold stroke to programme 'My Favorite Things' with two-thirds of John Coltrane's rhythm section working behind him as they did on *Matador*, but it served to illustrate first how adventurous Green could be, even within his harmonically uncomplicated idiom, and also how very different that modernist staple could be made to sound. Cranshaw is a funkier bassist than Jimmy Garrison and he probably makes the biggest overall difference to the sound. Tyner provides a near-perfect pianistic echo of Green's combination of delicacy, structural awareness and understated power. The guitarist already knew Jones from Chicago and from a 1959 Jimmy Forrest session, which was Green's recording debut. A fine album that shouldn't just be valued for the contributions of the supporting cast. Green himself is still very much at his peak.

*****(*) Talkin' About**

Blue Note 21958 *Green; Larry Young (org); Elvin Jones (d).* 9/64.

There is a mild discographical anomaly attached to this record because, though definitely led by Green, it was included in Mosaic's complete set of Larry Young's Blue Note sessions. Inevitably, Larry captures much of the attention, with huge, swirly figures on 'Talkin' About J.C.', 'Luny Tune' and 'I'm An Old Cowhand', but Green is also in fine form, spinning out some unusually complex lines for him. We've always loved the sound on this record, like fudge ice-cream sitting on ice cubes. Green plays rich and simple by turns, and even Elvin Jones is cool and abstract under all the intensity.

****** Street Of Dreams**

Blue Note 21290 *Green; Bobby Hutcherson (vib); Larry Young (org); Elvin Jones (d).* 11/64.

Another exceptional record, though this time it is very much the group set-up that makes the difference. Though hooked into that easily overcooked guitar, organ, drums format, the personnel is such that one can reasonably expect a blend of power grooves and subtlety. Young is exceptional, very much on form, and Hutcherson makes an enormous contribution to a slower-paced and more meditative session than he'd normally favour. There are no originals, but the choice of material, from Charles Trenet's 'I Wish You Love', the staple 'Lazy Afternoon', the Victor Young-written title-track and closing with 'Somewhere In The Night' (often referred to as 'The "Naked City" Theme') is spot-on. The alternation of solos on the title-track, with Green springing off from Larry Young's ever more intense chord-patterns, is the most impressive, but the quality never drops for an instant. Unusually, Capitol haven't added any alternatives or unreleased material. Perhaps there was none suitable; 35 minutes is short rations by present-day standards, though.

***** His Majesty King Funk**

Verve 527474-2 *Green; Harold Vick (ts, f); Larry Young (org); Ben Dixon (d); Candido Camero (perc).* 5/65.

This comes from Verve's 'Roots of Acid Jazz' series and compiles Green's record and *Up With Donald Byrd*, a joyous swinger from the trumpeter. 'The Cantaloupe Woman' was a hit for Green, but his section of the album is dominated by a wonderful, long 'Willow Weep For Me' and a cracking original called 'The Selma March'. Vick may not be known to many people. He is very much in the same mould as Mobley, though at moments he might almost be mistaken for Stanley Turrentine as well. He pretty much falls in with what's expected of him, neither surprising nor disappointing. By this stage, though, Young sounds as if he might want to be doing other things, and on 'That Lucky Old Sun (Just Rolls Around Heaven All Day)' he is positively lethargic. Dixon is a less than satisfactory replacement for Jones, who at this point was having 'personal problems' and was otherwise committed to the Coltrane group.

*****(*) I Want To Hold Your Hand**

Blue Note 59962 *Green; Hank Mobley (ts); Larry Young (org); Elvin Jones (d).* 3/65.

The reintroduction of a horn makes the music seem very linear and a touch unvaried. Coupled to a less enterprising programme of songs, the impact is much reduced. Leading off with a Beatles tune – the title-track – was pretty much par for the course at this time, and it's a strong enough idea to feed Green and Young with some interesting lines. 'Stella By Starlight' is rather weak, sounding as if it's been round the circuit too many times, but Steve Allen's 'This Could Be The Start Of Something' (Allen was a favourite of Green's) is excellently done. Mobley isn't deficient in ideas, but he does seem surplus to requirements for much of the set, and it would have been interesting to hear just Green, Young and Jones tackle exactly the same material. Again, the total duration seems stingy at less than 45 minutes. What has happened to all the stuff that wasn't released?

***** Blues For Lou**

Blue Note 21438 *Green; John Patton (org); Ben Dixon (d).*

***** Iron City**

32 Jazz 32048 *As above.* 67.

This trio was one of Green's most durable associations. Reissued in 1999, *Blues For Lou* is definitive organ–guitar jazz. Patton is strictly no-nonsense and stamps his personality on the album right from the start, a swirling, voluptuous reading of 'Surrey With The Fringe On Top'. Patton's own composition, 'Big John', isn't merely an organ feature. It also includes one of Green's most effective solos, not to be topped until the trio of tracks at the end of the album which represent his most direct but also most subtle approach to the blues. Dixon is something of a bystander and occasionally overcompensates with unnecessary power, but as a group it hangs together very well and this is a welcome reappearance.

Green moonlighted for Muse in 1967, during what now looks like a fallow period. The trio makes up for lost time with a steaming and utterly rhythmic set, dominated by 'Samba De Orpheus' and two finely executed spirituals, given the full treatment. Dixon is more alert here than on *Blues For Lou* and the sound suits him better.

**** Carryin' On**
Blue Note 31247 2 *Green; Claude Bartee (ts); Neal Creque, Clarence Palmer (p); Billy Bivens (vib); Jimmy Lewis (b); Idris Muhammad (d).* 9/69.

**** Green Is Beautiful**
Blue Note 28265 2 *As above, except omit Palmer, Bivens; add Blue Mitchell (t), Emmanuel Riggins (org), Candido Camero, Richard Landrum (perc).* 1/70.

A particularly dull spot. Green arguably suffered more than most of his peers from the growing dominance of rock, and his response to the challenge wasn't convincing. Both discs are very repetitive, tunes built on long, unvarying vamps and little imagination. *Beautiful* opens strongly enough with 'Ain't I Funky Now', which at least has some strong work from the horns, but there is little else to stir any excitement and the horns sound like men whistling in a wind. These albums have their admirers (and all of Green's Blue Notes have a certain cult standing) but these are hardly priority purchases.

***** Live At The Lighthouse**
Blue Note 4 93381 *Green; Claude Bartee (ts, ss); Gary Coleman (vib); Shelton Laster (org); Wilton Felder (b); Greg Williams (d); Bobbye Porter Hall (perc).* 4/72.

Green spent his last few years playing on autopilot, but he was occasionally capable of turning in a gig that combined the old class with a sufficiently contemporary spin to fill a house. This Hermosa Beach session is a case in point. He sounds in excellent fettle and, while he isn't doing anything either new or special, the group-sound is exactly what the punters have come to hear. On the original LP there were a number of disc jockey announcements which have been eliminated here, but for an introduction by Hank Stewart. The live feel is maintained, though, and a long version of Donald Byrd's 'Fancy Free' is worth the wait. Laster's 'Flood In Franklin Park' contains no surprises, but it's an entertaining enough piece. Unlike some recent reissues, there is at least some value for money here, a solid hour of uncomplicated funk.

*****(*) Street Funk & Jazz Grooves: The Best Of Grant Green**
Blue Note 789622 *As for Blue Note releases above.* 64–72.

***** The Best Of Grant Green: Volume Two**
Blue Note 37741 *Green; Blue Mitchell, Lee Morgan, Joe Newman, Victor Paz, Jimmy Sedlar, Joe Wilder (t); Harry DiVito (tb); Dick Hickson (btb); Phil Bodner, John Leone, George Marge, Romeo Penque, Jimmy Buffington (frhn); Claude Bartee, George Coleman (ts); Willie Bivens, Billy Wooten (vib); Neal Creque (p); Emmanuel Riggins, Reuben Wilson (org); Wilton Felder, Jimmy Lewis, Chuck Rainey (b); Stix Hooper, Idris Muhammad (d); Ray Armando, Candido Camero, King Ericson, Richard Landrum (perc).* 3/69–4/72.

***** Blue Breakbeats**
Blue Note 94705 *Green; Irwin Markowitz, Blue Mitchell, Marvin Stamm (t); Harold Vick (ss); Phil Bodner (woodwinds); Claude Bartee (ts); Clarence Palmer, Emmanuel Riggins (p); Richard Tee (ky); Neal Creque, Ronnie Foster (org); William Bivens, Billy Wooten (vib); Cornell Dupree (g); Gordon Edwards, Jimmy Lewis, Chuck Rainey (b); Idris Muhammad, Grady Tate (d); Ray Armando, Joseph Armstrong, Candido Camero, Richard Landrum, Ralph MacDonald (perc).* 69–72.

The first of these was unashamedly targeted at the club dance scene and won Green some new admirers when it was released. The second volume is a touch more jazz-orientated, and it usefully includes material from unavailable records (or expensive Japanese imports) like *Carryin' On*, *Green Is Beautiful*, *Visions*, *Shades Of Green* and *The Final Comedown*. Only 'Sookie Sookie' from *Alive!* and 'Windjammer' from *Live At The Lighthouse* can be found among the records above. So, from a purely practical point of view, this is a useful compilation, arranged chronologically, which helps the continuity considerably. A couple of songs are reduplicated from the first volume, 'Sookie Sookie' and shorter, studio versions of 'The Final Comedown' and 'Windjammer', but for the most part these are separate releases. *Street Funk & Jazz Grooves* has the more obvious stuff, like 'Grantstand' and 'A Walk In The Night', but now that more material has returned to the catalogue it's a less appealing purchase. The second volume brings in one track from a Reuben Wilson album on which Green featured strongly.

The recently reissued *Breakbeats* is equally pitched at a young, dance-orientated audience. Compiled by DJ Smash, it's intended to cement Green's standing as one of the presiding deities of the club scene. As such, it's a very persuasive set indeed, including the long version of 'Sookie Sookie' and one of 'Ain't I Funky Now'. The shorter tracks, including 'Final Comedown', are less convincing in this context, but it's easy to see why Green has been so respectfully sampled by the young hip-hoppers.

Thurman Green (1940–97)

TROMBONE

Bebop trombone was defined by J.J. Johnson, but Green has managed to combine boppish articulation with an older swing style and a leaven of avant-garde freedoms.

***** Dance Of The Night Creatures**
Mapleshade 1025 *Green; Hamiet Bluiett (bs, cbcl); John Hicks (p); Walter Booker, Steve Novosel (b); Steve Williams (d).* 94.

Green worked here and there, ranging from the boppish swing of the Clayton–Hamilton Orchestra to the modernist concepts of the Horace Tapscott group. The radical West Coast pianist leaves a mark on Green's belated debut as leader, contributing three strong themes to a thoroughly inventive set. Producer Hamiet Bluiett knew Green from the Navy School of Music in Washington, DC, but he remains pretty much in the background as a player except on 'Cross Currents', where he locks horns with Green, and on the improvised 'Searching For Peace'.

'Cross Currents' apart, this is a relatively conventional, changes-led session. The rhythm players put the emphasis squarely on chordal progressions and straightforward metres, and Green seems to thrive in this environment, with a biting, full-bellied tone that doesn't immediately recall either J.J. Johnson or

Curtis Fuller, but which draws from a longer history of slide horn playing. Sad that this should be the beginning *and* end of a potentially fascinating story.

Green Room

GROUP

Scottish improvising trio, mixing acoustic and electric idioms.

*****(*) Hidden Music**

Leo LAB CD 007 *Chick Lyall (p, elec, f); David Baird (vn, g, elec, perc); David Garrett (p, perc).* 7/94.

****** Live Trajectories**

Leo LAB CD 025 *As above, plus additional instruments.* 2/96.

Refreshing to come across an improv group who eschew the longer-is-better philosophy and work in digestible, almost song-like durations which imply structure even when it is not overt. With the exception of the slightly tedious 'Flux' and 'Satellites', both of which exceed 15 minutes and the patience of most listeners, the debut album consisted of one-and-a-half- to five-minute pieces. The live sequel inevitably stretches durations quite considerably but, if anything, Lyall, Baird and Garrett have pared down their operational language even further and there is no sense of clutter or playing to fill time. Interestingly, the group's jazz roots are slightly more evident on the 1996 album, which was recorded at Edinburgh's famously experimental Traverse Theatre, and there is a discernible logic to almost all the pieces. Lyall's reputation as a 'straight' player hasn't yet reached much beyond Scotland, but one suspects that here is a group who have paradoxically thrived on working on a relatively undersubscribed scene. There is a freshness and individuality to the music, a total absence of cliché, that is hugely encouraging. There isn't a desultory moment on either record. 'Flux II', the best track on *Live Trajectories*, is a wonderful synthesis of electronic styles and acoustic voicings, and 'Divertimento' plays with the unexplored border-zone between classical music and a spectrum of other idioms, highbrow and popular. Green Room have been functioning for more than a decade. Even if opportunities to play have been sparse, the trio has built up an impressive understanding and empathy.

Burton Greene (born 1937)

PIANO

Studied classical music in Chicago, then with Dick Marx, going to New York in the early '60s and forming the Free Form Improvisation Ensemble in 1963. Joined the Jazz Composers Guild and recorded for ESP. Moved to Paris in 1969, then divided his time between Europe and America, while also studying Indian music.

****(*) Shades Of Greene**

Cadence CJR 1087 *Greene (p solo).* 4/92–12/97.

***** Throptics**

CIMP 182 *Greene; Wilber Morris (b); Lou Grassi (d).* 7/98.

Greene has had a strange time of it in jazz, to say the least: a pioneer spirit in the free jazz of the early '60s, his ESP quartet album ('uninformed by any apparent communicative purpose' – Max Harrison) was reviled and applauded in about equal proportion, though it was ignored altogether in far greater numbers. Subsequent bulletins have been spasmodic and not much more enlightening. *Shades Of Greene* collects material from three solo concerts, two long pieces in Toronto, seven from Hilversum and a much earlier version of 'Off Minor' from a 1992 Amsterdam broadcast. As ever, Greene rambles away to some strange agenda of his own – he can be as long-winded as the most bloody-minded of improvisers, but he can also be pithy and almost epigrammatic when he wants to be – and it's this unpredictability which makes him either intriguing or exasperating, according to taste. We are somewhere in the middle.

The trio set at least allows Wilber and Grassi to centre him to some extent. 'Lennie Lives', for Tristano, and 'Tilo Akandita Brikama', by Pierre Dørge, for Johnny Dyani, are characterful excursions which Greene hurls himself into, but there is a good deal of chaos as well: the opening 'Light Blue' may well finish off some listeners at the first hurdle. A maverick spirit, to be sure!

Jimmy Greene (born 1975)

TENOR AND SOPRANO SAXOPHONES, FLUTE

Born in Connecticut, Green studied at Hartford and has played in the Boston area and in New York.

***** Introducing Jimmy Greene**

Criss Cross 1181 *Greene; John Swana (t, flhn); Steve Davis (tb); Aaron Goldberg (p); Darrell Hall (b); Eric McPherson (d).* 10/97.

***** Brand New World**

RCA 09026-63564-2 *As above, except add Darren Barrett (t, flhn), Dwayne Burns (b), Khalil Bell (perc); omit Swana and Hall.* 6/99.

Greene made a few waves as a runner-up in one of the Monk Institute competitions and his stint with Horace Silver has given him some dues. Neither of these records is going to have hats thrown in the air, but they're a solid enough start. The RCA debut has had its teeth drawn slightly by the simultaneous appearance of the Criss Cross set, actually recorded some two years earlier. *Introducing* feels like just another Criss Cross record for the most part, although here and there Greene is a degree more personal: with the rather dark and sidelong arrangement of 'I Love You', for instance. Swana and Davis sound as if they've just turned up to do the date and they don't add very much.

The RCA set is stronger, but not so much as to make a huge difference. Greene has an attractively light and unemphatic sound on tenor, but this makes it more difficult for him to create a whizz-bang impression over a single set. The band is much the same and the leader's composing takes more prominence, which seems to fuse the front line into a more characterful sound. Future releases may see Greene in a more purposeful light.

Sonny Greenwich

GUITAR

Canadian guitarist looking for challenging turf in an otherwise broad-based post-bop idiom.

***** Bird Of Paradise**

Justin Time JUST 22-2 *Greenwich; Fred Henke (p); Ron Seguin (b); Andre White (d).* 11/86.

****(*) Live At Sweet Basil**

Justin Time JUST 26-2 *As above.* 9/87.

Greenwich's guitarist's approach veers between guitar-driven jazz in a contemporary vein and an attempt to capture the sound of the late John Coltrane Quartet. This is not quite as misguided as it might sound, but it works only intermittently. The studio setting of *Bird Of Paradise* allows Greenwich more scope for experimentation and he produces some fascinating ideas on 'Of Stars And Strings' and the deeply felt 'Only One Earth' (which recalls his work with Paul Bley), lapsing into sentiment only on two out-of-place standards. He uses guitar synth sensitively and creatively, not just as a source of vague orchestral washes, and puts to shame most attempts to make something of this item of technology. The band, as will be seen above, is an established one, each member very responsive to the others. Most of the material on the live session, too, is original but without on this occasion being remotely innovative; the one attempt at a standard, 'You Go To My Head', misfires badly. 'Libra Ascending' is a heartfelt tribute to Coltrane but all the passion in the world doesn't make up for a wayward conception, and the recording is grim throughout, though Seguin can comfort himself with the realization that no one could ever hear Jimmy Garrison either. The drummer splashes about noisily and should be made to play in cuffs for three months after what he does to Greenwich's best tune, 'The Sky's The Limit'. Greenwich clearly has a good deal to say for himself, but it will take a sensitive producer and engineer to make it happen.

Guillermo Gregorio

SAXOPHONES, CLARINET

A saxophonist of understated brilliance, Gregorio has taken striking liberties with the harmonic language of classic jazz and swing. His approach is less ironic than that of others in the field, but is no less successful for that.

***** Ellipsis**

hatOLOGY 511 *Gregorio; Gene Coleman (bcl); Jim O'Rourke (g, acc); Carrie Biolo (vib); Michael Cameron (b).* 2/97.

***** Red Cube(d)**

hatOLOGY 531 *Gregorio; Mat Maneri (vn); Pandelis Karayorgis (p).* 3/98.

The language of these records will not seem strange to anyone who has experienced the *avant*-Cool of Franz Koglmann, another one-time hat ART recording artist, with whom Gregorio has worked in the past. At first blush, the first of these albums is more directly influenced by the Fluxus group and by modernist composers such as Earle Brown and Giacinto Scelsi, with whose pure-sound approach Gregorio has something in common.

After a little exposure, and certainly after one hears what he does with jazz-based material on *Red Cube(d)*, it becomes evident that he has roots in that tradition as well. The later album was seemingly inspired by a batch of lost Red Norvo discs from the 1940s. Vibes played a part in the earlier album, though paradoxically not in the second, but their presence on *Ellipsis* and Gregorio's reworkings of Fletcher Henderson's 'Red Dust', 'Ghost Of A Chance' (or 'Chu's Spectre') and 'These Foolish Things' suggest just how much he has tried to combine jazz and other harmonic languages within a rhythmic conception which is not drum-led. The most remarkable piece of all is 'Woodchopper's Nightmare', a veritable palimpsest of themes by Norvo, Shorty Rogers, Woody Herman, Flip Phillips and others. Its concentration is highly impressive and the interplay of saxophone, piano and violin is virtuosic.

Gregorio is unlikely to be for every taste. Some of his work veers perilously close to navel-gazing but, like Koglmann, he has important things to say about the jazz tradition, things which we ignore at our peril.

Stan Greig (born 1930)

PIANO

Edinburgh-born, Greig worked as a teenager with Sandy Brown and joined the Ken Colyer band as a drummer in 1954. He worked extensively with Humphrey Lyttelton, the Fairweather–Brown group and, for most of the '60s, Acker Bilk, before rejoining Lyttelton in the '80s and leading his own Harlem Blues and Jazz Band.

***** Boogie Woogie**

Lake LACD97 *Greig; Johnny Hawksworth (b); Richie Bryant (d).* 71.

Though Greig's main calling is as the archetypal mainstream-band pianist, this set features him in boogie mode. For the most part it's a reissue of an obscure 1971 set for Rediffusion. The piano sound is rather hard, but the playing – of chestnuts such as 'Shout For Joy' and 'Death Ray Boogie', as well as a few appropriate originals – is delightfully bright and bumptious. We are not sure that we agree with the sleeve-note assertion that there aren't many players left who can play 'authentic' boogie woogie, since it's more that the style has simply gone out of fashion. In a way, this set explains why: well done though it is, it tends to pall over album length through the repetitiveness of the idiom. Three 'new' tracks, featuring Greig solo in 1997, are more sedate and even surprisingly hesitant.

Al Grey (1925–2000)

TROMBONE, VOCAL

Joined Benny Carter after military service, then was with various groups until a key period with Count Basie, 1957–61. Afterwards freelanced, often with old friends Jimmy Forrest and Buddy Tate, and led some record dates of his own.

***** Al Grey–Jesper Thilo Quintet**
Storyville STCD 4136 *Grey; Jesper Thilo (ts); Ole Kock Hansen (p); Hugo Rasmussen (b); Alex Riel (d).* 8/86.

Al Grey will always be remembered as a Basie sideman, even though he spent more years away from the Count's band than with it. His humorous, fierce style of improvising is more in the tradition of such colleagues as saxophonist Lockjaw Davis than in the rather more restrained trombone lineage, although Grey is especially accomplished with the plunger mute. He came to seem like the successor to Vic Dickenson's mantle as the great trombone individualist.

Last time we were pleased to note that his discography had expanded but, as is so often the case, it's shrunk again as far as availability is concerned. The Storyville session, made on one of his many European sojourns, is typical of his usual manner: brisk mainstream with some sterling blues playing, although Thilo and the rhythm section accommodate rather than compel Grey into his best form.

***** The New Al Grey Quintet**
Chiaroscuro CD 305 *Grey; Mike Grey (tb); Joe Cohn (t, g); J.J Wiggins (b); Bobby Durham (d).* 5/88.

*****(*) Al Meets Bjarne**
Gemini GM 62 *Grey; Bjarne Nerem (ts); Norman Simmons (p); Paul West (b); Gerryck King (d).* 8/88.

***** Fab**
Capri 74038-2 *Grey; Clark Terry (t, flhn, v); Don Sickler (t); Mike Grey, Delfeayo Marsalis (tb); Virginia Mayhew (as); Norman Simmons (p); Joe Cohn (g); J.J Wiggins (b); Bobby Durham (d); Jon Hendricks (v).* 2/90.

The quintet date for Chiaroscuro features a 'family band': Mike is Al's son, Joe is Al Cohn's son, and J.J. Wiggins is pianist Gerald's offspring. Although the group sound a little rough-and-ready at times, and the absence of a pianist is probably not quite as useful a freedom as it might have been, it works out to be a very entertaining record. Mike is almost as ripe a soloist as his father, and the sound of the two trombones together leads to a few agreeably toe-curling moments; but Joe Cohn's playing is equally spirited, and Wiggins and Durham sound fine. The set-list includes some standards and a few pleasingly obscure choices, such as Hank Mobley's 'Syrup And Bisquits' and Art Farmer's 'Rue Prevail'.

The session with Nerem was cut on a visit to Norway. The title-blues is almost indecently ripe, and 'I'm In The Mood For Love' is taken at surely the slowest tempo on record, but there are meaty blowing tunes as well and Nerem, a player in the kind of swaggering swing tradition that Grey enjoys, has the measure of the trombonist. Outstandingly good studio sound.

The Capri record is a bit self-consciously 'produced' around Grey, with a number of guessable routines in place – mumbling duet with Clark Terry, all-bones-together blues, and so on. Al still sounds robust and comfortably on top of the situation. Capri also have a seasonal album featuring Grey, *Christmas Stocking Stuffer* (Capri 74039-2 CD), for those with a taste for yuletide jazz.

***** Matzoh And Grits**
Arbors ARCD 19167 *Grey; Cleave E Guyton (as, f); Randolph Noel (p); Joe Cohn (g); J.J Wiggins (b); Bobby Durham (d).* 4/96.

*****(*) Me N' Jack**
Pullen PULL 2350 *Grey; Jerry Weldon (ts); Jack McDuff (org); Joe Cohn (g); Jerome Hunker (b); Bobby Durham (d).* 96.

Al seemed ageless, even when he was playing the sly old man, and these two show no falling-off in quality. *Matzoh And Grits* is let down a bit by the band: Cohn and Durham are favourite stagers with Grey and they're fine, but Guyton and Noel are a little ordinary and here and there the music droops, although the Ellington tunes are very good value. *Me N' Jack* is much more like it. Pairing Grey with McDuff was an inspired move. The organist refuses to do any showboating and instead takes his turn in the ensembles while offering support to anyone who needs it. Weldon has some good turns, Cohn is terrific, and Grey is in marvellous heart, with his ballad showpiece on 'God Bless The Child' a treat. The rest of the material is nearly all blues, but it doesn't hurt.

Carola Grey

DRUMS

Munich-born drummer playing in a stretch of styles from hard bop to fusion.

***** Noisy Mama**
Jazzline 11130-2 *Grey; Ralph Alessi (t); Peter Epstein (ss, as); Craig Handy (ts); Mike Cain (p); Lonnie Plaxico, Ron McClure (b).* 1–7/92.

*****(*) The Age Of Illusions**
Jazzline 11139-2 *Grey; Ralph Alessi (t, flhn); Peter Epstein (ss, as); Ravi Coltrane (ts); Carlton Holmes, Dario Eskenazi (p); Mike Stern (g); Ed Schuller, Calvin Jones, Gregg Jones, Gene Perez (b); Cafe, Bobby Sanabria (perc).* 6/94.

***** Girls Can't Hit!**
Lipstick 8945-2 *Grey; Rick Keller (ts); Martin Kalberer (ky); Werner Neumann, Paul Koji Shiighara (g); Paul Tietze (b).* 6/96.

Grey can play with great *brio* in a number of styles, but she's basically moving from straight-ahead to fusion over the course of these three interesting records. *Noisy Mama*, which is mostly self-penned (like all three discs), offers a sheaf of good themes to a particularly brainy and adept band of New Yorkers and, although it feels a bit like a self-conscious debut, Grey gets some fine work out of all the players. She does better still with *The Age Of Illusions*. 'The Colour We Create' is a ballad written over some very attractive changes which Coltrane takes full advantage of; Stern is usefully employed on two tracks and the rest is colourfully paced and illuminated by the leader, with Alessi and Epstein injecting some comely solos. The rocking groove of the title-track sets her up for *Girls Can't Hit!*, which returns her to her native Germany and a 'local' band. This is something of a step sideways and arguably a less impressive record than the others but, with some taut, individual playing from Neumann in particular, she once again gets a cogent response from a group that could as easily have settled for filibustering.

Johnny Griffin (born 1928)

TENOR SAXOPHONE

If saxophone playing had a Formula One division, Johnny Griffin would have pole position every start – or he would have had before he discovered a gentler and more lyrical side to his musical personality. Born in Chicago, the Little Giant was part of the first bebop generation, but he only really found his true voice in the '50s and very often in partnership with Eddie 'Lockjaw' Davis, with whom he duelled to often spectacular effect. Griffin spent some time in Europe in the '60s but has enjoyed a resurgence back home in more recent years.

*** A Blowing Session

Blue Note 99009 *Griffin; Lee Morgan (t); John Coltrane, Hank Mobley (ts); Wynton Kelly (p); Paul Chambers (b); Art Blakey (d).* 5/57.

This is the period when Griffin's youthful rep as the fastest tenor on the block was made official. In the company of Coltrane and Mobley, neither of them slouches, he rattles through 'The Way You Look Tonight' like some love-on-the-run hustler with his mates waiting out in the car. Only Trane seems inclined to serenade, and it's interesting to speculate how the track might have sounded had they taken it at conventional ballad tempo; 'All The Things You Are' begins with what sounds like Reveille from Wynton Kelly and then lopes off with almost adolescent awkwardness. This was a typical Griffin strategy. For much of his most productive period Griffin more or less bypassed ballad-playing and only really adjusted his idiom to the medium and slower tempos as he aged; 'It's All Right With Me' is way over the speed limit, as if Griffin is trying to erase all memory of Sonny Rollins's magisterial reading of a deceptively difficult tune. *Blowing Session* is oddly unsettling and by no means the most appealing thing Griffin put his name to. The new special edition is nicely packaged but doesn't overcome our unease.

***(*) Way Out

Original Jazz Classics OJCCD 1855 *Griffin; Kenny Drew (p); Wilbur Ware (b); Philly Joe Jones (d).* 2/58.

Recorded by Orrin Keepnews in New York City, this is a set that nevertheless breathes Chicago. In some respects, it isn't the 'person we knew'; Griffin sounds quieter, more measured and contained and, but for a blaze through 'Cherokee' at high tempo, content to play a much gentler set. Items like 'Where's Your Overcoat, Boy?' and 'Teri's Tune' centre on Ware's hugely expansive bass line, with Drew in close proximity, leaving Griff to develop and embellish. 'Little John' is distinctive for Drew's solid chording and interchanges with the drummer. The rhythm section could hardly be faulted, and CD transfer has improved sound-quality tenfold.

**** Johnny Griffin Sextet

Original Jazz Classics OJC 1827 *Griffin; Donald Byrd (t); Pepper Adams (bs); Kenny Drew (p); Wilbur Ware (b); Philly Joe Jones (d).* 2/58.

Despite the drummer's name, this was a Chicago group *par excellence.* Everything seems just a little magnified, and tunes like 'Stix' Trix' and 'Woody'N'You' are gloriously pumped-up and brazen. A pity that Griffin didn't record more with this line-up. They sound like they're just about to hit proper stride when the record ends. Ware is magnificent as always, and Kenny Drew stretches himself ambitiously.

*** The Little Giant

Original Jazz Classics OJC 136 *Griffin; Blue Mitchell (t); Julian Priester (tb); Wynton Kelly (p); Sam Jones (b); Albert 'Tootie' Heath (d).* 8/59.

This isn't the only album bearing this title (which refers to the diminutive saxophonist's nickname), so it might be worth checking that you're getting the right one. Heath finds it harder than Blakey to keep up, but the rhythm section get it just about right, opening up the throttle for Griffin and two rather underrated brass soloists with just the right amount of brassiness in their tone to match the leader's.

*** The Big Soul-Band

Original Jazz Classics OJC 485 *Griffin; Clark Terry, Bob Bryant (t); Julian Priester, Matthew Gee (tb); Pat Patrick, Frank Strozier, Edwin Williams, Charles Davis (sax); Harold Mabern, Bobby Timmons (p); Bob Cranshaw, Vic Sproles (b); Charli Persip (d).* 5–6/60.

A little like standing out in a high wind. Griffin wasn't necessarily the most subtle of bandleaders but he knew how to make a group swing, and that's what he brings to this. An alternative version of 'Wade In The Water' on the CD suggests that this was a group always teetering on the brink of self-destruction, in the musical if not the personal sense. Griffin's frontmanship was pretty tenuous – but when it worked, it worked wonderfully.

*** Studio Jazz Party

Original Jazz Classics OJCCD 1902 *Griffin; Dave Burns (t); Norman Simmons (b); Vic Sproles (b); Ben Riley (d).* 9/60.

The deal here was that the band would play live, not in a club, but before an invited studio audience. The atmosphere is loose and relaxed, and Babs Gonzales MCs in an attempt to authenticate the live atmosphere, but the freshness and novelty wear off very quickly after 'Good Bait' and 'There Will Never Be Another You'. The band is rather anonymous but, with Griff occupying the spotlight throughout, that isn't so much of an issue. One simply hankers after something a little subtler and more modulated.

**(*) Lookin' At Monk

Original Jazz Classics OJCCD 1911 *Griffin; Eddie 'Lockjaw' Davis (ts); Junior Mance (p); Larry Gales (b); Ben Riley (d).* 2/61.

There is something amiss here. Much as the latter history of ragtime piano was ruined by a refusal to look even cursorily at Scott Joplin's intended tempi, so Griffin and Lockjaw race through a set of Monk compositions with lights blazing and tyres squealing, and with no real indication that they have a feel for a tune as delicately nuanced as 'Ruby, My Dear' or 'Well, You Needn't', let alone that old warhorse, 'Round Midnight'. The two saxophones attack each tune like a pair of drag-racers, and there's not much more satisfaction to be had from the performances, unless you have an appetite for empty displays of virtuosity. Not, in our view, any great surprise that this 1999 reissue has taken so long to reappear.

***** White Gardenia**

Original Jazz Classics OJCCD 1877 *Griffin; Ernie Royal, Clark Terry (t); Nat Adderley (c); Jimmy Cleveland, Paul Faulise, Urbie Green (tb); Ray Alonge (frhn); Barry Harris (p); Ron Carter, Barry Galbraith, Jimmy Jones (b); Ben Riley (d); strings.* 7/61.

A delightful, smoothly orchestrated tribute to Lady Day that manages to be more than just pastiche. Griff is no Lester Young, and he isn't perhaps the obvious soloist for a gig of this sort. Even so, he makes a wonderful job of 'God Bless The Child' and 'Left Alone', though it's 'That Old Devil Called Love' which allows him to be most fully and obviously himself. The band is not so smooth as to blur some real jazz feel, and the strings are there mainly for depth of focus and harmony, rather than as emotional treacle.

****(*) Tough Tenor Favourites**

Original Jazz Classics OJCCD 1861 *Griffin; Eddie 'Lockjaw' Davis (ts); Horace Parlan (p); Buddy Catlett (b); Ben Riley (d).* 2/62.

A drably generic two-tenors duel, without a shard of sophistication. For some, that will be the highest possible recommendation and 'Ow!' and 'Tin Tin Deo' will be meat and drink. For us, though, this is a dispiriting low in the Little Giant's career, redeemed by Parlan's mournful chords and sudden scampers into the light. This was Griff's last full year in America before beginning his European exile and it's hard to avoid the impression of a man who thinks that something is closing in on him.

****(*) Do Nothing 'Til You Hear From Me**

Original Jazz Classics OJCCD 1908 *Griffin; Buddy Montgomery (p, vib); Monk Montgomery (b); Art Taylor (d).* 63.

At the tag end of his Riverside contract, Griffin seemed to be marking time and, while there was some comfort in the realization that the time in question was less hectic than of yore, it was still outside most saxophonists' comfort zone. The blowing themes are less convincing than they once were, and less convincingly executed. The Montgomery brothers, with Monk (unusually for the time) on an upright bass, do a manful job, and Buddy's switch to vibes is very effective, but it's hard to avoid the feeling of creative stalemate that surrounds this session.

***** The Man I Love**

Black Lion BLCD 760107 *Griffin; Kenny Drew (p); Niels-Henning Orsted Pedersen (b); Albert 'Tootie' Heath (d).* 3/67.

In the Black Lion catalogue this immediately follows Wardell Gray's *One For Prez*, which includes three takes of 'The Man I Love'. There could hardly be a sharper contrast. Where Gray's tone and delivery drew heavily on Lester Young's pre-bop idiom, Griffin swoops on the same material with an almost delinquent energy that comes direct from Charlie Parker. It isn't the most settling of sounds, but the technical control is superb and only a rhythm section of the quality of this one could keep the tune on the road.

**** Blues For Harvey**

Steeplechase SCCD 31004 *Griffin; Kenny Drew (p); Mads Vinding (b); Ed Thigpen (d).* 7/73.

**** The Jamfs Are Coming**

Timeless SJP 121 *Griffin; Rein De Graaff (p); Henk Haverhoek, Koos Serierse (b); Art Taylor (d).* 12/75, 10/77.

Both these sessions mark something of a low point in Griffin's generally even output. There's something slightly numbed about the solos on *Blues For Harvey* (compare the title-track with the lovely version on *The Man I Love* (above)) and some questionable material which includes a mercifully rare jazz reading of Gilbert O'Sullivan's 'Alone Again (Naturally)'. Griffin takes the theme at his natural clip but makes nothing significant of it. He constantly overshoots the measure on 'Rhythm-A-Ning', another slightly surprising choice which wrong-foots the band on a couple of measures. De Graaff is an interesting player with a steady supply of unhackneyed ideas, but he's only a questionable partner for Griffin and the two never catch light on *The Jamfs Are Coming*. Griffin fans with some practice in mentally editing out dodgy backgrounds might well want to have both of these, but everyone else might as well hang on to their cash.

*****(*) The Return Of The Griffin**

Original Jazz Classics OJCCD 1882 *Griffin; Ronnie Mathews (p); Ray Drummond (b); Keith Copeland (d).* 10/78.

*****(*) Live / Autumn Leaves**

Verve 523261-2 *As above, except Kenny Washington (d) replaces Copeland.* 7/80, 5/81.

The Griffin 'returned' without ever really having been away. The 1978 album was, though, the product of his first visit to the USA since 1963. Griffin's brand of saxophonics had been at something of a discount Stateside for a time, and the Galaxy recording was understandably intended to revive his fortunes. Mathews is a bright and responsive accompanist, and 'A Monk's Dream' and 'Autumn Leaves' are both strong performances, with a slightly altered melody statement on the latter which gives it a wry ambiguity. Copeland has never been a highly regarded player, except by other musicians, and this is further proof of his considerable powers. He is replaced by Washington on the live set, carefully selected from a week-long residency at the New Morning in Paris – except for 'Autumn Leaves' itself, which was recorded the summer before at the Antibes–Juan-les-Pins festival, where the song has had an iconic status since Miles's band gave a near-definitive version there. Griffin's attack is more abrasive on the live version, but he softens his delivery very considerably for 'Prelude To A Kiss', a melting performance which again significantly reworks the melody in places.

****(*) Tough Tenors Back Again!**

Storyville 8298 *Griffin: Eddie 'Lockjaw' Davis (ts); Harry Pickens (p); Curtis Lundy (b); Kenny Washington (d).* 7/84.

As far as we can tell, this is the last recorded encounter between Johnny and Locks. It's pretty much par for the course. Any slowing of pace on Griffin's case over recent years is pretty much cancelled out in a programme of straight – some would say unrelieved – blowing themes. There are a few entertaining moments, though unfortunately the best of them is the conversational rap on 'Blues Up And Down'. An excellent rhythm section almost saves the day, with the little-known Pickens in decent if unspectacular form, but we remain unconvinced. On the night, in the Jazzhus Montmartre, it must have been exciting. As a recording, it's very one-dimensional.

***** In Copenhagen**

Storyville 8300 *Griffin; Kenny Drew (p); Niels-Henning Orsted Pedersen (b); Art Taylor (d).*

****(*) Catharsis**

Storyville 8306 *Griffin; Kenny Drew (p); Jens Melgaard (b); Ole Streenberg (d).*

Griffin wasn't the only American exile working in Copenhagen. Kenny Drew proved to be an able and sympathetic partner and their dates at the Jazzhus Montmartre were widely admired. We like the first of these records very much. 'What Is This Thing Called Love?' and 'Body And Soul' are very good indeed, but there are persistent problems with the source tape. The playing is generally very good and the band is in cracking form on 'Wee Dot' and 'A Night In Tunisia' which begins with a strange, almost warlike chant. NHOP is his reliable and inventive self, and Taylor's crackling cymbal figures and furious cross-rhythms seem to mark a bridge between classic bebop and the complexities of the Coltrane quartet.

Issued only recently and received shortly before press time, we haven't had an opportunity to listen to the oddly titled *Catharsis* more than cursorily, but it seems like standard later-period Griffin, ably abetted by the late Kenny Drew. Separated in time though they are, these two albums do seem to belong together. 'If I Should Lose You' is ably done with altered chords and the traditional 'Hush-A-Bye' provides an attractive setting for Johnny's quieter approach. It's hard to make a monkey of the classic Hodges feature, 'Isfahan', but Griff almost manages. Fortunately, his sheer musicality wins the day.

***** Grif'N'Bags**

Ubiquity 19303 *Griffin; Idrees Sulieman (t); Sahib Shihab (bs); Milt Jackson (vib); Ake Persson (b); Kenny Clarke (d).*

An absolutely fascinating selection of mostly little-heard tunes on this 1999 reissue. Apart from Hefti's 'Lonely Girl' and Griff's 'The Jamfs Are Coming', all the material is markedly obscure. George Duvivier's 'Foot Patting' – not, as far as we are aware, frequently covered – is a gift for the vibes–horn combination, and there is a healthy representation of Francy Boland material which suits the almost big-band configuration very well. Jackson isn't on the best form in his solos, which mainly build on either short melodic cells or slightly disengaged harmonic sequences, but his ensemble work is awesome, and even Griffin trims down the flow of notes in respect. The set ends with a Griffin rarity, 'Lady Heavy Bottom's Waltz', a grand dowager of a tune that rounds out a packed and very good set.

Tiny Grimes (1916–89)

PIANO, VOCAL

A four-string guitar player, Grimes was a sensation in the Art Tatum Trio and then elsewhere in New York clubs of the '40s. Later he tried his luck with rock'n'roll. Illness slowed him in the '60s, but he recovered and was on the festival circuit again in the '70s and '80s.

***** Callin' The Blues**

Original Jazz Classics OJC 191 *Grimes; J.C Higginbotham (tb); Eddie 'Lockjaw' Davis (ts); Ray Bryant (p); Wendell Marshall (b); Osie Johnson (d).* 7/58.

***** Blues Groove**

Original Jazz Classics OJC 817 *Grimes; Coleman Hawkins, Musa Kaleem (ts) ; Ray Bryant (p); Earl Wormack (b); Teagle Fleming Jr (d).*

***** Tiny In Swingville**

Original Jazz Classics OJC 1796 *Grimes; Jerome Richardson (ts, bs, f); Ray Bryant (p); Wendell Marshall (b); Art Taylor (d).* 8/59.

At one time Grimes's standing with fans and fellow-musicians utterly confounded his diminutive nickname. One of the midwives of popular music, he attended bebop's first contractions (the earliest of the legendary Charlie Parker Savoy sessions were under Grimes's leadership) and then, in the early 1950s, slapped rock and roll firmly on the bottom with his bizarrely kilted (*sic.!*) Rockin' Highlanders, who can be heard on the now-deleted *Rock The House*.

In Swingville dispenses with the theatricals. Though there's still a novelty element to the music, which includes 'Annie Laurie' (hoots, mon!) and 'Frankie And Johnnie', frontman Richardson is a completely convincing player and Grimes himself glides through some parallel sections that would do Kenny Burrell proud. The earlier *Callin' The Blues* has the improbable pairing of Higginbotham and Davis for the front line, while *Blues Groove* summons the great Hawkins to the studio (as well as Kaleem, a Blakey sideman back in 1947). The material is either blues or obvious standards on both occasions, and nothing feels very substantial, but Grimes likes being in charge and he gets sterling work out of all hands on each occasion.

Grismore/Scea Group

GROUP

A group of Massachusetts-based musicians with their distillation of various contemporary methods.

****(*) Just Play**

Accurate AC 5003 *Tim Hagans (t); Paul Scea (ts, f); Steve Grismore (g); Matt Wilson (b); John Turner (d).* 8/93.

***** Of What**

Accurate AC 5022 *As above.* 12/95.

Entertaining sessions by a keen band, seemingly based around the Massachusetts conclave which Accurate has been documenting. Hagans will be the familiar name to most, and predictably enough he's the most impressive soloist, but Grismore and Scea, who share the writing credits, play with great enthusiasm and know their jazz. With no keyboards, and with the guitarist taking a linear approach, the music stays harmonically open and light, and what comes out is a mix of free bop, modal playing and the odd piece of almost Zappa-esque convolution. The first disc is a bit thin and self-conscious, but the second is altogether tougher, louder, harder and more inventive – without quite suggesting that the Group is ready for immortality yet.

Martin Groeneveld

VARIOUS (OFTEN HOME-MADE) INSTRUMENTS

German instrument-maker, touching on free improvisation principles.

****(*) Friends**

JKL 9401 *Groeneveld; Jim Fulkerson (tb); Gregg Moore (tb, tba, bjo); Hans Mekel (as, cl, chanter); Jan Hallema (b, perc).* 12/93.

This one might go down as an interesting failure. Groeneveld seems to be coming from a sound-sculpture perspective, with his instruments described as items such as Volkswagen-Beetle-harp, sea-machine, electric-wicker-basket, and so forth. Fulkerson, Moore and Mekel come and go across the seven tracks, while Hallema is a regular participant. The result is a potentially fascinating mix, since the horn players assuredly come from a free-improv background and use what they have to engage with the more abstracted sounds coming from Groeneveld. Problem is, too much of the music seems to get bedded down in slow-moving scratchings and scrapings which are seldom more than enervating, and the initial promise of the opening 'Mr Trombonus, I Presume?' is eventually dissipated.

Don Grolnick (1947–96)

PIANO, KEYBOARDS

Grolnick became one of the most creative figures on the American studio scene of the 1980s and '90s, working with many of his peers as an arranger-performer and blending interests and influences from rock, jazz and South American music. His early death was a sad end to a career which should have had much great music in its future.

***** Hearts And Numbers**

VeraBra 2016-2 *Grolnick; Michael Brecker (ts); Jeff Mironov, Hiram Bullock, Bob Mann (g); Will Lee, Marcus Miller, Tom Kennedy (b); Peter Erskine, Steve Jordan (d).* 86.

****** The Complete Blue Note Recordings**

Blue Note 57197-2 2CD *Grolnick; Randy Brecker (t); Barry Rogers, Steve Turre (tb); Michael Brecker, Joe Lovano (ts); Marty Ehrlich, Bob Mintzer (bcl); Dave Holland (b); Bill Stewart, Peter Erskine (d).* 92.

***** Medianoche**

Warners 946287-2 *Grolnick; Michael Brecker (ts); Dave Valentin (f); Mike Mainieri (vib); Andy Gonzalez (b); Don Alias, Steve Berrios, Milton Cardona (perc). n.d.*

Grolnick's standing as producer/arranger/Svengali to some of the leading lights of the studio circuit obscured his own music to some extent, but these very fine records ought to have a wider hearing. The VeraBra album (originally released on the tiny Hip Pocket label) is dominated by Brecker's characteristically muscular tenor solos, and Grolnick contents himself with small touches. The result is thoughtful, smart, flexible fusion. Grolnick's two Blue Note albums, *Weaver Of Dreams* and *Nighttown*, have been repackaged as a two-disc set. These are superb sessions, utilizing a starry personnel with exemplary finesse, sharing out duties with democratic insight but letting each man test the weight of the music. Grolnick might have been saving his best writing for the second date, since the compelling 'Heart Of Darkness', for one, cuts anything on his previous records, good though they are, and the brilliant update on 'What Is This Thing Called Love' is a recurring surprise. Brecker, Turre and Lovano play to their best, but it's Ehrlich's bass clarinet which is the key voice in the ensemble. Grolnick himself plays shrewd composer's piano as the icing on a considerable cake.

Medianoche reshapes some of Grolnick's material (there is a new version of 'Heart Of Darkness') in a more Latinized environment. The three percussionists and the light timbres of flute and vibes which predominate give the music a deceptively slight and sunny air. Actually, there is a good deal more going on than at first seems apparent, with Grolnick finding all sorts of harmonic and textural nuances in the situation. Brecker, almost the faithful disciple at this point, plays some gracefully measured solos. An intriguing continuation; but Grolnick's early death has left his discography sadly unfinished.

Richard Grossman (died 1992)

PIANO

Though he recorded comparatively little, Grossman was an influential figure in the recent West Coast tradition of free improvisation, and his reputation has increased since his death in 1992.

****** Trio In Real Time**

Nine Winds NWCD 0134 *Grossman; Ken Filiano (b); Alex Cline (d).* 10/89–1/90.

****** In The Air**

Nine Winds NWCD 0146 *As above, except add Vinny Golia (sno, ss, bcl), John Carter (cl).* 10–12/89.

Grossman's death silenced a valuable piano voice too soon. He managed the rare feat of distilling structure and freedom, lyricism and astringency, in a tough yet profoundly sensitive way. His playing from moment to moment evokes most of the post-Taylor masters without ever sounding much like any of them, and he secures a very fine interplay with Filiano (who suffers a bit here and there on these recordings, all done at various concerts) and the virtuosic Cline, who really does run the gamut from whispered skin-strokes to screaming clatter. The trio album revises piano-trio dimensions, taking in a pulsing, Evans-like quietness along with the more customary energetics, ideas appearing and evolving with formidable speed. Seventy minutes are sustained here without much trouble. The quintet date is even longer, and is cleverly programmed around one theme, an opening improvisation, a very long sequence of overlapping solos and a sardonic encore entitled 'Henny Youngman's Bird Imitation'. Golia and Carter are wonderfully loquacious in their playing, which acts as a neat contrast to the more rigorous piquancy of Grossman's manner: his solo passage on 'Everything Else Is Away' merits close attention.

*****(*) Even Your Ears**

Hatology 515 *Grossman; Ken Filiano (b); Alex Cline (d).* 1/90–3/92.

***** Remember**

Magnatone 512MGT *As above.* 12/89–3/92.

These survivals from various Californian concerts are a valuable addition to Grossman's meagre discography. The Hatology disc is the superior one. 'Fresh Vegetables' and 'The Switchbacks At Big Sur' are piano solos which underline his originality: a flinty, decisive touch and a reluctance to use much sustain spell out how prodigious his imagination was, each phrase a complete entity while still a building-block in a bigger conception. The four trio tracks are slightly less interesting since Cline is for once a bit too loud and fierce for the balance of the group to hold together. But these are still way, way ahead of most piano–bass–drums situations, as the supernal glow of 'Rubidoux Twilight' suggests.

Grossman's admirers will want to try and find the Magnatone disc, obscure though it is. There is one solo, two duets and one long trio piece. 'Afternoon Full Of Hummingbirds' is a typically fascinating solo, laden with Grossman's unique harmonic thinking, and the delicate piano–drums tracery of 'Green Of The East' matches it, but the long trio piece, 'Like Godzilla', is less interesting, and the recording quality is far from terrific.

Steve Grossman (born 1951)

SOPRANO AND TENOR SAXOPHONES

A New Yorker, Grossman's precocious start found him playing with Miles Davis as early as 1969. He worked with different leaders during the '70s and has operated mostly as a freelance since, often basing himself in Europe.

***** Hold The Line**

DIW 912 *Grossman; Hugh Lawson (p); Juni Booth (b); Masahiro Yoshida (d).* 4/84.

***** Way Out East Vol. 1**

Red 123176-2 *Grossman; Juni Booth (b); Joe Chambers (d).* 7/84.

***** Way Out East Vol. 2**

Red 123183-2 *As above.* 7/84.

***** Love Is The Thing**

Red 123189-2 *Grossman; Cedar Walton (p); David Williams (b); Billy Higgins (d).* 5/85.

****(*) Standards**

DIW 803 *Grossman; Fred Henke (p); Walter Booker (b); Masahiro Yoshida (d).* 11/85.

****(*) Bouncing With Mr A.T.**

Dreyfus 36579-2 *Grossman; Tyler Mitchell (b); Art Taylor (d).* 10/89.

***** Reflections**

Musidisc 500212 *Grossman; Alby Cullaz (b); Simon Goubert (d).* 9/90.

Grossman was working with Miles Davis when still only a teenager, and it's tempting to suggest that his career peaked too early. He has a prodigious command of the saxophone and a fearless energy, which puts him in the same class as Michael Brecker and Bill Evans. But Grossman's sometimes faceless facility can also make him appear as just another Coltrane/Rollins disciple. Most of these entries from the 1980s make no attempt to evade the appropriate comparisons, since they all stand as hired-gun blowing dates, Grossman peeling off suitably muscular solos against a conventional post-bop rhythm section. The two trio sessions for Red offer perhaps the most exciting music, since Grossman gets more space to work in, and *Vol. 1* provides some impressively characterized standards. *Love Is The Thing*, though, has the players setting themselves a few challenges by turning a ballad recital upside down in a couple of places with, for instance, an almost brutal 'I Didn't Know What Time It Was'. A later return to the trio format in *Reflections* is also a shade more interesting than the very plain *Standards*, while *Hold The Line* has an uninvolving rhythm section, though Grossman's own playing is sometimes quite ferocious. *Bouncing With Mr A.T.* could have been a great one: trouble is, the sound abominably mistreats both Mitchell and Taylor, the result of a club setting in Genoa. Grossman sounds terrific here, and his beautiful treatment of 'Soultrane' should be heard.

***** My Second Prime**

Red 123246-2 *Grossman; Fred Henke (p); Gilbert Rovere (b); Charles Bellonzi (d).* 12/90.

****(*) Live At Café Praga**

Timeless SJP 314 *As above.* 12/90.

My Second Prime and *Live At Café Praga* were recorded on an Italian sojourn. The Red album is another grandstanding festival set, with the time of year marked by Grossman's choice of 'The Christmas Song' as one of the tunes. His tone has a dusky, almost chargrilled feel to it, and there are some improvisations of expansive power, but the rhythm section merely mark time. The *Café Praga* set is marred by indifferent sound, Bellonzi's snare having a tinny quality and Grossman seemingly too far back, though he plays with his customary authority.

***** Do It**

Dreyfus 191032-2 *Grossman; Barry Harris (p); Reggie Johnson (b); Art Taylor (d).* 4/91.

*****(*) In New York**

Dreyfus 1910867-2 *Grossman; McCoy Tyner (p); Avery Sharpe (b); Art Taylor (d).* 9/91.

*****(*) A Small Hotel**

Dreyfus FDM 36561-2 *Grossman; Cedar Walton (p); David Williams (b); Billy Higgins (d).* 3/93.

*****(*) Time To Smile**

Dreyfus 36566-2 *Grossman; Tom Harrell (t, flhn); Willie Pickens (p); Cecil McBee (b); Elvin Jones (d).* 2/93.

Persistence is making Grossman into an impressive character. He still doesn't seem ambitious so far as record-making is concerned: *In New York* is live, the other three are both studio dates; but all four seem cursorily organized and find him reeling off standards and easily picked jazz themes, seemingly at a moment's notice. For consistency, he's hard to beat. But if the sheer strength of his playing usually transcends any banalities, he seldom goes for broke either. The difference with these records is in the calibre of his accompanists. *Do It* is all heartland bebop – 'Cherokee', 'Dance Of The Infidels', 'Oblivion', 'Chi Chi' – possibly at Harris's request. The pianist doesn't seem quite at his best, though, and it's Taylor's incisive work that stimulates Grossman into his best moments. Though at times it suffers from club-set longueurs, the session with McCoy Tyner is on a more intense level: when they dig into 'Impressions', it's as if Tyner has found the man to replace his old boss after all this time. Some great playing here. *A Small Hotel* is more mediated, civilized by Walton's urbane playing and the more rounded feel to the performances; but again Grossman plays with real purpose and feel. *Time To Smile* sets up a meeting with another great drummer and, with Harrell sitting in on some tracks and a smart set-list to work with, the music is mature and satisfying. If these are all, in the end, further chapters in a hard-bopper's blowing book and little more, it's still exhilarating jazz.

***** Quartet**

Dreyfus FDM 236602-2 *Grossman; Michel Petrucciani (p); Andy McKee (b); Joe Farnsworth (d). 1/98.*

One of Petrucciani's last dates, and he surely brings a note of distinction to the event. So much so, actually, that Grossman himself sounds oddly heavy and even fatigued here and there, his solos often leading down some strange byways. 'Body And Soul' is positively laboured. Petrucciani shines as always and, even though he often plays more circumspectly than he would in a solo or trio situation, his solos are worth paying attention to.

Marty Grosz (born 1930)

GUITAR, BANJO, VOCAL

Born in Berlin, Grosz began making a name for himself as a rhythm guitarist and sometime group-leader in Chicago in the 1950s, playing in an old-fashioned style formed out of a balance of the '20s and the '30s. In recent years he has become a great favourite on the club circuit, working with a variety of mainstreamers, singing, strumming and playing his favourite role, raconteur.

*****(*) Swing It!**

Jazzology JCD-180 *Grosz; Peter Ecklund (t); Dan Barrett (tb); Bobby Gordon (cl); Loren Schoenberg (ts); Keith Ingham (p); Murray Wall (b); Hal Smith (d). 6–7/88.*

***** Extra!**

Jazzology JCD-190 *Grosz; Peter Ecklund (c); Bobby Gordon (cl, v); Ken Peplowski (cl, as); Murray Wall, Greg Cohen (b). 8–9/89.*

****** Unsaturated Fats**

Stomp Off CD1214 *Grosz; Peter Ecklund (c); Dan Barrett (tb); Joe Muranyi (cl, ss); Keith Ingham (p); Greg Cohen (b); Arnie Kinsella (d). 1–2/90.*

***** Songs I Learned At My Mother's Knee And Other Low Joints**

Jazzology JCD-220 *Grosz; Randy Sandke (t); Peter Ecklund (c); Bob Pring, Joel Helleny (tb); Ken Peplowski (as, cl); Dick Meldonian (cl, ts); Keith Ingham (p); Greg Cohen (b); Chuck Riggs (d). 3–6/92.*

***** Live At The L.A. Classic**

Jazzology JCD-230 *Grosz; Peter Ecklund (c); Bobby Gordon (cl); Greg Cohen (b); Hal Smith (d). 6/92.*

***** Thanks**

J&M CD 502 *Grosz; Peter Ecklund (c); Dan Barrett (tb); Bobby Gordon (cl); Scott Robinson (ts, bs, bsx); Mark Shane, Keith Ingham (p); Murray Wall, Greg Cohen (b); Hal Smith (d). 4–5/93.*

*****(*) Keep A Song In Your Soul**

Jazzology JCD-250 *As above, except add Dan Levinson (as, C-mel), Joel Helleny (tb), Dan Block (cl, as), Chris Dawson (p), Arnie Kinsella (d); omit Barrett, Shane, Wall. 10/94.*

*****(*) Ring Dem Bells**

Nagel-Heyer 022 *Grosz; Jon-Erik Kellso (t); Scott Robinson (cl, ss, bs); Martin Litton (p); Greg Cohen (b); Chuck Riggs (d). 2/95.*

*****(*) Rhythm For Sale!**

Jazzology JCD-280 *Grosz; Peter Ecklund (t, c); Dan Block (cl, as); Bobby Gordon (cl); Scott Robinson (ts, bs); Jack Stuckey (cl, as, bs); Vince Giordano (bsx, b); Pierre Calligaris (p); Keith Ingham (cel); Greg Cohen, Murray Wall (b); Hal Smith, Arnie Kinsella (d). 5/93–1/96.*

***** Just For Fun!**

Nagel-Heyer 039 *Grosz; Alan Elsdon (t, v); John Barnes (cl, as, bs, v); Murray Wall (b). 4/96.*

Grosz has been industriously documenting hot and sweet tunes of pre-war vintage on the basis that they don't write 'em like that any more. He is a master jazz entertainer who takes everything – and nothing – seriously, so even the corniest relics in his set-list are usually funny and convincingly hot at the same time. His genuine affection for this kind of music takes it out of the museum bracket, and it is all performed with much aplomb. Grosz has assembled a favourite repertory of players, and some or all of them are guaranteed an appearance on all of these records. The hot, wistful Ecklund, the charming Gordon, the ineffable Barrett and the mysteriously versatile Robinson chime in with playing that has freshness and bloom. The above discs are variously credited to the Orphan Newsboys, The Collectors Item Cats and Destiny's Tots; but the best of them is probably *Unsaturated Fats*, by the Grosz–Ingham Paswonky Serenaders. This is dedicated entirely to Fats Waller tunes, all but one of them obscurities which Waller himself never recorded: Ingham's spry arrangements put new life into melodies unheard for decades, and there some real discoveries such as 'Dixie Cinderella' and 'Asbestos'.

Of the others, *Swing It!* is a shade hotter, and *Songs I Learned At My Mother's Knee* has the best title. The Jazzology live album might have been the most fun but the sound is less than ideal and Grosz has suppressed all his between-song patter (probably so that he can recycle it at future gigs). *Ring Dem Bells* is completely fired up from the opening 'Rose Of The Rio Grande'. The occasionally restrained Robinson really lets himself go on the likes of 'Old Man Blues', Kellso plays livelier horn than he ever has, and Grosz seems to relish every moment. *Keep A Song In Your Soul* and *Rhythm For Sale!* are the most recent studio sets and include everything from 'Satan Takes A Holiday' to 'Sentimental Gentleman From Georgia'. Since Grosz never changes his act much, one could argue that this is starting to seem like a lot of records in a similar guise; on the other hand, one could say the same about Coltrane.

Just For Fun! is a bit different, anyway. Marty's on stage with Elsdon and Barnes from the old country and favourite bass confederate Murray Wall. Some lovely stuff, though they play more familiar standards than usual, and docked a notch for letting both Elsdon and Barnes have a vocal each.

George Gruntz (born 1932)

PIANO, BANDLEADER

Gruntz studied in his native Basle and Zurich, and worked in European obscurity – though a spell with Phil Woods brought him wider exposure – until forming The Band, an orchestra which he co-led with fellow Swiss players. It became the Gruntz Concert Jazz Band in 1978, a large orchestra which is still active from time to time.

*****(*) The MPS Years**

MPS 533552-2 *Gruntz; Art Farmer, Benny Bailey, Dusko Goykovich, Franco Ambrosetti, Virgil Jones, Woody Shaw, Jon Faddis, Palle Mikkelborg, Earl Gardner, Americo Bellotto, Allan Botschinsky, Lew Soloff, Charles Sullivan, Tom Harrell (t, flhn); Jiggs Whigham, Albert Mangelsdorff, Erich Kleinschuster, Jimmy Knepper, Eje Thelin, Mike Zwerin, Ake Persson, Runo Ericksson, Peter Herbolzheimer, Slide Hampton (tb); Herb Geller, Leo Wright, Heinz Bigler, Dexter Gordon, Don Byas, Sahib Shihab, Phil Woods, Eddie Daniels, Flavio Ambrosetti, Joe Henderson, Alan Skidmore, Ferdinand Povel, Jerry Dodgion, Lew Tabackin, Bennie Wallace, Bob Malach, Seppo Paakkunainen, Ernst-Ludwig Petrowsky, Charlie Mariano (reeds); Howard Johnson (bs, bcl, tba); Jasper Van't Hof (ky); Lois Colin (hp); John Scofield (g); Niels-Henning Orsted Pedersen, Mike Richmond, Gordon Johnson, Isla Eckinger (b); Daniel Humair, Tony Inzalaco, Elvin Jones, Peter Erskine (d); Dom Um Romao (perc).* 9/71–4/80.

****(*) Theatre**

ECM 815678-2 *Gruntz; Marcus Belgrave, Tom Harrell, Palle Mikkelborg (t, flhn); Julian Priester (tb); Dave Bargeron (tb, euph); Dave Taylor (btb); Ernst-Ludwig Petrowsky, Charlie Mariano, Seppo Paakkunainen (reeds); Howard Johnson (bs, bcl, tba); Dino Saluzzi (band); Mark Egan (b); Bob Moses (d); Sheila Jordan (v).* 7/83.

Gruntz has been running his gigantic Concert Jazz Band since 1972. Formidably weighted with famous names in each of its editions, the group is a live phenomenon which perhaps hasn't translated quite so well to record, since none of their albums is well known – although the excellent MPS best-of, culled from several discs for that label, is a fine introduction. Gruntz's persona as writer/arranger is difficult to perceive, since he cheerfully plunders various aspects of big-band tradition for his charts, but he has an unusual way of bridging the kind of freedoms one associates with, say, the Globe Unity Orchestra and the grand language of Ellington and Kenton. Perhaps the CJB is most like a liberated successor to the Clarke–Boland Big Band.

The MPS disc is full of fine music, from the huge voicing of 'Lonely Woman' to a light, almost dancing treatment of Joe Henderson's 'Black Narcissus' that must have pleased its composer, who's also the main soloist. 'Destiny' and 'Morning Song Of A Spring Flower' include solos by the young John Scofield, but there are plenty of fine cameos sprinkled among the tunes and the record is consistently rewarding. The ECM album catches them in 1983, but the programme is a bit portentous – a long and rather worthy 'The Holy Grail Of Jazz And Joy' takes up the bulk of it – and the results are disappointing.

***** Blues 'N Dues Et Cetera**

Enja 6072-2 *Gruntz; Marvin Stamm, Bob Millikan, Randy Brecker, Michael Mossman, Jon Faddis, John D'Earth, Wallace Roney (t); Ray Anderson, Art Baron, Dave Taylor, Dave Bargeron (tb); John Clark, Jerry Peel (frhn); Chris Hunter, David Mann (as); Bob Mintzer, Bob Malach, Jerry Bergonzi, Alex Foster (ts); Roger Rosenberg (bs); John Scofield (g); Howard Johnson (tba); Mike Richmond (b); Adam Nussbaum (d); DJ A.D (turntables).* 91.

*****(*) Beyond Another Wall**

TCB 94102 *Gruntz; Lew Soloff, John D'Earth, Tim Hagans, Jack Walrarth (t); Ray Anderson, Art Baron, Dave Taylor (tb); Chris Hunter, Sal Giorganni, Bob Malach, Larry Schneider (reeds); Howard Johnson (bs, tba); Carl Weathersby (g); Mike Richmond (b); Danny Gottlieb (d); Billy Branch (v, hca).* 11/92.

***** Sins 'N Wins 'N Funs**

TCB 96602 *Full personnel unlisted, but similar to discs above, plus Tim Berne (as), Seamus Blake (ts), Django Bates (whistle).* 3/81–4/95.

Although more inclined towards modern big-band convention than the MPS music, these are still vivid examples of Gruntz's music-making. The Enja album is the result of a number of studio sessions in New York, with the usual starry cast (the trumpet section by themselves make up a formidable roll-call). 'Q-Base' and 'Rap For Nap', with daft vocals and uneventful scratching by turntable artist DJ A.D., are the kind of pieces which are going to make the record seem foolish a few years hence; but more encouraging are the sonorous scores, 'Forest Cathedral' and 'General Cluster'.

Beyond Another Wall was made on a ground-breaking (if not epoch-busting) tour of China. The concerts seem to have brought out the best in the band: the playing has terrific energy and élan, standouts including Ray Anderson's 'Literary Lizard', once a quartet piece but here brilliantly realized by the brass section, and Mike Richmond's 'Giuseppi', much more electric than it was on the Enja album. Bluesmen Billy Branch and Carl Weathersby are unlikely imports for the occasion, but they fit right in.

Sins 'N Wins 'N Funs collects tracks from some 15 years' worth of concerts, in New York, Rome, Israel, Tokyo and wherever else they've hung their collective hat. Although the collective personnel isn't listed, the soloists by themselves – from Eje Thelin and Sheila Jordan to Tim Berne and Seamus Blake – are testament to the kind of groups Gruntz has managed to put together down the years, the kind of wish-lists which even George Russell and Gil Evans couldn't have matched. As a record, it doesn't really hang together but, as a jumble of mightily entertaining bits and pieces, it's fine.

***** Mock-Lo-Motion**

TCB 95552 *Gruntz; Franco Ambrosetti (flhn); Mike Richmond (b); Adam Nussbaum (d).* 5/95.

Gruntz in much more modest surroundings. He takes only a deferential role as an instrumentalist on the orchestral records, and here he's a much more garrulous presence. The music has a splashy quality, not without charm, and when Ambrosetti sits in on three tunes the results are a melodious kind of post-bop, never as original as the band records but pleasing enough.

*****(*) Liebermann**

TCB 99452 *Gruntz; Marvin Stamm, Alexander Sipiagin, Scott Wendholt, Matthieu Michel (t, flhn); Luis Bonilla, Clark Gayton (tb); Chris Hunter (as, ss, f); Sal Giorgianni (as, ts, f); Larry Schneider (ss, ts, f); Donny McCaslin (ts, f); Steffen Schorn (bs, bsx, bcl); Mike Richmond (b); John Riley (d).* 11/98.

Here they go again, this time at the 1998 Berlin Jazz Festival. The dedicatee is Rolf Liebermann, composer and polymath, whose 1954 'Symphony For Jazz Ensemble' is the centrepiece of this set (and who died just as the record was being prepared for release). Besides this, there are three new pieces and a version of Wayne Shorter's 'Footprints'. The band are in great heart. Among the soloists, none surpasses Marvin Stamm, usually deemed a pro's pro among sessionmen but rarely acknowledged as an improviser. Blessed also by an excellent location recording, this is a fine place to make the group's acquaintance.

Gigi Gryce (1927–83)

ALTO SAXOPHONE, FLUTE

Worked with Tadd Dameron and Lionel Hampton in 1953, then with Oscar Pettiford, the Jazz Lab Quintet and his own small group; but it was his writing which established his reputation. Drifted from sight in the early '60s and didn't record again.

***** And The Jazz Lab Quintet**

Original Jazz Classics OJCCD 1774 *Gryce; Donald Byrd (t); Wade Legge (p); Wendell Marshall (b); Art Taylor (d).* 2–3/57.

***** Sayin' Somethin'**

Original Jazz Classics OJCCD 1851 *Gryce; Richard Williams (t); Richard Wyands (p); Reggie Workman (b); Mickey Roker (d).* 3/60.

***** The Hap'nin's**

Original Jazz Classics OJCCD 1868 *As above, except replace Workman with Julian Euell (b).* 5/60.

*****(*) The Rat Race Blues**

Original Jazz Classics OJCCD 081 *As above.* 6/60.

Joe Goldberg's perceptive liner-note for *The Hap'nin's* makes the perceptive point that, however good a player Gryce was, his real talent and contribution was as a leader, a figure who catalysed talent in others. He is certainly a victim of what might be called Rodin's Syndrome, an artist recognized for just one or two not necessarily representative works. Of the many pieces he wrote for a variety of ambitiously proportioned projects – not big in numbers, but in conception – the only ones which have really entered the jazz mainstream are 'Nica's Tempo' and, to a lesser extent, 'Speculation' and 'Minority'. The former was given a definitive statement in a group that also included Thelonious Monk and Art Blakey, which gave it something of a leg-up into the mainstream. In the year of Charlie Parker's death, the pretenders to the throne were thrown into unusually high profile. Gryce was never a virtuosic player, but these sessions suggest that he was more interesting than is often supposed, certainly not a Bird copyist. His tone was darker and with a broader vibrato, the phrasing less supple but with an emphatic, vocal quality that carries over into his flute playing. 'Laboratory' and 'workshop' have always been weasel terms, useful camouflage for the well-founded jazz tradition of rehearsing – or experimenting – at the public's expense. Gryce, though, was a genuine experimenter, even if a relatively modest one. He never stopped trying to find new colorations and new ways of voicing chords, and the set from 1957 is no exception. No great revelations, but Byrd is a responsive partner in the front line and the rhythm section is less hung-up on its own ideas, more aware, one suspects, of what Gryce himself is looking for.

Hard to put any real distance between the later dates. As before, the writing is often a good deal more interesting than the playing. Gryce is often overshadowed by Williams, and the rhythm section boil away as if on their own private date. We still find *The Rat Race Blues* the best set, track by track, from this rather crowded vintage, but there are good things, too, on *The Hap'nin's* (love that punctuation!), including an excellent 'Nica's Tempo', which was originally written for the Messengers, and two lovely standards in 'Lover Man' and 'Summertime'. The picture is now a good deal fuller than it was, though it's unlikely that any but convinced enthusiasts will find space for more than one of these.

Vince Guaraldi (1928–76)

PIANO

Born in San Francisco, and working there for most of his career, Guaraldi had an uneventful time with various leaders in the 1950s but found his niche as a pop-jazz composer in the '60s. His Charlie Brown music won him a big audience. A smooth jazzer, ahead of his time.

****(*) Vince Guaraldi Trio**

Original Jazz Classics OJC 149 *Guaraldi; Eddie Duran (g); Dean Reilly (b).* 4/56.

****(*) Jazz Impressions**

Original Jazz Classics OJC 287 *As above.* 4/56.

****(*) A Flower Is A Lovesome Thing**

Original Jazz Classics OJC 235 *As above.* 4/57.

**** Jazz Impressions Of Black Orpheus**

Original Jazz Classics OJC 437 *Guaraldi; Monty Budwig (b); Colin Bailey (d).* 62.

****(*) In Person**

Original Jazz Classics OJC 951 *Guaraldi; Eddie Duran (g); Fred Marshall (b); Colin Bailey (d); Benny Valarde (perc).* 5/63.

****(*) The Latin Side Of Vince Guaraldi**

Original Jazz Classics OJC 878 *Guaraldi; Eddie Duran (g); Fred Marshall (b); Jerry Granelli (d); Bill Fitch, Benny Valarde (perc); string quartet.* 64.

**** The Grace Cathedral Concert**

Fantasy 9678 *Guaraldi; Tom Beeson (b); Lee Charlton (d); St Paul's Church Of San Rafael Choir.* 5/65.

(*) From All Sides
Original Jazz Classics OJC 989 *Guaraldi; Bola Sete (g); Fred Marshall, Monte Budwig (b); Jerry Granelli, Nick Martinez (d).* 65.

*** **Greatest Hits**
Fantasy FCD-7706-2 *Guaraldi; various groups as above.*

*** **A Boy Named Charlie Brown**
Fantasy FCD-8430-2 *Guaraldi; Monty Budwig (b); Colin Bailey (d).*

(*) A Charlie Brown Christmas
Fantasy FCD-8431-2 *As above, except add* Fred Marshall *(b),* Jerry Granelli *(d).*

Guaraldi was a harmless pop-jazz pianist, not as profound as Dave Brubeck, not as swinging as Ramsey Lewis, but capable of fashioning catchy tunes from favourite licks; the most famous example remains his Grammy-winning 'Cast Your Fate To The Wind'. If this kind of music appeals, the best way to sample it is through the *Greatest Hits* collection, which gathers together his most characteristic moments. The earlier trio dates offer mild, unambitious variations on standards, with Eddie Duran figuring rather more strongly than Guaraldi himself. *In Person* is live, and at a slightly higher temperature than the studio dates, while *The Latin Side* is about as hot-blooded as a game of dominoes. *The Grace Cathedral Concert* finds him jazzing the liturgy to a less than holy-rolling effect.

As a composer, Guaraldi will always be best represented by his music for the Charlie Brown TV-cartoon series (it certainly made an impact on Wynton Marsalis, who has himself done what is effectively a tribute album). The first record in particular includes some charming miniatures, performed with surprising delicacy. The second is merely more of the same with less of the freshness, though it is stuck with Yuletide material. One might dismiss Guaraldi as the lightest of lightweights, but look how many records he has in print.

Johnny Guarnieri (1917–85)

PIANO

Took up jazz piano after hearing some of the stride players in New York, then worked with Benny Goodman and Artie Shaw at the end of the '30s. Various associations, including staff job at NBC, and solo recordings, during the '40s. Much studio work until a move to California in the '60s. Occasional later appearances and non-stop composing: he reckoned to have written 5,000 tunes in his lifetime.

*** **Johnny Guarnieri 1944–1946**
Classics 956 *Guarnieri; Billy Butterfield (t); Hank D'Amico (cl); Lester Young, Don Byas (ts); Dexter Hall (g); Billy Taylor, Slam Stewart, Leo Guarnieri, Bob Haggart (b); Cozy Cole, Sammy Weiss, J.C Heard (d).* 4/44–1/46.

*** **Johnny Guarnieri 1946–1947**
Classics 1063 *Guarnieri; Tony Mottola (g); Bob Haggart, Trigger Alpert, Leo Guarnieri (b); Cozy Cole, Morey Feld (d); Rosemary Calvin (v).* 5/46–47.

The kind of musician whose name is drifting into obscurity, not through wilful neglect but because he never had his name on any significant recordings. Guarnieri's consummate professionalism, unselfish attitude (he became a generous and much-liked teacher later in life) and robust energy made him a fixture in his milieu – New York club jazz of the '40s – although various big-band leaders tried to squirrel his talent away in the confines of their own orchestra. His own-name LP recordings are minor works which have never been reissued, and at present these Classics compilations of various and mostly minor-league dates are all that will be found under his stamp. His 1944 Savoy trio sessions form the bulk of Classics 956, and they show how much of his right hand came from Waller and Tatum: these are frothy, mischievous dates which also highlight Slam Stewart's hokum. But the first session has Lester Young hiding in the shadows, and a later one has some splendid work by Don Byas. Aside from a couple of vocals by Rosemary Calvin, Classics 1063 is all solo, trio or (with Mottola's guitar) quartet material. There's a novelty element to much of this music: the pianist isn't interested in touching great depths of feeling, preferring to make his point through a precise, almost dainty paraphrase of his melodic material. He sings on 'Bobo, The Bowery Barber', which makes one glad that he didn't do it too often. The transfers are no more than adequate and there's very little sparkle in the sound.

Lars Gulliksson (born 1967)

TENOR SAXOPHONE, FLUTE

Another young saxophonist from Sweden, performing post-bop of his own writing.

*** **Bumps Ahead**
Dragon DRCD 298 *Gulliksson; Magnus Broo (t); Torbjorn Gulz (p); Mattias Svensson (b); Leroy Lowe (d).* 8/96.

Gulliksson's rather wayward sound and off-centre phrasing are certainly nonconformist, and he sounds even more unusual next to the crisp modern swing of this rhythm section. Broo has his oblique moments, too, and they make an interesting front line. If there's a drawback, it's that it's not in the leader's nature to characterize the playing as strongly as he should, and the record seems to dawdle and lack conviction at key points. There are 13 originals by the leader, none of them exactly gripping.

Lars Gullin (1928–76)

BARITONE SAXOPHONE, PIANO

A major figure in Scandinavian modernism as player, leader and composer, Gullin's stature is eminent in European circles, but he is still little known elsewhere. His career tailed off somewhat in the '70s and his early death denied him the chance to enjoy the retrospective acclaim which has gone to several of his generation.

*** **Lars Gullin Vol. 1 1955–56**
Dragon DRCD 224 *Gullin; Chet Baker (t); George Olsson (tb); Arne Domnérus (cl, as); Rolf Berg, Bjarne Nerem (ts); Lennart Jansson (bs); Dick Twardzik, Gunnar Svensson (p); Georg Riedel,*

Jimmy Bond (b); Peter Littman, Bosse Stoor, Egil Johansen (d); Caterina Valente (v). 4/55–5/56.

****** Lars Gullin Vol. 2 1953**

Dragon DRCD 234 *Gullin; Weine Renliden, Conte Candoli (t); Frank Rosolino (tb); Lee Konitz (as); Zoot Sims (ts); Kettil Ohlsson (bs); Putte Lindblom, Bob Laine, Mats Olsson (p); Yngve Akerberg, Georg Riedel, Simon Brehm, Lars Petersson, Tauno Suojärvi, Don Bagley (b); Jack Noren, Bosse Stoor, Stan Levey (d); Rita Reys (v).* 3–12/53.

Gullin has been gone for over 20 years now, but he remains among the most creative of European voices. After working in big bands as an alto player, he took up the baritone at the age of 21, and his utterly distinctive sound – delicate, wistful, pensively controlled – is the linchpin of his music: when he wrote for six or eight or more instruments he made the band sound like a direct extension of that big, tender tone. He seems like neither a bopper nor a swing stylist. The first volume in Dragon's reissue programme includes a meeting with Baker's quartet, with a few precious glimpses of Twardzik, a very melancholy 'Lover Man' and Caterina Valente vocalizing on 'I'll Remember April'; there are also three charming octet scores. The second disc includes the superb tracks that were issued as a 10-inch album by Contemporary in the USA: Gullin sustains a steady, effortless flow of ideas on all his solos and plays alto on two tunes. The rest of the disc includes various studio sessions with other leaders, and three tracks with the visiting Americans, in which Gullin holds his own comfortably.

***** 1954/55 Vol. 3 Late Date**

Dragon DRCD 244 *Gullin; Leppe Sundevall (bt); Kurt Jarnberg (tb); Rolf Billberg (ts); Jutta Hipp, Bengt Hallberg, Claes-Goran Fagerstadt (p); Rolf Berg (g); Georg Riedel, Simon Brehm (b); William Schiopffe, Bosse Stoor (d); The Moretone Singers (v).* 9/54–6/55.

Lower marks only because the seven tracks with the cooing Moretone Singers may disenchant some supporters – even though Gullin's own playing remains impeccable (consult the fine improvisation on 'Lover Man' for one example). Four brief tracks with Hipp's trio are unremarkable, but two tracks by the Gullin sextet, 'Late Summer' and 'For F.J. Fans Only', are superb.

*****(*) Vol. 4 Stockholm Street**

Dragon DRCD 264 *Gullin; Bengt-Arne Wallin (t, flhn); Andreas Skjold, Eje Thelin (tb); Putte Wickman (cl); Rolf Billberg (as); Harry Backlund (ts); Lars Bagge (p); Sune Larsson (g); Lars Pettersson, Claes Lindroth, Erik Lundborg (b); Sture Kallin, Bosse Skoglund, Robert Edman (d).* 1/59–9/60.

The series picks up again with the contents of four EP sessions plus four other tracks from the same period. The brief playing-time afforded by the medium concentrates Gullin's writing, the harmonic weight offset by the plain rhythmic language. Arguably not his best work as a player – there is a bonus in two tracks from an abandoned session, including a longer treatment of 'Darn That Dream', which have extended but somewhat desultory solos by the leader – but some of these miniatures are hauntingly effective, especially 'Nightshade' and the bittersweet gem, 'The Yellow Leaves' Love To The Earth'.

*****(*) Portrait Of My Pals**

EMI (Swed) 7924292 *Gullin; Jan Allan, Torgny Nilsson (tb); Rolf Billberg (as); Harry Backlund (ts); Lars Sjøsten (p); Bjorn Alke, Kurt Lindgren (b); Bo Skoglund (d); strings.* 6/64.

*****(*) Aeros Aromatic Atomica Suite**

EMI (Swed) 4750752 *Gullin; Bertil Lövgren, Leif Hallden, Jan Allan, Maffy Falay (t); Håkan Nyqvist (t, frhn); Bertil Strandberg (tb); Sven Larsson (btb, tba); Arne Domnérus, Claes Rosendahl, Lennart Aberg, Erik Nilsson (woodwinds); Bengt Hallberg (p); Rune Gustafsson (g); Stefan Brolund, Georg Riedel (b); Egil Johansen (d).* 72–73.

***** Bluesport**

EMI (Swed) 1364612 *Gullin; Maffy Falay (t, flhn); Bertil Strandberg (tb); Lennart Aberg (ss); Lennart Jansson (as); Bernt Rosengren (ts); Gunnar Lindqvist (f); Lars Sjøsten (p); Amadeo Nicoletti (g); Jan Bergman, Bjorn Alke (b); Fredrik Norén, Rune Carlsson (d); Ahmadu Jarr, Okay Temiz (perc).* 9/74.

Though released only in Sweden, these reissues are essential parts of the Gullin canon. *Portrait Of My Pals* includes some of Gullin's most skilful writing, with strings appended to six tracks; the versions of 'Prima Vera' (alias 'Manchester Fog') and 'Decent Eyes' are among his best work, the timbres of the ensemble beautifully handled. Remastering hasn't helped the original sound, which was never very clear, and the presence of two basses in the rhythm section imparts a rather odd, off-centre feel to the rhythms. The CD includes three alternative takes and one newly issued tune.

Aeros Aromatica Atomica Suite was a project close to Gullin's heart, and this fine performance by a team of Swedish mainstays must be counted one of his strongest records. If one isn't always convinced that the composer truly has hold of the thematic thread running through the three parts, the textures and contrasts are still absorbing, and there is always the solo work by the horns (and the perennially undervalued Gustafsson). Excellent sound this time. *Bluesport*, though recorded later, has an inferior mix, and this time some of the music sounds only half finished. But the vibrant title-track alone is compellingly done and Gullin's own powers as an improviser, if less sharp than in his youth, remained a notable force. There is more Gullin waiting to be reissued: let's have it soon!

Peter Gullin (born 1959)

BARITONE AND TENOR SAXOPHONES

The son of Lars is no mean saxophonist himself, playing able post-bop horn in these contemporary settings.

***** Tenderness**

Dragon DRCD 222 *Gullin; Jacob Fischer (g); Ole Rasmussen (b).* 2/92.

***** Transformed Evergreen**

Dragon DRCD 266 *As above, except replace Fischer with Morten Kaargard (g).* 3/94.

*****(*) Untold Story**

Dragon DRCD 315 *As above.* 3/97.

Gullin himself likens the approach on these records to that of the Dutch national soccer team in the 1970s. They espoused 'total football', in which every player was expected to perform in every position – attack, defence, back, wide, forward – as circumstances dictated. Some may feel that the likelier analogy lies with the Swedish national side: correct, rather polite, almost apologetic in the tackle, not much aggression – though aggression wasn't in the nature of Peter Gullin's father, the legendary Lars, either. It's somewhat brave for a son to follow quite so closely in the parental footsteps, though a couple of Coltranes have tried it. Peter's baritone sound is fuller and throatier, though something of the difference must surely be explained by modern recording techniques. What the old man wouldn't have given for the bright top-notes and rich bottom-end Peter (whose birth was celebrated in 'Peter Of April') gets on *Tenderness* and its two sequels. The classical references pall after a while, but they are handled with some taste both on the first album and on the recent *Untold Story*, where Prokofiev and Rimsky-Korsakov are both name-checked on 'Incognito'. Gullin Jr has stuck with the same drummerless concept from the beginning. With a piece like 'Men Stig In' on the same record he shows that he has begun to write themes which sit comfortably with it. Kaargard (a Dane, like Rasmussen) is also a gifted writer, and his three pieces include the title-track. Gullin himself is only now beginning to develop convincingly in this direction. The three 'Fantasias' on the previous disc border on the pedestrian, while 'The Hollow Clown' (and we still think it ought to be 'crown') suggests he's been listening to Mingus. There isn't a note here that isn't played with taste and conviction, but it may yet be a touch too dry and accommodating for some tastes.

Gully Low Jazz Band

GROUP

A one-off band of young and old traditionalists led by David Ostwald.

***** Down To Earth**

GHB BCD-233 *Dan Barrett (c, v); Joel Helleny (tb); Clarence Hutchenrider (cl); David Ostwald (tba); Frank Vignola (g, bj); Fred Stoll (d).* 4/85.

David Ostwald's group plays happy, skilful, traditionally styled jazz. The band has a curious mix of players – Barrett is usually renowned as a trombonist, Vignola wasn't long out of college, and Hutchenrider, a veteran of the Casa Loma Orchestra, is in his eighties and played with Beiderbecke. But they work together with fine grace and aplomb. Barrett's cornet lead is as strong and flexible as it has to be, and Helleny and Hutchenrider play more idiosyncratic but no less authoritative solos. The others provide an unflappable, at times even velvety beat, a rarity in this kind of group. The live recording favours some instruments over others (Vignola's virtuoso banjo comes through loud and clear) but it falls easily on the ear.

Russell Gunn (born 1971)

TRUMPET, FLUGELHORN, KEYBOARDS, PERCUSSION

Raised in St Louis, Gunn was a trumpet-competition winner in 1989 and a rapper in high school. He played with the Oliver Lake group before going to New York and featuring in Buckshot LaFonque and the Lincoln Center Jazz Orchestra.

****(*) Gunn Fu**

High Note HCD 7003 *Gunn; Greg Tardy (ts, f); Sherman Irby (f); James Hurt (p); Stefon Harris (vib); Eric Revis (b); Ali Jackson (d).* 12/96.

****(*) Love Requiem**

High Note HCD 7020 *Gunn; Myron Walden (as); Mark Turner (ts); Gregory Tardy (f, ts); James Hurt, Shedrick Mitchell (p); Stefon Harris (vib); Eric Revis (b); Cindy Blackman (d).* 8/97.

***** Ethnomusicology Vol. 1**

Atlantic 7567-83165-2 *Gunn; Andre Heyward (tb); Bruce Williams (as, cl); Gregory Tardy (ts, f, bcl); James Hurt (ky); Chieli Minucci (g); Rodney Jordan (b); Woody Williams (d); Khalil Kwame Bell (perc); DJ Apollo (turntables).* 7/98.

Gunn looks destined to go places and will look back on his early discs as 'prentice work. His debut record for Muse, *Young Gunn*, was a cautious, promising start, but the record has already disappeared. *Gunn Fu* seems like much more Gunn's own situation, with a young band and arrangements that belong to his own experience, such as the surprising version of 'Invitation' sprung off Revis's compelling bass vamp. Gunn has a big, almost noisy style on up-tempo tunes and there's an interesting gambit in Harris, whose vibratoless vibes are an unpredictable colour. However, the record seems sabotaged by its sound-mix which muddles and takes the edge off all the sharpest aspects of Gunn's music.

Love Requiem is much more achieved, though it has a curiously inappropriate aura for a set coming out of the usually down-home High Note label. Structured as a nine-part sequence on the rise and fall of a relationship, it does feel ponderously solemn, underscored by episodes such as 'Torment' and 'Psychosis'. Walden, Tardy and Turner make the best of it, but this is another one that the leader may look back on with a little embarrassment when he's no longer young Gunn.

Signed to Warners, Gunn came up with the modish, wise-guy stew of this and that which is *Ethnomusicology Vol. 1*. He's a lively player, and this variation on the styles of Branford Marsalis's *Buckshot LaFonque* has much to entertain, the horns strutting over hip-hop beats, playing rasping R&B charts against turntable scratching, or putting a contrastingly sweet line over a stone-faced funk beat. But it doesn't feel like a record that's built to last.

John Gunther

ALTO, TENOR AND SOPRANO SAXOPHONES, BASS CLARINET

Contemporary free-bop multi-instrumentalist and composer.

***** Permission Granted**
CIMP 136 *Gunther; Leo Huppert (b); Jay Rosen (d).* 1/97.

Melodious free-bop of an unassuming disposition. This is the kind of record CIMP has set its stall up to accommodate: Gunther is a thinker's saxophonist, almost a Tristano-ite in his reluctance to plumb false registers or end up on a squeal and, with Huppert often hidden in the music, the propulsion all comes from Rosen, whose drum parts, for all their invention, often overwhelm everything else. The tunes are quirky things, but the record seems to get quieter and more remote as it goes on, with the rather lonesome 'Lines' and the bass–tenor duet, 'Us', particularly well focused. Gunther ends on a tenor solo of 'Stardust', played with the minimum of elaboration: an affecting coda.

*****(*) Healing Song**
CIMP 163 *As above, except add Ron Miles (t).* 9/97.

*****(*) Above Now Below**
CIMP 176 *As above, except add Rob Thomas (vn).* 6/98.

Better and better. Gunther's composing is the thread that makes these discs work, with 21 pieces across the two discs – and scarcely one of them less than memorable, as well as useful provocation for the improvisers. He's helped greatly by the arrival of the admirable Miles, who can get all over the horn (especially the lowest register, out of which he gets an unearthly growl) and, on the second disc, Thomas, who bides his time between barn-dance figures and a Stuff Smith-like swing. There's a lot of humour in this music (not a commodity this label trades in much) and pieces such as 'BooBoo Joins The Circus', 'The Collective' or several of the episodes in the three 'suites' which fill the second disc should provoke a grin. He's in hock to Ornette Coleman some of the time – 'Sound Byte' is pure Coleman, and 'Colemanation' makes a homage out of it – but there's nothing wrong with that. Very engaging music altogether.

Gush

GROUP

Swedish improvisers at work in a group context, from which the peripatetic Gustafsson has since moved on.

*****(*) ... From Sounds To Things**
Dragon DRCD 204 *Mats Gustafsson (sax); Sten Sandell (p, ky, v); Raymond Strid (d, perc).* 5 & 10/90.

*****(*) Gushwachs**
Bead 002 *As above, except add Philip Wachsmann (vn, vla, elec).* 5/94.

Presumably not a coincidence that this trio should bear a name alphabetically very close to saxophonist Mats Gustafsson's. Given that this is very much a collaborative trio, it seems only proper to list it separately. Much of the impetus comes from Strid's big-hearted approach to the kit and associated percussion, a drummer with the rare capacity to suggest a pulse without laying down the rhythmic law. Sandell is a suprisingly fleeting and fugitive figure in this context, often seeming to come in at the last moment to smooth the music into a more finished shape. He is more prominent (or perhaps easier to identify) on the first record. On *Gushwachs*, he blends into the electronic soundscape established by Wachsmann. The addition of the violinist brings an extra dimension to the music. Interesting to compare it with the less successful addition of Marilyn Crispell to the Barry Guy/Gustafsson/Strid trio which has been working concurrently. Whereas Crispell brought an over-the-top expressionism to what was already a very tight-knit group, Wachsmann alters the emphasis dramatically and creates a dark *mise-en-abîme* effect, like a multiple reflection in a hall of cracked mirrors. Two very strong records from a highly intelligent and likeable group, and a good introduction to Gustafsson, of whom more in a moment ...

Mats Gustafsson (born 1965)

BARITONE, TENOR, SOPRANO, AND SOPRANINO SAXOPHONE, FLUTEOPHONE, OTHER INSTRUMENTS

A Swedish improviser, playing in comparative obscurity at the beginning of the '90s, but latterly becoming more familiar through work with the group Gush, Barry Guy and Ken Vandermark.

***** Nothing To Read**
Blue Tower Records BTCD 03 *Gustafsson; Paul Lovens (d, perc, saw).* 3/90.

****** Mouth Eating Trees And Related Activities**
Okkadisk OD 12010 *As above, except add Barry Guy (b).* 12/92.

*****(*) Parrot Fish Eye**
Okkadisk OD 12006 *Gustafsson; Gene Coleman (bcl); Jim O'Rourke (g, acc, perc); Michael Zerang (perc).* 10/94.

*****(*) Impropositions**
Phono Suecia PSCD 99 *Gustafsson (sax solo).* 6/96.

*****(*) Frogging**
Maya 9702 *Gustafsson; Barry Guy (b).* 6/97.

Gustafsson has the capacity to become one of the giants of European improvisation. Blessed with a seemingly effortless technique, a wittily deconstructive approach to his instrument(s), and a generous intelligence, he never produces work that is less than thoughtful or other than exuberant. The duos with Lovens are not very well recorded but there is some terrific playing from both men, and the CD case is a first example of Gustafsson's interest in design; the session was recorded at the Blatornet antiquarian bookshop in Stockholm's Rorstrandsgatan, but, apart from five pictures of the setting, there is not a single word to read, just thick, blank card.

Impropositions is just the opposite. Released on the (mainly) classical label, Phono Suecia, this enhanced CD, suitable for Mac or PC, also has a beautifully designed book, containing notes on each of 13 solo improvisations and a collection of elegant abstract paintings. The emphasis as ever is on baritone. Gustafsson's lineage is now clear, though Serge Chaloff seems to have been a greater influence than the young Swede's compatriot, Lars Gullin. On 'Just A Slice Of Acoustic Car', the horn is modified with a beer-can inside the bell. 'Out Of IF' is dedicated to Lovens and has an edgy, percussive attack, flurries of notes and pungent, stabbing phrases. 'Long Titles – NO WAY!' sees him shift to tenor, changing the sound by pressing the bell against his knee. One of the most interesting pieces, particularly given what Gustafsson and Barry Guy have discussed regarding the place that movement has in their collaborations, is 'Bevllohallat Hhu/o', which introduces the fluteophone as well as baritone, intended to accompany an improvised dance by choreographer Lotta Melin. The fluteophone is basically a normal flute played through a saxophone mouthpiece and part-muted by a clarinet stand wedged in the other end. It's not an immediately identifiable sound, except in so far as it has become an integral part of Gustafsson's work.

His duo with Guy is celebrated on *Frogging*. Like Gustafsson, the bassist has a great interest in the visual arts, using a drawing by a Scottish abstract expressionist and mythological painter on the cover; Guy is also very interested in the relationship between player and instrument, which seems to be a major concern of Gustafsson's as well. The title of the CD and of individual tracks makes reference to a metaphor on the pair's trio record with drummer Raymond Strid, *You Forget To Answer*, on the same label. The long 'Hyla gratiosa' is memorable for Guy's exquisitely balanced long-form line and his delicacy of touch, even when playing with some force. There is nothing remotely aggressive, though, about either man.

Mouth Eating Trees rather squares the circle, a trio performance of great concentration and one which, despite the extraordinary title, gives away little more about itself, creating a sequence of five enigmatic numbered canvases, each with a sweep out of all proportion to actual size. Numbers one and five are tiny and yet seem to contain an extraordinary amount of musical information. The very long part four, on the other hand, makes a whole out of tiny elements, almost like a mosaic, but with much less sense of developing, unfolding structure. *Parrot Fish Eye*, recorded on an early visit to Chicago, is perhaps the most fun of all his records and might be the easiest place to start with Gustafsson. There's an almost zoological feel to eight duos with percussionist Zerang, whistles, chitterings and unidentified sounds creating an aura of animal-house nuttiness. Five trios with Coleman and O'Rourke are more stealthy in the way they unfold and, if Gustafsson is comparatively reserved here, he and Coleman make an interesting 'front line', if that term's appropriate.

Barry Guy (born 1947)

BASS

The London-born bassist has kept up a parallel career in classical and new-music work and in improvisation. He was a pioneer figure in SME, Amalgam and Iskra 1903, and is the motivating force behind the London Jazz Composers Orchestra.

***(*) Arcus

Maya MCD 9101 *Guy; Barre Phillips (b).* 90.

Guy's activities in recent years have been largely focused on composition for the London Jazz Composers Orchestra, which is listed separately. He has, however, kept up his improvisational work, and the items here are well worth pursuing, even if they prove difficult to track down. Though recorded as if on the other side of the veil of Maya, *Arcus* is improvised music of the very highest order. Guy's productive trade-off of freedom against more formal structures is constantly in evidence, and there is enough music of straightforward, digestible beauty to sustain listeners who might otherwise find an hour and a quarter of contrabass duos more than a little taxing. It ends, appropriately enough, on the quiet majesty of 'New Earth', where Phillips's purged simplicity and dancer's grace sound out ahead of Guy's more formal and sculpted delivery. Twice wonderful, but may call for patience.

***(*) Fizzles

Maya MCD 9301 Guy (*b* solo) 9/91.

Fizzles is not so immediately appealing, but it has a quiet charm that reveals itself over repeated listenings and it is certainly better-recorded than its predecessor. Guy uses a conventional contrabass on only three tracks, switching for the others to a small chamber bass. In his liner-note, John Corbett relates this to Guy's stated desire to make his instrument as small as possible while he is improvising. One can hear this effect on 'Five Fizzles', a sequence dedicated to Samuel Beckett in which, using both his basses, Guy concentrates on the tiniest details with an almost hallucinatory intensity, much as Beckett would concentrate on a single word, sound or gesture. Pitched higher than a conventional bass, the concert instrument has a cello-like warmth of tone and speed of response that is very attractive, and the drone-like effects in 'Afar' and 'Tout Rouge' are reminiscent of devices in the work of cult Italian composer, Giacinto Scelsi. Significantly or not, the most compelling track is for double bass. Dedicated to a Native-American friend, 'She Took The Sacred Rattle And Used It' is one of Guy's finest moments as an instrumentalist.

***(*) Study – Witch Gong Game 11/10

Maya MCD 9402 *Guy; John Korsrud (t); Ralph Eppel (tb); Saul Berson (as); Coat Cooke (ts, bs, f); Graham Ord (ts, ss, picc); Bruce Freedman (ss); Paul Plimley (p); Ron Samworth (g); Peggy Lee (clo); Paul Blaney, Clyde Read (b); Dylan Van der Schyff (d); Kate Hammett-Vaughan (v).* 2/94.

This is a project that takes Guy back closer to the kind of formal-free experiment promulgated and sustained with the London Jazz Composers Orchestra. Recorded in Canada, *Witch Gong Game 11/10* is a musical realization of certain signs and symbols in paintings by Alan Davie, another of the visual artists to have provided Guy with a rich vein of inspiration in recent years. Guy reads Davie's work as a floating, by no means determinant, system of archetypes which can be interpreted so as to create dense polyphonies, lighter, more textural passages, or else entirely free improvisational areas. The music is as vividly present as Davie's curiously totemic images, and the young orchestra respond to it very openly and sympathetically.

**** You Forget To Answer

Maya MCD 9601 *Guy; Mats Gustafsson (ss, ts, bs, fluteophone); Raymond Strid (d, perc).* 11/94, 7/95.

***(*) gryffgryffgryffs

Music & Arts CD 1003 *As above, except add Marilyn Crispell (p).* 1/96.

A tremendous trio which helped to bring the brilliant young Swedish saxophonist to attention outside his native country. Gustafsson, who has also established a strong recording career of his own, is the obvious star, using his whole range of saxophones, adding devices like a crumpled beer-can in the bell of his baritone, and pioneering the fluteophone, which is basically a flute with a saxophone mouthpiece stuck on one end, and a clarinet stand jammed in the other (the latter a device he discovered by accident, as you may have guessed). His sound is very strong and, in partnership with the barrel-chested Strid, who always plays as if he's having a whale of a time, he generates considerable excitement. It takes a couple of hearings before one realizes that Guy is the fulcrum and the driving force of this group, creating a complex fabric of sound and pushing the two younger men out into areas that don't so much suggest total abstraction as a kind of mathematical abstractness, a rapid computation of possibilities that is, as mathematics always is, deeply exciting. 'Schrödinger's Cat' (named after a philosophical puzzle which seems to intrigue improvising musicians) is the most vibrant track: playful, wry and not taking itself too seriously. All but three short tracks on *You Forget To Answer* were recorded by the BBC in London for the now defunct *Impressions* programme. There are slight problems here and there with the balance of Strid's drums, but the sound-quality is excellent and every tiny buzz and resonance on both bass and saxophone can be heard clearly.

The Swedish Broadcasting Corporation take a more conventional approach on *gryffgryffgryffs*, a broader and less detailed group sound. Admittedly, the inclusion of Crispell makes a significant difference to the sheer density of the group but, even so, this is a blunter, denser product. The key sequence consists of three tracks, 'Org', 'Ghast', 'Orghast', which seem to explore a carefully delimited range of ideas, except that Crispell is never content to remain within narrow harmonic or rhythmic bounds. It works, despite her overblown expressionism.

Bobby Guyer (died 1988)

TRUMPET, VOCAL

An experienced lead man in several major big bands, Guyer was born in Richmond, Indiana. As the big bands declined, he worked in clubs and casinos in northern Kentucky.

*** Bobby Guyer And Friends

Jazzology JCD-213 *Guyer; Bill Gemmer (tb); Paul Thatcher (cl); Ted Des Plantes (p); Tom Cahall (b); Dee Felice (d).* 85.

An affectionate lightning-sketch of a good journeyman trumpeter who never found any kind of real acclaim. The gentle Guyer played lead trumpet with Goodman, Herman and the Dorseys without quite making a particular name for himself. This stray session as a leader comes from late in his life and was obviously a happy and swinging affair, even if Bobby leaves much of the solo work to Thatcher, Des Plantes and the excellent Gemmer. His Beriganesque lead horn still sounds strong and clear, and the music is a pleasing souvenir of what is a forgotten jazz community based around Cincinnati and Kentucky.

Bobby Hackett (1915–76)

CORNET

One of the best-liked men in the business, Hackett was born in Providence, Rhode Island, and began as a guitarist on the local scene. Influenced by Bix Beiderbecke and Louis Armstrong, he eventually formed his own group in 1938 and played at Benny Goodman's celebrated Carnegie Hall concert. He worked with Glenn Miller in addition and then disappeared into the studio for almost a decade, making occasional appearances thereafter and almost up to his death.

*** Bobby Hackett And His Orchestra, 1938–1940

Classics 890 *Hackett; Sterling Bose, Harry Genders, Joe Lucas, Bernie Mattison, Jack Thompson, Stan Wilson (t); Jerry Borshard, George Brunies, Cappy Crouse, John Grassi, George Troup (tb); Brad Gowans (vtb, as); Bob Riedel (cl); Pee Wee Russell (cl, ts); Jerry Caplan, Louis Colombo (as); Bernie Billings, George Dessinger, Hank Kusen, Hammond Rusen (ts); Jim Beitus, Ernie Caceres (bs); Dave Bowman, Frankie Carle (p); Eddie Condon, Bob Julian, Bob Knight (g); Sid Jacobs, Eddie McKinney, Clyde Newcombe (b); Johnny Blowers, Don Carter, Andy Picard (d); Lola Bard, Linda Keene, Claire Martin, The Tempo Twisters (v).* 2/38–2/40.

Louis Armstrong liked to keep the opposition under the closest observation and so, for much of the 1940s, Bobby Hackett played second trumpet under the wing of the man who had influenced his style almost as much as Bix. Hackett was probably too modest for leadership, but in 1938 he made the first recordings under his own name for the Vocalion label, with whom he stayed for the next two years, typically when there were more lucrative possibilities elsewhere.

Hackett had worked in a trio with Pee Wee Russell in the early days and, though temperamentally they were very different indeed, to put it mildly, the clarinettist and guitarist Eddie Condon were first-call recruitments to the Hackett orchestra which recorded four sides in February 1938. Of these the best is the pairing of 'At The Jazz Band Ball' and 'If Dreams Come true', the latter a vehicle for vocalist Lola Bard. A different band but the same formula for the November session that same year, with 'Poor Butterfly' the best showing for Hackett's sweetly melancholy cornet.

Thereafter he tended to use slightly larger bands with augmented saxophones. The sound is closer to the easy swing of the Miller Orchestra he would shortly join, and the romantic tension seems to have deserted the leader for a time. Here and there, there are flashes of brilliance, as on 'Bugle Call Rag' and 'I Surrender, Dear' from July 1939, the latter with a vocal by an earlier-generation Claire Martin, but the latter half of the disc is disappointing and a little flat.

*** 1943 World Broadcasting Jam Session

Jazzology JCD 111 *Hackett; Ray Conniff (tb); John Pepper (cl); Nick Caizza (ts); Frank Signorelli (p); Eddie Condon (g); Bob Casey (b); Maurice Purtill (d).* 12/43.

The title is more or less self-explanatory, a recording set up by Milt Gabler for the WBS Inc. Though not a vintage band, the playing is of a high order, even if some may find the false starts and incompletes irritating. Coniff is a robust presence and some of his fills and countermelodies are worth studying, but it's very much Bobby's gig and, while he doesn't grandstand or posture, he makes the most of the spotlight.

***** Dr Jazz: Volume 2 – 1951–1952**
Storyville STCD 6042 *Hackett; Vic Dickenson (tb); Gene Sedric (cl); Teddy Roy (p); John Giuffrida, Irv Manning (b); Buzzy Drootin, Morey Feld, Kenny John (d).* 2/52.

*****(*) Off Minor**
Viper's Nest VN 162 *Hackett; Dick Oakley (t); Jack Teagarden (tb); Ernie Caceres (cl, bs); Tom Gwaltney (cl, vib); Dick Cary (p, ahn); Don Ewell (p); Stan Puls (b); John Dengler (bb); Buzzy Drootin, Ronnie Greb (d).* 7/57, 7/58.

The Dr Jazz sessions were originally broadcast from Lou Terassi's on West 47th Street as part of a WMGM series. Again, it's very much Hackett's gig, though Dickenson is also a strong presence, underlining how much Bobby liked the cornet and trombone to interweave at the front, using the reeds for depth of focus and sometimes merely as wallpaper.

The best was still to come, and with a still more substantial partner. His association in the '50s with Jack Teagarden produced some of the best jazz of the post-war years, with Hackett's supremely elegant legato and deceptive force perfectly matched by the man who virtually invented modern jazz trombone. The Viper's Nest disc brings together two live concerts exactly a year apart. The second is by Teagarden's sextet, with Hackett as the main soloist. The earlier set includes some surprising material. Alongside the more predictable 'Fidgety Feet' and 'Royal Garden Blues', Hackett approaches Monk's 'Off Minor' with understanding and control and he makes a profound contribution to it.

*****(*) Bobby Hackett Sextet & Quintet**
Storyville STCD 8230 *Hackett; Vic Dickenson, Urbie Green (tb); Bob Wilber (cl); Dave McKenna, John Ulrich (p); Franklin Skeets, Nabil Totah (b); Morey Feld, John Mead (d).* 1/62, 1 & 2/70.

The first six tracks on this fine CD were originally made for a film by the Goodyear Rubber Company. Along with a further half-dozen they were released on a Storyville LP, now augmented with sessions from 1970 with Dickenson back on board as trombonist. Green is a fine player, but it is clear from the very simple themes chosen for the programme (perhaps sop to the sponsors) that Hackett is playing more notes and relying less on Green for elaborated material than he would on the more formidable Dickenson. Vic is astounding on 'Wolverine Blues', which is very much pitched at his range, and then Bobby comes in with strength and delicacy and makes a small masterpiece of 'Satin Doll'. Why these tracks, along with 'I Can't Get Started' and 'Original Dixieland One-Step' weren't released at the time is something of a mystery. To be sure, they aren't flawless technically, but musically they seem well up to scratch. Good to hear big Dave McKenna making an early appearance on the 1962 session and already playing with his trademark two-handed style. Bob Wilber is also instantly recognizable, with that faintly hollow-toned, very reedy sound coming through on 'Sentimental Blues' and 'When The Saints', where he sounds like one of the old-time New Orleans guys.

***** Milton Jazz Concert 1963**
IAJRC 1004 *Hackett; Vic Dickenson (tb); Edmond Hall (cl); Evans Schwartz (p); Champlin Jones (b); Mickey Sheen (d).* 4/63.

The Milton Concert was released by the International Association of Jazz Record Collectors, which has done a great service to Hackett fans and to jazz by making this Massachusetts gig available. The tape-quality isn't tip-top and there are moments when Hall drifts way out of picture but, given the circumstances, the record is very good indeed. Hackett and Dickenson play out of their respective skins, and the rhythm section, which we failed to note before, is in splendid supportive form.

***** Melody Is A Must: Live At The Roosevelt Grill**
Phontastic PHONT 7571 *Hackett; Vic Dickenson (tb); Dave McKenna (p); Jack Lesberg (b); Cliff Leeman (d).* 3 & 4/69.

This actually pre-dates the later material on *Sextet & Quintet*, but it feels very much of the same vintage. McKenna is still in the band and the association with Dickenson seems tighter than ever. *Melody Is A Must* is a perfect example of Hackett's grace-without-pressure. There are no steam-valve emotional tantrums; nor is there casual verbosity. According to Whitney Balliett, Duke Ellington once spoke, apparently in approval, of Dickenson's 'three tones'. Like the trombonist, Hackett kept the music simple and direct, remarkably uncluttered by ego or undue embellishment. There is still not enough of him around on CD and we'd still like to hear again some of the beautiful sessions with strings which Hackett recorded in the 1950s and '60s.

Charlie Haden (born 1937)

DOUBLE BASS

Born in Shenandoah, Haden was a child performer who began working in Los Angeles circles in 1957. Joined Paul Bley and then Ornette Coleman in 1958. In the '60s, was associated with Keith Jarrett and his own Liberation Music Orchestra. Since 1980 he has been a free-jazz eminence who has worked mainly in post-bop, particularly with his own Quartet West. His daughters perform rock music.

*****(*) Liberation Music Orchestra**
Impulse! 051188-2 *Haden; Don Cherry (c, f); Michael Mantler (t); Roswell Rudd (tb); Bob Northern (frhn, perc); Howard Johnson (tba); Perry Robinson (cl); Gato Barbieri (ts, cl); Dewey Redman (as, ts); Sam Brown (g, thumb p); Carla Bley (p, perc); Andrew Cyrille, Paul Motian (d, perc).* 69.

The man from Shenandoah, Indiana, helped redefine modern jazz with Ornette Coleman's quartet, and gave a new impetus to jazz bass without ever once pretending that he was playing a horn. Haden is the ultimate timekeeper, bending and stretching the pulse like a true relativist, but never once forgetting his duties. This, coupled with a heartbeat tone, has placed him at the centre of literally hundreds of important sessions.

Ten years after making *The Shape Of Jazz To Come*, his best performance with Coleman, Haden recorded under the collectivist banner of the Liberation Music Orchestra a suite of revolutionary songs from the Spanish Civil War (arranged by Carla Bley),

Ornette's 'War Orphans' and Haden's own 'Song For Che'. Everything else on the record is transitional, gateposts and entryways. Like the almost contemporary Jazz Composers Orchestra (of which most of these players were members), the LMO was a blend of collectivism and radical individualism. Ensemble was everything – but solos were everything, too. On the long suite of anarchist songs begun by 'El Quinto Regimiento', Brown, Cherry and Haden himself are featured, followed by Rudd in the middle section and the almost caustically toned Barbieri in the conclusion, 'Viva La Quince Brigada'. The bassist dominates the brooding 'Song For Che', with Cherry and Redman in support.

Recording quality has been improved immeasurably, and the ensembles now sound open-grained and present, not lost in a backwash of overtones. The orchestra, or a descendant of it, was to return in the early 1980s with *The Ballad Of The Fallen* and *Dream Keeper*. They are certainly more polished, but this has the ring of truth.

***(*) The Golden Number

A & M 390825-2 *Haden; Don Cherry (pkt-t, f); Ornette Coleman (t); Archie Shepp (ts); Hampton Hawes (p).* 6–12/76.

*** Closeness

A & M 397000-2 *Haden; Ornette Coleman (as); Keith Jarrett (p); Alice Coltrane (hp); Paul Motian (d).* 76.

*** As Long As There's Music

Verve 513534-2 *Haden; Hampton Hawes (p).* 1–8/76.

Perhaps only Eddie Gomez, Gary Peacock and George Mraz, all of whom draw something from Haden's example, sound as convincing in duo performance. These are all head-to-head pairings with musicians who have been close to the bassist in one form or another. Inevitably, Coleman is the most powerful single presence, though interestingly he sticks to trumpet on 'The Golden Number', giving the piece a stark, unembellished quality which Haden makes no attempt to soften or mitigate.

The piece with Cherry, 'Out Of Focus', is double-tracked and is more richly textured for that reason. Haden immediately adjusts his focal length, playing small-scale, detailed figures against long drones. Something similar happens in his duet with Alice Coltrane, where he is content to cede the foreground to someone else. With Shepp he is required to be a good deal more forceful, setting up the sort of rising, chromatic figures the saxophonist loves to play, and then weaving free passages with ironic bebop flourishes and delicate upper-register trills. Jarrett is a challenging partner, but one already feels that the relationship is competitive rather than collaborative, and when the Jarrett material is set against the session with Hawes the difference is almost flagrantly evident. In the last months of his life, the pianist was moving back towards a more radical conception, having exhausted his interest in fusion. The partnership on Ornette's 'Turnaround' is a high point from this period in Haden's career, and there is a further version on *As Long As There's Music*. The title-track of the last record includes one of the best solos of Haden's recorded career: everything one needs to know about him is there in miniature: hand-speed, strength, delicacy and an innate musicality.

**(*) Duo

Dreyfus Jazz Line 365052 *Haden; Christian Escoudé (g).* 9/78.

This would be entirely forgettable if it didn't afford advance notice of Haden's gentler side. Though he could be pretty combustible in other contexts, there was always a romantic core to his playing, a fondness for dipping, minor-key themes and meltingly ambiguous cadences. The material is unimaginative, including a drab version of 'Nuages', and only some clever lyrical interplay spares it the 'Reject' button.

*** Magico

ECM 823474-2 *Haden; Jan Garbarek (ts, ss); Egberto Gismonti (g, p).* 6/79.

***(*) Folk Songs

ECM 827705-2 *As above.* 11/79.

This trio was presumably a going concern for a time. One of the authors was present at some of the sessions for *Folk Songs* and what was obvious there was that, though Garbarek tends to dominate the sound on almost every record he is involved with, it was Haden who called the shots musically. He sounds more sombre than usual, perhaps in reaction to Gismonti and the saxophonist swooping like gulls overhead. *Folk Songs* endures, retaining an uncomplicated charm that wasn't to surface again until Haden's Quartet West records.

***(*) The Ballad Of The Fallen

ECM 811546-2 *Haden; Don Cherry (pkt-t); Michael Mantler (t); Gary Valente (tb); Sharon Freeman (frhn); Jack Jeffers (tba); Jim Pepper (ts, ss, f); Dewey Redman (ts); Steve Slagle (as, ss, cl, f); Mick Goodrick (g); Carla Bley (p, glock); Paul Motian (d).* 11/82.

There were seismic shifts in both music and politics between 1969 and 1982, an entire decade of retrenchment and renewed attachment to order. The reconvened Liberation Music Orchestra was never going to sound as it had. What's immediately clear from this is that the LMO was in essence a small group, Redman, Bley, Haden and Motian, augmented *ad hoc* by low brass, additional horns and percussion. Almost all the energy comes from that axis and, if this time around the solo spots are less vibrant, even inflammatory, the big difference is that the arrangements are structural rather than decorative.

As before, and as again on *Dream Keeper* in 1990, the arrangements are by Bley. Most of the tracks are extremely short, building towards 'Too Late' (a superb bass–piano duet), 'La Pasionaria' and 'La Santa Espina'. The climax is as fiery as it has been long in coming.

***(*) Quartet West

Verve 831673-2 *Haden; Ernie Watts (as, ts, ss); Alan Broadbent (p); Billy Higgins (d).* 12/86.

***(*) Charlie Haden's Private Collection: Volume 1

Naim CD 005 *As above.* 8/87.

The Liberation Music Orchestra was an ambitious *ad hoc* venture. Haden's diary had long been packed with dates for other leaders. The one thing seemingly not catered for was a regular, working small group. That changed with the formation of Quartet West, a lyrical – sometimes almost sentimentally so – ensemble featuring two unsung heroes of the mainstream and, with the recruitment of Larance Marable later, a third; one must assume that Billy Higgins's credentials are unimpeachable

The first of the Quartet West discs is still the best. Haden wanted to recapture something of the musical atmosphere he had soaked up in childhood, when he had starred in a family radio show. The later *Haunted Heart* was a rather mannered exercise in nostalgia. The 1986 record is in the style of the '40s, beautifully and idiomatically played. Watts and Broadbent are as aware of contemporary harmonics as one would expect, but they aren't prepared to dismiss an older language either. Haden himself straddles the broad highway that runs from Jimmy Blanton to Jimmy Garrison, and some of the phrase shapes irresistibly recall Wilbur Ware. Even allowing for the crystalline quality of the record, who could with confidence have dated these performances of 'Body And Soul' or 'My Foolish Heart'? 'Taney County' is a solo feature, an evocation of the days when he played and sang on the family show; the playing is firm, sure and very expressive.

The *Private Collection* disc, first of a pair, celebrates the bassist's fiftieth birthday. Not a bad way to notch up the start of a new decade in the business than to call in a few friends for a jam. The recording sounds as if it was made on the fly, but the playing is good enough to make up for any technical insufficiencies. Haden programmes future associate Pat Metheny's 'Hermitage' and 'Farmer's Trust' (which also surfaces on Volume Two), with two little-known Parker tunes, 'Passport' and 'Segment', Miles Davis's 'Nardis' and Tony Scott's 'Misery'.

**** Silence**

Soul Note 121172 *Haden; Chet Baker (t, v); Enrico Pieranunzi (p); Billy Higgins (d). 11/87.*

Not so very surprising, given the context of the Quartet West material, but still a surprise and something of a blip in Haden's recorded progress. By this stage in his slow downward spiral, Chet was playing with just about everyone who'd have him. There's a strange enervation and lack of focus to most of the material, and it's Pieranunzi (a strong and creative presence on the European scene) who wins out. Haden is poorly recorded, recessed and muffled.

*****(*) Charlie Haden's Private Collection: Volume 2**

Naim CD 006 *Haden; Ernie Watts (ts); Alan Broadbent (p); Paul Motian (d). 4/88.*

***** In Angel City**

Verve 873031-2 *As above, except omit Motian; add Alex Cline, Larance Marable (d). 6/88.*

This time the 'private' tapes come from a public event, and a stirring version of Quartet West reuniting Haden with Motian. Drummer and live setting affect the music more than a little, and Watts responds with an angular, sometimes almost caustic approach that diverges sharply from the other recordings by this group.

Angel City is a mannered pastiche, an attempt to paint in sound the city of Raymond Chandler. The best is very good indeed. The less successful flirts with kitsch. Marable is an excellent foil, in character moody and unforced. Cline actually plays on only one track.

*****(*) The Montreal Tapes: Volume 1**

Verve 523260-2 *Haden; Don Cherry (pkt-t); Ed Blackwell (d). 7/89.*

****** The Montreal Tapes: Volume 2**

Verve 523295-2 *Haden; Paul Bley (p); Paul Motian (d). 7/89.*

*****(*) The Montreal Tapes: Volume 3**

Verve 537486-2 *Haden; Geri Allen (p); Paul Motian (d). 7/89.*

****** The Montreal Tapes: Volume 4**

Verve 537670-2 *Haden; Gonzalo Rubalcaba (p); Paul Motian (d). 7/89.*

Over eight nights, straddling the end of June and the first week of July 1989, the Montreal International Jazz Festival in collaboration with Canadian Radio pitched Haden in some wonderfully creative settings, mainly trios but also including a duo with Egberto Gismonti and a final-night reunion with the Liberation Music Orchestra, who were to return to the studio the following April.

Of the trios, that with Cherry is the only one which isn't uniformly excellent. There is a touch of Hamlet-without-the-Prince in what otherwise sounds like a version of the classic Ornette Coleman quartet, a seam Haden had already mined in the Old and New Dreams group. These are stirring performances, but there is something lacking, and it becomes more and more obvious on repeated hearings. Cherry is certainly the weak link, plunging off on his own. 'The Sphinx', 'The Blessing' and 'Lonely Woman' have great strengths, and the other covers are clean-limbed and unfussy: 'Art Deco' and 'Mopti' are excellent.

One of the fascinating aspects of this superb series is the opportunity to hear Haden reworking the same material with different piano players. 'When Will The Blues Leave' misfires with Cherry, but the version with Bley is sterling. 'The Blessing' is the star track on the disc with Rubalcaba, which is an absolute cracker, also including long versions of Haden originals, 'Bay City', 'Silence' and 'La Pasionaria', and a slightly tentative working of fellow-bassist Gary Peacock's 'Vignette'.

The trio with Geri Allen is already well attested, but one suspects that here competing conceptions and some awkward shifts of impetus between pianist and her older partners have compromised the music somewhat. 'Dolphy's Dance' is excellent, but most of the rest seems bracketed with self-consciousness, even a touch of irony. Bley, by contrast, is in his element: relaxed, magisterial, wry and funny. The version of 'Turnaround', Ornette's masterpiece despite itself and himself, is glorious.

A fantastic week of music. The good news is that there is still more to come: Haden with Gismonti, with Pat Metheny and Jack DeJohnette, and with Joe Henderson and Al Foster. Somewhere down the road, a boxed set beckons. Pictures, please, and every onstage announcement, song and squeak.

****(*) Dream Keeper**

Verve 847876-2 *Haden; Tom Harrell (t, flhn); Earl Gardner (t); Ray Anderson (tb); Sharon Freeman (frhn); Joe Daley (tba); Ken McIntyre (as); Branford Marsalis, Dewey Redman (ts); Joe Lovano (ts, f); Amina Claudine Myers (p); Juan Lazzaro Mendolas (wooden f, pan pipes); Mick Goodrick (g); Paul Motian (d); Don Alias (perc); Oakland Youth Chorus. 4/90.*

Whatever anyone may have thought, there was no less reason to sing about liberation in 1990 than in 1980 or even 1970. The problem for the Liberation Music Orchestra was that the world and music – and above all music – had changed in the interim. The reconvened orchestra was a curious mixture of old and new generations. This time Bley conducted, leaving the piano parts to the earthy Myers, while the horns battle it out for dominance. Great to hear Ken McIntyre (who had worked with Eric Dolphy) featured on 'Canto del Pion' and on the African National Congress anthem, 'Nkosi Sikelel'i Afrika'. Harrell is typically powerful on 'Feliciano Ama', while Lovano and Redman on tenors whirl in the 'tail of the tornado' – 'Rabo de Nube'.

'Dream Keeper' derives from a poem by Langston Hughes. Bley's suite is a vast palimpsest of anarchist songs. Sung by the Oakland Youth Chorus, it has a sombre, almost apocalyptic cast. 'Sandino' is a latter-day version of 'Song For Che', with a powerful statement from Goodrick. Unfortunately, not everything is up to this standard, and the overall impact is decidedly drab.

*****(*) First Song**

Soul Note 121222-2 *Haden; Enrico Pieranunzi (p); Billy Higgins (d).* 4/90.

No Chet this time, for the saddest and most obvious of reasons, but a set that grows in stature almost every time it's heard. Pieranunzi stakes an ever stronger claim for major league status with a well-structured and resonant performance, dark-toned lyricism that chimes with Haden's romantic attack and with the clipped swing dictated by the drummer. Lennie Tristano doesn't look to be the most obvious source for any of these players, but 'Lennie's Pennies' focuses the entire set.

***** Haunted Heart**

Verve 513078-2 *Haden; Ernie Watts (ts); Alan Broadbent (p); Billy Higgins (d); Billie Holiday, Jeri Southern, Jo Stafford (v on record).* 90.

***** Always Say Goodbye**

Verve 521501-2 *As above, except omit vocalists; add Stéphane Grappelli (vn).* 7 & 8/93.

Flagrant exercises in nostalgia, utterly beyond the pale, but for the complete lack of irony and detachment. *Haunted Heart* is Haden's 'Radio Days' set, a reconstruction that uses old vocal recordings as scene-setting. *Always Say Goodbye* further underlines Haden's passion for Jo Stafford, adding material by Duke, Coleman Hawkins, Chet Baker and Django Reinhardt, which helps explain the charmingly unexpected addition of the late Stéphane Grappelli. Watts is in very good form.

The palimpsests on Lady's 'Deep Song' and Jeri Southern's 'Every Time We Say Goodbye' – and indeed Jo Stafford's 'Haunted Heart' – are cleverly conceived and executed, but the idea is a trifle overcooked and one almost yearns for some interactive medium which allows performance with or without the archive material, and at will.

***** Steal Away: Spirituals, Hymns And Folk Songs**

Verve 527249-2 *Haden; Hank Jones (p).* 7/94.

Depending on your point of view, Jones is either an elegant master of standards jazz, an expressive balladeer with the delivery of an urbane, big-city preacher, or he's an increasingly formulaic purveyor of catechistic ideas. Any way, this recording doesn't comfortably stand the test of time.

Behind the record is the recent loss of Haden's mother, Virginia May, and also his desire to rescue from historical oblivion the makers of spirituals and vernacular hymns. In performance terms, though, this is the start of a slide into a worryingly complacent New Age sensibility, a jazz equivalent of so-called 'faith minimalism'. Done with as much calm professionalism as you would expect, it palls with distance.

***** Now Is The Hour**

Verve 529827-2 *Haden; Ernie Watts (ts); Alan Broadbent (p); Larance Marable (d).* 95.

Vintage product from a settled band, perhaps a little anonymous and lacking in focus, but pulling things together with an excellent closing sequence: 'Palo Alto', 'Marable's Parable' and the title-piece. As a Haden performance it isn't so very outstanding, but it reaffirms our growing conviction that this is the Ernie Watts group under an alias.

****** Beyond The Missouri Sky**

Verve 537130-2 *Haden; Pat Metheny (g, sitar).* 96.

This has sold like SnoCones in the desert, a record that obviously appeals to Metheny fans first and foremost, but also to a cohort of New Agers who are hipped to the unguarded frontiers of jazz. The original intention was to record a set of acoustic duets, but these have been embellished with guitar overdubs and with Metheny's previously unveiled acoustic guitar/sitar.

At the heart of the set, two tunes dedicated to Haden's late parents: Roy Acuff's country classic, 'The Precious Jewel', and the traditional 'He's Gone Away'. Also in the line-up, Jim Webb's 'The Moon Is A Harsh Mistress' and two themes from the movie *Cinema Paradiso*. It's easy enough to dismiss this music as undemanding, pastelly and soft-focus. As ever, it's also formidably disciplined, and there's a hint of rock only just under the surface.

*****(*) Night And The City**

Verve 539961-2 *Haden; Kenny Barron (p).* 9/96.

Liner-notes by novelist Rafi Zabor, author of *The Bear Comes Home*, one of the finest fictional creations ever with jazz as its background. That alone will recommend it to some, but it's an imprimatur that is hardly needed. Haden is playing exquisitely and in Barron he has a partner who knows the repertoire with the intimacy of a genuine creator. Dedicated to Manhattan, it's another atmospheric album built around luminous versions of 'For Heaven's Sake', 'Spring Is Here' and a slow, ardent 'Body And Soul'. Each man has an original, Barron's lovely 'Twilight Song', which gets the sun down and the lights on at the start of the set, and Haden's often-covered 'Waltz For Ruth' towards the end.

If it has a down side, it is that the artistry often seems too easy, too unflustered. There is not much risk in any of these tracks. At this stage in both careers that may not be surprising, but it is a little disappointing.

****** None But The Lonely Heart**

Naim CD022 *Haden; Chris Anderson (p).* 7/97.

Anderson is not only blind but a victim of the same brittle-bone ailment that afflicted Michel Petrucciani. A veteran of the Chicago scene, he has played with everyone from Bird to Sonny Rollins and along the way has acquired a formidable grasp of jazz harmonics. There isn't a single track on this magnificently recorded album of standards that doesn't bring something new to the original melody. Even 'Alone Together', that tiredest of all duo chestnuts, takes on a new resonance, while 'Body And Soul' and 'The Things We Did Last Summer' should henceforward be in the study file of every young jazz pianist.

Both voices are recorded in a big, alert acoustic (Cami Hall in New York City) which brings out every detail in both bass and piano. Hard to fault on any count.

***(*) The Art Of The Song

Verve 547403-2 *Haden; Ernie Watts (ts); Alan Broadbent (p); Larance Marable (d); Bill Henderson, Shirley Horn (v); orchestra, Murray Adler (cond). 2/99.*

Brave to lay down a first public vocal recording for 45 years (aside from the scarcely noticed cameo on Carla Bley's *Escalator Over The Hill*); braver still to do it in the company of Shirley Horn and Bill Henderson. Shirley's opening reading of Bernstein's 'Lonely Town' establishes the note of nostalgic longing that has surrounded Haden's work for some years. Concert master Murray Adler's violin solo offers the perfect balance to her breathy intimacy. Adler returns as soloist on Haden's own composition, 'Ruth's Waltz'; Henderson delivers the lyric with a sardonic poise which never sounds remotely cynical. His reading of 'Why Did I Choose You?' from *The Yearling* is no less arresting, a song that requires great maturity if it isn't to sound either immature or offhand. There follows a remarkable arrangement of Rachmaninov's 'Moment musical, Opus 16' which features just Haden (stately, precise and full-voiced) and Watts over strings. The other classical arrangement is Ravel's 'Prelude in A minor', a perfect tonality for Haden.

Broadbent and Watts team up with the orchestra on Jeri Southern's 'Theme For Charlie', which is thereby recast as a tribute to the leader and a prelude to his first recording vocal since the Haden family show days. Interesting that his choice should be the traditional 'Wayfaring Stranger', with its mournfully upbeat 'going over Jordan' conclusion. Another deftly crafted album from a great romantic.

Dick Hafer (born 1930)

TENOR SAXOPHONE

He played lead tenor for Barnet, Thornhill and Herman in the 1950s, then spent many years in TV bands and in studios. He lives and plays in the Los Angeles area, after moving there in 1974.

**(*) In A Sentimental Mood

Progressive PCD-7094 *Hafer; Johnny Varro (p); John Leitham (b); Gene Estes (d). 12/91.*

*** Prez Impressions

Fresh Sounds FSR 5002 *Hafer; Ross Tompkins (p); Dave Carpenter (b); Jake Hanna (d). 2–3/94.*

Sideman and studio pro for decades, these are indian-summer dates for Dick Hafer as a leader. Since there's no pressing reason for them to exist, perhaps, they don't really cut much of an impression. *In A Sentimental Mood* is the gentlest of jogs through 12 pieces of swing-to-bop, and most of the playing honours go to Leitham, who always swings. The Fresh Sounds disc is well named since Hafer sounds much like Lester Young in his most dawdling mood, and this is the slightly better record.

Tim Hagans (born 1954)

TRUMPET

Although his profile as a leader has come about only recently, Hagans has been in jazz for many years. He worked with Stan Kenton and Woody Herman in the 1970s, before moving to Sweden, playing and teaching there until his return to the USA in 1981. He played in Cincinnati and Boston before becoming a fixture on the New York scene.

*** No Words

Blue Note 789680-2 *Hagans; Joe Lovano (ts); Marc Copland (p); John Abercrombie (g); Scott Lee (b); Bill Stewart (d). 12/93.*

***(*) Audible Architecture

Blue Note 831808-2 *Hagans; Bob Belden (ts); Larry Grenadier (b); Billy Kilson (d). 12/94.*

Hagans has become sought after for all kinds of work, and his own records for Blue Note expose a mercurial, accomplished trumpeter with perhaps a significant discography ahead of him. He has an elegant tone and a penchant for long, rococo lines which he seems able to deliver without undue strain. *No Words* is a rather cautious start in that he's a little crowded by the top-notch band, and none of the compositions makes a special mark (interestingly, his sleeve-notes to the second disc reveal that he wrote all the tunes here on piano, accounting for the harmonic rather than melodic interest, whereas the themes on disc two came straight off the horn). Lovano and Abercombie do their usual sterling work and, though Hagans sounds more like a bandsman than a leader, it's still an enjoyable record.

Audible Architecture is much more a trumpet showcase – he even sounds further forward in the mix. Two standards are thoughtfully done, but it's the snap and hustle of the up-tempo originals that one remembers, and when Belden sits in on four tracks the music takes on a cast that moves from bright free bop to a funky groove. Kilson plays as Hagans instructed him, as if the whole thing were a continuous drum solo, and, while he sometimes goes too far, it's an exciting response. The leader's own playing sounds sharper and riskier, without trading in his fundamentally calm eloquence.

*** Hubsongs

Blue Note 837628-2 *Hagans; Marcus Printup (t); Vincent Herring (as); Javon Jackson (ts); Benny Green (p); Peter Washington (b); Kenny Washington (d). 8/97.*

Another concept album, this time a dedication to Freddie Hubbard by two prominent disciples. The two trumpeters create some piquant if scarcely arresting contrasts in their playing: Hagans tends to be more of a rhythmic thinker, varying the pace and emphases in his solos, while Printup likes the dazzle and flash which is one of Hubbard's bequests. The band is suavely accomplished (the sax role is shared out between Herring and Jackson) and the ten pieces affirm Hubbard's place in the hard-bop heartland rather than his fusion-bound phase. But it's unconvincing as any kind of personal project, and certainly sidles back into orthodoxy after the grace notes of the previous discs.

***** Animation – Imagination**

Blue Note 495790-2 *Hagans; Bob Belden (ss, ky); Scott Kinsey (syn); Kevin Hays (p); Kurt Rosenwinkel (g); Ira Coleman, David Dyson (b); Billy Kilson (d); DJ Smash, DJ Kingsize (programming).* 5/98.

Just as, 30 years before, Freddie Hubbard left hard bop behind with his own kind of fusion, Hagans here pitches camp inside crossover lines. The music, cannily produced by Bob Belden, mediates a line somewhere between the Miles Davis of *Bitches Brew*, the Davis of 15 years after that, and the exotic ambience of Jon Hassell and Chris Botti. When Hagans keeps his mute in and the rhythm tracks secure a slinky kind of funk-fusion, the music is intensely Milesian. But he doesn't want to relinquish his bebop skills: his improvisations bypass the textural virtues of the players mentioned above and look for a more specific musical consequence. The mood changes between frenetic, spacious and colouristic, and Hagans is on top of all of it, but it still seems more like a parade of interesting episodes than a particular statement.

Jerry Hahn (born 1940)

GUITAR

An important figure in jazz guitar. He made his name with John Handy and Gary Burton. For many years thereafter, he devoted his time to teaching and writing a column for Guitar Player, but the compulsion to perform returned and Hahn moved to Oregon and then to Denver in pursuit of an active improvising scene.

***** Time Changes**

Enja ENJ 9007 *Hahn; David Liebman (ss); Art Lande, Phil Markowitz (p); Steve LaSpina (b); Jeff Hirshfield (d).* 10/93.

Though hardly a household name, Hahn is a significant player, and this record, which for many will be a first glimpse of the man, oozes maturity and, after 20 years without a record as leader, seems bursting with ideas. Perhaps because of this, the trio tracks with LaSpina and Hirshfield are far and away the most interesting. Liebman adds next to nothing beyond curlicues and furbelows, and the piano players are both too quirky to make much sense of music that anticipates the work of contemporary icons such as Abercrombie and Scofield. The arrangement of Dolphy's '245' is fascinating, as is the resolutely unmournful 'Goodbye Pork Pie Hat'. Hahn wrote 'Oregon' before moving to the North-West, and it doesn't seem to have any direct relation to the place; it is, though, one of his most moving pieces and, for once, Markowitz sounds like the right man for the job.

Al Haig (1924–82)

PIANO

Acknowledged as a master of bebop piano, Haig has nevertheless suffered in comparison to many of his peers through his neglect as a recording artist in later years; he never made a single album for a major label. His work with Parker, Gillespie, Getz and others shows how fine an accompanist and group pianist he was, but his 'name' work is even finer and implies a rare mastery: he was effectively an understated, 'cool' stylist inside the hot medium of bebop. He enjoyed a revival of interest in the 1970s but died before he could reap any great rewards from it.

♛ ** The Al Haig Trio Esoteric**

Fresh Sound FSR-CD 38 *Haig; Bill Crow (b); Lee Abrams (d).* 3/54.

****** Al Haig Trio**

Fresh Sound FSR-CD 45 *As above.* 3/54.

***** Al Haig Quartet**

Fresh Sound FSR-CD 12 *Haig; Benny Weeks (g); Teddy Kotick (b); Phil Brown (d).* 9/54.

***** Al Haig Today!**

Fresh Sound FSR-CD 6 *Haig; Eddie De Haas (b); Jim Kappes (d).* 65.

Al Haig was deplorably served by records in the earlier part of his career, and as a result he is almost the forgotten man of bebop piano. Yet he was as great a figure as any of the bebop masters. If he denied himself the high passion of Bud Powell's music, he was still a force of eloquence and intensity, and his refined touch lent him a striking individuality within his milieu. The first trio album, originally released on the Esoteric label, is a masterpiece that can stand with any of the work of Powell or Monk. Haig's elegance of touch and line, his virtually perfect delivery, links him with a pianist such as Teddy Wilson rather than with any of his immediate contemporaries, and certainly his delivery of an unlikely tune such as 'Mighty Like A Rose' (on FSR-CD 45) has a kinship with the language of Wilson's generation. Yet his complexity of tone and the occasionally cryptic delivery are unequivocally modern, absolutely of the bop lineage. Voicings and touch have a symmetry and refinement that other boppers, from Powell and Duke Jordan to Joe Albany and Dodo Marmarosa, seldom approached. The second *Trio* album, originally released on Period, dates from the same day of recording and is virtually as good – but it could just as easily have fitted on to the same CD as its companion-piece. Still, Haig's bittersweet reduction of 'Round Midnight', present here, is unmissable, even among the many versions of that tune.

The *Quartet* and *Today!* albums are flawed by their circumstances. On *Quartet*, his accompanists are no more than adequate, even though the pianist's subtle touch on a typical programme of standards is impeccable. The sound, though, is inadequate. *Today!* is a stray bulletin from the mid-1960s, originally very rare on vinyl, and several of the tunes sound foreshortened. 'Bluesette' and 'Polka Dots And Moonbeams' still show that Haig's powers were undimmed.

***** Ornithology**

Progressive PCD 7024 *Haig; Jamil Nasser (b); Frank Gant (d).* 77.

Haig went through a burst of recording late in his life, and he remained a marvellous musician to the end. So far, though, most of the vinyl has yet to make it to CD, outside of Japanese issues. This one is so-so. Nasser and Gant are no more than workmanlike, and Haig himself is sometimes content to take it easy, though his version of Strayhorn's 'Daydream' reminds us how he might have been the premier poet of bebop. Incredibly, we're still waiting for (among other later records) Spotlite's beautiful *Invitation* to make it to general CD release.

Pat Halcox (born 1930)

TRUMPET

A Londoner by birth, Halcox has been known for his entire career for one playing association, as the trumpeter in many editions of the Chris Barber Band since 1954.

**** Pat Halcox All Stars**

Lake LACD84 *Halcox; Campbell Burnap (tb, v); John Crocker (as, ts, cl); Johnny Parker (p); Johnny McCallum (g); Vic Pitt (b); Pete York (d).* 7/78–7/79.

****(*) There's Yes! Yes! In Your Eyes**

Jazzology JCD-186 *Halcox; John Beacham (tb); Bruce Turner (cl); Ray Smith (p); Jim Douglas (g); Vic Pitt (b); Geoff Downes (d).* 6–7/89.

Halcox will for ever be associated with Chris Barber's band, and these are rare examples of records under his nominal leadership. The Lake CD reissues a 1978 session by his then-regular group but it's an ignoble survivor. The ten tunes are insufferably polite trad-to-mainstream, and why Burnap insists on singing in his phoney American accent, we don't know. Four live tracks from the same period, used as a makeweight, at least have a bit more go in them.

The Jazzology disc offers a sensible and mildly persuasive set of performances on a group of mostly very old tunes, several of them exceptionally obscure even by trad standards. If not quite as courteous as the earlier disc, this is still deeply uneventful, with the rhythm section clunking along and Halcox sounding too gentlemanly to take a serious lead. The recording (at the Bull's Head, Barnes, God save it) sounds authentically British. Halcox has deserved better opportunities at leadership than these, but perhaps he simply isn't interested.

Edmond Hall (1901–67)

CLARINET

A native New Orleans man, Hall has often been unfairly eclipsed in discussions of jazz clarinettists. His three brothers all played clarinet too, but it was Ed who took most of the jazz-playing honours, spending several years with Claude Hopkins in the 1930s and then freelancing, mostly around New York, for the rest of his life.

****** Edmond Hall 1936–1944**

Classics 830 *Hall; Billy Hicks (t, v); Sidney De Paris, Emmett Berry (t); Vic Dickenson, Fernando Arbello (tb); Meade Lux Lewis (cel); Cyril Haynes, Teddy Wilson, Eddie Heywood, James P Johnson (p); Red Norvo (vib); Leroy Jones, Jimmy Shirley, Al Casey, Carl Kress (g); Al Hall, Israel Crosby, Billy Taylor, Johnny Williams (b); Arnold Boling, Big Sid Catlett (d); Henry Nemo (v).* 6/37–1/44.

***** Edmond Hall 1944–1945**

Classics 872 *Hall; Irving Randolph (t); Benny Morton, Henderson Chambers (tb); Harry Carney (bs); Teddy Wilson, Don Frye, Ellis Larkins (p); Everett Barksdale (g); Johnny Williams, Alvin Raglin, Billy Taylor (b); Big Sid Catlett, Arthur Trappier, Jimmy Crawford (d).* 5/44–45.

****** Profoundly Blue**

Blue Note 821260-2 *Similar to above discs.* 2/41–5/44.

Hall was one of the most popular musicians in the Eddie Condon circle, but his experience – with big bands in the 1920s and '30s and with Louis Armstrong's All Stars – was much wider than that. He played in a driving manner that married the character of his New Orleans background with the more fleet methods of the swing clarinettists. Classics 830 starts off with an obscure session by Billy Hicks and his Sizzlin' Six, with Hall as a sideman, but the meat of it is in Hall's first three sessions for Blue Note and a stray Commodore date. This is outstandingly fine midstream swing, with superb contributions from de Paris, Berry, the incomparably refined Wilson, Lewis (on celeste), James P. Johnson and, above all, the magnificent Dickenson, whose solos on the blues are masterful statements of jazz trombone. And there is Hall himself. Sound is mainly excellent, but the final Blue Note date is a bit scruffy. The next Classics disc is less involving: the first session, with Morton and Carney, is more fine small-group swing, but eight tracks in a quartet with Wilson are comparatively sedate and the two final band sessions merely agreeable.

Collectors will surely welcome Blue Note's own edition of their three Ed Hall sessions on *Profoundly Blue*. The sound is, surprisingly, not much better than on the Classics discs, with a lot of surface noise on several tracks, but the music stands tall and three alternative takes are well worth having. The May 1944 session is especially pleasing here, with Carney and Morton getting turns in the spotlight which are as rare as Hall's own.

***** Edmond Hall With Alan Elsdon**

Jazzology JCD-240 *Hall; Alan Elsdon (t); Phil Rhodes (tb); Andy Cooper (cl); Colin Bates (p); John Barton (g); Mick Gilligan (b); Billy Law (d).* 66.

***** Edmond Hall Quartet**

Jazzology JCD-207 *Hall; Colin Bates (p); Mick Gilligan (b); Billy Law (d).* 11/66.

****** Edmond Hall In Copenhagen**

Storyville STCD 6022 *Hall; Finn Otto Hansen (t); Arne Bue Jensen (tb); Jorgen Svare (cl); Jorn Jensen (p); Bjarne 'Liller' Petersen (bj); Jens Solund (b); Knud Ryskov Madsen (d).* 12/66.

***** Edmond Hall's Last Concert**

Jazzology JCD-223 *Hall; Bobby Hackett, George Poor (c); Joe Robertson (tb); Joe Battaglia, Evans Schwartz, Marie Marcus (p); Wally Livingston, Russell Best (b); Dale Pearman, Bob Saltmarsh (d).* 4/64–3/67.

Hall toured in the 1960s until he died, and there is a rash of recordings from his final year or so. The first two Jazzology discs come from a British tour with Elsdon's band: one with the horns, one without. The date with horns just has it for the better variety, though this is in the main an unremarkable line-up of performers, and Hall's careful heat and elegant, supple parts outclass his surroundings, even in his final year. *Last Concert* comes from only days before he died. Sitting in with Hackett and some local players from South Byfield, MA, Hall still sounds in great shape. So does Hackett: but the indifferent band and low-fi sound make this for fans only. Three stray tracks from another occasion fill it out.

The Copenhagen date makes the best memorial to him. 'I like to work in different contexts, but I can only play one style': hot, fluent, swinging, pinching the odd note here and there, but mostly displaying a remarkably clean and supple line, here is Ed Hall at his best. The Papa Bue band play on two tracks, the rhythm section and Hall on most of the others and, while the Swedish players are no great masters, they know how to respect a player who is. Hall even turns in a lovely *a cappella* treatment of 'It Ain't Necessarily So'. Splendid remastering of a beautiful record.

G.P. Hall (born 1943)

GUITAR, BASS, VIOLIN, AUTOHARP, PIANO, SOPRANO SAXOPHONE, PERCUSSION

Born in London, Hall worked in beat groups and moved into the British alternative scene of the '70s, working with the music-theatre group, The Welfare State, and recording solo and small-group works based around his guitar playing. Studied flamenco with Manitas De Plata and evolved his own kind of 'world music'.

****(*) Fragments Of Imagination**
FMR CD31-VO796 *Hall; David Ford (t); Paul Rutherford (tb); Lol Coxhill, Vicky Burke (ss); Tim Hill (as, bombarde); Lyn Dobson (f); Diana Van-Lock (vn); Jeff Clyne (b); Sam Brown, Richard Marcangelo, Matt Lewis (d).* 1/74–5/95.

***** Mar-Del-Plata**
FMR CD46-VO997 *Hall; Paul Dunderdale (cl); Alison Fox (p frame, dulcimer); Leo Khan, Paivi Hall (vn); Gus Garside (g, perc); Richard Hogan, Ilbert Stubbs (b); Rob Pusey (d); Steve Symes (perc).* 75–8/95.

***** Steel Storms & Tender Spirits**
FMR CD58-VP998 2CD *Hall; Andy Hague, David Ford (t); Vicky Burke (ss, ts); Diana Van-Lock (vn); Sam Brown (d).* 87–2/98.

Hall has taken flamenco guitar as a starting point and developed it into an all-encompassing style that takes in jazz, improvisation and world music. These records are scrapbook-like testaments to what he does: aimless and rambling much of the time, but not without a ramshackle charm, and occasionally finding something exceptionally vivid and arresting. *Fragments Of Imagination* goes back to some commissioned works of the 1970s (not very well recorded) and includes groups with noted improvisers Coxhill and Rutherford, although they play atypically. Much of it is rather doomy and gloomy in a style of old progressive rock. *Mar-del-Plata* has a hippie travelogue feel to it: the very pretty 'Spirit Sky Montana' seeks to evoke Copland's wide-open spaces, but was recorded in Kewstoke, North Somerset. 'Charmouth Beach' ('this track is often played on Japanese radio') is an awful lot of strange noise to come out of a single 12-string guitar. 'The Estates' goes as far back as 1975 and is a group piece about developers destroying old communities – a musical equivalent of kitchen-sink melodrama, perhaps.

Steel Storms & Tender Spirits goes all the way with two and a quarter hours of music, a dedicated old muso's book of memories. In the notes, G.P. talks about what he remembers of being in Spain, Finland, Africa, Egypt and Wiltshire (where he saw a UFO!). Overdubbed solo performances, industrial clank, electronic storms and more spiral in and out of earshot. It's all too much, but every so often a track jumps out and sticks in the mind. A very likeable oddball.

Jim Hall (born 1930)

GUITAR

Played on the West Coast with Chico Hamilton and Jimmy Giuffre in the '50s, then returned east to work with Sonny Rollins and Art Farmer. Many years were spent in studio work, but in his fifties and sixties Hall became much more prominent as a leader, and is now recognized as a subtle master of his instrument.

***** Where Would I Be?**
Original Jazz Classics OJC 649 *Hall; Ben Aronov (p); Malcolm Cecil (b); Airto Moreira (d).* 7/71.

Hall's smooth, gentlemanly approach got seriously interesting only once he had passed his sixtieth birthday and started to work with larger groups. The problem with these early sessions boils down, as the title implies, to their unvarying niceness. Totally professional, Hall delivers reliably every time, with no apparent difference in approach between live and studio sessions. He can certainly never be accused of pointless redundancy, for his solos are always unimpeachably controlled.

****(*) Alone Together**
Original Jazz Classics OJC 467 *Hall; Ron Carter (b).* 8/72.

A live set without a single rough edge or corner, and with almost no improvisational tension either. The slight surprise of Rollins's 'St Thomas' quickly evaporates as Hall negotiates its contours with almost cynical ease – is there really no more to it than that? The rest is more caressingly familiar. There are moments of genuine beauty, notably on 'Softly As In A Morning Sunrise' and 'Autumn Leaves', but there's something fatally lacking in the conception.

***** Circles**
Concord CCD 4161 *Hall; Don Thompson (p, b); Rufus Reid (b); Terry Clarke (d).* 3/81.

There's still a big gap in Hall's discography, accounting for much of the 1970s, an admittedly fallow period for the guitarist. *Circles* finds him more conventionally swinging than for some time, but in a rather oddly weighted group in which Thompson doubles on piano and bass (Reid's only in for the fine 'All Of A Sudden My Heart Sings' – did he show up late?). There's not a lot of substance to it, and it would be as flat as a pancake if it weren't for Clarke's peppy drumming, a feature of most Hall records from here on.

****(*) Jim Hall's Three**
Concord CCD 4298 *Hall; Steve LaSpina (b); Akira Tana (d).* 1/86.

Ironically, Clarke isn't on hand for this rather drab standards session; but LaSpina, another regular, is and he takes a fairly strong hold on things from the off. Tana's too busy and energetic for the general pace of things and he tends to go round and round in pointless loops on 'All The Things You Are', which might have benefited from a subtler approach. Hall himself isn't bad, but the jaded familiarity of a lot of his solos, now seemingly composed of strings of favourite figures and runs, may put some listeners off.

*****(*) All Across The City**

Concord CCD 4384 *Hall; Gil Goldstein (p, ky); Steve LaSpina (b); Terry Clarke (d).* 5/89.

This contains some of Hall's most innovatively 'contemporary' playing. Certainly, no one thrown into the deep end of 'R.E.M. Movement' – a Gil Goldstein composition with free passages from all the players – would suspect the provenance. Elsewhere the material is more familiar. 'Young One (For Debra)' consciously recalls Bill Evans and 'Waltz For Debby'. Of the other originals, the gentle 'Jane' is dedicated to Mrs Hall, composer in turn of 'Something Tells Me'; 'Drop Shot' and 'Big Blues' are tougher but also more humorous in conception, the former featuring Goldstein's electronic keyboards to good effect, the latter an unexpected tribute to Stanley Turrentine. The title-track, a gentle and slightly wondering cityscape, also recalls Hall's association with Bill Evans. Hall, though, is much more than an impressionistic colourist. His reading of Monk's 'Bemsha Swing' confirms his stature as one of the most significant harmonic improvisers on his instrument.

***** Live At Town Hall**

Musicmasters 65066-2 *Hall; Gil Goldstein (p, syn); John Scofield, Mick Goodrick, John Abercrombie, Peter Bernstein (g); Gary Burton (vib); Steve LaSpina (b); Terry Clarke (d).* 6/90.

A guitar summit in New York City to mark Hall's sixtieth birthday. It's perhaps a measure of his level of performance that the most striking track on the disc is a duo version of 'My Funny Valentine', performed by Goodrick and Abercrombie. Elsewhere, the main man is upstaged by Scofield and even by Bernstein, and Gary Burton briefly steals the show on 'Careful', where he has to contend with all five guitarists. It must have been a good night (and there was an earlier volume from the same session), but as a record it's not much more than an interesting souvenir for jazz guitar fans.

***** Subsequently**

Musicmasters 65078-2 *Hall; Rasmus Lee (ts); Toots Thielemans (hca); Larry Goldings (p, org); Steve LaSpina (b); Terry Clarke (d).* 92.

****(*) Something Special**

Musicmasters 518 445 *Hall; Larry Goldings (p); Steve LaSpina (b).* 3/93.

There are signs that, having passed the sixty mark, Hall shook himself down and tried to look at his playing and his repertoire afresh. Anchored by the regular rhythm section of LaSpina and Clarke, *Subsequently* is quite an adventurous record. Though outwardly a rather lightweight programme of mid-tempo themes, Hall's approach is quite different from his usual laid-back stroll, and Lee gives it a bit of unflustered pace, sounding a lot like Zoot Sims. Thielemans is an asset to any set, and one can imagine duets with Hall working well. Here, they're a bit cramped, but the combination yields some lovely moments.

Just to prove or disprove our earlier point about drummers, *Something Special* dispenses with a percussionist. There's probably more straightforward guitar playing on this than on any of the recent things, but it's neither inventive nor particularly well recorded, and the balance of the trio sounds all wrong; odd, because producer Gil Goldstein normally does these things exceptionally well.

*****(*) Dedications & Inspirations**

Telarc CD 8365 *Hall (g solo).* 10/93.

... or not entirely solo, since on this fascinating record he experiments with a multi-playback system that allows him to overlay rich contrapuntal patterns and often surprisingly austere textures in a set that reflects his love of the visual arts as much as his lifelong passion for jazz. The telling thing is that at no point does the technology ever render it difficult to recognize Jim Hall in there. The voice is his from start to finish, and what he does with 'Bluesography' (which might have made a good alternative title for this session) and 'In A Sentimental Mood' could bear no other stylistic signature. It's perhaps a little too much sheer technical virtuosity to absorb at album length, but track by track it's hard to beat in this superb player's output.

****** Dialogues**

Telarc CD 83369 *Hall; Tom Harrell (flhn); Joe Lovano (ts); Bill Frisell, Mike Stern (g); Gil Goldstein (acc); Scott Colley (b); Andy Watson (d).* 2/95.

Something of a dream-team package. There are actually only two duet tracks, both with Goldstein on his regular and bass accordion; the rest are small-group performances designed to highlight horns and guitar, and with Colley and Watson taking pretty much a back seat. With the exception of the closing 'Skylark', which features Harrell in exquisite form, all the tunes are Hall originals, written with a playing partner in mind – 'Frisell Frazzle', 'Calypso Joe', and 'Stern Stuff' – and it is Mike Stern who delivers the surprise of the session with an offbeat blues sound on 'Uncle Ed'. Frisell is in typically playful form on the opening dedication, reappearing on 'Simple Things', which has more of a country feel. The saxophonist has had more convincing days, but he manages to give his two appearances enough of a personal slant to distinguish him from A.N. Other guest hornman. Telarc recordings are famously good, but on this occasion John Snyder and Jane Hall have outdone themselves. Holding back a notch on the rhythm section was a risky stratagem, but what they have produced has near-perfect balance and no loss of definition. Plaudits all round.

*****(*) Textures**

Telarc CD 83402 *Hall; James Finegan, Ryan Kisor (t); Claudio Roditi (flhn); Conrad Herwig, Jim Pugh (tb); Alex Brofsky (frhn); Marcus Roja (tba); Joe Lovano (ss); Louis Schulman (vla); Myron Lutzke (clo); Scott Colley (b); Terry Clarke (d); Derek DiCenzo (steel d); Gordon Gottlieb (perc); strings.* 9/96.

As he neared seventy, Hall grew ever more adventurous, rather than less. The main drawback of this record – easily as well crafted as its predecessor – is that it attempts too much in too short a span. A brass-dominated 'Fanfare' with Hall, Roditi and Pugh all featured; a couple of tracks with strings; a 'string quartet'; and the curious multi-cultural 'Sazanami', with its steel pans part. 'Ragman' is a further dialogue with Lovano, a plaintive evocation of urban loneliness and decay, beautifully constructed. 'Quadrologue', with Hall's electric standing in for first violin and Scott

Colley's bass shifting the tonality downward, is a piece of latter-day Third Stream, while 'Passacaglia' is in near-classical form, a little soft-centred on repeated hearings, but an elegant line. Jim's daughter, Devra, contributes an illuminating liner-note.

*****(*) Panorama**
Telarc CD 83408 *Hall; Art Farmer (flhn); Slide Hampton (tb); Greg Osby (as); Kenny Barron, Geoff Keezer (p); Scott Colley (b); Terry Clarke (d).* 12/96.

Cut live at the Village Vanguard, Hall invites various masters to sit in with his own trio. It makes for a bitty album, but there are some specific highlights, most particularly Osby's two turns: his blues playing on 'Furnished Flats' is as fine as anything he's set down on record (and paved the way for Hall to feature on one of Osby's own sets). All-original material keeps the situation from turning into a series of walk-on cameos and the results are more than pleasing.

***** Jim Hall And Pat Metheny**
Telarc CD 83442 *Hall; Pat Metheny (g).* 7–8/98.

Nothing untoward about this collaboration: Hall is an obvious reference-point for much of Metheny's methods, and the pairing is as *simpatico* as one would expect. Probably too much so: the tracks are so sweetly choreographed, every affinity carefully underscored, that in the end it's little more than a pleasant distraction, and unlikely to make much appeal to anyone who isn't a dedicated guitar-follower.

Bengt Hallberg (born 1932)
PIANO, ORGAN, ACCORDION

Born in Gothenburg, Hallberg was playing on the Swedish swing scene when a teenager, before adapting to bop styles and working with Stan Getz and other Americans. While familiar to foreign audiences, his local status endures as one of the major figures in Swedish jazz, with numerous composing duties, soundtracks and other credits, along with a big discography and a style that seems to encompass most of jazz piano history.

***** Hallberg's Happiness**
Phontastic PHONT 7544 *Hallberg (p solo).* 3/77.

*****(*) The Hallberg Treasure Chest: A Bouquet From '78**
Phontastic NCD 8828 *Hallberg (p solo).* 8–10/78.

***** The Hallberg Touch**
Phontastic PHONT 7525 *Hallberg (p solo).* 8/79.

Bengt Hallberg is a major part of Swedish jazz and has been active since the 1940s; not much of his earlier work is currently in print, though. The pianist made only a few albums under his own name in the 1960s and '70s, and most of those have disappeared; but these three solo sessions are engaging, if a little lightweight compared to some of his earlier discs. *Happiness* is a packed collection of miniatures, some dispatched in a few breaths, others lingered over: there is a measured look at 'Sophisticated Lady' as well as a couple of jolly, faintly ludicrous ragtime pieces. The presence of the traditional 'Herdesang' is a reminder that Hallberg looked into the possibilities of improvising on native Scandinavian tunes before many more publicized attempts. *Touch* is another mix of unpredictable choices – 'In A Little Spanish Town', 'Charleston' – but plays out with a more thoughtful élan overall. The 1978 *Treasure Chest* set includes an 'Erroll Garner Joke', some judiciously picked standards and a couple of particularly fine ballads – 'I Couldn't Sleep A Wink Last Night' is one.

**** Hallberg's Hot Accordeon**
Phontastic PHONT 7553 *Hallberg; Arne Domnérus (as, cl); Rune Gustafsson (g); Georg Riedel (b).* 5/80–6/81.

****(*) Kraftverk**
Phontastic PHONT 7553 *As above.* 5/80–9/83.

Some of Hallberg's projects suggest an oddball streak that is perhaps more interesting for him than for anyone listening. The appeal of the *Accordeon* set hinges entirely on how much one likes the piano-accordion, since all involved play the Dixie-to-swing repertoire with charming commitment. *Kraftverk* finds Hallberg at the organ of the Stockholm Konserthus, abetted by Domnérus on alto (there are a couple of stray tracks with the quartet from the earlier record, this time with Hallberg on piano). There's a certain creaking grandeur about their readings of 'God Bless The Child' and 'Blood Count', but a few tune choices ('Just A-Sittin' And A Rockin''?) seem almost bizarre, and one is often reminded of Frank Zappa's decision to play 'Louie Louie' on the Albert Hall organ.

***** Hallberg's Yellow Blues**
Phontastic PHONT 7583 *Hallberg (p solo).* 84.

*****(*) Hallberg's Surprise**
Phontastic PHONT 7581 *Hallberg (p solo).* 3–5/87.

Few would credit Hallberg with leading the march from jazz to any kind of 'world music'. Yet the sleeve-note author for *Surprise* opines that it 'is not a jazz record', and the other disc consists of traditional folk material. Hallberg has studied and composed in the European tradition, and he moves through non-jazz mediums with the same ease with which he slips from swing to bop and after. These records feature him improvising on music remote from conventional jazz repertory, but they sound unequivocally comfortable, the familiar songful touch brought to bear on a surprising range of themes. The folk pieces are dealt with a little more discreetly, and the pianist trusts the inner lights of the material rather than imposing too much of himself on it; but the *Surprise* record is considerably more adventurous, with 'Take The "A" Train' sandwiched between Paganini's 'Caprice No. 24' and Handel's 'Sarabande', and Neal Hefti lining up with Corelli and Chopin. Hallberg plays on and around each of the pieces, never unduly respectful but sticking to his essential thriftiness and grace as an improviser: some pieces work superbly, others sound curiously abstracted, yet it's an altogether intriguing record.

***** Spring On The Air**
Phono Suecia PSCD 51 *Hallberg; Jan Allan, Gustavo Bergalli, Bertil Lövgren, Magnus Johansson (t, flhn); Lars Olofsson, Olle Holmqvist, Ulf Johansson (tb); Sven Larsson (btb); Arne Domnérus, Krister Andersson (cl, as); Lennart Aberg (ss, ts, af); Jan Kling (ts, f); Erik Nilsson (bs, bcl, f); Stefan Nilsson (p); Rune Gustafsson (g); Sture Akerberg (b); Egil Johansen (d).* 5/87.

Hallberg's writing for big band hasn't been widely documented on record, which makes this CD the more welcome. Nearly an hour of music is devoted to a sequence of impressionist themes meant to evoke aspects of his country and, while it's hard to know if the sax writing for 'Göta River' is any kind of accurate picture, there's a vividness in the writing which the players respond to with the kind of sober relish that's characteristic of them. Old friends such as Jan Allan and Arne Domnérus are provided with features which suggest either Ellington or Gil Evans; but a piece such as 'Night In The Harbour', with its virtuoso trombone part by Ulf Johansson, sounds like Hallberg through and through. The recording lacks a little punch, but the clarity illuminates all the strands of the writing.

(***) Skansen In Our Hearts
Aquila CD 3 *Hallberg; Gustaf Sjokvist (p); Gavleborg Symphony Orchestra.* 91.

(***) 5 × 100
Improkomp IKCD 1 *Hallberg; Ad Libitum Choir.* 6/94.

Two of Hallberg's 'outside' projects, touched by jazz but primary examples of how far afield he's explored. *Skansen In Our Hearts* collects five of his orchestral pieces, some concerto-like in form (he sees little reason to exclude himself from any of his own works) and all firmly in a Scandinavian symphonic tradition. Some might wish for some extra gravitas, but there's no questioning the sonority and inventiveness of the composer's writing. *5 × 100* features his writing for choir – psalm settings, Shakespeare, Schubert, Swedish folksong and something of himself. He can't resist the occasional bit of mischief but some of the music is disarmingly lovely, and admirers of his piano will be partial to the four solo interludes. Rather remote recording from the Linkoping Cathedral School.

***** The Tapdancing Butterfly**
Aquila CD 4 *Hallberg; Ronnie Gardiner (b); Sture Akerberg (d).* 92.

Hallberg's trio music has an element of kitsch about it: he likes tempos and rhythms that suggest a kind of jazz vaudeville at times, and the queer setting chosen for 'Poor Butterfly', for instance, will raise either a smile or a wince of irritation. The butterfly theme drifts through these pieces, and the best of them are vintage Hallberg, but it's as well to be tuned in on his wavelength.

****** Time On My Hands**
Improkomp IKCD 2-3 2CD *Hallberg (p solo).* 2/94–4/95.

Hallberg played a radio concert in which he performed nothing but written requests from the audience, and he liked it so much that he repeated the method at two subsequent sessions. This two-disc set takes the pick of the three occasions. Non-Swedish speakers are denied the chance to savour the pianist's amusing introductions (his first number is the theme from *Dallas*!), but nobody will mistake the elegance, wit and lucidity on show in the playing itself. This is vintage Hallberg, and probably the ideal introduction to one of Europe's most eminent masters.

***** In A Mellow Tone**
Improkomp IKCD 5 *Hallberg; Hans Backenroth (b).* 3/96.

This time Hallberg is in conversation with a young bassist, and they tackle a typical programme for the pianist: three traditional Scandinavian pieces, three originals and a group of standards. In case one expected Hallberg to take a perfunctory route, have a listen to what he does with 'Out Of Nowhere'. Maybe this isn't one of his great ones – the sound is a bit reverberant, and some of the tunes are dispatched almost too quickly – but admirers will enjoy all the same.

Lin Halliday (1936–2000)

TENOR SAXOPHONE

Though not from Chicago, Halliday's residency there established him as one of the local heroes of the hard-bop scene in the 1980s and '90s.

***** Delayed Exposure**
Delmark DE 449 *Halliday; Ira Sullivan (t, flhn, f); Jodie Christian (p); Dennis Carroll (b); George Fludas (d).* 6/91.

***** East Of The Sun**
Delmark DE 458 *As above.* 4/92.

The title of the first disc is suitably pointed, since this was Halliday's debut as a leader: 'An extremely likeable tenor saxophonist,' says the sleeve-note writer, and there's little here to make one disagree. Halliday emerges as a well-practised Rollins disciple. He'd been living and working in Chicago for a little over a decade at that point, and Delmark's minor crusade to record the city's less sensational but worthy constituents pays off with a muscular, well-fashioned blowing date. Some standards and a blues give everyone a chance to hold down some choruses and, if Sullivan's trumpet turns are the most distinctive things here, Halliday acquits himself with the comfortable assurance of a veteran player. The second album is a plain-and-simple second helping, but one can't expect fresh initiatives from a seasoned campaigner at this stage: just good, genuine jazz. Sullivan brings out his tenor for the final 'Will You Still be Mine', and it's a splendid joust that results. An unassuming testament to the player who died as we were preparing this edition.

Jimmy Halperin

TENOR SAXOPHONE

Young American saxophonist working in the Tristano idiom of improvising.

*****(*) Psalm**
Zinnia 110 *Halperin; Sal Mosca (p).* 1/97.

This is the Tristano doctrine in its coolest and most concentrated form. The disc consists of seven lines written by Halperin, played as a series of formal duets and followed by improvisations on six of them: it runs as 49 minutes of uninterrupted music. The lines are utterly remote from their standard chords, as serpentine as any composing in this manner, and the improvising is enacted completely in the spirit of the occasion: oblique, far-sighted, completely self-absorbed yet drily compelling. Halperin suggests an unswerving dedication to the idiom and Mosca is the ideal partner. Scarcely to every jazz taste, and all the better for it.

Chico Hamilton (born 1921)

DRUMS

A native Los Angeles man, Hamilton played in the city through the '40s and '50s, forming his own band in 1955, which won much acclaim. Studio credits as writer and performer took up much of his time until the '80s, when he began touring and recording with his own groups again. An undervalued and considerable influence and performer.

*** Gongs East

Discovery DSCD 831 *Hamilton; Eric Dolphy (as, f, bcl); Dennis Budimir (g); Nathan Gershman (clo); Wyatt Ruther (b).* 12/58.

*** Featuring Eric Dolphy

Fresh Sound FSCD 1004 *As above, except add Ralph Pena (b).* 5/59.

A less celebrated drum-led academy than Art Blakey's, and yet Hamilton has always surrounded himself with gifted young musicians and has helped bring forward players as inventive as Eric Dolphy, Larry Coryell, Charles Lloyd and, much later, Eric Person as well. Hamilton has always taken an inventive and even idiosyncratic approach to the constitution of his groups, and often the only identifying mark is his own rolling lyricism and unceasing swing. Anyone who has seen the classic festival movie, *Jazz On A Summer's Day*, will remember the almost hypnotic concentration of his mallet solo.

Hamilton poses rather self-consciously on the cover of *Gongs East* like a pre-Charles Atlas, 110-lb.-weakling version of J. Arthur Rank's trademark gong-beater. By 1958, though, nobody was kicking sand in the face of this band, which was commercially one of the most successful modern-jazz units of its day. The recruitment of Dolphy in place of previous multi-reedmen Buddy Collette and Paul Horn came just in time for the Newport Jazz Festival appearances, captured in the evergreen movie, *Jazz on a Summer's Day*, and gave the album, his second with Hamilton, the kind of unexpectedly pointed resonance that has always characterized the drummer's slightly Europeanized chamber jazz.

Dolphy's later enthusiasm for cello in place of piano may have been inspired by Gershman's distinctive passage-work, but the album is now primarily of interest for his own increasingly confident soloing; check out 'Passion Flower'. His bass clarinet work on the title-track and the alto-led ensembles on 'Tuesday At Two' are particularly distinctive. Budimir makes a few successful interventions and Hamilton's drumming is as adventurous as always.

The May 1959 session – previously released as *That Hamilton Man* – is darker and more angular. On his last studio appearance with the Quintet, Dolphy chips in with his first recorded composition; the moody 'Lady E' largely avoids the folkish sentimentality of parts of *Gongs East* and helps sustain the later album's prevailing air of appealing melancholy.

***(*) The Dealer

Impulse! 547 958-2 *Hamilton; George Bohanon (tb); Arnie Lawrence (as); Jimmy Woods (ts); Charles Lloyd (ts, f); Archie Shepp (p); Ernie Hayes (org); Larry Coryell, Gabor Szabo (g); Richard Davis (b); Albert Stinson (b, v); Willie Bobo (perc).* 9/62–9/66.

There is still a huge gap, several decades wide, in the Hamilton discography, but at least the reappearance of this fine set signals an intent to backfill some of his excellent work for Bob Thiele at Impulse!. The CD includes the original album, with earlier material from *Chic Chic Chico* and *Passin' Thru*, as well as a single track – the not entirely representative 'Big Noise From Winnetka' – from the label compilation, *Definitive Jazz Scene: Volume 3*.

As ever, much of the emphasis falls on young and relatively untried players. Coryell is treated as the remarkable discovery he undoubtedly was, with generous solo space on almost every track. His soulful blues line and rock intensity are best sampled on 'Thoughts', which begins with an echoed vocal from Chico himself; Larry's spot is punctuated with sharp, pots-and-pans accents from the leader, before giving way to arguably Richard Davis's best solo on record, a wonderfully constructed thing. On his jazz debut Coryell also makes his presence felt with his first recorded jazz composition; 'Larry Of Arabia' is a pretty basic rise-and-fall idea, but it spurs the drummer into a fabulous solo. Too bad the track fades away so lamely; so much so that one suspects there must have been a tape problem.

Shepp stops by to add a piano line to his own 'For Mods Only', as quirky and self-possessed as ever. There is uncredited percussion on the closing 'Jim-Jeannie', a tribute to the Cheathams. Jimmy provides the arrangements for 'The Dealer' and 'Baby, You Know' and conducts 'A Trip', so it's not inconceivable that he was persuaded to shake a tambourine as well. Arnie Lawrence is virtually unknown. A Brooklynite who moved to the West Coast in search of work, he sounds superficially like Charlie Parker, but has a rawer tonality and an almost eccentric approach to phrasing that could never be confused with Bird.

The additional material is marked by the very different guitar-sound of Gabor Szabo, and Charles Lloyd's floatier saxophone and flute. Good as it is to have these things back in circulation, the real weight falls on *The Dealer* itself. Heard afresh, it confirms Hamilton's standing as one of the most original bandleaders around. A few more reissues will perhaps speed up the process of rediscovery.

*** Reunion

Soul Note 121191 *Hamilton; Buddy Collette (f, cl, as); Fred Katz (clo); John Pisano (g); Carson Smith (b).* 6/89.

No longer 110 lb., the latter-day Hamilton packs an impressive punch. This was a brief album-and-tour reunion of the original Hamilton Quintet, with Pisano in for the otherwise-engaged Jim Hall, and it reveals Hamilton as one of the most underrated and possibly influential jazz percussionists of recent times. Rather than keeping up with any of the Joneses, he sustains a highly original idiom which is retrospectively reminiscent of Paul Motian's but is altogether more abstract. The spontaneously improvised 'Five Friends' might have worked better as a duet with Collette (like 'Brushing With B' and 'Conversation'), but the immediately preceding 'Dreams Of Youth', dedicated by its composer, Fred Katz, to the dead and betrayed of Tiananmen Square, is one of the most moving jazz pieces of recent years, drawing out Hamilton's non-Western accents. *Reunion* is confidently exploratory and powerfully effective.

*****(*) Arroyo**
Soul Note 121241 *Hamilton; Eric Person (as, ss); Cary DeNigris (g); Reggie Washington (b).* 12/90.

That Hamilton should christen this band Euphoria is testimony to his continued appetite for music-making. Though it's as far in style as it is in years from the 1950s Quintet, there are clear lines of continuity. Hamilton's preference for a guitarist over a piano player helps free up the drums, allowing Hamilton to experiment with melodic improvisation. Typically, DeNigris is given considerable prominence – much as Jim Hall, Larry Coryell and John Abercrombie were at different times – with Person assigned a colourist's role.

The long opening 'Alone Together' is a vibrantly inventive version of a wearying warhorse. Hamilton's polyrhythms open the tune to half a dozen new directions and Washington produces some of his best work of the set. The other standard, Lester Young's and Jon Hendricks's 'Tickle Toe', has the drummer scatting with the same relaxed abandon he applies to his kit. His writing on 'Sorta New', 'Cosa Succede?' and the intriguingly titled 'Taunts Of An Indian Maiden' is still full of ideas, exploiting band textures to the full. DeNigris and Person both claim at least one writing credit, and the guitarist's 'Stop' is ambitious and unsettling. The mix doesn't favour the leader unduly, but Washington is slightly submerged on some of the up-tempo numbers. Hamilton's inventiveness seems unstinted; this is impressive stuff.

*****(*) Trio!**
Soul Note 121246 *Hamilton; Eric Person (as, ss, sno); Cary DeNigris (g).* 5/92.

At 71, Hamilton still produces a beefy sound and still refuses to stay rooted in the styles of his youth. The 'heavy metal' mannerisms of his late-'80s bands have mellowed a bit, though both Person and DeNigris let rip when the need arises. The trio had been around for some time when the record was cut, and they play as if they're used to one another. DeNigris and Hamilton combine effectively on 'C & C' but the outstanding track is Person's long '10th Vision', which calls in M-Base mannerisms, the oozing funk of old-time organ trios, and hints of a free-ish idiom.

Hamilton simply can't stay still and has obviously decided to play until he drops. Be assured, there's plenty more to come.

*****(*) My Panamanian Friend**
Soul Note 121265 *As for Arroyo, except omit Washington; add Kenny Davis (b).* 8/92.

To mark the thirtieth anniversary of the saxophonist's death, this is a tribute to former employee Eric Dolphy, whose tragically foreshortened career after leaving the Hamilton band is still one of the major, if unassimilated, achievements of contemporary jazz. Predictably, perhaps, Hamilton selects from among the least wiggy areas of Dolphy's output: 'South Street Exit', 'Springtime', the blues 'Serene', the inevitable 'Miss Ann' (perhaps Dolphy's best-known composition), 'Mandrake', 'Miss Movement' and, from *Out To Lunch*, 'Something Sweet, Something Tender'. Dolphy's young namesake plays decently, but a lot of the emphasis falls on Hamilton, whose rather enigmatic title relates to Dolphy's Panamanian ancestry, of which Eric Dolphy senior was so proud.

***** Dancing To A Different Drummer**
Soul Note 121291 *Hamilton (solo perc).* 3–4/93.

There haven't been many drummers who could sustain this level of interest unaccompanied. Hamilton has always been a highly melodic player and, though there are moments among these ten tracks when he seems to be striving *too* hard for that effect, there is no mistaking the innate musicality of his approach. Some of the tracks – like 'Dance Of The Tympanies' and 'The Snare Drum' – would be mere technical exercises in other hands, but Chico carries them through, logically, smilingly and lovingly. Not perhaps the most instantly accessible of his records, but certainly one for Hamilton enthusiasts.

***** Timely**
All Points Jazz 3001 *Hamilton; Eric Person (ss, as, f); Cary DeNigris (g); Paul Ramsey (b).* 99.

As if to mock us for our premature obituary of a couple of editions back, Hamilton continues to create vivid, tireless jazz. Having enjoyed his moment in the foreground on *Different Drummer*, he holds back from the foreground to provide a potent accompaniment to Person and DeNigris. 'Malletdonia' is the exception, but it comes right at the end of the album. The switch to electric jazz and funk is a surprise, given the times and given Hamilton's recent recorded output, but these tracks are every bit as idiomatic and personalized as the more conventional acoustic tunes. We particularly liked 'Cheeks' Groove' and the two-part 'These Are The Dues'. The Salvador Dalí cover (melting watches, predictably) is perhaps a bit of a false note. Hamilton isn't so much bending and distorting time as taking the hurry out of it.

Scott Hamilton (born 1954)

TENOR SAXOPHONE

Born and raised in Providence, Rhode Island, Hamilton has helped redefine mainstream jazz for two decades. To say that he plays like Ben Webster or Don Byas is to miss the point, for Hamilton has always been more resolutely contemporary than conservative.

*****(*) Scott Hamilton Is A Good Wind Who Is Blowing Us No Ill**
Concord CCD 4042 *Hamilton; Bill Berry (t); Nat Pierce (p); Monty Budwig (b); Jake Hanna (d).* 77.

***** Scott Hamilton 2**
Concord CCD 4061 *As above, except omit Berry; add Cal Collins (g).* 1/78.

*****(*) Tenorshoes**
Concord CCD 44127 *Hamilton; Dave McKenna (p); Phil Flanigan (b); Jeff Hamilton (d).* 12/79.

He doesn't double on soprano, bass clarinet or flute. He probably doesn't know what multiphonics are. He has never been described as 'angular', and if he was ever 'influenced by Coltrane' it certainly never extended to his saxophone playing. And yet Scott Hamilton is the real thing, a tenor player of the old school who was born only after most of the old school were dead or drawing bus-passes. His wuffly delivery and clear-edged tone are definitive of mainstream jazz, and the affection in which Hamilton is held on both sides of the Atlantic is not hard to understand. And yet what he does is utterly original and un-slavish, not in thrall to anyone.

Concord boss, the late Carl Jefferson, remembers Hamilton turning up for his first session for the label, looking 'like a character in Scott Fitzgerald', with a fifth of gin tucked into his jacket, and playing, as it turned out, like a veteran of the first Jazz Age, a style which drew on Coleman Hawkins, Chu Berry, Lester Young, Don Byas and Zoot Sims, resolutely unfashionable in 1977 but completely authentic and unfeigned.

Hamilton's Concord debut, named after Leonard Feather's enthusiastic imprimatur, wasn't perhaps quite forceful enough to be described in terms of wind but it was certainly a breath of fresh air, and it refocused attention almost immediately on the undischarged possibilities of jazz before the bebop revolution. From the opening lines of 'That's All', it was clear that a special new talent was at work. At twenty-two Hamilton had the poise and the patience of a much more experienced player. Quite how he had learnt so much so quickly remains something of a mystery and, though there are one or two instances of him coltishly running ahead of the group, what is most impressive is the sheer discipline of his playing.

As the unimaginative title suggests, the follow-up was recorded almost immediately afterwards, given the enthusiasm for the first record. It was perhaps too soon for Hamilton to have settled down and thought about what he was going to do. The absence of Berry was unfortunate, and the addition of guitar makes for a rather smoother and less pungent product. For once, Hamilton seems content to fall back on predetermined ideas. Though everything on the record is played with exemplary professionalism, it never seems to get beyond that point and remains rather formulaic.

The cover of *Tenorshoes* features a pair of basketball boots (a Hamilton signature at the time) bronzed like a baby's first shoes, and beside them a dish of chocolates. However tired Hamilton must have been about constant references to his age – a veteran at twenty-five – he might usefully have sued over the sweets, because his saxophone playing is fat-free and low-cholesterol. However saccharine some of the tunes – 'I Should Care', 'The Shadow Of Your Smile' and 'The Nearness Of You' might all have come from the confectionery counter – Hamilton explores the changes with a fine, probing intelligence that is every bit as intellectually satisfying as it is emotionally fulsome. The unaccompanied intro to 'I Should Care' and an energetic reading of 'How High The Moon' bespeak a rapidly developing sense of structure and dynamics. McKenna is superb (a duo album would have been a worthwhile investment) and the recording is bright and unfussy, even if Hamilton seems a little too forward on occasion.

***** With Scott's Band In New York City**

Concord CCD 4070 *Hamilton; Warren Vaché (c); Chris Flory (g); Norman Simmons (p); Phil Flanigan (b); Chuck Riggs (d).* 78.

One of the less well-known items in the Hamilton catalogue, and pretty largely hijacked on this occasion by his front-line partner. Vaché's crisp, bright-toned cornet is endlessly attractive and this is one of his very best recordings of the period. 'Darn That Dream' and 'There Will Never Be Another You' are sterling performances from both men. Ideas are exchanged at a furious pace. But for the later swing-era tonality of Hamilton's tenor, this might almost be a throwback to something by the Austin High School gang.

*****(*) Groovin' High Live At E.J.'s**

JLR 103.607 2CD *Hamilton; Rick Bell (ts); Johnny O'Neal (p); Dewey Sampson (b); James Martin (d).* 10/81.

A rare release away from Concord, and presumably part of some contractual deal with the Atlanta, Georgia, club who have released some excellent live sets, though unfortunately the club closed its doors only months after this recording (which didn't see the light of day for 15 years) was made. Because of the lapse in time, hearing it for the first time in 1996 required a certain resetting of expectations. It did, though, underline how much rougher and edgier Hamilton could be in a live context. The opening 'Stella By Starlight' has some extraordinarily gruff, passionate wails, though most of the set is light and limber, with an emphasis on Lestorian cool. Hamilton is joined for three numbers by fellow tenorman Rick Bell, not widely known but a fast and accurate player who is no slouch as a soloist. His approach to 'I'll Remember April' is tougher and more abrasive than Hamilton, with a hard, sandblasted tone that you wouldn't want to listen to all night. He's more in place on the next two tunes, 'Things Ain't What They Used To Be' and 'Lester Leaps In', after which he leaves Hamilton to it. We're not convinced that there was really enough in this for a two-CD set. The second disc has a couple of beauties – the boppish title-theme and a more than routine 'Body And Soul' – but the essence of this set could certainly have been captured on a single disc.

***** Close Up**

Concord CCD 4197 *Hamilton; John Bunch (p); Chris Flory (g); Phil Flanigan (b); Chuck Riggs (d).* 2/82.

***** In Concert**

Concord CCD 4233 *As above, except add Eiji Kitamura (cl).* 6/83.

***** The Second Set**

Concord CCD 4311 *As above.*

The early 1980s saw Hamilton consolidating his position as a torchbearer for mainstream jazz. In doing so, he turned himself into a seemingly tireless tourer. The band with John Bunch, Chris Flory, Phil Flanigan and Chuck Riggs was the first that seemed moulded to his particular conception, and they gave him the basis for some more adventurous playing. Some of the harmonic excursions on *Close Up* are significantly bolder and more risky than anything he'd been able or prepared to do before that point. 'Mr Big And Mr Modern' might be read as a reply to some of the critics who, by 1982, were almost routinely dismissing Scott as a young fogey who perversely refused to fall in with the Coltrane tendency; at least some of his solos might usefully have been transcribed and sent round the papers (if indeed some of these critics knew how to read black dots).

On the live records it is Hamilton who dominates, understandably enough. Bunch and Flory, though, do seem to be rather out of things, which is a pity. Setting aside the irritation value of a Japanese audience who seem determined to applaud themselves every time they recognize an intro, the two Tokyo sets are marvellous and the occasion certainly merited the release of two discs; five years on, and Concord would probably have paired them up. *The Second Set* begins with a reading of 'All The Things You Are' that within a few bars confirms that Hamilton is much more than a mellow stylist; he is also an improviser of real stamina and character. Flory has his moment on big flag-wavers like Basie's 'Taps Miller' (*Second Set*) and 'One O'Clock Jump' (*In Concert*), and Bunch, though mixed down, has his couple of moments in the sun. That audience should have been shot, though: enjoyment is one thing, self-congratulation another.

*** Major League

Concord CCD 4305 *Hamilton; Dave McKenna (p); Jake Hanna (d).* 5/86.

A grower, and one we feel much more sanguine about this time round. Our anxiety stemmed from the more fiery pace Hanna brought to the set. The trio had played together under McKenna's leadership on *No Bass Hit* for Concord, one of big Dave's themed projects, and it may be that he wriggled slightly at the thought of handing over the reins to the youngster. He's certainly still the playing star of this set, turning in a magnificent solo on 'It All Depends On You' and running a powerful, low-register left-hand line that more than amply takes up any slack from the missing bassist. And remember that this is the configuration Cecil Taylor liked to work with.

**** Plays Ballads

Concord 4386 *Hamilton; John Bunch (p); Chris Flory (g); Phil Flanigan (b); Chuck Riggs (d).* 3/89.

Still for some Hamilton's best record, not because the ballad programme allows him any paths of least resistance but simply because this is the sort of material which allows him to show off his strengths: harmonic subtlety at slow tempos, delicate, almost seamless transitions between ideas, and an ability to invest a simple, familiar melody with maximum expression. 'Round Midnight' and 'In A Sentimental Mood' are read with an intriguing slant which freshens up the Monk tune considerably. 'Two Eighteen', dedicated to Hamilton's wife (and we suspect it may refer to the number of a honeymoon suite), is surprisingly his first recorded composition; at first blush, it doesn't suggest a writing talent commensurate with his playing skills, but it's a fine piece nevertheless. The Don Byas-associated 'Laura' and an oblique 'Body And Soul' (also considerably freshened) were added only when *Ballads* was transferred to CD. This seems odd, because these are the outstanding performances on the record and, we hear, are much enjoyed by Don and Bean up in heaven.

***(*) Radio City

Concord CCD 4428 *Hamilton; Gerald Wiggins (p); Dennis Irwin (b); Connie Kay (d).* 2/90.

This was a smashing band. The defining difference from previous ensembles was the much-lamented Kay's springy, joyous drumming, though Wiggins is also a hugely undervalued player who merits close attention. The material is the usual mix of the familiar – 'Yesterday', 'My Ideal', 'The Touch Of Your Lips' – and the less familiar – Duke and Mercer Ellington's 'Tonight I Shall Sleep With A Smile On My Face' and Woody Herman's 'Apple Honey', which was an inspired choice, a tune that might almost have been written for Hamilton. The title-track is the most accomplished original to date, a vigorous, bouncing theme with an appealing rawness of tone, and again a tune that wears its nostalgic heart openly on its sleeve. Wiggins and Kay meld impeccably, the pianist's big, generous delivery built right on top of the count, pushing Hamilton along gently but firmly.

**** Race Point

Concord CCD 492 *Hamilton; Gerald Wiggins (p); Howard Alden (g); Andy Simpkins (b); Jeff Hamilton (d).* 9/91.

Another wonderful record, and certainly the most adventurous one to date. Carl Perkins's 'Groove Yard' was a fascinating choice of opener, an evocative, left-field theme with an insistent drive to the chords. Again Hamilton gives the lie to any suggestion that he is unwilling to experiment; his solo has its 'outside' moments, and very convincing they are. Interspersed with the quartet tracks are four duets with guitarist Alden. 'Chelsea Bridge' is outstanding and so is 'The Song Is You', which closes the set. Alden's low string figures and Hamilton's squeezed harmonics give the duos a tremendous range. Of the quartet tracks, 'Race Point' itself is notable; Wiggins opens up the middle section with a wild clamber up the scale that feeds the leader (and writer) a powerful solo. Jeff Hamilton plays immaculately, if a touch stiffly in places. We were initially disappointed with the sound, but in retrospect a more compressed mix probably makes sense. A very strong record. Surprise yourself with it or, better still, surprise a Hamilton sceptic.

*** Groovin' High

Concord CCD 4509 *Hamilton; Ken Peplowski, Spike Robinson (ts); Gerald Wiggins (p); Howard Alden (g); Dave Stone (b); Jake Hanna (d).* 9/91.

This could have gone either way: down the same road as many of those formulaic tenor battles of the past, or it could have opened up an increasingly needed outlet for Hamilton, an opportunity to play with other like-minded horn players. As things turn out, it's a bit of both. Sensibly, the three-tenor front-line is called for on every track. Hamilton himself sits out 'What's New', Peplowski powders his nose during 'That Old Devil Called Love' and the excellent Robinson takes a powder for 'I'll See You In My Dreams'. It might have been interesting to let the one doubler in the line, Peplowski, air his clarinet at some point, but that doesn't seem to have been part of the deal. They open, Musketeer fashion, with Sonny Stitt's 'Blues Up And Down', after which there's a fairly predictable round of solo spots, culminating in 'Body And Soul' which they manage to knock off with a solo each in five and a half minutes. There's certainly no hint of the kind of shapeless jamming that overtakes many multiple-horn sessions. The heads are relaxed and bitty enough to suggest that there wasn't much time for advance preparation, but there's sufficient empathy and hands-on experience for that not to matter.

**(*) Scott Hamilton With Strings

Concord CCD 4538 *Hamilton; Alan Broadbent (p); Bob Maize (b); Roy McCurdy (d); strings.* 10/92.

We can't find any justification for a more positive assessment of this, beyond the point that it seems a bit of a waste of a player like Broadbent to have him backed by not very impressive string-textures. The usual drill otherwise: highly professional, inevitably not very swinging, trio bits fine, Scott good out in front, but definitely hampered by the format.

****** East Of The Sun**

Concord CCD 4583 *Hamilton; Brian Lemon (p); Dave Green (b); Allan Ganley (d).* 8/93.

*****(*) Live At Brecon Jazz Festival**

Concord CCD 4649 *As above.* 94.

Perhaps a touch of cis-Atlantic pride in our rating for these. A devoted Anglophile, Hamilton was spending more and more time playing in the UK, where he has a more-than-loyal following and where in this group he has found like-minded players of great experience. Just to complicate the geography a little, the tunes on *East Of The Sun* were the result of a readers' poll in the Japanese *Swing Journal*. Hamilton had long wished to record with a British group, and one can see why. Lemon is one of the finest accompanists around, and he solos with such bluff confidence that he often masks the subtlety of what he is playing. Ganley and Green combine effectively, and both of them are accurately caught.

The live session from Brecon (a small but growing festival in Wales that has always managed to attract top talent) is inevitably more relaxed and free-flowing, though there are hints here and there – 'Come Rain Or Come Shine', 'Blue Wales' – that Hamilton is working on autopilot and not thinking through his ideas. These are quibbles, though. The whole thing gives off an air of matey enjoyment, and the standard of musicianship from the trio suggests one more reason than English beer why Scott might yet settle here.

Just for the record (so to speak), the programme *SJ* readers wanted to hear from Hamilton went as follows: 'Autumn Leaves' (big-toned and romantic), 'Stardust', 'It Could Happen To You', 'It Never Entered My Mind' (one of the loveliest recordings of it since Miles's classic), 'Bernie's Tune' (mysteriously), 'East Of The Sun (And West Of The Moon)', 'Time After Time', Hamilton's own 'Setagaya Serenade', 'That's All', 'All The Things You Are' and 'Indiana'. Full of surprises, the Japanese.

****** Organic Duke**

Concord CCD 4623 *Hamilton; Mike LeDonne (org); Dennis Irwin (b); Chuck Riggs (d).* 5/94.

This instantly superseded *Ballads*, *Race Point* and *East Of The Sun* as our favourite Hamilton album. A couple of years on, it's probably slipped back a little in our affection, but it's still a remarkable and very beautiful record. The use of organ is a surprise – and a very effective one – but it might have been an idea to replace string-bass with guitar and vary the textures a little. As it is, some tracks are a touch monochrome. It helps more than a little that the material is of such high quality, from robust swingers like 'Jump For Joy' and 'Castle Rock' (a favourite Hodges vehicle) to 'Moon Mist' and 'Isfahan', which Hamilton gives a strong Yankee accent, taking away something of its melting 'Eastern' quality. This was one of the last records supervised by Concord boss, Carl Jefferson, before his death, and all those years after that improbable debut it must have given him considerable satisfaction to see how well the kid had turned out.

*****(*) My Romance**

Concord CCD 4710 *Hamilton; Joel Helleny (tb); Norman Simmons (p); Dennis Irwin (b); Chuck Riggs (d).* 2/95.

Rare indeed to hear Hamilton working with a brass player. Helleny appeared with the saxophonist at the Fujitsu-Concord Jazz Festival not long before this (the results are documented on a live Concord set) and they seemed to get along famously there. The unexpected effect is to make Hamilton sound harder-edged and more pungent in attack than usual. Presumably he is playing no differently, but the context of a slide trombone makes that much difference.

The other big difference on this set is Simmons who, of all Hamilton's piano players of recent years, seems less concerned with his own thing and most able to buckle down to the job. He is an elegant stylist in his own right, with a firm, sure touch and a lovely tone. His original composition, 'Abundance', gets the album off to an arresting start. He also contributes a gentler theme, 'Jan', towards the end. Hamilton throws in his usual token theme, the joyous 'Sugarchile', but for the most part this is a set of old standards like 'Poor Butterfly' and 'Lullaby In Rhythm', though the rather startling opening is compounded by Blue Mitchell's 'Blue Caper' and Pettiford's 'Swingin' Till The Girls Come Home', neither of them things you would expect to find in Scott's bag.

*****(*) The Red Door**

Concord CCD 4799 *Hamilton; Bucky Pizzarelli (g).* 3/95.

Ah, but who's playing the bass? The answer is Bucky himself, whose seven-string guitar – with low A string – and nimble technique make it sound as if there is at least a trio at work here. The idea of the album was a tribute to Zoot Sims and it includes material that would have been familiar to the great saxophonist. Zoot and Bucky appeared in this configuration on a 1975 album for Classic Jazz; we can't comment on it, but there is no doubt that each and every item on this set has Zoot's signature all over it, and Bucky frequently quotes his distinctive phrases. There are some fascinating moments on this. 'Gee Baby, Ain't I Good To You' is astonishing, pitched high and fast, but it's a subtly transposed interpretation of 'Jitterbug Waltz' that really catches the attention; virtuosic, intelligent jazz, played at a very high level. Buy and enjoy this record.

*****(*) After Hours**

Concord CCD 4755 *Hamilton; Tommy Flanagan (p); Bob Cranshaw (b); Lewis Nash (d).* 96.

So effortless and smooth that it could almost pass by unnoticed. To our eternal shame, we have regularly taken the title all too literally and used this one to chill out after a session at the screen. This is very close to late-nite-and-lite, exquisitely done as you would expect, given the personnel, but curiously lacking in bite and chew. 'Woody'N'You' is a great group performance, a real meeting of minds. Nothing that follows comes close to its elegant pace. Flanagan is in magisterial form, leading a rhythm section that is recorded with gentle authority, a Concord strength.

***** Christmas Love Song**

Concord CCD 4771 *Hamilton; Alan Broadbent (p); Dave Cliff (g); Dave Green (b); Allan Ganley (d); London String Ensemble; etc.* 4/97.

It's almost axiomatic that we'll pretend to hate Christmas albums. How many do you know that are really worth hearing? Ella's, maybe, and this one. Hamilton is ironic enough to cut through the schmaltz, and Broadbent is an intelligent enough arranger to give these familiar tunes an extra level of interest. It would be redundant to list them all, since you know them anyway.

*****(*) Concord Jazz Heritage**
Concord CCD 4819-2 *As above.* 77–98.

A useful and attractive selection of the saxophonist's work for his home label. Anyone who's been on board from the start will find it a rather predictable trawl, but for anyone who's new to Hamilton it's going to be a delightful surprise.

***** Blues, Bop & Ballads**
Concord CCD 4866 *Hamilton; Greg Gisbert (t); Joel Helleny (tb); Norman Simmons (p); Duke Robillard (g); Dennis Irwin (b); Chuck Riggs (d).* 2/99.

As the title hints, this is an eclectic survey, too various to work entirely successfully as an album. As ever, Scott picks some fascinating material. He programmes Ike Quebec's 'Blue Harlem' alongside Eldridge's 'Fish Market', Hawk's 'Stuffy' and Dameron's 'Good Bait', but we really like 'Smile', the Charlie Chaplin song which has rarely sounded more joyous and more philosophically supple. The band isn't quite the unit you'd expect to hear round Scott. Gisbert is a leader himself and some of the others are all too obviously journeymen, leaving the album sound like a cobbled-together club or festival set. Not a classic and some way short of exceptional, but as ever a solidly executed jazz record.

Atle Hammer

TRUMPET AND FLUGELHORN

Norwegian trumpeter who follows a conservative hard-bop method.

**** Joy Spring**
Gemini GMCD 49 *Hammer; Harald Bergersen (ss, ts); Eivin Sannes (p); Terje Venaas (b); Egil Johansen (d).* 6/85.

***** Arizona Blue**
Gemini GMCD 65 *Hammer; Jon Gordon (as); Red Holloway (ts); Egil Kapstad (p); Terje Venaas (b); Egil Johansen (d).* 8/89.

Honest and workmanlike music fronted by a self-effacing brassman. Hammer's affection for Clifford Brown's music is evident, but he is a long way short of his model here. The first session, co-led with tenorman Bergersen, is done decently enough, but the material, an interesting set of jazz themes, is woefully under-characterized and nobody seems eager to take advantage of the solo limelight. *Arizona Blue*, hurriedly organized to take advantage of the presence of Holloway on a visit to Oslo, works out much better. Kapstad contributes two memorable themes, with the 3/4 'Remembrance Of Eric Dolphy' particularly strong, and Hammer, though still no match for the other horns, makes his careful style sound appropriate to 'Stranger In Paradise' and 'Portrait Of Jenny'. Gordon's blues, 'Rainbow Rabbit', is the other playing highlight.

Gunter Hampel (born 1937)

COMPOSER, VIBRAPHONE, PIANO, REEDS

Born in Göttingen, he studied music and architecture before firing up much of the German free scene of the early '60s. Formed his own Birth label in 1970, which has documented a broad span of work since; vibes and reeds vie for first place in his own playing.

****(*) The 8th July 1969**
Birth 001 *Hampel; Anthony Braxton (as, ss, sno, f, cbcl); Willem Breuker (ss, as, ts, b cl); Arjen Gorter (b); Steve McCall (d); Jeanne Lee (v).* 7/69.

Virtually all of Hampel's work since 1969 has appeared on the fissiparous Birth label (and virtually the whole Birth catalogue consists of Hampel's work, in small groups and in various versions of his improvisation collective, the Galaxie Dream Band; the only two exceptions are duos nominally led by singer Jeanne Lee, who is Mrs Hampel, and by the alto saxophonist, Marion Brown). Birth has transferred some of a substantial back-catalogue to CD, though collectors will still have to rely on vinyl bins and auctions. Completists can probably still find factory-condition LPs at specialist shops.

There are obvious and misleading parallels between Hampel's work and that of the similarly cosmically obsessed Sun Ra, but Hampel is typically saturnine rather than Saturnian and he lacks the ripping, swinging joy of Ra's various Intergalactic Arkestras. There is another obvious connection, another American one, which has the beauty of having a basis in this discography. However deeply absorbed he has appeared to be in Afro-American music, multi-instrumentalist composer Anthony Braxton learned a great deal from the European collective/free movement of the late 1960s, and particularly from Hampel, who has written pieces with numbered and coded titles reminiscent of Braxton's own later practice.

8th July 1969 was the first Birth disc to become available on CD. It isn't quite as time-warped as some of his work of the time, but nor is it quite as individual. Lee's voice is one of the most significant in contemporary improvisation; only Linda Sharrock, Diamanda Galas and Joan La Barbara match her for sheer strength and adaptability. Willem Breuker is already an imaginative and powerful soloist. Braxton, who in 1969 had just completed the epochal solo *For Alto* (which then had to wait three years for commercial release), still sounds as if he's fishing for a music commensurate with his remarkable talent. It's not at all clear that he found it with Hampel.

*****(*) All The Things You Could Be If Charles Mingus Was Your Daddy**
Birth 031 *Hampel; Perry Robinson (cl); Thomas Keyserling, Mark Whitecage (as, f); Martin Bues (d, perc); Jeanne Lee (v).* 11/78, 7/80.

The reference, of course, is to Mingus's own elaborate contrafact on 'All The Things You Are'. Scored for just percussion and woodwinds (with Lee very much part of the horn section), it's a sprawling and contrary piece with moments when the ensemble perversely stretches taut as a hawser. Recording quality isn't the very best and some of the instruments are recessed or distorted.

Robinson's clarinet is the main sufferer and there are a couple of moments on one of his main statements when there might also be tape problems.

This isn't music for hi-fi fiends. Its sheer energy and self-possession are what create the magic, and anyone who has yet to hear Hampel will find this an appealing place to start. The additional tracks, recorded two years earlier, were originally to be found on the Birth LP, *All Is Real*.

***** Jubilation**
Birth 0038 *Hampel; Manfred Schoof (t); Albert Mangelsdorff (tb); Perry Robinson (cl); Marion Brown (as); Thomas Keyserling (as, f, af); Barre Phillips (b); Steve McCall (d); Jeanne Lee (v).* 11/83.

***** Fresh Heat – Live At Sweet Basil**
Birth CD 0039 *Hampel; Stephen Haynes, Vance R Provey (t); Curtis Fowlkes (tb); Bob Stewart (tba); Perry Robinson (cl); Thomas Keyserling, Mark Whitecage (as, f); Bob Hanlon (ts, f); Lucky Ennett (ts); Bill Frisell (g); Kyoto Fujiwara (b); Marvin 'Smitty' Smith (d); Arthur Jenkins, Jeanne Lee (v).* 2/85.

*****(*) Dialog – Live At The Eldena Jazz Festival, 1992**
Birth CD 041 *Hampel; Mathias Schubert (ts).* 7/92.

*****(*) Time Is Now – Live At The Eldena Jazz Festival, 1992**
Birth CD 042 *Hampel; Mike Dietz (g); Jurgen Attig (b); Heinrich Kobberling (d).* 7/92.

***** Celestial Glory – Live At The Knitting Factory**
Birth CD 040 *Hampel; Perry Robinson (cl); Mark Whitecage (as, ss); Thomas Keyserling (as, f); Jeanne Lee (v).* 9/91.

Promising signs that Hampel, now in his mid-fifties, is branching out in new directions and at the same time attracting a wider following. *Jubilation* is an excellent album – 'Little Bird' is particularly strong – which lacks some of the instinctive empathy of the Galaxie Dream Band but also some of its increasingly hermetic inwardness. The live New York City set smacks of no one more forcibly than Charles Mingus, who was at the very least a conscious presence in Hampel's thinking as far back as 1980 and the double reference of *All The Things You Could Be* ... (Birth 0031). Mingus's legacy is still largely unexplored and Hampel, now that he has abandoned the more indulgent aspects of free music, may be the man to do it.

The Knitting Factory would seem on the face of it to be a potential home away from home for Hampel, the kind of place where his approach to improvisation meets with a ready acceptance and understanding. Unfortunately, the three pieces included on *Celestial Glory* are a bit drab and slabby. Robinson is always interesting, and his solo passages and duets with the leader provide much of the interest. Lee is recorded very close, which introduces some ugly pops and squawks, and there is an overall lack of good production which CD cruelly exposes.

The duos with Schubert at Eldena are very good indeed and 'After The Fact' is one of the best-documented performances by any of the Hampel 'family'. The other record, taped a day earlier at the same festival, has a less familiar line-up but is marked by 'Serenade For Marion Brown', a heartfelt tribute to a loyal ally who seems to have been ill with dental problems at the time. One wouldn't wish the same thing on Hampel but, at this stage in the game, it may be time for him to lay down the bass clarinet and concentrate his attention exclusively on vibes.

Collectors may be interested to note that there are also videos of some of Hampel's activities, also available from Birth, and that he has also published four books of music and interviews which offer important insights into one of Europe's most independent improvisers.

***** Next Generation**
Birth 0043 *Hampel; Christian Weidner (as, ts); Mike Dietz (g); Christoph Busse (p); Fritz Feger (b); Michael Verhovec (d); Barbara Studemann, Shaun Vargas, Rumi, Spax, One Soul (v).* 9/95.

Subtitled 'Concepts in Jazz-Rap-Hip-Hop', which rather makes the flesh crawl in anticipation, this turns out to be no more self-consciously fashionable than anything else this determined individualist has ever done. The rappers do a creditable job with some pretty cumbersome words, though things like 'Paradise Of The Haves And Hell Of The Have Nots' are so completely *sui generis* that no one is likely to compare them with similar syntheses Stateside. Hampel is unmistakably a European and, though he remains devoted to what he sees as the anarchic dimension in jazz, he is also a passionate believer in order.

As before, Weidner is the key instrumentalist, but the new rhythm section functions with ferocious intensity and drummer Verhovec deserves special mention for combining freedom and control. Hampel is still hard to pin down as an instrumentalist. His vibes work is incomparable – which is not to say that he is greater than Bags or Hamp or Hutcherson, simply that he can't be compared to anyone, living or dead. His bass clarinet playing has become more conventional over the years, perhaps as his technique has grown sounder, but it is still broodingly effective.

***** Solid Fun**
Birth 044 *Hampel; Christian Weidner (as, ts).* 9/95, 1/96.

All but one of these eight tracks were recorded live at Auerbach Jazznight. 'Solid Fun' itself bears relation to pieces like 'Iron Fist In A Velvet Glove' and 'You Ever Saw Birds Gather And Lift Off?' but is freshly conceived and executed. Once again, Weidner is responsive and intelligent, but Hampel himself rarely rises to his usual level of imagination and some of his solo playing is pedestrian in the extreme.

*****(*) Legendary**
Birth 045 *Hampel; Manfred Schoof (t, flhn); Alexander von Schlippenbach (p); Arjen Gorter (b); Pierre Courbois (d).* 5/97.

A reunion for Hampel's late-'60s band, the same line-up which recorded *Heartplants*. It is now – seemingly – available as a Japanese CD issue. For the rest of us, this latter-day encounter will have to do. 'Legendary' is a flute solo by Hampel, as lateral and sardonic as ever, but with his usual romantic burnish. There is also a reprise of 'Spielplatz', a group composition with a rough-hewn architecture that is entirely Hampel's own. The album is bulked out with a new reading of 'All The Things You Could Be If Charles Mingus Was Your Daddy', a perverse, jolly idea that cements Hampel's open-form approach.

Schlippenbach's contribution is considerable. He is courtly and thoughtful but swings outrageously even when the metre is almost uncountable. Schoof is the Darth Vader of contemporary trumpet playing, a sweet and accommodating talent who has turned to the dark side. His tone is expansive, but with an astringent, tobacco-y quality. Hampel's multi-instrumentalism is no longer a surprise, but his adaptability and ability to shift between idioms is consistently impressive.

***** Köln Concert: Part 1**
Birth CD 047 *Hampel; Christian Weidner (as, ts); Smudo, Christian Vargas, Nuclear B, Sprite, Nore (v); other instrumentation not specified.* 5/97.

****(*) Köln Concert: Part 2**
Birth CD 048 *As above.* 5/97.

Recorded just a day after *Legendary* and at the same festival. It was a good wheeze, naming these records after one of the best-selling jazz records of all time. Unfortunately, instead of Keith Jarrett's tortured intensity and virtuosic handling of technical problems and instead of the thoughtful penetration of the *Legendary* quintet, the Next Generation band indulge themselves mercilessly. It's no accident that the most impressive music here is instrumental, the beautiful 'Jazz Life' on Volume One, and the equally touching 'Sun Down' on the sequel. Jeanne Lee's role seems restricted these days to writing. She has a hand in 'You Ever Saw Birds Gather And Lift Off?' which opens the set, but one misses that rising, potent voice and the sense of danger she always brings. There is nothing on either of these discs that doesn't sound processed, pre-formed and entirely formulaic. Hampel fans will treasure them for the jazz playing but will be put off by some nonsensical trend-chasing. What a contrast to *Next Generation*.

Lionel Hampton (born 1908)

VIBES, PIANO, DRUMS, VOCAL

Born in Louisville, Kentucky, Hampton went to Chicago as a boy and learned drums in a boys' band. He went on to work with various bands – including Les Hite's, backing Louis Armstrong – before switching to vibes and leading his own group in Los Angeles, where Benny Goodman heard him and invited him to join his band. RCA Victor let him lead pick-up dates in New York, 1936–40, and he ran his own big band from 1941, dominated by his own showmanship on vibes, piano and drums alike. That show-stopping style anticipated R&B and let the band survive even the lean rock'n'roll years, although he also recorded in many small-group situations. In the '80s and '90s he was also a major figure in education and publishing, and he assisted in housing programmes. At the end of the century, though suffering some poor health, Hamp continued to be one of jazz's grandest elder statesmen.

***** Lionel Hampton 1929 To 1940**
Jazz Classics In Digital Stereo RPCD 605 *Hampton; Benny Carter (t, as); Ziggy Elman, George Orendorff, Jonah Jones, Cootie Williams, Walter Fuller, Dizzy Gillespie, Henry 'Red' Allen (t); Bobby Hackett (c); J.C Higginbotham, Lawrence Brown, Vernon Brown (tb); Benny Goodman, Eddie Barefield, Pee Wee Russell, Buster Bailey, Edmond Hall, Mezz Mezzrow (cl); Marshal Royal, Omer Simeon (cl, as); Vido Musso (cl, ts); Johnny Hodges, Earl Bostic, Toots Mondello, Buff Estes, George Oldham (as); Arthur Rollini, Paul Howard, Bud Freeman, Budd Johnson, Robert Crowder, Ben Webster, Chu Berry, Coleman Hawkins, Jerry Jerome (ts); Edgar Sampson (bs); Jess Stacy, Joe Bushkin, Clyde Hart, Harvey Brooks, Dudley Brooks, Sir Charles Thompson, Nat Cole, Spencer Odun (p); Ray Perry (vn); Allan Reuss, Charlie Christian, Freddie Green, Ernest Ashley, Oscar Moore, Irving Ashby, Eddie Condon (g); Thomas Valentine (bj); James Jackson (bb); Billy Taylor, Artie Shapiro, Jesse Simpkins, Milt Hinton, Artie Bernstein, Vernon Alley, Mack Walker, Johnny Miller, John Kirby, Wesley Prince (b); Cozy Cole, Alvin Burroughs, Big Sid Catlett, Zutty Singleton, Sonny Greer, Gene Krupa, Lee Young, Nick Fatool, Al Spieldock (d).* 4/29–12/40.

*****(*) Lionel Hampton 1937–1938**
Classics 524 *Hampton; Ziggy Elman, Cootie Williams, Jonah Jones (t); Lawrence Brown (tb); Vido Musso (cl, ts); Mezz Mezzrow, Eddie Barefield (cl); Johnny Hodges, Hymie Schertzer, George Koenig (as); Arthur Rollini (ts); Edgar Sampson (bs); Jess Stacy, Clyde Hart (p); Bobby Bennett, Allan Reuss (g); Harry Goodman, John Kirby, Mack Walker, Johnny Miller, Billy Taylor (b); Gene Krupa, Cozy Cole, Sonny Greer (d).* 2/37–1/38.

*****(*) Lionel Hampton 1938–1939**
Classics 534 *Hampton; Cootie Williams, Harry James, Walter Fuller, Irving Randolph, Ziggy Elman (t); Rex Stewart (c); Lawrence Brown (tb); Benny Carter, Omer Simeon (cl, as); Russell Procope (ss, as); Hymie Schertzer (as, bcl); Johnny Hodges, Dave Matthews, George Oldham (as); Herschel Evans, Babe Russin, Jerry Jerome, Chu Berry (ts); Edgar Sampson, Harry Carney (bs); Jess Stacy, Billy Kyle, Spencer Odun, Clyde Hart (p); Allan Reuss, Danny Barker (g); Billy Taylor, John Kirby, Jesse Simpkins, Milt Hinton (b); Sonny Greer, Jo Jones, Alvin Burroughs, Cozy Cole (d).* 1/38–6/39.

*****(*) Lionel Hampton 1939–1940**
Classics 562 *Hampton; Dizzy Gillespie, Henry 'Red' Allen, Ziggy Elman (t); Benny Carter (t, as); Rex Stewart (c); Lawrence Brown (tb); Edmond Hall (cl); Toots Mondello (cl, as); Earl Bostic, Buff Estes (as); Coleman Hawkins, Ben Webster, Chu Berry, Jerry Jerome, Budd Johnson (ts); Harry Carney (bs); Clyde Hart, Nat Cole, Joe Sullivan, Spencer Odun (p); Allan Reuss, Charlie Christian, Al Casey, Ernest Ashley, Oscar Moore (g); Billy Taylor, Milt Hinton, Artie Bernstein, Wesley Prince (b); Sonny Greer, Cozy Cole, Big Sid Catlett, Slick Jones, Zutty Singleton, Nick Fatool, Al Spieldock (d).* 6/39–5/40.

***** Lionel Hampton 1940–1941**
Classics 624 *Hampton; Karl George, Ernie Royal, Joe Newman (t); Fred Beckett, Sonny Craven, Harry Sloan (tb); Marshal Royal (cl, as); Ray Perry (as, vn); Dexter Gordon, Illinois Jacquet (ts); Jack McVea (bs); Nat Cole, Sir Charles Thompson, Marlowe Morris, Milt Buckner (p); Oscar Moore, Teddy Bunn, Irving Ashby (g); Douglas Daniels (tiple, v); Wesley Prince, Hayes Alvis, Vernon Alley (b); Al Spieldock, Kaiser Marshall, Shadow Wilson, George Jenkins (d); Rubel Blakey, Evelyn Myers (v).* 7/40–12/41.

Lionel Hampton's Victor sessions of the 1930s offer a glimpse of many of the finest big-band players of the day away from their usual chores: Hampton creamed off the pick of whichever band was in town at the time of the session and, although most of the tracks were hastily organized, the music is consistently entertaining. If one has a reservation, it's to do with Hampton himself: if you don't enjoy what he does, these discs won't live up to their reputation, since Hampton takes every lead offered. He'd already worked with Louis Armstrong in Les Hite's band as far back as the late '20s, and he came to New York in 1936, following an offer from Benny Goodman. The Victor dates began at the same time, and Hampton cut a total of 23 sessions between 1936 and 1941. The personnel varies substantially from date to date: some are like small-band sessions drawn from the Ellington or Goodman or Basie orchestras, others – such as the extraordinary 1939 date with Gillespie, Carter, Berry, Webster and Hawkins – are genuine all-star jams. Carter wrote the charts for one session, but mostly Hampton used head arrangements or sketchy frameworks. The bonding agent is his own enthusiasm: whether playing vibes – and incidentally establishing the dominant style on the instrument with his abrasive accents, percussive intensity and quickfire alternation of long and short lines – or piano or drums, or taking an amusing, Armstrong-influenced vocal, Hamp makes everything swing.

In the end, surprisingly few tracks stand out: what one remembers are individual solos and the general climate of hot, hip good humour which prevails. One might mention Benny Carter on 'I'm In The Mood For Swing', Chu Berry on 'Shufflin' At The Hollywood', Dizzy Gillespie on 'Hot Mallets', J.C. Higginbotham on 'I'm On My Way From You' or Buster Bailey on 'Rhythm, Rhythm'; but there are few disappointments amid an air of democratic enterprise, despite the leader's showboating. Hamp's drum and piano features are less than enthralling after one has heard them once, but they don't occupy too much space.

The availability of this important music is still less than ideal. While the Classics CDs take a full chronological look up to December 1941 and the start of Hamp's own big band, the sound is inconsistent: some tracks field too much surface noise, others seem unnecessarily dull. Bluebird's series seems to have disappeared altogether: it is surely time for a comprehensive box of this music. The final disc in the Classics sequence includes the final 13 tracks for Victor and, while these are a shade less interesting than the earlier dates, it's useful to have them in sequence. The European label, Memoria, has also issued four discs covering the same material. Robert Parker's compilation starts with a few early tracks featuring Hampton as sideman, but then concentrates on his pick of the 1930s dates. The music is fine and vital enough to demand a general four-star rating for most of these compilations, but we would issue a caveat that collectors might wish to audition the various editions and judge for themselves as to the most preferred transfers.

***** Lionel Hampton 1942–1944**

Classics 803 *Hampton; Snooky Young, Wendell Culley, Joe Morris, Dave Page, Lamar Wright, Ernie Royal, Karl George, Joe Newman, Roy McCoy, Cat Anderson (t); Booty Wood, Vernon Porter, Andrew Penn, Fred Beckett, Sonny Craven, Allen Durham, Al Hayes, Harry Sloan (tb); Herbie Fields (cl, as); Gus Evans, George Dorsey, Ray Perry, Marshal Royal, Earl Bostic (as); Arnett Cobb, Fred Simon, Jay Peters, Dexter Gordon, Illinois Jacquet, Al Sears (ts); Charlie Fowlkes (bs); Milt Buckner (p); Billy Mackel, Irving Ashby, Eric Miller (g); Charles Harris, Ted Sinclair, Vernon King, Vernon Alley, Wendell Marshall (b); George Jenkins, Fred Radcliffe, Lee Young (d); Rubel Blakey (v).* 3/42–10/44.

***** Lionel Hampton 1945–46**

Classics 922 *As above, except add Joe Morris, Al Killian (t), Abdul Hamid, John Morris, Al Hayse (tb), Bobby Playter, Ben Kynard (as), Johnny Griffin (ts), Dardanelle Breckenridge, John Mehegan (p), Dinah Washington, Bing Crosby (v); omit Anderson, Newman, Dorsey, Royal, Bostic, Gordon, Jacquet, Miller, King, Alley, Marshall, Radcliffe, Young, Blakey.* 1/45–1/46.

****(*) Lionel Hampton 1946**

Classics 946 *Mostly as above, except add Jimmy Wormick (tb), Jack Kelso (cl), Joe Comfort (b), Curley Hamner (d).* 1–9/46.

***** Lionel Hampton 1947**

Classics 994 *Hampton; Wendell Culley, Duke Garrette, Jimmy Nottingham, Kenny Dorham, Leo Sheppard, Snooky Young, Teddy Buckner, Walter Williams, Benny Bailey (t); Britt Woodman, James Wormick, Sonny Craven, Andrew Penn, James Robinson (tb); Jackie Kelson (cl, as); Bobby Player, Ben Kynard (as); Morris Lane, Johnny Sparrow (ts); Charlie Fowlkes (bs); Milt Buckner, Dodo Marmarosa (p); Billy Mackel (g); Charles Harris, Joe Comfort, Charles Mingus (b); Curley Hamner, Earl Walker (d); The Hamptonians, Wini Brown, Roland Burton (v).* 4–11/47.

*****(*) Swingsation**

GRP 059922-2 *As appropriate discs above.* 42–47.

Hampton's big bands of the 1940s were relentlessly entertaining outfits, their live shows a feast of raving showstoppers which Hampton somehow found the energy to replenish time and again. He tended to rely on a repertoire – including 'Flying Home', 'Hamp's Boogie Woogie' and a few others – which he has stuck by to this day, but his ability to ignite both a band and an audience prevailed over any doubts concerning staleness. The studio sessions are inevitably a lot tamer than what happened on stage, but there's still some good, gritty playing, which opened the book on a blend of swing and R&B which other bandleaders followed with some interest. Classics 803 gets a bit stuck on some dull material – there are four different takes on 'Flying Home' in all, including a two-part V-Disc version – but there are also some strong charts by Clyde Hart and Milt Buckner. Classics 922 is another mixed bag, but there is a lovely Dinah Washington vocal on 'Blow Top Blues', two bits of fun with Bing Crosby, a couple of bacchanalian V-Disc sides and a thumping 'Rockin' In Rhythm'. The 1946 disc has fewer pickings and is really only for Hampton nuts, although Arnett Cobb gets off a couple of superheated solos. The 1947 set picks up a bit with the arrival of Dorham and Mingus, and some good set-pieces such as 'Three Minutes On 52nd Street', 'Red Top' and 'Mingus Fingers', ending on a vigorous sextet date. The *Swingsation* compilation usefully brings together the big hits of this era of Hamp and will do fine for anyone wanting to sample this period.

*****(*) Hamp: The Legendary Decca Recordings**

Decca GRD 2-652 2CD *As above discs, plus various other groupings, including Charlie Teagarden, Charlie Shavers (t), Willie Smith (as), Corky Corcoran (ts), Jerome Richardson (f), Buddy Cole (org), Barney Kessel (g), Slam Stewart (b), Betty Carter (v).* 5/42–3/63.

One could take issue with the 'legendary' description, but this is a very fair sifting-through of Hampton's years with Decca, starting with the May 1942 'Flying Home' and closing on two amusing small-group tracks from a Las Vegas club show of 1963 with, of all people, Charlie Teagarden. The main bonus of this set is the inclusion of Hamp's quite classic treatment of 'Star Dust' from a

1947 Gene Norman Just Jazz show: combative and lyrical in equal measure, this is a rare chance to hear Hamp at length in his prime and away from his big band. The second disc includes the swagger of 'Three Minutes On 52nd Street', Charles Mingus's dramatic composing debut with 'Mingus Fingers' and the lustrous treatment of 'Midnight Sun', as well as Betty Carter's improbably sexy vocal on 'The Hucklebuck' and another fine Hamp set-piece on 'Moonglow' – as well as a few less-than-immortal selections. After the respectable but uninvolving sound on the Classics discs, these tracks come over with tremendous punch, which is just as it should be.

***** The Complete Lionel Hampton Quartets And Quintets With Oscar Peterson On Verve**

Verve 559797-2 5CD *Hampton; Buddy DeFranco (cl); Oscar Peterson (p); Herb Ellis (g); Ray Brown (b); Buddy Rich (d).* 53–54.

***** Just One Of Those Things**

Verve 547437-2 *As above.* 54.

*****(*) Jazz Masters 26: Lionel Hampton With Oscar Peterson**

Verve 521853-2 *Hampton; Roy Eldridge, Dizzy Gillespie (t); Bill Harris (tb); Buddy DeFranco (cl); Flip Phillips, Ben Webster (ts); Oscar Peterson (p); Herb Ellis (g); Ray Brown (b); Buddy Rich (d).* 53–54.

Hampton's early sessions for Norman Granz were originally spread over some 15 LPs, so this comprehensive five-disc set from Verve clears up what was for many years something of a discographical muddle. Hampton and Peterson clearly enjoyed each other's company, and the generous solos, jocular interplay and general bonhomie which prevails is certainly uplifting from track to track. That said, we offer only a low rating since the music quickly starts to seem all the same, with very little variation in manner. There are great things to enjoy, such as a second classic treatment of 'Star Dust', but one wishes these discs had been made available separately in a more economical way. DeFranco arrives for one session and offers some useful contrast, but as a block of music this is one of those sets to dip into very sparingly. The ugly packaging is another minus.

The Jazz Masters package has been around for a while and is still the best place to hear Hampton with Verve. *Just One Of Those Things* fillets sundry 1954 tracks from the complete set.

***** Rare Recordings Vol. 1**

Telarc CD-83318 *Hampton; Woody Shaw, Clark Terry, Jack Walrath, Thad Jones (t); J.J Johnson (tb); Lucky Thompson, Steve Marcus (ss); Ricky Ford, Dexter Gordon, Coleman Hawkins (ts); Gerry Mulligan (bs); Earl Hines, Hank Jones, Barry Kiener, Teddy Wilson, Bob Neloms (p); Bucky Pizzarelli (g); Tom Warrington, Arvell Shaw, Charles Mingus, Milt Hinton, George Duvivier (b); Oliver Jackson, Buddy Rich, Dannie Richmond, Teddy Wilson Jr, Grady Tate, Osie Johnson (d); Candido Camero, Sam Turner (perc).* 4/65–11/77.

Hampton's late-'50s and '60s recordings are almost a no-show on CD at present. This is a peculiar set of tracks, mostly from the mid-'70s, but with a 'Stardust' from 1965 that includes Hawkins, Hines and others. Hampton stars with Mingus, Mulligan, Wilson Sr and Hines in various small-to-medium group situations: the two tracks with Mingus, 'Slop' and 'So Long Eric', are dynamic workouts that Hampton fits right into, and the pairings with Hines and Wilson are effective. Less interesting are those with Mulligan and Gordon, and the 'Stardust' is a tail-dragger.

**** Live At The Muzevaal**

Timeless SJP 120 *Hampton; Joe Newman, Victor Paz (t); Eddie Chamblee (as, ts); Paul Moen (ts); Wild Bill Davis (p, org); Billy Mackel (g); Barry Smith (b); Frankie Dunlop (d).* 5/78.

**** All Star Band At Newport '78**

Timeless SJP 142 *Hampton; Cat Anderson, Jimmie Maxwell, Joe Newman (t, flhn); Doc Cheatham (t); Eddie Bert, John Gordon, Benny Powell (tb); Earl Warren (cl, as, f); Bob Wilber (cl); Charles McPherson (as); Arnett Cobb, Paul Moen (ts); Pepper Adams (bs); Ray Bryant (p); Billy Mackel (g); Chubby Jackson (b); Panama Francis (d).* 7/78.

**** Hamp In Harlem**

Timeless SJP 133 *Hampton; Joe Newman, Wallace Davenport (t); Curtis Fuller (tb); Steve Slagle (as); Paul Moen (ts); Paul Jeffrey (bs); Wild Bill Davis (p, org); Billy Mackel (g); Gary Mazzaroppi (b); Richie Pratt (d).* 5/79.

This is a disappointing batch of records. The three albums by smaller bands set only a functional setting for Hampton and, although there's some interesting material – 'Giant Steps', 'Moment's Notice' and Joe Henderson's 'No Me Esqueca' on *Muzevaal*, for instance – the arrangements are stolid and the playing routine. Nor is the recording very good, poor in balance and detail. It's worse on the *All Star Band* record, though, which is a weak souvenir of what must have been a fine tribute concert. Panama Francis is too far up-front – his hi-hat sounds louder than the brass section – and some instrumentalists disappear altogether, while the final 'Flying Home' is a mess. There are some good moments from the soloists – especially Cheatham's pointed improvisation on 'Stompin' At The Savoy' – but only hardcore Hampton enthusiasts will get much out of it.

***** Made In Japan**

Timeless SJP 175 *Hampton; Vince Cutro, John Marshall, Barry Ries, Johnny Walker (t); John Gordon, Chris Gulhaugen, Charles Stephens (tb); Thomas Chapin, Ricky Ford, Paul Jeffrey, Yoshi Malta, Glen Wilson (saxes); John Colianni (p); Todd Coolman (b); Duffy Jackson (d); Sam Turner (perc).* 6/82.

The opening charge through 'Air Mail Special' makes it clear that this was one of the best of Hampton's latter-day big bands: accurate, attacking section-work, a set of virile soloists and a hard-hitting rhythm section fronted by the useful Colianni. The choice of material spotlights the interesting paradox in the leader's direction – while he seems content at one moment to rely on the most familiar warhorses in his repertoire, uncompromising 'modern' scores such as Ricky Ford's 'Interpretations Opus 5' and James Williams's 'Minor Thesis' sit just as comfortably in the programme and Hampton takes to them with the same enthusiasm. Ford stands out on his own tune, and there are worthy efforts from Jeffrey, Wilson and others. The sound is big and strong, although the vibes have a less attractive dryness in their timbre.

**** Mostly Blues**

Musicmasters 65011-2 *Hampton; Bobby Scott (p); Joe Beck (g); Bob Cranshaw, Anthony Jackson (b); Grady Tate, Chris Parker (d).* 3–4/88.

***(*) Mostly Ballads**

Musicmasters 65044-2 *Hampton; Lew Soloff (t); Harold Danko, John Colianni (p); Philip Markowitz, Richard Haynes (ky); Bill Moring, Milt Hinton (b); James Madison, James D Ford (d).* 9–11/89.

****(*) Two Generations**

Phontastic NCD 8807 *Hampton; Lars Estrand (vib); Kjell Ohman (p, org); Tommy Johnson (b); Leif Dahlberg (d).* 3/91.

**** Live At The Blue Note**

Telarc Jazz CD-83308 *Hampton; Clark Terry (t, flhn); Harry 'Sweets' Edison (t); Al Grey (tb); James Moody, Buddy Tate (ts); Hank Jones (p); Milt Hinton (b); Grady Tate (d).* 6/91.

**** Just Jazz**

Telarc Jazz CD-83313 *As above.* 6/91.

Hampton's recent recordings are, with the best will in the world, echoes of a major talent. Since he isn't the kind of artist to indulge in autumnal reflections, one has to use his earlier records as a yardstick, and these sessions inevitably fall short in energy and invention. No one can blame Hamp for taking things steady at this stage in what's virtually a 70-year career. The *Blues* and *Ballads* collections are both taken at an undemanding tempo throughout, and both – particularly the soporific *Ballads* – sound as if they'd prefer to stay well in the background. The session recorded at New York's Blue Note is an expansive all-star session by musicians whose best work is, frankly, some way behind them: only the seemingly ageless Terry and the exuberant Grey defy the circumstances and muster a sense of commitment. Everyone else, including Hampton, falls back on simple ideas and tempos which give no cause for alarm. The second volume, *Just Jazz*, is more of the same. The nicest record in this batch is the hastily organized meeting with the group led by fellow vibesman, Lars Estrand: lots of chummy dialogue between the two musicians on harmless material. A pity that they didn't have enough time to get a better sound in the studio, though.

Slide Hampton (born 1932)

TROMBONE

Locksley Hampton played with Lionel Hampton before joining Maynard Ferguson as an arranger in 1957. Freelanced in the '60s before a spell with Woody Herman and a long stint in Europe, though he returned to the USA in 1977. His arranging has often taken precedence over his playing, but he remains a quick and skilful trombonist.

***** Slide!**

Fresh Sound FSR-CD 206 *Hampton; Freddie Hubbard, Booker Little, Hobart Dotson, Willie Thomas, Burt Collins (t); Bernard McKinney (euph); George Coleman (ts, cl); Jay Cameron (bs, bcl); Eddie Kahn, George Tucker (b); Pete LaRoca, Lex Humphries, Charli Persip, Kenny Dennis (d).* 59–61.

The personnel, with Hubbard, Little and Coleman, looks mouth-watering, but the horns have an ensemble role; Hampton gives himself most of the solos, which is fair enough: they were his dates, now usefully combined on to a single CD. The earlier date has a fine 'Newport', among some smart originals; the second mixes five tunes from *Porgy And Bess* with a dance suite called 'The Cloister'. Hampton depends mainly on brass sound, the reeds used for low tone colours, and the absence of piano gives unusual weight to the front lines. An interesting survival.

****(*) World Of Trombones**

Black Lion 60113 *Hampton; Clifford Adams Jr, Clarence Banks, Curtis Fuller, Earl McIntyre, Douglas Purviance, Janice Robinson, Steve Turre, Papo Vasquez (tb); Albert Dailey (p); Ray Drummond (b); Leroy Williams (d).* 1/79.

This kind of band is a logical development for Hampton, who has always loved trombone sound and has developed a rare fluency in his own playing, yet has made his significant mark as an arranger. An arranger's band featuring an all-trombone front line is, not surprisingly, long on texture and short on much excitement or flexibility. The massed horns gliding through 'Round Midnight' and 'Chorale' are impressive, but the record isn't very involving overall.

****** Roots**

Criss Cross Jazz Criss 1015 *Hampton; Clifford Jordan (ts); Cedar Walton (p); David Williams (b); Billy Higgins (d).* 4/85.

A session in which everything worked out right. Hampton and Jordan are perfectly paired, the trombonist fleet yet punchy, Jordan putting a hint of dishevelment into otherwise finely tailored improvisations; and Walton has seldom played with so much vitality, yet without surrendering his customary aristocratic touch. Williams and Higgins are asked to play hard throughout the four long titles, and they oblige without flagging. Although a very fast 'Solar' is arguably the highlight, it's a fine record altogether.

*****(*) Dedicated To Diz**

Telarc 83323 *Hampton; Jon Faddis, Roy Hargrove, Claudio Roditi (t, flhn); Steve Turre (tb, shells); Douglas Purviance (btb); Antonio Hart (as, ss); Jimmy Heath (ts); David Sanchez (ts, ss, f); Danilo Perez (p); George Mraz (b); Lewis Nash (d).* 2/93.

Having Faddis in a Gillespie tribute guarantees a certain authenticity of sound. The idea of founding the Jazz Masters, as this group is known, was to record larger-scale arrangements of work associated with the greats. A great charts man as well as player, Hampton handles this one with entirely characteristic discretion and charm. Our only quibble is that it might have sounded better done in a studio than live at the Village Vanguard. There are moments when the sound is imperfect, and one or two of the ensembles could – and probably should – have been touched up. The high points are 'Lover Man' and (surprise, surprise) 'A Night In Tunisia'. Faddis is quite properly the star, but Hargrove, Roditi and Turre, Heath and Sanchez also have their moments in the sun on this thoroughly sun-warmed date.

Herbie Hancock (born 1940)

PIANO, KEYBOARDS

One of the most significant composers in modern jazz, the creator of 'Watermelon Man' and 'Dolphin Dance' as well as the unforgettable 'Rockit'. Chicago-born Hancock was something of a child prodigy, playing Mozart as a youngster. He has embraced bebop, funk and elements of classical form and, though his work of recent years has lacked the sheer, unselfconscious brilliance of his early records, he is still a formidable technician.

***(*) Takin' Off

Blue Note 37643 *Hancock; Freddie Hubbard (t, flhn); Dexter Gordon (ts); Butch Warren (b); Billy Higgins (d).* 5/62.

Takin' Off was a remarkable debut. He had made his professional debut, following master's work at the Manhattan School of Music, just two years earlier with Coleman Hawkins, before signing up with trumpeter Donald Byrd and coming to the attention of Alfred Lion of Blue Note, who agreed to allow the 22-year-old to record with a horn-led group rather than as a trio. The result is astonishingly mature and poised. 'Watermelon Man' digs back into memories of Chicago's South Side, a gospelly roller which prompts a full-hearted solo from Hubbard; not the obvious choice for the gig, perhaps, with Byrd a more likely candidate, but he fits right in. As does Gordon, who was only getting back to serious work after his tribulations; he sounds earthy and intense, and much more focused than on the alternative take, which has been added to the CD. The collaboration was to firm up a friendship that would last till the end of Gordon's life; in the Tavernier movie, *Round Midnight*, Hancock would accompany 'Dale Turner' in his pomp. 'Three Bags Full' is a curious piece, almost Eastern in harmony and apparently intended to underline the stylistic differences between the three soloists. This might almost be something by the 1950s Miles Davis group, with Gordon emulating Coltrane. 'The Maze' is a puzzle-piece, and 'Driftin'' is a relaxed blowing tune featuring Hubbard's flugelhorn. Perhaps the most effective track of all is the ballad, 'Alone Am I', moody and philosophical, with a superb solo from Hancock. Can there ever have been a more auspicious debut?

*** My Point Of View

Blue Note 21226 *Hancock; Donald Byrd (t); Grachan Moncur III (tb); Grant Green (g); Chuck Israels (b); Tony Williams (d).* 3/63.

My Point Of View was the second of Hancock's records for Blue Note. It's never been the most celebrated, despite including the wonderful 'Blind Man, Blind Man', which is now represented in an extra take. Herbie's relationship with Tony Williams is often regarded as the key to this fine record, and revisiting it in this special Rudy Van Gelder edition merely reinforces that view. 'King Cobra' is a brilliant synthesis of Williams's rhythmic genius and Hancock's structural gifts. Herbie's passing interest in R&B surfaces on 'And What If I Don't', which most blindfold testees would be hard pressed to identify. Second albums are notoriously tricky, but Hancock made the best of his opportunity by casting his net wider still. It wasn't a format that he was to return to in later years, so *My Point Of View* remains one of a kind.

*** Inventions And Dimensions

Blue Note 84147 *Hancock; Paul Chambers (b); Willie Bobo (d); Chihuahua Martinez (perc).* 8/63.

The forgotten album. Hancock wanted to experiment and, short of going entirely free and outside, he pushed his personal concept as far as it would go. It seems that the leader gave his musicians nothing more than a time-signature and some general idea about the shape of the piece, and the session went from there. 'Succotash', named after the sound of Willie Bobo's brushes rather than the beans-and-corn mix, is in double waltz-time. 'Triangle' falls into three distinct sections, with the feel of the blues but no obvious blues content. 'For Jack Rabbit' and 'A Jump Ahead' were effectively co-written by Paul Chambers, who determined much of the content; on the former track he drives the improvisation along with a repeat figure, while the title of the latter derives from his four-note pedal at the start. Few Blue Note sessions of the time were created with such freedom, and *Inventions And Dimensions* does stand somewhat apart from the mainstream of Hancock's work. However, it remains to this day testimony to his restless, exploratory nature and it certainly shouldn't be overlooked.

♛ **** Maiden Voyage

Blue Note 95331 *Hancock; Freddie Hubbard (t); George Coleman (ts); Ron Carter (b); Tony Williams (d).* 64.

**** Empyrean Isles

Blue Note 98796 *As above, except omit Coleman.* 6/64.

***(*) Cantaloupe Island

Blue Note 29331 *As above, except add Donald Byrd (t), Grachan Moncur III (tb), George Coleman, Dexter Gordon (ts), Butch Warren (b), Billy Higgins (d).* 5/62, 3/63, 6/64, 3/65.

Maiden Voyage has been tussled over more than once. Revisionists will argue that it is glib and superficial, not at all the masterpiece it has been claimed to be. We increasingly disagree and have no hesitation this time round in promoting it to the premier league. Particularly when, considered as a pair with *Empyrean Isles*, it represents a colossal achievement from a man still just 24 years old. Both are quiet records, likened by Joachim Berendt to Debussy's *La Mer*. Coleman plays with delicate understatement and Hancock never puts a foot wrong. No great surprise that the chemistry was so good for, with the obvious exception of Hubbard, this was Miles's group.

Empyrean Isles is almost as good. 'Cantaloupe Island' is a glorious piece of quartet jazz, and 'Dolphin Dance' has seldom been out of the repertoire in the last 30 years. The absence of Coleman puts ever greater emphasis on piano and, though one misses his slightly breathy delivery, there's an amazing clarity to the other record from 1964.

Cantaloupe Island is a compilation of material from *Takin' Off*, *Empyrean Isles* and, from the now-deleted *My Point Of View*, a single track called 'Blind Man, Blind Man' which highlights Hancock's not yet fully developed skills as an arranger for larger ensembles.

**** The Complete Blue Note Sixties Sessions

Blue Note 4 95569 2 6CD *As above, except add Melvin Lastie (c), Johnny Coles, Thad Jones (flhn), Garnett Brown (tb), Jack Jeffers, Tony Studd (btb), Jackie McLean (as), Jerry Dodgion (as, f), Jerome Richardson (bcl, f), Romeo Penque (bcl), Hubert Laws (f), Stanley Turrentine (ts), Eric Gale, Billy Butler (g), Bob Cranshaw (b), Albert 'Tootie' Heath, Bernard Purdie, Mickey Roker (d).* 12/61–4/69.

Immaculately and expensively packaged, this is a set to die for and it is denied the coveted crown only on cost grounds. As well as the Blue Notes issued above, the set includes the whole of the deleted *My Point Of View*, *Speak Like A Child* and Herbie's last album for the label, *The Prisoner*. Though little known now in comparison to the rest, this was much more than a contract filler. Herbie had been poached by Warner Bros, but he and Alfred Lion took the opportunity to create a unique sound for the last LP, augmenting the sextet with horns and allowing Herbie to experiment with a Fender Rhodes instrument during the en-sembles. 'He Who Lives In Fear' and the title-piece are outstanding Hancock conceptions and the sound is awesome, yet the album has an air of hurry and unfinish as well, which is evident in some of the alternatives.

My Point Of View is a recent reissue, but it is deeply regrettable that *Speak Like A Child* is still available only patchily. If resources stretch, both are available in this edition, and there are also unissued versions of 'Riot' and 'Goodbye To Childhood' from the latter album, which also includes a couple of tracks, notably 'Toys', for just piano and rhythm. Blue Note have included some interesting filler material as well to round out the profile of Herbie's time with the label. There are early tracks recorded under the leadership of Donald Byrd and Jackie McLean, some material with Bobby Hutcherson from *Blow-Up* (see below), and 'The Collector' from Wayne Shorter's *Adam's Apple* date, issued only in Japan. At the very end of the set, a rarity: Herbie's one and only serious dabbling in R&B, in a band fronted by Melvin Lastie and Stanley Turrentine. That was a road not taken. This magnificent set compresses the real journey, its byways and stumbles; what a trip it was.

*** Blow-Up

Soundtracks 852280 *Hancock; other personnel not specified.* 66.

Hancock's brilliant soundtrack is a near-perfect correlative to the funky, ambiguous world of Michelangelo Antonioni's film. It could hardly be improved upon, and it's a wonder – though perhaps a blessing – that it didn't lead to more and yet more offers from directors. The album includes a song by The Yardbirds, who actually appeared in the film, and also the two songs commissioned from the band Tomorrow but not used. These are curiosities. It is unmistakably Hancock's album, and as transitional a work as Miles's moody score for *L'Ascenseur pour l'échafaud.*

*** Speak Like A Child

Blue Note 746136 *Hancock; Thad Jones (flhn); Peter Phillips (btb); Jerry Dodgion (af); Ron Carter (b); Mickey Roker (d).* 3/68.

An experiment in sound-texture, this was the first of Hancock's records to suggest that he might welcome a swing towards electronics. The sound is slithery and quite abstract, certainly not dance-orientated but full of intimations of what was to come in the 1970s. Jones was an unexpected recruitment, but he plays with delicate beauty and some muscle throughout. An easy record to overlook; well worth hearing.

***(*) Mwandishi: The Complete Warner Bros Recordings

Warner 245732 2CD *Hancock; Johnny Coles, Eddie Henderson, Joe Newman, Ernie Royal (t); Garnett Brown, Bennie Powell, Julian Priester (tb); Ray Alonge (frhn); Bennie Maupin (ss, bcl, picc, af, perc); Joe Farrell (as, ts); Joe Henderson (ts, af); Arthur Clarke (bs); Patrick Gleason (syn); Billy Butler, Eric Gale, Ron Montrose (g); Jerry Jermott, Buster Williams (b); Billy Hart, Albert 'Tootie' Heath, Bernard Purdie (d); Ndugu Leon Chancler (d, perc); Jose Areas, George Devens, Victor Pontojoa (perc); Candy Love, Sandra Stevens, Della Horne, Victoria Domagalski, Scott Beach (v).* 10/69–2/72.

Working with Miles Davis suggested the possibilities of an electric band. When he moved on, Hancock immediately experimented with his own version. The three albums for Warner Bros were *Fat Albert Rotunda*, *Mwandishi* (the Swahili name he had adopted for himself) and *Crossings*. The first, from 1969, was based on themes for Bill Cosby's TV cartoon series, and it marks a first use on his own date of the Fender Rhodes, which was to become something of a Hancock trademark over the next few years. With the criminally under-recorded Johnny Coles on trumpet and Joe Henderson on tenor and alto flute, the session has a surging, almost breathless power that takes it far beyond its origins.

Mwandishi is altogether more thoughtful and personal. On tunes like 'Wandering Spirit Song', Hancock experiments for the first time with sheer duration, and it's hard to believe that this album did not exert some sort of reciprocal influence on Miles Davis, notably the saturnine *Agharta* and *Pangaea*. Maupin's multi-instrumentalism has already become a key element, but the other Henderson's melancholic trumpet (like Miles without the strut and swagger) is the dramatic focus of a lot of the music. 'You'll Know When You Get There' is a long journey across the Kalahari, punctuated by harmonic mirages and sudden changes of pace.

The final disc of the Warner period more or less consolidates what has gone before, but Hancock has introduced a synthesizer and already seems a step closer to the funk/soul idiom of *Headhunters.* Warners allowed him to experiment and gave him the technical support he needed at a time when it would have been quite easy to have slipped into self-parody, turning out ever paler versions of *Maiden Voyage* or perhaps funking up older tunes with a conventional, horn-led instrumentation. The remote, beautiful *Sextant* is still not securely available in all territories, but with these reissues a missing link in Hancock's development has been filled.

*** Sextant

Columbia CK 64983 *Hancock; Eddie Henderson, Julian Priester (tb, atb, btb, perc); Bennie Maupin (ss, bcl, picc, perc); Jaco Pastorius, Buster Williams (b); Billy Hart (d, perc); Buck Clarke (perc); Scott Beach, Delta Horne, Candy Love, Sandra Stevens (v).* 72.

The joyous dancing figures on the cover of Hancock's Columbia debut convey some of its lasting charm and appeal. In retrospect, it's hard to think of *Sextant* as anything other than a transitional phase in Hancock's career, and a shift towards the electronic funk of mind-decade, but it has an infectious freshness and lack of elaboration which is typical of the composer, if not of the label he had just signed to. 'Rain Dance' is one of his most delightful themes, shifting between metres and harmonically agile as well. 'Hidden Shadows' and 'Hornets' are more like long-form jams, though the basic architecture of the second track particularly is very impressive. Obviously influenced by Miles, it points in very different directions; where the trumpeter was interested in abstraction and pure sound, Hancock was devoted to melody. The doubling of lines, often by Priester and Maupin in conjunction with the bassist, was also a key element of Hancock's approach, and it's deployed to great effect here. In future, his groups would be much more obviously electrified. This carries over personnel from one phase to another, but it leaves behind a very definite period and ushers us on to the next. Out of circulation or available only as an import for some time, it fills in an important part of the Hancock story.

****** Head Hunters**
Columbia CK 65123 *Hancock; Bennie Maupin (ts, ss, saxello, bcl, af); Paul Jackson (b); Harvey Mason (d); Bill Summers (perc).* 73.

*****(*) Thrust**
Columbia CK 64984 *As above, except Mike Clark (d) replaces Mason.* 74.

***** Man-Child**
Columbia 471235-2 *Hancock; Wilbur Brisbois, Jay DaVersa (t); Garnett Brown (tb); Dick Hyde (btb, tba); Jim Horn, Ernie Watts (sax, f); Wayne Shorter (ss); Bennie Maupin (ts, ss, saxello, bcl, af); Stevie Wonder (hca); Blackbird McKnight, David T Walker (g); Henry Davis, Paul Jackson (b); Mike Clark, James Gadson (d); Bill Summers (perc).* 1/76.

****(*) Secrets**
Columbia CK 34280 *Hancock; Bennie Maupin (ts, ss, bcl, lyricon, perc); Wah Wah Watson (g, syn, v); Ray Parker (g); Paul Jackson (b); James Levi (d); Kenneth Nash (perc).* 76.

Miles legitimized a view of black musical history that made room for Sly Stone and James Brown, as well as Charlie Parker and John Coltrane. *Head Hunters* – and yes, it is two words at this stage – was the direct result, an infectiously funky and thoroughly joyous record; only the closing 'Vein Melter' hints at melancholy. Hancock includes 'Watermelon Man', not because he is short of ideas, but because he wants to demonstrate the essential continuity of his music. Earlier albums may have seemed a 'departure', as critics like to say. This one was confidently on the main line. For the simplest point of comparison, listen to Butch Warren's line on *Takin' Off* and then compare the toppling, dotted rhythm Paul Jackson brings to it on *Head Hunters*. A later generation, weaned on stuff like this and disillusioned with the designer gloss of the 1980s, would disagree, but Hancock's electric keyboards sound pretty one-dimensional here and there; the Hohner Clavinet is very much an acquired taste. The latest remastering, coupled to budget release and including a new essay by Hancock, gives the biggest-selling jazz record of all time a new gloss and impetus, and once again 'Chameleon' and 'Sly' are thudding club walls up and down the country and coast to coast. Maupin performs a role much like Wayne Shorter in Weather Report, not soloing at length or necessarily carrying the line but placing brushstrokes and punctuating moods much as Miles did. 'Vein Melter', which is perhaps his best moment on the record, is to some extent a throwback to the more introverted music of the very early 1970s, but it is no less effective in this context, a much-needed counterbalance. Hancock provides most of the colours, but he is also improvising with genius. Some of his very finest keyboard work can be heard during the quarter-hour span of 'Chameleon'.

Thrust was conceived as a near-exact replica, but this time the bank of Arps – Odyssey, Soloist, 2600 synth and string synth – lack creative personality. 'Palm Grease' is unmistakable Hancock, oozing with class and a politely ironic menace. Jackson's bass is a little like a truncheon round the head and ribcage, not quite in earnest, but not quite easy to listen to either. Mike Clark is your basic Rock Skool drummer, but quite effective in this context and capable of some delicacy, as on 'Butterfly'.

Vividly textured and awash with new ideas of instrumental colour, *Man-Child* now sounds like Hancock's shade-card for the bands of the mid-'70s. He wasn't to use quite such a broad spectrum again, and on occasion he trades in drive and energy for surface tone. The work of the early '70s was influenced by Indian and African idioms and makes much use of doubled instruments, out-of-synch transitions and rhythmic overlaps that seem to happen in phase rather than at once. The horns are uniformly good, if a little too uniform in focus. The fast, semiquaver patterns were to become a little irritating later. Here they are modulated more carefully. Veering close to the 'space music' that was to be his commercial, if certainly not his critical, nadir, *Man-Child* isn't the easiest album to locate in the continuum. Even so, it remains eminently listenable.

Secrets dispensed with the sci-fi covers in favour of a more outdoor, sunlit look. The appearance of 'Cantaloupe Island' was further sign that Hancock wanted to accommodate his own back-catalogue to the new instrumentation, and yet what emerges is barely the same tune, pumped up and oddly aggressive. Despite a general simplification of texture over its predessors, this is the mood of the album. 'Doin' It' (co-written with Ray Parker and Wah Wah Watson, who was shortly to join the Headhunters crew) is a slice of rather crude funk and, before long, guitars were to dominate the band. This is the first album on which Hancock ceded compositional control. It's no better for it.

***** V.S.O.P.**
Sony 34688 *Hancock; Freddie Hubbard (t); Eddie Henderson (t, flhn); Julian Priester (tb); Wayne Shorter (ss, ts); Bennie Maupin (af); Ray Parker Jr, Wah Wah Watson (g); Ron Carter, Paul Jackson, Buster Williams (b); James Levi, Tony Williams (d); Kenneth Nash (perc).* 7/76.

****(*) V.S.O.P.: The Quintet**
Sony 65462 *Hancock; Freddie Hubbard (t); Wayne Shorter (ss, ts); Ron Carter (b); Tony Williams (d).* 7/77.

A pre-Internet grapevine buzzed with rumour before Hancock's retrospective at the 1976 Newport Jazz Festival. Could it really be that the great Miles Davis Quintet would take the stage with the great man himself (by then famously mired in his own dark agenda) playing trumpet *sans* pedals, fuzzes, wah-wahs and all the rest of his post-1969 paraphernalia? In the event, it was left to Freddie Hubbard, and probably it had been planned that way all along, but the gig had a disproportionate impact on modern jazz, inspiring younger-generation players who were tiring of electro-funk to revisit the classic Prestiges and Blue Notes.

'Maiden Voyage' and 'Nefertiti' are performed without much dynamism, and the complex line of the latter tune almost unfurls onstage. Hancock is playing an electric instrument, albeit the closest thing yet devised to a genuine Steinway, and, partly as a result, the sound of the band is hard and brittle. Hubbard is, as ever, unwilling to play himself in and blasts away; in comparison to the more reflective Eddie Henderson, who crops up later, he sounds almost vulgar and brusque. Almost perversely, the concert and album also reflect the changes that had overtaken jazz, with a final performance by the recent Hancock sextet (which included Henderson) and some post-*Headhunters* funk from the new unit. The sextet is represented by just two tracks – but this, equally perversely, given that it was a farewell gig, is where the real musical action is. 'Toys' is a splendid piece of post-Miles jazz, and Henderson's part indicates the direction Miles might have gone in had he not opted for the dark, turbid landscapes of *Agharta* and *Pangaea*. The Headhunters stuff at the end is engaging enough but overlong and excessively indulgent. The abiding impression is of an immensely gifted player who had perhaps peaked too soon and who found himself desperately pursuing change to seem ahead of – or at least up with – a game that was already changing rules again. Much came of this moment, and it's the moment that's important rather than the rather patchy record.

Inevitably, it was too good and too money-spinning an idea to leave as a one-off so, in the summer of 1977, the quintet went on the road. Many bootlegs of these concerts have been circulated and those we have heard – which are of wildly variable quality – suggest that the band was no less consistent in delivery. This is one of the middling sets, recorded at two Californian venues. Unlike the retrospective event, this was a project of leaders, and so there are compositions by Hubbard ('One Of A Kind'), Shorter ('Dolores'), Williams ('Lawra') and Carter ('Third Plane') in a shapeless set. The band was clearly pulling in too many directions at once and, given the number of powerful egos on the stand, it's a wonder they got it together at all.

**(*) An Evening With Herbie Hancock & Chick Corea

Columbia C2K 65551 2CD *Hancock; Chick Corea (p).* 2/78.

The most alarming thing here is what has gone wrong with 'Maiden Voyage', that exquisite tune turned into a sequence of rolls and fakes as Hancock tries to wrest something new out of it. This was a public shaking of hands as much with Mr Steinway as with Mr Corea. Hancock had certainly not given up playing acoustic piano in favour of Fenders, Hohners, Moogs, Mellotrons and Arps, but one might be forgiven for thinking so. Corea wipes the floor with him, and there is a further, rather better selection of material from the same night issued on Polydor, on which Chick majors.

It should be noted that Hancock endeavoured to keep his jazz playing going in parallel with his other interests. There was a solo piano album, recorded for Columbia in Japan. There were the duos with Corea, and there was the ongoing V.S.O.P. project. However, they were doomed to take second place in discographical terms, for the moment at least.

*** Sunlight

Columbia 486570 *Hancock; Bennie Maupin (ss); Ray Parker Jr, Wah Wah Watson (g); Paul Jackson, Byron Miller, Jaco Pastorius (b); Leon Ndugu Chancler, James Levi, Harvey Mason, Tony Williams (d); Raul Rekow, Bill Summers (perc).* 78.

** Feets Don't Fail Me Now

Columbia CK 35764 *Hancock; Bennie Maupin (ss); Ray Obiedo, Ray Parker Jr (g); Eddie Watkins (b); James Gadson, James Levi (d); Coke Escovedo, Sheila Escovedo, Bill Summers (perc); Julia Tillman Waters, Maxine Willard Waters, Oren Waters, Luther Waters (v).* 79.

**(*) Monster

Columbia 486571 *Hancock; Randy Hansen, Ray Parker Jr, Carlos Santana, Wah Wah Watson (g); Freddie Washington (b); Alphonse Mouzon (d); Sheila Escovedo (perc); Oren Waters, Bill Champlin, Greg Walker, Gavin Christopher (v).* 80.

The later 1970s saw Hancock laying siege to the discotheque market, making singles rather than structured albums, and increasingly reliant on vocals. Much of the material that came out of this period is unlikely to be of sustained interest to jazz purists, though the one-off pairing of Tony Williams and Jaco Pastorius on 'Good Question' is eminently collectable. Some will find it all hard to square with *Maiden Voyage*. On its own terms, though, Hancock's output was consistent, utterly professional and very successful. The big hit was still to come in 1983, but 'I Thought It Was You', which kicked off *Sunlight*, was one of the ubiquitous sounds of 1979.

Feets ..., which was recorded in that summer, is an extended promotional tape for the Sennheiser Vocoder, which had played a less prominent role on the earlier disc. Players like Maupin have been relegated to bit parts and the compositions are disturbingly anonymous. *Monster* is rather better; the rhythm section has a new bustle and urgency, and Carlos Santana's appearance on 'Saturday Night' lends a fresh touch as well.

** Magic Windows

Columbia 486572 *Hancock; Michael Brecker (ts); Adrian Belew, George Johnson, Al McKay, Ray Parker Jr, Wah Wah Watson (g); Louis Johnson, Freddie Washington, Eddie Watkins (b); James Gadson, Alphonse Mouzon, John Robinson (d); Paulinho Da Costa, Kwasi Dzidzornu, Juan Escovedo, Pete Escovedo, Sheila Escovedo, Kwazu Ladzekpo, Moody Perry III (perc); Gavin Christopher, Dede Dickerson, Vicki Randle, Ngoh Spencer, Sylvester, Jeanie Tracy (v).* 81.

** Lite Me Up

Columbia 486573 *Hancock; Jay Graydon, Steve Lukather, David Williams (g); Randy Jackson, Louis Johnson, Abe Laboriel (b); Jeff Porcaro, John Robinson, Narada Michael Walden (d); Wayne Anthony, Patrice Rushen (v).* 82.

By the turn of the 1980s there were signs that Hancock had almost exhausted the funk/disco seam and was turning his attention back towards jazz forms and instrumentations. Far be it from us to suggest that these two records represent rock bottom. It's almost inevitable that a great artist will produce something interesting in whatsoever form he chooses to work, and there isn't a moment on either disc that falls below that threshold. However, these are likely to be dispiriting moments for Hancock fans. A cameo from Brecker on 'Help Yourself' points a way forward.

***(*) Mr Hands

Columbia 471240 *Hancock; Bennie Maupin (ts); Wah Wah Watson (g); Ron Carter, Paul Jackson, Byron Miller, Jaco Pastorius (b); Leon Ndugu Chancler, Harvey Mason, Tony Williams (d); Sheila Escovedo, Bill Summers (perc).* 82.

A similar line-up to *Sunlight*, but behind it a strong recognition on Hancock's part that the funk experiment is over, both creatively and commercially. The first sign of change is that once again the leader is credited with all the material. 'Calypso' isn't 'Cantaloupe Island', but it is Hancock's strongest jazz writing for some years, and the attack is strong and pianistic. Other tracks, notably 'Just Arour 1 The Corner' and the gloriously danceable 'Shiftless Shuffle', are still at the fusion end of things, but with a less one-dimensional beat and a growing harmonic flexibility grafted on. And doesn't Maupin sound like the George Coleman and Dexter Gordon of the early Blue Notes? A conscious homage, no doubt, but not so slavish that his own slightly formal style doesn't emerge.

***** Quartet**
Columbia 465626 *Hancock; Wynton Marsalis (t); Ron Carter (b); Tony Williams (d).* 82.

As his interest in rock and pop receded, Hancock made carefully selected forays back into the world of straight jazz. Only his enduring enthusiasm for the Yamaha Electric Grand struck an unlikely chord. Perversely, the chops don't sound nearly as good as they did on *Head Hunters*, and the standard and repertory material, like 'I Fall In Love Too Easily' and a couple of Monk tunes, don't afford him much respite. Fortunately for the album, Marsalis is feeling his oats, dispatching his solos with testy arrogance, and of course the other two rhythm players are in superb shape. Only on 'Round Midnight', which was to become a career leitmotif from the moment Hancock got involved in the Tavernier project, does he sound much like his old self.

***** Future Shock**
Columbia 471237 *Hancock; Michael Beinhorn (ky); Pete Cosey (g); Bill Laswell (b); Grandmixer DST (turntables); Sly Dunbar (d, perc); Daniel Ponce (perc); Bernard Fowler, Dwight Jackson, Lamar Wright (v).* 83.

****(*) Sound-System**
Columbia CK 39478 *Hancock; Wayne Shorter (lyricon); Henry Kaiser, Nicky Skopelitis (g); Bill Laswell (b, syn, elec); Johnny St Cyr (turntables); Will Alexander, Bob Stevens (elec); Anton Fier (d, perc); Aiyb Dieng, Hamid Drake, Daniel Ponce (perc); Jali Foday Musa Suso (doussn'gouni, balafon); Bernard Fowler, Toshinori Kondo (v).* 84.

A decade on from *Head Hunters*, Hancock was to have one last throw of chart success with 'Rockit', a number-one single that propelled *Future Shock* up the album charts as well. Working with Bill Laswell put him in touch with elements of the New Wave, a more brooding sound that once again kindled memories of Miles's organ bands (and the presence of Pete Cosey brought the connection into even sharper focus).

Sound-System is equally unmistakably of its moment, the new supporting cast again in evidence, and Shorter, the only familiar jazz face in the line-up, involved in his own rock'n'roll transformation and restricted to the characterless lyricon. Compared to *Future Shock*, it's a lumbering, ungainly affair – but, as always, it has its moments, and it provides further evidence of Hancock's restless shape-shifting in pursuit of the new commercial *Zeitgeist*.

***** A Tribute To Miles**
Qwest/Reprise 45059 *Hancock; Wallace Roney (t); Wayne Shorter (ts); Ron Carter (b); Tony Williams (d).* 9/92.

Hancock founded the jazz quintet V.S.O.P. in 1976, mainly as a festival outfit; the name stood for 'Very Special One-time-only Performance', but of course it was a one-off idea that was going to be in considerable demand. The tantalizing prospect that one night Miles would square the circle and complete the reunion kept the group going almost until his death, and there was always speculation who – when the inevitable happened – would take his place. Roney makes a creditable job of it, pungent, agile and a good deal more acerbic on 'So What' and 'All Blues' than the onlie begetter had ever been. Both are recorded live and seem a touch lifeless. The rest of the material was taped in studio, and it would be fascinating to hear the out-takes of something like 'Pinocchio', which is executed so smoothly it's hard to believe that it wasn't fully written out beforehand. Hancock seems increasingly in charge, not just of his own acoustic technique but of the overall shape of the music. The process of re-mainstreaming himself hasn't really stopped since.

***** Dis Is Da Drum**
Mercury 528 185 *Hancock; Wallace Roney (t); Bennie Maupin (ts); Mars Lasar, Darrell Smith (ky); Darrell Bob Dog Robertson, Wah Wah Watson (g); Armand Sebal Leco, Frank Thibeaux (b); Guy Eckstine, Will Kennedy, Bob Strong (d); Will Roc Griffin (samples); Niayi Asiedu, Skip Bunny, Bill Summers (perc); Lazaro Galarraga, Marina Bambino, Yvette Summers, Lynn Lyndsey, Louis Verdeaux, Felicidad Ector, Huey Jackson (v); Chil Factor (rap); The Real Richie Rich (scratches).*

What were we saying about the mainstream? Just when it seemed that Hancock had realigned himself with jazz, along came this odd mish-mash. The only conclusion is that Herbie really does still want to be a pop star. 'Butterfly' reappears from *Thrust*, albeit with a pungent '90s beat, and the other material is a catch-all synthesis of bebop and the gentler end of hip-hop. Even the raps sound polite. This is the first time, alarmingly, that he has seemed out of his depth with a new trend, all the more ironic in that Hancock is a father figure to a new cohort of youngsters who regard *Head Hunters* and *Thrust* as Holy Writ and the Mini Moog as the Ark of the Covenant. Always a gracefully purposeful player, he certainly doesn't relate to the almost nihilistic drive of the new generation, and he has little success getting even seasoned hands like Maupin, Watson and Summers to come along with him. Call us old-fashioned, but a record that needs a 'sound designer' is in trouble.

*****(*) The New Standard**
Verve 527715-2 *Hancock; Michael Brecker (ts, ss); John Scofield (g, sitar); Dave Holland (b); Jack DeJohnette (d); Don Alias (perc); woodwinds, brass.* 96.

Moving away from Columbia prompted a further re-examination of repertoire and market range from an artist who by this stage was certainly not scuffling for gigs. The notion of what constituted a 'standard' seemed to ossify in the aftermath of bebop: Broadway tunes, a few torchy ballads, a few novelty items, but a pretty consensual playlist of material. It was John Coltrane and, as ever, Miles who blew that away, deconstructing tunes like 'My Favorite Things', 'Chim Chim Cheree' and 'The Inch Worm' almost with savagery, and then in Miles's case digging into chart pop for 'Time After Time' (the Cyndi Lauper version) and Michael Jackson's 'Human Nature'. Hancock takes a very similar line on *The New Standard*, programming tunes like British soul diva Sade's 'Love Is Stronger Than Pride' (a lush, big-band interpretation) and Kurt Cobain's 'All Apologies', T.A.F.K.A. Prince's irrepressibly funky 'Thieves In The Temple' and Peter Gabriel's

'Mercy Street'. The essential approach is no different from any other standards recording, except that Hancock is obviously aware that some of these songs will not stand too much harmonic deconstruction at this stage in their public histories. They are not as yet true contrafacts, except for the more familiar 'Scarborough Fair', and the limitations of the record, excellently performed as it is, lie in the reliance on melodic variation of songs that in some cases are fairly cut-and-dried and not really susceptible to this treatment. One suspects that Brecker probably has a pop and rock collection at home; he revels in the challenge and turns in some fresh-voiced and unhackneyed solos. Holland and Scofield (who switches to electric sitar for 'Norwegian Wood') are masterful, and only DeJohnette, normally the most adaptable of players, seems to strain at the leash.

***** 1 + 1**
Verve 537564-2 *Hancock; Wayne Shorter (ss).* 96.

'The artists call upon the full palette of their musical resources to paint life's stories with all the texture of emotion and intensity of color – a process demanding the performance equivalent of a leap into the unknown.' Tosh. For a start, the palette is all too limited. Shorter's tenor remained in its case and there is a limit to how much of his eccentric soprano voice one wants to hear at a sitting. And there is no sense whatsoever that this is an ex-ploratory, existential encounter. What one hears is two now-middle-aged players of huge ability and scope conversing idly, eliding much of the middle ground, elevating slight ideas to spurious grandeur. Nothing wrong with that, but a mistake surely to make extravagant claims for such a lightweight session. 'The evanescent made eternal'? Don't think so.

*****(*) Gershwin's World**
Verve 557797-2 *Hancock; Eddie Henderson (t, flhn); James Carter, Wayne Shorter (ss, ts); Kenny Garrett (as); Marlon Graves (g); Stevie Wonder (hca, v); Ron Carter, Stanley Clarke, Ira Coleman (b); Terri Lyne Carrington, Gene Jackson (d); Cyro Baptista, Massamba Diop (perc); Kathleen Battle, Joni Mitchell (v); Orpheus Chamber Orchestra.* 98.

Hancock has not generally been thought of an interpreter of other composers' music, but the centenary of George Gershwin was too significant an occasion to miss. Herbie delivers one of the most elegant and thoughtful records of his career, some of it on the fringes of jazz proper, but all of it marked by a profound musicianship and a genuine empathy with Gershwin's world and music. There are some additional, non-Gershwin items: a revival of the old duo with Chick Corea for James P. Johnson's 'Blueberry Rhyme', Duke's 'Cottontail', Ravel's Piano Concerto and W.C. Handy's 'St Louis Blues'. It features the unmistakable voice of Stevie Wonder, whose equally unmissable harmonica accompanies Joni Mitchell on 'Summertime'; Shorter's soprano solo on the same track completely transforms the song into something delicate and otherworldly. From a younger generation, James Carter makes his presence felt in a style derived from Shorter's Blue Note period, but with a distinctly contemporary edge. Kenny Garrett and Eddie Henderson keep the blues very squarely on the agenda and block any risk of drifting off into 'classics lite' mode. By blending together Gershwin originals and related material, Hancock has created a mini-musical that links the great man back and forward in time, and across the divide between 'popular' and 'classical' music. It is a bold and by no means obvious programme, and this album shouldn't be missed on any account.

Captain John Handy (1900–1971)

ALTO SAXOPHONE, CLARINET

A New Orleans musician working in the city from the 1930s, Handy started on clarinet but preferred alto; when he became internationally known as a touring hired-gun in the '60s, his broad-based style suggested a synthesis of revivalism and a down-home R&B.

****(*) The Very First Recordings**
American Music AMCD-51 *Handy; Jimmy Clayton (t); Dave Williams, Louis Gallaud (p); George Guesnon (g, bj); Sylvester Handy, McNeal Breaux (b); Alfred Williams, Josiah Frazier (d).* 7/60.

*****(*) Capt. John Handy & His New Orleans Stompers Vol. 1**
GHB BCD-41 *Handy; Kid Thomas Valentine (t); Jim Robinson (tb); Sammy Rimington (cl); Bill Sinclair (p); Dick Griffith (bj); Dick McCarthy (b); Sammy Penn (d).* 12/65.

***** Capt. John Handy & His New Orleans Stompers Vol. 2**
GHB BCD-42. *As above.* 12/65.

***** Very Handy!**
GHB BCD-325 *Handy; Clive Wilson (t); Bill Bissonette (tb); Sammy Rimington (cl, g); Bill Sinclair (p); Dick Griffith (bj); Dick McCarthy (b); Art Pulver (d).* 5/66.

***** John Handy With Barry Martyn's Band**
GHB BCD-377 *Handy; Teddy Fullick (t); Pete Dyer (tb); Sammy Rimington (cl, ts); Graham Paterson (p); Brian Turnock (b); Barry Martyn (d).* 3/68.

***** Television Airshots 1968–1970**
Jazz Crusade JCCD-3008 *Handy; Punch Miller, George 'Kid Sheik' Cola (t, v); Homer Eugene, Louis Nelson (tb); Andrew Morgan (cl, ts); Dick Wellstood, Bill Sinclair (p); Dave Duquette (bj); Sylvester Handy, Chester Zardis (b); Lester Alexis, Sammy Penn (d).* 3/68–6/70.

It still seems strange that John Handy should have had so much flak from New Orleans purists for so long. He seldom worked very far from the city and had been a fixture in local bands since 1919. But because he preferred to play alto over clarinet – there is just a single track of the smaller horn on the American Music CD – and his style anticipated such R&B players as Earl Bostic, he was almost ostracized for many years. Yet he is always the most interesting player on all these records, and the bounce and wit of his playing can sometimes be phenomenal in the strict channels of New Orleans playing.

Actually, many listeners will be reminded of the alto playing of Earl Fouche with Sam Morgan. One can't hear Handy that well on the *First Recordings* disc since he seems to be at the back of the band, but when he breaks through – as on the animated 'Panama' – he makes the music bristle. Most of the disc consists of previously unreleased music, but the band is clumsy and the final three tracks, where Handy works with a different rhythm section, slightly disappointing. The two live shows from 1965 are much more like it and a strong document of the New Orleans movement at its most spirited. Valentine's jabbing trumpet spars with Handy's almost pirouetting lines, with Rimington the elegant voice in the middle. This is great stuff and, though raggedness sometimes takes over – more often on the second volume – these are records to play if one wants to sample how vibrant this kind of jazz can be. *Very Handy!* has the Captain on board with Bill Bissonnette's band, and though the leader wasn't very happy with the results, as detailed in his curmudgeonly sleeve-note, the music has plenty of fizz. Handy plays with quite herculean abandon on such as 'Give Me Your Telephone Number', and the tempos seem to quicken towards helter-skelter as a result. The sound is a bit thin and strangled but it's not hopeless, and five previously unissued tracks take the CD over 60 minutes.

Recorded on tour with the Barry Martyn group, Handy seems in good spirits. The cover photo of six young Englishmen and the weatherbeaten New Orleans veteran seems redolent of an era of pre-history, but the music, driven along by Kid Martyn's unquenchable enthusiasm from the kit, has a gutsy excitement. Fullick, who was a new recruit to the group, has a tone that's even shakier than Kid Thomas Valentine on an off-day, but Rimington and Handy make a good team. The TV recordings are from two shows with different groups, though there's little between them in terms of either playing or sound, which is decent if flat. Miller and Kid Sheik divide honours about even and, though the presence of Wellstood on the first date is a surprise, neither pianist has much to do. Handy weathers all storms with soldierly fortitude and gets in some good blows on the way.

John Handy (born 1933)

ALTO SAXOPHONE, FLUTE, OTHER REEDS

Born in Dallas, Texas, 30 years before John F. Kennedy's fateful, fatal visit, Handy moved to New York in his mid-twenties and found work with Charles Mingus and others. The 1965 Monterey Jazz Festival was his coming-out, and perhaps a premature climax.

*****(*) Live At The Monterey Jazz Festival**

Koch KOC 3-7820-2 *Handy; Mike White (vn); Jerry Hahn (g); Don Thompson (b); Terry Clarke (d).* 9/65.

***** The Second John Handy Album**

Koch CD 7812-2 *As above.* 7/66.

Not to be confused with the much older alto saxophonist, 'Captain' John Handy, the Texan is one of the few contemporary players who sounds as though he had listened carefully to Eric Dolphy, an enthusiasm that must have been encouraged during his association with Charles Mingus.

The 1965 Monterey Jazz Festival appearance was a roaring success and should have created more critical momentum than the work of later years suggests. The CD reissue has put the two long tracks back in the original order of performance, with 'If Only We Knew' placed ahead of 'Spanish Lady'. Handy's intriguing harmonics and ravelling lines are supplemented by White and Hahn, but it's the leader who really commands attention.

The studio follow-up has its dead spots, not least in the over-long 'Scheme #1', but there is no mistaking Handy's originality and desire to plough his own furrow. The CD adds three splendid tracks, an alternative version of 'Blues For A Highstrung Guitar' and two unissued items, 'A Bad Stroke Of Luck' and 'Debonair'. Once again, White is a key performer, used in ways that recall the violin parts in Albert Ayler's bands, only rather gentler. Hahn is more audible in the studio and seems more relaxed than at Monterey.

****** New View!**

Koch CD 7811-2 *Handy; Bobby Hutcherson (vib); Pat Martino (g); Albert Stinson (b); Doug Sides (d).* 6/67.

Handy's masterpiece, caught at the Village Gate in New York. The opening 'Naima', performed in the last month of composer John Coltrane's life, has a particular synchronicity, and a flavour that the unusual instrumentation hammers home. The real plus, though, is the restoration to full length of 'Tears Of Ole Miss (Anatomy Of A Riot)', which now comes in at a full half-hour. Also on the album, 'A Little Quiet', which also shows John Hammond's gifts as a producer, the live mix balanced with genuine taste.

***** Projections**

Koch KOC CD 7865 *Handy; Michael White (vn); Mike Nock (p); Bruce Cale (b); Larry Hancock (d, perc).* 68.

Ambitious, but deeply flawed, *Projections* was the work of Handy's pretentiously named Concert Ensemble, a group that was required to generate a bigger and fuller sound. Nock and White contribute compositions, and this perhaps allows Handy to concentrate on his playing. He doubles on flute and the rarely heard saxello, and he seems to be experimenting with a spectrum of sound-sources, something Dolphy did. The flute playing, rather like Dolphy's, is more enthusiastic than accomplished, but on saxello Handy finds a fascinating tonality that he doesn't reach on alto. 'Dance To The Lady' is glorious, but far in advance expressively of anything else on the disc.

***** Two Originals: Karuna Supreme / Rainbow**

MPS 519195 2CD *Handy; Ali Akbar Khan (sarod); L Subramaniam (vn); Zakir Hussain, Shyam Kane (tabla); Mary Johnson, Yogish S Sahota (tambura).* 11/75, 9/80.

Handy's interest in Indian music is evident on *Musical Dreamland*, but its most idiomatic and effective expression comes on the MPS twofer which brings together the 1975 LP, *Karuna Supreme*, with *Rainbow*, recorded five years later. Unlike John Mayer's much over-praised *Indo-Jazz Fusions*, rather more like some of Charlie Mariano's crossover experiments, Handy seems to have found a way to combine and blend jazz and Karnatic harmonic language and rhythms. The association with Ali Akbar Khan and, on the second record, Dr L. Subramaniam proved to be immensely fruitful, and Handy's playing always sounds secure and relaxed.

Roland Hanna (born 1932)

PIANO

Sir Roland Hanna, as he should more properly be addressed (he was knighted by the President of Liberia in 1970), is one of the finest living piano improvisers. Bud Powell was the single most important influence on Hanna's playing style, but the Detroit man has also taken careful note of Tommy Flanagan and Teddy Wilson.

*****(*) Perugia**
Freedom 741010 *Hanna (p solo).* 7/74.

In these superb solo cuts there are echoes of Tatum's tightly pedalled, rapid-fire runs and crisply arpeggiated chords. *Perugia* begins with a superb rendition of Strayhorn's 'Take The "A" Train' and a clever 'I Got It Bad And That Ain't Good', before moving off into original material. The influence of Teddy Wilson is also evident, but there are boppish passages and elements of free jazz as well. Anyone unfamiliar with Hanna's work should certainly begin with *Perugia*, not least for the insight it offers into Sir Roland's stylistic sources.

***** Bird Tracks**
Progressive 7031 *Hanna (p solo).* 2–3/78.

The Parker material fizzes and bounces in a convincing pianistic impersonation of the album's inspiration. Hanna's ability to capture the cadence of horn lines is something that again he shares with Tommy Flanagan, but he does it with his own distinctive spin.

****(*) Glove**
Storyville STCD 4148 *Hanna; George Mraz (b); Motohiko Hino (d).* 87.

*****(*) Round Midnight**
Town Crier 513 *Hanna (p solo).* 3/87.

****(*) This Time It's Real**
Storyville STCD 4145 *Hanna; Jesper Thilo (ts); Mads Vinding (b); Aage Tanggaard (d).* 6/87.

****(*) Persia My Dear**
DIW 8015 *Hanna; Richard Davis (b); Freddie Waits (d).* 8/87.

The solo album is the highpoint of a vintage year for Sir Roland. Mostly original material, and including 'Prelude' (originally written for solo cello) and 'Century Rag', it's a sepia-hued session recorded close up and very warmly.

Hanna sounds most obviously like Flanagan when duetting with the excellent Mraz. Formerly listed on Black Hawk, *Glove* is a set of tunes with 'love' in the title, a thematic approach more associated with another pianist, Dave McKenna. The sound is nothing like as exact as that on the DIW, also from Japan, and the drummer is all over the music, like a cheap suit. Surprisingly, perhaps, with Richard Davis, normally the most classically inclined of bassists, Hanna opts to groove. 'Persia My Dear' has a Monkish quality, but the stand-out tracks are 'Summer In Central Park' and 'Manhattan Safari', tributes to the city that has been the Detroit-born Hanna's working home for many years and focus of his long-standing New York Jazz Quartet.

Saxophonist Thilo gets equal billing on the Storyville and takes his full ration of solo space. Hard to begrudge him it, but he isn't the most terrifically interesting of players, lacking the harmonic sophistication of, say, Bernt Rosengren, whom he occasionally resembles. It's a safe programme for the Tivoli Gardens punters – 'Stella', 'Cherokee', 'Body And Soul', 'Star Eyes' – and the only really startling bit is Hanna's segue between the title-track and the last of these, a glimmer of pure invention on an otherwise rather overcast night.

*****(*) Duke Ellington Piano Solos**
Musicmasters 65045-2 *Hanna (p solo).* 3/90.

Opening with 'In My Solitude', Hanna brings a calm, meditative quality to a gently paced programme. 'Isfahan' and 'Single Petal Of A Rose' mark the mid-point and a slight change of direction. By the end, Hanna seems to be taking more liberties (though they're probably there from the off) and 'Caravan' has a curiously remote air that defamiliarizes the theme.

*****(*) Maybeck Recital Hall Series: Volume 32**
Concord CCD 4604 *Hanna (p solo).* 8/93.

The Maybeck setting seems to reawaken Sir Roland's interest in the classics. There is a rich chromaticism, worthy of Debussy and, in its extreme form, pointing on to Schoenberg, lurking behind more than a few of these solo performances. The opening 'Love Walked In' is a good example, though the more obvious sources for it are Monk and Garner. As Grover Sales notes in an appreciative liner-comment, it is Hanna's sense of structure that is so impressive. Not a single track carries on past its logical conclusion, and even the long, seemingly episodic Gershwin medley has a firm anchoring logic. Above all, too, it's a witty set. A charge through 'Oleo' and a technically brilliant coda to 'This Can't Be Love' are both done with a smile, which makes the romantic-tragic strains of 'Lush Life' all the more convincing.

***** Plays Gershwin**
Delta 17123 *Hanna; Bill Easley (sax); Jon Burr (b); Ronnie Burrage (d).* 4/97.

The very clever and unexpected 'Variations on Concerto in E' sets the tone for a thoroughly individual approach to the Gershwin canon. The remaining selections are pretty much greatest hits, opening with 'Summertime' and 'Lady Be Good' and ending with a twinkle on 'Strike Up The Band'. You don't often hear Hanna with a horn, and Easley is spot-on for this material. A word, too, for Burrage, who exudes delight from start to finish.

Mick Hanson

GUITAR

British guitarist working in a conservative modern idiom.

***** Do You Have A Name?**
Spotlite SPJ-CD 555 *Hanson; Kevin Flanagan (ts); Mike Carr, Jay Denson (org); Gordon Beck, Brian Dee (p); Len Skeat (b); Chris Dagley, Bobby Worth (d).* 12/95–1/96.

Hanson is a veteran British guitarist, although this is his first disc as a leader. The music's a docile blend of organ–guitar combo jazz, pastel-toned quartet tracks and – a country mile ahead of the rest – three exemplary duets with Gordon Beck. If these three stand out, it's because the other music simply ticks along, with little help from the rhythm sections. Hanson has a featureless tone, in the classic jazz-guitar manner, and he plays very well. As so often, though, the record's too long.

Bill Hardman (1933–90)

TRUMPET

Born in Cleveland, Hardman had several major associations in his career, playing with both Charles Mingus and Art Blakey in the 1950s, '60s and '70s. Co-led a small group with Lou Donaldson in the early '60s and latterly one with Junior Cook.

*** What's Up

Steeplechase SCCD 1254 *Hardman; Robin Eubanks (tb); Junior Cook (ts); Mickey Tucker (p); Paul Brown (b); Leroy Williams (d).* 7/89.

Bill Hardman was a Jazz Messenger, a staunch sideman, and the long-time front-line partner of Junior Cook. A tough, no-nonsense hard bopper of the second division, he usually raised the temperature of whatever date he was on. Early records such as *Jackie's Pal* (briefly available as an OJC) and a fine date for Savoy are in need of revival. *What's Up* was his final album and it was made not long before his sudden death. It's a typically likeable statement. Eubanks, who can play in almost any kind of modern setting, fits in comfortably alongside Hardman's regular colleagues and, as well as the customary hard bop and blues, there are a couple of sober ballads in 'I Should Care' and 'Like Someone In Love' which, in the circumstances, enact a poignant farewell to the trumpeter's art. Exceptionally well recorded by the Steeplechase team: Hardman's sound was probably never captured better.

Roy Hargrove (born 1970)

TRUMPET, FLUGELHORN

Raised in Dallas, Hargrove emerged as something of a wunderkind at the end of the '80s, making a string of albums for BMG and subsequently signing to Verve. He leads his own touring band and has guested on many recent albums.

***(*) With The Tenors Of Our Time

Verve 523019-2 *Hargrove; Ron Blake (ss, ts); Johnny Griffin, Joe Henderson, Branford Marsalis, Joshua Redman, Stanley Turrentine (ts); Cyrus Chestnut (p); Rodney Whitaker (b); Gregory Hutchinson (d).* 1/94.

While much of the new jazz of the 1990s attracted criticism for excessive orthodoxy or mere executive showmanship, it's less often remarked that many of today's younger players exhibit a rhythmic bravado and harmonic lucidity which are a natural step forward from (and within) the tradition. After the sideways evolutionary paths of fusion, the so-called 'neo-classicism' which players like Hargrove represent offers a dramatic refocusing, if not any particular radicalism. Hargrove is a highly gifted trumpeter whose facility and bright, sweet tone bring a sense of dancing fun to his music. But he is steadily working towards a gravitas that places him in the trumpet lineage as surely as Marsalis or Faddis. Antonio Hart, a friend and college colleague, is equally impressive on his early records, his searingly pure tone placed at the service of a canny understanding of bebop alto.

After five records for Novus there was still no classic on the shelves, and Hargrove departed for Verve (some of his Novus albums may still be available in some territories, but basically they're gone). *With The Tenors Of Our Time* is no masterwork, but the trumpeter rises to the challenge of having five grandmasters sit in on the different tunes – although Blake holds his own with real class on 'Once Forgotten' and with Redman on 'Mental Phrasing'. Branford gets off a good one on 'Valse Hot' and Hargrove and Turrentine enjoy themselves on 'Soppin' The Biscuit'; but the trumpeter plays with fresh resolve throughout, and his flugelhorn solo on 'Never Let Me Go' is a quiet showstopper.

*** Family

Verve 527630-2 *Hargrove; Wynton Marsalis (t); Jesse Davis (as); David 'Fathead' Newman (ts, f); Ron Blake (ts); Stephen Scott, John Hicks, Ronnie Mathews (p); Rodney Whitaker, Walter Booker, Christian McBride (b); Gregory Hutchinson, Lewis Nash, Karriem Riggins (d).* 1/95.

***(*) Parker's Mood

Verve 527907-2 *Hargrove; Stephen Scott (p); Christian McBride (b).* 4/95.

Family is a sequence of dedications to personal and spiritual kin that opens out into an interesting meditation on Hargrove's possible future course. Fats Navarro's 'Nostalgia', delivered as a duet with Marsalis, sounds like two parallel reflections on bebop tradition, and the ruminative pieces which open the disc include some of the trumpeter's most skilful and personalized playing. His regular band provides decisive support, but the line-up of guest stars rocks the record at some moments where it ought to be steady, and in the end this still feels like a transitional disc.

Recorded in Parker's 75th anniversary year, *Parker's Mood* is a delightful meeting of three young masters, improvising on 16 themes from Bird's repertoire. Hargrove's luminous treatment of 'Laura' provides further evidence that he may be turning into one of the music's pre-eminent ballad players, but it's the inventive interplay between the three men that takes the session to its high level: Scott, sometimes burdened by the weight of his conceptions on his own records, plays as freely as he ever has, and McBride is simply terrific.

*** Habana

Verve 537563-2 *Hargrove; Frank Lacy (tb); Gary Bartz (as, ss); David Sanchez (ts, ss); Chucho Valdes (p); Russell Malone (g); John Benitez (b); Horacio Hernandez (d); Jose Luis Quintana, Miguel Diaz (perc).* 1/97.

Although the packaging seems to suggest that this was cut on a long weekend in Cuba, Hargrove's Latin project emanates from an Italian concert, even if the idea was germinated by his visiting and playing with Cuban musicians. Jostling with rhythms, plangent in its solos, this is a fun, lightweight record which isn't so much a departure for the trumpeter as a sunny vacation. There's little to suggest any profound commitment to the local style, or indeed anything beyond a good-natured piece of opportunism, and some of the elements (particularly Lacy's misguidedly awry trombone parts) just sound wrong; but it remains an enjoyable piece of hokum, whatever the subtext. As he approaches thirty, isn't it time Hargrove took time out to make a masterpiece, though?

****(*) Moment To Moment**
Verve 543540-2 *Hargrove; Sherman Irby (as); Larry Willis (p); Gerald Cannon (b); Willie Jones III (d); strings.* 99.

Nothing doing here, either. A strings album is something that Hargrove might well aspire to in the fullness of time; at this point, it suggests a career that's lacking purpose and direction. His current working band is terrific, and much of it plays here, but they're swamped by arrangements which at best are serviceable and, over the course of an album, merely anodyne for much of the time. Docked a further notch for taking an expensive soft option.

Harlem Jazz Camels

GROUP

Swedish repertory outfit dedicated to the small-group jazz of the 1930s.

***** Drop Me Off In Harlem**
Phontastic PHONTCD 8832 *Bent Persson (t); Jens Lindgren (tb, v); Goran Eriksson (as); Claes Brodda (cl, ts, bs); Ulf Lindberg (p); Goran Stachewsky (g, bj); Lars Lindbeck (b); Sigge Dellert (d).* 1/93.

***** Blue Interlude**
Phontastic PHONTCD 8851 *As above, except Stephan Lindstein (tb) replaces Lindgren; add Marit Elfstrom (v).* 3–4/96.

The Camels have been around long enough to have pre-dated the more fashionable interest in this area of jazz in America. The speciality of the day here is Ellington's small-unit music, which brings the likes of 'The Jeep Is Jumpin'', 'Love In My Heart', 'Back Room Romp' and 'Barney Going Easy' into the book on the first disc, and 'Diga Diga Doo', 'Rexatious', 'Downtown Uproar' and 'Stompy Jones' on the second. Persson's uncanny ability with bygone styles is becoming well known; but equally impressive here is Eriksson's stroll in Hodges' footsteps, and Brodda's spirited playing on baritone in particular is very effective. The later set suffers slightly from a sound-balance that puts the rhythm section in the middle distance, but it's not too troublesome.

Cathy Harley

PIANO

Contemporary Australian pianist.

*****(*) Tuesday's Tune**
Rufus RF028 *Harley; Warwick Alder (t); Bernie McGann (as); Craig Scott (b); Alan Turnbull (d).* 2/95.

Entirely without frills or pretension, Harley's record is typical of the kind of modern hard bop that develops away from any obvious jazz limelight and exists on its own hard-won virtues and modest inspirations. The band are a group of (if they'll excuse us) veteran Australian modernists, with McGann the name that will be most familiar to those of us listening from afar: as ever, he's a wild card, solos full of unexpected incident and strange light and dark. Everybody else keeps up, though, and Harley herself writes tunes that are both functionally effective and naggingly memorable. Particularly gratifying: the ballad 'Old Heart'.

Billy Harper (born 1943)

TENOR SAXOPHONE, ALTO SAXOPHONE

Born in Houston, he studied at North Texas State before moving to New York in 1965. A regular sideman with Art Blakey, Jones–Lewis and Gil Evans and sometimes a leader, he is a conservative radical with a formidable command of most aspects of post-bop.

***** Capra Black**
Strata East 660 51 022 *Harper; Jimmy Owens (t); Dick Griffin, Julian Priester (tb); George Cables (p); Reggie Workman (b); Billy Cobham, Elvin Jones, Warren Smith (d); Barbara Grant, Laveda Johnson, Gene McDaniels, Pat Robinson (v).* 73.

Initially influenced by Sonny Rollins, Harper got his chops playing in church before going on to work with Art Blakey, Max Roach and Gil Evans, for whom he wrote 'Priestess' and 'Thoroughbred', two of the best modern-jazz compositions in the book. Coupled to his gifts as a writer, Harper's big, gospelly solo style should have made him a star, but he has never quite achieved the breakthrough his talents deserve, and the absence of major-label interest in his work remains a serious disgrace.

Capra Black, like a good deal of the Strata East catalogue, now feels very much of its time, and in the 1970s even experiment had a formula. The title-piece makes plentiful use of double time and skewed passages in unexpected keys. By contrast, the other tunes are more broadly emotional and very much in the line of 'Priestess', bearing witness with passion and the fullest sound since Coltrane. 'New Breed' is a blues which never leaves the groove Cobham chisels out for it. 'Soulfully I Love You' is a spiritual with voices, a slightly sentimental idea which nevertheless redeems itself on the grounds of sheer beauty. 'Cry Of Hunger', another important original, brings the session to a close with the leader wailing righteously under Barbara Grant's urgent voice.

*****(*) Black Saint**
Black Saint 120001 *Harper; Virgil Jones (t); Joe Bonner (p); David Friesen (b); Malcolm Pinson (d).* 7/75.

***** In Europe**
Soul Note 121001 *Harper; Everett Hollins (t); Fred Hersch (p); Louis Spears (b); Horace Arnold (d).* 1/79.

Like many of his countrymen, Harper had to look to Europe for recognition, and to the Black Saint/Soul Note stable (good trivia question: which artist kicked off both imprints?) for the beginnings of a discography. *Black Saint* is still the album people associate with Harper, a strong, eclectic blend of blues, hard-edged rock patterns and the by-now-familiar preaching style. Jones and Bonner are greatly admired in Europe, too, and the pianist makes his mark on the record from the very start with his tersely romantic approach and elastic chord-patterns which add fuel to the perfervid intensity of the leader.

The Soul Note is faintly disappointing, albeit full of potential and marked by pretty much the same strengths as Harper's other work. Hersch still hadn't quite come into his own at this point and he sounds a little acid here and there, but it's a good night's work for Everett Hollins, who had also recorded with Archie Shepp and who makes a strong case for himself here. 'Calvary' is superb. Launching two important contemporary labels is no mean feat. Both albums are well worth having.

***** Destiny Is Yours**
Steeplechase SCCD 31260 *Harper; Eddie Henderson (t); Francesca Tanksley (p); Clarence Seay (b); Newman Baker (d).* 12/89.

There is a bit of a hole in the discography at this point, almost a decade in which Harper was mainly involved in other projects, and other people's projects. This, though, unveils what was to be a working band. Henderson very nearly steals it, but it is the solid, melodic playing of Chessie Tanksley that holds the date together. The other two members of the group are somewhat mechanical – but, oddly, this contributes to our abiding feeling that this date is reminiscent of the Ayler brothers' association.

*****(*) Live On Tour In The Far East**
Steeplechase SCCD 31311 *Harper; Eddie Henderson (t); Francesca Tanksley (p); Louis Spears (b); Newman Baker (d).* 4/91.

****** Live On Tour In The Far East: Volume 2**
Steeplechase SCCD 31321 *As above.* 4/91.

***** Live On Tour In The Far East: Volume 3**
Steeplechase SCCD 31331 *As above.* 4/91.

This documents a poised and confident band. Having Henderson and Tanksley on the strength must have made an enormous difference, and both horns and piano are playing at full stretch for most of the first two volumes. It's a set which palls when less compelling material is brought in, and only then because the rhythm section is far from inspiring. The version of 'Priestess' on *Volume Two* is definitive, for now and all time, and there is a wonderful cover of 'My Funny Valentine'.

****** Somalia**
Evidence ECD 22133 *Harper; Eddie Henderson (t); Francesca Tanksley (p); Louis Spears (b); Horace Arnold, Newman Baker (d); Madeleine Yayodele Nelson (shekere).* 10/93.

The introduction of a second drummer here gave Harper a rhythmic base on which he was able to build some of his most inventive and focused improvisations for years. The long 'Thy Will Be Done' is outwardly the sort of thing Trane and Pharoah Sanders were doing in later years, except that Harper clings to the security of simplicity, investing a hymn-like idea with ambiguities that help create a long-form improvisation of genuine subtlety. The two tunes that bracket it, 'Somalia' and 'Quest', are more straightforward, though the title-piece is a return to some of the things he was doing at the time of *Capra Black*, a hint of unfinished business.

The band now sounds thoroughly played-in and responsive, and Tanksley's comping is hugely impressive – more so than her solo work, which still lacks a single informing idea to give it coherence.

*****(*) If Only Our Hearts Could See**
DIW 931 *As above, except omit Arnold, Nelson.* 2/97.

Pretty much a continuation of recent form. Henderson is used on only three tracks, though his contributions to 'The Seventh Day' and 'Egypt' are sterling, some of the best playing he's done for years. Unusually, there is a standard, 'My One And Only Love', performed with a high level of concentration and a rich sound which owes as much to the engineer as to the players. This is the most elegantly finished album Harper has yet to make. We are still finding new things in it after many hearings.

Herbie Harper (born 1920)

TROMBONE

Worked in big bands during the 1940s but settled on the West Coast from 1950 and appeared on countless studio dates as a reliable pro from that point onwards.

***** Five Brothers**
VSOP 9 *Harper; Bob Enevoldsen (vtb, ts); Don Overburg (g); Red Mitchell (b); Frank Capp (d).* 55.

***** Two Brothers**
VSOP 80 *Harper; Bill Perkins (ts, bs, f); Larry Koonse (g); John Leitham (b); Larance Marable (d).* 9/89.

Harper's buttery high notes and mellifluous mid-register have been poured over numerous Californian record dates for 40 years and more. These rare excursions into the limelight are good to have in the catalogue, though neither makes a pressing claim on the casual listener. The 1955 date is one of those clipped West Coast schedule-fillers which succeeds in spite of itself: the two horns plait their lines together with beguiling finesse, though they don't give themselves much space – even with three alternative takes on the CD reissue, the music doesn't crack the 40-minute barrier.

A generation later, Harper revisited the same instrumentation. Koonse shares solo honours with the others, playing with great fluency, and Perkins sounds good, too. A couple of the arrangements – such as the misplaced funk of Neal Hefti's 'Fred' – are a strain. But Harper's lovely sound is a pleasure to hear all the same.

Winard Harper (born 1962)

DRUMS

Born in Baltimore, Harper was already playing drums by the time of his teens and was with Dexter Gordon in 1982. He spent four years with Betty Carter, then worked with his brother Philip in the Harper Brothers Band, before leading his own dates.

****(*) Trap Dancer**
Savant SCD 2013 *Harper; Patrick Rickman (t); J.D Allen (ts); George Cables (p); Eric Revis (b); Cecil Brooks (d).* 12/97.

***** Winard**
Savant SCD 2021 *As above, except add Abdou Mboup (perc).* 12/98.

Harper is a strong and capable drummer, but there's little here to suggest that he has any great talents as a group leader. Both discs are filled with brief, taster-like pieces which hint at directions without fulfilling them. Each has a quota of hard-bop hits such as 'Work Song', along with originals from band members that never receive any kind of development (possibly with radio play in mind). The second disc is ahead of the first, but that's not saying a great deal, and what Cables is doing in this company isn't clear. Of the participants, Allen, who gets some clear space to work in on some tracks, is easily the standout performer.

Tom Harrell (born 1946)

TRUMPET, FLUGELHORN, PIANO

Born in Urbana, Illinois, he was influenced by Clifford Brown and, later, John Coltrane. After service with Woody Herman and Stan Kenton, he started playing bop with Horace Silver, an association which added Blue Mitchell to his roster of influences. Despite often disabling illness, Harrell has created a substantial career as sideman and leader. His limpid tone in ballads is balanced by a ferocious attack on up-tempo numbers, with a round, full and very brassy timbre. Harrell is also a fine composer.

***** Moon Alley**

Criss Cross 1018 *Harrell; Kenny Garrett (as, f); Kenny Barron (p); Ray Drummond (b); Ralph Peterson (d).* 12/85.

****(*) Open Air**

Steeplechase SCCD 31220 *Harrell; Bob Rockwell (ts); Hal Galper (p); Steve Gilmore (b); Bill Goodwin (d).* 5/86.

Anyone who has seen Tom Harrell perform live will understand the transformative power of music. When not playing, he stands slumped and bowed, stock-still in what looks like mute agony. When it comes time to take a solo, it is as if an electric charge has passed through him. Harrell is one of the finest harmonic improvisers in jazz today, a player with a fierce tone who is also capable of playing the most delicate ballad with almost unbearable feeling.

We have been criticized for pointing out that he has battled with psychiatric illness for many years. It does not define him, either personally or creatively, but schizophrenia has been a shaping influence for much of his adult life. Schizophrenics never make any bones about it, and Harrell has even been known to joke about his condition, once commenting as he entered a hotel suite that there was a room for each of his personalities. There are two playing personalities. They are not yet dramatically separated on the two early records as leader. *Moon Alley* has its slightly morose side, but this has as much to do with the recording as with Harrell's temperament. He is hugely secure in technique, already a veteran, evoking everyone from Kenny Dorham when at full tilt, to Freddie Hubbard when doubling on flugelhorn, to Miles inevitably. Teamed with Kenny Garrett, one of Miles's last saxophone players, he sounds bred in the bone, slightly out of synch with the rapid progressions of 'Scrapple From The Apple'. *Open Air* is a little flat. Galper is too lush and fulsome, and the rest of the rhythm section hangs back. Rockwell is a liability in the ensembles, though a fresh and often provocative soloist.

*****(*) Stories**

Contemporary C 14043 *Harrell; Bob Berg (ts); Niels Lan Doky (p); John Scofield (g); Ray Drummond (b); Billy Hart (d).* 1/88.

****** Sail Away**

Contemporary C 14054 *Harrell; David Liebman (ss); Joe Lovano (ts); John Abercrombie (g, g syn); James Williams (p); Ray Drummond (b); Adam Nussbaum (d).* 3/89.

*****(*) Form**

Contemporary C 14059 *Harrell; Joe Lovano (ts); Danilo Perez (p); Charlie Haden (b); Paul Motian (d).* 4/90.

****** Visions**

Contemporary C 14063 *Harrell; George Robert (as); Joe Lovano (ts, ss); Bob Berg, David Liebman (ss); Cheryl Pyle (f); Niels Lan Doky (p); John Abercrombie (g, g syn); Ray Drummond, Charlie Haden, Reggie Johnson (b); Bill Goodwin, Billy Hart, Paul Motian, Adam Nussbaum (d).* 4/87–4/90.

The records for Contemporary were something of a purple patch. *Visions* is actually a compilation of material recorded over a span of time during which Harrell recovered some of the snap and pointed delivery people noted during his sojourn with Horace Silver. Every now and then, as on 'Visions Of Gaudi' with Liebman and Abercrombie, he delivers something that is as hard-edged and as finely detailed as mosaic. He spends most of the album on flugelhorn, but 'Suspended View', with Berg on soprano, is a trumpet performance of magical skill, fleeting, ambiguous and endlessly replayable. Only 'April Mist' seems conventional.

Of the group, *Sail Away* is probably the most coherent. 'Glass Mystery' and the more driving 'Buffalo Wings' are model performances, and the balance of form and function, which also seems to be the underlying emphasis of the small-scale 1990 album, is well judged. The Haden/Motian axis functions well behind Perez, as might be expected, but the set lacks a certain spark.

***** Sail Away**

Musidisc MU 500252 *Harrell; Kenny Werner (p); Paul Imm (b); André Ceccarelli (d).* 4/91.

Confusingly titled, given the 1989 Contemporary set, and not a patch on it. It's a perfectly decent record, and Harrell seems to have discovered new timbral areas that he's anxious to explore, but these aren't the players to inspire him and, though Werner is an able and sensitive accompanist, he has an irritating predilection for dotting 'i's and crossing 't's, a surplus of detail that muddles some of Harrell's strongest lines.

****** Passages**

Chesky JD 64 *Harrell; Joe Lovano (as, ts, ss); Danilo Perez (p); Peter Washington (b); Paul Motian (d); Cafe (perc).* 10/91.

*****(*) Upswing**

Chesky JD 103 *As above, except add Phil Woods (as), Bill Goodwin (d); omit Cafe, Motian.* 6/93.

Who knows what personal agony lies behind a title like *Upswing*, however wry and ironic it is? These are marvellous records, polished, forceful, beautifully recorded and absolutely fresh. Harrell's ability to shift up through the changes without losing the momentum of a song is uncanny and seems to be done with ideas to spare. On the second outing Motian is missed for the sheer subtlety with which he colours a phrase and the almost miraculous way that he can appear to be playing free while sustaining an absolutely metronomic line underneath the horns. Harrell and Lovano have struck up one of the great jazz partnerships and seem genuinely to enjoy teasing out each other's idiosyncrasies. Perez might quibble about the sound (and possibly the piano) he has been given, but he too has become an integral part of the trumpeter's concept. Woods is there to return a compliment, another former employer who has publicly acknowledged Harrell's gifts. And they are manifest; first-rate modern jazz.

****** Labyrinth**

RCA Victor 09026 68512 *Harrell; Steve Turre (tb); Don Braden, Joe Lovano (ts); Gary Smulyan (bcl); Rob Botti (ob); Kenny Werner (p); Larry Grenadier (b); Billy Hart (d); Leon Parker (perc).* 1/96.

Fine as the two Cheskys were, *Labyrinth* was Harrell's real coming out as a major figure. Just turning fifty, he came to it with renewed fire. In a sense, the album takes him full circle, teaming him with players who were part of the Criss Cross operation almost a decade earlier. Braden and Smulyan have gone on to their own projects, and Turre is now an established star. Harrell writes all the tunes, with the exception of 'Darn That Dream', which is an overdubbed duet with himself on piano – and a piano formerly used by Bill Evans at that. The larger-scale arrangements with horns, like 'Majesty', 'Sun Cycle' and 'Blue In One', take him to a new phase of musical organization, a sequence of shifting themes which often defy major/minor distinction and which resolve in the most unexpected ways, though individual parts sound perfectly logical. Harrell sticks mainly to trumpet, reserving flugelhorn for 'Marimba Song', with the basic group of Braden, Werner, Grenadier and Hart, and for 'Darn That Dream'. An essential modern record: the superlatives have pretty much been exhausted.

*****(*) The Art Of Rhythm**

RCA Victor 09026 68924 *Harrell; Dewey Redman (ts); David Sanchez (ts, ss); Greg Tardy (cl, ts); Gary Smulyan (bs, bcl); David Kassoff (ob); Romero Lubambo, Mike Stern (g); Danilo Perez (p, harmonium); Regina Carter (vn); Ron Lawrence (vla); Akua Dixon (clo); Bryan Carrott (mar); David Finck, Ugonna Okegwo (b); Duduka Fonseca, Leon Parker (d); Waltinho Anastacio, Milton Cardona, Adam Cruz, Natalie Cushman (perc).* 5–7/97.

What was becoming increasingly obvious over time is how ebullient and rhythmic a player Harrell is. Listening back to some of the darker and more subdued tracks on previous albums, having heard this pungent set, one understands that he has learnt a good deal from Dizzy's Afro-Hispanic experiments. *The Art Of Rhythm* isn't, though, a soaraway south-of-the-border set. It might equally be subtitled 'the art of colour' or 'the art of arrangement'. Never before has Harrell, who is the composer of all ten tunes, experimented more freely with instrumental combinations. The string and guitar writing, for both Lubambo and Stern, is exquisite. He opens in gentle mode with clarinet, acoustic guitar and string trio on 'Petals Danse', builds in woodwinds elsewhere, but also allows himself a hefty dose of jazz horns on 'Oasis' (sharing solo space with Dewey Redman), 'Doo Bop' (a feature for Tardy's tenor) and 'Madrid'. He leans heavily on flugelhorn, perhaps too much so, though Harrell has always been able to give the bigger horn the bite and attack of trumpet when so required. A wonderful, accomplished record from an important player. The success of *Labyrinth* has given him considerable artistic leverage; here, he has used it to maximum effect.

***** Time's Mirror**

RCA Victor 09026 63524-2 *Harrell; Joe Magnarelli, Chris Rogers, David Weiss, James Zollar (t, flhn); Earl Gardner (t); Conrad Herwig, Mike Fagan, Curtis Hasselbring (tb); Douglas Purviance (btb); Craig Bailey, Mark Gross, Alex Foster, Don Braden, David Schumacher (reeds); Xavier Davis (p); Kenny Davis (b); Carl Allen (d).* 3/99.

Our rather miserly rating shouldn't deter Harrell admirers from investigating this big-band set, but it does feel a little careful and even antiseptic here and there. It's a selection of Harrell charts which in some cases go back a long way ('Autumn Leaves' is dated to 1964) and, as thoughtful and accomplished as the writing is, it's sometimes too thoughtful and accomplished: some of the music looks inwards at the point where it should surely sound welcoming. 'Time's Mirror' itself is a handsome piece, which acts as a gorgeous setting for Tom's flugelhorn playing, yet only occasionally does that lustre spread through the rest of the music.

Joe Harriott (1928–73)

ALTO SAXOPHONE

A Jamaican who came to London in 1951, Harriott played bebop alto but formulated a method of free jazz somewhat independent of Coleman's music. Recorded with his own quintet, and later in a collaboration with Indian violinist John Mayer, but he was marginalized by his times and eventually was killed by cancer.

****** Free Form**

Redial 538 184-2 *Harriott; Shake Keane (t, flhn); Pat Smythe (p); Coleridege Goode (b); Phil Seamen (d).* 60.

*****(*) Abstract**

Redial 538 138-2 *As above, except add Bobby Orr (d); Frank Holder (perc).* 11/61, 5/62.

***** Indo Jazz-Fusions I & II**

Redial 538 048-2 *As above, except omit Seamen and Holder; add John Mayer (vn, hpd); Kenny Wheeler (t, flhn); Chris Taylor (f); Jackie Dougan, Alan Ganley (d); Diwan Motihar (sitar); Chandrahas Paigankar (tambura); Keshav Sathe (tabla).* 67, 68.

***** Indo-Jazz Suite**

Koch KOC CD 8512 *As above.*

Believers in the theory of simultaneous evolution always mention Joe Harriott, who seems to have worked out free jazz for himself, just as controversial Americans like Ornette Coleman were making similar noises. Unlike Coleman, Harriott played with a transparent emotion, like a blues man. Apart from Kippie Moeketsi, Dudu Pukwana and Jackie McLean on his day, no one has ever blown an alto saxophone with such obvious pain *and* joy.

Harriott suffered ill-health, and tuberculosis compromised his recording career substantially. Nevertheless, he has left at least these astonishing memorials to his genius. *Indo-Jazz Fusions* was a project more often cited and discussed than actually heard. Its reappearance on CD and Polygram's generous repackaging of Harriott's classic Jazzland sessions push past the mythology of the brilliant West Indian as a doomed tragedian. Like Charlie Parker, Harriott at his most typical is an effortless melodist. Look past the more forbiddingly abstract titles on *Free Form* and *Abstract* – 'Subject', 'Parallel', 'Straight Lines', 'Idioms' – and hear something altogether different. 'Calypso' on the 1960 session is the most obvious pointer, but almost everywhere Harriott blends freedom and abstraction with blues-inflected changes jazz in a way that has become almost definitive of British improvisation. These sessions are also a showcase for two of the lost legends of British jazz, pianist Pat Smythe, much missed, and the intense, self-destructive power of Phil Seamen, who sounds instinctively attuned to what Harriott is trying to do, even if he is often asked to play the most conventional role.

Abstract is split over two sessions, with some change of focus over the set. *Free Form* has more of the drama of a single creative moment. By later standards, Harriott's experiments seem cautious. On every track, at least one of the familiar parameters – tonality, regular rhythm, timbre – is retained as Harriott weighs anchor and pushes off into deep waters. The reading of Sonny Rollins's 'Oleo' on *Abstract* is probably the clearest expression of what is special and different about these records, but the opening 'Subject' on the same album jumps straight into a sound-world which is both more alien and more traditional than anything Ornette ever dared.

Indo-Jazz Fusions is more properly a John Mayer record, but Harriott is its defining presence. Much discussed, it remains a slightly unsatisfactory experience, not so much a synthesis as an awkward juxtaposition. It is performed by a double quintet of jazz and subcontinental players, somewhat on the model of Ornette's *Free Jazz* group. But whereas there the logic of the thing was the individual personality of the soloists, here the problems are more deep-rooted. Rhythms and tonalities lie alongside one another but fail to gel. After 30 years the original excitement of hearing these unexpected sounds has faded somewhat, but partly because the scalar experiments Mayer was making, building jazz improvisations on raga forms and on unfamiliar nine- and ten-beat patterns, have since 1968 become part of an extended jazz syntax. Once again, British-based musicians seemed to be moving in parallel to their American colleagues and in some cases ahead of them; the highly sophisticated rhythmic patterns John Coltrane and Rashied Ali were using as foundation blocks on some of Trane's last recordings are deployed here with great ease. By the same token, Harriott and Mayer sound untroubled about abandoning conventional changes.

The reissue includes original liner-notes by Max Harrison and Ian Carr and a retrospective essay after 30 years by Professor John Mayer. Taken together with the music, they establish a context for a historically significant record. New listeners simply shouldn't expect too much from it.

Here and elsewhere, the key voice is Harriott's. Its kinship to other British players of the time and after – to Trevor Watts and Mike Osborne – is unmistakable, but Harriott also brought the swing and abandon of the islands, introducing a spicy leaven to British jazz which has never really gone away.

Barry Harris (born 1929)

PIANO

One of the leading Detroit pianists, Harris subsequently arrived in New York in the late 1950s and has remained there ever since. The preferred accompanist of both Coleman Hawkins and Sonny Stitt, Harris's bebop methodology owes much to both Powell and Monk, while mining his own gentler persuasions. In the '80s and '90s he became revered as one of the great teachers in the music, although this has largely kept him away from recording.

***** At The Jazz Workshop**
Original Jazz Classics OJC 208 *Harris; Sam Jones (b); Louis Hayes (d). 5/60.*

***** Preminado**
Original Jazz Classics OJC 486 *Harris; Joe Benjamin (b); Elvin Jones (d). 12/60–1/61.*

*****(*) Listen To Barry Harris**
Original Jazz Classics OJC 999 *Harris (p solo). 7/61.*

*****(*) Chasin' The Bird**
Original Jazz Classics OJC 872 *Harris; Bob Cranshaw (b); Clifford Jarvis (d). 5/62.*

*****(*) Luminescence!**
Original Jazz Classics OJC 924 *Harris; Slide Hampton (tb); Junior Cook (ts); Pepper Adams (bs); Bob Cranshaw (b); Lennie McBrowne (d). 4/67.*

The career of Barry Harris suggests a self-effacing man for, although he is among the most accomplished and authentic of second-generation bebop pianists, his name has never excited much more than quiet respect among followers of the music. Musicians and students – Harris is a noted teacher – hold him in higher esteem. One of the Detroit school of pianists which includes Tommy Flanagan and Hank Jones, Harris's style suggests Bud Powell as an original mentor, yet a slowed-down, considered version of Powell's tumultuous manner. Despite the tempos, Harris gets the same dark timbres from the keyboard.

His records are perhaps unjustly little known. There is no masterpiece among them, just a sequence of considered, satisfying sessions which suggest that Harris has been less interested in posterity via recordings and more in what he can give to jazz by example and study. Nevertheless, he cut several records for Prestige and Riverside in the 1960s, and most are now back in the catalogue. The live date from 1960 finds him with the ebullient rhythm section of Cannonball Adderley, and the music is swinging if not especially absorbing. Rather better is the date with Elvin Jones, which features some fiery interplay between piano and drums, although the highlight is probably an uncommonly thoughtful solo reading of 'I Should Care'. *Listen To Barry Harris* is that rarity, a bebop pianist by himself, and while one sometimes misses the buzz of the rhythm section this is a thoughtful and focused example of Harris's music, from standards such as 'I Didn't Know What Time It Was' to characteristic excursions like 'Teenie'. *Chasin' The Bird* is a smart exercise in bebop piano: unfussy, unpretentious, but carried off with a distilled intensity that keeps the attention. *Luminescence!* brings together a fine group. We were rather cool about this in our last edition, but further acquaintance has revealed a thoroughgoing commitment which transcends the regulation professionalism of these players. Adams, Cook and Hampton solo with a taut assertiveness that makes a 1967 bebop date seem entirely relevant, despite its time and place.

****** Magnificent!**
Original Jazz Classics OJC 1026 *Harris; Ron Carter (b); Leroy Williams (d).* 11/69.

Hard to argue with the title on this immaculate recital. Turning forty, Harris is musing on his uncluttered bebop roots in 'Bean And The Boys' and seeing how far he can push the envelope in the ingenious fresh voicings of 'Ah-Leu-Cha', in which Carter is a willing partner. 'Just Open Your Heart' is a Monkian original that Harris subjects to a playful twist. 'Dexterity' takes us back to first-generation bebop, but again Harris casts it in a darker, more evasive setting. A neglected classic of its day.

****** Live At Maybeck Recital Hall Vol. 12**
Concord CCD 4476 *Harris (p solo).* 3/90.

In the 1980s and '90s Harris has been active mainly as a teacher, but this solo date is an exemplary account of his stature in the book of bebop piano. He finds just the right pace and programme: a leisurely but not indolent stroll through bop and after, with Powell and Parker represented as composers and influences, and a lovely choice of tunes including 'Gone Again', 'Lucky Day' and 'Would You Like To Take A Walk'.

Beaver Harris (1936–91)

DRUMS, PERCUSSION

Played with several of the '60s free leaders, including Shepp and Ayler, before moving into a more conventional kind of post-bop, although his interest in the roots of his music remained constant.

*****(*) Beautiful Africa**
Soul Note 121002 *Harris; Grachan Moncur III (tb); Ken McIntyre (as, f, bsn); Rahn Burton (p); Cameron Brown (b).* 79.

Harris called his group the 360° Music Experience, a title that refers to his search for a multi-perspectival and non-hierarchical approach that goes beyond styles and, to a degree, distinctions between leaders and sidemen. To a degree only, because his music is always focused on the drums, as in African performance. The opening track on *Beautiful Africa* is a statement of that ideal, a stately theme in 3/4 time with solo space for all the players. However, only this and a brief percussion solo, dedicated to the team at Soul Note in Milan, are written by Harris. Moncur, Burton and bassist Cameron Brown contribute material. Brown had never recorded his own work before. At the heart of his 'Baby Suite' is a wonderful duet for Moncur and McIntyre, two depressingly under-exposed musicians who demonstrate their pedigree in every bar. McIntyre's multi-instrumentalism is clearly in keeping with the ethos of 360° Experience. He is the only one without a composition credit, but the sheer range of sound he produces on his three horns makes him central to all the performances and recalls his own *Looking Ahead*. Moncur's fat, brassy sound is the perfect complement, and Burton moves around in modalities that are subtly shifting and uncertain, utterly consistent with Harris's own conception. An idiosyncratic but strong testament from a player who has, in the end, left little behind him.

Bill Harris (1916–73)

TROMBONE

Born in Philadelphia, Harris had an anonymous time of it until joining Woody Herman in 1944, with whom he stayed on and off until 1959. He disappeared into Las Vegas bands in the '60s and eventually retired from music.

****** Bill Harris And Friends**
Original Jazz Classics OJC 083 *Harris; Ben Webster (ts); Jimmy Rowles (p); Red Mitchell (b); Stan Levey (d).* 9/57.

Harris was always among the most distinctive and sometimes among the greatest of jazz trombonists. His style was based firmly on swing-era principles, yet he seemed to look both forward and back – his slurred notes and shouting phrases recalled a primitive jazz period, yet his knowing juxtapositions and almost macabre sense of humour were entirely modern. But he made few appearances on record away from Woody Herman's orchestra and is now a largely forgotten figure. This splendid session should be known far more widely. Both Harris and Webster are in admirable form and make a surprisingly effective partnership: Ben is at his ripest on 'I Surrender, Dear' and 'Where Are You', and Harris stops the show in solo after solo, whether playing short, bemused phrases or barking out high notes. A fairly hilarious reading of 'Just One More Chance' caps everything. The remastering favours the horns, but the sound is warmly effective.

Craig Harris (born 1954)

TROMBONE

Harris has played with Sun Ra, Abdullah Ibrahim, Henry Threadgill and David Murray, and has led bands which have bridged post-bop with funk. None of his own discs have really broken through to an audience, though, and he seems somewhat in shadow at present.

*****(*) Black Bone**
Soul Note 121055 *Harris; George Adams (ts); Donald Smith (p); Fred Hopkins (b); Charli Persip (d).* 1/83.

Harris plays in a strong, highly vocalized style which draws directly on the innovations of former Mingus sideman, Jimmy Knepper, and on players like Grachan Moncur III and Roswell Rudd who, in reaction to the trombone's recent desuetude, have gone back to the New Orleans and Dixieland traditions in an attempt to restore and revise the instrument's 'natural' idiom.This early set finds him in genial post-bop company. Adams was the perfect partner in any modern/traditional synthesis, and the rhythm section (Smith occasionally excepted) is rock-solid on such pieces as 'Conjure Man' and 'Song For Psychedelic Souls', which could almost have been by Roland Kirk. Excellent.

*****(*) F-Stops**
Soul Note 121255 *Harris; John Stubblefield (ts); Hamiet Bluiett (bs); Bill White (g); Darrell Grant (p, ky); Calvin Jones (b); Tony Lewis (d).* 6/93.

A fascinating interconnected suite of themes and observations, realized by the best band Harris has had in a decade, if one leaves aside the more mainstream/crossover Tailgater's Tales (responsible for several JMT albums, currently lost). Using trombone and didgeridoo, he conjures up dark, roiling shapes that confirm his growing interest in John Coltrane's music. Bluiett is the ideal partner in this enterprise and Stubblefield, having done some similar things as a dep with the World Saxophone Quartet and on his own account, seems absolutely across the music. Nothing new from him in several years, though.

Eddie Harris (1934–96)

TENOR SAXOPHONE, KEYBOARDS, TRUMPET, VOCAL

A Chicagoan, Harris learned several instruments in his youth and finally settled on sax as the main one. Scored a million-selling hit with a version of 'Exodus' in 1960, then made many records and experimented with electronic sax, a reed trumpet and other stylistic quirks. A great crowd-pleaser, but often at odds with critical acceptance, Harris remained a master technician, and in his final years, touring as a solo, he proved his enduring toughness as an improviser.

***** Exodus To Jazz + Mighty Like A Rose**
Vee Jay VJ-019 *Harris; Willie Pickens (p); Joe Diorio (g); William Yancey (b); Harold Jones (d).* 1–4/61.

***** A Study In Jazz + Breakfast At Tiffany's**
Vee Jay VJ-020 *As above, except add John Avant (tb), Charles Stepney (vib), Roland Faulkner (g), Donald Garrett, Richard Evans (b), Marshall Thompson, Earl Thomas (d).* 61–62.

Harris got off to a tremendous start with his first album, *Exodus To Jazz*, with the title-theme selling a million in single form. It rather knocked his jazz credibility, but Harris was a complex talent anyway and his range of ideas was a peculiar mix of the ingenious and the bizarre. His tenor sound was high – so high that he once received votes in a 'Best Alto' poll – and his tonalities suggested a kinship with the avant-garde which he actually had nothing to do with, preferring soft hard-bop or boogaloo situations that drew on the blues and gospel strains of his native Chicago. The first four Vee Jay albums have been reissued in these two-in-one discs, and they're a pleasing, likeable lot, if hardly immortal documents. 'Down' (*A Study In Jazz*) shows how useful a blues player he was, but the amusing 'Olifant Gesang' from the same album shows his wild side: blowing through the neckpiece, blowing without the neckpiece, using a trombone mouthpiece on the body of the sax. The earlier set is slightly preferred, since the *Tiffany's* disc is one of those jazz-at-the-movies albums that were fashionable at the time and is nothing special at all.

***** Here Comes The Judge**
Columbia 492533-2 *Harris; others unlisted, but may include Kenny Burrell (g), Bob Cranshaw (b), Billy Brooks (d), unknown organist.* 64–65.

A mild-mannered set of standards and current pop themes ('Goldfinger', 'People') cut during Harris's brief stay with Columbia. The one track he gets to stretch out on is 'That's Tough' at the end, a good one. Shoddily packaged with no information about the date.

***** The Electrifying Eddie Harris / Plug Me In**
Rhino/Atlantic R2 71516 *Harris; Melvin Lastie, Jimmy Owens, Joe Newman, James Bossy (t); Garnett Brown, Tom McIntosh (tb); King Curtis, David Newman (ts); Haywood Henry (bs); Jodie Christian (p); Chuck Rainey, Ron Carter, Melvin Jackson (b); Richard Smith, Grady Tate (d); Ray Barretto, Joe Wohletz (perc).* 4/67–3/68.

*****(*) Artist's Choice: The Eddie Harris Anthology**
Rhino/Atlantic R2 71514 2CD *As above, except add Ray Codrington, Don Ellis, Benny Bailey (t), Willie Pickens, Cedar Walton, Muhal Richard Abrams, Milcho Leviev, Les McCann (p), Ronald Muldrow, Joe Diorio (g), Leroy Vinnegar, Rufus Reid, Bradley Bobo (b), Billy Higgins, Billy James, Billy Hart, Harold Jones, Donald Dean, Paul Humphrey (d), Felix Henry, Marshall Thompson (perc).* 1/61–2/76.

*****(*) Greater Than The Sum Of His Parts**
32 Jazz 32067 2CD *Similar to above two discs.* 65–68.

When he moved to Atlantic, Harris continued experimenting with electric saxes, trumpets played with sax mouthpieces and other gimmicks, with varying levels of success. The *Artist's Choice* compilation picks tracks from 16 albums, the best of them making a good case for Harris's eminence: he's no genius improviser, and many a solo seems to get too pooped to continue, but he had a knack for making simple licks and phrases fit on shuffling rhythms and have it all sound great. There's the extravagant range which became his trademark: the straightahead post-bop of 'Freedom Jazz Dance', pretty pop-jazz with 'The Shadow Of Your Smile', a growling big-band chart in '1974 Blues', the knockout funk of 'Is It In' and the ragbag electric sax treatment of 'Giant Steps'. Much of it sounds hopelessly dated in the age of digital keyboards, but that only adds to the charm of Harris's futurism. The individual albums from the period are a patchy lot, evidenced by the two-in-one reissue on the second disc: the tracks from *The Electrifying Eddie Harris* are often hot stuff, especially the choogling 'Sham Time', but those from *Plug Me In* are more like a downright mess, the sax hollering against the brass to little purpose.

32 Jazz have stepped into the fray by coupling up four of Harris's original Atlantics in their entirety, *The In Sound*, *Mean Greens*, *The Tender Storm* and *Silver Cycles*, on the double-disc *Greater Than The Sum Of His Parts*. This is arguably the best set of vintage Harris material, since the albums in question start with his more conventional side (*The In Sound* is basically a straight-ahead set of standards, which Harris makes a fine job of), before moving towards electric sax and ending up with the entertaining nuttiness of the *Silver Cycles* tracks, an eccentric mix of soul-jazz, big-band hooting and prototype urban funk.

****(*) I Need Some Money**
Atlantic 7567-80781-2 *Harris; Ronald Muldrow (g, guitorgan); Bradley Bobo (g); Rufus Reid (b); Calvin Barnes (d); Frederick Walker (perc).* 75.

One of the later Atlantics and an uninspiring selection for the label's fiftieth anniversary release. Eddie's gimmicks – which include singing through the electric sax and playing his reed trumpet – overwhelm the musical content here, and the thin production makes the keyboards and rhythm sections sound even weedier than they were. The final 'That's It' gets a nice groove going, but it's too late. Either *Excursions* or *Is It In* would have been a better choice.

***** Listen Here**

JLR 103.611 2CD *Harris; Dan Wall (p); Neil Starkey (b); Al Nicholson (d).* 2/82.

Going out as a single, Harris was caught live at EJ's with the house rhythm team for a couple of sets. This might not have been his finest period, but he sounds in great shape and there are almost two hours of gruffly swinging music here. A knockout 'Love For Sale' and swaggering 'Listen Here' highlight the first disc; 'Cherokee' is a solo *tour de force* on the second. His off-kilter tonalities and unique use of the high tenor register have seldom been heard to such purpose at this kind of length. The band are good enough, with Wall having some strong moments, but it has to be docked at least a notch for the very indifferent sound, which isn't much better than bootleg quality.

***** The Real Electrifying Eddie Harris**

Ubiquity URCD038 *Harris; Bill Henderson (p); Larry Gales (b); Carl Burnett (d).* 8/82.

**** People Get Funny ...**

Timeless SJP 228 *Harris; William S Henderson III (ky, perc); Larry Gales (b); Carl Burnett (d).*

****(*) Eddie Who?**

Timeless SJP 244 *Harris; Ralphe Armstrong (b, v); Sherman Ferguson (d, v).* 2/86.

Harris had a wry take on the ups and downs of his career, and on the title-track of *Eddie Who?* he gets some fun out of it. Both of the Timeless records suffer from the leader's modest attention-span: on the earlier disc, he switches from alto to tenor to electric sax to piano to clavinet and then sings a little, and on the 1986 session he works through some strong material with the same diffuse results. *The Real Electrifying Eddie Harris* is a boisterous work-out on some of his favourite themes, harmonized on multiple horns, and although the rhythm section is over-recorded and Burnett often pushes too hard, it's a spirited session for sure.

***** There Was A Time (Echo Of Harlem)**

Enja 6068 *Harris; Kenny Barron (p); Cecil McBee (b); Ben Riley (d).* 5/90.

This seemed almost like a departure from Harris's earlier work, a concentrated tenor-and-rhythm date, and the results are good enough to make you wonder why he spent time on the other music. There's a courageous solo reading of 'The Song Is You', but the rest is adeptly supported by the no-nonsense rhythm team and, although Harris's rubbery tone and pinched expressiveness won't be to all tastes, there's no denying his energy.

****(*) For You, For Me, For Evermore**

Steeplechase SCCD 31322 *Harris (ts, p).* 10/92.

The idea was to do a duo session with another pianist but, when the second musician never turned up, Harris volunteered to set down his own piano parts first. While he's scarcely a dunce at the keyboard, having played professional piano in the past, the impromptu nature of the date forbade much preparation; too many of the pieces sound hesitant and the 'dialogue' is clumsily realized. There are some beguiling passages, and Harris's tenor tone was taking on a querulous, affecting frailty, but this is no solo masterwork.

****(*) Listen Here!**

Enja 7079-2 *Harris; Ronald Muldrow (g); Ray Peterson (b); Norman Fearrington (d).* 11/92.

Harris's brand of funky jazz retained plenty of potency in it. On record, the music loses much of its grit and snap: what endures is the easy-going intimacy of the Harris groove. It helps that old buddy Ronald Muldrow is back on the team here, and they remake 'Funkaroma' from the great *Is It In* (still not reissued by Atlantic) to start the session off. But too much of the music is merely OK.

****(*) The Battle Of The Tenors**

Enja 9336-2 *Harris; Wendell Harrison (ts, cl); Alex Rigowski (g); Ralphe Armstrong (b); Tom Starr (d).* 9/94.

A good-humoured bout between two tenormen – though Harrison picks up the clarinet for the second half and Harris moves to the piano, where he rolls out another version of his crowd-pleaser, 'Eddie Who?'. Recorded at the Montreux-Detroit Festival of 1994, and it must have been fun if you were there, but the music survives only patchily on CD.

*****(*) Vexatious Progressions**

Flying Heart FH-343D *Harris; Thara Memory (t); Peter Boe, Janice Scroggins (p); Phil Baker (b); Ron Steen (d).* 4/94.

This tough and uncompromising record is the last great Eddie Harris album. Jan Celt asked Harris to make a no-frills straight-ahead record (in Wilsonville, Oregon!), with mainly local players and few familiar names (Boe is recognizable from his work with Robert Cray). Harris came up with ten originals, and the band play the hell out of them. Whatever it may lack in finesse (Memory won't be challenging anyone's recollections of their favourite trumpet playing), the music has a gutsiness which most of Harris's later records have had brushed away. It's a classic 'local' jazz record, of a sort which hardly ever comes to any prominence now, but which has a far more natural feel than most major-label dates.

***** Freedom Jazz Dance**

MusicMasters 65164 *Harris; Jacky Terrasson (p); George Mraz (b); Billy Hart (d).* 6/94.

**** The Last Concert**

ACT 9249 *Harris; Nils Landgren, Andy Haderer, Bob Bruynen, Klaus Osterloh, Rudiger Baldauf, John Marshall (t); Dave Horler, Henning Berg, Bernd Laukamp, Roy Deuvall (tb); Heiner Wiberny, Harald Rosenstein, Olivier Peters, Rolf Römer, Jens Neufang (reeds); Frank Chastenier, Gil Goldstein (p); John Goldsby (b); Bernard Purdie (d); Haywood J Gregory (v).* 3/96.

Harris's farewell dates, one studio, one live, make moving listening, not for his weaknesses but for his strengths. The MusicMasters date is one of his best latter-day sessions. Here is 'Freedom Jazz Dance' yet again, but also 'Stars Fell On Alabama', 'Little Sunflower' and the poignant goodbye of 'For All We Know'. *The Last Concert* is nothing like as good, but that's not Harris's fault: the WDR Big Band clump along in support, and for some reason there's a three-song coda featuring the self-regarding vocals of Haywood Gregory, a glaringly inappropriate touch. A shame, since the saxophonist himself sounds very game and his solos are definitively Eddie Harris, the odd, vocalized tone and strange flurries of notes still entirely his own.

Gene Harris (1933–99)

PIANO

Played in army bands in the early '50s, then formed a trio with Andy Simpkins and Bill Dowdy, The Three Sounds, which made many albums and was very successful. Lasted till 1974, then after a quiet spell Harris reappeared as a small-group and big-band-featured performer, making many records for Concord in a style that mixed simple bop, blues and gospel styles.

***** Gene Harris Trio Plus One**

Concord CCD 4303 *Harris; Stanley Turrentine (ts); Ray Brown (b); Mickey Roker (d).* 11–12/85.

***** Listen Here!**

Concord CCD 4385 *Harris; Ron Eschete (g); Ray Brown (b); Jeff Hamilton (d).* 3/89.

Gene Harris finally assumed an 'own-name' reputation in the '80s and '90s via his work for Concord, specifically with big bands, but latterly with small groups as well. These small-band dates are good in their way – simply resolved light blues on the second record, a handful of standards on the first with Turrentine sitting in – but polish and good manners tend to stand in for genuine excitement. Brown, Roker and Hamilton can certainly cover their tasks here without having to try very hard. But it's agreeable enough to service those moments when the last thing one wants on the sound-system is some monumental masterwork. Turrentine sounds like his then sensible, middle-aged self on *Trio Plus One*.

***** Tribute To Count Basie**

Concord CCD 4337 *Harris; Jon Faddis, Snooky Young, Conte Candoli, Frank Szabo, Bobby Bryant (t); Charles Loper, Bill, Thurman Green, Garnett Brown (tb); Bill Reichenbach (btb); Marshal Royal, Bill Green, Jackie Kelso (as); Bob Cooper, Plas Johnson (ts); Jack Nimitz (bs); Herb Ellis (g); James Leary III, Ray Brown (b); Jeff Hamilton (d).* 3–6/87.

***** Live At Town Hall, N.Y.C.**

Concord CCD 4397 *Harris; Joe Mosello, Harry 'Sweets' Edison, Michael Philip Mossman, Johnny Coles (t); Eddie Bert, Urbie Green, James Morrison (tb); Paul Faulise (btb); Jerry Dodgion, Frank Wess (as, f); James Moody (ts, cl, f); Ralph Moore (ts); Herb Ellis (g); Ray Brown (b); Jeff Hamilton (d); Ernestine Anderson, Ernie Andrews (v).* 9/89.

***** World Tour 1990**

Concord CCD 4443 *Harris; Johnny Morrison (t, flhn); Harry 'Sweets' Edison, Joe Mosello, Glenn Drewes (t); Urbie Green, George Bohannon, Robin Eubanks (tb); Paul Faulise (btb); Jeff Clayton, Jerry Dodgion (as, f); Plas Johnson (ts, f); Ralph Moore (ts); Gary Smulyan (bs); Kenny Burrell (g); Ray Brown (b); Harold Jones (d).* 10/90.

Like the latter-day records of such bandleaders as Basie and Herman, these discs tend to be enjoyable more for their gold-plated class and precision than for any special inventiveness. The first session, credited to Gene Harris and The All Star Big Band, is, in those circumstances, a very truthful kind of tribute to Basie's band, the eight charts offering a fair approximation of the familiar sound. The two discs by the later bands – now known as The Philip Morris Superband – are, we find, rather more entertaining. The *Town Hall* set boasts a vast digital presence, the brass particularly bright and all the soloists well catered for, but some may find its showbiz atmosphere less than ingratiating. Andrews and Anderson have some enjoyable vehicles and there are appropriately outgoing solos from Edison, Ellis, Dodgion and others. *World Tour 1990* reprises the situation, with a somewhat different cast but much the same atmosphere.

***** At Last**

Concord CCD 4434 *Harris; Scott Hamilton (ts); Herb Ellis (g); Ray Brown (b); Harold Jones (d).* 5/90.

***** Black & Blue**

Concord CCD 4482 *Harris; Ron Eschete (g); Luther Hughes (b); Harold Jones (d).* 6/91.

****(*) Like A Lover**

Concord CCD 4526 *As above.* 1/92.

***** At Maybeck Recital Hall**

Concord CCD 4536 *Harris (p solo).* 8/92.

***** A Little Piece Of Heaven**

Concord CCD 4578 *Harris; Ron Eschete (g); Luther Hughes (b); Paul Humphrey (d).* 7/93.

***** Funky Gene's**

Concord CCD 4609 *As above.* 5/94.

***** Brotherhood**

Concord CCD 4640 *As above.* 8/92.

Scott Hamilton's unwavering consistency is somewhat akin to Harris's own, but the tenorman has a slightly greater capacity to surprise and, while the material could have stood a couple of less familiar inclusions, the quintet plays with great gusto on *At Last*. Even 'You Are My Sunshine' is listenable. *Black & Blue* introduces a new Harris group: Eschete returns on guitar, but Hughes and Jones are first-timers, and they dig into the programme – dependent on traditional blues of the order of 'C C Rider' – with the same infectious enthusiasm as Harris. *Like A Lover* continues along the same path, but the ballads sound almost soppy in comparison with the upbeat tunes – Harris wasn't made to be tenderized. *A Little Piece Of Heaven* restores order by dropping the group into a live situation. This must be one of the most rollicking treatments of 'Take The "A" Train' on record, and there are somewhat bacchanalian treatments of 'Old Dog Blues' and 'Blues For Sainte Chapelle' (appropriately, since this is one of Concord's live-at-the-winery dates). Harris is always going to end up making the same record, but so far it still sounds pretty good.

His entry in the Maybeck Recital Hall series is typically straight-ahead and without frills. There are four more blues in the programme, but this time the ballads don't seem quite so ponderously tender, and he is assuredly enjoying himself throughout.

The next two Concords (*Brotherhood* apparently dates from 1992 but didn't get a release until '95) continue a solid if scarcely arresting run. *Funky Gene's* is comfortably in the usual pocket and, although 'Children Of Sanchez' is a mistaken choice, most of the tunes fit Harris like his favourite tuxedo. *Brotherhood* is pretty much the same. Eschete's solo on 'I Remember You' makes one sit up and wish that perhaps he had more space than he usually gets; Harris, on the other hand, has never sounded more swinging than he does on Frank Loesser's 'The Brotherhood Of Man'. If you have some Gene Harris albums already, you probably won't need this one, but it's still a very good place to start.

****(*) It's The Real Soul**

Concord CCD-4692 *Harris; Frank Wess (ts, f); Ron Eschete (g); Luther Hughes (b); Paul Humphrey (d). 3/95.*

****(*) In His Hands**

Concord CCD 4758 *As above, except add Jack McDuff (org), Gregg Field, Steve Hockel (perc), Nikki Harris, Ralph E Beechum, Cherie Buckner, Curtis Stigers (v); omit Wess. 12/96.*

***** Down Home Blues**

Concord CCD-4785 *As above, except omit Field, Hockel, Beechum, Buckner. 12/96.*

Concord seem ready to let Harris record whenever he wants. It was scarcely worth the effort on *It's The Real Soul*, which simply re-runs one of his concert sets. The band are as usual, but guest Wess coasts through a couple of blues and a couple of flute features to negligible effect. Docked a notch for pointlessness.

Gospel and blues take up the next two, recorded at the same sessions. *In His Hands* partakes of the spirit well enough, even if Stigers and Nikki Harris are more Hallelujah-Hollywood than anything, but the material is groaningly obvious. The most interesting presence is McDuff, and he shares the billing with Harris on the next one, which is nearly all blues. Nikki Harris and Stigers again have cameos, but the meat of it is in the interplay between piano and organ. A bit airbrushed in the Concord style, but enjoyable.

***** All-Stars Live**

Concord CCD 4808-2 *Harris; Harry 'Sweets' Edison (t); Stanley Turrentine (ts); Kenny Burrell (g); George Mraz (b); Lewis Nash (d); Ernie Andrews (v). 4/95.*

****(*) Alley Cats**

Concord CCD-4859-2 *Harris; Ernie Watts (ts, as); Red Holloway (ts); Jack McDuff (org); Frank Potenza (g); Luther Hughes (b); Paul Kreibich (d); Nikki Harris (v). 12/98.*

The concert recording is a sweet-natured reunion of old-timers. Everybody does their usual, but the one who puts in a little more elbow-grease is Turrentine, continuing his recent good run with a fine 'Time After Time'. *Alley Cats* is yet another live one, and the hero this time is the failsafe Watts, who burns up the changes on 'Bird's Idea' and completely outclasses the razzle of Holloway. Gene himself does his usual yet again; if Concord have anything unreleased in the can, we imagine that will be the same.

Stefon Harris (born 1973)

VIBRAPHONE

Young vibes player at the forefront of new New York music, and already much in demand as a star sideman.

*****(*) A Cloud Of Red Dust**

Blue Note 23487 2 *Harris; Steve Turre (tb); Greg Osby (as); Steve Wilson (ss, as); Kaoru Watanabe (f); Mulgrew Miller, Jason Moran (p); Dwayne Burno (b); Alvester Garnett (d); Kimati Dinizulu (perc, 1-string hp); June Gardner (v). 10/97.*

****** BlackActionFigure**

Blue Note 99546 2 *Harris; Steve Turre (tb); Greg Osby (as); Gary Thomas (ts, af); Jason Moran (p); Tarus Mateen (b); Eric Harland (d). 2/99.*

Our Penguin colleague Jonny King, writing in his book, *What Jazz Is*, very perceptively notes how often the vibraphone attracts the most talented and versatile musicians. This is perhaps because the instrument, whether played with two mallets or four, demands such a perfect balance of melodic, harmonic and rhythmic awareness. It has long been our view that players as diverse as Lionel Hampton, Milt Jackson and Bobby Hutcherson (to say nothing of Joe Locke, Khan Jamal and Walt Dickerson) would be regarded far more highly if they were playing almost any other instrument.

It's a great pleasure to encounter a young player just about to join those august ranks. Harris has worked with an array of leaders, including Buster Williams and Steve Turre, but he is already a highly developed musical personality. His debut album is interestingly structured. Rather than a sequence of discrete tracks, Harris has woven them together with short interludes to create an almost continuous suite. It grips the attention from the very start and flags only very briefly, with June Gardner's vocal feature on 'In The Garden Of Thought', which seems to come from a different session altogether. Some of the shorter pieces, like 'One String Blues', co-written with Kimati Dinizulu, are quirky and playful, but Harris's most characteristic sound is a flowing lyricism, grafted on to a swinging shuffle beat, a combination of metres that is always threatening to fall apart but never quite does. There is something of Hutcherson's tightrope daring in his solo on 'Of Things To Come' on the second album.

The sequel builds on the strengths of its predecessor. As before, the writing is strong and archetypal, vindicating Harris's idealist belief that all music is pre-ordained, that it can't be composed, merely transcribed. 'The Alchemist' and the stately 'Chorale' which follows are perfect illustrations of this: timeless-sounding compositions that seem to exist in the mind before they're heard. This has the odd effect of making the album's two standards, 'There Is No Greater Love' and 'You Stepped Out Of A Dream', sound as if they might be brand-new conceptions. The only other repertory piece is a version of Onaje Allan Gumbs's 'Collage'.

A Cloud Of Red Dust established Harris as one of the most exciting prospects for years. It was slightly marred by inconsistent production – Greg Osby took over from Billy Banks for the follow-up and delivered a much more graceful product – but it put a new name on the distinguished Blue Note roster.

Donald Harrison (born 1960)

ALTO SAXOPHONE, SOPRANO SAXOPHONE, BASS CLARINET

Born in New Orleans, he studied with Ellis Marsalis and joined Art Blakey in 1982. Co-led a quintet with Terence Blanchard and has subsequently freelanced.

*** For Art's Sake

Candid CCD 79501 *Harrison; Marlon Jordan (t); Cyrus Chestnut (p); Christian McBride (b); Carl Allen (d).* 11/90.

Perhaps the key story in the jazz of the 1990s has been the revival of New Orleans, the legendary cradle of the music, as a vital, thrusting, experimental location. Much of the credit goes to the Marsalis family and in particular to the patriarch, Ellis, who was one of Donald 'Duck' Harrison's teachers at NOCA. Like many of the younger generation, Harrison has tried to fuse traditional idiom with a thoroughly contemporary style, and this early album ('early' isn't quite right for a player already thirty) reflects the instincts that pushed the Messengers as far as Art Blakey ever allowed the group to go. Harrison had been active for a good few years before this record was released and had worked out a strong, uncompromising voice.

For Art's Sake is a classic instance of a leader upstaged by his sidemen. Harrison has assembled a powerful young band (McBride was only eighteen) who know the tradition inside out and are brimming with their own ideas. The opening 'So What' helps settle the players and establish credentials. Chestnut's semi-autobiographical 'Nut' is the pianist's feature, elegantly sculpted, formal and unaffected. Harrison gives most of the opening statements to the nineteen-year-old Jordan, who emerges as a rawer version of Wynton Marsalis. The trumpeter comes into his own on a superb reading of 'In A Sentimental Mood', which he gradually cranks up from a melancholy ballad into a funky swinger. Offered as 'proof' that 'hard bop is the basis of '90s jazz', the record does no more than confirm that there are still lots of youngsters around who are willing to take it on. Not the same thing at all.

*** Indian Blues

Candid CCD 79514 *Harrison; Cyrus Chestnut, Mac Rebennack (Dr John) (p, v); Phil Bowler (b, v); Carl Allen (d, v); Bruce Cox, Howard Smiley Ricks (perc, v); Donald Harrison (v).* 5/91.

Hard bop is still the basic language here, but Harrison has also tried to combine the sound of the Messengers with that of a more literal father-figure. Donald Harrison Sr has been leader of the Guardians of the Flame, who also feature on the album. 'Hiko Hiko' and 'Two-Way-Pocky-Way' are traditional (the former is credited to the legendary Black Johnny); 'Ja-Ki-Mo-Fi-Na-Hay' and the opening 'Hu-Tan-nay' are credited to the Harrisons. Dr John sings and plays piano on the two originals, sings on Professor Longhair's 'Big Chief' and plays piano on 'Walkin' Home' and Big Chief Jolly's 'Shave 'Em Dry'.

If it's part of Harrison's intention to reflect the continuity of the black music tradition, he does so very convincingly, and there's no sense of a break between the densely rhythmic N'w'Orleans numbers with their chattering percussion and the more orthodox jazz tracks. He plays 'Indian Red' pretty much as a straight alto feature, but then adds a rhythmic line to the prototypical standard 'Cherokee' that gives it an entirely new dimension. His own 'Indian Blues' and 'Uptown Ruler' reflect a decision in 1989 to 'mask Indian' again and join the feathered throngs that march on Mardi Gras. In touching his roots, he's brought them right up to date.

***(*) Nouveau Swing

Impulse! 051209-2 *Harrison; Anthony Wonsey (p); Christian McBride, Reuben Rodgers (b); Carl Allen, Dion Parson (d).* 8/96.

As close to a summation as this restless artist will ever achieve. The only thing wrong with *Nouveau Swing* is that it attempts to touch too many bases at once: jazz, soul, reggae, R&B – all of them, though, melded and blended into a continuous and evolving sound that for the first time sounds like Harrison's own voice.

Allen has for some time been a responsive and intelligent foil; the revelation here is Wonsey, emerging as a star in his own right but absolutely in sympathy with the leader. Much of the serious action takes place late in the set, and the combination of 'New Hope', 'Christopher Jr', the tiny 'South Side People' (one of three miniatures) and 'Dance Hall' concentrates as much musical information into 20 minutes as Harrison has achieved in a decade and a half of active performance. Excellent, stirring stuff.

**** Free To Be

Impulse! 051283-2 *Harrison; Brian Lynch (t); Teodross Avery (ts); Andrew Adair, Mulgrew Miller (p); Rodney Jones (g); Vicente Archer, Christian McBride, Reuben Rogers (b); Carl Allen, John Lamkin (d); Jose Claussell (perc).* 8/98.

Harrison follows up his Impulse! debut with a vocal reprise of 'Nouveau Swing' but, by the time it heaves into view, this superb album has already established its magic. The title-track and a softly rasping, Dolphy-tinged interpretation of 'Softly, As In A Morning Sunrise' establish a tone of plangent lyricism that dominates the whole album, seeing Harrison kick back and revisit some of his influences even as he consolidates a mature expressionism. Harrison deploys two basic groups: his own working band of Adair, Rogers and Lamkin and, on five tracks, a line-up of '80s Young Turks with and without guest stars. Avery adds a beefy presence to 'Indian Blues' and Lynch to the unexpected 'Again, Never', which negotiates some tricky inversions.

Antonio Hart (born 1969)

ALTO SAXOPHONE

Based in New York from 1991, notably as a Roy Hargrove sideman, Hart made a string of albums for Novus, but has since signed to Impulse! for his one listing here.

*****(*) Here I Stand**

Impulse! IMP12082 *Hart; Patrick Rickman (t); Robin Eubanks (tb); Mark Gross (as, f); Amadou Diallo (ts); Jay Brandford (bs); James Hurt, Shirley Scott (p, org); John Benitez, John Ormond (b); Nasheet Waits (d); Pernell Saturino (perc); Jessica Care Moore (v).* 96.

It takes its title from Paul Robeson's defiant autobiography, and it sees Hart for the first time throwing down the gauntlet: *this* is what I want to do, *this* is how I intend to do it, *like* it, *don't* like it. The basic group – Hurt, Benitez and the excellent Waits (son of the late Frederick and Hart's right-hand man) – is absolutely right for what he is doing, and the guest slots on 'True Friends', 'Brother Nasheet', 'Ven Devorame Otra Vez' and 'Riots – The Voice Of The Unheard', all arranged for horns and rhythm, and 'Flamingo', a steaming organ trio with Scott and Waits, are well judged and serve the music rather than making up for its structural insufficiencies, as has been the case in the past. Scott reappears on piano on 'Like My Own', and vocalist Jessica Care Moore is held in reserve for the closing 'The Words Don't Fit In My Mouth', which clinches a very strong disc. Hart seems to have found his voice, but it remains to be seen whether the label will back him: his previous sets for Novus are already in the cutout racks, and there's been no new report since our last edition.

John Hart (born 1961)

GUITAR

Hart is a contemporary guitarist who cut two apparently unsuccessful albums for Blue Note; he is now recording for Concord.

***** High Drama**

Concord CCD 4688 *Hart; Chris Potter (ss, ts); Marc Copland (p); Jay Anderson (b); Jeff Hirshfield (d).* 6/95.

*****(*) Bridges**

Concord CCD 4746 *Hart; Chris Potter (ss, ts, bcl); Bill Moring (b); Andy Watson (d).* 7/96.

Hart walks an interesting line between a very traditional mainstream and contemporary guitar language. He's much more in debt to Montgomery and Hall than to the rock-flavoured stylists, yet he can get in a lick or two from that bag when he wants, and at fast tempos he sounds quite individual. There were two 1980s albums on Blue Note that went nowhere, and these Concord dates seem more propitious. *High Drama* is good if a little rote, with a rhythm section of hired guns and Potter arriving for four tracks. The more successful record is *Bridges*, which features a quartet that have worked often, if at irregular intervals. 'Under The Influence' is a terrific start, cleverly swinging between structure and improvisation, and there's a startling chunk of acoustic funk in 'Urban Appalachia', where Potter switches to bass clarinet. Inevitably, he's a star partner, coming on like Lovano with Frisell or Scofield, and if Hart isn't quite on his level as an improviser he clearly draws inspiration from the saxophonist. Moring and Watson are virtual unknowns but perform with great skill.

Johnny Hartman (1923–83)

VOCALS

Hartman's rich, lustrous baritone was really suited to only one tempo, slow enough for every syllable to be enunciated with loving attention. Oddly, having worked with Earl Hines, Errol Garner and Dizzy Gillespie, he is nowadays best remembered for a somewhat unlikely Impulse! pairing with the giant of modernism, John Coltrane.

*****(*) All Of Me**

Bethlehem CDGR 137 *Hartman; Howard McGhee, Ernie Royal (t); Frank Rehak (tb); Anthony Ortega (as); Jerome Richardson (ts, f); Lucky Thompson (ts); Danny Bank (bs); Hank Jones (p); Milt Hinton (b); Osie Johnson (d).* 11/56.

Until recently, Hartman owed his small corner in the awareness of modern-jazz fans to his role in Bob Thiele's attempt to prettify John Coltrane by having him work with a singer. It was a relatively successful experiment on its own terms, but it did tend to obscure Hartman's own achievement. Possessed of a rich, full baritone, somewhere between Nat Cole and Al Hibbler, Hartman had the ability to caress even a banal lyric into shape, infusing it not so much with emotion as with a sort of intelligence. This is the quality most evident on *All Of Me*, reissued with four alternative takes which show how carefully, but also how instinctively, Hartman improvised on a melody. On this occasion, too, he had at his disposal a band of bop craftsmen who give him some challenging backgrounds to work against. The arrangements on 'I'll Follow You' and the much-reworked 'Blue Skies' (included as a bonus is take 13) allow him to go a good deal vocally, and he rises to the challenge every time. On the other hand, he gives take 1 of 'Birth Of The Blues' a resonant responsiveness which isn't quite there on the more polished issue take.

****(*) And I Thought About You**

Blue Note 57456 *Hartman; unknown personnel.* 60.

For some reason, Hartman recorded only once between the Bethlehem sessions and his contract with Impulse!. There are scant pickings on this unaugmented reissue which weighs in at just over the half-hour. The voice is as rich as ever and the arrangements by Rudy Traylor are highly professional but there is too little to bite on, and not even the delicious cadences of the title-track right at the end are enough to make this a compelling addition to the Hartman discography.

*****(*) I Just Stopped By To Say Hello**

Impulse! IMP 11762 *Hartman; Illinois Jacquet (ts); Hank Jones (p); Kenny Burrell, Jim Hall (g); Milt Hinton (b); Elvin Jones (d).* 10/63.

***** Unforgettable**

Impulse! IMP 11522 *Hartman; Bud Brisbois, Conte Candoli, Jules Chaikin, Freddie Hill, Ollie Mitchell, Melvin Moore, Al Porcino (t); Mike Barone, Billy Byers, John Ewing, Lester Robertson, Ernie Tack (tb); Gabe Baltazar, Anthony Ortega (as); Curtis Amy, Teddy Edwards, Bill Green, Plas Johnson, Harold Land (ts); Jack Nimitz (bs); Mike Melvoin (p); Dennis Budimir, Herb Ellis, John Gray, Howard Roberts (g); Jimmy Bond, Ray

Brown, Joe Mondragon (b); Stan Levey, Shelly Manne (d); James Lockert (perc); strings. 2 & 9/66.

Hartman was a graceful interpreter of ballads particularly, and the later Impulse! albums succeed in direct ratio to the success of the slower songs. The earliest is enhanced by the musicians, while on the second they fulfil a pretty workmanlike function. Listen to Jones's accompaniment on 'Stairway To The Stars' and the Sinatra-associated 'Wee Small Hours Of The Morning', both on *I Just Stopped By* … for a sense of how invaluable he could be to a singer. He'd shown a similar touch on the Bethlehem set, but it's here that he really comes into his own as an accompanist.

Unforgettable is a more recent reissue, consisting of 12 songs from the ABC Paramount release, *Unforgettable Songs By Johnny Hartman*, and a further five from a set called *I Love Everybody*, which was taped in a studio but with a substantial audience of invited guests who help give it its live ambience. It includes 'Girl Talk', one of Hartman's increasingly self-indulgent spoken monologues and certainly a little overcooked in this case. However, it's good to hear him work a room, even a room as acoustically unresponsive as the LA studio. Technically, the better stuff comes from the three-day February session. Presumably, as throughout his career there were a lot of abandoned or rejected takes, Hartman seems to have been something of a perfectionist, and once or twice even on issued material one hears him wandering slightly off the pitch. No evidence (unless it's been done very well indeed) of any internal splicing. Everything sounds like a complete and integral performance. All the songs are short and emphatic, with no room for instrumental embellishment or for vocal gymnastics. That isn't what Hartman was about. He liked to let the song do the work, and mostly that's what happens. A remarkable vocal talent, only now beginning to be recognized for his own achievement, rather than for that one-off association with one of the giants of modernism.

***** For Trane**

Blue Note 35346 *Hartman; Terumasa Hino (t); Masabuma Kikuchi, Mikio Masuda (p); Yoshio Ikeda, Yoshio Suzuki (b); Motohiko Hino, Hiroshi Murakami (d).* 11 & 12/72.

Recorded in Tokyo and very misleadingly titled, since most of the album consists of material with no Coltrane association at all but comes from a separate session. 'Violets For Your Furs', 'Nature Boy' and 'My Favorite Things' betray not the slightest hint that the singer is aware of Trane's versions, but the singing is good, and Hartman's voice still has a melting intensity on ballads. One for collectors, but don't be misled by the spurious Coltrane connection.

**** Today / I've Been There**

Collectables 5619 *Hartman; George Coleman (ts); Herman Foster (p); Roland Prince (g); Earl May (b); Billy Higgins (d); a.o.* 72, 75.

Despite the sterling line-up, these two LPs for Perception were pretty forgettable affairs, an attempt to put Johnny across a pop repertoire that in no way suited his voice. 'By The Time I Get To Phoenix' might be by any one of half a dozen lounge singers of the time, and even the indestructible 'The First Time Ever I Saw Your Face' shows signs of abuse. Best avoided unless you are absolutely addicted to Johnny's voice.

***** Thank You For Everything**

Audiophile 165 *Hartman; Loomis McGlohon (p); Terry Lassiter (b); James Lackey (d).* 78.

****(*) This One's For Tedi**

Audiophile 181 *Hartman; Tony Monte (p); Lorne Lofsky (g); Chris Conner (b); Buff Allen (d).* 8/80.

Thank You consists of live performances from Alec Wilder's regular radio programme, and they find an older-sounding Hartman in very good form indeed. The band is nothing special, but they have little to do except nudge the singer through the melody and changes of 'Lush Life' and a couple of other Ellington–Strayhorn numbers. The title-track is a version of Strayhorn's 'Lotus Blossom' set for voice and it is very effective, though it would have been interesting to hear Hartman shadowed by a horn; his vocal line is a touch one-dimensional for such a glorious tune.

Hartman's final recording came three years before his death. It's an attractive but low-key set and there is nothing on it which suggests it should be part of anyone's vocal collection. 'Send In The Clowns' always seems to go best when the singer is a bit world-bitten and off the money. As farewells go, this isn't too bad, but this certainly isn't the Hartman who was to become such a posthumous hero in the wake of his association with Trane.

Jim Hartog

BARITONE SAXOPHONE

Baritone saxophonist and founder-member of the 29th Street Saxophone Quartet.

***** Time And The City**

Planet X 010 *Hartog; Terrell Stafford (t); Pete McCann (g); Essiet Okun Essiet (b); Steve Johns (d).* 10/94.

This is Hartog's second disc as a leader in his own right. It takes its piquancy in the contrast between Stafford's elegant, almost dapper phrasing and the leader's less precise, more unpredictable solos. It never gets better than the opening 'The Sport', an original line that lingers in the memory; a perhaps deliberately messy 'I Hear A Rhapsody' doesn't really work. Hartog's other choice of standard, 'Autumn In New York', is done as an edgy baritone solo.

Mark Harvey Aardvark Jazz Orchestra

GROUP

Big-band vehicle for the writing and arranging of Bostonian Mark Harvey.

*****(*) Aardvark Steps Out**

Nine Winds NWCD 0155 *Mark Harvey (t, p); Mike Peipman, Frank London, Jeanne Snodgrass, Raj Mehta (t); Bob Pilkington, Jay Keyser, Jeff Marsanskis (tb); Marshall Sealy (frhn); Arni Cheatham, Peter Bloom, Tom Hall, Phil Scarff, Brad Jones, Vinny Golia (reeds); Rick Nelson (g); Diana Herold (vib); Ken Filiano, Joe Higgins, Brian McCree (b); Jerry Edwards (b, v); Harry*

Wellott (d); Craig Ellis (perc); Donna Hewitt-Didham (v). 4–8/91.

(***) **Paintings For Jazz Orchestra**
Leo Lab 014 *As above, except add K.C Dunbar (t), John Patton (frhn), Eric Hipp, Joe Springer (reeds), John Funkhauser (b, p); omit Peipman, London, Mehta, Golia, Herold, Higgins, McCree.* 4/93–4/94.

Intriguing big-band music from the Boston underground, masterminded by Harvey who's been running the group on and off for some 20 years. His writing on *Aardvark Steps Out* ransacks various disciplines and forms, with huge, prodigious pieces juxtaposed with single ideas: 'Mutant Trumpets' is a brief brass feature, 'A Zippy Manifesto' is a 24-minute sprawl that is actually an episode from a work called 'American Zen', which Harvey describes as 'much larger'! Blues and impressionistic pieces touch base with jazz scoring traditions, but the ideas are opened out by an adventurous team of soloists, and the gospel chords and celebratory union of 'Blue Sequence' bring about a rousing climax. It's a pity that the sometimes cloudy sound doesn't do the Orchestra full justice. That problem is exacerbated by *Paintings*, which comes in fidelity that isn't much above bootleg quality. This is a critical weakness, since Harvey and his team put so much into detail and texture – and it's pretty poor for a record made in the 1990s anyway. Harvey's admiration for the twin poles of Ellington and Ives remains well served by the Orchestra across two more sprawling works and, despite the numerous interesting solo contributions, it's the band that counts. But next time someone should record them in a decent studio.

*** **Psalms & Elegies**
Leo Lab 028 *Mark Harvey (t, p); Jeanne Snodgrass, K. C Dunbar, Greg Kelley, Frank London, Mike Peipman (t); Bob Pilkington, Jay Kyser (tb); Jeff Marsanskis (btb); Marshall Sealy, John Patton (frhn); Arni Cheatham (as, ts, ss, f); Phil Scarff, Mark Messier (ts, ss, cl); Vinny Golia (bs, ss, cl); Brad Jones (ts, bs); Peter Bloom (as, f, picc); Walter Thompson (as); Joel Springer (ts); Sheila Waxman (p); Diana Herold (vib); Richard Nelson (g); Tomas Ulrich (clo); Bill Lowe, Jim O'Dell (tba); Ken Filiano, Jim Whitney, Harold Anderson, Jerry Edwards (b); Harry Wellott (d); Craig Ellis, Hollis Headrick (perc); Donna Hewitt-Didham (v).* 8/90–4/96.

(*) **An Aardvark Christmas
Nine Winds NWCD 0201 *Basically as above, except add Daniel Smith, Stan Strickland, Tom Hall (reeds), John Funkhouser (b, v).* 12/92–7/97.

Both these discs are patched together from sessions in some cases several years apart. Four long pieces on *Psalms & Elegies* – four around the 15-minute mark, one at almost 30 minutes – touch on the Orchestra's grand range, even as Harvey frequently breaks it down into small, sometimes almost nebulous units. The hymn-like climax of 'Other Angels/Other Voices' emerges out of a scuffling, scurrying section of improvisation. 'Tiananmen Elegy' is suitably sombre. 'Psalms', recorded in 1990, is the oldest piece in the discography, and one of the most freewheeling: it starts as chamber-ensemble music, Hewitt-Didham's vocals against bass clarinet and a steadily growing ensemble, before developing into a sequence of settings for three of the Psalms. Perhaps this disc is best seen as a sampler of the Orchestra's work.

The Christmas collection is an unlikely pendant to the other records, a genuine attempt at translating Christmas melodies from English, Appalachian, West Indian, Catalan, French and other backgrounds into a feasible, jazz-inflected whole. It needs a degree of sympathy, with its dependence on a genuflection to the melodies, and it makes a curious adjunct to the other records, but if you partake of the spirit you may find it their most appealing record.

Michael Hashim (born 1956)

ALTO AND SOPRANO SAXOPHONES

Made his reputation when he joined – and later became leader of – the Widespread Depression/Jazz Orchestra, working out of Rhode Island. His New York experience in the '80s found him working with many senior figures, and he is a modern 'repertory' player of great skill.

**** **Lotus Blossom**
Stash ST-CD-533 *Hashim; Mike LeDonne (p); Dennis Irwin (b); Kenny Washington (d).* 90.

*** **A Blue Streak**
Stash ST-CD-546 *Hashim; Mike LeDonne (org); Peter Bernstein (g); Kenny Washington (d).* 91.

*** **Transatlantic Airs**
33 Records 023 *Hashim; David Newton (p); Dave Green (b); Clark Tracey (d); Tina May (v).* 11/94.

Hashim is that rarity, a passionate, humorous and quick-witted repertory player. His alto recalls Hodges, Carter and Willie Smith without placing himself entirely in anyone's debt, and his sound and phrasing have a mercurial, breezy assurance. From the opening measures of 'Grievin'' from *Lotus Blossom*, which is entirely dedicated to Billy Strayhorn themes, it's clear that the material is at Hashim's service rather than the other way round. He has often worked with the Widespread Depression/Jazz Orchestra and sounds entirely at home with pre-bop material: the excellently produced first record captures his rich timbre with eloquent clarity, and his quartet – especially the outstanding Washington – shadow him with exact aplomb. Since *Lotus Blossom* is so consistently delivered, honouring Strayhorn's familiar pieces and refurbishing such lesser-known ones as 'Juniflip' and 'Sunset And The Mockingbird', it's easily the superior record. *A Blue Streak* is slightly disappointing, with Hashim turning to more bop-directed music on some tracks; Le Donne's switch to organ, on which he doesn't have much to say, is another drawback, as is the somewhat bass-heavy sound. But tracks such as a fine soprano reading of 'Brother, Can You Spare A Dime?' are still substantial.

Transatlantic Airs catches him on one of his visits to England and in the context of a British rhythm section. Hashim sounds as good as ever, with a very fine meditation on 'Love Song' from Weill's *Threepenny Opera* as the standout. The local team aren't truly a match for the Americans, but it's a record that holds the attention.

*** **Guys And Dolls**
Stash ST-CD-558 *As A Blue Streak, except Peter Washington (b) replaces Bernstein.* 5/92.

The concept this time is Frank Loesser's musical. Hashim is on bumptious form on the up-tempo numbers, and he plays the ballad, 'I'll Know', with great tenderness: unfussily done, it's closely reminiscent of countless similar projects that filled jazz recording dates in the late 1950s and early '60s. The one to start with, though, remains the Strayhorn album.

**** Keep A Song In Your Soul

Hep 2068 *Hashim; Claudio Roditi (t); Richard Wyands (p); Dennis Irwin (b); Kenny Washington (d).* 5/96.

Doing a Fats Waller repertory record in a contemporary idiom is about as tough a conceptual undertaking as one can imagine. Hashim's astonishing achievement is all the more praiseworthy in that he even gets new life out of the normally intractable 'Jitterbug Waltz' and the roasted 'Honeysuckle Rose'. This is the best band he's ever fronted in a studio: Roditi is his usual cavalier self, and he's a splendid foil for the leader. 'Get Some Cash For Your Trash' is improbably thoughtful and elegant, 'E Flat Blues' never stops cooking, 'Two Sleepy People' is mildly gorgeous, but the pinnacle comes on an extraordinarily dark and baleful 'Black And Blue', which Hashim does on soprano. The further back he looks for material, the more modern he seems to sound: there are bits and pieces on the record that, say, Oliver Lake might have used. One of Hep's best-ever productions and catnip for Hashim's admirers.

***(*) Multicoloured Blue

Hep CD 2075 *Hashim; Joe Temperley (bs); Mike LeDonne (p); Peter Washington, John Webber (b); Kenny Washington (d).* 7–10/98.

Hashim continues to set a fine standard – the only quibble here being that he's done Strayhorn before, and with a similar personnel. But there are rarities of the order of 'Triple Play', 'Suite For The Duo' and 'Strange Feeling', alongside 'Chelsea Bridge', which may be getting a bit tired as everyone's piece of Strayhorn impressionism. Temperley trades phrases on the title-piece.

George Haslam

BARITONE SAXOPHONE, TAROGATO

Emerged in the '80s as a can-do organizer, group leader and own-label boss, recording many venturesome players. His own work on baritone has taken him round the world in search of fellow spirits.

*** 1989 – And All That

Slam CD 301 *Haslam; Paul Rutherford (tb).* 4/89.

*** Level Two

Slam CD 303 *Haslam; Paul Rutherford (tb); Howard Riley (p); Marcio Mattos (b); Tony Marsh (d); Liz Hodgson (v).* 6/92.

A relatively late starter on the saxophone, Haslam was quick to see the potential of free or spontaneous music. The solos and duos on the record with Rutherford are, with the exception of a surprisingly subtle solo baritone version of Ellington's 'Come Sunday', improvised without predetermined structure. The record launched Haslam's own label, an operation which broadly reflects the range of his musical interests.

He has continued to play in a more conventional jazz context, concentrating largely on West Coast material, and, like other British free players, has shown a strong awareness of folk forms. The name of his regular improvising group, Level Two, reflects an interest in performance that falls between the realization of scored compositions – level one – and complete abstraction – level three. If Riley introduces a strong compositional element, Rutherford is again on hand to prevent the music drifting into a settled groove or fixed direction. Mattos and Marsh impart a constantly unpredictable swing, while Haslam himself and (on two tracks only) singer Hodgson provide a vigorous melodic focus that cements the interplay of otherwise disparate elements.

Haslam's baritone has the husky uncertainty of pitch one expects of a folk instrument, and in some respects the tarogato (a Hungarian instrument of parallel antiquity to the saxophone) is the horn that provides his definitive voice. Its graininess is ideally suited to the open-ended songs and quasi-pastoral themes on *Level Two*.

***(*) Argentine Adventures

Slam CD 304 *Haslam; Enrique Norris (t); Sergio Paulucci (as, v); Daniel Harari (ts, ss); Ruben Ferrero (p); Quique Sinesi (g); Pablo Blasich, Mono Hurtado (b); Horacio López, Sergio Urtubei (d); Fernando Barragan, Tim Short, Horacio Straijer (perc); Mirta Insaurralde (v).* 3/91–8/93.

**** Duos East West

Slam CD 309 *Haslam; Ruben Ferrero, Vladimir Solyanik (p); Mono Hurtado (b).* 6–8/97.

Haslam's enterprise and creative initiative are remarkable. He was the first British jazz musician to play in Argentina (and, earlier, in Cuba) and he has kept up contacts and a working association with musicians there. When plans to take his regular quintet in 1991 fell through, Haslam went as a single. The first track is an unaccompanied tarogato solo. Thereafter, *Adventures* consists of collaborations with Argentinian players, tracing Haslam's exploration of forms like the elegiac *vidala* – sung by Insaurralde – and rhythms like the *malambo* and *carnavalito*. The session ends with a remarkable trio performance of John Coltrane's 'Affirmation', for saxophones and bass, with Paulucci also adding a vocal component. Highly recommended.

The association has continued and *Duos East West* finds him back in Buenos Aires, playing three numbers with pianist Ruben Ferrero and one trio with double bassist Mono Hurtado. Recorded on the night Diana, Princess of Wales died, against the stormy background of the Santa Rosa, heavy humidity, lightning and apocalyptic rain, they sound appropriately fiery and intense, in marked contrast to the folksier sound of Vladimir Solyanik. Recorded some weeks earlier on Haslam's second visit to the Ukraine, these improvised performances include a gloriously busked version of the English folksong, 'Barbara Allen'. 'Bi-Bop' is a slightly breathless work-out, apparently recorded at the very end of the session, but programmed first on the disc. Intriguing as these tracks are, it's the Latin American vector which seems to work best for George. His baritone is full-voiced on 'Rio De La Plata', a broad, weighty sound that seems to have no less buoyancy than Ferrero's. The pianist is a real discovery, capable of shifts from quite abstract sonic gestures, often inside the piano, to the most elemental swing. Solyanik's common-time playing has a touch of the metronome about it – notably on 'Waltzes With Wolves' – but Ferrero has the loose-limbed grace required of the tango dancer. Another intriguing record from Haslam and his now solidly established label.

Gabriele Hasler

VOCALS

German vocalist tickling the boundaries of freedom.

*** OrganIC VoICes

Leo Lab CD 003 *Hasler; John Wolf Brennan (org); Peter Scharli (t, flhn); Christian Muthspiel (tb).* 2/90, 9/92, 6/91, 9/92, 5/93.

*** Rosenstucke

Foolish Music FM 211 096 *Hasler; Thomas Heberer (t); Jorg Huke (tb); Wollie Kaiser (ts, ss, bcl, cbcl); Susanne Muller-Hornbach (clo); Martin Wind (b); Jorn Schipper (perc).* 6/96.

Her work veers towards the new music end of things, but she merits a place here for the sheer, intuitive fluency of her singing and its more than subliminal links to blues, spirituals and to the great jazz vocalists. The partnership with Brennan is a longstanding one, as can be seen. The capitalized 'IC' in the title refers to 'integrated circuit', a notion of voice and instrument, words and music working in the closest harmony, though not always a comfortable harmony. Brennan is an expert surrealist, using the organ's huge range to confirm and subvert its religious and liturgical associations. The two 'PaniConversations' are his work; elsewhere the lyrics are by Oskar Pastior, Avi Rosenthal, Shakespeare ('T.N.T. (Twelfth Night Tango)') and Hasler herself.

Brass and organ make for an irresistible combination and it's hard not to focus on the four tracks that included Scharli or Muthspiel, though Brennan's 'Dorian Elegy' is the most substantial single piece and the one that remains in the consciousness longest. Fine, indefinable music that transcends its materials.

The later set involves a more familiar-sounding ensemble and a set of songs celebrating the mystical and folkloric (and plain personal) associations of the rose. Hasler comes into her own here.

Ake 'Stan' Hasselgård (1922–48)

CLARINET

Despite his modest legacy of recordings, Hasselgård is widely recognized as a major player and one of the very few to make a convincing case for the clarinet as a bop instrument. After his apprentice years in his native Sweden, he went to New York in the 1940s and worked for a time with his original idol, Benny Goodman. The evidence is that he was able to outplay the master when it came to bebop. But his life ended in a road accident while driving to California.

*** At Click 1948

Dragon DRCD 183 *Hasselgård; Benny Goodman (cl); Wardell Gray (ts); Teddy Wilson (p); Billy Bauer (g); Arnold Fishkind (b); Mel Zelnick (d).* 5–6/48.

***(*) The Permanent Hasselgård

Phontastic NCD 8802 *As above, except add Tyree Glenn (tb), Red Norvo, Allan Johansson (vib), Thore Swanerud (p, vib), Hasse Eriksson, Lyman Gandee (p), Sten Carlberg (g), Rollo Garberg, Jud DeNaut (b), Uffe Baadh, Nick Fatool (d), Louis Tobin (v).* 10/45–11/48.

*** Cottontop 1946–1948

Dragon DRCD 332 *Similar to above discs, except add Mary Lou Williams, Per-Erik Sperrings, Barbara Carroll (p), Chuck Wayne (g), Simon Brehm, Clyde Lombardi (b), Bertil Frylmark (d), Jackie Searle (v).* 1/46–11/48.

Stan Hasselgård left only a handful of legitimate recordings at the time of his death, but the diligence of Lars Westin of Dragon Records in Sweden has ensured that his legacy has been enriched by many airshots and private records. There is something like five CDs' worth of material to be issued. Dragon originally issued four LPs, and the *At Click* CD begins a programme of CD transfers, while the Phontastic release covers the broad spectrum of the clarinettist's work.

His precocious talent and early death have made Hasselgård something of a folk hero in Swedish jazz circles, and the evidence of the surviving tracks is that he was an outstanding player. He worshipped Goodman and never tried to evade comparisons with his guru, but the traces of bebop in his playing hint at a stylistic truce which he never had the opportunity to develop further. The Goodman septet, which featured Hasselgård, is comprehensively covered on *At Click*, where the Swede worked with his idol in a two-week engagement. The contrast between the two players isn't as interesting as the similarity: often it's quite hard to tell them apart, and whatever Hasselgård is reputed to have taught Goodman about bop isn't clear from this music. In fact, Hasselgård often gets short shrift in these tracks, with Goodman getting the lion's share of the solos, and Gray and Wilson taking their share. But it's surprising to hear Goodman playing on the likes of 'Mary's Idea' and even 'Donna Lee'. The sound varies, but the meticulous remastering has done the best possible job.

Anyone wanting a one-disc primer on Hasselgård, though, is directed to the Phontastic compilation, which includes many of the tracks on the earlier Dragon releases as well as four fine quintet tracks led by the clarinettist (in excellent sound), a feature for Tyree Glenn and a sextet track with Red Norvo. A generously filled and respectful memorial to a fine player.

Cottontop, the latest retrieval work by Dragon (Lars Westin is clearly a concerned guardian of Hasselgård's spirit), is something of a hotch-potch. Some rare private recordings and acetates are in poor shape aurally, and on some tracks there's no more than a glimpse of Hasselgård. Yet the solos on two takes of 'Patsy's Idea', taken down only weeks before his death, and a few other passages, all point to his mastery.

Greg Hatza

ORGAN

Post-bop organ stylist with a classic approach to the Hammond B-3.

****(*) The Greg Hatza Organization**

Palmetto PM-2012 *Hatza; Major Boyd (ss); Jim Snidero (as); Paul Bollenback (g); Gary Jenkins (d).* 3–4/93.

***** In My Pocket**

Palmetto PM-2019 *Hatza; Ralph Lalama (ts); Paul Bollenback (g); Gary Jenkins (d).* 5/96.

The first album falls prey to routine: plenty of organ–guitar combo licks rearranged in an appropriate order, but nothing special, too many familiar tunes, and Snidero sounds a bit tight and pinchy. Things get considerably better with *In My Pocket*. Hatza has a boppish way with his solos, fleet lines individually fingered, and this time the tempos never feel rushed or wrong. The situation is meat and drink to a player like Lalama, who blows some cheerful solos over the top, while Bollenback always finds an interesting turn in his own playing. Hatza wrote all but one of the tunes, and they're a worthwhile lot.

Havana Flute Summit

GROUP

A one-off celebration of the flute, from Havana.

***** Havana Flute Summit**

Naxos Jazz 86005 *Jane Bunnett, Richard Egues, Celine Valle, Orlando Maraca Valle (f); Hilario Duran (p); Oscar Rodriguez (b); Adel Gonzalez, Juan Carlos Rojas, Robert Vizcaino (perc).* 4/96.

Naxos have cast their net far and wide for acts to sign. This is an engaging enough session, distinguished by the presence of Hilario Duran, one of the key figures on the Cuban scene, and Jane Bunnett, who has hitched her wagon ever more securely to the Havana scene. The original aim was to team her with Orlando Valle, who is a legendary figure in Cuban music. The addition of Richard Egues turned what might have been an interesting pairing into a genuine summit conference. Three of the compositions are by Valle, two by Duran, one by Egues, two by Bunnett (including another tribute to her mentor, Don Pullen, the beautiful 'Sunshower') and one by her partner, Larry Cramer, who doesn't play trumpet on this one but produces with his usual sensitive touch. The results are a mite too smooth and unruffled, and one might have preferred to hear a rawer and more spontaneous sound on things like 'Kamikaze Kat' and the closing 'Latin Jane', Valle's tribute to the *norteamericana* who has taken their music to her heart. It would have been interesting to hear a greater mix of horns and, though the styles are somewhat different, the flute-only approach is a bit hard to sustain.

Hampton Hawes (1928–77)

PIANO

Born in Los Angeles, where he stayed, Hawes was a major player in West Coast '50s jazz, his career foundering when he was imprisoned for narcotics offences but quickly revived on his release in 1963. Combined blues and bebop forms with rare energy and acumen and, though he toyed with fusion-lite towards the end, he remained a prodigious player.

****(*) Piano: East/West**

Original Jazz Classics OJCCD 1705 *Hawes; Larry Bunker (vib); Clarence Jones (b); Larance Marable (d).* 12/52.

Hampton Hawes is still something of a well-guarded secret, a name known to jazz piano fans but still to break through to a wider audience. Given the sheer exhilaration and lyrical intensity of his music, it is strange that he is not better known. All the more so, given the spectacularly self-destructive mythology he sketched out in his autobiography, *Raise Up Off Me*, one of the most moving memoirs ever written by a musician, and a classic of jazz writing.

An Angelean, Hawes worked with Charlie Parker on the West Coast and learned a huge amount from him. This set, shared with Freddie Redd, who represents the opposite seaboard, is a reasonable representation of the 24-year-old at work, still not quite settled into a personal idiom, still drawing more than he would later from a saxophone sound. He gets off a good solo on 'Hamp's Paws' and on 'I'll Remember April', but he never quite blends convincingly with vibraharpist Bunker, and Jones is too understated a player to give the group sound much presence.

****** The Trio**

Original Jazz Classics OJCCD 316 *Hawes; Red Mitchell (b); Chuck Thompson (d).* 6/55.

****** The Trio**

Original Jazz Classics OJCCD 318 *As above.* 12/55.

*****(*) Everybody Likes Hampton Hawes**

Original Jazz Classics OJCCD 421 *As above.* 1/56.

These were really Hawes's first serious statements as leader and they are still hugely impressive, combining long, demanding passages of locked-hands chording and fast, unpredictable melody lines. The bebop idiom is still firmly in place but already Hawes is demonstrating an ability to construct elaborate out-of-tempo solo statements which seem almost detached from the theme being approached but which are drawn entirely from its chord structure.

Mitchell is a wonderful accompanist, already experimenting with his trademark tuning and getting a huge sound out of the bass. Thompson is a resolute and often sophisticated player, who has been quite extensively recorded and always manages to catch the ear.

*****(*) All Night Session: Volume 1**

Original Jazz Classics OJCCD 638 *Hawes; Jim Hall (g); Red Mitchell (b); Bruz Freeman (d).* 1/56.

*****(*) All Night Session: Volume 2**

Original Jazz Classics OJCCD 639 *As above.* 11/56.

***** All Night Session: Volume 3**

Original Jazz Classics OJCCD 640 *As above.* 11/56.

Hawes's recording of the night of 12/13 November 1956 remains one of his very best. The material was mainly familiar bop fare – 'Groovin' High', 'I'll Remember April', 'Woody'N'You' – but cuts like 'Hampton's Pulpit' are a reminder of the pianist's church background and the curious underswell of gospel, Bach and Rachmaninov that keeps refreshing the topwaters of his harmony. Hall is magnificent, picking out clear, uncluttered lines against the leader's brisk chords.

The pace has certainly slackened and the quality fallen away by Volume Three, but this is a hugely enjoyable set which one day will doubtless be compiled and perhaps edited down in an affordable double-CD set. Roll on.

*****(*) Four!**

Original Jazz Classics OJCCD 165 *Hawes; Barney Kessel (g); Red Mitchell (b); Shelly Manne (d).* 1/58.

Kessel's rather conventional approach has always put us off *Four!* Renewed acquaintance suggests that it's a transitional record. Hawes was responsive enough to hear the first whispers of a new style coming in off the air and he tries to toughen up his delivery, sounding more like the great swing pianists (Teddy Wilson, especially) than boppers like Bud and Monk. If that seems ironic, it also makes sense, for Hampton was always trying to broker a style which combined the strengths of old and new, and this was one of the places where the synthesis worked *and* showed the joins.

****** For Real**

Original Jazz Classics OJCCD 713 *Hawes; Harold Land (ts); Scott LaFaro (b); Frank Butler (d).* 3/58.

A strong album from an exceptional band. LaFaro's short career had many spectacular moments, but few as sheerly joyous as this one. 'Wrap Your Troubles In Dreams' and 'Crazeology' use altered chords and passing notes to create a subtle harmonic environment in which piano and bass are equal front-line partners with the saxophone. Land is in cracking form and exuberantly feeds on cues in the leader's own solos. The closing 'I Love You' is one of Hawes's most completely satisfying recorded performances, every element balanced and communicative.

*****(*) The Green Leaves Of Summer**

Original Jazz Classics OJCCD 476 *Hawes; Monk Montgomery (b); Steve Ellington (d).* 2/64.

Hawes spent the early 1960s in jail, a tough woodshed for anyone; but, as he explains in the autobiography, one that gave him a new philosophy which couldn't help but come out in the playing. From here on, he seems devoted to a robust beauty and to an approach to ballad playing that would almost become a mannerism towards the end but which is still new at this stage: opening a tune with a long rubato introduction, unaccompanied, and as yet uninvolved with the melody. Later it could seem mannered, but at this stage it has all the resonance and the chastened passion of a man who has not had his liberty or his voice for some time.

Monk Montgomery is the elder brother of guitarist Wes, a solid, dependable player without much sparkle or brio but constant in his task and capable of surprise here and there.

***** Here And Now**

Original Jazz Classics OJCCD 178 *Hawes; Chuck Israels (b); Donald Bailey (d).* 5/65.

***** I'm All Smiles**

Original Jazz Classics OJCCD 796 *Hawes; Red Mitchell (b); Donald Bailey (d).* 4 & 5/66.

***** The Seance**

Original Jazz Classics OJCCD 455 *As above.* 5/66.

The later of these, recorded in perormance at Mitchell's Studio Club in Hampton's native LA, marked his last recordings with the other Mitchell. 'The Shadow Of Your Smile' is quite exceptional, an elegantly crafted and intelligent response to the theme from *The Sandpiper*, which has often tempted even otherwise tasteful players into schmaltz. *Here And Now*, with the underrated Israels, still betrays some shades of the prison-house, a slight stiffness and irresolution, but it's difficult to make an absolute distinction between these records, which are pretty much form-guide performances from Hawes.

His touch is as good as it was ever to be, with variations in that familiar locked-hands approach that allowed him to roll chords and arpeggiate some of the more significant of them. He is also audibly listening to his bass player much more, drawing and feeding ideas, back and forth. Exhilarating music, marred only here and there by slightly tired formulae, like anecdotes told once too often.

***** Piano Improvisation**

91 Vintage CRCJ 10009 *Hawes; Martial Solal (p); Gilbert Rovere, Jimmy Woode (b); Kenny Clarke, Daniel Humair (d).* 67, 68.

Live recordings from Rome, a setting which must have been close enough to California for Hawes, who plays with relaxed intensity throughout. Two versions of 'Autumn Leaves' with Woode and Clarke are magnificent, almost as good as anything he did in his career. The rest (apart from a version of his poppy favourite, 'Fly Me To The Moon') is less compelling, though a duo with Solal on 'Godchild' is to be treasured, two masters at work.

The recording, licensed in Japan, is very good for its time, with all the instruments coming through faithfully and without distortion, except for a few piano top notes, which are slightly metallic.

***** Blues For Bud**

Black Lion BLCD 760126 *Hawes; Jimmy Woode (b); Art Taylor (d).* 3/68.

***** Live At Memory Lane**

Fresh Sound FSRCD 406 *Hawes; Harry 'Sweets' Edison (t); Sonny Criss (as); Teddy Edwards (ts); Leroy Vinnegar (b); Bobby Thompson (d); Joe Turner (v).* 70.

****(*) Live In Montreux 71**

Fresh Sound FSRCD 133 *Hawes; Henry Franklin (b); Michael Carvin (d).* 6/71.

Live, Hawes was maddeningly inconsistent, but he usually managed to produce some diamonds out of the silt. The first and third of these are pretty much definitive of what the Hawes trio was about in the last decade of his life: funky, lyrical jazz, with a mixture of bop and pre-bop elements. The Montreux set has a verbose, grandstanding quality that might be explained by the glitzy setting; Hawes often sounded portentous away from what he regarded as his natural turf, as if compensating for his own insecurity.

The other Fresh Sound is interesting in teaming him with some of the other stalwarts of the Los Angeles scene. Good, too, to hear him with horns. Jazz has never been well served by television on either side of the Atlantic, but this record stands as a reminder of what could be done. Hawes and his group were captured at a beat-up club in LA as part of a series of short films made by Jack Lewerke. The combination of Criss and Hawes is irresistible and their blues interpretations are impeccable. The entry of Joe Turner dilutes the musical content a little, but the audience love it and the sound of cheering must have attracted Teddy Edwards, who sits in for a final extended blues jam on which Edison is rather disappointing. Good, clubby sound, though.

****(*) Plays Movie Musicals**

Fresh Sound FSR CD 65 *Hawes; Bobby West (b); Larry Bunker (d); strings.* 8/68.

The strings kill it, reducing Hawes's crisp lines to mush. There is plenty of attractive music on the record and the sound is above average for the vintage, but it's lost in the background. By this, given how short time was, anything and everything was precious, and Hawes was spending much of his time in a slew of electronic instruments which brought him much-needed work and cash but reduced him to a middle-order funkster.

***** High In The Sky**

Fresh Sound FSR 59 *Hawes; Leroy Vinnegar (b); Donald Bailey (d).* 70.

The final few years of Hawes's life saw a simultaneous resurgence and retreat from experiment. Heard out of context, this 1970 session is almost anonymous. As often as not, it is Vinnegar's distinctive walking style which catches the attention and only on 'Evening Trane' – an interesting exercise in altered changes – and 'High In The Sky' itself does the leader sound as if he is wholly engaged.

Fresh Sound releases are never the most glittering of recordings, and this one has a rather flat and unresonant ambience; not unattractive, but far from flattering.

***** Live At The Montmartre**

Black Lion BLCD 760202 *Hawes; Dexter Gordon (ts); Henry Franklin (b); Michael Carvin (d).* 9/71.

Other – and, we initially thought, better – music from the same date appeared formerly on an Arista LP, *A Little Copenhagen Night Music.* In retrospect, these performances are pretty decent for this vintage. Hampton's articulation is unusual here and there. Was he dodging a dead key? Or was there something amiss with his right hand? 'This Guy's In Love With You' is delivered with a gloriously insouciant swing, but the following 'South Hampton' [*sic*] is surely a version of Wayne Shorter's 'Footprints' and not as listed on some issues. There is also some doubt about the labelling of Dexter Gordon's solitary guest appearance, which sounds to us like 'Long Tall Dexter', though it is given as 'Dexter's Deck'.

We'd happily trade this for a record the same trio made less than a month earlier with British altoist Peter King under the title *Anglo-American Jazz,* but it's a good enough representation of Hampton on the road in his later years.

*****(*) As Long As There's Music**

Verve 513534-2 *Hawes; Charlie Haden (b).* 1/76.

This was released only after Hawes's death in 1977, and the CD has three alternative takes which bring it up to decent length as well as filling out the story of this unexpected collaboration, which dates from the same sessions as the *Closeness* and *The Golden Number* duets issued under Haden's name. The chemistry between the two is very evident and Hawes plays wonderfully on what sounds like a big, resonant studio piano; his original 'Irene' is outstanding, as is the quasi-bossa nova, 'Rain Forest', but the best thing in the session is a lope through Ornette Coleman's 'Turnaround'. Here the partnership could hardly be better balanced. An attractive record full of long-lasting treasures. One we've gone back to many times.

***** Something Special**

Contemporary CCD 14072 *Hawes; Denny Diaz (g); Leroy Vinnegar (b); Al Williams (d).* 6/76.

Hawes kept super-busy right to the end. There is certainly no deterioration and no sense of fated hurry about his work during the summer of 1976. This is a particularly relaxed session, recorded almost on the beach at a club in Half Moon Bay, California. He had been working in commercial settings for some time and it was only on occasions like this that he could afford to slip back into straight jazz, though 'Fly Me To The Moon' has a quasi-pop feel to it. Also on the date was Denny Diaz, who had been working with Steely Dan and Al Williams, an undersubscribed player who eventually gave up performance to manage Birdland West (now sadly defunct). Vinnegar, as ever, is poised and resourceful, and it is often he who provides the musical stimulus to the leader, prodding him on rhythmically (Williams is too accommodating) and throwing in fresh melodic ideas. Great time-keeper, too; set your watch by him. Not a classic, but a valuable document and meat and drink to Hawes fans.

***** At The Piano**

Original Jazz Classics OJCCD 877 *Hawes; Ray Brown (b); Shelly Manne (d).* 8/76.

Indian summer. Hawes seemed to find a measure of calm and contentment in the last year of his life, at least when there was a decent piano on offer. This is as good a place as any to take our leave of him. The second round of duos with Charlie Haden was still ahead, with its promise of more inventive improvisation, but this is in effect the last session as leader and as generous a send-off as he could have organized. As so often over the last few years, Hampton relied on a powerful bass player to reinforce the architecture of his changes playing. There are moments here, even on the relatively straight reading of 'Killing Me Softly With His Song', when the harmonic floor seems to drop out of the music. It's Brown who comes to the rescue every time.

'Blue In Green' and 'When I Grow Too Old To Dream' are sterling performances and the sound is balanced to perfection there and throughout. Farewell, gentleman ranker.

Coleman Hawkins (1901–69)

TENOR SAXOPHONE, VOCAL

Born in St Joseph, Missouri, Hawkins played in Chicago as a teenager and joined singer Mamie Smith's band in 1921. His reputation took off after joining Fletcher Henderson in 1924, and he stayed for ten years, before a European sojourn which lasted until 1939. That same year he recorded one of the biggest of all jazz hits, 'Body And Soul'. Ran small groups (with a nod towards bop) in the '40s and also played with Jazz At The Philharmonic. Worked as a solo artist in the '50s and '60s, often with compadres like Roy Eldridge, and maintained an elder-statesman aplomb, although he finally succumbed to a poor diet and a taste for brandy in 1969, having done everything he could in jazz. Hawkins modelled the saxophone for everyone who came after him, and he remained its most statesmanlike exponent.

**** Coleman Hawkins 1929–1934

Classics 587 *Hawkins; Henry Allen, Jack Purvis (t, v); Russell Smith, Bobby Stark (t); Muggsy Spanier (c); Glenn Miller, J.C Higginbotham, Claude Jones, Dicky Wells (tb); Russell Procope, Hilton Jefferson, Jimmy Dorsey (cl, as); Pee Wee Russell (cl); Adrian Rollini (bsx); Red McKenzie (comb, v); Frank Froeba, Jack Russin, Horace Henderson, Buck Washington (p); Bernard Addison, Jack Bland, Will Johnson (g); Pops Foster, Al Morgan, John Kirby (b); Gene Krupa, Charles Kegley, Josh Billings, Walter Johnson (d).* 11/29–3/34.

The first great role-model for all saxophonists began recording in 1922, but compilations of his earlier work usually start with his European sojourn in 1934. This valuable cross-section of the preceding five years shows Hawkins reaching an almost sudden maturity. He was taking solos with Fletcher Henderson in 1923 and was already recognizably Hawkins, but the big sound and freewheeling rhythmic command weren't really evident until later. By 1929 he was one of the star soloists in the Henderson band – which he remained faithful to for over ten years – and the blazing improvisation on the first track here, 'Hello Lola' by Red McKenzie's Mound City Blue Blowers, indicates the extent of his confidence. But he still sounds a little tied to the underlying beat, and it isn't until the octet session of September 1933 that Hawkins establishes the gliding but muscular manner of his 1930s music. The ensuing Horace Henderson date of October 1933 has a feast of great Hawkins, culminating in the astonishing extended solo on 'I've Got To Sing A Torch Song', with its baleful low honks and daring manipulation of the time. Three final duets with Buck Washington round out the disc, but an earlier session under the leadership of the trumpeter Jack Purvis must also be mentioned: in a curious line-up including Adrian Rollini and J.C. Higginbotham, Hawkins plays a dark, serious role. Fine transfers throughout.

*** The Hawk In Europe

ASV AJA 5054 *Hawkins; Arthur Briggs, Noel Chiboust, Pierre Allier, Jack Bulterman, George Van Helvoirt (t); Benny Carter (t, as); Guy Paquinet, Marcel Thielemans, George Chisholm (tb); André Ekyan, Charles Lisée, Alix Combelle, Wim Poppink, Sal Doof, Andre Van der Ouderaa, Jimmy Williams (saxes); Stanley Black, Stéphane Grappelli, Nico De Rooy, Freddy Johnson (p); Albert Harris, Django Reinhardt, Jack Pet, Fritz Reinders, Ray Webb (g); Tiny Winters, Len Harrison, Eugene D'Hellemmes, Toon Diepenbroek (b); Maurice Chaillou, Kees Kranenburg, Tommy Benford, Robert Montmarche (d).* 11/34–5/37.

***(*) Coleman Hawkins 1934–1937

Classics 602 *As above, except add Henk Hinrichs (t), Ernst Hoellerhagen (cl, as), Hugo Peritz, Omer De Cock (ts), Ernest Berner, Theo Uden Masman (p), Billy Toffel (g), James Gobalet (b), Benny Peritz (d), Annie De Reuver (v); omit Carter, Williams, Johnson and Webb.* 11/34–37.

Hawkins arrived in England in March 1934 and stayed in the old world for five years. Most of his records from the period have him as featured soloist with otherwise strictly directed orchestras, and while this might have been occasionally discomforting – the routines on such as 'What Harlem Is To Me' with the Dutch group The Ramblers aren't much better than a suave variation on Armstrong's contemporary struggles – Hawkins was polishing a sophisticated, rhapsodic style into something as powerful as his more aggressive, earlier manner. Two sessions with Benny Carter, including the four tumultuous titles made by the All Star Jam Band, are included on the ASV set, while the Classics sticks to the chronology; but the ASV sound is much more mixed. Classics begin with four titles made in London with Stanley Black at the piano, continue with dates in The Hague, Paris and Laren, and add the little-known Zurich session which finds Hawkins singing on the fairly awful 'Love Cries'! A spirited 'Tiger Rag' makes amends, and there's a curiosity in an unidentified acetate (in very poor sound) to close the disc. 'I Wish I Were Twins', 'What A Difference A Day Made' and 'Netcha's Dream' are three examples of the lush but shrewdly handled and often risky solos which Hawkins creates on an instrument which had still only recently come of age.

**** Coleman Hawkins 1937–1939

Classics 613 *Hawkins; Jack Bulterman, George Van Helvoirt (t); Benny Carter (t, as); Maurice Thielemans (tb); Wim Poppink (cl, as); Alix Combelle, Andre Van der Ouderaa (cl, ts); Sal Doof (as); Nico De Rooy, Stéphane Grappelli, Freddy Johnson (p); Fritz Reinders, Django Reinhardt (g); Jack Pet, Eugene D'Hellemmes (b); Kees Kranenburg, Tommy Benford, Maurice Van Cleef (d).* 4/37–6/38.

**** Coleman Hawkins In Europe

Timeless CBC 1-006 *As above discs.* 11/34–5/39.

The last of Hawk's European recordings. The All Star Jam Band titles turn up here again, as well as a further session with The Ramblers, but otherwise the main interest is in ten titles with just Freddy Johnson (and Maurice van Cleef on the final six). 'Lamentation', 'Devotion' and 'Star Dust' are masterclasses in horn technique, Hawkins exploring the registers and feeling through the harmonies with complete control. The sound is good, although the engineers aren't bothered about surface hiss. Vinyl followers should be aware of *Dutch Treat* (Xanadu 189, LP), which includes all the tracks with Johnson and van Cleef (including two alternative takes) and the 1936 Zurich session, in respectable transfers.

The Timeless CD cherrypicks some of the best Hawkins of the 1930s: the London quartet session of 1934, four tracks with The Berries, one with Reinhardt, five with The Ramblers, and a London pair with Jack Hylton from 1939. The very fine remastering is by John R.T. Davies: enough said.

*****(*) Coleman Hawkins 1939–1940**

Classics 634 *Hawkins; Tommy Lindsay, Joe Guy, Tommy Stevenson, Nelson Bryant (t); Benny Carter (t, as); Earl Hardy, J.C Higginbotham, William Cato, Sandy Williams, Claude Jones (tb); Danny Polo (cl); Eustis Moore, Jackie Fields, Ernie Powell (as); Kermit Scott (ts); Gene Rodgers, Joe Sullivan (p); Ulysses Livingston (g, v); Lawrence Lucie, Bernard Addison, Gene Fields (g); William Oscar Smith, Artie Shapiro, Johnny Williams, Billy Taylor (b); Arthur Herbert, George Wettling, Walter Johnson, Big Sid Catlett, J.C Heard (d); Thelma Carpenter, Jeanne Burns, Joe Turner, Gladys Madden (v).* 10/39–8/40.

****** Body And Soul**

Bluebird ND 85717 *As above, except omit Bryant, Cato, Williams, Powell, Scott, Fields, Taylor, Turner, Madden and Burns; add Fats Navarro, Jimmy Nottingham, Bernie Glow, Lou Oles, Ernie Royal, Charlie Shavers, Nick Travis (t), J.J Johnson, Urbie Green, Jack Satterfield, Fred Ohms, Tom Mitchell, Chauncey Walsh (tb), Jimmy Buffington (frhn), Budd Johnson, Hal McKusick, Sam Marowitz (as), Zoot Sims, Al Cohn (ts), Marion De Veta, Sol Schlinger (bs), Phil Bodner (ob), Julius Baker, Sid Jekowsky (f), Hank Jones (p), Marty Wilson (vib), Chuck Wayne, Barry Galbraith (g), Jack Lesberg, Milt Hinton (b), Max Roach, Osie Johnson (d).* 10/39–1/56.

***** Body And Soul**

Topaz TPZ 1022 *As various discs above, plus tracks with McKinney's Cotton Pickers, Spike Hughes, Fletcher Henderson and Mound City Blue Blowers.* 29–41.

Hawkins didn't exactly return to the USA in triumph, but his eminence was almost immediately re-established with the astounding 'Body And Soul', which still sounds like the most spontaneously perfect of all jazz records. Fitted into the session as an afterthought (they had already cut 12 previous takes of 'Fine Dinner' and eight of 'Meet Doctor Foo'), this one-take, two-chorus improvisation is so completely realized, every note meaningful, the tempo ideal, the rhapsodic swing irresistible, and the sense of rising drama sustained to the final coda, that it still has the capacity to amaze new listeners, just like Armstrong's 'West End Blues' or Parker's 'Bird Gets The Worm'. A later track on the Classics CD, the little-known 'Dedication', revisits the same setting; although masterful in its way, it points up how genuinely immediate the greatest jazz is: it can't finally compare to the original. If the same holds good for the many later versions of the tune which Hawkins set down – there is one from 1956 on *Body And Soul* – his enduring variations on the structure (and it's intriguing to note that he only refers to the original melody in the opening bars of the 1939 reading – which didn't stop it from becoming a huge hit) say something about his own powers of renewal.

The Classics CD is let down by dubbing from some very surfacey originals, even though it includes some strong material – two Varsity Seven sessions with Carter and Polo, the aforementioned 'Dedication' and a 1940 date for OKeh which features some excellent tenor on 'Rocky Comfort' and 'Passin' It Around' – and those who want a superior-sounding 'Body And Soul' should turn to the Bluebird CD, *Body And Soul*, which also includes the full, remarkable date with Fats Navarro and J.J. Johnson, who are superb on 'Half Step Down, Please' and 'Jumping For Jane', as well as the 1956 tracks, which suffer from schmaltz-driven arrangements but feature the Hawkins tone in the grand manner.

The Topaz disc offers a wide cross-section of Hawkins recordings through the 1930s but starting as far back as McKinney's Cotton Pickers in 1929. In the end it seems like a bit of a jumble, but the music sounds good enough.

****** The Complete Coleman Hawkins**

Mercury 830960-2 4CD *Hawkins; Roy Eldridge, Joe Thomas, Buck Clayton, Charlie Shavers (t); Jack Teagarden, Trummy Young (tb); Hank D'Amico (cl); Tab Smith (as); Don Byas (ts); Harry Carney (bs); Teddy Wilson, Earl Hines, Johnny Guarnieri, Herman Chittison (p); Teddy Walters (g); Israel Crosby, Billy Taylor, John Kirby, Al Lucas, Slam Stewart (b); Cozy Cole, Denzil Best, Big Sid Catlett, George Wettling (d).* 1–12/44.

*****(*) Rainbow Mist**

Delmark DD-459 *Hawkins; Dizzy Gillespie, Vic Coulson, Ed Vandever (t); Leo Parker, Leonard Lowry (as); Georgie Auld, Ben Webster, Don Byas, Ray Abrams (ts); Budd Johnson (ts, bs); Clyde Hart, Bill Rowland (p); Hy White (g); Oscar Pettiford, Israel Crosby (b); Max Roach, Specs Powell (d).* 2–5/44.

*****(*) Coleman Hawkins 1943–1944**

Classics 807 *As above, except add Cootie Williams, Roy Eldridge (t), Edmond Hall, Andy Fitzgerald (cl), Art Tatum, Ellis Larkins, Eddie Heywood (p), Al Casey, Jimmy Shirley (g), Shelly Manne, Max Roach (d).* 12/43–2/44.

***** Coleman Hawkins 1944**

Classics 842 *Similar to above discs.* 2–5/44.

1944 was a busy year for Hawkins in the studios. His Keynote recordings have been reissued in various editions over the years, but the Mercury set includes the whole series and has no fewer than 27 alternative takes. The eight sessions have a number of all-star line-ups; particularly outstanding are two quartet dates with Wilson, the Sax Ensemble session with Smith, Carney and Byas and a Cozy Cole group with Earl Hines. Hawkins plays on a consistently high level and there is treasure on all four discs. Delmark's *Rainbow Mist* includes three sessions for Apollo. The first includes what's thought of as the first bop recording, 'Woody'N'You', which also features Gillespie's first modern solo, and 'Rainbow Mist' itself is a little-known but superb variation on the 'Body And Soul' chords. A sextet with Auld and Webster is the makeweight. Sound is quite good, though these weren't the liveliest of recordings.

The Classics discs cover similar territory, but Classics 807 includes some other excellent material: an Esquire All Stars date with Tatum in imperious form, and three sessions for Signature, with Hawk outstanding on 'The Man I Love', 'Sweet Lorraine' and 'Lover Come Back To Me'.

*****(*) Coleman Hawkins 1944–1945**

Classics 863 *Hawkins; Charlie Shavers, Jonah Jones, Buck Clayton, Howard McGhee (t); Eddie Barefield (cl, as); Edmond Hall (cl); Hilton Jefferson (as); Walter Foots Thomas (ts); Clyde*

Hart, Thelonious Monk, Teddy Wilson, Sir Charles Thompson (p); Tiny Grimes (g); Billy Taylor, Edward Bass Robinson, Oscar Pettiford, Milt Hinton, Slam Stewart (b); Denzil Best, Cozy Cole (d). 7/44–1/45.

****** Coleman Hawkins 1945**

Classics 926 *Hawkins; Howard McGhee, Dick Vance (t); Vic Dickenson, Tyree Glenn (tb); Hilton Jefferson (as); Sir Charles Thompson, Billy Taylor, Art Tatum (p); Allan Reuss, Al Casey (g); Oscar Pettiford, John Simmons (b); Denzil Best, Big Sid Catlett (d); Matthew Meredith (v).* 1/44–10/45.

The merit of the Classics discs is the way they catch sessions that have been missed off other Hawkins collections. Classics 863 includes some of the final dates for Keynote, but adds four tracks where Hawkins guested with a Walter Thomas group, a septet date with Shavers and Hall (lovely rhapsodizing on 'All The Things You Are'), four quartet tracks with Monk (though the pianist is disappointingly unexceptional) and a final date where Howard McGhee begins the fruitful association that would blossom on the Capitol sessions.

These form the bulk of Classics 926 and make it essential. The dozen titles were made on a recording trip to Los Angeles, with McGhee an ebullient and *simpatico* partner: 'Rifftide' and 'Stuffy' show the older man relishing the challenge of McGhee's almost-bop pyrotechnics, although the sly intrusions of Vic Dickenson on four other titles are just as effective, and Pettiford and Best are a crackling rhythm section. Excellent sound on these sessions. Four titles with a Sid Catlett group are less valuable, but there are two intriguing bonuses: a two-part *a cappella* solo for the Selmer label, comprising some themeless variations (though 'Body And Soul' never seems far away), and a glimpse of Hawkins with Art Tatum on a V-Disc of 'My Ideal'.

*****(*) Body And Soul Revisited**

GRP 051627-2 *Hawkins; Benny Harris, Idrees Sulieman, Joe Wilder (t); Rex Stewart (c); Tyree Glenn, Matthew Gee, Jimmy Knepper (tb); Tony Scott (cl); Cecil Payne (bs); Duke Jordan, Hank Jones, Sanford Gold, Tommy Flanagan, Claude Hopkins (p); Bill Doggett, Danny Mendelsohn (ky); Al Casimenti, Billy Bauer, George Barnes (g); Wendell Marshall, Gene Casey, Conrad Henry, Arvell Shaw, Trigger Alpert (b); Art Taylor, Bunny Shawker, Jimmy Crawford, Cozy Cole, Shadow Wilson, Walter Bolden (d).* 10/51–10/58.

This sweeps up miscellaneous Decca sessions of the 1950s. Hawk is here with strings, with small groups, at a live date, with an odd group featuring Cozy Cole, Rex Stewart and Tyree Glenn, playing a two-minute unaccompanied solo and delivering a final (previously unreleased) blues with Tony Scott. Some tracks are little more than filler, but much excellent Hawkins too.

*****(*) The Genius Of Coleman Hawkins**

Verve 539065-2 *Hawkins; Oscar Peterson (p); Herb Ellis (g); Ray Brown (b); Alvin Stoller (d).* 57.

****** Coleman Hawkins Encounters Ben Webster**

Verve 521427-2 *As above, except add Ben Webster (ts).* 3/59.

***** Coleman Hawkins & Confreres**

Verve 835255-2 *As above, except add Roy Eldridge (t), Hank Jones (p), George Duvivier (b), Mickey Sheen (d).* 10/57–2/58.

***** At The Opera House**

Verve 521641-2 *Hawkins; Roy Eldridge (t); J.J Johnson (tb); Stan Getz, Lester Young (ts); John Lewis, Oscar Peterson (p); Percy Heath (b); Connie Kay (d).* 9–10/57.

*****(*) Coleman Hawkins: Verve Jazz Masters 34**

Verve 521586-2 *As above Verve discs, except add Cecil Payne (bs), Al Haig, Tommy Flanagan, Teddy Wilson (p), John Collins (g), Major Locke, John Kirby, Israel Crosby, Nelson Boyd (b), Big Sid Catlett, Buddy Rich, Eddie Locke, Shadow Wilson, Cozy Cole (d).* 44–62.

Hawkins and Webster are incomparable together. On some of *Encounters* they seem to be vying to see who could sound, first, more nasty and, second, more charming. But there's an undercurrent of mutual feeling that makes 'It Never Entered My Mind' as moving as anything in Hawkins's discography. Ben is alternately respectful and keen to make his own points, and the rhythm section play up to their names. The new Master Edition of this session sounds very handsome. *The Genius Of* is only marginally less appealing: too many ballads, perhaps, when a couple of stompers would have put some more beef in the session, but the playing is very fine and, with a raft of extra material – three previously unissued tracks and various mono versions – that makes this Master Edition in Verve's series particularly attractive. *And Confreres* takes a couple of tracks off those sessions and puts them with a studio date with Eldridge: not a classic encounter, and Hawkins's tone sounds like solid granite on 'Hanid', but some agreeable music. Their Opera House meeting was actually recorded at two shows, one in stereo and one in mono, and the horns are in jousting mood, with the imperturbable MJQ rhythm section as a bonus. A 15-minute jam on 'Stuffy', with Getz and Young, comes from another JATP show.

The *Jazz Masters* disc rounds up Hawkins from various Verve and Keynote dates, with an especially valuable addition in the 'Picasso' *a cappella* solo from 1947.

****** The Hawk Flies High**

Original Jazz Classics OJC 027 *Hawkins; Idrees Sulieman (t); J.J Johnson (tb); Hank Jones (p); Barry Galbraith (g); Oscar Pettiford (b); Jo Jones (d).* 3/57.

*****(*) Soul**

Original Jazz Classics OJC 096 *Hawkins; Ray Bryant (p); Kenny Burrell (g); Wendell Marshall (b); Osie Johnson (d).* 1/58.

***** Hawk Eyes**

Original Jazz Classics OJC 294 *Hawkins; Charlie Shavers (t); Ray Bryant (p); Tiny Grimes (g); George Duvivier (b); Osie Johnson (d).* 4/59.

*****(*) Coleman Hawkins With The Red Garland Trio**

Original Jazz Classics OJC 418 *Hawkins; Red Garland (p); Doug Watkins (b); Charles 'Specs' Wright (d).*

*****(*) At Ease With Coleman Hawkins**

Original Jazz Classics OJC 181 *Hawkins; Tommy Flanagan (p); Wendell Marshall (b); Osie Johnson (d).* 1/60.

***** Night Hawk**

Original Jazz Classics OJC 420 *Hawkins; Eddie 'Lockjaw' Davis (ts); Tommy Flanagan (p); Ron Carter (b); Gus Johnson (d).* 12/60.

***** The Hawk Relaxes**

Original Jazz Classics OJC 709 *Hawkins; Ronnell Bright (p); Kenny Burrell (g); Ron Carter (b); Andrew Cyrille (d).* 2/61.

***** Jam Session In Swingville**

Prestige 24051 *Hawkins; Joe Newman (t); Vic Dickenson, J.C Higginbotham (tb); Jimmy Hamilton, Pee Wee Russell (cl); Hilton Jefferson (as); Al Sears, Buddy Tate (ts); Claude Hopkins, Cliff Jackson (p); Danny Barker, Tiny Grimes (g); Joe Benjamin, Wendell Marshall (b); Bill English, J.C Heard (d).* 4–5/61.

****(*) In A Mellow Tone**

Original Jazz Classics OJC 6001 *Variously as above.* 58–61.

***** Blues Wail**

Prestige 11006 *Variously as above.* 57–61.

Hawkins's records for Riverside and Prestige revived a career that was in decline and reasserted his authority at a time when many of the older tenor voices – Lester Young, Don Byas – were dying out or in eclipse. Hawkins could still feel at home with his immediate contemporaries – the same year he made *The Hawk Flies High*, he cut tracks with Henry 'Red' Allen and a Fletcher Henderson reunion band – but the younger players represented by J.J. Johnson and Idrees Sulieman on *Flies High* were a greater challenge; the tenorman responds, not by updating his style, but by shaping it to fit the context. The rhythm sections on these records are crucial, particularly the drummers: Jo Jones, Osie Johnson and Gus Johnson were men after Hawk's own heart when it came to the beat, and their bass-drum accents underscore the saxophonist's own rhythmical language.

Hawkins keeps abreast of the times, but he doesn't really change to suit them. *The Hawk Flies High* was an astonishingly intense beginning, almost a comeback record and one in which Hawkins plays with ferocious spirit. The notes claim that he picked all his companions on the date, and Sulieman and Johnson were intriguing choices: it brings out the bluesman in each of them rather than the bopper, and both seldom played with this kind of bite. 'Laura' is a peerless ballad, but it's the blues on 'Juicy Fruit' and 'Blue Light' which really dig in. *Soul*, though sometimes rattling uneasily over prototypical soul-jazz grooves courtesy of Burrell and Bryant, isn't much less intense, and 'Soul Blues' and the bewilderingly harsh 'I Hadn't Anyone Till You' are classic set-pieces. Unfortunately, the similar *Blues Groove* with Tiny Grimes is currently deleted, but *Hawk Eyes* brings in Grimes and Charlie Shavers, though to sometimes hysterical effect: Hawkins's opening solo on 'C'mon In' seems to be carved out of solid rock, but Shavers's preposterous bawling soon takes the pith out of the music. Still an exciting session overall, though.

The trio sessions with Garland and Flanagan are hot and cool respectively, and they prove that Hawkins could fill all the front-line space a producer could give him. The force he puts into his phrasing in this period sometimes undoes the flawless grip he once had over vibrato and line, but these are living sessions of improvised jazz. *Night Hawk* is a good-natured five-round contest with Lockjaw Davis, who was virtually suckled on the sound of Hawkins's tenor, and there's plenty of fun if no great revelations and little of the intuitive empathy with Webster (see above). *The Hawk Relaxes* puts him back with Kenny Burrell on a more peaceable programme, and there are no problems here. As a sequence of tenor albums, there aren't many this strong, in whatever jazz school one can name. *Jam Session In Swingville* is more lightweight and finds Hawkins in a situation – a studio jam – which he had more or less given up. The two bands involved (Hawkins is the only man common to both) each have their share of mavericks and straight men and, if the results are inevitably patchy, Hawkins, Russell and Dickenson in particular all have moments worth savouring.

The best-of, *In A Mellow Tone*, gets only moderate marks for an imbalance of ballads: there are already two fine ballad records listed above. Another compilation, *Blues Wail*, concentrates on Hawk handling the blues and is very enjoyable if a little one-noted.

****(*) The Hawk Swings Vol. 1**

Fresh Sound FSR-CD 14 *Hawkins; Thad Jones (t); Eddie Costa (p, vib); Nat Pierce (p); George Duvivier (b); Osie Johnson (d).* 60.

****(*) The Hawk Swings Vol. 2**

Fresh Sound FSR-CD 15 *As above, except omit Pierce.* 60.

***** Coleman Hawkins & His All Stars**

Fresh Sound FSR-CD 88 *Hawkins; Emmett Berry (t); Eddie Bert (tb); Billy Taylor (p); Milt Hinton (b); Jo Jones (d). n.d.*

The two 1960 discs have been out on various labels in the past: Fresh Sound are docked a notch for spreading this 60-odd-minute session over two CDs, though. The band sound unfamiliar with the material but there is some fine playing, with Jones a compatible front-line partner for Hawkins and the mercurial Costa sounding good. The *All Stars* date comes in aircraft-hangar sound but, for all that, this is a swinging session, powered by Taylor, Hinton and Jones to terrific effect and with the undervalued Berry taking some strong solos. Hawkins is his consistent self.

***** Perdido**

Uptown UPCD 2745 *Hawkins; Ted Donnelly (tb); Norman Lester (p); Leon Spann (b); Jerry Potter (d).* 4/58.

***** Bean Stalkin'**

Pablo 2310-933 *Hawkins; Roy Eldridge (t); Benny Carter (as); Don Byas (ts); Lou Levy, Lalo Schifrin (p); Herb Ellis (g); Max Bennett, Art Davis (b); Gus Johnson, Jo Jones (d).* 10–11/60.

*****(*) Hawkins! Eldridge! Hodges! Alive! At The Village Gate**

Verve 513755-2 *Hawkins; Roy Eldridge (t); Johnny Hodges (as); Tommy Flanagan (p); Major Holley (b); Eddie Locke (d).* 8/62.

***** Masters Of Jazz Vol. 12: Coleman Hawkins**

Storyville SL4112 *Hawkins; Billy Taylor, Bud Powell, Kenny Drew (p); Oscar Pettiford, Niels-Henning Orsted Pedersen (b); Kenny Clarke, Albert 'Tootie' Heath, Jo Jones (d).* 11/54–2/68.

Live recordings from this period find Hawkins in variable but usually imposing form. His tone had hardened and much of his old fluency had been traded for a hard-bitten, irascible delivery which placed force over finesse. But he was still Hawkins, and still a great improviser, weatherbeaten but defiant. The meeting with Bud Powell found him in flag-waving form (the rest of the Storyville album is made up of odds and ends), and the two European sets on *Bean Stalkin'* are strong sessions. With Eldridge and Hodges at New York's Village Gate, Hawkins sounds in ripe good humour: four of the tracks are tenor-and-rhythm, and he bullies his way through 'Bean And The Boys'. 'Satin Doll' is a very slow warm-up, but 'Perdido' and 'The Rabbit In Jazz', a sprawling blues, get the best out of the horns; and one shouldn't forget Flanagan, unobtrusively in the pocket.

The most remarkable of all these sets is the Uptown disc, *Perdido*. The music itself is relatively unremarkable, Hawkins playing with an out-of-town group at a students' ball in Jamestown. But the documentation is absolutely fascinating. The producers have trascribed the (often barely audible) onstage talk between the musicians and run it in the booklet, almost as a stage play; as an insight into the working musician's lot it must get a priority mark (Hawkins was clearly unhappy about the six-hour drive to the gig, the band and the circumstances, but his kingly demeanour ensured that he still gave a great performance and refused to undersell his own work). Donnelly died only weeks after the gig and the rest of the band are obscure but, for its presentation, it is nevertheless a remarkable disc.

**** Hawk Talk**

Fresh Sound FSR-CD 130 *Hawkins; Hank Jones, Dick Hyman (p); Milt Hinton, George Duvivier (b); Jimmie Crawford, Osie Johnson (d); Frank Hunter Orchestra.* 3/63.

****** Today And Now**

Impulse! 051184-2 *Hawkins; Tommy Flanagan (p); Major Holley (b); Eddie Locke (d).* 9/62.

***** Desafinado**

Impulse! 051227-2 *Hawkins; Tommy Flanagan (p); Barry Galbraith, Howard Collins (g); Major Holley (b); Eddie Locke (d); Willie Rodriguez (perc).* 10/62.

The great record in this batch is *Today And Now*. Despite the unpromising material, Hawkins is at his most engaging throughout. He seems to love 'Put On Your Old Grey Bonnet' and sounds as if he could play all night on it. 'Love Song From Apache' is distinguished by the loveliest of introductions by Tommy Flanagan, and Hawkins only has to breathe through the melody to make it work. There is little of the quaver in his tone that makes some of his later records bothersome, and nobody's coasting.

There was probably a great Hawkins-with-strings album to be made, but *Hawk Talk* wasn't really it. The pieces are trimmed too short to give the tenorman much space to rhapsodize, and too many of them sound foreshortened. Nor are Hunter's strings particularly well handled. *Desafinado* is disappointing in its way. Hawkins gets a sympathetic setting and a sense of time passing at just the pace he wants; still, like most such records of the period, it's finally little more than an easy-listening set with the saxophonist adding a few characteristic doodles of his own.

***** Supreme**

Enja 9009-2 *Hawkins; Barry Harris (p); Gene Taylor (b); Roy Brooks (d).* 9/66.

****(*) Sirius**

Original Jazz Classics OJC 861 *Hawkins; Barry Harris (p); Bob Cranshaw (b); Eddie Locke (d).* 12/66.

There's no need to be sentimental about Hawkins's later recordings: it's not as if his life was a tragic spiral, the way Young's or Holiday's was, and if his playing was audibly impaired in his final years he was doing his best not to reveal it. *Supreme*, a live session released for the first time, finds him in Baltimore, still playing chorus after chorus on 'Lover Come Back To Me' to open with. If this 'Body And Soul' has only a halting majesty about it, the phrasing broken into pieces, majesty there still is. Harris comps with the utmost sensitivity and, by the time of the playful treatment of 'Ow!' at the close, it sounds as though the players have enjoyed it. *Sirius* is more hesitant still, and perhaps this isn't the way to wind up a Hawkins discography; but that is what it currently does.

Erskine Hawkins (1914–93)

TRUMPET

Alabama-born, Hawkins made his start as an Armstrong disciple, and he began fronting his own group from the mid-'30s onwards. They were good enough and successful enough to outlast the decline of the swing era, and Hawkins switched to a small-group format only in the middle of the 1950s. He worked the 'society' end of big-band music until the 1970s and made occasional guest appearances as a soloist at festivals.

***** Erskine Hawkins 1936–1938**

Classics 653 *Collective personnel for first five discs: Hawkins; Sammy Lowe, Wilbur Bascomb, Marcellus Green, James Harris, Charles Jones, Willie Moore, Robert Johnson (t); Edward Sims, Robert Range, Richard Harris, Norman Greene, David James, Donald Cole (tb); William Johnson, Jimmy Mitchelle, Bobby Smith (cl, as); Julian Dash, Paul Bascomb, Aaron Maxwell (ts); Haywood Henry (cl, bs); Avery Parrish, Ace Harris (p); William McLemore, Leroy Kirkland (g); Leemie Stanfield (b); James Morrison, Edward McConney, Kelly Martin (d).* 7/36–9/38.

***** Erskine Hawkins 1938–1939**

Classics 667 *Similar to above.* 9/38–10/39.

***** Erskine Hawkins 1939–1940**

Classics 678 *Similar to above.* 10/39–11/40.

***** Erskine Hawkins 1940–1941**

Classics 701 *Similar to above.* 11/40–12/41.

***** Erskine Hawkins 1941–1945**

Classics 868 *Similar to above.* 12/41–11/45.

***** Erskine Hawkins 1946–1947**

Classics 1008 *Similar to above, except add Bill Flood, Reunald Jones (t), Matthew Gee, Bob Range, Ray Hogan (tb), Frank Derrick (as), Aaron Maxwell (bs, ts), Ace Harris, Don Michael (p), Joe Murphy (d), Ruth Christian, Laura Washington (v).* 4/46–12/47.

They called him the 'Twentieth-century Gabriel' and, although Erskine Hawkins was at heart only a Louis Armstrong disciple, his big band's records stand up remarkably well, considering their comparative neglect since the orchestra's heyday. They were certainly very popular with black audiences in the 1930s and '40s, staying in residence at Harlem's Savoy Ballroom for close to ten years and delivering a smooth and gently swinging music that was ideal for dancing. Hawkins's rhapsodic high-note style has been criticized for excess, but his was a strain of black romanticism which, interestingly, predates the work of later Romeos such as Billy Eckstine, even if he did sing with his trumpet. Besides, the band had a number of good soloists, including Julian Dash, Paul

Bascomb and Avery Parrish, who, with Sam Lowe, arranged most of the material.

The Bluebird compilation listed in previous editions has now gone, so swing specialists may want to invest in the chronological series on Classics. If the character of the music is comparatively bland, it was absolutely reliable, and playing through even this many tracks is a painless experience. The first CD documents Hawkins's sometimes uncertain but still swinging early sessions for Vocalion (as 'Erskine Hawkins And His 'Bama State Collegians') and goes up to his first session for Bluebird in 1938. Given the limited number of tracks on the Bluebird set, and the real consistency of Hawkins's individual records, there are many fine tracks to discover, including 'Hot Platter' (Classics 667), 'Baltimore Bounce' and 'Uptown Shuffle' (Classics 678) and 'No Use Squawkin'' (Classics 701); but it's the high professionalism of the section playing and the crisp, no-waste arrangements that make one wonder why Hawkins has been neglected in favour of Jimmie Lunceford or even Basie. Admittedly, his vocalists were never up to much. Classics 868 takes the sequence up to November 1945 and, although that includes the 30-month gap of the recording ban, Hawkins's style scarcely bothers to change. The outstanding tracks here are, as usual, the instrumentals: Sammy Lowe's excellent chart for 'Bear Mash Blues', one of the great Hawkins records, 'Tippin' In' and 'Drifting Along'. The certitude which is supposed to be a virtue of Basie's records is certainly here in abundance. Classics 1008 shows that, even though its era was slipping away, the Hawkins band was far from finished. 'Sneakin' Out' and 'Feelin' Low' are Ellingtonian in their execution, Bobby Smith's alto adopting the Hodges style to his own ends, and though there are plenty of the inevitable vocal features, a couple of pleasing charts such as 'Coast To Coast' and 'Sammy's Nightmare' sneak by. Throughout this sequence, the transfers are the usual mixture from Classics: mostly solid enough, some from less than perfect sources. Overall, we must confess to a considerable fondness for this seldom-remembered band even if, record for record, there are few truly memorable tracks.

Edgar Hayes (1904–79)

PIANO

Hayes studied music at college and led his own bands in the south during the 1920s, eventually joining the Mills Blue Rhythm band in 1932. He led his own orchestra again, 1937–41. His final years were spent in California, where he continued to play in clubs into the 1970s.

***** Edgar Hayes 1937–1938**
Classics 730 *Hayes; Bernie Flood (t, v); Henry Goodwin, Shelton Hemphill, Leonard Davis (t); Robert Horton, Clyde Bernhardt, John Haughton, David 'Jelly' James, Joe Britton (tb); Rudy Powell (cl, as); Roger Boyd, Stanley Palmer, Alfred Skerritt (as); Joe Garland (ts, bs); Crawford Wethington, William Mitchner (ts); Andy Jackson, Eddie Gibbs (g); Elmer James, Frank Darling (b); Kenny Clarke (d, vib); Orlando Roberson, Earlene Howell, Bill Darnell, Ruth Ellington (v).* 3/37–1/38.

***** Edgar Hayes 1938–1948**
Classics 1053 *Hayes; Bernard Flood, Henry Goodwin, Leonard Davis (t); Robert Horton, David James, Clyde Bernhardt (tb); Rudy Powell (cl, as); Roger Boyd (as); William 'Happy' Mitchner (ts); Joe Garland (bs, ts); Eddie Gibbs, Teddy Bunn (g); Frank 'Coco' Darling, Willie Price (b); Kenny Clarke (d, vib); Bryant Allen (d); James Clay Anderson (v).* 2/38–48.

Hayes led a very good orchestra, following his stint with the Mills Blue Rhythm Band. They had a big hit with 'Star Dust' – ironically, not one of their best records – which is on Classics 1053. There were good soloists: trombonist Robert Horton was exemplary on both muted and open horn, Joe Garland could play tenor, baritone and bass sax with equal facility, and Henry Goodwin's trumpet shines here and there. Garland was also a very capable arranger, and the rhythm section could boast the young Kenny Clarke, already restlessly trying to swing his way out of conventional big-band drumming: all of the band's records benefit from his presence. There are too many indifferent vocals, and some of the material is glum, but many of the 24 tracks on the first volume stand up to a close listen. The second disc picks up the story with their final Decca session from February 1938, but that was more or less the end of the Hayes story as far as big-band records were concerned. There are four titles made in Stockholm a month later under Kenny Clarke's nominal leadership, a sextet date where Clarke plays only vibes and Goodwin and Powell sound fine – but Anderson's unfortunate vocals take up too much time. The rest are tracks by Hayes and rhythm section alone, for V-Disc, Exclusive and Modern, obscure pieces that depend heavily on the blues and are features for Teddy Bunn as much as Hayes, though that's no bad thing. An intriguing rediscovery.

Louis Hayes (born 1937)

DRUMS

Born in Detroit, Hayes spent long periods as drummer with several of the key hard-bop leaders: Yusef Lateef, Horace Silver and especially Cannonball Adderley, with whom he stayed for six years. In the 1980s he also emerged as a leader of considerable if relatively unassuming stature, and his seniority in the style makes him one of the grandmasters of this kind of drumming.

***** Light And Lively**
Steeplechase SCCD 31245 *Hayes; Charles Tolliver (t); Bobby Watson (as); Kenny Barron (p); Clint Houston (b).* 4/89.

*****(*) Una Max**
Steeplechase SCCD 31263 *Hayes; Charles Tolliver (t); Gerald Hayes (as); John Stubblefield (ts); Kenny Barron (p); Clint Houston (b).* 12/89.

***** The Crawl**
Candid CCD 79045 *Hayes; Charles Tolliver (t); Gary Bartz (as); John Stubblefield (ss, ts); Mickey Tucker (p); Clint Houston (b).* 10/89.

*****(*) Nightfall**
Steeplechase SCCD 31285 *Hayes; Eddie Allen (t); Gerald Hayes (as); Larry Willis (p); Clint Houston (b).* 1/91.

*****(*) Blue Lou**
Steeplechase SCCD 31340 *Hayes; Eddie Allen (t); Gerald Hayes (as); Javon Jackson (ts); Ronnie Mathews (p); Clint Houston (b).* 4/93.

***** The Super Quartet**
Timeless SJP 424 *Hayes; Javon Jackson (ts); Kirk Lightsey (p); Essiet Okun Essiet (b).* 2/94.

Louis Hayes remains one of the master drummers in the hard-bop idiom, a key figure in the Detroit-based community and a player whose undemonstrative virtue of playing for the band has perhaps told against his wider reputation. The fine sequence for Steeplechase finds him making a serious mark as leader for the first time. Besides Hayes's own playing – and he is probably the star performer overall – the first point of interest is the return of Tolliver to active duty after a number of years away. He sounds in need of some further woodshedding on *Light And Lively*, but the two later records are better showcases for him. Watson sounds a shade too slick for the company on the first record, but *Una Max* is a record that grows in stature on repeated hearings: Stubblefield is in the mood for some grand oratory, Tolliver's spacious solos accumulate strength as they go forward, and the rougher, unpredictable alto of the younger Hayes is an interesting wild card. The Candid set, recorded live, could use some editing, but it's an atmospheric occasion and, although Bartz sounds a little sour at some moments, there is still some fiery hard bop in the programme. Going back into the studio for *Nightfall*, Hayes assembles a fresh front line: Allen's trumpet is less immediately distinctive than Tolliver's, but he has a very impressive solo on 'I Waited For You', and Hayes and Willis are in buoyant form. Besides that, the drummer's evolving command of the leader's role seems to be inspiring his own playing to new heights.

Blue Lou continues the exceptional run at Steeplechase. Still not quite in the absolute top bracket, but all three horns have some fine contributions to make, and what registers most strongly is the bustle and impetus of Hayes's group – a Blakey trademark which Louis seems intent on following through. 'Quiet Fire' is a classic example of what Hayes's bands can do, the soloists brimming with fire and excitement without surrendering the improviser's control. The distinguished Mathews is a valuable recruit to the team, too.

The Super Quartet is perhaps not quite as super as some of the preceding discs. With Jackson as sole horn, the date is more of a potboiler tenor-plus-rhythm affair – although the saxophonist is nobody's slouch. But the familiar material and relatively routine performances don't lift it above average.

*****(*) Louis At Large**
Sharp Nine 1003-2 *Hayes; Riley Mullins (t); Javon Jackson (ts); David Hazeltine (p); Santi Debriano (b).* 4/96.

***** Quintessential Lou**
TCB 99652 *As above, except Abraham Burton (ts) replaces Jackson.* 3/99.

Louis At Large was Hayes's first American set as leader for many years. Mullins and Jackson are keen to please in the front line, but perhaps the most interesting performer here is Hazeltine, who builds on the good impression of his own records. The tunes offer some surprisingly strong originals from various hands – no simple hard-bop blues lines but genuine themes – and Hayes is clearly delighted at the shape the band's in.

Quintessential Lou is a shade less involving, though it's hard to say why – Burton is a characterful substitute for Jackson and the combo is on its mettle as standard-bearers of a hard-bop tradition. But there's a rote feel to some of this. Only two originals from within the ranks of the band and, although they choose such genre rarities as Sonny Rollins's 'Decision', the playing has settled into a measure of routine for the moment.

Tubby Hayes (1935–73)

TENOR SAXOPHONE, FLUTE

Born in London, Hayes was a prodigy who took up saxophone at eleven and made his recording debut at sixteen with Kenny Baker. The most forceful of soloists, he was completely at home in the virtuosity of bebop, and he also became an adept vibes player. He co-led the Jazz Couriers with Ronnie Scott in the 1950s and visited New York in 1961 to play and record. His eminence on the British scene in the '60s was insufficiently recognized, partly through the eclipse of modern jazz by pop, and his final years were troubled by illness. Many of his records have yet to appear on CD.

****** Late Spot At Scott's**
Redial 558183-2 *Hayes; Jimmy Deuchar (t); Gordon Beck (p); Freddie Logan (b); Allan Ganley (d).* 5/62.

****** Down In The Village**
Redial 558184-2 *As above.* 5/62.

***** Night And Day**
Jazz House JHAS 602 *As above, except add Terry Shannon, Mike Pyne (p), Jeff Clyne, Bruce Cale (b), Benny Goodman, Phil Seamen (d).* 12/63–8/66.

***** Jazz Tête A Tête**
Progressive PCD-7079 *Hayes; Les Condon (t); John Picard (tb); Tony Coe (ts); Mike Pyne, Colin Purbrook (p); Frank Evans (g); Ron Mathewson, Peter Ind (b); Jackie Dougan, Tony Levin (d).* 11/66.

*****(*) For Members Only**
Mastermix CDCHE 10 *Hayes; Mick Pyne (p); Ron Mathewson (b); Tony Levin (d).* 1–10/67.

***** Live 1969**
Harlequin HQ CD 05 *As above, except Spike Wells (d) replaces Levin.* 8–12/69.

Tubby Hayes has often been lionized as the greatest saxophonist Britain ever produced. He is a fascinating but problematical player. Having put together a big, rumbustious tone and a delivery that features sixteenth notes spilling impetuously out of the horn, Hayes often left a solo full of brilliant loose ends and ingenious runs that led nowhere in particular. Most of his recordings, while highly entertaining as exhibitions of sustained energy, tend to wobble on the axis of Hayes's creative impasse: having got this facility together, he never seemed sure of what to do with it in the studio, which may be why his studio records (all currently missing in action) ultimately fall short of the masterpiece he never came to make.

His live albums are, nevertheless, sometimes breathtaking in their impact and excitement. The most famous are the two Fontana discs now reissued on Redial, dating from a pair of nights at the Ronnie Scott Club. On vibes, as in the title-track to *Down In The Village*, he is coolly melodic, but on tenor his playing is a rollercoaster of power and excitement. There is little to choose between the two records; perhaps we slightly prefer *Down In The*

Village. But there is also some exemplary support from Deuchar, Beck, Logan and Ganley, in what was one of the strongest groups of its era. *Night And Day* offers material from five dates at Ronnie's over a period of three years: the tenor playing on 'Night And Day', to choose one, is unquenchably vivid, even electrifying. But the issue offers little more than bootleg sound, and one is sometimes reminded of some of the old tapes of Coltrane that used to circulate among collectors.

Jazz Tête A Tête will be nostalgic for many British readers as a souvenir of one of the concerts promoter Peter Burman organized in the 1960s, this one at Bristol University, with groups led by Les Condon (with Tubby sitting in), Tony Coe and Frank Evans. Hayes followers will welcome his rhapsodic ballad, 'When My Baby Gets Mad'; the rest is more routine, but Coe's playing is a reminder that there was more than one great tenorman at work in Britain then. The recording quality – the original album was issued on Doug Dobell's 77 Records – is of documentary standard, but isn't too bad, and there is a previously unheard version of 'Tenderly' by Coe.

The Mastermix CD has some 70 minutes of music drawn from three broadcasts, with a couple of rare excursions on flute and plenty of rousing tenor, as well as a nice glimpse of Hayes the composer. The CD suffers from some occasional blinks and drop-outs, but nothing too distracting. *Live 1969* sounds pretty dusty, drawn from a couple of London gigs, and Hayes is too generous with everybody else's solo space. But the second date, with a tumbling reading of 'Where Am I Going' and a couple of Hayes originals, is a degree more intense.

***** A Tribute: Tubbs**

Spotlite SPJ-CD 902 *Hayes; Jimmy Deuchar (t, mel); Terry Shannon (p); Freddy Logan (b); Allan Ganley (d).* 12/63.

***** Quartet In Scandinavia**

Storyville STCD 8251 *Hayes; Staffan Abeleen (p); Niels-Henning Orsted Pedersen (b); Alex Riel (d).* 2/72.

A couple of memories to add to the legacy of Tubbs on record. He is in his prime on the Spotlite set and, although the music isn't up to the electrifying standard of the two Redial albums, it's a valuable glimpse of the man in exuberant form. The sheer ebullience of his solo on 'Don't Fall Off The Bridge' is breathtaking. Deuchar doesn't have quite such a good night, but there is also little enough around of him in his pomp to make this a keeper.

The Storyville disc comes from a Swedish broadcast. This is typical visiting-soloist stuff with the local rhythm section, and Hayes – who had already suffered more than one serious illness – probably approaches this as just another gig. As a quartet, though, this is a class act and, if there are too many long solos shared around the band, the music has spirit as well as polish.

Roy Haynes (born 1926)

DRUMS

Roy Haynes worked with Charlie Parker, Miles Davis, Bud Powell, Sarah Vaughan, Thelonious Monk and Eric Dolphy, and was dep for the classic John Coltrane Quartet. If power and swing were measured relative to physical size, the little man from Roxbury, Massachusetts, would be one of the major figures of the music. Recent years have seen him establish himself ever more confidently as a leader, with what is now a substantial and consistently inventive discography.

***** We Three**

Original Jazz Classics OJC 196 *Haynes; Phineas Newborn Jr (p); Paul Chambers (b).* 11/58.

*****(*) Out Of The Afternoon**

Impulse! IMP 11802 *Haynes; Roland Kirk (ts, manzello, stritch, f); Tommy Flanagan (p); Henry Grimes (b).* 5/62.

***** Cracklin'**

Original Jazz Classics OJC 818 *Haynes; Booker Ervin (ts); Ronnie Mathews (p); Larry Ridley (b).* 4/63.

Haynes's output as leader has been disappointingly small. Few contemporary drummers have been so precise in execution, and what Haynes lacks in sheer power – he is a small man and has generally worked with a scaled-down kit – he gains in clarity, playing long, open lines that are deceptively relaxed but full of small rhythmic tensions. In 1958 his work still clearly bears the mark of stints with Thelonious Monk and Miles Davis. Bar lines shift confidently or else are dispensed with altogether, without violence to the underlying pulse. Phineas Newborn's recent association with Charles Mingus had helped pare down his slightly extravagant style; he plays very differently against Haynes's slightly staccato delivery than with, say, Elvin Jones much later in his career or Philly Joe Jones in 1961, where Chambers again provided the harmonic substructure. Haynes himself sounds wonderful on 'Sugar Ray' and the romping 'Our Delight', where he is almost tuneful.

The Impulse! record is a splendid one-off. After a big, dramatic opening on cymbals, Kirk blasts off on the Artie Shaw theme, 'Moon Ray', using both manzello and tenor (beautifully in tune), doubling his lines against a big reverb that makes him sound like a whole section. Haynes's solo is low, slow and dramatic, halving the basic tempo at one point. That is not Kirk's bent. On 'If I Should Lose You', he squalls his way through a magnificent stritch solo which pulls the standard apart. (The original liner-note by Stanley Dance was slightly misleading about Kirk's two non-canonical horns; any misconceptions are corrected on this otherwise intact reissue by Michel Cuscuna.) 'Snap Crackle' was an expression coined by bassist Al McKibbon to describe Haynes's sound. The drummer adopts it here as a song title and, coupled to Kirk's weird vocalized flute and nose-flute solo, it rather stands out from the rest of the album.

Cracklin' is more mainstream but the fizz and pop are still very much there, and Haynes's polyrhythms are all the more evident for not being eclipsed by such an idiosyncratic front man. Which isn't to say that Ervin is less than exemplary. His solo on 'Under Paris Skies' is first rate and Mathews's accompaniment pushes a rather slight vehicle to the limit.

***** Live At The Riverbop**

EPM Musique FD 152032 *Haynes; Ricardo Strobert (as, f); Marcus Fiorillo (g); David Jackson (b).* 12/79.

After a long gap in his recording career, Haynes sounds as urgent and provocative as ever, albeit in the context of a lumpy and uninspired band. Roy's compositions, 'Little Sun Flower', 'I'm So High', 'Bull Fight' and 'Riverbop Blues', are convincingly performed, though one might have preferred a more developed version of Shorter's 'Footprints', which is the best moment on the album. Lousy recording.

****** True Or False**

Evidence 22171 *Haynes; Ralph Moore (ts); David Kikoski (p); Eddy Howard (b).* 86.

***** Homecoming**

Evidence 22092 *As above, except omit Moore; add Craig Handy (ts).* 6/92.

*****(*) When It's Haynes It Roars**

Dreyfus 191151 2 *As above.* 7/92.

The basic saxophone quartet was to be Haynes's preferred format for most of his career. Never a confident or particularly inventive big-band drummer, he functions best when the configuration is quite simple and untextured, and he takes responsibility himself for filling out the background with detail. In the mid-'80s, after a couple of decades of quiet and self-effacement, Haynes returned to the studio as a leader and created a tough and able session that very sensibly touched on as many sources and influences as possible. 'True Or False' had featured on *Live At The Riverbop* and here it's reduced to the simplest contour. The big tracks are Chick Corea's 'Psalm' and 'Bud Powell', Wayne Shorter's 'Fee-Fi-Fo-Fum' and Sonny Rollins's 'Everywhere Calypso'. Tough and joyous hard bop with real intelligence in the engine-room.

The later band isn't particularly exciting or starry on paper, but the choice of material is interesting as ever on *Homecoming* – Trane's 'Equinox', Corea's 'Powell, Bud', Monk's 'Green Chimneys' and a version of 'Star Eyes' – and Roy coaxes the band to some genuinely inventive re-exploration of those three dominant composers. What's impressive is that he makes them sound as if they're working to *his* rhythmic agenda, with lots of seven and five patterns thrown in to break up the symmetry. Anonymous as the line-up might initially appear, Kikoski is an intelligent player and Handy one of the more underrated tenor players around, well versed from Mingus days in playing along the edge of the predictable.

Craig comes to the fore even more strongly on the second disc, which was recorded in Paris shortly thereafter. Chick's 'Steps' and Monk's 'Bye Ya' continue the homage, but otherwise it's a more evenly paced standard- and repertory-set, with greater concentration on tight ensembles and crisp unisons. Howard's bass is anonymous on the earlier record and really booms through here. These are Haynes records that shouldn't be overlooked.

*****(*) Te Vou!**

Dreyfus FDM 36569 *Haynes; Donald Harrison (as); Pat Metheny (g); David Kikoski (p); Christian McBride (b).* 94.

Te Vou! is absolutely consistent with past form. Haynes dares to play quietly and delicately, and his solo on 'Trigonometry' is exquisite. He has some interesting companions here, not least Metheny, who quite clearly revels more in this setting than in the bombast of Denardo Coleman on *Song X*. The guitarist features strongly on 'John McKee', a beautiful thing made out of perfectly balanced parts. The recording is flatteringly balanced and very true, with no artificial heightening of the soloists.

***** My Shining Hour**

Storyville 4199 *Haynes; Tomas Franck (ts); Thomas Clausen (p); Niels-Henning Orsted Pedersen (b).* 3/94.

Recorded with Clausen's Jazz Participants, *My Shining Hour* is a Jazzpar project and a disappointing one by comparison with other records from the prestigious event. Haynes is in a show-boating mood and there's too little of interest coming from the horn of Tomas Franck to balance up the drama. The saxophonist does contribute one lively composition to the set, but otherwise it might as well have been a trio session. Clausen and NHOP are fascinating in themselves and some of the best exchanges on the record are quite simply for piano and bass. 'Bessie's Blues' isn't the most covered of Coltrane compositions and it's good to hear it handled with such imagination. Otherwise, though, a border-line item.

****** Praise**

Dreyfus 36598 *Haynes; Graham Haynes (c, flhn); Kenny Garrett (ss, as); David Sanchez (ts); David Kikoski (p); Dwayne Burno (b).* 98.

Haynes plays one of his most persuasive recorded solos on the closing 'Shades Of Senegal', a performance that is as expressive as it is rhythmically astute. The album covers every possible permutation, from solo percussion to septet, and at every level it is Roy who dominates. Son Graham and the two saxophone players each have interesting things to say, but it is the rhythm section, with Kikoski very much in the foreground, that makes things happen. Some of the selections, like John Carisi's 'Israel', are less than ideally suited to this personnel but 'My Little Suede Shoes', the Charlie Parker classic, and the traditional 'Morning Has Broken' are both sterling performances, and Roy has rarely sounded more gleefully in charge.

***** The Roy Haynes Trio**

Verve 543534-2 *Haynes; Danilo Perez (p); John Patitucci (b).* 99.

This arrived right on press time and we've had only limited time to sample it. Roy, though, sounds strong and inventive, and the new trio fits him like a glove. Two sets – studio and live – include compositions by Miles Davis, Pat Metheny, Chick Corea, Duke, Monk and a couple of standards. The live sound is more convincingly three-dimensional – and by contrast the studio tracks sound anonymous. We'd like to hear this group settled in a club for a couple of weeks and then skim off the cream. *That* would be worth hearing.

Kevin Hays (born 1968)

PIANO

Born in New York, Hays listened to Oscar Peterson and George Shearing as a teenager and was soon playing in clubs. He has been a frequent sideman in the Tri-State area.

*****(*) Sweet Ear**

Steeplechase SCCD 31282 *Hays; Eddie Henderson (t); Vincent Herring (ss, as); James Genus (b); Joe Chambers (d).* 1/91.

***** Ugly Beauty**
Steeplechase SCCD 31297 *Hays; Larry Grenadier (b); Jeff Williams (d).* 8/91.

*****(*) Crossroad**
Steeplechase SCCD 31324 *Hays; Scott Wendholt (t, flhn); Freddie Bryant (g); Dwayne Burno (b); Carl Allen (d).* 11/92.

Hays is a gifted young American pianist whose three Steeplechase albums include a lot of satisfying jazz: they're arguably still his best calling-card. The leader is sometimes a rather demure performer: his touch, if not exactly diffident, is a little reticent in making an impact on the keys, and rhythmically he tends to organize solos around certain patterns – halving the tempo or working a sequence of arpeggios – which crop up often enough to hint at routine. But his writing offers some interesting situations and on, say, the trio reading of 'You And The Night And The Music' on the first album he manages to create a logical and inventive development far away from the melody.

The first album is arguably the best by dint of some excellent teamwork: Henderson takes some very fine solos, Herring manages to step out of his Adderley impersonation for most of the date, and Chambers is as eccentrically inventive as ever (sample his solo on 'Neptune'). The quintet with Wendholt is notable for the trumpeter's beautiful solos, expertly paced and tonally exquisite, as well as fine covers of Ray Bryant's 'P.S. The Blues' and Duke Pearson's 'Gaslight'. The trio record is inevitably less absorbing, given Hays' light grip, but is still worth hearing. Hays subsequently signed to Blue Note and recorded three albums, but they have since been deleted.

David Hazeltine (born 1958)

PIANO

Born in Milwaukee and based there for many years, Hazeltine is a 'local' hard-bop pianist who has been making more frequent and prominent appearances on record of late.

***** 4 Flights Up**
Sharp Nine 1002-2 *Hazeltine; Slide Hampton (tb); Peter Washington (b); Ray Appleton (d).* 7/95.

*****(*) The Classic Trio**
Sharp Nine 1005-2 *Hazeltine; Peter Washington (b); Louis Hayes (d).* 8/96.

***** How It Is**
Criss Cross 1142 *Hazeltine; Jim Rotondi (t, flhn); Steve Wilson (as); Peter Washington (b); Joe Farnsworth (d).* 10/97.

Hazeltine's comments draw a list of influences which are a key to his style, and to an interesting take on modern jazz piano: Oscar Peterson, Barry Harris, Buddy Montgomery, Cedar Walton. He's a communicator in the Peterson manner, voicing melodies in a recognizable yet inventive way, adding just enough rhythmic nuance to take an interpretation out of the ordinary, and placing absolute trust in his rhythm-section sidemen – Washington in particular, common to all three records. *4 Flights Up* has Hampton as the sole horn but, though he performs likeably enough, his solos add a note of blandness and sometimes get in Hazeltine's way. *The Classic Trio*, with lovely, grooving work from Washington and Hayes, is a peach of a trio date. Though Hazeltine says he prefers to work with more modern material ('Betcha By Golly Wow', from the songbook of the Stylistics, is on the previous disc) he still does very well out of standards such as 'Sweet And Lovely' and 'These Foolish Things', an unerring sense of tempo helping to swing the melodies and set the pace for constructions that are intricate without seeming fussy or deliberately complex. 'My Stuff's On The Street' is a witty blues, Bud Powell's 'The Fruit' is bebop cooled off in a delightful setting, and 'One For Peter' is an adroit feature for Washington.

The Criss Cross date is disappointingly prosaic in comparison. Rotondi and Wilson play well enough, but they add little aside from extra weight to some of the tunes. The pianist's 'Nuit Noire' is a fine set-piece and his treatment of 'Pannonica' comes off with an expert flourish, but it's all a little ordinary.

Jon Hazilla

DRUMS

Contemporary drummer moving from bop to freer forms.

***** The Bitten Moon**
Cadence CJR 1058 *Hazilla; James Williams (p); Ray Drummond (b).* 3/94.

Hazilla's ingenuity sets the tone for this session. He likes to dominate but realizes that a domineering drummer can be a bore, so he plays intrusively rather than giving himself lots of solos. Williams and Drummond are personalities in their own right, and they hold their own, but it must have been Hazilla's decision to do a snappy, up-tempo version of 'Naima', for one. There are two short but interesting solo pieces – one, 'Pancakes From Meductiv', is actually a cymbal solo – and the overall result is a sharp, out-of-the-ordinary rhythm-section record with some bite to it.

****** Form And Function**
CIMP 142 *Hazilla; John Pierce (tb); Jim Odgren (as); Greg Badolato (ts); Tim Mayer (bs).* 3/97.

This is the band Hazilla calls Saxabone – for obvious reasons – and their resonant, freshly peeled sound comes across wonderfully via CIMP's no-frills recording. The record is a sequence of eight drum solos interspersed with four hard-bop chestnuts performed by the band ('Eternal Triangle' appears in two takes). The result is a compelling and wholly original meditation on hard-bop form and, indeed, function, with the drummer's set-pieces pointedly breaking down aspects of the group player's art while the horns create a superbly expressive argument for the 'modern' possibilities in 'Our Man Higgins', 'Crepuscule With Nellie', 'A Little Brazil' and the aforementioned Stitt tune. Played end to end, it's a fascinating document and a notable essay on jazz tradition. Bravo!

Jimmy Heath (born 1926)

TENOR, ALTO AND SOPRANO SAXOPHONES

Born in Philadelphia, the middle Heath brother led big bands and bebop groups in the original bebop era but did more writing than playing in the '50s. Since then, much more active as player-leader and a renowned teacher. A major contributor to the hard-bop book and a great patrician influence.

****** The Thumper**

Original Jazz Classics OJC 1828 *Heath; Nat Adderley (cl); Curtis Fuller (tb); Wynton Kelly (p); Paul Chambers (b); Albert 'Tootie' Heath (d).* 9/59.

***** Blue Soul**

Original Jazz Classics OJC 765 *As above.* 9/59.

***** The Riverside Collection: Nice People**

Original Jazz Classics OJC 6006 *Heath; Donald Byrd, Freddie Hubbard, Clark Terry (t); Nat Adderley (c); Curtis Fuller, Tom McIntosh (tb); Dick Berg, Jimmy Buffington, Don Butterfield (tba); Julius Watkins (frhn); Cannonball Adderley (as); Pat Patrick (bs); Herbie Hancock, Wynton Kelly, Cedar Walton (p); Kenny Burrell (g); Paul Chambers, Percy Heath (b); Albert 'Tootie' Heath, Connie Kay (d).* 12/59-64.

*****(*) Really Big!**

Original Jazz Classics OJC 1799 *Heath; Clark Terry, Nat Adderley (t); Tom McIntosh, Dick Berg (tb); Cannonball Adderley, Pat Patrick (sax); Tommy Flanagan, Cedar Walton (p); Percy Heath (b); Albert 'Tootie' Heath (d).* 60.

The middle of the three Heath brothers is perhaps and quite undeservedly now the least known. Jimmy Heath's reputation as a player has been partly overshadowed by his gifts as a composer ('C.T.A.', 'Gemini', 'Gingerbread Boy') and arranger. *The Thumper* was his debut recording. Unlike most of his peers, Heath had not hurried into the studio. He was already in his thirties and writing with great maturity; the session kicks off with 'For Minors Only', the first of his tunes to achieve near-classic standing. He also includes 'Nice People'. The Riverside compilation which bears that name was until recently the ideal introduction to the man who was once known as 'Little Bird' but who later largely abandoned alto saxophone and its associated Parkerisms in favour of a bold, confident tenor style that is immediately distinctive. Now that *The Thumper* is around again, the compilation album is a little less appealing.

Also well worth looking out for is the big-band set from 1960. Built around the three Heath and the two Adderley brothers, it's a unit with a great deal of personality and presence. Sun Ra's favourite baritonist, Pat Patrick, is in the line-up and contributes fulsomely to the ensembles. Bobby Timmons's 'Dat Dere', 'On Green Dolphin Street' and 'Picture Of Heath' are the outstanding tracks, and Orrin Keepnews's original sound is faithfully preserved in Phil De Lancie's conservative remastering.

Heath's arrangements often favour deep brass pedestals for the higher horns, which explains his emphasis on trombone and french horn parts. The earliest of these sessions, though, is a relatively stripped-down blowing session ('Nice People' and 'Who Needs It') for Nat Adderley, Curtis Fuller and a rhythm section anchored on youngest brother, Albert, who reappears with Percy Heath, the eldest of the three, on the ambitious 1960 'Picture Of Heath'. Like Connie Kay, who was to join Percy in the Modern Jazz Quartet, Albert is an unassuming player, combining Kay's subtlety with the drive of Kenny Clarke (original drummer for the MJQ).

More than once in these sessions (and most noticeably on the 1964 'All The Things You Are' with Kenny Burrell and the brilliant Wynton Kelly) it's Albert who fuels his brother's better solos. This is a fine set, though chronological balance occasionally dictates a less than ideal selection of material. Well worth investigating.

*****(*) The Quota**

Original Jazz Classics OJCCD 1871 *Heath; Freddie Hubbard (t); Julius Watkins (frhn); Cedar Walton (p); Percy Heath (b); Albert 'Tootie' Heath (d).* 4/61.

***** On The Trail**

Original Jazz Classics OJCCD 1854 *Heath; Wynton Kelly (p); Kenny Burrell (g); Paul Chambers (b); Albert 'Tootie' Heath (d).* 64.

The Quota perfectly underlines Jimmy's ability to make three contrasting horns sound like a big band, or very nearly. This is a cleverly arranged session, and an agreeably fraternal one, with Percy and Tootie on hand as well. Hubbard was a killer at 23, soloing with fire and conviction, but it is Jimmy's own work, on his own title-track and on 'When Sonny Gets Blue', that stands out, arguably some of his best tenor-playing on record.

On The Trail is less arresting; more of a straight blowing session, it doesn't play to Jimmy's real strengths and the production seems oddly underpowered, as if everything has been taken down a notch to accommodate Burrell's soft and understated guitar lines. 'All The Things You Are' has some moments of spectacular beauty, as when Jimmy floats across Wynton Kelly's line with a soft restatement of the melody and a tiny fragment of the 'Bird Of Paradise' contrafact patented by Charlie Parker. Good, straightforward jazz, but not a great Jimmy Heath album.

*****(*) Triple Threat**

Original Jazz Classics OJCCD 1909-2 *Heath; Freddie Hubbard (t); Julius Watkins (frhn); Cedar Walton (p); Percy Heath (b); Albert 'Tootie' Heath (d).* 1/62.

A dry run for the Heath Brothers project and another object lesson in how to give a relatively small unit an expansive sound. Jimmy takes a couple of numbers with just rhythm and even there manages to suggest a massive structure behind his elegantly linear melody lines. Watkins has an enhanced role and demonstrates once again what an exciting player he can be on an instrument usually consigned to a supportive role.

Jimmy's blues waltz, 'Gemini', is probably better known in the version recorded by Cannonball Adderley, but the little man's own solo statement confirms ownership rights. Hubbard is in quiet form, but already gives notice of what he was capable of.

*****(*) Swamp Seed**

Original Jazz Classics OJCCD 1904-2 *Heath; Donald Byrd (t); Jimmy Buffington, Julius Watkins (frhn); Don Butterfield (tba); Herbie Hancock, Harold Mabern (p); Percy Heath (b); Albert 'Tootie' Heath, Connie Kay (d).* 63.

Jimmy's genius as an arranger is evident here, where he manages to make three brass sound like a whole orchestra. With no supplemental reeds to support his own muscular lines, Jimmy is the most prominent voice. On 'Six Steps', 'Nutty' and 'D Waltz', he creates solo statements of genuine originality, relying on the subtle voicings given to Butterfield, Buffington and Watkins to support his more adventurous harmonic shifts. As 'D Waltz' demonstrates, Jimmy learned a lot from listening to Charlie Parker, but also to the older bandleaders like Lunceford and Eckstine, who understood how to give relatively simple ideas maximum mileage.

****** Changes**

Camden 74321 61086 2 2CD *Heath; Tom Williams (t, flhn); Curtis Fuller, Benny Powell (tb); Bob Routch, John Clarke (frhn); Howard Johnson (tba); Stanley Cowell, Tommy Flanagan, Larry Willis (p); Pat Martino, Tony Perrone (g); Sam Jones, Stafford Jones, Rufus Reid (b); Al Foster, Billy Higgins, Akira Tana (d); Mtume (perc).* 6/74, 6/85, 2/87.

***** The Professor**

32 Records 32096 *As above.*

Jimmy's playing career has been marked by a number of hiatuses, usually when he was busy writing and arranging for others. The sabbaticals seem, if anything, to have sharpened his appetite for performance. The valuable Camden discs are culled from three Muse LPs spanning more than a decade: *The Time And The Place*, *New Picture* and *Peer Pleasure*. It sees him straddle a generational change in jazz with consummate ease, pulling into shape a younger and less orthodox band on the 1987 session with complete authority. The 32 Records is a more selective trawl through the same material, preferable only for a slightly sharper remastering and for some few additional tracks. The Camden is typically sloppy on documentary detail – Tommy *Flannigan*, indeed! – but good value nevertheless.

The chanted opening and drones on Kenny Dorham's 'No End' (originally on *The Time And The Place*) give way to a performance of great elegance, graced by a double-time solo from Pat Martino. Orrin Keepnews curated the two '80s sessions and gave Jimmy a sound that highlighted his diversity; for a change, he doubles on alto and soprano on these sessions, though for some reason there is no reprise of the elegant flute-playing on *The Time And The Place*. 'Lush Life' is masterly, grand as well as very moving. This fine compilation is heartily recommended to newcomers and settled fans alike.

***** You've Changed**

Steeplechase SSCD 31292 *Heath; Tony Purrone (g); Ben Brown (b); Albert 'Tootie' Heath (d).* 8/91.

In the early 1990s he was still playing with great character. The opening solo on *You've Changed* delivers 'Soul Eyes' at an easy lope that scarcely varies for the remainder of the set. Heath can now say more in half a dozen notes than most young players can in three choruses. He places accents so carefully that even straightforward theme statements become objects of considerable interest. The group – even Tootie on this occasion – is rather dull and sluggish, but Jimmy sails on regardless, often quite blatantly ignoring key shifts and rhythmic downshifts to follow an interesting thought to its destination.

****** You Or Me**

Steeplechase SCCD 31370 *Heath; Tony Purrone (g); Kiyoshi Kitagawa (b); Albert 'Tootie' Heath (d).* 4/95.

A session tinged with real sadness, after Jimmy learned of his elder sister's death just as they were about to record. Whether Elizabeth was on his mind when he set out to re-create the Ben Webster solo on Ellington's 'All Too Soon' isn't certain, but it's a performance of great gentleness and soft regret, one of his more open-hearted ballads. Hearing him in this, albeit rather exceptional, context is a reminder of how cool and detached he has often sounded in the studio.

Not here, though. There is a real bounce and bluster to the closing 'Hot House' and the work-out on Blue Mitchell's 'Fungi Mama' is anything but diffident. The album begins with three Heath originals, including 'The Quota', and thereafter sticks to repertory material, including the Ellington and Mitchell tunes, and Duke Pearson's seldom covered 'Is That So?', which was probably recorded at least once in the old Steeplechase studio. The new digital set-up is flattering to Jimmy's sound, highlighting its glacial harmonics and filling out its bass register. Guitarist Purrone is a bit distant in places and doesn't seem to fall into any definite role, neither second 'horn' nor accompanist. As before, the understanding with Tootie is sensitive and subtle and some of their exchanges are wickedly clever.

The Heath Brothers

GROUP

Among the first families of jazz, only the Joneses can have racked up anything like the list of credits put together in the Heaths' 150 collective years in the business. Older brothers Percy and Jimmy left Philadelphia in 1949 to join Howard McGhee's band; Albert is almost a decade younger but quickly became one of the ablest and busiest drummers on the circuit.

*****(*) As We Were Saying ...**

Concord CCD 4777-2 *Jimmy Heath (ts, ss); Percy Heath (b, clo); Albert 'Tootie' Heath (d); Jon Faddis (t, flhn); Slide Hampton (tb); Stanley Cowell, Sir Roland Hanna (p); Mark Elf (g); James Mtume (perc).* 97.

****** Jazz Family**

Concord CCD 4846-2 *Jimmy Heath (ts, ss); Percy Heath (b, clo); Albert 'Tootie' Heath (d); Earl Gardner, Joe Wilder, Tom Wiliams (t, flhn); Benny Powell (tb); John Clark (frhn); Bob Stewart (tba); Jeb Patton (p); Tony Purrone (g).* 98.

The Heath Brothers recorded several albums in the 1980s, but these are the first fraternal offerings since then. It would be nice to report that there are strong family traits in their playing. The fact is that all three brothers have very different styles and approaches, *except* when they play together, and then the Heaths seem to draw on a shared background and experience from the heyday of bebop. Jimmy's writing and playing have developed in many different directions since then, but as 'Bop Again' on *As We Were Saying* ... suggests, this is where their hearts lie. The title is obviously meant to suggest that the boys have just picked up where they left off, as brothers do, and there is nothing in the set to indicate that this was a historic reunion rather than a new album from a working band. In Sir Roland Hanna and Stanley Cowell, Percy and Albert have two perfect rhythm section partners, players who mix the almost classical precision of Percy's bass and cello work with Tootie's African-tinged rhythms. Just to make the family gathering complete, Jimmy's son, James Mtume, adds percussion on 'South Filthy'. The presence of Jon Faddis might lead you to think you were listening to some otherwise undocumented Dizzy project, an effect that seems to encourage Jimmy's now unabashed Parkerisms. They used to call him Little Bird; he switched to tenor but now he manages to sound like Parker's happy shade.

The follow-up album is better still, but it's hard to think of it as anything other than a Jimmy Heath project. Percy contributes one tune, 'Move To The Groove' (actually the weakest thing on the roster), but the rest is dominated by the middle brother. His writing and arrangements are endlessly inventive. '13th House' is one of the best things he has written, not a classic on a par with 'CTA' or 'Gingerbread Boy', but a richly constructed tune nonetheless. 'A Harmonic Future' and 'Wind Print' are a little more schematic, the former an intriguing but slightly dry exercise on neo-bop, the latter more impressionistic. Yet, wedged as they are in between 'Easy Living', Otis René's 'I'm Lost' and Kenny Dorham's lovely 'None Shall Wander', they add to the texture of a wonderfully well-crafted album.

Mark Helias (born 1950)

DOUBLE BASS, ELECTRIC BASS

New Jersey-born and Yale-educated, Helias combines a streetwise toughness with real musical intelligence. Recent years have seen him as busy as ever, but somewhat diverted towards production and a consequent hiccup in his own recording career.

**(*) The Current Set

Enja 5041 *Helias; Herb Robertson (t, c, flhn); Robin Eubanks (tb); Tim Berne (as); Greg Osby (ss); Victor Lewis (d); Nana Vasconcelos (perc, v). 3/87.*

*** Desert Blue

Enja 6016 *Helias; Herb Robertson (t, c); Ray Anderson (tb); Marty Ehrlich (as, ts, cl, bcl); Anthony Davis (p, syn); Pheeroan akLaff (d). 4/89.*

***(*) Attack The Future

Enja 7019 *Helias; Herb Robertson (t, flhn, c); Michael Moore (cl, bcl, as); David Lopato (p); Tom Rainey (d, perc). 3/90.*

**** Loopin' The Cool

Enja 9049 *Helias; Ellery Eskelin (ts); Regina Carter (vn); Tom Rainey (d, perc); Epizo Bangoura (djembe, perc). 12/94.*

There is now a fully fledged generation of jazz musicians for whom rock is a simple fact, part of the background of contemporary music, and not a hard place to be defiantly or submissively negotiated. Helias is one of the more influential of the Young Turks; as well as his own impressive work, he has recorded with Barry Altschul and with Ray Anderson, who makes a welcome appearance on *Desert Blue*.

Helias is capable of boiling intensity or an almost desolate abstraction. The currently deleted *Split Image* was the most tightly structured and arranged of Helias's records until *Attack The Future* was released, largely due to Hemingway's inspirational drumming. The combination of Tim Berne, who is much less effective on *The Current Set*, with the veteran Dewey Redman is particularly enjoyable.

Helias is rhythmically not the most sophisticated of players and he seems to rely quite heavily on his drummers. Lewis is in some respects too oblique and elided and it's akLaff's every-which-way explosions around a solid beat which lift *Desert Blue*. Helias is, though, constantly aware of texture and resonance, and of his own technical limitations, deploying instrumental voices with great subtlety. Regular cohort Robertson is a less than virtuosic player but he makes up for any purely mechanical shortcomings with a clever disposition of brasses.

Attack The Future is committed and venturesome, benefiting hugely from the presence of Robertson and Moore. There are signs here, and even more clearly on *Loopin' the Cool*, that Helias is moving out into new territory, refining his own sound quite considerably and putting ever greater emphasis on highly dissonant ideas and unsettling rhythms. 'Loop the Cool' is a long line that sets Eskelin's wonderfully relaxed tenor against Regina Carter's violin; it's a compelling combination, and Carter is first to the punch again on the following 'One Time Only', which is the most rhythmically challenging thing on the session. Some of the ideas have resurfaced from other contexts, like the Ed Blackwell Project, but here they seem to have found their ideal expression. Helias has long been a respected sideman. This, though, lifts him up into the top league.

Paul Heller

TENOR SAXOPHONE

A member of the NDR Big Band, Heller is a young German saxophonist in the post-bop milieu.

***(*) Paul Heller

Mons LC 6458 *Heller; Ack Van Rooyen (flhn); Roberto Di Gioia (p); Ingmar Heller (b); Wolfgang Haffner (d). 94.*

Nothing wrong with this. Heller is a skilful, unselfconscious tenorman: he plays the opening blues with beguiling confidence, sidestepping cliché but standing foursquare in the Rollins lineage. Most of the date comes off around mid-tempo, which evades any hard-bop breathlessness, and Heller (with his brother, Ingmar, on bass) rings the changes throughout – each of the two horns has a ballad to itself, but both disappear on 'Song For Bea', and the drums are out on the suitably thoughtful 'Contemplation'. Ack van Rooyen was a good choice for frontline partner, mellow but incisive on the big brass horn. The writing is a shade lacking in any ambition, but the playing is full of rewarding things.

Bob Helm (born 1914)

CLARINET, ALTO CLARINET, ALTO SAXOPHONE, VOCALS

A veteran of the Californian revivalist scene for more than 50 years, Helm began playing with Lu Watters in 1940 and with Turk Murphy from the mid-'40s until 1980.

*****(*) Hotter Than That**
Stomp Off CD1310 *Helm; Leon Oakley (c, v); Charlie Sonnanstine (tb); Ted Des Plantes (p, v); Vince Saunders (bj, g); Bill Carroll (tba); Marty Eggers (b); Bob Raggio (wbd).* 10/94–1/95.

***** Ma 'N' Bessie's Greater Tent Show Act 1**
Stomp Off CD1331 *As above, except add Ray Skjelbred (p), John Gill (bj, g, d, tb, v), Craig Ventresco (bj, g), Mike Walbridge (tba), Pete Devine (wbd, jug), Carol Leigh (v).* 10/94–9/97.

***** Ma 'N' Bessie's Greater Tent Show Act 2**
Stomp Off CD1332 *As above.* 10/94–9/97.

Bob Helm's matchless knowledge of traditional styles serves these records well, the first under his leadership since a Riverside session in 1954. *Hotter Than That* rounds up some of the best of the Stomp Off repertory company for a marathon 20-song session that almost bursts the CD's boundaries. Although here and there the band take things easy so as not to overwhelm the leader, some of the slower tempos suit the material better: 'Everybody Loves My Baby' is taken at an almost menacing slow jog, and Natty Dominique's 'Too Tight' sounds less clockwork at this pace. In any case, the likes of 'Hotter Than That' itself steam along.

The other two records are culled from sessions meant to recreate the style and feel of the sort of tent shows which Ma Rainey and the young Bessie Smith would have toured with, with the various aggregations listed as The Rabbit Foot Hoppers, The Barbary Coasters, The Banjo Papas and so on. Excellent fun, although Carol Leigh's singing may not be to all tastes and not all the pieces succeed as well as they might.

Gerry Hemingway (born 1955)

DRUMS, PERCUSSION

An important collaborator – with Anthony Braxton, Marilyn Crispell and others – and lately a considerable leader, as well as a solo-percussion performer, Hemingway has been a significant part of the mainstream avant-garde in the USA since the late '70s.

***** Acoustic Solo Works**
Random Acoustics RA 016 *Hemingway (perc solo).* 12/83, 7/85, 10/90, 8/93.

***** Electro-Acoustic Solo Works**
Random Acoustics RA 017 *Hemingway (perc, elec solo).* 6/84, 5/90, 4/95.

Gerry Hemingway is still a little weighed down in critical terms by his part in what for a significant number of listeners remains *the* Anthony Braxton group, the 1985 quartet with Marilyn Crispell and Mark Dresser. A lot of water, as Sam Goldwyn used to say, has been passed since then. Hemingway has gone on to assert himself as a fine individual talent with a strong sense of tradition, incidentally revealing in the process, one suspects, that his attunement to Braxton's vibrational philosophy was an act of will rather than of instinct and conviction.

These solo records are a good representation of a drummer and composer whose earliest musical encounters were with rock music, but who quickly saw beyond backbeats and basic fours to a more adventurous rhythm. However, the sheer force and energy of rock remains embedded in all these performances, even when they seem quite rarefied. There is a tremendous consistency of sound material both within and between these discs. Hemingway has always explored restlessly, re-examining aspects of his work in contexts which emphasize time and ritual components, pure sonics and, on occasion, expressive and programmatic elements. 'Dance Of The Sphygmoids' (on the acoustic disc) was included on his debut solo disc, *Tibworks*, and is substantially reworked here, more obviously dance-based, but also more abstract in contour. The two 'Trance Tracks' are intriguing in the light of later developments in breakbeats and drum'n'bass, and Hemingway shows himself to be well ahead of the game on both counts. 'For Buhaina' is a straightforward tribute to Art Blakey, an example of Hemingway the less-is-more kinsman of the great novelist, while on 'Tyrolienne', he uses glockenspiel bars to create an almost vocalized sound, extending the range of the kit enormously.

This is clearly the purpose of the electro-acoustic compositions as well. The earliest of these, 'Waterways', is a fairly conventional piece for tape and percussion. It is only with the work of the 1990s, perhaps influenced by Braxton, that the drummer begins to demonstrate an idiomatic understanding of the power and range of electronic processes. 'Polar' from 1990 and for two simultaneous tapes, is chill and acerbic, but the later 'Chatterlings', which combines live percussion and a Midi-triggered sampler, is much more responsive.

*****(*) Slamadam**
Random Acoustics RA 012 *As above, except add Ernst Reijseger (clo).* 11/91, 2/93, 2/94.

****** Perfect World**
Random Acoustics RA 019 *As above.* 3/95.

The spanking *Slamadam*, which appears on Georg Graewe's ambitious small label, brings together material over quite some time, but the bulk of the recording was done within days of *The Marmalade King*, and it's interesting to hear how different the group sounds in concert, a lot fresher and more immediate and with a fire that the studio discipline seems to bank down and even extinguish. The closing 'Pumbum' was a quartet performance because Reijseger was in hospital with a slipped disc, and if you ever saw the way he waves a cello around ...

He was available for duty again for the quintet's European tour of spring 1995, a vintage spell for Hemingway. The deal with hat ART now seems to be over, but this more casually assembled set (which was fraught with packaging problems) is perhaps the best thing currently available under Hemingway's name. The long 'Little Suite' and 'Perfect World' itself, recorded in England by the BBC, are the key to the record, occupying more than half its length and again suggesting how strong a grasp of large-scale structures Hemingway can call on. The only non-original item is Ellington's 'Village Of The Virgins', a startling inclusion but one that fits the group like a glove.

****** Waltzes, Two-Steps And Other Matters Of The Heart**
GM Recordings Inc GM 3043 *As above.* 11/96.

The Hemingway Quintet toured tirelessly during 1996, at one point playing 27 concerts in a 28-day period. Two of those dates are sampled here. Hemingway has recently taken charge of his own management and distribution, an overload which might have been disastrous had one happenstance not lightened his load. The electronic samples which were to have accompanied the tour were lost when a computer crashed. The mishap threw Hemingway back on the band's internal resources, and *Waltzes* is a superb representation of its improvisational versatility. There are duos and trios, solo spots and areas of near silence as all five ponder decays in the markedly different acoustics of the Berlin Jazz Festival and Fasching in Sweden.

Hemingway had been writing a lot of material in waltz time, though in practice the count is often 7/4 or 9/4 rather than a strict three-quarter. That is acknowledged on the opening 'Waltz In Seven', with its mournful *rubato* opening. The first of the long tracks is the slow, stately 'Gitar', which opens with Hemingway on harmonica, albeit an instrument so oddly pitched that he sounds like a consort of Tibetan Buddhists playing shawms. The main melody could almost be Aaron Copland in a melancholic mood, with Wierbos playing in the lower reaches of his register.

By contrast to the open-form pieces, 'Gospel Waltz' is a relatively straight-ahead blowing piece, though each of the group approaches its changes and melodic form in a quite different way. 'XI' is an arrangement of a madrigal by Gesualdo, further evidence of how tirelessly Hemingway ranges for new inspiration. 'Ari' is a traditional German waltz and an ideal curtain-piece.

Julius Hemphill (1940–95)

ALTO AND SOPRANO SAXOPHONES

No one talks about 'Texas alto' but Hemphill's most obvious kinship is with Ornette Coleman, and yet he is a very different style of composer and the resemblance is somewhat superficial. The complex polyphony of the World Saxophone Quartet, of which he was a founding member, leaches into all his work, which is urgent and thoughtful. Hemphill's early death was a grievous loss.

*****(*) Live In New York**

Red RR 123138 *Hemphill; Abdul Wadud (clo).* 5/76.

***** Blue Boyé**

Screwgun 70008 *Hemphill (sax solo).* 77.

****** Flat-Out Jump Suite**

Black Saint 120040 *Hemphill; Olu Dara (t); Abdul Wadud (clo); Warren Smith (perc).* 6/80.

Hemphill was the chief composer for the World Saxophone Quartet, and his signature style was lean – some said 'raw' when his Texas roots were showing – and often quite drastically pared-down. Seemingly inspired by Dolphy's collaborations with Ron Carter, he favoured cello as an alternative harmony instrument, enjoying a fruitful relationship with Wadud. Like Dolphy, his alto sound was piercing and intensely vocalized, and always locked into very clear musical logics. Hemphill exerted a major influence on the following generation of American musicans – people like Tim Berne especially – and his premature death was a significant loss.

It was Berne who reissued *Blue Boyé* on his own Screwgun label. Not the most successful or satisfying of Hemphill's records, it first appeared on Mbari and doesn't sound any better recorded on transfer to CD. Some of the saxophonist's most idiomatic compositions are included, though: 'Hotend', the Ornettish 'C.M.E.' and 'Homeboy Tootin' At The Dog'.

Initially a more abstract session than Hemphill's later output, the *Flat-Out Jump Suite* builds to a rousing funk climax on 'Body'. Hemphill intones the title to each part as it begins, starting with the soft, percussion-led figures of 'Ear', plunging into the complexities of 'Mind' (which is dominated by Wadud) and then picking up a more continuous rhythm with 'Heart', on which Hemphill begins to string together his light, slightly floating textures into a more continuous, jazz-based improvisation. On the original LP, 'Mind, Part 2' opened the second side with a brief coda to the long central piece. It makes more sense as an integral drum solo, typically understated. It is, until the very end, a remarkably quiet album that requires some concentration. Dara uses his mute a good deal and otherwise plays quite softly. Hemphill seems to play a wooden flute and gives his saxophone a soft-edged quality that is very attractive. An excellent record, easily overlooked.

The duos are not so well recorded, a little too loud and indistinct (certainly not as faithfully rendered, even in the studio, as the 1992 concerts on *Oakland Duets*, covered below), but the long 'Echo 2 (Evening)' offers a clear sense of how Hemphill's ears worked, harmonically speaking. There are moments when his stark lines seem to be light years away from Wadud's chocolatey chords and faster, more rhythmic devices. Then suddenly the whole improvisation clicks into focus as a whole. Ironically, it is these four pieces which, despite the limited personnel, offer the best introduction to Hemphill the composer, even in the context of the most basic personnel. Virtually all the later things, including his 'saxophone opera', *Long Tongues*, and his larger ensemble and big-band projects stem from this.

***** Chile New York**

Black Saint 120146-2 *Hemphill; Warren Smith (vib, mar, perc).* 5/80.

Chile New York was devised as a sound environment for a sculpture and poetry installation by Jeff Schlanger (whose ceramics were to be used for later Hemphill album covers) and James Scully. The inspiration was the overthrow of the democratic Marxist government in Santiago and the subsequent killing of President Salvador Allende and singer Victor Jara. After 20 years, the music stands somewhat apart from its occasion, and one doesn't need to know much about the programme or its setting to appreciate Hemphill's slow, meditative themes which are gathered into three long pieces and three very short ones. Smith is a veteran of the Chicago free scene and he provides the scampering backgrounds, redolent of rat alleys and paper-strewn streets, through which Julius walks, alone and troubled. It's a powerful record, and its posthumous release fills in another corner of the Hemphill story.

****(*) Big Band**

Elektra/Asylum 60831 *Hemphill; David Hines, Rasul Siddik (t); Frank Lacy (t, tb); David Taylor (btb); Vincent Chancey, John Clark (frhn); Marty Ehrlich (ss, as, f); John Purcell, John Stubblefield (ss, ts, f); J.D Parran (bs, f); Bill Frisell, Jack Wilkins (g); Jerome Harris (b); Ronnie Burrage (d); Gordon Gottlieb (perc).* 2/88.

Though the later Sextet had the texture and depth of a big band – and was presumably easier to convene – this is the only real chance to hear how Hemphill's arduous procedures sound at full scale. Coming across this record again after a lapse of time is disillusioning. What had seemed effusive and controlled now sounds chaotic and much too discursive. There are a couple of very strong tracks, notably the closing 'Bordertown', which features Bill Frisell, and the delicately cadenced 'For Billie', but even the shorter tracks soon go the way of 'Drunk On God', which rambles on past the quarter-hour point and shows no sign of reaching any convincing destination. Not an easy record to find now, and recommended only to those already sold on Hemphill's music; better to try one of the later saxophone ensembles.

*****(*) Fat Man And The Hard Blues**
Black Saint 120115 *Hemphill; Marty Ehrlich (as, ss, f); Carl Grubbs (as, ss); James Carter, Andrew White (ts); Sam Furnace (bs, f).* 7/91.

***** Live From The New Music Café**
Music & Arts CD 731 *Hemphill; Abdul Wadud (clo); Joe Bonadio (d, perc).* 9/91.

***** Oakland Duets**
Music & Arts CD 791 *As above, except omit Bonadio.* 11/92.

****** Five Chord Stud**
Black Saint 120140 *Tim Berne, James Carter (as, ts); Marty Ehrlich, Andrew White (ss, as, ts); Fred Ho, Sam Furnace (ss, as, bs).* 11/93.

'The Hard Blues', the last and longest track on Hemphill's first post-WSQ recording, is an old tune which seemed finally to have found its appropriate setting in Hemphill's all-horn groups of the early '90s. The sextets were an obvious extension of his work with the Quartet, with the emphasis on Hemphill's composition and arranging, and on a distinctive variation on conventional theme-and-solo jazz; often the group will improvise round a theme stated quite simply and directly by the 'soloist'.

The same process can even be heard in the duos with Wadud, still going strong after more than a decade. What's different this time around, perhaps reflecting the wider change in Hemphill's self-definition, is that the pieces are shorter and more self-contained, and they obey a more obvious structural logic. Good to have a live version of one of the 'Dogon' pieces. The longest single item, significantly, is Wadud's dull 'Sigure'; Hemphill palpably loses interest, and blares his impatience. Bonadio isn't the most virtuosic drummer, but he's right for this music precisely because he doesn't want to plug every hole, fill every silence with sound.

This has a bearing on the music for the larger, horn groups, which do tend to become rather heavy round the middle. Hemphill avoids extremes of pitch, often building long passages on minor seconds and quasi-microtonal ideas, scoring in such a way that small variations of register and timbre take on considerable significance. That stands out on the sinuous 'Tendrils', one of the more linear themes and written chiefly for the two flautists. The piece actually seems to unravel, in contrast to the melting, blurry quality of most of the other tracks. Unwise to review an album by recourse to its sleeve, but the deceptively liquescent lines of ceramic artist Jeff Schlanger's blue stoneware saxophone suggest something of Hemphill's hard centre. *Fat Man And The Hard Blues* was both an intelligent continuation of the last decade's work and a challenging new departure.

Unfortunately, Hemphill's health subsequently deteriorated to the extent that he was no longer able to perform. There is no error in the personnel detailed for *Five Chord Stud*. Even in his absence as a player – he was recovering from open heart surgery (alas, not successful in the long term) – this is unmistakably Hemphill's group and Hemphill's music. The title-piece is fascinating not least for an apparent lack of interest in textural and timbral variation: two tenor solos, three alto solos, sopranos and baritones reserved for ensembles. There is strong evidence that Hemphill has been listening to Ornette on harmolodics; 'Mr Critical' is a tribute and there are frequent allusions to Ornette themes throughout the session. It isn't absolutely clear whether the composer/conductor is directing the two collective improvisations (in which Ehrlich for one cuts loose) but he certainly puts his stamp very firmly on the rest. As with *Fat Man*, the back cover illustration is a ceramic figure: a saxophone player, languid but compact, dark, atavistic, and absolutely concentrated on his music.

*****(*) At Dr King's Table**
New World 80524 *Hemphill; Marty Ehrlich (ss, as, cl, bcl, f, af); Sam Furnace (as, ts); Andy Laster (as, f); Eugene Ghee, Andrew White (ts); Alex Harding (bs).*

Posthumously released, and a salutary reminder of Hemphill's powers as a composer and performer. *At Dr King's Table* is a sequence of 15 mostly very short tunes, arranged in different configurations, and calling on the full multi-instrumental permutation of the group. At first hearing it sounds like an Anthony Braxton project working in a more than usually settled groove, but within a couple of tracks Hemphill's signature-phrases and use of raw thirds and sevenths begins to come through. 'Holy Rockers' is the only long track, a dense, preachy song. 'Sojourner's Blues: "Ain't I A Woman?"' and 'At Dr King's Table/Ascension' are more condensed but equally powerful. Ehrlich and Hemphill inevitably dominate the foreground, but the supporting players are very much part of the mesh of an album that requires close and careful attention.

Eddie Henderson (born 1940)

TRUMPET, FLUGELHORN

Henderson studied trumpet at the San Francisco Conservatory before embarking on medical studies; he has combined the two disciplines ever since. His sound is typically soft-edged, with a certain emotional rawness and a resistance to cut-and-dried resolutions.

***** Phantoms**
SteepleChase SCCD 31250 *Henderson; Joe Locke (vib); Kenny Barron (p); Wayne Dockery (b); Victor Lewis (d).* 4/89.

***** Think On Me**
SteepleChase SCCD 31264 *As above, except replace Lewis with Billy Hart (d).* 12/89.

Twenty years ago, Eddie Henderson had a pop hit with the disco-influenced 'Comin' Through'. It was just the latest twist in a career which had started with every ambitious parent's nightmare moment, when Henderson – having completed his medical studies – listened to Miles Davis and went off to become a professional musician instead. Actually, Miles was a Henderson house-guest during a residency at the Blackhawk and, while obviously impressed by young Eddie's ability to play through *Sketches Of Spain* without a fluff, pointed out that that was *him*; Eddie was going to have to work out his own approach and voice. That he has certainly done; though his tone and phrasing irresistibly recall Woody Shaw, Henderson is a highly distinctive stylist.

Despite gigs with Miles, Herbie Hancock and Joe Henderson and with his own group, he has remained essentially a part-time player, a fiercely difficult discipline to maintain. After working with Hancock, who is perhaps the most significant single influence after Miles on his general musical conception, Henderson made two records for the Capricorn label. Libra or Gemini might seem to be more likely sources for a player of admirable balance and sympathy.

The association with SteepleChase has been a very fruitful one, not least in throwing him up against another of the label's unsung heroes, Joe Locke. The vibist dominates *Think On Me* with the extraordinary 'Seven Beauties' and with the long opening piece; as so often on his own records, Henderson seems perfectly content to remain in the background, listening, not judging or forcing a conclusion, the disinterest required of the practising psychiatrist. One is always impressed by Henderson's equanimity, which sits well beside Locke's often quite fulsome expressions. Henderson is perhaps a little too detached here and there on *Phantoms*, perhaps because the thrust of the rhythm section is more assertive than seems to suit him.

***(*) Flight Of Mind

SteepleChase SCCD 31284 *Henderson; Larry Willis (p); Ed Howard (b); Victor Lewis (d).* 1/91.

Equanimity and emotional balance of an almost superhuman sort must have been required to record *Flight Of Mind*, which followed very soon after the death of Henderson's son. Whatever else, it brings a fragile grace and philosophical calm to a set which includes a performance of Freddie Hubbard's 'Lament For Booker' (covered later on *Dark Shadows*) and a magnificent interpretation of 'Un bel dì vedremo' from *Madama Butterfly*, a solo worthy of Miles himself. There is no overblown emotion, no grandstanding, just simple and direct statement. Locke would have been wrong for this particular session; fine as he always is, this needed something different.

*** Inspiration

Milestone MCD 9240 *Henderson; Grover Washington Jr (ss); Joe Locke (vib); Kevin Hays (p); Ed Howard (b); Lewis Nash (d).* 7/94.

Vivid, emotive playing apart, Locke's other contribution to this slightly patchy but thoroughly accomplished session was to bring in the Bobby Hutcherson composition, 'Little B's Poem', which, though treated somewhat briefly, is one of the high points of the record. Otherwise the choice of material is fairly routine, even rather conventional, with 'On Green Dolphin Street', 'Surrey With The Fringe On Top' and 'When You Wish Upon A Star' all played in a rather perfunctory way. Henderson's seeming preference for putting the main piece at the centre of the album on this occasion dictates a pairing of another Hancock masterpiece, 'Oliloqui Valley' (a guest slot for Washington), with a re-run of Kenny Barron's 'Phantoms'. Washington also figures, rather less successfully, on 'I Remember Clifford', a tune that doesn't seem quite tailor-made for Henderson, but to which he brings quiet counsels of his own.

***(*) Dark Shadows

Milestone MCD 9254 *Henderson; Joe Locke (vib); George Colligan, Kevin Hays (p); Ed Howard (b); Billy Hart, Lewis Nash (d); Steve Berrios (perc); Lee Menzies (v).* 9/95.

Another Henderson family connection – and a happier one this time – attaches to this album. During the making of the record, Henderson's daughter Lee Menzies turned up unexpectedly after not seeing her old man for 15 years. It was decided on the spot that they would record the spiritual 'The Water Is Wide', which she knew from her vocal arts course. The result is a thing of delicate, almost glassy beauty, bringing to a close an album that manages to combine pain with a redemptive purity of expression.

Henderson has never sounded more like Woody Shaw, and the interplay of trumpet and vibes here unshakeably recalls Shaw's work with Bobby Hutcherson. The centrepieces of the disc are Gordon Jenkins's relatively little-known 'Goodbye' (which had also featured so poignantly on *Flight Of Mind*), followed by Locke's glorious 'Cerulean Blue', on which Hays switches to Fender Rhodes, and then the big Henderson statement. 'Dark Shadows' is one of the finest things he has ever written, rhythmically and thematically complex, and calling on a second drummer in the shape of Billy Hart. Its juxtaposition with namesake Joe Henderson's 'Punjab' is a brilliant piece of programming. The closing sequence begins with a new and reconciled version of 'Lament For Booker', continues with Locke's gloriously optimistic 'Dawning Dance' and then ends with the spiritual. Hugely satisfying and creating a sense of closure that has been present only sporadically in Henderson's work since *Flight Of Mind*. Something laid to rest, perhaps? Countermagic against those very shadows?

**** ReEmergence

Sharp Nine Records CD 1012-2 *Henderson; Kevin Hays (p); Joe Locke (vib); Ed Howard (b); Billy Drummond (d).* 3/98.

Dominated by the long and graceful 'Gershwin Suite', this is a triumphant record, a near-perfect articulation of Henderson's skills not just as a trumpet player but also as a bandleader. One of his great gifts is to allow his players to complete the process of creation by leaving themes, notably his own composition 'Dreams', open-ended and only loosely arranged, so that performance actually completes the process of composition and arrangement.

This time around, there are only a couple of Henderson originals in the set, which ends with the brief 'Natsuko-san', played straight and without solos, a simple message of love to his wife. Joe Locke is, as ever, a key element and he brings the epic sweep of 'Saturn's Child' to the date, a wonderful theme that would work for anything from solo piano to full symphony.

The Gershwin material is pitched just right for Henderson: clever, warm, life-aware and sardonic without a hint of cynicism. 'Summertime' needs something a bit special these days, and the trumpeter gives it a soaring presence that blows the clichés away. 'Embraceable You' is equally good at the end of the sequence, expressive but highly disciplined, not quite a politically correct hug, perhaps more a fraternal one. Everything on the album, from the opening 'This Is For Albert' (a Wayne Shorter theme) to the close, seems to be in exactly the right place and pitched dead on. A great place to make the acquaintance of Eddie Henderson if you haven't already.

Fletcher Henderson (1897–1952)

PIANO, BANDLEADER

Born in Georgia, Henderson arrived in New York in 1920, seeking scientific work but ending up as an A&R man in the fledgling black record industry. He played piano behind many blues singers and began leading an orchestra at the Roseland Ballroom, filling it with the best players he could find, including Louis Armstrong and Coleman Hawkins. It was the top band of its day, but a car crash in 1928 seemed to dissipate Henderson's interest and thereafter the orchestra went into a slow decline. He was a good arranger whose scores for Benny Goodman in the '30s helped the clarinettist establish his eminence. He still ran bands and small groups in the '40s, but a stroke in 1950 effectively finished him.

****(*) Fletcher Henderson 1921–1923**
Classics 794 *Henderson; Elmer Chambers, Russell Smith, Joe Smith (c); George Brashear (tb); William Grant Still, Edgar Campbell, Ernest Elliott, Don Redman, Billy Fowler (reeds); Leroy Vanderveer, Charlie Dixon (bj); plus various unknowns.* 6/21–6/23.

***** Fletcher Henderson 1923**
Classics 697 *Henderson; Elmer Chambers, Howard Scott (c); Teddy Nixon (tb); Don Redman (cl, as); Coleman Hawkins (ts, bsx, cl); Billy Fowler (bsx); Allie Ross (vn); Charlie Dixon (bj); Ralph Escudero (bb); Kaiser Marshall (d).* 6/23–4/24.

***** Fletcher Henderson 1923–1924**
Classics 683 *As above, except omit Ross.* 12/23–2/24.

***** Fletcher Henderson 1924**
Classics 673 *As above.* 2–5/24.

****(*) Fletcher Henderson 1924 Vol. 2**
Classics 657 *As above, except add Charlie Green (tb), Lonnie Brown (as), Rosa (v).* 5–8/24.

***** Fletcher Henderson 1924 Vol. 3**
Classics 647 *As above, except add Louis Armstrong (c, v), Buster Bailey (cl, as); omit Nixon, Brown, Rosa Henderson.* 9–11/24.

***** Fletcher Henderson 1924–1925**
Classics 633 *Henderson; Louis Armstrong, Elmer Chambers, Howard Scott, Joe Smith, Russell Smith (t, c); Charlie Green (tb); Don Redman (cl, as, v); Buster Bailey (cl, as); Coleman Hawkins (cl, Cmel, ts, bsx); Charlie Dixon (bj); Ralph Escudero (bb); Kaiser Marshall (d); Billy Jones (v).* 11/24–11/25.

****** The Complete Louis Armstrong With Fletcher Henderson**
Forte F38001/2/3 3CD *As above.* 24–25.

Henderson drifted into both music and bandleading after casually working for the Black Swan record label, and his first records as a leader are frequently no more than routine dance music. The arrival of Louis Armstrong – whom Henderson first heard in New Orleans at the turn of the decade – apparently galvanized everyone in the band and, eventually, every musician in New York. But it's hard to make assumptions about Henderson's band. He already had Don Redman and Coleman Hawkins working for him prior to Armstrong's arrival, and there are too many good records prior to Louis's first session of October 1924 to dismiss the group as jazz ignoramuses. The sequence of Classics CDs has now been expanded into a complete run of Henderson's recordings (though there remain a number of blues accompaniments yet to find their way to CD). These were skilful if not particularly outward-looking musicians, and even as early as 1923 – on 'Shake Your Feet' or '31st Street Blues' – there are fragments of solos which work out. The very first disc in the sequence is of no more than historical interest: only at the very end does the band begin to stir into life beyond the most ordinary dance music, though there are three interesting early solos by Henderson himself. Classics 697 includes Coleman Hawkins's first session, where he played what's an extraordinary solo for 1923 on the Vocalion version of 'Dirty Blues'. The next three CDs are inevitably mixed affairs: Henderson cut some songs in a completely straight manner, barely allowing the musicians any leeway, and he let them have their head on others. From session to session, though, there is usually something of interest. The weakest disc is probably Classics 657, which includes a preponderance of dull tracks – although even here there is Redman's interesting chart for 'The Gouge Of Armour Avenue', which features Green's rasping trombone, and two good versions of 'Hard Hearted Hannah'. Classics 647 goes up several gears with Armstrong's arrival and, while he doesn't exactly dominate, the music always catches fire when he takes a solo, even on an early piece like the Pathé version of 'Shanghai Shuffle'. He is present on most of Classics 633 and, luckily, gets a solo on most of the tracks. His cornet improvisations – often set against Marshall hitting the off-beat to heighten the dramatic effect – are breathtaking, especially on what would otherwise be dreary tunes, such as 'I'll See You In My Dreams' or the amazing 'I Miss My Swiss', where he electrifies the whole band. But some of the other musicians were getting into their stride, too: Redman delivers some strong early arrangements, Hawkins and Bailey sneak through some breaks, and the best of the material – 'TNT', 'Money Blues', 'Carolina Stomp' and, above all, their hit version of 'Sugar Foot Stomp' – lets the best black band in New York play to their strengths.

Transfer quality is unfortunately often indifferent. Classics appear to have opted for a variety of sources and, while the original 78s differ strikingly in terms of their sound from label to label, the remastering is often less than ideal: the Vocalion originals sound a touch too heavy in the bass, and a comparison between the Classics Pathé tracks and those on Fountain's *The Henderson Pathés* (listed in our first edition but now out of print) shows a cleaner, lighter sound on the LP version. Classics, though, offer the only edition of many of the earlier tracks, which scholars should welcome.

For Henderson with Armstrong, the clear winner is the Forte three-disc collection: the 65 tracks include all known original and alternative takes, and the remastering by John R.T. Davies is of the very best.

***** Fletcher Henderson 1925–1926**
Classics 610 *As above, except Rex Stewart (c) replaces Armstrong, Scott and Chambers.* 11/25–4/26.

*****(*) Fletcher Henderson 1926–1927**

Classics 597 *As above, except add Tommy Ladnier (t), Jimmy Harrison (tb), Fats Waller (p, org), June Cole (bb, v), Evelyn Thompson (v).* 4/26–1/27.

*****(*) Fletcher Henderson 1927**

Classics 580 *As above, except add Jerome Pasquall (cl, as); omit Escudero, Thompson.* 1–5/27.

*****(*) Fletcher Henderson 1927–1931**

Classics 572 *Henderson; Bobby Stark, Tommy Ladnier, Russell Smith, Rex Stewart, Cootie Williams (t, c); Jimmy Harrison (tb, v); Charlie Green, Claude Jones, Benny Morton (tb); Jerome Pasquall, Benny Carter, Harvey Boone (cl, as); Coleman Hawkins (cl, ts); Charlie Dixon, Clarence Holiday (bj, g); John Kirby, June Cole (bb, b); Kaiser Marshall, Walter Thompson (d); Lois Deppe, Andy Razaf (v).* 11/27–2/31.

By the mid-1920s Henderson was leading the most consistently interesting big band on record. That doesn't mean all the records are of equal calibre, and the title of a famous earlier retrospective of Henderson's work – 'A Study In Frustration' – gives some idea of the inconsistencies and problems of a band that failed to secure any hit records and never sounded on record the way it could in person (at least, according to many witnesses). But Henderson's best records are classics of the period. Don Redman was coming into his own, and his scores assumed a quality which no other orchestral arranger was matching in 1926–7 (though it is tantalizing to ponder what Jelly Roll Morton could have done with the same band): 'The Stampede', 'The Chant', 'Henderson Stomp', the remarkable 'Tozo' and, above all, the truly astonishing 'Whiteman Stomp' find him using the colours of reeds and brass to complex yet swinging ends. Luckily Henderson had the players who could make the scores happen: though Armstrong had departed, Hawkins, Ladnier, Joe Smith, Jimmy Harrison and Buster Bailey all had the stature of major soloists as well as good section-players. The brass sections were, indeed, the best any band in New York could boast – the softer focus of Smith contrasting with the bluesy attack of Ladnier, the rasp of Rex Stewart, the lithe lines of Harrison – and any group with Hawkins (who was loyal enough to stay for ten years) had the man who created jazz saxophone. Henderson's own playing was capable rather than outstanding, and the rhythm section lumbered a bit, though string bass and guitar lightened up the feel from 1928 onwards. It took Henderson many records to attain a real consistency: in 1925 he was still making sides like 'Pensacola' (for Columbia), which starts with a duet between Hawkins and Redman on bass sax and goofus! But there weren't many vocals, and this let the band drive through their three-minute allocation without interruption and, if Henderson never figured out the best use of that time-span (unlike Ellington, who grew to be his most serious rival among New York's black bands), his team of players made sure that something interesting happens on almost every record.

The Classics CDs offer chronological surveys which Henderson specialists will welcome, although no alternative takes are included (there are actually relatively few in existence). We would single out the 1926–7 and 1927 discs as the most important, but there are so many fine moments scattered through even second-rate pieces that any who sample the series may well find that they want them all. Remastering is again variable: the tracks made under the name 'The Dixie Stompers' were made for Harmony, which continued to use acoustic recording even after most other companies had switched over to the electric process in 1925, and some may find these tracks a little archaic in timbre. Mostly, we find that the transfers are acceptable, though they don't measure up to the relentlessly high standards of John R.T. Davies, whose JSP compilation is currently out of print. The 1927–31 disc marks the departure of Redman, the first steps by Henderson himself as arranger, guest appearances by Fats Waller (who reportedly gave Henderson a dozen tunes in trade for a plate of hamburgers at a Harlem eaterie) and Benny Carter, and the arrival of the fine and undervalued trumpeter, Bobby Stark, whose solos on 'Blazin'' and 'Sweet And Hot' find a lyrical streak somewhere between Joe Smith and Rex Stewart. But the band was already in decline, especially following Henderson's car accident in 1928, after which he was never the same man. They cut only three record dates in 1929 and three in 1930 (compared with 17 in 1927).

***** Fletcher Henderson 1931**

Classics 555 *As above, except add Sandy Williams (tb), Russell Procope (cl, as), Edgar Sampson (cl, as, vn), Horace Henderson (p); George Bias, Dick Robertson (v); omit Ladnier, Green, Pasquall, Dixon, Cole, Marshall, Deppe, Razaf.* 2–7/31.

****(*) Fletcher Henderson 1931–1932**

Classics 546 *Henderson; Russell Smith, Bobby Stark (t); Rex Stewart (c); Sandy Williams, J.C Higginbotham (tb); Russell Procope (cl, ss, as); Edgar Sampson (cl, as, vn); Coleman Hawkins (cl, ts); Clarence Holiday, Ikey Robinson (bj, g); John Kirby (bb, b); Walter Johnson (d); John Dickens, Harlan Lattimore, Baby Rose Marie, Les Reis, Dick Robertson (v).* 7/31–3/32.

*****(*) Fletcher Henderson 1932–1934**

Classics 535 *As above, except add Henry 'Red' Allen, Joe Thomas, Irving Randolph (t), Keg Johnson, Claude Jones, Dicky Wells (tb), Buster Bailey (cl), Hilton Jefferson (cl, as), Ben Webster (ts), Horace Henderson (p), Bernard Addison, Lawrence Lucie (g), Elmer James (b), Vic Engle (d), Charles Holland (v); omit Robinson, Holiday, Lattimore, Marie, Reis and Robertson.* 12/32–9/34.

***** Fletcher Henderson 1934–1937**

Classics 527 *Henderson; Russell Smith, Irving Randolph, Henry 'Red' Allen, Dick Vance, Roy Eldridge, Joe Thomas, Emmett Berry (t); Ed Cuffee (tb, v); Keg Johnson, Claude Jones, Fernando Arbello, George Washington, J.C Higginbotham (tb); Omer Simeon (cl, as, bs); Jerry Blake (cl, as, v); Buster Bailey, Hilton Jefferson, Russell Procope, Jerome Pasquall (cl, as); Benny Carter, Scoops Carey (as); Ben Webster, Elmer Williams, Chu Berry (ts); Horace Henderson (p); Bob Lessey, Lawrence Lucie (g); Elmer James, John Kirby, Israel Crosby (b); Walter Johnson, Big Sid Catlett (d); Teddy Lewis, Georgia Boy Simpkins, Dorothy Derrick (v).* 9/34–3/37.

****(*) Under The Harlem Moon**

ASV 5067 *As above two discs.* 12/32–6/37.

**** Fletcher Henderson 1937–1938**

Classics 519 *Henderson; Russell Smith, Emmett Berry, Dick Vance (t); George Washington, Ed Cuffee, Milt Robinson, George Hunt, J.C Higginbotham, Albert Wynn, John McConnell (tb); Jerry Blake (cl, as, v); Eddie Barefield (cl, as); Hilton Jefferson (as); Chu Berry, Elmer Williams, Ben Webster (ts); Lawrence Lucie (g); Israel Crosby (b); Walter Johnson, Cozy Cole, Pete Suggs (d); Chuck Richards (v).* 3/37–5/38.

Henderson's music was already in decline when the 1930s began, and by the end of the decade – as illustrated on the rather sad final disc in the Classics sequence – the orchestra was a shadow of what it had been in its glory days. Ironically, it was Henderson's own work as an arranger in this period which set off the swing era, via the charts he did for Benny Goodman. The 1931 and 1931–2 discs offer sometimes bewildering juxtapositions of corn (Henderson employed some excruciating singers at this time) and real jazz: the extraordinary 'Strangers', on Classics 546, includes an amazing Coleman Hawkins solo in the middle of an otherwise feeble record, while some of the tunes which the Hendersonians might have been expected to handle well – 'Casa Loma Stomp' (Classics 546) and 'Radio Rhythm' (Classics 555) – turn out poorly. Yet the band was still full of fine ensemble players and soloists alike, and some of the Horace Henderson arrangements from this time – especially 'Queer Notions', 'Yeah Man' and 'Wrappin' It Up' (all on Classics 535) – are as well managed as any band of the period could do. Besides, while players of the calibre of Hawkins, Allen and (subsequently) Webster, Berry and Eldridge were on hand, there can't help but be fine moments on many of the records. Classics 535 is certainly the pick of these later discs, with a dozen excellent tracks included. Classics 527 and 519, which were recorded mainly after Henderson temporarily disbanded for a while in 1934 and worked with Goodman, show the vitality of the band sagging, and the final dozen sides they made might have been done by any competent dance orchestra (as a postscript, there are four nondescript 1941 tracks which wind up the Horace Henderson disc listed below). Transfers are usually reasonably good and clear, although as usual it's the later discs that sound cleaner and less prone to track-to-track fluctuations in quality. The ASV disc compiles 23 of the better tracks from the 1932–7 period, but the sound appears muddier than on the Classics issues.

***** Fletcher Henderson & His Orchestra**
Topaz TPZ 1004 *As appropriate discs above.* 4/27–8/36.

****** A Study In Frustration: The Fletcher Henderson Story**
Columbia 57596 3CD *As appropriate discs above.* 8/23–5/38.

The Topaz compilation is a sensible if sometimes arbitrary compilation of Henderson's later material, concentrating on the 1930s and missing out on most of his best early work. The remastering is respectable if rather bass-heavy. The reappearance of the famous Columbia set, though, is to be welcomed. Originally a four-LP set, it's been smartly remastered across three CDs. It misses very few of the best Henderson tracks from the crucial mid- to late-1920s period, and the choice of Vocalion sides from the 1930s is never less than sound. Remastering is consistently clean and clear, and the packaging is splendid.

Horace Henderson (1904–88)

PIANO

Fletcher's brother never had a career of the same stature but he was a gifted pianist and a fine arranger. He was still working as a musician in Denver in the late 1960s.

****** Horace Henderson 1940**
Classics 648 *Henderson; Emmett Berry, Harry 'Pee Wee' Jackson, Gail Brockman, Nat Bates (t); Harold 'Money' Johnson (t, v); Ray Nance (t, vn); Edward Fant, Nat Atkins, Joe McLewis, Leo Williams, Archie Brown (tb); Delbert Bright (cl, as); Willie Randall, Howard Johnson, Charles Q Price (as); Elmer Williams, Dave Young, Mosey Gant, Bob Dorsey, Lee Pope (ts); Leonard Talley (bs); Hurley Ramey, Leroy Harris (g); Jesse Simpkins, Israel Crosby (b); Oliver Coleman, Debo Williams (d); Viola Jefferson (v).* 2–10/40.

'One of the most talented yet most neglected and enigmatic figures in all of jazz' – Gunther Schuller's verdict on Horace Henderson sounds over-enthusiastic, but the 1940 tracks collected on this important CD go a long way towards bearing out his verdict. Fletcher's brother was a fine, Hines-like pianist, but it was his arranging that was outstanding: the 16 themes collected here include charts by both brothers, and the contrasts between Fletcher's stylized call-and-response figures and the fluid, overlapping ideas of Horace are remarkable. Horace's band was full of fine soloists who received sometimes unprecedented space: Nance has two full choruses of violin on the engaging 'Kitty On Toast' and Berry is generously featured throughout: his 'Ain't Misbehavin'' melody is beautifully sustained. But it's the section-work, the saxes full and rich, the brass outstandingly punchy, which brings complex charts to life: 'Shufflin' Joe', the very first track here, is a little masterpiece of varied dynamics and interwoven tone-colours. The rhythm players – including the young Israel Crosby on some of the later sides – are as good as their colleagues. This Classics CD displaces the Tax LP listed in our last edition, and though the sound is, as so often with discs from this source, a little inconsistent, the CD remains a very good buy. There are four tracks by the 1941 Fletcher Henderson band tagged on at the end, but these are a somewhat doubtful bonus.

Joe Henderson (born 1937)

TENOR AND SOPRANO SAXOPHONES

Born in Lima, Ohio, Henderson arrived in New York in 1962 a fully formed stylist. He had stints with Horace Silver, Freddie Hubbard and Herbie Hancock before a brief but high-profile stay with Blood, Sweat And Tears. He moved to San Francisco in the '70s and made a string of albums for Milestone, before re-emerging in the mid-'80s, first on Blue Note and then with a sequence of acclaimed and best-selling albums for Verve. He is acknowledged as one of the last great tenormen to emerge from the original hard-bop generation.

****** Page One**
Blue Note 98795 *Henderson; Kenny Dorham (t); McCoy Tyner (p); Butch Warren (b); Pete La Roca (d).* 6/63.

Joe Henderson has become one of the surviving jazz icons, and as a consequence his back pages have been extensively released on CD. He's a thematic player, working his way round the structure of a composition with methodical intensity, but he's also a masterful licks player, with a seemingly limitless stock of phrases that he can turn to the advantage of any post-bop setting: this gives his best improvisations a balance of surprise, immediacy and coherence few other saxophonists can match. His lovely tone, which combines softness and plangency in a similar way, is another pleasing aspect of his music. *Page One* was his first date as a leader, and it still stands as one of the most popular Blue Notes of the early 1960s. Henderson had not long since arrived in New York after being discharged from the army, and this six-theme set is very much the work of a new star on the scene. 'Recorda-Me', whose Latinate lilt has made it a staple blowing-vehicle for hard-bop bands, had its debut here, and the very fine tenor solo on Dorham's 'Blue Bossa' explains much of why Henderson was creating excitement. But everything here, even the throwaway blues, 'Homestretch', is impressively handled. Tyner, Warren and La Roca are a rhythm section who seldom played together but they do very well here, as does the erratic Dorham. The new Rudy Van Gelder Edition brings even more weight and power to the music.

*****(*) In 'N Out**

Blue Note 29156 *Henderson; Kenny Dorham (t); McCoy Tyner (p); Richard Davis (b); Elvin Jones (d).* 4/64.

****** Inner Urge**

Blue Note 84189 *Henderson; McCoy Tyner (p); Bob Cranshaw (b); Elvin Jones (d).* 11/64.

*****(*) Mode For Joe**

Blue Note 84227 *Henderson; Lee Morgan (t); Curtis Fuller (tb); Bobby Hutcherson (vib, mar); Cedar Walton (p); Ron Carter (b); Louis Hayes, Joe Chambers (d).* 1/66.

Inner Urge, which features Henderson as sole horn, is dark and intense music. The title-tune, commemorating Henderson's experiences of trying to make a living in New York, is a blistering effort at a medium tempo, and it's interesting to compare Tyner and Jones as they are with Henderson rather than with Coltrane. While the atmosphere isn't as teeth-grittingly intense, it's scarcely less visceral music. Even the sunny reading of 'Night And Day' musters a terrific urgency via Jones's continuously glittering cymbals.

Mode For Joe plants Henderson in a bigger environment, and at times he sounds to be forcing his way out: the solos on the title-track and 'A Shade Of Jade' make a baroque contrast with the otherwise tempered surroundings. Chambers drums with pile-driving intensity in places and, though the large number of players tends to constrict the soloists at a time when Henderson could handle all the stretching out he was given, it's still a fine record.

The earlier *In 'N Out* is a welcome restoration. Henderson's three tunes are the standout pieces, the quizzical title-track, the haunting theme of 'Punjab', the charming 'Serenity'. Dorham seems to be thinking through his solos rather than punching them out and, while in general the temperature seems rather lower than on Henderson's other Blue Notes, it's fascinating music.

***** Four!**

Verve 523657-2 *Henderson; Wynton Kelly (p); Paul Chambers (b); Jimmy Cobb (d).* 4/68.

***** Straight No Chaser**

Verve 531561-2 *As above.* 4/68.

A historical curiosity, brought to life courtesy of Henderson himself. He played these sets with the old Miles Davis rhythm section at an unrehearsed show at Baltimore's Left Bank. The sound is sometimes muddy, without much top end, but listenable. The quartet work through six themes on *Four!* with a mix of intensity and doggedness which leaves the music a bit colourless at times, yet the feeling of three old masters in conversation with a younger one comes through, and it's interesting to hear Henderson on standard material which he otherwise never plays. *Straight No Chaser* is a second helping from the same source, and with similar results.

***** The Milestone Years**

Milestone 4413-2 8CD *Henderson; Mike Lawrence, Woody Shaw, Oscar Brashear (t); Grachan Moncur III, Julian Priester, Curtis Fuller (tb); Jeremy Steig, Ernie Watts (f); Haldey Caliman (ts, f); Lee Konitz (as); Kenny Barron, Don Friedman, Joe Zawinul, Mark Levine, Joachim Kühn, Herbie Hancock, George Cables, Hideo Ichikawa, George Duke, Alice Coltrane, Patrick Gleason (ky); Michael White (vn); George Wadenius, James Blood Ulmer, Lee Ritenour (g); Ron Carter, Victor Gaskin, Stanley Clarke, Kunimitsu Inaba, Dave Holland, Charlie Haden, Jean-François Jenny-Clark, David Friesen, Alphonso Johnson (b); Louis Hayes, Jack DeJohnette, Roy McCurdy, Lenny White, Motohiko Hino, Leon Ndugu Chancler, Daniel Humair, Harvey Mason (d); Airto Moreira, Carmelo Garcia, Bill Summers (perc); Flora Purim (v).* 67–76.

While there are many rewarding things in this exhaustive collection of Henderson's work for the Milestone operation, it's finally let down by the indifferent calibre of the early 1970s sessions which he made for the label. Sessions such as *If You're Not Part Of The Solution*, *Live At The Lighthouse* and *In Japan* find him in sharp, creative form, adapting to rhythm sections that remained rooted in hard bop but which fed in the kind of groove playing that would lead to jazz-rock. Later sets like *Canyon Lady* find Joe fighting a losing battle with his backings, and the final set, *Black Miracle*, is close to disaster. Henderson fanatics will want this, and the packaging and annotation are exemplary, but there is too much driftwood to elicit a general recommendation. The discs listed below will be useful samplers of this period for most.

****(*) The Kicker**

Original Jazz Classics OJC 465 *Henderson; Mike Lawrence (t); Grachan Moncur III (tb); Kenny Barron (p); Ron Carter (b); Louis Hayes (d).* 8/67.

*****(*) Tetragon / In Pursuit Of Blackness**

BGP CDBGPD 084 *Henderson; Woody Shaw (t, flhn); Curtis Fuller (tb); Pete Yellin (as, f, bcl); Kenny Barron, Don Friedman, George Cables (p); Ron Carter, Ron McClure, Stanley Clarke (b); Louis Hayes, Jack DeJohnette, Lenny White (d).* 9/67–5/71.

***** Multiple**

Original Jazz Classics OJC 776 *Henderson; Larry Willis (ky); James Blood Ulmer, John Thomas (g); Dave Holland (b); Jack DeJohnette (d); Arthur Jenkins (perc).* 1/73.

****(*) The Elements**

Original Jazz Classics OJC 913 *Henderson; Alice Coltrane (p, hp, harmonium, tamboura); Michael White (vn); Charlie Haden (b); Leon Ndugu Chancler (d); Baba Duru Oshun (perc); Kenneth Nash (perc, v).* 10/73.

****(*) Canyon Lady**

Original Jazz Classics OJC 949 *Henderson; Oscar Brashear, John Hunt, Lou Gasca (t); Julian Priester, Nicholas Ten Broeck (tb); Hadley Caliman (ts, f); Ray Pizzi, Vincent Dengham (f); George Duke, Mark Levine (p); John Levine (b); Eric Gravatt (d); Carmelo Garcia, Victor Pantoja, Francisco Aguabella (perc).* 10/73.

A disheartening step after the Blue Note albums, *The Kicker*, Henderson's debut for Milestone, is respectable but prosaic stuff, with Lawrence and Moncur adding little of interest and the tracks sounding short and 'produced'. BGP's coupling of two later albums on a single CD is a much better choice: the sessions for *Tetragon* offer some very hard-edged playing by the leader, with a riveting dissection of 'Invitation', and the four Henderson originals from the *Blackness* date are blown open over polyrhythmic bases that the horns meet head-on. The sound and feel are sometimes a little more dated than the straight tenor-and-rhythm tracks – Cables uses a tinkly electric piano, and there are elements of fashionable freak-out in some of the ensembles – but it's a valuable CD. *Multiple* is another that has worn less well: Henderson doubles on soprano, flute and percussion (and even does some chanting), Willis plays electric keyboards, and the guitarists strum to no great purpose; yet the saxophonist still earns the stars for the surprising tenor solos. *Tetragon* is also now available by itself on Original Jazz Classics OJC 844.

The Elements presses Henderson into the kind of role John Coltrane might have taken up, had he lived, with a world-music feel swirling around Alice Coltrane's exotic settings. *Canyon Lady* is more Latinized, with Henderson asked to be the soloist on some light, sweet arrangements in the idiom. The problem with both situations is that, as gamely as he responds, this was hardly useful employment for one of the premier jazz improvisers in what should have been one of his greatest periods.

****(*) Barcelona**

Enja 3037-2 *Henderson; Wayne Darling (b); Ed Soph (d).* 6/77–11/78.

Not bad – but, for Henderson, this is notably second-rate. The main piece is the title-cut, recorded live, and it presents a chance to hear him in the trio format he's favoured of late; there is some typically magisterial playing, but Darling and Soph can't centre the music the way the saxophonist's current groups can. Two brief studio pieces beef up the playing time.

*****(*) Relaxin' At Camarillo**

Original Jazz Classics OJC 776 *Henderson; Chick Corea (p); Tony Dumas, Richard Davis (b); Peter Erskine, Tony Williams (d).* 8–12/79.

*****(*) Mirror, Mirror**

MPS 519092-2 *Henderson; Chick Corea (p); Ron Carter (b); Billy Higgins (d).* 1/80.

Henderson and Corea made an improbable but productive team: Joe's doggedly unpredictable lines asked the pianist to concentrate, and a fundamentally lyrical bent is something they both share, even if Corea usually oversweetens his playing. The OJC reissue just has the edge for a long, firmly sustained treatment of 'Y Todavia La Quiero', one of the best of Henderson's Latin tunes – but there is excellent jazz on both discs.

****** The State Of The Tenor Volumes One And Two**

Blue Note 828779-2 2CD *Henderson; Ron Carter (b); Al Foster (d).* 11/85.

Although they had a mixed reception on their release, these records now sound as authoritative as their titles suggest. Henderson hadn't recorded as a leader for some time, and this was his return to the label where he commenced his career, but there is nothing hesitant or routine about the playing here. Carter and Foster provide detailed support – the dates were carefully prepared, the themes meticulously chosen and rehearsed, before the recordings were made at New York's Village Vanguard – and the bassist in particular is as inventive as the nominal leader. Henderson takes an occasional wrong turning, noted perhaps in a recourse to a favourite lick or two, but he functions mainly at the highest level. The intelligent choice of themes – from Silver, Monk, Mingus, Parker and others, none of them over-familiar – prises a rare multiplicity of phrase-shapes and rhythmical variations out of the tenorman: as a single instance, listen to his manipulations of the beat on Mingus's 'Portrait' (on *Volume Two*), with their accompanying subtleties of tone and attack. Both discs have now been coupled as a mid-price two-disc set.

***** An Evening With Joe Henderson**

Red 123215-2 *Henderson; Charlie Haden (b); Al Foster (d).* 7/87.

More of the same, with Haden substituting for Carter and the four longish tracks opening out a little further. The music isn't as comprehensively prepared, and Haden's flatter sound and less flexible rhythms make him no match for Carter; but Henderson himself plays with majestic power. Decent concert recording, from the Genoa Jazz Festival of 1987.

*****(*) The Standard Joe**

Red RR 123248-2 *Henderson; Rufus Reid (b); Al Foster (d).* 3/91.

*****(*) Lush Life**

Verve 511779-2 *Henderson; Wynton Marsalis (t); Stephen Scott (p); Christian McBride (b); Gregory Hutchinson (d).*

There is very little to choose between the two 1991 recordings, though they're very different from each other. The trio session for Red is an off-the-cuff blowing date, but it's obvious from the first measures of 'Blue Bossa' that all three players are in peak form, and the matching sonorities of Reid and Henderson create a startlingly close level of empathy. There is almost 70 minutes of music, including two long but quite different takes of 'Body And Soul', and the invention never flags. *Lush Life* is a programme of Billy Strayhorn compositions done as one solo ('Lush Life'), three duos (one with each member of the rhythm section), a lovely quartet reading of 'Blood Count' and three pieces with Marsalis joining the front line, of which 'Johnny Come Lately' is especially spirited. If Henderson's delivery sounds a fraction less assured than he does at his best, the quality of his thinking is as outstanding as always and, though there is the odd tiny blemish – Scott's treatment of 'Lotus Blossom' seems too irritatingly clever – it's a splendid record.

****** So Near, So Far (Musings For Miles)**

Verve 517674-2 *Henderson; John Scofield (g); Dave Holland (b); Al Foster (d).* 10/92.

Great music. Henderson's virtual rebirth continued with a tribute to Miles Davis from four former sidemen (Henderson played with Davis briefly in the mid-'60s) that stands as a masterclass of top-flight improvising. Impeccably prepared charts for the likes of 'Miles Ahead', boiled down from the original Gil Evans arrangement to a setting for four-piece, directed the players to a particularly acute yet heartfelt memorial. Many of the tunes associated with Davis as composer have scarcely been covered by other players, which adds a note of unusual freshness, but the scope and calibre of the improvising by all four men is what one remembers. Scofield's runs of melody are a match for Henderson's own, and Holland and Foster – the latter in some of his finest playing – are a dream team.

***** Double Rainbow**

Verve 527222-2 *Henderson; Eliane Elias, Herbie Hancock (p); Oscar Castro-Neves (g); Christian McBride, Nico Assumpção (b); Paul Braga, Jack DeJohnette (d).* 95.

Though conceived as a collaboration with Antonio Carlos Jobim, this turned out to be a memorial to the composer after his death, a dozen tunes shared between one Brazilian and one all-American rhythm section. Everybody plays well and Henderson sounds supremely relaxed, but sometimes one longs for a really outstanding solo or for something to intrude on the general sunniness of the music: lush, charming, this is essentially high-calibre light-jazz.

*****(*) Shade Of Jade: Joe Henderson Big Band**

Verve 533451-2 *Henderson; Lew Soloff, Marcus Belgrave, Freddie Hubbard, Idrees Sulieman, Jimmy Owens, Jon Faddis, Virgil Jones, Nicholas Payton, Byron Stirling (t); Robin Eubanks, Jimmy Knepper, Kiane Zawadi, Douglas Purviance, Conrad Herwig, Keith O'Quinn, Dave Taylor, Larry Farrell (tb); Craig Handy, Joe Temperley, Bob Porcelli, Pete Yellin, Dick Oatts, Steve Wilson, Tim Ries, Gary Smulyan (reeds); Chick Corea, Ronnie Mathews (p); Christian McBride (b); Louis Nash (d); Bob Belden (cond).* 92–96.

A half-finished project in 1992, this was completed in 1996 and is almost Henderson's forgotten album. Yet it's one of his best. He did much of the scoring himself, in association with Belden, and his own solos have much of his old *brio* allied with the gravitas he has latterly assumed. The various orchestras involved offer a generational mix that doesn't seem to confound the continuity of the album, and in 'Shade Of Jade' and 'Without A Song' they frame the saxophonist with a sophistication that makes one wish that these expensive projects were less of a rarity.

***** Porgy And Bess**

Verve 539048-2 *Henderson; Conrad Herwig (tb); Stefon Harris (vib); Tommy Flanagan (p); John Scofield (g); Dave Holland (b); Jack DeJohnette (d); Sting, Chaka Khan (v).* 5/97.

Gimcracked around Henderson as soloist (and chorus?), here is yet another jazz *Porgy And Bess*. Line by line there is much to enjoy, but the guest vocalists reek of bought-in stardom, the playing has a somewhat elephantine grace, and there is nothing here that Henderson hasn't done better in other circumstances. Recently, Joe has been out of the public eye and ear.

Jon Hendricks (born 1921)

VOCALS

Born in Newark, Ohio, Hendricks was spotted by Charlie Parker and advised to make music his career. With Dave Lambert and Annie Ross, he founded a stylish vocal trio devoted to vocalese, setting jazz arrangements to words. After its final break-up, he spent some time in England and as a music critic, but has continued to record into his seventies.

***** Boppin' At The Blue Note**

Telarc 83320 *Hendricks; Wynton Marsalis (t, v); Al Grey (tb); Red Holloway (as); Benny Golson (ts); Mark Elf (g); Ugonna Okegwa (b); Andy Watson (d); Kevin Fitzgerald Burke, Judith Hendricks (v).* 12/93.

Nothing ever quite added up to the sheer *esprit* of Lambert, Hendricks & Ross, but there are flashes on the later records that allow one to gauge the size and scope of Hendricks's remarkable talent. It is a full, forceful voice, with near-perfect control right through its range and with a speed of articulation only matched by Ross in her heyday. Nonsensical too to suggest that he lacked either accuracy or expressiveness (these are common enough quibbles) when he bends notes with the same freedom as any saxophone player or trumpeter who would receive immoderate praise for what in Hendricks is considered to be uncertain technique.

The Blue Note disc offers an unexpected chance to hear Wynton Marsalis scatting like Dizzy Gillespie, which he does with great humour and some dexterity. Ranged alongside Jon and Michele on 'Everybody's Boppin'', he sounds in great form. Hendricks himself is in powerful and affecting voice on originals like 'Contemporary Blues' and the classic 'Roll 'Em Pete'. He hasn't quite the agility of yore, but the depth of expression is unmistakable, and the reprise of Basie-inspired Lambert, Hendricks & Ross material with the family and Kevin Burke is delightful. The instrumental support is also impressive, with a lovely contribution from Al Grey and sweet-toned choruses from Red Holloway.

Ann-Marie Henning

PIANO

Swedish pianist and composer-arranger, with rock, folk and blues experience before turning to jazz.

***** Tidal Dreams**

Dragon DRCD 279 *Henning; Fredrik Norén (t, flhn); Jan Kohlin, Peter Asplund, Gustavo Bergalli (t); Bertil Strandberg, Mats Haermansson, Urban Wiborg (tb); Anders Wiborg (btb); Johan Alenius (ss, ts, cl); Johan Horlen (as); Ulf Andersson (ts); Ingalill Hogman (ts); Alberto Pinton (bs); Semmy Stahlhammer (vn); Tommy Johnson, Jan Adefeld (b); Henrik Wartel, Martin Lofgren (d); Häkan Landgren (perc); Berit Andersson (v).* 5–8/96.

The cool-toned small-group jazz of the first few tracks gives way to the orchestral score of 'April Light', although this is in some ways the least effective piece here. Henning has a delicate touch both at the piano and with her compositions, but the big band comes out a bit blustery and routine. It's the quintet pieces, with excellent work by Norén and Alenius, that go deepest.

Ernie Henry (1926–57)

ALTO SAXOPHONE

A Brooklynite, Henry was on the periphery of a major career in bebop, having worked with Tadd Dameron as far back as 1947, and also with Gillespie, Monk and Mingus. But his early death cut him off from a wider reputation.

***** Presenting Ernie Henry**

Original Jazz Classics OJC 1920 *Henry; Kenny Dorham (t); Kenny Drew (p); Wilbur Ware (b); Art Taylor (d).* 8/56.

***** Seven Standards And A Blues**

Original Jazz Classics OJC 1722 *Henry; Kenny Dorham (t); Wynton Kelly (p); Wilbur Ware (b); Philly Joe Jones (d).* 9/57.

Henry left few records in a very brief career, but those he did make reveal a limited but vividly creative post-Parker altoist. His intense tone points towards Jackie McLean, even as his phrasing mixes the wistfulness of Tadd Dameron (with whom he made some of his early records) and Parker's high drama. *Presenting Ernie Henry* is sloppy in its execution, with Dorham sounding unsure of himself and the rhythm section seemingly unfamiliar with Henry's originals: the lingering power is in the leader's assertive and slightly off-centre improvising. *Seven Standards And A Blues* is arguably his best record: not quite fast enough to stand next to the best boppers, Henry instead makes a mark through the plangency of his phrases. On these show-tunes (and the Dameron-like blues, 'Specific Gravity') he leaves a telling impression.

The Herbie Nichols Project

GROUP

A vivid, inventive tribute band which goes way beyond the vague, wannabe gestures of less thoughtful projects.

*****(*) Dr Cyclops' Dream**

Soul Note 121333 *Ron Horton (t, flhn); Ted Nash (ts, bcl, af); Michael Blake (ss, ts); Frank Kimbrough (p); Ben Allison (b); Tim Horner (d).* 2/99.

Gone are the days when it was possible to describe Herbie Nichols and Sonny Clark as 'neglected' relative to the giants of bebop piano, Thelonious Monk and Bud Powell. Pianist Kimbrough and his colleagues have gone as far into the Nichols *œuvre* as anyone, recording five tunes straight from manuscript, pieces that have not been put on record before. Some of the tracks are very short, almost vestigial: 'Cro-Mag At T's' weighs in at less than a minute, while 'Dreamtime' and 'I've Got Those Classic Blues' are only about two. Yet the remainder are pretty substantial further evidence for Nichols's overlooked genius. 'Riff Primitif', 'The Bebop Waltz' and the title-tune bear comparison with Monk's work. The use of blues and non-blues intervals is utterly distinctive and these players know exactly what they're dealing with.

Peter Herborn

ARRANGER, CONDUCTOR, TROMBONE, EUPHONIUM

Combining the sophisticated voicings of European composer/arrangers like Mike Gibbs with something of the boiling intensity of John Coltrane's large-scale bands, Herborn has updated and personalized a big-band style that seemed dead in the water.

****** Large One**

Jazzline JL 1154-2 *Herborn; Dave Ballou, Taylor Haskins, John Swana (t, flhn); Dontae Winslow (t); Robin Eubanks, Clark Gayton, Dan Gottshall, Jeff Nelson (tb); Greg Osby (ss, as); Miriam Kaul (as, f); Gary Thomas (ts, f); Adam Kolker (ss, ts, cl); Alex Stewart (bs, bcl); Uri Caine (p); Mike Herting (ky); Marvin Sewell (g); John Hebert (b); Gene Jackson (d).* 5/97.

The title of Herborn's first record – now unfortunately deleted – has it just about right: *Subtle Wildness*. Herborn's music habitually achieves a balancing act between academic formality and the improvisational freedom still largely demanded of jazz. Though it is on the surface a very 'European' sound, its roots are always to be found in American jazz (and rock) of the 1960s. Like another erstwhile trombonist-turned-composer, Mike Gibbs, he has a brilliant melodic instinct and a sure feel for unexpected voicings.

The recent *Large One* is poised and elegant, but also restlessly exploratory. Herborn leans heavily on Caine, Osby and Thomas, the last of whom is the composer of two pieces. Of perhaps greatest interest are the opening piece, a turbulent overture called 'The Blizzard', and a sequence of repertoire pieces, including McCoy Tyner's 'Contemplation', Monk's 'Misterioso' and Jackie McLean's all too rarely covered 'Omega'. It features Thomas and Eubanks and a solo from guitarist Sewell, who is a new name to us, but a fine and distinctive performer. Thomas and Eubanks collide again on the saxophonist's own 'The Kold Kage'. It comes at the centre of the record and reinforces its sombre swing.

Some of the recording balance is a bit off, with piano mixed very far forward, and perhaps an over-emphasis on the percussion, but it suits Herborn's purpose for a large ensemble to have the punch and immediacy of a small combo. Herborn always has stories to tell, new variations on relatively familiar procedures. It is a pity, though hardly unexpected, that he should have had so few opportunities to record.

Heritage Hall Jazz Band

GROUP

New Orleans jazz of the 1990s, played like-it-was.

****(*) Cookin!**

GHB BCD-287 *Teddy Riley (t, v); Fred Lonzo (tb); Manuel Crusto (cl); Ellis Marsalis (p); Walter Payton Jr (b); Freddie Kohlman (d, v).* 92.

Swinging new jazz from New Orleans in the old style, even if it was recorded in New York. The problem might be that, personable as these stylists are, they don't make up a convincing ensemble. Riley and Crusto are old-school players, with the trumpeter's powers in some decline, and their leads are sometimes a little overwhelmed by Marsalis's sweeping piano and Kohlman's spirited drums. Lonzo, one of the best of the younger New Orleans traditionalists, plays more of a cameo role. The material is old hat, even if these oldish heads have the right to wear it.

Woody Herman (1913–87)

CLARINET, ALTO AND SOPRANO SAXOPHONES, VOCAL

A child performer in vaudeville, Herman took over the Isham Jones band in 1936 and kept it afloat until the mid-'40s. His Second (1947–9) and Third (1952–4) Herds were star-studded big bands which he led with indomitable showmanship, his singing and playing a diehard element in all of his groups. He constantly updated his repertoire while never neglecting his library of swing-era hits and was still leading small groups and larger bands into his seventies, although his last years were troubled by desperate tax problems as a result of financial mismanagement.

***** At The Woodchoppers' Ball**

ASV AJA 5143 *Herman; Clarence Willard, Kermit Simmons, Steady Nelson, Mac MacQuordale, Bob Price, John Owens, Ray Linn, Cappy Lewis, George Seaberg, Billy Rogers, Charles Peterson (t); Joe Bishop (flhn); Neal Reid, Toby Tyler, Buddy Smith, Vic Hamann, Tommy Farr, Walter Nimms (tb); Murray Williams, Don Watt, Joe Estrin, Ray Hopfner, Herb Tompkins, Joe Denton, Eddie Scalzi, Jimmy Horvath, Sam Rubinowich (as); Saxie Mansfield, Bruce Wilkins, Pete Johns, Ronnie Perry, Nick Caiazza, Sammy Armato, Mickey Folus, Herbie Haymer, Pete Mondello (ts); Skippy DeSair (bs); Horace Diaz, Tommy Linehan (p); Nick Hupfer (vn); Chick Reeves, Hy White (g); Walter Yoder (b); Frank Carlson (d).* 3/36–1/42.

***** Woody Herman 1936–1937**

Classics 1042 *Similar to above.* 2/36–8/37.

***** Woody Herman 1937–1938**

Classics 1090 *Similar to above.* 10/37–12/38.

Woody Herman didn't secure his principal fame until after these early tracks were made, but as an instrumentalist and vocalist he was already a characterful performer, and the pre-war sides – by a band that came together out of the Isham Jones Orchestra in 1936 – were centred mainly on him. There was some light pop fodder in among them and, while the band is short on strong soloists – trombonist Reid and flugelhorn player Bishop, who also contributed several of the charts, are about the best of them – the arrangements make the most of simple blues resources, one reason why the orchestra was called 'The Band That Plays The Blues'. By the 1940s, though, Herman was seeking out superior material and hiring sharper musicians. Woody himself was a clarinettist whose easy-going playing lacked the brilliance of Goodman or Shaw but who made up in affable, on-the-beat timing. A few tracks on the ASV set are by the small band of The Four Chips and the immortal 'Woodchoppers' Ball' is here in its original version, a Joe Bishop head arrangement. ASV's reproduction isn't ideal but it will have to do as the sole compilation of the period.

Classics have begun their usual chronological survey with two volumes that start with some of the Isham Jones tracks and get as far as the small-group 'River Bed Blues' on Classics 1090. Herman sounds undecided at times whether to go for a Crosby-like Dixieland feel or choose the smooth Dorsey route. Either way, at this time he was still short on star soloists and took a lot of the weight himself. He sings on most of the early tracks, too, revealing an appealing mid-range voice that had to deal with songs such as 'I Wanna Be In Winchell's Column' and 'Broadway's Gone Hawaii'. Decent sound, although some of the very early tracks have a lot of surface noise.

****(*) At The Hollywood Palladium 1942–1944**

RST 91536-2 *Herman; Cappy Lewis, George Seaberg, Chuck Peterson, Neal Hefti, Chuck Frankhauser, Ray Wetzel, Pete Candoli, Carl Warwick (t); Neal Reid, Tommy Farr, Walter Nimms, Bill Harris, Ralph Pfeffner, Ed Kiefer (tb); Sam Rubinowich, James Horvath, Mickey Folus, Pete Mondello, Skippy DeSair, Sam Marowitz, John LaPorta, Flip Phillips (reeds); Tommy Linehan, Ralph Burns (p); Marjorie Hyams (vib); Hy White, Billy Bauer (g); Chubby Jackson, Walter Yoder (b); Dave Tough, Frank Carlson (d); Carolyn Grey, Frances Wayne (v).* 8/42–11/44.

A couple of broadcast shows, the first in quite good sound, the second very scrappy; and the pity is that the latter features the really interesting band. '125th Street Prophet' is a glimmer of what the band could do. Too many vocals, but the playing remains swinging.

****** The V-Disc Years Vols 1 & 2**

Hep CD2/3435 2CD *Herman; Sonny Berman, Shorty Rogers, Cappy Lewis, Billy Rogers, Pete Candoli, Conte Candoli, Chuck Frankhauser, Carl Warwick, Ray Wetzel, Neal Hefti, Irv Lewis, Ray Linn, Marky Markowitz (t); Bill Harris, Ed Kiefer, Ralph Pfeffner, Neal Reid, Bob Swift, Rodney Ogle, Tommy Pederson (tb); Sam Marowitz, John LaPorta, Les Robinson, Jimmy Horvath (as); Mickey Folus, Flip Phillips, Pete Mondello, Vido Musso, Ben Webster (ts); Sam Rubinowich, Skippy DeSair (bs); Ralph Burns, Fred Otis, Tony Aless (p); Margie Hyams, Red Norvo (vib); Chuck Wayne, Billy Bauer, (g); Joe Mondragon, Chubby Jackson, Walt Yoder (b); Dave Tough, Don Lamond, Johnny Blowers (d); Martha Raye, Frances Wayne, Carolyn Grey (v).* 2/45–12/47.

*****(*) This Is Jazz**

Columbia CK 65040 *Similar to above.* 3/45–11/64.

A brilliant rhythm section, a brass team that could top any big-band section on either coast and arrangements that crackled with spontaneity and wit: Herman's 1945 band was both a commercial and an artistic triumph. With Burns, Bauer, Tough and Jackson spurring the horns on, the band handled head arrangements and slicker charts such as Neal Hefti's 'Wild Root' with the same mixture of innate enthusiasm and craft. There was a modern edge to the group that suggested something of the transition from swing to bop, even though it was the Second Herd that threw in its lot with bop spirit if not letter.

Until Columbia do their Herman recordings justice in a full CD reissue (and when will that be?), this collection of V-Discs will have to do. Impeccably restored by Jack Towers and John R.T. Davies, the music comes flag-waving through with most of its original punch intact. Showstoppers such as 'Red Top' and 'Apple Honey' still impress and, if the soloists don't always have the finesse of some of Woody's later section stars, there is still some superb playing from most hands, with rare glimpses of Berman, Burns, Bauer and others. The rather modest collection in Columbia's *This Is Jazz* series at least puts together some of the best of Woody's hits – 'Bijou', 'Northwest Passage', 'Four Brothers', 'Caldonia' – along with one stray track from the 1964 band. Docked a notch for not putting out a proper and full-scale best-of.

***** Woodchoppers' Ball Live 1944 Vol. 1**

Jass 621 *Herman; Neal Hefti, Billy Robbins, Ray Wetzel, Pete Candoli, Conte Candoli, Charlie Frankhauser, Carl 'Bama' Warwick (t); Ralph Pfeffner, Bill Harris, Ed Kiefer (tb); Sam Marowitz, Bill Shine, John LaPorta (as); Flip Phillips, Pete Mondello (ts); Skippy DeSair (bs); Ralph Burns (p); Margie Hyams (vib); Billy Bauer (g); Chubby Jackson (b); Dave Tough (d); Frances Wayne (v).* 8–10/44.

*****(*) Northwest Passage Live 1945 Vol. 2**

Jass 625 *As above, except add Sonny Berman, Ray Linn (t), Tony Aless (p); omit Robbins and Shine.* 7–8/45.

Live material by Herman was reissued in a somewhat haphazard way in the LP era, and these two CDs sort out a few broadcasts with good sound and sensible programming. The first includes a V-Disc version of 'Flying Home' and two broadcast sessions. Herman, Harris, Phillips and Pete Candoli take the lion's share of the solo features and the band sound in exuberant form. But the second disc, with this edition of the Herd really getting into its stride, is even better: Frances Wayne has two of her best features in 'Saturday Night' and 'Happiness Is A Thing Called Joe' and the band rocket through 'Apple Honey', 'Bijou' and 'Red Top'. A valuable supplement to the studio sessions.

*****(*) Keeper Of The Flame**

Capitol 984532-2 *Herman; Ernie Royal, Bernie Glow, Stan Fishelson, Red Rodney, Shorty Rogers, Charlie Walp, Al Porcino (t); Earl Swope, Bill Harris, Ollie Wilson, Bob Swift, Bart Varsalona (tb); Sam Marowitz (as); Al Cohn, Zoot Sims, Stan Getz, Herman Marowitz, Gene Ammons, Buddy Savitt, Jimmy Giuffre (ts); Serge Chaloff (bs); Lou Levy (p); Terry Gibbs (vib); Chubby Jackson, Joe Mondragon, Oscar Pettiford (b); Don Lamond, Shelly Manne (d); Mary Anne McCall (v).* 12/48–7/49.

Finally a CD reissue for some of the best tracks by Herman's Second Herd. A look through the personnel reveals a formidable roll-call, and the obvious stand-out is the famous reading of 'Early Autumn' with Getz's immortal tenor solo. Chaloff is memorable in his outings, especially 'Lollipop', and 'That's Right' and 'Lemon Drop' are minor Herman classics; but there is some commercial chaff too, which reminds that this was a band that was looking for an audience as well as trying to swing.

*****(*) At Palladium Hollywood / Commodore Hotel New York 1948**

Storyville STCD 8240 *Similar to above.* 3–5/48.

Herman's Second Herd in full flow in two broadcasts from early in its existence – actually before the arrival of Bill Harris and Lou Levy. To that extent the band is not quite as strong as it would be, but these are still performances full of interest and, with soloists like Getz, Cohn and Chaloff on some inventive charts, the music has genuine class. Also more than noteworthy is the overlooked but splendid Mary Ann McCall, one of the most gracious vocalists of the late swing era. Broadcast-quality sound but not at all bad.

***** The Great Soloists 1945–1958**

Blue Flame BFCD-1003 *Personnels unlisted.* 45–58.

A scattering of mostly heated big-band workouts covering a 15-year period, this has scrappy documentation but is full of great music. There are starring moments for Getz, Sims, Berman, Chaloff and many more, with the extraordinary workout on Shorty Rogers's chart, 'More Moon', hitting a pinnacle of big-band energy. Sound varies widely – several bright and clean tracks, but a lot suffer from hiss, surface noise or general wear and tear.

***** The Third Herd**

Storyville STCD 8241 *Herman; Don Fagerquist, Doug Mettome, Roy Caton, Shorty Rogers (t); Herb Randel, Urbie Green, Jerry Dorn (tb); Phil Urso, Bill Perkins, Jack Dulong, Kenny Pinson (ts); Sam Staff (bs); Dave McKenna (p); Red Wooten (b); Sonny Igoe (d); Dolly Houston (v).* 5–6/51.

Herd number three still mustered a string of great names in the personnel and there were fine charts in the book by Al Cohn, Ralph Burns, Neal Hefti and more. These three broadcasts from the Palladium in Hollywood have their share of features for Dolly Houston and some dull pieces, but there are good spots for Perkins and Urso and young Dave McKenna gets a piece of the action on 'Leo The Lion'. In reasonable sound.

*****(*) Songs For Hip Lovers**

Verve 559872-2 *Herman; Harry Edison, Charlie Shavers (t); Bill Harris (tb); Hal McKusick (as); Jerry Cook, Bob Newman, Ben Webster (ts); Jack Nimitz, Sol Schlinger (bs); Jimmy Rowles, Lou Stein (p); Billy Bauer, Barney Kessel (g); Milt Hinton, Joe Mondragon (b); Larry Bunker, Jo Jones (d).* 1–3/57.

This vocal album for Woody might seem a strange choice for Verve to reissue first, given that they have plenty of excellent big-band material which has yet to reappear. But it's a delightful set. Herman's singing was enduring and unpretentious, and he made a lyric line swing without manhandling it. Marty Paich wrote some decent charts and it's a great band, with handsome work from Webster, Edison, Kessel and the rest.

*****(*) Live At Peacock Lane Hollywood 1958**

Fresh Sound FSCD 2011 *Herman; Danny Stiles, Bobby Clark, John Cappola, Andy Peele, Hal Posey (t); Bill Harris, Archie Martin, Roy Weigand (tb); Joe Romano, Jay Migliori, Arno Marsh (ts); Roger Pemberton (bs); Pete Jolly (p); Jimmy Gannon (b); Jake Hanna (d).* 1/58.

*****(*) The Herd Rides Again**

Evidence ECD 22010-2 *Herman; Ernie Royal, Al Stewart, Bernie Glow, Nick Travis, Burt Collins, Marky Markowitz, Joe Ferrante, Willie Thomas (t); Bob Brookmeyer, Billy Byers, Frank Rehak (tb); Sam Marowitz (as); Al Cohn, Sam Donahue, Paul Quinichette (ts); Danny Blake (bs); Nat Pierce (p); Billy Bauer (g); Chubby Jackson (b); Don Lamond (d).* 7–8/58.

*** Herman's Heat And Puente's Beat

Evidence ECD 22008-2 *Herman; Willie Thomas, Danny Stiles, Hal Posey, Al Forte, Bobby Clark, Ernie Royal, Steve Lipkins, Nick Travis, Marky Markowitz (t); Willie Dennis, Jimmy Guinn, Roger DeLilio, Bill Elton, Billy Byers, Frank Rehak (tb); Marty Flax, Joe Romano, Jay Migliore, Pete Mondello, Danny Bank, Al Cohn, Herman Marowitz, Paul Quinichette, Al Belletto (reeds); Al Planck (p); Major Holley, Robert Rodriguez (b); Jimmy Campbell (d); Tito Puente, Ray Barretto, Raymond Rodriguez, Gilbert Lopez (perc).* 9/58.

While Woody's records for Capitol and Verve from the 1950s have nearly all slipped from circulation, these sets offer some testimony to how fine the band could be. The ballads have a smooth, perfectly cooked texture, the brass almost gliding from *piano* to *forte*, but the swingers hit home with astonishing precision. Bill Harris had already been with Herman for many years, but only now was he genuinely asserting himself as the band's major soloist, his playing utterly unpredictable and individual from phrase to phrase. The Peacock Lane session is in fine sound: there is a spellbinding feature for Harris in Ralph Burns's arrangement of 'Gloomy Sunday', but the reeds have a very good night of it as well.

The Evidence reissues restore two more good Herman dates to the catalogue. Harris is replaced by Brookmeyer, and he brings his more ascetic wit to his features, while both reed and rhythm sections exude class. The programme on *The Herd Rides Again* is mostly remakes of old Herman hits, which are revised as frequently as the Ellington band's staples. Half of *Herman's Heat* is the band alone on six charts; the rest is a bang-up meeting with Tito Puente's percussion team, period stuff but engagingly done.

*** 1963 Summer Tour

Jazz Hour JH-1006 *Herman; Bill Hunt, Dave Gale, Bill Chase, Gerry Lamy, Paul Fontaine (t); Bob Rudolph, Phil Wilson, Henry Southall (tb); Sal Nistico, Carmen Leggio, Bobby Jones, Jack Stevens (ts); Frank Hittner (bs); Nat Pierce (p); Chuck Andrus (b); Jake Hanna (d).* 63.

The Fourth Herd in action. The swinging delivery of 'The Preacher' sets a notable tone from the start and, though sound is indifferently mixed and the programme is still reliant on some Herman warhorses, this is a tough and hard-hitting edition.

**(*) Wild Root

TKO Magnum Collectors Edition CECD 018 *Herman; various groups and personnel, sometimes unlisted.* 53–67.

Sixteen live or broadcast performances, culled from all over the place, and it makes for something of a dog's breakfast, with wild variations in audio quality and style. Some exuberant playing as usual, but it's a string of tracks that makes little sense as an album. For hardcore Hermanites only.

**(*) The Raven Speaks

Original Jazz Classics OJC 663 *Herman; Al Porcino, Charles Davis, John Thomas, Bill Stapleton (t); Bill Byrne, Bob Burgess, Rick Stepton, Harold Garrett (tb); Frank Tiberi, Greg Herbert, Steve Lederer, Tom Anastos (reeds); Harold Danko (p); Pat Martino (g); Alphonso Johnson (b); Joe LaBarbera (d); John Pacheco (perc).* 8/72.

*** Feelin' So Blue

Original Jazz Classics OJC 953 *Herman; Dave Stahl, Nelson Hatt, Buddy Powers, Dennis Dotson, Bill Byrne, Larry Pyatt, Gil Rathel, Walt Blanton, Bill Stapleton, Tony Klatka (t, flhn); Jim Pugh, Steve Kohlbacher, Harold Garrett, Geoff Sharp, Dale Kirkland, Vaughan Wiester (tb); Greg Herbert, Frank Tiberi, Steve Lederer, Harry Kleintank, Gary Anderson, Jan Konopasek (reeds); Andy LaVerne (p); Joe Beck (g); Chip Jackson, John Paley, Wayne Darling (b); Jeff Brillinger, Ron Davis, Ed Soph (d); John Rae, Ray Barretto, Kenneth Nash (perc).* 4/73–1/75.

Herman's 1970s bands were still impressive outfits, but their studio records tended towards a fashionable and ultimately pretty indifferent eclecticism. *The Raven Speaks* has a top-notch cast largely wasted on some dreary tunes and so-so charts which just occasionally flicker or burst into life. *Feelin' So Blue* has some deeply unpromising material – 'Killing Me Softly With His Song', James Taylor's 'Don't Let Me Be Lonely Tonight' – yet turns out surprisingly well. The rock rhythms and modish figures don't completely undercut the strength of the band, which breaks through on 'Brotherhood Of Man', 'Evergreen' and 'Echano' to surprising effect, considering that the original album was patched together from three sessions over a two-year period.

**(*) Live In Warsaw

Storyville STCD 8207 *Herman; Jeffrey Davis, Nelson Hatt, John Hoffman, Dennis Dotson, William Byrne (t); Jim Pugh, Dale Kirkland (tb); Vaughan Wiester (btb); Frank Tiberi, Gary Anderson, Salvatore Spicola, John Oslawski (reeds); David Mays (p); Wilbur Stewart (b); Stephen Houghton (d).* 2/76.

A typical late-period Herman concert, cut in Poland in 1976. The programme relies heavily on the Herman hits with an overblown 'MacArthur Park' there to test the stamina of some. Amazing, really, that the band could attack what were very old charts and tunes with such spirit.

*** The 40th Anniversary Carnegie Hall Concert

RCA Victor 74321 591512 2CD *Herman; Alan Vizutti, Nelson Hatt, John Hoffman, Dennis Dotson, Bill Byrne, Pete Candoli, Conte Candoli, Danny Styles (t, flhn); Jim Pugh, Dale Kirkland, Jim Daniels, Phil Wilson (tb); Frank Tiberi, Gary Anderson, Joe Lovano, John Oslawski, Al Cohn, Stan Getz, Jimmy Giuffre, Zoot Sims, Flip Phillips (saxes); Nat Pierce, Jimmy Rowles, Ralph Burns, Pat Coil (p); Billy Bauer (g); Chubby Jackson, Rusty Holloway (b); Don Lamond, Jake Hanna, Danny D'Imperio (d).* 11/76.

To celebrate Woody's anniversary, the 1976 Herd was joined at this concert by numerous old boys of the band, including Cohn, Sims, Giuffre and Getz being the Four Brothers, Getz doing his 'Early Autumn' set-piece and Phil Wilson doing the Bill Harris part on 'Bijou'. On the second disc, the regular Herd struts its stuff. It must have been a great occasion but, as so often, it doesn't make for such a great record to go back to, although Herman himself makes everything rattle along in style. Getz returns on the second disc for a couple more numbers.

*** Woody And Friends

Concord CCD 4170 *Herman; Dizzy Gillespie, Joe Rodriguez, Tim Burke, Kitt Reid, Jim Powell, Bill Byrne, Woody Shaw (t); Birch Johnson, Nelson Hinds, Larry Shunk, Slide Hampton (tb);*

Frank Tiberi (ts, f, bsn); Dick Mitchell (ts, f, af, ob, picc); Bob Belden, Stan Getz (ts); Gary Smulyan (bs); Dave Lalama (p); Dave LaRocca (b); Ed Soph (d). 9/79.

***** Woody Herman Presents ... Vol. 1: A Concord Jam**

Concord CCD 4142 *Herman; Warren Vaché (c); Eiji Kitamura (cl); Dick Johnson (as, f); Scott Hamilton (ts); Dave McKenna (p); Cal Tjader (vib); Cal Collins (g); Bob Maize (b); Jake Hanna (d).* 8/80.

***** Woody Herman Presents ... Vol. 2: Four Others**

Concord CCD 4180 *Herman; Al Cohn, Sal Nistico, Flip Phillips, Bill Perkins (ts); John Bunch (p); George Duvivier (b); Don Lamond (d).* 7/81.

****(*) Live At The Concord Jazz Festival**

Concord CCD 4191 *Herman; Brian O'Flaherty, Scott Wagstaff, Mark Lewis, George Rabbai, Bill Stapleton (t, flhn); Gene Smith, John Fedchock, Larry Shunk (tb); Bill Ross (ts, f, af, picc); Paul McGinley (ts, f); Randy Russell (ts, f); Al Cohn, Zoot Sims (ts); Nick Brignola (bs, bcl); John Oddo (p); Mike Hall (b); Dave Ratajczak (d).* 8/81.

****(*) World Class**

Concord CCD 4240 *As above, except Bill Byrne (t, flhn), Randy Hawes (tb), Sal Nistico, Jim Carroll, Med Flory, Flip Phillips, Frank Tiberi (ts), Dave Shapiro (b), Jeff Hamilton (perc) replace Stapleton, Shunk, Ross, Russell, Sims and Hall.* 9/82.

***** 50th Anniversary Tour**

Concord CCD 4302 *Herman; Roger Ingram, Les Lovitt, Mark Lewis, Ron Stout, Bill Byrne (t); John Fedchock, Paul McKee (tb); Mark Lusk (btb); Dave Riekenberg (ts, f); Frank Tiberi, Jerry Pinter (ts); Nick Brignola (bs); Brad Williams (p); Lynn Seaton (b); Jim Rupp (d).* 3/86.

****(*) Woody's Gold Star**

Concord CCD 4330 *As above, except George Baker, Jim Powell (t, flhn), Joe Barati (btb), Joel Weiskopf (p), Nick Carpenter (b), Dave Miller (d), Pete Escovedo, Poncho Sanchez, Ramon Banda (perc) replace Lovitt, Lewis, Lusk, Williams, Seaton and Rupp.* 3/87.

Herman's final years were capably documented by Concord and, although there are no truly outstanding records in this stint, there are sound standards of big-band playing on the orchestral records and plenty of characteristic Herman dudgeon on the small-group discs. Though his final years were tragically marred by problems with the IRS, he somehow found the spirit to play jazz with much of his old fire. What had changed – as it did for Ellington, Basie and Goodman, his fellow survivors from a bygone era – was the traditional big band's place in the music. As a repertory orchestra, filled with good, idiomatic players but few real characters, Herman's last Herd had no more going for it than precision and automatic punch. *Woody And Friends* finds them at the 1979 Monterey Festival, with Gillespie, Hampton, Shaw and Getz (doing a lovely 'What Are You Doing The Rest Of Your Life') as guest stars, and the occasion is atmospherically recalled by the record. The *Concord Jam* session mixes young and older players and everyone is in strong voice, with features for everybody. *Four Others* lines up four tenor stalwarts to so-so effect. The remaining big-band records all have their moments without securing any serious candidacy for any collection that already has plenty of vintage Herman in it.

Vincent Herring (born 1964)

ALTO AND SOPRANO SAXOPHONES

One of the best of the younger generation of post-boppers, Herring's similarity to Cannonball Adderley was reinforced by a long and happy stay in brother Nat's band. His own work as leader has tended to be less blues-driven and more lyrical, but the influence is still there.

***** American Experience**

Music Masters 5037-2 *Herring; Tex Allen, Dave Douglas (t); Clifford Adams (tb); John Hicks, Bruce Barth (p); James Genus, Marcus McLaurine (b); Marc Johnson, Beaver Harris (d).* 4/86–12/89.

***** Scene One**

Evidence ECD 22170 *Herring; Darrell Grant (p); Kris Defoort (syn); Robert Hurst (b); Jack DeJohnette (d).* 12/88.

These records are a pretty fair résumé of a career on the move. It would be hard to top Vince's solo on the opening 'The Athlolete' on *American Experience* as an example of here-I-am *brio* – firing through the changes with an attack that blows past any doubts about his experience. This is 'prentice work, all the same, and, though there is a youthful exuberance about the two sessions that make up the record, the bands are comparatively ordinary and Herring stands out like a beacon.

A couple of years later, Herring is playing with the same relaxed exuberance, but with maturity as well. 'Elation' is the right mood to start the second of these records, and Vince's crisp, dry solo is a model of controlled excitement. Jack DeJohnette is at his best on the faster tracks and Darrell Grant plays with admirable authority.

*****(*) Early On: Evidence / Dawnbird**

32 Jazz 32086 *Herring; Wallace Roney, Scott Wendholt (t); Kevin Hays, Mulgrew Miller (p); Dwayne Burno, Ira Coleman (b); Carl Allen, Billy Drummond (d).* 90, 10/91.

Two of Herring's deleted Landmark albums, brought together in a single, highly attractive set. *Evidence* was the proverbial 'transitional album'. Concentrating on material from other composers, the saxophonist turns in a series of strong and provocative performances that have a bright and boppish edge. Monk's 'Evidence' is an easy number to miscue, but Vince nails it true first time, with a freshness and spontaneity that were missing from the earlier records. The band, which in different permutations was to be a regular working unit, sounds in sharp form, and the second half of the disc is pretty nearly flawless.

Dawnbird was the work of two different groups though, apart from Mulgrew's distinctive chording and Billy Drummond's easy offbeats, there is not much to choose between them. This was Herring's most adventurous session yet and on 'Soundcheck' and 'Almost Always' he stretches out and pushes at the rhythm. On paper, Roney is a more interesting player than Wendholt, but it's Scott who does the mettlesome work on this occasion.

***** Secret Love**

Music Masters 65092 *Herring; Renee Rosnes (p); Ira Coleman (b); Billy Drummond (d).* 92.

One can see why he wanted to make the more easy-going and ballad- or mid-tempo-orientated *Secret Love* – nobody wants to be seen as a mere speed merchant – but one misses Herring's quota of derring-do and the hint of dark deeds in his distinctive minor-key compositions.

****(*) Folklore: Live At The Village Vanguard**
Music Masters 65109 *Herring; Scott Wendholt (t); Cyrus Chestnut (p); Ira Coleman (b); Carl Allen (d).* 11/93.

As a club set or, rather, as the best of three nights at the Vanguard, this is a pretty respectable showing, but it lacks the emphasis and presence that will make even Herring enthusiasts return to it again and again, which is the mark of a significant album. Chestnut is an able accompanist and his composition 'Romantic Journey' is certainly the most strikingly original piece on the record. Unfortunately, Vince seems unwilling to let go and try something adventurous, even in front of an obviously sympathetic crowd. His compositions, 'Folklore', 'Theme For Dolores' and 'Fountainhead', are solid and thoughtful but lack spirit, as does his playing. There is an interesting version of Hank Mobley's 'This I Dig Of You' which briefly makes things interesting, but it doesn't redeem a very flat set.

***** Days Of Wine And Roses**
Music Masters 65152 *Herring; Cyrus Chestnut (p); Jesse Murphy (b); Billy Drummond (d).* 6/94.

Originally released in Japan, where Vince has been far more widely recognized than back home, *Days* is a thoughtful and laid-back session that needs a little more punch. The quality playing comes from the rest of the band. Chestnut is in great form on 'Body And Soul' and 'Come Rain Or Shine', and the two rhythm players are well on the case. The saxophonist picks up the pace later on, but not enough to make this an urgent purchase.

*****(*) Don't Let It Go**
Music Masters 65121 *Herring; Scott Wendholt (t); Cyrus Chestnut (p); Jesse Yusef Murray (b); Carl Allen (d).* 10/94.

Don't Let It Go seemed to mark a jump in maturity, a beautifully crafted and unfussily executed session that ends on a 'Blueprint For A New Tomorrow'. Even when the mood is upbeat, though, the familiar shadows remain and few young players (this marked his thirtieth birthday) can convey such immense world-weariness. The combination with Wendholt has been proven before, but it is Chestnut who adds the necessary leaven on this occasion.

***** Sterling Place All-Stars**
Metropolitan 1117 *Herring; Ronnie Mathews (p); Richie Goods (b); Carl Allen (d).* 8/99.

Vince and Ronnie hit it off instinctively, and though the record is somewhat formulaic in formal terms, sticking to theme–solos–recapitulation almost all the way through, the sheer drive and quality of playing lifts tracks like 'Salima's Dance', one of the pianist's best compositions, and Carl Allen's tricky 'Alternative Thoughts'. Vince takes it on soprano, which he otherwise seems to be resting. 'Summer Night' and 'In A Sentimental Mood' are both quality performances. This is a group that rates a long residency somewhere; when the music catches fire, it's as exhilarating as anything currently going the rounds, but it's too apt to drift off into conventional forms.

Fred Hersch

PIANO

Born in Cincinnati, Hersch worked in his local scene as a young man, went to the New England Conservatory, and subsequently gained a wide range of experience under different small-group leaders, including Stan Getz and Joe Henderson. He has recorded for numerous labels as both leader and sideman.

***** Horizons**
Concord CCD 4267 *Hersch; Marc Johnson (b); Joey Baron (d).* 10/84.

***** Sarabande**
Sunnyside SSC 1024 *Hersch; Charlie Haden (b); Joey Baron (d).* 12/86.

*****(*) Etc**
Red 123233-2 *Hersch; Steve LaSpina (b); Jeff Hirshfield (d).* 5/88.

***** Heartsongs**
Sunnyside SSC 1047 *Hersch; Mike Formanek (b); Jeff Hirshfield (d).* 12/89.

In the past we have routinely characterized Fred Hersch as a Bill Evans follower, but as his discography has grown it's clear that there's much more to him than that. He's actually a profoundly attentive scholar of many styles of jazz piano and a lucid and perceptive analyst of the forms that solo, trio and group playing can take for a pianist. His writing, which may be less important to him than his powers of interpretation, has something of Evans about it, as in originals such as 'Lullabye' (*Heartsongs*) and 'Child's Song' (*Sarabande*). But Hersch has an energy of his own, and all these records have something to commend them.

His first album, *Horizons*, has only recently made it to CD. It's a confident and typically catholic programme, with standards, Ellington, Shorter and one tune of his own, the stormy 'Cloudless Sky'. *Heartsongs* is one of the best integrated, since it's by a regular trio: Haden is a little too stodgy to make *Sarabande*'s liveliest tunes break out. *Heartsongs* also has the most individual approach to the material, and Hersch chooses good covers: Wayne Shorter's 'Fall' is done in *passacaglia* form, and Ornette Coleman's 'The Sphinx' casts the composer in an impish light. But a few of the freer pieces sound more effortful than they should: Hersch may be an impressive conservative, but at this stage he's a conservative all the same. *Etc* is a more straight-ahead date, and this time the music works out beautifully: a fine programme of jazz themes, with LaSpina and Hirshfield both constructive and challenging in support, the bassist in particular coming up with some quick ideas and agile lines.

*****(*) At Maybeck Vol. 31**
Concord CCD 4596 *Hersch (p solo).* 10/93.

Hersch's turn at Maybeck might not be his finest hour, but it sets up a near-perfect balance of his meditative and argumentative sides. The percussive, almost stabbing treatment of Coleman's

'Ramblin'' and the breezy lyricism of his own 'Heartsong' are set beside a glowing 'If I Loved You' and a very ambitious approach to 'Haunted Heart' which opens the song out into a long *fantaisie*. As usual, impeccable sound.

****** Last Night When We Were Young**

Classical Action 1001 *Hersch; Jane Ira Bloom (ss); Bobby Watson, Craig Bailey (as); Phil Woods (as); Dan Faulk (ts); Toots Thielemans (hca); Andy Bey (p, v); George Shearing, Rob Schneiderman, Dave Catney (p); Oscar Castro-Neves (g); Gary Burton (vib); Drew Gress, Rufus Reid (b); Tom Whaley, Akira Tana (d); Leny Andrade, Mark Murphy, Janis Siegel (v).* 94.

Recorded for the label set up by Performing Arts Against AIDS, this remarkable record was organized by Hersch and he plays on eight of the 13 tracks. As a sequence of ballad interpretations there can be few recent records to come even close to it, with some of the artists giving career performances: Leny Andrade on 'Quiet Nights', Jane Ira Bloom on 'Wee Small Hours Of The Morning', the Tana–Reid group on 'Memories Of You'. Bobby Watson does a memorable one-take exploration of 'Soul Eyes', Janis Siegel eclipses most memories of 'More Than You Know', and Toots Thielemans is typically superb on 'Estate'. Fred, who is himself HIV-positive, has a very fine 'Somewhere', and he accompanies elsewhere with a sympathy that lifts everyone's game, with the closing duet with Mark Murphy leaving the listener very quiet. Despite the melancholy subtext, this is a superlative and ultimately uplifting record.

***** Beautiful Love**

Sunnyside SSC 1066 *Hersch; Jay Clayton (v).* 5/94.

Rather different from Hersch's occasional collaboration with Janis Siegel, but no less rewarding in its way. Clayton's adventurous ways with time and space lend occasionally over-startling timbres to some of these standards, and it's not an approach for all tastes. But any who admire the kind of sensibility that Betty Carter has brought to jazz will surely warm to this: try their version of 'Footprints' to start.

*****(*) Point In Time**

Enja 9035-2 *Hersch; Dave Douglas (t); Rich Perry (ts); Drew Gress (b); Tom Rainey (d).* 3/95.

A rare example of Hersch as nominal leader in a band situation, although the horns are on only half the tracks – and it's the trio pieces that are the real highlights: 'You Don't Know What Love Is' configured over a rephrasing of the melody and 'The Peacocks' a quite superb treatment. Perry shines on 'Infant Eyes', his solo a frank nod to the composer's style.

*****(*) Passion Flower: Fred Hersch Plays Billy Strayhorn**

Nonesuch 9395-2 *Hersch; Nurit Tilles (p); Drew Gress (b); Tom Rainey (d); Andy Bey (v); strings.* 7–8/95.

****** Fred Hersch Plays Rodgers And Hammerstein**

Nonesuch 79414-2 *Hersch (p solo).* 1/96.

****** Thelonious: Fred Hersch Plays Monk**

Nonesuch 79456-2 *Hersch (p solo).* 2/97.

The Strayhorn collection is limpidly beautiful and, while these are marginally less impressive features for the leader's piano than the discs listed below, it's difficult to carp at the lustre of Fred's string charts, even if 'Day Dream' and 'Lush Life' flirt with mush. The programme is a blend of solos, trios and three settings for the strings; Bey adds a lubricious vocal to 'Something To Live For', with the almost unknown verse an extra pleasure; Tilles joins Hersch for a duet on 'Tonk', which comes out sounding almost like ragtime.

Hersch's approach to Rodgers and Hammerstein is that of a recitalist. He doesn't try to 'swing' the tunes – and in any case many of them are vehicles which jazz musicians have seldom turned to. As familiar as they are, few improvisers have looked at 'A Cock-Eyed Optimist', 'Shall We Dance?', 'Getting To Know You' or 'I Have Dreamed'. The pianist plays them in a musing, respectful manner, rarely letting the melody drift too far from sight, and parading the structure of the song as he goes: one can almost see the choruses unfolding as he walks through them. Where he makes his mark is in the voicings and harmonies: with his immaculate touch and exacting delivery, the songs are recast as rich, graceful arias, parlour songs made modern by their fresh clothes. Fred's note tells of how he learned many of the tunes through Broadway cast albums played on the family gramophone, and that domestic memory is honoured by these wonderful treatments.

His Monk recital is more of the same, yet quite different. These are tunes which pianists have mulled over and covered until there's very little of the original flesh left. Hersch starts with 'Round Midnight', done first as a raindrop dance in the highest register, before the music thickens and grows dark. And then it's over – Hersch leaves no waste in these interpretations, and his judgement rarely fails him. The five choruses he takes on 'Misterioso', each a pristine investigation of that curious melody line, are a unique insight; but so is what happens to 'Let's Cool One' or 'Ask Me Now'. Rather than relying on Monk's rhythmic staggering for flavour, as so many pianists do, Hersch evens out the pulse and places the emphasis on the substance and colour of his chords. It's a fascinating essay on the master, and further proof that Hersch himself must now be counted among the contemporary giants of the instrument.

***** Songs We Know**

Nonesuch 79468-2 *Hersch; Bill Frisell (g).* 98.

It's possible to find Frisell's eclecticism a little tiresome, and these 11 standards and jazz tunes might have been overpowered by his signature methods. But Hersch keeps him on planet Earth. The pianist's incisive parts curb the guitarist's taste for outrageous harmonics and there's some terrific interplay. But the record doesn't sustain its running-time. As with all of Frisell's records, there's a novelty element which turns either cute or folksy at points, and the shameless romanticism which Hersch is partial to is something that the guitarist can't commit to without a lick of irony.

*****(*) Let Yourself Go**

Nonesuch 79558-2 *Hersch (p solo).* 10/98.

A concert recording from Jordan Hall, Boston. Hersch enjoyed this gig and he is in fine form. As ever, it's his ballads which highlight the best of his style: 'Black Is The Colour/Love Theme From Spartacus' is an almost transcendant treatment of the two melodies, and when he gets to an encore of 'The Nearness Of You' his reading scarcely ruffles the feathers of the tune. One or two pieces seem a bit overly calculated, such as the awkward gait chosen for 'Speak Low', but Hersch's admirers shouldn't be disappointed.

John Hicks (born 1941)

PIANO

The elegant Georgian studied music at Lincoln University across the State line in Missouri, and has retained an urbane intelligence in his approach to form and structure. His time with Art Blakey and with Betty Carter significantly enhanced his public profile and in the 1970s allowed him to explore the fringes of avant-garde jazz, while retaining his own essentially lyrical and melodic approach. Recent years have seen him work with Arthur Blythe, Oliver Lake and Bobby Watson. His composition, 'Naima's Love Song', is a modern classic.

***(*) **Inc. 1**
DIW 817 *Hicks; Walter Booker (b); Idris Muhammad (d).* 4/85.

**** **In Concert**
Evidence ECD 22048 *As above, except add Elise Wood (f), Bobby Hutcherson (vib).* 8/84.

*** **Luminous**
Evidence ECD 22033 *Hicks; Elise Wood (f); Clifford Jordan (ts); Walter Booker (b); Jimmy Cobb, Alvin Queen (d).* 7/85, 9/88.

*** **I'll Give You Something To Remember Me By**
Limetree MCD 0023 *Hicks; Curtis Lundy (b); Idris Muhammad (d).* 3/87.

***(*) **East Side Blues**
DIW 8028 *Hicks; Curtis Lundy (b); Victor Lewis (d).* 4/88.

**** **Naima's Love Song**
DIW 823 *As above, except add Bobby Watson (as).* 4/88.

***(*) **Two Of A Kind**
Evidence ECD 22017 *Hicks; Ray Drummond (b).* 8/88.

***(*) **Is That So?**
Timeless SJP 357 *Hicks; Ray Drummond (b); Idris Muhammad (d).* 7/90.

Hicks has been the pianist of choice on so many fine recordings that it's often overlooked how compressed his own career has been. Early sessions for Strata East are now available only irregularly, as with everything on that twilight label. This string of albums from the mid-'80s onwards tells a detailed story of his progress since. He favours bassists with a low, dark tone and straightforward delivery. Similarly, he looks to drummers for a firm, reliable count. Even on ballads, Hicks enunciates very strongly and makes effective use of the damper pedal, trimming off chords tidily but with none of the staccato bite one hears from Bud Powell, one of his stylistic models and a more dominant one than Monk. The Monk themes on *Inc. 1* are stretched out to an unfamiliar extent, something that happens to 'Rhythm-a-Ning' on the Maybeck set (below). Though the performances themselves are not long, Hicks seems determined to unpack the melody as much as possible. Though essentially a chordal player, he resembles Mal Waldron in his attention to melody.

The mid-'80s sessions with Booker and Muhammad on DIW and on Evidence were the most searching that Hicks ever made, though not necessarily always the most polished or satisfying. The partnership with Lundy and then with Lewis merely iced the cake. The bassist plays an understated but vital role on the Limetree, with lovely phrasing on Paul Arslanian's 'Pas De Trois' and big, bold sound on Rollins's 'Airegin'. The same combination occurs on *In Concert*, though this time the Rollins tune is 'Paul's Pal' and Hicks is pushed along by Bobby Hutcherson's often hectic vibes. Elise Wood sounds pretty, but hasn't much to say for herself, certainly not enough to sustain her role on the rather odd *Luminous*.

After *In Concert*, the real highspots are *East Side Blues* and the associated *Naima's Love Song*, which Bobby Watson nearly pinches with a display of flawlessly lyrical alto. Brightly recorded and balanced, these should be considered priority items, though it would be worth finding a space for the two sessions with Drummond which, for sheer beauty of playing, are hard to beat. The duos include Ellington's 'Take The Coltrane' (a favourite with the Booker/Muhammad axis) and a late-night 'Parisian Thoroughfare'; the trios work seasonal variations on a carefully limited palette.

**** **Sketches Of Tokyo**
DIW 812 *Hicks; David Murray (ts, bcl).* 4/85.

This has, not surprisingly, been seen as another Murray album and, despite the saxophonist's respectful nods to past masters – Coltrane's 'Naima', Dolphy's bass clarinet version of 'God Bless The Child' – Hicks can equally claim it as a quiet exorcism of some of his own ghosts: Monk in 'Epistrophy', Bud Powell, and even Ellington. It's a superb record, but it's the pianist who impresses most on later hearings, once Murray's almost casual brilliance has been absorbed.

**** **Live At Maybeck Recital Hall, Volume 7**
Concord CCD 4442. *Hicks (p solo).* 8/90.

The opening 'Blue In Green' has a relaxed, untroubled quality and helps check out both the piano and a lovely acoustic. 'All Of You' is so bouncy that one isn't quite prepared for the fulsome sweep of 'After The Rain'. Hicks has shown a considerable understanding of and sympathy for Coltrane's harmonic ideas, and Coltrane compositions appear regularly throughout his work. His own composition, 'Naima's Love Song', has a strong Coltrane resonance, and echoes of the original 'Naima', heard on the duos with David Murray, frequently insinuate themselves into solos. The set continues with an improvised 'Blues For Maybeck' and with material by Billy Childs, Kurt Weill, Monk, Mingus and Wayne Shorter. Bud Powell's 'Oblivion' is a long-standing favourite (also included on *In Concert*) and 'Straighten Up And Fly Right' has been Hicks's curtain-piece for some time.

***(*) **Beyond Expectations**
Reservoir RSR CD 130 *Hicks; Ray Drummond (b); Marvin 'Smitty' Smith (d).* 9/93.

Drummond's introduction to 'There Is No Greater Love' on the Reservoir disc captures in just a few bars what a valuable player he is. Drummond's statement of the Isham Jones theme tees Hicks up for a firmly unsentimental set of variations that gains in stature (despite an uncertain beginning) with virtually every bar. The piano is recorded with a lot of presence, and the recording as a whole has Rudy van Gelder stamped all over it: lively, resonant, utterly musical. By this point in his career, Hicks records come with all sorts of expectations attached (the actual reference is to a composition with Elise Wood) and this one confounds none of them, an utterly professional performance from a seasoned performer.

***** Single Petal Of A Rose**

Mapleshade 02532 *Hicks; Jack Walrath (t); Elise Wood (f); Curtis Lundy (b).* 94.

Wood is still an acquired taste, but she makes some pretty sounds here and there, and it might be that there's a bit more stuff to her playing of late. She's strongly featured on the Mapleshade session (Walrath has a guest role only) and there is considerable lyric invention in her statement on the title-piece. Working without percussion gives it all a very light, chamber-jazz feel, but there is enough substance to keep the level of interest high. For more recent examples of Hicks in peak form, turn to the Keystone Trio entry.

Billy Higgins (born 1936)

DRUMS, VOCALS, GUITAR

Higgins began his career playing R&B and rock'n'roll, but he has become one of the most-recorded jazz players of all time, as our index will bear out. His recording career under his own name has been intermittent but consistently inventive.

***** Soweto**

Red RR 123141 *Higgins; Bob Berg (ts); Cedar Walton (p); Tony Dumas (b).* 1/79.

*****(*) The Soldier**

Timeless SJP 145 *Higgins; Monty Waters (as); Cedar Walton (p); Walter Booker (b); Roberta Davis (v).* 12/79.

****(*) Once More**

Red RR 123164-2 *As Soweto.* 5/80.

***** Mr Billy Higgins**

Evidence ECD 22061 2 *Higgins; Gary Bias (sax); William Henderson (p); Tony Dumas (b).* 4/84.

***** 3/4 For Peace**

Red RR 123258 *Higgins; Harold Land (ts, ss); Bill Henderson (p); Jeff Littleton (b).* 1/93.

Raised in LA, Billy started playing in his early teens and came of age professionally as a jazz drummer in Red Mitchell's quartet. Since then, Higgins has been a drummer of choice in a huge variety of playing contexts, bringing a brisk, bright swing and an ability to work in a variety of metres from the very simple and forceful to the complex and delicate. Like many busy rhythm players, he's had relatively few opportunities to record under his own name. Higgins generally doesn't compose his own material and the records are often only as good as the charts he's given to play. That's what holds back the Evidence set. Gary Bias has a lovely tone but can't write for toffee. Only W.J. Lee's 'John Coltrane' gives the leader the push he needs. Othewise, even in the signature solo on bassist Henderson's oddly familiar 'Dance of the Clones' he remains rather static.

The early Red session opens on the powerful statement, 'Soweto', on which Higgins sings. His vocal skills are pretty limited, but the vocal has an unmistakable power, more so than the closing feature, 'Bahia Bahia Bahia', on which he's also credited with guitar, taking a leaf out of Elvin Jones's book. The rest of the session is given over to tunes by Cedar Walton, who was to become his most reliable co-conspirator, and by the oddly reticent Bob Berg, who has an off-day, not even rising to the attractive hook on his own 'Neptune'. *Once More* has never been one of our favourites, either of Billy's or out of the Red catalogue. Berg and Walton are quality players and good writers, but neither is in strong form. Billy's own solo spots seem detached from the ensembles and sections like Dumas's feature on 'Lover Man' require an effort of will. A rather dreary disc.

The Soldier is plagued by disappointing sound. One has to listen actively for Booker, one of those big, booming string players who sound good alongside Higgins, and the drummer's own sounds lacks the crispness and power one normally expects of him. However, the playing is uniformly good, particularly on 'Midnight Waltz' and 'Peace', where Walton excels himself.

The military theme returns, albeit negatively, in *3/4 For Peace*, which is interesting mainly for Land's rich, full-voiced tenor and the interplay between horn and drums. A subtle, insistent record that recalls aspects of Max Roach's association with Clifford Brownie, a perfect axis. The drum suite dedicated to Juno Lewis is one of Higgins's most personal statements on record, though it makes slightly uncomfortable listening at the second and third attempt.

Eddie Higgins (born 1932)

PIANO

Higgins was born in Cambridge, Massachusetts, but spent 20 years working in Chicago, recording with Lee Morgan and Wayne Shorter. He now bases himself in Fort Lauderdale, plays in a swing-to-bop mainstream, and has a particular interest in Brazilian music.

***** By Request**

Solo Art SACD-104 *Higgins; Milt Hinton (b); Bobby Rosengarden (d).* 8/86.

*****(*) Those Quiet Days**

Sunnyside SSC 1052D *Higgins; Kevin Eubanks (g); Rufus Reid (b).* 12/90.

*****(*) Zoot's Hymns**

Sunnyside SSC 1064D *Higgins; John Doughten (ts); Phil Flanigan (b); Danny Burger (d).* 2/94.

Higgins has been making occasional visits to the studio since the 1950s. *By Request* sticks to well-trodden paths, so far as material is concerned, though the pianist's approach has a verve that takes it out of routine: he has some of the rocking ebullience of the great Chicago pianists, and touches of stride and boogie are integrated into a wide-ranging taste. Hinton and Rosengarden provide flexible support, and a couple of original Higgins rags round out the picture. The irreproachable *Those Quiet Days* is one of his most recent records and surely one of his best. The interplay of piano, guitar and bass has a natural litheness and melodic and harmonic tang and, with Eubanks and Reid sounding both attentive and inventive throughout, the ideas have a seamless momentum. Higgins is no great original, with a style much indebted to the deceptively easy swing of Hank Jones, but he has a calm authority perfectly suited to this kind of date. Eubanks continues his double life as a traditional modernist and a fusioneer with another distinguished turn in the former category, and Reid hunkers down on all the bass lines.

Zoot's Hymns – the dedication is obvious – is another unassuming beauty. Doughten can't quite live up to the Sims and Getz comparisons that come in the sleeve-notes, but he's still darn good: easy swing, good head for melody and prototypical big tone. Higgins sounds more relaxed than ever, but he can't help coming up with ingenious turns in solos that never quite resolve into any of the clichés one expects in this setting. He also picks great tunes: three uncommon A.C. Jobim pieces are highlights to go with his pair of originals.

***(*) **Haunted Heart**

Sunnyside SSC 1080D *Higgins; Ray Drummond (b); Ben Riley (d).* 6/97.

A meeting of masters, and the fact that the material is so well-worn – the only remotely unusual choice is a medley of 'Stolen Moments' and 'Israel' – is the only hindrance to unqualified enjoyment. Measured but never outstaying their welcome, these nine interpretations are about as classic as a piano trio can be. Higgins exposes nothing new in these tunes: he simply reminds us why the likes of 'My Funnay Valentine' and 'Isn't it Romantic?' have endured in the jazz canon, and why playing of this unassuming excellence will always be worth listening to.

Andrew Hill (born 1937)

PIANO

Born in Chicago and not on Haiti as is sometimes reported, Hill draws on his Caribbean ancestry and always sounds torn between cultures – on the one hand analytical, on the other powerfully visceral. Influenced by Bud Powell and Thelonious Monk, but also thoroughly individual, Hill is both an avant-gardist and a loyal traditionalist whose basic language remains close to bebop.

♛ **** **Point Of Departure**

Blue Note 99007 *Hill; Kenny Dorham (t); Eric Dolphy (as, f, bcl); Joe Henderson (ts); Richard Davis (b); Tony Williams (d).* 3/64.

Hill's whole career has been marked by the silences that punctuate his compositions. Of the important bop and post-bop pianists – Bud Powell, Horace Silver, Mal Waldron, Paul Bley, Cecil Taylor – he is the least known and most erratically documented; even Herbie Nichols enjoys a certain posthumous cachet.

Point Of Departure is one of the very great jazz albums of the 1960s and is now available in a new edition dedicated to engineer Rudy van Gelder. Hill's Blue Note debut, *Black Fire*, was available briefly on CD but seems to be out of circulation at the moment. It is an altogether more conservative record than this magnificent statement. Hill's writing and arranging skills matured dramatically with *Point Of Departure*. Nowhere is his determination to build on the example of Monk clearer than on the punningly titled 'New Monastery'. Hill's solo, like that on the long previous track, 'Refuge', is constructed out of literally dozens of subtle shifts in the time-signature, most of them too subliminal to be strictly counted. Typically, Hill is prepared to hold the basic beat himself and to allow Williams to range very freely. 'Spectrum' is the one disappointment, too self-conscious an attempt to run a gamut of emotions and instrumental colours; an extraordinary 5/4 passage for the horns almost saves the day. Henderson at first glance doesn't quite fit, but his solos on 'Spectrum' and 'Refuge' are exemplary and in the first case superior to Dolphy's rather insubstantial delivery. The mood of the session switches dramatically on the final 'Dedication', a dirge with a beautiful structure that represents the sharpest contrast to the rattling progress of the previous 'Flight 19' and brings the set full circle. Unfortunately, Hill was offered few opportunities to record with similar forces in years to come and suffered long neglect, pigeon-holed with the awkward squad. The new Rudy van Geller Edition is a fine improvement on the previous CD, and it includes three alternative takes.

*** **Live At Montreux**

Freedom FCD 741023 *Hill (p solo).* 7/75.

(*) **Faces Of Hope

Soul Note 121010 *As above.* 6/80.

Marked by a forceful dissonance, unusual and unsettling harmonic intervals, Hill's dark, incantatory manner as a solo performer sometimes obscures a lighter, folksy side. Like Monk's, his gammy melodic patterns work better either solo or with horns; conventional trio playing represents only a surprisingly small proportion of his output. The Montreux set is marred by some unevenness of tone and *Faces Of Hope* by some of Hill's least compelling charts. There is an introverted and brooding quality to these records that will not win over uncommitted listeners. However, both are essential purchases for Hill enthusiasts and disappoint only relative to an astonishingly high career standard.

*** **Invitation**

Steeplechase SCCD 31026 *Hill; Chris White (b); Art Lewis (d).* 10/74.

Like many of his contemporaries, Hill enjoyed greater visibility in Europe than in the USA during the 1970s. This was one of his consistently good performances for the Danish label, a studio session rather than one of Steeplechase's notoriously unselective club recordings. Hill is playing well, albeit with a rather stiff and foot-soldierish rhythm section who don't seem altogether easy with the material.

*** **Spiral**

Freedom FCD 741007 *Hill; Ted Curson (t, flhn, picc t); Robin Kenyatta (as); Lee Konitz (as, ts, ss); Stafford James, Cecil McBee (b); Barry Altschul, Art Lewis (d).* 12/74, 1/75.

Spiral is very mixed, featuring two quite different bands. The sessions with Konitz, Curson, McBee and Lewis are smoother and outwardly less oblique, but without cost to the harmonic interest. The disposition of Curson's and Konitz's three horns apiece (it's often now forgotten how adept Konitz was on tenor and even baritone saxophones) invest 'Laverne', 'The Message' and the title-track with maximum variety, and the solos are extremely effective. By no means an afterthought on this session, there is a duo, 'Invitation', by Hill and Konitz, spontaneously done and strongly recalling Hill's Waldron-like talents as an accompanist.

In contrast to the variety he achieves with Konitz, the sessions with alto saxophonist Robin Kenyatta, another adoptive New Yorker with a highly individual musical background, are much more direct and to the point, with less self-conscious manipulation of mood. Kenyatta is a fine and restless player who nevertheless prefers to get down to business, doing most of his soul-searching and experimentation on his own time.

*****(*) Strange Serenade**

Soul Note 121013 *Hill; Alan Silva (b); Freddie Waits (d).* 80.

This is as dour and dark as anything Hill has committed to record. Silva and Waits are ideal partners in music that isn't so much minor-key as surpassingly ambiguous in its harmonic language. Hill seems on occasion to be exploring ideas that can be traced back to Bud Powell – not the straight bebop language so much as the more impressionistic things. There are curious little broken triplets and wide-interval phrases which seem to come straight from Bud's last recordings, and it would be interesting to know if Hill had been studying these at the time *Strange Serenade* was recorded.

*****(*) Verona Rag**

Soul Note 121110 *Hill (p solo).* 7/86.

The mid-'80s saw something of a revival in Hill's critical fortunes and 1986 was one of his busiest years in two decades. Of the available solo albums, by far the best is *Verona Rag*, a gloriously joyous set full of romping vamps, gentle ballad interludes and Hill's characteristic harmonic ambiguities. Not recognized as a standards player, he invests 'Darn That Dream' with an almost troubling subtext in the bass and stops just short of reinventing the tune wholesale. The whole album has the sound of a man who is enjoying his music and who is no longer troubled by the idea of experimentation.

****** Shades**

Soul Note 121113 *Hill; Clifford Jordan (ts); Rufus Reid (b); Ben Riley (d).* 7/86.

Far from settling back into a comfortable accommodation with a 'personal style', Hill's work of the later '80s was as adventurous as anything he had done since *Point Of Departure.* Reid and Riley create exactly the right background for him, taut but undogmatic, elastic around the end of phrases, constantly propulsive without becoming predictable. His kinship with Monk (whom Riley had accompanied) was always obvious, but it was increasingly clear that the differences were more important (some have suggested Herbie Nichols and Ellington as more fruitful sources) and that Hill was nobody's follower. *Shades* is one of the very best jazz albums of the decade. The two trio tracks – that is, with the pungent Jordan absent – are probably the finest since his debut on *Black Fire*, one of the missing Blue Notes. Hill has been inclined to avoid the conventional trio format. Like Monk, he operates better either solo or with horns, but on 'Tripping' and 'Ball Square' he is absolutely on top of things, trading bass lines with Reid and constantly stabbing in alternative accents. 'Monk's Glimpse' pays not altogether submissive homage to Hill's spiritual ancestor. The one slight misgiving about the album is its sound, which is a trifle dark, even on CD.

Buck Hill (born 1928)

TENOR SAXOPHONE

Roger Hill began playing saxophone in his teens and has hardly ever played outside his Washington, DC, home base; his reputation is high with a few musicians but negligible with the wider jazz audience.

***** This Is Buck Hill**

Steeplechase SCCD 31095 *Hill; Kenny Barron (p); Buster Williams (b); Billy Hart (d).* 3/78.

***** Scope**

Steeplechase SCCD 31123 *As above.* 7/79.

***** Easy To Love**

Steeplechase SCCD 31160 *Hill; Reuben Brown (p); Wilbur Little (b); Billy Hart (d).* 7/81.

***** Impressions**

Steeplechase SCCD 31173 *As above.* 7/81.

Buck Hill is one of the most notable 'regional' jazzmen in America. Like Von Freeman, who has never strayed far from his Chicago base, Hill has spent the largest part of his career with local players on local bandstands, the locale in question being Washington, DC. He has a big, Hawkins-like sound but says he prefers Lester Young, and inside a bluff manner is a certain elliptical way with phrasing a tune. The Steeplechase albums feature Hill with two different rhythm sections, although each winds up with the same result: honest, proficient blowing that has its individual clout without quite persuading that it's music of great moment which is being created. He has made more recent records but, with the elimination of the Muse catalogue, Buck is rather out in the cold at present as far as CDs are concerned. Spot a fine recent appearance as sideman with Shirley Horn, though.

Teddy Hill (1909–78)

TENOR SAXOPHONE, BANDLEADER

A competent saxophonist, but Hill was better as a bandleader, and his New York outfit of the mid-'30s was a fine one. It broke up in 1940 and Hill took over Minton's Playhouse, the bebop crucible.

***** Uptown Rhapsody**

Hep CD 1033 *Hill; Bill Dillard, Bill Coleman, Shad Collins, Roy Eldridge, Dizzy Gillespie, Frank Newton (t); Dicky Wells (tb); Russell Procope (cl, as); Howard Johnson (as); Chu Berry, Robert Carroll (ts); Cecil Scott (ts, bs); Sam Allen (p); John Smith (g); Richard Fulbright (b); Bill Beason (d); Beatrice Douglas (v).* 2/35–5/37.

(*) **Teddy Hill 1935–1937
Classics 645 *As above.* 2/35–5/37.

Nowadays Hill is guaranteed his slight fingerhold on lasting celebrity for his custodianship of Minton's Playhouse in New York City, the most pungent crucible of the bebop movement. By that point, his own musical career was pretty much over, but he had led a short-lived but quite significant big band which numbered among its most illustrious alumni Chu Berry, Bill Coleman, Roy Eldridge and Dizzy Gillespie. These two items are in pretty direct competition, and it behoves us to say that the Hep, intelligently and very faithfully remastered by John R.T. Davies, is the only one to consider. The 26 tracks in question, from 'Lookie, Lookie, Lookie, Here Comes Cookie' in February 1926 to 'Blue Rhythm Fantasy' a decade and a few months later, are the entire output of the orchestra. The first track is dominated by a blistering Eldridge solo; the last session marks Diz's first recorded solo, on 'King Porter Stomp'. This may seem a by-way in the history of the music, but it is one worth exploring.

Earl Hines (1905–89)

PIANO, VOCAL

Raised in Pittsburgh, Hines began leading groups in Chicago and soon teamed with Louis Armstrong in the later Hot Five. From 1929 he ran the band at the Grand Terrace Ballroom for 12 years. Ran another big band (with many prototype boppers in the ranks), then joined the Armstrong All Stars but left in 1951. More club work followed, but Hines was at a low ebb when a series of New York concerts made him a star all over again in 1964. Thereafter he worked constantly until his death. Along with Tatum, the greatest piano innovator and stylist of the pre-bop era, who outlived most of his contemporaries.

***(*) **Earl Hines 1928–1932**
Classics 545 *Hines; Shirley Clay, George Mitchell, Charlie Allen, George Dixon, Walter Fuller (t); William Franklin (tb, v); Lester Boone, Omer Simeon (cl, as, bs); Darnell Howard (cl, as, vn); Toby Turner (cl, as); Cecil Irwin (cl, ts); Claude Roberts (bj, g); Lawrence Dixon (g); Quinn Wilson (bb, b); Hayes Alvis (bb); Wallace Bishop (d).* 12/28–6/32.

**** **Earl Hines 1932–1934**
Classics 514 *As above, except add Louis Taylor, Trummy Young, Kenneth Stuart (tb), Jimmy Mundy (cl, ts), Herb Jeffries (v); omit Clay, Mitchell, Boone, Turner, Roberts and Alvis.* 7/32–3/34.

***(*) **Earl Hines 1934–1937**
Classics 528 *As above, except add Milton Fletcher (t), Budd Johnson (ts), The Palmer Brothers, Ida Mae James (v); omit Franklin.* 9/34–2/37.

**** **Earl Hines Collection: Piano Solos 1928–1940**
Collector's Classics COCD 11 *Hines (p solo).* 12/28–2/40.

Earl Hines had already played on some of the greatest of all jazz records – with Louis Armstrong's Hot Five – before he made any sessions under his own name. The piano solos he made in Long Island and Chicago, one day apart in December 1928, are collected on the first Classics CD – a youthful display of brilliance that has seldom been surpassed. His ambidexterity, enabling him to finger runs and break up and supplant rhythms at will, is still breathtaking, and his range of pianistic devices is equalled only by Tatum and Taylor. But these dozen pieces were a preamble to a career which, in the 1930s, was concerned primarily with bandleading. The remainder of the first Classics disc is filled with the first recordings by the orchestra which Hines led at Chicago's Grand Terrace Club for ten years, from December 1928. Their 1929 sessions struggle to find an identity, and only the leader cuts any impressive figures.

The 1932–4 sessions on the second record are better played, better organized and full of brilliant Hines. The surprising thing may be Hines's relatively subordinate role within the band: he had few aspirations to compose or arrange, entrusting those duties to several other hands (including Fuller, Mundy, Johnson, Crowder and Wilson); he revelled instead in the role of star soloist within what were increasingly inventive frameworks. By 1934 the band was at its first peak, with fine Mundy arrangements like 'Cavernism' (including a startling violin solo by Darnell Howard) and 'Fat Babes' and Wilson's vigorous revisions of older material such as 'Maple Leaf Rag' and 'Wolverine Blues'. It's a pity that the chronology has split the 1934 sessions between the second and third Classics volumes. Hines is a wonder throughout, both in solo and in the commentaries with which he counters the arrangements. The other principal soloist is Walter Fuller, a spare, cool-to-hot stylist whose occasional vocals are agreeable copies of Armstrong. The 1934–7 disc shows an unfortunate decline in the consistency of the material, and their move to Vocalion to record coincided with a dissipation of the band's energy.

All three records feature transfers which are respectable rather than notably effervescent, which is disappointing – the sound of the original recordings is excellent, as John R.T. Davies had shown on some earlier LP transfers for Hep, currently yet to emerge on CD. However, Davies has also done the remastering for the piano solos collection on Collector's Classics, which covers all the 1928 pieces, five takes of two solos from 1932/3, and a pair of titles from 1940. Excellent sound and strongly recommended.

*** **Earl Hines 1937–1939**
Classics 538 *Hines; Walter Fuller (t, v); Milton Fletcher, Charlie Allen, Freddy Webster, George Dixon, Edward Sims (t); Louis Taylor, Trummy Young, Kenneth Stuart, Joe McLewis, Ed Burke, John Ewing (tb); Omer Simeon (cl, as, bs); Leroy Harris (cl, as, v); Darnell Howard (cl, as); Budd Johnson (cl, as, ts); William Randall, Leon Washington (cl, ts); Robert Crowder (ts); Lawrence Dixon, Claude Roberts (g); Quinn Wilson (b); Wallace Bishop, Alvin Burroughs, Oliver Coleman (d); Ida Mae James (v).* 37–39.

*** **Earl Hines 1939–1940**
Classics 567 *As above, except add Shirley Clay, Harry Jackson, Rostelle Reese, Leroy White (t), Edward Fant (tb), Scoops Carey (as), Franz Jackson, Jimmy Mundy (ts), Hurley Ramey (g), Truck Parham (b), Billy Eckstine, Laura Rucker, Madeline Green (v); omit Allen, Taylor, Young, Stuart, Howard, Randall, Washington, Dixon, Bishop and James.* 10/39–12/40.

*** **Earl Hines 1941**
Classics 621 *Hines; Harry Jackson, Tommy Enoch, Benny Harris, Freddy Webster, Jesse Miller (t); Joe McLewis, George Hunt, Edward Fant, John Ewing, Nat Atkinson, Gerald Valentine*

(tb); Leroy Harris (cl, as, v); Scoops Carey (cl, as); William Randall, Budd Johnson, Robert Crowder, Franz Jackson (ts); Hurley Ramey (g); Truck Parham (b); Rudolph Taylor (d); Billy Eckstine, Madeline Greene, The Three Varieties (v). 4–11/41.

****** Fatha**

Topaz TPZ 1006 *Similar to above, except add Sidney Bechet (ss).* 32–42.

***** Piano Man!**

ASV AJA 5131 *Similar to above.* 28–40.

It wasn't until the emergence of Budd Johnson as an arranging force that the Hines band recovered some of its flair and spirit. The most renowned of the later pieces – 'Grand Terrace Shuffle' and 'G.T. Stomp' – are both on the 1937–9 CD, which follows the band as it tries to recapture its earlier zip. Johnson himself is a significant soloist, and Hines softens into a more amiable version of his daredevil self. The important thing about the 1940 tracks, on Classics 567, is the arrival of Billy Eckstine, who would influence the band's move towards modernism and first provide it with a couple of major hits, starting with the 1940 'Jelly, Jelly'. He is featured further on the final Classics CD in the sequence, which also features arrangements from several hands – Johnson, Benny Harris, Jackson – and which includes a couple of imposing Hines features in 'The Father Jumps' and 'The Earl'. These tracks haven't been reissued very often, and they deserve to be better known.

The best single-disc compilation of Hines in the 1930s comes with the Topaz set, *Fatha*. An excellent choice of tracks by both the early and later bands comes in clear, lively sound, with only an occasional surface swish to betray their 78 origins. *Piano Man!* also sounds good for the most part, though some of the later Bluebird sides are inexplicably gritty, and the choice of tracks – including Armstrong Hot Fives and Bechet's 'Blues In Thirds', which is also on the *Fatha* set – concentrates more on Hines the soloist than on Hines the bandleader.

****(*) Earl Hines 1942–1945**

Classics 876 *Hines; George Dixon (t, as); Pee Wee Jackson, Maurice McConnell, Jesse Miller, Charlie Shavers, Palmer Davis, Billy Douglas, Willie Cook (t); Ray Nance (t, vn); George Hunt, Joe McLewis, Gerald Valentine (tb); Druie Bess, Walter Harris, Gus Chappell (tb); Rene Hall (tb, g); George Carry, Tab Smith, Johnny Hodges, Lloyd Smith, Leroy Harris, Scoops Carey (as); William Randall, Budd Johnson, Flip Phillips, Robert Crowder, Kermit Scott, Wardell Gray (ts); John Williams (bs); Skeeter Best, Tommy Kay, Al Casey (g); Red Norvo (vib); Truck Parham, Al Lucas, Oscar Pettiford, Gene Thomas, Al Hall (b); Rudy Traylor, Jo Jones, Big Sid Catlett, Chick Booth, Specs Powell (d); Billy Eckstine, Betty Roche, Madeline Green, The Three Varieties (v).* 3/42–1/45.

***** Earl Hines And The Duke's Men**

Delmark DD-470 *Hines; Rex Stewart (c); Cat Anderson, Lee Brown, Don Devilla, Archie Johnson, Joe Strand (t); Lawrence Brown, Joe Britton, Floyd Brady, LeRoy Hardison, George Stevenson (tb); Curby Alexander, Vince Royal, Johnny Hodges (as); Jimmy Hamilton (cl, ts); John Hartzfield, Vincent McCleary, Flip Phillips (ts); Harry Carney (bs); Marlowe Morris, Horatio Duran (p); Al Casey, Teddy Walters (g); Oscar Pettiford, Bob Paige (b); Sonny Greer, Big Sid Catlett, Bobby Donaldson (d); Betty Roche (v).* 4/44–5/47.

The *1942–1945* Classics set is a motley set of tracks where Hines seems more sideman than leader. A final and fairly undistinguished big-band date for Bluebird is followed by a trio date for Signature with Al Casey and Oscar Pettiford, Hines uncharacteristically quiet; a brash quintet session led by Charlie Shavers for Keynote; and the more interesting sextet date for Apollo, which is also on the Delmark disc. Hines then returns to big bands for two tracks for Bluebird from 1945.

The Delmark disc is more interesting. Besides the sextet tracks with Hodges and Nance, the other groups are led by either Sonny Greer or Cat Anderson (Anderson's mysterious line-up of unknowns may actually be pseudonymously hiding more famous names). Some of these are minor mixtures of swing and jump-band R&B, but there are many nice touches – from Hodges, Stewart, Nance and Hines himself, though Anderson's usual top notes are a bore – and it's a useful sweep through an otherwise obscure period for many of these players. Good transfers.

***** Earl Hines 1945-1947**

Classics 1041 *Hines; Arthur Walker, Vernon Smith, Willie Cook, Palmer Davis, Geechie Smith, Charlie Anderson (t); Bennie Harris, Joe McLewis, Clifton Small, Druie Bess, Walter Harris, Gordon Alston (tb); Scoops Carry, Lloyd Smith, Thomas Crump (as); Wardell Gray, Kermit Scott, Erbie Wilkins, Budd Johnson (ts); John Williams, Wallace Brodis (bs); Bill Thompson (vib); Bill Dougherty (vn); Skeeter Best (g); Gene Thomas, Oscar Pettiford (b); Calvin Ponder (b); Chick Booth, Rudy Traylor, Gus Johnson (d); Lord Essex, Johnny Hartman, Dolores Parker, Arthur Walker, Melrose Colbert (v).* 9/45–47.

Hines's 1947 big band isn't well known for its records, and this is an interesting sweep through the surviving recordings. Wardell Gray gets some solos as well as the leader, but there's nothing very forward-looking in the arrangements, and the performances aren't so much lacking in spirit as directionless. Vocal admirers will enjoy the four handsome contributions from Johnny Hartman, very much in the Eckstine mould, and Hines himself remains inimitable. Hard to say how good the transfers are from what are probably indifferent original recordings, but don't expect hi-fi: some of them are distinctly rough.

*****(*) Another Monday Date**

Prestige 24043-2 *Hines; Eddie Duran (g); Dean Riley (b); Earl Watkins (d).* 55–56.

Hines entered the LP era rather cautiously, and the 1950s weren't his greatest decade on record. After several years with the Louis Armstrong All Stars, he found himself somewhat adrift as hard bop took over the jazz mainstream; but the mainstream itself was beginning a revival as swing-era musicians found their feet in the microgroove era, and in 1956 the pianist cut a pair of sessions for Fantasy which showed his old powers intact and unfettered by time constraints. One set of Waller interpretations is coupled with a collection of originals and, though the sidemen are almost a distraction from his own mercurial way with time, Hines sweeps through the music.

****(*) Earl Hines' Dixieland All-Stars**
Storyville STCD 6036 *Hines; Marty Marsala (t); Jimmy Archey (tb); Darnel Howard (cl); Red Garland (b); Joe Watkins (d).* 9/55.

Three broadcasts from The Hangover Club in San Francisco. This isn't the place to hear Hines, who seems very low in the balance, but there's some effusive if inelegant playing from Marsala and Archey.

***** Grand Reunion**
Verve 528137-2 *Hines; Roy Eldridge (t); Coleman Hawkins (ts); George Tucker (b); Oliver Jackson (d).* 3/65.

****** Blues In Thirds**
Black Lion CLCD 760120 *Hines (p solo).* 4/65.

*****(*) Spontaneous Explorations**
Columbia/Red Baron JK 57331 2CD *Hines; Richard Davis (b); Elvin Jones (d).* 3/64–1/66.

****(*) Live! Aalborg, Denmark, 1965**
Storyville STCD 8222 *Hines; Morten Hansen (b); Jorgen Kureer (d).* 4/65.

****(*) Blues So Low (For Fats)**
Stash ST-CD-537 *Hines (p solo).* 4/66.

*****(*) Blues And Things**
New World 80465 *Hines; Budd Johnson (ss, ts); Bill Pemberton (b); Oliver Jackson (d); Jimmy Rushing (v).* 7/67.

***** At Home**
Delmark DD-212 *Hines (p solo).* 69.

Hines really came back into his own in the '60s. He was able to unleash all the rococo elements in his methods at whatever length he chose, and the so-called 'trumpet style' – using tremolo to suggest a horn player's vibrato and taking a linear path even when playing an ensemble role – began to sound modern by dint of its individuality. Nobody played like Hines, as influential as he had been. He was more or less rediscovered in 1964, following New York concerts that were greeted as a sensation, and thereafter embarked on regular tours and records. *Grand Reunion* effectively replaces an earlier issue on Xanadu. Eldridge and Hawkins were guests with Hines and they play on 8 of the 11 tracks, while Hines elaborates on a stack of tunes via three medleys. Recording is less than ideal, with Jackson's cymbals sounding all too loudly in the mix, but it isn't too bad. There is better playing by all three masters on other records, but the meeting has plenty of charisma and some genuinely inspired playing in patches.

It's hard to go wrong with Hines on record, but one should be a cautious in approaching some of his live recordings: the fondness for medleys and a weakness for an over-extended right-hand tremolo betray a hankering for applause which, merited though it may be, occasionally tips his style into excess. *Spontaneous Explorations*, though unnecessarily reissued as a two-disc set (it runs less than 70 minutes), has much classic Hines. The first half is a solo date cut on the occasion of a famous 'comeback' concert in New York; the second matches him with Davis and Jones in a session that recalls the Ellington *Money Jungle* date. These are brimming performances which reach a climax of sorts in the trio version of 'Shoe Shine Boy', where the empathy in the trio is superb. The Danish concert is much less substantial and is compromised by the noisy recording. Medleys take up much of the set, and Hines's closing party piece of 'St Louis Blues' is best heard only once. The 1966 concert, in dedication to Waller, has as much overcooked Hines mannerism as inspiration.

Blues And Things has a regular Hines band of that moment in the studio with Jimmy Rushing guesting, to noble effect, on four tracks. The quartet have two almost classic performances in the ever-modulating 'Changing The Blues' and 'Louisiana', where Johnson turns in one of his calmly definitive statements.

The best portrait is provided by the one solo studio set, *Blues In Thirds*, which adds three extra tracks to the original LP release. The 'Tea For Two' here is an overwhelming *tour de force* and the blues playing on 'Black Lion Blues' and 'Blues After Midnight' is even more luxuriant than Art Tatum's essays in the method. In comparison, *At Home* is a mild disappointment. There are too many slow tunes and too much meditation, perhaps brought on by the relaxed surroundings (he was recorded on his own piano, at home), and only when he gets to the marvellous finale of 'The Cannery Walk' does the best of Hines break through.

*****(*) Four Jazz Giants**
Solo Art SACD 111/2 2CD *Hines (p solo).* 7/71.

Not quite on the exalted level of the Ellington set listed below, but this was still an unusually well-prepared and handsome set of sessions, one each in dedication to W.C. Handy, Hoagy Carmichael and Louis Armstrong – the latter recorded only days after Pops's death. Hines chooses his favourite rocking mid-tempo for many of the tunes, but when he goes up a gear, as in the labyrinthine 'Struttin' With Some Barbecue', he's miraculous. There's a huge exploration of 'Star Dust', many of the Handy themes contain some of his most detailed examinations of the blues, and the Armstrong tunes find him at his most lyrical. In full and lifelike sound (though with a degree of tape hiss), this fine package is top-notch Hines.

***** In Paris**
Musidisc 500562 *Hines; Larry Richardson (b); Richie Goldberg (d).* 12/70.

****** Tour De Force**
Black Lion BLCD 760140 *Hines (p solo).* 11/72.

****** Tour De Force Encore**
Black Lion BLCD 760157 *Hines (p solo).* 11/72.

***** Live At The New School**
Chiaroscuro CRD 157 *Hines (p solo).* 3/73.

*****(*) Plays George Gershwin**
Musidisc 500563 *Hines (p solo).* 10/73.

*****(*) One For My Baby**
Black Lion BLCD 760198 *Hines (p solo).* 3/74.

*****(*) Masters Of Jazz Vol. 2**
Storyville STCD 4102 *Hines (p solo).* 3/74.

*****(*) Plays Cole Porter**
New World 80501-2 *Hines (p solo).* 4/74.

A spate of solo recording meant that, in his old age, Hines was being comprehensively documented at last, and he rose to the challenge with consistent inspirational force. The two *Tour De Force* discs are among his very best records, since the studio sound is fine, if a little hard, and Hines seems completely relaxed and under his own orders (although Stanley Dance's discreet supervision must have assisted). The CD versions include previously unheard tracks but, since alternative takes are spread across the pair of discs, most will choose one or the other. The single take of 'Mack The Knife' on each disc is Hines at his most extraordinary, however: his variation of time, ranging from superfast stride to wholly unexpected suspensions, is bemusing enough, but the range of dynamics he pushes through each solo is more so. He seldom lingers in thought – one of the things he bequeathed to later players such as Oscar Peterson and Cecil Taylor was the bruising speed of the process by which ideas are executed – but the essentially tuneful stamp he puts on every improvisation (and the different takes underline his spontaneity) humanizes what might otherwise be a relentless, percussive attack. *One For My Baby* isn't too far behind the other Black Lion discs: the expected fireworks are ignited on the up-tempo pieces, but the most telling interpretation is arguably the slow and handsomely detailed 'Ill Wind', which distils a gravity unusual in Hines, who never forgot to be an entertainer. The Storyville disc strings together six standards, and again the playing is extravagantly strong and elaborate, with a couple of tunes that Hines seldom recorded ('As Long As I Live' and 'My Shining Hour') adding some spice.

The 16-minute Fats Waller medley on *New School* and other flag-wavers let down the superior aspects of the set, but it has a share of Hines in regal form: he liked to play for people, and some of the pyrotechnics are *echt*-Hines. The two Musidisc sets are both worth while. *In Paris* has a desultory rhythm section accompaniment and is merely very good, but the solo meditations on Gershwin tunes are more substantial. The two extravagances are long versions of 'Embraceable You' and 'They Can't Take That Away From Me', but there are also several tunes that Hines didn't cover elsewhere, such as a boisterous 'Let's Call The Whole Thing Off', and his opening and closing versions of 'Rhapsody In Blue' – which Gershwin himself once complimented Hines on – are a neat piece of dovetailing. *Plays Cole Porter* is another 'songbook' tackled with relish, 'Night And Day' pushing close to ten minutes of invention, and the other pieces finished with hard, polished clarity.

***** Back On The Street**

Chiaroscuro CD(D) 118 *Hines; Jonah Jones (t); Buddy Tate (ts, cl); Jerome Darr (g); John Brown (b); Cozy Cole (d).* 3/72.

****(*) Swingin' Away**

Black Lion BLCD 760210 *Hines; Doc Cheatham (t); Rudy Richardson (cl, as, ts); Jack Wilkins (g); Jimmy Leary (b); Ray Mosca (d).* 12/73.

A couple of band dates with mixed results. *Back On The Street* is a frowsy set of blues and standards which the protagonists sometimes trudge through. Hines does 'You Can Depend On Me' yet again (and he does it on the Black Lion disc as well) but otherwise he takes something of a back seat to the horns, who have their moments, though both Jones and Tate have sounded better. *Swingin' Away* is almost ruined by terrible studio sound, and even the CD remastering hasn't got rid of the distortion all over it. Still, there's one lovely track, where Cheatham rhapsodizes on 'Don't Take Your Love From Me', earning the stars on his own.

****** Earl Hines Plays Duke Ellington**

New World NW 361/2 2CD *Hines (p solo).* 12/71–4/75.

*****(*) Earl Hines Plays Duke Ellington Vol. 2**

New World 80532 *Hines (p solo).* 12/71–3/74.

Made over a period of four years, these are much more than casual one-giant-nods-to-another records. Hines was cajoled by Stanley Dance into looking into many unfamiliar Ellington tunes and creating a memorial (Ellington died around the time of the final sessions) which is surely among the best tributes to the composer on record. Since Hines's more aristocratic touches are close in feeling to Ellington's own, there is an immediate affinity in such pieces as 'Love You Madly' and 'Black And Tan Fantasy'. But Hines finds a wealth of new incident in warhorses such as 'Mood Indigo' and 'Sophisticated Lady' and he turns 'The Shepherd' and 'Black Butterfly' into extravagant fantasies which go far beyond any of Ellington's own revisionist approaches. Even a simple piece such as 'C Jam Blues' receives a fascinating, rhythmic treatment, and the voicings conjured up for 'I'm Beginning To See The Light' upset conventional wisdom about Ellingtonian interpretation. In his variety of resource, Hines also points up all the devices he passed on to Powell, Monk and virtually every other post-swing pianist. A memorable lesson, and a fine tribute to two great piano players, spread over two hours of music. New World have now released a second volume, which covers the remainder of the sessions. This is just slightly less interesting as far as tune titles and interpretations go, but Hines collectors will surely want both.

*****(*) Hot Sonatas**

Chiaroscuro CR(D) 145 *Hines; Joe Venuti (vn).* 10/75.

***** In New Orleans**

Chiaroscuro CR(D) 200 *Hines (p solo).* 11/77.

Hines's final years offered fewer recording opportunities. *In New Orleans* would not be our first choice for one of his solo dates, but there are still felicities to savour, such as the almost demure warmth of 'I'm A Little Brown Bird'. *Hot Sonatas*, though, is an invigorating display by two inveterate swingers. With no previous meetings and no rehearsals, the results are just occasionally scatty, but more often each man is swept along on the jubilation of the other's playing. 'C Jam Blues' becomes almost Byzantine in its ramifications. Bravo, Joe and Earl! Five extra rehearsals and alternatives are taken from a TV video track which was made at the sessions.

Motohiko Hino (1946–99)

DRUMS

Tokyo-born, the brother of trumpeter Terumasa moved to the USA in 1978 and played with a wide range of musicians. A promising career was cut short by his early death.

*****(*) Sailing Stone**

Gramavision R2 79473 *Hino; Terumasa Hino (c); Dave Liebman (ss, ts); Karen Mantler (org, hca); Mike Stern, Marc Muller (g); Steve Swallow (b).* 11/91.

'Satisfaction', 'Lady Jane', 'Angie' and 'Continental Drift' are the Stones tunes rolling through this fetching set, helmed by the lesser-known of the Hino brothers (Terumasa turns 'Lady Jane' into a lovely, cracked lament). The insistent drone of Mantler's organ and the buoyancy of Swallow's bass-lines give the varying instrumentations a firm identity, and Liebman and Stern play up to their best: Stern's 'Satisfaction' is a winning revamp. Nor is the leader in the shadows: he plays with restraint but is always varying the pace and density of the rhythms, and there are four good themes of his own.

***(*) **It's There**
Enja 8030-2 *As above.* 3/93.

Same again – same band, same concept, but different source, since Hino this time tackles (sharp intake of breath) the Led Zeppelin songbook. He makes the likes of 'The Rain Song', 'The Ocean' and 'Thank You' into lovely things, too, the guitarists setting the melodies all a-shimmer. 'Dazed And Confused' is the rave-up, though whether Jimmy Page approved is a mystery. His own themes, 'Tok O' The Town' and 'Hangin' Out', are fine enough to hope for an all-original date, but sadly it was not to be.

Milt Hinton (born 1910)

BASS

A great witness to most eras of the music, Hinton was playing with Tiny Parham in Chicago in the '20s. He has gone on to play and record with thousands of others, from Eddie South to Branford Marsalis, and since he's a dedicated photographer he has a picture of most of the occasions too.

*** **Old Man Time**
Chiaroscuro CRD 310 2CD *Hinton; Doc Cheatham (t); Eddie Barefield (as, ts); Buddy Tate (ts); Red Richards (p); Al Casey (g); Gus Johnson (d); Dizzy Gillespie (v).*

Hinton is a great entertainer, playing, singing and rapping about the good old days with undiminished vigour into his eighties. He is quite at ease working with players almost two generations below him. He has such an accumulated head of experience that he can pick – or, failing that, talk – his way out of almost any situation. Like a great many rhythm players, the discography is huge, but very little is credited to him, so the slightly overcooked two-volume *Old Man Time* has to be seen as a kind of *This Is Your Life* accolade. The band, arranged and conducted by Buck Clayton, gives him plenty of room for his party pieces on the big bull fiddle, while the Mississippi voice spins its yarns. Entertaining but lightweight. A great celebration is planned for his ninetieth in 2000.

Erhard Hirt

GUITAR

German guitar experimentalist.

(****) **Gute Und Schlechte Zeiten**
FMP OWN-90003 *Hirt (g solo).* 12/91–5/93.

The bracketed qualification is only to warn any who might expect something in the tradition of Herb Ellis or Tal Farlow – or, indeed, of anyone who's played guitar before. Hirt's attitude seems to be to start from scratch and treat it as a new instrument. He gets a different sound on every one of 18 tracks, most of them over in three or four minutes. The sonic range seems inexhaustible, from bizarre dinosaur roars to radio static to feedback banshees to staccato blips and blats. His deadpan titles – 'Percussion', 'Drone', 'Flute', 'Axes' – give nothing away beyond a bare programmatic description. One is occasionally reminded of the work of Fred Frith or Hans Reichel, but only through casting around for comparisons: Hirt is after new sound-worlds, and it's a challenge keeping up with him. 'Please think of Magritte, Duchamp, Broodthaers,' sleeve-note writer Markus Muller pleads. Absolutely.

Jeff Hittman

TENOR SAXOPHONE

Contemporary New York-based saxophonist.

*** **Mosaic**
Soul Note 121 137 *Hittman; Valery Ponomarev (t); Larry Willis (p); Dennis Irwin (b); Yoshitaka Uematsu (d).* 1/86.

Hittman is a Rollins-influenced New Yorker with broad, catholic tastes. Two of the tracks are originals, but it is the choice of material by Hank Mobley ('The Opener'), Steve Grossman ('New York Bossa') and two versions, quick and slow, of 'Cedar's Blues' by pianist Cedar Walton that underlines the saxophonist's versatility and taste. The performances have a relaxed, clubby feel, but they are expertly and sympathetically recorded. Uncontroversial, mainstream-modern jazz with just enough individuality to lift it above the mass.

Fred Ho

BARITONE SAXOPHONE, CHINESE INSTRUMENTS, BANDLEADER

Ho's brand of engaged and ebullient big-band jazz has obvious ties to Charles Mingus, but there are many other influences at work as well, not least a desire to synthesize modern jazz and Eastern influences. This is most effective when it is least self-consciously signalled and when music is given priority over protest and ideology. Ho's baritone isn't a virtuosic voice; drawing somewhat on Carney, it's intended as the sheet anchor of the ensemble, holding the middle together and giving shape to ambitious structures.

*** **Tomorrow Is Now**
Soul Note 121117 *Ho; Sam Furnace (as, ts); Sayyd Abdul Al-Khabyyr, Al Givens (ss, ts, f); Richard Clements (p); Jon Jang (p); Kyoto Fujiwara (b); Taru Alexander (d); Carleen Robinson (v).* 85.

****(*) We Refuse To Be Used And Abused**
Soul Note 1211167 *Ho; Sam Furnace (as, ss, f); Hafez Modir (ts, f); Jon Jang (p); Kyoto Fujiwara (b); Royal Hartigan (perc).* 11/87.

*****(*) The Underground Railway To My Heart**
Soul Note 121267 *Ho; Martin Wehner (tb); Sam Furnace, James Norton (as, ss); David Bindman, Hafez Modirzadeh, Allen Won (ts); Francis Wong (ts, f, picc); Peter Madsen (p); Kyoto Fujiwara, John Shifflet (b); Royal Hartigan (d, perc); Pei Sheng Shen (sona, ob); You Qun Fu (erhu); Pauline Hong (san shuen); Cindy Zuoxin Wang (v).* 90–93.

This is powerfully advocated music from a 'rainbow coalition' of fine young players, Afro- and Asian-Americans in the main. Houn, who has more recently phoneticized his name to Ho, has a big, powerful sound reminiscent of Harry Carney, and this sets the tone for ensembles with a strongly Ellingtonian cast. The title of the first album sets up all sorts of different expectations – from Ornette Coleman's *Tomorrow Is The Question* to Max Roach's *Freedom Now* suite – which are not so much confounded as skirted. There would seem to be little place for prettiness in music as aggressively programmatic as this, but the band plays with surprising delicacy and unfailing taste. CD transfer flatters Ho's skills as an orchestrator.

The second album is more bitty and has a much less coherent sound. There is also an unwonted and mostly unwelcome stridency. Unlike Charlie Haden and his Liberation Music Orchestra, Ho still hadn't quite found a way of synthesizing political urgency with lyricism. That's largely addressed in the excellent *Underground Railway*. It starts unpromisingly with a noodling ethnic jam featuring the double-reed *sona* over bass and drums. What follows is the title-piece: a long, elegantly communicated suite which Ho describes as 'anti-bourgeois boogie-woogie'. Here the Ellington (and Carney) influence is unmistakable and in character. Too much of the remainder is bland *chinoiserie*: full, unfamiliar sonorities used for their own sake. There is, though, an interesting 'revisit' to Billie Holiday's 'Strange Fruit' and a glorious reading of Tizol's 'Caravan'. They make it possible to forgive the multilingual 'Auld Lang Syne' (oh, go on, it's not that bad), or the two closing selections from an 'epic' score called *Journey Beyond The West: The New Adventures Of Monkey*. Nuts to that. Otherwise excellent.

Jim Hobbs (born 1968)

ALTO SAXOPHONE

Free-bop saxophonist working with his trio, the Fully Celebrated Orchestra.

***** Babadita**
Silkheart SHCD 133 *Hobbs; Timo Shanko (b); Django Carranza (d).* 1/93.

***** Peace And Pig Grease**
Silkheart SHCD 136 *As above.* 1/93.

A sparky set of trio workouts. The group is more regularly known as the Fully Celebrated Orchestra, but *Babadita* appears under Hobbs's name – he writes most of the material and hits a point somewhere between Ornette Coleman and (he claims) Willie Nelson. He squeaks his way through a lot of these brief vignettes (there are 15 in 70-odd minutes): interestingly, he claims to have been inspired more by Don Cherry than by the leader on the early Coleman recordings. Shanko and Carranza play boisterously in support and the music is fun, but it doesn't go anywhere particular – three guys in search of a context, which the deliberately quirky and jagged writing doesn't always allow for. *Peace And Pig Grease* is more, from the same time, and is ... more of the same.

Art Hodes (1904–93)

PIANO

Hodes was brought to Chicago from his native Ukraine when he was only a few months old. As player, writer and broadcaster, he was a lifelong devotee and exponent of classic jazz, blues, stride and ragtime. Better known in later years as a solo performer, he began his career in groups run by Wingy Manone, Joe Marsala and Sidney Bechet. For a time Hodes ran his own label and magazine, both called Jazz Record. In origins, temperament and longevity, he was the Irving Berlin of jazz.

***** Vintage Art Hodes**
Solo Art Records SACD 20 *Hodes; Benny Moylan (v).* 30–50.

***** Art For Art's Sake**
Jazzology JCD 46 *Hodes; Freddie Greenleaf (t); Dave Remington (tb); Bill Reinhardt (cl); Truck Parham (b); Freddy Moore (d, v).* 8/39, 8/40, 6/57.

*****(*) The Jazz Record Story**
Jazzology JCD 82 *Hodes; Duke DuVal (t); George Brunies (tb); Rod Cless, Cecil Scott (cl); Pops Foster (b); Joe Grauso, Baby Dodds (d).* 43–46.

Until recently it was believed that, apart from a couple of cuts with Wingy Manone, Art didn't record on his own account before the summer of 1939, though it was known that he had used a Victor Home Recording machine to make half a dozen discs at a gig in Racine, Wisconsin. These were thought to be unplayable and incapable of being dubbed, but Barry Martyn has managed to reconstruct four of them here. 'Ain't Misbehavin'' and 'I Ain't Got Nobody' are indeed vintage Hodes, and no one will particularly mind the scrappy recordings of 'Tin Roof Blues' and 'Cherry', which is a vocal feature for saxophonist Benny Moylan. There is then a wonderful recording of Johnson's 'Snowy Morning Blues', recorded some time in the very early '40s, and a further array of solo sides cut in or around 1944, with two tracks at the end – 'Slow Boogie', 'Fast Boogie' – from 1949 or 1950. All dates are pretty uncertain, but there is no mistaking the importance of these tracks historically. They help to fill in the early history of a player whose awareness and understanding of jazz history were unequalled and priceless.

There are more early solo performances on *Art For Art's Sake*, though by far the best of the material comes later in the span of the compilation. There is a notably good version of Duke Ellington's 'The Mooche' from 1957, and there are group tracks from the same date. Freddy Moore sings on 'None Of My Jelly Roll' and 'Blues And Booze' (a title that chimed very strongly with Art) and Freddy also adds a touch of washboard to 'Tiger

Rag'. Art's solo playing, though, is as ever the key element. His ballad touch is as sure as on faster tempos, and 'Someone To Watch Over Me' is a delight.

The Jazz Record material restores to circulation many of the sides Art cut and released with his own label. The very first tracks, '103rd Street Boogie' and 'Royal Garden Blues', appeared at the end of 1943, credited to the Columbia Quintet, which had played a residency at Childs' Restaurant in New Haven. The wonderful trio with Pops Foster and Baby Dodds is a little later, and there are further group recordings made by the band co-led by Art and three horns, including big Cecil Scott (who had 13 children, eating in shifts and sleeping in tiers). The performances are peppy and joyous, an unalloyed delight for anyone who loves traditional jazz.

*** Parlor Social

Solo Art Records SACD 50 *Hodes; Fred Higginson (p); Russel Roth (d); Buddy Smith (perc).* 51.

The first six numbers, with Art and percussionist Buddy Smith, were recorded during a supper party at Chadwick Hansen's house in Minneapolis. While playing some Jelly Roll Morton records, Smith, who was Art's drummer at the time, revealed that he was the nephew of Andrew Hilaire, who had drummed for Morton. Using a beer case with newspaper taped over the top and a pair of whisk brooms, he improvised a drum kit and sat down to jam with the pianist. Naturally, they began with Morton and 'Granpa's Spells'. There were also versions of Johnson's 'Carolina Shout', Art's 'Stuff And Nonsense' and 'Plain Old Blues', and a wonderful theme called 'Blues Keep Calling', which reaffirms Art's decision to give up alcohol; he was to be a member of Alcoholics Anonymous in the second half of his life. The assembled guests add handclaps and there are sounds of drinking – except, touchingly, on 'Blues Keep Calling' – and train and street sounds from outside. As a document of musicians relaxing and playing for their own enjoyment and edification it is priceless, reminiscent of Bud Powell's recordings in François Paudras's Paris flat. The remaining cuts are by Fred Higginson, a literature scholar and college professor who was an admirer and disciple of Art's. Most of the tunes he tackles are Hodes arrangements, though his own 'Sapient Sutlers' Stomp' (we said he was a college professor) bespeaks an intelligent composer in his own right.

*** All Star Stompers

Jazzology JCD 20 *Hodes; Larry Conger (t); Charlie Bornemann (tb); Tony Parenti (cl); Johnny Baynes (b); Cliff Leeman (d).* 66.

A session recorded at Dreher High School in Columbia, South Carolina, and a relatively unknown band. Bornemann is the strongest of the sidemen; though not a strong soloist, his ensemble work is sparky and brisk, with a lovely tone. 'Willie The Weeper' merits comparison with the Louis Armstrong original, not because it is up to that galactic standard, but because it shows how much Art rethinks and colonizes a familiar theme. The set includes four previously unissued takes and an alternative ending to 'Shake That Thing'. Together with the eight main tracks, they represent an important contribution to a major body of work.

*** Recollections From The Past

Solo Art SACD 41/42 2CD *Hodes (p, v).* 7/71.

Unlike Jelly Roll Morton, Art never claimed to have invented jazz, or to have imported the music from his native Ukraine, but here he does something very similar to Ferdy's Library of Congress recordings. Taking the part of Alan Lomas is Dr Van Velser of Wilmington, North Carolina. Art narrates the story of his engagement with jazz and some of its leading personalities: Sidney Bechet, Bunk Johnson, Eddie Condon and others. There are reminiscences aplenty: of being picked up for speeding, of meeting Hollywood stars, and of drinking with Condon. The playing is illustrative rather than central this time out, but the playing is very good indeed and, though this isn't a set you'll play straight through that often, it's an irresistible self-portrait.

*** Up In Volly's Room

Delmark DE 217 *Hodes; Nappy Trottier (t); George Brunies (tb); Volly DeFaut (cl); Truck Parham (b); Barrett Deems (d).* 3–4/72.

When this was recorded, back in 1972, the clarinet *was* pretty much in abeyance as a jazz instrument and traditional jazz was at its lowest ebb commercially. A great deal has happened since then, of course. There is far greater respect for the tradition, and the emergence of a whole generation of young traditionalists has reduced the impact of this record's special pleading. On its own terms, as relaxed and matey old buzzards meet, it sounds pretty good. DeFaut is a decent player of the Dodds school, with traces of Jimmie Noone and even of Goodman thrown in. He actually appears on only four tracks; the rest are duets with Parham, and the whole thing is topped off like a rather wobbly sundae with two pieces featuring the splendidly monikered Trottier and George Brunies. Poorly recorded, but well worth a listen.

*** Indianapolis Concert

Solo Art SACD 20 *Hodes; Herb Guy (b).* 8/77.

At seventy-plus, Art was in his pomp, utterly confident and articulate and capable of navigating an imaginative course through the repertoire. The highlights are 'C Jam Blues', 'I Can't Get Started' (unusually modernist in conception), 'Mood Indigo' and – an old favourite – Morton's 'Granpa's Spells'. The sound is of intermittent quality, but the playing is good enough to overcome all but the most obsessive quibbles.

*** Echoes Of Chicago

Jazzology JCD 79 *Hodes; Ernie Carson (t); Charlie Bornemann (tb); Herman Foretich (cl); Spencer Clark (bsx); Jerry Rousseau (b); Spider Ridgeway (d); Maxine Sullivan (v).* 2/78.

Haunted by the Windy City, but recorded in the softer chill of Atlanta in February, this is a valuable addition to the roster of Hodes albums with full ensemble. The pairing of string bass and bass saxophone is unusual and stretches the tonality to the limit, with cornet and clarinet at the top end of the range. Maxine Sullivan contributes a vocal to 'It's The Talk Of The Town'. There are two alternatives to 'Sunday', which add little of substance but represent more than a footnote to Art's art.

***(*) Pagin' Mr Jelly

Candid CCD 79037 *Hodes; Nappy Trottier (t); George Brunies (tb); Volly DeFaut (cl); Truck Parham (b); Barrett Deems (d).* 11/88.

****** Keepin' Out Of Mischief Now**

Candid CACD 79717 *As above.* 11/88.

****** The Parkwood Creative Concept Sessions: Volume 1**

Parkwood PWCD 114 *Hodes (p solo).* 4/87–7/89.

If consistency and regularity are the keys to longevity, Hodes seems to have survived by *not* bending to the winds of fashion. His records – solos in particular – tend to be comfortably interchangeable, and only real enthusiasts for his rather throwaway style or for the South Side pianists in general will want shelf-loads. *Real* enthusiasts will already have the Mosaic box, *The Complete Art Hodes Blue Notes*, which remains the most important single item in his catalogue. Though over-represented as a solo performer in comparison with his group work, Hodes conjures some interesting variations on Jelly Roll Morton, his greatest single influence, on *Pagin' Mr Jelly*, and this, or the remaining material from that session on *Mischief*, is perhaps the place for fans of either to start. Hodes's only originals, the title-tune and the related 'Mr Jelly Blues', are virtually impossible to pick out from a session that sticks to only the most sanctified of early jazz tunes: the march 'High Society', 'Wolverine Blues', 'Mr Jelly Lord', 'Winin' Boy Blues', 'Buddy Bolden's Blues' and 'The Pearls'. What's wonderful about Hodes's approach to this material, the Morton stuff in particular, is how *natural* he sounds. There's no pressure or effort, no hint of pastiche, just straightforward playing of magnificent music. For a change, he's playing on a really decent piano, and that is perversely disconcerting.

The Parkwood disc pulls together two sessions from the late 1970s, the second of which, *Art's Originals*, has never been available on vinyl. The earlier of the pair, *Christmastime Jazz and Blues* (or *Joy To The Jazz World*), is the sort of 'concept' package that makes many purists and even fans with more adulterated tastes spit blood. Wrong on this count. The Christmas tunes are beautifully executed and jazzed up. Hodes manages to turn 'Silent Night' into a softly swinging quasi-blues, and even 'Jingle Bells' works. The originals set is less startling but of no less quality. 'Selections From The Gutter', 'Gipsy Man Blues' and 'Russian Ragu' contain unusual harmonic elements that will throw off unwary blindfold listeners. The remainder has Hodes's signature through it like a stick of rock.

***** Art Hodes Jazz Trio**

Jazzology JCD 307 *Hodes; Reimer Von Essen (cl, as); Trevor Richards (d).* 86.

****(*) Art Hodes Trio**

Jazzology JCD 237 *Hodes; Trevor Whiting (reeds); John Petters (d); Dave Bennett (v).* 9/87.

***** Art Hodes Blue Five And Six**

Jazzology JCD 172 *Hodes; Al Fairweather, Pat Halcox (t); Wally Fawkes (cl); Fapy Lapertin (g); Andy Brown (b); Dave Evans, Stan Greig (d); Johnny Mars (v).* 9 & 10/87.

Hodes's trip to Britain in 1987 was as a laying-on of hands, a chance to make contact with someone who belonged to an apostolic line going back to the origins of jazz. Traditional jazz players of all sorts made their way to listen to and sit in with the great man. The results are pretty uniform, with most of the best music coming in solo performances by Hodes himself. There is no apparent stylistic distinction between the Trio and the Jazz Trio; the latter is simply better. The larger groups called on more seasoned and experienced musicians and the playing is better in proportion, with some excellent moments from that Chris Barber stalwart, Pat Halcox. Fawkes is still underrated and Greig is as good in this style as one could hope to find.

****(*) Live From Toronto's Café Des Copains**

Music & Arts 610 *Hodes; Jim Galloway (ss, bs).*

Music & Arts have a slightly odd approach to matchmaking on disc, alternating avant-garde couplings (Anthony Braxton and Marilyn Crispell, Jane Bunnett and Don Pullen) with the likes of this Odd Couple set. Galloway, like Davern, is an instinctive revivalist and seems blissfully unaware of the incongruity of much of the stuff he plays. Though the material doesn't always seem to suit Hodes, he responds imaginatively to some of the Scotsman's more probing cues and plays like a man on monkey glands.

Johnny Hodges (1907–70)

ALTO SAXOPHONE, SOPRANO SAXOPHONE

Born in Massachusetts, Hodges studied with Sidney Bechet and took his place in Willie 'The Lion' Smith's group. In 1928 he joined the Ellington orchestra and remained with Duke for the next four decades, despite occasional forays into leadership himself. Rabbit's intense, bluesy tone is one of the most distinctive instrumental voices in jazz. Though he started out essentially as a soprano specialist, it is his alto playing, ever more pared down as the years went by, that is remembered.

***** Classic Solos: 1928–1942**

Topaz TPZ 1008 *Hodges; Bunny Berigan, Freddy Jenkins, Bubber Miley, Ray Nance, Arthur Whetsol, Cootie Williams (t); Rex Stewart (c); Lawrence Brown, Joe 'Tricky Sam' Nanton, Juan Tizol (tb); Barney Bigard (cl, ts); Harry Carney (bs, as, cl); Otto Hardwick (as, bsx); Ben Webster (ts); Duke Ellington, Teddy Wilson (p); Fred Guy (bj); Lawrence Lucie, Allan Reuss (g); Hayes Alvis, Jimmy Blanton, Wellman Braud, John Kirby, Grachan Moncur, Billy Taylor (b); Cozy Cole, Sonny Greer (d); Mildred Bailey (v).* 10/28–7/41.

***** Jeep's Blues: His Greatest Recordings: 1928–1941**

ASV CD AJA 5180 *As above, except add Buck Clayton, Louis Metcalf (t), Buster Bailey (cl), Lester Young (ts), Edgar Sampson (bs), Jess Stacy (p), Lionel Hampton (vib), Artie Bernstein, Harry Goodman (b), Gene Krupa (d), Billie Holiday (v).* 6/28–6/41.

*****(*) Johnny Hodges And His Orchestra, 1937–1939**

Black & Blue 59.239 *Hodges; Cootie Williams (t); Lawrence Brown (tb); Harry Carney (bs); Duke Ellington, Billy Strayhorn (p); Billy Taylor, Jimmy Blanton (b); Sonny Greer (d).* 3/38–10/39.

There are probably no voices in jazz more purely sensuous than that of John Cornelius Hodge (the extra 's' was added later). Subtract Hodges's solos from Duke Ellington's recorded output and it shrinks disproportionately. He was a stalwart presence right from the Cotton Club Orchestra through the Webster–Blanton years and beyond. Sadly, perhaps, for all his pricklish dislike of sideman status in the Ellington orchestra (he frequently mimed counting bills in the Duke's direction when receiving his usual ovation for yet another perfectly crafted solo), Hodges was a rather unassertive leader, and his own recordings under-represent his extraordinary qualities, which began to dim only with the onset of the 1960s.

The ASV and the Topaz do a fairly good job of compiling a representative profile and doing so with very little overlap. Probably the best guide to these is not personnel but session dates. Topaz ignore things like the 1940 'Good Queen Bess' and the slightly earlier 'Warm Valley', but material from the 1929 Cotton Club Orchestra *is* included, filling in an important gap in the transition from blues and jump to the lyrical majesty of later years. Hodges's alto (and occasionally soprano) stand out strongly wherever featured, and The Black & Blue selection (which overlaps only on half-a-dozen tracks, inevitably including 'The Jeep Is Jumping') is a good option, selecting the better material and skipping some of the fluff. Despite the date given in the title, the dates all come from 1938 and 1939. All this leaves room for a dozen tracks from 1939. Hodges switches to soprano again for 'Rent Party Blues' (Topaz) and 'Tired Socks' (ASV).

***(*) Passion Flower

RCA 66616 *Hodges; Cat Anderson, Harold Baker, Willie Cook, Roy Eldridge, Clark Terry (t); Ray Nance (t, vn); Lawrence Brown, Quentin Jackson, John Sanders, Britt Woodman (tb); Russell Procope (as, cl); Paul Gonsalves, Ben Webster (ts); Jimmy Hamilton (ts, cl); Harry Carney (bs, cl, bcl); Call Cobbs, Duke Ellington, Raymond Fol, Lou Levy, Billy Strayhorn (p); Herb Ellis (g); Les Spann (g, vn); Al Hall, Sam Jones, Wendell Marshall, Earl May, Wilfred Middlebrooks, Jimmy Woode (b); Butch Ballard, Louie Bellson, Gus Johnson, Jo Jones, Ed Thigpen, Sam Woodyard (d).* 11/40–7/46.

Hodges recorded eight sides for Bluebird in 1940, including the classic 'Good Queen Bess' (two takes), 'Squatty Roo', and Strayhorn's 'Passion Flower'. Hodges is buoyant and alert, though not yet in possession of the intense romantic tone of later years. The compilation is filled out with a baker's dozen of tracks with the Ellington orchestra.

***(*) Caravan

Prestige PRCD 24103 *Hodges; Taft Jordan, Cat Anderson, Harold Baker (t); Lawrence Brown, Juan Tizol (tb); Willie Smith (as); Paul Gonsalves, Al Sears (ts); Jimmy Hamilton (ts, cl); Harry Carney (bs); Duke Ellington (p); Billy Strayhorn (p, org); Wendell Marshall, Oscar Pettiford (b); Wilbur De Paris, Louie Bellson, Sonny Greer (d).* 6/47–6/51.

The sessions on *Caravan* were originally recorded for the short-lived Mercer label. Long unavailable, they include some classics, like 'Charlotte Russe' (aka 'Lotus Blossom'), for which Hodges, Duke and Strayhorn all claimed some credit at varying times. Recorded in 1947, it is one of the most graceful of Hodges's solos. 'Caravan' itself is performed by a band that includes Duke Ellington and the composer, Juan Tizol, himself. Hodges isn't featured on the later stages of what was originally a double LP, lest anyone mistake Willie Smith for him.

***(*) Jazz Masters 35: Johnny Hodges

Verve 521857-2 *Hodges; Cat Anderson, Shorty Baker, Emmett Berry, Willie Cook, Roy Eldridge, Dizzy Gillespie, Eddie Mullens, Ernie Royal, Charlie Shavers, Clark Terry, Snooky Young (t); Ray Nance (t, v); Lawrence Brown, Chuck Connors, Vic Dickenson, Quentin Jackson, John Saunders, Britt Woodman (tb); Tony Studd (btb); Russell Procope, Jerome Richardson, Frank Wess (cl, as); Jimmy Hamilton (cl, ts); Danny Bank (cl, bs); Benny Carter, Charlie Parker (as); Paul Gonsalves, Flip Phillips, Al Sears, Ben Webster (ts); Harry Carney, Gerry Mulligan (bs); Earl Hines, Jimmy Jones, Hank Jones, Leroy Lovett, Junior Mance, Oscar Peterson, Billy Strayhorn, Claude Williamson (p); Everett Barksdale, Kenny Burrell, Barney Kessel, Les Spann (g); Aaron Bell, Ray Brown, Buddy Clark, Richard Davis, Milt Hinton, Sam Jones, Lloyd Trottman, Jimmy Woode (b); Sonny Greer, J.C Heard, Lex Humphries, Mel Lewis, Joe Marshall, Grady Tate, Sam Woodyard (d).* 2/51–8/67.

***(*) Johnny Hodges With Billy Strayhorn And The Orchestra

Verve 557543-2 *Hodges; Cat Anderson, Shorty Baker, Bill Berry, Howard McGhee, Ed Mullens (t); Lawrence Brown, Quentin Jackson, Chuck Connors (tb); Russell Procope (cl, as); Jimmy Hamilton (cl, ts); Paul Gonsalves (ts); Harry Carney (bs, cl); Jimmy Jones (p); Aaron Bell (b); Sam Woodyard (d).* 61.

Only Verve and Bluebird have done anything to bring Hodges into the CD era. At least the Verve Jazz Masters compilation is an ideal representation of later Hodges, at his most magisterial. Usually working with Ellingtonians, there is little to distinguish most of these settings from Ducal ones, except for the fact that Rabbit is even more generously featured than usual. It is wonderful to hear him in the company of a baritonist other than Carney on the 1959 session with Mulligan, and the compilation reprises the July 1952 Norman Granz jam which saw Hodges on stage with Benny Carter, Ben Webster and Charlie Parker.

A more recent arrival is the set arranged by Strayhorn and rather coyly credited to 'The Orchestra', in other words, Ellington with the Duke on holiday. Rabbit could hardly have been in more familiar company for a concerto-like situation and, if he doesn't exactly put himself out to make the most of the opportunities, that isn't what such a hardened pro would have done anyway.

***(*) Johnny Hodges At Sportpalast, Berlin

Pablo 2620 102 2CD *Hodges; Ray Nance (t); Lawrence Brown (tb); Harry Carney (bs); Al Williams (p); Aaron Bell (b); Sam Woodyard (d).* 61.

Still associating largely with Ellingtonians, Hodges entered his final decade possessed of a magisterial voice which was like no other in jazz and which increasingly seemed the ancestor of everyone from John Coltrane to Bobby Watson. A surprising dearth of live material makes the return of the 1961 Sportpalast recording doubly welcome. Hodges was in magnificent voice on this occasion, playing with the moody grace that was his stock-in-trade. A few moments into 'Satin Doll' one realizes how wonderful it would have been to have seen this complex, rather difficult man perform as he does on these discs.

**** Everybody Knows Johnny Hodges

Impulse! GRP 11162 *Hodges; Cat Anderson, Rolf Ericson, Herbie Jones, Ray Nance (t); Lawrence Brown, Buster Cooper, Britt Woodman (tb); Harry Carney, Paul Gonsalves, Jimmy Hamilton, Russell Procope (reeds); Jimmy Jones (p); Ernie Shepard (b); Grady Tate (d).* 2/64.

Perhaps the best known of his latter-day records, the lovely *Everybody Knows Johnny Hodges* has reappeared in a bright CD issue that captures the saxophonist's distinctive combination of tough jump tunes and aching ballads. Billy Strayhorn composed '310 Blues' specially for the session; Hodges is somewhat upstaged by both Gonsalves and the on-form Brown, but he has the final word. Strayhorn's other credit is the evergreen 'A Flower Is A Lovesome Thing', given a brief and tender reading. It's one of four small-group pieces from within the full band. 'Papa Knows' and 'Everybody Knows' represent a pair; the first is something of a ragbag of familiar Hodges materials, the latter a fine opening blues. Other tracks include a big-band 'Main Stem' and a medleyed 'I Let A Song Go Out Of My Heart'/'Don't Get Around Much Anymore'.

**** Johnny Hodges With Lawrence Welk's Orchestra**

Ranwood 8246 *Hodges; Lawrence Welk Orchestra; Vic Schoen Orchestra.* 12/65.

Eh? After Ellington, where would you go? Not most obviously to the smoothnesses of Lawrence Welk, except that the much-maligned bandleader, with his passion for the polka, was a lifelong lover of beautiful music. The settings are lush and neutral enough to act as mere backdrops to Hodges's soloing, which is of typically high quality.

Jan Gunnar Hoff (born 1958)

KEYBOARDS

Born in Bødo, Hoff has been playing and working in relative isolation in the north of Norway. He played a 'debut' solo concert at the 1992 Harstad Festival.

***** Syklus**

Odin 4046-2 *Hoff; Knut Riisnaes (ss, ts); Tor Yttredal (ss); Bjorn Kjellemyr (b); Audun Kleive, Trond Kopperud (d); Celio De Carvalho (perc).* 10/92–2/93.

*****(*) Moving**

Curling Legs CLP CD 16 *As above, except add Per Jorgensen (t, v); omit Yttredal, Kopperud, de Carvalho.* 4/94–2/95.

Hoff is from the far north of Norway and his music sounds like the result of a lot of meditation – not necessarily profound, but there's not a note that doesn't seem considered. A track on *Syklus* called 'New York City' sounds like the fantasy of a man who's never been far from home. Actually, these are calm, lucid examples of a blueprint which the region has long since perfected, and inevitably they were set down by Jan Erik Kongshaug at Rainbow Studio. The earlier disc is a shade undeveloped, the promise of the opening and closing improvisations never quite fulfilled, but there's some lovely playing – Riisnaes is absolutely the man for the sax role, and Yttredal's two appearances only underline that. Hoff picks out his solos with obsessive care, but his use of electric keyboards – as sparing as desert rainfall – is very effective. *Moving* moves on via some superior themes and the surprisingly effective use of Jorgensen, whose three (wordless? – certainly hard to decipher) vocals add an emotive, almost a shamanistic colour to four tracks.

Jay Hoggard (born 1954)

VIBRAPHONE

On the fringes of the New Haven new-music scene in the '70s, then moved to New York and played in more straight-ahead, post-bop surroundings. Some profile as a leader in the '80s, but has rather slipped from sight of late.

***** Solo Vibraphone**

India Navigation IN 1040 *Hoggard (vib solo).* 11/78.

****(*) Rain Forest**

Original Jazz Classics OJC 800 *Hoggard; Chico Freeman (ts); Kenny Kirkland (ky); John Koenig (clo, g); Roland Bautista (g); Francisco Centeno (b); Harvey Mason (d); Paulinho Da Costa, Jose Guico (perc); Maxayn Lewis, Patryce Banks, Sybil Thomas (v).* 11/80.

There's a fierceness about Hoggard – 'the little tiger', the name of one of his albums, seems a perfect description – that communicates itself through almost everything he does, not just the more avant-garde aspects. His exposure is currently thin due to the disappearance of all his Muse albums, and this pair are merely worthwhile. The solo India Navigation set, now reissued with extra tracks, is one side of Hoggard's musical personality. Titles like 'May Those Who Love Apartheid Rot In Hell' give a sense of the burning intensity that fuels his work, but even here it's worth noting that such pieces sit alongside 'Toe Dance For A Baby' and a markedly jovial reading of 'Air Mail Special'. Recorded live, the disc doesn't give the best representation of Hoggard's clean, exact delivery. Technically, he sounds closer to Hamp than to Milt Jackson or Bobby Hutcherson. *Rain Forest*, a Contemporary date now reissued in the OJC series, is muddled by the Latin percussion and misguided vocals, and often seems inappropriately lightweight for such a dignified performer; but the sparkle of Hoggard's best playing glints through what looks suspiciously like a session he was talked into leading. Currently he seems disappointingly out of favour as a recording artist.

John Högman (born 1953)

TENOR AND BARITONE SAXOPHONES, SYNTHESIZER

Based in Uppsala, Högman was turned on to jazz by hearing an Edmond Hall record. He got to know Thomas Arnesen, Ulf Johansson and others as a youth and deleoped as a swing-to-bop player through the 1970s and '80s.

*****(*) Good Night Sister**

Sittel SITCD 9202 *Högman; Ulf Johansson (tb); Knud Jorgensen (p); Thomas Arnesen (g); Nils-Erik Sparf (vn, vla); Bengt Hansson (b); Johan Dielemans (d).* 10/92.

***** 203 Park Drive**

Sittel SITCD 9229 *Högman; Bosse Broberg (t); Jens Lindgren (tb); Gosta Rundqvist (p); Bengt Hansson (b); Martin Lofgren (d); Omnibus Wind Ensemble.* 9/95.

Good Night Sister is hugely enjoyable. Högman's opening tune, 'Theodore', is a Sonny Rollins dedication that makes clear his primary influence, but it's Rollins without the soul-searching and the inner demons: what one hears is a confident unfurling of fine melodic ideas, etched in a big, shapely sound. He plays baritone on two cuts, and that sounds just as impressive. 'Look For The Silver Lining' is another Theodore-like performance, but the exquisite ballad-work on the title-piece and the wry, ambivalent bounce of 'Hiccup' prove his range. Johansson and Arnesen take cameo roles; more important is Jorgensen, who plays very well but who sadly died only weeks after the session.

203 Park Drive doesn't quite match up. Maybe Högman is just being too self-effacing here: he doesn't even start playing until three minutes into the first track, and guest spots for Broberg, Lindgren and the Omnibus Wind group take the focus off him when what we want to hear is his own playing, which remains full of charm and light. Unhurried at any tempo and gently smouldering on the ballads, Högman earns the stars by himself. But the disc is a bit too long, and the space offered to everyone else takes some of the appeal off what is still a good record.

Billie Holiday (1915–59)

VOCAL

Born in Baltimore, Holiday had a wretched childhood, but she was singing early and made her first records in 1933. Her pre-war sessions with Teddy Wilson established her reputation, followed by stints with Basie and Artie Shaw, before choosing to work as a soloist. Drink and narcotics problems, which attended the rest of her life, held her back, but she worked through the '40s, despite a spell in prison, and began recording for Decca in 1944. She tried but largely failed to make a career in films, and eventually signed to Norman Granz's operation in 1952. Her voice declined to a croak, but her musicianship stayed intact.

***** The Quintessential Billie Holiday Vol. 1 1933–35**
Columbia 450987-2 *Holiday; Charlie Teagarden, Shirley Clay, Roy Eldridge, Dick Clark (t); Benny Morton, Jack Teagarden (tb); Cecil Scott, Benny Goodman, Tom Macey (cl); Johnny Hodges (as); Art Karle, Ben Webster, Chu Berry (ts); Joe Sullivan, Teddy Wilson (p); Dick McDonough, Lawrence Lucie, John Trueheart, Dave Barbour (g); Artie Bernstein, Grachan Moncur, John Kirby (b); Cozy Cole, Gene Krupa (d).* 11/33–12/35.

*****(*) The Quintessential Billie Holiday Vol. 2 1936**
Columbia 460060-2 *Holiday; Chris Griffin, Jonah Jones, Bunny Berigan, Irving Randolph (t); Rudy Powell, Artie Shaw, Irving Fazola, Vido Musso (cl); Harry Carney (cl, bs); Johnny Hodges (as); Ted McCrae, Ben Webster (ts); Teddy Wilson (p); John Trueheart, Allan Reuss, Dick McDonough (g); Grachan Moncur, John Kirby, Pete Peterson, Artie Bernstein, Milt Hinton (b); Cozy Cole, Gene Krupa (d).* 1–10/36.

****** The Quintessential Billie Holiday Vol. 3 1936–37**
Columbia 460820-2 *Holiday; Irving Randolph, Jonah Jones, Buck Clayton, Henry 'Red' Allen (t); Vido Musso, Benny Goodman (cl); Cecil Scott (cl, as, ts); Edgar Sampson (cl, as); Ben Webster, Lester Young, Prince Robinson (ts); Teddy Wilson (p); Allan Reuss, Jimmy McLin (g); Milt Hinton, John Kirby, Walter Page (b); Gene Krupa, Cozy Cole, Jo Jones (d).* 10/36–2/37.

***** Billie Holiday 1933–37**
Classics 582 *As above three discs.* 33–37.

****** The Quintessential Billie Holiday Vol. 4 1937**
Columbia 463333-2 *Holiday; Cootie Williams, Eddie Tompkins, Buck Clayton (t); Buster Bailey, Edmond Hall (cl); Johnny Hodges (as); Joe Thomas, Lester Young (ts); Harry Carney (bs); Teddy Wilson, James Sherman (p); Carmen Mastren, Freddie Green, Allan Reuss (g); Artie Bernstein, Walter Page, John Kirby (b); Cozy Cole, Alphonse Steele, Jo Jones (d).* 2–6/37.

*****(*) The Quintessential Billie Holiday Vol. 5 1937–38**
Columbia 465190-2 *Holiday; Buck Clayton (t); Benny Morton (tb); Buster Bailey (cl); Prince Robinson, Vido Musso (cl, ts); Lester Young (ts); Claude Thornhill, Teddy Wilson (p); Allan Reuss, Freddie Green (g); Walter Page (b); Jo Jones (d).* 6/37–1/38.

*****(*) The Quintessential Billie Holiday Vol. 6 1938**
Columbia 466313-2 *Holiday; Bernard Anderson, Buck Clayton, Harry James (t); Dicky Wells, Benny Morton (tb); Buster Bailey (cl); Edgar Sampson, Benny Carter (as); Lester Young (cl, ts); Babe Russin, Herschel Evans (ts); Claude Thornhill, Margaret 'Queenie' Johnson, Teddy Wilson (p); Al Casey, Freddie Green (g); John Kirby, Walter Page (b); Cozy Cole, Jo Jones (d).* 5–11/38.

****(*) The Quintessential Billie Holiday Vol. 7 1938–39**
Columbia 466966-2 *Holiday; Charlie Shavers, Roy Eldridge, Hot Lips Page, Frankie Newton (t); Bobby Hackett (c); Trummy Young, Tyree Glenn (tb); Tab Smith (ss, as); Benny Carter, Toots Mondello (cl, as); Teddy Buckner (as); Kenneth Hollon, Ernie Powell, Bud Freeman, Chu Berry, Stanley Payne (ts); Teddy Wilson, Sonny Payne, Kenny Kersey (p); Danny Barker, Al Casey, Jimmy McLin, Bernard Addison (g); Milt Hinton, John Williams (b); Cozy Cole, Eddie Dougherty (d).* 11/38–7/39.

***** Billie Holiday 1937–1939**
Classics 592 *As above four discs.* 37–39.

***** The Quintessential Billie Holiday Vol. 8 1939–1940**
Columbia 467914-2 *Holiday; Charlie Shavers, Buck Clayton, Roy Eldridge, Harry 'Sweets' Edison (t); Tab Smith, Earl Warren, Jimmy Powell, Carl Frye, Don Redman, Georgie Auld (as); Kenneth Hollon, Stanley Payne, Lester Young, Kermit Scott, Jimmy Hamilton, Don Byas (ts); Jack Washington (bs); Sonny White, Teddy Wilson, Joe Sullivan (p); Bernard Addison, Freddie Green, John Collins, Lawrence Lucie (g); John Williams, Walter Page, Al Hall (b); Eddie Dougherty, Jo Jones, Harold 'Doc' West, Kenny Clarke (d).* 7/39–9/40.

***** Billie Holiday 1939–1940**
Classics 601 *As above two Columbia discs.* 39–40.

***** The Quintessential Billie Holiday Vol. 9 1940–42**
Columbia 467915-2 *Holiday; Bill Coleman, Shad Collins, Emmett Berry, Roy Eldridge (t); Benny Morton (tb); Jimmy Hamilton (cl); Benny Carter (cl, as); Leslie Johnakins, Hymie Schertzer, Eddie Barefield, Ernie Powell, Lester Boone, Jimmy Powell (as); Lester Young, Georgie Auld, Babe Russin (ts); Sonny White, Teddy Wilson, Eddie Heywood (p); Ulysses Livingston, John Collins, Paul Chapman, Gene Fields, Al Casey (g); Wilson Meyers, Grachan Moncur, John Williams, Ted Sturgis (b); Yank

Porter, Kenny Clarke, J.C Heard, Herbert Cowens (d). 10/40–2/42.

Billie Holiday remains among the most difficult of jazz artists to understand or study. Surrounded by a disturbing legend, it is very difficult to hear her clearly. The legendary suffering and mythopoeic pain which countless admirers have actively sought out in her work make it difficult for the merely curious to warm to a singer who was an uneven and sometimes baffling performer. There is occasionally a troubling detachment in Holiday's singing which is quite the opposite of the living-every-line virtue which some have impressed on her records; and those that she made in her later years often demand an almost voyeuristic role of any listener determined to enjoy her interpretations. Nevertheless, Holiday was a singular and unrepeatable talent whose finest hours are remarkably revealing and often surprisingly – given her generally morose reputation as an artist – joyful. New listeners may find the accumulated weight of the Holiday myth discouraging, and they may be equally surprised at how much fun many of the earlier records are.

Virtually all of her music is now available on CD: the nine-record sequence on Columbia is perhaps the most desirable way to collect the pre-war material, although, as with the Classics discs, the transfers don't have much sparkle but homogenize the often superb accompaniments into a dull blend that lacks dynamics, although even the original 78s admittedly don't have as much zip as they might. The standard of these records – particularly considering how many tracks were made – is finally very high, and the best of them are as poised and finely crafted as any small-group jazz of the period. One of Holiday's innovations was to suggest a role for the singer which blended in with the rest of the musicians, improvising a line and taking a 'solo' which was as integrated as anything else on the record. On her earlier sides with Wilson as leader, she was still credited as responsible for the 'vocal refrain', but the later titles feature 'Billie Holiday and her Orchestra'. She starts some records and slips into the middle of others, but always there's a feeling of a musician at ease with the rest of the band and aware of the importance of fitting into the performance as a whole.

Her tone, on the earliest sides, is still a little raw and unformed, and the trademark rasp at the edge of her voice – which she uses to canny effect on the later titles – is used less pointedly; but the unaffected styling is already present, and there are indications of her mastery of time even in the tracks on *Quintessential* Volume 1. While the most obvious characteristic of her singing is the lagging behind the beat, she seldom sounds tired or slow to respond, and the deeper impression is of a vocalist who knows exactly how much time she can take. She never scats, rarely drifts far from the melody, and respects structure and lyrical nuance, even where – as has often been remarked – the material is less than blue-chip. But her best singing invests the words with shades of meaning which vocalists until that point had barely looked at: she creates an ambiguity between what the words say and what she might be thinking which is very hard to distil. And that is the core of Holiday's mystique. Coupled with the foggy, baleful, sombre quality of her tone, it creates a vocal jazz which is as absorbing as it is enduring.

Like her fellow musicians, she had good and bad days, and that's one reason why it's difficult to pinpoint the best of the records listed above. Some may prefer to have those albums featuring the best-known songs; but one peculiarity of these sessions is that her attention seldom depends on the quality of the material. An otherwise forgotten Tin Pan Alley novelty may give rise to as great a performance as any of the best-known standards. The constantly changing personnel is also a variable. The tracks with Lester Young on tenor (and occasionally clarinet) have been acclaimed as the greatest of her collaborations, and those on Volumes 3 and 4 of the Columbia sequence are certainly among the best tracks: but some may find them occasionally lachrymose rather than moving. 'This Year's Kisses' (Volume 3), for instance, may be a serenely involving treatment of the song, with Holiday and Young seemingly reading each other's minds, but it points towards the bathos which blights much of her later work. Other accompanists do equally fine work in their way: Roy Eldridge, who suppresses his wildest side to surprisingly controlled effect on his appearances; Ben Webster, whose solo on 'With Thee I Swing' (Volume 2) is memorably sustained; Bunny Berigan, who plays superbly on Volume 2 and contributes (along with Artie Shaw) a classic solo to 'Billie's Blues', one of the greatest performances in the series; Irving Fazola, Buck Clayton, Tab Smith and Hot Lips Page, who all play with knowing insight; and, above all, Teddy Wilson, who organized many of the sessions and who finesses his playing into little masterpieces of economy and apposite counterpoint, whether in solo or ensemble terms.

Holiday herself is at her freshest and most inspirational in these pre-war recordings and, whatever one may think about the later albums, these sessions surrender nothing in gravitas and communicate a good humour which is all their own. The session producers – John Hammond or Bernie Hanighen – encouraged an atmosphere of mutual creativity which the singer seldom fails to respond to and, even on the less immortal songs, Holiday makes something of the situation: there is no sense of her fighting against the material, as there often is with Armstrong or Waller in the same period. On some sessions she sounds less interested: much of the music on Volume 7 fails; and elsewhere she reacts against a tempo or simply lets her interest flag, sometimes within the parameters of a single tune. If we single out Volumes 3, 4 and 5 of the Columbia series, it's purely because some of the tracks – such as 'I Must Have That Man', 'My Last Affair' (3), 'Foolin' Myself', 'Mean To Me' (4), 'Trav'lin' All Alone' and 'I Can't Believe That You're In Love With Me' (5) – reach a special peak of creativity from all involved. The Classics CDs cover all the material which isn't also included on their Teddy Wilson series: a useful way to fill gaps if the other discs are already in the collection, but splitting the music between Wilson and Holiday separates much of the best material. The transfer quality is mixed.

Other compilations from the period include: *The Early Classics 1935–40* (Flapper CD-9756), a decent cross-section in bright if sometimes thin sound; *Greatest Hits* (Columbia CK 65757), a recent and enjoyable pick of this period; *16 Most Requested Songs* (Columbia 474401-2), an excellent choice; and *Lady Day's 25 Greatest Hits* (ASV AJA5181), an ambitious title but a sound choice, which underlines that it's difficult to go wrong in choosing the tracks for early Holiday compilations.

*** The Legacy (1933–1958)

Columbia 469049-2 3CD *As above Columbia discs, plus Duke Ellington Orchestra, Benny Goodman Orchestra, Martha Tilton, Johnny Mercer, Leo Watson (v).* 33–58.

An unsatisfactory mixture of Columbia's pick from the nine-volume 'Quintessential' series and various obscure airshots, including 'Saddest Tale' with Ellington and two pieces with Goodman's band. There are 70 tracks, and most of them come from the 1936–41 period; only a few from her final years are here, and they sound wretched in comparison. Ornately packaged in an oversize box, this seems awkward and unnecessarily over-bearing as a compilation, but the best of the music is, of course, splendid.

***** The Complete Commodore Recordings**

Commodore CMD 24012 2CD *Holiday; Frankie Newton, Doc Cheatham, Freddy Webster (t); Vic Dickenson (tb); Lem Davis, Tab Smith (as); Stan Payne, Kenneth Hollon (ts); Eddie Heywood, Sonny White (p); Jimmy McLin, Teddy Walters (g); John Williams, John Simmons (b); Eddie Dougherty, Big Sid Catlett (d).* 4/39–8/44.

Holiday's Commodore sessions account for only 17 titles all told, but the numerous multiple takes make up enough music for a two-disc set, and this is the definitive edition. It opens on her signature set-piece, 'Strange Fruit', which sets a sombre tone for the first session, and though there's then a jump of some five years the rest of the tracks tend to follow the pattern of subdued tempos and rather severe interpretations. The ultra-slow speed of 'How Am I To Know' is startling in itself, and so in its way is the gently entreating 'Lover Come Back To Me'. The accompaniments include some excellent players, but Eddie Heywood's charts give them precious little chance to shine. This is one of the least well-known periods in the Holiday discography, and with the over-abundance of rejected takes it's very much a set for hardcore collectors only. The remastering is good enough, even if the original recording left something to be desired.

*****(*) The Complete Original American Decca Recordings**

GRP 052601-2 2CD *Holiday; Russ Case, Joe Guy, Gordon Griffin, Rostelle Reese, Billy Butterfield, Jimmy Nottingham, Emmett Berry, Buck Clayton, Bernie Privin, Tony Faso, Dick Vance, Shad Collins, Bobby Williams, Bobby Hackett (t); Dicky Wells, George Matthews, Henderson Chambers, Mort Bullman, George Stevenson (tb); Milt Yaner, Bill Stegmeyer (cl, as); Hymie Schertzer, Jack Cressey, Lem Davis, Toots Mondello, Al Klink, Rudy Powell, George Dorsey, Johnny Mince, Pete Clark, Sid Cooper (as); John Fulton (ts, cl, f); Dick Eckles (ts, f); Larry Binyon, Paul Ricci, Dave Harris, Hank Ross, Armand Camgros, Bob Dorsey, Art Drelinger, Lester Young, Joe Thomas, Budd Johnson, Freddie Williams, Pat Nizza (ts); Eddie Barefield (bs, cl); Stan Webb, Sol Moore, Dave McRae (bs); Dave Bowman, Sammy Benskin, Joe Springer, Charles LaVere, Bobby Tucker, Billy Kyle, Horace Henderson, Bernie Leighton (p); Carl Kress, Tony Mottola, Everett Barksdale, Bob Bain, Mundell Lowe, Tiny Grimes, Jimmy Shirley, Dan Perry (g); Haig Stephens, Bob Haggart, Billy Taylor, John Simmons, Thomas Barney, George Duvivier, Joe Benjamin, Jack Lesberg, Lou Butterman (b); Johnny Blowers, George Wettling, Specs Powell, Big Sid Catlett, Kelly Martin, Denzil Best, Kenny Clarke, Norris 'Bunny' Shawker, Shadow Wilson, Cozy Cole, Wallace Bishop, Jimmy Crawford, Nick Fatool (d); Louis Armstrong (v); strings and choir.* 10/44–3/50.

***** Billie Holiday 1944**

Classics 806 *Similar to above, except add Roy Eldridge, Doc Cheatham, Freddy Webster (t), Vic Dickenson (tb), Barney Bigard (cl), Lem Davis (as), Al Casey, Teddy Walters (g), Oscar Pettiford (b).* 3–11/44.

Holiday's Decca sessions have been impeccably presented here, in a double-CD set which has been remastered to make the music sound as big and clear as possible. Some may prefer a warmer and less boomy sound, but the timbre of the records is impressively full and strong. These sessions were made when Holiday had established a wider reputation, and their feel is very different from the Columbia records: carefully orchestrated by a multitude of hands, including Sy Oliver and Gordon Jenkins, the best of them are as good as anything Holiday did. Many listeners may, indeed, find this the single most entertaining set of Holiday reissues on the market, for the polish and class of the singing and playing – while less spontaneously improvisational in feel – are hard to deny. Her own songs, 'Don't Explain' and 'God Bless The Child', are obvious highlights, even if they mark the beginning of Holiday's 'victim' image, and here is the original reading of the subsequently famous 'That Ole Devil Called Love', two duets with Louis Armstrong, slow and emotionally draining readings of 'Porgy' and 'My Man' (from the one session with the sole accompaniment of a rhythm section), and a lot of pleasing, brightly paced readings of superior standards. Few players stand out the way Young and Wilson do on the pre-war sides, but these aren't the same kind of records.

The Classics sequence continues with various 1944 tracks. It starts with three numbers from a Metropolitan Opera House show, with Eldridge and Tatum in the band, then goes through material with Eddie Heywood's Orchestra and finally reaches the first of the sessions on the MCA set. A useful in-between compilation.

***** Billie Holiday 1945–1948**

Classics 1040 *Holiday; Louis Armstrong (t, v); Joe Guy, Rostelle Reese, Billy Butterfield (t); Henderson Chambers (tb); Bill Stegmeyer (cl, as); Edmond Hall (cl); Toots Mondello, Al Klink, Lem Davis (as); Hank Ross, Armand Camgros, Bob Dorsey, Art Drellinger, Bernie Kaufman (ts); Stan Webb (bs); Sammy Benskin, Joe Springer, Billy Kyle, Bobby Tucker, Charlie Bateman (p); Mundell Lowe, Tiny Grimes, Jimmy Shirley, Dan Perri (g); John Simmons, Bob Haggart, Billy Taylor, Thomas Barney, Johnny Williams, John Levy (b); Specs Powell, Kelly Martin, Kenny Clarke, Big Sid Catlett, Denzil Best, Jimmy Crawford, Bunny Shawker (d); The Stardusters (v); strings.* 8/45–12/48.

An unhappy period, during which Holiday served time for narcotics possession, but there were nevertheless some fine records. 'Don't Explain' and 'Good Morning Heartache' appear in their definitive versions. 'The Blues Are Brewin'' is a beauty. The comeback date of December 1948 is saddled with the cooing Stardusters singing on two tracks, but 'Porgy' and 'My Man' are vintage Billie. Two V-Discs with Louis Armstrong fill out the disc. Excellent sound.

****** Billie's Love Songs**

Nimbus NI 2000 Holiday; various personnel as appropriate discs above, 35–49.

Robert Parker's new remastering series for Nimbus gets off to a tremendous start with what is surely the finest single-disc collection of Holiday on the market. Twenty tracks, excellently chosen, show all sides of the great voice, from 'Lover Man' to delicious upbeat material such as 'Twenty-Four Hours A Day'; but the real joy of the set is how immaculate the transfers are. Ten of the tracks are from pre-war Columbia masters and they've never sounded better than this. On this evidence, Parker should immediately be given the job of remastering all of Holiday's Columbia output, since his work shames the company's own efforts.

*****(*) Solitude**
Verve 519810-2 *Holiday; Charlie Shavers (t); Flip Phillips (ts); Oscar Peterson (p); Barney Kessel (g); Ray Brown (b); Alvin Stoller (d).* 52.

***** Recital By Billie Holiday**
Verve 521868-2 *Holiday; Harry 'Sweets' Edison, Joe Newman, Charlie Shavers (t); Willie Smith (as); Paul Quinichette (ts); Oscar Peterson (p, org); Bobby Tucker (p); Herb Ellis, Freddie Green, Barney Kessel (g); Ray Brown, Red Callender (b); Chico Hamilton, Gus Johnson, Ed Shaughnessy (d).* 7/52–9/54.

***** Lady Sings The Blues**
Verve 521429-2 *Holiday; Charlie Shavers (t); Tony Scott (cl, p); Budd Johnson, Paul Quinichette (ts); Wynton Kelly, Billy Taylor (p); Billy Bauer, Kenny Burrell (g); Aaron Bell, Leonard Gaskin (b); Cozy Cole, Lennie McBrowne (d).* 2/55–6/56.

*****(*) Music For Torching**
Verve 527455-2 *Holiday; similar to above.* 8/56.

****** All Or Nothing At All**
Verve 529226-2 *Holiday; Harry 'Sweets' Edison (t); Ben Webster (ts); Jimmy Rowles (p); Barney Kessel (g); Joe Mondragon (b); Alvin Stoller (d).* 8/56–1/57.

****** Songs For Distingué Lovers**
Verve 539056-2 *As above, except add Larry Bunker (d).* 7/56.

*****(*) The Billie Holiday Songbook**
Verve 823246-2 *Holiday; Joe Newman, Charlie Shavers, Roy Eldridge, Buck Clayton, Harry 'Sweets' Edison (t); Tony Scott (cl); Willie Smith (as); Paul Quinichette, Al Cohn, Coleman Hawkins (ts); Wynton Kelly, Carl Drinkard, Mal Waldron, Oscar Peterson, Bobby Tucker (p); Kenny Burrell, Herb Ellis, Freddie Green, Barney Kessel (g); Aaron Bell, Ray Brown, Carson Smith, Milt Hinton, Red Callender (b); Gus Johnson, Chico Hamilton, Ed Shaughnessy, Don Lamond, Lennie McBrowne (d).* 7/52–9/58.

*****(*) Verve Jazz Masters: Billie Holiday**
Verve 519825-2 *Holiday; various groups.* 52–8/56.

***** Jazz Masters 47: Sings Standards**
Verve 527650-2 *As above.* 2/45–3/59.

*****(*) Lady In Autumn**
Verve 849434-2 2CD *Holiday; Buck Clayton, Joe Guy, Charlie Shavers, Joe Newman, Harry 'Sweets' Edison, Roy Eldridge (t); Tommy Turk (tb); Tony Scott (cl); Romeo Penque (as, bcl); Willie Smith, Gene Quill, Benny Carter (as); Ben Webster, Lester Young, Coleman Hawkins, Al Cohn, Paul Quinichette, Budd Johnson (ts); Oscar Peterson (p, org); Milt Raskin, Bobby Tucker, Mal Waldron, Carl Drinkard, Jimmy Rowles, Hank Jones, Wynton Kelly (p); Irving Ashby, Barney Kessel, Kenny Burrell, Barry Galbraith, Freddie Green (g); Janet Putnam (hp); Milt Hinton, Carson Smith, Joe Mondragon, Red Mitchell, Red Callender, Aaron Bell, Leonard Gaskin, John Simmons, Ray Brown (b); Dave Coleman, Alvin Stoller, J.C Heard, Ed Shaughnessy, Chico Hamilton, Larry Bunker, Lennie McBrowne, Osie Johnson (d); strings.* 4/46–3/59.

****** First Issue: The Great American Songbook**
Verve 523003-2 2CD *Similar to above.* 52–59.

Holiday's last significant period in the studios was with Verve in the 1950s, and this is the best-known and most problematical music she made. Her voice has already lost most of its youthful shine and ebullience – even a genuine up-tempo piece like 'What A Little Moonlight Can Do', where Oscar Peterson does his best to rouse the singer, is something she only has the energy to glide over. Whether this makes her music more revealing or affecting or profound is something listeners will have to decide for themselves. There are songs where the pace and the timbre of her voice are so funereal as to induce little but acute depression; others have a persuasive inner lilt which insists that her greatness has endured. And the best of the interpretations, scattered as they are through all these records, show how compelling Holiday could be, even when apparently enfeebled by her own circumstances.

Although there is a complete edition available (see below), Verve have now released Holiday's output in seven separate sets (the last, *All Or Nothing At All*, is a two-disc set, while the live records are listed below). Preference among the discs depends mainly on song selection and accompanists: whatever her own physical well-being, Norman Granz always made sure there were top-flight bands behind her. *Solitude* has some lovely things: a classic 'These Foolish Things', a marvellous 'Moonglow'. *Recital* has some happy work, including 'What A Little Moonlight Can Do' and 'Too Marvellous For Words', but there are some sloppy pieces too. *Lady Sings The Blues* (which basically replaces the previous disc under that title) has three or four of her best-known heartache songs and includes the rehearsal tape with Tony Scott where they work up 'God Bless The Child' – intriguing, but probably for scholars only. *Music For Torching* is small-hours music of a high, troubling calibre. *All Or Nothing At All* rounds up seven long sessions across two discs and includes some magnificent work from Edison and Webster (there is even a warm-up instrumental cut while they were waiting for her to arrive at the studio on one date) as well as what is probably Holiday's most regal, instinctual late work. It all seems to come to a peak on the very last track on disc two, the definitive version of 'Gee Baby, Ain't I Good To You?'.

Songs For Distingué Lovers has now been made available by Verve in their Master Edition series and, with the original programme expanded to 12 tracks, putting the entire session in one place, this is another front-rank recommendation, the music in its latest remastering sounding particularly handsome. In comparison, the compilations seem superfluous, except for those who prefer just the odd Holiday record in their collection. Both discs in the Jazz Masters series would do fine for that, though the *Standards* selection rather inevitably comes off second best. The *First Issue* two-disc set is, though, a beautifully chosen retrospective which eschews Holiday's tortured epics and lines up the choicest examples of Tin Pan Alley instead. Remastering has been done to a very high and meticulous standard.

****(*) Masters Of Jazz Vol. 3: Billie Holiday**
Storyville 4103 *Holiday; Hot Lips Page, Roy Eldridge, Neal Hefti (t); Herbie Harper, Jack Teagarden (tb); Barney Bigard (cl); Herbie Steward (cl, ts); Coleman Hawkins (ts); Teddy Wilson, Jimmy Rowles, Art Tatum (p); Al Casey (g); Iggy Shevack, Oscar Pettiford (b); Blinkie Garner, Big Sid Catlett (d).* 44/49.

****(*) At Storyville**
Black Lion BLCD 760921 *Holiday; Stan Getz (ts); Buster Harding, Carl Drinkard (p); John Fields, Jimmy Woode (b); Marquis Foster, Peter Littman (d).* 10/51–10/53.

***** Billie's Blues**
Blue Note 748786-2 *Holiday; Monty Kelly, Larry Neill, Don Waddilove (t); Skip Layton, Murray McEachern (tb); Buddy DeFranco (cl); Alvy West, Dan D'Andrea, Lennie Hartman (reeds); Haywood Henry (ts, bs); Carl Drinkard, Bobby Tucker, Buddy Weed, Sonny Clark, Beryl Booker (p); Jimmy Raney, Mike Pingitore, Tiny Grimes (g); Red Mitchell, Artie Shapiro (b); Elaine Leighton, Willie Rodriguez (d).* 42–54.

***** Jazz At The Philharmonic**
Verve 521642-2 *Holiday; Buck Clayton, Roy Eldridge, Howard McGhee (t); Tony Scott (cl); Illinois Jacquet, Wardell Gray, Al Cohn, Coleman Hawkins, Lester Young (ts); Carl Drinkard (p); Kenny Burrell (g); Charles Mingus, Carson Smith (b); Dave Coleman, J.C Heard, Chico Hamilton (d).* 2/45–11/56.

***** 1949–52 Radio and TV Broadcasts**
ESP 3002 *Holiday; other personnel uncertain, but includes Mal Waldron (p), Milt Hinton (b), Osie Johnson (d).* 49-52.

***** 1953–56 Radio and TV Broadcasts**
ESP 3003 *As above.* 53–56.

***** At Carnegie Hall**
Verve 527777-2 *Holiday; Buck Clayton, Roy Eldridge (t); Al Cohn, Coleman Hawkins (ts); Tony Scott (cl, p); Carl Drinkard (p); Kenny Burrell (g); Carson Smith (b); Chico Hamilton (d).* 11/56.

Holiday left a fair number of live recordings, most of them unauthorized at the time, and they can make a rather depressing lot to sort through. Unlike, say, Charlie Parker's live music, this presents a less than fascinating portrait, often of a musician in adversity. Club recordings such as the *Storyville* disc find her in wildly varying voice, almost from song to song: truly affecting performances may sit next to ragged, throwaway ones. The 'Masters Of Jazz' series disc includes some good material from the 1940s. *Billie's Blues* is an interesting cross-section of tracks: several from a European tour which was a mixed success, including three with Buddy DeFranco's group that feature some fine clarinet by the leader, and four from an obscure session for Aladdin with a group that puts the singer into a jump-band blues situation. She handles it unexpectedly well.

The ESP discs make an interesting pair, but we are still waiting for the new issue of what was the third volume in this series, which includes the famous 'Fine And Mellow' from the 1957 *Sound Of Jazz* telecast, as well as an excellent 'Porgy' from 1956. Look for ESP 3005 when it reappears. Her JATP appearances are collected on the Verve album, plus material from other (somewhat less inspiring) appearances from the 1950s. *At Carnegie Hall* is the record of one of her last great live performances. The notes reveal she was scarcely in any fit state to perform and, with the music interspersed with readings from her book, there is a macabre quality which her artistry somehow rises above.

****** The Complete Billie Holiday On Verve 1945–1959**
Verve 517658-2 10CD *Holiday; various groups as above.* 45–59.

*****(*) Billie's Best**
Verve 513943-2 *As above.*

*****(*) The Very Best Of Billie Holiday**
Verve 547494-2 2CD *As above.*

With the appearance of this set, the circle is closed on Holiday's career: the various multi-disc packages impose an order which allows anyone to follow her from the beginning to the end. There are rarities in this major collection which includes what are often wryly funny rehearsal tapes with Jimmy Rowles (it seems strange to hear this famously tormented woman laugh and tell jokes), but its main purpose is to provide first-to-last coverage of her major studio years. There is splendid documentation to go with the records. *Billie's Best* is a useful pocket edition that samples the big box. *The Very Best Of Billie Holiday* is a UK release and is a generous and splendid representation of her Verve years, although the necessary absence of any Columbia material means that it inevitably can't match up to the title.

(***) Lady In Satin
Columbia CK 65144 *Holiday; strings.* 58.

(***) Last Recordings
Verve 835370-2 *Holiday; Harry 'Sweets' Edison, Joe Wilder (t); Jimmy Cleveland, Bill Byers (tb); Romeo Penque (as, ts, bcl); Gene Quill (as); Al Cohn (ts); Danny Bank (bs); Hank Jones (p); Kenny Burrell, Barry Galbraith (g); Milt Hinton, Joe Benjamin (b); Osie Johnson (d); strings.* 3/59.

A troubling farewell which for some has a certain grim fascination. The croaking voice which barely gets through *Lady In Satin* has its admirers, and there is arguably some of the tormented revelation which distinguishes such earlier works as Parker's 'Lover Man', but we suggest that it be approached with care. Columbia have prepared a new edition that includes a fresh remastering, but frankly we see little reason to revise our earlier opinion; it's hard to find any artistic triumphs here, more a voyeuristic look at a beaten woman. *Last Recordings* emerges in much the same way, if it is in sum rather less harrowing.

Dave Holland (born 1946)

DOUBLE BASS, CELLO

Studied in London in the '60s, then joined Miles Davis, 1968–70. Has been constantly in demand ever since and has built a huge discography. Teaches and leads his own quintet when other demands allow. Occasional work on cello or electric bass, but basically a stand-up man with a peerless sound.

****** Conference Of The Birds**
ECM 829373-2 *Holland; Anthony Braxton, Sam Rivers (reeds, f); Barry Altschul (d, perc).* 11/72.

In 1968, the 22-year-old Holland recorded *Karyobin* with the Spontaneous Music Ensemble and *Filles de Kilimanjaro* with Miles Davis. Even given Miles's left-field enthusiasms and seeming Anglophilia, even allowing for most bassists' wide and varied CV, this is a pretty broad musical spectrum to pack into a few months. Holland has been spoken of in the same breath as the legendary Scott LaFaro; he shares the American's bright, exact intonation, incredible hand-speed and utter musicality.

If he had never made another record as leader, *Conference Of The Birds* would still stand out as a classic and as one of the finest things in the nascent ECM catalogue. The title-piece, marked out by Altschul's marimba figures and the two reedmen interweaving basket-tight, was inspired by the morning chorus outside Holland's London flat and not, as is sometimes suggested, by Attar's great mystical poem. Mystical much of the music is, however, indivisible and remarkably hard to render verbally.

On flutes, Rivers and Braxton are hard to separate; on saxophones, the differences are salutary. Altschul is at his very best. Perhaps the responsiblities of leading and writing weighed subtly on Holland himself. Though he is never less than audible, his contributions are more muted and reticent than usual. A quiet masterpiece nevertheless.

*** Emerald Tears

ECM 529087-2 *Holland (b solo).* 8/77.

*** Life Cycle

ECM 829200-2 *Holland (clo solo).* 11/82.

Though solo bass (and cello) performances were to become something of an ECM staple, with work by David Darling, Barre Phillips and Miroslav Vitous, Holland's two early solo discs stand out. *Emerald Tears* is a quiet and meditative album. Though it sustains interest for a full three-quarters of an hour (and after 20 years), it does on occasion begin to seem like a series of exercises. The eight tracks are more or less the same length, even when some, like the opening 'Spheres' or the beautiful 'Under Redwoods', seem to call out for further development, while others – the *arco* 'Combination' and 'Flurries' – seem to linger unnecessarily. One Miles Davis tune is included; 'Solar' sits comfortably for a bass player and it brings out Holland's singing tone. There is also a piece by Anthony Braxton, with whom the bassist worked in Circle.

The cello record is not quite such a tough listen, perhaps because it has an internal consistency *Emerald Tears* largely lacks. It is difficult to separate real echoes from simple association of ideas, but much of the language seems to be classical rather than jazz-based; some moments will suggest Bach, others Kodály, though there are also parallels with Oscar Pettiford and Ron Carter. For sheer musicianship, these records probably merit higher ratings; for most listeners, they demand a pretty substantial loyalty.

***(*) Jumpin' In

ECM 817437-2 *Holland; Kenny Wheeler (t, pkt-t, c, flhn); Robin Eubanks, Julian Priester (tb); Steve Coleman (as); Steve Ellington (d).* 10/83.

*** Seeds Of Time

ECM 825322-2 *As above, except replace Ellington with Marvin 'Smitty' Smith (d).* 11/84.

*** The Razor's Edge

ECM 833048-2 *As above, except omit Priester.* 2/87.

Holland's 1980s bands were the antithesis of what he had been doing 15 years before, whether with the SME or with Miles. Tightly arranged, with much of the drama enacted between bass and brass, they manage to steer a path between freedom and the fixity of detail that, say, Braxton's music demanded. Holland also seemed to be much concerned with texture, and Kenny Wheeler's range of horns on *Jumpin' In* suggests a desire for subtle coloration that was to be developed, albeit less obviously, over the next couple of albums.

One obvious influence at this time was the Mingus Jazz Worskhop. 'Blues For C.M.' on *Razor's Edge* is the only fully explicit reference and, while it's difficult to reconcile the quiet and unassuming Holland with the volcanic American, the voicings and the interplay of structure and freedom come from the same root. The sound has paled a little by 1987, but these are all strong statements by a highly accomplished player and composer.

*** Triplicate

ECM 837113-2 *Holland; Steve Coleman (as); Jack DeJohnette (d).* 3/88.

**(*) Extensions

ECM 941778-2 *Holland; Steve Coleman (as); Kevin Eubanks (g); Marvin 'Smitty' Smith (d).* 9/89.

There may be no such thing as an 'ECM sound', but there are certainly reference-points, career-wise, and one of the most obvious – it's also happened to Ralph Towner, to Jan Garbarek, even to the seemingly untouchable Keith Jarrett – seems to be a desire at some point to get back to jazz basics. At the end of the 1980s, Holland – or Manfred Eicher – seemed to want a more mainstream approach. In prospect, *Triplicate* promised to be a stripped-down swinger, a deliberate increase in temperature. In reality, it appeared rather tame, even when Coleman bit down hard and vied with his namesakes. Passing time suggests it was a stronger and more durable exercise than it initially seemed. The follow-up was pretty duff, though. Eubanks is untameable and Smith can be ruthlessly self-indulgent. Poor old Holland found himself out of things at his own party.

***(*) Dream Of The Elders

ECM 529084-2 *Holland; Eric Person (as, ss); Steve Nelson (vib, mar); Gene Jackson (d); Cassandra Wilson (v).* 95.

This was Holland's first ECM record as leader for eight years. Our initial reaction was disappointment, but it wears better than expected. Despite the personnel, it has a strongly European feel, settled into a slightly dated folkish idiom. Person sounds very much like Coleman, albeit sharper and less groove-orientated, and he fits very comfortably into Holland's concept. As he was to do on the following record as well, Nelson is the one who pulls the sound closer to what Holland was doing a decade before: creating open-ended harmonies and a softly percussive pulse. Individual compositions are less clearly differentiated than they might have been, but perhaps because Holland was looking for something that had more of a unified feel.

Cassandra Wilson plays the wild card, and a rather effective one, bringing a delicate touch and a steely strength to the Maya

Angelou lyric, 'Equality'. On this form, it's a performing relationship one would like to see developed. Holland has a sure, delicate touch around singers, strongly reminiscent of Ray Brown, whose example was to be honoured on *Points Of View* a couple of years later.

Our hesitant valuation first time round now seems too grudging. *Dream Of The Elders* may not belong in the front rank of Holland records, but it is a very impressive statement nevertheless.

****** Points Of View**

ECM 557020-2 *Holland; Robin Eubanks (tb); Steve Wilson (ss, as); Steven Nelson (vib, mar); Billy Kilson (d).* 9/97.

From the faintly mournful opening of 'The Balance' to the soaring delight of 'Herbaceous', a dedication to Herbie Hancock, this is an altogether more even and generous record. Once again, Holland floats comfortably on top of the implicit pulse established by Nelson and secured by the new drummer. Kilson won't be to every taste and his solo on the Ray Brown tribute, 'Mr B', is lacking in substance, but he has a very secure time-feel, even when everything around seems to be drifting off-line. Reminiscent of a more mainstream Paul Motian, his has been a valuable recruitment.

Ironically, the strongest compositions on the album are by Eubanks and Wilson. The trombonist's 'Metamorphos' stands as a dark, ambiguous tailpiece to Holland's own 'Bedouin Trail'. Wilson creates his own mysteries on 'The Benevolent One', an idea which seems to draw on the same harmonic language as Coltrane's 'Alabama' and 'Wise One'. Nelson's feature comes right at the end, his own *faux*-Latin 'Serenade', which relegates the horns in favour of a gently swinging trio that cues up Holland's most relaxed playing of the set; unwary listeners might think they'd stumbled across one of Charlie Haden's romantic song projects. That good.

Rick Hollander (born 1956)

DRUMS

Detroit-based, Hollander works in a modern hard-bop idiom, having served time under such leaders as Woody Shaw and Warne Marsh, as well as leading his own groups.

***** Private Ear**

yvp music CD 3013 *Hollander; Tim Armacost (ts, ss); Walter Lang (p); Jos Machtel (b).* 12/88.

***** Out Here**

Timeless SJP 309 *Hollander; Tim Armacost (ts); Walter Lang (p); Will Woodard (b).* 6/91.

***** Accidental Fortune**

Concord CCD-4550 *As above.* 9/92.

****(*) Once Upon A Time**

Concord CCD 4666 *As above.* 4/94.

Midstream post-bop, served with all the usual accomplishments. The most interesting and effective item on both *Private Ear* and *Accidental Fortune* is a drum-and-bass-only version of 'Star Eyes'. As a performance, it suggests that Hollander has also paid attention to the great bebop drummers: Clarke, Roach and, to a lesser extent, Blakey. He is, *rara avis*, a drummer who might be interesting enough on his own account to sustain a whole record. His performance on 'My Old Flame' on *Accidental Fortune* is leerily satirical, though this time he is supported by a long-established group which is undeniably capable; but there are sour touches that sit uncomfortably with the listener. When tackling standards, they seem to go for self-consciously different approaches: 'I've Grown Accustomed To Her Face' is almost torpedoed by Lang's preposterous introduction (also on *Accidental Fortune*). They treat the original material with far more respect, and Armacost's snaky lines often grab the limelight. *Once Upon A Time* is a programme of Hoagy Carmichael material, but this time it's Hollander's own playing that lets the group down, fussily working through what are often very slow tempos that don't suit either band or material very well.

Red Holloway (born 1927)

ALTO AND TENOR SAXOPHONE, VOCAL

Originally from Arkansas, James Holloway got his start in the blues and R&B bands which were all over Chicago in the late 1940s and early '50s. He later worked in the sax–organ-combo format and has lately turned up in big-band and mainstream situations.

***** Brother Red**

Prestige 24141-2 *Holloway; Alvin Red Tyler (ts); Brother Jack McDuff (org); George Benson (g); Wilfred Middlebrooks (b); Joe Dukes (d).* 2/64.

***** Legends Of Acid Jazz**

Prestige 24199-2 *Holloway; John Patton, Lonnie Smith (org); Norman Simmons (p); Eric Gale, George Benson (g); Leonard Gaskin, Charles Rainey, Paul Breslin (b); Herbie Lovelle, Ray Lucas, Frank Severino (d).* 10/63–12/65.

***** Nica's Dream**

Steeplechase SCCD 31192 *Holloway; Horace Parlan (p); Jesper Lundgaard (b); Aage Tanggaard (d).* 7/84.

****(*) Red Holloway & Company**

Concord CCD 4322 *Holloway; Cedar Walton (p); Richard Reid (b); Jimmie Smith (d).* 1/87.

*****(*) Locksmith Blues**

Concord CCD 4390 *Holloway; Clark Terry (t, flhn, v); Gerald Wiggins (p); Phil Upchurch (g); Richard Reid (b); Paul Humphrey (d).* 6/89.

***** Live At the 1995 Floating Jazz Festival**

Chiaroscuro CR(D) 348 *Holloway; Harry Edison (t); Dwight Dickerson (p); Richard Reid (b); Paul Humphrey (d).* 11/95.

This Chicago alto and tenor veteran now has a better showing of his early work in the racks. *Brother Red* is basically the *Cookin' Together* collaboration with Jack McDuff, and a sturdy if unexceptional example of the sax/organ genre of the time. *Legends Of Acid Jazz* doubles up the original sets, *The Burner* (with Patton and Gale) and *Red Soul* (with Smith and Benson). Nothing ambitious, just sound, beefy playing by all hands.

More recent records have been somewhat mixed. The Steeplechase session reissues a mid-'80s date, and here Holloway hits a swinging groove that hardly lets up for 40-odd minutes: since he likes the high parts of the tenor and the middle range of the alto, it often sounds like he's playing a hybrid of the two horns, lean, many-noted and decidedly cheerful – he plays blues as if they were fun, and ballads tend to be amiable rather than deeply felt. Parlan and the Scandinavians do well for him. Although the 1987 session is a pleasing enough collection, Holloway sounds perfunctory in the company of players who are content to perform to order. With nobody pushing him much and with a pro's pro like Walton at the piano, the music is just another set of standards and blues. But the meeting with Clark Terry is very different, suggesting that Holloway is always happier with another horn to joust with. The title-blues is lavishly done, 'Red Top' is a terrific swinger, and the Ellington tunes are delivered with a finesse that normally eludes Holloway's records.

Red's stint on board the S.S. *Norway* is captured on the Chiaroscuro CD. Sweets Edison sits in on three leisurely standards, and Red is in good enough spirits to sing one somewhat dubious love song.

Ron Holloway

TENOR SAXOPHONE

Holloway is a saxophonist who's played in countless situations in and out of jazz, a journeyman who's worked with everybody, from Dizzy Gillespie to Gil Scott-Heron.

****(*) Slanted**

Milestone MCD-9219-2 *Holloway; Chris Battistone, Tom Williams (t); Reuben Brown, Bob Butta, George Colligan (p); Paul Bollenback, Larry Camp (g); Lennie Cuje (vib); Keter Betts, James King, Tommy Cecil, Pepe Gonzalez (b); Lenny Robinson, Steve Williams, John Zidar (d).* 8–9/93.

***** Struttin'**

Milestone MCD-9238-2 *Holloway; Mac Gollehon (t, flhn); John Bell (f, sitar); Kenny Barron, Larry Willis, Lonnie Liston Smith (p); Paul Bollenback, John Scofield, Marlon Graves, Ray Tilkens (g); David Williams, Gary Grainger, Lamar Brantley (b); Victor Lewis (d); Steve Berrios, Broto Roy (perc).* 2/95.

**** Scorcher**

Milestone MCD-9257-2 *Holloway; Chris Battistone (t); Mark Wenner (hca); Vince Evans (ky); Joey DeFrancesco (org); Paul Bollenback, Pye Williams (g); John Evans (sitar); Vince Loving, Tommy Cecil (b); Byron Landham, Rod Youngs (d); Alex Jones, Eric Jones, Gil Scott-Heron, Sunny Sumpter, Rachel-Ann Cross, Neeta Ragoowansi, Jaqui Macmillan (v).* 2–3/96.

****(*) Groove Update**

Milestone BCD-9276-2 *Holloway; Chris Battistone (t, flhn); Larry Willis (p); Benjie Porecki (ky); Paul Bollenback (g); Andy Kochenour (tba); James King, Vince Loving, Gary Grainger (b); Lenny Robinson, Andre 'Blues' Webb, Rod Youngs (d); Lizabeth Flood, Gil Scott-Heron (v).* 10–11/97.

Holloway's manifest authority on tenor is let down by a lack of purpose on the first record. His experience adds up to a faceless consistency on this date. Standards like 'Pent-up House' and 'Autumn Leaves' are loaded with calories but short on any kind of individuality.

Struttin' offers some improvement. Todd Barkan's production involves the band as something more than bystanders, and a few tracks – like the bare-bones treatment of 'Where Are You?' or the unusual choice of 'I've Found A New Baby' – stand aside from cliché. But Holloway still gives only modest evidence that he merits a leadership role – and the east–west fusion of 'Cobra' sounds like a cast-iron clinker.

Scorcher goes completely the wrong way. By drafting in rappers (on one track), Gil Scott-Heron (on two) and material that can't be personalized ('The Sidewinder', 'Red Clay'), Holloway sounds completely at sea, for all the energy of his playing and the worthy sidemen.

So, what of *Groove Update*? Holloway picks interesting material all right – Monk, Silver, Jimmy Heath and Herbie Hancock are among the composers called upon – but his own playing has taken on an almost vaudevillian cast. Sample his absurd solo on 'Epistrophy' or the stab at a New Orleans march for 'Lulu's Back In Town'. There are decent players on the record and when they hunker down and find a groove it's appealing enough, but much of this seems plain silly.

Bill Holman (born 1927)

TENOR SAXOPHONE, ARRANGER

One of the most gifted of big-band arrangers, Holman studied music in California and then scored music for Stan Kenton in the early 1950s. Though much of his work from the '60s onwards was in TV and session situations, he kept his hand in as a jazz writer and formed an 'occasional' big band to play his own charts beginning in 1975. His records in the 1990s were few but memorable.

***** Jive For Five**

VSOP 19 *Holman; Lee Katzman (t); Jimmy Rowles (p); Wilfred Middlebrooks (b); Mel Lewis (d).* 6/58.

Holman is known these days as a grandmaster arranger. He has also been a more than useful saxophonist, tonally similar to the red-wine sound of Al Cohn, and this relic from a West Coast vintage has some particularly sinewy playing from the co-leader. Rowles is his customary splendid self and the almost forgotten Katzman holds his place without turning a hair, in the manner of the California movement. Lewis, who co-led the group, is discreet.

*****(*) Bill Holman Meets The Norwegian Radio Big Band**

Taurus TRCD 826 *Holman; Christian Beck, Atle Hammer, Bernt Anker Steen, Finn Eriksen, Gunnar Andersen (t, flhn); Jens Wendelboe, Tore Nilsen, Harald Halvorsen, Steffan Stokland, Frode Thingnaes (tb); Oivind Westby (btb); Harald Bergersen, Helge Hurum, Knut Riisnaes, Vidar Johansen, Nils Jansen, Johan Bergli (reeds); Erling Aksdal (ky); Steinar Larsen (g); Bjorn Kjellemyr (b); Svein Christiansen (d).* 6/87.

****** A View From The Side**

JVC 2050-2 *Holman; Carl Saunders, Frank Szabo, Ron Stout, Bob Summers (t, flhn); Andy Martin, Jack Redmond (tb); Bob*

Enevoldsen (vtb); Kenny Shroyer (btb); Lanny Morgan (as, f); Bill Perkins (as, ss, f); Pete Christlieb (ts, f); Ray Herrmann (ts, ss); Bob Efford (bs, bcl); Rich Eames (p); Doug Macdonald (g); Dave Carpenter (b); Bob Leatherbarrow (d). 4/95.

****** Brilliant Corners**

JVC 9018-2 *As above.* 2/97.

Seldom in receipt of the kind of plaudits some other arrangers seem swamped in, Holman has quietly put together an awesome body of work, and recent records find him in peerless form. The Norwegian record was cut over a week's stay in Oslo: six new pieces plus a typically ingenious revision of 'All The Way'. The group rise to a challenge difficult enough to defeat many an ensemble, and on a piece such as 'A Separate Walking' the colours of brass, reeds and rhythm spin in perfect accord.

If the Norwegians did a fine job, they don't quite compare to Holman's own regular band, responsible for the two stunning JVC discs which testify not only to his undimmed creativity but to the ageless zest of West Coast jazz as a whole. Players such as Enevoldsen and Perkins are among the more notable survivors from the era's golden age, but this is a band almost indecently weighted with experience and they eat up whatever Holman can throw at them. *A View From The Side* is replete with frighteningly elaborate scores dispatched with the utmost elegance: to cite a mere two examples, sample the almost fantastical interplay of the sections on 'I Didn't Ask' or the rich, sobering treatment of 'The Peacocks', a concerto for Bob Efford's bass clarinet. *Brilliant Corners* is no less of an achievement and, considering the difficulty of arranging Monk tunes for big band, these ten charts seem like the work of a magician: has anyone dared score the title-piece in such a way? Here is one of the genuine masters doing his greatest work.

Richard 'Groove' Holmes (1931–91)

ORGAN

Discovered in Pittsburgh by Les McCann, who plays on his first records, Groove Holmes played organ in an old-fashioned swing style that was accommodating enough to any kind of soloist who happened to be out front. He stuck with his tested horn-plus-rhythm format and contiued to work until his death, a few weeks after his sixtieth birthday.

*****(*) Groove**

Pacific Jazz 94473-2 *Holmes; Lawrence 'Tricky' Lofton (tb); Ben Webster (ts); Les McCann (p); George Freeman (g); Ron Jefferson (d).* 3/61.

****(*) Somethin' Special**

Pacific Jazz 55452-2 *As above, except add Clifford Scott (as, ts), Joe Pass, Gene Edwards (g), Leroy Henderson (d).* 3/61–4/62.

***** Groovin' With Jug**

Pacific Jazz 92930-2 *Holmes; Gene Ammons (ts); Gene Edwards (g); Leroy Henderson (d).* 8/61.

***** After Hours**

Pacific Jazz 37986-2 *Holmes; Joe Pass, Gene Edwards (g); Leroy Henderson, Larance Marable (d).* 61–62.

***** Soul Message**

Original Jazz Classics OJC 329 *Holmes; Gene Edwards (g); Jimmie Smith (d).* 10/66.

**** Misty**

Original Jazz Classics OJC 724 *Holmes; Gene Edwards (g); Jimmie Smith, George Randle (d).* 4–7/66.

*****(*) Blues Groove**

Prestige PRCD-24133-2 *Holmes; Blue Mitchell (t); Harold Vick, Teddy Edwards (ts); Pat Martino, Gene Edwards (g); Paul Chambers (b); George Randle, Freddie Waits, Billy Higgins (d).* 3/66–5/67.

***** Legends Of Acid Jazz**

Prestige PRCD 24188-2 *Holmes; Rusty Bryant (as, ts); Earl Maddox, Billy Butler (g); Billy Jackson, Herbie Lovelle (d).* 2–8/68.

Holmes was one of the most big-sounding organists. A sometime bassist, he liked earthy, elemental bass-lines, and he decorated melodies with something like reluctance: he made the organ sound massive and implacable. He recorded most prolifically in the 1960s, and he now has a fair showing on CD – though British readers will have to ask their importer for most of what's listed above. The Pacific Jazz discs were his earliest and are rather a mixed bag. *Groove* still stands up well, if only for the unlikely presence of Ben Webster, who rouses himself sufficiently to huff and grumble his way past the swelling chords of the Hammond. It's a bit like two huge men tossing bodacious remarks at each other across the floor. Lofton walks on as comic relief. McCann is present, but he comes into his own more on *Somethin' Special*, which has its moments but gets tarnished by Scott's ludicrously overheated solos. Collectors may want it for the out-take from the *Groove* session, a nice 'Satin Doll'. *Groovin' With Jug* is mostly live, with Ammons chewing over his bluesiest licks to, in the end, rather limited purpose. Maybe the best place to hear Holmes himself is on *After Hours*, where he has only guitar and drums to contend with.

Soul Message is a fat, funky album which opens on the blues workout, 'Groove's Groove', seven minutes that just about sum up Holmes's entire style. *Misty* is a ballad-orientated collection and the kind of thing that organists were obliged to make as songs for sedentary lovers: purely on those terms, it's rather good, but the formula is still boring over the long haul. A better choice is *Blues Groove*, which doubles up two Prestige albums, *Get Up And Get It!* and *Soul Mist!*. The first offers Edwards a guest role which he makes the most of: there's a long, expansive treatment of the tenorman's set-piece, 'Body And Soul'. Mitchell and the unimpressive Vick sit in on two tracks of the second set, but this is Groove's show, and he's at his best on the light touch of 'Up Jumped Spring'. *Legends Of Acid Jazz* is a modish disguise for two Prestige dates from 1968, *The Groover* and *That Healin' Feelin'*. Rusty Bryant livens up the latter session and Holmes rumbles and stomps his way around the likes of 'See See Rider' and some standards.

****(*) Plenty Plenty Blues**

RCA Camden 74321 610732 2CD *Holmes; Cecil Bridgewater (t); Houston Person (ts); Gerald Smith, Jimmy Ponder (g); Wilbur Bascomb (b); Bobby Ward, Cecil Brooks III, Greg Bandy (d); Ralph Dorsey (perc).* 12/80–9/89.

****(*) Broadway**

32 Jazz 32085 *Holmes; Houston Person (ts); Gerald Smith (g); Bobby Ward (d); Ralph Dorsey (perc).* 12/80.

Late Groove. The big man was still in hearty form on his Muse albums – *Broadway* is the one of that title, and the Camden set adds all of *Blues All Day Long* and *Hot Tat* to its two-disc programme – but frankly these are pretty average repasts, routine slabs of funk and R&B combo music, and they'll satisfy only the mildest appetite.

Yuri Honing

TENOR SAXOPHONE

Dutch saxman, trying out unusual material in a post-bop vernacular.

***** Gagarin**

A Records AL 73025 *Honing; Tony Overwater (b); Jost Lijbaart (d).* 9/95.

***** Star Tracks**

Jazz In Motion 992102 *As above.* 7/96.

Just don't mention Candy Dulfer ... The Netherlands' second-most famous saxophonist could equally and quite legitimately trade on his looks; spaghetti-thin, cheekbones you could shave parmesan on (please insert the appropriate Dutch equivalent, if you know it), a wonderful beauty spot on his cheek, and a look of Harry Connick Jr. In addition, damn and blast him, Honing is immensely talented, both as a player and composer.

The earlier of the two records consists entirely of moody, exploratory originals. Honing favours the lower end of the tenor range, and he works largely outside the chords, in the sort of free-but-controlled language Eric Dolphy may have bequeathed to Holland in his final days. The slower-tempo pieces, like 'Nuku'Alofa' and 'The Beauty Of Reason', almost suggest Warne Marsh at his most subtly seductive, while 'Gagarin' itself and the intriguingly titled 'Nelson's Victory' (Lord? Oliver? Louis? Steve?) are upbeat boppers.

On both albums, Lijbaart and the gifted Overwater (who has toured with David Murray) are equal and active partners, powering along the faster material, supporting and augmenting the gentler things. They are perhaps less prominent on *Star Tracks*, a fascinating attempt to generate a canon of new standards, 'West European pop music from the period 1974–1995', which explains Bjork's 'Isobel', Abba's 'Waterloo', and the Police's 'Walking On The Moon', but not 'Body And Soul'. As on *Gagarin*, Overwater contributes an edgy composition, but the later record's emphasis is on stripping away all the production values of contemporary pop, exposing the basic theme and then examining its potential. As such, it succeeds very well indeed.

If there is a criticism of these records, it is that the first is rather too one-dimensional, and that much of the material on the second doesn't really stand up to repeated scrutiny. Honing, though, looks and sounds like a man for the future.

William Hooker (born 1946)

DRUMS, VOCAL

A veteran of New York's avant-garde of the '80s and '90s, Hooker is a poet, drummer and bandleader, always with projects on the go.

**** Lifeline**

Silkheart SH 19 *Hooker; Masahiko Kono (tb); Alan Michael, Claude Lawrence (as); Charles Compo (ts); Mark Hennen (p); William Parker (b).* 2/88.

***** The Firmament / Fury**

Silkheart SH 123 *As above, except add Donald Miller (g); omit Hennen and Parker.* 4/89.

***** Shamballa**

Knitting Factory Works KFW 151 *Hooker; Thurston Moore, Elliott Sharp (g).* 93.

****(*) Tibet**

Ummo 1 *Hooker; Charles Compo (ts); Mark Hennen (p); Donald Miller (g).* 3/94.

****(*) Envisioning**

Knitting Factory Works KFW 159 *Hooker; Lee Renaldo (g, syn, v).* 4/94.

*****(*) Joy (Within!)**

Silkheart SHCD 147 *Hooker; Billy Bang (vn, f).* 6/94–6/95.

***** Armageddon**

Homestead HMS 223-2 *Hooker; Lewis Barnes (t); Blaise Siwula, Richard Keene (ts); Doug Walker (syn); Kickwad, David First, Letha Rodman, Jesse Henry (g).* 2/95.

***** Great Sunset**

Warm-O-Brisk WD3 *Hooker; Lewis Barnes (t); Richard Keene (ss, ts); Charles Compo (ts, bs, f).* 6/96.

Hooker typifies New York's avant-garde while standing at a tangent to it. His records tend to feature his repertory cast of players and an occasional 'star' name or two, yet he dominates all of them, with a drumming style born out of Sunny Murray's freedoms, an endless solo that seems to go on and on. His companions either surf on his breakers or try to stand up and fight them. It can be an exhilarating confrontation or a boring one. He has managed to get out a fair number of records, and the above are the ones we've managed to hear.

The two early Silkhearts are messy affairs, the first spoiled by indifferent sound, the second an advance though still subject to a classic case of free-form incoherence. Miller's typically gothic guitar adds some cruel gusto to the second one. *Shamballa* is made up of two long duets, one with Sonic Youth's Thurston Moore, the other with ubiquitous, eclectic Sharp: where Moore builds great walls of fuzz and feedback, Sharp comes to the same ends by much more cerebral means. These are enjoyably bleak and propulsive encounters. *Envisioning*, with Renaldo, follows a similar pattern but suffers from some pretentious commentaries by the guitarist.

Tibet is also a bit of a mess and underlines how important good recording is to this kind of music. There are lots of interesting intensities which the band work up in a timeless, free-jazz language, yet they're undercut by the bad sound – even the usually cataclysmic Miller seems restrained here. *Great Sunset*, another one done live at the Knitting Factory, is briefer and more concentrated, with some splendid ensemble work, though Barnes, Compo and Keene never signal that they're particu-larly strong voices in their own right. *Armageddon* is a studio disc that finds Hooker by himself, in duet, in trio and with a trumpet–sax–guitar team. The closing 'State Secrets' with Rodman and Henry is a fine show of crawling feedback over thundering drums, although some of the other pieces seem unreasonably skinny for something that was done in a studio.

The feel of all of these discs is *audio vérité*, which is probably as it should be, and no different with *Joy (Within!)*, a duet concert with Billy Bang drawn from two shows a year apart. Here, though, Hooker is working with a master improviser, and the results muster eloquence along with the enthusiasm which the other records work from. By now Bang's playing has acquired a furrowed majesty, which Hooker's rough-and-tumble rhythms throw into a special relief. The other records will appeal to those searching for the conversation of underground voices; this one deserves a wider audience.

Bertha Hope (born 1936)

PIANO

Wife of the pianist Elmo Hope, Bertha is no mean talent herself at the keyboard, and she once cut an album of duets with her husband before these late-flowering examples of her work.

****(*) In Search Of ... Hope**

Steeplechase SCCD 31276 *Hope; Walter Booker (b); Billy Higgins (d). 10/90.*

***** Elmo's Fire**

Steeplechase SCCD 31289 *Hope; Eddie Henderson (t); Junior Cook, Dave Riekenberg (ts); Walter Booker (b); Leroy Williams (d). 1/91.*

***** Between Two Kings**

Minor Music 801025 *Hope; Walter Booker (b); Jimmy Cobb (d). 92.*

Elmo Hope's widow makes no attempt to disguise her fealty to his music: there are two of his tunes on the first album, four on the second, one on the third; and Bertha's own style is a gentle extrapolation of Elmo's off-centre lyricism. She is no great executant, happiest at a steady mid-tempo and unwilling to risk any flourishes in a solo, but her improvisations have a patient and rather beguiling beauty about them, a bebop vocabulary fragmented into very small pieces which she seems to turn over and over in her phrases. *In Search Of ... Hope* is a little too tasteful and laid-back, Higgins as solid as ever, Booker quiescent, and it bows before the superior quintet date (Riekenberg appears on only one tune). Eddie Henderson walks a measured line between elegance and real fire, with a remarkable improvisation on the blues 'Bai Tai'. Junior Cook is patchy, but Hope herself sounds convincing, and her treatment of Sonny Fortune's wistful 'For Duke And Cannon' is splendid. *Between Two Kings* returns her to the trio format and blends standards with her own writing, which comes out best on the charming 'Hokkaido Spring' and the inverted tribute to sardine salad, 'De La Senidras'.

Elmo Hope (1923–67)

PIANO

Elmo's finest moment was probably as a sideman on Harold Land's 1959 album, The Fox. Drug problems and a certain lack of self-assurance hampered his own career, but nevertheless there is a substantial body of work.

****** Trio And Quintet**

Blue Note 784438 2 *Hope; Freeman Lee, Stu Williamson (t); Frank Foster, Harold Land (ts); Percy Heath, Leroy Vinnegar (b); Frank Butler, Philly Joe Jones (d). 6/53–10/57.*

*****(*) Meditations**

Original Jazz Classics OJC 1751 *Hope; John Ore (b); Willie Jones (d). 6/55.*

Hope managed to sound sufficiently different from both his main influences, Bud Powell (with whom he went to school) and Thelonious Monk, to retain a highly individual sound. His reputation as a composer is now surprisingly slight, but he had a strong gift for melody, enunciating themes very clearly, and was comfortable enough with classical and modern concert music to introduce elements of fugue and canon, though always with a firm blues underpinning. Like a good many pianists of his generation, he seems to have been uneasy about solo performance (though he duetted regularly with his wife Bertha) and is heard to greatest effect in trio settings. The early *Meditations* sounds remarkably Monk-like in places and John Ore's slightly limping lines confirm the resemblance (Ore was a long-standing member of the Thelonious Monk quartet and Jones was one of Monk's favourite drummers, a rating passed on to Charles Mingus). 'Elmo's Fire' and 'Blue Mo' are deft originals.

The Blue Note sessions are taut and well disciplined, though the trio tracks are very much better than the quintets, where the sequence of solos begins to seem rather mechanical and Hope progressively loses interest in varying his accompaniments of others. Originals like 'Freffie' and 'Hot Sauce' come across well, and the sound stands up down the years.

***** Hope Meets Foster**

Original Jazz Classics OJC 1703 *Hope; Freeman Lee (t); Frank Foster (ts); John Ore (b); Art Taylor (d). 10/55.*

***** The All Star Sessions**

Milestone M 47037 *Hope; Donald Byrd, Blue Mitchell (t); John Coltrane, Jimmy Heath, Hank Mobley, Frank Wess (ts); Paul Chambers, Percy Heath (b); Philly Joe Jones (d). 5/56–6/61.*

Hope responded well to the challenge of Coltrane's developing harmonic language and the Milestone sessions contain some provocative indications of Trane's early willingness to deconstruct standard material, in this case a bold reading of 'Polka Dots And Moonbeams'. The sessions with Foster are rather more conventional, but 'Georgia On My Mind' demonstrates Hope's original and uncompromising approach to standard ballad material, and Foster is only able to embellish a very strong conception.

***** Elmo Hope Trio**

Original Jazz Classics OJC 477 *Hope; Jimmy Bond (b); Frank Butler (d).* 2/59.

*****(*) Plays His Original Compositions**

Fresh Sound FSR CD 181 *Hope; Paul Chambers, Butch Warren (b); Granville Hogan, Philly Joe Jones (d).* 61.

*****(*) Homecoming**

Original Jazz Classics OJC 1810 *Hope; Blue Mitchell (t); Jimmy Heath, Frank Foster (ts); Percy Heath (b); Philly Joe Jones (d).* 6/61.

***** Hope-Full**

Original Jazz Classics OJC 1872 *Hope; Bertha Hope (p).* 11/61.

The 1959 trio, which was for Contemporary, is rather disappointing, but Hope had by this stage moved to the West Coast (which he found professionally conducive – i.e. more gigs – but artistically a little sterile) and had become further involved in drugs, for which he was eventually jailed. His fortunes were on a roller-coaster from then until his untimely death, aged only 43. The Fresh Sound is an excellent way of getting Hope's most interesting compositions on one disc, though the Blue Note *Trio And Quintet* album remains the item of first choice.

However, the very fine *Homecoming* is still available, restoring material from the trio and sextet dates in June 1961 and unveiling another batch of intelligent arrangements. Another return is the hitherto very rare *Hope-Full*, which includes three duets with Bertha and five solos. It would have been more interesting to hear the pianist improvising alone on some of his own themes: these are mainly standards, with the odd choice of 'When Johnny Comes Marching Home' the only real surprise; Hope sounds interesting but lacking in the confidence to really assert himself on this material.

*****(*) The Final Sessions**

Evidence ECD 22147-2 2CD *Hope; John Ore (b); Clifford Jarvis, Philly Joe Jones (d).* 3–5/66.

The Final Sessions, released in 1966 shortly before his death, help to fill in another corner of the picture. It was thought that he had made his last recordings as far back as 1963, but these tapes see him back in the company of Philly Joe, with whom he had worked in Joe Morris's R&B band, and with Ore. Jarvis was also a sensitive collaborator, and he is the drummer on two-thirds of these cuts.

At the end, Hope sounds thoughtful and technically sound, recording long takes (which are now issued unedited) that are jam-packed with ideas. His ability to reshape a standard like 'I Love You' and the bebop classic, 'A Night In Tunisia', is undiminished by time; but the real meat of the two discs comes in originals: a long version of 'Elmo's Blues', with altered changes and a curious long-form structure, the terse 'Vi-Ann', and the excellent 'Toothsome Threesome' and 'Punch'. The recordings are somewhat rough and ready. Though a certain degree of electronic sweetening has taken place, much of the texture of the original has been preserved, which is appropriate to music of historical importance. However frustrating the Elmo Hope discography still seems, it is in better shape than for years.

Claude Hopkins (1903–84)

PIANO

Hopkins was bandleading by the early 1920s. He had much success in New York from 1930 onwards and as a touring attraction from 1937. Hopkins did staff-arranging for CBS and switched to small-band work from 1947 when the big bands died. He carried on into old age, but his principal legacy is his 1930s material.

***** Claude Hopkins 1932–1934**

Classics 699 *Hopkins; Ovie Alston (t, v); Albert Snaer, Sylvester Lewis (t); Fred Norman (tb, v); Fernando Arbello, Henry Wells (tb); Ed Hall (cl, as, bs); Gene Johnson (as); Bobby Sands (ts); Walter Jones (bj, g); Henry Turner (b); Pete Jacobs (d); Orlando Roberson (v).* 5/32–12/34.

***** Claude Hopkins 1934–1935**

Classics 716 *As above, except add Snub Mosley (tb), Hilton Jefferson (cl, as); omit Wells.* 1/34–2/35.

****(*) Claude Hopkins 1937–1940**

Classics 733 *Hopkins; Shirley Clay, Jabbo Smith, Lincoln Mills, Sylvester Lewis, Robert Cheek, Albert Snaer, Russell Jones, Herman Autrey (t); Floyd Brady, Fred Norman, Vic Dickenson, Ray Hogan, Norman Greene, Bernard Archer (tb); Gene Johnson, Chauncey Haughton, Ben Smith, Floyd Blakemore, Ben Richardson, Howard Johnson, Norman Thornton (as); Bobby Sands, Cliff Glover, Benny Waters (ts); Walter Jones, Rudolph Williams (g); Abe Bolar, Elmer James (b); Pete Jacobs, George Foster, Walter Johnson (d); Beverley White, Froshine Stewart, Orlando Roberson (v).* 2/37–3/40.

Hopkins was a skilful pianist and he liked to get a lot of solos with his band – so much so that the demands of arranging around him may have told against the ambitions of the group. It certainly never worked as well as the Earl Hines orchestra and, though Hopkins had fewer imposing soloists – the brief stays by Smith and Dickenson in 1937 were wasted – the group's ensemble sound lacked character and the arrangements were often second rate. These chronological CDs tell the story in decent if unexceptional transfers. Some of the music on the early disc promises more than is eventually delivered: 'Mad Moments', 'Shake Your Ashes', 'Hopkins Scream' and especially Jimmy Mundy's arrangement of 'Mush Mouth' are exciting and surprising pieces. But the two later discs, while interesting, never break very far out of swing-era clichés. There is also a serviceable compilation of the earlier material on *Monkey Business* (Hep CD1031).

Johan Horlen (born 1967)

ALTO AND SOPRANO SAXOPHONES

Young Swedish saxophonist, making his leadership debut in a post-bop style.

***** Dance Of Resistance**

Dragon DRCD 260 *Horlen; Torbjorn Gulz (p); Christian Spering (b); Jukkis Uotila (d).* 6/94.

Playing alto on all but one of the seven themes, the Swede is equal parts lyricism and passion here. The title-piece exemplifies this tightrope walk: continually skirling up towards a false note, he keeps pulling himself back in line before matters get out of hand. That reserve makes the still waters of 'To Miss', a lovely duet for soprano and piano, and the contrary position of 'The Best Things In Life Are Free', an argument for alto and drums, the more effective. But some of his ideas go nowhere, and the closing blow-out on 'Everything I Love' is perhaps a step too far. Another horn shouldering some responsibility might have balanced out the session better, though Horlen will be worth watching.

John Horler (born 1947)

PIANO

British pianist and composer, a regular with John Dankworth and Cleo Laine, and an occasional leader.

****(*) Gentle Piece**
Spotlite SPJ-CD 542 *Horler; Phil Lee (g); Dave Green (b); Spike Wells (d).* 93.

Horler's amiable playing owes much to his acknowledged mentor, Bill Evans, though encouragingly it's Evans's tougher side that he comes closest to, and while some of this music is a bit wispy, as on Kenny Wheeler's title-track, there's an underlying assertiveness ever present. This comes out most effectively in the surprising *fast* version of 'My Funny Valentine', done as a hard-bitten duet for piano and guitar. Not much else makes a terrific impression, though, and the date is let down by Spike Wells's splashy drumming and a particularly ungracious studio sound.

Shirley Horn (born 1934)

PIANO, VOCAL

A native of Washington, DC, Horn studied piano at college and was leading her own small groups from 1954. She remained a well-kept Washington secret until the 1980s, when she began touring Europe, and a contract with Verve marked her belated coming-out.

***** Loads Of Love / Shirley Horn With Horns**
Mercury 843454-2 *Horn; Jimmy Cleveland (tb); Hank Jones, Bobby Scott (p); Kenny Burrell (g); Milt Hinton (b); Osie Johnson (d); rest unknown.* 63.

A reissue of the two albums Horn made for Mercury in 1963. They're modest, pleasing records, much like many another light-jazz vocal record of the period, and, while Horn's voice is transparently clear and warm, she was used to accompanying herself; placed in the studios with a stellar but unfamiliar band, she occasionally sounds stilted. Nor was she allowed to work at her favourite dead-slow tempos on ballads. Fine remastering.

*****(*) A Lazy Afternoon**
Steeplechase SCCD 1111 *Horn; Buster Williams (b); Billy Hart (d).* 7/78.

***** At Northsea**
Steeplechase SCCD 37015/16 2CD *Horn; Charles Ables (b); Billy Hart (d).* 7/81.

***** The Garden Of The Blues**
Steeplechase SCCD 1203 *Horn; Charles Ables (b); Steve Williams (d).* 11/84.

Horn's first Steeplechase set broke a long silence; if anything, it was effectively a debut album. The manner here, and throughout these three fine and under-recognized records, is reflective and sparsely evocative. Horn establishes her liking for intensely slow tempos with a compelling treatment of 'There's No You', but she feels able to contrast that immediately with the hipsterish reading of 'New York's My Home', and the long trio instrumental on 'Gentle Rain' displays a piano method that works with the simplest materials and makes something distinctive. Williams and Hart – the latter an old friend who might understand Horn's music better than anyone – play with complete empathy. If anything, the remaining discs are a slight letdown after *A Lazy Afternoon*, since Horn had already made a nearly definitive statement in this context; but *At Northsea*, which catches the best from several sets at the 1981 Northsea Jazz Festival, is an attractive souvenir of Horn on stage and blends together many of her favourite set-pieces.

***** Softly**
Audiophile 224 *Horn; Charles Ables (b); Steve Williams (d).* 10/87.

***** I Thought About You**
Verve 833235-2 *As above.* 87.

*****(*) Close Enough For Love**
Verve 837933-2 *Horn; Buck Hill (ts); Charles Ables (b); Steve Williams (d).* 11/88.

*****(*) You Won't Forget Me**
Verve 847482-2 *Horn; Miles Davis, Wynton Marsalis (t); Buck Hill, Branford Marsalis (ts); Toots Thielemans (hca, g); Charles Ables (b, g); Buster Williams (b); Billy Hart, Steve Williams (d).* 6–8/90.

***** Here's To Life**
Verve 511879-2 *Horn; Wynton Marsalis (t); Steve Kujala, James Walker (f); Alan Broadbent (p); John Chiodini (g); Charles Ables, Chuck Domanico (b); Steve Williams, Harvey Mason (d); strings.* 91.

*****(*) Light Out Of Darkness**
Verve 519703-2 *Horn; Gary Bartz (as); Charles Ables (g, b); Tyler Mitchell (b); Steve Williams (d).* 4–5/93.

***** I Love You, Paris**
Verve 523486-2 *As above, except omit Bartz and Mitchell.* 3/92.

*****(*) The Main Ingredient**
Verve 529555-2 *As above, except add Roy Hargrove (flhn), Joe Henderson, Buck Hill (ts), Steve Novosel (b), Elvin Jones (d).* 5–9/95.

What amounts to Horn's second comeback has been distinguished by a perfect touch and luxury-class production values. Actually, in terms of her own performances or those of her trio – Ables and Williams have been faithful and diligent disciples – there's no special advance on her Steeplechase albums, or on the single Audiophile set, which is an especially slow and thoughtful disc. The first two Verves continue to work at favourite standards, and Hill's presence adds a useful touch of salt to proceedings that may sound a little too sweetly sensuous for some listeners. But *You Won't Forget Me* is a step forward in its pristine attention to detail, awesome array of guest-star soloists – Davis was a great Horn admirer, and he sounds like himself, if well below his best – and the faithfulness with which Horn's voice is recorded. Marsalis turns up again on two tracks on *Here's To Life*, which is otherwise dedicated to arrangements by Johnny Mandel, and again there's a hint of overdoing the sentiment: some may find the title-track far too wobbly in its emotional appeal. But the particular qualities of Horn's singing – the eschewal of vibrato, the even dynamic weight – are given full rein. *Light Out Of Darkness* is pitched as a tribute to Ray Charles, and after the heavyweight emoting of the previous record Horn sounds almost carefree on the likes of 'Hit The Road Jack' and 'I Got A Man'. Bartz lends a few swinging obbligatos, but the emphasis here is on Horn's understanding of the beat, her dry, almost elemental phrasing, and the intuitive touch of her regular group.

I Love You, Paris comes from a French concert. Shirley makes no concessions to the occasion in terms of turning up her tempos, and 'It's Easy To Remember' is about as slow as it will ever get. But she has the art of making the time move, even at this kind of tempo: 'Wouldn't It be Luvverly' is luvverly indeed. The disc is perhaps overlong at almost 75 minutes, but the best of it is top-flight Horn. Same applies to *The Main Ingredient*, cut mainly at her home, with famous names sitting in to add variety to what's now a long string of similarly inclined dates. Buck Hill outdoes Joe Henderson, and Hargrove is untypically laid back on his flugelhorn feature. Yet the highlight is surely her gorgeous version of 'The Look Of Love', done alone with her regular team of Ables and Williams, which suggests that Shirley can probably play this way for ever and still make it sound good.

*****(*) Loving You**

Verve 537022-2 *Horn; George Mesterhazy (ky, g); Steve Novosel (b); Steve Williams (d); Alex Acuna (perc).* 11/96.

*****(*) I Remember Miles**

Verve 557199-2 *Horn; Roy Hargrove (t); Toots Thielemans (hca); Charles Ables, Ron Carter (b); Al Foster, Steve Williams (d).* 97.

The inevitable complaint is that Horn goes on making the same record and, nine albums into her Verve contract, little seems ready to change. Yet nobody grumbled much about the sameness of Ella, Billie or Sarah in their various careers. Shirley's difficulty is that her preference for achingly slow tempos and sung-spoken lyrics doesn't chime very easily with the modern attention-span. *Loving You* may be no masterpiece but it's probably as good as any record she's made: the tunes impeccably chosen, the delivery perfectly judged. Of course Lil Green never meant 'In the Dark' to sound like this; but it's just as sexy, maybe more so. The title-tune is bathos made bearable by the refinement of her methods, and 'It Amazes Me' might even amaze you.

Miles Davis was always a Shirley Horn fan, and the singer repays the compliment with a homage album that sounds a lot more genuine than most of the rash of tribute discs. Whether doing Gershwin, other standards or 'Blue In Green', this is a smoke-filled reminiscence that has the feel and weight of something real, and the spare charts (Hargrove plays the obvious role on four tracks and Thielemans is inspiring on 'Summertime') replicate something of the skeletal intensity of Davis in his golden age.

*****(*) Ultimate**

Verve 547162-2 *Horn; as various Verve and Impulse! albums above.* 62–97.

Chosen by Diana Krall, the tracks on Horn's entry in the Verve *Ultimate* series make up a sensible cross-section of her records in this series, although none of our particular favourites are here. But that is always the way with somebody else's compilations.

Wayne Horvitz

PIANO, KEYBOARDS

Horvitz was one of the leading personalities of the New York downtown circle and is now based in Seattle. He is a strong, even idiosyncratic player and composer who has roved back and forth between situationist improvisation and more generic grooves, as in his organ group, Zony Mash.

***** Some Order, Long Understood**

Black Saint 121159 *Horvitz; Butch Morris (c); William Parker (b).* 2/82.

***** The New Generation**

Elektra Nonesuch 60759 *Horvitz; Robin Holcomb, Doug Wieselman (ky); Bill Frisell (g); Elliott Sharp (g, b); Jon Rose (clo); David Hofstra (b, tba); Bobby Previte (d, ky); Jim Mussen, Joey Peters (elec d); Chris Brown (gazamba, wing); Nica (v).* 9/85.

*****(*) Miracle Mile**

Elektra Nonesuch 7559 79278 2 *Horvitz; J.A Deane (tb, elec); Denny Goodhew (sax); Doug Wieselman (ts, cl); Stew Cutler, Bill Frisell, Elliott Sharp (g); Ben Steele (g syn); Kermit Driscoll (b); Bobby Previte (d).* 91.

Horvitz got off to a brisk start with a clattery sound that wasn't too proud to make use of user-friendly electronics and pop-punk dynamics. *Some Order, Long Understood* consists of just two long tracks, spun out of seemingly nothing by a surprisingly lyrical trio. Morris is revelatory in his use of classic-jazz shapes and modernist accents, and Parker's *arco* work is superb. It's possible to hear in this session embryonic intimation of everything that was to follow.

Horvitz's wife, Robin Holcomb, has had a rough ride from jazz critics. She has a brief part on *The New Generation*, the disc that established Horvitz as a recording artist. It consists of 13 brief excusions with various permutations from the line-up shown. The best tend to be those with Frisell and Previte, and the duos with Wieselman are merely dull.

Miracle Mile offers moody and slightly threatening music from Horvitz's band, The President. Horvitz is an impressive melodist, but tunes are constantly set in front of rather sinister guitar and synth backgrounds as if to suggest that the 'kinder, gentler America' of George Bush, apostrophized in an interesting 'Open Letter', merely caps the kind of violence implied by the dramatic smoke-pall on the cover. The horns don't do much of interest, but Previte is absolutely superb, giving one of his best performances on record.

***** Pigpen: V As In Victim**
Avant AVAN 027 *Horvitz; Briggan Krauss (as); Fred Chalenor (b); Mike Stone (d).* 5/93.

Pigpen is an extra-curricular project of Horvitz's, a band which tries to make associations between jazz, advanced rock and country music, often in near-unrecognizable forms. The 'Portrait Of Hank Williams Jr' and the long title-piece are the heart of a session which bears the A&R stamp of label guru John Zorn, who also has a hand in production. Not much to say about the other players, beyond the obvious point that they execute Horvitz's wishes competently and with an authentic lack of feeling.

***** Cold Spell**
Knitting Factory KFW 201 *Horvitz; Timothy Young (g); Fred Chalenor (b); Andy Roth (d).* 97.

*****(*) Brand Spankin' New**
Knitting Factory KFW 223 *As above.* 98.

Horvitz's organ group specializes in moody cyber-funk. The later album drifts between genres like the soundtrack to some ironic comedy show about creatives in an unspecified city. It's not all atmosphere and SFX, though. As ever, Horvitz's line is rich in associations and as driving as any hard-bop master of the '50s. Even on Hammond B3, he always sounds like a piano player, and both records reveal a linear development very far removed from the average organ/guitar group.

Young is a fine player, reminiscent of Bill Frisell only in the loosest sense, because he lacks Bill's interest in great washes of sound and in competing lines and countermelodies. Roth has probably listened to his fair share of Tony Williams records down the years and has profited by them. He has much of Horvitz's own ability to combine power and propulsion with a real delicacy of touch.

****** 4 + 1 Ensemble**
Intuition INT 3224-2 *Horvitz; Julian Priester (tb); Eyvind Kang (vn); Tucker Martine (processing).* 98.

Martine has been Horvitz's *éminence grise* for some time, co-producing and adding effects to previous albums. Here, though, he really does seem to be part of a group project, transforming a remarkably well-balanced instrumentation into something surreal and delightful. Priester is, as ever, a thoughtful and atmospheric presence, playing low and slow in a tonality that often recalls french horn. The revelation is Kang, shadowing and bridging trombone and piano and often repeating the same melody higher in register, as he does on the mournful, penultimate 'Take Me Home'. Horvitz sticks to steam piano throughout, revealing himself again as a player of slightly limited dexterity but nimbler in thought than he is at the keyboard. This is a quietly powerful record from a group of genuine originality.

Hot Stuff!

GROUP

Old rascals of British trad get together.

****(*) Hot Stuff!**
Lake LACD40 *Chez Chesterman (c, v); Mike Pointon (tb); Dick Charlesworth (cl, ss, ts, v); Barney Bates (p); Jim Forey (g); John Rodber (b); Graham Scriven (d).* 2/94.

This is good fun, though one needs a tolerance for some of the nuttier aspects of British trad. Charlesworth (senior readers may recall his group, The City Gents) seems to be the leader, but all seven men have records as long as your arm at this kind of thing, and such misdemeanours are second nature to the lot of them. Several interesting obscurities among the 17 tracks, and there's actually some fine playing: Chesterman's gracious if slightly ashthmatic-sounding cornet on 'Will You Or Won't You Be My Babe', Pointon's brawling trombone on 'Sunset Café Stomp', and so on. But docked a notch for the sound, which has so little bottom-end it makes Bates sound like he's playing tack piano. And docked another for the vocals, which are a large side-order of ham.

François Houle

CLARINET, SOPRANO SAXOPHONE

Vancouver-based, Houle studied the classics and is a thoroughgoing clarinet technician, looking to explore improvisatory worlds.

***** Hacienda**
Songlines 1501-2 *Houle; Brad Muirhead (btb, euph); Saul Berson (as, cl, f); Tony Wilson (g); Ian McIntosh (tba, didgeridoo); Joe Williamson (b); Dylan Van der Schyff (d).* 3/92.

*****(*) Schizosphere**
Red Toucan RT 9203 *Houle; Tony Wilson (g, khaen, aktira); Dylan Van der Schyff (perc).* 8/94.

***** Any Terrain Tumultuous**
Red Toucan RT 9305 *Houle; Marilyn Crispell (p).* 9/95.

Houle is a classically trained Canadian who has been turned on to improvised music by the likes of Evan Parker and Steve Lacy. In sound, he is immediately reminiscent of another latter-day clarinet master, Michael Moore, but Houle is perhaps less interested in structures and navigable harmonies. *Hacienda* was recorded live at Vancouver's The Glass Slipper and was an early release on the enterprising Songlines label. Houle leads an energetic and enthusiastic septet through a barnstorming set. There's a rickety quality to some of the ensembles and the favoured low brass (an odd touch) lend a marching-band feel to some of the tunes, particularly 'Gospells'. Splashy recording and the sense that this is just a night at the club caught by chance mean that it's no masterpiece, but an interesting find.

The trio on *Schizosphere* is beautifully balanced; Houle's richly grained sound blending perfectly with Wilson's sudden electrical storms and van der Schyff's Bennink-inspired drumming. There is a lot of gestural playing, passages of simul-instrumentalism *à la* Roland Kirk, and abstract effects from Wilson as he rubs the strings with his forearms while playing a Khmer mouth-organ.

The record with Crispell is inevitably very different, and the pianist does tend to dominate. However, she shows her partner considerable respect, and as time goes by it is Houle's voice which commands attention. His sheer quality of sound, clean, unfailingly accurate at the register break (though, as often as not, played *chalumeau* in the Giuffre style), is highly attractive, but it is the quiet urgency of the ideas which increasingly comes across.

***** Nancali**

Songlines SGL 1519-2 *Houle; Benoit Delbecq (p).* 4/96–5/97.

Having gone down the duo route with Crispell, Houle takes another trip with another pianist. Delbecq covers more abstract, unclaimed ground than his illustrious predecessor, with the rattle and twang of 'Early Dance' one example of using the piano's innards, and the contrary music-box rhyme of 'Late Dance' cast as a rejoinder to his own experiments. But the duo wire in strands from other disciplines too, such as the title-piece, where Delbecq turns his instrument into a simple thumb-piano, and the result feels like a Bedouin dance. Houle is sometimes outshone by his partner but, when he does assert, his beautiful tone keeps taking the ear, no matter how much he disfigures it in the line of duty.

*****(*) In The Vernacular**

Songlines SGL 1522-2 *Houle; Dave Douglas (t); Peggy Lee (clo); Mark Dresser (b); Dylan Van der Schyff (d).* 10/97.

Two brief interludes apart, this is a set of interpretations of John Carter's music – including, in 'Three Dances In The Vernacular', a debut recording. But Carter's music without Carter proves at times to be a surprisingly dour and difficult undertaking. Deprived of the composer's own gravitas, the more taxing pieces cry out for something more inspiriting than this quintet provides. Yet they compensate with the fleet rush of 'Sticks And Stones', a marvellous collective throw of the dice, and the 'Juba's Run' section of 'Fields Medley'.

Karsten Houmark (born 1951)

GUITAR

Danish guitarist, working in a light style of modal fusion.

****(*) Four**

Storyville STCD 4197 *Houmark; Thomas Clausen (ky); Lennart Ginman (b); Jonas Johansen (d).* 9/94.

*****(*) Dawn**

Storyville STCD 4211 *As above, except John Taylor (p) replaces Clausen.* 10/96.

Four has excellent playing by a talented quartet: Houmark is a nimble improviser and unselfish enough to let his accomplished team have plenty of space, with the reliable Clausen in his usual thoughtful form. But the music fails to make any impact in the end. None of Houmark's nine originals impresses, his various guitar sounds are blandly derivative, and the faceless production closes off the inspiration.

In comparison, *Dawn* seems like a huge step forward, but it's mainly down to Taylor's splendid playing and what seems to be an inspiring empathy with Houmark. The nominal leader came up with some eloquent tunes for the date, with 'Serenity' and 'Sirens Song' outstanding; and the improvised 'A Drop Of The Ocean' duet with Taylor is an unaffected piece of melodic freedom. In the end, this sounds very like a good John Abercrombie date, with Houmark's sound mirroring the American's, but there's nothing much wrong with that.

Avery 'Kid' Howard (1908–66)

TRUMPET, VOCAL

He began as a drummer but switched to trumpet in the 1930s, joining the George Lewis group in the following decade. In the last ten years of his life he was a much-loved regular at Preservation Hall.

(***) Prelude To The Revival Vol. 1

American Music AMCD-40 *Howard; Andrew Anderson, Punch Miller (t, v); Duke Derbigny (t); Joe 'Cornbread' Thomas (cl, v); Martin Cole (ts); ? Harris (p, v); Joe Robertson (p); Leonard Mitchell (g, bj, v); Frank Murray (g); Chester Zardis (b); Charles Sylvester, Junious Wilson, Clifford 'Snag' Jones (d); Matie Murray (v).* 37–41.

So little jazz was recorded in New Orleans during the 1930s that any archive material from the period is valuable. Sam Charters, perhaps not the most reliable judge, reckoned that Kid Howard would have been the next King of New Orleans trumpet after Joe Oliver. He is only on the first four tracks here, in barely passable sound, but they show a mature, hard-hitting musician displaying the inevitable debt to Armstrong but resolutely going his own way. Anderson and Derbigny are less individual but they bridge the older and younger New Orleans traditions unselfconsciously enough. The sleeve-notes detail the detective work that went into finding and restoring the original acetates, and ears unused to prehistoric sound must beware. The five tracks by Miller are discussed under his name.

****(*) Kid Howard's La Vida Band**

American Music AMCD-54 *Howard; Eddie Sommers (tb); Israel Gorman (cl); Homer Eugene (bj); Louis James (b); Josiah Frazier (d).* 8–9/61.

Recorded on the cusp of the oncoming revival of the 1960s, this date went some way to re-establishing Howard's standing. It's a pity, though, that there's some rustiness, not only in his playing but with most of the band too: fluffs and sloppiness are a distraction, even in the name of authenticity. But there are great moments, such as the tribute to Chris Kelly, Howard's early idol, in 'The Three Sixes', or the opening ensemble of 'Nelly Gray', and New Orleans scholars will welcome an important record on CD. The sound has attracted some haziness in the digital remastering. Howard can also be heard on several records with George Lewis.

Noah Howard (born 1943)

ALTO SAXOPHONE

Howard grew up in New Orleans and had his first experience of music as a chorister. Moving to California in his late teens exposed him to the avant-garde in the shape of Dewey Redman and Sonny Simmons, but he never quite shook away his soulful, churchy quality.

***(*) Patterns / Message To South Africa

Eremite MTE019 *Howard; Chris McGregor, Misha Mengelberg (p); Jaap Schoonhoven (g); Earl Freeman, Johnny Dyani (b); Noel McGee (d); Han Bennink (d, perc, Tibetan hn); Steve Boston (perc); Zusaan Kali Fasteau (v, sheng).* 10/71, 79.

Message To South Africa was written in the week that Steven Biko was killed and it features two of the Cape's most powerful and evocative exiles. It's a stunning performance, laden with passionate vocals from Howard, the magnificent Dyani and Zusaan Kali Fasteau. Howard is always sensitive to the *yin* aspects of the music, its feminine side, and even in the midst of violence and despair it sings.

The earlier material was originally released on Howard's own AltSax label. It was commissioned by Dutch Radio, just as that country nurtured the last wisdom of Eric Dolphy. As with Eric back in 1964, Bennink is magnificent: swinging, dark and funny. Mengelberg is more uncomfortable in the context, and at moments he treats the African material almost dismissively.

McGregor quotes the African National Congress anthem, 'Nkosi Sikeleli Afrika', once explicitly and once in inverted form on *Message To South Africa*. It's a tiny reminder of the political context against which this music is created. At this point, almost anything of Howard's is welcome. These, though, are genuinely important points in the story.

***(*) In Concert

Cadence CJR 1084 *Howard; Bobby Few (p); James Lewis (b); Calyer Duncan (d).* 9/97.

The two FMP LPs of 1975 and 1977 have yet to reappear, leaving a ridiculous gap in the still underweight Howard discography which even the reappearance of the '70s material above doesn't quite put right. 'Schizophrenic Blues' puts in an appearance on this 1997 live recording from Amsterdam. The saxophonist likes to introduce himself with the words 'I'm Noah Howard – of the world', and much of his travelling is compressed into this performance, with European and African elements blended into the mix. Mongo Santamaria might be surprised to see 'Afro-Blue' credited to John Coltrane, but he'd certainly be gratified by what has been done with his most famous theme. 'We Remember John' is presumably also for Coltrane, a long, clattering performance that throws into focus how good a drummer Duncan is. Bobby Few always responds well to gigs like this, his natural bluesiness mediating his rather dry attack.

Freddie Hubbard (born 1938)

TRUMPET, FLUGELHORN

Born in Indianapolis, Hubbard first worked with the Montgomery brothers and arrived in New York in 1959. He joined the Jazz Messengers in 1961 and was involved in important recordings with Ornette Coleman and Oliver Nelson, as well as leading his own dates for Blue Note and Impulse!, and later Atlantic. In the '70s he moved in a lite-fusion direction at CTI and sold many records but by the end of the decade he was out of fashion, and he spent much of the next two decades trying to decide what situation to play in. Recently, lip trouble has kept him away from playing at all.

**** Goin' Up

Blue Note 59380 *Hubbard; Hank Mobley (ts); McCoy Tyner (p); Paul Chambers (b); Philly Joe Jones (d).* 4/61.

**** Hub-Tones

Blue Note 99008 *Hubbard; James Spaulding (as, f); Herbie Hancock (p); Reggie Workman (b); Clifford Jarvis (d).* 10/62.

*** Minor Mishap

Black Lion BL 60122 *Hubbard; Willie Wilson (tb); Pepper Adams (bs); Duke Pearson (p); Thomas Howard (b); Lex Humphries (d).* 8/61.

Freddie Hubbard was one of the liveliest of the young hard-bop lions of the late 1950s and early '60s. As a Jazz Messenger, and with his own early albums for Blue Note, he set down so many great solos that trumpeters have made studies of him to this day, the burnished tone, bravura phrasing and rhythmical subtleties still enduringly modern. He never quite had the quickfire genius of Lee Morgan, but he had a greater all-round strength, and he is an essential player in the theatre of hard bop. His several Blue Note dates seem to come and go in the catalogue, but we are listing *Goin' Up* (though it is a 'Connoisseur' limited edition) and the new Rudy van Gelder edition of *Hub-Tones*, each a vintage example of Blue Note hard bop. *Goin' Up* was his second record for the label and its youthful ebullience is still exhilarating, the trumpeter throwing off dazzling phrases almost for the sheer fun of it. *Hub-Tones* includes one of Hubbard's most affecting performances in the tribute to Booker Little, as well as his first jousting with James Spaulding (repeated in *Breaking Point*, listed below). Both of these number among Hubbard's choicest albums. The Black Lion CD is of a similar vintage, but nothing like as good. The band is less enthusiastic than Hubbard, who plays well, if a little within himself. Extra takes of all but one of the seven titles pad it out to CD length, but to no special advantage.

***(*) The Artistry Of Freddie Hubbard

Impulse! 33111 *Hubbard; Curtis Fuller (tb); John Gilmore (ts); Tommy Flanagan (p); Art Davis (b); Louis Hayes (d).* 7/62.

*** The Body And The Soul

Impulse! 11832 *Hubbard; Clark Terry, Ed Armour, Richard Williams (t); Melba Liston, Curtis Fuller (tb); Bob Northern, Julius Watkins (frhn); Eric Dolphy (as, f); Seldon Powell, Wayne Shorter (ts); Jerome Richardson (ts, bs); Charles Davis (bs);*

Cedar Walton (p); Reggie Workman (b); Philly Joe Jones, Louis Hayes (d); strings. 3–5/63.

Hubbard made two appearances as a leader for Impulse!. The 1962 sextet session is unusual for Gilmore's presence, one of the few small-group albums he made away from Sun Ra in the early 1960s. The music offers a slightly more expansive setting than Hubbard was used to at Blue Note and, though Fuller and Gilmore are perhaps at less than their best, the music has a forceful presence, with Flanagan offering a dapper counterpoint to the horns. *The Body And The Soul* is a quirkier offering, thanks mostly to Wayne Shorter's sometimes peculiar arrangements, for septet, big band and strings. Hubbard plays with beautiful alacrity, his quicker solos dancing over the charts, his slower ones underscoring what melody he can find; but Shorter's arrangements have their problems: audible fluffs betray a lack of rehearsal, some of the tunes seem cut off before they're properly developed, and moments like Eric Dolphy's alto squiggle on 'Clarence's Place' seem to have strayed in from another situation altogether.

*****(*) Breaking Point**

Blue Note 84172 *Hubbard; James Spaulding (as); Ronnie Mathews (p); Eddie Khan (b); Joe Chambers (d).* 5/64.

One of the most 'out' of Hubbard's Blue Notes, but not so far out that it gives the trumpeter any real problems as regards sounding convincing when improvising on the material. 'Far Way', for instance, is a complex piece but not so difficult that it undercuts his natural virtuosity. 'D Minor Mint' is the kind of bebop swinger which he eats up. Spaulding is exemplary, and the unusual rhythm section do nothing amiss.

****(*) Backlash**

Atlantic 7567-90466-2 *Hubbard; James Spaulding (as, f); Albert Dailey (p); Bob Cunningham (b); Ray Appleton (d); Ray Barretto (perc).* 10/66.

A good enough session, but the emphasis on backbeats, riff tunes and squared-off solos is a broad hint at the lighter direction Hubbard was already looking towards, as jazz faced its slump in popularity. Perhaps he can't be blamed. A likeable 'Up Jumped Spring', the most enduring of the trumpeter's compositions, adds a little extra weight.

***** Straight Life**

CTI EPC ZK 65125 *Hubbard; Joe Henderson (ts, f); Herbie Hancock (p); George Benson (g); Ron Carter (b); Jack DeJohnette (d); Weldon Irvine, Richie Landrum (perc).* 11/70.

Hubbard's CTI catalogue is also in disrepair, with new editions being prepared of some of the discs; this is still all we have so far. It was an erratic period for him, and for many of his generation, trying to come to terms with jazz's commercial eclipse, and though this album and the slightly earlier *Red Clay* owe much to the contemporary work of Miles Davis, this is really a simpler, far less formidable equation the band is working on. The title-piece and 'Mr Clean' are almost themeless blow-outs for the players, and in most hands this would be a complete mess, especially with DeJohnette crashing around the mix and the two percussionists adding little but further noise. But the soloists are Hubbard, Henderson, Hancock and Benson, not a bad band in anybody's book, and they take vociferous but plausible routes to some kind of catharsis. The disc is completed with a sweetly handled 'Here's That Rainy Day' on flugelhorn. *Red Clay* (still out of print) is a better bet – but add it to this and you have the best of Hubbard's CTI work: the later discs dive headlong into early fusion, sometimes calamitously.

**** Born To Be Blue**

Original Jazz Classics OJC 734 *Hubbard; Harold Land (ts); Billy Childs (ky); Larry Klein (b); Steve Houghton (d); Buck Clark (perc).* 12/81.

***** Outpost**

Enja 3095-2 *Hubbard; Kenny Barron (p); Buster Williams (b); Al Foster (d).* 2–3/81.

****(*) Face To Face**

Original Jazz Classics OJC 937 *Hubbard; Oscar Peterson (p); Joe Pass (g); Niels-Henning Orsted Pedersen (b); Martin Drew (d).* 5/82.

All of Hubbard's 1970s albums for Columbia are currently out of print. These records for Pablo are a disappointing lot. *Born To Be Blue* was recorded live on a European tour and, while the leader plays with much of his old energy, the group musters little distinction: Land sounds largely uninterested and Childs adds nothing special of his own. While there is the usual quota of virtuoso fireworks on the meeting with Peterson, the session is, like so many involving Peterson's group, built on technical bravura rather than specific communication. Interesting to hear Hubbard tackling 'All Blues', but this version is about a hundred degrees hotter than any Milesian treatment and the tune wilts in the furnace. The quartet session for Enja, though, is much more worthwhile. Hubbard sometimes sounds bland and, talented though the rhythm section is, they don't ask him to be demonstrative; but there are some glowingly executed solos and a particularly rapt flugelhorn treatment of 'You Don't Know What Love Is'. Excellent recording.

***** Keystone Bop: Sunday Night**

Prestige 24146-2 *Hubbard; Joe Henderson (ts); Bobby Hutcherson (vib); Billy Childs (p); Larry Klein (b); Steve Houghton (d).* 11/81.

***** Keystone Bop, Vol. 2: Friday And Saturday**

Prestige 24163-2 *As above.* 11/81.

A smoking live date, now spread across two discs. Hubbard sets a cracking pace on the Sunday show with his own blues, 'Birdlike', which leads to inspired solos from Henderson and Hutcherson too. Thereafter the pressure drops a little and the rest is merely very good, but it's a pleasure to hear three great improvisers, all on resolute form, and this time Hubbard's intensity actually counts for something. The second volume has a less-than-immortal 'Round Midnight', but there's enough headstrong blowing to keep the spirits up.

*****(*) The Freddie Hubbard And Woody Shaw Sessions**

Blue Note 32747-2 2CD *Hubbard; Woody Shaw (t); Kenny Garrett (as); Mulgrew Miller (p); Cecil McBee, Ray Drummond (b); Carl Allen (d).* 85–87.

In a way, these were comeback dates for both men: Shaw had to endure personal fallibilities which always stood in the way of his career, and Hubbard was still trying to shake off the aftermath of years of nonsense. They cut two albums for the 'new' Blue Note which found each man, if not at his best – Hubbard has never recaptured his youthful sparkle, and Shaw's inconsistencies are palpable – at least in keen and lucid voice. There is some merriment in the various jousts they put together, and with Garrett kibitzing very effectively there is enough here to overcome any awkwardness of delivery. Hubbard also reminds of his talents as a balladeer in 'Lament For Booker'.

***** Feel The Wind**

Timeless SJP 307 *Hubbard; Javon Jackson (ts); Benny Green, Mulgrew Miller (p); Lonnie Plaxico, Leon Dorsey (b); Art Blakey (d).* 11/88.

***** Topsy**

Enja 7025-2 *Hubbard; Kenny Garrett (as); Benny Green (p); Rufus Reid (b); Carl Allen (d).* 12/89.

*****(*) Bolivia**

Musicmasters 65063-2 *Hubbard; Ralph Moore (ss, ts); Vincent Herring (ss, as); Cedar Walton (p); David Williams (b); Billy Higgins (d); Giovanni Hidalgo (perc).* 12/90–1/91.

***** Live At Fat Tuesday's**

Musicmasters 65075-2 2CD *Hubbard; Javon Jackson (ts); Benny Green (p); Christian McBride (b); Tony Reedus (d).* 12/91.

Hubbard sessions dating from the last ten years or so have been hit-and-miss, but there's often something interesting going on, even when the leader isn't at his peak. *Feel The Wind* breezes along without a great deal to show for it, though Green and Jackson are always good value, and they're in sterling form on the live session from Fat Tuesday's, where Freddie manages some solid improvisations. The sound is a bit unfavourable, particularly to Jackson. *Topsy* is a batch of standards, beautifully recorded: Kenny Garrett comes in for three tracks, there is a 'Cherokee' which must be one of the fastest on record, and Hubbard keeps the mute in for the whole session, often a sign that he's a bit unsure about his tone that day. All rather so-so for Freddie himself, but every so often Hubbard does a session like *Bolivia*, and all his old virtues fall back into place. The major props here are Cedar Walton and Billy Higgins, two men who've little time for frippery; they play with such class that it obliges Hubbard to work hard and return the favour. Moore is a little in shadow (and Herring makes only one appearance), but the weight rests on Hubbard, and he seems to be feeling good about it.

****(*) M.M.T.C. (Monk, Miles, Trane, Cannon)**

Musicmasters 65132-2 *Hubbard; Robin Eubanks (tb); Vincent Herring (as); Javon Jackson (ts); Gary Smulyan (bs); Stephen Scott (p); Peter Washington (b); Carl Allen (d).* 8–12/94.

If Hubbard had been able to hold his own with this all-star assemblage, this could have been a classic encounter. As it is, it sounds like a contrived tribute concept covering the poor form of a man who by the sound of it can't play too well any longer. The five-horn front line gets in some good blows and the rhythm section is A-1. It seems a pointless exercise, nevertheless. Recent reports of Hubbard's capabilities have been conflicting, but at present nobody is entrusting him to his own date.

Spike Hughes (1908–87)

BASS, PIANO, CELESTE, REED ORGAN

A Londoner by birth, Hughes taught himself bass and worked as an arranger and composer in the British dance music field of the late 1920s and early '30s. He visited New York in 1933 and organized recording sessions featuring some of the best black players on the scene. But he quit jazz altogether for classical music in 1934.

*****(*) Spike Hughes Vols 1 & 2**

Kings Cross Music KCM 001/002 2CD *Hughes; Sylvester Ahola, Jack Jackson, Max Goldberg, Norman Payne, Bill Gaskin, Leslie Thompson, Arthur Niblo (t); Muggsy Spanier (c); Jock Fleming, Lew Davis, Bernard Tipping (tb); Danny Polo, Rex Owen (cl); Max Farley (cl, as, f); Jimmy Dorsey, Philip Buchel, Harry Hines (cl, as); Bobby Davis (cl, bs); Buddy Featherstonehaugh (cl, ts); Eddie Carroll, Claude Ivy, Gerry Moore (p); Stan Andrews, George Hurley (vn); Leslie Smith, Alan Ferguson (g); Val Rosing (d, v); Bill Harty (d).* 3–12/30.

****** Spike Hughes Vols 3 & 4**

Kings Cross Music KCM 003/004 2CD *As above, except add Jimmy Macaffer, Chick Smith, Billy Higgs, Billy Smith, Bruts Gonella (t), Freddy Welsh, Don Macaffer, Bill Mulraney (tb), Billy Amstell (cl, as), Harry Hayes, Dave Shand (as), Billy Munn, Billy Mason (p), Ronnie Gubertini (d), Elsie Carlisle, Joey Shields (v); omit Ahola, Jackson, Goldberg, Spanier, Polo, Owen, Dorsey, Davis, Moore, Andrews, Hurley, Smith.* 11/30–11/32.

****** Spike Hughes & Benny Carter 1933**

Retrieval RTR 79005 *As above, except add Henry 'Red' Allen, Leonard , Shad Collins, Bill Dillard, Howard Scott (t), Dicky Wells, Wilbur De Paris, George Washington (tb), Benny Carter (as, ss, cl), Howard Johnson (as, cl), Wayman Carver (as, cl, f), Coleman Hawkins (ts), Chu Berry (ts), Luis Russell, Nicholas Rodriguez (p), Lawrence Lucie (g), Ernest Hill (b), Big Sid Catlett, Kaiser Marshall (d).* 11/31–5/33.

Spike Hughes had a brief affair with jazz: 'I left jazz behind me at the moment when I was enjoying it most, the moment when all true love-affairs should end.' It was just after the sessions with the all-star American line-up which features on the Retrieval. But he had already made an extraordinary mark on the music in Britain. His early 78s, handsomely collected on the four discs on the Kings Cross label, are intensely sought after and contain some of the best British music of the period. Even on the earliest sessions Hughes was looking for hot material to put in a dance context – 'Zonky', 'The Man From The South'. Soon enough he was on to 'The Mooche', 'Harlem Madness' and 'Blue Turning Grey Over You'. Jimmy Dorsey appears as guest soloist on one 1930 session and, as adept as he is, the best British horn-players aren't outclassed: there are fine moments for Payne, Davis, Farley and others. If British players had been under the sway of the Red Nichols school, Hughes's interest in Ellington especially was bringing in a new slant on playing hot, and when he *did* tackle a New York piece such as Joe Venuti's 'Doing Things', the results were rather different from those of some years before. The second set includes nuggets like 'A Harlem Symphony', 'Six Bells Stampede' and 'Blues In My Heart', and both collections, expertly remastered and neatly packaged, are outstanding bargains for anyone interested in the second age of British jazz. But the Retrieval disc, which includes all the American recordings that Hughes made on a visit to New York, is indispensable. Though the band was really the Benny Carter orchestra, Hughes did the writing and arranging, and in pieces such as 'Donegal Cradle Song', a luminous feature for Hawkins, and 'Sweet Sorrow Blues', with superb Henry Allen, Hughes closed his jazz career on an amazing high note.

Daniel Humair (born 1938)

DRUMS

Though often assumed to be a Frenchman, the big drummer was born in Geneva and moved to Paris only when he was twenty. His most important association was with pianist Martial Solal, but Humair also became a respected sideman for a roster of visiting Americans. He also became the regular drummer of the George Gruntz band.

****** Daniel Humair Surrounded**

Blue Flame 40322 *Humair; Eric Dolphy (as, bcl); Phil Woods (as); Johnny Griffin (ts); Gerry Mulligan (bs); Jane Ira Bloom (ss); Kenny Drew, Michel Graillier, Joachim Kühn, Tete Montoliu, Martial Solal, Maurice Vander (p); Eddie Louiss (org); Dave Friedman (vib); René Thomas (g); Jean-François Jenny-Clark, Ron Mathewson, Gus Nemeth, Guy Pedersen, Mike Richmond, Gilbert Rovere, Henri Texier (b).* 5/64–7/87.

It's often a little difficult when Gato Barbieri is playing in his characteristic hyperthyroid manner, to hear much else that is going on in the band. But sometime try to follow the drumming behind Barbieri on the classic *Last Tango In Paris*, for it illustrates in convenient miniature the qualities that have made Humair one of the finest European drummers. He has all the rhythmic subtlety and inventiveness one associates with Philly Joe Jones, but also some of the inherent tunefulness of Roy Haynes. *Surrounded* is a superb introduction, documenting almost a quarter-century of sterling performance. The roster of names is testimony to Humair's pedigree as a drummer. The 1983 session with Johnny Griffin is not quite as hectic as earlier encounters, but 'Wee' is still taken at a respectable gallop. On Dolphy's blues, 'Serene', a session under Kenny Drew's leadership, he sounds appropriately thoughtful and never hurries the delivery. And so on, down the years, taking in the funky organ trio of Eddie Louiss (see below), the cool swing of Gerry Mulligan, and the abstract folkiness of Martial Solal. Appropriately, the most recent piece is a solo percussion work, 'L'Espace Sonore', a strongly constructed piece with scarcely a wasted gesture.

*****(*) Humair–Louiss–Ponty: Volume 1**

Dreyfus 191018-2 *Humair; Eddie Louiss (org); Jean-Luc Ponty (vn).* 67.

***** Humair–Louiss–Ponty: Volume 2**

Dreyfus 191028-2 *As above.* 67.

Fascinating as much as anything for a glimpse of the 25-year-old Ponty, who takes the lead on a good few of these picturesque but undeniably swinging sessions. Louiss has an emphatic touch, with a lot of dissonance thrown in for sheer colour. Humair keeps things pretty neat, except on 'Bag's Groove' (*Volume 2*), which is a bit of a mess. The outstanding performances are all on the first set, with 'You've Changed', a shameless 'Summertime' and 'Round About Midnight', and a chipper 'So What' that manages to hang on to a thread of pure romance.

*****(*) Akagera**

JMS 012-2 *Humair; François Jeanneau (ts, ss, f, bcl, syn); Henri Texier (b, oud, perc); Gordon Beck (p).* 10 & 11/80.

An African-inspired session (the title is an alternative or mythical name for the Nile), this eases Humair out of straight jazz playing and allows him to focus on more exotic rhythms. Jeanneau frequently sounds as if he's playing some exotic shawm or wood flute, and Texier's use of *oud* is both idiomatic and highly personal. Gordon Beck pops up for a brief outing on 'Nebbia'. A good idea to reserve him for that. The rest of the session is spacious, even sparse, and works all the better for light and air. One or two other Humair sessions for JMS, including a couple of early all-solo dates, have drifted in and out of circulation lately; admirers may like to keep their eyes peeled for them.

***** Pépites**

CELP C3 *Humair; André Jaume (reeds).* 4/87.

Like all duo records, this could just as easily have been listed under the other partner, except that here Humair does seem to be the driving force, increasing the energy levels on what might otherwise have been a rather stiffly filigreed session and adding his own wry awareness to pseudo-classical skits like 'Les oiseaux sont marteaux', which has nothing whatever to do with either Messiaen or Boulez. Jaume turns in a splendid solo version of Coltrane's 'Naima'. All the other tunes are originals, with both men putting up pieces.

****** 9–11 p.m. Town Hall**

Label Bleu LBLC 6517 *Humair; Michel Portal (sax, bcl, bandoneon); Joachim Kühn, Martial Solal (p); Jean-François Jenny-Clark (b).* 6/88.

Humair's own records have the same thoroughgoing musicality that he brings to work with artists as different as Anthony Braxton, Stéphane Grappelli and Lee Konitz. *Town Hall* is a superb introduction to all the participants, and if the veteran Solal's part isn't as large as one might wish for, it's none the less significant as an exercise in the genealogy of the 'new' French jazz, whose roots actually strike a lot deeper than first appears. That is nowhere more evident than here and on ...

***** Up Date 3.3**

Label Bleu LBLC 6530 *Humair; François Jeanneau (as, ss, ts, f); Henri Texier (b).* 2/90.

... where Humair teams up with Texier (a bassist with a more folkish and structured approach than the more freely orientated Jenny-Clark) in an album of looser compositions and improvisations. Jeanneau more than makes up for any slight technical shortcomings by an intelligent disposition of his four horns, but the real foundation of the music is the interaction in the bass and drums. Both come highly recommended.

***(*) Edges

Label Bleu LBLC 6545 *Humair; Jerry Bergonzi (saxes); Aydin Esen (p); Miroslav Vitous (b).* 5/91.

Much of the interest here settles again on the interplay between Humair and another great European bassist. Vitous's own 'Monitor' is a strange stop-start theme that downplays Esen's rippling accompaniments and Bergonzi's full-ahead Coltranism in order to explore the complex times and sonorities that are meat and drink to both 'rhythm' players. Something of the same goes on throughout the very long 'Genevamalgame' (co-written by Joachim Kühn and the drummer, his only compositional credit on the album). The title suggests a much more exploratory, risk-taking endeavour. Humair's out-of-tempo sequences and dramatic *rallentando* passages must be extremely challenging to his players. There may be a hint of compromise to the market in Bergonzi's and Esen's dramatic soloing, but they are both capable of abstraction, too, and the net effect of their more obvious strategies is to concentrate attention on the drummer and bassist. The mix is nicely horizontal, though Vitous could have done with a slight lift, particularly on the early tracks.

***(*) Quatre Fois Trois

Label Bleu LBLC 6619/20 *Humair; Hal Crook (tb); George Garzone (ts); David Liebman (ss); Michel Portal (bcl); Joachim Kühn (p); Marc Ducret (g); Bruno Chevillon, Jean-François Jenny-Clark (b).* 4/96–3/97.

After experimenting with larger-scale units for some time, Humair came to believe that the trio, with its balance of responsibilities and forces, was still the most satisfying equation for his music. The title is then explained easily enough: four very different triumvirates of improvising musicians, playing a repertoire very much dominated by Humair material. The best of the groups is the one with Dave Liebman and Jean-François Jenny-Clark. They open with a segue from Humair's 'Casseroles' to the Joachin Kühn tune, 'More Tuna', and pick up the story later with Daniel's 'Bas de Lou'. Then there is a string-based group with Bruno Chevillon and Marc Ducret, an intriguing association between Kühn and Michel Portal, and last – and, in some respects, least satisfactory – the enigmatic George Garzone and Hal Crook. The drummer plays very differently in each of these contexts, though it is always clear who the percussionist is and that he is very much the fulcrum of performance. Humair's fertile and eclectic imagination can be gauged from his arrangement of the famous Massenet 'Méditation' from *Thaïs*, deeply felt and well thought out. Garzone might have been more comfortable with his own material. He sounds ill at ease on the almost folksy theme of 'La Galinette', though he turns in a brisk and powerful performance on Franco Ambrosetti's 'For Flying Out Proud', which makes the most of the unusual instrumentation. A fine record and, like all good projects of this sort, one that might have yielded four different albums.

Helen Humes (1913–81)

VOCAL

Sang in Chicago while still a teenager and worked with various bands in the '30s before being hired by Count Basie in 1938. Stayed until 1941, then sang as a solo and in package tours. Moved to Australia in 1964 but returned home three years later after her mother became ill, then began singing again, and was a grande dame of the scene in the '70s.

*** Helen Humes 1927–1945

Classics 892 *Humes; Dizzy Gillespie, Bobby Stark, Ross Butler (t); Jimmy Hamilton (cl); Herbie Fields (cl, as); Pete Brown, John Brown (as); Prince Robinson, Wild Bill Moore (ts); J.C Johnson, De Loise Searcy, Sam Price, Leonard Feather, Bill Doggett (p); Lonnie Johnson, Sylvester Weaver, Walter Beasley, Chuck Wayne, Elmer Warner (g); Charlie Drayton, Oscar Pettiford, Alfred Moore (b); Ray Nathan, Denzil Best, Charles Harris (d).* 4/27–45.

Remarkably, Helen Humes made her first records in the 'classic' blues idiom when she was only thirteen. That OKeh coupling, and the results of two sessions a few months later, open this fascinating CD of her early work. She sounds amazingly confident for her youth, and tracks such as 'Garlic Blues' and 'Alligator Blues' are handled with assurance and a degree of adventure. A 15-year jump leads to a fine session with a Pete Brown band (including Gillespie, who unfortunately gets very little space), before a rather extraordinary date with a Leonard Feather group, pairing old-timers Stark and Robinson with what is almost a bebop rhythm section! Five titles with a chunkily swinging Bill Doggett jump band round off the disc. Helen sounds a bit prosaic here and there, but the sweetness of her voice and her gift for swinging enliven what would otherwise be mostly ordinary sides. Transfers are surprisingly clear and clean: only the first 1927 coupling sounds really rough.

***(*) Helen Humes 1945–1947

Classics 1036 *Humes; Snooky Young, Buck Clayton (t); George Matthews (tb); Scoville Brown (cl); Edward Hale, Willie Smith (as); Wild Bill Moore, Maxwell Davis, Lester Young, William Woodman, John Hardee, Rudy Wiliams (ts); Arnold Ross, Jimmy Bunn, Meade Lux Lewis, Eddie Beal, Ram Ramirez, Teddy Wilson (p); Allen Reuss, Dave Barbour, Irving Ashby, Mundell Lowe (g); Red Callender, Jimmy Rudd, Walter Page, Jimmy Butts (b); Henry Tucker Green, Chico Hamilton, Jo Jones, Denzil Best (d).* 45–12/47.

Some excellent line-ups behind Helen on this scattering of Los Angeles and New York dates for Philo, Black & White and Mercury. The material is mostly a workable mix of blues, jump tunes and the odd novelty piece, with only the dreary 'Please Let Me Forget' coming out of the ballad bag. Snooky Young gets some great moments, Lester Young ambles slowly through a solo, and Buck Clayton is in charge of the last three dates. The trumpeter on 'Married Man Blues' is unidentified but he's useful. Helen is mistress of all this material and she sounds terrific on the Mercury dates in particular. A few tracks are surfacey, but it's mostly clear and very listenable.

**** 'Tain't Nobody's Biz-ness If I Do

Original Jazz Classics OJC 453 *Humes; Benny Carter (t); Frank Rosolino (tb); Teddy Edwards (ts); André Previn (p); Leroy Vinnegar (b); Shelly Manne, Mel Lewis (d).* 1–2/59.

****** Songs I Like To Sing**

Original Jazz Classics OJC 171 *Humes; Al Porcino, Ray Triscari, Stu Williamson, Jack Sheldon (t); Harry Betts, Bob Fitzpatrick (tb); Art Pepper (cl, as); Ben Webster, Teddy Edwards (ts); Bill Hood (bs); André Previn (p); Barney Kessel (g); Leroy Vinnegar (b); Shelly Manne (d).* 9/60.

*****(*) Swingin' With Helen**

Original Jazz Classics OJC 608 *Humes; Joe Gordon (t); Teddy Edwards (ts); Wynton Kelly (p); Al Viola (g); Leroy Vinnegar (b); Frank Butler (d).* 7/61.

Helen's sessions with Count Basie in the 1930s established her career, but she never lost her way. Her three albums for Contemporary have luckily all been reissued in the OJC series, and they make a powerful argument for her standing as one of the finest (and most overlooked) jazz vocalists of the swing era and after. Recorded in stereo for the first time, her voice's natural mix of light, girlish timbre and hard-hitting attack creates a curiously exhilarating impact. She's like a less matronly Ella Fitzgerald, yet she can phrase and change dynamics with more inventiveness than Ella. The 1959 session, organized almost as a jam session by Benny Carter, has a rare grip and immediacy; although almost everything on it is fine, special mention should be made of a superbly structured 'Stardust' and 'I Got It Bad And That Ain't Good' and a perfectly paced 'You Can Depend On Me'. The band, a strange mix of players, work unexpectedly well together, with the rhythm section's modern grooving offsetting terrific solos by Carter, Rosolino and Edwards.

Swingin' With Helen is just a shade less impressive, but the 12 standards here are all delivered with great charm and aplomb. The pick of the three, though, is *Songs I Like To Sing*, which arranger Marty Paich built very specifically around Humes's talents. The singer has no problem dealing with scores which would have taxed such a modernist as Mel Torme, and these eight tracks define a modern approach to swing singing. But the other four, with Humes set against a rhythm section and the sole horn of Ben Webster, are equally beautiful, particularly a glorious reading of 'Imagination'. Although Humes's voice isn't as forward in the sound-balance as it might be, the remastering of all three records is very crisp and strong.

***** 'Deed I Do**

Contemporary 14071-2 *Humes; Don Abney (p); Dean Reilly (b); Benny Barth (d).* 4/76.

A late entry for Helen, cut during her '70s comeback. *'Deed I Do* only has a plain old rhythm section for company and the material is only too familiar, but the intimacy is nice and she sounds like she enjoyed it.

Percy Humphrey (1905–95)

TRUMPET

The middle one of the Humphrey brothers started out as a drummer before switching to trumpet. He worked with George Lewis in the 1950s and led the Eureka Brass Band for many years, as well as the Preservation Hall Jazz Band and the New Orleans Joymakers. He seldom played outside the city and also had a day job selling insurance for many years.

***** Percy Humphrey's Sympathy Five**

American Music AMCD-88 *Humphrey; Waldron Joseph, Jack Delany (tb); Willie Humphrey, Raymond Burke (cl); Stanley Mendelson, Lester Santiago (p); Johnny St Cyr (g, bj, v); Blind Gilbert (g, v); Richard McLean, Sherwood Mangiapane (b); Paul Barbarin (d).* 1/51–6/54.

****(*) Sounds Of New Orleans Vol. 1: Paul Barbarin & His Band / Percy Humphrey's Jam Session**

Storyville STCD 6008 *Humphrey; Joe Avery (tb); Ray Burke (cl); Sweet Emma Barrett (p); Billy Huntington (bj); Ricard Alexis (b); Cie Frazier (d).* 5/54.

***** New Orleans The Living Legends: Percy Humphrey's Crescent City Joymakers**

Original Jazz Classics OJC 1834-2 *Humphrey; Louis Nelson (tb); Albert Burbank (cl); Emanuel Sayles (g, bj); Louis James (b); Josiah Frazier (d).* 1/61.

***** Climax Rag**

Delmark DE-233 *Humphrey; Jim Robinson (tb); Albert Burbank (cl); George Guesnon (bj); Alcide Slow Drag Pavageau (b); Cie Frazier (d).* 2/65.

***** Percy Humphrey's Hot Six**

GHB BCD-85 *Humphrey; Louis Nelson (tb); Albert Burbank (cl); Lars Edegran (p); Chester Zardis (b); Barry Martyn (d).* 11/66.

The middle one of the three Humphrey brothers was a substantial figure in New Orleans jazz. His most significant playing was usually done with the city's brass bands, and he became leader of the Eureka Brass Band in the early 1950s until its disbandment some 20 years later. The 1954 jam session, one-half of a disc shared with a Paul Barbarin set, is relatively slight music, but Humphrey plays with the characteristically short-breathed phrasing of the New Orleans brassman and makes all his notes count: his solo on 'Everybody Loves My Baby', decorated with the familiar wobble which is the New Orleans vibrato, sums up his style, a mixture of abrasiveness and raw melody. The sound is quite good, although Sweet Emma Barrett, a minor legend who wore bells on her hat and round her ankles, is almost inaudible at the piano.

The Sympathy Five (the name derives solely from the handwritten title on a discovered reel of tape) offer six 1954 titles on the American Music CD. Humphrey sounds in good spirits and his solos have a lean, almost wiry quality; but he is if anything outshone by Burke and the splendid Delany. The remainder of the disc is filled out with four strong titles by a Paul Barbarin group (with both Humphrey brothers) and three odd pieces by a trio with Burke, Mangiapane and the mysterious Blind Gilbert, who sings and strums a guitar in questionable tune. The Sympathy Five tracks aren't exactly hi-fi but they sound a lot better than some American Music discoveries.

Most of Humphrey's later records are hard to locate, but this 1961 date in Riverside's Living Legends series is worth remembering, recorded in far superior sound to that often granted this kind of jazz. Humphrey himself is rather overpowered by Albert Burbank, whose clarinet predominates with an eagerness that recalls Boyd Senter, and Frazier's drumming is crashingly resonant; but the band live up to their name at many points.

Climax Rag is a good if somewhat uneventful session for Delmark, recorded at San Jacinto Hall on the day after Cie Frazier's birthday (they play a brief 'Happy Birthday' for him).

Tight, rigorous playing, and for once Burbank is somewhat recessed in the sound. No fewer than eight alternative takes beef up the CD reissue, although if anything this dilutes the impact of the original LP.

The 1966 date captured on the GHB CD is a memento of one of Barry Martyn's trips to New Orleans – though Humphrey is the nominal leader, the date was organized by the drummer. The front line may have been a little tired (Jim Asman's notes record that they'd been playing the previous night till 7 a.m.) and the playing is ragged, though ably policed by Martyn's beat. The rough, open-hall ambience reeks of vintage New Orleans music and it's a charismatic disc.

Willie Humphrey (1900–1994)

CLARINET

A New Orleans forefather, he took up clarinet at fourteen and five years later was playing in Chicago with Joe Oliver and Freddie Keppard. He drifted around through the 1920s and '30s but returned to his home town after the war and became a mainstay of the revivalist movement thereafter.

****(*) In New Orleans**

GHB BCD-248 *Humphrey; Norbert Susemihl (t); Mari Watanabe (p); Emile Martyn (d).* 4/88.

***** Two Clarinets On The Porch**

GHB BCD-308 *Humphrey; Brian O'Connell (cl); Les Muscutt (g, bj); Frank Fields (b); Ernie Elly (d).* 8/91.

**** A Kiss To Build A Dream On**

GHB BCD-428 *Humphrey; Joruis De Cock (t, v); Gerhard 'Doggy' Hund (tb); Klaus-Dieter George (cl); Rowan Smith (p); Büli Schöning (bj, g); Peter Wechlin (d).* 10/92.

Only a few months younger than George Lewis, Willie Humphrey harked back to an ancient New Orleans tradition. He didn't start recording until 1926, but these records come from over six decades later. *In New Orleans* puts him up with a German trumpeter, a Japanese-American pianist and a British drummer, and the youngsters play with an affectionate energy that Willie seems to enjoy being involved with. It's let down, though, by a sense that these are keen amateurs keeping the old man company, and there are some errors of judgement (such as Susemihl's four vocals) which tarnish the occasion.

Three years later, Humphrey palled up with another clarinet man 60 years his junior. His phrasing and gargled tone persuade the other players to walk a little gingerly round him: the seven trio pieces, which Willie and Ernie Elly sit out, probably account for the best music, deftly sprung round Muscutt's deferential banjo and O'Connell's sweet-toned clarinet. But 'I Want To Be Happy' or 'China Boy' feature some amusing interplay, and it's pleasant to hear an unalloyed New Orleans legend raising his voice in the 1990s on what turned out to be a sprightly farewell.

Except it wasn't quite his last recording. That distinction goes to *A Kiss To Build A Dream On*, released by GHB in 2000, one hundred years after Willie was born. It features him guesting with the Maryland Jazz Band of Cologne. Willie sounds like he's having fun, but one has to make allowances for the occasion, and on its own terms this is pretty ramshackle music.

Charlie Hunter

8-STRING GUITAR

Part of a community of jamming musicians who emerged from the Bay Area in the early 1990s, Hunter is a virtuoso guitarist playing an eight-string model, with bass and lead lines combined.

***** Bing ... Bing ... Bing**

Blue Note 31809-2 *Hunter; Jeff Cressman (tb); Dave Ellis (ts); Bing Goldberg (cl); David Phillips (pedal steel g); Jay Lane (d); Scott Roberts (perc).* 95.

***** Ready ... Set ... Shango!**

Blue Note 37101-2 *Hunter; Calder Spanier (as); Dave Ellis (ts); Scott Amendola (d).* 96.

****(*) Natty Dread**

Blue Note 52420-2 *As above, except replace Ellis with Kenny Brooks (ts).* 97.

It's always worth pointing out to anyone who laments the populist derelictions of the 'new' Blue Note that since the mid-1980s renaissance the label has done nothing more than go back some way towards its own rhythm-and-blues roots. Hunter's ability to make his 8-string guitar sound like – and occasionally *remarkably* like – a Hammond B-3 reinforces the historical link. The earliest of the group is probably the most guitaristic, if we may be forgiven the term, a brisk, bright session with more external input than the latter pair. Hunter sounds good with brass, and it's a shame that Cressman's contribution (and Goldberg's, for that matter) is so limited. Some of Hunter's own best songs are on the debut: 'Greasy Granny' and 'Scrabbling For Purchase' are excellent, but the outstanding track is a wholly unexpected cover of Nirvana's 'Come As You Are'.

The middle album sounds great, a thick, swampy performance which ironically is diluted only by the crispness and clarity of Lee Townsend's production. Inevitably, the two saxophone players occupy much of the foreground, interestingly trading their differences of approach, Ellis's dark, raw-edged tone and Spanier's lighter, bop-orientated delivery most effectively juxtaposed on 'Let's Get Medieval', less so on the not-quite-urgent '911'.

Natty Dread is an oddity, a track-by-track gloss on Bob Marley and the Wailers' classic reggae record, issued as part of Blue Note executive Bruce Lundvall's 'Cover Series'. Leaving aside the slightly uneasy relationship between jazz and reggae, Hunter's approach seldom adds much to the original. On what might be thought the most pristine and untouchable of the Marley compositions, 'No Woman No Cry', he does, however, import an opening section and some of the harmonic material from 'The Tennessee Waltz', which was a clever stroke. Here, the pristine sound makes more sense, a gentle, sometimes buoyant listen, but seldom as moving or inflammatory as the original. Be grateful that Hunter decided against Carole King's *Tapestry* or the Beach Boys' *Pet Sounds*, which – for entirely different reasons – would have made less sense.

*****(*) Return Of The Candyman**

Blue Note 23108-2 *Hunter; Stefon Harris (vib); Scott Amendola (d); John Santos (perc).* 98.

The big bonus here is Harris, the most exciting vibraharpist to appear on the scene since Hutcherson. His tight, ringing sound and long, pattering runs give the line-up – now going out as Pound For Pound – a heavily percussive emphasis which provides the perfect launch-pad for Hunter's increasingly idiosyncratic 8-string work.

Punctuated by five short interludes which serve no very obvious purpose beyond punctuation, the tunes are tough, funky and hit the mark every time. The title-track, 'Pound For Pound' and 'Enter The Dragon' are the ones to sample if you happen across it on a listening post.

*****(*) Duo**

Blue Note 99187-2 *Hunter; (d, perc).* 99.

Our earlier comments about the Beach Boys have come back to haunt us because Hunter includes a Brian Wilson song here. Most of the material is self-written, though, including the swinging 'Belief' by Parker, and the guitarist has never sounded jazzier, using his thick low strings to generate simple bass lines against those now familiar 'organ' chords and single-note lines, so that this almost sounds like a trio recording.

Wilson's 'Don't Talk (Put Your Head On My Shoulder)' is a lovely thing, laden with shimmering reverb and every bit as tender as the original. The pair also tackle one standard, 'You Don't Know What Love Is'. Parker's roots are more firmly in classic jazz than Hunter's, but he has a solid rock backbeat at his disposal as well. Nothing here to set the heather on fire, but an intriguing, low-key album.

Bobby Hutcherson (born 1941)

VIBRAPHONE, MARIMBA, PERCUSSION

If Hutcherson were a saxophonist, trumpeter or pianist, he would be regarded as a major figure in modern jazz, but the vibes still have a slightly eccentric standing, a prejudice which has kept Bobby on the margins. Born in California, he was inspired by another undervalued genius, Milt Jackson, and took up vibraphone in preference to piano. Hutcherson's distinctive style is intensely rhythmic and harmonically subtle. Though extensively recorded, until recently his back-catalogue was very patchy indeed.

*****(*) Components**

Blue Note 29027 *Hutcherson; Freddie Hubbard (t); James Spaulding (as, f); Herbie Hancock (p, org); Ron Carter (b); Joe Chambers (d).* 6/65.

****** Stick Up!**

Blue Note 59378 *Hutcherson; Joe Henderson (ts); McCoy Tyner (p); Herbie Lewis (b); Billy Higgins (d).* 7/66.

*****(*) The Kicker**

Blue Note 21437 *Hutcherson; Joe Henderson (ts); Grant Green (g); Bob Cranshaw (b); Al Harewood (d).*

Few have developed such a consistently challenging language for the instrument as Hutcherson. In the 1960s he made a series of superb albums for Blue Note, the equal of any of the classic dates from that label. Their availability has been very intermittent, although some have recently returned fleetingly as limited editions. *Dialogue* is an astonishing album by any standard, but once again it's in the deletion file.

Components continues the purple patch with a set of short lyrical themes. The title-track is a cracker, and 'Little B's Poem' was to become a modern classic, a softly articulated but totally convincing modern ballad. Anyone who hasn't encountered Hutcherson before might do well to start with this one, but just to get into training for the glories of *Dialogue*. *Stick Up!* opens with Ornette's 'Una Muy Bonita', demonstrating how much of Bobby's conception came from that source. The remainder of the set is closer to the harmonic experimentation that was shortly to become an orthodoxy. 'Verse' is masterly and 'Summer Nights' a lusciously coloured and textured tone-poem, shaded (as Hutcherson compositions almost always are) with obliquely related tonalities.

The Kicker wasn't made available until 1999, an astonishing oversight on Blue Note's part. Even if Hutcherson's standing were thought to be marginal, the presence of Joe Henderson should have been enough to see this fine, imaginative session into the light of day. The saxophonist is the main composer and Bobby is represented only by the rather slight 'For Duke P.', a tribute to Blue Note's musical director. Joe's 'Kicker' and 'Step Lightly' are cracking tunes and blistering performances from all concerned. Hutcherson's fleet, ringing lines have rarely sounded more buoyant and persuasive, and it remains a mystery that this record should have been considered so marginal that it lay in the vault for 30 years.

***** Un Poco Loco**

Koch 7868 *Hutcherson; George Cables (p); John Abercrombie (g); Chuck Domanico (b); Peter Erskine (d, perc).* 79.

Restored to circulation after 20 years, this is uncomfortably time-locked and awkwardly registered relative to Bobby's earlier records. The rock rhythms, bass guitar, and electric piano shimmers are only superficially distracting, though. The recording doesn't help, but Hutcherson's angle on the Bud Powell title-track is utterly captivating, and his solos are as convincing as ever throughout.

***** Solos / Quartet**

Original Jazz Classics OJC 425 *Hutcherson solo and with McCoy Tyner (p); Herbie Lewis (b); Billy Higgins (d); John Koenig (bells).* 9 & 10/81, 3/82.

*****(*) Farewell Keystone**

Evidence 22018-2 *Hutcherson; Oscar Brashear (t, flhn); Harold Land (ts); Cedar Walton (p); Buster Williams (b); Billy Higgins (d).* 7/82.

The 1980s saw something of a revival in Hutcherson's fortunes: uncompromised recording opportunities, sympathetic collaborators and, one suspects, a consequently renewed faith in his own abilities. *Farewell Keystone* reunites him with Harold Land, and the encounter still sounds pretty incisive more than ten years on, with a truly fantastic rhythm section propelling the front men. Hutcherson's multi-directional contrapuntal imagination, with melodic, harmonic and rhythmic parameters all intelligently controlled, makes solo performance more than commonly feasible, particularly with the use of multi-tracking; where Lionel Hampton required a great surfer's wave of chords and riffs piled up behind him, Hutcherson creates his own internal impetus.

The tone is by no means as percussive as it was on *Out To Lunch*, though ironically Hutcherson has put increasing emphasis on xylorimbas at the same time as smoothing out his vibraphone lines in what looks like a degree of accommodation with Milt Jackson.

The quartet sessions, which include a sparkling 'Old Devil Moon' and 'My Foolish Heart', simply underline Tyner's astonishing eclecticism and adaptability. Those with longer memories will automatically track back to Hampton's interplay with Teddy Wilson in the classic Benny Goodman Quartets of 1936 and 1937. That good.

***** Vibe Wise**

32 Jazz 32037 *Hutcherson; Branford Marsalis (ss, ts); George Cables, Mulgrew Miller (p); Ray Drummond, John Heard (b); Billy Higgins, Philly Joe Jones (d); Airto Moreira (perc).* 8/84, 10/85.

A great value set; another of 32's excellent twofers, bringing together *Good Bait* and *Color Scheme*, two of the best of Bobby's non-Blue Note records. The compilation finds him straddling two jazz generations, with Branford Marsalis and Mulgrew Miller picking up the challenge of Bobby's complex charts on the second disc. Unusually, and perhaps because for a time he found it difficult to find players who'd empathize with his demanding direction, the first half of the programme consists mainly of standard and repertory material, with fine versions of Golson's 'Whisper Not', John Carisi's 'Israel', Monk's 'Bemsha Swing' and McCoy Tyner's 'Love Samba'. As always, Cables is a stal-wart presence, but he is constantly attempting to normalize Hutcherson's harmonics, ease them back into a more straightforward groove. Miller – with his strong Tyner influence ever in view – is perhaps more sympathetic, but the recording bumps vibes and piano up close and blurs the edges of Bobby's more detailed lines as well as losing some definition on the keyboard. A good buy, though.

*****(*) In The Vanguard**

32 Jazz 32170 *Hutcherson; Kenny Barron (p); Buster Williams (b); Al Foster (d).* 12/86.

In our last edition, we lamented the disappearance of Hutcherson's recordings for Landmark. The estimable Joel Dorn of 32 Jazz has guaranteed that at least this fine set survives for the moment. Dominated by long versions of 'Young And Foolish' and a Miles-influenced 'Some Day My Prince Will Come', this live set from the Village Vanguard catches him in adventurous and sometimes mischievous mood. Though the avant-garde gestures of previous years have disappeared, there is still an edgy intelligence and experimental edge to these seven cuts. Bobby's original 'I Wanna Stand Over There' is rather orthodox post-bop and won't frighten any but the most conservative of horses. Buster Williams is huge-toned and compelling and, as he would again on *Skyline*, Al Foster demonstrates what a master he is.

***** Skyline**

Verve 559616-2 *Hutcherson; Kenny Garrett (as); Geri Allen (p); Christian McBride (b); Al Foster (d).* 99.

Much was hoped for when the news broke of Hutcherson's long-belated new contract for Polygram/Universal, but *Skyline* is a disappointment. Smooth and accomplished, it lacks the edgy brilliance of Bobby's earlier career. Garrett and Allen are in great form. The saxophonist has some strong interchanges with Bobby on the opening 'Who's Got You', and Geri is terrific on the vibes/piano duet, 'Candle', which winds things up on a high. Generally, though, the dynamic is very restrained and there is a slick and settled cast to the playing which doesn't recall the Hutcherson of old. Other tracks include 'Delilah', done softly and with feeling, and 'I Only Have Eyes For You', which is nicely done, but oddly placed on an eccentrically programmed disc. Great to see the big man having some money spent on him, but not the most compelling of label debuts.

Ken Hyder (born 1946)

DRUMS, PERCUSSION, ELECTRONICS, VOICE

Born in Dundee, he had '60s experience in jazz and folk, forming Talisker at the beginning of the '70s to explore a fusion of the two. In the '90s he collaborated with folk and jazz players from all parts of the planet, engaged in the deepest kind of fusion.

****** The Known Is In The Stone**

Impetus IMP CD 17932 *Hyder; Dave Brooks (bagpipes); Pete McPhail (low whistle); Don Paterson (g); Marcio Mattos (b); Maggie Nicols (v).*

If the term 'world music' has any validity at all then it surely must apply to the work of Ken Hyder, whose career in recent years has taken in the music of Siberian shamans, Tibetan Buddhist monks, Tuvan throat-singers and Russian improvisers, as well as the music he grew up with in Scotland. In recent editions we have followed his work with the Bardo State Orchestra. Here, though, he goes back to roots.

The personnels above are slightly misleading. *The Known Is In The Stone* includes just one track by the long-standing Celtic jazz outfit, Talisker. Otherwise it consists of two duo projects: Hoots & Roots with singer Maggie Nicols (herself of mixed Scottish-Berber parentage), and The World's Smallest Jazz Pipe Band with piper Dave Brooks. Hyder and Brooks begin with a traditional strathspey played with great rhythmic freedom. This contrasts with the bluesy abandon of 'Gallus Grannie Goes Her Mile' (untranslatable for English and North American readers) and the real pathos of 'Drum Salute And Lament For Stevens' with whom Hyder worked at the legendary Little Theatre Club.

It is followed by an improvised pibroch in Stevens's memory by Hyder and Nicols. Their working relationship is further cemented by political commitment, and two of the songs here are based on poems by the militant Dundee jute worker, Mary Brooksbank, who is a central figure in her city's tradition of politically committed art. Nicols is also an extraordinary ballad and jazz singer and her version of 'My Love Is Like A Red, Red Rose' suggests it shouldn't be overlooked by singers looking for 'standards' to cover. Hyder and Brooks also adapt a traditional lament about the Highland Clearances, a passionate enough piece rendered even more powerful by Hyder's Tuvan-style throat-singing and Brook's dismantling of half-inflated pipes.

Everyone remembers that Samuel Barber's 'Adagio For Strings' was played at JFK's funeral. Fewer remember John Cameron of Ballachulish's '*Chi Mi Na Morbheanna*' ('I See The High Mountains') on which Jim McLean based his song 'Smile In Your Sleep', another Clearances lament. This is performed by Talisker, a switch of register at the end of a remarkable album. Don't be put off by the prospect of the pipes. Remember how the blues began.

Dick Hyman (born 1927)

PIANO, ORGAN, VOCAL

He studied with Teddy Wilson but became a staff player at NBC in the 1950s and an organizer of concerts dedicated to the jazz repertory – a rarity at the time. He was playing synthesizers early on and, with the growing interest in jazz repertory, has assumed a central role in propagating a wider understanding of the music's history. In the '80s and '90s he recorded in a broad range of situations, on several kinds of keyboard.

***** The Kingdom Of Swing And The Republic Of Oop Bop Sh'Bam**

Musicmasters 60200 *Hyman; Joe Wilder (t); Warren Vaché (c); Urbie Green (tb); Buddy Tate (cl, ts); Derek Smith (p); Milt Hinton (b); Butch Miles (d).* 7/87.

***** Plays Harold Arlen**

Musicmasters 60215 *Hyman (p solo).* 4/89.

***** 14 Jazz Piano Favourites**

Music & Arts CD 622 *Hyman (p solo).* 6/88.

***** Plays Fats Waller**

Reference RR-33 *Hyman (p solo).* 8/89.

*****(*) Music Of 1937**

Concord CCD 4415 *Hyman (p solo).* 2/90.

***** Stride Piano Summit**

Milestone 9189 *Hyman; Harry 'Sweets' Edison (t); Ralph Sutton, Jay McShann, Mike Lipskin (p); Red Callender (b); Harold Jones (d).* 6/90.

***** Plays Duke Ellington**

Reference RR-50 *Hyman (p solo).* 90.

****** All Through The Night**

Musicmasters 5060-2 *Hyman (p solo).* 91.

***** Gershwin Songbook: Hyman Variations**

Musicmasters 5094-2 *Hyman (p solo).* 9/92.

***** Concord Duo Series Vol. 6**

Concord CCD 4603 *Hyman; Ralph Sutton (p).* 11/93.

Dick Hyman has had a pretty paradoxical career in many ways. In the 1940s he was playing with both Charlie Parker and Benny Goodman. Working as a studio musician through much of the 1950s and '60s, he also recorded novelty tunes under various pseudonyms, as well as Scott Joplin's complete works. He loves early jazz, is an expert on the jazz-piano tradition, can re-create pit-band orchestrations or ragtime arrangements to order – yet he was also one of the first to record an album of tunes played on prototype synthesizers. For a long time there was very little 'strict' jazz in the catalogue under Hyman's name, but recent times have found him busy on repertory albums of one sort or another. Most of these discs validate his findings with their exuberance as well as their attention to detail. *The Kingdom Of Swing* provides a record of a New York show in which Hyman enlisted various swing-era types (authentic and modernist) for an evening of good-hearted fun. Vaché is on his mettle and there is a charming duet between Hyman and Tate, on clarinet instead of his shakier tenor. The four-man *Stride Piano Summit* sets Hyman against two other masters (Lipskin is rather less of a giant) in another multi-combination show: he does his Fats Waller pipe-organ bit on 'Persian Rug' and roisters through 'Sunday' with McShann and Edison. Lightweight but entertaining.

The solo albums are the best place to examine the range of Hyman's interests. He goes back as far as ragtime and Jelly Roll Morton on the Café des Copains recital for Music & Arts, making light of any rhythmical squareness in the likes of 'Frog-I-More Rag' and freshening up 'Blue Skies' until it sings. *Music Of 1937*, an early entry in the Maybeck Recital Hall series, concentrates on a single year in songwriting: by no means exceptional, but the best of these pre-war hits – 'The Folks Who Live On The Hill', 'Some Day My Prince Will Come', 'Thanks For The Memory' – tend to prove the subtext that they don't write 'em like that any more, which would be a curmudgeonly verdict if it weren't for the sprightly and glowing readings that Hyman gets.

His five composer-dedicated records are unfailingly entertaining, if mixed in their profundities. Hyman is an excellent mimic when he wants to be, and for the Arlen record he sounds like an urbane, less fulsome copy of Art Tatum, an impressive trick to be sure. When he sets 'Over The Rainbow' to a bossa rhythm, the humour too is Tatumesque. This is a bright, ingenious collection, and it works out rather better than the Waller set: Hyman loves this music, but sometimes even he must feel that it sounds a little dated and, since he has little of Waller's genial uproar in his bones, he can't always bring it to life. Ellington also eludes him to some extent, since Duke's intimacies are just as personal to himself; but both records still have a degree of sophistication and elegance that set them some way above everybody's routine tribute record. The very best of this sequence, though, is *All Through The Night*, which is all Cole Porter. Hyman's delivery seems an exact match for Porter's own blend of sophistication and sardonicism, with the romantic undertow of his warmest music still on hand. The opening 'Easy To Love' seems like an encyclopedia of stride and swing piano in 18 choruses and ten minutes. 'Were Thine That Special Face' is as placid as motionless water. 'Brush Up Your Shakespeare' is the most light and swinging 3/4 time imaginable, and 'Let's Do It' is perky without once seeming cute. This is all Hyman at his best. Piano sound (from live shows in Cambridge Springs, Pennsylvania) is less than ideal, but not troublesome.

The Gershwin disc features Hyman playing 18 pieces of the composer straight off the sheet-music before adding his own variations to each. This kind of formal lesson is meat and drink to Hyman, but as a record it palls just a little over the long haul, despite his many ingenuities. The same could be said of his duets with Ralph Sutton, indomitably swinging but falling into patterns, if not routines, across a dozen tunes. Taken a couple of tracks at a time, this is delightful, but the earlier disc with Kellaway is just a fraction better.

*****(*) Elegies, Mostly**

Gemini GMCD 90 *Hyman; Niels-Henning Orsted Pedersen (b).* 8/95.

*****(*) Cheek To Cheek**

Arbors ARCD 19155 *Hyman; Howard Alden (g); Bob Haggart (b).* 6/95.

Hyman is not in the business of making grand statements and, for all his virtuosity and insuperable accomplishment, his records are cast as almost modest affairs – conversations with good friends or with like-minded masters. That is the case on both of these recent discs and, while one regrets that a man of this eminence has made no single masterpiece album, perhaps this is the more appropriate way. *Cheek To Cheek* is an enchanting mix of material: Thelonious Monk, John Lewis, Irving Berlin, Flip Phillips and more. The triologue with Alden and Haggart is delightfully underplayed, so a test piece like 'Misterioso' (and who would ever have thought they'd hear Bob Haggart playing on this?) becomes charmingly restrained – it seems to glow, putting a new shine on Monk. Sometimes the bass parts aren't so helpful to the splendid guitar–piano interplay, but there's really nothing here to dislike. *Elegies, Mostly* may be a bit quiescent for some tastes, and perhaps they could have added a couple more tunes with the same pep as 'We're In The Money', the closer. But it's hard to argue with a duo this strong, and imaginative, and lyrically inventive. As a single sample, hear the gorgeous treatment of 'Some Other Time'.

***** Dick & Derek At The Movies**

Arbors ARCD 19197 *Hyman; Derek Smith (p).* 4/98.

Hyman has recorded duets with Smith before. Two-piano records are an odd breed and, since both men have a virtuosic streak, showmanship is frequently the order of the day. There are flashes of stride, ragtime, parlour-piano and more, and what grabs the attention are the set-piece quick tempos and superfast fingering. Fifteen tracks of this kind of thing are probably a few too many for most listeners, although from moment to moment the music is certainly joyful.

Susie Ibarra

DRUMS

This gifted young percussionist really came to notice on saxophonist David S. Ware's contemporary classic, Godspellized, and since then has started to carve out a voice and place of her own.

*****(*) Home Cookin'**

Hopscotch HOP 1 *Ibarra; Assif Tsahar (ts).* 2 & 7/98.

****** Radiance**

Hopscotch HOP 2 *Ibarra; Charles Burnham (vn); Cooper-Moore (p, hp).* 7/99.

Are they destined to be the Geri and Wallace of the new decade? Ibarra and husband Assif Tsahar have arrived on the scene with the uncomplicated confidence of a shared mission. Ibarra will inevitably be compared to other female percussionists, earlier on the scene, players like Cindy Blackman and Marilyn Mazur, but she has moved the game along considerably. Her roots would seem to be in the avant-garde of the 1960s, in the work of Rashied Ali and Andrew Cyrille, but she already plays with a highly distinctive voice: a light, pattering articulation which often disguises its punch; a musicianly ability to play or imply melody on the kit; and an unerring ear for pulses which go deeper than conventional metre.

The duos with Assif are perhaps closer to Archie Shepp's work with Max Roach than the more obvious example of Trane's *Interstellar Space* duets with Ali. They're interleaved with eight 'Dream Songs', played at home on a recently acquired array of Afro-Asian 'little instruments'. Nine times out of ten, such pieces would be an annoying distraction, but these work very well, and in intriguing ways they anticipate the language of *Radiance*.

An unusually constituted trio, it offers an even richer harmonic background for Ibarra's complex percussion. Burnham has long been an undervalued talent, and in tandem with the less familiar Cooper-Moore (no other name) he creates an intriguing dialogue which – if further analogy isn't redundant – recalls Billy Bang's duos with Dennis Charles. The inclusion of alternative versions of 'Dreams' and 'Laughter', two sections of the opening suite, 'Radiance', suggests how inventive and responsive a player Ibarra is. Pointless to talk of promise and potential. She has already arrived.

Abdullah Ibrahim (born 1934)

PIANO, SOPRANO SAXOPHONE, CELLO, VOICE

Ibrahim left his native South Africa in the aftermath of the Sharpeville massacre, settling first in Europe, latterly in the United States. He converted to Islam in 1968, but his given name, Dollar Brand, still has considerable currency and, however improperly, is apt to be used interchangeably. Along with Hugh Masekela and Kippie Moeketsi, Brand was a member of the epochal Jazz Epistles, the first black South African jazz group and a legendary catalyst on the scene there. Though influenced by Ellington, he has a distinctive keyboard style, rocking bass tone ostinati punctuated by stabbing or more lyrical right-hand figures and melodies.

****** Voice Of Africa**

Camden CDN 1007 *Ibrahim; Kippie Moeketsi (as); Robbie Jansen (as, f); Basil Coetzee (ts, f); Duke Makasi (ts); Sipho Gumede, Basil Moses, Paul Richards (b); Gilbert Mathews, Monty Weber (d).*

The first of Camden's reissue of the African recordings is, like the rest, frustratingly lacking in detail, most obviously session dates, but *Voice Of Africa* documents some of the earliest material in all its plangent, swinging glory. Brand's rapid-fire chording behind Moeketsi on the opening 'Black Lightning' is instantly identifiable and, though it would be good to have some of the material with Masekela, the supporting horns here do more than justice to their role, with Coetzee's flute the key element. The quartet tracks with Coetzee (on tenor), Moses and Weber are not so powerful, but the reissue of this material as a whole, and the later volumes under the Camden Africa imprint, help fill in an important aspect of recent jazz history.

***** Reflections**

Black Lion 760127 *Ibrahim (p solo).* 3/65.

****(*) African Sketchbook**

Enja 2026 *As above.* 5/69.

****** African Piano**

Japo 835020-2 *As above.* 10/69.

Brand came to the attention of Duke Ellington after he went into exile in Switzerland, and it was Ellington who gave him the opportunity to make his first American recordings. Ellington had been his greatest single influence, though there are perhaps stronger traces of black church music, African folk themes and hints of Thelonious Monk and the 1960s free movement in his solo performances. These have a hypnotic intensity and a surprising level of formality, which lends an often-repeated tune like 'Bra Joe From Kilimanjaro' (on the surviving Japo and *African Portraits*, for instance) an almost ritual quality.

African Piano is certainly still the best of the solo records, even though the CD robs the music of some of its full-hearted resonance. The Enja (*Sketchbook* is as bitty as it sounds) offers valuable insights into some of Ibrahim's stylistic debts, with tributes to Ellington, Coltrane (just one of a rash of memorials marking the fifteenth anniversary of the saxophonist's death) and Monk. Ibrahim plays 'A Flower Is A Lovesome Thing', 'Blue Monk' and an inventive, firmly contoured 'Round About Midnight' that strips the tune down to more authentically Monkish basics. The early *Reflections* develops a similar range of material, applying Brand's drumming lyricism to 'Don't Get Around Much Any More' (an astonishing performance), 'Mood Indigo', 'Take The "A" Train' and 'Monk's Mood'.

***** Round Midnight At The Montmartre**

Black Lion BLCD 760111 *Ibrahim; Johnny Gertze (b); Makaya Ntoshko (d).* 1/65.

****(*) Anatomy Of A South African Village**

Black Lion BLCD 760172 *As above.* 1/65.

'Round About Midnight' takes on a more conventional outline in the first of the trio performances, recorded at the Café Montmartre. There's a short version of 'Tintinyanna', and two solo tracks, which are much jazzier than usual and don't initially sound typical of Brand's work of the time. Ntoshko plays in the post-Elvin Jones idiom favoured by Billy Higgins and Hart. Like his fellow-countryman, Louis Moholo, he has the ability to range between freedom and strict (but complex) time and can blur the line between polyrhythmic playing and complete abstraction so much that it often sounds as though Brand is keeping time for the drummer. The mix is rather uneven and the bass is often lost altogether, though what one can hear isn't that interesting.

Taken from the same set, *Anatomy* sounds perversely much more like a mainstream jazz album. With the exception of the title-track, Brand seems content to work his way through some mildly Africanized changes. The fact that he does so with fire doesn't quite eliminate the essential blandness of what he is doing. A disappointing follow-up, but a sure sign that they got the selection right first time. This material is also available on the German label DA Music CDs under the titles *Pre Abdullah Ibrahim* and *Anatomy Of An African Village*. We are unclear what arrangement has been arrived at concerning these CDs.

****** African Sun**

Camden CDN 1007 *Ibrahim; Dennis Mpale (t); Robbie Jansen, Kippie Moeketsi, Barney Rachabane (as); Basil Coetzee, Arthur Jacobs, Duke Makasi (ts); Sipho Gumede, Paul Michaels, Basil Moses, Victor Ntomi (b); Timmy Kewbulana, Nelson Magwaza, Gilbert Mathews, Peter Morake, Monty Weber (d).* 71, 74, 75, 77, 79.

***** Tintinyanna**

Camden 1009 *Ibrahim; Blue Mitchell, Dennis Mpale (t); Buster Cooper (tb); Harold Land, Duke Makasi (ts); Basil Coetzee (ts, f); Lionel Beukes, Sipho Gumede, Victor Ntoni (b); Nelson Magwaza, Peter Morake, Doug Sydes (d).* 71, 75, 79.

***** Blues For A Hip King**

Camden 1010 *Ibrahim; Blue Mitchell (t, flhn); Buster Cooper (tb); Robbie Jansen, Kippie Moeketsi (as); Basil Coetzee (ts, f); Arthur Jacobs, Duke Makasi (ts); Lionel Beukes, Sipho Gumede, Victor Ntoni (b); Nazier Kapdi, Gilbert Mathews, Makaya Ntoshko, Doug Sydes (d).* 74, 76, 79.

It was Moeketsi who took Brand out of District Six and off to Jo'burg, where the former was an indomitable opponent of apartheid racism, consistently refusing to knuckle under to white supremacism and being steadily ground down for his pains, dying in 1983 with his real musical potential still unfulfilled. These are marvellous discs, full of treasures that have remained buried for too many years. Moeketsi's unpolished wail and directness of statement and Brand/Ibrahim's deceptively simple accompaniments are the main elements, but Coetzee is also a wonderful player who deserves wider recognition. As with the earlier disc, documentation is very poor indeed. The liner to *Blues For A Hip King* suggests he performs (with fellow-American Blue Mitchell) on that disc, when in fact both appear on *Tintinyanna*. They take part in a wonderful version of the Brand classic, 'Bra Joe From Kilimanjaro', which is also covered by the earlier band with Moeketsi, and the contrast is a fascinating one, showing how much Brand and the other Epistles had learned from the Americans, but also how much of what they were doing – both harmonically and rhythmically – was utterly original. 'King Kong' on *Blues For A Hip King* is a reference to the musical which Brand refused to take part in in South Africa, preferring to woodshed and (in effect) prepare himself for exile. The title-piece is dedicated to the Swazi ruler, King Sobhuza, a jazz fan and a sponsor of many of the South African musicians when they wanted to leave the country for a respite from the rigours of apartheid. Once again, the only thing marring these records is the appalling documentation. The painted covers, familiar from Kaz releases, are appealing, the music is as vibrant as ever, but one looks to the label for a little more consistency and a little more factual information.

***** African Space Program**

Enja 2032 *Ibrahim; Cecil Bridgewater, Enrico Rava, Charles Sullivan (t); Kiane Zawadi (tb); Sonny Fortune, Carlos Ward (f, as); Roland Alexander (ts, hca); John Stubblefield (ts); Hamiet Bluiett (bs); Cecil McBee (b); Roy Brooks (d).* 11/73.

A rare opportunity to hear Ibrahim fronting a substantial, hand-picked band. Six months before Duke's death, the parallels are once again strongly evident, with Ward sounding like an Africanized Hodges and Hamiet Bluiett slipping easily into the Harry Carney role. 'Tintinyanna' falls into two parts, its progress clarified by the leader's piano statements and percussive breaks. The sound is somewhat better on CD than on the original release, but it's still very bottom-heavy and leaden.

*****(*) Good News From Africa**

Enja 2048 *Ibrahim; Johnny Mbizo Dyani (b, bells, v).* 12/73.

****** Echoes From Africa**

Enja 3047 *As above.* 9/79.

Dyani towers on these fascinating and often moving duos, which move between a dark, almost tragic pessimism to a shouting, joyous climax. 'Saud' is a dedication to McCoy Tyner (the title reflects the other pianist's more briefly adopted Islamic name) and interestingly suggests how some of Ellington's modal explorations of the 1960s filtered into the vernacular via younger piano players. Ibrahim adds some flute colours to the earlier album, and the two voices entwine in celebration of the homeland. *Echoes* was originally released as an audiophile direct-to-disc recording. CD makes the music even more immediate and penetrative.

***** Africa Tears And Laughter**

Enja ENJ 3039 *Ibrahim; Talib Qadr (ts, ss); Greg Brown (b); John Betsch (d).* 3/79.

*****(*) African Marketplace**

Discovery 71016 *Ibrahim; Gary Chandler (t); Craig Harris, Malindi Blyth Mbityana (tb); Carlos Ward (as, ss); Dwayne Armstrong, Jeff Jawarrah King (ts); Kenny Rogers (bs); Lawrence Lucie (bj); Cecil McBee (b); Andre Strobert (d, perc); Miguel Pomier (perc).* 12/79.

There were signs that at this point in his career Ibrahim wanted to take stock of his progress so far. The Enja date examines its Africanness almost clinically, holding itself up to the light in a way that he either couldn't or wouldn't do in the company of Johnny Dyani later that same year. This – along with the Shepp encounter – is one of the only points in Ibrahim's career when the relentlessness of his approach begins to sound like self-parody, or at least self-pastiche.

A little later again, *Marketplace* contains a pretty substantial reworking of much of his work since coming to America and, ending on 'Anthem For The New Nation', with its pounding, cyclical *ostinati* and another soaring statement from Ward, seems to look forward to the next stage and to a future for South Africa that in 1979 was still unimaginably distant. The title-piece is the most substantial, expressing a movement from African community – signalled by drums – through fragmentation and pain to reintegration. It contains one of Ibrahim's most significant saxophone solos of recent years. There is plenty of unaffectedly raucous blowing. 'The Homecoming Song' is a throwback to the shebeens and clubs of his homeland; one almost expects to hear Kippie Moeketsi instead of Ward. 'Mamma' is a straight blowing theme with a gospelly chorus. A fine, if occasionally shambolic record.

*****(*) Montreux '80**

Enja 3079 *Ibrahim; Carlos Ward (as, f); Craig Harris (tb); Alonzo Gardner (b); Andre Strobert (d).* 7/80.

***** Zimbabwe**

Enja 4056 *Ibrahim; Carlos Ward (f, as); Essiet Okun Essiet (b); Don Mumford (d).* 5/83.

***** South Africa**

Enja 5007 *As above, except add Johnny Classens (v).* 7/83.

****** Water From An Ancient Well**

Tiptoe 88812 *Ibrahim; Dick Griffin (tb); Carlos Ward (as, f); Ricky Ford (ts); Charles Davis (bs); David Williams (b); Ben Riley (d).* 10/85.

*****(*) The Mountain**

Camden CDN 1002 *As above, except omit Williams.*

The association with Carlos Ward has been the most productive and sympathetic of Ibrahim's career. The saxophonist has a high, exotic tone (superficially reminiscent of Sonny Fortune's, but much less raucous) that is ideally suited to his leader's conception. Working with Ward has reinforced Ibrahim's preference for song-like forms built over harmonically unvarying *ostinati* but has allowed him to develop a more abstract, improvisational feel, which reaches its peak on *Water From An Ancient Well.* This was made by Ibrahim's band, Ekaya (the word means 'home'); an earlier, eponymous disc on Black Hawk has disappeared. *Water* is a carefully structured album with something of the feel of Ellington's *Far East Suite*, and most of the drama comes from the interplay between Ibrahim and the horns. It includes another heartfelt tribute to Sathima Bea Benjamin, 'Daughter Of Cape Town'.

In their earlier encounters, Ward seemed willing to play Charlie Rouse to Ibrahim's Monk, but increasingly he develops his own approach, and by 1983 is putting his own stamp on the music. *South Africa* is the most self-consciously African of the group, an impression heightened by Classens's effective vocal contributions. *Zimbabwe* is less original in either content or treatment, but it contains some of Ibrahim's best group-work on record, and Essiet's bass-work (clearly drawn from the example of Johnny Dyani) is very fine.

***** Mindif**

Enja 5073 *Ibrahim; Benny Powell (tb); Ricky Ford (ts, ss); Craig Handy (f, ts); David Williams (b); Billy Higgins (d, perc).* 3/88.

****** African River**

Enja 6018 *Ibrahim; Robin Eubanks (tb); John Stubblefield (fl, ts); Horace Alexander Young (ss, as, picc); Howard Johnson (bs, tba); Buster Williams (b); Brian Adams (d).* 6/89.

Ward is immediately missed on *Mindif* (which was written as the soundtrack to Claire Denis's atmospheric film, *Chocolat*; see also below) but Powell and Handy are both exciting players, and Higgins's drumming is so imaginative as often to become the focus of a piece like 'African Market' or 'Thema [sic] For Monk'. The later album is absolutely superb and a vivid extension of the kind of arrangements Ibrahim had attempted on *African Space Program.* 'The Wedding' reappears from 1980 (*Montreux* and *Duke's Memories*) and receives a definitive performance, with Eubanks to the fore. Stubblefield and Young more than make up for the departure of Ricky Ford, and Howard Johnson does his usual patented stuff in the bottom half of the chart. Williams is a rather significant addition, playing big, singing lines that are occasionally reminiscent of Ibrahim's own early experiments on cello. Anyone with the solo *African Piano* and *African River* in their possession (the titles are uniquely repetitive and rather unimaginative) can feel confident of a reasonable purchase on his best work.

*****(*) No Fear, No Die / S'en fout la mort**

Tiptoe 88815 *Ibrahim; Frank Lacy (tb); Ricky Ford (ts); Horace Alexander Young III (as, ss, f); Jimmy Cozier (bs, cl); Buster Williams (b); Ben Riley (d).* 7/90.

Where *Mindif* was intended to evoke the magnificent spaciousness of the African landscape which forms the backdrop to

Chocolat, No Fear, No Die is a more brooding and troubled score. Claire Denis's film concerns cockfighting in France among the African community. Its edgy unease was immediately likened to Louis Malle's quasi-*vérité* thriller, *L'Ascenseur pour l'échafaud*, and to Miles Davis's score for that film. There are parallels (as there are to Duke's *Anatomy of a Murder* music) but they are more apparent than actual. Ibrahim's music is actually more effective on record than in the film because the individual pieces are better made, more carefully constructed than is usually considered either necessary or desirable for a film score. So where Miles's magnificent improvisations sound like snippets out of a longer continuum, *No Fear, No Die* behaves very much like a consciously produced album, programmed to work on its own and without images. The group performs brilliantly, with Ford as always delivering far more on someone else's record than on his own. Williams and Riley keep Monk very much in the stylistic frame. One suspects that dedicated Ibrahim fans may reject the record as 'untypical' or a second-order project. The first it may be; the second it's not.

*** Mantra Mode

Tiptoe 88810 *Ibrahim; Johnny Mekoa (t); Basil Coetzee (ts); Robbie Jansen (as, bs, f); Errol Dyers (g); Spencer Mbadu (b); Monty Weber (d).* 1/91.

*** Desert Flowers

Enja 7011 *Ibrahim (p, ky solo).* 12/91.

These were meant to express a sort of homecoming to what was, even then, being hailed as the 'new' South Africa; Ibrahim had spent much of his creative life in exile. *Desert Flowers* is a very personal programme of music and there are moments when emotion (and the synthesizer) blur the focus badly. Ibrahim actually uses synth only on the first and last tracks, an uneasy welcome and farewell that completely belies the warmth radiating from the heart of the set. Significantly, middle position is occupied by Duke's 'Come Sunday', a gorgeous performance preceded by a breath of the past in 'Ancient Cape', followed by 'District Six', 'Sweet Devotion', and a passionate vocal tribute to John Coltrane. Though far from a classic Ibrahim album, it contains enough of real merit to lift it to the fringes of the first division.

Mantra Mode is less inward and more buoyant, but one can't quite ignore the feeling that these men don't play with the bounce and gusto one hears in South African recordings of the late 1950s, from groups like the Jazz Epistles. The joy of playing appears to be assumed rather than completely spontaneous, and there is a thread of melancholy through even the upbeat numbers.

***(*) Knysna Blue

Tiptoe 888816 *Ibrahim (p solo).* 9 & 10/93.

Frankly celebratory, and intended as a mystical reconsecration of post-apartheid South Africa as a country at the world's apex, between two great oceans and focusing the cultural energies of four continents. All this is probably too much freight for one piano album, and sometimes one feels Ibrahim is trying too hard to express the inexpressible, to catch the ineffable in a combination of heavy chords and floating melody lines. There is, though, no mistaking the joy with which it comes and the total identification in Ibrahim's mind of personal and political/cultural liberation. It is, very simply, an extended love song, and the closing Monk cover, 'Ask Me Now', is as nakedly personal and unguarded as Ibrahim has ever been.

**** Yarona

Tiptoe 888820 *Ibrahim; Marcus McLaurine (b); George Johnson (d).* 1/95.

A truly magisterial performance by the sixty-year-old, bringing the house down at Sweet Basil in New York City. Ibrahim was on record around this time, reinforcing his conviction that the piano-trio format permitted the most fundamental representation of the African source; and it is very hard to argue with that on the basis of these performances. He still hits the piano very hard, using the bass almost as a drone, alternating narrow intervals and often allowing the drummer considerable licence to range outside the metre. The left hand is relentless and, in the other sense, timeless, the melody lines stripped down and ritualized. 'Duke 88' once again acknowledges a personal debt. 'Nisa' is an exclamatory hymn to another, the womenfolk of South Africa. There is a reworking of 'African Marketplace' and a concert outing for 'Stardance', one of the lovelier themes from the *Chocolat* soundtrack. The love song, 'Cherry' (not, as one critic assumed, a tribute to the trumpeter), shows his more lyrical side.

***(*) Cape Town Flowers

Tiptoe 888 826 *Ibrahim; Marcus McLaurine (b); George Gray (d).* 97.

As Hans-Hurgen Schaal perceptively points out in his liner-note, Ibrahim is above all a great storyteller. These 11 narratives in jazz take the story on a step in time and in the context of a free country. Few artists have been as relentlessly consistent in style as Ibrahim and yet as endlessly changing. What's obvious here is that some of the anger and some of the sense of loss has already faded from his music. This, on something like 'Joan – Cape Town Flower' in particular – is the work of a man reconciled to his world, not complacent, still questioning, but certainly not in the throes of alienation. It is arguably Ibrahim's most peaceful album to date. Newcomers should still explore the earlier work, but this makes a delightful place to begin.

***(*) African Suite

Enja/Tiptoe TIP 888 832 2 *Ibrahim; Belden Bullock (b); George Gray (d); strings.* 11/97.

Beautifully arranged by Daniel Schnyder, this project opens out the orchestral dimension of Ibrahim's rich and multi-textured compositions and does so without swamping the music. The young players from the Youth Orchestra of the European Community (a Claudio Abbado brainchild) have obviously all come through as part of a generation that no longer makes hard and fast distinctions between 'classical', 'jazz' and 'world' styles. Their playing is accurate but not stiff and the ensembles are relaxed enough not to sound like a paid-by-the-hour session orchestra. Long-established favourites like 'Tintinyanna' mean there are familiar reference-points, and Ibrahim takes a delightful piano solo on 'Aspen'. A very lovely record.

***(*) Cape Town Revisited

Enja/Tiptoe TIP 888 836 2 *Ibrahim; Feya Faku (t); Marcus McLaurine (b); George Gray (d).* 12/97.

Dominated by stunning performances of 'Tintinyanna', 'Water From An Ancient Well' and by the jazz suite, 'Cape Town To Congo Square', this is a summation of much of Ibrahim's musical experience and exploration over the last 20 years. Playing at Spier Estate in Cape Town and with Feya Faku on three tracks echoing the sound of Hugh Masekela all those years before, it is both the most backward-looking and one of the most sanguinely optimistic and exploratory of Ibrahim's recent discs. The sound is very good for a live recording, very present and alert, and the southern hemisphere summer warms and colours every track.

ICP Orchestra

GROUP

Named after the pioneer LP label which recorded many of the Dutch free players of the '60s and '70s, the orchestra offers a cross-section of American and European performers for this collection.

***** Herbie Nichols / Thelonious Monk**

Bvhaast 026 *Toon De Gouw (t); Wolter Wierbos, George Lewis (tb); Steve Lacy (ss); Michael Moore (cl, as); Paul Termos (as); Ab Baars (ts, ss, cl); Sean Bergin (ts); Misha Mengelberg (p); Ernst Reijseger (clo); Maurice Horsthuis (vla); Larry Fishkind (tba); Han Bennink (d).* 84–87.

A larger-scale version of the tributes which Mengelberg, Lacy and others recorded for Soul Note at much the same time, this highly coloured and generous programme makes light of the difficulties in both composers' work. Monk tributes have become commonplace, but Baars, Moore and Wierbos are soloists with an idiosyncratic accent, and Lewis appears on a few tracks for an extra brassiness. Mengelberg and Bennink, the most practised of in-to-out rhythm sections, make Monk's rhythmic eccentricities their own property, too. But the Nichols tracks are more interesting, since his tunes are less familiar, and the larger group – which includes Termos, Horsthuis, Bergin and Lacy – lends a firmer substance to music which is difficult to characterize.

Klaus Ignatzek (born 1954)

PIANO

German pianist in a conventional post-bop idiom, with a wide range of recordings and compositions to his credit.

****(*) Don't Stop It**

Timeless SJP 271 *Ignatzek; Claudio Roditi (t, flhn); Paulo Cardoso (b); Mario Gonzi (d).* 5/87.

*****(*) Jacaranda**

Timeless SJP 292 *As above.* 5/87.

**** New Surprise**

Timeless CD SJP 324 *As above, except add Tim Armacost (ts).* 11/88.

****(*) The Klaus Ignatzek Trio**

yvp 3020 *Ignatzek; Jean-Louis Rassinfosse (b); John Engels (d).* 7/89.

*****(*) The Answer!**

Candid CCD 79534 *Ignatzek; Claudio Roditi, Gustavo Bergalli (t); Jean-Louis Rassinfosse (b); Jorge Rossy (d).* 12/92.

Ignatzek has immersed himself so completely in the idioms of Horace Silver, Bill Evans, Sonny Clark and Wynton Kelly as to claim almost apostolic understanding of the roots of hard bop. Like some clairvoyant transcriber of 'posthumous' Mozart symphonies, he has produced a steady stream of rather unconvincing pastiche that may sound good in a club setting but which seems a thoroughly dull option when set against a random sample of late-1950s Blue Notes.

Ignatzek has been singularly fortunate in his access to saxophone players of the quality of Dave Liebman, Joe Henderson and, on a deleted LP, Bobby Watson; but most of that work is now in the deletions office. Ignatzek's regular band of the late 1980s was of very intermittent quality. *Jacaranda* is remarkably good, with trumpeter Roditi leading a Messengers line on standards such as 'Softly As In A Morning Sunrise' and 'There Is No Greater Love', along with an original 'Blues for Lee M.' and a take of 'Day For Night'. Neither the earlier *Don't Stop It* (with the same group) nor the ghastly *New Surprise*, which adds Tim Armacost's inept tenor, sounds like the same band at all, and the charges of bland revivalism, to which Ignatzek has always replied hotly, very definitely stick. The most recent sets show something of a consolidation, with Roditi giving the music a hint of sparkle and edge, but they still seem terribly rootless. Just as clichés are clichés because they communicate some pretty basic truths, standards are standards because they contain something over and above the normal run of songs. Even the most ambitious of the boppers knew that they had to negotiate the standards first.

The most recent of the above records, *The Answer!*, is probably the best of all, a tight, well-disciplined set with a minimum of fuss, but with some sharp arrangements that make maximum use of the two horns and exploit the more percussive side of this saxophone-less band.

***** Silent Horns**

Candid CCD 79729 *Ignatzek; Claudio Roditi, Gustavo Bergalli (t); Jean-Louis Rassinfosse (b); Jorge Rossy (d).* 94.

Ignatzek seems to like this curious instrumentation, and there's certainly some élan about this homage to deceased bebop trumpeters (that explains the title). If only Bergalli and Roditi were more individual than proficient, the music might be genuinely challenging, but what tends to emerge is a series of skilful set-pieces rather than an absorbing record.

***** Reunion**

Acoustic Music 319.1084.2 *Ignatzek; Florian Poser (vib, mar).* 8/95.

***** Live**

Acoustic Music 319.1097.21 *Ignatzek; Claudio Roditi, Gustavo Bergalli (t); Jean-Louis Rassinfosse (b); Chip White (d).* 10/95.

****(*) Obrigado**

Acoustic Music 319.1113.2 *Ignatzek; Martin Wind (b).* 6/96.

***** Springdale**

Acoustic Music 319.1166.2 *Ignatzek; Florian Poser (vib, mar).* 6–7/98.

Now on a new label, Ignatzek continues to work prolifically. The live album by the quintet goes off at a furious pace with 'Quasi-Modal' and, though it rarely stirs the blood beyond the expected muscle-flexing, it's a group which here makes the most of its collective chops, although the material offered by the leader isn't very inspiring. The duo album with Martin Wind benefits from the bassist's sonorous tone: they make a lovely, big, rich sound together and, although the record is far too long at over 70 minutes, much of it (taken a track at a time) is appealing in a lightweight way. The same goes for the two discs which pair Ignatzek with vibist Poser. There's very little to say about this music except to note its neat, dovetailed interplay and *simpatico* nature: everything falls where one expects, and the pleasure in it comes not from any kind of surprise but from professional inevitability.

Ove Ingemarsson

TENOR SAXOPHONE

Swedish saxophonist, much in demand as a sideman with post-bop outfits and here leading his own record.

***** Heart Of The Matter**
Imogena IGCD 051 *Ingemarsson; Lars Jansson (p); Lars Danielsson (b); Adam Nussbaum (d).* 1/95.

After numerous exemplary turns as a sideman, Ingemarsson steps out on his own with a typically considered set. His grand saxophone tone and heavyweight manner come off best on the slower pieces: the fine title-track, Danielsson's pretty ballad, 'Alma', and a thoughtful 'Seems Like Yesterday'; while the rhythm section relish the quicker pieces, Ingemarsson himself sounds less engaging when he has to turn on the heat. The fast pace of 'The Masquerade Is Over' results in a stolid variation on the melody, and if Nussbaum enjoys the ska licks in 'Hotel Trianon', they don't suit the leader at all. A mixed success.

Keith Ingham (born 1942)

PIANO

Born in London, Ingham was a familiar face in British mainstream in the '60s and early '70s, then he moved to New York in 1978, originally as an accompanist to Susannah McCorkle. He is a prime mover in the field of reviving hot jazz and dance from the '20s and '30s, often with Marty Grosz.

***** The Music Of Victor Young**
Jump JCD12-16 *Ingham; Bob Reitmeier (p); Frank Tate (b); Vernell Fournier (d).* 3/89.

***** Out Of The Past**
Sackville SKCD 2-3047 *Ingham (p solo).* 11–12/90.

*****(*) Donaldson Redux**
Stomp Off CD 1237 *Ingham; Peter Ecklund (c); Dan Barrett (tb); Bobby Gordon, Billy Novick (cl); Loren Schoenberg (ts); Vince Giordano (bsx, tba, b); Marty Grosz (g, bj, v); Greg Cohen (b); Hall Smith, Arnie Kinsella (d).* 6–11/91.

Ingham is the archetypal Englishman in New York (though the solo album was cut mainly in Toronto). He plays a history of jazz piano with unflinching finesse, taste and skill, and unearths tunes that few would think of trying. The 18 tracks on *Out Of The Past* cover composers from Richard M. Jones to Barry Harris, and resuscitate such cadavers as 'Just Like A Butterfly' and Rube Bloom's 'Truckin''. It is all beautifully played, the variations improvised with rag-like precision, but the unobtrusive nature of Ingham's talent is eventually frustrating. After a dozen tracks one wonders if there ought to be greater difference between such diverse sources than Ingham allows, and his version of, say, Jimmy Yancey's 'At The Window' is very pale next to the composer's own. The Jump CD is also all *politesse*, one of a series of composer-dedicated sessions: everyone sticks very closely to the melodies and it seldom seems like more than mood music. Very gracefully done, though, and musicians may like to hear some neglected melodies ('Golden Earrings', 'A Love Like This', 'Got The South In My Soul') played straight.

The Stomp Off album is another matter, since it documents the further adventures of Marty Grosz in hot-dance music. The songs are all by Walter Donaldson, and some of this archaeology is almost preposterously rarefied. Grosz does his usual update of Ukulele Ike at the microphone, and the band play a lilting approximation of old-time hot music with a few knowing modern licks. Ingham is co-credited as leader and no doubt approves of all the fun.

***** My Little Brown Book**
Progressive PCD 7101 *Ingham; Harry Allen (ts); Chris Flory (g); Dennis Irwin (b); Chuck Riggs (d).* 3/93.

*****(*) The Intimacy Of The Blues**
Progressive PCD 7102 *As above.* 3/93.

***** Music From The Mauve Decades**
Sackville SKCD2-2033 *Ingham; Bobby Gordon (cl); Hal Smith (d).* 4/93.

***** Just Imagine ...**
Stomp Off CD1285 *Ingham; Peter Ecklund (c, t); Dan Barrett (tb); Dan Levinson (cl, Cmel); Scott Robinson (cl, ts, bs, bsx); Marty Grosz (g, v); Greg Cohen (b); Joe Hanchrow (tba); Arnie Kinsella (d).* 4/94.

***** New York Nine Vol. 1**
Jump JCD12-18 *Ingham; Randy Reinhart (c, tb); Dan Barrett (t, tb); Phil Bodner (cl, as); Scott Robinson (ss, ts, bs); James Chirillo (g); Vince Giordano (bsx, b); Murray Wall (b); Arnie Kinsella (d).* 5/94.

***** New York Nine Vol. 2**
Jump JCD12-19 *As above.* 5/94.

*****(*) The Back Room Romp**
Sackville SKCD2-3059 *Ingham; Peter Ecklund (t); Scott Robinson (cl, ss, bs); Harry Allen (ts); James Chirillo (g); Murray Wall (b); Jackie Williams (d).* 1/95.

Ingham has been busy in the 1990s. The two albums of Billy Strayhorn tunes on Progressive are a light, floating collaboration with the classically styled tenor of Harry Allen. This is Strayhorn done straight, the melodies softly enunciated, the improvisations taken only a few feline steps away from the melodies. Ingham varies the arrangements between groupings of musicians and plays a few tracks solo. Scarcely an adventurous approach to repertory, but very satisfyingly done: the second disc just edges ahead since it has the less frequently encountered material.

Music From The Mauve Decades covers 1900–1920 in terms of material. Some of it is a little too musty, and the normally reliable Smith doesn't always sound appropriate in some of the tunes: a simple duet between Gordon and Ingham might have worked better. But there are still some exquisite moments, such as the lulling 'Just A-Wearyin' For You'. The remaining discs are all by bigger ensembles, and they whistle in several of the top repertory players in the field. *Just Imagine ...* is mostly infectious fun, though a shade below the Walter Donaldson set listed above. The two New York Nine albums slip between the 1920s and '30s without any pain and, though the band could still use a little more heat on the fiercer tunes, the playing is impeccably crafted. Best of them is perhaps *The Back Room Romp*, which concentrates on the small-band swing repertory of the 1930s. They rescue a couple of Rex Stewart rarities in the title-piece and 'San Juan Hill', and Allen continues his progress from Ben Webster and Paul Gonsalves to something approaching an individual style. Ecklund is irreproachable as usual. Ingham is often content to stay in the shadows on these records, but his calm hand on the arranging tiller seems rock-solid.

*****(*) Going Hollywood**
Stomp Off CD1323 *Ingham; Peter Ecklund (c, t); Joel Helleny (tb); Scott Robinson (cl, ss, as, ts, bs, bsx); Dan Block (cl, ss); Andy Stein (vn); Marty Grosz (g, bj, v); Vince Giordano (tba); Brian Nalepka, Greg Cohen (b); Arnie Kinsella (d).* 5–9/96.

***** A Star Dust Melody**
Sackville SKCD 2-2051 *Ingham; Randy Reinhart (t); Bobby Gordon (cl); Scott Robinson (reeds); James Chirillo (g); Greg Cohen (b); Arnie Kinsella (d).* 8–11/97.

Going Hollywood sees Ingham and Grosz pal up with their 'Hot Cosmopolites' to excellent, if by now familiar, effect. Grosz digs up spectacular forget-me-nots such as 'The Wedding Of The Painted Doll' and 'The Woman In The Shoe', and the ensemble hit the right note of reverent irreverence.

The Sackville album is a more respectful saunter through the Hoagy Carmichael songbook. Gordon gets a starring role and, although some of it is rather plain-spoken, the quality of the melodies endures.

Didrik Ingvaldsen

TRUMPET, PICCOLO TRUMPET, FLUGELHORN

Scandinavian trumpeter leading the jazz-rock group, Pocket Corner.

***** By-Music**
Da-Da 3 *Ingvaldsen; Stale Storlokken, John Erik Kaada (ky); Stein Ornhaug (g); Tor Mathisrud (b); Paal Nilssen-Love, Borge Fjordheim (d).* 5–6/97.

Ingvaldsen calls his band Pocket Corner and they play a likeable stew of old-fashioned (as in early Miles Davis) jazz-rock with more modern ingredients tipped in here and there. This is the Davis method trimmed into palatable cuts. Nothing goes on for very long, solos emerge out of the fabric with complete logic, and a basic sparseness belies the fact that there are seven people in the group. Keyboards sound like nice old analogue synthesizers, and Ingvaldsen himself leads rather bashfully from the front. Most intriguing piece is 'I'm On Air', with its quirky fanfare and brooding middle section.

Kjeld Ipsen

TROMBONE

Danish mainstream trombonist.

***** Ipsen / Markussen Jazz Code**
Storyville STCD 4208 *Ipsen; Uffe Markussen (ts); Ben Besiakov (p); Lennart Ginman (b); Jonas Johansen (d).* 4/95.

Very much all right and a genial hour's music from a skilful group. Skill is what one thinks of, hearing the brisk interweaving of trumpet and tenor (very like the old Getz/J.J. group) and, while there's little to rouse the spirits beyond a certain smooth appreciation, only a churl would dismiss Ipsen's swing through 'Hello Young Lovers' or the purring momentum of 'Isn't It Romantic'.

Sherman Irby (born 1968)

ALTO SAXOPHONE

A native of Tuscaloosa, Alabama, Irby came to New York in 1994 and has become part of the young corps of contemporary jazzmen in the city.

***** Full Circle**
Blue Note 852251-2 *Irby; James Hurt (p); Eric Revis (b); Dana Murray, Charli Persip (d).* 5/96.

'Melodies are important, man. Don't clutter tunes with stuff they don't need.' Irby is as good as his word, and his playing adopts an unusually cool and clear-headed posture for what's otherwise a familiar show of post-bop sax-and-rhythm. He really displays his fastest chops only on a very fine 'Wee' (which has Persip sitting in for Murray), and this comes after a beautifully stark and heart-sore ballad called 'How Strong Is Our Love?'. He has a pliable tone and a fine sense of what to leave out. A pity, then, that he seems a step or two ahead of his group: one could call Hurt's style a contrast, but his fussy elaborations don't sit all that comfortably with Irby's to-the-point approach. 'Giant Steps' is an off-colour bit of revisionism, and the blues, 'Mamma Faye', sounds too smart by half. For Irby's playing alone, though, the record works.

***** Big Mama's Biscuits**
Blue Note 856234-2 *Irby; Roy Hargrove (t); James Hurt (p); Ed Cherry (g); Gerald Cannon (b); Clifford Barbaro, Dana Murray (d).* 2/98.

Fractured and disjunctive, Irby's second record is a surprisingly dark effort, with the cheeriness of the debut traded for some striking if sometimes uncertain explorations of the sax–bass–drums format (Hargrove and Hurt are present on only one track, and Cherry is on three). 'Take The "A" Train', for instance, is stripped down to a stark, even bleak reading at a funereal tempo.

It's not all that way: a spirited take on Stevie Wonder's 'Too High' and the closing pick-me-up of 'We're Gonna Be Alright' bring a Cannonball-like feel to the proceedings.

Italian Instabile Orchestra

ENSEMBLE

Founded in 1990 by trumpeter Pino Minafra and the poet Vittorino Curci, but functioning as a co-operative, the Orchestra was an attempt to create an Italian ensemble with the eclectic range of the Vienna Art Orchestra, the Willem Breuker Kollektief or one of the more theatrical of the Russian free-jazz groups.

*****(*) Italian Instabile Orchestra**
Leo CD LR 182 *Pino Minafra (t, flhn, didjeridu); Guido Mazzon (t, flhn); Alberto Mandarini (t); Giancarlo Schiaffini (tb, tba); Sebi Tramontana (tb, v); Lauro Rossi (tb); Martin Mayes (frhn); Mario Schiano (as, v); Eugenio Colombo (as, ss, f); Carlo Actis Dato (ts, bs, bcl); Daniele Cavallanti (ts, bs); Gianluigi Trovesi (as, cl in A, bcl); Renato Geremia (vn); Paolo Damiani (clo, b, v); Bruno Tommaso (b); Giorgio Gaslini (p); Vincenzo Mazzone, Tiziano Tononi (d, perc).* 6/91, 1/92.

****** Skies Of Europe**
ECM 1543 *As above.* 5/94.

*****(*) European Concerts '94–'97**
NEL Jazz 0968 *As above.* 10/94, 9 & 11/96, 1/97.

***** Festival: Pisa Teatro Verdi December 1997**
Leo CDLR 292/293 2CD *As above, except add Luca Calabrese (t).* 12/97.

The Italian Instabile Orchestra is uncategorizable, not so much because it goes in for promiscuous genre-bending, but because it is a genuine convocation of equals, and because individual members and sub-groups are likely to go off in whatever direction takes their fancy. Like ARFI in France (of which Louis Sclavis is an adherent), the Orchestra seeks to articulate an 'imaginary folklore', an improbable common ground between popular forms, formal composition and free improvisation. There shouldn't be a strong enough gravitational field to hold it all together but, miraculously, there is. All but one of the pieces were recorded at Radio France's international jazz festival at Rive-de-Gier. The exception is perhaps the key to the whole enterprise. Giorgio Gaslini's 'Pierrot Solaire' proposes a sunshine cure for the moonstruck icon of musical modernism. Relaxed, funny, joyous, you're meant to think it's a long way from Schoenberg, except, of course, he's in there too.

Eugenio Colombo's 'Ippopotami' is a typically amphibian theme; satirically cumbersome ashore, it shows considerable if improbable grace once in the freer element of improvisation. There's also an element of that in Giancarlo Schiaffini's 'La Czarda dell'Aborigeno', which manages to graft a didjeridu introduction on to a Hungarian dance and which features fine soloing from Carlo Actis Dato on baritone and transplanted Scot, Martin Mayes, on horn.

Pachyderms reappear in Minafra's 'Noci ... Strani Frutti', a title that contains one of the Orchestra's carefully veiled allusions to jazz. This has less to do with Billie Holiday's 'Strange Fruit' than with the improbable pickings of surrealist art. Divided into 'African' and 'Indian' sections, it sets Afro-American jazz off against the other major improvisational tradition with a flute *raga* by Colombo. Dato (wearing rubber elephant ears, allegedly) rants a tale of Latin intrigue and passion.

The set opens with cellist Paolo Damiani's 'Detriti', a Noah's ark of musical and textual specimens rescued from the latter-day flood of genres and styles. It ends with 'I Virtuosi de Noci', a free-jazz piece reminiscent of Globe Unity or the Berlin Jazz Orchestra, and a powerful statement of belief in the stabilizing and cohesive power of improvisation.

The orchestra benefits more than a little from the ministrations of ECM, and Steve Lake's meticulous production opens up dimensions and strata which simply aren't accessible on the Leo. The CD is divided into two long suits, 'Il Maestro Muratore', by Tomasso, which is inspired by the great Sard sculptor, Constantino Nivola, who took his genius and his passionate defence of Sardinia's place at the international table to the United States. The opening portrait features a powerful solo statement from Minafra and Dato, and a superb string duet between the composer and Damiani. Most of the other movements are short ensembles, but 'Meru lo snob' is another free-blowing track, with Gaslini bracketed by Schiano and Cavallanti.

The pianist is also the composer of 'Skies Of Europe', an extended meditation on some of the great outsiders of European culture – Duchamp, Satie, Antonioni and Fellini – and is also intended to echo the orchestral ambitions of Ornette Coleman's *Skies Of America*. As ever, Gaslini's ideas are simultaneously rooted in jazz and orthodox composition, and the texture of his orchestrations is very detailed. He structures the opening 'Du Du Duchamp' (a pun on the old Dubonnet advert) round a sequence of duets, which gives a first airing of the set to Martin Mayes's fruitily-toned horn. Mayes reappears on 'Il suono giallo' to equally strong effect. The brasses tend to dominate elsewhere as well, with Minafra and Mazzon trading ideas on the Antonioni tribute and trombonist Schiaffini catching the ear on 'Quand Duchamp joue du marteau', which also has Gaslini moving back and forth from piano to anvil.

Like the VAO, the orchestra have never found their eclecticism a problem, putting them between the anvil of classicism and the hammer of jazz. The touring material on the NEL Jazz disc is quite various in style, sound and quality, but it offers a decent representation of the band in what has been a period of quite intense activity. Mazzon's 'Fall In Jazz', recorded in Rome in 1994, is the earliest of the pieces included, and certainly the closest to jazz proper. Later items, and particularly Tononi's 'La leggenda del lupo azzurro', have their premises elsewhere. As before, the soloing is virtuosic and cheerfully idiosyncratic. The Italian Instabile Orchestra has established a place and a very distinctive sound-palette.

The latest discs were an attempt to make a festival record sound like anything but a festival record. The usual running order – small groups and solo spots first, then the full orchestra – makes logistic sense on the ground but none on disc, so the material is generously redistributed. Equally, unless a particularly wonderful solo was likely to be lost, technically suspect recordings were excluded. It isn't as pristine as the ECM disc, but it suffices. We just wonder whether a touch more judicious editing of excerpts and the quiet disappearance of a couple of less-than-riveting tracks might not have yielded just one powerful CD rather than dissipating the attention across two. Even committed listeners will dwell longer on CD one. Schiaffini and Tramontana's trombone duet with electronics is fascinating, and Dato's concluding 'AEIO' is powerful enough for many spins, but the second half definitely loses pace.

The trombonists are eclipsed by Rava and Minafra on 'Dialogo instabile' and by the formal vigour of the Moers Brass Quintet. Trovesi's opening 'Scarlattina' (which refers to the composer and not the juvenile ailment) is rousing enough for any festival. Even so, we remain only partially convinced. This is a disc to dip in and out of.

Ethan Iverson

PIANO

New York-based pianist, born in Wisconsin – 'like my great compatriot, Liberace'. An original thinker and likely to be a very considerable force.

***(*) **Construction Zone (Originals)**
Fresh Sound FSNT 046 *Iverson; Reid Anderson (b); Jorge Rossy (d).* 4/98.

**** **Deconstruction Zone (Standards)**
Fresh Sound FSNT 047 *As above.* 4/98.

**** **The Minor Passions**
Fresh Sound FSNT 064 *As above, except Billy Hart (d) replaces Rossy.* 5/99.

Iverson seems implacably opposed to anything predictable, conventional or otherwise previously-done in the area of the piano trio, which is a pretty ambitious stance for someone working in this area of the literature. He has swinging rhythm-sections but doesn't want them to swing in the expected ways, if at all. His own material seems cryptic, even baffling, but what he does to standards can be even more unsettling. He plays melodically, uses harmonies that are rarely outlandish, yet is always pushing a new, untried sound in the listener's direction. The first two records were made at the same sessions but they have been deliberately divided between the pianist's own compositions and a group of very familiar standards. If the latter set gets the nod as the more striking portrayal of Iverson's methods, it's only because, with a familiar framework to start from, the originality of the trio's playing is all the more apparent. There are so many ingenuities in the revision of the seven pieces on *Deconstruction Zone* that one is at a loss to catalogue them all. 'The Song Is You' is cast as a furious swinger, but Iverson teasingly holds back from stating the melody until he's turned the opening phrase into a tattoo. 'This Nearly Was Mine' is reharmonized and refashioned as a sepulchral waltz. 'All Of Me' hovers mischievously between metres. 'I'll Remember April' is anointed with a stunningly virtuosic intro before a deceptively constrained treatment that gets darker and more oblique as it progresses. Rossy is superb, but the key dialogue in all these pieces is between piano and bass: Iverson and Anderson have worked together for a long time, and it shows. The 'originals' record needs more time and more study, but much of it repeats the prestidigitation of the other disc, with all sorts of fascinating twists on perceived piano-trio routines in the likes of 'New Chimes Blues' and 'The Inevitable Wall'.

The Minor Passions is a snapshot of 'the state of our art, 28 and 29 May 1999' (the recordings are drawn from a couple of gigs at Greenwich House Music School in New York). Iverson's notes here are useful. He likens his intro on an enigmatic version of 'Milestones' to Herbie Nichols, and that is one shade who does seem to be manifest in an otherwise unclassifiable bag of influences. Iverson also cites the incomparable blues master, Jimmy Yancey, 'my hero', with 'Blues For The Groundskeeper'. One can go through these records track by track and pick out extraordinary things, but that would be an unnecessarily piecemeal analysis of a performer who needs to be heard at length and in the luxury of repeated listening to let his merits break through fully. Anderson is once again an admirable assist on *The Minor Passions*, but Hart, even more than Rossy on the previous sets, brings his best attention and all the skills of both swinging drummer and soundscaping percussionist to bear on this music. These are outstanding records which Fresh Sound deserve the strongest praise for sponsoring.

D.D. Jackson (born 1967)

PIANO

At the end of jazz's first century, there was an understandable search for figures who combined tradition and innovation, the heartland of the music and its new, global diaspora. Jackson seemed a better contender than most and his steady output of crafted, intelligent jazz confirmed all the hype and promise.

***(*) **Peace-Song**
Justin Time JUST 72-2 *Jackson; David Murray (ts); John Geggie (b); Jean Martin (d).* 11/94.

**** **Rhythm Dance**
Justin Time JUST 89-2 *Jackson; John Geggie (b); Jean Martin (d).* 95.

Jackson is a Canadian of mixed race and unadulterated gifts, one of the most sheerly exciting piano players to emerge in a decade. A regular associate of violinist Billy Bang, saxophonist David Murray, and jazz *auteur* Kip Hanrahan, he brings a performing style which is both classically aware and uninterruptably swinging, and a writing concept which is similarly eclectic and unforced. Influences are easy enough to spot: Monk, Don Pullen, Jaki Byard. Where they give way to a more original conception is harder to specify.

Peace-Song is an impressive debut. Murray's presence is obviously advantageous, but not definitive. It's the sheer confidence of Jackson's writing and playing that commands attention. 'Waltz For A New Life', 'Seasons' and the title-piece are all strong statements, very much group efforts; only on 'Canon' and the closing 'Funerale' does Jackson seem a touch self-indulgent, too self-consciously eclectic.

The second album was a resounding coming-of-age, with Jackson responsible for all the compositions and for a startling range of expressive formats, from the roistering swinger 'No Boundaries', to a gentle ballad like 'For Mama'. His ease and poise are breathtaking, and even at speed his articulation and phrasing are inch-perfect, though never too precise to be unmusical.

*****(*) Paired Down: Volume 1**
Justin Time JUST 99-2 *Jackson; Hugh Ragin (t); James Carter (ts, Cmel); David Murray (ts); Hamiet Bluiett (bs); Billy Bang (vn); Santi Debriano (b).* 11 & 12/96.

*****(*) Paired Down: Volume 2**
Justin Time JUST 104-2 *Jackson; Ray Anderson (tb); David Murray (ts); Don Byron (cl); Jane Bunnett (f); Santi Debriano (b).* 97.

There are moments on the first volume of *Paired Down* when Jackson seems at some risk of disappearing into a private conversation with former employers, not so much over-respectful as too eager to please. Highlights are a pair of tunes with Hamiet Bluiett (including a wonderful tribute to the late Don Pullen), a trio of tracks with trumpeter Hugh Ragin (high skittering figures pitched against the busy action of the piano) and two with James Carter, who opens the disc on C melody saxophone, a harmonically awkward sound that nevertheless works. As ever, Jackson sounds aware and responsive to his playing partners, a fast, very melodic technique that seems unembarrassed by harmonic theory.

A second volume of duets reprises the association with Murray and also puts Jackson in the company of another former leader saxophonist (and here flautist) Jane Bunnett. Perhaps the best track of all, though, is a duet with bassist Debriano which recalls some of the late Red Mitchell's encounters with piano players.

*****(*) ... So Far**
RCA Victor 09026 63549 2 *Jackson (p solo).* 5/99.

Jackson's first solo album is somewhat well behaved, an exercise in form rather than virtuosic grandstanding. Debts to fellow-pianists – Don Pullen, Michel Camilo, Jackie Byard, Duke Ellington, Bud Powell and John Hicks – are uppermost in his mind, though Jackson makes it clear from the outset that he wishes to pay respects in his own voice and terms and not in a pastiche of 'influences'. Nods of respect to Debussy and Horowitz are less convincing, not because Jackson lacks the chops but rather because his classical mannerisms are worn too self-consciously.

Generally, though, one simply marvels at the fluency and sophistication of his playing. 'Suite New York' suggests the influence of fellow-Canadian Paul Bley, the only obvious ancestor not namechecked on the record, which may or may not be significant. It's a flowing, shapely composition, unreadable by anyone less comfortably two-handed than Jackson, whose bass chords are as featherlight as his melody lines are resonant and massive.

The piano (a modern Yamaha?) is in impeccable shape, accurate and without undue idiosyncrasy but with genuine character. The record flows easily from idea to idea, almost as if the whole session were a continuous performance. Jackson has already staked his place at the high table. The next few years are going to be very exciting indeed.

Duffy Jackson

DRUMS, VOCAL

Big-band drummer in a modern-mainstream style, from a famous jazz family.

****(*) Swing! Swing! Swing!**
Milestone MCD-9233-2 *Jackson; Bill Prince, Ken Faulk, Luis Aquino, Jeff Kivit, Riley Mullins, Barry Rios, John Bailey (t); Phil Gray, Dana Teboe, Greg Cox (tb); Billy Ross, Ed Calle, Chip McNeil, Ed Maina, Neal Bonsanti, Rob Scheps, Gary Campbell, Todd Del Giudice (reeds); Mike Levine, Larry Ham, Roger Wilder (p); Joe Cohn (g); Jay Leonhart, Jeff Grubbs (b); Bobby Thomas (perc); Chubby Jackson (v).* 95.

Duffy is Chubby Jackson's son, and he doesn't let us forget it – 'I'm Just A Son Of A Bass Player' is the second tune, and Jackson Senior steps up to scat on 'Lemon Drop'. This is showbiz jazz of a modestly entertaining mien. A few boppish scores get out from under Jackson's grasp and a few soloists have their say, which is about as far as it goes. Bob Weinstock continues a seemingly inauspicious second-time-around career as producer.

Franz Jackson (born 1912)

CLARINET

A veteran reed player on the Chicago scene from the 1930s onwards, Jackson played in countless groups until forming his Original Jass All-Stars in 1957, a very successful group which toured and worked residencies for many years. He was still touring Europe in the 1980s.

***** Franz Jackson's Original Jass All-Stars**
OJC 1824-2 *Jackson; Bob Shoffner (t); John Thomas (tb); Rozelle Claxton (p); Lawrence Dixon (bj); Bill Oldham (tba); Bill Curry (d).* 9/61.

One of the best in this series of revivals from the Riverside catalogue's 'Chicago Living Legends' sequence. Jackson was something of a modernist compared to the others – he worked with Earl Hines in the 1940s, playing mainly tenor sax – and he approaches the ten warhorses in this programme with gusto, thick-toned and hard-hitting. Shoffner and Thomas, much older hands, play with comparative reserve but, while Jackson is right up in the front of the mix, they seem to be at the back of the room. Nevertheless Shoffner, who was already in his sixties, sounds well, and Thomas plays better than he ever did with Louis Armstrong. The steady-rolling rhythm is maintained throughout by the other four, and they all kick their feet up on a spiffing 'King Porter Stomp'.

Javon Jackson

TENOR SAXOPHONE

A later member of the Jazz Messengers, Jackson has since graduated to a position in New York's hierarchy of hired-gun tenormen, with a string of Blue Notes to his name.

***** Me And Mr Jones**
Criss Cross CRISS 1053 *Jackson; James Williams (p); Christian McBride (b); Elvin Jones (d).* 12/91.

***** Burnin'**

Criss Cross CRISS 1139 *Jackson; Billie Pierce (ts); Kirk Lightsey (p); Christian McBride (b); Louis Hayes (d).* 12/91.

*****(*) For One Who Knows**

Blue Note 30244-2 *Jackson; Jacky Terrasson (p); Fareed Haque (g); Peter Washington (b); Billy Drummond (d); Cyro Baptista (perc).* 95.

Mr Jones is, of course, drummer Elvin, with whom Jackson worked a productive internship after his stint in the Messengers. Whatever else he learnt from these luminaries, he has emerged as a leader of tremendous resourcefulness and self-confidence. Even if his soloing still doesn't sound completely mature, his sense of purpose is unmistakable. The first disc leans heavily on a restricted range of ideas and tempos and could sound a little formulaic compared to the later Blue Notes. Here Jackson benefits from more thoughtful production and a more relaxed approach to the material. His writing is quite blunt and un-ambiguous, sometimes a little too assertive, but that too will sort itself out when the time is right.

Burnin' is officially co-led by fellow tenorist Pierce, but it is Jackson who commands attention, opening and closing the record with two strong originals, 'So The Story Goes' and 'Not Yet'. The rhythm section is impeccable and, though the sound is rather dry and studio-based, Jackson has a warmth and fullness of sound, as well as his trademark responsiveness, which put Pierce in the shade. What the session really lacks is a sharp, acidulous brass voice to counter the tenor.

For One Who Knows finds him, as it should, developing strongly and moving out into new areas of concern. There is a splendid trio version of Rollins's seldom-covered 'Paradox' which suggests another source for a young player who has done his utmost to steer clear of bargain-basement Traneism. That the best of the tracks should be a trio is perhaps suggestive. For all Jackson's progress, the band simply isn't right for the gig. Terrasson has his own ideas now and is unwilling to be held in check. Good as Drummond is, in a School of Blakey way, he doesn't quite suit the more lyrical and legato new style and is apt to chop up the time feel rather than letting it breathe. Hard to fault any of these on more serious counts, though. Jackson is a happening player who will make a substantial career for himself.

*****(*) A Look Within**

Blue Note 36490-2 *Jackson; Lonnie Smith (org); Fareed Haque (g); Peter Washington (b); Billy Drummond (d); Cyro Baptista (perc); Cassandra Wilson (v).* 96.

*****(*) Good People**

Blue Note 56680-2 *Jackson; Fareed Haque, Vernon Reid (g); John Medeski (org); Peter Sash (b); Billy Drummond (d); Cyro Baptista (perc).* 96.

Recorded live and spontaneous into what Jackson himself describes as an 'antique tape machine', *A Look Within* has the oily analogue sound of an earlier Blue Note era. The roster of material is almost bizarrely varied. Opening once again with a tribute to Elvin Jones, the composers thereafter are (in order) Egberto Gismonti, Frank Zappa ('Zoot Allures'), Muddy Waters (a vocal on 'Country Girl' from Cassandra Wilson), Freddie Hubbard, Charles Mingus (a medley of 'Peggy's Blue Skylight' and 'Duke Ellington's Sound Of Love'), Serge Gainsbourg and Hank Mobley, with Jackson's own obeisance to 'Hamlet's Favourite Son' (a reference to John Coltrane) thrown in.

Lonnie Smith figures on the Zappa and the Mingus, a roiling, dark sound that is unmistakable and very attractive. Apart from that, harmonic duties are down to guitarist Haque, who sounds much like a cross between Paul Metzke and Vernon Reid. Drummond holds the sound together, giving way to Blue Note favourite Baptista on 'Country Girl' and the Mobley bossa nova which ends the album. A strong set, ably and unfussily produced by Craig Street, this is the closest yet to how Jackson sounds in a live context.

Good People is also a strong set, with effective guest performances by Reid and Medeski. Baptista comes into his own when the recording picks up more detail, and he sounds entirely at ease here. Jackson makes it clear that this is a highly personal statement, a poem of respect and praise to the family and to the values he grew up with. He's done them proud.

*****(*) Pleasant Valley**

Blue Note 99697-2 *Jackson; (g); (org); (d).* 1/99.

Though a sharp-eared listener might pick out the tenor/organ/guitar instrumentation and hazard a guess at the now well-documented Jackson, the opening of *Pleasant Valley* is a complete surprise, a soft ballad interpretation of Duke's 'Sun Swept Sunday', with Stryker on acoustic guitar and Goldings using some toy instrument effect to create a gentle ringing sound not unlike a celeste.

The pace picks up from there. The title-track is a relaxed swinger that carries over something of the Ellington feel of the opening track. Its harmonics are nevertheless far from straightforward and suggest how far Jackson has come as a writer since mid-decade. Stryker's solo is full of guile and invention. Perhaps the standout track is a boppish version of Joe Zawinul's 'Hippodelphia'. Drummond is superb on it, seeming to quote the infamous 'Birdland' riff in passing, a wry nod and wink from a hugely accomplished and thoroughly musical drummer.

Attention wavers a little on later tracks. The saxophonist seems to retread ideas and some of the cohesion slips out of the ensembles. There are, though, inventive versions of Stevie Wonder's 'Don't You Worry 'Bout A Thing' and Al Green's 'Love And Happiness', which suggest that Jackson may also be looking at other areas of resource in Black American music. So much the better if he does, because on this showing alone he has inscribed his own name in the tradition.

Milt Jackson (1923–99)

VIBES, PIANO, VOCAL

Born in Detroit, Jackson moved to New York after his studies and joined Dizzy Gillespie at the start of recorded bebop in 1945. He was with various leaders before rejoining Gillespie in 1950, then with his own quartet, which became the MJQ in 1954. Played with that group throughout its career but also made many records of his own. The master vibesman of jazz after the swing era, Jackson established the instrument in a competitive bop environment, at the same time introducing a new elegance into its sound via his ballad playing, and reaching back to basic jazz elements by remaining a peerless improviser on the simplest blues forms. His work inside and outside the MJQ is a model of consistency, without settling into a rut.

****(*) In The Beginning**

Original Jazz Classics OJC-1771 *Jackson; Russell Jacquet (t); J.J Johnson (tb); Sonny Stitt (as); Leo Parker (bs); Sir Charles Thompson, John Lewis (p); Al Jackson (b); Kenny Clarke (d); Chano Pozo (perc).* 47–48.

Obscure beginnings, though Jackson had already made a remarkable debut with Dizzy Gillespie on the sextet session for Victor which produced the astonishing 'Anthropology'. But there is nothing primitive about the playing on the four quartet tracks with three-quarters of the MJQ, from 1948, where Jackson's ballad playing on 'In A Beautiful Mood' matches the title. An earlier sextet date is more conventional bebop.

****** Milt Jackson**

Blue Note 81509-2 *Jackson; Lou Donaldson, Sahib Shihab (as); Thelonious Monk, John Lewis (p); Percy Heath, John Simmons, Al McKibbon (b); Shadow Wilson, Art Blakey, Kenny Clarke (d).* 6/48–4/52.

Six of these tracks can also be found on records under Monk's name, while a quintet date with Donaldson and what was to become the MJQ was first issued as a 10-inch LP. The tracks with Monk are flawless classics, rising to their greatest height with the riveting version of 'I Mean You', while the other date, though at a less exalted level, finds Jackson quite at home with Donaldson's uncomplicated, bluesy bop.

***** MJQ**

Original Jazz Classics OJC 125 *Jackson; Henry Boozier (t); Horace Silver (p); Percy Heath (b); Kenny Clarke (d).* 6/54.

***** Milt Jackson**

Original Jazz Classics OJC 001 *Jackson; Horace Silver (p); Percy Heath (b); Connie Kay (d).* 5/55.

MJQ features four titles by the personnel listed (the remainder are by a first-generation MJQ). Though no more than a pick-up date, all concerned play well. *Milt Jackson* is more substantial, but the preponderance of slow tempos lends a rather sleepy air to the date: the exception is 'Stonewall', a blues with a 13-chorus vibes solo that effectively defines the principles of Jackson's art. Remastering up to the strong OJC standard.

***** Bags Meets Trane**

Atlantic 1553-2 *Jackson; John Coltrane (ts); Hank Jones (p); Paul Chambers (b); Connie Kay (d).* 1/59.

We are waiting for new editions of Jackson's excellent work for Savoy, so there's currently a gap between the Prestige and Blue Note material and this survivor from his Atlantic sessions of the late '50s. It's a genial if relatively unambitious meeting of giants. Always the most unprejudiced of collaborators, Milt simply goes ahead and blows, and though Coltrane is on the verge of his first great breakthroughs he responds to the less fearsome blues situations with his usual majestic command.

****** Bags Meets Wes**

Original Jazz Classics OJC 240 *Jackson; Wynton Kelly (p); Wes Montgomery (g); Sam Jones (b); Philly Joe Jones (d).* 12/61.

****(*) Invitation**

Original Jazz Classics OJC 260 *Jackson; Kenny Dorham, Virgil Jones (t); Jimmy Heath (ts); Tommy Flanagan (p); Ron Carter (b); Connie Kay (d).* 8–11/62.

***** Big Bags**

Original Jazz Classics OJC 366 *Jackson; Clark Terry (t, flhn); Bernie Glow, Ernie Royal, Snooky Young, Doc Severinsen, Dave Burns (t); Jimmy Cleveland, Melba Liston, Paul Faulise, Tom McIntosh (tb); Willie Ruff (frhn); James Moody (as, ts, f); Earl Warren, George Dorsey, Jerome Richardson (as); Jimmy Heath (ts); Tate Houston, Arthur Clarke (bs); Hank Jones (p); Ron Carter (b); Connie Kay, Philly Joe Jones (d).* 6–7/62.

***** At The Village Gate**

Original Jazz Classics OJC 309 *Jackson; Jimmy Heath (ts); Hank Jones (p); Bob Cranshaw (b); Albert 'Tootie' Heath (d).* 12/63.

***** For Someone I Love**

Original Jazz Classics OJC 404 *Jackson; Clark Terry, Thad Jones, Dave Burns, Snooky Young, Bill Berry, Elmon Wright (t); Quentin Jackson, Jimmy Cleveland, Jack Rains, Tom McIntosh (tb); Bob Northern, Julius Watkins, Ray Alonge, Willie Ruff, Paul Ingraham (frhn); Hank Jones, Jimmy Jones (p); Major Holley (tba); Richard Davis (b); Connie Kay, Charli Persip (d).* 3–8/63.

Jackson was firmly ensconced in the MJQ by this time, but occasional blowing dates were something he obviously enjoyed, and his association with Riverside led to some more challenging situations. *Invitation* is somewhat disappointing, given the personnel: some of the tunes are cut off short, and Dorham and Heath never quite get into it as they might. Heath fares better on the live date from the Village Gate, which works mostly from a blues base. *Big Bags* puts Jackson to work in some Ernie Wilkins arrangements for orchestra, and there is a puissant 'Round Midnight' among the charts (an alternative take is also included on the CD reissue), although the vibraphonist's impassive assurance isn't ideal for this situation. *For Someone I Love* is another try at the same sort of thing, though here the front lines are all brass, working from charts by Melba Liston. Jackson approaches it in just the same way, digging in hard on 'Extraordinary Blues', rhapsodic on 'Days Of Wine And Roses'. The best of this group is the meeting with Wes Montgomery. This time the tunes seem just the right length, even on a miniature like the ballad, 'Stairway To The Stars', and the quintet lock into an irresistible groove on the up-tempo themes. The CD includes three alternative takes, all worth having.

***** In A New Setting**

Verve 538620-2 *Jackson; Jimmy Heath (ts, f); McCoy Tyner (p); Bob Cranshaw (b); Connie Kay (d).* 12/64.

'Hard-hitting and concise jazz statements' – the Limelight label, for which this set was originally recorded, wasn't much interested in the open-ended jamming of hard bop, and most of its jazz output was like this – crisp, restricted tracks with just a chorus or two per man on the blues (most of the originals here) and a few standards. It suited Jackson well enough, and he has an excellent team on hand, with Tyner enjoying himself on 'Slow Death' and Heath big and bold throughout. Still, there's little here that one could call memorable jazz.

***** The Big Three**
Original Jazz Classics OJC 805 *Jackson; Joe Pass (g); Ray Brown (b).* 8/75.

***** Montreux '77**
Original Jazz Classics OJC 375 *Jackson; Clark Terry (t); Eddie 'Lockjaw' Davis (ts); Monty Alexander (p); Ray Brown (b); Jimmie Smith (d).* 7/77.

**** Feelings**
Original Jazz Classics OJC 448 *Jackson; Hubert Laws, Jerome Richardson (f); Tommy Flanagan (p); Dennis Budimir (g); Ray Brown (b); Jimmie Smith (d); strings.* 4/76.

***** Soul Fusion**
Original Jazz Classics OJC-731 *Jackson; Monty Alexander (p); John Clayton (b); Jeff Hamilton (d).* 6/77.

*****(*) Milt Jackson + Count Basie + The Big Band Vol. 1**
Original Jazz Classics OJC 740 *Jackson; Waymon Reed, Lyn Biviano, Sonny Cohn, Pete Minger (t); Bill Hughes, Mel Wanzo, Fred Wesley, Dennis Wilson (tb); Danny Turner, Bobby Plater (as); Eric Dixon (ts, f); Kenny Hing (ts); Charlie Fowlkes (bs); Count Basie (p); Freddie Green (g); John Clayton (b); Butch Miller (d).* 1/78.

*****(*) Milt Jackson + Count Basie + The Big Band Vol. 2**
Original Jazz Classics OJC 741 *As above.* 1/78.

***** All Too Soon**
Original Jazz Classics OJC 450 *Jackson; Joe Pass (g); Ray Brown (b); Mickey Roker (d).* 1/80.

***** Night Mist**
Original Jazz Classics OJC 827 *Jackson; Harry Edison (t); Eddie 'Cleanhead' Vinson (as); Eddie 'Lockjaw' Davis (ts); Art Hillery (p); Ray Brown (b); Larance Marable (d).* 4/80.

*****(*) Ain't But A Few Of Us Left**
Original Jazz Classics OJC 785 *Jackson; Oscar Peterson (p); Ray Brown (b); Grady Tate (d).* 11/81.

*****(*) It Don't Mean A Thing If You Can't Tap Your Foot To It**
Original Jazz Classics OJC 601 *Jackson; Cedar Walton (p); Ray Brown (b); Mickey Roker (d).* 7/84.

***(*) Soul Believer**
Original Jazz Classics OJC 686 *Jackson; Plas Johnson (ts); Cedar Walton (p); Dennis Budimir (g); Ray Brown (b); Billy Higgins (d).* 9/78.

****(*) Bags' Bag**
Original Jazz Classics OJC 935 *Jackson; Cedar Walton (p); Vaughan Andre, John Collins (g); Ray Brown (b); Billy Higgins, Frank Severino (d).*

***** Jackson, Johnson, Brown And Company**
Original Jazz Classics OJC 907 *Jackson; J.J Johnson (tb); Tom Rainier (p); John Collins (g); Ray Brown (b); Roy McCurdy (d).* 5/83.

***** A London Bridge**
Pablo 2310-932 *Jackson; Monty Alexander (p); Ray Brown (b); Mickey Roker (d).* 4/82.

***** Mostly Duke**
Original Jazz Classics OJC 968 *As above.* 4/82.

***** Memories Of Thelonious Sphere Monk**
Original Jazz Classics OJC 851 *As above.* 4/82.

***** The Best Of Milt Jackson**
Pablo 2405-405 *Compilation from the above.* 77–82.

Jackson's signing to Pablo – which also snared the MJQ for a time – brought forth a flood of albums, nearly all of which are now available on CD. Just as he did with Count Basie, Granz basically set Milt up in the studio and let him go, which means that all these records are solidly entertaining without ever quite going the extra distance and becoming a classic.

One of the most obvious mix-and-match situations, though, proved to be a winner: the two albums with Basie, cut at a single session in 1978. Here are two kindred spirits, both in love with playing the blues, giving it their best shot, and with the orchestra in towering form behind them. There are a few small-group tracks, but it's mainly the big band with Jackson taking most of the solos, Basie restricting himself to the occasional rejoinder. The only disappointment must be that the material is nearly all Basie warhorses; but it gives Jackson the unshakeable platform which his previous records with a big band never finally secured. On 'Lil' Darlin'' he sounds gorgeous, and on a stomper like Ernie Wilkins's 'Basie' the studio nearly goes up in smoke, even if it's always a controlled explosion with this band.

Most of the other records keep to a high standard. *The Big Three*, a typical Granz set-up of masters, works pretty well – there is a lovely 'Nuages', and Pass digs in unusually strongly on a fast 'Blue Bossa' – without making a very deep impression. *Soul Believer*, where Jackson sings, is eminently avoidable, and the strings album, *Feelings*, is pretty but disposable. The Montreux jam session is slightly above par for this kind of course. Of the remainder, another standout is the quartet date on *It Don't Mean A Thing*. Cedar Walton and Jackson inspire each other to their best form, and an intensely swinging 'If I Were A Bell' and the Ellington near-title-track, taken at a daringly relaxed tempo, are marvels. *Ain't But A Few Of Us Left* is as swinging as the best Peterson records can be, and Jackson seems to have enjoyed his meeting with the great man: 'Body And Soul', set off with a bossa feel, is impressive, and they take a luxurious time over 'If I Should Lose You'. *All Too Soon* is a little too laid-back as an Ellington tribute. *Jackson, Johnson, Brown And Company* has some lovely moments between Milt and J.J., although the record feels a bit stilted at points where they might have really stretched out. The rest of the band sometimes get in Jackson's way on *Night Mist*, an all-blues programme, but – pro that he is – Bags settles into the situation and takes some typically collected solos. *A London Bridge* and *Mostly Duke* were cut at the same engagement at Ronnie Scott's in London, and Alexander's carousing piano parts are an interesting foil for Jackson's imperturbable solos. *Memories Of Thelonious Sphere Monk*, from the same occasion, is also good, but in a sense a wasted opportunity. A full-scale meditation on Monk by Jackson, one of his canniest interpreters, should have been set down before now; here, though, three of the four themes are tossed to the other members of the quartet as features, and Bags tackles only the comparatively straightforward 'In Walked Bud'.

***** High Fly**
JLR 103.602 2CD *Jackson; Johnny O'Neal (p); Steve Novosel (b); Vinnie Johnson (d).* 7/80.

Another set from the Atlanta club e.j.'s, dating from 1980, with Jackson guesting with the house rhythm section on a comfortable set of standards, blues and bebop. It's typical of Bags that he doesn't stop swinging across both discs, from 'Close Your Eyes' to 'Good Bait', and the trio work alongside with plenty of gusto. Held back, though, like all the discs from this source, by the amateurish location recording, which does the vibes very few favours.

****(*) Reverence And Compassion**

Qwest/Reprise 945204-2 *Jackson; Oscar Brashear (t); George Bohannon (tb); Jeff Clayton (as); Gary Foster (ts, f); Ronald Brown (ts); Jack Nimitz (bs, bcl); Cedar Walton (p); John Clayton (b); Billy Higgins (d); strings.* 92.

Hugely overproduced, with thunderous orchestral arrangements draped over and round the music, but Jackson and his rhythm section still manage to make worthwhile music when the smoke clears. 'Young And Foolish' and the dreaded 'How Do You Keep The Music Playing' may sound like high-class mood music, but when the quartet digs into 'Bullet Bag' and 'Reverence' it sounds like the real thing.

***** The Prophet Speaks**

Qwest/Reprise 945591-2 *Jackson; Joshua Redman (ts); Cedar Walton (p); John Clayton (b); Billy Higgins (d); Joe Williams (v).* 93.

***** Burnin' In The Woodhouse**

Qwest/Reprise 945918-2 *Jackson; Nicholas Payton (t); Jesse Davis (as); Joshua Redman (ts); Benny Green (p); Christian McBride (b); Kenny Washington (d).* 94.

Milt's tenure with Qwest/Reprise offered him some nice opportunities to play, but these are still largely unremarkable records. *The Prophet Speaks* features guest Redman on several tracks, and when they take on Monk's 'Off Minor' the intensity goes up a notch. The magisterial Walton is also good value: try his sly blues deconstruction on 'Five O'Clock In The Morning'. But the music has no real fire, and Joe Williams sounds past it on his three features. The horns play on only three tracks of *Burnin' In The Woodhouse*, which is more like a slow simmer than anything with flames in it. Jackson's vibes sound different on all three of his records for this company, and they're notably muffled on the last two.

***** Sa Va Bella**

Qwest/Warners 46607 *Jackson; Mike LeDonne (p); Bob Cranshaw (b); Mickey Roker (d); Etta Jones (v).* 96.

The atmosphere here is rosy with reminiscence as Bags pays fetching homage to the female jazz singers. Etta Jones does the honours on three tracks (though not, interestingly enough, her own 'Don't Go To Strangers') but this is mostly about the vibes master playing with a congenial team on eight tunes he knows well, one blues and a customized 'tribute' track. If there's nothing to exactly stir the blood here, it showed that one of the great jazz figures of the past half-century was still just that.

*****(*) Explosive!**

Qwest/Warners 9362-47286-2 *Jackson; Byron Stripling, Snooky Young, Oscar Brashear, Clay Jenkins, Bobby Rodriguez (t); Ira Nepus, George Bohanon, Isaac Smith (tb); Maurice Spears (btb); Jeff Clayton, Keith Fiddmont (as, cl, f); Rickey Woodard, Charles Owens (ts, cl); Lee Callet (bs, bcl); Bill Cunliffe (p); Jim Hershman (g); John Clayton Jr, Christoph Luty (b); Jeff Hamilton (d).* 6/99.

'Bags' Groove' – one more time. It's a splendid farewell for the old man, teaming up with a band (the Clayton–Hamilton Jazz Orchestra) full of old friends, still swinging with an absolutely indomitable assertion on tunes that he loved to blow on, such as 'Since I Fell For You', 'Indiana' and 'Along Came Betty'. Good, functional charts by John Clayton, and engineer Joel Moss gives everybody a big and illustrious sound, with Milton fashioning solos of such elegance that they celebrate a magnificent life of music.

Ronald Shannon Jackson (born 1940)

DRUMS, PERCUSSION, OTHER INSTRUMENTS

Born in Fort Worth, Texas, Jackson studied history before receiving a music scholarship to New York. Played drums for Ayler, Mingus and Betty Carter; then, after a sabbatical, played with Ornette Coleman and Cecil Taylor in the late '70s and formed The Decoding Society in 1981. Also toured with Last Exit.

***** Raven Roc**

DIW 862 *Jackson; Jef Lee Johnson, David Fiuczynski (g); Dom Richards (b).* 2/92.

***** What Spirit Say**

DIW 895 *Jackson; James Carter (ts, ss); Martin Atangana, Jef Lee Johnson (g); Ngolle Pokossi (d).* 12/94.

The sound of Shannon Jackson's Decoding Society is characteristically an unsettling amalgam of dark, swampy vamps, huge, distorted chorales and sudden outbursts of urban noise. Decoded, it yields up a grand range of putative influences, from Albert Ayler's increasingly abstract and fissile music (Shannon played with the saxophonist in the early 1960s), to Mingus's open-ended compositional style, to Ornette Coleman's harmolodics, to black and white thrash-metal music; it was James Blood Ulmer's brutal funk *Are You Glad To Be In America?* that helped establish the drummer's reputation in Europe. He in turn has had a powerful impact on such once-fashionable outfits as Decoding Society guitarist Vernon Reid's Living Colour and the Black Rock Coalition, while his work with the heavyweight Last Exit spawned a shoal of imitators.

The early albums – for Antilles, About Time and Caravan Of Dreams – are still not around at present, so much of his work in the '80s has been rather unfairly overlooked by the CD era. Jackson had spent much of the 1970s in obscurity and has had to suffer oversights and unimaginative marketing throughout his career. *The* drummer of the late 1980s looked like making only a slow and uneasy accommodation to the new decade, but *Raven Roc* found him in pleasingly murky and bad-tempered form, battering out themes of authentic unpleasantness like 'Sexual Drum Dance' and 'Hatched Spirit Blues'. The upgraded Decoding Society lacks some of its predecessors' metallic blare, but Jackson makes it clear that he doesn't need horns, and the guitarists demonstrate that they don't need optional extras like technique.

What Spirit Say is more from the same dark place, though the addition of saxophone in place of a second guitar gives the music a more vocalized and thus more humane sound. There is always a twinkle about Jackson, a slimmed-down, pawky version of the fat boy who 'wants to make yer flesh creep'. There's more sheer fun and soul food in his 'Sorcerer's Kitchen' than he'd like to pretend.

***** Shannon's House**
DIW-913 *Jackson; Rachella Parks (ss, ts); Thomas Reese (ky); Jef Lee Johnson (g); Ramon Pooser (b).* 3/96.

Here he goes again with another new band, although Johnson is a confederate who seems to have stayed the course as well as Vernon Reid once did. 'Julius Is Gone' and 'Hymn For Mandela' are thoughtful openers, the old thunder tamed in favour of the lyricism which has always been shining out of the corners of Shannon's music, and, although Reese's keyboards temper much of the edginess and buff the corners of the music, the undercurrent of menace in the likes of 'Blackegg' is still around. Some of the old Decoding Society discs ended up by settling for a brainy kind of fusion, and maybe this band goes much the same way, but it's still resolutely Jackson's show and there are plenty of moments when he is definitively in the house.

Willis Jackson (1928–87)

TENOR SAXOPHONE

Born in Miami, Jackson made his name with the Cootie Williams small group of the early '50s and thereafter toured and recorded mostly in small-combo R&B-styled settings.

**** Call Of The Gators**
Delmark DD-460 *Jackson; Andrew Fats Ford, Bobby Johnson (t); Booty Wood, Bobby Range (tb); Haywood Henry, Ben Kynard, Reuben Phillips (bs); Bill Doggett, Arnold Jarvis, Duke Anderson (p); Leonard Swain, Leemie Stanfield (b); Joe Murphy, Panama Francis (d).* 1–5/50.

***** Please Mr Jackson**
Original Jazz Classics OJC 321 *Jackson; Jack McDuff (org); Bill Jennings (g); Tommy Potter (b); Alvin Johnson (d).* 5/59.

***** Legends Of Acid Jazz**
Prestige 24198-2 *Jackson; Jack McDuff (org); Bill Jennings (g); Wendell Marshall, Tommy Potter, Milt Hinton (b); Alvin Johnson, Bill Elliot (d); Buck Clarke (perc).* 5/59–8/60.

****(*) Gentle Gator**
Prestige 24158-2 *Jackson; Jimmy Neely, Richard Wyands, Gildo Mahones, Tommy Flanagan (p); Kenny Burrell, Bucky Pizzarelli, Jose Paulo (g); Wendell Marshall, Peck Morrison, George Tucker, Eddie Calhoun (b); Roy Haynes, Bobby Morrison, Gus Johnson, Mickey Roker (d); Juan Amalbert, Montego Joe (perc).* 1/61–12/62.

***** Willis Jackson With Pat Martino**
Prestige 24161-2 *Jackson; Frank Robinson (p); Pat Martino (g); Carl Wilson (b); Joe Hadrick (d).* 3/64.

Willis 'Gator' Jackson made a lot of records for Prestige and Muse, most of them in the tenor-and-organ format, and they've trickled back into circulation. Delmark have reminded us of where he began with a compilation of ancient R&B sides: leathery, honking solos coughed out over sloppy-joe rhythms, good fun provided you don't have to hear more than a couple of tracks at a time. His long stint as a soul-sax man at Prestige has lately been rewarded with a couple of reissues, one with the young Pat Martino: reliably gritty playing by all hands, and – again – taken a few minutes at a time, this stuff can sound great. But don't expect a CD to have staying power. *Gentle Gator* has him turning the juice on with the ballad format, and this is frankly even slighter: no need to put this record on when there's a Lockjaw Davis, let alone a Ben Webster, album to hand. His entry in the *Acid Jazz* series couples the Prestige originals, *Blue Gator* and *Cookin' Sherry*. Old favourites like McDuff and Jennings do their duty, and this might be the record to get if you want a single Jackson in your house: too bad about the silly psychedelic cover-art, though.

****(*) Bar Wars**
32 Jazz 32018 *Jackson; Charles Earland (org); Pat Martino (g); Idris Muhammad (d); Buddy Caldwell (perc).* 12/77.

Jackson's Muse albums seem set for reissue by 32 Jazz, but they're hardly priority purchases. This one, though, has a sound, hard-hitting band, and Willis blows the blues with enough gusto to keep the customer something like satisfied.

C. W. Jacobi's Bottomland Orchestra

GROUP

A tribute band dedicated to the music of Clarence Williams, led by German arranger-saxophonist Jacobi.

***** A Tribute To Clarence Williams**
Stomp Off CD1266 *Roland Pilz (c, v); René Hagmann (tb); Matthias Seuffert (cl, as); Claus Jacobi (cl, as, ts); Rurik Van Heys (p); Gunter Russel (bj); Dietrich Kleine-Horst (tba); Gunter Andernach (wbd, perc); Gaby 'Ottilie' Schulz (v).* 3/93.

***** A Tribute To Clarence Williams Vol. 2**
Stomp Off CD1336 *As above, except Norbert Kemper (p) replaces Van Heys; omit Schulz.* 11/97.

Despite Williams's widespread influence on early jazz, only three of the 18 tunes on the first disc – 'Baby Won't You Please Come Home', 'I Wish I Could Shimmy Like My Sister Kate' and 'Old Folks' Shuffle' – could be called standards. Yet the entire programme is played with easy panache and fluency by this splendid outfit of German connoisseurs. The remarkable Hagmann is on loan from The Dry Throat Fellows, playing trombone this time, and the reed players get very close to the warbling style of their 1920s counterparts; Pilz, too, makes a good fist of the Ed Allen cornet parts. The result is a bright, happy session which flirts with the novelty flavour that Williams himself traded on without succumbing to it: symbolic in this regard is the ferocious trashing of 'Anywhere Sweetie Goes (I'll Be There)', but almost anything here would have sounded just fine on an original Vocalion of 65 years earlier. *Volume 2* continues where they left off four years earlier and, with a superior studio sound and a confident band, this one may edge out the earlier disc, though Williams fans may find this a less gratifying set of tunes. Unencumbered by any American affiliation – they never sound like they're following the Murphy/Watters line, which many an American traditionalist does – they make this stuff sound very fresh. Perfection: the loco feel of 'Railroad Rhythm'.

Illinois Jacquet (born 1922)

TENOR SAXOPHONE, BASSOON, VOCALS

Jacquet made his reputation with a solo on Lionel Hampton's 'Flying Home' and condemned himself to playing it for the next 40 years. The quintessential Texas tenor, Jacquet was a stalwart of the Basie orchestra and later of Norman Granz's Jazz At The Philharmonic, sometimes generating more heat than light, but always playing inventive, full-toned jazz.

***** Illinois Jacquet, 1945–1946**

Classics 948 *Jacquet; Emmett Berry, Russell Jacquet (t); Henry Coker (tb); John Brown (as); Tom Archia (ts); Arthur Dennis (bs); Bill Doggett, Sir Charles Thompson (p); Freddie Green, Ulysses Livingston (g); Billy Hadnott, Charles Mingus, John Simmons (b); Johnny Otis, Shadow Wilson (d).* 7/45–1/46.

****** Illinois Jacquet, 1946-1947**

Classics 1019 *Jacquet; Miles Davis, Marion Hazel, Russell Jacquet, Fats Navarro, Joe Newman (t); Gus Chappell, J.J Johnson, Ted Kelly, Fred Robinson, Trummy Young, Dickie Wells (tb); Porter Kilbert, Ray Perry (as); Leo Parker (bs); Bill Doggett, Leonard Feather, Sir Charles Thompson (p); John Collins, Freddie Green (g); Al Lucas, John Simmons (b); Denzil Best, Shadow Wilson (d).* 8/46–11/47.

***** Flying Home**

Bluebird ND 90638 *Jacquet; Russell Jacquet (t, v); Joe Newman (t); J.J Johnson (tb); Ray Perry (as); Leo Parker, Maurice Simon (bs); Milt Buckner, Cedric Haywood, Sir Charles Thompson (p); Lionel Hampton (vib); John Collins (g); George Duvivier, Al Lucas (b); Alan Dawson, Jo Jones, Shadow Wilson (d).* 12/47–7/67.

Born in Broussard, Louisiana, and raised in Houston, Texas, you somehow just know how Illinois Jacquet is going to sound. It's a big, blues tone, edged with a kind of desperate loneliness that somehow underlines Jacquet's status as a permanent guest star, an unbreakable mustang of a player who was never really given either the right amount of room or genuinely sympathetic sidemen. He learned his showmanship in the Lionel Hampton band of the early 1940s, trading on his remarkable facility in the 'false' upper register and on sheer energy.

Jacquet seems permanently saddled with the largely meaningless 'Texas tenor' tag. In fact, his playing can show remarkable sensitivity and he is one of the fastest thinkers in the business. His ability to take care of his own business was obvious from the shrewd self-management that kept him in the forefront of Norman Granz's Jazz At The Philharmonic, a story that has yet to be told in revealing detail. Just a few days after his triumphant debut with JATP, Jacquet cut the first of the sides included on the Classics compilation. Inevitably, given the huge success he'd had with the Good–Hampton–Robin tune which propelled him to early fame, he includes another version of 'Flying Home', accompanied this time by brother Russell (who takes the vocal on 'Throw It Out Of Your Mind, Baby'), trombonist Henry Coker and Sir Charles Thompson. The four July sides for Philo are pretty forgettable, and there isn't a chance to hear what Jacquet is really made of until he starts recording for Apollo in August. 'Jacquet Mood' and 'Bottoms Up' are both impressive up-tempo numbers, and there is an early sighting of Jacquet the balladeer, an exquisite performance of 'Ghost Of A Chance'. He's back in the same mood early the following year, recording for Savoy in a band with Emmett Berry, who was credited as leader on half the releases. This time, it's 'Don't Blame Me' that reveals the romantic in him. The only other items on this first Classics compilation are a couple of obscurities recorded by the August 1945 band for ARA. The sharp-eyed will have noted a credit for the 23-year-old Charles Mingus, playing bass on the Apollo sessions.

Classics move in their typically dogged way, hoovering up everything that has been done under the artist's name, month by month, session by session. Jacquet was still with Basie in the summer of 1946, and used many of his day-job colleagues for his recordings for Apollo. These and what followed make the next Classics volume a near-essential buy for Jacquet fans and a highly recommended one for swing enthusiasts. A measure of the excitement generated by his newly configured big band of January 1947 (which doesn't seem to have performed live, simply as a studio line-up) can be judged by the quickest scan of the personnel. Four outstanding cuts, with Leonard Feather sitting in as pianist on 'Big Dog'. Illinois with big-toned, confident solos and the ensembles, on 'For Europeans Only' in particular, can't be faulted, all the more so if this really wasn't a regular working band.

The spring of 1947 saw the saxophonist back working with a smaller group, but no less impressive a personnel, with Russell Jacquet, Newman, J.J., Leo Parker, Sir Charles Thompson *and* Freddie Green on board to record just one rather scanty idea; the other cut, from April Fool's Day, is for saxophone and rhythm only. As so often, Jacquet is the only lead woodwind, with Parker used largely to fill out the mid-end of the ensembles when he is present. Larger and smaller versions of the All Stars line-up were to be Jacquet's working group for the rest of the year, and there are excellent things from May ('Robbin's Nest' and 'Jumpin' At The Woodside'), September (another sax-and-rhythm track, 'It's Wild', with one of his most intense solos on disc) and November (for some reason, 'I Surrender Dear' was issued only in France). A cracking vintage for the saxophonist and, despite the usual technical quibbles, a fine compilation.

*****(*) Flying Home: The Best Of The Verve Years**

Verve 521644-2 *Jacquet; Roy Eldridge, Russell Jacquet, Joe Newman, Elmon Wright, Lamar Wright Jr (t); Henry Coker, Matthew Gee (tb); Ernie Henry, Earl Warren (as); Count Hastings, Ben Webster (ts); Cecil Payne (bs); Johnny Acea, Carl Perkins, Hank Jones, Jimmy Jones, Sir Charles Thompson (p); Count Basie, Wild Bill Davis, Gerry Wiggins (org); Irving Ashby, Kenny Burrell, John Collins, Herb Ellis, Freddie Green, Oscar Moore, Gene Ramey, Joe Sinacore (g); Ray Brown, Red Callender, Curtis Counce, Al Lucas (b); Al Bartee, Art Blakey, Jimmy Crawford, J.C Heard, Osie Johnson, Jo Jones, Johnny Williams, Shadow Wilson (d); Chano Pozo (perc).* 1/51–4/58.

Jacquet's work for Verve is gathered on the later of two compilations here called *Flying Home*, named after the Benny Goodman–Lionel Hampton–Sid Robin tune that became his calling card. Brian Priestley has made an intelligent selection and sequence of the Granz recordings, placing quite a bit of emphasis on the 1951 and 1952 sessions that made up the two volumes of *Illinois Jacquet Collates*, which were issued on Verve's elder sibling, Clef, like all the other tracks on offer. It's a selection of big-band and small-group settings (the latter featuring a diversity of accompanists, covering the elegant Hank Jones and the eccentric Carl Perkins). Only 'No Sweet', from the 1958 *Cool Rage*, and some of the material from the less reflective organ groups disappoint. Jacquet's style didn't really develop in the accepted sense. His great virtue was consistency and, while this is a plus in a gigging musician, it is somewhat at a discount in the studio, where surprises, new wrinkles and out-and-out rethinks are called for.

***** The Kid And The Brute**

Verve 557096-2 *Jacquet; Russell Jacquet (t); Matthew Gee (tb); Cecil Payne (bs); Leo Parker (bs, v); Ben Webster (ts); John Acea (p); Al Lucas (b); Osie Johnson, Shadow Wilson (d); Chano Pozo (perc).* 12/53, 12/54.

The kid is Jacquet, the brute Ben Webster; the occasion a challenge to the kind of tenor sax duel that was to become their stock in trade for some time to come, often to the detriment of Jacquet's subtler side. The opening piece, 'I Wrote This For The Kid', is a long, actually co-written jam, tedious at almost 12 minutes, but the rationale for the whole session. Webster appears on only one other track, 'The Kid And The Brute', which manages to get its business done a touch more briskly. All the rest of the material is from Jacquet's regular group of the time. A few dodgy vocals here and there, and on 'JATP Conga' the curious sound of Jacquet's mouth percussion. Not much to excite the unconverted, though collectors of Webster material and enthusiasts for heavyweight title-fights will enjoy the two long tracks. The sound is superb, probably undeservingly so.

*****(*) Illinois Jacquet**

Columbia EK 64654 *Jacquet; Roy Eldridge, Ernie Royal (t); Matthew Gee (tb); Charlie Davies, Leo Parker, Cecil Payne (bs); Sir Charles Thompson (p); Kenny Burrell (g); George Duvivier, Jimmy Rowser (b); Jimmy Crawford, Jo Jones (d).* 2–5/62.

Recording for Epic, Jacquet called together the players who had stood him in good stead since the mid-1940s, and created perhaps the best music of his career. It was a period not unmarked by tragedy, because the session of 5 February 1962 was the last before the death of Leo Parker, who'd been a kingpin of the group. From the opening 'Frantic Fanny', which isn't quite as wild and woolly as the title suggests, to the superb 'Stella By Starlight', which is played by saxophone and rhythm, Jacquet doesn't put a foot wrong. A large-scale arrangement by Ernie Wilkins of 'Satin Doll' puts the saxophonist in the midst of the fuller, brassier sound he had grown to distrust a little. It's very close to the original Ellington version, but both Jacquet and Eldridge rework significant elements of it. Throughout these sessions, Thompson is masterful, playing deadly choruses and fills, and always swooping in right underneath the soloist, the best possible accompanist. One intriguing element of the work for Epic is Jacquet's return to the alto saxophone. He roars through an upbeat 'Indiana' on the smaller horn and returns to it for an exquisite arrangement of Debussy's 'Reverie', which draws out his romantic strain again.

***** Bottoms Up**

Original Jazz Classics OJC 417 *Jacquet; Barry Harris (p); Ben Tucker (b); Alan Dawson (d).* 68.

***** The King!**

Original Jazz Classics OJC 849 *Jacquet; Joe Newman, Ernie Royal (t); Milt Buckner (org); Billy Butler (g); Al Lucas (b); Jo Jones (d); Montego Joe (perc).* 68–69.

***** The Soul Explosion**

Original Jazz Classics OJC 674 *Jacquet; Russell Jacquet, Joe Newman, Ernie Royal (t); Matthew Gee (tb); Frank Foster (ts); Cecil Payne (bs); Milt Buckner (org); Wally Richardson (g); Al Lucas (b); Al Foster (d).* 3/69.

***** The Blues, That's Me!**

Original Jazz Classics OJC 614 *Jacquet; Wynton Kelly (p); Tiny Grimes (g); Buster Williams (b); Oliver Jackson (d).* 9/69.

Jacquet seldom played the blues better than on these good sets, which were originally released on Prestige. As so often on that label, a period of concentrated activity with sympathetic colleagues gave a slightly directionless career a significant boost. Not much to be said about the music, except that the large-group material on *The Soul Explosion* is more sophisticated than might be supposed. Fine versions of 'Still King' and 'Round About Midnight' on *The Blues, That's Me!*, both of which demonstrate, in markedly different ways, the delicacy of Jacquet's touch. *The King!* is a bit of a rag-bag, but it has some strong work from Newman and Royal and the doubled-up CD bonuses, extra takes of 'A Haunting Melody' and 'Blue And Sentimental', are well worth having.

***** The Comeback**

Black Lion BLCD 760160 *Jacquet; Milt Buckner (org); Tony Crombie (d).* 4/71.

Of all the organists Jacquet worked with, it was Buckner with whom he worked up the closest rapport. Their exchanges on the two Ellington tunes that form the bulk of this Ronnie Scott's session from 1971 (not a comeback at all – that's the title of one of the pieces) are full of the sort of understanding that lifts this above the immediately apparent roar-and-rave. Recorded in the presence of Stan Getz, though not of Ella Fitzgerald, as Jacquet claims (the scat vocal on 'I Wanna Blow' is his own), it reflects little of Getz's legendary finesse, but it's undoubtedly energetic and entertaining stuff, and one shouldn't be too condescending about its more unsophisticated elements.

***** Birthday Party**

Groove Note 1003 *Jacquet; Joe Newman (t); Art Farmer (flhn); Jimmy Smith (p); James Moody (ts, f); Gerry Mulligan (bs); Kenny Burrell (g); Jack Six (b); Roy Haynes (d).* 72.

Given a little simple arithmetic, the title becomes self-explanatory: an all-star cast get together to celebrate the saxophonist's fiftieth in style. To borrow a title from trumpeter Joe Newman, it was a grand night for swingin', but as ever Jacquet marshals the band with all the discipline and rigour that characterized his large ensembles. He is out on his own for 'Polka Dots And Moonbeams' and his solo on 'The "Sandpiper" Theme' is all schmaltz, with a strong blues pulse beating through it. The other soloists are well presented, too. Moody has his moment on flute with 'Ebb Tide' and elsewhere complements the leader's gruffer excursions with his own strangely feminine tonality. Burrell is outstanding from start to finish and Newman shines. There must surely be more material from this great event still awaiting release. What's on offer is wonderful but rather scant for the money.

Jean-Marc Jafet

BASS, PERCUSSION

French bassist-composer looking for new ideas with post-bop ensembles.

*** Agora

JMS 18639 *Jafet; Stéphane Belmondo (t); Denis Leloup (tb); Eric Seva (ss); Jean-Yves Candela (p, syn); Sylvain Luc (g); Marc Berthoumieux (acc, syn); Thierry Eliez (syn); Thierry Arpino, André Ceccarelli (d); François Constantin, François Laizeau (perc).* 7/93–9/94.

Jean-Marie Salhani's JMS label has been an important sponsor of new talent in France, giving players enough time and resources to develop ideas that might not otherwise see the light of day. Jafet is very much in the Henri Texier mould and there might be some doubt about the originality of some of his compositional ideas. However, his real skill, and Salhani's, is in collaging a wide range of sounds (and the synths expand the palette considerably) to create new entities that seem to be much larger than the basic band. Belmondo and Leloup are both gifted players, with an accent on sonority over straight harmonic blowing, and Jafet's devotion to Miles Davis and Jaco Pastorius opens up areas of contemporary non-jazz usage.

Ahmad Jamal (born 1930)

PIANO

Originally Fritz Jones of Pittsburgh, Jamal may well have adopted a more exotic name, but stylistically he went in the opposite direction, carving out a spare, spacious piano style, characterized by a subtle use of silence and much admired by Miles Davis. His recordings from the Pershing Lounge are among the commercially most successful in modern jazz, despite which he remains something of a coterie enthusiasm.

*** Ahmad's Blues

Chess 051803-2 *Jamal; Israel Crosby (b); Vernell Fournier (d).* 9/58.

But for his enormous influence on Miles, Ahmad Jamal might by now have fallen into the pit dug for him by tin-eared critics, dismissed as an inventive cocktail pianist or (still more invidiously) as an entertainer rather than an artist. As Brian Priestley has pointed out, pianists who achieve a modicum of commercial success tend to move closer to the entertainment mainstream than any other musicians, except possibly singers, who are often thought to belong there anyway. For many years, Jamal gave much of his attention to running a chi-chi club, the Alhambra, rather than to playing.

He is certainly not a studio-friendly pianist and almost always sounds better caught live. The former Fritz Jones had launched his career seven years earlier as part of The Three Strings and had caught the ear of the intuitive John Hammond with the subtlety and sophistication of his work. His technique has scarcely changed over the years and remains closer to Errol Garner than to anyone else, concentrating on fragile textures and calligraphic melodic statements, rather than the propulsive logic of bebop piano. *Ahmad's Blues* is enjoyable unless one is looking for starburst virtuosity and a hint of romantic agony.

**** Cross Country Tour: 1958–1961

Chess GRP 18132 2CD *Jamal; Israel Crosby (b); Vernel Fournier (d).* 1/58–6/61.

The contents of four Argo LPs on a double-CD set, filling out the picture of this hugely successful trio considerably. Volume One covers material from the Pershing in Chicago in January and September 1958, previously issued as *Ahmad Jamal At The Pershing* and *Jamal At The Pershing: Volume 2*. Other material comes from the Spotlite in Washington, DC (*Portfolio*), his own Alhambra back in Chicago (*All Of Me*) and at the Black Hawk in San Francisco (and so titled), though here the exact date of recording is unclear and, *pace* the subtitle of the set, might be 1962.

The outstanding performance on Volume One, improbably, is 'Music! Music! Music!', to which Jamal gives the kind of spin that intrigued Miles Davis and influenced him in his approach to popular material. It is both faithful and deeply subversive. He does the same with 'Cherokee' and the traditional 'Billy Boy' on Volume Two. The remaining cuts are more conventionally provenanced, show-tunes in the main but with the usual deep understanding of melody and harmony in active interplay. Performances are rarely very long, often sticking to the dimensions of the original song; but here and there, as on 'Broadway' at the Alhambra, Jamal will cut loose and venture out into uncharted territory. It's perhaps his most searching performance of the period and, oddly, the least idiomatic, or at least the only one that couldn't immediately be identified as his work.

As ever, Crosby and Fournier are utterly sympathetic and responsive, bringing real feeling to the songs and sticking tight to the leader at every turn, so that the group really does function as a three-in-one rather than a loose coalition.

***(*) The Awakening

Impulse IMP 12262 *Jamal; Jamil Nasser (b); Frank Gant (d).* 2/70.

The reappearance of this record more or less rounds out the picture of Jamal as a polished stylist, highly pianistic but disinclined to emote. What is once again clear, though, is how integrated and even-handed a Jamal group is; Nasser and Gant are no mere accompanists, but significant performers in their own right, and the drummer brings a depth of focus to the music, a touch of darkness and danger even to a joyous theme like 'Dolphin Dance'. Apart from the title-track, with its dramatic four-note cell, and the more abstract 'Patterns', everything is by other hands. Oliver Nelson's 'Stolen Moments' is the outstanding item.

*** Live 1981

Black Label 8031 *Jamal (p solo).* 81.

*****(*) Live In Concert**

Black Label 8006 *Jamal; Gary Burton (vib); Sabu Adeyola (b); Payton Crossley (d).* 1/81.

*****(*) Live At The Montreal Jazz Festival**

Atlantic 81699 2 *Jamal; James Cammack (b); Herlin Riley (d).* 85.

***** Crystal**

Atlantic 81793 2 *Jamal; James Cammack (b); David Bowler (d); Willie White (perc).* 87.

The 1981 solo session is an obscure item in the Jamal discography, rescued from the Chiaruscuro catalogue. It and the live disc with Burton nevertheless fill in an otherwise barren period in the discography, as does the smoother and more reflective Atlantic studio session, which is a useful time-capsule of the pianist's compositional ideas of the time. 'Perugia', 'Swahililand' and the more obviously formal 'Arabesque' are cleverly constructed, if a little dry. The Montreal tracks are looser and more extended and are distinguished by a fine closing section which sequences 'Round Midnight' along with Wayne Shorter's 'Footprints' and Jack DeJohnette's 'Ebony', which is meat and drink to Jamal, combining rhythmic intensity at a medium count with a lot of harmonic detail.

The live set with Burton is a superficially unlikely combination that works rather well. Gary hijacks the set with a solo version of Jobim's classic 'No More Blues', which is slightly discomfiting for the leader, but the interplay between vibes and piano works very well on 'The Night Has A Thousand Eyes' and Duke's 'African Flower'. As to the other Black Label set, real enthusiasts will certainly want to track it down and will be unconcerned by its technical shortcomings.

****** Chicago Revisited**

Telarc CD 83327 *Jamal; John Heard (b); Yoron Israel (d).* 11/92.

***** The Essence: Part 1**

Birdology 529 327 *Jamal; George Coleman, James Cammack, Jamil Nasser (b); Idris Muhammad (d); Manolo Badrena (perc).* 94–95.

The 1990s saw a startling renaissance. Jazz piano became fashionable again, and Jamal started to play with something like the poise and brilliance of the 1950s. *Chicago Revisited* could hardly be bettered as an example of contemporary jazz piano. The elegance of his line on 'All The Things You Are', with which the set opens, is such that it could be balanced on a pin. Clifford Brown's 'Daahoud' recalls a whole era in just a few bars. The remainder of the set is typically eclectic, tunes by Irving Ashby, Harold Adamson and Jimmy McHugh, Nick Brodszky and Sammy Cahn, and John Handy, closing with a 'Lullaby Of Birdland' that is concentrated songfulness.

These days, he has the wise, thoughtful look of an African parliamentarian, and a measured, slightly unrevealing delivery, well represented on *The Essence*. It runs counter to the prevailing expectation that Jamal can still easily be dismissed as shallow and clinical, unemotional and even unexpressive. Nonsense; there are more things to be expressed than anguish and despair, or roaring delight. Jamal has chosen to refract a misunderstood band of the jazz spectrum, and the music would be poorer without him.

***** I Remember Duke, Hoagy & Strayhorn**

Telarc 83339 *Jamal; Ephraim Wolfolk (b); Arti Dixson (d).* 6/94.

A slow and stately performance, though Jamal often experiments in double-time improvisations over very stately rhythm tracks. The mood is almost bizarrely even and elegiac. This works less well, perversely, on material like 'Prelude To A Kiss', which sounds enervated rather than swooningly passionate, than on 'Skylark' and 'I Got It Bad ...' The Carmichael material is the scantest, though 'I Remember Hoagy', derived from the changes to 'Stardust', is a delightful conceit and a perfect showcase for Jamal's cool and playful approach. We know little about Wolfolk or Dixson, but they sound like competent and uncomplicatedly expressive players; and the trio sound, with Jamal pitched well to the forefront, is nicely recorded.

*****(*) Nature: The Essence, Part 3**

Atlantic 83115 *Jamal; Stanley Turrentine (ts); James Cammack (b); Idris Muhammad (d); Othello Molineaux (perc).* 6/98.

For us the best of the *Essence* sequence, this shifts between dense, rhetorical piano solos – 'Chaperon', 'And We Were Lovers' – and quartet tracks like 'Devil's In My Den', which features a walk-on from the rejuvenated Stanley Turrentine. There is also an intriguing role for the steel drum player, Othello Molineaux. The rhythm section is well up to form and Cammack, as the junior partner, seems to have come on in leaps and bounds. Strongly recommended.

Khan Jamal (born 1946)

VIBRAPHONE, MARIMBA

Began playing vibes in the middle '60s and since then his various associations – with Byard Lancaster, Sunny Murray, Charles Tyler and others – suggest a restless but accommodating spirit.

*****(*) Dark Warrior**

Steeplechase SCCD 31196 *Jamal; Charles Tyler (as, bs); Johnny Dyani (b); Leroy Lowe (d).* 9/84.

***** Three**

Steeplechase SCCD 31201 *Jamal; Pierre Dørge (g); Johnny Dyani (d).* 10/84.

***** The Traveller**

Steeplechase SCCD 31217 *Jamal; Johnny Dyani (b); Leroy Lowe (d).* 10/85.

The dedication to Cal Tjader on *Three* suggests one (outwardly unlikely) source for Jamal's firmly rhythmic but freely pulsed vibraphone style. Almost all of his albums, which have now returned to circulation on CD, have a dark freedom and surge which is curiously Europeanized, the kind of thing one hears when passing an African tea-house or café in the Paris Zone, in Hamburg or Copenhagen. The partnership with Dyani was an immensely fruitful one, and on *Dark Warrior* the additional presence of Tyler's sour-sweet alto and bossy baritone delivers some fascinating music, which isn't quite matched on the two later Steeplechases. There is just a hint of Tjader's pattering approach, and vibes fans may hear echoes of just about everyone from Bobby Hutcherson to Steeplechase stablemate Walt Dickerson, to Karl Berger, and it may be that the lack of a settled identity and idiolect is the main problem with Jamal's work. Though his approach to a standard, like the usually saxophonic 'Body And Soul' on *The Traveller*, is reminiscent of Hutcherson's free counterpoint, in terms of diction it is even less horn-like, closer to Dickerson's abstract theme formulations.

*****(*) Percussion And Strings**
CIMP 143 *Jamal; Dylan Taylor (clo); Ed Crockett (b); Craig McIver (d, mar); Pete Vinson (d, perc).* 3/97.

This is probably the sound Jamal has heard in his head for years but only now been able to evoke in real time, when he found a set-up willing to give him his head. The combination of instruments is very powerful, with strings acting as rhythmic accompaniment to the percussion players. Vinson is involved on only a couple of tracks, playing cowbell on 'Return From Exile' and switching to drums for 'Round About Midnight', allowing Craig McIver to switch to marimba. Monk and Johnny Dyani are the presiding presences, with 'Blue Monk' and 'Witch Doctor's Son' the outstanding tracks. The sound, as always from CIMP, is raw and unvarnished, but very faithful to the performances.

Harry James (1916–83)

TRUMPET

Born into a family of musicians who played in a circus band, James joined Ben Pollack in 1935 and quickly became a hot property, switching to Benny Goodman as star soloist in 1937, then leading his own band from 1939, with Sinatra as vocalist. His taste for show-off virtuosity brought him million-selling records but the derision of many jazz followers. He moved into small-group work as the swing era declined and remained popular on the West Coast and in Las Vegas, having sold more records than most other jazz musicians. Eventually he moved back into big-band work.

*****(*) Harry James 1937–1939**
Classics 903 *James; Jack Palmer (t, v); Tommy Gonsoulin, Claude Bowen, Buck Clayton (t); Eddie Durham, Vernon Brown, Russell Brown, Truett Jones (tb); Earl Warren, Dave Matthews, Claude Lakey (as); Jack Washington (as, bs); Herschel Evans, Arthur Rollini, Drew Page, Bill Luther (ts); Harry Carney (bs); Jess Stacy, Pete Johnson, Albert Ammons, Jack Gardner (p); Bryan Kent (g); Walter Page, Thurman Teague, Johnny Williams (b); Jo Jones, Dave Tough, Eddie Dougherty, Ralph Hawkins (d); Helen Humes, Bernice Byers (v).* 12/37–3/39.

***** Harry James 1939**
Classics 936 *James; Jack Schaeffer, Tommy Gonsoulin, Claude Bowen, Jack Palmer (t); Russell Brown, Truett Jones (tb); Dave Matthews, Claude Lakey (as); Drew Page, Al Sears, Bill Luther (ts); Jack Gardner (p); Bryan Kent (g); Thurman Teague (b); Ralph Hawkins (d); Frank Sinatra, Fran Haines, Bernice Byers (v).* 4–10/39.

***** Harry James 1939–1940**
Classics 970 *As above, except add Dalton Rizzotto (tb), Mickey Scrima (d), Dick Haymes (v); omit Gonsoulin, Palmer, Sears, Hawkins, Byers.* 11/39–4/40.

****(*) Harry James 1940–1941**
Classics 1014 *James; Claude Bowen, Nick Buono, Jack Palmer, Al Stearns (t); Truett Jones, Dalton Rizzotto, Bruce Squires, Hoyt Bohannon, Harry Rodgers (tb); Dave Matthews, Claude Lakey, Johnny Mezey (as); Vido Musso (ts); Chuck Gentry (bs); Jack Gardner, Al Lerner (p); Ben Heller (g); Thurman Teague (b); Mickey Scrima (d); Fran Haines, Dick Haymes (v).* 5/40–1/41.

***** Harry James 1941**
Classics 1052 *Similar to above, except add Sam Rosenblum, Stan Stanchfield, William Schumann, George Koch (vn).* 1–4/41.

****(*) Harry James 1941 Vol. 2**
Classics 1092 *James; Claude Bowen, Al Stearns (t); Dalton Rizzotto, Hoyt Bohannon, Harry Rodgers (tb); Claude Lakey, Sam Marozwitz (as); Vido Musso, Johnny Fresco (ts); Chuck Gentry, Clint Davis (bs); Al Lerner (p); Sam Rosenblum, Glenn Herzer, Leo Zorn, Alex Pevsner, Al Friede, Paul Lowenkron, Lou Horvarth, Bill Spears (vn); Ben Heller (g); Thurman Teague (b); Mickey Scrima (d); Helen Ward, Dick Haymes, Lynn Richards (v).* 5–8/41.

***** Harry James And His Orchestra Featuring Frank Sinatra**
Columbia CK 66377-2 *James; Jack Schaeffer, Claude Bowen, Tom Gonsoulin, Jack Palmer, Claude Lakey (t); Russell Brown, Truett Jones, Dalton Rizzotto, Bruce Squires (tb); Dave Matthews, Claude Lakey, Bill Luther, Drew Page (saxes); Jack Gardner (p); Brian Kent (g); Thurman Teague (b); Ralph Hawkins, Mickey Scrima (d); Frank Sinatra (v).* 7–10/39.

James's early period is now well represented on CD (at the time of our first edition he had almost nothing available in the medium) and there is plenty for admirers to choose from. The Classics discs start him off with three terrific sessions, two in which he fronts a small group drawn from the Basie band, one where he repeats the trick using Goodman sidemen (plus Harry Carney!). Unabashed by the heavy company, James often blows the roof off. Four tracks with Albert Ammons and Pete Johnson spotlight his tersest, hottest playing before the sessions with his proper big band close the disc, opening on his theme-tune, 'Ciribiribin', which exemplifies what James was about: no better trumpet technician, a great capacity to swing, but with a penchant for schmaltz mixed with bravado which has been his critical undoing. Classics 936 follows the band through six sessions in six months. Sinatra arrives for eight vocals and, though the band sound quite impressive on the likes of 'King Porter Stomp', James is the only soloist of any consequence and the arrangements are workmanlike. One is reminded of the Bunny Berigan big band, except that James has all of Berigan's technique and little of his judgement. The remastering on both discs is all right, if a little grey. *Featuring Frank Sinatra* is a good set of the young crooner's vocals with James and, though jazz followers will be disappointed at the low temperature, it remains a classy edition of smooth playing and singing. Transfers are mostly good, though one or two masters sound inexplicably rough.

Classics have continued their sequence, but those searching for hot music will be disappointed by these discs. Vocals by Sinatra and subsequently Haymes tend to dominate the band's output (James was reported as saying that he saw singers as 'a necessary evil', but he certainly wasn't shy about featuring them) and Classics 970 introduces such infamous showpiece hits as

'Ciribiribin', 'Concerto For Trumpet' and 'Carnival Of Venice', the sort of material which ruined James's reputation with many jazz followers. With hindsight, these are actually entertaining enough, but it's disappointing that the leader didn't see fit to balance such music out with some decent flag-wavers that could show off the chops of the band. Classics 1014 starts with 'Flight Of The Bumble Bee' and, unless one enjoys the Haymes features, pickings here are pretty slim. Classics 1052 at least has the likes of 'Duke's Mixture' and 'Jeffries' Blues', but the addition of a violin section allowed little but extra schmaltz and James recut new versions of 'Carnival Of Venice' and 'Trumpet Rhapsody'. Classics 1092 again has little to offer beyond the vocal features. Transfers are all right, but they're mysteriously inconsistent, on the last volume in particular.

*** James With Haymes – 1941

Circle CCD-5 *James; Claude Bowen, Al Stearns (t); Hoyt Bohannon, Dalton Rizzotto, Harry Rogers (tb); Claude Lakey, Vido Musso, Sam Marowitz, Chuck Gentry (saxes); Al Lerner (p); Ben Heller (g); Thurman Teague (b); Mickey Scrima (d); Dick Haymes (v); strings.* 41.

*** Jump Sauce

Vipers Nest VNG-201 *James; Jimmy Campbell, Nick Buono, Vincent Badale, Al Cuozzo (t); Murray McEachern, Don Boyd, Harry Rogers, Ray Heath (tb); Philip Palmer (frhn); Johnny McAfee, Sam Marowitz, Claude Lakey, Corky Corcoran, Hugo Lowenstein, King Guion, Sam Sachelle (saxes); Al Lerner (p); Ben Heller (g); Thurman Teague (b); Mickey Scrima (d); Helen Forrest, Buddy Moreno (v); strings.* 6–12/43.

**(*) Spotlight Bands Broadcast 1946

Jazz Hour JH-1046 *Personnel unlisted, but includes Willie Smith (as), Helen Forrest (v).* 43–46.

*** Feet Draggin' Blues

Hep CD 62 *James; Jimmy Campbell, Al Ramsey, Uan Rasey, Red Berken, Jim Troutman, Jimmy Grimes, Lenny Corris, Hal Moe, Darl Berken, Zeke Zarchy, Paul Geil, Mannie Klein, Pinky Savitt, Nick Buono, Gene Komer, Ralph Osborn (t); Vic Hamann, Charlie Preble, Ray Heath, Dalton Rizzotto, Ed Kusby, Ziggy Elmer (tb); Juan Tizol (vtb); Willie Smith (cl, as, v); Eddie Rosa (cl, as); Claude Lakey, Les Robinson (as); Polly Polifroni (cl, ts); Corky Corcoran, Clint Davis, Herbie Haymer, Babe Russin, Sam Sachelle (ts); Stuart Bruner, Bob Poland (bs); Arnold Ross, Stan Wrightsmann, Bruce MacDonald (p); Allan Reuss, Hayden Causey, Tiny Timbrell (g); Ed Mihelich, Artie Bernstein (b); Carl Maus, Nick Fatool, Buddy Combine, Lou Fromm (d); Ginnie Powell (v); strings.* 11/44–11/47.

*** There They Go

Fresh Sound FSRCD 2014 *James; Nick Buono, Pinky Savitt, Ralph Osbourne, Gene Komer, Everett Macdonald, Neal Hefti (t); Juan Tizol, Ziggy Elmer, Charlie Preble, Dave Robbins (tb); Eddie Rosa, Al Pellegrini, Willie Smith, Bob Walters (c, as); Jimmy Cook, Sam Sachelle, Corky Corcoran (ts); Bob Poland (bs); Bruce McDonald (p); Tiny Timbrell (g); Joe Mondragon (b); Don Lamond, Frank Bode, Louie Bellson (d).* 48.

*** Big John Special '49

Hep CD 24 *Similar to above, except add Phil Cook (t), Tommy Greco (tb), Musky Ruffo (as), Bobby Bain (g), Norman Seelig (b).* 6/49–11/50.

***(*) Bandstand Memories 1938–1948

Hindsight HBCD503 3CD *As all discs above, probably with numerous others!* 38–48.

The easiest way to get a feel for James's better music at present is to listen to some of these numerous aircheck recordings. James seemed to remain popular on radio throughout the 1940s, and plenty of material has survived in pro-am recordings. The cleanest of the lot is certainly the *Jump Sauce* disc of two 1943 broadcasts, in very clear sound from acetates. Though there were no real stars in the band at this point other than James himself, they play with a crisp and surprisingly limber swing which – on the occasional interesting chart, like 'The Gravy Train' – musters a fair attack. The strings weren't used with anything like the imagination that Artie Shaw employed, but they still create some impressive effects, especially on a fine transformation of 'Chelsea Bridge'.

The disc with Dick Haymes luxuriates in the singer's impeccable vocals – extraordinarily deep and resonant for a man of 21. Not much jazz here, but a beguiling disc. The 1946 Spotlight Bands disc is rougher and, though the band take a good romp through 'King Porter Stomp' and generally give the impression that they're waking up rather more often, the sound tells against it – even more so on six pretty horrible-sounding transcriptions from 1943, here as a dubious bonus. *There They Go* is a better bet. James seemed to get more rather than less adventurous as the big-band era wore down, and there are some fine charts here from Neal Hefti in particular. The programme is rather exhaustingly fast and sometimes it seems the other soloists have caught James's showstopping infection to their detriment, but the music's exciting. Quite clean sound from airshot sources.

First choice must go to the handsomely boxed, three-disc set on Hindsight. This covers ten years of material and is as good a summary of James as we're likely to get for now. The first disc, with the earliest material, has many rough spots, but the next two range from good to excellent, and the third in particular is a strong manifesto for the band. James himself remained the main soloist, his style an idiosyncratic blend of schmaltz, practised routine and surprising twists. Some part of the young firebrand who started with Goodman remains, but the broad tone and sometimes broader taste of his later work is in there too.

It has some stiff competition now from the two Hep discs which are in excellent sound and which between them cover most of James's stylings from 1944 onwards. *Big John Special* duplicates much of what is on *There They Go*, but this is a superior edition. Track for track, there is nothing to get really excited about on any of these discs: James's modernism was always going to be cautious, and he valued precision as much as heat in his players. But they will confound listeners who expect the dreary routines of his hit records.

***(*) Trumpet Blues

Capitol 521224-2 *James; full personnel unlisted, but soloists include Willie Smith (as), Corky Corcoran (ts), Jack Perciful (p), Buddy Rich (d), Helen Forrest (v).* 7/. 55–7/58.

A compilation from the Capitol originals, *Harry James In Hi-Fi* and *More Harry James In Hi-Fi*, part of the label's initiative in asking swing-era bandleaders to redo their hits for LP. The warmest pieces have been chosen and they make a good fist of re-creating James's work, with a few nods to his more contemporary direction, the new Ernie Wilkins charts in particular. The Capitol engineers got a very grand sound out of the sessions and the sections play with fine panache.

*****(*) Jazz Masters 55: Harry James**

Verve 529902-2 *James; John Audino, Ollie Mitchell, Nick Buono, Bob Rolfe, Rob Turk, Larry Maguire, Vince Guertin, Jack Bohannon, Dick Cathcart, Sam Conte, Mike Conn, Bill Mattison, Fred Koyen (t); Ray Sims, Bob Edmondson, Ernie Tack, Vince Diaz, Joe Hambrick, Dick Leith, Joe Cadena, Dick McQuary (tb); Matty Matlock (cl); Willie Smith, Herb Lorden, Pa Cahrttrand, Joe Riggs, Larry Stoffel (as); Corky Corcoran, Sam Firmature, Bob Poland, Jay Corre, Modesto Brisenio, Dave Madden (ts); Ernie Small, Bob Achilles (bs); Jack Perciful (p); Dave Koonse, Terry Rosen, Guy Scalise, Dempsey Wright (g); Joe Comfort, Russ Phillips, Red Kelly (b); Charli Persip, Jackie Mills, Buddy Rich, Tony DeNicola, Jake Hanna (d).* 59–3/64.

****(*) 1964 Live! Holiday Ballroom, Chicago**

Jazz Hour JH-1001 *James; Buddy Rich (d); rest unlisted.* 64.

**** The Golden Trumpet Of Harry James**

London 820178-2 *James; rest unknown.* 68.

The Verve *Jazz Masters* compilation of some of the best of James's MGM tracks will be a revelation to any who thought the bandleader a swing-era relic. This was some of the best music of his career: excellent charts by Thad Jones, Ralph Burns (including two previously unheard ones) and Ernie Wilkins; an impeccable band enjoying a catholic choice of material, from 'Walkin'' to 'Cornet Chop Suey'; and James himself still without peer as a trumpet executant. His solos on 'I Surrender Dear' would be enough to defeat most rivals, and his delivery is tempered by a certain thoughtfulness.

The 1964 show was obviously a happy occasion, with the band playing with real fire on some excellent charts and Rich firing everyone up from the drums. But the sound is very trebly, with a lot of top end that lends a shrillness to everything from the hi-hat downwards. Tune that out and anyone will enjoy.

The Golden Trumpet is pure Las Vegas. James reprises some of his old hits in front of a suitably faceless orchestra.

Jon Jang

PIANO

Originally Jang Jian Liang, Jang is a young Chinese-American who was first recognized when a member of Fred Ho's Afro-Asian Ensemble. He took up piano rather late and still has a fairly limited range as an instrumentalist – but in any case his main strength lies elsewhere, in composition and cultural activism. In 1987 he co-founded AsianImprov Records, devoted to what might realistically be called frontier music

*****(*) Self Defense!**

Soul Note 121203 *Jang; John Worley Jr (t, flhn); Jeff Cressman (tb, perc); Melecio Magdaluyo (as, ss, f, perc); Jim Norton (bcl, ss, f, dizi); Mark Izu (b, sheng); Anthony Brown (d, perc); Susan Hayase, James Frank Holder (perc).* 6/91.

*****(*) Tiananmen!**

Soul Note 121223 *Jang; Liu Qi-Chao (suona, erhu, sheng, v); Zhang Yan (guzheng); John Worley Jr (t, flhn); Jeff Cressman (tb); James Newton (f); Melecio Magdaluyo (as, ss, f); Francis Wong (ts, f); Jim Norton (cl, bcl, af); Mark Izu (b); Anthony Brown (perc).* 2/93.

It was widely assumed that the title of Jang's Arkestra was a reference to Sun Ra's intergalactic academy of musicians. In fact, it relates to the Pan African People's Arkestra, led by radical Californian composer, Horace Tapscott. Like Tapscott, Jang is an activist. The pieces on *Self Defense!* relate to issues such as anti-Japanese violence in America, the demand for reparations for Japanese-Americans interned during the war, Jesse Jackson's pan-ethnic Rainbow Coalition. Even 'A Night In Tunisia' has a political resonance; Dizzy Gillespie was once put forward as a write-in candidate for the presidency. Jang gives it a huge programme that links it to 'The Butterfly Lovers Song' and Jang's own 'Never Give Up!'. The original pieces may depend too heavily on exclamation marks, but 'Concerto For Jazz Ensemble And Taiko' demonstrates Jang's ability to give large-scale structures a quietly appealing directness that doesn't depend on either volume or a ready-to-wear outfit of worthy slogans. Even in live performance (and this is a recording of a festival appearance in Seattle), there is no tendency to hector. There are fewer actual references to Asian music on *Self Defense!* than on *Tiananmen!*, a magnificent suite of pieces dedicated to the activists and martyrs of the Chinese democracy movement. Jang repeats the 'Butterfly Lovers Song' and calls repeatedly on Chinese folk-tunes, but the main influences are Charles Mingus (for his integration of polemical ideas with jazz) and Duke Ellington (particularly the later 'world music' suites); 'Come Sunday, June 4, 1989' contains an explicit homage, when Ellington's tune is played in counterpoint to Jang's theme by James Newton, a long-time supporter of the Asian jazz movement.

Jang's use of Asian instruments like the *taiko* drums on 'Concerto', the *guzheng* zither, the double-reeded *suona*, the two-stringed *erhu* and harmonica-like *sheng* is never purely for local effect. Frequently, as in 'Come Sunday', he exploits them to highlight a dramatic contrast between East and West, or to effect an integration between jazz and non-Western styles and concerns. The effect is less shambolic, more carefully marshalled than Ho's collective, and ultimately more satisfying.

*****(*) Two Flowers On A Stem**

Soul Note 121253 *Jang; James Newton (f); David Murray (ts, bcl); Chen Jiebing (erhu); Santi Debriano (b, Chinese gong); Billy Hart (d).* 6/95.

At last a group that is commensurate with Jang's gifts and which allows him to probe deeper into contemporary jazz while preserving his passionate interest in synthesizing Eastern and Western styles. The presence of Murray and Newton gives the music both gravity and a wonderful lightness of spirit, and there can rarely have been such a sanguine interpretation of Mingus's 'Meditation On Integration'. Most of the material is Jang's own, a suite of pieces dedicated to family members and friends, but there is also a closing reprise of the 'Butterfly Lovers Song', which is as exquisitely beautiful as the title-piece, dedicated to his mother.

Guus Janssen

PIANO, HARPSICHORD

Dutch pianist who's investigated the spectrum of the keyboard repertoire and how it can be adapted to playing entirely free.

***** Pok**

Geestgronden 3 *Janssen; Paul Termos (as); Wim Janssen (d).* 1/88–7/89.

***** Harpsichord**

Geestgronden 7 *Janssen (hpd solo).* 90.

****(*) Klankast**

Geestgronden 9 *Janssen (p solo).* 6/87–8/91.

*****(*) Lighter**

Geestgronden 11 *Janssen; Ernst Glerum (b); Wim Janssen (d).* 11/92–4/95.

****** Zwik**

Geestgronden 19 *As above.* 3/96–9/97.

Janssen's music is funny and accomplished. *Pok*, which starts with a dedication to Sandy Nelson and moves on through nods to boogie-woogie and swing time, tends to crash around various points, suggesting free jazz but always tied to a quite strict, formal aesthetic. The pianist's playing incorporates many styles, and Wim Janssen's drums are similarly diverse, but Termos's rather spindly alto parts could use an ounce more determination. The recording is rather distant. *Harpsichord* is a possibly unique example of solo free music on a keyboard that scarcely ever enters into the field. As with the previous disc, Janssen's taste runs to odd, wide-ranging ideas within a distinct formal grasp, and there are perhaps unsurprising echoes of the baroque repertory within an otherwise unpredictable record.

Klankast does much the same for the piano, though in a piece like 'Hi-Hat' Janssen seems to be back to guying the swing tradition. Some of the tunes run out of steam before they're done, and this set is perhaps not the one to try first. *Lighter*, on the other hand, is consistently good. Though pieced together from sessions over a three-year period, this is a more thoroughgoing exploration of jazz and free playing and how the two might work together. Janssen's use of silences, long form and satire makes the most of these sketched (not sketchy) frameworks and, when they get to a version of 'Lennie's Pennies', the connection between this kind of free playing and the Tristano-ite school suddenly seems clear. Glerum and the other Janssen add a merry accompaniment.

This trio is surely his best set-up, because *Zwik* is a tremendous continuation. Janssen does nothing less than reinvent the piano-trio record with this one. The first piece, 'I Mean', sounds like Thelonious Monk having a go at 'The Song Is You' and not getting beyond the first few bars. After that, the pianist lights on bebop, swing, various classical traditions and whatever else he can find to make the music new. Every one of the 12 pieces is quite different from every other one – listen to 'Pollux' and follow that with 'Azuur' and you'll wonder if it's the same group playing. Glerum and Wim Janssen seem completely in tune with the pianist's cliff-hanger choices, so nothing sounds wayward or merely cute. Brilliant.

Lars Jansson (born 1951)

PIANO, KEYBOARDS

A frequent visitor to the studios from the late '70s onwards, Jansson is a charter member of the contemporary Swedish movement, though currently he spends much of his time teaching.

*****(*) Trio 84 / The Eternal Now**

Dragon DRCD 301 *Jansson; Lars Danielsson (b, clo); Anders Jormin (b); Anders Kjellberg (d).* 84–87.

***** A Window Towards Being**

Imogena IGCD 019 *Jansson; Brynjar Hoff (ob); Lars Danielsson (b); Anders Kjellberg (d).* 2/91.

***** Invisible Friends**

Imogena IGCD 055 *As above, except omit Hoff.* 1/95.

Jansson is an excellent post-bop pianist whose affection for Bill Evans's manner is wedded to an attractive way with melody in his writing: it means that his music comes out with a little more brightness than that of the typical Evans disciple. The fine *Trio 84* on Dragon is now back in print, coupled with the subsequent *The Eternal Now* in an excellent package. Far from the willowy impressionism one might expect, this was a vital and attacking trio (Danielsson subs for Jormin on the second set), lighting up all the instinctive lyricism of the leader by playing with unaffected *brio* on the likes of 'Långtans Berg' and 'Yanina'. 'To Bill Evans' is a muscular workout, not a weepy requiem, with Jansson carrying the improvisation on a Moog synthesizer. At the same time, Jansson isn't afraid to darken the harmonic substance of pieces such as 'At Once Always' and 'After The Storm'.

A Window Towards Being picks up where the earlier set left off. Hoff is used for instrumental colour on three atypically lightweight tracks; but the main interest is in the piano improvisations on Jansson's own originals. *Invisible Friends* is four years on and in the same impeccable vein. Here and there Jansson drifts off a little, but his playing partners pilot a firm rhythmic course that admits of no rambling. The portentousness of some of the titles seems to be nicely deflated by the penultimate one: 'I Have Nothing To Say And I Am Saying It'.

Lena Jansson

VOCAL

Swedish vocalist tackling swing repertory.

***** Lena Jansson Nils Lindberg Stockholm Big Band**

Bluebell ABCD 3005 *Jansson; Johnny Olsson, Stefan Johansson, Per-Olof Hjort, Stefan Gustavsson, Kina Sellergren, Markku Johansson, Peter Bjork, Martin Lundberg, Magnus Jedermalm, Asa Bystrom (t); Andreas Carpvik, Mikael Anderfjard, Mats Lundberg, Sven Lob, Anders Evaldsson, Hans Backman, Stefan Hjelmberg (tb); Henrik Blome, Patrik Westin, Hector Bingert, Annica Carlsson, Jan Levander (as); Lennart Jonsson, Joakim Milder, Michael Trense, Patrik Edgren (ts); Erik Nilsson, Hans*

Olofsson (bs); Nils Lindberg (p); Joakim Jennefors, ,Hans Larsson (b); Martin Erikson, Birger Torelli (d). 4/83–6/86.

***** That Certain Feeling**

Bluebell ABCD 061 *Jansson; Johan Setterlind (t); Torgny Nilsson (tb); Putte Wickman (cl); Lennart Jonsson (ts); Nils Lindberg (p); Sture Nordin, Dan Berglund (b); Rune Carlsson, Martin Lofgren (d).* 4/84–3/95.

Jansson's small-girlish voice may remind some of the young Blossom Dearie, had she been raised in Sweden. She sings in English throughout with no attempt to hide her accent, and in these comfortable settings she can be surprisingly effective on the right song: 'Pay Some Attention To Me' on the second disc and a plain, wistful 'Lost In The Stars' on the first. The big-band recordings are lifted from two Bluebell albums, with Lindberg's arrangements finding a few subtleties in the harmonies. There is a fine treatment of a song Lindberg wrote with Red Mitchell, 'As You Are', and a charmingly naïve version of 'Shall I Compare Thee To A Summer's Day'.

That Certain Feeling is all Gershwin, and it adds six tracks from a new session to five from what was Lena's first album. It's the same as before, only scaled down to a small group, and the sweetness of tone and gentle touch remain very likeable.

Rolf Jardemark

GUITAR

Danish guitarist moving from fusion to modal bop styles.

**** Jungle Crunch**

Imogena IGCD 027 *Jardemark; David Wilczewski (ss, ts); Jan Zirk (ky); Fredrik Bergman (b); Terje Sundby (d).* 5/91.

***** Guitarland**

Imogena IGCD 044 *Jardemark; Lars Danielsson (b); Anders Kjellberg (d).* 5/93.

Jardemark started as if meaning to take on the GRP guitarists at their own game: *Soft Landing* (Liphone LiCD 3095) was a noisy and flavourless fusion bash. *Jungle Crunch* suffers from the hangover of that approach, with Zirk's keyboards spread over everything and Jardemark and Wilczewski getting in a few interesting points in spite of it all; 'Half Spanish' survives as a pleasing theme. But *Guitarland* is down-the-line guitar, bass and drums, and all the better for it. Danielsson is the ideal man to have on hand, firming up all the lines and feeding Jardemark with good cues, and Kjellberg fits right in. The leader leaves his fuzz and effects boxes at home and gets a cool, limpid sound that suits the tones of 'Freddie Freeloader' and a few decent tunes of his own, with nimble solos on top.

Joseph Jarman (born 1937)

SAXOPHONES, OTHER REEDS, FLUTE

He grew up in Pine Bluff, Arkansas, but found himself serendipitously in Chicago at a moment when the very foundations of jazz were being rethought. He worked with Muhal Richard Abrams and made the acquaintance of Roscoe Mitchell, playing Eric Dolphy-influenced saxophone in Mitchell's jazz group. He is best known, though, for his work with the Art Ensemble Of Chicago, for which his needle-sharp tone and vivid alternation of free and melodic ideas were a key element.

****(*) Song For**

Delmark DD 410 *Jarman; Bill Brimfield (t); Fred Anderson (ts); Christopher Gaddy (p, mar); Charles Clark (b); Thurman Barker, Steve McCall (d).* 10 & 12/66.

Art Ensemble of Chicago fans are apt to regard record projects by Joseph Jarman or Roscoe Mitchell much as Rolling Stones fans might regard a new solo record by Mick Jagger or Charlie Watts: worthy of notice and support, but essentially a distraction from the main matter at hand. In the former case, at least, they're quite wrong. Whether or not the Art Ensemble members feel disinclined to record or tour together, there's no doubt that most of their interesting work since 1975 has been apart. This is particularly true of Jarman who, depending on your viewpoint, is either the quintessential voice of the AEC or else its squarest peg. The reissued *Song For* is relatively standard AACM fare, intercut with neo-Dada recitations and characterized by a lack of formal shape. The supporting performers, with the exception of the two drummers, are not always up to scratch, though Clark produces some wonderfully sonorous bass on 'Adam's Rib', which certainly benefits considerably from CD transfer. The long tracks – 'Non-Cognitive Aspects Of The City', 'Song For' and a second and longer unissued take of Fred Anderson's 'Little Fox Run' with its skittering marimba patterns – pall slightly on repeated hearings. Of great documentary and historical significance, it's unlikely to effect any dramatic conversions.

***** Connecting Spirits**

Music & Arts CD 964 *Jarman; Marilyn Crispell (p).* 1/96.

It must be indicative of something that the liner of this fine live CD, recorded at the First Universalist Unitarian Society Meeting House in Madison, Wisconsin, should list no fewer than five discs with Crispell as leader, while it does not note a single one under Jarman's name. Though much of his career has been subsumed under the activities of the Art Ensemble, it might be thought that a player of his skills would have a reasonable catalogue of work by this stage. How much the reverse depends on diffidence, how much on indifference, remains unclear. Somewhat like Julius Hemphill, Jarman has never shown a huge ambition for recording but, unlike Hemphill, he does not have a parallel life as a composer. Most of the material here is credited to Crispell. 'Structure I' and 'Connectivity' are improvised duets, 'Dear Lord' is by Coltrane, and only 'Upper Reaches' and the closing 'Meditations On A Vow Of Compassion' actually bear the saxophonist's name. Like everything he does, it is thoughtful, passionate and somewhat enigmatic, a lateral approach to fairly basic material, and a technically modest exercise in saxophone artistry.

***** Pachinko Dream Track 10**

Music & Arts CD 1040 *Jarman; Francis Wong (ts, f, erhu, perc, v); Glenn Horiuchi (p, shamisen, erhu, perc); Elliot Humberto Kavee (d, perc).* 5/96.

Four overlong but mostly riveting live performances by a thoroughly inventive group, recorded at the annual Asian

American Jazz Festival in San Francisco. Most of the action is between Jarman and Horiuchi, and their confident synthesis of jazz and Asian tonalities is most evident on the pianist's 'Dew Drop', which just avoids self-conscious orientalism. 'Another Space' is collectively improvised and a little ragged at the edges. By contrast, Jarman's title-track has an almost classical control and discipline.

Keith Jarrett (born 1945)

PIANO, ORGAN, SOPRANO SAXOPHONE, OTHER INSTRUMENTS

It's often forgotten by those who wish to do down Keith Jarrett's jazz credentials that he was a member of the unimpeachable Messengers before he joined Charles Lloyd's crossover quartet and long before he began to experiment with long-form piano improvisation. The young Pennsylvanian was, like Chick Corea, something of a child prodigy. He learned his craft in the Boston area. Jarrett is a restless experimenter whose more extravagant flights seem to have won uncritical acclaim while his more straightforward work is overlooked. His standards trio of the 1980s and '90s has rewritten the American songbook every bit as thoroughly as Jarrett has reworked the idiom of jazz piano.

****** Life Between The Exit Signs / El Juicio**

Collectables COL CD 6254 *Jarrett; Dewey Redman (ts); Charlie Haden (b); Paul Motian (d).* 5/67, 7/71.

***** Restoration Ruin**

Collectables COL CD 6274 *Jarrett (all instruments); string quartet.* 3/68.

****(*) Somewhere Before**

Atlantic 7567 81455 *Jarrett; Charlie Haden (b); Paul Motian (d).* 8/68.

****** El Juicio (The Judgement)**

Atlantic 7567 80783-3 *Jarrett; Dewey Redman (ts); Charlie Haden (b); Paul Motian (d).* 7/71.

***** The Mourning Of A Star**

Atlantic 8122 75355-2 *Jarrett; Charlie Haden (b); Paul Motian (d).* 71.

****** Foundations: The Keith Jarrett Anthology**

Rhino R2 71593 *Jarrett; Chuck Mangione (t); Joe Farrell, Hubert Laws, Charles Lloyd (f); Frank Mitchell, Jim Pepper, Dewey Redman (ts); George Benson, Sam Brown (g); Gary Burton (vib); Ron Carter, Charlie Haden, Reggie Johnson, Cecil McBee, Steve Swallow (b); Art Blakey, Bill Goodwin, Bob Moses, Paul Motian (d); Airto Moreira (perc).* 66–75.

Having passed his half-century, Jarrett is now a senior figure, and some kind of revised perspective seems in order. Inevitably, for an artist of his range and ambition, he divides critical opinion wildly and is himself, as every great artist must be, wildly inconsistent. The sheer momentum of early success has allowed him to experiment freely, but it has also allowed an unusual and not always desirable licence to experiment in public. (Many artists might have attempted the material documented on *Spirits*, below; few would have expected to see it make the shops.)

It's tempting to suggest that the essential Jarrett is to be found in the solo performances and that these are the place to begin. He now, though, reached the position where there is more than one essential Jarrett, and it is worthwhile backtracking a little. The appearance of *Foundations* and now the re-emergence of Jarrett's original Atlantic recordings make this possible. The compilation is a remarkably modest selection, just two discs to cover the seven years from his tough New York apprenticeship to the much-underrated and very ambitious Atlantic session, *El Juicio*, with the Redman/Haden/Motian quartet. It remains one of the high points of his career. The joyous countrified swing of 'Gypsy Moth' and 'Toll Road' could hardly be more infectious, at the opposite remove to the dour atmosphere of 'El Juicio' itself, a strange, brooding tone poem, or indeed to the experimental melodism of 'Piece For Ornette'. It exists in two forms, one at nine and a quarter minutes, the other at twelve seconds! A sly nudge from Jarrett: this is all it's about, this little idea, but see what we do with it!

Collectables have been putting out a strange but appealing array of material over the last year or so. Pairing Jarrett's early *Restoration Ruin* with the Art Ensemble of Chicago's *Bap-Tizum* is a little strange, but it is good to have this early example of multi-instrumentalism back in the catalogue. The pieces are all very short, sometimes almost perfunctory, but there is no mistaking Jarrett's gifts and, as an exercise in instrumental eclecticism, it is a much more appealing and convincing performance than the later *Spirits*.

The other Collectables set brings together *El Juicio* and the fine early trio, *Life Between The Exit Signs*. Interesting to compare this unit with the later 'standards' trio. It is immediately apparent how much more straightforwardly rhythmic Jarrett sounds in 1967, but as yet how uncomfortably co-ordinated he is with the group. 'Lisbon Stomp' is a cracking opener. The two tunes called 'Love No. 1 and No. 2' are extremely individual and 'Life ...' itself has the distinctive jazz/pop/country feel one associates with Jarrett. What is as yet unformed is his ability to shape a group as if it were a single instrument compounded of different personalities, rather than a contending alliance bent on similar ends.

The early *Somewhere Before* is for trio, reuniting the line-up that made *Life Between The Exit Signs*. Heavily rock-influenced and still reminiscent of the methodology of the Charles Lloyd Quartet, of which Jarrett had been a member, it includes a version of Bob Dylan's 'My Back Pages' and two delightfully cadenced rags. Recorded live and slightly rough in texture, it has a freshness of approach that Jarrett quickly lost and was slow to regain.

The Mourning Of A Star is an odd, offbeat record that never quite fixes itself in the mind. Returning to it is both a surprise and a slight disappointment. Its main problem is a bittiness that was presumably supposed to cohere into something larger and grander. Good though it is to have the Atlantics back in catalogue again, for many purchasers the compilation set will be enough. What is immediately striking, listening to Jarrett play a standard, 'Smoke Gets In Your Eyes', in Bob Moses' group behind the gruff, squally tenor of Jim Pepper, is how fully formed he already sounds. 'Love No. 3', nominally a Charles Lloyd Quartet cut, is actually a Jarrett solo, played in front of a first-house crowd at the Fillmore West; again, it's the same voice, not even in embryo, but already working out its own priorities. Go back a further year (the tracks aren't in strict chronological order on the disc, either) and listen to the 21-year-old hold his own with Art Blakey, albeit in a non-vintage Messengers. It all reinforces the impression of a young man who came of age with his artistic and creative agenda already in place and who has spent the last quarter-century working through all of its ramifications and by-ways.

He is perhaps the most sophisticated technician working today outside the 'straight' repertoire (and he has, of course, crossed that boundary, too). The early piano style – the Lloyd group apart – is less obviously influenced by rock and country music than by the jazz mainstream, but then he was playing for other leaders at this stage and was required to do so in the idiom, a discipline that has paid colossal dividends in the recent 'Standards Trio'. Lloyd's influence and tolerance shouldn't be underestimated; that extraordinary group was clearly the catalyst. From 'Love No. 3' to the closing selection on disc two, the improvised 'Pardon My Rags', there is plentiful evidence of Jarrett's gifts as an 'instant composer', an instinctive melodist who seems able to find a match and a harmonic logic for almost any musical given. As his premisses become more searching, then with almost Wagnerian logic the improvisations grow proportionately longer and more intense. He's still capable, even at his most intense, of throwing in cheesy little songs or marking time with big, time-killing exercises straight out of h&c class at the conservatory. There is also a slightly fluffy track under Airto's leadership and some sub-standard material with Gary Burton, a partnership that might have been better represented.

There is an unavoidable problem with an output of this bulk – a cash problem if nothing else. ECM have arguably released too much material, more than 50 hours' worth in the present catalogue, of which perhaps only one-third has the stamp of greatness. It's a fascinating story all the same and, for newcomers or seasoned enthusiasts alike, *Foundations* is an excellent way of getting up to speed.

****** Expectations**

Columbia/Legacy C2K 65900 2CD *Jarrett; Dewey Redman (ts, perc); Sam Brown (g); Charlie Haden (b); Paul Motian (d); Airto Moreira (perc); brass; strings.* 9 & 10/71.

Not for the first time, Columbia hesitated about how to deal with a major and challenging artist, and Jarrett was dropped less than a month after this record was released, even though they are now claiming it as his breakthrough disc. Perhaps inevitable on both counts, given corporate expectations at the time and recent rewrites of the label's own history, but a dismal miscall, given the quality of this record, which is now restored to its full length over two CDs and with accurate track-listing.

There are few better places to sample Jarrett's uncanny ability to make disparate musical ideas work together. It's possible to argue for *Expectations*' breakthrough status rather more disinterestedly by pointing to the pianist's increasingly confident synthesis of jazz ('Circular Letter'), rock ('Sundance'), gospel ('There Is A Road') and Latin ('Common Mama') themes into a passionate, occasionally ecstatic mix. Some of the more extravagant freedoms relate closely to his work with a man who stayed with Columbia a while longer. Jarrett learned – or allowed himself – to play free on Miles Davis's *Live–Evil* and there is ample evidence of that here. Redman plays on only half the tracks, Brown on six; Jarrett plays soprano saxophone in addition to piano, but also (and despite Columbia's silence on the matter) organ and percussion. The new issue restores the strings piece, 'Visions', and revises the running order to its original form, ending on 'There Is A Road (God's River)'. Much as we liked the revised order, this makes better sense. Everything else now leads up to it. The logic of the session is impeccable, with seemingly abstract tonalities deployed chorally, much like the raw and unvarnished singing of the Black Church, and yet always anchored in something much more formal and familiar. 'Nomads' is the only really long track and it – appropriately, perhaps – meanders quite a bit, its climaxes a little hollow relative to what now follows. The best of the session lies in well-crafted tunes and textures. The addition of guitar changes the feel more than a little. Brown wasn't yet or wasn't here doing the single-note sustains that he made an integral part of Paul Motian's group sound but, even when playing the distorted chords typical of fusion music at the time, he sounds wholly convincing. It's taken a while to establish this record at the heart of Jarrett's output. This issue, with its generous documentation, surely does that.

***** Rutya And Daitya**

ECM 513776-2 *Jarrett; Jack DeJohnette (d).* 5/71.

It will sound like a slice of bland promotional puff to say that here DeJohnette plays like the piano man he also is and that Jarrett plays with a percussive edge which is not always heard in his work. This isn't so much a matter of timbre and attack as of general approach. Jack is one of the most musical drummers ever, and his phrasing constantly recalls his other instrument. Jarrett varies his playing accordingly, and the result is a very happy collaboration, much stronger with every hearing.

*****(*) Facing You**

ECM 827132-2 *Jarrett (p solo).* 11/71.

*****(*) Solo Concerts**

ECM 827747-2 2CD *As above.* 3 & 7/73.

****** The Köln Concert**

ECM 810067-2 2CD *As above.* 1/75.

***** Spheres**

ECM 827463-2 *Jarrett (org solo).* 9/76.

****(*) Staircase**

ECM 827337-2 2CD *Jarrett (p solo).* 11/76.

**** Sacred Hymns Of G. I. Gurdjieff**

ECM 1174 *As above.* 11/79.

***** Sun Bear Concerts**

ECM 843028-2 6CD *As above.* 3/80.

**** Invocations**

ECM 1201/2 2CD *Jarrett (p, pipe org, ss solo).* 7–10/80.

***** Concerts**

ECM 827286-2 *Jarrett (p solo).* 5 & 6/81.

**** Book Of Ways**

ECM 931396-2 2CD *Jarrett (clavichord solo).* 7/86.

***(*) Spirits**

ECM 829467-2 2CD *Jarrett (assorted instruments).* 4/87.

**** Dark Intervals**

ECM 847342-2 *Jarrett (p solo).* 10/88.

**** Paris Concert**

ECM 839173-2 *As above.* 10/88.

*****(*) Vienna Concert**
ECM 513437-2 *As above.* 7/91.

There was an uneasy giantism in Jarrett's work of the later 1970s, culminating in the release of the infamous *Sun Bear Concerts*, hours of densely personal piano improvisations in a 10-LP box, and only slightly less cumbersome on CD. It's clear that these episodically remarkable performances occupied a very significant, slightly chastened place in Jarrett's rather lonely and dogged self-exploration, but that doesn't automatically make for good music. Without being excessively Dr Johnsonish ('It is not done well; but you are surprised to find it done at all') about music so naked and questing, one wonders how much of the critical excitement it garnered was simply a response to its size and to Jarrett's brass neck in releasing product on a scale usually only accorded the great and the dead.

The jury needn't stay out quite so long on the preposterous *Spirits*, a double (of course) album of overdubs on a bizarre variety of ethnic instruments. To be fair, the album has its serious proponents (including Jarrett's biographer, Ian Carr) but, for all its healing and restorative intent and putative impact on the music that followed, it occupies only a marginal place in Jarrett's output. Other offences to be taken briefly into consideration are the thin *Gurdjieff* essays, the jangly clavichord improvisations on *Book Of Ways* (which is also burdened by the fact that the clavichord is an inherently unpleasant instrument to listen to at any length) and the dismal *Invocations*, executed in part on the same organ as *Spheres* but lacking that album's extraordinary experimental intensity and concentration. *Spheres* derives from the double-LP set, *Hymns Spheres*. It is by no stretch of the imagination a jazz record, but it does belong to another great improvisatory tradition, and it may be significant that, in contrast to the critical spanking it received in the United States, the album was favourably reviewed in Europe, though without quite enough leverage to see it transferred in full to compact disc. A great shame. Jarrett's approach to the unfamiliar keyboards and their associated pedals and stops is quite remarkable and generates one of his finest ever performances, easily the equal in conception and intelligence of the best-selling *Köln Concert*.

This is perhaps Jarrett's best and certainly his most popular record. ECM has been dining out or, to be fairer, recording others on the proceeds for two decades. Made in conditions of exceptional difficulty – not least an audibly unsatisfactory piano – Jarrett not for the first time makes a virtue of adversity, carving out huge slabs of music with a rare intensity. His instrument does sound off-puttingly bad-tempered, but his concentration on the middle register throughout the performance has been a characteristic of his work throughout his career.

The Bremen and Lausanne sets on *Solo Concerts* are almost equally good. Jarrett's first multi-volume set was extraordinarily well received on its release and stands up particularly well now (by contrast, *Facing You* seems slightly time-locked for some reason). These are friendlier, less intense performances than the *Köln* sides, but no less inventive for that, exploring Jarrett's characteristic blend of popular and 'high' forms. The 1981 *Concerts* was also recorded in Germany and in slightly easier circumstances (Jarrett suffered agonizing back pain throughout the Bremen *Solo Concert*) and perhaps as a consequence there's far less tension in the music; this is the surviving half of a two-LP release from Germany, of which the Munich half was probably better. That same quality of tension is noticeable on both *Facing You*, the earliest of the solo recordings and the best place to get a feel of Jarrett's characteristic method before tackling the multi-volume sets, and *Staircase*, where he seems to range across a multiplicity of idioms (many of them identifiably classical rather than popular) with no apparent urgency.

Much has been made of the cohesion and unity of Jarrett's solo performances. They are often likened to multi-movement suites rather than collections of discontinuous tunes or numbers. This is certainly true of *Facing You*, which shares with the *Köln Concert* a satisfying roundness; it certainly isn't true of *Staircase* or of the recent *Dark Intervals* and *Paris Concert*. The former is a moody, sonorous affair, recorded live in Tokyo and interspersed with thunderously disciplined applause. Apart from 'Fire Dance' – track titles are rare or *ex post facto* in the improvised performances – the music has a very formal, concertizing solemnity. The *Paris Concert*, by contrast, is lively at least but is also disturbingly predictable. The idiomatic shifts have become mannered almost to the point of self-parody, and there's a slightly cynical quality to Jarrett's apparent manipulation of audience expectations. The notorious grunting and moaning, with which he signals ecstasy and effort, have never been more intrusive.

By the turn of the 1990s Jarrett's solo concerts had their own terms of reference; it is hard to imagine where one might find a critical language larger than the music itself. The *Vienna Concert* is at once more formal and more coherent than the disappointing *Paris Concert*. If there is a dominant influence it is Bach, who is explicitly (though possibly unconsciously) quoted at a number of points, as is Shostakovich, whom Jarrett has also been recording. It opens with a quiet, almost hymnic theme which develops very slowly over sombre pedals for just over 20 minutes, before opening out into a broken-tempo country theme that still preserves the original material in inverted form. The second and third pieces seem to develop material from the first, but in such a way that one wonders if they have been released in the order of the original concert. Long-standing Jarrett fans will find all the required elements in place; newcomers may find this more approachable than *Köln* or *Sun Bear*, but only if they're not put off by the classical resonances of the opening movement.

***** Fort Yawuh**
Impulse! 547 966-2 *Jarrett; Dewey Redman (ts, perc); Charlie Haden (b); Paul Motian (d); Danny Johnson (perc).* 2/73.

*****(*) The Survivor's Suite**
ECM 827131-2 *Jarrett; Dewey Redman (ts, perc); Charlie Haden (b); Paul Motian (d).* 4/76.

***(*) Eyes Of The Heart**
ECM 825476-2 *As above.* 5/76.

Jarrett's American quartet probably never reached the heights or achieved the almost telepathic understanding of the European group responsible for the classic *Belonging*, below. The addition of Dewey Redman to the basic trio on *Fort Yawuh* (another of Jarrett's irritating pun-anagrams, this time of 'Fourth Way') gives that album a dark power. The new edition of *Fort Yawuh* includes unedited performances of all tracks and the addition of one more from the session, the long 'Roads Travelled, Roads Veiled', which previously appeared on *Impulse! Artists On Tour*.

Survivor's Suite, two years further down the road, is a masterpiece, with the quartet pulling together on an ambitiously large-scale piece, each member contributing whole-heartedly and passionately. By the sharpest of contrasts, *Eyes Of The Heart*, a live exploration of much the same material, is a near-disaster. The original release was as a double LP with one blank side. What it documents – and the format is in every way symbolic – is the final break-up of a rather fissile band; Dewey Redman contributes scarcely anything, and the album ends with Jarrett playing alone.

***** Silence**

Impulse! GRP 11172 *Jarrett; Dewey Redman (ts); Charlie Haden (b); Paul Motian (d).* 75.

A sensible compilation of two previous Impulse! LPs, *Bop-Be* and *Byablue*, dropping 'Pyramids Moving' from the former and concentrating on those tracks on *Byablue* that featured the whole group, with the exception of a piano solo reading of 'Byablue' itself. This was the last of Jarrett's records for the label and it's a slightly uneasy affair, reflecting not just a measure of strain that had grown up within the group but also (a matter of months after the Cologne concert) Jarrett's increasing interest in solo performance. As such, it's of considerable historical importance, but it can't be considered one of the more important albums.

****** Mysteries: The Impulse Years 1975–1976**

Impulse! IMPD 4 149 4CD *Jarrett; Dewey Redman (ts, musette, perc); Charlie Haden (b); Paul Motian (d); Guilherme Franco (perc).* 12/75, 10/76.

Superseding the earlier *Silence* compilation, which put together most of *Bop-Be* and *Byablue*, this handsome package also includes two slightly earlier and better albums, *Shades* and *Mysteries*, and a significant amount of previously unissued material from the sessions. The albums were recorded in pairs, in December 1975 and October 1976, and it's quite clear that by the later date the group, always more volatile than the 'European quartet' reviewed below, was now in a pretty terminal state, which Jarrett has likened to an attempt to save a rocky marriage. It's always a mistake to personalize or psychologize music, but the contrast between Jarrett's joyous, sometimes bumptious, and still country-tinged vamps and improvisations and Redman's sour-toned and often rather grouchy solos on the later sessions is very striking. The more important difference, though, is that for the October 1976 studios, Jarrett very largely ceded writing credits to Haden, Redman, Margot Jarrett and, in particular, Motian. Though he and the drummer clearly hold a good deal of musical territory in common, Jarrett doesn't sound much at ease on 'Yallah' or 'Byablue', and his soloing is schematic and at times unwontedly laboured.

The big plus on these transfers is being able to hear Haden in full voice and in a sensible stereo position, unexpectedly foregrounded and bridging saxophone and piano with great dexterity. The 11 unreleased tracks are of mixed interest. The unissued version of 'Everything That Lives Laments' (*Mysteries*) stretches to more than a quarter of an hour without adding anything of substance, but there is much to ponder in three versions of 'Rose Petals' from *Shades*, flawed but subtly modulated performances in each case.

****** Belonging**

ECM 829115-2 *Jarrett; Jan Garbarek (ts, ss); Palle Danielsson (b); Jon Christensen (d).* 4/74.

*****(*) My Song**

ECM 821406-2 *As above.* 1/77.

***** Personal Mountains**

ECM 837361-2 *As above.* 4/79.

***** Nude Ants**

ECM 829119-2 2CD *As above.* 5/79.

Both *Belonging* and *My Song* have also been covered in the entry on Jan Garbarek, because the saxophonist's contribution to both albums seems particularly significant. The 'European Quartet' was probably the most sympathetic grouping Jarrett ever assembled and *Belonging* in particular is a superb album, characterized by some of the pianist's most open and joyous playing on record; his double-time solo on 'The Windup' is almost Tatum-like in its exuberance and fluency. The country-blues feel of 'Long As You Know You're Living Yours' is a confident reflection of his music roots. The ballads 'Blossom', 'Solstice' and the title-piece – the first two powerfully extended, the last uncharacteristically brief – are remarkable by any standards; Garbarek's slightly out-of-tune opening statement on 'Solstice' and Danielsson's subsequent solo are masterful, while Jarrett's own split chords accentuate the mystery and ambiguity of the piece.

Nude Ants is a live set from New York City (the title is a metathesis of the bouncing 'New Dance'). It's a valuable documentation of the European Quartet outside the studio, but the performances are somewhat below par and Garbarek (who admits dissatisfaction with the performances) sounds alternately forced and diffident. Recording quality is also disappointing and well below ECM's usual standard. *Personal Mountains* sounds very much better, but the playing has a sleepy, jet-lagged quality (it was taped in Tokyo) that blurs the impact of the title-piece and the momentarily beautiful 'Prism', 'Oasis' and 'Innovence'.

****(*) In The Light**

ECM 835011-2 2CD *Jarrett; Ralph Towner (g); string quartet; brass quintet; strings.* 73.

****(*) Luminessence**

ECM 839307-2 *Jarrett; Jan Garbarek (ts, ss); strings.* 4/74.

****(*) Arbour Zena**

ECM 825592-2 *Jarrett; Jan Garbarek (ts, ss); Charlie Haden (b); strings.* 10/75.

***(*) The Celestial Hawk**

ECM 829370-2 *Jarrett; symphony orchestra.* 3/80.

If it's every jazzer's dream (it was certainly Charlie Parker's) to play with strings, then it seems hard to deny Jarrett his moment. Hard, but not impossible. These mostly sound like the indulgences of a star figure unchecked by sensible aesthetic criteria and doubtless encouraged by sheer bankability. And why not? The *Köln Concert* is still shifting units like a life-jacket sale before the Flood.

Jarrett would doubtless argue that critical sniffiness about these albums is the result of sheer prejudice, the jazz community's snotty, elbows-out attitude to anything scored or on the grand scale and, on the other hand, the sheer exclusivism of the 'straight' music cartel. *Arbour Zena* and *Luminessence* contain some beautiful moments, but what an opportunity missed for a stripped-down duo with Garbarek. The overall mood of *Arbour Zena* is elegiac and slightly lorn, and the strings melt like marshmallows over some of the sharper flavours; the later album has simply been left cooking too long.

The earlier *In The Light* was a composer's showcase and, as such, a forerunner of ECM's much-admired New Series. The individual works struggle to stay in focus, but as a whole the album has surprising consistency. *The Celestial Hawk* is pure tosh ... with some nice bits.

*****(*) Standards: Volume 1**
ECM 811966-2 *Jarrett; Gary Peacock (b); Jack DeJohnette (d).* 1/83.

***** Changes**
ECM 817436-2 *As above.* 1/83.

****** Standards: Volume 2**
ECM 825015-2 *As above.* 7/85.

***** Standards Live**
ECM 827827-2 *As above.* 7/86.

*****(*) Still Live**
ECM 835008-2 2CD *As above.* 10/86.

*****(*) Standards In Norway**
ECM 521717-2 *As above.* 10/89.

****(*) Tribute**
ECM 847135-2 2CD *As above.* 10/89.

*****(*) Changeless**
ECM 839618-2 *As above.* 4/90.

****** The Cure**
ECM 849650-2 *As above.* 4/90.

One of the less fair subtexts to the widespread critical acclaim for Jarrett's 'Standards Trio' is the implication that he is at last toeing the line, conforming to an established repertoire, finally renouncing the extravagances of the *Köln Concert* and the other multi-volume sets.

In practice, nothing could be much further from the truth. Jarrett's approach to standards is nothing if not individual; for all his obvious respect and affection for the material, he consistently goes his own way. The main difference from the solo performances is the obvious one: Peacock's firmly harmonic bass and DeJohnette's astonishingly imaginative drumming adjust his improvisatory instincts to the degree that they simplify his articulation and attack and redirect his attention to the chords and the figuration of melody.

It doesn't always come off. There are moments on *Standards: Volume 1* which are simply flat and uninspired, as on 'God Bless The Child'. *Volume 2* immediately feels more confident. The themes, which are less familiar anyway, are no longer an embarrassment; Jarrett clearly feels able to leave them implicit a little longer. That is even more obvious on the fine *Standards Live* and *Still Live*, though it's a pity – from the point of view of comparison – that Jarrett hasn't repeated any of the studio titles. The only occasion where this is possible is on the strangely patchy *Tribute*, which repeats 'All The Things You Are' from *Standards: Volume 1*. The later version is more oblique, but also simpler. Like the rest of the tracks, it is intended as a *hommage*, in this case to Sonny Rollins, which is pretty typical of the curious but doubtless very conscious matching of standards and dedicatees. Typically, perhaps, Jarrett adds two of his own compositions to an already rather overblown and diffuse set, as if to inscribe himself more legibly into the tradition he is exploring and rediscovering.

In that same vein, the 'Standards Trio' hasn't limited itself to existing repertoire. *Changes* and *Changeless* contain original material which is deeply subversive (though also respectfully aware) of the whole tradition of jazz as a system of improvisation on 'the changes'. Typically, Jarrett invests the term with quite new aesthetic and philosophical considerations. On *Changeless*, there are no chord progressions at all; the trio improvises each section in a single key, somewhat in the manner of an Indian *raga*. The results are impressive and thought-provoking, like everything Jarrett has attempted. Even his failures, of which two more are listed below, are never less than interesting.

(As a footnote, the same trio has also recorded under Gary Peacock's leadership. The fine *Tales Of Another* is reviewed more fully under the appropriate heading.)

*****(*) Bye Bye Blackbird**
ECM 513074-2 *Jarrett; Gary Peacock (b); Jack DeJohnette (d).* 10/91.

*****(*) At The Deer Head Inn**
ECM 517720-2 *Jarrett; Gary Peacock (b); Paul Motian (d).* 9/92.

Bye Bye Blackbird is Jarrett's tribute to the late Miles Davis, with whom he worked in the 1960s and about whom in later years he had made some decidedly snitty comments. It is certainly startling to hear him talk in a rare ECM liner-note about Miles's 'purity of desire' (the phrase, or a version of it, is repeated) when the burden of on- and off-stage comments in the 1980s had been that Miles had seriously compromised the music – to electricity, to mere fashion, and so on.

Taken on its own merits, *Bye Bye Blackbird* is a wonderful record. The choice of material is refreshingly unobvious (how often is Oliver Nelson's 'Butch And Butch' covered?) and immaculately played, as this group always does. The two originals, 'For Miles' and a coda 'Blackbird, Bye Bye', are as intensely felt as anything Jarrett has done in recent years, and the level of abstraction that has crept back into the music is well judged and unobtrusive. DeJohnette performs wonders, changing metre subtly with almost every bar on 'Straight No Chaser'. An excellent record, beautifully packaged. What one wouldn't have given for an LP-sized print of Catherine Pichonnier's magnificent silhouette cover-photo.

It's a recurrent craving of superstars that they should turn their backs on the big halls and all the paraphernalia of stardom and play small venues again. The Dear Head Inn in Allentown, Pennsylvania, was the scene of Keith Jarrett's first serious gig on piano. It has now sustained a jazz policy for more than 40 years, a dedication passed on by the original owners to their daughter and son-in-law. In order to re-launch the club in 1992, Jarrett agreed to play a gig there, taking along Paul Motian, with whom he had not worked since the time of *Silence*. Motian brings a lighter and more flowing pulse to the music than DeJohnette. The obvious point of comparison is 'Bye Bye Blackbird', which glides along without wires or other obvious support for more than ten minutes, a beautiful, airborne performance. This might almost be a second tribute to Miles. It opens with a superb reading of 'Solar', but then follows with skilful readings of 'Basin Street Blues' and Jaki Byard's 'Chandra', two pieces that belong to an entirely different musical realm, but which take on a similar coloration to the Miles tune. As so often, Peacock is more forceful and less complex out of the studio. He drives 'You And The Night And The Music', giving it a pugnacious edge one doesn't normally hear. It seems unlikely that Jarrett will ever need to go back to bar-room gigs, but here he's demonstrated his ability to work a small audience with powerful, unpretentious jazz. Anyone who has never heard him could hardly be better advised than to start with one of these.

****** At The Blue Note: The Complete Recordings**
ECM 527638-2 6CD *As above.* 6/94.

This is an extraordinary piece of documentation, two sets from each of three consecutive nights at the New York club. It might be considered warts-and-all but for the fact that there are no warts. Nor is there any repetition or aimless noodling. It's fascinating, given sufficient time and attention, to hear Jarrett import ideas – harmonic resolutions, phrases, improbable interval jumps like elevenths and thirteenths – from one piece to another on different nights. As an insight into how spontaneously creative he can be, it is unparalleled even in this extraordinary discography.

It was played, one suspects, with the recording very much in mind. One might almost prefer more repetition of tunes, but he goes his own individual way, leaning a little more than previously on top-ten standards – 'Autumn Leaves', 'Alone Together', 'On Green Dolphin Street' – and on jazz repertory pieces like Rollins's 'Oleo'. There may ultimately be a scaled-down compilation from this, but if you can afford the cash and patience to get the full set, don't hesitate for a moment. One of the high points of jazz playing in the 1990s.

*****(*) La Scala**
ECM 537268-2 *Jarrett (p solo).* 2/95.

There were already rumours of ill-health at this stage, over and beyond Jarrett's chronic lower back problems. A certain weary simplicity creeps into this immaculately recorded solo set, which is certainly the best for some time. Jarrett's improvisations are as long and as densely textured as ever, but there is a modesty and philosophical calm about the music which seems new. The second part of 'La Scala', the generic title for the two main pieces, has outbreaks of quiet violence, but nothing that doesn't have its own resolution. The instrument is immaculate, warm and full-voiced. As so often, Jarrett encores with 'Over The Rainbow', a touchingly uncomplicated performance that will stand comparison with anyone's cherished private C90.

***** Tokyo '96**
ECM 539955-2 *Jarrett; Gary Peacock (b); Jack DeJohnette (d).* 3/96.

The story continues, unstaunchable, maddeningly indulgent and selflessly brilliant by turns. There are moments of pure genius here, like the tiny treble figures on 'Autumn Leaves' or the bass vamp that underpins 'My Funny Valentine', but the overall impression is of low-key predictability. Jarrett has always exposed his own creative facility to new challenges, but this group now sounds too comfortable with its language. Interesting to compare it with the Haden/Motian line-up of years gone by, where beauty of form never precluded enterprise and a hint of danger.

****** The Melody At Night, With You**
ECM 547949-2 *Jarrett (p solo).* 98.

And just when you thought the story would simply run '... and so on', Jarrett pops up with a record of fragile magnificence, a sequence of filigreed songs from a common musical past. Hearing him do 'My Wild Irish Rose' and 'Someone To Watch Over Me' back to back is to hear a musician who recognizes no tension between improvisation and 'tradition', between the recalled and the intuitive. It is a quite simply magnificent record, swinging in a way that Jarrett has rarely before been swinging ('I Got It Bad And That Ain't Good'), and sweetly melodic ('Shenandoah'). The totality of his work for ECM now amounts to one of the most significant in the whole literature of piano jazz, however uneasily some of it sits in that particular bin.

Jayne Jarvis

PIANO

Growing up in Indiana, Jarvis began working as a pianist and organist at several musical levels – she was intermission organist for the Milwaukee Braves and the New York Mets and was even a vice-president of the Muzak Corporation. Despite these unlikely affiliations, her jazz work remains uncompromisingly in the swing mainstream.

***** Cut Glass**
Audiophile ACD-258 *Jarvis; Joe Beck (g); Jay Leonhart (b); Grady Tate (d).* 85.

***** The Jayne Jarvis L.A. Quartet**
Audiophile ACD-248 *Jarvis; Tommy Newson (ts); Monty Budwig (b); Jake Hanna (d).* 2/88.

****** Jayne Jarvis Jams**
Arbos SRCD 19152 *Jarvis; Dan Barrett (c, tb); Bob Haggart (b); Grady Tate (d).* 6/95.

***** Atlantic–Pacific**
Arbors ARCD 19189 *Jarvis; Bill Berry (t); Benny Powell, Dan Barrett (tb); Frank Wess, Tommy Newsom (ts); Earl May, David Stone (b); Jackie Williams, Jake Hanna (d).* 7/97–12/98.

Jarvis's style comes from the generous, big-handed swing stylists of Erroll Garner's generation, though when she actually tackles a Garner theme ('One Good Turn' on *Cut Glass*) she sounds curiously unlike him. Both Audiophile discs offer an assured programme of standards and a very occasional original: the title blues on *Cut Glass* is a delightful one, and her funky modification of 'Bali Ha'i' on the same session is an instance of how wittily she varies the pace. The quartet date (Beck sits in on only a single track of the earlier disc, which is otherwise all trio) offers fewer surprises, but Newsom's romantic tenor flourishes fit the bill very comfortably.

There could hardly be a better example of four old pros enjoying themselves than *Jayne Jarvis Jams* (even if Barrett isn't so old). The level of sheer good spirits in this programme of standards is completely infectious and, when coupled with Jarvis's skill at renewing fusty old tunes, it makes the record irresistible. The pep and swing in 'Mountain Greenery' ('It's so clean that I feel like I've brushed my teeth every time I play it'), 'Begin The Beguine' and 'Lady Be Good' are enough to rattle the floor, and there are deep-toned treatments of 'For Jess' (for Jess Stacy), Haggart's own immortal 'What's New?' and 'I Get Along Without You Very Well'. Barrett chimes in when he has to with some delicious choruses, and Haggart and Tate are marvellous. As is the piano player.

Atlantic–Pacific is something of a disappointment. Jarvis settles in for a session on each coast, with Powell her principal Atlantic partner (Wess contributes only a few solos) and Barrett, Berry and Newsom handling horn duties in the second half. Powell's contributions (there are three of his own tunes included) feature his whispery, conspiratorial style, but the tempos are a bit slack, and ballad settings also dominate the second half. Jarvis floats stylishly through it, but one longs for a couple more steamers to perk up each session.

Bobby Jaspar (1926–63)

TENOR SAXOPHONE, FLUTE

Born in Liège, Jaspar made his name in Paris in the 1950s, and he moved to the USA when he marrried Blossom Dearie. His most famous association was a brief spell with Miles Davis in 1957. He died in 1963 following heart surgery.

***** Bobby Jaspar With George Wallington, Idrees Sulieman**
Original Jazz Classics OJC 1788 *Jaspar; Idrees Sulieman (t); George Wallington (p); Wilbur Little (b); Elvin Jones (d).* 5/57.

***** Bobby Jaspar With Friends**
Fresh Sound FSRCD-166 *Jaspar; Mundell Lowe, René Thomas (g); George Duvivier, Monty Budwig, Jean Marie Ingrand (b); Ed Shaughnessy, Jean-Louis Viale (d).* 58–62.

Jaspar sounded like Lester Young might have done if Lester had been Belgian. His pale tone and amorphous phrasing on tenor were matched with an agile and exceptionally pointed flute style, abjuring the mere prettiness which normally attends that instrument. He has two flute features on the agreeable if unexceptional 1957 session: Sulieman sits out on four of the seven numbers, but Jaspar is quite confident enough to handle the front line by himself. *With Friends* is a motley but absorbing collection of mainly live tracks, most with a small group under Mundell Lowe's leadership, but two were cut in Paris with René Thomas – excellent, sinuous bebop workouts. The tracks with Lowe are a mixed lot: Jaspar has a gorgeous flute feature on 'It Could Happen To You' and generally uses this horn over the tenor. Lowe's own work shouldn't be discounted: he has a fine improvisation on 'Gal In Calico'. Still not much Jaspar around at present : there are sessions for Vogue, Barclay and Columbia that could stand CD reissue. He is becoming very much a forgotten figure.

André Jaume (born 1940)

TENOR SAXOPHONE, FLUTE, CLARINET, BASS CLARINET

After beginning with Dixieland groups, Jaume sought out more modern company in the 1960s, and since then his work on record has been rather unpredictable, with solo and duo recordings (with Joe McPhee, a long-time associate) sequenced with more large-scale efforts. He is also much interested in gamelan music and is a close associate of Jimmy Giuffre.

*****(*) Pour Django**
CELP C1 *Jaume; Raymond Boni (g).* 6/85.

***** Songs And Dances**
CELP C4 *As above, except add Joe McPhee (t, ss).* 5/87.

****** Cinoche**
CELP C7 *Jaume; Rémi Charmasson (g); François Mechali, Claude Tchamitchian (b); Daniel Humair (d).* 1/84–3/88.

*****(*) Piazza Di Luna**
CELP 10 *Jaume; Rémi Charmasson (g); Jean-Marc Montera (g-syn); Claude Tchamitchian (b); Fredy Studer (d); Jackie Micaelli, Jean-Pierre Lanfranchini, Jean-Claude Albertini, Jean-Etienne Langianni, Francis Marcantei (v).* 8–9/89.

***** Standards**
CELP 12 *Jaume; Jean-Sebastien Simonoviez (p); François Mechali (b); Olivier Clerc (d).* 4/89.

****(*) Something ...**
CELP 15 *Jaume; Joe McPhee (ss, vtb); Clyde Criner (p); Anthony Cox (b); Bill Stewart (d).* 4/90.

*****(*) Peace/Pace/Paix**
CELP 19 *Jaume; Charlie Haden (b); Olivier Clerc (d).* 5/90.

*****(*) Abbaye De L'Epau**
CELP 20 *Jaume; Charlie Mariano (as, f).* 3/91.

****** Giacobazzi, Autour De La Rade**
CELP 25 *Jaume; Barre Phillips (b); Barry Altschul (d).* 6/92.

Jaume's sequence of records for the French CELP company is a superb body of work, as well as his only representation in the catalogue, since his old hat Art albums have now gone. His own playing has acquired tremendous stature: the tenor is still his primary instrument, and he gets a granitic, almost Gothic tone out of it when he wishes, though he's as likely to play quietly, almost deferentially. The alto he picks up only occasionally, but his bass clarinet and flute work are also distinctive: lyrical, but with a dark, sometimes misshapen side to them. His tribute to Django casts only a sidelong look at Reinhardt's material: he and Boni play 'Mélodie Pour Julie' relatively straight, but there are also abstract originals here that honour the guitarist's spirit as well as the letter of his music. Boni's effects colour much of the festival set recorded on *Songs And Dances*, where they play Coleman's 'Blues Connotation' as well as Otis Redding's 'Dock Of The Bay' and do three solos in tribute to Jimmy Lyons. *Cinoche* is a masterful record, music for '*un film policier qui n'existe pas*': split between one group with Humair and Mechali and another with Charmasson and Tchamitchian, Jaume's playing has a Rollins-like authority on tenor, with the superb 'Ballade A Perdre Le Temps' outstanding. *Piazza Di Luna* documents a project with

Tavagna, a group of Corsican polyphonic singers. An unlikely collaboration, with two of the vocalists reciting the words of Andrée Canavaggio as well as singing; but Jaume makes it work by choosing to create two contrasting vistas rather than a fusion.

The *Standards* collection seems to set Jaume off on a new mid-stream course. Aside from a single original, 'Escapade', the programme offers nine familiar songs to work with, and Jaume's querulous tone and slightly tortuous phrasing make deliberately unsettled work of the music. He takes out the bass clarinet as often as the tenor and soprano, and it lends a mooching air to 'Nancy'. Jaume's first recording with an American rhythm section is a little disappointing. Criner, Cox and Stewart play as if this were just another post-bop date, and that's how it ends up sounding: with compositions by Jackie McLean and Grachan Moncur in the programme, as well as four Jaume originals, the feel is reminiscent of Blue Note's experimental mid-1960s period. But Jaume and McPhee give the impression of being tranquillized by the setting. An austere reworking of Moncur's 'Love And Hate' is rather effective, and Jaume's terseness works well with the splashier playing of McPhee, but the record is slack overall.

On the next two records Jaume sounds as if he's growing ever more quiet and introspective. He seldom raises his saxophone voice on either one, yet both make a firmer impression than some of the earlier discs. The trio session establishes a line of descent from Ornette Coleman, which 'Peace' and 'Blue Connotation' make manifest, but Jaume's playing has little of Coleman in it: he's too quirkily himself, and the steady-rolling pulses devised by Haden and Clerc support what's now a very personal kind of melodic improvisation. *Abbaye De L'Epau* is more soberly reflective, and the very even pacing of the music makes this sequence all-of-a-piece, with Mariano turning his own light down a little to remain in keeping with the occasion. Both discs are well recorded (the second is from a concert session) and gently absorbing.

Any fear that Jaume might be heading towards silence is dispelled by the most recent trio session, a series of dedications to painter Jean Pierre Giacobazzi, performed in collaboration with the sombre, earth-solid bass of Phillips and the magnificent Altschul, whose exacting, intensely detailed playing is remarkable by itself. Jaume makes the most of all his horns, with the soprano and bass clarinet finding new depth; but his tenor continues to impress the most, and the best music here is as absorbing as Coleman's great Golden Circle sessions.

*****(*) Team Games**

CELP 31 *Jaume; John Medeski (p).* 5/94.

A very improbable meeting, with the keyboardist of Medeski, Martin And Wood producing some inspired playing. Steve Lacy's 'Blues For Aida' is a favourite of Jaume's (it appears on *Borobodur Suite*, listed below) and the alternately harsh and gentle treatment it gets here is memorably invigorating. Otherwise it's Monk and Coltrane on the set-list, and unhackneyed choices at that, with a beautifully irreverent 'Ba-Lue Bolivar Ba-Lues Are' to highlight what they can do.

***** Borobodur Suite**

CELP 30 *Jaume; Septo Raharjo, Setyaji Dewanto, Gatot Djuwito, Poernomo Nugruho, Sonny Suprapto (gamelan orchestra).* 2/95.

***** Merapi**

CELP 34 *As above, except add Rémi Charmasson (g); S.P Joko and Azied Dewa replace Dewanto and Djuwito.* 4/96.

There's no gainsaying Jaume's inquisitive spirit, and these two collaborative meetings with Septo Raharjo's gamelan orchestra are handled with great confidence by all the players. Jaume is the central figure throughout the first disc; he shares improvising duties with Charmasson – low-key but very sympathetic – on the second. Raharjo and his men play to the letter of their music, creating a rustling, river-like flow of sound that complements what the jazz players are doing without subsuming them. In the end, though, one finds it all rather interesting and very seldom fascinating. As graciously as the players share their space, there seems to be very little genuine interaction, and saxophones and clarinets don't sit all that well with gamelan instruments (Charmasson does rather better in that respect).

*****(*) Clarinet Sessions**

CELP 40 *Jaume; Rémi Charmasson (g); Bruno Chevillon, Alain Soler (b); Randy Kaye, Barry Altschul (d).* 1–6/96.

*****(*) A Portrait Of Jimmy Giuffre**

CELP 39 *Jaume; Jean-François Canape (t, bugle); Rémi Charmasson (g); Bob Harrsion (b); Randy Kaye (d).* 6/98.

Jaume's fascination with the clarinet and with Jimmy Giuffre gets full rein on these two. *Clarinet Sessions* has its misfires, such as the misjudged duets with Altschul which open the disc, but there are also some sublime moments: 'Mountain By The Sea', a fine mood piece, and the three duets with Chevillon. The conventionally swinging 'Bonne Course' and the feathery duet with Kaye, 'West Stockbridge Impression', round out a quietly provocative set.

The set in dedication to Giuffre finds a ground common both to its dedicatee and to Jaume's more abstract side. 'Apes', for instance, is taken further out than the composer himself would probably sanction, but Harrison and Kaye (himself a former Giuffre sideman) know just how far to push their roles without surrendering the chamberish feel of the group, and the three principal soloists make any journeys from inside to out entirely logical within what is a carefully designed group framework. Cut live at two Avignon concerts, this was a splendid event.

The Java Quartet

GROUP

Contemporary Australian foursome.

***** Glow**

Rufus RF026 *Jason Cooney (ts); Michael Galeazzi (p); Greg Coffin (b); Mike Quigley (d).* 6/96.

Nothing riveting about the way this quartet plays, but they find themselves in the writing – eight attractive originals – and the way they bring it to life, sometimes with a caress ('God's Gift', haunting in its impassive way), more often with an accomplished post-bop attitude. Another interesting bulletin from Australia courtesy of the adventurous Rufus label.

Jazz At The Philharmonic

SUPERGROUP

Instigated by Norman Granz, this took its name from a single concert at the Philharmonic Theater in Los Angeles in 1944, but became a generic title for multi-artist package shows or tours, promoted by Granz and featuring an evolving repertory cast of players. It was a phenomenon which lasted into the 1980s.

****** The Complete Jazz At The Philharmonic On Verve 1944–1949**

Verve 523893-2 10CD *Shorty Sherock, Al Killian, Neal Hefti, Charlie Shavers, Buck Clayton, Ray Linn, Dizzy Gillespie, Howard McGhee, Roy Eldridge, Joe Guy (t); J.J Johnson, Bill Harris, Tommy Turk (tb); Charlie Parker, Willie Smith, Georgie Auld, Pete Brown (as); Illinois Jacquet, Lester Young, Flip Phillips, Coleman Hawkins, Bumps Meyers, Babe Russin, Corky Corcoran, Charlie Ventura, Joe Thomas, Jack McVea (ts); Meade Lux Lewis, Garland Finney, Buddy Cole, Nat Cole, Milt Raskin, Arnold Ross, Hank Jones, Bobby Tucker, Kenny Kersey, Ralph Burns, Oscar Peterson, Teddy Napoleon, Mel Powell (p); Slim Gaillard (g, p, v, d); Tiny 'Bam' Brown (g, p, v); Les Paul, Irving Ashby, Barney Kessel, Dave Barbour, Bill De Arango, Ulysses Livingston, Tiny Grimes (g); Johnny Miller, Red Callender, Curley Russell, Ray Brown, Charles Mingus, Billy Hadnott, Al McKibbon, Rodney Richardson, Charlie Drayton, Benny Fonville (b); Lee Young, Joe Marshall, Dave Coleman, Gene Krupa, J.C Heard, Jo Jones, Alvin Stoller, Dave Tough, Big Sid Catlett, Jackie Mills (d); Carolyn Richards, Billie Holiday, Ella Fitzgerald (v).* 44–49.

***** The First Concert**

Verve 521646-2 *Shorty Sherock (t); J.J Johnson (tb); Illinois Jacquet, Jack McVea (ts); Nat Cole (p); Les Paul (g); Lee Young (d).* 7/44.

***** Norman Granz's Jazz At The Philharmonic, Hartford, 1953**

Pablo 2308240 *Charlie Shavers, Roy Eldridge (t); Bill Harris (tb); Benny Carter, Willie Smith (as); Flip Phillips, Ben Webster (ts); Oscar Peterson (p); Herb Ellis (g); Ray Brown (b); Gene Krupa (d).* 5/53.

*****(*) JATP In Tokyo**

Pablo PACD 2620 104 2CD *As above, except add Raymond Tunia (p), J.C Heard (d), Ella Fitzgerald (v).* 11/53.

***** The Exciting Battle: JATP, Stockholm '55**

Pablo 2310713 *Roy Eldridge, Dizzy Gillespie (t); Bill Harris (tb); Flip Phillips (ts); Oscar Peterson (p); Herb Ellis (g); Ray Brown (b); Louie Bellson (d).* 2/55.

*****(*) JATP In London, 1969**

Pablo 2620119 *Dizzy Gillespie, Clark Terry (t); Benny Carter (as); Coleman Hawkins, Zoot Sims (ts); James Moody (ts, f); Teddy Wilson (p); T-Bone Walker (g); Bob Cranshaw (b); Louie Bellson (d).* 3/69.

*****(*) JATP At The Montreux Festival, 1975**

Pablo 2310748 *Clark Terry (t, flhn); Benny Carter (as); Zoot Sims (ts); Joe Pass (g); Tommy Flanagan (p); Keter Betts (b); Bobby Durham (d).* 7/75.

***** Return To Happiness: JATP At Yoyogi National Stadium, Tokyo**

Pablo 2620117 *Harry 'Sweets' Edison, Clark Terry (t); J.J Johnson, Al Grey (tb); Zoot Sims, Eddie 'Lockjaw' Davis (ts); Joe Pass (g); Oscar Peterson, Paul Smith (p); Keter Betts, Niels-Henning Orsted Pedersen (b); Louie Bellson, Bobby Durham (d); Ella Fitzgerald (v).* 10/83.

Jazz At The Philharmonic dates from 2 July 1944 at the Philharmonic Auditorium in Los Angeles, when Norman Granz mounted a concert headlined by Nat Cole, Illinois Jacquet, Meade Lux Lewis and others who will probably sound slightly unfamiliar in this context at least. A decade later, when JATP had reached the peak of its international celebrity, there was a relatively fixed roster of stars, all from within Granz's recording empire, who took part in these events – part concerts, part public jams – which gained him such success and which lasted, virtually uninterrupted, over the span of these records and beyond.

Granz was a passionate believer in the racial integration of jazz. He was also shrewd enough to recognize that more very definitely meant more so far as marketing big jazz names was concerned. There is often a sense of 'never mind the quality, count the names' on a JATP record, and finesse and expressive sophistication were very often lost in polite cutting sessions which put high note playing and amicably fiery exchanges at a premium. The JATP discography has always been something of a shambles, the records issued and reissued in all manner of combinations, and very little of the kosher Verve material has even made it to CD – until, that is, the long-awaited and much-delayed set of all the '40s material, displayed in an elaborate construction which includes ten CDs and a huge booklet. Considering that so many of these dates are little more than institutionalized jam sessions or platforms for showmanship, listening through the discs is unexpectedly easy and rewarding. As the JATP package was formulating itself, it still accommodated a great variety: there is Slim Gaillard and Bam Brown (doing their pretty hilarious schtick on 'Opera In Vout'), solos by Meade Lux Lewis, Nat Cole groups, a trio of Gene Krupa, Charlie Ventura and Teddy Napoleon, Ella and Billie in their own sets, Coleman Hawkins with Hank Jones, Buddy Rich and Ray Brown (here with three previously unheard numbers), features for Bill Harris and Charlie Shavers ... the range of jazz on offer is in the end pretty extraordinary. Every so often someone such as Roy Eldridge goes too far, but that is also part of the atmosphere. There's a lot of newly discovered material and, although the sound is basically rather thin, everything comes through clearly. As a feat of re-organization alone, the set has merit, but it's hard to see anyone being disappointed with a glorious set of performances too.

That high standard persisted through the later JATP survivals, the rest of which are currently available through Pablo (Verve will presumably tackle their remaining material in due course, but since it took them many years to get the first set out, we advise readers against holding their breath). It's difficult to identify highs and lows or to make qualitative judgements about the playing. There are no bad or even disappointing records. The earlier Japanese session recommends itself on grounds of sheer length and also because there is a winning freshness to everybody's playing; but that might also be said of the 1969 London concert or the triumphant return to Japan (and 'to happiness') which neatly rounds off the 40-year span of these particular discs.

An astonishing feat of organization, JATP also made great marketing sense, and Granz has to be complimented for keeping the music going during a period when in market terms it was more than embattled. Mainstream fans will love any of these.

Jazz Composers Orchestra (founded 1967)

GROUP

An American ensemble formed by Michael Mantler, part of an initiative to commission and perform new large-scale jazz compositions. It gradually became, effectively, a Carla Bley–Mantler orchestra.

***(*) Communications

JCOA 841124-2 *Michael Mantler (dir); Don Cherry (c); Randy Brecker, Stephen Furtado, Lloyd Michels (flhn); Bob Northern, Julius Watkins (frhn); Jimmy Knepper, Roswell Rudd (tb); Jack Jeffers (btb); Howard Johnson (tba); Al Gibbons, Steve Lacy, Steve Marcus (ss); Bob Donovan, Gene Hull, Frank Wess (as); Gato Barbieri, George Barrow, Pharoah Sanders, Lew Tabackin (ts); Charles Davis (bs); Carla Bley, Cecil Taylor (p); Larry Coryell (g); Kent Carter, Ron Carter, Bob Cunningham, Richard Davis, Eddie Gomez, Charlie Haden, Reggie Johnson, Alan Silva, Steve Swallow, Reggie Workman (b); Andrew Cyrille, Beaver Harris (d).* 1–6/68.

The JCO was formed to give improvising musicians an opportunity to play extended structures in larger formations than were normally considered either economic or artistically viable. Its best-known product is still the massive opera – or 'chronotransduction' – *Escalator Over The Hill*. From the same period came *Communications*, if anything a more ambitious work. It consists of four enormous slabs of orchestrated sound and a brief 'Preview' (which comes fourth of five), each with a featured soloist. Or, in the case of the opening 'Communications No. 8', two soloists: Don Cherry and Gato Barbieri. Mantler's scoring is interesting in itself. Cherry's squeaky cornet is the only high-pitched brass instrument; the sections are weighted towards french horns and trombones, with flugelhorn accents generally located in the middle register and the higher-pitched parts assigned to soprano saxophones. In addition, Mantler scores for five double basses on each track (perm from the list above), which gives each piece a complex tonal rootedness for the soloists' (mostly) unrestrained excursions. Restraining Gato Barbieri would be pointless. He tends to begin a solo where most saxophonists climax. It's redundant to say he sounds strained on 'Communications No. 8' but, tone apart, he seems to be straining for ideas. By contrast, Pharoah Sanders has to squeeze everything into a brief three and a half minutes on 'Preview' and nearly achieves meltdown in the process. On 'Communications No. 9' Larry Coryell is used as a sound-effects department. If Barbieri seems slightly short of ideas, Coryell is a *tabula rasa*. Fortunately, the best is still to come. Roswell Rudd's playing on the longer 'No. 10' is some of the best he has committed to record; Steve Swallow's bass introduction establishes its parameters with great exactness, and again the dark scoring works superbly. The final two-part section fully justifies Cecil Taylor's top billing. His solo part is full of huge, keyboard-long runs and pounded chords and arpeggios that leave Andrew Cyrille sounding winded and concussed. Very much of its time, and betraying occasional signs of a dialogue of the deaf, *Communications* is still an important historical document. However demanding its headlong progress may be on the intellect and the emotions, Mantler – like Barry Guy, who followed his example in the United Kingdom – has a considerable musical intelligence and shapes performances that have logic, form and a sort of chastening beauty.

Jazz Group Arkhangelsk

GROUP

Russian new-music ensemble, active at the beginning of the '90s.

***(*) Live In Japan

Ninety One CRCJ 9102 *Vladimir Rezitsky (as, f, melodica, perc); Vladimir Turov (syn); Nikolai Klishin (b, vn, hca); Oleg Yudanov (d, perc); Nikolai Yudanov (perc); Konstantin Sedovin (v).* 11/91.

*** Portrait

Leo CDLR 180 *As above, except omit Sedovin.* 11/91.

On the downside of the 'liberation' of Eastern Europe and Russia is a dramatic change in the status of creative artists in the former people's democracies. The Jazz Group Arkhangelsk is a perfect instance of a creatively adventurous ensemble that won official sanction, playing regular 'workers' concerts' in and around the northern port of Arkhangel. Typical of Russian new music – see entries on the Ganelin Trio and Sergey Kuryokhin – the JGA combined an accelerated historiography of jazz (they include 'Afro Blue' in the Tokyo concert) and a welter of native and imported popular musics. Leader Rezitsky is a deceptively smooth player, sounding almost as if he is still doing the restaurant gigs that supported the band until they received State backing. That isn't quite the case on *Portrait*, recorded at an impromptu concert at a community college in Leicester, with most of the band suffering from viruses. Generally, though, the overall blend is headlong, buoyant and joyous. The huge 'Sound Of The World' that makes up most of *Live In Japan* is the most characteristic performance currently on record. Unfortunately, like the Art Ensemble of Chicago, the JGA are difficult to assess on record. Unlike the Chicagoans, they have also been difficult for Westerners to see in the flesh.

Jazz Jamaica

GROUP

The impact of Caribbean music – ska, calypso, reggae, mento – on British jazz has been considerable. Figu es like Shake Keane, Harry Beckett and guitarist Ernest Ranglin ave left a substantial legacy; Gary Crosby, the former Jazz Warrior and de facto leader of Jazz Jamaica, is Ernest's nephew.

*** Skaravan

Skazz Records SKACD 001 *Eddie Thornton (t); Rico Rodriguez (tb); Michael Rose (ts, f); Cedric Brooks (ts); Clifton Morrison (ky, hca); Alan Weekes (g); Gary Crosby (b); Kenrick Rowe (d).* 93.

A unique and infectious fusion of musical styles, Jazz Jamaica's brand of 'skazz' sounds as if it's been around for ever. The best testimony to its naturalness is the title arrangement of the Juan Tizol/Duke Ellington tune, which joins Charlie Parker's 'Barbados' and a couple of Skatalites songs in a joyous programme of blowing tunes. The rhythms may be a little unvaried and the solos lacking somewhat in subtlety, but the impact of players like Rico Rodriguez, the legendary trombonist of the Skatalites, and of Clifton 'Bigga' Morrison, is unmistakable, and Crosby and Rowe hold the rhythm section together with great poise. Rico's solo on his own 'Ramblin'' is definitive. Hard to dislike, any of it, but possibly a bit one-dimensional for repeated hearings; almost inevitably, Jazz Jamaica are considerably more impressive as a live outfit.

The Jazz Passengers

GROUP

A New York band which seeks a measure of cabaret-theatre to go along with the expected post-modern shenanigans.

****** Implement Yourself**

New World/Countercurrents NW 398 *Curtis Fowlkes (tb); Roy Nathanson (as, ts, ss); Bill Ware (vib); Bill Nolet (vn); Marc Ribot (g, E flat horn); Bradley Jones (b); E. J Rodriguez (d, perc); Waldwick High School Marching Band.* 3/90.

***** Live At The Knitting Factory**

Knitting Factory KFWCD 107 *As above, except omit Ribot, band; add Marcus Roja (tba), Dave Fiuczinski (g), Dougie Bowne (d), Yuka Honda (samples).* 1/91.

***** Plain Old Joe**

Knitting Factory KFWCD 139 *As above, except omit Fuczinski, Roja, Bowne, Honda; add Michael Dorf (hca), Helen Wood (v).*

****** In Love**

High Street Records 72902 10328 *As above, except omit Dorf, Wood; add Marc Ribot, David Tronzo (g), Anthony Coleman (harm), Mary Wooten (clo), Bob Dorough, Mavis Staples, Deborah Harry, Jimmy Scott, Elisheba Fowlkes, Abie Rodriguez, Jenni Muldaur, Freddy Johnston, Manuel Oliveras, D.K. Dyson, Leopoldine Core, Carter Spurier, Wilbur Pauley, Marc Bleeke, Jeff Buckley, Kate Silverman, Laurie Gallucio (v).* 94.

The original idea was a trombone/saxophone duo consisting of Curtis Fowlkes and Roy Nathanson, but it has steadily expanded into a flexible ensemble that does what can only be described as a form of jazz cabaret. Many of the vocal arrangments are reminiscent, weirdly, of Carla Bley's *Escalator Over The Hill*, or one of Frank Zappa's jazzier projects, which may or may not be enticing news. If one could imagine an avant-garde or post-modern Crusaders, that might be even nearer the mark. The drill is not to expect anything too much like the last track/album. Fortunately, it's all done with too much wit and intelligence to risk the charge of mere perversity, and the playing, from Fowlkes and Nathanson especially, is so good that one seldom pauses to wonder why? or even what?

With impeccable illogic, the Passengers' first recording appeared on the Crepuscule label, which hails from Belgium and enjoys a somewhat twilit reputation elsewhere. Since the turn of the 1990s, the group has had a fairly regular berth at the Knitting Factory in New York City and their live album was cut there. It's by far the weakest of the available records and the only one to which the charge of self-indulgence sticks. Though they seem on the surface to be the quintessential live act, the Passengers are brilliant exponents of studio performance, and *Implement Yourself* manages to combine a relaxed 'live feel' with astonishing discipline and exactness. As befits a group that has grown organically, there is no obviously dominant voice, though Fowlkes and Nathanson are clearly the guiding personalities, somewhat like Zawinul and Shorter in Weather Report. Even so, Jones, Ware, Rodriguez and, somewhat episodically, Nolet add their two cents' worth, and it is difficult to conceive of the group (unlike the Report) other than as a unit. That being so, guests are absorbed into the unit quite seamlessly, rarely sticking out or intruding. *Implement Yourself* has much less vocal material than most, but Ribot's vocalized guitar-line intercutting with the vibes on the Dolphyish 'Peace In The Valley' takes the place of a conventional lyric. As a whole, it's a bruising but constantly fascinating listen. *Plain Old Joe* is somewhat closer to the group's music-theatre vein and doesn't come across so well on disc. There is a lack of presence, which certainly doesn't trouble *In Love*, one of those records that demand complete surrender and a suspension of all normal generic expectations. It starts off with a chaotic dialogue between the Angels, Mr Strawhat and the Underground Man, before segueing into the Ellingtonish 'Imitation Of A Kiss', sung 'straight' in Billie Carter/Peggy Lee manner over a late-nite vibes accompaniment, before Nathanson takes it away in a gloriously distraught tenor solo. The guest singers are extraordinary: Mavis Staples, Jeff Buckley and Deborah Harry – perhaps the only person on the planet who could deliver with conviction lines like: 'Just this mornin' I met a strange old man / A distant cousin at a taxi stand / The half-blind stepson of my weird aunt Flo.' Harry is now a regular vocalist with the band on their concerts, which are frequently unmissable.

The Jazz Tribe

GROUP

Co-led by percussionist Ray Mantilla and altoist Bobby Watson, the Tribe is effectively the Red Records house band, a dazzling collection of soloists matched by a first-rate rhythm section.

****** The Jazz Tribe**

Red RR 123254-2 *Jack Walrath (t); Bobby Watson (as); Steve Grossman (ts); Walter Bishop Jr (p); Charles Fambrough (b); Joe Chambers (d); Ray Mantilla (perc).* 12/90.

*****(*) The Next Step**

Red RR 123285-2 *Jack Walrath (t); Bobby Watson (as); Ronnie Mathews (p); Curtis Lundy (b); Victor Lewis (d); Ray Mantilla (perc).* 2/99.

Any useful definition of a tribe will talk about common origins and customs and above all a common language or group of dialects, and that is exactly what you get with this confederation of talents. Bobby Watson's understanding of bebop has always included a strongly Latin tinge, and he and Mantilla – who is the other axis of the group – seem to be linked telepathically. Walrath is a deliberately capricious player, but his witty take on jazz is grounded in an ironclad technique and in the wry, ironic approach to song one hears in 'The Straight Caballero' on the 1990 album. There are few clues that it was recorded live. One assumes it was taped through the desk, which isn't always ideal, but producers Alberto Alberti and Sergio Veschi have taken pains to balance the sound and only faint smatters of applause betray the tape's origins. In fact, it sounds more like a good studio recording than the later record. A decade on, the empathy is still very much there. Changes in personnel have made some difference to the balance of the group. Lewis is a drummer with strong ideas of his own, evident on his composition, 'Ella Dunham', and he doesn't work entirely easily alongside Mantilla. Chambers is more receptive and the balance of percussion is better on the earlier disc.

Overall, *The Jazz Tribe* has more musical substance. Watson's hotly uxorious 'Pamela' features one of his best ever solos, punctuated by idiosyncratic articulation – like the '*pa-pa-pa*' that presumably signals the lady's name – and his trademark smears of sound, halfway between Hodges and Coltrane. Everyone solos to wonderful effect on the long 'Caballero' and the middle of the set is dominated by a Mantilla *tour de force*, the well-known 'Synergy' followed by the rhythmically demanding 'Six For Kim'. Walter Bishop has ancestral ties to this music and he writes and plays with immense maturity. Grossman only stops by for the sole standard 'Star Eyes', but it's a guest spot that helps take the album up on to a new plane.

David Jean-Baptiste (born 1969)

BASS CLARINET, ALTO SAXOPHONE, CLARINET, KEYBOARDS

A generation after the legendary Joe Harriott and Shake Keane, Jean-Baptiste put new life into the Anglo-Caribbean connection in jazz. Keen to assert his British background, he has studiously avoided the faux-Americanism of some of his contemporaries. A confident and steady voice.

***** Feeling Tones**

Candid CCD 79744 *Jean-Baptiste; Rowland Sutherland (f, af); Alex Wilson (p, ky); Mervyn Africa, Jonathan Gee (p); Orphy Robinson (vib, mar); Morten Gronvad (Midi vib, kys); Alec Dankworth (b); Kenrick Rowe, Frank Tontoh (d); Richard Ajileye (perc); Phillip Jamma Stuart (steel d); Enyoman Gbesemete, Sabine Schmidt (v).* 97.

*****(*) Neuriba**

Candid BCCD 79204 *Jean-Baptiste; Ingrid Laubrock (ss); Tony Kofi (bs); Rowland Sutherland (f); Julian Joseph (p); Orphy Robinson (vib); Daniel Berdichevsky (g); Ricardo Dos Santos (b); Kenrick Rowe (d); Richard Ajileye (perc); Sandra Phenis, Mallissa Read (v).* 5/98.

Influenced by Eric Dolphy and, at somewhat closer hand, by saxophonist David Murray, Jean-Baptiste is nevertheless an individualist. His concentration on bass clarinet for five of the eleven tracks on *Feeling Tones* is only the most obvious homage. In his writing, too, he is marked by Dolphy's desire to work both 'inside' and 'outside' the logic of the chords. Marimba and piano lines abut but fail to interlock as expected on 'Murray's Montclaire Blue', and the beautifully voiced opposition of bass clarinet and flute on 'Cause And Effect', a tribute to Charles Mingus, drifts over a soft electronic shimmer from the keyboards. Jean-Baptiste shows a bold touch with a standard as well, interchanging bass and E-flat clarinets on 'You Don't Know What Love Is', as Alex Wilson (a responsive partner throughout) moves from piano to keys and back. They take the David Murray blues, 'Monarchs', absolutely straight as a duo, a performance topped only by the Mervyn Africa tune, 'No Way Home', on which Jean-Baptiste duets with the composer, bass clarinet again. The title-track is a Dolphyish epic, percussive and blunt but with an underlying lyricism; 'Jitterbug Waltz' departs significantly from Dolphy's famous 1963 version, but it's clear that Jean-Baptiste is aware of it.

The first album lacked nothing in either confidence or craft, but the follow-up is in every way a more assured statement. The real pay-off is the five-part 'Euro-Carib Classicism Suite', a title which sums up Jean-Baptiste's stylistic origins, but which also points to a musicological discursiveness entirely missing in the music. Joseph and Robinson and drummer Kenrick Rowe are the core of a highly accomplished band that sounds aware and technically astute even while it grooves. Jean-Baptiste plays with a calm authority (and an occasional flicker of black and red in the tonality) and his ability to shape a solo across a swing beat is ever more obvious. We're not entirely convinced by Mallissa Read's 'jazzoetry', but Sandra Phenis's vocal on 'Mysti' is tastefully done, very much in the spirit of the classic jazz singers. The real action, though, is between saxophone, piano and drums.

Eddie Jefferson (1918–79)

VOCALS

Along with King Pleasure, and Lambert, Hendricks and Ross, Eddie Jefferson was the big star of jazz vocalese, a style which involved putting lyrics to famous jazz solos; in Jefferson's case, the starting point was Coleman Hawkins's classic 'Body And Soul'. Originally a dancer, Eddie sang with a gruff grace and sustained a career as a member of James Moody's and then Richie Cole's groups right through to the end of his life.

*****(*) The Jazz Singer**

Evidence ECD 22062 *Jefferson; Frank Galbreath, John McFarland, Howard McGhee (t); Matthew Gee, Tom McIntosh (tb); Sahib Shihab (as); James Moody (ts); Musa Kaleem (ts, bs); Bill Graham (bs); Johnny Acea, Gene Kee, Tommy Tucker (p); Louisiana Red (g); John Latham, Peck Morrison (b); Clarence Johnson, Osie Johnson (d); Babs Gonzales, Honi Gordon, Ned Gravely (v).* 64–68.

***** Letter From Home**

Original Jazz Classics OJC 307 *Jefferson; Ernie Royal, Clark Terry (t); Jimmy Cleveland (tb); James Moody (as, f); Johnny Griffin (ts); Arthur Clarke (bs); Junior Mance, Joe Zawinul (p); Barry Galbraith (b); Louis Hayes, Osie Johnson, Sam Jones (d).* 12/61.

*****(*) Body And Soul**

Original Jazz Classics OJC 396 *Jefferson; Dave Burns (t); James Moody (ts, f); Barry Harris (p); Steve Davis (b); Bill English (d).* 9/68.

*****(*) Come Along With Me**

Original Jazz Classics OJC 613 *Jefferson; Bill Hardman (t); Charles McPherson (as); Barry Harris (p); Gene Taylor (b); Bill English (d).* 8/69.

A death sentence is a pretty harsh review, as Ralph Ellison wrote of Salman Rushdie. In 1979, the sixty-year-old Jefferson was shot dead outside the Detroit club in which he'd been appearing. Like most of the bebop vocalists – and despite a brief recent revival in the critical fortunes of King Pleasure, who successfully co-opted Jefferson's style – he is little known among younger jazz fans, and various attempts at revival in recent years have fallen rather flat. A Muse disc, currently out of circulation with the rest of that label, dubbed him 'The Godfather Of Vocalese', and there is some justice in this. There is a widespread belief that Pleasure wrote the lyrics to 'Moody's Mood For Love', a vocalized transcription of James Moody's alto saxophone solo on 'I'm In The Mood For Love'; Pleasure certainly made it a monster hit, but the song was Jefferson's.

The early material on *The Jazz Singer* is taken from an Inner City LP, augmented by six rare tracks, some of which have not been available before. There are interesting duets from 1964 and 1965 with pianist Tommy Tucker ('Silly Little Cynthia') and guitarist Louisiana Red ('Red's New Dream'), but the key material is the well-known stuff: Parker's 'Now's The Time', Jimmy Forrest's 'Night Train' and, of course, 'Moody's Mood For Love' and the intelligent and inventive 'Body And Soul' (later revived by Manhattan Transfer as a tribute to Jefferson), which are also included on the fine 1968 session, also featuring Moody and a brilliant version of 'Filthy McNasty'.

Letter boasts a heavyweight line-up and some sure-footed – Jefferson was also a dancer – vocal arrangements. Four of the tracks are for sextet, but the better pieces use the full breadth of the band, with Jefferson high-wiring it over the 29-year-old Joe Zawinul's spry comping; check out Jefferson's version of the pianist's 'Mercy, Mercy, Mercy' on the 1968 *Body And Soul*. The singer's longest-standing partnership, with saxophonist Moody, is reflected in a dozen cuts, one of the best of which is a lively 'So What' (again on *Body And Soul*). Their relationship had rekindled in the 1960s when Jefferson, who had been eclipsed by smoother talents like Jon Hendricks, staged something of a comeback; the later sessions (*Come Along With Me*) with Bill Hardman and Charles McPherson on staples like 'Yardbird Suite' and 'Dexter Digs In' are well worth catching, though the voice has lost some of its elasticity and bounce. Like King Pleasure, Jefferson improvised and wrote lyrics to some of the classic bop solos; precisely because they worked such similar turf, there was a constant risk of copyright wrangles, which explains why 'Body And Soul' is sometimes retitled 'I Feel So Good', 'Parker's Mood' and 'Bless My Soul'.

Vocalese has never recaptured the success it enjoyed when these sides were recorded. In recent years, though, it has shaken off something of the stigma it had acquired and is again being taken seriously. Eddie Jefferson commands a place – albeit a small one – in any comprehensive collection.

Billy Jenkins (born 1956)

GUITAR, PIANO, VOICE

Basing himself in Bromley, Kent, Jenkins has progressed from his pub-rock roots into a visionary figure whose embrace of jazz, rock and other musics is intensely personal and creative, even if it is constantly undercut by his satiric bent and bravura eccentricity. He recorded constantly in the '80s and '90s, mainly on his own labels, and has employed most of the best of the younger British jazz musicians to play on them at some point.

****** Scratches Of Spain**

Babel BDV 9404 *Jenkins; Chris Batchelor, John Eacott, Skid Solo (t); Dave Jago (tb); Ashley Slater (btb, tba, v); Iain Ballamy, Steve Buckley, (sax); Dai Pritchard (sax, cl); Dave Cooke (g); Django Bates (ky); Jimmy Haycraft (vib); Jo Westcott (clo); Tim Matthewman, Simon Edwards (b); Steve Arguëlles, Roy Dodds (d, perc); Dawson (perc).* 87.

***** Entertainment USA**

Babel BDV 9401 *Jenkins; John Eacott (t); John Harborne (tb); Mark Lockheart (ts); Martin Speake (as); Django Bates (ky); Maria Lamburn (vla); Huw Warren (acc, clo); Steve Watts (b); Roy Dodds (d); Dawson, Martin France (perc); Lol Graves, Suzy M, Lindy Lou, Tina G, Tony Messenger (v).* 94.

***** Mayfest '94**

Babel BDV 9502 *Jenkins; Rainer Brennecke (t); Jorg Huke (tb); Thomas Klemm (ts, f); Huw Warren (p, acc, glockenspiel); Steve Watts (b); Martin France (d).* 5/94.

****** First Aural Art Exhibition**

VOTP VOCD 921 *Jenkins; John Eacott, Skid Solo (t); John Harborne, Dave Jago (tb); Ashley Slater (btb, tba); Iain Ballamy, Mark Ramsden, Martin Speake (as); Steve Buckley, Mark Lockheart (ts); Dai Pritchard (bs, bcl); Stuart Hall, Andy McFarlane (vn); Jo Westcott (clo); Dave Cooke, Robin Aspland (g); Jim Haycraft (vib); Steve Berry, Winston Blissett, Tim Matthewman, Steve Watts (b); Roy Dodds, Martin France (d); Dawson (perc).* 84–91.

*****(*) Still ... Sounds Like Bromley**

Babel BDV 9717 *Jenkins; Claude Deppa (t); Roland Bates (tb); Iain Ballamy (as, ts); Dai Pritchard (bcl); Django Bates (ky); James Taylor (org); Davey Williams (g); Steve Watts, Mike Mondesir (b); Martin France (d); David Vine (perc); strings.* 95.

Billy Jenkins is a musical anarchist. Notably resistant to ideology, he espouses a version of the kitchen-sink Situationism which lay behind the British punk movement. If music has become business (an equation he rejects), then the only refuge is a kind of unselfconscious anti-technique Jenkins has christened 'Spazz', which encourages the retention of 'wrong' notes and false starts, and the propagation of lo-fi recordings on the least sophisticated of formats. Jenkins is uniquely concerned with the packaging of music, not just in the cardboard-and-laminate sense but in terms of its perceived contours and limits. His 'Big Fights' encounters restrict duo improvisation to 12 three-minute 'rounds', the antithesis of the open-ended approach of most 'free' improvisers, but which also levels pertinent comment at their tacit belief that sheer duration is an end in itself. More satirically, Jenkins has presented 'uncommercial' samples of his work in chocolate wrappers, a neat comment on music's consumable nature, and has mimicked ECM and Windham Hill colophons and the ubiquitous 'Nice Price' cover to Miles Davis's *Sketches Of Spain*. *Scratches of Spain* is, rightly, Jenkins's most celebrated single record, a frantic, un-Cool exposition of 'Spazz' technique and his deployment of a ragged army of co-religionists known as the Voice of God Collective. *Scratches*' arrival on CD doesn't for a moment diminish its brutal simplicity or its deceptive sophistication as a piece of 'product'. Jenkins's transfer to CD is not yet total, and a good deal of his work, including the 'Big Fights', may still be found on Voice of the People cassettes, but we have not listed these this time round. Jenkins has been around on the British scene long enough now for pieces like 'Benidorm Motorway Services' and 'Cooking Oil' to have become minor classics, albeit harder to hum than the adagio from *Concierto de Aranjuez*. In place of the 'Spanish tinge', a pervasive greasy taste. In place of Gil Evans's limpid orchestration, the 'ensemble' sound of a dozen lager louts going home at 2 a.m., like the discoboats that used to compromise Jenkins's rest in his studio home at Greenwich.

His gift for pastiche and even meta-pastiche is more evident still on the brilliant *Entertainment USA*, a collection of bilious and affectionate tributes to great American entertainers like Ronald Reagan, Oliver North, daffy-haired boxing promoter and philanthropist Don King, and Charles Manson, to say nothing of weightier individuals like Doris Day, Elvis Presley and Johnny Cash. Both the excellent *First Aural Art Exhibition* and the live Glasgow gig with the Fun Horns offer a chance to hear earlier Jenkins opus numbers on CD, in advance of some of the earlier vinyl and cassettes being reissued entire. The former includes 'Brilliant', 'Expensive Equipment', 'Fat People', 'The Blues', 'Sade's Lips', 'Discoboats At Two O'Clock', 'Cooking Oil', 'Donkey Droppings', and 'Elvis Presley', which – initiates will confirm – is a pretty fair representation. The Glasgow session has, *inter alia*, 'Arrival Of The Tourists', 'Greenwich One Way System' and 'Fat People', delivered in a rough-and-ready taping straight off the mixing desk at the old Renfrew Ferry. *Still ... Sounds Like Bromley* is a definitive Jenkins band line-up and seems to some extent like a dry run for the conceptual masterpiece which is listed below, although this is more specifically prepared for jazz band: David Vine's steel pan solo on 'High Street/Part Pedestrianized' virtually invents a jazz vocabulary for that instrument, and throughout there are marvellously vivid moments of Jenkinsization. As always, genres and the whole idea of 'genre' are turned upside down. It may be that Frank Zappa is the nearest measurable equivalent to Jenkins, but it seems unlikely that he would be flattered by the comparison and it may yet be that he is a more significant figure.

****** Suburbia**

Babel BDV 9926 *Jenkins; Rainer Brennecke (t); Jorg Huke (tb); Mark Lockheart (saxes); Volker Schlott (as); Thomas Klemm (ts); Kit Packham (bs); Dave Ramm (ky); Huw Warren (p); David Le Page, Matt Sharp (vn); Neil Catchpole (vla); Chris Allen (clo); Steve Watts (b); Martin France, Roy Dodds, Steve Noble (d); Nicky Kemp, Gem Howard, Cassidy Howard-Kemp, Alice Jenkins, Harriet Jenkins, Daisy Lockheart, Rita Lockheart, Grace Messenger, Roxanne Messenger, Kati Tighe, Sophie Tighe (v); Suzy M (chorus mistress).* 99.

Jenkins has been busy, as usual, and while some may cavil at even including him in the book, it would be an outrage to omit this Home-Counties masterpiece, a concept album about Bromley as a home of the blues, with all its attendant irritations and virtues alike. The titles of some of these pieces – 'The Unknown Car Across Your Drive', 'Corner Shop With Security Grills' and so on – make manifest the subtext of the record, but the music is vintage Jenkins, bits and pieces from all over the place, fused by great playing and sheer determination. American readers will be baffled by him; but he is, along with the Princess Royal and Walthamstow dog stadium, one of our national treasures.

Leroy Jenkins (born 1932)

VIOLIN, VIOLA

Jenkins spent some time away from his native Chicago, teaching in the south, before returning to Chicago and becoming part of the influential AACM. His extended approach embraces classical violin of the Heifetz era with contemporary free jazz. Jenkins has been a member of the Revolutionary Ensemble and was leader of the advanced group, Sting.

***** Lifelong Ambitions**

Black Saint 120033 *Jenkins; Muhal Richard Abrams (p).* 3/77.

***** The Legend Of Ai Glatson**

Black Saint 120022 *Jenkins; Anthony Davis (p); Andrew Cyrille (d, perc).* 7/78.

*****(*) Mixed Quintet**

Black Saint 120060 *Jenkins; John Clark (frhn); James Newton (f); J.D Parran (cl); Marty Ehrlich (bcl).* 3/79.

****(*) Urban Blues**

Black Saint 120083 *Jenkins; Terry Jenoure (vn, v); James Emery, Brandon Ross (g); Alonzo Gardner (b); Kamal Sabir (d).* 1/84.

*****(*) Live!**

Black Saint 120122 *Jenkins; Brandon Ross (g); Eric Johnson (syn); Hill Greene (b); Reggie Nicholson (d).* 3/92.

Leroy Jenkins and George Lewis share one often-forgotten characteristic that makes them ideal improvising partners. Though both are given to very forceful and even violent gestures, they are also capable of great lyricism; the same has to be said of Andrew Cyrille. In a period when Billy Bang is, rightly or wrongly, the benchmark jazz violinist, critics have often missed the fact that Jenkins's percussive, rasping delivery rarely departs from an identifiable tonal centre or melodic logic. His preference is for looping statements, punctuated by abrupt rhythmic snaps; the most obvious influence is Stuff Smith, but there are also parallels with the way saxophonist Anthony Braxton used to deliver improvised lines. Like pianist Anthony Davis, Jenkins has an almost 'legitimate' technique and a tone that one can imagine negotiating with Bartók or Stravinsky.

Davis is present on *The Legend Of Ai Glatson*, which was recorded shortly after the Revolutionary Ensemble disbanded. It is one of the few places in contemporary jazz where the direct and unassimilated influence of Cecil Taylor can be detected, and it remains strongly reminiscent of Cecil's Café Montmartre sessions. Jenkins is in stunningly good form, and his solo play on tributes to two modern saxophone players, 'Brax Stone' and 'Albert Ayler (His Life Was Too Short)' is as good as anything in his catalogue. *Legend* isn't the prettiest of recordings, but it has all the intensity Jenkins brings to live performance.

The *Mixed Quintet* session is a foretaste of the classical configurations that were to follow. Some of the titles might sound restrainedly formal – 'Quintet #3', 'Shapes, Textures, Rhythms, Moods' – but none of these are merely abstract études or exercises, and all of them have Jenkins's trademark blend of intense expression and admirable control. The four wind players who join him are all, of course, masters in their own right, and Ehrlich is revelatory, a player as strongly rooted in classic jazz as he is in European art music.

Jenkins released no commercial recordings between 1984 and 1992, and his back-catalogue is in a rather threadbare state. Jenkins's working band, Sting, were capable of great things in a live setting, but they're nothing compared to the new Computer Minds. The live session completely merits the exclamation mark. It's a fierce, urgent session, recorded in a New York public school, and sounds appropriately in contact with what's going on in the streets. To an extent, Jenkins is a traditionalist rather than a radical. His interests, though, have always reached well beyond jazz, and his band tackles a whole range of black musics.

The duos with Abrams are also both traditionally minded and innovative. All the compositions are from the violinist, even the closing 'The Father, The Son, The Holy Ghost', which clearly isn't the same as the Albert Ayler piece. Like their titles – 'The Blues', 'Meditation', 'Happiness' – the pieces are kept pretty abstract (and are all almost exactly the same length). There's a patient, almost schoolmasterly side to Abrams's playing. Jenkins moves off into pan-tonality a few times, but he stays firmly anchored in an identifiable key for most of the set, even when his partner has dissolved the normal ties of melody and accompaniment. It's difficult to tell when they're improvising and when reading, and the abiding impression is of formality rather than freedom.

Urban Blues is a less-than-representative account of a band that on its night could be wildly exciting. Recorded live in Sweet Basil in New York City (on 2 January, which might explain the liverish playing), it comes across as muddled rather than waspy. Terry Jenoure's vocals were a luxury that Sting could have dispensed with, and the twinned guitars (great players when on their own turf) are often repetitive and unilluminating. The CD brightens up the sound considerably, but doubts remain.

****** Themes & Improvisations On The Blues**

CRI 663 *Jenkins; Frank Gordon (t); Jeff Hoyer (tb); Henry Threadgill (f); Don Byron (cl); Janet Grice (bsn); Myra Melford (p); Jane Henry, David Soldier (vn); Ron Lawrence, Laura Seaton (vla); May Wooton (clo); Lindsay Horner (b); Thurman Barker (d).* 4/92.

Poised with ever more confidence between classical composition and free jazz, this ambitious session consists of four long pieces. The title-track is an object lesson in the extension of blues forms into large-ensemble writing. The other tracks, 'Panorama I', 'Off Duty Dryad' and 'Monkey On The Dragon', are similarly conceived but more loosely constructed. Where 'Themes & Improvisations' is solo-plus-ensemble, the remainder of the album is more of a collective performance. Jenkins is recorded rather quietly and somewhat off to one side, but his command of the project is undoubted.

****** Solo**

Lovely Music 134 *Jenkins (vn solo).* 98.

There is a grizzled majesty to this unaccompanied set, a confident conflation of traditions. Tackling 'Giant Steps' and Dizzy's 'Wouldn't You' on solo fiddle and viola bespeaks some courage, but Jenkins skates across those familiar harmonics with breathtaking ease. The recording is up-close and very personal, and anyone who has not encountered his work previously will be captivated.

Ingrid Jensen (born 1969)

TRUMPET, FLUGELHORN

Jensen's musical progress has been astonishing. At 25, she became the youngest faculty member at the Bruckner Conservatory in Linz, adding academic honours to a growing list of performing and recording credits with the likes of Kenny Barron, the Mingus Big Band and the Maria Schneider Orchestra. Her trumpet tone is highly distinctive, like oiled silk.

***** Vernal Fields**

Enja ENJ 9013-2 *Jensen; Steve Wilson (as, ss); George Garzone (ts); Bruce Barth (p); Larry Grenadier (b); Lenny White (d).* 10/94.

*****(*) Here On Earth**

Enja ENJ 9313-2 *Jensen; Gary Bartz (as, ss); George Colligan (p); Dwayne Burno (b); Bill Stewart (d); Jill Seifers (v).* 9/96.

*****(*) Higher Grounds**

Enja ENJ 9353-2 *Jensen; Gary Thomas (ts, f); Dave Kikoski (p, el p); Ed Howard (b); Victor Lewis (d).* 98.

Jensen is a young Canadian propelled on to an international stage by the growing confidence and adventurousness of the scene back home. It's perhaps significant, though, that she should have been picked up by a European label, fruit of a period of study in Vienna with pianist Hal Galper. Purely in terms of sound, she resembles a cross between Woody Shaw (an acknowledged hero) and Art Farmer, with whom she has also taken classes. The latter debt is predictably most evident when she switches to flugelhorn; when she does so on the title-track of *Here On Earth*, it is immediately evident that she intends to do things her own way, as she did on the debut album, where 'Every Time We Say Goodbye' sounds like a Farmer pastiche only until Jensen is ready to make her own statement. Though 'Here On Earth' is pianist George Colligan's composition and though Jensen is sharing the front line with the veteran Gary Bartz (who has rarely sounded better, incidentally), she stamps her personality even on this rather slight, Latinized waltz. On 'Woodcarvings', the other debt is made explicit, a dense but curiously floating theme that one might imagine Woody playing himself. This time Bartz is on soprano, masterfully negotiating a theme that sits awkwardly for the horns but which is made to sound as natural as breathing. Stewart is a calm and steady presence throughout, less showy than White in the way that Bartz is less emphatically expressive than Wilson, but unfailingly musical all the same.

What sets the second album apart more than anything isn't the playing – which is superlative – so much as the choice of material. It's a beautifully judged set: just the one original, and this time one by sister Christine Jensen (who wrote four of the tunes on *Vernal Fields*); alongside this, themes by Cole Porter, Hank Mobley, Kenny Wheeler, Miles Davis and Gil Evans's 'The Time Of The Barracudas', and Mercedes Rossi's 'Ninety-One', the latter an unexpectedly lyrical gem. Jill Seifers's two vocals are somewhat dispensable, but they do contribute an intelligent change of pace and add a new range of colours to a beautifully modulated set. One simply basks in Gary Bartz's warm-hearted wisdom, and in Jensen's own poise and confidence.

The third album simply builds on its predecessors, but there are signs that Jensen is increasingly thinking of the band as a unit, a collective instrument, rather than as an aggregate of individuals. The arrangements, especially on 'Litha' and the closing 'Land Of Me' are very tight and highly organized, though not so excessively programmed that they lose the feeling of improvisational looseness which is also a characteristic of her work. The rhythm section is utterly sympathetic, and in Gary Thomas she has found a second horn who challenges her in the most positive way. *Higher Grounds* includes some of his best work of recent times. Jensen continues to impress.

Jeff Jerolamon (born 1955)

DRUMS

Mainstream-modern drummer with a penchant for the stylings of the great swing players.

***** Introducing Jeff Jerolamon**

Candid CCD 79522 *Jerolamon; George Cables (p); Javier Colin (b). 10/91.*

***** Swing Thing!**

Candid CCD 79538 *Jerolamon; Randy Sandke (t); Doug Lawrence (ts); George Cables (p); Harvie Swartz (b). 7/93.*

Jerolamon's heart is on his sleeve. His household gods are not Elvin Jones or even Klook, but the drummers of the swing generation, men like Gene Krupa, Buddy Rich and Louie Bellson. The second record is much more obviously in that line and – retrospectively at least – one detects Jerolamon's slight discomfort with some of the settings on *Introducing*; too far down the bebop road for this most mainstream of drummers. Recorded in Valencia at the end of a highly successful Spanish tour, the debut set has a sun-warmed spontaneity that has at least as much to do with Cables's confident swing as with the drummer's undoubted skills. The pianist contributes two originals, 'Dark Side/Light Side' and 'Quiet Fire', which sit very comfortably alongside such well-worn standards as 'Round Midnight', 'Straight, No Chaser', 'A Night in Tunisia' and 'You Stepped Out Of A Dream'. It might have been better to have placed more emphasis on original themes, for Jerolamon comes out of a tradition that isn't strictly jazz-based. It's still possible to hear the narrow-gauge steadiness of a rock beat from time to time, and that sits slightly awkwardly with the Monk tunes especially. He takes to Bobby Hutcherson's 'Little B's Poem' so adroitly that you almost wish he could switch to vibes for the duration.

Swing Thing! is less laid back, a little pushier, and it suits the rhythm section well. While Randy Sandke (featured on just three tracks, two Charlie Shavers tunes and the Goodman/Christian 'Seven Come Eleven') contributes very little, Lawrence has the deceptively lazy swing and dramatic bite of Paul Gonsalves. Cables is heroic throughout, and especially good on 'Nancy With The Laughing Face' and the Monk medley, for our money the heart of an otherwise slightly directionless set.

Jerry Jerome (born 1912)

TENOR SAXOPHONE, CLARINET

Busy since the 1930s, Jerome has had a long jazz life, working as a section-player with Miller, Goodman and Shaw and as a studio regular thereafter.

*****(*) Something Old, Something New**

Arbors ARCD 19168 2CD *Jerome; Yank Lawson, Chris Griffin, Bobby Hackett, Dale McMickle, Mel Davis, Randy Sandke (t); Henry 'Red' Allen (t, v); George Masso, John Messner, Frank Sirocco, Vernon Brown, Ray Coniff (tb); Tyree Glenn (tb, vib); Bill Stegmeyer (cl); Toots Mondello, Paul Rickey, Wolfie Tannenbaum (as); Arthur Rollini, Hymie Schertzer (ts); Joe Grim (bs); Teddy Wilson, John Potoker, Dick Hyman, Johnny Guarnieri, Frankie Hines, Dick Cary, Bill Clifton (p); Phil Kraus (vib); Charlie Christian, Johnny Smith, Allen Hanlon (g); Oscar Pettiford, Bob Haggart, Sid Weiss, George Roumanis, Tommy Abruzzo (b); George Wettling, Joe Ascione, Mousie Alexander, Dave Tough, Specs Powell (d). 9/39–3/96.*

Jerome's name appears several times in our index, but this was his first jazz album for 40 years. The first disc is almost a 'bonus' album, since it consists of Jerry reminiscing on his career – with Glenn Miller, Goodman and Shaw, and as a studio regular. There are some fascinating fragments from many years of work – a 1939 jam with Charlie Christian, small groups with Charlie Shavers and Teddy Wilson, commercials featuring Bobby Hackett and Henry Allen and plenty more besides. Not a record to hear often, but an engaging audio-documentary. The 'New' section is a delight. Jerome was almost 84 when he made the date, but his tenor sound is still big and unfaltering, and none of the tempos trouble him. Arbors assembled one of their repertory casts for the session and, with Sandke and Masso at their best, it's a fine hour or so of blue-chip mainstream, and a beguiling tribute to a likeable old pro.

Bjorn Johansen (born 1940)

TENOR SAXOPHONE

A senior member of Norway's mainstream jazz movement, Johansen's music has rarely got much further than his native scene and his gracious playing is in consequence little known to the wider jazz audience.

***** Dear Henrik**

Gemini GMCD 52 *Johansen; Erling Aksdal (p); Carl Morten Iversen (b); Ole Jacob Hansen (d). 2–5/86.*

***** Take One**

Odin 21 *Johansen; Cedar Walton (p); David Williams (b); Billy Higgins (d).*

A Norwegian with much local experience but with little exposure overseas, Johansen is one of the many cases of European jazz musicians who ought to be better known outside their local base. His leathery tone and sometimes gnarled phrasing remind one of Clifford Jordan, and it's no surprise to find a tune on the Gemini album dedicated to the American saxophonist. Johansen works a furrow which is much like other post-bop – but, as conventional as it may be, the music never quite settles into cliché or routine. 'Beside', on *Dear Henrik*, opens as a ballad yet gathers power and momentum in a surprising way, with Aksdal proving a match for Walton on the 'American' session. Higgins gives an ounce or two of extra lift to the Odin record, but there is really little to choose between them, although the Gemini is recorded a little more modestly in terms of sonic punch.

Henrik Johansen (1935–92)

CLARINET

Danish clarinettist who began as a strict trad performer, playing some sessions in London in the '50s, before moving into a more mainstream style in his later years.

***** Og Det Var Så Det!**

Storyville STCD 5501 *Johansen; Gunnar Johnsson, Theis Egil Jensen (c); Al Fairweather, Chris Bateson, Jorn Thomsen, Valdemar Rasmussen (t); Peter Nyegaard, Arne Bue Jensen, John R.T Davies, Ole Toft (tb); Sandy Brown (cl); Adrian Bentzon, Bent Eriksen, Hans Otto Jorgensen (p); Russell Quay (g, kz, v); Jack Elliott, Hylda Sims (g, v); Diz Disley (g); Knud Fryland (g, bj); Freddy Poulson, Anthony Buguet, Per Krogh (bj); Fridolin Bentzon (bj, b); Ole Christiansen, Major Holley, Jens Solund, Heinz Carstens, Hugo Rasmussen, Henrik Hartmann (b); Ole Karn, Henrik Eigil Jensen, Graham Burbidge, Niels Bodker, Poul Jensen, Ole Streenberg (d); Alan Sutton (wbd).* 54–81.

A splendid memorial to a musician whose sympathies stretched well across the jazz spectrum. The opening track, a 1954 version of 'Careless Love', sets the Danish clarinettist down as a classic-jazz stylist, but the final tracks find him in more mainstream company and, though his strong tone and agile phrasing show preference for the New Orleans masters, he holds his own with the maverick Sandy Brown on four tracks where they cross liquorice sticks. There is a nice 'New Orleans Hop Scop Blues' with Fairweather, Davies and Disley, a track with the City Ramblers Skiffle Group and a very fine 'Cool Water' from a 1963 session with his own band. Johansen is always at least as good as the best man on the date, and he's usually better. Excellent sound throughout from diverse source material.

Jan Johansson (born 1944)

GUITAR

Guitarist and teacher based in Stockholm, playing in a modern-midstream style.

***** Blaus**

Dragon DRCD 272 *Johansson; Red Mitchell (b, p, v).* 9/89.

Johansson is a music teacher and occasional performer who struck up a friendship with Red Mitchell that resulted in their working as a duo in the last years of the bassist's life. This disc of duets was cut at Red's Stockholm apartment and is the only souvenir of their work together. The easeful charm and sly intelligence which Mitchell injected into every date holds this one together: Johansson plays very capably, but his twangy sound and spidery inflexions are made to sound even thinner by Red's characteristically boomy parts. There is a lovely treatment of 'Lover Man' among the five standards on display, and 'In A Sentimental Mood' is nearly as good. Sound isn't bad, but it would have been good to have heard the duo in a proper studio situation.

Jan Johansson (1931–68)

PIANO, ORGAN, VIBES

Born in Söderhamn, Johansson studied piano from the age of eleven. He moved to Copenhagen in the late '50s and then to Stockholm in 1962. He became a prolific composer and performer in the Swedish modern scene of the '60s and wrote music for film, radio and TV, as well as recording his own albums, but a meteoric career was cut short by his death in a car accident en route to a concert.

****(*) En Resa I Jazz Och Folkton**

Heptagon HECD-0101 *Johansson; Bernt Rosengren (ts); Rune Gustafsson (g); Sture Akerberg, Roman Dylag (b); Egil Johansen (d); Rupert Clemendore (perc).* 2/61–8/66.

****** 8 Bitar Johansson / Innertrio**

Heptagon HECD-005 *Johansson; Gunnar Johnson, Georg Riedel (b); Ingvar Callmer, Egil Johansen (d).* 2/61–7/62.

****** Folkvisor**

Heptagon HECD-000 *As above, except add Bosse Broberg (t), Arne Domnérus (cl), Lennart Aberg (ts); omit Johnson and Callmer.* 2/62–9/67.

***** Spelar Musik Pa Sitt Eget Vis**

Heptagon HECD-012 *Johansson; Andreas Skjold (tb); Arne Domnérus (as, cl); Claes Rosendahl (cl, f); Rune Gustafsson (g); Sture Nordin (b); Egil Johansen (d); Rupert Clemendore (perc).* 10/64–11/66.

*****(*) Jazz Pa Ungerska / In Pleno**

Heptagon HECD-014 *Johansson; Svend Asmussen (vn); Rune Gustafsson (g); Palle Danielsson, Georg Riedel (b); Egil Johansen (d); Rupert Clemendore (perc).* 64.

*****(*) Live In Tallinn**

Heptagon HECD-007 *Johannson; Rune Gustafsson (g); Georg Riedel (b).* 6/66.

***** Spelar Musik Pa Sitt Eget Vis**

Megafon MFCD-2021 2CD *Johansson; Andreas Skjold (tb); Arne Domnérus (cl, as); Claes Rosendahl (cl); Bjarne Nerem (ts); Rune Gustafsson (g); Georg Riedel, Sture Nordin, Sture Akerberg (b); Egil Johansen, Rupert Clemendore (d).* 9/64–11/66.

****** Den Korta Fristen**

Heptagon HECD-001 *Johansson; Bertil Lövgren, Rolf Ericson, Jan Allan, Bosse Broberg, Lars Samuelsson (t); Runo Ericksson (btb); Arne Domnérus, Claes Rosendahl, Lennart Aberg, Erik Nilsson, Rune Falk (reeds); Rune Gustafsson (g); Georg Riedel (b); Egil Johansen (d).* 67–68.

***** 300,000**

Heptagon HECD-006 *Johansson; Lennart Aberg (ts); Georg Riedel (b); Egil Johansen, Rupert Clemendore (d); Gote Nilsson (elec).* 8/67–7/68.

***** Musik Genom Fyra Sekler**

Heptagon HECD-002 2CD *Johansson; Claes Rosendahl (cl, f); Sven Berger (f, ob, bsn); Rune Gustafsson (g); Georg Riedel (b); Arne Wilhelmsson, Sture Akerberg (b).* 9–10/68.

Johansson was badly neglected by CD reissue until comparatively recently – so much so that many outside Sweden may scarcely be aware of this pioneering composer-pianist whose inquiring mind was extraordinary enough to demand a place for him among the modern masters of the music. Heptagon's initiative has done much to bring back several of Johansson's major albums. Though most of his recording was compressed into an eight-year period, he was prolific enough to have cut some 20 LPs, and several of the best are now back in circulation. Many may know him for his work with Stan Getz on some of the saxophonist's recordings in Scandinavia, but that seems like mere 'prentice-work compared with the two marvellous discs reissued on *8 Bitar Johansson/Innertrio*. Beautifully shaded between differing jazz styles, the music seems entirely fresh and unjaded, even after almost 40 years. The standards include a lovely 'She's Funny That Way' and a remarkable revision of Morton's 'The Chant', while the originals drift placidly between bebop and swing tempo, improvisations falling out of the set patterns, tamed by the lucidity of Johansson's touch and the variety of his voicings. *Folkvisor* is, if anything, even more impressive, bringing together the original albums, *Jazz Pa Svenska* and *Jazz Pa Ryska*. The 12 variations on Swedish folksong, with only the solid Riedel for company, make up a heartfelt meditation that equals any fusion of jazz and folk music so far committed to disc and, if the Russian themes that make up the rest of the disc are less affecting, they're a delightful makeweight. Johansson's insights are uniquely valuable and it's fitting that his own notes mention Jimmy Giuffre, since one is reminded of the American folklore which Giuffre inculcated into his own masterpiece, *The Jimmy Giuffre Clarinet*.

A recent reissue couples *Jazz Pa Ungerska*, where Johansson's usual team are joined by Svend Asmussen for another investigation of local themes, this time from Hungary, and the almost experimental *In Pleno*, where strange pieces such as 'Musik' and 'Mitt Piano' mingle with Coleman's 'Una Muy Bonita' and a tremendous fast blues, 'Pleno'. With the Asmussen tracks a fine legacy, this is another strong issue. Less successful is the patched-together *En resa I Jazz Och Folkton*, which includes some early mischief-making – 'Tea For Two' is double-tracked with a backwards-tape solo, and 'Tico Tico' is ludicrously fast – as well as an unexpected appearance by Rosengren on one track, a waltz, a couple of polkas and some unfunky Hammond organ. For Johansson collectors only.

The live album suffers from indifferent sound but gains from the intense communication among the three men, Gustafsson sounding especially involved: sample the interplay on 'Blues For Lange', or the jaunty treatment given to Oscar Pettiford's 'Laverne Walk'. *Spelar Musik Pa Sitt Eget Vis* is comparatively disappointing, a hotch-potch of bits and pieces from various radio sessions: there's a fine 'Django' with strings and some other telling fragments, but some of the experiments take on an unappealing cast – a strange 'Camptown Races', for instance. Half of this set is also available on the one-disc *Spelar Musik Pa Sitt Eget Vis*, now also available on Heptagon. This is completely outdone by the compelling scores for Radiojazz Gruppen on *Den Korta Fristen*, music of real power and originality that makes one realize why his fellow-musicians held Johansson in such high regard. The almost shocking revision of 'A Night In Tunisia', set up as a feature for Nilsson's superb baritone, is a revelation – but so is 'Hej Blues', a haunting feature for Domnérus, the sparse setting for Gustafsson on 'Samba Triste' and several of Johansson's own scores, crowded with ideas.

Another live album, *300,000*, is less essential: Johansson had a taste for flirting with the edges of the avant-garde, and the two pieces which involve electronics and radio static sound as dated as most such adventures of the period. *Musik Genom Fyra Sekler* is a curious coda to the rest, a double-CD covering further explorations into Swedish traditional music. Johansson handles his group like a chamber ensemble, the reed players switching between instruments from track to track, melodies given a poker-faced treatment or just slightly subverted by the leader's variations. 'Ack Varmeland Du Skona', which every Swedish jazzman has played at some point, is given a soberly attractive reading, but some of the other tunes run dangerously close to kitsch. An odd if intriguing end: Johansson's death was only weeks away.

Ulf Johansson (born 1957)

PIANO, TROMBONE, VOCAL

A Swedish jazz Everyman, Johansson is a strong piano player who likes to play trombone and manages to be convincing in styles ranging from Dixieland to post-bop, although most of his records find him in some kind of mainstream setting.

****(*) Trackin' The Wulf**

Phontastic PHONT 8809 *Johansson (p solo); Kicki Werre-Johansson (v).* 1/91.

*****(*) The Wobbling Woodwinds – Solo Flight**

Phontastic NCD 8829 *Johansson; Tord Larsson, Peter Lindqvist, Jan Lundberg, Stefan Lindberg, Jan-Eric Sundqvist (woodwinds); Tor Holmstrom (p); Stefan Nordgaard (g); Stefan Karlsson (b); Ulf Degerman (d).* 5/93.

***** Hot Time In Umea!**

Phontastic NCD 8833 *Johansson; Antti Sarpila (cl); Ronnie Gardiner (d).* 8/93.

Johansson plays good trombone, but he sticks to the piano on *Trackin' The Wulf* for a bright recital of swing-styled piano. Despite his comparative youth, it's the earlier generation of Wilson, Waller and perhaps Nat Cole that Johansson seems to admire, and he likes a striding left hand more than any bebop triplets. The 16 tracks include plenty of pre-war chestnuts as well as four originals of his own, and he usually has a fresh idea for most of them: listen to the way he sidles into 'Sweet Georgia Brown', for instance. Beautiful piano-sound, but docked a notch for the singing that he mistakenly decides to contribute to four tracks. Ms Werre-Johansson sings only on 'Until The Real Thing Comes Along', nicely enough.

Solo Flight offers a trim programme of swing-era settings for the very accomplished Swedish woodwind team. They open with seven Benny Carter tunes – none of them obvious choices, aside from 'When Lights Are Low' – and then work through 11 other charts with no concessions to cliché. The playing is uniformly impeccable, and Johansson, on trombone this time, peppers the ensemble with some splendidly agile solos. *Hot Time In Umea!* is a festival set in which Johansson returns to the piano and Finnish clarinet maestro Sarpila and drummer Gardiner dig into a bag of Benny Goodman chestnuts. This is skilful repertory playing and, though the musicians choose not to impose too much of themselves on the situation, it's beguiling stuff, and a useful blindfold test for swing-jazz pundits.

Budd Johnson (1910–84)

TENOR, SOPRANO AND ALTO SAXOPHONE, CLARINET

Born in Dallas, Johnson was on the road as a drummer at fourteen and then switched to saxophone. Worked in a Kansas City band in the late '20s and then co-led a band with Teddy Wilson in Chicago. Joined Louis Armstrong, 1933, then Earl Hines, 1935, for whom he wrote many arrangements. Stayed until 1942, then was with Dizzy Gillespie, Boyd Raeburn and Billy Eckstine. In the '50s he toured with Benny Goodman and Quincy Jones. Then often in a small band with Earl Hines. A classic stylist in the Hawkins mould and an outstanding arranger, Johnson is often overlooked, but he was a figure of real stature. He continued playing until his death in 1984.

***** Budd Johnson And The Four Brass Giants**

Original Jazz Classics OJC 1921 *Johnson; Nat Adderley (c); Ray Nance (t, vn); Clark Terry (t, flhn); Harry Edison (t); Jimmy Jones, Tommy Flanagan (p); Joe Benjamin (b); Herbie Lovelle (d).* 8–9/60.

*****(*) Let's Swing**

Original Jazz Classics OJC 1720 *Johnson; Keg Johnson (tb); Tommy Flanagan (p); George Duvivier (b); Charli Persip (d).* 12/60.

***** The JPJ Quartet**

Storyville STCD 8235 *Johnson; Dill Jones (p); Bill Pemberton (b); Oliver Jackson (d).* 69 or 70, 6/71.

Budd Johnson was a jazz giant for over five decades, yet he made comparatively few recordings under his own leadership, and it's sad that fewer still are currently in circulation. The OJC reissues are a thin representation, but at least a couple of good records are restored to the catalogue. Johnson was already a veteran when he made these, having been an arranger for big bands throughout the 1930s and '40s, involving himself in many of the pioneering bebop gatherings and generally slotting comfortably into almost any setting. His tone was in the classic Hawkins mould: big, broad, soaked in blues feeling. 'Blues By Budd', on *Let's Swing*, is an inimitable example of Johnson at his best. There is a certain dry humour in his playing which never spills over into parody or flippancy: listen to the way he opens his solo on 'Uptown Manhattan' on the quintet album, and hear how he intensifies his playing from that point. His brother Keg plays some cheerful solos, but it's Budd's record – try the lovely reading of 'Someone To Watch Over Me', in which the saxophonist composed a unison passage for himself and Duvivier.

Four Brass Giants was a session instigated by Cannonball Adderley, who'd been listening to some of Johnson's scores for the Hines band. Johnson swings almost blandly through this one and the brassmen aren't given the most compelling of duties to perform, but it has its moments.

The later quartet was recorded in the studio (exact date not reliably known) and at the Montreux Jazz Festival in 1971. Of the two, the live performances are immeasurably superior, and one wonders whether there wasn't more material from the same event to make the record a concert set without recourse to what could justifiably be dismissed as rehearsal material. The group has a seasoned, familiar sound, as if used to working together, and Johnson obviously thrives on a conducive harmonic environment.

Bunk Johnson (1889–1949)

TRUMPET

Though he originally claimed a birthdate of 1879, Johnson was born in New Orleans ten years later. He was a frequent second-trumpet man in the city's pioneer ragtime-to-jazz groups, but left in 1915 to tour the South, and in the '30s more or less quit music. Rediscovered in 1942, he became emblematic of the New Orleans revival, cantankerous and difficult but playing in a style which many found moving and mystically primeval.

***** Bunk Johnson And His Superior Jazz Band**

Good Time Jazz 12048 *Johnson; Jim Robinson (tb); George Lewis (cl); Walter Decou (p); Lawrence Marrero (bj); Austin Young (b); Ernest Rogers (d).* 6/42.

***** Bunk And Lou**

Good Time Jazz 12024 *Johnson; Lu Watters, Bob Scobey (c); Turk Murphy (tb); Ellis Horne (cl); Wally Rose, Burt Bales (p); Clancy Hayes, Russ Bennett, Pat Patton (bj); Dick Lammi (bb); Squire Girsback (b); Bill Dart (d).* 2/44.

A difficult and contentious man, Bunk Johnson remains mysterious and fascinating, still the figurehead of 'revivalist' jazz even though his records remain difficult to find and have been marginalized where those by, say, George Lewis have kept their reputation. Deceitful about his age – he was long thought to have been born in 1879, which would have made him even older than Buddy Bolden – Johnson was rediscovered in 1942 and, after being fitted out with new teeth, began making records. He had never recorded before, even though he'd played in Bolden's band, had moved on from New Orleans at some time in his mid-teens and had gone on to play all over the South. But many records came out of the next five years. Those for Good Time Jazz were among the earliest. *Bunk Johnson And His Superior Jazz Band* establishes the best-remembered Johnson line-up, with fellow veterans Robinson, Lewis and Marrero, and the material is mostly New Orleans staples such as 'Down By The Riverside'. *Bunk And Lou* pits him against the Lu Watters band, who mix 'modern' items such as 'Ory's Creole Trombone' with a number of truly ancient ragtime pieces like 'Smokey Mokes' although, frustratingly, Johnson plays on only the more recent material. While neither is a really satisfactory record – Watters and company sound too slickly amateur to suit an original like Johnson, and the other record lacks the awareness which Johnson would quickly develop – both establish the tenets of his own trumpet style: a polished, almost courtly sort of phrasing, the elimination of 'hot' tricks such as growls or shakes or needless vibrato, a bright and optimistic open tone and a way of swinging which sounds like a development out of ragtime and older brass traditions than jazz. Something, perhaps, between swing and syncopation.

*****(*) Bunk Johnson In San Francisco**

American Music AMCD-16 *Johnson; Mutt Carey (t); Jim Robinson, Kid Ory, Turk Murphy (tb); Wade Whaley, Ellis Horne (cl); George Lewis (cl); Buster Wilson, Burt Bales, Bertha Gonsoulin (p); Frank Pasley (g); Lawrence Marrero, Pat Patton (bj); Sidney Brown (bb); Ed Garland, Squire Gersback (b); Everett Walsh, Clancy Hayes, Edgar Moseley (d).* 9/43–1/44.

***** The King Of The Blues**

American Music AMCD-1 *Johnson; Jim Robinson (tb); George Lewis (cl); Lawrence Marrero (bj); Sidney Brown (b, bb); Alcide Slow Drag Pavageau (b); Baby Dodds (d).* 44–45.

****** Bunk Johnson 1944**

American Music AMCD-3 *Johnson; Jim Robinson (tb); George Lewis (cl); Sidney Brown (bb); Lawrence Marrero (bj); Alcide Slow Drag Pavageau (b); Baby Dodds (d).* 8/44.

****** Bunk Johnson 1944 (2nd Masters)**

American Music AMCD-8 *As above.* 8/44.

****** Bunk's Brass Band And Dance Band 1945**

American Music AMCD-6 *Johnson; Louis 'Kid Shots' Madison (t); Jim Robinson (tb); George Lewis (cl); Isidore Barbarin (ahn); Adolphe Alexander (bhn); Joe Clark (bass hn); Lawrence Marrero (bj, d); Alcide Slow Drag Pavageau (b); Baby Dodds (d).* 5/45.

Johnson's American Music recordings are his most substantial legacy, even if there is occasionally indifferent sound-quality and various incompatabilities with sidemen and material. Robinson and Lewis may have been New Orleans's finest, but Johnson didn't seem to like them all that much, and he frequently plays much better than Lewis on these sessions. Nevertheless *The King Of The Blues* and *1944* – as well as its subsequent CD of alternative takes on AMCD-8 – feature much fine music, the first all on blues themes, the second a mix of the obvious ('Panama' and so forth) and tunes which show Johnson's weakness for popular novelties, such as 'There's Yes Yes In Your Eyes'. It is mostly an ensemble music, leads being passed around the front line and small inflexions making each performance unique to itself; but there is a freshness and intensity here (Johnson had, after all, been waiting a long time to make serious records) which give the music a real cumulative power that grows with each listening. Any raggedness in the playing or flaw in the sound is made to seem insignificant by the surpassing rigour of Johnson's men and their fierce craftsmanship, especially on the 1944 discs (recorded on a hot day: a photo of the session shows everyone in their undershirts). Bill Russell's session notes make fascinating reading in the booklet with AMCD-8.

The other two discs are at least as interesting. *In San Francisco* includes a This Is Jazz broadcast with an all-star band including, intriguingly, Johnson's trumpet contemporary, Mutt Carey, and though Johnson sounds unhappy on 'Dipper Mouth Blues' it's absorbing music. Even better, though, are the six trumpet–piano duets with Bertha Gonsoulin. Nowhere else can one hear Johnson's silvery tone and proper phrasing so clearly. *Bunk's Brass Band And Dance Band* is a fine introduction to Johnson's music, since it features what would have been a regular parade band line-up on 11 tracks and a further nine by a typical Johnson dance group (recorded at George Lewis's home). Lewis sounds a little shrill on the *Brass Band* tracks, which makes one wonder about the pitching, though there is a credit for 'pitch rectification' on the CD. It is a pioneering record nevertheless, as the first authentic, New Orleans brass-band session. The 'dance' tracks are very sprightly and feature some fine Lewis, as well as some of Johnson's firmest lead and even some respectable solos. The sound is quite clean as these sessions go, though some of the *Brass Band* acetates are in less than perfect shape.

*****(*) Bunk Johnson And His New Orleans Band 1945–1946**

Document DOCD-1001 *Johnson; Jim Robinson (tb); George Lewis (cl); Alton Purnell (p); Lawrence Marrero (bj); Alcide Slow Drag Pavageau (b); Baby Dodds, Red Jones (d).* 11/45–1/46.

Four Decca titles, eight for Victor and two V-Discs, plus eight alternative takes. Compared to the original American Music sessions, these are less heavy with authenticity, and some may prefer them for that. Even so, the band still stumbles along at times (listen to the opening ensemble on 'Maryland, My Maryland') and one can sometimes understand Johnson's own frustrations, even if he is as frequently to blame as everyone else. The Victor dates have a chugging intensity which the rather close recording tends to accentuate. The two V-Disc tracks are surprisingly expansive and relaxed. Fascinating music.

***** Bunk & Leadbelly At New York Town Hall 1947**

American Music AMCD-46 *Johnson; Jimmy Archey (tb); Omer Simeon, Edmond Hall (cl); Ralph Sutton (p); Huddie 'Leadbelly' Ledbetter (g, v); Danny Barker (g, bj); Cyrus St Clair (bb); Freddie Moore (d, v); Mama Price (v).* 9/47.

***** Bunk Johnson & Mutt Carey In New York 1947**

American Music AMCD-45 *Johnson; Mutt Carey (t); Jerry Blumberg (c); Jimmy Archey, Bob Mielke (tb); Albert Nicholas,*

Jack Sohmer (cl); James P Johnson, Dick Wellstood (p); Pops Foster, Charles Treager (b); Baby Dodds, Irv Kratka (d). 10/47.

Two souvenirs from Johnson's stay in New York during 1947. The *Town Hall* concert with an all-star group is sound, spirited Dixieland: Johnson isn't on his best form but he plays decently enough. Leadbelly's billing is a bit misleading since he sings for only four minutes on the entire record. The sound, drawn from previously bootlegged acetates, has been cleaned up very respectably.

The other disc finds Bunk at the Caravan Ballroom, once with a team of old hands, the other time with a very young group of white Dixielanders including the twenty-year-old Wellstood. Mutt Carey replaces Bunk on four tracks, rather than sitting in with him. None of this counts as 'authentic' Johnson, but it shows that he was more adaptable than his roots following might wish to think, since there's nothing that disgraces him.

*****(*) Last Testament**

Delmark DD 225 *Johnson; Ed Cuffee (tb); Garvin Bushell (cl); Don Kirkpatrick (p); Danny Barker (g); Wellman Braud (b); Alphonse Steele (d).* 12/47.

Johnson's farewell was reportedly the only session in which he really got his own way, choosing both sidemen and material; and New Orleans purists must have been surprised on both counts: he lined up a team of players quite different from the American Music cronies, and he chose rags and pop tunes to perform. 'The Entertainer', 'Kinklets' and 'The Minstrel Man' have a rather wistful animation about them, while a tune such as 'Till We Meet Again' has a (perhaps inevitable) air of valediction about it. Cuffee and Bushell play with more fluency and zip than Robinson and Lewis ever did, but their slightly anonymous quality stops them from overwhelming Johnson himself, who sounds far from finished. He plays a firm lead and takes simple, bittersweet solos. The sound is a drawback: though recorded in the Carnegie Recital Hall, the quality is indifferent, often boxy and without much definition, and Jack Towers and Bob Koester haven't been able to do much with it in the remastering.

Charlie Johnson (1891–1959)

PIANO

An unremarkable pianist, but Johnson led one of the best bands in Harlem, resident at Small's Paradise, 1928–38. They recorded little and, after the band broke up, Johnson worked around New York but became ill and gradually drifted from sight.

****** The Complete Charlie Johnson Sessions**

Hot 'N Sweet FDC 5110 *Johnson; Gus Aiken, Leroy Rutledge, Jabbo Smith, Thomas Morris, Sidney De Paris, Leonard Davis (t); Regis Hartman, Charlie Irvis, Jimmy Harrison, George Washington (tb); Ben Whittet, Benny Carter (cl, as); Benny Waters (as, ts); Edgar Sampson (cl, as, vn); Bobby Johnson (bj); Cyrus St Clair, Billy Taylor (tba); George Stafford (d); Monette Moore (v).* 10/25–5/29.

Charlie Johnson was a major name in Harlem in the 1920s and '30s, and it's mystifying that he recorded only 14 titles in all that time. All of them are collected here, along with 10 alternative takes, and the calibre of the music is strong enough to regret that Johnson didn't do more in the studios. He lured some top sidemen into the band, including Jimmy Harrison, Jabbo Smith and Sidney De Paris; Benny Carter contributed some arrangements and played on one date; Benny Waters, who was still recording 60 years later, made some of his earliest appearances here. If the earlier pieces such as 'Meddlin' With The Blues' sound like rough-and-ready examples of black dance music of the day, there is a greater polish by the time of the superb 1928–9 sessions. The rhythms are still a little old-fashioned, tied to St Clair and Taylor, but the music seems to have rocket fuel in it on the likes of 'Walk That Thing'; and their farewell tracks, 'Harlem Drag' and 'Hot Bones And Rice', are front-rank examples of hard-swinging Harlem dance music. De Paris, Smith and Waters all have their moments, but Harrison stands out even more remarkably than he does with Fletcher Henderson. The remastering is inconsistent, some tracks being much louder than others, but no serious reservations on an important reissue.

Howard Johnson (born 1941)

TUBA, BARITONE SAXOPHONE, PENNY WHISTLE

A veteran 'specialist' player, Johnson started on baritone sax and soon picked up the tuba as well. He's subsequently been a frequent section-man on both horns, but these records are by his mass-tuba band, Gravity.

*****(*) Gravity!!!**

Verve 531021 *Johnson; Dave Bargeron, Joe Daley, Nedra Johnson, Carl Kleinsteuber, Earl McIntyre, Tom Malone, Marcus Rojas, Bob Stewart (tba); Raymond Chew, Paul Shaffer, James Williams (p); George Wadenius (g); Bob Cranshaw, Melissa Slocum (b); Kenwood Dennard, Kenny Washington (d); Victor See Yuen (perc).* 96.

****** Right Now!**

Verve 537801 *Johnson; Dave Bargeron, Joe Daley, Carl Kleinsteuber, Earl McIntyre, Bob Stewart (tba); Raymond Chew (p, syn); James Cammack (b); Kenwood Dennard (d); Taj Mahal (v).* 97.

As Johnson points out, the tuba is the youngest of the brasses to evolve, an instrument unknown to Beethoven, and the last to acquire the sophisticated valving required for a full chromatic range. In the United States, William Bell of Toscanini's NBC Symphony Orchestra was the first to give the tuba a prominent profile, but it was the legendary Henry 'Bass' Edwards who, with Ellington *and* the London Symphony Orchestra, made it a viable solo instrument and is thought to have inspired Vaughan Williams's Tuba Concerto. Jazz tubists and french horn players, though, are more inclined to offer up a prayer to the memory of Gil Evans, who brought them a new prominence and a new sophistication of approach. 'Svengali's Summer/Waltz' on *Right Now!* is the most obvious tribute, a reworking of Evans's own 'Summertime' charts, but his touch can be heard almost everywhere.

The later of these records actually helps document the origins of Johnson's remarkable all-tuba (or, these days, mostly tuba) band, Gravity. In 1971, along with Bob Stewart, Joe Daley and Earl

McIntyre (Dave Bargeron was to have been involved but had just joined Blood, Sweat & Tears), Johnson recorded a live album with Taj Mahal at the Filmore East. *The Real Thing* still pops up here and there and still makes for good listening, which makes it a little surprising, even given their crowded diaries, that neither man thought to repeat the experiment for close on a quarter of a century. *Right Now!* features only three vocal tracks, but they're strong enough to suggest that this is a relationship that could have been developed.

Gravity was by no means the first of Johnson's own groups, but *Gravity!!!* was a big step forward. We previously suggested that Anthony Braxton had produced more idiomatic writing for tuba ensemble, and there's no particular reason to go back on that now. There was never any doubt that Johnson and his fellow-tubists had the vision and the chops to avoid a one-dimensional sound and approach. However, whereas the earlier record concentrates largely on varying and expanding the sonority, the more recent disc takes a much more imaginative approach to the material. Opening with Charles Tolliver's 'Right Now' was a master-stroke. What follows is equally enterprising. Slide Hampton's 'Frame For The Blues' is made for tubas and, with Earl McIntyre and Joe Daley stretching the range as high and as low as possible, it doesn't just sound like a piece pinched from someone's trombone section. Johnson has varied the sound further by reintroducing his baritone on South African pianist Caiphus Semenya's 'MaMa' and on his own 'Raggedy Man' (a rare Johnson composition, used, without rhythm section, as a Gravity encore piece); while for an extraordinary arrangement of Herbie Hancock's 'Tell Me A Bedtime Story', he plays penny whistle. The arrangements are tighter and more adventurous than ever; the other brassmen in the band are exceptional players and idiosyncratic enough not to sound homogenized.

J.J. Johnson (born 1924)

TROMBONE

The dominant bebop trombonist, Johnson's saxophone-influenced sound has been criticized as unidiomatic and insufficiently 'brassy' – whatever that means – but there is no mistaking his pre-eminence in the recent history of jazz. Born in Indianapolis, Johnson emerged in Benny Carter's orchestra and as part of Jazz At The Philharmonic, but he left an indelible mark as half of Jay and Kai with fellow-trombonist Winding.

*****(*) Trombone By Three**

Original Jazz Classics OJC 091 *Johnson; Kenny Dorham (t); Sonny Rollins (ts); John Lewis (p); Leonard Gaskin (b); Max Roach (d).* 5/49.

♛ ** The Eminent Jay Jay Johnson: Volume 1**

Blue Note 81505 *Johnson; Clifford Brown (t); Hank Mobley (ts); Jimmy Heath (ts, bs); Wynton Kelly, John Lewis, Horace Silver (p); Paul Chambers, Percy Heath, Charles Mingus (b); Kenny Clarke (d); Sabu Martinez (perc).* 6/53–6/55.

****** The Eminent Jay Jay Johnson: Volume 2**

Blue Note 81506 *As above.* 6/53–6/55.

J.J. Johnson is one of the most important figures in modern jazz. Once voguish, the trombone, like the clarinet, largely fell from favour with younger players with the faster articulations of bebop. Johnson's unworthily low standing nowadays (his partnership with Kai Winding, as 'Jay and Kai', was once resonantly popular) is largely due to a perceived absence of trombone players with whom to compare him. In fact, Johnson turned an occasionally unwieldy instrument into an agile and pure-toned bop voice; so good was his articulation that single-note runs in the higher register often sounded like trumpet. He frequently hung an old beret over the bell of his horn to soften his tone and bring it into line with the sound of the saxophones around him.

The first volume of the Blue Note set is one of the central documents of post-war jazz and should on no account be missed. Johnson – who was working as a blueprint checker at the time of the earliest sessions recorded, apparently dissatisfied with his output to date – sounds fleet and confident, and he has a marvellous band round him, including a young Clifford Brown. 'Turnpike' and 'Capri' exist in two versions each and show Johnson's ability to rethink his phraseology, adjusting his attack on the original-release versions to accommodate Clarke's powerful but unemphatic swing (which is rather swamped on the sessions of September 1954 by Mingus's chiming bass and the slap-happy Martinez); even on the slow-tempo 'Turnpike', Clarke provides an irresistible moving force underneath the melody. 'Get Happy' is appropriately up-beat and joyous, with notes picked off like clay pipes at a shooting gallery. In contrast, 'Lover Man' is given a mournful, drawn-out statement that squeezes out every drop of emotion the melody has to offer. The 1954 session yields some fine exchanges between Johnson and Kelly, notably on 'It's You Or No One' and 'Too Marvellous For Words', where the leader's tone and attack are almost as perfect as on 'Turnpike'. Volume 2 is filled out with a less than inspiring 1955 date featuring Hank Mobley and Horace Silver, neither of whom seems attuned to Johnson's taxing idiom.

***** Kai Winding And Jay Jay Johnson**

Bethlehem BET 6026 *Johnson; Kai Winding (tb); Dick Katz (p); Milt Hinton, Wendell Marshall (b); Al Harewood (d).* 1/55.

*****(*) Jay and Kai + 6**

Columbia 480990 *Johnson; Kai Winding (tb, trombonium); Urbie Green, Bob Alexander, Eddie Bert, Jimmy Cleveland (tb); Bart Varsalona, Tom Mitchell (btb); Hank Jones (p); Milt Hinton, Ray Brown (b); Osie Johnson (d); Candido Camero (perc).* 56.

***** Trombone Master**

Columbia CK 44443 *Johnson; Victor Feldman (p, vib); Tommy Flanagan (p); Paul Chambers, Wilbur Little, Sam Jones (b); Albert 'Tootie' Heath, Max Roach (d).* 57–60.

*****(*) The Great Kai And J.J.**

Impulse! 051225-2 *Johnson; Kai Winding (tb); Bill Evans (p); Paul Chambers, Tommy Williams (b); Roy Haynes, Art Taylor (d).* 60.

The Impulse! recording was a commercially motivated reunion, some time after the partnership had been amicably dissolved. Perhaps because the band behind them was so good, J.J. and Kai very quickly rediscovered their old groove. The two horns are exactly in balance, and the vibrato, which in Winding's case was apt to get wider as he aged, is exactly co-ordinated. There is much good-natured four-bar swapping which might pall after a while, were it not so sweetly and tunefully done. There is nothing like

Bill Evans's brief but elegantly articulated solos on the first record, and he makes an enormous difference to the overall feel of the Impulse!, which sounds like a proper group project rather than a trombone feature with accompaniment. That's the problem with the Bethlehem, where even on CD the band sounds very far back. The best point of comparison, before-and-after, is 'Going, Going, Gong', which refers back to the lively 'Gong Rock' on the 1955 Bethlehem session. If this is qualitatively representative, and we tend to feel it is, then the later sessions have gained considerably in sophistication and sheer class and, though dedicated J.J. and Kai fans will think the suggestion heretical, the Impulse! is the one to go for, though trombone nuts will find themselves drawn to the earlier Columbia, which features eight – count 'em – of the sliding fellows, often in jubilant unison. The two frontmen vary the sound a bit on the self-explanatory 'Piece for Two Tromboniums', which is interesting enough to suggest that these admittedly less limber valved horns could have been developed a step further. The arrangements are very good indeed and the material (with the exception of 'Surrey With The Fringe On Top') highly original and exciting. George Avakian's production is, as always, faultless. *Trombone Master* corrals material from four different albums, so it isn't much more than a sampling compilation from a relatively quiet period in J.J.'s career. There are some fine moments, notably his solo on 'Misterioso' and the almost eponymous 'Blue Trombone', but it isn't a particularly coherent or satisfying album.

*** Four Trombones: The Debut Recordings

Prestige PCD 24097 *Johnson; Willie Dennis, Bennie Green, Kai Winding (tb); John Lewis (p); Charles Mingus (b); Art Taylor (d).*

Originally recorded for the short-lived independent label co-run by Mingus and Max Roach, this suffers slightly from its own ungainly format, which buries Johnson a little. There are, though, fine and fresh performances all round, including a stirring account of 'Now's The Time'. Mingus takes charge more than once. The sound is a shade too bright on the transfer and the top notes are inclined to be a bit vinegary.

***(*) The Birdlanders

Fresh Sound FSRCD 170 *Johnson; Jerry Lloyd (t); Al Cohn (ts); Gigi Gryce (bs); Milt Jackson (vib, p); Henri Renaud (p); Percy Heath, Curley Russell (b); Walter Bolden, Charlie Smith (d).* 2 & 3/54.

***(*) Live At The Café Bohemia

Fresh Sound FSRCD 143 *Johnson; Bobby Jaspar (ts, f); Tommy Flanagan (p); Wilbur Little (b); Elvin Jones (d).* 2/57.

Among the best of the surviving albums, both are beautifully transferred to CD, avoiding the awkward chiming effect that plagues much trombone of the period, particularly on live recordings. The first is very nearly hi-jacked by the vibraharpist, whose soloing on another supposedly cumbersome instrument is dazzlingly self-confident. Cohn is actually rather muted, and the later sessions with Gryce and trumpeter Jerry Lloyd aren't up to standard. Despite Jaspar's shortcomings as a soloist (he's still a block ahead of Henri Renaud) and a degree of unease in the ensembles, the Café Bohemia sessions provide an ideal blowing context for Johnson; he lets go joyously on 'Angel Eyes', 'Old Devil Moon' (see also *Eminent*, Volume 1) and, a favourite, 'Solar'. Flanagan's chording and fills are as near perfect as they could be. A constant delight.

*** At The Opera House

Verve 847340-2 *Johnson; Stan Getz (ts); Oscar Peterson (p); Herb Ellis (g); Ray Brown (b); Connie Kay (d).* 9–10/57.

Later the same year as the Café Bohemia session, Johnson and Stan Getz co-led a band at the Civic Opera in Chicago, and then again at the Shrine in LA. Someone had the nous to get the first one down in stereo, but the West Coast tracks, which are probably the better musically, are in very four-square mono. It's fascinating to be able to compare versions of 'Billie's Bounce' (which Getz doesn't really treat as a bebop tune either time), 'Crazy Rhythm', 'Blues In The Closet' and 'My Funny Valentine', though of course the variance in recording means that some of the apparent stylistic differences are artefacts. One great beauty of the session is the opportunity to hear both front men playing songs not normally associated with them. As such, it has to be considered a footnote rather than a centrally important record. Even so, it's well worth the investment.

***(*) J.J. Inc

Columbia Legacy CK 65296 *Johnson; Freddie Hubbard (t); Clifford Jordan (ts); Cedar Walton (p); Arthur Harper (b); Albert 'Tootie' Heath (d).* 8/60.

'Aquarius' is the best evidence yet of J.J.'s great skills as a composer-arranger. As fellow-trombonist Steve Turre points out in a thoughtful liner-note to this augmented reissue, it's a work that is almost orchestral in conception, making full use of the three-horn front line, and also Walton's elegant accompaniment. Brasses are pitched against saxophone and piano in a wonderful contrapuntal development, and Tootie Heath gets a rich sound out of the kit. Apart from this piece and 'Minor Mist', most of the material is deeply rooted in the blues. The reissue includes a longer version of 'Fatback', which shows just how funky J.J. could be when he let go. 'Blue'N'Boogie', another of the extra tracks, is no less down-home and basic, and the leader's ease in a minor blues is evident from the off on 'Mohawk'. The sound has been considerably enhanced on this 20-bit digital remastering. The rhythm section, who sounded a bit remote on LP, are now absolutely central to the music, and the horns are much better balanced than previously. A valuable addition to the story.

***(*) The Total

BMG 74321 47791 2 *Johnson; Bert Collins, Art Farmer, Ernie Royal, Danny Stiles, Snooky Young (t); Paul Faulise, Benny Powell (tb); Ray Alonge, Jimmy Buffington (frhn); Jerome Richardson (as, cl, f); Phil Bodner (ts, cl, f, ob); Tom Newsom (bs, bcl, f); Hank Jones (p); Ron Carter (b); Grady Tate (d); Bobby Rosengarden (perc).* 12/66.

Recorded over the course of an intense week in New York City and a showcase for some thoughtful and adventurous new material, including sections from J.J.'s *Euro Suite*, which was written for Friedrich Gulda's Eurojazz Orchestra earlier the same year. The opening 'Say When' sets a tough tempo and puts a well-coached band through its paces. J.J. solos strongly on 'Blue' and is then upstaged by the consistently undervalued Jerome Richardson. 'Short Cake' and 'Space Walk' suggest how advanced the trombonist's harmonic thinking was at the time, two really strong ideas done full justice, while 'Ballade', originally for Art Farmer, probably needs a more intimate setting and a closer recording to pull it off. Otherwise, though, a most welcome reissue from a time when Johnson was still experimenting with hybrids of jazz.

*****(*) Yokohama Concert**

Pablo 262019 *Johnson; Nat Adderley (c); Billy Childs (ky); Tony Dumas (b); Kevin Johnson (d).* 4/77.

J.J. had spent most of the preceding decade working as a full-time arranger, and this was his first recording for the better part of a decade. Since he had also been writing extensively over that period, it's less surprising than it might have been that he should have opted to go mainly for originals, though the gig also includes a version of Nat's 'Work Song', Tony Dumas's clever 'It Happens' and the standard 'Walkin''. The live sound is very good indeed and J.J.'s solos are strong enough to suggest that he'd never really been away.

***** Pinnacles**

Original Jazz Classics OJCCD 1006 2 *Johnson; Oscar Brashear (t); Joe Henderson (ts); Tommy Flanagan (p, ky); Ron Carter (b); Billy Higgins (d); Kenneth Nash (perc).* 9/79.

Dated to a degree by the sound of Tommy Flanagan on Fender Rhodes and clavinet, and by J.J.'s use of pitch-shifters on a couple of tracks, *Pinnacles* is nevertheless a very fine record that has been out of circulation for too long. His solo on the opening 'Night Flight' is fleet and eloquent, and his arrangement of the traditional 'See See Rider' suggests how hard he was working to keep up with a prevailing taste for blues and rock. Flanagan switches to synth on the cheesy 'Mr Clean', which doesn't benefit from being cluttered with additional percussion. It also lacks the sterling presence of Joe Henderson, who's probably the most effective soloist on the set, playing with calm authority and a sharper than usual edge to his tone for this period. J.J. has a reasonably quiet time of it but makes his choruses count.

***** Concepts In Blue**

Original Jazz Classics OJC 735 *Johnson; Clark Terry (t, flhn); Ernie Watts (ts, as); Pete Jolly (ky); Victor Feldman (vib, ky); Ray Brown (b); Tony Dumas, Kevin Johnson (d).* 9/80.

What's obvious again, even before a note is played, is Johnson's ability to put together great bands. Despite a few 1970s giveaways (like electric keyboards) and a rather busy mix, it's a terrific disc. A sameness starts to creep in before the end, particularly from Watts, who seems to have only a handful of ideas in his bag, but Terry's clear upper-register notes and broad smears are an ideal complement to Johnson, and it might even have been possible to dispense with a saxophonist altogether. Recommended.

*****(*) We'll Be Together Again**

Pablo 2310911 *Johnson; Joe Pass (g).* 10/83.

***** Things Are Getting Better All The Time**

Pablo Today 2312141 *Johnson; Al Grey (tb); Kenny Barron (p, ky); Ray Brown (b); Mickey Roker (d).* 11/83.

Johnson kept out of sight for most of the 1970s, composing and arranging for the movies and television. Within five weeks in 1983, however, he made two sterling albums that belied the full stop some critics had put after his name. The sanguinely titled *Things* looks suspiciously like another attempt to reduplicate the Jay and Kai sound, but it comes across much more individually. Grey, a year younger than Johnson, is a more traditional stylist; a genius with the plunger mute, he has a big, belting tone that goes well with Johnson's increasingly delicate fills and recapitulations. 'Soft Winds', 'Paper Moon' and 'Softly, As In A Morning Sunrise' are particularly good. Pianist Barron is contained and exact, but Brown and Roker are uncharacteristically listless, perhaps recognizing that the two principals (who shared the billing) play to their own inner metre. Good stuff.

Like Johnson, Joe Pass represents an extraordinary cross-section of modern jazz idiom, all carefully assimilated and absorbed. His constant lower-string pulse makes him particularly adaptable to solo and duo performance, and *Together Again* has the fullness of texture that might be expected of a larger group. The performances – 'Nature Boy', 'Bud's Blues', 'Solar', 'When Lights Are Low' and six others – have a fresh-minted sparkle and immediate currency. Strongly recommended.

*****(*) Vivian**

Concord CCD 4523 *Johnson; Rob Schneiderman (p); Ted Dunbar (g); Rufus Reid (b); Akira Tana (d).* 6/92.

A gentle ballad set, dedicated to the trombonist's late wife who succumbed to a stroke after more than 40 years of marriage. The band is just right for the job. Reid and Tana are almost telepathically linked, and Schneiderman and Dunbar strike up a rapport and a partnership that feeds Johnson a huge range of colours and dynamic variations, even within a gentle and slightly melancholy programme. A lovely record; for hopeful romantics everywhere.

*****(*) The Brass Orchestra**

Verve 537321-2 *Johnson; Danny Cahn, Jon Faddis, Earl Gardner, Eddie Henderson, Lew Soloff, Byron Stripling, Joe Wilder (t); Joe Alessi, Robin Eubanks, Jim Pugh, Steve Turre (tb); Dave Taylor, Douglas Purviance (btb); John Clark, Bob Carlisle, Chris Komer, Marshall Sealy (frhn); Bruce Bonvissuto, Alan Ralph (euph); Howard Johnson, Andy Rodgers (tba); Dan Faulk (ts, ss); Francesca Corsi (hp); Renee Rosnes (p); Rufus Reid (b); Victor Lewis (d); Milton Cardona, Kevin Johnson, Freddie Santiago (perc).* 9/96.

Should you ever tire of the ubiquitous sound of the saxophone, this is a delicious antidote, massed brass of a sort that seemed to have gone out of fashion a generation and a half ago. With compositions by Miles, Robin Eubanks, Jimmy Heath, J.J. himself and Dimitri Tiomkin's 'Wild Is The Wind' for good measure, pace and sheer intensity of sound don't flag from the opening 'El Camino Real' to the final notes of Miles's 'Swing Spring'. Dan Faulk's solo spots on soprano and tenor mitigate the acidity here and there, and Eddie Henderson's Harmon-muted solo on 'Ballad For Joe' has all the frail beauty of its stylistic inspiration, as well as providing a counter to dedicatee Joe Wilder's more acerbic attack. Faulk, Henderson and J.J. combine to great effect on Heath's classic 'Gingerbread Boy'. By far the most unfettered thing J.J. has done for a long while is 'If I Hit The Lottery', a skittery march with maximum brouhaha. The leader takes the lion's share of solos but provides generous scope for Eubanks, both as front man and as composer/arranger. The other charts were prepared by Robert Farnon and the irrepressible Slide Hampton. As one would hope and expect from this source, the sound is superlative, full of body and nicely balancing orchestral mass with the character of individual instruments. If there is a down side, it isn't a very exciting record. J.J. has never been a man for histrionics, but he could have done with a few outbursts or a couple more aggressive soloists here.

*****(*) Heroes**
Verve 528864-2 *Johnson; Don Sickler (flhn); Wayne Shorter (ts); Renee Rosnes (p); Rufus Reid (b); Victor Lewis (d).* 96.

A rather self-conscious attempt to re-inscribe J.J. in the continuum of modern jazz, *Heroes* works only episodically. Wayne Shorter's walk-on is effective enough, and there are some nice exchanges between J.J. and Sickler, who possesses a liquid, floating tone that might at moments almost be trombone. Generally, though, it's a rather muted and unexciting set which drifts by at its own patient gait. The rhythm section is first rate, and Rosnes plays it as tough as anyone, adding Monk-like accents and counter-melodies to the softer arrangements, giving them just enough edge to sustain interest.

James P. Johnson (1894–1955)

PIANO, COMPOSER

An enormously versatile and subtle player who played jazz and composed classical music, Johnson is the inventor of stride piano, a mixture of ragtime and other styles. He came to New York as a youngster and was exposed to a huge range of music in the ghetto region known as 'the Jungles', where rent parties and shebeen provided regular work for talented players. His interest shifted to formal composition during the 1930s and '40s, but he left a body of more than 250 small-scale compositions and his influence on jazz piano is inestimable.

***** Carolina Shout**
Biograph BCD 105 *Johnson (p rolls).* 5/17–6/25.

***** Hot Piano**
Topaz 1048 *Johnson; Henry 'Red' Allen, Max Kaminsky, Frankie Newton, Cootie Williams (t); J.C Higginbotham, Dicky Wells (tb); Mezz Mezzrow, Pee Wee Russell, Omer Simeon (cl); Pete Brown (as); Al Gold, Gene Sedric (ts); Fats Waller (p); Al Casey, Eugene Fields, Freddie Green (g); Wellman Braud, Pops Foster, John Kirby, Joe Watts (b); Big Sid Catlett, Cozy Cole, Zutty Singleton (d); Perry Bradford (v).* 21–44.

*****(*) Harlem Stride Piano, 1921–1929**
Hot'N'Sweet 151032 *Johnson; Louis Metcalf (c); King Oliver, David Nelson, Cootie Williams (t); James Archey, Geechie Fields (tb); Ernest Elliott (cl); Bobby Holmes (cl, as); Charles Frazier (ts); Fats Waller (p); Teddy Bunn, Bernard Addison (bj, g); Harry Hull, Joe Watts (b); Edmund Jones, Fred Moore (d); Perry Bradford (d, v); other personnel unidentified.* 8/21–11/29.

*****(*) James P. Johnson, 1921–1928**
Classics 658 *As above, except omit Oliver, Archey, Fields, Elliott, Frazier, Addison, Hull, Jones, Moore.* 8/21–6/28.

***** James P. Johnson, 1928–1938**
Classics 671 *Johnson; Louis Metcalf (c); King Oliver (t); James Archey, Geechie Fields, Joe 'Tricky Sam' Nanton (tb); Ernest Elliott (cl); Barney Bigard (cl, ts); Johnny Hodges (as, ss); Charles Frazier (ts); Clarence Williams (p, v); Bernard Addison (bj, g); Harry Hull (b); Sonny Greer, Edmund Jones, Fred Moore (d); Perry Bradford, Gus Horsley, Andy Razaf (v).* 10/28–3/38.

Too little is known now about James P. Johnson's orchestral music (of which much has been lost) to make any settled judgement about his significance as a 'straight' composer. Ironically, though, his enormous importance as a synthesizer of many strands of black music – ragtime, blues, popular and sacred song – with his own stride style has been rather eclipsed by the tendency to see him first and only as Fats Waller's teacher. Johnson was in almost every respect a better musician than Waller, and perhaps the main reason for his relative invisibility has been the dearth of reliable recorded material. The early Biograph brings together Johnson's rather staccato and lumpy piano rolls, an acquired taste but of unmistakable significance for the history and development of jazz in the period. 'Charleston' is a rarity, and 'Carolina Shout' had a profound impact on Duke Ellington.

As so often, the French Classics label has made up a considerable deficit. The early material overlaps at around the dates indicated with the Hot'N'Sweet compilation and the Topaz. This is as close as anyone is going to get to the sound of Harlem rent parties – if there were an additional quarter-star for quality of sound, *Harlem Stride Piano* might just nip it – and it's a pity that some of these sessions are not more fully documented. The group that recorded the autumn 1921 'Carolina Shout' (there is a solo version from the same period, different label) goes unidentified. Johnson is unmistakable from the first moments of 'Harlem Strut', a subtle, propulsive player with bags of ideas.

The Topaz compilation offers an excellent introduction to the pianist's work, covering a generous sweep of material from the middle of his career. Most of the tracks that a seasoned Johnson listener would expect to find are present – 'Snowy Morning Blues', 'Harlem Strut', 'Worried And Lonesome Blues', 'Mule Walk' – but with two dozen tracks on the disc, well mastered and clearly documented, there is something for everyone at a budget price.

Classics omit a piano-roll 'Charleston (South Carolina)' from June 1925 but fill in with four Original Jazz Hounds numbers from March 1927 and March 1928. The second volume takes the story on a full decade, opening with a couple of numbers by the Gulf Coast Seven (an uncertain personnel but possibly including Ellingtonians Nanton and Hodges) before covering the overlap with Hot'N'Sweet. Among the highlights here are two duets and chirpy *kvelling* with Clarence Williams, together with three songs from 1931 with Andy Razaf (co-author of 'Honeysuckle Rose') as vocalist. As on Classics 658, Johnson tends to get buried in the group recordings. Ultimately it is the solo tracks, including little gems like 'You've Got To Be Modernistic' and the earlier 'Riffs', that are most significant. The disc ends with a session by Pee Wee Russell's Rhythmakers; Johnson solos on a second take of 'There'll Be Some Changes Made'.

*****(*) James P. Johnson, 1938–1942**
Classics 711 *Johnson; Henry 'Red' Allen (t); J.C Higginbotham (tb); Pee Wee Russell (cl); Gene Sedric (ts); Albert Casey, Eugene*

Fields (g); Pops Foster, Johnny Williams (b); Big Sid Catlett, Zutty Singleton (d); Anna Robinson, Ruby Smith (v). 8/38–7/42.

*****(*) The Original James P. Johnson, 1942-1945**

Smithsonian Folkways 40812 *Johnson (p solo).* 42–45.

***** James P. Johnson, 1943–1944**

Classics 824 *Johnson; Sidney De Paris (t); Vic Dickenson (tb); Ben Webster (ts); Jimmy Shirley (g); John Simmons (b); Big Sid Catlett (d).* 7/43–4/44.

***** James P. Johnson, 1944**

Classics 835 *Johnson; Frank Newton, Sidney De Paris (t); Vic Dickenson (tb); Albert Casey, Jimmy Shirley (g); Pops Foster, John Simmons (b); Big Sid Catlett, Eddie Dougherty (d).* 4–6/44.

***** James P. Johnson, 1944 – Volume 2**

Classics 856 *Johnson; Sterling Bose, Max Kaminsky (t); Frank Orchard (vtb); Rod Cless (cl); Eddie Condon (g); Bob Casey, Pops Foster (b); Eddie Dougherty, George Wettling (d).* 44.

***** James P. Johnson, 1944-1945**

Classics 1027 *Similar to Classics above.* 44–45.

The picture is getting steadily more patchy as the decade advances. Classics 711 is significant because it contains a lot of band material which scarcely saw the light of day during the LP era and which is now heard for the first time since its first release. One of these features vocals by Ruby Smith, a niece of the great Bessie. The disc overlaps with Classics 671 in the shape of a trio with Pee Wee Russell and Zutty Singleton, apparently recorded at the end of the August 1938 date. There are excellent solo performances from the following spring, made for Columbia.

The Smithsonian Folkways release is of excellent quality. The remastering, by Malcolm Addey and Alan Yoshida, is clean and unfussy, and classics like 'Yamekraw', 'Snowy Morning Blues' (two versions), and 'Daintiness Rag' come through clear and unwavering alongside tunes by Handy, Joplin and Pickett.

The later Classics anthologies have filled in much of the rest of the picture, inevitably with some further overlap with earlier releases. Some of the 1944 and later cuts already betray signs of the ill-health that, as a series of mild but progressively debilitating cerebral haemorrhages, was to overtake Johnson later in the decade, finally incapacitating him in 1951. The basic elements of the style are still in place, though, and on the most recent Classics volume there is an opportunity to hear several versions of themes like 'Blue Moods' and 'Yamekraw', as well as a session devoted to Handy material. The subtly varied bass figures and the forward motion of his sophisticated melodic variations place him closer to later jazz than to the increasingly basic syncopations and repetitions of ragtime. For that reason alone, and for his incorporation of jazz and blues tonalities, Johnson sounds much more 'modern' than many of his contemporaries, and a far more compelling musician than the overrated Waller. As so often with the Classics reissues, the transfers are seldom as meticulous as they might be and they are from unlisted sources, although for the most part the music comes through clearly enough.

****(*) James P. Johnson, 1945-1947**

Classics 1059 *Johnson; Albert Nicholas (cl); Danny Barker (g, v); Pops Foster (b).* 6/44–6/47.

These few cuts round out Classics' documentation of Johnson. Only serious collectors will be troubled by these rather lame performances, recorded for Folkways, Riverside and Circle, with a couple of tracks rejected by Moses Asch, including the recently rediscovered 'Woman Blues' and the two-part 'Jazzamine Concerto'. Though only just turned fifty, Johnson sounds tired and slightly disorientated. His recovery from a stroke sustained while working with Eddie Condon (which couldn't have been anyone's idea of a rest cure) was temporary and this compilation marks a sad conclusion to such a distinguished and influential career.

Marc Johnson (born 1953)

DOUBLE BASS, ELECTRIC BASS

Made his first mark with the final Bill Evans trio, 1978–80, then with various leaders and fronting his own Bass Desires band. In the '90s he was among the most sought-after of bassists and proved adaptable to most jazz situations.

***** Bass Desires**

ECM 827743-2 *Johnson; Bill Frisell (g, g syn); John Scofield (g); Peter Erskine (d).* 5/85.

****(*) Second Sight**

ECM 833038-2 *As above.* 3/87.

Johnson is a magnificent bass stylist, with all the limitations such a description suggests. Everything he does has an inbuilt grandeur and seriousness; even a tune like the well-worked 'Samurai Hee-Haw', which has immense potential, is treated with undue seriousness. The original *Bass Desires* was a record of immense potential which failed to deliver a real punch. Frisell's disciplined surrealism was an interesting foil to Scofield's more logically organized play. The John Jacob Niles song, 'Black Is The Colour Of My True Love's Hair', is freshly reworked, but Johnson the stylist is never far from centre stage and constantly rumbles front and centre. No reason whatever why a bass player shouldn't occupy the foreground, but on both these records it's underlined so heavily that one's only just finished getting to one's feet in respectful attention when the idea is over.

Second Sight lacks the freshness and the occasional flash of wry humour. In their place, a slightly wishy-washy sound, replete with high-note twiddles and drab rock effects that would have had the late Sonny Sharrock hiding his head in shame. While its predecessor wears well, this palls steadily.

****** The Sound Of Summer Running**

Verve 539299-2 *Johnson; Bill Frisell, Pat Metheny (g); Joey Baron (d, perc).* 97.

Exquisite. A set of delicate responses to Americana, reminiscent of Frisell's *Have A Little Faith* and Metheny's set of duets with Charlie Haden, *Missouri Skies*. Johnson has finally found an idiom and a group of collaborators who give his lovely sound a proper context. Every one of these ten tracks opens up on an inscape: childhood, unsentimental innocence, a forgotten and abandoned America. Frisell's and Metheny's folksy lines have very little to do with jazz harmony, but the ease and freedom of their playing are the real thing.

***** If Trees Could Fly**

Intuition INT 3228 2 *Johnson; Eric Longsworth (clo).* 11/96, 6/97.

Though Johnson's name is listed first, most of the material is by the young cellist. It sounds a very comfortable collaboration – Johnson describes it as 'effortless', which is slightly worrying – obviously aimed at overturning preconceptions about both instruments. Longsworth plays an electric cello, which allows him to articulate more quietly and softly than on a conventional instrument. His strums and double stops resemble baritone guitar, while Johnson favours single lines and interwoven counter-melodies. His only compositional credit comes with 'Ton Sur Ton' which is reprised right at the very end, almost as if to remind us which of the pair is the ranking star. Johnson can be forgiven everything for the delicate, bowed melody on 'Lullaby'. This is the kind of music Jaco Pastorius might have played if he had managed to find some peace and tranquillity in his life. As a place to be, that sounds fine. As a listening experience, this lacks a certain edge.

Pete Johnson (1904–67)

PIANO

Born in Kansas City, Johnson became prominent during the boogie-woogie craze of the late '30s, with Albert Ammons and Meade Lux Lewis. He faded rather quickly from sight in the '40s, but was still playing until his death.

****** Pete Johnson 1938–1939**

Classics 656 *Johnson; Harry James, Hot Lips Page (t); Buster Smith (as); Albert Ammons, Meade Lux Lewis (p); Lawrence Lucie, Ulysses Livingston (g); Abe Bolar, Johnny Williams (b); Eddie Dougherty (d); Joe Turner (v).* 12/38–12/39.

*****(*) Pete Johnson 1939–1941**

Classics 665 *Johnson; Hot Lips Page (t); Eddie Barefield (cl, as); Don Stovall (as); Don Byas (ts); Albert Ammons (p); John Collins, Ulysses Livingston (g); Abe Bolar, Al Hall (b); A.G Godley, Jimmy Hoskins (d).* 12/39–6/41.

***** Central Avenue Boogie**

Delmark DD-656 *Johnson; Arnold Wiley (p, v); Charles Norris, Carl Lynch (g); Bill Davis, Al McKibbon (b); J.C Heard, Jesse Price (d).* 4–11/47.

Johnson's mastery of boogie-woogie and blues piano is given a near-definitive airing on these CDs. The chronological survey on Classics begins with the Kansas City pianist accompanying Joe Turner on the singer's first studio date, before two quartet tracks with Harry James: 'Boo-Woo' is an outright classic. His complete 1939 date for Solo Art is another memorable occasion, nine solos that go from the Tatum-like elaborations on Leroy Carr's 'How Long, How Long Blues' to the furious 'Climbin' And Screamin'' and 'Shuffle Boogie'. The sound here is rather thin, but Johnson's energy and invention shine through. There are four more tracks with a small band including Page and Turner, a solo 'Boogie Woogie', two trio pieces and the first trio with Albert Ammons and Meade Lux Lewis on 'Café Society Rag'. There are shortcomings in the remastering, but this is a marvellous disc.

His 1939 session for Blue Note is, unfortunately, split across the end of Classics 656 and the beginning of Classics 665, which opens on the stunning 'Holler Stomp', the most audacious of boogie showcases. 'You Don't Know My Mind', from the same date, is contrastingly dreamy and may remind blues aficionados of pianists such as Walter Davis and Lane Smith. Aside from another track with Joe Turner's Fly Cats and a small group with Page and others, the rest of the disc is made up of duets with Ammons; as elegant as these sometimes are, they also fall prey to routine from track to track.

Delmark's compilation sets Johnson back in front of guitar, bass and drums, and includes several previously unheard takes. He still sounds best by himself, but there is some virtuoso stuff on 'Margie' and the several takes of 'Hollywood Boogie'.

Plas Johnson (born 1931)

ALTO AND TENOR SAXOPHONES

Johnson's work ties him only peripherally to jazz: he was a mainstay of R&B in the 1950s, then did countless sessionman chores in the '60s and '70s.

***** The Blues**

Concord CCD 4015 *Johnson; Mike Melvoin (p); Herb Ellis (g); Ray Brown (b); Jake Hanna (d); Bobbye Hall (perc).*

Johnson has an appealingly sharp and direct approach to the blues. His sole Concord disc benefits from the presence of a highly professional rhythm section which glosses over his more obvious deficiencies. Not a player for the over-extended solo, Johnson tends to make a few points forcefully, with a tendency to repeat ideas a little louder just to make sure they've sunk home. Not a classic, but entertaining enough in its limited way.

Philip Johnston

ALTO SAXOPHONE, SOPRANO SAXOPHONE

During the '80s, Johnston was leader of the Microscopic Sextet, a medium-sized band with big ideas. No less a personage than John Zorn was a charter member. The group combined modern ideas with the sound and feel of a swing band and a cinematic vividness in the colours. Johnston declared a self-imposed 'recording ban' between 1988 and 1992, but returned with Big Trouble and an impressive bag of unrecorded tunes.

*****(*) Philip Johnston's Big Trouble**

Black Saint 120152-2 *Johnston; Bob DeBellis (ss, bs, bcl); Jim Leff (tb); Marcus Rojas (tba); Joe Ruddick (ky, as); Adam Rogers, David Tronzo (g); David Hofstra (b, tba); Kevin Norton (d, perc, mar); Richard Dworkin (perc).* 6 & 7/92.

***** The Unknown**

Avant AVAN 037 *Johnston; Steve Swell (tb); Bob DeBellis (f, af, bcl, bs); Joe Ruddick (p, syn); David Hofstra (b); Kevin Norton (d, perc, vib).*

*****(*) Normalology**

Eighth Day Music EDM 80006 *Johnston; Allan Chase (as); Paul Shapiro (ts); Bob DeBellis (bs); Joe Ruddick (p, org); Stew Cutler (g); David Hofstra (b); Richard Dworkin (d).* 5/96.

Big Trouble was formed following the demise of the Microscopic Sextet, one of the more original of the saxophone-based 1980s bands, which drew much of its inspiration from the tight arrangements of the swing era but added a beat that was often coloured by contemporary rock and pop. In the new band, Johnston has pushed even further his offbeat arranging skills. 'Chillbone' on the Black Saint is scored for soprano saxophone, tuba and marimba, set over a stark wind *ostinato*. The set also includes notably complex compositions by Steve Lacy (the brief but awkwardly structured 'Hemline') and by Herbie Nichols, who's credited with both 'Step Tempest' and 'Twelve Bars'. The addition of slide guitar gives the last of these and the closing 'Powerhouse' an entirely unexpected dimension.

Johnston uses space brilliantly, often leaving yawning gaps precisely where one expects to hear fills or returns to a head theme. The obvious comparison is with John Zorn, who is the mastermind behind Avant, except that Big Trouble play in a more structured and less ironic idiom. *The Unknown* is packed with strange Zornish titles and weird staccato music that never allows the listener more than a moment's complacent comfort before breezing on to the next idea. On this showing the prospects are good, and anyone who enjoyed what the Micros did should certainly check it out.

Normalology gets up to date with a lot of material written some years ago but left unrecorded. As ever, the tunes flirt confidently with dissonance. There are moments when one might almost be listening to an out-of-whack Grover Washington gig. Johnston's soprano is very much in that territory, and the arrangements are expansive and generously proportioned. All four horn-players have an individual touch, and the rhythm section (augmented by guitar on three numbers) is as elastic and flowing as the original band. Johnston's touch as a film composer comes out on things like the tiny 'My Grey Heaven', a melancholy celebration of everyday heroism. Our favourite tracks are 'Spilled Perfume' (which seem to come from an unperformed musical), 'Lobster Leaps In' and the closing blues 'No Mistakes In Hell'. Gloriously mad music by a greatly underrated performer.

Joint Venture

GROUP

Early work by leading free players Smoker and Eskelin.

*****(*) Joint Venture**

Enja 5049 *Paul Smoker (t); Ellery Eskelin (ts); Drew Gress (b); Phil Haynes (d).* 3/87.

***** Ways**

Enja 6052 *As above.* 1/89.

***** Mirrors**

Enja ENJ 7049 *As above.* 9/91.

Jointly fronted by Smoker and Eskelin, this group performs more straightahead material than either man does on solo records. 'Chorale And Descendance', which Smoker has also recorded on his own, is a choppy but curiously formal piece that takes up ideas which lie all over the place in contemporary jazz and weaves them all into a satisfyingly ironic shape. The second album is less successful, largely because it is too easy to hear Smoker and Eskelin working out ideas from their own projects, but also because Gress and Haynes seem to have settled into a predictable groove that does the front line no favours whatever. If there were hairs to split, *Mirrors* might be considered something of an advance. It is certainly a more polished and professional product, but the sheer intelligence and control required to drive music like this are not conducive to warm, uncomplicated expressiveness, and again the album is slightly forbidding.

Pete Jolly (born 1932)

PIANO, ACCORDION

A veteran West Coast man of the 1950s and '60s, Jolly made countless sideman dates, but his own work as a leader is rather infrequent and mostly of little account. He has also made a go of jazz on the accordion.

****(*) Jolly Jumps In**

RCA Victor 74321 592632 *Jolly; Shorty Rogers (t); Jimmy Giuffre (ts, bs); Howard Roberts (g); Curtis Counce (b); Shelly Manne (d).* 3/55.

**** Pete Jolly And Friends**

VSOP 78 *Jolly; Howard Roberts (g); Chuck Berghofer (b); Larry Bunker, Nick Martinis (d); strings and brass.* 11/62–8/64.

****(*) Yeah!**

VSOP 98 *Jolly; Chuck Berghofer (b); Nick Martinis (d).* 10/95.

A definitive West Coast man, Jolly has spent most of his professional life in studios and on soundtracks. He likes to use his right hand at the very top of the keyboard and the insistently dinky phrasing which results gets a bit tiresome over CD length. The RCA album is a relic of vintage West Coast days, and not one of the better ones: the three sextet tracks put Pete to work on the accordion, and the trio pieces seem oddly melodramatic. Manne, though, plays as superbly as ever. *And Friends* pulls together tracks from three rather obscure early-'60s dates, and they're an indifferent lot with hack orchestral arrangements on seven tracks and a thin sound on all of them. A generation later, he is still playing with Berghofer and Martinis, and *Yeah!* isn't bad – some nice choices of tune, and the trio are as comfortable as an old pullover. But it's a potboiler.

Chris Jonas

SOPRANO SAXOPHONE

New York-based, Jonas has worked with Anthony Braxton and with young Turks Assif Tsahar and Susie Ibarra. Superficially reminiscent of Steve Lacy at his freest, he has perhaps also learnt from Braxton and Julius Hemphill.

*****(*) The Sun Spits Cherries**

Hopscotch Hop 4 *Jonas; Chris Washburne (tb); Joe Fiedler (ts); Andrew Barker (d).* 9/99.

The poetic title refers to the fact that four and a half pounds of sunlight strike the earth every second, and there is a juicy warmth to be extracted from these spare and uncomplicated sounds. Jonas exploits the interesting textures available from saxophones and trombone, with no bass or harmony instrument. Some of it is little more than old-fashioned musical pointillism, but it is clear that the leader's imagination is more capacious and more structured than that. Heard as a continuous suite, *The Sun Spits Cherries* has a compelling logic that repays many hearings. With more to come from Jonas, including a solo soprano record on NuSonic, he is a name to watch.

Ed Jones (born 1961)

TENOR SAXOPHONE, SOPRANO SAXOPHONE, FLUTES

Busy British saxophonist, with lots of bands, projects, scores and activity.

***** Piper's Tales**

ASC CD2 *Jones; Jonathan Gee (p); Wayne Batchelor (b); Brian Abrahams (d).* 7/91, 12/92.

*****(*) Out Here**

ASC CD 17 *Jones; Byron Wallen (t); Jonathan Gee (p); Max Beasley (vib); Geoff Gascoyne (b); Winston Clifford (d, perc).* 9/96.

The main quibble regarding Jones's debut on ASC was the quality of the sound, which torpedoed a promising set of tunes. That seems to have been addressed for the second, which is an altogether more ambitious project, calling for a fuller, more thoroughly arranged sound. The addition of a second horn, and of vibes on the four best tracks, opens up the texture considerably and gives Jones something to play off. His soloing on 'Silverlining' and 'Very Urgent' is exemplary and he gives a promising account of himself on two takes of 'New Swing', a deceptively conventional idea with some unexpected variations.

The earlier album is wearing well, and the better tracks – 'Kindred Spirit' and 'The Piper's Tale' – manage to survive a winsome performance and a thin, unemphatic sound.

Elvin Jones (born 1927)

DRUMS, GUITAR

The kid brother of the Jones family, and almost a decade younger than Hank, Elvin started his career in Detroit, before moving to New York City, and established himself as an intense bebop drummer, adding a new and complex dimension to the rhythmic language of bop. His key musical encounter was with John Coltrane, with whom he worked for five intense years, before Trane's desire to introduce a second percussionist severed the relationship. Elvin has continued to tend the flame, but also to develop his own fiery brand of jazz.

***** Elvin!**

Original Jazz Classics OJCCD 259 *Jones; Thad Jones (c); Frank Wess (f); Frank Foster (ts); Hank Jones (p); Art Davis (b).* 7/61–1/62.

Elvin remains an enigma; a shy but affable man whose exterior masks a turbulent and often self-destructive nature, he transformed modern jazz drumming like no one else since the early heyday of Max Roach. Jones's introduction of African 'polyrhythms' became a key feature of the John Coltrane quartet, of which he was arguably the key member, and it has fed into a long recording history as a leader.

Elvin! is noisy, heated bop, with some good interplay between Jones and a front line that refuses to play by the rules. The trio tracks with elder brother Hank and Art Davis are particularly good, at once fiery and lyrical, stretched out rhythmically and yet sounding quite accommodating. Wess and Foster are perhaps too strait-laced for this session, but both are adventurous enough to go along for the ride, and Wess in particular turns in some lovely ideas.

*****(*) Illumination!**

Impulse! IMP 12502 *Jones; Prince Lasha (cl, f); Sonny Simmons (as, eng hn); Charles Davis (bs); McCoy Tyner (p); Jimmy Garrison (b).* 8/63.

A side project for the Coltrane rhythm section, with not one but three saxophones making up the deficit and, as it turns out, three of the most consistently neglected figures on the modern scene. Lasha is best known from his brief involvement with Eric Dolphy and from a couple of collectable records of his own, but it has taken Sonny Simmons many, many years to break through to the major status he so thoroughly deserves. They and Davis, who has two composition credits on the disc, are responsible for all but two of the tracks, with Tyner and the nominal co-leader Garrison chipping in with one apiece.

Lasha's opening 'Nuttin' Out Jones' is notable for a long cor anglais solo from Simmons and an extraordinary duet with the drummer. Tyner's ballad, 'Oriental Flower', is very much his own feature, but it underlines what a brilliant technician Jones could be with brushes when he chose. The two Davis tunes are pretty basic material, though 'Half-And-Half' is rhythmically subtle and again uses the unexpected timbre of Simmons's English horn. Sonny is the composer of 'Aboriginal Dance In Scotland', a four-minute demonstration of the often-cited theory that the blues and jazz were inspired by the sound of bagpipes (the horns in some weird intervals) over African percussion. Wacky and splendid, as indeed is the whole album.

*****(*) Live At The Village Vanguard**

Enja 2036 *Jones; Hannibal Marvin Peterson (t); George Coleman (ts); Wilbur Little (b).*

This was a tough gig in terms of its abrasive, compellingly forceful soundscapes, but also more technically, since what we are hearing for most of the time is a pianoless trio, a form Jones was to experiment with for some years. Working without a harmony instrument, and leaning very heavily on big George's very sophisticated and often lateral harmonic sense, Jones, as ever, plays as if he's conducting an entire orchestra – but also on occasion as if he has a personal grudge against each and every member. Little is something of a passenger in this setting and spends most of his time laying down steady, patient figures with just the odd embellishment to keep himself interested. Peterson gatecrashes on 'Mr Jones', taking the shine off another perfectly good trumpet.

** Heavy Sounds

Impulse! 547959-2 *Jones; Frank Foster (ts); Billy Green (p); Richard Davis (b).* 6/67.

Billed as a collaboration between Jones and Davis, this breaks down into a series of feature spots, stitched together with some suspect ensemble play which suggests that this wasn't a regular working band. Foster is responsible for two compositions, 'Raunchy Rita', on which Davis indulges a curious out-of-tempo excursion, and the classic 'Shiny Stockings', and these are actually rather good, if it weren't for bassist and drummer constantly vying for attention like overgrown schoolkids. Green is a very decent accompanist, not someone who will be widely recognized but a creditable player. Jones's one composition credit is the dismal 'Elvin's Guitar Blues' on which he strums the opening choruses like a teenager who's just learnt about Bert Weedon. 'Summertime' is spoiled by rain, and not until 'Here's That Rainy Day' does the sun come out. Too late by then.

*** At This Point In Time

Blue Note 93385 2 *Jones; Frank Foster, Steve Grossman (ss, ts); Pepper Adams (bs); Jan Hammer (p, syn); Cornell Dupree (g); Gene Perla (b); Candido Camero, Omar Clay, Richie Pablo Landrum, Warren Smith (perc).* 7/73.

The tone of this album – intense, collective and dark – sets it apart from most of Elvin's solo albums. His introduction to 'Currents/Pollen' is astonishing and is the equal of anything he has ever done. Though Foster takes the lead on his own piece, the title-track, it is Jan Hammer who dominates the remaining solo space, switching to piano only for ensemble passages but shaping some fantastic sweeping figures on the synth. The two other horns are less compelling, but Adams's rich, middle-register sounds give the longer tracks a weighty presence. Jones uses the additional percussionists the way an arranger might use woodwinds or strings. The middle of the album is dominated by Omar Clay compositions, of which 'Whims Of Bal' is the most impressive. Clay is also the session producer, and he has mixed up the drums rather more than one might like. The playing is funky stuff, but the album could do with some judicious remixing.

**(*) Live In Japan

Konnex 5041 *Jones; Frank Foster (ts); Pat LaBarbera (ts, ss); Roland Prince (g); Andy McCloud (b).* 4/78.

*** Very R.A.R.E. / Love & Peace

Konnex 5036 *Jones; Pharoah Sanders (ts); Art Pepper (as); Roland Hanna (p); Jean-Paul Bourelly (g); Richard Davis (b).* 6/79, 4/82.

Around this time in his career, Jones seemed to attempt the impossible (and certainly undesirable) by cranking up his bands to maximum impact and volume. Prince won't win any poll citations for Most Understated Artist but, unfortunately, he has very little to say, and to find him in company with real players like Foster and LaBarbera is disappointing to say the least; his own 'Antigua' rambles desperately. Fine as they are, the two horns sound consistently mismatched and even out of tune with each other; a long version of 'A Love Supreme' is little short of embarrassing.

The later Konnex compilation puts the good, the bad and the ugly side by side. *Love & Peace* has also been available as *Reunited* on Black Hawk. Hanna is a star and makes his presence felt on 'The Witching Hour', exuding the same graciousness and intelligence Sanders was beginning to display as he got over his Coltrane fixation and his seeming conviction that he was a court musician during the Middle Kingdom. Here he is peerlessly melodic and to the point, a bright spot that lifts an otherwise shambolic set.

***(*) When I Was At Aso-Mountain

Enja 7081 *Jones; Sonny Fortune (as, f); Takehisa Tanaka (p); Cecil McBee (b).* 12/90.

This is a smashing record, as lyrical and centred as Jones's records had habitually been noisy and unfocused. Eight shortish tracks flow comfortably from one to the next without a hint of strain. Fortune emerges as an ideal voice for this sort of Eastern-tinged music, and Tanaka (who is well known in Japan, still pretty marginal in the West) proves to be a more than competent soloist; a little wishy-washy on 'You Don't Know What Love Is' and 'Stella By Starlight', more robust on his own tunes. The real star of the session – no surprise to his admirers – is McBee, who sounds like Garrison reborn; rewarded with a handful of solo spots, he turns in elegant playing that concentrates on low strings, double stops and big, fat sounds, so rich they might almost be *arco* tones.

*** The Elvin Jones Jazz Machine In Europe

Enja 7009 *Jones; Sonny Fortune (ts, f); Ravi Coltrane (ts, ss); Willie Pickens (p); Chip Jackson (b).* 6/91.

Predictably, there was great excitement at the thought of Jones playing with a Coltrane again. Ravi was born just a year before his father's death and he isn't an entirely convincing chip off the family block. The tone is still very wayward, lacking the old man's iron authority, and there is a worrying dearth of ideas as well. In the event, almost all the solo emphasis falls on Fortune, a player who has been relegated (by ourselves as well; guilty as charged) to a colourist's role, when in fact he has a confident and often very sophisticated grasp of harmonics and solo development. His flute introduction to 'Doll Of The Bride', a traditional Japanese tune arranged by Jones's wife, Keiko, is one of the best things on a thinly recorded record that grows only very slowly and still requires too much of an adjustment in mood to appeal to most mainstream tastes.

**(*) Youngblood

Enja 7051 *Jones; Nicholas Payton (t); Javon Jackson, Joshua Redman (ts); George Mraz (b).* 4/92.

*** Going Home

Enja 7095 *Jones; Nicholas Payton (t); Ravi Coltrane, Javon Jackson (ts, ss); Kent Jordan (f, picc); Willie Pickens (p); Brad Jones (b).* 10/92.

Inevitably, perhaps, Jones turned 65 and almost immediately acquired Grand Old Man status. He had become a latter-day Blakey, breaking in bright and gifted young players, though without Art's boisterous self-confidence, without his gift for balancing temperaments within a band, and without any real sense of how a group was supposed to sound. The Messengers were unmistakable through a dozen incarnations, not because Blakey imposed his personality as an instrumentalist but because he allowed others to develop theirs. The reverse is true with Jones, and these records almost always sound like chaotic attempts on the part of younger men to keep up with the old fellow.

Going Home has some of the harnessed energy that went into big-band projects of the time, a strong and peppy session that is one of the strongest statements Jones was to make as leader. 'East Of The Sun' is original and affirmative, while brother Thad's 'Cross Purpose' is subtler and more finely crafted than first appears. What's most encouraging here is that with Rudy van Gelder in the frame again, you can actually hear what is going on. The other plus-point is that Coltrane junior has acquired a touch of experience and is beginning to find things to say, especially with the soprano, on which he sounds not unlike a latter-day version of his father. No surprises there, perhaps, but a pity he doesn't carry over some of that same strength to his tenor playing.

On *Youngblood*, it's Jackson who dominates proceedings, knocking the already over-hyped Redman back into his corner. The best tracks on the earlier record are trios – 'Angel Eyes' and 'Body And Soul' – with just Redman and Mraz. The lack of a harmony instrument now seems less surprising than it was, and with players of this calibre it hardly makes a difference. Not much white space around the edges; everything is filled in, packed with detail to the point of redundancy. A duo with Mraz is neither here nor there, and the solo percussion feature, 'Ding-A-Ling-A-Ling', is so well named it's scary. Tosh and nonsense of the worst sort.

****** Live At Pit Inn, Tokyo**

Columbia 487899 *Jones; Wynton Marsalis (t); Marcus Roberts (p); Reginald Veal (b). 12/92*

Supergroup, ahoy. Convened to mark the 25th anniversary of John Coltrane's death, this remarkable group (rightly described as the 'Special Quartet') turned in a quite wonderful version of the 'Love Supreme' suite and 'Dear Lord' and a couple of other items, including a Wynton blues. It's the Coltrane masterpiece which catches the ear, though; unusual to hear it with a trumpet out front. It marks precisely because of the oddity of timbre, the absence of more than notional pedal-notes and because Wynton is such a drivingly logical soloist. He doesn't let things slide for a moment, pushing as hard as Jones could possibly want, the two of them often leaving bass and piano to flounder for a chorus or so, while they race away ahead to the next idea. Oddly recorded, but undoubtedly atmospheric, and certainly a historic encounter worthy of documentation.

***** It Don't Mean A Thing**

Enja ENJ 8066 *Jones; Nicholas Payton (t); Delfeayo Marsalis (tb); Sonny Fortune (ts, f); Willie Pickens (p); Cecil McBee (b); Kevin Mahogany (v).* 10/93.

A mixed band of Young Turks and old guard, and the most settled unit Jones has had for some time. McBee is again the key element, filling, commentating, holding back the pace just a shade here and there, and adding a wedge of lyricism to 'Lush Life'. The important component on most of the set is Jones's unwonted and very attractive restraint. Nothing too upfront, and a version of 'A Change Is Gonna Come' to die for, modest, simple and sincere when it would have been all too simple to turn it into a great marching epic.

Etta Jones (born 1928)

VOCAL

Touring with Buddy Johnson at sixteen, later with Earl Hines, and eventually making a solo success with her Don't Go To Strangers album. A big, bluesy voice and an in-my-own-time relationship to the beat.

***** Etta Jones 1944–1947**

Classics 1065 *Jones; Joe Thomas, Hot Lips Page, Jessie Drakes, George Treadwell, Joe Newman (t); Clyde Bernhardt, Dickie Harris (tb); Barney Bigard (cl); Joe Evans, Floyd Williams, Don Stovall, Pete Clarke (as); Georgie Auld, Budd Johnson, Big Nick Nicholas (ts); Leonard Feather, Duke Jordan, Pete Johnson, Jimmy Jones, Luther Henderson (p); Chuck Wayne, Jimmy Shirley, John Collins, Herman Mitchell (g); Billy Taylor, Eugene Ramey, Abe Bolar, Al McKibbon, Trigger Alpert (b); Stan Levey, J.C Heard, Jack Parker, Denzil Best (d).* 12/44–10/47.

*****(*) Don't Go To Strangers**

Original Jazz Classics OJC 298 *Jones; Frank Wess (ts, f); Richard Wyands (p); Skeeter Best (g); George Duvivier (b); Roy Haynes (d).* 6/60.

****(*) Something Nice**

Original Jazz Classics OJC 221 *Jones; Lem Winchester (vib); Richard Wyands, Jimmy Neely (p); George Duvivier, Michael Mulia (b); Roy Haynes, Rudy Lawless (d).* 9/60–3/61.

***** Lonely And Blue**

Original Jazz Classics OJC 702 *Jones; Gene Ammons, Budd Johnson (ts); Patti Bown (p); Wally Richardson (g); George Duvivier (b); Ed Shaughnessy (d).* 4–5/62.

***** So Warm**

Original Jazz Classics OJC 874 *Jones; Ray Alonge (frhn); Eric Dixon, Jerome Richardson, Phil Bodner, Arthur Clarke (reeds); Mal Waldron (p); George Duvivier (b); Charli Persip, Bill English (d); strings.* 61.

***** Love Shout**

Original Jazz Classics OJC 941 *Jones; Jerome Richardson (ts, f); Kenny Cox (p); Sam Bruno (p, org); Larry Young (org); Kenny Burrell, Bucky Pizzarelli (g); Peck Morrison, Ernest Hayes, George Tucker (b); Oliver Jackson, Bobby Donaldson, Jimmie Smith (d).* 11/62–2/63.

Jones began recording as a teenager in the 1940s, and her earliest sides have been collected on the Classics compilation. She was singing lightweight blues at this point, even if one of the tracks is called 'Blues To End All Blues' (other titles include 'Osculate Me Daddy' and 'Misery Is A Thing Called Moe'!). Some pretty useful groups backed her up on these sessions, for Black & White, Chicago, Savoy and Victor, with Budd Johnson in several of the bands and Pete Johnson leading a group with Lips Page. A rediscovery of some largely forgotten tracks.

By the time she came to make *Don't Go To Strangers*, Jones was already a veteran. But the title-song from the LP became a gold record, and she subsequently made several albums for Prestige. In its modest way the album remains a fine achievement, with Jones's heavy, blues-directed voice piling extra substance on to fluff such as 'Yes Sir, That's My Baby', with rolling support from an excellent band. The subsequent *Something Nice* is more quiescent, the 11 songs dispatched matter-of-factly, although Jones's regal delivery makes such as 'Through A Long And Sleepless Night' into sometimes heady stuff. *Lonely And Blue* was a prescient suggestion of the kind of albums she would make for Muse, a generation later: small-hours, lonesome music which is barely a step away from outright blues. Johnson handles most of the tenor chores (as Houston Person would later do) and his wry rejoinders on 'Gee Baby Ain't I Good To You' are delightful. *So Warm* tips the scales towards MOR, but Etta's natural warmth heats up the string charts, and it's a beguiling result. *Love Shout* goes back to a small-band setting: Jerome Richardson turns in a great solo on the fine 'The Gal From Joe's', and the twin guitars of Burrell and Pizzarelli are a bonus on 'Hi-Lilli, Hi-Lo'. Some of the rest is fluff.

***** The Melody Lingers On**

Highnote HCD 7005 *Jones; Houston Person (ts); Tom Aalf (vn); Dick Morgan (p); Keter Betts (b); Frankie Jones (d).* 11/96.

Etta recorded steadily through the '80s and early '90s. She seems comfortable back with a band on *The Melody Lingers On*, a sequence of tribute songs to departed singers, and with Person returned to her side it's a pleasing if unexceptional occasion. Like Shirley Horn, Jones prefers a slow-to-ambling tempo that she can take her own time with, and though some of the songs are a bit obvious, on a less frequently encountered tune like 'For Sentimental Reasons' she's very good.

Hank Jones (born 1918)

PIANO

The eldest of the three brothers, Hank Jones is as quiet and unassuming as drummer Elvin is extrovert, but he shares something of the late Thad Jones's deceptive sophistication. After working in territory bands, Hank became part of the first bebop generation and has retained much of that complex idiom in his recent solo and small-group recordings.

***** Urbanity**

Verve 537749-2 *Jones; Johnny Smith (g); Ray Brown (b).* 47, 53.

The early material on *Urbanity* reappears on CD, over 50 years after the original solo tracks were recorded. Six light-footed standards, dispatched with Hank's usual grace and lack of fuss. Some find him lacking in substance, but there is such ease in the playing that it is hard to criticize it on those grounds. Unfortunately, the CD is padded out with an inordinate amount of unissued material from a 1953 trio session, unusual for being drummerless. There are no fewer than five takes of 'Things Are So Pretty In The Spring' (none of them revelatory) and four of 'Thad's Pad'. It requires a certain commitment to listen to these in sequence, and only the subtlest and most highly attuned listener will find much essential difference between them.

****** Hank**

All Art AAJ 11003 *Jones (p solo).* 1/76.

***** Tiptoe Tapdance**

Original Jazz Classics OJC 719 *As above.* 6/77, 1/78.

****(*) Just For Fun**

Original Jazz Classics OJC 471 *Jones; Howard Roberts (g); Ray Brown (b); Shelly Manne (d).* 6/77.

***** Jones–Brown–Smith**

Concord CCD 4032 *Jones; Ray Brown (b); Jimmie Smith (d). n.d.*

Like everyone else, Jones had a quiet time of it in the 1960s, but he re-emerges with a bang in the following decade, which really marks the beginning of his now substantial output of high-quality solo and trio jazz. Never much of a composer, a fact often adduced to downplay his significance, Jones is not given to wholesale reassessment of standard progressions but prefers to concentrate on the *sound* of a tune. *Hank* is certainly the place to start; the songs are all very brief – and there are 14 of them squeezed into less than 45 minutes – but it's worth listening closely to the way Jones colours every chord and fine-brushes his own solo contributions. His delicacy and balance, that tiptoeing, tap-dancing feel, are among the qualities which have enhanced and prolonged his reputation as a great accompanist, but (unfairly) only a rather lightweight soloist. *Hank* is full of gospel and hymn tunes, which receive sensitive and sometimes quite oblique interpretations. There are some inconsistencies of sound, but nothing untoward.

The Concord and *Just For Fun* are both growers, records that initially come across as rather superficial, but gradually yield up subtleties not audible first time around. Despite the presence of Manne (the players actually split into two – drummerless and guitarless respectively – trios) the results are slightly uncertain. Jones is too straightforward an executant to be able to rely on irony, and pieces like 'A Very Hip Rock And Roll Tune' and 'Kids Are Pretty People' fall flat on that account. Though they perhaps lack the inventive fire of the Savoys (currently waiting to be repackaged), the 1970s sets are to be preferred for their almost magisterial calm and command.

***** Ain't Misbehavin'**

Original Jazz Classics OJCCD 1027 *Jones; Teddy Edwards (ts, cl); Kenny Burrell (g); Richard Davis (b); Roy Haynes (d).* 8/78.

Hank pays his dues to the spirit of Fats Waller on six elegantly crafted themes. The title-piece gets the record off to a rollicking start, but it's only with 'Joint Is Jumpin'' and 'Honeysuckle Rose' that it hits top form. Edwards is also in very good form and Burrell's guitar playing is both elegant and propulsive, and Roy Haynes is masterful at the kit. Arranged by Bill Holman and produced by Ed Michel, the set lacks nothing but a touch of fire and passion.

***** The Incredible Hank Jones**

Stash ST CD 553 *Jones; Jon Faddis (t, flhn); Ira Sullivan (t, flhn, as, ts, f); Bob Malach (ts); Bucky Pizzarelli (g); Eddie Gomez, Milt Hinton (b); Louie Bellson, Duffy Jackson (d).* 79, 5/80.

This became a Jones record only by sleight of hand. The material had formerly been released on two LPs under the names of Louie Bellson and the irritatingly eclectic Ira Sullivan. It isn't as if Jones is such a prominent soloist on either of them, and Bellson is certainly strongly favoured on the sound-mix. Taken on their merits, though, these are both highly desirable selections, and a worthy inclusion in any collection.

*****(*) Master Class**
32 Jazz 32022 *Jones; Thad Jones (c); Charlie Rouse (ts); George Duvivier, Sam Jones (b); Ben Riley, Mickey Roker (d).* 1/77–1/78.

Originally recorded for Muse, these two LPs, *Bop Redux* and *Groovin' High*, were reissued in 1998. The former title is a useful shorthand for what Jones was doing at the time. The basic tonality is still bebop but toned down so many notches that it sounds closer in idiom to an early generation of piano players, Teddy Wilson especially. Jones's take on 'Yardbird Suite' and other Parker themes is almost as smoothly uncomplicated as the original versions, though without their subversive punch. The emphasis shifts to Monk on the second LP, though both 'Groovin' High' and 'Anthropology' point to the Bird/Diz axis of bebop again and as well. The later set features Hank's brother, Thad, playing as well as he had for years, a tight, intense tone on 'I Mean You' and 'Jackie-ing'. A most valuable and timely reissue.

*****(*) Duo**
Timeless SJP 283 *Jones; Red Mitchell (b).* 12/87.

Two master-craftsmen left to their own devices with a pile of music. Mitchell's singing tone fulfils the same function as Holland's slightly more robust approach. Jones works around and under the bassist's lines like the great accompanist he is. 'Wee' and 'I'll Remember April' are almost consciously misremembered returns to bebop, freshly and inventively conceived. 'Like Someone In Love' draws freely on Coltrane's reading. Gorgeous.

****** Lazy Afternoon**
Concord CCD 4391 *Jones; Ken Peplowski (as, cl); Dave Holland (b); Keith Copeland (d).* 7/89.

Lazy Afternoon is a peach: warm, vibrant jazz with the modulation and pace of a good club date. Jones is generous with solo space for his sidemen, though his unusual approach to Kurt Weill's 'Speak Low', a striking choice for openers, is marred by an intrusive Copeland solo. Holland and Copeland had acted as the pianist's performing trio, with an evident empathy; quite properly, the bassist is featured strongly, with particularly fine excursions on the J.J. Johnson composition, 'Lament', and the succeeding 'Comin' Home Baby'. Jones's fine touch as a colourist is evident on the title-track, where a hint of Ellingtonish celeste under Ken Peplowski's smooth clarinet spices a slightly bland approach. Warmly recommended.

*****(*) Live At Maybeck Recital Hall, Volume 16**
Concord CCD 4502 *Jones (p solo).* 90.

*****(*) Jazzpar 91 Project**
Storyville STCD 3091 *Jones; Mads Vinding (b); Al Foster (d).* 3/91.

*****(*) Handful Of Keys**
Emarcy 513 737 *Jones (p solo).* 4/92.

****** Upon Reflection**
Verve 514898-2 *Jones; George Mraz (b); Elvin Jones (d).* 2/93.

Jones entered the 1990s one of the music's elder statesmen. His Maybeck recital was, predictably, one of the high points of the series, and his recent recording has all been of a tremendously high standard. There are inconsistencies in the discs from the Danish Jazzpar project (otherwise a signal moment of recognition) and the Waller songbook on Emarcy, where he simply doesn't know what to do with some of the songs but play them straight and then ... play them straight again. There is, however, a second masterwork to sit alongside the Maybeck. *Upon Reflection* is devoted to the music of his brother, Thad, who died in 1986. Quite properly, the drummer's job went to Elvin rather than to Foster or Higgins, who might have been more suitable musically. It's a tender, but by no means sentimental, record. However, if you can listen to 'A Child Is Born' without a tear, tear up your donor card; they can't transplant hearts of stone.

***** Sarala**
Verve 528783-2 *Jones; Cheick-Tidiane Seck (org, perc, v); The Mandinkas.* 4/95.

The result of Jones's desire to record an album of traditional African music, *Sarala* tends to marginalize him slightly, so powerful and compelling is the playing and sheer presence of Cheick-Tidiane Seck and his Mandinkas. Mixing flutes, guitars, other native instruments and intense vocalization, they generate textures of close, grainy detail that frequently capture the foreground from Jones. If one is looking for jazz 'roots' in the contemporary world, this is as close and as deep as it gets.

*****(*) Favors**
Verve 537316-2 *Jones; George Mraz (b); Dennis Mackrel (d); Winds Jazz Orchestra, Osaka.* 5/96.

Since 1992, Jones has been guest professor at Osaka College of Music and has been responsible for a spring recital which puts his Piano Workshop alongside work by student orchestras. Predictably, the standard of work is very high, crisp and professional. Following six tracks by the trio, it has its work cut out, but the set gets better with each succeeding number until the closing 'Armageddon', a Wayne Shorter composition that makes an intriguing tailpiece to brother Thad's 'A Child Is Born'. The recording is curiously dry, as if recorded in a very flat acoustic, but the standard of playing carries it through.

Jo Jones (1911–85)

DRUMS

Jones is credited with shifting the basic drive of the rhythm section from the bass drum to the hi-hat and to a softer, more legato sound. As such, he represents the single most important bridge between classic jazz and bebop. Typically for a rhythm player, he is poorly represented as a leader.

***** Jo Jones Trio**
Fresh Sounds FSR-CD 40 *Jones; Ray Bryant (p); Tommy Bryant (b).* 5/59.

***(*) Percussion And Bass**
Fresh Sound FSR-CD 204 *Jones; Milt Hinton (b).* 5/60.

The master drummer of the swing era became widely celebrated after he left Count Basie in 1948, but thereafter he seldom found the best contexts for his work, at least on record. His great sessions for Vanguard seem to be back in limbo for the moment. But don't bother with *Percussion And Bass*. The idea of a supposedly improvised duo record with Hinton was fascinating, but the results – Papa Jo noodling away on chimes, skins and even vibes at one point, while Milt booms alongside – are pretty laughable, and made worse by the ridiculous studio sound, which suggests that both men were recorded at the bottom of separate wells. Avoidable.

Jonah Jones (1908–2000)

TRUMPET

Born in Louisville, apprenticed in various territory bands, then worked with Lunceford, Stuff Smith and, through most of the 1940s, Cab Calloway. Eventually scored a huge hit with the album Jonah Jones At the Embers, yet to see any kind of reissue, and became a cabaret star. Worked through the 1960s, '70s and '80s and, though basically retired, he could still play useful trumpet even at the end of his life.

****(*) Jonah Jones 1936–1945**
Classics 972 *Jones; Tyree Glenn (tb, vib); Joe Marsala, Buster Bailey, Al Gibson (cl); Edgar Sampson, Hilton Jefferson (as); Ike Quebec (ts); Dick Porter (p, v); Clyde Hart, Buster Harding, Dave Rivera (p); Eddie Condon, Bobby Bennett, Danny Barker (g); Wilson Myers, John Kirby, Milt Hinton (b); George Wettling, Cozy Cole, J.C Heard (d).* 10/36–7/45.

Jones began as a minor Armstrong disciple. His big, blowsy style tends to dominate the groups he's in, and these rather motley sessions are more like swing-era footnotes than anything. Six tracks with the Fats Waller copyist, Dick Porter, are scarcely worth remembering, and two sessions for Keynote and one for Commodore form the meat of this CD. They have their moments, but the slow tunes are dreary and the most interesting player is Tyree Glenn, whose sleepy-sounding solos have the odd quirk in them. The Porter tracks have very indifferent sound; the later ones are all right. Jonah passed away as this edition was going to press, and it would be nice for Capitol to reissue some of his hit albums again.

Oliver Jones (born 1934)

PIANO

Born in Montreal, Jones was playing in local clubs when he was still in high school. He formed a showband which played in Puerto Rico, where Jones stayed for some years, before returning to Canada in 1980 and releasing a steady stream of records, mostly in the trio format. He retired from full-time playing in 1995.

****(*) The Many Moods Of Oliver Jones**
Justin Time JUST 3 *Jones (p solo).* 2–3/84.

**** Lights Of Burgundy**
Justin Time JUST 6 *Jones; Fraser McPherson (ts); Reg Schwager (g); Michel Donato (b); Jim Hillman (d).* 4/85.

****(*) Requestfully Yours**
Justin Time JUST 11 *Jones; Skip Beckwith (b); Anil Sharma (d).* 11/85.

***** Speak Low Swing Hard**
Justin Time JUST 17 *Jones; Skip Beckwith (b); Jim Hillman (d).* 7–9/85.

***** Cookin' At Sweet Basil**
Justin Time JUST 25 *Jones; Dave Young (b); Terry Clarke (d).* 9/87.

****(*) Just Friends**
Justin Time JUST 31 *Jones; Clark Terry (t); Dave Young (b); Nasyr Abdul Al-Khabyyr (d).* 1/89.

****(*) Northern Summit**
Justin Time JUST 34/Enja 6086-2 *Jones; Herb Ellis (g); Red Mitchell (b).* 6–9/90.

***** A Class Act**
Justin Time JUST 41 *Jones; Steve Wallace (b); Ed Thigpen (d).* 4–5/91.

Oliver Jones is destined to be no more than the the second most famous piano export from Canada, after Oscar Peterson. Although he actually studied with Daisy Peterson and grew up in Montreal, he didn't get serious about a jazz career until after he'd spent 20 years directing music in Puerto Rican tourist shows. Maybe his showmanship derives from that experience; either way, he clearly aspires to being a communicator the way Peterson himself does, and his closeness to the master's methods extends to his composing. Original tunes such as 'Blues For Helene' (*Just Friends*) or 'Fulford Street Maul' (*Lights Of Burgundy*) are exactly the kind of up-tempo blues which Peterson himself writes.

Jones is an engaging enough soloist, filling his records with good-hearted, swinging music, but they seldom add up to a very convincing whole and there always seem to be stretches of sheer professionalism in place of genuine feeling. His ballads are glossy rather than introspective, but perhaps one listens to Jones for his generous virtuosity, not his tenderness. He worked away from any limelight until the 1980s, but since then he has recorded regularly for Justin Time.

Since his playing scarcely varies in intensity or prowess from record to record, preferred sessions are more a matter of the setting. The solo set is slightly less interesting since, like Peterson, Jones thrives on a propulsive rhythm section. Both *Speak Low Swing Hard* and the *Sweet Basil* concert set find everyone playing with huge enthusiasm, and the earlier of these sessions is distinguished by some interesting material, including Ferdie Grofé's 'On The Trail' and a reading of 'I'm An Old Cowhand' that sounds as if it was played on tiptoes. *Lights Of Burgundy* is let down by the unattractive studio-sound and rote performances. Clark Terry sparks a few tracks on *Just Friends*, although he's not quite at his best; but the meeting with Mitchell and Ellis takes a ponderous course, with so much space allotted to each man that the music lacks Jones's usual ebullience. *A Class Act*, though, might be the best of these discs, with two of his best originals in 'Mark My Time' and 'Peaceful Time', and a couple of mature embellishments on Kenny Wheeler's 'Everybody's Song But My Own' and Bill Evans's 'Very Early'. Thigpen and Wallace offer seamless support.

***** Have Fingers, Will Travel**
Justin Time JUST 102-2 *Jones; Ray Brown (b); Jeff Hamilton (d).* 5/97.

Here's a recent set by Oliver to set beside the others. The essential sameness and predictability of his output suggests, in its way, something about jazz's commercial dilemma: it's often those qualities which have brought his audience to him. The difference with this disc is the rhythm section, the best he has ever recorded with: Brown has more gravitas than any bassman alive, Milt Hinton excepted, and Hamilton is a drummer whose merits far outweigh his wider recognition. On a medium-tempo groove, they're close to peerless, and Jones revels in the situation. There's surely nothing here that the pianist hasn't played for us before, somewhere or other, but it's as smiling and warm-blooded as he's ever been, and it feels fine.

*****(*) Just In Time**

Justin Time JUST 120/1-2 2CD *Jones; Dave Young (b); Norman Marshall Villeneuve (d).* 11/97.

Jones may have gone into semi-retirement but he's still enjoying his jazz. He's always fun to hear in person, so this in-person set, replete with the usual dazzle, is a nice place to make his acquaintance. Two and a quarter hours is far too much, but there's nothing that's less than enjoyable and swinging and, since our grades have been rather harsh with Jones in the past, he deserves the extra point.

Philly Joe Jones (1923–85)

DRUMS

So called to distinguish him from 'Chicago' Joe Jones, he became one of the key modern-jazz drummers, despite succumbing to heroin abuse at intervals. Originally influenced by Sid Catlett, he had a ferociously powerful delivery which blended with modernist cross-rhythms to dazzling effect, though his jazz-rock group, Le Grand Prix, turned into self-parody. Philly Joe's work with Miles Davis in the mid-'50s was definitive of an era and a style.

***** Blues For Dracula**

Original Jazz Classics OJC 230 *Jones; Nat Adderley (c); Julian Priester (tb); Johnny Griffin (ts); Tommy Flanagan (p); Jimmy Garrison (b).* 9/58.

***** Drums Around The World**

Original Jazz Classics OJCCD 1792 2 *Jones; Blue Mitchell, Lee Morgan (t); Curtis Fuller (tb); Cannonball Adderley (as); Benny Golson (ts); Sahib Shihab (bs); Herbie Mann (f, picc); Wynton Kelly (p); Jimmy Garrison, Sam Jones (b).* 5/59.

***** Showcase**

Original Jazz Classics OJCCD 484 2 *Jones; Blue Mitchell (t); Julian Priester (tb); Bill Barron (ts); Pepper Adams (bs); Charles Coker (p); Jimmy Garrison (b).* 11/59.

****(*) Mo'Joe**

Black Lion BLCD 760154 *Jones; Les Condon, Kenny Wheeler (t); Chris Pyne (tb); Pete King (as); Harold McNair (ts, f); Mike Pyne (p); John Hart, Ron Mathewson (b).* 10/68.

These bracket a torrid decade in Philly Joe's personal life, but his most productive as a musician. *Blues For Dracula* was recorded towards the end of the drummer's main association with Miles Davis's touring band, a period in which he was much in demand musically, but also making absurd demands on himself by means of a well-developed habit. There are some signs of strain on a mainly good-natured blowing album, with Jones well up in the mix and his characteristic rimshots slightly overloud; 'Two Bass Hit', which inspired some of Philly Joe's best moments on Davis's *Milestones*, is particularly strong. The three horns were well chosen but sound ragged in some of the less frenetic ensembles. The 'European' sessions sound altogether less certain, though Wheeler and King in particular produce an acceptable synthesis of their own slightly abstract idiom with Jones's whacking verve and oblique intelligence. *Showcase* is notable for a multi-tracked trio, 'Gwen', on which Philly Joe plays piano, bass and drums and does so very swingingly. The other tracks are strongly coloured by the horn players, Mitchell's raw earth colours, Priester's slightly surreal tinge, Garrison's magnificently centred bass playing. By contrast, the drummer is something of a bit-player.

The 1959 large-ensemble record was intended to show off rhythm styles from around the world and it reflected Philly Joe's fascination with the multi-culturalism of another of his great influences, Max Roach. It isn't entirely successful, but the playing is uniformly good – as well it might be, given such a dream band. Two versions of Benny Golson's 'Stablemates' stand out strongly, as does the long, Dameron-composed 'Philly J.J.', but quite how 'Cherokee' fits into the global perspective isn't clear. None of these can be said to be absolutely essential to a good modern collection; nevertheless, Philly Joe was a significant presence for three decades, and his influence can be heard today in the likes of Andrew Cyrille.

Quincy Jones (born 1933)

ARRANGER, BANDLEADER, TRUMPET

Jones played trumpet with Lionel Hampton in 1951–3, then did freelance arranging, including a stint in Europe. Toured with his own big band, 1959–61; arranged for Basie and several singers; then took an industry job at Mercury Records. He has since scored many film soundtracks, run his own record label, Qwest, and overseen numerous high-profile projects at the very top end of the music business. All of his projects include at least a nod to his jazz roots, no matter how remote they may become.

***** Free And Easy**

Ancha ANC 9500-2 *Jones; Lennie Johnson, Benny Bailey, Floyd Standifer, Clark Terry (t, flhn); Ake Persson, Melba Liston, Quentin Jackson, Jimmy Cleveland (tb); Julius Watkins (frhn); Porter Kilbert, Phil Woods, Jerome Richardson, Budd Johnson, Sahib Shihab (reeds); Patti Bown (p); Les Spann (g, f); Buddy Catlett (b); Joe Harris (d).* 2/60.

***** Q Live In Paris Circa 1960**

Qwest 946190-2 *As above.* 2/60.

***** Swiss Radio Days Jazz Series Vol. 1**

TCB 02012 *As above, except Roger Guérin, Clyde Reasinger (t), Harold McNair (as) replace Terry, Lennie Johnson and Budd Johnson.* 6/60.

***** The Quintessence**

Impulse! 051222 *Jones; Jerry Kail, Clyde Reasinger, Clark Terry, Joe Newman, Thad Jones, Freddie Hubbard, Al De Risi, Snooky Young, Ernie Royal (t); Bill Byers, Melba Liston, Paul Faulise, Rod Levitt, Curtis Fuller, Tony Mitchell (tb); Julius Watkins, Jimmy Buffington, Earl Chapin, Ray Alonge (frhn); Phil Woods, Jerome Richardson, Eric Dixon, Oliver Nelson, Frank Wess (reeds); Gloria Agostini (hp); Bobby Scott, Patti Brown (p); Milt Hinton (b); Harvey Phillips (tba); Buddy Catlett, Stu Martin, Osie Johnson (d).* 11–12/61.

***** Strike Up The Band**

Mercury 830774-2 *Joe Newman, Clark Terry, Ernie Royal, Snooky Young, James Nottingham, Al Perisi, Jimmy Maxwell, John Bello, Benny Bailey (t); Curtis Fuller, Urbie Green, Richard Hixson, Bill Byers, Quentin Jackson, Tony Studd, Paul Faulise, Jimmy Cleveland, Kai Winding, Thomas Mitchell, Santo Russo, Melba Liston (tb); Zoot Sims, Roland Kirk, Walter Levinsky, James Moody, Phil Woods, Frank Wess, Al Cohn, Jerome Richardson, Seldon Powell, Romeo Penque, Walter Kane, Sahib Shihab, Eric Dixon, Stanley Webb, Budd Johnson, Seldon Powell (reeds); Jimmy Buffington, Tony Miranda, Bob Northern, Ray Alonge, Julius Watkins, Earl Chapin, Bob Ingraham, Fred Klein, Willie Ruff (frhn); Charles McCoy (hca, perc); Toots Thielemans (hca); Lalo Schifrin, Bobby Scott, Patti Bown (org, p); Gary Burton (vib); Wayne Wright, Sam Herman, Kenny Burrell, Jim Hall, Vincent Bell, Mundell Lowe, Don Arnone (g); Bill Stanley, James McAllister (tba); Milt Hinton, Art Davis, George Duvivier, Major Holley, Ben Tucker, Chris White (b); Rudy Collins, Osie Johnson, Ed Shaughnessy, Stu Martin, Jimmy Crawford (d); Tito Puente, Carlos Patato Valdes, Mike Olatunji, Martin Grupp, Philip Kraus, James Johnson, Carlos Gomez, Jack Del Rio, Jose Paula, Bill Costa, George Devins (perc).* 1/61–2/64.

***** Bossa Nova**

Verve 557913-2 *Jones; Clark Terry (t); Roland Kirk, Jerome Richardson (f); Phil Woods, Paul Gonsalves (as); Lalo Schifrin (p); Jim Hall (g); Chris White (b); Rudy Collins (d); Jack Del Rio, Carlos Gomez, Jose Paula (perc).* 62.

Jones has been among the most charismatic figures in black music in the past 40 years. His specific jazz records have been few, since he's chosen to make his mark as a producer/Svengali to countless other artists, involving himself in some of the most successful recording projects of recent years with Michael Jackson and others. But his best music assuredly deserves a place in a comprehensive jazz collection.

Disastrously, his best CD, *This Is How I Feel About Jazz*, which combined the original album of that name with most of *Go West, Man* has been consigned, temporarily we hope, to jazz limbo. Currently, his story on record starts with the three releases from his 1960 sojourn in Europe with a big band. The Ancha disc, recorded for Swedish Radio in Goteborg, is marginally more hi-fi, though the performances here sound more buttoned-up; the similar (and slightly longer) programme in Lausanne swings with greater abandon, though ensembles are paradoxically more secure. Interesting to compare solo spots between the two shows: Clark Terry and Benny Bailey each take a crack at 'I Remember Clifford' (Terry wins), while Melba Liston and Quentin Jackson go through 'The Phantom's Blues' (honours even). The Qwest album is another one from Europe and is another spirited set of performances from what was often a less-than-happy tour; sound is not much better than on the other discs, though.

The Quintessence is something of a disappointment after *This Is How I Feel About Jazz.* The tracks are concise and undeveloped, the charts considerably less imaginative and, though the players (all top studio pros) don't stint of themselves, there's little to turn the head other than a few breezy passages of section-work. With hindsight, *Bossa Nova* now looks like a typical piece of Jones opportunism, arranging pop hits and 'genuine' bossa nova pieces in a light, pleasing froth, although the excellent band can't help but do a good job on what is high-class fluff. *Strike Up The Band* is culled from various Mercury albums of a commercial bent, though Jones again assembles several remarkable orchestras and persuades them to make the most of 'Baby Elephant Walk' and 'Cast Your Fate To The Wind'.

****(*) Gula Matari**

A&M 393030-2 *Jones; Freddie Hubbard, Danny Moore, Ernie Royal, Marvin Stamm, Gene Young (t, flhn); Wayne Andre, Al Grey, Benny Powell, Tony Studd (tb); Jerome Richardson (ts, f); Danny Bank (bs, bcl); Pepper Adams (bs); Herbie Hancock, Bob James, Bobby Scott (ky); Milt Jackson (vib); Eric Gale (g); Ron Carter, Ray Brown, Richard Davis, Major Holley (b); Grady Tate (d); Don Eliott, Jimmy Johnson, Warren Smith (perc).* 3–5/70.

****(*) Smackwater Jack**

A&M 393037-2 *Similar to above.* 71.

***** Straight No Chaser: The Many Faces Of Quincy Jones**

Universal 541542-2 2CD *Jones; as all discs above, plus other unlisted personnel.* 61–81.

By the late '60s, Jones was leaving jazz to other hands, though he usually found room for soloists in his prolific film and TV scoring. *Gula Matari* has a simpering treatment of 'Bridge Over Troubled Water', but it also has 'Walkin'' and, although Jones was clearly already in hock to the pop market, at least he was giving well-paid studio gigs to quality jazz musicians. *Smackwater Jack* walks a similar line, but it has a certain metropolitan flash to it which Jones liked to keep hold of.

Universal's two-disc compilation concentrates on his pop/lounge-music side, and within that brief it's very entertaining, getting as far as 1980s hits such as 'Ai No Corrida' and 'Razzamatazz'. But since it ignores all of his most interesting early material – it includes two and a half minutes of 'Straight No Chaser' and then calls the album after it, thus raising false hopes among those hoping for more of Jones's best jazz scores – it seems disappointingly likely that we now won't get a compilation that genuinely explores the breadth of Jones's work.

Richard M. Jones (1889–1945)

PIANO, VOCAL

Jones worked in New Orleans as a teenager and was an important A&R man for OKeh in Chicago, often doubling as pianist and session-leader. He was still working in a similar capacity for Mercury in the 1940s.

***** Richard M. Jones 1923–1927**

Classics 826 *Jones; Shirley Clay, Eddie Mallory, Don Nelson, Willie Hightower (c); Preston Jackson, Henry Clark, John Lindsay (tb); Albert Nicholas (cl); Artie Starks, Fred Parham (cl, as); Warner Seals (ts); Johnny St Cyr, Ikey Robinson, Bud Scott, Leslie Corley (bj); Rudy Richardson (d); Lillie Delk Christian (v).* 6/23–7/27.

***** Richard M. Jones 1927–1944**

Classics 853 *As above, except add Jimmy Cobb, Elisha Herbert (c), Jimmy McLeary, Eddie McLaughlin, Milton Fletcher, Thomas Gray, Lee Collins, Bob Shoffner (t), William Franklin, Roy Palmer, Edward Fant, Albert Wynn (tb), Darnell Howard (cl), Omer Simeon (cl, as), John Davis, John McCullin (as), Otha Dixon, Herschel Evans (ts), Dave Peyton, Gideon Honore, George Reynolds (p), Huey Long, Hurley Ramey (g), Quinn Wilson (tba), John Lindsay, Bob Frazier, Oliver Bibb (b), Wallace Bishop, Eddie Green, Roy Slaughter, Baby Dodds (d); George D Washington (v); omit Nicholas, St Cyr, Corley, Seals, Nelson, Hightower, Scott, Parham and Richardson.* 11/27–3/44.

Composer, talent scout and studio A&R man, Jones did much for jazz in the Chicago scene of the 1920s. As a performer, though, he is all but forgotten. He might have helped bring about the Armstrong Hot Five sessions in the OKeh studios, but his own records are relatively mild and undistinguished. The best tracks are on the first disc listed above. After a couple of doughty 1923 piano solos there are six good tracks by a trio of Jones, St Cyr and the young Albert Nicholas. Various tracks by Jones's Jazz Wizards, with the indifferent lead cornet of Shirley Clay, don't amount to much, although a stray 1927 trio date for Paramount – of cornet, clarinet and piano! – is surprisingly hot and furious. Scholars of the period will nevertheless want this CD for the presence of just two tracks: the incredibly rare sides by Hightower's Night Hawks featuring the somewhat legendary Willie Hightower, whose cornet lead is for once becoming that of a legend.

The second disc features some very obscure music. After four sessions at the far end of the '20s there's a leap forward to 1935, and the remaining dozen tracks offer an anachronistic survival of old-style Chicago hot music in a swing era that had gone light-years ahead. The final session, made some 18 months before Jones's death, is a competent if pointless attempt at recalling what had been happening 20 years before. 'Jazzin' Babies Blues', which Jones had cut solo at his first date in 1923, appears again in what with hindsight seems a poignant farewell.

Sam Jones (1924–81)

BASS, CELLO

His most important association was with Cannonball Adderley, working with him during 1956–7 and 1959–66. He then led occasional groups (including a 12-piece band), worked often with Cedar Walton, and mostly as unassuming but rock-solid hard-bop rhythm player. Sometimes doubled on cello.

***** The Riverside Collection: Sam Jones – Right Down Front**

Original Jazz Classics OJC 6008 *Jones; Nat Adderley (c); Blue Mitchell, Clark Terry, Snooky Young (t); Melba Liston, Jimmy Cleveland (tb); Cannonball Adderley, Frank Strozier (as); Jimmy Heath, Jimmy Smith (ts); Charles Davis, Tate Houston, Pat Patrick (bs); Bobby Timmons, Victor Feldman, Joe Zawinul, Wynton Kelly (p); Les Spann (g, f); Keter Betts, Ron Carter, Israel Crosby (b); Louis Hayes, Ben Riley, Vernell Fournier (d).* 3/60–6/62.

***** The Soul Society**

Original Jazz Classics OJC 1789 *Jones; Nat Adderley (c); Blue Mitchell (t); Jimmy Heath (ts); Charles Davis (bs); Bobby Timmons (p); Keter Betts (b); Louis Hayes (d).* 3/60.

***** The Chant**

Original Jazz Classics OJC 1839 *As above, except add Melba Liston (tb), Cannonball Adderley (as), Tate Houston (bs), Wynton Kelly (p), Victor Feldman (p, vib), Les Spann (g); omit Davis, Timmons.* 1/61.

Sam Jones had a beautiful sound on bass – fat, resonant, fluid without any loss of body – and he was among the first to make the cello sound plausible in post-bop jazz. The compilation is chosen from five sessions he made during his time with Cannonball Adderley and, although the settings are mostly rather ordinary – two tracks by a big band with Melba Liston charts are more challenging – Jones's quiet good humour gives as much buoyancy as his bass to the music. A quintet reading of 'Round Midnight' with Jones on cello is a little fluffy, and 'Some Kinda Mean' gives a better idea of his powers on that instrument. That track is drawn from The Soul Society sessions, which has also been reissued as a single album. The cello tracks (there are four with Sam on that instrument, where Keter Betts takes over bass duties) are a little gimmicky in the fashion of the day, but the band is a rousing one, and the other session with Mitchell in for Adderley boils water on 'All Members' and 'The Old Country'.

The Chant is another good session. Cannonball takes a back-seat role, but most of the other horns get in a blow, and the studio sound gets a nice burnish on the section-work. Jones himself has a number of features, but what one remembers is his drive in the ensembles and alongside old partner, Louis Hayes.

****(*) Visitation**

Steeplechase SCCD 31097 *Jones; Terumasa Hino (c); Bob Berg (ts); Ronnie Mathews (p); Al Foster (d).* 3/78.

Sam's few sessions as a leader in the 1970s found him pursuing a lyrical kind of hard bop. *Visitation* is dependable rather than especially exciting, although Hino's peculiar mix of rhapsody and restlessness is as engaging as usual.

Thad Jones (1923–86)

TRUMPET, CORNET, FLUGELHORN, VALVE TROMBONE, BANDLEADER, ARRANGER

Joined Count Basie in 1954 and stayed for some ten years, while also cutting some small-group records. Began arranging and composing and formed an orchestra with drummer Mel Lewis in 1965, which lasted until Jones left for Denmark in 1978. Ran the Basie band after its leader's death for a spell but himself died not long afterwards.

*****(*) The Fabulous Thad Jones**

Original Jazz Classics OJC 625 *Jones; Frank Wess (ts, f); John Dennis, Hank Jones (p); Charles Mingus (b); Kenny Clarke, Max Roach (d).* 54.

***** After Hours**

Original Jazz Classics OJC 1782 *Jones; Frank Wess (ts, f); Kenny Burrell (g); Mal Waldron (p); Paul Chambers (b); Art Taylor (d).* 6/57.

*****(*) Mad Thad**

Fresh Sound FSR CD 117 *Jones; Henry Coker (tb); Frank Foster (ts); Frank Wess (ts, f); Tommy Flanagan, Jimmy Jones (p); Eddie Jones, Doug Watkins (b); Elvin Jones, Jo Jones (d).* 12/56.

***** Mean What You Say**

Original Jazz Classics OJC 464 *Jones; Pepper Adams (bs); Duke Pearson (p); Ron Carter (b); Mel Lewis (d).* 4–5/66.

***** Three And One**

Steeplechase SCS 1197 *Jones; Ole Kock Hansen (p); Jesper Lundgaard (b); Ed Thigpen (d).* 10/84.

Though better known than the quiet Hank, the middle Jones brother has been consistently underrated as a soloist, recognized mainly as an arranger for the band he co-led with drummer Mel Lewis (see below). Not usually considered a small-group player, or even a soloist of any unusual interest, Jones's recorded output on this scale is disappointingly slight, relative to his significance as a composer. On the measure of the late *Three And One* alone, this is a pity. He's a subtle and vibrant player with a cornet tone similar to Nat Adderley but able to sustain big transitions of pitch with absolute confidence, much as he demands of his big bands. 'But Not For Me' is marred by a slightly tentative accompaniment, but Thigpen splashes in sensuous slo-mo, almost tuneful.

Mad Thad is even better. The trumpeter was signed to Basie for most of the late 1950s and early '60s, a period that firmed up his reputation as an arranger but afforded regrettably few solo flights. He'd recorded on Mingus's demanding *Jazz Experiment* and won the bassist's heart for ever with his bustling, opportunistic runs and confident entanglements in and around the theme. On *Mad Thad*, playing trumpet only, he sounds full-throated and sure of himself; there are what appear to be very minor articulation problems on a couple of tracks, but these are incidental stammers in some beautifully crafted ('Whisper Not' especially) solos.

The sessions done for Mingus's and Roach's Debut label are very good indeed; these are also to be found in the 12-CD Debut compilation. Mingus admired the trumpeter inordinately and Jones was the only artist to record twice under his own name for Debut. Their duo on 'I Can't Get Started' is interesting first of all for Mingus's restructuring of the harmony, but Jones's response to this bare-boned setting and to the quasi-modal 'Get Out Of Town' is full confirmation of his ability to improvise at the highest level. Wess's flute makes a fine contrast on 'Sombre Intrusion'. The slighter *After Hours* has nothing quite so daring, but it's a solidly inventive session nevertheless, and the CD sound on both is very good.

Mean What You Say comes just after the formation of the Jones–Lewis big band. Though it casts the trumpeter in what should be completely sympathetic company, it's a rather uncertain affair, with most of the honours going to baritonist Pepper Adams, named as co-leader on the session. The sound is exemplary, though, with a representation of bass and percussion that was better than average for the time.

***** Eclipse**

Storyville STCD 4089 *Jones; Jan Glasesel, Tim Hagans, Egon Petersen, Lars Togeby, Erik Tschentscher (t); Richard Boone, Ture Larsen, Niels Neergaard, Bjarne Thanning, Axel Windfeld (tb); Michael Hove, Bent Jaedig, Ole Thoger Nielsen, Jorgen Nilsson, Sahib Shihab (sax); Horace Parlan (p); Jesper Lundgaard (b); Ed Thigpen (d).* 9/79.

After leaving Mel Lewis in 1978, Jones spent most of his remaining years in Scandinavia, where he formed and led the Eclipse big band, an outfit which reflected some of the old partnership's combination of power and complexity. For all his virtues, Thigpen is no Lewis, but the band sounds well drilled and the charts are razor-sharp. In the late 1970s, Jones took up valve trombone as an alternative horn. It sounds fleet and subtle, and it lends him a breadth of tone he could not have achieved with trumpet. The sound doesn't hold up to current digital standards, but it's big and warm and preserves enough of the grain in the ensembles to afford a hint of what this band was like in concert.

****** Live At Montmartre**

Storyville STCD 4172 *Jones; Benny Rosenfeld, Palle Bolvig, Idrees Sulieman, Allan Botschinsky, Perry Knudsen (t); Vincent Nilsson (tb); Erling Kroner, Richard Boone (tb); Ole Kurt Jensen (btb); Axel Windfeld (btb, tba); Jesper Thilo (ss, as, cl, f); Per Carsten Petersen (ss, as, f); Bent Jaedig (ts, f); Uffe Karskov (ts, as, f, cl); Flemming Madsen (bs, cl, bcl); Ole Kock Hansen (p); Bo Sylven (g); Niels-Henning Orsted Pedersen (b); Bjarne Rostvold (d); Ethan Weisgard (perc).* 3/78.

One of the authors was present at the concert recorded here and can confirm that this is an authentic documentation of one of the very finest concerts of Jones's later career, made on the eve of his departure from the long-standing Jones–Lewis band, and the trumpeter (or, rather, cornetist) played his socks off. His tone on the ballad, 'Old Folks', on his own 'Tip Toe' and 'A Good Time Was Had By All' is pure and bell-like and the solos are relaxed enough to allow digressions into other themes and harmonic displacements without losing the thread.The sound is considerably better than in the rather cramped acoustic of the Jazzhus Montmartre. Bass trombonist Jensen co-produced and gets the brasses sounding as shiny as Gabriel's. Completely enjoyable, and one of the best big-band records of that period.

Cennet Jonsson

SOPRANO SAXOPHONE, BASS CLARINET

Based in Lund, Sweden, Jonsson is a saxophonist and teacher who plays in the Tolvan Big Band and has worked as a leader only rarely.

***** Ten Pieces**

Phono Suecia PSCD 94 *Jonsson; Staffan Svensson (t); Sven Berggren (tb); Joakim Milder (ts); Dan Malmqvist (bcl, cbcl);*

Jacob Karlzon (p); Mats Rondin (clo); Christian Spering (b); Peter Danemo (d); Lisbeth Diers (perc). 1/96.

Written as a suite – for ten players, in celebration of a festival's tenth birthday – Jonsson's music is a formidably assured compendium of ideas. The best of it comes in the truly remarkable fantasy on bebop melody, 'Bebopmania', which springs from an endlessly elongated riff into a brilliant sifting-together of the ensemble, highlighted by outstanding solos from Milder, Rondin and Malmqvist. Almost as good are 'The Larch' and the worldly fusion of 'Dance Children, Dance!', the latter elevated by Svensson's terrific solo. Jonsson has a great team here and they give him their best, but there are a few false steps – 'Funkypunky' turns out to be an ominously awful title, and 'Dark Clouds' is merely dreary – which let down the substance of the rest of it a little.

Clifford Jordan (1931–93)

TENOR SAXOPHONE

Jordan went to school in Chicago with Johnny Griffin and John Gilmore, a detail that bears out the pointlessness of talking in terms of 'Chicago tenor'. His characteristic sound was warm and breathy, with something of both Ben Webster and Lester Young in it, and only rather later a hint of the harmonic innovation of John Coltrane.

****(*) Cliff Craft**
Blue Note 81582 *Jordan; Art Farmer (t); Sonny Clark (p); George Tucker (b); Louis Hayes (d).* 11/57.

****** Spellbound**
Original Jazz Classics OJC 766 *Jordan; Cedar Walton (p); Spanky De Brest (b); Albert 'Tootie' Heath (d).* 8/60.

*****(*) Bearcat**
Original Jazz Classics OJC 494 *Jordan; Cedar Walton (p); Teddy Smith (b); J.C Moses (d).* 10/61, 62.

At first blush, Jordan is 'just' another Chicago tenor. That was very much the way he was perceived and marketed. His Blue Note debut, *Blowin' In From Chicago*, is still in limbo, as is the OJC *Startin' Time*, but the reissue of *Cliff Craft* is a step in the right direction. For some reason, Jordan didn't seem to find much favour at Blue Note, perhaps because his style in these years did seem to reflect an interest in the swing era. Forty years ago, his style was much closer to the tempestuous approach associated with such natives of the Windy City as Johnny Griffin and – in timbre particularly – Von Freeman. And yet *Cliff Craft* is a markedly laid-back session, almost taken at a stroll. Never a true bebopper, Jordan takes his own route through 'Confirmation' and 'Anthropology', pulling the teeth of both somewhat but managing to make the results sound logical and engaging. Art Farmer is the co-star, playing with all the grace and sensitivity that was to be his stock in trade in later years.

Bearcat is the perfect characterization of Jordan's sound, sometimes growling, sometimes purring. This old Jazzland set isn't particularly well recorded and the bassist is prone to sudden surges towards the mike, but the music is fine and Jordan is in good voice on 'How Deep Is The Ocean?' and the original 'Middle Of The Block'. The old home town is eulogized in 'Dear Old Chicago', a performance that name-checks one or two distinguished ancestors. A word of praise is in order for Walton and Moses, both of whom play exceptionally well.

Spellbound contains one of Jordan's very finest recorded performances, on 'Lush Life'. His understanding with Walton was only to grow and deepen with the years, but their level of communication here is most impressive and they hurtle through 'Au Privave' with almost cavalier abandon. The sound – originally a Riverside – is very full and authentic. A recommended purchase.

***** These Are My Roots: Clifford Jordan Plays Leadbelly**
Koch 8522 *Jordan; Roy Burrowes (t); Julian Priester (tb); Cedar Walton (p); Chuck Wayne (g, bjo); Richard Davis (b); Albert 'Tootie' Heath (d); Sandra Douglass (v).* 1/65.

Clifford Jordan and Huddie Ledbetter aren't the most obvious bunkmates, but this 1960s album of interpretations of classic blues songs works better than it has any right to. Recorded for Atlantic, it was very much part of an ongoing rediscovery of American folklore, though it was mainly rock musicians who explored this strand of black American music. Jordan assembled a very fine band and got a big, brash sound from engineer Phil Iehle and producer Donald Elfman. Intriguingly, the saxophonist includes his own signature-piece, 'Highest Mountain', in the middle of the set as if to indicate Leadbelly's influence on it. The connection isn't entirely clear, but each of the ten performances – which include 'Yellow Gal', 'Silver City Bound' and the classic 'Goodnight Irene' – are beautifully handled and, though almost all the tracks are very short, nothing longer than four and a half minutes, the solos are compressed and effective. Of the supporting cast, Priester is excellent and fans of the trombonist will welcome a chance to hear this little-known selection. Bassist Richard Davis, another schoolmate of Jordan's, simplifies his playing markedly for the occasion and doesn't seem hampered by the idiom. We've heard little of singer Sandra Douglass, but she makes a very decent shift of 'Black Girl' and 'Take This Hammer'.

***** On Stage: Volume 1**
Steeplechase SCCD 31071 *Jordan; Cedar Walton (p); Teddy Smith (b); Billy Higgins (d).* 3/75.

***** On Stage: Volume 2**
Steeplechase SCCD 31092 *As above.* 3/75.

***** On Stage: Volume 3**
Steeplechase SCCD 31104 *As above.* 3/75.

***** The Night Of The Mark VII**
32 Records 32118 *Jordan; Cedar Walton (p); Sam Jones (b); Billy Higgins (d).* 3/75.

***** The Highest Mountain**
Steeplechase SCS 1047 *As above.* 3/75.

***** Firm Roots**
Steeplechase SCS 1033 *As above.* 4/75.

It was having such firm roots that allowed Jordan to drift through a theme as cavalierly as he often did. Throughout the highly productive mid-1970s, he was probably playing more 'legitimately' than at any other time in his career, but there are constant reminders of his Mingus-influenced tendency to regard the note as a dartboard (which, of course, you don't always want to hit dead centre) and a progression as a series of mentally totted-up scores that always come out right in the end. Though he had a fair change of pace, he was definitely more successful at a medium-to-slow clip. He was a consummate ballad-player (see 'Stella By Starlight' on *On Stage: Volume 2*), with the kind of articulation and presence that suggest unused gears. Throughout these sets, it is the romantic ballads that consistently score high points. Compared to, say, Griffin, he never quite convinces at a gallop.

The mid-'70s were a very good time for Clifford Jordan. He was playing regularly with Cedar Walton, Sam Jones and Billy Higgins under the name The Magic Triangle, gigging pretty steadily and recording a substantial amount. *Night Of The Mark VII* was a Muse LP and is also known as *The Highest Mountain*, a title that has been hijacked elsewhere. Cedar's 'Midnight Waltz' is a high point of the album. Jones and Higgins are equally sympathetic to the concept, and Sam's big, booming lines come through magnificently in Joel Dorn's remastering.

Much has been said about Jordan's supposed John Coltrane influence – some find it dominant by this stage; some profess not to hear it at all – so Bill Lee's 'John Coltrane' seems a reasonable place to test the hypothesis. Unlike Trane, Jordan strays over bar lines and stretches theme statements out, without seeming to elaborate unnecessarily. His solos on 'Highest Mountain' and on 'Blue Monk' suggest influences from an earlier generation, combined with a phraseology that is entirely his own. Excellent news that this fine album is back in the catalogue. It further fills out documentation of what was to be a busy year.

Firm Roots was more prosaic, but the evocative title captures something like the equidistance and responsiveness that Jordan, a great arranger, achieved with his colleagues. They work hard for one another, creating spaces and textures, laying off chords that lead whoever is soloing out into new territory, then gently pulling on the strings.

***** Adventurer**

32 Records 32181 *Jordan; Tommy Flanagan (p); Bill Lee (b); Grady Tate (d).* 2/78.

Helping to fill out the picture, this valuable reissue of Cliff's 1978 Muse LP finds him approaching the end of a long and productive decade in good form and spirits. It's a business-like rather than inspired record and Tommy Flanagan seems eager to get things wrapped up in the briefest possible time, restricting himself to terse and understated solo statements. Jordan is the featured player but even he hangs back, as if unwilling to let fly. Joel Dorn's label is giving sterling service in bringing material of this vintage back to the light. *Adventurer* is perhaps one of the less compelling items in the current catalogue.

***** Repetition**

Soul Note 121084 *Jordan; Barry Harris (p); Walter Booker (b); Vernell Fournier (d).* 2/84.

***** Two Tenor Winner**

Criss Cross Criss 1011 *Jordan; Junior Cook (ts); Kirk Lightsey (p); Cecil McBee (b); Eddie Gladden (d).* 10/84.

*****(*) Royal Ballads**

Criss Cross Criss 1025 *Jordan; Kevin O'Connell (p); Ed Howard (b); Vernell Fournier (d).* 12/86.

In later years Jordan perfected a ballad style that was strikingly reminiscent of Wardell Gray's. *Royal Ballads* is a lovely record; if it steers close to easy listening on occasion, a more attentive hearing uncovers all manner of subtleties and harmonic shifts. The opening 'Lush Life' is almost lost in Fournier's constant cymbal-spray, but the drummer – who has worked to great effect with Ahmad Jamal – is a great ballad player and every bit as adept as Jordan at varying an apparently sleepy beat with odd, out-of-synch metres and quiet paradiddles. As Jordan quotes 'Goodbye Pork Pie Hat' on the original 'Royal Blues', Fournier squeezes the tempo almost subliminally, so that the reference evades identification as the mind subconsciously readjusts to the beat. Subtle and intelligent jazz, and a sure sign that ballads albums are not just the preserve of MOR acts.

The slightly earlier *Repetition* and *Two Tenor Winner* have more variation of pace (though no less inventive a trawl of material). Fournier doesn't seem quite so much at ease, but Harris is a much subtler player than O'Connell. Cook plays with a loose-limbed ease, but he lacks the chops to go head to head with Jordan in this way. Once again, nothing to choose between them. Late-nighters might prefer the ballads.

*****(*) Four Play**

DIW 836 *Jordan; James Williams (p); Richard Davis (b); Ronnie Burrage (d).*

It's not quite clear who's supposed to be leader here. A companion DIW set, *sans* Jordan, and either deliberately or misleadingly entitled *I Remember Clifford*, is reviewed under Richard Davis's name. Jordan contributes two fine compositions to *Four Play* and kicks off the session on his 'Tokyo Road' with a dark, Coltranish wail that lightens steadily as the set progresses. There's an excellent reading of Monk's 'I Mean You', one of the less exploited items in the canon, and a superb long version of Randy Weston's 'Hi-Fly', which leads in to Richard Davis's moving 'Misako – Beautiful Shore', a theme that brings back some of the sombre quality to Jordan's voice. Impeccably recorded, and laurels for the unsung Williams and the prodigious Burrage. Well worth what might seem a pricey investment.

*****(*) Live At Ethell's**

Mapleshade 512629 *Jordan; Kevin O'Connell (p); Ed Howard (b); Vernell Fournier (d).* 10/87.

Ethell's is – or was, we don't know – a club in Baltimore. Jordan's October 1987 residency yielded some of his most impressive small-group playing on American soil. As relaxed and unhurried as ever, he strolls through a set comprising jazz staples – 'Lush Life', 'Round Midnight' – some originals – 'Blues In Advance' and the intriguingly titled 'Little Boy For So Long ... Little Boy ... But' – and a Stanley Cowell eulogy to the brilliant trumpeter and composer, Cal Massey. Cliff's solo on the Monk tune says much about the man; he tackles it pretty much straight, remaining close to the melody but all along the way finding new variants and chord changes which lift a tune that probably deserves a moratorium of at least five years on to a new and original plane. The band Jordan brought to Baltimore was talented without being surprising. With no other horn, the emphasis is very much on the leader.

****** Masters From Different Worlds**

Mapleshade 01732 *Jordan; Julian Priester (tb); Windmill Saxophone Quartet: Clayton Englar, Jesse Meman, Tom Monroe, Ken Plant (sax); Ran Blake (p); Steve Williams (d); Alfredo Mojica (perc); Claudia Polley (v).* 12/89.

A most unusual record: Jordan in duo and in an assortment of slightly unlikely settings with composer and pianist Blake, one of the most analytical of contemporary players. Much of the material is Blake's, including the contemporary classic, 'Short Life Of Barbara Monk'; but there are also interpretations of 'Mood Indigo', Billy Strayhorn's 'Something To Live For' played as a moody duo, and even John Lennon's song to his mother, 'Julia'. There's nothing overtly 'Third Stream' about the set, except that Blake does seem to slide into occasional reveries and lets the rhythm go completely to pot. On 'Arline', Jordan makes a rare shift to soprano, sounding very polished indeed; with Priester beside him, the sound is wonderful. To what extent, and with what success, they've sunk their differences really isn't clear, but this is an extraordinary record nevertheless.

***** Play What You Feel**
Mapleshade 3232 *Jordan; Joe Gardner, Dean Pratt, Dizzy Reece, Don Sickler (t); Benny Powell, Kiane Zawadi (tb); John Jenkins (as); Junior Cook, Lou Orenstein, Willie Williams (ts); Robert Eldridge (bs); Ronnie Mathews (p); Ed Howard (b); Tommy Campbell (d).* 12/90.

****** Down Through The Years**
Milestone MCD 9197 *Jordan; Dizzy Reece, Stephen Furtado, Dean Pratt, Don Sickler (t); Brad Shigeta (tb); Kiane Zawadi (euph); Jerome Richardson, Sue Terry (as); Lou Orenstein, Willie Williams (ts); Charles Davis (bs); Ronnie Mathews (p); David Williams (b); Vernell Fournier (d).* 10/91.

Jordan rarely had an opportunity to play with a big band but, late in life, opportunities presented themselves from time to time. The Mapleshade set was recorded live and has atmosphere in buckets, as a thoroughly sympathetic band work through Dizzy Reece's arrangements. Monk's 'Evidence' has rarely been given this kind of broad-brush treatment and the old rogue responds very positively indeed. Cliff throws in 'Bearcat' and 'Charlie Parker's Last Supper' from his own catalogue and, for a curtain call, Duke's 'Don't Get Around Much Any More'.

The hand-picked orchestra on *Down Through The Years* was the fulfilment of considerable planning and thorough rehearsal. Recorded at Condon's in New York City, the disc captures the sound of an excellent ensemble playing at full stretch. The programme includes such long-standing favourites as 'Highest Mountain', on which the saxophonist is, appropriately, the only soloist, singing away on his solitary eminence, 'Japanese Dream', which provides an outlet for Dizzy Reece, and the strangely moving 'Charlie Parker's Last Supper', which brings the set to a close. Jordan played better many times, but rarely in such a completely sympathetic setting. His phrasing is almost always right on the beat, but he manages to avoid sounding mechanical.

***** The Mellow Side Of Clifford Jordan**
Mapleshade 5032 *Jordan; Kenny Reed (t); Julian Priester (tb); Carter Jefferson (ts); Larry Willis, Chris Anderson (p); Mike LeDonne (org); Edison Machado (d); Nassser Abadey (perc).*

We have no reliable recording date for this 1997 release, but presumably it came towards the end of Cliff's long and distinguished career. A mainly standards set, it hinges on a titanic journey through the soulful chords and mood shifts of Mal Waldron's 'Soul Eyes'. All the other songs are quite brief – disappointingly so, given the richness of the orchestration and the moody, reflective quality of Jordan's solos. Old friends Chris Anderson, Carter Jefferson and Julian Priester were all on hand and, as so often, Cliff plays easily and adventurously when in familiar company. The association with Mapleshade was a happy one for the saxophonist, and the final flourish on the Ellington/Strayhorn classic, 'Daydream', is a delightful curtain call.

Duke Jordan (born 1922)

PIANO

Jordan was recruited from the Three Deuces by Charlie Parker and became a bit player in the bebop movement. His style is an amalgam of Art Tatum and Bud Powell, the parts not always cohering with absolute authority. A player of great facility, he may have recorded too much to be absolutely distinctive.

****(*) Flight To Denmark**
Steeplechase SCCD 31011 *Jordan; Mads Vinding (b); Ed Thigpen (d).* 11/73.

***** Two Loves**
Steeplechase SCCD 31024 *As above.* 12/73.

Duke Jordan's career has an odd trajectory. At 25, with an apprenticeship under Coleman Hawkins behind him, he was thrust into the limelight with Charlie Parker and proved himself an able and frequently imaginative accompanist. Thereafter, though, his progress has been curiously elided, with long disappearances from the scene. Perhaps as a consequence, he is by far the least well-known of the bebop pianists, surprisingly diffident in performing manner and little given to solo performance. Though he is a fine standards player, he has from time to time preferred to rework a sizeable but tightly organized body of original compositions. These have been documented by the Danish Steeplechase label with a thoroughness bordering on redundancy and seemingly quite inconsistent with the pianist's rather marginal reputation. There are very many recorded versions of some of the pianist's most successful themes. 'Jordu', in particular, has become a popular repertoire piece. A Jordan theme tends to be brief, tightly melodic rather than just a launching-pad of chords, and disconcertingly unmemorable, in the positive sense that they resist being hummed.

Unlike his later work for Steeplechase, these are essentially albums of standards, and in some sense an attempt to come to terms with the legacy of bebop. There are finely judged readings of 'Here's That Rainy Day', 'On Green Dolphin Street' and 'How Deep Is The Ocean?' on *Flight*, 'I'll Remember April' and 'Embraceable You', 'Blue Monk' and 'My Old Flame' on *Two Loves*, which also includes the ubiquitous 'Jordu' and 'Lady Dingbat', an unaccountably popular original. Jordan's career had been rather stop–start since the mid-'50s and there are occasional rust-spots on his faster runs and a slight stiffness in his octaves. The CD transfers aren't perfect. There are alternative takes of several tracks; newcomers might find *Two Loves* preferable.

****(*) Misty Thursday**
Steeplechase SCCD 31053 *Jordan; Chuck Wayne (g); Sam Jones (b); Roy Haynes (d).* 6/75.

***** Lover Man**
Steeplechase SCCD 31127 *Jordan; Sam Jones (b); Al Foster (d).* 11/75.

*****(*) Duke's Delight**
Steeplechase SCCD 31046 *Jordan; Richard Williams (t); Charlie Rouse (ts); Sam Jones (b); Al Foster (d).* 11/75.

***** In Concert From Japan**
Steeplechase SCCD 37005/6 2CD *Jordan; Wilbur Little (b); Roy Haynes (d).* 9/76.

****(*) Flight To Japan**
Steeplechase SCCD 31088 *As above.* 9/76.

***** Duke's Artistry**
Steeplechase SCCD 31103 *Jordan; Art Farmer (flhn); David Friesen (b); Philly Joe Jones (d).* 6/78.

***** The Great Session**
Steeplechase SCCD 31150 *As above, except omit Farmer; add Paul Jeffrey (bells).* 6/78.

****(*) Tivoli One**
Steeplechase SCCD 31189 *Jordan; Wilbur Little (b); Dannie Richmond (d).* 11/78.

****(*) Wait And See**
Steeplechase SCCD 31211 *As above.*

*****(*) Duke Jordan Solo Masterpieces Vol. One**
Steeplechase SCCD 31299 *Jordan (p solo).* 1 & 2/79.

*****(*) Duke Jordan Solo Masterpieces Vol. Two**
Steeplechase SCCD 31300 *Jordan (p solo).* 2–11/79.

***** Double Duke**
Steeplechase SCCD 37039/40 *Jordan; Niels-Henning Orsted Pedersen (b); Billy Hart (d).* 10/79.

****(*) Midnight Moonlight**
Steeplechase SCCD 31143 *Jordan (p solo).* 79.

*****(*) When You're Smiling**
Steeplechase SCCD 37023/24 2CD *Jordan; Jesper Lundgaard (b); Billy Hart (d).* 79–7/85.

The late 1970s were a remarkably productive time for Jordan. In Billy Hart and Dannie Richmond he found drummers with the kind of rhythmic tension he required on which to sound his taut melodic figures. The mix of material is much as usual, but some mention should be made of 'Light Foot' and 'The Queen Is Home To Stay' on *Double Duke*, which brings together two single albums – *Thinking Of You* and *Change A Pace* – and makes an attractive package out of them, though one wonders sometimes at the logic of this recent bout of rationalization at the Danish label.

Compare the studio version of 'Night Train To Snekkersten', one of his best compositions, on *Misty Thursday* with the live versions recorded in Osaka 15 months later. Sam Jones has a more contained approach and lacks Little's strength, but he is absolutely right for the lovely 'Hymn To Peace'. The sound is a little flat.

The *Tivoli* sessions with Richmond are again standards-based, with an accent on bebop-associated themes. Jordan adds vocals to *When You're Smiling* (which brings together two single albums, *Time On My Hands* and *As Ditto Goes By*) but in all conscience we can't recommend him as a singer. Much as Ahmad Jamal is popularly supposed to, Jordan occasionally skirts a Vegas-style 'entertainment' approach that obscures his more interesting ideas to all but the most attentive listeners. *Duke's Delight* has long been one of our favourites among the Steeplechases, an inventive set by an interesting band.

Jordan was warmly received in Japan. As with much of the catalogue, Steeplechase have rationalized scattered material on a double-CD set. Since favourites like 'Misty Thursday', 'Jordu' and 'Flight To Jordan' are all included, it might make a sensible introduction to the pianist's work. The recording quality is very good, if a bit cavernous in places.

'Lady Bird' on *The Great Session* helpfully points to Tadd Dameron as a further factor in the development of Jordan's approach (Lennie Tristano, at the opposite pole from bebop, is another). These are unexceptionable sessions; Philly Joe plays with his incomparable verve and exactness, and Friesen sounds confident and aware.

What all this amounts to is very difficult to judge. Though there are later recordings from the mid-'80s on *When You're Smiling* and the playing sounds as solid and untroubled as ever, Jordan's *annus mirabilis* had been and gone. Nils Winther of Steeplechase was a sympathetic and attentive patron, but it must be said that few collectors will want more than two or three of these discs at best, and none of them makes a genuinely pressing demand on the casual listener. This is a vast body of work, with only the most obvious reference-points in the shape of oft-repeated themes and compositions. Doubtless there are aficionados who can speak with authority on the question of their respective merits. However, since we are dealing with records and not tracks, only a rather impressionistic valuation is feasible. Perhaps the two *Masterpieces* discs offer the best music.

***** One For The Library**
Storyville STCD 4194 *Jordan (p solo).* 10/93.

What an odd, even cynical title for a record. One does begin to wonder how much of the Jordan discography has been merely 'for the library', documentation for the sake of it. The galling thing is that this is a perfectly respectable record, swinging in the rather restrictive mode of solo piano records, packed with melody and invention (18 tracks in 65 minutes) and beautifully recorded in the studio on a responsive, big-hearted piano. But ask us to differentiate it blindfold from half a dozen others of Duke's records and we'd have to bow out.

Louis Jordan (1908–75)

ALTO AND BARITONE SAXOPHONES, CLARINET, VOCAL

Jordan, who came from Arkansas and had a father in vaudeville, quit playing in big bands in the early 1940s to form his Tympany Five, one of the most successful small bands in jazz history. The Five lasted until 1951, and thereafter Jordan toured and often guested with local bands, such as Chris Barber in Britain. He helped to father R&B with his mix of jive, jump music and small-band swing.

***** Louis Jordan 1934–1940**
Classics 636 *Jordan; Mario Bauza, Bobby Stark, Taft Jordan, Courtney Williams, Charlie Gaines (t); Ed Allen (c); Claude*

Jones, Sandy Williams, Nat Story (tb); Pete Clark (cl, as, bs); Cecil Scott (cl, as); Lem Johnson (cl, ts); Ted McRae, Stafford 'Pazuza' Simon (ts); Wayman Carver (ts, f); Stafford Simon (ts); Tommy Fulford, Clarence Johnson, James P Johnson (p); John Trueheart (g); Cyrus St Clair (tba); Beverley Peer, Charlie Drayton (b); Chick Webb, Walter Martin (d); Floyd Casey (wbd); Rodney Sturgis, Clarence Williams (v). 3/34–1/40.

***** Louis Jordan 1940–1941**

Classics 663 *Jordan; Courtney Williams, Freddy Webster, Eddie Roane (t); Stafford Simon (cl, ts); Kenneth Hollon (ts); Arnold Thomas (p); Charlie Drayton, Henry Turner, Dallas Bartley (b); Walter Martin (d); Mabel Robinson, Daisy Winchester (v).* 3/40–11/41.

*****(*) Louis Jordan 1941–1943**

Classics 741 *Jordan; Eddie Roane (t); Arnold Thomas (p); Dallas Bartley, Jesse Simpkins (b); Walter Martin, Shadow Wilson (d).* 11/41–11/43.

***** Louis Jordan 1943–1945**

Classics 866 *As above, except add Idrees Sulieman, Aaron Izenhall (t), Freddie Simon, Josh Jackson (ts), William Austin, Wild Bill Davis (p), Carl Hogan (g), Al Morgan (b), Slick Jones, Razz Mitchell, Eddie Byrd (d), Bing Crosby (v); omit Bartley.* 11/43–7/45.

***** Louis Jordan 1945–1946**

Classics 921 *As above, except add James Wright (ts), Joe Morris (d), Harry Dial, Vic Lourie (perc), Ella Fitzgerald (v); omit Roane, Thomas, Sulieman, Simon, Martin, Wilson, Jones, Mitchell, Crosby.*

*****(*) Louis Jordan 1946–1947**

Classics 1010 *Jordan; Aaron Izenhall (t); James Wright, Eddie Johnson (ts); Wild Bill Davis (p); Carl Hogan (g); Jesse Simpkins, Dallas Bartley (b); Joe 'Chris Columbus' Morris (d); The Calypso Boys (perc).* 10/46–12/47.

****** Swingsation**

GRP 059951-2 *As above discs.* 39–53.

Jordan was an incomparable funster as well as being a distinctive altoman and smart vocalist. His hit records, 'Five Guys Named Moe', 'Choo Choo Ch'Boogie', 'Caldonia' and many more, established the idea of the jump band as a jiving, irrepressible outfit which persists to this day. Rightly so: Jordan was a pro's pro, tirelessly seeking out fresh songs and constantly touring. But, surprisingly, the music seldom suffered, which is why his best sides still sound fresh. Most of the hits – which mixed comic lyrics with spirited swing-style playing and paved the way for R&B – are collected on the GRP record, an irresistible platter to warm up a room. The Classics series tells much of the story. Classics 636 starts with an obscure 1934 Clarence Williams date where Jordan croons 'I Can't Dance, I Got Ants In My Pants'. The usual approach of chronological order is then followed through to the end of the 1945–6 disc and, though some of the material is just a tad strained – try 'Sam Jones Done Snagged His Britches' – there is some unbeatable jive here too. Classics 741 is probably the first choice, given that there are the first versions of some of Jordan's most enduring hits: 'Five Guys Named Moe' (also present in a V-Disc version), 'The Chicks I Pick Are Slender, Tender And Tall' and so on. But Classics 921 has 'Choo Choo Ch'Boogie' and 'That Chick's Too Young To Fry' plus a couple of duets with Ella Fitzgerald. Classics 866 includes eight tracks made for V-Disc, a radio ad for Oldsmobile and the sublime duet with Bing Crosby on 'Your Socks Don't Match'. Classics 1010 has a sublime put-down in 'You're Much Too Fat And That's That', as well as Jordan's first two versions of 'Open The Door Richard!'. These and few other favourites of ours, such as 'Boogie Woogie Blue Plate' and the straight blues, 'Roamin' Blues' and 'Inflation Blues', persuade us to award an extra point. Excellent sound on these later tracks, although by and large most of these discs are in decent fidelity.

***** Rock 'N' Roll**

Mercury 838219-2 *Jordan; Ernie Royal (t); Jimmy Cleveland (tb); Budd Johnson (ts, bs); Sam 'The Man' Taylor (ts); Ernie Hayes (p); Jackie Davis (org); Mickey Baker, Irving Ashby (g); Wendell Marshall, Billy Hadnott (b); Charli Persip, Marvin Oliver (d); Francisco Pozo (perc); Dorothy Smith (v).* 10/56–8/57.

***** No Moe!**

Verve 512523-2 *As above.* 10/56–8/57.

Jordan's later recordings were remakes of his old ones. On the Mercury sessions it worked out well, since Quincy Jones's arrangements brought in some sterling instrumentalists and updated Jordan's sound just enough without prettifying it too much. As a result, the likes of 'Is You Is Or Is You Ain't My Baby' become rejuvenated, and Louis never sounded wilder than he did on 'Salt Pork, West Virginia'. The Verve disc is almost the same: five fewer tracks, but three from a later small-group session which *Rock 'N' Roll* misses.

**** Louis Jordan And Chris Barber**

Black Lion BLCD 760156 *Jordan; Pat Halcox (t); Chris Barber (tb, v); Ian Wheeler, John Crocker (cl, as); Steve Hammond, Johnny McCallum (g, bj); John Slaughter (g); Eddie Smith (bj); Dick Smith, Jackie Flavelle (b); Graham Burbidge (d).* 12/62–12/74.

Nine tracks with the 1962 Barber band and five more by Barber's men without Louis. Jordan does his best, but these Englishmen aren't much good at jiving.

Marlon Jordan (born 1970)

TRUMPET

New Orleans trumpeter playing a local spin on the new jazz of the '90s.

***** Marlon's Mode**

Arabesque AJO 127 *Jordan; Alvin Batiste (cl); Victor Goines (ss, ts); Victor Atkins (p); David Pulphus (b); Jason Marsalis, Troy Davis (d).* 8/96.

After two desperately self-conscious albums for Columbia, this is effectively Jordan's comeback record, for a small independent label. He is a New Orleanian, the son of Kidd Jordan, and the band is full of local players, with Batiste a welcome addition where he appears. Instead of the immature writing of the earlier albums, this is a cautious homage to Miles Davis (three tunes) and John Coltrane (another three), with 'Caravan' and Kidd Jordan's 'Ballad For Trane' as the fill-up. What comes out is a good repertory record. Inevitably, these versions of 'Agitation', 'Equinox' and 'Freddie Freeloader' hardly challenge the originals, but there is a pleasing thoughtfulness about much of the music, without it seeming over-deliberate. Some of the trumpeter's solos still sound a bit effortful, such as the somewhat pretentious statement on 'Equinox', but when he relaxes he sounds very good, and Goines makes a serious, shrewd foil. Work in progress, though enjoyable on its own terms.

Sheila Jordan (born 1928)

VOICE

Born in Detroit, Jordan was turned on to modern jazz by hearing Charlie Parker, and her first work was with vocalese groups, singing lyrics to Bird material. She was married to pianist Duke Jordan for a decade, studied under Lennie Tristano and worked with George Russell, Roswell Rudd and others. Her style covers an enormous range, from scat and ballads to art song.

****** Portrait Of Sheila**

Blue Note 789902-2 *Jordan; Barry Galbraith (g); Steve Swallow (b); Denzil Best (d).* 9 & 10/62.

Sheila Jordan shows much of her former husband's concentration on the melodic progress of a song and much of his intelligent, unhistrionic and almost diffident delivery. Like the truly great instrumentalists, Sheila Jordan is content to explore all the potential of the middle register, where words are more likely to remain intact (with lesser talent, prosaically so), rather than overreach a range which is nevertheless greater than sometimes appears. At the end of phrases, she deploys a superbly controlled vibrato.

On *Portrait*, her most complete artistic statement, she ranges between the rapid and slightly alienating 'Let's Face The Music And Dance' (which anticipates the surrealism of her contributions to Roswell Rudd's remarkable *Flexible Flyer* (Affinity)) and the fragile beauty of 'I'm A Fool To Want You' and 'When The World Was Young' with its extraordinary, ambiguous ending. The instrumentation is highly subtle. Bobby Timmons's 'Dat Dere' is given just to voice and bass (and Swallow is superb), 'Who Can I Turn To?' to voice and guitar, while 'Hum Drum Blues' and 'Baltimore Oriole' are set against rhythm only, as if she were a horn.

***** Sheila**

Steeplechase SCCD 31081 *Jordan; Arild Andersen (b).* 8/77.

*****(*) Songs From Within**

M.A. Recordings M014A *Jordan; Harvie Swartz (b).* 3/89.

***** The Very Thought Of Two**

M.A. Recordings M018 *As above.* 93.

If one is looking for an exact instrumental analogy for Sheila Jordan's voice, it's probably the round, precariously controlled wobble of the flugelhorn. Tom Harrell was an ideal foil on *The Crossing*, a fine Black Hawk record from 1984, since deleted but worth looking out for. The sparser landscape of *Sheila*, where she is accompanied only by double bass, suits her much better, and this has been her preferred format for many years. Andersen is a much more interesting player, and appears more responsive, than Swartz, but the later session with Swartz is a winner; that despite the 'acoustically unfriendly' heating system, put on in the Japanese hall where *Songs From Within* was recorded to counteract the effects of cold on Swartz's bass. It has lovely versions of 'Waltz For Debby', 'St Thomas', 'A Child Is Born' and a walk through the classic bop changes, 'I Got Rhythm/Anthropology'. (The disc also includes a bonus track by the Marty Krystall Spatial Quartet.) The connection is sustained on *Very Thought Of Two* but, though technically fine, there are signs of archness and cuteness here, unbecoming to either musician. Few singers have been as consistently inventive and challenging in an era dominated by horns and guitars; few, predictably, have been so little appreciated. Sheila Jordan is an essential figure in modern jazz and *Portrait* should be in every collection.

Theo Jörgensmann (born 1948)

CLARINET

Though he has always been a clarinet man, Jörgensmann started out in hard bop and in the '70s made a string of albums for independent German labels, in a modal free-bop style (they are all out of print). He later led a clarinet quartet, CL-4, and in the '90s worked with chamber groups and string players. These discs represent his new quartet.

***** Ta Eko Mo**

Z.O.O. 29-1 *Jörgensmann; Christopher Dell (vib); Christian Ramond (b); Klaus Kugel (d).* 97.

*****(*) Snijbloeman**

hatOLOGY 539 *As above.* 1–4/99.

He might have stuck by the clarinet, but Jörgensmann followed few of his forebears on the instrument, preferring Coltrane as an influence. He is, nevertheless, a performer of classical rigour: he likes shapely, well-modelled lines, rarely resorts to tonal distortion, and projects a clean, full-bodied sound. Rarely sighted in the CD era, these recent records mark a return to action with a new quartet of young German players. The key combination is with Dell: much of the music feels like a dialogue for vibes and clarinet, with Ramond and Kugel working sometimes as a means of propulsion, sometimes as colourists. Both records are rather short and compact (the hatOLOGY disc is longer by dint of offering two alternative takes) and they offer up their ideas sparingly. Which doesn't stop the likes of 'Kospi' (with an extraordinary solo by Dell) and 'Wiesengrund' from emerging as eventful and dense pieces, packed with ideas. A welcome return for a singular voice.

Anders Jormin (born 1957)

BASS

Though still relatively young, Jormin is a long-standing leader and catalyst in Swedish post-bop. Raised in Jönköping, he came to prominence with the important '70s group, Rena Rama. Although he has a number of sideman credits, he has worked extensively as a leader and has several large-scale commissions to his credit as composer.

*****(*) Nordic Light**

Dragon DRCD 305 *Jormin; Thomas Gustafson (ss, ts); Bobo Stenson (p); Christian Jormin (d).* 5/84.

***** Eight Pieces**

Dragon DRCD 306 *Jormin; Staffan Svensson (t); Dave Wilczewski, Thomas Gustafson (ss, ts); Thomas Jäderlund (as, f); Bobo Stenson (p); Harald Svensson (ky); Göran Klinghagen (g); Audun Kleive (d).* 2/88.

These entries from Dragon's LP era have recently made it to CD. *Nordic Light* has certainly worn the better of the two. The quartet plays seven pieces based around Scandinavian compositions of the past, from Grieg, Peterson-Berger, Sjöberg, Nielsen and Ekström. Stenson is his usual powerful self and the quartet has much in common with the Garbarek–Stenson group. The original themes are elaborated on thoughtfully, rather than bowdlerized or turned into something else, and if this sounds conservative next to other such projects, the musicians clearly have the spirit of these pieces in their bones.

Next to this, *Eight Pieces* actually sounds more dated: Harald Svensson's keyboards, as so often with synthesizers, now sound timelocked to their period, and the blending of styles seems more effortful. But the writing still has many points of interest, and it's a good band.

***** Alone**

Dragon DRCD 207 *Jormin (b solo).* 91.

***** Jord**

Dragon DRCD 243 *Jormin; Per Jorgensen (t, perc, v); Harald Svensson (ky); Severi Pyysalo (vib); Lisbeth Diers (perc, v).* 10/94.

***** Opus Apus**

LJ 5212 *Jormin; Mats Gustafsson (ts, bs, f); Christian Jormin (d).* 5/96.

Jormin's entries purvey a catholic sense of adventure keyed in to a fundamental restraint. On the solo album he says he aimed for something 'naked, pure and lyrical', cutting the 40-odd minutes of music in a single evening with a DAT machine, and the unaffected qualities of the playing lend the music much charm – where most bass albums are deliberately cumbersome and sombre in texture, this one is songful and optimistic. Jormin plays only three brief tunes of his own: the rest is dominated by three burnished melodies by Silvio Rodriguez and the unforgettable melody of A. Ramirez's 'Alfonsina'. Those hoping for the kind of sumptuous bass-sound which hallmarks studio bass albums may be disappointed in the relatively light and 'live' atmosphere here, but it emphasizes the calibre of the playing over any mere hi-fi experience.

Jord is a live-in-the-studio group record, carefully balanced between the four musicians. Svensson's keyboards provide melting electronic textures which Pyysalo's vibes dance gently over; Jorgensen comes on as principal soloist, and Diers and Jormin create elliptical rhythms. A bit shapeless, but some exquisite passages.

The trio record with Gustafsson and brother Christian is typically refined, detailed improvisation. There are a handful of climactic moments but otherwise this is nearly *pointilliste* in feel, the percussionist working almost in microtones and even the normally boisterous Gustafsson apparently reined in. Most of the pieces are dedicated to birds, with 'Lagopus Lagopus' (a willow grouse, ornithologists will note) pecking and scratching out a plausible miniature. As with all of Jormin's music, there is a dedication to beauty which seems to shine through even in abstraction.

*****(*) Once**

Dragon DRCD 308 *Jormin; Thomas Gustafson (ss, ts); Jarle Vespestad (d); Jeanette Lindström (v).* 8/96.

Beautifully pitched between something formal and something quite abstract, this quartet's music is complex without being demanding of anything more than a sympathetic ear. Vespestad is crucial to the freeness of the playing, frequently doing anything but playing straight time and using the kit in its most percussive form, often getting a tympani-like sound out of the bass and floor toms. Gustafson is alternately dramatic and respectful, and Jormin brings in some good themes as well as choosing works by Ornette Coleman, Evert Taube and Kurt Weill. But it's Lindström's singing, in English, Swedish or wordless, which mollifies any danger of stepping too far into formlessness. She is at least as good here as she is on her Caprice albums.

***** Silvae**

Dragon DRCD 338 *Jormin; Arve Henriksen (t); Fredrik Ljungkvist (cl, ss, ts); Severi Pyysalo (vib, marim); Marc Ducret (g); Christian Jormin (d, p).* 1/98.

Drawn from a commission for two hours of music, *Silvae* (forests) is typically imaginative music, but the success of the record may depend on your response to Ducret. For us, he unbalances the rest of the group, his rockier solos too splashy to fit in with Jormin's concept. For once, a Jormin record seems stitched together out of disparate pieces, with his usual impeccable flow suffering too many changes of mood; but much of it, such as the cod-Japanese 'Koto', with lovely trumpet from the under-exposed Henriksen, is still more than worthwhile. Had Henriksen and Pyysalo (the latter employed largely as a colourist) been made more use of, this might have been a classic.

Ekkehard Jost (born 1938)

BARITONE SAXOPHONE, BASS SAXOPHONE, CONTRABASS CLARINET

Author of one of the best books on European jazz, Jost presides over a much-underrated jazz scene in the college town of Giessen, south of Hanover, and is a considerable player himself. He also runs his own record label.

***** Weimarer Balladen**

Fish Music FM 004 *Jost; Herbert Hellhund (t, flhn); Detlef Landeck (tb); Wollie Kaiser (ss, ts, bsx); Uli Orth (ss, as); Martin Pfleiderer (ts); Dieter Glawischnig (p); Gerd Stein (g); Manfred Becker (acc); Dieter Manderschied (b); Joe Bonica (d); Fredericke Nicklaus (v).* 11/91.

*****(*) Von Zeit zu Zeit**

Fish Music FM 005 *Jost; Reiner Winterschladen (t); Detlef Landeck (tb); Dieter Manderschied (b); Joe Bonica (d, perc).* 4/93.

***** Out Of Jost's Songbook**

Fish Music FM 006 *As above, except add Frank Gratkowski (ss, as); Wollie Kaiser (ss, ts, bsx, cbcl); Dieter Glawischnig (p); Manfred Becker (acc).* 6/94.

*****(*) Deep**

Fish FM 007 *Jost; Reiner Winterschladen (t); Ewald Oberleitner (b); Tony Oxley (d).* 1/97.

The town of Giessen lies approximately midway between Hanover and Frankfurt, a small college town which fills up during term time and empties in the summer and winter. It supports a lively jazz and improvisation scene, stiffened by visiting and exiled Americans like Bonica, who anchors most of these sessions.

Jost is an interesting composer, influenced by Mingus and Ornette Coleman and by free music. His sound is characteristically low, dark and intense, with extensive use of chromatic harmonies and dissonant voicings. A tribute to Ornette Coleman on *Von Zeit zu Zeit* (along with *Deep*, the best of these records) suggests where some of his ideas come from, and there is a fine version of Mingus's 'Oh Lord, Don't Let Them Drop That Atomic Bomb On Me' on *Weimarer Balladen*, medleyed with 'Das Gaslied'.

The earlier pair of records demonstrate Jost's interest in short, almost song-like forms. The 1993 album is credited to the group, Chromatic Alarm, and this is Jost's core unit. Comparable to Gunter Hampel's Galaxie Dream Band, it combines dense, sophisticated structures with free-form playing. Landeck is a key component, as the trombones always were in Mingus bands, and he and Jost very often provide the basic musical language.

The more recent set with Oxley is predictably freer in conception, a powerful, roiling album marked by some of the drummer's most relaxed and reflective playing on disc.

Vic Juris (born 1953)

GUITAR

Juris took up the guitar in 1963 and began playing in fusion situations in the 1970s. He has begun to record as a leader in the 1990s.

***** Night Tripper**

Steeplechase SCCD 31353 *Juris; Phil Markowitz (p); Steve LaSpina (b); Jeff Hirshfield (d).* 4/94.

***** Pastels**

Steeplechase SCCD 31384 *Juris; Phil Markowitz (p); Jay Anderson (b); Matt Wilson (d).* 11/95.

***** Moonscape**

Steeplechase SCCD 31402 *Juris; Dick Oatts (as, ts, f); Jay Anderson (b); Jeff Hirshfield (d).* 10/96.

*****(*) Music Of Alec Wilder**

Double-Time DTRCD 118 *Juris; Tim Hagans (t, flhn); Dave Liebman (ss, ts); Steve LaSpina (b); Jeff Hirshfield (d).* 9/96.

Having worked extensively with Larry Coryell and Bireli Lagrene as duet partners and with fusion bands in the 1970s, Juris has rather belatedly begun to acquire a leadership profile. He's a keen technician and likes to vary the pace on all his own albums: one tune done on open electric might be followed by another on nylon acoustic, before the guitar-synth comes out for the next. All the Steeplechases are nicely rounded and there's little to choose between them – though one could complain that there's not much that stands out either. *Night Tripper* has a lovely take on 'Estate', and Markowitz's 'Dekooning' is a clever and challenging piece; *Pastels* pulls out another charmer in 'Berlin', and Anderson and Wilson, if less ambitious than the other rhythm sections, do great service to the soloists. Oatts is a welcome addition to *Moonscape* and they open with the terrific 'Vampicide', but some of the other tunes seem a touch routine in the delivery. On balance, *Pastels* is our favourite of the three.

The Double-Time release is better still, though mostly for the superb horn-players. Liebman and Hagans could have had a more gracious sound in the studio, but they steal this date from Juris, who sounds more like the good and true sideman that he is here. The material, all Alec Wilder tunes and plenty of interesting obscurities among them (such as his extraordinary valedictory song for Sinatra, 'A Long Night'), is a bonus and the treatments are consistently imaginative.

*****(*) Remembering Eric Dolphy**

Steeplechase SCCD 31453 *Juris; Dick Oatts (as, ts, f); Jay Anderson (b); Jeff Hirshfield (d).* 4/98.

A provocative concept for a guitarist to essay, and this set of four Dolphy tunes and five in-the-spirit originals by Juris doesn't shirk any comparisons. Oatts gets a lean, almost rubbery sound, not much like the dedicatee but observant of the master's abstracted bebop roots, and the accuracy of the playing on the likes of 'Miss Ann' and 'Out There' – not to mention Oatts's own original 'Emphasizing Eric', which Juris admits is the hardest thing he's ever tried to play on the guitar – is a pleasure in itself. Anderson and Hirshfield create a free-flowing and open-minded pulse which is very suitable for the occasion. An excellent record.

Richie Kamuca (1930–77)

TENOR SAXOPHONE

Born in Philadelphia, where he was spotted by Roy Eldridge, Kamuca worked with Stan Kenton and Woody Herman and with smaller West Coast groups, notably Shelly Manne's. Despite a late flurry of discs for Concord, he recorded very little as leader despite an appealing freshness and a tender ballad style.

***** Richie Kamuca Quartet**

VSOP 17 *Kamuca; Carl Perkins (p); Leroy Vinnegar (b); Stan Levey (d).* 6/57.

***** Jazz Erotica**

Fresh Sound FSR 500 *Kamuca; Conte Candoli, Ed Leddy (t); Frank Rosolino (tb); Bill Holman (bs); Vince Guaraldi (p); Monty Budwig (b); Stan Levey (d).* 58.

***** West Coast Jazz In Hi-Fi**

Original Jazz Classics OJC 1760 *As above.* 58

Apart from his late recordings for Concord, which were packed into the final year of Richie's life, this is pretty much the sum of his work as leader. The reappearance of the 1957 session, unfortunately without additional takes, offers a better measure of his quality than the two slightly later discs. The tracks are mostly very short and to the point, with just one original in a nicely judged set. 'Rain Drain' is closer to the quirky modernism of his big-band work, but it's an appealing enough tune. Perkins puts up two ideas of his own, 'Early Bird' and 'Fire One', and here and there steals the show with his terse, unshowy phrasing and offbeat ideas.

The title of the Fresh Sound (not the 'Jazz' part) is perhaps a shade misleading, though Kamuca favoured an intimate, close-to-the-ear murmur which comes direct from Lester Young, seductive with little hint of Pres's native ambivalence. The 'Jazz' part in the title is important because there isn't much sign either of the gimmicky Kenton approach in which much of the band was schooled. Kamuca's approach to standards – 'Star Eyes', 'Angel Eyes', 'Stella By Starlight' – is direct and unsentimental, and for combined impact and sophistication there's little to choose between the four quartet tracks and Holman's arrangements for the larger group. There are one or two minor technical quibbles about the transfer, and the identical OJC sounds a little brighter and cleaner, but, in the absence of three excellent Concords, *Drop Me Off In Harlem*, *Richie* and *Richie Kamuca's Charlie* (where he explores the Parker legacy), this makes for a highly desirable introduction to the saxophonist's work.

Misako Kano

PIANO

A native of Yamaguchi in Japan, Kano studied classical and jazz piano in the United States and has taken lessons with Richie Beirach, Harold Danko and others. A robust chordal player, she favours quite percussive, single-note melody lines in solos.

*****(*) Breakthrew**

Jazz Focus JFCD 027 *Kano; Thomas Chapin (as, f); Ron McClure (b); Jeff Williams (d).* 1/96.

*****(*) 3 Purple Circles**

Jazz Focus JFCD 034 *Kano; Dave Liebman (ss, ts); Mark Helias (b); Satoshi Takeishi (d).* 5/99.

Originally released only in Japan, *Breakthrew* was the product of a fruitful relationship with saxophonist Chapin, who succumbed to leukaemia before the record was made available in the West. His sharp, keening tone, false fingerings and offbeat ideas are a distinctive component of the record, a contrast to Dave Liebman's more measured approach on the second disc. Surprisingly, Chapin contributes no titles to the set, most of which is original material by Kano, with just two standards and a piece by Ron McClure.

Her playing is emphatic and percussive, reminiscent of no one else in particular, and while she is not a particularly dramatic soloist she does have a gift for creating atmospheres with a great simplicity of gesture. 'Mao' isn't a political statement but a song for Ron McClure's cat (who, we understand, is a Brad Pitt among felines). 'Freezing Drizzle' is a nod to the Canadian weather, and occasion for some of Chapin's most exuberantly wacky styling. 'Timeless Craving' starts with Kano inside the piano and Chapin on flute; very effective. Some signs of Richie Beirach's influence on the title-tune, which is a an elegant waltz, while the album ends as quietly and as reflectively as it had begun in ramping confidence. Kano plays 'Longing' as a solo piece; following on from Cole Porter's 'I Love You', it marks an exquisite point of rest while promising new departures.

Dave Liebman is probably the only senior saxophonist who might have joined this group and fitted in with comfort. His formidable musical intelligence clearly identifies with elements of Kano's thinking, and the two together make some fascinating leaps of imaginative sympathy. 'Choker' was written for Chapin, but Tom didn't live to play it, so Liebman takes it on with a quirky shift of register that must represent a nod in his predecessor's direction. His soprano duet with Kano on 'Tinge' is also exquisite.

The inclusion of Ornette's 'Ramblin'' and the dirge, 'Broken Shadows', is something of a surprise but, given the slightly sombre mood of the session, the latter piece fits perfectly and Kano's bright intuition turns it into a New Orleans processional. Those 'Three Purple Circles' are the underground symbol in Tokyo, which here finds some subterranean connection to the NY subway, a wonderful meeting of voices and registers. As before, Kano closes solo with a reading of 'Prelude To a Kiss', a performance that only confirms what we thought already: that she is a player to watch or, better still, a player to listen to very carefully.

Seppo Kantonen

PIANO, KEYBOARDS

Finnish pianist, working in free-form, post-bop, mostly whatever takes his fancy.

*****(*) Klang**

Impala 001 *Kantonen; Uffe Krokfors (b); Markku Ounaskari (d). n.d.*

Kantonen isn't well known, but some may be familiar with his CD of duets with Jarmo Savolainen, *Phases* (Love BECD 4020), as well as sideman work with Eero Koivistoinen and Rinneradio. This excellent record shows how much mileage there still is in the piano trio. The writing is consistently intriguing, always looking to vary the dynamics of the group, the way the players move between form and freedom, the tonal colours available. Krokfors must take a big share of the credit, since he wrote four of the nine themes. 'Good Things', one of them, bounces off the simplest of bass riffs into a sizzling workout for the trio. Ounaskari can work up a terrific amount of noise, as he does on the climax of 'Lammen Haltija', without toppling the group over, but at least some of the time he's working in tiny strokes, or playing the kit – as on 'The Way In' – as if he's got a set of tuned tympani. Kantonen is quick and thoughtful and he uses what sounds like an old-fashioned analogue synth on a couple of pieces. Some of this music calls to mind a certain old-fashioned European elegance, as in some of the early ECM sessions. The impression is of a group that's thought long and hard about their music, without desiccating the essential spontaneity of their interaction.

Ori Kaplan (born 1969)

ALTO SAXOPHONE

The young Israeli and his colleagues first came together at the New School in New York, playing bebop. They've moved on a bit since then.

***** Realms**

CIMP 190 *Kaplan; Tom Abbs (b, tba); Geoff Mann (d, t).* 1/99.

This is as raw a piece of jazz vérité as even CIMP have ever released, but when it eventually does come together it delivers on its promise. Abbs doubles very effectively on bass and tuba and Mann even does his own version of British drummer John Stevens's bugle things, but the emphasis falls pretty squarely on the young saxophonist from Tel Aviv. Kaplan is a vivid, intelligent player who has obviously listened closely. He keens like Ornette but likes a gentler and more harmonic approach as well. Definitely someone to watch.

Egil Kapstad (born 1940)

PIANO

Kapstad learned piano as a child and was working in the Oslo jazz scene by 1960. He performed with Karin Krog and in a long association with Bjørn Johansen, as well as writing choral and orchestral music and pieces for TV and theatre.

*****(*) Cherokee**

Gemini GMCD 61 *Kapstad; Terje Venaas (b); Egil Johansen (d).* 11/88.

A beautiful and typically individual record by a modern master of Norwegian jazz. Kapstad's thoroughgoing absorption of the requisite piano influences lets him put a personal spin on what is actually his first-ever trio date: the nine standards all have a novel point of view, such as the piano/bass duet on 'Autumn Leaves' or the dreamily slow treatment of 'Cherokee' itself. His solo reading of 'Darn That Dream' is modelled out of a simple but detailed look at the harmonies, and the opening run through 'When You're Smiling' freshens even that tune. Venaas and the redoubtable Johansen are perfectly in step, and the only disappointment is that there isn't more of Kapstad's own writing. He restricts himself to a blues and the brief, charming 'Our Autumn Waltz'.

****** Remembrance**

Gemini GMCD 82 *As above.* 10/93.

Even more remarkable. Kapstad's record is, in effect, a celebration of Norwegian jazz, since it draws from the work of eight native composers (including the members of the trio). The abiding factor is his meticulous technique: even in the middle of a fast piece such as 'Big Red', he displays a refinement of touch that elevates the composer without relinquishing his own stamp on the piece. If the overall feel of the session is romantic, even a trifle forlorn, the exacting lyricism which he gets out of most of the tunes is intensely satisfying. Venaas and Johansen take honours, too.

Jacob Karlzon (born 1970)

PIANO

Based in Malmö, Karlzon follows the modern mainstream of Swedish jazz.

***** Take Your Time!**

Dragon DRCD 276 *Karlzon; Mattias Svensson (b); Peter Danemo (d).* 5/95.

Karlzon has done some fine work as a sideman, and this is his first as a leader. The ingenious examination of Cole Porter's 'Everything I Love' which opens the record is a little misleading, since thereafter the trio move into bigger territory: the processional title-track, the crashing 'For Crying Out Loud', the rather elephantine 'Contre Tens'. Karlzon appears to like big gestures and he lets Svensson and Danemo have plenty of space, but the music could use some centre and a more profitable direction, for all its absorbing moments.

Larry Karush

PIANO

Contemporary US pianist with eclectic leanings.

***** The Art Of The Improviser**

Naxos 86026 2 *Karush (p).* 5/97.

Perhaps too eclectic to appeal to all tastes, this is nevertheless an immensely impressive exercise in comparative pianism. From the opening 'Banjo Variations', which attempts to capture on the keyboard the clean-edged articulation of clawhammer banjo technique, to the closing threnody of 'Reach' – a memorial to Karush's father – the album commands admiring attention. 'L's P's' is an obvious reference to Tristano's 'Lennie's Pennies', though the material has been considerably transformed. A long set of variations on a theme by James P. Johnson includes some quite wonderful left-hand work, while 'Country' recalls some of the C&W ideas on Keith Jarrett's early records.

The two-track DAT source lacks presence but isn't off-puttingly dry, and once again plaudits to Naxos for showcasing a talent that almost certainly would have seemed too various and experimental for the majors.

Chris Kase (born 1964)

TRUMPET, FLUGELHORN

Raised in Connecticut, Kase studied at Berklee and played in various situations before arriving in New York in 1992.

***** Starting Now**

Mons MR 874-659 *Kase; Bob Mintzer (ts); Tom Varner (frhn); John Stetch (p); Johannes Weidenmuller (b); Adam Nussbaum (d).* 6/94.

Essentially this is a good, thoughtful, trumpet-and-rhythm date: Mintzer is on only three of eight tunes and Varner appears only for colour. Kase is a confident if self-effacing soloist who drops painterly lines (especially on flugelhorn) on to a deft setting provided by a sound team. 'Evening At Sympathy', quiet and lyrical without being lachrymose, is particularly fine, and the 3/4 of 'True Or Waltz?' has the rhythm almost floating around the melody lines which all the players seem able to pose to the listener. 'King Of Jazz', with the horns really digging in, comes on like a shocking contrast. It doesn't linger long in the memory, perhaps because of Kase's reluctance to push clear of his backgrounds: one has to go back and listen again for the felicities.

Jan Kaspersen (born 1948)

PIANO

A contemporary Danish pianist, composer and bandleader, with a distinguished record of work since 1970 and a penchant for leopardskin hats and Thelonious Monk.

***** Memories Of Monk**

Olufsen DOCD 5208 *Kaspersen; Peter Danstrup (b); Ole Romer (d).* 11/86.

*****(*) Space And Rhythm Jazz**

Olufsen DOCD 5060 *Kaspersen; Anders Bergcrantz (t); Simon Cato Spang-Hanssen (ss, ts); Fredrik Lundin (ss, ts); Michael Hove (as, bs); Peter Danstrup (b); Ole Romer (d).* 10/87.

***** Ten By Two**

Olufsen DOCD 5053 *Kaspersen; Simon Cato Spang-Hanssen (ss, ts).* 7/87.

*****(*) Special Occasion**

Olufsen DOCD 5111 *Kaspersen; Peter Danstrup (b); Ole Romer (d).* 9/90.

****** Live In Sofie's Cellar**

Olufsen DOCD 5136 *Kaspersen; Anders Bergcrantz (t); Bob Rockwell (ts); Peter Danstrup (b); Ole Romer (d).* 8/91.

*****(*) Heavy Smoke**

Olufsen DOCD 5188 *As above.* 12/92.

Marvellous records from a Dane whose music is a beautifully personal, inventive and humorous response to the particular influence of Thelonious Monk. This is made crystal-clear by the Monk tribute album (DOCD 5208) which distils a nice blend of homage, celebration and evolution from the model. Kaspersen has done better since and perhaps he can be a shade too slavish in some of his tribute, but the sense of enjoyment shines through. *Space And Rhythm Jazz* is a skilful, all-original programme that makes the music of a quirkily expressive cast of horn players and creates consistently absorbing ideas within what is broadly a post-bop framework. *Ten By Two* relies in the main on Monk and Ellington and is a bit po-faced, perhaps because Spang-Hanssen is a little pedestrian in places, but there are still some pleasing variations on the material. The pianist gets a fuller rein on the second trio set, which has some mischievous originals ('Bird Goes Cuckoo') and a couple of nicely reflective ballads. Kaspersen's heavily rolling manner will strike a chord of recognition in British listeners who've heard Stan Tracey, but his sense of humour is a little more impish than our man's. The great one here is the glorious live session: Bergcrantz reveals himself as a major (and so far shamefully under-recognized) soloist, Rockwell is only a beat behind, and Kaspersen directs with great exuberance from the piano. There is the third version of his favourite 'I Mean Monk' and this is surely the best. *Heavy Smoke* returns the band to the studio and, while the music is unimpeachably inventive, we slightly prefer the dash of the live session.

***** Joinin' Forces**

Olufsen DOCD 5184 *Kaspersen; Horace Parlan (p).* 4/94.

*****(*) Special Occasion Band Live In Copenhagen Jazzhouse**

Olufsen DOCD 5303/4 2CD *Kaspersen; Lars Vissing (t); Erling Kroner, Lis Wessberg (tb); Simon Cato Spang-Hanssen (as); Bob Rockwell, Fredrik Lundin (ss, ts); Henrik Sveidahl-Hansen (ts, bs); Aske Jacoby (g); Peter Danstrup (b); Ole Romer (d); Jacob Andersen (perc).* 9/94.

The duo with Parlan is an enjoyable if lightweight meeting in which the two keyboards bump and jostle over some familiar ground. The big-band set is much more exciting. With seven horns in the front line, Kaspersen marshals a serious force to get the most out of his writing and, in what's almost a greatest-hits set of his own tunes, the band play with unquenchable enthusiasm and flair. Sound is just a little rough, but the ambience of the occasion – recorded when the band were flying at the end of a tour – communicates a tremendous amount of fun.

***** Portrait In Space And Rhythm**

Olufsen DOCD 5356 *As above discs.* 11/86–6/95.

A useful best-of, culled mostly from the above sessions, although there is a track apiece from Kaspersen's two solo sets of Satie piano music. Fans will also welcome two out-takes from the live record at Sofie's Cellar, not quite up to the rest of the programme but still splendid. A pocket portrait of a man who loves his jazz.

*****(*) Live At Copenhagen Jazzhouse**

Olufsen DOCD 5355 *Kaspersen; Jan Kohlin, Benny Rosenfeld, Palle Bolvig, Henrik Bolberg Pedersen, Lars Togeby (t); Vincent Nilsson, Steen Hansen, Kjeld Ipsen (tb); Axel Windfeld (btb, tba); Giordano Bellincampi (btb); Michael Hove (ss, as, cl); Christina Von Bülow (ss, as); Uffe Markussen, Tomas Franck (ts); Flemming Madsen (bs, bcl); Anders Lindvall (g); Thomas Ovesen (b); Jonas Johansen (d); Ole Kock Hansen (cond).* 10/95.

Kaspersen meets the Danish Radio Jazz Orchestra and together they give eight of his tunes a good going-over. 'Roll Jelly Roll' is a clever slant on Morton's music; 'Duke Directions' is an exuberant boogaloo for the rhythm team and is not as Ellingtonian as 'Naja's Dream', which features Hove as Hodges. This is colourful, easy-going music, inventive without feeling the need to be too incessantly clever, and the DRJO, stacked with talent as it is, brings it all to vivid life. Kaspersen gets plenty of solos, but it's his scores which are the thing. Very good location sound, too.

***** Den Blå Munk**

Scanbox/Music Mecca 2072-2 *Kaspersen (p solo).* 11/97.

Kaspersen was the obvious choice to do this music for a film soundtrack concerning his beloved idol, Thelonious. He starts and finishes with a slow 'Blue Monk', plays a livelier version as track two, then ruminates through six of his own themes. A brief, not especially heavyweight record, but Kaspersen's admirers will surely enjoy.

Bruce Katz

PIANO, ORGAN

Energetic post-bop keyboardist, at home on both piano and organ.

***** Transformation**

Audioquest AQ CD 1026 *Katz; Tom Hall (ts); Kevin Barry (g); David Clark (b); Lorne Entress (d).* 11/93.

This band's favoured groove is a medium funk shuffle, but with lots of unexpected elements – weird bent notes, busy little percussion outbreaks from co-founder Entress, top-line/bass-line swaps – that lift it a little out of the ordinary. Katz's piano and organ sound had been heard for a while in and around Boston (including recordings with Ronnie Earl and the Broadcasters) before he and the drummer unveiled this project of their own. The organ tracks, beginning with 'Boppin' Out Of The Abyss', are generally more energetic and forceful, but it is Katz's piano playing that is the key to his sound. He's an active, multi-directional player, often building solo ideas out of fast, narrow-interval arpeggios, with occasional excursions out into free time, almost like the young Cecil Taylor. Sensibly, he seldom dwells on an idea past its due time, preferring to spin off in a new direction. Saxophonist Tom Hall is just a cut above the average bar-room honker and he turns in some very nifty solo work, as do the guitarist and super-solid bassist. The real axes of the group, though, are Katz and Entress, the latter contributing one composition to a set of lively, thoughtful originals.

Shake Keane (1927–97)

FLUGELHORN

Born in St Vincent, Keane came to the UK in 1952 and worked extensively with Joe Harriott. Back in St Vincent he was Minister of Culture for a time, but the job bored him. Poetry occupied him more than trumpet playing, and he spent his last years in Brooklyn, succumbing to cancer in 1997.

***** Real Keen: Reggae Into Jazz**

LKJ CD 001 *Keane; Henry Holder (ky); John Kpiaye (g); Dennis Bovell (b, ky, d machine); Jah Bunny, Angus Gaye (d); Geoffrey Scantlebury (perc).* 91.

He was christened Ellsworth McGranahan Keane, and he derived his nickname from a passion for Shakespeare, which was reinforced during a spell at the University of London. Keane never acquired the legend that attached to his fellow West Indian, Joe Harriott, with whom he played in the Harlem All-Stars after leaving college. Quite simply, Keane survived and went off to work with various big bands in Europe, including the Clarke–Boland outfit and Kurt Edelhagen's. Not such a romantic story.

This disc came 30 years after his excellent Columbia session, *In My Condition*, which British jazz collectors greatly prize. The reggae grooves have become something of a cliché in recent years, but Keane's lyrical style and expansive musical understanding make something out of a rather restrictive set of formulae. On 'Gorby Gets Them Going' (one of several politically tinged titles) he moves outside the rhythm altogether, while on 'Prague 89' and the very differently paced 'Rift', he floats or bounces along on top of the basic metre, creating a curious tension that is resolved only in the melody. The youngish band plays this sort of stuff pretty much by-the-yard, professionally but scarcely passionately; in the final count, it's hard to get over-excited about *Real Keen*. Perhaps his early work will return on CD soon: it would be a better memorial to him.

Geoff Keezer (born 1970)

PIANO, KEYBOARDS

Born of two piano-teacher parents, Keezer was in the final edition of the Jazz Messengers when only seventeen. He worked in other sideman situations before joining the Ray Brown group in 1997.

*****(*) Waiting In The Wings**

Sunnyside SSC 1035D *Keezer; Bill Mobley (t); Billy Pierce (ss, ts); Steve Nelson (vib); Rufus Reid (b); Tony Reedus (d).* 9/88.

***** Curveball**

Sunnyside SSC 1045D *Keezer; Steve Nelson (vib); Charnett Moffett (b); Victor Lewis (d).* 6/89.

Keezer is a formidable talent. Both of these records were made before he was twenty. While he's a vivid executant, synthesizing such influences as Ahmad Jamal and Phineas Newborn into the kind of broad post-bop style which is the contemporary norm, he's also an unusually thoughtful composer, organizing a small band into a distinctive ensemble and building rhythmic licks into convincing melodies. Examples here include the title-tunes of *Waiting In The Wings* and *Curveball*, and 'Accra', a blistering waltz-tune; but Keezer's thoughtful programming of rare Ellington and Monk themes adds a piquant variety to his own writing. He greatly admires Steve Nelson's playing, and the vibes player in turn does some of his best work here. While some may see these discs as 'prentice work, the sheer energy of the debut in particular remains very satisfying.

***** World Music**

DIW 609 *Keezer; James Genus (b); Tony Reedus (d); Rudy Bird (perc).* 1/92.

***** Other Spheres**

DIW 871 *Keezer; Bill Mobley (t, flhn); Bill Pierce (ss, ts); Bill Easley (as, f, af, cl, bcl); Peter Bernstein (g); Steve Nelson (vib, mar); John Lockwood (b); Leon Parker (d); Rudy Bird (perc); Jeanie Bryson (v).* 11/92.

These are ambitious records, the trio set no less demanding than the subsequent *Other Spheres*, and, while they're impressive in their way, they also suggest a leader overplaying his hand. *World Music* starts with an ingenious revision of 'It's Only A Paper

Moon' and moves into an ominously bleak 'Black And Tan Fantasy', but Keezer's originals aren't quite as fresh as before and the trio tend to push too hard as a unit, Reedus piling on detail when a simpler, more directly swinging beat would do better. *Other Spheres* is an all-original programme that brims with complexity, the three Bills creating a continually shifting front line of horn sounds, Nelson meshing loyally with the leader's piano, and the studio used to add a few deft overdubs. But while it makes for some intriguing arranger's jazz, notably on 'Little Minu' and 'Serengeti Stampede', pieces such as 'Auntie Matter' and 'Event Horizon' sound overwritten, their energy a little stifled by their complexity.

*****(*) Trio**
Sackville SKCD2-2039 *Keezer; Steve Nelson (vib); Neil Swainson (b).* 11/93.

Recorded at Toronto's Montreal Bistro, this live set overflows with playing and, though Swainson is a useful anchor, it's mainly about the prodigious outpouring of two men in full command. Keezer and Nelson run delighted rings round each other on tunes by Parker and Monk, settle into a mellifluous rendition of Nelson's 'There Are Many Angels In Florence' and end on a blow-out with 'Eternal Triangle'. Maybe not the most subtle or elevated record either man has been involved with, but basically a delight, in excellent location sound.

****** Turn Up The Quiet**
Columbia 488830-2 *Keezer; Joshua Redman (ts); Tony McAnany (ky); Laura Bontrager, Maria Kitsopoulos, Maureen McDermott, Caryl Paisner (clo); Christian McBride (b); Cyro Baptista, Scott Frankfurt (perc); Diana Krall, Nona Hendryx (v).* 12/96.

This doesn't feel like a breakthrough record, and its piecemeal nature may not appeal to some. But the best performances here are so strong, and the playing so accomplished, that it seems churlish to withhold a top rating. Signed to another major label – a Blue Note entry is missing in action – Keezer plays a restrained hand for his Columbia debut. Old friends Redman and McBride contribute to three fine trio pieces, the opening 'Stomping At The Savoy' being a model of revisionist thinking. There's an underlying Japanese theme, with two Ryuichi Sakamoto songs included, and a very effective piece of impressionism called 'Island Palace', where Keezer's keyboards set a swirling tone. Sakamoto's 'Bibo No Aozora', with the four-woman *cello* quartet, may emerge as little more than mood music, but it's awfully pretty, and Keezer handles the substance quotient with three exemplary solos – one of them an improbable look at My Bloody Valentine's 'Lose My Breath'. Everything, though, is put in the shade by Krall's quite stunningly beautiful treatment of 'The Nearness Of You', which surpasses almost anything on her own records. Disappointingly, though, it seems that Columbia have chosen not to persevere with Keezer.

Roger Kellaway (born 1939)

PIANO

He studied at New England Conservatory in the late 1950s, spent the early '60s in New York, then moved to California in 1966, playing in jazz and rock session situations. Most of his subsequent work has been as composer, arranger and producer, often in TV and film, and straight-ahead jazz appearances have unfortunately been rare.

****** A Portrait Of Roger Kellaway**
Fresh Sound FSR-CD 147 *Kellaway; Jim Hall (g); Steve Swallow, Ben Tucker (b); Dave Bailey, Tony Inzalaco (d).* 63.

*****(*) The Roger Kellaway Trio**
Original Jazz Classics OJC 1897 *Kellaway; Russell George (b); Dave Bailey (d).* 5/65.

Kellaway's early records are buried treasure. He has a scholar's approach to jazz history, bundling together stride, boogie and swing devices into a manner which was and is otherwise entirely modern. *Portrait* is a forgotten classic. 'Double Fault' calls to mind such contemporaries as Andrew Hill, yet the off-centre lyricism and abstracting of melody mark Kellaway as very much his own man. Tucker and Bailey offer prime, swinging support on four tracks, which keeps the composer's ideas in accessible domain, while the trio of Hall, Swallow and Inzalaco create a contrapuntal music of sometimes bemusing intricacy to go with the pianist's work. Two solos are equally rich and detailed, and there is a brilliant transformation of 'Crazy She Calls Me'. Slightly brittle sound doesn't mar a very fine record.

The trio record for Prestige has recently been restored to circulation. If not quite as fine as *Portrait*, there is still some outstanding music. His treatment of the then-contemporary Lennon and McCartney tune, 'I'll Follow The Sun', is a rare example of successfully jazzing the Beatles. The blues waltz, 'Signa: O.N.', is indecently rich and 'Ballad Of The Sad Young Men' is as sober as Kellaway is playful elsewhere – especially on the prepared-piano knockabout 'Brats'. A pity that the remastering couldn't get a better sound out of the piano.

*****(*) Fifty-Fifty**
Natasha NI-4014 *Kellaway; Red Mitchell (b); Brad Terry (whistling).* 2/87.

***** Alone Together**
Dragon DRCD 168 *Kellaway; Red Mitchell (b).* 7/88.

*****(*) Live At Maybeck Recital Hall Vol. 11**
Concord CCD 4470 *Kellaway (p solo).* 3/91.

Kellaway has been sighted on and off, away from studio and film-score work, and his records are always welcome. The two earlier duos with Red Mitchell are very like the ideal of eavesdropping on a couple of old friends after hours. The Dragon album sounds better all the time, though Mitchell's whimsical search for the lowest note a bass can produce may still irritate some listeners, and sometimes they ramble, as after-hours sessions will. But there are beautiful deconstructions of choice standards on both records, with the Natasha set edging ahead for a fantastical 'Gone With The Wind' and a funky 'St Thomas' to wrap things up. Brad Terry whistles on 'Doxy', for some reason. The solo set is a winner, far more satisfying. Perhaps the pianist is sometimes a little too relaxed, with three tunes running around nine minutes and the tempos more often stately than up, but there is much marvellous pianism here. He takes three minutes over the first chorus of 'How Deep Is The Ocean', before moving into an intense, labyrinthine exploration, and his bitonal ventures are so completely assimilated that the most outré gestures become a plausible part of his flow. Especially fine is the resplendent version of Hoagy Carmichael's 'New Orleans'.

*** **That Was That**

Dragon DRCD 201 *Kellaway; Jan Allan (t); Red Mitchell (b).* 1/91.

While this is something of a re-run of the earlier session with Mitchell, the presence of Jan Allan seems to focus the music much more and, though most of the tracks run to seven or eight minutes in length, there's no sense of excessive meandering. Mitchell's amusing vocals on 'Leavin' Blues' and the title-track add to the fun and there are some very pleasing solos by Allan, whose unassuming and rather frail playing suits this context very well.

***(*) **Roger Kellaway Meets Gene Bertoncini And Michael Moore**

Chiaroscuro CR(D) 315 *Kellaway; Gene Bertoncini (g); Michael Moore (b).* 2/92.

***(*) **Life's A Take**

Concord CCD-4551 *Kellaway; Red Mitchell (b).* 5/92.

The trio session is a densely packed series of performances that can seem a bit much over CD length, given the high, concentrated interplay among the three men. On 'All The Things You Are' their contrapuntal thinking is astonishing, yet their simple, songful treatment of Moore's sweet-natured 'Old New Waltz' is as charming as it is naggingly memorable. Kellaway continues to surprise, improvising on the melody or the chords just when one expects the opposite, turning the device of 'locked hands' into something ingenious. Bertoncini's acoustic guitar never sounds altogether right in the context, and Rudy van Gelder's somewhat eccentric studio sound might be the cause.

Life's A Take is another meeting with Red Mitchell, cut only months before the bassist's death. If you have either of the studio dates listed above, this one is a luxury. But there's an extra sting with the live setting, and there are some beautiful introductions from both men that make an affecting memorial to Mitchell. Sound doesn't favour him as much as it does on the studio recordings, though.

Gary Keller

TENOR AND SOPRANO SAXOPHONES

A Miami-based musician, Keller is a post-bop foot-soldier with wide experience in big bands and section-work who has only recently been afforded his own leadership.

***(*) **Blues For An Old New Age**

Double-Time DFTRCD-147 *Keller; Scott Wendholt (t); John Fedchock (tb); Kenny Werner (p); Drew Gress (b); Billy Hart (d).* 9/98.

An unusual record, for a debut or indeed anything else: Keller is an old hand at playing and performing, but instead of showcasing his talents as writer-leader he chose to do an entire CD based around the compositions of his former teacher and colleague at Miami University, Ron Miller, who is just as much an unknown to the general audience as is Keller himself. But the saxophonist assembled a very strong band, and Miller's tunes are an exemplary bunch, with a variety of clever and provocative turns of phrase on such standard idioms as AABA hard bop, the blues, modalism and standard reharmonization. The result is an unemphatic, almost deferential record but a thinker's delight. Wendholt and Fedchock are the kind of players who are perfectly attuned to the ideals of the date, forthright but unselfish, and the rhythm section is superb; the only thing that holds us back from a top rating is the comparative modesty of Keller himself, an engaging soloist but one whose inclinations are not to collar any limelight. Just here and there, that strategy stops the record from making a deeper impression. But it's extremely well done.

Jon-Erik Kellso (born 1964)

TRUMPET, CORNET

Kellso is from Dearborn, Michigan, and began playing in symphony orchestras before playing hot cornet and trumpet in traditional-to-swing groups.

*** **Chapter 1**

Arbors ARCD 19125 *Kellso; Scott Robinson (ts, C-mel, cl); Jeremy Kahn (p); Frank Vignola (g); Milt Hinton (b); Chuck Riggs (d).* 4/93.

*** **Chapter 2: The Plot Thickens**

Arbors ARCD 19160 *Kellso; Harry Allen (ts); Scott Robinson (reeds, theremin); John Bunch, Jeremy Kahn (p); Howard Alden (g); Mike Karoub (clo, b); Paul Keller (b); Joe Ascione (d)* 12/95.

Kellso is a gifted hot cornetist in the tradition of his avowed hero, Ruby Braff. These sessions are characteristic Arbors mainstream dates, with a group of cronies putting a few fresh twists on some familiar, sometimes hoary material. The earlier date has the more interesting list of tunes but is a bit taut, and Kellso's growl playing on the likes of the Ellington obscurity, 'Pelican Drag', is in the shadow of the masters of the style. *The Plot Thickens* benefits from Allen's suave presence, and the group sounds more relaxed and able to stretch, although Karoub's cello isn't a very engaging ingredient. Kellso doesn't really stamp either disc with his personality, and in the end they both sound like strong but often anonymous records.

Ed Kelly

PIANO

Rarely sighted on record, Kelly moved to Oakland when he was eight and has seldom strayed far from the local scene, where he used to play with Sanders in the early '60s.

*** **Ed Kelly And Pharoah Sanders**

Evidence ECD 22056-2 *Kelly; Larry Jones, A.J Johnson (t); Anthony Sidney (tb); Pharoah Sanders (ss, ts); Don Ramsey (as); Junius Simmons (g); Peter Barshay, Harley White (b); Eddie Marshall, Mark Lignell (d); strings.* 12/78–12/92.

Kelly has spent many years teaching in Oakland, but this genial record is a pleasing documentation of his rolling, two-handed gospel style. Half of it was cut in 1978, the remainder 14 years later: some of the earlier tracks have some dubious pop leanings, but the entire disc rates three stars for the superb tenor-and-piano duet on Sam Cooke's 'You Send Me' alone, where Sanders sounds like a slowly boiling volcano. The 1992 tracks offer some local hard bop in unaffected good humour.

Wynton Kelly (1931–71)

PIANO

Born in Jamaica, Kelly also ended his life outside the United States, perhaps symbolically, because he has also seemed strangely marginal to the main thrust of bebop. And yet it was he more than anyone other than Charlie Parker who sustained its origins in the blues. Some of Kelly's finest work was for Miles Davis, but he also left behind a substantial body of work as leader.

***** Wynton Kelly – Piano**

Original Jazz Classics OJC 401 *Kelly; Kenny Burrell (g); Paul Chambers (b); Philly Joe Jones (d).* 1/58.

On the face of it, Kelly didn't seem the most obvious replacement for Bill Evans and Red Garland in the Miles Davis group, but he had a lyrical simplicity and uncomplicated touch that appealed enormously to the trumpeter, who hired him in 1959; Kelly played on only one track on the classic *Kind Of Blue*, but 'Freddie Freeloader' is enough to show what distinguished him from Evans's more earnestly romantic style and to establish his quality. *Piano* is a full-voiced quartet that makes full use of Burrell's boppish grace.

****** Kelly Blue**

Original Jazz Classics OJC 033 *Kelly; Nat Adderley (c); Bobby Jaspar (f); Benny Golson (ts); Paul Chambers (b); Jimmy Cobb (d).* 2 & 3/59.

The gentle but dynamic bounce to his chording comes to the fore on the marvellous *Kelly Blue* (which also reunites the *Kind Of Blue* rhythm section). On the title-track and 'Keep It Moving', the addition of Adderley and Jaspar makes perfect sense, but Benny Golson's robust contributions tend to unbalance the delicate strength of Kelly's arrangements. The trio cuts are far superior.

***** Kelly Great**

Vee Jay 003 *Kelly; Lee Morgan (t); Wayne Shorter (ts); Paul Chambers (b); Philly Joe Jones (d).* 60.

*****(*) Kelly At Midnite**

Vee Jay 006 *As above, except omit Morgan and Shorter.* 60.

***** Wynton Kelly**

Vee Jay 011 *Kelly; Paul Chambers, Sam Jones (b); Jimmy Cobb (d).* 61.

Something of a Bill Evans influence (unless the route is in the opposite direction) creeps into Kelly's playing at this time, and it is possible also to hear echoes from the market dominance of Ahmad Jamal, who was being talked up by Miles Davis at every available opportunity. The three Vee Jays are good, strong albums, though the hard-bop horns on the first of the trio sit uneasily with the leader's conception.

***** It's All Right!**

Verve 557750-2 *Kelly; Kenny Burrell (g); Paul Chambers (b); Jimmy Cobb (d); Candido Camero (perc); Tommy Rey Caribe Street Band.* 3/64.

*****(*) Full View**

Original Jazz Classics OJCCD 912 *Kelly; Ron McClure (b); Jimmy Cobb (d).* 66.

Leaving in some studio noise on *It's All Right* adds a touch of atmosphere but doesn't add much to the musical presence. The musicianship is beyond question and will probably appeal to some far more than the rougher sound of the earlier date, but for us it is a dilution of an important and still unregarded artist.

Ron McClure replaced Paul Chambers in 1966 and brought an immediate change of dimension to the music. *Full View* is an excellent record, an eclectic mix of styles and genres, with a much more balanced feel to the trio, not just piano and rhythm. Cobb is an asset, too, with a relaxed, springy pulse and the ability to cut in behind the melody line with near instantaneous response figures.

***** Last Trio Session**

Delmark 441 *Kelly; Paul Chambers (b); Jimmy Cobb (d).* 8/68.

This had been a long-standing unit since leaving Miles Davis and spending a further tenure as Wes Montgomery's rhythm section. As a curtain-call, it's deeply disappointing and is rendered all the more poignant by the early death of Paul Chambers (just five months after these cuts were made) and then of Kelly. The choice of material is suspect. The Doors' 'Light My Fire' isn't a comfortable theme for a trio of this sensitivity, though the version of Aretha's 'Say A Little Prayer For Me' is very affecting. Chambers is in good, if slightly detached form, and Jimmy Cobb rarely slipped below standard.

Kelly's death, still on the wrong side of forty, robbed jazz of one of its most inventive and hard-working figures. He deserves wider recognition.

Chris Kelsey

SOPRANO SAXOPHONE

Contemporary American free-bop saxophonist; also active as a critic.

***** The Ingenious Gentlemen Of The Lower East Side**

CIMP 139 *Kelsey; Dominic Duval (b); Ed Ware (d).* 3/97.

Kelsey's garrulous soprano is well matched with the busy, pattering free-bop rhythms set up by Duval and Ware. The result is an enjoyable if unexceptional session that retains the interest without suggesting any special creative peaks or intensities. The earnestness of the playing, somewhat aggravated by CIMP's increasingly self-important 'unadorned' presentation, is undercut by a New York sense of humour: hence titles such as 'The Pitiful Tale Of A Battle To Death That Ended In A Draw'.

Stacey Kent (born 1968)

VOCAL

Kent is a New Yorker who came to London and studied at Guildhall School. She is an unapologetic mainstreamer in terms of material and approach.

***** Close Your Eyes**
Candid CCD 79737 *Kent; Jim Tomlinson (ts); David Newton (p); Colin Oxley (g); Andy Cleyndert (b); Steve Brown (d).* 11/96.

*****(*) The Tender Trap**
Candid CCD 79751 *As above, except Dave Green (b), Jeff Hamilton (d) replace Cleyndert and Brown.* 2/98.

*****(*) Let Yourself Go**
Candid CCD 79764 *As above, except Simon Thorpe (b), Steve Brown (d) replace Green and Hamilton.* 7/99.

Kent's curiously lean voice and unmannered phrasing have become very addictive to British audiences, and these neatly tailored records are a fine calling-card for her work. There's hardly a song on any of these records which is less than familiar from the American songbook – and this may discourage collectors familiar with the classic vocalists – but at least she makes no self-conscious attempt at crossing over into pop material. The band, directed largely by saxophonist Thompson, is absolutely assured and glances off and around the singer's vocals. The third record is dedicated to music associated with Fred Astaire and is arguably the pick of the three, although both *Close Your Eyes*, with its sexy-samba title-track, and *The Tender Trap*, a graceful smooch record of a high order, have had a profusion of admirers. Where she takes it from here is hard to say, but there ought to be another dozen or so records in this mould before she runs low on material.

Stan Kenton (1911–79)

PIANO, VOCAL, BANDLEADER

Born in Wichita but raised in California, Kenton learned piano early and was touring with bands as a teenager. Formed his own band in 1940 and through tours and broadcasts became widely known, yet had a yen to experiment and tried to create a 'progressive jazz'. Ran a 40-strong 'Innovations' orchestra in the early '50s, with strings, but gradually reverted to more conventional big-band music, though he later tried a Neophonic Orchestra and the so-called Mellophonium Orchestra (early '60s). Many of the principal West Coast soloists passed through his band, and many leading arrangers did their early work for Kenton. Often dismissed as pretentious, but his orchestra and their records still have a huge following.

***** Stan Kenton 1941–1944**
Classics 828 *Kenton; Franck Beach, Chico Alvarez, Earl Collier, Ray Borden, John Carroll, Buddy Childers, Karl George, Dick Morse, Mel Green, Gene Roland (t); Harry Forbes, Dick Cole, George Faye, Bart Varsalona, Bill Atkinson, Freddie Zito, Milt Kabak, Lory Aaron (tb); Jack Ordean, Ted Romersa, Eddie Meyers, Art Pepper, Boots Mussulli, Al Harding, Bill Lahey, Chester Ball (as); Red Dorris (ts, v); Maurice Beeson, Dave Matthews, Stan Getz, Emmett Carls (ts); Bob Gioga (bs); Bob Ahern, Ralph Leslie (g); Buddy Hayes, Clyde Singleton, Gene Englund, Bob Kesterson (b); Chauncey Farre, Jesse Price, John S Bock, Joe Vernon (d); Anita O'Day, Gene Howard (v).* 11/40–12/44.

***** Broadcast Transcriptions 1941–45**
Music & Arts 883 *Similar to above.* 41–45.

Kenton remains a controversial figure and while his discography on CD is gradually coming into focus – there are still a lot of latter-day vinyl discs which are unavailable, particularly from his own Creative World enterprise – it's still hard to evaluate as a whole. He often had the biggest of big bands and, with his penchant for symphonic uproar, grandiose conception and a demanding menu, it's a curious achievement. Given the 'modernist' tag which stuck to him, it's odd how at this point a lot of his music can seem almost quaint in its methods and matter. Kenton seemed to believe in principles which often had little to do with musical substance: volume, power, weight, noise. Much of the orchestra's output seems to derive from half-assimilated ideas of twentieth-century orchestral composition, and it always sat uneasily next to more familiar notions of jazz scoring. Later editions of the band pilfered from rock and soul idioms, with another batch of mixed results, even if Kenton seemed more at home in that milieu than Woody Herman ever did. His best music still swung mightily, was brilliantly played, and went to exhilarating extremes of both musicianship and showmanship.

The very early sessions for Decca and Capitol are collected on the Classics disc. 'Artistry In Rhythm', Kenton's theme, turns up in the fourth session, but otherwise these are often run-of-the-mill swing arrangements, and the main point of interest is the early vocal features for Anita O'Day. *Broadcast Transcriptions* is a livelier mix, with a teenage Getz taking a solo on 'Pizzicato' among other odds and ends of interest, and a very appreciative crowd on hand on some of the dates. Classics have fair if erratic sound, from unlisted sources; Music & Arts have the usual variable aircheck quality, but the band come through with plenty of spark.

***** On AFRS 1944–1945**
Status DSTS 1019 *Kenton; Buddy Childers, Ray Wetzel, John Anderson, Russ Burgher, Bob Lymperis, John Carroll, Karl George, Gene Roland, Mel Green, Dick Morse (t); Harry Forbes, Freddie Zito, Milt Kabak, Jimmy Simms (tb); Bart Varsalona (btb); Bob Lively, Boots Mussulli, Al Anthony, Eddie Meyers, Chet Ball (as); Stan Getz, Dave Matthews, Emmett Carls, Vido Musso, Bob Cooper (ts); Bob Gioga (bs); Bob Ahern (g); Eddie Safranski, Bob Kesterson, Gene Englund (b); Jesse Price, Ralph Collier, Jam Falzone (d); June Christy, Gene Howard, Anita O'Day (v).* 5/44–11/45.

***** The Transcription Performances 1945–1946**
Hep 47 *Kenton; Buddy Childers, Ray Wetzel, John Anderson, Russ Burgher, Bob Lymperis, Chico Alvarez, Ken Hanna (t); Freddie Zito, Jimmy Simms, Ray Klein, Milt Kabak, Kai Winding, Miff Sines (tb); Bart Varsalona (btb); Al Anthony, Boots Mussulli (as); Vido Musso, Bob Cooper (ts); Bob Gioga*

(bs); Bob Ahern (g); Eddie Safranski (b); Ralph Collier, Shelly Manne (d); June Christy (v). 11/45–7/46.

***** Live At The Café Rouge & Hollywood Palladium 1945**
Jazz Unlimited JUCD 2055 *Similar to above.* 9–11/45.

Not so different from the studio dates, although here and there on these transcriptions the band stretch out a little. Musso's tenor treatment of 'Body And Soul', for instance, features an extended coda on the version on Status, whereas it's briefer and sharper on the Hep disc – though both times he ends it with the Hawkins tag. The earlier tracks on Status mean that O'Day is still present for a couple of features and there's a couple of interesting rarities – 'Conversin' With The Brain', for one. Sound on the Hep disc is superior; the Status transfers tend to sound their age rather more. Jazz Unlimited jump in with a generous 70 minutes of material from three September 1945 broadcasts. The programmes aren't terribly interesting but the sound is more than fair for the period.

***** Stan Kenton 1945**
Classics 898 *Basically similar to above discs.* 12/44–5/45.

*****(*) Stan Kenton 1946**
Classics 949 *As above.* 1–8/46.

Anita O'Day left the band at the beginning of 1945 (her last two features open the *1945* disc) and the introduction of June Christy brought a sweeter, brighter sound to Kenton's palette. The other key import was arranger Pete Rugolo, who charted several staples and hits for Kenton's book. Classics 898 has its share of novelties, which Kenton himself probably detested, such as 'Shoo Fly Pie And Apple Pan Dowdy', and Christy's big hit, 'Just A-Sittin' And A-Rockin''. More typical is the protoype of 'Opus In Pastels' (rejected from a May 1945 date and not cut again until August 1946) and six titles from a hard-hitting V-Disc session. Classics 949 sees Rugolo flexing his muscles and the debut of several Kenton classics: 'Intermission Riff', 'Artistry In Boogie', 'Artistry In Bolero' and the brooding 'Concerto To End All Concertos', a good deal more reflective in its original incarnation than in some subsequent versions. It ends on the accepted version of 'Opus In Pastels'. Remastering is mostly good, if a little harsh on some tracks.

*****(*) Stan Kenton 1947**
Classics 1011 *Kenton; Buddy Childers, Ray Wetzel, Chico Alvarez, John Anderson, Ken Hanna, Al Porcino (t); Kai Winding, Skip Layton, Milt Bernhart, Harry Forbes, Bart Varsalona, Eddie Bert (tb); Eddie Meyers, Boots Mussulli, George Weidler, Frank Pappalardo (as); Red Doris, Bob Cooper, Vido Musso, Warner Weidler (ts); Bob Gioga (bs); Bob Ahern, Laurindo Almeida (g); Eddie Safranski (b); Shelly Manne (d); Jack Costanzo (perc); June Christy, Don McLeod, The Pastels (v).* 2–9/47.

***** Stan Kenton 1947 Vol. 2**
Classics 1039 *As above, except add Dizzy Gillespie (t), Bill Harris (tb), Buddy DeFranco (cl), Art Pepper (as), Flip Phillips (ts), Nat Cole (p), Billy Bauer (g), Buddy Rich (d), Carlos Vidal, Machito (perc); omit Winding, Layton, Meyers, Mussulli, Doris, Musso, Ahern, Mcleod, The Pastels.* 9–12/47.

Kenton was busy in the studios in 1947 and there are 13 sessions for Capitol spread across these two discs. There are many surprising things in what was an adventurous period for the band. Rugolo's 'Machito' is an astonishing explosion. 'Collaboration' (here in both the rejected and issued versions), the two-part 'Rhythm Incorporated', George Weidler's virtuoso turn on 'Elegy For Alto', Kenton's own curiously effective playing on 'How Am I To Know' and a couple of gorgeous Christy vocals make Classics 1011 a priority for Kentonians. Classics 1039 includes the issued version of Rugolo's 'Monotony' (Charlie Parker: 'Very weird, marvellous idea!'), a fine Pepper solo in 'Unison Riff', Christy at her best in 'I Told Ya I Love Ya, Now Get Out' and 'Lonely Woman', several more full-on Rugolo scores and the kitsch masterpiece that is 'The Peanut Vendor'. Pretty good sound throughout. The Metronome All Stars sit in on one track, which accounts for the presence of the starry names listed in the personnel.

****** The Innovations Orchestra**
Capitol 59965-2 2CD *Kenton; Buddy Childers, Maynard Ferguson, Shorty Rogers, Chico Alvarez, Don Paladino, Al Porcino, John Howell, Conte Candoli, Stu Williamson, John Coppola (t); Milt Bernhart, Harry Betts, Bob Fitzpatrick, Bill Russo, Eddie Bert, Dick Kenney (tb); Bart Varsalona, Clyde Brown, George Roberts (btb); John Graas, Lloyd Otto, George Price (frhn); Gene Englund (tba); Bud Shank, Art Pepper, Bob Cooper, Bart Caldarell, Bob Gioga, Bud Shank (reeds); Laurindo Almeida, Ralph Blaze (g); Don Bagley, Abe Luboff (b); Shelly Manne (d); Carlos Vidal, Ivan Lopez, Stenio Orozo, Jose Oliveria, Jack Costanzo (perc); strings.* 2/50–10/51.

***** Carnegie Hall – October '51**
Hep CD 68 *Similar to above.* 10/51.

This is all of the LPs *Innovations In Modern Music* and *Stan Kenton Presents*, along with 14 extra tracks, offering a detailed look at Kenton's 1950–51 orchestra – one of his finest. With the swing era gone, and with the harsher propensities of bebop acclimatizing jazz to more oblique areas of expression, there was no need for Kenton to be shy about the kind of scores he offered here; 'Mirage', 'Conflict', 'Solitaire' and 'Soliloquy', where the orchestra was carefully sifted with strings, are intriguing little tone-poems which, for all their occasionally arch details and overreaching style, work well enough to survive the years. There is one of Christy's finest vocals in 'Lonesome Road'; smart scores by Shorty Rogers like 'Jolly Rogers' and 'Round Robin'; Bob Graettinger's eerie 'House Of Strings'; skilful features for Manne, Pepper, Rogers and Ferguson; Bill Russo's lovely 'Ennui', one of four live tracks used to round off the second disc; and the feel of a very considerable orchestra entering its most challenging period, with soloists befitting an important band. Along with *City Of Glass*, this is surely Kenton's most valuable CD entry.

The Hep transcription of a couple of Carnegie Hall concerts emerges as an interesting pendant to the studio sessions. There are the inevitable sonic shortcomings compared to the Capitol dates, and much of it is no more than secondary versions of the studio sides, but there's a movement from 'City Of Glass' and the soloists – Pepper, Candoli, Cooper, Betts – make their mark.

*****(*) New Concepts Of Artistry In Rhythm**
Capitol 92865-2 *Kenton; Conte Candoli, Buddy Childers, Maynard Ferguson, Don Dennis, Ruben McFall (t); Bob Fitzpatrick, Keith Moon, Frank Rosolino, Bill Russo (tb); George Roberts (btb); Lee Konitz, Vinnie Dean (as); Richie Kamuca, Bill*

Holman (ts); Bob Gioga (bs); Sal Salvador (g); Don Bagley (b); Stan Levey (d); Derek Walton (perc); Kay Brown (v). 9/52.

Laden with top-flight musicians, this was another of Kenton's best bands. There is one arrangement by Bill Holman – the intriguing 'Invention For Guitar And Trumpet' – but most of the scores were penned by Bill Russo, including the glorious kitsch of the opening 'Prologue: This Is An Orchestra!', a kind of Young Person's Guide with Kenton himself narrating and characterizing each member of the band (considering the personalities he's describing, it's both funny and oddly moving at this distance, especially when he calls Frank Rosolino – who would later take his own life – 'this fellow who has few if any moody moments'). The brass section is top-heavy and blows all else before it, but the rhythm section swings hard, and there are some wonderful interjections on almost every piece by the major soloists, especially Salvador on 'Invention', Konitz on 'Young Blood' and 'My Lady', Rosolino on 'Swing House'. The remastering is bright and just a little harsh in places, but it makes the band sound grandly impressive, which is as it should be.

****** City Of Glass**
Capitol 832084-2 *Similar to above discs.* 12/47–5/53.

The 16 pieces arranged by Bob Graettinger which make up this CD number among the most exacting works Kenton was ever responsible for. Graettinger's two major pieces, 'City Of Glass' and 'This Modern World', are extraordinary works – Ellingtonian in their concentration on individuals within the band, yet using the bigger resources of the orchestra to create its own sound-world. All of his 14 originals (there are two arrangements on standards) create their own kind of jazz, and its suitability to Kenton's orchestra might almost be likened to Strayhorn's music for Ellington – except Graettinger was by far the more original thinker. Splendidly remastered, this is an important memorial to a man often forgotten in the annals of jazz composition, and Max Harrison's typically elegant sleeve-note supplies the fine context.

*****(*) Kenton In Hi-Fi**
Capitol 84451-2 *Kenton; Ed Leddy, Dennis Grillo, Lee Katzman, Phil Gilbert, Tom Slaney (t); Archie LeCocque, Kent Larsen, Jim Amlotte (tb); Ken Shroyer (btb); Irving Rosenthal, Joe Mariani (frhn); Lennie Niehaus (as); Bill Perkins, Richie Kamuca (ts); Pepper Adams (bs); Ralph Blaze (g); Jay McAllister (tba); Don Bagley (b); Mel Lewis (d).* 2/56–7/58.

****(*) Live At The Macumba Club Vol. 1**
Magic DAWE 48 *As above.* 11/56.

****(*) Live At The Macumba Club Vol. 2**
Magic DAWE 49 *As above.* 11/56.

***** Rendezvous Of Standards And Classics**
Music For Pleasure 833620-2 2CD *Similar to above discs.* 43–57.

***** Cuban Fire**
Capitol 96260-2 *Kenton; Ed Leddy, Sam Noto, Phil Gilbert, Al Mattaliano, Bud Brisbois, Dalton Smith, Bob Rolfe, John Audino, Steve Hofsteter (t); Bob Fitzpatrick, Carl Fontana, Kent Larsen, Don Kelly, Dick Hyde, Ray Sikora (tb); Jim Amlotte, Bob Knight (btb); Dwight Carver, Joe Burnett, Bill Horan, Tom Wirtel, Gene Roland (mel); Gabe Baltazar, Lennie Niehaus (as); Bill Perkins, Lucky Thompson, Sam Donahue, Paul Renzi (ts); Wayne Dunstan (bs, bsx); Billy Root, Marvin Holladay (bs); Ralph Blaze (g); Jay McAllister, Albert Pollan (tba); Curtis Counce, Pete Chivily (b); Mel Lewis, Art Anton (d); Sol Gubin, George Gaber, Tommy Lopez, George Laguna, Roger Mozian, Maro Alvarez, George Acevedo (perc).* 5/56–9/60.

The mid-1950s found Kenton somewhat in transition, from the more stylized West Coast touches of the early-'50s band to another kind of progressive-orchestral music which he had tried in the 1940s with mixed results. Live sessions were customarily a blend of straightahead swing variations on standards, the Afro-Cuban element, and Kenton's penchant for orchestral bombast.

The 1956 albums are a patchy lot. The three discs from the Mocamba Club are a rather motley lot in no more than respectable sound. The two original studio albums are the most important. *Kenton In Hi Fi* was a hit album for the bandleader and offered a reworking (almost Ellingtonian in intent) of many of his early successes, seeking the crisper definition of LP-era sound. If hardly a dramatic improvement or a startling revision (Kenton kept many of the patterns intact), it reasserts the orchestra's clout on its staple themes. The CD is beefed up with three 1958 tracks. *Cuban Fire* chronicles the arrival of arranger Johnny Richards, who had been studying Latin rhythms and came up with a series of charts which incorporated a six-man percussion team. The results catch much of the undertow of explosive kitsch which Latin bands love, although how 'authentic' it is in other ways is harder to judge. The six later tracks, from 1960, document one of Kenton's so-called 'mellophonium' bands, with five men playing that instrument among what is incredibly a band with 16 brass. Much of it sounds like mood or movie music, taken at tempos which tend towards trudging. The remastering is strong on the brass, but the bass frequencies are less well handled and the percussion section is mixed well off-mike on the earlier session.

Rendezvous Of Standards And Classics is a two-disc set (at bargain price) which collects no fewer than five Capitol albums: *Milestones, Sketches On Standards, Kenton Classics, Portraits On Standards* and *Rendezvous With Kenton*. Familar material and some of the hits dominate the first disc, but most of the rest offers often relatively subdued arrangements of songbook tunes. A nice package for fans, though one slight caveat on the remastering: very shrill on some tracks, with the brass deafening, and misty on others – the power of the band comes through, but not very subtly.

***** Live At The Patio Gardens Ballroom Vol. 1**
Magic DAWE 56 *Kenton; Ed Leddy, Sam Noto, Billy Catalano, Lee Katzman, Phil Gilbert (t); Kent Larsen, Archie LeCocque, Don Reed, Jim Amlotte (tb); Kenny Shroyer (btb); Lennie Niehaus, Bill Perkins, Bill Robinson, Wayne Dunstan, Steve Perlow (reeds); Red Kelly (b); Jerry McKenzie (d).* 8/57.

****(*) Live At The Patio Gardens Ballroom Vol. 2**
Magic DAWE 57 *As above.* 8/57.

****(*) Live At The Patio Gardens Ballroom Vol. 3**
Magic DAWE 58 *As above.* 8/57.

Music from a two-night engagement in Salt Lake City. These are typical Kenton sets for a dancing audience, which means less ambitious programmes, many standards, brief interpretations, careful solos. Given all that, the playing is still pointed and skilful, and Niehaus, Perkins and Noto have many good moments. Sound isn't as good as on some of the Status CDs, but isn't bad. *Volume One* has the best material.

***** The Ballad Style Of Stan Kenton**

Capitol 56688-2 *Kenton; Jules Chaikin, Bill Catalano, Lee Katzman, Phil Gilbert, Ed Leddy, Don Fagerquist (t); Bob Fitzpatrick, Kent Larsen, Archie LeCocque, Jim Amlotte, Don Reed (tb); Kenny Shroyer (btb); Lennie Niehaus (as); Bill Perkins, Richie Kamuca (ts); Bill Robinson, Steve Perlow (bs); Red Kelly (b); Mel Lewis, Jerry McKenzie (d).* 5–6/58.

Or 'Kenton Plays Pretty'. In a way this isn't so different from the kind of easy-listening records that were going under Jackie Gleason's name for Capitol, with the leader the principal soloist and most of the melodies only slightly Kentonized. But it *is* a very pretty record of big-band ballads.

***** Live From The Las Vegas Tropicana**

Capitol 35245-2 *Kenton; Frank Huggins, Bud Brisbois, Jack Sheldon, Joe Burnett, Roger Middleton (t); Archie LeCocque, Kent Larsen, Jim Amlotte (tb); Bob Olsen, Bill Smiley (btb); Lennie Niehaus (as); Richie Kamuca, Bill Trujillo (ts); Billy Root, Sture Swenson (bs); Red Kelly (b); Jerry McKenzie (d).* 2/59.

Stan opens with a self-deprecating announcement to the effect that they're going to try and make a record that sells. Admittedly, there's little from his obviously progressive side to the programme: mostly standards, a few Gene Roland originals, and the band are relatively quiescent, but the playing is up to scratch and a few nice routines, like the piano–bass embellishments on 'Bernie's Tune', give it plenty of appeal.

*****(*) Standards In Silhouette**

Capitol 94503-2 *Kenton; Bud Brisbois, Clyde Reasinger, Dalton Smith, Bill Chase, Rolf Ericson, Roger Middleton (t); Archie LeCocque, Don Sebesky, Kent Larson (tb); Jim Amlotte, Bob Knight (btb); Charlie Mariano (as); Bill Trujillo, John Bonnie (ts); Jack Nimitz, Marvin Holladay (bs); Pete Chivily (b); Jimmy Campbell (d); Mike Pacheco (perc).* 9/59.

***** Adventures In Blues**

Capitol 20089-2 *Kenton; Dalton Smith, Marvin Stamm, Bud Brisbois, Bob Rolfe, Bob Behrendt, Sam Noto, Steve Huffsteter, Norman Baltazar (t); Bob Fitzpatrick, Dee Barton, Bud Parker, Jack Spurlock, Dick Hyde, Ray Sikora (tb); Jim Amlotte, Ray Knight, Dave Wheeler (btb); Gene Roland (mel, ss); Dwight Carver, Joe Burnett, Bill Horan, Tom Wirtel, Keith La Motte, Carl Saunders, Ray Starling (mel); Gabe Baltazar (as); Buddy Arnold, Paul Renzi, Sam Donahue (ts); Marvin Holladay, Allan Beutler (bs); Wayne Dunstan (bsx); Albert Pollan (tba); Pat Senatore, Red Mitchell, Pete Chivily (b); Jerry McKenzie, Art Anton (d).* 9/60–12/61.

***** Adventures In Jazz**

Capitol 21222-2 *As above, except add Joel Kay (bsx); omit Noto, Huffsteter, Hyde, Sikora, Knight, Burnett, Horan, Wirtel, Pollan, Chivily, Anton.* 7–12/61.

Standards In Silhouette is a modest gem in this period of Kenton. The charts were by the 22-year-old Bill Mathieu, and they fashion 'concert' settings for nine ballads, from 'Little Girl Blue' (which is barely recognizable) to John Lewis's 'Django', which survives Kentonization mainly through a beautiful contribution from Charlie Mariano. There are some other good soloists – LeCocque in 'Ill Wind', Roger Middleton on 'The Thrill Is Gone'. It still makes a long haul over CD length, but track by track this is an accomplished and handsome big-band record.

The two *Adventures* records have their moments. The *Blues* set was arranged by Gene Roland, who seldom bothers to tax the resources of this over-resourced band, although he does what he can to vary the sonorities coming out of this brass-heavy orchestra. There were fewer interesting soloists in the band at this point, though, and both this and *Jazz* could use a maverick spirit to cut loose here and there.

****(*) Live In Biloxi**

Magic DAWE 30 *Kenton; Frank Huggins, Bud Brisbois, Jack Sheldon, Billy Catalano, Bob Ojeda (t); Archie LeCocque, Kent Larsen, Jim Amlotte (tb); Bob Olsen, Bill Smiley (btb); Lennie Niehaus (as); Bill Perkins, Bill Trujillo (ts); Bill Robinson, Steve Perlow (bs); Red Kelly (b); Jerry McKenzie (d). c.* 60.

****(*) Return To Biloxi**

Magic DAWE 35 *As above. c.* 60.

***** Live At Barstow 1960**

Status DSTS1001 *Kenton; Bud Brisbois, Dalton Smith, Bill Chase, Rolf Ericson, Danny Nolan (t); Bob Fitzpatrick, Kent Larsen, Bill Smiley (tb); Jim Amlotte, Bob Knight (btb); Lennie Niehaus (as); Bill Trujillo, Ronnie Rubin (ts); Jack Nimitz, Marvin Holladay (bs); Pete Chivily (b); Jimmy Campbell (d); Mike Pacheco (perc).* 1/60.

There is a rash of live material by the Kenton band from this period but several of the better Status CDs seem to have been deleted. The two Biloxi sets – the first is the more progressive material, the second a more standards-orientated session – are recorded mistily and the orchestra comes over rather waywardly. *Live At Barstow* is nearly all standards, with many nice solo spots for Niehaus, Ericson and Trujillo, and the band sound strong on what must have been a dance date for the marine corps.

*****(*) Mellophonium Moods**

Status STCD 106 *Kenton; Dalton Smith, Marvin Stamm, Bob Behrendt, Keith La Motte, Bob Rolfe (t); Gene Roland, Ray Starling, Dwight Carver, Carl Saunders (mel); Bob Fitzpatrick, Dee Barton, Bud Parker (tb); Jim Amlotte (btb); Dave Wheeler (btb, tba); Gabe Baltazar (as); Charlie Mariano, Ray Florian (ts); Allan Beutler (bs); Joel Kaye (bsx); Val Kolar (b); Jerry McKenzie (d).* 3/62.

****(*) One Night Stand**

Magic DAWE 66 *Similar to above.* 9/61–7/62.

***** More Mellophonium Moods**

Status DSTS1010 *As above, except add Bill Briggs (t), Lou Gasca (mel), Tom Ringo (tb), Bucky Calabrese (b), Bill Blakkested (d), Jean Turner (v); omit Rolfe, Roland, Kolar, McKenzie.* 8/62.

****(*) At The Holiday Ballroom, Northbrook, Chicago**

Status DSTS1018 *As above.* 5/62.

Kenton's 'mellophonium' band took his fascination with brass to new lengths: there are 14 brass players in both of these bands. The leader's verdict was that the band represented 'the New Era in Modern American Music', but it actually sounds like a beefier, more metallic edition of the old Kentonian machine. By this time

Kenton had become entirely *sui generis*, and the prevailing winds of jazz fashion had little effect on the orchestra's direction. But he was still usually on the dinner-dance circuit, and both these discs contain somewhat rueful admissions from the leader that they'll play something people can dance to, but he wouldn't mind if some people also wanted to listen. No false pride: this was a great, swinging band and, if Kenton had lost most of his best soloists, the features for Baltazar, Mariano and some of the brassmen are handled with great aplomb. The *Mellophonium Moods* set is the best one in terms of fidelity – the sound is quite superb for a supposedly private recording – and, with a higher degree of original material, including a number of Kenton rarities, it's marginally the most interesting musically, too. The two concerts on *One Night Stand* are from AFRS broadcasts from New Jersey, something of a throwback; while the band still sound well, the sound is far below that achieved on the Status CDs. *More Mellophonium Moods* doesn't quite have the hi-fi of the other one, but it still sounds pretty good, and there is some lovely playing: Ray Starling takes a perfectly poised solo on 'Misty', and 'Maria' is a resplendent treatment of Johnny Richards's arrangement. The comedy version of 'Tea For Two' is a drawback, though. The same band took to the boards at Northbrook, Chicago, and this time the sound is muzzier and the programme a little lacking in lift. Nevertheless, Status should be congratulated for unearthing so much by this edition of the band.

***** Adventures In Time**

Capitol 55454-2 *Kenton; Dalton Smith, Bob Behrendt, Marvin Stamm, Keith La Motte, Gary Slavo (t); Bob Fitzpatrick, Bud Parker, Tom Ringo (tb); Jim Amlotte (btb); Ray Starling, Dwight Carver, Lou Gasca, Joe Burnett (mel); Dave Wheeler (btb, tba); Gabe Baltazar (as); Don Menza, Ray Florian (ts); Allan Beutler (bs); Joel Kaye (bs, bsx); Bucky Calabrese (b); Dee Barton (d); Steve Dweck (perc).* 9/62.

One of the studio entries by the mellophonium band. The charts are all by Johnny Richards, neither the best nor the worst of Kenton's arranging clique, and their particular trait is a hankering to use as much of this 24-strong band as possible, as much of the time as possible. There's an awful lot of *fff* in the scoring and some of the crescendoes are apocalyptic, even by Kenton's standards. Soloists make their mark – Gabe Baltazar's alto in particular – but this isn't about the jazz improviser, it's about Kentonian hosannas. On those terms, a great one.

***** Stan Kenton Conducts The Los Angeles Neophonic Orchestra**

Capitol 94502-2 *Kenton; Dalton Smith, Frank Higgins, Gary Barone, Ronnie Ossa, Olie Mitchell (t); Bob Fitzpatrick, Vern Friley, Gil Falco (tb); Jim Amlotte (btb); Vince DeRosa, Bill Hinshaw, John Cave, Richard Perissi, Arthur Maebe (frhn); Bud Shank, Bill Perkins, Bob Cooper, Don Lodice, John Lowe (reeds); Claude Williamson (p); Emil Richards (vib); Dennis Budimir (g); John Worster (b); Nick Ceroli (d); Frank Carlson (perc).* 9/65.

The Neophonic Orchestra was to be permanently based in Los Angeles and would use some of the mass of former Kentonians who'd gone on to regular studio work there. As it happened, this session was a mix of the regular men with old hands such as Shank, Cooper and Perkins. The music came from various hands, including Hugo Montenegro, Jimmy Knight and John Williams, but the only really interesting piece is the bonus track which wasn't even on the original album, Clare Fischer's 'Piece For Soft Brass, Woodwinds And Percussion'. The rest is standard if accomplished Kentonian grandiloquence. Excellent sound.

**** At Fountain Street Church Part One**

Status DSTS 1014 *Kenton; Mike Price, Jim Kartchner, Jay Daversa, Carl Leach, John Madrid (t); Dick Shearer, Tom Whittaker, Shelley Denny (tb); Joe Randazzo (btb); Bob Goodwin (btb, tba); Ray Reed (as, f); Mike Altschul, Bob Crosby (ts); Earle Dumler (bs); Bill Fritz (bs, bsx); John Worster (b); Dee Barton (d); Efrain Logreira (perc).* 3/68.

**** At Fountain Street Church Part Two**

Status DSTS 1015 *As above.*

There are some good things here, particularly among the more shaded sections of the arrangements, which catch the band midway between its subtler middle period and the supposed populism of the 1970s. But for once Dave Kay's source material let him down: the sound isn't much better than an average bootleg, with balances off and the drums booming like an artillery range.

****(*) Live At Redlands University**

Creative World STD 1015 *Kenton; Joe Ellis (t, v); Mike Vax, Jim Kartchner, Dennis Noday, Warren Gale (t); Dick Shearer, Mike Jamieson, Fred Carter, Tom Bridges (tb); Graham Ellis (btb, tba); Quin Davis (as); Richard Torres, Norm Smith, Jim Timlin (ts); Willie Maiden (bs); Gary Todd (b); John Von Ohlen (d); Efraim Logreira (perc).* 10/70.

****(*) Live At Brigham Young University**

Creative World STD 1039 *Kenton; Mike Vax, Gary Pack, Jay Saunders, Joe Marcinkiewicz (t); Dick Shearer, Fred Carter, Mike Jamieson, Mike Wallace, Graham Ellis (tb); Quin Davis, Kim Frizell (as); Willie Maiden (ts, bs); Richard Torres (ts); Chuck Carter (bs); Gary Todd (b); John Von Ohlen (d); Ramon Lopez (perc).* 8/71.

**** Live At Butler University**

Creative World STD 1059 *Kenton; Jay Saunders, Dennis Noday, Mike Vax, Mike Snustead, Raymond Brown (t); Dick Shearer, Mike Jamieson, Fred Carter, Mike Wallace (tb); Phil Herring (btb, tba); Quin Davis (as, f); Richard Torres, Chris Galuman (ts, f); Chuck Carter (bs, ss, f); Willie Maiden (bs); John Worster (b); Jerry McKenzie (d); The Four Freshmen (v).* 6/72.

***** Birthday In Britain**

Creative World STD 1065 *Kenton; Dennis Noday, Paul Adamson, Frank Minear, Mike Snustead, Robert Winiker (t); Dick Shearer, Harvey Coonin, Lloyd Spoon (tb); John Park (as); Chris Galuman (ts, f); Richard Torres, Willie Maiden (ts); Roy Reynolds (bs); John Worster (b); Peter Erskine (d); Ramon Lopez (perc).* 2/73.

****(*) At The Pavilion, Hemel Hempstead**

Status DTS1017 *As above.* 2/73.

***** Live At London Hilton 1973 Vol. I**

Status DSTS1005 *As above.* 2/73.

***** Live At London Hilton Vol. II**

Status DSTS1006 *As above.* 2/73.

****(*) 7.5 On The Richter Scale**

Creative World STD 1070 *As above, except add Mike Barrowman (t), Gary Pack, Dale Devoe, Bill Hartman, Mike Wallace (tb), Mary Fettig (ts), Kim Park (ts, as), Kirby Stewart (b); omit Minear, Winiker, Coonin, Maiden and Worster.* 8/73.

***** Live At Carthage College Vol. One**

Magic DAWE 69 *Kenton; Mike Barrowman, Kevin Jordan, Glenn Stuart, John Harner, Mike Snustead (t); Dick Shearer, Lloyd Spoon, Brett Stamps (tb); Bill Hartman (btb); Mike Wallace (btb, tba); Terry Cooke (as); Richard Torres, Dick Wilkie (ts); Roy Reynolds, Rich Condit (bs); Kirby Stewart (b); Peter Erskine (d); Ramon Lopez (perc).* 2/74.

****(*) Live At Carthage College Vol. Two**

Magic DAWE70 *As above.* 2/74.

****(*) Plays Chicago**

Creative World STD 1072 *Kenton; John Harner, Dave Zeagler, Mike Barrowman, Mike Snustead, Kevin Jordan (t); Dick Shearer, Lloyd Spoon, Brett Stamps, Bill Hartman (tb); Tony Campise, Greg Smith, Rich Condit, Dick Wilkie, Roy Reynolds (reeds); Mike Wallace (tba); Mike Ross (b); Peter Erskine (d); Ramon Lopez (perc).* 6/74.

*****(*) Fire, Fury & Fun**

Creative World STD 1073 *As above, except Tim Hagans (t), Dave Keim, Greg Sorcsek, Mike Suter (tb), Dan Salmasian (reeds) replace Snustead, Stamps, Hartman and Wilkie.* 9/74.

****(*) Kenton '76**

Creative World STD 1076 *Kenton; John Harner, Jay Sollenberger, Steve Campos, Jim Oatts, Tim Hagans (t); Dick Shearer, Dave Keim, Mike Egan (tb); Alan Morrissey (btb); Douglas Purviance (btb, tba); Terry Layne (as, f); Roy Reynolds, Dan Salmasian (ts, f); Alan Yankee, Greg Smith (bs, f); Dave Stone (b); Gary Hobbs (d); Ramon Lopez (perc).* 12/75.

****(*) Journey Into Capricorn**

Creative World STD 1077 *As above, except Dave Kennedy (t), Jeff Uusitalo (tb), Dave Sova (ts), Bill Fritz (bs), John Worster (b) replace Oatts, Keim, Salmasian, Smith and Stone.* 8/76.

Like any bandleader working through this period, Kenton had to change and compromise to survive, and the orchestra he worked with through the 1970s became as modish and subject to fads as any big-band survivor. But at least Kenton had always stood by his 'progressiveness' and, subject to trashy material and clockwork charts though many of the later records are, the orchestra is no less predictable or bombastic than, say, the Basie band in the same period. Kenton had no charmed team of soloists by now but, as with the Buddy Rich band, he valued precision and overall effect, and all the surviving records (on CD – presumably there is much more that will be reissued) have virtues of their own.

The various university concerts (where Kenton was always in favour, it seems) are sometimes bizarre mixtures of old and new: at Redlands he plays 'Hey Jude' and 'Macarthur Park' alongside 'Here's That Rainy Day' and 'Artistry In Rhythm'. At Brigham Young, it's 'Theme From Love Story' and 'Rhapsody In Blue'. Most peculiar of all is the Butler University set, where the band play 'Surfer Girl' (in 1972?) and 'Brand New Key', and then have the Four Freshmen join them! But the usual assertiveness of the brass section introduces moments of both grandeur and genuine excitement into all of these sets. The best of them is *Fire, Fury And Fun*, which has splendid features for Reynolds ('Roy's Blues') and Erskine ('Pete Is A Four-Letter Word') and is let down only by Campise's silly 'Hogfat Blues'. *Birthday In Britain* has a superior set of charts (with the young Peter Erskine driving them), and *7.5 On The Richter Scale*, despite opening with the theme from *Live And Let Die* and going on to 'It's Not Easy Being Green', isn't a bad set of punch-ups for the sections. *Plays Chicago* refers not to the town but to the group, a modish attempt at playing thin, rocked-up tunes – insulting to Kenton, really – and the fact that he and the band make as good a fist of it as they do is surprising. *'76*, with another new band, is merely OK big-band fare, and *Journey Into Capricorn* bogs down on the ponderous 'Celebration Suite', though 'Too Shy To Say' (also on *Street Of Dreams*, listed below) is a warm revision of a Stevie Wonder tune.

More live material has appeared on Status and Magic. The British concerts from February 1973 appear in good sound on their respective discs, but since the programme at Hemel Hempstead is largely duplicated on the Hilton show, which is spread across two discs (with a lot of chat, banter and introductions), only fanatics would consider getting both. Each is a decent set, though, with some of Kenton's most jazz-directed charts and Park, Winiker and Torres all taking good turns – Park's feature on 'Street Of Dreams' at the Hilton is a gem. The Carthage College date also sounds full and vivid, with occasional bass-heaviness. The programme is a typically catholic mixture, with 'Peanut Vendor' sitting next to 'Macarthur Park'. Probably for hardcore fans only, well though the band play.

***** Live At Sunset Ridge Country Club Chicago**

Magic DAWE 59 *Kenton; Jay Sollenberger, Dave Kennedy, Steve Campos, Tim Hagans, Joe Casano (t); Dick Shearer, Dave Keim, Mike Egan (tb); Allan Morrisey (btb); Doug Purviance (btb, tba); Terry Layne (as); Roy Reynolds, Dan Salmasian (ts); Greg Smith, Alan Yankee (bs); John Worster (b); Gary Hobbs (d); Ramon Lopez (perc).* 5/76.

****(*) Live In Cologne 1976 Vol. One**

Magic DAWE 64 *As above, except Jeff Uusitalo (tb), Teddy Andersen (ts), Greg Metcalf (bs) replace Keim, Salmasian and Smith.* 9/76.

***** Live In Cologne 1976 Vol. Two**

Magic DAWE 65 *As above.* 9/76.

Two concerts from towards the end of the band's life. Kenton is still reprising his remarks about music for dancing versus music for listening at the start of the Chicago dance date, but he's humorous enough about it, and the band sound very full and strong (though the sound-mix shoves Worster to the very front). Terry Layne sounds good on alto and, though the tempos are easy-going, they don't get slack. The Cologne date is more ambitious, though not necessarily more enjoyable: sound is a bit less palatable, and 'Intermission Riff' on the first disc is a bit of a never-ending story, but the band sound fit and Kenton enjoys it, even though his own health was in serious decline.

*****(*) Street Of Dreams**

Creative World STD 1079 *As above discs.* 73–76.

A rather good and well-chosen compilation from some of Stan's latter-day sessions. It's mostly ballads, which lets the great sonority of the Kenton brass assert itself one final time, and Chuck Carter's baritone on 'Rhapsody In Blue', Tim Hagans on 'My

Funny Valentine' and John Park's exquisite alto on 'Street Of Dreams' honour the arrangements.

Freddie Keppard (1890–1933)

CORNET

A bandleader in New Orleans at sixteen, Keppard was touring by the 1910s, his massive sound shaking up the pre-jazz scene. Secretive about his own playing, he missed the chance to record early and in the '20s was overtaken by Armstrong and others, alcoholism adding to his decline. He died of TB in Chicago.

***** The Legend**

Topaz TPZ 1052 *Keppard; Elwood Graham, James Tate (c); Fred Garland, Eddie Vincent, Fayette Williams, Eddie Ellis (tb); Jimmie Noone (cl, as, v); Clifford King (cl, as); Johnny Dodds, Angelo Fernandez (cl); Joe Poston (as); Jerome Pasquall, Norval Mortroin (ts); Arthur Campbell, Antonia Spaulding, Adrian Robinson, Jimmy Blythe (p); Jimmy Bell (vn); Stan Wilson, Erskine Tate (bj); Bill Newton (tba); Bert Greene, Jasper Taylor, Jimmy Bertrand (d); Papa Charlie Jackson (v).* 6/23–1/27.

*****(*) The Complete Set 1923–1926**

Retrieval RTR 79017 *As above.* 6/23–1/27.

One of the great unsolved questions in jazz is how good Freddie Keppard really was. The second 'King' of New Orleans horn, after Buddy Bolden and before Joe Oliver, his handful of records offer scant evidence for his stature and suggest a musician who cottoned on to ragtime but never quite got a grip on jazz, or at least where it was going. He has a big, jabbing sound (when you can hear him at all – more often than not he's hidden in several of these groups) and when he cuts loose from his surroundings he can work up some genuine excitement. That happens only a few times on the 24 tracks which are his entire legacy – and even then his presence is doubtful on a few of them. The bigger-band sides with Doc Cook and Erskine Tate are often a disappointing lot, and one has to turn to the small-group sides with Jimmy Blythe, Jasper Taylor and Keppard's own Jazz Cardinals to hear him working at something like optimum level, in rough-and-ready Chicago jazz of the day.

The Topaz disc is decent enough, but the new Retrieval edition is so well remastered that it asked us to reconsider our verdict on Keppard. The Doc Cook band sides have never sounded finer, and even the Erskine Tate tracks from 1923 stand up much better than before. One still needs ears sympathetic to the music of that day but, more than any other previous issue, this brings Keppard back to life.

Barney Kessel (born 1923)

GUITAR

Born in Muskogee, Oklahoma, Kessel was playing in big bands in Los Angeles in the mid-'40s. He spent much of the next two decades doing studio work but also led many sessions of his own, and he formed The Pollwinners Trio with Ray Brown and Shelly Manne. He continued touring until 1992, when he suffered a stroke.

***** Easy Like**

Original Jazz Classics OJC 153 *Kessel; Bud Shank, Buddy Collette (as, f); Harold Ross, Claude Williamson (p); Harry Babasin (b); Shelly Manne (d).* 11/53–2/56.

***** Plays Standards**

Original Jazz Classics OJC 238 *Kessel; Bob Cooper (ts, ob); Claude Williamson, Hampton Hawes (p); Monty Budwig, Red Mitchell (b); Shelly Manne, Chuck Thompson (d).* 6–7/54.

*****(*) To Swing Or Not To Swing**

Original Jazz Classics OJC 317 *Kessel; Harry 'Sweets' Edison (t); Georgie Auld, Bill Perkins (ts); Jimmy Rowles (p); Al Hendrickson (g); Red Mitchell (b); Irv Cottler (d).* 6/55.

***** Music To Listen To Barney Kessel By**

Original Jazz Classics OJC 746 *Kessel; Buddy Collette, Jules Jacob, George Smith, Howard Terry, Justin Gordon, Ted Nash (reeds); André Previn, Jimmy Rowles, Claude Williamson (p); Buddy Clark, Red Mitchell (b); Shelly Manne (d).* 8–12/56.

'The blues he heard as a boy in Oklahoma, the swing he learned on his first band job and the modern sounds of the West Coast school': Nesuhi Ertegun's summary of Kessel, written in 1954, still holds as good as any description. Kessel has often been undervalued as a soloist down the years: the smoothness and accuracy of his playing tend to disguise the underlying weight of the blues which informs his improvising, and his albums from the 1950s endure with surprising consistency. *Easy Like*, with flute by Shank and Collette, is a little too feathery, but the guitarist's clean lines spare little in attack and the terrific 'Vicky's Dream' emerges as furious bop. The two subsequent albums suggest a firm truce between Basie-like small-band swing – hardly surprising with Edison on hand – and the classic West Coast appraisal of bop. The inclusion of such ancient themes as 'Louisiana', 'Twelfth Street Rag' and 'Indiana' suggests the breadth of Kessel's interests and, although most of the tracks are short, nothing seems particularly rushed. Lester Koenig's superb production has been faithfully maintained for the reissues: Manne, especially, is well served by the engineering. *Music To Listen To Barney Kessel By* sweetens the mix by sticking to cute woodwind and reed arrangements of familiar tunes while Kessel swings smilingly through it; nothing demanding, but it's done so breezily that it cuts most of the so-called easy-listening jazz of recent years.

*****(*) The Poll Winners**

Original Jazz Classics OJC 156 *Kessel; Ray Brown (b); Shelly Manne (d).* 3/57.

***** The Poll Winners Ride Again**

Original Jazz Classics OJC 607 *As above.* 8/58.

*****(*) Poll Winners Three**

Original Jazz Classics OJC 692 *As above.* 11/59.

Since Kessel, Brown and Manne regularly scored high in jazz fans' polls of the day, Contemporary's decision to record them as a trio was commercially impeccable. But they were a committed musical group too. *The Poll Winners* includes jamming on 'Satin Doll' and 'Mean To Me' which is sophisticated enough to imply a telepathy between Kessel and Manne. But the group push harder on the remaining records, although *Ride Again* includes some weak material. The superb studio sound highlights inner detail.

**** Plays Carmen**

Original Jazz Classics OJC 269 *Kessel; Ray Linn (t); Harry Betts (tb); Buddy Collette (cl, f); Bill Smith (cl, bcl); Jules Jacobs (cl, ob); Pete Terry (bcl, bsn); Herb Geller (as); Justin Gordon (ts, f); Chuck Gentry (bs); André Previn (p); Victor Feldman (vib); Joe Mondragon (b); Shelly Manne (d).* 12/58.

***** Some Like It Hot**

Original Jazz Classics OJC 168 *Kessel; Joe Gordon (t); Art Pepper (cl, as, ts); Jimmy Rowles (p); Jack Marshall (g); Monty Budwig (b); Shelly Manne (d).* 3–4/59.

***** The Artistry Of Barney Kessel**

Contemporary 60-021 *As OJC albums listed above.*

The *Carmen* album was a cute idea that might best have stayed as no more than that, although Kessel gives it enough dedication to create some typical swinging blues out of the likes of 'Carmen's Cool'. *Some Like It Hot* works much better, since this set of tunes from the then-hit film offered the kind of new-lamps-for-old which Kessel had already been trying on earlier records. Pepper shines on all three horns, Gordon contributes some acrid solos on one of his rare appearances on record, and Kessel experiments with three different guitars and a couple of duo-only tunes. 'Runnin' Wild', taken at a blistering pace, is a tiny gem. *The Artistry Of* is a user-friendly selection from the OJC albums and is an effective sampler of the period.

**** Aquarius**

Black Lion BLCD 760222 *Kessel; Kenny Salmon, Steve Gray (org); Ike Isaacs (g); Tony Campo (b); Barry Morgan (d).* 11/68.

****(*) Autumn Leaves**

Black Lion BLCD 760112 *Kessel; Teddy Edwards (ts); Jimmy Rowles (p); Kenny Napper (b); John Marshall (d).* 10/68–9/69.

***** Yesterday**

Black Lion BLCD 760183 *Kessel; Danny Moss (ts); Stéphane Grappelli (vn); Brian Lemon (p); Kenny Baldock (b); Johnny Richardson (d).* 7/73.

***** The Poll Winners / Straight Ahead**

Original Jazz Classics OJC 409 *Kessel; Ray Brown (b); Shelly Manne (d).* 7/75.

Kessel spent most of the 1960s as a studio session guitarist. *Aquarius* has him sounding like he's doing sessionman chores, covering ten tunes from the score of *Hair*. This is really more of an instrumental rock record than a jazz date, and it needn't detain most readers, but, pro that he is, Barney gets off a few strong solos and the tunes are good enough to remind that the original score is rather more than a period piece. Most of the music on *Autumn Leaves* is with the sole support of Napper and Marshall, who play perfunctorily, which leaves Kessel to toy with ideas; it's still a pretty record, with three odd tracks with Edwards and Rowles as makeweight. *Yesterday* replays Kessel's Montreux Festival appearance from 1973, with a guest appearance apiece by Moss and Grappelli, the latter on his patented sashay through 'Tea For Two'. 'Laura' and 'Old Devil Moon' are vintage Kessel, the former building from a featherdown exposition of the tune through progressively burning choruses. Moss sits in on a gruffly swinging blues and, though the music has the ad hoc feel of a typical festival set, it was worth keeping. *The Poll Winners* re-union is as good as their earlier records, yet looser, less drilled. 'Caravan' and 'Laura' become springboards for playing as freely as they ever could together.

****(*) Three Guitars**

Concord CCD 6004 *Kessel; Herb Ellis, Charlie Byrd (g); Joe Byrd (b); Johnny Rae (d).* 7/74.

****(*) Barney Plays Kessel**

Concord CCD 6009 *Kessel; Herbie Steward (ss, as, f); Victor Feldman (vib); Jimmy Rowles (p); Chuck Domanico (b); Jake Hanna (d); Milt Holland (perc).* 4/75.

***** Soaring**

Concord CCD 6033 *Kessel; Monty Budwig (b); Jake Hanna (d).* 77.

****(*) Poor Butterfly**

Concord CCD 4034 *Kessel; Herb Ellis (g); Monty Budwig (b); Jake Hanna (d).* 77.

****(*) Live At Sometime**

Storyville STCD 4157 *Kessel; Kunimitsu Inaba (b); Tetsujirah Obara (d).* 2/77.

***** Jellybeans**

Concord CCD 4164 *Kessel; Bob Maize (b); Jimmie Smith (d).* 4/81.

The Concord albums are all right, but a bit quiescent, and admirers of Barney's most virile playing may find they're put to sleep. The duos and trios with Byrd and Ellis offer only routine virtuosity, and his first programme of originals isn't much of an event when the accompanying band play them as politely as they do on *Plays Kessel*. *Soaring* creates some pretty music but is laid-back enough to raise itself barely above the horizontal. Much the same with *Poor Butterfly*: gentlemanly interplay between Barney and Herb, but it's something of a snooze. *Jellybeans* is the best of this lot, often due to the inventive support from Maize and Smith: when they get a groove going, as on 'Stella By Starlight', everything starts swinging.

The Storyville record catches him on a globe-trotting expedition to Japan, where two local players offer respectful support on a sometimes banal programme of ready-mades: Barney strolls through it.

***** Solo**

Concord CCD 4221 *Kessel (g solo).* 4/81.

Kessel's only solo album isolates the virtues and the vulnerabilities of his art. In an age of superfast guitarists and everyday eclectics, Kessel's simplicity and trust in his touch seem almost elemental. On a ballad like 'What Are You Doing The Rest Of Your Life?' he treats the melody like a recitalist, brushing through it, the soul of discretion. His finger technique makes you feel the physicality of the guitar, and the strumming on the up-tempo section of 'Manha De Carnaval' reminds one that he helped establish the grammar for rock'n'roll guitar, playing on some of the Coasters' classic sides. He touches on bebop almost as an aside, and one can hear him thinking back to Charlie Christian some of the time. This is the most unpretentious of solo records and, while nothing like a masterpiece, it affords much pleasure.

***** Spontaneous Combustion**
Contemporary 14033 *Kessel; Monty Alexander (p); John Clayton (b); Jeff Hamilton (d).*

*****(*) Red Hot And Blues**
Contemporary 14044 *Kessel; Kenny Barron (p); Bobby Hutcherson (vib); Rufus Reid (b); Ben Riley (d).* 88.

Poor health has curtailed Kessel's playing, and these are likely to be his farewells. The tempestuous Alexander is not an ideal partner, although at a more amiable pace the music has plenty of substance to it. *Red Hot And Blues* puts him in front of a superb band and, with Hutcherson and Barron in aristocratic form, the music teases Barney out of his shell a little on the likes of 'Barniana', while the blues themes get a timeless treatment. A great one to close on.

Keystone Trio

GROUP

Top-of-the-line piano trio, living up to its on-paper promise.

****** Heart Beats**
Milestone MCD 9256 *John Hicks (p); George Mraz (b); Idris Muhammad (d); Freddy Cole (v).* 12/95.

****** Newklear Music**
Milestone MCD 9270 *As above, except omit Cole.* 2/97.

The odd, electric-motor sound is the authors purring. This is piano-trio jazz of the very highest quality, two records which just beg to be played again and again. Hicks has his critics, some of whom condemn him for insubstantiality. This, we think, is missing the point. Almost always, he is more concerned to work within the dimensions of a song than to go off into the stratosphere. On *Heart Beats* he is admirably disciplined, relying on the exquisitely toned Mraz for counter-lines and embellishment. The opening 'Speak Low' is a *tour de force* and 'How Deep Is The Ocean?' wrings more feeling out of that rather tired song than any group we have heard in years.

As the awkwardly punning title suggests, the later record is a tribute to the music of Sonny Rollins, and a highly adventurous sampling of Newk's workbook at that: 'O.T.Y.O.G.', 'Times Slimes', 'Wynton', the inevitable 'Airegin', and others. The initial idea for the project came from session producer Todd Barkan, who is responsible for a pristine sound, and it comes to mark the great man's 25 years with the label. If people think of him as a saxophonist first and foremost and a composer only in a somewhat pragmatic sense, this is the record which may reshape that consensus. What is immediately clear is that Newk writes *songs*, not chord shapes. Hicks and Mraz intuit that and build on them gracefully. Muhammad provides the appropriate rhythmic impulse, and the results could hardly be better. The pianist signs off with 'Love Not For Sonny', a piece that bears more than a passing resemblance to his own classic 'Naima's Love Song', and none the worse for that.

Steve Khan (born 1947)

GUITAR

Born in Los Angeles, Khan arrived in New York in 1970 and did sessionman chores on both pop and jazz records. Made several fusion records in the '80s, but subsequently returned to straight-ahead guitar styles.

*****(*) Tightrope**
Columbia 496852-2 *Khan; Randy Brecker (t); David Sanborn (as); Michael Brecker (ts); David Spinozza, Jeff Mironov (g); Bob James, Don Grolnick (ky); Will Lee (b); Steve Gadd (d); Ralph McDonald (perc).* 77.

***** The Blue Man**
Columbia 496853-2 *As above, except add Rick Marotta (perc).* 78.

****** Got My Mental**
Evidence ECD 22197-2 *Khan; John Patitucci (b); Jack DeJohnette (d); Cafe (perc, v); Don Alias, Bobby Allende, Marc Quinones (perc).* 9/96.

Khan's occasional adventures in fusionland are far behind him by now, but his progress through the '80s and '90s is now hard to follow since many of his records have recently been deleted. However, Columbia have unexpectedly restored two of his earliest efforts to the catalogue. These were heady days for this kind of fusion, and the music holds up surprisingly well, particularly on *Tightrope*. Khan rounded up the princes of the New York studio gang for these sessions and, with Sanborn and both Breckers at their (comparatively) youthful best, the music has a tough urban edge to go with the top-of-the-line chopsmanship. Maybe the subsequent *The Blue Man* is a little more standardized (how quickly fusion tumbled into clichédom!) but both discs are frequently electrifying in all senses.

Khan's Verve albums have been given the axe, but his newer label has brought off his best record for years in *Got My Mental*. The nucleus of Khan, Patitucci and DeJohnette play with stunning authority. Ornette Coleman's 'R.P.D.D.' is beautifully stretched out, light yet intense. 'The Last Dance' and 'I Have Dreamed' are gorgeous ballads, the latter glimpsed through a pollen drift of percussion that seems unlikely yet works superbly. 'Paraphernalia' and 'Cunning Lee' are full-blooded jazz performances that are perfectly weighted. DeJohnette, who can often be overpowering in the studio, is at his most subtle and searching throughout and Patitucci seems twinned with the guitarist's lines. A very fine disc.

Talib Kibwe

ALTO SAXOPHONE, SOPRANO SAXOPHONE, FLUTE

Has worked with Abdullah Ibrahim and Randy Weston and spent a significant period of time in Europe, with a view to closer contact with African culture. Previous bands include Taja (a collaboration with pianist James Weidman) and T.K. Odyssey, with which he recorded more than a decade ago.

***** Introducing Talib Kibwe**

Evidence ECD 22145 *Kibwe; Benny Powell (tb); Aaron Graves, Randy Weston, Jerome Weidman (p); Lonnie Plaxico (b); Cecil Brooks III (d).* 96.

***** Another Blue**

Arkadia Jazz 70351 *Kibwe (as 'T.K. Blue'); Eddie Henderson, Tony Branker (t); Bob Ferrel (tb); James Weidman, Michael Cochrane, Onaje Allan Gumbs, Randy Weston (p); Lenny Argese (g); Santi Debriano, Calvin Hill (b); Cecil Brooks III, Greg Bufford (d); Guilherme Franco (perc).* 5/97–12/98.

Introductions are perhaps slightly overdue, for the gifted New Yorker, whose parentage is Afro-Caribbean, has been around for some time. The Evidence disc, though, was the first example of his work to receive wide distribution. It's a competent, nicely modulated set. Kibwe stamps his personality on the opening 'Is That So?', a Duke Pearson composition which is given an upbeat reading, highlighting the saxophonist's bright, slightly keening sound; think somewhere midway between Jackie McLean and Marion Brown. Brownie's 'Joyspring' is equally buoyant, and then a surprise on the first of the originals. 'Heaven Scent' is backed by a multi-tracked trombone choir, played and arranged by Benny Powell, who returns for a romp through 'Star Eyes' at the end. Kibwe shifts to flute for 'The Lady In White', and to soprano for 'Kim', not Bird's but a love song for Mrs Kibwe. One-time employer Randy Weston lopes in for a guest appearance, kicking off the perennial 'Hi Fly' with a wonderfully fresh but unexpectedly thoughtful introduction. Thereafter, what turns out to be the longest thing on the album slips into a sure-footed groove that is tremendously appealing. Plaxico is immense throughout, soloing strongly on 'Hot House' and confident enough to drop out here and there and open up the texture.

Another Blue is credited to his alias, T.K. Blue. Over the basic team of Weidman, Debriano and Brooks (the other rhythm players arrive for guest appearances), he makes a good if workmanlike second set for Arkadia. His own tunes make no great impression next to standards such as 'Solar', but the playing has enough assertiveness to take the ear even if it doesn't leave much trace behind it.

Franklin Kiermyer (born 1956)

DRUMS

Canadian drummer, starting with post-bop and '60s free stylings and moving to take in other worlds of ethnic musics too.

***** Break Down The Walls**

Konnex KCD 50444 *Kiermyer; Chris Gekker (t); John Rojak (tb); Russ Rizner (frhn); Dave Braynard (tba); Peter Madsen (p); Tony Scherr (b).*

*****(*) In The House Of My Fathers**

Konnex KCD 5052 *As above, except omit Scherr; add Dave Douglas (t), John Stubblefield (ts), Anthony Cox (b).*

*****(*) Solomon's Daughter**

Evidence ECD 22083 *Kiermyer; Pharoah Sanders (ts); John Esposito (p); Drew Gress (b).* 93.

*****(*) Kairos**

Evidence ECD 22144 *Kiermyer; Eric Person (as, ss); Sam Rivers (ss); Michael Stuart (ts, ss); John Esposito (p); Drew Gress, Dom Richards (b).* 2/95.

Someone listening to a late Coltrane group with Pharoah Sanders in the line-up said that they sounded as if they were trying to demolish Jericho; one hears the same Hebraic intensity in Albert Ayler's work. This is the musical birthright of a powerful Canadian whose interests have broadened in recent years into ritual and shamanistic musics from around the world. *Kairos* is interspersed with such oddities (in jazz terms) as Angolan circumcision rituals, rainforest Pygmy chants, M'buti Congo drums, Native-American medicine chants and Pontic Greek pipes. The basic inspiration, however, remains the New Thing of the 1960s. The two Konnexes have the turbulent horn-and-drum sound of Coltrane projects like *Ascension*, though with a much more evident melodic edge. On *Solomon's Daughter* Sanders abandons the warm ballad tones he has adopted in recent times for the shrieking fury of his 1960s work with Coltrane. It's all rather ancestral and backward-looking until, on *Kairos* with what has become his regular band, Kiermyer begins to allow more straightforwardly expressive themes to assert themselves. Eric Person's soprano solo on 'In Your Presence I Behold' is a delight, topped only by Sam Rivers's sinuous and frenzied counter-statement on the following track, 'Basheret', where he sounds as if he's playing in a pool of muffled reverb. It is testimony to Kiermyer's standing that he is able to call in players of this calibre. No recorded progress since, though.

Rebecca Kilgore

VOCAL

A former computer programmer, Kilgore took up singing part-time in 1980 and worked in and around Portland, Oregon. She now sings full-time and specializes in vintage repertory.

***** I Saw Stars**

Arbors ARCD 19136 *Kilgore; Dan Barrett (t, tb); Scott Robinson (cl, ts, bsx); Chuck Wilson (as); Dave Frishberg (p); Bucky Pizzarelli (g); Michael Moore (b).* 4/94.

*****(*) Not A Care In The World**

Arbors ARCD 19169 *Kilgore; Dave Frishberg (p); Dan Faehnle (g).* 11/95.

****** Rebecca Kilgore**

Jump JCD 12-22 *Kilgore; Dan Barrett (c, tb); Bob Reitmeier (cl, ts); Keith Ingham (p).* 10/98.

Becky Kilgore isn't a profound singer, at least not in the way we understand Billie Holiday and Sarah Vaughan to be; but she has enormous charm and a sweet control over her material that make these entries unfailingly enjoyable. The first finds her matched with one of Dan Barrett's swing groups, and they sparkle on his canny arrangements of standards and obscurities. If it all sounds a fraction precise and calculated, it must be because this kind of repertory date has become a commonplace in its craft and sunny expertise: labels like Arbors, Concord and Nagel-Heyer have done so many similar projects of late.

We prefer the duets with Frishberg (Faehnle sits in on about half of the record). Pianist and singer work regularly together and there is a free-flowing empathy between them that makes the music almost sing itself. Out of 22 songs, several of them medleyed, more than half are rarely encountered nuggets from long ago, and Kilgore's fresh voice renews their acquaintance with perfect *brio*. When she gets to a wistful one, 'Talkin' To Myself About You', it's surprisingly affecting. Frishberg proves himself again to have no peers as an accompanist.

Appropriate that the Jump CD was recorded at the Manchester Craftsmen's Guild. The music is sheer unpretentious class, as close to perfect as a repertory CD can be. Barrett and Ingham confect little arrangements for 18 songs, of which only 'Just You, Just Me' could be called even close to hackneyed, and Becky's clear, melodious voice sings through the lyrics without any trace of routine. She finds a poignancy in 'Very Good Advice' which makes one wonder why this song is so obscure, and even the cutesy 'Ain't We Got Fun' has a dignity about it. And the instrumentalists are in superb fettle.

Jonny King (born 1965)

PIANO

American contemporary pianist, sometime jazz author, and attorney-at-law.

*****(*) In From The Cold**

Criss Cross CRISS 1093 *King; Vincent Herring (as, ss); Mark Turner (ts); Ira Coleman (b); Billy Drummond (d).* 1/94.

****** Notes From The Underground**

Enja ENJ 9067 *King; Joshua Redman (ts, ss); Steve Nelson (vib); Peter Washington (b); Billy Drummond (d).* 9/95.

There are many roads to Damascus. Some people are turned on to jazz by hearing a fragment of Charlie Parker doing 'Now's The Time' drifting up from the flat below; some graduate from the wilder shores of rock music, or like to slum away from opera; others still may simply be seduced by the sinuous outlines of a saxophone. For Jonny King, it was seeing *The Sting* and hearing Joshua Rifkin's hyped-up ragtime soundtrack and meeting both Earl Hines and Teddy Wilson. Though his career has also been touched with tragedy, King seems to have got off to a blessed start.

Even now, he is a part-time jazz musician, devoting his daytime energies to the law and specializing in the increasingly knotty business of copyright. *In From the Cold* is perhaps a deliberate echo of Out Of The Blue, the New York band he joined before going up to Harvard. It's a record deeply coloured by the premature death of his girlfriend Rosanna, whose passing is the inspiration for 'Condundrum', a wise and strongly felt piece with as many twists and turns as life itself. The other strong track is the opener, 'El Jefe', a deceptively straightahead theme which, like much of King's work, disguises its subtleties.

Joshua Redman was a college friend of King's, and the pianist has played in Redman's quartet for some time. He makes a significant difference to *Notes From The Underground*, as does the addition of Steve Nelson in place of a second horn, but it's King's own playing that commands attention, highlighted much more starkly than before. The solo introduction to 'Soliloquy' is superb, and his mysterious figures on 'Gnosis' again turn a fairly conventional head into a freighted, intense meditation. Drummond, another old friend, is immaculate throughout, playing cymbals only on 'Gnosis', driving along the Afro-tinged 'Notes From The Underground'. The dominant influence on the title-track is McCoy Tyner, and King seems to have left behind his initial devotion to Mulgrew Miller, with whom he used to work out, for a more varied sampling of the modern piano canon. Impressive progress for a man who has had more commanding imperatives to deal with along the way.

Peter King (born 1940)

ALTO SAXOPHONE, SOPRANO SAXOPHONE, CLARINET

Born in Kingston, Surrey, King was still a teenager when he opened at the Ronnie Scott Club in 1959. For many years a straightforward bebopper, playing in countless bands and situations as a sideman, King has gradually taken on more recent influences and has begun to assemble a body of recorded work under his own leadership.

*****(*) East 34th Street**

Spotlite SPJ-CD 24 *King; John Horler (p); Dave Green (b); Spike Wells (d).* 1/83.

***** Brother Bernard**

Miles Music MM CD 076 *King; Guy Barker (t); Alan Skidmore (ts); John Horler (p); Dave Green (b); Martin Drew, Tony Levin (d).* 88–89.

***** Tamburello**

Miles Music MM CD 083 *King; Steve Melling (p, ky); James Hellawell (ky); Alec Dankworth (b); Stephen Keogh (d, perc).* 10/94.

King remains Britain's most eminent keeper of the bebop alto flame, although his recent work has sought wider fields and a way out of perceived restrictions. In fact, the best and most convincing music on most of the available records under his own name remains broadly in the bebop idiom.

It's good to have the Spotlite LP back in circulation. This presented King's working group of the period and is the best of four Spotlite records. If it seemed comparatively plain in its time, the resounding impact of King's playing seems more impressive at this distance. There are six originals, each just individual enough to take the context out of the ordinary, and the saxophonist's brimming virtuosity goes in tandem with an inner calm that gives the music a satisfying depth.

Brother Bernard includes extended solos on 'Overjoyed' and 'But Beautiful' which offer intensely lucid thinking on fertile melodies, but the rhythm section contribute facelessly admirable support and the guest spots by Barker and Skidmore add little except extra weight. *Tamburello* is a deal more ambitious yet doesn't hang together very well as an album. Fine improvisations on Wayne Shorter's 'Yes And No' and McCoy Tyner's 'You Taught My Heart To Sing' sit alongside a couple of diffident King originals and arrangements on Bartók and Purcell, with the final four tracks standing as a linked meditation on the death of Ayrton Senna. Touchingly effective in parts, but too much of the music is compromised by the electric keyboards. It's not that their presence is disagreeably 'modern', but that they're just not recorded or mixed with any subtlety. When King gets clear space and plays, he still sounds terrific.

***** Lush Life**

Miles Music MM CD085 *King; Gerard Presencer (t); Steve Melling, Gordon Beck (p); Steve Hamilton (ky); Jeremy Brown (b); Stephen Keogh (d); Lyric String Quartet.* 7/98.

King's own playing remains a marvellous burst of saxophone sound. But he is still searching for something which suggests a more meaningful context as far as records are concerned, and we are unconvinced by some of these settings. For a bebop disciple, it's noticeable how much King is taking on later influences: Coltrane looms large over the intense soprano improvisation on 'Ronnie's Sorrow', and the solo treatment of 'Lush Life', if a bit rehearsed in feel, is something new in his work on record. Yet it's still the straightahead burners such as 'Flying Scotsman' which carry the most pleasure. Perhaps Peter's version of 'Nefertiti', a clever paraphrase of the composer's ideas, is the track which best suggests how he might make the recorded masterpiece which he must have in him.

Colin Kingwell's Jazz Bandits

GROUP

Formed by Kingwell in 1956, this is a die-hard trad outfit and one of the few to work regularly in the London area. Current members include some long-standing veterans of the British trad scene, particularly the rhythm team of Knight and Murphy. Kingwell himself played early on with Mick Mulligan, Pat Halcox and Steve Lane.

***** Always For Pleasure**

Lake LACD59 *Dave Clennell (t, v); Colin Kingwell (tb); Rod Chambers (cl, as, v); Doug Kennedy (bj); Terry Knight (b); Malc Murphy (d, v).* 11/95.

***** Spreading A Little Happiness**

Lake LACD103 *As above, except Ian Parry (bj, g) replaces Kennedy.* 3/98.

More or less fundamentalist trad in the New Orleans manner, although never as grim as the style has sometimes been in British hands (the titles of the CDs are suitably upbeat). We slightly prefer the later of the two sets; it seems to have an ounce more spring in its step (perhaps Parry is a more forceful presence), but there's little to choose. Each has a pleasing share of unusual titles from what is clearly a capacious band-book and, while Kingwell himself is an unambitious rasper, Clennell and Chambers play inventively within their chosen styles. Recorded at The White Lion, Little Chalfont.

John Kirby (1908–52)

BASS

Joined Fletcher Henderson in 1930 and then in various bands until scoring a big hit with a small group at the Onyx Club in 1937, with Charlie Shavers and latterly vocals by Maxine Sullivan. Very successful until the '40s, then drifted into a decline which ended with his death from diabetes in California.

*****(*) John Kirby 1938–39**

Classics 750 *Kirby; Charlie Shavers (t); Buster Bailey (cl); Russell Procope (as); Billy Kyle (p); O'Neil Spencer (d, v).* 10/38–10/39.

*****(*) John Kirby 1939–41**

Classics 770 *As above.* 10/39–1/41.

They played in white ties and tails – and they often sounded that way – but the Kirby Sextet has exerted a small and subtle influence on the jazz of the 1980s and '90s, a cool, sometimes almost chill sound that was utterly unfashionable for the better part of 40 years. The original septet, led by Buster Bailey, shed a member and Kirby (a better organizer and front man, despite his instrument) was appointed leader. Many of the early arrangements are, surprisingly, credited to Charlie Shavers, and it's fascinating to hear him sound so well-mannered, both with horn and with pencil. Titles like 'Opus 5', 'Impromptu' and 'Nocturne' on the first Classics set point to classical sources and ambitions for some of the material; the earlier 'Anitra's Dance' sounds like Grieg, and there are borrowings from Schubert, Chopin ('The Minute Waltz', alas) and Dvorák elsewhere.

***** John Kirby 1941–43**

Classics 792 *Kirby; Charlie Shavers (t); Buster Bailey (cl); George Johnson, Russell Procope (as); Clyde Hart, Billy Kyle (p); Bill Beason, Specs Powell, O'Neil Spencer (d, v).* 7/41–12/43.

***** John Kirby 1941–44**

Tax CD 3714 *As above, except omit Powell; add Ben Webster (ts).* 5/41–8/44.

The Kirby group sustained a stable membership over a remarkably long span of time. This gave the group a strong if slightly formulaic identity into which outsiders fitted only rather awkwardly. For serious collectors, the Tax compilation includes some valuable radio transcriptions which are not available elsewhere and, while the sound is rather remote and there are significant drop-outs here and there, they don't entirely answer the question of how much of the material is improvised. There's no great variation to suggest that it was; only Bailey exacts a measure of freedom.

*****(*) John Kirby 1945–46**

Classics 964 *Kirby; Emmett Berry, Clarence Brereton, George Taitt (t); Buster Bailey (cl); Hilton Jefferson, George Johnson (as); Budd Johnson (ts); Billy Kyle, Ram Ramirez, Hank Jones (p); Bill Beason (d); Shirley Moore, Sarah Vaughan (v).* 4/45–9/46.

At the end of the war the Kirby band reinvented itself, with a new, fuller sound that combined some of the strengths of the old line-up, but also with a richer and darker palette. Budd Johnson's tenor is oily and intensely coloured, perfectly suited to 'Mop Mop' and 'K.C. Caboose' on the solitary 1945 session, less so to 'Passipied'. Kirby had made some V-Discs during the war, but he found his activities a little restricted at war's end. The following year began with a session backing Sarah Vaughan on four sides for Crown. She is very much the focus, and the arrangements are unusually formulaic in response; they're a little off the money on 'It Might As Well Be Spring', but Sassy more than makes up the deficit. Working from a lower league, Shirley Moore is included on two tracks from the April session, and there is also a single track ('Freedom Blues', which was done for Danish Baronet) on which the nominal leadership reverts to Buster Bailey. The final session – indeed the final date under Kirby's name – is an oddity, reworked versions of Sextet staples like 'Schubert's Serenade' and 'Sextet From Lucia', as well as the Jones/Kirby 'Ripples'. The main point of interest is the participation of Hank Jones, sounding very different indeed from his mature self.

Andy Kirk (1898–1992)

BANDLEADER, BASS SAXOPHONE, TUBA

Kirk took over Terrence Holder's Dark Clouds of Joy in 1929 and turned the band into a successful touring and recording unit, very largely dependent on the magnificent writing and arranging of Mary Lou Williams. His biggest success was with 'Until The Real Thing Comes Along' in 1936, after which the band did little more than consolidate and deliver more of the same material.

***** Andy Kirk 1929–1931**
Classics 655 *Kirk; Clouds of Joy (various personnel).* 29–31.

****** Andy Kirk 1936–1937**
Classics 573 *Kirk; Paul King, Harry Lawson, Earl Thomson, Clarence Trice (t); Ted Donnelly, Henry Wells (tb); John Harrington (cl, as, bs); John Williams (as, bs); Earl Miller (as); Dick Wilson (ts); Claude Williams (vn); Mary Lou Williams (p); Ted Brinson, Ted Robinson (g); Booker Collins (b); Ben Thigpen (d); O'Neil Spencer, Pha Terrell (v).* 3–12/36.

*****(*) Andy Kirk 1937**
Classics 581 *As above.* 2–12/37.

*****(*) Andy Kirk 1937–1938**
Classics 598 *As above.* 2–12/38.

****** Andy Kirk, 1929-1940**
ASV 14321 2 *As for the above.* 29–40.

*****(*) Kansas City Bounce**
Black & Blue 59.240 *As above, except add Harold Baker (t); Fred Robinson (tb); Edward Inge (cl, ts); Rudy Powell (as); Don Byas (ts); Floyd Smith (g); June Richmond (v).* 11/39–7/40.

***** Andy Kirk 1939–1940**
Classics 640 *As above.* 39–40.

***** Andy Kirk 1940–1942**
Classics 681 *As above.* 40–42.

***** Andy Kirk 1943-1949**
Classics 1075 *Kirk; Art Capehart, Talib Daawood, Claude Dunson, Harry Lawson, John Lynch, Howard McGhee, Fats Navarro, Fip Ricard, Clarence Trice (t); Joe Baird, Bob Murray, Wayman Richardson, Milton Robinson, Henry Wells (tb); Reuben Phillips, Ben Smith (as); Eddie Davis, Jimmy Forrest, John Harrington, J.D King, John Taylor (ts); Ed Loving, John Porter (bs); Hank Jones, Johnny Young (p); Floyd Smith (g); Lavern Baker, Booker Collins, Al Hall (b); Ben Thigpen (d); Jimmy Anderson, Bea Booze, Billy Daniels, June Richmond, Beverley White, Kenny White, Joe Williams, The Four Knights, The Jubalaires (v).* 12/43–5/49.

Though he was often out front for photo opportunities, Andy Kirk ran the Clouds of Joy strictly from the back row. The limelight was usually left to singer June Richmond or vocalist/conductor Pha Terrell; the best of the arrangements were done by Mary Lou Williams, who left the band in 1942; as a bass saxophonist, Kirk wasn't called on to take a solo. All the same, he turned the Clouds of Joy into one of the most inventive swing bands. His disposition was sunny and practical and he was a competent organizer (who in later life ran a Harlem hotel, the legendary Theresa, and organized a Musicians' Union local in New York City).

Inevitably, given Kirk's low musical profile, critical attention is more usually directed to other members of the band. The classic Clouds of Joy cuts are those that feature Mary Lou Williams's arrangements and performances, and for these the three earliest Classics compilations are essential, though many of the best tracks can be found on compilations under Williams's own name. The earlier material is still the best, with 'Moten Swing', 'Until The Real Thing Comes Along' and the hit 'Froggy Bottom' prominent. There are, though, fine performances from 1937 and 1938, most notably 'Mary's Idea' from December 1938. Sound-reproduction is reasonable if not startling.

As the lengthening chronology suggests, opportunities to record were fewer and further between in the mid- to late-1940s, though Kirk successfully negotiated the band through the draft and a recording ban. As ever, the outfit sounds like a proving ground for artists who were to make the grade on their own account in future years. Players like Fats Navarro, Howard McGhee and Jimmy Forrest enjoyed a valuable apprenticeship with Kirk. But the writing was already on the wall and gigs were becoming more sporadic. By the end of the war, the musical and commercial impetus was elsewhere and Kirk's later bandleading career was very much *ad hoc.*

Kansas City Bounce will answer most non-specialist needs. It offers a reasonable selection from arguably the most significant period of the Clouds' activity. The CEDAR noise-reduction process has made some of the louder passages a bit shrill and unnatural, but it's no worse than average for music of the period. The ASV sampler is a reasonable alternative, again with significantly better sound than the notoriously muddy and hissy Classics.

Rahsaan Roland Kirk (1936–77)

TENOR SAXOPHONE, MANZELLO, STRITCH, FLUTE, ASSORTED INSTRUMENTS

Lost his sight as an infant, and learned clarinet and sax at a blind school. Learned to play three saxophones at once, and tinkered with hybrid instruments; began recording under his own name at twenty, and worked with Charles Mingus but otherwise as a soloist-leader. Records and performances alike were extravagant carnivals of sound, often only intermittently successful, but always full of indomitable spirit. Fought back from a debilitating stroke in 1975, but a second one killed this much-loved maverick at 41.

***** Introducing Roland Kirk**
Chess 051821-2 *Kirk; Ira Sullivan (t, ts); William Burton (p, org); Don Garrett (b); Sonny Brown (d).* 6/60.

This is perhaps the first time the real Kirk can be heard on disc, the first time that his astonishing range is put to real use. With the remarkable Sullivan on hand, and with Burton providing big, raw organ chords on some tracks, the harmonic spectrum sounds far bigger than a quintet date would normally offer. The opening track is 'The Call', and it immediately identifies itself as Kirk's work, a haunting blues-derived theme with weird polytonal appendages as all three of the leader's horns are called into play. As ever, though, he varies the texture and timbre by modulating from tenor to tenor-plus-manzello to manzello alone during his solo. 'Soul Station' follows, a more straightforward blowing theme that demonstrates his credentials as a mainstream jazz musician. On 'Our Love Is Here To Stay' he opts for the manzello alone, a forlorn, emotional sound that is unlike anything or anyone else. Sullivan's trumpet feature on 'Spirit Grill' is backed by two of Kirk's horns, presumably tenor and stritch, but sounding like a whole section. The rhythm section is fairly run-of-the-mill and Burton's closing tune, 'Jack The Ripper', really isn't up to the quality of the rest of the session, a refugee from an R&B date.

***(*) **Kirk's Work**

Original Jazz Classics OJC 459 *Kirk; Jack McDuff (org); Joe Benjamin (b); Art Taylor (d).* 7/61.

'Skater's Waltz' is one of Kirk's best bits of surreal kitsch, combined with his familiar inventive ambiguity. He clearly enjoys the big, bruising sound of McDuff's electric organ and boots furiously on all three saxophones and flute. On 'Three For Dizzy' he executes difficult tempos with quite astonishing dexterity. A largely forgotten Kirk album, but one which generally deserves the classic reissue billing.

***(*) **We Free Kings**

Mercury 826455 *Kirk; Richard Wyands, Hank Jones (p); Art Davis, Wendell Marshall (b); Charli (d).* 61.

This is the first major Kirk record, and the opening 'Three For The Festival', a raucous blues, is the best evidence there is on record of his importance, even greatness. Kirk's playing is all over the place. He appears out of nowhere and stops just where you least expect him to. On 'You Did It, You Did It', he creates rhythmic patterns which defeat even Persip and moves across the chords with a bizarre crabwise motion. A wonderful record that every Kirk fan should have.

**** **Rahsaan**

Mercury 846630 10CD + bonus *Kirk; Nat Adderley, Al Derisi, Freddie Hubbard, Virgil Jones, Jimmie Maxwell, Joe Newman, Jimmy Nottingham, Ernie Royal, Clark Terry, Richard Williams, Snooky Young (t); Martin Banks (flhn); Garnett Brown, Billy Byers, Jimmy Cleveland, Paul Faulise, Curtis Fuller, Charles Greenlee, Dick Hixon, Quentin Jackson, J.J Johnson, Melba Liston, Tom McIntosh, Tom Mitchell, Santo Russo, Tony Studd, Kai Winding (tb); Ray Alonge, Jimmy Buffington, Earl Chapin, Paul Ingraham, Fred Klein, Tony Miranda, Bob Northern, Willie Ruff, Julius Watkins (frhn); Don Butterfield, Jay McAllister, Henry Phillips, Bill Stanley (tba); Benny Golson, Lucky Thompson (ts); Tubby Hayes (ts, vib); James Moody (ts, f; as 'Jimmy Gloomy'); Pepper Adams (bs); Al Cohn, Jerry Dodgion, Budd Johnson, Walt Levinsky, Romeo Penque, Seldon Powell, Jerome Richardson, Zoot Sims, Stan Webb, Frank Wess, Phil Woods (reeds); Walter Bishop Jr, Jaki Byard, Hank Jones, Wynton Kelly, Harold Mabern, Tete Montoliu, Bobby Scott, Horace Parlan, Richard Wyands (p); Andrew Hill (p, cel); Patti Brown, Lalo Schifrin, Bobby Scott (p, org); Eddie Baccus (org); Gary Burton, Milt Jackson, Bobby Moses (vib); Vincent Bell, Kenny Burrell, Mose Fowler, Jim Hall, Wayne Wright (g); Sonny Boy Williamson (hca; as 'Big Skol'); Charles McCoy (hca); Bob Cranshaw, Art Davis, Richard Davis, George Duvivier, Michael Fleming, Milt Hinton, Sam Jones, Wendell Marshall, Vernon Martin, Eddie Mathias, Don Moore, Niels-Henning Orsted Pedersen, Major Holley, Abdullah Rafik, Ben Tucker, Chris White (b); Art Blakey, Sonny Brown, George Cook, Rudy Collins, Charles Crosby, Henry Duncan, Steve Ellington, Louis Hayes, Roy Haynes, Albert 'Tootie' Heath, Osie Johnson, Elvin Jones, J.C Moses, Walter Perkins, Charli Persip, Ed Shaughnessy (d); Bill Costa, Jack Del Rio, George Devens, Charles Gomez, Phil Kraus, Montego Joe, Jose Paula, Manuel Ramos (perc); Crystal Joy Albert (v); others unidentified.* 61–64.

***(*) **Verve Jazz Masters 27**

Verve 523489-2 *As above.* 61–64.

*** **Does Your House Have Lions?**

Rhino R2 71406 2CD *Kirk; Ron Burton, Jaki Byard, Hank Jones, Charles Mingus, Trudy Pitts, Lonnie Smith, Sonelius Smith, Richard Tee (p); Ron Carter, Major Holley, Vernon Martin, Steve Novosel, Henry Pearson, Henry Metathias Pearson, Bill Salter, Doug Watkins (b); Sonny Brown, Charles Crosby, Jimmy Hopps, Oliver Jackson, James Madison, Khalil Mhridri, Bernard Purdie, Robert Shy, Harold White (d); woodwinds, strings.* 61–76.

Potential purchasers shouldn't be misled into thinking that *Rahsaan* is a 'Complete' or 'Collected' Kirk. It represents only the – admittedly marvellous – recordings he made for the Mercury label during five of his most productive years. Serious collectors will also want to have later material like *The Inflated Tear*, and a group of unpredictable Atlantics, *Volunteered Slavery*, *Rahsaan Rahsaan*, *Natural Black Invention: Roots Strata*, *Left And Right* and *Here Comes The Whistleman*.

Disc 1 of the Mercury set is a repackaging of the popular *We Free Kings* with a good alternative take of Parker's 'Blues For Alice' and an unissued 'Spring Will Be A Little Late This Year'. This is roughly the pattern observed throughout the set: alternatives have been included on merit, not (as with some Parker compilations) merely for the sake of checking matrix numbers. The other original releases are *Domino* (MG 20748, now disc 2), *Reeds And Deeds* (MG 20800, discs 3–4), *The Roland Kirk Quartet Meets The Benny Golson Orchestra* (MG 20844, now 4) where Kirk sounds quite at home in Golson's rich, Gil Evans-like arrangements; there is the live *Kirk In Copenhagen* (MG 20894, now discs 5–6, with nine unissued tracks) featuring Sonny Boy Williamson, *Gifts And Messages* (MG 20939, now disc 7), *I Talk With The Spirits* (LM 82008, now disc 8), *Rip, Rig And Panic* (LM 82027, now disc 9 – but see below), and *Slightly Latin* (LM 82033, now disc 9). In addition to an uncredited and mostly unissued 1964 session on disc 7, there are also cuts made under the leadership of Tubby Hayes, organist Eddie Baccus (one track only) and Quincy Jones.

The Jones tracks bear much the same relation to the better material as the Bird-with-strings sessions to the classic Verve small groups. Jones's advocacy – like Ramsey Lewis's – was critical to the hornman's career and helped overcome a dead-weight of industry suspicion, but the mid-market pitch was unfortunate. Eminently professional, the arrangements smooth out Kirk's eldritch sound in a way that Golson's imaginative charts don't.

Of the small groups, the *We Free Kings* session is still as fresh as paint; Kirk's mildly irreverent reworking of the Christmas carol sounds hokey at first hearing but makes increasing sense on repeated exposure, much like Thelonious Monk's 'straight' 'Abide With Me'. 'Three For The Festival' became one of his most frequently performed compositions. There are marvellous things, too, on the 1962 and 1963 sessions with Andrew Hill (his first working group) and Harold Mabern slip-anchoring sympathetic rhythm sections. Some of the real surprises come in the one-off collaboration with Tubby Hayes. Also featuring James Moody (under the contractual *nom de studio*, 'Jimmy Gloomy'), the pairing of flutes over Hayes's vibes on 'Lady "E"' is masterful. The tenor-chase effects recall 'Three For The Festival'. Elsewhere, Kirk and Moody play off against the visitor's less abstract bop style. During a superb ballad medley, Kirk attacks 'For Heaven's Sake' without a reed in his tenor saxophone; the sound is both startling and beautiful.

The live Copenhagen sessions with bluesman Williamson are credited with two bassists, Don Moore and the ubiquitous NHOP. They don't seem to play together, but it isn't always easy to pick detail out of a raucous, clubby recording which has Montoliu optimistically bashing an out-of-tune and tinny piano much as his model, Bud Powell, had to do in later years. Needless to say, Kirk remains triumphantly unfazed.

Inevitably expensive but beautifully packaged, and with an intelligently detailed booklet by critic Dan Morgenstern, *Rahsaan* nevertheless affords unparalleled detail on perhaps the most significant single phase of Kirk's career. Newcomers should certainly start elsewhere, ideally with the well-selected but inevitably very selective *Jazz Masters* set; but enthusiasts will find these ten discs (and the brief bonus 'Stritch In Time' from the 1962 Newport Festival) essential acquisitions.

The smaller *Does Your House Have Lions?* covers his recording for Atlantic and is both more selective and less richly funded in the first place. The label deliberately encouraged his more maverick side on the assumption that Kirk unfettered was the only Kirk anyone really wanted, when in fact he was an artist who, more than most, needed a sympathetic but steadying hand. As a result, these discs are patchy and sometimes downright disappointing. But Kirk is Kirk, and it would be a mistake to expect smoothly crafted mainstream jazz.

*** I Talk With The Spirits

Verve 558076-2 *Kirk; Bobby Moses (vib); Horace Parlan (p); Michael Fleming (b); Walter Perkins (d); Crystal Joy Albert (v).* 9/64.

The flute album. As Edith Kirk attests, Roland had a heavy, sometimes massive sound, often vocalized and multiphonic, that contrasted sharply with the thin, skittery voicings of players who were saxophonists first and foremost and who used the flute solely for colour. The title-track and the opening 'Serenade For A Cuckoo' are essential Kirk. The rest is fine, but rather wearisome, even over the scant 40 minutes the CD offers. Whether any more from these sessions – if indeed the tapes exist – would be welcome is very much a matter of taste.

I Talk is a fascinating exercise, as perverse and quirky as anything he ever put on tape. As a concept album, it's right up there. As a listening experience, it's a little unrelieved and shrill, but let's be clear: listening to Rahsaan playing a kettle for 40 minutes was always going to be more interesting than listening to the average jazz player on a Selmer Mark V.

*** Dog Years In The Fourth Ring

32 Jazz 32032 2CD *Kirk; Henry Rogers (bs); Ron Burton, George Gruntz, Tete Montoliu, Hilton Ruiz, Donald Smith (p); Vernon Martin, Henry Metathias Pearson, Niels-Henning Orsted Pedersen (b); Jerome Cooper, Richie Goldberg, John Goldsmith, Daniel Humair, Alex Riel, Robert Shy (d); Arthur Perry, Anthony Scott, Joe Habao Texidor (perc).* 10/63–75.

There was Dean Benedetti, and there was George Bonafacio: collectors both of live jazz music. Dean collected Charlie Parker, so obsessively that he would spare the wire when Bird was resting for a chorus. George Bonafacio showed up with a bunch of Rahsaan Roland Kirk tapes, and this generously proportioned set is testimony to his enthusiasm. Kirk live was a different proposition even from Kirk in the studio (as the item below also attests). His visit to Europe in 1964 and subsequent visits must have been an exercise in the paranormal for strait-laced jazz fans, but the 28-year-old Kirk was playing with such authority and such imagination that only the hardest of hearts could fail to be melted.

Kirk programmes Miles's 'Freddie Freeloader', Bird's 'Blues For Alice' and Horace Silver's 'Sister Sadie' alongside a brilliant version of Burt Bacharach's 'I Say A Little Prayer', which comes from later, in 1972. Disc 2 begins with an excerpt from 'Three For The Festival' from the 1964 tour, an overture to another quirky sequence of performances, highlighted by Trane's 'Giant Steps'. Also included in the set is Kirk's most singular recording, *Natural Black Inventions: Root Strata* which saw him add a weird array of devised instruments to his already wide range. It is a baroque and extravagant session. Almost entirely played solo, with just Joe Texidor on hand – and washboard – it attests to Kirk's innate musicality. The man who'd started out on rubber hose was still able to create a whole musical universe on 'black mystery pipes' and do it with an unfailing instinct for what jazz and the blues were about.

*** Gifts And Messages

Ronnie Scott's Jazz House JHAS 606 *Kirk; Stan Tracey (p); Rick Laird (b); Allan Ganley (d).* 10 & 11/64.

On the opening tune, 'Bags' Groove', Kirk shouts at Stan Tracey to 'Play them blues', something the Englishman has always done with absolute authenticity. This band was something of a gift for an American musician 'going single' through Europe. Poor Eric Dolphy, who had died in Berlin in the summer of 1964, had had to make do with much less. The understanding between group and leader was cemented by Tracey's familiarity with material like Tadd Dameron's 'On A Misty Night' and Duke's 'Come Sunday', which receives a rather short performance.

There's more emphasis on vocal devices than was usual for the time, perhaps because Kirk's lip doesn't seem to be in tip-top working order. He does a good deal of singing through the flute and on 'It Might As Well Be Spring' he pioneers the 'saxophonium', a sax without mouthpiece. The whole set is peppered with quotes, allusions and tags from other songs, sometimes punning, sometimes surreal, always absolutely musical. Not the best recording (the first in the Jazz House to use the same machine the original tapes were made on), but the music more than makes up for any technical deficiencies.

***(*) Rip, Rig And Panic / Now Please Don't You Cry, Beautiful Edith

Emarcy 832164 *Kirk; Lonnie Liston Smith, Jaki Byard (p); Ronnie Boykins, Richard Davis (b); Elvin Jones, Grady Tate (d).* 1/65, 4/67.

Now included on the Emarcy CD twofer, *Now Please Don't You Cry, Beautiful Edith* revives one of Kirk's unaccountably least-known recordings; it was his only record for Verve, made between contracts. Kirk's usual approach to schmaltz was to pepper it furiously. Brief as it is, 'Alfie' is given a half-ironic, half-respectful reading that is genuinely moving, with a typically ambiguous coda. Elsewhere, Kirk ranges from big Ellingtonian themes to out-and-out rock'n'roll.

Rip, Rig And Panic justifies single-CD release in this packaging (it's also to be found in the *Rahsaan* compilation, above) by its sheer energy and popularity (a British-based funk band named themselves after the album). The opening 'No Tonic Pres' is a tribute to Lester Young developed without definite key resolution. Like the succeeding 'From Bechet, Fats And Byas', it underlines Kirk's allusive invention and ability to make music with the most attenuated materials. Both 'Slippery, Hippery, Flippery' and the furious title-track develop Kirk's interest in 'found' or chance effects; Byard's piano playing switches between Bud Powell, the rhythmic fractures of Monk and the uncentred tonality of Cecil Taylor. Elvin Jones's drum solo on 'Rip, Rig And Panic' is one of his very best on record. On the final 'Mystical Dream', Kirk plays stritch, tenor and, incredibly, oboe at the same time, posing articulation and harmonic problems that would have sunk a less complete musician.

Fine as it is, there seems little point in going for the vinyl *Now Please Don't You Cry* unless you've already invested in the ten-CD *Rahsaan*. If not, *Rip, Rig And Panic* is a must.

*** Talkin' Verve: Roots Of Acid Jazz

Verve 533101-2 *Personnel as for Verve, Mercury and Emarcy items above.* 61–67.

A shrewd piece of marketing, aimed at a younger audience whose experience of this music is filtered through the club scene and an on-again/off-vogue for acid jazz and rare groove. The selection is pretty uncontroversial, including favourites like 'A Sack Full Of Soul', 'Theme From Peter Gunn' and the ridiculously groovey 'Dyna-Soar'. Again, anyone who owns the box set or who has a run of Polygram material won't be bothered, but a decent compilation and a fairly representative sample of what the great man is all about. Was he cool? Does it snow in Greenland?

*** Here Comes The Whistleman

Atlantic 7567 80785-2 *Kirk; Jaki Byard, Lonnie Smith (p); Major Holley (b); Charles Crosby (d).* 66.

The Inflated Tear was Roland Kirk's first studio album for Atlantic. This, though, was the result of determined coat-tugging by Kirk fans. Recorded live, it has a raw immediacy which is instantaneously beguiling. Kirk's tenor solo on 'I Wished On The Moon', which he introduces as something he used to busk with washboard players and phonebook drum at house parties, has an almost unbearable simplicity of feeling. The title-track is a more virtuoso performance, doubled on tenor and nose flute, and 'Making Love After Hours' sees him run the whole range of his horns; but by and large *Here Comes The Whistleman* gives the lie to any impression of Kirk as a gimmicky showman. Most of the horn playing is straight and unadorned, almost deliberately minimal. Of particular interest is his alto work on the closing 'Step Right Up'. At first hearing he might almost be Eddie Cleanhead Vinson: the same boppish, bluesy phrasing, but behind it a dark and almost tearful intensity of feeling. Not a classic album, but a most enjoyable representation of Kirk in a club setting, and working with a player of Byard's roots-aware sophistication.

***(*) The Inflated Tear

Rhino R2 75207 *Kirk; Ron Burton (p); Steve Novosel (b); Jimmy Hopps (d).* 5/68.

One of the finest of all Kirk's albums, his first studio cut is also one of the most contained and straightforward, establishing his gifts as an improviser beyond all contradiction. It's also now available in an enhanced digital version. The title-track relates to his blindness and conveys the dreamlike oddity and human passion of his music to perfection. The band are by no means top-drawer, but Kirk had a happy knack not just of getting the best out of players but also of subtly adapting his own delivery to the men round him. An ideal place to begin if you've never heard a note of Kirk; but prepare for surprises elsewhere. The CD sound is pretty good.

** The Case Of The Three-sided Dream In Audio Color

Atlantic 1674 *Kirk; Pat Patrick (bs); Cornell Dupree, Keith Loving, Hugh McCracken (g); Arthur Jenkins, Hilton Ruiz, Richard Tee (ky); Francisco Centeno, Henry Metathias Pearson, Bill Salter (b); Sonny Brown, Steve Gadd, John Goldsmith (d); Lawrence Killian; Ralph McDonald (perc).*

This later album is disappointing. The much-hyped *Three-sided Dream* was a self-conscious bid to bring Kirk to the attention of rock audiences. The cover-art was a good match for his surrealist approach, but the arrangements are too flabby for the imaginative suite-like approach, and the performance as a whole tumbles between two stools. Given that Kirk could almost always levitate in exactly that position, its failure is all the more galling.

*** Aces Back To Back

32 Jazz 32060 4CD *Kirk; Charles McGhee, Richard Williams (t); Dick Griffin (tb); Pepper Adams (bs); Harry Smiles (ob, eng hn); Ron Burton, Trudy Pitts, Hilton Ruiz (p); Henry Metathias Pearson (b); Selwart Clarke, Sanford Allen, Julien Barber, Gayle Dixon (vn); Al Brown (vla); Kermit Moore (clo); Gloria Agostini, Alice Coltrane (hp); Roy Haynes, Robert Shy (d); Sonny Brown (d, perc); Arthur Jenkins, Ralph MacDonald, Joe Habao Texidor (perc); Dee Dee Bridgewater, Jeanne Lee (v); strings.* 68–76.

Some fascinating material buried here, but very much a specialist collector's album. *Aces* brings together material from four Kirk records for Atlantic. *Left And Right* is mainly a strings session and far from compelling fare, but it does include 'Expansions', which has Alice Coltrane on harp, Pepper Adams on baritone and the neglected Richard Williams on trumpet. Rahsaan's solo playing on the string selections is predictably more lyrical than usual, less strident and emphatic. *Rahsaan, Rahsaan* features another distinctive band, with trombone, tuba, violin and celeste alongside a conventional rhythm section. Kirk's ability to stretch themes out and segue between harmonically unrelated material has rarely been better represented, but there is something rather desiccated about these cuts.

By 1972, Kirk was programming lots of pop tunes in his set, but *Prepare Thyself To Deal With A Miracle* concentrated on original material and included pieces like 'Saxophone Concerto' (which isn't that, whatever it is) and the lovely two-part 'Seasons', which suggest that Kirk was simultaneously exploring large-scale structures as well as standards improvisation. The remaining space on this compilation is the 1976 album, *Other Folks' Music*. It doesn't in any way stand up on its own account in terms of this discography, but these tracks offer a particular leaven to the reissue. Ruiz is as ever a strong presence, but the otherwise little-known Trudy Pitts does some fascinating work as well on both acoustic and electric piano.

Even enthusiasts tend to regard these late sessions as the wilderness years. Kirk was ill and tired, and physical disability had restricted his more baroque techniques, but the sheer feeling of his blues and the delicacy of touch he brings to ballads cannot be denied.

*****(*) Volunteered Slavery**

Rhino R2 71407 *Kirk; Charles McGhee (t); Dick Griffin (tb); Ron Burton (p); Vernon Martin (b); Charles Crosby, Sonny Brown, Jimmy Hopps (d); Joe Habao Texidor (perc); Roland Kirk Spirit Choir (v).* 7/69.

*****(*) Blacknuss**

Rhino R2 71408 *Kirk; Charles McGhee (t); Dick Griffin (tb); Richard Tee, Sonelius Smith (p); Mickey Tucker (org); Cornell Dupree, Billy Butler, Keith Loving (g); Henry Metathias Pearson, Bill Salter (b); Bernard Purdie, Khalil Mhridri (d); Richard Landrum, Joe Habao Texidor, Arthur Jenkins (perc); Cissy Houston, Princess Patience Burton (v).* 8 & 9/71.

***** (I, Eye, Aye)**

Rhino R2 72453 *Kirk; Ron Burton (p); Henry Pete Pearson (b); Robert Shy (d); Joe Habao Texidor (perc).* 6/72.

***** Bright Moments**

Rhino R2 71409 2CD *As above, except add Todd Barkan (syn, perc).* 6/73.

Blacknuss, Volunteered Slavery and *Bright Moments* are the records which brought Kirk to a wider audience in the 1970s but which maintained a degree of creative integrity that was lost on nonsense like *The Case Of The Three-sided Dream*. There were signs of failing powers even before the debilitating stroke of 1975. *Bright Moments* is disconcertingly bland (and overlong, scarcely justifying two CDs-worth) and for the first time Kirk's multi-instrumentalism began to seem a mere gimmick. Ironically, the most obvious effect of the stroke was to throw him back into much straighter playing.

He is at his best on *Volunteered Slavery*: five powerful studio tracks, followed by a set from the 1968 Newport Festival, at which Kirk played a deeply felt and touching 'Tribute To John Coltrane' before finishing with his own 'Three For The Festival'. There is nothing quite so powerful on *Blacknuss*, but it holds up triumphantly as a record. Kirk was playing a lot of pop tunes at this point. On *Blacknuss* he includes Marvin Gaye's 'What's Goin' On' and 'Mercy Mercy Me'; on *Slavery*, Burt Bacharach's 'I Say A Little Prayer' and Stevie Wonder's 'My Cherie Amour'. Though doubtless under a certain amount of pressure from the label to do so, he sounds completely comfortable with the slight change of emphasis, and throws in old spirituals and hymn tunes as well. What it essentially does is reassert the continuity of Afro-American music; to give just one example, the Cissy Houston who sings on 'Never Can Say Goodbye' and 'Blacknuss' itself is the mother of present-day pop star Whitney Houston. Some of the arrangements are a little guitar-heavy and the backbeats are decidedly uncouth, but Kirk can transcend difficulties of that sort. These are by no means peripheral to his main output.

(I, Eye, Aye) – another reference to sight and self – was recorded at the 1972 Montreux Jazz Festival, an occasion which has also been documented and released on commercial video. At this point Kirk had a young band who were responsive to his every need and forbearing enough to allow him the full glare of the spotlight. If this was jazz showmanship, the straight men were there as well. The passage from 'Balm In Gilead' to a rousing version of 'Volunteered Slavery' is one of the best of this period, and this is a record rich in period feel. For some the video version will be more entertaining, but there is more than enough strong musicianship to sustain interest on CD alone.

The remaining years were to be marked by illness and failing powers, but in the early 1970s Kirk worked tirelessly to propagate his version of 'black classical music'. This is it at its rawest and most immediate.

****(*) A Standing Eight**

32 Jazz 32479-2 2CD *Kirk; Edie Preston (t); Steve Turre (tb); Jimmy Buffington (frhn); Howard Johnson (tba); Romeo Penque (bs, ob); Kenneth Harris (f); Hilton Ruiz (p, cel); Hank Jones, Sammy Price, Richard Tee (p); Trudy Pitts (org); William S Fischer (syn, p); William Butler, Cornell Dupree, Tiny Grimes (g); Sanford Allen, Doreen Callender, Regis Iandiorio, Kathryn Kienke, Harold Kohon, Yoko Matsuo, Tony Posk (vn); Julien Barber, Alfred Brown, Selwart Clarke, Linda Lawrence (vla); Jonathan Abramowitz, Charles Fambrough, Percy Heath, Kermit Moore, Eugene Moye (clo); Phil Bowler, Gordon Edwards, Milt Hinton, Henry Metathias Pearson, Arvell Shaw, Milton Suggs, Buster Williams (b); Sonny Brown, Bill Carney, Jerry Griffin, Gifford McDonald, Jason Madison, Walter Perkins, Charli Persip (d); Fred Moore (wbd); Sonny Barkan (d, perc); Ruddley Thobodeaux, Tony Waters (perc); Warren Smith, Joe Habao Texidor (perc, v); Wilton Eaton (whistler); Adrienne Albert, Francine Caroll, Milt Grayson, Hilda Harris, Michael Hill, Randy Peyton, Maeretha Stewart, Arthur Williams (v); Betty Neals (recitation).* 76, 77, 78.

It would be naïve and pointless to claim that Kirk's very late work for Atlantic was anything other than self-pastiche. He was tired and unwell, full of spirit and capable of some very emotive single-horn playing, but he had all the signs of a man who stayed on the road to pay the bills, lacking Chet Baker's disinterest but occasionally rising to something like Chet's tragic grace.

This compilation brings together three albums: chronologically *Return Of The 5000 Pound Man*, *Kirkatron* and *Boogie-Woogie String Along For Real* – none of which would ever find themselves in anyone's A-list of Kirk's work. *Kirkatron* itself was a muddled assemblage of diverse material. By this stage, though, Kirk was much less concerned with eclectic display than with holding together the song. He makes an effective job of the staple, 'Serenade To A Cuckoo', at the Montreux Jazz Festival, but for once the studio material is more securely registered. The bands are very mixed, not so much in quality as in basic sound. By this stage in the game, simply playing with Kirk must have been regarded as a strange rite of passage and one senses not so much hostility or indifference as a polite reserve in his colleagues.

Completists will by definition want this material. Most everybody else can take it as read that Roland Kirk is better heard in other contexts. Even heroism sometimes best goes unrecorded.

Yoshiko Kishino (born 1960)

PIANO

Japanese contemporary pianist recording in America with the local talent.

*****(*) Photograph**

GRP 98842 *Kishino; Romero LuBambo (g); Marc Johnson (b); Bill Stewart, Paul Motian (d).* 3/96.

Kishino's style has been characterized as belonging to Bill Evans, but she sounds nothing like him. She has an interestingly proper, formal way with a tune's structure. *Photograph* is superior to her first record (the deleted *Fairy Tale*) and is altogether very handsomely done. 'Scarborough Fair' is an unpromising choice which she builds into an intense portrait. 'All Blues' and 'On Green Dolphin Street' are interpreted with surprising freshness. She still plays very deliberate, full-voiced lines, yet rhythmically she is prepared to create lots of space, and at times she seems to be listening to the sonorities of dying chords before moving on to the next thing. The closing 'Autumn' is a piano solo of stark, slow elegance. There's unblemished support from Johnson, Motian and Stewart, with LuBambo's gently nimble guitar a bonus on three pieces.

Ryan Kisor (born 1973)

TRUMPET

Already a veteran of New York's contemporary jazz scene, Kisor made albums for Columbia before he'd turned 21. A much-in-demand player for big-band and small-group gigs alike.

*****(*) Battle Cry**

Criss Cross 1145 *Kisor; Sam Yahel (org); Peter Bernstein (g); Brian Blade (d).* 10/97.

***** Point Of Arrival**

Criss Cross 1180 *Kisor; Justin Kisor (t); Peter Zak (p); John Webber (b); Willie Jones III (d).* 12/98.

Kisor has some of the ebullience of the young trumpet masters of hard bop yore. He doesn't have that measure of originality or capacity to surprise, but there's a kindred energy in his playing, and he has quite a personal, immediate sound. His two Columbia albums put him in more heavyweight company, but none of these guys are exactly slouches either, and if both dates are quickly organized blowing sessions, they're cultured with it. He's a schooled player, so he treats a melody such as 'Falling In Love With Love' or 'I'm Old Fashioned' with a kind of old-fashioned respect. Those are both on *Battle Cry*, which isn't quite the stormy affair suggested by the title, based around several long ballad features, but it has a lot of beguiling trumpet, and Bernstein and Yahel are excellent.

Point Of Arrival seems that bit more ordinary, a rather plain trumpet-and-rhythm outing. Kisor is always worth hearing, even on a prosaic blues such as 'Smoke Signal', but the date needs an extra spark from somewhere. Brother Justin arrives for one duet, his own 'Sir Lancelot'.

Alf Kjelling

COMPOSER

A veteran modern-mainstream saxman from Norway, Kjelling has led bands there for many years but has only rarely been sighted on record.

***** You'll Always Need Friends**

Gemini GMCD 94 *Kevin Dean (t); Frode Nymo (as); Jørn Oien (p); Harald (b); Ole Jacob Hansen (d); Inge Stangvik (v).* 8/97.

Kjelling is a saxophonist, but he didn't feel that his own playing was up to being featured on this session of his own tunes. That reticence, apparently a tonic-note in his career, also seeps into the writing, which has its charms but lacks a positive centre. Some of the charts are little more than straightforward bebop heads, and some look for a more searching quality. He has a melancholy streak which emerges frequently enough to make the ballads a bit lachrymose: but the (mostly young) group on hand plays the music with enough involvement to shed some attractive light on the raw material. Stangvik sings on two tracks, with lyrics by herself.

Miriam Klein

VOCAL

Originally from Basle, Klein began a singing career in Vienna in the late 1950s. Few of her records received international exposure, but this set, made for MPS in Munich, has been reissued on CD.

***** Ladylike**

MPS 523379-2 *Klein; Roy Eldridge (t); Slide Hampton (tb); Dexter Gordon (ts); Vince Benedetti (p); Oscar Klein (g); Isla Eckinger (b); Billy Brooks (d).* 5/73.

Klein's singing was almost irresponsibly close to that of Billie Holiday, and with this band and a set of Billie-associated tunes the illusion is close to complete. But this is still a worthwhile record. She has the dawdling phrasing, lazy vibrato and vague slur captured perfectly, but she avoids the abject pathos – and many will welcome that, at least. This was a one-off for the MPS label and the reissue revives the excellent original sound. Eldridge, Hampton and Gordon were hired guns for the occasion and all played rather well, the trumpeter in particular forgoing much of the inconsistency that marred his later work.

John Klemmer (born 1946)

TENOR AND SOPRANO SAXOPHONES, FLUTE, PIANO, VOCAL

Born in Chicago, Klemmer's conservative beginnings – working in dance bands and big bands – provide few clues to his big success with a hybrid of jazz, electronics and a prototype world-music in the early 1970s. He drifted off the scene in the '80s, and little has been heard of him since.

****(*) Priceless Jazz Collection**

GRP 059946-2 *Klemmer; Dave Grusin, Mike Nock, Mike Lang (p); Larry Carlton (g); Phil Upchurch (b); Shelly Manne, Jim Keltner (d); Victor Feldman (perc).* 67–72.

**** The Best Of John Klemmer Vol. One**

GRP 059838-2 *As above, except add Jorge D'Alto, Milcho Leviev (p), Richard Thompson (org), Oscar Castro-Neves (g), Abe Laboriel, Chuck Domanico, Bernie Fleischer (b), John Guerin, Lenny White, Harvey Mason, Morris Jenning (d), Joe Porcaro, Emil Richards, Airto Moreira, Alex Acuna, Chino Valdez (perc); omit Nock, Lang, Manne, Keltner and Feldman.* 75–78.

***** Simpatico**

JVC 9025-2 *Klemmer; Oscar Castro-Nueves (g, v). n.d.*

This pioneer of the kind of smooth-sax meandering which has become a commonplace in American radio in the 1990s has some CD representation again. Klemmer made a stack of records in that style in the '70s, and they – along with a few sessions of even earlier vintage – have been filleted for the two GRP compilations. Vaguely exotic (hence the large number of percussionists getting credits) but laden with cornball romanticism, Klemmer comes on like Gato Barbieri's soft country cousin. He blows quite fiercely at times, and *Priceless Jazz Collection* has its moments, especially on the earlier tracks where he hadn't yet patented on the successful formula. But the later stuff is more like sucking on cotton wool, and the quaint echoplex and electric-sax effects do little now except date the music. Titles such as 'My Love Has Butterfly Wings' and 'Poem Painter' tell their own story.

The series of duets with Castro-Nueves is another matter. While the guitarist provides the most basic of chordal (and hummed) accompaniments, Klemmer investigates such standards as 'My Funny Valentine' and 'Moonlight In Vermont', often going to almost baroque lengths along the way. There is an inevitable recall of Getz with Gilberto, but Klemmer's fulsome statements walk a peculiarly nervous line between rhapsody and something a lot darker and deeper. The bareness of the format palls after a while, and the dubbed-in sounds of the ocean and its attendant seagulls are an unfortunately phoney touch of New Age. Klemmer's own playing, though, is impressive in its energy and fortitude. Does this date from his commercial golden age? What is he doing now?

Goran Klinghagen (born 1955)

GUITAR

A stalwart guitarist on the modern Swedish scene, Klinghagen worked with Lars Danielsson in the early-'80s group, Time Again, and has since played with numerous different groups and soloists.

***** Time Again**

Dragon DRCD 247 *Klinghagen; David Wilczewski (ss, ts); Lars Jansson (p); Bruno Raberg (b); Magnus Gran (d).* 6/93.

The opening track, 'Include', is one of those set-pieces that linger long in the mind. After a rambling introduction, the music settles into a shifting groove in which Wilczewski's soprano picks out a melody against Klinghagen's lonesome guitar arpeggios. The record is never quite as haunting as this again, though it's an interesting showcase for the guitarist's range, from Hendrix licks to the kind of windswept impressionism that Terje Rypdal made his own 20 years earlier. Jansson guests on one track only.

***** Triometric**

Dragon DRCD 325 *Klinghagen; Christian Spering (b); Leroy Lowe (d); Lina Nyberg (v).* 12/97.

Klinghagen's second Dragon CD is much more of a group record, closely argued between himself and the superbly talented Spering in particular. Their lengthy investigation of 'Hello Young Lovers', where the bassist contributes a roving, virtuosic line, repays many listens. Lowe seems content to take a more quiescent role, but his more reserved style is just what's needed. Tonally, though, the record becomes a bit monochromatic after a while, the soft articulations a little too lulling. Nyberg comes in right at the end for a duet on 'Prelude To A Kiss'.

Eric Kloss (born 1949)

ALTO AND TENOR SAXOPHONES

Born blind, Kloss was something of a prodigy who was working as a teenager in Pittsburgh and cut his first album at sixteen. A flurry of albums in a similar flurry of styles followed, but he has not been heard from much in recent years.

*****(*) Eric Kloss And The Rhythm Section**

Prestige PRCD-24125-2 *Kloss; Chick Corea (ky); Pat Martino (g); Dave Holland (b); Jack DeJohnette (d).* 7/69–1/70.

****(*) One, Two, Free**

32 Jazz 32094 *Kloss; Ron Thomas (p); Pat Martino (g); Dave Holland (b); Ron Krasinski (d).* 8/72.

Kloss caused ripples of excitement when he arrived on the American scene in the late 1960s, but most of his ten Prestige albums have been in limbo for many years. The first CD doubles up two of them, *To Hear Is To See!* (a discreet reference to Kloss's blindness) and *Consciousness!*, both faintly reminiscent of the beatific aspirations of the day but filled with hard-edged blowing that teeters on a line between bop and the oncoming explorations of Miles Davis's electric music. Given the rhythm-section personnel, this was hardly a surprise: Holland and DeJohnette lay down some of their funkiest parts (and they're recorded rather better than they were by Teo Macero with Miles), and Corea's almost minimalist electric piano cushions the harshness of Kloss's solos. Martino arrives for the second session, which opens on the bizarre choice of Donovan's 'Sunshine Superman'. No problem, though, since the quintet pile into it, Kloss lets go with some of his greasiest licks and they almost succeed in turning it into a blues. Most of the music bumps along on this path, and perhaps the souped-up tightness palls a little in the way that some of Gene Ammons's records do, but it's a superior example of the style.

32's album reissues a Muse date by an interesting-looking group, which unfortunately labours under the pretensions of the time. The title-piece is an elephantine three-part work that goes nowhere and expends a lot of hot air doing it. Carole King's 'It's Too Late' gets a spirited workout but goes on far too long and Martino's solo is tiresome. When Kloss gets some clean air to blow in, he sounds fine, but the album is weighed down with needless stuff.

Jim Knapp

ARRANGER, COMPOSER

Californian trumpeter and arranger, here directing rather than performing.

***** On Going Home**

Sea Breeze SB-2078 *Jay Thomas, Jack Halsey (t, flhn); Brad Allison (t); Jeff Hay, Jim Christensen (tb); Karen Halsey (frhn); Hans Teuber, Mark Taylor, Rick Mandyk, Jon Goforth, Greg Metcalf (reeds); John Hansen (p); Chuck Deardorf, Doug Miller (b); John Bishop, John Wikan (d); Gary Gibson (perc).* 1/95.

Knapp is a trumpeter, but he's content here to direct and arrange an unusually literate and persuasive set of scores for this skilled team of Californians. Maybe none of the pieces especially stands out as a classic, but the sections are combined in numerous ingenious ways, the soloists – especially the excellent Thomas, whose playing has an aristocratic mien – are more than capable, and the whole has an elegance somewhat different from the familiar machine-tooled power of many West Coast big bands.

Jimmy Knepper (born 1927)

TROMBONE

Born in Los Angeles, he spent time in various big bands before going to New York and joining Charles Mingus in 1957. Injured in a contretemps with Mingus, he then worked in pit bands from 1962, returning to various jazz situations in the '60s and '70s. A considerable technician but an unassuming figure, he has a small and rather scarce discography as a leader.

***** Cunningbird**

Steeplechase SCCD 31060 *Knepper; Al Cohn (ts); Roland Hanna (p); George Mraz (b); Dannie Richmond (d).* 11/76.

***** Special Relationship**

Hep CD2012 *Knepper; Bobby Wellins (ts); Joe Temperley (bs, ts); Pete Jacobsen, Derek Smith (p); Dave Green, Michael Moore (b); Billy Hart, Ron Parry (d).* 10/78–11/80.

*****(*) I Dream Too Much**

Soul Note 121092 *Knepper; John Eckert (t); John Clark (frhn); Roland Hanna (p); George Mraz (b); Billy Hart (d).* 2–3/84.

***** Dream Dancing**

Criss Cross Jazz 1024 *Knepper; Ralph Moore (ts); Dick Katz (p); George Mraz (b); Mel Lewis (d).* 4/86.

Long associated with Charles Mingus, Knepper has an astonishingly agile technique (based on altered slide positions) which allows him to play extremely fast lines with considerable legato, more like a saxophonist than a brass player. Doing so has allowed him to avoid the dominant J.J. Johnson style and to develop the swing idiom in a direction that is thoroughly modern and contemporary, with a bright, punchy tone. A dramatic contretemps with Mingus drove him out of active jazz performance for some time, and much of the next decade was spent in the relative obscurity of recording sections and theatre work. *Cunningbird* effectively marked his renaissance as a soloist and leader. It's a strong enough album, though Knepper's tone isn't quite as assured here as it became in the 1980s, and Al Cohn is below par. Mraz's firm melodic sense makes him the ideal accompanist, but Knepper has also been shrewd or lucky in his choice of drummers. Hart has the right kind of swing and Richmond is endlessly adaptable; an initial question mark about Lewis's big sound on *Dream Dancing* resolves into an ignorable quirk of the mix, which could be rectified on what would be a welcome CD transfer. It's not quite the best of the bunch, but it's still a fine album. Ralph Moore still had some growing to do, but he didn't make the mistake of doing it in the studio, concentrating on playing within his perfectly respectable limits. The beautifully arranged brass tonalities of *I Dream Too Much* make it Knepper's most ambitious and fulfilling album. Hanna's comping is first rate throughout.

Special Relationship, as the name and personnel imply, is a transatlantic project, two quintets of respectively Americans and Brits, though Joe Temperley really falls into both categories. Bobby Wellins (strictly speaking, a Scot) is the star turn here. His tone is as airy as ever and his soloing on 'Round About Midnight' and 'Latterday Saint' underlines once again what a loss his absences from the scene always were. Knepper plays against him with great delicacy and control, reserving his more expansive gestures for the sessions with an engagingly gruff and even impatient-sounding Temperley.

Jonas Knutsson

SOPRANO, ALTO, TENOR AND BARITONE SAXOPHONES, PERCUSSION

Contemporary Swedish saxophonist, primarily a soprano player, touching on other musics at least as often as jazz.

***** Views**

Caprice CAP 21426 *Knutsson; Lars Lindgren (t, flhn); Mikael Raberg (tb); Joakim Milder (ss); Jan Levander (as); Johan Soderqvist, Mats Oberg (ky); Anders Persson (p); Per Westerlund, Max Schultz, Hakan Wyoni (g); Olle Steinholtz, Christian Spering (b); Magnus Gran, Martin Lofgren, Michael Hedenquist (d); Bengt Berger, Rafael Sida (perc); Lena Willemark (v).* 1–2/92.

***** Lust**

Caprice CAP 21459 *Knutsson; Mats Oberg (ky, hca); Hakan Wyoni (g, perc); Mikael Berglund (b); Michael Hedenquist (d); Rafael Sida (perc).* 9/94.

***** Flower In The Sky**

ACT 9248-2 *As above, except add Johan Soderqvist (ky), Anders Persson (p), Christian Spering (b), Magnus Gran (d), Lena Willemark (v).* 1/92–9/94.

Knutsson's is a kind of digital folk music. His themes and arrangements suggest an ancient Swedish strain – and there are three traditional tunes on the second record and two on the third – but the timbre of the music is modern, electric and high on texture. His main instrument is soprano sax and he uses it as a piper might, chanting elegant melodies against a backdrop of keyboards, resonant electric bass and occasional other horns: the first track on *Views* finds him alongside Milder, Levander, Lindgren and Raberg in a bracing swirl of voices. But his own writing tends towards an impressionism that goes soft some of the time. The only other memorable piece on the first disc is the lovely duet with Oberg's piano and bubbling synthesizer on 'Vadring'; elsewhere, Knutsson relies heavily on programmatic effects.

The second set is more of a fusion-band session, even settling into a little gentle funk on 'Loff', although it's the more restrained and songful pieces, like the mildly affecting 'Hymn', which linger longest in the mind. *Flower In The Sky* puts together a compilation of tracks from the first two records, though it scarcely stands as a best-of, since some of the most interesting pieces are absent.

***** Malgomaj**

Atrium 0630-17710-2 *Knutsson; Ulrik Dahl (flhn); Stephan Jonsson, Thomas Hulten (tb); Per Sjöberg (tba); Johan Soderqvist (ky); Ale Möller (mand); Monica Ramos (hp); Tomas Gustafsson, Jennie Sandborg (vn); Jakob Rutberg (vla); Magnus Ekenborn, Johanna Sjunesson (clo); Anders Löfgren, Christian Spering (b); Jonas Sjoblom (perc).* 96.

Knutsson goes deeper into an imaginary world-music, with 14 pieces that seem like lightning flashes on a Nordic past, present and future. His piercing soprano (with occasional excursions into baritone sax) is the constant, and it's paired with harp, a string section, a brass team, percussion. Each episode is a little glittering world of its own, but as a record the album unfolds like a travel brochure, moving quickly on before a mood or a musical result is really given time to settle. Not so far removed from what a musician such as Garbarek has set out to achieve, but he takes his time – Knutsson seems unnecessarily impatient.

Hans Koch

SAXOPHONES, CLARINETS

Similar in configuration to the Clusone 3, but very different in conception, the Swiss reedman's long-standing trio with cellist Schutz and percussionist Studer generates a rich amalgam of jazz, classical and folk forms. Koch's saxophone sound is slightly raw and unfinished, but always profoundly evocative.

**** Acceleration**

ECM 833473-2 *Koch; Martin Schutz (b, clo); Marco Käppeli (d).* 6/87.

****** Uluru**

Intakt CD 014 *Koch (solo).* 1/89.

****** Duets, Dithyrambisch**

FMP CD 19/20 *Koch; Louis Sclavis (ss, bcl); Evan Parker (ts); Wolfgang Fuchs (sno, cbcl).* 7/89.

In the fullness of time, Koch will be recognized as one of the most significant and certainly one of the most adventurous improvisers on the European scene. Until the appearance of the utterly marvellous *Uluru*, Koch was heard to best advantage on the FMP record, *Duets, Dithyrambisch*, with Evan Parker and Louis Sclavis. The Englishman is, of course, a completely intuitive and sympathetic partner, but Sclavis also has things to say for himself, and Koch revels in the moment. On the 1989 record he creates a bewildering variety of voices with his three horns. 'Whirly Bird' and 'Tongue Salad' are both virtuosic, but there are more accessible things as well. There is some harsh, interesting music on the well-named *Acceleration*. Schutz and Käppeli play a subsidiary but highly interactive role: on the ECM album, against some ponderous improvising by Koch on a variety of horns, they work up a vivid rhythm partnership. But the programming of that album, with dreary interludes such as the clarinet solo on 'Loisada', lets it down.

***** Chockshut**

Intakt CD 031 *Koch; Andreas Marti (tb); Martin Schutz (clo); Jacques Demierre (p); Stephan Wittwer (g); Fredy Studer (d, perc).* 12/91.

*****(*) Hardcore Chambermusic**

Intakt CD 042 *As above, except omit Martin, Demierre, Wittwer.* 10/94.

****** Heavy Cairo Traffic**

Intuition INT 3175-2 *As above, except add El Nil Troop.* 95.

***** Fidel**

Intakt CD 056 *As above, except add Musicos Cubanos.* 3 & 4/97.

*****(*) With DJ M. Singe and DJ I. Sound**

Intakt CD 062 *As above, except add DJ M. Singe, DJ I. Sound (turntables).* 99.

Koch, Schutz and Studer take on all-comers; they are among the most fearless and welcoming collaborators in European jazz. The boldest association is the encounter with El Nil Troop on *Heavy Cairo Traffic*, a haunting musical soundtrack that draws inspirations from Sun Ra to Grace Jones and which is invested with the passionate improvisational spirit of the great Omm Kholsoum.

'Belly Button Rave' and the Sun Ra-dedicated title-track are great jazz, and there are moments on 'Vice Versa' which recall Herbie Hancock at his most extreme ... in the days when Herbie flirted with extremes. The mix is heavy with found sounds and overlaid vocal and horn lines from the members of El Nil Troop. Live, this must be an awesome conjunction, and it's almost as powerful on record.

The Cuban album is a disappointment by comparison, a messy, sprawling postcard from another culture that never quite rises above its own limited premisses. Episodically, it sounds gorgeous, but there's little cohesion and it's a hard album to absorb other than in fragments. Perhaps the best place to start, and before plunging into the dense sound-world of *Heavy Cairo Traffic*, is the trio performance on *Hardcore Chambermusic*, on which the individual contributions of the three members is most straightforwardly evident. Koch's squalling, fervid saxophone harks back to an early age in European free jazz, but he is also aware of how and what that idiom took from other disciplines and he makes an entirely convincing synthesis. He is responsible for all compositions except the closing 'Airglow' and 'Megalith', which seem to be spontaneously created, and his use of samplers and sequencers generates much of the background ambience.

Chockshut is more straightforwardly instrumental, but Koch uses the harmonic range of the 'shadow' trio to create a spacious background of effects which is more open-textured than the electronics-laden vistas of *Hardcore* and *Heavy Cairo Traffic* but no less effective. Something of its energy is carried over into the recent trio set with DJs, a logical step for Koch and the trio and a highly effective one. 'Thai Speed Parade' is a nervy, twittering thing, built round an insistent pulse which seems to be the dominant metre for the album as a whole. Other tracks are less compelling and mostly a touch overlong, but the eight tracks are packed with musical ideas.

Franz Koglmann (born 1946)

TRUMPET, FLUGELHORN

The Austrian trumpeter believes that jazz, as an active and developing genre, is dead. This doesn't rule out – indeed, the example of Bach and the Baroque suggests the opposite – that great jazz may still be created, but that it now requires to move in new directions. Koglmann's own work is a quiet, understated hybrid of classic jazz and classical modernism.

*****(*) We Thought About Duke**

hatOLOGY 543 *Koglmann; Rudolf Ruschel (tb); Raoul Herget (tba); Lee Konitz (as); Tony Coe (cl, ts); Burkhard Stangl (g); Klaus Koch (b).* 6/94.

***** Make Believe**

Between The Lines btl 001 *Koglmann; Tom Varner (frhn); Tony Coe (ts, cl, v); Brad Shepik (g); Peter Herbert (b).* 11/98–99.

*****(*) An Affair With Strauss**

Between The Lines btl 006 *As above.* 6/99.

Until the end of the '90s and the formation of his own label, Between The Lines, Koglmann's recorded output was exclusively on the hat ART label. With the deletion of its 6000 series, almost all of the trumpeter's records have disappeared and only the Ellington tribute, which has Konitz as co-leader, has survived the transition to the new hatOLOGY imprint. The saxophonist has worked in very similar territory – cool to abstract – over recent years and he sounds like a soulmate, albeit better adjusted, to the so-called Monoblue Quartet of Koglmann, Coe, Stangl and Koch than to the stripped-down Pipe Trio who are credited with the other five tracks. Koglmann contributes three original compositions under the generic heading, 'Thoughts About Duke', and otherwise explores the less familiar reaches of the Ducal canon. 'Dirge' and 'Zweet Zurzday' bear the counter-signature of Billy Strayhorn and 'Pyramid' is a Tizol tune; otherwise, it's 'Lament For Javanette', 'Ko-Ko', 'Love In My Heart' and 'The Mooche'. All are beautifully played and atmospheric, as you'd expect by now.

The first releases on Koglmann's new label continue the project of recent years and the work with hat ART. *Make Believe* is a quiet and thoughtful set, not easily assimilated at first hearing. Koglmann has cited writer and film-maker Jean Cocteau before, but *Make Believe* is a series of meditations on the Frenchman's classic *Les Enfants Terribles.* It represents an attempt to demonstrate by musical means 'the hidden world of dreams, the intoxication of fantasy and the artificial reality of life in closed spaces'. As such, it succeeds pretty well. Koglmann, Coe and Varner evoke a world of claustrophobic intimacy. As ever, it is a world governed by rules and forms, but also prey to irruptions from elsewhere, slashed across by the opium nightmares and sudden estrangements of Shepik's effects-laden guitar. An instrumental 'Interlude', led by Coe in his Pink Panther mode, seems to lead out into a more brightly lit world, but then 'Rue Montmartre' (home to Elisabeth, Agathe, Paul and Gérard) re-establishes the mood of threat and existential danger. Set as *faux*-rock, it bears just one instruction to the players, the simple, devastating 'Stupid'. Rarely has he allowed players even the freedom to be dumb. This is certainly the least predetermined and written-out project Koglmann has released. In addition to the material based on *Les Enfants Terribles*, there is a new appearance of an old Koglmann composition, 'Der Vogel', and, as a final tag, a flugelhorn interpretation of a rare Cocteau poem written in German, 'Blut', a dark, suave lullaby with a hint of menace under the midnight blue. *An Affair With Strauss* again imaginatively hybridizes classical procedures and standards jazz in a way that sparks new ideas. Coe is, as ever, such a brilliant technician with such a remarkably poised and focused tone that he dominates proceedings; and yet Koglmann, always a slightly diffident player, asserts himself more completely on 'A Metropolitan Affair' and 'Out Of Strauss' than he ever has before. The remaining members of the group are also highly responsive to Koglmann's needs and the whole project is sophisticated and very aware.

Eero Koivistoinen (born 1941)

TENOR SAXOPHONE

One of a richly talented generation of Finnish horn players, Koivistoinen studied at Berklee in the early '70s when already an accomplished and distinctive player. His recorded output is relatively small but of a consistently high standard.

***** Picture In Three Colors**

Core Records/Line COCD 9.00515 *Koivistoinen; Tom Harrell (t, flhn); John Scofield (g); Jim McNeely (p); Ron McClure (b); Jack DeJohnette (d).* 10/83.

***** Altered Things**

Timeless SJP CD 367 *Koivistoinen; Randy Brecker (t); Conrad Herwig (tb); John Scofield (g); David Kikoski (p); Bugge Wesseltoft (syn); Ron McClure (b); Jack DeJohnette (b).* 9/91.

Koivistoinen has a pungent, spicy tone that is deceptively 'American' in accent. His kinship with the dominant Garbarek approach is only incidental and he veers towards a free style that dispenses with orthodox changes. The line-ups alone are a virtual guarantee of quality on these. DeJohnette is relaxed and attentive to the spaces in Koivistoinen's impressive charts, creating abstract figurations within the basic sequence. Harrell has rarely sounded more haunted than he does on *Picture* but is in excellent voice, and Brecker is only a rather one-dimensional replacement. The only quibble is the co-presence of McNeely and Scofield. Given the nature of the music, it might have been preferable to dispense with a keyboard instrument and rely more heavily on the less formalized chording and high accents of the guitarist who is replacing John Abercrombie as the player of choice for this kind of gig. Sco makes a big impact on the second record, but without theatricals. He's rarely been so contained and subtle, and the whole set is very much lighter in touch than its predecessor, though this may also have something to do with the first-rate production.

***** Sometime Ago**

A Records AL 73139 *Koivistoinen; Seppo Kantonen (p); Severi Pyysalo (mar); Jesper Lundgaard, Ron McClure (b); Jeff Hirshfield (d).* 10/92–10/94.

Koivistoinen has always been an attractive ballad-player, but this is the first time he has made a whole album of slower and mainly standard tunes. The sessions involved three separate units, all of them anchored on Kantonen. Trio X is completed by Severi Pyysalo on marimba, a warm and responsive sound that works wonderfully on the title-piece and on the only original 'Relation'. Koivistoinen concentrates on soprano for both these tunes, spreading the sound as broadly as possible. The quartet with McClure and Hirshfield revives an association that goes all the way back to Berklee days. 'Where Are You' begins the album with an authoritative tenor solo, very clean-lined and uncomplicated. 'Every Time We Say Goodbye' is masterly, with some detailed interplay between saxophone and bass. The third group is a drummerless trio with Lundgaard, similar in conception to Trio X but more boppish in conception. They do a version of Duke Pearson's 'You Know I Care' and Kurt Weill's 'My Ship'. Rounding out the album, two Monk compositions, 'Monk's Mood' and 'Crepuscule With Nellie', the latter played as a straight melody without soloing, bringing to an end an impressively varied and textured album.

*****(*) Dialog**

L + R CDLR 45094 *Koivistoinen; Anders Bergcrantz (t); Seppo Kantonen (p); Jesper Lundgaard (b); Leroy Lowe (d).* 1/94.

On *Dialog*, Koivistoinen shares the honours with trumpeter Bergcrantz, an agile enough player whose real ace is a big rich tone that sits beautifully with saxophone. On the evidence of 'Home', 'Sinuhe' and 'All Those Dreams', he also writes well. The (nominal) leader takes a more relaxed attitude on this date, lying back a bit and easing into solos with a conversational quality that is as attractive as it is unexpected. The rhythm section, anchored on Lowe, who looks as though he might have considered pro basketball as an alternative, is solid through and through. The only problem is Kantonen's tendency to use every good idea at least three times, as if we might have misheard.

Krzysztof Komeda (1931–69)

PIANO

Komeda is the Lost Leader of Polish jazz. A brilliant composer rather than a virtuosic player, he remained better known in the West for film scores like Knife In The Water and Rosemary's Baby for his friend, Roman Polanski. Komeda's death remains mysterious but recent years have seen him emerge from an almost conspiratorial cult to wider and more intelligent appreciation.

****(*) Volume 1: Ballet Etudes / Breakfast At Tiffany's**

Power Bros PB 00155 *Komeda; Tomasz Stankon (t); Eje Thelin (tb); Zbigniew Namyslowski (as); Michal Urbaniak (ts); Jerzy Lesicki (f); Janusz Sidorenko (g); Roman Dylag, Jacek Ostaszewski (b); Rune Carlsson, Adam Jedrzejowski (d); Wanda Warska (v).* 10/62, 1/63.

***** Volume 2: Memory Of Bach**

Power Bros PB 00157 *Komeda; Tomasz Stankon (t); Zbigniew Namyslowski (as); Michal Urbaniak, Jan Ptaszyn Wroblewski (ts); Jerzy Milian (vib); Roman Dylag, Jozef Stolarz, Maciej Suzin (b); Czeslaw Bartkowski, Rune Carlsson, Jan Zybler (d).* 56–67.

***** Volume 3: Nightime, Daytime Requiem**

Power Bros PB 0159 *Komeda; Tomasz Stankon (t); Zbigniew Namyslowski (as); Roman Dylag (b); Rune Carlsson (d).* 11/67.

***** Volume 4: Moja Ballada**

Power Bros PB 0161 *Komeda; Tomasz Stankon (t); Michal Urbaniak (ts); Adam Skorupka, Maciej Suzin (b); Czeslaw Bartkowski, Adam Zielinski (d); other personnel.* 11/61, 67.

♛ ** Volume 5: Astigmatic**

Power Bros 00163 *Komeda; Tomasz Stankon (t); Zbigniew Namyslowski (as); Günter Lenz (b); Rune Carlsson (d).* 12/65.

****** Volume 6: Crazy Girl**

Power Bros PB 00165 *Komeda; Bernt Rosengren (ts); Roman Dylag (b); Leszek Dudziak, Adam Skorupka, A Zielinski (d).* 60, 61.

***** Volume 7: Sophia's Tune**

Power Bros PB 00167 *Komeda; Tomasz Stankon (t); Michal Urbaniak (sax); Bo Stief (b); Simon Kopel (d).* 65.

***** Volume 8: Roman Two**

Power Bros PB 00169 *As above.* 65.

***** Volume 9: What's Up Mr Basie?**

Power Bros PB 00171 *As above, except omit Stief, Kopel; add Maciej Suzin (b), Czeslaw Bartkowski (d).* 63.

***(*) **Volume 10: Astigmatic In Concert**

Power Bros PB 0173 *Komeda; Tomasz Stankon (t); Michal Urbaniak (ts); Janusz Kizlowski, Bo Stief (b); Rune Carlsson, Simon Kopel (d).* 65.

***(*) **Knife In The Water**

Power Bros PB 00175 *Komeda; other musicians unidentified.* 57–62.

Komeda was born Trzcinski and trained as an ear, nose and throat specialist. He changed his name to avoid the attentions of both the political and medical authorities, neither of whom would have taken kindly to his extracurricular activities; later, in America, he was to anglicize his first name to Christopher. In 1956 he made his musical debut at a small, semi-official jazz festival at the coastal town of Sopot in Poland, the forerunner to the now annual Jazz Jamboree in Warsaw. In 1960 he recorded a standards album with Adam Skorupka and Andrzej Zielinski.

The following year Komeda wrote the music for *Knife In The Water*, using the gifted Swedish saxophonist, Rosengren, who reappears in wonderful form on *Crazy Girl*. The title-piece became a favourite concert-piece and is included in a rather rambling version on the Copenhagen live set. It also includes disappointingly lax interpretations of themes from his masterpiece, *Astigmatic*, which in our view (now reinforced by expert remastering) is not just one of the best Polish or European jazz records, but quite simply one of the best jazz records, full stop. Komeda was at the height of his powers when he made the disc in 1965 and he had with him a sympathetic and highly gifted group of young Poles, including trumpeter Stanko, then making his professional debut. 'Kattorna' and 'Svantetic' are both highly original, combining jazz tonality with folk and classical idioms; however, it is 'Astigmatic' itself, a swirling, multi-part suite with a skewed, elusive quality, that represents his masterpiece. There is not so very much solo space devoted to Komeda himself and it is one of the ironies of his career that his importance is less as a performer than as a composer and catalyst.

The second soloist, Zbigniew Namyslowski, was replaced on the Scandinavian tour by Michal Urbaniak, who was then still playing saxophone. The Danish tapes were released by Komeda's widow to mark the 25th anniversary of his death. In our last edition, all that was generally available of Komeda's work was the mighty *Astigmatic* and these very unsatisfactory live sessions. The initiative did, though, spark off a major reassessment and reissue of his work, a digitally remastered Komeda edition with excerpts from an extended interview with Zofia Komeda included on each handsomely packaged disc. The best of the music from the live Copenhagen set – a cracking reading of 'Svantetic' – is incorporated into other discs in the sequence – notably *Sophia's Tune* and *Roman Two* – and it demonstrates how Komeda's working band handled the *Astigmatic* material out on the road. Unfortunately the tape quality is diabolical, with extraneous noise and unignorable dropouts. In addition, Urbaniak is playing poorly, leaving Stanko again to carry much of the weight of the music, which he does with characteristic fire. And yet there is no mistaking either the quality of the music or its jazz fire.

The series – which is not chronological – begins with a set of ballet studies Komeda made for an experimental troupe at Cracow Engineering College, together with a score for a theatre production of Truman Capote's *Breakfast At Tiffany's*. Both suggest a musician with a clear but idiosyncratic understanding of American jazz, and also a composer with a wonderful gift for suggestive musical drama. Some of that comes out again on Volume 11, where the famous score for *Knife In The Water*, a chillingly effective piece of writing, is paired with soundtracks for two avant-garde films, *Two Men And A Wardrobe* and *When Angels Fall*. These discs and *Memory Of Bach* bracket the series very effectively indeed, offering the clearest possible picture of Komeda as a composer whose early style was delineated by swing, the Baroque and silent movies.

Memory Of Bach includes material written for Komeda's Sopot debut and the title-track is the original version of an important piece for the composer, one that established him as an original, albeit respectful voice. In addition to the title-track, the record includes one of the Copenhagen tracks, a version of 'Crazy Girl', one of the tunes on *Knife In The Water*. For comparison, there is an earlier version from the Sopot Jazz Festival in 1961 (*Crazy Girl*, Volume 6); this is an important disc because it offers early and alternative readings of key pieces – 'Moja Ballada' is another – and because it also offers a glimpse of Komeda playing a standard, two very different versions a year apart, of 'Stella By Starlight'. 'Crazy Girl' was a dedication to Zofia, who emerges as the composer's muse. 'Sophia's Tune' appears in another slice of the Copenhagen concert on Volume 7. The remainder occupies the whole of *Roman Two*. The sound is still appalling, the quality of music unexceptionable.

'Nighttime, Daytime Requiem' on the album of that name is a good example of Komeda's otherworldly impressionism. This is unmistakably the composer of the film music, a musician with a keen but maverick sense of structure. Mood almost always dictates the dimensions and pace of a piece and subtly invests the harmonic language as well. For once it is easy to pick out his further debt to Polish Romanticism.

What's Up Mr Basie? is the Komeda set from the 1963 Warsaw Jazz Jamboree, the gathering which evolved out of Sopot and which is now the world's longest continuously running jazz festival. The group is by now a familiar one. Stanko, who later felt snubbed by the festival organizers, is in cracking form, and the only pity is that the piano is so far back in the mix, not at all true to the balance of the group.

Which leaves *Astigmatic*, in both studio and live forms. We cannot recommend this record highly enough and we envy anyone who can come to it fresh, ideally with no prior knowledge or expectations of Komeda. It is a record that never fails to repay close attention, but one that has an engrossing emotional physicality. Stanko's tone is lustrous and intense and the great Namyslowski projects his complex bop-derived lines in phrases that link together like pieces of DNA into living wholes. One misses him on the live version, where again the spotlight falls on Stanko. As ever, Komeda is a presence and a unifying element rather than a commanding soloist. The studio sound favours his rather unemphatic touch, and he certainly had a better piano in Warsaw than on the road – though, listening to it again, we wonder if the instrument wasn't perhaps tuned a little dark. Deliberately? There is no indication that tape speed is the problem, but it raises the interesting possibility that Komeda was already experimenting with the kind of detuning and pure sound that would resurface on *Rosemary's Baby*. The soundtrack album to that still-frightening film can probably be found in good film music sections and in specialist stores; it merits comparison with these records. It also hints at the tragic aura that seemed to hang round

Polanski and his circle. Scarcely was Komeda established in Hollywood than he was brought home to Poland in an irreversible coma. The exact circumstances have never been clear, but even without conspiracy theories and a whiff of martyrdom his death was to be a symbolic moment in the assimilation of jazz in Eastern Europe. Whether he would have succumbed to the lure of Hollywood or whether the embryo of another *Astigmatic* perished with him can never be known. What is certain is that he created one permanent masterwork.

Jan Erik Kongshaug

GUITAR

Internationally renowned as an engineer, mainly through his work for ECM, he also plays guitar, as here.

***** The Other World**
ACT9267-2 *Kongshaug; Svein Olav Herstad (p); Harald Johnsen (b); Per Oddvar Johansen (d).* 4 & 6/98.

If the name seems familiar, but not quite familiar in this context, then let us tell you that *The Other World* was recorded at the Rainbow Studio and that guitarist, producer and engineer are all one and the same fellow. Responsible for working the faders on literally dozens of sessions for ECM and other labels at the Oslo studio, Kongshaug now steps briefly into the limelight himself.

Over the years he has continued to perform club dates and the occasional studio session, but this is the first time he has put together a group to record his own material. It's a set shrewdly sandwiched with standards, from the opening 'If I Should Lose You', which establishes his bouncy, clean-cut attack, to Rollins's 'Airegin', Brubeck's 'In Your Own Sweet Way', and a delicate reading of 'Like Someone In Love'. Jan Erik's own writing won't melt any glaciers, but 'Mina's Waltz', 'Going West', 'July First' and the title-track all bespeak a comfortable facility for melody, while the closing 'When I Met You' is genuinely affecting.

The trio is well drilled and rather precise. A slightly rougher delivery probably wouldn't have done the album any harm, but how likely was it that Mr Kongshaug was going to settle for a run-down and a first take?

Klaus König (born 1959)

TROMBONE, COMPOSER, CONDUCTOR

A remarkable, intricate musician of great originality, König studied classical composition and trombone, and he worked with Mauricio Kagel before turning to modern jazz. He founded his orchestra in 1989. Somewhat like Kip Hanrahan, he is an auteur rather than a conventional composer.

***** Times Of Devastation / Poco A Poco**
Enja ENJ 6014 2CD *König; Kenny Wheeler, Reiner Winterschladen (t, flhn); Ray Anderson, Bruce Collings (tb); Frank Struck (frhn); Michel Godard (tba); Marty Ehrlich (cl, bcl, as); Frank Gratkowski (f, bcl, as, ss); Mathias Schubert (ts, ob); Renato Cordovani, Michel Pilz (bcl); Simon Nabatov (p); Tim Wells (b); John Betsch, Frank Kollges (d).* 6/89.

***** At The End Of The Universe: Hommage A Douglas Adams**
Enja ENJ 6078 *König; Kenny Wheeler, Reiner Winterschladen (t); Conrad Bauer (tb); Horst Grabosch (frhn); Michel Massot (tba); Louis Sclavis (cl); Jane Ira Bloom (ss); Frank Gratkowski (as, f); Mathias Schubert (ts, ob); Wollie Kaiser (bs); Simon Nabatov (p); Dieter Manderschied, Tim Wells (b); John Betsch, Tom Rainey (d).* 3/91.

*****(*) Song Of Songs**
Enja 7057 *König; Reiner Winterschladen (t); Herb Robertson (t, flhn); Bruce Collings, Jorg Huke (tb); Michel Godard (tba); James Newton (f); Frank Gratkowski (ss, as, f, bcl); Michael Moore (cl, as); Mathias Schubert (ts, ob); Wollie Kaiser (bsx, cbcl); Marc Ducret (g); Simon Nabatov (p); Mark Dresser (b); Tom Rainey (d); Jay Clayton, Phil Minton, Montreal Jubilation Gospel Choir (v).* 11/92.

****** Time Fragments**
Enja ENJ 8076 *König; Reiner Winterschladen (t); Kenny Wheeler (t, flhn); Jorg Huke (tb); Michel Godard (tba); Frank Gratkowski (as, ss, f); Mathias Schubert (ts, ob); Wollie Kaiser (ss, bcl); Robert Dick (f, picc); Mark Feldman (vn); Stefan Bauer (mar); Mark Dresser (b); Gerry Hemingway (d).* 5/94.

***** Reviews**
Enja 9061 *König; Reiner Winterschladen (t); John D'Earth (t, flhn); Ray Anderson, Jorg Huke (tb); Michel Massot (tba); Claudio Puntin (cl); Frank Gratkowski (as, f, picc); Mathias Schubert (ts); Wollie Kaiser (ts, ss, bsx, cbcl); Mark Feldman (vn); Markus Wienstroer (g, bj, vn); Dieter Manderschied (b); Gerry Hemingway (d); David Moss, Joe Bob Finetti, Richard Bob Greene, Janie Bob Scott, Matthew Bob Stull (v).* 9–10/95.

The individual sections of *Time Fragments* are dedicated to some of Klaus König's heroes, past and present: Alban Berg and Charles Mingus, Thelonious Monk and Béla Bartók, Igor Stravinsky and Anthony Braxton, Duke Ellington and Charles Ives, Henry Threadgill and Gustav Mahler, Scott Joplin and Maurice Ravel. Pausing only to wonder what Threadgill and the Gloomy Gus of classical music might find to talk about, mix and serve.

These are remarkable records, conceived and confected by a genuine original. König's charts are multi-layered, poly-stylistic and densely detailed. The Braxton/Stravinsky/Ellington/Ives axes are probably the most helpful to an understanding of what is going on. There is a kind of neo-classical purity to the overall conception of what König describes as a cycle, now completed by a piece originally to be called *Reviews Reviewed Revue*, but going out under the more modest version listed above. There is also a hint of Braxton's open-ended jazz codes and of Ives's wonderful compression of tunes-from-unusual-angles. In terms of orchestration and *dramatis personae*, Duke is the significant forebear. Everything is written with a player in mind. The opening piece on *Time Fragments* has a wonderfully idiomatic solo for Michel Godard's tuba. It retrospectively establishes the parameters of the sound-world that is still chaotic and unshaped on *Times Of Devastation*. The first of the bunch is, properly, the weakest, an occasionally hesitant prolegomenon to the main action, though the hesitation is the players' and not the composer's.

At The End Of The Universe may be the weakest of the bunch, not because it is ostensibly tied to Douglas Adams's irritating stories or because the playing is off, which it isn't, but because the overall logic of the album fails to cohere as the others do with increasing confidence and definiteness. *Song Of Songs* also has an underlying programme, and the presence of a gospel choir gives the biblical subtext additional impact. The really successful piece, though, is *Time Fragments*, a marvellous (literal) romp through jazz and 'straight' styles. For once, a CD booklet actually turns out to be useful. A graphic schema of the piece really does help make sense of its overlapping layers, and it folds out to reveal a beautifully shot mini-poster of the band in action. The expression on Gerry Hemingway's face as he looks at the composer/conductor is worth a thousand words. And this is a man who played for Anthony Braxton night after night. Challenging, adventurous music; a little chill and formal for some tastes, but full of meat.

Reviews is the most skittish and satirical of the sequence. Dedicated to the spirit of Frank Zappa, its basic premiss is one that inevitably must give the present writers some pause: that the language of criticism is formulaic, repetitive, reductive, and so on, basic artists' chants against the evils of *Uberkritik*. (No more formulaic, repetitive, etc., we say, than what some musicians try to get away with in the name of art; but that's from another day.) Moss is the sonorous narrator, supported by The Bobs, and the libretto consists very largely of lines and tags pulled from press reviews of the earlier pieces in the cycle. There is, as ever, a varied and playful score, and plenty of solo space for the likes of Hemingway, Kaiser and Manderschied. It's difficult to get a purchase on something as heavily ironic and there is a risk of being too po-faced reviewing the revue of the reviews. The playing is accurate, highly drilled and, once again, a little chill. A Zappa dedication should somehow have more of a whiff of anarchy, and arguably more of an eye to the market.

***** The H.E.A.R.T. Project**

Enja ENJ 9338-2 *König; Claus Stötter (t, flhn); Frank Gratkowski (as, cl); Claudius Valk (ss, ts, f); Werner Neumann, Markus Weinstroer (g); Dieter Manderschied (b); Thomas Alkier (d).* 12/97.

Following the conclusion of his great orchestra project, König returned to the kind of octet he'd run with great success in the '80s and which was then known as Pinguin Liquid. The new band is effectively an orchestra in miniature, the two guitarists weaving complex polyphonic lines and the four horns often pushing off in quite different directions.

Perhaps surprisingly, König emerges as a quite significant trombone player, reminiscent of Albert Mangelsdorff in his ability to appropriate and naturalize many different styles, but thoroughly idiomatic and free of the saxophone-influenced voicings that most 'bone players seem to have opted for. The writing is as challenging as ever, and in Stötter and Gratkowski he has two interpreters who rise to every challenge. A promising new direction after the rigours of the '90s suites.

Lee Konitz (born 1927)

ALTO SAXOPHONE, SOPRANO SAXOPHONE

The redoubtable Chicagoan worked with Miles Davis but came under the influence of Lennie Tristano quite early in his career, thereby avoiding the overdetermining sound of Charlie Parker on the alto saxophone. Along with tenorist Warne Marsh, Konitz created the definitive cool saxophone sound. He was out of active music-making for some years, but came back and increasingly – but entirely at his own pace – assimilated bebop to his personal style. He also flirted with the avant-garde and has dabbled in free improvisation as well as harmonic jazz. Konitz has been a prodigal recording artist, with a huge number of records to his name, many of them on very small labels.Even three years after the release of Anthony Braxton's ground-breaking For Alto, solo saxophone performance was still considered a radical strategy. Konitz's unaccompanied treatment of just two standards – 'Cherokee' and 'The Song Is You' – contains some of his very best playing. Smooth legato passages are interspersed with harsher, almost percussive sections in which his pads snap down impatiently on the note. There are few if any hints of the free playing he essayed during a thoroughly unexpected collaboration with Derek Bailey's improvising collective, Company, in 1987; but there is a further dimension of freedom in his playing on the record that is rarely encountered elsewhere in his work. Even so, nowhere does he lose contact with the source material, which is transformed with a robust logic that never degenerates into pointless noodling. Recording quality is unexceptional and the CD sounds rather metallic.

*****(*) Subconscious-Lee**

Original Jazz Classics OJC 186 *Konitz; Warne Marsh (ts); Sal Mosca, Lennie Tristano (p); Billy Bauer (g); Arnold Fishkind (b); Denzil Best, Shelly Manne, Jeff Morton (d).* 1/49–4/50.

***** Jazz At Storyville**

Black Lion BCD 760901 *Konitz; Ronnie Ball (p); Percy Heath (b); Al Levitt (d).* 1/54.

***** In Harvard Square**

Black Lion BLCD 760928 *As above, except add Peter Ind (b), Jeff Morton (d).* 4/54, 2/55.

****(*) Konitz**

Black Lion BLCD 760922 *As above, except omit Heath and Levitt.* 8/54.

Most of the more casual generalizations about Lee Konitz – cool, abstract, passionless, untouched by bebop – were last relevant about 40 years ago. A stint in the Stan Kenton band, the musical equivalent of Marine Corps boot camp, toughened up his articulation and led him steadily away from the long, rather diffuse lines of his early years under the influence of Lennie Tristano, towards an altogether more pluralistic and emotionally cadenced approach. Astonishingly, Konitz spent a good many of what should have been his most productive years in relative limbo, teaching when he should have been playing, unrecognized by critics, unsigned by all but small European labels (on which he is, admittedly, prodigal). Despite (or because of) his isolation, Konitz has routinely exposed himself over the years in the most ruthlessly unpredictable musical settings, thriving on any challenge, constantly modifying his direction.

Subconscious-Lee brings together material made under Lennie Tristano's leadership in January 1949, with quartet and quintet tracks made a few months later, featuring the wonderful Warne Marsh on the anything but redundant 'Tautology' and four other numbers. The remaining group material with Mosca and Bauer is less compelling (and certainly not as good as the 1951 sessions with Miles Davis on the deleted *Ezz-thetic*), but there is a fine duo with the guitarist on 'Rebecca' which anticipates some of the saxophonist's later intimacies.

Konitz is a useful reminder of how the saxophonist sounded on demob from the Kenton orchestra. Multiple cuts of 'Mean To Me', 'Bop Goes The Leesel' (ouch!) and 'Nursery Rhyme' show to what extent he'd already reached an accommodation with some of the more intractable lessons of bebop and how far behind he'd left his initial thrall to Lennie Tristano. Morton and Ind are too mannerly even for this company. The *Storyville* band has some of the edge Konitz thrives on. 'Lee' puns abound in the track titles but 'These Foolish Things' and 'Foolin' Myself' are both first rate.

In Harvard Square, issued in 1996, fills out the story with seven tracks from April 1954 and three from the following spring, longer and more adventurous improvisations on 'If I Had You', 'Foolin' Myself' and the original 'Ablution'. Of these, the first is titanic, a great slab of music with little finesse or grace beyond the weaving, endless line of the saxophone part. In a story so punctuated with frustrating gaps, any additional material is welcome, and this reissue adds considerably, if without controversy, to a key period in the saxophonist's career.

*****(*) From Newport To Nice**

Philology W 65 *Konitz; Warne Marsh (ts); Russ Freeman, Roland Kovac, Misha Mengelberg, Jimmy Rowles (p); Jimmy Raney, Johnny Smith, René Thomas, Attila Zoller (g); Frank Carroll, Bob Carter, Johnny Fischer, Henry Grimes, Rob Langereis, Red Mitchell, Barre Phillips (b); Han Bennink, Buzzy Drootin, Don Lamond, Ed Levinson, Shelly Manne, Stu Martin, Rudi Sehring (d).* 7/55–7/80.

An odd but very valuable compilation of festival appearances from Newport in 1955 to the Grande Parade in the south of France 25 years later. The style has undergone some significant changes, of course, but it's less noticeable than one might expect. He's perfectly full-voiced on 'Two Not One' with Marsh at Newport, and he's perfectly capable of sounding dry and abstract when it suits his purpose in later years. Outstanding tracks? A long 'Lover Man' from Turin in 1978, with Jimmy Rowles in support, and a devilishly subtle and ironic 'All The Things You Are' with René Thomas, Misha Mengelberg and Han Bennink (the Low Countries Mafia) in 1965.

*****(*) The Lee Konitz Duets**

Original Jazz Classics OJC 466 *Konitz, with Marshall Brown (vtb, euph); Joe Henderson, Richie Kamuca (ts); Dick Katz (p); Karl Berger (vib); Jim Hall (g); Ray Nance (vn); Eddie Gomez (b); Elvin Jones (d).* 9/67.

****** I Concentrate On You**

Steeplechase SCCD 1018 *Konitz; Red Mitchell (b, p).* 6/74.

*****(*) Windows**

Steeplechase SCCD 31057 *Konitz; Hal Galper (p).* 77.

****(*) Once Upon A Line**

Musidisc 500162 *Konitz; Harold Danko (p).* 6/90.

Improvising duets fall somewhere between the intimacies of a private dinner and the disciplines of the boxing ring. If there are minor embarrassments in being overheard with, so to speak, the emotional gloves off, that's nothing to being caught out by a sudden rhythmic jab or harmonic cross from your partner; there's no band waiting in the corner. In a very real sense, the duo is Konitz's natural constituency. Perhaps only fellow alto saxophonist Marion Brown gets near him for sheer quality in a demanding setting that perfectly suits Konitz's balancing of almost conversational affability with a gimlet sharpness of thought.

On the 1967 record, Konitz comes on like a cross between an all-comers' booth boxer and a taxi dancer: a lover, not a fighter. The album pivots on five versions of the classic duo piece, 'Alone Together'; the first is solo, the next three are duets with Karl Berger, Eddie Gomez and Elvin Jones (with whom he made the marvellous *Motion*), culminating in a fine quartet reading. The pairings with saxophonists Joe Henderson ('You Don't Know What Love Is') and Richie Kamuca ('Tickle Toe'), and with trombonist Marshall Brown are astonishing, as far as possible from the comforting horn-plus-rhythm options, most of them refused, of the tracks with Dick Katz, Jim Hall and even Ellingtonian Ray Nance (who plays his 'second' instrument). It all culminates in a fine, all-in nonet, an intriguing numerical anticipation of one of Konitz's best later bands.

Hal Galper's lush, velvety backgrounds inspire some of Konitz's most lapidary performances. There is very little harmonic tension in the pianist's approach, in contrast to Red Mitchell (on either double bass or piano), and the result is to focus Konitz very much on the tune rather than on its changes. That is particularly noticeable on 'Stella By Starlight'. Each man has one (improvised) solo slot; Konitz's 'Soliloquy' is a lean, unself-indulgent exercise in low-fat improvisation and, as such, an illustration of the album's considerable strengths; Galper's 'Villainesque' is exactly the opposite, clotted like some multilayered Viennese confection.

The duos with Harold Danko are more assured, but they suggest a polished concert performance rather than the more exploratory intrigues that Konitz foments with one-off partners, as if sounding them out and challenging them to try something different, come across to his bit of turf. 'Hi, Beck', based on the chords of 'Pennies From Heaven', has become an established set-opener, perhaps too familiar now to Konitz-watchers to reveal all the finessing he does on the top line. Danko is an adequate partner but a desperately unexciting one; it's by no means the only instance of Konitz playing well in less than challenging contexts.

The Cole Porter readings with Red Mitchell explore equally familiar territory, but as if by night. Konitz clearly enjoys this kind of dead-reckoning performance and steers through the chords with finely tuned instinct. He also seems to like the extremes of pitch he gets opposite the notoriously straight-backed Mitchell, a man who prefers to play bass-as-bass, and it's a pity that the saxophonist wasn't currently toting a soprano instrument as well. Minor quibbles can't detract from the unfailing quality of the performances, which are absolutely top-notch. An essential Konitz album.

*****(*) Jazz A Juan**

Steeplechase SCCD 1072 *Konitz; Martial Solal (p); Niels-Henning Orsted Pedersen (b); Daniel Humair (d).* 7/74.

Top-of-the-range standards jazz by a marvellously Esperantist quartet. Solal is one of the great harmonists, with the ability to find anomalous areas of space within the most restrictively familiar themes; his statement and subsequent excursions on 'Round About Midnight' are typical of his innate resistance to cliché.

NHOP is the Terry Waite of jazz: big and bearded; willing to go anywhere; able to communicate in almost any company; a reconciler of opposites, gentle, but with a hard centre. His low notes behind 'Autumn Leaves' merit at least one listen with the 125-Hz slide on the graphic equalizer up at +10 and the rest zeroed. Konitz sounds relaxed and easy, flurrying breathy top notes and leaving space round the brighter middle register.

*****(*) Lone-Lee**

Steeplechase SCCD 31035 *Konitz solo.* 8/74.

Even three years after the release of Anthony Braxton's ground-breaking *For Alto*, solo saxophone performance was still considered a radical strategy. Konitz's unaccompanied treatment of just two standards – 'Cherokee' and 'The Song Is You' – contains some of his very best playing. Smooth *legato* passages are interspersed with harsher, almost percussive sections in which his pads snap down impatiently on the note. There are few if any hints of the free playing he essayed during a thoroughly unexpected collaboration with Derek Bailey's improvising collective, Company, in 1987; but there is a further dimension of freedom in his playing on the record that is rarely encountered elsewhere in his work. Even so, nowhere does he lose contact with the source material, which is transformed with a robust logic that never degenerates into pointless noodling. Recording quality is unexceptional and the CD sounds rather metallic.

****** Satori**

Original Jazz Classics OJCCD 958 *Konitz; Dick Katz, Martial Solal (p); Dave Holland (b); Jack DeJohnette (d).* 9/74.

Long out of circulation, this was the last of four important albums Konitz made for the Milestone label. With a top-flight rhythm-section who had seen service with Miles Davis, he dips a toe into rock-influenced free funk, adding producer Dick Katz on second (electric) piano on the long title-track. Solal also uses a Fender Rhodes on 'Sometime Ago', a rare chance to hear him flirt with technology, and a not entirely happy blend. The mix of material is determined by the instincts of the group, not just the leader. 'What's New' and the closing 'Free Blues' are geared to Holland in particular and he makes a sterling job of yoking together sometimes incompatible elements. DeJohnette strains at the leash, clearly wanting to inject more power and pace than the session calls for, but never for a moment breaking the bounds of taste. A most welcome reappearance in what is now an impressive output.

***** Yes Yes Nonet**

Steeplechase SCCD 31119 *Konitz; Tom Harrell (t, flhn); John Eckert (t, picc t, flhn); Jimmy Knepper (tb); Sam Burtis (btb, tba); Ronnie Cuber (bs, cl); Harold Danko (p); Buster Williams (b); Billy Hart (d).* 8/79.

****(*) Live At Laren**

Soul Note 121069 *Konitz; Red Rodney (t, flhn); John Eckert (t, picc t, flhn); Jimmy Knepper (tb); Sam Burtis (btb, tba); Ronnie Cuber (bs, cl); Ben Aronov (p, electric p); Harold Danko (p); Ray Drummond (b); Billy Hart (d).* 8/79.

The Nonet was one of Konitz's more successful larger groups. The brass settings were well ventilated and open-textured and Konitz soloed confidently, often oblivious to the constraints of metre. The Steeplechase is the better of the two (though the title is unforgivable), largely because Harrell sounds more sympathetic to Konitz's own conception; Wayne Shorter's 'Footprints' is the outstanding cut. On *Live At Laren*, generally a good concert rendering, the saxophonist rather too generously accommodates Rodney's rather backward-looking bop manner with what occasionally sound – on 'April' and 'Moon Dreams' – like pastiches of himself.

***** Dovetail**

Sunnyside 1003 *Konitz; Harold Danko (p); Jay Leonhart (b).* 2/83.

How a 'terzet' differs from a trio isn't clear, though we'd argue that the geometry of this set is very different from the average jazz threesome. Rhythm duties are distributed round the group and, particularly on tunes like 'Alone Together' (a Konitz favourite) and 'Cherokee', it is hard to differentiate between melodic, harmonic and time-keeping roles. Delightful stuff.

*****(*) Art Of The Duo**

Enja ENJ 5059 *Konitz; Albert Mangelsdorff (tb).* 6/83.

It's a pity that Konitz hadn't made the soprano saxophone a routine part of his travel-kit at this point. There's a slight lack of variation in pitching on these fascinating tracks, and there is certainly a tendency for Mangelsdorff to cleave to the same range as his partner. The pieces range from brief, song-form duets to more antagonistic and searching confrontations in which Konitz's acerbic wit and the trombonist's dry romanticism clash fruitfully.

*****(*) Dedicated To Lee**

Dragon DRCD 250 *Konitz; Jan Allan (t); Gustavo Bergalli (t, flhn); Torgny Nilsson (tb); Hector Bingert (ts); Gunnar Bergsten (bs); Lars Sjøsten (p); Lars Lundstrom (b); Egil Johansen (d).* 11/83.

A decade before this session, Konitz had played on one of the last studio sessions by Lars Gullin. Though the great Swedish baritonist, who died in 1976, is widely acknowledged as one of the best European players of his day, his compositional output is still very little known. Hence the happy idea of putting Konitz together with Lars Sjøsten's octet and a group of Gullin pieces. Sjøsten was Gullin's regular accompanist during the last decade-and-a-half of his career, and he knows this material inside out. 'Dedicated To Lee' and 'Late Date' had actually been written for Konitz 30 years before, when the two saxophonists recorded in Stockholm; the originals are included on a Gullin composition issued by Dragon. The immediate reaction to these tracks is that Gullin was a deceptively simple melodist. Pieces like 'Fine Together' and 'Happy Again' may be generic, and might have been written by any one of a dozen American song-writers, but 'Peter Of April' (dedicated to his son) is a subtle and masterful conception that is very difficult to reduce to its essential parts. A couple of pieces have been reconstructed from piano scores, which partly explains the inclusion of Jan Allan, a guest spot in thanks for bringing in the chart for 'Peter Of April'. Anyone who hasn't made Lars Gullin's acquaintance would be well advised to start sampling the Dragon discs (see above), but this is a very worthwhile piece on its own account, and the combination of Gullin and Konitz is, as ever, irresistible.

****** Wild As Springtime**

Candid CCD 79734 *Konitz; Harold Danko (p).* 3/84.

Recorded in Glasgow by Elliot Meadow, this pairs Konitz with his most responsive accompanist of the '80s. The big plus on this carefully mastered CD issue is an unreleased track, 'It's You', and two alternatives, Chick Corea's 'Hairy Canary' and George Russell's classic 'Ezz-thetic', his elaborate contrafact on the changes to 'Love For Sale'. This is the territory Konitz loves, and his own 'Hi, Beck', which is mined from 'Pennies From Heaven' takes on a startling new profile in this version. Meadow's liner-note makes it clear that the session wasn't just a tired souvenier of what had been a long tour but a patiently crafted and very thoughtful session. Including 'Hairy Canary' is certainly a sign that they weren't coasting; it's certainly a very different Corea from the wistful composer of 'Duende', also represented here, and the release take is certainly a couple of degrees more accomplished and polished than the rejected one. Danko weighs in with a couple of typical themes, both dance-based: 'Silly Samba' is an invitation to Konitz to step and slide away on one of his fugitive lines, while 'Spinning Waltz', a Danko favourite, is delicately woven out of the lightest of materials. Perhaps the best place to judge the empathy between these two remarkable players is the spontaneously composed 'Ko', its title derived from the first two letters of the saxophonist's name and the last two of the pianist's. Hard to believe that no element of this exquisite performance was predetermined; Danko sweeps the open strings of the piano, creating a shimmering backdrop to one of Konitz's most formally perfect off-the-cuff statements. Utterly delightful from start to finish.

***** Ideal Scene**

Soul Note 121119 *Konitz; Harold Danko (p); Rufus Reid (b); Al Harewood (d).* 7/86.

***** The New York Album**

Soul Note 121169 *Konitz; Harold Danko (p); Marc Johnson (b); Adam Nussbaum (d).* 8/87.

Danko's exact chording and fine grasp of durations on *Ideal Scene* open up the challenging spaces of George Russell's 'Ezz-thetic' and the more familiar, but inexhaustible, 'Stella By Starlight'. He is more conventional but no less inventive on *The New York Album*. Constant duo performance tended to reinforce Konitz's early preference for very long, unpunctuated lines. Working with a band as closely attentive as both of these allows him to break up his development and give it an emotional directness which is reminiscent – in mood if not always in tonality – of the blues. Johnson's and Reid's moody delivery, and Nussbaum's almost casual two-fours on the later album, reinforce the slightly darker sound – 'Limehouse Blues' included! Hard to choose between them.

***** Medium Rare**

Label Bleu LBLC 6501 *Konitz; Dominique Cravic (g); Francis Varis (acc); Hélène Labarrière (b); Jean-Claude Jouy (d).* 86.

Positively undercooked in places, but there's enough juicy substance from the mid-point 'Monk's Mood' onwards to keep eyes on the plate. 'Ezz-thetic' is marvellous again, one of the most imaginative covers the piece has ever received; 'Chick Came Round' also reappears from *Ideal Scene* (and is worth a brief comparison); and Dominique Cravic's three originals (notably the name-checking 'Blue Label', with its fine intro from Hélène Labarrière) are all excellent. The accordion functions very differently from a piano or even a vibraphone in the mix, keeping the harmonies from tightening up, laying on areas of colour, accentuating a softly shuffling rhythm. Konitz ranges between alto and soprano saxophones, with a tight clarinet sound in the higher registers which is exactly right for this company. Unusual and fine.

*****(*) 12 Gershwin In 12 Keys**

Philology W 312 *Konitz; Franco D'Andrea (p).* 12/88.

Exactly what it says it is. A round dozen Gershwin tunes in all the keys from A round to A♭, again with, tacked on, another Gershwin medley also recorded live, this time at Massalombarda. The Vicenza concert is utterly fascinating. Apparently the format was decided (by Konitz) at a pre-gig meal. Listening to Konitz drill his way through the familiar melodies, it's clearly the piano player who is having to think ahead, and he doesn't seem to know 'Our Love Is Here To Stay' or 'Love Walked In' as well as the rest, but D'Andrea has a secure technique and doesn't sound fazed. Something funny happens in 'But Not For Me'. Nominally in E♭, it starts somewhere else and finishes up nowhere in particular, in an odd version of the atonal exercises Konitz must have done all those years ago with Lennie Tristano. A splendid disc, all the same.

***** Blew**

Philology W 26 *Konitz; Enrico Pieranunzi (p); Enzo Pietropaoli (b); Alfred Kramer (d).* 3/88.

A studio recording by the have-sax-will-travel Konitz and the highly professional Space Jazz Trio. The set has the feel of one put together in rather a hurry, though it seems to have followed a short residency at Rome's Big Mama club. Pieranunzi's 'From E To C' sounds a little like a back-of-envelope run-down (though the pianist plays it with great conviction and development) and the two standards at the end sound as if they have been tacked on *faute de mieux*. Konitz's tone is sharp and resonant, and very well captured by producer Piangiarelli.

***** Solitudes**

Philology W 28 *Konitz; Enrico Pieranunzi (p).*

In contrast with his earlier performances with Pieranunzi's Space Jazz Trio, Konitz plays with a rather thin detachment that doesn't quite fit in with the Italian's very proper phrasing and tight rhythmic control. Konitz almost sounds as if he has gone back to a version of the Lester Young-influenced cool he espoused at the beginning of his career. It would be interesting to hear him do it in a rather more promising context than this.

*****(*) Zounds**

Soul Note 121219 *Konitz: Kenny Werner (p, ky); Ron McClure (b); Bill Stewart (d).* 5/90.

Konitz continues to surprise with three remarkable free improvisations on which he abandons chord changes, conventional melody and straightforward rhythmic computations in favour of an exploration of pure sound. These tracks are interspersed with two staple items ('Prelude To A Kiss' and 'Taking A Chance On Love'), an original samba and the astonishing 14-minute 'All Things Considered', which sounds like a summation of what

Konitz has been doing for the last 25 years. The whole set has a freewheeling, spontaneous feel that confirms the saxophonist's status as one of the most original players on the scene. As a free player, Konitz has well-attested credentials, having worked in unscripted formats with Lennie Tristano, four decades before his surprise inclusion in Derek Bailey's Company collective for 1987. 'Synthesthetics' is a set of duets over Werner's highly individual synthesizer lines (an individual player, he brings a doom-laden atmosphere even to the Ellington tune); Konitz vocalizes with surprising self-confidence. His soprano saxophone playing on 'Soft Lee' is probably the best he's yet committed to record. Werner and McClure are both magnificent, but there has to be a slight hesitation over Bill Stewart, who seems to fall in and out of synch with the music, overcompensating furiously when a more regular groove is re-established. Otherwise absolutely sterling.

*****(*) Lullaby Of Birdland**
Candid CCD 79709 *Konitz; Barry Harris (p); Calvin Hill (b); Leroy Williams (d).* 9/91.

As with *Jazz Nocturne*, below, this is valuable for showing Konitz on home turf and with a front-rank *jazz* accompanist. Harris plays the changes immaculately, eschewing fancy modulations and non-canonical key-changes. If it sounds boringly conventional, it ain't. Both men are at the top of their craft, and the solos on a totally standards-based programme are packed with invention. Konitz's solo on 'Cherokee' even manages to squeeze in a couple of Ornette phrases, just as he inverts a Parker idea, stretching out its metre in the process, on 'Anthropology'. The only quibbles about *Lullaby Of Birdland* concern the rhythm section, who are either playing too loud or else have been badly balanced in Mark Morganelli's final mix. Otherwise, hard to fault.

***** Friends**
Dragon DRCD 240 *Konitz; Gunnar Bergsten (bs); Lars Sjøsten (p); Peter Soderblom (b); Nils Danell (d).* 12/91.

The performances of two Lars Gullin compositions – 'Lars Meets Jeff' and 'Happy Again' – suggest that Konitz may have been studying the great Swede's records, since he quotes from original solos in a couple of places. This sort of gig is now pretty run-of-the-mill for him, but there's never a moment when the attention seems to flag or waver. Sjøsten's quartet is highly professional and very musical, and the permutation of alto/soprano with baritone saxophone works delightfully.

***** Lunasea**
Soul Note 121249 *Konitz; Peggy Stern (p); Vic Juris (g); Harvie Swartz (b); Jeff Williams (d); Guilherme Franco (perc).* 1/92.

Stern's a gutsy, uncomplicated player with a very individual delivery that somehow recalls Tommy Flanagan. Konitz clearly enjoys the settings Stern and Juris lay out, for he plays with great freedom and relaxation, compressing ideas into short, slightly enigmatic, solo statements that frequently drift outside the confines of the song in question. Swartz and Williams keep things securely moored, but Franco is mixed up way too loud and his busy percussion intrudes more than once.

***** Leewise**
Storyville STCD 4181 *Konitz; Jeff Davis (t); Allan Botschinsky (t, flhn); Erling Kroner (tb); Niels Gerhardt (btb, tba); Jens Sondergaard (ss, as, bs); Peter Gullin (ts, bs); Butch Lacy, Peggy Stern (p); Jesper Lundgaard (b); Svend-Erik Norregaard (d); Brigitte Frieboe (v).* 3/92.

Konitz was the 1992 winner of the prestigious Jazzpar Prize, an accolade which brings with it the opportunity to record with a hand-picked Danish group. Only the first three tracks – 'Partout', 'Alone Together' and 'Body And Soul' – were recorded at the Jazzpar concert. The All-Star Nonet, directed by Jens Sondergaard, is exemplarily professional but lacks a little in relaxed expressiveness. As probably befits a celebratory event, the emphasis is on playing rather than on ground-breaking new material. There are a couple of more improvisatory duets, with saxophonist Sondergaard and with Botschinsky, but these are less focused than usual, even a little casual and bland.

*****(*) Jazz Nocturne**
Evidence ECD 22085 *Konitz; Kenny Barron (p); James Genus (b); Kenny Washington (d).* 10/92.

Great to hear Konitz in a straight jazz context and in such a good band. Though his younger European collaborators deserve every credit and respect for their musicianship, these are the saxophonist's peers – Barron at least – and this is the kind of music where his gifts are best deployed. It's entirely a standards session: 'Misty', 'Body And Soul', 'You'd Be So Nice To Come Home To', 'Everything Happens To Me', 'Alone Together', 'In A Sentimental Mood'. Impeccably played and engineered with taste and discretion by Peter Beckerman, who's managed to iron out some shaky moments with discreet edits (or so it sounds on a very careful listen). All of the material was laid down in a day, but it does sound as if the studio was rearranged at least once; Genus certainly moves in the mix.

*****(*) So Many Stars**
Philology W 45 *Konitz; Stefano Battaglia (p); Tiziana Ghiglioni (v).* 11/92.

Chet Baker's spirit rests heavily on this strangely intense vocal set. Much care has been taken in the *construction* of the record – much more, certainly, than on the average small-label session. The saxophonist's second-take solos on the title-track and 'O Cantador' have been grafted on to the first complete takes, making composite pieces. There are two gorgeous takes of 'My Funny Valentine' (a jazz anthem in Italy), with totally different inflexions by Ghiglioni and Battaglia, and a superb reading of 'It Never Entered My Mind' which in addition pays homage to Miles. Konitz sounds brassier than usual, leaving the floatier lines to Ghiglioni, who gets better every time she records.

***** The Jobim Collection**
Philology W 68 *Konitz; Peggy Stern (p, syn).* 1/93.

Elegantly crafted and typically individual readings of 14 Jobim songs, of which the majority are likely to be unfamiliar to all but bossa nova collectors. 'Corcovado', 'How Insensitive' and 'The Girl From Ipanema' are all included and given just enough spin to rescue them from banality. The saxophonist's attachment to Stern makes more sense each time they record, but she is still a rather enigmatic player, as likely as he is to throw something unexpected into the mix. Her synth work is very expressive.

***** A Venezia**

Philology W 53 *Konitz; Paolo Fazio, Marlon Nather, David Boato (t); Giuseppe Calamosca, Dario Prisco, Umberto De Nigris, Roberto Rossi (tb); Massimiliano Tonello (tba); Piero Cozzi, Euro Michelazzi (as); Massimo Spiro, Massimo Parpagiola (ts); Michele Magnifichi (bs); Tatiana Marian, Carolina Casciani (cl); Roberto Rossetti (bcl); Stefano Benini, Loris Trevisan, Margherita Mesirca, Giuliana Cravin (f); Paolo Birro (p); Walter Lucano, Sandro Gibellini (g); Lello Gnesutta (b); Davide Ragazzoni (d); Renzo Zulian (v).* 3/93.

***** Free With Lee**

Philology W 46 *Konitz; Augusto Mancinelli, Danny Mixon (g).* 3/93.

The first finds Konitz in a Venetian television studio with the Suono Improvviso big band and a hatful of originals by director Giannantonio De Vicenzo, Marco Castelli and Paolo Birro. It's very much an honoured-guest role (he solos on all but three of the tracks) and he doesn't sound as comfortably across the charts as some of the young Italians, who play with uniform precision. Trombonist Rossi establishes his presence from the word go, and he is perhaps the most compelling voice on the set, though Castelli's soprano (on the opening number again and on De Vicenzo's 'Eros Detritus') has a quiet forcefulness that recalls the younger Steve Lacy. A great deal of emphasis is placed on the flutes and Benini has a prominent part, coming in behind Konitz on the long 'Solo Sogni'. Not strictly a part of Lee's own discography, but it's always good to see him working with musicians of a generation he helped to foster. His sponsorship of Mancinelli and Mixon at this stage in their respective careers is also interesting. Working as a trio and as two duos, they run down some demanding and unexpected stuff, and the existence of alternatives for Wayne Shorter's 'Nefertiti', Bruno Martino's 'Estate' and the improvised original, 'Free With Lee', permits a glimpse of the two younger players learning from the master on the spot. Certainly guitar players will want to study this one, not least for the difference between Mixon's Wes-influenced octaves and the Italian's floatier, less anchored approach.

*****(*) Dearly Beloved**

Steeplechase SCCD 31406 *Konitz; Harold Danko (p); Jay Anderson (b); Billy Drummond (d).* 10/96.

****** Out Of Nowhere**

Steeplechase SCCD 31427 *As above, except omit Danko; add Paul Bley (p).* 4/97.

In many respects, Paul Bley is a musician whose career trajectory has been broadly similar to Konitz's: a huge output, almost unfeasibly large, and yet with only a rather vague and insubstantial purchase on popular recognition. Listen to the two veterans negotiate 'Lover Man' and you realize how much of this business depends on experience, not just technical facility but the ability to distil sound from the brute business of getting by. The two other long numbers, 'Sweet And Lovely' and 'I Can't Get Started', are more abstract, but no less effective. Anderson and Drummond provide unflagging support, and Nils Winther's production skills are once again evident, as they are on the slightly earlier *Dearly Beloved*. Danko is more of a melodist than Bley, and on 'The Way You Look Tonight' and 'Bye Bye Blackbird' he sticks close to the basic code, only really breaking loose on the closing 'Night Has A Thousand Eyes'. By then, though, the spell has been cast; a less venturesome and cerebral album than *Out Of Nowhere*, but no less vibrantly exciting for all that.

*****(*) Unaccompanied In Yokohama**

PSFD 83 *Konitz; Kazuo Imai (g).* 10/96.

The title is quite accurate, for Imai joins in only for two untitled duo improvisations at the end, and these are frankly dispensable in this context. The real meat of the record is the solo stuff, most of it familiar: 'Thingin'', 'Darn That Dream', 'Subconscious-Lee', 'Kary's Trance' and 'The Nearness Of You'. Lee plays with a quietly plangent intensity, rarely allowing any sense of urgency to overtake him, and working steadily at the themes and their superstructure of chords. The items with Imai should perhaps have been held over for a separate project. Paired with a ringing electric guitar, he toughens up his delivery, adding an edge that at moments suggests he has switched to soprano, and at others to some curiously tuned member of the Adolphe Sax family.

****** Alone Together**

Blue Note 57150 *Konitz; Brad Mehldau (p); Charlie Haden (b).* 12/96.

*****(*) Another Shade Of Blue**

Blue Note 98222 *As above.* 12/97.

At this point, Konitz seemed to have his pick of the major labels and was issuing records with prodigal self-assurance. This live session is one of his best ever. Turning seventy, he was playing with magisterial calm and an elder statesman's mischief, as when he turns more than one of these chestnuts inside out. 'Round Midnight' is the most thoroughly subverted, with every cliché going registered and passed over almost mockingly. 'Cherokee', 'The Song Is You', 'What Is This Thing Called Love' and the title-tune are the other standards covered but, lest this suggest a pedestrian run-through of familiar changes, nothing is taken for granted in any of these performances. Everything, from the basic harmony to the final detail of the tune, is open to question and to rearrangement. Mehldau and Haden are equal partners, the latter not unexpectedly so, given his immense experience; but the pianist too has things to say and is temperamentally resistant to easy options, creating a sense of space and relaxed time whenever he is featured, accompanying his seniors with a solid musical scaffolding.

The sequel certainly doesn't match up to the original record, but the long, thoughtful versions of 'Body And Soul' and 'What's New' are packed with musical detail and with some drama as well.

***** Self Portrait**

Philology W121 *Konitz (as solo and multitracked).* 2/97.

Not quite, as producer Paolo Piangarelli claims, Konitz's only solo recording since *Lone-Lee*, but an unexpectedly rare return to such a successful and technically uncomplicated formula. The difference here is that the saxophonist is heard in counterpoint with himself and in canonical groups of up to four lines. The effect is actually quite mechanical, and when one turns to the central 'Self Portrait In Blues', a wry, self-effacing diary entry in an idiom that hasn't always been Konitz's most comfortable, it's clear that much of the multi-tracked material relies too much on technical trickery and not quite enough on straightforward expression. Made to celebrate the saxophonist's seventieth birthday, it lifts another corner on a fascinating career. The 'Self Portrait', a long 'Dearly Beloved' and parts of 'Subconscious-Lee' are worth having. The rest is for dedicated collectors only.

***(*) Dig Dug Dog

Columbia 488831 *Konitz; Laurent De Wilde (p); Ira Coleman (b); Dion Parson (d); Keiko Lee (v).* 3/97.

Coming off the end of a short tour in Japan, Konitz sounds played in, confident and at ease. His scatted vocal on the final item, 'Dug', is a tiny thank you to the Shinjuku club where the group had its residency. Elsewhere, on three tracks at least, he leaves vocal duties to Keiko Lee (the set was nearly called *Lee Meets Lee*) who has the good sense not to try to sound American and for that reason brings to 'Body And Soul', 'Gee, Baby' and 'I Got It Bad' a touching simplicity of diction which is often lost in more self-conscious renditions. There are three originals on the set, of which 'Thingin'' has been recorded before, but the key items are 'Ruby My Dear', Monk performed with a wry detachment equal to the master's own, and the Tony Williams tune, 'Sister Cheryl', which was included on the drummer's last studio record. Here, as elsewhere, Konitz strips it down to basics, refusing to make a grand romantic statement of it, but showing an instinctive understanding of its structure and its mood all the same. Konitz has had to wait an unconscionably long time for a studio sound as good as this, strong, burnished and absolutely faithful to his now familiar dry but far from unexpressive delivery. De Wilde and Coleman come out equally well.

***(*) Three Guys

Enja ENJ 9351 2 *Konitz; Steve Swallow (b); Paul Motian (d).* 5/98.

A trio of radical individualists, doing their several and collective thing on a set of clever and challenging themes, most of them originals. 'Thingin'', Lee's version of 'All The Things You Are', is now a central component of his repertoire, and this is a fabulous performance of it, with the trio weaving and interlocking in the most imaginative way. The really interesting writing is Swallow's, 'Ladies' Wader' and 'Eiderdown', but Motian delivers two cracking themes on 'From Time To Time' and 'Johnny Broken Wing'. Beautifully recorded and mixed, a high-gloss showcase for three astounding players.

*** Saxophone Dreams

Koch International 6900 *Konitz; Metropole Orchestra.* 98.

'Effortless' is insulting; 'seemingly effortless' is just about OK, because it implies that there may have been a sheen of sweat at some point. Konitz is a player of surpassing elegance and polish, but in recent years he has introduced more and more grit and passion, and these delightful orchestrations are a basis for some of his most effective improvisations, brief but very effective.

**** Sound Of Surprise

RCA Victor 69309 *Konitz; Ted Brown (ts); John Abercrombie (g); Marc Johnson (b); Joey Baron (d).* 99.

The key track here is the classic 'Subconscious-Lee', played by each of the players individually, then as an ensemble, then as a more orthodox theme-plus-solos. Brown has something of Warne Marsh's smooth, cool, thoughtful tone, and the echoes are confirmed time and again, on 'Blues Suite', 'Hi Beck' and 'Thingin''. Johnson and Baron are magnificent and Joey's pattering, rapid-fire percussion is the key to a thoroughly enjoyable and endlessly thought-provoking set.

Krakatau

GROUP

Much sound and fury from this Finnish blending of improvisation and dark rock music, led by guitarist Björkenheim.

*** Ritual

Cuneiform RUNE 86 *Raoul Björkenheim (g, shekere, talking d, rebab); Jorma Tapio (as, bcl, bf, perc); Tapani Rinne (ts, bs, wood f); Sampo Lassila (b); Michael Lambert, Heikki Lefty Lehto (d).* 88–90.

*** Volition

ECM 511983-2 *Raoul Björkenheim (g, shekere); Jone Takamaki (ts, krakaphone, toppophone, whirlpipe); Uffe Krokfors (b); Alf Forsman (d).* 12/91.

*** Matinale

ECM 523293-2 *As above, except Ippe Kätka (d) replaces Forsman.* 12/93.

Krakatau is essentially guitarist Björkenheim's band, hived off from percussionist Edward Vesala's Sound & Fury collective in the mid-1980s. Where Vesala mixed free playing with '60s psychedelia, tangos and straight composition, Björkenheim has a declared interest in Hendrix, Cream, Zappa, and a line of post-bop jazz that takes in Coltrane, Eric Dolphy, and the Miles of *Agharta*. The debut *Ritual* suggests a folkier edge to the music than will be familiar to those who first heard the group in a later incarnation, and the continuity with Vesala's workshop bands is more obvious. 'Ritual' and 'Relentless' perhaps too neatly sum up the overall impact. Björkenheim is a very concentrated musician, but he does occasionally leave his foot on the pedal too long, sometimes literally so.

Volition is a cheerfully noisy record with remarkably little of the big-biceps nonsense that often comes with guitar-fronted groups. In Sound & Fury, Vesala had used Björkenheim a little aside from the main thrust of a composition, often asking him for explosively abstract sound-shapes that encouraged non-standard techniques: bowed and scrabbled strings, electronic distortion, 10+ volume readings. A dedicated instrument-hunter, like Vesala, saxophonist Takamaki supplies his own fair share of unusual sonorities, most notably the 'krakaphone', a copper organ pipe two feet taller than the performer and fitted with a baritone saxophone mouthpiece and reed. It lends its bulk most effectively to 'Little Big Horn', a title that's also been used by Gerry Mulligan. It's a not entirely absurd parallel, for there is a softer and more lyrical side to Krakatau, most obviously heard on the soothingly oriental 'Changgo' and the folkish 'Nai', but clearly audible too on the closing ballad, 'Dalens Ande', which has a cool modality far removed from the all-out impact of the title-track.

Matinale is a second helping of the ECM-era band, the music again somewhat mediated by the studio but recorded with a handsome degree of clarity and body that helps punch up the impact. When they're going for the visceral, that is – pieces such as 'Unseen Sea Scene' and 'Rural' are more about brooding atmosphere than any sonic fisticuffs. 'Sarajevo' and 'Matinale' itself even echo some of Terje Rypdal's old work for the label. Attractive in a sluggish, world-weary way, the music finally doesn't seem to go anywhere much.

Diana Krall

VOCALS, PIANO

A Canadian from Nanaimo, Krall was a teenage prodigy who studied with Jimmy Rowles and began recording for the local label, Justin Time, in 1992. She has since signed to Impulse!/Verve and has become a major crossover star, helped by shrewd marketing.

***** Stepping Out**

Justin Time 50-2 *Krall; John Clayton (b); Jeff Hamilton (d).* 93.

*****(*) Only Trust Your Heart**

GRP 059810-2 *Krall; Stanley Turrentine (ts); Ray Brown, Christian McBride (b); Lewis Nash (d).* 94.

***** All For You**

Impulse! 051164-2 *Krall; Benny Green (p); Russell Malone (g); Paul Keller (b); Steve Kroon (perc).* 10/95.

Vocally and stylistically, Krall sounds a generation older than her chronological age. She has a rich, resonant contralto and a preference for standard repertoire. The most obvious influences on her singing are Carmen McRae and Shirley Horn, who has also doubled vocals and piano. As 'Straighten Up And Fly Right' and 'Frim Fram Sauce' on the first of these suggest, Krall has also listened attentively to Nat Cole, and the third album is intended as a tribute to his great trio, hence the basic instrumentation of piano, guitar and bass, with just a touch of percussion thrown in on 'Boulevard Of Broken Dreams'. What the third album lacks, inevitably, is musicianship of the sort guaranteed by Brown, McBride and Nash. Turrentine does more than just show up, contributing hugely on his three tracks. Our preference for *Only Trust Your Heart* is based solely on their roles; Krall's singing is impeccable throughout. The debut set has been remastered with an extra track, an ebullient 'Sunny Side Of The Street'; listening again, it's surprising to hear how much piano she was playing – compared with the recent records at least.

*****(*) Love Scenes**

Impulse! 051234-2 *Krall; Russell Malone (g); Christian McBride (b).* 97.

Krall has become the warmest commercial property in the music. It can be difficult to evaluate her music in light of the attention she has received, but at least (unlike Cassandra Wilson) she seems unencumbered by her status. Where Wilson already seems to have invested in the hype surrounding her, Krall – so far – has hardly let it invade her records. This one may be cannily pitched at an audience hungry for a sexy young jazz singer, but the performances are hard to fault and Malone and McBride are more than willing partners in the affair. The obvious killer is Dave Frishberg's 'Peel Me A Grape', cheekily done; but more demurely effective are 'The Gentle Rain' and 'Garden In the Rain'. Krall's understatement is part of her strength and she hasn't given up on it yet.

***** Only Trust Your Heart**

Verve 050304-2 *Krall; Larry Bunker (vib); Russell Malone (g); Ben Wolfe, John Clayton (b); Lewis Nash (d); strings.* 98.

... although, on this evidence, she may eventually have little choice in the matter. This is still just about a jazz record, but it's pitched to make Krall a vocal star, and the accompaniments are almost peripheral. Johnny Mandel contributes some of his most weeping arrangements to seven tracks (the title-piece is almost glutinous) and, although Krall is still at home with her small group, mannerism is clearly being encouraged to excess by her producer.

Wayne Krantz

GUITAR

Born in Oregon, Krantz came to New York in the mid-1980s and has been a regular on the scene there ever since.

***** Signals**

Enja 6048-2 *Krantz; Jim Beard (ky); Leni Stern (g); Hiram Bullock, Anthony Jackson (b); Dennis Chambers (d); Don Alias (perc).* 5–6/90.

*****(*) Long To Be Loose**

Enja 7099-2 *Krantz; Lincoln Goines (b); Zach Danziger (d).* 3/93.

*****(*) 2 Drink Minimum**

Enja 9043-2 *As above.* 2–4/95.

Krantz works an interesting furrow somewhere between Frisell's displaced ruralisms and a bluesier improvisation that sounds plausible as either jazz-rock or, well, rock-jazz. In other words, another good guitar player who's hard to slot in. What he enjoys is the resonant sound of strong lead guitar: he's not much interested in FX, delay, fuzz, or whatever. The starry cast on the first record suggests a typical fusion slugging match, but the support team is used rather sparingly (drums and percussion on only five out of ten tracks) and, though the pieces are rather short and curtailed, they're an entertaining bunch. The trio-orientated records put Krantz in a setting that plays tight or loose as he pleases and has a lot of fine, unassumingly accomplished guitar. The studio set is structured piece by piece, even though the titles tell a story if you read them end to end; but to get a handle on what this group is about, the live *2 Drink Minimum* is an even better choice. Though spliced together from various shows at New York's 55 Bar, the disc plays like a single, well-paced, explosive concert set: the cumulative intensity of 'Whippersnapper' and the lyricism of 'Isabelle' work despite (or because of) their rough edges, the occasion adding a pinch of seasoning to music that a studio might have dried out a little. The fine, interlocking work of Goines and Danziger comes over with the same power as Krantz's.

*****(*) Separate Cages**

Alchemy ALCD 1007 *Krantz; Leni Stern (g, v).* 96.

Although this is more in tune with Stern's aesthetic than Krantz's, it's a charming and very playable series of duets, performed with a two-way sympathy that is very fetching. 'King's Cross', in dedication to Emily Remler, and Stern's softly effective vocal on 'Something Is Wrong In Spanish Harlem' are but two highlights in a programme that goes quietly and thoughtfully without meandering.

*****(*) Greenwich Mean**
Wayne Krantz Records no number *Krantz; Timothy Lefebvre, Will Lee (b); Keith Carlock (d).* 7–8/99.

A return visit to New York's 55 Bar for Wayne's regular gig, although this set is a distillation of many hours of gigs into what's effectively a single piece. The new trio is playing harder, faster and louder, but Krantz still surrenders nothing in sophistication or harmonic elegance, making only sparing use of effects such as wah-wah and relying on his own imagination to meld his rock and country interests into what's an unequivocally modern approach to jazz guitar. As fine a soloist as he is, it's also very much a group music. The slightly unkempt sound (recorded on portable DAT machines) may trouble some, but the music's terrific. However, the record is available only directly from Wayne himself. Contact him at www.waynekrantz.com.

Ernie Krivda (born 1945)

TENOR SAXOPHONE, VOCAL

His father was a swing-era reedsman, and he followed in those steps in the 1970s with an individual approach to hard-bop orthodoxy.

***** Ernie Krivda Jazz**
Cadence CJR 1049 *Krivda; Dennis Reynolds, Mike Hazlett (t); Pat Hallaran (tb); Joe Hunter (p); Pete Selvaggio (acc); Jeff Halsey, Gary Aprile, Roger Hines, Chris Berger (b); Paul Samuels, Scott Davis (d).* 1–8/91.

***** So Nice To Meet You**
Cadence CJR 1056 *Krivda; Joe Hunter (p); Bill Plavan, Chris Berger (b); Val Kent, Mark Gondor (d); Paula Owen (v).* 6/93–1/94.

***** Sarah's Theme**
CIMP 102 *Krivda; Bob Fraser (g); Jeff Halsey (b).* 9/95.

Krivda has a markedly individual approach to the tenor: wildly elongated lines with barely a pause for breath, a hiccupy kind of rhythm that abjures conventional hard-bop phrasing, and a tone that evades obvious comparison, though he sometimes gets a scuffling sound that is rather like Warne Marsh. The ingredients tend to make his music exciting but unresolved. On *Ernie Krivda Jazz*, the three duets with bassist Halsey are the most interesting things: two pieces with accordionist Selvaggio are unusual but not terribly involving, 'The Bozo' is a more complicated chart involving the two trumpeters, and the final quartet/quintet tracks are lively but let down slightly by the modest support. The album is further compromised by the scrawny, indifferent production. The pairing with singer Paula Owen is even stranger: Owen's basically straightforward style is embellished by Krivda's jaw-breaking solos, everything pitched in double-time, each solo a blitz on its surroundings. It's oddly exhilarating stuff, but over a CD's duration a little exhausting. One could say the same about *Sarah's Theme*: the title-track runs just over 20 minutes and, aside from the three subsequent interludes, each of the tracks seems obsessively long. Halsey and Fraser play a shadowy role, but Krivda himself is actually in comparatively restrained mood on this set. CIMP's two-track digital sound, designed for 'realism', tends to sound rather dry and unappealing, but in some ways it suits Krivda's tough and uncompromising approach.

*****(*) The Art Of The Ballad**
Koch 7806 *Krivda; Bill Dobbins (p).* 6/93.

*****(*) Golden Moments**
Koch 37310 *Krivda; Dan Wall (p).* 6/95.

Krivda doesn't mind the most exposed situations, but on the face of it he seems an unlikely choice for two duo albums of ballads for horn and piano. The dryness of his sound, the oddball phrasing and the refusal to colour a melody with any of the horn's bell notes are scarcely food for Ben Webster addicts. Both Dobbins and Wall – the latter especially, with a flourish and a readiness to quicken the pace – push and prod him all the way, but each of these belongs to Krivda as a self-challenging performer. 'Darn That Dream' on the first disc and 'Angel Eyes' on the second are model instances of making a new song out of an old one, which for some is what jazz is meant to be about. These absorbing (and swinging, it should be added) records will be a tonic for anyone bored with hushabye tenor recitals.

*****(*) The Band That Swings**
Koch 7880 *Krivda; Keith Powell, Joe Miller, Steve Enos, Brad Goode (t); Garney Hicks, George Carr, Chris Anderson (tb); Paul Abel (btb); Dave Sterner (as); George Shernit (as, cl, f); Chris Burge, Tom First (ts); Dick Ingersoll (bs); Joe Hunter (p); Lee Bush (g); Sherry Luchetti (b); Rick Porello (d).* 11/98.

Krivda as frontman for a '40s-style big band, sometimes playing sweet (listen to the Lawrence Welk chords in 'I Should Care', actually a Billy May chart) as well as hot? We didn't believe it either. But the record is great fun, and Krivda is clearly having a ball with this group (the Fat Tuesday Big Band, here recorded in Cleveland). There's nothing modern in the sound, but it doesn't feel especially retro either and, with Krivda's tenor taking on a new swagger in his features, this baker's dozen tunes will raise spirits wherever they're played.

Karin Krog (born 1937)

VOCALS

Karin Krog apparently dodged school one afternoon to see Billie Holiday perform in Oslo. What she learned or absorbed by osmosis that day has stood her in better stead than many hours of bokmal or civics. Krog is an expressive, technically astute singer with advanced musical ideas of her own. Her recordings, now largely on her own label, are thoughtful, utterly musical and desperately underrated.

****** Jubilee: The Best of 30 Years**

Verve 527316-2 2CD *Krog; Don Ellis, Bob Harman, Palle Mikkelborg, Glenn Stuart, Ed Warren, Alan Weight (t); David Sanchez, Terry Woodson (tb); Per Carsten, Tom Scott, Ira Schulman, Ron Starr, Ruben Leon, John Magruder (f, sax); Dexter Gordon, Bjorn Johansen, Warne Marsh, Archie Shepp (ts); John Surman (bs, ss, syn); Bent Larsen (f, as, bf); Niels Peters (ob); Kenny Drew (p, org); Jon Balke, Bengt Hallberg, Ole Koch-Hansen, Egil Kapstad, Roger Kellaway, Mike Lang, Arild Wickstrom (p); Jan Berger, Philip Catherine (g); Arild Andersen, Niels-Henning Orsted Pedersen, Kurt Lindgren, Per Loberg, Red Mitchell, Ray Neapolitan, Frank De La Rosa (b); Jon Christensen, Beaver Harris, Alex Riel, Epsen Rud (d); Steve Bohannon, Mark Stevens, Chino Valdes, Kasper Vinding (perc); strings.* 3/64–6/94.

*****(*) Some Other Spring**

Storyville STCD 4045 *Krog; Dexter Gordon (ts); Kenny Drew (p); Niels-Henning Orsted Pedersen (b); Epsen Rud (d).* 5/70.

*****(*) Gershwin With Karin Krog**

Meantime MR4 *Krog; Egil Kapstad (p); Arild Andersen (b); Jon Christensen (d).* 74, 89.

***** You Must Believe In Spring**

Meantime MR5 *Krog; Palle Mikkelborg (t); Per Carsten (as, f); Bent Larsen (f, af, bf); Niels Peters (ob); Ole Koch-Hansen (p); Philip Catherine (g); Niels-Henning Orsted Pedersen (b); Alex Riel (d); Kasper Vinding (perc); strings.* 5/74.

Krog is one of Europe's most stylish and significant jazz singers. The early work documented on the capacious *Jubilee* finds her working an idiosyncratic swing vein, with strong intimations of bebop, perhaps of Annie Ross's vocalese. Her first recordings are with Arild Wikstrom's group, professional, swinging and sufficiently offbeat to seem individual. There is a significant shift at the time of the first American recording, made in LA with Don Ellis's eclectic orchestra. Perhaps the bandleader's open-mindedness encouraged Krog's folkish-classical vein, for there is a very different approach to basic changes on 'In Your Arms' and 'Spring Affair'. Her work with Dexter Gordon, with the refiguring of bop that that entailed, is also documented on the Storyville; most listeners would be satisfied to have the well-packaged and -documented Verve. It takes the story forward, overlapping with a good deal of the stuff also available separately on other labels, the association with Shepp and Hallberg, for instance. Much of Krog's best work has been with her companion, John Surman. However, her own catalogue has undergone a significant boost over the last two years, largely as a result of her own initiative in releasing material on the Meantime imprint which is usually quite easy to track down.

****** One On One**

Meantime MR7 *Krog; Nils Lindberg (org); Bengt Hallberg (p); Red Mitchell (b).* 7 & 10/77, 2/80.

Krog made a number of recordings in the late '70s for Frank Heman's Bluebell label. Three of those duo performances are compiled here. Mitchell's lyricism is immediately evident on 'Blues In My Heart' and his subtle sense of structure is the key to 'God Bless The Child', a beautifully plain and untheatrical reading by Krog. The set with Hallberg begins – unexpectedly – with Leon Russell's all too rarely covered 'A Song For You'. The pianist is discretion itself, touching in the harmonies without fuss or undue embellishment. The real treat of the set is the duets with Lindberg. One rarely hears organ in this context, and his accompaniments to 'Sometimes I Feel Like A Motherless Child' and 'Psalm' from Coltrane's *A Love Supreme* are striking in their rich simplicity. A wonderful collection of songs, accompanied by three master musicians.

***** Hi-Fly**

Meantime MR3 *Krog; Archie Shepp (ts); Charles Greenlee (tb); Jon Balke (p); Arild Andersen, Cameron Brown (b); Beaver Harris (d).* 6/76.

***** Two Of A Kind**

Meantime MR1 *Krog; Bengt Hallberg (p).* 4/82.

*****(*) Freestyle**

Odin NJ 4017 *Krog; John Surman (ss, syn, perc); Brynjar Hoff (ob).* 8/85, 4/86.

***** Something Borrowed ... Something New**

Meantime MR2 *Krog; Kenny Drew (p); Niels-Henning Orsted Pedersen (b); Alex Riel (d).* 6/89.

A fine technician, Krog doesn't allow an impressive understanding of 'extended technique' to over-reach itself, keeping the words and their attendant emotions in view. Perhaps because of this, she sounds best in small-scale and rather intimate surroundings. The session with Surman is quite exotic in sonority, with overdubbing and electronic treatments on some tracks, unusual percussion and synth patterns on the original material. The repertoire is pretty ambitious, even including 'Raga Variations' by the composer Arne Nordheim, who writes brilliantly for voice. A Fran Landesman medley strongly recalls the work of the late Radka Toneff, a Norwegian compatriot of Krog's, but is even more musical in conception.

Something Borrowed is more straightforwardly jazz-orientated, as is the Gershwin record. A gap of 15 years between them (or the contrast between the 1974 and 1989 material on *Gershwin With Karin Krog*) demonstrates how completely the singer has absorbed the basic repertoire and made it her own. Krog's versions of well-tramped turf like 'Summertime' and 'Someone To Watch Over Me' (*Gershwin*, later sessions) or 'I Get A Kick Out Of You' and 'Everytime We Say Goodbye' (*Borrowed*) are entirely her own. Hallberg is a graceful accompanist who gives her a softly insistent beat as a springboard into her vocal, and there isn't a track that one wouldn't want to listen through again, so subtle is some of her phrasing and her awareness of harmony. That's at more of a premium in the Legrand session, *You Must Believe In Spring*, where the outstanding track is 'Once Upon A Summertime' (also on the Verve). She's a little swamped here by Mikkelborg's dense orchestration but manages to rise above the waves most of the time.

She's under a different sort of pressure on the session with Shepp, a player who turned himself from a screamer into a (relatively) sensitive balladeer rather later in the day. Krog adds lyrics to Carla Bley's 'Sing Me Softly Of The Blues' and makes an impressive job of Mal Waldron's 'Soul Eyes' (a singer's tune if there ever was one) and Randy Weston's affirmative 'Hi-Fly'. The horns are too dominant and Harris is slightly overpowering in places; Krog also sounds uncomfortable on Shepp's own 'Steam', though their duet, 'Solitude', suggests that there was more than enough common ground.

The group on *Borrowed* is much better attuned to what Krog is doing. NHOP emerges as the dominant voice, easing aside a rather lacklustre and uncharacteristically heavy-handed Drew. The sound is far from ideal, pinching some of the top notes, but the vocal performances are generally of a very high standard. Excellent as all these records are, we would emphasize that *Jubilee* will answer all but the most dedicated requirements.

****** Bluesand**

Meantime MR9 *Krog; John Surman (ss, bs, bcl, cbcl, p, syn).* 99.

Immaculately recorded by Jan Erik Kongshaug at the legendary Rainbow Studio in Oslo, this fine duo set conjures up a huge range of timbres and tonalities, the product of now twenty years working as a duo. Krog's voice has rarely sounded better and Surman's finely developed accompaniments are deployed as effectively here as on his own solo records. The longer tracks are the most powerful, allowing both performers to stretch out, but the shorter pieces, like the mysterious 'Hidden Dreams', are equally effective. The title-track is equally enigmatic, a terse central theme strung out across a rich, almost orchestral backdrop. Even when the arrangements are stripped down to basics, there is so much grain and texture to Surman's playing that one senses much larger forces at work. An exceptional record.

Gene Krupa (1909–73)

DRUMS

Born in Chicago, Krupa joined Benny Goodman's orchestra and stayed for the better part of half a decade before striking out on his own. His sheer energy is infectious, and he remained a master drummer to the end of his life.

*****(*) Gene Krupa, 1935–1938**

Classics 754 *Krupa; Tom Di Carlo, Tom Gonsoulin, Dave Schultze, Roy Eldridge, Nate Kazebier (t); Chuck Evans, Joe Harris, Charles McCamish, Bruce Squires (tb); Benny Goodman (cl); Murray Williams, George Siravo (as); Chu Berry, Dick Clark, Vido Musso, Carl Bleisacker (ts); Milton Raskin, Jess Stacy (p); Ray Biondi, Allan Reuss (g); Israel Crosby, Horace Rollins (b); Helen Ward, Jerry Kruger (v).* 11/35–7/38.

***** Gene Krupa, 1938**

Classics 767 *Krupa; Tom Di Carlo, Ray Cameron, Tom Gonsoulin, Nick Prospero, Dave Schultze (t); Charles McCamish, Bruce Squires, Toby Tyler, Chuck Evans (tb); Murray Williams, Mascagni Ruffo, George Siravo (as); Vido Musso, Carl Bleisacker, Sam Musiker, Sam Donahue (ts); Milton Raskin (p); Ray Biondi (g); Horace Rollins (b); Irene Daye, Leo Watson (v).* 7–12/38.

There is a memorable photograph of the young Gene Krupa at the kit, hair slick, tux sleeves and collar soaked with sweat, mouth and eyes wide and hungry, his brushes blurred to smoke with the pace of his playing. Received wisdom has Krupa down as a showman who traded in subtlety for histrionic power. George T. Simon, in the hopped-up prose that was almost *de rigueur* in the *Metronome* of the late 1930s, referred to the drummer's 'quadruple "f" musical attacks'; it's interesting to speculate how many people read that as 4F (that is, unfit for military service) rather than as some battering dynamic above *molto fortissimo*, for there is no doubt that Krupa's film-star looks and superb technique also made him a target. During the war, which he spent as a very combative non-combatant, he was twice set up for police arrest and spent part of his 35th year waiting on remand until a witness contracted amnesia. The critics have taken much the same route, sniping, then forgetting. Even in neglect, Krupa's impact on the jazz rhythm section is incalculable. He himself said, 'I made the drummer a high-priced guy.' Though black percussionists who had worked for years in the shadow of the front men had some cause to be resentful, Krupa's respectful investigation of the African and Afro-American drumming tradition was of tremendous significance, opening the way for later figures as diverse as Max Roach, Elvin Jones, Andrew Cyrille and Milford Graves.

The documentation is in much better shape these days with the issue of Classics' typically detailed job. Krupa joined the Benny Goodman band in 1934 and stayed till 1938, when his boss finally decided there was room for only one of them on stage. The drummer recorded under his own name only twice during the Goodman years. The sessions of November 1935 (made for Parlophone UK) and February 1936 kick off the first Classics volume on a high. Being able to call on Goodman, Jess Stacy and the remarkable Israel Crosby offered some guarantee of quality, and 'Three Little Words' and Krupa's own 'Blues For Israel' are spanking performances, driven along by that dynamic drumming. The following session included Chu Berry and Roy Eldridge, an established double-act in the Fletcher Henderson outfit and always ready to try something new. Berry cheekily weaves in and out of Goodman's line, while Eldridge dive-bombs from above. Great stuff.

There is then a chronological hiatus until Krupa's break with Goodman and the chance to capitalize on his own rising stardom. The April 1938 Brunswicks also signalled a move to New York City, which seems to have put a slight brake on Krupa's invention for a while, unless it was the new burden of managing his own orchestra. Not yet the banked strings of the later band but a slightly cumbersome feel nevertheless, and the fourth item ('The Madam Swings It') of an uninspired session was eventually rejected. Singers Helen Ward, Jerry Kruger and Irene Daye fail to add very much, but vocals were commercially essential and these discs did big business right through 1938, with the band averaging a session a month. Leo Watson's scats were lively and often very musical, but Krupa must have felt partly inhibited by the formula and there's an audible sense of relaxation and renewed vigour about the sessions recorded back in Chicago in October, when he is able to lay down a couple of fine instrumentals, including the excellent 'Walkin' And Swingin''. November and December saw the band on the West Coast, where a new audience was conquered and three excellent recording sessions laid down. Watson's 'Do You Wanna Jump, Children?' brought the year to a happy close.

***** Gene Krupa, 1939**

Classics 799 *Krupa; Ray Cameron, Charles Frankhauser, Tom Gonsoulin (t); Toby Tyler, Bruce Squires, Dalton Rizzotto (tb); Bob Snyder, Mascagni Ruffo (as); Sam Musiker, Sam Donahue (ts); Milton Raskin (p); Ray Biondi (g); Horace Rollins (b); Irene Daye (v).* 2–7/39.

*****(*) Gene Krupa, 1939–1940**

Classics 834 *Krupa; Johnny Martel, Corky Cornelius, Torger Halten, Nate Kazebier, Johnny Napton, Shorty Sherock (t); Al Sherman, Floyd O'Brien, Red Ogle, Al Jordan, Sid Brantley (tb);*

Bob Snyder, Clint Neagley (as); Sam Donahue (ts); Sam Musiker (cl, ts); Tony D'Amore, Milt Raskin (p); Ray Biondi (g); Biddy Bastien (b); Irene Daye, Howard DuLany (v). 7/39–2/40.

The following year was no less busy and there is a strong sense of consolidation in the band, which begins to sound like a more solidly integrated unit. Krupa's leadership is tight and very musical. A new version of 'The Madam Swings It' is cut and this time passes muster. Nate Kazebier returns to the fold and Floyd O'Brien signs up to stiffen the brasses. Apart from a couple of novelty instrumentals made for dancing ('Dracula' and 'Foo For Two') the standard is very high and Krupa can increasingly be heard to experiment with rhythmic embellishments, off-accent notes, single beats on the edge of his cymbals, and with the dynamics. Even with such a powerful group, he was always prepared on occasion to play quietly and to contrast *fff* and *pp* passages within a single song, relatively unusual at that time when up was up and a ballad was a ballad. Into 1940, it's pretty much a question of steady as she goes, even with the inevitable personnel changes. By this point Krupa can be heard to be shaping the band to his new requirements, which were much more musicianly and much less histrionic. The Benny Carter piece, 'Symphony In Riffs', recorded for Columbia in September 1939, and the majestic two-part 'Blue Rhythm Fantasy' (nearly seven minutes in total) stand out as representative masterpieces, making this, along with the first volume, essential buys.

***** Gene Krupa, 1940 – Volume 1**

Classics 859 *Krupa; Corky Cornelius, Torg Halten, Nate Kazebier, Rudy Novak, Shorty Sherock (t); Al Jordan, Jay Kelliher, Babe Wagner (tb); Clint Neagley, Bob Snyder (as); Walter Bates, Sam Donahue, Sam Musiker (ts); Tony D'Amore (p); Ray Biondi (g); Biddy Bastien (b); Irene Daye, Howard DuLany (v).* 3–5/40.

***** Gene Krupa, 1940 – Volume 2**

Classics 883 *As above.* 11/39, 1–9/40.

***** Gene Krupa: 1940 – Volume 3**

Classics 917 *As above, except omit Jordan and d'Amore; add Pat Virgadamo (tb), Bob Kitsis (p).* 9–11/40.

Annus mirabilis, or what? Krupa could hardly have been busier during 1940, churning out a series of slick, pop-orientated sides for OKeh, milking a market that could hardly have been more responsive. The element of showmanship is inevitably missing on record, and most of these extended solos drag their feet. The bands increasingly seem to be foils for the soloist, chugging away anonymously and with little of the personality that made the Goodman, Dorsey and James units so distinctive. Collectors of this sort of material will find much to enjoy, including two rarities on Volume Two from November 1939 and January 1940, rejected takes of 'Time Out' and 'The Birth Of Passion' for Columbia. More of the material for the label is collected on the item below.

***** Drum Boogie**

Columbia Legacy 473659 *Krupa; Norman Murphy, Torg Halten, Rudy Novak, Shorty Sherock (t); Pat Virgadamo, Jay Kelliher, Babe Wagner (tb); Clint Neagley, Mascagni Ruffo (as); Walter Bates (ts); Sam Musiker (cl, ts); Bob Kitsis (p); Ray Biondi (g); Biddy Bastien (b); Irene Daye (v).* 40–41.

It would be hard to ignore the Columbia compilation, which affords a glimpse of the band in a somewhat more reflective mood. Jimmy Mundy's arrangements often cleave to a rather mechanical shuffle-beat that doesn't suit a group of this size or inclination, but the horns are nicely voiced and there is a lot more space round the music than in earlier days. Irene Daye is still the singer, still leaning on ballads rather than faster numbers. She was soon (in 1941) to be replaced by one of the great presences in the band. Anita O'Day refused to wear a spangly frock and turned out in a band jacket like the rest of them, emphasizing that she was part of things and not just a walk-on. (Re)joining with her was Eldridge, who helped transform the group yet again, into a less poppy, more jazz-based and improvisational unit.

***** Gene Krupa, 1941**

Classics 960 *As above.* 41.

***** Gene Krupa, 1941 – Volume 2**

Classics 1002 *Krupa; Roy Eldridge (t, v); Torg Halten, Norman Murphy, Graham Young (t); John Grassi, Jay Kelliher, Babe Wagner (tb); Sam Listengart, Jimmy Migliore, Clint Neagley, Mascagni Ruffo (as); Walter Bates, Sam Musiker (ts); Bob Kitsis, Milton Raskin (p); Ray Biondi (g); Biddy Bastien, Ed Mihelich (b); Johnny Desmond, Howard DuLany, Anita O'Day (v).* 6–10/41.

***** Gene Krupa, 1941-1942**

Classics 1006 *As above, except add Al Beck, Mickey Mangano (t), Ben Feman, Rex Kittig (as), Don Brassfield (ts), Joe Springer (p).* 10/41–2/42.

This was the period of maximum productivity, with the band going into the studio virtually every month in the period before Pearl Harbor. The key recruitment during 1941 was singer Anita O'Day; her presence tends to distract attention from the band itself, which is steamingly powerful. Roy Eldridge is the featured soloist and singer elsewhere, and the vocals certainly can't be dismissed. Gene doesn't vary much from an alternation of 4/4 and 6/8, but his sheer presence is infectious and his attack unfailingly dramatic. The vocal contributions tend to predominate, but Gene's own playing is revelatory for anyone who thinks that polyrhythms began with Elvin Jones and the Coltrane quartet.

***** Gene Krupa: 1946 – Volume 1**

Hep CD 26 *Krupa; Ed Badgley, John Bello, Gordon Boswell, Richard Dale, Don Fagerquist, Vince Hughes, Jimmy Milazzo, Al Porcino, Red Rodney, Joe Triscari, (t); Bob Ascher, Nick Gaglio, Urbie Green, Tasso Harris, Cley Hervey, Emil Mazanec, Emil Melnic, Dick Taylor, Jack Zimmerman (tb); Charlie Kennedy, Tommy Lucas, Sam Marowitz, Harry Terrill (as); Mitch Melnic, Charlie Ventura, Buddy Wise (ts); Joe Koch, Larry Patton, Jack Schwartz (bs); Bob Lesher, Mike Triscari (g); William Baker, Buddy Neal, Teddy Napoleon (p); Irv Lang, Bob Strahl (b); Carolyn Grey, Dolores Hawkins, Buddy Hughes, Anita O'Day, Buddy Stewart (v).* 46.

***** Gene Krupa: 1946 – Volume 2**

Hep CD 46 *Similar to above.* 46.

***** Gene Krupa: 1946–1947 – Volume 3**

Hep CD 51 *Similar to above.* 46–47.

Krupa was almost forced out of the music business altogether in 1943 when he was charged with 'contributing to the delinquency of a minor'; in our view, this is what jazz music is all about, but marijuana was involved and musicians presented a soft target at the time. Typically, the drummer bounced back and the following year formed his second orchestra, an outfit which achieved a rare peak of popularity for the time, consistently outperforming its rivals not just by showmanship but by the sheer force and concentration of the ensembles. Krupa regulars like Sherock, Neagley, Bondi and Bastien became instinctive interpreters. Not much in the way of musical subtlety was required and only genuine devotees of this style and period will have much use for three volumes, albeit disc mastered with a care that puts the Classics to shame. The presence of Anita O'Day made this a rather special band. Her replacement, Carolyn Grey, was a reasonable band singer, but she entirely lacked Anita's sense of drama and swing. There are a group of interesting trio tracks, Krupa with Teddy Napoleon and Charlie Ventura, recorded in February 1946, on which the crash and bash give way to something a little more spacious; these make Volume Three perhaps the most worthwhile of the sequence. Not much in it, though.

***** Krupa And Rich**

Verve 521643-2 *Krupa; Roy Eldridge, Dizzy Gillespie (t); Illinois Jacquet, Flip Phillips (ts); Oscar Peterson (p); Herb Ellis (g); Ray Brown (b); Buddy Rich (d).* 5 & 11/55.

Krupa and Rich shouldn't be confused with an earlier Compact Jazz compilation on Verve which included some of the material. This record documents a typical Norman Granz summit, bringing together the younger Rich and probably the only man who could properly be said to have influenced his own fiercely swinging style. Given the nature of the occasion, this wasn't nearly as arid and tiresome as the majority of contemporary 'drum battles'. Each takes a big solo spot – 'Gene's Blues', 'Buddy's Blues' – and, for the rest, it's a matter of trading fours and eights until the customers are satisfied. Fortunately the band is good enough to assert itself and nobody will feel percussed out of countenance when they hear Oscar Peterson's sweepingly elaborate accompaniments or Dizzy poking gentle fun at the vanities of drummers.

Steve Kuhn (born 1938)

PIANO, KEYBOARDS

A piano pupil of the celebrated teacher Margaret Chaloff (Serge's mother), Kuhn worked the New York jazz scene from the late '50s onwards, living in Stockhom in the late '60s and frequently accompanying Sheila Jordan as well as leading his own groups.

*****(*) Looking Back**

Concord CCD 4446 *Kuhn; David Finck (b); Lewis Nash (d).* 10/90.

*****(*) Live At Maybeck Recital Hall: Volume 13**

Concord CCD 4484 *Kuhn (p solo).* 11/90.

*****(*) Years Later**

Concord CCD 4554 *Kuhn; David Finck (b); Lewis Nash (d).* 9/92.

***** Remembering Tomorrow**

ECM 529035-2 *Kuhn; David Finck (b); Joey Baron (d).* 3/95.

Unrelated to Rolf and Joachim Kühn – though occasionally confused with the latter – Steve Kuhn is an older and more traditionally minded player whose roots reach back as far as Tatum and Waller, but who most immediately recalls Bill Evans. Kuhn has worked with Kenny Dorham, Stan Getz and Sheila Jordan, and he is often at his best comping for a very lyrical player or singer. With a left hand that is less than sturdy, he is more than usually dependent on a strong bass player and has tended to recruit very dominant bass-fiddlers to his trios; his solo work can sound a little ungrounded and introspective.

Recorded a month after *Looking Back*, the Maybeck recital underlines once again the differences between Kuhn's solo and trio work. Where the latter is increasingly a partnership of equals, the solo work opens up a remarkable amount of space in the middle of the music. The Maybeck Hall series, recorded in a warm but uncomplicated acoustic in Berkeley, California, has tended to feature meditative and/or lyrical piano music rather than the wilder shores of improv, and this is no exception. Kuhn's sometimes extreme opposition of left and right hands (if you like, the exact antithesis of Keith Jarrett's normal strategy) still betrays a certain crudity towards the bass end. The marvellous, Bird-influenced melodic figures on 'Old Folks', the opening cut, are made over an almost childishly simple left-hand alternation that very quickly palls (if it isn't intended to make a satirical comment about the song). Much the same happens on an otherwise beautiful and very thoughtful 'I Remember You', where a rumbling bass-line suddenly and disconcertingly gives way to an abstract passage over the basic chords.

Of the available trios – the fine *Trance* with Steve Swallow and Jack DeJohnette is deleted – by far the best is heard on *Looking Back* where, perhaps ironically, the pianist is working with a much less dominant rhythm section and gives signs of having broadened his own intonation and sharpened his attack. Finck is not a bass player one hears much about, but he clearly provides Kuhn with what he needs and, in company with a drummer of Baron's wit and acumen, he can sound very good indeed. *Years Later* is an excellent repeat, with some surprising and almost defiantly individual takes on 'Good Bait', 'Silver's Serenade' and 'In A Sentimental Mood'. The most recent ECM is just a little lacking in spark and variety. The pianist sounds thoughtful and relaxed but, despite Baron's playfulness, it never quite catches light.

Joachim Kühn (born 1944)

PIANO, KEYBOARDS

Born in Leipzig, Joachim is the brother of clarinettist Rolf Kühn. He studied and performed as a classical pianist through his teens. He then worked with his brother but has been most widely recognized for virtuosic solo and duo performance in which he calls upon a wide range of advanced compositional ideas and a greatly expanded palette of sound derived from his interest in playing direct on the piano strings

****(*) Kiel / Stuttgart Live!**

Inak 868 *Kühn; Jan Akkerman (g, el g, syn).* 79.

*****(*) Nightline New York**

Inak 869 *Kühn; Michael Brecker, Bob Mintzer (ts); Eddie Gomez (b); Billy Hart (d); Mark Nauseef (perc); collective personnel.* 4/81.

Joachim Kühn has a prodigious, rather 'legitimate' technique that reflects a solid grounding in classical practices and sometimes cramps his improvisational instincts. These, though, are considerable and they're perhaps better heard in a group or duo context than in solo performance. A couple of appearances from the 1980s for the Inak label are still in circulation. Star of the once-fashionable progressive-rock band, Focus, Jan Akkerman manages to sound both fleet and stiff, not at all an instinctive improviser, and he is best at colouring backdrops for Kühn's lavishly voiced chord-structures and thoughtful lines. To gauge Kühn as an improviser in the Euro-American contemporary mainstream, one needs to turn to *Nightline New York*, where he sounds quite at ease with a quick-witted two-tenor front line.

*****(*) Music From The Threepenny Opera**

Verve 532498-2 *Kühn; Jean-François Jenny-Clark (b); Daniel Humair (d).* 95.

****** Triple Entente**

Mercury 558690-2 *As above.* 12/97.

A good deal of Kühn's best work from the 1980s is missing with the rest of the CMP catalogue. These wonderful sets redress the balance comprehensively. Interesting to hear Kühn tackle the Weill–Brecht standards, which must have been almost second nature to him, so pervasive do they now seem. And yet he manages to bring a freshness to them that suggests they haven't just been plucked out of the standards bag but have been rethought very carefully from first principles, not least the chilling 'Moritat' (aka 'Mack The Knife'), which has rarely had such a sinister freight. Humair and Jenny-Clark are a formidable rhythm section and bring an intelligent and responsive touch to Kühn's compositions on the second album. 'Missing A Page' and 'Sunny Sunday' are extraordinary performances, somewhat reminiscent of Paul Bley's trio with Kent Carter and Barry Altschul, but much less dependent on *ostinati* and on sheer power. Kühn plays lines off against one another at a level of integration that would defeat most orchestral conductors. There is a single collective improvisation, 'Croquis', that suggests even more interesting things might come from that direction, and there is a composition apiece from bassist and drummer, worthy recognition of their immense contribution to this album and to European jazz in general. Strongly recommended.

Rolf Kühn (born 1929)

CLARINET, SYNTHESIZER

The elder Kühn brother played in '40s dance orchestras before going to America, where he depped for Benny Goodman and formed his own group. Latterly returned to Germany and has gone through swing, bop, cool, free and fusion styles without any apparent awkwardness, even on the awkward clarinet.

*****(*) Rolf Kühn**

Blue Flame 40162 *Kühn; Joachim Kühn (p, syn); Klaus Blodau, Larry Elam, Paul Kubatsch, Mannie Moch (t); Wolfgang Ahlers, Egon Christmann (tb); Ronald Piesarkiewicz (tba); Herb Geller, Charlie Mariano (reeds); Klaus-Robert Kruse, Thilo Von Westernhagen (ky); Philip Catherine, Peter Weihe (g); Niels-Henning Orsted Pedersen (b); Alphonse Mouzon (d); strings.* 78, 80.

***** Don't Split**

L + R 40016 *Kühn; Bob Mintzer (ts); Joachim Kühn (p); Peter Wiehe (g); Detlev Beier (b); Mark Nauseef (d, perc).* 6/82.

*****(*) As Time Goes By**

Blue Flame 40292 *Kühn; Joachim Kühn (p); Detlev Beier (b).* 4/89.

Clarinet is still sufficiently rare an item in contemporary jazz to render exact location of Rolf Kühn's style rather difficult. Leonard Feather, though, was in no doubt when he called the young German the 'new Benny Goodman'. Like his pianist brother, Joachim Kühn, who makes intelligent contributions to all three albums, and, of course, much like Goodman, Rolf Kühn has a well-schooled and sophisticated approach that suits both small groups and larger orchestral settings. In 1959 he played some memorable sessions with the great American bassist Oscar Pettiford, and they can still be found on a good Jazzline CD called *Jazz Legacy – Baden-Baden Unreleased Radio Tape.*

The fusion impulse that underlines much of the music on *Don't Split* and the earlier big-band album is handled with considerable intelligence and a fine grasp of dynamics and textures, but it was encouraging to find Kühn making a more direct approach to jazz in the late 1980s. *As Time Goes By* is a fine combination of standard material – 'When I Fall In Love' and the title-track – with originals and some elements of free-form playing. Not plugging in his once-ubiquitous synthesizer allows him to develop a much more direct discourse which is extremely impressive and well worth the effort of discovery.

Sergey Kuryokhin (1954–96)

PIANO, OTHER INSTRUMENTS

Born in Murmansk, Kuryokhin barnstormed his way through music, ejected from conservatories, playing in rock bands, forming vast and unwieldy 'Pop Mechanics' ensembles, creating musical-theatre events and playing a lot of piano along the way. Cancer killed this mercurial man at 42.

*****(*) Divine Madness**

Leo CD LR 813–816 4CD *Kuryokhin; Igor Butman (as, ss); Vladimir Chekasin (sax, v); Boris Grebenschikov, Yuri Kasparyan, Alexander Pumpyan, Victor Sologub, Igor Tikhomirov, Alexander Titov, Viktor Tzoi (g); Elvira Shylkova (acc, v); Seva Gakhil (clo); Sergey Panasenko (b, tba); Sergey Belischenko, Alexander Kondrashkin (d); Anatol Adasinsky, Gustav Gurianov, Leonid Leykin, Valentina Ponomareva (v).* 3/80–10/86.

***** Some Combinations Of Fingers And Passion**

Leo LRCD 178 *Kuryokhin (p solo).* 91.

Classically trained, and capable of playing quite legitimately in the midst of an otherwise chaotic performance, Kuryokhin was easily the most charismatic of the younger Russian players. He fronted his own 'Pop Mechanics' performances, mixed-media pieces that ape Western forms in a deliberately exaggerated, 'Martian' fashion that is not so much satirical as clownishly respectful. His Leo discs still crop up on disc and are noted in previous editions of this *Guide*. Since his death, though, the major source for Kuryokhin enthusiasts is *Divine Madness*, a multiple CD set of mostly unreleased material which covers his solo piano work and his Pop Mechanics projects in some detail.

Disc one includes two long piano improvisations, a 15-minute track from 1980 with the Creative Ensemble, and a 12-minute 'Opera' with the Vladimir Chekasin Big Band. The saxophonist was already chafing against what he saw as the limitations of the Ganelin Trio and was looking for a more overtly theatrical formulation. Kuryokhin helped steer him in that direction. The second disc features solo piano material formerly released on the Leo LP, *Popular Zoological Elements*, as well as *Pop Mechanics No. 17*, a key development in Kuryokhin's multi-genre theatre. The disc begins with a performance recorded in Novosibirsk with Valentina Ponomareva, Sergey Belischenko and Sergey Panasenko, who were the mainstays of Pop Mechanics.

There is a story attached to the late-night improvisations on disc three. Allegedly, Kuryokhin and guitarist Grebenschikov bribed their way into the Kirov Ballet and Opera Theatre in Leningrad with bottles of vodka, in order to record 'Subway Culture' on the theatre organ. The technical difficulties of taping pipe organ and guitar (which is played with a razor blade) were scarifying, but the result is grandly operatic. A middle section with the addition of saxophonist Igor Butman was recorded two years earlier. The final disc is the big-band *Introduction To Pop Mechanics*, which was released as Leo LP 146. Taped live in Leningrad, in a country on the brink of disintegration and political realignment, it has a quality compounded of optimism and nostalgia, a sense that things are never going to be quite the same again. And so it proved. Whether Kuryokhin was a dissident who used irony as a polemical weapon or one of the *yurodivye* – the holy fools – who work outside the bland logics of politics and establishment culture is never going to be clear, any more than Shostakovich's or Solzhenitsyn's exact aesthetic and political orientation can now be decoded. What remains is an extraordinary legacy of recorded work and the memory of a man constantly on the move, burning oxygen faster than seemed possible, let alone advisable. *Divine Madness* is too concentrated and too personal a testament to unpick. Anyone who has fallen under his spell should experience it. Anyone who remains sceptical should perhaps start with his one current solo album on CD.

Kuryokhin was more likely to refer to Rachmaninov than to Art Tatum in his solo performances, and he seemed to make it a point of principle to avoid direct reference from the jazz tradition. 'Blue Rondo A La Russ – A Tribute to Dave Brubeck' on *Some Combinations* is an apparent exception; Brubeck is perceived in a very different way in Russia than in his native United States and he enjoys honorific status as one of the first major jazzmen to appear there, but Kuryokhin's tribute is typically oblique.

Technically, his technique is interesting largely for its avoidance of the usual jazz-piano dichotomy between the left hand, with its rhythmic chording, and the right, which carries the melody and the subsequent improvisation. In addition, Kuryokhin was a virtuosic user of the pedals (a sharp contrast to Cecil Taylor, who uses them very sparingly indeed), creating some quite remarkable two-piano illusions. Rapidly pedalling also creates an occasional sense, as on the long 'Passion And Feelings' section of the later session, that tiny segments of music are being edited together at very high speed, creating the studied artificiality of tone one hears throughout his earlier work, an apparent refutation of conventional pianistic 'passion', whether of the Horowitz or the Taylor variety.

Kuryokhin's is very difficult music to characterize, because it consistently undermines its own premisses. These are quite alien to Western ears in any case. Kuryokhin is on record as believing that the end of State suppression of improvised music is an aesthetic disaster on a par with the death of Satan. There is certainly a slackness of purpose to the later record which one does not associate with Kuryokhin and which dilutes its considerable technical achievements.

Billy Kyle (1914–66)

PIANO

Philadelphia-born, Kyle worked with Tony Bradshaw and Lucky Millinder before a four-year stint with John Kirby, ending only with his being drafted. He joined the Louis Armstrong All Stars in 1953 and stayed there until his unexpected death while on tour with the group.

*** Billy Kyle 1937–1938

Classics 919 *Kyle; Charlie Shavers, Billy Hicks (t); Rex Stewart (c); Tyree Glenn (tb, vib); Buster Bailey (cl); Eddie Williams (cl, as); Tab Smith, Rudy Williams, Russell Procope (as); Harold Arnold, Don Byas, Ronald Haynes (ts); Danny Barker, Brick Fleagle (g); John Williams, Walter Page, John Kirby (b); O'Neil Spencer (d, v); Fran Marx, Jo Jones (d); The Palmer Brothers, Leon Lafell, Jack Sneed, Inez Cavanaugh (v).* 3/37–9/38.

*** Billy Kyle 1939–1946

Classics 941 *Kyle; Nat Gonella (t, v); Dick Vance, Charlie Shavers (t); Trummy Young (tb); Buster Bailey (cl); Benny Carter, Lem Davis (as); John Hardee (ts); Milt Herth, Bob Hamilton (org); Teddy Bunn (g, v); Brick Fleagle, Dave Barbour, Jimmy Shirley (g); John Kirby, Marty Kaplan, John Simmons (b); O'Neil Spencer (d, v); Jack Maisel, Buddy Rich (d).* 1/39–9/46.

The Philadelphian was a great acolyte of Earl Hines, so much so that his best work sounds like Hines on a good day: for a blindfold-test teaser, try the solo on 'The Song Is Ended' on the first record. Eventually, Kyle replaced Hines in the Louis Armstrong All Stars. But he also had a touch of Teddy Wilson urbanity in his playing, and the two trio sides he made for Decca in 1939, on the second disc, are beautiful examples of how elegant he could be. Classics have gathered together a group of sometimes obscure small-group swing dates which have Kyle's presence as their common element and, while some of them are forgettable – the feeble tracks with Bob Hamilton and Milt Herth on the second set especially – most have some bright moments on even a routine chart. There is a very agreeable 1938 date for Victor with Rex Stewart and (making their debuts) Tyree Glenn and Don Byas, while four tracks find Kyle turning up in support of Nat Gonella with Benny Carter and Buster Bailey. There is an intriguing 'Afternoon In Africa', from a trio date with Bailey and O'Neil Spencer, and the closing 1946 session includes the idiosyncratic tenorman, John Hardee. A trio session from the same year includes some splendid music but is marred by poor-sounding masters. The backwaters of swing on some almost-forgotten recordings.

Charles Kynard

ORGAN

Los Angeles-based organist of the 1960s who made a string of albums for Prestige during the period.

****(*) Reelin' With The Feelin' / Wa-Ta-Wa-Zui**

BGP CDBGPD 055 *Kynard; Virgil Jones (t); Wilton Felder, Rusty Bryant (ts); Joe Pass, Melvin Sparks (g); Carol Kaye, Jimmy] Lewis (b); Paul Humphrey, Idris Muhammad, Bernard Purdie (d).* 8/69–71.

Kynard, who is from Kansas City, was perhaps the last of the jazz organists to emerge in the 1960s. This British reissue doubles up two of his five Prestige albums. The first session is sagging with organ-combo clichés and Humphrey is a pedestrian drummer; the second adds electric piano to Kynard's instrument-list and is a bit brighter, thanks to the reliable Jones and Bryant, who can play the legs off a blues when they feel like it. Nothing fancy, but a good one to cheer up a traffic jam with the in-car stereo.

L.A.4

GROUP

One bossa nova pioneer, one cool West Coaster, one of the key bebop bass players, and a drummer who must have been a Time Lord; result: a genuine supergroup. The L.A. 4's lifespan was just long enough. It endured two changes of personnel in the percussion department; Chuck Flores gave way to Shelly Manne, who moved over for Jeff Hamilton. The group was ever smooth and accessible but with formidable musical intelligence in every bar.

***** The L.A.4**

Concord CCD 4018 *Bud Shank (as, f); Laurindo Almeida (g); Ray Brown (b); (d).* 74.

****(*) Just Friends**

Concord CCD 4199 *As above.* 75.

****(*) The L.A.4 Scores!**

Concord CCD 6008 *As above, except omit Manne; add (d).* 75.

***** Watch What Happens**

Concord CCD 4063 *As above.*

***** Zaca**

Concord CCD 4131 *As above.* 6/80.

***** Montage**

Concord CCD 4156 *As above.* 4/81.

***** Concord Jazz Heritage Series**

Concord CCD 4827 *As above discs.*

This West Coast supergroup foundered only when bassist Ray Brown's own career as a bandleader under his own name began to take off. The quartet's legacy of material is rather muted in hindsight. While it shares something of the Modern Jazz Quartet's intelligent conflation of jazz with classical forms, it hasn't had the same staying power. Even though the palette and dynamic range are greater, it's hard to recall an L.A.4 album in the way one remembers the classic MJQs.

The obvious difference was the hefty infusion of Latin-American themes and rhythms which came from Almeida, and the two influences fruitfully collide on the eponymous Concord in an excerpt from Rodrigo's *Concierto de Aranjuez*, a piece which it is now difficult to hear unmediated by either Segovia or Miles Davis and Gil Evans, but which is performed with intelligence and fire. Some of these experiments, like 'Prelude Opus 28, No. 4' on *The L.A.4 Scores!* and 'Nouveau Bach' on *Just Friends*, the two most disappointing of the albums, drift towards pretentiousness. By and large, though, the quartet has a strong jazz feel and is capable of playing, as on the excellent (but currently deleted) *Montreux* set, with a robust swing; the Ellington medley – or 'melange' – is beautifully done.

As well as a few residual Parkerisms, Shank has something of the tendency of his next model, Art Pepper, to float free of the rhythm section, which in this context permits some interesting counterpoint with Almeida. Shank's flute-playing is usually more challenging but tends to accentuate a vapidity which overtakes Almeida on slower ballads, as on his (mostly forgettable) Concord albums with Charlie Byrd. The rhythm section are unimpeachable and, though Manne was a more interesting drummer, Hamilton is a better blend with the overall sound. *Watch What Happens* is a good alternative to the *Montreux* set, with sensitive readings of 'Summertime', 'Mona Lisa', 'Nuages' and 'Misty'.

Of the two recent reappearances, there is not much to say except: steady as she goes. *Montage* is perhaps the drier and more academic of the pair, with its snatch of Villa-Lobos and the reedy chromaticism of 'Syrinx'. Brown plays out of his skin on this record and is, by some ironic contrast, rather far back on *Zaca*. As often, it is his contribution that anchors the group. To make up the deficit, Shank is masterful on the 1980 record.

As an introduction, or as an alternative to the group's eight discs on Concord (not all of them still around), the Jazz Heritage Compilation is a very attractive buy. It covers a fairly uneventful waterfront, but with a nice variation of pace and emotional temperature that is probably better than any of the individual albums.

Pat LaBarbera (born 1944)

SOPRANO AND TENOR SAXOPHONE

An American who settled in Canada, LaBarbera was a major soloist in the Buddy Rich band in the late 1960s and early '70s, subsequently playing with Elvin Jones.

***** JMOG**

Sackville SKCD2-2301 *LaBarbera; Don Thompson (p); Neil Swainson (b); Greg Joe LaBarbera (d).* 4/87.

Though he grew up in New York State, LaBarbera moved to Canada many years ago and is now seldom heard from on record. His most renowned stint was with Buddy Rich in the 1960s and '70s. *JMOG* is an acronym for Jazz Men On The Go, with brother Joe at the drums and the experienced team of Thompson and Swainson handling the middle row. It's not a rote blowing date since the seven originals all come from the pens of LaBarbera, Swainson or Thompson and, though there's nothing fancy in the construction, the lack of standard melodies asks a little more than usual from such seasoned pros. Swainson's nocturne, 'Dark Ocean', and Thompson's thoughtful tunes are the best. But LaBarbera's tenor blows along too many familiar paths to make the record transcend the usual tenor-and-rhythm virtues.

Steve Lacy (born 1934)

SOPRANO SAXOPHONE

The staggeringly prolific Lacy is almost unique in his dedication to the treacherously pitched soprano saxophone. Inspired by Sidney Bechet, he in turn inspired John Coltrane to turn to the small horn. Born Steven Lackritz in New York, he began his career playing Dixieland but was recruited by Cecil Taylor to the nascent avant-garde and subsequently became a Monk disciple, regularly returning to Monk compositions over the years. Lacy has performed in many contexts, from solo saxophone, small groups with his wife Irène Aëbi, to larger, almost classically configured ensembles.

***** Axieme**

Red RR 123120 *Lacy (ss solo).* 9/75.

***** Straws**

Cramps CRSCD 066 *As above.* 77.

*****(*) Only Monk**

Soul Note 121160 *As above.* 7/85.

****(*) Solo**

In Situ 590051 *As above.* 85.

****** More Monk**

Soul Note 121210 *As above.* 4/89.

There are, at a (now very) conservative estimate, more than 100 recordings in the Lacy discography, with a substantial proportion of those as leader or solo performer. His prolific output anticipates that of Anthony Braxton, consisting as it does of group performances with a relatively conventional – if Thelonious Monk can ever be considered conventional – 'standards' repertoire, large-scale compositions for ensembles and mixed-media groups, right down to solo improvisation. In one significant respect, though, the two part company utterly. Where Braxton has been promiscuously eclectic in his multi-instrumentalism, tackling all the saxophones from sopranino to contrabass, and all the clarinets as well, Lacy has concentrated his considerable energies throughout his career on the soprano saxophone, which is why we have listed this group of solo performances first and out of chronological sequence. Drawing his initial inspiration from Sidney Bechet, he has combined a profound interest in Dixieland jazz with an occasionally extreme modernism. In a typical performance there may be short, almost abecedarian melodic episodes, repeated many times with minimal variation; there will be passages of free, abstract sound, often produced by sucking through the reed; there may even be strange, onomatopoeic effects, bird-calls and toneless shouts. The 1975 *Axieme* is probably the best available example of his more abstract style. *Straws*, recorded in Italy and available on CD only somewhat recently, is more eclectic in its inspiration, with pieces dedicated to Stravinsky (who had died some time before) and Janis Joplin, dedicatee of the moving 'Hemline'. Recorded in extreme close-up, it's one of the most revealing of the records in terms of the microstructure of Lacy's saxophone sound, exposing all the gritty little resonances, breath sounds and clicks.

Lacy favours tremendously long lines with no obvious developmental logic – which might be reminiscent of Lee Konitz's work, but for Lacy's insistence on long, sustained notes and modestly paced whole-note series. The weakness of *Solo*, caught live in the mid-1980s and perhaps best left in the vaults, is that such devices do untypically seem to be in default of anything larger. A melodist rather than an orthodox changes player – those unfamiliar with his music can find it deceptively simplistic, almost naïve, on first exposure – Lacy has been obsessed with the compositions of Thelonious Monk for more than 30 years and has become perhaps the foremost interpreter of Monk's music. The two solo Monk albums are among the finest of Lacy's multifarious and often interchangeable recordings. If the earlier of the pair is less immediately appealing, it is also more challenging and requires a closer acquaintance with the source material; with the exception of 'Pannonica' and 'Misterioso', the pieces are less well known than those established favourites on *More Monk*: 'Ruby My Dear', 'Straight No Chaser', 'Trinkle Tinkle', 'Crepuscule With Nellie'. Lacy has turned to Monk's music many times during his career. (There is more of it, alongside work by fellow-Monastics, on DIW's four-CD *Interpretations Of Monk*.) It represents a source of inexhaustible inspiration for him.

However, Lacy also draws on many other musics, both formal and popular. In his solo improvisations he often accelerates essentially simple 12-tone figures to the point of disintegration, allowing each piece to end unresolved. The antithesis of bebop expressionism or the huge inscapes of John Coltrane (whose use of soprano saxophone was directly inspired by Lacy's example), the solos are cold and impersonal but not without a certain broad humour that skirts burlesque. There are perhaps more completely achieved recordings than these, but there's no better place to make acquaintance with one – or perhaps two – of the music's great originals.

***** Soprano Sax**

Original Jazz Classics OJC 130 *Lacy; Wynton Kelly (p); Buell Neidlinger (b); Dennis Charles (d).* 11/57.

****** Reflections**

Original Jazz Classics OJC 063 *Lacy; Mal Waldron (p); Buell Neidlinger (b); Elvin Jones (d).* 10/58.

As with *The Straight Horn*, below, there was some attempt at the end of the 1950s to market Lacy as the soprano saxophone specialist, trading on the instrument's relative unfamiliarity. *Soprano Sax* is somewhat atypical in that it consists of rather more developed harmonic improvisations on open-ended standards. Kelly's time-feel and exuberant chording aren't obviously suited to Lacy's method, and 'Rockin' In Rhythm' sounds much as if a lion were playing see-saw with a swan. There is, though, an excellent, slightly off-beat reading of 'Alone Together'. Some hints still of the problems recording engineers faced in miking Lacy's horn.

Reflections was the first of Lacy's all-Monk recordings. Waldron was one of the few piano players who understood how such intractable material could be approached, and there are hints already of what he and Lacy were capable of in duo performance. Neidlinger has an attractively firm sound on both records, but Jones sounds slightly out of place, reinforcing Lacy's characteristic tendency to ignore the explicit metre. The sound is not altogether well balanced, and Neidlinger's lower-register fills are lost on the vinyl format. Lacy, on the other hand, sounds rather acid on the CD, but the performances more than make up for minor cosmetic defects.

*** The Straight Horn Of Steve Lacy

Candid 9007 *Lacy; Charles Davis (bs); John Ore (b); Roy Haynes (d).* 60.

One of the best-known and certainly most accessible of Lacy's records, *The Straight Horn* sounds rather muted and tentative after the passage of four decades. In conception it marks a bridge between bebop (which was never Lacy's natural constituency) to the New Thing, as represented by two Cecil Taylor compositions. Monk again provides the keystone, but whereas the saxophonist sounds in complete sympathy with this material – 'Introspection', 'Played Twice' and 'Criss Cross' – his approach to Charlie Parker's 'Donna Lee' sounds remarkably hesitant, all the more so given Roy Haynes's palpable delight in the accelerated metre. Nor is it certain that Lacy or his sidemen have got a firm purchase on Taylor's 'Louise' and 'Air'; compare Archie Shepp's handling of the latter on *The World Of Cecil Taylor*, also Candid. Nevertheless, this is a significant and not unattractive record. Davis's throaty baritone fulfils much the same timbral function as Roswell Rudd's or George Lewis's trombone on later recordings, and the pianoless rhythm section generates a more sympathetic context than Elvin Jones's wilder rush. Recommended, but with reservations.

***(*) Evidence

Original Jazz Classics OJC 1755 *Lacy; Don Cherry (t); Carl Brown (b); Billy Higgins (d).* 11/61.

Lacy's associations with Monk and Cecil Taylor are well known, and there was an intriguing attraction-of-opposites in his impact on John Coltrane. Rarely, though, is he ever mentioned in the same breath as the other great modernist, Ornette Coleman. In part, this is because they worked on parallel tracks, rarely intersecting but concentrating on a similar redistribution of melody and rhythm. *Evidence* is the closest Lacy comes to the sound if not the substance of Coleman's great quartets. On 'The Mystery Song' and 'Evidence', he achieves something like Ornette's lonely stillness. Cherry, on trumpet rather than one of his squeaky miniatures, provides a strong tonal contrast (but wouldn't it have been interesting to pair Lacy's soprano with cornet or pocket trumpet?) and the rhythm section, pianoless again and with the little-known Carl Brown standing as acceptable substitute for Charlie Haden, plays with good understanding.

**** Scratching The Seventies / Dreams

Saravah SHL 2082 3CD *Lacy; Enrico Rava (t); Lawrence Butch Morris (c); Italo Toni (tb); Steve Potts (as, ss); Claudio Volonte (cl); Takashi Kako (p); Michael Smith (p, org); Derek Bailey, Boulou Ferre, Jack Treese (g); Irène Aëbi (clo, v); Jean-Jacques Avenel (b, kora, cheng, autoharp); Kent Carter (b, clo); Kenneth Tyler (d, perc, f); Oliver Johnson, Carlo Tonaghi (d).* 6/69–77.

A rich garnering of material from a period and an association that yielded one of Lacy's classic records, *The Owl*, and also some of his least-known material. To deal with the latter first, there are two long parts to 'Roba', from the 1969 group featuring Enrico Rava and recorded by arch-modernist Alvin Curran. This includes a rare excursion by Lacy on sopranino saxophone, a dry, bat-squeak sound that floats outside the harmonic scale, and a 1971 solo performance, chronologically the next thing on the record, which makes inventive use of tape.

The material on *Scraps* and *Dreams* (which features Derek Bailey) is more familiar in conception and execution, and the latter includes a wonderful version of what is still one of the saxophonist's most durable compositions, 'The Wane'. 'The Uh Uh Uh' is inspired by Monk and could almost pass for a composition of the master's except that it is so far removed from the blues.

The Owl is masterly, and the inclusion of these seven bands is what makes this compilation indispensable. Morris is present only for part of the set, but his urgent, pungent tone makes a huge difference. Lacy has not worked much with trumpeters and, apart from Roswell Rudd, has not demonstrated much kinship with brass. Here, though, he feeds off Butch's delivery and flow of ideas, and weaves himself into a double helix with the cornetist.

*** Cinco Minutos de Jazz

Strauss ST 1087 *Lacy; Steve Potts (as); Irène Aëbi (clo, hca, radio); Kent Carter (b); Noel McGhie (d, perc).* 72.

Recorded in Lisbon to celebrate the sixth anniversary of a radio show which dedicated the same length of time to jazz that orthodox psychoanalysts give to their patients. And just to sustain that improbable analogy, Lacy digs deep into the collective unconscious (uh oh, that's Jungian) to create a network of allusions and references that tap back into the early history of jazz, something that Lacy was to do at moments of maximum confidence. He tags Hodges and Bechet, there is a brief nod to Johnny Dodds on 'No Baby', and lots of ironic pastiche elsewhere.

**** Weal & Woe

Emanem 4004 *Lacy; Steve Potts (as, ss); Irène Aëbi (v, vl, clo); Kent Carter (b); Oliver Johnson (d).* 72, 73.

Two important components to this very valuable reissue of Emanem and Quark LP material. The earlier recording is a document of Lacy's first ever solo soprano saxophone concerts, made in Avignon. Just four years after Anthony Braxton's pioneering *For Alto*, it is fascinating to hear Lacy take a very different course, sinuously melodic, less antagonistic in attack than Braxton but no less percussive and definite, and no less willing to superimpose different rhythmic shapes over a pretty basic line. *The Woe* was Lacy's anti-war suite, a powerfully advocated protest that gave this classic group something to get their teeth into. The recording is a little unfriendly to Aëbi and to some of the quieter soprano saxophone parts, but there is so much meat and meaning to the performances that one hardly notices any such shortcomings.

***** Saxophone Special**

Emanem 4024 *Lacy; Enrico Rava (t); Lawrence Butch Morris (c); Italo Toni (tb); Steve Potts; Trevor Watts; (ss, as); Evan Parker (ss, ts, bs); Derek Bailey (g); Michel Waisvisz (syn); Kent Carter (b); John Stevensl (d).* 7/73, 12/74.

These are tapes recorded in concert at the 100 Club in London's Oxford Street and the more up-market Wigmore Hall a year and a half later. At the time, Lacy was experimenting with saxophone harmonics based on seconds; Potts, who came to Britain with Lacy and Kent Carter, is supremely confident in the idiom. '38', performed at the 100 Club with Bailey and Stevens, is a tribute to Coleman Hawkins, and it's followed by 'Flakes' and 'Revolutionary Suicide', the latter derived from a damaged tape. The whole session was originally released in faulty stereo, but the reissue uses a single good mono channel. The 1974 session makes use of pure noise and found sounds, on LP on 'Dreams' and from Michel Waisvisz's crude by expressive synth effects. Essentially, though, it's a saxophone quartet spread out across the stereo picture, and dramatically different from the kind of work done by a conventional SATBar line-up. When all four players are on soprano, the overtone field is immensely complex, and one wishes for a chance to hear this same grouping recorded with more up-to-date technology.

***** Trickles**

Black Saint 120008 *Lacy; Roswell Rudd (tb, chimes); Kent Carter (b); Beaver Harris (d).* 3/76.

With his brief, substantive titles, Lacy almost seems to be attempting a new generic definition with each succeeding album. There is certainly a sense in which *Trickles* works by the slowest accumulation, like the slow accretions of limestone. There is also, unfortunately, an obduracy and resistance in this music that one doesn't often find elsewhere. The fault is not with the band. Rudd plays wonderfully, carving big, abstract shapes that are shaded in by Carter and Harris, coaxing a more intense sound from the saxophonist. It's Lacy who seems unyielding. On sabbatical from his lifelong study of Monk, he seems at something of a loss, stating ideas without rationale or conviction, redeeming them only by the absolute consistency of his playing. Utterly fascinating, like all of Lacy's work, and perhaps all the more significant for being less entire and achieved, but certainly not his most successful recording.

****** Chirps**

FMP CD 29 *Lacy; Evan Parker (ss).* 7/85.

By the turn of the 1980s, Lacy appears to have regarded total improvisational abstraction as a way-station rather than a long-term direction in his work. Nevertheless, in *Chirps* he and fellow soprano saxophonist Evan Parker produced one of the best and most significant free albums of the decade. Concentrating on high, brief sounds that are more like insect-twitter than bird-song, the two players interleave minimalist episodes with a level of concentration that seems almost superhuman. Endlessly demanding – and a quarter of an hour longer on CD reissue – it's unlikely to appeal to anyone primed for hummable melody or more than usually susceptible to sounds at the dog-whistle end of the spectrum. It is, though, curiously involving and has considerably more accessible charm than the sere whisperings of the now-deleted duos with British guitarist Derek Bailey.

****(*) Troubles**

Black Saint 120035 *Lacy; Steve Potts (as, ss); Kent Carter (clo, b); Oliver Johnson (d); Irène Aëbi (v, vl, clo).* 5/79.

This was the period when Lacy characterized his music as 'poly-free', an attempt to categorize his still rather ramshackle combination of unfettered group improvisation with scored or predetermined passages. One of the problems with the album is that it sounds precisely like that: uneasy alternations with little coherence or flow other than the sidewinding motion of Lacy's own lines.

*****(*) The Flame**

Soul Note 121035 *Lacy; Bobby Few (p); Dennis Charles (d).* 1/82.

Whenever he plays, Few emerges as the fulcrum of Lacy's groups. His composition, 'Wet Spot', is the briefest and the only non-Lacy number on the album, but it's a particularly clear example of how Lacy and his loyal group of collaborators have rationalized the stretched-out improvisations of Cecil Taylor and the tautness of Monk. In timbre and tonality these sessions strongly resemble Taylor's 'bass-less' trios, but with the emphasis switched unequivocally to the saxophone. Lacy's four compositions form part of an ongoing series of dedications to 'eminent source figures', or what Lacy calls his 'Luminaries'; 'The Match' is for the surrealist Man Ray, 'Gusts', 'Licks' and 'The Flame' for an assortment of instrumentalists from around the world whose music has inspired him. In the trio context, Lacy sounds much more rhythmic than usual and appears to adapt his line to the drummer's beat, punching his own little toneless accents at appropriate moments.

***** The Condor**

Soul Note 121135 *Lacy; Steve Potts (ss, as); Bobby Few (p); Irène Aëbi (vn, v); Jean-Jacques Avenel (b); Oliver Johnson (d).* 6/85.

*****(*) The Window**

Soul Note 121185 *Lacy; Jean-Jacques Avenel (b); Oliver Johnson (d).* 7/87.

Two fine hat ART albums from this period, *Morning Joy* and *Flim Flam*, have both disappeared from the catalogue, which is sad, since the former is perhaps the best single Lacy album, and certainly one of the most straightforward. 'Morning Joy' also kicks off the fine 1985 *The Condor*, where the balance of written-out passages and freer improvisation seems almost ideal; it also features some of the best interplay between the two saxophones, with Potts in exceptionally good form. If one of the great pleasures of investigating Lacy's mammoth output is the comparison of (sometimes drastically, sometimes only minimally) different versions of the same repertoire piece or 'instant standard' (his term), then these are critical performances for an understanding of how unconventionally he relates to a 'rhythm section'.

Stripped down to just saxophone, bass and drums on *The Window*, he reveals just how unconventional a player he actually is, refusing all the obvious rhythmic and chordal clues, playing lines so oblique as almost to belong to another piece altogether. 'Flakes' is another of those apparently self-descriptive compositions that resist all external reference. Again, very fine.

*****(*) One Fell Swoop**
Silkheart SHCD 103 *Lacy; Charles Tyler (as, bs); Jean-Jacques Avenel (b); Oliver Johnson (d).* 6/86.

***** The Gleam**
Silkheart SHCD 102 *As above, except omit Tyler; add Steve Potts (as, ss).* 7/86.

Lacy's two Silkheart recordings throw up some interesting contrasts. It's fascinating to hear him working with a lower horn, as he had with Charles Davis way back. There are signs on *One Fell Swoop* that he is looking back and re-running some ideas from his own bottom drawer, reviving that Dixieland counterpoint which had tended to get unravelled and spun out at unrecognizable length in more recent years. The title-track (two versions) and 'Ode To Lady Day' are splendid performances. Nothing quite as striking on *The Gleam*, but it's another perfectly acceptable quartet performance for enthusiasts, and the two takes of 'Napping' provide much to think about.

****** Sempre Amore**
Soul Note 121170 *Lacy; Mal Waldron (p).* 2/86.

*****(*) Let's Call This ... Esteem**
Slam CD 501 *As above.* 5/93.

****** Communique**
Soul Note 121487 *As above.*

The dedication to Waldron signals one of the most productive partnerships in Lacy's career. The pianist's name comes first on the wonderful *Sempre Amore*, but the honours are strictly shared. Waldron's big, dark left-hand chords and single-note statements take some of the acid out of Lacy's frail and thinly voiced takes on a bag of Ellington and Strayhorn themes. The opening 'Johnny Come Lately' is appealingly off-centre and 'Prelude To A Kiss' sounds at the edge of sleep. It's worth comparing 'A Flower Is A Lovesome Thing' to the version Waldron recorded with Marion Brown the previous year on *Songs Of Love And Regret*, where his accompaniment is little more than a sequence of moodily recessed pedals. With the undemonstrative Lacy, he's all over the place, arpeggiating and trilling furiously, like Wordsworth trying to explain to Newton what a flower really is.

Let's Call This ... Esteem shouldn't be confused with the hat Art *Let's Call This*, which still hasn't made it to CD. The Slam disc was recorded during a concert at Oxford Playhouse, compèred by another soprano specialist, Lol Coxhill. The sound is oddly cavernous but the performances are uniformly excellent. Another version of 'Johnny Come Lately' suggests how much they've grown into the partnership. The Monk tunes – 'Let's Call This', 'Monk's Dream', 'Evidence' and the inevitable 'Epistrophy' – are expertly co-ordinated and by no means soulless. Waldron's own 'Snake Out' sounds great without a larger band, and the pianist has his moment again on 'In A Sentimental Mood'. The Soul Note disc catches the duo in one of their better latter-day encounters.

****(*) Image**
Ah Um 001 *Lacy; Steve Arguëlles (d).* 10/87.

Arguëlles may be outclassed; Lacy may have done just one gig too many of this sort. The effect is of two players conversing politely over slightly too great a distance, like friends spotting each other by chance at opposite corners of a restaurant and refusing to get up and walk over to the other's table, thus spending the evening mouthing deafly over the gap. Lacy generally takes the lead, easing his way through Monk's 'Evidence' with almost magisterial calm, leaving the drummer to patter out completely autonomous lines and figures (how might Steve Noble have faced the same challenge?). Only towards the end of the set, which goes up a gear after the second track and then over-revs in it until almost too late, is there any real dialectic. Lacy has some fine moments, like the solo intro to 'Art', but it's not a classic.

***** Packet**
New Albion NA1349 *Lacy; Frederic Rzewski (p).*

Rzewski is a composer/improviser of great experience who shares something of Lacy's cool, unemphatic approach. The main problem here is the balance between piano and saxophone. They seem to fight more than is strictly necessary and, though the recording has great clarity, there's too artificial a balance. One shouldn't feel distracted from the music by technical considerations, but that's what happens here.

*****(*) Revenue**
Soul Note 121234 *Lacy; Steve Potts (as, ss); Jean-Jacques Avenel (b); John Betsch (d).* 2/93.

****** Vespers**
Soul Note 121260 *As above, except add Ricky Ford (ts), Tom Varner (frhn), Bobby Few (p), Irène Aëbi (v).* 7/93.

Betsch's arrival on board gave the Lacy group a less raw, slightly more delicate rhythmic feel. Even so, as he proves on 'The Rent' and the title-track, the new drummer is no slouch when it comes to sticking his foot in the door and demanding a hearing. He powers these tracks along very crisply and, on 'Gospel', subtly stretches and compresses the time exactly in keeping with Lacy's own elastic pulse. Potts more than ever brings in ideas of his own and a range of contributions that might be likened to Don Cherry's in the classic Ornette quartet: responsive, aware of the leader's intentions and requirements, but still absolutely individual and effortlessly taking up point on 'The Uh Uh Uh'. Now in the middle of a long purple patch, Lacy seems incapable of making an indifferent album. *Vespers* is focused on Blaga Dimitrova's lyrics for Aëbi; the songs are softly melancholy farewells and remembrances of departed friends and idols: Miles Davis, Corrado Costa, the artists Arshile Gorky (whose 1946 abstract graces the cover) and Keith Haring (whose bold, stark lines had something in common with Lacy's saxophone sound), clarinettist John Carter, John Coltrane, Charles Mingus and Stan Getz. This is perhaps the most personal music we've heard from Lacy, and it is all the more affecting in coming from a man normally so reticent about inward states. Aëbi is magnificent, as is Ricky Ford, who now notoriously plays better on other people's records than on his own.

****** 5 × Monk 5 × Lacy**
Silkheart SHCD 144 *Lacy (ss solo).* 3/94.

Having spent a good deal of time over the past few years working with the group and with larger-scale arrangements, Lacy shows every sign of wanting to return to unaccompanied performance. This one is exactly as described, five tunes by the master and five originals, including the familiar 'The Crust' and 'Deadline', both of them well-established Lacy repertory tunes. The Monk compositions are also things Lacy has covered in detail in the past, but this time his take on 'Pannonica' and 'Evidence' is notable for subtle shifts in the geometry of the tune, as if he is trying some virtual recomposition, changing internal relationships without changing the components, rather like one of those relativity diagrams in which time-space is presumed to be gridded on a sheet of rubber which can then be stretched and folded but not cut or torn. All the material was recorded during an improvisation festival in Stockholm. It isn't clear whether these ten tracks were the whole of Lacy's performance or an edited segment. At 45 minutes – and this is a hobby-horse of ours – it seems perfectly balanced as a CD. Any more material would simply blur the lines.

**** Actuality

Cavity Search CSR 24 *Lacy (ss solo).* 4/95.

The liner-note begins with a useful comparison. It was Anthony Braxton who pioneered the solo saxophone record and, as we have noted elsewhere, Braxton is perhaps the only other performer on the planet to have had his career so thoroughly documented. However, Pierre Coussault of Cavity Search is more and rightly concerned to point up differences rather than similarities, and he is probably right in claiming priority for Lacy in developing the art of solo reed improvisation. 'Actuality' is an interesting word because – as this European exile understands – it doesn't mean 'real', the opposite of false or imaginary, but 'here and now', as in the French word for news, *actuelles.* And what this live record documents is Lacy's commitment to the thought of the moment, to a kind of articulation in which a phrase or a note is not predetermined and then not analysed or debated, but simply articulated and allowed its moment in the air. As usual, Lacy draws on compositions from the span of his career. 'Revolutionary Suicide' is dedicated to the life of Black Panther Huey Newton, but was called back to mind by news of violent struggle elsewhere. 'Moms' is exactly what it says, a song of affection and thanks to Steve's and Irène Aëbi's mothers. 'The Door', with its knocking sounds, is devoted to Joseph Haydn, perhaps the most at-hand of all the classical composers; for Lacy, the knock at the door (something of a twentieth-century bogey) is also the moment of maximum immediacy, a challenge. Challenging music this is. With the exception of the final club track, *Actuality* was recorded in a Portland, Oregon, church, an acoustic that throws a wrap round Lacy's chill tone. Congratulations to Cavity Search for having the foresight to tape and issue one of the best performances of recent years.

*** The Joan Miró Foundation Concert

New Contemporary Music NCM 10 *Lacy; Irène Aëbi (v).* 6/95.

This was never intended for release and there are flaws and inconsistencies of pitch on the source tape which haven't been successfully addressed, but the Lacys' Barcelona concert was one of those magical occasions where the yin–yang of Steve's dry, cerebral line and Irène's floating melodism mesh perfectly. The opening sequence is Monk material, the closing section settings of poetry by Robert Creeley and an excellent example of the couple's response to literary texts. There is also a fantastic arrangement of Herman Melville's literary credo, 'Art'.

**** Five Facings

FMP CD 85 *Lacy; Marilyn Crispell, Ulrich Gumpert, Misha Mengelberg, Vladimir Miller, Fred Van Hove (p).* 4/96.

Five nights at the 1996 Workshop Freie Musik and five confrontations with piano players of markedly different disposition. Four of the eight performances are Lacy compositions. Two rather short items with Crispell open the record and fail to catch light, mainly because she tends to think in great massy blocks of sound and doesn't seem prepared to follow the saxophonist's long, weaving lines. At the opposite end, Miller is perfectly content to act as accompanist on 'The Wane', making no attempt to stamp his personality on the music.

The real meat of the record lies in between, a magnificent duo improvisation with van Hove, a long meditation on 'Art' with the classically inclined and suitably dry Gumpert (a collaborator on the 1985 *Deadline*), and three Monk tunes performed with the redoubtable Mengelberg. Of these, 'Ruby, My Dear' is a masterpiece that almost justifies the price on its own; 'Off Minor' and 'Evidence' are a little drier, but no less thoughtful and accomplished. A wonderful record, in what has become Lacy's favourite and most successful setting.

*** Solo: Live At Unity Temple

Wobbly Rail WOB 003 *Lacy (ss solo).* 11/97.

Unity Temple is an ecumenical religious building in Chicago, designed by Frank Lloyd Wright. As such, and given its humane acoustic, it's the perfect setting to run through an unusual, comfortable and familiar set of themes, including his now well-attested Monk medley and the delightfully wry 'Revenue'. 'Crust' and 'Art' are textbook Lacy, and this is the kind of record with which you might win round someone who's previously found his unaccompanied performances hard to follow.

***(*) The Rent

Cavity Search 44 *Lacy; Jean-Jacques Avenel (b); John Betsch (d).* 98.

A cracking trio record that retreads some of Lacy's most distinctive themes, 'Door', 'Flakes', 'Shuffle Boil (Monk)', and re-energizes them considerably. His playing has of late taken on a warmer and more expressive cast, a more vocalized tone than in the past, and it suits this context extremely well. Avenel and Betsch are entirely in tune with the approach and the recording is very plain and faithful.

*** Sands

Tzadik 7124 *Lacy; Irène Aëbi (v).* 98.

Pages from Lacy's musical workbook, spun out at leisure and with admirable concentration at home. Steve's tone is warm, precise and refreshingly ambiguous. There are more exciting solo performances, but this is well up to scratch.

*** The Cry

Soul Note 121315 2CD *As for small-group albums above.* 99.

Lacy is the key presence on this highly developed and intelligently programmed set of his own compositions. Aëbi is, as so often, his most responsive and sympathetic partner, but on tracks like 'The Cry' and 'Rundown', which end the album, Steve is away out on his own, rapt and lost in the intricacies of his music. The difficulties of recording Lacy lie in the sharpness and intensity of the high harmonic he achieves, and here and there the saxophone tone distorts and flattens, but the music comes through strongly nevertheless.

Bireli Lagrene (born 1966)

GUITAR

Born to a Sinti gypsy family, Lagrene began playing guitar at four and quickly became a prodigy. He was touring as a teenager and showed a style that went back to Django as well as taking in the recent past and the present.

***** Routes To Django**

Jazzpoint JP 1003 *Lagrene; Jorg Reiter (p); Wolfgang Lackerschmidt (vib); Gaiti Lagrene, Tschirglo Loeffler (g); Scmitto Kling (vn); Jan Jankeje (b).* 5/80.

***** Bireli Swing '81**

Jazzpoint JP 1009 *As above, except omit Reiter, Lackerschmidt and Kling; add Bernd Rabe (ss), Allen Blairman (d).* 4/81.

If Django Reinhardt were to have a spiritual heir, it would surely be Lagrene, who emerged from a gypsy community in the 1980s to stun European and American audiences with his virtuosity. Both of the above were recorded in concert, with Lagrene's electrifying improvisations (all done on acoustic guitar) conducted on a range of material which includes swing, blues, bop and original themes, all of it mastered with effortless aplomb, even when it sounds as if the guitarist isn't sure of his ground.

That hint of flying blind gives the greatest excitement to the debut album, *Routes To Django*, which includes a nerve-racking romp through the tune identified as 'Night And Day' (actually 'Don't Worry 'Bout Me'). The 1981 session is nearly as good, although Rabe is an irrelevance; but from this point Lagrene began to fall foul of seeming like a novelty act.

****(*) Stuttgart Aria**

Jazzpoint JP 1019 *Lagrene; Vladislaw Sendecki (ky); Jaco Pastorius (b, p, v); Jan Jankeje (syn, v); Peter Lubke (d); Serge Bringolf (perc, v).* 3/86.

Lagrene meets Pastorius. This souvenir of a European tour is good-humoured but tends to go the way of all live fusion albums: a noisy dead-end. Salvaged by flashes of brilliance by both frontmen, including a ferocious 'Donna Lee', it doesn't amount to very much. Lagrene's subsequent Blue Note albums all seem to be missing in action at present.

***** Blue Eyes**

Dreyfus Jazz FDM 36591-2 *Lagrene; Maurice Vander (p); Christian Minh Doky (b); André Ceccarelli (d).* 6/97.

The discography is in an unsatisfactory state at present. This recent entry by Lagrene is a bit of a shock, a Sinatra tribute which features the guitarist turning in vocals on four tracks. Sensibly, he sings only on chucklesome tunes like 'Luck Be A Lady' and doesn't go for the heartbreakers, since he's scarcely the crooning type. The guitar playing remains heroic in a dashed-off sort of way, but this is a relentlessly swinging rhythm section and they're pushing him pretty hard. Rather pin-bright a lot of the time; he could relax a little more on the ballads.

Oliver Lake (born 1944)

ALTO SAXOPHONE, OTHER SAXOPHONES, FLUTE

One of the few alto saxophonists who has whole-heartedly taken up the challenge of Eric Dolphy, not in terms of multi-instrumentalism, but in striving to play 'inside' and 'outside' at the same time. Still best known as a member of the World Saxophone Quartet, Lake has created a substantial body of recordings as leader, almost all of them reflecting that sometimes schizophrenic but profoundly adventurous ambition.

***** Heavy Spirits**

Black Lion BLCD 60209 *Lake; Olu Dara (t); Joseph Bowie (tb); Donald Smith (p); Al Philemon Jones, Steven Peisch, C Panton (vn); Stafford James (b); Victor Lewis, Charles Bobo Shaw (d).* 1–2/75.

A founding member of the pioneering World Saxophone Quartet, Lake has been rather neglected in the rush to sanctify his WSQ partner, David Murray. A player of great power who touches bases in funk and free improvisation, Lake is also capable of great sophistication and a sort of convulsive beauty that requires a little time to assimilate. *Heavy Spirits* seems, at this distance, like a relic of an exciting period in the American avant-garde, a sort of grab-bag of possibilities: group tracks, three pieces for alto and three violins, a brusquely contemplative alto solo and a bustling trio with Bowie and Shaw. Hit and miss, but untempered and often intriguing.

***** Prophet**

Black Saint 120044 *Lake; Baikida Carroll (t, flhn); Donald Smith (p); Jerry Harris (b); Pheeroan akLaff (d).* 8/80.

***** Clevont Fitzhubert**

Black Saint 120054 *As above, except omit Harris.* 4/81.

*****(*) Expandable Language**

Black Saint 120074 *Lake; Geri Allen (p); Kevin Eubanks (g); Fred Hopkins (b); Pheeroan akLaff (d).* 9/84.

Expandable Language sets Lake alongside Geri Allen and Kevin Eubanks for six provocative explorations, alternately fierce and lyrical, almost a mainstream situation for this powerful voice. *Prophet* is a less cohesive album but also a far bolder one, and it's interesting to track the path of Lake's engagement with free procedures over this (almost) five-year period. The tension between orthodox, changes-based jazz and abstraction has always been a creative one for him; in his interchanges with Carroll one can detect distant echos of Parker and Gillespie duelling at Massey Hall, and indeed Ornette and Cherry trading ever sharper phrases on the early Atlantics. The middle record with its enigmatic dedication to a 'good friend' is packed with intriguing themes and counter-themes, not least the title-track. 'November '80' is also finely judged and there is a single composition by the fiery Carroll, who features on his own 'King'.

***** Boston Duets**

Music & Arts CD 732 *Lake; Donal Fox (p).* 8/89.

The present listing is depleted by the disappearance of *Zaki*, one of the saxophonist's best albums, which has gone the way of all of hat ART's influential 6000 series. It's to be hoped that it will return soon. Lake scarcely ever returned to this freewheeling free-bop style, though there are echoes of it, paradoxically, in the slightly formal setting of the duos with Donal Fox. The pianist is a restless and highly intelligent improviser who also works in more formal structures, and it's easy to hear why the two men found the partnership congenial.

*****(*) Virtual Reality: Total Escapism**
Gazell 4004 *Lake; Anthony Michael Peterson (g); Santi Debriano (b); Pheeroan akLaff (d).* 10/91.

Not always the easiest label to track down, but still in print and well worth the hunt. This was Lake's working quartet and perhaps the most pungent band he'd had for a decade. Having dipped a toe into more formal, 'sheet-driven' composition, this marked a return to post-Dolphy jazz. Eric is represented by 'Prophet', which follows a version of Mingus's 'Fables Of Faubus' even more deeply rooted in Dolphy's style. Bobby Bradford's 'Shedetude' is also meat and drink to Lake, who is in very fine form indeed, relaxed but poised and thinking fast on his feet. A very fine album.

***** Edge-ing**
Black Saint 120104 *Lake; Charles Eubanks (p); Reggie Workman (b); Andrew Cyrille (d).* 6/93.

***** Dedicated To Dolphy**
Black Saint 120144 *Lake; Russell Gunn (t); Charles Eubanks (p); Belden Bullock (b); Cecil Brooks (d).* 11/94.

Lake has a powerful enthusiasm for the work of Eric Dolphy and, on *Prophet*, includes two of Dolphy's most vibrant compositions, 'Hat and Beard' and 'Something Sweet, Something Tender', both from the classic *Out to Lunch!*. They're imaginative re-readings, not just pastiches, and certainly a good deal more inventive than the very straight versions of those same two tracks (plus 'Miss Ann', 'G.W.', '245' and Mal Waldron's 'Fire Waltz') on *Dedicated To Dolphy*, which is a disappointment. The one quantifiable plus is the trumpet-work of Russell Gunn from St Louis, sounding brisk and bright and very like the young Freddie Hubbard.

Lake veers towards lyricism again on *Edge-ing*, rejigging 'Zaki' for a fuller-voiced band and bringing in material like John Hicks's almost schmaltzy 'Peanut Butter' and Curtis Clark's unexpected 'Verve Nerve'. His bluesy tone is eloquent enough to sustain some rather bland arrangements, and the bass and drum interactions are consistently interesting. Which leaves the finger pointing at Eubanks, a rather dull accompanist who doesn't quite have the Hicks trick of playing spikily *and* lyrically off pat.

*****(*) Movement, Turns & Switches**
Passin' Thru 41210 *Lake; Kenyatta Beasley (t); Donal Fox (p); Sandra Billingslea, Ashley Horne, Regina Carter (vn); Maxine Roach (vla); Eileen Folson (clo); Belden Bullock (b).* 8/96.

***** Matador Of 1st & 1st**
Passin' Thru 40709 *Lake (ss, as, f, bells, v).* 97.

These records signal a new label and a new phase in Lake's career. *Matador* is a strange montage of instrumental miniatures, some of them only a matter of seconds long, others shaped almost like scaled-down bebop tunes. It's not the easiest or most accommodating of listens, but it reveals a great deal about the microstructure of Lake's playing and compositions. Increasingly he seems to cast himself in the latter role. The saxophonist doesn't play at all on the title-track of the earlier album, which is a duo for Carter and Fox. The remainder of the album is credited to his String Project, with additional instrumentalists added on *ad hoc*. The album begins with stunning simplicity on 'Fan Fare Bop', a sharp, declamatory theme which is catchier than you'd imagine possible. The role of Kenyatta Beasley is all too brief. It might have been better to have included bassist Bullock on more of the tunes as well. He adds bottom to a sound that is a little shrill and unsupported. Otherwise, though, a fascinating record that constantly throws up new insights.

Ralph Lalama (born 1951)

TENOR SAXOPHONE

The son of a drummer and a singer, Lalama began playing at fourteen. He studied at Youngstown State and moved to New York in 1975. Stints with Woody Herman, Buddy Rich and the Jones–Lewis band followed, and he is a regular on the city's scene.

*****(*) Feelin' And Dealin'**
Criss Cross 1046 *Lalama; Tom Harrell (t, flhn); Barry Harris (p); Peter Washington (b); Kenny Washington (d).* 11/90.

***** Momentum**
Criss Cross 1063 *Lalama; Kenny Barron (p); Dennis Irwin (b); Kenny Washington (d).* 12/91.

***** You Know What I Mean**
Criss Cross 1097 *Lalama; George Cables (p); Dennis Irwin (b); Leroy Williams (d).* 12/93.

A former section-player with the Jones–Lewis big band, Lalama plays with iron in his tone. His choice of composer credits gives his idols away – Rollins, Dexter, Mobley – and, though he sometimes falls prey to the habitual anonymity of the great section-man, his improvising has real class and substance from moment to moment. A very fine solo on Mobley's 'Third Time Around' on the first record shows what he can do: the way he masters the rhythmic suspensions in the tune, throws in a couple of unexpected, whistling high notes and takes in a timbral exploration along the way suggests both technical and conceptual mastery. The record isn't consistently good, and Harrell doesn't seem quite at his best, but there is a lot to enjoy. *Momentum* is a degree more ordinary: Lalama handles the casting as sole horn with aplomb, but the session ends up as merely decent hard bop. *You Know What I Mean* follows a similar pattern, although Lalama's playing continues to give much pleasure: his persuasive handling of 'This Love Of Mine', where his solo manages to get all over the horn without any apparent effort, is very beguiling, and nearly every track has its own satisfactions.

***** Circle Line**
Criss Cross 1132 *Lalama; Peter Bernstein (g); Peter Washington (b); Kenny Washington (d).* 12/95.

***** Music For Grown-Ups**

Criss Cross 1165 *As above, except Richard Wyands (p) replaces Bernstein.* 12/98.

Circle Line is something of a homage to *Bridge*-era Sonny Rollins: listen to the way Lalama swaggers into 'My Ideal'. 'Giant Steps' is ordinary and, while Lalama and the others are never less than assured, one waits in vain for some kind of surprise along the way. Despite the somewhat snobbish title, *Music For Grown-Ups* has a welcoming atmosphere, four pros flexing their collective muscle. Lalama has spent many years in sections and his tone has been buffed to a hard matt surface: he wouldn't do anything to unbalance either band or listener and, while his stability is un-arguable, it means that his records will rarely collar the attention. Best shot: a gruff, feisty stroll through 'Lullaby Of The Leaves'.

Lambert, Hendricks & Ross

GROUP

Along with Eddie Jefferson and King Pleasure, the original trio cemented a brief fashion for vocalese, a style in which instrumental jazz is replicated in sung lines and invented lyrics. The trio came together in 1957 with other singers to record an album of Basie tunes. The results were unsatisfactory and the material was re-recorded by just LH&R, using overdubs. Five years later, with Ross ailing, the group was reconvened with Bavan.

***** Live At Basin Street East**

BMG International 25756 *As above, except replace Ross with Yolande Bavan (v); add Pony Poindexter (as); Gildo Mahones (p).* 5/63.

***** At Newport '63**

RCA 68731 *As above, except add Clark Terry (t), Coleman Hawkins (ts), George Tucker (b), Jimmie Smith (d).* 63.

****(*) Havin' A Ball At The Village Gate**

BMG International 22111 *As above, except add Thad Jones (c), Booker Ervin (ts).* 63.

Jazz vocalese may have began with the Mills Brothers and their clever vocal mimicry of brass and saxophones, developed along very different lines when Jefferson and then King Pleasure and Annie Ross began to fit words to famous jazz solos. Jefferson's vocalization of James Moody's solo on 'I'm In The Mood For Love' was perhaps better known in the King Pleasure version. Ross's virtuoso interpretation of Wardell Gray's 'Twisted' was a huge hit. Perhaps the finest exponent of vocalese, though, was Jon Hendricks, who seemed to have an unfailing facility for words to fit instrumental effects and for glib rhymes to link lines together.

The group continued for a little time with Bavan standing in for the indisposed Ross; and currently, ironically, there is more stuff from this line-up than from the wonderful original. We have always found it hard to put a value on these records. Bavan's accent always militated against convincing solo performance, and the group sounds more and more like Hendricks-plus-rhythm. Technically, Bavan is unexceptionable; expressively, she leaves a good deal to be desired.

The first record, which (like the others) is a live recording, includes a fine version of Coltrane's 'Cousin Mary', and a clever, debunking version of 'This Here'. The second, recorded at Newport, is probably more distinguished for the guest spots by Hawkins and Terry than for the singers, who sound a touch overwhelmed by the occasion. The final disc is clever, bordering here and there on novelty vocal territory, as 'Three Blind Mice' and 'With 'Er 'Ead Tucked Underneath 'Er Arm' suggest. A further version of 'Jumpin' At The Woodside' merely underlines how good the LH&R line-up had been.

Lammas

GROUP

A band fusing various strands of British folk music with jazz.

****(*) The Broken Road**

EFZ 1015 *Tim Garland (ss, ts, f, ky); Steafan Hannigan (uillean pipes, whistle, perc); Don Paterson (g); Mark Fletcher, Roy Dodds (d); Christine Tobin (v).* 8/95.

***** Sourcebook**

EFZ 1022 *As above, except add Karen Street (acc), Nic France (d); omit Dodds.* 2/97.

This balmy, lilting music makes a good case for itself, just through the woodsy feel of its textures and the plausible mix of styles; but it's scarcely anything more than a distraction for Garland, a saxophonist of distinction in other contexts. Tobin sounds too blandly appeasing as the group's singer, mixing wordless vocals with poetry and folk lyrics. *Sourcebook* is a more decisive and vigorous record; the earlier *The Broken Road* tends to drift away on the breeze. Jazz is in here, but only just.

Harold Land (born 1928)

TENOR SAXOPHONE, FLUTE, OBOE

Born in Texas but raised in San Diego, Land worked with Max Roach before becoming a fixture on the West Coast scene of the later '50s and '60s. Later sightings in the Timeless All Stars and on the Postcards session suggest his durability.

***** Harold In The Land Of Jazz**

Original Jazz Classics OJC 162 *Land; Rolf Ericson (t); Carl Perkins (p); Leroy Vinnegar (b); Frank Butler (d).* 1/58.

Made towards the end of his stint with bassist Curtis Counce's band, this is the first of a series of fine Land records. A still underrated player, hampered by a rather dour tone, Land favoured – or happened across – unusual piano players, giving more than one of his albums a harmonic unease that is more disconcerting than genuinely attractive. Perkins's crab-wise gait across the keyboard is mitigated by the vibrant rhythm-work of Vinnegar and Butler, and the best track on the album is the quartet, 'You Don't Know What Love Is', which the showy Ericson sits out (Land made some interesting brass appointments as well).

*****(*) The Fox**

Original Jazz Classics OJC 343 *Land; Dupree Bolton (t); Elmo Hope (p); Herbie Lewis (b); Frank Butler (d).* 8/59.

Jazz history has drawn something of a veil over the subsequent career of trumpeter Dupree Bolton. Though this is his solitary appearance in the current catalogue, he plays with confidence and some fire, seemingly at ease at the accelerated tempo of 'The Fox' and the easier flow of 'Mirror-Mind Rose'. If Carl Perkins recalls a crab, then Elmo Hope has to be, yes, a butterfly. His touch was as light as his ideas and colours were fleeting. One of the least dynamic of players (and singularly dependent on drummers of Butler's kidney), he was nevertheless able to keep track with a rhythm line he wasn't actually playing, laying out astonishing melody figures on 'One Down' in what is probably his best recorded performance, certainly a step ahead of *Harold In The Land Of Jazz*. Land is an underrated composer with a deep feeling for the blues, who never quite translated his most compelling ideas into practice. *The Fox*, tricky and fugitive as much of it is, must be thought his finest moment.

****(*) Eastward Ho!**

Original Jazz Classics OJC 493 *Land; Kenny Dorham (t); Amos Trice (p); Joe Peters (d).* 7/60.

Pianist Trice was briefly known for his work with Wardell Gray and, heard blindfold, this rather unusual session might well suggest Gray's work. Land and Dorham are both in fine voice but rarely seem to be thinking along the same lines. 'Slowly' and 'On A Little Street In Singapore' (the latter well known to Glenn Miller fans) are both engagingly handled. Not one of Land's best records, though.

***** Mapanzi**

Concord 4044 *Land; Blue Mitchell (t, flhn); Kirk Lightsey (p); Reggie Johnson (b); Albert 'Tootie' Heath (d).* 77.

The two-decade gap in the current catalogue sees the saxophonist emerging from a long and not always coherent examination of John Coltrane's harmonics with a new, mature style that retains much of the temper of his late-1950s work, but with added strength in the upper register. *Mapanzi* is *almost* a terrific record, but Mitchell seems ill at ease with the saxophonist's new-found modernism and catches light only on his own 'Blue Silver'. Land and Lightsey work well together, and the leader's 'Rapture' is a finely etched confessional that pitches his adapted 'sheets of sound' approach against the pianist's highly wrought but never overwrought chords.

***** A Lazy Afternoon**

Postcards POST 1008 *Land; Bill Henderson (p); Alan Pasqua (syn); James Leary (b); Billy Higgins (d); orchestra conducted by Ray Ellis.* 12/94.

Comfy, pipe-and-slippers settings for the old chap. Ellis's arrangements are lush and uncomplicated, and Land responds with some of his most soulful playing in years. All the themes are standards, and one only wonders how it would have panned out if the saxophonist had worked with rhythm section alone. There are intermittent question marks about his intonation, and the pacing of some of the songs is a little odd, though mostly on the fast side. A lovely record, though, if you have an appetite for strings dates.

Art Lande (born 1947)

PIANO, PERCUSSION

American pianist-composer whose brief tenure with ECM was responsible for the major part of his reputation. In the '80s he moved into full-time teaching.

***** Rubisa Patrol**

ECM 519875-2 *Lande; Mark Isham (t, flhn, ss); Bill Douglas (b, f); Glenn Cronkhite (d).* 5/76.

The first of Lande's two albums for ECM with this band (the second record is deleted) has now been reissued on CD. Renewed acquaintance with the music suggests that it is rather more durable than we had previously allowed. Isham, who has spent most of his time subsequently in film music, plays with a steely elegance and contributes two of the best themes, 'Many Chinas' (which opens the record after Douglas's remarkable bamboo flute solo) and 'For Nancy'. Although Lande's improvising is unremarkable, his own music displays a sense of nocturnal quiet that the group distil with great skill. The sound remains limpidly beautiful on CD.

***** Skylight**

ECM 531025-2 *Lande; Paul McCandless (ss, cor, ob, bcl, f); David Samuels (vib, mar, perc).* 5/81.

Another charming record, though more of a co-operative venture: Lande contributes two tunes, and one of them, 'Dance Of The Silver Skeezix', is pure floss. It's McCandless's pair of compositions that suit the trio best. But the music as a whole is unaffectedly sweet: a bright summer's day after the cool evening of *Rubisa Patrol*.

Nils Landgren (born 1956)

TROMBONE, TRUMPET, VOCAL

His father played cornet and his grandfather was a pastor: the music of both influenced him. Worked with Thad Jones, 1981–3, then theatrical work as singer and dancer. Wide experience as a sideman, then formed his own Funk Unit.

**** Follow Your Heart**

Caprice 21393 *Landgren; Leif Lindvall, Lars Lindgren (t); David Wilczewski (ts); Johan Stengard (as, bs); Stefan Blomqvist, Peter Ljung, Pal Svenre (ky); Staffan Astner, Johan Folke Norberg, Henrik Janson (g); Lars Danielsson (b); Per Lindvall, Andre Ferrari (d); Sharon Dyall (v).* 90.

***** Gotland**

ACT 9226-2 *Landgren; Tomasz Stankon (t); Anders Eljas, Claus Bantzer (org).* 96.

****(*) Paint It Blue**

ACT 9243-2 *Landgren; Till Bronner (t); Randy Brecker (t, flhn); Michael Brecker (ts); Per Johansson (saxes); Steffen Schorn (bcl);*

Esbjörn Svensson (ky); Henrik Janson (g); Lars Danielsson (b); Bernard Purdie (d); Airto Moreira, Marcia Doctor (perc). 96.

The first and third records would barely even qualify Landgren for entry here. *Follow Your Heart* is an inoffensive but entirely unremarkable set of softcore pop tunes with the slightest lite-jazz flavour. Landgren actually sneaks in some good fills, but he's hardly a commanding vocalist. *Paint It Blue* sets his Funk Unit to work on a Cannonball Adderley tribute. There's some perfectly serviceable playing, although the samples of Cannonball's voice scarcely anoint the occasion with any distinction, and there's nothing that isn't done better on a Maceo Parker or Fred Wesley record.

Gotland could hardly be a greater contrast. Landgren soliloquizes on some beatific melodies – most of his own writing, though two are adapted from ancient Swedish folk-tunes – in churches in Stockholm and Hamburg; Stanko joins him on some pieces, and there are lowering commentaries from the organists. Spare and contemplative, there is some lovely music from the trombonist, even if the situation at times seems a touch too calculated.

***** Ballads**

ACT 9268-2 *Landgren; Joakim Milder (ts); Bobo Stenson, Esbjörn Svensson (p); Johan Norberg (g); Palle Danielsson, Dan Berglund (b); Anders Kjellberg, Magnus Oström (d).* 3/93–5/98.

*****(*) Swedish Folk**

ACT 9257-2 *Landgren; Esbjörn Svensson (p).* 8/97.

***** Live In Montreux**

ACT 9265-2 *Landgren; Per Johansen (ss, as); Esbjörn Svensson (p); Henrik Janson (g); Magnum Coltrane Price (b, v); Janne Robertson (d).* 7/98.

***** 5000 Miles**

ACT 9271-2 *As above, except add Till Brönner, Roy Hargrove (t, flhn), Tim Hagans (t), Fred Wesley (tb), Robert Ostlund (g, org), Johan Norberg (g), Dan Berglund (b), Ake Sundqvist, Magnus Oström (perc), Viktoria Tolstoy (v).* 3/98–7/99.

The appeal of all Landgren's records depends on how much one warms to each of the styles he works in. *Ballads*, a slightly augmented reissue of a 1993 CD, has him as a vocal stylist on a range of standards and pop tunes: the supporting cast play with typical acuity, and Svensson's trio do back-up on the bonus tracks, 'You Stole My Heart', but the singing is enough of an acquired taste to offer a reservation. The two records by the Funk Unit, one live at the '98 Montreux Festival, the other a studio set with several star guests, have a problem shaking off the sense that the manner of the music is too old-fashioned – it holds back sophisticated players such as Landgren and Svensson, or at least encourages them to settle for easy routes to resolution. Which doesn't stop both men turning in some hard and exciting solos on the live material, jazz-funk licks toasted to a righteous frazzle. *5000 Miles* takes advantage of studio crispness, and Hargrove, Hagans and the others have fun on their sit-in assignments. It's not that material such as 'Da Fonk' and 'In A Fonky Mood' is beneath jazz musicians, more that they sit awkwardly beside their more demanding material (and a 'genuine' funk record would be produced differently too).

Next to these, *Swedish Folk* seems a bizarre alternative. Although there are a couple of pieces drawn from the classical Swedish repertoire, the material is otherwise all by Landgren and Svensson, a deeply felt meditation on their country's roots music. Played with the barest of detail, the musicianship is impeccable and often bewitchingly beautiful.

Eddie Lang (1904–33)

GUITAR

Born Salvatore Massaro in Philadelphia, Lang began his partnership with violinist Joe Venuti in school. They worked the New York dance-band scene throughout the 1920s. Lang visited London with the Mound City Blue Blowers, duetted with bluesman Lonnie Johnson, and became Bing Crosby's favourite accompanist. He also recorded with Louis Armstrong, King Oliver and the Ponce Sisters, though not at the same time. His bell-like tone is always audible on the records he plays on. He died as a result of complications following a tonsillectomy.

*****(*) A Handful Of Riffs**

ASV AJA 5061 *Lang; King Oliver (c); Leo McConville, Andy Secrest, Bill Margulis (t); Tommy Dorsey, Bill Rank (tb); Jimmy Dorsey (cl, as); Charles Strickfadden, Bernard Daly (as); Issy Friedman (cl, ts); J.C Johnson, Frank Signorelli, Arthur Schutt (p); Hoagy Carmichael (p, cel); Henry Whiteman (vn); Lonnie Johnson (g); Joe Tarto, Mike Trafficante (b); George Marsh, Stan King (d); Justin Ring (perc).* 4/27–10/29.

***** Jazz Guitar Virtuoso**

Yazoo 1059 *Lang; Frank Signorelli, Rube Bloom, Arthur Schutt (p); Lonnie Johnson, Carl Kress (g); Justin Ring (chimes).* 27–29.

****** The Quintessential Eddie Lang 1925–1932**

Timeless CBC 1-043 *As above discs, except add Bix Beiderbecke (c), Tommy Gott, Fuzzy Farrar, Ray Lodwig, Manny Klein, Bill Moore, Louis Armstrong, Harry Goldfield (t), Boyce Cullen, Miff Mole, Wilbur Hall, Loyd Turner (tb), Arnold Brilhart, Alfie Evans, Harold Sturr, Don Murray, Doc Ryker, Frankie Trumbauer, Andy Sannella, Tony Parenti, Happy Caldwell, Chester Hazlett, Red Mayer (reeds); Otto Landau, Matty Malneck (vn); Roy Bargy, Clarence Williams, Itzy Riskin, Joe Sullivan, Irving Brodsky (p); Cliff Edwards (uke, v); Harry Reser, Tony Colucci, Mike Pingitore (bj); Red McKenzie (comb); Dick Slevin (kz); Arthur Campbell, Min Leibrook (tba); Steve Brown, Ward Lay (b); Neil Marshall, Vic Berton, Kaiser Marshall (d); Bessie Smith, Noel Taylor, The Rhythm Boys, Bing Crosby (v).* 1/25–2/32.

*****(*) Pioneers Of Jazz Guitar 1927–1939**

Retrieval RTR 79015 *Lang; Arthur Schutt, Frank Signorelli, Rube Bloom (p); Carl Kress, Dick McDonough (g); Justin Ring (perc).* 4/27–8/39.

Eddie Lang was the first guitarist to make a major impact on jazz away from the blues, and even there he took a hand by recording many duets with the 'authentic' bluesman, Lonnie Johnson. Lang's polished, civilized but swinging art was worked out in dance bands and as an accompanist – after joining Paul Whiteman in the late 1920s, the guitarist struck up a professional kinship with Bing Crosby, who hired him until his early death. He was an important member of the white New York school of the period and can be found on records by Beiderbecke, Joe

Venuti and the Dorseys; but the sides made under his own name were also plentiful and, for all his restraint and good taste, he was a jazzman through and through. His most characteristic playing is as rhythmically driving as it is harmonically deft and inventive.

We are beter served by Lang reissues now than we have been for some time, although there is annoying duplicaton between all of these. As a general cross-section, the Timeless disc sweeps the board for now: quite beautifully remastered by John R.T. Davies, and with a shrewd and wide-ranging set of tracks, it's a very strong introduction. Lang is immediately identifiable on the early piece by the Mound City Blue Blowers, from 1925, and he turns up elsewhere in dance bands led by Fred Rich, Jean Goldkette, Roger Wolf Kahn and Paul Whiteman, backing Ukulele Ike and Bessie Smith, partnering Lonnie Johnson, sitting in with Louis Armstrong and King Oliver, and taking a solo turn on Rachmaninov's Opus 3 Prelude. Could any other musician of the era claim such a CV? Twenty-four tracks and not a dud among them.

Eight of the Yazoo tracks are also included on the ASV set. Yazoo concentrate on Lang the soloist, including all eight of the sides he made in that context, plus two tracks with Carl Kress and three with Johnson. There isn't much jazz in 'April Kisses', but showpieces like 'Eddie's Twister' and the luxuriant duet with Johnson on 'Blue Guitars' show all of Lang's beauty of touch, harmonic shrewdness and rhythmical dexterity. A couple more spirited tracks wouldn't have come amiss here, and the ration of 14 tracks is somewhat short measure.

The ASV issue offers a wider choice of 21 pieces, including the famous session with King Oliver on cornet and the five tracks by an orchestra led nominally by Lang. Sound on both issues is generally very good: the Yazoo is a little livelier but has a higher level of surface hiss.

Retrieval's new edition contains all of Lang's solo and guitar–piano pieces, the two duets with Carl Kress, and a further ten tracks featuring Kress, either by himself or with Dick McDonough. For those who want to hear the guitar away from any band situations, this is excellent, although over CD length it palls a bit unless you're a confirmed guitar-lover. Kress and McDonough are a shade more modernistic, but they had the benefit of Lang going before them.

Steven Lantner

PIANO

An associate of saxophonist Joe Maneri, Lantner helped set up the Boston Microtonal Society. In addition to acoustic piano, he uses a digital electronic instrument which allows variation of pitch, thus getting round the fixity of conventional or even altered piano tuning.

***** Reaching**

Leo Lab 062 *Lantner; Mat Maneri (vn).* 8/97.

Lantner has performed extensively with Maneri's son, whose application of microtonality is highly sophisticated on both his conventional and extra-stringed violins. The best sample track from which to get an impression of their collective aims is 'In The River', a slow, dirge-like theme using pitch-shifting on the keyboard and changes of string tonality. There is something of a sameness to the dozen tracks, but anyone who has listened to Ornette Coleman will have some familiarity with the language; use of piano apart, this is very much the territory that Ornette mapped out in the '60s. As such, it is less radical than its admirers would suggest but is no less intriguing for that.

Lou Lanza (born 1970)

VOCAL

Born in Philadelphia, Lanza's parents are professional classical musicians. This is his third CD as a vocalist-leader.

*****(*) Shadows And Echoes**

A Records AL 73131 *Lanza; Dick Sudhalter (t, flhn, c); Allen Farnham (p); Jimmy Bruno (g); Pete Colangelo (b); Ari Hoenig (d).* 5/98.

Lanza's earlier records are on independent labels and have eluded us. This is a sweet-natured set of standards. Lanza has a smooth, clean-shaven sort of voice, moving easily up and down the scale and most gracious in a high tenor register. Excellent choice of songs, with only 'Get Happy' and 'Lover Come Back To Me' even approaching the obvious. Farnham is an old hand at arranging this kind of date, and there is a wonderful flugelhorn solo by Dick Sudhalter on Jerome Kern's 'Make Believe'. Lanza isn't a familiar styling of male jazz singer – 'I feel that I'm a bit of a wild card', he says in the notes – but he's fundamentally a conservative, and those who prefer something less idiosyncratic than Kurt Elling will go for this in a big way.

Ellis Larkins (born 1923)

PIANO

Larkins was a child prodigy in his native Baltimore, graduating from Peabody and Juilliard before turning to a jazz career in the clubs of New York. He has recorded most frequently as a favoured accompanist to singers, but he has occsional discs where he is in the spotlight himself.

****(*) Duologue**

Black Lion BLCD 760911 *(p solo).* 54.

****(*) A Smooth One**

Black & Blue 591232 *Larkins; George Duvivier (b); J.C Heard (d).* 7/77.

*****(*) At Maybeck Recital Hall**

Concord CCD 4533 *Larkins (p solo).* 3/92.

Larkins's mastery is so understated that his reputation lags some way behind his abilities. Although he has been active for 60 years there are relatively few records under his own name. *Duologue* offers four brief solos from 1954 (the rest of the record features Lee Wiley with a Ruby Braff group). *A Smooth One* is Larkins's only available trio date. Several of the eight pieces remind one of his judgement that with some songs 'you just play them and get out'; but there are some bewitching moments hidden behind his professional excellence.

The Maybeck recital finds him back in the spotlight at last, and seemingly bemused by it: the monochrome photograph on the front sleeve looks like an old blues daguerrotype, with Larkins posing in his old-fashioned suit and tie. The music exists in a state of old-world elegance, too. He chose a rarefied selection of songs – 'Howdja Like To Love Me', 'I Don't Want To Cry Any More', 'Leave Me Alone' – as well as some Ellington and a tune of his own, 'Perfume And Rain', that really does sound like raindrops on the keys. His proper technique, off-kilter humour and very slow, stately swing make up a kind of jazz that has almost vanished; here is a reminder of it. For more recent appearances, check the Ruby Braff entry.

Prince Lasha (born 1929)

ALTO SAXOPHONE, FLUTE

Born in Texas, Lasha moved to California in the '50s and to New York in the '60s, before a brief spell in London – where he cut a little-known CBS LP with Stan Tracey – and a return to California. Intermittently visible since, he has recorded only rarely.

*****(*) Firebirds**

Original Jazz Classics OJC 1822 *Lasha; Sonny Simmons (as); Bobby Hutcherson (vib); Buster Williams (b); Charles Moffett (d).* 65.

Lasha – pronounced 'Lashay' – was in the same Fort Worth high school band as Ornette Coleman and King Curtis. There are elements of both in his playing, should you wish to look for them, but the dominant influence is Eric Dolphy, with whom Lasha played on *Iron Man*. That session also featured Hutcherson and Simmons, who both appear on the one surviving record. Lasha has a frail, slightly thin tone on alto saxophone, explained in part by his choice of a plastic instrument (this was inspired not so much by Ornette Coleman as by Charlie Parker's use of a bakelite horn at the famous Massey Hall concert); as a result, he often sounds as if he may be playing a North African or Asian wind instrument of variable pitch. Following the same instinct for unusual colours, he also uses a wooden flute which gives a softer, slightly 'dead' timbre; though again influenced by Dolphy, it is a markedly individual sound which anticipates the later work of multi-instrumentalists like Oliver Lake, Douglas Ewart and, above all, Henry Threadgill. *Firebirds* is enough to suggest that Lasha is a figure who deserves wider acknowledgement.

Steve LaSpina (born 1954)

BASS

Born in Texas but growing up in Chicago, LaSpina followed his father, also a bassist. He went to New York in 1979 and became a regular on the scene there, teaching and performing; subsequently moved to Milford, PA.

***** New Horizon**

Steeplechase SCCD 31313 *LaSpina; Billy Drewes (ss, as, ts); Marc Copland (p); Jeff Hirshfield (d).* 4/92.

***** Eclipse**

Steeplechase SCCD 31343 *As above.* 4/93.

***** When I'm Alone**

Steeplechase SCCD 31376 *As above, except add Vic Juris (g).* 95.

*****(*) The Road Ahead**

RAM RMCD 4526 *As above, except Jim McNeely (p) replaces Copland.* 12/95.

*****(*) Story Time**

Steeplechase SCCD 31396 *As above, except omit McNeely; Drewes also plays cl.* 3/96.

***** When Children Smile**

Steeplechase SCCD 31419 *As above, except add Dave Ballou (t).* 10/96.

A very good run of records by the accomplished bassist-leader. He writes most of the material, which tends towards soft-focus harmonies and elliptical melodic lines, and the basic band is well attuned to the feel: Drewes especially gets the mood right with his rather light sound (he usually favours the upper reaches of the horn) and patient delivery. *New Horizon* and *Eclipse* are solidly inventive without being startling, and the originals on the latter pass dreamily by (Drewes plays alto for much of the record, contrary to the sleeve). Juris arrives for *When I'm Alone* and adds some piquant weight, although if there's a problem with these discs it's Copland, who's effective enough but tends to add a pretentious note with some of his solos. There's a noticeable upping of the ante with the arrival of McNeely on the RAM date: he's a superior player, and the trio version of 'Body And Soul' is just one instance of why this is the pick of the five discs. That said, *Story Time* is only just behind. With Juris handling what might have been the piano parts, the harmonic base expands further and some of LaSpina's originals are deliciously songful. There's also a rather surprising clarinet turn by Drewes on the curious 'Scott's Bop'.

When Children Smile continues the sequence and adds Ballou as a new voice in the group. Nothing wrong with it, but LaSpina's tunes here are so laid-back and uneventful that the music starts to seem tranquillizing. In this company, Coleman's 'Ramblin'' sounds almost raw, even in a relatively tame treatment.

Last Exit

GROUP

A supergroup of the avant-garde, organized by bassist Laswell in the 1980s.

****** Last Exit**

Enemy EMY 101 *Peter Brötzmann (reeds); Sonny Sharrock (g); Bill Laswell (b); Ronald Shannon Jackson (d, v).* 2/86.

***** The Noise Of Trouble**

Enemy EMY 103 *As above, except add Akira Sakata (cl, as), Herbie Hancock (p).* 10/86.

Last Exit now seem like an almost nostalgic holdover from the avant-garde of the 1980s, though the group has long since ceased to be active, and Sharrock has gone in the interim. Heard live, they were a scabrous pleasure, and we remember their concert appearances with the kind of warmth one associates with bad behaviour in one's youth. Listening back to the records, which are now only spottily available, one feels a little disappointed that the music only rarely matches up to what is now a sizeable legend. Their warts-and-all first record remains their best legacy, a testing blow-out which is something like a bedevilled jam session for four virtuoso, cussed spirits. While Jackson's polyrhythmic parts establish a single, ever-evolving drum solo, Laswell anchors the pieces with huge, juddering bass-lines, obsessively decorated by Brötzmann and Sharrock.

Perhaps this should have been a one-disc-only band, for *The Noise Of Trouble* has worn much less well than we expected; or maybe the continually evolving avant-garde of rock and jazz alike has simply done what it has to do, and rendered a previous era's outrage as something merely *passé*.

Yusef Lateef (born 1921)

TENOR SAXOPHONE, OBOE, FLUTE, OTHER SAXOPHONES, COR ANGLAIS, OTHER INSTRUMENTS, VOCALS

Born Bill Evans in Chattanooga, Lateef was taught in Detroit and went to New York in 1946, later moving back to the Detroit area after a spell with Dizzy Gillespie. He then played with Mingus and with Cannonball Adderley for three years, before leading his own groups and teaching and studying philosophy as well as music. He taught in Nigeria during the 1980s and now teaches at Amherst College, running his YAL label for his own music.

***** Cry! – Tender**

Original Jazz Classics OJC 482 *Lateef; Lonnie Hillyer (t); Wilbur Harden (flhn); Hugh Lawson (p); Ernie Farrow, Herman Wright (b); Frank Gant, Oliver Jackson (d).* 10/59.

*****(*) The Centaur And The Phoenix**

Original Jazz Classics OJC 712 *Lateef; Clark Terry, Richard Williams (t); Curtis Fuller (tb); Tate Houston (bs); Josea Taylor (bsn); Barry Harris, Joe Zawinul (p); Ernie , Ben Tucker (b); Lex Humphries (d); Roger Sanders (perc).* 10/60, 6/61.

*****(*) Eastern Sounds**

Original Jazz Classics OJC 612 *Lateef; Barry Harris (p); Ernie Farrow (b); Lex Humphries (d).* 9/61.

*****(*) Live At Pep's Vol 2**

Impulse! 547961-2 *Lateef; Richard Williams (t); Mike Nock (p); Ernie Farrow (b); James Black (d).* 6/64.

***** The Blue Yusef Lateef**

Atlantic 82270 *Lateef; Blue Mitchell (t); Sonny Red (as); Buddy Lucas (hca); Hugh Lawson (p); Kenny Burrell (g); Cecil McBee, Bob Cranshaw (b); Roy Brooks (d); Selwart Clarke, James Tryon (vn); Alfred Brown (vla); Kermit Moore (clo); Sweet Inspirations (v).* 4/68.

****(*) The Diverse Yusef Lateef / Suite 16**

Rhino Atlantic R2 71552 *Lateef; Richard Tee, Joe Zawinul, Hugh Lawson, Barry Harris (p); Neil Boyar (vib); Eric Gale (g); Chuck Rainey, Bob Cunningham (b); Albert 'Tootie' Heath, Roy Brooks, Bernard Purdie, Jimmy Johnson, Ray Lucas (d); Ray Barretto (perc); strings, voices.* 5/69–4/70.

****(*) The Man With The Big Front Yard**

32 Jazz 32059 3CD *Lateef; Danny Moore, Snookie Young, Joe Wilder, Leonard Goines, Jimmy Owens, Thad Jones (t); Jack Jeffers (tb); Jimmy Buffington (frhn); Hugh Lawson, Kenny Barron, Ray Bryant (p); Al White (org); Dana McCurdy (syn); David Nadien (vn); Eric Gale, David Spinozza, Billy Butler, Cornell Dupree, Keith Loving (g); Kermit Moore (clo); Jonathan Dorn (tba); Cecil McBee, Chuck Rainey, Bob Cunningham, Ron Carter, Anthony Jackson, Bill Salter (b); Roy Brooks, Albert 'Tootie' Heath, Bernard Purdie (d); Sylvia Shemwell, Norman Pride, Ray Barretto, Dom Um Romao (perc); Monroe Constantino, The J.C. White Singers, Cissy Houston, Judy Clay (v); strings.* 67–76.

***** The Gentle Giant**

Atlantic 1602 *Lateef; Bill Campbell (as); Ray Bryant (p); Kenny Barron (electric p); Eric Gale (g); Neal Boyer (vib, chimes); Sam Jones, Chuck Rainey (b); Bob Cunningham, Bill Salter (b); Albert 'Tootie' Heath, Jimmy Johnson (d); Sweet Inspirations (v).* 74.

Lateef avoided the confusion of yet another Evans in the catalogue by adopting a Muslim name in response to his growing and eventually life-long infatuation with the musics of the Levant and Asia. One of the few convincing oboists in jazz and an ancestor of East–West outfits like Oregon (whose Paul McCandless has, consciously or unconsciously, adopted some of Lateef's tonal devices), he has suffered something of Rahsaan Roland Kirk's fate in finding himself dismissed or marginalized as a 'speciality act', working apart from the central dramas of modern jazz. Like Kirk's, Lateef's music was cartoonized when he came under Atlantic's wing, making albums that were enthusiastically promoted and received, but which rarely represented the best of his work.

The two early Savoy reissues find him blowing rough, burly tenor alongside two solid, hard-bop rhythm sections, together with the elegant Harden on one album and the bluff Fuller on the other. Already, though, there are the exotic touches: 'A Night In Tunisia' gets off to a suitably authentic start with the muezzin-like wail of the *argol*, and the same thing happens with 'Metaphor' on *Jazz Moods*. The OJC records are consistently interesting, with relatively unfussy arrangements leavened by unusual timbres and instrumental colours. *The Centaur And The Phoenix* isn't well known, despite the presence of critically OK names like Terry and Fuller. The vocal 'Jungle Fantasy' is dire, but the large-group pieces are as good as anything on the earlier *Cry! – Tender*, and 'Summer Song' is among the most straightforwardly lyrical things in Lateef's whole output. *Live At Pep's Vol. 2* has returned to the catalogue recently, and it stands up extremely well, substantiating Lateef's often queried jazz credentials. He plays with great spirit and an authentically bluesy drive that makes the exact choice of instrument (oboe, saxophone, shenai, flute) pretty much irrelevant.

Like Kirk, the tenor saxophone is Lateef's 'natural' horn, but in his best period he made jazz whatever he was playing. In approach, he is somewhat reminiscent of the pre-bop aspect of Sun Ra's long-time associate, John Gilmore, working in a strong, extended swing idiom rather than with the more complex figurations of bebop. Just occasionally this spilled over into something schmaltzier. The *Eastern Sounds* session also included film music from *The Robe* and *Spartacus*, on flute and oboe respectively, that borders on kitsch, but the tenor-led 'Snafu', a thoroughly occidental expression of fatalism, has a surging energy that has Lateef's very good band panting.

There are good things on *Blue*, with an orchestra fronted by Lateef, Mitchell and Lucas and anchored on two basses (upright and electric) and the power drumming of Brooks. However, the vocal tracks and the string arrangements on 'Like It Is' are pretty shallow, or only rather shallowly pretty in a *Summer Of Love*-ish way, and the album as a whole lacks focus. Matters worsen with the terribly mixed double-reissue of *The Diverse Yusef Lateef/Suite 16*: the first album is a strange blend of funk, a lot of Lateef flute, some pseudo-gospel singing and oddball string charts, ending on a blowsily exotic 'When A Man Loves A Woman'. *Suite 16* is an extended concerto for Lateef that veers wildly from passionate improvising to mere pretentiousness and exposes some of his wider ambitions as fatally dilettantish: there is much of interest in the writing which is sunk by the wrong-headed parts.

The Man With The Big Front Yard is even more of a rag-bag, spreading the original albums, *The Complete Yusef Lateef*, *Yusef Lateef's Detroit*, *Hush 'N' Thunder* and *The Doctor Is In ... And Out* across three CDs. Only the first of these has any sustained blowing by Yusef: the others are a baffling mix of funk, gospel (a rather grand 'His Eye Is On The Sparrow', with Lateef blowing in front of the J.C. White Singers), cop-show instrumentals, chamber music, hard bop, synthesizers making ghostly noises, poetry recitations, grunting and strange exhortations of foreboding about the future. All very early '70s, but it doesn't amount to much. The third CD is worth sitting through, though, just to get to the marvellous finale, Lateef wailing in front of an ancient vocal-group recording of 'In A Little Spanish Town'!

Lateef's vocal contributions on some of the earlier records merely anticipate the grosser insult of 'Hey, Jude' on *The Gentle Giant*. In turning Lateef into a marketable crossover performer, Atlantic took most of the bite out of his playing. There are four good tracks on the mid-'70s album, most notably 'Nubian Lady', but there was an awful thinness to much of the rest that boded ill for the future.

****(*) Heart Vision**

YAL 900 *Lateef; Everett Haffner (syn); Christopher Newland (g); Adam Rudolph (perc); Nnenna Freelon, Tsidii Le Loka, Richard Ross, Mount Nebo Baptist Church Choir (v).* 1/92.

****** Tenors**

YAL 977 *Lateef; Archie Shepp (ts); Tom McLung (p); Avery Sharpe (b); Steve McCraven (d); Adam Rudolph, Mulazimuddin Razool, Tony Vacca (perc).* 1/92.

***** Plays Ballads**

YAL 333 *As above, except omit Razool and Vacca.* 12/92.

*****(*) Tenors**

YAL 911 *Lateef; Von Freeman (ts); John Young (p); John Whitfield (b); Terry Morrisette (d).* 7/92.

*****(*) Tenors**

YAL 019 *Lateef; René McLean (ts); Andrew Hollander (p); Avery Sharpe (b); Kamal Sabir (d).* 5/93.

*****(*) Metamorphosis**

YAL 100 *As above, except omit McLean and Hollander.* 12/93.

***** Woodwinds**

YAL 005 *Lateef; Ralph M Jones (ts, ss, f, bf, hirchirki); Andrew Hollander (p); Avery Sharpe (b); Adam Rudolph (d).* 7/93.

***** Tenors**

YAL 105 *Lateef; Ricky Ford (ts); Avery Sharpe (b); Kamal Sabir (d).* 94.

****(*) Suite Life**

YAL 111 *Lateef; Andrew Hollander (p); Marcie Brown (clo).* 94.

***** In Nigeria**

YAL 707 *Lateef; Shittu Iskyaku (d); P Adegboyega, Salisu I Mashi, Awwalu Adamu (perc); voices.* 7/83.

In his seventies, Lateef's energy and commitment are astonishing. He has now formed his own label and has released a stack of records in the 1990s. They are a fascinating sequence. *Heart Vision* has the closest links with Lateef's recent work: the use of voices and choir, the shimmering electronics and Lateef's occasional bursts of tenor flirt with pretension but as often return to planet earth. The next four discs, though, are all about the tenor saxophone. *Ballads* is a slow, almost ritual unpeeling of the ballad form, with the rhythm players seemingly itching to get at the kernel but Lateef consistently holding them back: a tense, sometimes strange session, but the saxophonist has some imperious improvising on what are all original themes. The four meetings with other tenormen are all remarkable in their way. He challenges Shepp into his best form: there's little of the bleariness which has tarnished all of Archie's later music, just irascible, grouchy saxophone playing: Lateef with his eyes on higher things, Shepp always dragging matters back to worldly affairs. It's like a sour re-run of a Hawkins/Webster date, and it's splendid music. With McLean, all taut, biting lines, Lateef sounds sagacious; with Freeman, whose ragged phrasing and street-fighter tone crowd into the microphone like a swelling bruise, he ducks and weaves in what sometimes sounds like a punch-drunk cutting contest. But the extraordinary thing about all three encounters is that all the material is new, abstract, almost no more than a few sketchy lines: this is anchorless free playing much of the time, and the gutsy performances by all the rhythm players are compelling too. *Metamorphosis* is also much about rhythm: stripping the cast back to himself, Sharpe and Sabir, Lateef looks for a free kind of funk, the pulse staggered across an indeterminate time. Lateef rails away on tenor but adds a chorus of murmuring flutes as well: a workshop date, perhaps, but full of energy and surprise.

The *Tenors* meeting with Ricky Ford is another good blow-out, cast as a sequence of tributes to other saxmen. *In Nigeria* is an archive piece from an African visit, a slowly simmering backdrop of percussion and voices framing the leader's improvisations, some simple, some deceptively complex. *Suite Life* is a sequence of chamberish pieces of no great weight or import, while *Woodwinds* is more about the hushed whisper of confiding flutes than reeds: only on the closing 'Brother Man' do Jones and Lateef get stuck into a tenor duel. An effective set. YAL has its share of indulgences, but overall this is an absorbing body of work from a man who clearly has a lot of music in him.

***** The World At Peace**

YAL 753 2CD *Lateef; Charles Moore (t, dumbek, kudu horn); Ralph Jones (ss, ts, f, bcl, musette); Jeff Gauthier (vn); Federico*

Ramos (g, kudu horn); Susan Allen (hp); David Johnson (vib, mar, perc); Bill Roper (tba, kudu horn); Eric Von Essen (b); Adam Rudolph, Jose Luis Perez (d). 6/95.

****(*) Full Circle**

YAL 000 *Lateef; Tom McLung (p); Avery Sharpe (b); Steve McCraven (d). 5/96.*

**** Earth And Sky**

YAL 794 *As above, except add Sayyd A Al-Khabyyr (ts, f), Kamal Sabir (d); omit McCraven. 1/97.*

**** CHNOPS, Gold And Soul**

YAL 497 *Lateef; Avery Sharpe, Mark Saltman (b); Adam Rudolph (d). 97.*

These are frankly disappointing and YAL is suddenly beginning to seem like another of Lateef's indulgences (though one could complain that if you have your own label, you can do anything you like with it – including giving the records apparently random catalogue-numbers). *Earth And Sky* finds the group mooching around some of Lateef's open-ended structures to no feasible purpose, while he sort of sing-raps over the top for quite a lot of the time. *CHNOPS, Gold And Soul* is a bit more listenable but wanders off to no avail, usually with Lateef noodling away on the keyboards: what are these tracks about, with so little melodic, textural or rhythmic interest? *Full Circle* is a bit more pointed, and one has to give Yusef some marks for choosing to sing 'When The Saints Go Marching In' as a dirge! The 12-strong group on *The World At Peace* were recorded in concert and, while it doesn't justify its two-disc status, it's interesting to hear Lateef and Rudolph (co-credited as leaders) trying to make a world-jazz concept work as a live performance. The ensembles tend to have a wheezing, chamberish feel to them, and more illuminating are the moments when a soloist (Lateef himself, in particular) takes off from the intricate patterns that Rudolph, Perez and Johnson weave through the whole event. Worth experiencing, by no means unmissable.

Christof Lauer (born 1953)

TENOR SAXOPHONE

Born in Melsungen, Germany, he studied piano and took up sax at eighteen. Played with Austrian bands of various stripes and has since freelanced, cut occasional leadership dates, and done big-band work, all in a tough post-Coltrane style.

*****(*) Fragile Network**

ACT 9266-2 *Lauer; Michel Godard (tba, serpent); Marc Ducret (g); Anthony Cox (b); Gene Jackson (d). 9/98.*

One of the younger generation of European players who have stepped beyond the overpowering influence of John Coltrane, Lauer has assimilated such a range of styles – from Stan Getz's smooth *legato* to Albert Ayler's all-out fury – that it is impossible to accuse him of being derivative of anyone. Engineer Walter Quintus is on hand on *Fragile Work* and creates a brooding but brightly registered canvas of sound for Lauer and tubist Godard, who emerges here in the Stewart role but with a much more developed solo part. His serpent feature on 'Ferma L'Ali' is breathtaking, and his virtuosity on tuba transforms 'Vernasio' and steals it from under the saxophonist's nose. Guitarist Ducret is sometimes a little overcooked, but on 'Human Voice' he shows what a delicate touch he also has at his disposal. This time out, Lauer is much more obviously part of a group rather than a horn player-plus-rhythm. His placement of lines and phrases is exact and always telling and, though it is Godard who commands much of the foreground, the saxophonist continues to produce compelling jazz.

Cy Laurie (born 1926)

CLARINET

A major figure on the London trad scene of the '50s, Laurie's groups won admiration among hardcore revivalists since he refused to go mainstream. In 1960 he left to live in India until the end of the decade. Since then, he has decamped to Southend but continues to lead groups on the surviving trad circuit.

*****(*) Blows Blue Hot**

Lake LACD122 *Laurie; Al Fairweather, Alan Elsdon (t); John Picard, John R.T Davies (tb); Alan Thomas, Dick Hughes (p); Johnny Potter, Brian Munday (bj); Dave Wood, Stan Leader (b); Ron McKay (d, wbd). 7/54–1/55.*

***** Chattanooga Stomp**

Lake LACD61 *Laurie; Alan Elsdon, Sonny Morris, Ken Sims (t); Graham Stewart, Terry Pitts (tb); Tedd Ramm, Ian Armit, Anne Varley (p); Brian Munday, Diz Disley (bj); Stan Leader (b); Peter Mawford (d); Viv Carter (d, wbd). 6/55–5/57.*

Laurie is in some ways the forgotten man of British trad clarinet, but he was as good a player as any of his peers. His style walked a rather awkward line between imitation and individuality: very much in thrall to Johnny Dodds, he led a band that, on the *Chattanooga Stomp* tracks, mostly taken from Esquire masters, could play with surprising heat. Dodds favourites like 'Goober Dance' and 'Perdido Street Blues' emerge unscathed, but rather more interesting is the way they recompose 'Twelfth Street Rag', a variation on the Armstrong Hot Five version. 'St Phillips Street Breakdown' has nothing of George Lewis in it, and two amusing bits of Mozart (including 'Minuet Wobble'!) are entertaining features for the leader. Morris is the pick of the three trumpeters and, although mastered from vinyl and shellac rather than the original tapes, the sound is bright and lively.

The earlier sessions on *Blows Blue Hot* have now also been reissued in another conscientious Lake release. The first eight tracks comprise the original Esquire ten-inch of the same title, with the balance made up of one 78 and three EP sessions. We slightly prefer these intense and full-blooded tracks, with the excellent Fairweather out front and Picard's blasting trombone just about manageable.

Anna-Lena Laurin

KEYBOARDS, VOCAL

Based in Malmö, Laurin has ended up in jazz after playing in rock and folk situations.

*** **Dance In Music**

Dragon DRCD 262 *Laurin; Anders Bergcrantz (t, flhn); Rolf Nilsson (g); Hans Andersson (b); Kristofer Johansson (d).* 5–6/94.

Laurin's light and appealing voice is the keynote here, with a wordless vocal line following a melody taken up by the trumpet or guitar. The music is a similarly airy, dancing kind of pop-jazz; with splendid work by Bergcrantz and an intelligent mediatory role played by Nilsson, there's nothing shallow or throwaway about the results, which find a pleasing balance between songs and playing. 'Blunda Och Njut' features some rather startling multi-tracked singing by Laurin, and Bergcrantz's solos on 'All By Myself' are worth the ticket-price by themselves. An agreeable surprise.

Andy LaVerne (born 1947)

KEYBOARDS

A pianist born in New York, LaVerne studied at Berklee for only weeks before turning professional and joining Woody Herman in 1973 and Stan Getz in 1977, the latter job lasting almost four years. He has since recorded extensively as a leader.

(*) **Another World

Steeplechase SCCD 31086 *LaVerne; Mike Richmond (b); Billy Hart (d).* 9/77.

***(*) **Frozen Music**

Steeplechase SCCD 31244 *LaVerne; Rick Margitza (ss, ts); Marc Johnson (b); Danny Gottlieb (d).* 4/89.

** **Fountainhead**

Steeplechase SCCD 31261 *LaVerne; Dave Samuels (vib).* 6/89.

*** **Standard Eyes**

Steeplechase SCCD 31280 *LaVerne; Steve LaSpina (b); Anton Fig (d).* 10/90.

LaVerne is a dedicated, accomplished player, but we've found difficulty getting excited about his records in the past. His considerable technique and prolific output as a composer are unarguable. The problem is finding any character at the heart of it all. Rhythmically he can be a little four-square, and he plays so many notes that his solos can get hung up on a rush to reharmonize. His earlier Steeplechase albums tend to be worthy rather than exciting sessions. *Frozen Music* offers a glimpse of the useful young Margitza, but the LaVerne originals are disappointingly unmemorable. The meeting with Samuels creates a lot of pretty music and not much more. *Standard Eyes*, though, is better, and benefits from LaSpina and Fig, who make an excellent team for LaVerne to work with.

** **Natural Living**

Musidisc 500092 *LaVerne; John Abercrombie (g).* 11/89.

*** **Nosmo King**

Steeplechase SCCD 31301 *As above.* 12/91.

** **Pleasure Seekers**

Triloka 320186 *LaVerne; Bob Sheppard (ss, ts, cl, f); John Patitucci (b); Dave Weckl (d).* 1/91.

** **Buy One Get One Free**

Steeplechase SCCD 31319 *LaVerne (p solo).* 4/92.

(*) **Double Standard

Triloka 320198 *LaVerne; Billy Drewes (ss, ts); Steve LaSpina (b); Greg Hutchinson (d).* 1/93.

*** **Plays Bud Powell**

Steeplechase SCCD 31342 *LaVerne (p solo).* 2/93.

(*) **At Maybeck Recital Hall Vol. 28

Concord CCD 4577 *LaVerne (p solo).* 4/93.

***(*) **First Tango In New York**

Musidisc 500472 *LaVerne; Joe Lovano (ss, ts); Steve LaSpina (b); Bill Stewart (d).* 5/93.

LaVerne and Abercrombie work well together, and *Natural Living* should have been a promising collection of standards and originals. But the bass-heavy sound smudges detail and sensitivity, and one tune soon comes to sound like another. Only on the title-piece, where Abercrombie switches to acoustic guitar, does the music become fully expressive. *Nosmo King* is a good deal better, sensibly varied in pace; but several of the pieces meander past their natural climax and LaVerne's heavy voicings make one wish for a lighter touch. The main highlight is the rarefied treatment of 'I Loves You, Porgy'. *Pleasure Seekers* is a competent, dull, reeds-and-rhythm date, and the more interesting *Double Standard*, where LaVerne takes his penchant for reharmonizing standards to the extreme of adding a new melody to go with them, doesn't benefit much from Walter Becker's big-screen production.

The solo albums seem only to indulge the pianist's temptations to overdo things. *Buy One Get One Free* double-tracks him with piano parts recorded earlier on a Disklavier, and it all gets fulsome beyond words on the endless glisses of 'Fine Tune'. His contribution to the Maybeck series is similarly ponderous: this is impressive pianism, and some of the pieces make a more substantial showing, but too often one longs for a more filigree touch. *Plays Bud Powell* is a smart idea, since Powell is still surprisingly neglected as a composer, and for once LaVerne says his piece on each of the tunes briskly and without undue ornamentation: probably the best of his solo sessions to this point.

LaVerne has top billing on *First Tango In New York* but, as usual, the session is dominated by Lovano's splendid playing. Six good standards are topped off with two LaVerne originals, but the material takes second place to the playing, which is primed by Lovano's furry tone and circuitous lines.

***(*) **Severe Clear**

Steeplechase SCCD 31273 *LaVerne; Tim Hagans (t); Rick Margitza (ts); Steve LaSpina (b); Anton Fig (d).* 3/90.

A great band for sure, and this time LaVerne brought some of his best writing to the date, eight provoking if not exactly memorable originals that the musicians swarm all over. Fig's powerhouse display on 'No Guts, No Glory' or the flowing melodies of 'Plasma Pool' catch the ear, and Margitza and Hagans play up to their reputations.

*** **Glass Ceiling**

Steeplechase SCCD 31352 *LaVerne; Steve LaSpina (b); Anton Fig (d).* 10/93.

***(*) **Time Well Spent**
Concord CCD 4680 *LaVerne; George Mraz (b); Al Foster (d).* 12/94.

What seems to be the final album with LaSpina and Fig benefits from a strong tune selection, with LaVerne finding new muscle in Corea's 'Litha' and 'Tones For Joan's Bones', and the specific empathies which the group had developed: it really is an all-of-a-piece session. Yet it's actually surpassed by the feel of *Time Well Spent*. LaVerne gets into such a productive groove with Mraz and Foster that, even though the music feels lighter, the results are the more impressive. 'On A Misty Night' has seldom been so finely judged, 'I Should Care' is a model of carefree swinging, and LaVerne saves one of his wittiest originals, 'Rhythm And Blues', for last.

(*) **Tadd's Delight
Steeplechase SCCD 31375 *LaVerne (p solo).* 5/95.

A reader took us to task for saying in our last edition that 'Tadd Dameron's legacy as a composer is ultimately slight'. What we should have said was that only a handful of his works figure much in repertory exercises, and this interesting idea for a homage includes most of the familiar pieces. Unfortunately this one's a disappointment. He seems to make heavy weather out of most of the melodies, as if deliberately stepping away from bebop velocity, and while some of the harmonizations are thought-provoking, one hardly feels that 'Hot House' or 'The Chase' really emerge in the spirit of the composer. Steeplechase also opt for a heavy 'classical' piano sound and it tends to add needless weight to an already hefty conception.

*** **Serenade To Silver**
Steeplechase SCCD 31388 *LaVerne; Tim Hagans (t); Rick Margitza (ts); Steve LaSpina (b); Billy Drummond (d).* 11/95.

Not bad, but this is a bit thin when one remembers how tough and attacking *Severe Clear* was – and on a set of tunes that should have cued up a little vim and vigour. LaVerne's tribute to Horace Silver takes up the pretty rather than the funky side of the hard-bop master and, while it pays dividends on an interesting reworking of 'Song For My Father' and the sweet 'Peace', the other tunes sound merely polite.

*** **Four Miles**
Triloka 536186-2 *LaVerne; Randy Brecker (t, flhn); George Mraz (b); Al Foster (d).* 2/96.

*** **Bud's Beautiful**
Steeplechase SCCD 31399 *LaVerne; Peter Washington (b); Billy Hart (d).* 3/96.

*** **Stan Getz In Chappaqua**
Steeplechase STCD 31418 *LaVerne; Don Braden (ts); Dave Stryker (g); Steve LaSpina (b); Danny Gottlieb (d).* 10/96.

Randy Brecker's a logical choice for the hornman on a Miles Davis tribute: since he can play in any style he wants, doing Miles is no problem, and here he gets just close enough without it seeming like a rip. The tunes are either Davis favourites or second-cousin choices like 'Mr Syms' and 'Cantaloupe Island'. It's done graciously without seeming in any way essential and, if anything, Brecker is a distraction from the good work of the trio.

LaVerne never seems short of a concept, and he has another go at Bud Powell with another new rhythm section on *Bud's Beautiful*. There are half a dozen rarities here and simply as a piece of scholarship this has its virtues. LaVerne, Washington and Hart swing through the programme with suitable energy and, if no surprises are sprung, it has a bopper's tautness about it, something LaVerne hasn't always found in this kind of material.

The Getz album is his inevitable nod to his former boss. The quartet (Stryker appears only on the 'Bossa Nova Medley') tackles a plausible set of tunes, from 'Early Autumn' to 'Windows'; but Braden, stylistically a useful alternative to the Getz sound, doesn't seem especially engaged with the material, and the session turns out as a potboiler.

John Law

PIANO

Law first emerged as a force to be reckoned with in 1989 as one-third of Atlas, a group that also featured percussionist Mark Sanders. The gifted Englishman straddles modern/free jazz and a lightly worn classical learning. He is capable of almost violently percussive rhythms alternated with a meditative lyricism.

**** **Exploded On Impact**
Slam CD 204 *Law; Alan Wilkinson (as, bs); Roberto Bellatalla (b); Mark Sanders (d).* 2 & 7/92.

(*) **Talitha Cumi
FMR CD06 081994 *Law (p solo).* 8/93.

Law is an improviser whose background in and understanding of classical piano language alternately fuels and haunts him. His harmonics and sense of structure are unexceptionable, but there are moments on *Talitha Cumi*, a set of meditations on the *Dies irae*, when he sounds much too correct and self-absorbed. Compared to the group and duo work, it is a disappointing appearance.

On *Exploded On Impact* Law's writing breathes intelligence through and through, and is distinguished by a firm architecture seldom encountered in free bop of this type. It's often difficult to discern what is predetermined and what is spontaneously improvised, particularly on the two main statements, 'Mothers' Lament' (a threnody for Yugoslavia), and the punning 'A Pissed-Off Tree', which nods in the direction of a 'felonious monk'. Bellatalla is a less percussive and somewhat less energetic player than some others, and much of the harder-edged stuff has been consigned to Wilkinson, one of the unsung heroes of new music in Britain. Sanders plays briskly and with humour, as he does with Jon Lloyd's similarly disposed group. Law himself develops relatively small harmonic areas with great intensity, building up climaxes that are as logical as they are explosive.

***(*) **The Boat Is Sinking, Apartheid Is Sinking**
Impetus IMP CD 19322 *Law; Louis Moholo (d).* 11 & 12/93.

The association with Moholo might seem surprising at first glance, but it is a happy combination of opposites: the pianist's careful sense of order providing a solid, provocative base for Moholo's fierce, highly directed drumming. The South African is a model improviser, pushing on forcefully with the sort of deceptive intelligence that marked the 'Freedom Tour' documented on *Boat/Apartheid*. The recording is somewhat off-balance: the drums peaking too high and the piano overloading at the top end. Such shortcomings are incidental, though; this is a very worthwhile modern record from an unexpectedly fruitful pairing.

****** Giant Leaves (Autumn Steps)**
FMR CD 32 *Law; Tim Wells (b); Paul Clarvis (d, perc).* 12/95.

Giant Leaves (Autumn Steps) provides a welcome opportunity to hear Law in a conventional trio setting. The most obvious precedent is Howard Riley's elegantly freewheeling trio of the mid-'60s. What Law brings in addition is a quasi-classical expansiveness that has more in common with Keiths Jarrett and Tippett, great rolling figures and pure sound. The toy keyboard 'Rockaby' at the start of 'Playground … So There!' kicks off an irritatingly memorable theme that flounces and taunts all the way to the finish. A beautiful 'Sarabande' is dedicated to the late John Stevens and is well worthy of reprise at the close. What relation 'Giant (Steps)' bears to the Coltrane theme and 'Autumn (Leaves)' to the standard isn't always clear. Both are meditations rather than strict covers, but the coda to 'Giant (Steps)', in which the theme is played absolutely straight, makes it perfectly clear how close to the original Law had been working. A splendid record, full of invention, wit, sadness and fire.

*****(*) Pentecost**
FMR CD27 0396 *Law (p solo).* 2/96.

***** The Hours**
FMR CD 41 V0697 *As above.* 9 & 10/96.

These two records complete Law's cycle of improvisations based on monastic plainchant. The earlier of the pair was recorded at a solo concert which happened to fall on the Feast of Pentecost, which suggested the thematic material to Law. In contrast to *The Hours*, it's a single large slab of music, relatively static and curiously reminiscent of similar – and similarly spiritual – performances by the South African, Bheki Mseleku. In contrast to *Talitha Cuma*, whose success suggested the series, it's not a performance that wears its classical antecedents openly on its sleeve. It isn't strictly a jazz performance, either. Law develops ideas in an impressively logical way, building by accretion and occasionally indulging changes of direction which suggest a *coup de théâtre* rather than anything inherent to the music itself. His use of the 'Veni Creator Spiritus' is highly intelligent and highly spontaneous. There is very little outward evidence that much was predetermined. Perhaps oddly, *The Hours*, which is based on the eight hours of prayers observed in the monastic tradition, sounds more organized and deliberate, though Law himself concedes that he benefited from earlier performances of the piece in festival settings (including one in an abbey at Le Mans). Divided into two parts – 'The Exposition of the Chants' and 'The Hours' – it's a work with an unexpectedly grand internal architecture, which is somewhat mitigated by the rather clinical sound of the studio piano. Nevertheless, a substantial achievement and a piano sequence which invites the closest study and reflection.

Claude Lawrence

ALTO SAXOPHONE

A sometime sideman with William Hooker, Lawrence has a long association with Morris and Charles.

***** Presenting**
CIMP 147 *Lawrence; Wilber Morris (b); Dennis Charles (d).* 4/97.

Lawrence plays with the kind of wounded lyricism that used to belong to Jimmy Lyons; he nags at certain phrases and makes whole pieces out of them. Some of this feels like little more than a man running up and down the horn, but the music is redeemed by the wonderful team of Morris and Charles, who make even simple free rhythms fascinating. Although Lawrence apparently played with them many times in the 1980s, this CIMP disc is his first as a leader. It's not unworthy.

Hugh Lawson (born 1935)

PIANO

One of the school of Detroit pianists who emerged during the hard-bop era, Lawson has only rarely been recorded as a leader. He spent a period with Charles Mingus and has lately been more active as a teacher.

***** Colours**
Soul Note 121052 *Lawson; Calvin Hill (b); Louis Hayes (d).* 1/83.

Better known as a sideman with George Adams–Dannie Richmond, Turk Mauro and Yusef Lateef, Lawson has a strong, slightly dry delivery that lends itself better to the ironies of 'Pictures At An Exhibition' and 'If' than to the more conventional changes of '23rd Street Blues'. Hayes raises the temperature, and Hill, who has also recorded with Max Roach and McCoy Tyner, keeps the multilinear feel going. Worth checking out.

Yank Lawson (1911–95)

TRUMPET

Born John Rhea Lawson in Trenton, Missouri, he joined Ben Pollack's New York band in 1933, then spent a famous period (interrupted by an argument) with Bob Crosby. In the 1950s and '60s he often worked with Crosby sideman Bob Haggart, and they formed the World's Greatest Jazz Band together in 1968. In the '80s, he and Haggart were still co-leading bands. He is somewhat taken for granted as a master of Dixieland trumpet.

****** Something Old, Something New, Something Borrowed, Something Blue**
Audiophile APCD-240 *Lawson; George Masso (tb); Johnny Mince (cl); Lou Stein (p); Bucky Pizzarelli (g); Bob Haggart (b); Nick Fatool (d).* 3/88.

***** Jazz At Its Best**

Jazzology JCD-183 *Lawson; George Masso (tb); Kenny Davern (cl); Al Klink (ts); John Bunch (p); Bucky Pizzarelli (g); Bob Haggart (b); Jake Hanna (d).* 2/89.

*****(*) Singin' The Blues**

Jazzology JCD-193 *As above, except Joe Muranyi (cl, ss) replaces Davern; omit Klink; add Barbara Lea (v).* 3/90.

***** With A Southern Accent**

Jazzology JCD-203 *As above, except add Kenny Davern (cl); omit Muranyi and Lea.* 3/91.

Yank Lawson and Bob Haggart played together for almost 60 years. Their Lawson–Haggart Jazz Band of the 1950s was one of the best Dixieland outfits of its kind; their World's Greatest Jazz Band repeated the trick in the 1960s and '70s. Their records for Audiophile and Jazzology maintained a formidable standard: Yank Lawson's tough, growling solos have a bite and pungency which he retained, even into his eighties, and Haggart's steady propulsion never faltered at all. This is a splendid group of discs and only the relatively tame repertoire on the latter three keep them out of the top bracket: the mostly recent material on the first disc is so fresh and is played so enjoyably that one wishes the group had stuck to originals over warhorses. A lovely 'Blues For Louise', a Spanish-sounding 'Bumps', played by a trio of Lawson, Stein and Fatool, and a swaggering 'Come Back, Sweet Papa' are only three highlights from a very fine set. The next three all rely for the most part on Dixieland and traditional staples and, though all are played with gusto and panache, there's a trace of weariness here and there in tunes that might be laid to a comfortable rest. *Jazz At Its Best* dispatches its tunes capably, with extended explorations of 'Willow Weep For Me' and 'Mandy Make Up Your Mind', as well as a memorial to Maxine Sullivan, 'Lonesome Yank'. *Singin' The Blues* finds Yank in tremendous form on the title-song, on a slow, sturdy 'Tin Roof Blues' and a fine 'Blue, Turning Grey Over You'. *With A Southern Accent* peaks on an intensely felt 'Creole Love Call'. This and *Jazz At Its Best* are somewhat pointlessly padded out with a couple of alternative takes.

Daunik Lazro

ALTO AND BARITONE SAXOPHONES

A free improviser who recorded rather more widely on the cusp of the '80s, Lazro has only recently got himself on to CD in any significant way.

*****(*) Hauts Plateaux**

Potlatch P 498 *Lazro; Carlos Zingaro (vn, elec).* 2/95.

*****(*) Dourou**

Bleu Regard CT 1954 *Lazro; Joe McPhee (pkt-t, ss, ts); Didier Levallet, Paul Rogers (b); Christian Rollet (d).* 11/96.

Lazro can't prevent himself from playing songful, temperate lines, even in the midst of an otherwise wild collective passage or a temptingly open canvas. He often shows a Lacy-like restraint on the alto (he plays baritone too, but it's clearly his secondary voice). The duets with Zingaro were recorded at a Marseilles concert and feature some interplay which has as much Gallic charm as ferocity. Zingaro dusts some of the sound with a ripple of electronics; but what you mostly hear is the melodious ache of the alto against the gymnastic tarantella of the violin.

Dourou is a good deal darker, with the yin and yang of Levallet and Rogers underscoring McPhee's characteristically tough tenor. But this is full of colour and energy. Lazro's 'Africa Lab', which derives in part from some traditional melody-lines, is a long piece that brilliantly shows off the individual and collective strengths of the band, the music changing from solo to duo to trio and quintet passages as it evolves through a full 20 minutes in which nothing feels overcharged or underpowered. The Levallet–Rogers combo proves to be the most inspired ingredient to this playing, from their delicious *arco* groaning under 'Catty' to the double-solo on 'Candide'. Lazro should take credit for a singular and original group record.

Nguyen Lê (born 1959)

GUITAR, DANH TRANH, GUITAR SYNTHESIZER

Vietnamese guitarist seeking a fusion of his musical roots with a more worldly jazz-rock synthesis.

*****(*) Miracles**

Musidisc 500102 Lê; Art Lande (*p*); Marc Johnson (*b*); Peter Erskine (*d, perc*) 11/89.

***** Zanzibar**

Musidisc MU 500352 *Lê; Paul McCandless (ss, ob, eng hn, bcl); Art Lande (p, thumb p); Dean Johnson (b); Joel Allouche (d).* 5/92.

***** Million Waves**

ACT 9221 *Lê; Dieter Ilg (b, v); Danny Gottlieb (d, perc).* 12/94.

Something about the overall packaging leads one to expect a hybrid of rock and world music from these records. The reality is quite otherwise. Lê favours soft, clean-picked lines and delicately arpeggiated chords, often using a nylon-strung electric guitar to get a rich 'acoustic' sound that is quite squarely in the jazz tradition. The synths are reserved for delicate background traceries or gently insistent ostinati.

If this is world music, it is unusually well focused and assimilated. The presence of Oregon's Paul McCandless on the later and more diffuse *Zanzibar* gives a reasonable impression of its provenance; the spontaneously improvised 'Sarugaku' might almost have been an early Oregon piece. Much of the material is credited to assistant producer Dominique Borker, who also turns up as co-writer on the earlier and better *Miracles*, a surprisingly tight and jazzy set that recalls Joe Zawinul's stronger post-Weather Report projects.

Lê's habit of alternating longer and more developed tracks with short impressionistic sketches (the dread term *haiku* turns up towards the end of *Miracles*) runs a risk of becoming too mannered. The brief 'Cerf Volant', for Vietnamese zither or dulcimer, is too slight to have been worth including, leading one to wonder why the guitarist hadn't been tempted to use the *danh tranh* more extensively. One obvious answer is that his guitar sound is attractive enough in itself. Lande, Marc Johnson and Erskine prove to be sympathetic interpreters, and McCandless produces moments of chilling beauty on the later disc.

Lê seemed to have gone as far as he could with this approach after two albums. *Million Waves* is both more of the same and very different. It isn't quite a conventional jazz trio, but the rudiments are quite definitely there and the long, spontaneously improvised 'Trilogy', the only track not recorded at Walter Quintus's state-of-the-art CMP studios, opens up sufficient files for a decade's-worth of experimentation; excellent stuff. The high gloss that Quintus brings occasionally diverts attention away from less than stirring material. 'Butterflies And Zebras' is a short gloss on Jimi Hendrix's 'Little Wing', which follows it, without adding much to the original. Dominique Borker is co-credited again on the attractive 'Moonshine', confirming the fruitfulness of that relationship. Surprisingly, Lê plays out on James Brown's 'I Feel Good'; perhaps the jazz-funk album is just around the corner.

***** Tales From Viêt-Nam**

ACT 9225-2 *Lê; Paolo Fresu (t, flhn); Simon Spang-Hanssen (sax, f); François Verly (p, ky, mar, perc); Michael Benita (b); Hao Nhien (danh tranh, dan bau, sao, perc); Thai An (dan nguyet); Joël Allouche, Steve Arguëlles (d); Trilok Gurtu (d, perc); Huong Thanh (v).* 10–11/95.

*****(*) Three Trios**

ACT 9245-2 *Lê; Renaud Garcia-Fons, Dieter Ilg, Marc Johnson (b); Peter Erskine, Danny Gottlieb (d); Mino Cinelu (d, perc).* 11/96.

***** Maghreb And Friends**

ACT 9261-2 *Lê; Paolo Fresu (t); Wolfgang Puschnig (as); Stefano Di Battista (as, ss); Alain Debiossat (ss); Hao Nhien (Vietnamese f); Aly Wagué (African f, v); Bojan Zulikarpasic (p); Cheb Mami (acc syn); Djemaï Abdenour (mandola, Algerian bjo); Jean Jacques Avenel (kora); Mejdoub Ftati (vn); Michel Alibo (b); Mokhtar Samba (d); Karim Ziad (d, perc, v); Mehdi Askeur, Gaëlle Hervé, Marielle Hervé, Aziz Sahmaoui, Huong Thanh (v); Zahra Bani, B'net Houariyat, Kadija Haliba, Saïda Madrani, Mohamed Menni, Malika Rhami, Halima Zaiter (v, perc).* 11/97–3/98.

Like Anouar Brahem and Rabih Abou-Khalil, Lê has already gone some considerable way towards broadening the constituency of 'world jazz'. No sign of the jazz-funk album we feared, but instead a steady consolidation of the different aspects of his work so far. *Maghreb And Friends* is an interesting attempt at synthesizing different traditions, probably too many and too different to pull off with absolute conviction. A hybrid like 'Funk Raï' is of questionable valuable, given that *raï* is a form with its own subtly propulsive dynamic, much of which is lost when rendered down into lumpy fours.

Much of the material here comes from percussionist Karim Ziad, who acts as co-leader. His 'Louanges' – a near-untranslatable word for ecstatic praises favoured by composer Olivier Messiaen – is the most beautiful track on the album, an exquisite blending of Maghrebi, Vietnamese and Guinean voices. The horns are used only sparingly throughout the album and really come into their own only on the closing 'Guinia' (Mahmoud Guinia is one of the greatest exponents of *gnawa* singing) and the closing love-chant, 'Nesraf'. An album of many elements, all of them fascinating and most of them rendered immaculately but without coherence.

Tales From Viêt-Nam was the album that allowed Lê to break through to a wider audience, partly because of the successful touring project that bore the same name. It is probably our least favourite of all so far, for most of the same reasons as *Maghreb And Friends*. Where its attempt to unite white and black Africa had a certain fresh logic, *Tales* sounds very much like an attempt to import new cuisine. Relying almost entirely on traditional material, it's a record that appears to struggle somewhere in the dead zone between 'authenticity' and the players' palpable desire to shake loose and pursue fascinating lines of inquiry. Arguëlles and Allouche share percussion responsibilities, and it's the Englishman (if he still considers himself such) who shows the more penetrating insight into the source material, playing brilliantly on an early trio of wistful narratives. The drummers alternate on the two-part 'Mangustao', the name of a strange, dual-natured fruit whose rugged exterior and delicate flesh seem to hold a symbolic importance for Lê. Trilok Gurtu adds chipper, slightly pointless cameo percussion to 'Hen Ho' and 'Ting Ning'.

By contrast to the others, *Three Trios* is coherent, expressively focused and brimming with extraordinary playing. The best of the three line-ups is, predictably, the reunion with Johnson and Erskine. It is also the most straightforwardly jazz-based. Lê characterizes the groups according to the titles of the first three tunes: 'Silk', 'Silver', 'Sand' – delicate but strong threads bind him to Marc and Peter; there is a shiny metallic edge to the group with Dieter Ilg and Danny Gottlieb; and a shifting, rhythmically looser quality to the performances with Garcia-Fons and Cinelu.

Some familiar themes are aired. 'Idoma' refers to an African tribe who wear white masks with slanting eyes, which strongly suggests Asian origin; the melody sounds Oriental but is actually a pygmy song. 'Woof' for Dieter and Danny and 'Foow' for Renaud and Mino are the same theme, a quick way of unpicking the differences in approach. The closing 'Straight, No Chaser', played *à l'argent*, is a complete surprise and a provocative close to a thoroughly unexpected and completely enjoyable jazz record.

The Leaders

GROUP

Conceived as a touring group trading on the starry nature of the line-up, this turned into a regular band for several years and went some way to developing an aesthetic of its own.

*****(*) Out Here Like This**

Black Saint 120119 *Lester Bowie (t); Arthur Blythe (as); Chico Freeman (ts, bcl); Kirk Lightsey (p); Cecil McBee (b); Famoudou Don Moye (d).* 6/86.

***** Slipping And Sliding**

Sound Hills SSCD 8054 *As above.* 6/93.

Occupying a mid-point between the now almost parodic anarchy of the Art Ensemble of Chicago and the more professional musical showmanship of Lester Bowie's Brass Fantasy, and offering a left-of-centre balance between Chico Freeman's freer style and the soul-funk of his Brainstorm band, The Leaders also helped redeem Arthur Blythe's skidding career. Never as impressive on record as they were live, *Out Here Like This* is nevertheless a powerful and varied sampling of contemporary styles. There's a better balance of sound between the front-row voices and a more prominent role for McBee, who shares some of Ron Carter's ability to style-shift while maintaining a basic consistency of tone. Bowie's theatrical approach manages to compress a huge acreage of jazz history, calling in references to Armstrong, Bix Beiderbecke and Miles Davis. The more recent *Slipping And Sliding* reinforces the Art Ensemble analogy more than we might have expected, with an emphasis on showmanship and pure theatre that might dismay some listeners. However, the sheer range of musicianship is what sustains this band and there is enough quality playing from just about every position to satisfy even the most finicky. With Bowie now gone, it feels nostalgic, too.

The Leaders Trio

GROUP

A one-off session by the rhythm section of the all-star aggregation.

*****(*) Heaven Dance**

Sunnyside SSC 1034 *Kirk Lightsey (p); Cecil McBee (b); Famoudou Don Moye (d).* 5/88.

Not the least of *Heaven Dance*'s merits is that it sends us back to the original Leaders sets with a heightened awareness of what was going on in the warp-factor engine-room. Which is not to say that *Heaven Dance* is not a substantial achievement on its own terms. Though it may masquerade as a conventional piano trio, the balance of emphasis favours McBee (particularly) and Don Moye. The title-track is an intriguing pattern of melorhythms with some fine piano; 'Cecil To Cecil' and a tribute to the great bassist, Wilbur Ware, also catch the eye.

Joelle Léandre (born 1951)

DOUBLE BASS, VOICE

The French bassist and vocalist has produced a huge body of work, much of it with other leaders, in the anonymity of collectives and on small and hard-to-find labels. Consequently, her dramatic presence and stunning bass-work are less well known than they should be. She plays resonantly but with a great deal of detail.

***** Urban Bass**

Adda 581254 *Léandre; Sylvie Altenburger (vla).* 90.

***** Ecritures**

Adda 590038 *Léandre; Carlos Zingaro (vn).*

*****(*) Blue Goo Park**

FMP CD 52 *Léandre; Rüdiger Carl (acc, cl).* 7/92

A good proportion of Léandre's concert and recorded output consists of new music. She has either commissioned or received dedication of speciality pieces for double bass from composers such as Betsy Jolas, Jacob Druckman, Sylvano Bussotti and especially Giacinto Scelsi, and has adapted other materials, including John Cage's song, 'The Wonderful Widow of Eighteen Springs', for bass and voice; all of these are on Adda 581043. This work apart, though, Léandre is a formidable improviser. She has appeared as part of Derek Bailey's Company project and has a number of improvisation-based recordings to her credit.

Violinist Zingaro (another occasional Company shareholder) is a sympathetic collaborator, offering the same wild and unrestrained string-playing she experienced with maverick Australian fiddler/inventor, Jon Rose. On a single track from the *Urban Bass* session, she looks to Altenburger for a rich viola sound. Léandre and Eric Watson (on the deleted hat Art, *Palimpseste*) explore the idea of palimpsest improvisation, overlaying composed structures with freehand materials, much as she does with Carl on the FMP session, which is probably her most concentrated to date. Consisting of 23 tracks, at just over an hour's tracking time, it emphasizes Léandre's interest in brief, almost song-like forms.

***** Contrabasses**

Leo CD LR 261 *Léandre; William Parker (b).* 97.

****(*) E'Vero**

Leo CD LR 275 *Léandre; Sebi Tramontano (p).* 97.

It would be hard to imagine a more compelling meeting between two contemporary improvisers than *Contrabasses*. Parker is a modern master and a musician of vast resource and intelligence. As on the duets with Tramontano which make up the slightly disappointing *E'Vero*, Léandre is comfortable enough to cede musical territory to her playing partners. With Parker, though, she is as forceful and full-voiced as we have ever heard her on disc. His sense of structure is without peer, and Léandre might seem a miniaturist by comparison, except that here she lengthens her line and adds weight to every stroke of the strings. A marvellous record; don't be put off by the rarefied instrumentation.

*****(*) Joelle Léandre Project**

Leo CD LR 287 *Léandre; Marilyn Crispell (p); Richard Teitelbaum (ky, elec); Carlos Zingaro (vn); Paul Lovens (d).* 1/99.

This is the group record that Léandre has threatened for a long time. Her past associations with all these players guarantee a strong empathy and, as with the Parker duets, she has a partner of equal force and expression in Marilyn Crispell. Using Zingaro and Teitelbaum allows her to create broad and complex soundscapes, but much of the music is unexpectedly spacious and detailed; there is no clutter anywhere on the nine numbered improvisations which made up the midwinter performance at Sons d'Hiver.

LeeAnn Ledgerwood

PIANO

Born in Ohio, Ledgerwood studied classical piano but was won over by a Bill Evans LP. After studying at Berklee, she arrived in New York in 1982, where she plays and teaches.

****(*) You Wish**

Triloka 187 *Ledgerwood; Bill Evans (ts, ss); Jeremy Steig (f); Eddie Gomez, Steve LaSpina (b); Danny Gottlieb (d).* 1/91.

LeeAnn Ledgerwood was first noticed by Marian McPartland and received enthusiastic acclaim for her role on McPartland's 'Piano Jazz' broadcasts in 1990. Buoyed up by that success, Ledgerwood recorded her debut record with a degree more haste and enthusiasm than judgement. There's a nervy edge to *You Wish* that a more interventionist producer (Walter Becker is an avowed fan) might have tried to temper. She solos on every track but seems to play the same solo at least four times over. The record also leans rather heavily on Evans and Steig, neither of whom is a charismatic soloist. Better, surely, to have essayed a modest trio album with Gomez (for whom she had already recorded) and the estimable Gottlieb, who stands out like a beacon in this.

*****(*) Now And Zen**

Steeplechase SCCD 31432 *Ledgerwood; Jon Gordon (ss, as); Matt Penman (b); Heinrich Köbberling (d).* 9/97.

***** Transition**

Steeplechase SCCD 31468 *Ledgerwood; Matt Penman (b); Jaz Sawyers (d).* 4/98.

These rather belated follow-ups to the debut are a lot more confident and settled. Gordon was an excellent choice for the horn on the quartet date, smoothly assertive in his solos but conservative enough not to bruise the reflexes of a rhythm section that had already worked together a lot. Ledgerwood doesn't write much – there are a meagre four originals spread over the two discs – and the focus here is on getting a group result. Even so, Ledgerwood's theme, 'Now And Zen', sparks what's perhaps the best performance on that disc, the group gradually raising the intensity until Gordon's alto fireworks seem like a logical outburst. Some of the pieces, such as Wayne Shorter's 'Water Babies', are under-coloured, but it's an assured set.

The trio set isn't quite as convincing. Some of the tracks are too long, such as the smart but overbuilt revision of 'Night And Day'. She does better by the frantic but under-control scamper through McCoy Tyner's 'Four By Five'. Penman and the youthful Sawyers are more than keen in keeping up.

Mike LeDonne

PIANO

He worked early on as the house pianist at Jimmy Ryan's in New York and played with many of the swing-to-mainstream masters there. Sideman duties include Benny Goodman, Art Farmer, James Moody and Sonny Rollins.

***** 'Bout Time**

Criss Cross 1033 *LeDonne; Tom Harrell (t, flhn); Gary Smulyan (bs); Dennis Irwin (b); Kenny Washington (d).* 1/88.

****(*) The Feeling Of Jazz**

Criss Cross 1041 *As above.* 1/90.

****(*) Common Ground**

Criss Cross 1058 *As above, except omit Harrell and Smulyan.* 12/90.

*****(*) Soulmates**

Criss Cross 1074 *LeDonne; Ryan Kisor (t); Joshua Redman (ts); Jon Gordon (as); Peter Washington (b); Lewis Nash (d).* 1/93.

*****(*) Waltz For An Urbanite**

Criss Cross 1111 *LeDonne; Steve Nelson (vib); Peter Bernstein (g); Peter Washington (b); Kenny Washington (d).* 6/95.

***** To Each His Own**

Double Time DTRCD 135 *LeDonne; Peter Washington (b); Mickey Roker (d).* 1/98.

LeDonne leads some very capable groups here. The first two discs are typical, consistent, slightly soft Criss Cross dates, despite the skilful team involved. Tunes, charts and solos all bespeak an unflagging but rather charmless dedication to hard-bop routine. Four of the themes on the second record are handled by the rhythm section alone, but otherwise there's little to tell the two records apart. *Common Ground* gives LeDonne the spotlight with only bass and drums in support; though the tunes are way out of the ordinary – Wes Montgomery, some rare Ellington – they sound as if they were meant to show off his ingenuity. *Soulmates* is a different matter. Kisor and Redman are an indecently talented front line and they finesse the material to a degree that takes this out of the usual neat-and-tidy sessionman bag. Come to that, Gordon is quite up to their level. LeDonne himself doesn't do anything awesomely different from the other records, but it all sounds very accomplished.

Waltz For An Urbanite continues the good form. LeDonne is used to playing alongside vibes after many years with Milt Jackson, and he makes a seamless team with the typically elegant and quick-witted Nelson. His originals have a flavoursome touch – the title-piece is especially smart – and the music as a whole has a sexier, more lilting feel than some of the earlier records. One or two tunes take a longer route than they might have done, but the playing has real sass, and it sustains the disc.

Moving to Double Time, LeDonne turns in another genuine date. Wes Montgomery's 'Movin' Along', an inspired choice, shows how much he can get out of the basic material of the blues. He's never a filigree player, but he rarely wastes a note, and the almost spidery lines he extracts out of this one are compelling to follow as he unfolds them. Roker, less often sighted these days, is a fine choice for the drum role, and Peter Washington is his usual blameless self.

Phil Lee (born 1943)

GUITAR

British guitarist associated with the London modern-jazz movement of the 1960s and fusion and art-rock in the '70s, subsequently moving into a more straight-ahead position.

*****(*) Twice Upon A Time**

Cadillac SGCASCD 1 *Lee; Jeff Clyne (b).* 12/86–1/87.

Quiet, often subliminal guitar-and-bass music. Both men light on points of harmonic detail rather than pushing for a rhythmic result, and the consequence is a series of improvisations of delicate, exacting finesse. The tunes are very well chosen, with composers from Mercer Ellington to Steve Swallow in the list.

Soren Lee

GUITAR

Guitarist in a conventional, accomplished post-bop setting.

***** Soren Lee Quartet**

L + R CDLR 45073 *Lee; Thomas Clausen (p); Ray Brown (b); Alvin Queen (d).* 2/90.

*****(*) Soren Lee Trio**

L + R CDLR 45072 *Lee; Jesper Lundgaard (b); Adam Nussbaum (d).* 2–4/92.

Nothing fancy, nothing spare or wasted; just excellent guitar jazz, with fleet, horn-inflected lines and a generous harmonic range, many of the tunes cast in keys which don't sit entirely comfortably for the instrument. Lee calls on top-flight sidemen for both these sessions. Having Ray Brown in the studio is a bit of luxury and the great man is mixed a little high, as is drummer Queen. On purely acoustic grounds, the live sessions are preferable – compare 'Dr Jeckyll' for confirmation – though some of the sharper guitar attacks come through a little harshly. Lee sticks in the main to familiar material – 'My Favorite Things', 'Bemsha Swing', 'All The Things You Are' – and it is easy to be caught napping by this, for there is some thoughtful music-making going on, especially again in the numbers recorded at the Jazzhus Montmartre, where he is a much-admired regular.

Cliff Leeman (1913–86)

DRUMS

A drummer who worked with many of the great swing-era orchestras, Leeman later spent most of his career playing in superior Dixieland bands. He rarely aspired to even a nominal leadership.

****(*) Cliff Leeman And His All-Stars**

Jazzology JCD-112 *Leeman; Tom Saunders (c); Spiegel Wilcox, Al Winters (tb); Nick Sassone (cl, ts); Dill Jones, John Eaton, Larry Eanet (p); Butch Hall, Steve Jordan (g). Late 70s.*

This is a raggedy live date – made in Manassas, Virginia, on an uncertain date – with Leeman directing a Dixieland group of sometimes uncertain personnel. The playing has great good humour and some spirited solos, but it's nothing special, and the perfunctory location recording doesn't make the most of it. Leeman's own playing, though, merits attention: he drives the band hard without sounding remorseless.

Michel Legrand (born 1932)

PIANO, ORGAN, VOCAL

Studied at Paris Conservatoire, then began film-composing in 1957 and has written numerous themes and songs which have entered the jazz repertory. A capable jazz pianist, he has been involved in several major recording projects involving jazz musicians, and he occasionally works in small-group situations.

****** Legrand Jazz**

Philips 830074-2 *Legrand; Miles Davis, Ernie Royal, Art Farmer, Donald Byrd, Joe Wilder (t); Frank Rehak, Billy Byers, Jimmy Cleveland, Eddie Bert (tb); James Buffington (frhn); Gene Quill, Phil Woods (as); Ben Webster, John Coltrane, Seldon Powell (ts); Jerome Richardson (bs, bcl); Teo Macero (bs); Herbie Mann (f); Bill Evans, Hank Jones, Nat Pierce (p); Eddie Costa, Don Elliott (vib); Betty Glamann (hp); Major Holley (b, tba); Paul Chambers, George Duvivier, Milt Hinton (b); Don Lamond, Kenny Dennis, Osie Johnson (d).* 6/58.

***** Le Jazz Grand**

Castle PACD 027 *Legrand; Joe Shepley, Burt Collins, John Gatchell, John Clark, Albert Richmond, Jon Faddis, Brooks Tillotson, Tony Price (t); Phil Woods (as); Gerry Mulligan (bs); Bernie Leighton, Tom Pierson (ky); Harry Leahey (g); Ron Carter, Don Elliot (b); Jimmy Madison, Grady Tate (d).* 78.

*****(*) After The Rain**

Original Jazz Classics OJC 803-2 *Legrand; Joe Wilder (t, flhn); Phil Woods (as, cl); Zoot Sims (ts); Gene Bertoncini (g); Ron Carter (b); Grady Tate (d).* 5/82.

Legrand's name is so widely known as a pop composer that his jazz leanings are largely ignored. But this small discography is worth much more than a passing look. The sessions for the *Legrand Jazz* album are uniquely star-studded, and the quality of the writing matches up to the cast-list. Legrand chose many unexpected tunes – including ancient history such as 'Wild Man Blues', as well as the more predictable 'Nuages' and 'Django' – and recast each one in a challenging way. 'Night In Tunisia' is a controlled fiesta of trumpets, 'Round Midnight' a glittering set-piece for Davis, 'Nuages' a sensuous vehicle for Webster. The latter is placed alongside a trombone section in one of the three groupings devised by the arranger; another is dominated by a four-man trumpet group. The third has the remarkable situation of having Davis, Coltrane and Evans as sidemen, playing Fats Waller and Louis Armstrong tunes. Many of the arrangements are tellingly compact, seven not even breaking the four-minute barrier, and it ends on a *fast* treatment of Beiderbecke's 'In A Mist'.

The 1978 *Le Jazz Grand* is comparatively lightweight, with Woods, Faddis and Mulligan as featured soloists: interesting, and the brass writing is carefully worked through, though it's hardly on a par with its predecessor. *After The Rain* was done almost off the cuff and stands as a ballad album, the group working casually through six lesser-known Legrand tunes – yet the playing by the three front-liners is so exquisitely done that the music glows. 'Nobody Knows', in which Sims and Woods luxuriate through the lovely chords as if taking a bath in them, is an impromptu classic.

*****(*) Legrand Grappelli**

Verve 517028-2 *Legrand; Stéphane Grappelli (vn); Marc Michel (b); André Ceccarelli (d); strings.* 92.

***** Douce France**

Verve 529850-2 *Legrand; Stéphane Grappelli (vn); Marc-Michel Lebevillon (b); Umberto Pagnini (d); strings.* 8–10/95.

Grappelli loved these records, which were among his last, and both he and Legrand had reason to be proud of the collaboration. Steph plays the jazz while Michel sets the most gorgeous, chocolate-box arrangements he can think of to swirl around the violin. Lots of sugar, spiced just a little by the wilier aspects of each man's art; when they do such Gallic heart-tuggers as 'La Vie En Rose' or 'Je Tire Ma Révérance', dry eyes are at a premium. The first set edges ahead for having the best of Legrand's own tunes.

Johan Leijonhufvud (born 1971)

GUITAR

Began playing guitar at twelve, and performing in the local scene around Malmö.

***(*) Speaks The Local Bebop

Sittel SITCD 9215 *Leijonhufvud; Anders Bergcrantz (t); Mattias Hjorth (b); Kristofer Johansson (d); Sofia Pettersson (v).* 11/93–5/94.

A winner. Leijonhufvud gets a huge sound out of his (untreated) electric instrument and, as the title suggests, he prefers the rules and language of hardcore bop – without sounding encumbered by any of it. The result is a fresh, excitable session that has the trio playing as if they're just discovering this new music. Bergcrantz sits in on four tunes, and he sounds terrific on 'Vals', the pairing of trumpet and guitar emerging as sonorously beautiful. Some of the tunes are on the glib side but, if the playing ever strays in that direction, their enthusiasm sees them through it. Pettersson takes a cameo role on one tune and sounds a little uneasy with the lyrics.

**** Happy Farm

Sittel SITCD 9231 *As above, except Jacob Karlzon (p) replaces Bergcrantz and Pettersson.* 4/96.

A great one. Karlzon proves to be a superbly effective foil to Leijonhufvud, and there's nothing prosaic about what looks like a routine instrumentation. No mid-tempo ballad could sound more poignantly beautiful than 'Kattis', and the absolutely barnstorming 'Backwoods' shows how much power-with-finesse the group can muster. There's a knockout run across Joe Henderson's 'The Kicker', a meditative passage through Phil Markowitz's 'Sno Peas' and excellent writing by everyone bar Johansson.

Urs Leimgruber

TENOR SAXOPHONE, SOPRANO SAXOPHONE, BASS SAXOPHONE, FLUTE

Leimgruber is a post-Coltrane saxophonist who has explored other dimensions of contemporary jazz as well. His use of dynamics and timbre can be quite abrasive, but he is unfailingly musical and never resorts to empty gesture.

*** Reflexionen Live

Timeless SJP 234 *Leimgruber; Don Friedman (p); Bobby Burri (b); Joel Allouche (d).* 11/85.

*** Reflexionen

Enja 5057 *Leimgruber; Don Friedman (p); Palle Danielsson (b); Joel Allouche (d).* 2/87.

In tonal range and diversity of concerns, Leimgruber somewhat resembles Briton John Surman. Surman, though, has only rarely ventured into total freedom and utilizes extremes of pitch rather sparingly. Leimgruber's Reflexionen is far from being a conventional horn-and-rhythm unit. The Timeless session, recorded live in Switzerland, finds him working with space and extended structures like the 'Rotsee Suite'.

Friedman is an interesting name to come across in company like this, though like many adventurous Americans he has had to look to Europe for a sympathetic audience. He is not well recorded on the live album, which favours the saxophonist to the detriment of the others, but he comes through very strongly indeed on *Reflexionen* and the partnership with Danielsson is consistently inventive and thoughtful.

***(*) No Try No Fail

hatOLOGY 509 *Leimgruber; Joelle Léandre (b); Fritz Hauser (d, perc).* 3/96.

*** Live

SR2 *Leimgruber; Fritz Hauser (d, perc).* 4/98.

***(*) Quartet Noir

Victo CD 067 *Leimgruber; Marilyn Crispell (p); Joelle Léandre (b); Fritz Hauser (d, perc).* 5/98.

The partnership with Hauser is a long-standing one, perhaps to the detriment of communicability. An earlier duo on hat ART, *L'Enigmatique*, is currently deleted, though it might reappear under the new hatOLOGY umbrella. The live duo appears to be self-released, but is reasonably widely available and is certainly well worth checking out. At times, the improvisations are so intensely personal that the listener feels shut out of a conversation in which most of the obvious reference points are omitted; but after a while even this begins to exert a fascination. A challenging record, with much to ponder.

In his liner-note to *No Try No Fail* Bert Noglik expresses surprise that the duo should countenance the addition of a third member. That is precisely what was needed. Léandre brings her usual intelligence to the session and breaks up what was beginning to seem like a huddle. No singing from her, unfortunately, but some gloriously rich-toned bass playing, especially on the first and third tracks, which are helpfully called 'First' and 'Third'. Not programme music, then, but certainly less abstract than of yore.

The quartet with Marilyn Crispell was one of the best-received sets at the 1988 Festival International de Musique Actuelle at Victoriaville, and it's a performance that comes across fully and persuasively on record as well. There seem to have been no preset themes or ideas, with everything improvised spontaneously. Crispell seems like the outsider – which in effect she was – but she makes a virtue of that, working in parallel, and not trying to inveigle her way into an extremely tight unit. It isn't clear whether the pieces were played in the order given on the CD, but if they were, it suggests that she found herself on a fast learning curve; by the last two longish tracks, she is very much in tune with the other three and, if anything, occupies the driving seat. Her Coltraneisms are less evident than usual, though on a couple of occasions she and Leimgruber seem to exchange reminiscences of Trane's phrasing and solo formation. A fine performance all round.

Peter Leitch

GUITAR

Drawing on every available aspect of the guitar tradition, Leitch is a smooth and accomplished performer whose very facility sometimes disguises the sophistication of what he is doing. Easy in the studio, he has created a substantial body of recorded work.

***(*) **Red Zone**

Reservoir RSR CD 103 *Leitch; Pepper Adams (bs); Kirk Lightsey (p); Ray Drummond (b); Marvin 'Smitty' Smith (d).* 11/84, 11/85, 7/88.

*** **Exhilaration**

Reservoir RSR CD 118 *Leitch; Pepper Adams (bs); John Hicks (p); Ray Drummond (b); Billy Hart (d).* 11/84, 12/88.

*** **On A Misty Night**

Criss Cross Criss 1026 *Leitch; Neil Swainson (b); Mickey Roker (d).* 11/86.

***(*) **Portraits And Dedications**

Criss Cross Criss 1039 *Leitch; Bobby Watson (as); Jed Levy (afl); James Williams (p); Ray Drummond (b); Marvin 'Smitty' Smith (d).* 12/88, 1/89.

*** **Mean What You Say**

Concord CCD 4417 *Leitch; John Hicks (p); Ray Drummond (b); Marvin 'Smitty' Smith (d).* 1/90.

***(*) **Trio / Quartet '91**

Concord CCD 4480 *Leitch; John Swana (t, flhn); Neil Swainson (b); Marvin 'Smitty' Smith (d).* 2/91.

***(*) **From Another Perspective**

Concord CCD 4535 *Leitch; Gary Bartz (as); Jed Levy (afl, ts, ss); John Hicks (p); Ray Drummond (b); Marvin 'Smitty' Smith (d).* 6/92.

A glance at the personnel on Leitch's records gives a quick summary of his standing in the jazz community. One moment the young guitarist was hacking a living in his native Canada, the next – or so it seemed – he was pumping out a steady flow of top-flight jazz albums. In a recording career stretching back just over a decade, Leitch has evolved from an essentially horn-based style to a much more guitaristic (his own word) approach. The tracks with Pepper Adams on the November 1984 session worked because of the degree of separation between the baritone and Leitch's own lines. A couple of duos with Drummond explore a similar contrast. Hicks and Lightsey are both quite dominant, dark-toned piano players, and that contributed to the overall feel of these sessions.

When he came to Criss Cross, Gerry Teekens gave him the breadth and leeway he wanted to make swinging but intelligent records which refused to sit neatly in any currently agreed niche. *On A Misty Night* betrays some signs of having been his debut. Leitch tries to pack in too much and falls rather flat, caught between opposites rather than using them to fuel one another. Leitch has, though, always known what he wants. The change of emphasis on *Portraits And Dedications* was quite striking. It would be difficult to imagine a saxophonist who sounds less like Pepper Adams than Bobby Watson, and the switch to James Williams marked a clear recognition that Leitch was increasingly capable of sustaining a broader, self-accompanied sound, the very thing that seemed lacking on the first Reservoir's solo tracks. Jed Levy's alto flute is used very sparingly on *Portraits*, for the softly romantic 'Visage De Cathryn' and 'Portrait Of Sylvia'. His moment was to come later.

The three Concords are uniformly excellent. *Mean What You Say* pared the sound down again. Leitch plays ringingly on 'Blues On The East Side' and 'Stairway To The Stars', but he's always prepared to step aside for Hicks. On the *Trio/Quartet* record, he brings in a horn for three tracks and modernizes the material considerably; Joe Henderson's 'Inner Urge' and Chick Corea's 'Tones For Joans Bones' present new challenges. Leitch has devised a new way of playing chords which also allows him to pick off clean top-string lines; as a technique, it comes down through Jim Hall and Joe Pass, but Leitch makes it his own, and in the absence of piano it serves him wonderfully well. Smitty Smith's presence is an important factor throughout the decade, but this is his best moment. His sheer control at low tempi and softer volumes is exemplary.

The subsequent release is very much a re-run of the *Portraits* concept. Bartz is magnificent and Jed Levy gets to show off his considerable skill. The charts are perhaps tighter than before, and original material like 'For Elmo, Sonny And Freddie' and '91-1' is well organized and unfussy. Leitch clearly hasn't run out of ideas yet. For relatively straight-ahead guitar jazz, his work has been remarkably unpredictable and always fresh.

*** **Duality**

Reservoir RSRCD 134 *Leitch; John Hicks (p); Ray Drummond (b); Marvin 'Smitty' Smith (d).* 7/93.

*** **A Special Rapport**

Reservoir RSRCD 129 *Leitch; John Hicks (p).* 6/94.

Leitch gets on well with Hicks, and both these discs are full of appeal. The quartet date sometimes settles down too comfortably, though one can hardly blame Leitch for enjoying his surroundings, and in a medley of Strayhorn tunes the music reaches a peak of gentle but firm lyricism. In the pure duo situation, there's the same sageness of utterance and fertility of invention, although again there's a sense that the two men are basking in their abilities rather than going so far as to actually push each other. To that extent, the records don't compel the same attention. But they're equally hard to resist.

***(*) **Colours And Dimensions**

Reservoir Music RSRCD 140 *Leitch; Claudio Roditi (t); Gary Bartz (as); Jed Levy (ts); John Hicks (p); Rufus Reid (b); Marvin 'Smitty' Smith (d).*

Elegant and tasteful jazz from what sounds like a very settled group. Bartz is in excellent form, hot, intense and bluesy. 'Bluesview' is magnificent and 'Round Lake Burnt Hills' highlights the leader's smoothly elegant approach, with the big Zoller guitar ringing and singing in every chorus.

***(*) **Up Front**

Reservoir RSRCD 149 *Leitch; Sean Smith (b); Marvin 'Smitty' Smith (d).* 96.

*****(*) Blues On The Corner**
Reservoir RSRCD 160 *Leitch; Bobby Watson (ss, as); Renee Rosnes (p); Dwayne Burno (b); Billy Hart (d); Kendra Shank (v).* 97.

By this stage in the game, Leitch is such a reliable commodity that it is difficult to make meaningful distinctions between his records; they sound like an ongoing session with a steady procession of guests. Watson's plangent approach is even better suited to this material than is Bartz, and on 'The Hillary Step', 'Wendy's Shoes' and the title-piece he is magisterially good.

The trio album is an all too rare opportunity to hear Leitch out on his own, with just rhythm. 'You're My Everything' and 'Sea Change' are noteworthy for the interplay of guitar and percussion, underlining Leitch's strong rhythmic instincts. As a showcase for a quiet and understated talent, it comes highly recommended.

John Leitham

BASS

As his album titles tend to trumpet, Leitham is a left-handed bassist, based in California. His major gig in the 1980s and '90s was in the trio backing Mel Torme. A straight-ahead player with a big sound.

***** Leitham Up**
USA CD-725 *Leitham; Tom Ranier (ts, bcl, p); Jake Hanna (d).* 5/89.

***** The Southpaw**
USA CD-765 *Leitham; Buddy Childers (t, flhn); Bob Cooper (ts); Tom Ranier, Milcho Leviev (p); Roy McCurdy (d).* 9/92.

***** Lefty Leaps In**
USA CD-940 *Leitham; Bill Watrous (tb); Pete Christlieb, Rickey Woodard (ts); Tom Ranier (p); Barry Zweig (g); Jeff Hamilton (d).* 4–5/96.

***** Live!**
CARS CP 0020 *Leitham; Pete Christlieb, Rickey Woodard (ts); Shelly Berg (p); Joe LaBarbera (d).* 3/97.

A gifted and exceptionally skilful player, Leitham is one of those mercurial sessionmen who have been filling West Coast studios for the past 40 years. None of these records really makes its way to the essential shelf, but they're all full of swinging and attention-grabbing playing. The trio album sometimes stalls on Leitham's virtuosity: he can play awfully fast, and rapid-fire bass solos can get boring all too quickly; but the on-the-toes gumption of his companions keeps the music from growing mundane. Ranier plays piano for most of the date, but his two horn features – including, oddly, 'Moose The Mooche' on bass clarinet – are respectable enough. *The Southpaw* is mostly trio, too (Leviev takes the piano stool on three tracks), though Childers and the great Bob Cooper sit in for four affable numbers. 'Scrapple From The Apple' is a fine slug of straightforward bebop, and Leitham has the *chutzpah* to play the melody of 'Jitterbug Waltz' on bass. *Lefty Leaps In* benefits from a greater variety of settings: there are two-tenor fisticuffs from Woodard and Christlieb on four tracks, including a breathtakingly fast 'Oleo', and some trio pieces with Ranier and Hamilton; but perhaps the best music is with Watrous and Zweig – a lovely 'Zingaro' highlights the trombonist's peerlessly singing tone. Leitham still probably gives himself too much space but, hey, it's his date.

The live album extends the set-up tried on the previous studio album. Christlieb and Woodard have at it for an hour's worth of virile and often exciting blowing. There's little in it if you're looking for the winner out of the two horns: both play it big and hearty. Lots more bass solos and Leitham treats himself to a solo *arco* piece as well.

Brian Lemon (born 1937)

PIANO

This stalwart of the British scene grew up in Nottingham and first came to prominence in the legendary group fronted by Sandy Brown and Al Fairweather. He has often worked as a jobbing sideman, often accompanying visiting Americans; with the advent of the Zephyr label he has also emerged – belatedly – as a regular recording star, often sharing billing with horn players.

***** But Beautiful**
Zephyr ZE CD 1 *Lemon; Dave Cliff (g); Dave Green (b); Allan Ganley (d).* 1 & 3/95.

****(*) A Beautiful Friendship**
Zephyr ZE CD 4 *Lemon; Warren Vaché (c); Roy Williams (tb); Dave Cliff (g); Dave Green (b); Martin Drew, Allan Ganley (d).* 2/95.

***** How Long Has This Been Going On?**
Zephyr ZE CD 5 *As above, except omit Vaché, Drew; add Scott Hamilton (ts).* 8/95.

The answer to the third of these is: six decades now, or four at least as an active musician. At sixty, Lemon is a stalwart of the British scene, a figure easily overlooked only because he seems always to have been there, turning out classy, unpretentious jazz with an effortless swing. Appearing on a 1993 Concord disc by American saxophonist Scott Hamilton (whose anglophile stance can be at least partly explained by his enthusiasm for working with Lemon) brought him to the notice of a bigger international audience, but it was the launch of John Bune's lemon-liveried Zephyr label (the only imprint around to give credits for 'benign gophery') that cemented Lemon's class and standing with record buyers.

The first of the bunch is quality product. The title-track is a model of its kind, and the medley of 'Exactly Like You' and 'I Thought About You' is hard to fault. A version of Sonny Rollins's 'St Thomas' doesn't sit quite as obviously for Lemon's technique but, following as it does the one original on the set, 'Blues For Suzanna', it underlines his other gift, the pacing and direction of a set. The session with Vaché and Roy Williams is a little too polite and matey: 'After you, Claude', 'No, after you, Cecil', as they used to say in ITMA (apologies to non-British readers for a momentary descent into parochialism). However, the brass is nicely recorded and there are splendid readings of 'Moten Swing', 'Up With The Lark' and 'Skylark', further evidence of Lemon's skill in pacing a record. Hamilton makes a big contribution to *How Long?*, smooth, relaxed, but still challenging. The tracks are notably longer here, more stretched out and teasing, and 'Tenderly' is probably the best thing in the catalogue so far.

Other early titles in the Zephyr catalogue feature Lemon's group with star soloists and are listed under their names, trumpeter Derek Watkins, reed maestro Alan Barnes and Vaché again; *A Beautiful Friendship* really belongs in that category as well, but we've made an entirely arbitrary exception – that's the kind of people we are.

***** Old Hands – Young Minds**

Zephyr ZECD 12 *Lemon; Alan Barnes, Gerard Presencer (t); Ian Dixon, Andy Panayi (reeds); Anthony Kerr (vib); Alec Dankworth, Dave Green (b); Clark Tracey (d).* 97.

Though most of the younger players on the roster are associated with a more contemporary approach to jazz, at least two of them – Tracey and Dankworth – have direct blood-ties to the older generation and grew up in the presence of this kind of music. Lemon and Barnes quite properly share the honours between them, but the excitement of the set comes when the two approaches rub up against each other, not aggressively, but with affectionate rivalry.

***** Lemon Looks Back – Just For Fun**

Zephyr ZE CD 14 *Lemon; Roy Williams (tb); Alan Barnes (as, cl); Ken Peplowski (ts, cl); Dave Cliff (g); Dave Green (b); Martin Drew (d).* 4/96.

A relaxed and utterly enjoyable programme of standards, distinguished by an elegant guest-slot from Peplowski, who has been going through a purple patch. Lemon lies back a bit more than usual and leaves much of the running to the horns. Again, though, the pacing of the set is immaculate, with 'When It's Sleepy Time Down South', 'When Your Lover Has Gone' and 'Cottontail' rounding out the album. Not a classic, but a gift for Lemonheads everywhere.

***** Brian Lemon And David Newton**

Zephyr ZECD 20 *Lemon; David Newton (p).* 98.

Once again, Lemon puts himself in the company of a younger player with a very definite stance on the tradition. Newton is an elegant melodist with a deceptively light left hand. However gentle and indefinite the chords might sound at first glance, there is no mistaking how surely Dave constructs a song. Hoagy Carmichael seems an ideal source for them both, and this songbook project will appeal to anyone who cherishes the originals or who simply likes piano jazz.

Harlan Leonard (1905–83)

CLARINET, ALTO AND BARITONE SAXOPHONES, BANDLEADER

Leonard was born in Kansas City and took a job with the Bennie Moten band in 1923. He stayed until 1931, joined the Kansas City Sky Rockets, and took that band over in 1934. A new group, Harlan Leonard's Rockets, became the major Kansas City orchestra from 1938 until the mid-'40s, but it broke up in 1945 and Leonard left the music business.

*****(*) Harlan Leonard And His Rockets 1940**

Classics 670 *Leonard; James Ross (t); Edward Johnson, William H Smith (t); Fred Beckett, Walter Monroe, Richmond Henderson (tb); Darwin Jones (as, v); Henry Bridges (cl, ts); Jimmy Keith (ts); William Smith (p); Efferge Ware, Stan Morgan (g); Winston Williams, Billy Hadnott (b); Jesse Price (d); Myra Taylor, Ernie Williams (v).* 1–11/40.

The forgotten men of Kansas City jazz. When Basie left for New York, Leonard's orchestra took over many of the Count's local engagements. But he didn't make many records; all 23 surviving tracks are here, in quite good transfers. It was a good band rather than a great one, lacking something in individuality: some of the tracks are built round the kind of devices which Basie was personalizing to a much greater degree, the section work is occasionally suspect, and the KC rocking rhythm is something they fall back on time and again. But something good is to be found in nearly all these tracks, and some fine soloists, too – Henry Bridges is an outstanding tenorman, Fred Beckett (whom J.J. Johnson admired) a surprisingly agile trombonist, and the trumpets hit the spot whenever they have to. Scholars will prize the six early arrangements by the young Tadd Dameron, an intriguing hint of things to come, and one shouldn't miss the blues-inflected vocals of Ernie Williams, a lighter Jimmy Rushing.

Marilyn Lerner

PIANO

Born in Montreal, Lerner has been a presence on the Candian jazz scene since the early '80s, although few recordings have broken out of local appreciation.

****** Birds Are Returning**

Jazz Focus JFCD 022 *Lerner; Jane Bunnett (ss, f); Yosvanny Terry (as, ts); Javier Falbo (bs); Kieran Overs (b); Dafnis Prieto (d); Carlos Francisco Hernandez Mora, Ogduardo Diaz Anaya, Atonio Martinez Campos, Inor Sotolongo (perc).* 1/97.

Lerner's music demands a far wider hearing than it has so far received. This brilliant collection derives from a project to visit and record with local players in Havana. Unlike most such collaborations, Lerner's material refuses to simply lie back and get inundated with Cuban rhythm and the sunny (and, the less sympathetic might argue, sappy) sweetness of the country's music. While there is much that could be identified as Cuban – hardly avoidable, given the phalanx of local players that appear alongside visiting confederates Kieran Overs and Jane Bunnett – Lerner makes sure that what she wants comes first. The opening 'Runaround' may work off Latin polyrhythms, but the off-kilter melody and simple but dark harmonies are pure Lerner. 'I Loves You, Porgy' is set to a very stately bolero rhythm, fleshed out by thick, swelling chords. None of the original themes seems to fall in quite the places one expects: 'Imogene', set to a pulse that seems to snake alongside the melody, and 'Condensation', with its curious twinning of soprano and baritone, are striking in and of themselves, and the superb playing of the soloists – especially Bunnett and local man Terry – heightens their impact. For Lerner's own best moment, go to the tranquil but haunting 'Say Now Always'.

Carl Leukaufe

VIBRAPHONE

A veteran local man on the Chicago scene, Leukafe finally got his name on the marquee with this solid midstream bop session.

***** Warrior**

Delmark DE 491 *Leukaufe; Kevin Quail (tb); Lin Halliday (ts); Jodie Christian, Joe Iaco (p); Dan Shapera (b); Robert Barry (d).* 8/95 & 7/96.

Not quite 50 years of endeavour to become an overnight success, but not far off it. The veteran Chicagoan has left it late in the day to record under his own name. *Warrior* doesn't sound like the work of a young man in a hurry. Alternating two bands, the one led by saxophone, the other (and better) by Kevin Quail's Fuller-like trombone and with the excellent Iaco on piano, Leukaufe strikes a balance between Milt Jackson's horn-lines and a harder-edged, more percussive sound that anticipates some of the avant-gardists. Halliday is, as ever, a hard-blowing soloist, but his features tend to be on the more mainstream, standards-based material ('The Man I Love', 'Come Rain Or Come Shine', 'Star Eyes'). Iaco is composer of the brisk, lateral 'Before You Know It', and drummer Barry offers up a discordant 'Blues For John Gilmore'. The two most positive tracks from the trombone group, though, are Monk's 'Pannonica' and Pettiford's 'Tricotism': finely focused performances.

Jed Levy

TENOR SAXOPHONE

Studied at New England Conservatory, then played with the Jaki Byard and Don Patterson groups. Now works in and around the New York City area.

*****(*) Sleight Of Hand**

Steeplechase SCCD 31383 *Levy; George Colligan (p); Ron McClure (b); Gerry Gibbs (d).* 11/95.

Very impressive and about as inventive a departure from the standard tenor-and-rhythm conventions as one can hope for. Levy's broad-shouldered tone and confident delivery give him the kind of full-on swing one associates with an earlier generation, but he's soaked in bebop and hard-bop practice. The super-fast title-track and the closer, a recasting of the 'Cherokee' chords, show off his chops without just showing off. 'Three And Me' is an ingenious use of 3/4 and it's the setting for a quite extraordinary solo by Colligan, who takes the McCoy Tyner method to its limit here. Colligan is as imposing as Levy himself, with his playing on 'Nice And Easy' (a clever choice of standard) as humorous as it is inventive. McClure is his usual tower of strength and Gibbs is marvellously fluent and powerful. This is a great band and they change setting and pace throughout with no loss of interest: there's a bit of a dead spot in the middle with the long and uneventful 'Desert Church', but otherwise it's a first-class session.

George Lewis (1900–1968)

CLARINET

One of the great primitives of early and classic jazz, Lewis had a raw and untutored tone and an impassioned, technically unembellished approach to soloing. Lewis was very much part of the postwar revival in traditional jazz and in later years became an indefatigable touring artist, bringing his vision of New Orleans jazz to Europe and Japan.

*****(*) And His New Orleans Stompers: Volume 1**

American Music AMCD 100 *Lewis; Avery 'Kid' Howard (t); Jim Robinson (tb); Lawrence Marrero (bj); Sidney Brown (bb); Chester Zardis (b); Edgar Moseley (d).* 5/43.

****** And His New Orleans Stompers: Volume 2**

American Music AMCD 101 *As above, except omit Brown.* 5/43.

****** George Lewis With Kid Shots**

American Music AMCD 2 *Lewis; Bunk Johnson, Louis 'Kid Shots' Madison (t); Jim Robinson (tb); Lawrence Marrero (bj); Alcide 'Slow Drag' Pavageau (b); Baby Dodds (d).* 7 & 8/44.

****** Trios And Bands**

American Music AMCD 4 *Lewis; Avery 'Kid' Howard, Louis 'Kid Shots' Madison (t); Jim Robinson (tb); Lawrence Marrero (bj); Ricard Alexis, Alcide 'Slow Drag' Pavageau, Chester Zardis (b); Baby Dodds, Edgar Moseley (d).* 5/45.

***** At Herbert Otto's Party**

American Music AMCD 74 *Lewis; Herb Morand (t); Jim Robinson (tb); Albert Burbank (cl); Lawrence Marrero (bj); Alcide 'Slow Drag' Pavageau (b); Albert Jiles, Bob Matthews, Joe Watkins (d).* 11/49.

Rarely has a traditional jazz musician been documented on record in so concentrated a way as clarinettist George Lewis was in the early 1950s. American Music's patient documentation, which now extends beyond the capacity of this listing, even gives street numbers and times of day for the earliest material here. Having been coaxed out of a 'retirement' working as a dockhand at the start of the war, Lewis was by the mid-'50s the surviving pillar of 'serious' revivalism, which he'd helped kick off with Bunk Johnson, working what looked like a politician's itinerary across the United States; Johnson is featured on three tracks of the early *With Kid Shots* compilation.

The early material is absolutely pristine and comes across on CD with remarkable freshness. The first tracks on Volume One of the 1943 material were recorded in the drummer's house and, though they're more raggedy than the later sessions at the Gypsy Tea Room (high point: two takes each of 'Climax Rag' and 'Careless Love'), they provide an excellent starting-point for serious examination of this remarkable musician. Lewis's solo breaks are oddly pitched (and there are a couple where this might be down to tape yaw) but the pitching remains consistent relative to other players so it has to be considered an idiosyncrasy rather than poor articulation. The *Trios & Bands* compilation includes some second takes from the group sessions with 'Shots' (including a marvellous second try on 'San Jacinto Blues' and the first, presumably rejected, take of 'High Society'). He was apparently unhappy about the quality of some of the performances and asked to make some more discs with just banjo and bass. These contain some of his best-ever improvisations, all delivered in that plaintive, singing style that is among the most imitated of jazz sounds. The bounce and economy of 'Ice Cream' and the brief, gentle optimism of 'Life Will Be Sweeter' contain in four minutes the essence of Lewis's music: clear melodic statement, rhythmic simplicity and straightforward emotion.

***** Jazz Band Ball**

Good Time Jazz GTCD 12005 *Lewis; Elmer Talbert (t); Jim Robinson (tb); Alton Purnell (p); Lawrence Marrero (bj); Alcide 'Slow Drag' Pavageau (b); Joe Watkins (d).* 6/50.

Not strictly a Lewis record, and not, as sometimes hinted, documentation of a single evening. Nevertheless, this affords a valuable opportunity to hear Lewis in company with bands led by trombonists Turk Murphy and Kid Ory, and cornetist Pete Daily, thus providing a clear diagnostic section of what was going on in revivalist jazz between the end of the war and 1950, when the Lewis tracks were recorded. Talbert is a surprise, a little-recorded player with a fine individual tone and some interesting ideas to contribute on 'Willie The Weeper', where he keeps his main influence firmly in view.

*****(*) George Lewis With Red Allen**

American Music AMCD 71 *Lewis; Alvin Alcorn (t); Henry 'Red' Allen (t, v); Bill Matthews, Jim Robinson (tb); Lester Santiago (p); Lawrence Marrero (bj); Alcide 'Slow Drag' Pavageau (b); Paul Barbarin (d).* 8/51.

It's very rare that anyone catches American Music out in an error, but the Alcide Marrero playing bass on these tracks has to be old 'Slow Drag' Pavageau who is listed for one session and garbled for the other. Nor would we accuse the label of short measure, but Allen fans should be aware that he appears on only five tracks, albeit five excellent ones. 'Hindustan' and the two versions of 'St James Infirmary' are up with the trumpeter's best recorded work and, if Lewis sounds a little shadowed, he makes up for it later (presumably) that same day with Alcorn. These are studio recordings, a little boxy but not unpleasantly so, and the quality of the music – other highlights include 'Bourbon Street Parade' and 'Who's Sorry Now', taped a fortnight later – more than makes up for any technical deficit.

*****(*) Jazz In The Classic New Orleans Tradition**

Original Jazz Classics OJC 1736 *Lewis; Alvin Alcorn (t); Bill Matthews (tb); Alton Purnell, Lester Santiago (p); Lawrence Marrero (bj); Alcide 'Slow Drag' Pavageau (b); Paul Barbarin (d).* 8/51–9/53.

This introduces bandleader and drummer Paul Barbarin, a nearly exact New Orleans contemporary of Lewis, and one of the great originals in the music. The band is familiar enough by now, and the ability to extract the maximum expression from the most minimal of settings has rarely been better documented than here, coupled to an above-average standard of recording. Heard side by side, Lewis and Barbarin underline many of the contradictions that underlay the revivalist movement. To a degree it was exploitative and naïve, as the blues boom of the 1960s was to be, but it was also a living source, and few were as angrily in thrall to its political dimensions as Barbarin. Utterly obsessed, where Lewis was innocently untroubled (and thus manipulable), about the status of black musicians, Barbarin dropped dead on his first appearance at the hitherto segregated Proteus parade; Lewis beat him to the farm by a mere two months.

*****(*) The George Lewis Ragtime Band Of New Orleans: The Oxford Series – Volume 1**

American Music AMCD 21 *Lewis; Percy G Humphrey (t); Jim Robinson (tb); Alton Purnell (p); Lawrence Marrero (bj); Alcide 'Slow Drag' Pavageau (b); Joe Watkins (d).* 52.

*****(*) The George Lewis Ragtime Band Of New Orleans: The Oxford Series – Volume 2 (Concert, First Half)**

American Music AMCD 22 *As above.* 52.

*****(*) The George Lewis Ragtime Band Of New Orleans: The Oxford Series – Volume 3 (Concert, Second Half)**

American Music AMCD 23 *As above.* 52.

***** The George Lewis Ragtime Band Of New Orleans: The Oxford Series – Volume 4 (Recording Session)**

American Music AMCD 24 *As above.* 3/53.

****(*) The George Lewis Ragtime Band Of New Orleans: The Oxford Series – Volume 5 (Concert, First Half)**

American Music AMCD 25 *As above.* 3/53.

***** The George Lewis Ragtime Band Of New Orleans: The Oxford Series – Volume 6 (Concert, Second Half)**

American Music AMCD 26 *As above.* 3/53.

***** The George Lewis Ragtime Band Of New Orleans: The Oxford Series – Volume 7 (Concert, First Half)**

American Music AMCD 27 *As above.* 3/53.

***** The George Lewis Ragtime Jazz Band Of New Orleans: The Oxford Series – Volume 8 (Concert, Second Half)**

American Music AMCD 28 *As above.* 3/53.

****(*) The George Lewis Ragtime Jazz Band Of New Orleans: The Oxford Series – Volume 9 (Church Service, Rehearsal And Party)**

American Music AMCD 29 *As above.* 3/53.

****(*) The George Lewis Ragtime Jazz Band Of New Orleans: The Oxford Series – Volume 10 (Party)**

American Music AMCD 30 *As above.* 3/53.

***** The George Lewis Ragtime Jazz Band Of New Orleans: The Oxford Series – Volume 11 (Concert – First Half)**

American Music AMCD 31 *As above.* 3/53.

****(*) The George Lewis Ragtime Jazz Band Of New Orleans: The Oxford Series – Volume 12 (Concert – Second Half)**

American Music AMCD 32 *As above.* 3/53.

In 1952, Lewis was recorded by the American Folklore Group of the English department at Miami University, an institution rather confusingly situated in Oxford, Ohio. The 'Oxford Series' CDs are well mastered and sound amazingly fresh for recordings nearly five decades old. Lewis made a studio recording of seven quite extended pieces, including a long 'Tin Roof Blues' (on which Humphrey makes his presence felt) and a rousing 'Saint' to finish. The subsequent concert discs are better still, with excellent performances of Lewis staples like 'Over The Waves', 'Darktown Strutters' Ball' and 'Careless Love', closing with a vintage 'Sheikh Of Araby'. It seems unlikely that anyone other than stoneground experts will want to have the later rehearsal and party volumes, though these contain some of the most unfettered playing in the set. The concert of 21 March on Volumes Seven and Eight is superior to that of the day before only because the band now sounds played in and relaxed. Lewis is soloing well and Howard plays with great dexterity on 'Glad When You're Dead, You Rascal You'. The sound may also be a shade brighter in places, though that is probably a function of Lewis lifting his enunciation to compensate for a generally more buoyant en-semble. Purely as an experiment, it's fascinating to listen to this material continuously from start to finish. There are literally dozens of tiny changes of inflexion and emphasis (countless fluffs and missed cues, too, which might be overlooked on a more casual listen), but also a growing sense that the presumed spontaneity and freshness of this music are actually much less than its advocates might like to think. Lewis is prone to fall back on a set of stock phrases (though Howard is not) and there are very few real surprises. A double-CD of the very best performances would be welcome, particularly now that the series has been extended further, though discs one to three will already suffice for most tastes.

***** The George Lewis Ragtime Jazz Band Of New Orleans: The Oxford Series – Volume 13 (Concert – First Part)**
American Music AMCD 33 *Lewis; Avery 'Kid' Howard, Johnny Lucas (t); Jim Robinson (tb); Alton Purnell (p); Alcide 'Slow Drag' Pavageau (b); Joe Watkins (d).* 2/55.

*****(*) The George Lewis Ragtime Jazz Band Of New Orleans: The Oxford Series – Volume 14 (Concert – Second Part)**
American Music AMCD 34 *As above, except add Jan Carroll (bj).* 2/55.

These were the last of Lewis's Ohio stopovers, which had acquired an almost hysterical following. There is certainly no sign of tiredness, either in the formula or in the playing, but larger projects beckoned and, over succeeding years, Lewis was to become an international superstar, albeit a modest and occasionally bewildered one. The later volume is the better of the pair, albeit dominated by Watkins vocals. 'Loveless Love' is a singing feature for Johnny Lucas, whose lip doesn't seem to have been in the best of order. 'Closer Walk With Thee' and 'Walking With The King' are both magnificent, feeling performances, sacred and profane in near-perfect balance. As always, Barry Martyn gets the sound as good as this sort of thing can get. There are clinkers, mic noises, and assorted shuffles and bumps, but nothing that doesn't positively add to the atmospherics.

****** The Beverley Caverns Sessions**
Good Time Jazz GTCD 12058 *Lewis; Avery 'Kid' Howard (t, v); Jim Robinson (tb); Alton Purnell (p); Lawrence Marrero (bj); Alcide 'Slow Drag' Pavageau (b).* 5/53.

*****(*) Jazz At Vespers**
Original Jazz Classics OJC 1721 *As above.* 2/54.

*****(*) Jass At Ohio Union**
Storyville STCD 6020/1 2CD *As above.* 3/54.

***** Sounds Of New Orleans: Volume 7**
Storyville SLP 6014 *Lewis; Avery 'Kid' Howard (t); Jim Robinson (tb); Alton Purnell (p); Lawrence Marrero (bj); Alcide 'Slow Drag' Pavageau (b); Joe Watkins (d); Lizzie Miles (v).* 12/53 & 1/54.

***** George Lewis Of New Orleans**
Original Jazz Classics OJC 1739 *Lewis; Avery 'Kid' Howard, Peter Bocage (t); Jim Robinson, Harrison Barnes, Joe Howard (tb); Alcide 'Slow Drag' Pavageau (b); Baby Dodds (d); Sister Berenice Phillips (v).*

***** George Lewis In Stockholm, 1959**
Dragon DRCD 221 *Lewis; Avery 'Kid' Howard (t); Jim Robinson (tb); Joe Robichaux (p); Alcide 'Slow Drag' Pavageau (b); Joe Watkins (d, v).* 2/59.

By contrast with the folksy, homely quality of most of his tours, including later ones to the United Kingdom, Lewis's appearances in Scandinavia and in Japan had all the appearance of an imperial progress. What this essentially quiet and modest man could have made of the adulation he received is anyone's guess. It certainly didn't always have a positive effect on his playing. Lewis seemed to strain for volume in larger halls, presumably largely unused to sophisticated amplification, and there are occasions on the otherwise excellent Stockholm disc, too, where he squeaks and overblows.

Lewis's almost studied primitivism and simplicity of tone beguiled even self-consciously sophisticated audiences, who often made the mistake of thinking that Lewis himself was a primitive. So many of these live discs, rough as they are, underline the extraordinary variety and depth of his playing, that disconcerting ability to invest almost subliminal changes of emphasis or diction with a disproportionate significance. The Beverley Caverns record, made in Hollywood, is a good case in point. A now familiar band, hardly a surprise in the set-list, and yet something to listen to and ponder in virtually every chorus. This is easily the most desirable of all the later sessions, and it should be a high priority for anyone who wants to get to grips with Lewis and his music.

***** George Lewis And His New Orleans Stompers**
Blue Note 7243 8 21261 2 *Lewis; Avery 'Kid' Howard (t, v); Jim Robinson (tb); Alton Purnell (p); George Guesnon (bj); Alcide 'Slow Drag' Pavageau (b); Joe Watkins (d, v).* 4/55.

Richly textured and thoroughly authentic traditional jazz from a group who could and often did play this material in their sleep. Lewis himself is most impressive on 'Gettysburg March', 'See See Rider' and 'High Society', where the pace and pitching suit his still raw technique. A bywater in Lewis's recorded output, attractive enough in its way, but not a classic.

***** The Spirit Of New Orleans: Volume 1**
Music Mecca CD 1014 *Lewis; Avery 'Kid' Howard (t, v); Jim Robinson (tb); Charlie Hamilton (p); Emanuel Sayles (bj); Alcide 'Slow Drag' Pavageau (b); Joe Watkins (d, v).* 61.

****** Endless The Trek, Endless The Search**
American Music AMCD 59 *Lewis; Kid Thomas (t); Jim Robinson (tb); George Guesnon (bj); John Joseph (b); Cie Frazier (d).* 8 & 9/62.

*****(*) George Lewis In Japan: Volume 1**
GHB BCD 14 *Lewis; Punch Miller (t); Louis Nelson (tb); Joe Robichaux (p); Emanuel Sayles (bj); John Joseph (b); Joe Watkins (d).* 63.

***** George Lewis In Japan: Volume 2**
GHB BCD 15 *As above.* 63.

***** George Lewis And The Barry Martyn Band**

GHB BCD 37 *Lewis; Cuff Bilett (t); Pete Dyer (tb); Graham Paterson (p); John Coles (bj); Terry Knight (b); Barry Martyn (d).* 3/65.

***** Classic New Orleans Jazz: Volume 1**

Biograph BCD 127 *Lewis; George Blod (t); Jay Brackett (tb); J.R Smith (tba); Ronnie Bill (bj); Alex Bigard (d).* 4/65.

***** George Lewis With Ken Colyer's Jazzmen**

Lake LACD 27 *Lewis; Ken Colyer (t, v); Geoff Cole (tb); Tony Pyke (cl); Johnny Bastable (bj); Bill Cole (b); Ryan Hetherington (d).* 9/66.

In later life, Lewis was a celebrity, a living link back to the pre-history of the music. As such he toured Japan and Europe, turning up in such unlikely places as the White Horse Inn, Willesden, and the Dancing Slipper, Nottingham, both occasions documented on the GHB set, above.

Endless The Trek, Endless The Search rounds out a session recorded by Ken Mills for Icon. The two new tracks, 'Tiger Rag' and 'Icon Blues', are quite properly given pride of place at the front of the CD, rather than tacked on at the end, and it's difficult to see why they were rejected first time out. This date saw Lewis working with banjoist Guesnon's 'authentic' New Orleans band, an outfit which only deserves the protective quotation marks because by this stage it was almost impossible to gauge what the word means. The presence of Kid Thomas is a virtual guarantee of unvarnished realism, and Lewis himself plays with a raw and unpolished vigour. The legendary Josiah 'Cie' Frazier occupies the drum chair with his usual poise and confidence, and the sound is very good indeed.

In the autumn of 1963 the Lewis band played more than a hundred concerts during an extended tour of Japan, arriving to a rapturous welcome in August, and leaving on the same flight as the Japanese prime minister, who was travelling to the USA for the funeral of John F. Kennedy. Most of the concerts seem to have been in Osaka, a fanatical jazz centre. No exact date is given, but the big hall was obviously packed. Lewis sounds in excellent form, and only Punch Miller sounds jaded and slow-fingered, though his vocal on 'Sister Kate' (Volume 1) is characteristically vital. More material from the tour is in circulation and should be sampled as and when it becomes available. Lewis, who was in his early sixties by this stage, made little or no attempt to leave hotel rooms, preferring to nap and prepare for these long, carefully staged events. In contrast to the Oxford, Ohio, sessions, these are pure showbiz, but they are no less attractive for that.

His appearance with Ken Colyer's Jazzmen in Manchester over 30 years ago must have seemed a little like the Road to Emmaus for these very purist believers and their fans. It is perhaps ironic that clubs and concert halls in the British midlands and north should have become the last bastions of strict constructionism while players back in New Orleans were beginning to tinker with rock'n'roll. With that in mind, it's easy to see why Lewis became the icon and his work the sacred texts of the revivalist movement, susceptible as both are to myth-making and picayune analysis. Are occasional bent notes the result of carelessness or a gesture of experiment from a seemingly conservative man whose putative conservatism was what made him famous? Were rephrased licks the result of new ideas or, as appears to be the case on 'Walk Through The Streets Of The City' at Beverley Caverns, a combination of faulty memory and fast reflexes? The *Times-Picayune* in his native city became inclined to harshness about Lewis's technical shortcomings in succeeding years, and there is no doubt that constant performance of a severely limited repertoire seriously overstretched his abilities. The life, in a curious way, was always more interesting than the music. Lewis's residency at the Hangover Club in San Francisco was the high-water mark of revivalism, and the many recordings from this period have a joyous optimism which it is hard not to like; even so, it's equally hard to get over-excited about them. Lewis's fame largely depends on his willingness to be cast in a particular role.

***** Reunion With Don Ewell**

Delmark DE 220 *Lewis; Jim Robinson (tb); Don Ewell (p); Cie Frazier (d).* 6/66.

***** A Portrait Of George Lewis**

Lake LACD 50 *As above, except add Lars Edegran (p), Chester Zardis (b), Alex Bigard (d).* 3 & 5/66.

Both discs contain material from a June 1966 high-school gig in Salisbury, North Carolina. There's no overlap, so plenty of motivation to buy the Lake disc as well, which includes eight tracks recorded with Robinson at Preservation Hall in March of the same year. These are pretty standard fare for this vintage and may well be known from earlier Center and Biograph releases; these same labels also covered the Salisbury gig. The unacknowledged star of this late session is drummer Frazier, who died in 1985 and took with him at least some of the secrets of New Orleans drumming. At this age, he wasn't capable of the same flexibility as in his under-documented youth, and he has cut back on some of the elements of sheer noise (untuned woodblocks, and so on) which were a part of his sound. Ewell is interesting in that he incorporated large elements of Harlem stride into the Morton-influenced New Orleans style that was his basic staple. The hybrid approach is most evident on tracks like 'Yes, Yes, In Your Eyes', one of four numbers here for which alternatives have been included on this CD reissue. Recorded in a high-school gym in North Carolina, it's further testimony to the sheer mileage Lewis put in over the decade, not just abroad, but within the United States as well. Something of a curiosity, this one, but meat and drink to more specialist collectors.

George Lewis (born 1952)

TROMBONES, SOUSAPHONE, TUBA, COMPUTER

The Chicagoan – strictly George E. Lewis, to distinguish him from the great clarinettist – taught himself improvisation while still in his early teens by transcribing Lester Young solos for trombone. He later did formal study at Yale, but his real musical education was with the Association for the Advancement of Creative Musicians, whose ethos and aesthetics have remained with him. Lewis is technologically astute, but also profoundly subversive, making music on computer, but also dismantling his horn to get at its spectral sound-colours.

****** Shadowgraph, 5 (Sextet)**

Black Saint 120016 *Lewis; Roscoe Mitchell (as, ss, bs, cassette recorder); Douglas Ewart (cl, bcl, sno, f, bsn, cassette recorder, perc); Muhal Richard Abrams, Anthony Davis (p); Leroy Jenkins (vn, vla); Abdul Wadud (clo).* 77.

***** Jila – Save! Mon – The Imaginary Suite**

Black Saint 120026 *Lewis; Douglas Ewart (as, f, perc).* 78.

♛ ** Homage To Charles Parker**

Black Saint 120029 *As above, except add Anthony Davis (p), Richard Teitelbaum (syn).* 79.

It is significant that, as a trombonist growing up in a period marked by the dominance of the saxophone, George Lewis should have taken saxophone players as his primary models. His rather emotional *legato* is reminiscent of both Lester Young and, depending on context, virtually all the evolutionary stages of John Coltrane's style. Context is of considerable importance, because Lewis has played in a bewildering variety of musical settings, from relatively conventional section-playing (a brief stint with the mid-1970s Basie band) to technically adventurous free playing. Lewis habitually plays either with intense and surprisingly gentle lyricism or with a deconstructive fury that has led him to dismantle his trombone in mid-performance, producing non-tempered and abstract tones on mouthpiece and slide. He has also taken a close interest in electronics, using computers with increasing technical assurance to provide backgrounds and to create a much-needed dialectical tension in improvised performances.

Lewis's discography as leader is scandalously thin, but the quality is very high indeed. *Shadowgraph* and the duos with Ewart are characteristic of the free abstract jazz that emerged out of AACM's explorations in the 1960s and early '70s. Listening to them, one is aware how little of this music has been assimilated into the mainstream of either jazz or improvisation. 'Monads' is almost a philosophical primer for free players, an oblique and sometimes violent outburst of sound in which ideas fly around almost too fast to be absorbed. One wonders how it would ever have been possible to assimilate this music in live performance. 'Triple Slow Mix' is a more spacious and accommodating piece, with Abrams and Davis (in opposite channels) suggesting different points of focus for Lewis's gloriously flatulent sousaphone. 'Cycle' recalls the duos, but the real meat of the record is the title-track, part of a series of compositions written by Lewis under a grant from the National Endowment for the Arts. Though the sonic landscape is much more exotic, 'Shadowgraph' is identifiably in the line of one of Ellington's noise pieces. The main soloists are Mitchell and Abrams, with Lewis himself eschewing his synths in favour of an exotic selection of brasses, including Wagner tuba. The tension is almost palpable as potential grooves rise up and are systematically extinguished in a mass of sound that includes cassette players and (from Ewart) incidental percussion of the home-made variety favoured at the time. It's a wonderful record to have back in the lists, but it scarcely reaches the heights of what was to follow.

Ewart is Jamaican-born and 'Save! Mon' is his dedication to the poeple of his homeland. It features him on alto, which is more immediately appealing but less idiomatic and challenging than his work on flute and 'Ewart flutes'. 'Jila' is a more straightforward and expressive piece, indeed unexpectedly so, written as a posy for his daughter. Lewis is much more obviously in command on the two parts of *The Imaginary Suite* included on the record. These are inspired by figures or icons of ancient mythology and some of their modern counterparts; Anthony Braxton may or may not be pleased to learn that 'Charon' is dedicated to him. The addition of electronics greatly expands the available sound-palette and the playing is more expansive and sustained, rather than the staccato, pointillistic approach of the other two pieces. It is in this sense much closer to the blues-tinged world of Lewis's best work, *Homage To Charles Parker*.

The latter represents a further triumphant extension and synthesis of the same basic language premises, combining improvisation with predetermined structures – rather in the manner of Lawrence 'Butch' Morris or pianist-composer Anthony Davis, who plays on the date – and reintroducing a strong programmatic element to abstract music. As he shows in the fine duets with Ewart, using predetermined structures in indeterminate juxtapositions and dynamics can create a music of considerable resonance. 'Homage To Charles Parker' and 'Blues', the two long sides that made up the original LP, are among the most profound and beautiful performances of recent times and certainly rank in the top dozen or so jazz/improvised records made since 1960. Lewis's rather stilted liner-notes somewhat undersell the emotional impact of both pieces. 'Blues' consists of four independent diatonic 'choruses' of absolute simplicity which are played in shifting configurations by the four musicians. Despite the fact that there are no conventional resolutions and no predictable coincidence of material, the piece evokes order as much as freedom. Although none of the material conforms to the blues, its 'feel' is absolutely unmistakable and authentic. If 'Blues' is a triumphant extension of the black tradition in music, 'Homage To Charles Parker' concerns itself intimately with the saxophonist's putative afterlife and musical real-presence. There is a long opening section on electronics, synthesizers and cymbals which evoke Parker's 'reality'. Reminiscent of evocations of primeval Chaos by Marilyn Crispell on *Gaia* (Leo Records) and the electronic composer Bernard Parmegiani, it gradually yields place to a series of apparently discontinuous solos on saxophone, piano and finally with no ensemble backing beyond the synthesizer sounds, which recast and project Parker's life and language. There are no explicit bebop references and, indeed, the piece seems to serve as a healing response to the fractures that separated bop from the earlier history of black American music, of which it was also the apotheosis. The music is calm and almost stately, occasionally suggesting a chorale. Lewis's concluding statements are unbearably plangent but also forceful and intelligent. In their refusal of tragedy, they also have to be seen as political statements. This is an essential modern record.

*****(*) Voyager**

Avant AVAN 014 *Lewis; Roscoe Mitchell (ss, as).* 2/93.

Fine musician though Douglas Ewart is, he seems a beginner compared to the mighty Roscoe Mitchell, who comprehensively outclasses even the nominal leader here. There is a sense in which this is intended as a musical autobiography of the trombonist. Enthusiasts will hear lots of references to earlier work, including the Ewart duos, and will wonder, on occasion, why it wasn't tackled as an entirely solo project, with or without electronic enhancements. The eight parts of 'Voyager' and the single-part 'Homecoming' are by far the most accessible things Lewis has attempted in years, and it is Mitchell who introduces a level of complexity that on occasion really does prompt one to stop and rethink what is going on. Not necessarily a good sign with music of this type.

*** Changing With The Times

New World NW 80434 *Lewis; Douglas Ewart (as, cl, bcl, shakuhachi, didjeridu, perc); Jeannie Cheatham (p, org, v); Daniel Koppelman, Ruth Neville (p); Mary Oliver (vn, vla); Peter Gonzales III (perc); Bernard Mixon, Ned Rothenberg, Quincy Troupe (v).* 3/93.

Recorded just a month later, this music-and-poetry session with its unlikely-looking participants (Jeannie Cheatham?) is a most untypical Lewis record, unless of course it signals a move – 'changing with the times' – in this rather mild-mannered direction. Lewis has always been concerned with the dramatic dimension of what he is doing, and the trombone is a highly dramatic instrument; but there is a flimsiness here and a lack of focus which will disconcert those who have been turned on by the above.

***(*) The Usual Turmoil And Other Duets

Music & Arts CD 1023 *Lewis; Miya Masaoka (koto).* 2/97.

It starts with a fart and a twang as one feared it might, given this instrumentation, but thereafter it is sublime. Masaoka is an extremely intelligent musician and a recording artist in her own right. Her role here is not so much to provide harmonic support and a rhythmic peg as to create distinct lines of development which contrast with and complement Lewis's characteristic shards and fragments. The first ten pieces are recorded in studio and are inspired by lines in the autobiography and letters of black leader George Jackson. They're mostly short and highly concentrated, pitched in a variety of registers, from frenetic and scratchy to near-lyrical. The two longer tracks at the end, recorded live at Koncepts in Oakland, don't have the same bite and lapse into flabby self-parody. Oddly, these shapeless final tracks serve to point up the real effectiveness of the earlier tracks, but they're really interesting only as repositories of sound.

*** Conversations

Incus CD 32 *Lewis; Bertram Turetzky (b).* 11/97.

Bert Turetzky is less well known than one of his pupils, Mark Dresser, but much of his personality and artistic presence can be deduced from Dresser's intentness, humour and openness to experiment. *Conversations* is always a discouraging title for an improvised record, suggesting off-the-cuff musings and private dialogues. Nothing of the sort here. Lewis hasn't played such fine trombone – and indeed so much trombone – on record for a while. He deliberately remains in the upper register of his instrument for much of the time, leaving Turetzky to explore the depths. Though the tonality varies little, the pieces are quite different one from the other. 'After Dark' is the only item that wanders off course and, significantly, it's the longest item on a set composed largely of short forms and dedications – to Lester Bowie, more apologetically to Paul Desmond for 'Take One', and to 'The Ecumenical Blues'. A demanding listen, as these things often are, but the sheer musicianship of both participants and the openness of the musical language make it a delightful experience as well.

John Lewis (born 1920)

PIANO

Born in Illinois, Lewis joined the Dizzy Gillespie band in 1946 and became an important figure in the bebop scene. He worked with numerous leaders until a stint with Milt Jackson in 1951 led to the formation of the MJQ, which he has been associated with as the pianist and prime composer ever since. Away from the MJQ, he has composed several film soundtracks, played Bach, and composed and scored pieces which are a unique blend of classical and jazz sympathies.

♛ **** The Modern Jazz Society Presents A Concert Of Contemporary Music

Verve 559827-2 *Lewis; J. J Johnson (tb); Stan Getz, Lucky Thompson (ts); Tony Scott, Aaron Sachs (cl); Gunther Schuller (frhn); Manuel Zegler (bsn); Janet Putnam (hp); Percy Heath (b); Connie Kay (d).* 3/55.

One of the great forgotten masterpieces of the 1950s, this brilliant date is still available only as a limited-edition reissue in Verve's Connoisseur Edition. Collectors are advised to snap up any copies they see, although it's disgraceful that this classic should not be more easily available. The Modern Jazz Society was an initiative by Lewis and Schuller to present new works and new arrangements, broadly in the 'Third Stream' vein which Schuller encouraged. Lewis was only the supervisor of the original LP, but new discoveries – a rehearsal of a previously unheard J. J. Johnson piece, 'Turnpike' and a run-through of 'Queen's Fancy' – find him at the piano.

The five principal pieces are all Lewis compositions, and they are among the finest treatments of 'Little David's Fugue', 'Django' and 'Queen's Fancy' ever set down. 'Django', with its final coda taken at the stately pace of a cortège, is so bewitching that it can silence a room. 'Midsömmer', which has not been performed or recorded in the intervening 45 years, is a gorgeously evocative piece. The arrangements and ensembles are intoxicatingly beautiful, but there are also the most handsome solos from Getz, Johnson and Thompson – the latter, especially, reminding us how poorly he was served by most of his recording opportunities.

***(*) The Wonderful World Of Jazz

Atlantic 90979-2 *Lewis; Herb Pomeroy (t); Gunther Schuller (frhn); Eric Dolphy (as, f); Benny Golson, Paul Gonsalves (ts); Jimmy Giuffre (bs); Jim Hall (g); George Duvivier (b); Connie Kay (d).* 7–9/60.

Lewis has been making occasional discs under his own name since the mid-1950s. Scandalously few of them are currently in print. Although the above two have made at least some appearance on CD, we would respectfully suggest that *The John Lewis Piano* (Atlantic), *Animal Dance* (Atlantic) and *European Windows* (RCA) are brought to CD at an early opportunity.

The Wonderful World Of Jazz is another great one. It opens with a superb Gonsalves solo on a 15-minute 'Body And Soul' and then works through a short programme of jazz standards, including a new '2 Degrees East, 3 Degrees West'. Newly available on the CD are 'The Stranger', precious for Eric Dolphy's solo, and a long quartet version of 'If You Could See Me Now'; but the whole disc is a thoughtful reflection on the jazz tradition as it was standing in 1960.

***(*) Afternoon In Paris

Dreyfus 849234-2 *Lewis (p solo). 11/79.*

*** Kansas City Breaks

DRG Disques Swing 8430 *Lewis; Frank Wess (f); Howard Collins (g); Joe Kennedy Jr (vn); Marc Johnson (b); Shelly Manne (d). 5/82.*

**** Private Concert

Emarcy 848267-2 *Lewis (p solo). 9/90.*

Regrettably few of Lewis's later own-name projects are currently in print, too. The 1982 session features an unlikely combination of players, though the music has some beautiful touches: Lewis has pursued an amalgam of jazz and chamber music on many levels, and this instrumentation is one more example, even if Kennedy's almost bluegrass violin and Wess's pretty flute make strange bedfellows. Manne is as swinging as usual, and there is a fine 'Milano', a smooth 'Django'. The sound is rather clattery.

Lewis's solo albums are never alike. The 1979 session is a very short, almost clipped recital, his favourite themes skimmed through, a series of lightning sketches rather than the full oils of the Emarcy date. Yet there are fascinating revisions, the almost perky 'Django' for one, and a reverent take of Ellington's 'Come Sunday'. Eleven years later, with the Lewis Steinway shipped into New York's Church of the Ascension for the occasion, the pianist created one of the most refined and memorable piano records of recent times. The programme is much the same as always, with some particular favourites from his own book, yet each interpretation sounds different: his latest thoughts on 'Round Midnight' shed new light on that faded masterpiece, while 'Milano', 'Afternoon In Paris' and 'Midnight In Paris' bring European elegance and charm into a direct fusion with the blues that Lewis has always loved. Superlative sound.

**** Evolution

Atlantic 7567-83211-2 *Lewis (p solo). 1/99.*

Lewis is by now one of the most senior survivors of the bebop era, and this marvellous solo album underscores what an extraordinary figure he has been in jazz for the past 50 years. As a composer, he is mysteriously neglected when it comes to source material for other players, but perhaps only Lewis's Lewis really hits the mark. He revisits five of his own favourites, and each is an affectionate new look at an old friend: 'Django', for instance, is elegantly recast around a left-hand bass that sounds almost like a tango. 'Sweet Georgia Brown' and 'Cherokee' are sketches that suggest a summing-up of both swing and bebop. 'Afternoon In Paris' muses on his lifelong affinity with the old world. Moving yet wonderfully fresh and unaffected, this is a consummate recital by the master.

Meade Lux Lewis (1905–64)

PIANO, CELESTE, HARPSICHORD

A Chicagoan who made his name in the city, Lewis created a signature-piece in 'Honky Tonk Train Blues' and his teaming with Albert Ammons and Pete Johnson at the 1938 Spirituals To Swing concert at Carnegie Hall started a craze for boogie woogie. Although he worked on until his death, most of his few later recordings suggest a jaded spirit.

**** Meade Lux Lewis 1927–1939

Classics 722 *Lewis; Albert Ammons, Pete Johnson (p). 12/27–1/39.*

***(*) Meade Lux Lewis 1939–1941

Classics 743 *Lewis; J.C Higginbotham (tb); Albert Ammons (p); Teddy Bunn (g); Johnny Williams (b); Big Sid Catlett (d). 1/39–9/41.*

*** Meade Lux Lewis 1941–1944

Classics 841 *Lewis (p, cel, hpd solo). 4/41–8/44.*

**** Boogies And Blues

Topaz TPZ 1069 *Lewis; Frankie Newton (t); J.C Higginbotham (tb); Sidney Bechet (ss, cl); Edmond Hall (cl); Teddy Bunn, Charlie Christian (g); Johnny Williams (b); Israel Crosby (b); Big Sid Catlett (d). 1/36–2/41.*

**(*) The Blues Piano Artistry Of Meade Lux Lewis

Original Jazz Classics OJC 1759 *Lewis (p solo). 11/61.*

Lewis encapsulated his contribution to jazz in his first three minutes as a soloist with his 1927 Paramount record of 'Honky Tonk Train Blues'. He recorded it again at his second session, and again at his fourth. All three are on the first Classics CD, along with 15 other variations on the blues and boogie woogie. His signature-piece remains a marvellous evocation of a locomotive rhythm, perfectly balanced through all its variations, and, if he became tired of it, his listeners never did. It's a pity, though, that it's about the only piece he's much remembered for, since there is plenty more excellent music among his various sessions and the first Classics CD brings together much of it. His 1936 session for Decca includes two extraordinary pieces on celeste, 'I'm In The Mood For Love' and 'Celeste Blues', and his 1939 session for Blue Note – which supplied the first Blue Note issue, 'Melancholy' and 'Solitude' – opens with a five-part investigation of 'The Blues', all rejected at the time but a remarkable sequence, at least as personal and imaginative as his train pieces. The sound on the CD is frequently muffled, sloppily remastered or otherwise imperfect, but the music is marvellous. There's a modest decline on Classics 743: the 1940 version of 'Honky Tonk Train Blues' goes off at a faintly ludicrous tempo, and some of Lewis's boogie pieces end up as all the same. But three duets with Ammons and the rest of the Blue Note session tracks offer rewards, while the 1939 Solo Art session is mostly at a slow tempo and spotlights Lewis the bluesman to stunning effect. Sound here is far less than ideal once again, though the Blue Note tracks (from an unidentified source) are better, if brittle.

That disc ends on two rather nutty harpsichord solos, and the next one starts with the other two from the same session. A single V-Disc finds Lewis playing piano and celeste simultaneously on 'Doll House Boogie' before nine tracks cut at a date for the Asch label. Again, the fast pieces suggest a sinking into boogie clichés, but there are still some startling things, notably 'Denapas Parade' and above all the previously rejected 'Special No. One', with its melody carried in the left hand. There is yet another 'Honky Tonk Train', and this one is taken at a farcical pace. He must have been fed up with it.

Collectors are now offered a further choice with the Topaz compilation, which cherrypicks (mostly) from the Blue Note sessions, although there's a stray track by the Port of Harlem Seven – a blues with Bechet and Newton – and four tracks from a quartet date led by Edmond Hall in which Lewis plays celeste and, intriguingly, Charlie Christian is the guitarist. The 18 tracks include the first four parts of 'The Blues' plus both 'Solitude' and 'Melancholy' and, from the earlier Decca sessions, 'Yancey Special' and 'Celeste Blues'. The sound here offers only the slightest of improvements over the Classics issues – surely better can be done with these tracks? – but measure for measure this is probably the finest single-disc representation of Lewis.

His 1961 Riverside session, now reissued in the OJC series, wasn't a milestone or a major rediscovery. Lewis had clearly grown tired of his own work over the years, and this group of remakes is done professionally, without much joy. He died three years later, following a car accident.

Mel Lewis (1929–90)

DRUMS

Lewis was drumming with Boyd Raeburn in 1948, when still only nineteen, and later with Stan Kenton. His most famous association is with Thad Jones: their big band ran from 1965 to 1978 and, when Jones left, Lewis kept at it, playing weekly at the Village Vanguard until his final illness.

***** Got'cha**

Fresh Sound FSR-CD 73 *Lewis; Ed Leddy (t); Richie Kamuca, Jerry Coker (ts); Pepper Adams (bs); Johnny Marabuto (p); Dean Reilly (b).* 11/56.

****(*) Naturally!**

Telarc 83301 *Lewis; Earl Gardner, Ron Tooley, Larry Moses, John Marshall (t); John Mosca, Lee Robertson, Lolie Bienenfeld (tb); Jim Daniels (btb); Dick Oatts, Steve Coleman (ss, as, f); Bob Rockwell, Richard Perry (ts, f); Gary Brown (bs); Jim McNeely (p); Bob Bowman (b).* 3/79.

Lewis was a master of big-band drumming, less relentlessly driving than Buddy Rich but as capable of swinging a big ensemble from the kit. His enduring achievements in that respect were with the band he led for many years with Thad Jones; yet little from their (admittedly rather sparse) discography is currently available. These two sessions, almost a generation apart, show some of his mettle. *Got'cha*, cut in San Francisco, is characteristic of certain aspects of West Coast jazz of the day without capitulating to the clichés of the style: Bill Perkins's arrangement of 'In A Mellowtone', for instance, is interestingly lugubrious, even sour; and with Coker and Leddy – otherwise neglected players – often in the solo limelight, this is a refreshing cut above several such sessions.

Naturally! is distinguished by the excellent reed section, with Oatts and Coleman sounding young and hungry, and the lacerating punch of the brass is undeniable; but the degree of flair that Jones could interpolate is missed.

*****(*) The Definitive Thad Jones Vol. 1**

Musicmasters 5024-2 *Lewis; Earl Gardner, Joe Mosello, Glenn Drewes, Jim Powell (t, flhn); John Mosca, Ed Neumeister (tb); Douglas Purviance, Earl McIntyre (btb); Stephanie Fauber (frhn); Dick Oatts, Ted Nash, Joe Lovano, Ralph Lalama, Gary Smulyan (reeds); Kenny Werner (p); Dennis Irwin (b).* 2/88.

***** The Definitive Thad Jones Vol. 2**

Musicmasters 5046-2 *As above.* 2/88.

A double tribute to Thad, with the Lewis band breezing through a selection of the trumpeter's tunes at a Village Vanguard engagement. Lewis's band sounded friendlier than many a big ensemble, with the reed section having a wide range of tones and the horns securing a fine attack without undue brassiness. They sound in top fettle on both discs: the first has a very good 'Three In One' and, though the second is a mite more ordinary, they finesse the material rather than bang it about.

*****(*) The Lost Art**

Musicmasters 6022-2 *Lewis; Jim Powell (flhn); John Mosca (tb); Dick Oatts (ss, as, ts); Gary Smulyan (bs); Kenny Werner (p); Dennis Irwin (b).* 4/89.

The sextet date was one of Lewis's final recordings. The music is skilfully arrranged by the idiosyncratic Werner – who cites such influences here as Andrew Hill and Bob Brookmeyer – into a rounded portrait of the options for small-group jazz in the aftermath of hard bop. On the face of it, Lewis is an unlikely choice as drummer for such an occasion, but he never played better, embellishing march or 4/4 or intensely slow pieces with the same assiduous craft and subtlety. 'The Lost Art' itself refers to his use of the brushes. Mosca is too bland, but Oatts, Smulyan and Werner are an absorbing team of improvisers, and they were all masterfully recorded by producer John Snyder. A fine farewell for Lewis in the studios.

Ramsey Lewis (born 1935)

PIANO, KEYBOARDS

Lewis is comparable to guitarist – later singer – George Benson, a musician whose genuine jazz gift has been at least partly eclipsed by enormous commercial success. The Chicagoan has a deft and understated touch at the keyboard, and echoes of past association with vibist Lem Winchester and master percussionist Max Roach might lie in his softly pattering, often consciously repetitive delivery.

***** Down To Earth**

Verve 538329-2 *Lewis; Eldee Young (b); Red Holt (d).* 58.

*****(*) In Person, 1960–1967**

Chess 051 814 2 2CD *As above, except add Cleveland Eaton (b), Maurice White (d).* 60–67.

***** Wade In The Water**

Jazz Time 6115 *As above.* 5 & 6/66.

Failure to include Ramsey in some earlier editions has been interpreted as snobbery on the editors' part. Not a bit of it. We are as convinced as any of his greatness. His million-seller, *The In-Crowd*, was a remarkable record and one that still repays listening. One suspects that Lewis had himself been listening to it when he decided to turn legit and return to acoustic piano in the 1980s. Unfortunately, most of his latter-day material is drab, formulaic funk, sounding like a Herbie Hancock project gone disastrously wrong. These early records are now very curious to place when heard out of context. There is already more than a hint of the smoothed-out funk of later years, and a tendency to build in big show-stopping tunes, like the *Spartacus* theme, or else current pop ('Hang On Sloopy'), but at moments it's difficult to forget, apart from Lewis's characteristic attack, that the soloist isn't Ahmad Jamal. Lewis's happy-clappy soul-jazz is less harmonically resonant, but the connection is there. Though he doesn't seem to have been vocal about it, it would be good to know how many times Miles Davis – who adjudged Jamal a significant performer – had listened to these early records. 'The "In" Crowd' is still a crowd-pleaser on the Chess compilation, but Lewis has perhaps gone too far in the obvious A&R direction and built in too much chart pop, much of it unsuited to piano trio.

His gospel roots are most clearly heard on the well-named *Down To Earth*. 'Sometimes I Feel Like A Motherless Child' is played with genuine feeling, and there are moments on the live discs when pomp and 'style' are put aside to permit some unalloyed improvisation. 'Django' is splendid and 'Come Sunday', with its unexpected harmonic shifts, could hardly be bettered.

*** Classic Encounter

Columbia MK 42661 *Lewis; Bill Dickens (b); Frank Donaldson (d); Philharmonia Orchestra.* 88.

Easy to dismiss as mere mood music, this orchestral 'encounter' is slightly edgier and less formulaic than expected. James Mack's orchestral arrangements are full and unctuous, but interesting things start to happen when orchestra and trio get together. A version of the seventeenth-century William Byrd's 'Earl of Salisbury Pavan' is an astonishing *tour de force* and almost sounds like some lost rarity of Latin jazz. A version of Johnny Mandel's 'Time For Love' is very strong, as is 'Spiritual', on which Ramsey finally lets loose his cool, gospelly sound.

*** We Meet Again

Columbia 44941 *Lewis; Billy Taylor (p).* 88.

Superficially reminiscent of Chick Corea and Herbie Hancock's celebrated double-headers. Ramsey and Billy cement the old pals act with Chick's 'We Meet Again', Horace Silver's 'Cookin' At The Continental', Oscar Peterson's 'Nigerian Marketplace' and John Lewis's 'Django'. Attractive and often quite pungent piano-jazz, though Taylor certainly takes the laurels.

*** This Is Jazz: Volume 27

Sony 65043 *Lewis; Rahm Lee (flhn); Louis Satterfield (tb); Don Myrick (sax); Bill Dickens (ky, b); Kevyn Lewis (ky, perc); Larry Dunn (ky); Byron Gregory, Fareed Haque, Al McKay (g); Cleveland Eaton, Ron Harris, Byron Miller (b); Leon Ndugu Chancler, Frank Donaldson, James Gadson, Morris Jennings (d); Steve Cobb (d, v); Philip Bailey, Paulinho Da Costa, Pennington McGee, Fred White (perc); Dert Recklaw Raheem (perc, v).*

A valuable gathering-in of Lewis's work for Columbia, much of which is otherwise out of catalogue. One measure of his stance on contemporary jazz-piano is the version of Bill Evans's 'Waltz For Debby'. It's clear you're not listening to the *Village Vanguard Sessions*, but Lewis has plans of his own for the tune.

** Sky Islands

GRP 059745-2 *Lewis; Art Porter (as); Henry Johnson (g); Mike Logan (ky); Chuck Webb (b); Steve Cobb (d, perc); Tony Carpenter, Eve Cornelious, Carl Griffin, Brenda Stewart (v).*

** Ivory Pyramid

GRP 059 688 2 *Lewis; Mike Logan (ky); Henry Johnson (g); Charles Webb (b); Steve Cobb (d, perc); vocalists.* 92.

**(*) Between The Keys

GRP 059 843 2 *Lewis; Orbert Davis (t); Grover Washington Jr (ss); Michael Logan, Kevin Randolph (ky); Keith Henderson (g); Charles Webb (b); Oscar Seaton (d); Frayne Lewis (d prog); Tony Carpenter (perc); orchestra, vocalists.* 95–96.

**(*) Dance Of The Soul

GRP 059 904 2 *Lewis; Orbert Davis (flhn); Michael Logan (ky); Fareed Haque, Henry Johnson (g); Maurice Fitzgerald, Charles Webb (b); Oscar Seaton (d); Alejo Poveda (perc); vocalists.* 97.

The 1990s 'revival' and 'return to mainstream' are very much in the ear of the behearer. Lewis is still a fleet and effective piano player, but he has spent far too much time in discotheques to understand the fundamental differences between jazz and pop, and *Sky Islands* in particular is a macaronic mish-mash of styles.

The records of the '90s have, though, been uniformly expert in execution and often surprisingly subtle in detail, but they are on the fringes of jazz and probably involve a casual listener in too much hard work, filleting deft piano lines out of vast washes of orchestral and vocal colour. The presence of Grover Washington greatly enlivens *Between The Keys*, but Ramsey's own love affair with the '88 monsters' now seems too settled and comfortable a business and there is little of the old authority left. As ever, though, there are flashes of what might be, and the closest listen to *Dance Of The Soul* discovers Lewis attempting things which in quite other acoustic contexts would seem advanced but which are simply lost here. We all ended up saying of Miles Davis that one day he would again appear in a small club with just an upright bass and acoustic piano. It never happened, but who's to say whether Lewis's instincts might yet veer in that direction?

***(*) Priceless Jazz

GRP 059 898 2 *As for the above.* 58–95.

It could be that this excellent and thoroughly representative compilation contains all the Ramsey Lewis you'll ever need. 'The "In" Crowd' is included (of course), as are 'Django' and 'Since I Fell For You'. Of the later material, 'Sun Goddess 2000' from *Between The Keys* is by far the best, the sort of tune Grover Washington used to specialize in and which can warm up the drabbest urban day.

**(*) Appassionata

Narada 47996 *Lewis; Larry Gray (b); Ernie Adams (d).* 99.

A new label and something of a shot-in-the-arm artistically. As often recently, the material is drawn from classical music and opera as much as from jazz and pop. Some of this is cringingly overdone, like the *arco* bass intro to 'Nessun Dorma', but some, like the opening version of Fauré's 'Pavane', is arresting, percussive jazz and shouldn't be too quickly dismissed. At 65 Lewis is still capable of surprise, and this retrospective of the tunes that helped shape his passion for music (hence the title) is very revealing.

Ted Lewis (1890–1971)

CLARINET, VOCAL, BANDLEADER

Born Theodore Leopold Friedman in Circleville, Ohio, Lewis was a vaudevillian who broke into jazz when he began playing clarinet with Earl Fuller's Famous Jazz Band in 1917, in the wake of the success of the ODJB. He ran a hugely popular and jazz-flavoured dance band throughout the 1920s, with many important sidemen in its ranks. His own clarinet playing and singing, though, remained in the realm of vaudeville. He continued to tour almost until his death in 1971.

*****(*) The Jazzworthy Ted Lewis**

Retrieval RTR 79014 *Lewis; Muggsy Spanier (c); Dave Klein, Manny Klein, Red Nichols (t); George Brunies (tb, kz); Harry Raderman, Sammy Blank (tb); Benny Goodman, Rod Cless (cl, as); Frank Teschemacher, Donald 'Slats' Long (cl, ts); Jimmy Dorsey (cl, as, bs); Hymie Wolfson (ts); Louis Martin (bs); Sol Klein, Sam Shapiro (vn); Fats Waller (p, v); Jack Aaronson (p); Tony Girardi (g); Jimmy Moore (b); Bob Escamilla, Harry Barth (tba); John Lucas, Rud Van Gelder (d); The Four Dusty Travellers, The Bachelors (v).* 8/29–7/33.

The defensive title will raise a smile among those who know Lewis's work; he is unfortunately remembered as much for Eddie Condon's remark – 'Lewis could make the clarinet talk, and usually it said "put me back in the case"'– as for his merits as bandleader. The hammiest of showmen, he nevertheless ran a very fine dance band throughout the 1920s and early '30s, and there are numerous great spots for the heavyweight names listed in the personnel – particularly Spanier, who is magnificent on the likes of 'Lonesome Road' and 'Aunt Hagar's Blues'. This compilation cherrypicks the best of Lewis's later Columbia sessions, up until his final date for them in July 1933, the very rare (and surprisingly fine) 'Here You Come With Love'. The four tracks where Fats Waller sat in with the band are here; George Brunies lets rip on kazoo on 'San'; and Ted himself is, for all his egregious mannerisms, not too hard to take when there is a lot of good music surrounding him. Top-notch transfers, and with JSP's Lewis CD now out of circulation, what we need next are the best of the early Lewis tracks.

Vic Lewis (born 1919)

BANDLEADER AND WEST COAST ALL STARS (FOUNDED 1963)

Playing guitar in London clubs in the '30s, then he worked in the USA before RAF service. Formed a Kenton-styled big band in the '40s and ran it on and off into the '60s, while pursuing a career as manager of many major names. In the '90s he was recording with famous names once again.

**** Play Bill Holman**

Candid CCD 79535 *Conte Candoli, Jack Sheldon (t); Andy Martin, Rob McConnell (tb); Ron Loofbourrow (frhn); Lanny Morgan, Lennie Niehaus, Bud Shank (as); Bob Cooper (ts, cl, f); Bill Perkins (bs, ss, f, as, bcl); Alan Broadbent, Mike Lang, Dudley Moore (p); John Clayton (b); Jeff Hamilton (d); Ruth Price (v).* 8/89, 3/93.

***** Shake Down The Stars**

Candid CCD79526 *Andy Martin (tb); Bob Cooper (ts); Bill Perkins (ts, bs, ss, cl, f); Mike Lang (p); Joel Di Bartolo (b); Paul Kreibich (d).* 4/92.

***** A Celebration Of West Coast Jazz**

Candid CCD 7971/2 *Steve Huffstetter (t, flhn); Andy Martin, Charlie Lopez, Alex Eyles, Bob McCheskie (tb); Don Shelton (as, cl, picc, f); Bill Perkins (f, cl, as, ts, bs); Bob Cooper (ts, cl, f); Bob Efford (bs, ob, ts, cl); Jack Nimitz (bs, bcl); Clare Fischer, Christian Jacob, Frank Strazzeri (p); John Leitham, Tom Worthington (b); Paul Kreibich, Bob Leatherbarrow (d); Sue Raney (v).* 4/93, 2/94.

Short, on the round side, and with hair even blacker than near-contemporary Ronald Reagan's, Lewis cuts an improbable figure in the jazz world. The most prominent of his more recent projects has been the West Coast All Stars, who have previously recorded for Candid. As always, his role on this project – beyond having his picture taken standing alongside featured trombonist Martin – seems to have been purely fiscal. Even joint arranging (with Lang) and co-production credits with the reliably sharp-eared Perkins have to be regarded with some scepticism. He does, though, manage to persuade top-flight players to turn out and record for the same rates as session men, which implies a gift of the gab if nothing else.

So what of the records themselves? *Shake Down The Stars* is attributed to Lewis's favourite songwriter, Jimmy Van Heusen. Among the tracks: 'But Beautiful', 'Here's That Rainy Day', the warhorse 'Polka Dots and Moonbeams', 'I Thought About You' and the title-track. Lewis had himself once turned to trombone, so featuring Martin on every track except 'I'll Only Miss Her' (a welcome outing for the stalwart Cooper, who is the only ever-present All-Star) smacks of surrogacy or wishful thinking. Martin has a nice old-fashioned sound and isn't troubled by too many fancy ideas, and there it really ends.

The Bill Holman set is pretty messy, padded out with an alternative version of 'Oleo' and a re-recorded vocal by Ruth Price. It sounds as if not one of them cares even remotely about what they're playing, and the solos, such as they are, fail to register. Dudley Moore has played better solos off the cuff in the middle of comedy programmes, but at least he sounds as if he's enjoying himself.

The *Celebration* was also a fly way of marking Lewis's own 75th birthday. The box actually contains two sessions, recorded almost a year apart. Given that the band on the very first All Stars date included Shorty Rogers, Bud Shank, Laurindo Almeida, Victor Feldman and Shelly Manne, it might be thought that we have drifted into a Silver Age. The silvery quality of Perkins's flute playing only serves to underline that. Everything is bright and polished, very clean-edged and not very involving. Martin's solos are increasingly routine, and it is really only Perkins who continues to put some emotion into the playing; his 'Waltz For Coop' on disc two is lovely. But where are the trumpet-players of yesteryear?

A rather disappointing record from a player who has anchored some of the best albums of recent times.

Victor Lewis

DRUMS

Recognized for his work with Bobby Watson and others, Lewis is the repertory jazz drummer of his generation, a significant stylist who has branched out as a composer and bandleader.

***** Family Portrait**
Audioquest 1010 *Lewis; John Stubblefield (ss, ts); Eduardo Simon (p); Cecil McBee (b); Don Alias, Jumma Santos (perc); Pamela Watson, Bobby Watson, Yvonne Hatchet, Shani Phillpotts, Michael Moses, Melissa Thomas, Raymond Cruz (v).* 11–12/92.

*****(*) Know It Today, Know It Tomorrow**
Red 123255-2 *Lewis; Eddie Henderson (t, flhn); Seamus Blake (ts); Eduardo Simon (p); Christian McBride (b).* 4/92.

Lewis is one of the leading drummers of today, but his recent showing as a composer has been confined to a few themes turning up on other people's dates. These two sessions give him a better opportunity, and some of the material is interesting enough to suggest that Lewis could be as involved in writing as, say, Joe Chambers. The Audioquest album is sometimes obscured by an ambitious game-plan, with massed voices used on three tracks (offering a slight recall of Max Roach's work in this area) and the percussionists building over, rather than especially complementing, Lewis's own work. Stubblefield, though, is as authoritative as always and Simon's Herbie Hancock touches make modest waves. *Know It Today, Know It Tomorrow* is less self-consciously striving but more detailed and meticulous. It's as much a showcase for the youthful Blake as it is for Lewis: aside from the slow crescendo at the climax of 'Swamp Dog', there is very little grandstanding from the drums. Blake's diffident, slightly hollow sound can be very affecting on slow pieces such as 'The Loss Of A Moment', a scrupulous, Shorterish ballad by Lewis, or 'The Truce', but he has no trouble keeping up a flow of ideas at quicker tempos, and the long melody lines of his own tune, 'Gotta Start Somewhere', are intriguing. The only gripe would be that Henderson, going through a memorable patch of playing, appears only occasionally on the date. The phenomenal McBride gels perfectly with Lewis, as ever.

***** Eeeyyess!**
Enja ENJ 9311-2 *Lewis; Terell Stafford (t); Seamus Blake (ts); Stephen Scott (p); Ed Howard (b); Don Alias (perc).* 7/96.

Not quite the revelatory explosion that the title suggests. This is a workmanlike performance from Lewis and his band. Mortgaged to a latter-day version of Blue Note hard bop, it would have sounded more interesting if the dateline had been 20 years earlier. The components are all perfectly respectable, and Stafford plays some wonderful stuff in the key of Lee, but Morgan pastiche is a touch passé at the end of the century.

Lewis's grasp of metre is impossible to fault but, apart from 'Alter Ego' and 'Stamina', he shows too little of his melodic side.

Steuart Liebig

BASS

Bass guitarist based in California and recording in the Nine Winds community of West Coast improvisers and free-bop players.

***** Hommages Obliques**
Nine Winds NWCD 0158 *Liebig; John Fumo (t, flhn); Jeff Gauthier (vn); Jeff McCutchen (d).* 5/93.

*****(*) Lingua Obscura**
Nine Winds NWCD 0173 *As above, except Dan Morris (d) replaces McCutchen.* 5/95.

***** Pienso Oculto**
Nine Winds NWCD 0191 *As above.* 2/97.

*****(*) No Train**
Cadence CJR 1086 *Liebig; Vinny Golia (ss, bs); Billy Mintz (d).* 8/97.

We have been a while catching up with these records, but they're worth seeking out. Steuart Liebig plays what he calls ContraBass-Guitars, getting a fluid, melodious sound that has plenty of air as well as boom in it. The three records by his Quartetto Stig are full of his own writing. Gauthier and Fumo are familiar from their own Nine Winds projects and, if this is a somewhat rarefied instrumentation, it presents many opportunities for the four men (McCutchen, who subsequently died, was replaced by Morris after the first disc) to play within structure while still getting good improvising space. Liebig's tunes aren't terrifically memorable, mixing brief pieces with what are in some cases hugely long tracks, such as 'Commedia' and 'Overcoming Goingunder', which seem to touch on all sorts of stylistic bases. *Lingua Obscura* might be our favourite of the three: 'Plums And Apricots Falling From The Sky' shows what they can do in a tiny episode, and the laments of 'Nef' and 'Coda', in dedication to McCutchen, are played with great feeling.

No Train is more of a free-jazz blowout, with long-time mainstays of the area Golia and Mintz digging in alongside. With Golia concentrating on baritone for much of the way, the music has a great rumbling feel that should blow away a few cobwebs as it goes. Fine and hard-headed virtuosity.

David Liebman (born 1946)

TENOR SAXOPHONE, SOPRANO SAXOPHONE, FLUTES

Liebman studied with Lennie Tristano and saxophonist Charles Lloyd and founded his own group, Lookout Farm, while still working with Miles Davis. He was one of the few Coltrane-influenced saxophonists to go back to first principles and explore a parallel line of inquiry, attempting to synthesize jazz and Indian music. For a time, he abandoned tenor saxophone in favour of the soprano.

****(*) One Of A Kind**

Core/Line COCD 9.00887 *Liebman (ss solo).* 81–84.

***** The Tree**

Soul Note 121195 *As above.* 4/90.

It's one of the paradoxes of David Liebman's career that an improviser who has put such emphasis (in bands such as Lookout Farm and Quest) on collective improvisation and non-hierarchical musical tradition should so frequently evoke solitariness. In 1980 Liebman, perhaps tired of reading about the 'dominant Coltrane influence' on his work, decided to give up tenor saxophone and flute in order to concentrate on the horn that best expressed his individuality. It's interesting that the soprano saxophone (which was always the least Coltrane-accented of his horns) should also be associated, via John Surman and Steve Lacy, with solo performance. *One Of A Kind* is a curious act of self-restitution. Multi-tracked, like some of Surman's or Alfred 23 Harth's solo projects or Keith Jarrett's restorative *Spirits*, it has something of the same self-probing intensity; track-titles like 'Ethnic Suite: The Semites', 'Real Self', 'Relentless', 'Words', 'Spirit', 'The Power Of The Cross', and even the Satie 'Trois Gnossiennes', give some sense of Liebman's curiously referential approach to improvisation.

In contrast, *The Tree* is for unaugmented soprano saxophone, with none of the overdubs of the previous disc. Liebman solemnly intones, 'Roots – take one,' gradually building up his image of jazz tradition as a vegetative organism with taproots and trunk representing origins and mainstays, giving way to branches and twigs of lesser structural or more individual significance, and finally the transitory leaves of fashion. Palindromic in structure, the second takes occur in mirror order, leading back to the roots. In its lonely oddity and *faux-naïf* simplicities, it's reminiscent of Joyce Kilmer's great-awful poem about trees. In sharp contrast to the creeping pretentiousness of the earlier sets, it's simple and direct, and the mimetic references – wind, mainly – are logical and unintrusive. Far removed from either Coltrane or Lacy, Liebman's sound is vocalized in a much more straightforwardly humane way, and one can easily reconstruct the impact it has had on the French saxophonist and clarinettist, Louis Sclavis. Remarkable as these albums may be, they're probably best approached via Liebman's more conventional group work.

***** The Dave Liebman Quartet in Australia**

Enja ENJ 3065 *Liebman; Mike Nock (p); Ron McClure (b); Ed Soph (d).* 2/79.

And why should the Antipodes be denied the multi-active Liebman? At least some of the material is site-specific: 'The Opal Hearted Aborigine' and 'Down Under' have much of Liebman's desire to synthesize many styles and forms. In retrospect, McClure comes to seem ever more important to the overall sound, but Nock is an impressive accompanist and soloist, and he responds as instinctively as Richie Beirach had to Liebman's challenging melodic ideas and tonalities.

*****(*) Doin' It Again**

Timeless SJP 140 *Liebman; Terumasa Hino (t, flhn); John Scofield (g); Ron McClure (b); Adam Nussbaum (d).* 80.

***** If They Only Knew**

Timeless SJP 151 *As above.* 80.

This was Liebman's touring band of the late 1970s, and one of his very best. Some of the rhythmic energy of his early rock experience (with the otherwise forgettable Ten Wheel Drive and in Miles Davis's fusion experiment) had crept back into his work, and he seems liberated by the absence of piano, playing off and against the high-energy pairing of Hino and Scofield. The first of the CDs is marginally the better, but both are worth having; the writing and playing are of high quality and there's one great standard on each, 'Stardust' and a wholly unexpected 'Autumn In New York'.

****** Double Edge**

Storyville STCD 4091 *Liebman; Richie Beirach (p).* 4/85.

***** Nine Again**

Red RR 123234 *Liebman; Franco D'Andrea (p).* 89.

At first glance, not at all the kind of set one would expect to find on the rather traditionalist Storyville. At second, Liebman's approach to an obvious-looking set of standards – 'Naima', 'Lover Man', 'Round Midnight', 'On Green Dolphin Street' – is even less likely to attract conservatives. It's the very lushness of Beirach's chording and the frequent but almost subliminal displacements of the rhythmic pattern that cue Liebman for his more adventurous explorations. On 'Naima', which became a pianist's tune in any case, he moves outside the chords; on 'Green Dolphin Street' he all but ignores them. Throughout, he sounds quizzical, as if reading from an early and much-revised manuscript of the tune. Liebman at his best.

D'Andrea is a less troubled romantic than Richie Beirach, but he's well up to Liebman's by now almost routine respraying of standards. 'Autumn Leaves', a tune that creaks with the weight of bad interpretations, sounds as if it was written yesterday. Repertoire pieces, like the once fashionable 'Freedom Jazz Dance', are given a fresh gloss. The problem is that these brightened-up covers contain absolutely no suggestion of depth. With Beirach, Liebman seemed to reach down into a tune; with D'Andrea, it's all brushwork and no perspective or dimensionality. A lot more interesting than just watching paint dry, all the same.

***** Quest II**

Storyville STCD 4132 *Liebman; Richie Beirach (p); Ron McClure (b); Billy Hart (d).* 4/86.

The liner image of four intensely staring and mustachioed figures gives away something about the music inside, which is almost too intense and inward. Certainly less dynamic than other Quest sets, this one has a pervasive melancholy quality, even a touch of bleakness. It isn't unattractive – there's an unmistakable edge of humour to the opening 'Gargoyles' – but it palls a bit after half an hour. The shortest track, 'The Hollow Men', is one of the toughest things Liebman has written for this line-up, and it's a pity that it wasn't developed further.

*****(*) Trio + One**

Owl 051 *Liebman; Caris Visentin (ob); Dave Holland (b, clo); Jack DeJohnette (d, syn).* 5/88.

*****(*) Quest / Natural Selection**

Core/Line 9.00748 *Liebman; Richie Beirach (p); Ron McClure (b); Billy Hart (d).* 6/88.

The slightly calculated eccentricity of Liebman's approach surfaces only peripherally on *Trio + One* with the ironic 'All The Things That ...'. For the most part, this is an intelligent set of straightforwardly conceived originals, given flesh and complexion by the top-flight rhythm-section and a heightened emotional profile by the interplay of the horns. (Ms Visentin is Mrs Liebman in private life.) DeJohnette is in powerful form, but it's odd that other leaders don't find room for his outstanding synthesizer work.

Liebman's band, Quest, a more settled outfit with a more exploratory ethos, steered an unsteady course between starchy music logics and inspired nonsense. At their best, as on most of *Natural Selection*, they seemed able to find a reasonable middle ground with a configuration that represented an at least partial return to conventional horn–piano–rhythm hierarchy, with which Liebman – no instinctive radical, one suspects – seems happiest.

***** Plays The Music Of Cole Porter**

Red RR 123236 *Liebman; Steve Gilmore (b); Bill Godwin (d).* 88.

This is a very sparse setting for Porter. Without a piano, Liebman is required to play very melodically and to spin new lines out of the songs. This is the sort of thing he can do standing on his head – and unfortunately, after about 25 minutes, one begins to hope that he will stand on his head, just to vary the pace and timbre a bit. Beautifully done, but decidedly passionless, a Porter flaw which most of his more intelligent interpreters have managed to work around.

*****(*) Classic Ballads**

Candid CCD 79512 *Liebman; Vic Juris (g); Steve Gilmore (b).* 12/90, 1/91.

****** Setting The Standard**

Red RR 123253 *Liebman; Mulgrew Miller (p); Rufus Reid (b); Victor Lewis (d).* 5/92.

The ballads album is dedicated to Liebman's mother-in-law, Natalie Visentin. She chose the material from the songs that she loved in her teens. Liebman plays them pretty straight but is still willing to introduce material from outside the basic sequence in a romantic version of bebop technique. It's a pity there isn't a track in common with the Red recording, which is more rhythmic and changes-based. Juris is used as a second lead as well as a harmony instrument, which means that Gilmore is also called into play as an accompanist. That's clearly the case on 'Angel Eyes' and 'If I Should Lose You', the two most developed tracks.

Setting The Standard is probably the straightest recording Liebman's made in years, and it suits him. Miller has the same rolling, harmonically dense quality that McCoy Tyner brought to the Coltrane quartet ('Grand Central Station' is a nod in that direction) and he pulls Liebman along more insistently than Beirach, say, or d'Andrea. Liebman's tendency to play in rather fixed metres is less evident with a rhythm section as probing as this, and on several of the tracks the pace changes quite dramatically, forcing the saxophonist to vary his phrasing and often his dynamics accordingly. The studio sound is full but not especially flattering.

*****(*) Joy**

Candid CCD 79531 *Liebman; Gregory Oaks, Donna Ott, Brian Garland, Christopher Breault, Kevin Lewis (t); Tom McKenzie, Michael Mosley, Kim Zitlau (tb); Steve Coonly (btb); Bill Schnepper, Mike Fansler (as, bcl); Jed Hackett, Kenny Flester (ts, bcl); Jim Wingo (bs); Kristi Blalock, Mary Kay Adams, Margaret Ross, Tracie Vies, Melinda Gryder, Kerry O'Connor, Jen Kuk, Dawn Rhinehart, Jennifer McQueen, Mandy Harris, Grace P. Manuel, Elisabeth L. Boivin, Susan L. Walker, Carrie Scattergood, Miranda Hopkins, Christine Fry (f); Butch Taylor (p); Michael Souders (ky); Jim Roller, Pete Spaar (b); Mike Nichols (d); R.J Geger (perc).* 3/92.

In the later 1980s, Liebman became much obsessed with the legacy of Coltrane. He'd already made one tribute album. *Joy* was recorded just after what would have been Coltrane's 65th birthday. It's an altogether more positive and coherent session, backed by a forward-looking and utterly competent campus jazz orchestra (from James Madison U. in Harrisonburg, Virginia) under the directorship of the impressive Mossblad, who solos himself on 'Alabama' and 'India'. On the latter, both he and Liebman switch to ethnic flutes, Mayan and Indian respectively. They collaborate on an astonishing arrangement of 'After The Rain' which uses the university flute choir, a strange but stirring sound. 'Alabama' is the only small-group track, and it exposes Spaar a little, though Taylor is an exceptional accompanist, capable of a thoughtful solo, as he proves on 'Naima', 'Untitled Original' and 'Joy/Selflessness'. Liebman more or less surrenders himself to the music, playing unaffectedly in a lower register than normal. The recording, made (catch this) by the Multitrack Recording Class, is first rate and puts a good many so-called professional efforts to shame.

***** The Seasons**

Soul Note 121245 *Liebman; Cecil McBee (b); Billy Hart (d).* 12/92.

Big on the concepts, is Liebman. This interweaves some Vivaldi quotes, some pretty straight-ahead jazz and some free-form impressionism, with a few compositional ideas that have floated around for years in the Liebman canon. His dry, almost Lacy-like delivery suits this line-up very well indeed, though the fullness of accompaniment sometimes overpowers his lighter passages.

****(*) Besame Mucho**

Red RR 123260 *Liebman; Danilo Perez (p); Tony Marino (b); Bill Goodwin (d); Mark Holen, Scott Cutshall (perc).* 3/93.

The Latin Album. Had to happen eventually, and of course Liebman handles it with consummate professionalism. It isn't the most inspiring group he's ever recruited, and there are *longueurs*when the focus is off the saxophone. Not much in the way of atmosphere, which may be the result of doing a south-of-the-border record in Saylorsburg, Pennsylvania. The rhythmic vigour of the leader's playing has never been more evident, but the overall sound is rather flat and uninflected.

***** Songs For My Daughter**

Soul Note 121295 *Liebman; Vic Juris (g); Phil Markowitz (p); Tony Marino (b); Jamey Haddad (d); Scott Cutshall (perc).*

Very much better, but still oddly focused and amazingly sloppy in execution here and there. Liebman's flute playing is the main revelation, and there is some nice interplay between it and Juris's smoothly articulate guitar. A very enjoyable record, but still down the list of priorities for this artist.

**** Miles Away

Owl 078 830485 *As above, except add Caris Visentin (eng hn).* 3/94.

There has been a veritable rash of Miles memorials since the trumpeter's death, but few would question Liebman's right to his moment. His tenure with Miles's band was one of the least clearly understood of all. Liebman seemed to understand his boss's desire for a sound that was both lyrical and mysterious, and these are the qualities he brings to this imaginatively mixed set, which includes late things like 'Code M.D.' (actually written by Robert Irving III), Mingus's 'Smooch', Wayne Shorter's 'Fall' and Gil Evans's 'Pan Piper' (with its lovely feature for Caris Visentin's cor anglais), as well as 'Wili', which Miles wrote for Liebman himself. This is the regular '90s band, and Liebman (still on soprano) sounds completely at ease, musing and laughing, attacking the material playfully. A gorgeous record, and one of the best of the recent crop.

*** John Coltrane's Meditations

Arkadia 71042 *Liebman; Tiger Okoshi (t); Caris Visentin (ob); Phil Markowitz (ky); Vic Juris (g); Cecil McBee, Tony Marino (b); Jamey Haddad, Billy Hart (d).* 12/95.

How brave it was to go back to Trane's classic album with a very different instrumentation, one that included brass, an extra woodwind, guitar and electric keys, as well as doubled-up bass and drums. The result is faithful to the spirit of the original tracks. 'The Father And The Son And The Holy Ghost', 'Compassion', 'Love' and the somewhat shorter but climactic 'Consequences' and 'Serenity' are integrated even more than on the original record, and Liebman, admittedly with the benefit of hindsight and long exposure to Coltrane's music, is able to import themes and ideas from one track to another, underlining the coherence of the project.

***(*) Return Of The Tenor / Standards

DoubleTime Records DTRCD 109 *Liebman; Phil Markowitz (p); Vic Juris (g); Tony Marino (b); Jamey Haddad (perc).* 1/96.

Liebman put away his tenor because he wasn't sure there was anywhere to go in the 'post-Coltrane' idiom he had been identified with. Returning to it brings a new simplicity and rawness to his sound, and a programme of familiar tunes – 'All The Things You Are', 'Summertime', 'Yesterdays', 'There Will Never Be Another You', and so on – encourages him to play with a minimum of embellishment and a refreshingly straightforward attack. The band is nothing exceptional. Markowitz is amiable and – for the most part – very appealing, leaving much of the straight rhythmic work to Juris. Bass and drums don't so much drive things along as punctuate and sustain the beat. It's left to Liebman himself to provide the surface interest and the deeper ideas, and for the most part that is exactly what he achieves.

**(*) New Vista

Arkadia 71041 *Liebman; Phil Markowitz (syn); Vic Juris (g).* 7/96.

Though there are interesting interpretations of 'Estate' and a second standard piece, 'Zingaro', this is a thoroughly disappointing set, overcooked and overladen with electric textures. Liebman is as thoughtful and as responsive to nuance as ever, but the chemistry is uncertain.

***(*) Monk's Mood

Double Time 154 *Liebman; Eddie Gomez (b); Adam Nussbaum (d).* 98.

Wonderfully pared down and spacious, these 11 Thelonious Monk compositions are both entirely idiomatic and entirely recast in Liebman's own distinctive voice. The set is bracketed by two cleverly differentiated versions of 'Monk's Mood', but the outstanding performance is the leader's tenor solo on the relatively little-known 'Gallop's Gallop'. Eddie Gomez is in stunning form throughout, and the duet version of 'Monk's Mood' at the end of the record is hijacked by the great bassist. Among the other tracks included are 'Introspection', 'Nutty', 'Skippy' and a revelatory account of 'Ugly Beauty' which should become a standard study-piece for all Monk students.

*** Elements: Water

Arkadia Jazz 71043 *Liebman; Pat Metheny (g, syn); Cecil McBee (b); Billy Hart (d).* 98.

Oddly concluded by a interview with Liebman on the theme of water, this opens a sequence of four records coming up on Arkadia celebrating the elements. Mercifully, *Water* isn't just a sequence of knocked-down Debussy, but a tough and surprisingly varied sequence of originals, which range from sparkly neo-bop on 'Storm Surge' to the more impressionistic 'Reflecting Pool' (which borders on mood music), to the surprising formal control of 'Ebb And Flow'. McBee and Metheny are both featured in solo interludes which help to give the record a valuable change of pace. It will be interesting to hear how Dave tackles fire, air and earth.

***(*) Souls & Masters

Cactus CAC 9901 *Liebman; Michael Gerber (p).* 99.

Dedicated to the music of a young composer called Rhoda Averbach, *Souls & Masters* is one of the most sheerly astonishing records of recent times, an enigmatic modern classic that depends for its impact on strange time-signatures, symmetrical scales on 'For Nanda' and an overdetermining concern with the spiritual and psychological power of music. However impressive Averbach's ideas might be (and we are convinced that they are), it is the playing of Gerber and Liebman which holds the attention here. A difficult album to describe, other than very technically, which somehow defeats the object.

Lifetime

GROUP

A 'power trio' which presaged the fusion of the '70s and came to be used as the name for subsequent Tony Williams-led groups.

*****(*) Emergency!**

Verve 539117-2 *Tony Williams (d); John McLaughlin (g); Larry Young (org).* 5/69.

*****(*) Turn It Over**

Verve 539118-2 *As above, except add Jack Bruce (b, v).* 70.

*****(*) Ego**

Verve 559512-2 *Tony Williams (d); Ted Dunbar (g); Larry Young (org); Ron Carter (b, clo); Don Alias, Warren Smith (d, perc); Jack Bruce (v).* 2–3/71.

****** Ultimate Tony Williams**

Verve 559704-2 *As above.* 69-71.

*****(*) Spectrum: The Anthology**

Verve 537075-2 2CD *As above, except add Tillmon Lewis (ts); David Horowitz (p, vib, syn); Webster Lewis (org, clavinet); Ted (g); Tequila (g, perc, v); Ron Carter (b, clo); Herb Bushler (b); Don Alias, Warren Smith (perc).* 69–73.

****(*) The Collection**

Columbia 468924 *Tony Williams (d); Allan Holdsworth (g); Tony Newton (b, v).* 7/75–6/76.

If all the people who claim to have seen Lifetime live during the band's relatively brief incarnation really had, they'd probably still be going. This was the power trio to end all trios, strictly known as the Tony Williams Lifetime, and it might be thought to be more appropriately discussed under the same heading as the late and much-lamented Williams's other work. On the other hand, whatever the official title, the original Lifetime was a collaborative group. John McLaughlin and Larry Young contributed substantially to its roiling, intense sound. Later additions didn't add much, and for most enthusiasts the only albums worth bothering about are *Emergency!* and *Turn It Over.* In the latter, Jack Bruce was brought in as bassist and vocalist. The first job had been done more than adequately by Young's pedals and, as 'Once I Loved' and 'This Night This Song' underlined on the second album, Williams himself could invest his light, almost toneless vocals with a curious poignancy which he traded on more forcefully later.

Acoustically, *Emergency!* was always a disgrace and it is scarcely improved on CD, though for some reason it sounds rather crisper on *Spectrum*, which is only a good buy if you respond positively to the latter-day material. Disc two begins with Lifetime's single, 'One Word', a monotonously rising figure with a strained vocal from Bruce.

By the time *Ego* was made, the band was explicitly 'The Tony Williams Lifetime' and there was a sharp move towards a more percussion-orientated sound. The addition of Alias and Smith took care of that. Dunbar's guitar playing was much more linear and blues-based than McLauglin's, and Ron Carter's bass work provided a solider spine than Bruce's blub-a-lib slurs. They had their place, but the new band was moving in different directions. Bruce returns for a solitary vocal on 'Two Worlds', but it is Williams's vocal on the storming 'Lonesome Wells' which haunts the mind. The record opens with a minute of virtuosic hand-clapping (presumably by the whole group) which would put the Steve Reich Ensemble to shame. It and the solo 'Some Hip Drum Shit' find their way on to *Ultimate Tony Williams*, a selection of Lifetime (and only Lifetime) material by the only drummer of the succeeding generation who can hold a candle to him, Jack DeJohnette. DeJohnette really was at the trio's first gig, at Count Basie's in Harlem, and immediately recognized that what was radical about it was that it was centred on the drumkit. Important to register that, whatever the title suggests, this isn't a career-best compilation but merely the Williams material held by Polygram. For a wider view of Williams, his work for Blue Note and elsewhere also need to be taken into account, and is reviewed under his name.

The bands after *Ego* frankly aren't worth a damn. Fans of Allan Holdsworth (and, to be fair, there are many) will value the 1975 and 1976 recordings on *The Collection*, though this must count as one of Williams's drabbest performances ever. These sessions were originally released as *Believe It* and *Million Dollar Legs* and promptly disappeared from sight. The real stuff comes right at the start of the group's life.

Young's swirling, piercing clusters on the organ are the key to the group's shifting polytonality. McLaughlin sounds almost linear by contrast, whipping out licks and lines almost like an illusionist pushing swords through a box. Williams, as ever, is both intensely driven and fierce, and romantically expressive. On 'Sangria For Three' (*Emergency! / Spectrum*) he sounds not unlike the great swing-era drummers, but hyped up to the maximum. Elsewhere, and notably on the more brooding and introspective *Turn It Over*, he doesn't seem to be keeping time at all, but pushing out beyond such considerations. We *did* catch them live. They *were* extraordinary, probably in ways that never could have been caught on record. Even given their technical limitations, the two first albums are soberingly powerful.

Terry Lightfoot (born 1935)

CLARINET, ALTO SAXOPHONE, VOCAL

Born in Potters Bar, Lightfoot was bandleading by the mid-'50s and became one of the big names during the ensuing trad boom. He weathered the leaner years of the late '60s and '70s, kept a pub, then went back to pro bandleading in the mid-'80s.

***(*) When The Saints Go Marching In! / Varied Jazz**

C5 MCD 566 *Lightfoot; Ian Hunter-Randall (t); Mickey Cooke (tb); Paddy Lightfoot (bj, v); Peter Skivington (b); Ian Castle (d).* 71–75.

****(*) Down On Bourbon Street**

Timeless TTD 581 *Lightfoot; Ian Hunter-Randall (t); Phil Rhodes (tb); Bruce Boardman (p); Tony Pitt (g, bj); Andy Lawrence (sou, b); Johnny Armatage (d).* 8/93.

Popular as he often was, Lightfoot is an also-ran in British trad. A few years younger than the Ball/Barber/Bilk axis, he never had quite the same impact and has never altogether won the authenticity which those groups marked out for themselves. The C5 compilation is a frightful set of crusty trad staples and indifferent originals, played as if everyone in the group was on buttoned-down best behaviour. Lightfoot's prim vocals don't help.

Down On Bourbon Street isn't too bad. 'Grandpa's Spells' is an attempted carbon of Morton's original and was ill-advised. 'Bourbon Street Parade' itself sounds more like a march down Wandsworth High Street. But 'A Closer Walk With Thee', taken apart by Rhodes's comically over-the-top trombone, and Lightfoot's gentle examination of 'Petite Fleur' are more encouraging, and Hunter-Randall usually has some decent points to make, even after 25 years with the band.

***** Strictly Traditional**
Lake LACD117 *Lightfoot; Paul Lacey, Alan Gresty (t); Ian Bateman (tb); Richard Simmons (p); Tony Pitt (g, bj); Andy Lawrence (b); Johnny Richardson (d).* 1–2/99.

Lightfoot's best for years is a re-creative look at some of the favourites from his heyday, done by a band which mixes old hands (Richardson goes back to the original 1956 Lightfoot band!) with younger heads, and the results have an infectious good humour and chutzpah. It's just solid old British trad, but they're swinging.

Kirk Lightsey (born 1937)

PIANO

Kirk Lightsey's career began with Ernestine Anderson and Melba Liston, and he made something of a speciality of working with singers, a discipline that may well have had some influence on his unfussily evocative improvisations, which always speak confidently but without excess. He has been a member of the Leaders and of the hornless Leaders Trio.

***** Shorter By Two**
Sunnyside 1004 D *Lightsey (p solo) and with Harold Danko (p).* 7/83.

*****(*) Lightsey Live**
Sunnyside 1014 D *Lightsey (p solo).* 6/85.

Beginning, middle and end: Lightsey's compositions and solo performances have a well-made, almost narrative quality that is the antithesis of free-form 'blowing'. It's a characteristic he shares with Wayne Shorter, and Lightsey has long shown an interest in the saxophonist's unusually gnomic small-group compositions (which Miles Davis once likened to short stories). Transcribing Shorter pieces for solo piano presents quite particular difficulties. These are partially overcome in the duos with Danko, whose rich articulation is a softer version of Lightsey's, but a good many of these pieces are over-egged and compare rather poorly with the wonderful 'Fee Fi Fo Fum' on *Live*. The solo album also takes in Monk – a finger-bending 'Trinkle Tinkle' – Cole Porter, Rodgers and Hart, and Tony Williams, whose 'Pee Wee' (from the drummer's 1988 *Angel Street*, Blue Note 748494 CD) gets the album off to a deceptively stately start. Lightsey's delivery is quite formal, and improvisations unfold with an absence of histrionics, which means that tracks often make their full impact only on subsequent hearings.

*****(*) Isotope**
Criss Cross Criss 1003 *Lightsey; Jesper Lundgaard (b); Eddie Gladden (d).* 2/83.

***** Everything Is Changed**
Sunnyside SSC 1020 *Lightsey; Jerry Gonzalez (t, flhn); Jerry Routch (frhn); Santi Debriano (b); Chico Freeman, Famoudou Don Moye (perc).* 6/86.

***** From Kirk To Nat**
Criss Cross Criss 1050 *Lightsey; Kevin Eubanks (g); Rufus Reid (b).* 11/90.

Only deceptively in opposition to Lightsey's interest in Shorter is a liking for broad vamps over repeated figures, a device strongly reminiscent of Abdullah Ibrahim (Dollar Brand), who has something of Shorter's enigmatic brevity. *Everything Is Changed*, but the significant addition of Jerry Gonzalez further restricts Lightsey's multi-linear instincts. Gonzalez's brass lead flatters 'Blues On The Corner' but tends to muffle Lightsey elsewhere. There are, though, interesting experiments in tone-colour, notably the french horn on 'Nandi' and the augmented percussion (featuring, of all people, Chico Freeman, *sans* saxophone, and Don Moye).

Debriano and Gladden serve the pianist no less well than Moye and McBee in the hived-off Leaders Trio (*q.v.*) but with less emphasis on a democracy of voices; the bassist is often a shade recessed and his role is certainly more functional than McBee's. The earlier and excellent *Isotope* has transferred predictably well to CD, gaining in resolution as a result; the performances are very fine indeed, with an unexpected 'Oleo', some more Monk stylings, and another fine version of Williams's 'Pee Wee' (the CD has 'I'll Never Stop Loving You' as a bonus track).

The immediate inspiration for *From Kirk To Nat* is Nat Cole's wartime piano–guitar–bass trio with Oscar Moore and Johnny Miller (see *The Early Forties*, Fresh Sound FSR CD 139). One of the most copied of piano and vocal stylists, Cole has rarely been imitated successfully, and Lightsey steers well clear of pastiche. His singing on 'Never Let Me Go' and 'Close Enough For Love' is growly and soft, almost spoken, and it draws something from late Chet Baker. On piano he is already individual enough not to risk unconscious echo, and his firm touch on the opening 'You And The Night And The Music' sets the tone for the whole album. Guitarist Eubanks, always more impressive on other people's albums, presents a useful latter-day version of Oscar Moore's single-note runs and softly strummed counter-melodies; it's Rufus Reid who dominates the longest single track, a subtle 'Sophisticated Lady', with a resonant solo that is mixed too loud but which is as purposeful and strongly outlined as anything by Jimmy Blanton.

****** Goodbye Mr Evans**
Evidence 22165 *Lightsey; Tibor Elekes (b); Famoudou Don Moye (d).* 5/94.

There have been many tributes to Bill Evans and this one is so-named only really because of its final track, but Lightsey's humble respect for other musicians suffuses a graceful trio record, with nods to Jimmy Heath, Dave Brubeck, Monk, Coltrane, Shorter (again) and Chopin along the way. Elekes is not well known, but he has the firm, melodic touch of a Red Mitchell or a George Mraz (who may well be a compatriot) and he has the taste to remain quiet when Lightsey explores the bottom end of the scale. Moye is not often heard away from the Art Ensemble, and this is an ideal opportunity to check his colourful and expressive approach, most notably on the sole Lightsey original, 'Habiba'. A very fine, understated record.

Abbey Lincoln (born 1930)

VOCALS

Worked as a singer in California under the name Anna Marie, then began recording for Prestige. Recorded with Max Roach (her husband, 1962–70), but her career faded in the '70s until a revival of interest in Europe in the '80s led to a new and successful contract with Verve. Now a matriarchal influence on a younger generation of female vocalists.

(*) **That's Him!

Original Jazz Classics OJCCD 085 *Lincoln; Kenny Dorham (t); Sonny Rollins (ts); Wynton Kelly (p); Paul Chambers (b); Max Roach (d).* 10/57.

*** **It's Magic**

Original Jazz Classics OJCCD 205 *Lincoln; Kenny Dorham, Art Farmer (t); Curtis Fuller (tb); Benny Golson (ts); Jerome Richardson, Sahib Shihab (bs, f); Wynton Kelly (p); Paul Chambers, Sam Jones (b); Philly Joe Jones (d).* 8/58.

***(*) **Abbey Is Blue**

Original Jazz Classics OJCCD 069 *Lincoln; Kenny Dorham, Tommy Turrentine (t); Julian Priester (tb); Stanley Turrentine (ts); Les Spann (g, f); Wynton Kelly, Cedar Walton, Les Wright (p); Bobby Boswell, Sam Jones (b); Philly Joe Jones, Max Roach (d).* 59.

Lincoln's own emancipation proclamation turned her from a conventional club singer into one of the most dramatic and distinctive voices of the day. To suggest that she owes her creative freedom to one-time husband Max Roach is to say no more than she has herself. Before working with Roach on the powerful *We Insist! Freedom Now Suite*, she had notched up a number of sessions under her own name.

She was never a conventional standards singer, indicating her individuality and occasionally her disaffection in subtle ironies, almost subliminal variations and, even more occasionally, hot blasts of fury. Like John Coltrane and Billie Holiday, she was both respectful of her material and inclined to manipulate it without mercy or apology. 'Afro Blue' with the Max Roach Sextet on *Abbey Is Blue* is one of her strongest performances at any period, though slightly hectoring in tone. The unaccompanied 'Tender As A Rose' on *That's Him!* is more than a little mannered but, like so many Lincoln performances, succeeds through sheer force of personality. Dorham is one of the most naturally vocal of the bop trumpeters and as such is a natural partner, though it's the still underrated Kelly who carries the day, and it's a shame that there are not more voice–piano duets in the catalogue.

*** **Straight Ahead**

Candid CCD 79015 *Lincoln; Booker Little (t); Julian Priester (tb); Eric Dolphy (as, bcl, f); Walter Benton, Coleman Hawkins (ts); Mal Waldron (p); Art Davis (b); Max Roach (d); Roger Sanders, Robert Whitley (perc).* 2/61.

Just look at the line-up. *Straight Ahead* brought together players from two distinct generations in jazz. If Hawkins was the sole representative of older cohorts, he was more than balanced by Little, Priester and Dolphy, who were just beginning to make waves with the turn of the 1960s. Lincoln herself isn't quite on top of her game yet; 'expressive' flatting of notes has to be handled with great care if it isn't to sound like incompetence.

Three tracks stand out: 'When Malindy Sings', based on a Paul Laurence Dunbar poem, a vocalization of 'Blue Monk' (made with the composer's blessing), and the closing 'Retribution', co-written with Julian Priester. This is significantly placed. For the first time, Lincoln seems willing to confront her music rather than stand up-stage of it. 'Retribution' is raw, responsive and aware. It boded well for what was to come.

** **People In Me**

Verve 515246-2 *Lincoln; David Liebman (ts, ss, f); Hiromasa Suzuki (p); Kunimitsu Inaba (b); Al Foster (d); James Mtume Heath (perc).* 6/73.

The one moment where Lincoln's unflinching self-determination founders, rendered null by a ridiculously self-conscious *négritude*. The album finds herself possessed by the spirits of Bessie Smith, Billie Holiday, Betty Carter and even, God bless her, Diana Ross; and, while there is no reason to believe that all these styles can't be subsumed and synthesized, that isn't what's happening here.

Two tracks stand out: Max Roach's 'Living Room', a song that seems to be rooted in real experience, and 'You And Me Love', a Johnny Rotalla song to which Lincoln has written lyrics. The version of Coltrane's 'India' seems less awful with age, but a singer who depends so much on a meaningful lyric needs to be sure that it does mean something before launching off into territory like this.

** **Talking To The Sun**

Enja ENJ 4060 *Lincoln; Steve Coleman (as); James Weidman (p); Bill Johnson (b); Marc Johnson (d); Jerry Gonzalez (perc); Bemshee Shirer, Naima Williams (v).* 11/83.

This is astonishingly passionless and glib, a real low point. One doesn't want to underestimate the level of resistance a musician of Lincoln's stamp must have encountered in the business, but one can only really judge on results, and *Talking To The Sun* touches bottom. Coleman has moments of fire, and voice and saxophone engage in some promising dialogue. Nothing develops, though.

(*) **A Tribute To Billie Holiday

Enja ENJ 6012 *Lincoln; Harold Vick (ts); James Weidman (p); Tarik Shah (b); Marc Johnson (d).* 11/87.

*** **Abbey Sings Billie: Volume 2**

Enja ENJ 7037 *As above.* 11/87.

It isn't clear what is intended here. Lincoln seems torn between paying tribute to her single most obvious influence and subverting it. There are moments, as in an overcooked 'Strange Fruit', when she almost sounds sarcastic, indulging in shifts of pitch and rhythm that in other contexts would require a major change of perspective. 'Lover Man', by contrast, sounds almost dismissive, though the singer's grasp of dynamics has never been more straightforwardly challenged.

If anything, Volume Two is the better. 'God Bless The Child', something of a Holiday crux, is lovingly and creatively revisited, and there may even be a reference to Eric Dolphy's extraordinary solo bass clarinet deconstruction hidden in a few bars of low-register phrasing.

There still isn't more than one solid album's worth of material here. Perhaps Enja might think of editing down.

*** The World Is Falling Down

Verve 843476-2 *Lincoln; Clark Terry (t); Jerry Dodgion, Jackie McLean (as); Alain Jean-Marie (p); Charlie Haden (b); Billy Higgins (d).* 2/90.

A fine return to form. Lincoln came to the notice of a whole new audience when she guested on Steve Williamson's Verve debut, *A Waltz For Grace*, and everything she did from the turn of the decade seemed to be touched with that energy. The combination of Terry and McLean is irresistible and, with the session anchored by Haden and Higgins, it's hard to get the tunes back out of your head. As so often before and since, she manages to acidulate a ballad without making it sound either sardonic or cynical. 'How High The Moon' answers its own question astronomically, and 'African Lady' is perfectly judged.

***(*) You Gotta Pay The Band

Verve Gitanes 511110 *Lincoln; Stan Getz (ts); Hank Jones (p); Charlie Haden (b); Maxine Roach (vla); Marc Johnson (d).* 2/91.

Having once adopted the tough, survivalist persona, Lincoln found it hard to shrug off. This was the first indication that she was also willing to open the shutters a chink and let in a little sunlight and irony. With the sole exception of 'Bird Alone', which is dud, the material is excellent, and it's the sort of band singers will die for. After three previous albums, a word is due for drummer Johnson; not a fire-merchant like Roach or Higgins, but an elegant and subtle performer who knows where to place an accent and how to weight it. Getz was already ailing by this stage, but he still performs with consummate grace; 'A Time For Love' could hardly be improved upon.

*** Devil's Got Your Tongue

Verve 513574-2 *Lincoln; J.J Johnson (tb); Stanley Turrentine (ts); Rodney Kendrick (p); Maxine Roach (vla); Marcus McLaurine (b); Yoron Israel, Grady Tate (d); Keninde O'Uhuru, Sole O'Uhuru, Babatunde Olatunji, Gordy Ryan (perc); The Noel Singers, The Staple Singers (v).* 2/92.

*** When There Is Love

Verve 519697-2 *Lincoln; Hank Jones (p).* 10/92.

Two albums within a year, but exhibiting the greatest possible contrast. *Devil's Got Your Tongue* goes in umpteen directions at once. It also begins to underline growing doubt about Lincoln's direction as a lyricist, never quite managing to combine a sophisticated and faintly surreal language with the urgently inflected repetitions of the blues. 'Story Of My Father' is ponderously rhymed and is marred by bathetic repetitions. Another family story, 'Evelina Coffey (The Legend Of)', fares better, perhaps because it doesn't have the Staple Singers wallpapering the arrangement. Vocally and musically, the material is too dense, almost as if she is trying to recapture the contours of the old Candid sessions, but not recognizing that modern recording and production will tend to swamp arrangements like this. 'People In Me' and 'Rainbow' had been heard before, but these too seem cloyingly sentimental. Only when Lincoln switches to Thad Jones's 'A Child Is Born' and Alex Wilder's lyric do we begin to hear her true voice.

The duets with Jones are not all they might have been. Hank is a superb accompanist, but this isn't one of his better dates. 'C'est Si Bon' is badly misjudged, but the main objection to the set is the mannered way it's been put together: showbizzy segues, big shouters followed by torchy ballads. Abbey tones down her more histrionic excesses, not having to compete with horns or percussion, but she overcompensates in other ways, on occasion enunciating the words as if she was reciting fire exits. A more satisfying set than many, all the same.

**** A Turtle's Dream

Verve Gitanes 527382 *Lincoln; Roy Hargrove (t); Julien Lourau (ts, ss); Kenny Barron, Rodney Kendrick (p); Pat Metheny, Lucky Peterson (g, v); Charlie Haden, Christian McBride (b); Victor Lewis (d); strings.* 5–11/94.

There has been a tension throughout Lincoln's years with Verve between letting her build a band of young, responsive players who can be moulded to her idiosyncratic vision, and surrounding her with established stars on the label's roster. The 1994 album is an almost perfect illustration of the point. One of the joys of the record, as with some of its predecessors, is flicking through and identifying one dream line-up after another – Metheny and house pianist Kendrick, or Metheny and Barron with Haden and Lewis – only to find that the saxophone solo you've just swooned to on 'A Turtle's Dream' or 'Not To Worry' is by the relatively unknown Lourau.

Like Betty Carter, Lincoln has always had the ability to bring on young players. Like every great musician, she has the gift of making everyone around her play better.

***(*) Who Used To Dance

Verve Gitanes 533559 *Lincoln; Graham Haynes (c); Riley T Bandy III, Steve Coleman, Oliver Lake, Frank Morgan, Justin Robinson (as); Julien Lourau (ts); Marc Cary, Rodney Kendrick (p); Michael Bowie, John Ormond (b); Taru Alexander, Alvester Garnett, Aaron Walker (d); Bazzi Bartholomew Gray, Arthur Green (v).* 4–5/96.

This very much picks up where the last album left off, except that it sounds an altogether better-integrated concept. The basic group is Cary, Bowie and Walker, teaming Lincoln with three of the brightest young instrumentalists around. The only track on which they don't appear at all is 'The River', a fantasia whose humour fails to overwhelm a certain melancholy. 'Love What You Doin'' is a big arrangement for three alto saxophones, and fine, terse solos from Coleman, Lake and the as-yet-unknown Bandy. Frank Morgan does alto duty on 'When Autumn Sings', one of two songs by R.B. Lynch. The only dud track is 'Mr Tambourine Man', a good enough idea but executed far too knowingly and redeemed only by Lourau's saxophone. The title-piece is intriguing in that it features tap-dancer Savion Glover, a young man in the great tradition of jazz hoofers, but with moves all his own; don't dismiss the concept out of hand – it works.

Only a label with Verve's resources could possibly put together a session of this range and diversity. The question still remains whether the money wouldn't be better spent letting Abbey hole up with a young group for a few months, try out some gigs, run some song ideas and ditch those that don't shout to be sung again, and only then take it all into the studio. Only then is she going to produce the jazz record that's been threatened for thirty-plus years now.

*****(*) Wholly Earth**

Verve Gitanes 559538 *Lincoln; Nicholas Payton (t, flhn); Marc Cary, James Hurt (p); Bobby Hutcherson (vib, mar); Michael Bowie, John Ormond (b); Alvester Garnett (d); Daniel Moreno (perc); Maggie Brown (v).* 6/98.

The pairing of Lincoln with vibist Hutcherson is irresistible, two entirely opposite rhythmic concepts working together more comfortably than they have a right to. Abbey's reworking of the Johnny Mercer–Lionel Hampton song, 'Midnight Sun', is one of the truly great things in her catalogue. The title-track, which follows, is one of only a couple which don't include Bobby, but it illustrates her ability to invest a slightly banal, almost poppy idea with unmistakable conviction.

The voice is now so confidently intimate, so easily conversational, that it becomes difficult to think of Lincoln in terms of 'performance'. Her ability to make large harmonic shifts and reshuffle the tempo allows considerable leeway in the songs 'Conversation With A Baby' and 'Caged Bird', both of which sound considerably less artful than they actually are.

Cary continues to offer sympathetic support, and the pairing of Ormond and Garnett is tailor-made for Abbey's laid-back approach. The group interplay on 'If I Only Had A Brain' is a model for anyone attempting vocal jazz of this sort.

Lincoln Center Jazz Orchestra

GROUP

Founded by Wynton Marsalis as part of his artistic input at Lincoln Center in New York, this repertory orchestra tackles the jazz of the past on today's terms – as they see it.

****(*) Portraits By Ellington**

Columbia 472814-2 *Marcus Belgrave (t, flhn); Wynton Marsalis, Umar Sharif, Lew Soloff, John Longo (t); Art Baron, Britt Woodman, Wycliffe Gordon (tb); Chuck Connors (btb); Michael White (cl); Bill Easley (cl, ts); Frank Wess, Norris Turney (as); Todd Williams (ts); Joe Temperley (bs); Sir Roland Hanna (p); Steve Nelson (vib); Andy Stein (vn); Paul Meyers (g); Reginald Veal (b); Kenny Washington (d); Milt Grayson (v).* 8/91.

While this must be an exhilarating experience in a concert situation (where it was recorded), on CD it emerges as a sometimes pointless exercise in re-creating some eventful Ellington scores. Whatever sleeve-note writer Stanley Crouch claims, too much of the music here sounds like slavish duplication, especially the three themes from 'New Orleans Suite'. The sound may be better engineered than on most Ellington albums, and the best things happen when the orchestra musters a resonant grandeur of delivery, but there are no new insights into Ellington's music. Among the soloists, Todd Williams tries to come on as both Paul Gonsalves and Coleman Hawkins and succeeds in sounding like nobody in particular, while Wynton does a credible Cootie Williams on 'Portrait Of Louis Armstrong'. The best music comes in the 'Liberian Suite', where vocalist Grayson's sonorous baritone is startling. Overall, though, this is nothing like as good as the American Jazz Orchestra's Ellington tribute.

***** The Fire Of The Fundamentals**

Columbia 474348-2 *Wynton Marsalis, Joe Wilder, Marcus Belgrave, Umar Sharif (t); Britt Woodman, Wycliffe Gordon, Freddie Lonzo (tb); Michael White (cl); Jimmy Heath (ss); Charles McPherson, Norris Turney, Wessell Anderson, Jerry Dodgion (as); Todd Williams, Frank Wess, Bill Easley (ts); Joe Temperley (bs); Marcus Roberts, Cyrus Chestnut, Kenny Barron, Mulgrew Miller (p); Don Vappie (g); Reginald Veal, Curtis Lundy, Chris Thomas (b); Herlin Riley, Lewis Nash, Clarence Penn, Kenny Washington (d); Betty Carter, Milt Grayson (v).* 7/92–2/93.

***** They Came To Swing**

Columbia 477284-2 *As above, except add Lew Soloff, Jon Faddis, Nicholas Payton, Marcus Printup, Ryan Kisor, Russell Gunn, Roger Ingram (t), Art Baron, Jamal Haynes, Ronald Westray (tb), Herb Harris (ss), Jesse Davis (as), Joshua Redman, Victor Goines, Robert Stewart, Walter Blanding Jr (ts), James Carter (bs), Kent Jordan (picc), Sir Roland Hanna, Eric Reed (p), Billy Higgins (d); omit Wilder, Sharif, Lonzo, White, Heath, McPherson, Turney, Wess, Chestnut, Barron, Miller, Vappie, Lundy, Penn, Washington, Carter.* 10/92–4/94.

Though the 'official' Orchestra is responsible for much of the music on these two discs, they're really various-artists albums accredited to 'Jazz At Lincoln Center', with material culled from a number of shows, some of them by the Orchestra on tour. *Fire Of The Fundamentals* stretches from piano solos to big-band episodes. Kenny Barron's 'Trinkle Tinkle' is terrific and Marcus Roberts does all right by 'Bolivar Blues', but his version of Morton's 'The Crave' is a massacre. Betty Carter's group follow her through her gorgeous set-piece, 'You're Mine You', and Michael White leads the New Orleans homies on 'Jungle Blues'. The Marsalis group tackle two chunks of classic repertory and Wynton just gets away with his Miles parts on 'Flamenco Sketches', while the Orchestra close on a rare piece of Strayhorn, 'Multi-Colored Blue'. An entertaining mixed bag. *They Came To Swing* is more consistently about the big band, though some of the repertory is ponderous: a hugely overheated 'Black And Tan Fantasy' at a tempo Ellington would never have allowed, and a similarly melodramatic 'Things To Come'. Better is Marsalis's fast, funny locomotion sketch, 'Express Crossing', and Grayson does his Eckstine bit in 'Jelly, Jelly'. Rich and sonorous at its best, the Orchestra is quite something, but these are more like show souvenirs.

***** Live In Swing City – Swingin' With Duke**

Columbia CK 69898 *Wynton Marsalis, Marcus Printup, Ryan Kisor, Seneca Black (t); Wycliffe Gordon, Ronald Westray, Wayne Goodman (tb); Wessell Anderson, Ted Nash (as); Victor Goines (ts, cl); Walter Blanding Jr, Illinois Jacquet (ts); Joe Temperley (bs); Cyrus Chestnut (p); Rodney Whitaker (b); Herlin Riley (d); Dianne Reeves, Milt Grayson (v).* 12/98.

Recorded to cue up the Ellington centenary celebrations, this is the LCJO making a return visit to the repertoire on their less-than-enthralling debut CD. It's better, but not much better. Whitaker and Riley can be terrific small-group players but they don't swing this orchestra, and there's a self-congratulatory feel to many of the set-pieces and solos which Ellington would have grimaced at. Grayson is as enjoyably ripe as ever in 'Multi Colored Blue' although listeners will be divided over that one, and Reeves is wasted on 'Bli-Blip'. Ellingtonians have tut-tutted over the record, but it has its enjoyable aspects – when the sections swing into a familiar passage, there's some real exhilaration.

Ove Lind (1926–91)

CLARINET

Born in Stockholm, Lind played in swing-styled small groups such as the Swinging Swedes in the early '50s, as well as in his own sextet (1956–62). After some years away from jazz, he helped spearhead a revival of interest in swing mainstream in the '60s and '70s.

****** One Morning In May**

Phontastic PHONTCD 7501 *Lind; Bengt Hallberg (p); Lars Estrand (vib); Staffan Broms (g); Arne Wilhelmsson (b); Egil Johansen (d). 4/75–5/76.*

*****(*) Summer Night**

Phontastic PHONTCD 7503 *As above. 4/75–5/76.*

There was something of a revival of swing-styled jazz in Sweden in the 1970s, a rehabilitation of a manner that Swedish musicians had helped to pioneer in Europe the first time around, and these records – the very first Phontastic LPs, now transferred to CD – are mildly historic in their way. They're also very fine, irresistibly swinging small-group sessions. Lind was cast entirely in Benny Goodman's image and was proud of it. There are obvious echoes of the Goodman small-band records, but an extra degree of inventiveness takes this well beyond any copycat concept. Hallberg and Estrand are inspired throughout, thinking almost telepathically when their improvisations run together, and the utterly relaxed pulse of the rhythm section is both unobtrusive and indispensable. Little to choose between the two records, but *One Morning In May* has a slight edge for the freshness of the material as it features standards of a less familiar stripe.

John Lindberg (born 1959)

DOUBLE BASS

As a nineteen-year-old, Lindberg was a member of the Human Arts Ensemble with Charles Bobo Shaw and Joe Bowie. Later associations included a demanding stint in Anthony Braxton's group and charter membership of the String Trio of New York. In recent years, he has become increasingly prominent as a composer.

****** Dimension 5**

Black Saint 120062 *Lindberg; Hugh Ragin (t, picc t); Marty Ehrlich (as, f); Billy Bang (vn); Thurman Barker (d). 2/81.*

Lindberg jumped to notice 20 years ago with a solo recording for the Leo label and since then has produced a steady sequence of thoughtful, intelligent records. This is not the sort of music you're going to hear in a club or bar; it repays attention and repeated hearings. Its very calm and orderliness may sometimes count against it, but Lindberg also knows how to harness musical chaos.

Dimension 5 is a live recording from New York City with a working group centred on two pairs of winds and strings. Bang and Lindberg do most of their head-to-head stuff on the opening 'Eleven Thrice', leaving the shorter middle numbers, 'Twixt C And D', as ensemble pieces. The sound is far from ideal, betwixt CD and some other carrier, very fuzzy at the lower end and decidedly peaky and percussive when Ragin and Ehrlich hit the upper registers.

Untypically for a bassist, Lindberg is a miniaturist, most successful when on a restricted canvas and dealing in tiny, almost calligraphic gestures. It's a style that was often lost on vinyl, not just the outer shadows, but some of the smaller motions as well.

*****(*) Trilogy Of Works For Eleven Instrumentalists**

Black Saint 120082 *Lindberg; Hugh Ragin (t); Mike Mossman (t, picc t); Ray Anderson (tb); Vincent Chancey (frhn); Marty Ehrlich (as, f, picc); J.D Parran (ts, cl); Pablo Calogero (bs); Alan Jaffe (g); Eric Watson (p); Thurman Barker (d, perc, xyl). 9/84.*

Large-scale works of considerable sophistication that perhaps steer Lindberg away from jazz proper and towards the new music end of his bag. The closing 'Dresden Moods' is too long and episodic in this version, but it contains some beautiful voicings. The opening 'Holler' is more direct and again suggests a synthesis of classic jazz and new wave ideas. The whole band plays well and is beautifully caught by engineer Gennaro Garone, with the balance of brass and woodwinds exactly right and in perspective. It seems unlikely that Lindberg will have many opportunities to record on this scale, so the record is to be valued all the more.

****** Luminosity**

Music & Arts CD 970 *Lindberg (b solo). 2/92, 8/96.*

Bassist David Izenzon died suddenly in 1979. He had attained a certain celebrity in Ornette Coleman's Golden Circle trio with Charles Moffett, and he also recorded with Paul Motian before devoting himself to a second career as a psychiatrist, specializing in the rehabilitation of marijuana abusers, and to the care of his brain-damaged son, Solomon. Lindberg helped in the boy's care while he was studying contrabass with Izenzon, which doubtless helped to cement the association.

Some of the material on *Luminosity*, which is a tribute to Lindberg's teacher, was written during their years of contact; other pieces are more recent. As he points out, neither 'In My Mind's Eye' nor the enigmatically titled 'I Am A Leaf For Today', both Izenzon compositions, was originally written with solo bass performance in mind, but as regular jazz songs with chord changes, melodies and even lyrics. They work fine in this context, though, as do Lindberg's own more obviously idiomatic ideas. 'Utter Sanity' and the closing title-piece are the most substantial, the latter a long-after recollection of a lost friend and mentor. There is just one standard, 'Softly As In A Morning Sunrise', which nails the suggestion that Lindberg is incapable (as was said of Izenzon as well) of playing a swinging line.

****** Dodging Bullets**

Black Saint 120108 *Lindberg; Albert Mangelsdorff (tb); Eric Watson (p). 6/92.*

*****(*) Quartet Afterstorm**

Black Saint 120162 *As above, except add Ed Thigpen (d).* 94.

*****(*) Resurrection Of A Dormant Soul**

Black Saint 120172 *As above.* 2/95.

The deleted *Give And Take* with George Lewis is one of the best things in Lindberg's catalogue, suggesting that he relishes playing against the broad legato lines and the full, low-end timbre. Like the Lewis date, these are wonderfully open and uncluttered, and they suggest a fruitful synthesis between Lindberg's more avant-garde approach and a jazz tradition. Mangelsdorff is one of the true stars of European jazz, but there is nothing abstractly 'European' in his strong-toned playing or in writing like 'Dots, Ditches and Scratches' on *Resurrection* … The addition of Thigpen on *Quartet Afterstorm* and the later record is as effective as it is unexpected. No sense that any of this is chamber jazz, but Ed's rootsy, funky approach slots in without a join. He solos joyously on 'X.1' and brings in his own 'E.T.P.' to the *Resurrection* date, and Lindberg turns into Ray Brown before your startled ears. A splendid group of records.

****** Bounce**

Black Saint 120192 *Lindberg; Dave Douglas (t); Larry Ochs (sax); Ed Thigpen (d).* 2/97.

The new Lindberg Ensemble combines advanced ideas with sheer firepower. Thigpen's designation as 'Mr Taste' doesn't prevent him from cutting loose on occasion, but here he keeps the reins fairly tight, suggesting contained energy, but rarely breaking out into the open. Douglas's contribution is as distinctive and idiosyncratic as ever. His use of extended technique and non-standard timbres, some of them remarkably close to saxophone tonality, is a constant delight and his soloing on these taxing themes is perceptive to a degree not even suspected from his own recordings. 'Fortone On A Sphere' and 'The Terrace' are the two main pieces. Each negotiates a path between through-composition and improvisational freedom. Lindberg himself sounds roomy and relaxed and the recording gives due weight to each individual voice. A further step in a fascinating career.

Nils Lindberg (born 1933)

PIANO

A giant of Swedish jazz through his composing and pianism, Lindberg has also worked as a composer in modern classical idioms, and his jazz recordings are comparatively few. He also pioneered the coupling of traditional Swedish music with jazz expression.

****** Sax Appeal & Trisection**

Dragon DRCD220 *Lindberg; Jan Allan, Idrees Sulieman, Lars Samuelsson (t); Sven-Olof Walldoff, Eje Thelin (tb); Rolf Billberg (as); Harry Backlund, Allan Lundstrom (ts); Lars Gullin (bs); Sture Nordin (b); Olle Holmqvist (tba); Sture Kallin, Conny Svensson (d).* 2/60–1/63.

*****(*) Symphony No. 1 & Jazz From Studio A**

Dragon DRCD 331 *Lindberg; Jan Allan, Benny Bailey (t); Ake Persson (tb); Rolf Billberg (as); Bjarne Nerem, Harry Bäcklund (ts); Lars Gullin, Erik Nilsson (bs); Sture Nordin, George Riedel (b); Sture Kallin, Egil Johansen (d); Swedish Radio Orchestra.* 6/61–8/63.

*****(*) Saxes Galore / Brass Galore**

Bluebell ABCD 3004 *Lindberg; Jan Allan, Allan Botschinsky, Markku Johansson (t, flhn); Torgny Nilsson (tb); Sven Larsson (btb, tba); Herb Geller (as, ss, f); Claes Rosendahl (ts, f); Bernt Rosengren (ts, as, f); Lennart Aberg, Erik Nilsson (bs, f); Mads Vinding, Red Mitchell (b); Rune Carlsson (d).* 5/79–5/81.

*****(*) Melody In Blue**

Dragon DRCD 245 *Lindberg; Anders Paulson (ss, ts); Johan Horlen (as); Joakim Milder, Krister Andersson (ts); Charlie Malmberg (bs); Jan Adefeld (b); Bengt Stark (d).* 5/93.

*****(*) Lindberg Mitchell Paulsson**

LCM C-128 *Lindberg; Anders Paulsson (ss); Dan Almgren, Torbjorn Bernhardsson (vn); Hans Lindstrom (vla); Ulrika Edstrom (clo); Red Mitchell (b).* 92.

***** Alone With My Melodies**

Dragon DRCD 277 *Lindberg (p solo).* 4/95.

Nils Lindberg plays piano, but what he loves to do is to write for horns, especially saxophones. His current CD listing has a rather unique distinction in that he has written saxophone records for three generations of Swedish reed players. The first, *Sax Appeal*, has been reissued in tandem with the slightly later *Trisection* on a single Dragon CD. In Jan Olsson's words, Lindberg's sound is 'the sound of Swedish summer nights and 52nd Street at the same time' – although, more accurately, it's the timbre of West Coast saxes that he gets here and on the later *Saxes Galore*. There are superb sequences not only for the whole section but also for Gullin and Billberg, and the subsequent *Trisection* brings in brass for a Gil Evans-like exploration of timbre.

The first track, 'Curbits', turns up again as the first on *Saxes Galore*, where Lindberg repeated his formula with another all-sax team, and this time inveigled a genuine West Coast man (Herb Geller) to participate. The sound he gets out of the section is a haunting drift that seems to float between traditions, with solos emerging from the ensemble like smoke drifting through clear, cold air. *Brass Galore* is coupled with this session on the Bluebell reissue: not quite as impressive, but there are still some inventive charts here, especially the 3/4 ballad, 'Waltz For Anne-Marie'.

The *Symphony No. 1* was a commission from Swedish television (those were the days). Lasse Sarri's very entertaining notes recall all the circumstances surrounding the preparation of the music (such as Lars Gullin's hospitalization, which meant he had to walk into the recording completely unprepared), yet they do not prepare one for the lovely freshness of the score and the uncomplicated melding of the soloists with the radio orchestra. Lindberg's writing might not always stand up to the most merciless scrutiny, but it is beautifully realized by the players, and at this distance is effortlessly nostalgic of a different time in European music-making. Making up the CD are five tracks from another all-but-impromptu session for Stockholm television, two years earlier, comprising five warm-natured tracks by a septet with Bailey, Billberg, Persson and Nerem in the front line. Hard to resist.

Melody In Blue puts together a third reed team, made up of the latest generation of Swedish saxophonists, and, if anything, this sounds like the best of the three, given a modern studio mix and vivid, energetic playing from all hands. One or two of the pieces sound comparatively ordinary, and Lindberg doesn't always set out to have the band swing; but 'Blue Bop' defies that judgement, and in the extraordinary miniature of 'Polska With All My Love' – once a student work of Lindberg's – the poise of the playing is breathtaking.

Lindberg Mitchell Paulsson is a typically beautiful session from this supreme melodist. Lindberg arranges parts for a string quartet, has old friend Mitchell (on one of his final dates) play a roving bass line, and adds embellishments by himself and the lyrical voice of saxophonist Paulsson. There are several pieces inspired by Swedish folksong, from the Dalarna district, plus reworkings of two pieces from his 'Seven Darlecarlian Pictures' and some new originals. Where other Scandinavian composers get an autumnal chill from their heritage, Lindberg seems to find only warmth and light. The charm and radiance of these settings is very hard to resist.

His solo piano album is a slow and reflective set, a bit ponderous in parts, and perhaps one of those records which means more to the maker than to his audience. Worth hearing, though, for his deeply felt 'In Memoriam', the piece he wrote on the untimely death of Rolf Billberg in 1966 – which brings this discography full circle for now.

Lasse Lindgren

TRUMPET

Swedish trumpeter working in a midstream between post-bop and fusion.

***** To My Friends**

Dragon DRCD 227 *Lindgren; Mikael Raberg (tb); Esbjorn Svensson (ky); Jan Adefelt (b); Raymond Karlsson (d).* 4/92.

Walking a line between post-bop and something like abstruse jazz-funk on some tracks, Lindgren's group keep their options attractively open. The leader has a good tone – which even comes through on the couple of points when he uses a little electronic alteration – and in tandem with the splendidly forceful Raberg he creates an all-brass front line that bounces off the rather hard rhythms of the trio. Svensson's lyrical side comes out to good effect on the slow tunes, and in 'Two Bass Fishers Walking Down The Line' and 'Ice Eyes' they fashion some plausible impressionism.

Magnus Lindgren

TENOR SAXOPHONE, FLUTE

Young Swedish saxophonist with a post-modern take on post-bop.

***** Way Out**

Caprice 21609 *Lindgren; Patrik Skogh, Magnus Thorell (t); Karin Hammar (tb); Magnus Petersson (frhn); Mathias Algotsson (p); Fredrik Jonsson (b); Jonas Holgersson (d).* 5/99.

A good record, but Lindgren suffers from an overabundance of knowing: he makes these themes seem flimsy, even jokey. A flippant flute-run through 'Polka Dots And Moonbeams' and the closing saunter across 'Goodbye Pork Pie Hat' find him all but making fun of the tradition, but with nothing to put in its place. The originals, though, have a pinch more substance in their treatments: the other four horns are used as a sparky chorus on their few appearances, and the rhythm section is strong and alert. Lindgren seems to use the flute as a kind of novelty instrument, but his tenor playing shows a commanding technique.

Jeannette Lindstrom

VOCAL

A Swedish composer-vocalist performing songs that touch on jazz and other areas of popular song.

*****(*) Another Country**

Caprice CAP 21480 *Lindstrom; Orjan Hulten (ss, ts); Torbjorn Gulz (p); Dan Berglund (b); Magnus Ostrom (d).* 6/95.

*****(*) I Saw You**

Caprice CAP 21549 *As above, except Christian Spering (b), Anders Kjellberg (d) replace Berglund and Ostrom.* 6/97.

As a performer, Lindstrom belongs rather more to the world of art-song than to jazz, and her compositions – with lyrics by Robert Creeley, Steve Dobrogosz and Elizabeth Bishop, as well as her own – sit a little awkwardly beside the handful of standards on the first disc. But there is nothing wrong with the music or the interpretations on either disc. Lindstrom has a rather flighty voice which she controls very carefully, and on quieter pieces like 'My Hands' and Radka Toneff's 'It Don't Come Easy' she can be surprisingly moving. The first disc starts with Frank Loesser's 'Never Will I Marry' and when, at the other end of the record, she does a version of 'Wives And Lovers', it's almost a sour bit of irony: but it works. Both records sustain such an equivocal mood that it's almost impossible to choose between them, and the two quartets are wonderfully responsive and *simpatico* with the singer; but perhaps the second, with its intoxicating title-track and Steve Dobrogosz's lyric for 'Stockholm', which will surely strike a chord with anyone who has visited the city, has the edge.

Rudy Linka

GUITAR

Hard to categorize, Linka draws on mainstream jazz guitar, folk and classical elements, with an occasional rock tinge to his electric work.

***** Czech It Out!**

Enja ENJ 9001-2 *Linka; George Mraz (b); Marvin 'Smitty' Smith (d).* 94.

*****(*) Always Double Czech**

Enja ENJ 9301-2 *As above.* 1/96.

The check/cheque/Czech puns are going to run thin very quickly, but it seems unlikely that the versatile Linka will run out of ideas. The talented Czech has apparently made six records under his own name. These are the only ones we know and are the only ones likely to be widely available. He convened a brilliant trio for his

Enja debut. Mraz is the most purely singing of bassists, certainly since the death of Red Mitchell, and he works an indefinable magic with the guitarist, whether Linka is playing smooth but faintly acidic chords or single-note lines. Smitty is his usual bustling self, perhaps a little too insistent on the first record, in terms both of his playing and his position in an unnecessarily democratic mix; guitar, particularly gut-strung, is apt to be swamped in a context like this.

The balance and the material both seem better judged on *Always Double Czech*. As before, it's a mixture of new and standard material, again coloured by any number of musical styles, from folk to classical. 'Come Rain Or Come Shine' is a moment of relaxation in the middle of a terse and sometimes quite clipped performance. Again, it's Mraz who provides much of the romance, but Linka imposes himself with authority and good humour. We hardly need say that he's well worth checking out.

Jukka Linkola (born 1955)

KEYBOARDS

Swedish composer who works in mixed-media and contemporary composition, at least as often as in a more formal jazz environment.

****(*) Jukka Linkola Octet**

Hi-Hat HICD 2 *Linkola; Esko Heikkinen (t); Tom Bildo (tb); Pentti Lahti, Teemu Salminen (reeds); Ilkka Hanski (b); Jukkis Uotila, Upi Sorvali (d); Mongo Aaltonen (perc).* 79–82.

***** Pegasos**

Imogena IGCD 050 *Linkola; Lars Lindgren, Jan Eliasson, Hildegunn Oiseth, Jan Anders Berger (t, flhn); Mikael Raberg, Christer Olofsson, Ralph Soovik (tb); Niclas Rydh (btb); Miklas Robertsson, Sven Fridolfsson, Erik Norstrom, Michael Karlsson, Janne Forslund (reeds); Jan Zirk (ky); Staffan William-Olsson (g); Yasuhito Mori, Fredrik Bergman (b); Marko Timonen (d).* 11/93.

****(*) Libau**

Syrene CD-5 *Linkola; Pentti Lahti (saxes); Antti Murto (ky); Markku Kanerva (g); Juha Tikka (b); Anssi Nykanen (d); Anna-Mari Kahara, Kaarle Manila (v).*

Linkola's sympathies aren't only with jazz: he's written operas, ballet and chamber music. The octet session is hardly an exciting discovery: a few good solos by an accomplished team can't overcome the foursquare arrangements and rhythm charts which are painfully clenched. *Pegasos* is a sequence of pieces for the Bohuslan Big Band – something of a co-operative between Swedish and Finnish musicians – and an extension of his work for his touring eight- and ten-piece groups. The round dozen arrangements are performed with great enthusiasm by the orchestra, and it's a pity there isn't more going on inside them. Linkola's melodies are a bit thin and he tends to let his guard down when leaving space for a soloist: several of the themes are no more than a tissue surrounding whoever steps out of the ensemble. He's interested in the texture of electric keyboards, so Zirk's parts are important, and on a few tunes – 'Boogie Woogie Waltz' and 'Syrene' – the music assumes more substance.

Libau is a fun fusion record by Linkola's band, EQ. 'Ne Me Nah Wah Ya' is a sly pastiche of one of Zawinul's world-jazz chants and, though a lot of the rest sounds like either nature-film music or elongated jingles, Linkola obviously has a sense of humour about it.

Staffan Linton (born 1916)

PIANO

Though seldom encountered outside of Swedish jazz circles, Linton worked in London as long ago as the 1940s. He plays in a modest distillation of swing and bebop styles.

***** Unfinished Affair**

Dragon DRCD 193 *Linton; Yasuhito Mori (b); Christian Jormin (d).* 3/90.

Linton spent some of his formative years abroad and actually broadcast for the BBC in the 1940s, cutting a few sides for Decca in 1948. He didn't make another record, though, until *Nevergreen* in 1984, which is still awaited on CD. That album had some problems, but they were overcome on the engaging *Unfinished Affair*. Jormin provides just the right balance of drive and sensitivity, and the session is beautifully recorded. The youthful gaiety of 'Song For Judith' belies Linton's age, and the trio even concoct a reggae-like syncopation for 'Heart Beat'. The leader composes plain but often affecting minor-key melodies, and the music is a refreshing antidote to the busy, overwrought attack of many contemporary pianists.

Booker Little (1938–61)

TRUMPET

Born in Memphis and started as part of that community of players, though he went to Chicago in 1957 and subsequently joined Max Roach, then Eric Dolphy. A career of great promise was cut short by his death from uraemia.

***** Booker Little 4 And Max Roach**

Blue Note 84457 *Little; Louis Smith (t); Frank Strozier (as); George Coleman (ts); Tommy Flanagan, Phineas Newborn (p); Calvin Newborn (g); Art Davis, George Joyner (Jamil Nasser) (b); Charles Crosby, Max Roach (d).* 58.

*****(*) Out Front**

Candid 9027 *Little; Julian Priester (tb); Eric Dolphy (as, bcl, f); Don Friedman (p); Ron Carter, Art Davis (b); Max Roach (d, timp, vib).* 3 & 4/61.

Some artists are simply in a hurry. It is probably pointless to mourn the waste and loss. With Booker Little, though, a scant 23 years really does seem like short change. More than Fats Navarro, more even than Clifford Brown, who put his stamp on the young man's bright, resonant sound and staunchless flow of ideas. What occasionally sounds like hesitancy, even inaccuracy in the harmonic language is probably something more positive, a rethinking of the syntax of bebop, parallel to what his friend and associate, Eric Dolphy, was doing. There was precious little chance to find out. When a creative life is as short as this one was, almost every survival is of value. The shapeless and technically flawed jams on 'Blue'N'Boogie' and 'Things Ain't What They Used To Be' on the Blue Note session would probably not be considered worth releasing if there had been more material around. (Even now, some good stuff on Time and the limited edition Jazz View is out of catalogue.) As it is, out-takes are required to fill out the picture to an undesirable degree, some of them falling short of the standard even the youthful trumpeter would have expected. The Blue Note reissue pairs him with fellow Memphisite George Coleman in a state-of-the-art 1950s front line that on tracks like 'Dungeon Waltz' and 'Jewel's Tempo' – both Little compositions – suggests something like what Ornette Coleman and Don Cherry (and Bobby Bradford) were doing over over on the West Coast. The whole set is marred by technical problems, though, which blunt its impact. There are showers of static and Flanagan's piano is signficantly under-recorded.

Out Front is one of the best albums of the period, and not just because it also adds a brick to the Dolphy discography. The opening 'We Speak' is a relatively straightforward blowing theme, but the balance of tonalities and the use of abrasive dissonance evokes Ornette's *Free Jazz* experiment, which was recorded a bare four months before, and about which Dolphy would surely have talked and enthused. Little and Roach are once again the axis of the music. The drummer adds timps and vibes to his armoury, and this makes up somewhat for the shortcomings in Don Friedman's playing, but it blurs the bass lines to the extent that one wonders whether some of this material might not have been done just with horns and percussion, a radical notion for the time but perfectly feasible, given the architecture of the music. The shifting signature of 'Moods In Free Time' stretches Little's phrasing and 'Hazy Hues' explores his interest in tone-colour. The closing 'A New Day', with its hints of freedom and its fanfare-like acclamations, is an ironic end to a short career, albeit a wonderfully positive one.

The Little Ramblers

GROUP

Basically a studio group which grew out of the parent band, the California Ramblers, originally organized by Ed Kirkeby, and involving some of the many session players in New York in the 1920s.

***** The Little Ramblers 1924–1927**

Timeless CBC 1-037 *Bill Moore, Red Nichols, Roy Johnston, Chelsea Quealey (t); Tommy Dorsey, Herb Winfield, Abe Lincoln (tb); Jimmy Dorsey (cl, as); Bobby Davis (cl, ss, as); Adrian Rollini (bsx, gfs); Irving Brodsky (p); Tommy Felline, Ray Kitchingman (bj); Stan King (d, kz, v); Herb Weil (d); Billy Jones, Arthur Fields, Ed Kirkeby (v). 9/24–7/27.*

The 'small' edition of the California Ramblers had the same pretensions as the principal orchestra – to play dance tunes of the day as warmly as possible – and because it was a leaner outfit their records were often hotter than those of the bigger Ramblers. This was the name they used, at any rate, on their Columbia sessions, capably collected and truthfully remastered here. Titles such as 'In Your Green Hat' and 'Those Panama Mamas' are these days recalled only by era connoisseurs, but a glance through the listing will tell anyone familiar with the field that these are all game and politely swinging performances that are liberally sprinkled with the kind of pertly inventive solos which the New Yorkers of the day could produce to order for eight or sixteen bars. Nichols and the Dorseys are the obvious names, but the true Ramblers stalwarts were Chelsea Quealey, Bobby Davis and Adrian Rollini, and they all turn in typically bright work. The first six tracks are acoustic, but the big sound of the electrical sessions is a nice reminder of how good the Columbia engineers were at that time.

Martin Litton (born 1957)

PIANO

Litton has worked in and around the established circle of British trad-to-mainstream for 20 years, with stints in the touring groups of Kenny Ball and Humphrey Lyttelton.

***** Falling Castle**

Asman Jazz 001 *Litton (p solo). n.d.*

Litton is a clever and accomplished practitioner of early jazz piano methods. His stride playing is rather light and graceful, seldom resorting to the hammer-fisted approach, and in the original 'Litton On The Keys' he even suggests a link between the Harlem stride masters and the 'novelty' pianists of the same period. 'Limehouse Blues' is busy in a scurrying way. 'Alice Blue Gown' is amusingly knocked about. 'For Rebekah' is a fetching piece of impressionism which ends the record on a note that Litton might well explore at greater length. The record is sometimes a victim of its own unemphatic nature and slips into the background, but it's a pleasing recital.

Fredrik Ljungkvist

TENOR, ALTO AND SOPRANO SAXOPHONES

Contemporary Swedish post-bop saxophonist.

***** Fallin' Papers**

Dragon DCD 267 *Ljungkvist; Torbjorn Gulz (p); Filip Augustson (b); Bo Soderberg (d). 8/94.*

A thoughtful set of originals, mostly by the leader and Gulz, although bassist Augustson sneaks in what might be the best tune in 'You Always Remember How'. Much of it is in the style of sombre lyricism which often characterizes music from this quarter, yet the unexpectedly spry 'Vilse I Fororten' is a smart change of pace. The title-track is an overwrought requiem, and Ljungkvist plays nothing that is strikingly individual, but there's much to enjoy in its cool way.

Charles Lloyd (born 1938)

TENOR SAXOPHONE, FLUTE, TIBETAN OBOE

There has been a tendency to suggest that Charles Lloyd appeared on the stage of the Fillmore West fully formed, like any one of the pop performers who were breaking into the West Coast scene in and around the Summer of Love. The truth is that the almost thirty-year-old Memphian had already had a rugged training and apprenticeship, with Gerald Wilson and Chico Hamilton and in the company of some of the most advanced musicians on the Coast. It's a strange-looking career now: pop adulation followed by silence and near-retirement followed by a latter-day re-emergence with a dark new sound.

****** Just Before Sunrise**
32 Jazz 327135 *Lloyd; Keith Jarrett (p); Cecil McBee, Ron McClure (b); Jack DeJohnette (d).* 66, 67.

*****(*) Journey Within / In Europe**
Collectables COL CD 6236 *As above.* 66, 67.

****(*) The Flowering Of The Original Charles Lloyd Quartet**
Collectables COL CD 6285. *As above, except omit McClure.* 7 & 10/66.

***** Forest Flower / Soundtrack**
Atlantic/Rhino 8122 71746 *As above, except add Ron McClure(b).* 2/67, 11/68.

***** Soundtrack / In The Soviet Union**
Collectables COL CD 6237 *As above.* 5/67, 11/68.

For a time Lloyd was so terminally uncool it was almost embarrassing to mention his name in mixed company. However, the leader who launched the careers of both Keith Jarrett and Jack DeJohnette, and who later was to propel Michel Petrucciani into a world-striding career, is worthy of a second look; since our last edition most of the work which established his career and reputation has returned to the catalogue. All to the good, and an intriguing balance to his recent records.

At one time, Lloyd was, along with Miles Davis, considered the saviour of jazz, the only performer who could get young people weaned on the Dead and the Airplane to attend a jazz gig, and he did, at the Fillmores especially. If he was the token jazzer of Haight-Ashbury, he more than kept the lamp alight and the jazz was often of very high quality. *Just Before Sunrise* pairs the two indispensable Lloyd records, the live *Love-In* which was recorded at the Fillmore West, and the marvellous *Dream Weaver* from the year before. What is immediately surprising is how thoroughly steeped in the language of John Coltrane Lloyd sounds at this point. 'Bird Flight' with its magnificent Jarrett solo, 'Love Ship' and the exquisite groove of 'Sombrero Sam' attest to a soloist and leader who managed to assimilate Trane's harmonics with pop prettiness. DeJohnette was a stunningly good beat drummer, and if this sounds curiously two-edged praise, consider how much of his later work owes to Ringo and Charlie Watts, as well as to Max Roach and Elvin Jones.

There is an unmistakable whiff of patchouli and joss around *Love-In*, and not just by association. It's a less inventive record all round, but the opening sequence of 'Tribal Dance' and 'Temple Bells' catches its moment just right, and Lloyd's flute reading of the Beatles' 'Here, There And Everywhere' is one of those rare occasions when the Fabs and the jazz fraternity did seem to speak the same language; it's the only tune the audience recognizes and they applaud themselves generously. Who says the '60s was all about amnesia? Inevitably looser and less generously recorded, *Love-In* still stands a monument to a special moment in American musical culture and easily passes the test of time.

Lloyd knew what a talent he had in Keith Jarrett and was generous with solo and unaccompanied spots; rich glimpses of future promise on 'Sunday Morning', an experiment repeated on 'Love No. 3', his feature on *Journey Within.* The album – also recorded in concert – also introduces Jarrett as a soprano saxophonist a year before his multi-instrumentalism was given its first full airing on his own *Restoration Ruin.* 'Lonesome Child' is a complex, multi-layered composition that requires concentration and flair from all four performers. 'Memphis Green' is a much more downhome idea, a nod back to the kind of stuff Lloyd grew up with in his home town.

In Europe was yet another live record, taped in Oslo in front of a crowd who were waking up fast to the new thing in both pop and jazz. 'Tagore' and 'Karma' underline how close Lloyd still was to the spiritualized voice of John Coltrane, but it's a looser and less assured performance than some. Perhaps the strain of touring – and by this stage the Quartet was mega – was taking its toll.

The opening 'Autumn Sequence' of *Dream Weaver* attests to Lloyd's interest in longer-form composition. On the strength of the material telescoped on *Forest Flower/Soundtrack*, he might well have made a decent living writing incidental music, film scores and dance suites – except that Lloyd thought of everything he wrote as a dance suite. Lloyd appeared, if not quite fully formed, then certainly already sounding like the light, uncertainly pitched but highly effective solo voice which was to re-emerge in the 1980s.

Even without benefit of hindsight, the Lloyd quartet was pretty exceptional. In 1967 Jarrett and DeJohnette were bursting with promise. Neither of them quite lives up to potential on *Forest Flower*, which remains unmistakably the leader's gig with accompaniment, but there is enough on show to suggest important things to come. Jarrett's composer credit on 'Sorcery' is an early foretaste, and McBee is the only other band-member to get his name under the line. The two-part title-piece remained a favourite, almost a signature-tune, until the band broke up. It's much more robust and much less impressionistic than one remembers. Never thought of as much of a standards player, Lloyd does have a crack at 'East Of The Sun' and shows off something of the blues coloration that crept into his more idiomatic work.

Soundtrack is also available paired with *In The Soviet Union*, but this version unfortunately omits 'Voice In The Night', a tune and title that Lloyd was to return to in 1999, the year that saw his catalogue finally take on a more comprehensive shape. The Russian set is probably the poorest of the bunch, so we'd recommend the 1994 reissue with *Forest Flower.* Tallinn *was* still in the Soviet Union in those days, but in May 1967 it was rare for any but the real heavyweight jazz ambassadors to secure the necessary visas, and the trip attests again to Lloyd's enormous international pull.

The Flowering is another of Collectables' rather strange pairings: the Lloyd album shares the space with an eponymous Warne Marsh record. Again, most of the material (which includes 'Speak Low') is recorded in Norway, but there is a single track from the

1966 Antibes Jazz Festival, which segues 'Goin' To Memphis' with 'Island Blues', the latter tune's second appearance on the disc, for it also appears with 'Love-In'.

*** Fish Out Of Water

ECM 841088-2 *Lloyd; Bobo Stenson (p); Palle Danielsson, Jon Christensen (d).* 7/89.

Despite commercial success on a level rivalled only by pop musicians, Lloyd turned his back on jazz performance (more gradually than is sometimes supposed) after the end of the 1960s. By the end of the following decade, the sabbatical was thought to be permanent and Lloyd was largely forgotten.

His return to performance has been much discussed. Whether it was at the behest of Michel Petrucciani or not is now a matter of question. The fact is that he came back, first at an event organized by Blue Note and then, somewhat later, as one of the most unexpected signings ECM ever made, though the presence of Jarrett and DeJohnette on the roster points to an obvious source for the suggestion. The comeback found him in much the same voice as before, more pastel and less rhythmically propulsive, but unmistakably himself. On *Fish Out Of Water* (a hugely unfortunate title for a new initiative) he takes six new but rather samey compositions at an easy pace, unhurried by the ECM house rhythm section, who can do most of this stuff with pyjamas on. Though there are flashes of increased intensity here and there, and an underlying urgency which impinges only rather gradually, it's mostly a rather enervated affair. Lloyd's tone, digitalized, has lost none of its soft burnish, but it is closer to the Coltrane of the 'sheets of sound' period and the great Atlantics than most people will remember. In the 1960s, he was something of a flute specialist, and that has not deserted him; the sound on 'Haghia Sophia' is deep and tremulous, almost as if he has switched to an alto instrument. Not a great album, but a very welcome return.

***(*) Notes From Big Sur

ECM 511999-2 *Lloyd; Bobo Stenson (p); Anders Jormin (b); Ralph Peterson (d).* 11/91.

This was a more varied and enterprising set, still dominated by the spirit of Coltrane but with a bedrock of invention underneath the rather melancholy delivery. It might have been preferable to start with the upbeat 'Monk In Paris'; it was certainly ill-advised to start with the rather melancholy 'Requiem', though this is the sort of programme that ECM have boldly essayed over the years, mostly succeeding, only sometimes miscueing. 'Sister', which comes second, is very similar in theme; and it's only really with Jormin's plangent introduction to 'Persevere', the first part of 'Pilgrimage To The Mountain', that interesting things start to happen. 'Sam Song' is a medium-tempo swinger underpinned by Peterson's gentle but unmistakably firm drumming and Stenson's impeccable accompaniment. After Christensen, it's a little hard to hear another drummer in this role, though Billy Hart was to come along later and make the gig his own.

The bassist introduces 'Takur' with horn-like harmonics down near the bridge, but the piece doesn't travel beyond its own opening bars. 'When Miss Jessye Sings', a tribute to opera singer Jessye Norman, begins disconcertingly close to Coltrane's most famous intro and, in the light of 'Pilgrimage To The Mountain: Persevere/Surrender', one almost wonders if Lloyd intends this album to be his *A Love Supreme*, a passionate personal statement in suite form rather than a collection of discontinuous pieces. If so, inevitably he falls short, but he has created something rather lovely in the attempt. Our favourite of the bunch.

*** The Call

ECM 517719-2 *Lloyd; Bobo Stenson (p); Anders Jormin (b); Billy Hart (d).* 7/93.

*** All My Relations

ECM 527344-2 *As above.* 7/94.

***(*) Canto

ECM 537345-2 *As above.* 12/96.

This is a group to match the line-up of the 1960s, a perfectly balanced combination of power and delicacy, and fronted by a man who is once again at the top of his considerable powers. It took time for us to appreciate *The Call*, which occasionally seemed like a turn full circle to the rather bland and unfocused style Lloyd seemed to have left behind with the '60s. It's a record that grows with time and familiarity, particularly once one begins to hear the interchanges between saxophonist and drummer.

Hart is the key addition to the band, a fiery but endlessly inventive player with a seemingly inexhaustible supply of rhythmic ideas. His work on *All My Relations* is superb. The 'Cape To Cairo Suite' is a tribute to Nelson Mandela, overlong and fuzzy in conception but episodically very good. The shorter cuts – 'Thelonious Theonlyus', 'Little Peace' and 'Hymne To The Mother' – are very much group efforts, played with a snap and crispness one would not have expected of the Lloyd of old. One almost wonders if he handed Stenson a stack of Monk LPs before the sessions. He is the overdetermining influence and a very fruitful one.

The most recent of the batch is desperately slow to get going, but 'Tales Of Rumi' repays the effort, and the tracks that follow (many of them apparently influenced by northern landscapes) have a bleak and uneventful majesty that oddly recalls another ECM master, Jan Garbarek. He is certainly in the background on 'Desolation Sound' and the title-piece, and it would have been simply wonderful had he been around Rainbow Studio just before Christmas 1996 to sit in on one of the sessions.

**** Voice In The Night

ECM 559445-2 *Lloyd; John Abercrombie (g); Dave Holland (b); Billy Higgins (d).* 99.

As he passed his sixtieth birthday, Lloyd seemed to pause and take stock. Here, having seemed for many years to have turned his back on much of his past work, Lloyd revisits past glories like 'Voice In The Night' and the glorious 'Forest Flower', as well as covering Strayhorn's 'A Flower Is A Lovesome Thing' and Elvis Costello's and Burt Bacharach's 'God Give Me Strength'. Also, much as he once did with 'Memphis Green' and similar down-home numbers, he gives himself the space to blow righteously on 'Island Blues Suite'.

Much has been said about the differences between the 'European' and 'American' quartets led by Lloyd's one-time pianist, Keith Jarrett. A similar comparison emerges here for, with his recent ECM group parked for the time being, Lloyd makes his first recording with an all-American group (Holland long since went Stateside) for almost three decades. And what a band it is! Higgins does very much the kind of job that DeJohnette did in the first group, a driving beat that also contributes to the innate musicality of the band, while Abercrombie and Holland bring their own insights, compounded of rock, free music and the latter-day atmospherics associated with the label's core roster, European or American. 'Forest Flower' is a delightful re-creation, unfolding the song's rich colours in a series of time-lapse shifts. There is even a tiny hint of a reference forward to the Strayhorn tune, thematically linked of course, but also bearing an interesting harmonic kinship. Perhaps an insight into its genesis? The Costello/Bacharach tune is the wild card, but just as Lloyd, like Miles, understood that 'standards' repertoire had to evolve and keep up if it was to remain viable, he gives it an authentic jazz feel while preserving the song's curious emotional climate.

The saxophonist sticks with tenor and uses a broader than usual tonality, which may have something to do with the way he's mixed up against Abercrombie rather than a piano player. Here and there he makes more or less explicit reference back to the early days, like the little down-in-the-mouth figure he inserts into his solo on 'Voice In The Night'. It will be familiar to Lloyd aficionados, and since that's what we are as well, what a shame they couldn't have fitted in 'Sombrero Sam'. Perhaps just a little too peppery for the latter-day Lloyd.

Jon Lloyd (born 1958)

ALTO SAXOPHONE, SOPRANO SAXOPHONE

British improviser who emerged in the late 1980s as a leader and London-based performer.

***** Syzygy**

Leo CDLR 173 *Lloyd; John Law (p); Paul Rogers (b); Mark Sanders (d).* 1 & 5/90.

*****(*) Head**

Leo CDLR 186 *As above.* 1/93.

****** By Confusion**

Leo CDLR 6198 *As above, except replace Rogers with Tim Wells (b).* 6/96.

Lloyd stands somewhat apart from musical fashions. His is an unmistakably British sound, related to Trevor Watts and Peter King, to Ray Warleigh and the troubled shade of Mike Osborne; but it also touches on darker – which is also to say blacker – sources, reaching into the deep blue centre which defines this music. There is no straightforward way to categorize this music. It flows over and round some notably strong compositional ideas which manage to hint at antecedents, particularly on *By Confusion*, without ever making them explicit, though the 1996 album does conclude with a rare cover, Eric Dolphy's 'Straight Up And Down'.

The earlier records are more obviously angular and, though one tended to think that Paul Rogers was a driving force, it turns out, following his replacement by Tim Wells, that he actually stopped up some of the music's energy. *Syzygy* – splendid word – is cross-grained, even perverse. By the time of *Head*, which was recorded live during a major Arts Council tour, Lloyd had not so much mellowed as allowed himself the time and space to let ideas breathe. The pay-off comes with the most recent of the three, a solid, provocative, completely achieved performance which begs the question why Lloyd isn't seen and heard much more often.

*****(*) Praxis**

FMR CD 47 V0198 *Lloyd; Marc Stutz-Boukouya (tb); Aleks Kolkowski (vn); Stan Adler (clo); John Edwards (b); Mark Sanders (perc).*

A significant change of direction for Lloyd, a move to a more harmonically grounded music and, in some respects, a more classically formal sound. *Praxis* is through-composed, with plenty of space for solo, duo and trio improvisation. The combination of horns and strings – which may have suggested itself because of Paul Rogers's resonant contribution to the Quartet – offers up a huge range of textures, counterpoints and independent lines. Stutz-Boukouya is a startling presence, perhaps registered a little too forcefully here and there, though the acoustic of Colchester Arts Centre could have something to do with that.

****** Four And Five**

hatOLOGY 537 *Lloyd; Stan Adler (clo); Marcio Mattos (b); Paul Clarvis (d, perc).* 12/98.

If *Praxis* had been the substantial recorded performance to date, *Four And Five* took Lloyd off on a new evolutionary direction, one in which even an implied pulse was very much central and the music behaved according to its own internal dictates rather than metrical and rhythmic road-signs. The title-tune works by a process of repetition and variation, as does the clever, classically inspired 'Zilch, Zero, Zed', which shuffles a parallel sequence of atonal ideas. 'Blues For' has no dedicatee and no underlying blues sequence either, while a version of Ellington's 'Take The Coltrane' underlines the technique involved more accurately than anything.

The new line-up maintains the sound and logic of earlier groups. As a cellist himself, Mattos understands the instrument's capacities and requirements and, though he doesn't play cello here, he slots into Adler's mood with precision. Clarvis is a less pungent player than Mark Sanders, more of an impressionist and certainly quite at ease where groove is at a discount. Lloyd himself sounds calm and thoughtful, feeding off the two string-players, spinning out intriguingly mathematical lines and commanding the sound with an air of patient authority.

Joe Locke (born 1959)

VIBRAPHONE

Journeyman vibes player whose versatility on an instrument which is difficult to pigeonhole has obliged him to make his own way: so far, he's been doing a fine job of it.

***** Restless Dreams**

Chief CD1 *Locke; Phil Markowitz (p); Eddie Gomez (b); Keith Copeland (d).* 6/83.

***** Present Tense**

Steeplechase SCCD 31257 *Locke; Larry Schneider (ts); Kenny Werner (p); Ron McClure (b); Ronnie Burrage (d).* 7/89.

*****(*) Longing**

Steeplechase SCCD 31281 *Locke; Mark Ledford (t, v); Johannes Enders (ss, ts); George Cables (p); Jeff Andrews (b); Ronnie Burrage (d).* 10/90.

****** But Beautiful**

Steeplechase SCCD 31295 *Locke; Kenny Barron (p).* 8/91.

****** Wire Walker**

Steeplechase SCCD 31332 *Locke; Danny Walsh (as, ts); David Kikoski (p); Ed Howard (b); Marvin 'Smitty' Smith (d).* 11/92.

Locke is a very gifted vibes player whose output, until recently confined to independent labels, has often been overlooked. While he can easily assert the kind of virtuosity associated with Gary Burton, it's Bobby Hutcherson's asymmetrical lines and dark, eruptive solos to which he sounds most in debt. Tonally, he gets an idiosyncratic sound from the notoriously faceless instrument – he keeps the sparkle of the vibes but loses their glassiness. As an improviser, he weaves very long lines out of open harmonic situations, maintaining a momentum over short or long distances – he can send up resonant clouds of notes or pare a trail back to its sparsest origins. He can also make the most of slow tempos: the duo album with Barron strikes a meditative pose that is remarkably well sustained for the 70-plus minutes it lasts.

The album co-led with Phil Markowitz is a strong if conventional vibes-and-rhythm date, but the Steeplechase discs are more adventurous. *Present Tense* is dominated by the interplay of Locke and the rhythm section (Schneider makes three somewhat cursory appearances), and Werner's probing accompaniments are particularly acute, although the sometimes inconclusive air of the music suggests that more preparation might have yielded a better result. *Longing* exchanges Werner for Cables, who's equally involved (Ledford and Enders are on only three tracks between them): 'The Double Up' and a profoundly felt 'A Child Is Born' offer very effective music. *But Beautiful*, as noted, is impeccably done, with Barron's felicities as telling as Locke's: this version of 'My Foolish Heart' is on a par with Hutcherson's classic set-piece. *Wire Walker* continues a memorable run: Smith stokes the fires on the burning title-track, Kikoski has seldom played with more point, and the leader's solos on 'A New Blue', 'A Time For Love' and the mesmerizingly complex introduction to 'Young And Foolish' figure among his best work. It scarcely matters that Walsh is little more than a bystander. A strongly recommended sequence.

****** Very Early**

Steeplechase SCCD 31364 *Locke; Ron McClure (b); Adam Nussbaum (d).* 10/94.

*****(*) Moment To Moment**

Milestone MCD 9243-2 *Locke; Billy Childs (p); Eddie Gomez (b); Gene Jackson (d).* 11/94.

Joe is still in great form here. The trio date with Nussbaum and McClure is another perfectly paced session, with the swinging tempo for 'You Don't Know What Love Is' giving way to a rapt 'I Loves You, Porgy', a dramatic 'Nature Boy' and on through eight tunes. McClure's bass lines are the ideal melodic/rhythmic counterweight, indecently rich but always on the right part of the chord, and Nussbaum is at his most subtle. *Moment To Moment* is really only a shade behind, starting with a terrific workout on 'Slow Hot Wind' and making the best of an ingenious choice of standards and connoisseur's pop. After McClure, Gomez can sound unnecessarily busy, and sometimes one wants to stop and revel in Locke's sound more, but this is basically another good 'un.

*****(*) Inner Space**

Steeplechase SCCD 31380 *Locke; Mark Soskin (p); Harvie Swartz (b); Tim Horner (d).* 4/95.

***** Sound Tracks**

Milestone 9271-2 *Locke; Olivier Ker Ourio (hca); Billy Childs (p); Rufus Reid (b); Gene Jackson (d).* 3/96.

Inner Space is no more or less than another report from a top-flight working band, even if it actually existed as such for no more than a year or so. Reunited in the studio, the group tackles chestnuts such as 'Django' and 'Skylark' alongside Andrew Hill's 'Tripping', Chick Corea's title-tune and Frank Kimbrough's 'Sanibel Island'. If Soskin seems less of an individual force than some of his predecessors, it doesn't stop Locke from delivering a typically eloquent and forceful performance on all the tunes.

Sound Tracks assembles nine Hollywood themes for Locke to investigate, going as far back as *Gone With The Wind* and as contemporary as *The English Patient*. Nothing wrong with the idea, and the leader seems as involved as usual, but Jackson's over-zealous drumming upsets the normally sensitive balance of Locke's music and some of the treatments seem a bit brash and over-heated.

*****(*) Slander (And Other Love Songs)**

Milestone 9284-2 *Locke; Billy Childs (ky); Vic Juris (g); Rufus Reid (b); Gene Jackson (d).* 3/97.

With pop tunes in the programme and Childs switching on his synth here and there, fears that Locke may have sold out to smooth jazz need to be allayed. Mostly, this is as tough and uncompromised as any record in his discography. The original tunes are the usual blend of lyrical and challenging, and he plays both Lalo Schifrin's 'Mission Impossible' and Joni Mitchell's 'Blue' without making them seem either kitsch or cute. He is a hard-nosed player and he's assembled a band that follows his instincts. Strong, intelligent playing from all hands – Juris especially thrives in the environment.

Mornington Lockett

TENOR SAXOPHONE, PIANO, BASS

British saxophonist in a mainstream-modern field.

***** Mornington Lockett**

EFZ 1006 *Lockett; Jonathan Gee (p); Jim Mullen (g); Laurence Cottle (b); Ian Thomas (d); Sarah Jane Morris (v).* 94.

Lockett came to notice with club owner/saxophonist Ronnie Scott's band, but he was immediately identified as a man who would go his own way. On the evidence of the more ambitious things on this debut disc, the complex 'P2C2E', and the deceptively straight-ahead 'Red Shift II' and 'Forca Al Canut', he is going to be a significant writer. He tackles the standard 'Lush Life' with conviction and a warmth of feeling. It comes two tracks after 'Laphraoig', the name of a wry, sardonic malt whisky whose distinctive flavour – iodine, seaweed, salt, smoke – seems to have found its way into Lockett's sound. Guitarist Jim Mullen guests on 'Lush Life' and one other track and fills out the harmony considerably; a pity he couldn't have been on hand for the whole session. Less enthusiasm for Sarah Jane Morris's vocal on the Etta James groaner, 'Don't Go To Strangers', which may have been a bid for airplay but fell flat if it was. A promising, thoughtful debut, perhaps too determined to show off a spectrum of ideas and styles rather than concentrating on good, straightforward playing, of which Lockett is demonstrably capable.

Mark Lockheart (born 1961)

TENOR AND SOPRANO SAXOPHONES

Studied classical saxophone in London, then worked the London scene and was a Loose Tubes charter member. Toured with Django Bates and Billy Jenkins, then formed Perfect Houseplants quartet.

***** Through Rose-Coloured Glasses**

Subtone ST 801 *Lockheart; Dave Priseman (t, flhn); Henry Lowther, Sid Gauld (t); Richard Henry (btb, tba); Jim Rattigan (frhn); Rob Townsend (as); Roland Sutherland (f, af); Huw Warren (p); John Parricelli (g, mand); Dudley Phillips (b); Martin France (d).* 4/98.

Perfect Houseplants has been Lockheart's principal recording vehicle, but this own-name album offers his writing for larger ensembles. Many of these pieces feel all but written-through: there are chances for more or less everyone on the record to step out at some point, but they're checked by the firm hand Lockheart keeps on the scheme of each composition. Sceptics won't be altogether convinced that this works out for the best, since some of the charts turn and twist so frequently that the music seems overburdened by its ingenuity: the title-track, for instance, seems to change tack every few bars. The limpid ballad, 'The Way Of The Road', is a notable exception, where Lockheart trusts his principal melody. The soft-focus sound doesn't always suit the music – some of these scores could triumph in a more aggressive mix. Reservations aside, an hour of quality time in the manner of new British jazz.

Didier Lockwood (born 1956)

VIOLIN

Born in Calais, Lockwood started with rock and blues and joined Magma in 1972, before trying mainstream jazz and then fusion. In the '80s and '90s he worked in numerous international post-bop settings.

****** Out Of The Blue**

JMS 037 *Lockwood; Gordon Beck (p); Cecil McBee (b); Billy Hart (d).* 4/85.

*****(*) 1 2 3 4**

JMS 041 *Lockwood; Thierry Eliez (ky, v); Jean-Michel Kajdan (g); Tom Kennedy (b); André Ceccarelli (d); Abdou M'Boup (perc); Nicole Croisille, Toure Kunda, Alex Ligertwood (v).* 87.

*****(*) New York Rendezvous**

JMS 075 *Lockwood; David Liebman (ss); David Kikoski (p, ky); Dave Holland (b); Gil Goldstein (acc); Mike Stern (g); Peter Erskine (d).* 1/95.

Lockwood is an immensely gifted player, combining a virtuosic technique with an attractive musicality. His association with Gordon Beck has been particularly fruitful. The earliest of the three JMS discs sees the two Europeans holding their own admirably in the company of two brilliant American rhythm players. Beck is in particularly good form and contributes the lovely 'November Song' to an exquisite session, revealing himself again as one of the finest accompanists Europe can provide. Unlike Michal Urbaniak or his fellow countryman, Zbigniew Seifert, Lockwood shows no desire to make the violin sound like a saxophone and is happy to explore the legacy of Stéphane Grappelli, albeit in a much updated form. It's hard to fault *Out Of The Blue* on any count, but the 1987 follow-up really is rather dull. The attempt to divide the album into four distinct 'chapters' simply doesn't make sense of the music, and the players are resolutely uninspired, with the exception of Ceccarelli and his occasional percussion partner, Abdou M'Boup, who make 'Aquamarine' a winning idea.

The New York session marks a welcome return to form. Holland and Erskine provide the solid foundation Lockwood thrives on, and the guests chip in with folksy melodic contributions that help temper the slightly monotonous sound of the violin as a front-line instrument. It's odd, given how good he is at it, that Lockwood hasn't capitalized more on his dazzling pizzicato work. He tried it on *Out Of The Blue* but has made precious little use of it since.

London Jazz Composers' Orchestra (founded 1970)

ENSEMBLE

A seminal ensemble of British free-music and modern-jazz figures, giving themselves a chance of working from a large-scale compositonal base. Barry Guy, the original founder, remains the central figure behind the LJCO.

♛ ** Ode**

Intakt CD 041 *Barry Guy (b, leader); Harry Beckett, Dave Holdsworth (t); Marc Charig (c); Mike Gibbs, Paul Nieman, Paul Rutherford (tb); Dick Hart (tba); Trevor Watts (as, ss); Bernard Living, Mike Osborne (as); Evan Parker, Alan Wakeman (ts, ss); Bob Downes (ts, f); Karl Jenkins (bs, ob); Howard Riley (p); Derek Bailey (g); Jeff Clyne, Chris Laurence (b); Paul Lytton, Tony Oxley (d, perc); Buxton Orr (cond).* 4/72.

The London Jazz Composers' Orchestra was directly inspired by the example of the American trumpeter and composer Michael Mantler's Jazz Composers' Orchestra, which afforded improvising players a rare opportunity to work outside the small-group circuit and to experiment with enlarged structures. The points of departure are, thereafter, much more interesting than the similarities. Whereas Mantler's group still remains audibly rooted in blues-based jazz, however subtly mediated by 12-tone music and other avant-garde inflexions, the LJCO is much closer in spirit to a European strain of collective improvisation. It also depends very heavily on the vision and eclecticism – and never has that overworked term been more apposite – of founder and leader, Barry Guy, who, in an age of hyper-specialization and stylistic antagonism, has been able to combine a passionate commitment to free improvisation with an interest in large-scale composition (something which remains anathema to some of his more dogmatic brethren) and also in Baroque music, an area which for a time at least he regarded as being every bit as radical in potential as free improvisation.

Ode is a landmark work. Conceived as a 'social framework' for improvisers, it is a brilliant response to the difficulty of combining what were considered to be irreconcilable musical philosophies. Inspired by Olivier Messiaen's masterpiece of orchestral coloration, *Chronochromie*, Guy devised and disguised structures, a series of philosophical quiddities to which the orchestra – both as collective and as a sum of expressive individuals – were asked to respond. The result is, as John Corbett suggests, not dense in the way that orchestral *tutti* are dense. It is dense in that the level of musical communication is such that every statement implies more than it states, creates networks of interaction between players, between constituent instrumental groups, and between types of musical response. If the latter sounds unclear, it is possible to hear players interacting vertically, rhythmically, timbrally, but also in constituent sub-groups, much as Guy was to do more formally much later in *Portraits*. *Ode* proved to be a little hard-boiled for most of the critics, and for some of the players, and at the time probably represented a blind alley in Guy's attempt to maximize soloists' freedom while maintaining a very cohesive overall argument. Hearing it many years on, and in the context of later and – in some ways – even more ambitious projects, what comes across most of all is that integrity of purpose and unity of musical language. It stands as one of the masterpieces of European improvisation.

*****(*) Zurich Concerts**

Intakt CD 005/1995 2CD *Barry Guy (b, leader); Anthony Braxton (leader); Jon Corbett, Henry Lowther (t); Marc Charig (c); Radu Malfatti, Paul Rutherford, Alan Tomlinson (tb); Steve Wick (tba); Paul Dunmall, Peter McPhail, Evan Parker, Simon Picard, Trevor Watts (reeds); Phil Wachsmann (vn); Howard Riley (p); Barre Phillips (b); Paul Lytton (d).* 11/87–3/88.

****** Harmos**

Intakt 013 *Barry Guy (b, leader); Jon Corbett, Henry Lowther (t); Marc Charig (c); Radu Malfatti, Paul Rutherford, Alan Tomlinson (tb); Steve Wick (tba); Paul Dunmall, Peter McPhail, Evan Parker, Simon Picard, Trevor Watts (reeds); Phil Wachsmann (vn); Howard Riley (p); Barre Phillips (b); |Paul Lytton (d).* 4/89.

*****(*) Double Trouble**

Intakt 019 *As above.* 4/89.

In the years that followed, the LJCO changed somewhat in ethos, opening up its repertoire to compositions other than those by Guy. These included challenging graphic scores by drummer Tony Oxley, looser structures from trombonist Paul Rutherford and, from outside the band, challenging works from 'straight' composers with an interest in improvisation, like Krzysztof Penderecki. Anthony Braxton was a thoroughly like-minded collaborator, and this is one of the few occasions when his contact with British and European improvisers has seemed to yield a genuinely communicative music. Whereas Guy likes to work with existing sub-groups of the orchestra, Braxton layers compositions – in this case 'Nos. 135 (+41, 63, 96)', 'No. 136 (+96)', 'No. 108B (+86, 96)' and 'No. 134 (+96)' – in dense palimpsests. There is a marked difference in the cast of sound during his pieces, a denser, less angular quality that doesn't always seem familiar from previous large-scale projects by the American. There is also a difference in ambience and acoustic which probably exaggerates the contrast.

Harmos and *Polyhymnia* (recorded at the earlier of the Swiss concerts) represent what Guy considers to be a third stage in the band's progress. The title alone aroused some anxiety before the fact that Guy was clambering on the bandwagon of neo-tonality. In fact, he interprets the Greek word in its original meaning of 'coming together'. It opens sharply enough with a broken fanfare from the trombones that is almost a station ident for British improvisation, a statement of jagged authority not unmixed with a tender joy. It's followed by a stately chorale which will inevitably bring to mind Guy's other musical enthusiasms, the Baroque filtered through a modern, radical consciousness. If the piece has a real centre, it is the long, winding saxophone melody played by Trevor Watts, a veteran of the band and in this composition its First Mate and co-pilot. Coming quite early (it's a long piece), Watts's solo nevertheless shapes the composition around itself, proposing some sort of rapprochement with harmony. No other player strays as far in this direction. Other individual contributions are, by comparison, harder-edged and more confrontational, but the piece does confirm what was to become a regular feature of Guy's LJCO work, a mutuality of effort between a single solo voice and the ensemble.

Double Trouble is a slightly tougher nut, originally conceived as a two-piano project for Howard Riley and Alex von Schlippenbach, whose Globe Unity Orchestra has trod similar territory. In the event, the recorded version is anchored on Riley alone, with a sequence of carefully marshalled instrumental groupings (notably two trios: Guy, Parker and Pytton, and Riley, Charig and Phillips) orbiting the centre. As a whole, the piece has a tremendous centrifugal coherence that balances the apparently anarchic but tightly organized behaviour of soloists and section players. If it's a less compelling record than *Harmos*, that's simply because it is also much less immediately accessible. On the other hand, it may pay a longer dividend.

****** Theoria**

Intakt CD 024 *As above, except omit Riley, Rutherford; add Conrad Bauer (tb), Irène Schweizer (p).* 2/91.

Theoria is effectively a piano concerto for Irène Schweizer, a player who had close contacts with the British avant-garde of the 1960s and who has since been a stalwart of Intakt's output. The difficulty presented was that of balancing individual and ensemble elements in a work of this scale and complexity; neither Guy nor Schweizer would have welcomed anything as fixed and definitive as a classical or Romantic concerto, yet clearly it would be undesirable to have a soloist improvise freely for nearly an hour against a fixed orchestral score. The solution is to demarcate very precisely the starting and finishing point for individual soloists and for internal sub-divisions of the orchestra, allowing the players a paradoxical degree of freedom within the basic structure. Guy attempts not to juxtapose blandly different styles of playing, but to overlap them creatively, creating diffraction patterns and points of maximum energy. In an orchestra of soloists, Schweizer stands out clearly but does not dominate; what happens is that her improvisations become the constitu entelements of other musicians' activity, a process parallel to but obviously very different from jazz musicians' reliance on chord sequences or standard tunes. It is a formidable achievement.

****** Portraits**

Intakt 035 2CD *As above, except omit Bauer; add Paul Rutherford (tb).* 3/93.

****** Double Trouble II**

Intakt CD 048 *As above, except omit Malfatti, Wick; add Chris Bridges (tb); Marilyn Crispell (p).* 12/95.

*****(*) Three Pieces For Orchestra**

Intakt CD 045 *As above, except add Maggie Nicols (v).* 6/96.

Portraits continues the line that began with *Ode*. Guy subdivides the orchestra into pre-existing and (in some cases) concurrent groups – Paul Rutherford's Iskra 1903, Evan Parker's Trio, John Corbett's Doppler – and thus to serve as a confederation rather than a vertically organized 'orchestra'. This posed fascinating problems and possibilities – in equal measure – which relate directly to Guy's running concerns. It is very much of its time, most obviously in the decision to include some explicitly melodic material (which seems to have antagonized some of the more dogmatic performers), which certainly makes *Portraits*, though long, one of the most approachable of the records. In the fifth of the main sections, which are interspersed by portrait subsections, there is a ballad, written for Simon Picard, an exquisite creation which is one of Guy's finest moments, let alone the saxophonist's. Alan Tomlinson is given a blues (words by Paul Rutherford, recited by the players), and there are other identifiable generic outlines as well. However, because of the internal configuration of languages and of personnels, none of these insists on anything like generic autonomy. Along with Guy himself, Evan Parker is the player who sustains the networks making up the piece, communicating at one point with several of the players around him, maintaining associations that would seem to be dispersed in time. It is a remarkable achievement. *Ode* may have a greater historical resonance, but *Portraits* is a work of masterful control and profundity.

Three Pieces continues in very much the same vein, uniting the distinct components in a way analogous to tensile structure, but once again using the existence of intra-relationships as a positive structural device. 'Owed To JS' is both an explicit homage to the late John Stevens and also a pun on *Ode* itself. It is written largely for Amalgam (Watts, Rutherford, Guy), for the long-standing duo of Parker and Lytton, and for the Howard Riley Trio (which also involves Guy in a prominent role). Generically, the material is distributed similarly to the previous project, though it seems that, having consulted with Crispell, Guy abandoned the idea of writing another ballad for her in favour of three more fractured, *haiku*-like figures. The American brings her usual serene strength to the music. The closing 'Strange Loops' is written for extraordinary improvising voice of Maggie Nicols and features Corbett, Charig, Phillips, McPhail, Hayward and Wachsmann. The textual dimension of *Portraits* is extended and developed, opening up new possibilities for the ensemble.

Double Trouble II is, naturally, a realization of the earlier work with something closer to the original conception of two pianists. They are, of course, very different pianists from those first intended, and the difference in texture and in harmonic sympathy is staggering. Crispell and Schweizer have collaborated in a number of contexts. This must be one of the most powerful. It is a culminating moment for the LJCO.

London Jazz Orchestra

GROUP

Orchestra of London-based players, crossing more than one jazz generation.

***** Dance For Human Folk**

Hot House HHCD 1016/7 2CD *Noel Langley, Andy Bush, Henry Lowther, Ian Carr, Sid Gauld (t, flhn); Scott Stroman, Paul Nieman, Brian Archer, Richard Edwards (tb); Dave Stewart, Andy Lester (btb); Stan Sulzmann, Martin Hathaway, Tim Garland, Pete Hurt, Jamie Talbot, Mark Lockheart, Alan Barnes (reeds); Pete Saberton (p); Phil Lee (g); Alec Dankworth (b); Paul Clarvis (d).* 1/94.

A 'mingling of generations' among London's jazz community, the LJO has Stroman as its MD and he wrote the four-part 'The Tradition' which takes up the first disc. The second features scores by Sulzmann, Hathaway, Hurt, Saberton, Lowther and Garland, which takes in a fair sweep of several of the major voices on the local scene from the past 25 years. The music is rather discouragingly ordinary at times, and as an orchestra the players don't really create a singular entity. But there are some lucid and worthwhile solos emerging from the scores, and of the 12 pieces Stan Sulzmann's pair of charts show an interestingly cluttered vision.

Jean-Loup Longnon

TRUMPET, VOCAL

French trumpeter in love with bebop but also looking much further afield.

*****(*) Cyclades**

JMS 18637 *Longnon; Tony Russo, Eric Giausserand, Michael Delakian, Christian Martinez, Philippe Slominski, Patrick Artero (t); Jacques Bolognesi, Denis Leloup, Jean-Louis Pommier, Jean-Marc Welch (tb); Patrice Petitdidier, Jacques Peillon (frhn); Didier Havet (tba); Lionel Belmondo, Christophe Laborde, Nicholas Montioer, Guillaume Naturel, Pierre Schirrer, André Villeger (sax); Pierre Mimran (f); Robert Persi (ky); Jean Michel Pilc (whistle); Stéphane Grappelli (vn); Hervé Sellin (p); Jeorgino Amorim, Khalil Chahine (g); Jean-Marc Jafet, Carlinho Verneck (b); Luis Augusto Cavani, François Laizeau (d); Americo Pintinho Da Silva (perc); Zabele Pidner (v); orchestra.* 11/92.

Epic, and satisfyingly naïve, a little like a Tintin story, translated and transposed on to a grand musical stage. The piece is actually subtitled *'Les Extraordinaires aventures de Barnabe, le petit cochon voyageur'*, the details of which need not detain us here. However, anything that ends with a booming, jazzy arrangement of the 'Marseillaise' can't be bad. There is just a hint of Maynard Ferguson about Longnon, but MF with a Gauloise in his mouth; he even has a four-valve flugelhorn to cement the parallel. The most surprising guest artist is Grappelli, who solos on 'Paros' with customary grace and enthusiasm, but without the slightest indication that he knows what the hell is going on. *Cyclades* is the kind of eclectic, non-generic, boundary-squelching thing that the French have become extremely good at. What it's about and how to describe it is beyond our critical capacity, but the noise it makes is terrific and hugely enjoyable. Do try.

*****(*) Bop Dreamer**

Pygmalion 591612 *Longnon; Flavio Boltro (t); Lionel Belmondo, Yannick Rieu (ts); Pierre De Bethmann (p); Christophe Wallemme (b); François Laudet (d); Anna Gramm Delirium Big Band.* 8/96.

Much more prosaic this time, but what a warm, lovable concert recording this is. Longnon recruits a top-notch septet (two trumpets, two tenors, rhythm) to play some of his bebop favourites and evoke his heroes, 'those peaceful birds with immense wings'. So here are 'Billie's Bounce', 'Tin Tin Deo', 'Daahoud' and Quincy Jones's 'For Lenna And Lennie', along with some in-the-spirit originals. The arrangements show plenty of care and thought went into it all, the playing has zest and grace, and Longnon presides (and sings on 'The Speech') with grandmasterly presence.

Louisiana Repertory Jazz Ensemble

GROUP

A band of 'authentic performance' players tackling the repertory of the 1920s.

*****(*) Uptown Jazz**

Stomp Off CD 1055 *Eddie Bayard (c); Leroy Jones Jr (t); Eddie Lonzo (vtb); Fred Starr (cl, ss, ts, Cmel); John Royen (p); John Chaffe (bj, g, mand); Curtis Jerde (helicon); Sherwood Mangiapane (b); Walter Payton Jr (sou); John Joyce (d).* 6/82–6/83.

****** Hot & Sweet Sounds Of Lost New Orleans**

Stomp Off CD 1140 *Roy Tate (t, c); Charlie Fardella (c); Tom Ebbert (tb); Jacques Gauthe (cl, ss, as); Henry Duckham (cl, as); Fred Starr (cl, Cmel, ts, bs); Vince Giordano (bsx); John Royen (p); John Chaffe (g, bj); Walter Payton Jr (b, E-flat helicon); John Joyce (d, wbd).* 6/86.

The vogue for authentic performance which has dominated the classical world in recent years has scarcely entered into jazz interpretation as yet, since trad groups the world over are content to savage the old repertoire to their own ends. This remarkable ensemble instead takes a purist's hand to original 1920s material. They use old instruments – the notes to CD 1140 reveal that six different cornets, made between 1895 and 1922, were used by Tate and Fardella – and arrangements taken straight from original records. Solos are probably patterned on routines – but it hardly matters, since this is basically an ensemble approach to the music. On these terms it's an extraordinary success. There are infinite variations in light and shade: on *Hot And Sweet Sounds* the players appear in ten different combinations across the 17 tracks, and they sound as comfortable in Jelly Roll Morton's music as in Freddie Keppard's or Richard M. Jones's. More importantly, they understand the differences among all the styles. On the key issue of tempo they consistently make it sound right: a very slow pace for 'Smoke House Blues', perfectly sprung rhythms (even without a bass instrument) on 'Original Dixieland One-Step' and 'Stockyards Strut'. The earlier record is perhaps just slightly the more static, and consequently more at the mercy of history, though the concept – to differentiate the pulse of Uptown as opposed to Downtown New Orleans classicism – is an intriguing one. But both discs are marvel-lously entertaining, as well as the most enjoyable kind of history lesson.

Eddy Louiss (born 1941)

ORGAN, PIANO

A Parisian, he played in his father's band in the '50s and studied at the Conservatoire. Sang with Double Six, 1961–3, then backed horn players on piano and moved to organ in the late '60s. He later worked with his own big band, Multicolour Feeling.

****** Trio**

Dreyfus FDM 36501-9 *Louiss; René Thomas (g); Kenny Clarke (d).* 68.

*****(*) Conférence De Presse**

Dreyfus FDM 36568-2 *Louiss; Michel Petrucciani (p).* 6/94.

*****(*) Conférence De Presse Vol. 2**

Dreyfus FDM 36573-2 *As above.* 6/94.

***** Louissiana**

Initial IN10951101 *Louiss; Jeremy Davenport (t); Mark Mullins (tb); Eric Traub (ts); Brian Stoltz, Anthony Brown (g); George Porter, Donald Ramsey, Anthony Hamilton (b); Raymond Weber, Herman V Ernest III, Russel Batiste (d); Kenyatta Simon (perc).* 2–8/95.

*****(*) Sentimental Feeling**

Dreyfus FDM 36600-2 *Louiss; Bernard Balestier, Georges Beckerich, Thierry Bienayme, Julien Buri, Pascal Epron, Michel Hamparsumyan, Eric Hupin, Jean-Yves Martyinez (t); Frédéric Cerny, Philippe Jacquiet, Christophe Jardin, Gueorgui Kornazov, Philippe Lapeyre, Anne Lété (tb); Daniel Huck, Jo Bennaroch, Jean-Marc Bouchez, Alain Brühl, Tina Charlon, Jean-Bernard Charlot, Christophe Dunglas, Bernard Hugonnet, Claude Montis, Alain Villanneau (as); Xavier Cobo (ts, f); Thierry Bellenger, Christophe Beuzer, Christian Bonnanfant, Guillaume Christophel, Jean-Christophe Cornier, Eric D'Enfert, Alexis Drossos, Sylvain Miller (ts); Armand Antonioli, Claude Georgel, Daniel Martinez, Georges Varenne (bs); Didier Havet, Philippe*

Laroza, Jean-Noël Rochut, Bastien Stil (tba); Julio Rakotonanahary (b); Paco Sery (d). 11–12/98.

Louiss's records have been in and out of circulation, but Dreyfus have restored some of his past as well as more recent activity. The 1968 session by his trio is a tremendous rediscovery. The six themes mix bop/hard-bop staples like 'Hot House' and 'No Smoking' with Thomas's haunting 'Blue Tempo' and a line by Clarke, and the playing has enormous power and energy. Louiss swarms all over the organ, charming out sweet melodies as well as thrashing together blues-drenched solos, Thomas plays with what is for him a rare intensity, and Clarke, recorded in hot close-up, is magnificent. This takes most similar Jimmy Smith and Jack McDuff records to the cleaners.

A big leap to 1994. Two sets of duets with the mercurial Petrucciani are full of interest. While there are the expected hard-swinging vehicles, each man thinks carefully about how best to accommodate the other, and the initiative is generously traded back and forth. Louiss comes up with lots of colouristic devices to underpin the pianist's lines ('Naissance', on the second disc, is a fine instance) but the excitement here is in two masters of the keyboard swapping notes.

Louissiana was recorded in New Orleans, and it gets stuck into Meters-styled grooves, second-line marches and other funky byways. Excellent fun, if not quite as imposing as the earlier discs. *Sentimental Feeling* is altogether more grand: three tracks are with a trio, but the others feature the enormous Fanfare band, 41-strong and not afraid to sound it. Louiss wrote all the music and he tends to use the orchestra, perhaps unsurprisingly, in great blocks or washes of sound. On 'Le Destin', in dedication to Michel Petrucciani, there's an effect where the big band seems to be stalking the organist, and the result is close to unforgettable. Sometimes the band seems too unwieldy to make sense: when the trio set up the slinky pace of 'La Scorpionne', it's hard to see how they'll accommodate the orchestra, and sure enough the mass of players tend to lumber alongside the action. But it's a courageous and unpredictable record and well worth trying.

Joe Lovano (born 1952)

TENOR SAXOPHONE, ALTO SAXOPHONE, ALTO CLARINET, PERCUSSION

Worked with Woody Herman in the late '70s, but it was not until the mid-'80s – and featured recordings with Paul Motian – that Lovano made a real mark. Since then, a sequence of acclaimed Blue Note albums and a fat book of star-guest engagements have made him a fans' favourite.

*** Tones, Shapes And Colors

Soul Note 121132 *Lovano; Ken Werner (p); Dennis Irwin (b); Mel Lewis (d).* 11/85.

*** Village Rhythm

Soul Note 121182 *Lovano; Tom Harrell (t); Ken Werner (p); Marc Johnson (b); Paul Motian (d).* 6/88.

Coming up for two decades into his recording career, Joe Lovano now stands at the heart of contemporary jazz, a figure who, solo by solo, album by album, demonstrates the continuing fertility of the genre, straddling innovation and tradition. He first came to wider prominence with the Lovano–Frisell–Motian trio, a unit which generated tile-melting excitement in a live setting but which on record revealed a few more subtleties, more opportunities for sophisticated interplay. Lovano started out a relatively straightforward technician, often relying on others to embellish his slightly throaty but plain-speaking lines. Long association with Motian has accustomed him to a very strong pulse embedded in a vibrant surface; he gets much the same thing from the late Mel Lewis, who is surprisingly reminiscent of Krupa in a small-group setting, and also from guitarist Frisell, whose chords and single-note figures are ever more clearly enunciated as his delay-and-distort effects become more dominant.

Experience, however, has turned Lovano into perhaps the most distinctive tenor player at work today, and a hectic recording schedule has greatly added to his discography. It must be said that Lovano is one of the few artists that Blue Note have handled with sympathetic intelligence in recent years, allowing him to work with an impressive cross-section of contemporary players. What's become obvious since the turn of the 1990s is how much of Lovano's mature style was present in germ in his earlier work.

Village Rhythm is as impressive for the writing as for the playing, and reveals Lovano to be a surprisingly accomplished bop melodist. 'Sleepy Giant' is particularly memorable. On a couple of tracks the saxophonist overdubs his own rather World Musical drumming. An indulgence? No more so than the ghastly poem to his father on ''Twas To Me'.

Bearish and slightly withdrawn of aspect, Lovano hadn't yet made a completely individual impact, but all three of these are worthwhile efforts, steering clear of clichéd effects and overworked material.

**** Landmarks

Blue Note 796108 *Lovano; John Abercrombie (g); Ken Werner (p); Marc Johnson (b); Bill Stewart (d).* 8/90.

This is Lovano's breakthrough record, a wholly satisfying set that shouts for the repeat button before the last raucous notes of 'Dig This' (with its curious, Monkish interruptions) have died away. Stylistically it's poised midway between Monk and Coltrane, but with a pungent sauce of latter-day urban funk poured over the top, as on the mid-point 'Here And Now', with Abercrombie's uncharacteristically vocalized guitar well to the fore. The (impeccable) production is by John Scofield, who might have been a more obvious choice for the guitarist's role, but Abercrombie seems to take in Scofield's virtues as well as his own, absolutely howling through 'Dig This'. Lovano's ballad-playing, as on the tribute to Elvin Jones, is increasingly impressive, with a virile focus that belies the slightly tremulous delivery.

**** Sounds Of Joy

Enja CD 7013 2 *Lovano; Anthony Cox (b); Ed Blackwell (d).* 1/91.

Working without a harmony instrument still places considerable demands on a horn player. The opening 'Sounds Of Joy' immediately recalls the stark, melodic approach of the classic Ornette Coleman Atlantics, a jolting, unpredictable saxophone sound that seems to select notes from all over the scale without reference to anything other than the simplest sequences of melody. There are clear signs that Lovano is anxious to broaden his sound as much as possible. In addition to tenor and soprano (the latter given its most thorough and demanding workout to date on the dedication 'This One's For Lacy'), he has also taken on the alto saxophone (giving it a sonority somewhere between Bird and Ornette) and the seldom-used alto clarinet, which he unveils on Judith Silverman's free-tonal 'Bass Space', an almost formal theme executed over a tense 7/8 beat from Blackwell (the actual count varies considerably) and huge, *arco* effects from the fine Cox, who solos magnificently on 'Strength And Courage'.

♛ **** From The Soul

Blue Note 798363 *Lovano; Michel Petrucciani (p); Dave Holland (b); Ed Blackwell (d).* 12/91.

Lovano's 'Body And Soul' wins him lifetime membership of the tenor club. Interestingly, though, he takes John Coltrane's rarely covered 'Central Park West' on alto, as if doing it on the bigger horn were unpardonable arrogance. What's wonderful about the record – aside from the playing, which is gilt-edged all round – is how beautifully modulated the tracks are. There's not a cliché in sight. Lovano's own writing – 'Evolution', 'Lines & Spaces', 'Modern Man', 'Fort Worth', and the closing waltz, 'His Dreams' – has a clean muscular edge and, from the opening fanfare of 'Evolution' onwards, it's clear that the album is going to be something special.

Petrucciani established such a presence as a recording artist in his own right that it's easy to forget how superb an accompanist he could be. The Frenchman's responses on 'Left Behind', un-familiar territory for him, are startling. He sits 'Fort Worth' out, leaving Holland and Blackwell to steer a markedly abrasive theme. Though ailing and by no means as dynamic as in former years, the drummer still sounds completely masterful. His delicate mallet figures on 'Portrait Of Jenny' are one of the instrumental high points of a thoroughly compelling record.

*** Universal Language

Blue Note 799830 *Lovano; Tim Hagans (t); Ken Werner (p); Scott Lee, Steve Swallow, Charlie Haden (b); Jack DeJohnette (d); Judi Silvano (v).* 6/92.

Whereas *Sounds Of Joy* seemed like a genuine attempt on Lovano's part to push himself out into rather edgier territory, *Universal Language* is rather self-consciously eclectic, an attempt to broaden the sound by bringing in all sorts of world-music touchstones and shifting the emphasis over heavily to Lovano the composer, an individual still much less resourceful than Lovano the player. Even the latter is somewhat compromised by the shift to a multi-instrumental approach that lacks the logic it undoubtedly had on the Enja session. 'Lost Nations', in memory of the late Jim Pepper, features Lovano on both soprano and alto clarinet. 'Cleveland Circle' has him moving off into Coltrane harmonics; but, significantly, the most effective piece on the record is the ballad, 'The Dawn Of Time', on which Jack DeJohnette is magnificent.

The rhythm section isn't quite as ambitiously constructed as might appear. Haden and Lee don't appear on the same tracks, and Swallow is used essentially as a guitarist, weaving lines round Werner's ramrod comping.

***(*) Tenor Legacy

Blue Note 827014 *Lovano; Joshua Redman (ts); Mulgrew Miller (p); Christian McBride (b); Lewis Nash (d); Don Alias (perc).* 6/93.

Even given the impossibility of topping *From The Soul*, this is a slightly muted set, with a tentative quality that hasn't been evident in Lovano's work before. Redman had been garnering a huge amount of press before this was recorded, and it may be that both men felt that reputations were at stake. Certainly Lovano sounds edgy and over-assertive, making a decidedly strange fist of 'Love Is A Many-Splendored Thing'.

The two-tenor front line gives the music a rather old-fashioned aspect that is accentuated by probably the straightest rhythm section Lovano's worked with in years. The centre-piece is a version of Monk's 'Introspection', delivered with few frills and patient development by all the soloists. Nothing else quite comes up to that standard, though, and the long ballad, 'To Her Ladyship', has a cloyingly soft centre.

At this stage in his career, Lovano's entitled to lay a couple of eggs. This isn't but, in the context of its predecessors, it's a bit of a disappointment.

***(*) Quartets

Blue Note 829125 2CD *Lovano; Tom Harrell (t, flhn); Mulgrew Miller (p); Anthony Cox, Christian McBride (b); Billy Hart, Lewis Nash (d).* 95.

A slightly worrying development, albeit a highly accomplished record. Why should either Blue Note or Lovano feel it was necessary at this juncture to confirm his bona fides in avant/progressive and mainstream jazz with these differently constituted quartets at the Village Vanguard? That he functions well in both realms has been beyond doubt for so long, who remained to be convinced?

**** Rush Hour

Blue Note 829269 *Lovano; Jack Walrath (t); James Pugh (tb); David Taylor (btb, tba); John Clark, Julie Landsman (frhn); Richard Oatts (f, ts); Charles Russo (cl, bcl, as, ts); Dennis Smillie (cbcl); Robert Botti (eng hn); Michael Rabinowitz (bsn, bcl); Gloria Agostini (hp); James Chirillo (g); Fred Sherry (clo); Mark Helias, Ed Schuller (b); George Schuller (d); Mark Belair (perc, vib); Judi Silvano (v); Gunther Schuller (cond).* 4–6/94.

Last time out, we were inclined to worry that *Quartets* represented anxiety on Blue Note's part about what to do with Lovano long term. Fortunately, there has been no sign of anything since but a continued commitment to experiment and diversification. In a sense, *Rush Hour* emerges directly out of the stylistic shifting of the previous record. Certainly, the long 'Headin' Out, Movin' In' is very largely concerned with moving in and out of conventional harmony and grooves, a superb orchestration by the piece's composer, Gunther Schuller, who also contributes the atmospheric 'Rush Hour On 23rd Street'.

There could hardly have been a more sympathetic or understanding collaboration. Whether there has been any direct influence or not, Lovano's liking for overlaid voices, parallel melody lines floated over low-toned brass and woodwind, and for extremes of sonority is remarkably close to Schuller's conception. It works triumphantly not just on the original piece but also on 'Peggy's Blue Skylight', 'Prelude To A Kiss', and 'Crepuscule With

Nellie', one of the most significant performances in Lovano's growing attachment to Monk. It works, too, in scaled-down form, on a version of Ornette's 'Katheline Gray', which features a small string and woodwind ensemble built on the Schuller rhythm section, Ed and George, and coasting Lovano's acerbic soprano; it might almost be some forgotten nugget from the Third Stream.

Lovano's multi-instrumentalism is well aired as well. 'Wildcat' is an overdubbed duet for tenor and drums; 'Juniper's Garden' is for soprano saxophone and Judi Silvano's voice; 'Chelsea Bridge' is a magnificent *a cappella* performance. A major restatement and consolidation rather than a substantial step forward, this is Lovano's best work since *From The Soul*.

***(*) Celebrating Sinatra

Blue Note 837718 *Lovano; John Clark (frhn); Billy Drewes (ss, bcl); Dick Oatts (ts, f); Ted Nash (ts, cl); Tom Christensen (ts, ob, eng hn); Michael Rabinowitz (bsn); Kenny Werner (p); Emily Mitchell (hp); Mark Feldman, Sara Perkins (vn); Lois Martin (vla); Erik Friedlander (clo); George Mraz (b); Al Foster (d); Judi Silvano (v).* 6/96.

Interest in the great singer's pedigree as a *jazz* artist grew during the last few years of his life, and there have been a number of tribute albums by improvisers. This is one of the very best, distinguished by fine arrangements from the veteran Manny Albam and by some extraordinary playing from Lovano. The formula is now pretty familiar: saxophone and soprano voice over a conventional rhythm section and imaginatively deployed horns and strings.

The selection of material is unexpected and persuasive. At the heart of the set, a seductive reading of Sinatra's own composition, 'This Love Of Mine', a favourite of Sonny Rollins. Wedged between 'I've Got You Under My Skin' and 'Someone To Watch Over Me', it's the best small-group performance Lovano has turned in for some time. On other tracks, though, the emphasis is on an ensemble feel, and Albam's great skill is to make these familiar tunes sound fresh-minted. Opening with 'I'll Never Smile Again' was a clever choice, giving the least familiar of the songs the most conventional setting of the set, before striking out into more obviously revisionist territory with 'Chicago' and 'I'm A Fool To Want You'.

For a change, Lovano plays tenor throughout, and it's good to hear him concentrate on the big horn. He sounds as if he's steeped himself in mid-period Rollins, the same loping pace, unpredictable changes of direction and constant fidelity to the melodic line. By now, though, Lovano is his own man and nothing here is anything less than fresh and unhackneyed. And no, he doesn't do 'My Way'.

***(*) Flying Colours

Blue Note 856092 *Lovano; Gonzalo Rubalcaba (p).* 97.

Speaking in interviews, Lovano was as enthusiastic about this encounter as about anything in his career to date. On the face of it, it sounds like a dream ticket for Blue Note, their most enterprising horn player of recent times and the irrepressible Cuban. For all that, it could have been a rather flat and uninspiring encounter, and what really lifts it is the selection of material. Monk's 'Ugly Beauty' and Ornette's 'Bird Food' were inspired, left field choices. There's a somewhat more conventional attack on 'How Deep Is The Ocean', an opportunity for both men to show off a more lyrical side, but the real payoff comes on a magnificent interpretation of 'Gloria's Step', on which Rubalcaba quotes Scott LaFaro's original bass line in the left hand, at which Lovano immediately counters with the response figure.

Lovano sometimes sounds recessed relative to the piano, and there are a couple of slightly erratic edits. Nothing, though, that dents the appeal of a wonderful album by two instinctive but highly intelligent players.

**** Trio Fascination (Edition One)

Blue Note 833114 *Lovano; Dave Holland (b); Elvin Jones (d).* 9/97.

Supergroup, ahoy. Lovano's early days in saxophone/organ trios and later dabbling in starker bass-and-drum settings are generously synthesized on this fine session. Lovano's ninth Blue Note session revived a happy association with Jones, who used the big man as a dep for Pat LaBarbera and Sonny Fortune on a European tour that must have been one of the steepest points on his learning curve.

'Cymbalism' is a tribute to another drummer – Paul Motian – but also to a raft of other percussionists from whom Lovano has learnt the supremacy of the drums in jazz. 'Impressionistic' is more obviously saxophone-orientated, a clever, wry history lesson that looks forward and back with relaxed self-confidence. The mood on 'Days of Yore' is more sombre, a reminder that, beyond his recent multi-instrumentalism, Lovano is a formidable tenor stylist, able to conjure everyone from Chu to Trane. 'Villa Paradiso' and '4 On The Floor' are as uncompromisingly straightahead as anyone could ask for, broad blowing themes with generous detail right through the trio. 'Studio Rivbea' recalls the loft scene of New York City and the brave days of the late '60s. The only standard, 'Ghost Of A Chance', sounds like an emotional moment for Jones, who plays like a dream.

*** Friendly Fire

Blue Note 499125 *Lovano; Greg Osby (as, ss); Jason Moran (p); Cameron Brown (b); Idris Muhammad (d).* 12/98.

The idea came from label boss, Bruce Lundvall: separate invitations to Lovano and Osby to put down something special for Blue Note's sixtieth anniversary. Each, it seemed, mentioned the other, and the result is a warm, uncompetitive jam that harks back to the kind of loosely congregated session the label issued by the shelfload in the 1950s and '60s. Much as Lovano has lengthened his operational radius over the years, Osby has shown a growing interest in mainstream harmonic jazz. *Friendly Fire* is a genuine meeting of minds.

Compositions are shared between the two saxophonists. Osby's opening 'Geo J Lo' is a free-form idea that could have turned up in a Ben Webster–Chu Berry workout. The middle of the set is occupied by three repertory pieces, Eric Dolphy's maverick blues, 'Serene', Ornette Coleman's 'Broadway Blues' and Thelonious Monk's 'Monk's Mood', all three of them performed with respectful *brio*. 'Idris', Lovano's tribute to the date's endlessly inventive drummer, lags a touch over the stretch, as does the closing 'Alexander the Great'.

The young pianist, a member of Osby's current working band, is endlessly inventive, working in an idiom that recalls a roster of Blue Note greats from Bud Powell to Andrew Hill. Brown and Muhammad are superbly matched; but it's the saxophonists who command attention, two guys not quite speaking the same dialect but happy to trade. Happy stuff for an auspicious occasion.

Love Cry Want

GROUP

A band of some legend, Love Cry Want set up some of the options for jazz fusion at the beginning of the 1970s.

***(*) Love Cry Want

New Jazz NJC 001 *Nicholas (g syn, ring modulator, etc); Larry Young (org); Joe Gallivan (d, steel g, syn, perc); Jimmy Molneri (d, perc).* 72.

Larry Young was a member of not one, not two, but three legendary bands in the late 1960s and early '70s. Having helped create the new Miles Davis sound on *Bitches Brew*, he co-founded Lifetime with John McLaughlin and Tony Williams, and following that was a member of one of the legendary jazz-fusion groups, Love Cry Want, who carried the sound of both a step further, and perhaps a step too far for either critics or public. LCW were even banned from the environs of the White House on the grounds that they might interfere in some obscure electronic way with Richard Nixon's head. A whole era of American history falls into place in an instant.

The group sound was not quite so heavily dependent on Young as Lifetime had been, largely because guitarist Nicholas (no other name) had at his disposal a prototype guitar synthesizer which greatly increased his range of sound. Drummer Gallivan, who remains one of the unsung heros of this music, was also to go on and pioneer a drum synth. At this stage, though he has a Moog, he is mainly working acoustically, the light, fast but curiously threatening sound one knows from his own records. It is usually possible to distinguish what he is doing from the more straightforward style of Jimmy Molneri. The music consists of big, intense washes, driving motoric rhythms and occasional moments of unexpected grace. The basic components are not too difficult to unpick: the white R&B of Blood, Sweat and Tears or Chicago, and the thicker, more intense sound of Miles's electric group. There is a blatant rip-off of 'In A Silent Way' early in the set, not credited but surely too close to be unconscious and unintentional; and there are other moments when the trumpeter's work seems to be the reference point. Recording quality is far from wonderful, but the session has an amazingly atmospheric period-quality, and audio buffs will have fun working out who is playing what. A remarkable document of a largely forgotten but seminal group.

Allen Lowe

TENOR SAXOPHONE

American saxophonist of abstruse and intriguing tastes who made these cultish records early in the '90s.

**** Dark Was The Night

Music & Arts CD 811 *Lowe; Robert Rumbolz (t); Roswell Rudd (tb); Paul Austerlitz (cl, bcl); Stacy Phillips (g); Jeff Fuller (b); Ray Kaczynski (d).* 4–11/93.

***(*) Woyzeck's Death

Enja ENJ 9005 *Lowe; Roswell Rudd (tb); Randy Sandke (t); Ben Goldberg (cl, bcl); Andy Shapiro (p, syn); Jeff Fuller (b); Ray Kaczynski (d).* 5/94.

Most of the attention devoted to these on release focused on the role of New Wave trombonist Rudd, effectively co-leader on both sessions, who had been far out of the limelight for several years at this point. Both projects are, however, essentially Lowe's concept, with just two Rudd compositions (albeit fascinating ones) tacked on at the end of *Woyzeck's Death*. The 'American Song Project' that yields *Dark Was The Night* is an intriguing business, the result of Lowe's fascination with an art form which is at the heart of jazz – all those standards – but which nevertheless is largely overlooked; lots of guys know the chords to 'Body And Soul', not so many nowadays could sing you the words and proper melody. This isn't, however, a collection of Americana. Most of the material is by Lowe himself, an impressive melodist with a dry, slightly acidulous character, and is intended as a tribute to Louis Armstrong, Blind Willie Johnson, Elvis Presley and other neglected (*sic*) American masters. Some of Lowe's own playing is imprecise, a problem he puts down to a broken finger on the July session in Providence, but audible elsewhere as well. Rudd plays magnificently and the bit parts, touches of clarinet, National guitar and trumpet, are all handled professionally.

The other is a different kind of concept album, inspired by Georg Büchner's two plays, *Woyzeck* and *Dantons Tod*. Once the liner-notes and the relevant contexts have been absorbed the exact programme scarcely matters. Suffice it to say that Lowe has captured something of the brittle gaiety and bleak despair that oscillate through Büchner. His saxophone sound, on the opening 'Cold As Ice', 'Hard Gray Sky' and the climactic 'Woyzeck's Death' itself, has a kind of muscular melancholy that recalls no earlier player, other than perhaps Chu Berry in darker mood. Mood is the weasel word here, for there is no ECM-ish picture-painting; every episode is carefully shaped and logically constructed. Rudd is the anarchic element, breaking across Lowe's argument, Goldberg's atmospheric reed sound, and even Sandke's patiently built solos, with abrupt, ironic intensity. On his own 'Bonehead' and 'Concentration Suite', which closes the album, the trombonist shows again how solidly grounded he still is in classic jazz idiom and how exciting a performer he can be in a straight blowing context. However, he shouldn't be allowed to steal more than his fair share of Lowe's thunder. This is a fascinating contemporary record, but *Dark Was The Night* probably offers more lasting satisfaction.

Frank Lowe (born 1943)

TENOR SAXOPHONE

Lowe comes from Memphis and has the same big, abrasive tone as fellow-Tennessean, George Coleman. What makes him interesting is that even back in the late 1960s, when he was coming through as an individual stylist, he had no truck with the scorched-earth radicalism of most of his generation, constantly asserting an unfashionable (it was then) interest in classic swing players like Chu Berry and proto-boppers like Don Byas. He remains rather thinly documented before the mid-'90s.

****** The Flam**

Black Saint 120052 *Lowe; Leo Smith (t, flhn, wood f); Joe Bowie (tb); Alex Blake (b); Charles Bobo Shaw (d).* 10/75.

A wonderful band and a very fine record which was unavailable for far too long. Unlike the generation that took Trane as its model, Lowe has never seemed to regard the length of a solo as any measure of its importance, and here he is admirably concise and to the point, driving home ideas one after the other, like a country boy driving in spikes at a fair. 'Sun Voyage', 'Be Bobo Be' and 'Third Street Stomp' are all wonderful ideas, executed with such flair and confidence that one has to assume they were well worked out in advance. Smith and Bowie are both in good heart and voice, and the drummer reminds us yet again what an inventive player he can be in the right context. A good place to start if you haven't encountered Lowe before.

*****(*) Fresh**

Black Lion BLCD 760214 *Lowe; Leo Smith (t, flhn); Joe Bowie (tb): Abdul Wadud (clo); Selene Fung (cheng); Steve Reid (d); Memphis Four.* 74–75.

Previously available on Affinity, this is one of the clearest available examples of Lowe's backward-looking modernism or radical conservatism, depending on how you choose to look at it. 'Chu's Blues' is the clearest possible statement of Lowe's ancestral loyalties, a raw-boned monster of a thing with an extended bar structure. The cheng and cello are used to give some colour and variation, and the Memphis Four come on to add to the impression of a very serious knees-up. Good to see this one back in catalogue after a long break.

****** Exotic Heartbreak**

Soul Note 121103 *Lowe; Lawrence Butch Morris (c); Amina Claudine Myers (p); Wilber Morris (b); Tim Plesant (d).* 10/81.

*****(*) Live From Soundscape**

DIW 399 *As above.* 82.

Lowe's turn-of-the-decade band traded in a curiously raw finesse. There is nothing here, either live or from the studio, which swaps subtlety for power. And both should help dispel any notion of Lowe as an unsubtle roarer. Though both the horns are strong voices, neither ever goes for the obvious option, and Morris always seems a more interesting player on other people's projects (Lowe's, David Murray's) than on his own increasingly overcooked 'conductions'. A live version of 'Exotic Heartbreak' on the DIW suggests how comfortably Lowe has assimilated older styles to the most abrasively contemporary of tones and how well he has adapted himself to a new diction in jazz. The earlier record is marginally our favourite, simply because a lot of rough edges have been buffed away, but the live session from New York is well worth having. There is a tough, competitive ethos at Soundscape which almost always pushes players to their best.

*****(*) Decision In Paradise**

Soul Note 121108 *Lowe; Don Cherry (t); Grachan Moncur III (tb); Geri Allen (p); Charnett Moffett (b); Charles Moffett (d).* 9/84.

Unlike most of his generation, there isn't much bebop residue in Lowe's thinking, and it's unusual to hear him turn to post-bop like 'Cherryco', an inclusion presumably suggested by the trumpeter present on this wonderful session. It doesn't suit Lowe's chops altogether well, though he slows it down a touch and smooths out a couple of the rougher harmonic shifts. A heavyweight rhythm section, led off by Allen's forcefully eclectic chords and runs, keeps the energy level high. Don is having one of his best outings for years, bright, warmly antagonistic and full of melody. Moncur plays as well as ever (why is he still so underexposed?), varying his slide positions and embouchure to stay just this side of multiphonics. Perhaps not the best introduction to Lowe, who has to make room for three very strong soloists and for the Moffetts, but a powerful group record and an approach that sits wide of most else that was going on in '84.

***** Inappropriate Choices**

ITM Pacific 970062 *Lowe; James Carter, Michael Marcus, Carlos Ward (sax); Phillip Wilson (d).*

This was a fascinating idea, bringing together four of the most interesting and offbeatly creative saxophonists around. We're inclined to think better of it than we did. It takes time to absorb what is going on, largely because the sound is muddy and indistinct, but there are ideas flying about in there. The tragic Wilson (later found murdered in his apartment) is wasted, and it might have been better to have gone out as a straight sax quartet. Separating them isn't too hard. Carter often sounds like son-of-Lowe, curiously enough, a connection no one seems to mention now. There are enough of Ward's Middle Eastern yowls and Marcus's bizarre harmonics on evidence to identify them, but it's Lowe who cements the whole thing, often gluing together the bottom line the way Dewey Redman did in the Ornette band. Worth a try.

****** Bodies & Souls**

CIMP 104 *Lowe; Tim Flood (b); Charles Moffett (d).* 11/95.

*****(*) Vision Blue**

CIMP 138 *Lowe; Steve Neil (b, Guinea hp); Anders Griffen (d).* 2/97.

As spare and stern as the great Ornette Coleman Trio of the 1960s, which Moffett also graced, the first of these is the Frank Lowe disc of choice. CIMP (Cadence Improvised Music Project) is dedicated to raw and unvarnished slice-of-life veritism, and there are no frills to either of these performances. A long set, with the usual intensity, *Bodies & Souls* mixes four originals with material by Pharoah Sanders, Don Cherry (who is also the dedicatee of two joyous, complex numbers by Lowe himself), Ornette ('Happy House') and, on the stirring 'Impressions' which opens the set, Coltrane himself. It stands first, one feels, because Lowe wants to demonstrate both his respect for and distance from Coltrane's and later Coleman's language. By placing 'Body And Soul' last, he demonstrates more clearly than ever before how much he sees himself standing on the shoulders of earlier giants. It's a delicate performance, unaccompanied, lighter-toned and more intimate than Lowe often is. Flood and Moffett combine well, and they represent the real difference between the first CIMP and *Vision Blue*. Again, there's a mix of original and repertory material. Rollins's theme from 'Alfie' is an unexpected choice, and Percy Mayfield's 'Please Send Me Someone To Love' doesn't often figure in this sort of setting. 'Softly As In A Morning Sunrise' contains a couple of references to Coltrane, just so that we know he knows, and the now-obligatory Coleman numbers ('Law Years' and 'The Blessing') have the usual mixture of respect and self-reliance. The final two numbers seem a bit throwaway, a duo performance of Lowe's 'Dream State' with the drummer, and the only other acoustic variation, Neil's Guinea harp on the last track, his own 'Bobbo's Face', a bit wasted in that position. Outstanding track? For us, a blistering run-through of Jackie McLean's 'Little Melonae', one of the best things Lowe has recorded. Even with an augmented catalogue, he still seems a marginal figure. Time he was taken with the seriousness he deserves.

Francine Luce

VOCALS

Martinique-born singer and improvising vocalist, based in the UK.

*****(*) Bò kay la vi-a**

Ogun OGCD 012 *Luce; Claude Deppa (t, flhn); Paul Rutherford (tb); Evan Parker (ss, ts); Keith Tippett (p, music box); Paul Rogers (b); Louis Moholo (d, perc).* 9/96.

Luce comes from Martinique, and the island provides an aural backdrop to the opening of this debut recording, location tapes of birds, insects and water. As the presence of six veteran British improvisers suggests (and these days Deppa has the authority and gravitas of a senior player), the idiom is freely lyrical, with considerable space for improvisation.

Patois is already an improvising language, dancing over the syntax of 'official' French. Most of these songs are poised somewhere between jazz scat and folk forms. Rarely is the whole band playing at once. The opening 'Lè la tè ka kléré' is performed by Luce, Rogers and Moholo; she is joined by Parker and Deppa on the exquisite 'Pokéya' and by Tippett alone on 'L'amour vaut bien une chanson', which is a glorious conception, suiting her light but resonant voice to perfection. The use of multi-tracking and superb production by Hazel Miller and Steve Beresford yields a record of great technical polish as well as musical beauty.

As well as establishing Francine as a musician to watch – and we say 'advisedly', since she is much more than a singer – the album also serves as a reminder of what a remarkable sonic poet Paul Rutherfored can be. His playing on 'Rencontres' and 'Déjà Vu' is breathtaking.

Luce immediately joins the ranks of British vocal improvisers like Maggie Nicols and Julie Tippetts (whose old man is rather quieter than usual here) but immediately carves out a new direction and a rich future of song.

Jimmie Lunceford (1902–47)

ALTO SAXOPHONE, BANDLEADER

Lunceford studied music in Denver and Fisk University and then taught in Manassas, forming a band there. After four years of scuffling, they played at New York's Cotton Club and made a big name as a touring act. Much of their show was almost vaudevillian, with band members singing and doing routines, but the records were very fine too. Lunceford toured relentlessly and took up flying. Disgruntled bandsmen left in the early '40s after feeling cheated over their pay, and the band went into a slow decline. Lunceford died of a heart attack while signing autographs.

****** Jimmie Lunceford 1930–1934**

Classics 501 *Lunceford; Sy Oliver, Eddie Tompkins, Tommy Stevenson, William 'Sleepy' Tomlin (t); Henry Wells (tb, v); Russell Bowles (tb); Willie Smith, Earl Carruthers (cl, as, bs); LaForet Dent (as); Joe Thomas (cl, ts); Edwin Wilcox (p, cel); Al Norris (g); Moses Allen (bb, b); Jimmy Crawford (d, vib).* 6/30–11/34.

*****(*) Jimmie Lunceford 1934–1935**

Classics 505 *As above, except add Paul Webster (t), Elmer Crumbley, Eddie Durham (tb, g), Dan Grissom (cl, as, v); omit Tomlin.* 11/34–9/35.

***** Jimmie Lunceford 1935–1937**

Classics 510 *As above, except add Ed Brown (as); omit Stevenson, Wells.* 9/35–6/37.

*****(*) Jimmie Lunceford 1937–1939**

Classics 520 *As above, except add Trummy Young (tb, v), Ted Buckner (as).* 6/37–1/39.

*****(*) Jimmie Lunceford 1939**

Classics 532 *As above, except omit Durham; add Gerald Wilson (t).* 1–9/39.

***** Jimmie Lunceford 1939–1940**

Classics 565 *As above, except add Snooky Young (t), The Dandridge Sisters (v); omit Tompkins.* 12/39–6/40.

****(*) Jimmie Lunceford 1940–1941**

Classics 622 *As above, except omit Dandridge Sisters.* 7/40–12/41.

****(*) Jimmie Lunceford 1941–1945**

Classics 862 *Lunceford; Snooky Young, Gerald Wilson, Paul Webster, Freddy Webster, Bob Mitchell, Pee Wee Jackson, Melvin Moore, William 'Chiefie' Scott, Russell Green, Ralph Griffin, Chuck Stewart (t); Elmer Crumbley, Russell Bowles, Trummy Young, Fernando Arbello, Earl Hardy, John Ewing, James Williams (tb); Willie Smith, Earl Carruthers, Dan Grissom, Joe Thomas, Benny Waters, Ted Buckner, Dan Grissom, Omer Simeon, Ernest Purce, Chauncey Jarrett, Kirkland Bradford (reeds); Edwin Wilcox (p, cel); Al Norris, John Mitchell (g); Charles 'Truck' Parham, George Duvivier, Moses Allen (b); Jimmy Crawford, Joe Marshall (d); Delta Rhythm Boys, Claude Trenier, Bill Darnell (v).* 41–45.

***** Jimmie Lunceford 1945–1947**

Classics 1082 *Lunceford; Melvin Moore, Ralph Griffin, William 'Chiefie' Scott, Russell Green, Chuck Stewart, Bob Mitchell,*

Reunald Jones, Joe Wilder (t); Trummy Young (tb, v); Fernando Arbello, Earl Hardy, John Ewing, James Williams, Russell Bowles, Willie Tompkins, Alfonso King, Al Grey, Al Cobbs (tb); Omer Simeon (cl, as); Kirkland Bradford (as); Joe Thomas (ts, v); Ernest Purce, William Horner, Lee Howard (ts); Earl Carruthers (bs, cl); Edwin Wilcox (p); John Mitchell, Al Norris (g); Truck Parham, George Duvivier (b); Joe Marshall (d); Nick Brooks (v). 12/44–5/47.

Lunceford's orchestra is doomed always to be remembered behind Ellington and Basie as the great also-ran big band of its day. Part of the reason for that is its sheer class: there were no special idiosyncrasies which lifted the Lunceford orchestra away from the consistent excellence which it aspired to. Its principal arrangers – Sy Oliver in particular, but also Edwin Wilcox (in the earlier days) and Willie Smith – built the section-sounds into superbly polished, interlocking parts which made their records exude a high professional élan. Soloists stepped naturally out of and back into this precision machine, and there was never much danger of a Rex Stewart or a Lester Young breaking any rule. Lunceford's virtues were very different from those of the rough-and-ready (early) Basie band, or from Ellington's unique cast of characters. Still, the records endure very well, even though – as so often with the big bands of the period – the later sides show a dramatic falling-off.

The first volume of the Classics chronological survey shows the band coming together – there is a single 1930 session in the discography, followed by an incongruous jump to 1934 – but the important hit coupling of 'Jazznocracy' and 'White Heat' is here, as well as the remarkably nonconformist versions of 'Mood Indigo' and 'Sophisticated Lady'; once under way in earnest, Lunceford turned out some very fine records. The first two CDs feature some of the best of Oliver and Wilcox – there is even the very rare instance of two Ellington compositions, 'Rhapsody Junior' and 'Bird Of Paradise', which were never recorded by Duke, on the 1934–35 disc – and the 1935–37 session includes one of Oliver's masterpieces, the chart for 'Organ Grinder's Swing'. But a certain staleness sets in to the band from about 1936 onwards, with the Lunceford precision taking on a formulaic feel that fast tempos and good soloists – Smith was a rival to Hodges and Carter was one of the great alto stylists of the day, and Joe Thomas and Eddie Tompkins were excellent half-chorus players – never quite overcame.

The band continued to develop in minor ways: new players such as Trummy Young and Snooky Young were given tasks that raise the overall game on several of the tracks. Trummy's extraordinary playing (and singing) on 'Annie Laurie' and 'Margie' (Classics 520) is enough to make one wonder whether this is the same man who was such a dullard with Louis Armstrong's All Stars. Nevertheless the band's records started to sound as if they were being churned out by the end of 1939 – although, considered track by track, there is still much eloquent and occasionally surprising music here. The departure of first Oliver and then Smith was a blow that Lunceford's orchestra never recovered from, though to its last records it still sounds like a skilful band, a tribute to Lunceford's meticulous preparations and his admiration for Paul Whiteman. There is some dreary material on the next two discs, particularly the 1940–41 set, but even here there are a couple of interesting arrangements by new arrival Gerald Wilson ('Hi Spook' and 'Yard Dog Mazurka') and the closing two-part 'Blues In The Night', though laden with kitsch, is effective in its way. The 1941–45 set, though, has very little going for it. The band lost several of its key members during this period, notably Willie Smith and Snooky Young, and even with arrangements by Tadd Dameron and Horace Handerson (a very tame 'Jeep Rhythm') there is little to set the orchestra apart from its rivals. Nothing embarrassing here, at least, but the music is very reserved. The even later set of 1945–47 performances is in some ways rather better and may surprise those who feel that Lunceford'a decline was irreversible. Though he had lost so many of his key personalities, this was still a strong and professional outfit. A V-Disc date from October 1945 offers four straight-ahead swing titles, and a final look at 'One O'Clock Jump' (with Joe Wilder and Al Grey as young recruits) closes the disc.

We recommend the first two discs as the essential Lunceford, with the next three still full of interesting music. Transfers are, as usual from this source, rather variable: some of the earliest sides sound scratchy, and some of the later ones have a reverberant feel which at times suggests dubbings from tape copies. For the most part, though, it's been cleanly done.

***** Swingsation**

GRP 059923-2 *As appropriate discs above.* 34–37.

Universal have so far made little of their Lunceford holdings. This compilation in their 'Swingsation' series of big-band samplers is all right, but neither 'White Heat' nor 'Jazznocracy' is here, and 'I'm Nuts About Screwy Music' is. Eighteen tracks isn't particularly bountiful measure, either, if this is all they're going to give us.

Jan Lundgren (born 1966)

PIANO

Danish pianist who has worked extensively in California as well as at home in the '80s and '90s.

***** Conclusion**

Four Leaf Clover FLCD 136 *Lundgren; Jesper Lundgaard (b); Alex Riel (d).* 5–6/94.

*****(*) Bird Of Passage**

Four Leaf Clover FLCD 145 *Lundgren; Anders Bergcrantz (t); Rich Perry (ts); Hans Andersson (b); P.A Tollbom (d).* 7/95.

***** California Connection**

Four Leaf Clover FLCD 148 *Lundgren; Peter Asplund (t); Dave Carpenter (b); Paul Kreibich (d).* 1/96.

***** Cooking! At The Jazz Bakery**

Fresh Sound FSR 5019 2CD *Lundgren; Chuck Berghofer (b); Joe LaBarbera (d).* 9/96.

Lundgren knows his post-bop piano, and he takes his time over tempos and in filling up space. *Conclusion* has nothing green about it (Lundgren spent much of the 1980s playing behind various giants) though nothing to make one gasp at the originality. His own tunes are cute enough, but the standout is a glowing 'I See Your Face Before Me', played with the utmost finesse. He also starts *Bird Of Passage* with a slow ballad, 'This Is All I Ask', before any of the horns come in. Perry is a reliable type for a date like this, and he even comes a little way out of his usually deferential shell on the title-track, where the hollowed-out honks he uses to climax his solo are a surprise. These are longer, more expansive performances, and the show is stolen by Bergcrantz, who comes in on only two tracks yet delivers two outstandingly fine improvisations on Lundgren's originals. Excellent record. After that, Asplund's perfectly agreeable playing is a slight anti-climax on the third record, cut on an American visit with a local rhythm section. Intelligently varied for pace and material, this peaks on a wistful trumpet–piano version of Thore Swanerud's 'Sodermalm'.

Lundgren is back for more with a couple of live sets from Los Angeles's Jazz Bakery. Spreading them over two CDs makes the set an expensive introduction on his methods, and all 20 tracks are prime cut of bebop, bar a farewell solo on 'Värmlandsvisan'. Still, the vigour of the playing is emphatically sustained across both discs, and Berghofer and LaBarbera play with enough vim themselves to suggest that they're giving the young man plenty of respect.

Carmen Lundy (born 1954)

VOCALS

Began working in New York in 1979 and, in a career which has made modest progress, she sings in a style that blends the classic jazz vocal with soul influences, and has a penchant for writing songs herself.

***** Self Portrait**

JVC 2047 *Lundy; Ernie Watts (ts); Gary Herbig (ss, f, af, bf, cl); Cedar Walton (p); John Clayton Jr, Nathan East (b); Ralph Penland (d); strings; woodwinds.* 11/94.

***** Old Devil Moon**

JVC 9016 *Lundy; Randy Brecker (t, flhn); Frank Foster, Bob Mintzer (ts); Billy Childs (p); Harry Whitaker (syn); Victor Bailey, Santi Debriano (b); Winston Clifford, Omar Hakim (d); Mayra Casales, Ralph Irizarry (perc); Tawatha Agee, Dennis Collins, Lani Groves, Gwen Guthrie (v).* 97.

A strong, instrumental singer rather than a great interpreter, Lundy has taken to heart Billie Holiday's overused line about 'playing a horn'. Clearly influenced by saxophone players, Carmen often doesn't seem to be unduly concerned about the programme or the theme of a song, just by its chords and melody. If this makes her sound detached, she isn't, but technique has tended to come before expression, and this is only slowly righting itself. The earlier album opens on a very strong reading of 'Spring Can Really Hang You Up The Most', continues with an excellent original – 'Better Days' – one of several in the set, and peaks with a truly special performance of Kurt Weill's 'My Ship'. Cedar Walton dominates the small group, a player who understands the dynamics of a song better than anyone around. The orchestrations are lusher than they strictly need to be and there are a couple of occasions when one wishes for a simpler, less fussy background, which is what she gets on 'I Don't Want To Love Without You', with Ernie Watts on tenor. The later record is very good, too, but the Billie-isms have become ever more noticeable and are hampering her approach. She opens with 'Star Eyes' this time, and gives it a big send-off. 'In A Sentimental Mood' is the killer-diller, pushed along by a tense, almost threatening rhythm-section. Fewer originals this time out, perhaps because they don't sell, perhaps because Carmen has hipped to the unavoidable recognition that she's never going to outwrite Rodgers and Hart or Donny Hathaway.

Claude Luter (born 1923)

CLARINET, SOPRANO SAXOPHONE

A Parisian, Luter led the French revivalist movement in the late '40s and recorded first with Bechet and later with other clarinettists including Mezzrow, Nicholas and Bigard. Has stuck to his idea of jazz ever since.

***** Red Hot Reeds**

GHB BCD-219 *Luter; Jacques Gauthe (cl, ss); Steve Pistorius, David Boeddinghaus (p); Neil Unterseher (g, bj); Amy Sharpe (bj); Tom Saunders (tba, b); Rick Elmore (tba); Ernie Elly, Dicky Taylor (d).* 4/86.

Not much survives of Luter's discography at present, but he was one of the leading forces in French traditional jazz for decades and this 1986 date, co-led with Jacques Gauthe, is more like a postscript to a ubiquitous career. The horns play in a manner that offers an inevitable echo of Luter's records with Sidney Bechet in the 1950s, and the set-list covers Morton, Handy, Bechet and Jimmy Blythe. Recorded on consecutive days in New Orleans, with entirely different accompanists each day, and performed with much *brio* and enjoyment by the two front-line veterans.

Chick Lyall

PIANO

Scottish pianist making his debut after much activity through the '80s and '90s.

***** Solitary Dance**

Caber 004 *Lyall (solo p).* 1/98.

Though until recently Scotland lacked a solid infrastructure for jazz, the country has continued to produce inventive players. Of the current generation of piano players – which numbers Dave Newton and Brian Kellock – Chick Lyall is the most exploratory and adventurous. A charter member of improvising ensemble Green Room, he has the ability to switch from playing changes to quasi-classical contexts to free.

Solitary Dance is his belated solo debut. Its appearance on Caber is a sign that Scottish jazz is beginning to devise its own flotation system. It's hard to imagine any major label taking on a record as calmly unfashionable and cliché-free. The title-tune is a dedication to Sir Michael Tippett, a slow, understated essay in spatial relationships. Other titles have a more tentative quality. There are three pianistic 'Epigrams' and two 'Objects Of Contemplation', all of them beautifully executed and flawlessly tasteful, but very much academic studies. Elsewhere, as in the pairing of 'Flow River Flow' and 'Blow Wind Blow', the language is more obviously jazz-based, and Lyall's exceptional metrical sense becomes evident. On this showing Lyall is perhaps too reflective to captivate a wider audience.

Brian Lynch (born 1955)

TRUMPET, FLUGELHORN

Lynch has worked with Art Blakey and The Artist Formerly Known As Prince and has a well-deserved reputation for free-blowing swing in a whole range of genres and styles. His own records are largely an outlet for long-lined, complex themes influenced by bebop but often using Coltrane changes in imaginative ways.

***(*) **Peer Pressure**
Criss Cross Criss 1029 *Lynch; Ralph Moore (ts); Jim Snidero (as); Kirk Lightsey (p); Jay Anderson (b); Victor Lewis (d).* 12/86.

(*) **Back Room Blues
Criss Cross Criss 1042 *Lynch; Javon Jackson (ts); David Hazeltine (p); Peter Washington (b); Lewis Nash (d).* 12/89.

*** **At The Main Event**
Criss Cross Criss 1070 *Lynch; Ralph Moore (ts); Mel Rhyne (org); Peter Bernstein (g); Kenny Washington (d); Jose Alexis Diaz (perc).* 12/91.

Peer pressure, indeed. One of the occupational horrors of the jazz musician's life is 'going single', travelling from town to town, playing with local rhythm sections. Eric Dolphy suffered profoundly by it, Lee Konitz seems to thrive on it; *Back Room Blues* would seem to put Brian Lynch squarely with the Dolphys. There's nothing amiss about the leader's playing. His bright, brassy sound – particularly vivid on the often smudgy flugelhorn – is well up to scratch. But the band seems entirely devoid of ideas and the sound might just as well be live.

The line-up on *Peer Pressure* makes weight-for-weight comparison of the two albums as uneven as a Don King boxing bill. Where Jackson is sophomoric, the British-born, Berklee-graduated Ralph Moore is right on the case, responding to Lynch's unpretentious hard bop with a mixture of fire and intelligence. Jim Snidero has less to say but says it with unapologetic verve; his own *Mixed Bag* (Criss Cross Criss 1032 – the label's titles are always curiously self-revealing!) also features Lynch and is worth checking out. Tommy Turrentine's roistering 'Thomasville' gets everybody in and warmed up for the subtler cadence of Benny Golson's 'Park Avenue Petite'. Horace Silver's 'The Outlaw' gets a slightly camp reading but, apart from the low-key CD bonus, 'I Concentrate On You', the rest of the material is by the trumpeter and is generally very impressive, both in conception and in execution. Amazing what a bit of peer pressure can do.

The latest of the Criss Crosses is a good-hearted, expansive, blowin'-in-from-Milwaukee date, which celebrates local club The Main Event. There's plenty of playing to enjoy, even if Lynch acts as not much more than the genial host, and the round-robin of solos on the seven tracks elicits nothing knockout from any of the musicians.

*** **Keep Your Circle Small**
Sharp Nine CD 1001-2 *Lynch; David Hazeltine (p); Peter Washington (b); Louis Hayes (d).* 95.

*** **Spheres Of Influence**
Sharp Nine 1007-2 *Lynch; Tony Lujan, Pete Rodriguez (t); Luis Bonilla, Conrad Herwig (tb); Chris Washburne (tba); Donald Harrison (as); Kavid Kikoski (p); Essiet Okon Essiet (b); John Benitez, Adam Cruz, Jeff Tain Watts, Milton Cardona (perc).* 6/97.

A change of label and signs of growing confidence from Lynch, whose writing is ever more ambitious and capacious. The earlier of the pair is relatively modest in scope and the quartet aren't unduly stretched by the charts. It's with *Spheres Of Influence* that Lynch signals a desire to move on to a new plane, debuting some of his larger-group compositions and arrangements. The opening track uses soulful jazz measures, set to a kind of relaxed reggae beat. Lynch's solo is punctuated with glorious blares and smears. 'Green Is Mean' seems to be a contrafact on 'On Green Dolphin Street', with adventurous changes that recall Coltrane. The Wayne Shorter-composed 'Oriental Folk Song' is an unexpected delight, tucked away at the end of the record but worth programming earlier now and again. The most ambitious performances of the set are the two with extra horns. 'Palmieri's Mood' is a delightful Latin swinger; but, for an insight into Lynch's skill as an arranger, a standard, 'I've Grown Accustomed To Her Face', is the point of reference. Subtly modulated and richly voiced, it makes no compromises, working through a sequence of subtle changes before triggering Lynch's typically elaborate solo. A fine, assured performance from an ever-better player. In support, Donald Harrison plays more freshly and with more bite than he has since the days with Terence Blanchard. Some tracks seem to dispense with bass altogether, which is an interesting tack; on the others, Essiet and Watts mesh as surely as ever.

Jimmy Lyons (1932–86)

ALTO SAXOPHONE, FLUTE

Emerged in the early '60s as a free-thinking alto player who became a key member of Cecil Taylor's group; he remained close with Taylor, besides teaching and playing in other groups, but was killed by lung cancer in 1986.

***(*) **Something In Return**
Black Saint 120125 *Lyons; Andrew Cyrille (perc).* 2/81.

***(*) **Burnt Offering**
Black Saint 120130 *Lyons; Andrew Cyrille (d).* 82.

*** **Wee Sneezawee**
Black Saint 120067 *Lyons; Raphe Malik (t); Karen Borca (bsn); William Parker (b); Paul Murphy (d).* 9/83.

***(*) **Give It Up**
Black Saint 120087 *Lyons; Enrico Rava (t, flhn); Karen Borca (bsn); Jay Oliver (b); Paul Murphy (d).* 3/85.

If Charlie Parker had a true heir – in the sense of someone interested in getting interest on the inheritance, rather than merely preserving the principal – it was Jimmy Lyons. Compared to his light-fingered onrush, most of the bop *epigoni* sound deeply conservative. He didn't have the greatest tone in the world, though it seems rather odd to describe a saxophonist's tone as 'reedy' as if that were an insult. Lyons's delivery was always light and remarkably without ego. Years of playing beside Cecil Taylor, in addition to accelerating his hand-speed, probably encouraged a certain self-effacement as well.

On *Give It Up*, Lyons seems quite content to remain within the confines of the group. Significantly pianoless and with only a rather secondary role for the bassist and drummer, it resolves into a series of high, intermeshed lines from the saxophone and horn, with the bassoon tracing a sombre counterpoint. Karen Borca's role might have been clearer were she not so close in timbre to Jay Oliver's bass, but it's worth concentrating for a moment on what she is doing; the effect is broadly similar to what Dewey Redman used to do behind Ornette Coleman and Don Cherry. She also appears to great effect on the earlier *Wee Sneezawee*, perhaps the most conventional of these discs in free-bop terms but a similarly invigorating session. Only on the brief, uncharacteristic 'Ballada', with which the album ends, does Lyons occupy the foreground. It's immediately clear that his fey, slightly detached tone doesn't entail an absence of feeling; the closing track is a sad monument to an undervalued career that had little more than a year left to run.

Among the most fruitful encounters of Lyons's sadly under-documented career were his duos with Cyrille, a fellow-alumnus of Cecil Taylor Academy. Cyrille is a one-man orchestra, conjuring layered energies that make a sax-and-drums 'Take The "A" Train' seem anything but absurd. One of the great modern drummers, Cyrille can play at astonishing volume (at one point almost sounding as if he was trying to re-create a Cecil Taylor trio *à deux*), but also with considerable subtlety and a user-friendly reliability of beat. 'Exotique', on the later session, is a superbly structured and emotionally committed performance. Both this and the concert recording, *Burnt Offering*, are superb examples of two masters in full flight.

Johnny Lytle (1932–96)

VIBES

Played drums with Ray Charles in 1950 but switched to vibes and led his own groups from the late '50s onwards.

***** The Village Caller**

Original Jazz Classics OJC 110 *Lytle; Milt Harris (org); Bob Cranshaw (b); Peppy Hinant (d); Willie Rodriguez (perc).* 64–65.

****(*) The Loop / New & Groovy**

BGP CDBGPD 961 *Lytle; unknown p, b and d.* 65.

If there is a classic record by this Ohio-born drummer-turned-vibesman, it's surely *The Village Caller*, where he lives out all the clichés of organ–vibes rhythm combos and delivers a perfectly cooked slice of soul-jazz in the title-tune. The rest of the album bumbles past inoffensively enough.

The BGP CD couples two very rare albums from the same period, originally issued on Tuba with no personnel details, and the music is even slighter (typical titles include 'The Snapper' and 'Screamin' Loud'). The formula wears thin after a number of tracks but, taken a few at a time, they certainly stir the feet. The pianist sounds very like Wynton Kelly here and there, and the remastering is good if a little overbright. Lytle's subsequent Muse albums were a mostly disappointing lot and his passing left his status sadly unrealized.

Humphrey Lyttelton (born 1921)

TRUMPET, CORNET, CLARINET, VOCAL

The doyen of post-war British jazz, Lyttelton has been active for more than 50 years as a performer, broadcaster, writer, wit and general man-about-jazz, a tireless force whose early links with trad jazz soon blossomed into a shrewd pan-stylistic outlook. His toff's background (Eton and the Guards) might have instilled certain qualities of leadership, but he has never been shy about his work and he still leads a band and runs his own record label.

***** Delving Back With Humph 1948–1949**

Lake LACD 72 *Lyttelton; Harry Brown, Ian Christie, Bobby Mickleburgh (tb); Wally Fawkes (cl); Ernie Mansfield (ts); George Webb, Dill Jones (p); Nevil Skrimshire, Bill Bramwell (g); Buddy Vallis (bj); Les Rawlings, John Wright, Bert Howard (b); Dave Carey (d, wbd); Bernard Saward, Carlo Krahmer (d).* 1/48–11/49.

This is almost prehistoric for Lyttelton, who is still on active duty both as musician and emcee for jazz on stage and in radio. A very fine discography attests to his command as a trumpeter (and clarinettist, though that side of his playing is less often remarked on). These early sessions are the prelude to the full-blown British trad movement of the early 1950s: six tracks with a Carlo Krahmer group of 1948, followed by 15 from the following year, each led from the front by Lyttelton's tight, crisp trumpet and Fawkes's serpentine clarinet, at this stage almost entirely in Sidney Bechet's debt. The rhythm sections range from awkward to competent, and the material is mostly Oliver, ODJB and the like; but the peculiarly British fierceness of the music hasn't gone stale, and even in less than ideal sound the enthusiasm of the band cuts through.

****** The Parlophones Volumes One–Four**

Calligraph CLG CD 035-1/2/3/4 *Lyttelton; Keith Christie, John Picard (tb); Wally Fawkes, Ian Christie (cl); Bruce Turner (ss, as, cl); Tony Coe (as, cl); Ade Monsbrough (as); Jimmy Skidmore, Kathy Stobart (ts); Joe Temperley (bs); George Webb, Johnny Parker, Ian Armit (p); Freddy Legon (g, bj); Buddy Vallis (bj); Mickey Ashman, Brian Brocklehurst, Jim Bray (b); Bernard Saward, Stan Greig, Eddie Taylor, George Hopkinson (d); Iris Grimes, Neva Raphaello (v).* 11/49–8/59.

At last, the bulk of Lyttelton's Parlophone sessions make it to CD. One hundred titles are neatly spread across the four discs (available only separately, though Humph might do you a deal at one of his gigs) and, although in absolutist terms it isn't complete – there are no alternative takes, and titles by the collaborative bands with Graeme Bell and Freddy Grant are being saved for a possible follow-up – what remains is a comprehensive picture of ten years of work by the leading jazz force of his day and arguably the most influential jazzman Britain has ever produced.

Even the earliest tracks show how Lyttelton wasn't content to regard jazz as any kind of routine and, although the 1949–50 sessions are relatively formulaic, the playing – these were among the best players the country could muster, after all – is consistently creative and supple, with the rhythm sections never resorting to the trudge of regulation trad. Lyttelton's own playing is wasteless and controlled, without losing the terminal vibrato which was a feature of the '20s stylists he admired. Fawkes and Christie were important elements in this band, and so was Bruce Turner, a notorious recruit when he arrived in 1953 but a crucial aide in assisting Lyttelton's move from trad to mainstream. The progress through the '50s is marked by milestones such as 'The Onions' and the great hit, 'Bad Penny Blues', before concluding with the 1957–9 sessions which suggest how far Lyttelton had progressed, from the sparky trad of 'Memphis Blues' to the sophisticated mainstream inflexions of the likes of 'Hand Me Down Love'. There are also glimpses of young tykes such as Tony Coe, Kathy Stobart, Jimmy Skidmore and Joe Temperley.

Throughout the four discs there are surprises, such as the extraordinary, haunting 'Jail Break' or Lyttelton's blues playing behind Neva Raphaello on 'Young Woman Blues'. As a record of a crucial chapter in British jazz, it's peerless stuff. Remastering, by Dave Bennett when tape masters haven't been used, is excellent, although some of the original engineering wasn't up to all that much.

***** Take It From The Top**

Black Lion BLCD 760516 *Lyttelton; Bruce Turner (cl, as); Kathy Stobart (ss, ts, bs); Mick Pyne (p); Dave Green (b); Tony Mann (d); Elkie Brooks (v).* 6/75.

***** Movin' And Groovin'**

Black Lion BLCD 760504 *Lyttelton; Roy Williams (tb); Bruce Turner (as); Kathy Stobart, John Barnes (ts, bs); Mick Pyne (p); Dave Green (b); Adrian Macintosh (d).* 1/83.

There's still a gap in Humph's discography, with all of his 1960s discs missing, and very little between there and the formation of his own label in the 1980s. We still have these two dates for Black Lion. *Take It From The Top* is a dedication to Ellington, always a benevolent influence on Lyttelton's music, and there are some charming originals by the leader penned in the great man's style: listen especially to 'Sprauncy' and 'Lion Rampant'. Four features for Elkie Brooks don't quite work out so well, even if she'd had little time to learn the music. *Movin' And Groovin'* is another bridge between trad ('Basin Street Blues', 'Aunt Hagar's Blues' – a beautiful chart by Alan Hall) and mainstream ('Never No Lament', 'One For Buck') and it shows how Lyttelton had kept faith with a catholic philosophy which few others – anywhere in the music – have cared to maintain. His own chops also sound little weathered by the years: a bright, middleweight sound, coloured by his affection for players from Armstrong to Clayton.

*****(*) Beano Boogie**

Calligraph CLG 021 *Lyttelton; Pete Strange (tb); John Barnes (cl, ss, ts, bs); Alan Barnes (cl, ss, as); Stan Greig (p); Paul Bridge (b); Adrian Macintosh (d).* 3/89.

***** Rock Me Gently**

Calligraph CLG 026 *As above, except Kathy Stobart (cl, ss, ts, bs) replaces John Barnes; add Dave Cliff (g).* 7/91.

The formation of Calligraph, his own label, has produced a steady stream of new records from Humph, and they maintain a standard which many jazz musicians should envy. Some fine records from the early 1980s, including *At The Bull's Head* and *Gigs*, have yet to acquire CD transfer, though there may still be some LP stocks in circulation. *Beano Boogie* is notable for the arrival of Alan Barnes, whose alto turns add fresh fizz to a well-established front line. Though the record gets off to a slow start, when it reaches 'Apple Honey', a nearly explosive reading of the Woody Herman tune, it lifts off. The elder Barnes departed with *Rock Me Gently*, but Kathy Stobart's return to the fold (35 years after they recorded 'Kath Meets Humph') means there is no drop in authority, and she delivers a grippingly unsentimental version of 'My Funny Valentine' on what's a generously filled CD.

*****(*) At Sundown**

Calligraph CLG 027 *Lyttelton; Acker Bilk (cl, v); Dave Cliff (g); Dave Green (b); Bobby Worth (d).* 1/92.

It seems little short of amazing that these two veterans had never recorded together before, but apparently not! The result is a warmly amiable meeting which holds up throughout CD length. Humph's own interest in the clarinet – there's at least one clarinet feature for him on most of the Calligraphs listed above – makes him a fine match for Bilk here on 'Just A Little While To Stay Here', but it's the easy give-and-take between trumpet and clarinet, over an almost lissom rhythm section, which gives the record its class; even Acker's vocals sound sunny enough, and his clarinet has become as idiosyncratic and engaging as Pee Wee Russell's.

***** Rent Party**

Stomp Off CD1238 *Lyttelton; Keith Nichols (tb, tba); John Beecham (tb); Wally Fawkes (cl); Stan Greig (p); Paul Sealey (bj, g); Jack Fallon, Annie Hawkins (b); Colin Bowden (d).* 8/91–1/92.

*****(*) Hear Me Talkin' To Ya**

Calligraph CLG CD 029 *Lyttelton; Pete Strange (tb); Jimmy Hastings (cl, as, f); Kathy Stobart (cl, ts, bs); Stan Greig (p); Paul Bridge (b); Adrian Macintosh (d).* 5/93.

These bulletins from Humph make a neatly contrasting illustration of the breadth of his interests. *Rent Party* is straight out of the traditional pocket, with ancient material such as 'Texas Moaner' and 'Viper Mad' given a lusty work-out. Fawkes, who goes, as they say, way back with Lyttelton, gets as close to Bechet-like authority as he ever has, and the banjo-driven rhythm sections find the necessary feel without resorting to caricature. *Hear Me Talkin' To Ya* is a pleasing jazz-history lesson, with obscure Ellington (one of Humph's specialities), Carla Bley and Buck Clayton in the set-list as well as carefully revised treatments of 'Beale Street Blues' and 'St James Infirmary'. Jimmy Hastings comes on board for the first time and makes a keen addition to what is now a very commanding front line. The joints may creak a bit here and there, but this is still excellent jazz.

***** Three In The Morning**

Calligraph CLG 30 *Lyttelton; Acker Bilk (cl, v); John Barnes (cl, as, bs); Dave Cliff (g); Dave Green (b); Bobby Worth (d).* 9/93–4/94.

After-hours with Humph and Acker. The newly established old firm sound fine again here, though the session droops a little in places, possibly because of the absence of the late Bruce Turner, who fell ill before he could play the parts which ultimately fell to John Barnes. As usual, Lyttelton has done some inspired work in choosing material: 'I'd Climb The Highest Mountain', Al Fairweather's 'Ludo' and Ida Cox's 'Last Smile Blues' are among the nuggets that nobody else would have thought of.

***** ... Lay 'Em Straight!**

Calligraph CLG 33 *Lyttelton; Pete Strange (tb); Jimmy Hastings (as, f); Alan Barnes (as); Kathy Stobart (ts, bs); Joe Temperley (bs, ss); Ted Beament (p); Paul Bridge (b); Adrian Macintosh (d).* 2–10/96.

Frankly, a bit of a disappointment. Humph recalls Alan Barnes and Joe Temperley as guests on some tracks, and they certainly lend extra merit, especially Temperley's lovely baritone on 'Echoes Of The Duke'. There are the customary small ingenuities, too, in the likes of 'Zoltan's Dream', the old favourite 'Late Night Final' and more. But here and there the playing sounds fallible.

Paul Lytton

DRUMS, PERCUSSION, LIVE ELECTRONICS

British improvising percussionist, often at work with contemporaries Evan Parker and Paul Lovens; something of a pioneer in playing an amplified and electronically altered kit.

*****(*) The Balance Of Trade**

CIMP 114 *Lytton; Herb Robertson (c, t, vtb, tba, horn, flageolet etc.); Phil Wachsmann (vn, vla, elec); Dominic Duval (b, elec).* 5/96.

Lytton's first disc as nominal leader for many years is, as usual in this area of music-making, both visionary in scope and piecemeal in its actuality. The individual items range from a couple of minutes to over 19 in length, but each seems to last as long as it ought to, or has to. Lytton, whose history stretches back to all the British and European free musics of the 1960s and '70s, continues to be one of the drummer-percussionists least hidebound by the idea of time, rhythm or determined pulse. His enormous kit (which apparently took several hours to set up) is something he uses as sparsely as possible: it seems that a lot of it might be there for the purpose of perhaps one tiny gesture somewhere in the music. Nobody has ever used electronics in the way he does; in fact, it's hard to hear how his electronics even affect the music. Wachsmann is someone fully attuned to this situation, but Duval and Robertson are Americans who are remote from what is a very European style of free music – yet they both handle themselves extraordinarily well, idiomatic to a 't'. About as difficult as it gets.

Harold Mabern (born 1936)

PIANO

Allegedly influenced by Phineas Newborn, the big man from Memphis has a far more beguilingly melodic approach and more muscular delivery than Phineas. He worked with Art Farmer and Benny Golson and with Lionel Hampton, and spent many years as an accompanist. There are few early recordings still in circulation, but Mabern has released several sessions as leader in the 1980s and '90s.

***** Wailin'**

Prestige PRCD 24134 *Mabern; Virgil Jones (t, flhn); Lee Morgan (t); George Coleman (ts); Hubert Laws (ts, f); Boogaloo Joe Jones (g); Buster Williams (b); Idris Muhammad (d).* 6/69, 1/70.

***** Philadelphia Bound**

Sackville SKCD 23051 *Mabern; Kieran Overs (b).* 4/91, 2/92.

***** The Leading Man**

Columbia 477288 *As above, except add Bill Mobley (t), Bill Easley (as), Kevin Eubanks (g), Ron Carter (b).* 11/92, 1, 3 & 4/93.

There is something about Harold Mabern that just breathes Memphis. Few jazz pianists have come so close to the essence of the blues, yet there is nothing crude or revivalist about his playing, which also indicates a heavy debt to Ahmad Jamal and Phineas Newborn Jr, both pianists who made a distinctive use of space. This is never more obvious than on the most recent of these sets. He brings a special touch to Carl Perkins's seldom recorded 'Grooveyard' and invests 'Baubles, Bangles And Beads' with a weighty, masculine charm. Working with lighter-touched trio partners only accentuates the effect.

Even when Philadelphia bound, as on the duos with that marvellous accompanist, Kieran Overs, he sounds like a man happily locked into his own corner of the world. There is much that can be learnt about Mabern from this record, not least his awesome flexibility and awareness within his chosen stylistic field. Being in Philly (they were actually in Toronto, but the mood-setting number was Ray Bryant's 'Philadelphia Bound'), he touches on Coltrane ('Dear Lord' and 'Lazybird') and plays a solo version of 'The Cry Of My People', written by Trane's friend Cal Massey. There are also two Benny Golson numbers ('Are You Real' and 'Whisper Not') which take him back to the kind of material he was doing a couple of decades earlier.

Wailin' brings together two Prestige sessions from the late 1960s. The electric piano dates it a little on 'Blues For Phineas'; however, like Kenny Barron, Mabern invests the instrument with a bit of character. *Wailin'* also traces his development as a composer of original themes, still largely blues-based but forward-looking and surprisingly memorable (surprising only in that they seem to be covered so rarely); 'Greasy Kid Stuff' and 'Waltzing Westward' sit up and ask to be played. Morgan is an essential component of the 1970 group and Mabern was to return the compliment in the trumpeter's last group before his untimely death. One of the better tunes on the 1969 record, 'Too Busy Thinking About My Baby', has been held out but is promised on a further compilation, which may well include a greater variety of standards.

The chap who wrote the sleeve-notes for the Columbia record suggests that Mabern resembles 'an aging offensive lineman', which is apparently a compliment in the United States. We'd suggest that he's much more like a mature dancing-master, a little thicker in girth than of yore, but still with that pungently graceful approach to the blues. As we've said, recent years have seen him experiment with more adventurous material, and there are tunes by Wayne Shorter, Parker ('Au Privave'), Wes Montgomery and Coltrane again ('Moment's Notice') on this record. The only drawback to it can be inferred from the session dates. Neither expressively nor acoustically does it hang together as a package. There are effectively two groups represented with a very different stance on the material. No serious problem with this, but it does demand a certain internal readjustment. *The Leading Man* appears as part of Columbia's Legendary Masters of Jazz series. No arguments with that.

****** Straight Street**

DIW 608 *Mabern; Ron Carter (b); Jack DeJohnette (d).* 12/89.

****** Lookin' On The Bright Side**

DIW 614 *Mabern; Christian McBride (b); Jack DeJohnette (d).* 2 & 3/93.

****** Mabern's Grooveyard**

DIW 621 *Mabern; Christian McBride (b); Tony Reedus (d).* 96.

The DIW trios establish Mabern as one of the most imaginative current players of repertoire material. His ability to invest a tune with new lights and shades and to transform relatively banal material into substantial music is deeply impressive. Working with sidemen of the quality of DeJohnette and Carter has undoubtedly made a difference, but on each of these records it is Mabern's commanding voice which makes the final difference. These are flawless records.

Teo Macero (born 1925)

TENOR SAXOPHONE

Though guaranteed his place in the jazz pantheon for his pioneering production work on Miles Davis's Bitches Brew and other records, a process which made creative use of tape editing, Macero is little known as a saxophonist. He did, however, record several times as leader and, following the end of his working relationship with Miles in 1983, returned to recording and released a much-admired tribute to his former boss, Charles Mingus.

***** The Best Of Teo Macero**

Stash 527 *Macero; Art Farmer, Clark Terry (t); Eddie Bert, Frank Rehak (tb); Lee Konitz, Phil Woods (as); Al Cohn (ts); Pepper Adams, Charles Mingus (b); Bill Evans, Mal Waldron (p); Ed Costa (vib); Ed Shaughnessy (d); a.o.* 55–83.

****(*) With The Prestige Jazz Quartet**

Original Jazz Classics OJCCD 1715 2 *Macero; Teddy Charles (vib); Mal Waldron (p); Addison Farmer (b); Jerry Segal (d).* 4/57.

Possessed of a tremendous technique – Teo can or could play the entire harmonic scale simply by adjusting his embouchure – he is not particularly individual as an improvising soloist and the strength of these tracks, which pretty much exhaust his recorded output before the early '80s, is in the compositions themselves. All the selections are by Macero, written in a vein that occasionally recalls some of Bob Graettinger's work for Kenton and sometimes the more relaxed and swinging end of the Third Stream. Some of the best pieces are the shortest; 'Heart On My Sleeve' is less than three minutes long and the witty '24 + 18 +' gets it equations worked through in less than four. There is more energy expended, though, on long-form composition in 'Time Plus Seven: Seven/Equals/Time/Plus', which breaks down into a number of sub-sections, none of them exciting in itself but adding to the brickwork of a fascinating musical edifice. As a soloist he is very limited and is reminiscent in tone and phrasing of the Belgian, Bobby Jaspar. Lester Young was the obvious model for both, and Teo also seems to have derived something from Warne Marsh. Minus the interest of his more challenging compositional side, the Prestige set is rather flat and conventional. Gently paced and consisting mainly of new ballads – 'Star Eyes' is the only standard – it moves at an even, thoughtful pace which allows Macero to unspool his solos. Neither is by an means a classic record, but together they offer an insight into the man behind not just *Bitches Brew* but the classic *Kind Of Blue* as well.

Vanessa Mackness

VOICE

British vocal improviser, working in and around the London free-music community.

*****(*) Respiritus**

Incus CD014 *Mackness; John Butcher (ss, ts).* 4–12/94.

A long-awaited debut from the British improvising vocalist, here with frequent partner Butcher, recorded at two concerts in 1994. This is funny, serious music, and the two musicians strike up a brilliant empathy at many moments. An operatic bark might come from Mackness in response to some entirely different gesture by Butcher, and yet the juxtaposition can sound exactly right. The singer's range is wide, if not quite as awesome as, say, Diamanda Galas's, and it's her acute grasp of dynamics which makes these ten duets sound vital and vivid. Mouth, glottal and dialect effects are used sparingly and effectively. Butcher, in many ways as vocal a performer himself, is sensitive but never submissive in the dialogues. A splendid encounter session.

Fraser MacPherson (1928–93)

TENOR SAXOPHONE

Born in Winnipeg, he worked on the Vancouver scene in dance bands and doing studio duties, latterly achieving some recognition as a soloist.

***** Indian Summer**

Concord CCD 4224 *MacPherson; Oliver Gannon (g); Steve Wallace (b); Jake Hanna (d).* 6/83.

***** Honey And Spice**

Justin Time JUST 23 *MacPherson; Oliver Gannon (g); Steve Wallace (b); John Sumner (d).* 3/87.

****(*) Encore**

Justin Time 8420 *As above.* 4/90.

He might have been the Canadian Getz, or Sims, or another Lestorian pupil; but Fraser MacPherson's name was seldom kept before the wider jazz public, and his decent, graceful sound and sure-footed delivery must be accounted as the work of another accomplished tenorman with a few records to his name. Anyone checking him out with no greater expectations will find these records good value. The Concord album is a little more refined in studio terms (there are two other deleted albums on the label) but the Justin Time discs benefit from complete understanding between MacPherson and his rhythm team, and *Honey And Spice*'s considered mixture of ballads and swingers is probably his best memorial.

Katrine Madsen

VOCAL

Danish singer working with the American songbook and some more contemporary material.

***** Dream Dancing**
Music Mecca 2044-2 *Madsen; Thomas Fryland (t, flhn); Lars Jansson (p); Jesper Bodilsen (b); Morten Lund (d); Steen Raahauge (perc).* 9/97.

***** You Are So Beautiful**
Music Mecca 2088-2 *Madsen; Carsten Dahl (p), Jesper Bodilsen (b); Ed Thigpen (d); Svante Thuresson (v).* 12/98.

It's a surprise when Madsen's voice enters on the slow, tropical beat of Meredith D'Ambrosio's 'August Moon': a heavy, low contralto that almost slouches through the lyrics. The lilting rhythms and Fryland's perky trumpet lighten the mood and make quite a peppery contrast with the singer's methods. The playing is, indeed, vital and expressive throughout, so much so that attention is often taken away from the singer. Much may depend on whether Madsen's diction – slightly wayward and slurred, as is often the case with Scandinavian voices singing in English – appeals. She does best on the slow to mid-tempo pieces, and the three D'Ambrosio lyrics all suit her well.

The second disc is a shade more inhabited by the singer. She's lucky with her pianists: after the excellent Jansson comes the admirable Dahl, whose solo on the opening 'Early In The Autumn' gives early notice that he's going to play a considerable part in the record. Thuresson comes in to sing a couple of duets but Madsen is not overshadowed, and her own writing appears in a few places. 'Speak Low' works from a slow pace which she handles in a way that's fatigued and sexy at the same moment. Recommended to the adventurous.

Peter Madsen

PIANO

New York pianist with a sequence of early-'90s dates that so far seem to be his contribution.

***** Snuggling Snakes**
Minor Music 801030 *Madsen; Chris Potter (as, ts, ss); Toninha Horta (g, v); Anthony Cox (b); Lewis Nash (d).* 12/92.

***** Three Of A Kind**
Minor Music 801039 *Madsen; Dwayne Dolphin (b); Bruce Cox (d).* 93.

****(*) Three Of A Kind Meets Mr T**
Minor Music 801043 *As above, except add Stanley Turrentine (ts).*

Madsen is the kind of piano player who will always get gigs. Tremendously adaptable and eclectic, he sounds quite at ease in a mainstream jazz setting, as in *Three Of A Kind*; he can push out the envelope a little bit, as in the more contemporary-sounding 1992 group; or he can function in the avant-garde, having recorded with Franklin Kiermyer. Whether one likes the third of these really depends on having or lacking a settled view of Turrentine, who comes in very much like Mr T on *The A Team* and dominates things. Madsen is a forceful enough player and a clear-sighted leader, and he manages to put his personal stamp even on this one. *Snuggling Snakes* is diluted a bit by having Horta on two tracks, but it is still a very effective modern-jazz record.

The Magnolia Jazz Band

GROUP

American trad group from Stanford, California.

****(*) The Magnolia Jazz Band And Art Hodes Vol. 1**
GHB BCD-171 *Jim Borkenhagen (t); Jim Klippert (tb); Bill Carter (cl); Art Hodes (p); Danny Ruedger (bj, v); Robbie Schlosser (b); Jeff Hamilton (d).* 1/83.

****(*) The Magnolia Jazz Band And Art Hodes Vol. 2**
GHB BCD-172 *As above.* 1/83.

The Magnolias play upright, big-sounding trad which comes swaggering off this session (somewhat inconveniently split over two CDs). Art Hodes knew them and sat in for this studio date which finds him suitably prominent in the mix and sounding in superior form. The material sticks to familiar staples of the trad book and a few blues and, while it's not hard to live without it, this won't disappoint fans of either Hodes or local American trad. Docked a notch for the singing, which is pretty awful.

Mahavishnu Orchestra

GROUP

After the death of Jimi Hendrix, the mantle fell on the shoulders of John McLaughlin. For a time, the known world seemed to be divided between his Mahavishnu Orchestra and Chick Corea's similarly Miles-influenced Return to Forever. Easy now to parody the Orchestra's uneasy shifts from gentle arpeggiation to flat-out screaming in un-jazzy metres. At the time, they really seemed like the last best hope.

****** The Inner Mounting Flame**
Columbia CK 31067 *John McLaughlin; Jan Hammer (p, syn); Jerry Goodman (vn); Rick Laird (b); Billy Cobham (d).* 71–72.

*****(*) Birds Of Fire**
Columbia 468224 *As above.* 72.

***** The Lost Trident Sessions**
Columbia CK 65959 *As above.* 6/73.

***** Between Nothingness And Eternity**
Columbia 468225 *As above.* 8/73.

**** Apocalypse**
Columbia 467092 *John McLaughlin; Jean-Luc Ponty (vn); Gayle Moran (ky, v); Carol Shive (vn, v); Marsha Westbrook (vla); Philip Hirschi (clo, v); Ralphe Armstrong (b, v); Narada Michael Walden (d); Michael Gibbs (arr); London Symphony Orchestra, Michael Tilson Thomas (cond).* 3/74.

**** Visions Of The Emerald Beyond**
Columbia 467904 *John McLaughlin; other personnel unidentified.* 75.

***** Best Of The Mahavishnu Orchestra**
Columbia 468226 *As above.* 71–75.

One of the few jazz-rock bands of the early 1970s whose work seems certain to survive, the Mahavishnu Orchestra combined sophisticated time-signatures and chord structures with drum and guitar riffs of surpassing heaviness. Wielding a huge double-neck incorporating 6- and 12-string guitars, McLaughlin produced chains of blistering high notes, influenced by Hendrix and by earlier R&B, but still essentially in a jazz idiom. Less obviously dominant than on *Extrapolation*, McLaughlin works his group collectively, like an orchestra rather than a theme-and-solo outfit. Billy Cobham's whirlwind drumming was and remains the key to the group's success, underpinning and embellishing McLaughlin's and Hammer's often quite simple lines. His opening press-roll and subsequent accents on (the still incorrectly titled) 'One Word' (*Birds Of Fire*) clear the way for Rick Laird's finest moment on record. Even where he is poorly recorded on the live album, he is still dominant. Goodman came from the American 'progressive' band, Flock, and is used largely for embellishment, but his rather scratchy sound contributed a great deal to the overall impact of *Inner Mounting Flame*, still the group's best album, and he has no apparent difficulty playing in 13/8.

The first Mahavishnu album was one of the essential fusion records, largely because it was more generously promoted and more obviously rock-derived than *Extrapolation*. Ironically, just as he was pushing the iconic guitar solo to new heights of amplification and creative abandon, McLaughlin was also working against the dominance of electricity and setting a new standard for 'acoustic' performance. 'Thousand Island Park' and 'Open Country Joy' on *Birds Of Fire* recall the beautiful acoustic 'A Lotus On Irish Streams' from the first album. They ought to have done more in that vein, and McLaughlin's subsequent work with Shakti strongly suggested that it was far from exhausted.

One of the most intriguing musical rediscoveries of recent years has been a pair of quarter-inch tapes, unearthed by record producer Bob Belden. These contained the 'lost' sessions which would have been the Orchestra's fourth studio album. In the event, personal and artistic differences had blocked progress with what would have been the follow-up to the successful *Birds Of Fire* and the last issued recording by the original Mahavishnu Orchestra. In the event, Columbia released the live recording, *Between Nothingness And Eternity*, which was taped in concert at Central Park. For Mahavishnu loyalists, it's quite difficult now to hear these tracks in any form other than the original issue. Word of bootleg copies of the studio session has circulated for some time, but we've never been offered a copy. Hearing it cold, it seems a little flat and unatmospheric, and whoever in the band it was who wanted a bit of sweetening and perhaps a few over-dubbed strings has some justification. The opening 'Dream' lacks the drama – heralded by gongs and hissing cymbals – which made the start of *Nothingness/Eternity* so compelling.

There was clearly some conflict regarding composition credits on what was supposed to be a co-operative band rather than McLaughlin's band. The 'lost' session includes Hammer's 'Sister Andrea' – also on the live record – but also two short tunes by Rick Laird ('Steppings Tones') and Jerry Goodman ('I Wonder'), though it seems that Billy Cobham was inclined to keep his counsel and retain new tunes for his own projects. Interesting as the Trident tapes are, we remain resolutely underwhelmed.

Unfortunately Columbia have not drawn the Great Veil of Kindly Oblivion over the expanded Orchestra's subsequent recordings, *Apocalypse* and *Visions Of The Emerald Beyond*; apart from flashes of quality from replacement violinist Jean-Luc Ponty, these were as drearily directionless as the three quintet albums were forceful, developing the line McLaughlin had begun with *Extrapolation* and *Where Fortune Smiles*. The *Best Of* compilation is, therefore, very nearly that, though most people would have swapped the live tracks for more from *Inner Mounting Flame*.

Jack Maheu (born 1930)

CLARINET

One-time veteran of The Dukes Of Dixieland and the Salt City Six, Maheu is a battle-hardened Dixieland pro who retired to New Orleans in 1990 – and decided to carry on.

***** In New Orleans**
Jazzology JCD-278 *Maheu; Kevin Clark, Duke Heitger (t); Charles Fardella (c); Al Barthlow (tb); Tom Fischer (ts); Tom Saunders (bsx); Tom McDermott, John Royen (p); Steve Blailock (g); Matt Perrine (b, sou); Richard Taylor (d); Big Al Carson (v).* 6/96.

Maheu is a dedicated traditionalist who has moved from his New York patch to New Orleans for this smart, entertaining set of updates on the classic repertoire. He assembled a local ensemble for the 13 tunes, and they perform with fine chops and good gusto, getting a sound somewhere between commercial Dixieland and the more respectful feel of the heartland style. An original like 'Bourbon Moon' fits snugly beside an uproarious 'Cakewalkin' Babies From Home' (with a terrific vocal by Carson) and a treatment of 'Just A Closer Walk With Thee' that chugs along to a dead-slow R&B shuffle. Plenty of good solos, and Maheu himself is in fine fettle, but docked a notch for a couple of fillers and a daft ending with a variation on 'Chopsticks'!

Kevin Mahogany (born 1958)

VOCALS

The heir of Al Hibbler and Johnny Hartman, Mahogany is a throwback to an older style of jazz singer, though sufficiently aware of more recent developments not to sound like a nostalgia act.

***** Double Rainbow**

Enja ENJ 7097 *Mahogany; Ralph Moore (ts); Kenny Barron (p); Ray Drummond (b); Lewis Nash (d).* 93.

****(*) Songs And Moments**

Enja ENJ 8072 *Mahogany; Michael Philip Mossman (t); Robin Eubanks (tb); Arthur Blythe (as); Steve Wilson (as, cl); Willie Williams (ts, cl); Phil Brenner (ss, af); Gary Smulyan (bs, bcl); John Hicks (p); Ray Drummond (b); Marvin 'Smitty' Smith (d); backing vocalists.* 3/94.

What a splendid name for a jazz singer! We'd say the voice was closer to ripe cherry wood, with a bright, slightly splintery grain and the ability to turn to almost anything. Enja obviously consider Mahogany something of a discovery and have thrown some top-ranking players at him. The earlier album is obviously intended as a technical showcase, while the second, with a much bigger orchestra, is more relaxed and expressive. Ironically, Mahogany is less convincing in the latter mode. Unlike a lot of fast, scatty singers, he does know how to pull down the tempo without sounding flabby; purely as a matter of pacing and balance, however, he does better on the former. The highlights include tongue-twisting versions of Parker's 'Confirmation', 'Dat Dere' and a very moving performance of Duke Ellington's 'Sound Of Love'. He also does a James Baldwin recitation which suggests some more challenging musical areas that he might productively move into.

The next record is fussier and more obviously 'produced', with arrangements that once or twice threaten to swamp even an over-miked singer. It's worth it for 'My Foolish Heart' alone, and the take on both 'Caravan' and '"A" Train' is joyous and provocative. A precious talent which will be hard to manage, one suspects, in an industry that still has weirdly fixed ideas about what singers are meant to do.

***** You Got What It Takes**

Enja ENJ 9039-2 *Mahogany; Benny Golson (ts); James Williams (p); Michael Formanek (b); Victor Lewis (d); Jeanie Bryson (v).* 5/95.

A great band and a fine guest appearance from Jeanie Bryson, but a less than sparkling set by Mahogany himself. Golson's dark-brown tone and deceptively nimble moves are what capture the attention most immediately and wholly, and his interchanges with Williams and Formanek upstage the two vocalists comprehensively. Mahogany is also miked rather remotely compared to earlier records, perhaps in an attempt to get a more even band sound. It does him few favours.

*****(*) Kevin Mahogany**

Warner Bros 9 46226 *Mahogany; Kirk Whalum (sax); Peter Bernstein (g); James Weidman (p); Larry Goldings (org, p); Rodney Whitaker (b); Greg Hutchinson (d); Bashiri Johnson (perc).* 1/96.

*****(*) Another Time, Another Place**

Warner Bros 9 46699 *Mahogany; Joe Lovano (ts); Cyrus Chestnut (p); Dave Stryker (g); Ben Wolfe (b); Clarence Penn (d).* 3/97.

Major-label follow-through can be a crashing disappointment, but both of these records, very different from each other, suggest that Warners are prepared to allow Mahogany time and space to develop his own thing. The funkier, R&B-tinged sound of the eponymous 1996 album contrasts sharply with the cooler and more lyrical approach on *Another Time, Another Place*. The addition of Lovano is a huge bonus, even if he is restricted (somewhat oddly) to the first three tracks.

Mahogany's take on 'Nature Boy' borders on the sarcastic and is all the stronger for it. He gives 'In The Wee Small Hours Of The Morning' a throaty resonance that seems to conjure up a host of influences from Frank Sinatra to Al Hibbler, a genuinely significant piece of jazz singing. Future projects will be well worth the wait.

*****(*) My Romance**

Warner Bros 9 66453 *Mahogany; Michael Brecker, Kirk Whalum (ts); Bob James (p); Charles Fambrough (b); Billy Kilson (d).* 98.

The final minutes of this, with Mahogany backed by just Bob James in a heartaching version of 'Lush Life', clinch the most openly emotive set so far. Eleven poignant ballads which call on the more obscure corners of the American songbook and include tunes by Lyle Lovett, Van Morrison and James Taylor. Mahogany has the gift of making almost any song convincing and personal. He gives 'Wild Honey' and 'I Apologize' a true jazz feel and at the same time invests 'My Romance' and 'Stairway To The Stars' with a contemporary, almost hard-edged sound. Another fine album, though by this stage Mahogany seems to be coasting and could do with a new challenge.

Adam Makowicz (born 1940)

PIANO

Studied in Cracow and worked with Tomasz Stanko on and off through the '60s and '70s; more familiar as a soloist and trio player in the '80s and '90s, with several American discs to his credit.

***** Live At Maybeck Recital Hall Series, Volume 24**

Concord CCD 4541 *Makowicz (p solo).* 7/92.

****** The Music Of Jerome Kern**

Concord CCD 4575 *Makowicz; George Mraz (b); Alan Dawson (d).* 9/92.

*****(*) My Favorite Things: The Music Of Richard Rodgers**

Concord CCD 4631 *As above.* 9/93.

***** Adam Makowicz / George Mraz: Concord Duo Series – Volume 5**

Concord CCD 4597 *Makowicz; George Mraz (b).* 5/93.

It has become almost a cliché to characterize Adam Makowicz's style as a hybrid of Tatum and Chopin. Technically at least, it's pretty near the mark, and there is a persistent romantic (even tragic) tinge to even his most exuberant playing that makes the parallel with his (adoptive) compatriot a reasonable one. His first jazz partnership was with the trumpeter, Tomasz Stanko. Together they explored modal forms and free jazz but, whereas

Stanko was a wild, instinctual risk-taker, Makowicz approached the music in a more orderly and conceptual way. In the 1970s he wrote perceptive music criticism while he was working with both Michal Urbaniak and his then wife, Urszula Dudziak, in a number of fusion projects. It's unfortunate that there should be nothing available from before Makowicz's 52nd year. In the formal surroundings of the Maybeck Hall, his more classical leanings are in greater evidence. He opens, heart on sleeve, with 'Tatum On My Mind' but gives the theme a precise, rather stiff enunciation one hasn't heard in it from him before. The Cole Porter material that makes up the rest of the set has a convincingly *soigné* air but it's sustained too resolutely, and the final couple of numbers are rather dull. Some of this spills over into the duos with Mraz, which again are rather academic, not quite swinging enough to sustain interest over the full stretch. There are, to be sure, very beautiful things, such as the long originals, 'Mito', 'Culebra', 'Concordance' and '400 West D-Flat', but much of the rest is a little drab and best sampled in smallish doses. Mraz sounds a great deal more comfortable in the trio with Dawson. The drummer has an easy-sounding but very exact swing which never lets him down and he gives the familiar material a lot of pep and sparkle which rubs off on Makowicz. We like the Kern selection better. No special reason; it just seems to work more coherently as an album.

Llanfranco Malaguti

GUITAR

Contemporary Italian guitarist, performing in a conservative but creative idiom.

***** Inside Meaning**

Splasc(h) 403-2 *Malaguti; Stefano D'Anna (ss, ts); Enzo Pietropaoli (b, perc).* 2/93.

*****(*) Percorsi**

Splasc(h) 419-2 *Malaguti; Umberto Petrin (p).* 5/93.

****(*) New Land**

Splasc(h) 443-2 *Malaguti; Dario Volpi (g, g-syn).* 1/95.

***** Aforismi**

Splasc(h) 606-2 *Malaguti (g solo).* 11/96.

Malaguti shies away from effects and noise. He plays with a clean, slightly pinched open tone and prefers spareness to lots of notes. Some earlier vinyl for Splasc(h) suggested a conventional stylist, but these are wide-open records with plenty of space and air around the music. *Inside Meaning* seems to take off from a group of standard harmonic bases and into a series of triologues where the normally tempestuous D'Anna is unusually restrained. These are sometimes rather piecemeal, but there are some bewitching moments and the entirety is oddly satisfying in a modest way. *Percorsi* is a duo concert from Slovenia with the splendid Petrin. They feel their way through a group of standards – the way the opening improvisation turns into 'Solar' is quite magical, and there's a similar transformation of 'Just Friends' – before each man takes a few solos and they climax with 'Autumn Leaves'. Petrin's abstruse but acute methods are an ideal partner for the guitarist's own delivery and, though the location sound isn't ideal, it's pretty good.

New Land is comparatively tame, almost finicky in parts, with Volpi very much a second fiddle. Malaguti's tunes have their virtues, but this one is too becalmed to sustain the attention. *Aforismi* is a solo record in which the improviser uses echo effects with a memory expander to create real-time multi-tracking. With only two pieces breasting the five-minute barrier, the guitarist again impresses with his reserve, eliminating flab from the music, even if some of it lacks a distinctive flavour. Guitarists may enjoy this more than the uncommitted, but Malaguti has an interesting agenda.

Raphe Malik

TRUMPET

Often working around Boston or with San Francisco-based saxophonist Glenn Spearman, Malik is a free-form trumpeter and group leader with an increasing exposure on record.

*****(*) 21st Century Texts**

FMP CD 43 *Malik; Brian King Nelson (Cmel); Glenn Spearman (ts); Larry Roland (b); Dennis Warren (d).* 6/91.

*****(*) Sirens Sweet And Slow**

Outsounds 01972 *As above, except add Jamyll Jones (b).* 94.

***** The Short Form**

Eremite MTE05 *As above, except omit Nelson, Jones, Roland; add George Langford (b).* 7/96.

***** Consequences**

Eremite MTE013 *Malik; Sabir Mateen (as); William Parker (b); Denis Charles (d).* 7/97.

Malik is a sometime Cecil Taylor sideman who has managed to derive something from the pianist's style without being swamped by it. On *21st Century Texts* he marshals a tight little posse of like-minded improvisers (Spearman inevitably dominant, as he is wherever he plays) in the sort of session ESP Disk used to have a corner in. Nelson's C-melody sax has a strikingly unfamiliar tonality but, with no piano or guitar as a reference point, it's able to find its own territory, often coming in under Malik in a series of call-and-response passages that are both alien and highly traditional. *Sirens Sweet And Slow* breaks up the unit a little, with two long duets, trumpet with bass, and trumpet with drums. Malik manages to play big and loud without losing focus: he rarely goes for the buzzy, spluttery effects that avant-garde brassmen often rely on, and his note choices are boldly decisive. 'Companions' is an impressive group piece and there's a sort of stop-start blowout on 'Tenor', to which Spearman makes his usual full-blooded contribution. The unvarnished sound suits the band.

Energy-music followers will love *The Short Form*, a concert recording that pares the band back to a quartet and lets them explode. It's exhilarating enough, but the more specific restraint which Malik uses so effectively on the studio discs is missed. Similar state of affairs on the following year's *Consequences*, rather dustily recorded, and although this is a chance to hear Denis Charles in one of his final recordings, and Malik and Mateen play some vociferous solos, a strong live performance transfers rather uneasily to CD.

Pete Malinverni (born 1957)

PIANO

Malinverni grew up in Niagara Falls but is based in New York, teaching and playing numerous sideman gigs. A post-bop stylist in the modern mainstream.

*****(*) A Very Good Year**

Reservoir RSR CD 158 *Malinverni; Dennis Irwin (b); Leroy Williams (d). 10/98.*

Malinverni's dedication to church music comes out here in the gospel mix of 'Steal Away/My Lord, What A Mourning'. It's one of several interesting slants on the piano-trio formula, which is respected but not slavishly adhered to. 'Courtin' The Muse', with its odd harmonic flavour, is an intriguing little piece, and so is 'Projection', which sounds like a bop tune played on a tilt. These originals are good enough for one to wish for an album's worth of the pianist's own tunes, but the others are standards and jazz themes. 'Blue In Green' is switched from B flat to D flat and done as a waltz. Ellington's 'Angelica' is about the liveliest track, but most of the record is quiet and thoughtful, swinging in a very understated way. Well worth a try.

Janni Malmi

GUITAR, KEYBOARDS

Finnish guitarist with a wide taste in rock, jazz and local music, looking to fuse electric instruments with acoustic rhythms.

***** One Leg Duck**

Renroc RRCD 0394 *Malmi; Jorma Ojanperä (b); Markku Ounaskari (d). 94.*

***** Pataljoona**

Quirk 2004 *As above, except add Yrjänä Sauros (hca). 96.*

Malmi's engaging music sounds wholly in debt to John Scofield on the first, live record, a brief set which sets out his juicy tone, rocking licks and simple writing in front of an audience of what seems to be no more than twelve people. He knows his rock history – there are versions of 'Love Potion No. 9' and Frank Zappa's 'Theme From Lumpy Gravy' – but the most impressive piece is an imaginative reworking of 'Footprints'.

We were a bit hard on the *Pataljoona* set last time, but further acquaintance suggests that Malmi's imagination wasn't misplaced. Some of the 14 pieces are no more than cute ideas, but the best of them show a genuinely creative use of the short form: the wide range of settings for the guitar, Sauros's harmonica and the 'conventional' rhythm section make for a surprising and entertaining diversion.

Russell Malone (born 1963)

GUITAR, VOCAL

A conservative among modern guitarists, Malone matches deep knowledge of his instrument's history with a stance that suggests an investment in old values. He has worked extensively with many leading names as sideman and was previously listed for two albums on Columbia.

***** Sweet Georgia Peach**

Impulse! IMP 12822 *Malone; Kenny Barron (p); Ron Carter(b); Lewis Nash (d); Steve Kroon (perc). 2/98.*

Malone's career was abetted early on by his featuring as a Harry Connick sideman, and it has subsequently found further impetus via his work in the Diana Krall group. Is he merely famous by association? In the crowded field of contemporary jazz guitarists, there's seemingly little to pick him out: clean straightahead tone, rock-solid member of the team, lively but not difficult to follow and rarely head-turning in his solos. Our verdict on his two earlier albums for Columbia was 'entertaining licks rather than congruous solos', and there seems little reason to change that opinion on the evidence of *Sweet Georgia Peach*. But Impulse! have paid for a very good band, the tunes are better than rote, and it's hard to dispute the class of the record. 'Strange Little Smile' is a solo worthy of Jim Hall in its sensitivity, and Herb Alpert's 'Rise' is beautifully transformed. Let's see what happens with him next.

Stefano Maltese

SOPRANO, ALTO AND TENOR SAXOPHONES, BASS CLARINET, FLUTE, PAN PIPES, VIOLIN

The Sicilian is a versatile multi-instrumentalist, but his own-name albums are exercises more concerned with composing and arranging, especially for big ensembles.

***** Sombra Del Sur**

Splasc(h) 406-2 *Maltese; Roy Paci (t, pkt-t, flhn); Sebastiano Dell'Arte (t, flhn); Paolo Reale, Rino Caraco (tb); Claudio Giglio (f, bamboo f); Giuseppe Bonanno (f, picc); Paola Ammatuna, Jasmin Avitabile Leva, Andrea Cianci, Barbara Forzisi, Paola Milazzo (f); Salvatore Carnemolla (cl); Angelo Ragaglia (bsn); Ciccio Tiné (acc); Michele Conti (vn, mand); Salvo Amore (g); Michele Salerno (clo); Pino Guarrella (b); Antonio Moncada (d); Walter Di Mauro (perc); Gioconda Cilio (v). 7/92.*

***** Book Of Yesterday**

Splasc(h) 438-2 *Maltese; Ray Paci (t, pkt-t); Rosario Patania (tb); Alfio Sgalambro (cl); Giovanni Di Mauro (ob); Michele Conti (vn); Salvo Amore (g); Nello Toscano (clo); Giuseppe Guarella (b); Antonio Moncada (d); Gioconda Cilio (v, perc). 2/95.*

***** Seven Tracks For Tomorrow**

DDQ 128025-2 *Similar to above, except omit Sgalambro, Di Mauro, Amore, Toscano. 3/97.*

***** Living Alive**

Leo LR 265 *Maltese; Arkady Shilkloper (flhn, bugle, frhn); Sophia Domancich (p); Paul Rogers (b); Antonio Moncada (d); Gioconda Cilio (v, perc).* 9/98.

A sprawling, sometimes malevolent-sounding work, the big-scale suite which is *Sombra Del Sur* is about the slowness and heat-saturated quiet of the Italian 'South'. Slowness seems apt, since Maltese started it in 1986, and much of it is in turn based on an earlier piece dating back to 1978. His reluctance to use keyboards and his interest in woodwinds and strings introduces a variety of tone which is unusual: the massed flutes which are brought in for two tracks, the curious effect of free percussion and tenor over the fixed handclap of 'Hombre Lobo', the unearthly chorales of 'Estrellas'. It's an odd construction, sometimes very arresting, but often plain turgid. *Book Of Yesterday* is a retrospective of Maltese's writing over 25 years, going back to the lumbering 1974 'Trois Petits Chevaux Pour Erik Satie' and ending on a new (1994) piece. You can't say Maltese doesn't try hard: he creates an orchestra of 16 bass clarinets through overdubbing on 'Dans Les Nuits', and assembles such groups as a soprano/clarinet/oboe trio and various chamberish quintets. The sleeve-notes call him 'a poetic of estranged visionariness'. Much of this carefully arranged and cockeyed music seems deliberately eccentric, but there are shafts of humour to go with the many po-faced passages.

One of his key collaborators is Cilio, who takes a significant role as wordless vocalist on *Seven Tracks For Tomorrow*, a set which pursues Maltese's composing interests without reaching any clear indication of progress: he seems to flit from episode to episode, never quite settling into a style and passing the initiative round his players so restlessly that it's hard to focus on what each is doing. That issue is sidestepped by the more *ad hoc* Leo record, which was an opportunistic date following the players' appearance at the 1998 Labirinti Sonori Festival. Maltese is reluctant to present himself as a full-on free improviser and he leaves much of the main space to both Shilkloper and Cilio, with piano, bass and drums taking their own independent parts. Untypical, though arguably this has the greatest share of satisfying music of the four discs. Maltese will be an acquired taste, but more adventurous spirits may find him not a little intriguing.

Junior Mance (born 1928)

PIANO

Junior Mance has been playing professionally for almost 60 years. His first lessons with Julian Mance Sr and his grounding in blues, stride and boogie woogie have stood him in good stead ever since. Though by no means widely documented or particularly well known, Mance has concentrated very largely on his own groups and projects. A significant proportion of the existing recorded material is live.

***** Live At The Village Vanguard**

Original Jazz Classics OJC 204 *Mance; Larry Gales (b); Ben Riley (d).* 61.

*****(*) Smokey Blues**

JSP CD 219 *Mance; Marty Rivera (b); Walter Bolden (d).* 6/80.

***** Junior Mance Special**

Sackville CD 3043 *Mance (p solo).* 9/86, 11/88.

*****(*) Softly As In A Morning Sunrise**

Enja ENJ 8080 *Mance; Jimmy Woode (b); Bobby Durham (d).* 7/94.

Unmistakable from a random sample of half-a-dozen bars as a Chicago man, Mance can be a maddeningly predictable player on record, resorting to exactly the figure one expects him to play rather too often to leave any interest for his often adventurous variations and resolutions. That's certainly evident on the live OJC, a rare available example of pre-1980 Mance. It's a notably self-confident performance, and it will be obvious to anyone who has hitherto heard only the recent stuff that Mance's expert chops and obvious awareness of the earlier literature did not appear magically on his fiftieth birthday. It's a fairly representative programme, with the favoured 'Smokey Blues' (see below) prominent, and a slot for Basie's '9.20 Special'. There's an immediate lift to the five live tracks on *Special*, recorded at Toronto's intimate and much-documented Café des Copains, which suggests that studio performance really isn't Mance's strong suit. Certainly the opening 'Yancey Special', done on a better-tempered studio piano, is remarkably flat and unvaried; the long interpretations of 'Careless Love', Billy Taylor's 'I Wish I Knew How It Would Feel To Be Free' (a theme familiar to British fans as the sig to a well-known TV movie programme) and Ivory Joe Hunter's 'Since I Lost My Baby I Almost Lost My Mind' are characteristically bluesy but also rather tentative; and it's only among the live tracks – which include 'Blue Monk', Golson's 'Whisper Not' and two Ellington numbers – that Mance really seems to let go, working towards those knotted climaxes for which he is rightly admired.

Rivera is a bassist who fits snugly into the pianist's conception of how the blues should be played: strongly, but with considerable harmonic subtlety. The trio album is perhaps the best of the recent recordings, despite a rather uncertain sound-mix. Mance's ability to suffuse relatively banal ballad material with genuine blues feeling (a characteristic noted by the late Charles Fox in a typically perceptive liner-note) is nowhere more obvious than on 'Georgia On My Mind', a melody that can sound footling and drab but which acquires something close to grandeur here. Bolden's 'Deep' is basically a feature for the rhythm players and doesn't add very much to the total impact, but the closing 'Ease On Down The Road' and 'Smokey Blues' are authentic Mance performances.

The recent *Softly* is just about everything one could ask for in a record of this sort (and that is an assessment that also acknowledges its limitations). Mance has predictably become less assertive, more thoughtful, but he is still capable of swinging out on an up-tempo theme. It is just that he takes more care and time over the ballads. The title-track positively sparkles with freshness and optimism. Excellent stuff.

***** Milestones**

Sackville SACD2-3065 *Mance; Don Thompson (b); Archie Alleyne (d).*

A typically rhythmic and well-paced set of standard and repertory tunes featuring Mance in his favourite playing context. Most of the tunes are quite long and developed, though nothing else on the set quite matches up to the expectations established by a thorough rethink of Nat Adderley's 'Work Song', a swingingly brisk opener that has more ideas per chorus than anything Junior has released for years.

***** At Town Hall**

Enja 9085 *Mance; Houston Person (ts); Calvin Hill (b); Alvin Queen (d).*

Uncomplicated and soulful hard bop from two players who are happy to get into a groove and swing until the management put the lights up and turf everyone out. A long version of 'I Cried For You' is the key performance, delivered with emphatic delight that somewhat belies the title. The success of the gig is also very much down to the still too little recognized skill and vision of Alvin Queen, who remains one of the best exponents of this kind of repertoire.

***** Floating Jazz Festival Trio**

Chiaruscuro 340 *Mance; Benny Golson (ts); Keter Betts (b); Jackie Williams (d).* 95.

*****(*) Live At The 1996 Floating Jazz Festival: The Music Of Duke Ellington**

Chiaroscuro 352 *As above, except omit Golson; add Joe Temperley (bs).* 96.

***** The Floating Jazz Festival Trio**

Chiaroscuro 359 *As above, except omit Temperley; add Red Holloway (as), Henry Johnson (g).* 98.

Very much in the 'nice work if you can get it' mould, these annual appearances on a Caribbean jazz cruise have been central to Junior's gig diary for a while now and they always yield up joyous, entertaining jazz. Inevitably, it's the guest performers who provide much of the leaven. Golson's presence on his own 'Blues Alley' is a major plus on the first set, but it's Joe Temperley's reincarnation as Harry Carney that makes the 1996 cruise such a delight. Here the tunes stretch out generously, allowing Junior to do his familiar overhaul of the entire composition and giving plenty of solo space to the rest of the group. Temperamentally, the third volume is probably the most representative of Junior's style and the kind of company he likes. Johnson and Holloway are less celebrated names, but the alto man has the blue-toned wail that suits Mance's playing to a 't', and the terser, more melodic tunes will suit those who don't go the whole bundle on the pianist's usual full-on approach.

Augusto Mancinelli

GUITAR

Italian guitarist who takes a highly individual line between different improvising disciplines.

*****(*) Extreme**

Splasc(h) H 303-2 *Mancinelli; Roberto Rossi (tb, shells); Valerio Signetto (cl); Pietro Tonolo (ts); Mario Arcari (ob); Giulio Visibelli (f); Piero Leveratto (b); Tony Oxley (d).* 10/88–3/90.

A fascinating set which will appeal to anyone interested in improvisation. Mancinelli includes three very precise and hair-fine compositions, 'Poiesis' consisting of 23 sounds and a dodecaphonic series, written for oboe, flute and clarinet and designed to go with a display of electronic art. The other 29 tracks are all free improvisations, some lasting less than a minute, none more than five. Some are guitar solos – Mancinelli uses everything from wide, Frisell-like sweeps to hectic fingerpicking and strangled-tone twangs – while others involve Oxley, Leveratto, Rossi and Arcari (but not Tonolo or Signetto) in various combinations. As fragmented as it all is, the even dynamic of the music binds the various pieces together, and several of the improvisations sound so whole and finished that they might as well be compositions in any case.

*****(*) Jazz Work**

Splasc(h) 494-2 *Mancinelli; Paolo Ghetti (b); Massimo Manzi (d).* 12/95–6/96.

On the face of it this is a more prosaic set and, with bebop set-pieces like 'Cherokee' and 'All The Things You Are' in the programme, one could be forgiven for thinking Mancinelli has soft-pedalled this one. Yet he gets more inventive and original improvising out of a classic open-tone electric than most players do with a battery of effects, and the title – *Jazz Work* – suggests that this is his dissertation on modern history and how it works for him. The four standards (plus Monk's 'Evidence') are all handsomely delivered, but it's his originals that hang in the mind: 'Sassi Neri', 'When Love Is Over' and 'Aria' seem like rare blends of jazz exercise and Italian song-form. There are six solo 'Interludio' pieces interspersed throughout, and the guitarist saves some of his most startling work for these miniatures. Ghetti and Manzi are relatively workmanlike in support, and it would be fascinating to hear what Mancinelli can do with a 'heavy-weight' rhythm section. Seven years between discs is surely too long to wait for this exceptional talent: as we said last time, more, please!

Joe Maneri (born 1927)

ALTO SAXOPHONE, TENOR SAXOPHONE, CLARINET, PIANO

Like Hal Russell before him, Maneri was 'discovered' only rather late in his career, having influenced a whole generation of students with his theories on microtonality. He was born in New York City and he played clarinet with an eclectic procession of bands, embracing Irish, Middle Eastern and Greek music and bebop. After the war, he began studying twelve-tone music and to experiment with microtones. He was appointed to the faculty of the New England Conservatory of Music and published Preliminary Studies In The Virtual Pitch Continuum, now almost as celebrated – and probably almost as rarely read – as his colleague George Russell's magnum opus. Only in the '90s did he become widely known as a player and recording artist.

***** Paniots Nine**

Avant AVAN 067 *Maneri; Don Burns (p); John Beal (b); Pete Dolger (d).* 63.

These early demos, roughly recorded and unvarnished as they are, confirm to what extent Maneri is the natural ancestor of off-beat syncretists like John Zorn and klezmer fiend Don Byron. The album mixes free-jazz material with Levantine grooves.

'Shift Your Tail' is influenced by the *syrto*, a Greek dance Maneri must have played hundreds of times in wedding bands; 'Jewish Fantasy – At The Wedding' comes out of the same experience, an inauthentic but convincing blend of klezmer rhythms. 'After Myself' by the *kalamentiano* is in 7/8, which is broadly typical of the rhythms he favours. The title-piece is a Dolger composition, this time in 9/8 and already featuring the microtonal language that was to be a trademark in later years. Maneri's clarinet playing blows just about everything else out of the water. He has a huge tone, at the opposite end of the instrumental galaxy from fellow-Bostonian Jimmy Giuffre. It's fierce, angular, often shawm-like in its drift between pitches. None of the other players registers with anything like the same intensity, but the playing is generally very good, with Dolger an important presence. Given what was to come, this is of historical interest rather than anything else; Maneri enthusiasts will want to know where the great man was coming from; newcomers now have the luxury of starting the story at the very beginning.

****** Get Ready To Receive Yourself**

Leo Lab CD 010 *Maneri; Mat Maneri (vn); John Lockwood (b); Randy Peterson (d).* 93.

*****(*) Let The Horse Go**

Leo CD LR 232 *As above.* 6/95.

Maneri's coming-out as a jazz star – 65 years to become an overnight success – was at the 1992 Montreal Jazz Festival, where he appeared alongside Paul Bley, an old associate from New York days. The buzz was immediate, and Ornette Coleman's name was dropped more than once by way of comparison. Ornette's eldritch, 'off-pitch' sound is certainly the closest parallel, but Maneri works very much further from the blues. In combination with son Mat Maneri's squalling fiddle and bassist John Lockwood, it generates a sound that is utterly unique and distinctive, and dismayingly hard to categorize. 'Let The Horse Go' on the second of the two Leo Lab releases (and how typical of Leo Feigin to be hip to what Maneri is doing) opens up more questions about jazz harmony in its near-quarter-of-an-hour span than anyone has since the early days of Cecil Taylor. The language is not so much atonal as polytonal. Almost anything might resolve; almost nothing does. It's hard, even at this distance, to recapture the sheer alienating wallop of the earlier record. 'Anton' is presumably a nod in the direction of Herr von Webern, but it's items like 'Skippin' Thru The Turnips', 'Evolve' and the title-track that signal something radically new, teeing up a truly outrageous cover of 'Body And Soul' which blows every saxophone solo cliché off the face of the earth. Inevitably the second album isn't quite so shocking. It's a consolidation rather than a radical departure. In both cases the sound is very direct and unadorned, something of a contrast with what was to come.

****** Coming Down The Mountain**

hatOLOGY 501 *Maneri; Mat Maneri (vn); Ed Schuller (b); Randy Peterson (d).* 10/93.

An earlier record for hat ART, *Dahabenzapple*, is now unfortunately deleted, but the surviving disc is also a live performance, recorded in a Boston synagogue in the autumn of 1993. It's a bittier record in some ways, but the opening and closing tracks, 'Swing High' and 'To End Or Not To End', frame a record of quite extraordinary rhythmic concentration. Often very slow, but intensely focused, the interplay is little short of telepathic, with Schuller – who always sounds absolutely right in this context – contributing more than usual, perhaps making up for lost time. 'Joe's Alto' is a caprice, but it says more in under two minutes than most saxophonists squeeze out in a year.

****** Three Men Walking**

ECM 1597 *Maneri; Joe Morris (g); Mat Maneri (vn).* 10 & 11/95.

As with Hal Russell, Maneri's belated apotheosis was signalled by a call from ECM. It was apparently Paul Bley, that tireless and selfless talent scout, who put the label in touch. The cathedral acoustic is all wrong, but Maneri sounds wonderful in this context. Excellent as Randy Peterson and John Lockwood were in the quartet setting, this is an exceptional line-up. The album title comes from a Giacometti sculpture of three attenuated figures, insecurely attached to the ground and heading off in different directions, yet for the moment bound to the same patch of earth. It's a lovely visual echo of music that is both airy and earthy, solid and insubstantial, jazz and something else. As with other ECM sessions of this vintage, the group breaks down into its constituents. Joe opens on unaccompanied clarinet, a sound harder and darker than Giuffre's, though superficially similar. The group improvisations, 'Bird's [*sic*] In The Belfry', 'Three Men Walking' and 'Arc And Point', are exceptional, but the features for Mat and Joe are equally impressive, underlining the different idioms and responses at work in this material. While Mat seems resolutely committed to his father's idiom, often using the lower end of his six-string electric violin as the bass and percussion voice, Morris often sounds detached and even remote – but companionably so, the most errant of those three bronze men. The one standard in the book at this point, 'What's New', was a revelation in performance and is again here, richly rethought and brightly played. 'For Josef Schmid' is a little bouquet to the man who taught Joe the 'Schoenberg method'. It brings a remarkable album to a satisfying close.

*****(*) In Full Cry**

ECM 537048-2 *Maneri; Mat Maneri (vn); John Lockwood (b); Randy Peterson (d).* 6/96.

Good to hear the Maneri Quartet together again, but now that the first shock has passed, does this music still sound as startling as it once did? Does Ornette's? Does Cecil Taylor's? The answer ought to be 'yes' in all three cases. It's a function of music as wholeheartedly cross-grained as this that it will never enter a comfortable mainstream. The opening string sounds and the first entrance of Joe's tenor on 'Coarser And Finer' are enough to convince anyone that the old fellow is still the wildest player on the block, for all his professorial hats. As before, Joe's included some standard material: a long, haunted reading of 'Tenderly', 'Prelude To a Kiss' to close the set and two spirituals, 'Nobody Knows' and 'Motherless Child', which bring out the folkier side of his playing. He's never stuck closer to melody than on this album, but the estranging microtones are still in evidence from start to finish. A superb record, even if doesn't quite meet the standard of its predecessor.

***** Blessed**

ECM 557365-2 *Maneri; Mat Maneri (vn, baritone vn, vla).* 10/97.

The immanence of blessing doesn't always keep at bay the imminence of boredom – or, perhaps fairer, a sense of exclusion. This is an intensely private dialogue between father and son, and only occasionally does the listener find much real purchase. Joe's piano work on the traditional 'Never Said A Mumblin' Word' and on the beautiful closing title-track are the high points, reinforcing the suspicion that this was really a set to showcase Mat, with the old man acting as accompanist and household god. Mat's string playing on a deconstructed 'Body And Soul' is tremendous and this is perhaps the first time on record that he has put his full range of fiddles to such coherent and sheerly musical use. No sign that he is merely switching axes for the sake of change. The long 'Is Nothing Near?' is a key Maneris performance, tense, but throbbing with some promised revelation, though again very private in idiom. Not a record for a newcomer.

***** Tales of Rohnlief**

ECM 559858-2 *Maneri; Mat Maneri (vn); Barre Phillips (b).* 99.

Punctuated with odd vocal performances and with Monkish outbreaks on the piano, notably on 'When The Ship Went Down', this is essentially a Maneri-and-strings session. Mat and Barre spend a good deal of time adding complex, squiggly accompaniments to Joe's increasingly elegant – or are we just getting used to them? – dances between the piano tones. The long title-track is an unvarnished delight and, though this isn't necessarily the best place to start with Maneri, it's varied enough and certainly beautiful enough to win over the uncommitted listener.

Mat Maneri (born 1969)

VIOLIN, VIOLA

The son of maverick saxophonist Joe Maneri, he is a distinctive and adventurous player on his own account with a sound that synthesizes the untutored genius of Ornette Coleman with the relentless swing of Stuff Smith.

***** In Time**

Leo Lab CD 002 *Maneri; Pandelis Karayorgis (p).* 4/93.

*****(*) Fever Bed**

Leo Lab CD 022 *Maneri; Ed Schuller (b); Randy Peterson (d).* 12/94, 1/96.

Mat began working in his father's quartet at the age of fourteen and has remained refreshingly loyal to the old man's concept ever since, even when playing on his own projects. Unlike Denardo Coleman, who also helps negotiate sometimes difficult transactions between paternal genius and an uncomprehending outside world, Mat has a very distinctive approach of his own. The knowledge that he has taken lessons with both Miroslav Vitous and Dave Holland will help point listeners to the number of times he is cast as a bass-line player in the Joe Maneri Quartet. On these two albums he is freer to shape his own abstractly romantic lines, which recall nothing so much as the more lyrical side of Elliott Carter.

The group with Peterson and Schuller has a remote, slightly eerie quality. Lacking a horn or piano, the music is very difficult to pin down. 'Fever Bed' itself is restlessly dissonant, tossing and turning, finding no place of rest either harmonically or rhythmically. Peterson provides what little chordal information is made explicit and, though throughout the whole 11 minutes he seems constantly on the brink of breaking out into a climactic, convulsive statement, it is kept at bay, remaining tantalizingly unarticulated. After such an arresting opening, the remainder is less compelling. The long 'Iris' is more personal and expressive, and it may be (there are a couple of almost subliminal allusions) that 'Almost Pretty' is an oblique reference to Monk's 'Ugly Beauty', which features on the duo album with Karayorgis. Interesting that while the old man name-checks Webern on one of his albums, Mat's final word is for Gustav Mahler.

Apparently proposed by Paul Bley, who has a significant role in the Maneris' story, *In Time* is delicately beautiful and thoughtful, almost like a classical duo in timbre and dynamics, but dealing with a language that is far from classical. There are actually two versions of 'Ugly Beauty', framing a set of originals by both men. Karayorgis's 'Speaking' and 'Part III Of A Name', and Mat's 'Blue Seven' are exceptional. This, though, is a much milder project than the trio and it's probably advisable to catch up with Mat Maneri's work either via his dad's records or on *Fever Bed.*

*****(*) Acceptance**

hatOLOGY 512 *Maneri; Gary Valente (tb); Joe Maneri (as); John Dirac (g); Ed Schuller (b); Randy Peterson (d).* 8/96.

The new element here is the warmly textured viola, which sits in behind Valente's raucous trombone and blends exquisitely with Dirac's clean, crisp guitar. Maneri kicks off with the rhythmically offbeat 'Dolphy Dance', a funky 5/4 theme which puns on a Herbie Hancock composition. Boldly, he follows with 'My Funny Valentine', a version that will startle even those who felt inured by a thousand covers. In this reading it is neither sentimental nor sour, but plain-spoken, even blunt. The long 'Shroud' follows, before an even more startling version of Rollins's 'East Broadway Run Down'. 'Fever Bed' makes a reappearance, before the title-piece, written by the gifted Dirac and co-starring Joe Maneri with a distinctive statement of his own which generously refuses to step on the lad's toes.

****** So What?**

hatOLOGY 529 *Maneri; Mathew Shipp (p); Randy Peterson (d).* 8/98.

As the title suggests, this is something of a homage to Miles Davis. There are four Miles compositions and five by Mat, sequenced in such a way as to suggest he has attempted to stretch the trumpeter's modal ideas into the twenty-first century. It's quite possible, listening to 'Solar' and 'No Blues', to imagine Maneri slipping into place in a never actually convened Miles group. Interestingly, the intuitive understanding between Shipp and Peterson is such that Maneri has to tread carefully to avoid breaking the spell. The result is a beautifully balanced trio performance, with no dominant personality.

Albert Mangelsdorff (born 1928)

TROMBONE

The younger Mangelsdorff brother is the virtual inventor of modern German jazz. Only with his post-war recordings is it possible to trace the emergence of a distinctive idiom, rather than a mere copy of British and American models.

*****(*) Purity**

Mood 33631 *Mangelsdorff (tb solo).*

Mangelsdorff's discography is still thinner than his importance to European jazz would suggest. The unaccompanied *Purity* stands out as an example of his radical approach. Few trombonists of any period could sustain interest over this length, but Mangelsdorff has such a range at his disposal, from caressing, saxophone-like sounds to hard, blatting snaps and vicious, stiletto-thin harmonics, that it is like listening to a whole group of players.

***** Tension**

L + R CDLR 71002 *Mangelsdorff; Gunther Kronberg (as, bs); Heinz Sauer (ts); Gunter Lenz (b); Ralf Hubner (d).* 7/63.

****(*) Now Jazz Ramwong**

L + R CDLR 71001 *Mangelsdorff; Heinz Sauer (ts, ss); Gunther Kronberg (as); Gunter Lenz (b); Ralf Hubner (d).* 6/64.

***** Room 1220**

Konnex LC 8718 *Mangelsdorff; John Surman (bs); Eddie Louiss (p, org); Niels-Henning Orsted Pedersen (b); Daniel Humair (d).* 10/70.

***** Live In Tokyo**

Enja 2006 *Mangelsdorff; Heinz Sauer (ts, ss); Gunter Lenz (b); Ralf Hubner (d).* 2/71.

****** Three Originals: The Wide Point / Trilogue / Albert Live In Montreux**

MPS 519213 2CD *Mangelsdorff; Palle Danielsson, Jean-François Jenny-Clark, Jaco Pastorius (b); Ronald Shannon Jackson, Elvin Jones, Alphonse Mouzon (d).* 5/75–7/80.

One of the least egocentric of musicians, Mangelsdorff has been a model proponent of collectivist improvisation, both in smaller units nominally under his leadership and in larger combinations like the Globe Unity Orchestra and the United Jazz and Rock Ensemble, with whom he has produced some of his most striking work. He has worked with everyone, from Lee Konitz to Barbara Thompson and Jaco Pastorius, who appears on the middle third of the sets collected on the second set of *Three Originals* listed. Alphonse Mouzon isn't any more likely as a partner, but a relationship forged for the 1976 Berliner Jazztage works suprisingly well. In addition to *Trilogue*, which documents that occasion, *Three Originals* also includes *The Wide Point*, a 1975 trio with Danielsson and Jones, and the later and rather better *Albert Live In Montreux* with Jenny-Clark and Jackson, both of whom are in powerful form on the closing 'Rip Off'.

The more aggressive side can be sampled on the 1970 session with Surman – which incidentally offers an interesting sample of the saxophonist's baritone work before he put it away for its long sabbatical. He isn't playing at full stretch for most of the disc, tending to work in flashes that never seem to go anywhere. Mangelsdorff is more concentrated and constructs a beautifully balanced solo on 'My Kind Of Beauty'.

***** Spontaneous**

Enja 2064 *Mangelsdorff; Masahiko Hito (p, ring modulator); Peter Warren (b); Allen Blairman (d).*

***** Internationales Jazzfestival Münster**

Tutu 88110 *Mangelsdorff; John Scofield (g).* 6/88.

***** Lanaya**

Plainisphare CH 1267 *Mangelsdorff; Reto Weber, Nana Twum Knketia, Djamchid Chemirani, Adama Drame (perc).* 11/93.

Whatever the context, Mangelsdorff always manages to sound both absolutely responsive and absolutely himself. The duo with Scofield, which is only part of a live recording from the 1988 Münster junket – a vintage year – works much better than it probably ought to; the version of 'Gray And Visceral' is a good deal more appealing than on Scofield's earlier *Live*.

At the opposite end of the list chronologically is the trombone and percussion project, *Lanaya*, admirable evidence that Mangelsdorff is still experimenting, still pushing at the boundaries of what he knows. It is actually worth while listening to this record in the context of the very earliest things, because the basic language hasn't changed a bit, merely the questions that he asks with it. The recording could have been a little more professional, but these are difficult permutations to register exactly, with instruments like *zarb* and *djembe* calling for close, accurate studio miking, rather than the haphazard live mix that Plainisphare are offering. Fascinating nevertheless.

*****(*) Shake, Shuttle And Blow**

Enja ENJ 9374-2 *Mangelsdorff; Bruno Spoerri (ss, as, elec); Christy Doran (g); Reto Weber (d, perc).* 1/99.

Mangelsdorff's most recent ensemble, Movin' On, began as far back as 1990, originally with cellist Ernst Reijseger in the line-up. He was replaced by the resourceful Doran. Himself is a one-man orchestra but he just about meets his match in Bruno Spoerri. The saxophonist is a crafty user of electronics, working in the same multiphonic territory Mangelsdorff has made his own.

This is the old master's most joyous and unfettered record for many years. 'Do You Like Pastrami?' and 'Bolghatty Dreams' get the disc off to a cracking start and, if the rest doesn't quite match up to the beginning, 'Saxobonia' is a hysterical, hilarious subversion of bop orthodoxy, a piece of satire that is more musical than the forms it tries to knock down. The sheer ease and delight of Mangelsdorff's playing are infectious, quite delightful, and this is a cracking modern-jazz record, pushing through to a new and fresh idiom that takes its inspiration from all over the shop.

Emil Mangelsdorff (born 1925)

SAXOPHONES, FLUTE

Emerged in the post-war Frankfurt environment, playing in a swing-to-bop style which he thoughtfully developed as jazz moved forward. Less visible on record than his brother, Albert, but a significant figure in his country's jazz history.

***** This Side Up**

L + R 45065 *Mangelsdorff; Thilo Wagner (p); Gerhard Bitter (b); Janusz Stefanski (d). 9/92.*

*****(*) Meditation**

L + R CDLR 45088 *Mangelsdorff; Jo Flinner, Bob Degen (p); Attila Zoller (g); Gerhard Bitter (b); Janusz Stefanski (d). 6/86–8/94.*

The suppression of jazz in both Germany and Japan before and during the Second World War resulted in a dramatic acceleration of interest as soon as the war ended. In Germany there was a particularly strong underground jazz movement during the war years; Frankfurt was the main centre, a detail which some observers have attributed to its being in the American zone of occupation, though groups like the Hot Club of Frankfurt were active during the war years. Emil Mangelsdorff and his younger brother, Albert, came through in this environment, sharing a broad grounding in the swing movement, followed by rapid exposure to bebop and the beginnings of free jazz. Emil retained more of the earlier style but achieved a highly intelligent synthesis of older and new techniques. Like Lee Konitz, whom he sometimes resembles, he has a cooler approach than the average bebop player, but he is also capable of sustaining quite extended passages of dissonance, and complex rhythms. The solo tracks on *Meditation*, recorded in Italy as Mangelsdorff approached his seventieth birthday, are squarely in the Konitz mould, without surrendering a scrap of their originality. Little of Mangelsdorff's recorded output is available (though the appearance of material from a Hessischer Rundfunk ensemble makes a welcome difference). Neither of these records offers an entirely rounded picture, though the second does change the picture considerably. The duos with Zoller and the rather anonymous Degen are full of interesting things, and the group-tracks, with their emphasis on flute and soprano saxophone, open up another aspect; but it's the unaccompanied improvisations which catch the attention. As for the other record, the raw lyricism one associates with the younger Mangelsdorff is present in a much diluted form. Unfortunately, the original material sounds like any one of an identikit procession of European mavericks. A pity; the earlier records are much better. But it will take an enterprising label to bring them back.

Chuck Mangione (born 1940)

TRUMPET, FLUGELHORN

Co-led The Jazz Brothers with brother Gap, then joined the Jazz Messengers in 1965. Began playing a kind of easy-listening jazz in the '70s and scored several big-hit albums and singles. Much less active in the '80s and '90s.

***** Hey Baby!**

Original Jazz Classics OJC 668 *Mangione; Sal Nistico (ts); Gap Mangione (p); Steve Davis (b); Roy McCurdy (d). 3/61.*

***** Spring Fever**

Original Jazz Classics OJC 767 *As above, except Frank Pullara (b), Vinnie Ruggieri (d) replace Davis and McCurdy. 11/61.*

****(*) Recuerdo**

Original Jazz Classics OJC 495 *Mangione; Joe Romano (ts); Wynton Kelly (p); Sam Jones (b); Louis Hayes (d). 7/62.*

**** Love Notes**

Columbia FC 38101 *Mangione; Chris Vadala (ss, ts, f, picc); Peter Harris (g); Gordon Johnson (b); Everett Silver (d). 82.*

Mangione worked his way out of small-time hard bop to big-band section-playing before settling for easy-listening jazz with a series of hugely successful albums in the 1970s (*Feels So Good* sold in the millions). None of this later music is worth listing here, although it's no more offensive than a typical lite-fusion date of today; *Love Notes* is still in American print for the curious. Back at the beginning, though, are some serviceable (and sometimes excitable) sessions for Riverside, now back in the racks as OJC reissues. The two albums with brother Gap offer a genial reworking of some of the boppish trends of the day, but in each case the album is stolen from under the brothers' noses by Sal Nistico, whose tenor tear-ups are just the kind of thing he would do with Woody Herman on some of the best of Herman's '60s dates. A similar situation occurs on the pick-up date, *Recuerdo*, where Joe Romano's irascible solos undercut Mangione's efforts at fronting the action. The leader has a rather thin tone on trumpet, which hints at why he later switched to flugelhorn as his sole instrument; but his best solos are bright enough.

***(*) The Feeling's Back**

Chesky JD 184 *Mangione; Gerry Niewood (f); Cliff Korman (ky); Jaz Azzolina (g); Sarah Carter (clo); David Finck, Kip Reid (b); Paulo Braga (d); Cafe (perc); Maucha Adnet, Jacki Presti, Annette Sanders (v). 10/98.*

It is? The feeling we have is a faint queasiness (nothing so strong as revulsion). Mangione spells out melodies which present as much challenge as a nursery rhyme, and the use of a largely acoustic, real-time band is a mere pretence: it's as contrived as the sappiest smooth jazz. Feeble.

Manhattan New Music Project

GROUP

A one-off session organized largely by guitarist–composer Paul Nash.

***** Mood Swing**

Soul Note 121207 *Jack Walrath (t, flhn); Ron Tooley (t); Tom Varner (frhn); David Taylor (btb, tba); Bruce Williamson (as, f, cl, bcl); Chuck Clark (ss, ts, f); Tim Reis (bs); Neal Kirkwood (p); Paul Nash (g); Jeffrey Carney (b); Jamey Haddad (d). 9/92.*

Directed by guitarist Nash, the Project is a tightly marshalled, rather wry and tongue-in-cheek outfit, as one would expect with prankster Walrath in the front row. Not to be confused with the Manhattan Project *tout court*, this outfit makes a little more of the reference to America's A-bomb programme, blasting out megaton arrangements that always suggest a much bigger band. In part, the intention is to highlight each of the main soloists, with Walrath prominent on his own 'Depressions of Eastern Europe', Nash on the weird 'Queen Of Din's New Religion' and

'Shadow', Varner on 'Shovel Man'. *Mood Swing* is the perfect title, because there is no real continuity from one track to the next and it's a record probably best sampled a track at a time, on a whim and as mood dictates.

Herbie Mann (born 1930)

FLUTE, ALTO FLUTE, PICCOLO SAXOPHONE, BASS CLARINET

Extensive tours abroad – to Europe, Africa and Brazil – helped to hone Mann's style and open him to a sometimes bizarrely eclectic range of influences, everything from bebop and bossa nova to rock and Japanese classical music. He is a brilliant flautist with a light, skipping attack and an unfailing rhythmic sureness.

*****(*) Herbie Mann Plays**

Bethlehem BET 6010 *Mann; Joe Puma, Benny Weeks (g); Keith Hodgson, Whitney Mitchell (b); Lee Rockey, Herb Wassermann (d). 12/54, 56.*

***** Flamingo: Volume 2**

Bethlehem BET 6007 *Mann; Joe Puma (g); Charles Andrus (b); Harold Cranowsky (d). 6/55.*

***** Herbie Mann With The Sam Most Quintet**

Bethlehem BET 6008 *Mann; Sam Most (f); Joe Puma (g); Jimmy Gannon (b); Lee Kleimann (d). 10/55.*

****(*) Love And The Weather**

Bethlehem BET 6009 *Mann; Joe Puma (g); Milt Hinton, Whitney Mitchell (b); Herb Wassermann (d); strings. 3/56.*

***** The Epitome Of Jazz**

Bethlehem BET 6011 *As above four items.*

Mann occupies a similar position to Charles Lloyd's in recent jazz history. Influential, but cursed by commercial success and an unfashionable choice of instrument, both have been subject to knee-jerk critical put-down. Where Lloyd's flute was his 'double', Mann's concentration slowly evolved a powerful and adaptable technique which gave him access to virtually every mood, from a breathy etherealism, down through a smooth, semi-vocalized tone that sounded remarkably like clarinet (his first instrument), to a tough, metallic ring that ideally suited the funk contexts he explored in the late 1960s.

These early recordings for Bethlehem are a useful corrective to a later view of Mann as a paisley-patterned hipster, a Pied Piper to the hippy movement. It is a little hard to draw exact distinctions between individual albums. Mann has not yet devised his favourite flute-plus-vibes sound and relies on Puma's softly ringing guitar to temper his own whistly, almost reed-like sound, most obviously on *Flamingo*, whose first volume doesn't seem to have made it back from the void. The two-flute front line of the record with Most is quite attractive, though it is clear which of the two has all the ideas. *Love And The Weather* calls for sou'westers and gumboots, and undoubtedly the best is the plain-spoken *Plays*, which puts the emphasis on Mann's attempts to adapt stray elements of contemporary idiom to a smoothed-out and mellifluous context. Originally a ten-inch LP, it has been augmented with alternative takes and material from a 1956 session. *Epitome* is useful as a sampler for this period.

*****(*) Just Wailin'**

Original Jazz Classics OJCCD 900 *Mann; Charlie Rouse (ts); Kenny Burrell (g); Mal Waldron (p); George Joyner (b); Arthur Taylor (d). 2/58.*

Originally issued on New Jazz, this is Mann at his best. The rhythm section and the choice of front-line partners gave him exactly the balance between rhythmic toughness and melodic delicacy that he needed, enough instrumental chiaroscuro and a bag of blowing tunes ('Minor Groove', 'Jumpin' With Symphony Sid', 'Gospel Truth' among them) to stave off any risk of pale whimsy. Arthur Taylor is the key man on this session, throwing out ringing accents and dark bass figures, pattering away at the melody and conjuring up a whole chain of islands on the lovely 'Trinidad'. The CD sound is very good indeed, with plenty of definition in the rhythm section (which had been a problem on vinyl) and with no hint of distortion on Mann's horn.

***** Flute Soufflé**

Original Jazz Classics OJC 760 *Mann; Bobby Jaspar (f, ts); Tommy Flanagan (p); Joe Puma (g); Wendell Marshall (b); Bobby Donaldson (d). 3/57.*

*****(*) Sultry Serenade**

Original Jazz Classics OJCCD 927 *Mann; Urbie Green (tb); Jack Nimitz (bs, bcl); Joe Puma (g); Oscar Pettiford (b); Charlie Smith (d). 4/57.*

***** Flute Fraternity**

VSOP 38 *Mann; Buddy Collette (as, ts, cl, f, afl); Jimmy Rowles (p, cel); Buddy Clark (b); Mel Lewis (d). 7/57.*

Flute Soufflé is unusual in not having a vibes player on the strength. Mann found that soft metallic chime an ideal complement to the flute and, for the most part, one would have to agree with him. Flanagan does a similar job on the early disc, moving out into pentatonic scales on 'Tel Aviv', pattering through 'Let's March' and controlling the tempo on 'Chasing The Bird', obliging his colleagues to bring the beat back a notch in the last chorus.

Sultry Serenade is a delicately modulated and totally jazz-centred set which makes use of attractive and unfamiliar sonorities and sees Mann make a rare switch to bass clarinet on 'Lazy Bones', one of two Hoagy Carmichael tunes in the programme. Nimitz and Puma are both in revelatory form; the guitarist is terse and sharp, while the saxophonist reveals a depth of expression which is out of all proportion to Jack's rather lowly reputation.

Flute Fraternity pitched Mann up against that oddly under-achieving multi-instrumentalist, Buddy Collette. Endlessly varied in tonality and timbre, it's also a low-key and undramatic set which will appeal mainly to those who like their jazz abstract and unflustered.

***** Jazz Masters 56**

Verve 529901-2 *Mann; Leo Ball, Jerry Kail, Ziggy Schatz (t); Jimmy Rowles (p); Laurindo Almeida, Tony Rizzi, Howard Roberts (g); Johnny Rae (vib, perc); Buddy Clark, Tony Reyes, Knobby Totah (b); Rudy Collins, Mel Lewis, Santo Miranda (d); Ray Barretto, Ray Mantilla, Babatunde Olatunji, Chico Guerrero, Milt Holland, Jose Mangual, Carlos Patato Valdes (perc); strings. 8/57–7/60.*

Before signing for Atlantic, Mann signed to Verve for three years and three records, a move that had important repercussions on his future career, for it pushed him away from straight jazz and in the direction of the crossover artist of the 1960s. *The Magic Flute Of Herbie Mann, Flautista!* And *Herbie Mann's Cuban Band* opened up a new constituency to him, but also helped him rethink his own playing by adding Latin jazz elements to the rhythmic mix and foregrounding the flute as a light singing voice with a soft metallic rasp rather than the saxophone-emulating sound he had become stuck with up to that point. 'Evolution Of Mann', included on *The Magic Flute*, was perhaps the single item which broke his new career. It was taken by Symphony Sid Torin and given considerable airplay in the New York region, establishing Mann as a figure on the nascent Afro-Cuban scene. Most of the material on these sides was standards-based – 'You Stepped Out Of A Dream' and 'Strike Up The Band' being the obvious examples – or else Latin-tinged jazz like Ellington and Tizol's 'Caravan'; but there are also signs that Mann is working his way towards a new hybrid idiom, on such pieces as 'A Ritual', 'Todos Locos' and 'Come On, Mule' (a rare glimpse of the leader's bass clarinet). These were transitional albums, with all that that overworked expression suggests.

(*) **Flautista!

Verve 557448-2 *Mann; Johnny Rae (vib, mar); Knobby Totah (b, perc); Carlos Patato Valdes (perc).* 59.

Mann goes Afro-Cuban and with some conviction, though for us this is a bland and formulaic set that doesn't show off Mann to the best advantage. Production values seem to take precedence over creative performance and, apart from Juan Tizol's 'Caravan', the charts chosen are relatively undemanding and somewhat one-dimensional, as is the production, which has the blurry indistinctness which was starting to become the norm (though not this Norm) for popular music. The band is just Mann plus rhythm and one feels there is nothing for him to play off, leaving the flautist to process rather routine gestures.

***(*) **At The Village Gate**

Atlantic 7567 81350 *Mann; Hagood Hardy (vib); Ahmed Abdul-Malik (b); Rudy Collins (d); Chief Bey, Ray Mantilla (perc).* 11/61.

*** **Memphis Underground**

Atlantic 7567 81364 *Mann; Roy Ayers (vib, perc); Bobby Emmons (org); Larry Coryell, Sonny Sharrock, Reggie Young (g); Bobby Wood (p, electric p); Tommy Coghill, Mike Leach, Miroslav Vitous (b); Gene Christman (d).* 68.

*** **The Best Of Herbie Mann**

Atlantic 7567 81369 *Mann; Marky Markowitz, Joe Newman (t); Jack Hitchcock, Mark Weinstein (tb); Quentin Jackson (tb, btb); King Curtis (ts); Pepper Adams (bs); Chick Corea, Charlie Palmieri, Bobby Wood (p); Bobby Emmons (org); Larry Coryell, Al Gorgoni, Charlie Macey, Sonny Sharrock (g); Roy Ayers, Hagood Hardy, Dave Pike (vib); Tommy Coghill, Juan Garcia, Mike Leach, Joe Macko, Ahmed Abdul-Malik, Knobby Totah, Ben Tucker (b); Bruno Carr, Gene Christman, Rudy Collins, Pretty Purdie (d); Chief Bey, Ray Mantilla, Warren Smith, Carlos Patato Valdes (perc); Tamiko Jones (v).* 4/61–8/68.

Though most of the Atlantics remain out of catalogue, the perennial *Memphis Underground*, one of the founding documents of the fusion movement, has made a successful transfer to CD. Though the recording quality would scarcely pass current muster, the music has survived unexpectedly well. The interplay of three guitarists, notably the Cain and Abel opposition of Sonny Sharrock and Larry Coryell, gives it a flavour that from moment to moment gives off a whiff of Ornette Coleman's *Prime Time*; the addition of Roy Ayers's vibes and Bobby Emmons's organ gives the background a seething quality that adds depth to Mann's slightly unemotional virtuosity. The presence of one-time Weather Report bassist, Miroslav Vitous, on a single track, the excellent 'Hold On, I'm Comin'', may also attract notice. Head and shoulders with Lloyd above most of the crossover experimenters of the time, Mann deserves to be heard, and it's a pity there isn't more around. The live performances are much more what we've come to expect of the flautist and, all prejudice aside, they're jolly good. His reading of 'Summertime' echoes some of Coltrane's trills and grace notes, and there are some telling moments on 'It Ain't Necessarily So'.

(*) **Stone Flute

Embryo 520 *Mann; Roy Ayers (vib); Sonny Sharrock (g); Peter Dimitriades, Manny Green, Gene Orloff (vn); Selwart Clarke (vla); Kermit Moore, George Ricci (clo); Ron Carter, Miroslav Vitous (b); Bruno Carr (d).* 70.

It would be difficult, out of context, to identify this as a Mann recording at all, certainly of this vintage. There are hints in the phrasing of the flute, but most listeners will naturally guess that they are listening to someone more closely associated with the avant-garde or with a kind of impressionistic and classically influenced jazz. The line-up gives a fair impression of the kind of sound-world that can be expected. Mann takes a very free role, drifting over William Fischer's very good and thoroughly idiomatic string arrangements. Virtually unheard for 30 years, *Stone Flute* offers an intriguing sidebar on Mann's career.

(*) **Push Push

Embryo 532 2 *Mann; Richard Tee (ky); Duane Allman, Cornell Dupree, David Spinozza (g); Gene Bianco (hca, hp); Donald Duck Dunn, Gerald Jemmott, Chuck Rainey (b); Al Jackson, Pretty Purdie (d); Ralph MacDonald (perc).* 7/71.

Whatever one thinks of the genre, Mann's musicianship always lifted sessions like this above the ordinary. He was already flirting more than a little with rock-and-rollers (the legendary Duane Allman plays here), but they are required to swing to his beat and there is no suggestion that he is trying to borrow their youthful cachet. The strongest tracks are his own compositions, 'Push Push' and 'Man's Hope', both of which feature some very powerful flute-playing. Other numbers are more dance-orientated and less convincing on record. Richard Tee is immense in support (no offence intended) and creates a vivid, often very subtle backdrop for the leader.

*** **Caminho De Casa**

Chesky JD 40 *Mann; Eduardo Simon, Mark Soskin (p); Romero LuBambo (g); Paul Socolow (b); Ricky Sebastian (d); Cafe (perc).* 3/90.

Mann calls his bossa-influenced band Jasil Brazz; fortunately the synthesis is slightly more elegant than the nomenclature. Like Gato Barbieri's more obviously Latin 'Chapters', this is pan-American music with a vigorous improvisational component, not just a collection of exotic 'stylings'. Guitarist LuBambo is particularly impressive, but it's the drummer who keeps the music rooted in jazz tradition, leaving most of the colour work to percussionist Cafe. Mann himself is in fine voice, particularly on the beautifully toned alto flute. Only one of the nine tracks – the rather weak 'Yesterday's Kisses' – is credited to him; the rest are substantial enough. Recommended.

**** Opalescence**
Kokopelli KOKO 1298 *Mann; Mark Soskin (ky); Robben Ford, Romero LuBambo, Ricardo Silveira (g); Paul Socolow (b); Cyro Baptista (perc).* 91.

****(*) Deep Pocket**
Kokopelli KOKO 1296 *Mann; David 'Fathead' Newman (ts); Les McCann (p, v); Richard Tee (p, org); Cornell Dupree (g); Chuck Rainey (b); Buddy Williams (d, perc).* 4, 5 & 7/92.

For the most part these are drab slices of Latinized fusion, played with absolute authority and professionalism but lacking more than an occasional spark of imaginative improvisation. Most of these, to be fair, come from Mann himself, who does still occasionally throw in an unexpected element, as in his response to Newman on 'Moanin''. But such moments are too rare and widely spaced out for most needs.

***** Peace Pieces**
Lightyear 54193 *Mann; Randy Brecker (flhn); Bruce Dunlap (g); Paul Socolow (b); Lewis Nash, Ricky Sebastian (d); Sammy Figueroa (perc).* 3/95.

Mann had something of a purple patch in 1995, recording this entirely jazz-based record and then going to mark a significant birthday with a residency that was also a career retrospective; see below. This record, which explores the compositions of Bill Evans, is something of a backward glance as well. Mann had recorded with the pianist as long ago as 1961. Working without piano, though with additional solos from Randy Brecker and with some elements of overdubbing (which, of course, had been an Evans device as well), Mann sounds as if he's turned back the clock and traced a path he moved off with his switch of Latin fusion in the '60s. The themes will be familiar to Evans admirers, though it's the relatively little-known 'Peri's Scope' and 'Interplay' which immediately catch the ear, rather than the more evenly trod 'Waltz For Debbie' and 'Blue In Green' (which is still the subject of a freehold dispute with Miles Davis). Mann's ability to play complex figures and sustain difficult harmonics will surprise those who know only his mid-period work.

*****(*) Celebration**
Lightyear 54185 *Mann; Randy Brecker, Claudio Roditi, Terell Stafford (t); Jim Pugh (tb); Paquito D'Rivera, Bobby Watson (as); David Newman (ts); Dave Valentin (f); David Leonhardt, Edward Simon, Mark Soskin (p); Bruce Dunlap, Romero Lubambo, Lou Volpe (g); Sergio Brandao, Ron Carter, Eddie Gomez, Frank Gravis, Larry Grenadier, Nilson Matta (b); Adam Cruz, Duduka Fonseca, Winard Harper, Victor Lewis, Ricky Sebastian, Buddy Williams (d); Cyro Baptista, Cafe, Milton Cardona, Ray Mantilla, Tito Puente (perc).* 4/95.

***** America / Brasil**
Lightyear 54233 *As above.* 4/95.

Mann turned 65 and celebrated with a residency at the Blue Note in New York, a week that seemed to revivify his career and sharpen up his appetite for playing. The intention clearly was to take in as much of his career – varied and eclectic as it has been – as humanly possible, touching on hits like 'Memphis Underground' along the way. With that in mind, the personnel was as adaptable as possible, there were a number of rhythm permutations on offer, and the guest spots were judiciously placed so as to complement the leader rather than steal his thunder. Mann's origins in bebop are acknowledged in a very good version of 'Au Privave', and his even deeper roots in jump and swing in a very good interpretation of 'Jeep's Blues', in the arrangement of which Bobby Watson may very well have had a hand. 'Memphis Underground' is played with wry affection and a more tailored approach than in the old days, but the really outstanding performance is 'Give And Take'. Mann obviously had the time of his life and sings on his flute. Strongly recommended.

The second album is also drawn from the same week of concerts, but the selection doesn't have the same impact. Mann is playing every bit as well, but the accompaniments seem more routine and the material, with the exception of 'All Blues' and another Lins/Martins composition, 'America / Brasil' (they also composed 'Give And Take'), is lacklustre.

Shelly Manne (1920–84)
DRUMS

One of the finest – and shrewdest – musicians in modern jazz, Manne is also one of the most fully documented, playing with everyone from Charlie Parker and Coleman Hawkins to modernists. He grew up in New York but became definitive of the West Coast sound, playing drums with a cool melodism and restrained dynamics. For a time, he ran his own club, the Manne Hole, and bred horses, but he was never anything other than a whole-hearted musician.

*****(*) The Three And The Two**
Original Jazz Classics OJC 172 *Manne; Shorty Rogers (t); Jimmy Giuffre (cl, ts, bs); Russ Freeman (d).* 9/54.

***** The West Coast Sound**
Original Jazz Classics OJC 152 *Manne; Bob Enevoldsen (vtb); Joe Maini (as); Bob Cooper (ts); Jimmy Giuffre (bs); Russ Freeman (p); Ralph Pena (b).* 9/55.

A useful wrong-footer for a jazz Trivial Pursuit is: Who played drums on Ornette Coleman's *Tomorrow Is The Question*? Shelly combined the classic qualities of reliability and adaptable time with a much more inventive side that has more to do with the *sound* of the drums, an ability to play melodically, than with self-conscious fractures and complications of the basic four-in-a-bar. In the same way, Manne's solos could hardly have been more different from those of important predecessors like Gene Krupa. Where Krupa made the drummer a 'high-price guy', giving him a prominence from which Manne benefited, Manne draws attention to himself not by showmanship but by the sophistication of his playing.

The trios with Rogers and Giuffre find the players working in parallel, not in a horns-and-rhythm hierarchy. On 'Flip', Manne plays in counterpoint with his colleagues. On 'Autumn In New York', the horns diverge almost entirely, giving the standard the same rather abstract feel that pianist Freeman brings to a notably unsentimental duo reading of 'With A Song In My Heart'. 'Three In A Row' is an experiment in serial jazz, giving a tone-row the same status as a 'head' or standard. Cool and almost disengaged it may be, but it's also compellingly inventive. The duos with Freeman have survived rather less well, but broadly the same instincts are at work. On 'The Sound Effects Manne', Freeman plays a sharply percussive line alongside Manne's 'theme statement'. 'Billie's Bounce' is compact, bluesy and very intense. Strongly recommended.

The mid-1950s saw Manne turning his back slightly on the experimentalism still evident on *The West Coast Sound* in favour of a more direct idiom which nevertheless incorporated quietly subversive harmonic devices and a much-enhanced role for the drummer. The material may be interesting, but there's that almost academic quality to the delivery which one associates with some of Giuffre's work of the time. 'Grasshopper' and 'Spring Is Here' are worth the money on their own, though.

***(*) Swinging Sounds

Original Jazz Classics OJC 267 *Manne; Stu Williamson (t, vtb); Charlie Mariano (as); Russ Freeman (p); Leroy Vinnegar (b).* 1–2/56.

*** More Swinging Sounds

Original Jazz Classics OJC 320 *As above.* 7–8/56.

Manne was also a prolific releaser of records, most obviously with the Blackhawk sessions, but also including this excellent early material from a notably light and vibrant band, fronted by the underrated Stu Williamson and the always inventive Mariano, who contributes 'Dart Game' and 'Slan', two of the most interesting pieces on an album notably free of familiar standards. Shelly plays as softly as he ever did, and with great control on the mallets.

'More' just about covers it. The later album has the slightly anonymous, kit-built feel of a hundred contemporary West Coast discs. The playing is fine, of course, and Williamson's valve trombone mixes richly with Mariano's more acid saxophone tonality to create an attractive sweet-and-sour front line on 'Quartet'. The remaining material is less distinctive. Like Rogers, Williamson isn't an agile and virtuosic player so much as a tasteful colourman with a good sense of the broader structure. Manne shows no signs of wanting to go further in the direction of polyrhythms than he had previously, but he is unmistakably calling the shots, and the shots are by no means routine.

***(*) Shelly Manne And His Friends: Volume 1

Original Jazz Classics OJC 240 *Manne; André Previn (p); Leroy Vinnegar (b).* 2/56.

***(*) My Fair Lady

Original Jazz Classics OJC 336 *As above.* 8/56.

***(*) My Fair Lady / West Side Story

Contemporary CDCOPCD 942 *As above.* 8/56.

The first and probably the best of these Contemporary reissues (now on OJC) establishes firmly what a fine trio this was. The two-piano *Double Play*, co-led by André Previn and Russ Freeman, with Manne on drums, and also on OJC, is well worth catching, as are Previn's *West Side Story* covers, now reissued as a twofer with Manne's outwardly less promising *My Fair Lady*. It has taken on a life of its own. The bonus of the Previn tracks could outweigh the slightly less vivid sound on the Contemporary double-set. Manne's handling of 'Get Me To The Church On Time' and the surprisingly swinging 'I Could Have Danced All Night' comes as no surprise, but he works a kind of magic on 'Ascot Gavotte', and the reading of the standard 'I've Grown Accustomed To Her Face' is exemplary.

***(*) The Gambit

Original Jazz Classics OJCCD *Manne; Stu Williamson (t, vtb); Charlie Mariano (as); Russ Freeman (p); Monty Budwig (b).* 1/57.

Dominated by Mariano's chess-inspired suite, this is one of the more unusual items in Contemporary's detailed documentation of Manne and the Men. It really is such a good record that it's surprising we haven't seen it transferred before now. The saxophonist is in cracking form, working several moves ahead like a good chess player, and, though the main section suffers from a slight loss of spontaneity, the musical ideas are interesting enough to hold the attention. The remainder is looser but still packed with intelligent jazz. Mariano's 'Blue Gnu' is a clever reworking of a basic blues, transposed into unfamiliar keys, and Russ Freeman's 'Hugo Hurwhey' underlines his great contribution to the band and to the library of strong West Coast themes.

*** Bells Are Ringing

Original Jazz Classics OJC 910 *Manne; André Previn (p); Red Mitchell (b).* 7/58.

*** Play Peter Gunn

Original Jazz Classics OJC 946 *Manne; Conte Candoli (t); Herb Geller (as); Victor Feldman (vib); Russ Freeman (p); Monty Budwig (b).* 1/59.

Manne on Broadway, and TV. These jazz versions of show tunes and television-via-Hollywood soundtracks were always a popular schedule-filler, and after the success of *My Fair Lady* there was bound to be a formula to follow. Manne's men do the *Peter Gunn* music with a kind of cartoon tough-guy expression, but this was a great combo anyway and Candoli and Geller seldom knew how to be boring. *Bells Are Ringing* is a lovely score, too, and the trio make the best of it.

♛ **** At The Blackhawk

Original Jazz Classics OJC 656–660 5CD (separately available) *Manne; Joe Gordon (t); Richie Kamuca (ts); Victor Feldman (p); Monty Budwig (b).* 9/59.

One of the finest and swingingest mainstream recordings ever made, *At The Blackhawk* benefits immeasurably from CD transfer. Feldman's slightly dark piano-sound is lightened, Gordon and Kamuca lose a little of the crackle round the edges, and Budwig reappears out of the vinyl gloom. From the opening 'Our Delight' to the previously unissued material on Volume Five, and taking in a definitive performance of Golson's 'Whisper Not' along the way, this is club jazz at its very best. 'A Gem From Tiffany', heard on *Swinging Sounds*, above, had become Manne's signature-theme and it is rather indifferently played and repeated. Otherwise, everything sounds as fresh as paint, even the previously rejected 'Wonder Why' and 'Eclipse In Spain'. Utterly enjoyable ... nay, essential.

****** Live At The Manne Hole, Volume 1**
Original Jazz Classics OJC 714 *Manne; Conte Candoli (t); Richie Kamuca (ts); Russ Freeman (p); Chuck Berghofer (b).* 5/61.

*****(*) Live At The Manne Hole, Volume 2**
Original Jazz Classics OJC 715 *As above.* 5/61.

Nothing matches up to the Black Hawk sessions, but these come pretty close, confirming beyond doubt Manne's quality and staying power in the toughest gig of all, regular club work. This was his home turf, the joint he opened a year earlier as a hedge against failing chops and capricious bookers. That may be why he sounds more relaxed, even a little lazy, breaking out of a pleasant reverie only for one or two rather contrived solos. Again, though, as with the similar band on *Peter Gunn*, above, it's the quality of the group as a whole that registers. Even on warhorses like 'Softly As In A Morning Sunrise' (*Volume 1*) and 'Green Dolphin Street' (the sequel), they have original and incisive points to make. Both discs have a place on the shelf alongside the Black Hawk stuff.

***** Boss Sounds**
Koch International 8539 *Manne; Conte Candoli (t); Russ Freeman (p); Monty Budwig (b).* 66.

This was not yet available on CD when we went to press but, judging by the original Atlantic LP, it's a cool and eloquent set with lots of expressive detail. We'd expect the balance of drums, bass and piano to be rather more even on the reissue, but it's a very decent piece of work, and 'Frank's Tune' and 'Breeze And I' are well worth having.

*****(*) Alive In London**
Original Jazz Classics OJC 773 *Manne; Gary Barone (t, flhn); John Gross (ts); Mike Wofford (p); John Morrell (g); Roland Haynes (d).* 7/70.

Recorded during a fondly remembered residency at Ronnie Scott's club, this saw Manne experimenting in a slightly freer idiom, relaxing the usually watertight rhythms, exploring areas of pure sound. With the exception of Wofford (who plays an electric instrument throughout), the band are not particularly well known, but they play with great vigour and application, and Manne's original production job gives them all a decent representation. A branch line, perhaps, in view of what went before and what ensued, but an interesting and thoroughly enjoyable set nevertheless.

****** Perk Up**
Concord CCD 4021 *Manne; Conte Candoli (t); Frank Strozier (as, f); Mike Wofford (p); Monty Budwig (b).* 6/67.

A powerful and often overlooked session that is something of a rarity in the Concord catalogue. For a start, Shelly and his new gang of men seem intent on exploring the more out-of-the-way dimensions of contemporary jazz. This is easily the most adventurous set he made under his own name. It opens, deceptively but tellingly, with Jimmy Rowles's title-track. After that, Wofford and Strozier are the main composers, each delivering two strongly challenging tunes. Shelly is in great form, understated and effortlessly melodic, and he must have purred at the sound the Concord engineers gave him. This is an early set from the label, one of the very few they seem to have brought out before the formal inception of the imprint. Thank goodness they did; it's a belter.

Wingy Manone (1900–1982)

TRUMPET, CORNET, VOCAL

Born in New Orleans, Joseph Manone based himself in Chicago around 1930 and developed a reputation for showmanship. Led his own groups in New York from 1934 and made many records. Worked in Hollywood and on radio in the '40s and '50s, in Las Vegas in the '60s, making occasional touring appearances. His nickname came from losing an arm in a streetcar accident.

***** The Wingy Manone Collection Vol. 1 1927–1930**
Collector's Classics COCD-3 *Manone; Bob Price, Ed Camden (t); Orville Haynes (tb); Hal Jordy (cl, as); Wade Foster, Benny Goodman, Frank Teschemacher, George Walters (cl); Bob Sacks, Bud Freeman, George Snurpus, Joe Dunn (ts); Frank Melrose (p, acc); Johnny Miller, Jack Gardner, Art Hodes, Joe Sullivan, Maynard Spencer (p); Steve Brou, Ray Biondi (g); Miff Frink (bj, tb); Herman Foster (bj); Arnold Loyacano, Orville Haynes (b); John Ryan, Gene Krupa, Augie Schellange, Bob Conselman, Dash Burkis, George Wettling (d); Earl Warner (v).* 4/27–9/30.

*****(*) The Wingy Manone Collection Vol. 2 1934**
Collector's Classics COCD-4 *Manone; George Brunies, Santo Pecora, Dicky Wells (tb); Matty Matlock, Sidney Arodin (cl); Eddie Miller, Bud Freeman (ts); Gil Bowers, Jelly Roll Morton, Teddy Wilson, Terry Shand (p); Nappy Lamare (g, v); Frank Victor (g); Harry Goodman, John Kirby, Benny Pottle (b); Ray Bauduc, Bob White, Kaiser Marshall (d).* 5–9/34.

***** The Wingy Manone Collection Vol. 3 1934–1935**
Collector's Classics COCD-5 *Manone; Russ Case, Phil Capicotta, Harry Gluck (t); Santo Pecora, Will Bradley, Charlie Butterfield (tb); Toots Mondello, Sid Trucker (cl, as); Matty Matlock, Sidney Arodin (cl); Eddie Miller (cl, ts); Arthur Rollini, Paul Ricci (ts); Terry Shand, Gil Blowers, Claude Thornhill (p); Joe Venuti, Nick Pisani, Tony Alongi (vn); Nappy Lamare (g, v); Jimmy Lewis (g); Benny Pottle, Harry Goodman, Charlie Barber (b); Bob White, Ray Bauduc, Chauncey Morehouse (d).* 10/34–5/35.

Wingy Manone was a New Orleans man, much in thrall to Louis Armstrong as both trumpeter and vocalist, and the leader of a great stack of records made in the 1930s. The first disc is very rough-and-ready, with the small groups offering glimpses of precocious youngsters such as Bud Freeman, Benny Goodman and Gene Krupa, yet stumbling on the scrappy recording quality, off-the-peg arrangements and other, second-rate sidemen. For those whose taste runs to the offbeat music of the day, this is worthwhile – it also features the famous first appearance of the 'In The Mood' riff on 'Tar Paper Stomp' – but non-specialists should start with the fine second record. Manone's derivative playing has grown in stature, his singing has a hip, fast-talking swagger about it, and the bands – with Miller, Matlock, Brunies and the excellent Arodin extensively featured – set a useful standard of small-group playing in the immediate pre-swing era. One remarkable session even has Teddy Wilson and Jelly Roll Morton sharing keyboard duties.

Volume Three has three more sessions in the same mode before the one that produced 'The Isle Of Capri', Wingy's big hit. By this time the run of material was shifting away from jazz and into novelty pop, and it's ironic that Manone's 'Capri' vocal sent up the genre, only to secure a hit (a previously unissued non-vocal version is also included). Even so, the group often mustered a surprisingly hard-bitten treatment on a tune such as 'March Winds And April Showers'. The transfers throughout are lifelike and vivid: some scratch, and some of the early records (from Champion and Gennett masters) will always sound harsh, but otherwise entirely listenable. True to form, the Classics label has commenced its own survey of Manone material (Classics 774, 798 and 828) which more or less follows the same sequence as these discs. Transfers, from unlisted sources, are certainly no improvement on these, and there seems little reason for this sequence to be displaced.

***** The Wingy Manone Collection Vol. 4: 1935–36**
Collector's Classics COCD-6 *Manone; Jack Teagarden (tb, v); George Brunies, Ward Silloway (tb); Matty Matlock, Joe Marsala (cl); Bud Freeman, Tony Zimmers, Eddie Miller (ts); Horace Diaz, Gil Bowers (p); Carmen Mastren, Nappy Lamare (g); Sid Weiss, Artie Shapiro (b); Sam Weiss, Ray Bauduc (d); Johnny Mercer (v).* 7/35–3/36.

***** Wingy Manone 1936**
Classics 849 *Manone; Ward Silloway (tb); Joe Marsala, Mike Viggiano (cl); Matty Matlock, James Lamare (cl, ts); Tommy Mace (as); Eddie Miller (ts); Gil Bowers, Conrad Lanoue (p); Nappy Lamare, Carmen Mastren, Jack LeMaire (g); Artie Shapiro (b); Ray Bauduc, Sam Weiss, Abby Fisher (d).* 3–7/36.

***** Wingy Manone 1936–1937**
Classics 887 *As above, except add Al Mastren, George Brunies (tb), Babe Russin (ts), George Wettling, Danny Alvin (d), Sally Sharon (v); omit Mace, Silloway, Bowers, Mastren, Lamare, Bauduc, Fisher.* 8/36–5/37.

***** Wingy Manone 1937–1938**
Classics 952 *Manone; Al Mastren (tb); Brad Gowans (vtb); Joe Marsala, Al Kavich (cl, as); Doc Rando (as); Babe Russin, Chu Berry (ts); Conrad Lanoue, Wilder Chase (p); Jack LeMaire, Bobby Bennett (g); Artie Shapiro, Sid Jacobs (b); Danny Alvin (d).* 5/37–5/38.

***** Wingy Manone 1939-1940**
Classics 1023 *Manone; Buck Scott (tb, v); Buster Bailey, Gus Fetterer, Phil Olivella (cl); Chu Berry (ts); Conrad Lanoue, Ernie Hughes (p); Zeb Julian, Danny Barker (g); Jules Cassard, Sid Jacobs (b); Cozy Cole, Danny Alvin (d).* 4/39–1/40.

***** Wingy Manone 1940-1944**
Classics 1091 *Manone; Marty Marsala (t); Babe Bowman, George Brunies, Pete Beilman, Jack Flores, King Jackson, Floyd O'Brien, Abe Lincoln (tb); Bill Cobey (cl, as); Joe Marsala, Archie Rosati, Matty Matlock (cl); Stan Wrightsman, Mel Powell (p); Russell Soule, Carmen Mastren, Nappy Lamare (g); Bill Jones, Al Morgan, Jim Lynch, Artie Shapiro, Phil Stevens (b); Dick Cornell, Zutty Singleton (d); Johnny Mercer (v).* 8/40–3/44.

As the 1930s progressed, Manone began to seem like Fats Waller, also on Bluebird, for most of these sessions: he didn't send up his material the way Waller did but he seemed to get stuck with a lot of cornball tunes, and the records soon become formulaic. That said, his exuberance and the contributions of the better players enliven many of the tracks and it's hard not to enjoy most of these sessions. Collector's Classics go up to the start of the Bluebird era with their fourth disc, which includes a session with Jack Teagarden and Wingy's version of 'The Music Goes 'Round And Around'. From here we pick up the Classics sequence, which starts with the final Vocalion date – and a very good one, with four very swinging tracks – before shifting into the first Bluebird sessions. Marsala and Miller are the principal interest besides the leader, and some of the other players seem a bit stiff but, when they get to either a rare instrumental ('Panama') or a superior jazz piece like 'Basin Street Blues' or 'Jazz Me Blues', the band noticeably perk up. Manone's singing is inventive in its way, and on an unlikely piece such as 'Formal Night In Harlem' he's genuinely creative.

Classics 952 offers a session with Chu Berry (though the material is disappointing here) and paves the way for the two 1939 dates which commence Classics 1023. The 'In The Mood' riff turns up again, this time as 'Jumpy Nerves', and although Bailey and Berry are somewhat subdued they do increase the musical interest in these titles. Much better material and more of a focus and playing small-group jazz makes this arguably the best of these later discs. Classics 1091 has two final dates for Bluebird with a reversion to less promising tunes: the very last title is 'Stop The War (The Cats Are Killin' Themselves)'! A single date for Decca produced the six-part(!) 'Jam And Jive', with a lot of chaff between Wingy and straight man Eddie Marr. After the record ban, he returned with a single date for Brunswick and then four Capitol titles, with a band that included three trombonists and Johnny Mercer guesting on 'The Tailgate Ramble'. An entertaining miscellany. Transfers on these later discs seem consistent enough.

**** Trumpet Jive!**
Prestige PCD-24119-2 *Manone; Ward Silloway, Frank Orchard (tb); Joe Marsala, Hank D'Amico (cl); Nick Ciazza (ts); Conrad Lanoue, Dave Bowman (p); Chuck Wayne (g); Irv Lang, Bob Haggart (b); George Wettling (d).* 12/44–7/45.

Wingy shares this record with a couple of Rex Stewart sessions. His eight titles aren't up to much: feeble novelty material ('Where Can I Find A Cherry?' is pretty lamentable) and scruffy recording. But when the band starts to swing, they manage to squeeze some life out of the situation, and Joe Marsala especially is always worth hearing.

Ray Mantilla (born 1934)

PERCUSSION

A little like Don Alias, the gifted New Yorker has made something of a speciality of transforming other people's albums, at some cost to his own profile. Though probably best known for his association with Max Roach and Max's percussion band, M'Boom, Mantilla founded the group, Space Station, more than 20 years ago.

***** Hands Of Fire**

Red RR123174-2 *Mantilla; Dick Oatts (ss, ts, f); Eddie Martinez (p); Peter Barshay (b); Joe Chambers (d, perc).* 1/84.

***** Synergy**

Red RR 123198-2 *As above, except omit Barshay, Chambers; add Steve Grossman (ts), Guillermo Edgehill (b), Steve Berrios (d, perc), Vivien Ara Martinez (v).* 2/86.

****** Dark Powers**

Red RR 123221-2 *As above, except omit Grossman, Edgehill; add Bobby Watson (as), Ruben Rodriguez (b).* 2/88.

When middleweight boxing champion Roberto Duran came to London to train and spar for his last-ditch title bid, one of the tapes played in the gym was a private tape of Ray Mantilla with the Latin band he led during his six-year sojourn in Puerto Rico: Fists of Stone weaving and jabbing to Hands of Fire. Mantilla's sense of time is uncanny. When even the most rhythmic players sound as if they are marching in boots, Ray floats.

The first of the Space Station albums for Red is the plainest rendition of what the group was all about. Lacking guest soloists of the calibre of Watson and Grossman, it sticks to basics, generating a groove that burns with passion and chills with sheer precision. The exhilaration Mantilla generates – as on his percussion 'Dialogue' with Berrios on *Dark Powers* – has always been matched with a mathematically precise registration. Anyone who has the facilities to run these records through a digital editing suite can do the maths themselves; it's awesomely accurate and elastically funky playing. The presence of Chambers in the first group is interesting. Unlike Berrios later, he doesn't sound as if he is working entirely in idiom and yet he manages to get a purchase every time. Martinez is also an ideal partner, here and throughout, treating his keyboard like a responsive marimba and blocking in the chords with elegance and authority. Grossman is a surprisingly sympathetic partner. He appears on only three tracks but makes a solid impact on Monk's 'Eronel' and the standard, 'Star Eyes', where his boppish delivery recalls some of the stuff Dizzy was doing with his Afro-Cuban bands. Oatts is no slouch, either, a deft tenor player with a big, meaty sound, and a considerable flautist who knows how to modulate and thicken the tone when required.

The outstanding album is the one with Bobby Watson. 'Dark Powers' itself serves Bobby up a context for a fiercely witty alto sermon. He also writes or co-writes two numbers, 'Catch Me If You Can' and 'The Things You Do', both of them tailored to his own slightly mournful groove. Mantilla is back to the fore on the original 'Curve Ball', a tricksy swinger which requires the whole group to play percussively.

Karen Mantler

HARMONICA, ORGAN, VOICE

Daughter of Carla Bley and Michael Mantler. Difficult to know how seriously her work should be taken.

****(*) My Cat Arnold**

XtraWatt 839093-2 *Mantler; Steven Bernstein (t); Pablo Calogero (bs, f); Marc Muller (g); Steve Weisberg (ky, syn); Jonathan Sanborn (b); Ethan Winogrand (d); Eric Mingus (v).* Spring 88.

***** Karen Mantler And Her Cat Arnold Get The Flu**

XtraWatt 847136-2 *As above, except add Michael Mantler (t), Steve Swallow (flhn), Carla Bley (Cmel).* Summer 90.

One of the most evocative sounds on Carla Bley's superb *Fleur Carnivore* (Watt/21 839 662) was daughter Karen's floating harmonica solo on 'Song Of The Sadness Of Canute'. As yet, it's an under-exploited voice. Her solo albums are basically song collections, alternately reminiscent of Laurie Anderson's half-spoken narratives and Carla Bley's own free-associating surrealism on *Escalator Over The Hill*, but influenced by 1930s popular song and basic rock rhythms. The most obviously Anderson-like of the songs is the nightmarish 'Flu', spoken with a wry lack of expression. 'Mean To Me' is pure pastiche, featuring Mom and Dad and 'Uncle' Steve Swallow on decidedly unfamiliar instruments. The instrumental 'Au Lait', which appears to have been recorded live, is the most obviously jazz-based, with beautiful harmonica and trumpet parts. Otherwise, this is no-category music that stands, sometimes sturdily, sometimes not, on its own merits. We have to note that Arnold has since passed away. His passing has been covered by the subsequent *Farewell* (XtraWatt 8), but frankly we're ready to cry enough on this one.

Michael Mantler (born 1943)

TRUMPET, COMPOSER

Born in Vienna and educated at the Akademie there, Mantler brought a species of bleak European modernism to America, where he settled at the age of nineteen. He married Carla Bley and founded the Jazz Composers Orchestra Association. His works are slow, dark and intense, an acquired taste but often a rewarding one.

****** No Answer / Silence**

Watt 2 / 5 2CD *Mantler; Don Cherry (t); Carla Bley (p, org, v); Chris Spedding (g); Clare Maher (clo); Ron McClure (b); Jack Bruce (b, v); Robert Wyatt (perc, v); Kevin Coyne (v).* 2/73–6/76.

***** The Hapless Child**

Watt 4 *Mantler; Terje Rypdal (g); Carla Bley (ky); Steve Swallow (b); Jack DeJohnette (d); Alfreda Benge, Albert Caulder, Nick Mason, Robert Wyatt (v).* 7/75–1/76.

Mantler's music inhabits a world of dark whimsy stretched somewhere between Edward Gorey (whose writings provide the text to *The Hapless Child*) and Samuel Beckett. Beckett's shorn morality pops up throughout the Mantler *œuvre*, almost all of which is released on a label named after the Irishman's jolliest character. There are moments when Mantler seems almost perversely bleak and unrelieved. Jack Bruce's tortured enunciation of texts from Beckett's *How It Is* on *No Answer* still makes for difficult listening after nearly 20 years, but it is undoubtedly compelling and the spare, almost static accompaniment provided by bass, keyboards and Don Cherry's tiny voiced trumpet conveys a cosmic loneliness. *Silence*, also reissued in the same package, is a reworking of Harold Pinter's Beckett-inspired play, with Robert Wyatt, Carla Bley and Kevin Coyne in the parts of Bates, Ellen and Rumsey respectively. As music drama it is absolutely compelling; whether it qualifies as jazz is not a question we're inclined to engage; but certainly one misses the terse, bleached sound of the composer's trumpet on both these discs. Looking forward, it's possible to see Mantler as a harbinger of the death-of-jazz scenarios of his fellow-Austrian, Franz Koglmann.

****** Movies / More Movies**

Watt 7/10 *Mantler; Gary Windo (ts); Carla Bley (p, org, syn, ts); Philip Catherine, Larry Coryell (g); Steve Swallow (b); D Sharpe, Tony Williams (d).* 3/77–3/80.

Time and distance have been kind to Mantler, and CD remastering has brightened up the sound on these two albums. They fall into the genre of imaginary soundtracks and are perhaps best heard individually rather than one after the other. As ever, there is more sheer musicality in a three-minute Mantler composition than in half a dozen jazz themes, but they require time and patience. 'Movie Four' from the first album is the place to set the cueing button, though the final pair of eight are equally compelling, hybrids of jazz harmony and the Second Viennese School.

Tony Williams is the drummer on the first set, but we aren't clear whose illustrious identity the (presumed) pseudonym of 'D. Sharpe' disguises on *More Movies*. The two bands are pretty much identical in configuration, except that Carla's ABC tenor saxophone part is handed to Gary Windo and the fiery Coryell is replaced by the much more lyrical Philip Catherine.

It's been some time since we listened to these albums and the reunion has been a happy one, confirming Mantler's standing as one of the most adventurous composers of recent times and a player who every now and then reaches in and tugs the heart strings.

*****(*) Something There**

Watt 13 *Mantler; Carla Bley (p); Mike Stern (g); Steve Swallow (b); Nick Mason (d).* 83.

***** Alien**

Watt 15 *Mantler; Don Preston (syn).* 3–7/85.

Presumably scaled down from writing for full ensemble, the dark meditations that make up *Alien* are – hard as it is to write this without suspicion of overstating the case – the bleakest and most nihilistic pieces in Mantler's canon. Compared even to the numerically coded group and orchestra works on *Something There* they seem almost unbearably sunless and yet, as on the earlier album, there are glints and gleams of sardonic humour and an engaging humanity which doesn't come through often or readily in Mantler's work. To that extent, he is not the true heir of Beckett and Pinter, and still less of Gorey, but it is best to be alert to those moments, as on *Alien* part three, and on 'Something There' itself, where he allows a gentler and more accommodating side to emerge. As ever, Michael Gibbs's string arrangements are immaculate, sophisticatedly simple but full of depth and texture.

*****(*) Live**

Watt 18 *Mantler; Don Preston (syn); Rick Fenn (g); John Greaves (b, p); Nick Mason (d); Jack Bruce (v).* 2/87.

The live record is certainly the best place to sample Mantler's music if you haven't come across it before. Though not intended as a career retrospective, it does range across the work of the previous decade, touching on some of the material from *The Hapless Child*, to which Bruce brings his usual querulous strength and jazzy unfixity of pitch. While Bley's touch is missed, Preston has his own strengths and Fenn is very much in the line of previous guitar players.

*****(*) Many Have No Speech**

Watt 19 *Mantler; Rick Fenn (g); Jack Bruce, Marianne Faithfull, Robert Wyatt (v); orchestra.* 5–12/87.

***** Folly Seeing All This**

ECM 517363-2 *Mantler; Wolfgang Puschnig (af); Rick Fenn (g); Karen Mantler (p, v); Dave Adams (vib); Balanescu Quartet; Jack Bruce (v).* 6/92.

Compared to *How It Is*, the more recent Beckett settings on *Folly Seeing All This* are positively humane and accommodating. Bruce still likes to skin a lyric until it shows the nerves and sinews beneath, but of late his voice has acquired a mellower timbre, and the strings here and on *Many Have No Speech* raise the temperature above the glacial. The Balanescu Quartet are able crossover performers, bringing a hint of swing to these rather dry scores. Puschnig has been appearing in all sorts of eclectic settings in recent times. He's also an asset here.

Many Have No Speech adds Philippe Soupault and Ernst Meister to the lyricists' roster and Marianne Faithfull to the singers'. Wyatt, for so many years a standby, is used disappointingly little. He has exactly the right level of sheer artlessness to make Mantler's ideas come convincingly alive. Faithfull's gravel larynx is certainly authentic; her French diction is emphatically not, and she's guilty of some nightclub histrionics which don't fit this particular bill.

****** Cerco un paese innocente**

ECM 1556 *Mantler; Bjarne Roupe (g); Marianne Sørensen (vn); Gunary Lychou, Mette Winther (vla); Helle Sørensen (clo); Kim Kristensen (p); Mona Larsen (v); Danish Radio Big Band.* 1/94.

A moody inscape, very much in the slow and dimensionless idiom of earlier orchestral writing. Mantler follows Luciano Berio in setting a group of poems by Giuseppe Ungaretti, and he makes a very convincing job of rendering these curious lyrics transparent. As with most of his projects in this vein, it depends wholly on the quality of the singer. Mona Larsen does a wonderful job, huskily beautiful and totally unaffected, delivering the words like a folk singer and not a diva. An unexpected classic.

***** The School Of Understanding**

ECM 537963-2 2CD *Mantler; Roger Jannotta (cl, bcl, f, ob); Bjarne Roupe (g); Mette Brandt, Marianne Sørensen (vn); Mette Winther (vla); Helle Sørensen (clo); Tineke Noordhoek (vib, mar); Kim Kristensen (p, syn); Don Preston (syn, v); Jack Bruce, John Greaves, Susi Hyldgaard, Per Jorgensen, Mona Larsen, Karen Mantler, Robert Wyatt (v).* 8–12/96.

At least he had the decency not to call it a 'chronotransduction', as his former wife did *Escalator Over The Hill*. 'Sort-of-an-opera' serves very well. This is a piece of ambitious music-theatre on the slippages and breaks that afflict meaning – a previous version was called 'The School of Languages' – and so almost inevitably the presiding spirit is that of Samuel Beckett, whose text, 'What Is The Word', ends the work.

Mantler is least comfortable when he is writing *récit* and basic dialogue. Some of the set-pieces, notably those involving Larsen as a refugee and Bruce as the far from omniscient 'Observer', are very good indeed, and the small ensemble plays with admirable delicacy and control. Like *Escalator*, the piece is probably best heard as a series of episodes, rather than as a continuous work. It might well gain from staging (and has been produced in Denmark), but it is hard to penetrate the rather stiff exterior off a record. One for confirmed Mantlerians only.

*****(*) Songs And One Symphony**
ECM 1721 *Mantler; Kim Kristensen (p, syn); Bjarne Roupé (g); Marianne Sørensen (vn); Gunnar Lychou, Mette Winther (vla); Helle (clo); Mona Larsen (v); Radio Symphony Orchestra Frankfurt; Peter Rundel (cond).* 10/93, 11/98.

Intriguing to hear a composer so utterly in thrall to the musical languages of the twentieth century square up to the twenty-first with a record so true to his own origins and yet so replete with new possibility. This time, for *Songs*, Mantler has taken his inspiration from the poems of Ernest Meister, texts that deal with the difficulties of 'relationships', not just in the bland, agony-column sense, but in a much more philosophical context. They are still uneasy and to a degree unrelieved, but there is a sanguine beauty that has not been heard overtly in Mantler's work before now. Mona Larsen's voice is very beautiful and her feel for space is in keeping with previous Mantler vocalists, except that here there is a hint of lyricism he would not have admitted previously.

We were tempted to suggest that *Alien* was his first symphony. This one – which is *One Symphony* rather than Symphony No. 1, note – is surprisingly orthodox in its modernism and played rather flatly by the Frankfurt orchestra. Jazz purists will run a mile, but they should listen up to Mantler's intuitive voicings, which still have the resonance of jazz in their root notes and a slowed-down after-echo of swing in every measure.

Frank Mantooth

KEYBOARDS, ARRANGER

Californian arranger-pianist who leads a big band for these Sea Breeze recordings.

***** Suite Tooth**
Sea Breeze SB 2055 *Mantooth; Bobby Shew, Danny Barber, Art Davis, Mike Steinel (t); Art Farmer (flhn); Scott Bentall, Tom Garling, Mark Bettcher, Mike Young (tb); Howie Smith (as, ss); Bill Sears (as, f); Ed Petersen, Jim Massoth (ts); Scott Robinson (bs, f); Sam LiPuma (g); Kelly Sill, Curt Bley (b); Louie Bellson, Steve Houghton (d); Tim Kitsos (perc).* 11/87.

***** Persevere**
Sea Breeze SB 2062 *As above, except add Clark Terry (t, flhn, v), Steve Wiest (tb), Pete Christlieb (ts), Jerry DiMuzio (bs, f, cl), Steve Erquiaga (g), Bob Bowman (b), Alejo Poveda (perc); omit Farmer, Massoth, Robinson, LiPuma, Sill, Bellson, Kitsos.* 10/89.

***** Dangerous Precedent**
Sea Breeze SB 2046 *As above, except add Jeff Jarvis (t), Paul McKee, Leland Gause (tb), Kim Park, Scott Robinson (reeds), Matt Harris, Ramsey Lewis (ky), Danny Embrey (g), Kelly Sill (b), Kevin Mahogany (v); omit Christlieb, Bentall, Sears.* 12/91.

***** Sophisticated Lady**
Sea Breeze SB 2074 *As above, except add Roger Ingram, Marvin Stamm, Randy Brecker (t), Tom Matta (tb), Pat LaBarbera, Pete Christlieb, Nick Brignola (reeds), Jon McLean (g); omit Terry, Jarvis, Steinel, Gause, Petersen, Robinson, Lewis, Embrey, Sill, DiMuzio, Erquiaga.* 94.

More mighty big-band music from the West Coast, charted by the genial Mantooth, whose arrangements bristle with energy and sometimes hit a note of invention that carries them past the often rote nature of this kind of jazz. The first three albums all trade in fusion-based licks to some extent, though Mantooth finds a surprisingly provocative balance between that kind of jazz-lite and a more demanding arranger's taste. The three-part title-piece on *Suite Tooth* has some terrific playing and writing alike, especially in the mini-concerto for Shew which opens the disc, and the vim and vigour of 'Scam And Eggs' goes well enough with the mood-jazz feel of 'Lauralisa'. *Persevere* goes much the same way: Terry has a bumptious 'Mean To Me' mainly to himself, but four other standards are shrewdly arranged and there are good spots for Shew, Christlieb and Steinel. Terry and Shew have some more good moments on *Dangerous Precedent*, and Mahogany comes on like a young Joe Williams on his two appearances; but again it's the crackle of the band that overcomes any sense of muzak which could have overtaken relatively conventional scores such as 'Imagination'. *Sophisticated Lady* is in some ways the most traditional of the four discs, with Mantooth sticking to piano, the bassist staying acoustic and the charts hewing close to, say, the Jones–Lewis style of delivery. Excitements nevertheless exist in the knockout tribute to Woody Shaw, 'The Messenger', three more very able vocals by Mahogany and Brignola's authoritative solo on the title-piece. Little to choose among the discs, though we might pick *Dangerous Precedent* as the best sampler, if pressed.

Guido Manusardi (born 1935)

PIANO

Somewhat nomadic Italian pianist who has spent time in several European locations but is known as a distinguished player in the Italian post-bop scene of the 1960s onwards.

***** Immagini Visive**
Right Tempo/Sound Hills RTCL 808 *Manusardi; Furio Di Castri (b); Gianni Cazzola (d).* 1/81.

****(*) Downtown**
Soul Note 121131-2 *Manusardi; Isla Eckinger (b); Ed Thigpen (d).* 5–6/85.

*****(*) Introduction**
Penta Flowers 009 *Manusardi; Paolino Dalla Porta (b); Giancarlo Pillot (d).* 11/87.

Guido Manusardi is well known in many parts of Europe and scarcely even recognized in many others: a perhaps typical fate for a journeyman (he spent long periods in both Sweden, where he made his first album in 1967, and Romania) whose often lovely music touches many bases. He revels in the kind of unabashed lyricism that one day will be acknowledged as the premier bequest of the post-bop Italian jazzmen, but his up-tempo playing has a lot of Oscar Peterson in it too, and he likes to swing hard on the blues and on favourite standards. *Immagini Visive* is the earliest of his many records currently on CD, with his favourite 'Oltremera' alongside four standards: a solid one. Rather dis-appointing was *Downtown*: four originals, two good standards, a fine rhythm-section and good Soul Note recording, but 'Alexandria' is a merely doleful ballad, and only the Red Garland-like manoeuvres of 'Downtown' find the pianist at his most resourceful. *Introduction* is the pick of these three. Manusardi has seldom played the blues with as much wit and flair as he does on 'Blue Face', but this programme of originals has at least a morsel of interest in every track and there is the crispest and most on-the-ball support from Dalla Porta and Pillot.

***** Together Again**

Soul Note 121181-2 *Manusardi; Red Mitchell (b).* 11/88.

***** So That**

Splasc(h) H 328-2 *Manusardi; Eddie Gomez (b); Gianni Cazzola (d).* 10/90.

Manusardi liked working with Red Mitchell and their duo session is very *simpatico*, though the bassist is as wilful as ever – eccentrically dawdling over figures but doing so in such a charming way that the music picks up an idiosyncratic lilt which the pianist also takes note of. 'But Not For Me' is a delightful game of cat-and-mouse. *So That* is more obviously open-handed, the trio barrelling through most of the tunes at a rapid-fire tempo; but Gomez crowds out Manusardi at times and it's the sly interjections of Cazzola (listen to his fours on 'There Is No Greater Love') which referee the playing. Gomez's singalong bass is irritatingly picked up by the microphones, but recording is otherwise excellent.

***** Colored Passages**

Ram CD4504 *Manusardi; George Garzone (ss, ts); John Lockwood (b); Bob Gullotti (d).* 3/93.

The encounter this time is with the trio known as The Fringe. Manusardi brought some fine compositions to the session, with the catchy 'The Winding Road' leaping out of the gates and two pretty ballads in 'Engadina Valley' and 'Anytime, Anywhere'. His three compatriots don't quite let go the way they do on their own, and there are a couple of tracks too many – no need for the second take of 'The Touch Of Your Lips', perhaps. Otherwise well worth hearing.

***** Concerto**

Splasc(h) 437 *Manusardi (p solo).* 6/90–6/92.

*****(*) Contrasti**

Penta Flowers 012 *Manusardi (p solo). n.d.*

Concerto offers excerpts from some recent solo concerts. Manusardi isn't one for doodling to himself in solo recitals: he plays for the audience, and there is some very energetic variation on his favourite standards here, though the prettiest moments come on originals like 'Velvet Sunset' and 'The Ruins Of Piuro'. Warm and good-natured piano. *Contrasti* is a lot tougher and more assertive, and the excellent upfront studio sound magnifies Manusardi's decisive playing. There's a darkly sonorous quality to the pianism with themes such as 'Fort Apache', 'Mingus Suggestion' and 'Alive' emerging with unpretentious conviction.

***** Between The Two Of Us**

Penta Flowers 038 *Manusardi; Gianni Bedori (ts, bcl, f).* 1/94.

This is nicely done without seeming essential. Bedori is a nonchalant partner, commenting rather than building on the music, and with him playing more bass clarinet than tenor he's a colourist for Manusardi's parts. This is pleasingly melodic music and no more than a diversion in the pianist's discography.

***** Within**

Soul Note 121281-2 *Manusardi; Jerry Bergonzi (ts); Dave Santoro (b); Victor Lewis (d).* 8/95.

If Bedori was an underachiever, Bergonzi does his characteristic overplaying. This is a forceful chunk of post-bop and it's wrapped up with few problems by the quartet but, despite the pianist bringing a couple of attractive themes to the studio, the results lack much individuality. Only when piano and tenor have 'Laura' to themselves does the music get personal.

****** The Village Fair**

Soul Note 121331-2 *Manusardi; Paolo Fresu (t, flhn); Roberto Rossi (tb); Gianluigi Trovesi (cl, bcl, as); Furio Di Castri (b); Roberto Gatto (d).* 10/96.

Not exactly a departure and not quite typical, this is a triumph for Manusardi and a magical example of European jazz at its most unaffectedly 'authentic'. Manusardi made a record based around Romanian folk music many years before. This time he's assembled the cream of Italy's front rank to deliver a brilliantly coloured suite of inspired-by pieces, with dance rhythms and folkish melodies made transcendent by the vibrant playing and his own impressionistic (though not vague) arrangements. He knows his materials and what he wants to evoke – this is hardly the travelogue of some tourist, after all – and, with Fresu, Rossi and Trovesi at their most persuasive, the results are joyously convincing.

Michael Marcus (born 1952)

SOPRANO AND SOPRANINO SAXOPHONES, MANZELLO, STRITCH, CONN-O-SAX, BASS CLARINET

Marcus began his apprenticeship out on the 'chitlin'' circuit, working with the likes of Bobby 'Blue' Bland and Albert King, and has always insisted that behind even free jazz, which he imbibed from Frank Lowe and Sonny Simmons and which he plays with fundamentalist zeal, there is always the blues.

*****(*) Under The Wire**

Enja ENJ 6064 *Marcus; Ted Daniel (t); Joseph Bowie (tb); William Parker (b); Reggie Nicholson (d).* 5/90.

*****(*) Here At!**

Soul Note 121243 *Marcus; Ted Daniel (t); Steve Swell (tb); Fred Hopkins, William Parker (b); Dennis Charles, Sadiq Abdu Shahid (d).* 9/93.

Marcus didn't get the idea of manzello and stritch directly from Roland Kirk, but from a musician called George Braith, a Rahsaan follower who figured briefly in the Blue Note and

Prestige catalogues in the 1960s. Michael's microtonal approach is a near equal hybrid of R&B and modernist polytonality. And though he's basically an incendiarist, he's happy to set firestarting aside now and again and indulge the odd weird ballad, like 'Hidden Springs' on *Here At!*, where he uses an even greater oddity, the conn-o-sax, a saxophonic version of the cor anglais, pitched in F. On *Under The Wire* he's still concentrating on soprano, using its notorious waywardness to full advantage, bouncing ideas off Daniel and Joe Bowie. It's an album that improves with age, marred more than anything by a slightly dead sound. *Here At!* is more spacious, as it needs to be, given the range of instrumentations. The title-piece is a highly organized workout for double trio; Marcus doubles up stritch and manzello to counterbalance Swell's portamento effects, Hopkins and Parker (a recorded first, it seems), Shahid and Charles creating a shifting *moiré* effect. In the absence of a harmony instrument, the trombonist or – more often – Hopkins is called on to touch in the chords, often quite implicitly. It's a shame that Parker doesn't feature in a trio context: 'This Happening' and 'Hurdles', perhaps the best things on the record, are both played by Hopkins and Charles, though the two bassists appear again on 'Ithem'. The final track, 'In The Centre Of It All', is an eye-of-the-hurricane roarer for reeds and bass, a brief, astonishing epilogue to a fine record.

****** This Happening**
Justin Time JUST 98 *Marcus; Jaki Byard (p).* 12/96.

***** Intuition**
Justin Time JUST 104 *As above.* 97.

These will either set your teeth on edge or warm your heart; no middle course seems likely. Justin Time have acquired an impressive knack of putting together intriguing duos – Paul Bley and Kenny Wheeler being a more obviously homegrown promotion for the Montreal label – and on this one they have excelled themselves. Byard's slightly weird barrelhouse-meets-free-style suits Marcus perfectly. On *This Happening* he sticks very largely to the stritch (a straightened-out alto, also in E flat) but on this occasion doubles on the saxello, an instrument perhaps most closely associated with Britain's Elton Dean. On just one track he reverts to bass clarinet, a medley of Coltrane's 'Giant Steps' and 'Naima' that will unfailingly suggest the influence of Eric Dolphy. The only other familiar tune is 'Darn That Dream', an eccentrically romantic end to a wonderful, offbeat record. Jaki's death in 1999 robbed Marcus of his most responsive playing partner to date, a musician who instinctively understood his balance of traditionalism and experiment. Given how brief the association was, and still occasionally tentative – the second record is less sure-footed – these recordings are all the more valuable.

***** In The Center Of It All**
Justin Time JUST 130 2 *Marcus; Gary Strauss (t); Clark Gayton (tb); Rahn Burton (org); Nasheet Waits (d).* 4/99.

With this trio set – the horns are present on only two tracks – Marcus digs back into the catalogue and to early Prestige and Blue Note work by saxophonists Eric Kloss and, once again, George Braith. He also draws quite explicitly on Larry Young and evokes Roland Kirk more overtly than ever before. The result is an intoxicating brew that moves from the heat and dust of Death Valley on 'Badwater' to the church aisle on 'In The Center Of It All'. Burton is a key element, supplying the same rich ambiguities as Jaki Byard, but with his own amiable spin. Young Waits is equally well suited to the project, a terse, unflappable player who sounds remarkably mature and seasoned on a glorious version of Monk's 'Pannonica' and behind the horns on the two augmented tracks. Marcus includes the trickily pitched sopranino this time out and manages to give the midget horn an uncommonly generous tone and bright attack. The waifs and strays of the saxophone family have never been so well appreciated.

Rick Margitza (born 1963)

TENOR AND SOPRANO SAXOPHONES

Margitza first made waves as the saxophonist in the Miles Davis group of 1987–9. He signed to Blue Note as a solo artist but left after three records, and is now based at independent labels.

****** Work It**
Steeplechase SCCD 31358 *Margitza; James Williams (p); George Mraz (b); Billy Hart (d).* 4/94.

*****(*) Hands Of Time**
Challenge 70021 *Margitza; Kevin Hays (p); George Mraz (b); Al Foster (d).* 12/94.

Margitza's recordings have rarely secured the attention they deserve. These two are filled with such exemplary work that one wonders at his apparent neglect. On the other hand, he's hardly a fashionable player: he takes a long, thoughtful time over his solos, resists any excess of double-time or scalar exhibitionism, and presents a sonorous yet rather oblique tone which puts an ambivalent edge on his improvising. The long, Rollinsish cadenza on 'My Foolish Heart', the compelling circles cast through 'Widows Walk', the neo-blues shapes of 'Steppin' Out' and the unexpectedly jaunty revision of 'It Could Happen To You' are four highlights of the Steeplechase disc; but there really isn't a bad passage on it and, with Williams in top form and Mraz and Hart perfectly comfortable, this is leagues ahead of the typical tenor-plus-rhythm date. If the Challenge album is just a shade behind, it's still very fine: more emphasis on his own writing here, with six out of the seven tunes, and an unpredictable set they make – 'Hip Bop' turns organ-band clichés inside out and 'Forty Five Pound Hound' does the same for the blues. 'Embraceable You' gets one of its bleakest treatments since Coleman's famous rendition. These are very strong entries from an outstanding saxophonist.

*****(*) Game Of Chance**
Challenge CHR 70044 *Margitza; Jeff Gardner (p); Lars Danielsson (b); John Vidacovich (d).* 10/96.

Less obviously centred around Margitza and often unassumingly reticent to make its mark, this compilation of tracks from two nights of live work in Amsterdam is nevertheless a fine and detailed set that needs a few plays to sink in. Gardner shares composing credits with the leader, and with intriguing pieces like 'Jazz Prelude #9' and 'Blades Run' he sets a high standard for Margitza himself to aim at. Danielsson and New Orleans drummer Vidacovich make a fascinating team and the balance of the quartet is beautifully poised, swinging but always suggesting a sense of reserve. Margitza himself is reluctant to dominate in the way he does on some of his earlier records but the music has its own, slightly abstruse character which only rarely has the attention wandering.

*****(*) Heart Of Hearts**

Palmetto PM 2058 *Margitza; Joey Calderazzo (p); Scott Colley (b); Ian Froman (d).* 11/99.

A balance of originals and standards. Margitza presents his music very plainly, a this-is-all-there-is manner which perhaps makes it hard for his records to stand out from the countless sax-and-rhythm dates which still constitute much of the jazz release schedules. '14 Bar Blues' has a soprano solo which, for controlled rigour at a fast tempo, takes some beating, but it's as unshowy as it is accomplished. The middleweight feel he gives to his tone on tenor makes it easy to miss the subtlety of the playing on the title-track. Calderazzo is a much more voluble performer and Froman is at least as busily propulsive as his predecessors on Margitza dates. Nothing to win new admirers here, but it should please those who've been following this gracious musician.

Charlie Mariano (born 1923)

ALTO SAXOPHONE, SOPRANO SAXOPHONE, FLUTE, NAGASWARAM

Mariano grew up in Boston, worked with Shorty Sherock and Stan Kenton, and then formed a small group with his then wife Toshiko Akiyoshi. He has long had an interest in Indian music and brought the nagaswaram into jazz. His reedy, slightly plaintive alto sound has deepened in intensity down the years, but there is a clear continuity from Mariano's cool, boppish early records to his more eclectic recent work.

***** Boston All Stars / New Sound From Boston**

Original Jazz Classics OJC 1745 *Mariano; Joe Gordon, Herb Pomeroy (t); Sonny Truitt (tb); Jim Clark (ts); George Myers (bs); Roy Frazee, Richard Twardzik (p); Bernie Griggs, Jack Lawlor (b); Gene Glennon, Carl Goodwin, Jimmy Weiner (d); Ira Gitler (bells).* 12/51, 1/53.

***** Boston Days**

Fresh Sound FSRCD 207 *Mariano; Herb Pomeroy (t); Jaki Byard (p); Jack Carter (b); Peter Littman (d).* 11/53.

****(*) Charlie Mariano Plays**

Fresh Sound FSR CD 115 *As above, except add John Williams (p).* 7/54.

Critics were quick to locate the much-underrated Mariano in the gaggle of post-Bird alto players. It's true as far as it goes. Mariano was born only three years after Parker, and his first and greatest influence remains Johnny Hodges. His studies in Indian music, and on the wooden, oboe-like *nagaswaram*, have helped emphasize the exotic overtones he absorbed from Hodges and which are already evident in the early, bop-inspired sessions on OJC. The wrenching intensity of later years is not yet apparent, though Mariano invests 'Stella By Starlight' on *New Sound From Boston* with entirely convincing and personal feeling. It's interesting to compare this performance with that on the Fresh Sound *It's Standard Time* (below), made after a long break from standards repertoire. In the 1950s, Mariano is still playing in a very linear way, without the three-dimensional solidity and textural variation that he developed later; he was also still more or less rooted in conventional bop harmony, an attachment that weakened as he came to understand Indian music. *New Sound From Boston* is excellent, if a little raw. *Boston Days* is good, too, though many will find it more useful for its insights into the under-recorded Pomeroy; he very nearly steals the show, and his solo on 'Sweet And Lovely' is definitive. Byard, who reappears on a later Mariano session, is in highly inventive form as well.

***** A Jazz Portrait Of Charlie Mariano**

Fresh Sound FSRCD 176 *Mariano; Bernie Glow, Himmy Sedlar, Jimmy Nottingham, Marvin Stamm (t); Wayne Andre, Bob Brookmeyer, Joe Ciarvadone, Paul Faulise (tb); Bob Abernathy, Dick Berg, Dave Clevenger, Aubrey Facenda (frhn); Don Butterfield (tba); Phil Bodner (reeds); Roger Kellaway (p); Bob Phillips (p, cel, vib); Jim Hall (g); Art Davis, Richard Davis (b); Albert 'Tootie' Heath, Mel Lewis (d); Ed Shaughnessy (perc).* 7/63.

This helps to fill the yawning gap in the Mariano discography a little. One doesn't usually think of him as a big-band player, though he had worked with Pomeroy's outfit (see him, above) and, of course, he had the closest association with Toshiko Akiyoshi, one of the best arrangers and band composers in America at the time. This was recorded after the couple had flitted to Japan. The saxophonist was back in America to teach at campus jazz clinics, and these sessions were put together over two days during a slack spell in the summer. 'To Taoho' shows the most obvious Oriental influence. A modal theme, like much of the stuff he was doing at this time, it uses some unexpected intervals, and again Mariano is slightly upstaged by one of his playing partners. Marvin Stamm's contributions are consistently excellent; this was billed as his coming-out gig and he certainly made best use of the opportunity. Don Sebesky's writing for the larger group is limited to 'Portrait Of An Artist', which sits for Charlie the way Mingus's 'Portrait Of Jackie' sat for McLean, a perfect opportunity to be at their best. The other stuff is nicely balanced, though the three tracks with Jim Hall, strings, harp and celeste err on the side of mush. Leaving Mariano as the only woodwind against trumpets and an array of french horns was a slightly risky strategy but it works, and the small-group material nicely modulates the session as a whole.

****(*) Blue Stone**

Black Lion 760203 *Mariano; Chris Hinze (f, etc.); Malcolm Walker (p); Roger Cooke (b); Andre Van de Water (d).* 7/71.

In the '70s, like everyone else, Mariano tried to give jazz some of the propulsion and market cachet of rock music. He had, though, long been in the field of synthesizing jazz and Indian music, and the most effective item on this rather dated set is the version of a South Indian song. Hinze has been rather swallowed up by musical history. Similar in style to Paul Horn, he moved between instruments with disconcerting ease, but without ever really stamping his personality on one of them. He does at least make an impressive start on his own 'Lullaby For Dewi', but he provides little more than exotic colours after that. Long out of print, an interesting curiosity for Mariano, but very much a footnote even in his progress.

***** Jyothi**

ECM 811548-2 *Mariano; Karnataka College of Percussion: R.A. Ramamani (v, tamboura, konakkol); T.A.S. Mani (mridamgam); R.A. Rajagopal (ghantam, morsing, konnakol); T.N. Shashikumar (kanjira, konakkol).* 2/83.

***** Live**

VeraBra 2034 *As above, except omit Rajagopal, add Ramesh Shotam (chatam, morsing, tavil).* 2/89.

Only fans of a certain age remember Joe Harriott's and John Mayer's *Indo-Jazz Fusions*, released by Columbia in 1966 and 1967, hailed as the Next Big Thing, and then consigned to collector status. With a tonal approach not unlike Harriott's and with a similar awareness of the boundaries of tonality and abstraction, Mariano's albums with the Karnataka College of Percussion make a perfectly valid comparison. The saxophone is paired with R.A. Ramamani's expressive voice, and it's unfortunately easy to ignore the intricate rhythmic canvas being stretched behind them by the other players; the live session is a little more even-handed in this regard, but on *Jyothi* (with the close-miked and lapidary sound typical of ECM), most of the emphasis is on Mariano's fervid upper-register playing.

***** It's Standard Time: Volume 1**

Fresh Sound FSR 97 *Mariano; Tete Montoliu (p); Horacio Fumero (b); Peer Wyboris (d).* 4/89.

*****(*) It's Standard Time: Volume 2**

Fresh Sound FSR 98 *As above.* 4/89.

Mariano has not been closely associated with standards jazz in recent years. Like Miles Davis (and only those who haven't heard the saxophonist play would consider the analogy absurd), he believes in confronting the 'music of today' rather than endlessly reworking changes. However, on the basis of a performance at the Kenton Festival in Oldham, Lancashire, where Mariano had played 'Stella By Starlight', producer Jordi Pujol persuaded him to cut a standards album in Barcelona with Catalan pianist Tete Montoliu and two other local players. Mariano is in perfect voice. On Volume 1, 'Stella' is wonderful, given a harmonically 'flatter' but more resonant reading than Lee Konitz tends to. He misfires briefly on 'Billie's Bounce' and makes a bit of a nonsense of 'Poor Butterfly', but it's a highly appealing album nevertheless, ideal for anyone who hasn't previously made contact with the saxophonist's work or who has a constitutional aversion to the *konakkol* or the *kanjira*.

Unusually, the follow-up volume, drawn from the same two nights, is even better. The songs are no more demanding, though 'I Thought About You' and a second take of 'Billie's Bounce' include some stretching harmonic notions. Perhaps it's taken a CD's worth to get used to the idea of Mariano back playing this kind of material; neither volume will disappoint.

*****(*) Mariano**

Intuition INT 3002 *Mariano; Paul Shigihara (g); Michael Herting (p, ky).* 87.

***** Innuendo**

Lipstick LIP 890082 *Mariano; Jasper Van't Hof (p, ky); Marilyn Mazur (d, perc).* 7 & 9/91.

*****(*) Adagio**

Lipstick LIP 890242 *As for Mariano.* 93.

Like Lee Konitz, Mariano has increasingly moved back towards a mainstream jazz position. Mazur's uncomplicated drumming leads *Innuendo* into a more orthodox jazz groove. Like the standards sessions above, it takes a moment to adjust, but there's no doubting Mariano's competence in this idiom. He relies heavily on high wails and big portamento effects and, while initially these are wearing, they also camouflage some fascinating harmonic activity that takes time to get across.

The drummerless trio on *Mariano* delivers a surprisingly focused and exact recording, and the music performed (which includes a version of Ravel's 'Pavane pour une infante défunte', previously tackled only by Larry Coryell) steers well clear of the drab New Age waffle such a programme might suggest. The follow-up on Lipstick is reminiscent of *Sleep, My Lovely*, a record for CMP recorded with guitarist Philip Catherine and Jasper van't Hof on keyboards. Shigihara and Herting are not so distinctive, but this is much more emphatically the saxophonist's date. At first glance, his choice of classical themes is questionable – can you really jazz up Dvořák's 'New World' *Adagio*, or the *Pathétique* or Villa-Lobos's *Bachianas Brasileiras*? The short answer is no, but that isn't really what Mariano is trying to do. His interpretations are admirably straight and unfussy, and no more alien to the language of jazz than 'My Romance' or Indian classical music.

***** Mariano & Friends**

Intuition 2149 *Mariano; Kenny Wheeler (flhn); Jasper Van't Hof, John Taylor (p); Mike Herting (ky); Dino Saluzzi (acc); Rabih Abou-Khalil (oud); Nicolas Fiszman, Jean-François Jenny-Clark (b); Jerry Granelli, Aldo Romano (d); Ramesh Shotham (perc).* 93.

If there is a generic ECM sound, this comes close to it, though producer Vera Brandes has to work with a less resonant timbre and still comes up with something that transcends the limitations of the source tapes. To celebrate his seventieth birthday, Charlie invited along as many pals as he could muster for a programme of long and fascinating musical explorations. Only two of the tunes bear his signature, and one of them is a variant on the traditional 'Deep River', but the saxophonist is the dominant solo voice throughout and he sounds in sparkling form.

With the exception of Aldo Romano's 'Il Piacere', everything is over the ten-minute mark, allowing for maximum interplay and some extended soloing. Mariano is magnificently poised on Kenny Wheeler's 'Everybody's Song', but it is the composer who steals the show with a delicately weighted and unusually sardonic performance on flugelhorn. Saluzzi is as open-hearted and eclectic as ever, and 'Seva La Murga' comes across as the classic it unquestionably is. A marvellous record that should win Charlie some new friends as well.

***** An American In Italy**

Timeless SJP 443 *Mariano; Andrea Pozza (p); Ares Tavolazzi (b); Fabio Grandi (d).* 4/96.

And, sure enough, recorded in Milan. However, the Italianate strand doesn't stop there, for almost everything on this odd but very likeable disc has either an Italian provenance or – like the theme from Mahler's Fifth Symphony – some connection with Italy. Other than to theme an album, it isn't clear quite what motivated the session beyond a desire to re-establish contact with his ancestral country. That desire notwithstanding, the desire can be read quite literally; even moving from Carlo Rusticelli to Alessandro Marcello and Nino Rota, Mariano sounds thoroughly American. His transcription of Marcello's C minor Oboe Concerto is a touch of genius. A shame he didn't put Sammy Cahn's 'Autumn In Roma' last. It's the real pay-off of the set and is slightly lost in first place. The group is very good and make light of the job; perhaps they know this stuff much better than the leader.

*****(*) Savannah Samurai**

Jazzline JL 1153 2 *Mariano; Vic Juris (g); Dieter Ilg (b); Jeff Hirshfield (d).* 98.

There are other Mariano releases in the pipeline, but the most recent just for the present is a fresh and uncomplicated session with a very bright band, co-fronted by Vic Juris's guitar. The simplicity of the opening 'Children Steps' doesn't quite prepare the way for the detailed exposition on saxophone and guitar, and it isn't until 'Dark Alley', the atmospheric third tune, that one starts to penetrate the emotional thickets. There is a reprise of the Juris tune at the end of the record and anyone interested in comparative science might usefully put this performance against the notorious Ornette/Metheny encounter on *Song X*. We know where our preferences lie. Whether on acoustic or electric instrument, the guitarist is a fine collaborator; Ilg, always an interesting writer, contributes the title-tune and the delightful 'Waltz For Dani', which tips its hat in the direction of Bill Evans. Charlie's high, plaintive tone is so pure one might almost be listening to an oboe or cor, perhaps the pay-off from his own dabbling with double-reeded horns. The final four tracks constitute a 'Climate Suite' – a 'Four Seasons' to you and me – and are collectively composed. Here again, Mariano combines an elemental straightforwardness of outline with real musical thought and expressiveness. The album is consistently delightful from start to finish, and it was cunning of Mariano to present so much adventurous music in such an accessible format.

***** Bangalore**

Intuition INT 3246 2 *Mariano; V.K Raman (f); Louis Banks (ky); Amit Heri (g); T.A.S Mani (mridangam); Dr K Raghavendra (veena); Jacob Williams (b); R.A Rajagopal (ghatam, konakkol); B.N Chandramouli (kanjira, konakkol); T.N Shashikumar (tavil); G Omkar (morsing, konakkol); S Sudashan (dholak); R.A Ramamani (v).* 98.

A fascinating multi-cultural montage, but not necessarily an album that Mariano fans will take on board wholeheartedly. The music comes accompanied by a booklet of sketches by Dorothée Mariano, and it is pretty thoroughly pictorial and impressionistic, with a heavy emphasis on instruments from the subcontinent. The other key dimension, apart from Charlie's alto, is the vocal style of R.A. Ramamani, a singer of considerable standing and great power. She tends to predominate wherever she appears, and the fact that her vocal line is always more limber than any conventionally keyed horn gives her a signal advantage. Listening to her wavering trills and scats, it's easy to hear what John Coltrane was drawn to in Indian classical music.

Michael 'Dodo' Marmarosa (born 1925)

PIANO

Born in Pittsburgh, Marmarosa worked with Krupa and Barnet while still a teenager, then moved to California and recorded on several important bebop sessions. He returned to Pittsburgh in the '50s and, despite a brief reappearance in the early '60s, has seldom been heard from since.

***** On Dial: The Complete Sessions**

Spotlite SPJ-128 *Marmarosa; Howard McGhee, Miles Davis (t); Teddy Edwards, Lucky Thompson (ts); Arvin Garrison (g); Harry Babasin (clo); Bob Kesterson (b); Roy Porter, Jackie Mills (d).* 46–12/47.

***** Dodo's Bounce**

Fresh Sound FSCD-1019 *As above, except add Barney Kessel (g), Gene Englund, Red Callender (b); omit Davis, McGhee, Edwards, Garrison, Kesterson, Porter.* 46–47.

***** Dodo Lives**

Topaz TPZ 1058 *Marmarosa; Al Killian, Peanuts Holland, Jimmy Pupa, Art House, Roy Eldridge, Lyman Vunk, Paul Cohen, Bernie Glow, George Schwartz, Carl Green, Ray Linn, Dale Pierce, Nelson Shalladay, Howard McGhee, Miles Davis (t); Eddie Bert, Ed Fromm, Spud Murphy, Bob Swift, Porky Cohen, Tommy Pedersen, Ben Pickering, George Dikson, Harry Rogers, Ollie Wilson, Britt Woodman (tb); Charlie Barnet, Buddy DeFranco, Artie Shaw, Lou Prisby, Rudolph Tanza, Ralph Roseland, John Walton, Ray De Geer, Milt Bloom, Mike Goldberg, Danny Bank, Chuck Gentry, Andy Pinbo, Harry Klee, Lucky Thompson, Charlie Parker, Ralph Lee, Gus McReynolds, Hy Mandel, Boyd Raeburn, Hal McKusick (reeds); Turk Van Lake, Barney Kessel, Slim Gaillard, Dave Barbour, Arvin Garrison (g); Russ Wagner, Morris Rayman, Sam Brown, Ray Brown, Vic McMillan, Andy Ricardi, Red Callender, Harry Babasin (b); Harold Hahn, Lou Fromm, Zutty Singleton, Jackie Mills, Roy Porter (d).* 10/43–46.

A bebop enigma. Marmarosa played an important minor role in bop's hothouse days, recording with Parker in Los Angeles; but less than two years later he was back in his native Pittsburgh and heading for an obscurity and silence that has seldom been broken since. He had a foot in swing as well as the modern camp, and his precise articulation and sweeping lines make one think of Tatum as much as any of his immediate contemporaries: a pair of solos from 1946, 'Deep Purple' and 'Tea For Two', are strikingly akin to the older man's conception. But he had a gentle, even rhapsodic side which colours the trio tracks on both of these discs and, while he flirts with an even more audacious conception – hinted at on the two 'Tone Paintings' solos from 1947 – one feels he never satisfactorily resolved the different strands of his playing. Much of his best playing is to be found on Parker's Dials (a solitary example, 'Bird Lore', is on the Spotlite CD), but the solo, trio and sextet (with Howard McGhee) tracks on *On Dial* include much absorbing piano-jazz. The Fresh Sounds CD duplicates 14 of the 22 tracks on the Spotlite disc, but also includes ten tracks cut for the Atomic label prior to the Dials, plus six quartet sides with Lucky Thompson. Neither disc solves the problem of the indifferent sound of the originals, and both feature an atrocious speed wobble on the two 'Tone Paintings' solos (which originally were privately recorded in any case).

The Topaz disc is fine on its own terms but features Marmarosa mainly as a sideman – with Artie Shaw, Charlie Barnet ('The Moose'), Slim Gaillard and Boyd Raeburn, plus the six titles with Lucky Thompson, 'Mellow Mood', 'Deep Purple', 'Tea For Two' and a stray track with a Lyle Griffin group. So it's not quite an addendum to the other discs, and anyone who has a smattering of 1940s swing will probably have the Barnet and Shaw tracks already.

*****(*) Dodo Marmarosa, Pittsburgh 1958**

Uptown UPCD 27.44 *Marmarosa; Danny Conn (t); Buzzy Renn (as); Carlo Galluzzo (ts); Danny Mastri, Jimmy DeJulio, Johnny Vance (b); Henry Sciullo, Chuck Spatafore (d).* 3/56–62.

An amazing discovery and enough to warrant a fresh look at this remarkable jazzman. The lion's share of the disc is a tape recorded by Danny Conn of Marmarosa playing at the Midway Lounge in Pittsburgh in 1958. Indifferent sound, but the piano comes through clearly, and Marmarosa's powers seem undiminished on a mix of bebop and standards. Even more interesting are three tracks from a 1962 TV broadcast with a quintet led by Conn: 'Horoscope, Vigo Movement' and 'Dodo's Blues' are intriguing glimpses of how Marmarosa might have developed after bop's heyday. There is also an after-hours tape from a few years earlier by a similar band, including a starkly effective 'You're My Thrill'. Robert Sunenblick's documentation is superb, with revealing notes on all the musicians and a 1995 interview with Mike Marmarosa (as he prefers to call himself). While this is basically a memoir of bits and pieces, reading through the notes and hearing the music evokes a deeply moving portrait of a community of jazzmen whose efforts will hardly be remembered by posterity, sustained mainly by the rewards of the music itself.

Joe Marsala (1907–78)

CLARINET, VOCALS

A Chicagoan, Marsala already had ten years in clubs and circus bands before taking a group which featured a mixed-race line-up into New York's Hickory House in 1937. Worked there for some ten years but retired in 1948 and went mainly into music publishing, though he played again in the '60s. A versatile swing stylist on reeds.

***** Joe Marsala 1936–42**

Classics 763 *Marsala; Pee Wee Erwin, Max Kaminsky, Marty Marsala (t); Bill Coleman (t, v); George Brunies (tb); Pete Brown, Ben Glassman (as); John Smith (ts); Dave Bowman, Joe Bushkin, Dick Cary, Frank Signorelli (p); Ray Biondi (vn); Adele Girard (hp); Eddie Condon, Carmen Mastren (g); Jack LeMaire (g, v); Jack Kelleher, Arthur Shapiro, Haig Stephens, Gene Traxler (b); Danny Alvin, Stan King, Shelly Manne, Buddy Rich, Zutty Singleton (d); Dell St John (v).* 1/36–7/42.

*****(*) Joe Marsala 1944–46**

Classics 902 *Marsala; Dizzy Gillespie, Bobby Hackett, Joe Thomas (t); Frank W Orchard (tb); Gene DiNovi, Leonard Feather, Cliff Jackson, Charlie Queener, Gene Schroeder (p); Eddie Condon, Chuck Wayne (g); Adele Girard (hp); Bob Casey, Irving Lang, Clyde Lombardi, Sid Weiss (b); Buddy Christian, Rollo Laylan (d); Linda Keene (v).* 3/44–11/45.

Armed with Wagnerian good looks (that's Robert rather than Richard Wagner) and a dark, winey tone, Marsala also claims an honourable place in jazz history for his efforts to break down the race divide. It was an endeavour that won the respect of Leonard Feather, a poacher rather than a gamekeeper in those days and composer of all the material on the April 1940 session. Though Marsala had the projection and the sense of structure to perform effectively in big bands, he functioned best in small groups, notably the band which maintained a residency at the Hickory House on 52nd Street. These sides represent most of his recorded output. A couple of early tracks were made for Decca under the name The Six Blue Chips; Pee Wee Erwin was the main attraction. In 1937 Marsala married harpist Adele Girard, who had brought an attractive balance and sense of space to a front line of clarinet, trumpet and violin. In later years, and particularly on the sessions of May and November 1945, she was given ever more prominent status, perhaps as a result of market pressure, and on the late pair made for Musicraft ('East Of The Sun' and 'Slightly Dizzy') she is pushed well forward.

The second volume is distinguished by some fine playing from trumpeter Joe Thomas and a brief glimpse of Dizzy Gillespie in 1945, doing 'My Melancholy Baby' and 'Cherokee'. Another reason for Marsala's appearance in the history books is his prescience in recruiting young players like Buddy Rich and Shelly Manne, who made their debuts as jazz players under Marsala's leadership in March 1938 and April 1941 respectively. These associations aside, there is no mistaking the quality of the jazz Marsala played. The Chicagoan's band, featuring brother Marty on trumpet and Eddie Condon on guitar, swings like fury, as does the later All Timers set-up which opens Volume Two, with Bobby Hackett sounding harder-toned than usual (to a degree which might puzzle Hackett buffs) but unmistakably himself on 'Clarinet Marmalade' and 'Tiger Rag'. Linda Keene's vocals add nothing much to the November 1944 date, and for the most part Marsala steered clear of singers; Dell St John has a bit part on the earlier set and Joe himself takes a brief turn at the mike on 'Gotta Be This Or That'. Otherwise, straight, driving small-group jazz.

Branford Marsalis (born 1960)

TENOR AND SOPRANO SAXOPHONES

The eldest of the Marsalis brothers started on alto saxophone and joined Art Blakey's Jazz Messengers in 1981. After a period in brother Wynton's group, he has been his own man in various situations ever since: sideman with Sting, leader of the Tonight Show band, guest with The Grateful Dead, movie actor, leader of the hiphop jazz band, Buckshot LeFonque, teacher at Michigan University and A&R consultant for Columbia Records – all this besides touring and making albums with his own quartet.

***** Scenes In The City**

Columbia 468458-2 *Marsalis; John Longo (t); Robin Eubanks (tb); Mulgrew Miller (p); Ray Drummond, Ron Carter, Charnett*

Moffett, Phil Bowler (b); Marvin 'Smitty' Smith, Jeff Tain Watts (d). 4–11/83.

****(*) Royal Garden Blues**
Columbia 468704-2 *Marsalis; Ellis Marsalis, Kenny Kirkland, Herbie Hancock, Larry Willis (p); Ron Carter, Charnett Moffett, Ira Coleman (b); Ralph Peterson, Marvin 'Smitty' Smith, Al Foster, Jeff Tain Watts (d).* 3–7/86.

***** Renaissance**
Columbia 40711 *Marsalis; Kenny Kirkland (p); Charnett Moffett (b); Jeff Tain Watts (d).*

****(*) Random Abstract**
Columbia 468707-2 *Marsalis; Kenny Kirkland (p); Delbert Felix (b); Lewis Nash (d).* 8/87.

Articulate, hip, funny, the eldest of the Marsalis brothers was almost as ubiquitous a figure as his trumpeter-sibling in the 1980s and '90s. His tenor playing is stonily powerful in the Rollins tradition, and he has stuck by the bigger horn on most of his solo records, with soprano – granted a sometimes reedy but usually impressive full tone – as second instrument. *Scenes In The City* was an entertaining debut, with a wry version of the Mingus title-tune (complete with dialogue), and the storming manifesto of 'No Backstage Pass' to show what he could do: but it's a bit of a jumble. *Royal Garden Blues* is a step down, the playing messy and subdivided among a bewildering variety of rhythm sections. *Renaissance* and *Random Abstract* emerge as accomplished but undecided sessions. On *Random Abstract* he seems to explore the mannerisms of a number of preceding tenor influences: Coltrane, Shorter, Coleman, even Ben Webster, whose celebration in a bathetic reading of 'I Thought About You' seems more of a parody than a tribute. The chief problem with all these sessions, though, is that Marsalis promises more than he delivers, both conceptually and in the heft and weight of his playing. While still sounding imaginative and technically top-line, he can't seem to focus an eloquent battery of remarks into a proper speech. Delfeayo Marsalis's production is idiosyncratic: his interest in 'more bass wood' tends to make the lower frequencies sound woolly and unclear.

***** Trio Jeepy**
Columbia 465134-2 2CD *Marsalis; Milt Hinton, Delbert Felix (b); Jeff Tain Watts (d).* 1/88.

A rambling jam session, illuminated by some brilliant moments. 'The Nearness Of You' is a mature ballad reading, 'Doxy' a convincing nod to Rollins, and 'Random Abstract' features the Marsalis–Felix–Watts trio in full, exhilarating flight (the amazingly durable Hinton plays on most of the other tracks). While hailed (mystifyingly) as a breakthrough masterpiece in some quarters, it's actually a lightweight, fun record.

***** Crazy People Music**
Columbia 466870-2 *Marsalis; Kenny Kirkland (p); Robert Hurst (b); Jeff Tain Watts (d).* 1–3/90.

***** The Beautyful Ones Are Not Yet Born**
Columbia 468896-2 *Marsalis; Wynton Marsalis (t); Robert Hurst (b); Jeff Tain Watts (d).* 5/91.

Hurst and Watts are musicians of resolute power and high craft, and they provide Marsalis with the bedrock he needs to contextualize his playing. *Crazy People Music* is a solidly realized tenor-and-rhythm date, full of elegant playing, but the music on *The Beautyful Ones Are Not Yet Born* is better yet: the recording sounds warmer and more specifically focused, and the long, stretched-out improvisations insist that Marsalis has his perfect, singular setting in the trio with Hurst and Watts (brother Wynton makes a brief cameo appearance on one track). 'Citizen Tain', which has some of the wit of Sonny Rollins working against Philly Joe Jones on *Newk's Time*, 'Gilligan's Isle' and the steeply driven title-tune are aristocratic improvisations in which the leader finds a path away from merely discursive blowing. His soprano sounds pretty good, too.

***** I Heard You Twice The First Time**
Columbia 472169-2 *Marsalis; Wynton Marsalis, Earl Gardner (t); Delfeayo Marsalis, David Sager (tb); Wessell Anderson (as); Kenny Kirkland (p); B.B King, John Lee Hooker (g, v); Russell Malone, Joe Louis Walker (g); Reginald Veal, Robert Hurst (b); Jeff Tain Watts, Herlin Riley, Bernard Purdie (d); Thomas Hollis, Roscoe Carroll, Carl Gordon, Charles Dutton, Linda Hopkins (v). n.d.*

*****(*) Bloomington**
Columbia 473771-2 *Marsalis; Robert Hurst (b); Jeff Tain Watts (d).* 9/91.

Branford's blues album is somewhat lighter than Wynton's three-volume dissertation, but there's still a tendency to ramble: the crackling 'Rib Tip Johnson', with superb guitar by Russell Malone, would have been better at five minutes rather than nine, and B.B. King's feature also runs into flab. 'Sidney In Da Haus' is an impeccably arranged small-group piece, 'Mabel' hires John Lee Hooker for one of his show-stealing cameos, and the rest is good Branford, swinging hard, often connecting. *Bloomington*, though, is his least adorned, maybe his best record. A snapshot of a live date from Indiana with his regular partners, the music makes a virtue of its open-ended situation: away from studio microphones, one can hear the terrific heat and tumbling spontaneity that this group can put out in a live situation. There is a treatment of 'Everything Happens To Me' that wipes out the song itself, all stark corners and cold stares; a bumping 'Friday The Thirteenth'; a vast 'Xavier's Lair'. Dead spots, too, and Delfeayo Marsalis's sound is as questionable as usual, but a fine record.

***** Buckshot La Fonque**
Columbia 476352-2 *Marsalis; Roy Hargrove, Chuck Findley (t); Matt Finders (tb); Delfeayo Marsalis (tb, p); Greg Phillinganes (ky); Kenny Kirkland (p); David Barry, Kevin Eubanks, Ray Fuller, Nils Lofgren, Albert Collins (g); Robert Hurst, Darryl Jones, Larry Kimpel (b); Jeff Tain Watts, Chuck Morris (d); Mino Cinelu, Vicki Randle (perc).* 94.

Branford's hiphop album. Wacky, ironic, full of in-jokes, sardonic, embracing the idiom and rising over it at the same time, these are fragments from a busy man's workbook and chips off an old block: black music from the streets, clubs and concert halls. Marsalis doesn't suggest that he has any real faith or interest in hiphop, but he likes the style and he's interested in a piece of it. There is some inventive use of sampling, cut-ups, whatever, and some great playing. But it never seems like anything more than an ingenious bag of filed-down pieces. It is also starting to sound very dated.

*****(*) The Dark Keys**

Columbia CK 67876 *Marsalis; Kenny Garrett (as); Joe Lovano (ts); Reginald Veal (b); Jeff Tain Watts (d).* 96.

Where Wynton's records become more precise, more finished, Branford's get looser, even wilder – or so it seems on the surface. Marsalis never quite surrenders himself to the music, even when, as in the tornado title-track, he gets as close as he ever has to Coltraneish outpourings. As free-flowing as this date is, the man's sense of control is ironclad. On gentler terrain ('A Thousand Autumns', 'Blutain') he plays with a kind of impassive stoicism. When challenged by Lovano or Garrett, as he is in one track apiece, he digs in and plants his feet. As usual, a record to admire, a tough one to warm to, but prolonged acquaintance has increased our admiration.

*****(*) Requiem**

Columbia 069655-2 *Marsalis; Kenny Kirkland (p); Eric Revis (b); Jeff Tain Watts (d).* 8–11/98.

Recorded shortly before the death of Kenny Kirkland, the pianist's demise came while the group was planning a third session to complete the album, and its 'unfinished' state is how it has been left. Marsalis has had a distinctly unfocused career on record, certainly compared with his trumpet-playing brother, and as ever this is an imperfect statement from a perfectionist musician. But its merits are powerful indeed. The sting of Kirkland's death is made more unhappy by the excellence of his playing here, from the forcefulness of 'Doctone' to the bittersweetness of 'A Thousand Autumns'; and in 'Lykief' he and Marsalis seem to be running virtuoso rings around each other. But there remains the sense that these are brilliant men playing for themselves, and these overlong tracks could use editing which a more detached producer might have encouraged. No gainsaying the often scathing virtuosity of the saxophonist in this situation. Whether the listener responds to it is more than ever a matter of individual taste.

Delfeayo Marsalis (born 1965)

TROMBONE

The youngest of the three leading Marsalis brothers (drummer Jason is younger still) is more renowned as a producer than as a performer, having handled desk duties on many of his brothers' records.

***** Musashi**

Evidence ECD 22187-2 *Marsalis; Bill Reichenbach (btb); Branford Marsalis (ss, ts); Mark Gross (ss, as); Yuichi Inoue, Ellis Marsalis (p); Shigeo Aramaki (b); Masahiko Osaka (d).* 7/96.

The trambonist (his word) sounds in good spirits on his most recent entry. Delfeayo still has the least imposing rep of the family as an instrumentalist but he takes a couple of lip-busting solos on the date to show he's no slouch, and the rest of the music is intermittently impressive. There are four standards, most of them reharmonized or otherwise tampered with as if they were too pat to start with, but the originals are a rather dull lot – only 'Queen Himiko' makes an impact, with its eerie counterpoint between the soprano and the bass instruments and the shimmer of Inoue's Fender Rhodes. Although Branford and Ellis turn up for guest spots, the most striking parts are played by Gross, mainly restricted to soprano but a thoughtful and inventive saxophonist. The sleeve-notes contain a lot of the usual gas.

Ellis Marsalis (born 1934)

PIANO

Marsalis played and taught for many years in his native New Orleans with no recognition whatsoever beyond his playing circles. But he also sired a family of musicians who have gone on to become the most famous jazz dynasty of their day. Their success has also afforded him some wider exposure.

***** The Classic Ellis Marsalis**

Boplicity CDBOP 016 *Marsalis; Nat Perrilliat (ts); Marshall Smith (b); James Black (d).* 1–3/63.

***** Piano In E**

Rounder 2100 *Marsalis (p solo).* 84.

***** Heart Of Gold**

Columbia CK 47509 *Marsalis; Ray Brown, Reginald Veal (b); Billy Higgins, Herlin Riley, Jason Marsalis (d).* 2–6/91.

***** Whistle Stop**

Columbia 474555-2 *Marsalis; Branford Marsalis (ss, ts); Robert Hurst (b); Jeff Tain Watts, Jason Marsalis (d).* 3–6/93.

The founder of the Marsalis dynasty is no mean player himself. One can hear where Wynton got his even-handed delineation of melody from and where Branford's aristocratic elegance of line is rooted. Marsalis *père* isn't beyond tossing in the occasional surprise, but mostly he favours careful interpretations of standards, sparsely harmonized and delicately spelt out, with a few simple but cleverly hooked originals to lend a little extra personality. *The Classic Marsalis* is a surprising rarity, a quartet date from the early 1960s in which the pianist leads a group featuring the Coltrane follower, Nat Perrilliat, and the jittery, post-Elvin Jones drums of James Black, whose unsettling beats keep the group teetering on the brink of a chaos that the others carefully navigate. The recording is monochromatic, but it's an interesting period-piece.

Of the contemporary sessions, *Whistle Stop* is one of the Marsalis family affairs, and this is impressive playing – perhaps a degree too impressive. The sleeve-notes belabour the point that the group are actually playing in 5 on some tunes, even though this is hardly the revolution the author suggests, and the quartet's resolve to make it all sound so easy gives the music a steeliness that detracts from the writing, much of which comes from former Marsalis sidemen, Black and Perrilliat: five of the tunes were previously covered on *The Classic Marsalis*.

*****(*) A Night At Snug Harbor, New Orleans**

Evidence ECD 22129-2 *Marsalis; Nicholas Payton (t); Tony Dagradi, Rick Margitza, Donald Harrison (ts); Bill Huntington (b); Art Blakey, David Lee Jr (d).* 4/89.

This is the best album Marsalis has put his name to, a wonderfully disciplined jam session of sorts that has amazingly few *longueurs* (even at over 70 minutes). Payton's only appearance is with Blakey sitting in on one track, and the trumpeter (then only fifteen!) does nothing special. It's the keen interplay of the three tenormen with a splendid rhythm section that makes the music happen. Dagradi is all muscle and intensity, Harrison (present on only three tracks) is the epitome of refinement, and Margitza finds himself somewhere between the two. The blend works beautifully, and Marsalis himself seems to quietly call the various changes of dynamic via his own playing. Harrison's ballad feature on 'I Can't Get Started' is gorgeous; Ellis has a notably graceful 'The Very Thought Of You' to himself; and the expected blowout on the closing 'A Night In Tunisia' actually has power in reserve all through. Engineer David Farrell also got a very handsome location sound.

**** Loved Ones**

Columbia 483624-2 *Marsalis; Branford Marsalis (ss, ts).* 8–9/95.

Ellis has five solos to himself, which are fair enough. But the nine duets with his son are about as rambling and self-indulgent as detractors always think jazz is. This is a low point for both men.

***** Duke In Blue**

Columbia CK 63631 *Marsalis (p solo).* 3/99.

A sequence of Ellington interpretations, with a blues coda in the form of the title-track. Marsalis is at his most thoughtful and wide-ranging: stride, boogie and even Latin-styled piano forms are on show at various points. Appearing in Duke's centenary year, this was a worthy homage, but it doesn't much stand out from many others.

Wynton Marsalis (born 1961)

TRUMPET

One of six brothers, he learned trumpet as a child in New Orleans, was already playing concertos in his teens – and in funk bands on the side – then studied at Juilliard. Joined Art Blakey in 1980, then formed his own band with brother Branford in 1982 and began recording as a leader for Columbia. Since then he has followed a meteoric course of recording, teaching, touring, composing, acting as Artistic Director of Jazz at Lincoln Center (since 1992), speaking out, accepting awards, attracting controversy, and playing the trumpet. The most powerful jazz musician in America today.

*****(*) Wynton Marsalis**

Columbia 468708 *Marsalis; Branford Marsalis (ts, ss); Herbie Hancock, Kenny Kirkland (p); Ron Carter, Charles Fambrough, Clarence Seay (b); Jeff Tain Watts, Tony Williams (d).* 81.

What a weight of expectation and responsibility fell on Wynton Marsalis's shoulders. At twenty, not quite overnight, though it perhaps seemed like that away from New Orleans, he became the nominate leader and mouthpiece of a new traditionalism in jazz. Easy to parody his platform as 'Forward to the 1920s!', but for the first time in many years a young man stood up and declared a commitment to the tradition and, as a corollary, a measure of hostility to the compromises (as he saw it) of fusion and the anarchic bloodletting of the avant-garde. In the passionately articulate Stanley Crouch he had his *éminence noire*, an able polemicist and spokesman with a voice as ringingly clear as Marsalis's trumpet.

A front-line role in the Jazz Messengers obviously doesn't constitute obscurity, but there was a dramatic turn from gifted apprentice to star-in-waiting. The earliest recordings, made at Bubba's in Fort Lauderdale, came a year after his recruitment to the Messengers and, though available only on small labels, they bespoke a great talent and – already – a great purity of vision. In 1981, he parted company from Art Blakey, with the boss's blessing, and went on the road with a quartet that immediately and controversially cemented his claim to the then discarded mantle of Miles Davis, who later spurned the young pretender at a bizarre showdown in Canada.

Record companies have often miscued by putting promising talent in the company of grizzled veterans, but Marsalis shows total class in the company of Hancock, Carter and Williams. It's clear, though, that he is also building his own cohort of like-minded players. The opening 'Father Time', which features elder brother Branford and the lyrical Kirkland, is an astonishing major-label debut, a beautifully structured piece which uncovers a slew of improvisational ideas in a short span. Marsalis himself never sounds as if he's up on a soapbox, as happened from time to time later on. He's always got something to say and he does so with a simplicity that is as refreshing as rain.

Perhaps inevitably, perhaps rightly, much of the critical attention was directed towards the tracks with the senior players. Carter's 'RJ' and Williams's melancholic 'Sister Cheryl' bracket a furious stop-action Marsalis composition called 'Hesitation', which is actually a neo-bop variation on 'I Got Rhythm' and was presumably got up for the Messengers. A near-perfectly weighted programme closes with 'Twilight', one of the loveliest things he has ever done.

***** Fathers And Sons**

Columbia CK 37574 *Marsalis; Branford Marsalis (ts); Ellis Marsalis (p); Charles Fambrough (b); James Black (d).* 82.

Given the publicity the whole Marsalis dynasty was receiving, it was inevitable that a project of this sort would float up sooner or later. Actually shared with a Chico and Von Freeman session, this is a pretty middling selection of material, distinguished by one of the rare occasions when elder brother upstages younger, a saxophone solo of real quality on 'A Joy Forever' which prompts some wonder why Branford doesn't turn it on more often. Father Ellis is calmly authoritative throughout, playing with delicate sophistication and just a hint of irony on 'Lush Life'. Wynton returns to the spotlight with an exactly crafted solo on 'Nostalgic Impressions', sounding very much like Pops in reflective mood.

***** Think Of One**

Columbia 468709 *Marsalis; Branford Marsalis (ts, ss); Kenny Kirkland (p); Phil Bowler (b); Jeff Tain Watts (d).* 83.

***** Hothouse Flowers**

Columbia 468710 *Marsalis; Branford Marsalis (ts, ss); Kent Jordan (af); Kenny Kirkland (p); Ron Carter (b); Jeff Tain Watts (d).* 5/84.

The younger players must indeed have felt like hothouse flowers, brought on unseasonally in a rich mulch of label enthusiasm and under a glare of media attention. Marsalis's tone, forged in the Messengers, is hard and unflawed, producing patterns of sound like petals made of some hard but malleable metal. On 'Later', one of the better tracks on the 1983 album, he manages to find an idiom that contrives to evoke connections from Bubber Miley all the way to Butch Morris.

A year on, he sounds curiously detached, even a little remote. *Hothouse Flowers* sounds like a man under a bell-jar; the colours are intense, the ideas as rich and exotic as one would wish, but there is no real emotional engagement with the music, just a series of brilliantly executed ideas. 'Stardust' is a *tour de force* and, like 'When You Wish Upon A Star', seems confected out of next to nothing, just the melody and a gently oscillating chord-pattern. Even by this stage, Branford seems to be on board as a result of sibling loyalty rather than anything else, increasingly pushed into the background, as Jordan is. Watts is a key element, bright and crisp, often echoing Kirkland's chordal patterns on his toms and cymbals. If he resembles anyone of an earlier generation, it must be Max Roach: the same devotion to threes, the same urgency, the same melodic facility.

****** Black Codes (From The Underground)**

Columbia 468711 *Marsalis; Kenny Kirkland (p); Ron Carter, Charnett Moffett (b); Jeff Tain Watts (d).* 1/85.

****** J Mood**

Columbia 468712 *Marsalis; Marcus Roberts (p); Robert Leslie Hurst III (b); Jeff Tain Watts (d).* 12/85.

As jazz vintages go, this twelvemonth has to be considered pretty special. Within a year, two of Marsalis's very best showings on record, neither of which he has ever bettered. Watts is again absolutely central to the sound, particularly given the not unexpected decision to dispense with a second horn. *Black Codes* is a highly committed record, not just in its referencing of nineteenth-century slave law, but also in the sheer commitment of Marsalis's playing. The title-piece is his strongest single performance since 'Father Time', sorrowful and full of unaffected wisdom. 'Phryzzinian Man' has him playing stately modes, almost classical in conception. 'Chambers Of Tain' is a Kirkland composition, a caustically intense feature for the drummer.

J Mood was perceived at the time as a key recording for Marsalis. It is the first time he sounds completely relaxed and in possession of his own language and, though it was a record that intensified the debate about neo-traditionalism against experiment and contemporaneity, the actual music gives no sense of having a part in that. 'Much Later' might just be a reference to Miles Davis's favourite exit-line; there are certainly a couple of moments when Marsalis appears to allude to the classic Davis performances of the 1950s. 'Skain's Domain' and the beautiful 'Presence That Lament Brings' touch the opposite boundaries of the trumpeter's range, suggesting that his great quality is not after all virtuosic flash and fire but a deep-rooted expressiveness which maintains its integrity all the way across the spectrum, from fiery individualism to elegiac regret.

*****(*) Marsalis Standard Time: Volume 1**

Columbia 468713 *Marsalis; Marcus Roberts (p); Robert Leslie Hurst III (b); Jeff Tain Watts (d).* 5 & 9/86.

***** Standard Time: Volume 2 – Intimacy Calling**

Columbia 468273 *Marsalis; Wes Anderson (as); Todd Williams (ts); Marcus Roberts (p); Robert Leslie Hurst III, Reginald Veal (b); Herlin Riley, Jeff Tain Watts (d).* 9/87–8/90.

*****(*) Standard Time: Volume 3 – The Resolution Of Romance**

Columbia 466871 *Marsalis; Ellis Marsalis (p); Reginald Veal (b); Herlin Riley (d).*

The first of these albums was wonderfully judged, a programme of pieces that distanced him from the modernists without ever consigning him to the ranks of the Old Believers. Even after more than a decade, *Marsalis Standard Time* retains its burnish and class. As ever, there is a faint suspicion that the trumpeter is thinking through his solos several choruses ahead, trading in spontaneity and fire for control, but nevertheless the ideas are always vivid. Two versions of 'Cherokee', the first with mute and one of his most uncomplicatedly inventive essays, the second more orderly and discursive, but left curiously unresolved. Roberts has an unaccompanied feature on 'Memories Of You', a fitting recognition of his part in the music and an obvious showcase for his developing solo career.

Marsalis has always shown tremendous loyalty and respect to his sidemen, qualities that significantly dent charges of arrogance and remoteness. He also sits out 'East Of The Sun (West Of The Moon)' on *Intimacy Calling*, the less effective of the two later *Standard Times*. The extra horns bring nothing of any great substance, and Roberts seems to have difficulty making his presence felt. The quartet with Marsalis Sr, Veal and Riley offers a different, quieter sound from that of the groups with Roberts and Watts, and this is the one of the three which most consistently surprises now. Marsalis himself is in reflective mood throughout, relying on soft, almost *sotto voce* harmony effects and a wonderfully lachrymose wah-wah on 'The Seductress'.

A remarkable group of records, which put paid to one cavil and pointed the way towards a new and more broad-based approach to the repertoire.

*****(*) Live At Blues Alley**

Columbia 461109 2CD *Marsalis; Marcus Roberts (p); Robert Leslie Hurst III (b); Jeff Tain Watts (d).* 12/86.

Exactly a year on from the breakthrough *J Mood*, Marsalis answered the other question and proved that black-tie gigs, classical concertos and the almost ingratiating attention of Columbia hadn't compromised the terse, fiery performer who'd appeared with the Messengers. Recorded in Washington, DC, these club cuts establish him as the heir of Fats Navarro, Lee Morgan, Freddie Hubbard, and even the uptight little cat who'd just frosted him off a stage in Vancouver and who had just quitted Columbia for Warners, leaving the field clear for the youngster.

As before, the actual sound of Marsalis's trumpet (as opposed to the idiom in which he was playing) seems to come from an even earlier age, from 'Sweets' Edison, Roy Eldridge and from Armstrong again, and yet everything about these rollicking performances is as contemporary as the morning newspapers. In particular, Marsalis seems to be enjoying a flirtation with dissonance, bending notes at the edges, teasingly suggesting that he is going to go outside and then punching the orthodox changes with dead-centre accuracy.

Virtually all the material is familiar from earlier records. 'Knozz-Moe-King' from *Think Of One* gets the set off to a ripping start and is reiterated as a band theme throughout. An excoriating 'Skain's Domain' gives that well-worked theme its definitive rendition, while 'Delfeayo's Dilemma' and 'Chambers Of Tain' are both strongly argued versions. 'Do You Know What It Means To Miss New Orleans' is puzzling, but it squares with Marsalis's admirable refusal to overcook classic material of this sort.

Only a sound-balance which does scant justice to our main-man Watts denies this one a fourth star. In performance terms, it's a key moment for Marsalis.

*** The Majesty Of The Blues

Columbia 465129 *Marsalis; Teddy Riley (t); Freddie Lonzo (tb); Michael White (cl); Wes Anderson (as); Todd Williams (ts, ss); Marcus Roberts (p); Reginald Veal (b); Herlin Riley (d); Rev. Jeremiah Wright (v).* 10/88.

A first glimpse of a new phenomenon: Marsalis the self-appointed guardian of the flame. It is inaccurate to call *Majesty* a revivalist album. As before, Wynton manages to combine a classical sound with a thoroughly modern diction, but this concept-piece, a celebration of the music and culture of New Orleans, is hog-tied by worthy ambitions. Dr Michael White, who is perhaps more convincing as a scholar than as a player, appears on 'New Orleans Function', a suite of authentic-sounding ideas which consigns Marsalis to second place behind Teddy Riley. White is a curious performer, consistently sharp in tone and not too agile, but somehow always able to make a significant contribution and here without any doubt adding something to a group sound that has moved on a step from the 'classic' quartet. Roberts's use of bebop harmonies on the title-track, also known as 'The Puheeman Strut', and 'Hickory Dickory Dock' helps draw attention to Marsalis's restorative concern for the continuity of jazz music, which he believes was betrayed by the scorched-earth aesthetics of the 1960s and by pop.

The long suite is essentially a funeral procession for 'The Death Of Jazz' and is dominated by a 17-minute sermon, 'Premature Autopsies', written by Stanley Crouch and delivered by the Rev. Wright. The sonorous text – a good deal more convincing than Crouch's usual one-note spiel – draws attention away from the instrumental backing, but this deserves attention, too, an excellent example of the way Marsalis's music retains its connections with impassioned speech. Crouch's tribute to the nobility of jazz, and in particular the example of Duke Ellington, is surprisingly moving. A little breathless and unargued, it reads pretty poorly but, as performed, has an undoubted majesty, even if it cleaves closer to William Bradford Huie than to Martin Luther King.

***(*) Crescent City Christmas Card

Columbia CK 45287 *Marsalis; Wycliffe Gordon (tb); Wes Anderson (as); Todd Williams (ts, ss, cl); Alvin Batiste (cl); Joe Temperley (bs, bcl); Marcus Roberts (p); Reginald Veal (b); Herlin Riley (d); Kathleen Battle, Jon Hendricks (v).* 89.

Any disposition to cynicism at 'Wynton's Christmas Album' is dispelled by even the most sceptical hearing. Interestingly, this is much more authentic New Orleans jazz than the previous record, and there are moments of real beauty. Marsalis's attempt to combine the awe and sheer fun of Christmas works very well indeed, and the arrangements are inventive from first to last. 'Hark! The Herald Angels Sing' is conceived as a dialogue between European harmony and a jazz groove, but it's 'The Little Drummer Boy' that takes the breath away; hear this and still claim that Wynton Marsalis is a dry technician without a sentimental corner of his soul. Vocal features for Jon Hendricks (wonderful on 'Sleigh Ride') and Kathleen Battle, though even this wonderful soprano is upstaged by Wynton's muted solo on 'Silent Night'. The supporting cast is excellent, and Roberts's feature this time out is 'O Come All Ye Faithful', to which he brings a characteristic spin and invention, characteristic both of himself and of the boss.

***(*) Thick In The South

Columbia 468569 *Marsalis; Joe Henderson (ts); Marcus Roberts (p); Robert Leslie Hurst III (b); Elvin Jones, Jeff Tain Watts (d). n.d.*

*** Uptown Ruler

Columbia 468660 *Marsalis; Todd Williams (ts); Marcus Roberts (p); Reginald Veal (b); Herlin Riley (d). n.d.*

***(*) Levee Low Moan

Columbia 468568 *Marsalis; Wessell Anderson (as); Todd Williams (ts); Marcus Roberts (p); Reginald Veal (b); Herlin Riley (d). n.d.*

Three simultaneous issues from Columbia's capacious vault, issued under the more or less meaningless rubric, 'Soul Gestures in Southern Blue'. Clearly it was felt that the market would support a blanket release of this kind. *Thick In The South* stands up best a few years further on, though mostly for Joe Henderson's wonderfully wise and unruffled performances. Marsalis himself sounds like a man casting about for things to say; that he manages to find and utter them can't be questioned, but there is an air of contrivance which isn't particularly attractive. Jones is the other senior guest, but he's over-emphatic and rather dull in comparison to Watts's muscular groove. Roberts seems ill-at-ease around this time – whether suffering from creative depletion or champing at the bit of his own ambitions isn't clear. As Sun Ra used to say of himself, the Marsalis jail was the best jail built, but it could still have been seen as a jail to a progressive young stylist with ideas of his own.

Uptown Ruler is one of the least attractive-sounding Marsalis albums in the catalogue, reasons unknown and obscure. The accompaniments seem very recessed and almost cloudy, perhaps to throw into high contrast the leader's strongly etched blues ideas. 'Down Home With Homey' seemed an interesting attempt to combine an old-fashioned idiom with the rhythmic and colouristic values of the M-Base generation. The third of the group is interesting largely for pointing the way forward to Marsalis's new mid-size band and a new, more obviously arranged sound. The saxophones are beautifully voiced and Roberts regains something of his accustomed vigour. 'Jig's Jig' is extraordinary.

***(*) Blue Interlude

Columbia 471635 *Marsalis; Wycliffe Gordon (tb); Wessell Anderson (as); Todd Williams (ts, ss, cl); Marcus Roberts (p); Reginald Veal (b); Herlin Riley (d).* 92.

At the turn of the '90s, Marsalis's sights were fixed on bigger game; one senses that a gigging quartet no longer interested him much and that he had largely exhausted the possibilities of 'guest' horns. The new septet was a breath of fresh air, a big, spacious sound, with plenty of incident, varied textures and a remarkable even-handedness when it came to handing out solo space.

Increasingly, Marsalis was being seen as the heir apparent to Duke Ellington, a composer/performer with the totalizing gift of absolute organization and a parallel ability to give his colleagues enough freedom to express themselves. Todd Williams's 'Jubilee Suite' is a good case in point, or not a *good* case in point since it emerges as a flabby and shapeless sequence of unrelated ideas. The trombonist's 'And The Band Played On' is infinitely more interesting, a tune that other bandleaders must surely have looked at with envy. Marsalis is playing astutely and with infinite assurance. His long monologue on 'Sugar Cane And Sweetie Pie' sets up the title-piece's very Ellingtonian opposition of motifs, moods and harmonic atmospheres, out of which develops one of the trumpeter's most flowing improvisations, a graceful, swirling thing which could not have been conceived by anyone else on the planet at this time.

As an album, *Blue Interlude* is most interesting for what it promised. The septet's subsequent live appearances were to be among the finest moments in an already remarkable career.

**** Citi Movement (Griot New York)

Columbia 473055 2CD *As above, except replace Roberts with Eric Reed (p). n.d.*

It says something about Marsalis's redefinition of himself as teacher, *griot* and *auteur* that the record which very nearly achieves greatness should have been made for a collaborative project with a strong extra-musical component. As the 1990s advanced, it was clear that he required dramatic and programmatic triggers to give the music the definition he demanded. *Citi Movement* was written for the brilliant choreographer, Garth Fagan, whose approach to the dance balances traditional and contemporary values in much the same way as Marsalis's music.

By this point, the septet is playing with a greased precision of movement which makes it communicate like a single entity. The first section, 'Cityscape', has an energy and drive that are reminiscent of Charles Mingus's Jazz Workshop projects, and surely Stanley Crouch's invocation of Mingus is no coincidence. It's a deeply stratified and textured piece, with an enormous inner propulsion. A further dimension of the score is Marsalis's new interest in the African components of Afro-American culture. 'Transatlantic Echoes' is searching and thoughtful and it resolutely refuses to lean on bland musicological borrowings. Instead, Marsalis has created his own sense of Africanism, one that is entirely conditioned by his personal circumstances and ideas, rather than being adopted like fancy dress. The final movement, 'Some Present Moments Of The Future', sketches out in ever more lifelike outline his vision of a viable jazz tradition.

*** In This House, On This Morning

Columbia 53220 2CD *As above, except add Marion Williams (v).* 5/92.

Given that, by this stage, Ellingtonian parallels were almost *de rigueur*, this was mentioned as the first Sacred Concert. In fact, it's not so very different from what Marsalis was doing on *Majesty Of The Blues*, plunging back into church music and the homely liturgy of the Afro-American communion to give an expressive impulse to the highly sophisticated sound of the septet.

Why this was released as a double CD is mystifying, since there simply isn't enough high-quality material to justify release on this scale. The ritual slowness of 'Call To Prayer' and 'Recessional' is doubtless deliberate, but it suggests creative uncertainty and, for the first time in his career, Marsalis sounds as if he may be relying on stock phrases. The band as a whole creaks through the sermon which begins the second disc, and it's only when the Sunday business is over and the 'Uptempo Postlude' and 'Pot Blessed Dinner' re-establish secular communion that the music regains something of its impetus.

There have, of course, been many earlier attempts to marry jazz and church ritual, Ellington's being only the grandest of them. One suspects that here, exceptionally, Marsalis isn't sufficiently engaged in the belief-system and that the rituals he observes survive in him only as abstract 'pieties'. This may sound incidental, even irrelevant, but – given the claims made for *In This House, On This Morning* when it was first performed – its credibility has to be questioned.

***(*) Joe Cool's Blues

Columbia 478250 *Marsalis; Chuck Findley (t); Wycliffe Gordon, Delfeayo Marsalis (tb); Wessell Anderson (as); Branford Marsalis (ts); Victor Goines (ts, cl); Tom Peterson (bs); Ellis Marsalis, Eric Reed (p); Reginald Veal, Benjamin Wolfe (b); Martin Butler, Herlin Riley (d); Germaine Bazzle (v).* 4–8/94.

Marsalis has said that the only jazz heard on television when he was a boy was in Charlie Brown cartoon themes, written by Vince Guaraldi. Guaraldi was a friend of Ellis Marsalis, and the latter performs with his trio – Reginald Veal and Martin Butler are his partners – four of the 13 numbers, with a fifth, 'Little Birdie', arranged for a larger group with vocalist. For the rest, this was a joyously nostalgic curtain-call for the septet. If Schulz seems an unlikely source for the blues, then consider how finely his world balances hope and pain, disappointment, frustration, sheer delight.

'On Peanuts Playground' is a wonderful piece, delightful and brooding by turns. With perverse inevitability, Marsalis's own themes sound more like the real thing than Guaraldi's familiar signatures. 'Little Birdie' should probably have ended proceedings, with just a return of 'Joe Cool's Blues' to round things out, but the weakest of the originals, 'Why, Charlie Brown' comes in at that point to blunt the impact just a touch. A shame, for this is one of Marsalis's most unaffected and affecting records.

***(*) Blood On The Fields

Columbia 57694 3CD *Marsalis; Russell Gunn, Roger Ingram, Marcus Printup (t); Wayne Goodman, Ron Westray (tb); Wycliffe Gordon (tb, tba); Wessell Anderson (as); Victor Goines (ts, ss, cl, bcl); Robert Stewart (ts); Walter Blanding (ss); James Carter (bs, bcl, cl); Michael Ward (vn); Eric Reed (p); Reginald Veal (b); Herlin Riley (d, perc); Miles Griffith, Jon Hendricks, Cassandra Wilson (v).* 94.

Written almost half a century after Ellington's *Black, Brown And Beige*, this is a work which sets out to rival that great Afro-American masterpiece. A huge achievement, inevitably patchy and in places overcooked, but filled with superb jazz writing. Indeed, one can imagine – and may yet hear – a magnificent instrumental or orchestral suite derived from the music in *Blood On The Fields*. As a meditation on Southern slavery, its human and cultural impact, it is most wholly convincing when it delivers its points simply and plainly. Some of the texts, though sung well by Wilson, Griffith and the veteran Hendricks, are a little too pointedly earnest, but the emotion and the depth of thought behind them cannot be questioned.

It starts on a slave ship on the notorious 'middle passage', and puts together two characters, Jesse and Leona, divided by birth but united by the shared circumstance of the 'peculiar institution' of slavery. The music digs deep back into the traditions, and is marked by dancing syncopations, deep blues and African songs, powerful chants and testimonies. The dramatic thread is simple enough to sustain conviction and not to overpower the more purely musical elements of the work. If *Blood On The Fields* is an 'opera', it is within a very American subdivision of the genre. It is tragic and joyous, a numbers piece with a powerful unifying thread.

Marsalis's soloing is central to the drama, but he has wisely chosen to treat this is as an ensemble piece, spreading the emphasis over a number of players, allowing them to underline the vocal line with sometimes literal, sometimes ironic motifs. As a recorded experience, it is too long and difficult to absorb comfortably. Anyone who saw either the Lincoln Center première on All Fools' Day 1994 or subsequent European performances will understand its sheer impact. Others may well have to navigate their own most effective course through three densely packed CDs, selecting tracks, passing over others, dwelling where the emotional and dramatic impact seems most concentrated.

***** The Midnight Blues**

Columbia CK 68921 *Marsalis; Eric Reed (p); Reginald Veal (b); Lewis Nash (d); orchestra.* 97.

Beautifully crafted, undeniably atmospheric, but a little cold. Bob Freedman's exquisite arrangements are the necessary leaven on this repertory set (the latest in the *Standard Time* sequence). The ballad playing is richly registered, with Wynton sounding as close as breathing in the mix. 'It Never Entered My Mind' contains a couple of phrases that suggest he has taken on board Miles's definitive version. 'Ballad Of The Sad Young Men' includes an unexpected – perhaps unintentional – spark of humour, and 'Glad To Be Unhappy' exactly catches the ambivalence of the title. The title-track – an original – is probably the weakest thing on the set, but it's established itself by then and fans will be delighted by it. We remain unmoved, if grudgingly impressed.

*****(*) Standard Time, Volume 4 – Marsalis Plays Monk**

Columbia CK 67503 *Marsalis; Wycliffe Gordon (tb); Wessell Anderson (as); Walter Blanding, Victor Goines (ts); Eric Reed (p); Reginald Veal, Ben Wolfe (b); Herlin Riley (d).* 9/93–10/94.

Fascinating that Wynton's stated intention for this near-inevitable but long-deferred encounter should be to recast Monk's music in the form of the ensemble jazz of Louis Armstrong's jazz orchestras of 1927 and 1928. A double homage, or a deliberate act of subversion of the great modernist? Marsalis's own characterization sums up the unexpected sound of the fourth *Standard Time* project: '... [T]extural changes. Thick ensembles, then a duet, or just a few people playing. Breaks. Surprises. Long solos. Very short ones. Strange tags on the end of tunes.'

At first hearing this is a hard record to date and a hard record to place instantly as Marsalis's work. We have listed it out of strict chronological sequence because these sessions lay in the vault for nearly six years before release and they do, to some extent, need to be heard in a different context because of that. Marsalis uses himself quite sparingly as a soloist, placing the emphasis very much on ensemble values. The problem is perhaps that he has not stamped an individuality and authority firmly enough on music that will always have the last laugh on any revisionist. The jaggy urgency of 'Evidence' and the almost skittish playfulness of 'We See' which follows point to the extremes the album skirts and hint at some of its oddity of mood, though this oddity is of a different sort from Monk's.

Perhaps predictably, Marsalis has chosen to include amid the 14 tracks some less well-known items: 'Worry Later', 'Brake's Sake' and 'Let's Cool One' may take some moments to provenance. The standard of playing is as high and as disciplined as ever. The melting unisons of 'Monk's Mood' are glorious, and Marsalis and Anderson weave some absolute magic on 'Hackensack', but it's as hard as ever to approach this with affection rather than admiration.

***** Standard Time, Volume 5: The Midnight Blues**

Columbia CK 68921 *Marsalis; Eric Reed (p); Reginald Veal (b); Lewis Nash (d); strings.* 9/98.

Interestingly, this time out, Stanley Crouch's liner-note steers sharply away from rhetorical underpinning of Marsalis's traditionalism. Instead, it's a miniature film treatment about a woman called Ardella Jefferson, who divides her time between 'reading Derek Walcott's Nobel Lecture, 'The Antilles: Fragments of Epic Memory', and musing on the sound of trumpet and strings.

Compare these dozen immaculately executed tracks with, say, Chet Baker's final concerts and it immediately becomes clear that Ardella's likening of the sound to 'a brass cherry' on top of orchestral cream is all too accurate. Even with busted chops and no great appetite for the struggle, Chet sounded lived-in, wearily passionate, precariously alive. Marsalis plays with total authority, but the effect is still hard and oddly virginal. 'Glad To Be Unhappy' touches neither end of the spectrum convincingly, and yet as an exercise in controlled articulation it is genuinely awe-inspiring. Only Frank Sinatra was ever able to pull off a whole album of such uniform melancholy, because Frank was able to invest loss and absence with a complex freight of experience. Marsalis can't quite avoid referencing Miles's classic 'It Never Entered My Mind' and thereby throwing up another unflattering point of comparison.

The muted solo on 'Baby, Won't You Please Come Home' is thin and weakly recorded, the only time that Steve Epstein and Todd Whitelock's open and unscreened 'live' recording at the Masonic Grande Lodge in New York City sounded underpowered. The emotional charge picks up almost at the end with a superb reading of 'My Man's Gone Now', four and a half minutes that are almost worth all the rest put together, but then Marsalis throws away the moment with the long and indulgent title-track, a mini-opera without conflict and without a convincing protagonist.

****** Mr Jelly Lord: Standard Time – Volume Six**

Columbia CK 69872 *Marsalis; Lucien Barbarin (tb); Wycliffe Gordon (tb, tba, t); Wessell Anderson (as); Victor Goines (ss, ts, cl); Michael White (cl); Harry Connick Jr, Eric Lewis, Danilo Perez, Eric Reed (p); Donald Vappie (bjo, g); Reginald Veal (b); Herlin Riley (d).* 1/99 (12/93).

Sometimes even Wynton must wish Stanley Crouch would keep his mouth shut. Likening these modern – but unmodernized – versions of Jelly Roll Morton tunes to actor/director Kenneth Branagh's Shakespearean films isn't necessarily the most helpful imprimatur. As it turns out, Wynton's performance needs no Mortonesque hyperbole. There is no attempt to lend these astonishing compositions any false grandeur; they have quite enough as it is.

Wynton's playing has rarely sounded so relaxed and so raw. Even his cover-picture, looking tired, slumped astride a packing crate and resting an elbow on his instrument, suggests a measure of artisanly relaxation, like a man just coming off shift rather than a man waiting backstage at Carnegie Hall. 'The Pearls' and 'Dead Man Blues' see him reach levels of expression that will astonish even admirers.

Perez and Connick have cameo parts only, but the basic line-up is by now a familiar one. We have never been persuaded by the clarinet playing of Dr Michael White, which almost sounds a quarter-note sharp, but the two trombone players are majestically idiomatic (as at least one of them should be, bearing a name like Barbarin) and the saxophonists never sound as if they are on day-release from Bebop Academy. Our only faint quibble would be the drumming of Herlin Riley, which occasionally seems anachronistic.

A must for blindfold tests of the future is track 15. On 6 December 1993, Wynton and pianist Eric Reed went to the Edison National Historic Site at West Orange, New Jersey, and recorded 'Tom Cat Blues' direct to a wax cylinder. The result is still unmistakably Marsalis, but the old technology helps provide a ghostly coda to a remarkable record.

****** Live At the Village Vanguard**

Columbia ACK 61408/14 7CD (US) / 8CD (Europe) *Marsalis; Wycliffe Gordon (tb); Wessell Anderson (as); Victor Goines, Todd Williams (ts); Marcus Roberts, Eric Reed (p); Reginald Veal, Ben Wolfe (b); Herlin Riley (d).* 3/90–12/94.

Priced as a bargain deal and presented as a parade of great sets at jazz's most celebrated venue, here's Wynton and his men across a four-year span, with some eight hours of music (European collectors have a bonus CD in their edition, although that runs to only some 25 extra minutes of music). The discs are programmed to represent a week's work, with each having a different character, of sorts. Besides new versions of some choice pieces from his own canon, there are standards, blues, plenty of Monk, 40 minutes of 'Citi Movement', and 55 minutes of 'In The Sweet Embrace Of Life'. Wynton chaffs with the audience, welcomes celebrities – Sweets Edison, Lionel Hampton – and generally sets out to make sure that everyone has a good time. It's a fun set to play through: the music always seems lively and on its toes, the band precise but flying on the flair of the leader and his appetite for work. Besides the leader's playing, perhaps the greatest pleasure comes in the efforts of Veal, Wolfe and Riley, an engine-room of superb polish and palpable swing.

There are some inevitable historical parallels – with Rollins at the Vanguard, or, more specifically, with the comprehensiveness of the Miles Davis *Plugged Nickel* set. Yet this is a more calculated scripture than those on-the-hoof documents, and it suits the moment of the Marsalis doctrine. What one hears is elegance and poise; there is little in the way of risk, even less in the way of danger. But that is Wynton's way, and for the duration of this set – and kudos to him for releasing a lot of music for a modest price – it sounds terrific.

Warne Marsh (1927–87)

TENOR SAXOPHONE

Marsh's death onstage was a strangely fitting end to a life that seemed to have been spent mid-solo, unweaving one of his long, linear improvisations set against a deceptively simple and unembellished beat. Born in Los Angeles, he came under the influence of Lennie Tristano and, along with Lee Konitz, was Lennie's most prominent disciple. His association with the altoist was close but not as long-standing as is often thought. Marsh's slightly dry, almost papery tone is instantly recognizable.

***** Music For Prancing**

VSOP 8 *Marsh; Ronnie Ball (p); Red Mitchell (b); Stan Levey (d).* 57.

By far the most loyal and literal of the Tristano disciples, Warne Marsh sedulously avoided the 'jazz life', cleaving to an improvisatory philosophy that was almost chilling in its purity. Anthony Braxton called him the 'greatest vertical improviser' in the music, and a typical Marsh solo was discursive and rhythmically subtle, full of coded tonalities and oblique resolutions. He cultivated a glacial tone (somewhat derived from Lester Young) that splintered awkwardly in the higher register and which can be off-putting for listeners conditioned by Bird and Coltrane.

The early quartet is witty and smooth-toned, though Marsh sounds much closer to Stan Getz than he was in later years. The warmth is leavened by a rhythm section led by the remarkable Mitchell, whose unusual tunings and almost offhand ability to turn out terse countermelodies are a key element of a fine record.

*****(*) Release Record – Send Tape**

Wave CD 6 *Marsh; Ronnie Ball (p); Peter Ind (b); Dick Scott (d).* 12/59–8/60.

Recorded largely at Peter Ind's home studio and consisting almost entirely of improvised solos played without the original melody, this was considered commercial suicide on first release in 1967, but Marsh's growing reputation since then and certainly posthumously has justified Ind's confidence. The lightness of the saxophonist's touch and the agility of his playing are reminiscent of his fellow Tristano pupil, Lee Konitz, but with more substance on open-ended tunes like 'Sweet Georgia Brown' and 'Alone Together', where the chords are susceptible of almost infinite variation. Konitz has always tended to favour tighter structures. What shines through here is a capacious musical intelligence which turns each of these brief performances – only the improvised 'Marshlight' is longer than five minutes – into something much more substantial.

*****(*) Warne Marsh / Lee Konitz: Volume 1**

Storyville STCD 4094 *Marsh; Lee Konitz (as); Ole Kock Hansen (p); Niels-Henning Orsted Pedersen (b); Svend Erik Norregaard (d).* 12/75.

***** Warne Marsh / Lee Konitz: Volume 2**
Storyville STCD 4095 *As above.* 12/75.

***** Warne Marsh / Lee Konitz: Volume 3**
Storyville STCD 4096 *As above.* 12/75.

***** Live At The Montmartre Club: Volume 1**
Storyville STCD 8201 *As above, except add Alex Riel (d).* 12/75.

***** Live At The Montmartre Club: Volume 2**
Storyville STCD 8202 *As above.* 12/75.

***** Live At The Montmartre Club: Volume 3**
Storyville STCD 8203 *As above.* 12/75.

Marsh's reputation still falls far short of that of his exact contemporary, Lee Konitz, with whom he interlocks gracefully like dancing master and pupil on the live sessions from Fasching in Stockholm and the parallel sets from the Jazzhus Montmartre in Copenhagen. Where Konitz changed down the years, Marsh remained a dogged strict-constructionist, perhaps the last major exponent of Tristano's 'Cool School'. By the time of this much-heralded tour, Lee had moved somewhat to the left in musical terms and was playing a personalized bebop, as is evident on 'Au Privave' and 'Chi Chi' (*Montmartre: Volume 3*). Marsh isn't left behind on the Parker tunes but they aren't quite his meat, and he attempts to spin the short, segmented themes out into longer, much more discursive and angular forms; by no means unattractive, but slightly alien to the concept.

***** Unissued 1975 Studio Recordings**
Storyville 8259 *Marsh; Dave Cliff (g); Niels-Henning Orsted Petersen (b); Alan Levitt (d).* 12/75.

*****(*) Unissued Copenhagen Studio Recordings**
Storyville 8278 *As above, except omit Cliff.* 12/75.

Marsh rarely played standards as straightforwardly as this, and these discs, released only in the late '90s, are a revelation for anyone who has tried to trace Marsh's course on record. The earlier disc, with Cliff providing harmonic accompaniment, is the less interesting, but there is no denying its attractiveness, and on 'God Bless The Child' the saxophonist touches areas of emotion rarely associated with him. The second album, recorded during the same sessions, comprises a dozen familiar tunes, from Parker's 'Confirmation' (already a contrafact) to 'When You're Smiling' and 'Every Time We Say Goodbye'. Supported by NHOP and the inventive Alan Levitt, he turns in a series of performances that confirm his brilliance as a melodic improviser. This is the kind of music that was to influence later avant-gardists like Anthony Braxton, who instinctively responded to Marsh's flow of ideas.

***** I Got A Good One For You**
Storyville STCD 8277 *Marsh; Kenny Drew (p); Jesper Lundgaard (b); Alex Riel (d).*

For some reason, Marsh seems haunted by the spirit of Charlie Parker on this fine quartet session, which comprises 11 tersely performed bebop and standard themes. His solos on 'Sippin' At Bell's', 'Ornithology' and 'Star Eyes' are bursting with melodic ideas. Drew's accompaniment is only slightly marred by what sounds like a rather dull piano.

*****(*) Star Highs**
Criss Cross 1002 *Marsh; Hank Jones (p); George Mraz (b); Mel Lewis (d).* 8/82.

***** A Ballad Album**
Criss Cross 1007 *Marsh; Lou Levy (p); Jesper Lundgaard (b); James Martin (d).* 4/83.

***** Newly Warne**
Storyville STCD 4162 *Marsh; Susan Chen (p); George Mraz (b); Akira Tana (d).* 3/85.

***** Back Home**
Criss Cross 1023 *Marsh; Jimmy Halperin (ts); Barry Harris (p); David Williams (b); Albert 'Tootie' Heath (d).* 3/86.

The Criss Crosses are a strong sequence, with *Star Highs* definitely the one to plump for. Listen to the straightened-out 'Moose The Mooche', on which Marsh does his patented elongation and simplification of the melody and its rhythmic accompaniment. So entire is it that theme and solos almost sound through-composed. Barry Harris and Albert 'Tootie' Heath are highly responsive on *Back Home*, with the pianist playing in a boppish blues idiom similar to that of Hawes 30 years before. Jimmy Halperin is a superfluous presence on *Back Home*, taking a second tenor part on 'Two, Not One', but adding nothing of substance to Warne's edgy solo.

***** Two Days In The Life Of ...**
Storyville STCD 4165 *Marsh; Ron Eschete (g); Jim Hughart (b); Sherman Ferguson (d).* 87.

Just before Christmas 1987, Marsh collapsed and died at Donte's; he was playing 'Out Of Nowhere'. *Two Days* was recorded late in the day and with no warning that the end is already in view. Marsh plays superbly to a very routine accompaniment, and only flashes of invention from the drummer relieve the one-dimensional nature of the group. Marsh, as ever, needs to be listened to patiently and carefully. The discography is in better shape than it used to be but someone needs to do some serious reconstruction work, and we still await CD reissue of important albums on Atlantic, Revelation and Wave.

Tina Marsh & CO2

GROUP

Founded around 1980, this Texas-based ensemble is directed by Marsh, a vocalist–composer, and works in a style that bridges free playing and contemporary orchestration.

****(*) The Heaven Line**
CreOpMuse 002 *Martin Banks, Dennis Gonzalez, Larry Spencer (t); Randy Zimmerman, James Lakey (tb); Alex Coke, John Mills, Greg Wilson (reeds); Bob Rodriguez (p); Jay Rozen (tba); Ken Filiano (b); Billy Mintz (d); Tina Marsh (v).* 1/92–11/93.

***** Worldwide**
CreOpMuse 005 *As above, except add Paul Armstrong (t), René Saenz, Jay Fort (reeds), Edwin Livingston (b), Mark Kusey (d), Oliver Rajamani (perc); omit Gonzalez, Coke, Wilson, Filiano, Mintz.* 6/97.

Marsh has been active with her Creative Opportunity Orchestra for some 20 years, although documentation has been only sparse. These CDs offer a mixed result. *The Heaven Line* is rather disappointing after a strong vinyl-only session for Daagnim. A concert recording from Austin, Texas, the sound is misty and the compositions, while they have their moments, are a shapeless group of pieces, boosted here and there by soloists of character. *Worldwide* is a studio recording and a good deal more convincing. John Mills's opening 'Flywheel' is almost a 'conventional' big-band swinger. But the tone of the music is set principally by Marsh herself, and the listeners' response will depend on how they react to her wordless vocalizing and forays into what we are (probably disrespectfully) hearing as New Age philosophizing. 'Milky Way Dreaming', which includes a text by schoolchildren, is one big example. We prefer Rodriguez's thoughtful 'Homage' and Fort's 'Ballad Borscht'.

Claire Martin (born 1967)

VOCALS

Relaxed, technically sound and able to invest a lyric with genuine drama, Martin was the most exciting female jazz singer to emerge in the '90s. As well as original and standard material, she has shown how contemporary rock and pop material is adaptable to her unfussy and emotionally nuanced approach.

***** The Waiting Game**

Linn AKD 018 *Martin; Jim Mullen (g); Jonathan Gee (p); Arnie Somogyi (b); Clark Tracey (d).* 12/91.

*****(*) Devil May Care**

Linn AKD 021 *As above, except add Rick Taylor (tb, perc), Nigel Hitchcock (as), Iain Ballamy (ts, ss).* 2/93.

*****(*) Old Boyfriends**

Linn AKD 028 *As for The Waiting Game, except replace Gee with Steve Melling (p).* 5/94.

Martin was an inspired signing for Linn, but one wonders how she would have developed if she'd been picked up by Blue Note or Concord. She has always surrounded herself with sympathetic players, but one does wonder to what extent they push her hard enough. The voice matures considerably between *The Waiting Game* and *Devil May Care*, not so much in range or articulation as in sheer expressiveness. Martin never overdramatizes or dwells indulgently on a lyric, but delivers it with commendable conviction. She brings a playful poise to Bob Dorough's 'Devil May Care', a song that can sound more arch than Broxburn Viaduct, and she gives Noël Coward's 'If Love Were All' just the right mixture of sentiment and stiff upper lip. The other significant factor about the second album was Martin's songwriting skill. She has absorbed enough from the masters to handle the idiom with some confidence, and 'On Thin Ice' is a superb creation. Puzzlingly, and with the exception of the boppish 'Chased Out', co-written with Arnie Somogyi, the songs on *Old Boyfriends* are all covers. A later reference to writer's block may explain the hiatus. They are, though, covers which are picked with taste and imagination. Harold Arlen's 'When The Sun Comes Out' is a relatively conventional warm-up, but it's followed by an emotionally eclectic range of material, including Rupert Holmes's tough 'Partners In Crime', Artie Shaw's 'Moon Ray' and Jonathan Blair's oddly affecting 'I've Got News', which is as moving an account of the end of an affair as anyone's ever put to music. The Tom Waits-composed title-song is one that was written for Coppola's *One From The Heart*, and Martin delivers it straight from Breast Central. Not quite a concept album, but one that has a satisfyingly melancholy coherence, capped by Jule Styne and the late, great Carolyn Leigh's 'Gentleman Friend'.

It should have been much harder to replace Jonathan Gee, but Steve Melling does an impressive job, paving the way for a more intimate, less hectic approach on subsequent outings with Gareth Williams, who may yet turn out – with producer Joel E. Siegel and enthusiastic patron Richard Rodney Bennett – to be Claire Martin's most significant collaborator.

***** Offbeat**

Linn AKD 049 *Martin; Mark Nightingale (tb); Gareth Williams (p); Martin Taylor (g); Anthony Kerr (vib); Arnie Somogyi (b); Clark Tracey (d).* 8/95.

****** Make This City Ours**

Linn AKD 066 *Martin; Gerard Presencer (t, flhn); Antonio Hart (as); Gareth Williams (p, v); Peter Washington (b); Gregory Hutchinson (d).* 10/96.

Martin approached her thirtieth birthday with a solid reputation on both sides of the Atlantic, but not yet with a statement on record that matches up to her live presence. *Offbeat* was recorded at Ronnie Scott's with a working group, but not even guest spots like label-mate Martin Taylor's superb cameo on 'Some Other Time', a delightful encore duo, lift what seems with hindsight a rather pedestrian album compared to what preceded it and what was to follow. 'Wishful Thinking', co-written by David Newton (who also scored 'Victim Of Circumstance' on *Devil May Care*), is perhaps the high spot, and there are some vivid exchanges between Williams and Tracey.

If one album deserves to establish Martin as a singer with real star potential, then it's *Make This City Ours*. Even the title sounds like a confident declaration of intent. Recorded in New York, with Washington, Hart and Hutchinson guesting, it has a more international sound, a more cosmopolitan feel than any of its predecessors. Presencer's trumpet playing conveys a nice mixture of innocence and faintly weary maturity, and Hart always sounds good around singers. There is a new Martin composition, 'Empty Bed', which bodes well for more from that source. There are still occasional lapses into formula: 'Another Night' doesn't sound entirely assured, and an arrangement of Bruno Martino's 'Estate' with words by Joel Siegel doesn't quite come off. For the most part, though, this is an ideal showcase. (A word, too, for William Claxton: at last, a photographer who can make Claire look as beautiful on her album covers as she is in person.)

*****(*) Perfect Alibi**

Linn AKD 122 *Martin; Duncan McKay (t); Nichol Thomson (tb); Mornington Lockett (ts, cl); Charlotte Glasson (bs, f); Jo Richards (f); Jason Rebello (p); Robin Aspland (ky); Paul Stacey (ky, g); Andy Wallace (org); Anthony Kerr (vib); Arnie Somogyi (b); Andrew Newmark, Mathew Skeaping, Jeremy Stacey (d); Luis Jardim (perc); John Martyn (v).* 11/99, 1 & 2/00.

A range of material from Hendrix and Todd Rundgren to Laura Nyro and Julia Fordham, and an astonishing duet with John

Martyn on his 'Man In The Station' make this Claire's most inventively adventurous album to date. It also takes her a half-step away from a conventional jazz repertoire, but so thoroughly is her style invested in the jazz tradition that the feel is consistent, improvisational and un-trendy. Phoebe Snow's 'Inspired Insanity' is the closest it gets to pure pop, a tendency nicely balanced by Al Kooper's 'More Than You'll Ever Know' and Hendrix's 'Up From The Skies'. The instrumentation and arrangements (largely by Paul Stacey and Charlotte Glasson) are varied from track to track and *Perfect Alibi* once again has the feel of a well-planned and modulated jazz set.

Stu Martin

DRUMS, ELECTRONICS

Drummer whose pioneer work in jazz-rock is documented with The Trio and a few other ensemble records from the early '70s.

***** Live At Woodstock Town Hall**

BGO CD 290 *Martin; John Surman (ss, bcl, syn).* 75.

We have also noted this record under John Surman's name, but Martin's is listed first and the music is based on a radio serial he devised with the House of Four. It tells the story of 'Harry Lovett – Man Without A Country' who is transformed by the Masters of the Universe into Mr Everything, a cross between Superman and John the Baptist. The opening is fabulously arresting: slamming synth chords and splashy drum sounds are the launch pad for a high-register soprano line that could hardly be simpler or more effective. Squalls of electronic distortion interrupt before the track settles down to a bluesy unravelling of the original idea.

To be honest, nothing else on the album quite matches up to its first four minutes. One very quickly ceases to care about Harry, and only Surman's intense, burning lines engage the attention, especially his linear solo on 'Professor Goodly's Implosion Machine'. Martin all too readily trades in subtlety for headachey power, though he is also capable of genuine poignancy. At just over 35 minutes, it's a skimpy delivery for a full-price CD; anyone seriously interested is directed to a good-value twofer with Surman's fine *Where Fortune Smiles*, reviewed under Surman's entry.

Pat Martino (born 1944)

GUITAR

Born In Philadelphia, Martino was working as a teenager in combos led by Jack McDuff, Willis Jackson, Don Patterson, 'Groove' Holmes and others. His career was interrupted by illness in 1980, following which he had to completely re-learn his playing technique, and it was not until 1984 that he began working again. Although seldom recognized as an influence, he has been a distinctive and resourceful figure in jazz guitar for many years, and his fine technique and determination have inspired many players.

****(*) El Hombre**

Original Jazz Classics OJC 195 *Martino; Danny Turner (f); Trudy Pitts (org); Mitch Fine (d); Abdu Johnson, Vance Anderson (perc).* 5/67.

***** Strings!**

Original Jazz Classics OJC 223 *Martino; Joe Farrell (ts, f); Cedar Walton (p); Ben Tucker (b); Walter Perkins (d); Ray Appleton, Dave Levine (perc).* 10/67.

***** East!**

Original Jazz Classics OJC 248 *Martino; Eddie Green (p); Tyrone Brown, Ben Tucker (b); Lennie McBrowne (d).* 1/68.

**** Baiyina (The Clear Evidence)**

Original Jazz Classics OJC 355 *Martino; Gregory Herbert (as, f); Bobby Rose (g); Richard Davis (b); Charli Persip (d); Reggie Ferguson (perc); Balakrishna (tamboura).* 6/68.

***** Desperado**

Original Jazz Classics OJC 397 *Martino; Eric Kloss (ss); Eddie Green (p); Tyrone Brown (b); Sherman Ferguson (d).* 3/70.

After graduating from soul-jazz organ combos and the John Handy group, Martino led his own bands on a series of records for Prestige, all of which have now been reissued in the OJC series. Both *El Hombre* and *Strings!* depend on blues-based formulas and are typical of the genre; but Martino's maturing style – heavily indebted to Grant Green and Wes Montgomery, but built for greater speed than either of those masters – is good enough to transcend the settings. *Strings!* is noteworthy for a long, burning treatment of Gigi Gryce's 'Minority', where Farrell's thunderous tenor solo is matched by equally flying statements by Martino and Walton. Aside from the prophetically 'mystical' title-track, *East* offers some of Martino's clearest and most articulate soloing against a straightforward rhythm section. *Baiyina* nodded towards incense and peppermints with its noodling rhythm parts, but Martino's own playing remained tough underneath, and the rambling themes sometimes dissolved in the face of his improvising. *Desperado* is a little-known stab at fusion: Martino plays electric 12-string against rumbling electric piano and bass, and the results are akin to a tighter, less violent Lifetime. 'Express' and 'Desperado' hit a particularly compelling movement, although Green isn't a very stimulating partner (Kloss plays on only one track, 'Blackjack'). All the OJC remastering is good, although *Desperado*'s original production betrays how engineers didn't really know how to deal with that sort of music at the time.

*****(*) Head And Heart**

32 Jazz 32050 2CD *Martino; Ron Thomas, Eddie Green (p); Tyrone Brown (b); Sherman Ferguson (d).* 9/72–10/74.

*****(*) Impressions**

Camden 74321 610802 2CD *As above, except add Gil Goldstein (p), Richard Davis (b).* 9/72–2/76.

Martino spent the early 1970s with Muse, producing another strong and undervalued series of records. Now folded into the new 32 operation, so far these have made a repackaged appearance. *Head And Heart* is a twofer that couples the original albums, *Live!* and *Consciousness*. *Live!* consists of three long, rocking workouts that show how the guitarist can rework simple material into sustained improvisations of elegant and accessible fire: even when he plays licks, they sound plausibly exciting. *Consciousness* was a little more ballad-orientated, with a charming solo 'Both Sides Now', but Martino is still in terrific shape on the sambafied version of 'Along Came Betty' and in quite a torrid treatment of 'Impressions'.

Very good; but even better is the (British) RCA Camden twofer, *Impressions*, which combines those albums and the 1976 *Exit*. These six extra tracks offer a fine quartet date with Gil Goldstein on piano, and they find Martino playing at full tilt with a very sympathetic rhythm section.

***** All Sides Now**

Blue Note 837627-2 *Martino; Charlie Hunter, Kevin Eubanks, Les Paul, Joe Satriani, Mike Stern, Tuck Andress, Lou Pollo (g); Paul Nowinski, Scott Colley (b); Ben Perowsky, Michael Hedges, Jeff Hirshfield (d); Cassandra Wilson (v).* 6/96–1/97.

Martino arrives at Blue Note for a typical example of the jazz concept album. An improbably eclectic team of guitarists line up for a series of duets, with the perhaps inevitable result that the album stops and starts, and ends up a bit of a mess. There are some genuinely compelling episodes: the sparring with Charlie Hunter on 'Too High', the tough virtuosity of the meeting with Eubanks on 'Progression', the purling lyricism of 'Two Of A Kind', with Tuck Andress. On the debit side are the ponderous 'Both Sides Now' with Cassandra Wilson, two fairly meaningless chunks of interplay with Joe Satriani and the OK-but-effortful tracks with Mike Stern. Martino himself can largely be exempted from criticism: he brings dedication and inventiveness to all the tracks and earns the stars on his own. But this isn't a great deal of fun as a whole album.

***** Stone Blue**

Blue Note 853082-2 *Martino; Eric Alexander (ts); Delmar Brown (ky); James Genus (b); Kenwood Dennard (d).* 2/98.

Concentrated around the band which Martino calls Joyous Lake, this is an energetic and spirited album which has a lot of fine Martino guitar on it, as well as lusty blowing from Alexander. But its merits are compromised by the vague nods towards modishness provided by Brown's keyboards, sound effects and so forth. Martino is a player's player, like, say, John Scofield or Jim Hall: whatever his roots in the soul-jazz of the 1960s onwards, he doesn't really need trappings which are going to date the record more quickly than it deserves. If you can filter out the smooth-jazz inflexions that surround him, you'll find Pat in gregarious mood here.

Barry Martyn (born 1941)

DRUMS, VOCAL

Formed his own band in London at sixteen and visited New Orleans in 1961, where he became a tremendous force for organizing tours and recordings for the local players and visitors, also bringing them back to Europe. In Los Angeles from 1972 and resident in New Orleans from 1984. A tireless promoter of original New Orleans jazz, with a special interest in the brass band medium.

***** Vintage Barry Martyn**

GHB BCD-75 *Martyn; Clive Blackmore, Dennis Jones, Cuff Billett (t); Mike Pointon, Pete Dyer, Freddy John (tb); John Defferary (cl, as); Sammy Rimington, Dick Douthwaite (cl); Bill Greenow (as); Ken Saunders (ts); Graham Paterson, John Marks (p); John Coles, Bill Stagg (bj); John Renshaw, Bill Cole, Terry Knight, Brian Turnock (b).* 11/59–70.

**** On Tour 1969**

GHB BCD-255 *Martyn; Clive Wilson (t); Frank Naundorf (tb); Dick Douthwaite (cl, as); Jon Marks (p); Brian Turnock (b).* 68.

****(*) Legends Of Jazz & Barney Bigard**

GHB BCD-338 *Martyn; Andrew Blakeney (t, v); Louis Nelson (tb); Barney Bigard, Joe Darensbourg (cl); Alton Purnell (p, v); Ed Garland (b).* 5/74.

***** Barry Martyn's Down Home Boys**

Sackville KCD2-3056 *Martyn; Wendell Eugene (tb); Chris Burke (cl); Ron Simpson (g).* 10/93.

This cigar-chomping Londoner went to New Orleans in 1961 and became an unlikely champion of the city's traditional jazz. Basing his own style around that of the New Orleans masters, he not only sought out his heroes but played with them, recorded them and conducted interviews that have become integral to the archives on the music. At the moment there are still only a few of his many records available on CD, and this handful is rather unrepresentative. *Vintage Barry Martyn* collars four different British sessions – from Southall, New Bond Street and Basingstoke! – starting with 'Kid' Martyn's early group (including Rimington, and Clive Blackmore lying on the floor to sing the vocal on 'Robert E. Lee') and getting as far as 1970. Some of it is little more than amateur enthusiasm, but the music gets stronger as it goes on and Martyn himself is unfailingly swinging in the New Orleans style. His own memories in the sleeve-note are a priceless record in themselves.

The 1968 set features a band of Brits whose ardour doesn't wholly make up for the lack of finesse on ancient history such as 'Dardanella'; the recording sounds rusty, too. Martyn formed his Legends Of Jazz with a crew of venerable old-timers in 1973, and they became something of a festival attraction. This is quite a spirited recording, with guest Bigard sounding much stronger than he does on the *Pelican Trio* sessions (listed under Bigard's name). Some of the pieces shake along rather than swing, and Purnell's two vocals sound like pure sandpaper, but somehow Martyn (who was some 40 years junior to all the others) makes the whole thing work. His playing is strong enough to lift the band but never rough enough to knock the players about.

The recent Sackville CD is a good-natured jazz beano and, though the interesting instrumentation is never used to any surprising ends, the way that the players seem to blend agility with amiable sloppiness is rather beguiling. Bonus marks for playing 'Blue Hawaii', 'Sail Along Silvery Moon' and 'Dolores' instead of the usual old scrolls.

***** On The Sophisticated Side**

Jazzology JCD-282 *Martyn; Freddy John, Mike Owen (tb); Chris Burke (cl); Jan Engebretsen (p); Les Muscutt (bj); Bill Evans (b).* 4/97.

Martyn having fun with this pair of 'bones (Burke and Muscutt make a single appearance only). The material stretches from 'Tuxedo Junction' to 'Sleepy Lagoon' and much of it is borderline novelty music, but the Kid's drumming swings as famously as ever and Engebretsen is a strong two-fisted pianist.

Hugh Masekela (born 1939)

TRUMPET, FLUGELHORN, VOCALS

Though a minor figure on his own terms as an instrumentalist, Masekela is significant as a South African jazzman who worked in both the US and British scenes, before returning to Africa and rooting his playing in its home soil.

*****(*) The Lasting Impressions Of Ooga Booga**
Verve 531630 *Masekela; Larry Willis (p); Harold Dotson (b); Henry Jenkins (d).* 65.

Masekela is one of the key figures in South African music, a passionate voice whose sound has the throaty urgency of a street-corner preacher and the delicacy of emotion associated with Miles Davis and Chet Baker. At twenty, Masekela was a founder member, with Dollar Brand and Kippie Moeketsi, of the Jazz Epistles, South Africa's first significant jazz group. Masekela then married singer Miriam Makeba and left South Africa for the United States, recording classic songs like 'Grazin' In The Grass' (which sold four million copies and climbed to the top of the pop charts) and becoming a spokesman and icon of the anti-apartheid movement. *The Lasting Impressions Of Ooga Booga* is a compilation of two records taped live at the Village Gate in the winter of 1965. The original LP release, *The Americanization Of Ooga Booga*, was not initially followed, and it was only after the success of Masekela's blend of township *mbaqanga* and what he himself dubbed 'township bop' that the remaining tracks were released as *The Lasting Impression Of Hugh Masekela*, one track of which has been omitted on this reissue for reasons of space. Masekela's plangent, vocalized tone is unmistakable and these tunes, written by himself, Makeba, Willis and Caiphus Semenya, are among the strongest he ever recorded. Herbie Hancock's 'Canteloupe Island' is a reminder of how different he was from American jazz musicians of the same generation; the familiar changes are utterly transformed, pushed out into new harmonic and rhythmic territory. A marvellous record, both of its time and timeless, two great continents in fruitful collision.

****(*) Notes Of Life**
Columbia 48450 *Masekela; Trevor Gordon, Tim Hoare (ky, b); Paul Haumer, Themba Mkhize (ky); Lawrence Matchizai, Miles Shannon (g); Fana Zulu, Peter Sklair (b); Cedric Samson (d, perc); Faith Kekana, Stella Khumalo, Mandisa Dlanga, Wendy Mseleku, Wings Segale, Bongani Masuku, Sipho Nxumalo, Zamo Mbutho (v).* 95.

***** Black To The Future**
Columbia 489477 *Masekela; Jasper Cook (tb); Khaya Mahlangu (ts, f); Bushy Seatlholo (p); Don Laka (ky); Kenny Mathaba, John Selolwane (g); Tuli Masoka (b); Jethro Shasha (d); Godfrey Mgcina (perc); Family Factory, Children of Mathaba Centre (v).* 97.

Masekela's best record, the Chisa recording, *Home Is Where The Music Is*, remains to be reissued, but recent years have seen a resurgence of activity, both in the back-catalogue and in new recording. A deal with Columbia yielded two recordings which might be thought of as Masekela's *Tutu* and *Amandla*, not because of their political agenda, which are quiet and understated, but because musically both sound recycled and off the pace. Returning to a changed South Africa was inevitably a charged and emotional experience, but for Masekela it also seemed to blunt the edge of his playing. Never before had he sounded so unfocused and prettified. *Black To The Future* is the stronger of the two, not because the writing is better, but simply because there is more convinced playing. *Notes Of Life* has a cheesy, Afro-pop quality which will disappoint Masekela's fans. The later album brings together some of the best musicians in present-day South Africa and, while there is no Mongezi Feza or Kippie Moeketsi coming through, Khaya Mahlangu is a forceful and exciting player, and there is no mistaking the professionalism of the ensembles. The kids' choir sounds fantastic on 'Strawberries', one of the best tracks on *Black To The Future*. Masekela released a *Greatest Hits* album as we went to press, but the feeling persists that this talented musician has only rarely been served well by his recordings.

Keshavan Maslak aka Kenny Millions

ALTO SAXOPHONE, BASS CLARINET, SYNTHESIZERS, OTHER INSTRUMENTS

Born in New York but claiming Ukrainian ancestry, Maslak is a mercurial performer in a somewhat wild variety of styles and on a wide range of instruments, acoustic and otherwise.

***** Loved By Millions**
Leo CD LR 105 *Maslak; John Lindberg (b); Sunny Murray (d).* 10/80.

***** Mother Russia**
Leo CD LR 177 *Maslak (solo) and with Misha Alperin (p); Anatoly Vapirov (ts); Vladimir Tarasov (d).* 89.

***** Not To Be A Star**
Black Saint 120149 *Maslak; Paul Bley (p).* 10/92.

*****(*) Romance In The Big City**
Leo CD LR 104 *As above.* 2/93.

***** Excuse Me, Mr Satie**
Leo CD LR 199 *Maslak; Katsuyuki Itakura (p).* 5/94.

A talented but slightly enigmatic figure, Maslak cultivates a broadly satirical tone, as in the rock-influenced fantasies of another disc called *Loved By Millions* (formerly on ITM, but not to be confused with the fierce free-bop session listed above) and in 'Kenny Meets Misha Meets Hieronymus Bosch' on *Mother Russia*. The second Leo set was recorded during a tour of Lithuania and Ukraine. His technique is boppish, but with elements of abstraction; the satire in no way deflects or compromises his virtuosity. An extraordinarily overblown passage in the duet with pianist Alperin is sustained over nearly a minute by circular breathing, punctuating a folksy romp, some funeral music and a couple of cheesy dance tunes. The duets with Vapirov, 'One/Two/Three/Four Million Little Russians', are more intense but sound very dated. The real core of the album, and best confirmation of Maslak's quality, is the long duet with percussionist Tarasov, recorded on the same remarkable tour of the then Soviet Union. Considerably more accessible than most native Russian improvisation, Maslak's work is worth a look, and *Mother Russia* is the ideal place.

The duos with Bley on *Not To Be A Star* and *Romance In the Big City* are extraordinary, if beset by Maslak's gimmickry. All freely improvised – sometimes over lyrics written by Maslak in his Kenny Millions guise – they are some of the most intense and abstract performances the pianist has ever recorded, surprisingly so at a time when he seemed to have rediscovered the jazz heartland. Access to a 24-track studio allowed the saxophonist to multi-track himself on clarinet at a couple of points, and overall the first disc has less sheer impact than the less crisply recorded *Romance In The Big City*. Reissue of the 1980 record shows how little Maslak's basic approach has changed in the interim. Murray pushes him further than usual in the direction of abstraction, but the saxophonist tends to stick to a fairly linear programme nevertheless, creating an impression throughout that he is accompanying his own rhythm section. As on the other records, the music remains difficult to categorize: 'everyday magic/very deep/almost impossible to understand'.

The Satie session combines straight performances of 'Gnossiennes', 'Le Piège de Méduse' and other compositions by the maverick Frenchman, with interpolated 'excuse mes', executed in the Kenny Millions persona. As usual, the range of stylistic registers is sufficiently bewildering to suggest that passive acceptance is the best stratagem. A clever, funny show, it loses a little on record.

Phil Mason (born 1940)

CORNET

A Londoner, Mason has freelanced on the trad scene since the middle 1960s, and he formed his New Orleans All Stars in 1992.

****(*) You Do Something To Me!**
Lake LACD33 *Mason; Martin Bennett (tb, v); James Evans (cl, ts); Jim McIntosh (bj); Trefor Williams (b); Colin Bowden, Pete Cotterill (d); Christine Tyrrell (v).* 8/93.

****(*) West Indies Blues**
Lake LACD93 *Mason; Martin Bennett (tb, v); Paul Harrison (cl); Alan Bradley (p); Jim McIntosh (bj); Trefor Williams (b); Ron McKay, Pete Cotterill (d); Christine Tyrrell, Pauline Pearce (v).* 7/97.

***** Hush Hush**
Lake LACD111 *As above, except add Jonny Boston (cl, ts), Ronald Andersen (g), Spats Langham (bj); omit Harrison, Bradley, Cotterill, Pearce.* 5/98.

Methodical trad from a band given to no frills and not much licence. On *You Do Something To Me!* Mason's lead is decent enough, but it's Bennett's rather less predictable trombone parts that stand out in the ensembles. The foot-dragging tempos don't assist much, though.

West Indies Blues carries on regardless, and doesn't do an awful lot better. Tyrrell and Pearce both have distinctive voices, but neither is much of a singer. The surprise piece here is eight minutes of 'Davenport Blues' by a quartet of Mason, Cotterill, Williams and guest Bradley.

Hush Hush sees the group getting more eccentric. Andersen guests and plays a tinny-sounding electric in an amusingly shambling fashion, and Boston is a comparative firebrand who has an explosive go at 'Lester Leaps In', which for this group is almost the equivalent of going avant-garde. Not bad, and the best sound of the three discs.

Rod Mason (born 1940)

CLARINET, CORNET, VALVE TROMBONE, ALTO SAXOPHONE

A trad veteran whose playing goes back as far as Cy Laurie in 1959 and has taken in Sunshine, Bilk and the Dutch Swing College Band since, as well as his own groups.

***** Struttin' With Some Barbecue**
Black Lion BLCD 760511 *Mason; Pete Allen (cl, ts, bs); Jonny Withers (bj, g); Chris Haskins (b, v); Jimmy Garforth (d).* 1/77.

****(*) Hot Five**
Timeless TTD 538 *Mason; Joe Wulf (tb); Engelbert Wrobel (cl, as); Rainer Oeding (tba); Ray Smith (p); Udo Jaegers (bj, g).* 12/86.

****(*) Rod Mason's Hot Music**
Timeless TTD 550/551 *Mason; Achim Sturm, Uwe Schmidt, Karl-Heinz Weinz (t); Joe Wulf (tb, v); Engelbert Wrobel (cl, as); Hans Zaehringer (cl, ts, bs); Gerhard Muller (cl, ts); Ralph-Michel Peyer (p); Udo Jaegers (bj, g); Rainer Oeding (b, tba, p); Marcel Van Maele (perc).* 7/88.

An unreconstructed traditionalist, Mason often manages to sound like a computer-generated model of what traditional jazz is supposed to sound like. His bands tend to be stiffly correct and only rather mechanically swinging. There is doubtless a large market for material of this sort, and we could not in conscience suggest that any of these are less than professionally done, in either playing or performing terms; but they will prove to be thin pickings for anyone who knows anything of the originals, Mason's sources.

Masqualero

GROUP

Based around Balke's composing, this Norwegian group was a significant presence in their time, roughly 1985–91.

*****(*) Bande A Part**
ECM 829022-2 *Nils Petter Molvaer (t); Tore Brunborg (ts, ss); Jon Balke (p, ky); Arild Andersen (b); Jon Christensen (d).* 8 & 12/85.

***** Areo**
ECM 835767-2 *As above, except Frode Alnaes (g) replaces Balke.* 11/87.

*****(*) Re-Enter**
ECM 847939-2 *As above, except omit Alnaes.* 12/90.

Rooted on one of the finest rhythm sections in Europe, Masqualero occasionally sound like a self-conscious pastiche of the ECM sound: bleak, atonal passages grafted on to rippling polyrhythms, interspersed with sound-for-sound's-sake patterns from the horns and quiet, folksy melodies. What is interesting about the group's development over three albums is the abandonment (tactical or enforced) of harmony instruments in favour of a very stripped-down melodic approach that casts the bassist and drummer into appropriately high profile. It's routine to say that the two young frontmen are not up to the quality of the 'rhythm section', but Molvaer and Brunborg sound fresh and unaffected on the first album and matured considerably in the five years since then. Their contributions to 'Li'l Lisa', 'Re-Enter' and 'Gaia' on the third album are quite adventurous and certainly far in advance of anything attempted on the atmospheric *Bande A Part*. Nevertheless, that one is still probably the best of the three. *Areo* is not so good, for indefinable reasons that don't have anything obvious to do with the change in personnel. *Re-Enter* sounds a little tentative again, though it does sketch out some promising ways forward. But the group has done nothing more, and Molvaer in particular has moved down quite a different road since.

Cal Massey (1928–72)

TRUMPET

A bit-player in Philadelphia hard bop, Massey wrote for several important sessions and later bridged hard-bop and free forms in his playing; but he is relatively undocumented.

*** Blues To Coltrane

Candid CCD 9029 *Massey; Julius Watkins (frhn); Hugh Brodie (ts); Patti Brown (p); Jimmy Garrison (b); G.T Hogan (d).* 1/61.

A solitary glimpse of a briefly influential but slightly tragic figure, Massey recorded only once under his own name, and that was largely due to Nat Hentoff's generosity. He did, however, write some powerful music around this time, most notably 'The Damned Don't Cry' for his friend John Coltrane's *Africa/Brass* sessions. In the event, perhaps symbolically, it wasn't included on the original release, and Massey disappeared back into the shadows. For a long time, Massey was consigned to that curious circle of limbo reserved for artists known only from compilations and samplers. An excerpt of 'Father And Son', the most substantial piece on *Blues To Coltrane*, was included on a set called *The Jazz Life*. Full out, at 11 minutes, it's an impressive achievement which finally has the band sounding together. The opening 'Blues To Coltrane' is a raggy and faintly incoherent tribute, with Massey sounding a sharper, more anguished version of Wilbur Harden; Brodie is no Coltrane but needn't feel saddled with the comparison, for on his own terms he has some interesting ideas to impart, and a light, responsive sound. 'Bakai' was also written for Trane, who recorded it with trumpeter Johnny Splawn and baritonist Sahib Shihab on the 1957 *Coltrane*. In a previous edition we suggested that Massey's own version was less smooth, but it does also reveal subtleties in the keening, Arab-tinged theme which Coltrane and his colleagues seem unaware of. The same is true of 'These Are Soulful Days', written for Lee Morgan, and on *Leeway* given a flatter and much less responsive reading. No one will pretend that Massey is a lost giant, even on a par with Herbie Nichols or Sonny Clark, but he is an intriguing second-rank figure who merits attention.

Zane Massey (born 1957)

TENOR AND SOPRANO SAXOPHONES

Son of trumpeter Cal Massey, he worked as a sideman with Ronald Shannon Jackson before leading these Chicago-based dates.

*** Brass Knuckles

Delmark DD-464 *Massey; Hideji Taninaka, William Parker (b); Sadiq M. Abdu Shahid (d).* 11/92.

*** Safe To Imagine

Delmark DE-487 *As above, except add Denton Darien (p), Dr Cuz (perc); omit Parker.* 11/94.

This tenorman has a great gruff sound and prodigious energy. These aren't marathon workouts, with both discs having as many short, concise pieces as long ones, and the leader works the parameters of inside/outside with plenty of skill. *Brass Knuckles* is all trio (Parker replaces Taninaka only on 'Trickle Down Economics') and is full of gutsy blowing. 'Walk Right In' turns from its tricky theme to a simple blues groove that Massey gives his all to, and it's very exciting. Elsewhere, though, he seems to fall back on stock phrases which momentum alone can't sustain. *Safe To Imagine* brings in Darien on several tracks, but he lacks the kind of finesse that would take the group to a higher level, and much of the disc is merely so-so – until the final two tracks. 'Myra's Maya' is a model of cumulative power, the group driving on while still holding down some reserves, and the concluding treatment of Cal Massey's 'Things Have Got To Change' adds a touch of exotica to old Chicago via Dr Cuz's congas and Zane's soprano – 'a micro-tonal thing that goes back to, like, snake-charming', as he says.

George Masso (born 1926)

TROMBONE

Son of a local trumpet player, Masso grew up in Rhode Island and mainly taught music before beginning full-time playing in the '70s. He has since built a considerable reputation in mainstream circles.

*** The Wonderful World Of George Gershwin

Nagel-Heyer 001 *Masso; Randy Sandke (t); Kenny Davern (cl); Danny Moss (ts); Eddie Higgins (p); Len Skeat (b); Jake Hanna (d).* 9/92.

*** Trombone Artistry

Nagel-Heyer 014 *Masso; Ken Peplowski (cl, ts); Brian Dee (p); Len Skeat (b); Jake Hanna (d).* 8/94.

***(*) **That Old Gang Of Mine**

Arbors ARCD 19173 *Masso; Lou Colombo (t, c); Dick Johnson (as, cl); Dave McKenna (p); Marshall Wood (b); Artie Cabral (d).* 11/96.

*** **Shakin' The Blues Away**

Zephyr ZECD6 *Masso; Roy Williams (tb); Brian Lemon (p); Dave Cliff (g); Dave Green (b); Allan Ganley, Martin Drew (d).* 11/95–11/96.

More examples of quality repertory jazz by men who know the style so well that they have to come up with something new – they'd be bored themselves otherwise. Masso, who started out with Jimmy Dorsey 50 years ago, has a generous, peppery, surprising sound on the trombone, some notes turning into an abrupt bark, others crooning across bar lines, and his solos are nearly always a pleasurable education. The two Nagel-Heyer CDs are both live sessions from the label's Hamburg base, and perhaps not quite out of the potboiler class. The *Gershwin* disc assembles a list of chestnuts for the band to blow on, which they do with gusto and without leaving much that's memorable behind them. The quintet date, *Trombone Artistry*, benefits from Peplowski's cunning playing, though when they get to 'Blue Monk' it seems like the band think they're just blowing on the blues. The Arbors CD is by a band in which all the hands come from southern New England, Rhode Island to Massachusetts, and it's genial regional jazz at its best, ten good tunes given an affectionate going-over. *Shakin' The Blues Away* transplants him to the other side of the Atlantic for some good-natured duelling with Williams over the Zephyr house rhythm section. Not quite as strong, perhaps, even though the solos are mostly great fun.

Mikio Masuda

PIANO

A triumph of spirit and determination, Masuda's story is a remarkable one. Heard out of context, he might sound unadventurous and somewhat unvaried in pace, but there are depths of expression in these albums that must reflect some of the trials the pianist has gone through to make music at all.

*** **Black Daffodils**

JVC 9030 2 *Masuda; Ron Carter (b); Lewis Nash (d).* 9/96.

***(*) **Blue Dumplings**

JVC 9040 2 *As above, except replace Nash with Grady Tate (d).* 3/98.

Masuda's career was threatened by a serious accident which all but destroyed his hands. He battled back to something like dexterity, only to be diagnosed as having multiple sclerosis. That the first album should have been recorded at all seems little short of miraculous; that it is as good as it is seems to defy rationale. Anyone who has been led by the conjunction of that rather strange title and a Japanese name to expect some dark epic of perverse sexuality will be startled to hear a set of light and lyrical love-songs and improvisations, played with a thoughtful hesitancy which doesn't seem so much physical or technical as born of a genuine desire not to overstate the case. The opening 'In A Sentimental Mood' almost sounds like a spontaneous composition and, by the same logic, the album's two improvised pieces have a remarkable formal finish. 'Black Daffodils' itself is a marvellous notion, executed with quick strokes and little embellishment, like an ink-and-wash drawing. Carter and Nash are a dream partnership, supporting, cajoling, running little parallel ideas of their own. The sound is as good as one could hope for.

Two years on, the same refinement is even more clearly in evidence. Tate's delicate gestures are picked up with great clarity, adding to the album's air of filigreed lyricism. There are a couple of originals, the Miles-and-Bill-influenced 'Yellow In Green' and the Monkian title-track which suggests that, whatever the present state of Masuda's health, he's venturing into more percussive territory. As with its predecessor, the only drawback is an overall lack of fire and drama. This is easy music to put on and forget about. Not everyone, even primed with Masuda's story, will want to find the time.

Ronnie Mathews (born 1935)

PIANO

A New Yorker, Mathews is a sideman of wide experience, spending periods with Max Roach and Art Blakey (1960s) and Johnny Griffin (1970s). In the '80s he began recording as a leader.

(*) **Song For Leslie

Red RR 123162-2 *Mathews; Ray Drummond (b); Kenny Washington (d).* 3/80.

***(*) **Selena's Dance**

Timeless SJP 304 *Mathews; Stafford James (b); Tony Reedus (d).* 1/88.

*** **At Café Des Copains**

Sackville SKCD 2-2026 *Mathews (p solo).* 2/89.

***(*) **Dark Before The Dawn**

DIW 604 *Mathews; Ray Drummond (b); Billy Higgins (d).* 10/90.

*** **Lament For Love**

DIW 612 *Mathews; David Williams (b); Frank Gant (d).* 6/92.

*** **Shades Of Monk**

Sound Hills 8064 *Mathews; Buster Williams (b); Kenny Washington (d).* 5/94.

A venerable sideman, Mathews has made only occasional excursions as a leader. He's an exemplar of the skilful and self-effacing modal pianists who came in the wake of McCoy Tyner's eminence in the 1960s. While there's nothing to pull listeners out of their seats on any of these records, most say a lot about the dedication and craft of the men involved. Mathews likes generously voiced chords and momentous rhythmic drive, and his various rhythm-section partners complement his playing with great insight. *Song For Leslie* gets lower marks mainly because of the very poor studio-balance: Mathews is behind both Drummond and Washington in the mix, and the bassist is given a rather ugly, rubbery sound. The title-track and 'It Don't Mean A Thing' are terrific swingers, and it's a pity that the music sounds the way it does.

With James – an old friend and playing companion – and Reedus, Mathews tries a wide variety of settings on *Selena's*

Dance: 'Stella By Starlight' becomes a bass feature after a lovely out-of-tempo intro by James, 'My Funny Valentine' is an unexpectedly hard-hitting swinger, 'Body And Soul' starts with an improvisation on the verse, and the title-track is built on locomotive rather than dance rhythms, sustained with terrific power by all three men. *Dark Before The Dawn* is less variegated but, if anything, even more accomplished, in part because Higgins – whose work on cymbals is particularly well caught by the sumptuous sound – is so masterful. This time Mathews builds 'Theme From M*A*S*H' on to a Tynerish vamp, starts a reading of 'You Don't Know What Love Is' with a solo section from 'Don't Explain' and freshens up two infrequently visited standards in 'The End Of A Love Affair' and 'You Leave Me Breathless', which open and close the record with decisive authority.

If *Lament For Love* is a fraction less satisfying, that's no disgrace: it's just that the nine themes here receive a treatment which relies more on solid, gracious routine than on the careful preparation which distinguished the earlier discs. 'Gee Baby Ain't I Good To You', a singer's vehicle and a rare one for the piano, touches a fine vein of wistful lyricism. Much the same applies to *Shades Of Monk*, which sets three of that composer's tunes beside a couple of unusual Wayne Shorter choices and a few other nuggets. Mathews sounds in good form and Williams and Washington are typically assertive.

Bennie Maupin (born 1946)

SAXOPHONES, BASS CLARINET, OTHER INSTRUMENTS

Studied in Detroit until 1962, then with many leaders – Roy Haynes, Horace Silver, Herbie Hancock. A failsafe sideman.

***** Driving While Black ...**
Intuition INT 3242 2 *Maupin; Dr Patrick Gleeson (ky, perc).*

A defiant restatement of jazz-rock by one of the most talented multi-instrumentalists on the scene. Always more than a spear-carrier in the movement, Maupin has never had the critical attention he is due. He exemplifies better than anyone the continuities between hard bop and fusion, having worked in one of trumpeter Lee Morgan's later groups, before helping to hybridize jazz and rock with Miles Davis and, crucially, with Herbie Hancock's Headhunters.

Even so, this is an odd record. It sounds old-fashioned, but at the same time suggests the retro-jazz styling of many contemporary drum'n'bass and jungle projects. Reiterating Miles's desire to make Stockhausen dance with Sly Stone, it runs some risk of reinventing the wheel but succeeds almost despite itself. The title-track is the drabbest thing on the set, a slice of processed funk with none of the anger the title implies and none of the boiling fury Miles brought to similar ideas.

Gleeson's rhythms are more than wallpaper for Maupin's plangent saxophone. Synth technology was in its infancy at the end of the 1960s and Gleeson has embraced high-spec keyboards and sampling equipment with great confidence, even though the sound is still close to what one might have heard in 1970. Maupin doesn't so much improvise solos as throw shapes and make expressive gestures, but he does so with great beauty. Try *Driving While Black* ... on someone and see if they can guess who – and, crucially, when – it was.

Turk Mauro (born 1944)

TENOR AND BARITONE SAXOPHONES

Section player with many big bands, including Dizzy Gillespie's and Buddy Rich's, Mauro is based on the West Coast.

****(*) Hittin' The Jug**
Milestone 9246-2 *Mauro; Dr Lonnie Smith (p, org); Jeff Grubbs (b); Duffy Jackson (d). 95.*

****(*) The Truth**
Milestone 9267-2 *Mauro; Pete Minger (t); Eric Allison (ts); Dolph Castellano, Dr Lonnie Smith, Billy Marcus (p); Jeff Grubbs (b); Danny Burger (d). 6–7/96.*

Mauro is an honest journeyman saxophonist. He can play whatever he wants on the horn, but both these professional albums lack a particular cast. Each disc is based around blowing vehicles smoothed out into palatable, radio-friendly jazz and, warmly though the players seem to respond, it feels like a very practised routine.

Bill Mays (born 1944)

PIANO

Born in Sacramento, Mays studied in San Diego and played in small groups, as an accompanist, and with his own outfit. Settled in New York in the mid-'80s.

***** Kaleidoscope**
Jazz Alliance TJA-10013 *Mays; Dick Oatts (ss, ts, f); Peter Sprague (g); Harvie Swartz (b); Jeff Hirshfield (d). 10/89.*

***** At Maybeck Volume 26**
Concord CCD 4567 *Mays (p solo). 9/92.*

***** Bill Mays / Ed Bickert: Concord Duo Series Vol. 7**
Concord CCD 4626 *Mays; Ed Bickert (g). 3/94.*

***** An Ellington Affair**
Concord CCD 4651 *Mays; John Goldsby (b); Lewis Nash (d). 7/94.*

***** Mays In Manhattan**
Concord CCD 4738 *Mays; Marvin Stamm (c, t, flhn); Ed Neumeister (tb); Jon Gordon (as); Sean Smith (b); Tim Horner (d). 5/96.*

Though he subsequently settled on the East Coast, Mays is a Californian whose dynamics and even-tempered skills suggest a natural disciple of the tradition of Lou Levy, Pete Jolly, Claude Williamson and Marty Paich. *Kaleidoscope* bustles through some clever arrangements, the centrepiece being the pretty if ultimately rather bland 'Adirondack': Sprague shows more muscle than he does on his own records, and the reliable Oatts puts in some pungent playing, but the record is still sunnily polite rather than passionate. Mays's contribution to the Maybeck series turns out in much the same way: there are some imaginative standards, such as a neatly embroidered 'Nightingale Sang In Berkeley Square' and 'Guess I'll Hang My Tears Out To Dry', but 'Jitterbug Waltz' is done prissily, and 'Grandpa's Spells', delivered as a party-piece encore, misses the gravity that Marcus Roberts can bring to a similar chestnut. The meeting with Bickert is a charmer, the guitarist's old-fashioned elegance settling nicely alongside Mays's rather more inquiring parts, and while nothing here really makes one sit up and listen there are moments – especially the almost luminous ballad improvising of 'Quietly' – which run deep.

The Ellington album has its share of ingenuities – 'Satin Doll' is a revisionist treatment to end them all, finding a vein of melancholy which the song has scarcely sustained in the past – without making one sure that Mays has an agenda of any conviction beyond impressing the listener. He approaches almost every theme with an unexpected idea, but the chosen path – such as the boogie undertow of 'I'm Just A Lucky So And So' – can seem as gimmicky as it is genuine. Goldsby and Nash lend pristine support, all the same. *Mays In Manhattan* strings together nine tunes about New York, four of them with the horns, five by piano and rhythm section. Mays still can't leave a good tune alone – his tricksy arrangement of 'Autumn In New York' does nothing for the song – but this is a smart band and at least they didn't do 'New York, New York'.

Louis Mazetier

PIANO

Stride-piano stylist from France.

***** If Dreams Come True**

Stomp Off CD1289 *Mazetier; Neville Dickie (p).* 5/94.

***** Harlem Strut**

Stomp Off CD1302 *As above.* 5/95.

These are albums of piano duets which should be credited to both Dickie and Mazetier, but it seems fair to list them under the Frenchman's name. Stride, boogie woogie and a blush of ragtime or blues add up to close to 80 minutes of four-handed fun on each disc. None of this cuts very deep, since the intention is to re-create the craftsmanship of the piano entertainers of decades ago, and it could hardly be entrusted to two more adept practitioners. Occasionally they get slow and wistful; mostly it's music to watch those cakewalkin' babies from home by.

Robert Mazurek

TRUMPET, CORNET

Chicago-based trumpeter who spent a period in Scotland before returning to the USA. Has moved from a basic hard-bop stance to more freely focused music with the Chicago Underground Trio and others.

***** Man Facing East**

Hep CD 2059 *Mazurek; Randolph Tressler (p); Tom Allen, John Webber (b); George Fludas (d).* 12/93.

***** Badlands**

Hep CD 2065 *As above, except omit Allen; add Eric Alexander (ts).* 9/94, 7/95.

***** Green & Blue**

Hep CD 2067 *As above.* 9/94, 7/95.

If you were dispensing sage career advice to a young jazz musician, it is unlikely that you would ever hear yourself say, 'Yes, pack up in Chicago, and come over to Edinburgh in August; there isn't much going on, and you're bound to get a gig.' That, though, is what Robert Mazurek, originally from Jersey City, decided to do. He teamed up with Flora Harrold, who booked him into one of the city's few jazz venues, and eventually married her. The first visit was in 1993; thereafter Mazurek became an Edinburgh Festival fixture.

Musically, at this point he comes straight out of late-1950s Blue Note hard bop, direct and unadorned, sounding not unlike drummer Tommy Chase's groups of the early '80s in London, but with a more brittle, less abrasive sound. Tressler, who hails from Detroit, provides a solid harmonic anchor, over which the trumpet skates and bounces with absolute conviction and authenticity. To say that this is a band that isn't going to 'develop' is a description rather than a criticism; Mazurek delivers, then delivers again: a fast up-tempo blues, a ballad, a mid-paced groove with a minor feel; and then the same again. No frills.

The debut album is unmistakably capable but somewhat one-dimensional. 'Flora's House' and the title-track stand out. The addition of saxophonist Eric Alexander on the two subsequent discs cements the Blue Note lineage and adds a richness of texture which is welcome indeed. *Badlands* kicks off with a tribute to 'Arthur's Seat', the volcanic lump which dominates his adoptive city, and it immediately suggests a musical personality that has matured in less than a calendar year. The inclusion of standards – 'Deep Purple', 'Every Time We Say Goodbye', 'Stranger In Paradise' and 'I Fall In Love Too Easily' – was a wise decision; though not the most melodic of players, Mazurek is absolutely across the chords, and Alexander trails him every inch of the way.

Green & Blue is interesting not least because Mazurek, whose sound can be one-dimensional, decides to double not on flugelhorn but on cornet, a tight, fat sound that suits him very well. Non-Scottish listeners will probably not understand the implications of a title like 'Streets Of Raith', the long opener. A football commentator, reporting on a Cup victory, declared that 'they'll be dancing in the streets of Raith tonight'. There is actually no such town. Raith Rovers play in Kirkcaldy, once the world capital of linoleum. Find Mazurek's later adventures under Chicago Underground Trio.

Giovanni Mazzarino (born 1965)

PIANO

Milan-based contemporary Italian pianist.

***** Silence, Please!**

Splasc(h) H 375-2 *Mazzarino; Flavio Boltro (t, flhn); Benedetto Modica (tb); Orazio Maugeri (as); Marcello Szocol (vib); Lello Panico (g); Riccardo Lo Bue (b); Paolo Mappa (d).* 1/91.

An engaging, cheerful atmosphere surrounds this melodious and unpretentious session, with the sunny version of Horace Silver's 'Barbara' typifying the good humour of the date. The other five compositions are by Mazzarino and, though nothing makes a resounding impression, the music benefits from the contrasts in the cast: Panico's wistfully rocking guitar is countered by Boltro's imperturbably cool trumpet and flugelhorn, and Maugeri has a nicely bluesy tone. The leader does nothing extraordinary at the piano, but it doesn't detract.

Guido Mazzon

TRUMPET, FLUGELHORN, POCKET-TRUMPET, SLIDE TRUMPET, VOICE, ELECTRONICS

Pioneer Italian free player, with a recording career stretching back into the early '70s.

***(*) Other Line

Splasc(h) H 317 *Mazzon; Umberto Petrin (p); Tiziano Tononi (d).* 4–5/90.

** Il Profumo Della Liberta

Splasc(h) H 377-2 *As above, except add Renato Geremia (vn, cl), Eleonora Nervi (tba), Ellen Christi (v).* 4/92.

Guido Mazzon has been seeking new forms for jazz trumpet for many years. He recorded an all-solo record as far back as 1975 and another with the sole support of vocalist Marco Magrini in 1979; but none of his albums has been much distributed outside Italy. All the more cause to recommend *Other Line*, a fine trio session for Splasc(h). While there is some studio doctoring – the multiple-horns effect on 'Secret Music' and a stern reading of Ornette Coleman's 'Lonely Woman' – it's mostly the highly detailed interplay among the three musicians which the album relies on to make its mark. Mazzon never comes on as a great virtuoso and prefers a more circumspect approach, picking over melodic fragments and using the false areas of the horn very sparingly. Petrin responds with a similarly restrained style, allusively hinting at tonalities in some pieces and taking a linear course in others; Tononi plays timekeeper and colourist with marvellously adept touches. A couple of the slower pieces perhaps outstay their welcome, but otherwise a fine encounter.

It's a pity that the augmented group on *Il Profumo Della Liberta* adds little but pretentious weight to Mazzon's music. Christi's vocalizations range from complementary to glaringly inappropriate, and the lyrics to 'Old Tales And New Songs' are insufferable. Nervi's tuba and Geremia's primitive violin also get in the way more than they help the music. Very disappointing.

*** Trumpet 'Buzz' Duo

Splasc(h) 466 *Mazzon; Alberto Mandarini (t, flhn, pkt-t, slide-t, perc, v); Enrico Bellati (frhn).* 12/94.

Back on form here, though. It's a recording of a concert in Rome where Mazzon was partnered by the similarly minded Mandarini (Bellati plays a mournful melody on one track only). The duo play trumpet tag for some 50 minutes, switching instruments, using echo and other devices, sometimes conjuring counterpoint out of the air, and effectively living up to the title of the record. They end on a punchline which we won't divulge. A light repast: perhaps something to savour between a couple of heavyweight records, like a particularly refreshing sorbet.

**(*) If

Splasc(h) 629 *Mazzon; Umberto Petrin (p); Michel Godard (tba); Maria Elena Moro (v).* 11/97.

A brittle and sometimes unwelcoming record of chamber jazz. Hard to say whether this format really suits Mazzon or not, even if he wrote all of it: Godard's tuba and Moro's voice are striking but not necessarily suitable fellow travellers, and sometimes the record seems almost pointlessly eccentric. At other moments, the music seems bold and new. But it's hard work.

Cecil McBee (born 1935)

DOUBLE BASS

Born in Tulsa and a musical alumnus of the US Army, McBee worked with an array of notably idiosyncratic and maverick musicians, from Grachan Moncur III to Wayne Shorter, Charles Lloyd to Yusef Lateef and Sam Rivers. Grounded in bebop and reminiscent on occasions of Curley Russell, to the extent that Bird's favourite bassist was ever audible, he has a punchy, well-rounded tone.

**(*) Alternate Spaces

India Navigation 1043 *McBee; Joe Gardner (t); Chico Freeman (as, ts, bcl, f); Don Pullen (p); Allen Nelson, Famoudou Don Moye (perc).* 77.

*** Unspoken

Palmetto Jazz PM 2023 *McBee; James Zollar (t); Randall Connors (as); David Berkman (p); Matt Wilson (d).* 10/96.

Tulsa-born McBee led a military band for a time (playing clarinet in those days) before moving to New York City in 1964 and beginning a career that took in most contemporary jazz styles and stints in bands led by the likes of Charles Tolliver, Jackie McLean, Charles Lloyd, Pharoah Sanders, Alice Coltrane and many others. He has recorded as leader before and habitually brings a strong sense of structure and form to his sessions. The surviving India Navigation set is a bit of a disappointment in retrospect. As a duet with the sharp-edged and endlessly inventive Pullen, it might have been fascinating but, even with the gifted Freeman on board, it never rises above a rather bland modernism. On the later disc, a brisk young quintet plays very well, tackling unfamiliar originals like 'Catfish' and 'Sleeping Giant' with great aplomb. They sound well rehearsed but not overprepared, and there is a relaxed confidence to Zollar's playing in particular that speaks well of him. The saxophonist recalls McLean more than anyone, but he has his own voice and personality and his phrasing is intelligent. McBee doesn't feature himself any more often than seems appropriate, but his broad, chocolatey tone dominates the ensembles.

Christian McBride (born 1972)

DOUBLE BASS

Emerged in the '90s as the young giant of the bass on the New York session scene, and he already has a big sideman discography. Leadership duties were inevitable, if at times uncertain on record so far.

***(*) Gettin' To It

Verve 523989-2 *McBride; Roy Hargrove (t); Steve Turre (tb); Joshua Redman (ts); Cyrus Chestnut (p); Ray Brown, Milt Hinton (b); Lewis Nash (d).* 8 & 9/94.

***(*) Number Two Express

Verve 529585-2 *McBride; Gary Bartz, Kenny Garrett (as); Kenny Barron, Chick Corea (p); Steve Nelson (vib); Jack DeJohnette (d); Mino Cinelu (perc).* 11/95.

**** Fingerpainting

Verve 537856-2 *McBride; Nicholas Payton (t, flhn); Mark Whitfield (d).* 4/97.

Not 30 until the new century is well under way, McBride has the potential to become one of the legends on his instrument, up with the likes of Ray Brown and Milt Hinton. By the time he signed his deal with Verve, he was already a first-call sideman for a huge variety of sessions, and to date he has appeared on something like 60 or 70 records, preferred for his big woody tone and fluent delivery. He is one of the few mainstream bass players who is *always* interesting to listen to and who always has things to say rather than merely changes to negotiate.

Brown and Hinton join him on the first record for a remarkable three-bass version of Nefti's 'Splanky', but for the most part the date is unreconstructed and unapologetic hard bop with very few self-consciously contemporary references. *Gettin' To It* might almost be a Blue Note disc of a previous generation, something by Paul Chambers perhaps, except that McBride's approach goes back a half-generation beyond Mr P.C. for its sources and influences. One of those most frequently adduced when the album was released was Oscar Pettiford, and there is something of that in the riveting track, 'In A Hurry', with Josh Redman and Steve Turre in support. McBride works a number of variations on the basic quintet, and for 'Sitting On A Cloud' and 'Stars Fell On Alabama' he dispenses with horns altogether and substantially rejigs piano-trio idiom with Chestnut and Nash. The last track of all is a pretty emphatic statement of intent, an unaccompanied trip on Jimmy Forrest's 'Night Train', with a magnificent bowed passage that makes one wish to hear more of his *arco* work.

The second album suffers only from the fact that McBride's quality is now so well attested that it is no longer a surprise. Again, he varies the line-ups, duetting with Barron on the Wayne Shorter tune, 'Mikayo', and with Cinelu (and using electric bass) on the closing 'Little Sunflower', another nod in the direction of Freddie Hubbard. Barron and Corea share piano duties, memorably on the latter's 'Tones For Joan's Bones' and, with Barron, on Ornette's 'Jayne'. Barron has always been a fine exponent of the Fender Rhodes; 'A Morning Story' is written for amplified instruments, a persuasive expansion of the language. The hornmen are not so much superfluous as something of a luxury in this company, and there are moments when one wonders whether they mightn't have been saved for another day, or whether a brass instrument mightn't have been a good idea. Bartz is, however, well up to his fine recent form and Garrett's uncluttered, bluesy lines are most attractive. Production by Richard Seidel and Don Sickler is absolutely top-drawer, with McBride placed centre and left and the others ranged round him very naturally. The bass is very full, but never tiresomely dominant, as so often on gigs like this.

Fingerpainting is devoted to the music of Herbie Hancock and performed by three of the brightest stars in Verve's latter-day firmament. Divided into two loosely organized sections, 'Suite Herbie I/II', the album covers much of the pianist's recording career, including such classics as 'Dolphin Dance', which features a magnificent cup mute solo from Payton, and 'Driftin'', on which McBride is out of this world. 'The Sorcerer' and 'Sly' recall Herbie's association with Miles Davis and, though the session is drummerless, the trio invests both with much of the energy of the originals. 'Speak Like A Child' is performed on bass, flugelhorn and electric guitar, and there are two delightful tracks from Hancock's *Blow Up* soundtrack. A fine record all round.

Les McCann (born 1935)

PIANO, VOCAL

Born in Lexington, Kentucky, McCann had an undistinguished career until the mid-'60s, when he wrote some crossover hits and became popular on the nascent jazz festival circuit. He later worked extensively with Eddie Harris, and their Swiss Movement album became a great success in its day.

*** Talkin' Verve: Les McCann

Verve 557351-2 *McCann; Lee Katzman (t); Plas Johnson, Seldon Powell, Jerome Richardson (ts); Warren Chiasson, Lyn Blessing (vib); Jimmy Georgantones, Vinnie Bell, Carl Lynch (g); Leroy Vinnegar, Victor Gaskin (b); Paul Humphrey, Frank Severino, Booker T Robinson (d); Ron Rich, Joseph Torries, Ric DeSilva, Aki Aleong (perc).* 12/64–9/67.

**(*) How's Your Mother?

32 Jazz 32088 *McCann; Leroy Vinnegar (b); Frank Severino (d).* 7/67.

*** Much Les

Rhino/Atlantic R2 71281 *McCann; Leroy Vinnegar (b); Donald Dean (d); Willie Bobo, Victor Pantoja (perc); strings.* 7/68.

**(*) Swiss Movement

Atlantic 781 365-2 *McCann; Benny Bailey (t); Eddie Harris (ts); Leroy Vinnegar (b); Donald Dean (d).* 6/69.

*(*) Layers

Rhino/Atlantic R2 71280 *McCann; Jimmy Rowser (b); Donald Dean (d); Ralph MacDonald, Buck Clarke (perc).* 11/72.

Les McCann has made dozens of albums, although there is still not that much in print – somewhat fortunately for his reputation, since far too much of his production has been disfigured by faddish vocals and arrangements and by feeble material. At least the *Talkin' Verve* compilation sifts together some of the livelier material from a generally undistinguished run of LPs made for

Limelight in the mid-1960s. There are some fun moments in the percussion-heavy 'Watermelon Man', an overcooked but entertaining 'Sunny' and an early version of what's practically his signature piece, 'Compared To What?' – even if, like much of his stuff, it was actually written by somebody else.

Perhaps we've been a bit harsh on him, since McCann's background is more about good-time, low-light entertainment than anything out of the 'serious' hard-bop book (even if, apparently, Miles Davis once recommended him for the piano chair in the Cannonball Adderley band). Even so, the albums are a bit thin on persistently strong music. *How's Your Mother?* catches a typical trio set from 1967 at the Village Vanguard – lively playing, very average sound and, while it must have sounded great if you were there, as a record it barely passes muster. *Much Les* isn't bad. There are some fairly unobtrusive strings on some tracks, but McCann sets up some grooving tempos that Vinnegar and Dean help him to keep moving, and some of it is as good as any soul-jazz of the decade. There's also a pleasing version of his charming ballad, 'With These Hands'. A hit album in its time, the appeal of *Swiss Movement* has faded fairly drastically. Cut live at Montreux, it's a ragged set of soul-jazz vamps, with a probably definitive version of 'Compared To What?', but the excitement is mitigated by what remains atrocious sound, even for a live session. Bailey's solo on 'You Got It In Your Soulness' offers the best moment, but overall the revival of interest in soul-jazz has uncovered many better records than this. *Layers* is a trashy relic of thin, early-'70s soul-jazz, barely worth reviving.

Ron McClure (born 1941)

DOUBLE BASS

A follower of Paul Chambers – whom he replaced in Wynton Kelly's group – McClure has also been a prolific recording artist in his own right. He worked in big bands for a time, before joining Charles Lloyd's highly successful group, after which he began to emerge as a significant composer and leader.

***** Yesterday's Tomorrow**

EPC 884 *McClure; John Abercrombie (g); Aldo Romano (d).* 7/89.

*****(*) McJolt**

Steeplechase SCCD 31262 *McClure; John Abercrombie (g); Richard Beirach (p); Adam Nussbaum (d).* 12/89.

McClure's fusion group, Fourth Way, extended the jazz-rock idiom he had helped create with Blood, Sweat and Tears and the Charles Lloyd Quartet into more adventurous compositional territory. A fine bassist, with an excellent *arco* technique (see 'Tainted Rose' on *Yesterday's Tomorrow*), he is also an exceptional composer who draws on non-jazz tonalities with great confidence. One of his most characteristic devices is a percussive, almost marimba-like thrum achieved by striking the strings against the fingerboard. McClure's preference for players with a similar sound is obvious from the trio session with Romano and Abercrombie (whose guitar synthesizer takes the place of an electric piano). This is more abstract, impressionistic music, and very different from the standards approach of *McJolt*, where McClure develops the LaFaro sound very impressively on tracks like 'Nardis', 'Stella By Starlight' and 'Once I Had A Secret Love'. The trio set, released on the Montpellier-based EPC, is slightly short on conventional jazz virtues but features some of McClure's best writing and some of his best *arco* work since 'Line' on *Descendants*. 'Midi Evil' presumably refers to the south of France rather than to MIDI technology. The set *is* rather dominated in places (on 'Panchito' to a great extent) by Abercrombie's effects, sometimes at the expense of McClure's and Romano's more delicate interchanges. The sound is also a bit overcooked.

***** Strikezone**

Steeplechase SCCD 31277 *McClure; Marc Copland (p); Dave Stryker (d).* 90.

***** Never Forget**

Steeplechase SCCD 31279 *McClure; Eddie Henderson (t); Vincent Herring (as); Kevin Hayes (p); Bill Stewart (d).* 10/90.

***** For Tonite Only**

Steeplechase SCCD 31288 *McClure; Randy Brecker (t, flhn); John Abercrombie (g); Adam Nussbaum (d).* 3/91.

*****(*) Sunburst**

Steeplechase SCCD 31306 *McClure; Tim Hagans (t); Conrad Herwig (tb); Joe Gordon (as, ss); LeeAnn Ledgerwood (p); Jeff Hirshfield (d).* 12/91.

*****(*) Inner Account**

Steeplechase SCCD 31329 *McClure; Rich Perry (ts); Kenny Drew Jr (p); Vic Juris (g); Sylvia Cuenca (d).* 11/92.

The bassist sounds less persuasive in a conventional horn-led quintet and Herring has an uneasy time of it on the later of the 1990 sessions. We have only been able to sample *Strikezone*, recorded around the same period. McClure's preferred instrumentation is one that trickily pairs guitar and piano, usually allowing the keyboard player long, developed lines, while the guitarist plays 'free' over the top. That's essentially what Abercrombie does on *For Tonite Only*, and what Juris attempts to do, less confidently but in some regards more successfully, on the impressive *Inner Account*.

That's two reasons why *Sunburst* registers so strongly. The recording is very bright and detailed, without too much rumble from the bass, and the playing is straightforward and to the point. McClure has rarely sounded better, but this was only the beginning of a streak that was to continue through the 1990s.

*****(*) Never Always**

Steeplechase SCCD 31355 *McClure; Don Friedman (p); Billy Hart (d).* 94.

Friedman's classically influenced approach is the key to this slightly deliberate set. Despite the presence of Hart, who seemed to be getting better by the session through the mid-'90s, it never achieves the sheer verve and excitement of McClure's other discs. Yet it is an album which grows with every hearing, and we recommend it to your patient attention.

*****(*) Concrete Canyon**

Steeplechase SCCD 31391 *McClure; Tim Hagans (t); Marc Copland (p); Billy Hart (d).* 3/96.

****** Closer To Your Tears**

Steeplechase SCCD 31413 *McClure; Jay Azzolina (g); Marc Copland (p); Billy Hart (d); Manolo Badrena (perc).* 9/96.

***** Pink Cloud**

Naxos Jazz 86002 *McClure; Rick Margitza (ts, ss); Jon Davis (p); Jeff Williams (d).* 9/96.

A busy year, with a surprise switch of label in the autumn, doubtless a one-off. Hagans's Miles-influenced (but *early* Miles-influenced) trumpet makes an attractive and unexpected contribution to *Concrete Canyon*. With the exception of the opening 'All That's Left', which was written by Copland, everything else on the set is a McClure original and, though there's not much variety in the thematic material, it's open-ended enough to be lifted in performance, as is emphatically the case on the long 'Lock', originally written for vibist Joe Lock, *before* Ron learned to spell his name. Much of the material has a minor-key feel, even when it appears to be in the major, and there is a constant drift towards polytonality on things like 'Deception', 'Ears' (a more than usually reflective idea), and the title-piece, which is a poem to McClure's beloved New York. Fine as Copland and Hagans are, one finds oneself listening out for the bass and drums most of the time. Hart is at the top of his powers and this is one of his best guest appearances for years.

He's back, and in form, on the lovely *Closer To Your Tears*, which has confusingly similar, indeed almost identical cover art to the other Steeplechase. The title-piece is the most movingly personal McClure has ever allowed himself to be on record. All of his writing and playing comes from the heart – he is an instinctive player above all – but this one seems to come from some inner recess he hasn't tapped before. If there is a drawback to the set, it's probably too deliberate a swing from bright, up-tempo tunes to more expressive themes, like the delightful 'Eli's Wine', inspired by the Jewish tradition of Elijah's Cup, and the closing 'He, Who Cares', which seems to include a string of subliminal references to Miles Davis. The album isn't quite solidly balanced but, unlike that extra cup of wine, it's one that will be tasted and refilled many times.

The Naxos disc maybe should have been left to stand and breathe a little longer. Whereas Azzolina and Copland seemed absolutely in tune with the session, the players on *Pink Cloud* sound a little awkward with the settings, which are even more varied, and perhaps a little mannered, this time out. 'Where's Manuel?' is a strange, almost militaristic evocation of the pursuit of the Panamanian dictator Noriega (famously driven out of hiding by high-volume David Bowie tapes, pumped into the Vatican consular compound by the CIA and US army). 'Milk And Cookies', on the other hand, is a tribute to the wholesome values of Pat Metheny, another of McClure's kind-words-in-a-troubled-world pieces. 'Little Big One' is a gently complex waltz. Margitza only really shows his mettle on the Coltrane-tinged 'Street Smart', but he shows a much more traditional turn of phrase on 'Day By Day', the only standard in the set. Williams and Davis combine well, but are absolutely straightahead and uncomplicated, lacking the subtlety Copland and Hart brought to the Steeplechases. The Naxos set was something of a homecoming and a reunion for the bassist. Almost his first act after the break-up of the Charles Lloyd group was to phone his friend, Mike Nock, who was forming Fourth Way; he promptly hired McClure and, 27 years later, he's on hand again as executive producer.

*****(*) Dream Team**

Steeplechase SCCD 31435 *McClure; Rich Perry (ts); Marc Copland (p); Billy Hart (d).* 98.

A fascinating set that gets off to a wonderful start with 'Denial's Goat', a double-waltz-time groove which has Perry snaking off into a strange, shawm-like solo. The title-track comes next, a floating minor feel with a hint of song form. Copland brings 'Darius Dance' to the set, but otherwise all the tunes are McClure's, united by his characteristic attention to voicings that work right through the band, including the drummer. Hart seems to get better every time he records, and his delicacy of touch here is a key element of the overall sound. A dream team it may very well have turned out to be.

Rob McConnell (born 1935)

TROMBONE, VALVE TROMBONE

Born in London, Ontario, McConnell began by working in the Canadian dance-band scene of the 1950s and '60s, before forming his first Boss Brass group in 1968 and writing in a style which involved the brass sections working in particularly close harmony, often in unaccompanied stretches. The group abides to this day.

***** Two Originals: Brass My Soul & Tribute**

MPS 539083-2 *McConnell; Guido Basso, Sam Noto, Dave Woods, Erich Traugott, Arnie Chycoski (t, flhn); Ian McDougall, Bob Livingston, Dave McMurdo, Ron Hughes (tb); George Stimpson, Brad Warnaar (frhn); Moe Koffman, Jerry Toth, Eugene Amaro, Rick Willkins, Dave Caldwell, Bob Leonard (reeds); James Dale (ky); Ed Bickert (g); Don Thompson (b); Terry Clarke (d); Marty Morell (perc).* 10/79–12/80.

***** Live In Digital**

Sea Breeze CDSB 105 *As above, except omit Caldwell.* 12/80.

****(*) All In Good Time**

Sea Breeze CDSB 106 *As above, except John McLeod (t, flhn), Jim McDonald (frhn), Brian Leonard (perc) replace Warnaar, Bickert and Morell.* 82.

McConnell has kept his Boss Brass together on and off for more than 30 years. Initially, they did without any kind of sax section, but by the time of these records the band had grown bigger. McConnell's charts suggest expansiveness as the band's signifying element: although the leader worked with Maynard Ferguson for a spell, the brassiness of the BB is exploited for sonority rather than clout, and there's a kind of reluctance to even their toughest arrangements. The music is skilfully handled, but the various editions of the orchestra never seem really to set light to the charts. Even where McConnell seeks to evade cliché, he can't altogether shrug off the MOR atmosphere that hangs round most of their records. The live disc is arguably their best, if only because the setting gives them a pinch of adrenalin which their studio records (there are several on Canadian labels) tend to miss. *All In Good Time* was a Grammy winner, but that tends to prove the even-tempered pitch of a band that ought to show a few more claws. The recent MPS reissue couples two of their earlier albums and, while hardly a barnstormer, there's a degree of freshness about the playing – although, comparing this 'Blue Hodge' with the one cut 16 years later on *Even Canadians Get The Blues*, it's hard to see how the band has ever really changed much.

**** The Rob McConnell Jive 5**
Concord CCD 4437 *McConnell; Rick Wilkins (ts); Ed Bickert (g); Neil Swainson (b); Jerry Fuller (d).* 8/90.

Away from the big band, McConnell reveals himself as a merely workmanlike soloist, and Wilkins is a carbon copy of Zoot Sims on an indifferent day.

**** The Brass Is Back**
Concord CCD 4458 *McConnell; Arnie Chycoski, Steve McDade, John MacLeod, Guido Basso, Dave Woods (t, flhn); Ian McDougall, Bob Livingston, Jerry Johnson (tb); Ernie Pattison (btb); Gary Pattison, Jim McDonald (frhn); Moe Koffman, John Johnson (ss, as, f, cl); Eugene Amaro (ts, cl, f); Rick Wilkins (ts, cl); Bob Leonard (bs, bcl, cl, f); Don Thompson (p); Ed Bickert (g); Steve Wallace (b); Terry Clarke (d); Brian Leonard (perc).* 1/91.

****(*) Brassy And Sassy**
Concord CCD 4508 *As above.* 2/92.

The 'return' album by the Boss Brass is as accomplished as before, but there's too much lingering over detail and texture for a band in which details tend to disperse its impact. Most of the scores unfold at far too languorous a pace, each track clocking in between 7 and 11 minutes. Moe Koffman's vigorous (in Boss Brass terms, splenetic) alto feature on 'All The Things You Are' is the most interesting event. *Brassy And Sassy* comes in at a slightly higher level: the notion of a 19-minute piece, 'Blue Serge Suit(e)', sounds frightening, but the band play with some aplomb here, and the opening 'Strike Up The Band' is about as sassy as this brassy lot will ever get.

***** Our 25th Year**
Concord CCD 4559 *As above, except Alistair Kay (tb) replaces McDougall.* 93.

***** Overtime**
Concord CCD 4618 *As above, except Alex Dean (cl, f, ts), David Restivo (p), Jim Vivian (b), Ted Warren (d) replace Amaro, Thompson, Wallace, Clarke and Brian Leonard.* 5/94.

****(*) Don't Get Around Much Any More**
Concord CCD 4661 *As above, except Judy Kay (frhn), Lorne Lofsky (g) replace Pattison and Bickert.* 4/95.

**** Trio Sketches**
Concord CCD 4591 *McConnell; Ed Bickert (g); Neil Swainson (b).* 5/93.

In and of themselves these are all plausible entries in McConnell's chosen genre – *Overtime* in particular will probably be as close as the band will ever come to making a top-flight record. It starts with the lip-busting title-track that takes off via Restivo's quirky solo and Johnson's hair-raising alto escapade, and moves on through a lovely 'Stella By Starlight' for Basso and a two-tenor beanfeast called 'This May Be Your Lucky Day'. The rest is no more than the usual. So is *Our 25th Year*, which is more business-like than celebratory, and by the time of *Don't Get Around Much Any More*, which really starts to roll out the clichés, one feels that the band might be ready for its collective pension. There's always the fire-power of the section-work to enjoy, but even that is missing on McConnell's small-band starring role, *Trio Sketches*. This is just plain dull.

****(*) Even Canadians Get The Blues**
Concord CCD 4722 *McConnell; John Mcleod, Guido Basso, Arnie Chycoski, Steve McDade (t); Alastair Kay, Bob Livingston, Jerry Johnston (tb); Ernie Pattison (btb); Gary Pattison, James McDonald (frhn); Moe Koffman, John Johnson, Alex Dean, Rick Wilkins, Bob Leonard (reeds); David Restivo (p); Ed Bickert (g); Jim Vivian (b); Ted Warren (d).* 4/96.

****(*) Three For The Road**
Concord CCD-4765 *McConnell; Ed Bickert (g); Don Thompson (b, p).* 10/96.

Yes, it's more of the same. It probably wasn't a great inspiration for the band to do a programme of blues, since the limitations on thematic material scarcely bring out the best in McConnell's charts. Perfectly adequate, and few will find this in any sense necessary. *Three For The Road* is a two-day vacation with two old friends, and not bad: this is a rare instrumentation, with Thompson switching between piano and bass, and the players offer only modest elaborations on the melodies, which are well chosen. That said, it's hardly a record to generate wild enthusiasm.

Susannah McCorkle (born 1946)

VOCAL

A Californian by birth, McCorkle moved to Europe in 1971 and began working as a jazz vocalist in London. She returned to the USA in 1977 and, after a spell with The Jazz Alliance, she has since made many records for Concord, crossing between mainstream, blues and Brazilian material.

****** The Quality Of Mercer**
Jazz Alliance TJA-10031 *McCorkle; Digby Fairweather (t, c); Danny Moss (ts); Keith Ingham (p); Ron Rubin (b); Derek Hogg (d).* 9/77.

*****(*) The People That You Never Get To Love**
Jazz Alliance TJA-10034-2 *McCorkle; Keith Ingham (p); Al Gafa (g); Steve LaSpina (b); Joe Cocuzzo (d).* 11/81.

***** How Do You Keep The Music Playing?**
The Jazz Alliance TJA-10036-2 *McCorkle; Al Cohn (ts); Ben Aronov (p); Gene Bertoncini (g); Steve LaSpina (b); Joe Cocuzzo (d).* 6/85.

*****(*) No More Blues**
Concord CCD 4370 *McCorkle; Ken Peplowski (cl, ts); Dave Frishberg (p); Emily Remler (g); John Goldsby (b); Terry Clarke (d).* 11/88.

*****(*) Sabia**
Concord CCD 4418 *McCorkle; Scott Hamilton (ts); Lee Musiker (p); Emily Remler (g); Dennis Irwin (b); Duduka Fonseca (d); Cafe (perc).* 2/90.

***** I'll Take Romance**
Concord CCD 4491 *McCorkle; Frank Wess (ts, f); Allen Farnham (p); Howard Alden (g); Dennis Irwin (b); Keith Copeland (d).* 9/91.

McCorkle's records in the 1970s, now returning via the Jazz Alliance imprint, established her as a major songbook interpreter, uncovering rarities and seldom-heard verses from some of the best American composers. But they did her few commercial favours. *The Quality Of Mercer* has made it back to CD, and it's an absolute gem: 14 choice Johnny Mercer songs done with wit, feeling and guile in perfect balance, the charm of 'Love's Got Me In A Lazy Mood' matched to the wistfulness of 'Skylark'. A peerless session, with deft support from Ingham, Fairweather and the rhapsodic Moss. *The People That You Never Get To Love* is nearly as good. This is a more modern set of songs, with Blossom Dearie, Dave Frishberg, Neil Sedaka and A.C. Jobim represented, and McCorkle handles all of the lyrics in a hip, intelligent way, the pose just slightly world-weary, but with a clear streak of emotion below the surface cool. The somewhat later *How Do You Keep The Music Playing?* is the weakest of these three. Although there are a couple of sublime glimpses of Al Cohn in one of his last dates, some of the songs seem mishandled: a slow 'There's No Business Like Show Business' starts well but ends up far too overwrought, 'By The Time I Get To Phoenix' was a poor choice, and she overplays 'Blizzard Of Lies'.

Her current tenure with Concord has provided her with what is now a wide variety of settings. *No More Blues* benefits from a superbly integrated band, with Peplowski and Remler chiming in with pithy solos and Frishberg adding the most alert and gracious of accompaniments: McCorkle's big, courageous voice, which has been compared to Doris Day, is huskily entreating on the ballads and assuredly swinging on the faster tunes. She's an interpreter rather than an improviser, which sees her through the Brazilian songs on *Sabia*: the task here is to drift through the coolly appealing melodies rather than swinging them to pieces, and McCorkle does it with perfect aplomb. A couple of the ballads sound too stretched, but her take on Astrud Gilberto on 'So Danço Samba' is wholly beguiling, and Hamilton (in the Stan Getz role) and Remler (in her final studio date) are marvellous.

I'll Take Romance is perhaps a shade disappointing as a follow-up. Nothing wrong with the arrangements or the players, with Wess defining his role as strong-but-tender tenorman. But the material – all of it very well known, and excessively so in the case of 'Lover Man' and 'That Old Feeling' – seems like a deliberate attempt to play down McCorkle's knack for discovering forgotten gems, and some of her interpretations sound like false trails towards 'new' transformations. 'My Foolish Heart' and 'I Concentrate On You' are studied enough to suggest caricature, although occasionally – as on a wonderfully sustained 'It Never Entered My Mind' – it works out, and the faster pieces are magical. All three discs are recorded with fine lustre.

*****(*) From Bessie To Brazil**

Concord CCD 4547 *McCorkle; Randy Sandke (t, flhn); Robert Trowers (tb); Dick Oatts (as, f); Ken Peplowski (ts, cl); Allen Farnham (p); Howard Alden (g); Kiyoshi Kitagawa (b); Chuck Redd (d).* 2/93.

Almost a classic – what holds it back, as always seems to happen with this tremendously gifted singer, is the odd, strange lapse of judgement as to the kind of song she can get away with. The flaws this time are an embarrassing 'My Sweetie Went Away', done as a misplaced tribute to Bessie Smith, and a wincingly cavalier 'Still Crazy After All These Years'. On the plus side are a dozen gorgeous interpretations. Her second attempt at 'The People That You Never Get To Love', Rupert Holmes's only memorable song, is as wryly affecting as Jobim's 'The Waters Of March' is coolly hypnotic, and she does Dave Frishberg ('Quality Time') and Mercer and Arlen as well as anyone today. Sound backing from one of the Concord repertory teams, with Allen Farnham directing.

***** From Broadway To Bebop**

Concord CCD 4615 *As above, except add Frank Vignola (g), Richard De Rosa (d); omit Alden and Redd.* 4/94.

It will take tolerance to get through the aged kitsch of 'Chica Chica Boom Chic', and if she can do Broadway then bebop isn't really her thing. But there are some great ones here: a Nancy Wilson-type drama called 'One Of The Good Girls', a fine 'Guys And Dolls'. And the husk in her voice is getting the more attractive, the older she gets. Farnham's group offer gold-plated support.

***** Easy To Love – The Songs Of Cole Porter**

Concord CCD 4696 *McCorkle; Randy Sandke (t); Robert Trowers (tb); Chris Potter (as); Ken Peplowski (ts); Allen Farnham (p); Howard Alden (g); Steve Gilmore (b); Richard De Rosa (d).* 9/95.

She's in good voice, and the songs are impeccable, if sometimes worn smooth: one wonders whether there's really anything more a singer can elicit from 'Night And Day' and 'Just One Of Those Things'. So she does the latter at an unsuitably slow tempo, while 'From This Moment On' sounds too fast, and the choice of tempos generally seems like her Achilles heel. The lesser-known songs, such as 'Goodbye Little Dream, Goodbye', are the ones that turn out for the best, although 'Weren't We Fools?' is overdone. Farnham's arrangements are fair enough, if blandly Concordian at times.

***** Let's Face The Music**

Concord CCD-4759-2 *McCorkle; Greg Gisbert (t, flhn); Conrad Herwig (tb); Jerry Dodgion (as, f); Chris Potter (ts, cl, f); Allen Farnham (p); Al Gafa (g); Steve Gilmore (b); Richard De Rosa (d, ky).* 10/96.

*****(*) From Broken Hearts To Blue Skies**

Concord CCD-4857-2 *As above, except John Fedchock (tb), Jon Gordon (as, f), Dick Oatts (ts, ss, f) replace Herwig, Dodgion and Potter.* 10/98.

The first is an Irving Berlin tribute, and the rarities are what emerge best: 'Love And The Weather', a beautifully spare 'Better Luck Next Time' and a languorous 'Supper Time'. She has another go at 'There's No Business Like Show Business' and again overdoes it, although Farnham's arrangement also leans towards bombast. Excellent band, all the same.

The subsequent *From Broken Hearts To Blue Skies* is her best for years. The only false note is 'I Ain't Gonna Play No Second Fiddle': McCorkle may harbour a great affection for the Bessie Smith style but it really doesn't suit her. 'Nuages' and a lovely 'Caminhos Cruzados' are impeccable, 'Laughing At Life' is wistful, 'A Phone Call To The Past' is a Henry Mancini nocturne that she handles supremely well, and even 'I Wish I Were In Love Again' isn't overdone.

Jack McDuff (born 1926)

ORGAN

'Brother' Jack McDuff – the familial prefix predated its fashionable use – was born in Champaign, Illinois, and made his name on the Chicago club circuit, subsequently touring with his own small combo. He has touched on soul music and now calls his band The Heating System, but it all remains based around his own style of bluesy organ jazz.

***** Brother Jack – Legends Of Acid Jazz**

Prestige 24220-2 *McDuff; Harold Vick (ts); Bill Jennings, Grant Green (g); Wendell Marshall (b); Alvin Johnson, Joe Dukes (d).* 1/60–61.

***** Tough 'Duff**

Original Jazz Classics OJC 324 *McDuff; Jimmy Forrest (ts); Lem Winchester (vib); Bill Elliot (d).* 7/60.

***** The Honeydripper**

Original Jazz Classics OJC 222 *McDuff; Jimmy Forrest (ts); Grant Green (g); Ben Dixon (d).* 2/61.

***** Brother Jack Meets The Boss**

Original Jazz Classics OJC 326 *McDuff; Harold Vick, Gene Ammons (ts); Eddie Diehl (g); Joe Dukes (d).* 1/62.

***** Screamin'**

Original Jazz Classics OJC 875 *McDuff; Leo Wright (as); Kenny Burrell (g); Joe Dukes (d).* 62.

***** Crash!**

Prestige 24131-2 *McDuff; Harold Vick, Eric Dixon (ts); Kenny Burrell (g); Joe Dukes (d); Ray Barretto (perc).* 1–2/63.

***** Live!**

Prestige 24147-2 *McDuff; Red Holloway, Harold Vick (ts); George Benson (g); Joe Dukes (d).* 6–10/63.

'Brother' Jack McDuff managed to shake loose from a basic Jimmy Smith influence to explore a subtler and less heavy-handed approach to organ jazz. The earlier stuff picked up by OJC has begun to reappear on CD and any of these discs will be welcomed into the library of any collector who feels they have sufficient Smith albums by now. Little to choose between the studio dates, though Harold Vick is rather unfairly made to play second fiddle to Ammons on *Brother Jack Meets The Boss*: his feature on 'Strollin'' is as good as anything the other tenorman comes up with. *Brother Jack* is in Prestige's 'Legends Of Acid Jazz' series and couples McDuff's first albums, *Brother Jack* and *Goodnight, It's Time To Go*. These are among his freshest records, the tightness of the earlier date blending with the excitement of the new band with Vick and Green, although Joe Dukes's messy drumming lets the second set down. 'McDuff Speaking' is a definitive rocker by the man. *Crash!* brings together the LPs *Somethin' Slick*, Kenny Burrell's *Crash!*, and a stray track from *Steppin' Out*. A generous selection, and the doubled-up punch of Vick and Dixon, who unite on the first two tracks, is a different twist. *Live!* gets the nod for an extra ounce of excitement, with the likes of 'Rock Candy' and 'Sanctified Samba' digging deep without losing sight of McDuff's inventiveness and willingness to pace himself through both a solo and a set. There are also interesting glimpses of the young George Benson at work.

***** The Re-Entry**

32 Jazz 32030 *McDuff; Cecil Bridgewater (t); Houston Person, Ron Bridgewater (ts); John Hart (g); Grady Tate (d).* 3/88.

***** Groovin'**

RCA Camden 74321 610922 2CD *As above, except add Randy Johnston (g), Buddy Williams, Cecil Brooks III (d).* 88–90.

****(*) Color Me Blue**

Concord CCD 4516 *McDuff; Red Holloway (as, ts); George Benson, Phil Upchurch, Ron Eschete (g); Kevin Axt (b); Joe Dukes (d); Denise Perrier (v).* 5/91.

***** Write On, Cap'n**

Concord CCD 4568 *McDuff; Byron Stripling, Joe Magnarelli (t); Herb Besson (tb); Andrew Beals (as); Jerry Weldon (ts); John Hart (g); Winston Roye (b); Van Romaine, Rudy Petschauer (d); Johnnie Lambert (v).* 6/93.

*****(*) Bringin' It Home**

Concord CCD 4855-2 *McDuff; Andrew Beals (as); Red Holloway, Jerry Weldon (ts); John Hart, George Benson, Mark Whitfield (g); Frank Gravis (b); Rudy Petschauer, Grady Tate (d).* 8/98.

McDuff's career – or mission – has revived in the 1980s and '90s, and there are several recent sets to savour. The musical equivalent of soul food, they're undemanding and curiously effective. The Concords are a bit smoother than some earlier Muse albums, which have now been filleted for the 32 Jazz and Camden reissues – the latter is coupled with some Shirley Scott material in a bargain two-disc set. There's duplication between these two and, since neither is fat-free, one or other would suffice even hardcore collectors.

The Concord dates are initially altogether lighter fare but as the Cap'n has settled in at the label they've grown in calibre. The latest, *Bringin' It Home*, is very much the one to get. Graduates from the McDuff school like Benson and Holloway are here for the reunion, along with younger hands Whitfield, Hart and Beals, and the whole show is a thick, rich stew of bluesy small-combo sound that feels intensely satisfying.

Gary McFarland (1933–71)

VIBES, ARRANGER

Studied music in the late 1950s after trying various instruments, then did much studio work as arranger/bandleader in New York in the '60s. Put together a small group featuring his own playing, but died young.

*****(*) How To Succeed In Business Without Really Trying / Gloomy Sunday And Other Bright Moments**

Verve 527658-2 *McFarland; Clark Terry (t, flhn); Bernie Glow, Doc Severinsen, Joe Newman, Herb Pomeroy, Nick Travis (t); Wayne Andre, Bill Byers, Willie Dennis, Bill Elton (tb); Alan Raph (btb); Bob Brookmeyer (vtb); Phil Woods, Gene Quill, Eddie Wasserman (cl, as); Eddie Caine (as, f, picc); Phil Bodner (ts, ob, cor); Al Cohn (ts, cl); Oliver Nelson (ts); Sol Schlinger,*

Gene Allen (bs, bcl); Wally Kane (bsn); Hank Jones (p); Eddie Costa (vib, xy, perc); Jim Hall, Kenny Burrell (g); George Duvivier, Joe Benjamin (b); Osie Johnson, Mel Lewis (d). 11/61.

McFarland was a ubiquitous figure in the studio jazz of the 1960s. At this distance, and with so little in the CD catalogue, he now seems a bit of a mayfly. He came to New York in 1960, met Bob Brookmeyer and started composing charts for the Gerry Mulligan Concert Jazz Band. *How To Succeed* is an early example of his writing, the arrangements using the score to Frank Loesser's musical; if the material isn't as familiar as it once was, the range and sonority of McFarland's writing are intriguing, if sometimes rather period-piece in feel. It's coupled here with Brookmeyer's *Gloomy Sunday*, which includes charts by several hands, including McFarland, and involves many of the same musicians. This is a more substantial record, with Ralph Burns's ingenious revision of 'Caravan', two excellent Brookmeyer pieces and, indeed, McFarland's 'Why Are You Blue?' all outstanding. Terry and Brookmeyer shine as soloists, though there are plenty of others. McFarland did much else for Verve and Impulse!, but the interested will have to be patient or search for original vinyl.

Bernie McGann (born 1937)

ALTO SAXOPHONE

One of the major figures in contemporary Australian jazz, McGann has accrued an international reputation only slowly, but his intense playing is a classic example of 'deserving wider recognition'.

***** Ugly Beauty**

Spiral Scratch 0010 *McGann; Lloyd Swanton (b); John Pochee (d).* 1/91.

***** McGann McGann**

Rufus RF011 *As above, except add James Greening (tb).* 8/94.

*****(*) Playground**

Rufus RF023 *As above, except Sandy Evans (ts) replaces Greening.*

McGann's base in Sydney isolates him from a wider awareness, but he's a powerful, surprising, individual player whose work deserves wider currency. By working without a piano he opens these sessions up harmonically, yet he's a rather chameleonic player, as much in debt to the hard-bop masters as to Dolphy or Coleman. The weight and heft of his playing sometimes make him sound like a tenor player who's picked up the alto almost by chance, and when he locks horns with Pochee, especially on the extended rumpus created out of 'Without A Song' on *Ugly Beauty*, the music attains a terrific intensity. For all its heat and light, though, the trio session could use a centre of gravity: here and there the music seems to be grinding forward, and there's a lot of weight on McGann's shoulders.

Some of that is solved by *McGann McGann* and the recruitment of Greening, who actually takes the first solo on the record. With a Brookmeyer-like sense of humour and a big, vocal (rather than vocalized) sound, he's an apposite foil to the altoman. Some of the tunes have a bucolic charm about them, such as 'Brownsville' and 'June Bug', which makes one think of some of Jimmy Giuffre's more spirited music. But the whimsicality doesn't always work to the music's advantage.

Playground, though, solves that problem by introducing the tenor of Evans. She's not in the same league as McGann when it comes to putting together a convincing solo, relying too heavily on licks here and there, but for all that she's a tough and clear-headed performer whose contributions throw McGann's own solos into a fresh light. He's seldom sounded better than here, as fierce as ever when he wants to be, but as often turning to a slippery kind of phrasing which – given that he refuses to trade in clichés – is intriguingly personal and in hock to nobody else's jazz history. Swanton and Pochee play up to their best and Evans brings some fine tunes to the date, especially 'Snap' and the unsentimental 'Eulogy To A Friend'.

Howard McGhee (1918–87)

TRUMPET

The iconic young man with a horn, brooding, intense and self-destructive, McGhee was born in Tulsa, Oklahoma, grew up in Detroit and won his spurs in territory bands. Less of an innovator than either Fats Navarro or Dizzy Gillespie, his rather light tone and legato phrasing reflect an apprenticeship on clarinet. Maggie's recreational habits were to cost him dear but he was also a survivor, still gigging until late in life.

***** Howard McGhee On Dial – The Complete Sessions: 1945–47**

Spotlite SPJ CD 131 *McGhee; Teddy Edwards, James D King, James Moody (ts); Vernon Biddle, Jimmy Bunn, Hank Jones, Dodo Marmarosa (p); Milt Jackson (vib); Ray Brown, Bob Kesterson (b); J.C Heard, Roy Porter(d).* 9/45–12/47.

Charlie Parker's infamous 'Lover Man' sessions were originally issued under McGhee's name, but the four sides recorded in Los Angeles in 1945 for the Philo Aladdin label (and subsequently taken up by Dial) were his first as leader. They feature the twin tenors of Teddy Edwards and James D. King, the latter a friend from the Andy Kirk band. These and the jam band cuts from July 1946 are raw and rather shapeless. McGhee shows early signs of the bruised lyricism that became his signature in later years, but his phrasing is often indistinct and the line isn't always entirely convincing.

The Hollywood sextet of October 1946, which again uses Dingbod Kesterson and Roy Porter, but with the perennially undervalued Dodo Marmarosa on piano, is the first time one can really hear how fruitful an association the McGhee/Edwards front line was going to be. 'Dialated Pupils' (*sic*) and 'Up In Dodo's Room' (of which two versions survive) are strong bebop performances, and these were the cuts that began to reinforce McGhee's reputation, which was also being fostered by appearances with Jazz at the Philharmonic.

The New York tracks from December 1947 are oddly unsatisfactory, and 'Sleepwalker Boogie' may be the most telling title of the bunch, for McGhee seems to be running on autopilot. 'Night Mist' is magnificent (and also in two versions), but much of the interest comes from tenor saxophonist Moody and from the interplay between Milt Jackson and Hank Jones.

***** Howard McGhee: 1948**

Classics 1058 *McGhee; Fats Navarro (t); Billy Eckstine (vtb); Kenny Mann, Jesse Powell (ts); Jimmy Heath (as, bs); Milt Jackson (vib); Will Davis, Hank Jones (p); Ray Brown, Percy Heath (b); Joe Harris, J.C Heard (d).* 2/48.

Until very recently, McGhee wasn't well represented on CD, but Classics have now moved forward into the bebop era and the early picture is now a lot clearer. These sides catch the trumpeter at a particularly tempestuous time, when music was taking a back seat to other imperatives. As ever, McGhee seems to alternate between intense, intuitive playing and banal passage-work, but the partnership with Milt Jackson is unexpectedly calm and centred, and there are half a dozen breathtaking moments from the trumpeter. 'I'm In The Mood For Love' is one of the finest things in Maggie's entire catalogue, but it is Jackson who shines on the opening 'Sweet And Lovely'.

The Classics compilation also includes material recorded in Paris for Vogue and Blue Star, working with Jimmy Heath, who was still on alto and not yet ready to shake off his 'Little Bird' tag. By the same analogy, Jesse Powell finds himself in the Lucky Thompson role, helping to anchor the top line but creating unexpected little paths of his own through the changes.

The set ends with one of the classic bebop encounters, the October 1948 one with the trumpeter who'd made the biggest impact on his developing style. These four sides are included on *The Fabulous Fats Navarro*, which anyone committed either to bebop or to the golden years of Blue Note will already have. As usual, the mastering does the music no favours, but hearing these numbers – 'The Skunk', 'Boperation' and two parts of 'Double Talk' – under McGhee's nominal leadership perhaps slants the emphasis away from Fats for a moment. Maggie's phrasing on the first track is intriguing, because again he seems to be imitating clarinet lines, a habit he shrugs off later on in the session in favour of a much crisper attack. Interesting as it is to approach these familiar tracks from an unfamiliar direction, the only real way to hear them is on the original Blue Note issue, which is reviewed under Fats Navarro's name.

***** Maggie's Back In Town!**

Original Jazz Classics OJC 693 *McGhee; Phineas Newborn (p); Leroy Vinnegar (b); Shelly Manne (d).* 6/61.

***** Sharp Edge**

Black Lion BLCD 760110 *McGhee; George Coleman (ts); Junior Mance (p); George Tucker (b); Jimmy Cobb (d).* 12/61.

****(*) Just Be There**

Steeplechase SCCD 31204 *McGhee; Per Goldschmidt (t); Horace Parlan (p); Mads Vinding (b); Kenny Clarke (d).* 12/76.

McGhee was out of circulation for much of the 1950s. On *Maggie's Back In Town!* he sounds straightened-out and clear-headed, tackling 'Softly As In A Morning Sunrise' and 'Summertime' at a hurtling pace that sounds good in the ensembles but flags a little when he is soloing. The opening 'Demon Chase', dedicated to Teddy Edwards's son, is similarly hectic, but is good-natured enough. 'Brownie Speaks', included in homage to Clifford Brown, stretches him a little more convincingly, but by then the set is over. There is really only one ballad, and 'Willow Weep For Me' takes a slightly hysterical edge (as do one or two of the other tracks) from Newborn's very tensed-up accompaniment. Coleman's presence on *Sharp Edge* takes the heat off McGhee somewhat, and he sounds the better for it.

***** Home Run**

Storyville STCD 8273 *McGhee; Benny Bailey (t); Teddy Edwards, Sonny Redd (ts); Barry Harris, Art Hillery (p); Lisle Atkinson, Leroy Vinnegar (b); Bobby Durham, Billy Higgins (d).* 10/78–10/79.

*****(*) Wise In Time**

Storyville STCD 8272 *As above, except omit Redd, Harris, Durham.* 10/79.

McGhee was still holding his act together at the end of the '70s. The tone was still light and almost fragile, but there was an obduracy and determination in the logic of the playing which is still very appealing. Thirty years on from his debut, McGhee is once again happy to work in a more or less straight bebop form on occasions, programming Parker tunes like 'Moose The Mooche', 'Yardbird Suite' and 'Relaxin' At Camarillo'.

These albums are slightly confusing in that both also include material from the related Storyville set, *Young At Heart*, which was reviewed on LP in our first edition. The 1978 tracks with Benny Bailey sound like an attempt to recapture something of the sabres-at-dawn excitement of the McGhee–Navarro records. And yet it is the lyricism the two men share which comes across, rather than a simulacrum of the heady days of bop. The quintet with Edwards is by this stage rather like a comfortable old shoe, still capable of tramping out the miles without a pinch, and still capable of putting in a burst of speed on something like 'Moose The Mooche'. Autumnal jazz, but very beautiful.

Jimmy McGriff (born 1936)

ORGAN

Philadelphia-born, he learned a variety of instruments before studying organ at Juilliard. Had some single hits in the early '60s and has worked steadily as a club attraction since.

***** Pullin' Out The Stops! The Best Of Jimmy McGriff**

Blue Note 830724-2 *McGriff; various unlisted groups.* 64–71.

**** Electric Funk**

Blue Note 84350 *McGriff; big band including Horace Ott (p).* 9/69.

McGriff has more in common with Booker T. Jones than with the Jimmy Smith school. His name will for ever be associated with his hits, 'I Got A Woman' and 'All About My Girl', chunks of organ funk that set a tone for instrumental soul in the same way (and at a similar moment) as The MG's were cooking up their stuff at Atlantic and Stax. Both of those are on the *Pullin' Out The Stops!* compilation, which adds a further 15 tracks of steadily diminishing virtue. By the time of the awful 'Fat Cakes', from 1970, McGriff's groove sounds pooped. *Electric Funk* is a whole album of sad-sack funk from 1969 and it's hardly anything to get excited about, on or off a dance floor.

****(*) Countdown**

Milestone 9116 *McGriff; Clifford Adams Jr (tb); Marshall Keys (as); Arnold Sterling (ts, as); Melvin Sparks (g); Vance James (d).* 4/83.

***** The Starting Five**

Milestone 9148 *McGriff; Rusty Bryant (as); David Fathead Newman (ts); Mel Brown, Wayne Boyd (g); Bernard Purdie (d).* 86.

***** Blue To The 'Bone**

Milestone 9163 *McGriff; Al Grey (tb); Bill Easley (as, ts); Melvin Sparks (g); Bernard Purdie (d).* 7/88.

****(*) Right Turn On Blues**

Telarc CD-83366 *McGriff; Hank Crawford (as); Rodney Jones (g); Jesse Hameen (d).* 1/94.

***** Blues Groove**

Telarc CD-83381 *McGriff; Hank Crawford (as); Wayne Boyd (g); Vance James (d).* 7/95.

***** The Dream Team**

Milestone 9268 *McGriff; David Fathead Newman (ts); Red Holloway (ts, as); Mel Brown (g); Bernard Purdie (d).* 8/96.

There seems little merit in differentiating between these records, since they're all basically the same. McGriff (these days playing Hammond's XB-3, which offers the old sound plus various MIDI tricks) pumps away at the blues in his filigree manner, rarely working up a head of steam and instead settling for a leaner line that carries the music on a slow simmer. He gets some of his favourite hornmen to keep him company, has either Vance James or Pretty Purdie thump out the beat, and that's it. Oh, and there's some guitar, too – Sparks, Boyd or Brown, what's the difference? Even Bob Porter, who produced *The Dream Team*, says that 'the best thing is to stay the hell out of the way and let them do their thing'. Well, yes and no. It wouldn't have hurt to have most of these records tuned up a bit: the studio sound is so polite that when the band hits a groove it sounds no different from when they're laying back and floating on the chords. Both the Telarcs (actually co-credited with old chum Crawford) and the Milestones are smooth enough to spread on toast, and if they'd piled everything right to the front of the mix it might actually sound exciting. But that isn't the way jazz records are made these days.

Kalaparusha Maurice McIntyre (born 1936)

TENOR SAXOPHONE, BASS CLARINET, PERCUSSION

One of the less well-known adherents of AACM in Chicago, McIntyre absorbed more from New York-based players like Coltrane and Ayler and still sounds very much in thrall to their intensely spiritual approach.

***** Forces And Blessings**

Delmark DE 425 *McIntyre; Sarnie Garrett (g); Fred Hopkins (b); Wesley Tyus (d); Rita Omolokun Worford (v).* 11/70.

*****(*) Peace And Blessings**

Black Saint 120037-2 *McIntyre; Longineu Parsons (t, flhn, f, recorders); Leonard Jones (b); King I Mock (d).* 6/79.

***** Dream Of**

CIMP 174 *McIntyre; Michael Logan (b); Pheeroan akLaff (d).* 6/98.

At first blush, McIntyre is a fairly orthodox New Things modernist, exploiting Coltrane's extended harmony and the hands-on, little-instrument approach which was the AACM approach. As time goes by, though, he seems a more individual figure, interested in African musics – most notably on *Forces And Blessings* – and in non-Western rhythms. The reissue of the 1970 album includes unissued alternatives of 'Behold! God's Sunshine' and 'Ananda', but neither is particularly revelatory.

Much more interesting is the Black Saint album, which is somewhat dominated by Parsons, a neglected figure. He is credited with probably the best number, 'Anyway You Want It', a tough, hard-edged piece with less improvisational hinterland than McIntyre's pieces. The album as a whole has the looseness and immediacy of a live set, but is crisply recorded.

The CIMP session is, as ever, taped with maximum veracity and no frills. McIntyre's first album in almost 20 years sounds like a throwback to an earlier age in jazz. Still a commanding voice, he has a hard and unforgiving sound which probably needs a gentler acoustic environment. 'Kalaparusha's Blues Changes' and 'Denise's Song' suggest he has veered closer to the mainstream over the years, but the overall impression is oddly forbidding.

Ken McIntyre (born 1931)

ALTO SAXOPHONE, FLUTE, OBOE, BASSOON

Studied in his native Boston and made some striking early records with Eric Dolphy, but moved into education after that and, aside from some Steeplechase sets from the '70s, that is largely where his energies have been directed since.

****(*) Stone Blues**

Original Jazz Classics OJCCD 1818 *McIntyre; John Mancebo Lewis (tb); Dizzy Sal (p); Paul Morrison (b); Bobby Ward (d).* 5/60.

*****(*) Looking Ahead**

Original Jazz Classics OJCCD 252 *McIntyre; Eric Dolphy (as, f, bcl); Walter Bishop Jr (p); Sam Jones (b); Art Taylor (d).* 6/60.

It remains McIntyre's misfortune to be remembered chiefly for his brief association with Eric Dolphy and to have been almost entirely overlooked for his work since, except in Scandinavia, where his stock remains high, partly due to the sponsorship of the Steeplechase label, who kept him from obscurity in the 1970s. *Stone Blues*, with its obscure line-up, is a pretty undistinguished record, and only someone already securely interested in McIntyre's work will find much in it. It reveals a musician deeply influenced by Parker, but sounding like his own man in the search for a language beyond the orthodoxies of bebop. With the like-minded Eric Dolphy in tow, McIntyre made a more promising excursion on the well-named *Looking Ahead*, which is one of the most progressive recordings of its time, though Bishop, Jones and Taylor are still obviously thinking in the older idiom. Dolphy is, of course, superb, if still raw, and McIntyre almost inevitably plays second fiddle, but the younger man has his own things to say and he makes significant contributions to 'Lautir', 'Geo's

Tune' and 'Dianna', not quite putting Dolphy in the shade but certainly making him wait in the shadows for a moment or two. The two saxophonists shared a joyous quality that was not much in evidence in the jazz of the time and there is an infectious exuberance to their side-by-side playing.

*****(*) The Complete United Artists Sessions**
Blue Note 57200 2CD *McIntyre; John Mancebo Lewis (tb); Jaki Byard, Ed Stoute (p); Ahmed Abdul-Malik, Ron Carter, Bob Cunningham (b); Edgar Bateman, Louis Hayes, Ben Riley, Warren Smith (d); Selwart Clarke (vn, cond).* 6/62–5/63.

For a period after recording his two discs for New Jazz, McIntyre had to go into teaching to make a living; he finally retired in 1996, with the promise that he would thenceforward concentrate on music again. In 1961 and 1962, though, gigs and recording opportunities were in perilously short supply. Of the few things that did emerge, *The Year Of The Iron Sheep* grabbed the attention, if only for its strange title and for the listing of a trombone player (John Mancebo Lewis) who didn't actually figure on the released disc. Michael Cuscuna, a McIntyre enthusiast, figured that there must be more material in the can and squirrelled away until he uncovered another half-dozen tracks from June 1962 which had not seen the light of day. They are included here on the second disc of this compilation of material produced by Alan Douglas and George Wein. The *Iron Sheep* session and the slightly earlier *Way, Way Out* should have established McIntyre as a significant player, but neither seems to have attracted more than sporadic attention, mainly from fellow musicians. *Way, Way Out* had come at the height of the enthusiasm for Third Stream crossovers; it features a largish string section under the direction of Selwart Clarke. 'Miss Ann', identified here as a McIntyre composition, makes some effort to swing, but the problem with the strings format is that the pace and sheer angularity of the material run counter to the players' ability to articulate it. It is, however, an intriguing experiment, and mostly successful. The group which made *Iron Sheep* was one that might well have served Dolphy, and the abiding impression of these sides is that they might well come from the older saxophonist, who at the time was just about to head off to his uncertain future in Europe. The previously unreleased material contains no great revelations, though 'Bootsie' and the long 'Turbospacey' are tracks that historians of the New Thing and believers in the continuum of African-American music should certainly look at with interest.

****(*) Hindsight**
Steeplechase SCCD 31014 *McIntyre; Kenny Drew (p); Bo Stief (b); Alex Riel (d).* 1/74.

***** Home**
Steeplechase SCCD 31039 *McIntyre; Jaki Byard (p); Reggie Workman (b); Andre Strobert (d).* 6/75.

***** Open Horizon**
Steeplechase SCCD 31049 *McIntyre; Kenny Drew (p); Buster Williams (b); Andre Strobert (d).* 11/75.

McIntyre recorded nothing for a decade, but came back when Steeplechase began to show an enthusiastic interest in progressive American jazz. These records have been out of circulation for some time but, as with much of the label's catalogue, are now reappearing on CD with vastly improved sound. Technical qualities apart, *Hindsight* still seems rather dull, and McIntyre's treatment of repertory material – 'Naima', 'Sonnymoon For Two', 'Body And Soul' and 'Lush Life' – is eccentric rather than creative. *Home* ranges from bouncy, Caribbean impressions to funkier 'portraits' and dark-toned essays which bring together Byard and Workman in tight, adventurous arrangements. *Open Horizon* covers a similar range of material (no standards) but with a wider improvisational purview, and McIntyre appears to use his alternative horns structurally rather than to cosmetic effect. One of the few jazz players to make convincing use of the bassoon (Illinois Jacquet is another), he generally keeps to the centre of its range, much as he does with the bass clarinet, eschewing Dolphy's furious overblowing.

***** Introducing The Vibrations**
Steeplechase SCCD 31065 *McIntyre; Terumasa Hino (t); Richard Harper (p); Alonzo Gardner (b); Andre Strobert (d).* 10/76.

*****(*) Chasing The Sun**
Steeplechase SCCD 31114 *McIntyre; Hakim Jamil (b); Beaver Harris (d).* 7/78.

The two later Steeplechases, which come just before McIntyre's effective retirement from recording, are interesting in comparison of scale. The larger group with second horn and piano sounds rather drab now, partly because the cast of players doesn't throw up a natural front man to stand alongside the saxophonist. The trio with Jamil and Harris is perhaps the best thing McIntyre ever did, a rather delicate, spacious sound which uses Jamil to generate a bit of harmonic width as well as keeping time, and allows Harris, always a busy player, to state melodies as well as sustain the count. All the tunes are McIntyre originals and are uniformly of a length, nicely structured and contained.

Randy McKean

ALTO SAXOPHONE, BASS CLARINET

Contemporary free-bop saxophonist.

***** So Dig This Big Crux**
Rastascan BRD-012 *McKean; Paul Smoker (t); Drew Gress (b); Phil Haynes (d).* 4/91.

The rest of the group are familiar from Smoker's Joint Venture band, but McKean is the leader, and he's a vigorous altoist in the post-Chicago manner of the American avant-garde. Since the record is dedicated to Anthony Braxton, it's appropriate that he has something of that great Chicagoan's fiercely deliberate phrasing and scalded tone at intense moments. But passages such as the bass clarinet and trumpet dialogue of 'Quilt' are also in the spirit, if not quite the manner, of Eric Dolphy with Booker Little. Some tracks, such as the 12-minute 'Marchling', don't justify their length, but the satirical gospel strokes of 'Wholly Roller' and disrespectful reading of Roscoe Mitchell's 'Line Fine Lyon Seven' show that all four know their onions. Besides, Smoker is always worth hearing.

Dave McKenna (born 1930)

PIANO

Born in Rhode Island, McKenna spent much of the '50s in quiet sideman roles and much of the '60s with Bobby Hackett. He was still relatively unknown before signing with Concord in the '70s, where he has blossomed into an international name, one of the most reliable and hard-swinging of mainstream piano stylists with an encyclopedic knowledge of songs.

***** No Bass Hit**

Concord CCD 4097 *McKenna; Scott Hamilton (ts); Jake Hanna (d).* 3/79.

***** Giant Strides**

Concord CCD 4099 *McKenna (p solo).* 5/79.

*****(*) Left Handed Complement**

Concord CCD 4123 *As above.* 12/79.

***** My Friend The Piano**

Concord CCD 4313 *As above.*

Dave McKenna hulks over the keyboard; *Giant Strides* it is. He is one of the most dominant mainstream players on the scene, with an immense reach and an extraordinary two-handed style which distributes theme statements across the width of the piano. That's particularly evident on the good (1979) *Left Handed Complement*, a mixture of moody ballads and sharp, attacking modern themes (there's also an original 'Splendid Splinter') which keeps turning up fresh ideas. He doesn't threaten, he just plays, and on the earliest of these he plays up a storm. Long a 'players' player', he has grown in popularity and stature in recent years, not least through his association with the young Scott Hamilton, who plays a forceful but unquestionably secondary role on *One Bass Hit*.

***** A Celebration Of Hoagy Carmichael**

Concord CCD 4223 *As above.* 5/83.

*****(*) Dancing In The Dark**

Concord CCD 4292 *As above.* 8/85.

*****(*) Live At Maybeck Recital Hall: Volume 2**

Concord CCD 4410 *As above.* 11/89.

***** No More Ouzo For Puzo**

Concord CCD 4365 *McKenna; Gray Sargent (p); Monty Budwig (b); Jimmie Smith (d).* 6/88.

*****(*) Shadows And Dreams**

Concord CCD 4467 *McKenna (p solo).* 3/90.

*****(*) A Handful Of Stars**

Concord CCD 4580 *As above.* 6/92.

***** Concord Duo Series: Volume 2**

Concord CCD 4552 *McKenna; Gray Sargent (g).* 6/92.

McKenna is that rare phenomenon, a pianist who actually sounds better on his own. Though he is sensitive and responsive in group playing, and the association with Hamilton proves that, he has quite enough to say on his own account not to need anyone else to hold his jacket. The Hoagy tribute, recorded at the Second Story Club and the Tubaranch in Bloomington, Indiana, demonstrates his ability both to tame an audience and illuminate some turgid material in the process. No such problems (the former, at any rate) at Maybeck Hall, where the audiences are famously well behaved and attentive. McKenna's first Berkeley recital – *Handful Of Stars* was also played on that warm-hearted piano – is among the latest and best of McKenna's solo performances. He medleys – a frequently tiresome practice – with considerable ingenuity and absolute logic, switching hands, reversing the direction of the new theme and carefully disguising the welds. The 'Knowledge Medley' sounds odd and contrived on paper – 'Apple For The Teacher', 'I Didn't Know What Time It Was', 'I Wish I Knew', 'You'll Never Know', but you get the idea? – and works superbly in performance. The final 'Limehouse Blues' is archetypal.

Jazz players owe Arthur Schwartz an enormous debt. There are well over 50 versions of 'Alone Together' in the current catalogue, a record that approaches old warhorses like 'Body And Soul' and 'All The Things You Are'. McKenna treats the tunes with considerable respect, preserving their shape rather than just winkling out the meat of the chords. 'A Gal In Calico' and 'I See Your Face Before Me', both routinely sentimentalized, are played with exemplary taste, and 'Dancing In The Dark' has almost as much innate energy as a much later composition of the same name by a Bruce Springbok or Springstream, something like that. *My Friend* is the weakest of the bunch. The two medleys – 'Summer' and 'Always' – are slacker, and McKenna's very physical relationship with his instrument is slightly off-balance. (Normally he sounds as if he might be able to pick it up and put it in his pocket.) The 1990 solo disc ends a bit that way. It's a 'Dreams' and 'Shadows' medley, but McKenna is as distinct and wide-awake as ever. One of his best.

The quartet might just as well be a solo performance. Gray Sargent isn't quite the death's head the opening number suggests, but *rigor* has set in somewhere. Budwig is as loose and flowing as ever, and Smith clatters along with more enthusiasm than finesse. There's a 'Talk' medley this time, but you'll have to guess what's in that.

Sargent reappears on an early Concord duo Maybeck ('Maybeck' has almost become generic) and this is altogether more satisfactory. The sound is as good as you could possibly hope for and the twosome are ideally matched on 'letter' and 'time' medleys which tax Sargent's harmonic abilities more than a little but out of which he emerges with the appropriate three stripes and a hearty round of applause.

***** Sunbeam And Thundercloud**

Concord CCD 4702 *McKenna; Joe Temperley (bs).* 3/95.

Sunbeam And Thundercloud offers an unlikely pairing which works well enough. Temperley has been much lionized in recent years but to our ears he is scarcely a match for the genuine masters of the horn, and a baritone–piano pairing – on an interesting but sometimes dull selection of tunes – is tough to sustain over CD length. The distinctive moments earn the stars.

McKinney's Cotton Pickers

GROUP

Originally led by drummer Bill McKinney, they were hired by Jean Goldkette for a residency at his Detroit Graystone Ballroom in 1927. Hugely popular, they eventually recorded several sessions in New York, but the band declined when several key players left in the early '30s, and it disbanded in 1934.

*****(*) McKinney's Cotton Pickers 1928–29**

Classics 609 *John Nesbitt, Langston Curl, Joe Smith, Leonard Davis, Sidney De Paris, George 'Buddy' Lee (t); Rex Stewart (c); Claude Jones, Ed Cuffee (tb); Don Redman, George Thomas (reeds, v); Milton Senior, Prince Robinson, Jimmy Dudley, Benny Carter, Coleman Hawkins, Ted McCord (reeds); Todd Rhodes, LeRoy Tibbs, Fats Waller (p); Dave Wilborn (bj, g, v); Ralph Escudero, Billy Taylor (tba); Cuba Austin, Kaiser Marshall (d); Jean Napier (v).* 7/28–11/29.

****** Put It There Vol. 1**

Frog DGF25 *As above.* 7/28–11/29.

*****(*) McKinney's Cotton Pickers 1929–1930**

Classics 623 *As above, except add James P Johnson (p).* 11/29–11/30.

****** Cotton Picker's Scat Vol. 2**

Frog DGF 26 *As above.* 1–12/30.

It was primarily John Nesbitt who built McKinney's Cotton Pickers (although Jean Goldkette, who booked the band into his Graystone Ballroom in 1927, gave them their name). Redman's arrival in 1928 brought his distinctive touch as arranger to the band's book, but Nesbitt's driving and almost seamless charts were as impressive, and they remain so, more than 60 years later. McKinney's Cotton Pickers were among the most forward-looking of the large bands of their era: while the section-work retains all the timbral qualities of the 1920s, and the rhythm section still depends on brass bass and banjo, the drive and measure of the arrangements and the gleaming momentum of their best records both suggest the direction that big bands would take in the next decade.

On the later, New York sides, guest soloists include Coleman Hawkins, Rex Stewart and Fats Waller, and Benny Carter has one of his sharpest early outings on 'I'd Love It'. But Nesbitt, Robinson and Redman himself are significant players on the earlier sides, and the precision and verve of the band *in toto* is the main point of most of these tracks. Some of the vocals are banal, but that's the price on many such discs of the period. The new edition on Frog is easily the first choice in this important music, top-notch remastering by John R.T. Davies from fine original copies, and the great power and swing of the band come through better than ever. Whatever sources Classics used, they weren't as good, and in any case these discs came out some years earlier.

Hal McKusick (born 1924)

ALTO SAXOPHONE, CLARINET, BASS CLARINET

Work with Claude Thornhill and Boyd Raeburn was followed by small-group recordings in the '50s, some of which McKusick led himself. A cool stylist on alto and quite an adventurous thinker, but much of his best work is currently out of print.

***** In A Twentieth Century Drawing Room**

RCA 125842 *McKusick; Barry Galbraith (g); Milt Hinton (b); Sol Gubin, Osie Johnson (d); Abram Borodkin, Milton Prinz, Lucien Schmidt, Harvey Shapiro (clo).* 9/55.

***** Triple Exposure**

Original Jazz Classics OJCCD 1811 *McKusick; Billy Byers (tb); Eddie Costa (p); Paul Chambers (b); Charli Persip (d).* 12/57.

It was meeting George Russell in the mid-1950s that set McKusick on a course which might have seemed deliberately perverse to other players, exploring the outer edges of harmony, a complex approach to counterpoint, unusual and sometimes awkward time-signatures, and instrumentations that are not normally associated with jazz. The quartet of cellos on *In A Twentieth Century Drawing Room* functions as an expanded harmony instrument, generating sometimes complex, sometimes unexpectedly straight-ahead grooves for the horn. McKusick mainly floats over an open-ended accompaniment, Manny Albam's arrangements allowing him to range across the chords but also pushing him into keys that don't sit well for woodwinds. Osie Johnson's 'Minor Seventh Heaven' is a case in point. This is very musicianly music, not likely to appeal to those who like their jazz ruler-straight.

McKusick always took a thoughtful, melodic approach to soloing, keeping the tune in view at all times, rarely straying far into vertical fantasies. He's still perhaps best known for his clarinet work with Charlie Parker, and for the fine *Cross Section Saxes*, where he mixes ballad standards, 'Now's The Time', and 'Stratusphunk' by George Russell, a composer with whom he had a close relationship. *Triple Exposure* is probably the most straightforward representation of his playing style. The two horns blend particularly well on 'Con Alma', which is the archetypal McKusick performance. With *Quintet* and *Cross Section Saxes* both in limbo, he's rather marginalized at present.

John McLaughlin (born 1942)

GUITARS, GUITAR SYNTHESIZER

The story of the Yorkshire-born guitarist's recruitment by Miles Davis is a modern musical legend. McLaughlin was very much part of the reinvention of jazz and its accommodation to rock in groups like Miles's, Lifetime and his own Mahavishnu Orchestra. An intense electric player, he has also been influenced by Indian philosophies and by the flamenco tradition.

♛ ** Extrapolation**

Polydor 841598 *McLaughlin; John Surman (bs, ss); Brian Odges (b); Tony Oxley (d).* 1/69.

***** My Goal's Beyond**

Rykodisc 10051 *McLaughlin; Dave Liebman (ss); Jerry Goodman (vn); Billy Cobham (d); Mahalakshmi, Airto Moreira, Badal Roy (perc).* 6/70.

***** Devotion**

Movie Play 74058 *McLaughlin; Larry Young (org); Billy Rich (b); Buddy Miles (d).* 9/70.

****** Where Fortune Smiles**

BGO 1006 *McLaughlin; John Surman (bs, ss); Karl Berger (vib); Dave Holland (b); Stu Martin (d).* 71.

Extrapolation is one of the finest jazz records ever made in Europe. Ranging between gently meditative runs, as on 'Peace Piece', and furious 13/8 scrabbles, it combines all of McLaughlin's virtues (accuracy, power, vision) on a single disc. It has transferred to CD reasonably well, though Odges and some of McLaughlin's lower runs sound slightly artificial. The band was state-of-the-art for 1969. Oxley's drumming has the firmness of a rock beat, even when the count is extremely irregular, and Surman's playing is cast midway between folksy melodizing and complete abstraction. Tie to a chair any British jazz fan who came of age between 1967 and 1972, and a substantial number will confess that 'Binky's Beam' is their favourite track of all time. Those who attempt to deny McLaughlin's *bona fides* as a jazzman or more generally as an improviser almost always refer to *Shakti*, pseudo-classical pieces like the *Mediterranean Concerto* or one of the duff Mahavishnu Orchestra records like *Visions Of The Emerald Beyond.* They generally keep stumm about *Extrapolation*. This is essential and timeless.

My Goal's Beyond is by no means as wet as the album's design and image might suggest, and it is also a great deal more securely lodged in a jazz tradition. The original side one is a series of brief blowing themes, most of them dispatched very crisply, with McLaughlin's acoustic lines almost abrasively focused. The remainder of the album is devoted to two longer pieces 'Peace One' and 'Peace Two'. The objection to these is not so much that they are 'Indian' rather than 'jazz' as that they are so slackly conceived. The punning titles strong suggest that these were worked up quickly and without much in the way of expressive focus and they make rather sorry listening 30 years on.

We've always been very drawn to *Devotion*, which is about as close as McLaughlin gets to straightforward rock'n'roll. Much in the vein of McLaughlin's power trio, Lifetime, it again features the churning organ of Larry Young, as well as members of Jimi Hendrix's controversial and underrated Band of Gypsies line-up. 'Dragon Song' was popularized by British organist Brian Auger and the Trinity, but this is an equally invigorating performance. 'Don't Let The Dragon Eat Your Mother' and 'Devotion' are very similar to the Mahavishnu Orchestra's extended rock but grittier than the later band was to be, more's the pity.

If anyone wants to trace back the lineage of the Orchestra, then the reissued *Where Fortune Smiles* is the place to look. Anticipations of Jan Hammer's rippling arpeggiations and electronic soars can be heard in Berger's vibes and Surman's deceptively plain-spoken saxophone lines. It would be stretching it a bit to suggest that Dave Holland fulfilled the violin part, except that he does play genuine counter-melodies and does so in a rich, stringy tone that was so different from the amplified bass playing of the time. When this record came along, a new idiom seemed securely in place. Later, as we've said, it became fashionable to deride it, but even after 30 years the musicianship is immediately impressive and the overall conception still valid. *Extrapolation* is still the masterwork, but its successor repays attention as well. Catch it while it's still around.

***** Shakti**

Columbia 467905-2 *McLaughlin; L Shankar (vn); R Raghavan (mridangam); T.S Vinayakaram (perc); Zakir Hussain (tabla).* 75.

Sweetly complex acoustic music that was initially hard to absorb after the fantastic energy of the original Mahavishnu Orchestra, but which was infinitely more impressive than the OTT gestures and uneasy syntheses of Mk II. Shankar quickly went on to personal stardom, but the real drama of this set (which is much superior to the later *Handful Of Beauty*) is the interplay between McLaughlin and the tabla and clay pot percussion. Though it appeared to many fans that McLaughlin had simply gone native, it's easier in hindsight to see the continuity of all his work, in bop-influenced advanced rock, fusion, flamenco and Eastern forms, rather than its apparent breaks and changes of direction.

***** Electric Dreams**

Columbia 472210 *McLaughlin; David Sanborn (as); Stu Goldberg (p, org, syn); L Shankar (vn); Fernando Sanders (b); Tony Smith (d, v); Alyrio Lima (perc).* 11 & 12/78.

The One Truth Band was the successor to Mahavishnu. It conspicuously lacked both the spiritual intensity and the sheer musicianship of the earlier band, though there was no longer any doubt as to who was in charge. This is much more obviously a lead instrument and rhythm, without much in the way of group improvisation. Echoes of John's first dabblings in electric jazz are reinforced by a piece dedicated to and named after 'Miles Davis', returning the trumpeter's *Bitches Brew* compliment. 'Dark Prince' is in similar vein. Stu Goldberg is revelatory on keyboards, and Sanborn as ever creates some emotional excitement, but by and large the group never rises above competent anonymity and a kind of pumped-up energy.

***** Friday Night In San Francisco**

Sony 53926 *McLaughlin; Paco DeLucia, Al DiMeola (g).* 80.

*****(*) Passion, Grace & Fire**

Sony 38645 *As above.* 10–11/82.

Though honours are very deliberately closed at even and the illusion of joint leadership scrupulously maintained throughout, we have always found these sets to be rather pointlessly adversarial. Separating the component voices is easier on the later session, where the separate strands of interaction can be teased out. All three contribute characteristic themes: McLaughlin with 'Aspen' and 'David', which come from the milder end even of his recent output. *Friday Night* has been a successful and very popular album, but it never rises above its occasion or the simple fact of having this distinguished trio on a single stage together. Appealing as they are, we've found that these sets pall even after a couple of visits to the CD player.

****(*) Adventures In Radioland**

Verve 519397-2 *McLaughlin; Bill Evans (sax, ky); Mitch Forman (ky); Abraham Wechter (g); Jonas Hellborg (b); Danny Gottlieb (d, perc).* 1–2/86.

Confusingly, McLaughlin revived the Mahavishnu name for this project which bears no discernible relation to the early-'70s group. Dropping the 'Orchestra' tag was a little ironic, because all the synclavier digital equipment and Sycologic PSP drum interfaces and synths give the band a b-i-g expensive sound that conjures up adjectives like 'orchestral' willy nilly, but not without some irony. It seems that these recordings lay in the vault for some time before release. If so, one can easily relate to the marketing problem. Having done the stratospheric electric god bit, McLaughlin had recolonized a corner of the acoustic empire, and it must have been difficult to know how this testosterone-dripping sound would take. The problem lies not so much with the playing as with the writing, which is uniformly drab and unconvincingly macho. Evans's squawking solos flap through chicken-coop effects from Forman's keyboards, while Hellborg and Evans plug away humourlessly in the background. There are flashes of the old McLaughlin on 'Reincarnation' (not just the title) and 'Florianapolis', but generally this is bankrupt stock, and the much-heralded return to electricity goes nowhere fast.

*** Live At The Royal Festival Hall

JMT 834436 *McLaughlin; Kai Eckhardt (b); Trilok Gurtu (perc).* 11/89.

Twenty years on, with Lifetime, the Mahavishnu Orchestra(s), Shakti, the One Truth Band, and a wobbly 1980s mostly behind him, McLaughlin again sounds on good form, punching out rows of notes which are almost as impressive for their accuracy as for their power. Eckhardt is a subtler and more involving player than his predecessor, Jonas Hellborg, and Gurtu, as with the revivified Oregon, gives excellent value. The themes are no longer as obviously visionary and Eastern-influenced and the guitarist seems content to re-run many of the stylistic devices he had adopted from the days with Miles Davis through the ringing harmonics of Shakti and back out into a more obviously jazz-grounded idiom. These days, though, they have a clear organic function in the music. Less indulgent than formerly, McLaughlin can afford to let his strengths show through.

**** Qué Alegría

Verve 837280-2 *McLaughlin; Kai Eckhardt, Dominique De Piazza (b); Trilok Gurtu (d).* 11 & 12/91.

Designer stubble on the liner-photo and the most robust set from McLaughlin in a long time. Gurtu has always been a pulse-driven percussionist, rarely content merely to provide exotic colours round the edges of the music, and he and the bassists (Eckhardt appears on 'Reincarnation' and '1 Nite Stand', the two most forceful tracks) push McLaughlin's acoustic but subtly MIDI'd lines almost to the limits. Very little sign of the rather soft-centred flamenco approach and Indo-fusions that have dominated his work for many years. Excellent.

**(*) Time Remembered

Verve 519861-2 *McLaughlin; Aighetta Guitar Quartet: François Szonyi, Pascal Rabatti, Alexandre Del Fa, Philippe Loli (g); Yan Maresz (b).* 3/93.

McLaughlin's equation of Bill Evans = romanticism = guitars is the first and most serious thing wrong with this record. The Aighetta Quartet have performed many of the finest works for guitar ensemble, including, trivia collectors, one by the late British novelist and composer *manqué*, Anthony Burgess. Though there is nothing inherently wrong with having an essentially classical group play Evans's music (after all, the Kronos Quartet had done it), this is just not the group. In a brief personal memoir of Evans, McLaughlin remembers the pianist performing at the Village Vanguard and going into what he, very perceptively, describes as a 'state of grace'. The point was that Evans's trances were hard-won, the result of a profound dialectical approach to his material, not just an on/off mysticism. *Time Remembered* drifts all too readily into such a state. The music (familiar and beautiful themes like 'Turn Out The Stars' and, of course, 'Waltz For Debby') has no tension. Lacking drama, it ultimately lacks interest, and a rather short set is beset with longueurs which eventually torpedo it.

*** Tokyo Live

Verve 521870-2 *McLaughlin; Joey DeFrancesco (org, t); Dennis Chambers (d).* 12/93.

***(*) After The Rain

Verve 527467-2 *As above, except replace Chambers with Elvin Jones (d).* 10/94.

McLaughlin calls this new group the Free Spirits. The organ/guitar/drums line-up has become modestly fashionable again; John Abercrombie has experimented with it, and McLaughlin really sounds as if he's having *fun* for the first time in a long while. He extends the big, chunky sound he was exploring again in the mid-'80s, throwing in Wes Montgomery octave-runs and some of his own old wobbly chords. 'JuJu At The Crossroads' is terrific, though it has to be said that some tracks, notoriously the closing 'Mattinale', drag their feet unconscionably in a way they couldn't have been allowed to do in a studio. Positive sign, though: wanting to play as long as that.

Still Free Spirited, but darker and more serious in tone and with one significant change of personnel, *After The Rain* is a set of Coltrane and Coltrane-associated pieces, with a couple of McLaughlin originals thrown in. The immediate reaction on hearing those organ bass-lines and every-which-way cymbal patterns is that this is some forgotten item from the McLaughlin–Larry Young–Tony Williams terror trio, Lifetime. Too cleanly recorded, though, and McLaughlin's guitar has a plainer, quasi-acoustic ring, not the full-choke distortion of earlier years. Like his predecessor, but with less competition, Jones is almost too much in this context. The opening work-out on 'Take The Coltrane' very nearly damps enthusiasm for what's to come, except that 'My Favorite Things' and 'Sing Me Softly Of The Blues' and then 'Naima' (in which Jones dramatically switches to big palpitating tattoos on his skins) are so damn beautiful that you'd forgive him anything.

The mood is more sombre in the second half, and the drummer is less dominant, as if satisfied by his spot on McLaughlin's 'Tones For Elvin Jones'. On the face of it, 'Crescent' and 'After The Rain' aren't the likeliest items for this treatment, but they are exquisitely re-imagined, and demand to be heard again and again. A lovely record; shame about the rock album fades, though.

*** The Promise

Verve 529828-2 *McLaughlin; David Sanborn (as); Michael Brecker (ts); Jeff Beck, Philippe Loli, Paco De Lucia, Al DiMeola (g); Joey DeFrancesco (org, t); Jim Beard, Tony Hymas (ky); Nishat Khan (sitar, v); Pino Palladino, James Genus, Yan Maresz, Sting (b); Dennis Chambers, Vinnie Colaiuta, Mark Mondesir (d); Don Alias, Trilok Gurtu (perc); Zakir Hussain (tabla); Susana Beatrix, Stephania Bimbi, Mariko Takahashi (v).* 95.

What is 'the promise'? The notion perhaps that, just as there are always new fields to explore, so too the past is never quite shut off, that there are always places to go, forward or back. McLaughlin has always been a restless explorer of his own past, unusually conscious of his own back-catalogue. In a sense, this record is a re-run of *Electric Guitarist*, a sampling of tracks by half-a-dozen different line-ups, collaged with readings from Dante, Lorca and haiku. The effect is bitty and slightly bewildering, but there are treasures to be found. The Free Spirits trio is convened for 'Thelonious Melodius'. It immediately follows a guitar work-out on John Lewis's 'Django', with Jeff Beck – of all people – as second guitar. An even less likely personnel credit is Sting, who joins McLaughlin and Vinnie Colaiuta for one minute and twelve seconds of head-down jamming; wonder if he kept the cab waiting. Another long-standing trio, with de Lucia and DiMeola, reappears for 'El Ciego', a slightly routine dip into their emotive contrapuntal bag. The really substantial stuff (and the bulk of the album) is contained in two saxophone-led tracks: 'Shin Jin Rui' with the guest performer *par excellence*, David Sanborn; and the long, long 'Jazz Jungle', with the even more ubiquitous Michael Brecker up front. The latter degenerates into a bit of a jam but, with saxophone and guitar swapping ideas at ever higher altitudes, it's sustained by sheer excitement and pace, even over 14 minutes. One fascinating oddity is 'No Return' (which is presumably not McLaughlin's philosophy). Here he swaps places with DeFrancesco, who gets out his trumpet while the boss doubles on keyboards. Most of the ideas have been heard before, but never in this configuration, and it might have been more effective to leave it to the end of the record, which concludes on an ultra-mellow acoustic reading of Jimmie Rowles's 'The Peacocks'. Though this is a minor miscall, what comes across throughout the album is the extent of McLaughlin's fascination with the studio and its potentialities. He clearly wants to create an integrated and emotionally supple product that cancels out the item-by-item approach. He hasn't quite succeeded, but with continued major-label backing he has the opportunity to experiment further. A valid experiment by a major artist.

***** The Guitar Trio**

Verve 533215-2 *McLaughlin; Paco De Lucia, Al DiMeola (g).* 5–7/96.

Divided by a common instrument, common language, or by a gentle ambition to make the strongest impact on this collaborative set? Composition, solo and production credits are divided with almost schoolboyish even-handedness, and the disc gives every indication of having been A&R'd by committee. Not that the playing isn't superlative. McLaughlin's two solos on 'Le Monastère Dans Les Montagnes' and his introduction on 'Midsummer Night', both his own compositions, are magisterial and quite beautiful. His partners contribute their share and more, with De Lucia sounding relaxed and unemphatic, but totally focused. DiMeola is the wild card, but for once he resists a long-standing tendency to grandstand and overstate; his composition, 'Azzura', is perhaps the best thing on the whole album, a rich soundscape that inspires a wonderful opening solo from McLaughlin as well. Despite a slightly contrived summit conference feel, this is a marvellous album and one that will appeal to jazz guitar fans of every persuasion.

***** Belo Horizonte**

WEA International 57001 *McLaughlin; François Jeanneau (ss, ts); Katia Labèque (syn); Tommy Campbell (d); Steve Sheman (d).* 97.

This lurches between the inspirational and the ineffably dull, without much ground in between. McLaughlin and Labèque indulge in some musical flirtation, leaving the others in the group little to do except shuffle uneasily round the perimeter. Jeanneau never quite integrates himself into the group, and the percussionists seem to belong to a tougher and more confrontational group.

*****(*) The Heart Of Things**

Verve 539153-2 *McLaughlin; Gary Thomas (ts, ss, f); Jim Beard (p, syn); Jean-Paul Celea, Matthew Garrison (b); Dennis Chambers (d); Victor Williams (perc).* 97.

****** Live In Paris**

Verve 543536-2 *As above, except omit Beard, Celea; add Romario Ruiz (ky).* 11/98.

Old question: What would Charlie Parker, Eric Dolphy, Jimi Hendrix, Jaco Pastorius, Emily Remler, whoever, be doing if he, she, it were alive in the late 1990s? In all but name, this is a Mahavishnu Orchestra for the end of the century, stripped of much of the Eastern philosophy, hooked into a more contemporary sound, but identifiable from the same balance of ensemble and individual playing, the same flyaway soloing, and the easily missed glint of steel amid the gentleness. Compared to previous horn players – Liebman, Evans – Gary Thomas is a tough customer, and he prompts a more abrasive and confrontational sound from McLaughlin who, as in recent years, alternates electric and acoustic with MIDI guitars. The last of these performs much the same function as Jan Hammer's Moog had in the Ork, leaving Beard and Thomas to round out the front line in the same top-heavy way. The best of the music is concentrated in three long tracks: 'Acid Jazz' (which ain't), 'Seven Sisters' and a beautiful idea called 'Fallen Angels', which does as the album-title suggests and cuts to the essential. These days, McLaughlin doesn't sound so chilled as to be uninvolving, but he has managed to broker a philosophical position which allows him to play relatively free without lapsing into free-jazz cliché, and to revisit aspects of his own past without succumbing to nostalgia or self-regard.

The live album may well be compared in future to Miles's classic set in the same city and it focuses the energies of what has become McLaughlin's repertory band to an impressive degree. If this is what they can reproduce on tour, the prospects are scarily good. 'Fallen Angels' and 'Acid Jazz' are again the standout tracks and there is a beautiful tribute to the late Tony Williams, who would have enjoyed music of this intensity and rhythmic complexity. With a Ruiz, a Garrison, a Chambers and a Williams in the line-up, to say nothing of the redoubtable Thomas, it's hard to see how John McLaughlin can go wrong.

***** Remember Shakti**

Verve 559945-2 2CD *McLaughlin; Hariprasad Chaurasia (bansuri); Zakir Hussein (tabla); T.H Vinayakram (ghatam).* 97.

Reconvened for a tour that included these British dates, Shakti is still a compelling unit, though lacking the sheer percussive impact of the original group. Split over two discs, the set is dominated by an hour-plus performance of Chaurasia's 'Mukti', and there are also long versions of the flautist's 'Chandrakauns' and McLaughlin's 'Wish'. The pace is inevitably rather slacker and more meditative than of yore, but there is plenty of virtuosic playing and a joyous abandon which fans of the original group will value.

Jackie McLean (born 1932)

ALTO SAXOPHONE

McLean's father worked with Tiny Bradshaw, and young John grew up surrounded by music, a discipline that he later passed on to his son René. During a spell in the finishing school known as the Jazz Messengers, Jackie struck out on his own, recording prodigiously with his own quartet and patenting a sound that was compounded equally of bebop and the new, free style. Raw and urgent, no one else sounds quite like him.

*****(*) Lights Out**

Original Jazz Classics OJC 426 *McLean; Donald Byrd (t); Elmo Hope (p); Doug Watkins (b); Art Taylor (d).* 1/56.

***** 4, 5 And 6**

Original Jazz Classics OJC 056 *McLean; Donald Byrd (t); Hank Mobley (ts); Mal Waldron (p); Doug Watkins (b); Art Taylor (d).* 7/56.

***** McLean's Scene**

Original Jazz Classics OJC 098 *McLean; Bill Hardman (t); Red Garland, Mal Waldron (p); Paul Chambers, Arthur Phipps (b); Art Taylor (d).* 12/56, 2/57.

***** Jackie's Pal**

Original Jazz Classics OJC 1714 *McLean; Bill Hardman (t); Paul Chambers (b); Philly Joe Jones (d).* 56.

***** Makin' The Changes**

Original Jazz Classics OJC 197 *McLean; Webster Young (t); Curtis Fuller (tb); Gil Coggins, Mal Waldron (p); Paul Chambers, Arthur Phipps (b); Louis Hayes, Art Taylor (d).* 2/57.

***** Alto Madness**

Original Jazz Classics OJC 1733 *McLean; John Jenkins (as); Wade Legge (p); Doug Watkins (b); Art Taylor (d).* 5/57.

***** A Long Drink Of The Blues**

Original Jazz Classics OJC 253 *As above.* 8/57.

****(*) Jackie McLean & Co.**

Original Jazz Classics OJC 074 *McLean; Bill Hardman (t); Ray Draper (tba); Mal Waldron (p); Doug Watkins (b); Art Taylor (d).* 2/57.

***** Strange Blues**

Original Jazz Classics OJC 354 *McLean; Webster Young (t); Ray Draper (tba); Gil Coggins, John Meyers, Mal Waldron (p); Arthur Phipps, Bill Salter (b); Louis Hayes, Larry Ritchie, Art Taylor (d).* 2 & 8/57.

***** Fat Jazz**

Fresh Sound FSR CD 18 *McLean; Webster Young (t); Ray Draper (tba) Gil Coggins (p); George Tucker (b); Larry Richie (d).* 12/57.

Charlie Parker once invited Jackie McLean to kick him in the ass as pay-off for some typically selfish transgression. There were those who felt that McLean in turn could have used similarly robust encouragement in the 1950s, when his life and career teetered towards the edge.

These come from a turbulent but productive period in McLean's career. The OJCs mine almost to exhaustion the mid-1956 and early-1957 sessions with Waldron, filling in with other Prestige and New Jazz materials. McLean's pure, emotive blues tone, characteristically taking off with a wail at the break, has already become a manner, but there is a searching, troubled quality to his work on 'Abstraction' (*4, 5 And 6*), 'Flickers' and 'Help' (*& Co.*), and the two takes of 'Long Drink Of The Blues' (OJC 253, which also includes desirable versions of 'I Cover The Waterfront', 'Embraceable You' and 'These Foolish Things'). Given the range and familiarity of material, this might seem a good place to start, but *Scene* ('Mean To Me' and 'Old Folks') and *Changes* ('I Hear A Rhapsody' and 'Chasin' The Bird') are more challenging, pointing a way out of the still-dominant Parker influence.

Perhaps the best of the group is the earliest. *Lights Out* has a directness and simplicity of diction that are not so evident elsewhere; where McLean does attempt something more adventurous, as in the 'bagpipe' introduction and carefully harmonized final chorus of 'A Foggy Day', he does so with taste and precision. As on *4, 5 And 6*, Byrd is a fine collaborator, soloing in a sweet, Dorham-influenced tone on the ballad, 'Lorraine', and 'Kerplunk', both of which were written by the trumpeter. Hardman, a 'pal' from the *Hard Bop*-vintage Jazz Messengers, is almost equally good and Philly Joe cooks up an accompaniment very nearly as forceful as Blakey's.

The Fresh Sound is desirable not least because of the CD format but also for freshly minted charts, and the inventive brass interplay of Young and Draper (who led his own session with John Coltrane a year later – *A Tuba Jazz*, Fresh Sound CD 20). 'Tune Up' is one of McLean's leanest and most daring performances of the period.

****** New Soil**

Blue Note 784013 *McLean; Donald Byrd (t); Walter Davis Jr (p); Paul Chambers (b); Pete LaRoca (d).* 5/59.

***** Vertigo**

Blue Note 22669 *As above, except add Kenny Dorham (t), Herbie Hancock (p), Butch Warren (b), Billy Higgins, Tony Williams (d).* 5/59, 2/63.

***** Swing, Swang, Swingin'**

Blue Note 56582 *McLean; Walter Bishop Jr (p); Jimmy Garrison (b); Art Taylor (d).* 10/59.

Transitional and challenging, *New Soil* seems reasonably tame by present-day standards. McLean had passed through difficult times and was visibly reassessing his career and direction. The extended 'Hip Strut' is perhaps the most conventional thing on the album, but the saxophonist is straining a little at the boundaries of the blues, still pushing from the inside, but definitely looking for a new synthesis. 'Minor Apprehension' has elements of freedom which are slightly startling for the period and wholly untypical of McLean's previous work. Davis contributes a number of compositions, including the previously unreleased 'Formidable' (which isn't). Byrd is still a more than viable player. The transfer isn't as good as usual, with a lot of mess on the drummer's tracks, but the music is important enough to be labelled historic.

Vertigo has more material from the May date, together with further tracks from a 1963 session which marked the recorded debut of Tony Williams. Historically, this makes the album more important than the quality of performance might suggest. As ever, McLean seems poised between innovation and conservatism, and it's often hard to pin down where the music is coming from, less fruitfully so than on other discs.

The October session is less immediately compelling, partly because Jackie sticks to standards, but more because he so obviously remains within his comfort zone. The record was presumably an attempt to recapture commercial success, for it is palpably less compelling than its predecessors and some of the sessions that followed. Only the closing '116th And Lenox' has any of the saxophonist's ability to meld new and old in a single blues-based theme.

*****(*) Bluesnik**

Blue Note 84067 *McLean; Freddie Hubbard (t); Kenny Drew (p); Doug Watkins (b); Pete LaRoca (d).* 1/61.

Tough, unreconstructed modern blues that reveal considerable depths on subsequent hearings. That's particularly noticeable on the outwardly conventional title-track, on which McLean's solo has a formidably unexpected logic. The other soloists tend to take up space that one might prefer to have seen left to the on-form leader, but Hubbard is dashing and Drew affectingly lyrical. A word, too, for the seldom-discussed Watkins, who gives his lines a lazy-sounding drag that nevertheless holds the beat solidly together. An excellent record that should be a high priority for anyone interested in McLean's music.

****** Let Freedom Ring**

Blue Note 46527 *McLean; Walter Davis Jr (p); Herbie Lewis (b); Billy Higgins (d).* 3/62.

A classic. Influenced by Ornette Coleman – with whom he was to record for Blue Note on *Old And New Gospel* – McLean shrugged off the last fetter of bop harmony and pushed through to a more ruggedly individual post-bop that in important regards anticipated the avant-garde of the later 1960s. McLean's phenomenally beautiful tone rings out on 'Melody For Melonae', 'I'll Keep Loving You', 'Rene' and 'Omega'. Higgins's bright, cross-grained drumming is exemplary and the band is generously recorded, with plenty of bass.

*****(*) Destination ... Out!**

Blue Note 32087 *McLean; Grachan Moncur III (tb); Bobby Hutcherson (vib); Larry Ridley (b); Roy Haynes (d).* 9/63.

Though he emerged as a relatively orthodox bebopper, McLean was deeply influenced by the free-jazz movement, as his collaboration with Ornette Coleman underlined. Its title was significant, though, because McLean was unwilling to throw over entirely a more traditional idiom. *Destination ... Out!* is a great album for the way it combines both idioms. Moncur has the bulk of the composing credits, with just 'Kahlil The Prophet' from the leader. Complex, tricky and thoroughly engaging, this is one of the forgotten records of the period but it is well worth a visit now. (It's a limited edition, so hurry!)

*****(*) Dr Jackle**

Steeplechase SCCD 36005 *McLean; Lamont Johnson (p); Scott Holt (b); Billy Higgins (d).* 12/66.

***** Tune Up**

Steeplechase SCCD 36023 *As above.* 12/66.

The later 1960s were a somewhat dead time for McLean, and it looked as though the huge strides he had taken at the beginning of the decade led nowhere. He acted in Jack Gelber's *The Connection* and played some of the script for real. His playing of the time has a slightly tired edge and a hesitancy that comes not from lack of confidence but from a seeming lack of motivation to develop ideas. *Dr Jackle* includes a take of 'Melody For Melonae' which is quite discouraging in its diffidence and defensive show; McLean clearly isn't helped by the rhythm section, but Higgins alone should have been enough to spur him to better things. *Tune Up* has an air of afterthought; an attractive enough session, it can safely be left to completists, though Higgins is a revelation throughout, a mischievous, endlessly inventive performance.

****** Live At Montmartre**

Steeplechase SCCD 31001 *McLean; Kenny Drew (p); Bo Stief (b); Alex Riel (d).* 8/72.

***** A Ghetto Lullaby**

Steeplechase SCCD 31013 *As above, except replace Stief with Niels-Henning Orsted Pedersen (b).* 7/73.

For sheer *joie de vivre*, albeit with a chastened edge, *Live At Montmartre* is hard to beat. Full-voiced and endlessly inventive, McLean romps through 'Smile', adding the 'shave-and-a-haircut-*bay-rum*' cadence to the end of his first statement with an almost arrogant flourish. 'Parker's Mood' is perhaps the best of his later bebop essays, shifting out of synch with Drew's excellent chording for a couple of measures. *Lullaby* is less immediately appealing, though NHOP adds a significant element to the group's harmonic output, and he is a much solider player than Stief. 'Mode For Jay Mac' is interesting, and the title-track calls up some of McLean's most purely emotive playing.

****(*) Ode To Super**

Steeplechase SCCD 31009 *McLean; Gary Bartz (as); Thomas Clausen (p); Bo Stief (b); Alex Riel (d).* 7/73.

A disappointing confrontation that recalls the *Alto Madness* session with John Jenkins from 1957. Bartz already sounds as if he has set his sights on a rock/fusion future and McLean battles against Clausen's apparent insistence on closing up the harmonies. 'Monk's Dance' makes a promising but unfulfilled opening, and 'Great Rainstreet Blues' bogs down rather too quickly.

***** The Meeting**

Steeplechase SCCD 31006 *McLean; Dexter Gordon (ts); Kenny Drew (p); Niels-Henning Orsted Pedersen (b); Alex Riel (d).* 7/73.

***** The Source**

Steeplechase SCCD 31020 *As above.* 7/73.

For once, Steeplechase's obsessive over-documentation makes sense. Recorded over two nights, this isn't a good album and a makeweight but a 'double' of genuine quality. Gordon and McLean were poles apart stylistically, but temperament and geography suggested such a meeting was inevitable. The first volume is darker and more sensitive, and the opening 'All Clean' hits close to home. McLean is usually quicker to the punch, but Gordon spins out his ideas (particularly on the standards) with confidence and some in reserve. 'Half Nelson' and 'I Can't Get Started' (*The Source*) depend to a large extent on Drew's teasing out of the chords. The sound isn't spectacularly good, with a tendency to fragment round the edges; no better on the CD unfortunately, but the playing makes up for it.

***** New York Calling**

Steeplechase SCCD 31023 *McLean; Billy Skinner (t); René McLean (ts, ss); Billy Gault (p); James Benjamin (b); Michael Carvin (d).* 10/74.

New York Calling is a respectable performance from a band capable of better. The Cosmic Brotherhood featured McLean's talented and indoctrinated-from-the-cradle son, René. Far from sounding like a chip, he shows considerable individuality on both his horns, carving out intriguing counter-melodies and straightforward responses, neither over-respectful nor wilfully defiant. The charts are impressively varied, but *New York Calling* isn't a first choice for CD transfer; the sound is unaccountably flat. McLean *père* takes his best solo early, on the title-track, and finds little to add to it. Skinner sounds as if he could do with a bottle of valve oil and has intonation problems throughout (unless he intends some of his middle-register notes to be flatted). Once again, it's the drummer who attracts positive attention. A couple of months before, McLean and Carvin had recorded a duo album, *Antiquity*, perhaps the most far-out thing the saxophonist has ever done.

***** Antiquity**

Steeplechase SCCD 31028 *McLean; Michael Carvin (d, perc, v).* 8/74.

The duo with Carvin is as far out as anything McLean has attempted. The core of the session is an impressionistic account of slave days, with the drummer's passionate vocals helping to fill out the story. McLean's own passions seem a little muted by contrast, but there are moments when the two spiral up on a single motif and the music starts to fire up. Then there's no mistaking McLean's mastery.

****** Dynasty**

Triloka 181 2 *McLean; René McLean (ts, as, ss, f); Hotep Idris Galeta (p); Nat Reeves (b); Carl Allen (d).* 11/88.

*****(*) Rites Of Passage**

Triloka 188 2 *As above, except add Lenny Castro (perc).* 1/91.

Both sessions start with McLean originals, but responsibility for producing new material for the Dynasty band has largely fallen on René and South African-born pianist Galeta. Their work introduces a range of altered changes and curious tonalities that are drawn from African and Asian musics ('Zimbabwe', 'Muti-Woman', Stanley Wiley's 'Third World Express' on *Dynasty*, 'Naima's Love Poem' and 'Destiny's Romance' on *Rites*) and to which McLean responds very positively, confirming how much on the outside of conventional bop language he always was. The unmistakable tone is still very much intact and infuses even a rather bland vehicle like Bacharach's 'A House Is Not A Home' with considerable feeling.

His son simply can't match him for either speed or articulation or beauty of tone, having a rather vinegary sound on his two main horns and a bleary version of Richie Cole's reedy whine on the alto. He is, though, a fine flute player and it would be good to hear him more often on that horn. Both albums are a must for McLean fans and the first (recorded in front of a studio audience) can be confidently recommended to anyone interested in the finest modern jazz.

René McLean (born 1947)

SAXOPHONES, FLUTE

Jackie's son is a capable player in the contemporary style, though he has had only a few opportunities as a leader on record.

***** Watch Out**

Steeplechase SCCD 31037 *McLean; Danny Coleman (t, flhn); Nathan Page (g); Hubert Eaves (p); Buster Williams (b); Freddie Waits (d).* 7/75.

***** In African Eyes**

Triloka 203 195 *McLean; Hugh Masekela, Prince Lengoasa (flhn); Moses Molelekwa, Themba Mkhize, Rashid Lanie (p); Jonny Khumalo, Jonny Chancho, Prof. Themba Mokoena, Bheki Khasa (g); Bakhiti Khumalo, Fana Zulu, Victor Masondo (b); Sello Montwedi, Ian Herman, Lulu Gontsana (d); Jon Hassan, Papa Kouyate, Bill Summers, Zamo Mbutho (perc).* 92.

Second generation in the family business, young René famously was given one of dad's old mouthpieces as a comforter. The early start (and lessons with Sonny Rollins) notwithstanding, he seemed slow to develop a genuinely individual voice on the saxophone. Though he was working and recording with his father for several years beforehand, René didn't make a record of his own until 1975. *Watch Out* is a lively, often very impressive session, wisely mixing Young Turk enthusiasm up front with a solidly experienced back-line. There are already intimations of the African interests that have become dominant more recently; 'Bilad As Sudan' makes for an arresting opening, and the pace doesn't slacken much before the close, though by then, one feels, Coleman is long out of ideas. There are moments when the accompaniments become unnecessarily cluttered.

Clutter is in a curious way the rationale of *In African Eyes*, which at this point may be difficult to find on the disappearing Triloka label. René allows the sound to build up in bright, inexactly matched layers, a patchwork effect that is often very rewarding. The record was actually made in South Africa, hence his access to Masekela and the other, rather lesser lights of the new Azanian jazz. It's a joyous sound, as befits a country and culture in rapid change. McLean might have thought of adding another saxophone to keep the symmetry and fill out his parts in ensembles. As it is, he can sound a little thin, and boosting his volume doesn't entirely address this.

Dave McMurdo

TROMBONE

Canadian trombonist and arranger specializing in modern-mainstream big-band music.

****(*) The Dave McMurdo Jazz Orchestra**

Jazz Alliance TJA-10001 *McMurdo; Arnie Chycoski, Chase Sanborn, Steve McDade, Mike Malone, Neil Christofferson (t, flhn); Rob Somerville, Terry Lukiwski, Ted Bohn (tb); Bob Hamper (btb); Mark Promane (ss, as, cl, f); Don Englert (ss, as, f); Pat LaBarbera, Michael Stuart (ts, cl, f); Bob Leonard (bs, bcl, f); Don Thompson (p); Reg Schwager (g); George Mitchell (b); Kevin Dempsey (d).* 10/89.

***** Live At The Montreal Bistro**

Sackville SKCD2-2029 *As above, except add Sandy Barter, Kevin Turcotte (t, flhn), Perry White (bs, bcl, f); omit Chycoski, McDade and Leonard.* 4/92.

***** Different Paths**

Sackville SKCD2-2034 *As above, except Paul Novotny (b) replaces Mitchell.* 6/93.

***** Fire And Song**

Sackville SKCD2-5004 2CD *As above, except Terry Promane (tb), Alex Dean (ts, cl, f) replace Lukiwski and Stuart.* 3/96.

McMurdo's Canadian big band features many exemplars of a largely unsung (in international terms) scene and, though the music is often content to stay within the parameters of a well-drilled big band blowing conscientious arrangements, they are very good at their tasks. The first record is a little too precise and buttoned-down: a long, complex reworking of '(All Of A Sudden) My Heart Sings' is a fine opening, but some of the other scores are faceless, and the programme could use an all-stops-out snorter. The live session opens with just that, a rollicking treatment of 'Straight No Chaser', and the upfront punch of the live sound and a strongly contrasting choice of scores make this the best album of the three, with McMurdo's own playing on 'A Nightingale Sang In Berkeley Square' and a terse arrangement of Wayne Shorter's 'Black Nile' among the standouts.

Different Paths is more of a writer's showcase. Since the orchestra uses several arrangers and propagates an ensemble sound of impeccable balance, it seldom aspires to a particular character, but Don Thompson's charts are some of its best: the sprawling 'Don't/Wintermist', 'a true concert piece', as McMurdo notes, is their most ambitious undertaking. The rest is interesting rather than outstanding.

Fire And Song is elaborately spread across two discs and clocks in at nearly two and a half hours. They are back at the Montreal Bistro and in ebullient form. When the orchestra get hot, as on 'Fast Eddie' or 'Fire', they can turn a score inside out with an almost fearsome aplomb, and if none of the soloists cuts a genuinely individual figure, that hardly seems the point of what is an enterprise dedicated to a collective result. All virtues considered, there's a perhaps inescapable anonymity which the music can't wholly shake off. Big-band admirers should nevertheless alight here.

Jim McNeely (born 1949)

PIANO, KEYBOARDS

Born in Chicago, he studied piano and saxophone, then from a New York base spent substantial periods with the Jones–Lewis Orchestra, Stan Getz and Phil Woods. Holds a conducting position with Danish Radio Big Band and is now composer-in-residence for Vanguard Jazz Orchestra.

***** Rain's Dance**

Steeplechase SCCD 31412 *McNeely; Larry Schneider (ss, ts); Mike Richmond (b); Bob Merigliano (d); Sam Jacobs (perc).* 10/76.

***** Winds Of Change**

Steeplechase SCCD 31256 *McNeely; Mike Richmond (b); Kenny Washington (d).* 7/89.

Having worked with Mel Lewis, Stan Getz and Joe Henderson, McNeely has long since acquired a substantial reputation which these albums confirm in their unfussy way. A clever writer and a mercurial though restrained soloist, McNeely likes a lot of space to develop ideas in. *Rain's Dance* was his first date as a leader and it has recently made its bow on CD with an alternative take of the long title-track as a bonus. There are elements of 'prentice work about it and some of the tracks overrun their welcome, but it's hard to fault the commitment of the playing (Schneider could burn along modal lines as capably as any tenorman of that moment) and McNeely was already flexing a composer's muscles.

Currently it's a long gap to *Winds Of Change*. Each of the five originals has a specific turn of phrase, while 'Bye-Ya' is a particularly fluent reading of a Monk piece that not many tackle. Richmond, whose voluble yet lightly weighted lines are entirely apt, is certainly his ideal bass partner.

***** East Coast Blow Out**

Lipstick LIP 89007-2 *McNeely; John Scofield (g); Marc Johnson (b); Adam Nussbaum (d); WDR Big Band.* 9/89.

As a big-band commission this seems like only a half-hearted exercise by McNeely. His scores for the WDR Big Band are more like interpolations into what is fundamentally a tightly arranged sequence for the quartet: Scofield has a marvellous, concerto-like feature on 'Do You Really Think ...?' and McNeely's own piano improvisations on 'Skittish' are impeccable, yet the orchestra always sounds as if it's trying to nudge its way in, rather than playing a full role. For the quality of the individual playing, though, it merits a recommendation.

****** Live At Maybeck Recital Hall Vol. 20**

Concord CCD 4522 *McNeely (p solo).* 1/92.

McNeely's entry in this quietly compelling series is one of the most 'modern' in the sequence. If these concerts offer no more than a mere snapshot of a pianist at work, their knack of creating an individual and vivid picture is exemplified by McNeely's brilliant playing, oddly diffident in its tone yet achieved with the greatest finesse and inventiveness. On the opening 'There Will Never Be Another You', for instance, he calmly plays the tune in all 12 keys, batting the melody and development alike between his two hands and completing the task with a shoulder-shrug ending. There are readings of Jobim, Monk and Powell that honour each composer by transforming him, and there are two fine themes of his own. Always one is conscious of a two-handed player: for all the clarity of his touch, he takes in more of the keyboard in each improvisation than many do over a whole recital. Highly recommended.

Marian McPartland (born 1920)

PIANO

Born in Windsor, Marian Turner went to the USA when she married her husband, Jimmy McPartland, in 1945. She worked as a soloist in Chicago and had a long trio residency at New York's Hickory House in the 1950s. A low period in the '60s was succeeded by three decades of prolific and successful work: as pianist, composer, pioneer jazz educator, writer, and – most effectively of all – as broadcaster, her Piano Jazz interviews with fellow pianists running for many years on American public service radio.

***(*) **A Sentimental Journey**
Jazz Alliance TJA-10025 *McPartland; Jimmy McPartland (c, v); Vic Dickenson, Hank Berger (tb); Jack Maheu (cl); Buddy Tate (ts, bs); Rusty Gilder (b); Gus Johnson, Larry Bell, Mike Berger (d).* 11/72–6/73.

Marian's earlier sessions – for Capitol, Savoy and others – seem to be in limbo again at the moment, though hopefully the Savoy material at least will feature in that label's latest series of reissues. So we have to start in 1973, with a lovely memento of two engagements by bands led by Jimmy, with Marian on piano and two entertaining front lines. Jack Maheu blends a spiralling virtuosity with Pee Wee-type licks, Tate is reliable (and picks up the baritone here and there), Dickenson is absolutely himself (his 'When You Wish Upon A Star' is priceless) and Jimmy leads with typical aplomb. The piano sounds a bit difficult here and there, but the pianist is obviously enjoying herself, and she contributes a delightful sleeve-note.

**** **Plays The Music Of Alec Wilder**
Jazz Alliance TJA-10016 *McPartland; Michael Moore, Rusty Gilder (b); Joe Corsello (d).* 6/73.

This is one of the great single-composer recitals and it should be far better known than it is. McPartland has been intensely involved in Alec Wilder's difficult, bittersweet music for decades and she gets closer to the heart of it than any jazz player ever has. 'Jazz Waltz For A Friend', the first track, was written for her, and several of the other pieces have scarcely been touched by other improvisers. The five pieces with the lone support of Michael Moore are wonderfully lyrical and searching and, though the remaining five with Gilder and Corsello are a shade less involving, it is a memorable occasion which has been long overdue for CD release. The only regret must be that she didn't play Wilder's unforgettable 'Where Do You Go?' at the date.

*** **From This Moment On**
Concord CCD 4086 *McPartland; Brian Torff (b); Jake Hanna (d).* 12/78.

**** **Portrait Of Marian McPartland**
Concord CCD 4101 *As above, plus Jerry Dodgion (as, f).* 5/79.

***(*) **Personal Choice**
Concord CCD 4202 *McPartland; Steve LaSpina (b); Jake Hanna (d).* 6/82.

*** **Willow Creek And Other Ballads**
Concord CCD 4272 *McPartland (p solo).* 1/85.

McPartland's playing and composing have remained amazingly fresh and interested. Besides performing, she has hosted a long-running American radio series which features her with a different jazz pianist on every edition; and, perhaps as a result, her own playing seems sensitive to all the possible directions in contemporary jazz piano. Even though this would be classed by most as ostensibly 'mainstream jazz', there are inflexions in it which would be unknown to most of McPartland's immediate contemporaries. *From This Moment On* offers a tight, generous reading of familiar standards, but *Portrait* goes a notch higher by adding Dodgion's bristling alto and beautifully articulated flute to the mix. An incisive version of Herbie Hancock's 'Tell Me A Bedtime Story', a tart Dodgion blues called 'No Trumps' and an ideal treatment of the pianist's gorgeous 'Time And Time Again' are the highlights. *Personal Choice* is another catholic programme, with tunes by Jobim, Brubeck and Pettiford, but a surprisingly tough 'I'm Old-Fashioned' and a reflective solo 'Melancholy Mood' turn out the best. If the solo set is a shade behind the others, it's only because McPartland uses the resources of a trio so intelligently that she seems relatively quiescent by herself. While her treatments of the likes of 'Someday I'll Find You' are typically original, it would be agreeable to hear her tackle an entire set of her own compositions.

*** **Plays The Music Of Billy Strayhorn**
Concord CCD 4326 *McPartland; Jerry Dodgion (as); Steve LaSpina (b); Joey Baron (d).* 3/87.

***(*) **Plays The Benny Carter Songbook**
Concord CCD 4412 *McPartland; Benny Carter (as); John Clayton (b); Harold Jones (d).* 1/90.

Two fine excursions into repertory by McPartland. Strayhorn's suave impressionism is hard to evoke, let alone sustain for an entire album, but this is at least as convincing as any similar homage. Despite a couple of less successful entries – 'A Flower Is A Lovesome Thing', for instance, is a little too doleful – the quartet have the measure of this deceptive music. There is a witty, unpredictable revision of 'Take The "A" Train', a springy 'Intimacy Of The Blues' and a purposefully crafted 'Lush Life' by the trio without Dodgion. The meeting with Carter, who plays on 6 of the 11 tunes chosen from his book, is flawlessly paced. Though his technique is still astonishing for a man in his eighties, Carter's sound and delivery are rather old-world compared to McPartland's astute command. Trio versions of 'When Lights Are Low', the beautiful 'Key Largo' and 'Summer Serenade' are probably the most distinguished moments on the record. Both sessions are recorded excellently.

*****(*) Live At Maybeck Recital Hall Vol. 9**
Concord CCD 4460 *McPartland (p solo).* 1/91.

This solo recital finds the pianist in characteristically adventurous mood. The composers represented here include Alec Wilder, Ornette Coleman, Mercer Ellington and Dave Brubeck; there are her latest reflections on the tune she startled Ellington himself with, 'Clothed Woman', and one of the most affecting of her own themes, 'Twilight World'. Each interpretation contains nothing unnecessary in the way of embellishment, yet they all seem ideally paced, properly finished. She makes it sound very easy. Ripe, in-concert recording, typical of this series from Concord.

****** In My Life**
Concord CCD 4561 *McPartland; Chris Potter (as, ts); Gary Mazzaroppi (b); Glenn Davis (d).* 1/93.

A marvellous record. This time Marian sets Coltrane and Ornette alongside Lennon and McCartney, quietly introduces a couple of her own tunes, and invites one of the sharpest new saxophonists on the scene to sit in. The result is as catholic and accomplished a jazz record as one can find among modern releases. Chris Potter's unfussy virtuosity is a serenely appropriate match for the pianist's diverse tastes, and he is as purposeful and convincing on 'Close Your Eyes' as he is on 'Naima'. To close, there is a deeply affecting solo treatment of 'Singin' The Blues', done as a memorial to Marian's late husband, Jimmy. Essential.

*****(*) Plays The Music Of Mary Lou Williams**
Concord CCD 4605 *McPartland; Bill Douglass (b); Omar Clay (d).* 1/94.

This must have been a project close to Marian's heart, and she does this still-little-known songbook fine justice. One of the striking things about the playing is how Marian has an unerring instinct for the right tempo on a particular piece: 'Easy Blues' and 'It's A Grand Night For Swinging' hit an ideal pace from the start, and 'Cloudy', probably the most famous of Williams's tunes, is a beauty. If the disc has a weakness, it's that Marian doesn't always convince the listener that Williams's themes are as strong as they might be: her own composition, 'Threnody', a delightful tune in three, actually outclasses several of the pieces here.

***** Live At Yoshi's Nitespot**
Concord CCD 4712 *McPartland; Bill Douglass (b); Glenn Davis (d).* 11/95.

*****(*) Silent Pool**
Concord CCD 4745 *McPartland; Andy Simpkins (b); Harold Jones (d); strings, arr. Alan Broadbent.*

The live album might not quite rank among Marian's best, but this is still a hugely enjoyable date. 'Pretty Women', 'Chasing Shadows' and her own 'Silent Pool' are beautiful rarities in the repertory, and her version of Ellington's 'Warm Valley' is exquisite enough to remind any who have forgotten that she is one of our great ballad interpreters. A couple of the standards are comparatively routine, though, and newcomers should perhaps start with one of the earlier discs.

Her strings album is handsomely arranged by Alan Broadbent and at last offers a showcase of 12 McPartland originals in one place, with 'Twilight World', 'Time And Time Again' and 'There'll Be Other Times' among the most beautiful pieces. The only quibble might be that the languorous tempos and Broadbent's luxury-class scores are just a shade too relaxed at times. But this should still be filed alongside her other classics in what is now a superlative discography.

*****(*) Just Friends**
Concord CCD 4805-2 *McPartland; Tommy Flanagan, Renee Rosnes, George Shearing, Geri Allen, Dave Brubeck, Gene Harris (p).* 9/97–1/98.

*****(*) Reprise**
Concord CCD 4853-2 *McPartland; Bill Crow (b); Joe Morello (d).* 9/98.

Marian's eightieth birthday was greeted with the warmest of affection throughout the jazz world, with several special concerts to mark the occasion, and a reunion of her trio from the Hickory House days at New York's new Birdland. *Reprise* is the delightful result, the old firm still in joyful form, and the pianist still picking the most pleasing tunes, here including Hoagy Carmichael's 'New Orleans', the same arrangement of 'I Hear Music' which once started one of their Capitol dates, Henry Mancini's 'Two For The Road', and a piano–drums dialogue on 'Cymbalism'.

Just Friends is an album of duets, of the sort which she has been spontaneously performing on her *Piano Jazz* broadcasts for many years. Though one or two don't really come off – such as, surprisingly, a rather doom-laden 'Twilight World' with George Shearing – there are many more good ones: stomping along with Rosnes on 'It's You Or No One', playing tag with Brubeck on 'Gone With The Wind'. She closes it with a simple, lovely solo on 'When The Saints', dedicated to Jimmy.

There are now more than 20 releases on Jazz Alliance drawn from editions of Marian's Piano Jazz series for NPR and, while some of them are perhaps more of documentary and historical interest, all feature some fine piano playing.

Joe McPhee (born 1939)

TENOR SAXOPHONE, POCKET-CORNET, FLUGELHORN, ELECTRONICS

McPhee is that rare doubler, a musician equally at ease on brass and woodwind. Only Benny Carter has sounded as comfortable and idiomatic, but Joe's fierce anger and political engagement provide an important additional element.

*****(*) Impressions Of Jimmy Giuffre**
Celp C 21 *McPhee; André Jaume (ts, bcl); Raymond Boni (g).* 4/91.

McPhee's discography is currently diminished by the disappearance of his substantial hat ART catalogue, at least some of which we hope to see resurrected. This disc stands a little apart from his normal line of work, but there is no mistaking how much pleasure he took in making it. The trio kicks off with a glorious version of 'The Train And The River', with McPhee in the Brookmeyer role, and carries on with a mixture of Giuffre originals and specially written pieces which might have been laid down by the clarinettist's slightly wacky brother. There's even a posy for

Juanita Giuffre, who has been a substantial influence on her husband's recent career. A sundae to balance the meatier side of McPhee's output.

****** As Serious As Your Life**
hatOLOGY 514 *McPhee (solo).* 5/96.

Twenty years after McPhee's first solo record, *Tenor*, this marks a return to unaccompanied performance, an aspect of his career which he regards as being of paramount importance, but which is almost unknown. McPhee has identified 1996 as an important transitional year in his career, a point at which he looks back and forward, with the oneiric logic that dominates 'Project Dream Keeper', his latest sequence of work. Working alone and with ambient sound welcomed rather than edited out, he creates a body of work which is as evocative and expressive as anything he has ever made. 'Tok' is a Coltrane-influenced tenor piece which harks back to the earlier solo performance. 'Conlon In The Land Of Ra' documents an imaginary meeting between Sun Ra and the radical composer Conlon Nancarrow, who spent much of his life writing for player piano. Dedicated to Marilyn Crispell, who has made the tune something of a speciality piece, Coltrane's 'After The Rain' is a piano solo played on the house piano of the Village Gate jazz club and played with the sustain pedal depressed throughout, giving it a floating, fugitive quality. On 'The Man I Love' McPhee brings a highly personal focus to the Gershwin standard, a similar tonality and language to the two parts of 'As Serious As Your Life', named after an important book by British jazz writer and photographer Val Wilmer. As well as these, there is the opening 'Death Of Miles Davis', a heartfelt tribute, and 'Haiku Study #1', a sketch for work included on the duets with violinst David Prentice, below.

****** Legend Street One**
CIMP 115 *McPhee; Frank Lowe (ts); David Prentice (vn); Charles Moffett (d).* 6/96.

*****(*) Inside Out**
CIMP 120 *As above, except omit Lowe and Prentice.* 6/96.

McPhee's openness to all sound, natural and instrumental, recommends him to the unvarnished, non-hierarchical aesthetic espoused by CIMP. These two sessions are very much in keeping with the 'Dream Keeper' project, broodingly surreal and expressive encounters which refuse to obey the jazz rulebook. Like Henry Threadgill, McPhee now seems to have evaded bebop altogether and to be playing in an idiom that is entirely his own and almost beyond critical analysis. The bald session details are slightly misleading because on *Legend Street One* there are actually only two quartet tracks. The rest are either duos, like the two-tenor encounter of 'Loweville', a couple of tracks with Prentice anticipating the head-to-head of *Inside Out*, and the extraordinary flugelhorn/drums confrontation of 'Not Yet'. 'For Panama' is a drum solo, Moffett's tribute to Panama Francis, and one of the drummer's very best recorded performances. Indeed, the album is notably selfless, with considerable time and space for the remaining members of the group to establish their own musical personalities. The long group-track, 'Up, Over And Out', is all the better for knowing more about how these remarkable men think and interact.

****** A Meeting In Chicago**
Okkadisk OD 12016 *McPhee; Ken Vandermark (reeds); Kent Kessler (b).* 96.

Like Henry Threadgill, McPhee is hard to pin down critically because he belongs to no identifiable generic niche. This extraordinary set could almost be the work of some as yet unknown, conservatory-trained but sceptical modernist who has written his thesis on the wind groups of early modernism, those experimenters who took a perverse delight in trying combinations that had not been heard during the classical era. As a meeting of minds, this one is hard to improve on. Vandermark's NRGetic style is more cautiously modulated here and Kessler is, almost in compensation, much more pungent and confrontational than usual. McPhee, doubling as ever on trumpet and reeds, sounds in charge, signalling changes of direction and conducting the transitions from full-on collaborative batter to a more delicate choice of brush-strokes.

***** The Brass City**
Okkadisk OD12025 *McPhee; Jeb Bishop (tb).* 10/97.

McPhee was to turn his back somewhat on brass after this astonishing *tour de force*. Brass duos are pretty rare in the canon, but this one sounds as straightforward and idiomatic as saxophone and piano or trumpet and organ, with Bishop providing much of the harmonic foundation. McPhee includes both soprano saxophone and valve trombone but concentrates for much of the time on pocket cornet, a tight, terse sound similar to Don Cherry's. Most of the record is taken up with a suite of dance exercises for two horns, but there are also tributes to Tom Guralnick, and a delightful nod to Roswell Rudd in the oddly spelt 'Rozwell Incident'. Touches of distortion here and there when the two horns are playing *forte*, but generally speaking the sound is very good.

***** The Watermelon Suite**
CIMP 183 *McPhee; Dominic Duval (b, elec); Jay Rosen (d, perc).* 5/98.

***** Rapture**
Cadence CJR 1106 *As above, except add Rosi Hertlein (vn, v).* 12/98.

The trio with Duval and Rosen has proved to be a fruitful one for McPhee, the relationship with Cadence even more so. The elements of 'The Watermelon Suite' itself – whole, rind, meat, seeds – are treated with a strangely analytical certainty, but the playing is as refreshing and raw as ever. McPhee these days restricts himself to saxophone, and mostly the soprano. It is most effective on the long 'Putter Piece', but his solo on the closing 'My Funny Valentine' is wry and touching. Rosen and Duval (who also uses a scaled-down Hutchins bass) take time out for a duet on 'Soundboard Safari'.

Rapture is hijacked by the astonishing violinist and singer, Rosi Hertlein, who is destined for great things. With Duval's deployment of live electronics, the sound-world is greatly expanded and McPhee's prominence is scaled down somewhat. The opening fragment was inspired by composer and diarist Ned Rorem's eulogy on his partner of more than 30 years, but the main component of the album is a centenary reinterpretation of James Weldon Johnson's magnificent Negro anthem, 'Lift Every Voice

And Sing', a performance that comes in at more than three-quarters of an hour.

***(*) In The Spirit

CIMP 199 *McPhee; Joe Giardullo (ss, bcl, f); Michael Bisio, Dominic Duval (b).* 3/99.

The 'Spirit' is, of course, the Spirit Room at Rossie, New York, where CIMP sessions are always recorded. But it also reflects the spiritual tradition that McPhee explores with his drummerless Bluette group. Almost all the material here – the only exceptions are McPhee's 'Astral Spirits' and his meditation on 'Come Sunday/Birmingham Sunday' – is from the church or its adherents. 'Deep River' and 'Just A Closer Walk With Thee' are performed alongside Curtis Mayfield's 'People Get Ready' and Billie Holiday and Arthur Herzog Jr's 'God Bless The Child'. In this context, and played with McPhee's usual fervour, they sound spiritually consistent one with another. Pairing off with a second horn has always had an interesting effect on McPhee's approach and here he often sits back out of the foreground, working on the deep melody while Giardullo embellishes and improvises in the foreground. Joe's gift for using an unmodified live acoustic to create very subtle effects, the kind of thing that would normally involve retakes, overdubbing and careful mixing, is as impressive as ever, as on 'Birmingham/Come Sunday', when he uses microphone positioning and altered articulation to suggest changes of instrument, creating his own horn section live and on the stand.

Charles McPherson (born 1939)

ALTO SAXOPHONE

McPherson's training took place in a tough school called Mingus, with whom he worked for almost 15 years, transforming what had been the Jackie McLean sound into something rather more purely derived from Charlie Parker. An inventive soloist and a very effective writer, he remains oddly unappreciated, perhaps written off as a Bird copyist.

*** Be Bop Revisited

Original Jazz Classics OJC 710 *McPherson; Carmell Jones (t); Barry Harris (p); Nelson Boyd (b); Albert 'Tootie' Heath (d).* 11/64.

***(*) Con Alma!

Original Jazz Classics OJCCD 1875 *McPherson; Clifford Jordan (ts); Barry Harris (p); George Tucker (b); Alan Dawson (d).* 8/65.

*** The Quintet Live!

Original Jazz Classics OJC 1804 *McPherson; Lonnie Hillyer (t); Barry Harris (p); Ray McKinney (b); Billy Higgins (d).* 10/66.

*** Live At The Five Spot

Prestige PRCD 24135 *As above.* 10/66.

McPherson credits the relatively unsung Barry Harris for his schooling in bebop, but it's clear that Parker has marked his saxophone playing so deeply that he will always be identified as a faithful disciple. *Con Alma!* was reissued in 1995, and it's immediately clear from 'In A Sentimental Mood' and the title-track that Johnny Hodges was also a strong influence on the youngster. The straightforward bop covers on *Revisited* and the slightly more individualized live material have an energy and clarity of tone that are completely missing from the later, overproduced sessions once reissued on Mainstream.

Of this early group, the Five Spot recording and *Con Alma!* are probably the most immediately approachable, but McPherson remains a performer who is hard to identify other than by his ancestral traits – which is a pity, because he has a lovely tone and seems constantly responsive to his colleagues. Some of the exchanges with Jordan, who takes a much more sceptical view of bop, are revelatory, though few of them are allowed to develop.

*** From This Moment On!

Original Jazz Classics OJCCD 1899-2 *McPherson; Cedar Walton (p); Pat Martino (g); Peck Morrison (b); Lenny McBrowne (d).* 1/68.

*** Horizons

Original Jazz Classics OJCCD 1912-2 *As above, except omit Morrison, McBrowne; add Nasir Hafiz (vib), Walter Booker (b), Billy Higgins (d).* 8/68.

McPherson's growing confidence was cemented by a new working relationship with the up-and-coming Cedar Walton and with Pat Martino, a guitarist of genuine originality. The alto/guitar duet on 'Lush Life' on the August 1968 session is a remarkable performance, mining new insights from the old song and turning it into something altogether more solid and durable than the average 'standards' reading. The later album starts stronger than it finishes, as if the summer heat of New York City gets to the players halfway and they lose pace and commitment.

From This Moment On! is a much more even album. If it lacks the excitement and sheer imagination of its successor, it is probably a more successful entity. McPherson has rarely sounded as briskly swinging, and the sheer drive and energy of these seven relatively short numbers is infectious. Again, Martino is a key element in a line-up with just a single horn, and his playing veers between rich chording and strong, saxophone-influenced lines. The rhythm section of Morrison and McBrowne is less graceful and sophisticated than that of Booker and Higgins (even Booker and Higgins on a slightly off-day) but it gets down to business with a will. Two excellent records from a player now completely in command of his voice and idiom.

***(*) First Flight Out

Arabesque AJ 0113 *McPherson; Tom Harrell (t, flhn); Michael Weiss (p); Peter Washington (b); Victor Lewis (d).* 1/94.

First Flight Out is a good example of McPherson's more recent style. He still does a lot of Mingus material, which he presumably knows like the back of his hand, and there is a version of Monk's 'Well You Needn't' which suggests he's spent a bit of time on that fruitful source as well. The playing is lighter in touch but fuller in tone than it used to be and here it sits perfectly with Harrell's lyrical flugelhorn, a rare example of McPherson deliberately pitching himself against another horn.

**** Come Play With Me

Arabesque AJ0117 *McPherson; Mulgrew Miller (p); Santi Debriano (b); Lewis Nash (d).* 3/95.

A smashing record from a dream band. McPherson still likes to pay homage on occasion, and 'Bloomdido' allows him to show

how much he still draws from Charlie Parker's complex legacy but also how well he's invested his inheritance in new ideas. Mulgrew has never sounded comfortable round orthodox bop (none of McCoy Tyner's progeny ever did), but here he slips easily into the idiom and creates a space for himself which is as fruitful as it is challenging. McPherson's originals are as inventive as ever. 'Lonely Little Chimes' might well sound banal in other hands, but he creates a touchingly poignant song that swings in its own individual way. Debriano and Nash are beautifully caught by engineers Malcolm Addey and John Reigart, who both deserve a bigger credit for the set. The romping conclusion, a run-in of three wonderful new songs, might have sounded muddy and confused with the four musicians so closely placed, but the separation is near-perfect and McPherson cuts through without sounding as if he's been recorded separately, which has occasionally happened in the past.

***(*) Manhattan Nocturne

Arabesque AJ 01189 *McPherson; Mulgrew Miller (p); Ray Drummond (b); Victor Lewis (d); Bobby Sanabria (perc). 97.*

Poised and quietly charismatic bop from a group which extends the new confidence that has suffused McPherson's recent work. 'Blue'N'Boogie' manages to sound both calm and hectic, and both 'How Deep Is The Ocean' and the title-track have a settled authority which even Bird never achieved. Lewis is in exceptional form and the only disappointment is the rather offhand playing of Mulgrew Miller.

Carmen McRae (1922–94)

VOCAL

Born in New York, she played piano and wrote songs at an early age. Sang with Benny Carter, Basie and Mercer Ellington in the 1940s, then began recording under her own name in 1953 and worked as a solo from the late '50s. Retired in 1991.

*** Sings Great American Songwriters

MCA GRP16312 *McRae; with groups led by Ray Bryant, Matt Mathews, Ralph Burns, Tadd Dameron, Fred Katz, Jack Pleis, Frank Hunter and Luther Henderson. 6/55–3/59.*

**** I'll Be Seeing You

GRP 050647-2 2CD *McRae; orchestras and groups led by Jack Pleis, Ralph Burns, Jimmy Mundy, Frank Hunter, Luther Henderson. 55–59.*

An accomplished pianist, Carmen McRae was something of a late starter as a featured vocalist, not recording a vocal session under her own name until 1954. Her fame has always lagged behind that of her close contemporaries, Sarah Vaughan and Billie Holiday, but eventually she did achieve something like the honour she deserved, and her commitment to jazz singing was unflinching. Thus far, her early work has been largely and unjustly ignored by CD reissues: until recently, virtually nothing was available from her Decca period of the 1950s, which means that great records like *Torchy* and *Carmen For Cool Ones* must languish as collectors' items. There's always a tigerish feel to her best vocals – no woman has ever sung in the jazz idiom with quite such beguiling surliness as McRae. GRP duck the issue of releasing Carmen's albums in their proper sequence by giving us *I'll Be Seeing You*, but this handsome compilation of her late-'50s work is splendid enough to merit a high recommendation anyway. The backings wobble between sympathetic jazz settings and the usual blustery orchestras which singers of her generation had to contend with, but McRae's feline approach and unique timbre overcome most of the shortcomings. An excellent buy.

**** Sings Lover Man

Columbia CK 65115 *McRae; Nat Adderley (c); Eddie 'Lockjaw' Davis (ts); Norman Simmons (p, cel); Mundell Lowe (g); Bob Cranshaw (b); Walter Perkins (d). 6–7/61.*

McRae's original tribute to Billie Holiday was something she had wanted to do during her Decca period. At Columbia, where she made only one other album, she got her chance. The deft arrangements are by the often undersung Norman Simmons, and Adderley and Lockjaw Davis take on the Harry Edison and Ben Webster roles. Though she follows Holiday's manner almost to the letter on some songs, notably 'Them There Eyes' and 'Trav'lin' Light', this is all Carmen McRae: she is quite imperious on 'Yesterdays', finds a deadly, almost sardonic note in 'Strange Fruit' and is ineffably tender on 'If The Moon Turns Green'. The musicians play superbly alongside her.

***(*) The Great American Songbook

Atlantic 781323-2 *McRae; Jimmy Rowles (p); Joe Pass (g); Chuck Domanico (b); Chuck Flores (d). 72.*

A couple of the songs are only questionably 'great', and some of the treatments seem surprisingly hurried or perfunctory. Otherwise this is blue-chip material, a top band, and Carmen in excellent voice, cut live at Donte's in Los Angeles. There are too few such occasions in the McRae discography, so it's a welcome reissue.

**(*) Heat Wave

Concord CCD 4189 *McRae; Al Bent, Mike Heathman (tb); Mark Levine, Marshall Otwell (p); Cal Tjader (vib); Rob Fisher (b); Vince Lateano (d); Poncho Sanchez, Ramon Banda (perc). 1/82.*

*** You're Lookin' At Me

Concord CCD 4235 *McRae; Marshall Otwell (p); John Collins (g); John Leftwich (b); Donald Bailey (d). 11/83.*

**(*) Fine And Mellow

Concord CCD 4342 *McRae; Red Holloway (ts); Phil Upchurch (g); Jack McDuff (org); John Clayton Jr (b); Paul Humphrey (d). 12/87.*

***(*) Ballad Essentials

Concord CCD 4877-2 *As above Concord albums, plus George Shearing (p). 82–87.*

Her records for Concord were mostly rather disappointing, even if there is something good on all of them. The session with Tjader is blemished by the vibesman's usual flavourless Latin-jazz stylings which offer no backbone to the singer's efforts, and the Stevie Wonder tunes on the record scarcely suit a vocal personality which has a pronounced streak of cussedness when she warms up. Yet *Fine And Mellow* goes to the other extreme without much more conviction: McRae is too sophisticated a stylist to convince as an earthy R&B singer, which this programme and these accompanists are tailored for. The other record is a tribute to Nat Cole and, while she doesn't sound very taken with the likes of 'I'm An Errand Girl For Rhythm', the ballads and the more subtle lyrics garner her full attention, with a cool, attentive rhythm section in support. However, the very shrewdly chosen compilation *Ballad Essentials* creams off all the best tracks from the three dates, plus three duets with George Shearing, and makes this definitely the one to get.

*****(*) The Carmen McRae–Betty Carter Duets**
Verve 529579-2 *McRae; Eric Gunnison (p); Jim Hughart (b); Winard Harper (d).* 1–2/87.

A one-off meeting inspired by an impromptu partnership at a club engagement, this is great fun and, though Carter remains the consummate bebop gymnast, McRae isn't outclassed once. What she does is bring her great gravitas to bear on a session that could have been mere frivolity. The opening 'What's New' sets an amiable tone, but there is some serious and superb singing in 'Glad To Be Unhappy', a virtuoso 'Sometimes I'm Happy', a lovely arrangement of 'Stolen Moments' where the two voices hit perfect accord, and the suitably climactic 'It Don't Mean A Thing'. Three bonus tracks feature Carmen by herself. The recording is rather remote and needs a bit extra on the volume switch.

Jay McShann (born 1916)

PIANO, VOCAL, BANDLEADER

It's often assumed that 'Hootie' hails from Kansas City, but he was born in Muskogee, Oklahoma, and attended the famous Tuskegee Institute. He worked with Don Byas as a fifteen-year-old and later moved to KC, where his famous big band became a recruiting centre for some soon-to-be-legendary names. McShann's unaffected playing and singing have remained durable through many comebacks.

*****(*) Jay McShann, 1941–1943**
Classics 740 *McShann; Harold Bruce, Orville Minor, Bernard Anderson, Bob Merrill, Willie Cook, Dave Mitchell, Jesse Jones (t); Joe Baird, Alonzo Pettiford, Alonso Fook, Rudy Morrison (tb); Charlie Parker, John Jackson, Rudolf Dennis (as); Bob Mabane, Harry Ferguson, Fred Culliver, Paul Quinichette, Bill Goodson (ts); Rae Brodely (bs); Leonard Enois (g); Gene Ramey (b); Gus Johnson, Harold Doc West, Bob Merrill (d); Al Hibbler, Walter Brown (v).* 4/41–1/43.

Historically, McShann's swing band will always be remembered as the incubator for Charlie Parker's raw talent to start to blossom. The orchestra pack a Kansas City punch that stands squarely as second-generation Basie, and the blues performances on 'Hootie Blues', 'Swingmatism' and 'Dexter Blues' still have an authentic tang of KC *brio*. The Classics includes material from December 1943, three tracks of no special consequence, not least in not including Parker, who had already taken the next step in his career. McShann, who was considered a footnote in that story ever since, scarcely sounds it here, chugging away at his own thing without a shred of anxiety about what might be going on elsewhere in New York City.

***** Jay McShann, 1944–46**
Classics 966 *McShann; Major Evans, Clarence Thornton, Oliver Todd (t); Tommy Douglas, Edmond Gregory, Theodore Smalls (as); Cleophus Curtis, Seeward Evans, Claiborne Graves (ts); Efferge Ware (g); Percy Gabriel, Walter Page, Raymond Taylor (b); Sam Lovett, Jesse Price, Albert Wichard (d); Numa Lee Davis, Julia Lee, Charles Waterford, Jimmy Witherspoon (v).* 45–11/46.

After his discharge from the army, McShann had to rethink his strategy more than a little, scaling down his working band to a small, workable combo. The group's return to Kansas City, his home town, in November 1944 yielded one of the best sessions of his career. Julia Lee's vocals were an integral part of the equation, but it is the quality of playing in this terse, taut small group that attracts the attention. Nothing else on this disc is as good. The vocal material with Witherspoon and others has its moments, but the verve and wit of 'Moten Swing' and 'On The Sunny Side Of The Street' aren't matched in the 1945 material for Philo and Premier, and the pace picks up again only after McShann signed for Mercury, using Witherspoon as front man on material like 'Voodoo Woman Blues', 'Have You Ever Loved A Woman' and 'Gone With The Blues'.

***** With Kansas City In Mind**
Swaggie CD 401 *McShann; Buddy Tate (ts, cl); Julian Dash (ts); Gene Ramey (b); Gus Johnson (d).* 6/69–3/72.

Just as Dollar Brand records routinely figure 'Africa(n)' in the title and there are umpteen Django reissues working permutations on 'Paris' and 'swing', so McShann has found it hard to shake off the KC tag, even though by this stage he is no longer strictly a Kansas City player but one who draws much more freely on a wide range of traditional and contemporary idioms. It is, nevertheless, a fine vintage. On the Swaggie, there are eight piano solos from two sessions, three years apart, and a small group featuring McShann with the two tenors of Tate and Dash, larruping through seven indolent blues or game swingers. Nothing terribly fancy and certainly nothing wrong.

***** Going To Kansas City**
New World NWCD 358 *As for With Kansas City In Mind (above).* 3/72.

***** The Man From Muskogee**
Sackville 2-3005 *McShann; Claude Williams (vn); Don Thompson (b); Paul Gunther (d).* 6/72.

Some readers will know the slightly earlier of these excellent records as a Swaggie release. New World have done it proud with a bright, warm-toned CD transfer that brings out the best of what sounds like a thoroughly amiable run through some old big-band material. Tate and Dash present a formidable front line, and it's a pity that there wasn't a good trumpeter and trombonist on hand to give the set even more of the feel of Hootie's classic bands. The closing version of 'Moten Swing' is pure nostalgia, a loving re-creation.

We very much like the Sackville as well. The track listing, which includes 'The Man From Muskogee', 'Hootie Blues' and 'Yardbird Waltz', might come off almost any McShann album of the last 25 years. This, though, is one of the best, a bright and often quite adventurous encounter between the pianist and the neglected fiddler Williams, who plays very much in the spirit of

Stuff Smith. McShann returned to the fray with terrific exuberance, and one can sense his sheer delight in being able to hammer out these old tunes in sympathetic company. A high point from the later years and an excellent place to start if you haven't heard the work of more recent years.

***** Vine Street Boogie**

Black Lion BLCD 760187 *McShann (p, v).* 7/74.

Rising sixty, McShann could still put on a show, as he proved at the 1974 Montreux Festival. It was a vivid, highly personal accomplishment, marked by sharply defined performances of 'Satin Doll' and 'Yardbird Waltz'. McShann hits the piano with absolute confidence and resolve, several times elegantly manoeuvring out of difficult corners and fluffed passages. The voice isn't much to write home about on this occasion, but there is no mistaking the rapport with the crowd or the warmth of the reception.

****(*) After Hours**

Storyville 8279 *McShann; Thomas Muller (g); Ole Skipper Mosgard (b); Thorkild Moller (d).* 4/77.

The personnel is slightly misleading because, apart from two tracks, *After Hours* is entirely solo. McShann is in good if unexciting form, knocking out a solid, blues-based performance which includes hits like 'The Man From Muskogee' and 'Yardbird Waltz'. The group are buoyant and competent enough, but it's very much a question of McShann taking care of business in the old familiar way.

*****(*) Last Of The Blue Devils**

Koch Jazz 8525 *McShann; Joe Newman (t); Paul Quinichette, Buddy Tate (ts); John Scofield (g); Milt Hinton (b); Jack Williams (d).* 78.

An astonishing line-up and a wonderful set. One of the problems with the McShann discography is the relatively limited range of tunes and songs on offer, but even familiar things like 'Hootie Blues', which he famously co-wrote with young Charlie Parker, and 'Jumpin' At The Woodside' are as fresh minted as if they'd just been written on the piano lid. The two tenors – a configuration which Jay has always loved – give even the lightest of tunes a resonance and warmth and both Tate and Quinichette get off some very fine solos. The surprise in the personnel is, of course, the young Scofield. Should you have cause to wonder, listening to his work of the 1990s, where and how he acquired such astonishing chops, this may well be the answer. A recommended album.

**** Best Of Friends**

JSP CD 224 *McShann; Al Casey (g); Kenny Baldock (b); Robin Jones (d).* 4/82.

***** Swingmatism**

Sackville 2-3046 *McShann; Don Thompson (b); Archie Alleyne (d).* 10/82.

***** Just A Lucky So And So**

Sackville 2- 3035 *McShann; Jim Galloway (ss, bs); Don Thompson (b); Terry Clarke (d).* 8/83.

****(*) Airmail Special**

Sackville 2-3040 *McShann; Neil Swainson (b); Terry Clarke (d).* 8/85.

***** At Café Des Copains**

Sackville 2-2024 *McShann (p solo).* 8/83–9/89.

McShann has recorded many albums for Sackville and they are starting to reappear on CD. At his best, he blends a wide variety of mannerisms into a personal kind of swing-stride-blues piano; at anything less than that, he can sound like a less-than-profound and overly eclectic performer. Most of these records feature moments when he's caught between those positions. The meeting with Al Casey is jolly, unprepossessing stuff, both men jogging along to no great end except to have a bit of fun. *Swingmatism* is rather better: focused by a decent rhythm section, McShann sets his mind to a programme that depends heavily on Ellington for source material, and 'The Jeep Is Jumpin'' and 'The Mooche' are good accounts of less frequently heard tunes. Jim Galloway is an engaging partner on *Lucky So And So*, which features some attractive playing from both men. McShann excels on 'Red Sails In The Sunset' and gives 'On A Clear Day You Can See Forever' an emotional impact that previously only Barbra Streisand has ever delivered. What a duet that would be.

Airmail Special is all right, if a bit uneventful, but the best disc is probably the solo set. McShann thinks through a wide spectrum of material – going as far back as Ferde Grofé's 'On The Trail' and ending up with Michel Legrand – and the good piano and live atmosphere elicit a sound series of interpretations, recorded during several visits over a period of six years.

***** Havin' Fun**

Sackville 2-2047 *McShann; Major Holley (b).* 91.

****(*) Some Blues**

Chiaroscuro CR(D) 320 *McShann; Clark Terry (t, v); Al Grey (tb); Major Holley (b, v); Milt Hinton (b); Ben Riley, Bobby Durham (d).* 2/90–9/92.

***** My Baby With The Black Dress On**

Chiaroscuro 345 *McShann (p, v).* 92.

***** The Missouri Connection**

Reservoir RSR CD 124 *McShann; John Hicks (p).* 9/92.

Now into his eighties, McShann remains amazingly spirited. His meeting with John Hicks is a discussion about the blues over two keyboards and, while it hardly says anything new about the form, it's a genial encounter, neither man having to compromise his ground to any extent.

In Major Holley he has a partner of the old school, a bassist who can 'walk' with the best of them, but who's also capable of playing strong melody lines. A completely engaging album. *Some Blues* is a hotchpotch that starts with more duos cut with Major Holley and two sessions with Terry, Grey and the others. The bass-and-piano tracks hit a characteristic McShann note of rough good humour, but the band titles are a bit thin. There's also a bonus track of the leader reminiscing for the microphone.

My Baby comes with a very racy cover and Hootie immediately whisks you back to a world of speakeasies, gin joints and women of easy virtue, a mini-musical of the old jazz world. The voice is in great shape, ever more intimate and confiding, and Jay plays the blues as brilliantly as ever.

***** Hootie's Jumpin' Blues**

Stony Plain 1237 *McShann; Bob Tildesley (t); Gordon Beadle (ts); Dave Babcock (bs); Marty Ballou (b); Marty Richards (d).* 98.

***** Still Jumpin' The Blues**

Stony Plain 1254 *McShann; Dave Babcock (as, ts); Dennis Taylor (ts); Duke Robillard (g); Marty Richards (d); Maria Muldaur (v).* 99.

'Still' because at 83 Hootie is turning into one of the elder statesmen of the music and a living link back to the days of classic jazz and blues. Which is why no one will begrudge him the final interview track on this excellent disc. He is almost as convincing a storyteller as he is a bluesman, but it's his playing, still vibrant and alert, that really recommends this album. The inclusion of Maria Muldaur will make some hearts beat faster and her slow, moody delivery is an exact foil to McShann. The best of the tracks are 'Goin' To Chicago' and 'Moten Swing', old stuff to be sure, but played with absolute conviction.

The slightly earlier release adds a touch of brass to the ensemble and puts a bit of punch into the old tunes. As ever, the material is straightforwardly generic, though 'Hootie Ignorant Oil' and 'Profoundly Blue' may surprise some listeners. The saxes are very good and the recording has a relaxed live feel. As McShann well knows and is shrewd enough to exploit, he's become a living monument. The life story is in the music, but it's good to have the old man tell it straight as well.

Medeski, Martin & Wood

GROUP

New York trio who built a nationwide audience in the '90s by back-of-the-bus touring, fashioning a Grateful Dead-style cult of followers. The music is organ, bass and drums, jazz, rock and whatever else they can stir in.

***** It's A Jungle In Here**

Gramavision R2 79495 CD *John Medeski (org, p); Billy Martin (d, perc); Chris Wood (b); Steven Bernstein (t, flhn); Josh Roseman (tb); Jay Rodrigues (ts, as); Dave Binney (as); Marc Ribot (g).* 8/93.

… and in that jungle called Noo Yawk strange cries and rhythms proliferate like orchids. Where else would anyone put Monk's 'Bemsha Swing' in on top of Bob Marley's 'Lively Up Yourself' and make it work? Or follow it with King Sunny Ade's 'Moti Mo', and make that seem like a perfectly sensible juxtaposition? The basic organ trio is steaming enough not to require the assistance of horns (though Ribot's guitar is a definite fillip, by turns abstract and funky).

***** Friday Afternoon In The Universe**

Gramavision GCD 79503 *As above, except omit Bernstein, Roseman, Rodrigues, Binney, Ribot.* 94.

***** Shack-man**

Gramavision GCD 79514 *As above.* 6/96.

We were initially disappointed by the second album, but it stands up well over time, and it's here that one can start to hear the subtle mix of jukebox r'n'b and modern jazz which would subsequently lead MMW into the arms of Blue Note. The trio also showed itself to be capable of adding a floaty impressionism to its armoury of styles. The absence of additional players oddly didn't seem to strip down the sound unduly. *Friday Afternoon …* is every bit as richly textured as its predecessor.

The third in line was recorded at the Shack in Hawaii and has a sun-warmed ease deep down in the grooves. Less spiky than its two predecessors, *Shack-man* is firmly located in an acid-jazz bag, but John Medeski's wry grasp of sonics and Billy Martin's tight beat, loose-wristed but absolutely on the button, lift it right up there. The opening take on 'Is There Anybody Here That Love My Jesus' is simply glorious. Think Brian Auger Trinity. Think 1990s, and you just about have it.

****** Combustification**

Blue Note 7243 4 93011-2 *As above, except add DJ Logic (turntables).* 98.

MMW were a gift to the new look Blue Note, and the trio paid back their advance with a subtle, swinging album which is not nearly as trendily accessorized as the presence of turntable whizz DJ Logic might suggest. Logic actually figures on only three numbers and is subtlety itself, creating fills and cross-grained beats round the trio.

The album gained extra currency by being sampled for a mobile phone company's television commercials, but there is a haunting *déjà-vu* quality to the album as a whole, a perseveration that hints at how thoroughly it is inscribed in the Blue Note idiom. All the same, it is a completely individual work, and tracks like 'Nocturne' and 'Whatever Happened To Gus' are haunting. The latter features a surreal, nostalgic narration by Steve Cannon, a Beat-inspired celebration of the great days of jazz. A pity it fades away so irresolutely.

More than ever the trio sound revolves round the polyrhythms and deceptive embellishments of Billy Martin, who has emerged as a drummer of real gifts. His introduction to 'Latin Shuffle' is virtuosic and John Medeski's piano solo just about tops it for sheer energy. Chris Wood holds the theme together with a sinewy ostinato. *Combustification* is where modern jazz is going.

Brad Mehldau (born 1970)

PIANO

Born in Florida, Mehldau arrived in New York in 1989 and was soon getting plenty of sideman work, with Jimmy Cobb, Cecil Payne and Joshua Redman. Worked in Europe with Perico Sambeat and the Rossys, then signed to Warners as a solo artist.

*****(*) New York–Barcelona Crossing**

Fresh Sound FSNT 031 *Mehldau; Perico Sambeat (as); Mario Rossy (b); Jorge Rossy (d).* 5/93.

***** New York–Barcelona Crossing**

Fresh Sound FSNT 037 *As above.* 5/93.

*****(*) When I Fall In Love**

Fresh Sound FSNT 007 *As above, except omit Sambeat.* 10/93.

****** Introducing Brad Mehldau**

Warner Bros 945997-2 *Mehldau; Larry Grenadier, Christian McBride (b); Jorge Rossy, Brian Blade (d).* 3–4/95.

Mehldau continues to excite enormous interest. In our last edition we suggested that he was set fair to become one of the major voices in the music, and he's done little to disappoint that expectation, although a fair number of voices have been nay-sayers on the issue. His Warners records are a formidable lot, but the Fresh Sounds releases, which he will probably look back on as mere student-work, are exceptional. Both of the *New York–Barcelona Crossing* discs were cut live in a Spanish club and, besides the exemplary alto of Sambeat (who was the real leader of the date) and fine work from both the Rossys, Mehldau plays some uncannily beautiful jazz. His introduction and improvisation on 'Old Folks' are quite breathtaking and it's clear that the pristine touch of the later discs was already in place. The second volume isn't quite so impressive, although 'It's Easy To Remember' is another gorgeous ballad performance, at a dangerously slow tempo.

The trio record is a good display of chops. 'Anthropology' goes off at a hurricane tempo. The title-ballad takes a very long, expansive time over itself, and it does ramble a bit. 'At A Loss' and 'Convalescent' are fascinating originals and, as much as he enjoys exploring standards, Mehldau does seem to save some of himself for his own writing. Recorded live, this doesn't have the polish of the later records, but it still cuts most piano trio sessions.

The first album for Warners was a flying start. Though Mehldau's playing is structured in a familiar post-bop mode, it's as if he were aware of jazz tradition but entirely unencumbered by it. That lends such freshness to, say, the opening 'It Might As Well Be Spring' that he seems to be uncovering a previously overlooked but brilliant piano interpretation. On Coltrane's 'Countdown' he creates a logical solo out of phrases and whole passages that seem superficially disparate from one another. His slow playing is distinguished by an exquisitely light touch – 'My Romance' is made to glow – and it's lightness that characterizes his manner. He shies away from dense voicings and will leave a daring amount of space in even a fast improvisation. His own writing fits in with the rest of his style: sample the unexpectedly jaunty 'Angst'.

****** The Art Of The Trio Vol. 1**

Warners 46260-2 *Mehldau; Larry Grenadier (b); Jorge Rossy (d).* 9/96.

****** The Art Of The Trio Vol. 2: Live At The Village Vanguard**

Warners 46848-2 *As above.* 97.

The titles suggest some heavyweight expectations, and the records deliver on them all. The studio disc is a focusing of some of the flights he looked into on *Introducing*. An original like 'Lucid' is a beautiful, sculpted miniature which suggests that composing is something that comes easily to Mehldau – but also something which he may not actually be all that interested in, since his greatest energy seems to be reserved for his improvising on standards. 'Blame It On My Youth' sparkles at a slow-to-medium tempo, 'Blackbird' is shaped into a glittering new song, but it's his celestial treatment of 'I Fall In Love Too Easily' which is the heart of the record.

At The Vanguard, he played another version of Coltrane's 'Countdown', which can act as a marker for his progress from the debut album on Warners. Where the earlier version was created out of disparate lines, this one is detailed and dense – he gets a long, long way into the piece, which his unaccompanied passage seems suddenly to illuminate, as if abruptly finding answers to a lot of questions. This is perhaps a more ambitious record, sparked by the live situation, and it's like a detailed addendum to the finished elegance of the first volume. Rossy and Grenadier are inevitably overshadowed, but to their credit they follow Mehldau without a stumble.

*****(*) Songs The Art Of the Trio Vol. 3**

Warner Bros 9362-476051-2 *As above.* 5/98.

****** Art Of The Trio Vol. 4 Back At the Vanguard**

Warner Bros 9362-47463-2 *As above.* 1/99.

Mehldau has been exciting a lot of conversation, both for and against him, and he seems keen to join in the fray if his sleeve-note to *Vol. 4* is anything to go by. In so far as every white pianist who does a good ballad gets compared to Bill Evans, he's right to complain about many of the comments (and he doesn't much sound like Evans at all). More germane may be the fact that he's on a major label: if all these records had come out on some worthy independent, they would most likely have received uniform approbation.

So to the music. The third volume sets his own songs alongside Rodgers and Hart, Nick Drake and Radiohead, the kind of juxtaposition – in a straightahead context – which a new generation of jazz players is making plausible. Mehldau takes what he wants from each of these songs and fashions it into a plausible improvisation, without entirely abstracting the original material. Admittedly, it works better with some pieces than with others – 'Bewitched' seems set in aspic – and his five originals, including new versions of 'At A Loss' and 'Convalescent', might sit better in an all-original programme. But the trio are growing more individual as a unit all the time, too. That's made even more clear by the return to the Village Vanguard for *Vol. 4*, another superbly effective session. The long 'Nice Pass' contains enough food for thought by itself, 17 minutes of steadily evolving trio music, with the pianist suddenly taking a solo part midway through that suggests a stride-piano fantasia, before the other players are cleverly reintegrated into the action. Marvellous, but there is also a superbly compact 'Solar', a brimming 'All The Things You Are' which is a genuinely enjoyable show-off piece, and a general sense that Mehldau and his companions are pushing themselves and their audience that bit harder to cast away any demons of excessive introversion.

***** Elegiac Cycle**

Warner Bros 9362-47357-2 *Mehldau (p solo).* 2/99.

No reason why Mehldau shouldn't be ready to do a solo record. But this one seems likes a severe disappointment after the bounty of the trio albums. As bullish (and entertaining) as his sleeve-notes are, he seems defensive about his right to play this way. He can play whatever and however he chooses, but the audience has the same option of listening or not. In the end, with its rather stiff truce between song form, jazz and classical piano, this seems like a recital in search of a context.

Dick Meldonian (born 1930)

TENOR AND SOPRANO SAXOPHONES, CLARINET

Stduied clarinet and sax as a teenager and worked on the road with numerous West Coast bands, before going east in 1953 and working with Herman, Johnny Richards and others. Broadway band work and hotel gigs through the '60s and '70s.

***** You've Changed**
Progressive PCD-7052 *Meldonian; Derek Smith (p); Milt Hinton (b); Ronnie Bedford (d).* 8/78.

***** Play Gene Roland Music**
Circle CCD-141 *Meldonian; Leo Ball, Spanky Davis, Chris Pasin, Phil Sunkel (t, flhn); Gene Hessler, Dale Kirkland, Jim Pugh (tb); Tony Salvatori (btb); Ed Wassermann (as); Gerry Cappuccio, Gary Keller (ts); Dick Bagni (bs); George Syran (p); Jack Six (b); Sonny Igoe (d).* 5/81.

***** 'S Wonderful**
Circle CCD-150 *Meldonian; Paul Cohen, Phil Sunkel, John Eckert, Johnny Glasel (t); Bob Pring (tb); Gary Klein, Cliff Hoff, Arthur Sharp, Chuck Fisher (ts); Dick Bagni (bs, bcl); Derek Smith (p); Marty Grosz (g); Frank Tate (b); Fred Stoll (d).* 3/82.

***** It's A Wonderful World**
Jazzology JCD-164 *Meldonian; Marty Grosz (g, v); Pete Compo (b).* 3/83.

A veteran of many big bands – Barnet, Kenton, Russo – Meldonian typifies the sax section pro: adept and at home on tenor and soprano, reliable solos, fluent delivery. There's no special distinction to the small-group date, *You've Changed*, which, surprisingly, has the leader taking out his soprano more often than the tenor; but it's very sure-footed in its demeanour. Smith and Hinton are about as solid as you can get for this situation, and Smith plays very wittily on *'S Wonderful* too (try his solo on 'Lullaby Of Birdland'). Here Meldonian leads a crack team through 14 charts by Gene Roland, some originals, some based on standards: if the music sometimes sounds like anonymous big-band greenstuff, Roland's charts throw in a little pepper just when blandness sets in. The slightly earlier *Gene Roland Music* wasn't released until 1999. Nothing to really grab the attention, but in their deferential way these charts have a lot more going for them than many a more fancy and ostentatiously dynamic big-band session. 'Abscam', the brisk 'Papa Come Home' and the delicately perky 'Voice Of the Virgo' are full of interest.

It's A Wonderful World pares things back to a trio, Meldonian sticking mostly to soprano but bringing out the clarinet for one tune. The three chaps chug through a set of old-timers with much fun, though if you don't care for the guitarist's singing style be warned that much of it is subject to Grosz-out. Beefed up to CD length with eight alternative takes, though this tends to detract from rather than abet the show.

Myra Melford

PIANO

New York-based pianist and composer, working on the cusp of completely free playing and post-bop composition.

*****(*) The Same River, Twice**
Gramavision GCD 79513 *Melford; Dave Douglas (t); Chris Speed (ts, cl); Erik Friedlander (clo); Michael Sarin (d).* 1/96.

Melford's discography is a bit foreshortened at present. This 1996 date came after some fine hat Art sessions and records for American independent labels. At first it seems like there's some surprising energy loss here, but by the time of the long closer, 'The Large Ends The Way', it's clear that Melford is in a more musing and sombre frame of mind. Using the horns as markers in a chamber ensemble, and having Friedlander play in his most mournful *arco* style, she unfolds various dedications – to the Balkans, Vietnam, and her own meditation practice – in ways that distil some of the concerns of her previous work. Some may prefer the jump and spit of the earlier records, but the group creates a lovely sonority at so many moments that it is hard not to partake of the spirit, if not all of the time. And if you prefer a little more excitemet, there's always the next record ...

*****(*) Eleven Ghosts**
hatOLOGY 507 *Melford; Han Bennink (d).* 2/94.

An unlikely match – although who *is* a likely partner for Bennink? Drummed up on a visit to Zurich, this meeting is terrific fun, from the funeral-march tempo for Leroy Carr's 'How Long Blues' to the farewell punchline of 'Maple Leaf Rag'. To enjoy to the max, follow John Cage's advice and play the record once, thereafter relishing the memory.

Mike Melillo (born 1939)

PIANO

American bop-and-after pianist whose records have mostly been on European labels.

***** Moonlight On The Ganges**
Red 123264-2 *Melillo; Michael Moore (b); Ben Riley (d).* 5/94.

Melillo's interesting earlier records haven't so far made it to the current format. This forthright trio set would make a useful companion-piece to *Alternate Choices* (Red NS 211). Melillo's idiosyncratic take on bebop piano has a stuttering bounce to it, but he swings through his material, and Moore and Riley are in good shape alongside. Highlight: the nutty variations on Ornette Coleman's 'Humpty Dumpty'.

Gil Melle

BARITONE SAXOPHONE, KEYBOARDS

Melle's picaresque life is a fanciful subject too involved to list here: it takes in aviation, science and, for some of the time, jazz. His 1950s recordings are neglected classics.

****** Primitive Modern / Quadrama**

Original Jazz Classics OJC 1712 *Melle; Joe Cinderella (g); Bill Phillips (b); Ed Thigpen, Shadow Wilson (d).* 4–6/56.

****** Gil's Guests**

Original Jazz Classics OJC 1753 *Melle; Art Farmer, Kenny Dorham (t); Hal McKusick (as, f); Julius Watkins (frhn); Don Butterfield (tba); Joe Cinderella (g); Vinnie Burke (b); Ed Thigpen (d).* 8/56.

Melle's original sleeve-note for *Primitive Modern* suggests that 'modern jazz at its best is a wedding of the classics with the more modern developments native to jazz'; while that implies third-stream dogma, at least Melle put the notion to very striking use. Anyone who lists Bartók, Varèse and Herbie Nichols as major influences is going to do something more than hard bop, and the leader's attempts at shifting the parameters of standard jazz form remain surprising and invigorating. The fast-moving complexities of 'Ironworks', the mysterious dirge, 'Dominica', and the Russell-like 'Adventure Swing' mark out a path very different from most other developments of the time. Cinderella reveals himself as a fine soloist and perceptive interpreter of Melle's needs, and the rhythm section are also fine; while Melle himself is content to play an often reserved role, although his improvisations are melodically as strong as those of Lars Gullin, the baritone player he admits to admiring most. There are a couple of drawbacks – the original studio sound is rather flat, with the leader a little remote in the mix, and some of the structures are delivered a little stiffly by the quartet – but otherwise this is a significant and too little-known record. The CD edition is greatly welcomed, especially since it includes the entire *Quadrama* album as a bonus on the original programme, another remarkable quartet date with two exceptional Ellington transformations and the fine original 'Rush Hour In Hong Kong'.

If anything, *Gil's Guests* is even better, thanks to Rudy van Gelder's superior engineering and the opportunities that a bigger ensemble permits for Melle to create heightened colours, more vivid texture and counterpoint, and a smoother transition between his classically inspired ideas and a jazz execution. Even a conventional feature such as 'Sixpence', written for Kenny Dorham, has an ingenious arrangement for tuba and guitar at the beginning. 'Ghengis' is a direct borrowing from Bartók, and the shifting voicings of 'Block Island' merge brilliantly into a theme that works just as well as a blowing vehicle. An outstanding record, well remastered.

Misha Mengelberg (born 1935)

PIANO, COMPOSER

Mengelberg comes from a deeply musical family and has always straddled musical styles with ease. His place in jazz history was secured when he appeared on Eric Dolphy's last recording. Later, he co-founded the Instant Composers Pool and became a key figure in the Dutch avant-garde. Mengelberg has continued to combine improvisation with notated composition.

*****(*) Change Of Season**

Soul Note 101104 *Mengelberg; George Lewis (tb); Steve Lacy (ss); Arjen Gorter (b); Han Bennink (d).* 7/84.

****** Impromptus**

FMP 7 *Mengelberg (p solo).* 6/88.

****** Mix**

ICP 030 *As above.* 4 & 5/94.

****** Who's Bridge**

Avant AVAN 038 *Mengelberg; Brad Jones (b); Joey Baron (d).* 94.

****** No Idea**

DIW 619 *Mengelberg; Greg Cohen (b); Joey Baron (d).* 96.

Robert Frost once characterized free verse as 'playing tennis with the net down'. Improvisers like Dutchmen Mengelberg and Bennink have been very largely concerned with putting the net back, sometimes up to badminton height, searching for ways of combining the freedoms of improvisation with traditional jazz and even more formal structures. Mengelberg is also a 'legitimate' composer, albeit one in the Louis Andriessen mould, with a very strong jazz influence in his work. The collectivism that was so strong a component of the Dutch 1960s avant-garde is evident in the autonomy granted to the performers (all of them expert players) on *Change Of Season*. Lewis seems most comfortable in the mixed idiom, though Lacy (a purist's purist) sounds a little glacial. Bennink whips up little rhythmic storms, but he plays with unwonted reserve and an often unrecognized sensitivity. Mengelberg plays with great assurance and a graceful disposition of apparently self-contained and discontinuous ideas that are more reminiscent of the Swiss Irène Schweizer than of his compatriots, Fred Van Hove and Leo Cuypers. Interesting, if for no other reason than that there are other directions for 'free' piano than the one taken and dominated by Cecil Taylor.

Impromptus makes a generic nod to a (minor) classical form. The 13 individual pieces aren't obviously linked by theme or as variations, but they follow a barely discernible logic that can be picked up via Mengelberg's untutored vocalese, which is of the Bud Powell/Keith Jarrett/Cecil Taylor persuasion. *Mix*, recorded at a couple of live solo concerts in Amsterdam and The Hague, is very much in the same territory: huge, quasi-tonal shapes and structures jumbled together in what at first glance seems disorder but which is suddenly pierced by light, a simple melodic line that pulls the whole 'mix' into symmetry; perhaps the effect of a magnet on iron filings would be a more effective analogy.

Who's Bridge is intriguing in that it takes Melgelberg much closer to jazz idiom than he normally attempts. He has two very adept sidemen, and Baron is, when one thinks of it, the only younger-generation American who might remind listeners of Bennink. There are even songs here: the Monkish 'Romantic Jump Of Hares', the skittish, Morton-influenced 'Rumbone' and the real surprise, 'Peer's Counting Song', which finds Mengelberg in unwontedly lyrical and expressive mood. The great man is playing well on the recent *No Idea* as well, greatly abetted by two more sterling sidemen. Baron's light touch and pattering, almost tuneful figures transform what might have been a slightly dour performance, though Mengelberg's own humour also shows through here and there.

****** The Root Of The Problem**

hat OLOGY 504 *Mengelberg; Thomas Heberer (t); Michel Godard (tba, serpent); Steve Potts (sax); Achim Kramer (perc).* 96.

Recorded in Cologne, this fine set pits Mengelberg in duo and trio settings with a group of fine and highly eclectic players. The sound of Godard's serpent is still one of the most unusual in contemporary music; however, contrasting as it does with Potts's drily vivid saxophone and Heberer's hard-edged, throaty trumpet, it makes perfect textural sense. Above all, one senses that Mengelberg is enjoying himself here. His touch is relaxed and light, his ideas suitably skittish, and there is not a hint of strain in the flow of ideas.

*****(*) Two Days In Chicago**

hatOLOGY 2-535 2CD *Mengelberg; Fred Anderson (ts); Ab Baars (ts, cl); Ken Vandermark (ts); Fred Lonberg-Holm (clo); Wilbert De Joode, Kent Kessler (b); Hamid Drake, Martin Van Duynhoven (d).* 10/98.

In October 1998 Mengelberg and a group of Dutch musicians met and created some of the best music of his career. His encounter with the locals was at Fred Anderson's Velvet Lounge and the live material on disc two is indicative of the understanding that developed between them during their stay. Misha's long opening solo is typical of his approach: highly detailed, pan-tonal and sophisticated. His take on 'Body And Soul' and 'Round Midnight' is more constrained but highly effective. The first disc, actually recorded the next day finds the group in the studio. There are two Monk tracks, 'Eronel' and 'Off Minor', but the bulk of the session is taken up with improvised trios and quartets, American and Dutch, that negotiate some common ground between the two improvising cultures. It's an impressive set, finely played, and it enhances Mengelberg's visibility considerably.

Ian Menzies & His Clyde Valley Stompers

GROUP

Scotland's most eminent trad outfit, the Clydes were formed in 1952 and Menzies took over leadership in 1954. They lasted till 1963, having been regulars at all the Scottish clubs and halls, but re-formed for a couple of albums in 1981.

****(*) Ian Menzies & His Clyde Valley Stompers**

Lake LACD79 *Malcolm Higgins (t); Ian Menzies (tb); Forrie Cairns (cl); John Cairns (p); Norrie Brown, (bj); Bob Bain, Andrew Bennie (b); Bobby Shannon (d); Fiona Duncan, Lonnie Donegan (v).* 4/59–5/60.

****(*) Traditional Jazz**

Lake LACD126 *As above, except add Pete Kerr (cl), Jim Douglas (bj), Robbie Winter (d).* 4/59–5/61.

The CVS did staunch duty for Scottish trad followers, and their surviving records are in some ways disappointing. Recorded for Pye, and issued mainly as singles and EPs (their single album is on LACD79), their output is mostly sub-three-minute tracks at sometimes unsuitably fast tempos, with the rhythm section thumping along. The standout player is Forrie Cairns, a clarinet player with a touch of Celtic fire about him. Fiona Duncan belts out several vocals, and Donegan, who produced the original sessions, sings on three tracks.

Helen Merrill (born 1930)

VOCAL

Born in New York, Merrill was associated with the first-generation boppers and began recording for Emarcy in 1954. She lived in Italy for some years, later in Japan, and returned to Chicago and New York in the 1970s. Many of her recordings were for smaller labels, but her albums for Verve in the '80s and '90s restored her eminence, and a style based around slow, considered ballad singing. She is married to the arranger, Torrie Zito.

****** Helen Merrill With Clifford Brown And Gil Evans**

Emarcy 838292-2 *Merrill; Clifford Brown, Art Farmer, Louis Mucci (t); Jimmy Cleveland, Joe Bennett (tb); John LaPorta (cl, as); Jerome Richardson (as, ts, f); Danny Bank (f); Hank Jones, Jimmy Jones (p); Barry Galbraith (g); Oscar Pettiford, Milt Hinton (b); Joe Morello, Osie Johnson, Bobby Donaldson (d); strings, horns.* 12/54–6/56.

*****(*) Dream Of You**

Emarcy 514074-2 *As above, except omit Brown, Bank, Jimmy Jones, Hinton and Johnson.* 6/56.

Helen Merrill has never made a bad record and, while she scarcely conforms to the image of a swinging jazz singer, she's a stylist of unique poise and sensitivity. Her early work is as involving as her mature records. She sings at a consistently slow pace, unfolding melodies as if imparting a particularly difficult confidence, and she understands the harmonies of the songs as completely as she trusts her way with time. That gives these lingering performances a sensuality which is less of a come-hither come-on than the similarly inclined work of a singer such as Julie London. Merrill thinks about the words, but she improvises on the music too. Her treatment of 'Don't Explain' is cooler yet no less troubling than Billie Holiday's exaggerated pathos, and 'What's New' is a masterpiece. Brown's accompaniments on seven tracks make an absorbing contrast to his work with Sarah Vaughan, and Evans's arrangements on the other eight songs are some of his most lucid work in this area. *Dream Of You* restores that entire session to the catalogue, with a couple of alternative takes for good measure.

*****(*) Helen Merrill In Italy**

Liuto LRS 0063/5 *Merrill; Nino Culasso, Nino Rosso (t); Dino Piana (tb); Gianni Basso (ts); Gino Marinacci (f); Piero*

Umiliani, Renato Sellani (p); Enzo Grillini (g); Berto Pisano, Giorgio Azzolini (b); Sergio Conti, Ralph Ferraro, Franco Tonani (d); strings. 59–62.

This is flawed by the sometimes unlovely sound, but it's otherwise a compelling collection of all the pieces Merrill recorded on various trips to Italy. Three songs by Umiliani for film scores have lyrics by the singer, and those for 'My Only Man' and 'Dreaming Of The Past' are original and hard to forget. Most of the others are standards, again treated to the most rarefied of ballad settings – 'The More I See You' is almost impossibly slow – but the four closing tracks, sung in Italian with an orchestra conducted by Ennio Morricone, have a *Lieder*-like quality that's disarmingly direct.

****** The Feeling Is Mutual**

Emarcy 558849-2 *Merrill; Thad Jones (c); Dick Katz (p); Jim Hall (g); Ron Carter (b); Arnie Wise, Pete Laroca (d).* 65.

****** A Shade Of Difference**

Emarcy 5558851-2 *As above, except add Gary Bartz (as), Hubert Laws (f), Richard Davis (b), Elvin Jones (d); omit Wise and Laroca.* 7/68.

*****(*) Chasin' The Bird**

Emarcy 558850-2 *Merrill; Pepper Adams (bs); Dick Katz (p); Joe Puma (g); Rufus Reid, Ron McClure (b); Mel Lewis (d).* 3/79.

***** Casa Forte**

Emarcy 558848-2 *Merrill; Urbie Green (tb); Jim Buffington, Peter Gordon, John Clark (frhn); Sal Nistico (ts); Torrie Zito (p); Joe Beck, Bucky Pizzarelli (g); George Mraz, Francisco Centeno (b); Grady Tate, Ron Zito (d); Steve Kroon, Rubens Bassini, Dom Um Romao (perc); strings.* 4–5/80.

These four albums fill a huge gap in Helen's discography and their reissue is very welcome. *The Feeling Is Mutual* and *A Shade Of Difference* are unique records in the jazz vocal canon. Co-credited to pianist-arranger Dick Katz, their extraordinary range of material, offbeat charts and intensely concentrated musicianship contribute to an atmosphere that would be hard to breathe if it weren't for Merrill's conviction. On the earlier disc, she makes 'It Don't Mean A Thing' swing at a tempo that would bemuse most singers, and her almost abstract 'Baltimore Oriole' challenges even Sheila Jordan's unforgettable version. 'The Winter Of My Disconent' is an Alec Wilder tune which suits her perfectly, and 'Deep In A Dream' is done as a motionless duet with Jim Hall. *A Shade Of Difference*, with its larger group, starts with an amazingly dark treatment of Coleman's 'Lonely Woman' with a baroque solo by Bartz, and proceeds through a pin-drop 'While We're Young', a boppish 'A Lady Must Live' and a coolly effective blues in 'I Want A Little Boy'. It ends with Wilder again and his numbing 'Where Do You Go?'. Besides Merrill herself, credit to the players – especially Jones and Hall – and to Katz, who clearly took great pains over the arrangements, which are tight-knit yet open and unconstricting.

Chasin' The Bird picks up where they left off, 11 years on. This one is all Gershwin. If Katz chose to make this just slightly more conventional in terms of its arrangement, it's still not much like other singers' records. Adams was a surprising but superb choice for the sole horn, and they make 'Embraceable You' and 'Summertime' into unstinting hard-bop workouts. But it's the two ballads, 'Isn't It A Pity' and especially the marvellous 'I Can't Be Bothered Now', which bring out the best in Merrill.

Casa Forte is altogether grander, arranged by Torrie Zito, and in the likes of 'Natural Sounds' it takes Merrill towards art-song rather than jazz. Other pieces such as 'Vera Cruz' and 'Antonio's Song' have a surprising Latin feel. Interesting; but, while the singer offers her usual committed performance, by the standards of the other three this is a lesser affair.

*****(*) Collaboration**

Emarcy 834205-2 *Merrill; Shunzo Ono (t, flhn); Lew Soloff (t); Jimmy Knepper (tb); Dave Taylor (btb); Chris Hunter (ss, as, f, cl, ob, picc); Jerry Dodgion (ss, f); Steve Lacy (ss); Danny Bank (bs, f, bcl); Phil Bodner (bcl, f, af); Wally Kane (bcl, bsn); Roger Rosenberg (bcl); Gil Goldstein (ky); Harry Lookofsky, Lamar Alsop (vn); Theodore Israel, Harold Colletta (vla); Jesse Levy (clo); Joe Beck, Jay Berliner (g); Buster Williams (b); Mel Lewis (d); Gil Evans (cond).* 8/87.

One of the strangest singer-and-orchestra records ever made. Merrill's voice has grown weightier over the years, and she casts it very slowly on the waters of Gil Evans's arrangements here, the charts laying down thick, barely moving textures which suggest a mildewing romanticism. Her favourite slow tempos recur throughout, and it's Evans's often magical way with three different ensembles (one with strings, one with trombone and woodwinds, another led by brass) that stops the music from trudging to a stop. Lacy appears for a tart commentary on two tracks, but otherwise it's the long, carefully held tones of the vocalist which act on the music. Sometimes, as in an arrangement of 'Summertime' which harks back directly to *Porgy And Bess*, Evans seems to be reminiscing on his own past, too.

***** Just Friends**

Emarcy 842007-2 *Merrill; Stan Getz (ts); Joachim Kühn, Torrie Zito (p); Jean-François Jenny-Clark (b); Daniel Humair (d).* 89.

Merrill's return to a small-group format brings forth some quietly resolute performances, their autumnal feel heightened by the appearance of Getz in his twilight phase. 'Cavatina' and 'It's Not Easy Being Green' were questionable choices of material, though.

****** Clear Out Of This World**

Emarcy 510691-2 *Merrill; Tom Harrell (t, flhn); Wayne Shorter (ss, ts); Roger Kellaway (p); Red Mitchell (b); Terry Clarke (d).* 6–9/91.

One of the finest vocal records of recent years – although integral to the success is the superlative playing by the instrumentalists. Kellaway, Mitchell and Clarke are ideally sensitive and supportive, and Kellaway's playing in particular is extraordinary: his one-man accompaniment on 'Maybe', one of three good contemporary songs on the disc, is a textbook example of saying a lot while playing a little. Harrell's pristine control is in evidence on a luminous 'When I Grow Too Old To Dream', and the last 30 seconds of this track are reason enough to acquire the record. Shorter contributes eccentric soprano to one tune, strange tenor to another; and there's even a comic duet between Merrill and Mitchell on 'Some Of These Days' that actually works. The singer herself delivers some of her best latter-day performances, with her technique of holding very low notes close to the microphone used to expose telling detail in the songs.

***** Blossom Of Stars**

Emarcy 514652-2 *Merrill; personnel drawn from above Emarcy discs.* 54–89.

A compilation of episodes from both ends of Merrill's career on record, culminating in the new 'We Are Not Alone', a film soundtrack song. Very worthwhile, of course, but the albums above are the place to start.

****** Brownie**

Verve 522363-2 *Merrill; Roy Hargrove, Tom Harrell (t, flhn); Lew Soloff, Wallace Roney (t); Kenny Barron (p); Torrie Zito (ky); Rufus Reid (b); Victor Lewis (d).* 2/94.

Another extraordinary record, which works perfectly both as a homage to Clifford Brown and as a vehicle for Merrill's intensely refined approach to time. No matter how slow the tempo, she makes the line flow, the words mulled over but always sung, not talked through. Any frailties of tone are used for dramatic effect, and on a piece such as 'Born To Be Blue' it can be devastating. The stellar gathering of trumpeters evokes Brown's own ghost, with some electrifying unison passages and memorable individual turns for each of the four players; Barron, as ever, follows and fills in spaces with imperturbable grace.

****** You And The Night And The Music**

Verve 537087-2 *Merrill; Tom Harrell (t, flhn); Bob Millikan (t); Torrie Zito, Masabumi Kikuchi (p); Charlie Haden (b); Paul Motian (d).* 6/96.

*****(*) Carousel**

Finlandia 0630-14914-2 *Merrill; Juhani Aaltonen, Pentti Lahti (reeds); Heikki Sarmanto (ky); Laura Hynninen (hp); Juha Bjorninen (g); Pekka Sarmanto (b); Terry Clarke (d); Tapio Aaltonen (perc); Tapiola Sinfonietta.* 3/96.

Maybe *You And The Night And The Music* is a shade more lightweight than its immediate predecessor. It's still a magnificent effort, with Merrill as absolute in her commitment and the other players responsive to every nuance in the music. Kikuchi is a remarkable addition to the repertory cast, and his introduction to 'My Funny Valentine' is just one of several sublime moments. Although there are two originals by Merrill and Torrie Zito, with 'Don't Leave Me Alone' particularly effective, as usual it's her reworkings of standards which linger in the mind – the closing 'Street Of Dreams' is very fine, but it's the heart-stopping version of 'Young And Foolish' that will silence the room.

The Finlandia album is the realization of a cherished project for composer Heikki Sarmanto, to write a series of songs for Merrill. Torrie Zito arranges for the Tapiola Sinfonietta and, if the results seem lighter and sweeter than one expects from one of her records, there's a wistful gaiety in the music which is very appealing. Pleasing also to hear the great Juhani Aaltonen taking several featured solos.

*****(*) Jelena Ana Milcetic A.K.A. Helen Merrill**

Verve 543089-2 *Merrill; Dennis Anderson (ob, cor); Steve Lacy (ss); Sir Roland Hanna (p); Gil Goldstein (p, acc); Jeff Mironov (g); Gloria Agostini (hp); Jesse Levy (clo); George Mraz (b); Terry Clarke (d); Steve Kroon (perc); strings, choir.* 4–9/99.

A remarkable exercise in seeking out the past, with Merrill choosing songs like Judy Collins's 'My Father' and 'Among My Souvenirs' – even 'I'll Take You Home Again, Kathleen'. These intermingle with glimpses of an East European folk heritage in the opening 'Kirje' and 'Imagining Kirk'. The key instrumental voice is Steve Lacy's; his soprano dialogue moves in and out of view like a passing acquaintance. The bloom is gone from Merrill's voice, but any who've followed her career to this point will be untroubled by that in what is clearly a profoundly personal record.

Pat Metheny (born 1954)

GUITAR

A Mid-Westerner, from Missouri, Metheny was a quick learner, and by the time he was nineteen he had already been teaching at Berklee and playing with the Gary Burton group, an important early association. He made a string of records for ECM and formed a hugely successful touring group, with keyboardist Lyle Mays the other key performer. His switch to Geffen, and subsequently to Warner Brothers, ensured that his records were given major exposure, and he has built an audience in both the jazz and rock camps. In the 1990s he increasingly returned to playing in straight-ahead situations as a sideman, while still pursuing his own muse as he pleased.

***** Bright Size Life**

ECM 827133-2 *Metheny; Jaco Pastorius (b); Bob Moses (d).* 12/75.

***** Watercolours**

ECM 1827409-2 *Metheny; Lyle Mays (p); Eberhard Weber (b); Danny Gottlieb (d).* 2/77.

****(*) Pat Metheny Group**

ECM 825593-2 *As above, except Mark Egan (b) replaces Weber.* 1/78.

***** New Chautauqua**

ECM 825471-2 *Metheny (g solo).* 8/78.

***** American Garage**

ECM 827134-2 *Metheny; Lyle Mays (ky); Mark Egan (b); Danny Gottlieb (d).* 6/79.

Metheny has become a key figure in the instrumental music of the past 20 years. His stature as a jazz musician is more open to debate, and it's interesting to muse on a career which has grown increasingly diverse and self-challenging, even as his global audience has grown. He sees nothing incompatible about his sometimes bewildering range of appearances on record, which now encompasses companions such as Ornette Coleman and Derek Bailey, yet he continues to create own-name group records which can sound as lightweight and undemanding as those of the leading smooth-jazz performers. Most would call this a double-life. Metheny sees it as doing whatever he wants.

When he first appeared, as a coolly melodic electric guitarist for the ECM label, originally discovered by Gary Burton (one of his best early appearances is with the Burton group on *Ring*), Metheny seemed content to drop his playing into whatever context it might find. The first two ECM albums are a little untypical – each depends more on its respective star bassist to give it some clout – but, like the ones that follow, they are pleasant, hummable records with a degree of fine playing which the high-grade production values and sometimes over-sensitive musicianship can occasionally block out with sheer amiability. At this time Metheny favoured a clean, open tone with just enough electronic damping to take the music out of 'classic' jazz-guitar feeling, but he clearly owed a great debt to such urban pastoralists as Jim Hall and Jimmy Raney, even if he seldom moved back to bebop licks.

The Metheny Group albums settled the guitarist's music into the niche which he is still basically working from: light, easily digested settings that let him play long, meticulous solos which can as often as not work up a surprising intensity. *Pat Metheny Group* and *American Garage* each have their ration of thoughtful improvising which the guitarist settles inside a gently propulsive rhythm, more ruralized than the beefy urban beats of the contemporary fusion bands. That strain also colours the playing and composing of Mays, who has been Metheny's principal collaborator for 20 years. Scarcely a major voice in his own right – his own solo records have been entirely inconsequential – Mays is the perfect second banana. He feeds Metheny all kinds of tasteful orchestration without getting too much in his way.

New Chautauqua is a rare all-solo album in the Metheny canon. A pleasant, sweet-toned diversion, it hints at the multifariousness – with various electric and acoustic settings, including a 15-string harp-guitar – which Metheny has grown fascinated with in recent times.

*** 80 / 81

ECM 843169-2 2CD *Metheny; Dewey Redman, Michael Brecker (ts); Charlie Haden (b); Jack DeJohnette (d).* 5/80.

At the time this sounded like an almost shocking departure, but Brecker and Redman adapt themselves to Metheny's aesthetic without undue compromise and Haden and DeJohnette play with great purpose. There's too much music here and some dreary spots, but some excellent moments too.

**(*) As Falls Witchita, So Falls Witchita Falls

ECM 821416-2 *Metheny; Lyle Mays (ky); Nana Vasconcelos (perc).* 9/80.

**(*) Offramp

ECM 817138-2 *As above, except add Steve Rodby (b), Danny Gottlieb (d).* 10/81.

*** Travels

ECM 810622-2 2CD *As above.* 7–11/82.

The Metheny band was by now an international concert institution. *As Falls Witchita* is basically a duo situation for Metheny and Mays, with guest Vasconcelos adding a little zest: lots of pastels. *Offramp* brings back the quartet for another mild-mannered sequence, although here Metheny's knack for the melodic hook starts to blossom: 'Are You Going With Me', over a gently percolating bass vamp, remains an enduring set-piece which he is still playing today. *Travels* effectively summed up the band's tenure with ECM with a studious and densely packed live set. There are the kind of longueurs that one associates more with the double-live-album in rock, rather than the creative stretch of the jazz concert disc, but Metheny's group had built up a charisma of its own by this time and this is a good souvenir.

***(*) Rejoicing

ECM 817795-2 *Metheny; Charlie Haden (b); Billy Higgins (d).* 11/83.

All right, it's all too obvious citing this capital-letter jazz album as Metheny's best up to this point, but he finds a loneliness in Horace Silver's 'Lonely Woman' and a happiness in Ornette Coleman's 'Rejoicing' which more severe interpreters of those composers don't seem to have time or room for. By itself the playing isn't so remarkable, but pairing him with Haden and Higgins, on a programme of mostly Coleman and Metheny originals, sheds new lustre both on himself and on music that's often somewhat neglected.

**(*) First Circle

ECM 823342-2 *Metheny; Lyle Mays (ky); Steve Rodby (b); Paul Wertico (d); Pedro Aznar (perc, v).* 2/84.

The last ECM album is no kind of departure and even some fans were disappointed, but its larger sonic palette was a clear indication of where Metheny wanted to go next: expanding his group to a quintet, he staked a place in a much bigger sound. Unlike his ECM contemporary, Steve Tibbetts, who has never secured Metheny's audience yet whose works are an absorbing counterpart to his contemporary's, the guitarist seemed set on mediating his group's music through a fundamentally conservative synthesis of jazz, Latin and rock flavours: a catholic taste put through a blender to take all the harmful pieces out. And then he made ...

**** Song X

Geffen 924096 *Metheny; Ornette Coleman (as, vn); Charlie Haden (b); Jack DeJohnette, Denardo Coleman (d).* 12/85.

Metheny's great departure still seems like a bolt from the blue after playing through the previous half-dozen albums. There is still a sense that some of the best and most extreme material was left off the record (which Metheny has subsequently confirmed). Otherwise it's the most astonishing move ever made by any musician perceived as a middle-of-the-road jazz artist. Not only does the guitarist power his way through Coleman's itinerary with utter conviction, he sets up opportunities for the saxophonist to resolve and he creates a fusion which Coleman's often impenetrable Prime Time bands have failed to come to terms with. Melody still has a place here, which suggests that Metheny's interest in the original Coleman legacy may be carrying forward in his own work more intently than it is in the composer's. Either way, on many of the more raving episodes here both men sound exultant with the possibilities. Highly recommended.

**(*) Still Life (Talking)

Geffen GED 24145 *Metheny; Lyle Mays (ky); Steve Rodby (b); Paul Wertico (d); Armando Marcal (perc, v); David Blamires, Mark Ledford (v).* 3–4/87.

*** Question And Answer

Geffen GED 24293 *Metheny; Dave Holland (b); Roy Haynes (d).* 12/89.

** Secret Story

Geffen GED 24468 *Metheny; Gil Goldstein (p, acc); Lyle Mays (ky); Toots Thielemans (hca); Charlie Haden, Steve Rodby, Will Lee (b); Steve Ferrone, Paul Wertico, Sammy Merendino (d);*

Nana Vasconcelos, Armando Marcal (perc); Mark Ledford (v); strings and brass. 91–92.

***** The Road To You**

Geffen GED 24601 *Metheny; Pedro Aznar (sax, vib, mar, perc, g, v); Lyle Mays (ky); Steve Rodby (b); Paul Wertico (d); Armando Marcal (perc, v).* 92–93.

Metheny's albums for Geffen have followed an inexorable course towards (excuse these labels) light-rock. *Still Life (Talking)* is an exemplar of the style, which peaks on the infectious 'Last Train Home'; but there's an awful lot of fluff that goes with it, often courtesy of Mays's noodling keyboards. The wordless vocals of Ledford and Blamires remove the final barrier to a crossover audience by getting the human voice in there somewhere, and, though the increased orchestration of the sound may have displeased some of Metheny's admirers, it waved in many more. *Question And Answer* – which seems to be the kind of periodic vacation that Metheny takes from his regular band, and may it continue – finds the guitarist, bassist and, especially, the drummer playing with great *brio* and suppleness. The tunes are another mix of standards, Coleman and Metheny tunes; and if some of the charm of the ECM trio date is missing and a few tunes seem to end up nowhere, it's well worth hearing.

Secret Story is hopelessly overblown and would feel intolerably pompous were Metheny himself not so likeable: he usually salvages something interesting to play, even when the music's obese with strings, brass and whatever. But this remains his least tractable and most overworked record. *The Road To You*, a concert album, is much livelier and is one of the best records by the regular group since the last live set. They are a fun group to see live (even if some of their sets go on longer than The Grateful Dead used to), and this pared-down souvenir will find plenty of appeal.

***** Zero Tolerance For Silence**

Geffen GED 24626 *Metheny (g solo).*

Here is Metheny's most difficult record. While the Metheny Group seems intent on mere pleasantry, the man himself seeks to peer over the edge and into the abyss with this one, some sort of riot of electronic howling. Hardcore souls might sniff at the pretensions here, and it's scarcely on a par with a Sonny Sharrock or Hans Reichel solo record. But Metheny earns stars for doing something other hit-makers pay lip-service to: going for the hard stuff and insisting it gets released. He does better on his encounter with Derek Bailey (see under Bailey's entry), but this has its sore-headed moments.

***** We Live Here**

Geffen GED 24729 *Metheny; Mark Ledford (t, flhn, v); Lyle Mays (ky); Steve Rodby (b); Paul Wertico (d); Luis Conte (perc); David Blamires (v).* 94.

Back on undeadly ground. A few tracks work off programmed drum beats, and Metheny gets to do a Bensonesque bit here and there, but by the middle of the disc he's returned to his favourite platform, the soft cadences of Brazilian beat. Once there, he actually sounds in very good form, confirming that, with the rotten *Secret Story* behind him, this is a good period for him.

***** Quartet**

Geffen GED 24978 *As above, except omit Ledford, Conte, Blamires.* 5/96.

Written and recorded quickly by the nucleus of the group, this is interesting if hardly substantial Metheny fare. The improvisation 'Badland' suggests that this is not an improvising group. They do far better by pristine miniatures such as 'Seven Days' and 'Oceania'. The feel is not so much acoustic, as intended, more softly electric in its resonance, and it's surely no concidence that the title suggests a record of chamber music.

***** Imaginary Day**

Warner Bros 46791 *As above, except add Mark Ledford (t, vtb, flhn, v), David Blamires (mel, g, vn, melod, v), David Samuels (vib), Glen Velez, Mino Cinelu, Don Alias (perc).* 97.

Metheny plays at least ten different kinds of guitar on this one, the kind of arsenal one might once have associated with, say, Steve Howe, and perhaps it suits the kind of widescreen, almost symphonic music he seems to be increasingly in search of. If the jazz elements continue to filter away, he still manages to squeeze in solos of considerable moment. 'Follow Me' is a near-classic piece of instrumental pop with overtones of the jazz disciplines that he started out with. But too much of the rest runs stickily into the kind of bombastic terrain which he should have left behind after *Secret Story*. A perplexing artist.

***** A Map Of The World**

Warner Bros 9362-47366-2 *Metheny; orchestra. n.d.*

*****(*) Trio 99–00**

Warner Bros 9362-47632-2 *Metheny; Larry Grenadier (b); Bill Stewart (d).* 8/99.

A Map Of The World is a soundtrack album, and since it consists of 28 brief tracks, this is Metheny as miniaturist, playing acoustic against a full orchestra. It suits him rather well: big and sweeping motifs for a film set in Wisconsin, and the disciplines of the form result in some of his most precise and unrambling playing. But it is, in the end, a film soundtrack, and a backwater in his discography.

The trio record is his most straight-ahead situation since *Question And Answer*, although as a sideman he's been doing plenty of this sort of playing elsewhere. It would be interesting to poll Metheny's following on how they rate this kind of record next to his Group albums. For us – call us predictable if you have to – it rates ahead because it affirms what a graceful and quick-witted improviser the man is, away from his big-sound predilections. His version of 'Giant Steps' is light and airy but full of notes and intensely played. That said, there are many good guitar records like this out there, and it assists him enormously to have Grenadier and the admirable Stewart on hand, since they're integral to the record's success.

Hendrik Meurkens

VIBRAPHONE, HARMONICA

Born in Holland, raised in Germany, and completely obsessed by Brazilian music, Meurkens moved to the USA in 1992 to build on a promising start as a recording artist for Concord. Almost impossible to believe that these melodic, swinging records aren't created and recorded in Latin America, except that Meurkens has tapped into a vivid Latin scene in New York and has called on like-minded players to help create his beguiling and danceable tapestries of sound.

***** Sambahia**

Concord CCD 4474 *Meurkens; Claudio Roditi (t, flhn); Paquito D'Rivera (as, cl); Tim Armacost (ts); Lito Tabora (p); Jacare (b); Cesar Machado (d); Reginaldo Vargas (perc).* 12/90.

****(*) Clear Of Clouds**

Concord CCD 4531 *Meurkens; Claudio Roditi (t, flhn); Osmar Milito (p); Fernando Merlino (p, ky); Claudio Jorge (g); Alceu Maria (cavaquinho); Jacare (b); Pascoal Meirelles (d); Dom Chacal (perc).* 2 & 6/92.

***** A View From Manhattan**

Concord CCD 4585 *Meurkens; Jay Ashby (tb, perc); Dick Oatts (af, as, ts, ss); Mark Soskin (p); Harvie Swartz, Leonard D Traversa (b); Carl Allen (d); Thelmo Martins Porto Pinho (d, perc).* 7/93.

***** Slidin'**

Concord CCD 4628 *Meurkens; Peter Bernstein (g); Dado Moroni, Mark Soskin (p); David Finck, Harvie Swartz (b); Tim Horner (d).* 6/94.

***** October Colors**

Concord CCD 4670 *Meurkens; Helio Alves (p); Rogério Botter Maio (b); Portinho (d, perc).* 11/94.

*****(*) Poema Brasileiro**

Concord Picante CCD 4728 *Meurkens; Claudio Roditi (flhn); Jay Ashby (tb, perc); Laura Dreyer (as, ts, f); Steve Sacks (as, f); Mark Soskin (p); Dario Eskenazi (p, ky); Romero Lubambo (g, cavaquinho); Marty Ashby (g); Kip Reed (b); Rogério Botter Maio (b); Portinho (d, pandeiro); Vanderlei Pereira, Valtinho (perc) Ivan Lins (v).* 5/96.

His name would hardly lead you to expect smoothly flowing Latin grooves, but that is what Meurkens delivers. Despite his Dutch ancestry, he was born in Hamburg, a seaport initiation that somehow always holds out the promise of eclectic enthusiasms to come. His Rio-Samba Jazz Group has been around for some time, delivering consistent product without ever having sparked much excitement. A little like Klaus Ignatzek, Meurkens responds very favourably to close attention; otherwise he is apt to pass the casual listener by on the assumption that the calm surface conceals shallowness rather than music of some depth and thought.

Slidin' is the exception; no vibraphone, no Roditi, but an obvious attempt to move into the jazz mainstream with elegant portrayals of 'Have You Met Miss Jones?' and 'Come Rain Or Come Shine'. Bernstein is the key element here, a very underrated player whose sweeping arpeggiations and clean, accurate runs offer an ideal foil to Meurkens's plangent mouth harp.

The fifth record for Concord is pretty much more of the same, distinguished by a lovely version of Wayne Shorter's classic 'Footprints' but otherwise unremarkable. The next again – significantly issued on the label's more specialist Latin imprint – marks something of a change of direction, not away from Brazilian themes and rhythms, but towards a more arranged and layered sound. The guest appearances by Lins are the key to the record. He is masterful on his own 'Desesperar Jamais' and the heart-wrenching 'Saindo De Mim', though there is also sterling musicianship from almost everyone concerned. Roditi returns for a very effective flugelhorn feature on 'Passarim'. Two ears and the tail for engineer Michael Brorby and co-producers Jay Ashby and Steve Sacks; the studio sound is flawless.

Mezz Mezzrow (1899–1972)

CLARINET, SAXOPHONES

If ever there was a real-life version of Norman Mailer's 'White Negro', it has to be Mezzrow, who turned his back on a respectable and well-off white Jewish background to pass as black. Mezz's skills as a clarinettist were limited; his skills as a fixer, self-mythologizer and acquirer of lifestyle sundries were beyond question. The autobiography, Really the Blues, ghosted by Bertram Wolfe, can't be trusted as far as it can be thrown, but it remains a great read.

***** Mezz Mezzrow, 1928–1936**

Classics 713 *Mezzrow; Muggsy Spanier (c); Max Kaminsky, Frank Newton, Freddy Goodman, Ben Gusick, Reunald Jones, Chelsea Quealey (t); Benny Carter (t, as, v); Floyd O'Brien (tb); Frank Teschemacher (cl, as); Rod Cless (as); Bud Freeman, Art Karle, Johnny Russell (ts); Joe Bushkin, Teddy Wilson, Willie 'The Lion' Smith, Joe Sullivan (p); Eddie Condon (bj); Albert Casey, Clayton Sunshine Duerr, Ted Tonison (g); Wellman Braud, Pops Foster, John Kirby, Louis Thompson (b); Jim Lannigan (bb); Gene Krupa, Jack Maisel, George Stafford, Chick Webb (d); Chick Bullock, Elinor Charier, Red McKenzie, Lucille Stewart (v).* 4/28–3/36.

***** Mezz Mezzrow, 1936–1939**

Classics 694 *Similar to above.* 36–39.

Eddie Condon nicknamed him 'Southmouth' in ironic recognition of his obsessive self-identification with black musicians and self-consciously disenchanted and un-ironic pursuit of a 'Negro' lifestyle. He claims to have insisted on being put in the black cells of a segregated police block, on the grounds that he was only 'passing for white'. His nickname also carries an echo of Louis Armstrong's soubriquet, 'Satchelmouth'. Mezzrow idolized the trumpeter and once worked for him as factotum and grass distributor. His music was considerably more 'authentic' than his personal manners: sinuous if slightly repetitive lines, a dry, sharp tone (compare George Lewis's) and a flow of ideas which, if not endless, were always imaginatively permed and varied. For the time being, the best sources for Mezzrow are the Classics discs, which exclude material made under Sidney Bechet's leadership. These concentrate on various (often motley) small-group swing dates from the 1930s in which Mezzrow took some kind of leading role. There's nothing here that requires a wholesale revision of Mezzrow's oddly unbalanced reputation.

***** Mezz Mezzrow, 1944–1945**

Classics 1074 *Mezzrow; Hot Lips Page (t); Sidney Bechet (ss); Art Hodes, Sammy Price, Fitz Weston (p); Danny Barker (g); Pops Foster (b); Danny Alvin, Big Sid Catlett, Kaiser Marshall (d); Douglas Daniels, Pleasant Joe (v).* 3/44–8/45.

Much of the Mezzrow discography was under the joint nominal leadership of Sidney Bechet, and the recordings of summer 1945, made for King Jazz and for Storyville, featured some of Sidney's best work of the period. 'Revolutionary Blues', 'Sheik Of Araby' and 'Perdido Stomp' (which also reappears on a later version, recorded in New York for the Royal Jazz label) are among the best of Bechet's performances of the period, and Mezz provides stalwart support, more enthusiastic than subtle.

***** Mezz Mezzrow, 1947**

Classics 1095 *Mezzrow; Sidney Bechet (ss, cl); Sammy Price (p); Sox Wilson (p, v); Wellman Braud (b); Baby Dodds, Kaiser Marshall (d); Coot Grant (v).* 9 & 12/47.

Rounding out the story of King Jazz, the sessions of September 1947 and those later sides for Royal and Storyville are pretty orthodox – but what fun they must all have had. The joyousness is tempered by the knowledge that drummer Kaiser Marshall was dead a matters of days after the sides were cut, which is why the final track is posthumously titled 'Kaiser's Last Break'. Many of those who praise Mezz's playing like the *idea* of him and would be dismayed if they were presented with a Mezzrow solo blindfold; by the same token, many of those who dismiss his playing out of hand do so because they have chosen to believe he is merely an ofay dabbler, indulging a species of *nostalgie de la boue*.

Barend Middelhoff

TENOR SAXOPHONE

Dutch post-bop saxman.

***** The River**

A Records AL 73103 *Middelhoff; Anton Goudsmit (g); Carlo De Wijs (org); Joris Teepe (b); Joost Kesselaar (d).* 5/97.

This starts out so laid-back and late-nite that one wonders if 'Voice Of Romance' represents the only gear the saxophonist has at his disposal. Goudsmit's gentle chording and guest star De Wijs's mild Hammond lines don't do much to change the impression. The set, though, picks up with the second and subsequent tracks; 'Thanks To St George' would have been a more typical starting-point. The guitarist is credited with 'The Barrons', an interesting idea strongly played, and bassist Teepe with both 'The Blue Force' and 'Congo', gutsy, deceptive performances. Middelhoff's title-track is an unashamedly romantic colour-piece, moody, slightly soft-edged, but beautifully executed. Too easy-going, taken all in all, to make a very strong case for itself. One of those jazz records for people who don't really like jazz; the aural equivalent of a chicken korma.

Palle Mikkelborg (born 1941)

TRUMPET, FLUGELHORN, COMPOSER

Although a professional since 1960, Mikkelborg's own playing has lately taken a secondary role to composing and conducting, often with big ensembles. Aura for Miles Davis is his best-known work. Unafraid of electronics, and he often uses them on his own instrument.

*****(*) Heart To Heart**

Storyville STCD 4114 *Mikkelborg; Kenneth Knudsen (ky); Niels-Henning Orsted Pedersen (b).* 86.

A player of enormous technical capability and lyrical strength, Mikkelborg has always worn his influences on his sleeve. The 1984 composition, *Aura*, was a harmonically coded dedication to Miles Davis (on which Davis was to play a guest role). Much of Mikkelborg's most important work in the late 1970s and '80s has been for large-scale conventional forces, much like his sometime collaborator, the guitarist–composer Terje Rypdal, but he remains more deeply rooted in jazz than the Norwegian, having served an impressively documented apprenticeship with the exiled Dexter Gordon. Mikkelborg is one of the few convincing exponents of electric trumpet, which he uses, unlike Don Ellis, to produce great sheets of harmonic colour against which he dabs acoustic notes of surprising purity. *Aura* underlined the Miles influence to the apparent exclusion of any other; but he is perhaps closer in conception to Chet Baker and, even on an impressionistic set like *Heart To Heart*, he can sound astonishingly like both Clifford Brown and Howard McGhee. The opening track is an unashamed Miles rip-off, though played with a clear, brassy resonance that is Mikkelborg's own. Fortunately, perhaps, it doesn't set a tone for the set, which is quite varied in temper, though mainly in a meditative mood. Knudsen's keyboard structures are always highly effective, and NHOP is far better recorded than usual.

Joakim Milder (born 1965)

TENOR SAXOPHONE

Studied at Stockholm Conservatory, then worked with Fredrik Norén and in the Stockholm Jazz Orchestra. Several records as a leader and many collaborations with his Swedish contemporaries.

*****(*) Still In Motion**

Dragon DRCD 188 *Milder; Steve Dobrogosz (p); Christian Spering (b); Rune Carlsson (d).* 9/89.

*****(*) Consensus**

Opus 3 CD 9201 *Milder; Johan Hölén (as); Anders Persson (p); Christian Spering (b); Magnus Gran (d).* 2/92.

Milder sounded like one of the most adventurous and least conformist of players to emerge from the Swedish scene in the 1980s. As an improviser he eschews both easy licks and long, heavily elaborate lines, preferring a scratchy tone to the open-voiced timbre of most tenor players and fragmenting his lines with silences, rushes and retards, anything he can think of that varies the attack. Yet there is Rollins-like logic to some of his melodic paths, and on some standards he keeps the sense of the song to hand even as he takes it crabbily apart. The all-original *Still In Motion* was a tiny disappointment after the memorable debut LP, *Life In Life*, which is still on vinyl only; a more unified but fractionally less compelling session, since nothing quite aspires to the interplay with Palle Danielsson and Carlsson on the earlier set. *Consensus* returns to standards – there are 12 of them here – and refuses to take any obvious routes. 'My Funny Valentine', for instance, hints only obliquely at its melody, 'Some Day My Prince Will Come' gets a notably sour treatment – the tune almost exploded by

Gran's crackling toms – and the use of a second saxophone to counterpoint some of the tenor parts is always different from what might be expected.

***** Ways**

Dragon DRCD 231 *Milder; Lasse Lindgren (flhn); Håkan Nyqvist (frhn); Staffan Martensson (cl); Steve Dobrogosz (p); Henrik Frendin (vla); Bertil Strandberg (euph); Christian Spering (b); Rune Carlsson (d); Peter Ostlund (perc); string section.* 12/90–8/92.

Milder has been turning up on other records, but his own discography as leader is progressing slowly, carefully and with absorbing results. That said, this album of low-key, chamber-like music will be a distraction for those more interested in Milder's straight-ahead saxophone. The 11 originals are directed by their textural and tonal qualities rather than by anything rhythmic, and only 'Apart' and 'Where Do Pies Go When They Die' push Milder into his most effective improvising form. Otherwise it's the contrasting brass and string sections that drive the content: lyrical and desolate in the almost typecast manner of Scandinavian jazz, it's a meritorious record, but one for reflective tastes.

*****(*) Sister Majs Blouse**

Mirrors MICD 002 *Milder; Bobo Stenson (p); Palle Danielsson (b); Fredrik Norén (d).* 1/93.

***** Remains**

Dragon DRCD 285 *Milder; Steve Dobrogosz (p); Max Schultz (g); Henrik Frendin (vn, vla); Mats Rondin (clo); Christian Spering (b); Peter Ostlund (perc).* 10/94–3/95.

***** Ord Pa Golvet**

LJ LJCD 5210 *Milder; Tobias Sjogren (g); Johannes Lundberg (b); Gunnar Ekelof (v).* 1/95.

Three interesting records, but no masterpiece, and Milder's work seems to be slipping into a love of texture and sonic intricacy which may disappoint those who admire his saxophone playing. The *Sister Majs Blouse* project is dedicated to the music of the late Swedish saxman, Borje Fredriksson, with his original rhythm section standing in behind Milder. Fredriksson's tunes are a fascinating lot, from mood pieces to a wedding waltz, and the quartet characterize them with superb skill: Stenson, Danielsson and Norén have seldom sounded better. Ironically, Milder himself doesn't quite get hold of some of the tunes; but as a quartet disc this is very fine. *Remains* is distilled from woodwind, piano and strings: bountiful in terms of texture and variation, but not terribly vital to listen to. A theme like 'Simply Drift' shows how skilled Milder has become at fashioning themes out of fragments (and harmonic hooks), but his own playing here sounds relatively becalmed. Much the same could be said of the trio project, *Ord Pa Golvet*, but this is rather more mysterious, pieces of *audio vérité* passing into the music via traffic sounds and the enigmatic spoken commentary of Gunnar Ekelof. The most striking player here is actually Sjogren, whose wide vocabulary of sounds and influences creates the palette which most of the music is drawn from. Since our last edition, Milder has been doing plenty of sideman work, but his own projects don't seem to have emerged on CD for a while.

John Miles

TENOR SAXOPHONE, FLUTE

British post-bop saxman.

***** The Enchanter**

Miles Music MMCD 082 *Miles; Neil Angilley (p); Phil Hudson (g); Julian Crampton (b, d); Laura Fairhurst (clo); Winston Clifford, Marc Meader, Dave Ohm (d).* 93.

The technical details note that some of these tracks were made in Julian's bedroom; that, plus the family tie-up, might lead some to suspect a shabbily amateur effort. Not a bit of it. Like much of his generation, Miles wears his Coltrane influence very prominently, but he has turned it into a quite personal voice. The title-track, which opens, is very distinctive with its cello colours and, though there is nothing quite as arresting later on (except perhaps a duet with Crampton, done in the self-same bedroom studio), it establishes a tone and a standard which the record does not relinquish. One would like to hear the same music rather better recorded. There are some problems of audibility, and at one or two spots what sound like awkward edits or tape flaws. Otherwise very acceptable indeed.

Ron Miles (born 1963)

TRUMPET

Born in Indianapolis, he studied in Colorado before working with the Mercer-led Ellingtonn Orchestra. Associations with Bill Frisell and Ginger Baker began in 1995.

*****(*) My Cruel Heart**

Gramavision GCD 79510 *Miles; Fred Hess (ts); Kari Miles (f); Eric Moon (p); Al Hammond Moore (org); John Stubbs (syn, samples); Marc McCoin (samples); Todd Ayers, Farrell Rowe, Eddie Turner, Dave Willy (g); Artie Moore (b); Rudy Royston (d).* 96.

****** Women's Day**

Gramavision GCD 79516 *Miles; Mark Harris (bcl); Eric Gunnison (p); Todd Ayers, Bill Frisell (g); Kent McLagen, Artie Moore (b); Rudy Royston (d).* 97.

His music is much like the Rockies themselves, at once harsh and gentle, troubling and yet bespeaking a kind of calm grace. The earlier album opens on a grinding electric guitar ostinato, across which Miles's first entrance spashes like ice-water. The basic group on *My Cruel Heart* is a trumpet–bass–drums trio, and that is the cool, uncluttered instrumentation for three excellent pieces: 'Howard Beach', 'Naked' and the closing 'Hosea & Gomer'. Other tracks build in saxophone or a single guitar, but on 'Erase Yourself', the opening number 'Finger Palace' and the title-piece, Miles uses carefully layered guitar sounds, organ, multi-tracked flute from Mrs Miles, and samples to create a shifting, detachedly funky environment for his solo passages. Saxophonist Hess seems the false note here, too rawly blues-orientated for music of this sophistication.

Women's Day follows an identical tack, except that Frisell is an omnipresent component, spreading those trademarked washes and dabs behind and occasionally across the trio sound. Miles now seems settled to an approach that hasn't yet solidified into a formula. The most striking tracks – 'Belly', 'Jesus, I Want To Go To Sleep', a moving tribute to 'Cobain' – are those which don't involve other personnel, but the addition of Todd Ayers's guitar on 'Mommy On Top' gives it a fresh dimension and tees the album up for an achingly beautiful 'Goodnight'. Miles is possessed of a limpid, slightly tremulous brass sound. He certainly benefits from Hans Wendl's hand on the controls during the *Women's Day* sessions (its predecessor was self-produced). The balance is near-perfect and some of the less elegant transitions of the first album have been ironed out.

Harry Miller (1941–83)

DOUBLE BASS

Much love and missed, Miller was the anchorman of the British free-jazz scene in the 1970s. His big, vocalized tone worked in every context, from solo performance to big bands. Born in Johannesburg, he came to London at the age of twenty and joined drummer Don Brown's Sounds Five. Harry died in a car accident in the Netherlands, where he was living in his last months.

****** The Collection**

Ogun HMCD 1/2/3 3CD *Miller; Mark Charig (c, ahn); Malcolm Griffiths, Radu Malfatti, Wolter Wierbos (tb); Mike Osborne (as); Trevor Watts (ss, as); Willem Breuker (ts, bcl); Sean Bergin (ts); Keith Tippett (p); Louis Moholo (d); Julie Tippetts (v).* 74–3/83.

Harry Miller was an inspirational presence wherever he played, a musician who spoke entirely in his own voice, and with a quiet passion. The gentleness of his solo bass on *Children At Play* was perfectly at ease with the rhythmic intensity of his section-work on group albums like *Down South* or *Family Affair*, which he made with his group, Isipingo. Most of his records as leader were released on the label he helped found, and *The Collection* has been put together with loving care by Hazel Miller and John Jack, keepers of the flame. In addition to the three albums already mentioned, the set includes *Bracknell Breakdown*, a set of duets with trombonist Radu Malfatti, and *In Conference*, with the two-saxophone front line of Trevor Watts and Willem Breuker. The box also includes a booklet of photographs and the memories of friends and fellow-players.

The best measure of Harry's gifts can be had from the solo record, which has overdubbed flute and percussion parts, played over a rolling township beat that conveyed Harry's profound immersion in the musics of his native country. As with many of the South African exiles who came to Britain in the 1960s, he found the transition from settled grooves to free music perfectly congenial, and his out-of-tempo work on *Bracknell Breakdown* and *Down South* (made during the last year of his life and the only record not released on Ogun) is suggestive of a player who worked to a deeper, inner rhythm. He always had a special understanding with trombonists, perhaps drawn to that low, vocalized tonality, and some of his best work was in the company of Malfatti, Wierbos and Griffiths.

Harry was often so busy that he had little time for his own projects; however, he did establish one extraordinary band. On its day, Isipingo was one of the most incendiary and compelling bands around and, caught live at Battersea Arts Centre, proved a compelling experience even on record. Much of Harry's finest work was under other leaders, and it might have been good to have included some of his other Ogun sessions under different leaders, most obviously Mike Osborne, who was in Isipingo but who also led one of the greatest jazz trios Britain has heard, with Harry and Louis Moholo. For the moment, though, cherish his extraordinary touch on 'Foregone Conclusion' and behind Julie Tippetts on 'New Baby'. 'Aitchy' lives.

Marcus Miller (born 1959)

BASS, BASS CLARINET, KEYBOARDS, GUITAR, VOCAL

Born in Brooklyn, he studied clarinet and took up the electric bass in the '70s. Played bass with Miles Davis in the early '80s and was the producer and arranger on several of Davis's final records. Subsequently worked extensively as a rock and all-purpose black-music producer, occasionally getting the time to make his own records.

***** The Sun Don't Lie**

Dreyfus FDM 36560-2 *Miller; Miles Davis, Michael Stewart, Sal Marquez (t); David Sanborn, Kenny Garrett (as); Everette Harp (ss, as); Kirk Whalum, Wayne Shorter (ts); Joe Sample (p); Christian Wicht, Philippe Saisse (ky); Jonathan Butler, Vernon Reid, Paul Jackson Jr, Dean Brown, Hiram Bullock (g); Poogie Bell, Michael White, Tony Williams, Andy Narell, Steve Ferrone, Omar Hakim, William Calhoun, Lenny White (d); Don Alias, Paulinho Da Costa, Steve Thornton (perc).* 90–92.

****(*) Tales**

Dreyfus FDM 36571-2 *Miller; Michael Stewart (t); Kenny Garrett (as); Joshua Redman (ts); Bernard Wright (ky); Hiram Bullock, Dean Brown (g); Poogie Bell, Lenny White (d); Lalah Hathaway, Me'Shell Ndege Ocello (v).* 94–95.

***** Live & More**

Dreyfus FDM 36585-2 *Miller; Michael Stewart (t, flhn); Kenny Garrett (as, ss); Everette Harp, Roger Byam (ts); Bernard Wright, David Ward, Dave Delhomme (ky); Hiram Bullock, Drew Zingg, Dean Brown (g); Poogie Bell (d); Lalah Hathaway (v).* 7–10/96.

Miller has had a relatively quiet time of it in the last couple of years, but he's still much in demand as a musician-producer. Scientific and punctilious in the studio, as likely to get out his bass clarinet as his bass guitar, he masterminded most of the final Miles Davis studio records, and there are some notes from Miles on one track from *The Sun Don't Lie*, along with bits and pieces from some of the most famous session names in the business. Typically, it ends up being an album of brilliant fragments that, for all its skill, has a peculiarly unfinished feel to it, shards of jazz, rock, funk and film music flying in all directions. The ghost of Jaco Pastorius also haunts Miller's work – 'Mr Pastorius' is a simple solo tribute on bass, but so is the note-for-note recreation of Weather Report's 'Teen Town'. If there's such a thing as post-modernist jazz-funk, it surely sounds like this. *Tales*, though strung around some sort of concept, works in much the same way: Garrett, Stewart and Redman toss in some jazz content, but some of the zing has also slipped away since the last record.

The live album has the aura of something that used to hang around many a live rock album, years ago: the necessary souvenir of a top live show that has little musical reason to exist. Certainly Miller's takes on his own 'Panther' and 'Tutu' add little to their various studio incarnations. But it's a formidable band behind him, and the leader is a chopsman of such strength that the music takes on a degree of character that the spotless studio work sometimes misses. His bass clarinet treatment of 'Strange Fruit' shows what a wide-ranging virtuoso he is. The vocals are relatively painless. And if you miss the elasticated funk of his homebound sound, there are two studio tracks to fill up the disc.

Mulgrew Miller (born 1955)

PIANO

Born in Greenwood, Minnesota, Miller emerged as a major pianist in the 1980s, following stints with Woody Shaw, the Duke Ellington Orchestra and Art Blakey's Jazz Messengers. He has since worked mostly as a small-group leader himself.

***** Milestones**

RCA Camden 74321 610772 2CD *Miller; Kenny Garrett (as, f); Steve Nelson (vib); Ira Coleman, Charnett Moffett (b); Marvin 'Smitty' Smith, Terri Lyne Carrington, Tony Reedus (d); Rudy Bird (perc).* 6/85–87.

***** Chapters 1 & 2**

32 Jazz 32055 *As above, except omit Garrett, Nelson, Reedus, Bird.* 85–86.

At the moment, Miller's showing on record seems to be going backwards: his early discs for Landmark have been reissued in different editions, but the splendid albums for Novus are in the deletions file. *Milestones*, a good-value British twofer, brings together *Keys To The City*, *Work!* and *Wingspan*, while the 32 Jazz puts the first two on to a single disc. These are relatively ordinary post-bop records, energetic and full of hearty playing, but altogether missing the extraordinary gravitas and eloquence of his subsequent Novus records. He made three further dates for Landmark before moving on, and there is better music on those, too, although some of his originals here have an inquiring frame of mind which sometimes takes the ear: 'Sublimity' and the solo 'The Sage' are two such.

Punch Miller (1894–1971)

TRUMPET, VOCAL

Miller made an early name with Kid Ory in New Orleans, then worked in Chicago and New York in the 1920s and '30s, before moving in revivalist circles and in show bands. He was still playing in his flashy, almost defiant style in the last year of his life, including a last appearance at the Newport Jazz Festival.

***** Prelude To The Revival Vol. 1**

American Music AMCD-40 *Miller; – Harris (p, v); Clifford 'Snag' Jones (d).* 1/41.

There are five tracks by this group on the CD (the rest are covered under Kid Howard's entry). It's a fascinating glimpse of a fine New Orleans hornman (Punch wasn't a native of the city, but he is closely associated with its music) in mid-life, following plenty of sideman appearances in the 1920s. Miller's quick-fingered lines and excitable attack are unencumbered by other horns on these rough but quite listenable recordings, made at the H&T Tavern in Chicago. Harris and Jones offer knockabout support to what are really trumpet and vocal showcases, an idiosyncratic adaptation of the Armstrong method.

****(*) Punch Miller's New Orleans Band 1957**

504 CD 34 *Miller; Eddie Morris (tb); Simon Frazier (p); Ricard Alexis (b); Bill Bagley (d).* 3/57.

**** 1960**

American Music AMCD-52 *Miller; Eddie Morris (tb); John Handy (cl); Louis Gallaud (p); Emanuel Sayles (bj); Sylvester Handy (b); Alex Bigard (d).* 7/60.

**** Punch Miller And Louis Gallaud**

American Music AMCD-68 *As above, except add Emanuel Paul (cl); omit Morris, Handy, Handy and Bigard.* 5–7/61.

It's hard to know how good a player Miller really was: he wasn't recorded very often in what should have been his prime, and by the time of these informal tracks he was clearly wavering. 504's CD is part of their 'Larry Borenstein Collection' and is probably the best of these, though that's not saying all that much: cobwebby sound, Frazier mostly almost inaudible, and Morris, not much of a soloist, taking a lot of solos. But the rhythm players set a hearty pace and Miller's best solos have much of his showmanship in good order (his vocals are hopelessly off-mike).

The *1960* disc suffers from a somewhat chaotic personnel – John Handy was unused to playing clarinet, Miller struggles at the often too-fast tempos, and Morris drifts in and out of focus – and a pinched, dry sound. The second disc sounds better, but Gallaud's stentorian piano is a lumbering partner for Punch – he sounds better in the oddball duet with Sayles, 'I Never Had A Chance' – and the trumpeter veers between lovely singing notes and fumbling lines that are barely linked together. Approach with caution.

Vladimir Miller

PIANO

British-born but based in Russia, Miller is a composer–pianist making his way in post-Soviet jazz.

***** Frontiers**

Leo LAB CD 016 *Miller; Vitas Pilibavicius (tb); Vladimir Tarasov (d).* 2/95.

Miller is also included below as composer/conductor of the Moscow Composers Orchestra, but this Ganelin-influenced trio affords a chance to hear him as a performer. He is generally romantic in a spare sort of way and, though this live recording from a theatre in Vilnius does not flatter him any more than the piano did, he comes across as a strong, assertive stylist with a very definite sense of direction. Tarasov was, of course, in the original Ganelin Trio. His starbursts of sound and unexpected silences are still very effective and against the rough-edged Pilibavicius (unknown to us until this record) he performs very cleverly indeed.

Lucky Millinder (1900–1966)

BANDLEADER, VOCAL

Grew up in Chicago and had all kinds of showbiz jobs – including a stint as a fortune-teller – before fronting bands, including the Mills Blue Rhythm Band before its demise. Made his own records, 1942–52, and later worked in the liquor business.

*** Lucky Millinder 1941–1942

Classics 712 *Millinder; William Scott, Archie Johnson, Nelson Bryant, Freddy Webster, Dizzy Gillespie (t); George Stevenson, Eli Robinson, Donald Cole, Floyd Brady, Edward Morant, Sandy Williams, Joe Britton (tb); Bill Bowen, George James, Ted Barnett, Tab Smith (as); Buster Bailey (cl, ts); Stafford 'Pazuzza' Simon, Dave Young (ts); Ernest Purce (bs); Bill Doggett, Clyde Hart (p); Trevor Bacon, Sister Rosetta Tharpe (g, v); Sterling Marlowe (g); Abe Bolar, George Duvivier, Nick Fenton (b); Panama Francis (d).* 6/41–6/42.

*** Lucky Millinder 1943–1947

Classics 1026 *Millinder; Joe Guy, Frank Humphries, Joe Jordan, Chiefie Scott, Curtis Murphy, Leroy Elton Hill, Lamar Wright, Henry Glover, Thomas Grider, Archie Johnson, John Bello, Harold Johnson, Leon Meriam (t); Joe Britton, Gene Simon, George Stevenson, Alfred Cobbs, Money Johnson, Frank Mazzoli (tb); Billy Bowen, Tab Smith, Preston Love, Bill Swindell, Burnie Peacock, John Harrington, Sam Hopkins, Big Nick Nicholas (as); Eddie 'Lockjaw' Davis, Michael Hadley, Sam 'The Man' Taylor, Bull Moose Jackson, Elmer Williams (ts); Ernest Purce (bs); Ray Tunia, Ellis Larkins, Bill Doggett, Sir Charles Thompson (p); Trevor Bacon (g, v); Lawrence Lucie, Bernard McKey (g); George Duvivier, Beverly Peer, Al McKibbon, Jerry Cox (b); Panama Francis(d); Sister Rosetta Tharpe, Wynonie Harris, Judy Carol, Leon Ketchum, The Lucky Seven, The Lucky Four, Annisteen Allen, Paul Breckenridge (v).* 8/43–4/47.

Millinder had been fronting bands for years before he finally got his own name on a record label in 1942. His sessions for Decca (there are a scant four titles for V-Disc on Classics 1026) are energetic but middleweight titles which the occasional bright solo brings to life. Much of it yearns to be slimmed-down to R&B small-band size, and Millinder's use of vocalists such as Rosetta Tharpe and Wynonie Harris – as well as instrumentalists like Sam Taylor, Bull Moose Jackson and Bill Doggett – tells its own story about the direction of the music. A solitary date right at the end of Classics 712 hints at a different direction: Dizzy Gillespie is in the band, and there's a spirited version of 'Little John Special' (alias 'Salt Peanuts'). But that was a moment of madness in the Millinder story. He sings here and there, but otherwise his great contribution – an almost maniacal energy in directing the band onstage – has been lost to posterity. These discs pall over the long haul, but in small doses they're a worthwhile reminder of a staple part of black music in the early '40s.

Mills Blue Rhythm Band

GROUP

One of the major Harlem orchestras of the 1930s. The 'Mills' was impresario Irving Mills, who took over the original band in 1930, but it subsequently had several different leaders, including Harry White, Edgar Hayes, Baron Lee and Lucky Millinder.

*** Blue Rhythm

Hep CD 1008 *Wardell Jones, Shelton Hemphill, Ed Anderson (t); Harry White, Henry Hicks (tb); Crawford Wethington (cl, as, bs); Charlie Holmes (cl, as); Ted McCord, Castor McCord (cl, ts); Edgar Hayes (p); Benny James (bj, g); Hayes Alvis (bb, b); Willie Lynch (d); Dick Roberston, Chick Bullock, George Morton (v).* 1–6/31.

*** Mills Blue Rhythm Band 1931

Classics 660 *As above.* 1–6/31.

***(*) Rhythm Spasm

Hep CD 1015 *As above, except add George Washington (tb), Gene Mikell (cl, as), Joe Garland (cl, ts, bs), O'Neil Spencer (d), Billy Banks (v).* 8/31–8/32.

*** Mills Blue Rhythm Band 1931–1932

Classics 676 *As above.* 7/31–9/32.

**** Mills Blue Rhythm Band 1933–1934

Classics 686 *Wardell Jones, Shelton Hemphill, Ed Anderson, Eddie Mallory, Henry Allen (t); George Washington, Henry Hicks, J.C Higginbotham (tb); Crawford Wethington, Gene Mikell, Joe Garland, Buster Bailey (reeds); Edgar Hayes (p); Benny James (bj, g); Lawrence Lucie (g); Hayes Alvis, Elmer James (b); O'Neil Spencer (d); Lucky Millinder, Chuck Richards, Adelaide Hall (v).* 3/33–11/34.

***(*) Mills Blue Rhythm Band 1935–1936

Classics 710 *As above, except add Tab Smith (cl, as); omit Anderson, Mallory, Hicks, James and Alvis.* 1/35–8/36.

Although it lacked any solo stars in its early years, the Mills Blue Rhythm Band was a very hot outfit when the first of these records were made, even though it was originally used by its boss, Irving Mills, as a substitute band for either Ellington or Calloway. The lack of a regular front-man and a rag-tag sequence of arrangers prevented the band from ever establishing a very clear identity of its own, but it still mustered a kind of fighting collectivism which comes through clearly on its best records. These chronological CDs tell the band's story. Cover versions of Ellington ('Black And Tan Fantasy') and Calloway ('Minnie The Moocher') reveal what the band's purpose was to start with, and the most interesting thing about the earlier tracks is usually the soloists' role, particularly the impassioned and badly undervalued trumpeter, Ed Anderson. But by the time the music on *Rhythm Spasm* was made, the band was energizing itself in splendid charts such as 'The Growl' and the overwhelmingly swinging 'White Lightning', which reveals the dynamism of Hayes Alvis and O'Neil Spencer in the rhythm section. There are some cringingly awful vocals from such experts as Billy Banks and Chick Bullock, but those used to music of the period will know what to expect. John R.T. Davies remasters with his usual care and attentiveness to the music on the Hep discs; the Classics counterparts are, as usual, more mixed.

The 1933–6 material shows a steady if unspectacular growth in the band's abilities, the personnel remaining surprisingly stable over the period, although the arrival of Henry Allen, Buster Bailey and J.C. Higginbotham, all from Fletcher Henderson's band, gave the orchestra a new team of star soloists. Classics 686 is one of the best of the series, with swinging scores in 'Kokey Joe', 'The Growl', the terrific 'The Stuff Is Here (And It's Mellow)' and Allen's debut with 'Swingin' In E Flat'. There is also Adelaide Hall's extraordinary treatment of Ellington's 'Drop Me Off In Harlem', although the Classics remastering seems to be faulty here. There are more vital pieces on the next disc – the superb 'Harlem Heat' is one of Will Hudson's best scores, and 'Cotton', 'Truckin'' and 'Congo Caravan' aren't far behind – but the occasional show of routine and Chuck Richards's consistently unappealing vocals let matters down. As a sequence of records, though, an important portrait of a great Harlem orchestra.

Pino Minafra

TRUMPET, BUGLE, DIDJERIDOO, OCARINA, PERCUSSION, VOCAL, ETC.

Italian brass player whose range spans post-bop, orchestral work and entirely free improvisation.

***** Noci ... Strani Frutti**
Leo LR 176 *Minafra; Ernst Reijseger (clo); Han Bennink (d).* 7/90.

****** Sudori**
Victo CD034 *Minafra; Lauro Rossi (tb, perc, v); Carlo Actis Dato (ts, bs, perc, v); Giorgio Occhipinti (ky, perc, v); Daniele Patumi (perc); Vincenzo Mazzone (d).* 1/95.

Look out: genius at work. Minafra's early LPs for Splasc(h) were enjoyable post-bop outings of a comparatively conventional bent, but these are something else. The Leo disc catches him on the hoof at a late-night festival set with Reijseger and Bennink: his confiding, sputtering sound reminds one at different moments of Miles Davis, Ted Curson and Donald Ayler; but it's a very personal manner, and it fits well over the tumbling dialogue of the other two. Forty-five minutes of strong improvisation.

Sudori is entirely different. Meticulously arranged yet spontaneously exciting, Minafra's Sud Ensemble must be among the smartest outfits in European jazz today. With daredevil spirits like Dato and Rossi on hand, matters could have descended into chaos, given Minafra's own taste for excitement. Yet everything is perfectly realized, from the mounting movie-score drama of 'Exorcism' to the astonishing blues fantasy of 'Au Fond Je Suis Un Africain Du Nord'. The ensemble playing is as impeccable as the solos are rich and detailed, and in meltingly beautiful pieces like the gorgeous 'Tango', dedicated to Federico Fellini, one can hardly credit that this is the same band responsible for the uproarious stuff. A major piece of work that deserves the widest attention. We are still waiting for an encore!

Dom Minasi (born 1943)

GUITAR

A New Yorker whose appearances on record are rare, Minasi plays electric guitar with a semi-acoustic sound on this 'comeback' session.

****(*) Finishing Touches**
CIMP 196 *Minasi; Michael Bocchiicchio (b); Jay Rosen (d).* 2/99.

A strange one. This is Minasi's return to recording after a hiatus of some 25 years: he cut a couple of lite-jazz albums in the twilight stages of Blue Note's Liberty period, but has done nothing visible since. He plays these open-ended pieces with dexterity and spirit, but his rather shapeless style suggests that fundamentally he wants to play pretty and is awkward with the wilder leanings which this setting encourages. His thin, light tone shies away from any effects and he sometimes sounds a bit intimidated by loud bass and drums. The record is far too long and is interesting as an unvarnished block of music, but it's scarcely a cogent statement.

Pete Minger (1943–2000)

FLUGELHORN, TRUMPET

Mainstream trumpeter with varied big-band experience.

***** Minger Painting**
Jazz Alliance 10005 *Minger; Dolph Castellano (p); Keter Betts (b); Bobby Durham (d).* 10/83.

***** Look To The Sky**
Concord CCD 4555 *Minger; John Campbell (p); Kiyoshi Kitagawa (b); Ben Riley (d).* 8/92.

Though cut almost ten years apart, there's little to choose between these dates: Minger, a long-time Basie sideman in the 1970s, turns to the flugelhorn more often than the trumpet and secures the big, warm, comfortable sound that is almost a cliché in brass playing. The earlier date is livelier, the second takes more of a bath in the handsome Concord engineering and benefits from Campbell's useful commentaries. Minger always takes his time, flowing over fast tempos with a relaxed assurance, and the consequence is a fundamentally tranquil but satisfying jazz.

Charles Mingus (1922–79)

DOUBLE BASS, PIANO, COMPOSER

The turbulent voice of Beneath the Underdog, Mingus's self-told story of life and hard times, is audible in every note of the music as well. He was born in Nogales, Arizona, and grew up in Los Angeles, in the combustible district of Watts. After learning cello and trombone, he took to double bass and almost at once started to write a workbook of compositions that was to continue developing through his life. Working with vibist Red Norvo was his first exposure to critical attention, and thereafter he became involved in the bebop scene, playing with Charlie Parker, Miles Davis and Bud Powell at the famous Massey Hall concert. In the '50s he devised a workshop approach to improvisation and started moving towards the ambitious large-scale work that yielded the classic Black Saint And The Sinner Lady. Mingus regularly fell foul of authority and fell out with colleagues, but he was a tireless activist for the music, founding Debut Records and starting the Jazz Artists Guild in opposition to the commercialization of jazz. This marginalized him, and in the later '60s Mingus more or less went into seclusion as Thelonious Monk had before him. Later years were happier, more productive and won him belated critical attention. Near the end of his life, disabled by illness, he was honoured by the White House, and by a president from the segregationist South. It was both a fitting and an ironic end to a fiery career.

****** The Complete Debut Recordings**

Debut 12DCD 4402 12CD *Mingus; Miles Davis, Dizzy Gillespie, Louis Mucci, Thad Jones, Clarence Shaw (t); Eddie Bert, Willie Dennis, Bennie Green, J.J Johnson, Jimmy Knepper, Kai Winding, Britt Woodman (tb); Julius Watkins (frhn); Charlie Parker, Lee Konitz, Joe Maini (as); Paige Brook, Eddie Caine (as, f); George Barrow, Phil Urso (ts); Frank Wess, Shafi Hadi, Teo Macero (ts, f); Danny Bank, Pepper Adams (bs); John LaPorta, Julius Baker (woodwinds); Spaulding Givens, Hank Jones, Wynton Kelly, Wade Legge, John Lewis, John Mehegan, Phyllis Pinkerton, Bill Triglia, Mal Waldron, Hazel Scott (p); Teddy Charles (vib); George Koutzen, Jackson Wiley (clo); Fred Zimmerman (b); Elvin Jones, Kenny Clarke, Al Levitt, Joe Morello, Dannie Richmond, Max Roach, Art Taylor (d); Phineas Newborn Jr, Horace Parlan (perc); Bob Benton, George Gordon, George Gordon Jr, Honey Gordon, Richard Gordon, Jackie Paris (v).* 4/51–9/57.

***** Debut Rarities: Volume 1**

Original Jazz Classics OJC 1807 *Mingus; Ernie Royal (t); Willie Dennis, Jimmy Knepper (tb); Joe Maini (as); Eddie Caine (as, f); Teo Macero (ts, f); John Lewis, Bill Triglia (p); Jackson Wiley (clo); Kenny Clarke, Dannie Richmond (d).* 10/53, 6/57.

*****(*) Debut Rarities: Volume 2**

Original Jazz Classics OJC 1808 *Mingus; Spaulding Givens (p); Max Roach (d).* 4/51, 4/53.

***** Debut Rarities: Volume 3**

Original Jazz Classics OJC 1821 *Mingus; Clarence Shaw (t); Shafti Hadi (as, f); Pepper Adams (bs); Wade Legge, Wynton Kelly (p); Henry Grimes (b); Dannie Richmond (d).* 9?/57.

****(*) Debut Rarities: Volume 4**

Original Jazz Classics OJC 1829 *Mingus; Lee Konitz (as); Paige Brook (as, f); John Mehegan, Hank Jones, Phyllis Pinkerton (p); George Koutzen, Jackson Wiley (clo); Al Levitt, Max Roach (d); Bob Benton, Jackie Paris, The Gordons (v).* 4/52, 4/53.

***** Jazz Composers Workshop**

Savoy SV 0171 *Mingus; John LaPorta (cl, as); George Barrow, Teo Macero (ts, bs); Mal Waldron (p); Rudy Nichols (d).* 10/54.

****(*) Jazzical Moods**

Original Jazz Classics OJCCD 1857 *Mingus; Thad Jones (t); John LaPorta (cl, as); Teo Macero (ts, bs); Jackson Wiley (clo); Clem De Rosa (d).* 12/54.

****(*) The Jazz Experiments Of Charlie Mingus**

Bethlehem BET 6016 *As above.* 12/54.

Huge, paradoxical and immensely influential, Mingus's true significance has taken a long time to be recognized, though most of his innovations have long since been absorbed by the modern/avant-garde movement. In that regard, he is very different from the broadly comparable Monk, whose work is still not fully assimilated and understood but who has been almost casually canonized. In addition to pioneering modern bass-playing, Mingus is responsible for some of the greatest large-scale compositions in modern 'jazz', beside which overblown efforts like Ornette Coleman's *Skies Of America* look positively sophomoric; Mingus also transformed the conception of collective improvisation, restoring the energies and occasionally the sound of early jazz to an identifiably modern idiom. He pioneered over-dubbing and editing, thereby paving the way for Miles Davis and Teo Macero, who appears on these curiously lifeless, virtually identical compilations from two albums recorded for Period.

These can really only be mined for pointers to more impressive work later. 'Four Hands' experiments with overdubbed piano (not quite like Claude Williamson's two-piano essays on the same label), and there are out-of-tempo sections that anticipate later, more radical experiments. 'What Is This Thing Called Love' undergoes interesting transformations, in keeping with Mingus's palimpsest approach to standards and new composition, and the use of cello (one of Mingus's first instruments) is intriguing. The problem lies in the playing. Macero – later to achieve his apotheosis as producer/arranger for Miles Davis – is unpalatably dry, and the drummer tackles his part with no discernible enthusiasm. The Fresh Sound and overlapping Bethlehem (which was formerly issued under the name *Abstractions*) also contain Macero's Third Streamish 'Abstractions', but that's a fairly minor plus. For serious Mingus scholars only.

The inevitably pricey Debut set, which covers the period 1951 to 1957, is a completist's dream. The musician-owned Debut was started by Mingus and Max Roach as a way of getting their own adventurous music recorded, and it was briefly influential. With nearly 170 individual tracks under 19 nominal leaderships, and including many alternative takes, it's an exhaustive and occasionally exhausting compilation, well out of the range and probable requirements of the average fan, who may have some of the material elsewhere. One example might well be Mingus's own tape-recording of the famous Massey Hall, Toronto, 'Quintet of the Year' gig of 15 May 1953, and it's good to know that even some of the lesser material remains in circulation. The four *Rarities* abstracts may well be enough for most people, particularly those who have other, more accessible stuff on LP. The duos with Givens on *Volume 2* are well worth dusting down, as are the 1957 Workshop pieces on *Volume 4*, which point the way forward to Mingus's 1960s masterpieces.

***** Mingus At The Bohemia**

Original Jazz Classics OJC 045 *Mingus; Eddie Bert (tb); George Barrow (ts); Mal Waldron (p); Willie Jones, Max Roach (d).* 12/55.

***** Plus Max Roach**

Original Jazz Classics OJC 440 *As above.* 12/55.

The Jazz Workshop in fine, searching form. Jones, who was to figure on the classic *Pithecanthropus Erectus* but who nowadays is little regarded, came to Mingus at Thelonious Monk's behest. The opening theme on *At The Bohemia* is a Monk dedication (with Waldron re-creating an authentic cadence) that underlines Mingus's increasing emphasis on the rhythm section as a pro-active element in improvisation. 'Septemberly' is a characteristic hybrid of 'Tenderly' and 'September In The Rain', and 'Percussion Discussion' a duet between Mingus, on bass and cello, and Max Roach, just one of a long line of challenging duos set up by or for the great drummer. The rest of the material from this session was issued on a Prestige album called simply *Charles Mingus* (HB 6042).

****** Pithecanthropus Erectus**

Atlantic 81227 5357-2 *Mingus; Jackie McLean (as); J.R Monterose (ts); Mal Waldron (p); Willie Jones (d).* 1/56.

One of the truly great modern jazz albums. Underrated at the time, *Pithecanthropus Erectus* is now recognized as an important step in the direction of a new, freer synthesis in jazz. To some extent, the basic thematic conception (the story of mankind's struggle out of chaos, up and down the Freytag's Triangle of hubris and destruction, back to chaos) was the watered-down Spenglerism which was still fashionable at the time. Technically, though, the all-in ensemble work on the violent C section, which is really B, a modified version of the harmonically static second section, was absolutely crucial to the development of free collective improvisation in the following decade. The brief 'Profile Of Jackie' is altogether different. Fronted by McLean's menthol-sharp alto, with Monterose (a late appointee who wasn't altogether happy with the music) and Mingus working on a shadowy counter-melody, it's one of the most appealing tracks Mingus ever committed to record, and the most generous of his 'portraits'. McLean still carried a torch for orthodox bebop and soon came to (literal) blows with Mingus; the chemistry worked just long enough. 'Love Chant' is a more basic modal exploration, and 'A Foggy Day' – re-subtitled 'In San Francisco' – is an impressionistic reworking of the Gershwin standard, with Chandleresque sound-effects. Superficially jokey, it's no less significant an effort to expand the available range of jazz performance, and the fact that it's done via a standard rather than a long-form composition like 'Pithecanthropus' gives a sense of Mingus's Janus-faced approach to the music.

***** The Clown**

Rhino/Atlantic R2 75590 *Mingus; Jimmy Knepper (tb); Shafi Hadi (as, ts); Wade Legge (p); Dannie Richmond (d); Jean Shepherd (v).* 2 & 3/57.

With the first appearance of 'Reincarnation Of A Lovebird' and the *mano a mano* simplicities of 'Haitian Fight Song' (which saw Mingus build a huge, swinging performance out of the simplest thematic material), this is not a negligible record. It has never, though, been a great favourite. 'Blue Cee' is a dedication to Mingus's wife and has an almost gloomy cast. Throughout the album, the bassist grunts and hollers encouragement to himself and his players; perhaps he was still thinking about Bud Powell, who was apt to vocalize over his solos, because he had planned a 'portrait' of Powell before these sessions. The title-track is a reminder of Mingus's obsession with words and texts; Jean Shepherd's narration is fine, but one quickly longs for the instrumental versions that Mingus included in club sets thereafter. This is one of the few quality albums of Mingus's which is routinely neglected. That seems a pity.

*****(*) Tijuana Moods Complete**

RCA Victor 74321 74999-2 *Mingus; Clarence Shaw (t); Jimmy Knepper (tb); Shafi Hadi (as); Bill Triglia (p); Dannie Richmond (d); Frankie Dunlop (perc); Ysabel Morel (castanets); Lonnie Elder (v).* 7 & 8/57.

*****(*) East Coasting**

Bethlehem BET 6014 *As above, except omit Triglia, Morel, Dunlop, Elder; add Bill Evans (p).* 8/57.

***** A Modern Jazz Symposium Of Music And Poetry**

Bethlehem 6015 *As above, except omit Evans; add Bill Hardman (t), Bob Hammer, Horace Parlan (p), Melvin Stewart (v).* 10/57.

Tijuana Moods Complete combines the original release with the complete (that is, unedited) performances from which the label not always successfully spliced together LP-length tracks. 'Ysabel's Table Dance'/'Tijuana Table Dance' is the classic track, with Mingus's structures constantly erupting into group improvisations. Nothing else quite compares with that track, though 'Dizzy Mood' is also very fine, and 'Los Mariachos' is an impressive piece of writing. There is inevitably a bit more room on the longer versions for the soloists to stretch out; but, apart from that, most seasoned listeners will probably still want to cue the original releases on their CD players rather than the restored versions. What *Tijuana Moods* called for was better editing, not no editing.

The atmospheric *East Coasting* and the similarly constituted *Symposium* are part of the same cycle of pieces and bear strong similarities, in construction, material and, of course, personnel. 'Conversation' and 'West Coast Ghost' and the gloriously expressive 'Celia' are brilliantly realized collective performances and, while none of the pieces is quite as ambitious as the *Tijuana* structures, they all pay tribute to Mingus's growing stature as a grand synthesizer of blues, bop and swing, with the shadow of something entirely new hovering on the music's inner horizons.

The *Symposium* – and how extraordinary that title now seems – was an opportunity for Mingus to experiment with texts and with pure sound. 'Scenes In The City' reworks some of the ideas he had sketched in 'Foggy Day' on *Pithecanthropus Erectus*, but with a much greater degree of finish. The 'New York Sketchbook' is a parallel piece, finely drawn and performed, with Shaw rising above himself and playing some of the best trumpet heard on a Mingus album for some time before or since.

*****(*) Jazz Portraits: Mingus In Wonderland**

Blue Note 827325 *Mingus; John Handy (as); Booker Ervin (ts); Richard Wyands (p); Dannie Richmond (d).* 1/59.

Mingus's appearance as part of the Nonagon Art Gallery Composers' Showcase series in 1959 was a significant moment of recognition for a man whose life was passed in resistance to the 'jazz musician' tag. Previous composers showcased there had been Virgil Thomson, Aaron Copland and Carlos Chavez, and in addition there had been notable appearances by the MJQ and Cecil Taylor.

Working with something of a scratch band (the all-important Horace Parlan wasn't available), more emphasis than usual fell on Mingus's bass playing, which is consistently marvellous from the opening moody strains of 'Nostalgia In Times Square', written as part of the soundtrack to John Cassavetes's movie, *Shadows*, to the closing 'Alice's Wonderland', which gave the record its first release title. 'I Can't Get Started' had become one of his favourite standards, indeed the only non-original that seemed to fire him up to the heights of invention audible here, fiery double-stops and intense lyrical passages alternating with softer, almost guitar-like strums. Until recently, this has been one of the less well-known Mingus records (and on a label not normally associated with him). It's a welcome addition to the catalogue.

*****(*) Blues And Roots**

Rhino/Atlantic R2 75205 *Mingus; Willie Dennis, Jimmy Knepper (tb); John Handy, Jackie McLean (as); Booker Ervin (ts); Pepper Adams (bs); Horace Parlan, Mal Waldron (p); Dannie Richmond (d).* 2/59.

♛ ** Mingus Ah Um**

Columbia CK 65512 *As above, except omit Waldron, McLean; add Shafi Hadi (ts).* 5/59.

A classic period. This was the point where, rising forty in just a couple of years and aware of the encroachment of younger and perhaps more accommodating musicians, he began to show his absolute understanding of the African-American musical tradition. *Ah Um* is an extended tribute to ancestors, cemented by the gospellish 'Better Git It In Your Soul', a mood that is also present on *Blues And Roots* with the well-loved 'Wednesday Night Prayer Meeting' in its doubled-up 6/4 time. Everything here has its place. The shouts and yells, the magnificently harmonized *ostinati* which fuel 'Tensions' and the almost jolly swing of 'My Jelly Roll Soul' (*Blues And Roots*), the often obvious edits and obsessive recycling of his own previous output, all contribute to records which are entire unto themselves and hard to fault on any count. Extra material from the *Ah Um* session was made available on a Columbia disc called *Nostalgia In Times Square*, but it would be sacrilegious to tamper now with something as perfectly balanced; three-quarters of an hour of sheer genius. The latest (digipack) reissue of *Blues And Roots*, however, contains four alternative tracks, perfectly viable performances in their own right, albeit lacking the indefinable dramatic tension of the release versions.

***** Mingus Dynasty**

Columbia CK 65513 *Mingus; Don Ellis, Richard Williams (t); Jimmy Knepper (tb); Jerome Richardson (f, bs); John Handy (as); Booker Ervin, Benny Golson (ts); Teddy Charles (vib); Roland Hanna, Nico Bunink (p); Maurice Brown, Seymour Barab (clo); Dannie Richmond (d); Honey Gordon (v).* 11/59.

Often, mistakenly but understandably, thought to refer to a posthumous album, *Mingus Dynasty* is a pretty obvious pun when looked at twice. It wraps up a period of activity that seems to catch Mingus in mid-mood-swing between fired up and confident and way down low. 'Strollin'' is a version of 'Nostalgia On Times Square' and the music written for the (mostly improvised) John Cassavetes film, *Shadows*, in which jazz almost takes the place of orderly narrative dialogue. There is also a version of 'Gunslinging Bird', a take each of 'Song With Orange', 'Far Wells, Mill Valley', 'Slop' and, memorably, 'Mood Indigo'. As with so many other Mingus albums, this is somehow better and more coherent than it ought to be. Though not intended to be put together in this form, it works as an entity, and one wouldn't want the original sessions to be reconstructed in any other way.

*****(*) The Complete 1959 Columbia Sessions**

Sony 65145 3CD *Mingus; Don Ellis (t); Willie Dennis, Jimmy Knepper (tb); John Handy (as, cl); Shafi Hadi (as, ts); Booker Ervin, Benny Golson (ts); Jerome Richardson (bs, f); Sir Roland Hanna, Horace Parlan (p); Teddy Charles (vib); Dannie Richmond (d); Honey Gordon (v).* 5 & 11/59.

***** Alternate Takes**

Sony CK 65514 *As above.* 5 & 11/59.

Lifted from the sessions that went to the making of *Ah Um* and *Mingus Dynasty*, this elegant three-CD set includes a good deal of unreleased and alternative material previously available only on the exhaustive Mosaic box. It's obviously good to have it all back together again, though it isn't clear why Sony decided to release the alternatives separately as a single CD. Of largely specialist interest, this compilation of rejected takes includes 'Better Git It In Your Soul', 'Bird Calls', 'Jelly Roll', 'Song With Orange', 'Diane' and 'New Now Know How'. Though almost any Mingus performance of almost any period is likely to contain music of interest, and very little of it merely routine, there isn't much here that changes the existing picture. For trainspotters only. The boxed set is more appealing, but no amount of extra material adds any gloss to the magnificence of the original albums.

***** Pre-Bird**

Verve 538636-2 *Mingus; Marcus Belgrave, Ted Curson, Hobart Dotson, Clark Terry, Richard Williams (t); Eddie Bert, Charles Greenlee, Slide Hampton, Jimmy Knepper (tb); Don Butterfield (tba); Robert DiDomenica (f); Harry Schulman (ob); Eric Dolphy (as, bcl, f); John LaPorta (as, cl); Yusef Lateef (ts, f); Bill Barron, Booker Ervin (ts); Jake Hanna (p); Dannie Richmond (d).* 60.

***** Mingus Revisited**

Emarcy 826 496 *As above, except add Danny Bank, Charles Greenlee (tb), Don Butterfield (tba), Joe Farrell, Harold Shulman (woodwinds), Paul Bley, Sir Roland Hanna (p), Charles McCracken (clo), Sticks Evans, George Scott (d, perc), Lorraine Cousins (v).* 5/60.

Mingus Revisited was originally released as *Pre-Bird* in 1960, before being reissued by the Limelight label five years later with a liner-note by Leonard Feather. With the exception of 'Half-Mast Inhibition', a piece written by Mingus when he was just eighteen, conducted by Gunter Schuller, all the material is in short-song form, opening with a strikingly original sandwich of 'Take The "A" Train' and Dorothy Fields' 'Exactly Like You' and continuing later with another Ducal interpolation, 'I Let A Song Go Out Of My Heart' amidst 'Do Nothing Till You Hear From Me'; this is a record that puts all its emphasis on ensemble playing rather than extended soloing. Verve have now reissued the original session as it was intended to be heard, though it seems slightly odd that both albums should remain in catalogue. All that is extra on *Revisited* are two songs, albeit two of Mingus's most important, 'Eclipse' and 'Weird Nightmare', sung with estranged passion by Lorraine Cousins, one of the few Mingus interpreters to understand the balance between music and text.

****** Mingus At Antibes**

Atlantic 7567 90532-2 *Mingus; Ted Curson (t); Eric Dolphy (as, bcl); Booker Ervin (ts); Bud Powell (p); Dannie Richmond (d).* 7/60.

Charles Delaunay memorably likened Mingus's performance in the mellow warmth of Juan-les-Pins to a 'cold shower'. Certainly in comparison with the rest of the Antibes line-up, the 1960s band was intellectually recherché and somewhat forceful. Unreleased until after Mingus's death – the tapes had lain, unexamined, in Atlantic's vault – the set contains a valuable preview of some of the material to be recorded that autumn for Candid, below, and for a thumping 'I'll Remember April' with the exiled Bud Powell guesting. Mingus himself gets behind the piano on a number of occasions, perhaps trying to give the slightly chaotic ensembles more shape. The essence of the performance lies in the solos. Ervin is fine on 'Better Git Hit In Your Soul', as is Dolphy, still sounding like a renegade Parker disciple, on a first version of the gospelly 'Folk Forms', which reappears on *Presents*, below. The bass/bass-clarinet sparring on 'What Love' isn't quite as over the top as the later, studio version, but it shows how far Dolphy was prepared to move in the direction of Ornette Coleman's new synthesis. Not just another 'previously unreleased' money-spinner, the *Antibes* set contains genuinely important material. The chance to hear a Mingus concert in its entirety offers valuable clues to his methods at the time.

****** Charles Mingus Presents Charles Mingus**

Candid CCD 79005 *Mingus; Ted Curson (t); Eric Dolphy (as, bcl); Dannie Richmond (d).* 10/60.

*****(*) Charles Mingus**

Candid CCD 79021 *As above, except add Lonnie Hillyer (t), Jimmy Knepper, Britt Woodman (tb), Booker Ervin (ts), Paul Bley, Nico Bunink (p).* 10/60.

***** Reincarnation Of A Love Bird**

Candid CCD 79026 *As above, except omit Woodman, Bunink; add Roy Eldridge (t), Tommy Flanagan (p), Jo Jones (d).* 11/60.

****(*) Mysterious Blues**

Candid CCD 79042 *As above.* 10 & 11/60.

Mingus's association with Candid was brief (though no briefer than the label's first existence) and highly successful. His long club residency in 1960 (interrupted only by festival appearances) gave him an unwontedly stable and played-in band to take into the studio (he recorded a fake – and uncommonly polite – nightclub intro for the set), and the larger-scale arrangement of 'MDM' negatively reflects the solidity of the core band. *Presents* is for piano-less quartet and centres on the extraordinary vocalized interplay between Dolphy and Mingus; on 'What Love' they carry on a long conversation in near-comprehensible dialect. 'Folk Forms' is wonderfully pared down and features a superb Mingus solo. 'All The Things You Could Be By Now If Sigmund Freud's Wife Was Your Mother' has a wry fury (Mingus once said that it had been written in the psych ward at Bellevue) which is more than incidentally suggestive of 'harmolodic' and 'punk' procedures of the 1980s. The 'Original Faubus Fables' was a further experiment in the use of texts, here a furious rant against what Mingus later called 'Nazi USA', and his later '60s brothers 'Amerika'. It's powerfully felt but less well integrated in its blend of polemic and music than Max Roach's *Freedom Now Suite* on the same label.

If *Presents* is a classic, *Charles Mingus* falls slightly short. The augmented band on 'MDM' sounds uninspired, either unfamiliar or unhappy with the material (which isn't exceptionally demanding). 'Stormy Weather', also released on *Candid Dolphy*, below, features a monster introduction by the saxophonist. Like 'ATTYCBBNISFWWYM' above, 'Lock 'Em Up' makes some reference to Bellevue (or to Charlie Parker's 'holiday' in Camarillo), if only because it's taken at the same hare-brained pace, and Mingus bellows instruction to his troops in a voice that sounds on the brink. At producer Nat Hentoff's suggestion, he had attempted to vary the existing band and re-create the energy of the 'Newport rebels' anti-festival by bringing in past associates. The most notable of these was Roy Eldridge, who is featured (with Knepper, Flanagan and Jo Jones also guesting, as the Jazz Artists Guild) on the long 'R & R', a superb 'Body And Soul', and a previously unreleased 'Wrap Your Troubles In Dreams'. 'Reincarnation Of A Love Bird' and 'Bugs' are both Parker-inspired. The title-track features Hillyer, McPherson and Ervin over Dolphy's uncredited bass clarinet (Curson isn't listed either, and is mentioned only in Brian Priestley's characteristically detailed liner-note). By no means a classic Mingus album, it restores some fascinating performances and alternatives from a critical period in his career. Needless to say, worth having (and enthusiasts should take note of another 'Reincarnation' along with the Dolphy-led 'Stormy Weather' on the label compilation, *Candid Dolphy* (CCD 9033)).

The descending order of stars gives a fair account of *Mysterious Blues*' place in this sequence. Not much more than a collection of bin-ends and alternatives, it's likely to appeal only to serious Mingus collectors. Taking up nine and a half minutes with a drum solo by Richmond (who was never an inspiring soloist) is the main symptom of padding. The rejected 'Body And Soul' has some nice Dolphy and Flanagan, but still isn't particularly compelling.

***** Oh Yeah**

Rhino/Atlantic R2 75589 *Mingus; Jimmy Knepper (tb); Rahsaan Roland Kirk (ts, manzello, stritch, f, siren); Booker Ervin (ts); Doug Watkins (b); Dannie Richmond (d).* 11/61.

The addition of Rahsaan Roland Kirk gave the Mingus band the kind of surreality evident on the spaced-out blues, 'Ecclusiastics', which Mingus leads from the piano. Kirk is also the main attraction on 'Wham Bam, Thank You Ma'am', a typically de-romanticized standard. On the closing 'Passions Of A Man' Mingus overdubbed a bizarre, associative rap, which is rather more effective than the instrumental backing. Odd. Damned odd, even; but a significant instance of Mingus's often desperate conflation of music and words in the search for some higher synthesis.

****** Passions Of A Man**

Rhino/Atlantic R2 72871 6CD *As for Atlantic albums.* 56–61.

As will have been seen from the above sequence, it doesn't make entire sense to talk about 'the Atlantic years', because the label was never an exclusive focus of attention, and there is a considerable amount of overlap with other imprints, often using identical line-ups. However, the albums the bassist made for the Erteguns are among the best in the canon: *Pithecanthropus Erectus*, *The Clown*, *Mingus At Antibes*, the little-known *Tonight At Noon*, *Mingus Oh Yeah!* and the user-friendly *Blues And Roots*. Some of the material from it turned up, reworked, on the earliest of Mingus's Columbia sessions, and *Ah Um* almost feels like a record from the same stable. This, though, was a period in which the creative and experimental fires were at their height; there is an astonishing level of creative interplay between projects. As throughout his career, it wasn't so much a case of plans going awry as of ideas becoming fragmented and being distributed across foreground and background of the discography. Rhino's compilation has restored *Tonight At Noon*, a two-part work, to its position amid the sessions that yielded *Oh Yeah!* and *The Clown*. The set contains about 30 minutes of previously unissued music, not much for a six-CD (or effectively five, since the last of the run is devoted to interview material, more than an hour of Mingus's blustery 'What, then, I contradict myself ...' observation of his life, music and milieu). Of the new material, the most important is alternative tracks from *Blues And Roots* which has itself recently been polished and reissued to the same crisp standard. Inevitably an expensive item, but one that every genuine Mingus fan will want to have, since so much of this music was, as another American poet put it, the 'cry of its occasion', less meaningful when heard out of context and out of chronology.

*** The Complete Town Hall Concert

Blue Note 28353 *Mingus; Snooky Young, Ernie Royal, Richard Williams, Clark Terry, Lonnie Hillyer, Ed Armour, Rolf Ericson (t); Britt Woodman, Quentin Jackson, Willie Dennis, Eddie Bert, Jimmy Cleveland (tb); Don Butterfield (tba); Charles McPherson, Charlie Mariano (as); Buddy Collette (as, ts, f); Eric Dolphy (as, bcl, f); Booker Ervin, Zoot Sims (ts); Dick Hafer (ts, cl, f, ob); Pepper Adams (bs); Jerome Richardson (bs, ss, f); Teddy Charles (vib); Toshiko Akiyoshi, Jaki Byard (p); Les Spann (g); Milt Hinton (b); Dannie Richmond (d, tim).* 10/62.

An object case in the extraordinary performance history of Mingus's music. These ambitious charts, which were related to the huge *Epitaph* suite performed only after his death, were being prepared for a recording or concert-recording (the ambiguity was never quite settled) at New York's Town Hall. (This shouldn't be confused with the later occasion listed and discussed below.) Preparations were chaotic and there was no proper run-through on the night, leaving a body of material which was significantly flawed and in some cases considered unreleasable. The original LP lasted only 36 minutes. This re-issue, digitally remixed from the original three-track tapes and produced by biographer Brian Priestley, restores the whole extraordinary occasion with one minor re-ordering of tracks. 'Clark In The Dark', a feature for trumpeter Terry, is marred by a completely skew-whiff mix; the engineer still apparently hadn't managed to effect a proper balance. The next piece, 'Osmotin', breaks off, much like some of the internal sections on *Blues And Roots* and *Ah Um*. The opening part of 'Epitaph' features a glorious solo from Dolphy, communicating with the leader on a level far beyond any of the other soloists. There are versions of 'Peggy's Blue Skylight', more from 'Epitaph' and a new contrafact, 'My Search', on 'I Can't Get Started'. With time marching on, and the audience – presumably unused to the disciplines of recording – becoming restless, Mingus was signalled to stop towards the end of 'Please Don't You Come Back From The Moon', one of the previously unissued tracks. At this point, with the leader heading offstage and many of the players winding up, Terry, who'd kicked the whole thing off, went into 'In A Mellotone', and brought the band together again.

It was, to be sure, something of a shambles, but a magnificent shambles. The reconstructed evening has its rough edges and unresolved parts, but it is an essential document in Mingus's progress, and who can say what might have happened had the record company been more accommodating and smart enough to realize that it was virtually impossible and also undesirable to tape so much brand-new music, some of it being (re)written on the spot in front of an audience. For all its frustrations and its rather shambolic feel, this is essential Mingus.

♛ **** The Black Saint And The Sinner Lady

Impulse! 051174-2 *Mingus; Rolf Ericson, Richard Williams (t); Quentin Jackson, Don Butterfield (tba); Jerome Richardson (as, bs, f); Booker Ervin (ts); Dick Hafer (ts, f); Charlie Mariano (as); Jaki Byard (p); Dannie Richmond (d).* 1/63.

***(*) Mingus Mingus Mingus Mingus Mingus

Impulse! 051170-2 *As above, except add Britt Woodman (tb), Jay Berliner (g).* 1 & 9/63.

Black Saint is Mingus's masterpiece. Almost everything about it was distinctive: the long form, the use of dubbing, the liner-note by Mingus's psychiatrist. On its release, they altered its usual slogan, 'The new wave of jazz is on Impulse!', to read 'folk', in line with Mingus's decision to call the group the Charles Mingus New Folk Band. Ellingtonian in ambition and scope, and in the disposition of horns, the piece has a majestic, dancing presence, and Charlie Mariano's alto solos and overdubs on 'Mode D/E/F' are unbelievably intense. There is evidence that Mingus's desire to make a single continuous performance (and it should be remembered that even Ellington's large-scale compositions were relatively brief) failed to meet favour with label executives; but there is an underlying logic even to the separate tracks which makes it difficult to separate them other than for the convenience of track listing. Absolutely essential.

Mingus etc. comes from the same and one later session. It includes 'Celia' and 'I X Love', both older pieces, both distinguished by great Mariano performances, with 'Theme For Lester Young', which is a variant on 'Goodbye, Pork Pie Hat', and 'Better Git Hit In Your Soul'. Nothing comes close to *Black Saint*, but the pair give an even better account of Mingus's thinking at the time. Whatever the compromises forced upon him in the past by musicians (or now by his label), he is creating music of classic scope and lasting value.

*** Mingus Plays Piano

Impulse! 051217-2 *Mingus (p solo).* 7/63.

Mingus played something more than 'composer's piano' throughout his career. His touch and harmonic sense were so secure that, though hardly virtuosic, he more than passes muster on a very resonant and richly toned instrument with what sounds like a very brisk action. It's interesting to hear themes like 'Orange Was The Color Of Her Dress, Then Blue Silk' reduced to their essentials in this way, though the true highlights are 'When I Am

Real' and a thoroughly unabashed 'Body And Soul'. Not in the front rank of Mingus albums, but certainly not just for collectors.

****** Town Hall Concert 1964**

Original Jazz Classics OJC 042 *Mingus; Johnny Coles (t); Eric Dolphy (as, fl, bcl); Clifford Jordan (ts); Jaki Byard (p); Dannie Richmond (d).* 4/64.

***** Mingus In Europe: Volume 1**

Enja 3049 *As above.* 4/64.

***** Mingus In Europe: Volume 2**

Enja 3077 *As above.* 4/64.

***** Live In Amsterdam: Volume 1**

Aroc 1204 *As above.* 4/64.

***** Live In Amsterdam: Volume 2**

Aroc 1205 *As above.* 4/64.

*****(*) The Great Concert, Paris 1964**

Musidisc 500072 2CD *As above, except add Johnny Coles (t).* 4/64.

This is undoubtedly the most heavily documented period of Mingus's career. The Town Hall concert predated the European tour, and this set consists of two long tracks which strongly feature Dolphy (the dedicatee) on each of his three horns. The release shouldn't be confused with a 1962 Blue Note recording of the same name, which contains entirely different material.

There is a vast amount of bootleg material from the European tour of April 1964. We have omitted all but respectably licensed releases. Dedicated collectors may want to check dates and itinerary in our second edition and argue about the respective merits of individual performances, for the repertoire overlaps very considerably. 'Peggy's Blue Skylight' is ubiquitous, only omitted on *Great Concert*; other staples include 'Orange Was The Color Of Her Dress, Then Blue Silk' and 'Fables Of Faubus'. 'So Long, Eric' is sometimes described as a threnody or epitaph to the multi-instrumentalist, who died on 29 June of that year, but there he is playing it; the piece was actually supposed to be a reminder to Dolphy (who'd decided to try his luck in Europe for a while) not to stay 'over there' too long. Sadly, it was all too soon to become a memorial.

A bonus on the Enjas (which were recorded in Wuppertal at the opposite end of the month to the Amsterdam material, which was taped on the 10th) is a flute–bass duo credited to Dolphy as 'Started', but actually based on 'I Can't Get Started'. 'Fables' was awkwardly split on the LP format, and is very much better for being heard entire.

***** Right Now**

Original Jazz Classics OJC 237 *Mingus; John Handy (as); Clifford Jordan (ts); Jane Getz (p); Dannie Richmond (d).* 6/64.

Two long cuts – 'Meditation (On A Pair Of Wire Cutters)' and a revised 'Fables Of Faubus' – which were originally released on Fantasy, featuring Mingus's Californian band of that summer. Handy comes in only on 'New Fables' but sounds funky and a lot more abrasive than McPherson. Jane Getz is by no means well known, and is certainly less individual than the otherwise-engaged Byard, but she acquits her piano duties more than adequately.

***** Charles Mingus In Paris, 1970**

DIW 326/7 2CD *Mingus; Eddie Preston (t); Charles McPherson (as); Bobby Jones (ts); Jaki Byard (p, arr); Dannie Richmond (d).* 10/70.

In Paris is a rather straightforward, almost bland, concert recording from the city and country where Mingus had some of his more torrid moments. The repertoire combines recent arrangements with the well-worn but constantly evolving Ellington medley, and yet another version of 'Orange Was The Color ... '.

*****(*) Live At Carnegie Hall**

Rhino/Atlantic R2 72285 *Mingus; Jon Faddis (t); Charles McPherson (t); John Handy (as, ts); George Adams (ts); Roland Kirk (ts, stritch); Hamiet Bluiett (bs); Don Pullen (p); Dannie Richmond (d).*

What deep satisfaction he must have felt to see his name bracketed with that of America's toniest concert hall, a small step forward in his insistence that jazz was Afro-America's classical music. There is nothing classically calm about the music, which rumbles threateningly, then hints at a sunnier mood and then, just when the sky seems clear, delivers bolts of lightning. If it was Duke Ellington who cleared the way for Afro-Americans to be recognized as full partakers in the country's musical culture, then the concert's apparent dedication to Duke and his spirit seems entirely appropriate, with 'C Jam Blues' and 'Perdido' delivered with respect. To be frank, there are better Mingus albums and even the more chaotic live appearances delivered more compelling music than anything here, but it was an important step for him and for creative jazz in general. Sometimes the event is bigger than any single element it contains.

*****(*) Changes One**

Rhino/Atlantic R2 71403 *Mingus; Jack Walrath (t); George Adams (ts); Don Pullen (p); Dannie Richmond (d).* 12/74.

*****(*) Changes Two**

Rhino/Atlantic R2 71404 *As above, except add Jackie Paris (v), Marcus Belgrave (t).* 12/74.

Long out of print, these are among the best of Mingus's later works. Recorded in a single session, they represent definitive performances by a group that had played and gradually transformed this material – 'Orange Was The Color Of Her Dress', 'Devil Blues', two versions of 'Duke Ellington's Sound Of Love', one instrumental, one vocal – over a longer period than almost any previous Mingus unit. Some of the fire has definitely gone, and there is a hint of studio polish that was never evident on the band's live dates; but they are powerful records nevertheless, and essential documents for Mingus enthusiasts.

****** Thirteen Pictures: The Charles Mingus Anthology**

Rhino R2 71402 3CD *Mingus; Jack Walrath, Marcus Belgrave, Hobart Dotson, Clark Terry, Bobby Bryant, Lonnie Hillyer, Melvin Moore, Eddie Preston, Richard Williams (t); Lou Blackburn, Jimmy Knepper, Eddie Bert, Jimmy Greenlee, Slide Hampton, Britt Woodman (tb); Don Butterfield, Red Callender (tba); Mauricio Smith (as, ss, f, picc); John Handy (as, ts); Eric Dolphy (as, f, bcl); Lee Konitz, Jackie McLean, John LaPorta, Charles McPherson (as); Buddy Collette (as, f, picc); Booker Ervin, Dick Hafer, Shafi Hadi, Roland Kirk, J.R Monterose, George Barrow, Bill Barron, Joe Farrell, Ricky Ford (ts); Paul*

Jeffrey (ts, ob); Yusef Lateef (ts, f); Danny Bank (bs); Bob Didomenica (f); Harry Schulman (ob); Jerome Richardson, Jack Nimitz (bs, bcl); Gary Anderson (bcl, cbcl); Gene Scholtes (bsn); Jaki Byard, Phyllis Pinkerton, Sir Roland Hanna, Wade Legge, Mal Waldron, Horace Parlan, Duke Ellington, Bob Neloms (p); George Koutzen, Charles McCracken (clo); Doug Watkins (b); Willie Jones, Al Levitt, Walter Perkins, Sticks Evans, Dannie Richmond, Max Roach (d); Candido Camero, Alfredo Ramirez, Bradley Cunningham (perc); Jackie Paris (v). 52–77.

An excellent compilation of Mingus's work for Atlantic, beautifully packaged in a box with a booklet of photographs. It contains material from *Pre-Bird, Chazz!/At The Bohemia, Plays Piano, Cumbia And Jazz Fusion, The Clown*, the immortal *Ah Um, Oh Yeah* and *Mingus Mingus Mingus Mingus Mingus, Pithecanthropus Erectus, Money Jungle, At Monterey* and a rare Debut single from 1952 with Jackie Paris as vocalist. The packaging and accompanying documentation are immaculate; the music is, of course, brilliant. One can hardly imagine a nicer present for someone who hasn't got all this stuff already.

***** Three Or Four Shades Of Blues**

Atlantic 7567 81403 *Mingus; Jack Walrath (t); Sonny Fortune (as); George Coleman (ss, ts); Ricky Ford (ts); Bob Neloms, Jimmy Rowles (p); Philip Catherine, Larry Coryell, John Scofield (g); Ron Carter, George Mraz (b); Dannie Richmond (d).* 3/77.

Despite Mingus's deep and vocal reservations, this was one of his most successful albums commercially. The addition of guitarists clearly pitched it in the direction of the younger rock-buying audience that Atlantic had targeted, and the record also included staples like 'Goodbye, Pork Pie Hat' and 'Better Git Hit In Your Soul' (presumably with a view to initiating that younger audience). The title-track, though, is rather too broad in its catch-all approach and sounds almost self-parodic. Mingus's health was beginning to break down in 1977, and there are signs of querulousness throughout, not least on 'Nobody Knows The Trouble I've Seen'.

****(*) Cumbia And Jazz Fusion**

Atlantic 8122 71785-2 *Mingus; Jack Walrath (t, perc); Dino Piana (tb); Jimmy Knepper (tb, btb); Mauricio Smith (f, picc, as, ss); Quarto Maltoni (as); George Adams (ts, f); Ricky Ford (ts, perc); Paul Jeffrey (ts, ob); Gary Anderson, Roberto Laneri (bcl); Anastasio Del Bono (ob, eng hn); Pasquale Sabatelli, Gene Scholtes (bsn); Bob Neloms (p); Danny Mixon (p, org); Dannie Richmond (d); Candido Camero, Daniel Gonzalez, Ray Mantilla, Alfredo Ramirez, Bradley Cunningham (perc).* 3/76–3/77.

'Cumbia And Jazz Fusion' is a slightly messy piece that levels some doubts at Mingus's remaining talents as arranger and instrumentator. The ensembles are all rather congested, which mars a fine and vibrant piece that ranks as one of his best late compositions. There is a regularity to the basic metre and a simplicity of conception which make the rather opaque surface all the more disappointing. The fault doesn't seem to lie with the recording, which is well transferred. 'Music for *Todo Modo*' was written (sight unseen) as soundtrack to the film by Elio Petri. The ten-piece Italo-American band works a typically volatile score, which includes a variant on 'Peggy's Blue Skylight' and some fine blues.

***** His Final Work**

Master Dance Tones 8471 *Mingus; Woody Shaw, Jack Walrath (t); Peter Matt (frhn); Ricky Ford (ts); Gerry Mulligan (bs); Lionel Hampton (vib); Bob Neloms (p); Dannie Richmond (d); additional personnel.* 11/77.

Arranged and led by Lionel Hampton, this was a last fling in the studio for the ailing Mingus, though he was to direct a couple more sessions from his wheelchair. To be frank, the music is rather routine. 'Fables Of Faubus' and 'Peggy's Blue Skylight' have lost their antagonism and eager passion respectively and now sound like well-structured charts, played with competence. The new things are a bit drab, almost pastiche Mingus. Arranger Paul Jeffrey has done a fine job, and even though the ever-mischievous Jack Walrath lobs a few well-aimed cherry bombs, the general impression is polite and unemphatic. Even so, it's remarkable that a player of Hampton's generation and persuasion should have chosen to be involved in this at all. The record has a rather complicated discographical history and there may be other versions of it in circulation. The version of 'So Long, Eric' certainly doesn't appear on them all.

Mingus Big Band

GROUP

A 'ghost' group playing the music of Charles Mingus, featuring ex-Mingusians and younger players in the spirit.

***** Nostalgia In Times Square**

Dreyfus FDM 36955 2 *Randy Brecker, Christopher Kase, Ryan Kisor, Lew Soloff, Jack Walrath (t); Art Baron, Sam Burtis, Frank Lacy (tb); Dave Taylor (btb, tba); Alex Foster, Steve Slagle (as); Chris Potter (as, ts); John Stubblefield, Craig Handy (ts); Ronnie Cuber, Roger Rosenberg (bs); Joe Locke (vib); Kenny Drew Jr (p); Michael Formanek, Andy McKee (b); Victor Jones, Marvin 'Smitty' Smith (d); Ray Mantilla (perc).* 3/93.

***** Gunslinging Birds**

Dreyfus FDM 36575 2 *As above, except omit Kase, Walrath, Baron, Burtis, Taylor, Cuber, Rosenberg, Formanek, Jones, Smith, Mantilla; add Philip Harper (t); Jamal Haynes, Earl McIntyre (tb); Gary Smulyan (bs); David Lee Jones (as); Adam Cruz (d).* 95.

****** Live In Time**

Dreyfus FDM 36583 2 2CD *Similar to above, except add Earl Gardner, Alex Sipiagin (t); Robin Eubanks, Conrad Herwig, Britt Woodman (tb); Gary Bartz (as); Seamus Blake, Mark Shim (ts).* 96.

***** Que Viva Mingus**

Dreyfus FDM 36593 2 *Similar to above, except add Ryan Kisor (t); Steve Turre (tb, shells); Earl McIntyre (btb, tba); Vincent Herring (as); David Sanchez (ts); Ronnie Cuber (bs); David Kikoski (p); Gene Jackson (d); Steve Berrios, Milton Cardona (perc); La Conja (v, perc).* 9/97.

*****(*) Blues And Politics**

Dreyfus FDM 36603 2 *Similar to above, except add Alex Sipiagin (t); Bobby Watson (as); John Hicks (p); Boris Kozlov (b); Jonathan Blake (d); Eric Mingus (v).* 1/99.

Of the projects dedicated to the great man's memory and legacy, this is perhaps the most important, and now the most durable as well, enjoying the active blessing of the composer's widow and access to tapes and manuscripts from the huge Mingus archive. The band began round a regular Thursday session at Fez under the Time Café in New York City. Mingus had shrewdly recognized that a band could rehearse at the public's expense if an event was labelled a 'workshop' rather than a concert, and so the Mingus Jazz Workshops were born. These days the task is perhaps less urgent, and less driven by constraint; the Big Band provides an opportunity to work through the scrolls, providing exegesis and commentary on a vast body of work, little of which received definitive performance during its creator's lifetime.

But what of the records themselves? The sleeve of *Gunslinging Birds* is misprinted Mingus Big Bang, which is just about right. Both the first records listed deliver with ferocious power and, when required, some delicacy as well. As usual, the material is taken from throughout the Mingus archive. *Nostalgia* is probably more interesting in terms of material – 'Don't Be Afraid, The Clown's Afraid, Too', 'Weird Nightmare', the title-piece – but the playing and the recording are sharper and more exact on the later album, which centres on a superb reading of 'Fables Of Faubus'.

Live In Time of course refers to the venue, but it also underscores the vital, ongoing nature of the project and the fact that all of this music is being worked out in real time, in the laboratories of the spirit rather than in the formaldehyde of musicological analysis. A huge slab of music spread over two discs, it comes the closest of the group to recapturing the spirit of Mingus himself. The opening is stunning; 'Number 29' was written by Mingus as a challenge to all the gunslinging trumpet players in town – and, as written, it was impossible. Arranger Sy Johnson has spread the part through the trumpet section and given it a hard, bi-tonal quality that is pure Mingus. Two early pieces, 'Baby, Take A Chance With Me' and 'This Subdues My Passion', are recorded here for only the second time since they were written in the 1940s. Conrad Herwig solos on the second, Frank Lacy and Gary Bartz on the first. 'So Long Eric' is a *tour de force*, a solo feature for the entire horn section and one of the most sheerly exciting jazz performances we have heard for years.

Disc two is not quite as powerful as the first, though Johnson's long arrangement on 'The Shoes Of The Fisherman's Wife Are Some Jive-Ass Slippers' and the superb 'E's Flat, Ah's Flat Too' are impeccably conceived and performed. The night ends a day late with 'Wednesday Night Prayer Meeting', a stunning solo from Randy Brecker, ably supported by Mark Shim and Robin Eubanks. A great jazz record and a worthy homage to one of jazz's greatest composers.

Que Viva Mingus can't hope to reach the same heights, and for some reason the band this time out doesn't sit quite right, sounding rather tired and lacking in lustre. There are some superb moments, needless to say. Lacy, Stubblefield and Brecker make a wondrous thing of 'Love Chant' and Sy Johnson's arrangement of 'Cumbia And Jazz Fusion' could hardly have been bettered by the man himself. Many of the other arrangements are by Michael Mossman, and he directs 'Tijuana Gift Shop', teeing off fine solos from Ryan Kisor and Vince Herring. Ysabel – in the boisterous form of La Conja – does her table dance to end the session. Satisfying to Mingus buffs in unfolding further aspects of the oeuvre, but it will perhaps appeal less to the uncommitted.

As the title suggests, *Blues And Politics* foregrounds Mingus's fierce activism. It begins with the great man's voice, reciting 'It Was A Lonely Day In Selma, Alabama' at the Tyrone Guthrie Theater in Minneapolis, with interjections from the band of the time. That segues into a new recording of 'Freedom', arranged by Mike Mossman and bracketed by archive and new recordings of the narration by Charles and Eric Mingus. Boris Kozlov plays the opening cadenza of 'Haitian Fight Song' on Mingus's own lion-head bass, and the young Russian steals the apostolic thunder of Andy McKee, who is relegated to a single solo on 'Pussy Cat Dues'. The Russian surfaces again on 'Goodbye Pork Pie Hat', which shifts the emphasis from politics to blues, and 'Meditations For A Pair Of Wire Cutters'.

The lament for Lester Young opens with a magnificent Seamus Blake cadenza which confirms his rising status, but he is upstaged by Bobby Watson's searingly beautiful statement on 'Pussy Cat Dues', a high point on the album. No sign that the legacy is in anything but the safest and most committed hands, and certainly no sign that Mingus's turbulent output will not continue to inspire big-band performance of the highest quality and the strongest passion.

Mingus Dynasty

GROUP

Those with first-hand experience, and later admirers, come to celebrate the music of Charles Mingus.

***(*) Reincarnation

Soul Note 121042 *Richard Williams (t); Jimmy Knepper (tb); Ricky Ford (ts); Sir Roland Hanna (p); Reggie Johnson (b); Kenny Washington (d).* 4/82.

*** Mingus's Sounds Of Love

Soul Note 121142 *Randy Brecker (t); Jimmy Knepper (tb); James Newton (f); Craig Handy (ts); Sir Roland Hanna (p); Reggie Johnson (b); Kenny Washington (d).* 9/87.

There have always been 'ghost bands', orchestras which continued trading after the leader's death, like *Hamlets* without the prince or, as *The Next Generation* may call to mind, *Star Trek* without Kirk and Spock. The best-known of these bands in jazz are the Duke Ellington and Count Basie orchestras, their posthumous life justified by the perfectly reasonable feeling that what makes a group distinctive is the bandbook and the soloists, not the physical presence of the leader. It's a view that can be pushed to absurdity; but, in the case of Charles Mingus, a man who regarded composition as a discipline which allowed others to discover their own musical language, it has a special significance. These are records by the 'first' Mingus ghost band; the Mingus Big Band sets, listed above, were the successors.

After Mingus's death, conscious that his artistic legacy required careful investment, his widow, Sue Graham, formed Mingus Dynasty in the hope of seeing the music continuing to develop. To sustain an element of apostolic succession, at least one or two members of each line-up were to be musicians who had either worked with or studied under Mingus. The studio version of 'Sue's Changes' on *Sounds Of Love* gives Reggie Johnson one of his most forthright parts. 'The I Of Hurricane Sue' and 'Ysabel's Table Dance' are both outstandingly good. The band on *Reincarnation* is, if anything, even better and the choice of material aimed to please, with 'Wednesday Night Prayer Meeting', 'East Coasting' and 'Duke Ellington's Sound Of Love' all featured. Williams solos with great pointedness.

*****(*) Big Band Charlie Mingus: Live At The Théâtre Boulogne-Billancourt, Volume 1**
Soul Note 121192 *Randy Brecker (t); Jon Faddis (c); Mike Zwerin, Jimmy Knepper (tb); John Handy (as); Clifford Jordan (ts, ss); David Murray (ts, bcl); Nick Brignola (bs); Jaki Byard (p); Reggie Johnson (b); Billy Hart (d).* 6/88.

****** Big Band Charlie Mingus: Live At The Théâtre Boulogne-Billancourt, Volume 2**
Soul Note 121193 *As above.* 6/88.

A related project, Big Band Charlie Mingus mercifully stopped short of all-out 'orchestral' arranging that would have taken the sting out of much of Mingus's music. As it is, this group is just an augmented version of the Dynasty groups. There are good things on *Volume 1*, 'Jump Monk' and 'E's Flat, Ah's Flat Too', but 'The Shoes Of The Fisherman's Wife Are Some Jive-Ass Slippers' doesn't give the band much to work on and it sounds very uncentred. For some reason, most of the really good stuff is on the second disc. Faddis and Murray solo pungently on 'My Jelly Roll Soul', and Murray returns on bass clarinet for the third of the wind solos on 'Goodbye Pork Pie Hat', giving ground to the superb Byard. 'Boogie Stop Shuffle' is aired again; this time Murray, obviously relishing the occasion, jumps in after Cliff Jordan with three rasping, joyous choruses that exactly capture the spirit of the man they all came to honour.

The Minstrels Of Annie Street

GROUP

A one-off project dedicated to San Francisco revivalist repertory.

***** Original Tuxedo Rag**
Stomp Off STCD1272 *Bob Schulz (c); Chris Tyle (t); John Gill (tb, v); Phil Howe (cl, ss); Ray Skjelbred (p); Carl Lunsford (bj); Bill Carroll (tba); Hal Smith (d).* 7/93.

Led by Gill, this is a sextet (Tyle and Smith sit in as guests) dedicated to San Francisco repertory, and therefore heavily in debt to the Lu Watters revivalists. They take the more nimble rhythmic approach of today, though, which leavens the music and gives an extra lift to tunes that might otherwise tend towards flat-footed thunder. Nice touches include Tom T. Hall's country song, 'The Day Clayton Delaney Died', and a couple of ancient rags. Neat solos, but the band's the thing.

Phil Minton (born 1940)

VOICE, TRUMPET

Worked with Mike Westbrook as singer and trumpeter in the '60s and '70s, but moved increasingly towards entirely free vocal music, often working with other singers in that context.

*****(*) A Doughnut In Both Hands**
Emanem 4025 *Minton (solo v).*

Minton is perhaps the most powerful vocal performer working in Europe today, and singing has virtually overtaken his trumpet playing. Associated with Mike Westbrook on a number of text-based projects, he is also a stunning vocal improviser, with a tonal and timbral range that seems quite uncanny.

Most of the material on this remarkable record was released in America years ago as a Rift LP. Its concentration is extreme, both technically and emotionally. Seemingly inspired by the literature of the First World War, which (if Paul Fussell is to be believed) is definitive of many of our twentieth-century attitudes and obsessions, 'Cenotaph' and 'Wreath' are only three-quarters of a minute apiece, but overflowing with pain and pride, anger and redemption. A group of five 'Wood Songs' aren't quite so compelling, but a tiny dedication to German revolutionist Emma Goldman and the stunning 'Notes On Avarice' and 'Blasphemy' demand frequent recourse to the repeat button. 'Blasphemy' is one of half a dozen additional tracks not included on the original album.

***** Songs From A Prison Diary**
Leo CDLR 196 *Minton; Veryan Weston (p).* 10/91.

***** Dada Da**
Leo CDLR 192 *Minton; Roger Turner (d, perc).* 1/93.

The duos with Weston seem much more formalized than Minton's improvised work with Peter Brötzmann and others on a deleted FMP album, and they lack the sheer power of the slightly earlier work with Roger Turner on *AMMO*, but they are compelling all the same. The Ho Chi Minh texts on *Songs From A Prison Diary* are intensely moving and Minton brings to them a natural actor's ability to deliver apparently banal lines with a weight of experience that far exceeds their ostensible meaning.

The duos with Turner are initially rather baffling, but they repay time and attention, confirming how carefully and intuitively Minton navigates the rhythm of a piece. These are probably best heard first as percussion duos. You even get the soundcheck as a bonus.

*****(*) Two Concerts**
FMP OWN 90006 *Minton; John Butcher (ts, ss); Erhard Hirt (g, elec).* 6 & 8/95.

*****(*) Mouthfull Of Ecstasy**
Victo CD 041 *Minton; John Butcher (ts); Veryan Weston (p); Roger Turner (perc, v).* 1/96.

The FMP record documents a long-standing (we think five or six years at least) group which has over time achieved an almost perfect balance and economy of means. Hirt is something of a miniaturist; he has been described as the Webern of improv guitar, and there is certainly something in that, splitting up a line into an array of different sounds, and then drifting in behind Minton's shredded semantics and Butcher's wonderfully elegant, almost courtly wooing of the saxophone. The surprising revelation about this music is how romantic it seems, how full of expressive meaning. There's an unevenness of quality between the two sets represented, one from Vandoeuvre in June, the other from the Antwerp Free Music Festival later in the summer. The five numbers from Musique Action are oddly scrappy and unformed, impressive in bulk but hard to come to terms with individually. The Antwerp set consists of a massive central movement, fiercely dramatic and delicately modulated by turns, surrounded by two shorter items, prologue and epilogue, introduction and peroration, fascinatingly discursive by the standards of this music and, as so often, hovering on the fringes of orthodox song form.

That side of Minton is always more obvious when Veryan Weston is in attendance, and the London recording on Victo is full of moments when some melodic revelation seems near. Butcher loves to toy with such shapes, but it is clear that – as with a performer like Lol Coxhill – familiar material is both intellectually present and very distant. What one is hearing is pre-standard material, shapes and anticipations of song. Minton himself does much the same thing, constantly reworking the timbral and dynamic envelope within which songs can exist, creating his own vast sound-bank, an archive which is not there to be exploited but simply to exist on its own magnificent terms.

****** A Doughnut In One Hand**

FMP CD 91 *Minton (v solo).* 1/96.

This category-stretching return to solo singing – which now seems to have been recorded earlier than the date cited in our last edition – has no intrinsic relation to the earlier disc that (almost) shares its title. Now one doughnut short (which makes better sense on the cholesterol front), Minton also has a spare hand free to conduct himself through a disciplined and rigorous sequence of miniatures, 30 tracks in an hour of spectacular vocal acrobatics.

Relations between groups of pieces – 'Dough Songs', 'Para Songs', songs about 'drainage' and a Mr Wilkins, and 'Tip Head' – are never made entirely explicit, but by sequencing the CD differently one gets a strong impression of areas of concern approached and developed organically and then re-ordered to create a fractured narrative. The voice has seldom been better and Minton's use of space and microphone distance (the only kind of processing on the record) adds dimensions that are entirely unexpected. Don't expect an easy ride if this is your first experience of Phil Minton, but do expect your expectations and anticipations to be substantially re-ordered.

Bob Mintzer (born 1953)

TENOR SAXOPHONE, BASS CLARINET

Mintzer's experience is primarily with big bands, from Tito Puente and Buddy Rich in the '70s onwards. He has played, written and arranged for many orchestral situations since, although his most significant small-group experience may have been his association with the pop-jazz group, The Yellowjackets, beginning in 1991.

***** Departure**

DMP CD-493 *Mintzer; Marvin Stamm, Laurie Frink, Tim Hagans, Bob Millikan, Michael Mossman (t, flhn); Dave Bargeron, Mike Davis, Keith O'Quinn, Dave Taylor (tb); Lawrence Feldman, Bob Malach, Roger Rosenberg, Peter Yellin (reeds); Phil Markowitz, Jim McNeely (p); Michael Formanek, Lincoln Goines (b); Peter Erskine, John Riley (d); Sammy Figueroa (perc).* 92.

***** Only In New York**

DMP CD-501 *As above, except Ron Tooley (t, flhn), Dave Panichi (tb), Jay Anderson (b) replace Mossman, Bargeron, McNeely, Formanek, Goines, Erskine and Figueroa.* 11/93.

Mintzer is an accomplished soloist and arranger who's been recording big-band albums for a more than a decade. Earlier albums have been hit-and-miss affairs, with too much piling on of effects and a certain cuteness standing in for wit or ingenuity. But the two most recent discs are more coherent, more integrated, better. There is still some irritating stuff on *Departure*, such as 'The Big Show'; but some more genuine material includes 'Horns Alone', a mildly arresting feature for the front line minus the rhythm section, and with a superb team of players the sheer chutzpah of the musicianship is rewarding. *Only In New York* is probably a shade better yet. We could have done without Mintzer's vocal on 'TV Blues' – although the lyrics will probably raise a grin – but otherwise this is almost foot-perfect as skilful big-band dates go. The oddly appealing sound of electric bass clarinet colours 'Modern Day Tuba', the stop-go 'I Want To Be Happy' is an interesting revision, and so it goes through the ten tracks. Soloists include the surpassingly fine Hagans as a standout and, though Mintzer himself is more agile than profound, he has a good feature on 'What Might Have Been'. Both discs feature DMP's 20-Bit High Resolution recording and they sound awfully strong.

***** Latin From Manhattan**

DMP CD-523 *Mintzer; Bob Millikan, Larry Lunetta, Scott Wendholt, Michael Mossman (t); Larry Farrell, Keith O'Quinn, Sam Burtsi, Dave Taylor (tb); Bob Malach, Lawrence Feldman, Pete Yellin, Roger Rosenberg (saxes); Phil Markowitz (p); Jay Anderson (b); John Riley (d); Louis Bauzo (perc).* 1/98.

***** Quality Time**

TVT Jazz TVT-3230-2 *Mintzer; Phil Markowitz (p); Russell Ferrante (ky); Jay Anderson, Jimmy Haslip (b); Peter Erskine, William Kennedy (d).* 3/98.

Mintzer is still making big-band records for DMP, and *Latin From Manhattan* is the latest in an ongoing sequence. Tom Jung's sleeve-note captures the flavour of their accomplishments pretty well: top-flight technique and musicianship, meticulous studio sound. For people who want a drilled, hi-fi experience out of a big-band record, Minzter's albums are hard to top. A glance through the personnel shows what a formidable team he's got. This one has nine new tunes and an agreeable revamp of Tito Puente's 'Oye Como Va'. In its way, though, this music is for specialized tastes, just as much as, say, a Vinny Golia large-ensemble record. It seeks a perfection which many will find hard to warm to.

His small-group records have been less than compelling in the past, but *Quality Time* is a rather surprising success. The rhythm section of Markowitz, Anderson and Erskine (the others appear on only two rather annoying smooth-jazz tracks) play with such relaxed good humour that they soften all the rather clenched virtuosity which Mintzer is otherwise prone to fall into as a soloist (Erskine must be the best drummer in the world at making a complex groove seem beatifically simple). The result is one of

Mintzer's most enjoyable dates – but docked a notch for including the electric tracks, obviously pitched for radio-play, which spoil the album's karma.

Blue Mitchell (1930–79)

TRUMPET, CORNET

A fair proportion of the Miami-born trumpeter's career was spent away from jazz in R&B and blues outfits led by artists as various as Earl Bostic and John Mayall, and as a soloist with the likes of Ray Charles and Lena Horne. His soulful delivery was an asset wherever it was deployed and Blue, having inherited the Horace Silver band, made some fine recordings on his own account.

****** Big Six**

Original Jazz Classics OJC 615 *Mitchell; Curtis Fuller (tb); Johnny Griffin (ts); Wynton Kelly (p); Wilbur Ware (b); Philly Joe Jones (d).* 7/58.

*****(*) Out Of The Blue**

Original Jazz Classics OJC 667 *Mitchell; Benny Golson (ts); Cedar Walton, Wynton Kelly (p); Paul Chambers, Sam Jones (b); Art Blakey (d).* 1/59.

****** Blue Soul**

Original Jazz Classics OJC 765 *Mitchell; Curtis Fuller (tb); Jimmy Heath (ts); Wynton Kelly (p); Sam Jones (b); Philly Joe Jones (d).* 9/59.

*****(*) Blues On My Mind**

Original Jazz Classics OJC 6009 *Mitchell; Curtis Fuller (tb); Benny Golson, Johnny Griffin, Jimmy Heath (ts); Wynton Kelly (p); Paul Chambers, Sam Jones, Wilbur Ware (b); Art Blakey, Philly Joe Jones (d).* 7/58–9/59.

A stalwart of the Horace Silver band, Mitchell took it over in 1964, replacing the former leader with the young Chick Corea. The debut recording isn't particularly memorable; though Corea has a fine grasp of the required idiom, which is blues- and gospel-drenched hard bop of the kind Silver pioneered, it never quite ignites. The heavy-duty line-up on the Riverside reissues on OJC is much more satisfactory and *Big Six* is unquestionably the trumpeter's finest achievement. It contains the first recorded version of Golson's classic 'Blues March', a punchy version of what was to become a chestnut. The *Blues On My Mind* compilation is, for most casual purchasers, a good buy, bringing together 'Brother Ball' and 'There Will Never Be Another You' from OJC 615 and 'It Could Happen To You' and a rousing 'Saints' from *Out Of The Blue.*

In many respects, *Blue Soul* is the best of the bunch, though here Mitchell is occasionally outclassed by his band; Heath in particular sounds as if he's trying not to muscle in and one or two of his solos are curtailed rather suddenly, perhaps lest he outstay his welcome. Jimmy Heath resurfaces to equally good effect on *A Sure Thing* (below), especially on 'Gone With The Wind', which is arranged for just trumpet, saxophone and rhythm, a welcome variation on the big-band material but rather wastefully tucked away at the end. The two baritones and french horn provide a solid bottom for Heath's arrangements.

***** Blue's Moods**

Original Jazz Classics OJCCD 138 *Mitchell; Wynton Kelly (p); Sam Jones (b); Roy Brooks (d).* 4/60.

***** Smooth As The Wind**

Original Jazz Classics OJC 871 *Mitchell; Burt Collins, Bernie Glow, Clark Terry (t); Jimmy Cleveland, Urbie Green, Britt Woodman, Julian Priester (tb); Willie Ruff (frhn); Tommy Flanagan (p); Tommy Williams (b); Philly Joe Jones, Charli Persip (d); strings.* 12/60, 3/61.

*****(*) A Sure Thing**

Original Jazz Classics OJC 837 *Mitchell; Clark Terry (t); Julius Watkins (frhn); Jerome Richardson (as, f); Jimmy Heath (ts); Pepper Adams, Pat Patrick (bs); Wynton Kelly (p); Sam Jones (b); Albert 'Tootie' Heath (d).* 3/62.

***** The Cup Bearers**

Original Jazz Classics OJC 797 *Mitchell; Junior Cook (ts); Cedar Walton (p); Gene Taylor (b); Roy Brooks (d).* 4/63.

At the start of the '60s, Blue was still with Horace Silver but was already branching out on his own. Like many of his contemporaries, Mitchell long nursed a desire to work with strings. *Smooth As The Wind* is the result, an on-again, off-again mish-mash of terse big-band jazz arranged by Tadd Dameron and Benny Golson with oddly distanced orchestral washes that neither add nor significantly detract but which over the entire session pall rather badly.

The Cup Bearers is a bit of a disappointment. Unlike the urbane Henderson on the earlier record, Cook is forever in a tearing rush to get back and have a further say, not quite knowing how to get out of what he's set up for himself. What it palpably needs is someone of Heath's intelligence to tie up the loose ends.

Blue's Moods suggests some forgotten Lee Morgan session with the leader sounding unusually raw and unsettled. It's an oddly inelegant performance from Mitchell. 'Scrapple From The Apple' settles any doubt about who is playing, a definitive performance on material that doesn't obviously suit him, though towards the end of his life he was to form a bebop group with Harold Land. Kelly was a long-time collaborator and he brings his usual fresh-faced composure to all these tracks. Another excellent record from Mitchell, an artist who needs to be experienced in depth before he starts to pay dividends.

***** Down With It**

Blue Note 54327 *Mitchell; Junior Cook (ts); Chick Corea (p); Gene Taylor (b); Al Foster (d).* 7/65.

Recently returned from soul-jazz limbo, *Down With It* is an undemanding and largely entertaining session that delivers on promise without scattering any pigeons. The soloists – Corea, Cook, Mitchell – are good enough to sustain attention over a rather scant 40 minutes, even though the material is fairly light and trite. 'Hi-Heel Sneakers' is pitched straight at the jukeboxes, while tunes like 'Perception' (credited to Blue and Chick) and 'March On Selma' are more demanding. The horns are beautifully separated and balanced, but the bass could be more emphatic, and Al Foster is wasted.

***** Graffiti Blues**

Sony 57120 *Mitchell; James Bossy, Jon Faddis, Irwin Markowitz (t); Frank Vicari (ts); Seldon Powell (ts, bs); Joe Farrell, Herman*

Riley (ts, f); Donald Bailey (hca); Walter Bishop Jr (p); Joe Sample (ky); Joe Beck, Sam Brown, Freddy Robinson, John Tropea (g); Wilbur Bascomb Jr, Darrell Clayborn, Michael Moore (b); John Guerin, James Madison, Raymond Lee Pounds (d). 73–74.

Blue made five albums for Mainstream which did some quiet but respectable business without ever matching up to his work for Blue Note. This is the fourth, recorded shortly before the trumpeter decided to abandon solo work and hire himself out as a session-man. It's a funky and uncomplicated set, perhaps too much coloured by rock sensibilities, but inventive enough. The studio sound is very bright and sensuous.

****(*) Live At Douglas Beach House, 1976**

Culture Press 2006 *Mitchell; Mike Morris (ts); Michael Levine (p); Smiley Winters (d).* 76.

A pedestrian and unarresting live session from late on in Blue's foreshortened career. The trumpeter sounds more than usually introspective and brooding, a mood which the band seems determined to break. The opening 'Pleasure Bent' and the terse 'Something Old, Something Blue' are worth revisiting, but there's little else to snare an uncommitted listener.

Red Mitchell (1927–92)

BASS, PIANO

Born Keith Moore Mitchell, he came from New York but did much of his most familiar work on the West Coast, from 1954. Left for Stockholm in the '60s and stayed there almost until his death. A humorous, energetic, clever musician with many important credits in his discography.

*****(*) Presenting Red Mitchell**

Original Jazz Classics OJC 158 *Mitchell; James Clay (ts, f); Lorraine Geller (p); Billy Higgins (d).* 3/57.

****(*) Chocolate Cadillac**

Steeplechase SCCCD 1161 *Mitchell; Idrees Sulieman (t); Nisse Sandstrom (ts); Horace Parlan (p); Rune Carlsson (d).* 12/76.

***** Red'N'Me**

Dreyfus Jazz Line 365042 *Mitchell; Jimmy Rowles (p).* 7/78.

***** Simple Isn't Easy**

Sunnyside SSC 1016 *Mitchell (p solo).* 9/83.

***** The Red–Barron Duo**

Storyville STCD 4137 *Mitchell; Kenny Barron (p).* 8/86.

Mitchell was known for a fluent improvising style in which pulled-off (rather than plucked) notes in a typically low register (Mitchell used a retuned bass) suggest a baritone saxophone rather than a stringed instrument; Scott LaFaro was later sanctified for a broadly similar technique. Mitchell is also an accomplished pianist, with a hint of the romantic approach of his former colleague, Hampton Hawes. The early stuff on OJC with the short-lived Geller instead of Hawes is decent, boppish jazz consistently lifted by Mitchell's singing lines. 'Scrapple From The Apple' is a joy and a delight. The Sunnyside originals – with titles like 'I'm A Homeboy' and 'It's Time To Emulate The Japanese' – quash any notion that Mitchell is merely a standards hack, though he is more approachable in that territory. *Simple Isn't Easy* is entirely for piano and voice, and to that extent isn't typical; even so, it suggests that most of the elements of Mitchell's shaping intelligence are at work: harmonically limber, melodically sophisticated and rhythmically just dynamic enough to be listenable.

On *Chocolate Cadillac* the writing is good and Mitchell is playing well (top form on a couple of tracks). Unfortunately, the band simply isn't behind him. Parlan, normally a stylistic chameleon, seems to have his mind on something else, and the two horns lock only infrequently. Disappointing.

The Red–Barron Duo is the closest Mitchell came to duetting with himself. The pianist shares Mitchell's harmonic and rhythmic preoccupations to a productive degree, and their exploration of quite basic themes ('Oleo', 'The Sunny Side Of The Street') is compellingly inventive. So, too, is the collaboration with Rowles, except that here there is an entirely surprising element of tension, most of it generated by Mitchell's taut ostinati and a fresh set-list, in which only 'There Is No Greater Love' sounds like a chestnut.

Roscoe Mitchell (born 1940)

REEDS, PERCUSSION

One of the key figures in the Chicagoan avant-garde, Mitchell is a native of the city and has been active as a musician and associated with the city's 'new music' for close to 40 years. His group was transmuted into the Art Ensemble Of Chicago; several of his records are among the significant documents of post-Coleman jazz. Some of his solo and small-group records have set the tone for both solo and ensemble-based improvisers in free jazz and beyond.

****** Sound**

Delmark DE 408 *Mitchell; Lester Bowie (t, flhn, hca); Lester Lashley (tb, clo); Maurice McIntyre (ts); Malachi Favors (b); Alvin Fielder (d).* 6/66.

What a vital, electrifying document this remains! Restored to an excellent CD edition (original Delmark vinyl was seldom very clean), with an alternative version of 'Ornette' and the title-track, originally a composite of two versions, heard as two separate takes, there is a lot more music and nothing to diminish the power of the occasion. The two key pieces, 'Sound' and 'The Little Suite', are a message of freedom quite different from that being communicated by the contemporaneous recordings of Albert Ayler and Peter Brötzmann. Mitchell organizes his group around the notion of sounds entering into – and interrelating with – silence. So there are tiny gestures and startling emptinesses alongside long lines and soliloquies. Bowie, Lashley and McIntyre work in overtones and distortions more than they do in 'true' tones, and in 'The Little Suite' the sound of toys and bells and other found instruments carries as much sensitivity as the horns do elsewhere. Both a manifesto and an unrepeatable event, *Sound* remains a marvel.

***** Roscoe Mitchell**

Chief CD 4 *Mitchell; Leo Smith (t, pkt-t, flhn); George Lewis (tb, sou, tba); Thurman Barker, Anthony Braxton, Don Moye,*

Douglas Ewart, Joseph Jarman, Henry Threadgill, Malachi Favors (perc). 7–8/78.

Several of Mitchell's crucial recordings have disappeared with the apparent demise of Chicago's Nessa label, but the above re-issue of one of them returns some of his most significant 1970s work to the catalogue. Away from the Art Ensemble Of Chicago, this dedicated reed theoretician and experimenter has sought out some very rarefied terrain. There are three long pieces here: a trio for woodwinds, high brass and low brass, with Smith and Lewis; a phantasmagoria for eight percussionists, 'The Maze'; and almost 18 minutes of Mitchell blowing as softly as he can through the soprano sax, 'S II Examples', drifting through a world of shadowy microtones. A remarkable programme, but there are drawbacks: the 'L-R-G' trio is full of fascinating juxtapositions and echoes of countless other composers, yet its deliberately piecemeal nature seems laboured next to the spontaneous structures conceived as a matter of course by European improvisers. 'The Maze' has a burnished, glistening quality, but the fact that only two 'genuine' drummers are among the percussionists makes one wonder what Mitchell could have achieved with the involvement of eight full-time drum exponents. As it stands, the piece is a matter of shifting textures, when it might have transcended that. 'S II Examples', too, is more of an intriguing idea than a valuable musical one – or, at least, one more important to Mitchell than to the listener. All that said, it's a rather bewitching set altogether, and a useful notebook on what Chicago's playing élite were looking into at the period. The equally significant *Nonaah* from the same period has yet to appear on CD.

***** 3 × 4 Eye**

Black Saint 120050-2 *Mitchell; Hugh Ragin (t, picc t, flhn); Spencer Barefield (g); Jaribu Shahid (b); Tani Tabbal (d).* 2/81.

****** Roscoe Mitchell And The Sound And Space Ensembles**

Black Saint 120070-2 *Mitchell; Mike Mossman (t, flhn); Gerald Oshita (ts, bs, Conn-o sax, contrabass srspn); Spencer Barefield (g, v); Jaribu Shahid (b, v); Tani Tabbal (d, v); Tom Buckner (v).* 6/83.

**** The Flow Of Things**

Black Saint BSR 0090 *Mitchell; Jodie Christian (p); Malachi Favors (b); Steve McCall (d).* 6–9/86.

***** Live At The Knitting Factory**

Black Saint 120120-2 *Mitchell; Hugh Ragin (t, picc t, flhn); Spencer Barefield (g); Jaribu Shahid (b); Tani Tabbal (d).* 11/87.

Two of the best of Mitchell's Black Saint records are now available on CD. *3 × 4 Eye* features a picked team tiptoeing around a number of themes, including his tribute to Jarman, 'Jo Jar', and the ironic 'Variations On A Folk Song Written In The Sixties'. Improvisation becomes almost ritualized, yet the leader's idiosyncratic deployment of sound and space renders the sequence of events as something extraordinary. The subsequent *Sound And Space Ensembles* is completely *sui generis*. The trio of Mitchell, Oshita – on some of the oddest reed instruments ever made – and the classical tenor Tom Buckner perform an eerie mixture of Kurt Schwitters and Wilton Crawley, before a pseudo-funk rave-up by the whole ensemble, which features probably the only recorded solo on the contrabass sarrusophone. The two ensembles go on to blend again in two long, beautiful tracks, the needle-fine 'Linefine Lyons Seven' and the scuttling-drifting 'Variations On Sketches From Bamboo'.

In the latter part of the 1980s, though, Mitchell seemed to lose his listeners. While a colleague such as Anthony Braxton worked out many directions through obsessive recording, Mitchell scarcely recorded at all. The only studio date, *The Flow Of Things*, is a static and tamely conventional reeds-and-rhythm date which yields little advance on his earlier experiments. *Live At The Knitting Factory* replaces the live album from 1988 on Cecma, which so far is not on CD. The group is in good shape, but Mitchell's notebook-like approach to recording tends to make for a fragmented listening experience: the short pieces and the two cut-out solos break up the impact of the powerful 'Almost Like Raindrops' and the blowout memorial, 'The Reverend Frank Wright'. Ragin's impassioned yet curiously selfless playing is as effective as Mitchell's own.

***** After Fallen Leaves**

Silkheart SHCD 126 *Mitchell; Arne Forsen (p); Ulf Akerhielm (b); Gilbert Matthews (d).* 10/89.

****(*) Songs In The Wind**

Victo 011 *Mitchell; Vartan Manoogian (vn); Vincent Davis, Richard Davis (d); Steve Sylvester (bullroarers, windwands).* 6–8/90.

The haphazardness of Mitchell's recording regimen has made it difficult to take a balanced view of a musician whose work, had it been documented more extensively, might have had a far more profound impact on the new music of the 1980s and '90s. As it is, Mitchell's marginalization has made records like these two seem like hurried odds and ends from his workshop. *After Fallen Leaves* features him with the Swedish Brus Trio, and there are many good moments – the boiling alto solo on 'Mr Freddie' and the long patchwork improvisation, 'Come Gather Some Things' – without the session really making a coherent impact, since the trio seem eager but too unfamiliar with Mitchell's methods. *Songs In The Wind* is even more fragmented, the 13 pieces ranging through solo, duo and trio explorations of mood and form: Mitchell is at his most unflinchingly austere here, and the oddball contributions of Sylvester seem like nothing more than a textural distraction. Hopefully, if Mitchell's plans to create a large repertory ensemble come to fruition, there'll be more opportunities to hear him at length on record in future.

**** Duets And Solos**

Black Saint 120133-2 *Mitchell; Muhal Richard Abrams (p).* 3/90.

****(*) This Dance Is For Steve McCall**

Black Saint 120150-2 *Mitchell; Matthew Shipp (p); William Parker (b, perc); Jaribu Shahid (b); Tani Tabbal, Vincent Davis (d).* 5/92.

The meeting with Abrams is a terrible disappointment. Each man's solo section rambles dutifully along to no great purpose, Abrams constructing a rolling but directionless panorama of piano styles, Mitchell practising some of his minimalist licks. Together they provide a few felicitous moments, but Abrams's decision to use a synthesizer for most of these passages pushes the music towards routine impressionism. *This Dance Is For Steve McCall* debuts a new group, The Note Factory, though not very auspiciously; aside from a thoughtful new treatment of Jarman's

'Ericka', several of the nine pieces sound half-realized or foreshortened, with the bass and percussion textures unclear. 'The Rodney King Affair', a stew of disquiet, is suitably blunt political art.

****(*) Hey Donald**
Delmark DE-475 *Mitchell; Jodie Christian (p); Malachi Favors (b); Albert 'Tootie' Heath (d).* 5/94.

Another largely disappointing affair. When the rhythm section are playing straight time and setting up a groove underneath, Mitchell's honking and mordant saxophone often sounds frankly ludicrous. On the Tab Smith-styled smoocher, 'Walking In The Moonlight', it's close to absurd. Yet there are still felicitous moments – the simple, sweet flute piece, 'Jeremy' – and four duets with Favors evoke some of the mystery of the old days. But this is, in sum, not much of a record.

***** Pilgrimage**
Lovely Music LCD 2022 *Mitchell; Joseph Kubera (p); Vartan Manoogian (vn); Thomas Buckner (v). n.d.*

This is by Mitchell's New Chamber Ensemble. There are settings of e.e. cummings and Byron (as well as Joseph Jarman and Thulani Davis), and they inspire some of Mitchell's most meticulous and sensitive playing and writing, with frequent collaborator Buckner in fine voice and Manoogian and Kubera diligent disciples. It's interesting to conjecture on its relationship both with Mitchell's other work and with his view on the jazz tradition, since its involvement with jazz materials is very slight: much of this is chamber music which needs judgement within a different milieu. For all the refinement, one sometimes misses the energy of Mitchell's most involving work.

***** Sound Songs**
Delmark 2DE-493 2CD *Mitchell (reeds solo).* 94–97.

No lack of energy here: in some of the longer pieces, such as the concert recordings, 'Full Frontal Saxophone', 'Near And Far' and 'Closer', Mitchell has never sounded more powerful and adroit. Elsewhere, particularly in the application of little instruments to a saxophone line, as in much of disc two, he harks back not only to his early soliloquies but also to some of Julius Hemphill's overdubbed solo music. But the record is simply too long. The more absorbing pieces sit next to what could be called sound-exercises, a useful notebook for the performer and a test for impatient listeners. Mitchell's music often seems to need a large-scale overview; as with Braxton, one tries to fathom out the big picture. As an individual component, this tends towards the inscrutable.

***** Nine To Get Ready**
ECM 539725-2 *Mitchell; Hugh Ragin (t); George Lewis (tb); Matthew Shipp, Craig Taborn (p); Jaribu Shahid (b, v); William Parker (b); Tani Tabbal (d, v); Gerald Cleaver (d).* 5/97.

The grand, expansive sound which this nonet is granted by ECM may divide some listeners. It surely benefits the processional feel of 'Leola', but does the luxurious reverb of the production suit the testy interplay of the following 'Dream And Response'? Mitchell notes on the sleeve that he wished for many years to put together 'an ensemble of improvising musicians with an orchestral range', but only rarely does this album suggest a palette denied to the leader of the Nessa sessions of 20 years earlier. Tracks such as 'For Lester B' and 'Bessie Harris' suggest, indeed, a preference for a middleweight ensemble that blends a bigger sonority with the mobility of a medium-sized group. The most notable thing about the band – the double-rhythm section – is something that Mitchell seems reluctant to make much of. The results are in keeping with much of Mitchell's recent music: lots of interesting threads but none of them tied into a truly memorable result.

***** In Walked Buckner**
Delmark DE-510 *Mitchell; Jodie Christian (p, bells); Reggie Workman (b, perc); Albert 'Tootie' Heath (d, f, didgeridoo).* 7/98.

A slight return to the terrain of the previous Delmark group-record, and this one is better. 'Off Shore' proposes the sort of elliptical, intuitive aesthetic which Mitchell has made something like his own, and when they shift from there into the bleary bop of the title-piece it seems like a discouraging retreat. But the record has more in common with Mitchell's taste for the baroque. He picks up the piccolo and the bass recorder as well as the saxophones and, if Christian and Heath couldn't help their orthodox tendencies on the previous album, they seem willing to chance their arm a little further here. It remains an awkward rapprochement, but it's working a little more easily.

Bill Mobley (born 1953)

TRUMPET

Born in Memphis, the brass-playing Mobley worked the local scene for a time before moving to Berklee and a place on the faculty, where he coached small groups for a five-year period. This is his leadership debut.

*****(*) Triple Bill**
Evidence ECD 22163 *Mobley; Billy Pierce (ts, ss); Bill Easley (as, cl, f); Kenny Barron (p); Christian McBride (b); Alan Dawson (d); Ron McBee (perc).* 6/93.

The three Bills of the title blend together well. Mobley's 'Prelude' airs his own slightly fragile tone, before Easley comes in on his favoured flute and Pierce on soprano, an unexpectedly quiet and easy-going start to a notably unassertive and reflective album. '49th Street', another original, is more upbeat, and might come from some blindfold-testable corner of the early-'60s Blue Note catalogue, except that the sound is so unmistakably modern. The saxophonists are certainly not going to be confused with their forebears, and Mobley himself is possessed of a delightful sound which owes something to Miles and also, less obviously, to Woody Shaw, but which completely avoids retro gestures, even on the standards. The remaining Mobley compositions, 'Three Gifts' and 'Panon Impressions', are well up to scratch. Needless to say, the rhythm section is straight out of the top drawer. Barron is everyone's safety net and, even at this stage, McBride sounds utterly assured and capable of almost anything, though he tends to disappear in a rather compacted mix. The bittersweet note is the splendid drumming of Alan Dawson, who died in 1996, before the disc was – somewhat belatedly – released.

Hank Mobley (1930–86)

TENOR SAXOPHONE

Mobley was playing in R&B bands before joining Max Roach in 1951. Came to prominence in the Jazz Messengers in 1954 and then worked on numerous Blue Note record dates, many of which he led. With Miles Davis, 1961–2, then toured in other hard-bop situations, but eventually left music in the late 1970s through ill-health. Brief attempt at a comeback in 1986 but died of pneumonia shortly after.

*****(*) Peckin' Time**

Blue Note 81574-2 *Mobley; Lee Morgan (t); Wynton Kelly (p); Paul Chambers (b); Charli Persip (d).* 2/58.

****** Soul Station**

Blue Note 95343-2 *Mobley; Wynton Kelly (p); Paul Chambers (b); Art Blakey (d).* 2/60.

*****(*) Workout**

Blue Note 84080-2 *Mobley; Wynton Kelly (p); Grant Green (g); Paul Chambers (b); Philly Joe Jones (d).* 3/61.

***** Dippin'**

Blue Note 46511 *Mobley; Lee Morgan (t); Harold Mabern (p); Larry Ridley (b); Billy Higgins (d).* 6/65.

***** A Caddy For Daddy**

Blue Note 84230-2 *Mobley; Lee Morgan (t); Curtis Fuller (tb); McCoy Tyner (p); Bob Cranshaw (b); Billy Higgins (d).* 12/65.

***** Reach Out**

Blue Note 59964-2 *Mobley; Woody Shaw (t, flhn); Lamont Johnson (p); George Benson (g); Bob Cranshaw (b); Billy Higgins (d).* 1/68.

Mobley's music was documented to almost unreasonable lengths by Blue Note, with a whole raft of albums granted to him as a leader, and countless sideman appearances to go with them. Yet his current representation on CD is still comparatively meagre. A collectors' favourite, his assertive and swinging delivery was undercut by a seemingly reticent tone: next to his peers in the hard-bop tenor gang, he could sound almost pallid. But it shouldn't detract from appreciating a thinker and a solidly reliable player. Despite frequent personal problems, Mobley rarely gave less than his best in front of the mircrophones.

Peckin' Time is typical Blue Note hard bop, fired up by the ebullience of Morgan and the persuasiveness of Mobley's solos. He made many records with Morgan as his partner and they already knew each other's moves so well that there's a symmetry to go with the regulation fireworks. Mobley fans are divided as to whether *Soul Station* or the currently absent *Roll Call* is his masterpiece, but the Rudy Van Gelder Edition of the former is a welcome reminder of how creative a player Mobley was, here transcending his normal consistency and making a modest classic. Good as the other drummers on his records are, Blakey brings a degree more finesse, and their interplay on 'This I Dig Of You' is superb. Hank seldom took ballads at a crawl, preferring a kind of lazy mid-tempo, and 'If I Should Lose You' is one of his best. 'Dig Dis' is a top example of how tough he could sound without falling into bluster. A virtually perfect example of a routine date made immortal by master craftsmen.

Workout is really only a shade behind. Listen to how Mobley flirts with stomping-tenorman clichés on 'Uh Huh' and still turns in a decisively individual solo. Green is a splendid assist and Philly Joe's beat is unstoppable. *Dippin'* and *A Caddy For Daddy* are, by the high standards of his best Blue Notes, relatively ordinary sessions, but they will still satisfy any appetite for authentic and hard-won hard bop. At least a dozen other Mobley Blue Notes are currently in limbo and, of his late-'60s records, only *Reach Out* has been back of late; but what a peculiar session. They start with jazzed versions of 'Reach Out (I'll Be There)' and 'Goin' Out Of My Head', which are as soft as a marshmallow cushion. Thereafter it's down to Blue Note business with four hard-bop nuggets. Hardly Hank's best, but enough to keep the flame just about lit.

Modern Jazz Quartet

GROUP

The MJQ was originally the rhythm section of Dizzy Gillespie's post-war band, originally with Ray Brown on bass and Kenny Clarke on drums. After 1955, Connie Kay became a permanent member, joining pianist John Lewis, vibraphonist Milt Jackson and bassist Percy Heath in what was to become one of the most enduring jazz groups of all time. Often quietly understated and with a conservative image, the MJQ nevertheless created thoughtful and often innovative structures, a reminder that the rhythm section has always been the engine-room of innovation in jazz.

*****(*) The Artistry Of The Modern Jazz Quartet**

Prestige 60016 *Sonny Rollins (ts); John Lewis (p); Milt Jackson (vib); Percy Heath (b); Kenny Clarke (d).* 12/52–7/55.

*****(*) Django**

Original Jazz Classics OJC 057 *As above, except omit Rollins.* 6/53–1/55.

*****(*) MJQ**

Original Jazz Classics OJC 125 *As above, except add Henry Boozier (t), Horace Silver (p).* 6/54, 12/56.

Frequently dismissed – as unexciting, pretentious, bland, Europeanized, pat – the MJQ has remained hugely popular for much of the last 30 years, filling halls and consistently outselling most other jazz acts. The enigma lies in that epithet 'Modern' for, inasmuch as the MJQ shifted more product than anyone else, they were also radicals (or maybe that American hybrid, radical-conservatives) who have done more than most barnstorming revolutionaries to change the nature and form of jazz performance, to free it from its changes-based theme-and-solos clichés. Leader/composer John Lewis has a firm grounding in European classical music, particularly the Baroque, and was a leading light in both Third Stream music and the *Birth Of The Cool* sessions with Gerry Mulligan and Miles Davis. From the outset he attempted to infuse jazz performance with a consciousness of form, using elements of through-composition, counterpoint, melodic variation and, above all, fugue to multiply the trajectories of improvisation. And just as people still, even now, like stories with a beginning, middle and end, people have liked the well-made quality of MJQ performances which, on their night, don't lack for old-fashioned excitement.

The fact that they had been Dizzy's rhythm section led people to question the group's viability as an independent performing unit. The early recordings more than resolve that doubt. Lewis has never been an exciting performer (in contrast to Jackson, who is one of the great soloists in jazz), but his brilliant grasp of structure is evident from the beginning. Of the classic MJQ pieces – 'One Bass Hit', 'The Golden Striker', 'Bags' Groove' – none characterizes the group more completely than Lewis's 'Django', first recorded in the session of December 1954. The Prestige is a useful CD history of the early days of the band, but it's probably better to hear the constituent sessions in their entirety. Some of the material on the original two-disc vinyl format has been removed to make way for a Sonny Rollins/MJQ set ('No Moe', 'The Stopper', 'In A Sentimental Mood', 'Almost Like Being In Love'), which is a pity, for this material was long available elsewhere.

***** Concorde**

Original Jazz Classics OJC 002 *As above, except Connie Kay (d) replaces Clarke; omit Boozier, Silver.* 7/55.

*****(*) Fontessa**

Atlantic 81329 *As above.* 1 & 2/56.

*****(*) Pyramid**

Atlantic 81340 *As above.* 8 & 12/59, 1/60.

****** Dedicated To Connie**

Atlantic 82763 2CD *As above.* 5/60.

*****(*) Lonely Woman**

Atlantic 81227 5361-2 *As above.* 62.

***** The Comedy**

Atlantic 81390 *As above, except add Diahann Carroll (v).* 10/60, 1/62.

Connie Kay slipped into the band without a ripple; sadly, his ill-health and death were the only circumstances in the next 40 years of activity necessitating a personnel change. His cooler approach, less overwhelming than Clarke's could be, was ideal, and he sounds right from the word 'go'. His debut was on the fine *Concorde*, which sees Lewis trying to blend jazz improvisation with European counterpoint. It combines some superb fugal writing with a swing that would have sounded brighter if recording quality had been better. Though the integration is by no means always complete, it's more appealing in its very roughness than the slick Bach-chat that turns up on some of the Atlantics.

The label didn't quite know what to do with the MJQ, but the Erteguns were always alert to the demographics and, to be fair, they knew good music when they heard it. One of the problems the group had in this, arguably their most consistent phase creatively, was that everything appeared to need conceptual packaging, even when the music suggested no such thing. Chance associations, like the celebrated version of Ornette's 'Lonely Woman', were doubtless encouraged by the fact that they shared a label, and this was all to the good; there are, though, signs that in later years, as rock began to swallow up a bigger and bigger market share, the group began to suffer from the inappropriate packaging. Though home-grown compositions reappear throughout the band's history (there's a particularly good 'Django' on *Pyramid*), there are also constant references to standard repertoire as well and some of these are among the group's greatest achievements.

By the same inverted snobbery that demands standards rather than 'pretentious classical rubbish', it's long been a useful cop-out to profess admiration only for those MJQ albums featuring right-on guests. The earlier Silver collaboration isn't as well known as a justly famous encounter with Sonny Rollins at Music Inn, reprising their encounters of 1951, 1952 and 1953, which were really the saxophonist's gigs, and though there is a certain perversity in its disappearance from the catalogue it may help re-inforce our conviction – one widely shared by MJQ fans – that the group did not require the services of horn players to produce legitimate, creative jazz.

Lewis's first exploration of characters from the *commedia dell'arte* came in *Fontessa*, an appropriately chill and stately record that can seem a little enigmatic, even off-putting. He develops these interests considerably in the simply titled *Comedy*, which largely consists of dulcet character-sketches with unexpected twists and quietly violent dissonances. The themes of *commedia* are remarkably appropriate to a group who have always presented themselves in sharply etched silhouette, playing a music that is deceptively smooth and untroubled but which harbours considerable jazz feeling and, as on both *Fontessa* and *Comedy*, considerable disruption to conventional harmonic progression.

Given Lewis's interests and accomplishments as an orchestrator, there have been surprisingly few jazz-group-with-orchestra experiments. More typical, perhaps, than the 1987 *Three Windows* is what Lewis does on *Lonely Woman*. One of the very finest of the group's albums, this opens with a breathtaking arrangement of Ornette Coleman's haunting dirge and then proceeds with small-group performances of three works – 'Animal Dance', 'Lamb, Leopard' and 'Fugato' – which were originally conceived for orchestral performance. Remarkably, Lewis's small-group arrangements still manage to give an impression of symphonic voicings.

Kay's ill-health finally overcame him in December 1994 and the following February, the MJQ issued in his memory a concert from 1960, recorded in what was then Yugoslavia, a relatively innocuous destination on the international tour. Whatever its historical resonance, it inspired (as John Lewis discovered when he auditioned these old tapes and has asserted ever since) one of the truly great MJQ performances, certainly one of the very best available to us on disc. It knocks into a cocked hat even the new edition of the so-called *Last Concert*. Jackson's playing is almost transcendentally wonderful on 'Bags' Groove' and 'I Remember Clifford', and the conception of Lewis's opening *commedia* sequence could hardly be clearer or more satisfying. *Dedicated To Connie* is a very special record and has always been our favourite of the bunch, but renewed acquaintance suggests a few glossed-over cracks in the edifice, which is why, this time at least, it's denied the ultimate accolade of a crown. Perhaps, like the group itself, a lay-off will restore the lustre.

***** In A Crowd**

Knit Classics 3002 *As above.* 9/63.

Unusual fare for Knitting Factory, but certainly something of a find. Released in 1998 on licence from Alan Douglas's label, *In A Crowd* documents the group's 1963 performance at the Monterey Jazz Festival. We have had a bootleg copy of the same performances for some time, arranged in a different order and minus the opening performance of Ray Brown's 'Pyramid'. The poorly pressed disc was undated and untitled and merely stated *MJQ Live*. We were never able to pin down its vintage, which is telling since these seven tracks could have come from almost any point in the group's career from 1955 to 1974. Collectors will be delighted to have another point in the chronology filled in.

****(*) Blues On Bach**
Atlantic 7831393 *As above.* 11/73.

Lewis was always suspended somewhere between Bach and the old blues, and this intriguing project alternates original blues tunes with adaptations of J.S. Bach which stop short of suggesting that he and not W.C. Handy was the father of jazz blues but which nevertheless point up the kinship between the styles. As a further tribute to the father of classical music, Lewis doubles on harpsichord and still manages to get a solid, flowing sound. Jackson is as masterful as ever and his own 'Blues in H (B)' even makes reference to the traditional B-A-C-H signature-theme.

*****(*) The Complete Last Concert**
Atlantic 81976 2CD *As above.* 11/74.

Given the closeness of the relationship and its prolific nature, it wasn't entirely surprising that the four should have decided after more than 20 years as a unit to give their individual careers a little space and air. What was billed as the last concert was very much considered to be just that, rather than a shrewd marketing ploy at the start of a short sabbatical. It would be wrong to say that the music was inspired or more intense than usual, but certainly these are all very fine performances. The short bebop section in the middle – 'Confirmation', 'Round Midnight', 'A Night In Tunisia' – gives the lie to any prejudice that the group were uneasy with those jaggy changes and rhythms; they had, after all, cut their professional teeth in such a context. But it's the other, more familiar MJQ material that is most impressive. There are several blues pieces carried over from *Blues On Bach*, versions of 'The Golden Striker' and 'Cylinder' and a few of Lewis's more impressionistic compositions, such as 'Skating In Central Park' and 'Jasmine Tree'. One additional outstanding performance was the arrangement of Rodrigo's Miles-blessed 'Concierto de Aranjuez'. Strongly recommended to anyone who values the group, and effortlessly representative of its ability to shift between styles and moods.

****(*) Together Again**
Pablo 2308244 *As above.* 7/82.

***** Together Again – Echoes**
Pablo 2312142 *As above.* 3/84.

***** Topsy – This One's For Basie**
Pablo 2310917 *As above.* 6/85.

There is little question that the energy and inventiveness of the band were diluted by time. By the early 1970s the MJQ had become stylists first and improvisers only then. They disbanded in 1974, after a final flourish; but after seven years in the wilderness, and they were notably uncreative years for each of the members, they got together again and continued to produce vital music, much of it written by Lewis and all of it, as before, technically and structurally challenging. *Together Again* was recorded at the Montreux Jazz Festival. After the hiatus, the group seems content to deliver a set of familiar material – 'Django', 'The Cylinder', 'Woody'N'You' and what is listed as 'Bags' New Groove', though how substantially it really differs from the old one isn't entirely obvious. It's a nice, light performance, typical festival fare. The 1985 disc isn't, as it has sometimes been advertised, a programme of Basie tunes, but a tribute to the Count written almost entirely by Lewis. The only exceptions are 'Topsy' itself, 'Nature Boy' (which is played, unaccompanied, b Jackson) and Milt's composition, 'Reunion Blues'. The playing is sharp and engaging and both Lewis and Jackson are in fine form.

***** Three Windows**
Atlantic 254833 *As above, except add New York Chamber Symphony.* 87.

Almost a John Lewis album, this beautifully executed orchestral project included music which had been written for the Roger Vadim film, *No Sun in Venice*, almost 30 years earlier. There is also a wonderful tone poem, 'Day In Dubrovnik', and one of the best-recorded arrangements of the evergreen 'Django'. Not an essential purchase, but a deeply satisfying record.

***** For Ellington**
East West 790926 *As above, except omit NY Chamber Symphony.* 2/88.

Lewis's explorations into the wider ramifications of jazz composition have drawn him closer and closer to Ellington, and the Ducal tribute on East West combines the original title-track and 'Maestro E.K.E.' (standing for Edward Kennedy Ellington) with classics like 'Ko-Ko', 'Jack The Bear', 'Prelude To A Kiss' and 'Rockin' In Rhythm'. Invigorated by that contact, the MJQ sounded as if they could go on for ever.

***** A Celebration**
Atlantic 782538 *As above, except omit Kay; add Wynton Marsalis, Harry 'Sweets' Edison (t), Freddie Hubbard (flhn), Phil Woods (as), Nino Tempo, Illinois Jacquet (ts), Branford Marsalis (ts, ss), Mickey Roker (d), Bobby McFerrin (v).* 6/92, 4/93.

The fortieth-anniversary celebrations had to continue without Connie Kay and with Mickey Roker standing in. The guest-star formula worked as well as ever, and the MJQ machine moved smoothly along, the Cadillac of jazz groups.

****** MJQ 40**
Atlantic 7 82330 2 4CD *John Lewis (p); Milt Jackson (vib); Percy Heath (b); Connie Kay (d); with Bernie Glow, Joe Newman, Ernie Royal, Clark Terry, Snooky Young (t); Paul Ingraham, Jimmy Buffington (frhn); Jimmy Cleveland, Garnett Brown, Tony Studd, Kai Winding (tb); Don Butterfield (tba); Jimmy Giuffre, Bill McColl (cl); Robert DiDomenica (f); Manny Ziegler (bsn); Paul Desmond, Charlie Mariano, Phil Woods (as); Sonny Rollins, Richie Kamuca, Seldon Powell (ts); Wally Kane (bs); Laurindo Almeida, Howard Collins (g); Joe Tekula (clo); Betty Glamann (hp); Diahann Carroll, The Swingle Singers (v).* 52–88.

****(*) The Best Of The Modern Jazz Quartet**
Pablo 2405 423 *John Lewis (p); Milt Jackson (vib); Percy Heath (b); Connie Kay (d).* 80s.

A magnificently packaged ruby-anniversary celebration which draws on all stages and aspects of the group's career. Fifty-four tracks on four CDs taking in music from such records as *Plastic Dreams, Live At The Lighthouse, Third Stream Music,* and from the fine 1966 concert in Japan. As an introduction to the group's music, the accompanying booklet (which includes a complete discography) could hardly be bettered. The Pablo sampler does a pretty good job of boiling down and reducing the group's work since the reunion of 1981, but most fans will have the bulk of this material anyway and the selection doesn't have the logic and pace of an original album.

Charnett Moffett

BASS

One of the sons of Charles Moffett, he was a bright young star in the New York scene of the '80s, although his career seems to have settled down fairly significantly since.

***** Planet Home**

Evidence ECD 22122 *Moffett; Bary Lynn Sternely (ss); Kenny Kirkland (p, ky); Charles Moffett, Codaryl Moffett (d); Don Alias (perc); Charisse Moffett (v).*

*****(*) Still Life**

Evidence ECD 22180 *Moffett; Rachel Z (p, syn); Cindy Blackman (d).* 6/96.

Lead bass-lines – on piccolo bass or guitar – are always a temptation, and the young man's much-prized hyperactivity, which made him a first-call player on the New York scene, occasionally tripped him up on his early records, including work for Blue Note that has gone into the deletion file. *Still Life* is a huge improvement. Looming over it are the spirits of Jimi Hendrix, Jaco Pastorius and Miles Davis. Miles's brooding, bass-heavy funk is perhaps the dominant style, but it's Jaco's almost in-humanly virtuosic, fretless bass which inspires the title-track and 'Jungle Travel'. Miles's cover of 'Human Nature' legitimized the Michael Jackson songbook for jazz improvisers, and Charnett weighs in here with a lovely version of 'Heal The World', un-expectedly affecting. Both Rachel Z, a Herbie Hancock discovery, and the now almost veteran Blackman play with great restraint and taste. No histrionics; no pointlessly show-off stuff; just lots of intelligent music. Thoroughly recommended.

Cody Moffett

DRUMS

Son of Charles and brother of Charnett, Cody is the third member of the Moffett clan to be a jazz leader on CD.

*****(*) Evidence**

Telarc CD-83343 *Moffett; Wallace Roney (t); Kenny Garrett (as); Ravi Coltrane (ss, ts); Antoine Roney (ts); Charnett Moffett (b).* 3/93.

Another Moffett makes a pleasing debut as leader. The provocative element here is Moffett's reluctance to tie his flag to one mast: there are nods to Coltrane ('Equinox'), Coleman ('Blues Connotation'), bebop ('Salt Peanuts'), Monk ('Evidence'), mid-stream hard bop ('Bolivia') and even Freddie Hubbard ('Red Clay'). Surprisingly, most of it works very well. Each of the horns makes a fist of their differing assignments – Garrett does an interesting take on Ornette, and Roney's spin through 'Salt Peanuts' is good fun – and the drummer's enthusiasm carries them over any bumpy spots.

Anders Mogenson

DRUMS, KEYBOARDS

Young Danish drummer with rock and jazz experience, here leading his own small groups.

***** Taking Off**

Storyville STCD 4198 *Mogenson; Rick Margitza (ss, ts); Gary Thomas(ts); Niels Lan Doky (p); Ron McClure (b).* 10/94.

****(*) Taking Off Again**

Storyville STCD 4227 *Mogenson; Hans Ulrik (ss, ts); Henrik Lindstrand (org); Niclas Knudsen (g); Anders Christiansen (b).* 2/98.

Good drummer, great band, five originals, one Monk, one standard. The complementary energies of Margitza and Thomas are smartly filtered through the session, each man having a ballad apiece, and Margitza just wins out with the tart soprano brooding on 'Lonely'. Lan Doky, who also produced, is in top fettle, and Mogenson drives without overpowering. Typical modern blowing, and typically impressive.

The second outing is by the group Mogenson had just been leading on tour. Some of this has a pop-jazz feel to it, Mogenson turning to rock-inflected beats at times, and, capably as Ulrik and Knudsen play, there isn't really enough character about the music to make this one stand out from a host of similar records.

Louis Moholo (born 1940)

DRUMS, PERCUSSION

Born in Cape Town, Moholo led his own big band before joining the mixed-race Blue Notes in 1962. Left with them for Europe in 1964. Toured with Steve Lacy before returning to London in 1967, which has been his base since. In numerous groups, from Brotherhood Of Breath to his own Viva La Black, Moholo has been a powerhouse of versatility and strength.

***** Exile**

Ogun OGCD 003 *Moholo; Sean Bergin, Steve Williamson (reeds); Paul Rogers (b).* 90.

***** Freedom Tour: Live In South Afrika, 1993**

Ogun OGCD 006 *Moholo; Claude Deppa (t, flhn, v); Sean Bergin (ts, f, concertina, v); Toby Delius (ts, v); Jason Yarde (as, ss, v); Pule Pheto (p); Roberto Bellatalla (b); Thebe Lipere (perc).* 93.

In the 1960s, radical American improvisers (with separatist agenda firmly in mind) renewed their interest in African percussion. What was quickly evident was that traditional African musics frequently anticipated the methodologies of free jazz and that the sometimes anarchic energies of contemporary African jazz were already more abstract than the prevailing American models. In Europe, for a variety of reasons, this was perceived much more readily, and there was a quicker and less ideological trade-off between African jazz and popular music on the one hand, and free music. Louis Moholo, more than most of the South African exiles active on the jazz scene in Britain (but much like the late Johnny Dyani and the late Dudu Pukwana), was able to make the transition without undue strain. His own bands – Spirits Rejoice, Viva La Black, the African Drum Ensemble – have always contained free or abstract elements, and Moholo has always been in demand as a more experimental improviser, where his drive and intensity are comparable to those of Americans Milford Graves and Andrew Cyrille.

Exile is a hot, dangerous session, with Bergin's ferocious statements in constant opposition to Williamson's much cooler delivery, and with Rogers and Moholo working independently of the horns most of the time. 'Wathinta Amododa' is the main piece, but most of its initial power is thrown away in an overlong development-cum-denouement.

Viva La Black's tour and roving workshop for young South African musicians was, inevitably, a powerfully moving experience for Moholo; much of that comes across on the live record, fighting through a not very good recording which resists even Steve Beresford's skill at the final mix. Many of the tracks are short song-forms, some of them traditional; only the opening 'Woza' is substantially longer than five minutes, but the whole thing has the feel of a long, continuous suite, mostly celebratory in nature but with a few, entirely expected, dark corners and ambiguities.

Miff Mole (1898–1961)

TROMBONE

Mole pioneered the development of the trombone as a viable jazz instrument, having mastered a fluency and mobility on the horn which was almost unprecedented at the time of his earliest recordings in 1921. He became one of the kingpin figures in the New York dance-band and session-scene of the '20s but moved into more anonymous studio work in the '30s. Later spells with the Condon gang and some '40s dates for Commodore have been largely forgotten, as was Mole himself, ill and up against it in the '50s. He died, in penury, in 1961.

****** Slippin' Around**

Frog DGF19 *Mole; Red Nichols (c, t); Leo McConville, Phil Napoleon (t); Dudley Fosdick (mel); Jimmy Dorsey (cl, as); Fud Livingston, Pee Wee Russell (cl, ts); Frank Teschemacher (cl); Babe Russin (ts); Adrian Rollini (bsx); Arthur Schutt, Lennie Hayton, Ted Shapiro, Joe Sullivan (p); Eddie Lang, Carl Kress (g); Dick McDonough (bj, g); Eddie Condon (bj); Joe Tarto, Jack Hansen (tba); Vic Berton, Ray Bauduc, Chauncey Morehouse, Gene Krupa, Stan King (d).* 1/27–2/30.

****** Slippin' Around – Again!**

Frog DGF20 *Similar to above, except add Gordon Griffin (t), Paul Ricci (cl), Toots Mondello (as), Frank Signorelli (p), Sid Weiss (b), Sam Weiss (d), Chick Bullock (v).* 2/27–2/37.

Miff Mole was one of the master jazz musicians of the 1920s. Though subsequently eclipsed by Teagarden, Dorsey and others, he was the first trombonist to make any significant impression as a soloist, sounding fluent and imaginative as far back as the early recordings of the Original Memphis Five and Ladd's Black Aces at the beginning of the decade. His partnership with Red Nichols was as interesting in its way as that of Armstrong and Hines or Beiderbecke and Trumbauer. Though sometimes seen as a kind of jazz chamber music, or at worst a white New York imitation of the real thing, their records were a smart, hard-bitten development out of their hot-dance environment and, with no vocals, little hokum and plenty of space for improvisation, the music has an uncompromising stance which may surprise those who've heard about it second-hand.

The first of these overdue compilations brings together most of the sessions by Miff's Molers for OKeh, along with four Victor titles by Red and Miff's Stompers and a further pair of tunes credited to the Red Nichols Orchestra. The earlier dates have no more than five or six musicians on them, and titles like 'Hurricane' and 'Delirium' are intense little set-pieces. The later sessions have more players and feel more orchestrated, less private, though no less intriguing: two versions of Fud Livingston's 'Feeling No Pain' are remarkable, and so is the furious charge through 'Original Dixieland One Step'. Nichols, Russell, Rollini and others all have their moments, but Mole himself, alert and quick-witted and always able to find a fruitful line, has no peers here. The final two sessions, with the much-praised 'Shim-Me-Sha-Wabble' among them, seem rowdier and less personal. John R.T. Davies has worked his usual magic with what sounds like a set of mint originals: these have never sounded better.

The second volume is handled to similar standards. There are six titles by Red & Miff's Stompers, 15 by the Molers, two interesting airshots from 1936 featuring Mole with an unidentified band, and most of the titles from a 1937 date for Vocalion by a 'new' set of Molers. As Max Harrison once remarked, the later sessions by the Molers are less private and more public, which makes them neither better nor worse, only different. Mole's solo on 'Moanin' Low', delicate and nuanced next to the rowdiness of the closing chorus, underlines his originality, and it's a small sadness in jazz history that this talented man was largely left behind by the music as it progressed.

Lello Molinari

BASS

Italian bassist at work on the indigenous contemporary Boston scene.

***** No More Mr Nice Guy**

Accurate QAC-4501 *Molinari; George Garzone (ss, ts); Douglas Yates (as, bcl); Luigi Tessarollo (g); Matt Wilson (d).* 9/91.

***** On A Boston Night**

Accurate AC-4502 *As above, except Rick Peckham (g), Bob Gulotti (d) replace Tessarollo and Wilson.* 3/94.

Molinari has hooked up with some of the interesting local voices on the Boston scene. The first album is a studio date and runs through a gamut of styles: clever post-bop on 'C'era Chi?', flat-out storming on 'Stunt Cars'. Yates (who, along with Wilson, comes from the Either/Orchestra) and the dependable Garzone make a useful, gregarious front line, with their four horns alternated for piquant contrast; Tessarollo is impressive but sometimes predictably noisy. The subsequent live album is looser, less frenetic in its up-tempo pieces, but sometimes dull: Garzone's attempted tone-poem, 'Echoes Of Rome', is a washout. Peckham takes a more modulated role, and the leader plays with terrific propulsion without stealing too much limelight on both records. An interesting note on Boston's fertile and under-appreciated jazz community.

T.S Monk (born 1949)

DRUMS

Thelonious Jr made his public debut with his dad at the age of just ten and, after some time away from jazz, has devoted himself to the old man's memory and to a sound that is intended to recapture the melodic energy of '50s Blue Note hard bop. Influenced by Max Roach and Tony Williams, T.S. has become a strong, clear-voiced exponent and a fine writer.

**** Take One**

Blue Note 99614 2 *Monk; Don Sickler (t); Bobby Porcelli (as); Willie Williams (ts); Ronnie Mathews (p); James Genus (b).* 10/91.

Crude hard bop which murders a trio of dad's tunes with the kind of blunt insouciance that might be forgivable were he no older than Denardo Coleman was when *he* entered the family trade. The parallel isn't entirely incidental. They both have a clubbing, broom-handle sound, derived from R&B.

We certainly don't court controversy deliberately, but few reviews in this guide have sparked quite so much debate as these admittedly unenthusiastic remarks about T.S. How much of this can be explained by familial loyalty, how much by genuine enthusiasm for these drab and formulaic records isn't clear. One hopes the former. The arrangements are largely the work of Don Sickler, who also turns up on the second record, below. Covers of Hank Mobley's 'Infra-Rae', Clifford Jordan's 'Bear Cat' and two Kenny Dorham tunes all go the same way as a double-, then quadruple-time 'Round Midnight'. Monk Sr had a subtle and often overlooked instinct for dynamic modulation; Jr hectors. That might make sense of Tommy Turrentine's 'Shoutin'', but the band sounds ragged and under-rehearsed, and Rudy van Gelder's engineering skills can't make up the deficit. Van Gelder had also been on hand 38 years earlier when the three-year-old T.S. Monk shouted out take numbers as his dad recorded 'Think Of One' with Sonny Rollins (see OJC 016) in November 1953. It might have been a nice touch to have included that little bit of studio business at the head of T.S.'s 1991 version.

***** The Changing Of The Guard**

Blue Note 789050 *Monk; Don Sickler (t); Bobby Porcelli (as); Willie Williams (ts); Ronnie Mathews (p); Scott Colley (b).* 2/93.

****** Monk On Monk**

N2K Encoded Music N2KW 10017 *Monk; Laurie Frink, Virgil Jones, Wallace Roney, Arturo Sandoval, Don Sickler, Clark Terry (t); Roy Hargrove (flhn); Eddie Bert (tb); David Amram, John Clark (frhn); Bobby Porcelli, Bobby Watson (as); Wayne Shorter (ts, ss); Jimmy Heath, Roger Rosenberg, Grover Washington, Willie Williams (ts); Howard Johnson (bs, tba); Geri Allen, Herbie Hancock, Ronnie Mathews, Danilo Perez (p); Ron Carter, Dave Holland, Christian McBride, Dave Wang (b); Nnenna Freelon, Kevin Mahogany, Dianne Reeves (v).* 2/97.

For the record, no rating in a previous edition caused as much dismay as a lowly two stars for *Take One*. It's encouraging to be able to note, also for the record, that takes two and three represent a signal improvement. Same band, but an altogether subtler approach for *The Changing Of The Guard*. Monk resists the urge to thrash, and the soloists – Sickler in particular – play with urgency *and* taste. The Monk Sr material is done with thought and some imaginative flair.

By the time *Monk On Monk* appeared, one might have expected the rising-fifty-year-old to have pushed out into territory he could legitimately call his own, rather than continue playing dad's work. The dedication and the affection that go with it are hard to fault and some of the playing is very fine indeed. On this occasion, too, T.S. has assembled a superband which must have been the envy of the block. All the songs are by Monk, though 'Ruby My Dear' and 'In Walked Bud' have been transformed into vocal vehicles for Kevin Mahogany and Nnenna Freelon respectively. Herbie Hancock and Ron Carter solo on 'Two Timer', but the best double act of the evening bouquet goes to Bobby Watson and Wallace Roney for their spirited and lyrical attack on 'Jackie-ing'. A big, stellar cast and an album that entirely lives up to its billing. Fair do's; whatever our misgivings about earlier outings and however much we might question T.S.'s continued devotion to the flame, this is a spendid recording, multi-dimensional, richly textured, carefully thought out and thoroughly satisfying.

****(*) Cross Talk**

N2K 4202 *Monk; Don Sickler (t, flhn); Willie Williams (ss, ts, cl); John Gordon (as); Bobby Porcelli (as, cl, af); Ray Gallon (p, syn); Gary Wang (b); Patricia Barber (v).* 5/99.

A turn towards a new and funkier sound. T.S. uses electric drums and relies somewhat on synthesizers as well as conventional horns. Don Sickler's arrangements are generous and tough-minded and 'Heart' is testimony to his skills, reminiscent of the work he has done with Bobby Watson. 'A Chant For Bu' pays a debt to an ancestral influence, though *Cross Talk* as a whole is as far from the Messengers as could be imagined.

Thelonious Monk (1917–82)

PIANO

One of the giants of music, Monk conforms to no school or movement, and to no known law of development. Far from being unrecognized in his lifetime, he was a major star who retired early, recording nothing in the last few years of his life, presumably in order that the rest of the musical world could catch up. His angular, asymmetrical themes are rooted in the blues, but they accord to no logic other than their own. A Monk performance was always an adventure.

****** Genius Of Modern Music: Volume 1**
Blue Note 781510 *Monk; Kenny Dorham, Idrees Sulieman, George Taitt (t); Lou Donaldson, Sahib Shihab, Danny Quebec West (as); Billy Smith, Lucky Thompson (ts); Milt Jackson (vib); Nelson Boyd, Al McKibbon, Bob Paige, Gene Ramey, John Simmons (b); Art Blakey, Max Roach, Shadow Wilson (d).* 10/47–7/48.

****** Genius Of Modern Music: Volume 2**
Blue Note 781511 *As above, except add John Coltrane (ts).* 10/47–5/52.

♛ ** The Complete Blue Note Recordings**
Blue Note 830363 4CD *As above, except add Ahmed Abdul-Malik (b), Kenny Hagood (v).* 47–58.

****** The Best Of Thelonious Monk: The Blue Note Years**
Blue Note 795636 *As above.* 47–51.

Monk is one of the giants of modern American music whose output ranks with that of Morton and Ellington, as *composition* of the highest order. Though no one questions his skills as a pianist (they were compounded of stride, blues and a more romantic strain derived from Teddy Wilson and filtered through Monk's wonderfully lateral intelligence), it is as a composer that he has made the greatest impact on subsequent jazz music. Even so, it is vital to recognize that the music and the playing style are necessary to each other and precisely complementary. Though he has attracted more dedicated interpreters since his death than almost any musician (Ornette Coleman and John Coltrane perhaps approach his standing with other players, but from very different perspectives), Monk tunes played by anyone else always seem to lack a certain conclusive authenticity. Frequently misunderstood by critics and fans (and also by the less discerning of his fellow musicians), he received due public recognition only quite late in his career, by which time younger pianists originally encouraged by him and his example (Bud Powell is the foremost) had recorded and died and been canonized. It's now questioned whether Monk was ever, as he once appeared, a founding father of bop. Though some of his work, like 'In Walked Bud' on *Genius Of Modern Music*, utilized a straightforward chord sequence, and though 'Eronel', one of the additional tracks from the critical July 1951 session with Milt Jackson, is relatively orthodox bop, Monk's interest in tough, pianistic melody, displaced rhythm and often extreme harmonic distortion (as in his treatment of 'Carolina Moon') rather sets him apart from the bop mainstream.

The Blue Notes are essential Monk recordings, no less achieved and magisterial for being his first as a leader. It isn't often that we demote a coronetted item, but the appearance of *The Complete Blue Note Recordings*, which takes in a rediscovered live recording with John Coltrane at the Five Spot in New York City (far from pristine but musical gold-dust), inevitably changes the picture slightly. It is tempting to say that all that the newcomer needs is here, expensive as it is. For those who can't quite stretch to it or who need convincing, the *Best Of* set is very acceptable indeed, with 'Epistrophy', 'Misterioso', 'Round About Midnight', 'Evidence', 'Ruby, My Dear' and 'Straight, No Chaser' all included from the classic performances.

Monk recorded only intermittently over the next ten years, which makes them particularly valuable. Thwarted first by an American Federation of Musicians recording ban and later by a prison sentence and a blacklisting, Monk took time to regain the highs of these remarkable sides. The earliest of the sessions, with Sulieman, Danny Quebec West and Billy Smith, is not particularly inspired, though the pianist's contribution is instantly identifiable; his solo on 'Thelonious', built up out of minimal thematic potential, is emotionally powerful and restlessly allusive. A month later he was working with a more enterprising group (the difference in Blakey's response between the two sessions is remarkable) and producing his first classic recordings – of 'In Walked Bud' and 'Round About Midnight'.

The addition of Milt Jackson exactly a year later for the session that yielded 'Epistrophy' and 'Misterioso' was a turning point in his music, enormously extending its rhythmic potential and harmonic complexity. Jackson who, because of his association with the Modern Jazz Quartet, is now rather apt to be dismissed as a player lacking in improvisational excitement, makes an incalculable contribution to the music, here and on the session of July 1951 which yielded the classic 'Straight, No Chaser'. The later recordings on the set are much more conventionally arranged and lack the excitement and sheer imaginative power of the earlier cuts, but they do help overturn the received image of Monk as a man who wrote one beautiful ballad and then so dedicated the rest of his career to intractable dissonance as to set himself apart entirely from the main currents of modern jazz. Between 1952 and 1955, when he contracted to Riverside Records, Monk's career was relatively in the doldrums. However, he had already recorded enough material to guarantee him a place in any significant canon. No jazz fan should be without these records.

****** Thelonious Monk Trio / Blue Monk: Volume 2**
Prestige CDJZD 009 *Monk; Ray Copeland (t); Frank Foster (ts); Percy Heath, Gary Mapp, Curley Russell (b); Art Blakey, Max Roach (d).* 10/52–9/54.

*****(*) Thelonious Monk**
Original Jazz Classics OJC 010 *Monk; Percy Heath, Gary Mapp (p); Art Blakey, Max Roach (d).* 10/52–9/54.

*****(*) Thelonious Monk / Sonny Rollins**
Original Jazz Classics OJC 059 *Monk; Sonny Rollins (ts); Julius Watkins (frhn); Percy Heath, Tommy Potter (b); Art Blakey, Willie Jones, Art Taylor (d).* 11/53–10/54.

*****(*) MONK**
Original Jazz Classics OJC 016 *Monk; Ray Copeland (t); Julius Watkins (frhn); Sonny Rollins, Frank Foster (ts); Percy Heath, Curley Russell (b); Art Blakey, Willie Jones (d).* 11/53–5/54.

The end of Monk's Prestige period included some remarkably inventive and adventurous music, which isn't always played as well as it deserves. The trios with Heath and Blakey remain among the best performances of his career, however, and should on no account be missed. The first of this group is a valuable twofer reissue of Prestige P7027 and 7848, with original liner-notes in each case; though it involves repetition with the OJCs, it's a useful way of getting the best of the material on a single CD. OJC 010 repeats all the material save for four quintet tracks from May 1954 featuring Copeland and Foster on 'We See', 'Smoke Gets

In Your Eyes', 'Locomotive' and the too-little-played 'Hackensack', all of which are taken from *MONK*. The latter album also includes additional material from the November 1953 recordings with Sonny Rollins which yielded OJC 059. That date was marked by the astonishing 'Friday The 13th', a brilliant use of simultaneous thematic statements which doesn't quite come off in this performance but which sufficiently survives the group's uncertainty to mark it out as daring. The September 1954 session with Heath and Blakey was originally the basis of the Prestige *Monk's Moods*, and it's good to have it filled out with the additional 'Work' and 'Nutty', which are also on *Monk/Rollins*. Even with a repeat of 'Blue Monk' (the definitive version) and the solo slot, 'Just A Gigolo', the Prestige is unbeatable value, clocking in at nearly 78 minutes.

Monk's treatment of standards is remarkable. When he strips a tune down, he arranges the constituent parts by the numbers, like a rifleman at boot camp, with the overall shape and function always evident. On 'These Foolish Things' and 'Sweet And Lovely' he never for a moment loses sight of the melody and, as with the originals, builds a carefully crafted performance that is light-years away from the conventional theme–solo–theme format into which even relatively adventurous jazz performance seemed to be locked. A vital episode in modern jazz; the precise format chosen will depend on level of interest and budget, for it's almost impossible to go wrong.

***(*) **Solo 1954**

Vogue 111502 *Monk (p solo). 6/54.*

There is now, of course, very little left in the chest for 'rediscovery'. These unaccompanied sides are a welcome exception. Claude Carrière's claim that these are the only solo pieces he 'ever' recorded is of course incorrect. However, they are rare enough to merit careful attention now. It's a fairly straightforward roster of compositions, with 'Smoke Gets In Your Eyes' (a standard the pianist very much liked to play and had just recorded with his quintet) thrown in for good measure. 'Evidence' and 'Off Minor' are played chunkily, with ironic trills round the end of the melody, and there are moments when one might be forgiven for thinking that Monk was sending the whole thing up. The last phrases of 'Hackensack' are certainly intended to be ironic, as he stomps round the key changes. There is no information about the studio set-up or the piano Monk was given. On the strength of this, it sounds rather boxy, but there are oddities with the recording in places, which may suggest that the original tape-speed was uncertain. This doesn't mar a thoroughly enjoyable and historically important reissue, however.

*** **Plays Duke Ellington**

Original Jazz Classics OJC 024 *Monk; Oscar Pettiford (b); Kenny Clarke (d). 7/55.*

*** **The Unique Thelonious Monk**

Original Jazz Classics OJC 064 *Monk; Oscar Pettiford (b); Art Blakey (d). 3–4/56.*

A curious start at Riverside. Orrin Keepnews remembers that Monk spent an age simply picking out the Ellington tunes at the piano and trying to get them straight. It's a respectful nod from one master to another, but not much more. *The Unique* is a standards album which doesn't quite go to the extremes of demolition which Monk chose when dropping a standard into one of his otherwise original dates, and Pettiford doesn't seem like the best choice for bassist.

**** **Brilliant Corners**

Original Jazz Classics OJC 026 *Monk; Clark Terry (t); Ernie Henry (as); Sonny Rollins (ts); Oscar Pettiford (b); Max Roach (d). 12/56.*

A staggering record, imperfect and patched together after the sessions, but one of the most vivid insights into Monk's music. The title-tune was so difficult that no single perfect take was finished (after 25 tries), and what we hear is a spliced-together piece of music. Full of tensions within the band, the record somehow delivers utterly compelling accounts of 'Pannonica', 'Bemsha Swing', 'Ba-Lue Bolivar Ba-lues Are' as well as the title-piece, and Monk ties it up with a one-take reading of 'I Surrender Dear'.

**** **Thelonious Himself**

Original Jazz Classics OJC 254 *Monk; John Coltrane (ts); Wilbur Ware (b). 4/57.*

**** **Thelonious Monk With John Coltrane**

Original Jazz Classics OJC 039 *Monk; Ray Copeland (t); Gigi Gryce (as); Coleman Hawkins, John Coltrane (ts); Wilbur Ware (b); Shadow Wilson, Art Blakey (d). 4–6/57.*

**** **Monk's Music**

Original Jazz Classics OJC 084 *Monk; Ray Copeland (t); Gigi Gryce (as); Coleman Hawkins, John Coltrane (ts); Wilbur Ware (b); Art Blakey (d). 6/57.*

Thelonious Himself is a solo album, and one of his definitive statements up to this point. Alone at last, Monk's prevarications on his own pieces begin to sound definitive as each progresses: he unpicks them and lays them out again with almost scientific precision, but the immediacy of each interpretation is anything but detached. 'Functional' was probably never given a better reading than here, and his accompanying interpretations of standards are scarcely less compelling, melody and rhythm placed under new lights in each one. Capping it is the trio version of 'Monk's Mood' with Coltrane and Ware, and again, even with all the many versions of this tune which are extant, this one is unlike any other.

The sessions which made up *Thelonious Monk With John Coltrane* and *Monk's Music* are arguably the most compelling records with horns that he ever made. The first is actually by the quartet with Coltrane, Ware and Wilson on three tracks (frustratingly, the only ones the quartet made, despite working together for no less than six months at a New York residency), which include a lovely reading of 'Ruby, My Dear', and throughout Coltrane seems to play humbly, in almost complete deference to the leader. This contrasts pretty strikingly with Hawkins on the second session, of which two alternative takes are also on OJC 039. The sonorous qualities of the horns make this one of the most beautiful-sounding of Monk sessions, and his inspired idea to start the record with an *a cappella* arrangement of 'Abide With Me' sets an extraordinary atmosphere at the very start. There are still problems: the group play stiffly on these rhythms, Hawkins comes in wrongly a couple of times and, as fiercely as everyone is trying, it often sounds more like six men playing at Monk rather than with him. But the flavour of the session is fascinating, and Monk himself sounds wholly authoritative.

(****) Live At The Five Spot: Discovery!

Blue Note 799786 *Monk; John Coltrane (ts); Ahmed Abdul-Malik (b); Roy Haynes (d).* 57.

On atmosphere, it can't be faulted. The music's pretty amazing, too. These tapes were made by Juanita Coltrane (better known to posterity as Naima) during the band's residency at the Five Spot. The track order has been altered only slightly from the original performance, putting 'Crepuscule With Nellie' at the end of the disc in order to give the opening a rather more cosmetic quality. Predictably, the quality of sound is thoroughly archaeological. The tapes were made on a portable machine with a single mike. The wonder is that so much does actually register. From the prominence of Abdul-Malik's bass it has to be assumed that Mrs Coltrane was in front of him, to her husband's left and at some distance from the piano, which actually registers most poorly of all the instruments, sounding like an out-of-tune clavichord. Collectors of Coltrane solos will be transfixed by his opening statement on 'Trinkle Tinkle', where Monk drops out to let him play with just bass and drums, a practice that is repeated later. This is still in the 'sheets of sound' period and that much-misapplied concept may well become clearer after a listen to this record. There are many electrical and mechanical noises on the tape, a huge dropout during 'Epistrophy', where a portion was accidentally over-recorded (imagine having done that!) and an odd, dissociated feel to the whole thing, not unlike the effect of listening to a sold-out gig through a fire-escape door or side window. A discovery, indeed. However, a remastered version of the tape, with a speed correction, is now available on the complete Blue Note edition listed above.

***(*) Thelonious In Action

Original Jazz Classics OJC 103 *Monk; Johnny Griffin (ts); Ahmed Abdul-Malik (b); Roy Haynes (d).* 8/58.

***(*) Misterioso

Original Jazz Classics OJC 206 *As above.* 8/58.

It might, on the face of it, seem improbable that such a headstrong and unmysterious character as Johnny Griffin could be such a masterful interpreter of Monk. But their partnership was an inspiring one, the tenorman unperturbed by any idea that Monk's music was difficult, and the quartet is on blistering form on these dates, recorded live at New York's lamented Five Spot.

***(*) At Town Hall

Original Jazz Classics OJC 135 *Monk; Donald Byrd (t); Eddie Bert (tb); Bob Northern (frhn); Phil Woods (as); Charlie Rouse (ts); Pepper Adams (bs); Jay McAllister (tba); Sam Jones (b); Art Taylor (d).* 2/59.

Although Monk regarded this Town Hall concert as a triumph, the results seem rather mixed now. The long and suitably grand attempt at 'Monk's Mood' sounds rather lugubrious, and in general the ensemble catches only elements of Monk's intentions: his peculiar truce between a sober gaiety, bleak humour and thunderous intensity is a difficult thing for a big band to realize and, while there is some fine playing – by Woods and Rouse in particular – the band could probably have used a lot more time to figure out the composer's vision. Still, it's a valuable document of Monk's one personal involvement on a large-scale reading of his music.

*** 5 By Monk By 5

Original Jazz Classics OJC 362 *Monk; Thad Jones (t); Charlie Rouse (ts); Sam Jones (b); Art Taylor (d).* 6/59.

A relatively little-known Monk session, but a very good one. Jones is another not much thought of as a Monk interpreter, but he carries himself very capably and commits a brilliant improvisation to 'Jackie-Ing', even though (as Orrin Keepnews remembers) he had to struggle with what was then a new piece that Monk attempted to teach everybody by humming it. The CD includes the first two (rejected) takes of 'Played Twice', another new tune.

**** Thelonious Alone In San Francisco

Original Jazz Classics OJC 231 *Monk (p solo).* 10/59.

Another ruminative solo masterwork. Besides six originals, here is Monk elevating (or destroying, depending on one's point of view) 'There's Danger In Your Eyes, Cherie' and 'You Took The Words Right Out Of My Heart'. As a primer for understanding his piano playing, there is probably no better introduction than this one.

*** The Art Of The Ballad

Prestige 11012 *Monk; Ray Copeland (t); Gigi Gryce (as); John Coltrane, Frank Foster, Coleman Hawkins (ts); Gerry Mulligan (bs); Oscar Pettiford, Curley Russell, Wilbur Ware (b); Art Blakey, Kenny Clarke, Shadow Wilson (d).* 55–62.

The album begins and ends – inspired selection – with interpretations of 'Ruby, My Dear', featuring respectively Coleman Hawkins and John Coltrane. 'Monk's Mood' is for trio without percussion, and there is a generous smattering of solo tracks as well. 'Sweet And Lovely', as so often, is an occasion for extended performance, but 'Monk's Mood' and 'Ruby, My Dear' are also the object of notably tender readings. This being Monk, the interpretation of 'ballad' is somewhat idiosyncratic, but this is a delightful compilation from the Riverside and Prestige Years.

*** At The Blackhawk

Original Jazz Classics OJC 305 *Monk; Joe Gordon (t); Charlie Rouse, Harold Land (ts); John Ore (b); Billy Higgins (d).* 4/60.

Live in San Francisco. Land and Gordon were late additions to the band but both men play well. It's not a classic Monk date by any means – despite another tune, 'San Francisco Holiday', making its debut – but there seems to be a good spirit in the playing and the leader sounds at his most genial.

***(*) San Francisco Holiday

Milestone 9199 *Monk; Joe Gordon (t); Johnny Griffin, Harold Land, Charlie Rouse (ts); Sam Jones, Ahmed Abdul-Malik, John Ore (b); Art Blakey, Frankie Dunlop, Billy Higgins, Art Taylor (d).*

A generous compilation of sessions on which Monk finds himself briefly outclassed by an in-form Griffin and an unexpectedly powerful Land. Not much here for anyone but a devoted Monkian, but a good buy for all that.

***(*) The Thelonious Monk Memorial Album

Milestone 47064 *As for OJC discs above.* 55–62.

***(*) **Thelonious Monk And The Jazz Giants**
Riverside 60-018 *As above.*

♛ **** **The Complete Riverside Recordings**
Riverside 022 15CD *As above.*

The two single-disc compilations are perfectly adequate snapshots of Monk's Riverside period, though casual listeners would be better off zeroing in on the four-star records listed above. *The Complete Riverside Recordings* is another monument for the shelves, but there is so little flab and so much music in this set that it defies criticism. Superbly annotated by producer Keepnews, and including many out-takes and extras absent from the original records (though many of those have now been restored to the CD reissues of the appropriate albums), this is enough for a lifetime's study. On that basis alone we award it our crown.

*** **Monk In France**
Original Jazz Classics OJCCD 670 *Monk; Charlie Rouse (ts); John Ore (b); Frankie Dunlop (d).* 4/61.

(*) **Monk In Italy
Original Jazz Classics OJCCD 488 *As above.* 4/61.

The last Riverside albums were recorded during a wide-ranging tour of Europe which has been pretty extensively documented. There are also recordings from the Scandinavian capitals (assessed below), and they are consistently better than the oddly dull and unresponsive effort from Italy which marked Monk's farewell to the label. These sound horribly like contract-fillers. The band don't seem to be getting along, with Dunlop in particular all over the place on 'Straight, No Chaser' and most of the work left to Monk and Rouse, who might have taken a couple of the tunes as an unaccompanied duet.

Three days earlier, the Paris date has much more light and shade. Riverside decided against any overlap of material, so there are no direct comparisons to be made; but the band as a whole seems to be well fed and harmonious, and firing on all cylinders. 'I'm Getting Sentimental Over You' was meant to strike a chord in the French audience, and the little right-hand Django figures in the second chorus are a delightful posy for the home crowd. It's not clear whether the date was intended as a recording session but, whatever the circumstances, the sound is fine – which perversely tends to point up the flat-line dynamic. Monk was on a creative and professional cusp when this session was taped, but it certainly shouldn't be used as a measure of where he was in the spring of that key year.

*** **Monk In Copenhagen**
Storyville 8283 *As above.* 5/61.

***(*) **Live In Stockholm**
DIW 315/6 2CD *As above.* 5/61.

The 1961 European tour and the subsequent Columbia contract put the seal on Monk's critical reputation. It's arguable that the end of his great association with Riverside marked the watershed in his creativity and that nothing he did after 1962 had the inventiveness and authority of the Blue Note, Prestige and Riverside years. Certainly the concert recordings from the 1961 tour (and there have been others in circulation, from both sides of the contractual blanket) have a strange *fin de siècle* quality, with a more than usually repetitive carry-over of ideas and very little sign of the pianist's usual ability to re-invent songs night after night. And yet, comparing these two concerts, which were recorded a day apart, it's easier to hear how subtly Monk re-inflects not so much his solos as his basic theme statement, adding notes to 'Well You Needn't' in Copenhagen and restructuring the second subject in 'Monk's Mood' with the help of the resourceful Ore. On balance, we favour the Swedish date (which was presumably also a radio broadcast) for its extra length and a rather sharper sound; but both give a flavour of the band on the road. It's ironic that he should have been so warmly received in Europe, for Monk's compositional sense and his playing style were largely overdetermined by American models, rarely (as was the case with Bud Powell) by direct or ironic reference to the European classical tradition. What may have appealed to European audiences, even to Swedes weaned on marathon blowing sessions by American exiles, was precisely his emphasis on *compositions*, rather than schematic chord progressions, as the basis of improvisation.

As so often, Rouse is the bellwether, uneasy and aggressive by turns in the presence of a rather diffident Monk on the first of the records (see 'Off Minor') but finding his feet with a vengeance in Bern and Stockholm. The DIW sound is very clear and pristine, but it lacks the warmth and sheer 'feel' of the Dragon, and those who already have that needn't feel they have to update urgently. Of the group, the Bern concert is perhaps the more rounded, with a wonderful, spiky-romantic version of 'I'm Getting Sentimental Over You' and the staple 'Blue Monk'. The Swedish date offers welcome performances of 'Ba-Lue Bolivar Ba-Lues Are' from *Brilliant Corners* and a fine 'Body And Soul'. 'Just a Gigolo' is a solo performance, played in a self-consciously distracted manner, as if saying, It's a *hell* of a job, but someone has to do it.

*** **Monk's Dream**
Columbia 460065-2 *Monk; Charlie Rouse (ts); John Ore (b); Frankie Dunlop (d).* 10 & 11/62.

This was Monk's first album for CBS and, as Peter Keepnews points out in the reissue notes, it established the pattern for those that followed. Each contained a mixture of originals – most of them now getting quite long in the tooth – and standards, and marked a slight softening of Monk's once rather alien attack. The standards performances – 'Body And Soul', 'Just A Gigolo', 'Sweet And Lovely' – are not always immediately identifiable with the brittle, lateral-thinking genius of the Blue Notes and Riversides and are increasingly dependent on rather formulaic solutions. 'Monk's Dream' and 'Bye-Ya' are slightly tame and the changes of title on 'Bolivar Blues' (weirdly phoneticized in its first version) and 'Five Spot Blues' (originally 'Blues Five Spot') suggest how much Monk was unconsciously and partially moving towards the mainstream. No one seems to have told Charlie Rouse, who really takes over on some of these tracks. The saxophonist sounds jagged and angular where the rhythm has been somewhat rationalized, intensely bluesy where the harmony begins to sound legitimate. Worthy of three stars for Rouse alone.

*** **1963: In Japan**
Prestige PRCD SP 202 *As above, except Butch Warren (b) replaces Ore.* 5/63.

***(*) **Monk In Tokyo**
Columbia 489771-2 2CD *As above.* 5/63.

Monk's reputation in Japan was cemented much more quickly even than in Europe, and these document his first successful visit. The first of the pair was recorded at the TBS television studios. The group initially sound wary and uninspired, but almost every track catches light at some point. The standout performances on *Tokyo* are 'Pannonica' and a marvellous 'Hackensack'. By his own high standard, Rouse is rather anonymous and plays surprisingly little of consequence, but the set as a whole is well worth hearing.

*****(*) Monterey Jazz Festival '63**

Storyville 8255 2CD *As above, except John Ore (b) replaces Warren.* 9/63.

Try to imagine having been there. The quartet was perfectly attuned to Monk's conception and, apart from two long standards – 'I'm Getting Sentimental Over You' and 'Sweet And Lovely' – all the tunes are originals and are dispatched with a sardonic insouciance. Rouse is in exceptional form, carving out blunt, massy solos that are a near exact corollary of the leader's. Unless the source tapes are compromised in some way, the piano is slightly off in the middle register, but Monk works round its limitations and dead spots.

*****(*) Big Band / Quartet In Concert**

Columbia 476898 2CD *Monk; Thad Jones (c); Nick Travis (t); Eddie Bert (tb); Charlie Rouse (ts); Steve Lacy (ss); Phil Woods (as, cl); Gene Allen (bs, cl, bcl); Butch Warren (b); Frank Dunlop (d).* 12/63.

The original LP release trimmed this important document in an irritatingly Procrustean manner, lopping off two long orchestral numbers, 'Bye-Ya' and 'Light Blue', a tiny quartet version of 'Epistrophy' and a long, magisterial 'Misterioso', also by Monk, Rouse, Warren and Dunlop. The sound has also been tweaked into something like acceptable form, reducing the cavernous boom of the Philharmonic Hall at Lincoln Center, where the concert was recorded the day before New Year's Eve 1963. Monk himself sounds very relaxed, and one can't help comparing his almost Zen-like calm on occasions like this with Charles Mingus's torrential outpourings. The pianist's exchanges with Rouse on 'Misterioso' are some of his gentlest on record, and his re-invention of the obscure 'When It's Darkness On The Delta', a pop song from 1932, is redolent of great predecessors like Tatum, Waller and, at one point near the end, usually unnoticed, Earl Hines. The orchestra plays vigorously and well, seemingly well acquainted with Hall Overton's charts and able to handle some of the quicker turns on 'I Mean You' and 'Oska T', neither of them unchallenging charts, with great aplomb. Fascinating to see (and occasionally hear) that most resolute Monkian, Steve Lacy, in the ensemble; what this must have meant to him. This is a valuable recording, long overdue for reissue and rehabilitation.

*****(*) It's Monk's Time**

Columbia 468405 *Monk; Charlie Rouse (ts); Butch Warren (b); Ben Riley (d).* 64.

One of the best sessions of the period, recorded at the height of Monk's critical standing. In 1964 he was the subject of a cover story in *Time* magazine, one of only three jazz artists (all piano players, but no more clues) to have been accorded that accolade. There's certainly nothing compromised or middle-market about this tough, abrasive set. Monk's sound had softened considerably over the past decade, partly as a result of playing on better instruments, partly because of more sensitive recording set-ups. He still sounds angular and oblique, but he does so without the percussive edge he was wont to bring to theme statements like 'Lulu's Back In Town', 'Stuffy Turkey' and 'Shuffle Boil', which stand out from the rest for the piquancy of the melodic invention.

****** Live At The It Club – Complete**

Columbia C2K 65288 2CD *Monk; Charlie Rouse (ts); Larry Gales (b); Ben Riley (d).* 10/64.

***** Live At The Jazz Workshop**

Columbia 4691832 *As above.* 11/64.

Established connoisseurs of live Monk material will value the latter of these for a fizzing performance of the challenging 'Hackensack' and for a rhythmically adroit 'Bright Mississippi', on which Monk calls the shots to his rhythm section. The earlier session is more convincing all round, though, with particularly fine readings of 'Misterioso', 'Blue Monk' and 'Ba-Lu Bolivar Ba-Lues Are'. As with several of these reissues, the sound reveals significantly more of the bass and drums than on earlier sessions. The It Club session, recorded live in San Francisco, is now available complete and as performed, with three tracks which were previously unreleased and another nine restored to their original length. What's restored isn't simply empty duration but the whole feel of a Monk gig, its texture and pace, and something of its enigmatic logic. The previously unavailable 'Teo', 'Bright Mississippi' and 'Just You, Just Me' aren't revelatory in themselves. What is, though, is the dynamic of the session as a whole and, with the sound also restored to present-day standards, this is as good as it gets for live jazz performance.

***** Straight, No Chaser**

Columbia CK 64886 *Monk; Charlie Rouse (ts); Larry Gales (b); Frankie Dunlop (d).* 66.

Recently restored to its full recorded length by Orrin Keepnews, this is a complete version of the sessions of November 1966 and January 1967. This impeccably remastered issue includes a full version of the intriguing 'Japanese Folk Song' (which had been reduced by almost six minutes to conform to LP length) and a spanking version of 'We See', which had lost almost three minutes for the same reason. There are two unacompanied piano solos, 'Between The Devil And The Deep Blue Sea' and the tiny 'This Is My Story, This Is My Song'. The two additional tracks are an alternative of 'I Didn't Know About You' and the original 'Green Chimneys', both of them well worth having. This is as late as Monk remains interesting. There are already *longueurs* and too many of the eccentricities seem carefully studied. Much of the material is derived from a film made about Monk that further raised his critical standing without contributing substantially to awareness of what truly made him distinctive.

***** The Nonet – Live!**

Le Jazz 7 *Monk; Ray Copeland, Clark Terry (t); Jimmy Cleveland (tb); Phil Woods (as); Johnny Griffin, Charlie Rouse (ts); Larry Gales (b); Ben Riley (d).* 11/67.

A rare chance to hear Monk work with a larger group on this November 1967 recording from Paris, which seems to contain all the music from the concert. Strictly, it isn't a Nonet date, but the usual touring quartet with guest contributions on some tracks.

Long versions of 'We See', 'Epistrophy' and 'Evidence' allow the solos to stretch out, though Clark Terry restricts himself to a rather cautious and perhaps even sceptical appearance on 'Blue Monk'. Woods is a revelation on this repertoire, his idiosyncratic tack on bop bringing something quite individual to the ensemble. The recording quality is unexceptional but mainly clear and certainly more faithful than the bootleg editions of the gig which circulated for some years.

***** Monk's Blues**
Columbia 475698 *Monk; Robert Bryant, Frederick Hill, Conte Candoli, Bob Brookmeyer (t); Bill Byers, Michael Wimberley (tb); Ernie Small, Tom Scott, Gene Cipriano, Ernie Watts, Charlie Rouse (sax); Howard Roberts (g); Larry Gales (b); Ben Riley (d); John Guerin (perc).* 11/68.

For some reason, this one was credited to Thelonious Sphere Monk, his full name. Given the cost of this Oliver Nelson-arranged and -produced session, perhaps Columbia wanted it to sound as black-tie as possible. Monk came out to the Coast to do the session and to pick up a few side-gigs at the same time. It had apparently been impossible for Nelson, who was a busy television and film music writer and arranger, to get over to New York. What isn't clear is whether the pianist was attracted first and foremost by Nelson or by the chance to work in the sunshine for a while. Nelson certainly gives the complex tunes highly convincing arrangements. The horn players have some lip-busting parts to negotiate on 'Little Rootie Tootie' and 'Brilliant Corners', but they seem to manage. There was only one non-Monk tune on the list, Teo Macero's wryly titled 'Consecutive Seconds', and it stands out very prominently. The CD is filled out with about ten minutes of new material, including a rather slushy 'Round Midnight' which was quite properly omitted from the original release.

****** Monk Alone: The Complete Columbia Solo Studio Recordings, 1962–1968**
Columbia 2K 65495 2CD *Monk (p solo).* 62–68.

Glorious. Unaccompanied performances pulled together from *Monk's Dream, Criss Cross, It's Monk's Time, Monk, Straight, No Chaser*, the less well-known *Always Know* and the whole of *Solo Monk*. In addition, there are 14 previously unreleased tracks, mostly alternatives, some of them clearly sub-standard, like the rejected 'Body And Soul' from 31 October–1 November 1962, but all of them absolutely packed with musical invention. Remastered to the highest quality, these brisk, bright sessions show how complete a musician Monk was, using his piano like a drum kit, horn and full orchestra. This is an essential purchase, uncategorizable and resistant to the adjectival attentions of critics; the work of an artist who was completely *sui generis*, it's the kind of record that needs to be lived with for a time.

***** Standards**
Columbia CK 45148 / 465681-2 *Monk; Charlie Rouse (ts); Larry Gales, John Ore (b); Frankie Dunlop, Ben Riley (d).* 62–68.

But, almost needless to say, not predictable standards. Selected from the Columbia years, this is the obvious counterbalance to the assumption that Monk played just Monk. Apart from 'Tea For Two' and 'Nice Work If You Can Get It', these are songs from down the Broadway bill. Gershwin's 'Liza (All The Clouds'll Roll Away)' and Eubie Blake's 'Memories Of You' are stunning re-inventions, but there isn't a dull track on the album. We'd still counsel turning to the original records but, as a sample of Monk as an interpreter, it's hard to fault.

*****(*) The London Collection: Volume 1**
Black Lion BLCD 760101 *Monk; Al McKibbon (b); Art Blakey (d).* 11/71.

***** The London Collection: Volume 2**
Black Lion BLCD 760116 *As above.* 11/71.

***** The London Collection: Volume 3**
Black Lion BLCD 760142 *As above.* 11/71.

*****(*) The Complete London Collection**
Black Lion 7601 3CD *As above.* 11/71.

The critical tide had perhaps turned away from Monk by the end of the '60s. Though his standing among fellow musicians grew with every passing year and all-Monk performances became a sub-genre of modern jazz, the labels were no longer convinced that he could be marketed even on the basis of surreal art-work and a certain studied eccentricity. Amazingly, a decade before his death, these are the last full-scale sessions of Thelonious Monk as a leader. All collectors will want to have the complete boxed set, which includes a couple of alternatives that missed the cut for the 'complete' Mosaic box, but the individual albums seem to be available as well. The solo performances on *Volume 1* offer a fair impression of Monk's ability to invest improvisations on self-written or standard ('Lover Man', 'Darn That Dream') themes with the same logical development and sense of overall form that one might look for in a notated piece. It isn't clear that Blakey was an entirely sympathetic accompanist, and some of the faster-paced numbers sound a little overpowered. Certainly McKibbon is difficult to hear over clustered accents on the bass drum. There is a wonderful improvisation, mockingly called 'Chordially' on *Volume 3*, which is presumably meant to refute the charge that Monk's apparent indifference to conventional changes-playing was a token of limited technique rather than a conscious strategy. Useful and often enjoyable sessions, these are still rather late in the day for genuine fireworks.

J. R. Monterose (1927–93)

TENOR SAXOPHONE, SOPRANO SAXOPHONE

Hard-bop stylist, in thrall to few influences, rarely recorded and often forgotten now. His Blue Note album remains unreissued.

*****(*) The Message**
Fresh Sound FSRCD 201 *Monterose; Tommy Flanagan (p); Jimmy Garrison (b); Pete LaRoca (d).* 11/59.

***** Live At The Tender Trap**
Fresh Sound FSCD 1023 *Monterose; Dale Oehler (p); Dick Vanizel (b); Joe Abodeely (d); Al Jarreau (v).* 63.

***** A Little Pleasure**
Reservoir RSR CD 109 *Monterose; Tommy Flanagan (p).* 4/81.

*** **T. T. T.**

Storyville STCD 8291 *Monterose; Hod O'Brien (p); Guffy Pallesen (b); Jesper Elen (d).* 7/88.

Detroit-born Monterose fell into none of the familiar tenor-playing niches and so fell out of jazz history. If there was a single strong influence, it was probably John Coltrane; but Monterose was anything but a slavish Trane copyist and forged his own odd but inimitable style: a slightly tight, almost strangled tone, delivered before and behind the beat, often in successive measures, thin but curiously intense and highly focused. He was also a pioneer of electric sax, an interest that few others have followed. And yet, just half a dozen years after his largely unreported death, a significant European jazz label is capable of releasing a valuable late live session with J.R.'s surname consistently misspelt on cover, in personnel and notes, all the while wagging an admonitory finger at those who confuse him with the slightly younger West Coaster, Jack Montrose.

Even neglected dogs have their day. Monterose made a considerable impression on Charles Mingus's *Pithecanthropus Erectus*, an understated foil to Jackie McLean's impassioned alto. Sadly, not even that remarkable session won him enough leverage to build a significant body of work as leader. On parts of *The Message* the resemblance to Warne Marsh is almost uncanny, even down to specific phrases on 'Violets For Your Furs' and 'I Remember Clifford', in which he uses simple arch shapes with altered harmonics to create a strange, slightly distanced quality. Garrison, as was his fate, remains poorly audible, but LaRoca is very good and totally musical.

The early-'60s session features J.R.'s regular band, an able if slightly colourless unit, based at The Tender Trap in Cedar Rapids, Iowa. The group (with minor variants) enjoyed a long residency at The Tender Trap. Occasional guest players were David Sanborn and the young Al Jarreau, who studied psychology at the University of Iowa. His vocals are a must for collectors, as an earnest of the subtle stylist he was to become in later years. Alas, no glimpse of the young Sanborn, who went on to make more money per record than J.R. did in his entire career.

A Little Pleasure is Monterose's recording debut with soprano saxophone, and it casts him in mostly reflective mood. There are two good originals: the 3/4 'Pain And Suffering ... And A Little Pleasure' and the less satisfying 'Vinnie's Pad'. Monterose stays with the straight horn for 'A Nightingale Sang In Berkeley Square' (with Flanagan playing the verse) and on 'Central Park West', whose solo underlines just how little dependent on Coltrane Monterose has been down the years. It's very intimately miked, and Monterose's breathing is very audible.

We'd be much more enthusiastic about the Storyville disc if they had taken the trouble to spell J.R.'s surname correctly. Late in life, and rather flatly recorded for Danish Radio in live performance at the Jazzhus Slukefter, it catches him sounding rather strained but still generating ideas at an impressive rate. As ever, the programme is largely standards-based, with a movingly querulous 'You Don't Know What Love Is' and 'All The Things You Are'. He covers 'Central Park West' once again but also Sonny Rollins's 'Airegin', two themes coming from very different musical premises. The house band is sound enough, but by this point J.R. seemed fated to spend his career working with groups who chugged ahead almost despite him.

Wes Montgomery (1925–68)

GUITAR, BASS GUITAR

The middle and most celebrated of the Montgomery brothers was born like the others in Indianapolis. He took to guitar late and only began his professional career – in Lionel Hampton's band – when he was 25. Influenced by Charlie Christian, he developed a style in which thumb-plucked single-note lines were backed with softly strummed octaves and chords. Wes worked with his brothers Monk and Buddy, and with groups of his own. Montgomery died unexpectedly, at the height of his commercial appeal if not of his creative powers.

***(*) **Fingerpickin'**

Pacific Jazz 8 37987 *Montgomery; Freddie Hubbard (t); Wayman Atkinson, Alonzo Johnson (ts); Buddy Montgomery (vib); Joe Bradley, Richie Crabtree (p); Monk Montgomery (b); Benny Barth, Paul Parker (d).* 12/57, 4/58.

A strong, assured set which benefits from a string of horns. Hubbard is in good form on his four tracks, though Buddy Montgomery's themes don't give him a great deal to bite on. The remaining tracks from the Christmas 1957 session are too short to establish much of a presence, and one is left feeling slightly short-changed by something like 'All The Things You Are', which bounces by in little more than it would take to deliver the song, and with much less going on. The remaining three tracks were taped at the Forum Theatre in Los Angeles the following spring, with Crabtree and Barth joining the brothers. 'Baubles, Bangles And Beads' is lovely, if a touch raggedy round the edges. The sound lets things down here and there, and there may be a couple of reconstructed dropouts on 'Not Since Nineveh'. Otherwise, though, a very collectable item.

*** **A Dynamic New Jazz Sound**

Original Jazz Classics OJC 034 *Montgomery; Mel Rhyne (org); Paul Parker (d).* 10/59.

**** **Incredible Jazz Guitar**

Original Jazz Classics OJC 036 *Montgomery; Tommy Flanagan (p); Percy Heath (b); Albert 'Tootie' Heath (d).* 1/60.

***(*) **Movin' Along**

Original Jazz Classics OJC 089 *Montgomery; James Clay (ts, f); Victor Feldman (p); Sam Jones (b); Louis Hayes (d).* 10/60.

***(*) **So Much Guitar**

Original Jazz Classics OJC 233 *Montgomery; Hank Jones (p); Ron Carter (b); Lex Humphries (d); Ray Barretto (perc).* 8/61.

***(*) **Full House**

Original Jazz Classics OJC 106 *Montgomery; Johnny Griffin (ts); Wynton Kelly (p); Paul Chambers (b); Jimmy Cobb (d).* 6/62.

(*) **Boss Guitar

Original Jazz Classics OJC 261 *Montgomery; Mel Rhyne (org); Jimmy Cobb (d).* 4/63.

*** **Portrait Of Wes**

Original Jazz Classics OJC 144 *Montgomery; Johnny Griffin (ts); Wynton Kelly (p); Paul Chambers (b); George Brown (d).* 10/63.

***** Fusion!**

Original Jazz Classics OJC 368 *Montgomery; Phil Bodmer (sax, f); Dick Hyman (p, cel); Hank Jones (p); Kenny Burrell (g); Milt Hinton (b); Osie Johnson (d); strings.* 4/63.

***** Guitar On The Go**

Original Jazz Classics OJCCD 489 *Montgomery; Melvin Rhyne (org); George Brown, Jimmy Cobb, Paul Parker (d).* 10–11/63.

****** The Complete Riverside Recordings**

Riverside 12 RCD 4408 12CD *As for the above, except add Nat Adderley (c), Joe Gordon (t), Cannonball Adderley (as), Johnny Griffin, Harold Land (ts), Barry Harris, George Shearing, Bobby Timmons (p), Victor Feldman, Milt Jackson, Buddy Montgomery (vib), Ray Brown, Monk Montgomery (b), Walter Perkins (d); woodwinds; strings.* 59–63.

***** The Artistry Of Wes Montgomery**

Riverside FCD 60 919 *As above.* 59–63.

***** Dangerous**

Milestone 9298 *As above.* 59–63.

Wes Montgomery gave off a sense of effortlessness that is always bad karma in jazz; a little *sweat* and preferably some pain are almost considered *de rigueur*. But Montgomery used to loose off solos as if he was sitting on his back porch talking to friends. He used a homely, thumb-picking technique, rather than a plectrum or the faster finger-picking approach. Stylistically, he copied Charlie Christian's Ur-bop and added elements of Django Reinhardt's harmonic conception. It's interesting and ironic that Montgomery's most prominent latter-day disciple, George Benson, should have made almost exactly the same career move, trading off a magnificent improvisational sense against commercial success. In career terms, Montgomery really did seem to prefer his back porch. During the 1950s, which should have been his big decade, he hung around his native Indianapolis, playing part time. When his recording career got going again, he was still capable of great things. The massive Riverside box, including everything he did under the auspices of the label, has turned this entry on its head. Though much of the best material was and still is available separately, access to it in this bulk, and with a huge range of material recorded for other leaders – the Adderleys, Shearing, Land – and with the Montgomery Brothers makes a substantial difference to our view of the guitarist, highlighting his awesome consistency, pointing a slightly accusing finger at his tendency to settle for the obvious and familiar on occasion, rarely pushing out into the more experimental mode that he had flirted with early on. The boxed set has a price-tag commensurate with its size, and many listeners will feel the need to pick one or more of the individual discs instead.

Guitar–organ trios take a little getting used to nowadays, but *New Sound* and *Boss Guitar* contain some of the guitarist's most vibrant recordings. While some of the best of the material – 'Round Midnight', 'Fried Pies', and so on – has been sampled on the Milestone sets, below, these are worth hearing and having in their entirety. For no readily discernible reason, *Boss Guitar* sounds flatter than the others.

Incredible Jazz Guitar is probably the best Montgomery record currently available. His solo on 'West Coast Blues' is very nearly incredible, though there are hints of banality even there, in his trademark octave runs, which he borrowed from Django. Flanagan may have slipped the engineer a sawbuck, for he's caught beautifully, nicely forward in the mix. His lines on Sonny Rollins's buoyant 'Airegin' are exactly complementary to the guitarist's. There's a 'D-natural Blues' and covers of 'In Your Own Sweet Way' and 'Polka Dots And Moonbeams', which further hint at Montgomery's eventual artistic inertia, but for the moment he sounds like a master, and this is the one to go for if you aren't investing in the big box.

On *So Much*, Montgomery's smooth and uncannily fluent lines and Jones's elegant two-handedness lift 'Cotton Tail' out of the ordinary. Never a blindingly fast player, Montgomery specialized in sweeping oppositions of register that lend an illusion of pace to relatively stately passages.

Guitar On The Go was Wes's last release on Riverside before the label went pear-shaped. The dating may seem odd, but there is just one track – 'Missile Blues' – from the 1959 album. It was a remarkable and powerful end to a very fruitful relationship and, as well as the extra track, there is a spankingly good alternative of 'The Way You Look Tonight' and an untitled solo-guitar improvisation which will intrigue established fans and make them wish there were more of Wes's rehearsal work and solitary musings available. *Dangerous* is a valuable compilation of alternatives and live tracks, issued at a price that is more approachable than the box set.

The title *Fusion!* is interesting because in a sense Wes was one of the figures who lay behind later attempts to integrate the rhythm and energy of rock with jazz harmonies. Ironically, there isn't much trace of that here. Jimmy Jones's arrangements are engagingly tight and spare – one has to admire the sheer workmanship of 'Baubles, Bangles And Beads' – but the one thing these sessions lack is energy. Wes sounds positively pipe-and-slippers and, but for 'God Bless The Child', rather detached and disengaged. As with all these later recordings, though, remastering significantly improves the overall balance of sound.

*****(*) Far Wes**

Pacific Jazz 94475 *Montgomery; Pony Poindexter (as); Harold Land (ts); Buddy Montgomery (p); Monk Montgomery (b); Tony Bazley, Louis Hayes (d); collective personnel.* 4/58, 10/59.

A welcome reissue (of the better 1958 sessions particularly). Montgomery plays fluently if a trifle dispassionately but emerges here as a composer of some substance. The title-track is in relatively conventional bop idiom but has an attractive melodic contour (which Land largely ignores) and a well-judged 'turn' towards the end of the main statement. The later sessions are a trifle disappointing, though the great Louis Hayes weighs in at the drum kit with characteristic confidence. It's worth buying for the first half-dozen tracks alone.

***** The Alternative Wes Montgomery**

Milestone M 47065 *Montgomery; Johnny Griffin (ts); James Clay (f); Victor Feldman, Wynton Kelly, Buddy Montgomery (p); Mel Rhyne (org); Milt Jackson (vib); Paul Chambers, Sam Jones, Monk Montgomery (b); George Brown, Jimmy Cobb, Louis Hayes, Philly Joe Jones, Bobby Thomas (d); orchestra.* 10/60–11/63.

A mass of material, and no maps. Some of Montgomery's better later performances were buried away on rather unselective, buffet-table Milestone LPs, but the cumulative impression is of incipient commercial *longueur*; certainly the extra takes on *Alternative* don't contain any real revelations. Montgomery himself claimed to have been at his best a full decade before, but he spent most of the 1950s out of the limelight. It's hard to think that any but the most dogged of fans would want all the alternatives if the original releases were freely available on CD. For the time being, though, they represent a decent purchase.

***** Encores: Volume 1 – Body And Soul**

Milestone 9252 *Montgomery; Milt Jackson (vib); Victor Feldman (vib, p); Wynton Kelly, Buddy Montgomery (p); Sam Jones, Monk Montgomery (b); Louis Hayes, Philly Joe Jones, Bobby Thomas (d).*

*****(*) Encores: Volume 2 – Blue'N'Boogie**

Milestone 9261 *Montgomery; Johnny Griffin (ts); Wynton Kelly (p); Paul Chambers (b); Jimmy Cobb (d).*

Two very different and inevitably rather patchy sets from the Milestone archive. The first album pulls together a disparate body of material and makes a certain sense of it. 'Body And Soul' is worthy of its title position, a smooth but not unsubtle reading. Volume Two has rather more bite. Under normal circumstances Griff is too incendiary for a gig like this, but he and Wes struck up a strong relationship, and the fruits are very impressive indeed, with strong, punchy choruses from both on 'Born To Be Blue' and the inevitable 'Baubles, Bangles And Beads'.

***** Body And Soul**

Ronnie Scott's Jazz House JHAS 604 *Montgomery; Stan Tracey (p); Rick Laird (b); Ronnie Stephenson (d).* 4 & 5/65.

Souvenirs from a fondly remembered British visit, on which the guitarist won round even an audience that was decamping by the score to rock'n'roll. His easy rapport, with listeners and fellow musicians alike, is evident long before the spoken-word coda. He perhaps finds Tracey slightly jagged and, on 'Wes' Easy Blues' and 'Body And Soul', he attempts to soften the attack a touch. There's just one unaccompanied track, the slightly inconsequential 'Solo Ballad in A Major', a familiar idea but not one we can peg down to a known source. Laird and Stephenson are, as ever, reliable in support, though neither is very well recorded on these tapes.

****** Impressions: The Verve Jazz Sides**

Verve 521690-2 2CD *Montgomery; Donald Byrd, Mel Davis, Bernie Glow, Danny Moore, Joe Newman, Jimmy Nottingham, Ernie Royal, Clark Terry, Snooky Young (t); Wayne Andre, Jimmy Cleveland, Urbie Green, Quentin Jackson, Melba Liston, John Messner, Tony Studd, Bill Watrous, Chauncey Welsh (tb); James Buffington (frhn); Don Butterfield, Harvey Phillips (tba); Jerome Richardson (ts, ss, f); Stan Webb (as, bs, cl); Ray Beckenstein (as); Bob Ashton, Jerry Dodgion, Romeo Penque (reeds); Danny Bank (bs, af, f, bcl); Walter Kane (bs, cl); Herbie Hancock, Roger Kellaway, Wynton Kelly, Bobby Scott (p); Jimmy Smith (org); Jack Jennings (vib); Al Casamenti, Bucky Pizzarelli (g); Paul Chambers, Bob Cranshaw, George Duvivier (b); Jimmy Cobb, Sol Gubin, Grady Tate (d); Ray Barretto, Willie Bobo (perc).* 11/64–11/66.

***** Movin' Wes**

Verve 810045-2 *Montgomery; Ernie Royal, Clark Terry, Snooky Young (t); Jimmy Cleveland, Urbie Green, Quentin Jackson, Chauncey Welsh (tb); Don Butterfield (tba); Jerome Richardson (sax, f); Bobby Scott (p); Bob Cranshaw (b); Grady Tate (d); Willie Bobo (perc).* 11/64.

***** Bumpin'**

Verve 539062-2 *Montgomery; Roger Kellaway (p); Bob Cranshaw (b); Helcio Milito, Grady Tate (d); strings.* 5/65.

****(*) Tequila**

Verve 831671-2 *Montgomery; George Devens (vib); Ron Carter (b); Grady Tate (d); Ray Barretto (perc); Bernard Eichem, Arnold Eidus, Paul Gershman, Emmanuel Green, Julius Held, Harry Lookofsky, Joe Malin, Gene Orloff (vn); Abe Kessler, Charles McCracken, George Ricci, Harvey Shapiro (clo).* 3 & 5/66.

*****(*) California Dreaming**

Verve 827842-2 *Montgomery; Mel Davis, Bernie Glow, Jimmy Nottingham (t); Wayne Andre, John Messner, Bill Watrous (tb); James Buffington (frhn); Don Butterfield (tba); Ray Beckenstein (as, picc, f); Stan Webb (as, bs, cl, eng hn); Herbie Hancock (p); Al Casamenti (g); Jack Jennings (vib); Richard Davis (b); Grady Tate (d); Ray Barretto (perc).* 66.

The 'jazz' in the title of the two-CD set is a careful hedge, in recognition of the unreconstructed commerciality of much that Wes was doing at the time. Just as the Riversides have realigned the pre-1963 material, this elegantly packaged compilation brings together the best of albums like *Willow Weep For Me, The Small Group Recordings, Just Walkin', Smokin' At The Half Note, California Dreaming, Goin' Out Of My Head* and *Movin' Wes*, which remains available in its own right. As an entity, it has a lot more presence than the majority of the later discs; remastering brings guitar and band into better balance than on the original release. The only soloist on the date, Wes is playing very smoothly indeed. Tunes like 'The Phoenix Love Theme', 'Moca Flor' and 'Theodora' are little more than beefed-up elevator music. The title-tune (which comes in two parts, 'Born To Be Blue' and 'People') is a bit more focused, but there still isn't much excitement.

Bumpin' was the record that established a working relationship between Wes, Creed Taylor and arranger Don Sebesky, who is responsible for the strings. As with much of the guitarist's work, it has acquired a new currency through the acid-jazz movement. Without those loyalties it isn't so much revelatory as pleasantly irrelevant. Restored to pristine condition, it's technically flawless and expressively a bit dead, though 'Bumpin'' itself is as lovely as ever.

Tequila is one of the sessions that Verve have plundered in order to reposition Wes as a founding father of both acid jazz and a smooth, ambient saloon funk. It finds Montgomery rather wearily putting in his time with the Claus Ogerman Orchestra. 'Bumpin' on Sunset' is of course a long-standing favourite (subsequently revived by Brian Auger's Oblivion Express in the jazz equivalent of minimalist trance music). Montgomery is still harmonically inventive, but the arrangements are too pre-packaged for very much in the way of surprises.

California Dreaming kicks off with another pop hit but the record contains some brief flashes of Montgomery the jazz master. They're not evident other than episodically but, heard over time, this is a more substantial record than first appears and we recommend it ahead of almost any of Wes's later records.

***** Jazz Guitar**

Laserlight 17180 *Montgomery; Harold Mabern (p); Arthur Harper (b); Jimmie Lovelace (d).* 65.

Neither the date nor the personnel is definite, since this budget reissue comes without notes or details. The outstanding track is John Coltrane's blues theme, 'Impressions', a harmonically inventive interpretation which gives the lie to any suggestion that Montgomery had settled into easy pop stylings by this late stage in his active career. Whoever the other players are, they respond with intelligence and understanding.

*****(*) Jazz Masters 14**

Verve 519826-2 *Montgomery; Wynton Kelly (p); Paul Chambers (b); Jimmy Cobb (d); Ray Barretto (perc); Oliver Nelson Orchestra; Don Sebesky Orchestra; Johnny Pate Orchestra.* 64–66.

***** Ultimate**

Verve 539787-2 *As above.* 64–66.

***** Talkin' Verve – Roots Of Acid Jazz**

Verve 529580-2 *As above, except add Jimmy Smith (org), Jack Jennings (vib), Kenny Davis (b), Claus Ogerman Orchestra.* 64–66.

Three strong compilations drawn from Verve's capacious catalogue of Montgomery material. Inevitably, there is some overlap of tracks: 'Bumpin' On Sunset' is on both *Jazz Masters* and the acid jazz genealogy; 'OGD (Road Song)' can be found on the latter and *Ultimate*, and so on. It seems unlikely, though, that anyone will be tempted by more than one of these, and our recommendation is the *Jazz Masters* disc. A crossover star of a later generation, George Benson, is responsible for curating the *Ultimate* collection, but he adds no real insight to what seems like a haphazard selection from Wes's Verve years.

**** Down Here On The Ground**

A&M 396994-2 *Montgomery; Hubert Laws, George Marge, Romeo Penque (f, ob); Mike Maineri (vib); Ron Carter (b); Grady Tate (d); Ray Barretto, Bobby Rosengarden (perc); strings.* 12/67, 1/68.

By the last year of his life, Montgomery was a pop star, and there is precious little jazz on these chart-orientated sessions. The familiar parallel octaves are there in plenty, but Montgomery does little more than register the melody, repeat it with some slight elaboration, negotiate a middle eight as straightforwardly as possible, and then on out to a faded ending. An attractive record but with little improvisational sustenance.

Montgomery Brothers

GROUP

The Montgomery 'family' group, which worked in San Francisco in 1960–61.

***** Groove Yard**

Original Jazz Classics OJC 139 *Buddy Montgomery (vib, p); Monk Montgomery (b); Bobby Thomas (d).* 1/61.

A little like the Jackson Five, it can be a bit difficult to maintain an even focus on all the members of this once rather successful group. Monk and Buddy doubtless gained considerably from their association with Wes, but he also gained a sympathetic, supportive group which never quite attained its full potential in the midst of Wes's Riverside period. This record (and another recorded in Canada, still not on CD) represent the group's best output. Buddy's vibes playing was not quite in the Milt Jackson class but it was more than workmanlike, and his piano playing, which developed in years to come, is bright and rhythmic, with a slightly melancholy quality which suits the group very well. Monk has always been overshadowed, but the CD transfer allows him to come through quite strongly and his passage-work on 'If I Should Lose You' and 'Groove Yard' is quite impressive.

Tete Montoliu (1933–97)

PIANO

Born blind – and subsequently hearing-impaired too – Montoliu was born in Barcelona and played and recorded with visitors to his local scene in the 1950s before being internationally discovered. He toured widely in the '70s and '80s but died from lung cancer in 1997.

*****(*) Songs For Love**

Enja 2040 *Montoliu (p solo).* 9/71.

***** That's All**

Steeplechase SCCD 31199 *Montoliu (p solo).* 9/71.

***** Lush Life**

Steeplechase SCCD 31216 *Montoliu (p solo).* 9/71.

Montoliu was a European maverick whose ebullient music could be tender, memorably exciting, gracefully virtuosic. Dazzlingly fast in execution, his improvisations are mostly based on a standard bebop repertoire, yet at his best he seemed driven to making his music fresh and new from record to record. From moment to moment he might suggest Tatum, Powell or Garner, and his feeling for blues playing is particularly sharp. He began recording in 1958, but until recently most of his '60s sessions as a leader are still hidden on obscure, out-of-print Spanish labels (for contemporaneous work as a sideman, see under Dexter Gordon's entry). Frustratingly, a live set for Impulse! at the Village Vanguard in 1967, with Richard Davis and Elvin Jones, has never been released.

Montoliu opened a prolific decade of recording with a single session in Munich, half of which was released at the time by Enja, the remainder turning up many years later on the Steeplechase albums. Little to choose among the three discs, but the first has a few originals by Tete and a thoughtful improvisation on 'Two Catalan Songs'. The question of Montoliu's employment of his Catalan roots in a jazz environment is an interesting one: his oft-quoted remark, 'Basically, all Catalans are blacks', isn't very helpful, but there's little doubt that he is exceptionally responsive to using his native music in a post-bop setting.

***** Temas Brasilenos**

Ensayo ENY-CD-3951 *Montoliu; Alberto Moraleda (b); Miguel Angel Lizandra (d).* 11/73.

***** Catalonian Fire**
Steeplechase SCCD 31017 *Montoliu; Niels-Henning Orsted Pedersen (b); Albert 'Tootie' Heath (d).* 5/74.

*****(*) Tete!**
Steeplechase SCCD 31029 *As above.* 5/74.

***** Music For Perla**
Steeplechase SCCD 31021 *Montoliu (p solo).* 5/74.

***** Boleros**
Ensayo ENY-CD-3473 *Montoliu; Manuel Elias (b); Peer Wyboris (d); Rogelio Juarez (perc).*

*****(*) Tete A Tete**
Steeplechase SCCD 31054 *Montoliu; Niels-Henning Orsted Pedersen (b); Albert 'Tootie' Heath (d).* 2/76.

*****(*) Tootie's Tempo**
Steeplechase SCCD 31108 *As above.* 2/76.

***** Words Of Love**
Steeplechase SCCD 31084 *Montoliu (p solo).* 3/76.

***** Yellow Dolphin Street / Catalonian Folk Songs**
Timeless SJP 107/116 *Montoliu (p solo).* 2–12/77.

***** Blues For Myself**
Ensayo ENY-CD-3954 *Montoliu; Eric Peter (b); Peer Wyboris (d).* 1/77.

Montoliu seemed to release a lot of records in the 1970s, but actually he had only a few concentrated bursts of recording. The four albums by the trio with NHOP and Heath remain among his most impressive offerings: played with both elegance and fire, his improvisations on favourite themes have a poise and dash that make one overlook the frequent appearance of many familiar runs and manipulations of the beat. Pedersen, who loves to play with a pianist of outsize technique, holds nothing back in his own playing, while Heath's rather gruff and unfussy drumming makes him a nearly ideal timekeeper for the situation. Of the Steeplechases, *Tootie's Tempo* and *Tete!* are particularly good, but any one is highly entertaining. The solo records are slightly less interesting, though the Timeless session – combining an LP of standards and one of Catalonian tunes – has some thoughtful moments.

The Ensayo albums, all recorded in Barcelona, feature Tete in congenial local company and offer some of his most relaxed playing. *Temas Brasilenos* is based around four long medleys of choice material by Jobim, Barroso and others, and there are unusual touches on well-worn tunes like 'La Chica De Ipanema' and 'Desafinado' to refresh jaded ears. *Boleros* is a set of Spanish compositions and as such is a rarity in Montoliu's discography. But the problem with both discs is the unimaginative rhythm section in each case, and neither is especially well recorded. *Blues For Myself*, a set of five blues and two standards, is marginally ahead, with Peter and Wyboris reading Montoliu's moves ably enough, though again the Steeplechase sets offer better work. *Words Of Love* is a sound if finally unremarkable solo session from the same period.

***** Boston Concert**
Steeplechase SCCD 31152 *Montoliu (p solo).* 3/80.

***** I Want To Talk About You**
Steeplechase SCCD 31137 *Montoliu; George Mraz (b); Al Foster (d).* 3/80.

***** Catalonian Nights: Volume 1**
Steeplechase SCCD 31148 *Montoliu; John Heard (b); Albert 'Tootie' Heath (d).* 5/80.

***** Catalonian Nights: Volume 2**
Steeplechase SCCD 31241 *As above.* 5/80.

***** Catalonian Nights: Volume 3**
Steeplechase SCCD 31433 *As above.* 5/80.

Another year that turned out to be a busy one. Mraz and Foster weren't Tete's ideal rhythm section but they don't get in his way too much, and the solo concert from Boston includes some of his most detailed and handsome playing. The concert session on the *Catalonian Nights* discs makes up an exciting meeting, but it's let down by an indifferent balance – Montoliu is almost drowned out by Heath at times – and a suspiciously battered piano. The second disc is worth having for the almost ecstatically driving 'I'll Remember April', but the music maintains a high standard throughout. New is the third volume, which has a further quota of his grandstand playing, as well as a pleasing original in 'Jo Vull Que M'Acariciis'.

***** Face To Face**
Steeplechase SCCD 31185 *Montoliu; Niels-Henning Orsted Pedersen (b).* 4/82.

***** The Music I Like To Play: Volume 1**
Soul Note 121180-2 *Montoliu (p solo).* 12/86.

***** The Music I Like To Play: Volume 2**
Soul Note 121200-2 *As above.* 12/86.

***** The Music I Like To Play: Volume 3**
Soul Note 121230-2 *As above.* 1/90.

***** The Music I Like To Play: Volume 4**
Soul Note 121250-2 *As above.* 1/90.

Face To Face suffers slightly from the abundance of virtuosity on show, and occasionally there's a sense of each man cancelling out the other. Otherwise, though, there's some music-making which at moments verges on the ecstatic.

The Soul Notes remind that Montoliu tended throughout his career to get maximum mileage from each session. It should be noted here, though, that the two later volumes are from a later date. The difference is immediately apparent, not so much qualitatively as in the nature of his playing, which is much more percussive and direct. The earlier Soul Notes number among the most finished of Montoliu's albums, with a superior studio sound and one or two unexpected choices: Bobby Hutcherson's 'Little B's Poem', for instance, on the first record. But some routine improvisations betray that the pianist can defer to familiar patterns on some tunes that he knew a little too well. There's a nice smattering of Monk tunes on the latter pair and some ballads that have not previously figured in the Catalan's discography. Though it might seem a hefty investment to spring for all four, these are better value than most.

***** Sweet 'N' Lovely: Volume 1**
Fresh Sound FSR-CD 161 *Montoliu; Mundell Lowe (g).* 9/89.

***** Sweet 'N' Lovely: Volume 2**
Fresh Sound FSR-CD 162 *As above.* 9/89.

The clean and persuasive interplay here suggests a friendly empathy that makes this unlikely combination work out very well:

Lowe keeps to his unassumingly skilful, swing-based style, and the ease with which it slips alongside Montoliu's playing suggests that the pianist is more of a conservative than his more ferocious moments suggest. Both discs were recorded on the same day and, as pleasing as they are, one will be enough for most listeners.

***** The Man From Barcelona**
Timeless SJP 368 *Montoliu; George Mraz (b); Lewis Nash (d).* 10/90.

***** A Spanish Treasure**
Concord CCD 4493 *Montoliu; Rufus Reid (b); Akira Tana (d).* 6/91.

Up-to-scratch trio dates: Reid and Tana sound a bit too boisterous for Montoliu's sprightly lines to cut through as they should, and the more reserved Mraz and Nash work out better. As capable as the playing here is, though, one wishes Montoliu had sought out a new format for his studio dates, which are sounding very much the same. The quintet session with Peter King and Gerard Presencer on *Morning '89* (Fresh Sound FRS-117, 2LP; still awaited on CD!) was a nice blast of fresh air.

***** Music For Anna**
Mas I Mas 002 *Montoliu; Hein Van der Geyn (b); Idris Muhammad (d).* 10/92.

Montoliu surfaced only rarely in the 1990s, but this club set suggests that his playing lost little of its flash or surprise. The dramatic deconstruction of 'I'll Remember April' is a single example, but it's something he does at some point on most of the tunes on offer. As with Solal, the pianist's uncommon syntax has become a commonplace with the wider currency of his work via recordings, yet the impact of his most vivid improvising remains startling, and it's good to have this recent reminder. Sound is decent – Van der Geyn comes through strongly – though the piano itself sounds like a sometimes unresponsive instrument.

Jack Montrose (born 1928)

TENOR SAXOPHONE

Born in Detroit, Montrose played on many West Coast sessions in the 1950s and led several records of his own, but he had to do session-work away from jazz in the '60s and was heard from only rarely thereafter.

***** The Horn's Full**
RCA Victor 74321 18521 2 *Montrose; Red Norvo (vib); Jim Hall, Barney Kessel (g); Max Bennett, Larry Wooten (b); Bill Dolney, Mel Lewis (d).* 9–12/57.

Montrose cut four good albums as a leader, when the West Coast was still hot, and this reissue is a timely reminder of a player who was drastically sidelined by the decline of the music in the 1960s. Two different quintets – Norvo is common to both – handle this programme, and the notes show how Montrose was at pains to create counterpoint and contrast between sax, vibes and guitar almost throughout. The result is a set that flows into a single piece, and the manner suits the leader's own playing: he nudges his solos along an even line, but there's a sense of invention which has survived the years. Some of the arranging is on the cute side, and a few of the up-tempo pieces seem a little gauche, but otherwise it's a worthwhile souvenir from a vanished part of jazz.

James Moody (born 1925)

TENOR, ALTO AND SOPRANO SAXOPHONES, FLUTE, VOCALS

'I'm In The Mood For Love' was a big hit for Moody after the war, in its turn inspiring one of the highlights of vocalese. Moody – and he prefers to be called that – was initially influenced by Lester Young, but he has utilized a harder and more abrasive tone since the '60s, as he responded to the challenge of younger players. Flute has from time to time been his major horn. In his seventies, his career has enjoyed a further resurgence.

*****(*) Moody's Moods For Blues**
Original Jazz Classics OJC 1837 *Moody; Dave Burns (t); William Shepherd (tb); Pee Wee Moore (bs); Sadik Hakim, Jimmy Boyd (p); John Latham (b); Joe Harris, Clarence Johnson (d); Eddie Jefferson, Iona Wade (v).* 1, 4 & 9/54, 1/55.

*****(*) Hi Fi Party**
Original Jazz Classics OJC 1780 *Moody; Dave Burns (t); Bill Shepherd (tb); Numa Moore (bs); Jimmy Boyd (p); John Latham (b); Clarence Johnson (d); Eddie Jefferson (v).* 9/54.

*****(*) Wail, Moody, Wail**
Original Jazz Classics OJC 1791 *As above, except omit Jefferson.* 1, 8 & 12/55.

'Moody, just call me Moody', he says to anyone who dares to use either 'Mr' or first name. Moody's affability and slightly zany vocals have led some to dismiss him as a lightweight. Even on the song with which he is now inextricably associated he demonstrates fine if unorthodox improvisational skills. His debut 'I'm In The Mood For Love', recorded with a Scandinavian group in 1949, was a big hit, establishing him as a bopper with a quirky sensibility and a sombre, tense side. Moody's distinctive sinuousness became even more obvious when he added soprano saxophone to his kit a little later in his career.

He's also joined on *Hi Fi Party* and on the extra 'I Got The Blues' on *Moods* by Eddie Jefferson, who reworked a vocal version of the hit, thereby (allegedly) giving King Pleasure the idea for adding his own lyrics to bebop tunes. Moody has a strongly vocalized tone and frequently appears to shape a solo to the lyric of a tune rather than simply to the chords or the written melody, and that vocalized sound is perhaps more evident on his alto playing, though he even adapts it later in his career to flute, using a 'legitimate' version of Roland Kirk's vocalization. The saxophonist was off the scene for much of the 1970s, certainly as far as significant recording was concerned, and his reputation went into something of a decline. Without star names, though, both *Hi Fi Party* and the rather less gimmicky and straightahead *Wail* establish a strong, individual sound that deserves to be more widely known and that certainly stands up very strongly alongside later works.

*** Moody's Mood For Love

Chess 051 823 2 *Moody; Johnny Coles, Donald Cole (t); Tate Houston (bs); Jimmy Boyd, Benny Golson (p); Johnny Latham (b); Clarence Johnston (d); Eddie Jefferson (v).* 12/56, 1/57.

Eddie Jefferson's classic vocalese response to 'I'm In The Mood For Love' is the main attraction on this buoyant and well-crafted set from Chicago. Moody alternates tenor and flute and plays with jovial skill, belying the dark shadows that were supposed to be stalking him at this period. The band was picked and produced to flatter the leader and Moody is the chief soloist, though Golson (on piano!) and Coles both have effective moments of their own. Briefly available on Jewel, this marks a welcome return for one of the happiest Moody sets; check out his playing on 'Billie's Bounce'.

*** Don't Look Away Now!

Original Jazz Classics OJCCD 925 *Moody; Barry Harris (p); Bob Cranshaw (b); Alan Dawson (d); Eddie Jefferson (v).* 2/69.

It was relatively unusual at this time for Moody to steer clear of flute, but the defining item of this session is the saxophonist's last ever recording with Eddie Jefferson, who turns up on 'Hey Herb! Where's Alpert!', not the best thing they ever did together, but an effective enough use of Eddie's vocal skills. Moody plays alto on 'When I Fall In Love' and 'Don't Look Away Now' and gives a superb performance on tenor on the long 'Hear Me'. There's a retread of 'Last Train From Overbrook', which will appeal to anyone who loves the song or who's hipped to Moody's extraordinary story of survival and growth. At just 40 minutes, one looks to more material, even if just a miscued alternative, but none is forthcoming. We have no idea how much – if any – of this session still lies in the vaults.

**(*) Blues And Other Colors

Original Jazz Classics OJCCD 954 *Moody; Johnny Coles (t, flhn); Tom McIntosh, Britt Woodman (tb); Jimmy Buffington (frhn); Cecil Payne (bs); Joe Farrell (as, ob); Kenny Barron, Dick Katz (p); Sam T Brown (g); Alfred Brown (vla); Charles McCracken, Kermit Moore (clo); Ron Carter, Ben Tucker (b); Connie Kay, Freddie Waits (d); Linda November (v).* 69.

For some reason, Moody decided to restrict himself to soprano and flute for this odd session. The nonet format, arranged by trombonist Tom McIntosh, gives the soloist a lot of harmonic support, and the strings are imaginatively deployed; even the tracks with vocalist Linda November are interesting, and 'Gone Are The Days' is an unexpected gem. It's not altogether surprising that Moody should have returned to soprano so rarely in future. It's a thin sound and only Duke's 'Main Stem', coming right at the start of the record, has much emotional resonance. At the opposite end, 'Old Folks' merely sounds clichéd; compare Charlie Parker's version with the Dave Lambert Singers.

*** Feelin' It Together

32 Jazz 32045 *Moody; Kenny Barron (p, hpd); Larry Ridley (b); Freddie Waits (d).* 1/73.

Recorded for Muse and now restored by Joel Dorn and 32 Jazz, this is Moody at the top of his powers. His tone on all three of his main horns is sharp and pungent, but also floatingly delicate. Jobim's 'Wave' is one of his more extraordinary solos, unusually pitched and hypnotic. Barron's use of electric piano and electric harpsichord gives the disc a greatly enhanced range of sonorities which the bassist and drummer adapt and personalize. Waits has rarely been caught better on record, effortlessly in metre but capable of implying alternative melody-lines and, on 'Anthropology', something of Max Roach's demanding solo style. A very fine album that has been out of circulation for a few years. It helps fill a blank spell in Moody's discography.

*** Moody's Party

Telarc 83382 *Moody; Arturo Sandoval (t); Grover Washington (ss); Mulgrew Miller (p); Todd Coolman (b); Terri Lyne Carrington (d); Roy Ayers (v).* 3/95.

The old dog turned seventy with a party at the Blue Note, compèred by the one and only Bill Cosby. The seven tunes selected for release are pretty familiar, but with an unexpected emphasis on bebop classics: 'Groovin' High', 'Parker's Mood', 'Bebop'. Moody is in sparkling form on all his horns and rises to the guest appearances of Washington and Sandoval with just the right mixture of challenge and graciousness. A lively, uncomplicated record to mark a significant anniversary.

***(*) Young At Heart

Warner Bros 9362 46227 *Moody; Alex Sipiagin (t); Slide Hampton, Avi Leibovitz, Jack Schatz (tb); David Bargeron (tb, tba); Alan Cox, Timothy Malosh (f); Jerry Dodgion (f, af); Frank Wess (af, bf); Larry Goldings, Mulgrew Miller (p); Gil Goldstein (p, cel); Sara Cutler (hp); Todd Coolman (b); Billy Drummond (d).* 2/96.

At seventy-plus, Moody entered what was to be his pomp, playing with a grace and confidence which blew away everything that had happened before. This tribute to Sinatra is hugely entertaining, but it's also one of the most thoughtful records in the Moody canon. Working with horns or with orchestra, he sounds absolutely on the case, with a relaxed, insouciant swing and the gentlest delivery you ever heard. He had been playing for half a century by this stage, and only a performer with that pedigree and those dues could possibly have delivered the solo he creates on 'The Song Is You' or manage the wistful splendour of 'It Was A Very Good Year', without sounding flat or ironic. Gil Goldstein's arrangements are *comme il faut*, note-perfect but also relaxed enough to suggest a live session. There might be too much emphasis on the orchestra on a couple of tracks, acoustically speaking, a rather overdone mix that blunts the impact of the basic quartet, but for the most part the sound is flawless.

**** Mainly Mancini

Warner Bros 9 46626 *Moody; Gil Goldstein (ky); Todd Coolman (b); Terri Lyne Carrington (d).* 97.

While attending a tribute dinner to Ella Fitzgerald, Moody talked to Henry Mancini about the possibility of a songbook album and thereafter received in the mail a collection of scores, with some marked as the composer's special preferences. In the event, this is a posthumous celebration of Hank's great music, but it is none the less a true celebration. Working with a small group allows Moody to follow the line of a song with a concentration he has not often been permitted in recent years. 'Silver Streak' and 'Charade' are small masterpieces of harmonic improvisation and should be required listening for all wind players. Moody takes the vocal on 'Moon River' and '(I Love You And) Don't You Forget It', dispensable but curiously touching. As on the previous Warner Bros release, Goldstein has a major impact on the overall sound. Here, though, he demonstrates a rare touch as an accompanist, caressing the themes with a sensuous understanding. It's Moody one hears, though, full-voiced, philosophical and full of sly wit.

Jemeel Moondoc

ALTO SAXOPHONE

Comparisons between Moondoc's alto style and those of Ornette Coleman, Marion Brown and Jimmy Lyons are useful as navigation lines, but they don't do justice to Moondoc's originality. A fiery player, but with much of Ornette's fragile vulnerability ...

***** Konstanze's Delight**

Soul Note 121041 *Moondoc; Roy Campbell (t); Khan Jamal (vib); William Parker (b); Dennis Charles (d); Ellen Christi (v).* 10/81.

***** Judy's Bounce**

Soul Note 121051 *Moondoc; Fred Hopkins (b); Ed Blackwell (d).* 11/81.

****(*) Nostalgia In Times Square**

Soul Note 121141 *Moondoc; Bern Nix (g); Ron Burton (p); William Parker (b); Dennis Charles (d).* 11/85.

It was Cecil Taylor who turned the young Moondoc on to modern jazz, and he's remained a devoted disciple ever since. His early group, Ensemble Muntu, which also included the ubiquitous William Parker, was very much in the Taylor mould, but Moondoc remained open to other influences as well. 'One For Ornette' on *Judy's Bounce* accounts for only the most obvious; his playing style sits somewhere between Ornette's country wail and Jimmy Lyons's street-corner preaching.

Konstanze's Delight consists of just three long pieces, the first of them an opportunity for the whole band to show its stuff. As so often in this context, Parker is the cement, setting off on a dark, seductive chant that gradually reels in Moondoc, Campbell and the underrated Jamal, who conjures up storms on this record. The two horns seem to be engaged in a game of one-on-one ball, chasing, dodging, body-checking and setting up half a dozen false climaxes before the whole thing unwinds. At longer than half an hour, it palls pretty seriously before time's up, but it's part of a live set and is doubtless pretty typical of what Moondoc was doing at the time. 'Chasin' The Moon' is high-octane stuff, a starring vehicle for Jamal and Christi.

Judy's Bounce was recorded only a month later, but it's a very different sound, reminiscent more than anything of Ornette's trio with David Izenzon and Charles Moffett. The Coleman tribute is based on an authentically simple march-based riff, over which Moondoc declaims like a man possessed. 'Echo In Blue' might be one of Ornette's dirges, except that it stays much closer to bebop harmonies. The opening 'Judy's Bounce' is terser and tighter, almost joyous, with Hopkins pushing things along at a brisk walk. The set closes as far out as Moondoc has been. 'Nimus' is one of Jupiter's shattered moons, and Moondoc responds to the idea with a lonely, plangent sound that might well serve as an interplanetary lament, one of his strongest ideas and a perfect vehicle for this particular trio.

The last album of the group is interesting for the addition of a guitar player and the abandonment of vibes for piano. It's certainly a conservative step and there's nothing on the set that really grabs attention. Nix is most closely associated with Ornette's Prime Time experiments, but he gets little chance to play outside an Ulmer-ish R&B groove, with a few abstract flourishes.

***** Tri-P-Let**

Eremite MTE01 *Moondoc; John Voigt (b); Laurence Cook (d).* 6/96.

***** Fire In The Valley**

Eremite MTE08 *As above.* 7/96.

Moondoc's absence from the recording spotlight has done nothing to damp down the fires. During recent years he has worked with the Jus Grew Orchestra, which has not yet – as far as we know – recorded. The trio represented on these two discs has been Moondoc's bread-and-butter group. *Tri-P-Let* pretty much carries on from work he was doing on *Judy's Bounce* and other earlier records. Inspired in almost equal measure by Ornette and Albert Ayler, it trades in fierce harmonic runs, bursting rhythms and intense, free-form essays like 'Improv. #61696', which was seemingly prompted by hearing Johnny Mbizo Dyani on a Kalaparush Maurice McIntyre record.

Recorded live at the Fire in the Valley Festival in Amherst, the latter of the pair is a tough, often abrasive and, to be honest, slightly unrelieved set which doesn't benefit from a recording which makes no effort to buff up the blunter edges. A single continuous piece plus minuscule encore, it gives a reasonable account of Moondoc's current position, which is not so very far from where he was last sighted. Voigt and Cook are unfamiliar names, and one can only imagine them slogging away at this uncompromising and slightly unfriendly music. Anyone who's already converted will find much to savour, even if only episodically. For the most part, though, this is a specialist item.

****** New World Pygmies**

Eremite MTE020 *Moondoc; William Parker (b).* 7/98.

This is Moondoc's first recorded encounter with bassist Parker since *Nostalgia In Times Square*, and is a revelatory moment in the saxophonist's recorded output. People talk about the conversational quality of duo performance, but this is more like twin preachers in the mission hall, playing hard priest, soft priest alternately, the one threatening brimstone, the other promising redemption. Most of the writing is by Parker and includes the magnificent 'Huey Sees A Rainbow' and 'Theme For Pelikan', as well as the brief, intense 'Another Angel Goes Home', a dedication to drummer Dennis Charles, whose presence would have made this record near perfect.

Moondoc's playing is most convincing on the opening title-track and the encore. It's Parker who holds the attention most securely, a master musician who continues to develop by the session.

Brew Moore (1924–73)

TENOR SAXOPHONE

A faithful Lester Young disciple, Moore played in New York in the 1940s, in San Francisco in the '50s and in Europe in the '60s. He made comparatively few records and his career was interrupted by drink problems.

*****(*) Svinget 14**

Black Lion BLCD 760164 *Moore; Sahib Shihab (as); Lars Gullin (bs); Louis Hjulmand (vib); Bent Axen (p); Niels-Henning Orsted Pedersen (b); William Schiopffe (d).* 9/62.

***** I Should Care**

Steeplechase SCCD 36019 *Moore; Atli Bjorn (p); Benny Nielsen (b); William Schiopffe (d).* 4/65.

Moore was a terrific but star-crossed tenor player, at his best as good as Getz and Sims but never able to get a career together as they did. He left only a small number of records behind him, and only two are on CD so far. The Black Lion disc originally appeared on Debut and is full of fine blowing: 'Ergo' and the title-piece are superb improvisations with Moore at full stretch, his lightly foggy tone rounding all the corners and easing through problems without a murmur, while two duets with Gullin and a fierce blow with Shihab on 'The Monster' are outstandingly fine. The only problem is with the sound, which seems to break up into distortion quite often. The Steeplechase album is a surviving memento from a stay in Copenhagen: solid, but not quite Brew at his best. The city turned out to be his nemesis: Moore died when he fell down some stairs in Copenhagen in 1973.

Glen Moore (born 1941)

DOUBLE BASS, PIANO

This gifted bassist spent his early years with Ted Curson and Jake Hanna, plus a stint in Paul Bley's Synthesizer Show, before joining the Paul Winter Consort and taking the step that would ultimately lead to the formation of Oregon.

****(*) Dragonetti's Dream**

veraBra 2154 *Moore (b, p solo).* 7/95.

***** Nude Bass Ascending**

Intuition INT 3192-2 *Moore; Carla Bley (org); Rabih Abou-Khalil (oud); Steve Swallow(b); Arto Tuncboyaciyan (perc).* 5/96, 4/97.

Dragonetti's Dream is a very mixed bag. There are fast, jazzy pieces, played with the fingers, slow sonorous *arco* chants, like 'Red And Black', and some thoroughly dismal New Age material. Unlike Towner, Moore is no piano player and most of his attempts to do so result in nothing more than indulgent noodling. That being said, there is much to admire here (including a wry dedication to skater Tonya Harding) and much of straightforward beauty.

As Patrick Hinely observes in his liner-note, the opening track of *Nude Bass Ascending* bears an uncanny resemblance to the Eagles' 'Hotel California'. If it's safe to assume that Moore may not have known that, it is harder to believe that Carla and Steve didn't recognize the debt and perhaps had a smile over it. The album, which is very much a side project from Oregan activities, is divided into quartets with Bley, Swallow and Tuncboyaciyan, and duo tracks with Abou-Khalil, on whose Enja recordings Moore has often played. The balance of emphasis is quite different here, with the bass very much in the forefront, but the language is still the same rich multicultural stew. Moore continues to make fascinating music, though how much of it belongs strictly on the jazz shelves is a moot point.

Michael Moore

CLARINET, BASS CLARINET, ALTO SAXOPHONE, ETC.

Moore is based in Europe, where he has found a more sympathetic outlet for his demanding music. A brilliant composer as well as instrumentalist, he mixes structural elements with passages of complete freedom and non-tempered sounds. He is a member of Gerry Hemingway's quintet and of the neo-traditionalist Clusone 3.

*****(*) Home Game**

Ramboy 02 *Moore; Herb Robertson (t, c); Fred Hersch (p); Mark Helias (b); Gerry Hemingway (d).* 10/88.

***** Négligé**

Ramboy 04 *Moore; Alex Maguire (p); Ernst Reijseger (clo); Michael Vatcher (perc).* 12/89, 5/92.

***** Klezmokum**

Ramboy 07 *Moore; Larry Fishkind (tba); Burton Greene (p, perc); Roberto Haliffi (d, perc).* 92.

****** Chicoutimi**

Ramboy 06 *Moore; Fred Hersch (p); Mark Helias (b).* 9/93.

****** Bering**

Ramboy 11 *As above.*

*****(*) Tunes For Horn Guys**

Ramboy 08 *Moore; Wolter Wierbos (tb); Frank Gratkowski (as, bcl); Ab Baars, Tobias Delius (ts, cl).* 4, 5 & 8/95.

*****(*) Mount Olympus**

Ramboy 13 *Moore; Alex Maguire (p).* 98.

Ramboy is Moore's own label, named for his son (apparently R.A. Moore or some such) and largely dedicated to disseminating his own music. *Home Game* was recorded in New York City with an intriguing quintet which embraces the avant-garde and mainstream jazz. As ever, Robertson is a dominant presence, squally and lyrical by turns, with a fierce attack and a gentle edge to temper it. On the long 'Suburban Housewives', he and Moore interact in an unexpectedly complex way, weaving together wind figures which might almost come from a more formal conservatory piece. Everything points to the record being an attempt to recapture early and family memories, but it's not just this that suggests a seemingly improbable similarity to some of Charlie Haden's Quartet West recordings. The relation of bass, piano and horns, together with old-fashioned, swing-influenced drumming from Hemingway, is very much the same, and Moore's clarinet has never again sounded so Goodman-like. Hersch is the surprise package, a notably eclectic player who moves freely between idioms and genres but who always maintains a consistency of presence and expression.

On *Négligé* Moore has assembled another like-minded group with a similar balance of sound. Maguire is completely at ease in environments like these, and his own 'Sparky' and 'Epigram' sit at the heart of the disc. There are 15 tracks, offering a good initial sample of Moore's music. *Chicoutimi* and *Bering* are the ones to have, exquisitely executed and thoughtfully expressed, poised between modernist and mainstream, wacky and sentimental by turns. The latter is intriguing for its choice of material, which ranges from Irving Berlin's 'The Best Thing For You' (probably worked up with the Clusone 3), Wayne Shorter's 'Albatross', John Lewis's '2 Degrees East, 3 Degrees West', Theodorakis's 'Vradiazi' and Jimmy Rowles's 'The Peacocks'. Either of these records will delight.

Klezmocum is superficially reminiscent of Don Byron's Mickey Katz project, but Moore is both a more serious and a more humorous musician, so the blend of moods is altogether more satisfactory. 'Oy Tate S'iz Gut' is spot on: emotive, wry and so totally ironic that it sounds entirely sincere. The presence of the legendary Burton Greene guarantees interest, and the two rhythm players yomp along with enthusiasm.

Moore's saxophone work on *Tunes For Horn Guys* is sterling, but the real meat of this still quite slim output (more may be found on Ramboy and on other small labels) is on the trio album with Hersch and Helias, where Moore is able to work in a free but strictly controlled environment, trading on that dry but not unexpressive tone.

The duos with Alex Maguire open up a new dimension again, drawing on free improvisation but also on formal composition. The Englishman is a stunningly good player, robust and muscular, who sounds as if he is climbing Olympus by some heroically self-reliant route. Moore is as quizzically lyrical as ever, popping question marks and inverted commas on top of even the simplest melodies. A beautiful album.

Ralph Moore (born 1956)

TENOR SAXOPHONE, SOPRANO SAXOPHONE

British-born Moore returned to America in his teens to live with his father. He turned from trumpet to saxophone and nourished an already impressive talent with a diet of hard bop. Coltrane is the most evident influence, but assimilated with a lightness of touch and tone that has characterized an impressive array of discs.

*** Round Trip

Reservoir RSR CD 104 *Moore; Brian Lynch (t, flhn); Kevin Eubanks (g); Benny Green (p); Rufus Reid (b); Kenny Washington (d).* 12/85.

*** 623 C Street

Criss Cross Criss 1028 *Moore; David Kikoski (p); Buster Williams (b); Billy Hart (d).* 2/87.

***(*) Rejuvenate!

Criss Cross Criss 1035 *Moore; Steve Turre (tb, conch); Mulgrew Miller (p); Peter Washington (b); Marvin 'Smitty' Smith (d).* 2/88.

Moore has always known who he is and where he is going, even if in the early days his self-confidence was not yet accompanied by much profundity. A hard-bopper in the approved retro style, he has demonstrated that there is still plenty of good music to squeeze out of the idiom. Moore does nothing to ironize it or spice it up with contemporary references (other, perhaps, than Kevin Eubanks's soupy guitar on parts of *Round Trip*, for which he also wrote the final track).

Rudy van Gelder has been engineering this kind of material for longer than even he cares to remember, and all the records are technically flawless. The performances are equally unexceptionable but may prove a little cool. Though his writing skills have sharpened considerably ('Josephine', 'C.R.M.' and 'Song For Soweto' on *Rejuvenate!*), he draws much of his material from piano-centred late bop – Bud Powell's 'Un Poco Loco' on *623 C Street* – though rarely anything as ambitious as Elmo Hope's inventively Monkish 'One Second, Please', which appears on the Landmark compilation below.

His soprano playing, restricted to 'Cecilia' and 'Christina' on *623 C Street*, still needs thinking out, and he seems to have some intonation and breath-control problems, neither of which are remotely evident in his supremely confident tenor playing.

***(*) The Complete Landmark Recordings

32 Jazz 32135 2CD *Moore; Terence Blanchard, Roy Hargrove (t); Benny Green (p); Peter Washington (b); Victor Lewis, Kenny Washington (d); Victor See-Yuen (perc).* 12/88, 3/90.

Moore's two records for the Landmark label, *Images* and *Furthermore*, have been unavailable for some time; renewed plaudits to Joel Dorn and 32 for restoring them to catalogue. The earlier record makes the Coltrane influence explicit in a heartfelt 'Blues For John', which also helpfully underlines how individual and by no means slavish is Ralph's appropriation of the great man's example. He also shows his familiarity with the less well-known corners of the modern repertoire with versions of Joe Henderson's all too rarely covered 'Punjab', and Elmo Hope's 'One Second, Please'. Blanchard is heard only on the opening original, 'Freeway', a typically unpretentious Moore idea, on Donald Brown's 'Episode From A Village Dance', on the Henderson tune and on a free-blowing interpretation of Hank Mobley's 'This I Dig Of You'. Benny Green is the hero of the set, playing some blistering solos and driving along the tempo.

The later album is in almost identical mould, kicking off with a breezy original, 'Hopscotch', before turning to imaginatively selected repertory material, 'Monk's Dream' and Neal Hefti's 'Girl Talk', though this time there are compositions by Hargrove and Green in addition. Once again, the trumpeter is used quite sparingly and the switch of drummers (Washington on three tracks, the powerful Lewis on four) gives the album additional texture and character. A most valuable compilation.

Tony Moore

CELLO

Since the days of Oscar Pettiford the cello has become a much more familiar voice in jazz and improvisation. Moore's practice has always been located at the free end of the spectrum, but with much of Pettiford's rapidity of attack and tonal sureness. Recently,

Moore has been involved in a new improvising unit, Kiln, shortly to record.

*****(*) Observations**
Matchless MRCD 22 *Moore (clo solo).* 8/93.

*****(*) Assessments And Translations**
Matchless MRCD 28 *Moore; Josep Vallribera (gesto-grafia).* 5/95.

According to a liner-note, the apparently abstract cover art is a detail of a portrait of Moore by the Catalan artist, Josep Vallribera. Putting together these 16 improvised 'observations' is a little like doing a jigsaw without the lid, and doing a jigsaw of a late Jackson Pollock at that. There is a strongly marked personality in every gesture, but even the longest and most discursive sections (only two exceed five minutes, four are less than two minutes) manage to be both lucid and elusive. Moore's use of extended techniques is less overt than Marie-France Uitti's, closer perhaps to another classically literate improviser with ties to Matchless, Rohan de Saram. As label founder Eddie Prévost perceptively suggests in his introduction, Moore's main focus of observation is the cello itself, which is observed historically, dialectically, and sometimes even subversively. Set these pieces alongside any of David Darling's ECM albums and the difference will immediately be evident. The results may, however, be less readily palatable and, though the performances were in many cases continuous, some listeners will want a little space round individual tracks.

Vallribera's contribution to the second album requires a tiny gloss: 'gesto-grafia' appears to be a method of non-notational scoring in which graphic gestures (Pollock again) are assessed and then translated into the extra-temporal dimension that music demands. These are very much longer and more developed pieces, just four of them on the CD. It may be that some listeners will find it easier to get a purchase on this second disc. Not that there is any commercial compromise on either.

Jason Moran

PIANO

A youthful New Yorker, Moran has come to prominence as the pianist with Greg Osby's current group, and here debuts as a Blue Note leader.

*****(*) Soundtrack To Human Motion**
Blue Note 97431-2 *Moran; Greg Osby (as, ss); Stefon Harris (vib); Lonnie Plaxico (b); Eric Harland (d).* 8/98.

That's *motion*, rather than emotion, and as another of Blue Note's family of young stars takes his turn in the limelight it's a hint that what he's about – as with many of the most interesting young players in this precinct – is the momentum and the dynamic of his music as much as its body-weight of 'feeling'. Pieces such as 'Gangsterism On Canvas' and 'Snake Stance', the opening two here, are self-consciously hip and trickily built, as if Moran was concerned that he might be seen not to present strong enough meat for a top dog like Osby to work on. The pianist isn't given to preening, though. The trio piece which comes next, 'Le Tombeau De Couperin/States Of Art', is thoughtful and generously lyrical without falling back on any sort of navel-gazing.

He has a lively imagination, for sure. He says that 'Retrograde' was 'created from an Andrew Hill piece playing backwards on my record player'. The tracks with Osby and Harris tend to be stolen from under him, since those players are so strong; so it's the three trio pieces that offer the most exposure for a style that's unexpectedly dignified and even grandmasterly: listen to the beautifully voiced lines of 'Release From Suffering'. The brief solo, 'Kinesics', is three fascinating minutes by itself. A compelling start overall.

Herb Morand (1905–52)

TRUMPET, VOCAL

Born in New Orleans, Morand started there but did most of his playing in Chicago, especially with The Harlem Hamfats. Returned to New Orleans in the 1940s, ran his own group and performed with George Lewis.

***** Herb Morand 1949**
American Music AMCD-9 *Morand; Louis Nelson (tb); Andrew Morgan (ts, cl); Albert Burbank (cl, v); Johnny St Cyr, Raymond Glapion (g); Austin Young, Eddie Dawson (b); Albert Jiles, Andrew Jefferson (d).* 5–7/49.

Morand wasn't a typical New Orleans brassman. He is best remembered as the trumpeter with The Harlem Hamfats in Chicago, and these recordings were done following his return to his native city in the 1940s. He sounds a little out of place with these old-school players, but his firm lead and terse solos give the music an extra ounce of assertiveness. Most of the music comes from a session recorded by Bill Russell, a large part of it too long for 78s and heretofore unreleased, but there are four rough and exciting tracks recorded at a dance at Mama Lou's Lounge two months earlier. The sound is a little muffled throughout but all the players come through clearly enough.

Frank Morgan (born 1933)

ALTO SAXOPHONE

Morgan grew up in Minneapolis but began his career in the nascent West Coast bebop scene. Drug problems interrupted his progress but also froze his Parker-indebted saxophone style at somewhere around the year Bird died. A passionate improviser, he organizes his solos in a songful, highly logical way.

***** Gene Norman Presents Frank Morgan**
Fresh Sound FSR CD 71 *Morgan; Conte Candoli (t); Wardell Gray (ts); Carl Perkins (p); Wild Bill Davis (org); Howard Roberts (g); Bobby Rodriguez, Leroy Vinnegar (b); Jose Mangual, Lawrence Marable (d); Ralph Miranda, Uba Nieto (perc).* 55.

Frank Morgan's story is not just about paid dues. Shortly after this record was made he was sentenced to a term in San Quentin for drug offences. He maintained his involvement in music while in jail, jamming with the likes of Art Pepper. Though he had worked locally following his release, he reappeared on a wider stage in the mid-1980s, purveying a brand of chastened bop, his initially bright and Bird-feathered style only slightly dulled by a spell in the cage.

In the mid-1950s, he was one of a group of saxophonists who hung on Charlie Parker's coat-tails. The currently deleted Savoy sessions aren't the best place to pick up on what Morgan was doing at the time, partly because the material is relatively unfamiliar and partly because the dominant figure on the session is Milt Jackson, who is already thinking in new directions. The Fresh Sound CD is a much better place to begin, though the septet tracks with Wild Bill Davis and three Latin percussionists are a touch crude; 'I'll Remember April' succumbs almost completely. Wardell Gray lends his easy swing to 'My Old Flame', 'The Nearness of You' and four other tracks, and Carl Perkins's bouncy clatter at the piano keeps the textures attractively ruffled. These were also Wardell Gray's last recordings before his untimely death (which may not have been drug-related as originally thought).

***** Easy Living**
Original Jazz Classics OJCCD 833 *Morgan; Cedar Walton (p); Tony Dumas (b); Billy Higgins (d).* 6/85.

After so long off the scene, it seems extraordinary that Morgan should have returned with something as confidently shaped and expressive as this. It's still some way short of the work he was to do in the later '80s, but of all Morgan's records *Easy Living* is least in thrall to the ghost of Charlie Parker, despite a wonderful version of 'Now's The Time'. Frank also picks up on material that had been written while he was away, tunes by Jobim ('Easy Living'), Wayne Shorter ('Yes And No') and Cedar Walton ('Third Street Blues'). A remarkable comeback, tougher and more pointed than the records that followed.

***** Lament**
Contemporary C 14021 *As above, except Buster Williams (b) replaces Dumas.* 4/86.

*****(*) Double Image**
Contemporary C 14035 *Morgan; George Cables (p).* 5/86.

***** Bebop Lives!**
Contemporary C 14026 *Morgan; Johnny Coles (flhn); Cedar Walton (p); Buster Williams (b); Billy Higgins (d).* 12/86.

***** Quiet Fire**
Contemporary CCD 14064 *Morgan; Bud Shank (as); George Cables (p); John Heard (b); Jimmy Cobb (d).* 3/87.

*****(*) Major Changes**
Contemporary C 14039 *Morgan; McCoy Tyner (p); Avery Sharpe (b); Louis Hayes (d).* 4/87.

San Quentin must have been a rough woodshed. Outwardly, there's no immediate sign of change. Modern recording makes his sound more intimate – grainier, anyway – so there's no reason to suppose that occasional huskiness is especially significant. Nor has Morgan forgotten where he came from. Almost the first thing he did on his comeback in 1985 was a brightly intelligent 'Now's The Time' (it's also excerpted on *Bird Lives!* (Milestone M 9166)), and there's a trawl of Parker-associated material on *Yardbird Suite*, with Jackie McLean's 'Little Melonae' thrown in on *Bebop Lives!*

What *is* noticeable, even with these closely focused recordings, is that he has grown quieter and more reflective. He seems rather hung up on favourite ballads, and some of that softness comes through on the duo, *Double Image*, which is reminiscent of Marion Brown's collaborations with Mal Waldron. Cables, though, lacks the broad harmonic grasp of a McCoy Tyner, who provides the focus of *Major Changes*.

Shank sounds more abrasive than of yore and offers some interesting textures in the ensembles. As a whole, *Quiet Fire* lacks bite and focus but contains enough emotion and warmth to satisfy all but the most detached listener.

***** Yardbird Suite**
Contemporary C 14045 *Morgan; Mulgrew Miller (p); Ron Carter (b); Al Foster (d).* 11/88.

*****(*) Reflections**
Contemporary C 14052 *Morgan; Joe Henderson (ts); Bobby Hutcherson (vib); Mulgrew Miller (p); Ron Carter (b); Al Foster (d).* 89.

Probably the best of the comeback albums is the complex *Reflections*. The straight-shooting thing Morgan does with Joe Henderson nudges him into a different gear, sometimes reminiscent of Jackie McLean, sometimes – unexpectedly – of Lou Donaldson. Of all the pianists Morgan has worked with since his return, though, Miller is the least sympathetic, ironically because he is not forceful enough. He sounds much too respectful on *Yardbird Suite*; at this point in time, isn't it legitimate to interrogate that material a bit more vigorously? Morgan's lifelong devotion to Bird is in danger of sounding slavish.

***** Love, Lost & Found**
Telarc 83374 *Morgan; Cedar Walton (p); Ray Brown (b); Billy Higgins (d).* 3/95.

***** Bop!**
Telarc 83413 *Morgan; Rodney Kendrick (p); Ray Drummond, Curtis Lundy (b); Leroy Williams (d).* 8/96.

The pace picks up refreshingly with the shift to Telarc and a more natural, less heavily produced sound. Morgan keeps it simple on *Love, Lost & Found*, with a heavy emphasis on ballads and a cleaner line than usual. 'All The Things You Are' is wonderful and even the easy swing of 'Someday My Prince Will Come' conceals some gentle surprises.

Bop! continues to plough a familiar furrow. The two dominant tracks are 'Lover Man' and Miles's 'Half Nelson', both of them elegantly extended improvisations. Kendrick is surprisingly good as an accompanist, but Williams is an awkward timekeeper and doesn't do much for the faster numbers. We very much liked 'A Night In Tunisia', one of the few occasions when Frank's tongue seems to be in his cheek.

Lanny Morgan (born 1934)

ALTO SAXOPHONE

Born in Des Moines, Morgan played in West Coast big bands in the 1950s and took the inevitable sessionman–sideman–teacher route.

*** Pacific Standard

Contemporary 14084-2 *Morgan; Tom Ranier (p); Dave Carpenter (b); Joe LaBarbera (d).* 9–10/96.

The cover shows him walking on water; although this West Coast veteran doesn't quite do that, there's little argument about his fleet phrasing, rubbery sound and hot swing. This is a plain old blow on ten standards with a professionally excellent rhythm section and, if it seldom touches great profundities, there's much to enjoy in Lanny's playing. He's a bit like Pepper without the salt – no anguish or anatomy-of-my-soul, just tough, honest jazz.

Lee Morgan (1938–72)

TRUMPET

Like fellow-trumpeters Fats Navarro, Booker Little and Clifford Brown before him, Lee Morgan lived fast and died young. He is arguably the defining figure of hard bop. Born in Philadelphia, he played with the Messengers and, at first in parallel and later as a solo artist, embarked on a long series of tight, vociferous solo sessions on which his punchy, out-of-kilter phrasing is always the main component. Though he is scarcely underdocumented, Morgan's early death was a serious loss to jazz.

*** Dizzy Atmosphere

Original Jazz Classics OJCCD 1762 *Morgan; Al Grey (tb); Billy Mitchell (ts); Billy Root (bs); Wynton Kelly (p); Paul West (b); Charli Persip (d).* 2/57.

Though he gets the month wrong, David H. Rosenthal's history of *Hard Bop* gives central symbolic place to the death of Lee Morgan, victim not of overdose or car crash like so many of his peers, but murdered by a jealous girlfriend. If Morgan's passing in 1972 felt like the end of an era in jazz, it was an era he can certainly claim to have helped define. Masaya Matsumara's painstaking website discography lists 151 sessions at which Morgan was present. We would not presume to suggest there were more, but there were certainly umpteen undocumented live dates in that same 16-year period, a prodigious outpouring of music. In 'The Sidewinder' he created what may usefully stand as the representative hard-bop tune. If he was to repeat the formula to the point of redundancy in years to come, he had the justification of having shaped the formula in the first place.

Morgan was one of the very few top-flight players to adopt former boss Dizzy's trademark 'bent' trumpet. It's only the most obvious gesture of homage to the other player, who made a big impact on his playing style. This tribute band, which seems to have been called Dizzy Atmosphere, balances him on top of a substantial front line, skiting ideas around like a superball on string. The release of alternative takes on the CD gave a reasonable indication of how Morgan rethought his solo approach. 'Whisper Not' is a particularly good example, a subtle reworking which on the issued take 5 has a much sharper and more emphatic delivery. This is not a classic album by any stretch of the imagination. It gives a good indication of what the young man was capable of and where he came from stylistically. Beyond that, it is only intermittently engaging.

*** Candy

Blue Note 46508 *Morgan; Sonny Clark (p); Doug Watkins (b); Art Taylor (d).* 11/57, 2/58.

Recorded around the time the twenty-year-old graduated from section duties with Dizzy Gillespie's group to featured soloist with the Jazz Messengers (with whom he was to record two classics, *Moanin'* and *A Night In Tunisia*), these quartet sessions have an attractive frosting of arrogance that doesn't quite disguise a callow romanticism on things like Buddy Johnson's 'Since I Fell For You' and 'Who Do You Love'. Unaccountably, one of the very best tracks by this group – 'All At Once You Love Her' – has only surfaced on Mosaic and a Japanese compilation (and it should be said that in Japan Morgan is treated with reverence) when it would have been easy enough to squeeze it on to the CD.

*** Expoobident

Le Jazz 39 *Morgan; Clifford Jordan (as, ts); Eddie Higgins, Wynton Kelly (p); Paul Chambers (b); Art Blakey (d).* 2 & 10/60.

Honed and sharpened by his first stint with the Messengers, Lee sounds tough, sassy and alert on a now-augmented LP session that pits the trumpeter against the strong-voiced Clifford Jordan. Pianist Eddie Higgins, otherwise uncelebrated, is the composer of the title-piece, and as an accompanist he is worthy of some attention. The original sound is flat and unresponsive, and untypical of the bright, burnished tone Morgan fans will expect on the basis of his Blue Note recordings; for fans of hard bop, however, this is a worthy addition to the collection, and the four extra tracks will please serious Morgan collectors.

*** Take Twelve

Original Jazz Classics OJCCD 310 *Morgan; Clifford Jordan (ts); Barry Harris (p); Bob Cranshaw (b); Louis Hayes (d).* 1/62.

The years 1958 to 1961 were taken up mostly with Messengers duties, though Morgan also fitted in sessions for Ernie Henry, Curtis Fuller and fellow-messenger Wayne Shorter. His own *Expoobident*, taped in October 1960, was a rare date as leader in this period. *Take Twelve* originally appeared on Jazzland, and it's one of the first places where one can assess Morgan the composer. It also offers evidence that he was developing as a performer as well, ironically by turning back to the work of older figures like Rex Stewart (who wrote the book on half-valving) and Roy Eldridge. 'Raggedy Ann', 'Lee-Sure Time' and 'A Waltz For Fran' all come pretty much from the basic lode: driven, blues-inflected themes with a brisk bounce. Hayes is a less dominant player than Blakey and he leaves more room for Morgan to develop his blues phrasing asymmetrically and with occasional unexpected nods in the direction of polytonality. Compositions like Elmo Hope's title-track suggest that Morgan was looking for something more than orthodox 'hard bop'. What was to follow the next year more or less guaranteed that he would never break the mould.

♛ **** The Sidewinder

Blue Note 95332 *Morgan; Joe Henderson (ts); Barry Harris (p); Bob Cranshaw (b); Billy Higgins (d).* 12/63.

The title-track was written in the heads towards the end of the session, a glorious 24-bar theme as sinuous and stinging as the beast of the title. It was both the best and the worst thing that was ever to happen to Morgan before the awful events of 19 February

1972. 'The Sidewinder' was an instant jazz hit, one of those themes, like 'So What', that insinuate themselves into the subconscious and remain there for ever. Unfortunately, it also established a more or less unbreakable pattern for future LPs, a bold, funky opener – often with a title intended to recall 'Sidewinder' – followed by half a dozen forgettable blowing themes, or, if you were lucky, another swinger to kick off the second side. The other pieces on the record have never been acknowledged to the same degree, but 'Totem Pole' and the superb 'Hocus Pocus' are the best available evidence for Morgan's gifts as a writer: vivid, often unexpectedly angled themes with every potential for extended blowing and not just off the back of a few algebraic chords. Of the other members of the group, Henderson stands out for his solo on the title-track and on 'Hocus Pocus'. Harris is rock solid from start to finish, and the bass-and-drums team can hardly be faulted.

****** Search For The New Land**

Blue Note 84169 *Morgan; Wayne Shorter (ts); Herbie Hancock (p); Grant Green (g); Reggie Workman (b); Billy Higgins (d).* 2/64.

This is the exception. Though much of Morgan's output for Blue Note after 1962 was pretty formulaic, *Search* was a musical exploration as much as a programmatic one. The presence of Shorter and Hancock guaranteed a measure of lyrical unpredictability, which is immediately registered on the title-piece. 'The Joker' might be thought to be the 'Sidewinder' piece this time around, except that it's a darkly playful, rather treacherous idea built on altered chords, and certainly not a theme that encourages a relaxed or lazy approach. Workman fits into this context particularly well, and the hyperactive Higgins drills away without a pause. 'Mr Kenyatta' may point towards one possible new inspiration for Morgan's music, though the two remaining numbers, albeit more than makeweights, are more off-the-peg: 'Melancholee' is a tight, bluesy ballad and 'Morgan the Pirate' another fairly orthodox improvising tune. A fine, questing record, and a pity that – *The Gigolo* apart – there weren't to be more like it.

****(*) Tom Cat**

Blue Note 84446 *Morgan; Curtis Fuller (tb); Jackie McLean (as); McCoy Tyner (p); Bob Cranshaw (b); Art Blakey (d).* 8/64.

With complete absence of irony, the final track is 'Rigor Mortis', for this is the least distinguished of Morgan's Blue Notes, and one of the very few that doesn't manage to lift itself even for a couple of tracks. The three-horn front line sounds cluttered, despite some great episodic playing from Fuller and McLean. The fault lies not so much with the pristine van Gelder recording as with the arrangements, which have no air in them.

*****(*) The Gigolo**

Blue Note 84212 *Morgan; Wayne Shorter (ts); Harold Mabern (p); Bob Cranshaw (b); Billy Higgins (d).* 6 & 7/65.

***** Cornbread**

Blue Note 84222 *Morgan; Jackie McLean (as); Hank Mobley (ts); Herbie Hancock (p); Larry Ridley (b); Billy Higgins (d).* 9/65.

****(*) Infinity**

Blue Note 97504 *Morgan; Jackie McLean (as); Larry Willis (p); Reggie Workman (b); Billy Higgins (d).* 11/65.

The Gigolo is relatively unusual at this point for the inclusion of a standard – 'You Go To My Head' – but again Morgan seems to be trying to pull himself at least halfway free of the coils of *The Sidewinder*. Mabern is a strong, funky player, ably supported by Cranshaw, but Shorter keeps things broken up and unpredictable. 'Yes I Can, No You Can't' plays a brisk game of musical catch, while 'Speedball', which was to become a live favourite, pushes at the limits of orthodox hard bop. The title-piece is a slinky and seductive tune, one of the better compositions of recent years in this idiom.

Cornbread is production-line Morgan, no more inspired than that. With the exception of 'Ill Wind', all the tunes are the trumpeter's and, with the exception of 'Ceora', most of them pretty forgettable. Morgan still sounds brash, brassy and full-toned, but the urgency has gone out of his playing and he seems to rely more and more on predigested licks. They're still a lot more compelling than most of his peers', but they are too conventionalized to be involving.

Infinity is no less generic and formulaic, but by this point Morgan was so utterly confident that one tends to forget that most of these ideas are already well trodden. The title-track is overlong and a touch lumpy and it's only Jackie McLean's 'Portrait Of Doll' that changes the tonality by a degree or two.

***** Charisma**

Blue Note 59961 *Morgan; Jackie McLean (as); Hank Mobley (ts); Cedar Walton (p); Paul Chambers (b); Billy Higgins (d).* 9/66.

By this point in his career, Morgan seemed to be on tramlines, writing and performing with an untroubled self-confidence that rarely deviated off course, and yet there are signs that he has sniffed the coming of fusion jazz grazing and taking on water just over the skyline. *Charisma* is the most formulaic of the Blue Notes, lifted by the delightful 'Rainy Night', a Cedar Walton composition, and including a bouncy version of Duke Pearson's 'Sweet Honey Bee'. The two saxophone players are in excellent form. If Herb Wong's 'original liner notes' are really that, then this set wasn't released until 1969, when Paul Chambers was no more. It may be that Blue Note were stockpiled with Morgan material and there wasn't slack in the market for any more.

***** The Procrastinator**

Blue Note 33579 *Morgan; Julian Priester (tb); George Coleman, Wayne Shorter (ts); Herbie Hancock (p); Bobby Hutcherson (vib); Walter Booker (b); Billy Higgins, Mickey Roker (d).* 7/67.

***** The Sixth Sense**

Blue Note 22467 *Morgan; Jackie McLean, Frank Mitchell (as); Harold Mabern, Cedar Walton (p); Victor Sproles (b); Billy Higgins (d).* 7/67.

The music on *The Procrastinator* isn't so very radical, and yet it was deemed sufficiently outside the market standard to justify holding if back for two years before release. Morgan was never dully formulaic, but it would take a seasoned listener or a dedicated Morgan fan to distinguish this from any other album of the period. *The Sixth Sense* is virtually unknown, even by Morgan fans. Almost axiomatically of albums from this period, it sounds like the work of an artist who has heard the future and is anxious to make it work. On 'Psychedelic' and 'Leebop', and on the Cal Massey tune, 'City Of My People', Morgan is nudging at the frangible boundaries of hard bop, which was always one of those categories that were more useful than significant. The recorded sound has also got funkier and more rock-orientated, with extra weight on the bass and a hefty backbeat.

***** Taru**

Blue Note 22670 *Morgan; Bennie Maupin (ts); John Hicks (p); George Benson (g); Reggie Workman (b); Billy Higgins (d).* 2/68.

***** Caramba**

Blue Note 53358 *Morgan; Bennie Maupin (ts); Cedar Walton (p); Reggie Workman (b); Billy Higgins (d).* 5/68.

Taru is certainly only an inch away from the kind of stuff with which Miles Davis was to revolutionize jazz in the next couple of years. The presence of George Benson has something to do with it, and underneath his smooth and unguent approach there is a whiff of cold steel. The recruitment of Maupin to Morgan's group was to be a significant one. After Shorter, he was perhaps the most adventurous saxophonist Morgan was to work with. Often dismissed as a colourist with no real jazz centre, Maupin always sounds completely convincing in the trumpeter's company. Among the tracks on *Caramba*, on 'Suicide City', 'Helen's Ritual' and another Cal Massey song, 'A Baby's Smile', he brings a dark-toned eloquence which fits the bill exactly. Morgan himself is more reticent than in the past and, one suspects, short on new angles.

*****(*) Standards**

Blue Note 23213 *Morgan; James Spaulding (f, as); Wayne Shorter (ts); Pepper Adams (bs); Herbie Hancock (p); Ron Carter (b); Mickey Roker (d).* 1/67.

A lovely – in some regards unexpected – record from a vintage group. The combination of Morgan and Shorter was always an unlikely one, the driving, linear approach of the trumpeter pitched against the more lateral and enigmatic musings of the saxophonist. Spaulding and Adams glue it all together, and Hancock is absolutely on the case throughout. Marked out by its choice of material, which includes a glorious version of Tim Hardin's 'If I Were A Carpenter' and a yearning but tough-minded reading of the Sondheim–Bernstein 'Somewhere', this is playing of the highest order. It also serves as a reminder of what an excellent drummer Mickey Roker is. Like Grady Tate, one almost expects him to break into song at any moment. One to watch out for.

***** Blue Breakbeats**

Blue Note 94704 *Morgan; Jackie McLean (as); Bennie Maupin, Hank Mobley (ts); Herbie Hancock, Barry Harris, McCoy Tyner, Cedar Walton (p); Bob Cranshaw, Reggie Workman (b); Billy Higgins (d).* 63–68.

Morgan was one of many artists whose work found a new audience with the rise of acid jazz and rare groove. These selections are very much with that market in mind, bringing together 'The Sidewinder', 'Cornbread', 'Caramba' and 'Nite Flight'. Superb party fare, but if you have the originals you can make your own party tape.

***** Live In Baltimore**

Fresh Sound FSR CD 1037 *Morgan; Clifford Jordan (ts); John Hicks (p); Reggie Workman (b); Ed Blackwell (d).* 7/68.

Jordan claimed joint leadership and, in the event, dominates proceedings with his strong sound and bearish impact. For a change, there are no Morgan originals in the set. 'Straight, No Chaser' is the most compelling single performance, a vigorous reading from both the horns. 'Like Someone In Love' is a little lacking in definition and emotional resonance, and Miles's 'Solar' lacks sophistication. On the other hand, this must have been a great band to encounter live, and the patrons of the Royal Arms in Baltimore must have gone home happy.

*****(*) Live At The Lighthouse**

Fresh Sound FSRCD 140/141 2CD *Morgan; Bennie Maupin (ts); Harold Mabern (p); Jymie Merritt (b); Mickey Roker (d).* 6/70.

****** Live At The Lighthouse**

Blue Note 35228 3CD *As above, except add Jack DeJohnette (d).* 7/70.

*****(*) We Remember You**

Fresh Sound FSR CD 1024 *Morgan; Jimmy Heath (ts); Billy Harper (ts, f); Barry Harris, Harold Mabern (p); Spanky De Brest, Jymie Merritt (b); Albert 'Tootie' Heath, Freddie Waits (d).* 11/62, 1/72.

The Fresh Sound live set is misnamed. For a long time it was believed that it consisted of material excluded from Blue Note's *Live At The Lighthouse* release, when it fact it was recorded some time earlier at a club called the Both/And. Some of the material from the same session appeared on a disc called *Speedball* which was issued in Japan, but the Spanish issue is pretty decent, sharing a few technical shortcomings with the official Blue Note release from the Lighthouse, but bringing together a lot of good live stuff. At this stage in the game, Morgan was doubling on flugelhorn, perhaps looking for a richer, fatter sound. It isn't always possible to tell what horn he's on, which is some testimony to his razor-sharp accuracy and the hardness of his tone.

DeJohnette is the guest drummer on 'Speedball' on the official Blue Note release, and his brisk, contemporary sound points to some of the directions the trumpeter might have followed had he been allowed another few years of activity. Certainly Jack offers rhythmic possibilities which are not available elsewhere. Maupin's 'Peyote' and an extended version of 'The Sidewinder' are stand-outs. There seems to be some confusion between 'Meo Felia' (credited to Morgan) and 'Neophilia' (which is ostensibly a Maupin composition) and between 'Ujamma' on Fresh Sound and 'Meo Felia'. Both sets are compromised by technical shortcomings, with some dropouts on the Blue Note, and one track on which the tape obviously ran out just before the finish. There are also some problems with the sound. The piano was pre-balanced and couldn't be altered, and there are some places where the bass seems to disappear. Blue Note seem to have been motivated by the existence – and the success – of bootleg sets from around this time to put the whole thing out, warts and all, and, given the quality of the music, who can blame them?

All the more reason to release it, when there was to be just one more session for the label, in September 1971, a large-group date which has never been released. Thereafter, Morgan recorded with flautist Bobbi Humphrey and, a mere two days before his death, with Charles Earland's orchestra. In January 1972 he was playing with Billy Harper, Mabern, Merritt and Freddie Waits, a set that included a fine latter-day version of 'The Sidewinder'. Not enough material for a whole disc, so Fresh Sound, whose provenances aren't always immaculate, have added three items from almost a decade before, a band co-fronted by Jimmy Heath. It isn't quite the headstone Morgan deserves, but it does provide an insight into the changes in his playing style over ten years. Something mellower and more thoughtful has crept in, something almost vulnerable. Underneath the incendiary nature, a more reserved individual.

*****(*) The Last Session**

Blue Note 493401 *Morgan; Grachan Moncur III (tb); Billy Harper (ts, af); Bobbi Humphrey (f); Harold Mabern (p); Reggie Workman (b, perc); Freddie Waits (d, perc).* 9/71.

Originally released as a double album called simply *Lee Morgan*, this captured a young man trying to find a new direction, to push out beyond the borders of hard bop. It's a big and rangy group sound with the addition of Moncur and Humphrey and with the talented Harper, composer of 'Capra Black' (which occupied the original side one) and 'Croquet Ballet', coming on very powerfully. Though very similar to the band which played at the Lighthouse, this is much more modern in focus; the title 'In What Direction Are You Headed?', written by Mabern, is quite readily directed at both Morgan and the music, for at this point he seems determined to try out a harmonic direction which is close to what Coltrane was doing a few years before he died. Harper is less of a colour player than Bennie Maupin, but he is certainly not a one-dimensional bopper, and almost all his solo spots are engagingly lateral. Freddie Waits is also a great revelation, a freely swinging but never mechanical stylist whose composition, 'Inner Passions Out', is the most radical thing on the record, and one of the most 'out' pieces Morgan ever recorded under his own name.

On 19 February 1972, Lee Morgan was shot dead by Helen More as he relaxed between sets at Slugs Saloon in New York City. For some at least, a whole generation in jazz playing was brought to an abrupt and tragic end.

Sam Morgan (1887–1936)

CORNET, VOCAL

Morgan led one of the classic New Orleans bands of the 1920s, and their records are historically important as well as enduringly powerful. Illness forced him out of the busines in 1932.

♛ ** Papa Celestin & Sam Morgan**

Azure AZ-CD-12 *Morgan; Ike Morgan (c); Jim Robinson (tb); Earl Fouche (as); Andrew Morgan (cl, ts); Tink Baptiste, O.C Blancher (p); Johnny Davis (bj); Sidney Brown (b); Nolan Williams, Roy Evans (d).* 4–10/27.

The eight titles by Morgan's band are among the classics of 1920s jazz. They are a very rare example of a New Orleans group recorded in the city during this period, and it's been claimed that these are the most truthful recordings of how such a band sounded in its prime. Morgan's music is ensemble-based, solos and breaks threaded into the overall fabric, the playing driven by the gusty slap-bass of Sidney Brown. Fouche might be the outstanding player, with his mile-wide vibrato, but it's as a band that these players have endured. There are few more exhilarating records from the period than 'Steppin' On The Gas' or 'Mobile Stomp'. Together with the Celestin tracks, this makes up one of the most essential reissues of early jazz, in outstandingly fine sound.

Joe Morris (born 1955)

GUITAR

After a troubled childhood and adolescence, Morris found a means of self-expression. The Boston-based guitarist has a highly distinctive playing style, almost always in fast, single-note lines, with distinctive mid-phrase trills which may be influenced by saxophone players. Morris rarely chords, unless one counts the rapid arpeggiations he builds into his more boppish ideas. His use of space is also characteristic, though his group improvisations rely heavily on dark accretions of sound.

***** Symbolic Gesture**

Soul Note 121204 *Morris; Nate McBride (b); Curt Newton (d).* 6/93.

***** Illuminate**

Leo Lab CD 008 *Morris; Rob Brown (as); William Parker (b); Jackson Krall (d).* 95.

****** No Vertigo**

Leo CD LR 226 *Morris (g, mand, banjouke solo).* 4/95.

A charter member of the Boston Improvisers' Group, Morris was an actively eclectic sideman and local star before he made it big as a recording artist. He has a facility for straight blues and fusion playing, but he works in a pumped-up free style that doesn't just put the emphasis on dynamics but also works in quite stark, abstract ways. The Soul Note is not a debut because Morris has put material out on his own Riti label for some time – though, alas, distribution is not exactly universal. As a first point of contact, it is slightly soft-centred, and it might be as well to move quickly on to *Illuminate* on Leo's radical Lab imprint, before coming to any settled conclusion. The quartet there is fresh and uncliché'd, but comes off the back of saxophonist Brown's Riti session with Morris and other associations for different labels. A clangorous, unfussy record, it will appeal not just to guitar-trio fans (who may feel more comfortable with *Symbolic Gesture*) but also to those who don't like their free jazz too vegetarian and mild.

The best record of the three is the solo *No Vertigo*. Morris has obviously been influenced by British improviser Derek Bailey. His acoustic work is very reminiscent of Bailey's 1970s work but with a hint of a jazz groove always hovering in the background, which Bailey seldom permits. He also includes tracks on an electric instrument (the long, very detailed 'For Adolphus Mica'), banjouke ('Long Carry') and even mandolin (a sequence called 'The Edges'). There is nothing slipshod about this music. Morris is a stern self-disciplinarian and the defining characteristic of the music on *Illuminate* is the responsiveness of the players to one another, a listening quality that extends not just to pitching but also to dynamics, rhythmic and para-rhythmic properties, even the use of space and (relative) silence.

***(*) Elsewhere

Homestead Records HMS233-2 *Morris; Matthew Shipp (p); William Parker (b); Whit Dickey (d).* 2/96.

The title-track was inspired by a sympathetic review of Morris's previous record and by the suggestion that music could take the listener to some super-real 'elsewhere'. Morris's dogged concentration on melody and his refusal to fall back on harmonic cushions and props is communicated to his three partners, all of whom also have a strong stake in this brand of rugged improvisation. Parker is, of course, already an established master and his contribution here is as calmly magisterial as always. Shipp occasionally sounds uneasy, but his great banging punctuations towards the end of 'Elsewhere' and his tremendous sense of structure are evident throughout, almost as if every phrase and every solo statement form the basis for some new, crystalline structure or architectural space; the pianist has often likened his own work to making buildings. Dickey is content to lay out here and there, perhaps with the sense that they are gravitating to his pulse. He doesn't so much keep time as generate new dimensions of it, within which the others can work. A still underrated talent, who will continue to make a mark.

*** Antennae

AUM Fidelity AUM 004 *Morris; Nate McBride (b); Jerome Dupree (d).* 7/97.

***(*) A Cloud Of Black Birds

AUM Fidelity AUM 009 *Morris; Mat Maneri (vn); Chris Lightcap (b); Jerome Dupree (d).* 6/98.

While Morris was attending a special school for troubled children in the Boston area, as he movingly relates, he spent a lot of time alone watching starlings flock and fly outside his bedroom window. Their movement – patterned, complex, only seemingly chaotic – made a great impression on Joe, and some of that experience comes out in the densely packed music on 'A Cloud Of Black Birds'. Reunion with Maneri sparks off a lot of shared experience, and their interaction, notably on the duo, 'Renascent', is close, intelligent and thoroughly sympathetic. The group tracks are inevitably denser in conception but no less powerful. The same language applies in the trio setting, except Morris is more obviously out front as a soloist. Here, Morris acknowledges a debt to the pianist and composer, Lowell Davidson, whose advanced notational ideas involved colour imaging, use of light and extremes of concentration. The tracks on *Antennae* are among the most intense Morris has produced. He seems more inclined to dwell on notes and to explore the light and shade that gather between attack and delay. His use of upstrokes affects the sound significantly and he varies pressure on the strings to create subtle harmonic overtones which also emerge on the sessions with Maneri and are perhaps influenced by Mat's father Joe Maneri's theories on microtonality.

Lawrence Butch Morris (born 1947)

CORNET, CONDUCTOR

Morris began as a cornetist in the Californian free scene of the early '70s, also playing in Europe, then moving to the loft-jazz scene of New York and working frequently with David Murray. Also a prolific composer, and more recently largely gave up playing in order to pursue conduction, a system of conducted-improvised music.

*** Dust To Dust

New World/Countercurrents 80408-2 *Morris; J.A Deane (tb, elec); Marty Ehrlich (cl); John Purcell (ob); Janet Grice (bsn); Vickey Bodner (cor); Myra Melford (p); Jason Hwang (vn); Jean-Paul Bourelly (g); Brian Carrott (vib); Wayne Horvitz (ky); Zeena Parkins (hp); Andrew Cyrille (d).* 11/90.

Most visible lately as the *éminence grise* behind some of saxophonist David Murray's most challenging music, Morris is an exponent of what he calls 'conduction', a kind of directed improvisation by which improvising players respond moment to moment to the conductor's signals. *Dust To Dust* is the first proper documentation of a Morris conduction, examined in much greater detail by the set listed below. In small, shapely episodes, this is a very approachable proposition, and a good taster for the feast which followed next.

***(*) Testament: A Conduction Collection

New World/Countercurrents 80479-2/80488-2 10CD *Morris; Hugh Ragin (t); J.A Deane (tb, elec); Wolter Wierbos, Daniel Raney, David Tatro (tb); Vincent Chancey (frhn); Jon Raskin, Larry Ochs, Dave Barrett, Dietmar Diesner, Kizan Daiyoshi, Bruce Ackley, Arthur Blythe, Kazutoki Umezu, Marion Brandis, Jemeel Moondoc, Yukihiro Isso, Shonosuke Okura, Makiko Sakurai, Jesse Canterbury, Mimi Patterson, Scott Deeter, Michel Titlebaum, Philip Gelb, Michael Barker, Peter Van Bergen, Michihiro Sato, Janet Grice, Hans Koch (reeds, woodwinds); Jon Jang, Guillaume Dostaler, Curtis Clark, Steve Colson, Steve Beresford, Haruna Miyake, Mickey Sheen, Myra Melford (p); Christian Marclay, Yoshihide Otomo (turntables); Chris Brown (ky); BlK Lion, Bill Horvitz, Brandon Ross, Hans Reichel, Wiek Hijmans, Elliott Sharp, Chris Cunningham, Gregor Harvey, Ethan Schaffner (g); Elizabeth Panzer, Zeena Parkins (hp); Pierre Dube, Brian Carrott, Damon Ra Choice, Reggie Nicholson (vib); Hikaro Sawai (koto); Ayuo Takahashi (zheng); Yumiko Tanaka (gidayu); Helmut Lipsky, Kaila Flexer, Hal Hughes, Yuji Katsui, Alison Isadora, Gregor Kitzis, Dana Friedli (vn); Edgar Laubscher (vla); Kash Killion, Martin Schutz, Eric Longsworth, Tom Cora, Tristan Honsinger, Michelle Kinney, Ken Butler, Dierdre Murray, Martine Altenburger (clo); Mike Milligan, Keizo Mizoiri, Peter Kowald, Motoharo Yoshizawa, William Parker, Mark Helias, Fred Hopkins (b); William Winant, Han Bennink, Thurman Barker, Taylor McLean, Gunter Muller, Ikue Mori, Sachiko Nagata, Le Quan Ninh, Michael Vatcher (perc); Catherine Jauniaux, Asuka Kaneko, Jannie Pranger, Elisabeth King, Tomomi Adachi (v); Shuichi Chino (computer); The Suleyman Erguner Ensemble.* 88–95.

Morris's steady evolution of his 'conduction' – in two words, conducted improvisation – has been documented in fine detail by this handsomely prepared ten-disc set. Morris outlines all the principles in the accompanying notes, which are a useful guide, since the music across this vast spread is difficult and challenging and not without its share of obfuscatory passages. While some of the individual pieces are only a few minutes long, others stretch to nearly an hour in length. There are groupings from America, Europe, Japan and (a memorable one) Turkey. In the main Morris favours large ensembles, but there is one group of no more than five players. This kind of thing needs to be superbly recorded, and most of the sets come in excellent fidelity, though the earliest isn't quite so clear.

If we withhold our highest recommendation, it's because the music isn't quite as satisfying as it might be to witness. The textures seem to aspire to a density which makes it difficult to hear what precisely may be going on and, if Morris appears to favour orchestral weight and gravity, he can't always sustain the kind of argument which would be second nature to a 'straight' composer. Some of the pieces follow surprisingly predictable forms of rise and fall, call and response; though soloists emerge from the ensembles with sometimes electrifying effectiveness, there is an innate sense of balance which a more free-flowing improvisation wouldn't admit. But perhaps that is the point.

Even so, there is much fascinating and rewarding music. Occasionally, as in the Tokyo set, which also involved Butoh dancers, nothing truly seems to communicate across. Other pieces have the vivacity and crackle of the best improvising. Others aspire to slow-moving sound-mountains. An accompanying video would be a useful source of further enlightenment, but for now the booklet will have to do.

*****(*) Burning Cloud**

FMP CD 77 *Morris; J.A Deane (tb, f, elec); Le Quan Ninh (perc).* 10/93.

With Morris turning away from performing himself, at least as an instrumentalist, good to have this reminder of his powers in a small-group context, done at one of Berlin's Total Music Meetings. The key player here is arguably Deane: besides his trombone lines, his meticulous use of electronics creates much of the backdrop, while Ninh and Morris step in and out of view. Morris plays a jazzman's role, tightly muted, dappling the canvas with tiny, stringent melodies. As modest as the instrumentation is, this is a rich and exciting music.

***** Berlin Skyscraper '95**

FMP CD 92/93 2CD *Morris; Axel Dörner (t); Marc Stutz-Boukova (tb); Gregor Hotz (ss); Kirtsen Reese (f); Johanne Braun (ob); Wolfgang Fuchs (bcl); Elisabeth Böhm-Christl (bsn); Bernhard Arndt (p); Albrecht Riermeier (vib); Dietrich Petzold (vn, vla); Alex Kolkowski (vn); Nicholas Bussman (clo); Tatjana Schütz (hp); Olaf Rupp (g); Davide De Bernardi (b); Stephan Mathieu, Michael Griener (perc).* 11/95.

From the 1995 Total Music Meeting in Berlin, these are numbers 51, 52, 55 and 56 in the numbered sequence of Morris conductions. As hard as these events are to evaluate from the cold evidence of a CD recording, this one seems like a considerable success, since it passes the litmus test of excellent sound, a team of skilful players and an ensemble willing to listen and be generous. Some truly fascinating and unpredictable textures arise from the instrumental combinations, often with a degree of refinement that makes it hard to believe that certain passages weren't entirely scored. If Morris can carry on securing documentation of these events, he's going to build up an astonishing archive before he's done.

Sonny Morris

TRUMPET, VOCAL

A founder-member of the Crane River Jazz Band, Morris has led his own Delta Jazz Band for many years, and they play fundamentalist revivalism, British style.

***** The Spirit Lives On**

Lake LACD46 *Morris; Bob Ward (tb, v); Terry Giles (cl); Ben Marshall (bj); John Sirett (b); Colin Bowden (d).* 9/94.

****(*) For The Good Old Boys**

Lake LACD 63 *As above, except add John Clark (p), Eric Webster (bj, g); omit Marshall.* 3/96.

***** Sonny Meets Pat**

Lake LACD81 *As above, except add Pat Halcox (t, v).* 11/96.

*****(*) Silver Bell**

Lake LACD102 *As above, except Chris Satterly (p, v) replaces Clark; omit Halcox.* 3/98.

*****(*) Near The Cross**

Lake LACD125 *As above.* 6/99.

The spirit in question is that of the Johnson/Lewis American Music groups of the 1940s, and this congenial group of veterans pay a likeable homage on *The Spirit Lives On*. Morris and Marshall have their own authenticity in spades, both being founder-members of the Crane River Jazz Band alongside Ken Colyer, and the rest of the group hardly put a foot wrong. The anti-virtuosic solos are scarcely the point of this music. What counts is the steady beat, the *simpatico* ensembles and the irresistible sense of inevitability about it all. Crucially, the rhythm section are exactly right, with Bowden in particular outstanding in the Baby Dodds manner. Excellent choice of material, and docked a notch only for the occasional shakiness and the vocals, dispensable as usual. For some reason, *For The Good Old Boys* isn't quite so good: a few of the tracks lumber along, and the tunes aren't so appealing.

Recorded at Farnham Maltings, *Sonny Meets Pat* is very good fun, with guest Pat Halcox sitting in with Sonny's Delta Jazz Band. The horn players all hit the odd clinker here and there and nobody's that bothered. Morris and Halcox don't so much duel in the front line as nudge each other, and the crowd love it.

On the evidence of the latest pair of discs, the band are getting better (except in the vocal department, so we'll gloss over what singing there is). Hard to say *how* it's better, since the playing isn't sharper or more accomplished as such: more that the ensembles gather momentum with an ounce more certainty, the tunes are carried with a shade more lightness. *Silver Bell* is the usual mixed bag but *Near The Cross* is all sacred material of some sort and, with many of the tempos extraordinarily slow, it's a tribute to the band that they muster so much conviction at that pace. Morris's little solo on 'Were You There?' is also a fine example of his perfectly appropriate improvising.

Thomas Morris (1898–date unknown)

CORNET

A frequent visitor to recording studios in New York during the 1920s, Morris thereafter joined a religious sect and gave up music during the 1930s. Nothing is known of him after that.

****(*) When A 'Gator Hollers ...**

Frog DGF-1 *Morris; Rex Stewart, Jabbo Smith (c); Geechie Fields, Joe Nanton, Charlie Irvis (tb); Ernest Elliott (cl, ts, bs); Happy Cauldwell (cl, ts); Bob Fuller (cl, ss); Mike Jackson (p, v); Phil Worde (p); Buddy Christian (g, bj); Lee Blair (bj); Bill Benford (tba); Wellman Braud (b); Helen Baxter, Margaret Johnson (v).* 7–11/26.

Hardcore collectors will welcome this lovingly assembled set of early-jazz rarities; everybody else should be warned that this is second-rate music, for all its undoubted charm and savvy at this great distance. Morris – peculiarly little is known about his life – was a frequent accompanist to singers, but the sides made under his own leadership for Victor are more notable for the sidemen than for his own distinctly average playing. The best moment on the whole record is Rex Stewart's thrilling solo on 'Charleston Stampede', and that's even more thrilling on the Fletcher Henderson original. Elsewhere there are some interesting fragments from names usually consigned to the lumber-room of jazz history. Some typical hokum – 'Who's Dis Heah Stranger' or 'Jackass Blues', again not a patch on the Henderson version – mingles with the title-piece, sung by Margaret Johnson, and some later tracks that feature Joe Nanton just before he joined Henderson. The remastering is done superbly and every known take is here.

Wilber Morris

BASS

Leading bassist in the new New York jazz of the '70s and '80s.

***** Wilber Force**

DIW 809 *Morris; David Murray (ts, bcl); Dennis Charles (d).* 2/83.

While flawed – there are too many bass solos for Morris to sustain with comfort, and the material is repetitive – this concert set has a fine intensity of spirit. The best piece is the opening number, 'Randy', which features some superb interplay between the three musicians over a series of shifting metres. Murray's characteristically rambling improvisations muster their usual ornery temperament, and his bass clarinet showcase on 'Afro-Amer. Ind' is marvellously articulated. The sound is rather restricted but not too distracting from the music.

Dick Morrissey (born 1940)

TENOR SAXOPHONE

Emerged on the London scene in the early '60s as a hard-bop tenorman, then investigated a jazz-rock fusion in If (1970), and the subsequent and very popular Morrissey–Mullen (1976–87). Recently silenced by illness.

*****(*) It's Morrissey, Man**

Redial 558 701-2 *Morrissey; Stan Jones (p); Malcolm Cecil (b); Colin Barnes (d).* 4/61.

For a younger generation of listeners the name Morrissey will conjure up nothing more than the image of a camp pop singer who favours Johnny Ray hearing aids, gladioli and songs about assignations at cemetery gates. For us, it will always conjure up the beefy Webster-inspired tenor of the man from Chorley. Dick Morrissey dabbled with clarinet and other horns before making the tenor his main instrument, and along with muscle and sinew his playing has something of Pres's delicacy of touch.

Morrissey came to prominence with the jazz-rock group If, and later with Morrissey–Mullen, a similarly conveived outfit with perhaps a greater jazz and blues component. His co-leader was guitarist Jim Mullen, who remains one of Britain's best guitar improvisers. In recent years, ill-health has seriously curtailed Morrissey's activities, which makes this reissue all the more welcome. Morrissey was 21 when it was made, and his maturity is astonishing. He works the changes on Johnny Griffin's 'Mildew', yet another jazz piece based on 'I Got Rhythm', with consummate ease and makes Rollins's 'St Thomas' sound fresh-minted. 'Happy Feet' is a fast-paced swinger that manages to stay in touch with Milton Ager and Jack Yellen's glorious piece of nonsense. It's also a bit of a sucker punch, for the end of the album is rawly melancholy. 'Where Is Love' and 'Dancing In The Dark' drop the pace significantly. 'Willow, Weep For Me' could perhaps have been full-voiced, but Mingus's 'Jellyroll', which closes the record, is mainstream jazz at its best, played unaffectedly and with real feeling for the tune.

Stan Jones is the only group member with any writing credits on the album, checking in with two originals, 'Puffing Billy' and 'Gurney Was Here', both of which deserve another moment in the sun. Neither he nor the rest of the rhythm section are well recorded, with Malcolm Cecil's bass very boxy and distant.

Jelly Roll Morton (1890–1941)

PIANO, VOCAL

Morton led a picaresque life in New Orleans in the earliest 1900s – as a pianist, pimp, billiards player, tailor, minstrel-show entertainer, hustler and more. Began recording in Chicago in 1923, then bandleading with his Red Hot Peppers, making some of the classic early jazz recordings. Arrived in New York in 1928 but found it hard to compete and gradually lost ground. Scuffled and fought over unpaid royalties during the '30s, then began recording his life story (and his history of jazz) for the Library of Congress in 1938. Various comebacks, 1939–41, but died in Los Angeles, bitter and unrewarded. A great legend and perhaps the first great jazz composer.

***(*) **The Piano Rolls**

Nonesuch 79363-2 *Morton (p roll).* 20–2/97.

(***) **Blues And Stomps From Rare Piano Rolls**

Biograph BCD111 *Morton (p roll).* 24–26.

The Nonesuch disc is one of the most fascinating retrievals of recent years. Morton's twelve original piano rolls have been analysed in the light of his other recordings by Artis Wodehouse, who has subsequently converted the information to computer data and edited a previously missing interpretative element into the way the rolls are reproduced. The subsequently annotated rolls were then played back on a nine-foot Disklavier piano, in a concert hall, and recorded. The remarkable outcome may be the closest we can ever get to hearing what Morton might truly have sounded like at this early peak of his career. Or they may not. Sceptics will point to the issue that, however meticulous the homework, this is still only somebody's idea of how the rolls should sound. Yet the results are exhilarating enough to suggest that Jelly's ghost is indeed seated at the keyboard. If there is an inevitable sense of something mechanical in the delivery, it's offset by the rocking syncopations, rips and general *brio* which always seem to be among the hallmarks of a Morton performance. The odd combination of ferocity and gentility in 'Grandpa's Spells', the dizzying double-time break in 'Midnight Mama' and the unbridled virtuosity of 'Shreveport Stomps' have certainly never sounded more convincing. It is altogether a memorable event and indispensable to anyone intrigued by the early steps of the master. The Biograph disc, unadorned renditions of the original rolls, is rendered somewhat redundant by the Nonesuch CD, but we list it anyway.

*** **Jelly Roll Morton 1923–1924**

Classics 584 *Morton; Tommy Ladnier, Natty Dominique (c); Zue Robertson (tb); Wilson Townes, Boyd Senter, Horace Eubanks (cl); Arville Harris (as); W.E Burton (d, kazoo); Jasper Taylor (d).* 6/23–6/24.

**** **Piano Solos**

Retrieval RTR 79002 *Morton (p solo).* 7/23–4/26.

Although we are listing the piano-roll discs first, most assessments of the self-styled originator of jazz and stomps commence with these mainly solo sessions. Morton's all-embracing mastery of the keyboard makes these 19 solos a sublimation of everything jazz had done up to this point. He combines the formal precision of ragtime with a steady melodic flow and a portfolio of rhythms that are tirelessly varied: if Louis Armstrong finally liberated jazz rhythms, Morton had already set out the possibilities to do so. As a series of compositions, this was a storehouse of ideas which has yet to be exhausted: here are the first versions of two of jazz's most enduring masterworks, 'King Porter Stomp' and 'Wolverine Blues', as well as such definitive Morton portraits as 'The Pearls' and the brilliantly delivered 'Shreveport Stomps'. His timing is ambitious yet miraculously secure: listen to the poetic elegance of 'New Orleans (Blues) Joys' or the famous 'Spanish Tinge' in 'Tia Juana'. Considering the roughness of the original recordings, the fact that the music remains utterly compelling is testament to Morton's greatness. The piano-sound is still pretty awful to modern ears, and some of the (often very rare) originals are clearly in less than perfect shape, but this is essential music. The Classics CD scarcely improves on the earlier Fountain/Retrieval LP, now on CD, although the individual tracks have not been remastered from their 1972 incarnation. Admittedly, it adds what were really some false starts in Morton's career – two very cloudy 1923 tracks for Paramount, with a band that may or may not include Tommy Ladnier, a not much better session for OKeh with the feeble Dominique, Robertson and Eubanks, and a fairly disastrous 'Mr Jelly Lord', where he's buried behind Boyd Senter and some kazoo playing – but some may feel that it simply devalues the consistency of the solos. Retrieval's reissue now also includes the four solos for Vocalion from 1926, and this is certainly our first choice.

*** **Jelly Roll Morton 1924–1926**

Classics 599 *Morton; Lee Collins, King Oliver, George Mitchell (c); Roy Palmer, Kid Ory, Ray Bowling (tb); Omer Simeon (cl, bcl); Barney Bigard (cl, ts); Balls Ball, Volly DeFaut, Darnell Howard (cl); Alex Poole (as); W.E Burton (kazoo); Clarence Black, J. Wright Smith (vn); Johnny St Cyr (bj, g); John Lindsay (b); Clay Jefferson, Andrew Hilaire (d); Edmonia Henderson (v).* 9/24–12/26.

**** **Jelly Roll Morton 1926–1928**

Classics 612 *Morton; Ward Pinkett (t); George Mitchell (c); Kid Ory, Gerald Reeves, Geechie Fields (tb); Omer Simeon, Johnny Dodds (cl); Stump Evans (as); Bud Scott, Johnny St Cyr (g); Lee Blair (bj); Bill Benford, Quinn Wilson (tba); John Lindsay (b); Andrew Hilaire, Tommy Benford, Baby Dodds (d).* 12/26–6/28.

**** **Jelly Roll Morton 1928–1929**

Classics 627 *Morton; Ed Anderson, Edwin Swayzee, Boyd 'Red' Rosser, Walter Briscoe, Henry 'Red' Allen, Freddy Jenkins (t); William Cato, Charlie Irvis, J.C Higginbotham (tb); Russell Procope, Albert Nicholas, Wilton Crawley, George Baquet (cl); Paul Barnes (ss); Joe Thomas, Johnny Hodges (as); Joe Garland, Walter Thomas (ts); Luis Russell, Rod Rodriguez (p); Lee Blair, Will Johnson (g); Barney Alexander (bj); Bill Moore, Harry Prather (tba); Pops Foster (b); Manzie Johnson, William Laws, Paul Barbarin, Sonny Greer (d).* 12/28–12/29.

*** **Jelly Roll Morton 1929–1930**

Classics 642 *Morton; Ward Pinkett, Bubber Miley (t); Geechie Fields, Wilbur De Paris (tb); Albert Nicholas, Barney Bigard, Ernie Bullock (cl); Bernard Addison, Howard Hill (g); Lee Blair (bj); Billy Taylor, Bill Benford, Pete Biggs (tba); Zutty Singleton, Tommy Benford, Cozy Cole (d).* 12/29–7/30.

*** **Jelly Roll Morton 1930–1939**

Classics 654 *Morton; Ward Pinkett, Sidney De Paris (t); Geechie Fields, Claude Jones, Fred Robinson (tb); Sidney Bechet (ss); Albert Nicholas, Eddie Scarpa (cl); Happy Caldwell (ts); Bernard Addison, Lawrence Lucie (g); Billy Taylor (tba); Wellman Braud (b); Bill Beason, Zutty Singleton (d).* 10/30–12/39.

Classics 599 starts with a 1924 date with Morton's (so-called) Kings Of Jazz, and horrible it sounds too, poorly transferred from grim originals and featuring diabolical clarinet from the suitably named 'Balls' Ball and even worse alto by Alex Poole. Trio versions of 'My Gal' and 'Wolverine Blues' with Volly DeFaut aren't much better, but a fine 1926 solo date for Vocalion *is* included, and these tracks (unavailable elsewhere) must make the disc attractive to Morton specialists. Two sides with (allegedly) King

Oliver and Edmonia Henderson are a further bonus. They then go into the Victor sequence, which continues through Classics 612 and 627, although the latter adds an unremarkable session at the end under Wilton Crawley's leadership, with (somewhat mystifyingly) a number of Ellingtonians present.

Morton's recordings for Victor are a magnificent body of work which has been done splendid but frustratingly mixed justice by the various reissues now available. His Red Hot Peppers band sides, particularly those cut at the three incredible sessions of 1926, are masterpieces which have endured as well as anything by Armstrong, Parker or any comparable figure at the top end of the jazz pantheon. Morton seemed to know exactly what he wanted: having honed and orchestrated compositions like 'Grandpa's Spells' at the piano for many years, his realization of the music for a band was flawless and brimful of jubilation at his getting the music down on record. Mitchell, Simeon and the others all took crackling solos, but it was the way they were contextualized by the leader that makes the music so close to perfection. The 1926–7 dates were a summary of what jazz had achieved up to that time: as a development out of the New Orleans tradition, it eschewed the soloistic grandeur that Armstrong was establishing and preferred an almost classical poise and shapeliness. If a few other voices (Ellington, Redman) were already looking towards a more modern kind of group jazz, Morton was distilling what he considered to be the heart of hot music, 'sweet, soft, plenty rhythm', as he later put it.

While the earliest sessions are his greatest achievements, it's wrong to regard the later work as a decline. There are the two trio tracks with the Dodds brothers, with Morton tearing into 'Wolverine Blues'. The 1928 sessions feature his ten-piece touring band on the fine 'Deep Creek' and a small group handling the beautiful 'Mournful Serenade', while 1929 saw a memorable solo session which produced 'Pep', 'Fat Frances' and 'Freakish', and an exuberant band date that uncorked swinging performances in 'Burnin' The Iceberg' and 'New Orleans Bump'. But the sessions from 1930 onwards suffer from personnel problems and a vague feeling that Morton was already becoming a man out of time, with New York and territory bands moving into a smoother, less consciously hot music. His own playing remains jauntily commanding but sidemen become sloppy, and a piece like the complex 'Low Gravy', from July 1930, never reaches its potential on record. His last session for Victor until 1939 produced a final shaft of Mortonian genius in 'Fickle Fay Creep'; but a feeling was now deep-set that the pianist was a declining force, and he didn't record for Victor again until the end of the decade.

The 1939 tracks show the old master in good spirits, singing 'I Thought I Heard Buddy Bolden Say' and 'Winin' Boy Blues' with his old panache and directing an authentic New Orleans band with resilient aplomb. It is very old-time music for 1939 but it's still very different from the early Peppers sides, and none the worse for either. Classics 654 covers these sessions and also includes four titles from an excellent solo date from 1938.

Morton's music demands a place in any jazz collection. At the moment, the availability situation is back to being less than ideal. RCA's complete edition seems to have gone for the moment. It is high time that a proper job was done in making these magnificent tracks available in a comprehensive, state-of-the-art remastering. The Classics CDs have the field to themselves, and it's a pity that their remastering is often spotty and unpredictable. To add to the glut of issues, there are also sets available from Memoria (*The Complete Jelly Roll Morton, 1926–1930*, 2 CDs), EPM (*Creole Genius*, 3 CDs) and Fremaux (*The Quintessence*, 2 CDs) which go over the same ground. *Sweet And Hot* (Topaz TPZ 1003) is another good single-disc collection in the Topaz series of compilations.

****** Kansas City Stomp**
Rounder CD1091 *Morton (p, v).* 5–6/38.

*****(*) Anamule Dance**
Rounder CD1092 *Morton (p, v).* 5–6/38.

****** The Pearls**
Rounder CD1093 *Morton (p, v).* 5–6/38.

****** Winin' Boy Blues**
Rounder CD1094 *Morton (p, v).* 5–6/38.

In the summer of 1938, broke and almost finished, Morton was recorded – almost by chance at first – by Alan Lomax at the Library of Congress, and when Lomax realized the opportunity he had on his hands he got Morton to deliver a virtual history of the birth pangs of jazz as it happened in the New Orleans of the turn of the century. His memory was unimpaired, although he chose to tell things as he preferred to remember them, perhaps; and his hands were still in complete command of the keyboard. The results have the quality of a long, drifting dream, as if Morton were talking to himself. He demonstrates every kind of music which he heard or played in the city, re-creates all his greatest compositions in long versions unhindered by 78 playing time, remembers other pianists who were never recorded, spins yarns, and generally sets down the most distinctive (if not necessarily the most truthful) document we have on the origins of the music. The sessions were made on an acetate recorder and, while the sound may be uncomfortably one-dimensional to modern ears, everything he says comes through clearly enough, and the best of the piano solos sound as invigorating as they have to be. The new remastering achieved by Rounder is the best attempt to date to reproduce the music in correct pitch and speed; while much talk has been omitted from the four CDs, it is a wonderfully illustrated lecture on Morton's music by the man who created it. Of the four discs, only Volume Two is slightly less than essential, with the final disc offering perhaps the best selection of solos, including his astonishing extended treatment of 'Creepy Feeling'. Indispensable records for anyone interested in jazz history.

(***) Jelly Roll Morton 1939–1940
Classics 668 *Morton; Henry 'Red' Allen (t); Joe Britton, Claude Jones (tb); Albert Nicholas (cl); Eddie Williams (as); Wellman Braud (b); Zutty Singleton (d).* 12/39–1/40.

*****(*) Last Sessions: The Complete General Recordings**
Commodore CMD 14032 *As above.* 12/39–1/40.

Morton's final recordings are relatively little-known, cut originally for General and later appearing on Commodore. The tracks by the Morton Six and Seven find him back with several sons of New Orleans, but the music lacks the authority of his great days; a couple of solo sessions from 1939 do, though, reassert his enduring powers at the keyboard, with several favourites still sounding like pieces of jazz legend. When one tracks through his legacy, there is actually little enough (compare him with Ellington or Armstrong for prolificity!) to make any survivals rather precious. The new Commodore edition is in very decent sound and comes across much better than the Classics disc. It also has a far superior documentation.

Mosaic Sextet

GROUP

One-off band of new New York players, 1988–90.

***** Today This Moment**

Konnex KCD 5058 *Dave Douglas (t); Michael Rabinowitz (bsn); Michael Jefry Stevens (p); Mark Feldman (vn); Joe Fonda (b); Harvey Sorgen (d).* 1/88, 2/89, 3/90.

Such was the buzz surrounding the trumpeter a couple of years back that we were inclined to treat this outfit as if it were another of his groups. Hindsight suggests that Stevens and Feldman (who have recorded in duo on Leo Records) may almost be more proactive and exert a greater influence on the overall sound. There's no mistaking this group for any other, and the 13-month intervals between the constituent sessions suggest that they're happy to wait for everyone to be on hand, rather than plug gaps with stand-ins. Douglas's manic schedule is doubtless the main obstacle.

The best of the material comes from the most recent encounter. 'Gang Wars For Sexter' and 'Superconductor' remain the outstanding tracks, representative of a strong, rich sound that combines a live feel with a very accurate division of voices.

Sal Mosca (born 1927)

PIANO

A kindred spirit to Lennie Tristano, Mosca has carried on Tristano-ite trends by making himself scarce and recording only very sparingly. As a pianist, he displays the inevitable fealty to his mentor's methods.

*****(*) A Concert**

Jazz Records JR-8 *Mosca (p solo).* 6/79.

Belatedly released in 1990, this is a rare example of one of the leading followers of Lennie Tristano in a solo situation. Because Mosca has made so few recordings, his appearances always seem eventful and, despite the dour atmosphere of the CD – which settles for the grimmest monochrome packaging and presentation, a characteristic refusal to distract from the music's inner qualities – it is played electrically. Though most of the tunes are 'originals', they usually follow the standard Tristano-ite practice of an abstruse variation on a standard. Mosca's approach is formidably varied, both from piece to piece and within individual treatments. 'Co-Play', which starts as a relatively simple variation on 'Sweet And Lovely', becomes a labyrinthine investigation of the properties of the song, and 'That Time' turns 'That Old Feeling' into a fantasy on a number of kinds of jazz rhythm. Sometimes he plays it straight, but unexpectedly so: 'Prelude To A Kiss' has voicings more dense than in any authentic Ellington version. Always he is prodigiously inventive: while the music sometimes takes on a painstaking quality, Mosca's spontaneity is genuine enough to pack the programme with surprises. An important record, docked a notch only for the sound-quality: it's clear enough, but the piano's tone is scarcely ingratiating, and there's a lot of tape-hiss.

***** Sal Mosca / Warne Marsh Quartet Vol. 1**

Zinnia 103 *Mosca; Warne Marsh (ts); Frank Canino (b); Skip Scott (d).* 81.

***** Sal Mosca / Warne Marsh Quartet Vol. 2**

Zinnia 104 *As above.* 81.

More problems with sound-quality here. Mosca taped these Village Vanguard sessions himself and, for a recording dating from the 1980s, it's pretty shabby, though Tristano-ites and other scholars will have their ears used to this sort of thing by now. Still, it does detract from music that is as refined and impeccable as chords-based improvising with no emotional agenda can get. Marsh's streaming elegance matches Mosca's slightly more fanciful playing to the expected 't'. As always, they are working on old staples such as '317 East 32nd' and the usual thinly disguised standards, and as always their inventiveness on material they'd mused on countless times already is enough to provoke disbelief. Canino and Scott are no more than functional, though that is presumably how the principals wanted it.

Moscow Composers Orchestra

ENSEMBLE

A convening of new-music composers and performers from the post-Soviet Russian scene.

***** Kings And Cabbages**

Leo Lab CD 005 *Vladimir Miller (p, cond); Yuri Parfyonov, Vyacheslay Guyvoronsky (t); Andrew Solovyov (t, flhn); Arkady Shilkloper (frhn, flhn); Oleg Ruvinov (tba); Alexander Voronin (ss, f); Edward Sivkov (as); Sergey Batov (ts); Sergei Letov (bs, bcl, f); Bram Groothoff (bs); Alexei Levin (p); Alexander Kostikov (g); Vladislav Makarov (clo); Vladimir Volkov, Victor Melnikov (b); Valentin Sokolov (d); Mikhail Zhukov (perc).* 1/93.

A slightly misleading designation, since the MCO is fronted by an Englishman (albeit of Russian extraction) and the orchestra includes players from outside Muscovy, and even as far afield as the Netherlands. Musically, it's an intriguing session, though a little chewy for some tastes. The new-music scene in post-Soviet Russia has had its ups and downs, and the survival of creative music has been largely due to dedicated promoters and broadcasters like Nick Dmitriev and Dmitri Ukhov, both of whom are loyal supporters of radical experimentation. A good deal of Leo's output has an unmistakable theatrical component and *Kings And Cabbages* is no exception, a latter-day fairy tale suspended in ironic narrative space which denies conventional beginnings and endings. There are whispers of Rimsky-Korsakov (the fairytale operas most obviously) in some places, but these may be accidental; they're certainly incidental to the main progress of the four long pieces. Miller gives his oneiric method a clear musical equivalence in titles like 'Theme No Theme Yet A Re-occurring Dream', but his airily shifting, restlessly ambiguous approach is best encountered on the title-track, which is worth playing first, before running the set through as a whole. A beautifully drilled band, recorded in an unusually reverberant and responsive studio acoustic. Given the situation in present-day Russia, it seems unlikely that the MCO will be convened very often; all the more reason to value this interesting disc.

Danny Moss (born 1927)

TENOR SAXOPHONE

Made his name in dance and swing bands in the late '40s, then known as a sideman and occasional leader in British mainstream groups. Left for Australia in 1990.

****(*) The Good Life**
Progressive PCD 7018 *Moss; Ted Ambrose (t, v); Mike Collier (tb); Jack Jacobs (as); Terry Whitney (p); Alan Kennington (b); Derek Middleton (d).* 10/68.

***** Weaver Of Dreams**
Nagel-Heyer 017 *Moss; Brian Lemon (p); Len Skeat (b); Butch Miles (d).* 11/94.

***** A Swingin' Affair**
Nagel-Heyer 034 *Moss; Heinz Buhler (t); Hans Meier (tb); Werner Keller (cl); Buddha Scheidegger (p); Peter Schmidli (g); Vinzenz Kummer (b); Carlo Capello (d).* 11/96.

***** Three Great Concerts**
Nagel-Heyer 019 *Moss; Tom Saunders (c); Bill Allred (tb); Chuck Hedges (cl); Brian Dee, Brian Lemon, Johnny Varro (p); Isla Eckinger, Len Skeat (b); Oliver Jackson, Butch Miles (d); Jeanie Lambe (v).* 11/3–9/95.

Moss has often been hidden by his surroundings on record, usually in sections or anonymous groups, and he's had only a few opportunities of clear space. These discs, almost a generation apart, give a decent idea of his powers. The Hawkins/Webster tradition is what he sticks closest to, and it comes out mainly on slow and medium tempos: the big, beefy tenderness on the two takes of 'The Good Life' itself, from the 1968 session, are enduringly impressive and affecting. Much of this date is taken up with time-wasting by the mixed British talents on hand: Ambrose insists on singing on some tracks, Jacobs's Willie Smith-styled alto falls into routine, and Moss simply doesn't get enough space, though he also has a Hawkins-like 'Star Dust' to himself.

Weaver Of Dreams finds him in Hamburg, delivering a faithful set of tenorman's staples – '9.20 Special', 'Smoke Gets In Your Eyes', 'Blue Lou' – and a small number of choice ballads. Utterly reliable playing, though some of the old facility has been worn away, and one regrets that Moss wasn't featured more in his prime.

He seems to have made up a fruitful relationship with the Nagel-Heyer enterprise. *A Swingin' Affair* finds him guesting with the German mainstream group, Buddha's Gamblers, and, while there's nothing remarkable, the group take great satisfaction in swinging through some fine old Basie, Goodman and Ellington staples. Moss is right at home here. *Three Great Concerts* works primarily as a feature for vocalist Lambe, whose big voice and buttonholing style may not be to all tastes but who can certainly make the most out of a lyric like 'You Came A Long Way From St Louis'. The other horns turn up on only one track: Moss and the rhythm sections make most of the running. Sound enough, although, nudging the 80-minute barrier, there's too much music, and the CD could as easily have been judiciously pruned.

Bennie Moten (1894–1935)

PIANO, BANDLEADER

Born in Kansas City, Moten was bandleading in the city by 1920, starting with a small group but expanding into a big band by the time of his first records. He built it into the best band in the region throughout the '20s and early '30s, but after visting Chicago in 1935 Moten died there, following a surgical accident.

****(*) Bennie Moten 1923–1927**
Classics 549 *Moten; Lamar Wright, Harry Cooper, Ed Lewis, Paul Webster (c); Thamon Hayes (tb, v); Harlan Leonard (cl, ss, as); Woody Walder (cl, ts); Jack Washington (cl, as, bs); LaForest Dent (as, bs, bj); Sam Tall, Leroy Berry (bj); Vernon Page (tba); Willie Hall, Willie McWashington (d).* 9/23–6/27.

Moten's band was the most important group to record in the American south-west in the period, and luckily it made a large number of sides for OKeh and Victor; but the quality of the music is very inconsistent, and much of the earlier material is of historical rather than musical interest. This first CD in the complete edition on Classics couples the band's 14 sides for OKeh from 1923–5 with the first recordings for Victor. The OKeh tracks are a curious mixture: the very first two, 'Elephant's Wobble' and 'Crawdad Blues', are little more than strings of solos, while the subsequent 'South' and 'Goofy Dust' are driving, rag-orientated tunes which emphasize the ensemble. Wright is the only really interesting soloist from the period, and Walder, the apparent star, indulges in some idiotic antics on the clarinet; but, even so, the lumpy rhythms and clattery ensembles yield some strong, hard-hitting performances, sometimes redolent of Sam Morgan's New Orleans band of a few years later. The early Victors don't show a very great advance, despite electrical recording, and one must wait for the later sides for Moten's band to really shine. Decent remastering of what are very rare originals, although not superior to the old Parlophone LP which first collected the OKeh tracks.

****(*) Bennie Moten 1927–1929**
Classics 558 *As above, except omit Wright, Cooper, Tall and Hall; add Booker Washington (c), Buster Moten (p, acc), James Taylor, Bob Clemmons (v).* 6/27–6/2

***** Bennie Moten 1929–30**
Classics 578 *As above, except Count Basie (p) replaces Buster Moten; add Hot Lips Page (t), Eddie Durham (tb, g), Jimmy Rushing (v).* 7/29–10/30.

Moten's band progressed rather slowly, handicapped by an absence of both truly outstanding soloists and an arranger of real talent. The surprisingly static personnel did the best they could with the material, but most of the tunes work from a heavy off-beat. Walder has barely improved, and the arrival of Bennie's brother, Buster, with his dreaded piano-accordion, was enough to root the band in novelty status. The second Classics CD still has some good moments – in such as 'The New Tulsa Blues' or 'Kansas City Breakdown' – but sugary saxes and pedestrian charts spoil many promising moments. Matters take an immediate upward turn with the joint arrival of Basie and Durham in 1929. 'Jones Law Blues', 'Band Box Shuffle' and 'Small Black' all show the band with fresh ideas under Basie's inspirational leadership (and soloing – here with his Earl Hines influence still intact). 'Sweetheart Of Yesterday' even softens the two-beat rhythm.

****** Bennie Moten 1930–1932**

Classics 591 *Moten; Ed Lewis, Booker Washington (c); Hot Lips Page, Joe Keyes, Dee Stewart (t); Thamon Hayes, Dan Minor (tb); Eddie Durham (tb, g); Harlan Leonard, Jack Washington, Woody Walder, Eddie Barefield, Ben Webster (reeds); Count Basie (p); Buster Moten (acc); Leroy Berry (bj, g); Vernon Page (tba); Walter Page (b); Willie McWashington (d); Jimmy Rushing (v).* 30-32.

Under Basie's effective leadership, the Moten orchestra finally took wing, and its final sessions were memorable. There were still problems, such as the presence of Buster Moten, the reliance on a tuba prior to the arrival of Page, and a general feeling of transition between old and new; but, by the magnificent session of December 1932, when the band created at least four masterpieces in 'Toby', 'Prince Of Wails', 'Milenberg Joys' and 'Moten Swing', it was a unit that could have taken on the best of American bands. Page, Rushing, Webster, Durham and especially Basie himself all have key solo and ensemble roles, and the sound of the band on 'Prince Of Wails' and 'Toby' is pile-driving. Ironically, this modernism cost Moten much of his local audience, which he was only recovering at the time of his death in 1935. Fair remastering, though one feels better could have been done with a set of mint originals.

Paul Motian (born 1931)

DRUMS, PERCUSSION

Born in Philadelphia, Motian is one of the most influential modern percussionists, having largely freed the drummer from strict time-keeping duties. He matured artistically as a member of pianist Bill Evans's trio. Later, he turned to composition as well; his work is atmospheric, unlinear and often complex under a deceptively calm exterior.

***** Conception Vessel**

ECM 519279-2 *Motian; Becky Friend (f); Sam Brown (g); Leroy Jenkins (vn); Keith Jarrett (p, f); Charlie Haden (b).* 11/72.

****** Tribute**

ECM 519281-2 *Motian; Carlos Ward (as); Sam Brown, Paul Metzke (g); Charlie Haden (b).* 5/74.

Time will tell how important Motian is ultimately considered to be in the development of jazz since the war; but if all revolutions in the music turn out to be upheavals in the rhythm section, then it seems likely that he will be seen as a quiet revolutionary, freeing the drummer from basic time-keeping service even more thoroughly than the radicals of the 1960s – Murray, Cyrille, Graves – did. Motian's phrasing has less to do with the basic pulse of a piece than with its melody line. This has meant that he works best with very strong bass-players – Charlie Haden most obviously – and that in his own music the drums are pitched front and centre, not aggressively but as an emphatic structural component.

Both these early recordings for ECM illustrate the point perfectly. They were startling records when they first appeared, and they have retained their vigour and freshness. The single unaccompanied track on *Conception Vessel*, 'Ch'i Energy', provides a good representation of his basic sound-palette: sweeping cymbals, soft, delicately placed accents, a sense of flow and togetherness that is difficult to break down into components. Max Roach is the only other modern drummer who can sound anything like this, but Roach is a soapbox orator by comparison. Most of the first record is devoted to duo settings. The title-track and 'American Indian: Song Of Sitting Bull' are duos with Keith Jarrett (who plays flute on the latter). There are two trios with Haden and Brown, and the set closes with 'Inspiration From A Vietnamese Lullaby', which uses Friend and Jenkins, and points to the drummer's fascination with musical traditions outside the European/American orbit.

The 1974 album is a small classic. Ward is used sparingly, but the twinned guitars are a key component and, given the prominence of Bill Frisell in later years, it's interesting to note how Motian was using the instrument as early as this. The session consists of three Motian tunes, of which 'Sod House' and 'Victoria' are the best known; also on the session, wonderful readings of Ornette's 'War Orphans' and Haden's 'Song For Ché'. The leader is seldom far from the centre of things, but as ever he plays with grace and composure.

*****(*) Dance**

ECM 519282-2 *Motian; Charles Brackeen (ts); David Izenzon (b).* 9/77.

***** Le Voyage**

ECM 519283-2 *Motian; Charles Brackeen (ts, ss); Jean-François Jenny-Clark (b).* 3/79.

Timbrally, these trios are very different from the earlier ECMs. Motian plays in a more linear way, pushing the ideas along, and it is interesting to hear him in the company of such an emphatic horn-player as Brackeen, who seems to anticipate much of what Joe Lovano would bring to a Motian trio in later years. Izenzon and Jenny-Clark both carry deep, rich voices and an unorthodox approach to chords. Though neither will ever be mistaken for Haden, there is at least a consistency of sound. The earlier of the records is probably the more sheerly involving, largely because of Izenzon's immense power and throbbing, almost tragic voice. However, 'Folk Song For Rosie' and 'Le Voyage' itself are both delightful compositions, and Motian enthusiasts should certainly track down these fine discs.

***** Psalm**

ECM 847330-2 *Motian; Joe Lovano (ts); Billy Drewes (ts, as); Bill Frisell (g); Ed Schuller (b).* 12/81.

There was to be a later recording for ECM (we aren't quite sure how the contractual position worked itself out), but this already has a slightly intermediate feel. The bones of the great trio with Frisell and Lovano are there, but muddied by the second saxophone (we can't offer much information about Drewes, or much enthusiasm for his playing) and by the rather undefined bass-playing of Schuller. That having been said, this record contains some of Motian's darkest and most intriguing compositions: 'Mandeville' and 'Second Hand' are superb, and it's a pity that they aren't played with greater clarity. Here, the contours are blurred and imprecise.

*** The Story of Maryam

Soul Note 121074 *Motian; Jim Pepper (ts, ss); Joe Lovano (ts); Bill Frisell (g); Ed Schuller (b).* 7/83.

*** Jack Of Clubs

Soul Note 121124 *As above.* 3/84.

Unusually for a rhythm-section player, Motian has preferred to work with a very small group of like-minded interpreters, rather than constantly experimenting with line-ups. With the brilliant folksy Pepper replacing the anonymous Drewes, this was a settled band for some years in the 1980s. *The Story Of Maryam* is probably the least well-known of Motian's recordings, and some might argue it's the least typical, driven by an edgy, boppish line. The addition of Pepper and the need to accommodate two horns made an impact, but one senses that Motian himself is rethinking aspects of his conception, perhaps trying to inject some gristle and fibre into the music. *Jack Of Clubs* seems self-consciously abrasive in places, though that may have something to do with production values at Soul Note. This is very different product from the ECM records.

***(*) It Should've Happened A Long Time Ago

ECM 823641-2 *Motian; Joe Lovano (ts); Bill Frisell (g).* 7/84.

What should? The end of the association with ECM coincided with the birth of a group that was to reshape Motian's thinking completely. A retake of 'Conception Vessel' gives some sense of how far the drummer had come in a decade. This a roller-coaster ride in comparison to what went before. Lovano and Frisell conjure up a storm of ideas, combative, stirring and to the point. The guitarist seldom sounds less dreamy than in this context.

**** Misterioso

Soul Note 121174 *Motian; Jim Pepper (ts, ss); Joe Lovano (ts); Bill Frisell (g); Ed Schuller (b).* 7/86.

Whereas in the past Motian had seemed anxious to match material to session without undue overlaps, he was increasingly tempted into reworking successful themes. 'Folk Song For Rosie' is the outstanding track here, a powerful, heart-filling version of one of his most unaffectedly beautiful ideas. He was also beginning to explore standards and repertory pieces with greater enthusiasm; Monk's 'Pannonica' glows with affection and imagination. The sound isn't pristine and some of the softer cymbal accents seem unduly hissy, but there is no mistaking the fact that Motian is playing with joy and enthusiasm.

*** One Time Out

Soul Note 121224 *Motian; Joe Lovano (ts); Bill Frisell (g).* 9/87.

Monk was the defining presence during this period, and he even stands behind some of the standard treatments on this disconcertingly mild and low-key recording. 'The Man I Love' is lent a jaggy, almost disillusioned quality that some will find troubling, while 'If I Should Lose You' and 'My Funny Valentine' are rethought almost from the bottom up. Lovano knows this material inside out, and one suspects that it's Frisell who's the sheet-anchor. The Monastic canon is explored direct via 'Monk's Mood', and you kind of suspect that an all-Monk set is only just around the corner.

**** Trioism

JMT 514 012 *Motian; Joe Lovano, Dewey Redman (ts); Bill Frisell (g).* 6/93.

An established working band by this stage, touring indefatigably, the trio pushes out into new territory. Our suspicion is that about this time Motian was beginning more or less systematically to reassess the legacy of Ornette Coleman and the enigmatic doctrine of 'harmolodics'. The lineaments are becoming overt on *Trioism*, a new and more abrasive sound in which the 'rhythm' players really do generate the lead line. What followed was merely to confirm the point.

**** Sound Of Love

Winter & Winter 910 008 *Motian; Joe Lovano (ts); Bill Frisell (g).* 6/95.

Just as JMT reached its tenth anniversary, with an enviable reputation for creative output (and a less enviable one for illegible design), it was decided to wind it up. Stefan F. Winter had begun the label as an independent before throwing in his lot with Polygram, and there are signs that he was already looking to secede even before the corporate wind turned chilly. No one looking at any of the first Winter & Winter releases would have doubted their parentage, though it seems clear that the brothers merely took back their own concept rather than stealing Polygram's. Fortunately, artistic and production values remain undimmed as well. This session clearly straddles the end of the affair. The first for the new label is a live session from the Village Vanguard, and it catches the trio in cracking form, opening with 'Misterioso' and Mingus's most yearning composition, 'Duke Ellington's Sound Of Love', before diving into two bright, effusive originals ('Once Around The Park' is menthol fresh) and closing on 'Good Morning Heartache'. There are some glorious moments of interaction between the three players. The obvious difference between now and 1984 is that in the interim Lovano and Frisell have become superstars in their own right. No sign of clashing egos. Every indication of complete creative understanding.

***(*) Flight Of The Blue Jay

Winter & Winter 910 009 *Motian; Chris Potter (as, ts); Chris Cheek (ts); Brad Schoeppach, Kurt Rosenwinkel (g); Steve Swallow (b).*

The Electric Bebop Band, minus the irrelevant Alias this time (how *does* he get so much work?), in a strong, mixed programme. The two saxophonists have settled down and are more sympathetically separated in the stereo mix. Monk is once again the dominant presence; of three tunes, 'Light Blue' is the most unusually paced and inflected. The title-track is a Motian tune, and it's getting harder to find any more superlatives for him either as writer or performer. The big plus this time out is that he's fronting a much more tightly integrated group, who're responsive to changes in mood and pace, and to subtleties of light and shade.

****** Monk & Powell**

Winter & Winter 910045 2 *As above, except omit Schoeppach; add Steve Cardenas (g).* 11/98.

A Bill Evans programme would in some respects have been less surprising, but Paul brings tremendous insight and an instinctive musicality to five Monk compositions, of which 'Brilliant Corners' is the most compelling, and three by Bud. It is unusual to hear these familiar themes, and particularly something like 'Parisian Thoroughfare', arranged for horns and guitars, but the Electronic Bebop Band pulls off the transition with unnerving skill. Motian himself is somewhat in the background acoustically, and it's our growing impression that the subtler dimensions of his playing are lost in the mix.

Mound City Blue Blowers

GROUP

A group name used by the kazoo player and vocalist Red McKenzie (1899–1948) for many years, although at present only their swing-era records are available on CD.

*****(*) Mound City Blue Blowers 1935–37**

Timeless CBC-018 *Bunny Berigan, Yank Lawson (t); Al Philburn (tb); Red McKenzie (kz, v); Eddie Miller, Forrest Crawford (cl, ts); Gil Bowers, Frank Signorelli (p); Nappy Lamare (g, v); Dave Barbour, Carmen Mastren, Eddie Condon (g); Sid Weiss, Harry Goodman, Bob Haggart, Pete Peterson, Mort Stuhlmaker (b); Ray Bauduc, Stan King, Dave Tough (d); Billy Wilson, Spooky Dickenson (v).* 5/35–2/36.

Red McKenzie led this group through various incarnations from the early '20s onwards. Their Brunswick sessions with Eddie Lang, when the group was no more than a quartet, would be welcome on CD, but in the meantime this third generation of the band gets a comprehensive airing on another fine John R.T. Davies mastering. By 1935 McKenzie's comb-and-paper solos and rather proper singing might have seemed anachronistic, but he was a surprisingly inventive performer and he sounds quite at home, even in the company of some illustrious sidemen. But the main point here is to catch glimpses of the superlative Berigan, frustratingly confined on some of the 15 tracks he appears on but a marvel nevertheless: sample the beautiful solo on 'You've Been Taking Lessons In Love'. There are eight tracks by what amounts to a prototype of the Bob Crosby Bob Cats, with Lawson and Miller in strong fettle, and the results overall are some of the most enjoyable examples of small-group swing of the time.

George Mraz

BASS

Mraz has a Czech background, but he has been a fixture in American rhythm sections for many years; the roll-call of his credits can be judged by a look at this book's index. He is based in and around New York.

***** Jazz**

Milestone MCD 9248-2 *Mraz; Rich Perry (ts); Richie Beirach, Larry Willis (p); Billy Hart (d).* 9–10/95.

***** My Foolish Heart**

Milestone MCD 9262-2 *As above, except omit Perry, Willis.* 6/95.

***** Bottom Lines**

Milestone MCD 9272-2 *Mraz; Rich Perry (ts); Cyrus Chestnut (p); Al Foster (d).* 4/97.

*****(*) Duke's Place**

Milestone MCD 9292-2 *Mraz; Cyrus Chestnut, Renee Rosnes (p); Billy Drummond (d).* 11/98.

After many years as the most dependable of rhythm men, Mraz suddenly has a small string of albums to his name. A bassist in the limelight is often not such good news, given the instrument's limitations as a solo force in the mainstream of the music, and Mraz seems aware of this – while still succumbing to temptation here and there. *Jazz* and *My Foolish Heart* are both basically trio dates (Willis and Perry have three guest appearances between them) with the bass given more prominence than usual. Beirach is a sympathetic confrère and Hart is appropriately discreet. There are some lovely things on both records: Beirach's almost motionless ballad, 'Sunday's Song', the steady investigation of 'Cinema Paradiso' and a surprisingly vivid *arco* reading of Strayhorn's 'Passion Flower'. But there's quite a lot of chaff, too. *Bottom Lines* introduces the concept of nine tunes all written by bassists. Perry is on hand throughout this time, and his rather gentle manner suits the occasion. 'Mr Pastorius', which Marcus Miller wrote for Miles Davis, has the original trumpet solo scored and played as a duo line by Mraz and Perry: handsomely done, if seemingly rather pointless. The best things come at the end, with a soft-centred 'Goodbye Porkpie Hat' and a very incisive reading of Steve Swallow's 'Falling Grace', surely the best thing on the record.

Duke's Place just shades the other records. Although it's yet another Ellington tribute, and at least half of it qualifies as over-familiar even by the standards of that songbook, the playing by Chestnut and Rosnes (they have five tracks each and share a mutual joust with 'Duke's Place' itself) affirms their individual eminence among today's pianists. Since they are featured on alternate tracks throughout the session, the record works nicely in terms of contrast, a fulsome Chestnut treatment of 'Come Sunday' followed by a quicksilver Rosnes version of 'Angelica', and so on. Mraz plays a somewhat more supportive role rather than a front-line one as on the other albums – and it doesn't hurt.

Bheki Mseleku (born 1955)

PIANO, ALTO AND TENOR SAXOPHONE, GUITAR, VOCAL

A South African pianist with a grand if unfulfilled reputation, Mseleku settled in London in the 1980s but didn't make a record until 1991, when his worldly mix of post-township music and modal jazz suddenly attracted terrific attention.

***** Celebration**
World Circuit WC 019 *Mseleku; Steve Williamson, Courtney Pine (ss); Jean Toussaint (ts); Eddie Parker (f); Michael Bowie (b); Marvin 'Smitty' Smith (d); Thebe Lipere (perc).* 91.

*****(*) Timelessness**
Verve 521306-2 *Mseleku; Joe Henderson, Pharoah Sanders (ts); Kent Jordan (f); Rodney Kendrick (p); Michael Bowie (b); Marvin 'Smitty' Smith (d); Abbey Lincoln (v).* 8/93.

The South African-born Mseleku waited a long time for his debut record. It's a positive and big-hearted set, full of grand major themes and impassioned playing from a distinguished local cast, although overall Mseleku added little to the firm base established by SA expatriates such as Louis Moholo and Dudu Pukwana. His piano playing owes its weight and impetus to McCoy Tyner – 'Blues For Afrika' might have come off any of Tyner's Milestone albums of the 1970s – and his tunes are full of the call-and-response ingredients of such writers as Abdullah Ibrahim and Randy Weston. Not that the music lacks inner conviction: Bowie and Smith lend transatlantic muscle which raises the temperature several degrees on the faster pieces, and Jean Toussaint comes off best among the sax stars, with a measured improvisation on 'The Age Of Inner Knowing'. The debut record for Verve, though, was pitched at a higher level, with an extraordinary gallery of guest players. It's impressive enough that Mseleku stands as tall as any of them, but the quality of his writing here is exceptional, with the title-track a towering feature for Henderson and Smith, and such themes as 'Yanini' and 'Ntuli Street' given extra weight by the calibre of the players. Flawed, arguably, by its undue length and one or two lesser efforts (notably Lincoln's appearance), the record augured well for a renewed affiliation of South African jazz with American currents. So far, though, Mseleku hasn't truly built on this foundation to any exceptional degree.

Mujician

GROUP

Devoted to free improvisation without predetermined structures or conventional musical architecture, Mujician are definitive of one important strain in British jazz. The group chemistry is intense and uncomplicated by egos.

***** The Journey**
Cuneiform RUNE 42 *Paul Dunmall (ts, ss, bs, E-flat cl, bagpipes, shenai); Keith Tippett (p); Paul Rogers (b); Tony Levin (d, perc).* 6/90.

Over the past decade, Mujician has established itself as absolutely central to creative music in Britain. Rogers and Levin have ensured that the group's free-jazz core remains in place, but Tippett has a more formal compositional side and Dunmall is also involved in folk musics: these elements all play a significant part in making up what increasingly seems a unified, idiosyncratic and indivisible sound. *The Journey* is a continuous, 55-minute improvisation, recorded at the Bath Festival. At this point in its history, it seems clear that Tippett is the *de facto* leader, certainly the most dominant performing presence. Rogers constantly breaks up the pulse, sounding astonishingly like Mingus on occasions in the way he slips across what would be bar-lines in metrical jazz. Dunmall is the soundsmith, adding exotic colours – shenai and bagpipes – to the second and third of these records, introducing surprise melodic ideas, some childishly simple figures (and 'childish' is by no means an insult in Mujician's world) to otherwise hectic passages, and a big-hearted bravura to the whole.

****** The Bristol Concert**
What Jazz WHAT7 *As above, except add Enver Khmirev, Dmitri Saladze, Vakhtang Sirbiladze (t), Grigol Meladze, Roman Pogoev (tb), George Bagdasarov, George Geridze (as), Chabuki Amiranashvili (ts), David Masteranov (g), Maya Meladze, Julie Tippetts, Manana Tsitladze (v).* 6/91.

Happy circumstance took the members of Mujician and Julie Tippetts to Georgia in 1991. There they met with players for whom the group's concept of total improvisation was entirely unknown, but Mujician's impromptu performances struck a chord and, a month after the trip, a group drawn from the state orchestra in Tbilisi came to Britain for a reciprocal visit. Given their unease with an aesthetic of absolute freedom, Keith Tippett prepared a selection of compositions for the joint concert in St George's, Brandon Hill, Bristol, a church now devoted to music-making. The results are astonishing. From the opening duet between Paul Rogers and trumpeter Enver Khmirev to the interaction of voices and saxophones on 'Dedicated To Mingus' (which includes a fragment of 'Goodbye, Pork Pie Hat') to the delicate beauty of 'A Loose Kite' and the climax of 'The Irish Girl's Tear' and 'Septober Energy', featuring David Masteranov and Paul Dunmall respectively, the music is of the highest quality, charged with emotion, but also impressively cool and contained. The political situation in Georgia since 1991 has meant that contact has been cut off again and the fate of some of the musicians involved remains uncertain. However, the communication between the cultures was direct and intense and yielded a concert and record of rare beauty.

*****(*) Birdman**
Cuneiform RUNE 82 *As for The Journey.* 5/95.

****** Colours Fulfilled**
Cuneiform RUNE 102 *As above.* 5/97.

Tippett is less obviously central to *Birdman*. No longer is he the leader-at-the-piano, but he increasingly provides the nexus through which everything else flows. His sound is wonderfully delicate and unassertive, as if every last drop of ego has been squeezed out of his playing. By the time of *Colours Fulfilled*, which is the group's masterpiece, he is part of an unanalysable compound, which confirms the Uncertainty Principle moment to moment. As soon as one attempts to work out what one member of the group is doing, attention is commanded by something else, and then by something else again. The 1997 album is effectively a single, almost symphonic piece, broken up into introduction, two massive central movements and a coda. There is hardly a moment when nothing is going on and yet the overall impression is of great stillness, an almost statuesque grandeur. This stands alongside the finest free music being performed on either side of the Atlantic.

Gerry Mulligan (1927–96)

BARITONE SAXOPHONE, PIANO, SOPRANO SAXOPHONE

He took what looks like a cumbersome horn and made it sound fleet and natural. Mulligan began his career as an arranger with Gene Krupa and created the classic 'Disc Jockey Jump' as early as 1947. He was a key presence in the Birth Of The Cool project (usually attributed to Miles Davis) and co-led the famous pianoless group with Chet Baker. Later years saw him combine sophisticated arrangements with cool, often tender baritone on a host of small-group and big-band sessions.

*** Mullenium

Columbia 65678 *Mulligan; Ed Badgley, John Dee, Don Fagerquist, Don Ferrara, Jerry Lloyd, Al Porcino, Red Rodney, Phil Sunkel, Joe Techner, Ray Triscari (t); Sy Berger, Warren Covington, Jim Dahl, Chuck Harris, Frank Hunter, Frank Rehak, Jim Seaman, Dick Taylor, Jack Zimmerman (tb); Bob Brookmeyer (vtb); Louis Giamo, Charlie Kennedy, Lee Konitz, Hal McCusick, Joe Soldo, Harry Terrill (as); Charlie Rouse, Zoot Sims, Phil Urso, Charlie Ventura (ts); Gene Allen, Jack Schwartz (bs); Elliot Lawrence, Teddy Napoleon (p); Mike Triscari (g); Joe Benjamin, Bob Strahl (b); Dave Bailey, Gene Krupa (d).* 46-57.

*** Legacy

N2K 10002 *Mulligan; Chet Baker, Pete Candoli, Miles Davis, Jon Eardley, Don Ferrara, Wallace Roney, Clark Terry, Nick Travis (t); Wayne Andre, Dave Bargeron, Kai Winding (tb); Bob Brookmeyer, Bob Enevoldsen (vtb); John Clark, Junior Collins, John Graas (frhn); Billy Barber, Ray Siegel (tba); Dick Meldonian, Bud Shank, Phil Woods (as); Gene Quill (as, cl); Zoot Sims (ts); Gene Allen, Don Davidson (bs); Al Haig (p); Dick Mathes, Greg Phillinganes (ky); Mike Renzi (syn); Joe Mondragon, Joe Shulman, Bobby Whitlock (b); Dave Bailey, Bernie Dresel, Mel Lewis, Max Roach (d); Patti Austin, Diva Gray, Darryl Tookes (v).* 49–96.

The most important baritone saxophonist in contemporary jazz, Mulligan took the turbulent Serge Chaloff as his model, but he blended his fast, slightly pugnacious delivery with the elegance of Johnny Hodges and Lester Young. This produced an agile, *legato* sound which became instinct with the cool West Coast style, the flipside of bebop. Mulligan's – and Claude Thornhill's – major role in what became known as Miles Davis's *Birth Of The Cool* is now increasingly acknowledged, as is his genius as a composer/arranger. On the model of the *Birth Of The Cool* nonet, his big bands have the intimacy and spaciousness of much smaller groups, preferring subtlety to blasting power. His small groups, conversely, work with a depth of harmonic focus that suggests a much larger outfit.

In his short story, 'Entropy', the novelist Thomas Pynchon takes Mulligan's early-1950s pianoless quartets with Chet Baker as a crux of post-modernism, improvisation without the safety net of predictable chords. The revisionist argument was that Mulligan attempted the experiment simply because he had to work in a club with no piano. The true version is that there was a piano, albeit an inadequate one, but he was already experimenting with a much more arranged sound for small groups (to which the baritone saxophone was peculiarly adaptable) and the absence of a decent keyboard was merely an additional spur.

The material on *Mullenium* surfaced in the '70s on an LP called *The Arranger*. It comprises a lost big-band session from 1957 and a number of arrangements made for Gene Krupa ('Disc Jockey Jump' and 'How High The Moon') and for Elliot Lawrence. These do not feature Mulligan much or at all as a player, but they offer a valuable insight into his skill as an orchestrator, with a distinctive emphasis on the middle register and a relaxed and easy swing. There are valuable insights to be gleaned here, but it is probably best to leave this album till later in your exposure to Mulligan and his music, since any epiphanies are likely to be retrospective.

The material on *Legacy* covers a similar span of time. Mulligan is beginning to emerge as a soloist of some power and confidence, but even here the emphasis is still on arrangement. The selections are familiar enough – 'Jeru', 'Bernie's Tune', 'Mainstream', 'Boplicity' and 'Walking Shoes', as well as later stuff – but as a single-volume sampling of Mulligan's career this is hard to beat, scamped as the chronology is.

*** Mulligan Plays Mulligan

Original Jazz Classics OJC 003 *Mulligan; Jerry Hurwitz, Nick Travis (t); Ollie Wilson (tb); Allan Eager (ts); Max McElroy (bs); George Wallington (p); Phil Leshin (b); Walter Bolden (d); Gail Madden (perc).* 8/51.

These early sessions already demonstrate what a fine composer and arranger the saxophonist was. In comparison to later work, they're slightly featureless and Mulligan's playing is very callow. It's perhaps best to come back to this stuff.

**** The Original Quartet

Blue Note 94407-2 2CD *Mulligan; Chet Baker (t); Bob Whitlock, Carson Smith, Joe Mondragon (b); Chico Hamilton, Larry Bunker (d).* 8/52–6/53.

***(*) The Best Of The Gerry Mulligan Quartet With Chet Baker

Pacific Jazz CDP 7 95481 2 *Mulligan; Chet Baker (t); Henry Grimes, Carson Smith, Bob Whitlock (b); Dave Bailey, Larry Bunker, Chico Hamilton (d).* 8/52–12/57.

Mulligan's pianoless quartet is one of the epochal jazz groups, even if it had no such aspirations, formed for nothing more than a regular gig at The Haig (where some of the tracks were recorded) and even though many of its sessions were recorded quickly and with little preparation. In retrospect, it's the simplest pleasures which have made the music endure: the uncomplicated swing of the varying rhythm sections, the piquant contrast of amiably gruff baritone and shyly melodious trumpet, the coolly effective originals like 'Nights At The Turntable' and the irresistible 'Walkin' Shoes', and the subtle and feelingful treatments of standards such as 'Lullaby Of the Leaves'. Cool but hot, slick but never too clever, these are some of the most pleasurable records of their time. The two-disc set includes the basic library of 42 tracks and is an indispensable part of Mulligan's legacy.

The Pacific Jazz compilation, drawn from singles (including the classic 'Soft Shoe'/'Walkin' Shoes' combination) and subsequent 10-inch LPs, is an excellent sampling of Mulligan's 11-month association with Chet, with a single item, 'Festive Minor', from the same December 1957 sessions that yielded *Reunion*. It's fair (to Chet, at least) to record that it was Mulligan, not the famously unreliable trumpeter, who brought the line-up to an end. In June 1953, Mulligan was jailed for several months on a drugs offence. It is perhaps as well that the group was folded at its peak. Generously recorded in a warm close-up, the sessions convey all of Mulligan's skill as a writer and arranger, with the saxophone and a very foregrounded bass filling in the space normally occupied by piano.

*** With The Chubby Jackson Big Band

Original Jazz Classics OJCCD 711 *Mulligan; Chet Baker, Don Ferrara, Howard McGhee, Al Porcino (t); J.J Johnson, Kai Winding (tb); Charlie Kennedy (as); Georgie Auld, Zoot Sims (ts); Tony Aless (p); Chubby Jackson, Carson Smith (b); Chico Hamilton, Don Lamond (d).* 5/53.

An odd, rather fudged release, pairing the classic quartet, with Mulligan as featured soloist, with the Chubby Jackson Big Band. Stellar as it was and magnificently organized, it seems to be in the wrong gear for Mulligan, who works through the dense, rather toppy arrangements like a man cheerfully walking through a rainstorm. Fascinating to hear so many remarkable soloists all pulling together, though they all sound as if they're protesting too much. Not an unqualified success, but a further interesting byway on Mulligan's recording career.

***(*) Pleyel Concerts 54: Volume 1

Vogue 113411 *Mulligan; Bob Brookmeyer (vtb); Red Mitchell (b); Frank Isola (d).* 6/54.

***(*) Pleyel Concerts 54: Volume 2

Vogue 113412 *As above.* 6/54.

*** California Concerts

Pacific Jazz 46860 *Mulligan; Jon Eardley (t); Red Mitchell (b); Chico Hamilton (d).* 11/54.

Post-Chet. As far as French fans and critics were concerned, this was how young America looked and sounded. Sunny, cooled-out, elaborated but determinedly un-profound, it smacks very strongly of a time and place. No less than the slightly epicene Baker, the crew-cut, square-jawed Mulligan became a kind of icon, in sharp counter-definition to the long-hair, goatee and beret image of jazz. Early in 1954, following Mulligan's release from jail, a version of the group with Bob Brookmeyer out front had played a series of gigs at the Salle Pleyel in Paris. The two discs are a little repetitive, punctuated by the 'Utter Chaos' signature-theme, but Mulligan's playing is so subtly inflected that it's possible to listen to his solos back to back and hear him working through all the implicit chord variants. The 3 June version of 'Makin' Whoopee' is joyous, as is Giuffre's 'Five Brothers' (or 'Mothers', according to some versions). That vintage gig spills over on to Volume Two, but the two discs are worth having anyway. This issue largely supersedes Vogue 655616, which also included material with Chet, recorded in LA in May 1953.

The California material showcases a bold and inventive group. Eardley sounds not a bit like Chet and shapes a solo entirely differently, and the whole rhythmic/harmonic cast of the group changes with the introduction of Mitchell and Hamilton, who mesh instantly on 'Blues Going Up' and turn in a remarkable rhythm performance on 'Yardbird Suite'. The inclusion of 'Darn That Dream' and 'Makin' Whoopee' only serves to highlight the originality of Mulligan's conception. Again one can hearing him working over chord variants which come out of bebop, but he may be influenced by classical precedents as well.

*** At Storyville

Pacific Jazz 94472 *Mulligan; Bob Brookmeyer (vtb); Bill Crow (b); Dave Bailey (d).* 12/56.

There is a romping self-confidence and camaraderie to this live date (from the Boston club rather than New Orleans). For all the buttoned-down sobriety of this group, it is also a fleet and powerful outfit, capable of generating a big, resonant sound. Mulligan takes the lion's share of solos, but Brookmeyer is often working softly just behind, his gentle attack and rhythmically relaxed delivery acting as counterpoise to the leader's unusually punchy articulation. It would have been interesting to hear an occasional switch to soprano at this stage; one can hear Mulligan striving for a tighter, more pinched tonality on occasion, though generally he favours a mid-range, playing a couple of solos which might just as easily have been done on tenor, but for a few tell-tale pedal points.

***(*) Mulligan Meets Monk

Original Jazz Classics OJC 301 *Mulligan; Thelonious Monk (p); Wilbur Ware (b); Shadow Wilson (d).* 8/57.

Not an entirely probable encounter, but Mulligan more than keeps afloat on the Monk tunes, sounding least at ease on 'Rhythm-A-Ning', but absolutely confident on 'Straight, No Chaser' and, of course, 'Round About Midnight'. The dark, heavy sound of Wilbur Ware's bass is sufficiently 'below' Mulligan's horn and his intervals sufficiently broad to tempt the saxophonist to some unusual whole-note progressions. Monk darts in and out like a tailor's needle, cross-stitching countermelodies and neatly abstract figures.

***(*) Gerry Mulligan–Paul Desmond Quartet

Verve 519850-2 *Mulligan; Paul Desmond (as); Joe Benjamin (b); Dave Bailey (d).* 8/57.

Another of Verve's summit conferences – and a felicitous one. There has probably never been a saxophone sound as finely blended as this, and our only quibble – 'Body And Soul' notwithstanding – is that the material is not really up to the playing. Some of the tunes are obscure enough to suggest that it wasn't just run down on the spot, but there is a lack of anything to get one's teeth into. The best moments are, as in 'Body And Soul', when Desmond moves to the front and Mulligan plays what are effectively piano chord-shapes behind him. Glorious.

***(*) Songbook

Blue Note 33575-2 *Mulligan; Lee Konitz (as); Allen Eager, Zoot Sims (as, ts); Al Cohn (ts, bs); Freddie Green, Paul Palmieri (g); Dick Wetmore (vn); Calo Scott (clo); Vinnie Burke, Henry Grimes (b); Dave Bailey (d).* 12/57.

The year 1957 was a busy one for Mulligan, which is perhaps why this largely forgotten session was arranged by Bill Holman. There is no discernible difference in the voicings, but of course the multi-saxophone line-up is already rather startling. Allen Eager was effectively lost to the music after this point, which seems all the greater pity given the strength and authority of his playing (like Zoot Sims, he also doubles unexpectedly on alto) and the calm, authoritative logic of his soloing. Mulligan is as ever the centre of attention, but only as the apex of a highly organized octet consisting of individualists. He reprises 'Disc Jockey Jump' in a new, more smoothly contoured form and he showcases 'Turnstile' and 'Venus De Milo', two of his best and most adaptable compositions. The CD also includes four boppish tunes recorded with bassist Vinnie Burke and what amounts to a non-classical string quartet: guitar, violin, cello, bass. Unusual and non-essential as far as a casual collector is concerned, but another aspect of Mulligan's eclectic brilliance.

***** Reunion With Chet Baker**
Pacific Jazz 46857 *Mulligan; Chet Baker (t); Henry Grimes (b); Dave Bailey (d).* 12/57.

For one reason and another, there weren't many opportunities to reconvene the classic group. After a gap of some years, there is a touch of reserve – and maybe suspicion – in this reunion recording. Chet's tone is reserved and his delivery rather wandery, and there is an oddly clenched quality to Mulligan's playing as well. There are still, though, wonderful moments to be had from the album. 'Ornithology' is unexpected in its freshness and vivacity, and the alternative takes of 'Trav'lin' Light' and 'Gee, Baby, Ain't I Good To You' are a measure of how intuitively these musicians responded to one another when given time and the right context. Also, the closing version of 'All The Things You Are' is very special and maybe stands as epigraph – if not epitaph – to Gerry's association with Chet.

****** What Is There To Say?**
Columbia 475699 *Mulligan; Art Farmer (t); Bill Crow (b); Dave Bailey (d).* 12/58, 1/59.

***** Americans In Sweden**
Tax CD 3711 *As above.* 5/59.

****(*) News From Newport**
Jazz Hour 73577 *As above.* 59.

Farmer doesn't quite have the lyrical poignancy of Chet Baker in this setting, but he has a full, deep-chested tone (soon to be transferred wholesale and exclusively to flugelhorn) which combines well with Mulligan's baritone. *What Is There To Say?* was Mulligan's first recording for Columbia. It's very direct, very unfussy, very focused on the leader, but with the same skills in evidence as on the earlier *The Arranger*, which was a dry run for the label. The first album proper is a small masterpiece of controlled invention. Mulligan's solos fit into the structure of 'As Catch Can' and 'Festive Minor' as if they were machine-tooled. Farmer responds in kind, with smooth *legato* solos and delicate fills.

The Swedish gig is just one of many taken legitimately or otherwise around this time. Browsers will find several more of the same vintage, but this is one of the best. Farmer is not Chet Baker, but he does have his own things to offer, notably a solid attack and a very full, broad sound which can make Chet's sound decidedly underpowered. The Newport tapes are technically flawed, with drop-outs and distortions on several tracks, but this was a wonderful performance from all concerned.

*****(*) The Complete Gerry Mulligan Meets Ben Webster Sessions**
Verve 539095-2 2CD *Mulligan; Ben Webster (ts); Jimmy Rowles (p); Leroy Vinnegar (b); Mel Lewis (d).* 11 & 12/59.

****(*) The Silver Collection: Gerry Mulligan Meets The Saxophonists**
Verve 827436-2 *Mulligan; Conte Candoli, Don Ferrara, Nick Travis (t); Bob Brookmeyer (vtb, p); Wayne Andre, Alan Ralph (tb); Paul Desmond, Johnny Hodges, Dick Meldonian, Gene Quill (as); Stan Getz, Zoot Sims, Ben Webster (ts); Gene Allen (bcl, bs); Lou Levy, Jimmy Rowles, Claude Williamson (p); Joe Benjamin, Ray Brown, Buddy Clark, Leroy Vinnegar (b); Dave Bailey, Stan Levey, Mel Lewis (d).* 57–60.

***** Verve Jazz Masters 36**
Verve 523342-2 *Mulligan; Conte Candoli, Don Ferrara, Doc Severinsen, Clark Terry, Nick Travis (t); Willie Dennis (tb); Bob Brookmeyer (vtb); Alan Ralph (btb); Gene Quill (as, cl); Bob Donovan, Dick Meldonian (as); Jim Reider, Zoot Sims (ts); Gene Allen (bs); Buddy Clark, Bill Crow (b); Gus Johnson, Mel Lewis (d).* 7/60–12/62.

In Mulligan's book, everyone (by which he presumably means soloists as well as punters) profits from the 'good bath of overtones' you get standing in front of a big band. The great saxophonists lined up on *The Silver Collection* sound mostly constrained rather than inspired by the small- to medium-scale arrangements, steered in the direction of Mulligan's recitalist's cool rather than towards any new improvisational heights. Webster is magisterial on the sessions of November and December 1959 ('Chelsea Bridge' and 'Tell Me When' are excerpted on *The Silver Collection*), and the two saxophones blend gloriously in the lower register. Any quibbles about some other aspects of the sound have been allayed by a new, digitally remastered edition which restores the whole of the session, complete with alternatives. There is probably a surplus of material for most tastes, but hearing these two remarkable figures, with their very different backgrounds and approaches, working in this proximity is a rare privilege. Of the other saxophonists sampled, Hodges probably sounds the happiest of the lot on the compilation, but then he was used to quite reasonable arrangements; these tracks were originally issued backed by the Paul Desmond sessions, which made perfect sense all round.

The *Jazz Masters* collection is an excellent buy but is relatively limited in scope. Drawn in the main from *The Concert Jazz Band* discs, *Gerry Mulligan '63* (albeit recorded a year earlier) and *A Concert In Jazz*, it nevertheless gives full measure from these and fills in an important stage in Jeru's progress.

***** Gerry Mulligan And The Concert Jazz Band**
RTE Europe 1 710382/83 2CD *As for Jazz Masters.* 60.

This is one of a pair of live airshots recorded and issued by RTE. The Concert Jazz Band was an extraordinary outfit, perhaps the best representation there was of Mulligan's music. Unfortunately, this recording is not especially good; it is muddy and indistinct in important areas, lacking in pep and definition at exactly the moment when one senses the music taking flight. The performances are mostly long and designed to give maximum exposure to the soloists, but there is enough tight ensemble work to confirm that, even in this environment, Mulligan was absolutely in the driving seat.

*** Night Lights

Mercury 818 271-2 *Mulligan; Art Farmer (t, flhn); Bob Brookmeyer (vtb); Jim Hall (g); Bill Crow (b); Dave Bailey (d).* 63.

A somewhat overlooked Mulligan session, but marked out by some super playing from both Farmer and Brookmeyer. Mulligan himself is somewhat muted and concentrates as so often on filling out the middle of the orchestration. Hall is perhaps the key to the whole thing, an endlessly inventive and subtle player who takes great chances without fanfare.

**** The Age Of Steam

A&M 396996-2 *Mulligan; Harry 'Sweets' Edison (t); Bob Brookmeyer (vtb); Jimmy Cleveland, Kenny Shroyer (tb); Bud Shank (as, f); Tom Scott (ts, ss); Ernie Watts (reeds); Roger Kellaway (p); Howard Roberts (g); Chuck Domanico (b); John Guerin (d); Joe Porcaro (d, perc).* 2–7/71.

Almost unrecognizably long-haired and bearded, posed in denims in front of one of the locomotives that were his other great passion, Mulligan might almost be a footplateman on some lonely Mid-West branch line. In 1971 he hadn't recorded on his own account for nearly seven years, and so *The Age Of Steam* was awaited with considerable anticipation by those who had followed Mulligan's career, and with delight by many who were coming to him for the first time. The instrumentation (and Stephan Goldman's fine production job) are both identifiably modern, with Mulligan making extensive use of electric piano and guitar. Both 'Country Beaver' and 'A Weed In Disneyland' include strong rock elements (notably Roberts's powerful solo on the latter) and there's a sturdy dash of country swing to the opening 'One To Ten In Ohio', which reunites him with Brookmeyer. The two finest tracks, though, are the long 'Over The Hill And Out Of The Woods', which Mulligan opens on piano, comping for an extensive range of horns, out of which Harry 'Sweets' Edison emerges for a strong solo, and the hauntingly beautiful 'Grand Tour'. The latter must be counted among the saxophonist's most beautiful compositions, its meditative theme and misty timbre explored by Mulligan and Bud Shank. 'Golden Notebooks' is a further statement of Mulligan's long-sustained feminism. It's a light, almost floating piece from the yin side of his imagination. Even allowing for the rather static dynamics of both tracks, the most striking characteristic of *The Age Of Steam* is its strongly rhythmic cast. Even when playing solidly on the beat, Mulligan's is an unmistakable voice, and this was an important return to form after awkward years in the creative wilderness.

** Gerry Mulligan / Astor Piazzolla 1974

Accord 556642 *Mulligan; Astor Piazzolla (bandoneon); Angel Pocho Gatti (pipe org); Alberto Baldan, Gianni Zilolli (mar); Filippo Dacci (g); Umberto Benedetti Michelangeli (vn); Renato Riccio (vla); Ennio Morelli (clo); Giuseppe Prestipino (b); Tullio Di Piscopo (d).* 74.

A nice idea that doesn't quite happen. The problem is not with the instrumentation or the arrangements, nor that Mulligan is not in sympathy with Piazzolla's *nueva tango* approach. It's simply that the performances are so drably uninflected (certainly in comparison to what the two principals do on their own account) as to render the experiment non-consequential.

*** Carnegie Hall Concert

Columbia ZK 64769 *Mulligan; Chet Baker (t); Ed Byrne (tb); Bob James (ky); John Scofield (g); Dave Samuels (vib, perc, v); Ron Carter (b); Harvey Mason (d).* 11/74.

This was only the second – and would be the last – reunion between Jeru and Chet, and it was by and large a happy one. If there were differences and ongoing problems, they were very largely kept off the stand and both frontmen respond to the gala occasion with impassioned and highly focused playing. The rhythm section was the obvious sign of the times, though it's discreet and under-amplified enough not to intrude. Anyone keen on tracing the early career and influences of John Scofield will be delighted to hear his clean, spacious lines. Needless to say, they did 'My Funny Valentine', but the tune which sounds most refreshed and urgent is 'Line For Lyons', one of the less celebrated products of their association. A strong album, and by no means an exhaustive document of the occasion.

*** Idol Gossip

Chiaroscuro 155 *Mulligan; Hank Jones, Tom Fay, Bill Mays (p); Lionel Hampton, Dave Samuels (vib); Bucky Pizzarelli, Mike Santiago (g); George Duvivier (b); Bobby Rosengarden, Grady Tate (d); Candido Camero (perc).* 11/76.

Chiaroscuro seems exactly the right label, for this one has remained in the shadows for a quarter of a century. Mulligan's New Sextet, of which two contrasting versions are heard, was a showcase for new and reworked material (including a second version of 'Song For Strayhorn') and an unexpected cover of 'Waltzing Matilda'. Dave Samuels and Bucky Pizzarelli are key structural elements, though neither has much to say in solos. A lost curiosity, too accomplished to be set aside as 'transitional' and yet not entirely satisfactory as a finished album. Mulligan's soprano still sounds like an uneasy double, but it's kept to a sensible minimum.

*** Walk On The Water

DRG CDSL 5194 *Mulligan; Mike Davis, Laurie Frink, Tom Harrell, Danny Hayes, Alan Raph, Barry Ries (t); Dave Glenn, Keith O'Quinn (tb); Gerry Niewood, Kenneth Hitchcock (as); Seth Broedy, Gary Keller, Ralph Olsen, Eric Turker (ts); Joe Temperley (bs); Mitch Forman (p); Mike Bocchicchio (b); Richard De Rosa (d).* 9/80.

Some years after the demise of the Concert Jazz Band, Mulligan reconvened a similar project with wonderful latter-day soloists of the quality of Tom Harrell and the long-overlooked Gerry Niewood. The set consists of four originals, among them the gorgeous 'Song For Strayhorn', a Mitchel Forman composition called 'Angelica' and Duke Ellington's 'Across The Track Blues'.

*** Soft Lights And Sweet Music

Concord CCD 4300 *Mulligan; Scott Hamilton (ts); Mike Renzi (p); Jay Leonhart (b); Grady Tate (d).* 1/86.

What a session this might have been with Dave McKenna at the piano. As it is, Mulligan is left to carry too much of the harmonic weight, and in consequence his solo excursions seem cautious, rarely straying far from the most logical progression. There is also a tendency for the next phrase to be exactly the one you thought he was going to play. Hamilton shows off, but with forgivable charm and adroitness.

***** Re-Birth Of The Cool**

GRP GRD 9679/059679-2 *Mulligan; Wallace Roney (t); Dave Bargeron (tb); John Clark (frhn); Bill Barber (tba); Phil Woods (as); John Lewis (p); Dean Johnson (b); Ron Vincent (d); Mel Torme (v).* 1/92.

There has been some rewriting of the history books on behalf of Mulligan and pianist/arranger John Lewis *vis-à-vis* the original *Birth Of The Cool*. Mulligan is on record as feeling that the project was subsequently hijacked in Miles Davis's name. Though Miles 'cracked the whip', it was Lewis, Gil Evans and Mulligan who gave the music its distinctive profile. In 1991, Mulligan approached Miles regarding a plan to re-record the famous numbers, which were originally released as 78s and only afterwards given their famous title. Unfortunately, Miles died before the plan could be taken any further, and the eventual session featured regular stand-in Roney in the trumpet part. With Phil Woods in for Lee Konitz, the latter-day sessions have a crispness and boppish force that the original cuts rather lacked. Dave Grusin's and Larry Rosen's production is ultra-sharp and perhaps too respectful of individual horns on 'Deception' and 'Budo', where a degree less separation might have been more effective (unless this is an impression based entirely on folk-memories of the original LP). The mix works rather better on the boppish 'Move' and 'Boplicity', and on the vocal, 'Darn That Dream'. An interesting retake on a still-misunderstood experiment, *Re-Birth* sounds perfectly valid on its own terms.

***** Paraiso: Jazz Brazil**

Telarc 83361 *Mulligan; Charlie Ernst, Cliff Korman (p); Emanuel Moreira (g); Rogerio Maio, Leonard D Traversa (b); Duduka Fonseca, Peter Grant (d); Waltinho Anastacio, Norberto Goldberg (perc); Jane Duboc (v).* 7/93.

*****(*) Dream A Little Dream**

Telarc 83364 *Mulligan; Bill Mays, Ted Rosenthal (p); Dean Johnson (b); Ron Vincent (d).* 4/94.

***** Dragonfly**

Telarc 83377 *Mulligan; Warren Vaché (c); Ryan Kisor (t); Grover Washington Jr (ss, ts); Dave Grusin, Ted Rosenthal (p); Dave Samuels (vib); John Scofield (g); Dean Johnson (b); Ron Vincent (d); brass.* 3–6/95.

*****(*) Triple Play**

Telarc 84353 3CD *As above three discs.* 93–95.

The final run of albums for Telarc have been boxed together, with no additional material, as *Triple Play*. Good value though it is, not every purchaser will be thrilled with *Paraiso* and might prefer to acquire the records individually. Mulligan towers head and shoulders above all the other musicians on this slightly cheesy Latin-American date. Jane Duboc's vocals are actually rather winning and grow with familiarity, but the arrangements lack the subtlety and depth of focus for which one always looked to Mulligan in the old days.

There had been rumours for some time about Mulligan's health, and most of them proved to be premature. Certainly there is no lapse in quality on the gloriously recorded *Dream A Little Dream*. Some of the best moments are the most intimate, a duo version with Rosenthal of Alec Wilder's 'I'll Be Around' and duet versions of 'My Funny Valentine' and 'As Close As Pages In A Book' with guest pianist Bill Mays, who had been a regular performer with the quartet. The closing 'Song For Strayhorn' pays tribute to one of the saxophonist's great friends and idols and the man who, perhaps more than any other – more than Ellington, arguably – influenced his approach to the jazz orchestra. But then, of course, Mulligan always thought of a small group, even a duo, as an orchestra in miniature, so the piece has the bigness of spirit and sound one would expect.

Mulligan's final studio recording was a compromise, boosted by overdubbed brass and redolent of nothing but failing powers. That said, Jeru remains very much the focus and is featured on most tracks, none of which is intrinsically arresting. We've returned to this record many times in the hope of catching some overlooked last wisdom, but in the final measure it's a competent and gently paced set, designed to flatter an ailing man.

Mick Mulligan (born 1928)

TRUMPET, VOCAL

A quixotic hero of the British trad boom, Mulligan was never much of a trumpet player, but his bandleading exploits have gone down in well-documented history. To non-British readers, his band's reputation will remain a mystery.

****(*) Meet Mick Mulligan And George Melly**

Lake LACD 66 *Mulligan; Frank Parr (tb); Ian Christie (cl); Ronnie Duff (p); Bill Bramwell (g, v); Gerry Salisbury (b, tb); Alan Duddington (b); Pete Appleby (d); George Melly (v).* 9/58–4/59.

Mulligan's band have gained a picaresque reputation via George Melly's memoirs; their records are frankly rather less interesting. Nobody's useless, there are some worthwhile solos – especially Christie's somewhat crazed version of 'All Of Me' – and Melly contributes some entertaining vocals. But the band never sound like much of a unit, tending to play at the same time rather than together, and the dull material and thin sound tell against them.

Mark Murphy (born 1932)

VOCAL

Worked in New York clubs in the 1950s and made records for Capitol and Riverside. Lived in Europe for many years from the mid-'60s, then returned to the USA in 1975. Many albums for Muse, 1972–91. Originally a cool-hipster stylist, Murphy's command increased and his chops allowed him to sing effectively in a wide range of settings.

*****(*) Rah**

Original Jazz Classics OJC 141 *Murphy; Ernie Wilkins Orchestra.* 9–10/61.

***** That's How I Love The Blues**

Original Jazz Classics OJC 367 *Murphy; Nick Travis, Snooky Young, Clark Terry (t); Bernie Leighton, Dick Hyman (org);*

Roger Kellaway (p); Jim Hall (g); Ben Tucker (b); Dave Bailey (d); Willie Rodriguez (perc). 62.

Mark Murphy's been hip all his professional life. His earliest records, of which these are two of the best, found him looking to emulate Eddie Jefferson rather than Frank Sinatra (or Bobby Darin – Murphy looked a little like a bobbysoxer himself back then) and, while his delivery is sometimes self-consciously cool in its use of dynamics and bent notes, he's always an impassioned singer – sometimes too much so, such as on an overwrought 'Blues In My Heart' on the *Blues* collection. That record may annoy some with its showmanlike approach to a set of downbeat material, but Murphy is no more overbearing than Billy Eckstine or Al Hibbler. *Rah*, pitched as a college man's text of hipsterism, is marginally more enjoyable, but both records benefit from the singer's strong, flexible tenor – he's enough his own man never to shoot for black pronunciation – and canny arrangements by Ernie Wilkins and (on *Blues*) Al Cohn.

***** Songbook**

32 Jazz 32105 2CD *Murphy; Tom Harrell, Randy Brecker, Warren Gale, Brian Lynch, Ted Curson, Claudio Roditi (t); Mark Levine, Slide Hampton (tb); Richie Cole, David Sanborn (as); Michael Brecker, Danny Wilensky, Gerry Niewood (ts); Ronnie Cuber (bs); Smith Dobson, Mike Renzi, Michael Austin-Boe, Kenny Barron (p); Pat Rebillot, Don Grolnick, Bill Mays, Jay Wagner, Ken Ascher, Ben Aronov, John Cobert, Larry Fallon, Cliff Carter (ky); David Braham (org); Lou Lausche (vn); Joe Puma, Sam Brown, Jim Nichols, John Basile, Claudio Amaral, Gene Bertoncini, John Tropea, Harry Leahy, David Spinozza (g); Ron Carter, Paul Breslin, Michael Formanek, Harvie Swartz, Chuck Metcalf, Luther Hughes, Dave Hughes, Steve LaSpina, George Mraz, Mark Egan, Francisco Centeno (b); Jimmy Madison, Vince Lateano, Ben Riley, Chris Parker, Jimmy Madison, Joey Baron, Jeff Hamilton, Peter Grant, Grady Tate, Adam Nussbaum, Rubens Moura (d); Jack Gobetti, Susan Evans, Sammy Figueroa, Michael Spiro, Chalo Eduardo (perc); Julia Stewart, Sheila Jordan (v).* 11/72–12/91.

Murphy made 19 albums for Muse, but this compilation is currently all that remains. Covering almost 20 years of work, it's a strange and often unsatisfacrtory hotch-potch of styles and material. Many of the '70s tracks sound very dated and lumbered with archaic keyboards and old-fashioned guitar sounds. There's a ludicrous 'Eleanor Rigby' and some other misguided attempts at transforming pop into jazz. But Murphy's artistry asserts itself often enough to make it worthwhile nevertheless, and it might have been better boiled down even further to a single disc. Material from his *Bop For Kerouac* and *Kerouac Then And Now* albums is more encouraging, and other nuggets do break through: 'I'll Close My Eyes', and 'The Best Thing For You' with Sheila Jordan.

****(*) Night Mood**

Milestone MCD 9145 *Murphy; Claudio Roditi (t); Frank Morgan (as); Jose Bertrami (ky); Alex Malheiros (b); Ivan Conti (d).* 86.

***** September Ballads**

Milestone MCD 9154-2 *Murphy; Art Farmer (t); Larry Dunlap (ky); Oscar Castro-Nueves (g); David Belove, Jeff Carney (b); Donald Bailey (d); John Santos, Vince Lateano (perc).* 87.

***** Another Vision**

September 5113 *Murphy; Ack Van Rooyen (flhn); Turk Mauro (ts); Jack Poll (p); Martin Wind (b); Hans Van Osserhout (d).* 7/92.

Night Mood and *September Ballads* both set him up with a light fusion of jazz and Latin rhythms (the group Azymuth back him on the former) and, although his singing is as accomplished as usual, the thin material on *Night Mood* is discouraging; and nothing really stands out on the pleasing but muted *September Ballads*. *Another Vision* is distinguished by a fine team of players, a gentle production and some useful solos by guests Mauro and van Rooyen. Murphy's scatting and fast pace can sound affected on the swingers, and his voice has lost a lot of its bloom, but the more quiescent music still has an evocative streak.

*****(*) Song For The Geese**

RCA Victor 74321 44865-2 *Murphy; Marc Seales (ky); Doug Miller (b); John Bishop (d); Full Voice (v group).* 97.

You have to be a Murphy believer to agree with the rating, since this is the man at his most idiosyncratic and personal. Few singers would dare mix up 'Baltimore Oriole' and 'You're Blasé' with Steely Dan's 'Do It Again', and fewer still would take as many liberties with time, intonation and phrasing. The truth is that Murphy is now as singular and daring a singer as Betty Carter. The pipes may not be as flexible and smooth as they once were, but the intelligence and charismatic power in the singing are fascinating. The arrangements stick to a trusted small-group formula, dappled a little by synths and the surprisingly effective use of the vocal group, Full Voice. We look forward to his promised Go Jazz album, scheduled for release at the end of 2000.

Turk Murphy (1915–87)

TROMBONE

Melvin 'Turk' Murphy is a sometimes exalted figure among followers of American jazz revivalism. He made his name while working alongside Lu Watters in the more celebrated Yerba Bunea Jazz Band and ran his Earthquake McGoon's Club in San Francisco for the rest of his playing life.

***** Turk Murphy's Jazz Band Favourites**

Good Time Jazz 60-011 *Murphy; Don Kinch, Bob Scobey (t); Bill Napier, Skippy Anderson, Bob Helm (cl); Burt Bales, Wally Rose (p); Bill Newman (g, bj); Pat Patton, Dick Lammi, Harry Mordecai (bj); Squire Gersback, George Bruns (b, tba); Stan Ward, Johnny Brent (d).* 49–51.

***** Turk Murphy's Jazz Band Favourites Vol. 2**

Good Time Jazz 60-026 *Similar to above, except add Claire Austin (v).* 49–51.

**** Turk Murphy And His San Francisco Jazz Band Vol. 1**

GHB 091 *Murphy; Leon Oakley (c); Jim Maichak (tb); Phil Howe (cl); Pete Clute (p); Carl Lunsford (bj).* 4/72.

**** Turk Murphy And His San Francisco Jazz Band Vol. 2**

GHB 092 *As above.* 4/72.

Murphy's music would be a little more credible if he hadn't gone on making it for so long. At the time of his earliest recordings, when he was a member of the Lu Watters circle, the Californian traditional jazz movement had some nous as revivalists of music which had lain, unjustly neglected, for many years. In that light, the two Good Time Jazz compilations, hammy though much of the playing is, and often painfully (as opposed to authentically) untutored, are both interesting and enjoyable. But after more than 20 years of this kind of thing, Murphy's one-track traditionalism sounds tiresome and soulless on the two GHB CDs, taken from a single 1972 session. It might be cheerful and boisterous enough, and Murphy's own playing has achieved a ready constituency, but there are many better arguments for revivalism than this music. Murphy's legacy is better handled by some of the superior outfits now recording for GHB and Stomp Off.

David Murray (born 1955)

TENOR SAXOPHONE, BASS CLARINET

The David Murray phenomenon seems less comet-like and fateful at the end of the decade than it did at the beginning when Murray albums were coming in threes. He was born in Berkeley, where his mother was a gospel piano-player. Murray was alerted to modern jazz by Stanley Crouch and Arthur Blythe but became known to a wider public as a member of the World Saxophone Quartet. His signature style is a mixture of bebop, swing and free elements, alternated with boogie and funk. Even if the initial impact has faded somewhat, he remains the most formidable tenor soloist of his generation.

****** Flowers For Albert**

India Navigation IN 1004 2CD *Murray; Lawrence Butch Morris (c); Don Pullen (p); Fred Hopkins (b); Stanley Crouch (d).* 9/77.

***** Live At The Lower Manhattan Ocean Club**

India Navigation IN 1032 *Murray; Lester Bowie (t); Fred Hopkins (b); Phillip Wilson (d).* 12/77.

Over the last two decades David Murray would seem to have confirmed Ornette Coleman's famous claim that the soul of black Americans is best expressed through the tenor saxophone. A pivotal figure in contemporary jazz (and one of the most comprehensively documented), Murray has patiently created a synthesis of the radical experimentation of John Coltrane and (particularly) Albert Ayler with the classic jazz tradition. These are very much the agenda of *Flowers For Albert*, as rousing and provocative a start to a major recording career as you'll find anywhere in this *Guide*. Crouch's historiography may have had as great an impact as his drumming, and even at this stage Morris was beginning his own exploration of the line between formality and freedom. It was an ideal context for a player of Murray's instincts. They render him virtually uncategorizable, exploring freedom one moment, locked in bright swing structures the next, moving without strain from astonishing aggression to openly romantic expression (much of it dedicated to his wife, Ming).

Perhaps the best measure of his stance on tradition and experiment is his unaccompanied assault-and-seduction on 'Body And Soul', the tenor man's Matterhorn. It's an intense and sometimes scarifying performance, unmarred by a very indifferent and unresonant recording, and it shows how naturally Murray mixes dissonances and pure noise into his harmonic development. To this extent, he is a descendant of the Dolphy who made 'God Bless The Child' a model for radical standards playing. *Ocean Club* introduces material – 'Bechet's Bounce' and 'Santa Barbara And Crenshaw's Follies' – that typically reappears later, very much transformed; remastered from the LPs, it has Murray doubling rather unconvincingly on soprano saxophone, though Bowie is on top form. Stanley Crouch, who has cornered the market in liner-notes for young traditionalists like Murray and Wynton Marsalis, has been one of the central personal influences on the saxophonist's career, as is the superb Fred Hopkins.

***** Interboogieology**

Black Saint 120018 *Murray; Lawrence Butch Morris (c); Johnny Dyani (b); Oliver Johnson (d); Marta Contreras (v).* 2/78.

Two compositions each by Murray and his most significant collaborator, Butch Morris. The opening 'Namthini's Song' is a stately procession, marked by Morris's typically unpredictable voicings. Marta Contreras sings wordlessly, somewhere up near the cornet's register; it's certainly a more convincing use of her voice than the Abbey Lincoln mannerisms of the title-track. 'Home' is a huge duet from Murray and Dyani, with the bassist's solid chant underpinning a free-flowing improvisation. 'Blues For David' is uncharacteristically direct for Morris, a fine blowing number with the leader's most shaped solo contributions of the set.

This album probably set the pattern for Murray's subsequent and now very substantial output. A tireless experimenter, he also has a strong and canny urge to communicate, and there is a thread of populism running through his music that belies the easy critical association with Ayler and makes a nonsense of many critics' professed surprise at his rejection of unmediated avant-gardism in favour of a 'back to the future' examination of the whole sequence of black musical tradition.

****** Sweet Lovely**

Black Saint 120039 *Murray; Fred Hopkins (b); Steve McCall (d).* 12/79.

Stripped down to basics, this anticipates *The Hill*. The first version of 'Hope/Scope', which has a slightly odd subsequent history, is the clearest, pivoted on Hopkins's booming bass. 'Coney Island' and 'The Hill' are at opposite ends of Murray's repertoire, but the trio gives them an unexpected coherence.

****** Ming**

Black Saint 120045 *Murray; Olu Dara (t); Lawrence Butch Morris (c); George Lewis (tb); Henry Threadgill (as); Anthony Davis (p); Wilber Morris (b); Steve McCall (d, perc).* 7/80.

*****(*) Home**

Black Saint 120055 *As above.* 11/81.

For many fans, *the* jazz album of the 1980s was recorded before the decade was properly under way. *Ming* is an astonishing record, a virtual compression of three generations of improvised music into 40 minutes of entirely original jazz. The opening 'Fast Life' has a hectic quality reminiscent of another of Murray's household gods, Charles Mingus. 'Jasvan' is a swirling 'Boston' waltz that gives most of the band, led off by the marvellous Lewis, ample solo space. 'Ming' is a sweet ballad which follows on from the troubling, almost schizophrenic 'The Hill', a piece that occupies a central place in Murray's output, perhaps an image of the jazz *gradus ad Parnassum* that he is so studiously and passionately scaling.

Recorded by the same octet, *Home* is very nearly the better album. The slow opening title-piece is a delicately layered ballad with gorgeous horn voicings. 'Last Of The Hipmen' is one of his best pieces, and the Anthony Davis vamp that leads out of Steve McCall's intelligent and exuberant solo is a reminder of how close to Ellington's bandleading philosophy Murray has come by instinct rather than design.

***** Murray's Steps**

Black Saint 120065 *Murray; Bobby Bradford (t); Lawrence Butch Morris (c); Craig Harris (tb); Henry Threadgill (as, f); Curtis Clark (p); Wilber Morris (b); Steve McCall (d, perc).* 7/82.

This hasn't quite the sharpness of Murray's other octets and has to be considered (absurd as this will sound to anyone who has heard the disc) an off-day. The retake of 'Flowers For Albert' is an important index of how unwilling Murray has always been to leave his own output alone; there are more convincing versions; but, if the dedicatee represents some sort of magnetic north for Murray, then the piece is a good navigational aid.

*****(*) Morning Song**

Black Saint 120075 *Murray; John Hicks (p); Reggie Workman, Ray Drummond (b); Ed Blackwell (d).* 9/83.

Compare the version of 'Body And Soul' – the tenor saxophonist's shibboleth – here with the unaccompanied one on the first item, above. It is more assured, less willed and less concerned with deconstructing a piece that has been rendered virtually abstract by countless hundreds of improvisations. Note how Murray restores the tune in segments during his later statements of a freely arrived-at counter-theme.

Hicks is a wonderfully supportive and sensitive partner, particularly on the standard (enthusiasts should check out their duo, *Sketches Of Tokyo*, DIW 8006 CD, which features a – then surprisingly rare, but now more frequent – take on Coltrane by the saxophonist), and Blackwell's drumming touches all the right bases. A pity they haven't done more together.

***** Live At Sweet Basil: Volume 1**

Black Saint 120085 *Murray; Olu Dara (c); Baikida Carroll, Craig Harris (t); Bob Stewart (tba); Vincent Chauncey (frhn); Steve Coleman (ss, as); John Purcell (as, cl); Rod Williams (p); Fred Hopkins (b); Billy Higgins (d); Lawrence Butch Morris (cond).* 8/84.

***** Live At Sweet Basil: Volume 2**

Black Saint 120095 *As above.* 8/84.

Volume 2 kicks off with a version of the wonderfully cheesy 'Dewey's Circle' from *Ming*, one of those compositions of Murray's that many listeners swear they have heard somewhere before. It's not quite the best piece on the set, but it's the one where most of the constituent elements are coming together. 'Bechet's Bounce' and 'Silence' on the first volume redirect some of Murray's increasingly familiar obsessions in quite new ways. The final track is a brief dedication to Marvin Gaye; by this stage in his career Murray is namechecking at an impressive rate.

The live context, with a hefty band pushing from behind, makes for some inventive conjunctions, but Murray's tone is uncharacteristically acid. There's no obvious explanation for this; the production is well up to Black Saint's careful standard.

***** Children**

Black Saint 120089 *Murray; Don Pullen (p); James Blood Ulmer (g); Lonnie Plaxico (b); Marvin 'Smitty' Smith (d).* 10 & 11/84.

Rededicated to his son, David Mingus Murray, this is one of the poorer 1980s albums. Smith and Plaxico dominate unnecessarily, and Ulmer and Pullen make only cameo appearances. That's another two bankable modern names to tick off against Murray's list, with 'All The Things You Are' for anyone who's birdwatching the standards.

***** Recording NYC 1986**

DIW 802 *Murray; James Blood Ulmer (g); Fred Hopkins (b); Sunny Murray (d).* 86.

*****(*) I Want To Talk About You**

Black Saint 120105 *Murray; John Hicks (p); Ray Drummond (b); Ralph Peterson Jr (d).* 3/86.

Those who were disturbed by Murray's apparent abandonment of the avant-garde might have been reassured by his firm rejection of the backward-looking stance of Wynton Marsalis and others. It's clear from the live *I Want To Talk About You* that, while the saxophonist is looking increasingly to an earlier generation of saxophone players, Sonny Rollins pre-eminently, but also synthesizers like the fated Ellingtonian Paul Gonsalves, he is doing so with instincts very explicitly conditioned by Coltrane and Ayler. His reading of 'I Want To Talk About You' has to be heard in the context of Coltrane's own version; as a ballad player, Murray is vibrant and expansive and 'Heart To Heart' (written by Hicks) is one of his most nakedly emotional recorded performances.

'Morning Song' reappears, its robust R&B stretched out into something altogether stronger than the album version. 'Quads' has him switch to bass clarinet; if the technique ultimately derives from Dolphy, Murray has managed to extend his great predecessor's somewhat predictable upper-register devices, making use of more of the horn.

Ulmer is another to have apparently turned his back on the avant-garde in pursuit of a more marketable neo-populism. In practice, of course, the more conservative Ulmer is also the one who digs deepest into black tradition, and so it turns out to be with Murray.

***** In Our Style**

DIW 819 *Murray; Fred Hopkins (b); Jack DeJohnette (d, p).* 9/86.

Murray played in DeJohnette's Special Edition band, notably on *Album Album* (ECM 1280), but their duo confrontation feels slightly uncomfortable, as if they're doing no more than sounding one another out. DeJohnette's piano backgrounds, though uncharacteristically basic, are more effective foils than the drummed tracks, where DeJohnette seems to restrict himself to a disappointingly narrow range of devices, some of them overpoweringly recorded. It all makes a bit more sense when Fred Hopkins comes in on the title-track and 'Your Dice'.

****** The Hill**

Black Saint 120110 *Murray; Richard Davis (b); Joe Chambers (d).* 11/86.

One of the peaks of Murray's career. The title-piece, pared down from eight voices to three, doesn't fall apart but retains its rather mysterious and troubling presence. Murray has significantly toned down his delivery from the immediately previous sessions and sounds altogether more thoughtful. The material, by now, is quite self-consciously programmed, with 'Chelsea Bridge' and 'Take The Coltrane' mixed in with the originals. 'Herbie Miller' contains Murray's best-recorded bass clarinet solo; pitched against Richard Davis's rich *arco*, he develops an intense thematic discourse that takes enough time to vary its accents in keeping with the changing emotional climate of the piece. By contrast, 'Fling' is exactly as throwaway as it sounds. This is an essential modern album.

***** Hope Scope**

Black Saint 120139 *Murray; Hugh Ragin, Rasul Siddik (t); Craig Harris (tb); James Spaulding (as); Dave Burrell (p); Wilber Morris (b); Ralph Peterson (d).* 5/87.

Released only in 1991 (by which time Murray was recording for DIW), this is a bright, exuberant album, full of the band's palpable delight in what they're doing. This version of 'Hope/Scope' is much less convoluted than the one on *Special Quartet*, below, but it inspires some raggedly spirited ensemble improvisations. The tributes to Lester Young and Ben Webster are closer to pastiche than usual (see also DIW 851, below), reflecting a rather lightweight side to the album that is initially appealing but increasingly puzzling as the layers come off it.

***** The Healers**

Black Saint 120118 *Murray; Randy Weston (p).* 9/87.

Though Weston's sense of structure is much like Murray's, which turns out to be inhibiting rather than particularly productive, he tends to conceive developments in discontinuous units rather than in Murray's uninterrupted flow. Several times the pianist falls back on set licks which make him sound a less sophisticated player than he is. 'Mbizo' is a further version of a dedication to Johnny Dyani, who died the previous year. A by-way on Murray's increasingly determined course, *The Healers* takes Murray down a road he has seemed disinclined to pursue. Which is a pity.

***** Lucky Four**

Tutu 888108 *Murray; Dave Burrell (p); Wilber Morris (b); Victor Lewis (d, perc).* 9/88.

Moonlighting under the alias of Lucky Four, Murray and two long-standing collaborators turn in a slightly lacklustre session that, despite interesting variants on both 'Valley Talk' and 'As I Woke', never seems to grab the attention firmly. 'Chazz', dedicated to Mingus, and 'Strollin'', to Michel Basquiat, are both slightly woolly.

*****(*) Deep River**

DIW 830 *Murray; Dave Burrell (p); Fred Hopkins (b); Ralph Peterson Jr (d).* 1/88.

****** Lovers**

DIW 814 *As above.* 1/88.

*****(*) Tenors**

DIW 881 *As above.* 1/88.

****** Ballads**

DIW 840 *As above.*

*****(*) Spirituals**

DIW 841 *As above.*

****** Special Quartet**

DIW 843 *Murray; McCoy Tyner (p); Fred Hopkins (b); Elvin Jones (d).* 90.

Murray's move away from the Italian-based Black Saint (who had generously supported his work in the absence of any major-label bites) to the Japan-based DIW did nothing to stem the flow of material. Releasing records in threes quickly became the norm. These albums, with their explicitly traditionalist agenda, all come from a single New York session and are not quite as varied as the 1991 batch. *Ballads* has become one of the most popular of the saxophonist's albums, with *Spirituals* also touching a popular nerve; but spare a moment for *Deep River*, with 'Dakar's Dance' and 'Mr P.C.'. The latter is topped only by a riveting version of another Coltrane track on the 1990 album. *Special Quartet*? It certainly is, and a fine piece of arrogance on Murray's part to put half the classic Coltrane band back together, but it's no better than the 1988 group, even if Tyner is in sparkling form.

Lovers for some reason was omitted from our original survey of this batch. It begins in almost quintessential Murray style with a gentle ballad form, dedicated to bassist Jimmy Garrison, before Burrell kicks the metre into double time and provokes a shower of multiphonic splinters from Murray. There is a new version of 'Ming' and a thoughtful revision of 'In A Sentimental Mood'. The highlight of the session, though, is the title-track, a weaving, persuasive line that recalls the example of Paul Gonsalves. A quiet and deceptively understated record.

*****(*) Tea For Two**

Fresh Sound FSRCD 164 *Murray; George Arvanitas (p).* 5/90.

Headed 'George Arvanitas Presents: The ballad artistry of ... David Murray', there's a rabbit-out-of-hat quality to the ellipsis. Though no one's surprised any more to find Murray playing 'in the tradition', it's still rare to find him doing it quite this uncomplicatedly. The menu of standards doesn't really stretch him technically and there's a hint of a more mannered approach in his takes of past giants, almost as though he's over-anxious to inscribe himself into the history of jazz saxophone before the fortieth birthday comes up. For the record (this is a relatively undiscovered Murray album), the track listing is 'Chelsea Bridge', 'Polka Dots And Moonbeams', 'Star Eyes', 'Body And Soul' again, 'Tea For Two', 'I'm In The Mood For Love', an original 'Blues For Two', and 'La Vie En Rose'.

****** Remembrances**

DIW 849 *Murray; Hugh Ragin (t); Dave Burrell (p); Wilber Morris (b); Tani Tabbal (d).* 7/90.

Remembrances digs down into the same influences that conditioned Murray's great predecessor, Albert Ayler. Much of this material is in the spirit of the black church (and thus of *Spirituals* and *Deep River*), its abstractions emerging out of impassioned witness, its resolutions an expression of acceptance rather than of will.

The tonal integrity of Ragin and Burrell is extraordinarily beautiful, with the trumpeter pealing away with a much fuller sound than he often uses and Burrell laying fat, rolling chords over the rhythmic pattern. Very lovely, very accomplished, and absolutely of its time and place.

***(*) Shakill's Warrior

DIW 850 *Murray; Don Pullen (org); Stanley Franks (g); Andrew Cyrille (d).* 3/91.

**(*) Shakill's II

DIW 884 *Murray; Don Pullen (org); Bill White (g); J.T Lewis (d).* 93.

A much more personal dredge of the past. *Shakill's Warrior* plugs Don Pullen into a Hammond B3 and Murray into his R&B roots. He even looked up his old pal, Stanley Franks, from their teenage band, Notations of Soul. Franks does damn-all on the album, but the remaining trio is red-hot. Pullen, working to a broadly similar concept, goes back virtually all the way with Murray; Cyrille is a new factor and, if he doesn't at first seem ideally suited to this line-up, it's the drummer's 'High Priest' which dominates the album.

The sequel is fairly dismal, Pullen apart. Murray waffles from one theme to the next, rarely sounding properly engaged and often falling back on staringly obvious ideas. A disappointing follow-up to a steaming record.

*** David Murray Big Band

DIW 851 *Murray; Graham Haynes, Hugh Ragin, Rasul Siddik, James Zollar (t); Craig Harris, Frank Lacy, Al Patterson (tb); Vincent Chauncey (frhn); Bob Stewart (tba); Kahlil Henry (f, picc); John Purcell (as); James Spaulding (as, f); Patience Higgins (ts, ss); Don Byron (bs, cl); Sonelius Smith (p); Fred Hopkins (b); Tani Tabbal (d); Joel A Brandon (whistle); Andy Bey (v); Lawrence Butch Morris (cond).* 3/91.

There are further versions of 'Lester' and 'Ben' from *Hope/Scope* and a dedication to Paul Gonsalves, acknowledged as an influence on Murray. The former pair are given an altogether more complex and detailed reading but, by and large, the performances on this album are disappointingly trite, and certainly lacking in the multi-layered obliqueness one expects from Morris (who, significantly or not, doesn't contribute as a composer, other than the shared credit on 'Calling Steve McCall').

The band is impressively constructed, on a scale Murray hasn't attempted before, but it seems a pity to have got them all together and fired up and then to give them so little of consequence to play.

*** The Jazzpar Prize

Enja CD 7031 *Murray; New Jungle Orchestra: Pierre Dørge (g); Per Jorgensen (t); Harry Beckett (t, flhn); Jörg Huke (tb); Jesper Zeuthen (as, bcl); Jacob Mygind (ts, ss); Horace Parlan (p); Irene Becker (ky); Jens Skov Olsen (b); Audun Kleive (d); Donald Murray (v).* 3/91.

In the spring of 1991 Murray was awarded the third annual Jazzpar Prize, perhaps the only major international jazz award in the world. It was a significant accolade for a man not yet forty. During the course of the prize project, Murray recorded with Pierre Dørge's New Jungle Orchestra. The two men share an interest in Ellingtonian composition and sounds, and Murray fitted into the band with his usual ease. The two opening pieces are by the guitarist; there follows a gospel medley, with vocals from Donald Murray, a beautifully constructed version of 'In A Sentimental Mood', finishing with full-throated performances of 'Shakill's Warrior' and 'Song For Doni'.

Murray's solo is more restrained than usual, and in this context his kinship with Paul Gonsalves becomes entirely unambiguous. Though he varies the melody of the Ellington tune to spark off his solo, ironically it's one of the straightest and most respectful repertoire performances to be found anywhere in his recorded output.

**** David Murray / James Newton Quintet

DIW 906 *Murray; James Newton (f); John Hicks (p); Fred Hopkins (b); Andrew Cyrille, Billy Hart (d).* 8/91.

Welcome as much as anything for its exposure of the brilliant Newton, this is a superb session, lyrical, intense, buzzing with intelligence and replete with fine compositional ideas. Newton takes the lion's share of composing credits, though Murray, Hicks and Cyrille all contribute material as well. The drummer's misterioso 'Moon Over Sand II' is one of his most effective ideas, and the two long numbers, Newton's 'Inbetwinxt' and Murray's 'Doni's Song' (dedicated to his younger brother), are exceptional in their range. Impossible to fault any of the players. Hart appears only on the opening tune and it would have been good to have heard more from him, as ever.

By this point in his career, Murray's instrumental virtuosity is unquestionable. Though less effusive and dramatic than, say, Chico Freeman, he gives the impression of being able to do almost anything on his horns, and his longer solos, on 'Akhenaten' and 'Blues In The Pocket', are models of their kind. A lovely recording, too, which gives Newton's flute its proper balance.

*** Death Of A Sideman

DIW 866 *Murray; Bobby Bradford (c); Dave Burrell (p); Fred Hopkins (b); Ed Blackwell (d).* 10/91.

Death Of A Sideman is a suite of pieces dedicated to the late clarinettist and educator, John Carter. It's relatively unusual for Murray to play quite so much work by another composer. He remains constantly open to Bradford's ideas, but his solos on this occasion are often little more than sets of alternative scalar structures which never seem to develop satisfactorily. Only on 'Woodshedetude' does he build up enough momentum to burst out of the confines of the written chart and play imaginatively. Bradford's post-Cherry sound, tight, small, almost folkish, presents such a startling contrast to Murray's broad vibrato that the pairing works quite well. The rhythm section never falters for a moment, but Blackwell, who was in very indifferent health at the time, sounds unusually robotic.

**** Fast Life

DIW 861 *Murray; Branford Marsalis (ts); John Hicks (p); Ray Drummond (b); Idris Muhammad (d).* 10/91.

Just to round out an extraordinarily productive month, this beautiful album by the quartet-plus-one. Branford's contributions to Dave Burrell's 'Crucificado' and the title-piece are astonishingly close in conception and execution to Murray's own work, suggesting an unsuspectedly large area of common ground. Murray himself is as definite as a shark, moving ever forward and laying off lyrical ideas at a rate that almost defies belief. It would be tempting to think that at least some of the solos had been pre-formed, but for the objection that Hicks so obviously throws curves. Drummond is as expansive as his own waistline, and the underrated Muhammad does a great job.

****** Ballads For Bass Clarinet**
DIW 880 *Murray; John Hicks (p); Ray Drummond (b); Idris Muhammad (d).* 10/91.

It was logical that one day Murray would record exclusively on bass clarinet. The wonder is how effective an album it turns out to be, and how close his phrasing on the big, cumbersome horn is to his tenor work. The opening 'Waltz To Heaven' has a glowing warmth and presence, as does 'New Life'. 'Portrait Of A Black Woman' introduces a note of anguish, but only briefly.

****** Real Deal**
DIW 867 *Murray; Milford Graves (d, perc).* 11/91.
***** A Sanctuary Within**
Black Saint 120145 *Murray; Tony Overwater (b); Sunny Murray (d); Kahil El'Zabar (perc, v).* 12/91.

This might almost have come from a decade previously, when Murray was firmly locked into his avant-garde phase. Yet he has become much more varied in his choice of sounds, plumbing not just the stoical moods of 'Ballad For The Blackman' but also the more buoyant and affirmative 'Waltz To Heaven', a theme that was to reappear over the succeeding couple of years in a number of playing contexts, not least the bass clarinet album, above.

El'Zabar, a founding member of the Ethnic Heritage Ensemble, creates a whirl of exotic tinges round the fringes of each piece, but he doesn't feel integral to the project and a couple of tracks would certainly be improved if he simply weren't there.

Perversely, it would be fascinating to hear Murray work in duo with the percussionist for an entire session, as he does with the completely wonderful Graves on *Real Deal*. One of the pioneering musicians of the 1960s avant-garde, Graves largely disappeared from the recording scene and has come back to attention only quite recently. His encounter with Murray is as titanic as might have been supposed. Working in structures that might be called indefinite rather than abstract, they weave great loops of music on which first one, then the other, is able to improvise more freely. It's marvellously tight and wholly effective. An essential purchase for Murray admirers.

*****(*) South Of The Border**
DIW 897 *Murray; Hugh Ragin, Rasul Siddik, James Zollar (t); Graham Haynes (c); Craig Harris, Frank Lacy, Al Patterson (tb); Vincent Chauncey (frhn); Kahlil Henry (f); James Spaulding (as, f); John Purcell (as); Patience Higgins (ts, ss); Don Byron (cl, bs); Sonelius Smith (p); Fred Hopkins (b); Tani Tabbal (d); Larry McDonald (perc); Lawrence Butch Morris (cond).* 5/92.

Located somewhere between Murray's smaller-group sound and the orderly anarchy of Butch Morris's 'conduction' process, this is a fascinating synthesis of opposites, one of the most exciting big-band records of recent times and one with the terse immediacy of an orthodox quintet. Murray by no means hogs the solo spotlight, giving most of the other horns a decent amount of space to express themselves. He is the only featured player on Morris's 'Fling', but almost everywhere else he shares the spotlight with Byron, Spaulding, Lacy and Higgins (on Rollins's calypso, 'St Thomas'), with Spaulding, Siddik and Lacy again (on 'Happy Birthday, Wayne Jr') and with Harris and Ragin on the closing 'Flowers For Albert', a staple Murray composition which has rarely sounded better.

It's known that the band rehearsed dedicatedly before the recording session and they sound pretty much note-perfect, piece to piece. There are hints here and there that things have gone beyond the given charts, but never that the ensemble is merely jamming on chords and melodies. A hugely impressive achievement and a key work of recent years.

*****(*) Live '93 Acoustic Octfunk**
Sound Hills SSCD 8051 *Murray; Fred Hopkins (b); Andrew Cyrille (d).* 7/93.

This was a very successful tour for Murray, artistically if not always at the box office. Trio playing encouraged him to play simply, in bold strokes and relatively unadorned. His solos, as here on 'Mr P.C.' and 'Flowers For Albert', are intense, but it is the interplay among the three members of the group that is so impressive, and it communicates itself even across a rather unforgiving recording that booms and thuds away awkwardly. Hopkins plays superbly, and Cyrille's fills and solo spots are packed with ideas.

***** Picasso**
DIW 879 *Murray; Hugh Ragin, Rasul Siddik (t); Craig Harris (tb); James Spaulding (as, f); Dave Burrell (p); Wilber Morris (b); Tani Tabbal (d).* 92.

****** Body And Soul**
Black Saint 120155 *Murray; Sonelius Smith (p); Wilber Morris (b); Rashied Ali (d); Taana Running (v).* 2/93.

By the end of the 1980s, Murray's traditionalism was expressing itself in unambiguously literal form. Time and again, he plunged back into the history of the music, dredging up performances that fell somewhere between wholesale revision and an oddly uncertain faithfulness to the originals. Because it always sounded like Murray, nobody minded; but much of that was superficial, disguising how little he was prepared to disturb ancestral ghosts.

It was odds-on that Murray would one day record an album called *Body And Soul*. His understanding of Hawkins's classic solo is obvious from the outset of his own interpretation, which works a very specific, palindromic variation on the opening phrases. However, Murray's solo has only a rather artificial shape, not the almost organic unity of Hawkins, and the unity comes largely from Taana Running's vocal. In *Picasso*, a loose suite of tunes in which the great painter and Hawkins again are put within a single abstract frame, Bean's great unaccompanied meditation on 'Picasso' has become one of the most influential performances in jazz, as significant to the present generation as 'Body And Soul' was to previous cohorts. As before, Murray has absorbed it wholly. The question is whether he is able to do anything with it. The suite itself is little more than a sequence of faintly incompatible elements blended together by artificial means. It certainly lacks vision. The band on *Picasso* is a good one, but that on *Body And Soul* is superlative, always just poised to take the music one stage higher.

****** For Aunt Louise**

DIW 901 *Murray; John Hicks (p); Fred Hopkins (b); Idris Muhammad (d).* 9/93.

Intriguing for the range of material covered – all the way from the traditional 'Boogie Real Slow' to Kenny Dorham's 'Asiatic Raes' to Brian Smith's 'Cancion De Amor En Espanol' – *For Aunt Louise* is rather too eclectically shapeless to be entirely successful as an album. Hicks is too literal to keep track of Murray's more extravagant digressions and here and there seems to be missing the ironies of David's approach. He is most commanding on the sole bass clarinet performance of the set, 'Fishin' And Missin' You', which is dedicated to the Aunt Louise of the title. Here, once again, Murray's debt to Dolphy is evident, and there is even a ghost of a phrase from the great man's 'Something Sweet, Something Tender'.

*****(*) Windward Passages**

Black Saint 120165 *Murray; Dave Burrell (p); Monika Larsson (v).* 12/93.

Not released for some time after recording, this basically duo session documents one of Murray's closest artistic partnerships. Burrell's range of influences, everything from calypso and reggae to the modernist avant-garde, fuels the saxophonist's own eclecticism. From the opening 'Sorrow Song', through two beautiful takes of Coltrane's 'Naima', to the vocal tracks, 'It Hurts So Much To See' and 'Cela Me Va', the partnership is flawlessly intuitive, a conversation in which ordinary niceties can be elided and both players get straight to the meat of a tune.

Murray has regularly expressed his desire to work with songs and singers. In Larsson he has found a lyricist who has just the right mixture of romanticism and sardonic bite. However, it might have been better to have saved her for another occasion. The chemistry with Burrell is strong enough to sustain a whole album and the vocal tracks here are more of a distraction than an asset.

*****(*) The Tip**

DIW 891 *Murray; Bobby Broom (g); Robert Irving III (org, syn); Darryl Jones (b); Toby Williams (d); Kahil El'Zabar (perc); G'Ra (poetry).* 5/94.

***** Jug-A-Lug**

DIW 894 *As above, except omit G'Ra; add Olu Dfara (c); Daryl Thompson (g).* 5/94.

It keeps being said; it remains the case. Murray plays with magisterial calm and exactness, shows an intelligent awareness of the jazz tradition (*passim*), of the continuum of African-American music ('Sex Machine') and of his own back-catalogue ('Flowers For Albert'). This is an altogether funkier, more plugged-in project than he has previously seen fit to release, and it divided critical opinion somewhat: on the one hand, the 'sell-out' crowd bayed and barked in dismay; others found it a logical step along a long-established course.

It's not the best Murray album, of course; some of the Miles-derived electronic settings are pretty drab or drably pretty, but there is no mistaking the sheer intensity and individuality of Murray's own role. Like strong players before him – Parker, Coltrane, Miles – he simply breezes through uncertain accompaniments and contexts, transforming them in the process into something grander and more timeless. Quite a talent to have in this business.

The second of the pair is one of the least compelling items in the Murray canon and one of the few occasions when the multi-release approach isn't fully justified. The addition of Dara on 'Ornette' enlivens the opening section, but even he sounds a little tacked on and after the fact. (Do note that on both records it is Toby, not Tony, Williams at the kit; *caveat emptor*.)

*****(*) Dark Star**

Astor Place TCD 4002 *Murray; Omar Kabir, Hugh Ragin, James Zollar (t); Craig Harris (tb); Robert Irving III (p, org, syn); Bob Weir (g); Fred Hopkins (b); Renzell Merritt (d).* 1/96.

It was David Crosby who described the Grateful Dead's music as 'Electronic Dixieland'. Listening to this tribute, recorded not long after Jerry Garcia's death, it's not hard to see what he means, and the only surprise is that no one had thought of turning the Dead's long, floating lines and open-ended aesthetic to jazz use before. The material is far from predictable. It includes things like the traditional 'Samson And Delilah' and Bob Weir's 'One More Saturday Night' but saves the real joys for what was the vocal entry on 'Dark Star'; if anyone has heard anything as mysterious and joyous, anything more completely *right* over the last couple of years, then we'd be delighted to hear about it. In keeping with the Dead's own philosophy, there is more emphasis on group interplay than on soloing as such, though Murray does tend to dominate the foreground, as you might expect. Sometimes the brasses don't seem quite right, but that has more to do with their position in the mix than anything else. Bob Weir is on hand on 'Shoulda Had Been Me' to add a seal of approval to the project. Call us old hippies if you will ... oh, you already did?

*****(*) Quintet With Ray Anderson And Anthony Davis**

DIW 908 *Murray; Ray Anderson (tb); Anthony Davis (p); Kenny Davis (b); Tommy Campbell (d).*

It's the combination of Anthony Davis at his most adventurous and the scandalously undersung Tommy Campbell at his best that makes this such an appealing record. It's also impeccably recorded with marginally more definition to the rhythm section than to the two horns, which gives it an interestingly different spin and emphasis.

Opening with Chick Webb's 'Stompin' At The Savoy' was a masterstroke that only Murray (or possibly Murray with Anderson) could have pulled off with such panache. It's a bluntly unsophisticated reading, and there is so much information coded into it that it seems like a new track every time it hits the CD player; and this is a record that asks to be played again and again, a real grower.

****(*) Fo Deuk Revue**

Justin Time JUST 94 *Murray; Hugh Ragin (t); Craig Harris (tb); Robert Irving III (p); El Hadji Bniancou Sembene (ky); Assane Diop (g); Abdou Karim Mane, Jamaaladeen Tacuma (b); Darryl Burgee, Ousseynou Diop (d); Omar Mboup (perc); Didier Awadi, Amiri Baraka, Amiri Baraka Jr, Amadou Barry, Tidiane Gaye, Hamat Mal, Doudou N'Diaye Rose, Moussa Sene, Junior Soul (v).* 6/96.

Canadian label, African recording: small wonder that there is an element of confusion here. The presence of Robert Irving III, who contributes a fair proportion of the music, suggests a parallel with Miles Davis's later albums and the possibility that Murray has simply swung in late in the day to add some personal twists and curlicues to an otherwise rather banal project. When Murray is actually playing, and there is less of that than anyone would like, things go pretty well; however, the disc is laden with leaden lyrics and drab Afro-urban beats and, while Murray has long expressed a desire to work in song form and with non-jazz partners, this was hardly the most flattering context in which to experiment.

The members of Senegalese bands Dieuf Dieul and Positive Black Soul in turn sound restrained in Murray's presence, and, instead of a genuine meeting of minds, what results is an overly polite exchange of cultural postcards. Murray fans will find enough of the saxophonist to win them over. For the rest, though, this is thin fare, unrepresentative and disturbingly low on jazz content, a lazy and unfocused record that relies heavily on predictable atmospherics.

*****(*) The Long Goodbye**

DIW 930 *Murray; D.D Jackson (b); Santi Debriano (b); J.T Lewis (d).* 10/96.

It goes without saying that Murray misses Don Pullen profoundly. The pianist, who worked with him on *Shakill's Warrior*, had a sensibility straddling the avant-garde and R&B, and for that reason had a big effect on the saxophonist. This is his memorial to a piano player and composer who echoed many of his own concerns. The album consists of four Pullen tunes, two by the rapidly developing Jackson and one ('Long Goodbye') by Butch Morris. Murray, sounding disconcertingly like George Adams here and there, sticks to tenor throughout and leaves plenty of room for Jackson to develop his harmonic soundscapes round these powerful ideas. There might have been a case for leaving this as a duo set, perhaps developing some of the numbers ('Gratitude' in particular) in other contexts. However, the performances are all strong enough to sustain interest, and there isn't a moment when any of the quartet falls back on cliché.

***** Créole Project**

Enja ENJ 9355-2 *Murray; James Newton (f); Gérard Lockel (g); D. D Jackson (p); Ray Drummond (b); Billy Hart (d); Max Cilla, Klod Kiavue, François Landreseau (perc, v).* 10/97.

Any thought that the cross-cultural experimentation of *Fo Deuk Revue* was merely a sideshow disappeared in October 1997 when Murray took a quintet co-fronted by flautist Newton to the Caribbean island of Guadeloupe, an important staging-post for Creole culture and a meeting-point of French and Spanish, African and South American influences.

There, he met guitarist Lockel and local singer and percussionist Kiavue, and it was these encounters which led to the *Créole Project*. Ironically, while Jackson, Drummond and Hart seem immediately attuned to the rhythms brought to the sessions by the local men, and while Newton goes his own sweet way as ever, Murray himself seems much less comfortable in this context and a good deal of the confident individuality leaches out of his playing. The two longest pieces, 'Gansavn'n' and 'Mona', work up a decent head of steam, but even here Murray seems to going along with the others rather than forging ahead as he usually does.

The recording is very good, with the percussionists arrayed in a very natural acoustic arc round the jazz band. Jackson is more intriguing every time he records and some of his solo excursions are worth comparing to Dave Burrell's work with similar material – much of it, of course, made in Murray's company.

*****(*) Speaking In Tongues**

Enja ENJ 9370-2 *Murray; Hugh Ragin (t); Jimane Nelson (org, p); Stanley Franks (g); Clarence Jenkins (b); Ranzell Merritt (d); Leopoldo Flemming (perc); Fontella Bass (v).* 98.

After trips to Senegal and Guadeloupe, this has Murray diving back into his own musical heritage in the most direct way yet. Murray's mother was a renowned gospel pianist and *Speaking In Tongues* mixes gospel-influenced originals with material that would have been deeply familiar to her, like 'Just A Closer Walk With Thee'. Musically, it is by far the most compelling of the recent trilogy of transcultural projects, perhaps because emotionally and expressively Murray has such a profound stake in it.

The idea came about when Hamiet Bluiett invited Fontella Bass to sing with the World Saxophone Project. Murray had himself been working with a gospel choir, and the ground seemed ready for a project of this sort. 'How I Got Over' establishes an atmosphere of passionate witness and has Murray make the first of his fiery, overblown solos. Ragin is another horn player who can move with comfort from R&B grooves and shuffle rhythms to free-form playing, and his contribution here shouldn't be underestimated. The guitar/organ/electric bass section has an honourable ancestry in this music, and Jimane Nelson emerges as an authentic voice with very definite ideas of his own, as he reveals on 'Jimane's Creation'.

Bass is one of the great American voices, emotional and resonant but without the hysterical edge that overtakes some sanctified singers. Her 1965 hit, 'Rescue Me', would have been a delightful addition to this set but, even without it, *Speaking In Tongues* is a marvellous album.

Dierdre Murray

CELLO

New-music cellist whose work in several contemporary groups offers a rare sighting of the instrument in a modern context.

***** Firestorm**

Victo CD 020 *Murray; Fred Hopkins (b, sticks).* 7/92.

****(*) Stringology**

Black Saint 120143 *As above, except add Marvin Sewell (g, dobro); Newman Baker (d, spoons); Ray Mantilla (perc).* 9/93.

One of a small group of improvisers who have specialized in the cello, Murray is a player who probably still functions best in the context of rather larger groups, bringing in new colours and identities. This is not to say that her duos with the effervescent Hopkins are not interesting, or that there are no merits in the larger group. It is simply that one feels she trades too heavily on certain rather limited ideas and these, especially on the skittish second album, can't quite be made to last the pace.

Sunny Murray (born 1937)

DRUMS

Sunny Murray is the real inventor of free-jazz drumming. He had an early exposure to Cecil Taylor's atonality, but he heard something new in John Coltrane's rhythm and built his approach on that, using the kit as a colour palette rather than a metronome. Like all genuine innovators, as opposed to consolidators, he has been scandalously overlooked and is only thinly recorded as leader.

*****(*) Illuminators**

Audible Hiss 008 *Murray; Charles Gayle (p, ts).* 96.

****** We Are Not At The Opera**

Eremite MTE 014 *Murray; Sabir Mateen (as, ts, f).* 6/98.

All revolutions in jazz are fuelled and driven by the rhythm section. For every horn player or pianist hailed as a 'revolutionary', you can assume that there is at least one bassist or drummer in the background, unacknowledged. The history of the 1960s' avant-garde is very largely the history of what Garrison and Jones, Haden and Blackwell or Higgins, Cyrille, Graves and Sunny Murray brought to it.

Despite his presence on some of the key recordings of the period, to wit Cecil Taylor's 1962 Café Montmartre sessions and Albert Ayler's *Spiritual Unity*, Murray has scandalously little under his own name. A trio of albums for BYG – including the wonderfully titled *Never Give A Sucker An Even Break* – and the remarkable *Apple Cores* for Philly Jazz are just about all there is, except for the obligatory ESP Disk recording, more or less a rite-of-passage thing for players of this vintage and disposition (and, anyway, it's not yet back in circulation).

The duo with Gayle was to provide some of the most ferociously beautiful live moments of the 1990s. Inevitably, it transfers to record only with an overall loss of drive, but these five pieces, all but one by Murray himself, are as clear a representation of his art as one could hope for. Less Afrocentric than either Jones or Cyrille, less abstract than Milford Graves, Murray still cleaves to a dark, punchy groove, the percussion equivalent of what Cecil Taylor was doing, but with more song in it.

Much has been said in even more recent times about how happy and chilled Sunny is in Europe. Paris suits him and there has been a new tranquillity in his work. However, there are still occasional opportunities to visit the USA, and the June 1998 recital at the Amherst Unitarian Meetinghouse is a reflection of how different the sixty-year-old is from his own younger self. Mateen is a much less incendiary partner than Gayle, and his almost boppish phrasing on 'Musically Correct' coaxes some inspired metrical drumming from Sunny. The opening 'Rejoicing New Dreams' is a much gentler piece, a duet for flute and the most delicately enunciated percussion. Apparently Sunny was so drawn to his kit that he started playing during an intended intermission, a sound which attracted Mateen out from the dressing-room to join him; 'Too Many Drummers, Not Enough Time'. We are most certainly not at the opera. The music is made in a spirit of sympathetic informality, unbuttoned and relaxed, and it includes some of Sunny's very best work on record. A gentle classic.

Music Improvisation Company

GROUP

An important group of improvisers from the iron age of British free music.

*****(*) The Music Improvisation Company 1968–1971**

Incus CD12 *Evan Parker (ss, autoharp); Hugh Davies (org, elec); Derek Bailey (g); Jamie Muir (perc).* 68–71.

British improvisers were already a determined if small and embattled community by the time these recordings were made. As documentary pieces, culled from years of occasional work, they are in some ways charming, with Davies's fiercely primitive electronics countering Bailey's resolutely un-guitar-like guitar playing, an ongoing dialogue that will seem nostalgic of a vanished era to some older listeners. Parker's soprano is years away from his major developments and discoveries, yet it still sounds startlingly original: like Bailey, he was set on searching out a new way to play. Muir's contributions are arguably the least impressive, at least when set beside what free percussionists have done both before and since, and he isn't so well served by the recording; yet the six pieces are in the main about a quartet thinking and speaking as freely with one another as they possibly could. CD transfer has brought up some of the detail lost in ageing vinyl pressings, and the chamber-like quality of much of the music is unsettled by harshness and strangeness. But it remains rather beautiful, too. A welcome return, to be set alongside Spontaneous Music Ensemble's roughly contemporary *Karyobin*, also recently reissued.

Music Revelation Ensemble

GROUP

An '80s–'90s supergroup, based initially around the talents of David Murray and James Blood Ulmer.

**** Music Revelation Ensemble**

DIW 825 *David Murray (ts); James Blood Ulmer (g); Amin Ali (b); Jamaaladeen Tacuma (b); Ronald Shannon Jackson (d).* 88.

Music Revelation Ensemble bears out Bill Shankly's famous dictum about football being played on grass, not on paper. *Music Revelation Ensemble*, on paper the most impressive-looking of their earlier discs (the fine Moers debut is now deleted), is actually a rather dismal supergroup session that takes an inordinately long time to catch light. Murray enters very late – and with some diffidence – on the opening 'Bodytalk', and throughout the album he sounds as if he's just sitting in on someone else's date. Only with the third track, 'Nisa', do things get moving, by which time more than 20 tedious minutes of abstract noodling have already gone by. 'Blues For David', like all the tracks, is an Ulmer composition, and not the Butch Morris tune of the same name on Murray's *Interboogieology* on Black Saint; the saxophonist plays a melancholy intro and then takes the front over a surprisingly bland accompaniment. The closing 'Burn!' is a silly pile-up.

Prime Time and Last Exit (and Murray) fans may be tempted, but they would be advised to leave well alone.

***** Elec. Jazz**
DIW 841 *As above, except omit Tacuma, Jackson; add Cornell Rochester (d).* 2/90.

With a change of personnel in the engine-room, *Elec. Jazz* is rather better and sounds more like the product of a working group. Organized almost like a suite, with two parts each to 'Exit' and 'Big Top', it has far more shape than the first album and affords a better balance of ensemble and solo work. The musicians too are arrayed more logically in the mix, with Murray and Ulmer front and centre, bass and drums nicely divided across the near background. (In contrast, *MRE* sounded as if all four players – stars to a man – were queueing or jostling for a single spotlight.)

***** After Dark**
DIW 855 *As above.* 92.

*****(*) In The Name Of ...**
DIW 885 *As above, except add Sam Rivers (ss, ts), Arthur Blythe (as), Hamiet Bluiett (bs).* 94.

*****(*) Knights Of Power**
DIW 905 *As above, except omit Rivers.* 4/95.

The more recent records keep up the standard, though it is the presence of Blythe and the huge, dark-toned Bluiett that lift *Knights Of Power* and its predecessor up a notch. Without them, one suspects, these would not have sustained the quality or the frantic pace of this fine contemporary band.

Michael Musillami

GUITAR

Moved from his Californian beginnings to the East Coast in the 1980s and garnered much experience on the organ-combo circuit, before recording these more adventurous sessions.

*****(*) The Young Child**
Stash ST-CD-556 *Musillami; Thomas Chapin (as, f); Kent Hewitt (p); Nat Reeves (b); Steve Johns (d).* 12/90.

****** Glass Art**
Evidence ECD 22060-2 *Musillami; Randy Brecker (t, flhn); Thomas Chapin (as, f); Kent Hewitt (p); Ray Drummond (b); Steve Johns (d).* 12/92.

Musillami works with an interesting blend of tonal and harmonic orthodoxy while encouraging the music to extend itself: that makes the tempestuous Chapin the key element in these records, since his taste for paint-stripping solos sets fire to what would otherwise be tastefully controlled post-bop. One interesting influence that the guitarist claims is Bill Barron, and his themes certainly manage to revise conventional forms in the way that Barron's compositions often would. The intricacies of 'Beijing' and 'Mohawk Mountain' on the first record typify his intentions. Both discs brim with strong improvising and there's little to choose between them, with Chapin's generously featured flute another reason to listen: he plays with a sweetness that is turned around by the fierceness of his articulation. Another fine memorial to a sadly departed musician.

Wolfgang Muthspiel (born 1965)

GUITAR, GUITAR SYNTHESIZER, VIOLIN

Austrian guitarist, working first in a duo with his trombonist brother, then as soloist-leader. His scope starts with bebop and goes to avant-garde fusion.

****** Work In Progress 89–98**
Emarcy 558 185 *As above, except add Bob Berg (ts); Mick Goodrick (g); Aydin Essen (p); Frank Rothkamm (sampler, filters).* 89–98.

The elegant complexities of Muthspiel's music are partly explained by his classical training. The young Austrian came to jazz only after a solid grounding in violin and then classical guitar at the conservatory in his native Graz; subsequently he studied on the jazz programme at the New England Conservatory and Berklee College. Any suspicion that such a route could result only in hidebound formality was dispelled instantly by his first Polygram release, *Timezones*, which was gloriously tuneful and swinging, and also jammed with intriguing compositional ideas.

At first blush, it seems a little early for a career compilation, but it's easy to forget that Muthspiel has been recording for more than a decade (and most of his albums are out of print now anyway). *Work In Progress* is a very good introduction, including material from *Timezones, Black and Blue, Loaded Like New, In And Out* and, to illustrate his work with brother Christian, a single track from *Muthspiel/Peacock/Muthspiel/Motian*, which is reviewed in the trombonist's entry. Promisingly, there are three additional tracks, not offcuts or alternative takes but new recordings. 'Falling Grace' is a fascinating duet with fellow-guitarist Goodrick, while 'Transit', parts one and two, is a brief set of acoustic soundscapes with electronics man Rothkamm. It's perhaps a little worrying that Amadeo are prepared to issue new material but not an entirely new album, but there is enough movement here and the selection of tracks is judicious enough to suggest a continuing investment in Muthspiel's career. Newcomers should take the opportunity to catch up with a genuinely interesting player.

Amina Claudine Myers (born 1943)

PIANO, ORGAN

Born in Arizona, Amina has forged her own hybrid of jazz, soul, gospel and blues, combined with a strong infusion of the avant-garde. Predictably, she has been largely ignored by the major labels and has recorded mainly in Europe.

****** Salutes Bessie Smith**
Leo CDLR 103 *Myers; Cecil McBee (b); Jimmie Lovelace (d).* 2/83.

*****(*) The Circle Of Time**
Black Saint 120078 *Myers; Don Pate (b); Thurman Barker (d).* 2/83.

Myers's discography is far thinner than it ought to be, but natural selection has thinned the output to these two records. The Black Saint catches Amina in free-ish mode, but sounding remarkably like her great predecessor, Mary Lou Williams. Barker is a player of ferocious intensity and great concentration and occasionally sounds as if he has stopped listening to what's going on around him. Myers refuses to be browbeaten, though, and punches out chords and melody lines. Pate is largely surplus to requirements – no disrespect to him, but indicative of how much Myers likes to shape her own bass lines.

She had kicked off the soon-to-be-influential Leo label with an album called *Song For Mother E*, which had teamed her with percussionist Pheeroan akLaff but no bass player. McBee is always a strong presence and, freed from the normal requirement to keep time and anchor the chords, he creates some pungent figures. Without attempting to pastiche the great blues singer, Myers gets inside Bessie Smith's music completely. It's doubly unfortunate that later work should have been so blandly commercial.

Terry Myers

TENOR SAXOPHONE

A full-time musician since the early 1970s, Myers has played a wide variety of studio work and has only recently stepped into any solo limelight.

***** Soul Mates**
Contemporary CCD-14078-2 *Myers; Dr Lonnie Smith (org); Nathan Page (g); Duffy Jackson (d).* 11/95.

If there's nothing new here, there's little that sounds old. Myers's base is Orlando, Florida, and he's worked up a huge, swinging sound on the tenor that seems perfectly suited to this whiskery format. Twelve tunes, mostly originals, no shopworn standards, and the group sound like they're raring to go: Smith's solos are prime bebop cut, Page is quick, and Jackson, who's been known to overpower big bands, is fat-free muscle. Not many holds barred here. It's too long, of course, like so many CDs; but take it a few tracks at a time and it hustles you along all right.

Mika Myllari

TRUMPET

Finnish trumpeter leading jazz-based music of several possible directions.

***** Les Ponts**
MMQ CD-2 *Myllari; Jari Perkiomaki (as, bcl, f); Samuli Mikkonen (p, acc, perc); Reijo Tunkkari, Virpi Taskila (vn); Anna-Leena Kangas, Esa Laasanen (vla); Jorma Ojanpera (b, perc); Markku Ounaskari (d).* 11/96.

The trumpeter and his group present a round dozen pieces recorded in Kokkola on one November day. Myllari himself admits that the record sounds 'slightly strange and raw', the music set down in an old wooden house, but it plays like real music, and the muddy mix (Ojanpera is the main sufferer) is only a mild hindrance. Inspired by a visit to France, Myllari's picturesque writing has some enchantingly lyrical twists, with Perkiomaki excelling as a colourist and the leader himself offering a solo perspective of thoughtful reserve. When the string quartet come in on 'Tankar' it's an unexpected but apposite switch. Rather than play diffidently, the rhythm section perform with great dynamic flair and they enliven passages which might have grown too quiescent. Modest but very enjoyable.

Simon Nabatov

PIANO

An 'American of Russian origin', Nabatov is a contemporary of Pletnev and Pogorelich who turned from the classics to jazz. He works out of Cologne and is a structured player who pushes the frame as far as it will go.

****** Tough Customer**
Enja 7063-2 *Nabatov; Mark Helias (b); Tom Rainey (d).* 1/92.

*****(*) Sneak Preview**
hatOLOGY 548 *As above.* 1/99.

Nabatov's classical studies and ongoing experimentation with metre are some of the trademarks of a complex, two-handed pianism. The best introduction to what he can do is *Tough Customer*, which has some electrifying improvisation on themes that can turn labyrinthine when he wants them to: the opening 'Puzzled' takes off from a dissonant figure into a wonderland of devices that Nabatov clearly has complete mastery over. 'Simple Simon', at the other end of the disc, mixes Chinese chords with a lovely sing-song melody. This is a fine blend of form and freedom, and what takes it into the top bracket is the superbly responsive work of Helias and Rainey: the bounce of the bass lines and the high detail and free time that the drummer creates bolster everything that Nabatov does.

Reconvened in a studio after seven years, the trio picks up where it left off. Nabatov's ideas are as extravagant as ever, in the elaborate dedication 'For Steve' (Lacy) no less than in the displaced accents and off-kilter harmonies of the otherwise almost dance-like 'Let's Go Baby'. Helias and Rainey are as reflexive and attentive as before. Just here and there Nabatov's ingenuities are almost too private to communicate, even to a sympathetic istener, but he's making exhilarating trio music for sure.

Alberto Nacci

TENOR SAXOPHONE

Contemporary Italian saxophonist working in a post-bop vein.

**** Isola Lontana**
Splasc(h) H 310-2 *Nacci; Fabrizio Garofoli (ky); Giuliano Vezzoli (b); Stefano Bertoli (d).* 1/90.

****(*) Colours**
Splasc(h) H 387-2 *Nacci; Davide Ghidoni (t, flhn); Stefano Colpi (b); Stefano Bertoli (d).* 5/92.

Nacci's compressed tone and slurred phrasing suit his impressionistic aims, but the music on *Isola Lontana* has little that's profound about it. The compositions fail to get below any surface prettiness – 'Van Gogh' has nothing in it that makes one think of the dedicatee – and Garofoli's pretentious solos are a wrong ingredient, along with the soft-focus production that suggests European film music. *Colours* is much better, with Colpi and Bertoli laying down a thoughtfully shifting base for the two horns. Ghidoni is a bit too reserved, but that makes the leader's improvisations take a firmer hold. The sound is still too soft round the edges, but at least the two long pieces, 'Danza Araba' (with a fine bass solo) and 'Nuvole', keep the attention.

***** Passing**
Splasc(h) H 480-2 *Nacci; Francesco Manzoni, Fabio Brignoli (t); Alessandro Brignoli, Claudio Barbieri (tb); Tino Tracanna (ss); Enrico Terragnoli (g); Sbibu (d).* 3/96.

Nacci calls this his Brass Project, and the whole thing is a lot tougher and more concentrated than anything he's put his name on before. 'Duel' immediately establishes an urgent, almost menacing feel, and the excess weight of horns – cleverly arranged, often as a kind of chorale, and spread across the stage – never feels cumbersome, abetted by Terragnoli's agreeably clunky guitar-sound and the pirouetting lines of the two saxophonists. Nacci himself makes only a modest impression as a soloist, but this is a progressive record for him.

Naked City

GROUP

John Zorn's small group, dedicated to compressed and meticulously organized aggression and noise.

***** Naked City**
Nonesuch 79238 *John Zorn (as); Bill Frisell (g); Wayne Horvitz (ky); Fred Frith (b); Joey Baron (d); Yamatsuka Eye (v).* 91.

***** Heretic: Jeux Des Dames Cruelles**
Avant AVAN 001 *As above.*

*****(*) Grand Guignol**
Avant AVAN 002 *As above, except add Bob Dorough (v).* 92.

****(*) Radio**
Avant AVAN 003 *As above.* 93.

**** Absinthe**
Avant AVAN 004 *As above, except omit Eye.* 93.

Zorn's group patented a stylish musical terrorism, favouring short explosions of sound that rarely last longer than a couple of minutes (there are 41 tracks on *Grand Guignol*). More controversially, these are coupled with pornographic and sadomasochistic imagery, drawn from a variety of sources; *Grand Guignol*'s cover features a pathology photograph of a severed foot and a cadaver's trepanned skull. Coupled with track-titles like 'Perfume Of A Critic's Burning Flesh' (cheers, lads), this prompted a small measure of moral panic around the group, although it has long since receded as yesterday's outrage becomes today's convention. Much of the group's confrontational stance can be dismissed as an ironic tactic. It was undoubtedly both ear- and eye-opening, and Zorn is intelligent enough to realize that shock is effective only when juxtaposed to something else. *Grand Guignol* – to make it something of a test case – also includes a swooningly romantic interpretation of 'Louange pour l'éternité de Jésus' from Olivier Messiaen's *Quatuor pour la fin du temps*.

For Zorn fans, the most approachable is *Heretic*, which poses as the soundtrack to a dominatrix film, *Jeux Des Dames Cruelles*, and is dedicated to the visionary film-maker, Harry Smith; *Grand Guignol* is dedicated to another fantasy director, his namesake, Jack Smith, who succumbed to the AIDS virus in 1989. *Radio* is the least appealing. Like the others, it's a complex, slightly self-indulgent package, but it seems to have lost even an ironic rationale and, though both musically and visually the least aggressive of the discs, nevertheless it shocks by virtue of its sheer persistence. By the time we reach *Absinthe*, the packaging, which is eerily glamorous, has become more important than the music which, for its part, is uniformly dull. There are not, alas, a million tunes in the *Naked City*.

Zbigniew Namyslowski (born 1939)

ALTO SAXOPHONE, SOPRANO SAXOPHONE, CELLO

Played trad trombone in his native Warsaw, then took up alto in 1960 and formed his own group. Toured Europe with it and recorded a session for Decca in London (never reissued), and has since worked prolifically at home, though his international profile tends to be limited.

***** Zbigniew Namyslowski Quartet**
Power Bros 33861 *Namyslowski; Adam Makowicz (p); Janusz Koslowski (b); Czeslaw Bartkowski (d).* 1/66.

****** Winobranie**
Power Bros 00121 *Namyslowski; Stanislaw Cieslak (tb, perc); Tomasz Szukalski (ts, bcl); Pawel Jarzebski (b); Kazimierz Jonkisz (d).* 2/73.

*****(*) Kujaviak Goes Funky**
Power Bros 33859 *Namyslowski; Tomasz Szukalski (ts, as); Wojciech Karolak (p); Pawel Jarzebski (b); Czeslaw Bartkowski (d).* 75.

*****(*) The Last Concert**
Polonia CD 002 *Namyslowski; Janusz Skowron (p); Maciej Strzelczyk (vn); Zbigniew Wegehaupt (b); Cezary Konrad (d).* 10/91.

If the highly compressed history of Polish jazz seems littered with significant 'firsts', then Namyslowski managed to be present at a good few of them. In 1964 in London, he and his quartet became the first Polish jazz musicians to make a record in the West, the elegant and often startling *Lola*, which was released on Decca. The following year he played on Krzysztof Komeda's epochal *Astigmatic*, one of the most important European jazz records of the period. Temperamentally, Namyslowski resembled Komeda rather than someone like the pianist's colleague, Andrzej Trzaskowski, whose approach to the music was first and foremost intellectual. Where Komeda was only a rather limited performer, though, Namyslowski had an instinctive facility that made him an exciting soloist from the first. His debut in 1957 was as a cellist. Thereafter, he switched to trombone and thence to saxophones, though his cello can still be heard on the 1973 *Winobranie* – 'Wine Feast' – a glorious record only recently restored to circulation thanks to Power Bros' enlightened programme of reissue. This is one of Namyslowski's major statements and, though it lacks the weird brilliance of Komeda's *Astigmatic*, it is still very listenable and at moments quite profound.

From the start Namyslowski was interested in unusual sounds and metres and, like Jan Ptaszyn Wroblewski, he drew considerable inspiration from Polish music. The 1966 band with Adam Matyskowicz (later Makowicz) has him hopping around in 7/4 and 5/8; as late as 'Kujaviak Goes Funky' and 'Appenzeller's Dance', on the third of the reissued discs, where he was absorbing elements of American pop and R&B, he is still resistant to basic fours. Though subsequent to *Kujaviak* Namyslowski went into something of a creative decline, he comes back with a bang on *The Last Concert*, a live recording from the closing night of the Warsaw Jazz Jamboree in 1991. The polyrhythms are still there in 'Half Done Chicken' and the aggressive 'Total Incompetence'. Violin has played a major role in Polish jazz, and Maciej Strzelczyk's contributions to 'Five In One', another metrical maze, and the long, dancing 'What's In Yemikoy' are highly idiomatic. One feels that Namyslowski doesn't play with quite the attack of yore, but in Skowron he has one of the best accompanists in Eastern Europe, and the standard of playing throughout the set is very high indeed.

Phil Napoleon (1901–92)

TRUMPET

A genine pioneer, Filippo Napoli was one of the earliest white hot trumpeters and his lead work in the Original Memphis Five, one of the key small groups of the 1920s, was profoundly influential on men such as Red Nichols and Bix Beiderbecke. He remained active as a musician, making many latter-day Dixieland sessions into the late '50s.

***** Live At Nick's, NYC**

Jazzology JCD-39 *Napoleon; Andy Russo (tb); Phil Olivera (cl); Joe Rand (p); Jack Fay (b); Tony Spargo (d).* 49–50.

Napoleon is today virtually forgotten, yet he is among the most prolifically recorded of all jazz trumpeters, beginning with the Original Memphis Five in 1921 and still making tight, accomplished Dixieland sessions for Capitol in the '50s. These airshots were taken from radio sessions at Nick's in New York and they find him in self-effacing mood: he gives almost all the solo space to Olivera and Rand and is content to play a firm, unshakeable lead horn himself. Besides the obvious staple tunes, strung together in medleys, there are some nice rarities such as 'In My Merry Oldsmobile', once recorded by Bix Beiderbecke with Jean Goldkette, and 'I Used To Love You'. There's nothing outstanding and the sound is about average for the source and period, but Napoleon's determined, unflashy leadership has its own rewards, and the sound the band makes (with the ODJB's drummer Spargo driving them along!) is very appealing. We still await the advent of some of Napoleon's Capitol sessions on CD.

Lewis Nash (born 1958)

DRUMS

A much-in-demand drummer for any post-bop situation, Nash has hundreds of album credits as sideman; this is a rare leadership outing.

***** Rhythm Is My Business**

Evidence ECD 22041 *Nash; Mulgrew Miller (p); Steve Nelson (vib); Peter Washington, Ron Carter (b); Steve Kroon (perc); Teresa Nash (v).* 10/89.

On what seems to be his only leadership credit so far, Nash opens with a rolling, Afro-tinged theme by Roland Hanna, cast in double waltz time. His own '106 Nix' is just a blowing head but it offers some attractive possibilities to both vibes and piano, and Washington gives the blues line an interesting twist; he does well generally, only briefly upstaged by Ron Carter's walk-on piccolo bass feature on 'Omelette'. Don Pullen's 'Sing Me A Song Everlasting' was played at Dannie Richmond's funeral. It's one of the pianist's loveliest compositions, and Miller (who plays out of his skin from start to finish) rounds it off to perfection. Nash switches to brushes for 'My Shining Hour'; it might have been nice to do this one as a vocal instead of the rather stolid 'When You Return'. Ms Nash – who presumably got the gig on merit alone – is too beefy a singer for this material and she makes a bit of a stew of it.

Fats Navarro (1923–50)

TRUMPET

The unfortunate but brilliant Navarro worked in Andy Kirk's band and in Billy Eckstine's legendary outfit, where he replaced the trumpeter whose style he had adopted and adapted. Fats was a more lyrical player than Dizzy Gillespie and sounded easier in the middle register of the instrument. His career was greatly foreshortened by a narcotic habit and tuberculosis, but he recorded some of the finest brass solos of the bebop era, many of them with bandleader Tadd Dameron.

***** Memorial**

Savoy SV 0181 2CD *Navarro; Kenny Dorham (t); Ernie Henry, Sonny Stitt (as); Morris Lane (ts); Eddie De Verteuil (bs); Bud Powell (p); Al Hall, Curley Russell (b); Kenny Clarke (d); Gil Fuller (arr).* 9/46, 10/47.

***** Goin' To Minton's**

Savoy 92681 *Navarro; Sonny Stitt (as); Leo Parker (as, bs); Eddie 'Lockjaw' Davis, Charlie Rouse (ts); Tadd Dameron, Al Haig, Bud Powell (p); Nelson Boyd, Gene Ramey, Curley Russell (b); Denzil Best, Art Blakey, Kenny Clarke (d).* 9/46–12/47.

*****(*) Nostalgia**

Savoy SV 0123 *Navarro; Kenny Dorham (t); Eddie 'Lockjaw' Davis, Dexter Gordon, Charlie Rouse (ts); Tadd Dameron, Al Haig (p); Huey Long (g); Nelson Boyd, Gene Ramey (b); Denzil Best, Art Blakey, Art Mardigan (d); Kay Penton (v).* 12/46–12/47.

****** The Complete Fats Navarro On Blue Note And Capitol**
Blue Note 33373 2CD *Navarro; Howard McGhee (t); Ernie Henry (as); Allen Eager, Wardell Gray, Sonny Rollins, Charlie Rouse (ts); Tadd Dameron, Bud Powell (p); Milt Jackson (p, vib); Nelson Boyd, Tommy Potter, Curley Russell (b); Kenny Clarke, Roy Haynes, Shadow Wilson (d); Chano Pozo (perc).* 9/47–8/49.

*****(*) Fats Navarro Featured With The Tadd Dameron Band**
Milestone M 47041 *Navarro; Tadd Dameron (p); Rudy Williams (as); Allen Eager (ts); Milt Jackson (vib); Curley Russell (b); Kenny Clarke (d).* 48.

***** Bird & Fats – Live At Birdland**
Cool & Blue C&B CD 103 *Navarro; Charlie Parker (as); Walter Bishop Jr, Bud Powell (p); Tommy Potter, Curley Russell (b); Art Blakey, Roy Haynes (d); Chubby Newsome (v).* 6/50.

Like Howard McGhee, Navarro came up through the Andy Kirk band, having already worked with Snookum Russell. Overweight, with a high, rather effeminate voice (and nicknamed either 'Fat Boy' or 'Fat Girl'), he had by 1945, when he replaced Dizzy Gillespie in the Billy Eckstine orchestra, developed a trumpet style which replaced Gillespie's burp-gun lines with a more elegantly shaped approach that emphasized a bright, burnished tone. The open texture of his solos was altogether better suited to the Tadd Dameron band, which became his most effective setting. Dameron is the accompanist on the best of the *Nostalgia* material, which provides an additional 20 minutes' top-flight Navarro, with four dispensable tracks from a drab December 1946 session alongside Lockjaw Davis and Al Haig. There's also a slice of pre-Dameron work on *Memorial*, credited to Gil Fuller's Modernists, together with later stuff by an equally good band (Henry, Dameron, Russell, Clarke) and marred only slightly by Kay Penton's inconsequential vocals.

Goin' To Minton's and the other Savoys mop up some of the best of the material Fats recorded before his Blue Note apotheosis. Covering mainly tracks cut over five sessions round the autumn of 1946 and through the following year, they catch him developing into an ever more confident and moving soloist. His empathy with Bud Powell on 'Boppin' A Riff' and 'Fat Boy' is extraordinary and, generally speaking, he sounds better when unaccompanied by more than a single saxophone. Such was Fats' ability to blow resonant middle-register phrases that there is none of Dizzy's skyscraping which often sounded very far removed from the basic melody and key centre. Lennie Tristano may have been right in his valuation of the two trumpeters: Lennie thought Diz was a fine enough player, but he was no Fats Navarro.

The Blue Note sessions are one of the peaks of the bebop movement and one of the essential modern-jazz records. Navarro's tone and solo approach were honed in big-band settings and he has the remarkable ability to maintain a graceful poise even when playing loudly and at speed. The contrast with McGhee (it seems extraordinary that some of their performances together have been misattributed) is very striking. Their duelling choruses on 'Double Talk' from a marvellous October 1948 session are some of the high points of the record; there is, as with several other tracks, an alternative take which shows how thoughtful and self-critical an improviser the young trumpeter was, constantly refining, occasionally wholly rethinking his approach to a chord progression, but more frequently taking over whole segments of his solo and re-ordering them into a more satisfying outline. Navarro is rhythmically quite conservative, but he plays with great containment and manages to create an illusion, most obvious on 'Boperation', from the same session, that he is floating just above the beat; by contrast, McGhee sounds hasty and anxious. One hears the same effect rather more subtly on both takes of 'Symphonette' and on an alternative take of 'The Squirrel'.

There is an excellent version of 'Symphonette', also from 1948, on the Milestone Navarro/Dameron compilation. Milt Jackson is again present, but these performances, which also include 'The Squirrel', 'Dameronia' and two fine versions of 'Anthropology', are not up to the standard of the Blue Notes.

It's worth looking out for the unfortunately named *Fat Girl* and *Fat Again* on Savoy/Vogue. There are problems with both (including a degree of uncertainty whether Navarro or Dorham is playing on some cuts and the known fact that some of Navarro's solos were spliced in), but the quality of his playing shines through time and again on these earlier cuts. That talent dimmed only slightly towards the end. The tracks on *Live At Birdland*, one with his own quartet and 15 more with Bird's group, document his last public appearance. They find him still poised and lyrical, but lacking the dramatic edge of the classic sessions, and unmistakably weary.

Navarro died a week later of tuberculosis exacerbated by drug abuse. As an artist he was already astonishingly mature, and it's slightly ironic that many of the stylistic innovations and developments attributed to Clifford Brown were actually instigated by Navarro. Small as his legacy is, it is one of the finest in all of jazz.

NDR Big Band

GROUP

Formed as a radio dance-band in 1945, the Nord Deutscher Rundfunk orchestra has been existence ever since, playing host to numerous star guests down the years and playing big-band music in its own right.

***** Bravissimo**
ACT 9232-2 *Lennart Axelsson, Manfred Niezgoda, Ingolf Burkhardt, Johannes Faber, Manfred Moch, Heinz Habermann, Paul Kubatsch, Klaus Stotter, Bob Lanese, Torsten Maas, Reiner Winterschladen, Chet Baker (t); Joe Gallardo, Wolfgang Ahlers, Ulrich Plettendorf, Arnold Schon, Hermann Breuer, Manfred Grossmann, Hermann Plato, Michael Danner, Albert Mangelsdorff (tb); Egon Christmann, Lucas Schmid (btb); Herb Geller, Emil Wurster, Lutz Buchner, Jochen Ment, Stephan Pfeifer, Andreas Boether, Ron Aspery, Fiete Felsch, Peter Bolte (as); Johnny Griffin, Heinz Sauer, Roman Schwaller, Gabriel Coburger, Alan Skidmore, Harald Ende, Peter Weniger, Tobias Schmidt-Relenberg, Christof Lauer, Stuart Curtis, Emil Wurster (ts); Howard Johnson (bs, tba); Edgar Herzog, Werner Ronfeld, Klaus Nagurski, Thomas Zoller (bs); Roberto Di Gioia, Vladislaw Sendecki, Walter Norris, Nils Gessinger, Lex Jasper, Bob Degen, Steve Gray, Stan Tracey (p); Wolfgang Schluter (vib, mar); Gary Burton (vib); Stephan Diez, Heinz Schultze, John Schröder (g); Lucas Lindholm, Gunter Lenz (b); Aage Tanggaard, Lennart Gruvstedt, Thomas Alkier, Wolfgang Haffner, Clark Tracey, Ronnie Stephenson, Hans Dekker (d); Marcia Doctor (perc).* 4/80–11/95.

A worthy tribute to the Nord Deutscher Rundfunk house orchestra, still alive after more than 50 years and performing material from a vast range of sources. These highlights from recent years cover a typically wide base, from the rather foolish version of 'Voodoo Chile' featuring Johnson's tuba to the fully achieved and impressive scores for 'Night In Tunisia', done as a concerto for Schluter's vibes, and Mike Gibbs's arrangement of 'Country Roads' for Gary Burton. There's one of Stan Tracey's homages to his beloved Monk and a particularly haunting and effective set-piece for Chet Baker and, although the orchestra tends to work as second fiddle to the guest soloists, not many in-house radio bands could handle something as far out as Christof Lauer's 'Descent' with the same aplomb reserved for the more traditional fare.

Don Neely's Royal Society Jazz Orchestra

GROUP

American hot dance music resuscitated by a contemporary orchestra.

***** Ain't That A Grand And Glorious Feeling**

Stomp Off CD1208 *Frank Davis (t, c); Kent Mikasa (c); Jon Schermer (tb); Don Neely (reeds, v); Mark Warren, Lin Patch (reeds); Frederick Hodges (p, bells, v); Dix Bruce (g); Jeff Wells (tba, b); Steve Apple (d); Carla Normand, The Jesters (v).* 4/90.

***** Don't Bring Lulu**

Stomp Off CD1250 *As above, except add Bob Schulz (c), Jeremy Cohen (vn); omit The Jesters.* 4/92.

***** Roll Up The Carpet**

Circle CCD 147 *As above, except Brent Bergman (tb) replaces Schermer; omit Schulz and Cohen.* 10/94.

Done with so much affection and enthusiasm that it's hard to dislike. This is the heart of hot dance music, original arrangements transcribed from records as often as not, with Neely's talented team of throwbacks playing in note-perfect re-creations of the best of such bandleaders as Paul Ash, Ted Weems, Paul Whiteman and Isham Jones. While they put in the occasional Henderson or McKinney's Cotton Pickers chart, this is mainly about the New York society bands of the 1920s. They sidestep some of the novelty element and concentrate on the gaiety of a style that takes its virtues from drollery and nuance rather than any camp affectation. Normand and The Jesters hit the right note in their vocal spots, but it's Neely's own half-spoken vocals that just about take the biscuit. Soloists seldom take any real limelight, yet here and there is a fine eight- or sixteen-bar interlude. Little to choose between the three records – period connoisseurs may wish to compare song-titles, but then they'll probably want all three anyway – though, if pressed, we pick the first for its marginally punchier sound.

Buell Neidlinger (born 1936)

DOUBLE BASS, CELLO

The New Yorker has had an eclectic career, to put it at its mildest. Classically trained, he switched to swing and traditional jazz before joining Cecil Taylor's radical group of the mid-'50s. Since then, he has continued to move between the avant-garde and the mainstream, and has even formed a bluegrass group – always, however, playing with a solid emphasis that is rarely quite where one expects it to be.

***** Locomotive**

Soul Note 121161 *Neidlinger; Marty Krystall (ts); Brenton Banks (vn); John Kurnick (mand); Billy Osborne (d).* 6/87.

At first glance, *Locomotive* is closer to what Neidlinger was doing with Buellgrass than to his work with Cecil Taylor, but a closer comparative look at 'Jumpin' Punkins' here and on the Candid Taylor compilation of that name suggests much about Neidlinger's contribution to Taylor's music. A strong, uncomplicated player, he drives this unusually shaped band through a roster of Monk and Ellington tunes in a way that emphasizes the two composers' similarities rather than their differences. Though the pace is as abrupt as a John Zorn record, there are few obvious modernist concessions. Banks plays like a folk fiddler rather than the scratchy microtonal style of Leroy Jenkins or Billy Bang and, since there are very few mandolin players in or around jazz, it doesn't answer much to offer comparisons, though Bill Frisell would certainly appreciate John Kurnick.

****(*) Thelonious**

K2B2 2 2569 *Neidlinger; Marty Krystall (as, ts); John Beasley (p); Billy Osborne (d).* 6/88.

***** Big Drum**

K2B2 2 3069 *Neidlinger; Hugo Schick (t); Marty Krystall (ts); Vinny Colaiuta (d).* 6/90.

*****(*) Blue Chopsticks**

K2B2 2 3169 *Neidlinger; Hugh Schick (t); Marty Krystall (as, ts); Richard Greene (vn); Jimbo Ross (vla).* 7/94.

***** Rear View Mirror**

k2B2 2 2969 *Neidlinger; Warren Gale (t); Marty Krystall (ts); Peter Ivers (hca); Jeremy Peters (org); Andy Statman (mand); Richard Greene (vn); John Beasley, Peter Erskine, Billy Higgins (d).*

After Buellgrass, Neidlinger had a couple more named groups, including the short-lived Thelonious, which dedicated itself to Monk compositions, and String Jazz, which made the wonderful set of Herbie Nichols tunes which is *Blue Chopsticks.* He also formed his own label.

Big Drum is not as startlingly unusual as *Locomotive* was, but it is a spanking record. Recorded live and with lots of atmosphere, it strongly features saxophonist Krystall, who engineered the session. As on the 1994 album, where the leader limits himself to cello, it's dedicated to Herbie Nichols but, unlike *Blue Chopsticks*, doesn't include a single one of the pianist's compositions, which seems a touch perverse. There's a taut and compact reading of Monk's 'Brilliant Corners', on which Colaiuta shines. The remainder are originals, written by Neidlinger and Krystall. 'Ming's Last Visit', a 14-bar blues, pays tribute to another great bass player. 'Tienanmen Bop' responds to the massacre of pro-democracy students in China.

The material on *Thelonious* is broadly similar. 'Trinkle Tinkle' is sublime, and a new version of 'Locomotive' also catches the ear, but this is a mostly low-key record by a group that seemed rather *ad hoc* and perfunctory.

The retrospective on *Rear View Mirror* is the closest one gets to a rapid summation of the bassist's career. All the material had been previously released on LP, but it offers a quick sense of a player who has gone through some exotic changes and paid homage to some great masters.

Louis Nelson (1902–90)

TROMBONE

Born in New Orleans, although he grew up in nearby Napoleonville, Nelson played trombone with the Sidney Desvigne band for 15 years. After war service, he played extensively with the Kid Thomas band and was a regular at Preservation Hall with many leaders. A fundamentalist of New Orleans trombone, he had a long and prolific career, working until his death in 1990.

***** Louis Nelson's Creole Jazz Band**
GHB BCD-173 *Nelson; Cuff Billet (t, v); John Defferary (cl); Richard Simmons (p); Paul Sealey (g); Brian Turnock (b); Barry Martyn (d).* 66.

***** Jazz At The Palm Court Vol. 1**
GHB BCD-551 *Nelson; Wendell Brunious (t, v); Sammy Rimington (cl); Butch Thompson (p); Danny Barker (bj, v); Chester Zardis (b); Stanley Stephens (d).* 4/89.

This is the 'other' Louis Nelson, who came to prominence almost a generation after Big Eye Louis. Although most regularly appearing as a sideman, Nelson has a few records under his own name – although, strictly speaking, the first GHB date features him as a guest with the Barry Martyn Ragtime Band, a souvenir of a British visit. The record was made in an old hall attached to the White Horse pub in Willesden. Nelson contributes his unchanging, gruff trombone parts to the enthusiastic playing of these young Brits, and the session has a degree of charm as well as a bluff, good-humoured spirit, kept up to speed by Martyn's doughty and tireless drumming.

Louis was still determined to blow the horn, even at 86, and the Palm Court Jazz Band had plenty of fun on their regular gig. Brunious and Rimington will always seem like youngsters in this company, but they were pretty experienced themselves by this point, and the music has all the pungency it needs. Nelson himself is taking it easy, and his solos sound like a old man's defiance, even with Father Time knocking at the door.

Oliver Nelson (1932–75)

ALTO SAXOPHONE, TENOR SAXOPHONE, CLARINET

Unremarkable sideman career until he began recording as a leader in 1959, then arranging for big-band settings, especially with Jimmy Smith and Wes Montgomery. His own playing featured less as he won commissions for film and TV work from the late '60s onwards. Died suddenly of a heart attack.

***** Meet Oliver Nelson: Featuring Kenny Dorham**
Original Jazz Classics OJC 227 *Nelson; Kenny Dorham (t); Ray Bryant (p); Wendell Marshall (b); Art Taylor (d).* 10/59.

***** Taking Care Of Business**
Original Jazz Classics OJC 1784 *Nelson; Lem Winchester (vib); Johnny Hammond Smith (org); George Tucker (b); Roy Haynes (d).* 3/60.

Nelson served his apprenticeship with Louis Jordan and the Erskine Hawkins and Quincy Jones big bands, and he probably learned most from working with Quincy, not least that ability to combine sophisticated intervals and expansive shapes with a raw blues feel. Sadly, Nelson was to spend his last few years in the same direction, writing TV themes like 'The Six Million Dollar Man', lucrative but an unsatisfactory legacy for a man with an impressive jazz discography.

These early records are nicely arranged, well textured, but ultimately a bit flat. Dorham's contributions to the earlier of the pair are exactly what you'd expect of him: fluid, punchy and lyrical in all the unexpected places. The second is much more of an arranger's record, and it's the interplay of timbres and textures that one remembers rather than anything in the themes.

*****(*) Screamin' The Blues**
Original Jazz Classics OJC 080 *Nelson; Richard Williams (t); Eric Dolphy (as, bcl, f); Richard Wyands (p); George Duvivier (b); Roy Haynes (d).* 5/60.

Nelson cottoned on to Dolphy before the latter began to make a mark as a solo artist, and he blatantly and quite forgivably used him as a colourist rather than a lateral improviser. Nelson's own solos weren't quite as pedestrian as they sometimes sounded (we suggested he played 'arranger's sax') but they were somewhat limited both in sound and ideas, so Dolphy was an ideal recruitment; Richard Williams, destined never to have much of a career under his own name, is excellent in this context, brighter and sharper than Dorham, though without the softer, lyrical quality. The rhythm section has an almost time-capsule quality. If one were played this in the dark, it would be possible to date it almost to the month. The bebop figures are less in evidence. There's a growing attraction to diminished and off-centre chords, and the drumming is beginning to sound multi-directional, free of the bomb-dropping aggression of a previous generation. Haynes is one of the key protagonists here in one of his best sessions of this vintage.

****(*) Soul Battle**
Original Jazz Classics OJC 325 *Nelson; King Curtis, Jimmy Forrest (ts); Gene Casey (p); George Duvivier (b); Roy Haynes (d).* 9/60.

We've never much liked this record. It's slightly hard to work out what Nelson is doing on it. He's clearly not up to the earthy bravura of Curtis and Forrest, and without that there's not much point putting in an appearance. The rhythm section drive it along without a great deal of conviction, though Haynes is again wonderful, and Nelson's solos would (almost without exception) have best been left on the editing-room floor.

*** Nocturne

Original Jazz Classics OJC 1795 *Nelson; Richard Wyands (p); George Duvivier (b); Roy Haynes (d).* 60.

*** Straight Ahead

Original Jazz Classics OJC 099 *As above, except add Eric Dolphy (as, bcl, f).* 3/61.

The title of the second of the pair notwithstanding, these are both notably subtle records, perhaps too much so to catch the ear of most fans. Nelson thought out his arrangements with more care than instinct, and one sometimes finds oneself listening as if to tumblers falling into place. All items in the Dolphy catalogue are precious, but *Straight Ahead* has to be accounted one of the few disappointments, a rather unresolved and undifferentiated set with little of the brimstone and treacle one got on *Blues And The Abstract Truth* later.

**** Blues And The Abstract Truth

Impulse! IMP 11542 *Nelson; Freddie Hubbard (t); Eric Dolphy (as, f); George Barrow (bs); Bill Evans (p); Paul Chambers (b); Roy Haynes (d).* 2/61.

Restored to its original cover artwork (a portrait of Nelson was substituted when the stereo version appeared), this is one of the classics of the period, and if there were one Nelson track to take away to a desert island it would have to be the one that starts the album, the lovely 'Stolen Moments' with its mournful Hubbard solo and a lovely statement from Dolphy on flute. The great man left his bass clarinet behind for this session, and it isn't missed. Nelson tended to arrange for higher voices, and for this record he didn't stray outside 12-bar blues and the chords of 'I Got Rhythm'. 'Stolen Moments' is a minor blues, opening in C minor, with some fascinating internal divisions. 'Hoe Down' is a 44-bar figure based on the opening two notes. 'Teenie's Blues' is dedicated to the composer's sister, a talented singer. It rests on just three intervals, with transpositions for the two altos to maintain a level of tension and release. The rhythm section is again very fine, with Haynes relishing this setting and Chambers producing some lovely countermelodies and stop-time figures under the basic changes. The sound is now as good as anyone could possibly want, close and sharp enough to hear Dolphy's breath across the embouchure of the flute. Lovely.

*** Main Stem

Original Jazz Classics OJC 1803 *Nelson; Hank Jones (p); George Duvivier (b); Charli Persip (d); Ray Barretto (perc).* 61.

At the end of a hectically busy period for Nelson, he sounds tired and short of ideas. His own writing had become slightly formulaic and there was a dearth of real ideas in the playing. Jones has always been a player who is flattered by his companions, and here, though he sounds lovely, almost courtly, he is upstaged by everyone around him. Nelson is not playing well, falling back on licks and riffs that have been around for years. A word for Persip, who has been a constant presence on the scene for years but who is rarely given his due of recognition.

*** Afro / American Sketches

Original Jazz Classics OJC 1819 *Nelson; Billy Byers, Jerry Kail, Joe Newman, Ernie Royal (t); Paul Faulise, Urbie Green, Melba Liston, Britt Woodman (tb); Don Butterfield (tba); Ray Alonge, Jim Buffington, Julius Watkins (frhn); Bob Ashton, Eric Dixon, Jerry Dodgion, Charles McCracken (sax); Peter Makis (p); Art Davis (b); Ed Shaughnessy (d); Ray Barretto (perc).* 62.

Nelson prepared very carefully for this; indeed, he insisted that such a project was possible only with a lot of preparation. Perhaps that is the problem, for what this record desperately lacks is a measure of spontaneity, and this is a rather stiff and ungiving set. The story is that Nelson was originally unwilling to take on the project but eventually agreed to do so on his own terms. The themes are all very much in his normal range and there is more than enough space for the soloists, but something about the way the record is voiced leaves a rather flat impression. Nelson himself is not much interested in soloing and responds only perfunctorily when he does.

*** More Blues And The Abstract Truth

Impulse! 051212-2 *Nelson; Thad Jones, Danny Moore (t); Phil Woods (as); Phil Bodner (ts, eng hn); Ben Webster (ts); Pepper Adams (bs); Roger Kellaway (p); Richard Davis (b); Grady Tate (d).* 9/64.

In this case, more means less. This lacks the impact and the punch of the original session, not because the players are lacking in fire (any session that boasts Thad Jones, Phil Woods *and* Ben Webster isn't struggling for charisma) but because the music is already drifting towards the formulaic television funk that was to occupy too much of Nelson's later life. 'Theme From Mr Broadway' and 'Blue For Mr Broadway' are the strongest things, both of them big, generous themes with more bottom end than is usual in a Nelson composition and arrangement

***(*) Jazz Masters 48

Verve 527654 *Nelson; Nat Adderley (c); Burt Collins, Ray Copeland, Bernie Glow, Jimmy Maxwell, Joe Newman, Ernie Royal, Marvin Stamm, Joe Wilder, Snooky Young (t); Clark Terry (t, flhn); Wayne Andre, Jimmy Cleveland, Willie Dennis, Urbie Green, Quentin Jackson, Benny Powell (tb); Bob Brookmeyer (vtb); Tony Faulise, J.J Johnson, Rod Levitt, Tony Studd (btb); Ray Alonge, Jimmy Buffington, Bob Northern (frhn); Don Butterfield (tba); Danny Bank, Phil Bodner, Al Cohn, Jerry Dodgion, Zoot Sims, Stan Webb, Phil Woods (reeds); Patti Bown, Albert Dailey, Hank Jones (p); Eric Gale, Jim Hall, Jimmy Raney (g); Harry Brewer (mar, cel); Ron Carter, George Duvivier, Milt Hinton (b); Ed Shaughnessy, Grady Tate (d); Phil Kraus, Bobby Rosengarden (perc).* 11/62–11/67.

A fine compilation of material spanning just five years but covering a huge amount of ground in stylistic terms. Nelson's skills as an arranger have never been in doubt, but this record brings them out triumphantly, a debt to Ellington and Bartók, and a swinging, uncomplicated approach which is at its best when faced with a full jazz orchestra. Pieces like the long 'Complex City' have a strong Ellingtonian strain and are nicely pitched between structure and freedom for the soloists (in this case Woods, Bown, Sims and Newman). Others, like the staple 'Hoe Down' and 'Full Nelson', are more straightforwardly conceived, less dependent on individual expression. Most tracks are short and to the point and Creed Taylor gets a very full and accurate sound from the band. A valuable compilation from a less than accessible period in Nelson's foreshortened career. Nelson made a lot of records for Impulse! and at present he has a rather scant showing in the catalogue.

'Big Eye' Louis Nelson (1885–1949)

CLARINET

Born in New Orleans, he played bass in the Buddy Bolden group in 1900 but switched to clarinet, later working with most of the major early groups in the city. Taught many up-and-coming talents and spent most of his life playing in cabaret and theatres, but was effectively rediscovered in the '40s and cut several tracks at the very end of his life.

***** Big Eye Louis Nelson Delisle**

American Music AMCD-7 *Nelson; Wooden Joe Nicholas (t, v); Charles Love (t); Louis Nelson (tb); Louis Gallaud (p); Johnny St Cyr, Louis Keppard (g); Austin Young, Albert Glenny (b); Ernest Rogers, Albert Jiles (d); William Tircuit (v).* 5–7/49.

The only record under the nominal leadership of a man who taught Bechet and was an acknowledged inspiration of Dodds and Noone. The CD consists of three informal studio or home sessions and seven tracks from a dance-hall date in New Orleans; ten tracks appear for the first time. Whatever the credentials outlined above, Nelson sounds like a man content to coast through his working life: the clarinet playing ambles along, mixing fluffs and good notes. The live tracks are a bit more animated, played over a very steady beat, and, though Love and Nicholas provide firm leads, the horns (the other Louis Nelson, on trombone, is no relation) play things very straight. Worth hearing by New Orleans scholars, but of limited appeal otherwise. The sound is able-bodied but muffled on most of the tracks.

Bjarne Nerem (1929–91)

TENOR SAXOPHONE

Born in Norway, Nerem began playing at the tail end of the swing era and subsequently, from the early '50s, spent most of his career in Sweden, although recording only rarely as a leader.

***** How Long Has This Been Going On**

Gemini GMCD 72 *Nerem; Nisse Skoog (t); Tore Nilsen, Frode Thingnaes, Harald Halvorsen, Jens Wendleboe, Oivind Westby (tb); Hasse Eriksson (p, v); Bengt Hallberg, Lars Sjøsten, Rolf Larsson, Yor Hellvin, Einar Iversen (p); Kjell Ohman (org); Rune Larsson, Sten Carlberg (g); Sture Nordin, Thore Jederby, Per Loberg (b); Rolf Svensson, Jack Noren, Svein Christiansen (d); strings.* 8/48–5/81.

***** Everything Happens To Me**

Gemini GMCD 71 *Nerem; Einar Iversen, Egil Kapstad (p); Jan Erik Kongshaug (g); Terje Venaas (b); Eyvind Olsen (d); strings.* 2/76–5/77.

Four tracks from 1948 on *How Long Has This Been Going On* suggest Nerem's rather unremarkable beginnings as a bopper (he was actually from Norway but lived and worked longest in Sweden). Most of the disc features him from 1971, in his late prime, as a tenorman more in the tradition of Coleman Hawkins and Chu Berry: big sound, unhurried delivery, and a conservative approach. These are mostly short tracks in which he does little other than embellish the melodies. Five tracks from a 1981 session with a five-man-trombone front-line have a novelty-like feel about them. *Everything Happens To Me* follows a similar pattern, with strings on nine tracks, and it's the four previously unissued live tracks with a quartet led by Kapstad that let him stretch out a bit – though to no especially insightful ends. Unassuming as it is, Nerem's playing has an almost naïve candour to it which makes these survivals worthwhile.

The New Jazz Wizards

GROUP

The traditionally-inclined band, led by C.H. 'Pam' Pameijer, specializing in recreative projects dedicated to (sometimes unsung) early jazz.

***** Good Stuff, Hot And Ready**

Stomp Off CD1244 *Peter Ecklund (c); Jim Snyder (tb); Reimer Von Essen (cl); Billy Novick (cl, as); Butch Thompson (p); Peter Bullis (bj); Vince Giordano (tba, bsx); Pam Pameijer (d).* 1/92.

***** Golden Lily**

Stomp Off CD1281 *As above, except John Otto (cl, as), Robin Verdier (p), Mike Walbridge (tba) replace von Essen, Thompson, Giordano; add Dick Wetmore (vn).* 3/94.

Excellent repertory, arranged and recorded with much panache by Pam Pameijer's group of revivalists. The first disc is dedicated to the music of Richard M. Jones; the second, to that of Tiny Parham. It presents two different faces of classic jazz in the 1920s – whereas Jones was a comparatively simple, blues-based, small-group man, Parham's more elaborate music hinted at an alternative to the arranged styles of Morton and Ellington. Oddly, the Wizards sound more formal and strait-laced on the Jones music, where the highly structured Parham tracks go off with a bang. Ted des Plantes (whose own disc of Parham interpretations has yet to make it to CD) describes the big man's music as 'stodgy and stompy rather than streamlined', yet the Wizards whistle it along. *Good Stuff, Hot And Ready* has much meticulously detailed hot playing but can't quite evade a certain stiffness. In their sincerity in dealing with both composers, the group makes no attempt at hiding the music's weakness as well as its strengths and, despite the fine solos by Ecklund and the others, their attention to the nuts-and-bolts of it holds a certain exuberance in check.

***** The Music Of Jelly Roll Morton Vol. 1**

Stomp Off CD1318 *Peter Ecklund (c); Jim Snyder (tb); Billy Novick (cl, as); John Otto (cl, ts); Ray Smith (p); Howard Alden (g, bj); Vince Giordano (tba, b); Pam Pameijer (d).* 2/97.

***** The Music Of Jelly Roll Morton Vol. 2**

Stomp Off CD1336 *As above.* 2/98.

This time, of course, they're dealing with a major jazz composer – and a notorious stickler for the correctness of the idiom at that. The 19 tunes on the first volume are (deliberately?) from the obscure end of Morton's repertoire, so, instead of the likes of 'Doctor Jazz', there is 'Try Me Out', 'Mushmouth Shuffle', 'Gambling Jack' and so on. Virtually all the pieces are extensions of Morton's originals, so they tend to last longer, and the various arrangers have fastened on rococo touches to Morton's music. It's played with great spirit, and there are fine players in the band: Alden and Giordano in particular make the rhythm section sound right and good. Novick and Otto, though, seem set on a style which tends to ape the old-time reed players rather than pay homage to them, and while there is by necessity an element of vaudeville in this kind of jazz, it's an awkward thing to re-create.

The second instalment is done just as punctiliously and again draws from the less familiar aspects of Morton's book, although it seems to us that they've moved a little closer to the frameworks of the prototype recordings. To that extent, this disc feels a shade livelier than the other one, though there's little to choose. If you want to hear Morton's group music in contemporary sound, there's surely no more able re-creation than this.

***** The Music Of Louis Armstrong – Hot 5 & 7, Vol. 1**

Stomp Off 1350 *Bent Persson (t); Jim Snyder (tb); Matthias Seuffert (cl); Tom Roberts (p); John Gill (bj); Vince Giordano (tba); Pam Pameijer (d).* 5/99.

This band never takes the easy option! After Parham, Jones and Morton, here come their translations of the Hot Five and Seven. Each treatment is stretched just sufficiently to allow an extra solo or chorus or elaboration which the Okehs didn't allow, and some of them are beautifully done – especially on titles such as 'I'm Gonna Gitcha' or 'You're Next', which are seldom remembered to start with. But Persson, for all his loyalty to the early Armstrong cornet sound, is really on a hiding to nothing: how can he compete with that original glorious explosion? To his credit, he doesn't try to; but the point of the originals is the grand exuberance of their leader: as group performances, many are relatively unremarkable. Still, this should interest any scholars, and modern ears will enjoy the excellent sound which the group has conferred on it.

New Orchestra Workshop

GROUP

Canadian 'workshop' group, active in the early 1990s, working in a free-form idiom and featuring some of the major players of the Canadian improvisation scene.

*****(*) The Future Is N.O.W.**

Nine Winds NWCD 0131 *Daniel Lapp, Bill Clark (t); Graham Ord, Coat Cooke, Bruce Freedman, Roy Stiffe (reeds); Paul Plimley (p); Clyde Reed, Paul Blaney, Ken Lister (b); Claude Ranger, Gregg Simpson, Roger Baird, Stan Taylor (d).* 90.

***** NOW You Hear It**

Nine Winds NWCD 0151 *Bruce Freedman (as); Graham Ord (ts, ss); Coat Cooke (ts); Joseph Danza (shakuhachi); Paul Plimley (p); Ron Samworth (g); Lisle Ellis, Clyde Reed, Paul Blaney (b); Gregg Simpson, Roger Baird, Buff Allen (d); Jack Duncan (perc); Kate Hammett-Vaughan (v).* 5–11/91.

Vancouver's New Orchestra Workshop is a co-operative venture inspired by Chicago's AACM. *The Future Is N.O.W.* offers the chance to sample the work of five different bands which have grown out of NOW. The outstanding piece is the opening track by Plimley's Octet, a swirling, compelling montage of rhythmic and melodic figures that is gripping throughout its nine-minute length; but there isn't a bad track among the six here. The harmolodically inspired quartet, Lunar Adventures, contribute two tracks; Chief Feature is a quartet that brews up a long, blustering workout reminiscent of early Archie Shepp; and Unity purvey a vivacious free improvisation, with excellent work by Lapp, Blaney, Ord and Baird. Only the muddled piece by Turnaround is in any way disappointing.

Their second report on *NOW You Hear It* is mildly disappointing: plenty of interest, but nothing that really stands out. The Plimley/Reed duo contribute three interactive duets, and MuseArt, a trio with Plimley, Ellis and Baird, offers a long abstraction of the blues. Lunar Adventures make brainy jazz-rock, Garbo's Hat are a chamberish trio featuring the singing of Kate Hammett-Vaughan; and the closing 'jam' by a group featuring Ord, Blaney and Baird, with Danza's shakuhachi hanging around the perimeter, isn't bad. Plimley and Ellis have since gone on to other projects, but little has been heard of most of the rest of these players.

New Orleans Classic Jazz Orchestra

GROUP

A one-off project dedicated to early New Orleans music.

****** Blowin' Off Steam**

Stomp Off CD1223 *Eddie Bayard (c); Bob Havens (tb); Tom Fischer (cl, as); Steve Pistorius (p); John Gill (bj); Hank Greve (tba); Hal Smith (d).* 8/90.

When jazz scholarship is carried off with this degree of skill, good humour and sheer aplomb, it stops being a history lesson and stands as great, timeless music. Bayard's group – several of the names will be familiar to followers of other Stomp Off productions – tackle 20 nuggets from the golden age with an élan that is quite unselfconscious, even when they're following 70-year-old arrangements. Their treatment of Morton's 'The Chant', for instance, makes light work of a classic difficult enough to be absent from almost everybody else's trad repertoire; even comparatively well-known chestnuts like 'Shim-Me-Sha-Wabble' come out as evergreens. At the heart of the disc are four tunes from the book of The Halfway House Orchestra and six from that of The New Orleans Owls, rarities that fan out into a joyful celebration of the less familiar side of old New Orleans. Bayard and Fischer are exemplary soloists, Pistorius is his usual accomplished self, and the lilt and swing of the ensemble is ideally caught by the dry, no-frills recording.

New Orleans Jazz Wizards

GROUP

A group of local NO veterans raise their voices in the 1990s.

****(*) Jambalaya**

504 CDS-55 *Lionel Ferbos (t, v); Lester Caliste (tb); Pud Brown (cl, saxes); Les Muscutt (g, bj); Peter Badie (b, v); Ernie Elly (d).* 8/95.

Fifteen staples of the N'Awlins repertoire played as gently and sweetly as one could imagine. The Wizards have decades of experience between them and this is old men's music, with the rest of the band deferring to Ferbos's terribly shaky lead. Yet after 20 minutes or so, one feels drawn in to this peculiarly genteel and dulcet jazz, as so often happens with this kind of record. Muscutt, solid as a rock, is the unobtrusive support for the others, and he knows how to get a result from these old guys.

New Orleans Rhythm Kings

GROUP

Paul Mares put the band together to play in Chicago, and they were hugely popular at the Friars Inn, refusing all offers to play elsewhere. Split up in 1925 but there was a brief re-formation in the '30s. A big influence on the early Chicago white school.

****** The New Orleans Rhythm Kings And Jelly Roll Morton**

Milestone 47020-2 *Paul Mares (c); George Brunies, Santo Pecora (tb); Leon Roppolo (cl); Don Murray (cl, as); Charlie Cordella (cl, ts); Jack Pettis (Cmel, ts); Elmer Schoebel, Mel Stitzel, Jelly Roll Morton, Kyle Pierce, Red Long (p); Lou Black, Bob Gillett, Bill Eastwood (bj); Arnold Loyacano, Chink Martin (b); Frank Snyder, Ben Pollack, Leo Adde (d).* 8/22–3/25.

One of the major groups of jazz records, from the first stirrings of the music in recording studios, the New Orleans Rhythm Kings' sessions still sound astonishingly lively and vital 75 years later. The band recorded in Chicago but had come from New Orleans: Mares was already a disciple of King Oliver (who hadn't yet recorded at the time of the first session here), Roppolo played fluent, blue clarinet, and even Brunies made more of the trombone – at that time an irresponsibly comical instrument in jazz terms – than most players of the day. The rhythms tend towards the chunky, exacerbated by the acoustic recording, but the band's almost visionary drive is brought home to stunning effect on the likes of 'Bugle Call Blues' (from their very first session, in August 1922), the relentlessly swinging 'Tiger Rag' and the knockabout 'That's A Plenty'. On two later sessions they took the opportunity to have Jelly Roll Morton sit in, and his partnership with Roppolo on 'Clarinet Marmalade' and 'Mr Jelly Lord' – something of a sketch for Morton's own later version – invigorates the whole band. 'London Blues' and 'Milenberg Joys' find Morton more or less taking over the band in terms of conception. The two final sessions they made, early in 1925, are slightly less impressive because of Brunies's absence, and there are moments of weakness elsewhere in the original records: the use of saxes sometimes swamps the initiative, Mares isn't always sure of himself, and the beats are occasionally unhelpfully overdriven. But this is still extraordinarily far-sighted and powerful music for its time, with a band of young white players building on black precepts the way that, say, Nick LaRocca of the ODJB refused to acknowledge.

The Milestone CD is decent enough, though it's still about time someone assembled a set of mint originals and did the best possible job of remastering: the music demands it, historically and aesthetically.

New Winds

GROUP

The original line-up brought together three players equally at ease in jazz and new music and developed an eclectic repertoire which might be characterized as a latter-day and almost punkish Third Stream. Each of the trio is a formidable solo voice and the spectrum of timbres is consistently impressive.

***** Digging It Harder From Afar**

Victo CD028 *Robert Dick (picc, f, bf); Ned Rothenberg (as, bcl, shakuhachi, ocarina); J.D Parran (cl, acl, contra-acl, ss, af); Gerry Hemingway (d, elec).* 94.

****** Potion**

Victo CD053 *As above, except omit Parran, Hemingway; add Herb Robertson (t, flhn, v).* 97.

Digging It Harder From Afar was the last recording with the original line-up, though it also expands to a quartet with Hemingway playing samples. It's difficult to see what is wrong, but there is something fragmentary about the music. Dick sounds out of focus and is too reliant on exotic timbres, and Rothenberg is curiously impatient.

We've always taken the view that any band including Herb Robertson was automatically worth listening to. Replacing Parran, Herb fits like an old shoe, provided that shoe is snappy, two-tone, co-respondent job. He adds bite and humour to any group and his tight, cornet-like tone and vocalized approach is an immense asset to New Winds. The centre of gravity is shifted and the timbre of the group sharpened considerably. The material sounds fresh and untarnished and, though it doesn't cut *The Cliff*, the latest one is top notch.

New York All Stars

GROUP

Led by Randy Sandke, this varying group of mainstreamers is heard in mostly live albums of material associated with several jazz giants.

***** The Bix Beiderbecke Era**

Nagel-Heyer CD 002 *Randy Sandke (t, c); Dan Barrett (tb, t); Ken Peplowski (cl); Scott Robinson (Cmel, bsx, c); Mark Shane (p); Marty Grosz (g, v); Linc Milliman (b, tba); Dave Ratajczak (d).* 5/93.

***** Broadway**
Nagel-Heyer CD 003 *As above, except omit Peplowski.* 5/93.

***** We Love You, Louis!**
Nagel Heyer CD 029 *Randy Sandke (t); Byron Stripling (t, v); Joel Helleny (tb); Kenny Davern (cl); Mark Shane (p); David Ostwald (tba); Greg Cohen (b); Joe Ascione (d).* 11/95.

***** Count Basie Remembered Vol. 1**
Nagel Heyer CD 031 *Randy Sandke (t); Dan Barrett (tb); Brian Ogilvie (ts, as, cl); Billy Mitchell (ts); Mark Shane (p); James Chirillo (g); Bob Haggart (b); Joe Ascione (d).* 11/96.

***** Count Basie Remembered Vol. 2**
Nagel Heyer CD 041 *As above.* 11/96.

***** Oh, Yeah!**
Nagel Heyer CD 046 *Randy Sandke (t); Byron Stripling (t, v); Joel Helleny (tb); Allan Vaché (cl); Johnny Varro (p); Bob Haggart (b); Joe Ascione (d).* 2/98.

***** Hey Ba-Ba-Re-Bop!!**
Nagel Heyer CD 9047 *Randy Sandke (t); Roy Williams (tb); Antti Sarpila (cl, as, ts); Thilo Wagner (p); Lars Erstrand (vib); James Chirillo (g); Dave Green (b); Ed Metz Jr (d).* 10/98.

We previously listed a couple of these discs under Sandke's name but, since they have swelled in number, the group rates an entry on its own. Though they start with Beiderbecke and Armstrong and go as far as Basie and Hampton, the band approaches each situation with the same groomed, knowledgeable style: seven or eight pieces playing chestnuts associated with the faces shown on the CD sleeves. Since (with the exception of *Broadway*) these are all concert souvenirs, they don't emerge as particularly convincing records. The Armstrong discs in particular seldom catch fire, since Sandke is so respectful of the material. The Basie discs have too many obvious choices of tune: Mitchell is a good guy to have around, but he takes his place in the gang and never cuts loose. *The Bix Beiderbecke Era* was done on the occasion of Bix's ninetieth birthday and, though the sound isn't ideal, here at least Sandke's team punch through the Beiderbecke repertoire with plenty of fizz. *Broadway* is a studio date, cut the next day: it was hot, the group were tired, and the material is an unpromising set of warhorses. That it still sounds good is some tribute to a jazzman's professionalism and, though there are a couple of duds, the band play with an unexpected attack. The best of the live sessions, though, is probably *Hey-Ba-Ba-Re-Bop!!*, Lionel Hampton tunes performed by a slightly more mixed and interesting band, with Erstrand and Williams shining in their solos. These are records that have been widely welcomed, particularly by some British commentators, but we can't hear much difference between this type of jazz and the often-reviled trad which is still playing to keen audiences in Europe.

New York Art Quartet

GROUP

Short-lived but intense and of constant interest, the Quartet came along a year after JFK's death and sum up much of the ambiguity and uncertainty of those years. The personnel and the playing are definitive of a short period in American culture.

***** New York Art Quartet**
ESP Disk ESP 1004 *Roswell Rudd (tb); John Tchicai (as); Lewis Worrell (b); Milford Graves (d); Leroi Jones (v).* 11/64.

The whole ESP catalogue has a time-capsule quality. What made this one interesting on re-release was a rare glimpse of Rudd on record, but subsequent years have seen the trombonist staging something of a revival. In any case, on this set he rarely upstages the splendid Tchicai, whose period in New York City was brief but intense. On 'No 6' and 'Short' he builds up short, almost spasmodic phrases, weaving them into longer and longer strings which always seem to have a harmonic logic, even when it can't reliably be identified. Graves is another who has resurfaced in recent times, and he isn't at all well served technically, but he is a powerful percussionist who never disappoints. 'Black Dada Nihilismus' is perhaps the most time-locked item of all, a recitation by Jones (himself subsequently reborn as Amiri Baraka) over an appropriately abstract and anarchic backdrop from the quartet. A curiosity, with some nostalgic appeal for aficionados of the New Thing.

New York Composers Orchestra

GROUP

A band of New Yorkers dedicated to performing large-scale compositions that would otherwise languish as scores. Active through the '90s, but currently less visible.

***** First Program In Standard Time**
New World CounterCurrents 80418 *Eddie Allen, Jack Walrath (t); Steven Bernstein (t, flhn); Butch Morris (c); Ray Anderson, Art Baron (tb); Vincent Chancey (frhn); Cleave E Guyton Jr (as, f); Robert DeBellis (as, ss); Doug Wieselman (ts, cl); Marty Ehrlich (ts, as, ss, cl, bcl); Sam Furnace (bs); Robin Holcomb (p); Wayne Horvitz (p); Lindsey Horner (b); Bobby Previte (d, mar).* 1/90, 1/92.

***** Music By Marty Ehrlich, Robin Holcomb, Wayne Horvitz and Doug Wieselman**
New World NW 397 *As above.* 93.

The composers represented on the first disc – Braxton, Holcomb, Horvitz, Lenny Pickett, Previte and Elliott Sharp – are all cutting-edge representatives of a movement that no longer takes 'jazz' as its baseline but moves out into the wider reaches of contemporary music in search of inspiration. Ironically, perhaps, Braxton's numbered palimpsests are the most jazz-like things in the entire set until one comes to Previte's 'Valerie, Explain Pollock', a slightly mysterious piece for ensemble which is just about the only thing on the record not intended to highlight individual voices; ironically, this is its shortcoming. One would like to hear more ensemble work, and yet what springs out and insists on attention is solo material, by Ray Anderson on Pickett's 'Dance Music' and Horvitz's 'Nica's Day', and by Wieselman (a little-appreciated writer and soloist) on Holcomb's title-piece and throughout the programme.

The other record is for some reason slightly less geared to solo-istic play, but with almost wilful perversity the compositions are not nearly so strong and the effect is rather bland and unstimulating. On a good night, the NYCO generates a formidable noise.

Even in the relative formality of the studio they manage to sound good.

New York Jazz Collective

GROUP

A band of adventurous spirits from the current New York firmament.

*****(*) I Don't Know This World Without Don Cherry**

Naxos Jazz 86003 *Marty Ehrlich (cl, bcl, as, f); Baikida Carroll (t, flhn); Frank Lacy (tb); Mike Nock (p); Michael Formanek (b); Pheeroan akLaff, Steve Johns (d).* 4/96.

When Naxos Jazz was first announced, the worry was that it would be nothing but an anodyne purveyor of middlebrow and mainstream sounds, with no attempt to encourage creative projects. Emphatically not the case on the evidence of this remarkable album, which seems to be under genuinely collective leadership. The title threnody to the departed trumpeter is written by Ehrlich, who is the dominant soloist on the album. That mournful, clangorous piece is followed by two Baikida Carroll compositions and four by pianist and producer Mike Nock, who is perhaps the most conventional player on the set, but still a formidable technician. Lacy's wonderfully singing tone is the key element on Nock's 'New Morning Of The Dream', a tune that should be of interest to anyone putting together a book for a band of this sort. Michael Formanek, the other composer, is represented by a single track – 'El Nino' – which once again underlines his sombre force and sense of drama. A few raw edges here and there, which may be down to limited rehearsal time, or perhaps to unfamiliarity with playing partners. Nothing, though, that stints the impact of a thoroughly riveting set.

Phineas Newborn Jr (1931–90)

PIANO

Technically, he was sometimes claimed to run a close second to Art Tatum. In reality, Newborn was a more effective player at slower tempos and with fewer notes; but he could be dazzling when he chose, even after illness and injury hampered his progress. A sensitive and troubled soul, even the lightest of his performances point to hidden depths of emotion.

***** Here Is Phineas**

Koch International 8505 *Newborn; Oscar Pettiford (b); Kenny Clarke (d).* 5/56.

***** Phineas' Rainbow**

RCA 7423 1421 2 *Newborn (p solo).* 10/56.

***** Phineas' Rainbow / While My Lady Sleeps**

Collectables 2737 *As above.* 10/56, 57.

***** Plays Jamaica / Fabulous Phineas**

Collectables 2740 *As above.* 57.

*****(*) Stockholm Jam Session Vol. 1**

Steeplechase SCCD 36025 *Newborn; Benny Bailey (t); Oscar Pettiford (b); Rune Carlsson (d); unidentified (tb) and (bs).* 9/58.

***** Stockholm Jam Session Vol. 2**

Steeplechase SCCD 36026 *As above.* 9/58.

A player of tremendous technical ability, often likened to Oscar Peterson (who had come on to the East Coast scene with similar suddenness and plaudits), the younger Newborn was flashy, hyped-up and explosive, eating up themes like Clifford Brown's 'Daahoud' and Rollins's 'Oleo' as if they were buttered toast. Underneath the super-confident exterior, though, there was a troubled young man who was acutely sensitive to criticism, particularly the charge that he was no more than a cold technician. Newborn suffered a serious nervous collapse from which he only partially recovered, and the remainder of his career was interspersed with periods of ill-health. His later recording output is spasmodic to say the least, marked by a chastened blues sound which contrasts sharply – in style and quality – with the early work.

The Koch reissue was originally made for Atlantic. A shameless display of technical virtuosity, it is almost too much technically and, like the RCA session, difficult to absorb at length. The *Plays Jamaica* session, now available on a twofer with *Fabulous*, is more measured and this good-value compilation contains some of the pianist's best work of the period, including the deathless 'Pamela'. And yet even here the tendency to elaboration won't be curbed. Absurdly fast octave runs follow one another in quick succession, and even in ballad performances Newborn seems compelled to scatter notes in every direction, when a degree of reticence would be far more effective. Piano players will marvel, but most casual listeners may find the sum effect excessive.

Fortunately, it transpired in 1992 that tapes of Newborn's 1958 visit to Stockholm had survived, unheard, for 34 years. Expertly cleaned up by Nils Winther, they sound fresh and bright enough to counterbalance the vagaries of a single-mike recording and a ropy piano. The music is of an unexpectedly high quality for a spontaneous session. Some other instruments can be heard during the ensembles, but these did not play a major role and the individuals cannot be identified. Newborn's opening solo on the first session (Volume One) is patient and unhurried, growing in expressiveness as he moves outside the basic chords. It's perhaps his most complete statement of the evening. Elsewhere, he solos with great clarity and occasional glimpses of irony, as on Dizzy Gillespie's 'Woody'N'You' where, with Bailey sitting out, he mimics the punchy attack of the original trumpet line. Though badly recorded, Oscar Pettiford nearly makes the session his own. The bass solos on 'Ladybird' (Volume One) and 'It's You Or No One' (Two) are equally valuable additions to the Pettiford canon, and Bailey's luminous account of 'Confirmation' (Two) deserves a star or two. Local man Carlsson does his thing politely and professionally.

*****(*) A World Of Piano!**

Original Jazz Classics OJC 175 *Newborn; Paul Chambers (b); Louis Hayes, Philly Joe Jones (d).* 61.

***** The Great Jazz Piano Of Phineas Newborn Jr**

Original Jazz Classics OJC 388 *Newborn; Sam Jones, Milt Turner, Leroy Vinnegar (b); Louis Hayes (d).*

*****(*) The Newborn Touch**

Original Jazz Classics OJC 270 *Newborn; Leroy Vinnegar (b); Frank Butler (d).* 64.

*****(*) Harlem Blues**

Original Jazz Classics OJC 662 *Newborn; Ray Brown (b); Elvin Jones (d).* 2/69.

***** Please Send Me Someone To Love**

Original Jazz Classics OJCCSD 947 *As above.* 2/69.

Newborn made a string of records for Contemporary during the 1960s, though he was also hampered by a hand injury that curtailed some of his more virtuosic effects. It might be argued that this, compounded by a growing self-doubt, made him a more expressive player. The best of these sides are genuinely moving, as when on 'Prelude To A Kiss' (*Great Jazz Piano*), he restates the theme in octaves and floats it away over his own restatement, like a ghost score. There are equally lovely moments on *Harlem Blues*, most obviously a version of 'Tenderly' that melts the heart.

Throughout this period, he benefited from superb rhythm players. Vinnegar and Butler weren't the right combination for him, but Jones's celebrated polyrhythms, coupled to Brown's resolute chording and fast runs, were an ideal match for his own omnidirectional approach. *Harlem Blues* remains our favourite of the bunch by just a whisker, though there isn't much in it. The remainder of the session was released as *Please Send Me Someone To Love*, and surely now there's a strong case for editing together a good single CD from this pair?

***** Back Home**

Original Jazz Classics OJCCD 971 *Newborn; Ray Brown (b); Elvin Jones (d).* 76.

***** Look Out – Phineas Is Back!**

Original Jazz Classics OJCCD 866 *Newborn; Ray Brown (b); Jimmie Smith (d).* 76.

Newborn enjoyed a brief resurgence in the 1970s and was taken up by Pablo for a time. Interestingly, this was the closest he ever came to delivering a straight bebop record. Though his hand-speed would have suggested that the rapid-fire changes of bop would be meat and drink to him, he never seemed enamoured of the Monk/Powell axis, continuing to draw sustenance from Tatum and Peterson. On *Phineas Is Back!* he gives 'A Night In Tunisia' and 'Salt Peanuts' exuberant airings and adds the now familiar touch of pathos, even a hint of anger, to 'You Are The Sunshine Of My Life'. Brown and Smith are not well recorded, but both are audible and both play well.

Though there was a smattering of later records, for us, these are the last on which Newborn plays like his old self. Stories were rife about his psychological frailty in these years and it is remarkable that he managed to sustain a career at all, let alone at this generally impressive level. The trio on *Back Home* was one that he had worked with in the late '60s and there is genuine enjoyment in each other's company. Brown is happy to fill when the pianist's thoughts wander or when inspiration deserts him, as it seemed to in latter days, but the closing four tracks – 'Back Home', 'On Green Dolphin Street', 'Pamela' and 'Love For Sale' – are almost back to classic form.

****(*) Tivoli Encounter**

Storyville 8221 *Newborn; Jesper Lundgaard (b); Bjarne Rostvold (d).* 7/79.

Newborn recorded almost nothing in the final decade of his life, and so this has to be regarded as some sort of farewell. Clearly frail and certainly not playing at anything like full stretch, Phineas battles manfully through old favourites like 'Daahoud' and 'Lady Be Good', as well as some classic bebop themes and a couple of clever medleys. The trio could hardly be more supportive, but the fires are almost out and some fans may prefer not to hear him this way.

David 'Fathead' Newman (born 1933)

TENOR, ALTO AND SOPRANO SAXOPHONES, FLUTE

Born in Dallas, Newman was recording with rhythm and blues bands in the early 1950s and spent many years as the principal saxophonist in the Ray Charles group. A forty-year career as a leader on record has brought about a relatively sparing number of albums; not very many are in print.

***** Bigger And Better / The Many Facets Of David Newman**

Rhino/Atlantic R2 71453 *Newman; orchestra.* 3/68–2/69.

*****(*) House Of David**

Rhino/Atlantic R2 71452 2CD *Newman; various groups.* 52–89.

*****(*) It's *Mister* Fathead**

32 Jazz 32053 2CD *Newman; Marcus Belgrave (t); Bennie Crawford (bs); Ray Charles, Wynton Kelly, Norris Austin (p); Kossie Gardner (org); Ted Dunbar (g); Paul Chambers, Edgar Willis, Jimmy Jefferson (b); Milton Turner, Bruno Carr, Charli Persip (d).* 11/58–3/67.

**** Back To Basics**

Milestone 9188 *Newman; Wilbur Bascomb, Jimmy Owens, Milt Ward (t); Earl McIntyre (tb); Babe Clark (ts); Clarence Thomas (bs); Kenneth Harris (f); Pat Rebillot, George Cables, Hilton Ruiz (ky); George Davis, Lee Ritenour, Jay Graydon (g); Abraham Laboriel (b); Idris Muhammad (d); Bill Summers (perc); strings.* 5–11/77.

***** Lone Star Legend**

32 Jazz 32014 *Newman; Marcus Belgrave, Charlie Miller (t); Hank Crawford| (as); Howard Johnson (bs); Steve Nelson (vib); Cedar Walton, Larry Willis (p); Ted Dunbar (g); Walter Booker, Buster Williams (b); Louis Hayes, Jimmy Cobb (d).* 9/80–4/82.

In spite of his unfortunate nickname (which doesn't seem to bother him), Newman is an ornery, driving saxophonist whose R&B background – including 12 years with Ray Charles – has left him with a consummate knowledge in the use of riffs and licks in a soul-to-jazz context. He always swings and his unmistakable Texan sound is highly authoritative but, like so many musicians of a similar background, he's had trouble finding a fruitful context. His early Atlantic albums have been filleted to produce the excellent *House Of David* compilation, which starts with a date by Texas bluesman Zuzu Bollinand and goes through to the late 1980s with Aretha Franklin, Dr John and others, taking in the years with Charles and the crossover albums of the 1960s along the way. Newman plays it all with consummate heart, and there is a share of real classics: the irresistible theme of his own piece of jazz immortality, 'Hard Times'; the straight-ahead bop of 'Holy Land'; the suavity and grit of 'The Clincher'. But the miscellany does tend to prove Newman's second-fiddle status: he's a fine sideman, seldom a leader. 32 Jazz's *It's* Mister *Fathead* duplicates much of the compilation since it is a straight reissue of the four Atlantic albums, *Fathead, Straight Ahead, Fathead Comes On* and *House Of David*. There isn't much, er, fat on the original albums and the remastering catches Newman's salty, evocative sound beautifully. 'Night Of Nisan' is a pungent feature for the flute and all of the *Straight Ahead* session spots Newman with the Kelly–Chambers–Persip rhythm section on what is arguably his best record. The material is slightly less convincing on the later dates and the *House Of David* titles are lumbered with Kossie Gardner's routine organ. But this is a very playable set.

The other Rhino disc is a double-header featuring Newman fronting a couple of albums of nice tunes and smoochy ballads, usually with a good rhythm section at bottom but with the whole always papered over with strings and brass. Newman's playing salvages the music time and again, but a little can go a long way. *Lone Star Legend* reissues his two albums for Muse, *Resurgence!* and *Still Hard Times*. The playing is spirited, but some of the tracks settle for undistinguished funk rhythms.

The Milestone album is a waste of his time: puling backings, strings and horns sweeten up already saccharine material, and Newman's surviving solos are the only reason to listen.

****(*) Blue Head**

Candid CCD 79041 *Newman; Clifford Jordan (ss, ts); Buddy Montgomery (p); Ted Dunbar (g); Todd Coolman (b); Marvin 'Smitty' Smith (d).* 9/89.

Not much of a showing for Newman here. *Blue Head* has some decent stuff, thanks to Jordan's energetic solos, Montgomery's dextrous piano, and the tremendously shifting rhythms laid down by Coolman and Smith. But six very long jam tunes are probably at least one too many.

***** Chillin**

High Note HCD 7036 *Newman; Bryan Carrott (vib); John Hicks (p); Steve Novosel (b); Winard Harper (d); Cadino Newman (v).* 12/98.

The old warrior's taking things easy here and, while not all the tempos are slow, none of them exactly canters out of the gate. Carrott takes rather more of the improvising honours, and son Cadino sings on two tracks, quite effectively too. A likeable reminder that Newman's still around.

Joe Newman (1922–92)

TRUMPET

A deep-thinking musician with a reflective sound in an age when lead trumpeters were supposed to sky-write in every solo, Newman was – mutatis mutandis – the Johnny Hodges of the Basie band. He also had stints with Illinois Jacquet and with Benny Goodman and continued to record under his own name until quite late in life. Newman was also a passionate jazz educator.

****** The Count's Men**

Fresh Sound FSR CD 135 *Newman; Benny Powell (tb); Frank Foster (ts); Frank Wess (f, ts); Sir Charles Thompson (p); Eddie Jones (b); Shadow Wilson (d).* 9/55.

****(*) I'm Still Swinging**

RCA 7432 160985 2 *Newman; Urbie Green (tb); Gene Quill (as); Al Cohn (ts); Dick Katz (p); Freddie Green (g); Eddie Jones (b); Shadow Wilson (d).* 10/55.

*****(*) I Feel Like A New Man**

Black Lion BLCD 760905 *Newman; Benny Powell, Bill Byers (tb); Gene Quill (as); Frank Foster (ts); Frank Wess (f, ts); Sir Charles Thompson, John Lewis (p); Freddie Green (g); Eddie Jones, Milt Hinton (b); Shadow Wilson, Osie Johnson (d).* 9/55, 4/56.

***** The Midgets**

RCA 7432 1609872 *Newman; Frank Wess (f); Hank Jones (p, org); Barry Galbraith, Freddie Green (g); Eddie Jones (b); Osie Johnson (d).* 7/56.

Newman was never a whole-hearted modernist. His sharp attack and bright sound were derived almost entirely from Louis Armstrong and, though he was chief cadre of the 'Basie Moderns' in the 1950s, he maintained allegiance to the Count's music over any other. That's perfectly obvious from the scaled-down arrangements on *I'm Still Swinging*, which sounds very much like what it is, a mid-size ensemble working at the sharp end of the Basie idiom. Though not, significantly enough, with Basie material. A broad-ranging and imaginative set includes Ellington and Cole Porter material, Irving Berlin's delightful 'Top Hat, White Tie and Tails' (one of three fine arrangements by Manny Albam) and Joe's own 'Slats!' and 'Daughter Of Miss Thing'. As always at this vintage, the solos are well developed, favouring the middle register, and rhythmically steady, though the trumpeter's ability to drift at will across the bar lines suggests a player of a later generation.

The Midgets suggests some of the ways in which Newman wanted to reshape the Basie sound. Much of the writing is by Ernie Wilkins, but it's the trumpeter and Wess who take control of things and shape an elegant programme of restless and provocative themes, imaginatively arranged for the refreshing line-up of horn, flute, piano and two electric guitars. Green, as ever, plays rhythm only, albeit with consummate control and taste, but it's the voicing of the group that is so impressive, and the original material – Wilkins's 'My Dog Friday' and 'Scooter' and Joe's long title-piece – still sounds fresh, more than four decades later.

Better to start with the Black Lion and Fresh Sound CDs from a pair of mid-1950s sessions, recorded while Newman was still Basie's trumpet star. 'East Of The Sun' on *New Man* is touched by Parker, but 'Difugality', with the larger Byers/Quill/Foster front line, seems to be hamstrung between two idioms, offering a slightly ironic slant to Leonard Feather's famous characterization of the trumpeter as 'neutralist modern'.

As a useful compare-and-contrast exercise, try 'A.M. Romp' on *The Count's Men* with the same tune on *Good'n'Groovy*, below. The later version is slightly wilder, but it's the tighter version with Sir Charles Thompson that really impresses, and newcomers to Newman's entertaining sound would do well to begin with the mid-'50s stuff.

***** Good'n'Groovy**

Original Jazz Classics OJC 185 *Newman; Frank Foster (ts); Tommy Flanagan (p); Eddie Jones (b); Bill English (d).* 3/61.

*****(*) Jive At Five**

Original Jazz Classics OJC 419 *Newman; Frank Wess (ts); Tommy Flanagan (p); Eddie Jones (b); Oliver Jackson (d).* 5/60.

Good'n'Groovy was recorded at about the time of Newman's departure from the Basie band, though it's pretty clear that Joe retains a considerable loyalty to a sound and conception that he himself did so much to shape. *Jive At Five* has very much the same feel, but it's a more relaxed and poised performance. Newman always sounds good round Frank Foster, and the album bounces along with enough vigour to cut through a rather flat mix.

***** At The Atlantic**

Phontastic NCD 8810 *Newman; Ove Lind (cl); Lars Erstrand (vib); Staffan Broms (g); Arne Wilhelmsson (b); Robert Edman (d).* 8/77.

*****(*) Hangin' Out**

Concord CCCD 4462 *Newman; Joe Wilder (t, flhn); Hank Jones (p); Rufus Reid (b); Marvin 'Smitty' Smith (d).* 5/84.

The Phontastic record, recorded live in one of Stockholm's leading restaurants, is essentially an Ove Lind disc with a prominent guest slot by Newman and, as such, isn't absolutely central to the story. The other newish one, though, is a must for fans of the trumpeter. His partnership with Wilder proved to be one of the most fruitful of his career. Though they share an approach, each is idiosyncratic and individual enough to stand out as a stylist, and what one gets is a clever dialogue between two wise heads.

A canny and enterprising musician (who represents a 'positive' counter-image to many of the musicians of his generation), Newman headed the educational/promotional Jazz Interactions trust in the later 1960s, a thin time for the music, and expanded his interests to include large-scale composition (a direction that reflected more of his New Orleans background than it did the turbulent classicism of his exact contemporary, Charles Mingus).

***** A Grand Night For Swingin': The Joe Newman Memorial Album**

Natasha 5012 *Newman; Ross Tompkins (p); Russell George (b); Roy Lundberg (d).* 92.

Released just after Joe's death, this fine record sums up his virtues. He could take a song like 'You Are My Sunshine' and turn it into an almost desolate act of longing, and he could make 'Lady's In Love With You' as complex as *Madame Bovary*, all of it done under the guise of a swing so confident you might be tempted to describe it as 'effortless', except that this is a notably hard-working group. Tompkins turned out to be a very able accompanist indeed, and the rhythm section meshes well on every track. As a send-off for one of the most distinguished players of the swing era, it could hardly be improved … except, perhaps, by a rather more generous sound-mix, and a little more than 42 minutes of music.

Sam Newsome (born 1965)

TENOR AND SOPRANO SAXOPHONES

Began on alto, moved to tenor and finally, in the mid-'90s, chose to concentrate on soprano sax. Studied at Berklee and moved to New York in 1988. Settled on music after trying out as a stand-up comic!

*****(*) Sam I Am**

Criss Cross Jazz 1056 *Newsome; Marcus Miller (p); Steve Nelson (vib); James Genus (b); Billy Drummond (d).* 11/90.

***** The Tender Side Of Sammy Straighthorn**

Steeplechase SCCD 31452 *Newsome; Bruce Barth (p); Ugonna Okegwo (b); Matt Wilson (d); Elisabeth Kontomanou(v).* 4/98.

Newsome emerged as a tenorman of unpretentious authority with the Criss Cross album. He courts trouble by framing tributes to both Coltrane and Rollins here, but 'In The Vein Of Trane', basically a simple F minor vamp, manages to reflect on Coltrane without slavishly copying him, and 'Pent-up House' settles for the brazen confidence rather than the delivery of the young Sonny. Actually, Newsome takes his time in his improvising, building solos methodically, savouring his best phrases and going for tonal extremes only when he sees their logical point. A rich, dark tenor tone and a penchant for fitting in with the band rather than dominating them give this record much bonhomie as well as a lot of rigorous playing. Nelson is in his most attacking form, throwing off some dazzling solos in single lines rather than multiple-mallet chords, and the rhythm section is as impressive as always on Criss Cross dates.

By the time of the Steeplechase date, Newsome had decided to switch exclusively to soprano. He's recorded in a somewhat distant way on the session, and the music never quite takes a grip. The reaction of most will depend on how they respond to Kontomanou's singing, wordless but not resorting to scat, instead singing open-throated counterpoint to the leader's soprano lines. It's a curious combination, although she appears on only three of the seven tracks. A long fantasy on 'All The Things You Are' is intermittently impressive, and the Japanese 'Lullaby Of Takeda' is attractive. Newsome has since signed to Columbia, but his *Global Unity* album is a misguided mishmash of idioms.

David Newton (born 1958)

PIANO

Born in Glasgow, Newton worked on the Edinburgh scene before a move to London helped establish him as one of the leading younger British pianists, much in demand as accompanist and sideman.

***** Eyewitness**

Linn AKD 015 *Newton; Dave Green (p); Allan Ganley (d).* 2/90.

(*) **Victim Of Circumstance

Linn AKD 013 *As above, except add Alec Dankworth (b), Clark Tracey (d).* 2 & 5/90.

Like the young Americans of the same generation – from Geri Allen to Cyrus Chestnut – Newton served his apprenticeship as accompanist and musical director to a singer, in David's case Carol Kidd. His technique is briskly correct, sometimes a little too formal and orderly, though the rhythm section is so full-on that he's never allowed to sound stuffy. Newton worked with Dankworth and Ganley on a Buddy DeFranco record, and one can't quite escape the sensation that *Victim Of Circumstance* is a superior play-along disc, with a horn line constantly implicit. It certainly needs something. Hard to put air between them, but *Eyewitness* is perhaps more straightforwardly swinging. Green and Ganley appear only once on the second disc, and their absence is duly noted. *Victim* is one false climax after another, and only the unaccompanied 'It Never Entered My Mind' stirs the blood.

***(*) **Return Journey**

Linn AKD 025 *Newton (p solo).* 2/92.

More like it. Newton will still be too self-dramatizing for some tastes, and the suite of pieces that makes up 'Return Journey' itself doesn't quite work. Even so, it's brave at this stage in a career to devote an entire solo disc to originals, and to work of such thoughtfulness. The technique is no less proper than before and, without the rough-hewn presence of Green and Ganley, something like the long 'While You're Away' does, indeed, become a protracted sojourn. Great sound; producer Elliot Meadow's ears are as acute as ever.

***(*) **In Good Company**

Candid CCD 79714 *Newton; Dave Green (b); Allan Ganley (d).* 9/94.

It was thought when Newton switched to Candid that he might go for broke and record with an American trio. No problems whatsoever with the line-up on this, as we've said before, but it does seem time to kick over the traces and take some chances on a wider stage. With almost any transatlantic pairing – and it would be invidious to throw names about – this would be a more compelling record. As played, it's chunky, cable-knit jazz which trades funk and attitude for a smooth sophistication that shortens its shelf-life considerably.

**** **Twelfth Of The Twelfth: A Jazz Portrait Of Frank Sinatra**

Candid CCD 79728 *Newton (p solo).* 8/95.

The key track here is 'All The Way', just over half-way through the set. Newton reworks the tune and invests it with a sardonic quality that was never detectable in the original but which makes perfect sense, whether one takes the original as a jumping-off point or a sacred text. The pianist's long meditation on the Sinatra voice and legend, the title-track, is the most substantial single track. Everything else is at song length and absolutely faithful to the great man's own conception. It's easy to pick holes in this. Sinatra's own light legato and almost conversational phrasing are extraordinarily difficult to reduplicate instrumentally, but it's hard to imagine them done better. Some will wish the choice of tracks were different – 'This Love Of Mine' in for 'It's Nice To Go Trav'lling', 'Fly Me To The Moon' instead of 'This Is All I Ask' – except that one suspects Newton might well return to the territory, now that Sinatra is no longer around.

***(*) **D N A**

Candid CCD 79742 *Newton; Iain Dixon (ts); Matt Miles (b); Steve Brown (d).* 11/96.

The first time on record that Newton has worked with a horn-led quartet – and, by and large, a success. Dixon is a seasoned player, a little anonymous in tone and a little obvious in his range of ideas, but capable of giving even a relatively uncomplicated theme a mature lift and presence. His own 'The Scribe' was apparently worked out during the sessions.

Newton chips in with three originals, 'DNA', 'Julia' and 'Feet On The Ground', but the real substance of the record comes in Chick Corea's 'Highwire', an exuberant performance, and a long version of Tristano's and Konitz's 'Ablution'. The sound is impeccable, faithful to the physical reality and convincingly detailed.

Frankie Newton (1906–54)

TRUMPET

Played in several New York bands in the early-to-middle 1930s, including Charlie Barnet's and John Kirby's, and led some record dates of his own, but he never made much of his career and recorded only rarely after 1940. After 1950 he more or less retired from music altogether.

***(*) **Frankie Newton 1937–1939**

Classics 643 *Newton; Cecil Scott (cl, ts); Edmond Hall (cl, bs); Mezz Mezzrow (cl); Pete Brown, Russell Procope, Tab Smith, Stanley Payne, Gene Johnson (as); Kenneth Hollon (ts); Don Frye, James P Johnson, Kenny Kersey, Albert Ammons, Meade Lux Lewis (p); Frank Rice, Al Casey, Ulysses Livingston, Teddy Bunn (g); Richard Fulbright, John Kirby, Johnny Williams (b); Cozy Cole, O'Neil Spencer, Eddie Dougherty, Big Sid Catlett (d); Clarence Palmer, Slim Gaillard, Leon LaFell (v).* 3/37–8/39.

Newton was an intriguing, unguessable player whose small number of recordings represents the rare strain of swing-era small groups at their most interesting. In some ways he was an old-fashioned hot player, using a terminal vibrato borrowed directly from Armstrong and turning in oblique, poetic solos on otherwise slight material. He worked extensively at New York's Onyx Club in the late 1930s, when these tracks were made. 'Who's Sorry Now' features a Newton solo which summarizes his style: the quirky lyricism and sudden bursts of heat make him exhilaratingly hard to predict. But it's his four choruses on 'The Blues My Baby Gave To Me' which are close to perfection, beautifully controlled and achingly lyrical reflections on the blues. There are other good solos from Brown and Hall scattered through these sides; Johnson is in fine form on the 1939 Bluebird session, and there are one or two strikingly unusual tunes, including 'Vamp' and the odd 'Parallel Fifths' from the final (1939) date. Classics take their material from unlisted sources and the sound is unfortunately very variable.

James Newton (born 1953)

FLUTE

Raised in California, Newton studied with Buddy Collette and dabbled in both funk and the avant-garde before devoting himself exclusively to flute. He characteristically projects a strong, very exact classical line, but he modifies it with various extended techniques, including multiphonics, flutter tonguing and toneless blowing.

****** Axum**

ECM 835019-2 *Newton (f solo).* 81.

One of the first contemporary players to foster a direct Eric Dolphy influence, Newton started out as a multi-instrumentalist but gave up alto saxophone and bass clarinet towards the end of the 1970s. As a virtuoso flautist, he has worked in both formal and improvised contexts and has developed a wholly original means of vocalizing while he plays. This is by no means new (Roland Kirk was exceptionally proficient at it), but Newton has taken the technique far beyond unisons and harmonies to a point where he can sing contrapuntally against his own flute line. The results are frequently dazzling, as on the African-influenced *Axum*. Newton's vocalizations allow his pieces to develop with unprecedented depth, and his tone is quite remarkable.

***** In Venice**

Celestial Harmonies 13030 *Newton (f solo).* 10/87.

Powerfully reminiscent of some of Sam Rivers's later flute-based works, these solos are strongly architectonic but with undoubted drive and impetus. The classical references are still there – 'Syrinx', 'Bartók Dream' – but the bulk of the set alludes to the blues and to jazz harmony, even if it diverges sharply from both. 'Spiritual Suite: Going' comes in at more than a quarter of an hour and is a major statement by any standard. The set is marred by unforgiving sound and some (presumably unintentional) distortion.

***** Suite For Frida Kahlo**

Audioquest AQ 1023 *Newton; George Lewis, George McMullen (tb); Pedro Eustache (f, bf, bcl, ts); Julie Feves (bsn); Kei Akagi (p); Darek Oleszkiewicz (b); Sonship Theus (d, perc).* 8/94.

This is an odd work which catches Newton once again in a stylistic no-man's land. The dedication is to one of the honoured figures of feminist art history, but precisely what Newton *does* draw from Kahlo's surreally honest canvases isn't entirely clear. Though the best of the non-suite pieces on the record – 'Elliptical' is essentially a duet with the marvellous Lewis – still shows something of the Strayhorn influence, the sequence devoted to the painter is much closer in spirit and conception to Mingus's work. It is there in the voicing of the horns, the twinned flutes and trombones, the expressive part given to bassoon, the unexpected dance movements of 'The Broken Column' and the awkward spiritual breakthrough of 'The Love Embrace Of The Universe' which provides the climax. Newton himself notes classical composers Heitor Villa-Lobos and Toru Takemitsu as sources (rather than influences) for elements of the suite, and concedes that its creation was greatly affected by the recent death of clarinettist and composer John Carter, one of the few contemporary musicians to have taken up the challenge of Mingus's large-scale approach. The warm, analogue recording captures Newton's own playing more truthfully than anything in recent years, just as the album's range of styles reflects his ambition. A good, if challenging, place to make this undersung master's acquaintance.

Albert Nicholas (1900–1971)

CLARINET

Bandleading in New Orleans in the early 1920s, he then played with King Oliver before going to the Far East, then returning to work in the Luis Russell band. Spent the '30s in New York in various gigs, then re-emerged as a revivalist in the '40s. Moved to France in 1953 and became an honoured and much-travelled elder statesman.

*****(*) The New Orleans–Chicago Connection**

Delmark 207 *Nicholas; Art Hodes (p); Earl Murphy (b); Fred Kohlman (d).* 7/59.

***** Albert Nicholas With Alan Elsdon's Band**

Jazzology JCD-269 *Nicholas; Alan Elsdon (t); Phil Rhodes (tb); Andy Cooper (cl, ts); Colin Bates (p); Johnny Barton (g, bj); Mick Gilligan (b); Billy Law (d).* 2/67.

*****(*) Baden 1969**

Sackville SKCD2-2045 *Nicholas; Henri Chaix (p); Alain Du Bois (b); Romano Cavicchiolo (d).* 9/69.

One of the least exposed of the New Orleans clarinet masters on record, Nicholas's surviving discs are mostly delightful. For a man who played with King Oliver and Jelly Roll Morton, he seemed quite at ease in the company of musicians generations younger than himself. Art Hodes at least was a contemporary, and their Delmark album is a spirited ramble through some of the old tunes, Hodes's Chicagoan blues meshing easily with Nick's pithy solos. He has an odd way of mixing a circumspect, behind-the-hand manner with a piercing attack: a diffident statement of the melody may suddenly blossom on a sudden high note with a fast vibrato, before the line drops back into the depths of his horn. 'He could always get you with that tone,' Barney Bigard remembered, and something of the young Bechet survives in Nicholas's most sprightly playing. The original Delmark album has been fleshed out with a stack of alternative takes, none of them especially meaningful, but the body of the music is fine.

Nicholas had fun with the Elsdon band, and this souvenir of a gig in Manchester stands up fine. Not a very good piano, the trombonist is a bit of a lad, and even Elsdon himself has his shaky moments, but the New Orleans man hardly puts a foot wrong: listen to his lovely work on 'Blue Turning Grey Over You'. In Switzerland, with local man Chaix and his group, Albert played what was by this time a rather stock guest-star role, with most of his favourite pieces turning up in much the way he would always play them. But the music is very genuine. 'Rose Room' and 'Lover Come Back To Me' are swung off the stage and, though bass and drums aren't given a very pleasing sound, clarinet and piano come through strongly.

Wooden Joe Nicholas (1883–1957)

TRUMPET, CLARINET

Albert Nicholas's uncle played brass and clarinet, starting with the latter. Played with King Oliver in 1915 and modelled his style on Bolden, but missed out on recording in the golden age and left only a few documents of his sound during the revival of the '40s.

*** Wooden Joe Nicholas

American Music AMCD-5 *Nicholas; Jim Robinson, Louis Nelson, Joe Petit (tb); Albert Burbank (cl); Johnny St Cyr (g); Lawrence Marrero (bj); Austin Young, Alcide 'Slow Drag' Pavageau (b); Josiah Frazier, Baby Dodds, Albert Jiles (d); Ann Cook (v).* 5/45–7/49.

A legend calls down the years. Wooden Joe's main idol was Buddy Bolden, and hearing him play may offer us the best idea of what Bolden himself might have sounded like. Nicholas blew a very powerful open horn, and was famous for dominating a dance-hall sound. These were his only recordings, and they are clustered together from a session at the Artesian Hall and two later dates. A lot of New Orleans history is tied up here: the fearsome blues singer, Ann Cook, is on one track, the legendary trombonist, Joe Petit, on another. Nicholas and Burbank are the main voices on all the tracks (Wooden Joe also played clarinet, and does so on two numbers): compared with the clarinettist's weaving lines, Nicholas is reserved in his phrasing and takes only a few breaks and solos. But much of his power and stately delivery was intact. The music has been remastered from acetates and, though the fidelity isn't as good as in some of the American Music series, the history still comes alive.

Herbie Nichols (1919–63)

PIANO

Worked largely in swing, mainstream and R&B settings from the late '40s, mostly for other leaders; but his few own-name recordings show an original mind playing very different music. Since his death from leukaemia, enthusiasts such as Roswell Rudd have been determined to bring his music to wider attention.

**** The Complete Blue Note Recordings

Blue Note 8 59355 2 3CD *Nichols; Teddy Kotick, Al McKibbon (b); Art Blakey, Max Roach (d).* 5/55–4/56.

'There is a kind of culpability in the discovery of dead artists', and in Herbie Nichols there is an almost perfect example of an artist who was (largely, and with one significant exception) ignored during his lifetime, only to be canonized as soon as he was gone. When Nichols died, he had been working professionally for a quarter of a century, ever since joining the Royal Baron Orchestra in 1937. Yet in all those 26 years, by A.B. Spellman's reckoning, there was not one during which he was able to earn a living making the music he loved. Nichols made his way 'playing grease', as he put it himself, in R&B bands like Horsecollar Williams's, backing singers (Sheila Jordan being the most creative) and even providing accompaniments for lesbian shows. Perhaps making the best of necessity, he claimed to prefer barroom uprights, liking the percussive attack and the way the sound came back at him so quickly. One can certainly hear something of that in Nichols's compositions, which typically begin with a call-and-response between piano and percussion, before moving off into often quite unexpected harmonic and rhythmic territory. Nichols was rooted in the blues but regularly name-checked Bartók and Shostakovich among his influences, as well as Villa-Lobos, though the Latin inflexion in tunes like the delightful 'Terpsichore' probably came more directly from his West Indian ancestry; his parents had emigrated from Trinidad and St Kitts.

Nichols scuffled as a recording artist, doing R&B sides here and there, until Alfred Lion of Blue Note decided to sign him up. Two 10-inch LPs were issued from the May 1955 sessions, both called *The Prophetic Herbie Nichols*. How forward-looking he was as a composer may be judged by his use in 'The Third World', the opening item on *The Complete*, of a chord progression that would still sound radical when John Coltrane experimented with it more than a decade later (nearer two from the date of composition, since it seems to have been written as early as 1947). Typically, Lion gave him generous rehearsal time, and neither McKibbon nor Blakey sounds as though he is running down unfamiliar material. The playing is crisp and buoyant, and even alternative takes are worth hearing.

Nichols and McKibbon reconvened in August 1955 with Max Roach at the kit, and they recorded his best-known composition, 'Lady Sings The Blues', as well as the joyous 'The Gig'; but it is tunes like '23 Skiddoo' and 'Shuffle Montgomery' from the earlier sessions which have restored him to favour, largely through the advocacy of younger players like Geri Allen, a devoted Nichols fan. The three-CD *Complete* is his testament. No one interested in the development of bebop, or indeed of jazz piano, should be without it.

Keith Nichols (born 1945)

PIANO, VOCALS

Born in Ilford, Essex, Nichols has a versatile background in acting and entertaining, but is primarily a practising scholar of ragtime and early jazz repertory. Previous groups included, from the 1970s on, the Ragtime Orchestra, Midnite Follies Orchestra and Paramount Theatre Orchestra. He records mainly on piano but also plays trombone, accordion and reeds.

*** I Like To Do Things For You

Stomp Off CD1242 *Nichols; Guy Barker (c); Gordon Blundy (tb); Mac White (cl, bcl, ss, as); Randy Colville (cl, as, ts); Mike Piggott (vn); Mike French (p); Martin Wheatley (g, bj); Graham Read (bsx, tba, sou, b); Barry Tyler (d); Janice Day, Johnny M, The Happidrome Trio (v).* 6–7/91.

*** Syncopated Jamboree

Stomp Off CD 1234 *Nichols; Bent Persson, Mike Henry (t); Alistair Allan (tb); Claus Jacobi, Mac White, Mark Allway, Randy Colville, Robert Fowler (reeds); Mike Piggott (vn); Martin Wheatley (g, bj); Graham Read (sou); Richard Pite (d); Janice Day, Johnny M, Tony Jacobs (v).* 9/91.

****** Henderson Stomp**

Stomp Off CD 1275 *Nichols; René Hagmann (c, tb); Bent Persson, Guy Barker, Mike Henry, Rolf Koschorrok (t); Alistair Allan (tb); Claus Jacobi (ss, as, bsx, cl); Nicholas Payton (as, cl); Michel Bard (ts, cl); Martin Wheatley (bj); Graham Read (sou); Richard Pite (d).* 11/93.

Nichols is a British specialist in American repertory: ragtime, hot dance music, New York jazz of the 1920s, Blake, Morton, Berlin, whatever. His piano playing and Hoagy Carmichael-like singing are less important than the mastery of old form that he successfully displays on these records. *I Like To Do Things For You* is more of a chamber-jazz session: the instrumentation varies, but the largest group has eight players, while 'I'm Nobody's Baby' cuts the cast to three. Familiarity with any Nichols/Mole session or even the Bix and Trumbauer dates will give the idea. Janice Day's rather plummy contralto is much featured and may be an acquired taste. There are plenty of tunes among the 20 tracks that have probably been unrecorded since the 1920s, and the irony of having a brilliant modernist like Barker on hand goes almost unnoticed (he is at least as good as Wynton Marsalis at this kind of thing). Recorded in a dry acoustic, but it has a very appropriate sound.

Syncopated Jamboree is by a bigger band and is more of a piece: Read, who moves between various bass instruments on the other record, plays strict brass bass here, and the section-work would surely have been good enough for Roger Wolfe Kahn. Another stack of obscurities, expertly reworked in a little over an hour of music. Sometimes it all seems like a pointless exercise – Nichols isn't trying to bring anything new to this music, he just loves to play it – but sympathetic ears will be rewarded.

Henderson Stomp, though, is surely his finest hour to this point and one of the most convincing pieces of authentic-performance jazz ever set down. Twenty-two of Fletcher Henderson's most effective pieces – from several hands, though many of Don Redman's somewhat familiar charts are bypassed in favour of other arrangements – are re-created by a picked team of some of the most talented repertory players and revivalists in Europe: the brass team alone is gold-plated, with the amazingly versatile Persson and Barker set alongside the brilliant Hagmann. The reed section sounds totally schooled in the appropriate section-sound of the period, and each of the tunes emerges with the kind of rocking swing that sounds properly flavoursome of the era. With such a strong team of soloists, the various breaks and carefully fashioned improvisations have the nous needed to transcend any scripted mustiness. Dave Bennett engineers an ideal sound-mix. Result: a modern work of art wearing old-fashioned duds.

****** Harlem's Arabian Nights**

Stomp Off CD1320 *As above, except add Bob Hunt (tb), Matthias Seuffert (cl, as, ts), Janice Day (v); omit Barker, Payton, Bard.* 9–10/96.

Outrageously good. This is the result of Nichols doing some digging for early manuscripts in the Library Of Congress – rarities by Ellington, James P. Johnson, Waller and others. So here are 'Yam Brown' and 'Rub A Dub-Lues' (Ellington), 'Mistuh Jim' and 'She's The Hottest Gal In Tennessee' (Johnson), 'Say It With Your Feet' (Waller) and 18 others, knocked out with stunning panache by Nichols's Cotton Club Orchestra, the finest assemblage of repertory players he could muster. As with the Henderson collection, they make it new by playing it old and, though some of the phrasing may suggest a vaudevillian bent, we prefer to hear it as old-fashioned virtuosity put to very specific ends. Dave Bennett once again gets an ideal sound in the 'ballroom' ambience of Pizza Express, Maidstone.

Red Nichols (1905–65)

CORNET, TRUMPET

Born Ernest Loring Nichols in Utah, he played in his father's brass band as a boy but soon turned to jazz. Arrived in New York in the early '20s and became one of the most recorded sessionmen as both bandleader and section-player. His 'Five Pennies' sessions resulted in scores of titles. Directed Broadway show bands and toured through the '30s, running his own big band. After a spell out of music, he returned with a small group in 1945. Worked on the West Coast through the '50s, the biopic The Five Pennies revitalizing his career, and was still successful when he died suddenly during a Las Vegas engagement.

***** Red Nichols On Edison 1924–27**

Jazz Oracle BDW 8007 *Nichols; Frank Cush, Leo McConville (t); Bill Trone (mel); Miff Mole, Tommy Dorsey (tb); Dick Johnson, Jimmy Dorsey, Arnold Brilhart, Phil Gleason, Fred Morrow (cl, as); Paul Cartwright (cl, ss, ts); Alfie Evans (as); Freddy Cusick (cl, ts); Jack Pettis (Cmel); Irving Brodsky, Arthur Schutt (p); Dick McDonough (g, bj); Tommy Felline (bj); Joe Tarto, Jack Hansen (bbs); Adrian Rollini (bsx); Stan King, Vic Berton (d).* 11/24–2/27.

*****(*) Red Nichols & Miff Mole 1925–1927**

Retrieval RTR 79010 *Nichols; Miff Mole (tb); Dick Johnson (cl, as); Jimmy Lytell, Alfie Evans, Jimmy Dorsey, Pee Wee Russell (cl); Rube Bloom, Frank Signorelli, Arthur Schutt (p); Tony Colucci (bj); Joe Tarto (tba); Vic Berton, Ray Bauduc (d); Irving Kaufman (v).* 11/25–9/27.

****(*) Rhythm Of The Day**

ASV AJA 5025 *Nichols; Manny Klein, Leo McConville, Donald Lindley, James Kozak, Charlie Teagarden, Wingy Manone, Johnny Davis (t); Miff Mole, Glenn Miller, Will Bradley (tb); Dudley Fosdick (mel); Ross Gorman (cl, as, bs); Alfie Evans (cl, as, vn); Harold Noble (cl, as, ts); Jimmy Dorsey, Benny Goodman (cl, as); Billy McGill, Fud Livingston (cl, ts); Pee Wee Russell (cl); Babe Russin (ts); Adrian Rollini, Barney Acquelina (bsx); Nick Koupoukis (f, picc); Murray Kellner, Joe Venuti, Jack Harris, Saul Sharrow (vn); Milton Susskind, Arthur Schutt, Edgar Fairchild, Jack Russin, Fulton McGrath (p); Eddie Lang, Tony Colucci, Carl Kress (g); Tony Starr (bj); Artie Bernstein, Art Miller (b); Victor Engle, Chauncey Morehouse, Vic Berton, David Grupp (d).* 10/25–2/32.

*****(*) His Best Recordings 1927–1931**

Best Of Jazz 4041 *Similar to above.* 3/27–6/31.

***** Original 1929 Recordings**

Tax CD5 *Nichols; Leo McConville, Manny Klein, Tommy Thunen, John Egan, Mickey Bloom (t); Jack Teagarden, Glenn Miller, Herb Taylor, Bill Trone (tb); Alfie Evans, Arnold Brilhart (cl, as, bsn, f); Benny Goodman (cl, as, bs); Jimmy Dorsey (cl, as);*

Pee Wee Russell (cl); Jimmy Crossan (ts, bsn, f); Babe Russin, Bud Freeman, Fud Livingston (ts); Murray Kellner, Joe Raymond, Lou Raderman, Henry Whiteman, Maurice Goffin (vn); Arthur Schutt, Rube Bloom, Irving Brodsky, Joe Sullivan (p); Carl Kress (g); Tommy Felline (bj); Joe Tarto (bb); Jack Hansen, Art Miller (b); Gene Krupa, Vic Berton, George Beebe, Dave Tough (d); Scrappy Lambert, Red McKenzie, Dick Robertson (v). 4–10/29.

****(*) Radio Transcriptions 1929–30**

IAJRC 1011 *Basically as above; add Adrian Rollini (bsx).* 8/27–8/30.

These days it's a cliché to see Nichols as a maligned figure since the popular heyday of the white New York school of the 1920s; but, with that era itself falling away into history, arguments about his stature *vis-à-vis* Beiderbecke or Armstrong (and for a long time he seems to have been more popular than either) seem even more academic. For a man who cut probably thousands of records in the 1920s, under his name and in numberless dance orchestras, he still remains neglected in the CD era. His own precise, lightly dancing work on either cornet or trumpet might seem to glance off the best of Beiderbecke's playing, and the scrupulous ensembles and pallid timbre of the Five Pennies or whatever he chose to call a group on its day in the studios now seem less appealing. But it is unique jazz and, in its truce between cool expression and hot dance music, surprisingly enjoyable when taken a few tracks at a time.

The Best Of Jazz compilation makes a go of selecting some of his best moments. As with the similarly inclined ASV CD, though, it falls too much in the area of the later, more conventional and less obviously hot music of 1929–30. While there are fine moments for the likes of Teagarden ('Rose Of Washington Square') and Goodman ('Chinatown'), this isn't the best place to hear Nichols himself, and it's time we had the likes of 'Boneyard Shuffle' available again. It still earns the best rating since the transfers are decent and track-for-track this is perhaps the best Nichols compilation. But it gets stiff competition from the Retrieval disc, which brings together 23 titles by The (Six) Hottentots, The Original Memphis Five and The Arkansas Travellers, all basically co-led by Nichols and Mole and certainly dominated by their playing. The OM5 session is a cracker and, while some of the other titles are more like hot dance music (and the Travellers sessions are acoustic recordings, and less imposing), the playing has something to take the ear on every track. Top-notch transfers as always from this label.

The ASV CD is something of a missed opportunity, since it purports to be a Five Pennies compilation yet includes two tracks by Mole's Molers and one by Ross Gorman's dance band, as well as including several of the later, lesser records. At least the 1925–7 selections – including 'Alabama Stomp', 'Buddy's Habits' and 'Cornfed' – are among the best of the Pennies. Sound is average, which is to say not good enough.

The Jazz Oracle disc collects some of the many sides Nichols cut for Edison: longer than the average 78, there are multiple takes of various sides from the Red And Miff's Stompers date of 1927, which forms the heart of the CD. Trim, elegant playing by Mole and Nichols, but Edison's comparatively thin sound isn't as good as the Brunswick sides, and there are more conventional hot-dance numbers by Don Voorhees, Golden Gate Orchestra and the Charleston Seven (on which Red's presence is anyway in doubt). A welcome set of some rare records, though.

Tax's compilation covers Nichols's 1929 sessions in chronological order. He was leaving the '20s with his best work already behind him, even though he wasn't yet 25 years old, and these sessions, studded with several future stars, are a little poignant because of that. Yet Nichols still sounds good when he emerges from what were good dance-band arrangements for a group larger than the early Pennies. Excellent remastering by John R.T. Davies. The IAJRC disc collects music made for radio broadcast, and it is beset by laughably stilted announcements and some feeble ballads. Yet when the band dig in and start to stomp, there's some terrific music, and the last 20 minutes or so include some superb Rollini and Goodman, as well as Nichols.

**** Red Nichols And His Orchestra 1936**

Circle CCD-110 *Nichols; rest unknown.* 11/36

***** Wail Of The Winds**

Hep CD 1057 *Nichols; Don Stevens, J. Douglas Wood, Hilton Brockman (t); Martin Croy, Robert Gebhart, Slim Wilbur, Al Mastren, Jack Knaus (tb); Harry Yolonsky, Ray Schultz, Conn Humphreys (as); Bobby Jones, Billy Shepherd, Heinie Beau (cl, ts); Billy Maxted (p); Tony Colucci, Mike Bryan, Merrit Lamb (g); Jack Fay, Frank Ray (b); Harry Jaeger (d, v); Victor Engle (d); Marion Redding, Bill Darnell (v).* 3/39–6/40.

The Circle CD offers some WBS transcriptions which are shared with a nondescript dance session by Will Bradley's orchestra. Not that Nichols's titles are much better: the music is so anonymous that this was long thought to be a session by the Ray Noble band. Red has a meagre number of solo spots, and the rest of the group are capable but unexceptional on routine arrangements. Good remastering, though, of what's a mere 28 minutes of music.

Hep's set plugs a big gap by bringing some of Red's big-band records on to CD for the first time. With all his experience behind him, Nichols was still only 33 when the first of these sessions was made. The band received good notices and was taking up a prestige engagement at New York's Famous Door, only to see the club abruptly close, whereupon Nichols broke up the band after losing some of his best men. These Victor sessions reveal a strong if not especially characterful outfit: Nichols and Jones take most of the solos, but at least the band gets the chance to dig into plenty of instrumental charts (mostly by Maxted), along with the expected vocal features. Excellent sound.

***** Red Nichols And His Five Pennies**

Jazzology JCD-90 *Nichols; Kingsley Jackson (tb); Reuel Lynch (cl); Joe Rushton (bsx); Bobby Hammack (p); Rollie Culver (d).* 3–10/49.

***** Red Nichols Vol. 2: Saints, Ramble And Sensation!**

Jazzology JCD-290 *As above.* 3–10/49.

None of Nichols's many records of Dixieland for Capitol have made it to CD so far. Jazzology's two sets of Lang–Worth transcriptions find Red and his team in good spirits, playing the kind of thing he did for the rest of his life. Those who see him as incontrovertibly wooden will be surprised to hear the soft-toned elegance of some of his playing and, though much of each disc is straight Dixieland, they play it with enough flexibility to give it freshness, and there's a nice chance to hear Joe Rushton's bass sax. Sound is clear, if a little metallic at times.

Giancarlo Nicolai

GUITAR

Swiss guitarist, here leading a group otherwise dominated by guest John Tchicai.

***** The Giancarlo Nicolai Trio And John Tchicai**

Leo CD LR 164 *Nicolai; John Tchicai (ts, ss, v); Thomas Durst (b); Ueli Muller (d).* 7/86–11/87.

Hard not to hear this as John Tchicai-plus-rhythm. Apart from on the closing track (the trio, 'Puppetdreams', recorded a year earlier than the rest), it's the Danish saxophonist who dominates with his blaring, folksy sound and wild, Aylerish excursions. The story behind the session is that during the winter of 1985–6 Tchicai was in Switzerland, *en route* to Liechtenstein for a concert but lacking his regular Danish band, who were snowbound. A group centred on Swiss guitarist Nicolai was convened, and this turned out to be so successful that Tchicai decided to repeat the experiment a year later. Nicolai is no more conventional a jazz instrumentalist than Tchicai himself, preferring big, open sweeps of sound to carefully defined lines, moving easily between a free polytonality and an all-out atonality. On 'Trilogia' and highlighted as leader on 'Puppetdreams', he manages to create a richly dimensioned sound-environment without grandstanding. Tchicai composes most of the material, ranging between the almost naïve simplicity of 'Nu Skal du Komme' and the rasping ferocity of 'Mushi Miyake'.

Lennie Niehaus (born 1929)

ALTO SAXOPHONE

Much of the St Louis-born saxophonist's career has been spent as a studio musician and arranger and as a composer for film and television. He studied music in California and had two stints with Stan Kenton before becoming a fixture on the West Coast cool scene. Though more important as a composer than as a performer, Lennie has an engagingly conversational approach to phrasing and solo development.

*****(*) Zounds**

Original Jazz Classics OJCCD 1892 *Niehaus; Stu Williamson (t); Frank Rosolino (tb); Bob Enevoldsen (vtb); Vincent DeRosa (frhn); James McAllister (tba); Jack Montrose, Bill Perkins (ts); Pepper Adams, Bob Gordon (bs); Lou Levy (p); Monty Budwig, Red Mitchell (b); Mel Lewis, Shelly Manne (d).* 8/54, 12/56.

****** The Octet No. 2: Volume 3**

Original Jazz Classics OJC 1767 *Niehaus; Bill Holman (t); Stu Williamson (t, vtb); Bob Enevoldsen (tb); Jimmy Giuffre (reeds); Pete Jolly (p); Monty Budwig (b); Shelly Manne (d).* 1–2/55.

***** The Quintets & Strings**

Original Jazz Classics OJCCD 1858 *Niehaus; Stu Williamson (t); Bill Perkins (ts); Bob Gordon (bs); Hampton Hawes (p); Monty Budwig (b); Shelly Manne (d); strings.* 3–4/55.

The smooth West Coast veneer belies a substantial portfolio of imaginative compositions and standards arrangements. He worked with Kenton before and after a period in the service and, though much of his recorded work is in the rather anonymous context of Stan's reed sections, his own most distinctive work has tended to be for mid-size bands. The two contrasting octets on *Zounds* are both meticulously balanced, horns and woodwinds in opposition. Of the two groups, the December 1956 octet with Rosolino, Perkins and Adams is by far the more accomplished; its readings of Hampton Hawes's 'The Sermon', the first track on the disc, is also the most arresting, though a later reworking of Miles Davis's 'Four' by the same personnel is almost as good. *The Octet* is excellent, full of inventive and sophisticated arrangements that make up for a hint of blandness and propriety in the performances. Sadly, these fine sessions coincided with the beginning of a second stint with the Stan Kenton band. Niehaus also appears on a wilderness of Kenton albums (though there's little point looking for him there), after which he turned his music into a day job, writing and arranging for television and the movies. A loss and a lack. Only one of four quintet records is currently available, and it's not the best, though presumably the best-selling. It's almost entirely a standards session, and Perkins is again the star turn, though the West Coast rhythm section are hard to fault on any count. 'All The Things You Are' is a superb version and the brisk, breezy 'Star Eyes' would charm down the constellations.

***** Patterns**

Fresh Sound FSR CD 100 *Niehaus; Bill Perkins (ts, bs, ss, bcl); Frank Strazzeri (p); Tom Warrington (b); Joe LaBarbera (d).* 8/89.

***** Seems Like Old Times**

Fresh Sound FSR CD 5016 *As above, except add Jack Nimitz (bs).* 89.

The Fresh Sound albums help to fill out a skimpy list, and they underline how thoroughly the saxophonist enjoyed playing in later years, having spent much of his career either behind the scenes or in the anonymity of big-band woodwind sections. As ever, Perkins does the work of ten men on these, but the revelation is Warrington, a huge-voiced bass player with an inexhaustible stock of ideas. The second album is weightier and more obviously arranged, with the three saxophones often functioning as a unit. Niehaus's compositions are quietly challenging, and on a piece like 'Yesterday's Gardenias' (which might contain a tiny Billie Holiday reference) he shows how well he can combine advanced harmonic ideas with straightforwardly beautiful melody.

Christina Nielsen

TENOR AND SOPRANO SAXOPHONES

A Swedish-Danish partnership which co-leads this otherwise all-Swedish quintet.

***** Heartflower**

Dragon DRCD 319 *Soderqvist; Nielsen; Mathias Algotsson (p); Hans Backenroth (b); Johan Löfcrantz (d).* 10/97.

The result of 'a spontaneous friendship between two people, despite their different temperaments' – on the evidence of the playing, Soderqvist is the more careful one, Nielsen the more impulsive. This is accomplished post-bop played with great naturalness, if not always a tremendous amount of flair. The improvising tends towards the measured, a mood underlined by Algotsson's attractively cultured piano; but the themes (nine originals by the principals, and no standards or blues as a safety net, either) are full of interesting propositions.

P. A. Nilsson

SOPRANO AND BARITONE SAXOPHONES, ELECTRONICS

Norwegian saxophonist investigating the parameters of jazz with free music and electronic composition.

***** Random Rhapsody**

LJ LJCD 5207 *Nilsson; Anders Jormin (b); Peeter Uuskyla (d); Karin Krog (v).* 8/92.

Nilsson is a saxophonist with an abiding interest in electronics. All the 12 pieces here are the result of various procedures involving computers and electronics: rhythms generated by fractals, quantized pulses, acoustic improvisations converted to electrical ones and – in the sole instance of Jormin's involvement – a bass solo created on the computer but played back by a bassist! Perhaps inevitably, the results are more like a workshop notebook than a record, but there are some fascinating bits and pieces. Krog's three features use her voice to startling ends, the bubbling 'Bifurcations' sounds like saxman meets Kraftwerk, and the desolate closer, 'Paleolitic Hunt', is even more stark and wind-blasted than one of John Surman's tone-poems.

Bern Nix

GUITAR

Still best known as a member of Ornette Coleman's Prime Time group, this is the only own-name project by the guitarist.

****** Alarms And Excursions**

New World 80437 *Nix; Fred Hopkins (b); Newman Baker (d).* 1/93.

After a dozen years with Ornette Coleman's Prime Time band, Nix is well versed in the philosophy and practice of harmolodics. The final track on *Alarms And Excursions* is an exceedingly useful point of reference for anyone who still hasn't come to terms with Ornette's rather circular logic. On 'Boundaries', Nix dispenses with conventional tonality and blurs bar-lines to the point where the music, though still intensely propulsive, has none of the expected reference-points. Very different from the abstract, pulseless approach of the avant-garde, Nix's strategy may be one of the first successful expressions of harmolodic ideas since Ronald Shannon Jackson's *Decode Yourself*. It's a great deal more listenable, an exciting, headlong set that constantly refers back to earlier jazz, as on 'Z Jam Blues', the standard transcription, 'Just Friends', or the boppish 'Acuity', which is played as a duet with the magnificent Baker. At the opposite extreme is 'Ballad For L', on which Hopkins takes a leading part, gradually withdrawing as Nix reconstructs the theme at an ever higher register. This is essential listening for anyone who has followed Ornette's latter-day progress with interest or puzzlement. Nix's vivid extensions of guitar technique, most of them without the use of electronic technology, are an additional dimension, contributing to a very fine record indeed.

Steve Noble

PERCUSSION

A familiar figure in London's free-music scene since the mid-'80s, Noble has worked frequently in partnership with pianist Alex Maguire, as well as in numerous other configurations.

*****(*) Ya Boo, Reel And Rumble**

Incus CD06 *Noble; Alex Ward (cl, as).* 3/89, 7/90.

***** Bad Gleichenberg Festival Edition: Volume 3**

Jazz Live n/n *Noble; Oren Marshall (tba); Steve Buckley (as, bcl, whistle).* 94.

Steve Noble came to wider notice during the 'Company Week' of 1987, when he joined one of Derek Bailey's most adventurous collectives for a week of improvisation. At the same time, Noble and his occasional partner, Alex Maguire, were winning a reputation in the London free-music community for improvised performances that combined intense, sometimes ferocious interplay with a rare infusion of wit. Another partner, reeds player Alex Ward, was only in his mid-teens when the first of the performances of *Ya Boo, Reel And Rumble* were recorded. A virtuosic player with a strong background in modernist formal repertoire, he plays with considerable authority, matched move for move by Noble's quick-witted percussion. The opening '8th And How' may still be Noble's best performance on record. The other CD is a live concert from the Bad Gleichenberg Festival of 1994. Much of the record is taken up with solo material, which means that the two others demand equal billing, but it really is Noble's session. He energizes it and brings it a focus and intelligence that his partners cannot quite muster.

Mike Nock (born 1940)

PIANO

A New Zealander by birth, Nock came to the USA in the 1960s and stayed until 1985: he is on some records by Yusef Lateef and John Handy from the 1960s, and he tried jazz-rock before reverting to acoustic music in the '70s. He has lately been making records in the USA again and has taken on A&R duties for the Naxos Jazz label.

****(*) In Out And Around**

Timeless SJP 119 *Nock; Michael Brecker (ts); George Mraz (b); Al Foster (d).* 7/78.

**** Ondas**

ECM 1220 *Nock; Eddie Gomez (b); Jon Christensen (d).* 11/81.

Nock's earlier music is either out of catalogue or is scattered on rather obscure albums. His more straightforward hard-bop style is eschewed on the trio record for a much windier, overcooked method which seeks to feel every note and succeeds in communicating very little. Gomez sounds bemused, and it's left to the Christensen to find a line to earth for Nock's airy meanderings. Brecker gets off some good solos on *In Out And Around*. In a subsidiary role, Nock sounds fine: like many a journeyman pianist, he sounds vulnerable only when exposed to a solo spotlight.

****(*) Dark & Curious**
VeraBra vBR 2074 *Nock; Tim Hopkins (ts, rec); Cameron Undy (b); Andrew Dickeson (d).* 90.

***** Touch**
Birdland BL001 *Nock (p solo).* 7/93.

Two bulletins from Nock's Antipodean base. Hopkins sounds like an accomplished saxophonist, with a sanded, morose tone and a way of undulating long lines through the rhythm section, but there's something wearisome about the way the quartet plays: it's too ponderous, too full of portent, even when worthwhile ideas – as on a steady, well-turned piece like 'Resurrection' – are clearly there. Nock's own improvisations suggest that he remains a little too hung-up on his delivery. Yet the solo album shows a clearing away of some of his affectations. He still plays with an effortful tread, and rhythmically these pieces seem lame, but for once his seeking out of the essence of the tune sounds effective. The stiffly elegiac 'Django', and the rolling lyricism of (ahem) 'The Sibylline Fragrance Of Gardenias' are personal and absorbing.

*****(*) Not We But One**
Naxos Jazz 86006-2 *Nock; Anthony Cox (b); Tony Reedus (d).* 4/96.

Nock has taken on some A&R duties for the new Naxos Jazz label, and the least they could do was give him his own session. Perhaps surprisingly, it's one of the best of the lot. With the unlikely team of Cox and Reedus, Nock reinvents his trio style: spacious, meditative pieces are measured out with sublime good judgement. A tune like 'Kiss' is traversed with a decision that Nock has rarely found on record before. Reedus has never played so subtly, rustling at a bell tree as often as he's hitting his snare, and Cox finds a noble role in his bass lines. Three apparently improvised pieces have the same inevitable flow as several originals by Nock.

***** Ozboppin'**
Naxos Jazz 86019-2 *Nock; Phil Slater (t, flhn); Tim Hopkins (ts); Cameron Undy (b); David Goodman (d).* 1/98.

***** The Waiting Game**
Naxos Jazz 86048-2 *Nock; Marty Ehrlich (ss, as, cl, bcl).* 7/99.

The title of the quintet record is a giveaway that this is Nock's homegrown band, caught on local turf in Sydney. They're a sturdy group and Nock brought some excellent originals to the date, with 'Five'll Getcha!' particularly memorable. Nothing else much stays in the mind, but they know their stuff.

With Ehrlich, Nock sets a chamberish tone. The title-piece is a beautiful duet on a bittersweet twist of melody, and there's some spirited playing on 'Break Time' and the improvised 'Three Postcards'. They fare less well on the Brubeck and James P. Johnson themes, sounding almost laboured at times, and some of the tracks fetch up in an unsuitably lugubrious tone.

Soren Norbo

PIANO

Danish contemporary pianist.

***** Soren Norbo & Joakim Milder**
Music Mecca 2012-2 *Norbo; Joakim Milder (ts).* 6–11/92.

Finding their way in and out of ten standards, most of the melodies bleeding into each other, Norbo and Milder suggest Konitz–Bley or Konitz–Solal in the way they prise open the material: cool but not perfunctory, this is thematic improvising of a very high order, the slight fog in Milder's tone accentuated by the library surroundings. A shame that the three free pieces are merely doleful, and rather let down the rest of the record.

Caecilie Norby

VOCAL

After working with Danish rock groups, Norby moved into a jazz idiom with her debut album for Blue Note, although she still draws material from some rock composers.

****** Caecilie Norby**
Blue Note 832222-2 *Norby; Randy Brecker (t); Rick Margitza (ss); Scott Robinson (ts); Ben Besiakov (p, org); Lars Jansson, Niels Lan Doky (p); Jakob Foscher (g); Lennart Ginman (b); Billy Hart (d).* 9/94.

*****(*) My Corner Of The Sky**
Blue Note 8968-2 *Norby; Randy Brecker (flhn); Michael Brecker (ts); Scott Robinson (f); David Kikoski, Lars Jansson (p, org); Joey Calderazzo (p); Lennart Gunman, Lars Danielsson (b); Terri Lyne Carrington, Alex Riel (d).* 96.

The Danish singer's international debut is distinguished by a brilliant production by Niels Lan Doky. He chooses an ingenious setting for almost every tune, deploying a crack team of players with spontaneous assurance, and the rich detail of the studio sound is a further embellishment. Inside all this, Norby isn't intimidated once. She has a big, rather awkward voice which she can use with great dramatic force, and on ballads she finds a low-key but steely power, with nothing downcast entering the interpretation. The songs are a fascinating lot, with initially unpromising things like Rod McKuen's 'I've Been Town' and Jimmy Webb's 'By The Time I Get To Phoenix' surprising successes, and a couple of oblique originals adding a further dimension.

The follow-up, *My Corner Of The Sky*, is more of a mixed success. This time the material is a shade too eclectic for the record's own good. She makes a fist of David Bowie's 'Life On Mars', for instance, but all it tends to display is how meaningless the lyric is; and Sting's 'Set Them Free' is no more than high-class jazz-pop. Yet there are again some impressive successes, such as her setting of Wayne Shorter's 'African Fairytale', the stark

'Suppertime' and 'The Right To Love', a beautiful lyric impeccably handled. And 'Snow' transfers her roots into a plausible New York framework. Dedicated fans might wish to try and locate the Japanese edition of the album, which includes 'Guess Who I Saw Today' as a bonus track.

Peter Nordahl (born 1966)

PIANO

Swedish pianist at work in the post-bop mainstream.

***** Crazy She Calls Me**
Sittel SITCD 9232 *Nordahl; Patrik Boman (b); Leif Wennerstrom (d). 11/95.*

Nordahl claims Wynton Kelly and Horace Silver as his masters, but one is reminded more of Red Garland and some of his trio sessions for Prestige. When they do 'Dear Old Stockholm', the analogy seems hard to refute. Still, Nordahl has an impeccable touch, and since he loves Stephen Sondheim and includes four of that composer's tunes – all rarities in terms of jazz interpretation – this trio date has its own character. The rather woody sound suits what's an old-fashioned record, and Boman and Wennerstrom play with selfless support.

Fredrik Norén

DRUMS

The Swedish answer to Art Blakey's Jazz Messengers, the Fredrik Norén Band was formed in 1978 and carries the flame for the region's hard bop.

***** City Sounds**
Mirrors MICD 001 *Norén; Magnus Broo (t); Robert Nordermark (ts); Torbjörn Gulz (p); Dan Berglund (b). 12/91.*

***** One Day In May**
Mirrors MICD 004 *As above, except Fredrik Ljungkvist (ts), Filip Augustson (b) replace Nordermark and Berglund; add Lina Nyberg (v). 5/95.*

*****(*) T**
Mirrors MICD 008 *Norén; Anders Garstedt (t); Jonas Kullhammar (ts); Daniel Karlsson (p); Torbjörn Zetterberg (b). 5/99.*

Norén's band is something of an institution at this point and, with his ever-changing line-up and steady evolution – not to mention his own push and shove from the kit – he deserves the title of Sweden's Jazz Messenger. These three are in a long line of records, lately for the Mirrors label. *City Sounds* is live, and the most dependent on mere good blowing, but the band is hot and, though it smoulders rather than burns, the best of it – as on Gulz's 'I'm Ready' – is more than good enough. *One Day In May* benefits from the piquant contrast of Broo's rather careful trumpet with the bluster of Ljungkvist's tenor. Nyberg comes in for a rather strangely tempestuous 'Someone To Watch Over Me'.

The best of the three – and evidence that Norén is quite capable of revitalizing his old format – is surely the latest, *T*. The leader's own 'Trane Mode' calls up a fiercely individual sequence of solos and, as the record progresses, it's clear that Fredrik has found some fresh voices again – both Garstedt and Kullhammar refuse to conform to the obvious dialects on their horns. As just one instance, the trumpeter's snapping improvisation on his own 'No Choice' really grabs the lapels. Excellent variations on the grand old formula, and plangently recorded too.

Charlie Norman

PIANO

A pioneer figure in post-war Swedish jazz, Norman was playing a kind of small-group swing at the time of his first recordings in 1943. Bop informs his later work to some extent, but he remains basically a mainstream man.

****(*) Charles Norman 1943–1947**
Ancha 9704-2 *Norman; Olle Hedberg, Rolf Ericson (t); Sven Hedberg (tb); Sven Gustafsson (as); Nils Blucker (ts); Kurt Johansson, Sten Carlberg, Kurt Warngren (g); Simon Brehm (b); Henry Wallin, Rolf Stahlberg, Pedro Biker, Sven Bollhem (d); Naemi Briese (v). 6/43–5/47.*

A little Swedish jump music, courtesy of Charlie Norman's first recordings. Nothing whatsoever of pressing interest, and some of it is a howler, notably Naemi Briese's vocal on 'Jitterboogie'. On the other hand, nobody's disgraced, Blucker and the Hedbergs have their moments, Ericson comes in for a couple of sessions and Charlie himself ran a good ship. Good remastering from originals which must be almost unheard outside Sweden.

***** Papa Piano**
Phontastic NCD 8830 *Norman; Arne Wilhelmsson (b); Ronnie Gardiner (d); Johan Lofcrantz (perc). 6/93.*

*****(*) Charlie Norman And His Aces Featuring John Hogman**
Phontastic NCD 8838 *As above, except add John Hogman (ts), Lars Erstrand (vib); omit Lofcrantz. 8/95.*

Here is a senior member of Sweden's mainstream school playing for pure enjoyment. Norman's spry good humour and sense of mischief inform all of the 16 miniatures on display on *Papa Piano*: he has 'Anything Goes' teetering on a locomotive stride rhythm, for instance, and has it over and done with in less than a minute and a half. 'The Eternal Three' and 'Tribute To Swais' are interesting originals, 'March Of The Dalecarlian Grooms' is a silly one, and he acknowledges his debt to Erroll Garner's records with a good-natured 'Misty'.

All great fun, but the concerts caught on the second disc are even more satisfying. Charlie's introduction to an indecently good-humoured 'Honeysuckle Rose' shows him in fine spirits, but there are touching and even profound moments elsewhere on the CD, and the playing of the four old pros – extraordinary that Norman and Erstrand had hardly ever played together before – is impeccable. Young pro Hogman comes on like the icing on the cake, and he's marvellous: sample his uncluttered, simple reading of the tenorman's test-case, 'Body And Soul'.

Norrbotten Big Band

GROUP

Based in Lulea, this Swedish big band has been in existence for some years and has a policy of appointing guest MDs.

***** Animations**

Phono Suecia PSCD 75 *Bo Strandberg, Dan Johansson, Magnus Ekholm, Magnus Plumppu (t, flhn); P.O Svanstrom, Magnus Puls, Tony Andersson, Anders Wiborg, Bjorn Hjangsel (tb); Hakan Brostrom, Christer Johnsson (ss, as); Jan Thelin (as, cl); Mats Garberg (ts, f); Bengt Ek (ts); Per Moberg (bs); Hans Andersson (ky); Hans-Ola Ericsson (org); Johan Granstrom (b); Christer Sjöström, Lennart Gruvstedt (d); Kjell Westerberg (perc); Orjan Dahlstrom (cond, arr, ky).* 9/92–2/93.

***** Norrbotten Big Band Featuring Nils Landgren**

Caprice CAP 21494 *As above, except add Tapio Maunuvaara (t, flhn), Nils Landgren (tb, v), Hans (ky), Johan Norberg (g).* 2/93–2/95.

***** Future North**

Double-Time DTRCD-140 *As above, except add Tim Hagans (t), Christian Spering (b), Jukkis Uotila (d); omit Plumppu, Andersson, Wiborg, Johnsson, Andersson, Ericsson, Sjöström, Gruvstedt, Westerberg, Dahlstrom, Norberg.* 6/97.

Demanding big-band charts played with panache and fastidious clarity by this typically impressive Swedish orchestra. Orjan Dahlstrom leads the first record and does most of the writing. *Animations* features two long works, a series of pieces to go with the silent film, *Witchcraft Through The Ages*, and the title-work, a full-scale concerto for pipe organ and big band. It's a little hard to see how the film scores really fit with Benjamin Christensen's startling old film, since they actually sound like an unlinked sequence of charts, but there's no denying the impact. 'Animations' is an impressive if finally improbable blending of the organ and the band: Klas Persson cleverly mixes the two factors, but the music is more a matter of competition than integration. The Caprice disc (which also includes a single left-over track from the previous sessions) is a sometimes unconvincing mixture, with a few rhythms straying towards rock. Landgren is the main soloist, but his singing on 'Stone Free' and 'Ticket To Ride' wasn't the smartest of ideas and the best music is on the more thoughtful scores: a big, punchy 'Impressions', a sonorous Philip Catherine tune, 'Twice A Week', and Landgren's mellifluous trip through 'The Midnight Sun Never Sets'.

Tim Hagans was an interesting choice as guest arranger/soloist, a post he held in 1996. The resulting record is an impressionistic programme of charts, suggesting his reaction to both the orchestra and its native environment in northern Europe. Some of it, such as 'Twist And Out' and 'Waking Iris', is almost too clever even for this expert band, but when Hagans settles things down a little – as in the impressive three-part title-piece – he does better.

Walter Norris

PIANO

Norris is a remarkable composer and performer, still discovering new areas of activity within what had begun to sound like an exhausted idiom. He is unfailingly romantic (though he might prefer the designation Neo-Baroque) and is as likely to cite a Bach chord progression as a Broadway tune, often in the same chorus.

*****(*) Drifting**

Enja 2044 *Norris; George Mraz, Aladar Pege (b).* 8/74–5/78.

***** Stepping On Cracks**

Progressive PRO 7039 *As above, except omit Pege; add Ronnie Bedford (d).* 78.

*****(*) Live At Maybeck Recital Hall, Volume 4**

Concord CCD 4425 *Norris (p solo).* 4/90.

A fine and sensitive pianist who worked with Ornette Coleman in the days when the saxophonist still had a use for piano players, Norris has a moody, intense delivery best suited to introspection. His favoured recording format – without drummer – heightens a sense of almost static harmony, though Norris can swing when he chooses. Stylistically, he is probably closest to George Mraz's better-known piano partner, Tommy Flanagan. A CD reissue brings together the original *Drifting* with a slightly later album, *Synchronicity*, another duo session but featuring Aladar Pege in place of the wonderful George Mraz. It's Mraz who really lifts the earliest of these sessions, subtly adumbrating Norris's occasional uncertainties. The versions of 'Spacemaker' and 'A Child Is Born', both Norris originals, are more clearly articulated than the performances on *Synchronicity* and the LP-only *Winter Rose*, which has now drifted (so to speak) out of the catalogue. Mraz's inside-out familiarity with a standard like 'Spring Can Really Hang You Up The Most' gives it a singing confidence. Pege's virtuosity (impressive enough to win him the late Charles Mingus's role in the Mingus Dynasty) sometimes clutters essentially simple themes and is in marked contrast to Mraz's clearness of line.

We are unsure whether the Progressive album still has wide availability. It is interesting not least as a somewhat rare trio with drummer, certainly of this period, though once again Norris puts greater emphasis on his interactions with Mraz. Well worth hunting down.

Norris's Maybeck recital is further out than most in the series. His reworkings of 'The Song Is You', with its softly ambiguous introduction, and of 'Body And Soul', which Norris claims was influenced by Teddy Edwards's version, are strikingly original. On his own 'Scrambled' and 'Modus Vivendi' he has the Maybeck Yamaha singing in unfamiliar accents. A delightful record.

****(*) Lush Life**

Concord CCD 4457 *Norris; Neil Swainson (b); Harold Jones (d).* 9/90.

*****(*) Sunburst**

Concord CCD 4486 *Norris; Joe Henderson (ts); Larry Grenadier (b); Mike Hyman (d).* 8/91.

Henderson is one of the few saxophone players around who share Norris's fragile and very thoughtful lyricism. They do a masterful 'Naima' together, one that avoids all the dreary clichés that have attached themselves to Coltrane's love-theme. It's not at all clear that the two rhythm players are necessary to this music, but they have the good sense to maintain a lowish profile, accenting choruses and rounding off each number. It would have been intriguing to have had just one track as a duet between saxophone and piano.

Swainson is such a gifted and tasteful player (very much in the line of Mraz and Pege) that by contrast he seems essential to the success of *Lush Life*. The problem here, ironically, is Norris, playing well below his best and resorting to pat and generalized forms rather than his usual incisive structures. Disappointing.

*****(*) Love Every Moment**

Concord CCD 4534 *Norris; Putter Smith (b); Larance Marable (d). 9–10/92.*

****** Hues Of Blues**

Concord CCD 4671 *Norris; George Mraz (b). 5/95.*

Hard to fault either of these records on any count, and they mark a fitting end to Norris's highly fruitful association with Concord. The title-tune of *Love Every Moment* is dedicated to a friend left widowed and is one of Norris's most affirmatively philosophical creations. For the rest, apart from 'Moonglazed' (which has obvious associations with 'Sunhazed' and other pieces) and 'Postscript Blues', the material is most repertory. 'Blue Lester' is unexpectedly funky, but infused with Pres's oblique personality. 'Laura' is a delightful ballad creation which gives room to the very fine bassist to stretch himself a little.

Smith is clearly not as rounded a player as George Mraz, but then few are. The duos on *Hues Of Blues* are almost telepathic. The title-song is a quite remarkable reworking of the sound-colour and rhythmic subdivisions of the slow blues, almost a suite of pieces rather than a single conception. More technical wizardry on 'Backbone Mode', so called because the performer has to cross hands constantly. Norris's love of complex waltz patterns emerges this time on 'Orchids In Green' which, like the closing 'Afterthoughts', is played unaccompanied. A master at work; anyone interested in the longevity of jazz piano should pay close attention.

****** From Another Star**

Sunburst SRCD 2001 2 *Norris; Mike Richmond (b). 10/98.*

Norris now has his own record label, perhaps aware that his approach is technically too focused for the average, standard-driven programming of mainstream imprints. As might be expected, he concentrates very largely on new material. The album opens with the title-track in a highly complex but very logical metre which imparts a symmetry to every measure, no matter how extended. 'Images Enhanced' is definitive Norris, harmonically rich and elusive without being unapproachable; Richmond maintains a steady, understated presence, touching in pedal notes and keeping the rhythm open. Two tunes in the middle of the record mark a switch of emphasis, not so much to standard or traditional material as to historical foreshadowings of what Walter has always been about. One is Sammy Myzel's delightful song, 'Yesterday's Gardenia', and the other is a chord sequence of Bach's melded with the standard song, 'No Moon At All', to create 'Elysium'. Later tracks are either reworkings of earlier compositions like 'Sunhazed' (formerly 'Enkephalins') or formal harmonic *études* (like 'Dark Brows'), and the album ends with a brisk, thoughtful take on Dizzy Gillespie's arrangement of 'Tiger Rag'.

Northern Arizona University Jazz Ensemble

GROUP

One of the numerous American college jazz orchestras, it makes occasional records, presumably of promising students.

***** The Year Of The Cow**

Walrus CDWR-4506 *James Gregg, Matt Walsh, Ralph Cuda, Nick Cooper, Bob Woosley (t); Steve McAllister, Danny McQuillin, Mike Hilditch, Fred Krueger, Jesse Ribyat, Peter Vivona (tb); Jason Collins, Jim Hughens, Jason Kerr, Jeff Kay (saxes); Stephanie Galloway (p); Rob Hutchinson (b); Frank Rosaly (d); Barb Burzynski (perc). 5/93.*

***** Herding Cats**

Sea Breeze SBV-4508 *As above, except David Reed, Chris Ecklund (t), Coln Mason, Kenson Nishino, Joshua Cook (saxes), Jorg Brosemann (p), Geoffrey Miller (g), Louis Presti (b), Dan Smithiger (perc) replace Gregg, Woosley, Ribyat, Collins, Hughens, Kerr, Galloway, Hutchinson and Burzynski. 5/94.*

The NAU Ensemble play their jazz with great spirit and panache and, while this kind of music ends up as something of an exercise in muscle-building, at least these records have some spit along with the polish. None of the soloists stands out, yet all of them impress; none of the charts is genuinely memorable, yet each holds the attention while it's being played. The penmanship is by genre favourites like Bob Florence, Tom Kubis and Matt Catingub, and there is a degree of inspiration along with the mere ingenuity: try Florence's explosive (yet carefully controlled) 'BBC' on the second disc, or the peppery section interplay on Kubis's 'Slauson Cutoff' on the earlier set. Each is recorded and mixed with pristine clarity.

Kevin Norton

DRUMS, MARIMBA

A composer-drummer and sometime sideman in Anthony Braxton's groups, Norton leads a prodigious Ensemble of his own, responsible for two of the three discs below.

*****(*) Integrated Variables**

CIMP 121 *Norton; George Cartwright (ss, as, ts); Mark Dresser (b). 7/96.*

****** Knots**

Music & Arts CD-1033 *Norton; Bob DeBellis (cl, bcl, as); David Krakauer (cl); David Bindman (cl, ts); Tomas Ulrich (clo); Joe Fonda (b). 9–10/97.*

***** For Guy Debord**

Barking Hoop 001 *As above, except Anthony Braxton (as, cbcl) replaces Krakauer.* 9/98.

Norton is that rarity, a free drummer who's also a precision merchant. On *Integrated Variables* he gets a fireball momentum going on many of the tracks, but it's always ready to stop on a dime, switch gears or change direction. His rolls are pristine in their exactness and when he moves over to the marimba, which is often, he plays with the same attention to detail. This is one of the best of the CIMP albums: Norton is well matched with the imaginative Cartwright and the virtuosic Dresser, and their music is quick and funny as well as passionate. There's a lot of it, at over 70 minutes, but very few dead-ends. The unfiltered sound works well for this group – the music sounds raw and live without getting unduly messy.

Knots is by Norton's Ensemble, and presents a more considered sound – detailed and balanced compositions, though the players have sufficient space to let fly when they're asked to improvise. 'Hammer Or Anvil?' has the meticulous feel of composed chamber music, carefully weighted around the colours of the horns and the changing dynamics of Norton's own rhythms (including an overdubbed vibes solo). There are quite brilliant treatments of two Monk tunes – 'Epistrophy', its melody camouflaged by alternative lines drawn from one of Monk's own solos, then blown open by Bindman's blitzkrieg tenor solo, and 'Brilliant Corners', a tough challenge to start with but here evolved into a scintillating essay on the composer's rhythm-plan. 'Three Movements For Solo And Ensemble' is a setting for guest clarinettist Krakauer, who suggests klezmer-like ebullience, and the swing beats of 'Walking The Dogma' frame horn solos that eventually send the music somewhere else entirely. Very rich, and this is only half of a fine and thought-provoking record.

For Guy Debord is a nine-part piece in dedication to the French *provocateur* of that name, and it's a concert recording with a rare sighting of Braxton as sideman. A continuous 37-minute piece, it has many of the ingenuities of the studio date but a rougher ambience, and somehow Braxton's presence unbalances the group: his trademark timbres seem to sideline Bindman and DeBellis, and the multifarious threads of *Knots* seem less abundant (to be fair, it is but a single piece in what is clearly an ongoing and ambitious corpus of work in progress). Admirers of the first two discs will surely want to hear this, though – and whatever Norton comes up with next.

Red Norvo (1908–99)

XYLOPHONE, VIBRAPHONE

Born Kenneth Norville in Beardstown, Illinois, Red started out playing marimba and graduated to vibes playing without vibrato and with a light and almost delicate sound. He was married to singer Mildred Bailey and worked with her for some years. Attracted by bebop, he managed to synthesize swing with the new language of jazz.

*****(*) Dance Of The Octopus**

Hep CD 1044 *Norvo; Stewart Pletcher (t); Eddie Sauter, Jack Jenney (tb); Jimmy Dorsey, Donald McCook, Artie Shaw (cl); Benny Goodman (bcl); Charlie Barnet (ts); Bobby Johnson, Dick McDonough, George Van Eps (g); Fulton McGrath, Teddy Wilson (p); Artie Bernstein, Hank Hayland, Pete Peterson (b); Billy Gussak, Gene Krupa, Bob White, Maurice Purtill (d); Mae Questal (v).* 4/33–3/36.

***** Red Norvo And His Orchestra, 1933-1936**

Classics 1085 *Similar to above.* 4/33–2/36.

***** Jivin' The Jeep**

Hep CD 1019 *Norvo; Bill Hyland, Stewart Pletcher, Louis Mucci, George Wendt (t); Leo Moran, Eddie Sauter (tb); Frank Simeone (as); Slats Long, Hank D'Amico (cl, as); Len Goldstein (as); Charles Lanphere (as, ts); Herbie Haymer (ts); Joe Liss, Bill Miller (p); Dave Barbour, Red McGarvey (g); Pete Robinson (b); Mo Purtill (d); Mildred Bailey, Lew Hurst (v).* 36–37.

*****(*) Red Norvo On Dial**

Spotlite SPJ 127 *Norvo; Dizzy Gillespie (t); Charlie Parker (as); Flip Phillips (ts); Teddy Wilson (p); Slam Stewart (b); J.C Heard, Specs Powell (d).* 6/45.

*****(*) The Red Norvo Trios**

Prestige 24108 *Norvo; Jimmy Raney, Tal Farlow (g); Red Mitchell (b).* 53–54.

*****(*) Red Norvo Trio**

Original Jazz Classics OJC 641 *Norvo; Jimmy Raney (g); Red Mitchell (b).* 53, 54.

*****(*) Music To Listen To Red Norvo By**

Original Jazz Classics OJC 1015 *Norvo; Buddy Collette (f); Bill Smith (cl); Barney Kessel (g); Red Mitchell (b); Shelly Manne (d).* 54.

***** Red Plays The Blues**

RCA 2113034 *Norvo; Harry 'Sweets' Edison, Don Fagerquist, Ed Leddy, Ray Linn, Don Paladino (t); Ray Sims (tb); Willie Smith (as); Harold Land, Ben Webster (ts); Chuck Gentry (bs); Jimmy Rowles (p); Jimmy Wyble (g); Bob Carter, Red Wooten (b); Bill Douglas, Mel Lewis (d); Helen Humes (v).* 55.

***** Live From The Blue Gardens**

Musicmasters 65090 *Norvo; Jimmy Saiko, Bob Kennedy, Jack King (t); Eddie Bert, Abe Noel, Leo Conners (tb); Freddy Artzberger (as); Sal Dettore (as, cl); Johnny Mazet (ts); Sam Spumberg (ts, ob, eng hn); Jimmy Gemus (bs, f); Bob Kitsis (p); Joe Kawchak (b); Frank Vesley (d); Helen Ward, Kay Allen, Fran Snyder (v).* 8/89.

Norvo's early recorded work, before he made the switch from xylophone to vibraharp, illustrates the problem of placing so self-effacing an instrument in a conventional jazz line-up; it's sometimes difficult to separate technical limitations and compromises from conscious dynamic strategies in Norvo's recorded work. The material on the xylophonic Heps (there used to be an Affinity compilation with the self-explanatory title, *Knock On Wood*, and Classics have now got on the case) is generally pretty good, though inevitably much of the interest stems from the fantastic line-ups Norvo commanded as a youngster; compare the rather drab arrangements and unconvincing soloing on *Live From The Blue Gardens*. The last year of the war was a good one for Norvo. The super-session with the young Gillespie and Parker from 1945 is a significant moment in the development of bebop and the music that came after it. Though as ragged as any jam session, it is full of life and energy.

In those early, 'hands-off' days, Norvo frequently encountered engineers who would unilaterally boost the sound on quieter numbers or adjust the balances to accord with conventional expectations. Most of those were overturned in the 1950–51 trio in which Charles Mingus was the outwardly unlikely replacement for Red Kelly. Just as Norvo made a pioneering contribution to the use of vibraphone in jazz, so too did the early trios contribute enormously to the development of a style of 'cool' or 'chamber' jazz that became dominant much later in the decade. One of the more significant aspects of the early trio (it may also reflect the bassist's personality to some extent, particularly in the context of an otherwise white group) is the unprecedentedly prominent role assigned to Mingus. Unfortunately, the Savoy material is awaiting a new edition.

The later trios with Raney and Mitchell are much less obviously adventurous, though again it's the bassist's singing lines that carry much of the interest. Sooner or later when dealing with so-called 'chamber jazz', the question of its supposed 'pretentiousness' is bound to come into play. Norvo's 1954 quintet with Buddy Collette on flute and Barney Kessel on guitar strongly recalls fellow-member Chico Hamilton's sophisticated chamber jazz, with its soft, 'classical' textures and non-blues material. Titles like 'Divertimento In Four Movements' on (now vinyl-only and scarce) *Music To Listen To Red Norvo By* are apt to be seen as red rags by hard-nosed boppers. It's clear, though, from the album title if not immediately from the music itself, that there is a hefty dose of humour in Norvo's work. Structurally, the 'Divertimento' is unexceptionable, with a beautiful division of parts and as lightweight as the genre demands. Other tracks, like 'Red Sails' and the boppish thematic puns of 'Rubricity', suggest a 'different' side to Norvo which is actually present throughout his work, even in his sixties.

Though by no means a one-dimensional figure, Norvo has held to a steady course from the early days of bebop to the beginnings of a swing revival in the 1960s and '70s. His technique is superb and prefigures much of Milt Jackson's best MJQ passage-work. The early trios are unquestionably the place to begin, but there's plenty of good music later and newcomers shouldn't be prejudiced by the instrumentation. Norvo plays modern jazz of a high order.

NRG Ensemble

GROUP

The band formed by Hal Russell persisted after his passing, mainly under the direction of saxophonists Williams and Vandermark.

*****(*) Calling All Mothers**

Quinnah Q05 *Mars Williams (ts, as, ss); Ken Vandermark (ts, cl, bcl); Brian Sandstrom (g, t, b); Kent Kessler (b, didjeridu); Steve Hunt (d, vib, mar, didjeridu).* 11/93.

***** This Is My House**

Delmark DE 485 *As above, except add Daniel Scanlan (vn), Don Meckley (short wave radio).* 1/95.

Hal Russell was nicknamed 'jazz's very own Charles Ives'. When he died in 1992, it was assumed that his group, the NRG Ensemble, would disappear with him, but it didn't. Everyone – players and producer Steve Lake alike – insist that this is not a 'ghost band'. Though Williams and Vandermark are understandably anxious to keep Russell's anarchic spirit alive, the Ensemble goes off in some fascinating directions of its own. Some of the material on both records is composed by the old fellow, but the bulk of it is attributed to Williams and Vandermark, and it's by no means subservient to anyone else's vision. The two saxophones blend – or decline to blend – with just the right mixture of harmony and dissonance. Vandermark is the main writer, contributing the long 'Bullseye Witness' to *This Is My House* and 'American Tan' to *Calling All Mothers*. In playing terms, Williams is closer to Russell's sound but he lacks the sheer waywardness and oddity. Two entertaining, effective albums, neither of them mainstream or unduly avant-garde, but both unmistakably in the spirit of Russell's best work; however, they are now best seen as early examples of Vandermark's work, which has in recent years been an explosion of creative activity.

Dick Oatts

ALTO AND TENOR SAXOPHONES

Raised in Iowa, Oatts is a latter-day bopper who saw service with Red Rodney in the trumpeter's late quintet, and in the Thad Jones–Mel Lewis Orchestra. He made some records with fellow Rodney sideman, pianist Garry Dial, but is now recording for Steeplechase as a leader, basing himself in the New England area.

*****(*) All Of Three**

Steeplechase SCCD 31422 *Oatts; Dave Santoro (b); James Oblon (d).* 4/96–1/97.

***** Standard Issue**

Steeplechase SCCD 31439 *As above, except add David Berkman (p).* 97.

*****(*) Simone's Dance**

Steeplechase SCCD 31458 *As above, except Bruce Barth (p) replaces Berkman.* 5/98.

Although Berkman and Barth play their parts on the two discs they appear on, this is really all about the trio of Oatts, Santoro and Oblon. Oatts has a classic bebop tone on alto (he picks up the tenor only occasionally) and his big, unwrinkled sound was born to fly across changes; but he builds a lot of what came after bop into his thinking, so there are often moments – as on the nearly free 'Single Line', on the trio disc – when he can sound very like the young Ornette Coleman, edging towards a free play of tonality. The three men work hard to find variations in their group sound throughout *All Of Three*, from a zydeco feel on one track to the stark march figures of 'In Love And Memory'. There's a lot of weight on Santoro, who gets a deal of solo space, but he acquits himself well enough. 'Alone Together' is sustained for over 11 minutes, and they aren't struggling.

Standard Issue is a live blowing date with six expansive workouts, five standards and a blues. Oblon really gives the quartet a push on the up-tempo tunes and it's hot and forthright music, if subject to the filler which seems unavoidable in such situations. Oatts plays the Keilworth straight alto on one track here, and he returns to it twice on the studio date, *Simone's Dance*. As he says in the sleeve-note, it gives him a funkier sound, the pitching reminiscent of a low soprano; on 'Reverse Locomotion', a mock-tribute to the Coltrane tune, only constructed backwards, his playing is superbly fired-up and inventive. Peter Kontrimas gives the quartet a big and convincing sound, and across the length of the date Oatts's playing is fierce and cultured in an even balance.

Hod O'Brien

PIANO

A veteran bebop pianist, O'Brien has surfaced only intermittently on record but made a handful of leadership dates in the '90s.

***** Opalessence**

Criss Cross Criss 1012 *O'Brien; Tom Harrell (t, flhn); Pepper Adams (bs); Ray Drummond (b); Kenny Washington (d); Stephanie Nakasan (v).* 9/84.

****(*) Ridin' High**

Reservoir RSR CD 116 *O'Brien; Ray Drummond (b); Kenny Washington (d).* 8/90.

***** So That's How It Is**

Reservoir RSR CD 155 *As above.* 9/97.

Forty years ago, Hod O'Brien made an impressive contribution to Belgian guitarist René Thomas's *Guitar Groove*, playing alongside mavericks like J.R. Monterose and Albert 'Tootie' Heath. Later years saw him associated with Chet Baker (on the Criss Cross *Blues For A Reason*) and with saxophonist Ted Brown, strong bop credentials with a label not exactly short of respectable pianists.

Unfortunately his work as leader hasn't matched up to his sterling reliability and propulsive strength as a sideman. His solos seem studied to the point of predictability and he suffers from an irritating odd-handedness that sees him switching almost on cue from 'rhythm' to 'lead' like an electric guitarist. With players of Harrell's elegance and with Adams beefing up the arrangements, *Opalessence* is the more interesting of the first two albums but, like the semi-precious sheen of the title, it seems all surface and no durability. The trio album reintroduces standards material. 'You And The Night And The Music' reflects O'Brien's innate romanticism, but at opposite extremes 'Willow Weep For Me' and 'Yardbird Suite' simply expose his limitations.

The return match on *So That's How It Is* gets by on the generous good humour of the playing and the players. O'Brien still touches no great depths and his phrases all seem to end up exactly where one expects, but it's a shapely act, and Drummond and Washington are the kind of gregarious professionals who are always good for a groove worth hearing.

Giorgio Occhipinti

PIANO

Italian pianist–composer with an amibitious agenda.

****** The Kaos Legend**

Leo LAB CD 012 *Occhipinti; Alberto Mandarini (t, flhn); Lauro Rosso (tb); Gianni Gebbia (as, ss); Eugenio Colombo (as, ss, f); Carlo Actis Dato (bcl, bs); Renato Geremia (vn); Giovanni Macioci (clo); Giuseppe Guarella (b); Vincenzo Mazzone (d, perc).* 10/93, 10/94.

Take our word for it, there is no need to be aware of or be distracted by the legend of primeval *kaos* to appreciate this remarkable record. It is, in any case, not a continuous performance, but two pieces from the studio and two from the Ibleo Festival. That two are live merely underlines what a thoroughly competent band this is and what excellent improvisers it includes. Of their number only Gebbia and Dato are otherwise discussed in these pages, and our enthusiasm for both speaks for itself. Occhipinti himself is not a dramatic soloist, though he does often generate considerable volume against the full ensemble. His style is difficult to pin down – which is probably a good thing. Do try *The Kaos Legend.* It is one of a kind.

Bill O'Connell

DRUMS

Drummer based in Chicago, leading modern big-band dates manned by studio pros.

****(*) Jazz Alive**

Sea Breeze CDSB-2056 *O'Connell; Chuck Kininmouth, Rex Richardson, Terry Connell, Jared Brame (t); David Gross, Edwin Williams, Dan Snyderman, Bill Curran (tb); Dave Creighton, John Schmitt, Michael Finnerty, Paul Kober, Ken Bender (saxes); Eric Scott (ky); Andy Meachum (g); Joe Bonadonna (b); Mike Marotta (perc); Sherrilyn Riley (v).* 11/93.

***** Unfinished Business**

Sea Breeze CDSB-2063 *O'Connell; Kirk Garrison, Jim Peterson, Steve O'Brien, Rex Richardson, Jared Brame (t); Mark Corey, Edwin Williams, Rich Lapka, Craig Kaucher (tb); Dave Creighton, Jim Johnson, Mark Tuttle, Mike Knauf, Kenny Bender (saxes); Eric Scott (p); John Elmquist (b); Sherrilyn Riley (v).* 9/94.

***** That Toddlin' Town**

Blue Birdland 72596 *O'Connell; Kirk Garrison, Terry Connell, Tito Carillo, Jim Peterson, Jared Brame (t); Russ Phillips, Mark Corey, Edwin Williams, David Gross (tb); Brad Payne (btb); Bob Frankich, Bill Horn, Ken Partyka, Mike Bazan, Brian Sjoertinga, Kent Lawson (saxes); Bobby Schiff, Ron Mills (p); Dave Ivaz (g); Steve Hashimoto, John Elmquist (b); Dave Rush (perc); Sherrilyn Riley, Byron Woods (v).* 5–9/97.

A Chicago-based outfit helmed by O'Connell, this big band seems to be made up of whichever local session players are available on the day – hence the dramatically different personnels in records only a year apart – yet their similarity says something about the generic path that contemporary big bands follow. There's nothing very striking or original about the first disc, and some of the scores sound glumly by-the-numbers, but the band hits a useful stride here and there and could (on this date) boast some interesting soloists – notably trombonist Gross, whose oddball turns on 'All Of Me' and 'I Get The Blues When It Rains' are refreshingly out of kilter. The second disc is a shade tighter, faster and more exciting, and some of the charts have an independent life: solid filler for ears that can't get enough big-band sound.

After a three-year break, O'Connell returned with a new set for another small label. He's kept on many of his best players, and the band is certainly improving disc by disc: it's still never far away from big-band routine, and we could have done without the wretched likes of 'How Do You Keep The Music Playing?', here with a soppy vocal duet to make things worse. But when the band really dig in and swing, it makes a great sound.

Anita O'Day (born 1919)

VOCALS

The legend of Billie Holiday and the huge, vocal presences of Ella Fitzgerald, Sarah Vaughan and Carmen McRae have tended to overshadow Anita's reputation. She remains, though, one of the toughest, most dramatic and most fiercely swinging of all jazz singers, with a personality like rough-cut diamond. A great survivor, she kept on past her real sell-by date, but energized by a sheer appetite for life and music.

*****(*) Anita O'Day: Volume 1**

Masters of Jazz 122 *O'Day; Al Beck, Don Fagerquist, Torg Halten, Vincent Hughes, Norman Murphy, Tony Russo, Shorty Sherock, Joe Triscari, Graham Young (t); Roy Eldridge (t, v); Leon Cox, Billy Cully, John Grassi, Jay Kelliher, Tommy Pedersen, Pat Virgadamo, Babe Wagner (tb); Ben Freeman, Rex Kittig, Sam Listengart, Clint Neagley, Mascagni Ruffo (as); Charlie Kennedy (as, ts); Adrian Tei (as, cl); Johnny Bothwell (as); Walter Bates, Don Brassfield, Jimmy Migliore Charlie Ventura (ts); Stewart Olson (sax); Sam Musiker (ts, cl); Bob Kitsis, Teddy Napoleon, Joe Springer (p); Ray Biondi, Edward Yance (g); Biddy Bastien, Irv Lang, Edward Mihelich (b); Joe Dale, Gene Krupa (d); Howard Dulany (v).* 3–6/41.

*****(*) Anita O'Day: Volume 2, 1941–1942**

Masters of Jazz 157 *As above, except add Joe Conigliaro (tb), Sam Musiker (as, cl), Walter Bates (ts), Johnny Desmond (v).* 8, 10 & 11/41, 2 & 4/42.

*****(*) Anita O'Day: 1941–1945**

L'Art Vocal 19 *As above, except add Jon Carroll, Buddy Childers, Karl George, Mel Green, Mickey Mangano, Pinky Savitt (t), Bill Atkinson, Harry Forbes, Nick Gaglio, Milt Kabak, Greg Phillips, Dick Taylor, Bart Varsalona, Freddie Zito (tb), Chet Ball, Bill Hitz, Bob Lively, Harry Terrill (as), Eddie Meyers (as, cl), Emmett Carls, Stan Getz, Dave Madden, David Matthews, Buddy Wise (ts), Sid Brown, Bob Gioga, Joe Koch (bs), Stan Kenton, Milt Raskin (p), Bob Ahern, Teddy Walters, Frank Worrell (g), Gene Englund (b), Jim Falzone, Jesse Price (d).* 41–45.

****** Let Me Off Uptown**

Columbia Legacy CK 65265 *As above.* 41–45.

****** The Big Band Years**

President 547 *As above.* 41–45.

Anita O'Day lived the jazz life. She tells about it in *High Times, Hard Times* (1983). As a young woman she worked as a singing waitress and in punishing dance-marathons. And she shot horse until her heart began to give out in the 1960s and she was forced to battle her demons cold. As is immediately obvious from her combative, sharply punctuated scatting and her line in stage patter, O'Day was a fighter. As a 'chirper' with the Gene Krupa band in 1941, she refused to turn out in ball-gown and gloves, and appeared instead in band jacket and short skirt, an unheard-of practice that underlined her instinctive feminism. With Stan Kenton, she gave a humane edge to a sometimes pretentiously modernist repertoire. O'Day's demanding style had few successful imitators, but she is the most immediate source for June Christy and Chris Connor, who followed her into the Kenton band.

These early cuts with the Kenton and Krupa bands are definitive of her desire (one more commonly and erroneously associated with Billie Holiday) to be one of the guys, not so much socially and chemically, as musically. She sings like a horn player, not only when scatting, but also when delivering a song-line straight. Her phrasing has a brassy snap and polish and, even through the acoustic fog that surrounds most of these transfers, her enunciation is exact and focused. The bands were among the most exciting of their day, or ever. Kenton's outfit called for more sheer strength, but the unvarnished vivacity and raw charm of the Krupa tracks are what recommends this material. 'Let Me Off Uptown' is the classic, of course, destined to become shopworn and hackneyed in later years, but right off the mint here. 'Bolero At The Savoy' is a band original, presumably worked up during rehearsals. The Columbia set recaptures the sound with great fidelity and compresses the very best of the material from Anita's two stints with Krupa, though oddly this reissue breaks the chronology to no real purpose, starting with false logic on 'Opus One' from 1945.

The Masters of Jazz sets are pretty complete, not to say exhaustive, and if anyone wants a fuller documentation of Anita's early work in those two packed years before America entered the war, then these are the sets to go for, though we have found the sound rather flat and muffled. Containing more than two hours of music, they should be enough for the most devoted enthusiast.

Much of the material is duplicated on the French compilation, which fills in the years in between. The work with Kenton is typically more sophisticated in conception and abrasive in delivery. A pair of tunes in the middle of the set – 'I'm Going Mad For A Pad', 'And Her Tears Flowed Like Wine' – emphasize both the strengths and the drawbacks. A valuable and thoroughly enjoyable reissue.

The Big Band Years is a catch-up volume for newcomers or for those with only a limited appetite for swing of this sort. Recently remastered, the sound is very good indeed, with a lot of presence in the woodwinds and some of the tizz taken off the brass and drums. The duet with Eldridge on 'Let Me Off Uptown' has rarely sounded better.

*****(*) Swings Cole Porter With Billy May**

Verve 849266-2 *O'Day; main tracks with Billy May Orchestra, unknown personnel; other tracks include Conte Candoli, Roy Eldridge, Lee Katzman, Al Porcino, Jack Sheldon, Ray Triscari, Stu Williamson (t); Milt Bernhart, Bob Edmondson, Lloyd Elliot, Bill Harris, Joe Howard, Lou McCreary, Frank Rosolino, Simon*

Zentner (tb); Kenny Shroyer (btb); Al Pollan (tba); Charlie Kennedy, Joe Maini (as); Budd Johnson, Richie Kamuca, Bill Perkins (ts); Jimmy Giuffre (reds, arr); Jack Nimitz, Cecil Payne (bs); Ralph Burns, Lou Levy, Jimmy Rowles, Paul Smith (p); Tal Farlow, Al Hendrickson, Barney Kessel (g); Monty Budwig, Buddy Clark, Al McKibbon, Joe Mondragon, Leroy Vinnegar (b); Larry Bunker, Don Lamond, Mel Lewis, Lawrence Marable, Jackie Mills, Alvin Stoller (d); Buddy Bregman, Bill Holman (arr). 1/52–4/59.

*****(*) Verve Jazz Masters 49**

Verve 517954-2 *O'Day; Conte Candoli, Lee Katzman, Jack Sheldon, Al Porcino, Ray Triscari, Stu Williamson, Roy Eldridge, Joe Ferrante, Bernie Glow, Herb Pomeroy, Doc Severinsen, Ernie Royal, Nick Travis (t); Milt Bernhart, Jimmy Cleveland, Bob Edmondson, Lew McCreary, Frank Rosolino, Billy Byers, Bill Harris, Joe Howard, Willie Dennis, J.J Johnson, Fred Ohms, Kai Winding, Lloyd Ulyate, Simon Zentner (tb); Bob Brookmeyer (vtb); Kenny Shroyer (btb); Al Pollan (tba); Richie Kamuca, Jerome Richardson, Zoot Sims, Bill Perkins, Budd Johnson, Eddie Shu (ts); Sam Marowitz, Hal McKusick, Charlie Kennedy, Joe Maini, Phil Woods (as); Walt Levinsky (as, cl); Aaron Sachs, Jimmy Giuffre (ts, cl); Bud Shank (as, f); Danny Bank, Jack Nimitz, Cecil Payne (bs); Dave McKenna, Joe Masters, Oscar Peterson, Bob Corwin, Lonnie Hewitt, Hank Jones, Arnold Ross, Jimmy Rowles, Paul Smith (p); Barry Galbraith, Herb Ellis, Barney Kessel (g); Morty Cobb, George Duvivier, John Drew, Ray Brown, Buddy Clark, Monty Budwig, Larry Woods, Al McKibbon, Joe Mondragon (b); Corky Hale (hp); Jo Jones, Gene Krupa, Mel Lewis, Don Lamond, Jackie Mills, Lawrence Marable, John Poole, Alvin Stoller (d); and as for Sings The Winners and Pick Yourself Up.* 4/54–2/62.

*****(*) Pick Yourself Up**

Verve 517329-2 *O'Day; Conte Candoli, Pete Candoli, Harry 'Sweets' Edison, Conrad Gozzo, Ray Linn (t); Milt Bernhart, Lloyd Elliot, Frank Rosolino, George Roberts (tb); Herb Geller (as); Georgie Auld, Bob Cooper (ts); Jimmy Giuffre (bs); Larry Bunker (vib); Paul Smith (p); Barney Kessel, Al Hendrickson (g); Joe Mondragon (b); Alvin Stoller (d); Buddy Bregman (cond); other personnels unknown.* 1–12/56.

*****(*) All The Sad Young Men**

Verve 517065-2 *O'Day; Bernie Glow, Herb Pomeroy, Doc Severinsen (t); Bob Brookmeyer (vtb); Billy Byers, Willie Dennis (tb); Walt Levinsky, Phil Woods (as, cl); Jerome Richardson, Zoot Sims (ts); Hank Jones (p); Barry Galbraith (g); George Duvivier (b); Mel Lewis (d); Gary McFarland (arr, cond).* 61.

***** Sings The Winners**

Verve 837939-2 *As above, except add Bill Catalano, Jules Chaikin, Phil Gilbert, Lee Katzman, Sam Noto (t), Bob Enevoldsen, Jim Amlotte, Kent Larsen, Archie LeCocque, Ken Shroyer (tb), Lennie Niehaus, Bud Shank (as), Richie Kamuca, Bill Perkins (ts), Jack Dulong (bs), Gene Harris, Lonnie Hewitt, Joe Masters, Marty Paich (p), Cal Tjader (vib), Red Kelly, Freddie Schreiber, Andy Simpkins, Larry Woods (b), Bill Dowdy, Mel Lewis, John Poole, Johnny Rae (d).* 9/56–10/62.

***** Time For 2**

Verve 559808-2 *O'Day; Cal Tjader (vib, d); Bob Corwin, Lonnie Hewitt (p); Freddy Schreiber (b); Johnny Rae (d, perc).* 62.

The most familiar image of O'Day is at the Newport Festival in 1958, a set preserved in the movie, *Jazz on a Summer's Day*. In a spectacular black dress and a hat that must have accounted for half the egrets in Louisiana, she resembles one of those subtly ball-breaking heroines in a Truman Capote story. The voice even then is unreliably pitched, but there's no mistaking the inventiveness of 'Tea For Two' and 'Sweet Georgia Brown'. The woman who sang 'The *Boy* From Ipanema' with a sarcastic elision of the 'aahhs' was every bit as capable as Betty Carter of turning Tin Pan Alley tat into a feminist statement.

O'Day never sounds quite as effective with a full band, and May's beefy arrangements tend to overpower her subtler rhythmic skills. Fortunately, the reissue of the Cole Porter set includes six bonus tracks, including band arrangements by Buddy Bregman and Bill Holman, together with a magnificent small-group 'From This Moment On', a second, rather smoothed-out version of 'Love For Sale' to compare with May's, and Jimmy Giuffre's superb, throbbing arrangement of 'My Heart Belongs To Daddy'. The May tracks are virtually all at accelerated tempos (in contrast to the Rodgers and Hart sequel) but varied with Latin ('I Get A Kick Out Of You') or 'Eastern' ('Night And Day') settings. Even so, one would much prefer to hear O'Day swing Porter to the basic accompaniment of bass and drums. She sounds unusually husky at extremes of pitch, as if from the effort of projecting over the band, but these are still more than worthwhile performances, and a great deal wittier and more stimulating than most of the 'songbook' sessions that were rife at the time.

The 1956 sessions with Bregman's orchestra amount to a survivor's testament, a hard-assed, driving gesture of defiance that is still completely musical. The version of 'Sweet Georgia Brown', which she was to include in the Newport programme, is buoyant and lightfooted like all the Bregman arrangements, but the best of the record surely has to be among the small-group tracks with Sweets Edison. An alternative take of 'Let's Face The Music And Dance' is much broader than the released version; O'Day was nothing if not subtle and rarely attempted to nudge her audience. The 1958 performances are well above average and perfect examples of O'Day's wittily daring rhythmic sense. From the mid-1950s, her closest musical associate was drummer John Poole, who anchors the bonus 'Star Eyes' on *Winners*; she sticks close by him, leaving the pitched instruments to do their own thing, and, but for the words, she might almost be involved in a percussion duet. *Winners* is a useful compilation of material from the Verve catalogue and complementary to the excellent *Jazz Masters*, which is probably the best disc for an introduction to O'Day. It includes 'Sweet Georgia Brown' with Bregman's band, a duo 'God Bless The Child' with Barney Kessel from *Trav'lin' Light*, Giuffre's 'Four Brothers' chart from *Sings The Winners* and the marvellous 'I've Got The World On A String' from *Sings The Most*, one of her best records.

All The Sad Young Men is a delicious set, perhaps more distinguished for the instrumental arrangements than for Anita's singing, which is a bit flat. The material with Tjader on *Time For 2* is every bit as imaginative, but more sparsely arranged and all the better for it. 'Mr Sandman', 'Peel Me A Grape' and 'Spring Will Be A Little Late This Year' are all classic performances, and the 1962 Hollywood session, coming at a difficult time in Anita's progress, is worth hearing and having.

*****(*) I Get A Kick Out Of You**

Evidence ECD 22054 *O'Day; Don Raffell (sax); Ronnell Bright (p); George Morrow (b); John Poole (d).* 4/75.

***** Live In Concert, Tokyo 1976**

Emily 7610 *O'Day; Norman Simmons (p); Robert Maize (b); John Poole (d).* 76.

They've always lapped her up in Japan, where Anita's mix of tough and tender is appealingly exotic. They were also fascinated by the detail of her battle with narcotics. Cleaned up and fit, by this stage she's getting a kick out of the music again. The Evidence disc, originally available only in the East, is a bold comeback statement, with a long, exploratory version of 'Gone With The Wind' and shiveringly effective versions of 'When Sunny Gets Blue' and 'What Are You Doing The Rest Of Your Life'. The band, cemented as on the second disc by the charismatic Poole, is happy to spear-carry for much of the time, but the accompaniments are thoughtful and developed enough to hold the ear, even when Anita isn't front and centre. A strong patch and a welcome return to form.

***** Mello'Day**

GNP Crescendo GNPD 2126 *O'Day; Ernie Watts (ts); Lou Levy (p); Laurindo Almeida, Joe Diorio (g); Paulinho Da Costa (perc).* 78.

Elegantly produced by Leonard Feather, but frankly more interesting for the *bossa*-tinged guest spots with Watts and Almeida than for Anita's singing, which sounds very much by the numbers which are by and large familiar standards. She peaks early with 'Old Devil Moon' and 'Lost In The Stars'; thereafter it tails off, and the main interest falls to the Lou Levy trio and the guests.

***** In A Mellow Tone**

DRG CDSL 5209 *O'Day; Gordon Brisker (ts, f, syn); Pete Jolly (p); Corky Hale (hp); Brian Bromberg (b); Frank Capp (d); Dave Black (perc).* 3/89.

****(*) At Vine Street: Live**

DRG 8435 *O'Day; Gordon Brisker (ts, f); Bob Maize (b); Danny D'Imperio (d).* 8/91.

Caught either side of her seventieth birthday, but still as game as a bantam. She sounds rejuvenated on *In A Mellow Tone*, projecting well and still up for the odd harmonic experiment; 'I Cried For You' is bold and unexpected. It's a generously proportioned set, with a clever balance of vocals and crisp, effective soloing. Corky Hale's guest spots are as engaging as ever, but it's very much Anita's day and the singer's album. Other standout tracks include 'Sleepin' Bee' and 'Anita's Blues'.

She brings more presence than convincing musicality to the club set. Engineer and producer David Kreisberg has done his best to give the voice some effective backlighting, but the band are mostly too loud, swamping some of the more delicately nuanced passages. Anita's most effective when she cuts loose on 'Is You Is ...' and 'You'd Be So Nice To Come Home To', where she sounds in control of the swing, rather than trying to keep on top of someone else's beat; but she does also score with a nice medley of the two 'Yesterdays' – Harbach & Kern, Lennon & McCartney – a familiar enough conceit, but very elegantly done.

*****(*) Rules Of The Road**

Pablo CD 2310 950 *O'Day; Jack Sheldon, Wayne Bergeron, Ron King, Ron Stout, Stan Martin (t); Andy Martin, Bob McChesney, Bob Enevoldsen, Bob Sanders, Alex Iles (tb); Sal Lozano, Danny House (sax, f, cl); Pete Christlieb, Jerry Pinter, Brian Williams (sax, cl); Christian Jacob (p); Trey Henry (b); Ray Brinker (d).* 3/93.

She was in great shape for this 1993 one-off, and there's none of Billie's morose self-pity in this nicely structured and immaculately played saga of life on the road. The great thing about O'Day is the fact that she survived without turning hard. She sings gamily and with wit on material like 'Here's That Rainy Day', 'Soon It's Gonna Rain' and the title-song, still pumping out that beat like she's always done. The band is absolutely Rolls-Royce, two generations of players who combine verve and expertise in almost equal proportions. The only quibble: a rather flat and unresponsive sound and a positioning that sets O'Day way out in front, not where she needed to be and always used to be – in among the guys.

Chico O'Farrill (born 1921)

COMPOSER, ARRANGER

Raised in Havana, he settled in New York around 1950 and did countless Latin-style arrangements for other bandleaders during the '50s and '60s, as well as leading his own Afro-Cuban Big Band. A seminal figure in the fusion of Cuban and American rhythms and the way they will work for an orchestra.

*****(*) Cuban Blues: The Chico O'Farrill Sessions**

Verve 533256-2 2CD *O'Farrill; Mario Bauza, Paquito Davilla, Harry 'Sweets' Edison, Roy Eldridge, Bernie Glow, Carlton McBeath, Doug Mettome, Jimmy Nottingham, Al Porcino, Dick Sherman, Al Stewart, Nick Travis, Bobby Woodlan (t); Eddie Bert, Carl Elmer, Vern Friley, Bill Harris, Bart Varsalona, Ollie Wilson, Fred Zito (tb); Vince De Rosa (frhn); Danny Bank, George Berg, Lenny Hambro, Ben Harrod, Leslie Johnakins, Gene Johnson, Charlie Kennedy, Jose Madera, Pete Mondello, Charlie Parker, Flip Phillips, Sol Rabinowitz, Wilbur Schwartz, Fred Skerritt, Howard Terry, Eddie Wasserman, Warren Webb, James Williamson (reeds); Ralph Burns, Gene DiNovi, Rene Hernandez, Fred Otis (p); Billy Bauer (g); Irma Clow (hp); Don Bagley, Ray Brown, Clyde Lombardi, Roberto Rodriguez (b); Jo Jones, Don Lamond, Buddy Rich (d); Candido Camero, Machito, Jose Mangual, Modesto Martinez, Luis Miranda, Ubaldo Nieto, Chano Pozo, Carlos Vidal (perc); Bobby Escoto (v).* 12/50–4/54.

The ideal background source for this attractive compilation is the atmospheric novel, *The Mambo Kings Sing Songs of Love*, whose author, Oscar Hijuelos, provides the liner-note. O'Farrill studied composition in Havana before coming to the USA in his later twenties, where he had considerable success writing charts for Benny Goodman, Stan Kenton, Charlie Parker and Dizzy Gillespie. On the strength of a powerful vogue for Afro-Cuban music, he built an orchestra of his own round Machito's rhythm section and recorded a series of 10-inch LPs for Norman Granz's Verve and Norgran labels. Technically, the material stands up better than it does artistically. The recordings are wonderfully present and alive, and the remastering offers extra breadth without distorting the syrupy warmth of the originals. At more than 150 minutes, these two discs are a treat for the Latin-jazz enthusiast. All but the very committed, though, might find the diet a tad unrelieved and the pace a little relentless. The two *Afro-Cuban Jazz Suites*, one recorded under Machito's leadership in December 1950, the other under O'Farrill's own name two years later, are relatively ambitious in scope and content, but O'Farrill was not a man to overlook a successful formula, and the harmonic spectrum is otherwise kept comfortably narrow, with a substantial emphasis on danceable rhythms. One can readily imagine the brothers in *The Mambo Kings* moping through charts like 'Flamingo' while keeping an eye on the girls at the bar. This is music that requires some other sensory attraction.

*****(*) Heart Of A Legend**

Milestone 9299-2 *O'Farrill; Arturo Sandoval, Alfredo 'Chocolate' Armenteros, Jim Seeley, Matt Hilgenberg, Robert Ingram, Kenny Rampton, Peter Olstad, David 'Piro' Rodriguez (t); Gary Valente, Sam Burtis, Papo Vasquez, Juan Pablo Torres, Jack Jeffers (tb); Maurizio Smith (f); Mario Rivera (ss); Paquito D'Rivera (cl, as); Jimmy Cozier, Marshall McDonald, Bobby Porcelli (as); Mike Milgore, Peter Branin, Gato Barbieri (ts); Pablo Calogero (bs); Arturo O'Farrill (p); David Orquendo (g); Ilmar Gavilan (vn); Andy Gonzalez, Joe Santiago (b); Horacio Hernandez, Willie Martinez (d); Joe Gonzalez, Eddie Bobo, Candido Camero, Orlando 'Puntilla' Rios, Carlos Patato Valdes (perc); Vivian Ara, Freddy Cole (v).* 12/98–7/99.

A smashing homage to the grand old man of Afro-Cuban music. With son Arturo at the piano and an all-star assembly of the great names in the genre, from Candido to Sandoval, it's a tumultuous affair. O'Farrill's tunes and arrangements won't win prizes for subtlety or restraint, but he has a very sure hand with the kind of massed forces on show here, and for sheer excitement a chart such as 'Locos De La Habana' is hard to beat. This a tradition of show music, and it's more about larger-than-life virtuosity and entertainment than musical profundity. It might also sound best on the kind of hi-fi systems which few can afford (and which few neighbours will tolerate). But a hearty huzzah all the same.

Dave O'Higgins (born 1964)

TENOR, SOPRANO AND ALTO SAXOPHONES

Birmingham-born, O'Higgins has been a fixture of the contemporary London scene since the mid-'80s, having worked in high-profile bands such as Roadside Picnic and having lately made his mark as a leader himself.

***** All Good Things**

EFZ 1002 *O'Higgins; Robin Aspland (p); Alec Dankworth (bass); Jeremy Stacey (d).* 8/92.

*****(*) Beats Working For A Living**

EFZ 1009 *O'Higgins; Joe Locke (vib); Joey Calderazzo (p); James Genus (b); Adam Nussbaum (d).* 94.

***** Under The Stone**

EFZ 1016 *As for All Good Things, except add Gerard Presencer (t); replace Stacey with Gene Calderazzo (d).* 95.

*****(*) The Secret Ingredient**

EFZ 1020 *O'Higgins; Robin Aspland (p); Alec Dankworth (b); Gene Calderazzo (d); woodwinds; The Electra Strings.* 8/96.

Unlike several of the younger British jazz players, who seemed to make the leap from nowhere at all to 'exciting new recording star' in a matter of weeks, O'Higgins is a time-served performer with an already impressive track-record. A graduate of NYJO, he was spotted and then recruited by the hard-to-fool John Dankworth and Cleo Laine (the Dankworths' son is an effective presence on *All Good Things*), before making a partial breakthrough with the much-touted Roadside Picnic, for whom O'Higgins wrote much of the better material. Since then, he's played a part in Sax Appeal, Gang of Three, the prizewinning Itchy Fingers, and in the Pizza Express Modern Jazz Sextet.

Backing singers is an excellent discipline for a horn man. A typical O'Higgins solo is crisp, direct and to the point and rarely lasts longer than two or three nicely balanced choruses. The material on *All Good Things* is more obviously jazzy than anything written for Roadside Picnic, and the band oozes unfussy professionalism, honed for the occasion on a week's residency at Ronnie Scott's. Dankworth and Stacey impress throughout. All the tunes are by O'Higgins, with the exception of 'Every Time We Say Goodbye' and, following it, Coltrane's 'Dear Lord', a pairing which ironically serves only to underline the saxophonist's slight unease with more romantic or emotive stuff.

The second album saw him take the plunge and record with top-flight New Yorkers, a move that had tripped up another promising young Brit, the Scot Tommy Smith. Locke turned out to be the key to the session; in conjunction with the fiery Calderazzo, whose London-based brother turns up on the third album, the vibist soars and thunders, throwing out fast melodic lines with seeming ease. O'Higgins sounds well within himself and plays magnificently on 'Duke Ellington's Sound Of Love', a Mingus composition that requires delicacy as well as strength. The third album might have been a cautious consolidation, but O'Higgins (and here the parallel with Smith holds up) decides to push out the envelope a little and try some new things in his writing. These charts are much more detailed and complex, and the addition of a second horn in places adds a wonderful new dimension ... but largely in potential. There is an odd unpreparedness to parts of the record, mistimed cues and entrances, ensembles which are not quite clicking. At 70 minutes, too, there is probably just a touch too much material. A more tightly structured hour would have been quite satisfactory.

The Secret Ingredient was eagerly awaited and does not disappoint – but what an extraordinarily, perhaps foolhardily, eclectic trawl of material it represents, everything from Coltrane's ballad, 'Naima', to Ralph Towner's 'Icarus' (a curious choice for a horn player), to Led Zeppelin's 'Moby Dick', once a feature for Bonzo Bonham's hand drums. That O'Higgins moulds it all into a satisfying unity is the best evidence for his development. He has put his stamp on every track here, having learnt much from study of Miles Davis's classic collaborations with Gil Evans. About half the tracks, those with strings and extra woodwinds, are arranged, produced and conducted by Mike Mower. These modulate the sound beautifully, and Mower's work on Neal Hefti's 'Girl Talk' is absolutely exemplary.

***** The Grinder's Monkey**

Short Fuse 001 *O'Higgins; Jim Watson (org, p); Mike Outram (g); Orlando Le Fleming (b); Winston Clifford (d).* 11/99.

At 35, O'Higgins is hardly a young hotshot of the saxophone any longer, and there's a sense that this set – on a new label – is a transitional step for a musician who's slightly unsure of how to place his considerable talent. The leader plays big and powerful saxophone throughout, but on many of these tracks it feels overly neat and tidied-away within the context of the rest of the music. Watson plays organ some of the time, piano the rest, and the setting switches between organ-combo grooving and more mediated post-bop. He's well worth your time, but O'Higgins has yet to deliver his major statement.

Kjell Ohman (born 1943)

ORGAN

A familiar name in Sweden's jazz mainstream, Ohman has played on countless sessions in both jazz and pop. Most renowned today as being the country's leading Hammond organist.

***** Organ Grinders**

Four Leaf Clover FLC CD 126 *Ohman; Ulf Andersson (as, ts); Thomas Arnesen (g); Tommy Johnson (b); Douglas Westlund (d); Claes Janson (v).* 5/93.

***** The Hammond Connection**

Opus 3 19402 *Ohman; Arne Domnérus (as); Rune Gustafsson (g); Mads Vinding (b); Leif 'Gus' Dahlberg (d).* 3/94.

These are easy-going records. The earlier set has more of a jump-band feel to it as the Organ Grinders tuck into the likes of 'Got My Mojo Working' and 'Red Top'. Arnesen and Andersson get their shout in and Janson strolls in like the Swedish Mark Murphy. The second is more like small-group swing: Ohman lets his fingers do the walking while the rhythm section amble along, and the tunes are an uncontroversial lot of old swing numbers. But the playing has many felicities along the way, with only four tracks breaking the five-minute barrier, and Domnérus strolls into the music with his usual aplomb: listen to the way he floats his sound over 'Misty', which he must have played many times.

Old And New Dreams

GROUP

Founded by a quartet of sometime Ornette Coleman collaborators, the group devoted itself almost entirely to Ornette repertoire, a gesture of obvious and generous appreciation, but also a subtle reminder of the part each played in the formulation of one of the most challenging aesthetics of the last 50 years.

*****(*) Old And New Dreams**

ECM 829379-2 *Don Cherry (t, p); Dewey Redman (ts, musette); Charlie Haden (b); Ed Blackwell (d).* 8/79.

***** Playing**

ECM 829123-2 *As above.* 6/80.

*****(*) One For Blackwell**

Black Saint 120113 *As above.* 11/87.

One wonders if this is how the classic Ornette Coleman Quartet might have sounded with modern recording techniques and a more democratic sound-balance. Since Coleman started to concentrate largely on his electric Prime Time band and on large-scale projects, Old and New Dreams became the foremost interpreters of his acoustic small-group music. The dirges – 'Lonely Woman' on the first album and 'Broken Shadows' on *Playing* – are by no means as dark as the composer made them, and Redman adheres much more closely to a tonal centre on all the pieces, a role he performed in the Coleman quintet of the late 1960s/early 1970s. Cherry also seems to be using orthodox concert trumpet on at least the majority of the tracks, and its fuller tone sits more comfortably alongside Redman than the squeaky pocket cornet. Redman's eldritch musette, a two-reed oboe with a sound not unlike a shawm, gives 'Song Of La-Ba' (*O&ND*) a mysterious timbre.

Ed Blackwell has always been prominently featured with the band; the tribute album, recorded live at a Blackwell festival in Atlanta, Georgia, is entirely appropriate, given his multifarious commitment to New Orleans music, modern free jazz and, of course, the work of Ornette Coleman, to which he often stood as *il miglior fabbro*. The live versions of Ornette's 'Happy House' (from *Playing*) and the Ghanaian theme, 'Togo' (from the first album), are slightly rawer and more extended but show no significant differences over the studio versions. Indeed, the main difference between the live album and the others is the extent to which the drummer solos. It's in his work that the 'old' and 'new' of the band title truly resonate. Drawn to the rough second-line drumming of the marching bands, he adds the sibilant accents familiar from bebop, and also a strong element of African talking drum. His rhythmic patterns are dense, coded and allusive but, taken whole, refreshingly entire and self-sufficient. Altogether, these three albums are a worthy monument to a great innovator, and to the men (two of them now deceased) who walked the pioneer trail with him.

Joe 'King' Oliver (1885–1939)

CORNET, TRUMPET

A key figure in the first period of jazz history, Oliver's career was a mix of triumph and miscalculation. He was bandleading in New Orleans in the early years of the century, but it wasn't until the 1910s that he really rose above the other local groups. He went to Chicago in 1919 and created what became the Creole Jazz Band around 1921, which Louis Armstrong joined in 1922. They were a sensation, and made the first important group of records by black jazzmen. His later band, the Dixie Syncopators, was less successful, and turning down an offer from New York's Cotton Club may have been a crucial mistake (it went to Duke Ellington). Though he was still touring and recording, he was out of fashion by the early '30s and was often barely able to play, owing to poor teeth. He died in Savannah, Georgia, reduced to working as a pool-hall janitor.

**** **King Oliver Volume One 1923 To 1929**

Jazz Classics in Digital Stereo RPCD 607 *Oliver; Louis Armstrong (c); Tommy Dorsey, Bob Shoffner (t); Honoré Dutrey, Kid Ory, Ed Atkins (tb); Johnny Dodds (cl); Albert Nicholas (cl, ss, as); Billy Paige, Darnell Howard (cl, as); Barney Bigard (cl, ts); Stump Evans (ss, as); Charlie Jackson (bsx); Lil Hardin, Jelly Roll Morton, Luis Russell (p); Arthur Schutt (harmonium); Eddie Lang, Lonnie Johnson (g); Bud Scott, Bill Johnson (bj, v); Bert Cobb (bb); Jimmy Williams (b); Baby Dodds, Paul Barbarin, Stan King (d).* 4/23–5/29.

**** **King Oliver 1923**

Classics 650 *Similar to above.* 4–10/23.

***(*) **King Oliver 1923–1926**

Classics 639 *Similar to above two discs, except add , (cl), Teddy Peters, Irene Scruggs (v).* 10/23–7/26.

♛ *** **King Oliver's Creole Jazz Band – The Complete Set**

Retrieval RTR 79007 2CD *As above discs, except add Clarence Williams (p), Jodie Edwards, Susie Edwards (v); omit Shoffner, Dorsey, Nicholas, Paige, Howard, Russell, Schutt, Lang, Lonnie Johnson, Williams, Barbarin, King.* 4/23–12/24.

The third King of New Orleans, after Buddy Bolden and Freddie Keppard, remains among the most stately and distinguished of jazz musicians, although newer listeners may wonder whether Oliver's records are really so important in the light of what his protégé, Louis Armstrong, would do in the years after the Oliver Jazz Band records of 1923. Joe Oliver was in at the inception of jazz and it's our misfortune that his group wasn't recorded until 1923, when its greatest years may have been behind it: accounts of the band in live performance paint spectacular images of creativity which the constricted records barely sustain. Yet they remain magnificent examples of black music at an early peak: the interplay between Oliver and Armstrong, the beautifully balanced ensembles, the development of polyphony. Oliver's tight-knit sound, fluid yet rigorously controlled, projects the feel of his New Orleans origins, vivified by the electricity of his Chicagoan success. There is the brightness of the young Armstrong, content to follow his master but already bursting with talent, and the magisterial work of both of the Dodds brothers (only the recording stops us from hearing Baby's work in its full intensity). Ragtime and brass-band music still guide much of what Oliver did, but the unsettled ambitions of jazz keep poking through too. If the music is caught somewhere between eras, its absolute assurance is riveting and presents a leader who knew exactly what he wanted. Oliver's subsequent band, the Dixie Syncopators, was far less successful, troubled by a feeble reed section and cluttered arrangements; but its best sides – such as the furiously paced 'Wa Wa Wa' – are as good as anything from their own period.

There are 37 surviving sides by the Oliver (Creole) Jazz Band, including a handful of alternative takes. The Retrieval two-disc set is the first to include all of them in one place (one disc, the Gennett coupling of 'Zulu's Ball' and 'Working Man Blues', is so rare that only a single copy of the original 78 is known to exist) and, while Robert Parker's stunning remastering in his first Jazz Classics volume will sound better to some ears, we have transferred our number one choice to Retrieval, for whom John R.T. Davies has done his usual outstanding job. They also include a pair of 1924 titles by the vaudevillians, Butterbeans And Susie, with accompaniment by Oliver and Clarence Williams, and the famous pair of duets by Oliver and Jelly Roll Morton. Modern ears are still going to find this primitive in audio terms, but surely the excitement, panache and inventiveness of this incredible band will speak to anyone with even the slightest sympathy.

Robert Parker's compilation remains astonishingly good. If these primitive recordings have been transferred many times, none has appeared in such fine sound as here: Parker's search for only the finest originals pays off handsomely, and as he gathers the missing discs he will surely proceed until the Oliver story is complete: but we are still waiting for him to finish the job! In the meantime, here are 'Dippermouth Blues' (the Gennett version), 'Riverside Blues', 'Sweet Lovin' Man' and other records which pace out the first distinctive steps of black jazz on record. Parker also adds one of the duets with Jelly Roll Morton, 'King Porter'; seven sides by the Dixie Syncopators; the pair of tracks by 'Blind Willie Dunn's Gin Bottle Four', a session with Eddie Lang and Lonnie Johnson where Oliver's presence is in some doubt; and a track with Tommy Dorsey on trumpet which allows scholars to compare his work with that of the hornman on the previous session. This remains a model reissue in almost every way.

For those who want the 1923 sessions on a single disc, the Classics survey is good enough, though remastering seems only average next to the painstaking work of both Parker and Davies. Classics 639 takes off from the end of the Creole Jazz Band sessions and includes both of the Oliver/Morton duets, seven titles by the Dixie Syncopators and three tracks in which the King accompanies blues singers Teddy Peters and Irene Scruggs.

***(*) **King Oliver Volume Two 1927 To 1930**

Jazz Classics in Digital Stereo RPCD 608 *Oliver; Tick Gray, Ed Allen (c); Dave Nelson, Henry 'Red' Allen (t); Jimmy Archey, Kid Ory, Ed Cuffee (tb); Omer Simeon, Arville Harris, Ernest Elliott, Barney Bigard, Benny Waters, Buster Bailey, Bobby Holmes, Glyn Paque, Hilton Jefferson, Charles Frazier, Walter Wheeler, Paul Barnes (reeds); Clarence Williams (p, cel, v); Luis Russell, Don Frye, Norman Lester, Henry Duncan, Eric Franker (p); Eddie Lang (g, vn); Bud Scott, Leroy Harris, Arthur Taylor (bj); Bert Cobb, Cyrus St Clair, Clinton Walker, Lionel Nipton (bb); Paul Barbarin, Edmund Jones, Fred Moore (d); Justin Ring (perc); Texas Alexander (v).* 4/27–9/30.

*** **King Oliver 1926–1928**

Classics 618 *Similar to above.* 3/26–6/28.

*** **King Oliver 1928-1930**

Classics 607 *Oliver; Dave Nelson, Henry 'Red' Allen (t); Jimmy Archey (tb); Bobby Holmes, Glyn Paque, Charles Frazier, Hilton Jefferson, Walter Wheeler (reeds); Don Frye, James P Johnson, Hank Duncan, Eric Franker, Norman Lester (p); Roy Smeck (steel g, hca); Arthur Taylor (bj, g); Clinton Walker (bb); Fred Moore, Edmund Jones (d).* 6/28–3/30.

*** **King Oliver And His Orchestra 1930–1931**

Classics 594 *As above, except omit Frye, Johnson, Smeck and Jones; add Ward Pinkett (t, v), Bill Dillard (t), Ferdinand Arbello (tb), Buster Bailey (cl), Henry L Jones, Bingie Madison, Fred Skerritt (reeds), Gene Rodgers (p), Goldie Lucas (g, v), Richard Fulbright (bb), Bill Beason (d).* 4/30–4/31.

Oliver's later recordings are a muddle in several ways. Illness and problems with his teeth steadily cut down his instrumental powers, and some celebrated career errors – such as turning down a New York engagement which subsequently went to Duke Ellington – ruined his eminence. The first 13 tracks on the second Jazz Classics compilation trace his decline in fortunes, with nine underrated tracks by the Dixie Syncopators to start, two obscure blues accompaniments with Sara Martin and Texas Alexander to follow, and a session with Clarence Williams and Eddie Lang to complete the picture. Oliver could still play very well: his phrasing is usually simple and unadorned, a very different tale from Armstrong's vaulting mastery, but the quality of his tone and the starkness of his ideas can be both affecting and exhilarating. Parker concludes the disc with seven tracks from the King's Victor sessions. The Classics series takes a chronological route from the first Dixie Syncopators sides to the final Vocalion session of 1931.

The Victor sessions were often plodding and routine orchestral jazz that ran aground on some inept material ('Everybody Does It In Hawaii' features a bizarre appearance by steel guitarist Roy Smeck), and Oliver's own contributions are in much doubt: it's very hard to know where and when he plays, for he may even have asked some of his trumpeters to play in his own style. Nevertheless there are still many records with interesting passages and a few genuinely progressive items, such as 'Freakish Light Blues' and 'Nelson Stomp'. On a piece such as 'New Orleans Shout', where the soloist does sound like Oliver, he shows he can still play with the kind of sombre authority which befits a King. We primarily recommend the second Jazz Classics compilation as an introduction to this period of Oliver's work. For completists, the Classics series can be safely recommended, although reproduction is, as usual, varied.

***** King Oliver 1926–1931**

Topaz TPZ 1009 *As appropriate discs above.* 26–31.

A plausible compilation of Oliver's later work. Topaz offer a blend of Dixie Syncopators and Victor material in clean and acceptable sound.

One For All

GROUP

A conglomerate of some of the regulars who record for Gerry Teekens's Criss Cross label in New York.

*****(*) Upward And Onward**

Criss Cross 1172 *Jim Rotondi (t, flhn); Steve Davis (tb); Eric Alexander (ts); David Hazeltine (p); Peter Washington (b); Joe Farnsworth (d).* 6/99.

The presence of such a band, and their record, proposes a question as to the viability and relevance of straight-ahead hard bop at the start of a new century. On this evidence, there's no need to question its existence, relevance or necessity. If the means and language of this jazz are at least 40 years old, its immediacy and intensity make a plangent case for its timelessness. The material is a flavoursome set of originals by various band-members, utilizing the blues, blowing-vehicle conventions and the like; but the sheer chutzpah of the playing militates against any sense of cliché or anything being past its sell-by date. Rotondi, Davis and Alexander all solo with fine aplomb, and the rhythm section swings on regardless. If there's nothing terribly memorable here, it's hard to see anyone who likes the sound of three horns and a rhythm section having anything less than a very enjoyable hour or so while playing this record.

Junko Onishi (born 1967)

PIANO, KEYBOARDS

A Japanese pianist who divides her time between Tokyo and New York, Onishi has already made an extensive inventory for Blue Note.

***** Cruisin'**

Blue Note 828447-2 *Onishi; Rodney Whitaker (b); Billy Higgins (d).* 4/93.

***** Live At The Village Vanguard**

Blue Note 831886-2 *Onishi; Reginald Veal (b); Herlin Riley (d).* 5/94.

*****(*) Live At The Village Vanguard II**

Blue Note 833418-2 *As above.* 5/94.

***** Piano Quintet Suite**

Blue Note 836483-2 *Onishi; Marcus Belgrave (t, v); Eiichi Hayashi (as); Rodney Whitaker (b); Tony Rabeson (d).* 7/95.

Onishi plays catholic modern piano: she can do bebop or swing, and make it fit to either Ornette Coleman or John Lewis tunes. She also likes Ellington: there is a sweet version of 'The Shepherd' and a funny one of 'Caravan' on the first album. She sounds like she comes from a background of high training, so Monk's 'Brilliant Corners', on the second live album, seems to hold few terrors for her, difficult though it is. But she performs with a lot of brio, and her respective rhythm sections play a swinging yet oddly subservient role on each disc. Veal and Riley keep her covered on the live albums while staying out of her way. The first live date includes a version of 'Blue Skies' that expands into an extravagant fantasy on the melody; but just as effective is a rare piano version of Mingus's 'So Long Eric' and Lewis's tolling ballad, 'Concorde'. If anything, though, we slightly prefer Volume Two, which has a stinging take on Gigi Gryce's blues, 'The House Of Blue Lights', and a smoothly caressed 'Never Let Me Go'. *Piano Quintet Suite* has lots of interesting music, especially the title-piece, carefully structured as a showcase for the keyboard, which still manages to involve the other four players to the hilt. But when she turns to Mingus and Ellington for some of the other material, the record takes on a repertory feel which is much less individual, potently though the musicians perform.

***** Fragile**

Blue Note 498108-2 *Onishi; Reginald Veal (b); Karriem Riggins, Motohiko Hino, Tamaya Honda (d); Peace (v).* 7/98.

A fun record for Onishi, although it sidles into self-indulgence at points, and it might come as a shock to those who prefer the well-mannered pianist of the earlier discs. She brings in electronic keyboards for several tracks and 'BWV', 'Hey Joe' and 'Sunshine

Of Your Love' are an unlikely mix of old-style jazz-rock, modal jazz and high-spirited nonsense. Veal picks up the electric bass as well as his stand-up, and the different drummers used lend some spicy variety: 'Complexions', where Riggins and Hino duet on brushes, is very effective. 'You've Lost That Loving Feeling' ('I heard that the Righteous Brothers did this song, but I never heard their version') is a striking bit of revisionism, but 'Compared To What', with a silly vocal by Peace, is awful. A mixed result!

Opeye

GROUP

A group of improvisers based on the American West Coast.

***** Moss 'Comes Silk**

Humming Bird CD 1 *Esten Lindgren (t, tb, conch, stg, uke, v); Henry Kuntz (ts, musette, f, vn, perc); Brian Godchaux (vla, perc); Ben Lindgren (b, perc); John Kuntz (stg, mand, uke, perc).* 9/95.

Despite the fearsome-looking banner ('Avant-Shamanic Trance Jazz') this is a good-natured and bountiful set of improvisations which will remind many of Company in one of its wilder incarnations, or some of the remoter shores of the US avant-garde of two decades ago – an area which Henry Kuntz often found himself in. Not to say that the music's beached by time: they play a round dozen improvs of high vividness and needling energy, with instruments from Java, Bolivia, Nepal, China, Hawaii, Mexico and Bali, to suggest a teeming, worldly vista. The emphasis on acoustic strings gives a frequent impression of a slightly berserk chamber ensemble and, with the exotic percussion on hand, it's a very flavoursome experience, graphically recorded.

Orange Then Blue

GROUP

Based around Boston, George Schuller's group is a defining 'post-modern' jazz ensemble which takes in everything it can as an influence. The revolving cast-list numbers many of the most adventurous players to emerge in the '90s.

***** Jumpin' In The Future**

GM 3010 *Roy Okutani, Andy Gravish, Ken Cervenka, Greg Hopkins, Richard Given (t, flhn); Rick Stepton, Curtis Hasselbring, Kenny Wenzel, Peter Cirelli (tb); Krista Smith, Mark Taylor (frhn); Robert Carriker (tba); Howard Johnson (tba, bcl); Matt Dariau, Allan Chase, Dave Finucane, Adam Kolker, George Garzone, Bob Zung (reeds); Katharine Halvorsen (ob); Andrew Strasmich (f); Bevan Manson (p); Ben Sher (g); Dave Clark (b); George Schuller (d); Gunther Schuller (cond).* 3–5/88.

****(*) Where Were You?**

GM 3012 *As above, except Matt Simon (t, flhn) replaces Given; omit Wenzel, Smith, Taylor, Carriker, Chase, Zung, Halvorsen, Strasmich and Sher; add George Adams (ts), Bruce Barth (p), Russ Gold (perc).* 5/87–3/88.

***** Funkallero**

GM 3023 *Roy Okutani, Andy Gravish, Ken Cervenka, Diego Urcola, John Allmark (t, flhn); Rick Stepton (tb); Peter Cirelli (btb); Matt Darriau, Stan Strickland, Allan Chase, Adam Kolker, Dave Finucane (reeds); Tim Ray (ky); Paul Del Nero (b); George Schuller (d); Russ Gold, Bob Weiner, Alain Mallet (perc).* 8–11/89.

***** While You Were Out ...**

GM 3028 2CD *Dave Douglas, Cuong Vu, Dave Ballou (t); Rick Stepton (tb); Peter Cirelli (btb, euph); Chris Speed, Matt Darriau, Bob Bowlby (reeds); Darcy Hepner (f); Mark Taylor (frhn); Tom Ray (ky); Seido Salifoski (dumbek); Paul Del Nero (b); George Schuller (d); Greg Runions, Frank Lockwood (perc).* 7/92.

The band is led by George Schuller, son of Gunther, and is based in the Boston area. Their records should tempt anyone interested in the development of post-bop jazz, since they consist mainly of 'historical' material as translated through a contemporary set of inflexions. *Jumpin' In The Future* is a set of Gunther Schuller's charts dating from the mid-1940s to the mid-1960s, conducted by the arranger himself: an uneasy but often revealing alliance between the essential period quality of the music and the freedoms of a more modern jazz vocabulary. Schuller's scores show a concern with form which tends to override individual contributions, but the slow and peculiarly bleak reading of 'When The Saints Go Marching In' and the misty voicings of 'Summertime' provide their own rewards.

The next record is in some ways less successful, drawn from three live concerts by the band: although the choice of material includes pieces culled from the books of Miles Davis and Paul Motian as well as Monk and Mingus, the band play a little stiffly, and the presence of George Adams on three tracks tends to show up the other soloists as merely workmanlike. But when the music takes off, as on Garzone's 'New York', it makes an impressive sound. *Funkallero* restores some of their qualities: the title-piece is a vivid revision of the Bill Evans tune, strung out over a hypnotic bass-vamp, with a terrific, brawling tenor solo by Finucane; there's a strange, almost eerie 'Moose The Mooche' and a sharp expansion of Jack DeJohnette's 'Ahmad The Terrible'.

The live two-disc *While You Were Out* ... is probably their most engaging record. Here Schuller has enlisted some high-calibre soloists – Speed and Douglas among them – and the best of the charts have real substance and integrity, notably Speed's 'Scatter', Schuller's own tribute to Gil Evans, 'Evanescent', and the giddy revision of Albert Ayler's 'Truth Is Marching In'. There are also some failures, though, and the best music could probably have been cut to a single CD.

*****(*) Hold The Elevator**

GM 3040 *Cuong Vu, Dave Ballou (t); Jim Leff (tb); Tom Varner (frhn); Andrew D'Angelo (as, bcl); Andy Laster (as, bs, f); Chris Speed (ts, cl); Peck Allmond (ss, t, al hn); Matt Dariau (ts, ss, f); Jamie Saft, Tim Ray (p); Rufus Cappadocia (clo); Marcus Rojas, Jose Davila (tba); Reid Andersson, Ben Street (b); George Schuller (d); Seido Salifoski (perc).* 4/94–11/95.

The records are taking a while to appear and this set of concert performances, from Berlin, New York and Nijmegen, feels like history already with several of these names establishing their potential by themselves. Schuller's choice of tunes shows off the band's somewhat madcap range fruitfully enough and, while some of these pieces don't really come off – Andy Laster's 'Stentor', for instance – others hit a high point of exuberance that really lifts listener and band alike. Have a listen to the ragbag blowout of 'Peregrinations'.

Oregon

GROUP

Ironic that Oregon should sit so close alphabetically to the Original Dixieland Jazz Band and Kid Ory, when the music the group played seemed so very far from classic jazz idiom. An offshoot of the Paul Winter Consort, Oregon was a hugely successful side-project that makes most 'crossover' music seem unbearably bland and unthoughtful.

****** Music Of Another Present Era**

Vanguard VSD 79326 *Ralph Towner (g, 12-string g, p, syn, c, mel, frhn); Paul McCandless (ob, cor, ss, bcl, tin f, musette); Glen Moore (b, cl, vla, p, f); Collin Walcott (perc, sitar, dulc, cl, v).* 73.

****** Distant Hills**

Vanguard VSD 79341 *As above.* 73.

Hugely talented in terms of individual inputs and completely *sui generis* as an ensemble, Oregon has always managed to stay just a step ahead of critical prejudice. The band was formed at a point of low commercial ebb for jazz. By the time the music had come to seem viably marketable again, the group had evolved far enough beyond their filigree'd chamber-music origins and towards much more forcefully pulsed instrumental combinations to avoid the charge that they were 'merely' a Modern Jazz Quartet for the 1970s. In much the same way, their assimilation of ethnic sources from Asian and Native American music was complete long before 'world music' became a marketing niche and a critical sneer.

The early records were largely, but not exclusively, devoted to Towner compositions and were characterized by delicate interplay between his 12-string guitar and Paul McCandless's equally 'classical' oboe. The music on *Music Of Another Present Era* and *Distant Hills* was widely perceived as ethereal and impressionistic, and there was a tendency (perhaps encouraged by intermittent sound-balance on the original vinyl releases) to underestimate the significance of Glen Moore's firm bass-lines (see 'Spring Is Really Coming' on *Present Era*) or the forcefulness of Collin Walcott's tablas. The music combined evocative thematic writing ('Aurora' on *Present Era*, recently re-recorded on the last item below; the classic 'Silence Of A Candle' and McCandless's 'The Swan' on *Distant Hills*) with abstract, collectively improvised pieces (like the 'Mi Chirita Suite' on *Distant Hills*; a neglected aspect of the band's career) and forcefully rhythmic tunes like 'Sail' (*Present Era*) which should have confounded a lingering belief that the band were too professorial to rock.

*****(*) Winter Light**

Vanguard VSD 79350 *As above.* 74.

*****(*) The Essential Oregon**

Vanguard VSD 109/110 *As above, except add Zbigniew Seifert (vn); David Earle Johnson (perc).*

****(*) Out Of The Woods**

Discovery 71004 *As above, except omit Seifert and Johnson.* 4/78.

****(*) Roots In The Sky**

Discovery 71005 *As above.* 12/78, 4/79.

***** Moon And Mind**

Vanguard VMD 79419 2 *As above.* 79.

Winter Light was in some respects a transitional album. Simpler in outline and in its commitment to song forms, it is nevertheless curiously muted, lifted only by 'Deer Path' and by a version of Jim Pepper's 'Witchi-Tai-To', an item that has remained a staple of Oregon performances ever since. The album is also interesting for its (relative) avoidance of so-called ethnic elements in favour of Native American elements; Pepper is a North American Indian.

The Essential Oregon compilation tends to highlight this side of the band's work, certainly at the expense of more abstract treatments, but offers a much less balanced picture of the band's work than the original releases; the additional tracks featuring Johnson and Seifert are something of a distraction.

Oregon went through something of a slump in the later 1970s. Two studio albums, originally for Elektra, *Out Of The Woods* and *Roots In The Sky*, represent perhaps their weakest moments on record, though a live double-album contained some excellent individual work and a further sample of the group's free mode. The way forward had, however, been plotted by an astonishing collaboration with drummer Elvin Jones, also in Vanguard's back-catalogue, an unlikely combination of forces that in retrospect seemed perfectly logical. Though received wisdom has it that Jones taught them how to swing, it's clear that his polyrhythmic method was *already* part of the group's language. During this same period, the most obvious changes of focus were a gradual subordination of Towner's guitar playing in favour of piano (and, later, synthesizer) and McCandless's decision to double on the much more forceful soprano saxophone.

Moon and Mind is something of a footnote to the Vanguard years and it's an odd mix of material, ranging from the band's trademark hybrid of folk, classical and ethnic styles to a relatively straight version of a jazz tune, Scott LaFaro's 'Gloria's Step', a piece which entered jazz history through Bill Evans's classic Village Vanguard performances. It's also not strictly an Oregon album, but a sequence of duets in every possible combination and with a very stripped-down approach to instrumentation and, with the exception of 'Elevator' (a Towner/Walcott collaboration), making little use of overdubs and studio sweetening. Depending on your point of view, either an imaginative new departure or a stalled moment in the band's stately progress.

***** Oregon**

ECM 811711-2 *As above.* 2/83.

****(*) Crossing**

ECM 825323-2 *As above.* 10/84.

Oregon represents a partial return to form in the new, upbeat manner. Clearly, too, the group-sound benefited enormously from ECM's state-of-the-art production. However, the writing seems remarkably tame and formulaic, a tendency reinforced on its successor. *Crossing* has acquired a slightly sentimental aura, since it is the last Oregon record on which Walcott appeared; between recording and release, he and the group's road manager were killed in an auto accident while on tour in Europe. It is, though, a very unsatisfactory record with few compelling themes and some of the group's most banal playing.

(*) **Ecotopia

ECM 833120-2 *As above, but Trilok Gurtu (tabla, perc) replaces the late Collin Walcott.*

*** **45th Parallel**

veraBra CDVBR 2048 *As above, except add Nancy King (v).* 8 & 9/88.

*** **Always, Never And Forever**

veraBra CDVBR 2073 *As for Ecotopia.* 90.

It is, of course, idle to speculate what might have happened had Walcott survived. A hugely talented musician, with a recording career of his own, he was in some senses the most wayward of the group's members. To some extent, the range of his skills was at a premium in the 'new' Oregon. However, he was a vital component of the group's sound, and his death was a shattering blow which almost sundered the band permanently. Trilok Gurtu was recruited only after much heart-searching and because he combined many of Walcott's strengths with an individuality of voice and technique. His group debut on *Ecotopia* is uncertain, though the album's flaws can hardly be laid to his account. The group were still in personal and artistic shock, and there is a nostalgic rootlessness inscribed in every aspect of the album, from the title onwards. *45th Parallel* is better and more firmly demarcated, with some swinging piano from Towner (and a partial return to form on guitar) and a better balance of material. It's marred by Nancy King's preposterous vocal on 'Chihuahua Dreams', but there's a clear sense that the band has re-established contact with its own past output (that is made clear in the brief 'Epilogue') and with its own sense of development. Whether that is signalled equally successfully in the new version of 'Aurora' on the second veraBra album is a matter of conjecture; but the turn of the group's third decade does seem to represent a promising new dawn.

***(*) **Troika**

veraBra 2078 *Ralph Towner (g, syn); Paul McCandless (ob, eng hn); Glen Moore (b).* 1–11/93.

The experiment with Gurtu seemed to founder despite successful tours. Whether this was as a result of artistic incompatibility or as a result of his own burgeoning solo career is difficult to judge. *Troika* would seem to find Oregon in their natural state again. The absence of a percussionist is partially compensated for by Towner's increasingly inventive touch on the Korg synth, and Moore seems to have devised ways of playing in a much more accented and forceful style. There are a couple of free pieces which hark back to the early days, but most of the tracks are short songs that concentrate on particular harmonic and textural areas. Only the longer 'Mariella' and 'Celeste' and, to a degree, 'Gekko' and 'Tower' show much emphasis on structure as a guiding principle. There is no mistaking Oregon's viability as a creative force. This isn't one of their classics, but it is a cracking good album.

***(*) **North West Passage**

Intuition INT 3191 *As above, except add Arto Tuncboyaciyan, Mark Walker (d, perc).* 97.

In a revealing liner-note, Towner meditates on 27 years of the band's progress, the corners turned, the understated life-changes and shifts of direction; but, underlining them all, a basic faith and confidence in the kind of music Oregon makes, which is complex, eternally unfashionable and all too susceptible to charges of portentousness. One of the key factors he identifies is the constantly renewed desire to work with percussionists. Though Walcott's name is not mentioned, he is once again the unspoken presence behind this record. The recruitment of Tuncboyaciyan and the young, talented Walker (who has a specialist interest in hand drums) was a bold and imaginative one. Arto is a more appropriate player for the group than Trilok Gurtu ever would have been, and his drumming on the opening 'Take Heart' helps demonstrate what a jazzy group Oregon could be at their peak.

McCandless once again varies his horns, introducing sopranino saxophone on 'Nightfall', but sticking pretty much to soprano saxophone and oboe. Towner more or less abandons guitar in the middle of the record to concentrate on piano and keyboards. Somehow this makes sense of the shifting pace of compositions, but one still thinks of him as a guitarist first and foremost, and it is unfortunate that he feels unwilling to concentrate on guitar for at least one Oregon disc.

Original Dixieland Jazz Band

GROUP

A group of young white players from New Orleans who hung around many of the local leaders such as Joe Oliver and picked up ideas. Under LaRocca's leadership they began working in Chicago in 1916, then went to New York and created a sensation at Resenweber's restaurant the following year. Arrived in London in 1919 and played in Hammersmith for nine months. Returned to the USA and continued popularity, but went into abeyance when LaRocca became ill in 1925. Re-formed for a brief comeback in 1936. LaRocca retired to become a builder, back in New Orleans. The records they made are acknowledged as the first jazz sessions and remained enormously influential.

***(*) **Sensation!**

ASV AJA 5023R *Nick LaRocca (c); Emil Christian, Eddie Edwards (tb); Larry Shields (cl); Bennie Krueger (as); J. Russel Robinson, Billy Jones, Henry Ragas (p); Tony Sbarbaro (d).* 2/17–11/20.

(****) **The 75th Anniversary**

RCA Bluebird ND 90650 *As above.* 2/17–12/21.

**** **The Original Dixieland Jazz Band 1917–1921**

Timeless CBC 1-009 *As above.* 2/17–12/21.

The ODJB, for all their anomalous position, remain the place to start in dealing with the history of jazz on record. Whatever effects time has had on this music, its historical importance is undeniable: the first jazz band to make records *may* have been less exciting than, say, the group that King Oliver was leading in the same year, but since no such records by Oliver or any comparable bandleader were made until much later, the ODJB assume a primal role. Harsh, full of tension, rattling with excitement, the best records by the band have weathered the years surprisingly well. Although the novelty effects of 'Barnyard Blues' may seem excessively quaint today, the ensemble patterns which the group created – traceable to any number of ragtime or march strains – have remained amazingly stable in determining the identity of 'traditional' jazz groups ever since. The blazing runs executed by Shields, the crashing, urgent rhythms of Sbarbaro and LaRocca's thin but commanding lead cornet cut through the ancient recordings. Although the band were at the mercy of their material, which subsequently declined into sentimental pap as their early excitement subsided, a high proportion of their legacy is of more than historical interest.

Fifty-four of their recordings between 1917 and 1922 have survived, but there is no comprehensive edition currently available. Their 1917 sessions for Aeolian Vocalion, very rare records, have yet to make it to CD. The ASV CD includes 18 tracks and offers a good cross-section of their work, although a couple of undistinguished later pieces might have been dropped in favour of the absent and excellent 'Mournin' Blues' or 'Skeleton Jangle'. One can hear the band grow in stature as performers as time goes on, but the excitement of their earliest dates remains crucial to the spread of the music.

The Timeless CD sweeps the board, since it covers all of their Victor sessions up to the end of 1921, a perfect duplication of the Bluebird CD – but in much livelier and more enjoyable sound, which gives the best idea of the sensation this remarkable group must have caused. The *75th Anniversary* CD remains a decent alternative, but Timeless's remastering is clearly superior.

Original Memphis Five

GROUP

Something of a generic group-name for white small groups of the 1920s, it was first used by Phil Napoleon for his small band in New York, commencing in 1920, then in scores of sessions from 1922, although it was also used occasionally by Red Nichols and Miff Mole. Napoleon carried on using it, even into the 1980s!

***** Original Memphis Five Collection Vol. 1**

Collectors Classics COCD-16 *Phil Napoleon (c, t); Charles Panelli, Miff Mole (tb); Doc Behrendsen, Jimmy Lytell, Sam Lanin (cl); Rudy Wiedoeft (as); Frank Signorelli (p); Ray Kitchingman (bj); Jack Roth (d).* 4/22–12/23.

With the Ladd's Black Aces LPs on Fountain/Retrieval now out of print, this is the only disc dedicated to the work of the group that came to be, usually, the Original Memphis Five, although many of the tracks here are credited to Jazbo's Carolina Serenaders or The Southland Six. Napoleon is on every track, Mole on most of them, and together they make one of the best front lines of the day: Mole's flexibility shines through even the early tracks and Napoleon's steady, unflashy lead is a thread that runs through all 23 tunes. Improvisation is done more in breaks than in solos, but this is primarily an ensemble music, still edging away from the ODJB. It would be admirable to see this huge group of titles (more than 400 78-r.p.m. masters) given a proper reissue: this is a good start! Remastering is excellent, but younger ears should beware: this is ancient-sounding music, even off the cleanest transfer.

*****(*) The Original Memphis Five, Napoleon's Emperor's, The Cotton Pickers 1928-1929**

Timeless CBC 1-049 *Phil Napoleon (t); Tommy Dorsey (tb, t); Glenn Miller (tb); Jimmy Dorsey (cl, as); Frank Signorelli, Arthur Schutt (p); Joe Venuti (vn); Eddie Lang (g, bj); Carl Kress (g); Perry Botkin (bj); Joe Tarto (b); Stan King, Vic Berton (d); Hoagy Carmichael, Marlin Hurt, Libby Holman, Scrappy Lambert, Dick Robertson (v).* 6/28–7/29.

Not really the OM5 as they stood several years earlier, this is more like the New York studio jazz of the later part of the decade. With few concessions to dance-orchestra feel, and some hardcore material, it's surprisingly uncompromising for that moment, when such discs weren't selling too well (and these are all rare originals). The expected excellence from Napoleon and the Dorseys, although our favourite moment is the outrageous duet between Hoagy Carmichael and Scrappy Lambert on 'St Louis Gal'.

The Original Victoria Jazz Band

GROUP

A band of London-based traditionalists.

**** Plays Chicago Classics**

London Jazz LMJ 024B *Alan Snook (t, c); David Chandler (tb); Pete Bennetto (cl, ts); Billy Boston (bsx); Colin Good (p); Greg Potter (bj); Steve Wick (sou); Arthur Fryatt (d, wbd).* 3–5/90.

****(*) More Chicago Classics**

London Jazz LMJ 025B *As above, except omit Wick.* 3/92.

Trad from London. The material is all straight out of the Chicago repertory, and the trouble is that you can hear better versions of any of the tunes elsewhere, without trying very hard. The earlier disc is all too polite and tasteful – their 'Sheikh Of Araby' is flat out and taking forty winks. But there's a smidgeon of extra bounce and vim in the second CD, which is really more of the same only a little hotter. None of the soloists has much to say, and the rhythm section could use some rocket assist. Best moment: an agreeably tousled 'See See Rider'.

Carl Fredrik Orrje

PIANO

Contemporary Swedish pianist making his debut.

***** 102 Greet St, NYC**

Arietta ADCD 12 *Orrje; Essiet Essiet (b); Tony Reedus (d).* 5/96.

The young Swede's date was cut at the address indicated by the title, and it has the inevitable flavour of European-goes-to-New York which besets many such records. Orrje is a good executant, involving both hands in improvisations dense with notes, and his composing is better still: he sounds more interested in his own 'The Beginner', 'Empty Streets' and 'Dark Skies' than in the six standards and jazz tunes. Essiet and Reedus play well without suggesting that they're especially engaged in the leader's music, and the sound of the rhythm section is a little cloudy. Worthwhile, though we would rather hear Orrje in a more individual setting.

Niels-Henning Orsted Pedersen (born 1946)

DOUBLE BASS

The great Dane is one of the most prolific recording artists in the music. A glance at the index will confirm the number and diversity of his associations, though he is probably best known for his work with near-namesake Oscar Peterson, but he also worked with a huge variety of visiting Americans when he was house bassist at the Jazzhus Montmartre in Copenhagen. Something of a prodigy, NHOP switched from piano to bass quite late and seemed to acquire his mature voice almost instantly, even receiving an offer to join the Basie orchestra.

***** Jaywalkin'**

Steeplechase SCCD 31041 *Orsted Pedersen; Philip Catherine (g); Ole Kock Hansen (p); Billy Higgins (d).* 9 & 12/75.

***** Double Bass**

Steeplechase SCCD 31055 *Orsted Pedersen; Sam Jones (b); Philip Catherine (g); Albert 'Tootie' Heath, Billy Higgins (d, perc).* 2/76.

****** Live At Montmartre: Volume 1**

Steeplechase 51083 *Orsted Pedersen; Philip Catherine (g); Billy Hart (d).* 10/77.

*****(*) Live At Montmartre: Volume 2**

Steeplechase 51093 *As above.* 10/77.

*****(*) Dancing On The Tables**

Steeplechase SCCD 31125 *Orsted Pedersen; Dave Liebman (ts, ss, af); John Scofield (g); Billy Hart (d).* 7 & 8/79.

Even though misspelt and mis-indexed (and we have been guilty of the odd inconsistency ourselves), NHOP's credits as a sideman almost defy belief. He plays on well over 100 currently available CDs, backing the likes of Chet Baker, Kenny Drew, Lee Konitz, Ben Webster and (crucially) Dexter Gordon and Oscar Peterson. He has recorded with younger-generation players as far apart in style as Niels Lan Doky and Anthony Braxton. If his playing on the two Steeplechases from the Club Montmartre in Copenhagen sounds particularly confident, that is because he spent much of his later twenties as house bassist there. His technique as a young man was staggering, combining forceful swing with great melodic and harmonic sense and a sure-fingeredness that gave his big, sonorous tone an almost horn-like quality.

Equally consistent as a leader, NHOP probably hasn't received his due of praise for his own records. They are all broadly of a piece, largely standards-based, with the group sessions placing greater emphasis on swing, and the duos on a more musing, intimate quality; the ratings above give a reasonable sense of their respective merits. The bassist has enjoyed a particularly fruitful relationship with guitarist Philip Catherine, who shares many of his virtues; the two in combination are responsible for some formidably beautiful music. The punning *Double Bass* is an interesting experiment that almost falters when a second drummer joins the group, doubling not just the bass lines but the whole rhythm section; Catherine is left with an unenviable continuity job, but 'Au Privave' (Oscar Peterson's favourite Charlie Parker theme) and Coltrane's 'Giant Steps' fare remarkably well. *Dancing On The Tables* explores less familiar materials and tonalities. Liebman's saxophone playing is sufficiently light and spacious not to swamp the foreground, and NHOP produces some intriguing rapid-fire counterpoints to the guitarist.

*****(*) Friends Forever**

Milestone MCD 9269 *Orsted Pedersen; Renee Rosnes (p); Jonas Johansen (d).* 8/95.

Recorded as a tribute to the late Kenny Drew, with whom NHOP recorded over many years, *Friends Forever* is unmistakably in the spirit of the great pianist. Drew would have loved the straightforward and funky version of 'The Shadow Of Your Smile' and he could not have failed to be intrigued by the unison line of 'Kenny', the bassist's most explicit memorial. Rosnes was the perfect choice for the job; she obviously knows Drew's work pretty well, and she quotes more than once from *Dark Beauty*, his duo record with NHOP. Johansen is inevitably a quieter partner, but his brushwork on the closing 'Future Child – Friends Forever', a delicate bass feature with a glorious piano/*arco* middle section, is exemplary. The sound is very good indeed and Phil De Lancie's mastering is everything you would expect from this good friend of jazz music.

****** Those Who Were**

Verve 533232-2 *Orsted Pedersen; Johnny Griffin (ts); Ulf Wakenius (g); Victor Lewis, Alex Riel (d); Lisa Nilsson (v).* 5/96.

*****(*) This Is All I Ask**

Verve 539695-2 *Orsted Pedersen; Phil Woods (as); Oscar Peterson (p); Ulf Wakenius (g); Jonas Johansen (d); Monique, Monica Zetterlund (v).* 7 & 9/97.

These two records are the work of a man entirely at peace with himself and his music. There is nothing to prove, no rival reputations to beat down. Niels Lan Doky's intuitive touch at the controls gives both a clarity and a warmth that make the music come alive. NHOP's opening on 'Our Love Is Here To Stay', first track on the faintly elegiac *Those Who Were*, demonstrates yet again what a master of harmony and time he is. As before, he programmes intelligently, including a Carl Nielsen theme, the title-song (a feature for the lovely Lisa Nilsson) and 'You And The Night And The Music', which is one of two guest spots for Griff, playing with his now familiar relaxed intensity. The other, 'The Puzzle', is marginally less successful. The second of the two albums is marked by a guest appearance from old boss Oscar Peterson, sounding fleet and unhampered on the traditional 'I Skovens Dybe Stille Ro', a tune that lends itself well to a jazz interpretation. As before, NHOP also includes a classical piece, this time a Bartók fantasia, played with completely idiomatic understanding as an unaccompanied solo. Elsewhere, Wakenius and Johansen are able companions and the guest saxophonist this time out is much more obviously in the bassist's bag. Woods sounds great on the title-piece, blowing with a warm, waxy quality. The vocals are attractive enough, but not particularly compelling. We remain Zetterlund sceptics, and her near-namesake Monique sounds ill at ease in a jazz context.

***** Hommage – Once Upon A Time**

Emarcy 513 189 2 *Orsted Petersen; Palle Mikkelborg (t, flhn); Palle Bolvig, Jan Kohlin (t); Axel Windfeldt (tb); Flemming Madsen, Jan Zum Vorde (sax); Mogens Durholm (v); Ars Nova Choir; other personnel.* 97.

A lovely collaboration between NHOP and trumpeter Mikkelborg, who brings a characteristic richness of tone and density of texture to these delightful sessions. There is an almost autumnal maturity and poise to the bassist's recent solo work. While still very much rooted in bebop harmony and the need to drive the line forward, he is much more inclined than of yore to dwell on ideas for their sheer beauty, and the session is marked by some of his very best playing on record. The closing 'September Song (Epilogue)' is masterly.

Anthony Ortega (born 1928)

ALTO AND SOPRANO SAXOPHONES, FLUTE

A sideman with Lionel Hampton, then a leader in and around Los Angeles, Ortega incorporated some Ornette-like thinking into his basic bebop grammar. His early albums for Revelation were reissued by Hat ART in the '90s. Later records are scarce but worth seeking out.

*****(*) Anthony Ortega On Evidence**

Evidence EVCD 213 *Ortega; Sylvain Kassap (bcl); Manuel Rocheman (p); Didier Levallet (b); Jacques Mahieux (d).* 4/92.

Ortega has lost none of his adventurousness. This welcome return to the studios finds him in ruminative rather than urgent mood: the tempos are often dreamily slow, the melodies (all originals by Ortega or his wife, bar Mal Waldron's 'Warm Canto') poignantly caressed, and his previously astringent tone has softened a little. But there are still improvisations of absorbing skill and cumulative power: he's again a trifle unconvincing on the 'out' moments of 'Gone Again', yet the spiralling trails of 'Avignon' or 'Norge' are bewitching in their quiet intensity, with a new interest in soprano offering a change of timbre. The rhythm section are fine, even if Rocheman is occasionally a shade too flowery in some of his solos, and Kassap appears only on the closing 'Warm Canto', a sparse, almost elemental treatment.

Kid Ory (1886–1973)

TROMBONE, VOCALS

Composer of the immortal 'Muskrat Ramble' and an innovative player who made much use of mutes, slurs and other devices, Ory has a tutelary place in the history of recorded jazz. He also confounds Scott Fitzgerald's famous dictum about there being no second acts in American creative lives; having helped usher in the first jazz generation, the Kid was there to take part in its great revival.

****** Ory's Creole Trombone**

ASV CD AJA 5148 *Ory; Mutt Carey, George Mitchell, King Oliver, Bob Shoffner (c); Louis Armstrong (c, v); Johnny Dodds, Dink Johnson, Omer Simeon (cl); Stump Evans, Albert Nicholas, Billy Paige (cl, as, ss); Darnell Howard (cl, as); Barney Bigard (cl, ts, ss); Joe Clarke (as); Lil Armstrong, Jelly Roll Morton, Luis Russell, Fred Washington (p); Bud Scott, Johnny St Cyr (bj); Ed Garland, John Lindsey (b); Bert Cobb (bb); Paul Barbarin, Ben Borders, Andrew Hilaire (d).* 6/22–4/44.

***** Kid Ory, 1922–1945**

Classics 1069 *Ory; Mutt Carey (c); Darnell Howard, Dink Johnson, Omer Simeon (cl); Joe Darensbourg (cl, v); Fred Washington, Buster Wilson (p); Bud Scott (g); Ed Garland (p); Ben Borders, Minor Ram Hall, Alton Redd (d); Cecile Ory (v).* 22–45.

****** Kid Ory's Creole Jazz Band**

GHB BCD 10 *Ory; Mutt Carey (t); Darnell Howard, Omer Simeon (cl); Buster Wilson (p); Bud Scott (bj, v); Ed Garland (b); Minor Ram Hall, Alton Redd (d).* 8/44–11/45.

***** New Orleans Legends**

Vogue 655603 *Ory; Teddy Buckner, Mutt Carey (t); Joe Darensbourg, Jimmie Noone (cl); Lloyd Glenn, Buster Wilson (p); Bud Scott (g); Ed Garland (b); Minor Ram Hall, Zutty Singleton (d).* 4 & 10/44.

*****(*) Kid Ory: '44–'46**

American Music AMCD 19 *Ory; Mutt Carey (t); Barney Bigard, Albert Nicholas, Joe Darensbourg, Wade Whaley (cl); L.Z Cooper, Buster Wilson (p); Huddie Leadbetter, Bud Scott (g, v); Edward Garland (b); Charlie Blackwell, Minor Ram Hall, Zutty Singleton (d).* 1/44–5/46.

***** At The Green Room: Volume 1**

American Music AMCD 42 *As above, except omit Bigard, Nicholas, Whaley, Leadbetter, Singleton, Blackwell.* 2/47.

***** At The Green Room: Volume 2**

American Music AMCD 43 *As above.* 2/47.

***** At Crystal Pier, 1947**

American Music AMCD 90 *Ory; Andrew Blakeney (t); Joe Darensbourg, Archie Rosati (cl); Buster Wilson (p); Bud Scott (g); Ed Garland (b); Minor Ram Hall (d).* 8/47.

***** King Of The Tailgate Trombone**

American Music AMCD 20 *As above, except add Andrew Blakeney, Teddy Buckner (t).* 48–49.

Kid Ory's 1940s albums (on Good Time Jazz) had Creole cooking tips printed on the sleeves. On his comeback, after nearly a decade out of music fattening up chickens, the trombonist's rhythmic tailgating style was still as salty as blackened kingfish and as spicy as good gumbo. Ironically, he spent much of his life away from Louisiana, going to California for his health just after the First World War, where he recorded the first ever sides by an all-black group, 'Ory's Creole Trombone' and 'Society Blues', in 1922. For some purists, these – collected on the ASV compilation, *Ory's Creole Trombone* – and not the Original Dixieland Jazz Band's earlier discs, mark the real start of jazz recording.

The Classics compilation contains only sessions recorded under Ory's name. Leadership switched to Mutt Carey in 1925, and it wasn't until 1944 that the trombonist tried to put together a revived version of the original group. Hence a large gap in the documentation which renders the chronology pretty redundant and enhances the desirability of the ASV set.

A man can learn a lot watching chickens forage, though. Ory's comeback coincided with the big Dixieland revival, and he turned an instinct for self-marketing to lucrative effect. Notoriously difficult to work for, he was particularly demanding of his trumpet players. When Mutt Carey died in 1948, Ory used the equally brilliant Teddy Buckner and later Alvin Alcorn in what was to be one of the best and most authentic of the revivalist bands. Kid Ory's Creole Jazz Band lasted until the 1960s, by which time his exemplary stamina was failing and the big glissandi and slurs were sounding slightly breathless. Ory was a fine technician who cultivated a sloppy, 'rough' effect and a loud, forthright delivery that led some listeners to dub him a primitive. Like all the great Delta players, though, he thought of the whole group as a single instrument into which his own voice slotted perfectly.

The ASV also includes some important sides from 1926 with King Oliver and Louis Armstrong, and a group called the New Orleans Wanderers which was effectively the Hot Five without Pops. There is also material from later that year with Jelly Roll Morton and a jump forward in time to the revivalist band of 1944. A very valuable collection indeed.

The first American Music disc is mostly airshot material from Standard Oil-sponsored broadcasts in the first half of 1946. There is a brief, fascinating encounter with Huddie Leadbetter, better known as Leadbelly, on 'Bye'N'Bye' and 'Swing Low, Sweet Chariot', but for the most part it's the group with Carey or Joe Darensbourg, with four studio tracks showing Albert Nicholas in particularly good lip. There is some excellent material from the Green Room in San Francisco; content-wise nothing out of the ordinary except for a rather moving version of the 'Rifle Rangers (1919 March)' which must have pleased any old soldiers in the room. *King Of The Tailgate Trombone* is less individual, Blakeney and Buckner (on this 1949 occasion) rather indistinct and waffly. Sound-quality varies on all these but isn't significantly better or worse than the norm for the period, and Ory himself always took care to come through at the front, loud and firm, just in case anyone forgot his name.

***** Plays The Blues**

Storyville STCD 6035 *Ory; Alvin Alcorn, Teddy Buckner, Rico Valesti (t); Phil Gomez, Bob McCracken, George Probert (cl); Harvey Brooks, Don Ewell (p); Ed Garland (b); Minor Ram Hall (d).* 5/53–2/55.

*****(*) This Kid's The Greatest**

Good Time Jazz GTCD 12045 *Ory; Teddy Buckner (c); Pud Brown, Phil Gomez, Bob McCracken, George Probert (cl); Don Ewell, Cedric Haywood, Lloyd Glenn (p); Julian Davidson, Barney Kessel (g); Wellman Braud, Morty Cobb, Ed Garland (b); Minor Ram Hall (d).* 7/53–6/56.

*****(*) Kid Ory's Creole Jazz Band, 1954**

Good Time Jazz GTJ 12004 *Ory; Alvin Alcorn (t); George Probert (cl); Don Ewell (p); Bill Newman (g, bj); Ed Garland (b); Minor Ram Hall (d).* 8/54.

***** Sounds Of New Orleans: Volume 9**

Storyville STCD 6016 *Ory; Alvin Alcorn (t); Albert Burbank, Phil Gomez, George Probert (cl); Don Ewell (p); Ed Garland (b); Minor Ram Hall (d).* 5/54–2/55.

***** Kid Ory's Creole Jazz Band**

Good Time Jazz GTJ 12008 *Ory; Alvin Alcorn (t); George Probert (cl); Don Ewell (p); Barney Kessel (g); Ed Garland (b); Minor Ram Hall (d).* 12/55.

*****(*) The Legendary Kid**

Good Time Jazz 12016 *Ory; Alvin Alcorn (t); Phil Gomez (cl); Lionel Reason (p); Julian Davidson (g); Wellman Braud (b); Minor Ram Hall (d).* 11/55.

***** Favorites!**

Good Time Jazz 60-009 *Ory; Alvin Alcorn (t); Phil Gomez (cl); Cedric Haywood (p); Julian Davidson (g); Wellman Braud (b); Minor Ram Hall (d).*

The Good Time Jazz catalogue is now pretty much up to date, and frankly there's very little to choose between individual items. The titles are confusingly unvaried but the GHB disc has all the legendary Crescent recording sessions, excellent readings of 'Maple Leaf Rag', 'Ory's Creole Trombone', 'Careless Love Blues' and 'Oh, Didn't He Ramble', though not, unfortunately, Ory's own 'Muskrat Ramble', which was one of the revival hits of the mid-1950s. It's to be found on the good Storyville, with Alvin Alcorn's trumpet going sharp as a tack in and out of the melody, and also on *1954*. There are also a couple of good tracks on the Vogue compilation, and the earlier material on *New Orleans Jazz*; despite the presence of Bigard and Carey, the later stuff is pretty tired.

Plays The Blues has been augmented with five tracks not included on the LP release. Of these, 'Blues For Jimmie Noone' and 'Wolverine Blues' are the most substantial, genuine additions to the Ory catalogue. Nothing else is as compelling and only serious collectors will feel the need for 'Wang Wang Blues' or 'Sugar Blues'.

***** In Denmark**

Storyville 6038 *Ory; Henry 'Red' Allen (t, v); Cedric Haywood (p); Wellman Braud (b); Minor Ram Hall (d).*

This wasn't the easiest of associations, though very bankable at a time when New Orleans jazz was once again in vogue. Allen's was a restless and exploratory group, while by this stage Ory had pretty much decided that his style was set in stone. Red pushes the pace along and still sounds vital and alert, while the Ory group seems happy to dodge along at a consistent tempo. There are even moments when the trumpeter jumps a measure ahead. The programme of material is unsurprising, with 'St James Infirmary' a high point and bright, breezy renditions of 'Clarient Marmalade', 'Muskrat Ramble' and 'Indiana/Sheik Of Araby'. Ory's rewritten lyrics to 'I Wish I Could Shimmy Like My Sister Kate' suggest that Katherine has gone to the bad entirely. Entertaining stuff.

Mike Osborne (born 1941)

ALTO SAXOPHONE

Born in Hereford, Osborne became a major figure in the British contemporary scene of the '60s and '70s, although most of his recorded work is out of print and he has been inactive through illness since the early '80s.

**** Outback

Future Music FMR CD 07 *Osborne; Harry Beckett (t, flhn); Chris McGregor (p); Harry Miller (b); Louis Moholo (d).* 70.

For close to 20 years illness has silenced one of the most powerful and emotionally stirring voices in British jazz. A Mike Osborne gig, with whatever line-up, was a furious dance of disparate parts: simple hymnic tunes, wild staccato runs, sweet ballad formations and raw blues, all stitched together into a continuous fabric that left most listeners exhausted, and none unmoved. Osborne's early album, *Outback*, was rarely seen and highly collectable in its original LP issue on Turtle. With the Ogun catalogue, *All Night Long, Border Crossing, Tandem* and *Marcel's Muse* out of print, this is a more than worthwhile reissue. Readers of *The Wire* magazine voted *Outback* one of the records they would most like to see on CD, and one can immediately hear why. Ossie's wailing, turbulent voice fills up the room. He was probably always heard to greater advantage in the pianoless trio with Louis Moholo and the late Harry Miller, but before this session he invited friends Harry Beckett and Chris McGregor (who also has since passed away) to join in. Beckett lightens the sound with blinks of pure sunshine, but he's capable of a darker, freer tonality as well. There are just two long tracks, the title-piece and the more sanguine 'So It Is'. On the original LP they occupied opposite sides. Here, though, it's possible to hear them as two sides of a single musical personality, undoubtedly troubled, fiercely questing, but full of quiet humour as well. What's now impossible is to judge what Osborne might have gone on to do. All that's left is to hear his music and wish him well.

Greg Osby (born 1960)

ALTO AND SOPRANO SAXOPHONES

Born in St Louis, Osby studied in Washington, DC, and Berklee, then moved to New York. Worked with Ron Carter and Jack DeJohnette, then closely involved in the M-Base movement of musicians with Steve Coleman. Signed to Blue Note in 1990, pursued mix of rap, hip hop and jazz, but more recently reverted to acoustic music.

***(*) Zero

Blue Note 493760-2 *Osby; Jason Moran (p, org); Kevin McNeal (g); Lonnie Plaxico, Dwayne Burno (b); Rodney Green (d).* 1/98.

**** Banned In New York

Blue Note 496860-2 *As above, except Atsushi Ozada (b) replaces McNeal, Plaxico and Burno.* 98.

**** New Directions

Blue Note 522978-2 *Osby; Mark Shim (ts); Jason Moran (p); Stefon Harris (vib); Tarus Marteen (b); Nasheet Waits (d).* 5/99.

***(*) The Invisible Hand

Blue Note 520134-2 *Osby; Gary Thomas (ts, f, af); Andrew Hill (p); Jim Hall (g); Scott Colley (b); Terri Lyne Carrington (d).* 9/99.

Osby's M-Base period and the early records which came after it now seem like distractions from his mature work. It's somewhat surprising that, for an artist whom Blue Note clearly have a lot of faith in, even such recent records as *Art Forum* and *Further Ado* have been cut from the catalogue. Even so, at present Osby is setting a formidable pace with records of the calibre of those listed above. *Zero* establishes Moran and Green as key presences in his working group, musicians who can handle whatever tough tasks he can throw at them as ensemble players. Some of these themes still feel like holdovers from his earlier work, occasionally too hung up on effortful time-signatures or excessively knotted melody-lines; but relentless work has softened the edges of his writing and opened up what was previously too cryptic a content. The brilliant Moran finds all sorts of nourishment in these pieces – check his 'Minstrale' solo, blooming with Monkian quirks but less angular, more melodious – and Osby's own playing seems fuller, more singing, but no less intense.

Banned In New York, sent out at mid-price and packaged like an official bootleg, documents a single gig by the quartet, set down on a DAT player and rush-released as a report on work in progress. Osby's own '13th Floor' starts things off, but from there he brings in Rollins, Ellington, Parker and Monk tunes and uses the material to fashion an utterly compelling treatise on the tradition and how it can fuel the playing of contemporary spirits on the bandstand, here and now. Each of the musicians makes his individual mark, but it's the way the quartet develops and processes ideas, caught on the hoof, that makes the record so powerful and immediate. Osby has said that he wishes he could release several records a year, in the manner of the old Blue Note performers, and, if the results are like this, it's a sentiment we echo.

New Directions is, strictly speaking, a co-operative effort, but it was picked and planned by Osby. The sextet examines nine pieces from the Blue Note past, along with three originals by the principals. Osby took care to confound expectations of a simple repertory project by creating dramatic revisions of each piece. 'The Sidewinder' is just slightly reharmonized, strung over a tauter pulse than it usually gets, and the result is something refined but unsettling. 'Song For My Father', originally jovially bluesy, is darkened and sprung off Nasheet Waits's ominous patterns. Mark Shim makes a piquant contrast to Osby's terse, metropolitan sound: his thick, foggy but mobile delivery gets a showcase in his tremendous tenor solo on Wayne Shorter's 'Tom Thumb'. A brilliant effort all round.

The Invisible Hand is slightly disappointing, given the mouth-watering line-up. Osby again creates some extraordinary new twists on such familiar material as 'Nature Boy', using Thomas mainly on flute for tonal colour in the ensembles. Hall, inquisitive as ever, does his best to negotiate the music, but he never really seems entirely at one with what he's asked to do, and Hill is at times apparently somewhere else altogether. On the trio performance of 'Indiana', where he counterpoints himself with some discreet clarinet lines, Osby remains magnificently creative. This is a musician at the peak of his endeavours, and he must be followed by anyone interested in where jazz is going.

Oslo 13

GROUP

Formed in 1980 as a forum for young Oslo-based jazz musicians to play new music, this group was for the most part directed by Jon Balke.

**** Off-Balance

Odin NJ 4022-2 *Nils Petter Molvaer (t); Torbjørn Sunde, Dag Einar Eilertsen (tb); Erik Balke (as, bs); Tore Brunborg (ts); Arne Frang (ts, bsx); Olave Dale (bs); Jon Balke (ky); Carl Morten Iversen (b); Audun Kleive (d).* 8/87.

The sound of a Norwegian sax section is surely a unique one in contemporary music, with the mournful vibrato and wind-chilled timbre seemingly a national characteristic – or cliché, depending on one's sympathies. Jon Balke, who arranges and composes most of the music for this band (first formed in 1980, although now seemingly in abeyance) makes the most of that sound. Much of their music is based on the textural possibilities of the reeds, either skirling in opposition to the brass and rhythm or drifting in still, barren space. *Off-Balance* is a superb effort: Balke's scores offer something different in every track, the soloists are uniformly excellent, the balance of the band – trombones in tart opposition to the reeds, Molvaer a strong lone voice on trumpet, and Kleive's drum parts never content with playing time – is radically out of synch with any other contemporary large ensemble. They are also served with brilliant recording by Jan Erik Kongshaug.

*** Nonsentration

ECM 849653-2 *Per Jorgensen, Nils Petter Molvaer (t); Torbjørn Sunde (tb); Morten Halle (as); Tore Brunborg, Arne Frang (ts); Jon Balke (ky); Audun Kleive, Jon Christensen (d); Finn Sletten, Miki N'Doye (perc).* 9/90.

Both livelier and more inert than the previous record, this is a vaguely disappointing continuation. Balke's interest in texture and line continues to create some fascinating music, and the group again plays with real finesse and cumulative intensity, but the addition of funkier percussion on several tracks contrasts uneasily with the motionless mood-pieces which still take up a lot of the record.

*** Oslo 13 Live

Curling Legs CD07 *Jens Petter Antonsen, Staffan Svennson (t); Torbjørn Sunde (tb); Morten Halle (as); Thomas Gustavsson (ss, ts); Trygve Seim (ts); Jon Balke (ky); Carl Morten Iversen (b); Audun Kleive, Jon Christensen (d).* 5/92.

Something of a stop-gap live album, though much of the music here is strong and there's nothing that's less than interesting. Balke's opening 'Taraf' and Halle's finale, 'Hvit Vei', are the best pieces, sounding somewhat like slow Nordic marches: Svennson is superb in the first, and the intense ensemble colours run right through the second. Much of what comes in between seems slight, though. Impeccable playing, and Balke's awareness of what the group can do is impressive; but one feels more could have been made of a rather brief live record.

Other Dimensions In Music

GROUP

Free-jazz ensemble formed by four veterans of the New York scene of the 1980s and '90s.

**(*) Other Dimensions In Music

Silkheart SHCD 120 *Roy Campbell (t, flhn, pkt-t); Daniel Carter (as, ts, f, t); William Parker (b); Rashid Bakr (d).* 4/89.

*** Now!

AUM Fidelity AUM006 *As above.* 3/97.

***(*) Time Is Of The Essence Is Beyond Time

AUM Fidelity AUM013 *As above, except add Matthew Shipp (p).* 12/97.

They are, by now, a veteran group themselves, having played together as a quartet since the late '80s, but so far only a few records have come out of this New York ensemble. Campbell and Carter share a common impulse to be lyrical rather than wrathful in their playing and, with both Parker and Bakr also taking a relatively pacific line, the quartet's music emerges as patient and slow-burning. One of the best examples of what they do is the 33 minutes of 'For The Glass Tear/After Evening's Orange', the opening track on *Now!*, which sees a large canvas methodically explored as the four men enter and leave and return in varying combinations, Carter picking up tenor, flute and alto, Campbell spinning long lines on first open and then muted horn. The rest of the record doesn't quite match up to that long exploration, which may say something about how a CD can find it difficult to catch the quiet intensity the group generates in concert. Certainly the earlier Silkheart record feels unfocused and often ragged in comparison.

The meeting with Shipp is excellent. The pianist, effortlessly versatile in free situations, takes his place in the ensemble without any awkwardness – remarkable in itself, considering how long the quartet has played together – and without any cathartic crashing and banging the five players are quick to create a complex and shifting whole. Campbell and Carter make the most of their range of horns, but it's the momentum that Parker and Bakr create which holds the music-making together.

Roberto Ottaviano

SOPRANO AND ALTO SAXOPHONE, MANZANO

Italian saxophonist specializing in soprano. Has performed in several pan-European outfits, including Franz Koglmann's group, besides leading his own bands.

*** Sotto Il Sole Giaguro

Solstice SOLCD 1000 *Ottaviano; Stefano Battaglia (p); Piero Leveratto (b); Ettore Fioravanti (d).* 5/89.

*****(*) Items From The Old Earth**

Splasc(h) H 332 *Ottaviano; Roberto Rossi (tb); Mario Arcari (ss, ob, cor); Martin Mayes (frhn); Sandro Cerino (cl, bcl, f, bf); Fiorenzo Gualandris (tba).* 12/90.

He has done significant work as a sideman with Ran Blake, Franz Koglmann and Tiziana Ghiglioni among others, but Ottaviano's albums as a leader offer some of the best indication of his powers. He sticks to the soprano for the well-sustained quartet record for Solstice. Clearly he has worked very hard on his tone, for he gets an unusually pure and unaffected sound on the horn, rarely going for a squawk or anything remotely expressionist, and it lends his improvisations a clear if somewhat terse intensity. Six of the nine themes are by him – the other players have one writing credit each – and although some are less impressive, such as the fractured free-bop of 'Our Kind Of Wabi', others work splendidly. 'Feu De Glui' concentrates the quartet into a single voice, 'Freaks' has an ingeniously jabbing theme which sets up some pithy improvising, while Leveratto's 'Memories Memories' has a soprano solo of lucid beauty over walking bass and brushes. Excellent digital sound.

Items From The Old Earth is by Ottaviano's all-horns group, Six Mobiles. The sonorities are hard to predict, brassy at some points, woody at others, and the compositions are crowded (perhaps excessively so at times) both with ideas and with techniques, some of which beg comparison with European composition rather than jazz. But Ottaviano's own solos add a sudden brightness at moments when the ensemble threatens to turn stiff and dry.

***** Above Us**

Splasc(h) H 330-2 *Ottaviano; Stefano Battaglia (p); Piero Leveratto (b); Ettore Fioravanti (d).* 11/90.

****(*) Otto**

Splasc(h) H 340-2 *Ottaviano (ss solo).* 1/91.

Ottaviano returns to more conventional ground on the quartet record, which matches him with the gifted Battaglia: loose modal blowing seems to be the mainstay of the date, and it's done with aplomb, although some of the music lacks anchor and compass. *Otto* takes a stab at a solo album but seems a mite too cleverly conceived: reverb and overdubs distract from the point of Ottaviano's improvising and some of the solos seem like mere technical points-winners. A pretty record, though, when the saxophonist locates an attractive line.

*****(*) Hybrid And Hot**

Splasc(h) 453-2 *Ottaviano; Gianluca Petrella (tb); Tom Varner (frhn); Michel Godard (tba); Marcello Magliocchi (d).* 7/95.

This seems influenced at least in part by Ottaviano's work with Franz Koglmann, and the mordant humour of, say, 'The Lightwarrior' is something that the Austrian would surely appreciate. But Ottaviano has his own agenda here, with three Carla Bley themes and a solo treatment of Lacy's 'The Raps' alongside five of his own pieces; and his careful sifting of the four horns in front of Magliocchi's drums is fascinating and an absorbing study in light and shade. There are some wryly apposite solos from all four men, with the little-known Petrella at least as outstanding as his colleagues, yet it's the leader's meticulous playing which shines most particularly. Surely his best to date.

***** Black Spirits Are Here Again**

DIW 917 *Ottaviano; Mal Waldron (p).* 1/96.

A surprise meeting, even if Waldron's an old hand at this sort of thing with Steve Lacy. One feels that it isn't really Ottaviano's bag, impeccably though he plays, and standards like 'Come Sunday' are more like recitations than interactive dialogues. 'A Night In Tunisia', though, works splendidly, a very elegant dissertation from two cultured minds.

Tony Oxley (born 1938)

DRUMS, PERCUSSION

Oxley's importance to free music in Europe can scarcely be exaggerated, and yet he rarely plays in his native Britain, preferring exile and work in Germany. His apprenticeship ranges from a stint in the Black Watch band to the house section at Ronnie Scott's. He is a pioneer of metal and amplified percussion, and has retained a sense of swing and pulse even when playing free.

♛ ** The Baptised Traveller**

Columbia 494438 2 *Oxley; Kenny Wheeler (t, flhn); Evan Parker (ts); Derek Bailey (g); Jeff Cline (b).* 1/69.

*****(*) Four Compositions For Sextet**

Columbia 494437 2 *As above, except add Paul Rutherford (tb).* 70.

Tony Oxley served an apprenticeship in pub bands and then learnt a more formal craft as a military conscript. He was a key player in the early days of the British free scene, notably the trio of Josef Holbrooke with Derek Bailey and Gavin Bryars. Later years saw another trio, sOH, with Alan Skidmore and Ali Haurand and the Celebration Orchestra, which reveals him to be a composer of some considerable sophistication. Most of his pieces move relatively slowly, even if there is a lot of surface detail. Large acoustic masses seem to operate in three dimensions, as if Oxley were rotating the musical material to examine its unconsidered aspects.

These albums have enjoyed legendary status for years, and if only *Ichnos*, an even more adventurous vehicle for Oxley's pin-sharp sound and ideas, had also been reissued, a whole generation of British free-ophiles would be celebrating. For us, *The Baptised Traveller* is the most representative and coherent expression of his gifts. Thirled to a quest for identity, its four themes are calmly questioning, the two horns restlessly ranging over Cline's and Oxley's unceasing shifts of direction. 'Crossing' and 'Arrival', which are segued into a single improvisation, wipe clean almost all formal expectations. The centerpiece of the album is, unusually, a theme by a jazz composer. Oxley's stately reading of Charlie Mariano's 'Stone Garden' is one of the masterworks of contemporary improvised music, a slow chorale rooted in Bailey's chiming guitar chords. Their almost orchestral quality provides a starting point for Parker's solemn quiddities and for virtuosic percussion from Oxley. The closing 'Preparation' isn't so much an anti-climax as an obvious afterthought.

Four Compositions was a title guaranteed to offend players and fans who wanted to set aside any implication of predetermined structures. In the event, Oxley's ideas are all geared to solo improvisation. The opening of 'Saturnalia' is a mordant fanfare that announces the arrival of Evan Parker (probably his best recorded solo to date), Kenny Wheeler and Derek Bailey. The long 'Amass' is constructed from a graphic score and gives Rutherford, the sole newcomer from the previous album, his most effective moments. The disc ends with the scratchy, slightly unattractive 'Megaera', an exercise in sonic conflict that doesn't entirely convince.

Even 30 years on, one marvels at Columbia/CBS investing in music like this. That it was a brief experiment is no surprise. That it was so commandingly creative is a source of renewed delight. Two albums to treasure from a long-gone age in British music, but one whose creative implications are still being worked out.

*****(*) The Tony Oxley Quartet**

Incus CD15 *Oxley; Pat Thomas (ky, elec); Derek Bailey (g); Matt Wand (drum machine, tape switchboard).* 4/92.

This quartet session (recorded by WDR, Cologne) is a memorable reunion with Bailey as well as a meeting with two talented younger members of British improv. There are three quartet pieces, one trio (minus Oxley) and a duet between each of the four players. The opening quartet is a mesmerizing feeling-the-way performance, the soundscape wide open, with every man vital, nobody overplaying, each sound of interest. Thomas varies between analogue-synth wheezes and crisp digital arpeggios, while Wand's bricolage of found sounds and drumbeats redefines notions of minimalism. Bailey remains imperturbably himself, and his duet with Oxley is a superb co-operative battle of wits. The leader, if such he be here, continues to make free rhythm and pulse out of crashings and bangings that in other hands would be, well, unmusical. A magnificent and important (as well as enjoyable) modern document.

*****(*) The Enchanted Messenger**

Soul Note 1231284 *Oxley; Bill Dixon (t, flhn); Johannes Bauer (tb); Ernst-Ludwig Petrowsky (sax, cl); Frank Gratkowski (sax, bcl); Philip Wachsmann (vn, elec); Alex Kolkowski (vn); Marcio Mattos, Alfred Zimmerlin (clo); Pat Thomas (p, elec); Stefan Hölker, Tony Levin, Joe Thönes (d, perc); Matt Wand (elec); Phil Minton (v).* 11/94.

A superb large-scale composition for Oxley's Celebration Orchestra, performed at the 1994 JazzFest Berlin, *The Enchanted Messenger* consists of 19 interrelated parts or sections. The ensemble is very percussion-heavy, though Oxley doubles as drummer and conductor. The key soloists are trumpeter Bill Dixon, whose spirit suffuses the occasion almost as much as Oxley's, and violinist Philip Wachsmann, who always seems entirely at home in large ensembles like this.

Some of the material is atonal or pantonal but, as ever, Oxley gives a strong impression of pulse and swing. The balance of strings and winds isn't quite ideal and the sections fight in the mix, but it is possible to follow the course of this intriguing performance as it gradually dismantles its own initial premisses and pushes out into areas of freedom which only the London Jazz Composers' Orchestra and Globe Unity Orchestra have been able to explore with similar conviction. The use of electronics is what sets Oxley's ensemble apart from either of these. Wand, Thomas and Wachsmann create richly abstract textures, against which the acoustic instruments sound oddly alienated and strange. Not an easy record to absorb in just one or two sittings, but one that repays careful and prolonged attention.

Hot Lips Page (1908–54)

TRUMPET, MELLOPHONE

Oran Thaddeus Page grew up in Texas and was bound for a medical career when his mother started him on music lessons. He worked at menial jobs in the oilfield before finding work as a trumpeter and being recruited by Bennie Moten to the Blue Devils, led by Walter Page (who, he sometimes claimed, was a kinsman). Page worked with Basie in his classic orchestra and was admired for his warm, full tone, hence his nickname. Despite his talent and popularity, he made few records under his own name.

*****(*) Pagin' Mr Page: His Greatest Recordings 1932–1946**

ASV CD AJA 5437 *Page; Bobby Hackett (c); Lee Castle, Buck Clayton, Shad Collins, Harry Edison, Max Kaminsky, Joe Keyes, Ed Lewis, Steve Lipkins, Bobby Moore, Eddie Mullins, Dink Stewart (t); Ray Conniff, Vic Dickenson, Eddie Durham, J.C Higginbotham, Jack Jenney, Lou McGarity, Dan Minor, Miff Mole, Benny Morton, Morey Samuel, George Stevenson, Jack Teagarden, Dicky Wells, Harry White, Sandy Williams (tb); Ernie Caceres, Edmond Hall, Pee Wee Russell (cl); Eddie Barefield, Ben Smith (cl, as); Earl Bostic, Charlie DiMaggio, George Johnson, Gene Kinsey, Les Robinson, Ulysses Scott, Don Stovall, Earl Warren, Floyd Horsecollar Williams (as); Jack Washington (as, bs); Georgie Auld, Don Byas, Nick Caiazza, Sam Davis, Herschel Evans, Mickey Folus, John Hartzfield, Ernie Powell, Ike Quebec, Sam Simmons, Benny Waters, Ben Webster, Lester Young (ts); Art Baker, Jack Washington (bs); Count Basie, Johnny Guarnieri, Clyde Hart, Cliff Jackson, Jimmy Reynolds, Rufus Webster (p); Danny Barker, Leroy Berry, Mike Bryan, Teddy Bunn, John Collins, Herb Ellis, Freddie Green, Tiny Grimes, Connie Wainwright (g); Abe Bolar, Wellman Braud, Bob Casey, Israel Crosby, Pops Foster, Al Hall, Bass Hill, Al Lucas, Eddie McKimmey, Al Morgan, Walter Page (b); Big Sid Catlett, A.G Godley, Harry Jaeger, Jo Jones, Ed McConney, Willie McWashington, Buford Oliver, Jack Parker, Specs Powell, Alfred Taylor, Dave Tough, George Wettling (d).* 12/32–46.

***** Hot Lips Page, 1938–1940**

Classics 561 *Page; Bobby Moore, Eddie Mullens (t); George Stevenson, Harry White (tb); Ben Smith, Buster Smith (cl, as); Jimmy Powell, Ulysses Scott, Don Stovall (as); Ben Williams (as, ts); Don Byas, Sam Davis, Ernie Powell, Sam Simmons, Benny Waters (ts); Pete Johnson, Jimmy Reynolds (p); John Collins, Connie Wainwright (g); Abe Bolar, Wellman Braud (b); A.G Godley, Ed McConney, Alfred Taylor (d); Romayne Jackson, Bea Morton, Delores Payne, Ben Powers, The Harlem Highlanders (v).* 3/38–12/40.

*****(*) Hot Lips Page, 1940–1944**

Classics 809 *Page; Jesse Brown, Joe Keyes (t); Vic Dickenson, Benny Morton (tb); Earl Bostic, Benjamin Hammond, George Johnson, Floyd Horsecollar Williams (as); Don Byas, Ike Quebec, Ben Webster, Lem Johnson, Lucky Thompson (ts); Ace Harris, Leonard Feather, Clyde Hart, Hank Jones (p); Sam Christopher*

Allen (g); Teddy Bunn (g, v); Al Lucas, John Simmons, Carl Flat Top Wilson (b); Ernest Bass Hill (b, bb); Big Sid Catlett, Jack Parker, Jesse Price (d). 12/40–11/44.

An Armstrong imitator who never quite made it out of that constricting sack, Page has always hovered just below the threshold of most fans' attention. Realistically, he is a much less accomplished player who wasted much of his considerable talent on pointless jamming and dismal but lucrative rhythm and blues. The material recorded for Bluebird in April 1938 features a band that might have gone places had Page not had to disband it. At the beginning of 1940 he was recording with the remarkable Buster Smith, a Texan out of Ellis County, who became a mainstay of the Kansas City sound during the war years and after. These are fine sides, not altogether improved by some very odd remastering wobbles, but they're surpassed by the four cuts made for Decca towards the end of the year with Pete Johnson and Don Byas, which (leaving aside an indifferent vocal by Bea Morton) are among the best of the period and unjustly neglected.

The title of the second Classics volume is slightly misleading. There is, to be sure, material from 1940 and from 1944, but nothing in between. Some of the interim period is covered in various bootlegged jam sessions which may be available. The drummerless 1940 group with Feather, Bunn and Hill is very good indeed, with Hill a considerable surprise for a bass player of his day. Page also shows off his touch on the now seldom-used mellophone. The real treat on this volume, though, is the later material featuring Byas. As Anatol Schenker's informative liner-notes suggest, 'These Foolish Things' is one of the high points of 1940s saxophone jazz, worth playing to unsuspecting experts for a guess at the saxophonist involved. There are giveaway phrases here and there but, at these sessions for Commodore, Byas excelled himself. There is some Savoy material from June 1944, a bigger group in which Byas has to give ground to the great Ben Webster; but it is the two dates for Milt Gabler's label which stand out. Even the quasi-novelty items like 'The Blues Jumped A Rabbit' are excellent. It wouldn't be a Classics volume without an early appearance from a star of the future. On the last session, from November 1944, Hank Jones makes his recording debut backing Page, Dickenson and the very fine Thompson on 'The Lady In Bed' and 'Gee, Baby, Ain't I Good For You?'.

The ASV compilation is able to range more widely than Classics because it takes in material made for other leaders – Moten, Basie, Chu Berry, Artie Shaw, Albert Ammons and Eddie Condon – but does also sample the sessions of April 1938, January, November and December 1940, and June and September 1944. The sound is very good but, given how much of this material is available from other sources, it will be of limited value to anyone who isn't simply looking for a quick introduction to Page's work. For a quick comparison of sound, compare the Classics transfer of 'I Let A Song Go Out Of My Heart' with this. No comparison at all, really.

***** After Hours In Harlem**
HighNote HCD 7031 *Page; Joe Guy (t); Rudy Williams (as); Herbie Fields (ts); Donald Lambert, Thelonious Monk (p); Tiny Grimes (g); other personnel unidentified.* 40, 41?

Originally released on Onyx in 1973, this fascinating set represents the work of jazz fan Jerry Newman who, like Dean Benedetti with Charlie Parker, staked out his favourite musicians and recorded them on a portable machine. Over the years, he accumulated an astonishing archive. Not the least remarkable of these recordings are the first documented performances of Thelonious Monk, heard with Page and Joe Guy on 'Sweet Georgia Brown' and 'Topsy'. The disc would be valuable for that alone but, coupled with its picture of Page at work away from the studio, it helps fill out some aspects of his playing style, not least how much more of an Armstrong imitator he seems on record than in front of a live audience when more of his wry, reckless nature comes through. The tones are bright enough to come off a shaky source-tape and Page's solo development has a nicely asymmetrical logic which is very different from Pops and from almost anyone else on the scene at the time. There is also a nice example of his singing, on 'Yazoo'; again very different from the master, but not without its charms.

****(*) Dr Jazz: Volume 6 – 1951–1952**
Storyville STCD 6046 *Page; Wild Bill Davison (c); Lou McGarity, Sandy Williams (tb); Eddie Barefield, Peanuts Hucko, Pee Wee Russell, Cecil Scott, Bob Wilber (cl); Dick Cary, Charlie Queener, Red Richards, Joe Sullivan (p); Eddie Safranski, Jim Thorpe (b); George Wettling (d).* 12/51–3/52.

These late airshots were broadcast from Stuyvesant Casino at 2nd and 9th in New York City, under the auspices of drummer Wettling's group. There is one great session here, featuring Page with Wild Bill Davison and Lou McGarity on what occasionally sounds like an alto trombone, a sharp, puncturing sound that sits wonderfully with the two trumpets. Otherwise, it's fairly run-of-the-mill. To a large extent Page was yesterday's man; he can only occasionally, as on 'St Louis Blues' from February 1952, summon up the old fire. A valuable addition for dedicated collectors, but pretty marginal stuff compared to the above.

Willie Pajeaud

TRUMPET, VOCAL

An ensemble brassman in the old New Orleans tradition, Pajeaud was a foot-soldier in the music's honourable past.

***(*) Willie Pajeaud's New Orleans Band 1955**
504 LP31 *Pajeaud; Raymond Burke (cl); Danny Barker (g, bj, v); Len Ferguson (d); Blue Lu Barker (v).* 55.

Pajeaud is best known as a principal in the Eureka Brass Band, but this memento of a jam session on Bourbon Street in 1955 finds him leading a small group of New Orleans stalwarts. Frankly, it's more of historical interest than anything else: Danny and Blue Lu Barker take three of the numbers virtually by themselves, and the remainder are enthusiastic but ragged accounts of the kind of tunes these men must have played every night of their professional lives. The recording is an amateur one and, unfortunately, sounds it.

Ed Palermo (born 1955)

ALTO SAXOPHONE, GUITAR, ARRANGER

Contemporary altoman with a fan's tribute to Frank Zappa.

***** The Ed Palermo Big Band Plays The Music Of Frank Zappa**

Astor Place TCD 4005 *Palermo; Ronny Buttacavoli, Jami Dauber, Liesl Whitaker (t); Jeff Williams (t, picc t); Dale Kirkland, Dan Levine (tb); Jack Schatz (btb); Bob Mintzer, Chris Potter (ts); Cliff Lyons (as, f, cl); Phil Chester (ss, as, f, picc); Chuck Fisher (ts, f, cl); Al Hunt (bs, ss, f, picc, bcl, ob); Bob Quaranta (p); Ted Kooshian (ky); Dave Samuels (vib); Mike Kenneally, Mike Stern (g); Paul Adamy (b); Ray Machica (d).* 7/96.

Given how much of it was jazz-based or at very least jazz-tinged, it seems odd that Frank Zappa's work should have been 'discovered' by the new-music establishment – most remarkably by Pierre Boulez and the Ensemble InterContemporain – before it was taken up by jazz arrangers. Jimi Hendrix tributes now seem ten-a-penny, though most of them simply follow in Gil Evans's footsteps, and there have even been attempts (David Murray's most successfully) to give the Grateful Dead's back-catalogue a jazz outing, but little of the otherwise much-admired Zappa so far. The obvious problem with these tunes is that they are not really blowing vehicles. Melodically quirky, they don't offer much harmonic grist for conventional jazz soloing, and most of the featured players, including special guests Mintzer, Potter, Stern, Kenneally and Samuels, restrict themselves to embellishing licks, much as Zappa himself did. On the face of it, the guitarists have the better end of the deal. Palermo joins Stern and Kenneally on his second instrument for 'We Are Not Alone', a strong piece which probably benefits from being less immediately familiar than 'Peaches En Regalia', 'Toads Of The Short Forest' or even 'King Kong'. The last of these, which Jean-Luc Ponty helped turn into a quasi-repertory piece, is a feature for Bob Mintzer, in strong voice; Chris Potter is handed the less promising 'Waka/Jawaka' and manages to make something of it. Palermo is a reasonably deft altoist, with the broad, salty tone that Zappa's music somehow requires. One feels, though, that this whole project could have done with an added sprinkle of irony. It's all a touch serious.

Papa Bue's Viking Jazz Band

GROUP

Led by clarinettist Papa Bue Jensen, this is one of the most popular and durable trad-to-Dixie outfits in Europe, with more than 40 years of faithful service to their enthusiastic following.

***** Greatest Hits**

Storyville STCD 836 *Arne Bue Jensen (tb); Finn Otto Hansen (t); Jorgen Svare (cl); Jorn Jensen (p); Bjarne Liller (bj, v); Jens Solund (b); Knud Ryskov Madsen (d).* 58–70.

*****(*) Featuring George Lewis**

Storyville STCD 6018 *As above, except add George Lewis (cl).* 2/59.

***** Featuring Edmond Hall**

Storyville STCD 6022 *As above, except omit Lewis; add Edmond Hall (cl).* 66.

***** Original Studio Recordings: Volume 1**

Storyville STCD 5502 *As above.* 66–69.

***** Original Studio Recordings: Volume 2**

Storyville STCD 5503 *As above.* 66–69.

*****(*) In The Sixties: Volume 1**

Music Mecca CD 1088 *As above, except omit Hall.* 67–69.

***** In The Sixties: Volume 2**

Music Mecca CD 1089 *As above.* 67–69.

The Viking empire once stretched as far south as the Mediterranean, and considerable ingenuity has been expended in attempting to prove that a Norseman beat Christopher Columbus across the Atlantic. Arne Bue Jensen represents circumstantial evidence that the Vikings made it not just to a slippery rock off Newfoundland, but all the way down to New Orleans. Under the eponymous Jensen's leadership, the band became a tireless gigging unit, establishing a big reputation in Eastern Europe, as had Chris Barber. Like the Barber band, the Vikings sell a fair proportion of their CDs at gigs, and some of these items may be difficult to find in mainstream and multiple record stores. Specialists will be able to track them down without difficulty, however, and Music Mecca in Copenhagen, a sort of Valhalla for traditional jazz fans, can be contacted for mail order. Dare we say, though, that to savour these guys, it is really necessary to catch them live. Nonsense about 'authenticity' apart, Papa Bue's long-running band is one of the finest revival outfits ever to emerge north of the Mason–Dixon line. The emphasis, inevitably, is on ensemble playing rather than soloing, and these are as confidently relaxed as anyone might wish for, with none of the stiffness that creeps into more studied revivalism. The rhythm players have a particularly good feel, the giveaway with most such bands.

The band was founded in 1956, but was baptized and confirmed three years later when George Lewis paid a visit to Denmark. The encounter is preserved on the Storyville CD, which is well worth tracking down, not just to fill out the already generous Lewis discography. A similar encounter with Edmond Hall is more disappointing. Exactly a decade after entertaining (and startling) George, the Vikings played at the New Orleans Jazz and Heritage Festival and won the admiration of the unfoolable Ira Gitler, who pointed out that the band were more than revivalists with a cod gimmick, but serious players who could knock out Ellington charts as well as trad material. The material on the two 1960s compilations comes from that period. Ellington staples 'Rent Party Blues' (a Johnny Hodges vehicle) and 'Misty Morning' are outstanding on Volume One, but the long version of 'St Louis Blues' is outstanding and could stand up against anything created on the other side of the Atlantic. Volume Two is less emphatic but, unless Music Mecca's claim that all these sides are 'previously unissued' is misleading, these are very important releases. They sound strikingly if implausibly modern, even if the sound-quality is boxy and unvaried.

***** On Stage**

Timeless CD TTD 511 *Jensen; Ole Stolle (t, v); Jorgen Svare (cl); Jorn Jensen (p); Jens Solund (b); Soren Houlind (d, v).* 4–9/82.

*****(*) In The Mood**

Timeless CD TTD 539 *As above.* 86.

***** Ice Cream**
Music Mecca CD 1000 *Jensen; Ole Stolle (t, v); John Defferary (cl); Jorn Jensen (p); Ole Olsen, Jens Solund (b); Didier Geers (d, v); Soren Houlind (d).* 10/86–8/89.

***** Live In Slukefter Tivoli**
Music Mecca CD 1028 *As above.* 91.

*****(*) On Visit At Chlosterhof**
Music Mecca CD 1064 *As above.* 91–93.

****(*) Everybody Loves Saturday Night**
Timeless CD TTD 580 *As above.* 12/92.

*****(*) Collection**
Music Mecca CD 2101 2CD *As above.* 86–93.

Personnel inevitably changed over the years. The key recruitment was of 'Englishman' (though we suspect Irish ancestry) John Defferary in 1985. He immediately became the key player, alongside the long-standing Jensen and Papa Bue himself, bringing a virile, Lewis-influenced sound to the group. *Ice Cream* is patchy because recorded over three years and several different sessions. The 1992 studio recording is a rather lacklustre introduction compared to what one knows the band can do at a regular gig. *In The Mood* is splendidly varied, our pick of the bunch, though some of the live recordings from the early '90s are almost as attractive. *On Stage* was recorded on the familiar turf of Copenhagen, and before a home crowd the Vikings play like they're all heading across the Rainbow Bridge, with a rousing 'Tiger Rag' and a genuinely affecting 'Just A Closer Walk With Thee'. *Collection* is a very fair summary of some of the high points of recent albums.

***** Canal Street Blues**
Music Mecca CD 1090 *Jensen; Joe Errington (t); John Defferary (cl, v); Jorn Jensen (p); Ole Olsen (b); Didier Geers (d, v).* 95, 96.

Though a studio setting never gets the best out of the Vikings, it's good on occasion to hear the band in a pristine acoustic and professionally balanced. Errington isn't quite the ticket, but he fits in nicely with Defferary and Jensen, and 'Grandpa's Spells' is a miniature masterpiece of ensemble jazz.

***** 40 Years Jubilee Concert**
Music Mecca 2010 *Jensen; Joe Errington, Finn Otto Hansen, Ole Stolle (t); Erik Andersen, John Defferary, Jorgen Svare (cl); Jorn Jensen (p); Ole Olsen, Mogens Seidelin, Jens Solund (b); Didier Geers, Soren Houlind, Ib Lindschouw, Knud Ryskov Madsen (d).* 7/96.

The Viking Jazz Band celebrated its fortieth birthday in 1996 with a gala performance in the Tivoli. Jensen got together some of the players who had passed through the group and they turned in a bright, buoyant evening of music that must have been a delight to the crowd. On disc, it's a little muted and sounds as if it has been recorded through the desk, without much in the way of rebalancing or sweetening. 'The Old Rugged Cross' and 'Big Butter And Egg Man' are splendid. Much of the rest has an old-pals feel that doesn't draw in the listener.

Paradox

GROUP

A cross between drummer Tony Williams's Lifetime and the Mahavishnu Orchestra (which also featured Cobham), Paradox brings a well-attested format up to date, combining vivid funk grooves with a genuine jazz feel.

***** Paradox**
Tiptoe TIP 888 824 2 *Bill Bickford (g); Wolfgang Schmid (b); Billy Cobham (d).* 4/96.

***** The First Second**
Tiptoe 888 833 2 *As above.* 3/97.

Cobham's ability to make complex metres like 13/8 sound as natural as a straight 4/4 is the key to this attractive group. Anyone who thought that seething jazz-fusion was *passé* will be converted by tunes like 'Finkey Donkey' and 'Walking In Five' (on the first album) and the longer, more reflective 'Subwayer' and 'Serengeti Plains' (on the equally good follow-up).

Cobham's 'Quadrant' is dusted down on the 1996 session and given a more immediate and abrasive sound than the over-produced original. His ability to play with genuine feeling is evident on 'Once In A Blue Mood' (*The First Second*), on which Bickford turns a slightly lumpy and rock-drenched sound to better advantage. Power trios come and go. This one has the legs to stay the course.

Paramount Jazz Band Of Boston

GROUP

Bostonian revivalists who started working together in 1980. They have since scattered to several locations so that, although the personnel remains constant, they get together less often than before.

****(*) Ain't Cha Glad?**
Stomp Off CD1205 *Jeff Hughes (c); Gary Rodberg (cl, ss, as); Steve Wright (cl, bcl, ss, as, ts, bs, c); Robin Verdier (p); Jimmy Mazzy (bj, v); Chuck Stewart (tba); Ray Smith (d).* 5–6/89.

***** ... And They Called It Dixieland**
Stomp Off CD1247 *As above.* 4/90–11/91.

***** March Of The Hoodlums**
Stomp Off CD1340 *As above.* 1–2/98.

Skilful if not very involving playing from another group of American revivalists. They avoid carbon-copying original arrangements on the first disc, preferring to try some new twists on Ellington, Dodds, Doc Cook and others; but the playing lacks much individuality and the ensemble work is too polite to muster any of the heat of hot dance. When they try a faded rose such as 'Yearning And Blue', it just sounds old. The second disc, recorded at two live shows, is a lot more energetic, if still a bit short on a style of their own, and the sound is a mixed bag – Mazzy's banjo often seems like the loudest instrument in the group.

The group have returned after something of a hiatus with *March Of The Hoodlums*. Their go at 'Singin' The Blues' tells how much they love the music: this is the Bix and Tram version treated to an affectionate update, Trumbauer's solo played in unison by the reeds before stately cornet and piano improvisations and a return to the original last chorus. While the group still rarely rises above its collective (and entirely honourable) amateur status, this sounds like their best to date.

Tony Parenti (1900–1972)

CLARINET

A prodigy in his native New Orleans, Parenti was offered a job to go north by the Original Dixieland Jazz Band – he was too young to go, and he regretted it. He went to New York in the 1920s and did a lot of non-jazz session-work for CBS in the '30s. From the mid-'40s onwards he worked in a sort of merger of Dixieland with more faithful New Orleans music, and he remained fascinated with the possibilities of ragtime.

****(*) Strut Yo' Stuff**

Frog DGF 4 *Parenti; Henry Knecht, Albert Brunies, Leon Prima, Johnny Wiggs (c); Russ Papalia, Charles Hartman (tb); Hal Jordy (ts, bs, b); Vic Lubowski, Buzzy Williams, Vic Breidis (p); Jack Brian (g, v); Mike Holloway (bj); Mario Finazzo (tba); Monk Hazel (d, v); George Triay (d).* 1/25–6/29.

****** Tony Parenti & His New Orleanians**

Jazzology JCD-1 *Parenti; Wild Bill Davison (c); Jimmy Archey (tb); Art Hodes (p); Pops Foster (b); Arthur Trappier (d).* 8/49.

***** Tony Parenti's New Orleans Shufflers**

Jazzology JCD-61 *Parenti; Jack Hine (c); Bob Thomas (tb); Hank Ross (p); Danny Barker (bj); Arnie Hyman (b); Arthur Trappier (d).* 54.

***** Parenti–Davison All Stars Vol. 1**

Jazzology JCD-91 *Parenti; Wild Bill Davison (c); Lou McGarity (tb); Eustis Tompkins, Ernie Carson (p); Jerry Rousseau (b); Bob Dean (d). n.d.*

***** Parenti–Davison All Stars Vol. 2**

Jazzology JCD-92 *As above. n.d.*

*****(*) Ragtime Jubilee**

Jazzology JCD-21 *Parenti; Wild Bill Davison (c); Larry Conger (t); Charlie Bornemann, Jimmy Archey (tb); Ralph Sutton, Kocky Parker (p); Edmond Souchon, Danny Barker (bj); Cyrus St Clair, Don Franz (tba); Baby Dodds, Pops Campbell (d).* 11/47–?

A New Orleans man who left the city in 1927, Parenti made many records but has frequently been overlooked. Never an original, he could still play with a ferocious intensity; though he approached the gaspipe manner at times, there was no little sophistication in an approach that seldom strayed far from Dixieland ideology. The Frog compilation gathers up rare early material and is a valuable if sometimes disappointing glimpse of New Orleans jazz recorded in its home city in the early years of the music: these were competent rather than capable players for the most part, and the acoustic tracks in particular have little distinction. Things improve on the electrical recordings, and the best session, from April 1928, features Parenti alongside the charmingly Bixian cornet of Johnny Wigg. The leader's own style progresses from merely tricksy playing to the showpiece 'Old Man Rhythm', a clarinet–piano duet (made after his arrival in New York) which closes the disc.

Jazzology JCD-1 was the one that started the Jazzology operation in 1949, and it still sounds hard-nosed and terrific: Davison was at his most vituperative-sounding, Parenti weaves his way round the front line with much invention, Hodes stomps through everything, and Foster slaps his strings harder than ever. Rough old recording, though that doesn't matter, and rather unnecessarily padded out with extra takes.

The All Stars session is of indeterminate date but was cut at a club in Atlanta. The balance is all off, the drums louder than everyone else; the other players are relatively undistinguished and Parenti himself sometimes sounds like he's playing on another stage. But the spirit comes through, and Wild Bill stops at nothing.

New Orleans Shufflers is from a 1954 session made in New York. Some of the names are unfamiliar but the music is a deft mix of the more hard-nosed traditionalism of New York and the sweeter feel of New Orleans music. Solos are generously shared out (and this exposes Thomas a bit) and, since he's very prominent in the mix, you can hear how hard Parenti really blew. Atmospheric and honest, and Trappier's excellent drumming is also worth paying attention to.

Ragtime Jubilee is an unusual example of two bands of traditionalists playing a pure ragtime repertoire, everything from 'Smokey Mokes' and 'Swipesy Cake Walk' to 'Grace And Beauty Rag' and '(That) Erratic Rag'. It starts with six tracks cut for Circle in 1947 by a group including Davison, Archey and Sutton and, if they found the music unfamiliar (Parenti had taken the trouble to write out a set of arrangements), the group bluster through it with rowdy excitement. The remaining tracks are from a much later (though undated) session, and again Parenti makes a dedicated effort at playing original rags without surrendering a Dixieland looseness. Good sound on these later tracks, and a very enjoyable reissue. This is a fine group of undeservedly little-known albums.

*****(*) Tony Parenti And His Downtown Boys**

Jazzology JCD-11 *Parenti; Dick Wellstood, Armand Hug (p); Chink Martin (b); Sam Ulano, Abbie Brunies (d).* 55–65.

Although the circumstances are difficult to decipher from the sleeve-notes, this disc is made up of three sessions. Two are with Wellstood and Hug, who cut seven titles in 1961 and added three more four (!) years later to complete the original LP. For the CD reissue, four titles from a 1955 Southland LP with Hug, Martin and Brunies have also been included. The trio sessions are boisterous and exciting music: all three musicians are right at the front of the mix, and when they dig in and start stomping it's hugely exciting music that comes out. Wellstood strong-arms the piano and Ulano seems to have a full percussion kit at his disposal: listen to the clatter he gets out of 'Chantez Las Bas'. Parenti sounds a bit off-key here and there, but clearly he's enjoying himself. The 1955 tracks are almost sedate by comparison but they swing along. Another terrific Parenti album.

***** The Final Bar**

Jazzology JCD-71 *Parenti; Max Kaminsky (t); Charlie Bornemann (tb); Bobby Pratt (p); Bill Payne (bj); Joe Tarto (tba); Buzzy Drootin (d). 5/71.*

Parenti's final session, made the year before he died, is another chunk of no-frills Dixieland. Veterans like Tarto and Kaminsky are welcome companions, and Parenti himself still sounds in hearty form. Rather noisily recorded and not exactly immortal, but as honestly delivered as the rest of this fine jazzman's music.

Tiny Parham (1900–1943)

PIANO

Born in Canada, the huge pianist (Tiny was his inevitable nickname: real name Hartzell Strathdene) was a busy man on the Chicago scene of the 1920s, arranging for contemporaries such as King Oliver and leading his own groups, which made some idiosyncratic and intriguing records for Victor. He worked through the next decade too, but was playing in hotels and movie-houses at the time of his death.

*****(*) Tiny Parham 1926–1929**

Classics 661 *Parham; B.T Wingfield, Punch Miller, Roy Hobson (c); Charles Lawson (tb); Junie Cobb (ss, as, cl); Charles Johnson (cl, as); Leroy Pickett, Elliott Washington (vn); Charlie Jackson (bj, v); Mike McKendrick (bj); Quinn Wilson (bb); Jimmy Bertrand, Ernie Marrero (d). 12/26–7/29.*

*****(*) Tiny Parham 1929–1940**

Classics 691 *As above, except add Dalbert Bright (cl, ss, as, ts), Ike Covington (tb), Darnell Howard (cl, as), Jimmy Hutchens (cl, ts), John Henley (g), Milt Hinton (bb), Bob Slaughter (d), Sam Theard, Tommy Brookins (v); omit Wingfield, Cobb, Pickett and Jackson. 10/29–6/40.*

****** Tiny Parham 1928–1930**

Timeless CBC 1-022 2CD *Similar to above discs. 7/28–11/30.*

Parham's jazz was an idiosyncratic, almost eccentric brand of Chicago music: his queer, off-centre arrangements tread a line between hot music, novelty strains and schmaltz. The latter is supplied by the violinists and the occasional (and mercifully infrequent) singing – but not by the tuba, which is used with surprising shrewdness by the leader. Some of his arrangements are among the more striking things to come out of the city at that time – 'Cathedral Blues', 'Voodoo' and 'Pigs Feet And Slaw' don't sound like anybody else's group, except perhaps Morton's Red Hot Peppers, although Parham preferred a less flamboyant music to Jelly's. The 'exotic' elements, which led to titles such as 'The Head Hunter's Dream' or 'Jungle Crawl', always seem to be used for a purpose rather than merely for novelty effect and, with soloists like Miller, Hobson and the erratic Cobb, Parham had players who could play inside and out of his arrangements. The two-beat rhythms he leans on create a sort of continuous vamping effect that's oddly appropriate, and Tiny's own piano shows he was no slouch himself. There is a lot of surprising music on these discs, even when it doesn't work out for the best.

The Timeless two-CD edition sweeps past the Classics discs: consistently fine mastering, and with all 12 known alternative takes, this is an exemplary reissue. Diehards might want the obscure first coupling on Classics 661, which Timeless omit. The stray final tracks on Classics 691 date from 1940, by which time he was playing the electric organ; it was at a smart hotel engagement where he was the organist that this 300-lb. giant died of a heart attack in 1943.

Paris Washboard

GROUP

Lively group of French traditionalists, well schooled in old hot music, who bag the occasional guest on their record dates.

***** ... Waiting For The Sunrise**

Stomp Off 1261 *Daniel Barda (tb); Alain Marquet (cl); Louis Mazetier (p); Gérard Bagot (wbd, perc); Michel Marcheteau (sou). 8/92.*

***** California Here We Come**

Stomp Off 1280 *As above, except Gérard Gervois (tba) replaces Marcheteau. 11/93.*

***** Truckin'**

Stomp Off CD1293 *As above, except add Peter Ecklund (t). 2/95.*

***** Love Nest**

Stomp Off CD1308 *As above, except add Olivier Lancelot (p); omit Ecklund. 4/96.*

*****(*) Love For Sale**

Stomp Off 1326 *As above, except omit Gervois and Lancelot. 12/96.*

Not since The Louisiana Five (in 1919!) has a group relied on a clarinet/trombone front line, and though the group is basically a quartet they tackle repertoire that's not dissimilar to The L5's output. There the comparisons stop. Mazetier is a play-anything stylist who can do Waller, James P., Morton or anybody, while Barda and Marquet are superbly lively on their horns, whether in ensemble, counterpoint or quickfire solos. Each of the discs is a smart mix of old-time classics and a sprinkle of rarities, with Mazetier helping himself to a couple of solos and originals. Yet the most important member may be Bagot: never has there been a washboard player this nimble and light with his fingers, working up a scurrying kind of rhythm that's light-years from the mistreatment this instrument received in skiffle bands or wherever. Some may find the general cheeriness an irritation; but if so, this kind of jazz won't appeal in the first place, and the group are actually at pains to differentiate their material.

Truckin' has Ecklund as guest on six tracks and he joins in the fun without blinking. *Love Nest* has Mazetier's occasional dep, Olivier Lancelot, on three tracks and he's awarded a solo version of 'Daintiness Rag'. As each of the discs has its own virtues, it's hard to make an individual choice, but we award a token extra notch to *Love For Sale*, which is their tenth-anniversary album and includes some of their best moments in 'Blue Because Of You', 'Grandpa's Spells' and the title-track – which they worry about sounding too modern.

*****(*) One More Time!**

Stomp Off 1338 *Daniel Barda (tb); Alain Marquet (cl, bcl); Louis Mazetier (p); Gérard Bagot (wbd).* 2/98.

Something of a celebration, this one, since it marks Daniel Barda's hundredth record session (he started in 1964 with Les Haricots Rouges). It seems fanciful to hear them as getting better but this is at least as good as the best of their earlier work, the tempos brighter, the solos popping with jubilation. Marquet picks up the bass clarinet for a soulful 'When It's Sleepy Time Down South' and Mazetier gets a couple of tracks to himself: he plays a sensational solo on 'Runnin' Wild' too. A wonderful group at the height of their powers.

Charlie Parker (1920–55)

ALTO SAXOPHONE, TENOR SAXOPHONE

For good or ill, Charlie Parker's now seems like the definitive jazz life, compounded of genius, drugs and early death. The reality is inevitably a lot more complex and mediated. That he was a genius there is no doubt, but the Kansan's genius was based on long, effortful study and some humiliation before coming into his true voice; similarly with drugs, they played a part, but not an over-determining part, in his life and music and, while they certainly contributed to Bird's early demise, his addiction is too easily demonized. Though he had periods of disturbance, Parker's career, which began in local blues groups before he joined Jay McShann's orchestra, was one of steady and concentrated work. His role in the invention of bebop was critical, though he was certainly not the only begetter. The recorded legacy is very substantial indeed. Leaving aside airshots and other broadcast transcriptions, his recordings are among the key documents of modern music.

****** The Complete Dean Benedetti Recordings**

Mosaic MD7-129 7CD *Parker solos, with Miles Davis, Howard McGhee (t), Hampton Hawes, Duke Jordan, Thelonious Monk (p), Addison Farmer, Tommy Potter (b), Roy Porter, Max Roach (d), Earl Coleman, Kenny Hagood, Carmen McRae (v); other unknown personnel.* 3/47–7/48.

Parker's innovation – improvising a new melody line off the top, rather than from the middle, of the informing chord – was a logical extension of everything that had been happening in jazz over the previous decade. However, even though the simultaneous inscription of bebop by different hands – Dizzy Gillespie, Charlie Christian and Thelonious Monk all have their propagandists – suggests that it was an evolutionary inevitability, any artistic innovation requires quite specific and usually conscious interventions. With its emphasis on extreme harmonic virtuosity, bop has become the dominant idiom of modern jazz and Parker's genetic fingerprint is the clearest.

The British saxophone virtuoso, John Harle, has spoken of the remarkable *clarity* of Parker's music, and in particular his solo development. Even at his most dazzlingly virtuosic, Parker always sounds logical, making light of asymmetrical phrases, idiosyncratically translated bar-lines, surefooted alternation of whole-note passages and flurries of semiquavers, tampering with almost every other parameter of the music – dynamic, attack, timbre – with a kind of joyous arrogance. Dying at 35, he was spared the indignity of a middle age given over to formulaic repetition.

Because, in theory at least, he never repeated himself, there has been a degree of fetishization of many of Parker's solos, like 'The Famous Alto Break' from the Dial recordings (below) or some of the later Verve material, in which a solo is either preserved out of the fullest context on an incomplete take or executed with insouciant disregard for bland or faulty accompaniments. There is, though, an explanation that usefully combines mythology with sheer pragmatism. In his faulty biography of Parker, *Bird Lives!*, Ross Russell introduced a composite figure called Dean Benedetti (the Kerouac resonance was inescapable) who follows Bird throughout the United States capturing his solos (and the solos only) on a primitive wire-recorder. Though unreleased until 1990, the Dean Benedetti archive has enjoyed cult reputation with Parker fans, the Dead Sea Scrolls of bebop, fragmentary and patinated, inaccessible to all but adepts and insiders, but containing the Word in its purest and most unadulterated form.

The real Benedetti, routinely characterized by Russell as a saxophonist *manqué*, remained a practising player, and these remarkable recordings fall into place ever more clearly if one starts towards the end, with Benedetti's amateurishly dubbed attempts to play along with Parker records, and then accepts the absoluteness of his identification with his idol. Dean Benedetti died of *myasthenia gravis* (a progressive weakening of the musculature) two years after Bird. Benedetti was already fatally ill when he heard of Charlie Parker's death. He wrote: '*Povero C. P. Anche tu. Dove ci troveremmo?*' (Poor Bird. You too. Where will we meet again?) The answer is: here. Benedetti's archive was left in the care of his brother, Rick, who in turn died just too soon to witness the release of these astonishing records.

The Mosaic set, lovingly restored and annotated by Phil Schaap, consists of 278 tracks and a boggling 461 recordings of Charlie Parker, made between 1 March 1947 and 11 July 1948 in Los Angeles and New York (a much smaller span of time and geography than legend finds comfortable). The famous wire-recorder certainly existed but was not used for recording Bird. Benedetti worked with 78-r.p.m. acetate discs, and only later with paper-based recording tape. A good many of the recordings are vitiated or distorted by swarf from the cutting needle (which an assistant was supposed to brush away as a recording progressed) getting in the way; since the cutter moved from the outer edge of the disc towards the centre, there was also a problem with torque, and the inner grooves are often rather strained and indistinct. The sound-quality throughout is far from impressive. What is remarkable, though, is the utter dedication and concentration Benedetti brought to his task. Some of the tracks offer fully developed solos occupying several choruses; others, to take two examples only from a recording made in March 1947 at the Hi-De-Ho Club in Los Angeles, last as little as three ('Night And Day'!!) or seven (possibly 'I Surrender Dear') *seconds*.

As an insight into how Parker approached the same tune with the same group on successive nights (there are six separate solos from 'Big Noise'/'Wee' between 1 and 8 March 1947) or how he continued to tackle less familiar material associated with pre-bop figures like Coleman Hawkins (three helpings of 'Bean Soup' in the same period), it is an unparalleled resource. There is also valuable documentation of a rare meeting with Thelonious Monk, recorded on 52nd Street in July 1948. The density of background material (titles, durations, key-signatures, in some cases transcriptions) is awesome and, though some of the material has been available for some time as *Bird On 52nd Street* (Original Jazz Classics OJC 114 LP), the vast bulk of it has not been in the public domain. As such, *The Dean Benedetti Recordings* represent the last step in the consolidation of Parker's once inchoate and shambolic discography. Though there is a vast muddle of live material and airshots, there is a surprisingly small corpus of authorized studio material. Parker's recording career really lasts only a decade, from 1944 to 1953, and is enshrined in three main blocks of material, for Savoy (1944–8), for Dial (1946 to December 1947) and for Norman Granz's Verve (1948–53); throw in the significant Royal Roost live sessions and, but for the Benedetti archive, the main pillars of Parker's reputation are in place.

The painter, Barnett Newman, once said that aesthetics was for artists like ornithology was for the birds, and the unintended reference can usefully be appropriated in this context. Though essentially for specialists (and rather well-heeled experts at that) who are untroubled by the abruptly decontextualized nature of these performances, the Benedetti material represents a quite remarkable auditory experience. The initially exasperating sequence of sound-bites gives way to an illusion of almost telepathic insight, a key to the inner mystery of who and what Parker was.

***** Early Bird**

Stash STCD 642 *Parker; Jay McShann Orchestra; other personnel unknown.* 40–44.

The archaeology and pre-history of bebop is a subject of intense fascination. These sides afford a chance to hear the young Parker, working with McShann in 1940 and already sounding remarkably like the giant of the post-war years. The articulation and the unique, asymmetrical but perfectly balanced phrasing are already in place, though there are no hints yet of the dizzying (no pun intended) harmonic swoops that took him a huge step on from his Lester Young-derived approach. This is an eminently collectable set, with decent sound, given the circumstances. It should be clear, though, that quite a number of tracks do not feature Parker at all, even in embryo.

*****(*) Charlie Parker, 1947**

Classics 1000 *Parker; Miles Davis (t); Duke Jordan (p); Tommy Potter (b); Max Roach (d).* 10, 11, 12/47.

Appropriate that Classics 1000 (phew!) should be devoted to Parker at the peak of his powers, recording his last three sessions for Dial in New York and, a mere five days after 'How Deep Is The Ocean', reconvening with Miles, Duke, Tommy and Max in Detroit to make his first four cuts for Savoy, of which more below. The usual quibbles apply to these reissues: poor sound and a too-literal chronology. There is – arguably – some merit in not dividing the oeuvre into discontinuous label blocks, Dial, Savoy, Verve, but to treat it as a continuous whole. It's hard to imagine much dramatic stylistic development between 17 December and 21 December. To that extent, this compilation is salutary, but we can't recommend it on aesthetic grounds.

*****(*) The Immortal Charlie Parker**

Savoy SV 0102 *Parker; Miles Davis, Dizzy Gillespie (t); Clyde Hart, John Lewis, Bud Powell (p); Tiny Grimes (g); Nelson Boyd, Jimmy Butts, Tommy Potter, Curley Russell (b); Max Roach, Harold Doc West (d).* 9/44–9/48.

♛ ** The Charlie Parker Story**

Savoy SV 0105 *Parker; Miles Davis (t); Dizzy Gillespie (p, t); Bud Powell (p); Curley Russell (b); Max Roach (d).* 11/45.

****** Charlie Parker Memorial: Volume 1**

Savoy SV 0101 *Parker; Miles Davis (t); Duke Jordan, John Lewis, Bud Powell (p); Nelson Boyd, Tommy Potter, Curley Russell (b); Max Roach (d).* 12/47.

****** Charlie Parker Memorial: Volume 2**

Savoy SV 0103 *As above.* 5/47, 9/48.

****** The Genius Of Charlie Parker**

Savoy SV 0104 *As above, except add Jack McVea (ts), Tiny Brown (bs), Sadik Hakim, Dodo Marmarosa (p), Slim Gaillard (p, g, v), Zutty Singleton (d).* 12/45–9/48.

The sides Parker cut on 26 November 1945 were billed by Savoy on the later microgroove release as 'The greatest recording session made in modern jazz'. There's some merit in that. The kitchen-sink reproduction of fluffs, false starts and breakdowns gives a rather chaotic impression. Miles Davis, who never entirely came to terms with Parker's harmonic or rhythmic requirements, doesn't play particularly well (there is even a theory that some of the trumpet choruses – notably one on a third take of 'Billie's Bounce' – were played by Dizzy Gillespie in imitation of Miles's rather uncertain style), and some of Bud Powell's intros and solos are positively bizarre; step forward, pianist Argonne Thornton, who remembers (though he's the only one who does) being at the sessions. Despite all that, and Parker's continuing problems with a recalcitrant reed, the session includes 'Billie's Bounce', 'Now's The Time' and 'Ko-Ko'. The last of these is perhaps the high-water mark of Parker's improvisational genius and the justification for a four-star rating.

Though this is undoubtedly the zenith of Parker's compositional skill as well (in later years he seems to have created fewer and fewer original themes), it is noticeable that virtually all of the material on these sessions draws either on a basic 12-bar blues or on the chord sequence of 'I Got Rhythm', the Ur-text of bebop. 'Ko-Ko' is based on the chords of 'Cherokee', as is the generic 'Warming Up A Riff', which was intended only as a run-through after Parker had carried out running repairs on his squeaking horn. The remainder of Parker's material was drawn, conventionally enough, from show tunes; 'Meandering', a one-off ballad performance on the November 1945 session, unaccountably elided after superb solos from Parker and Powell, bears some relationship to 'Embraceable You'. What is striking about Parker's playing, here and subsequently, is the emphasis on rhythmic invention, often at the expense of harmonic creativity (in that department, as he shows in miniature on 'Ko-Ko', Dizzy Gillespie was certainly his superior).

Availability on programmable CD means that listeners who find the staccato progression of incomplete takes disconcerting are able to ignore all but the final, released versions. Unfortunately, though these are usually the best *band* performances, they do not always reflect Bird's best solo playing. A good example comes on 'Now's The Time', a supposedly original theme, but one which may retain the outline of an old Kansas City blowing blues (or may have been composed – that is, played – by tenor saxophonist Rocky Boyd). There is no doubt that Parker's solo on the third take is superior in its slashing self-confidence to that on the fourth, which is slightly duller; Miles Davis plays without conviction on both.

None of the other three volumes contains a single recording session, nor do any of the constituent sessions match up to the erratic brilliance of 26 November 1945. There are seven other dates represented, notably intermittent in quality. The sessions with Slim Gaillard, creator of 'Vout', an irritating hipster argot, are pretty corny and time-bound; a bare month after 'Ko-Ko', Parker seems to have come down to earth. An early session with guitarist Tiny Grimes and an unusual August 1947 date (under Miles Davis's control) on which Bird played tenor saxophone have been excluded from this CD reissue. Of the remaining dates, that of 8 May 1947, a rather uneasy affair, nevertheless yielded 'Donna Lee' and 'Chasing The Bird'; by contrast, on 21 December 1947, Parker seems utterly confident and lays down the ferocious 'Bird Gets The Worm' and 'Klaunstance'; the sessions of 18 and 24 1948 yielded the classic 'Parker's Mood' (original take 3 is suffused with incomparable blues feeling) and 'Marmaduke' respectively.

The other key figures on these recordings are Max Roach, barely out of his teens but already playing in the kind of advanced rhythmic count that Parker required, and Dizzy Gillespie. Miles Davis was demonstrably unhappy with some of the faster themes and lacked Parker's ability to think afresh take after take; by the time of the 'Parker's Mood' date, though, he had matured significantly (he was, after all, only nineteen when 'Ko-Ko' and 'Now's The Time' were recorded). A word, too, for Curley Russell and Tommy Potter, whose contribution to this music has not yet been fully appreciated and who were rather sorely used on past releases, often muffled to the point of inaudibility.

The Genius Of Charlie Parker brings together original masters only from the six sessions, with an introduction by Al 'Jazzbeau' Collins. It's an attractive package, ideal for those who find the archaeology of recording sessions less than inspiriting. But for sheer majesty of performance and the best available representation of Parker's ability to pack the inner space of his phraseology with musical information, listeners should try to ignore the naff cover-art (one side features an unrecognizable portrait that makes him look like a hip dentist from Barksdale) and go for *The Charlie Parker Story*. *The Immortal* takes us into the anoraky world of the alternative take. Was matrix X better than matrix Y? Did you hear that reed squeak at the turnaround in the fourth chorus? Was that Bud's piano stool squeaking? It does no harm to have these on a separate disc. There's enough awesome music-making on it to have established three more reputations, but at least it's now possible to listen to the classic performances uncluttered and as the artists themselves originally intended.

****** Charlie Parker On Dial: The Complete Sessions**

Spotlite/Dial SPJ CD 4 4101 4CD *Parker; Miles Davis, Dizzy Gillespie, Howard McGhee (t); J.J Johnson (tb); Flip Phillips, Lucky Thompson, Wardell Gray (ts); Jimmy Bunn, Duke Jordan, Russ Freeman, Erroll Garner, George Handy, Dodo Marmarosa (p); Red Norvo (vib); Arvin Garrison, Barney Kessel (g); Ray Brown, Red Callender, Arnold Fishkind, Bob Kesterson, Vic McMillan, Tommy Potter, Slam Stewart (b); Don Lamond, Specs Powell, Jimmy Pratt, Stan Levey, Roy Porter, Max Roach, Harold Doc West (d); Teddy Wilson, Earl Coleman (v).* 6/45, 2, 3 & 7/46, 2, 10, 11, & 12/47.

♛ ** The Legendary Dial Masters: Volume 1**

Stash ST CD 23 *As above.*

****** The Legendary Dial Masters: Volume 2**

Stash ST CD 25 *As above.*

On 26 February 1946, Parker signed what was intended to be an exclusive recording contract with Dial Records, an outgrowth of the Tempo Music Shop on Hollywood Boulevard in Los Angeles. The co-signatory was Tempo owner Ross Russell, subsequently author of *Bird Lives!* and disseminator of some of the more lasting myths about Parker. A contemporary headline declared rather enigmatically: 'West Coast Jazz Center Enters Shellac Derby With Be-Bop Biscuits'. Russell's original intention to specialize in classic jazz (largely ignoring swing, in other words) had been confounded by an unanticipated demand for bop 78s. With typical perspicacity, he lined up Parker, Gillespie and others, gave them unprecedented free rein in the studio and backed his commitment with the best engineers available. The investment predictably took some time to recoup. Parker's Dial period straddles a near-catastrophic personal crisis and a subsequent period of almost Buddhist calm, when his playing takes on a serene logic and untroubled simplicity which in later years was to give way to a blander sophistication and chastened professionalism.

On Volume 1 of the Spotlite Dial, a solitary February 1946 cut ('Diggin' Diz') under Gillespie's leadership pre-dates the remarkable session seven weeks later which yielded 'Moose The Mooche', 'Yardbird Suite', 'Ornithology' and 'A Night In Tunisia', four of his classic performances. Parker's solo on the third take of 'Ornithology' is completely masterful, by turns climbing fiercely and soaring effortlessly, always on the point of stalling but never for a moment losing momentum; close study reveals the daring placement of accents and a compelling alternation of chromatic runs (first refuge of beginners or those suffering temporary harmonic amnesia, but never handled with such grace) and dazzling intervallic leaps. Multiple takes of virtually every item (the six Spotlite volumes take in 39 tunes but 88 separate performances) demonstrate the extent to which Parker was prepared to re-take at constantly shifting tempi, never wrong-footing himself but often having to pull some of the rhythm players along in his wake. 'The Famous Alto Break', 46 seconds of pure invention on the saxophone, is all that remains of a first take of 'A Night In Tunisia'; before the Benedetti materials were made available, 'The Famous Alto Break' was Parker's best-known cameo solo.

In contrast to Curley Russell and Max Roach, Vic McMillan and Roy Porter can sound a little stiff, but Dodo Marmarosa (an undervalued player whose present whereabouts are unknown) has a bright, sharp-edged angularity which suits Parker perfectly and which is picked up generously by good digital remastering. On 29 July 1946, Parker was in the C.P. MacGregor Studios, Hollywood, with Howard McGhee, a fellow addict, in for Miles Davis or Dizzy Gillespie. Bird was practically comatose during the recording of 'Lover Man' (but nevertheless managed a brutal, convoluted solo that is a rare converse to his usual formal clarity) and collapsed shortly after the session, setting off a train of disasters that landed him in the State Hospital at Camarillo. Heroin addiction permits surprisingly extended activity at a high level, but usually at a high rate of interest. There has been a tendency again to fetishize work born out of appalling physical and psychological anguish at the expense of less troubled performances.

In the summer of 1946 Parker was writing cheques that his body and normally indomitable spirit could no longer cash. 'Lover Man', like so many club and concert solos from the preceding years, was done on autopilot. Bird's headlong flight was briefly halted.

He emerged healthier than he had been for a decade. Rest (as in 'Relaxin' At Camarillo'), detoxification and the occasional salad had done him more good than any amount of largactil. A rehearsal session held at Chuck Kopely's house on 1 February 1947 is included, but the recording is very poor (Howard McGhee allegedly kept a hand-held mike pointing at Bird throughout); there are two more tracks from the same occasion on Stash ST CD 25, above. Parker's first post-release recording for Dial cast him in the unlikely company of Erroll Garner and the singer, Earl Coleman. Garner's intriguing two-handedness, offering apparent independence in the bass and melody lines, was a valuable prop for Parker, and he sounds remarkably composed. Coleman's singing on 'This Is Always' and 'Dark Shadows' is uncomplicated and rather appealing. The meat of the sessions comes with 'Bird's Nest' and the marvellous 'Cool Blues', again attempted at very different tempi. The fourth – or 'D' – take of 'Cool Blues' is positively lugubrious. The soloing is limpid and logical, and not much circumstantial knowledge is required to hear the difference between these tracks and the tortured 'Lover Man' of six months before.

A week later, Parker returned to the studio with McGhee and Marmarosa. 'Relaxin' At Camarillo' was allegedly written in the back of a cab *en route* to the date; it was cast in familiar blues form but with an intriguing tonality that suggested Bird was beginning to exercise greater inventiveness along the other, relatively neglected, axis of his work. Unfortunately, the 26 February performances are rather cluttered (Wardell Gray's tenor adds nothing very much; Barney Kessel sounds rather blocky) and the sound isn't up to previous standards.

Parker's last West Coast recording for Dial came towards the end of 1947. The selections from 28 October and 4 November are some of the most lyrical in Parker's entire output. 'Bird Of Paradise' is based on the sequence of 'All The Things You Are', with an introduction (Bird and Miles) that was to become one of the thumbprints of bebop. Parker reinvents his solo from take to take, never exhausting his own resources, never losing contact with the basic material. 'Embraceable You' and the gentle 'Dewey Square' (October; Volume 4), 'Out Of Nowhere' and single takes of 'My Old Flame' and 'Don't Blame Me' (November; Volume 5) don't reach quite the same heights, but the third (unissued) take of 'Out Of Nowhere' is further demonstration of how much magnificent music had to be picked off the editing-room floor. The November session also included two of Parker's finest originals, 'Scrapple From The Apple' and the bizarrely entitled 'Klactoveeseds-tene' (apparently a quasi-phonetic transcription of *Klage, Auf Wiedersehen* – some give it as 'Klact', meaning 'bad noise' – which could be taken to mean something like 'Farewell To The Blues'), which is a raw and slightly neurotic theme played entirely out of kilter.

Roach's grasp of Bird's requirements was by now completely intuitive. Only he seems to have been entirely in tune with the saxophonist's often weirdly dislocated entries, and there is a story that Roach had to shout to Duke Jordan not to elide or add beats or half-bars, knowing that Parker would navigate a course back to the basic metre before the end of his solo choruses. This intuitive brilliance is particularly easy to trace on the slower ballad numbers, where the saxophone's entry is often breathtakingly unexpected and dramatic, underlined by Miles Davis's increasingly confident ability to work across the beat, especially at lower tempi.

Bird's final recording session for Dial and with the great quintet was held in New York City on 17 December 1947, with the addition of trombonist J.J. Johnson. 'Crazeology' is fast and furious, and Parker's solos on both the 'C' and (released) 'D' takes are impeccable; he was allegedly playing with a new horn and his tone is more than usually full and precise. Johnson was certainly the first trombone player to understand bop completely enough to make a meaningful contribution to it. His solos on 'Crazeology' and 'Bird Feathers' are excellent, rhythmically much more daring than anyone had previously dared to be on slide trombone.

The Parker Dials, though perhaps of less concentrated brilliance than the Savoys, are among the greatest small-group jazz of all time; masters were cut in October 1949 and the album released shortly thereafter. They are also of considerable significance in that *Bird Blows The Blues*, formerly available as a separate LP, was the first long-playing record devoted to jazz performance. It was distinctive in two regards. In the first place, Russell favoured the 12-inch format, which maintained its hegemony (until the rise of tape cassette and the compact disc) over the more usual 10-inch format, which was the record dealers' preference. Dial later bowed to market pressure, but subsequent 10-inch releases were pressed on a poor-quality vinyl mix that created a great deal of background noise. In the second place, Russell began to include alternative takes of many tracks, setting in motion a discographical mania that has haunted Parker fans ever since. Solos are sipped like vintages and too often spat into a bucketful of matrix numbers rather than fully savoured and absorbed. For those who have problems on both counts, the availability of master performances on good-quality CD and without the distraction of multiple takes may well be a godsend, and the first volume of the Stash compilation should perhaps be considered essential to anyone building up a non-vinyl jazz collection from scratch. However, the fully documented Spotlite Dials are outstanding. There are, in the Dial documentation, a large number of alternatives, of which the following seem to be the most important and merit the closest attention: 'Yardbird Suite', 'The Famous Alto Break', 'Cool Blues', 'Relaxin' At Camarillo', 'Bird Of Paradise', 'Scrapple From The Apple', 'Out Of Nowhere', 'Drifting On A Reed' (another of Parker's themeless improvisations) and 'Bongo Beep' (a December 1947 track that shouldn't be confused with the slightly earlier 'Bongo Bop'). Volume 2 also takes in two themeless blues recorded at the same home rehearsal at Chuck Kopely's that yielded 'Home Cooking', three versions in all. The Stash also includes some other material that has already appeared elsewhere; the trumpeters (McGhee, Rogers, Broiles) are scarcely audible and sit it out on the Spotlite title-track. If listeners went no further down this entry, they could be assured of having the very best work that Parker did, the tracks that made him unequivocally great. They would, of course, also miss some wonderful music ...

***** Charlie Parker, 1945–1947**

Classics 980 *As for Savoy and Dial sessions above.* 11/45–5/47.

You can't quibble about the music, but you can, and most purchasers will, quibble about the quality of these transfers. If you are looking for a cheap alternative, Classics will always provide the option, but these sides can't have much hope in the marketplace, given the high-quality versions that are on offer.

****** Bird: The Complete Charlie Parker On Verve**

Verve 837141-2 10CD *Parker; Mario Bauza, Buck Clayton, Paquito Davilla, Kenny Dorham, Harry Edison, Roy Eldridge, Dizzy Gillespie, Chris Griffin, Benny Harris, Al Killian, Howard McGhee, Jimmy Maxwell, Doug Mettome, Carl Poole, Al Porcino, Bernie Privin, Rod Rodney, Charlie Shavers, Al Stewart, Ray Wetzel, Bobby Woodlan (t); Will Bradley, Bill Harris, Lou McGarity, Tommy Turk, Bart Varsalona (tb); Vinnie Jacobs (frhn); Hal McKusick, John LaPorta (cl); Benny Carter, Johnny Hodges, Gene Johnson, Toots Mondello, Sonny Salad, Fred Skerritt, Willie Smith, Harry Terrill, Murray Williams (as); Coleman Hawkins, Jose Madera, Pete Mondello, Flip Phillips, Hank Ross, Sol Rabinowitz, Ben Webster, Lester Young (ts); Manny Albam, Danny Bank, Leslie Johnakins, Stan Webb (bs); Artie Drelinger (reeds); Walter Bishop Jr, Al Haig, Rene Hernandez, Hank Jones, Ken Kersey, John Lewis, Thelonious Monk, Oscar Peterson, Mel Powell, Arnold Ross (p); Irving Ashby, Billy Bauer, Jerome Darr, Freddie Green, Barney Kessel (g); Ray Brown, Billy Hadnott, Percy Heath, Teddy Kotick, Charles Mingus, Tommy Potter, Roberto Rodriguez, Curley Russell (b); Kenny Clarke, Roy Haynes, J.C Heard, Don Lamond, Shelly Manne, Buddy Rich, Max Roach, Art Taylor, Lee Young (d); Machito, Jose Mangual, Luis Miranda, Umberto Nieto, Chano Pozo, Carlos Vidal (perc); Ella Fitzgerald, Dave Lambert Singers (v); woodwinds; strings.* 1/46–12/54.

After the extraordinary Savoys and Dials, the sessions for Norman Granz's label mark an inevitable diminuendo. However, it must never be forgotten that Granz was a passionate and practical advocate of better treatment for black American musicians, and it was he who brought Parker to the attention of the wider audience he craved. For the saxophonist, to be allowed to record with strings was a final rubber-stamp of artistic legitimacy. Just as his association with Granz's Jazz At The Philharmonic jamborees are still thought to have turned him into a circus performer, the Parker With Strings sessions (fully documented here and on the special single CD noted below) have attracted a mixture of outright opprobrium and predictable insistence that Bird's solos be preserved and evaluated out of context; the point, though, would seem to be that Parker himself, out of naïvety, a wakening sense of self-advancement, or a genuine wish to break the mould of 'jazz' performance, was every bit as concerned with the context as he was with his own place in it. There is a fair amount of saccharin in the first strings performances, but Parker is superb on 'April In Paris' and 'I Didn't Know What Time It Was', and the release of the material in January 1950 propelled Parker on to a new, national stage. From February he toured with strings opposite Stan Getz. These experiments weren't always a perceived success. A vocal set to Gil Evans arrangements foundered after 15 takes of just four numbers; there are major problems with balances (and Schaap has fulfilled Evans's wish by re-weighting the rhythm section), but the performances are by no means the disaster they're commonly thought to be.

Parker's signing with Verve almost coincided with a recording strike that was called by the AFM for 1 January 1948. Verve boss Norman Granz managed to fit in two hasty recordings before that time, both of which were for a compilation album called *The Jazz Scene*, but neither of them did Parker much justice. There is some controversy as to the exact circumstances of his recording 'Repetition' with Neal Hefti's orchestra. Some sources suggest that Bird is overdubbed; he sounds merely overpowered by a lush arrangement but manages to throw in a quote from *The Rite Of Spring* (Stravinsky was currently high on his playlist). 'The Bird' was recorded by a scratch quartet (Hank Jones, Ray Brown, Shelly Manne) and apparently done at speed. Parker fluffs a couple of times and the rhythm section accelerate and stutter like courtiers trying to keep an even 10 paces behind the king.

The same group (with the unsuitable Buddy Rich in for the elegant Manne) sounded much better two and a half years later. On 'Star Eyes', 'I'm In The Mood For Love' and 'Blues (Fast)' Parker plays remarkably straight and with little of the jagged angularity of earlier recordings. The CD compilation adds no new material or alternatives, in sharp contrast to a session recorded two months later, in June 1950, for which Granz, ever on the lookout for eye-catching combinations, brought together Dizzy Gillespie, Thelonious Monk (their solitary studio encounter), Curley Russell (Bird's most sympathetic partner on bass) and, again, the wholly unsuitable Buddy Rich, who thrashes away to distraction. The new material consists of little more than tiny canapés of studio noise, false starts and run-downs, but there are previously undiscovered or unreleased takes of 'Leap Frog' and 'Relaxin' With Lee', tunes Parker is said to have composed spontaneously when it was discovered that he had forgotten to bring sheets with him. 'Ballade', apparently recorded for use in a film by Gjon Mili, partners Bird with Coleman Hawkins, their only known studio recordings together.

The most substantial single item uncovered by Phil Schaap in his painstaking trawl through the vaults is an acceptable master of Chico O'Farrill's 'Afro-Cuban Jazz Suite', recorded in December 1950 with Machito. Less adept at Latin rhythms than Dizzy Gillespie, Parker had nevertheless experimented with 'south of the border' sessions (there's a fine 1952 session with Benny Harris, co-composer of 'Ornithology') and he solos with great flourish on the 17-minute 'Suite'.

There are more Latin numbers on disc 6, which encapsulates Parker's finest studio performances for Granz. It covers three sessions recorded in January, March and August 1951. The earliest, with Miles, Walter Bishop Jr, Teddy Kotick and Max Roach, featured the classic original 'Au Privave', 'She Rote', 'K.C. Blues', and 'Star Eyes'. The 'Au Privave' solos (two takes) are rapid-fire, joyous Bird, deliberately contrasting with Miles's soft touch; on the alternative, Parker really pushes the boat out and Miles cheekily responds with mimicry of the last couple of bars. The tune is now an influential bebop staple, but it was originally issued as the B-side to 'Star Eyes' which, like the later 'My Little Suede Shoes', recorded in March with a Latin beat, enjoyed enormous success as a single. The August sessions featured a racially integrated line-up fronted by Parker and the young white trumpeter, Red Rodney, whose fiery playing reflected his nickname and hair coloration much more than it did his race, which presented a problem to some 'authenticity'-obsessed critics. The most poignant moment is a re-run, played at first with great correctness but with a bubbling eagerness coming up from underneath, of 'Lover Man', which had been the on-mike flashpoint of Parker's disastrous collapse in 1946. It is said that Bird was upset that the Dial performance was ever released; five years later, he gets his own back with an airy, problem-free reading (he even anticipates his own entry) and a snook-cocking 'Country Gardens' coda, a device Parker used frequently but which he intended here to be deflationary.

Swedish Schnapps (which covers the original LP of that name, the wonderful January 'Au Privave' sessions, and three alternatives from the May 1949 sessions with Kenny Dorham) is available as a separate CD and is an excellent buy for anyone not yet ready or not well enough funded for the kitchen-sink approach of the 10-CD set.

The small-group material thins after this point. There is a good December 1952/January 1953 quartet recording ('The Song Is You', 'Laird Baird', 'Cosmic Rays', 'Kim') with Jones, Kotick and Roach, and two late flourishes from an increasingly erratic Parker in July 1953 and March and December 1954. The latter sessions, which were to be the last studio recordings of his life, were devoted to Cole Porter themes. Parker plays much more within the beat than previously and, but for a near perfection of tone, some of these later performances could safely be relegated. Schaap has found a long alternative of 'Love For Sale', however, which suggests how thoroughly Parker could still rethink his own strategies. It also conveniently brings the whole extraordinary package full circle.

Bird will already have superseded the eight-volume vinyl *Definitive Charlie Parker* in most serious collections. The most important additional material, apart from a couple of genuinely valuable alternatives and the restored 'Afro-Cuban Jazz Suite', is a substantial amount of live performance recorded under the umbrella of Granz's JATP. The earliest item in the collection is a live jam from January 1946 at which Parker encountered (and, on 'Lady Be Good', totally wiped out) his great role-model, Lester Young, then already in his post-war doldrums. The two men met once again at Carnegie Hall in 1949, but it's the earlier encounter that conveys the drama of Bird's precarious grasp on the highest perch. Absent at the beginning of the performance, he comes on stage to thunderous applause and tosses something on to Bud Powell's piano strings, creating a weird jangle. It may be his reed guard, but Phil Schaap suggests (rather improbably, one would have thought) that it was a hypodermic and spoon. The beauty of the 1946 concert lies in its spontaneity. The later, June 1952, 'alto summit' with Johnny Hodges and the veteran Benny Carter is by contrast rather stilted, with an 'after you' succession of solo appearances. (Oscar Peterson, being groomed for stardom by Granz, is also present.)

Pricey and perhaps a little overcooked for non-specialists, *Bird* is nevertheless a model of discographical punctiliousness. The sound is excellent, the notes detailed and fascinating (often backed by anecdotal material from interviews Schaap has conducted with surviving participants) and the packaging very attractive.

****** Charlie Parker**

Verve 539757-2 *Parker; Kenny Dorham (t); Tommy Turk (tb); Coleman Hawkins (ts); Al Haig, Hank Jones (p); Ray Brown, Percy Heath, Teddy Kotick, Tommy Potter (b); Buddy Rich, Shelly Manne, Max Roach (d); Carlos Vidal (perc).* 12/47–7/53.

The first single-disc release of the quartet recordings since the monumental ten-CD set and an excellent buy for anyone who is unwilling to go that far. From the opening of 'Now's The Time' to the end of 'Visa', this is vintage Bird. We'd question the need, on a compilation of this sort, for five alternatives and false starts on 'Chi-Chi'. However, if you haven't experienced this kind of documentation before, it may well be beguiling and fascinating. Repackaged with Verve's usual understated care and attention to detail, this is a hugely attractive issue and one that may well help pull in new listeners to this extraordinary music. Listening to these familiar tracks again, we were struck by how magnificent even the occasionally dispraised later Bird could be.

****** Confirmation**

Verve 527815-2 2CD *As above.* 2/49–7/53.

****** Bird's Best Bop**

Verve 527452-2 *Parker; Miles Davis, Kenny Dorham, Dizzy Gillespie, Red Rodney (t); Walter Bishop Jr, Al Haig, Hank Jones, John Lewis, Thelonious Monk (p); Ray Brown, Percy Heath, Teddy Kotick, Tommy Potter, Curley Russell (b); Kenny Clarke, Buddy Rich, Max Roach (d).* 5/49–7/53.

***** Jazz Masters 15: Charlie Parker**

Verve 519827-2 *As above.* 47–53.

***** Jazz Masters 28: Charlie Parker Plays Standards**

Verve 521854-2 *Parker; Buck Clayton, Roy Eldridge, Benny Harris, Jimmy Maxwell, Carl Poole, Al Porcino, Bernie Privin (t); Bill Harris, Lou McGarity, Tommy Turk, Bart Varsalona (tb); Willie Smith, Harry Terrill, Murray Williams (as); Coleman Hawkins, Flip Phillips, Hank Ross, Lester Young (ts); Danny Bank (bs); Walter Bishop Jr, Stan Freeman, Al Haig, Hank Jones, Oscar Peterson (p); Billy Bauer, Freddie Green (g); Ray Brown, Percy Heath, Teddy Kotick, Charles Mingus (b); Roy Haynes, Don Lamond, Buddy Rich, Max Roach, Arthur Taylor (d); Luis Miranda (perc); Butch Birdsall, Ella Fitzgerald, Dave Lambert, Jerry Parker, Annie Ross (v); woodwinds; strings.* 46–54.

****** Swedish Schnapps**

Verve 849393-2 *Parker; Miles Davis, Kenny Dorham, Red Rodney (t); John Lewis, Walter Bishop Jr, Al Haig (p); Ray Brown, Teddy Kotick, Tommy Potter (b); Kenny Clarke, Max Roach (d).* 49–51.

****** Bird: The Original Recordings Of Charlie Parker**

Verve 837176-2 *As above.* 2/49–7/53.

****** Now's The Time**

Verve 825671-2 *Parker; Hank Jones (p); Percy Heath, Teddy Kotick (b); Max Roach (d).* 12/52, 8/53.

*****(*) Gitanes Jazz – Round Midnight: Charlie Parker**

Verve 847911-2 *As above; various dates.*

***** Ultimate Charlie Parker**

Verve 559708-2 *Parker; Mario Bauza (t); Coleman Hawkins, Flip Phillips, Lester Young (ts); Hank Jones (p); Ray Brown, Curley Russell (b); Shelly Manne, Buddy Rich (d); Machito (perc); strings.* 46–52.

So humungous and expensive is the ten-CD set that all but the very well-heeled would be advised to pick and choose among these wallet-friendly repackagings of the Verve Parkers. Most of the titles are self-explanatory or have been glossed in some way above. *Confirmation* attempts a distillation of the whole shebang which is quixotic but admirable and done with excellent taste and sense of balance. The *Jazz Masters* series is irreproachably accurate and well documented, but the boxes are unattractive and the by-the-numbers approach to Verve's back-catalogue is a touch off-putting. More casual listeners might find it a helpful, if ultimately misleading way of building a library. *Swedish Schnapps* we have already commented on, and it should perhaps be a priority purchase. For the car stereo, mobile disc-player or the *pied-à-terre*, *Bird's Best Bop* would be a sensible investment, covering the strongest of the Verve tracks ('Now's The Time', 'Confirmation', 'Swedish Schnapps', 'She Rote' and the glorious 'Au Privave'); romantics will find the *Gitanes Jazz – Round Midnight* compilation a little more amenable.

The *Ultimate* series, each of them curated by a musician influenced by the artist concerned, offers no new insight. Jackie McLean's recollections of Parker are interesting in themselves, but most of his anecdotes have been told many times over, and his debt to Bird is so obvious as to require no restatement.

***** Talkin' Bird**

Verve 559859-2 *Parker; Miles Davis, Roy Eldridge, Dizzy Gillespie, Charlie Shavers (t); Tommy Turk (tb); Benny Carter, Johnny Hodges (as); Flip Phillips, Ben Webster, Lester Young (ts); Walter Bishop Jr, Al Haig, Hank Jones, Thelonious Monk, Oscar Peterson (p); Barney Kessel (g); Ray Brown, Percy Heath, Teddy Kotick, Curley Russell (b); Roy Haynes, J.C Heard, Buddy Rich, Max Roach (d); Machito (perc).* 49–53.

*****(*) Hi-Fi**

Verve 539757-2 *Parker; Kenny Dorham (t); Tommy Turk (tb); Coleman Hawkins (ts); Al Haig, Hank Jones (p); Ray Brown, Percy Heath, Tommy Potter (b); Shelly Manne, Buddy Rich, Max Roach (d); Carlos Vidal (perc).* 47–53.

***** Bird & Diz**

Verve 521436-2 *Parker; Dizzy Gillespie (t); Thelonious Monk (p); Curley Russell (b); Buddy Rich (d).* 50.

Given the sheer creative density of Verve's holding of Parker material, it is hardly surprising that the label should have repackaged the work so insistently. What is more startling is that the later batches have often been better than the first pickings. That is certainly true of *Hi-Fi*, which is overstuffed with alternative takes of 'Chi Chi' but might otherwise serve as a very good introduction to Bird's work of the period. It is also true of *Bird & Diz*, which aims to document one central association within a limited time-frame and offers an opportunity to hear three of the giants of bebop in one session. Again, there are too many alternatives for the newcomer, though as always one of the best ways of studying Parker is to listen to how thoroughly he rethinks a solo from take to take, even if the broad melodic contour remains the same.

Talkin' Bird is a more expansive compilation but lacks any real logic and sense of progression. There are better introductions in the entry above, but we would direct your attention to *Hi-Fi* and *Bird & Diz* if you don't already have this material.

*****(*) The Cole Porter Songbook**

Verve 823250-2 *Parker; drawn from Bird: The Complete Charlie Parker On Verve.* 7/50–12/54.

Parker was very drawn to Cole Porter's music and was contemplating another all-Porter session at the time of his death. The slightly dry, pure melodism gave him the perfect springboard for some of his most unfettered solos. A lovely record and an ideal purchase for Parker or Porter addicts.

***** South Of The Border**

Verve 527779-2 *Parker; Machito Afro Cuban Orchestra; Roy Haynes, Buddy Rich, Max Roach (d).* 48–52.

***** Charlie Parker With Strings – The Master Takes**

Verve 523984-2 *Parker; Tony Aless, Al Haig, Bernie Leighton (p); Art Ryerson (g); Ray Brown, Bob Haggart, Tommy Potter, Curley Russell (b); Roy Haynes, Don Lamond, Shelly Manne, Buddy Rich (d).* 12/47–1/52.

There is still some pointless controversy as to the merits of Parker's With Strings projects. Pointless, because it is clear from a single chorus of 'Repetition' from 1947 (made for *The Jazz Scene*) or 'Stella by Starlight' in 1952 that here is a master at work. Bird's solo construction is poised and tasteful, and much of the talk about his 'impatience' with these smooth settings is a sort of wishful thinking. He basked in them and if on occasion he anticipates the beat, that's no more than he did with Al Haig or Thelonious Monk.

We find more to question among the Machito sessions on *South Of The Border*, but this aspect of Parker is hugely popular, too, and there is no mistaking his own pleasure in these rhythms, which challenged him to widen his phrasing and open up his tone a touch. Time, surely, to put paid to snobbery about these lovely records.

****** The Bird Returns**

Savoy SV 0155 *Parker; Miles Davis, Kenny Dorham (t); Lucky Thompson (ts); Milt Jackson (vib); Al Haig (p); Tommy Potter (b); Max Roach (d).* 9/48–3/49.

*****(*) Newly Discovered Sides By The Immortal Charlie Parker**

Savoy SV 0156 *As above.* 9/48–3/49.

Anyone in possession of the Savoys, Dials, Verves, the Dean Benedetti collection (if they can afford it) and the Royal Roost recordings can reasonably feel they have a purchase on the major outcrops of Parker's career. Of the very many live sessions and airshots in circulation, only these should be considered absolutely essential. These CD reissues mark one significant advance over earlier vinyl issues in reducing to a minimum the announcements of 'Symphony Sid' Torin, who always manages to sound like an alternative comedian mimicking an American radio presenter. This may have the negative effect of spoiling the 'live atmosphere' of the LPs; atmospherics, though, represent a serious problem on vinyl, and the CDs deliver the music in a much cleaner signal, if a little sharply in places. What are missing from these are the dates from May 1950, also at the Roost, when Parker recorded the astounding 'Street Beat' with Fats Navarro, on which the ill-fated trumpeter, who died shortly thereafter, put together perhaps the most balanced solo of his whole career. This is now available on the very useful Cool & Blue (below). Dorham is much less convincing and sounds very jaded indeed in places on the early-1949 sessions (though a rocky sound-balance doesn't favour his middle-register work, which is more subtle than first appears), tending to play formulaically and in rather staccato, predetermined bites. At this period Miles Davis plays very much more consistently in club situations than under the stop-start discipline of the recording studio.

Parker, of course, is sublime. His career was powerfully in the ascendant at this point, whatever 'personal problems' skulked around the edges; the recording ban was lifted and the substantial backing he was getting from Norman Granz allowed him to think ever more expansively. In a club context, too, he was able to free-wheel in a way that wasn't possible in the studio and, though few of the individual performances are very long (the norm is still 3–5 minutes, perhaps a concession to commercial times), there is a palpable sense of relaxation about his playing that comes through even on these rather one-dimensional recordings.

***** Live Performances: Volume 1**

ESP Disk ESP 3000 *Parker; Kenny Dorham, Dizzy Gillespie (t); John LaPorta (cl); Billy Bauer (b); Al Haig, Lennie Tristano (p); Ray Brown, Tommy Potter (b); Max Roach (d).* 9/47, 12/48.

***** Broadcast Performances: Volume 2**

ESP Disk ESP 3001 *Parker; Miles Davis (t); Tadd Dameron, Al Haig (p); Tommy Potter, Curley Russell (b); Joe Harris, Max Roach (d).* 6 & 8/49.

Most of this material is already well known, though it's startling to find it on ESP Disk, a label more commonly associated with the 1960s avant-garde. Like Blue Note, though, ESP were anxious to cash in – artistically, if not commercially – on the greatest figure of the preceding generation. The 1947 material on Volume 1 is prized for an opportunity to hear Bird playing with the pianist who seemingly represented the opposite tendency in modern jazz, Lennie Tristano. It is immediately obvious on 'Tiger Rag', the solitary cut, that the differences between them were not entirely irreconcilable. The Christmas night 1948 material is also well known from the LP era. 'White Christmas' is a piece of pure hokum but it shows how readily Bird could be triggered by the slightest piece of musical fluff. His solo is breathtaking. The Royal Roost recordings included on Volume 2 have had a rather chequered discographical history, but they are very well documented here, sounding clean and remarkably noise-free, particularly given that this is not a label normally much concerned with the niceties of hi-fi. Parker tackles his solo on 'Groovin' High' with ferocious application, trying out ideas that don't turn up elsewhere in the discography. He's more relaxed on 'East Of The Sun', which features a lovely statement from Dorham.

*****(*) 1949 Jazz At The Philharmonic**

Verve 519803-2 *Parker; Roy Eldridge (t); Tommy Turk (tb); Flip Phillips, Lester Young (ts); Hank Jones (p); Ray Brown (b); Buddy Rich (d); Ella Fitzgerald (v).* 9/49.

*****(*) Charlie Parker Jam Session**

Verve 833564-2 *Parker; Charlie Shavers (t); Benny Carter, Johnny Hodges (as); Flip Phillips, Ben Webster (ts); Oscar Peterson (p); Barney Kessel (g); Ray Brown (b); J.C Heard (d).* 7/52.

The symbolic importance of these two jams was Parker's appearance on the same stage as fellow-saxophonists, Lester Young (in 1949) and Benny Carter, Johnny Hodges and Ben Webster on the later session. Prez and Bird nose round each other for a bit on 'The Opener', a routine B-flat blues, but things get a little tougher on 'Lester Leaps In', where the tenor master with the sound that made Bird's possible lets everybody know that he's still in charge and still able to cut it. Parker doesn't show as strongly again until 'How High The Moon'.

Norman Granz's *Jam Session* of July 1952 was more of a processional and, though there are some extremely fine moments, from Bird, Shavers (who has refined the Eldridge style) and the stalwart Phillips, the confrontation with Carter and Hodges is pretty anticlimactic, a dialogue of the deaf rather than a significant joust. Each plays completely in character, Hodges with the walk-on walk-off shrug he was prone to. The biggest summit since Yalta was every bit as much a diplomatic window-display. The future of the world – or of modern music – had been decided elsewhere.

*****(*) Charlie Parker In Sweden, 1950**

Storyville STCD 4031 *Parker; Rolf Ericson, Rowland Greenberg (t); Lennart Nilsson, Gosta Theselius (ts, p); Thore Jederby (b); Jack Noren (d).* 1/50.

Record of a hectic week during Parker's second visit to Europe. He had had great success at the Paris Jazz Festival the previous year and was revered in Scandinavia, where bebop took deep and lasting root. A measure of that is the quality of the local musicians, who more than hold their own (Rolf Ericson, of course, acquired a substantial American reputation later in his career). Though Parker also played in Stockholm and Gothenburg, the materials are taken from sets in the southern towns of Hälsingborg and Malmö, plus a remarkable restaurant jam session at an unknown location. This last yielded the most notable single track, a long version of 'Body And Soul', more usually a tenor saxophonist's shibboleth but given a reading of great composure. This item was previously known in an edited form (which dispensed with solos by Theselius, who plays piano on the other selections, and Greenberg); but the restored version is very much more impressive, again by virtue of relocating Parker's improvisation in the wider context of a group performance. The remaining material is pretty much a 'greatest hits' package, with two versions each of 'Anthropology' and 'Cool Blues'. Worthwhile, but not essential.

*****(*) Bird At St Nick's**

Original Jazz Classics OJC 041 *Parker; Red Rodney (t); Al Haig (p); Tommy Potter (b); Roy Haynes (d).* 2/50.

An attractively varied package of material (including 'Visa', 'What's New', 'Smoke Gets In Your Eyes' and other, more familiar themes) from a tight and very professional band who sound as if they've been together for some time. Haynes is no Max Roach, even at this period, but his count is increasingly subtle and deceptive, and he cues some of Rodney's better releases brilliantly. Worth watching out for, and much more compelling than the rag-bag of material on *Bird's Eyes: Volume 1*.

*****(*) Charlie Parker Live; February 14, 1950**

EPM Musique FCD 5710 *Parker; Red Rodney (t); J.J Johnson (tb); Al Haig (p); Tommy Potter (b); Roy Haynes (d).* 2/50.

A Valentine's Night airshot from a rather jaded and uncertain band. Bird is playing well, though there are reed problems and a constant mis-hitting of the octave button, but the two brass players sound remote and uncommunicative, and the rhythm section is much more sluggish than on the other recordings of the period.

****** Bird And Fats – Live At Birdland**

Cool & Blue C&B CD 103 *Parker; Fats Navarro (t); Walter Bishop Jr, Bud Powell (p); Tommy Potter, Curley Russell (b); Art Blakey, Roy Haynes (d); Chubby Newsome (v).* 6/50.

There are moments on this when Parker is very nearly eclipsed by Fats Navarro, whose death was not far away when they recorded the astounding 'Street Beat'. Somebody calls out, 'Blow, Girl!' (Navarro's nickname was Fat Girl) as he burns through an absolutely astonishing solo that combines fire and attack with near-perfect balance. On his day, there was no one to touch him. Unfortunately, there were very few days left. Elsewhere, he is superb on 'Ornithology' and 'Cool Blues'. A marvellous moment, captured with lots of atmosphere and not too much extraneous noise.

***** Inglewood Jam**

Fresh Sound FSRCD 17 *Parker; Chet Baker (t); Sonny Criss (as); Russ Freeman (p); Harry Babasin (b); Lawrence Marable (d).* 6/52.

A historic encounter, Parker playing with two hornmen who in dramatically different ways (but with equally tragic repercussions) would take his legacy forward into the next generation. Baker sounds a modestly accomplished bebopper, much like the young and hesitant Miles Davis, in fact; but Criss is much more individual and distinctive than all the Bird-and-water copy might suggest. There are moments of marvellous tension in this, as when Baker throws Gillespie phrases at Bird during 'Donna Lee'. Parker appears to ignore them, but during his final chorus stuffs them all together into a single hectic phrase and heaves them back. Fifteen-all.

***** The Legendary Rockland Palace Concert: Volume 1**

Jazz Classics JZCL 6010 *Parker; Walter Bishop (p); Mundell Lowe (g); Teddy Kotick (b); Max Roach (d); strings.* 9/52.

Not unknown, but previously available only on a home recording of execrable quality. This more professional taping restores a bit of definition, and some good interchanges between Bird and Mundell Lowe, and it makes available some tracks that didn't pass muster before. The occasion was a dance in honour of an American Communist Party official and *Daily Worker* staffer. Not too much should be read into Bird's involvement on such a gig, not because he was cynical enough to take anything on, but because even at this late date American attitudes to socialism were still (in advance of the McCarthyite freeze) fairly relaxed, and black musicians of less public stature than Paul Robeson were exempt from unwarranted attention. There are no classic tracks or performances, but the general standard is high and the string settings are not too egregious. Of the unissued material, a sequence of Cole Porter songs is perhaps the most compelling. What one wonders at, though, is Parker's ability to fire off solos of consummate grace on such an unpressured and, one would have thought, creatively stultifying occasion.

****** The Quintet / Jazz At Massey Hall**

Original Jazz Classics OJC 044 *Parker; Dizzy Gillespie (t); Bud Powell (p); Charles Mingus (b); Max Roach (d).* 5/53.

Perhaps the most hyped jazz concert ever, to an extent that the actuality is almost inevitably something of a disappointment. Originally released on Debut (a musician-run label started by Mingus and Roach), the sound, taken from Mingus's own tape-recording, is rather poor and the bassist subsequently had to overdub his part. However, Parker (playing a plastic saxophone and billed on the Debut release as 'Charlie Chan' to avoid contractual problems with Mercury, Norman Granz's parent company) and Gillespie are both at the peak of their powers. They may even have fed off the conflict that had developed between them, for their interchanges on the opening 'Perdido' crackle with controlled aggression, like two middleweights checking each other out in the first round. There is a story that they didn't want to go on stage, preferring to sulk in front of a televised big game in the dressing-room. Parker's solo on 'Hot House', three-quarters of the way through the set, is a masterpiece of containment and release, like his work on 'A Night In Tunisia' (introduced by the saxophonist in rather weird French, in deference to the Canadian – but the wrong city, surely? – audience). Perhaps because the game was showing, or perhaps just because Toronto wasn't hip to bebop, the house was by no means full, but it's clear that those who were there sensed something exceptional was happening. Powell and Roach are the star turns on 'Wee'. The pianist builds a marvellous solo out of Dameron's chords and Roach holds the whole thing together with a performance that almost matches the melodic and rhythmic enterprise of the front men. The Massey Hall concert is a remarkable experience, not to be missed. (A cassette version of the full concert, with Bud Powell's trio set, is still advertised.)

****** Charlie Parker At Storyville**

Blue Note 785108 *Parker; Herb Pomeroy (t); Red Garland, Sir Charles Thompson (p); Bernie Griggs, Jimmy Woode (b); Kenny Clarke, Roy Haynes (d).* 3/53, 9/53.

First released in 1985, the tapes of these Boston club dates, made on a Rube Goldberg home-made system by John Fitch (aka John McLellan, the compère), have been magically reprocessed by Jack Towers and are among the most faithful live recordings of Parker from the period. Of the performances it is necessary only to say that Parker is magisterial. Pomeroy strives manfully but seems to be caught more than once in awkward whole-note progressions which start well but then lapse back into cliché. Local bassist Griggs (who appears again on Stash's compilation of rarities, below) chugs along manfully on the March sessions, but Roy Haynes is a heavy-handed disappointment. The September quintets are generally less enterprising, and there are even signs that Parker may be repeating himself. In an interview recorded in June of the same year, McLellan pointed to an increasingly noticeable tendency for Parker to play old and established compositions. By the turn of the 1950s, the flow of new variations on the basic blues or on standards had virtually dried up. Despite that, Parker's ability to find new things to say on tunes as well worn as 'Moose The Mooche', 'Ornithology' and 'Out Of Nowhere' (March) or 'Now's The Time', 'Cool Blues' and 'Groovin' High' (September) is completely impressive. The addition of relatively unfamiliar pieces like 'I'll Walk Alone' and 'Dancing On The Ceiling' contributes to a highly attractive set. The McLellan interview concludes with one of Parker's most quoted articles of faith: 'You can never tell what you'll be thinking tomorrow. But I can definitely say that music won't stop. It will continue to go forward.'

***** Bird In Boston: Live At The Hi Hat, 1953/54**

Fresh Sound FSCD 1006 *Parker; Herb Pomeroy, Herbert J Williams (t); Dean Earle, Rollins Griffith (p); Bernie Griggs, Jimmy Woode (b); Marquis Foster, Billy Graham (d); Symphony Sid Torin (v).* 6/53, 1/54.

***** Bird At The High Hat**

Blue Note 799787 *As above, except omit Pomeroy, Earle, Graham.* 12/53, 1/54.

One gets so used to hearing Parker with Miles, Gillespie, Navarro or Dorham that the immediate reaction to this is to ask, 'Who the hell's that?' as Pomeroy starts to play on 'Cool Blues'. These were game professional bands who had spent hours listening to the classic Parker recordings. Griffith in particular cops riffs and runs from Bud Powell, and the two trumpeters have their own respective allegiances. The Blue Note corrals material from the same club on a different date, though there is doubt about precisely what dates are involved. Bird himself sounds tired but surprisingly focused, leaning into one or two choruses as if the clock had gone back half-a-dozen years. There is no mistaking the change in quality, though. There was a man called Billy Graham at the drumkit. Bird was already much nearer to God.

*****(*) The Complete Birth Of The Bebop: Bird On Tenor, 1943**

Stash STCD 535 *Parker; Chet Baker, Miles Davis, Billy Eckstine, Dizzy Gillespie (t); Jimmy Rowles, Hazel Scott (p); Milt Jackson (vib); Hurley Ramey, Efferge Ware (g); Red Callender, Oscar Pettiford, Carson Smith (b); Roy Haynes, Shelly Manne, Harold Doc West (d); Bob Redcross (brushes); Benny Goodman Trio and Quartet on record; other personnel unidentified.* 5/40–11/53.

(*(*)) The Bird You Never Heard**

Stash ST-280 *Parker; Herb Pomeroy, Bud Powell (p); Charles Mingus (b); Art Taylor (d); Candido (perc); other personnel unidentified.* 8/50.

Barrel-scrapings, perhaps, but with Parker there was valid music to record every time he put a reed between his lips. Among the earliest items on *Birth Of The Bebop* are two examples of Bird's rare use of tenor saxophone; his only 'official' tenor recording was on a Miles Davis Prestige date, where he appeared as 'Charlie Chan' for contractual reasons. The first is a jammed 'Sweet Georgia Brown' with Dizzy Gillespie and Oscar Pettiford, the second a fascinating hotel-room recording with Gillespie and Billy Eckstine on trumpets and the rhythm shuffled out on a suitcase lid. Of the remaining material, by far the most interesting are the solo 'Body And Soul' and 'Honeysuckle Rose' (which Stash date from May 1940), two sets of duos with guitarists Ware (Bird on alto) and Hurley Ramey (tenor), and remarkable recordings of Parker improvising over Benny Goodman 78s of 'Avalon' and 'China Boy'. The original LP included tracks from 1953 with the 24-year-old Chet Baker on 'Ornithology', 'Barbados' and 'Cool Blues', but this has not been carried over. Both these Stashes are marred by very poor airshot sound. *The Bird You Never Heard* is the poorer, but the performances are all first class. Four tunes ('Ornithology', 'Out Of Nowhere', 'My Funny Valentine', 'Cool Blues') come from Parker's January 1954 residency at the Hi-Hat in Boston (local trumpeter Pomeroy figures on the Blue Note *At Storyville* – see above – from the previous year, and obviously enjoyed Parker's confidence). The anonymous author of the liner-notes offers an interesting sidelight on Parker's behaviour during such performances, pointing to his joshing and 'kvelling' with MCs and implying that the image of Bird as a lonely genius who refused to don motley and clown for his audience is not borne out by the recorded facts. A point to ponder.

*****(*) Bird's Eyes: Last Unissued – Volume 1**

Philology W 5/18 *Parker; Miles Davis (t); Walter Bishop Jr, Duke Jordan (p); Tommy Potter (b); Roy Haynes, Max Roach (d); Candido (perc).* 40, 48, 11/52.

*****(*) Bird's Eyes: Last Unissued – Volumes 2 & 3**

Philology W 12/15 *Parker; Red Rodney (t); Al Haig (p); Tommy Potter (b); Max Roach (d).* 11/49.

…

***** Bird's Eyes: Last Unissued – Volume 10**

Philology W 200 *Parker; Kenny Dorham (t); Al Haig (p); Tommy Potter (b); Max Roach, Roy Haynes (d); strings.* 5/49.

*****(*) Bird's Eyes: Last Unissued – Volume 11**

Philology W 622 *As above, except omit Haynes and strings.* 5/49.

***** Bird's Eyes: Last Unissued – Volume 12**

Philology W 842 *As above, except add Aimé Barelli, Norma Carson, Bill Coleman, Miles Davis, Jon Eardley, George Jouvin Fassin, Roger Guérin, Hot Lips Page (t), Big Chief Russell Moore, Maurice Gladieu, Jimmy Knepper, André Paquinet (tb), Hubert Rostaing (cl), Joe Maini (as), Robert Merchez, Sidney Bechet (ss), Don Byas, Don Lanphere, James Moody, Bob Newman, Roger Simon, Gers Yowell (ts), Honoré True (bs), Robert Cambier, Gers Williams (p), Hazy Osterwald (vib), Buddy Jones, Henri Karen (b), Buddy Bridgeford, Roy Haynes, Pierre Loteguy (d).* 5/49, 6 & 11/50.

*****(*) Bird's Eyes: Last Unissued – Volume 14**

Philology W 844 *Parker; Miles Davis, Dizzy Gillespie, Fats Navarro, Red Rodney (t); J.J Johnson, Kai Winding (tb); Buddy DeFranco (cl); Charlie Ventura (ts); Ernie Caceres (bs); Lennie Tristano, Al Haig, Duke Jordan (p); Billy Bauer (g); Tommy Potter, Eddie Safranski (b); Shelly Manne, Max Roach (d).* 1/46, 11/47, 1 & 11/48, 1 & 11/49.

****(*) Bird's Eyes: Last Unissued – Volume 15**

Philology W 845 *Parker; Marty Bell, Don Ferrara, Dizzy Gillespie, Don Joseph, Jon Nielson, Al Porcino, Sonny Rich, Red Rodney, Neil Friez (t); Frank Orchard (vtb); Eddie Bert, Porky Cohen, Jimmy Knepper, Paul Seldon (tb); Joe Maini (as); Al Cohn, Don Lanphere, Tommy Mackagon, Flip Phillips, Zoot Sims (ts); Marty Flax, Bob Newman (bs); Harry Biss, Teddy Wilson (p); Sam Herman (g); Red Norvo (vib); Buddy Jones, Slam Stewart (b); Phil Arabia, Sam Gruber, Don Manning, Specs Powell, J.C Heard (d).* 6/45, 4/50.

***** Bird's Eyes: Last Unissued – Volume 16**

Philology W 846 *Parker; Kenny Dorham, Benny Harris (t); Lucky Thompson (ts); Milt Jackson (vib); Al Haig (p); Tommy Potter, Teddy Kotick (b); Roy Haynes, Max Roach (d).* 3/49, 6/51.

…

*** **Bird's Eyes: Last Unissued – Volume 19**

Philology W 849 *Parker; Dizzy Gillespie (t); Trummy Young, Clyde Bernhardt (tb, v); Don Byas, Flip Phillips (ts); Clyde Hart, Nat Jaffe, Tadd Dameron, Jay McShann (p); Bill De Arango, Mike Bryan (g); Al Hall, Gene Ramey, Curley Russell (b); Gus Johnson, Specs Powell, Max Roach (d); Sarah Vaughan, Rubberlegs Williams (v).* 1 & 5/45.

*** **Bird's Eyes: Last Unissued – Volume 20**

Philology W 850 *Parker; Red Rodney, Jon Nielson? (t); Charlie Kennedy? (as); Al Haig (p); Tommy Potter (b); Freddie Gruber, Roy Haynes (d); other personnel unknown.* 2/50, 52 or 53.

Bird's Eyes – Last Unissued is the general title of one of the most extraordinary jazz documentations of recent times. It now stretches to many, many volumes of extremely mixed but, for Parker completists, absolutely essential material. We have noted some of the most valuable CDs but must leave it to dedicated collectors to follow up the remainder, should they feel so moved (and they should be warned that availability is sporadic in some territories). As far as we are aware, the series has now moved towards 30 volumes, but attempts to track down some of the more recent issues were met with helpless looks from dealers. Good luck if you have set your heart on following through.

The most startling items on this collection are two unaccompanied recordings of 'Body And Soul' and 'Honeysuckle Rose', apparently made in a booth. Both are also included on Stash STCD 535, above, where they are improbably dated 1937; Philology's suggestion of May 1940 seems much more realistic. Parker had recently heard Art Tatum playing in New York City and had experienced the much-discussed epiphany while playing 'Cherokee' which led him to improvise on the higher intervals of the chord. Though the voice on these crude recordings is still unmistakably Parker's, the music (a fairly basic set of harmonic variations) is still unsophisticated and rhythmically unenterprising; of course solo performance was not the norm, and it's unrealistic to expect more from what was probably a very casual self-documentation.

The 1948 live material with the great quintet is well up to scratch, with Miles producing some distinctively fragile solos and Roach, when he is clearly audible, steadily elaborating the rhythmic vocabulary he had limned on the Dial sessions. The later Parker With Strings tracks (two takes of 'Just Friends' and a theme) are pretty forgettable.

The second volume is something of a rag-bag of long and short edits. Rodney had joined Parker only rather diffidently, uncertain of his own abilities. He was frequently ill during their earlier association but allowed himself to become addicted to narcotics (perhaps in a misguided gesture of identification). There's a degree of strain in these early sets that is much less evident on the Jazz Anthology and *At St Nick's* sessions, above.

Volume 10, where we pick up the run again, mixes some rather good quintet material from the Salle Pleyel in Paris, May 1949, with another strings project at the Apollo the following August. Sound-quality in both cases is average to somewhat below, but there are valuable choruses in both sessions from Parker and some very crisp playing from Dorham, who sounds immensely relaxed and poised in Paris. The French trip also forms the substance of Volume 11 and the better part of 12. The first of these brings together more stuff from the Pleyel with material from a side-trip to Roubaix. On the latter, the quintet is generously augmented by fellow-visitors, a sprawling jam featuring Miles, Hot Lips Page, Bill Coleman, Don Byas, James Moody, and (a valuable encounter) Sidney Bechet. The quality of the music is, frankly, nothing to write home about, but it's marvellous to have all these names together in the one space.

There is more jam material on 12, Parker with Maurice Moufflard's well-drilled but uninspired orchestra. The more interesting material is recorded back home in New York, at the home of saxophonists Joe Maini and Don Lanphere, where a regular jam seems on occasion to have been recorded. Bird is the dominant voice but there are lots of others clamouring for attention, and it's hard to keep the attention riveted.

The next volume can be skipped on the thin grounds that all the material is under Dizzy Gillespie's name. Volume 14, though, is back to the small groups and a single take from the Metronome All Stars in January 1949. The next volume is perhaps the weakest of the latter bunch from a documentary point of view; the Red Norvo material is available elsewhere, and the big-band material under Gene Roland's leadership finds Parker somewhat under the weather, misfingering a couple of times.

Anyone who is interested in this music more than casually should, however, attempt to have a listen to the next volume. It includes a nine-minute lecture or lesson from Parker with a fascinating insight into his work on scales, all recorded in Dick Meldonian's apartment. Beside this, all the other tracks melt into relative insignificance, though the pair from the Waldorf Astoria with Dorham and Thompson from 1951 are very good indeed, if a little early in the evening for fireworks. In the lecture, one hears very little speech from Parker, but one audible fragment contains the nugget 'all music is harmony, melody and rhythm'. Harmony with who? someone asks. Parker informs him he's a fool, presumably because of the grammar.

Milt Jackson is on hand at the Waldorf Astoria for a version of 'Anthropology' which runs some minor variations on previously familiar versions. By this point in the series, producer Paolo Piangiarelli is adding material from other musicians. Volume 16 is filled out with Louis Armstrong material. Volume 19 has some tracks from 1949 by a Miles/Dameron group, but this volume also has reconstruction of four legendary glass-based acetates by blues singer and trombonist, Clyde Bernhardt, who had been in the Jay McShann band at around the same time as Parker. It had long been believed that these discs, which were in the possession of Frank Driggs, were unplayable. Rough and ready as they are, and containing only homoeopathic amounts of recognizable Parker, they fill in an important part in the story. The Clyde Hart material is lacklustre but there are flashes of brilliance from all the horn players, and the Sarah Vaughan material from May 1945, with Parker in the octet, is worth checking out.

The last item (in the current run of releases, at least) is subtitled 'The Great Lie', an item included in a previously unissued 1952 or 1953 jam session about which there is little definite information. There is an Art Pepper recording of the tune but, so far as is known, Parker had not played it before. The identity of the second altoist is a matter for speculation. He is a disciple of sorts, but not in the premier league; someone has suggested Charlie Kennedy. Nor is the identification of Jon Nielson as trumpeter entirely secure, though this does seem like a good bet. There is a re-run of the St Nicks material from 1950, sounding well mastered and very musical, and, as with recent issues, a batch of tracks by the Tadd Dameron Tentet which help fill out that rather intermittent discography.

Much as the discovery of Shakespeare's rough notes would be a major discovery, there is a place in the overall picture for almost all the Philology material; the ratings given are intended to reflect its historical significance. Casual buyers are counselled to save their money for more highly finished product and to leave these admirable releases to those who make Parker and his immediate environment their special study and passion.

Errol Parker (1930–99)

DRUMS

A picaresque jazz career is extensively described in Parker's autobiography, A Flat Tire On My Ass. He spent time in big bands and small groups, lived all over America and in Africa, led groups, taught, composed, and hustled his way into getting a number of records out over the years. This is what's left.

***** A Night In Tunisia**

Sahara 1015 *Parker; Philip Harper, Michael Thomas (t); Tyrone Jefferson (tb); Doug Harris (ss); Donald Harrison (as); Bill Saxton (ts); Patience Higgins (bs); Cary De Nigris (g); Reggie Washington (b).* 4/91.

***** Remembering Billy Strayhorn**

Sahara 1016 *As above, except Kenny Sheffield (t), David Lee Jones (as) replace Harper and Harrison; add Jimmy Cozier (bs).* 9/94.

Parker had a rather extraordinary career, often as a drummer, which he became after many years as a pianist. But he's seldom had the opportunity to record. His own label, Sahara Records, has had some earlier vinyl releases and presumably ended with these two CDs. Parker's 'A Night In Tunisia' is dramatically different from almost any other version: he breaks down both the melody and the rhythm (his drumming uses a modified kit in which the snare is replaced by a conga and there are more tom toms and fewer cymbals in use) to make it more like a bouncing, dishevelled fantasy on the original theme. Since Parker is Algerian-born, it can scarcely be a more authentic recreation, though. Originals such as 'Daydream At Noon' and 'The Rai' move to rhythms and grooves unfamiliar to the contemporary mainstream, most of them drawn from Parker's African background, and it places a compelling new context on the otherwise familiar solos of Harrison, Harper and Jefferson. The unglamorous sound, with the drums mixed right at the front, will knock out its appeal for many; but in a way this rough-and-ready mix suits what is a deliberately nonconformist session from a leader who deserves respect and attention.

Remembering Billy Strayhorn pretty much picks up where he left off three years earlier. The band is almost the same horn-heavy aggregation as before, the brass and reeds not so much acting as sections as working as a talking-in-tongues ensemble that rumbles over and round Parker's themes. With typical audacity, the disc includes not a single Strayhorn composition, despite the title: instead, it opens with two pieces which were written at Duke Ellington's request, some 30 years before, as a souvenir for Strayhorn of a Paris visit. Parker coaxes a powerhouse performance out of his group and, though there are some failures – 'Reggae' is a wrong 'un, and 'Autumn In New York' seems unnecessarily sour – they end on a tumultuous thrashing of 'Straight No Chaser'. Along the way, a heap of good solos and Parker's own inimitable propulsion from his unique drum set-up. Enigmatic and, unless anything emerges posthumously, his last word.

Evan Parker (born 1944)

SOPRANO SAXOPHONE, TENOR SAXOPHONE

The saxophone can have had few more challenging exponents. The Englishman came through free jazz to the kind of radical improvisation associated with the Spontaneous Music Ensemble and other free-music groups flourishing in the 1960s. Increasingly thereafter, he turned his attention to solo performance, very often on soprano saxophone, which he regards as his first instrument. His ability to create complex overtone series by overblowing is the source of music of formidable intellectual challenge, but there is also a gruff immediacy to much of his work which is closer to the sound-world of classic jazz. John Coltrane is perhaps the only audible influence, though more in spirit than in style.

***** Three Other Stories (1971–1974)**

Emanem 4002 *Parker; Paul Lytton (d, perc, harm, elec).* 6/71–7/74.

***** Two Octobers (1972–1975)**

Emanem 4009 *As above.* 10/72–10/75.

****** Saxophone Solos**

Chronoscope CPE 2002 *Parker (ss solo).* 6–9/75.

If genius is the sustained application of intelligence, then Evan Parker merits the epithet. Over 30 years he has laid down a body of work which is both virtuosic in terms of saxophone technique and profoundly resistant to 'instrumentalism'; it is both abstract and rooted, deeply tinged with the English philosophical and scientific tradition. Parker has made significant contributions to improvising collectives like the Spontaneous Music Ensemble and the London Jazz Composers Orchestra; but he is perhaps best known as a solo improviser whose grasp of harmonics, derived initially from Coltrane, is entirely *sui generis*. An Italian enthusiast, Francesco Martinelli, has devoted considerable time and effort to documenting Parker's recorded and concert works over the years, much of it on small labels in out-of-the-way places; as will be seen here and in the index, the available discography is now very large indeed.

The unaccompanied material on the Chronoscope disc remains as fresh and urgent as it was 25 years ago. Parker named these pieces 'Aerobatics' and appended subtitles from Samuel Beckett, his favourite author. They take common cause with the playwright and novelist in addressing those moments when language cedes to silence, non-communication and sheer physicality; not for nothing was an earlier Parker LP called *The Topography Of The Lungs*. Parker can be heard experimenting with duration, changing the colour of sound even as pitches are sustained, but also using multiphonics to collapse the vertical organization of jazz – the province of ancestors like his namesake, Bird, and John Coltrane – in favour of sounds that have mass but no single obvious direction and destination.

The duets with Lytton are inevitably more directed. The material on *Three Other Stories* is a dense palimpsest of saxophone, percussion, other sound-sources and tapes of previous performances. The result is much denser and blockier than one normally expects from Parker, though recent electro-acoustic work suggests that there are elements here which he still considers valuable, perhaps as a dialectical response to unaccompanied saxophone. *Two Octobers* is sparser, autumnally stripped and surreal, taking its inspiration and titles ('Then Wept! Then Rose In Zeal And Awe', 'Two Horn'd Reasoning, Cloven Fiction', 'I Want! I Want!') from William Blake, the Blake of *An Island In The Moon* rather than the *Songs Of Innocence And Experience*. Parker's deployment of circular breathing still sounds a touch mannered and self-conscious, not yet integrated. Lytton responds with flawless intuition, stretching out his line and dropping blocks of sound in mid-stream. His own use of live electronics is more refined than the actual technology might be thought to allow. The sound on both records is above average for material of this vintage; albeit grainy and one-dimensional, it captures most of the detail.

*** 4,4,4

Konnex KCD 5049 *Parker; Paul Rutherford (tb, euph); Barry Guy (b, elec); John Stevens (d, v).* 8/79.

An unsatisfactory record in a number of respects. Space is shared with a performance by the Spontaneous Music Ensemble from more than a decade later, but what gives the music its odd imbalance is that Parker still seems to be fighting with the remnants of a jazz aesthetic – Trane and Rollins, to name the names – which he seemed to have transcended a decade before. Why this should be isn't clear, but there is no avoiding the conclusion that it is Rutherford and Guy who hold the session together. Stevens rambles inconsequentially and often sounds detached and enervated; compare the absolute focus of his work on the SME track.

*** Waterloo 1985

Emanem 4030 *Parker; Paul Rutherford (tb); Hans Schneider (b); Paul Lytton (perc, elec).* 8/85.

This helps to plug an unexpected gap in the Parker discography and affords a glimpse of an otherwise undocumented group. Schneider is the unfamiliar element and, though he is a bassist very much in the Barry Guy mould, his approach is different enough to give the music a different impetus. The disc contains a continuous, unedited one-hour improvisation. Sound-quality is not pristine and the horns distort at maximum dynamics, but most of the tape seems faithful to the music as played and there is a reasonable balance among the elements.

**** Atlanta

Impetus IMP 18617 *Parker; Barry Guy (b); Paul Lytton (d, perc).* 12/86.

A glorious example of Parker in absolute sympathy with his fellow players. This comes three years after the group's first Incus recording, but a lot further down the path of association than that. Parker has spoken of offering up his solo style in 'sacrifice' when working in the trio context, and certainly it lacks something of the multi-dimensional complexity of the solo records. Newk's pianoless group may hover in the background, for here Parker has refined and simplified his small-group playing to the point where one can almost reconstruct the possibility – and no more than the possibility – of melody. This is one of the most accessible documents he has ever issued, the one most likely to appeal to listeners devoted to jazz and suspicious of anything that departs from chords. Guy and Lytton fulfil every expectation of a conventional bass-and-drums configuration without once touching fixed base.

*** Conic Sections

Ah Um 015 *Parker (ss solo).* 6/89.

*** Duets: Dithyrambisch

FMP CD 19/20 2CD *Parker; Louis Sclavis (bcl, ss); Wolfgang Fuchs (bcl, cbcl); Hans Koch (ts, ss).* 7/89.

The availability of the solo disc from 1975 and the existence of a limited-edition set which includes such masterworks as *Monoceros* and *The Snake Decides* in retrospect blunts the impact of *Conic Sections*. By the end of the '80s, Parker's unaccompanied soprano recitals were becoming a touch formulaic and repetitive. Indications were that Parker thrived better in a more responsive environment. The wind duos with Sclavis, Fuchs and Koch sometimes seem mismatched, even awkward, but they allow him to work on levels which are simply not possible in solo performance, evincing a simplicity of line and a directness of statement which were lost in the later solo performances. As ever, though, the technique is utterly assured and the tone is ironclad.

*** Hall Of Mirrors

MM&T 01 *Parker; Walter Prati (elec).* 2/90.

*** Process And Reality

FMP CD 37 *Parker (ts, ss solo, with multi-tracking).* 91.

These might almost have swapped titles. It's the solo multi-tracked album that suggests the *mise-en-abîme* of a mirror gallery, while Walter Prati's delicate acoustic environments constantly draw attention to their own processes, as against the hard-edged 'reality' of Parker's saxophone. Some of the backgrounds suggest that simple ring modulation would have sufficed. Others are as delicately imprecise as one of Morton Subotnick's subliminal 'ghost scores'. After *Atlanta*, 'Diary Of A Mnemonist' is among the most reachable things Parker has ever committed to record, by far the most interesting thing on *Process And Reality* and a fascinating anticipation of the electro-acoustic work he was to record for ECM some years later.

**** Imaginary Values

Maya MCD 9401 *Parker; Barry Guy (b); Paul Lytton (d).* 3/93.

Named after the nine theorems of primary arithmetic in G. Spencer Brown's *Laws of Form*, this supremely orderly set of improvisations is no less communicative, no less susceptible than the earlier trio disc. 'Variance' might almost be a written-out idea, so logically does it shape and reshape itself out of the stately processional sounded by Guy and Lytton. 'Distinction' is closer to the whirling intensity of the solo soprano records, but the bassist (who, as ever, doubles on chamber or piccolo bass) is almost playing *continuo*, strumming chords which seem to reach out and anchor the reed sounds. Lytton's mastery of cymbal overtones has never been documented better. Hard to attribute music as collective and mutual as this to any individual but, since we are concentrating on Parker here, we can say this is one of his finest hours on record. His tenor playing on 'Invariance' is like seeing and hearing the instrument reinvented before the senses, from primal breaths and metal sounds to music of the highest organization.

*** Birmingham Concert

Rare Music RM 026 *Parker; Paul Dunmall (ts, bs); Barry Guy (b); Tony Levin (d).* 3/93.

An unusually jazz-flavoured sound for Parker of this vintage, perhaps because Levin and Dunmall are so joyously devoted to a groove, however complex. The two-saxophone front-line is hugely powerful and perhaps at its best when both are playing tenor, though Dunmall's swoops down the range on his baritone provide some of the most dramatic moments on the whole set. Recorded and mastered by the indefatigable Dave Bernez in a somewhat soggy acoustic, it isn't the prettiest of products, but immensely listenable all the same.

**** Corner To Corner

Ogun OGCD 005 *Parker; John Stevens (d, t).* 6/93.

In June 1977 Parker and John Stevens recorded an extraordinary two-LP set for the Ogun label called *The Longest Night.* It remains a benchmark performance in British free music, so much so that any attempt to reduplicate its fierce energies more than a decade later might be seen to be doomed to failure. *Corner To Corner* confounds any such expectation. Its titles – 'Angles', 'Incidence', 'Reflections', 'Acute' – gently mock the cliché'd honorific of angularity, for there's also immense warmth and trust in these performances, two friends who can now comfortably elide at least some of the niceties, who can cross-talk and interrupt without offence, or simply hold the floor to the momentary exclusion of the other. Parker has rarely sounded as emotional as on the closing 'Each/Other'.

*** Synergetics – Phonomanie III

Leo CD LR 239/240 2CD *Parker; George Lewis (tb, computer); Jin Hi Kim (komungo); Motoharo Yoshizawa (b, v); Carlo Mariani (launeddas); Thebe Lipere (imbumbu, perc); Walter Prati, Marco Vecchi (elec); Sainkho Namchylak (v).* 9/93.

*** Ghost-In-The-Machine Featuring Evan Parker

Leo Lab CD 018 *Parker; Christer Irgens-Moller (p, ky, v); Peter Friis Nielsen (b); Pere Oliver Jorgens (d, perc); Martin Klapper (amplified object etc.).* 9/93.

Like his early inspiration, Peter Kowald, Parker has become increasingly interested in the global dimensions of improvisation. At the same time he has developed a parallel involvement in electronics. The 1993 Phonomanie Festival in Ulrichsberg, Austria, provided an opportunity to put these aspects together. Parker's regular trio was not there, but Tuvan vocalist Sainkho Namchylak was, and so was another occasional collaborator, George Lewis, a pioneer of the interface between acoustic instrumentation and computers. Something of the same was involved in Parker's collaboration with the Danish improvising ensemble Ghost-In-The-Machine. The record is a mixture of concert and studio material, the best of the former being the very intense and focused 'Intertuba/Extremii', the bulk of the remainder sounding rather abrupt and unachieved, and certainly no more than the sum of its parts. In a sense, the Danish project negatively illustrates what the other record was intended to represent.

The notion of synergy comes from Buckminster Fuller, another of the scientific thinkers who has made a substantial impression on Parker's creative processes. It is defined roughly as the residue or surplus of behaviour in systems which cannot be defined or predicted by the behaviours of the constituent elements, a notion which has an obvious application to improvising ensembles. The Ulrichsberg project made use of Lewis's Voyager software, a computer system which interacts with human agents, but, throughout the project, unpredictable and *ad hoc* groupings are required to interact with electronic resources. Different players are asked to define areas of interest and interaction, with Mariani, komungun player Jin Hi Kim, Parker, Lewis, and Lipere defining the parameters on the first disc, Lipere, Yoshizawa, Namchylak, Lewis and Parker again establishing the defining relationships on the second. The music included represents two days of intensive activity and is, to be frank, very difficult to absorb in this form. For the vast majority of potential listeners who couldn't be at the Ulrichsberg event, it provides an opportunity to sample Parker in unfamiliar sonic contexts. One fears, though, that most will find it frustratingly enigmatic.

♛ **** 50th Birthday Concert

Leo CD LR 212/213 2CD *Parker: Alex von Schlippenbach (p); Barry Guy (b); Paul Lovens, Paul Lytton (d).* 4/94.

'The echoing border zones ...' Robert Graves's poetry seems the ideal source for titles for these performances, which again combine Parker's gritty involvement in ideas and history, this time his own. The two trios represented two of his most important long-term associations. Despite the essential Englishness of much of his aesthetic (not the Englishness of the pastoralists or the Georgians, but of those who built an empire on empiricism and craft), Parker has always gravitated to the European scene. As he describes in an unwontedly personal liner-note, bassist Peter Kowald, promoter and label boss Jost Gebers and pianist Alex von Schlippenbach were largely responsible for widening his musical horizons, in terms of playing partnerships. The Schlippenbach trio with Lovens is the perfect counterbalance to the more familiarly documented work with Guy and Lytton. The textures are more open and more concerned with radical harmonics. Lovens and Lytton are occasionally confused – verbally – even by people who know the scene well. They couldn't be mixed up even on the briefest hearing. Lovens is immensely detailed, a microsurgeon of the pulse, while Lytton tends to favour broader and more extended areas of sound, opening and unfolding like an anatomist. The long opening piece with Schlippenbach, 'Hero Of Nine Fingers', is supremely well argued, with Parker and the the pianist trading ideas at a dazzling pace. This isn't energy playing, but it generates its own energies moment to moment. The only quibble is that disc one is only 45 minutes in length (and disc two only 40); however, we are not awarding the ultimate accolade on durations, but on sheer brilliance of conception and execution. The remaining pieces with Guy and Lytton are closer to the language of *Atlanta* and *Imaginary Values*, but no less valuable for that. Guy seems particularly focused on this celebratory occasion. Rising fifty himself, he has regularly re-thought his musical parameters, and one can almost hear him refining his language as he plays. Lytton is flawless on the long 'In Exultation', though he's the one musician on the set who probably isn't well served by the sound. The occasion, recorded in Dingwalls Club in north London, was very special. These documents are no less so. It would be hard to imagine music less of its moment *and* less ephemeral.

****** Breaths And Heartbeats**

Rastascan BRD 019 *Parker; Barry Guy (b); Paul Lytton (d).* 12/94.

*****(*) Obliquities**

Maya MCD 9501 *Parker; Barry Guy (b).* 12/94.

Breaths And Heartbeats is unusual, not so much in the way it was performed, but in the way that it involves post-sequence editing. The trio recorded material in three blocks, two sessions with saxophone, bass and drums and one on orchestral percussion. After the event, the percussion 'breaths' were attached to the 'heartbeat' tracks according to a certain formal symmetry. Parker points out that the album can be played in a different order so long as the final track is number 12 each time. Performances are shorter and more uniform in duration here than usual, though 'Breath And Heartbeat 3' is over ten minutes in length. The sound is wonderful, as it is on *Obliquities*. Asking what difference Lytton's absence makes to the music is the wrong question. This is not the trio-minus-percussion. This is a very differently configured relationship, a free give-and-take of ideas founded on years of shared experience. Essentially, tenor and contrabass, soprano and chamber bass are paired in order to ensure that the tessitura – the basic pitch-range – is aligned to greatest effect. The exchange of material is so fast and responsive that it is difficult to keep track of where it begins and where it is going, a perfect musical correlative of the uncertainty principle. Both are records that require time and a certain suspension of expectation. They pay huge aesthetic dividends.

***** The Redwood Sessions**

CIMP 101 *Parker; Joe McPhee (t); Barry Guy (b); Paul Lytton (d).* 6/95.

Not a quartet record; McPhee guests on the final jam, 'Then Paul Saw The Snake', a performance that suggests future collaboration may yield something. As it is, this has the feel of afterthought. The trio sound less intensely focused than usual, perhaps because they were playing in baking heat. This was the disc that kicked off CIMP's *audio-vérité* series, recorded in the Spirit Room in Rossie, New York (Cadence is based in Redwood, hence the title), and it underlines the label's unvarnished sound more than later sessions were to do, perhaps because windows had to be left open. The twitcher among us surfaces to point out that an American robin and some kind of babbler can be heard singing outside. Low recording levels are part of the ethos, but a concert experience and a home-listening experience are different, and some may find it hard to focus sufficiently on some of the quietest passages. These, though, are wider questions, not to do with these performances; they are non-vintage Parker/Guy/Lytton, fine in their way but lacking the intellectual command of previous discs.

****** Chicago Solo**

Okkadisk OD12017 *Parker (ts solo).* 11/95.

Remarkably, after eight discs of solo soprano saxophone, this is the first time Parker has committed himself to a full programme of tenor playing. The results are, as one would expect by this juncture, extraordinary, music of intense focus and a fearsome weight and intensity of tone. Four of the tracks are dedications to musicians Parker has worked with or been associated with over the years – Chris McGregor, Lee Konitz, trombonist George Lewis and 'Mr' Braxton. No evident thematic connection to any of them, though the tiny Braxton tribute includes elements that are reminiscent of the American. Probably redundant at this point in time to start taxonomizing the differences between Parker's soprano and tenor work. The range of overtones is perhaps more restricted, the line more direct, the pace and delivery of ideas more measured. No mistaking, though, the integrity of the performances or the identity of the performer.

***** Tempranillo**

New Contemporary Music NCM 4 *Parker; Agusti Fernandez (p).* 11/95.

A measure of the international dimension of Parker's career is that, less than a week after the Chicago recording, he is in the studio again, this time in Barcelona. Probably hard to get hold of, but as heady as the vinous elixir of the title. Fernandez is a fiery Mallorcan who is superficially reminiscent of Borah Bergman and plays in a similar hinterland between jazz and new music. At moments, he sounds as if he might be playing scored pieces by Xenakis or Stockhausen; at others, some passionate folk theme seems about to announce itself. Parker goes about his music with the same intensity as ever, listening, responding, interpolating new ideas. The studio sound is very good, with a resonant piano and a vibrant space round the saxophone. It's to be hoped that a few of these at least get into general circulation.

****** Towards The Margins**

ECM 453514-2 *Parker; Phil Wachsmann (vn, vla, elec); Barry Guy (b); Paul Lytton (d); Walter Prati, Marco Vecchi (elec).* 5/96.

The triumphant representation of 'synergetics', stripped of the awkward eclecticism of the Ulrichsberg project. Here the system yields unexpected surpluses when the sound of Parker's long-established trio, now increasingly often augmented with other voices, is confronted by a responsive technology which behaves – within the limits of its capability – like a listening musician. Without Wachsmann's presence one suspects that the degree of actual interaction would seem secondary rather than central to this music, but his highly attuned sensibility helps move the electronic elements from the periphery to the centre, without in any way de-emphasizing Parker's instrumental role (soprano throughout), or that of Guy and, above all, Lytton, who seems ever more important in this context. Though there is no mistaking that the Electro-Acoustic Ensemble performs like a regular (rather than an *ad hoc*) agglomeration, these are still difficult performances to analyse. Relative to a jazz tradition, they seem to advance a long-standing exploration of the limits of time. Relative to contemporary composition, they seem to relate to the whole modernist rejection of linear progress in favour of simultaneity, the physical presence of music as masses. This was an exciting step in Parker's progress, magnificently recorded and mastered, and compelling from start to finish. None of the pieces is very long (only two are over seven minutes), but even in the tiny space of 'The Regenerative Landscape', a tribute to AMM who pioneered some aspects of the idiom, the amount of musical information is formidable. 'Field And Figure' and the closing

'Contra-Dance' are Parker/Guy collaborations and perhaps the strongest things on the set.

***(*) Natives And Aliens

Leo CD LR 243 *Parker; Marilyn Crispell (p); Barry Guy (b); Paul Lytton (d).* 5/96.

As on the set with Fernandez, interesting to hear Parker, so long devoted to the microtonal devastation of Western harmony, working in the context of an instrument with fixed pitches. Not that it holds Crispell back. She creates huge, resonant chords which are difficult to analyse with any precision but into which the entire trio seems to be subsumed, as if the sound-box of the piano has become an environment rather than another instrument.

Lytton continues to develop with almost every release. His work on 'Sumach' (many of the titles are named after trees, invasive species in particular) is compellingly musical, the leaf-work to the roots, trunk and branches suggested by Crispell, Guy and Parker. If any is the alien, then – by virtue of instrument, nationality and artistic temperament – one would have thought it was Crispell, except that she naturalizes so instinctively. There is a fierce melancholy to some of Parker's playing, which is new and slightly unsettling. On the basis of it alone, this isn't a vintage performance, but the group has almost never sounded more unified and of equal weight.

**** At The Vortex (1996)

Emanem 4022 *Parker; Barry Guy (b); Paul Lytton (d, perc).* 6/96.

Those who were there still talk about this midsummer encounter at North London's 'listening jazz club'. Those who weren't will probably have tired of hearing about it and will be relieved that they too can now sample this extraordinary session. Because Guy and Lytton both live abroad, this isn't a group that gets together very often and every chance to hear them is rather special. Parker has often said that he regards the soprano saxophone as his first instrument, but on the first set he once again demonstrates what a formidable tenor-player he is as well. His gruff, low tones are ideally complemented by Guy's floating harmonics and Lytton's impeccably musical percussion. The second opens on a long soprano solo, an introduction that unleashes the saxophonist's signature sound, a long, continuous line using circular breathing and high-order harmonics, whose partials would defy all but the most mathematically minded of analysts. For some reason, this set seems less of a group effort than its predecessor. Guy is rather low in the mix and here and there seems to lose definition on an otherwise well-recorded disc. As so often in the past, the real dynamic is between Parker and Lytton, now two generations on from the Coltrane/Ali sessions that established the modalities of this extraordinary music.

**(*) Monkey Puzzle

Leo CD LR 247 *Parker; Ned Rothenberg (as, bcl).* 5/97.

Recorded at a mini-festival organized in memory of the late Sergei Kuryokhin, this was a frank and flat disappointment, a dialogue of the deaf in which two hugely talented players conspicuously failed to trade in their artistic differences. The release was distinguished only by a cryptic crossword for which the label offered as prize an unreleased CD-R of further material from the concert. 1 down, Abominable snowman loses personal identity after going north. Russian declines! (4)

***(*) London Air Lift

FMP CD 89 *Parker; John Russell (g); John Edwards (b); Mark Sanders (d).* 12/96, 3/97.

This group only convened during the latter part of 1996, but it has become a reasonably regular ensemble since then. The title, and the quite brief second piece, are ironic references to British improvisers' continuing dependence on Jost Gebers's excellent label to have their work heard. The two younger players in the line-up have had very different musical experiences from Parker and Russell, but they fit into this concept seamlessly. Edwards solos on the title-track and leads off 'The Drop', a tough, stringy sound that owes nothing to rock music and electronics except density and expanse. 'Half And Half' is a reference to Sanders's mixed parentage, but it's started by Russell, an acoustic guitar loyalist who always manages to combine a classical delicacy with the fire of rock. As ever, Parker shifts from soprano to tenor, playing with a lightness and speed that sometimes get buried in the sheer density of detail he generates solo and in duo formats. Within a more conventional group configuration he is happier to allow the line to declare itself. His tone more than ever recalls the late Coltrane, iron-hard, harmonically free, rhythmically complex. An artist in his pomp.

**** Most Materiall

Matchless MRCD 33A/B 2CD *Parker; Eddie Prévost (perc).* 2 & 4/97.

Given his immense respect for the pioneering example of AMM, and their long experience of the British scene, it is surprising that Parker and Prévost have not recorded in a duo setting before. The immediate and obvious source of comparison is Coltrane's late masterpiece with Rashied Ali, *Interstellar Space*, which was recorded exactly 30 years before. For all his attraction to the stillness of Korean court music, Prévost has remained grounded in modern jazz, and recent experience in rock groups has greatly strengthened and simplified the sense of pulse he derived from Roach and Blackwell. Similarly, Parker has always been Coltrane's man. In practice, this is much as one would expect: a tough, extended exploration of sonorities and structures. The titles are all derived from the work of Francis Bacon, which explains the curious spelling of 'materiall', and they underline once again Parker's capacious understanding of English natural philosophy. Prévost bows cymbals to create complex harmonic shapes. Parker exploits his circular breathing to create huge, spooling lines, which then break up multiphonically. There are tongue-slaps and toneless sounds from the saxophone, richly tuned, quasi-melodic figures from the kit, an unfailing procession of vividly exploratory ideas. Essential listening for anyone interested in the work of either man.

***(*) Live At 'Les Instants Chavires'

Leo CD LR 255 *Parker; Noel Akchoté (g); Joel Casserley, Joel Ryan (elec).* 12/97.

Recorded in Montreuil just a few days before Christmas 1997, this continues Parker's recent exploration of electronic interfaces, pitching him in with the rich jazz sound of Akchoté (who has also appeared with The Recyclers) and with two sound-processors who are kitted up to respond in real time to Parker's powerful, pungent saxophone improvisations. This is a record which either needs to be swallowed whole, absorbed as if it were a straightforward monolith of sound, or else responded to with care and attention. It is both intensely physical and intellectually detailed, constantly challenging at every level.

*****(*) Toward The Margins**

ECM 453514 *Parker; Phillip Wachsmann (vn, vla); Barry Guy (b); Paul Lytton (perc, elec); Walter Prati, Marco Vecchi (elec).* 98.

Parker's growing interest in electronic manipulation of sound has been the most important development in his music over the last few years. Old debates about 'instrumentalism' seem far behind, and with these performances he underscores their irrelevance by creating a body of music which sounds alert, responsive and utterly in keeping with his complex, overtone-laden delivery on saxophone. To a large extent, he simplifies his own playing in the presence of electronic sounds, which are generated live and real-time by Lytton, Prati and Vecchi, but it would be a mistake to overlook the role that Wachsmann and Guy play in the process as well. Most of the tracks are very short, sometimes little more than sketches, found moments in the collective experience of six extremely gifted but also highly spontaneous musicians. Some of the material is addressed to figures who've exerted a particular influence on Parker – Buckminster Fuller, Idries Shah, the members of AMM – and there is a short, delightful 'Contra-Dance' with Guy. Anyone who has found Parker's work difficult or unapproachable in the past will find easier leverage here.

****** After Appleby**

Leo 283/284 2CD *Parker; Marilyn Crispell (p); Barry Guy (b); Paul Lytton (d, perc).* 99.

A free-music supergroup, playing in a number of internal permutations but coming together forcefully on three long pieces, 'Blue Star Kachina', 'Where Heart Revive' and 'Capnomantic Vortex'. Crispell has been quieter recently than half a decade before and it's tempting to suggest that this is really her album. Her duets with Guy and particularly with Lytton are masterpieces of delicate concentration. However, it's Evan who dominates the long pieces, locked in dialogue with the sounds around him, constantly listening and responding and wasting nothing on empty gesture. His powers of concentration remain formidable.

*****(*) The Two Seasons**

Emanem 4202 2CD *Parker; John Edwards (b); Mark Sanders (d).* 2 & 7/99.

*****(*) Foxes Fox**

Emanem 4035 *Parker; Steve Beresford (p); John Edwards (b); Louis Moholo (d).* 7/99.

Marking an unexpected return to a species of free bop, the *Two Seasons* trio has its stylistic lineage in '60s groupings like Amalgam and the more pulse-driven versions of SME. Parker plays tenor for most of the album, including just one soprano piece on the July set. The sound at London's Vortex club is quite busy and intense, and it suits this music particularly well. Edwards amplifies his double bass, which gives him a wide range of articulations, and Sanders has always been an extremely active player, setting off patterns in entirely unexpected directions.

Edwards is back on *Foxes Fox*, but it is unclear whether his bass has any amplification on this studio recording. The line seems straighter and the dynamics less varied, except on his opening duet with Moholo. This is a collective album rather than a Parker. There are four quartet numbers, but there are also four on which Evan does not appear at all. Beresford is as cleverly inventive as ever and is sparkling with ideas on his two duets with Edwards and Moholo. Emanem have generally been associated with archive releases, often of mixed sound-quality. Here the standard of recording and mixing is very good indeed.

Leo Parker (1925–62)

BARITONE AND ALTO SAXOPHONES

He was a kibitzer in first-generation bebop, with Eckstine, Gillespie, Navarro and others, and played R&B-style swing in the early '50s; but narcotics spoiled his career. A Blue Note session from 1961 was released just as he died from a heart attack.

***** Prestige First Sessions: Volume 1**

Prestige PCD 24114 *Parker; Al Haig (p); Oscar Pettiford (b); Max Roach, Jack Parker (d).* 7/50.

Like Zeppo Marx, Leo is the saxophone-playing Parker whom people tend to forget. Like Zeppo, too, he quit the scene early, dying of a heart attack aged only 37. His best-known recordings were with Fats Navarro and Illinois Jacquet, having switched under Billy Eckstine from alto to baritone; he plays both on an early Prestige compilation. Just as the Eckstine Orchestra was always known, *tout court*, as 'The Band', so Leo was 'The Kid' or 'Lad'; themes like 'Mad Lad Returns' on the Prestige debut compilation (which is shared with his accompanist, Al Haig, and Don Lanphere) were meant to show off the jollier side of his personality, often at the cost of turning Leo into a novelty act; the two cuts (alternatives of 'Mad Lad Returns') with Jack 'The Bear' Parker fall into that trap. At this stage, though, Leo was playing some useful alto as well as baritone, but comparisons with another Parker probably put him off and he tended to concentrate on the bigger horn thereafter. Though fate didn't give him much personal leeway, there's a sense in which he never entirely grew up musically. Either way, his modest Blue Note discography is currently back in limbo.

Maceo Parker (born 1943)

ALTO SAXOPHONE

Joined the James Brown group in 1964 and was with him on and off until 1990. Subsequently led his own groups, featuring his brand of low-fat jazz-funk, big on showmanship and a great live attraction.

***** Roots Revisited**

Minor Music 1015 *Parker; Fred Wesley (tb); Vince Henry (as); Pee Wee Ellis (ts); Don Pullen (org); Rodney Jones (g); Bootsy Collins (b); Bill Stewart (d).*

***** Mo' Roots**

Minor Music 801018 *As above, except omit Pullen, Collins, Henry; add Larry Goldings (org, ky).* 3/91.

*****(*) Live On Planet Groove**

Minor Music 801023 *Parker; Fred Wesley (tb); Candy Dulfer (as); Vincent Henry (as, b); Pee Wee Ellis (ts); Larry Goldings (prog); Rodney Jones (g); Kenwood Dennard (d); Kim Mazelle (v).* 92.

***** Southern Exposure**

Minor Music 801033 *Parker; Kermit Ruffins, Derek Shezbie (t); Stafford Agee, Fred Wesley (tb); Philip Frazier (tba); Pee Wee Ellis, Roderick Paulin (ts); Will Boulware (org); Rodney Jones, Leo Nocentelli (g); George Porter Jr (b); Herman Ernest III, Ajay Mallory, Keith Frazier, Bill Stewart (d); Michael Ward (perc).* 93.

***** Maceo**

Minor Music 801046 *Parker; Fred Wesley (tb); Pee Wee Ellis (ts); Will Boulware (org); Bruno Speight (g); Jerry Preston (b); Jamal Thomas (d); Rebirth Brass Band; George Clinton, Kim Mazelle (v).* 4/94.

Just what the world needs, another saxophone-playing Parker. All things considered, though, this one may turn out to be the most widely exposed of all. As a member of soul godfather James Brown's backing group, he created an instrumental sound – hard, funky, tight as a nut – that has been immensely influential in popular music. Parker's discs for Minor Music are certainly worthy of their place as well, and the live missive from *Planet Groove* just gets the nod because this is what Parker, Wesley and Ellis do best: getting down and having a ball in the process.

Qualitatively, the others are almost impossible to set apart. The first has a brash, almost unrehearsed immediacy that suggests (correctly or not) that the band simply set up and got going. Pullen, whose involvement in R&B predates his avant-garde activities, throws in some readily identifiable shapes, and guest star Collins does some brilliant slap bass guitar. The remainder are more polished and trimmed at the edges. *Southern Exposure* and *Maceo* (which also bears the enigmatic word 'Soundtrack' on its front cover, and is also – regrettably – sponsored by a tobacco company) feature members of the Rebirth Brass Band sounding not too revivalist. All these discs are beautifully packaged in laminate cases by the German label, who are probably very pleased with their investment.

***** Dial Maceo**

ESC 03665-2 *Parker; Ron Tooley, Bennie Cowan (t); Gregg Boyer (tb); Will Boulware (org); Bruno Speight (g); Rodney 'Skeet' Curtis (b); Jamal Thomas (d); Kevin Hupp (perc); Corey Parker, Prince, Diann Sorrell, Ani DiFranco, Charles Sherrell, James Taylor (v).* 9/99.

He's back – and he's not proud enough to be shy about hiring chart personalities such as Prince, Ani DiFranco and even James Taylor (well, he was in the charts *once*) to provide some celebrity lustre on what's otherwise the same old groove. Synthetics are starting to overcome any natch'l feel, but the boss carries this one on his shoulders without any Fred or Pee Wee to help out. He's so busy touring all the time, we're surprised he even found the time.

William Parker

DOUBLE BASS

The creative heir of Jimmy Garrison and Paul Chambers, and directly influenced by '60s avant-gardists like Sirone and Alan Silva, Parker has emerged as one of the most inventive bassist/leaders since Mingus. His brooding, sepia-tinted tone first emerged in the Improvisers Collective in New York, an experimental workshop which later transmuted into the Mingus-like Little Huey Creative Music Ensemble.

***** In Order To Survive**

Black Saint 120159 *Parker; Lewis Barnes (t); Grachan Moncur III (tb); Rob Brown (as); Cooper-Moore (p); Denis Charles (d).* 4 & 6/93.

*****(*) Compassion Seizes Bed-Stuy**

Homestead 231 *Parker; Rob Brown (as); Susie Ibarra (d).* 7/96.

Dominated by 'Testimony Of No Future', one of three tracks recorded at Club Roulette, and almost 40 minutes in length. Developed from the simplest ideas generated in a rhythm section dominated by Parker and Cooper-Moore (who has been an important and loyal associate), it is an immensely involving piece that opens up acres of improvisational territory for all the soloists. 'Anast In Crisis, Mouth Full Of Fresh Cut Flowers' is transparently and gloriously influenced by Cecil Taylor, an impression reinforced on 'Testimony Of The Stir Pot'. The closing piece, 'Square Sun', was recorded on another occasion at the Knitting Factory and is very different emotionally and stylistically. Parker uses his bow to good – even comic – effect, and trumpeter Barnes (reminiscent of Hugh Ragin in style) covers the generations, drawing in everything from Cootie Williams to Leo Smith. Moncur is as wise and philosophical as usual.

After the Black Saint album, Parker groups seem to have been known as In Order To Survive. *Compassion* is tighter, more focused and more obviously improvisational than parts of the previous disc, which seems workshopped round simple predetermined ideas. The tracks on the later album are more developed and feature some of the bassist's very best writing. The opening sequence of pieces, 'Compassion', 'Malcolm's Smile', 'For Robeson' and 'Holiday For Hypocrites', is worthy of Mingus, and the playing is strongly reminiscent of a Mingus Jazz Workshop until Parker's subtle bass overtones and harmonics start to come through. The later stretches of the album are more discursive.

***** Testimony**

Zero In [no number] *Parker (b solo).* 12/94.

Solo contrabass performance is a stern discipline, mastered by few. Parker pays full tribute to the great Barre Phillips as his mentor, and much of this live recording from the Knitting Factory recalls Barre's rich, balletic solo works. The album is, however, dedicated to the less well-known and now sadly deceased French bassist, Beb Guerin, and it is interesting to note how much in tonal colour and sense of musical architecture Parker resembles other European contrabass players like Jean-François Jenny-Clark and Henri Texier. The opening 'Sonic Animation' is in places not much more than a repository of sound-sources, animated by no other impulse. The sheer physical effort of playing Parker's favourite instrument, with its famously wide divide between strings and fingerboard, is balanced by the intensity and massiveness of his tone, and it's only with 'Testimony' itself, the brief sketch of 'Light #3' and 'Dedication' (a tribute to two more familiar spirits who died young) that this starts to pay real expressive dividends. By no means an undemanding listen, *Testimony* goes to the very core of what Parker is about, both musically and emotionally.

***** Sunrise In The Tone World**

Aum Fidelity 2 2CD *Parker; Lewis Barnes, Richard Rodriguez (t); Roy Campbell (t, flhn); Masahiko Kono, Alex Lodico, Steve Swell (tb); Dave Hofstra (tba); Chris Jonas (ss); Marco Eneidi (as); Ben Koen, Assif Tsahar (ts); Richard Keene (ts, ob); Joe Ruddick, David Sewelson (bs); Vinny Golia (reeds); Gregg Bendian (vib); Jason Hwang (vn); Akira Ando (clo); Susie Ibarra (d); Lisa Sokolov (v).* 97.

The bassist's work with the Improvisers Collective led directly to the foundation of the Little Huey Creative Music Ensemble, and these large-scale compositions and group improvisations are close to the heart of Parker's turbulent music. Their roots are in Trane's *Ascension*, in Mingus's sprawling big bands and Sun Ra's Arkestra; but they also have strong affinities with Butch Morris's conducted improvisation and with Anthony Braxton's mythic-realist fantasy pieces. The two long tracks, 'Bluest J' and 'Huey Sees Light Through A Leaf', are guilty of moments of lassitude and self-indulgence but for the most part they fulfil Parker's creative imperatives, and some of the shorter tracks like 'Sunship For Dexter' and 'Voice Dancer Kidd' are as beautiful as they are challenging, pointing out beyond the bassist's influences to a new aesthetic for large-band performance.

***** Lifting The Sanctions**

No More 6 *Parker (b solo).* 97.

As before on his solo projects, Parker favours the bow over pizzicato and creates a dazzling soundscape that shows once again how engaged and committed a player he is, not just technically but also emotionally and intellectually. Experiencing this album without preconception and with gently suspended attention is akin to listening to philosophical argument in an unfamiliar tongue. The logic and the wisdom are evident, even if the components of the language remain a secret. As before, too, there is a discursive quality to the opening piece, 'Emory', but this soon leads into deeper and more evocative territory in Rainbow Escaping', 'Mary Waiting' and, above all, the monumental 'Macchu Picchu'.

*****(*) Posium Pendasem**

FMP CD 105 *Parker; Rob Brown (as, f); Assif Tsahar (ts, bcl); Cooper-Moore (p); Susie Ibarra (d).* 4/98.

****** The Peach Orchard**

Aum Fidelity 10 2CD *As above.* 98.

This is the point at which Parker's massive investment in his instrumental technique, in thoughtful musicianship and in the collective aesthetic of In Order To Survive pays off, as one knew it would. Recorded during the Workshop Freie Musik in Berlin, the fascinating *Posium Pendasem* suggests how close Parker has always been to the very different and un-American freedoms of European improvisation. Peter Kowald's presence as author of the liner-notes is a further reinforcement. Divided into three pieces, at 51 minutes, 13 minutes and 30 seconds, and one and a half minutes respectively, the album gives a reasonable impression of how In Order To Survive function structurally over different durations. Inevitably, the longest track, 'Posium Pendasem #7', is the most intensely involving. There are acres of space for individual improvisation, but the real substance of the piece is evident when the group is improvising collectively, as in the middle section, when the horns seem to develop a strangely symmetrical counterpoint to what in a more conventional jazz line-up would have been the rhythm section. It's unfair at this stage in his career to heap more 'influences' on Parker, all the more so when he is showing not so much influence as a desire to continue the work of others; but these moments strongly recall Cecil Taylor's intense – and ironically bass-less – trios of the 1960s. Fabulous music, in every sense of the word, dense and thoughtful, brightly coloured and abstract by turns.

The Peach Orchard is better still and arrayed across two full CDs of complex, mediated performance. Ibarra's long introduction to 'Moholo' (a tribute to South African drummer, Louis) is fine testimony to her growing skills and vision, while Cooper-Moore, who now plays only in Parker's company, creates a vivid and almost skittish accompaniment to the otherwise dark-toned 'Leaf Dance'. The first disc ends with a passionate elegy for a lost Eden. 'The Peach Orchard' is, along with a repeated version of 'In Order To Survive' at the end, the closest one comes to the essence of the group, highly individualistic but also profoundly collective in approach. Tsahar joins the group at the start of the second half with a mournful bass clarinet/piano duet on 'Posium Pendasem #3', another page from that astonishingly fertile workbook. William Parker is at the peak of his powers, and these two recent albums should be priority purchases for anyone who wants to confirm the durability of creative jazz at the turn of a new century.

Horace Parlan (born 1931)

PIANO

Veteran Pittsburgh hard-bopper, active in the USA through the '60s but since 1973 an expatriate living in Denmark. His blues-based style is solidity incarnate.

***** Arrival**

Steeplechase SCCD 31012 *Parlan; Idrees Sulieman (flhn); Bent Jaedig (ts); Hugo Rasmussen (b); Ed Thigpen (d).* 12/73.

***** No Blues**

Steeplechase SCCD 31056 *Parlan; Niels-Henning Orsted Pedersen (b); Tony Inzalaco (d).* 12/75.

***** Frankly Speaking**

Steeplechase SCCD 31076 *Parlan; Frank Strozier (as); Frank Foster (ts); Lisle Atkinson (b); Al Harewood (d).* 2/77.

****** Blue Parlan**

Steeplechase SCCD 31124 *Parlan; Wilbur Little (b); Dannie Richmond (d).* 11/78.

***** Musically Yours**

Steeplechase SCCD 31141 *Parlan (p solo).* 11/79.

*** **The Maestro**

Steeplechase SCCD 31167 *Parlan (p solo).* 11/79.

*** **Pannonica**

Enja 4076 *Parlan; Reggie Johnson (b); Alvin Queen (d).* 2/81.

*** **Like Someone In Love**

Steeplechase SCCD 31178 *Parlan; Jesper Lundgaard (b); Dannie Richmond (d).* 3/83.

***(*) **Glad I Found You**

Steeplechase SCCD 31194 *Parlan; Thad Jones (flhn); Eddie Harris (ts); Jesper Lundgaard (b); Aage Tanggaard (d).* 7/84.

(*) **Little Esther

Soul Note 121145 *Parlan; Per Goldschmidt (bs); Klavs Hovman (b); Massimo De Majo (d).* 3/87.

Parlan's most moving single performance is arguably the unaccompanied 'Lament For Booker Ervin', posthumously tacked on to the Ervin album of that title. None of his other solo recordings evinces that much intensity or attention to detail. A middle-order bop pianist in a highly oversubscribed field, Parlan catches the attention only for his tough bass chords and highly restricted melody figures (an attack of infantile paralysis crabbed his right hand) which contributed substantially to *Mingus Ah Um* and accorded closely with the bassist/composer's preference for highly rhythmic and unorthodox pianists. Parlan has developed a blues-influenced repertoire, marked by a substantial inclusion of Thelonious Monk themes, heavily left-handed melodies like 'Lullaby Of The Leaves' and throbbing swingers like Randy Weston's 'Hi-Fly', both of which recur throughout his recorded work, and in particular a wilderness of minimally differentiated Steeplechase sessions. Most of these have now returned on CD.

Perhaps the best of Parlan's earlier group work was made for Blue Note in the 1960s. The pick of those, *Happy Frame Of Mind*, which featured his friend Ervin, was briefly available on CD (784134) but has subsequently disappeared again. The excellent 1960 sessions with the Turrentine brothers are no longer available. Like other American players of the time, facing a slackening demand for jazz recording, Parlan emigrated to Scandinavia, where he has pursued a workmanlike and unspectacular career, documented by Steeplechase from *Arrival* onwards with almost redundant thoroughness. The only high spots that call for separate treatment are the very fine 1978 trio with Wilbur Little and Dannie Richmond (also, of course, a Mingus man) and the much later *Glad I Found You*, where Parlan and the late Thad Jones shrug off a rather diffident setting to produce some sparkling performances. *Frankly Speaking* offers a rare glimpse of Frank Strozier, briefly visible as a Steeplechaser at the time; and the solo sets, *Musically Yours* and *The Maestro*, each have their felicities, particularly the gentler tracks on the second disc. For the rest, cautious sampling is perhaps the best bet. Although he rarely resorts to cliché, Parlan is still somewhat repetitive in the structuring of his solos, and he's rarely as challenging as like-minded figures such as Roland Hanna and Jaki Byard.

Rob Parton's Jazztech Big Band

GROUP

Contemporary Californian big-band music helmed by trumpeter Parton.

*** **Rob Parton's Jazztech Big Band Featuring Conte Candoli**

Sea Breeze CDSB-112 *Rob Parton, Conte Candoli, Mike McGrath, Steve Smyth, Tom Reed, Al Hood (t); Russ Phillips, Brian Jacobi, Jim Martin, Scott Bentall, Tony Garcia (tb); Mike Young (btb); Bob Frankich, Ian Nevins (as); Tony Vacca, Greg Mostovoy (ts); Kurt Berg (bs); Larry Harris (p); John Moran (g); Stewart Miller (b); Bob Rummage, Bob Chmel (d); Bill Elliot (perc).* 91.

*** **The Count Is In!**

Sea Breeze CDSB-2047 *As above, except add Mark Thompson (t), Jack Schmidt (tb), Mark Colby (ss, ts), Brian Budzik (ts, bs), Eric Montzka (d); omit Candoli, Phillips, Bentall, Garcia, Vacca, Berg, Moran and Chmel.* 7/92.

*** **What Are We Here For?**

Sea Breeze CDSB-2067 *Rob Parton, Mike McGrath, Scott Wagstaff, Art Davis, Corey Deadman (t); Jack Schmidt, Brian Jacobi, Dan Jonson, Antonio J Garcia (tb); Mike Meyers (btb); Bob Frankich, Ian Nevins (as); Mark Colby, Brian Budzik (ts); Kurt Berg (bs); Karl Montzka (p); Jeff Hill (b); Mark Walker (d); Krista Smith (v).* 11/94.

Big-band music comfortably dispatched by a likeable if not markedly individual orchestra. Parton likes to lead the trumpet section rather than compose or arrange, and most of the charts for the band follow familiar routes of punchy brass contrasting with sinewy reeds. Candoli is named as the featured man on the first album, but he actually solos on only three numbers; the other soloists rarely rise above the workmanlike, but there's a nice contrast between the effortful playing of Phillips and Frankich on 'Sentimental Journey' and the smooth reworking of the melody. *The Count Is In!* adds the brusquely authoritative tenor of Mark Colby, and his impact suggests that the band could use a few more soloists of this calibre. *What Are We Here For?* is a little better still. Colby has a couple of good turns once again; Parton treats himself to a feature on 'My Romance', and the band have gained a fine vocalist in Krista Smith, with a very swinging ''Deed I Do' as one result. Garcia's trombone feature on 'Loved One (To Maria)' is a neat departure. Their best calling-card to date.

Alan Pasqua (born 1954)

PIANO

A veteran session-player and sideman before he made his leadership debut, Pasqua is a New York pianist and composer.

**** **Milagro**

Postcards POST1002 *Pasqua; Willie Olenick (t, flhn); Jack Schatz (tb, btb); John Clark (frhn); Michael Brecker (ts); Roger*

Rosenberg (af); Dave Tofani (bcl); Dave Holland (b); Jack DeJohnette (d). 10/93.

****** Dedications**

Postcards POST1012 *Pasqua; Randy Brecker (t); Gary Bartz (as); Michael Brecker (ts); Dave Holland (b); Paul Motian (d). 12/95.*

Pasqua started late as a leader, but this pair of albums make such good listening that one wonders where he's been. His own playing as an improviser is comparatively unexceptional, but the compositions on *Milagro* stick in the mind on one hearing, and the arrangements are absolutely gorgeous. Pasqua varies the pace between trio tracks, features for Brecker, and arrangements where the brass glower in the background as the rhythm section works through a lush harmonic sequence ('Heartland') or a luminous melody ('Milagro'). The opening 'Acoma' is transcendentally beautiful, and Brecker, Holland and DeJohnette give unstintingly of their own talents throughout.

Dedications is marginally more conventional, the disc divided between trios and tracks where the horns join in; but again it's the quality of the writing that elevates the situations and brings out the best in Bartz and the Breckers. 'Ellingtonia', taken at a daringly slow pace, is among the most intelligent of tributes; 'Mr Softee' is a clever vamp; 'Homage' is a darkly fiery manifesto to open the album. Throughout, Pasqua holds his own in the kind of band that most dream about fronting. There is the odd indulgence on both records, but the results are so fine overall – and so well recorded – that it would be churlish to hold back a top recommendation.

Joe Pass (1929–94)

GUITAR

Already working with pro bands when in high school, Joseph Passalaqua toured with Charlie Barnet before naval service, then grappled with a drug problem and played small gigs in Los Angeles. Cleaning up in the early '60s, he worked with George Shearing and others and became internationally known after signing with Norman Granz's Pablo operation, for which he made scores of albums as leader and sideman. Revered by other players for a consummate technique, he helped restore a 'traditional' modernism as something valuable, after the inroads of rock had taken their toll on the respectability of the open-tone electric sound.

***** Joy Spring**

Pacific Jazz 835222-2 *Pass; Mike Wofford (p); Jim Hughart (b); Colin Bailey (d). 2/64.*

Pass became the most significant 'classic' guitar stylist since Wes Montgomery. He first recorded as a member of a Synanon Rehabilitation Centre house-band, and the string of albums he made for Pacific Jazz during the 1960s are all currently out of general circulation – except this one, which didn't even emerge until the '70s. It's a typical Los Angeles club date from 1964, handling some bop and standard set-pieces. Pass's style is fully formed: only the warmth and finesse of his later years are missing, and that may be as much due to the recording, which is no more than respectable. He builds long and quite fanciful lines out of 'Joy Spring' and 'Relaxin' At Camarillo' and comfortably overcomes some tuning problems on 'The Night Has A Thousand Eyes'. This is an inadequate look at this point in his career but, in the absence of *Catch Me!* and *For Django*, it's all there is.

***** Portraits Of Duke Ellington**

Pablo 2310-716 *Pass; Ray Brown (b); Bobby Durham (d). 6/74.*

****(*) Tudo Bem!**

Original Jazz Classics OJC 685 *Pass; Don Grusin (p); Oscar Castro-Nueves (g); Octavio Bailly (b); Claudio Slon (d); Paulinho Da Costa (perc). 5/78.*

*****(*) Chops**

Original Jazz Classics OJC 686 *Pass; Niels-Henning Orsted Pedersen (b). 11/78.*

***** Checkmate**

Pablo 2310-865 *Pass; Jimmy Rowles (p). 1/81.*

***** Ira, George And Joe**

Original Jazz Classics OJC 828 *Pass; John Pisano (g); Jim Hughart (b); Shelly Manne (d). 11/81.*

***** Eximious**

Pablo 2310-877 *Pass; Niels-Henning Orsted Pedersen (b); Martin Drew (d). 5–7/82.*

***** We'll Be Together Again**

Original Jazz Classics OJC 909 *Pass; J.J Johnson (tb). 10/83.*

**** Whitestone**

Pablo 2310-912 *Pass; Don Grusin, John Pisano (g); Abe Laboriel, Nathaniel West, Harvey Mason (d); Paulinho Da Costa (perc); Armando Compean (v). 2–3/85.*

***** One For My Baby**

Pablo 2310-936 *Pass; Plas Johnson (ts); Gerald Wiggins (p, org); Andrew Simpkins (b); Albert 'Tootie' Heath (d). 4/88.*

***** Summer Nights**

Pablo 2310-939 *Pass; John Pisano (g); Jim Hughart (b); Colin Bailey (d). 12/89.*

***** Appassionato**

Pablo 2310-946 *Pass; Jim Hughart (b); Colin Bailey (d).*

***** Duets**

Pablo 2310-959 *Pass; John Pisano (g). 2/91.*

***** Joe Pass In Hamburg**

ACT 9100-2 *Pass; NDR Big Band and Radio Philharmonic. 4/90–2/92.*

***** Live At Yoshi's**

Pablo 2310-951 *Pass; John Pisano (g); Monty Budwig (b); Colin Bailey (d). 1/92.*

***** Nuages – Live At Yoshi's Vol. 2**

Pablo 2310-961 *As above. 1–2/92.*

*****(*) Finally**

Emarcy 512603-2 *Pass; Red Mitchell (b). 2/92.*

***** My Song**

Telarc CD-83326 *Pass; John Pisano (g); Tom Ranier (p); Jim Hughart (b); Colin Bailey (d). 2/93.*

His long series of albums for Pablo helped Pass become both a major concert attraction and a benchmark player for jazz guitar.

Pass smooths away the nervousness of bop yet counters the plain talk of swing with a complexity that remains completely accessible. An improvisation on a standard may range far and wide, but there's no sense of him going into territory which he doesn't already know well. There's nothing hidden in his music, everything is absolutely on display, and he cherishes good tunes without sanctifying them. His tone isn't distinctive but it is reliably mellifluous, and he can make every note in a melody shine. Compared with Tal Farlow or Jimmy Raney, Pass took few risks and set himself fewer genuine challenges, but any guitarist will recognize a performer who has a total command over the instrument.

Pass effectively became the house guitarist for Pablo and, besides his own sessions, there are very many guest appearances with Oscar Peterson, Milt Jackson and the rest of the company stable. One could complain that Pass made too many records, but even taking a few deletions into account it amounts to only about one a year under his own name. The problem is more that his favourite context tended to be insufficiently various to make one want to own more than one of them.

Although he recorded extensively as a soloist, there are also many group albums in the catalogue. *Chops* is plenty of fun for the sheer expertise on display, Pass and NHOP basically doing little more than showing off how well they can play, but with enough nous to make it sound good. The meeting with J.J. Johnson on *We'll Be Together Again* is a little sleepy, but these are two sly old dogs, and you can almost hear them kidding each other on the blues, 'Naked As A Jaybird'. Johnson deadpans his way through it and for once Pass sounds like the assertive one; still, it's hard to think of a more sheerly mellifluous partnership. Shelly Manne is a useful presence on *Ira, George And Joe*, and this set of Gershwin tunes is nicely varied: Pass almost twangs his way through 'Bidin' My Time' and 'It Ain't Necessarily So', makes a waltz out of 'Love Is Here To Stay' and does a beautifully slow take on 'Lady Be Good'.

Of the trio sets, the Ellington album with Ray Brown and Bobby Durham is a shade disappointing. *Summer Nights* is something of a tribute to Django Reinhardt, and Pass sounds contented and thoughtful, while *Appassionato*, which benefits from a wider and more modern sound on CD, chooses terser material than usual – 'Grooveyard', 'Relaxin' At Camarillo', 'Nica's Dream' – and finds a cutting edge which some of Pass's records pass by. *Eximious* is a mixed set of standards and jazz themes, most of them adroitly handled, although Drew doesn't seem like the ideal drummer for the situation and the studio sound is a bit glaring. *Live At Yoshi's* is a solid club set, recorded in California, with a boppish tinge that gets a little extra juice out of 'Doxy' and 'Oleo'. The second helping on *Nuages* turns out much the same, with the closing 'Cherokee' a characteristic flourish from all hands.

The odd records out are *One For My Baby*, which sets the guitarist up in a sort of down-home kind of roadhouse band with mixed success, although Johnson contributes a few lively solos; the two Latin-styled albums, both of which have their finesse swamped by Don Grusin's penchant for light-music triviality, prettily though everyone plays; and *In Hamburg*, which sets Joe against both big band and strings on two occasions. Some of the charts are prosaic and this kind of situation isn't really Joe's thing, but he treats the occasion graciously enough and on a superior arrangement like Herb Geller's 'Love For Sale' there's a degree of excitement.

There is some poignancy about *Finally*, given that it's among the last recordings by both Pass and Mitchell, but the sheer good humour and craftiness of the playing make it a special item in the Pass list. Mitchell's knack of elevating an ordinary playing situation brings out the best in both men, and there's an extra twist in such staples as 'Blue Moon' and 'Have You Met Miss Jones?'. 'I Thought About You', done at a tempo that approximates syrup dripping off a spoon, is very fine. The other duo albums are equally effective and suggest how much Pass responded to the format. *Checkmate* is a typical Rowles session, with forgotten sweeteners like 'So Rare' and 'Marquita' in the programme, and since both men share an approach that mixes the respectful with the inventive they get along just fine. Pass plays with the minimum of amplification and it helps to offset any chord-clashing problems. There was a long-standing and fruitful liaison with fellow guitarist Pisano, and *Duets* documents their sympathies very candidly. Whether playing acoustic or electric, there's a good deal of bite about this pairing, with little of the sonorous fluff that sometimes gets stuck to guitar duets. Recorded very close up, the music has much presence and sting.

His first for Telarc reunited him with Pisano, and the rhythm section generate some civilized heat. It's still a bit restrained, but a couple more records by this group might have seen them reaching beyond the norm. Instead, Pass's passing closed the chapter.

****** Virtuoso**
Pablo 2310-708 *Pass (g solo).* 12/73.

*****(*) Virtuoso # 2**
Pablo 2310-788 *Pass (g solo).* 10/76.

***** Virtuoso # 3**
Original Jazz Classics OJC 684 *Pass (g solo).* 5–6/77.

***** Virtuoso # 4**
Pablo 2640-102 2CD *Pass (g solo).*

***** At the Montreux Jazz Festival 1975**
Original Jazz Classics OJC 934 *Pass (g solo).* 7/75.

***** Montreux '77**
Original Jazz Classics OJC 382. *Pass (g solo).* 7/77.

***** I Remember Charlie Parker**
Original Jazz Classics OJC 602 *Pass (g solo).* 2/79.

***** Blues Dues (Live At Long Beach City College)**
Original Jazz Classics OJC 964 *Pass (g solo).* 1/84.

***** University Of Akron Concert**
Pablo 2308-249 *Pass (g solo).* 85.

***** Blues For Fred**
Pablo 2310-931 *Pass (g solo).* 2/88.

***** Virtuoso Live!**
Pablo 2310-948 *Pass (g solo).*

***** Songs For Ellen**
Pablo 2310-955 *Pass (g solo).* 8/92.

***** Unforgettable**
Pablo 2310964-2 *Pass (g solo).* 8/92.

Pass's solo records are almost a category by themselves, and their importance in re-establishing the eminence of straightahead jazz guitar now seems clear. At a time when traditional jazz guitar playing was being sidelined by the gradual onset of fusion, Joe's solo work reaffirmed the virtues of the unadorned electric guitar, and the subtleties and harmonic shrewdness of his playing are like a long drink of water after much of the overheated guitar-playing of the 1970s and '80s. The original *Virtuoso* album remains definitive: Pass never sounded sharper or warmer on a set of standards, played with all the expertise the title suggests. The three subsequent volumes are replays with lightly diminishing returns; *Virtuoso #4* has now made it to a double-CD, with some extra tracks, although with the emphasis here on the acoustic guitar, some may see this as a makeweight to the others.

Concert situations don't seem to affect Pass's concentration: he played with the same careful diligence as in the studio, so the live solo albums sound much alike. Both Montreux albums are good, but *Montreux '77* is interesting for its emphasis on blues – four of the seven tracks – and how much Pass can get out of the form. *Blues Dues* includes a 'Round Midnight' which makes one wish that Pass had looked at this repertoire more often. *University Of Akron Concert* includes one of his extended Ellington medleys, a favourite device. *Virtuoso Live!* is in most respects just another solo album, but the pieces chosen reflect Pass's concern to try and wriggle free of his own routines. 'Mack The Knife' appears as a ballad, delivered with a superb touch, and the chopped rhythms of 'Stompin' At the Savoy' show how he could find a new tone, even in such a warhorse as that.

Of the other studio dates, *I Remember Charlie Parker* is a slight disappointment, Pass a little quiescent; *Blues For Fred* has some charming material, associated with Fred Astaire; and *Songs For Ellen* is Pass at his gentlest. From those same final sessions *Unforgettable* has just emerged. Played on a nylon-strung acoustic, it is Joe at his most winsome, even if rhythmically it's a little deliberate.

***** The Best Of Joe Pass**

Pablo 2405-419 *Pass; as albums above.*

****** Guitar Virtuoso**

Pablo 4423 4CD *Pass; as albums above.*

The Best Of is a respectable cross-section from the Pablo albums, but it has been superseded by the handsome, smartly chosen and very pleasurable four-disc collection, *Guitar Virtuoso*, which puts Pass's virtues into a clear light as both leader and sideman. Hard to argue with the suggestion that if you have this, you have all the Pass you need.

Jaco Pastorius (1951–87)

BASS GUITAR, STEEL DRUMS

Tried several instruments before settling on bass, and played rock, soul and reggae before looking at jazz. He acquired enough of a reputation to have cut a solo record before joining Weather Report in 1976, where he stayed until 1982. His fretless-electric bass style, soloistic and virtuosic, was hugely influential, but his personal life went dramatically downhill in the mid-'80s and he died following a beating outside a night club in 1987.

***** Jaco**

DIW 312 *Pastorius; Paul Bley (p); Pat Metheny (g); Bruce Ditmas (d).* 6/74.

Le demi-dieu de la basse: the unofficial subtitle of a recent compilation of Pastorius's music suggests the magnitude of the cult that has grown up around him after his pointless, wasteful death, beaten senseless by a club bouncer following one of his legendary binges. There was never any doubt about Jaco's brilliance, even before he became a member of Weather Report and became sanctified as the Jimi Hendrix of the bass guitar. The quartet with Metheny and Paul Bley is pretty much how you'd expect it to sound at that vintage. Metheny's playing is articulate but not profound, and a great pianist (albeit on an electric instrument) finds himself lost away in a rumbly sound-mix. Even so, Pastorius is the voice who commands the attention, nimble, precise and already experimenting with chords and harmonics.

*****(*) Jaco Pastorius**

Sony Jazz EK 64977 *Pastorius; Randy Brecker, Ron Tooley (t); Peter Graves (btb); Peter Gordon (frhn); Hubert Laws (picc); Wayne Shorter (ss); David Sanborn (as); Michael Brecker (ts); Howard Johnson (b); Alex Darqui, Herbie Hancock (p, ky); Richard Davis, Homer Mensch (b); Bobby Oeconomy, Narada Michael Walden, Lenny White (d); Don Alias (perc); Othello Molineaux, Leroy Williams (steel d); Sam and Dave (v); strings.* 75.

This was the first time anyone attempted to groom Jaco for big stardom. It puts him into an appropriately epic setting and demonstrates with tiny gestures just how completely in command he was when focused and straight, not just of his own instrument, but of an entire musical conception. But for oddities like the vocal contribution of soulmen Sam and Dave, which doesn't really work, and an understandable desire to show off as many different facets of his musical personality as possible, this might stand as Pastorius's best memorial. In the end, it doesn't quite add up to a great album. The solo 'Portrait Of Tracy' is exquisite and there is an early and very wonderful performance of the Charlie Parker tune, 'Donna Lee', a tune dedicated to a bassist of a previous age, and a very courageous one by all accounts. Perhaps too many different line-ups on show for one record.

*****(*) Word Of Mouth**

Warner Bros 3535 *Pastorius; Bill Reichenbach (tb); Tom Scott (bcl); Toots Thielemans (hca); Jack DeJohnette (d, perc).* 80.

A brilliant example of Jaco's gift for sound, with a rich blend of horn sounds within the confines of the small group. DeJohnette's drumming is the key additional element here, intensely musical and endlessly responsive to the long, winding bass-line. Jaco seems at ease and plays more quietly and with less percussive an attack. Some of his mid-range tones might almost be made by a cello. A lovely record, full of surprises.

****** Holiday For Pans**

Sound Hills SSCD 8001 *Pastorius; Peter Graves (tb); Wayne Shorter (ss); Toots Thielemans (hca); Mike Gerber (p); Ted Lewand (g); Craig Thayler (vn); Kenwood Dennard (d); Bobby Oeconomy (d, perc); Don Alias (perc); Othello Molineaux, Leroy Williams (steel d); Michael Gibbs Orchestra.* 80–82.

This is an oddity, but a marvellous one. The imaginative use of steel drums is a throwback to the bassist's Florida upbringing. The set opens with an atmospheric working of Alan Hovhaness's *Mysterious Mountain* symphony, and from there develops rapidly into a Weather Report sound-alike on 'Elegant People', soft calypso-reggae on 'Good Morning Annya' and from there into any number of stylistic sidetracks. Though idiosyncratic in the extreme, it's by far the most imaginative project Pastorius ever undertook.

***** The Birthday Concert**

Warner Bros 954290 *Pastorius; Dan Faulk, Brett Murphy, Melton Mustafa, Brian O'Flaherty (t); Russ Freeland, Peter Graves, Mike Katz (tb); Dave Bargeron (tb, tba); Peter Gordon, Jerry Peel, Steve Rothstein (hn); Dan Bonsanti, Neal Bonsanti, Michael Brecker, Greg Lindsay, Bob Mintzer (sax); Randy Emerick (bs); Paul Hornmuller, Othello Molineaux, Oscar Salas, Bobby Thomas (perc).* 12/81.

Jaco's thirtieth birthday, celebrated in a club in his native Fort Lauderdale. The band seems to have been a mixture of visiting guests, like Brecker, and local stalwarts. It's the usual mix of virtuosic grandstanding and ambitious ensemble playing. Perhaps moved by the occasion (though there are other possible explanations), Jaco plays less than usual and with less than usual precision. Not much more than five years later he would be dead. Perhaps if there had been more years, less weight would now be put on sessions like this. As it is, every crumb and every contrivance must be made to count. Not a great sound, with the brasses in particular recorded thinly and inadequately.

***** Jaco Pastorius**

Warner Bros 9548 35880 *As for Word Of Mouth and The Birthday Concert, except add Randy Brecker, Jon Faddis (t), Paul McCandless (ob, ss), Wayne Shorter (ss), Ron Tooley, Forrest Buchtel (sax), Hubert Laws (f), Herbie Hancock (p), Don Alias (perc).* 80–82.

A mostly effective compilation of material from the thirtieth birthday gig in Fort Lauderdale, and the earlier *Word Of Mouth*. 'Crisis' with the Shorter, Laws, Hancock, DeJohnette supergroup is as good as it gets. Originally issued in continental Europe, it has now been distributed widely elsewhere.

***** PDB**

DIW 827 *Pastorius; Hiram Bullock (g, ky); Kenwood Dennard (d).* 2/86.

*****(*) Live In New York City: Trio**

Big World BW 1002 *As above.*

***** Live In New York City: Promise Land**

Big World BW 1003 *As above, except add Jerry Gonzalez (t, perc), Alex Foster (sax), Michael Gerber (p, v), Delmar Brown (syn, v), Butch Thomas (d).*

This was the apotheosis of Jaco's power-trio leanings, a tough, tight band, much emulated and much bootlegged. The interplay among the three elements was probably better in reality, given a decent sound-balance, than it sounds on most of the existing records, lacking that very commodity. These tend to be rather difficult records to listen to, rough and unpolished but with some striking moments: 'I Shot the Sheriff' on the second New York volume, 'Alfie' and the ubiquitous 'Niema' on volume three, which opens with one of his best bass-and-percussion introductions. Bullock is a forceful, funky player, not obviously *simpatico* at first playing, but with a dark and abstract intelligence. Dennard is the foil and the fulcrum, the Ginger Baker to Bullock's Clapton and Jaco's Jack Bruce.

*****(*) Punk Jazz**

Big World BW 1001 *Pastorius; Jerry Gonzalez (t, perc); Alex Foster, Butch Thomas (sax); Michael Gerber (p); Delmar Brown (ky); Hiram Bullock (g); Kenwood Dennard (d).* 3/86.

Pastorius's wish to be considered a jazz man (albeit a punk jazz man) surfaced regularly through the final few years, when as often as not personal circumstances dictated a less sophisticated approach. 'Donna Lee' reappears here, but without the boppish authenticity of the Epic session (reissued on Sony). The remainder of the set is good, hot-sauce electric jazz, surprisingly conventional when set alongside the 'punk' aesthetic of Zorn, Lindsay, Marclay and company.

****(*) Honestly**

Jazzpoint JP 1032 *Pastorius (b solo).* 3/86.

*****(*) Live In Italy**

Jazzpoint JP 1037 *Pastorius; Bireli Lagrene (g); Thomas Borocz (d).* 3/86.

***** Heavy'N Jazz**

Jazzpoint JP 1036 *Pastorius; Bireli Lagrene (g); Serge Bringolf (d).* 12/86.

The untitled improvisations on *Honestly* frequently seem no more than a Sears catalogue of exotic harmonies and effects, put together with diminishing logic and questionable taste. Needless to say, the Italian crowd cheer it to the echo, although they don't respond at all to a quote from 'My Favorite Things', though they don't rise to 'America The Beautiful' or the riff from 'Purple Haze' either, so what does that suggest about their musical expectations? The trio was recorded at the same time, a very different line-up and sound from the group with Bullock and Dennard, but it has its own distinctive strengths. Lagrene's romanticism is closest in spirit, and the two guitarists trade lines with fire and discipline. In contrast to Metheny's Wes Montgomery fixation, Lagrene is in thrall to his countryman, Django. His opening improvisation more or less focuses the mind on what he's doing thereafter, to the virtual exclusion of a slightly subdued and acoustically recessed Pastorius. They do creditable versions of 'Satin Doll', Joe Zawinul's Weather Report theme, 'Black Market', and Bob Marley's reggae classic, 'I Shot The Sheriff', which underlines Pastorius's childhood closeness to Caribbean music of all sorts.

***** Jazz Street**

Timeless SJP 258 *Pastorius; Rick Smith (sax, d program); Jan Davis (p, syn); Paul Mousavizadeh (g); Keith Jones (b); Brian Melvin (d, perc, d program); Bill Keaney (perc, syn).* 10–11/86.

A very odd record, but a pleasing one, given a bit of effort. The presence of synthesized percussion is slightly problematic but, as with so many of his projects, Jaco manages to make gold out of acoustic dross. The other instrumental sounds are pretty much superfluous, and it might have made a more appealing package if they had been dropped altogether.

***** Golden Roads**

Sound Hills SSCD 8074 *Pastorius; Benjamin Germain (ky, perc).*

****(*) A Good Stretch For Golden Roads**
Sound Hills SSCD 8078 *As above.* 11/86.

Curious duo sessions on which Jaco's habit of running through his entire box of tricks, and then running through it again, lest we didn't catch all of it, becomes increasingly tedious. Germain doesn't emerge with any personality whatsoever, and these must be considered dispensable items in this rather oddly balanced run of discs. A lot of stuff around – Jaco is nothing if not a minor cult – but so much of it sub-standard either artistically or technically.

Don Patterson (1936–98)

ORGAN

Switched from piano to organ after hearing Jimmy Smith, and began recording for Prestige in the '60s. Particular associations included Sonny Stitt and, latterly, Al Grey, and he was still performing in the '80s.

***** Legends Of Acid Jazz**
Prestige 24178 *Patterson; Booker Ervin (ts); Leonard Houston (as); Billy James (d).* 5/64.

***** Boppin' And Burnin'**
Original Jazz Classics OJC 983 *Patterson; Howard McGhee (t); Charles McPherson (as); Pat Martino (g); Billy James (d).* 2/68.

***** Dem New York Dues**
Prestige 24149 *Patterson; Blue Mitchell, Virgil Jones (t); Junior Cook, Houston Person, George Coleman (ts); Pat Martino (g); Billy James, Frankie Jones (d).* 6/68–6/69.

Patterson was an also-ran in the Hammond gang, though he cut plenty of albums for Prestige as both leader and sideman, several of them sampled here. The *Acid Jazz* entry is his debut for the label, *The Exciting New Organ Of Don Patterson* with a couple of extras from the same session. Ervin is his usual blustery and beefy self and they work up a fair head of steam on the likes of ''S About Time'. *Boppin' And Burnin'* moves forward four years, but Patterson's style hasn't changed a whit. His huge and overcooked solo on 'Pisces Soul' defines his style, all the clichés piled on, one after another, but played with an intensity that persuades (or bludgeons) the listener into thinking that it's burnin', all right. McGhee, as ever in this period, is wildly inconsistent and makes 'Donna Lee' into a splashy mess, but McPherson is ironclad, and the most exciting player is probably Martino, who sounds ferociously hungry. *Dem New York Dues* pulls together the LPs *Opus De Don* and *Oh Happy Day!*. More of the same, although the two different horn line-ups make this perhaps the pick of the three, for variety at least.

Big John Patton (born 1935)

ORGAN

Born in Kansas, Patton played piano for Lloyd Price in the 1950s, then switched to organ and made a string of Blue Note records as leader and sideman. Less visible in later years, he made a minor comeback in the 1980s, appearing on some John Zorn dates.

***** Let 'Em Roll**
Blue Note 89795-2 *Patton; Bobby Hutcherson (vib); Grant Green (g); Otis Finch (d).* 12/65.

Patton was one of the most entertaining of the players who followed in Jimmy Smith's footsteps, and a pile of Blue Note albums became his principal legacy. Most of them are out of print again, although this somewhat atypical date from 1965 is in the catalogue. Hutcherson is a surprise presence, but Grant is on hand to make sure nothing too unusual happens. They all get particularly busy on 'The Turnaround' to good effect.

****(*) This One's For Ja**
DIW 919 *Patton; Dave Hubbard (ts); Ed Cherry (g); Eddie Gladden (d); Lawrence Killian (perc).* 12/95.

Patton has been back more than once on record of late. The style of this one suggests that little has changed for him and, although there are covers of Coltrane and even Archie Shepp tunes here, the leader settles them down in his customary laid-back blues vocabulary. Hubbard and Cherry get in some capable solos, but it's hard to shake off a feeling of pointlessness.

La Pause Del Silenzio

VOCAL GROUP

Italian jazz-vocal outfit, here directed by eminent pianist Giorgio Gaslini.

*****(*) Freedom Jazz Dance**
Soul Note 121247 *Lucia Pinetti, Michela Martelli, Paolo Lorenzi, Gabriella Rolandi, Laura Conti (v); Giorgio Gaslini (p); Roberto Bonati (b); Giampiero Prina (d).* 3-4/92.

Forget the Swingles and Manhattan Transfer. This is a jazz vocal group with imagination and, what's more, with jazz. Giorgio Gaslini directs with his usual precision and imagination, arranging the title-tune as if the voices were horns, peeling off one at a time to solo. He does the same on Bessie Smith's 'Hard Time Blues' and Sy Oliver's 'Opus One', but on each occasion adds a dark, brooding introduction, reminiscent of Monk. Elsewhere, it's Bonati's full-voiced bass that provides both counterpoint and shading to the female voices. Not unexpectedly, given Gaslini's own eclectic repertoire, there is a diversity of material. The Lennon/McCartney song, 'Here, There, And Everywhere', is systematically deconstructed, as is Dave Brubeck's 'In Your Own Sweet Way'. There are two pieces by Gino Paoli, 'Dormi' and 'Sassi'; jazz players would do well to look at them closely. There's a fine version of Horace Silver's 'Peace' and of 'Mean To Me'. Interestingly, given the harmonic bias of the set, there's also a group of tunes associated with John Coltrane: 'Softly As In A Morning Sunrise', 'Nature Boy', and his own 'Spiritual'.

Mario Pavone

DOUBLE BASS

A frequently encountered presence on New York's downtown scene and a familiar from a few of the steady groups of that environment.

***** Toulon Days**

New World 80420 *Pavone; Steve Davis (tb); Thomas Chapin (as, f); Marty Ehrlich (cl, f); Joshua Redman (ts); Hotep Idris Galeta (p); Steve Johns (d).* 11/91.

*****(*) Song For (Septet)**

New World 80452 *As above, except Peter McEachern (tb) replaces Davis; Peter Madsen (p) replaces Galeta; add Bill Ware (vib).* 3/93.

*****(*) Dancer's Tales**

Knitting Factory Works KFW 205 *As above, except omit Ware.* 2/96.

Pavone has a big, ringing sound and a seemingly bottomless supply of ideas. A regular in Thomas Chapin's trio, he is probably best known in that context, but he has also worked with Bill Dixon, Anthony Braxton and Paul Bley. The distinctive feature of the albums he has released under his own name is the prominence given to trombone, either Steve Davis or Peter McEachern; the latter is responsible for the arrangement of 'Recovery', perhaps the best track on *Dancer's Tales*, and he brings a sharp-edged, slightly sour quality to the solo work. As a soloist, Pavone doesn't really emerge until *Song For (Septet)*, but there his fleet, Mingus-influenced approach begins to pay dividends; 'George On Avenue A' might well be something from the great man's notebook. 'Foxwood Shuffle' on *Dancer's Tales* is an explicit homage and an exceptional piece of work, as is the piece for Julius Hemphill, 'Lunch With Julius'.

Cecil Payne (born 1922)

BARITONE SAXOPHONE, ALTO SAXOPHONE, FLUTE

The powerfully voiced New Yorker gave up playing alto and switched to the big horn in 1946 while working with J.J. Johnson. If bebop seemed resistant to the tenor saxophone, it was even more so to the baritone. Payne, though, established a limber, articulate approach while with Dizzy Gillespie, and he has continued to make convincing bop-tinged jazz ever since, albeit with a lighter tone which owes a debt to Lester Young.

***** Stop And Listen To ...**

Fresh Sound FSR CD 193 *Payne; Clark Terry (t); Bennie Green (tb); Duke Jordan (p); Ron Carter (b); Charli Persip (d).* 61, 3/62.

Payne cut his teeth as a soloist with Dizzy Gillespie's late-1940s Cuban-bop big band. Along with the lighter-sounding Leo Parker, he did much to adapt the hefty baritone to the rapid transitions and tonal extremities of bebop. *Stop And Listen To ...* does little more than confirm his authority and demonstrate how comfortably he could function in company as demanding as this. Both are New York City sessions, recorded at a time when Payne seemed to be bent on proving that Charlie Parker's music *could* be played convincingly on the big horn. You want him to be right, but there are moments when it all falls apart rather badly. The Kenny Drew material on the 1962 date is more his speed, but of course it lacks that whirling intensity one gets from Parker.

***** Cerupa**

Delmark DE 478 *Payne; Freddie Hubbard (t); Eric Alexander (ts); Harold Mabern (p); John Ore (b); Joe Farnsworth (d).* 93.

*****(*) Scotch And Milk**

Delmark DE 494 *As above, except omit Hubbard; add Marcus Belgrave (t), Lin Halliday (ts).* 96.

*****(*) Payne's Window**

Delmark DE 509 *As above, except omit Halliday, Ore; add Steve Davis (tb), John Webber (b).* 8/98.

Payne's recent work for Delmark has been something of an Indian summer. The formula is pretty much the same on all three records: a weighty, two-saxophone front line (with the addition of Halliday as a pacemaker on *Scotch And Milk*), and guest brass in the very different shapes of Freddie Hubbard, Marcus Belgrave and, most effective of all, Steve Davis. The rhythm section is anchored by Mabern, who is one of the great post-bop pianists, a bridge between Duke Jordan and the younger generation. Eric Alexander is a Mabern pupil and has absorbed much of the pianist's vast knowledge of the idiom, creating solos that bespeak historical awareness as well as formidable technique.

Cecil himself continues to plough his own thoughtful furrow. The skirling bebop reel that begins 'Scotch And Milk' is an indication of how receptive he is to ideas from outside the bebop mainstream, but his strength remains the driving swing of 'Et Vous Too, Cecil?' on the same album. The recent *Payne's Window* (title track courtesy of the impressive Davis) is probably the best of the bunch by a nose. Cecil reprises his King tribute from *Zodiac*, adds Miles's 'Tune Up' and Gershwin's 'Delilah' and restates his commitment to the Minton's generation in 'Spiritus Parkus'. But it's his solo on 'Lover Man' that confirms the 75-year-old is still in magisterial form and still finding new angles on material that he's been playing on the big horn for most of his life.

Nicholas Payton

TRUMPET

Payton's ripe, rather full trumpet-sound is markedly different from Wynton Marsalis's, and it is his writing that most resembles Wynton's, essays in traditional harmony with a hard, modern edge. Payton lacks both the skyrocketing movement between pitches and the other's delicacy of touch with a ballad, but he seems to be moving on a fruitfully parallel course and it will be interesting to see how he responds to the challenge.

***** From This Moment**

Verve 527073-2 *Payton; Mulgrew Miller (p); Monte Croft (vib); Mark Whitfield (g); Reginald Veal (b); Lewis Nash (d).* 95.

***** Gumbo Nouveau**

Verve 531199-2 *Payton; Jesse Davis (as); Tim Warfield (ts); Anthony Wonsey (p); Reuben Rogers (b); Adonis Rose (d).* 96.

Verve have taken a slightly odd route with Payton, pushing him into situations which are obviously intended to increase his profile, but which seem to do no more than blunt his real strengths. A head-to-head with the venerable Doc Cheatham is the most obvious example, but then there was *Fingerpainting*, a homage to the compositional genius of Herbie Hancock with Mark Whitfield and Christian McBride (under whose name it is reviewed). Then there was the music for Robert Altman's thoroughly bogus *Kansas City* (a kind of *Nashville* with heroin and horns); the fairest thing that can be said about it is that at least the music was exuberantly played. So, a strange start for Payton.

Produced by Delfeayo Marsalis on *From This Moment*, he could hardly fail to sound a *little* like Wynton. Payton is a traditionalist who, in addition to developing his own book of songs, has shown a deep interest in classic jazz, as witness the material on *Gumbo Nouveau.* Interestingly, by the time he gets into the swing (and swing is the word) of both these crisp, uncomplicated sets, one has forgotten all about the Marsalis connection and begun to concentrate on the young man's bright, storytelling voice. He makes no demands on himself that he can't comfortably fulfil, and his best solos occupy that middle register which so many younger players seem to think is either dull or sissy. The material is all carefully thought out and, having seen service with Elvin Jones, he has a brilliant grasp of how to pace a set, one of Elvin's less well-publicized gifts. The band are pretty familiar now and go about their business with precision and enthusiasm. Needless to say, the recordings are absolutely up to standard.

*****(*) Payton's Place**

Verve 557327-2 *Payton; Wynton Marsalis, Roy Hargrove (t); Joshua Redman, Tim Warfield (ts); Anthony Wonsey (p); Reuben Rogers (b); Adonis Rose (d).* 9/97, 1/98.

He was obviously going to make a record called *Payton's Place* sooner or later. This is more like the real thing, working with a tough young band and with the chance to blow alongside a more appropriate trumpet partner than Cheatham. Marsalis stops long enough for two tunes, 'Brownie A La Mode' and the self-explanatory 'The Three Trumpeteers' (on which Hargrove also guests). Roy is the unexpected choice of partner on 'With A Song In My Heart' and shows a side of his playing which rarely surfaces in his own work, bright, fleet and softly lyrical. Josh Redman comes in on 'A Touch Of Silver' and continues to prompt questions as to how great he really is. This is a very lacklustre performance. The basic group is in no way overshadowed by the visiting stars. Warfield and Wonsey are both developing by the session, and newcomer Adonis Rose (since embarked on a recording career of his own) is a great find. The interaction on Wayne Shorter's 'Paraphernalia' (a favourite of Payton's) suggests directions he might want to explore with a working band, some shift of emphasis that might allow him to broker a synthesis of classic jazz and the challenging harmonics of 1960s Blue Note and beyond. As things stand, he sounds as if he might just get prematurely stuck in a style and a market niche – the perils of early success.

*****(*) Nick@Night**

Verve 547598-2 *Payton; Tim Warfield (ss, ts); Anthony Wonsey (p, hpd, cel); Reuben Rogers (b); Adonis Rose (d).* 5/99.

The title might suggest an e-mail address, and there is an urgency of communication about this very fine set. Payton's writing has come on in leaps and bounds, utilizing unfamiliar registers and altered harmonic patterns to give the album a hint of strangeness. That's evident on the title-track, on the two improvisaed interludes and on material like 'Somnia' and 'Little Angel'. The crepuscular feel is sustained in pieces by Wonsey and Rose, both fine composers in their own right. The pianist makes use of harpsichord and celeste colours but concentrates on soft, minor intervals that leave several of the tracks melodically but not harmonically resolved, a tinge of ambiguity that suits Payton's developing style very well indeed.

Gary Peacock (born 1935)

DOUBLE BASS

Played bass in army bands before going to California in 1958, then to New York in 1962, where he became immersed in the new free scene, particular associations including Albert Ayler and Paul Bley. Studied macrobiotics and other sciences during a sabbatical from music. Most recently associated with the Keith Jarrett 'Standards' trio.

*****(*) Tales Of Another**

ECM 827418-2 *Peacock; Keith Jarrett (p); Jack DeJohnette (d).* 2/77.

***** December Poems**

ECM 531029-2 *Peacock; Jan Garbarek (sax).* 78.

****(*) Shift In The Wind**

ECM 829159-2 *Peacock; Art Lande (p); Eliot Zigmund (d).* 2/80.

Peacock's career has rarely hewn to the centre. After a brief apprenticeship in Europe, he moved to the West Coast and worked with the likes of Bud Shank and Shorty Rogers, before absorbing himself in the challenging formal structures of Don Ellis, Bill Evans, Jimmy Giuffre and George Russell, all the while maintaining a powerful involvement in avant-garde transformations of early jazz, notably with Albert Ayler, Roland Kirk and Steve Lacy. His playing style combines elements of Jimmy Blanton's and Wilbur Ware's sonority with something of Oscar Pettiford's rapid disposition of wide intervals. Peacock's own records have been rather mixed and can't be taken as representative of his abilities. The earliest, *Tales Of Another*, is performed by the band that was to become known as Keith Jarrett's 'Standards Trio' six years later. In the late 1960s, Peacock had turned his back on the music scene and gone to Japan to study macrobiotics. However uncertain he may have been about a return to bass playing (and he may have been persuaded by ECM chief, Manfred Eicher), there is a wonderful coherence to his solo work on 'Vignette' (with piano rippling underneath) and on 'Trilogy I/II/III' which quashes any suggestion that this is another Jarrett album, politely or generously reattributed; it is, in fact, his last appearance but one as a sideman. Even so, the pianist is clearly at home with Peacock's music and there is a level of intuition at work which became the basis of their later standards performances, but it is unmistakably Peacock's record.

December Poems is almost claimed by the saxophonist, who at this point in his career was rapidly settling into the stark, echoey style ECM cemented for him. It's interesting to hear him in this duo in a rather drier and less responsive acoustic and with a good deal more definition on the lower frequencies. Peacock sets the agenda throughout, though in performance terms he does find himself consistently overshadowed. Sadly, he never sounds quite so poised or concentrated again. *Shift In The Wind* is merely enigmatic, and there seems to be little positive understanding among the trio (beyond, that is, an agreement not to tread on one another's toes).

***** Voice From The Past / Paradigm**

ECM 517768-2 *Peacock; Tomasz Stanko (t); Jan Garbarek (ts, ss); Jack DeJohnette (d).* 8/81.

***** Guamba**

ECM 833039-2 *Peacock; Palle Mikkelborg (t, flhn); Jan Garbarek (ts, ss); Peter Erskine (d, d syn).* 3/87.

The later quartets further obscure Peacock's playing, and though *Voice From The Past* is particularly good, it is chiefly memorable for the atmospheric interplay of Garbarek and Stanko. Mikkelborg's hyperactive style dissipates much of the concentration of Peacock's writing on *Guamba*, and Erskine seems a poor substitute for DeJohnette's brilliant out-of-tempo colorations. However, the 1987 record stands up pretty decently after a decade, and renewed acquaintance prompts a reassessment of Erskine's contribution in particular. Cruder, yes, but perhaps deliberately so, an attempt to roughen up the texture of music that had become a little hidebound in his pursuit of esoteric harmonies. Peacock himself also comes through very strongly and is clearly pushing himself into new territory.

***** Oracle**

ECM 521350-2 *Peacock; Ralph Towner (g).* 5/93.

The comparison with Glen Moore rises with *Oracle*, which some listeners may find reminiscent of Towner's *Trios/Solos* project with his fellow Oregonian. And the contrast holds good. Peacock is driven and propulsive where Moore is happy to dwell on particular areas of sound. This isn't a criticism but a description. Where one might criticize *Oracle* is in its rather haphazard alternation of moods and its rather indistinct programme. There is a floaty, New Age quality to some parts, and then the duo throws in something almost violent as if to offer a sufficient contrast. This isn't an effective way to make records, and the final verdict has to be that, good as *Oracle* is in parts, it doesn't cohere. Lately, Peacock seems to have been happy enough to settle for a sideman role again.

Duke Pearson (1932–80)

PIANO

Named after Ellington and sharing some of the great man's piano chops and big-band sound, the Atlantan had a stint as MD and producer at Blue Note, but never entirely fulfilled his potential, drifting away from the music as multiple sclerosis progressively hampered his technique.

***** Bags Groove**

Black Lion BLCD 760149 *Pearson; Thomas Howard (b); Lex Humphries (d).* 8/61.

Pearson's stint at Blue Note has meant that his name is scattered through this book, though there is perplexingly little under his own name. His natural life was uncomfortably fated. As a young man he was thwarted in his ambitions to become a trumpeter by dental problems, and his health failed while he was still in his forties. This trio date, though it looks unpromising, is unexpectedly strong. Howard and Humphries are no more than adequate, but Pearson thrives in their simple settings. 'Say You're Mine' is one of his prettiest originals; he finds some interesting turns in 'I'm An Old Cowhand' and makes a salutary, powerful blues out of the already well-worn title-tune. Unfussy and swinging, this makes up in part for the absence of most of his Blue Notes, which occasionally pop up in reissue schedules but seem to disappear again all too quickly.

***** Honeybuns**

Koch 8519 *Pearson; Johnny Coles (t); Garnett Brown (tb); James Spaulding (as); George Coleman (ts); Les Spann (f); Bob Cranshaw (b); Mickey Roker (d).* 5/65.

Back in circulation after a long time in limbo, this Atlantic session isn't absolutely compelling, but it does suggest some of the ways in which the pianist makes a smallish band sound like a much bigger unit. Some of it comes from the arranging, which is very richly textured in the middle register, but the recording is also very impressive, the horns arranged in a V-formation that gives the soloist a lot of presence but with a lot of backweight from the ensemble. Duke's originals, 'Heavy Legs' and 'Is That So', are wonderfully imagined, as is the title-track, which features a strong contribution from trumpeter Coles. Big George Coleman is in great shape, blowing his trademark choruses with freedom and great harmonic control. Spaulding is a little more anonymous. Comparing the sound with the original LP, the remastering sounds a little muffled when the dynamics peak; even so, this is a welcome return for a long-absent record.

***** Introducing Duke Pearson's Big Band**

Blue Note 94508 *Pearson; Randy Brecker, Burt Collins, Joe Shepley, Marvin Stamm (t); Jimmy Cleveland, Julian Priester, Kenny Rupp (tb); Benny Powell (tb, btb); Garnett Brown (btb); Jerry Dodgion (as, f, picc); Al Gibbons (as, f, bcl); Pepper Adams (bs, cl); Bob Cranshaw (b); Mickey Roker (d).* 12/67.

Pearson was always more interesting on a larger scale. He has an idiosyncratic touch as an arranger, imposing a personal touch on material as varied as Chick Corea's 'Tones For Joan's Bones', tunes by Joe Sample and standards as varied as 'Days Of Wine And Roses' and 'Here's That Rainy Day'. Nicely voiced and crisply recorded with a strong live presence, this is an album that repays the closest attention.

Wayne Peet

ORGAN

California-based keyboard player, often associated with an introspective avant-garde, here in a less diffident role.

****** Fully Engulfed**

Nine Winds NWCD 0165 *Peet; G.E Stinson (g); Lance Lee (d, v).* 3/94.

Peet's listing in our first edition was for an acoustic solo piano record, and there could hardly be a greater contrast with this release. It's a power trio in the hallowed tradition of Lifetime. Peet's organ is matched blow for blow with Stinson's guitar, with Lee playing the Tony Williams part, and it's as exhilarating as any record cut in the wake of that original typhoon. Where other efforts at reviving this feel have floundered in the face of modern recording's cleanliness, Peet's group are mired in fuzz, feedback and a bottom-heavy studio mix that restores this ultimate kind of jazz-rock to its proper purgatory. Peet's only concession to modern times is to use a synth bass as well as the organ pedals, which adds some useful bandwidth in the lower frequencies; otherwise, it's a torrid show of sound, washes of chords flowing over each other, Stinson piling licks over the top while Lee thrashes out a relatively straightforward beat. In some ways, Lee's part is critical: where someone like Dennis Chambers would be filling up every available space with polyrhythms, Lee's simplicity is marvellously effective. It's for sure that John McLaughlin's Free Spirits band have come nowhere near this in building on the feel and excitement of Lifetime's old music, and it's fitting that Peet both dedicates the album to Larry Young and delivers a fine, sinister cover of Young's 'Visions' in the tracklist. Can't we have a second helping?

Ken Peplowski (born 1958)

CLARINET, ALTO SAXOPHONE, TENOR SAXOPHONE

Strongly influenced by Benny Goodman, Peplowski plays clarinet with the same acidity and precision. A soloist of some imagination, he favours short, percussive sequences interspersed with longer and more detailed elaborations of the theme.

****(*) Double Exposure**

Concord CCD 4344 *Peplowski; John Bunch (p); Ed Bickert (g); John Goldsby (b); Terry Clarke (d).* 12/87.

***** Sunny Side**

Concord CCD 4376 *Peplowski; David Frishberg (p); Howard Alden (g); John Goldsby (b); Terry Clarke (d).* 1/89.

***** Mr Gentle And Mr Cool**

Concord CCD 4419 *Peplowski; Scott Hamilton (ts); Hank Jones (p); Bucky Pizzarelli (g); Frank Tate (b); Alan Dawson (d).* 2/90.

***** Illuminations**

Concord CCD 4449 *Peplowski; Junior Mance (p); Howard Alden (g); Dennis Irwin (b); Alan Dawson (d).* 90.

***** The Natural Touch**

Concord CCD 4517 *Peplowski; Ben Aronov (p); Frank Vignola (g); Murray Wall (b); Tom Melito (d).* 1/92.

There was once a *Punch* cartoon of a balding pipe-and-slippers man drowsing in front of the fire and telly while his wife and a friend look on: 'Oh, yes, Ken *does* have another side, but it's exactly the same as this one.' Pure coincidence, of course, but there is something slightly one-dimensional about Peplowski's sweetly elegant saxophone and clarinet playing. Certainly in comparison with Scott Hamilton, doyen of the young-fogey swing-revivalist boom, he is a very limited technician who relies on rather meretricious cosmetic effects.

Mr Gentle And Mr Cool emphasizes just how much he could do with a little of Dr Jekyll's elixir. The two sextet tracks with Hamilton lift the album two notches. There's nothing comparable to lift *Illuminations* (from later the same year), though Junior Mance's piano playing impresses, as does the impeccable Hank Jones. A clarinettist first, with a method halfway between Benny Goodman and the great swing saxophonists, Peplowski seems locked on to a single dynamic wavelength.

The two earlier albums show slight leanings towards the harmonic upsets of bop, but Peplowski's solos are the musical equivalent of what used, disgustingly, to be called heavy petting, ending just when he seems to be getting somewhere. That's nowhere truer than on *Natural Touch*, which is even more reticent and uncommunicative than usual. There's a ready market for material like this, but it's by no means up to Concord's usual high scratch.

*****(*) Concord Duo Series: Volume 3**

Concord CCD 4556 *Peplowski; Howard Alden (g).* 12/92.

After the solos, the duos and, presumably still to come, the trios as well. This is a heaven-made partnership, of course, friendly and fruitful, and the quality of playing is just about out of this world. Like heaven, though, there is a risk of it becoming just a little boring over the long haul, and by the end one is almost longing for Concord to start the trios here and now and wheel in another star guest.

***** Steppin' With Peps**

Concord CCD 4569 *Peplowski; Randy Sandke, Joe Wilder (t); Ben Aronov (p); Howard Alden, Bucky Pizzarelli (g); John Goldsby (b); Alan Dawson (d).* 3/93.

By this stage in his career, it's clear that what turns Peplowski on is being challenged by new partners and new contexts. One can hear that happening only intermittently here, with Sandke throwing down the gauntlet a few times. It's an '& friends' date and the rivalry has an easy, joshing feel that doesn't really lend itself to fiery playing.

***** Live At Ambassador Auditorium**

Concord CCD 4610 *Peplowski; Harry 'Sweets' Edison (t); Ben Aronov (p); Howard Alden (g); Murray Wall (b); Tom Melito (d).* 2/94.

A lively, beautifully paced concert from the Ambassador in Pasadena, California. The ambassadorial figure from Columbus, Ohio, brings his trumpet on at just the right moment – like comedy, diplomacy is all about timing – and transforms what threatens to become a run-of-the-mill Peplowski Quintet workout into a rather special occasion. The old chap plays only on 'With You', 'The Best Things In Life Are Free' and 'Exactly Like You', but these stand head and shoulders above the rest. The sound isn't bad for a hall believed to have acoustic problems, and the group is often more evenly distributed than on the studio discs.

***** Encore! Live At Centre Concord**

Concord CCD 4654 *Peplowski; Howard Alden (g); Jeff Chambers (b); Colin Bailey (d).* 94.

Exclamation marks are a bad sign, usually that someone is protesting too much. This is a workmanlike and unexceptional date, the kind of thing that Peplowski and Alden can throw off without a second thought. Certainly not one to get excited about.

*****(*) It's A Lonesome Old Town**

Concord CCD 4673 *Peplowski; Tom Harrell (t); Marian McPartland (p); Howard Alden, Charlie Byrd (g); Allen Farnham (p); Greg Cohen (b); Alan Dawson (d).* 1/95.

It's probably no better a sign at this stage in an artist's career that an album needs to be spangled with guest slots, and it's symptomatic of something that the best tracks should be the ones featuring Harrell and McPartland. 'Last Night When We Were Young', which has them both, is far and away the most appealing thing on the record, though Harrell's opening 'More Than Ever' is exquisite, a stinging trumpet solo tempered by a fresh and lovely statement from Ken. One of the last sessions produced by the late Carl Jefferson, this is a fitting tribute to his ear and his unfailing taste.

(****) The Other Portrait

Concord Concerto CCD 42043 *Peplowski; Vladimir Slavchev, Atanas Karafezliev, Bimo Brustov (tb); Ben Aronov (p); Liudmil Nenchev (vn); Greg Cohen (b); Chuck Redd (d); Bulgarian National Symphony Orchestra; Ljubomir Denev (cond).* 3 & 4/96.

Not strictly a jazz album at all, but a stunning triumph on its own terms. Combining jazz compositions by Ornette, Miles, Duke, Billy Strayhorn and Parker and Gillespie with classical pieces by Milhaud, Plamen Djurov and Lutoslawski, it offers Peplowski a chance to explore the more legitimate side of his playing. On the Lutoslawski 'Dance Preludes', he sounds completely in command of a score that is technically if not emotionally demanding. Coming as it does straight off the back of an unaccompanied reading of 'Milestones' and 'Anthropology', it rather takes the breath away, but it only prepares the listener for another solo, 'Single Petal Of A Rose', an arrangement of the Strayhorn/Jimmy Hamilton 'Duet' (arranged for clarinet and three trombones) and for a stunning interpretation of Ornette's 'Lonely Woman' for quartet and orchestra. The Bucharest-based orchestra isn't the best around, but they have more inkling of what is required for the Milhaud concerto (originally for Benny Goodman) than most American bands, and they make a wonderful job of 'Lonely Woman'. Not to everyone's taste, but open-minded listeners will find it absorbing.

*****(*) A Good Reed**

Concord CCD 4767 *Peplowski; Loren Schoenberg (ts); Ben Aronov (p); Greg Cohen (b); Chuck Redd (d); Loren Schoneberg Big Band.* 1/97.

Three big-band pieces among the more conventional settings for Peplowski's clarinet and tenor, and it is the larger-scale arrangements that command attention. James Chirillo's 'Homage Concerto' is in part a memorial to John Carisi, who is remembered in a quiet central section, surrounded by two more vibrant movements that recall the 'Birth Of The Cool' bands. Increasingly, Peplowski seems to see himself in classical and quasi-classical settings like this, and even the jazz pieces on the albums have a formal quality, impressive but a long way from the looser swing of earlier days. If Peplowski is clever, he can balance both sides to advantage, provided he recognizes that they are calling on subtly different aspects of his talent. Another excellent record that will frustrate jazz purists but delight those for whom arbitrary borderlines are meaningless.

****** Grenadilla**

Concord CCD 4809-2 *Peplowski; Kenny Davern (cl); Marty Ehrlich (cl, bcl); J.D Parran (cbcl); Scott Robinson (acl); Ben Aronov (p); Howard Alden (g); Greg Cohen (b); Chuck Redd (d).* 12/97.

Grenadilla is the wood from which the majority of quality clarinets are made. Like any other rainforest tree, it is endangered, and Peplowski dedicates this remarkable album to its preservation. Perhaps even more importantly, though, he makes the record an expression of his own desire to preserve jazz tradition even as he pushes it forward into a new generation. Here, the guests represent wildly different aspects of contemporary clarinet playing.

Working together for the first time, Peplowski and the veteran Kenny Davern combine on the New Orleans Rhythm Kings' 'Farewell Blues', a tune first recorded in 1922. Davern's calm delivery complements Peplowski's own characteristically fervid statement; ironically, he has seldom sounded more like Benny Goodman's descendant. At the opposite end of the spectrum are Marty Ehrlich's 'The Reconsidered Blues' and 'The Soul In The Wood' and Greg Cohen's brief, powerful 'Variations', on which Parran, Robinson and Ehrlich again guest. At first blush, Ehrlich might seem the arch-modernist, but his moody clarinet and bass clarinet (no accident that his publishing imprint is called Dark Sounds) is hooked back into a long and remarkably conservative line. In Peplowski's company his roots show through strongly.

The rest of the original writing is credited to Ben Aronov, who continues to surprise. He is composer of the two quartet tracks and the opening 'Benny's Pennies' (no real relation to the Tristano number) on which Alden makes the first of several strong contributions. At the end of the album, 'Farewell Blues' is sandwiched between two classics which show the guitarist and the leader at their intuitive best: Victor Herbert's 'Indian Summer' and, done as a drummerless, pianoless trio, 'Cry Me A River'. An exquisite end to a remarkable album.

*****(*) Last Swing Of The Century**

Concord CCD 4864-2 *Peplowski; Conte Candoli, Bob Millikan, Randy Sandke (t); Eddie Bert, Bobby Pring (tb); Joe Romano, Jack Stuckey (as); Scott Robinson, Rickey Woodard (ts); Ben*

Aronov (p); Frank Vignola (g); Richard Simon (b); Frank Capp (d). 11/98.

Recorded in Japan as part of the fourteenth Fujitsu/Concord Jazz Festival, this is a tribute to the music of Benny Goodman, the artist who most thoroughly shaped Peplowski's increasingly protean style. Encouraging to note that, even on an occasion like this, he is much more than a respectful copyist. Listening to him shape a solo on 'Stealin' Apples', 'King Porter Stomp' and even 'Moon Glow', it becomes obvious that Ken is ever on the lookout for ways to recast classic idiom. He subtly reworks those now slightly shopworn phrases, sometimes subverts them entirely and then, just to prove that he's no wrecker, restates them with absolute fidelity to the originals.

The band sounds a touch under-rehearsed and perhaps not entirely at ease with the material. The redoubtable Candoli is the obvious exception; he delivers crisp, shining solos on 'Between The Devil And The Deep Blue Sea', 'Moon Glow' and 'Don't Be That Way'. Aronov is the anchor, as ever, and he lifts the ensembles more than once, though he isn't best placed in the mix. It would be fine to hear this same material performed just by a quartet, but *Last Swing* will more than do to be going on with.

Art Pepper (1925–82)

ALTO AND TENOR SAXOPHONES, CLARINET

Pepper's first notable jobs were with the Benny Carter and Stan Kenton big bands. After army service, he rejoined Kenton and stayed until 1951. He was a premier name among Californian saxophonists in the '50s, cutting several leadership records, but his career was constantly interrupted by his dependence on narcotics and several spells in prison. He was finally rehabilitated at Synanon at the end of the '60s. In 1975, he made his comeback album and gradually forged a new career as a surviving master of West Coast bebop alto, curtailed only by his eventual death in 1982. His book, Straight Life, is a definitive jazz autobiography.

****(*) Surf Ride**

Savoy SV-0115 *Pepper; Jack Montrose (ts); Russ Freeman, Hampton Hawes, Claude Williamson (p); Bob Whitlock, Joe Mondragon, Monty Budwig (b); Bobby White, Larry Bunker (d).* 2/52–12/53.

****(*) Two Altos**

Savoy SV-0161 *Pepper; Jack Montrose (ts); Claude Williamson, Hampton Hawes, Russ Freeman (p); Bobby Whitlock, Joe Mondragon, Monty Budwig (b); Larry Bunker, Bobby White (d).* 3/52–8/54.

***** The Art Pepper Quartet**

Original Jazz Classics OJC 816 *Pepper; Russ Freeman (p); Ben Tucker (b); Gary Frommer (d).* 8/56.

Pepper's remains one of the most immediately identifiable alto sax styles in post-war jazz. If he was a Parker disciple, like every other modern saxophonist in the 1940s and '50s, he tempered Bird's slashing attack with a pointed elegance that recalled something of Benny Carter and Willie Smith. He was a passionate musician, having little of the studious intensity of a Lee Konitz, and his tone – which could come out as pinched and jittery as well as softly melodious – suggested something of the duplicitous, cursed romanticism which seems to lie at the heart of his music. After a brief period with Californian big bands, he began recording as a leader and sideman on the Hollywood studio scene of the early 1950s. *Surf Ride* includes his earliest tracks as a leader: these clipped, rather brittle records find him a little wound up, and the six tracks with Jack Montrose in the front line – who sounds untypically hesitant on a couple of his solos – are standard West Coast fare. There are some leftovers on *Two Altos*, which is otherwise shared with some tracks led by Sonny Red, and, aside from a characteristically engaging trip through 'Everything Happens To Me' (a favourite throughout Pepper's career), this is slight stuff. The OJC release is drawn from a session for the Tampa label, with five alternative takes beefing up the playing time. This is Pepper entering his greatest period, and the quality of his thinking and playing is already nearing that of the remarkable Contemporary sessions, though the rather brief tracks clip the wings of some of the solos.

***** The Return Of Art Pepper**

Blue Note 46863-2 *Pepper; Jack Sheldon (t); Red Norvo (vib); Gerald Wiggins, Russ Freeman (p); Leroy Vinnegar, Ben Tucker (b); Shelly Manne, Joe Morello (d).* 8/56–1/57.

****** Modern Art**

Blue Note 46848-2 *Pepper; Russ Freeman, Carl Perkins (p); Ben Tucker (b); Chuck Flores (d).* 12/56–4/57.

****** The Art Of Pepper**

Blue Note 46853-2 *As above, except omit Freeman.* 4/57.

Pepper's sessions for Aladdin, collected on the three Blue Note albums, have been overshadowed by his records for Contemporary (below). *The Return Of Art Pepper* (the altoist had been in prison for narcotics offences, a problem that would plague his career) puts together a fair if patchy quintet session with Jack Sheldon – the two ballad features without Sheldon, 'You Go To My Head' and 'Patricia', are easily the best things – with a set originally led by Joe Morello, with Red Norvo in the front line. The really valuable records, though, are the two quartet discs. *Modern Art* is a deceptively quiet and tempered session: the opening 'Blues In' is a seemingly hesitant, improvised blues which typifies the staunchless flow of Pepper's ideas, and the following 'Bewitched' and a quite exceptional reworking of 'Stompin' At The Savoy' are so full of ideas that Pepper seems transformed. Freeman responds with superbly insightful support. Yet the succeeding *Art Of Pepper* is even better, with bigger and more up-front sound and with Carl Perkins spinning along in accompaniment. 'Begin The Beguine' is both beguiling and forceful, the dizzying lines of 'Webb City' are an entirely convincing tribute to Bud Powell, and the melodies unravelled from 'Too Close For Comfort' and 'Long Ago And Far Away' – which Pepper returns to on the Contemporary sessions – show a lyrical invention few players of the day could have matched.

*****(*) The Way It Was!**

Original Jazz Classics OJC 389 *Pepper; Warne Marsh (ts); Ronnie Ball, Red Garland, Dolo Coker, Wynton Kelly (p); Ben Tucker, Paul Chambers, Jimmy Bond (b); Philly Joe Jones, Gary Frommer, Frank Butler, Jimmy Cobb (d).* 11/56–11/60.

****** Meets The Rhythm Section**

Original Jazz Classics OJC 338 *Pepper; Red Garland (p); Paul Chambers (b); Philly Joe Jones (d).* 1/57.

****** Modern Jazz Classics**

Original Jazz Classics OJC 341 *Pepper; Pete Candoli, Jack Sheldon, Al Porcino (t); Dick Nash (tb); Bob Enevoldsen (vtb, ts); Vince DeRosa (frhn); Herb Geller, Bud Shank (as); Charlie Kennedy (ts, as); Bill Perkins, Richie Kamuca (ts); Med Flory (bs); Russ Freeman (p); Joe Mondragon (b); Mel Lewis (d).* 3–5/59.

*****(*) Gettin' Together**

Original Jazz Classics OJC 169 *Pepper; Conte Candoli (t); Wynton Kelly (p); Paul Chambers (b); Jimmy Cobb (d).* 2/60.

****** Smack Up**

Original Jazz Classics OJC 176 *Pepper; Jack Sheldon (t); Pete Jolly (p); Jimmy Bond (b); Frank Butler (d).* 10/60.

****** Intensity**

Original Jazz Classics OJC 387 *Pepper; Dolo Coker (p); Jimmy Bond (b); Frank Butler (d).* 11/60.

Pepper's records for Contemporary, all of which have been reissued in the OJC series, make up a superlative sequence. *The Way It Was!* remained unissued until the 1970s, but the first half of it – a session with Warne Marsh, which secures a brilliant interplay on 'Tickle Toe' and exposes all Pepper's lyricism on 'What's New' – is as good as anything in the series (the other tracks are outtakes from the succeeding sessions). The playing of the quartet on *Meets The Rhythm Section* beggars belief when the circumstances are considered: Pepper wasn't even aware of the session till the morning of the date, hadn't played in two weeks, was going through difficult times with his narcotics problem and didn't know any of the material they played. Yet it emerges as a poetic, burning date, with all four men playing above themselves. *Modern Jazz Classics* is in some ways more prosaic, with Marty Paich's arrangements of Monk, Gillespie, Giuffre, Mulligan and more working from the by now over-familiar West Coast glibness, yet the sound of the ensemble is beautifully rich; Paich conjures new things out of 'Bernie's Tune' and 'Anthropology', and Pepper – who also brings out his clarinet and tenor – alternately glides through the charts and dances his way out of them. There isn't a great deal to choose between the three remaining sessions: *Smack Up* finds Pepper playing Ornette on 'Tears Inside' as well as a memorable version of Duane Tatro's haunting 'Maybe Next Year', and the appropriately titled *Intensity* is a wistful series of ballads and standards in which Pepper, a peculiarly astringent romantic, seems to brood on the words of the songs as well as their melodies and changes: 'Long Ago And Far Away', for instance, seems a perfect transliteration of the song's message. Throughout these records, the saxophonist's phrasing, with its carefully delivered hesitations and sudden flurries, and his tone, which sometimes resembles a long, crying ache, communicate matters of enormous emotional impact. They demand to be heard. Remastering of all of them is well up to the fine OJC standards.

****(*) Art Pepper Quartet '64 In San Francisco**

Fresh Sound FSCD-1005 *Pepper; Frank Strazzeri (p); Hersh Hamel (b); Bill Goodwin (d).* 5–6/64.

Devastated by his personal problems, Pepper didn't make another studio record (aside from a Buddy Rich session) until 1973. These tracks come from a 1964 TV appearance and another at a San Francisco club. Not long released from prison, his style had changed dramatically: hung up on Coltrane and a fear that his older style would be out of touch, he sounds to be in a bizarre transition from the former, lyrically confident Pepper to a new, darker, often incoherent style based round tonal investigations and timbral distortions as much as anything. It's a trait he would rationalize with his 'normal' self in the 1970s, but here he's finding his way. He's still musician enough to make it an intriguing document, though, with the first version of 'The Trip' and a long 'Sonnymoon For Two'. The sound is rough, not much better than an average bootleg, but Pepperphiles will want to hear it. There is also an interview track with presenter Ralph Gleason.

**** I'll Remember April**

Storyville STCD 4130 *Pepper; Tommy Gumina (polychord); Fred Atwood (b); Jimmie Smith (d).* 2/75.

*****(*) Living Legend**

Original Jazz Classics OJC 408 *Pepper; Hampton Hawes (p); Charlie Haden (b); Shelly Manne (d).* 8/75.

***** The Trip**

Original Jazz Classics OJC 410 *Pepper; George Cables (p); David Williams (b); Elvin Jones (d).* 9/76.

****(*) A Night In Tunisia**

Storyville STCD 4146 *Pepper; Smith Dobson (p); Jim Nichols (b); Brad Bilhorn (d).* 1/77.

****(*) No Limit**

Original Jazz Classics OJC 411 *Pepper; George Cables (p); Tony Dumas (b); Carl Burnett (d).* 3/77.

***** Tokyo Debut**

Galaxy GCD-4201-2 *Pepper; Clare Fischer (p); Cal Tjader (vib); Bob Redfield (g); Rob Fisher (b); Peter Riso (d); Poncho Sanchez (perc).* 5/77.

Pepper's re-emergence blossomed into the most remarkable comeback of its kind. He became a symbol of jazz triumph-over-adversity, and though in the end it didn't last very long, there was a stubborn, furious eloquence about his later playing that makes all his records worth hearing, even when he struggles to articulate a ballad or has to fight to get his up-tempo lines in shape. The earlier sessions, following the *Living Legend* set, continue his struggle to digest Coltrane and reconcile that influence with his honourable past achievements: on both *The Trip* and *No Limit* he gets there some of the time, and the former at least includes his haunting blues line, 'Red Car'. But *Living Legend* itself is the one to hear first. 'Lost Life' is one of his gentle-harrowing ballads, a self-portrait rigorously chewed out, and the whole session seems imbued with a mixture of nerves, relief and pent-up inspiration which the other players – an inspiring team – channel as best they can. The two Storyville discs chronicle a couple of live dates with local players in the rhythm sections. *I'll Remember April* is marred by a gymnasium sound and Gumina's odd-sounding polychord, but Pepper blows very hard throughout. *A Night In Tunisia* is better – Dobson is a useful player, and there is another strong version of 'Lost Life' – but the studio albums merit prior attention.

Tokyo Debut documents Pepper's first tour of Japan, which started with the utmost trepidation and ended in triumph. The Cal Tjader group is the unlikely support, with Fischer playing an ugly-sounding electric piano; but Pepper, who was honoured by every audience throughout the trip, pours himself into the music. 'Cherokee' is chorus after chorus of ideas and, when Tjader joins in for three numbers, the altoist fits comfortably with the lite-bossa grooves.

*****(*) Thursday Night At The Village Vanguard**

Original Jazz Classics OJC 694 *Pepper; George Cables (p); George Mraz (b); Elvin Jones (d).* 7/77.

***** Friday Night At The Village Vanguard**

Original Jazz Classics OJC 695 *As above.* 7/77.

***** Saturday Night At The Village Vanguard**

Original Jazz Classics OJC 696 *As above.* 7/77.

***** More For Les: At The Village Vanguard Vol. 4**

Original Jazz Classics OJC 697 *As above.* 7/77.

*****(*) The Complete Village Vanguard Sessions**

Contemporary CCD-4417-2 9CD *As above.* 7/77.

Pepper's four nights at New York's Village Vanguard were filleted down to four single LPs (and, subsequently, CDs) in the past, but Contemporary have gone for broke and brought together every note of the engagement in a single nine-disc set. This provides more than five hours of extra music. The new material includes alternative versions of tunes played in other sets plus three entirely fresh pieces: a jangling 'Stella By Starlight', a notably impressive blues called 'Vanguard Max' and 'Live At The Vanguard'. Pepper specialists can compare the different versions of 'Goodbye', 'Blues For Heard' and 'For Freddie' at their leisure, but the main point of the set is the way it documents one of the major performers of the era with unflagging candour. Pepper was always a fascinating man to see and hear in concert – his sometimes obsessive talking with audiences is given full rein with the announcements here – and playing through these discs will remind all who saw him of his enduring struggle with his own demons, as well as the sometimes cruel beauty of his music-making. Besides him, there is the blue-chip rhythm section to listen to. The less committed will settle for the remaining single discs, of which the first is probably the single best. Excellent location recording.

***** Live In Japan Vol. 1**

Storyville STCD 4128 *Pepper; Milcho Leviev (p); Bob Magnusson (b); Carl Burnett (d).* 3/78.

***** Live In Japan Vol. 2**

Storyville STCD 4129 *As above.* 3/78.

***** Art Pepper Today**

Original Jazz Classics OJC 474 *Pepper; Stanley Cowell, Cecil McBee (b); Roy Haynes (d); Kenneth Nash (perc).* 12/78.

***** Landscape**

Original Jazz Classics OJC 676 *Pepper; George Cables (p); Tony Dumas (b); Billy Higgins (d).* 7/79.

*****(*) Straight Life**

Original Jazz Classics OJC 475 *Pepper; Tommy Flanagan (p); Red Mitchell (b); Billy Higgins (d); Kenneth Nash (perc).* 9/79.

****** Winter Moon**

Original Jazz Classics OJC 677 *Pepper; Stanley Cowell (p); Howard Roberts (g); Cecil McBee (b); Carl Burnett (d); strings.* 9/80.

***** One September Afternoon**

Original Jazz Classics OJC 678 *As above, except omit strings.* 9/80.

***** Art 'N' Zoot**

Pablo 2310-957-2 *Pepper; Zoot Sims (ts); Victor Feldman (p); Barney Kessel (g); Ray Brown, Charlie Haden (b); Billy Higgins (d).* 9/81.

***** Arthur's Blues**

Original Jazz Classics OJC 680 *Pepper; George Cables (p); David Williams (b); Carl Burnett (d).* 8/81.

***** Goin' Home**

Original Jazz Classics OJC 679 *Pepper; George Cables (p).* 5/82.

***** Tete-A-Tete**

Original Jazz Classics OJC 843 *As above.* 4–5/82.

The later records for Galaxy are in some ways all of a piece, and it's rather appropriate that the Fantasy group have chosen to issue a colossal boxed set of the whole output (see below). Pepper remained in fragile health, however robustly he played and carried himself, and the sense of time running out for him imparted an urgency to almost everything he played: ballads become racked with intensity, up-tempo tunes spill over with notes and cries. Studio and live dates are the same in that respect. Of these many late albums, the best should be in all general collections: *Straight Life*, with another fine quartet; *Landscape*, a sharp set by the band Pepper worked with most frequently in his last years; and above all the profoundly beautiful *Winter Moon*, a strings album which far surpasses the norm for this kind of record, Pepper uncorking one of his greatest solos against the rhapsodic sweep of Bill Holman's arrangement on 'Our Song'. The two Japanese live albums are also well worth seeking out.

The meeting with Zoot Sims is an oddity, a UCLA concert in which Zoot had three features, Art one, and they jammed together on a pair of tunes. Pepper's 'Over The Rainbow' is one of his typical slowburns on a ballad, while Zoot breezes affably through 'In The Middle Of A Kiss' and digs in surprisingly hard on 'The Girl From Ipanema'; but the main point of interest is hearing them together on the old bebop jam, 'Wee'. It's good. The sound is much better than it was on an unauthorized European release.

Arthur's Blues is a distillation of nearly an hour of previously unreleased music, taken from the complete Galaxy set listed below. Like so much later Pepper, it's full of interesting music while falling short of essential, although the gripping title-track is a prototypical blues workout by a man desperate to play his soul out in the time he had left. The two duo sessions with Cables, his favourite accompanist, are neither more nor less 'naked' than the quartet music, since Pepper never spared himself or his listeners from his versions of the truth. 'Over The Rainbow' (*Tete-A-Tete*) and 'Don't Let The Sun Catch You Cryin'' (*Goin' Home*) are among his final ballads and set down the closing thoughts of an unbowed spirit.

***** Laurie's Choice**

Fresh Sound FSR-CD 192 *Pepper; Milcho Leviev, George Cables (p); Bob Magnusson, David Williams, Tony Dumas (b); Carl Burnett (d).* 78–81.

Odds and ends from Laurie Pepper's tape collection, this is probably for Pepper fanatics only. There are three terrific performances out of five: an almost definitive disquisition on his ballad, 'Patricia', from a 1980 Georgia concert, a tough 'Kobe Blues' and a long and thoughtful handling of Joe Gordon's 'A Song For Richard', apparently the only existing live version. There's also some prime bebop in 'Allen's Alley'. On the down side is the sound, which is often amateurish and unbalanced, and we have to question whether some of these tunes have been mastered at the right speed: a Tokyo reading of 'Straight Life', for instance, sounds unreasonably fast.

*****(*) San Francisco Samba**

Contemporary 14086-2 *Pepper; George Cables (p); Michael Formanek (b); Eddie Marshall (d).* 8/77.

***** In Copenhagen 1981**

Galaxy 2GCD-8201-2 2CD *Pepper; Duke Jordan (p); David Williams (b); Carl Burnett (d).* 7/81.

Fantasy continue to turn up previously unreleased live tapes of Pepper, and both of these will please his admirers. The outstanding one is the Keystone Korner date from 1977. Following his Village Vanguard recordings, Pepper had flown to San Francisco with Cables, but Formanek (then not yet out of his teens) and Marshall were hired guns for the date. There are just four tunes on the disc, but it earns the stars for the stunning treatment of 'Blue Bossa' which opens proceedings, 16 minutes of staunchless invention. Marshall was an inspired choice for the drumstool. After Elvin at the Vanguard he's relatively straight-ahead, but he drives the group with such energy that the leader is obliged to think hard and play up to his best. There is a fast, hard blues and an intense 'Here's That Rainy Day', while the closing 'Samba Mom-Mom' is another powerhouse, if a slightly less convincing one. Dusty recording, but the feel comes through.

The Copenhagen session is also good, with Jordan guesting on piano, and a set-list that includes more bebop staples than Pepper would have liked. As a result, he is rather more focused and less wilful than on some of his regular dates of the period. But two discs and two and a half hours of music is too much, and there are unavoidable dead patches. Best shot is probably a marathon 'Besame Mucho' in which the playing has unanswerable vim.

****** The Complete Galaxy Recordings**

Galaxy 1016 16CD *As above OJC/Galaxy albums.* 77–82.

A vast and surprisingly playable archive – most such monuments seldom come off the shelf, but Pepper's resilience, febrile invention and consistency of commitment make this music endure far beyond expectations. There are dead spots, inevitably, and it's a costly undertaking, but there is also a lot of music still unavailable elsewhere, including many alternative takes, out-takes and Japanese-only issues.

****** The Art Of the Ballad**

Prestige 11010 *Pepper; as various OJC albums above.* 77–81.

Pepper at his best was one of the masters of ballad playing, and this skilful compilation offers a splendid selection of some of his most intense and heart-on-sleeve performances from Fantasy's catalogue. An excellent buy for those who'd wish for only a few Peppers.

Jim Pepper (died 1992)

TENOR SAXOPHONE

A hard-bop player with some Native-American roots, an aspect which he introduced into much of his playing and writing.

***** Dakota Sound**

Enja 5043 *Pepper; Kirk Lightsey (p); Santi Wilson Debriano (b); John Betsch (d).* 1/87.

*****(*) The Path**

Enja 5087 *As above, except add Stanton Davis (t), Arto Tuncboyaciyan (perc), Caren Knight (v).* 3/88.

***** Remembrance Live**

Tutu 888152 *Pepper; Bill Bickford (g); Ed Schuller (b); John Betsch (d).* 5/90.

Pepper is best known as the composer of 'Witchi-Tai-To', a jauntily haunting theme reflecting his Native-American roots and turned into an album and concert hit by Oregon (there is also a memorable treatment by the Garbarek–Stenson quartet). A melodic player with a strong roots feel and a resistance to abstraction, Pepper performed best against a highly lyrical background with a firm pulse. Lightsey seems an ideal accompanist and *The Path* (which includes 'Witchi-Tai-To' as well as the pianist's 'Habiba') is his most accomplished album. The urgency which Pepper brought to his best work is audible throughout the Münster set on *Remembrance* with his band, Eagle Wing. His early death and comparative scarcity on record has left him as something of a footnote in recent history.

Ivo Perelman

TENOR SAXOPHONE, CELLO, PIANO

Brazilian saxophonist marching towards the freest free jazz he can find, without letting go of some elements of both hard bop and his native song.

***** Children Of Ibeji**

Enja 7005-2 *Perelman; Don Pullen, Paul Bley (p); Brandon Ross (g); Fred Hopkins (b); Andrew Cyrille (d); Guilherme Franco, Manolo Badrena, Frank Colon, Mor Thiam (perc, v); Flora Purim (v).* 5–7/91.

***** Bendito Of Santa Cruz**

Cadence CJR 1076 *Perelman; Matthew Shipp (p).* 1/96

*****(*) Blue Monk Variations**

Cadence CJR 1066 *Perelman (ts solo).* 2/96.

***** Cama De Terra**

Homestead HMS237-2 *Perelman; Matthew Shipp (ts); William Parker (b).* 6–7/96.

*****(*) Geometry**

Leo LR 248 *Perelman; Borah Bergman (p).* 6/96.

****** Sad Life**

Leo Lab 027 *Perelman; William Parker (b); Rashied Ali (d).* 6/96.

***** Slaves Of Job**

CIMP 126 *Perelman; Dominic Duval (b); Jay Rosen (d).* 10/96.

***** Revelation**

CIMP 134 *As above, except add Rory Stuart (g).* 10/96.

***** Sound Hierarchy**

Music & Arts CD-997 *Perelman; Marilyn Crispell (p); William Parker (b); Gerry Hemingway (d, v).* 10/96.

***** En Adir**

Music & Arts CD-996 *As above.* 10/96.

**** Strings**

Leo LR 249 *Perelman; Joe Morris (g).* 12/96–4/97.

Perelman is a Brazilian who has burst into a prolific streak of recording almost from nowhere. He is already shrugging off comparisons with Gato Barbieri (perfectly plausible), Ayler (same syntax, different agenda) and David Murray (well, he made a lot of records to begin with, too). Perelman's methodology is to grab hold of a theme and shake it asunder via his hugely powerful tone: whatever the surroundings in terms of group or material, Perelman takes himself off into the red at a moment's notice. It's frequently exciting and at times enthralling, though one questions whether he needs to be documented at this length and in these sometimes indulgent circumstances.

Children Of Ibeji was an arresting start. The sound of the record is unfocused, but Perelman is already more than a match for the formidable rhythm section of Pullen, Hopkins and Cyrille, and the auxiliary percussionists add to the air of wildness. The most interesting piece, though, is a duet with Bley, cooler and restrained yet strikingly effective.

There were an astonishing nine albums recorded in 1996 alone. *Bendito De Santa Cruz* is mostly made up of Brazilian folk tunes, and it's hard not to recall the Barbieri–Dollar Brand session of many years earlier – though Perelman is strong enough to outface memories of the older saxophonist. Shipp is very much second fiddle here, as he is on the subsequent *Cama De Terra*, and Borah Bergman is a more creative partner (opponent?) on the subsequent *Geometry*; but all three records show how much Perelman enjoys having a pianist behind him. He clearly likes to be the single voice out front, but the harmonic anchors offered by a piano are a useful succour, and Bergman in particular is wily enough to find ways of both supporting and undercutting the mighty sound of the tenor. *Slaves Of Job* and the 'bonus' *Revelation*, cut on a whim as a jam session with Stuart sitting in, are strong entries which don't quite enter the front rank: Duval and Rosen are too busy and tend to overplay their hands, and Stuart is a distraction. Perelman plays lustily enough to earn the stars, but these are basically inadequate showcases for him. The two discs with Crispell, Parker and Hemingway also offer some fine playing without quite gelling as a good framework for the saxophonist. Crispell is too strong a personality to settle for the kind of subsidiary role that Perelman needs, and Hemingway's rhythms are too bracingly inventive – they offer Perelman a distraction rather than fed lines. *En Adir*, a collection of traditional Jewish songs, is an interesting departure, but it's only intermittently effective.

The one outright miss is *Strings*, where Perelman plays cello (his apprentice instrument) in a series of duets with Morris. The guitarist tries his best to make something of the situation, but Perelman is so self-absorbed in what he's playing that nothing very meaningful happens, and his cello playing is frankly not up to the tenor-work. *Blue Monk Variations* is a vivid footnote to the other records. Warming up by himself in a studio, Perelman came up with some 36 minutes of solo tenor based around 'Blue Monk' – three full interpretations and three variations. Unencumbered by the need to 'perform' as such, Perelman presents some of his least self-conscious and surprising playing. He turns the tune inside out three times, in quite distinct ways on each occasion, and while this is as plangent as the rest of his work there's a vein of introspection which is absent in the rest of what he's done so far.

The essential disc, though, is surely *Sad Life*. With Ali and Parker he is playing with musicians on the highest level, and they secure a propulsion and intensity which has its independent life without either overpowering or standing subservient to the leader. In the title-tune (which he starts by playing through a mouthpiece), 'Caiapo' and the ambivalent 'Hoedown', Perelman is giving us his most emotive and convincing playing.

*****(*) The Hammer**

Leo LR 286 *Perelman; Jay Rosen (d).* 3/98.

***** The Alexander Suite**

Leo LR 258 *Perelman; Jason Hwang (vn); Ron Lawrence (vla); Tomas Ulrich (clo); Dominic Duval (b).* 5/98.

***** Brazilian Watercolour**

Leo LR 266 *Perelman; Matthew Shipp (p); Rashied Ali (d); Guilherme Franco, Cyro Baptista (perc).* n.d.

Only three new records for this edition? Perelman has been having a quiet time of it, although one wouldn't know it from listening to these storming records. *The Hammer* is blissful uproar of the sort which Perelman the saxophonist was born to make. Coltrane and Ali never got anywhere near this much violence on *Interstellar Space*, and the duo compounds it by having most of these pieces run to only a few minutes each in duration, purist punk onslaught. The sleeve-notes are going a country mile too far when they say that at the end, 'there is exactly nothing left anywhere in the world'; but it is a splendid battle royal. We are less convinced by the often similarly inclined chaos of *The Alexander Suite*. This eight-part work runs more of a textural gamut, but the noisier sections tend to run aground on incoherence – mere fury is not necessarily an end in itself, even when played by virtuosos, and for once Perelman's force of character doesn't legitimize the results.

Brazilian Watercolour is, by Perelman's standards, easy listening. Half of it is leftovers from the *Bendito Of Santa Cruz* session with Shipp, half a set of interpretations of Brazilian favourites such as 'Desafinado', in which the saxophonist is surrounded by percussion. A game of two halves, with the expected mixed results.

Danilo Perez (born 1966)

PIANO

Born in Panama, Perez studied at the National Conservatory and then went to Berklee. Played with the Dizzy Gillespie group, 1989–92, and with his own groups from 1993.

***** Panamonk**

Impulse! 11902 / 051190-2 *Perez; Avishai Cohen (b); Terri Lyne Carrington, Jeff 'Tain' Watts (d); Olga Roman (v).* 1/96.

***** Central Avenue**

Impulse! 12812 / 051281-2 *Perez; Aquiles Baez (cuatro); John Patitucci, John Benitez (b); Jeff Ballard, Jeff 'Tain' Watts (d); Ray Spiegel, Pernell Saturnino, Aquiles Baez, Miguel Anga Diaz (perc); Raul Vital, Lyciana Souza (v).* 98.

Perez is the most convincing of the several pianists to emerge from South America to stake a place in contemporary American jazz. However, his technical expertise still sometimes gets the better of him, as it does with such contemporaries as Chucho Valdes. On *Panamonk*, which synthesizes Monk's music with Perez's own composing, he plays 'Evidence' and 'Four In One' side by side in what amounts to a circus performance. Perez's Monk isn't terribly convincing, since he hits the piano so hard that all the abruptness in Monk's music is intensified to the point of absurdity, but he does much better by some of his own themes: 'Hot Bean Strut' and the pretty 'September In Rio', with a wordless vocal by Roman, are worth returning to.

Central Avenue self-consciously strives for a pan-global-jazz effect: setting 'Impressions', for instance, to three different rhythms, or recording the Panamanian folk singer Raul Vital by himself and then constructing a jazz background in the studio. When he settles himself away from such persiflage and focuses on the piano, with the excellent Patitucci and either Ballard or Watts in support, the best music breaks out: the three-part 'Rhythm In Blue' suite, the opening 'Blues For The Saints', and the solo farewell of 'Smoke Gets In Your Eyes'. Perez looks to be having a hard job separating his music from its marketing.

Perfect Houseplants

GROUP

Centred on Mark Lockheart's tenor, this is a contemporary British group with a hint of local folk tradition.

***** Perfect Houseplants**

Ah Um 014 *Mark Lockheart (sax); Huw Warren (p, acc, clo); Dudley Phillips (b); Martin France (d).* 93.

***** Clec**

EFZ 016 *As above.* 94.

***** Snap Clatter**

Linn AKD 063 *As above.* 8/96.

This imaginative British group has never quite managed to dig itself out of the hole that yawns for intelligent 'name' bands (one thinks of Roadside Picnic and Itchy Fingers). They certainly deserve to. All four players are gifted craftsmen and, if Lockheart and Warren are the main writers, the balance of responsibilities seems very evenly shared around. In common with many of their contemporaries, they have introduced a folk element – sometimes almost subliminally – into a jazz context. Because it *is* almost subliminal, it works very well indeed. The first album was slightly mannered but unmistakably fresh and inviting. It isn't until *Snap Clatter*, though, that the mix of technical facility, informed writing and convincing playing seems properly balanced. Lockheart's saxophone sound has always had a beguiling quality, but it is on the more recent discs that it becomes central to the Houseplants' concept. As Warren grows in stature on his own account, he too becomes more significant, and the shift from the first to third records is very telling: lots of space, a steady flow of ideas and a relaxed, almost insouciant quality to the playing.

Bill Perkins (born 1924)

TENOR AND BARITONE SAXOPHONES, FLUTE, BASS CLARINET

Born in San Francisco, Perkins studied music and engineering after military service. Much touring with Kenton and Herman, and then much studio work in the late '50s, '60s and '70s. Latterly he has assumed much eminence as a surviving original West Coaster and as a faithful Lester Young descendant.

***** Quietly There**

Original Jazz Classics OJC 1776 *Perkins; Victor Feldman (p, org, vib); John Pisano (g); Red Mitchell (b); Larry Bunker (d).* 11/66.

This was one of only two sessions that the veteran West Coast reedman made under his own name in the 1960s. Gentle, pretty, but closely thought out, this is easy-listening jazz as it could be at its best. The nine tracks are all Johnny Mandel compositions, and Perkins devises a different setting for each one, some decidedly odd: baritone sax and organ for 'Groover Wailin'', for instance, which mainly proves that Feldman was no good as an organist. But Perkins's grey, marshy tone makes a charming matter of 'The Shining Sea', the flute-and-vibes treatment of 'A Time For Love' is ideal, and tempos and textures are subtly varied throughout. A welcome reissue of a little-known record.

***** The Front Line**

Storyville STCD 4166 *Perkins; Gordon Goodwin (ss, ts); Pepper Adams (bs); Lou Levy (p); Bob Magnusson (b); Carl Burnett (d).* 11/78.

Perkins plays tenor, flute and baritone here, with another baritone expert in attendance in the shape of Adams. The latter's memorable 'Civilization And Its Discontents' gets a stringent reading here, but space is otherwise evenly split between the horns, and one could use more of Perkins's own playing.

*****(*) Remembrance Of Dino's**

Interplay IPCD-8606-2 *Perkins; Alan Broadbent (p); Putter Smith, Gene Cherico (b); John Tirabasso (d).* 86.

***** The Right Chemistry**

Jazz Mark 108 *Perkins; James Clay (ts); Frank Strazzeri (p); Joel Di Bartolo (b); Billy Mintz (d).* 8/87.

***** I Wished On The Moon**

Candid CCD79524 *Perkins; Metropole Orchestra.* 11/89–4/90.

*****(*) Warm Moods**

Fresh Sound FSR-CD 191 *Perkins; Frank Strazzeri (p).* 11/91.

After long periods away from the studios, Perkins is almost ubiquitous again. The album recorded over various sessions at the Pasadena club, Dino's, is drawn from Perkins's own tapes of many nights' playing, and he has put together a relaxed but very swinging collection: Cedar Walton's 'Bolivia' is taken at a fantastic tempo, 'Naima' is as thoughtful and mature a reading as we've had in recent years, and bop from Monk and Bird is suitably hard-hitting. The sound is very immediate, if lacking in some finesse. The meeting with James Clay is slightly troubled by Clay's cloudy, unconvincing phrasing, and only on 'Take The Coltrane' is there real empathy; but Perkins and Strazzeri both sound very good. Rob Pronk's arrangements for *I Wished On The Moon* give Bill his chance at a big band/strings album and, though the arrangements have more mush than backbone, the saxophonist breezes through the charts with an old pro's ease. The *Warm Moods* session is altogether tougher. Perkins chooses to use baritone for most of the record (with two forays into bass clarinet and a single clarinet reading of 'Sweet Lorraine') and his faintly peevish sound on the horn sits nicely with Strazzeri's energetic bop lines. When they get to a ballad like 'You Know I Care' the leathery sound unravels into tenderness. Warmly recommended.

***** Our Man Woody**
JazzMark 110 *Perkins; Rick Baptist, Joe Davis, Wayne Bergeron, Bob Summers, Clay Jenkins (t); Charlie Loper, Andy Martin, Rich Bullock (tb); Bob Cooper (ts); Brian Nimitz (as, ts); Jack Nimitz (bs); Frank Strazzeri (p); Dave Stone (b); Paul Kreibich (d).* 1/91.

***** Frame Of Mind**
Interplay IP 8612 *Perkins; Clay Jenkins (t); Frank Strazzeri (p); Bob Leatherbarrow (vib); Tom Warrington, Ken Filiano (b); Bill Berg (d).* 5/93.

Perkins was a Herman sideman, and his tribute to Woody's band is a genuine and sometimes scintillating one. The swingers come off at a terrific clip – though brass-laden, the band's real colour is provided by the reed section, dominated by Perkins and Cooper – and the ballads are played with great aplomb. Soloists pop in and out of the ensemble in the finest West Coast tradition, and the sound is a proper update on the classic California texture.

Frame Of Mind, according to Perkins's own sleeve-note, granted him more control than he's ever had over a record. With a picked band, old compadre Strazzeri on hand and an intriguing programme – Strazzeri, Duke Pearson, Monk, Jimmy Heath – the band play with gusto and excellent chops, though in the final analysis nobody quite has the character of Perkins himself to take it into the top bracket. The leader's solos, with just a hint of tonal quirkiness, are still the most arresting thing.

***** Perk Plays Prez**
Fresh Sound FSR 5010 *Perkins; Jan Lundgren (p); Dave Carpenter (b); Paul Kreibich (d); Jack Sheldon (v).* 6/95.

Clearly a labour of love for Perkins and realized with great finesse, this tribute to his original inspiration has been very carefully handled. He is paying homage to the Lester Young specifically of the late 1930s, and he re-creates entire Young solos – such as those of 'Shoe Shine Boy', 'Taxi War Dance' and 'Let Me See' – before adding improvisations of his own. As gracefully as it's done, there's a vague sense of redundancy about the exercise, given that Perkins's own solos seem strong enough to stand alone – and to have their own context. A bigger problem is the studio sound, which puts the saxophonist too far back: delicate as his tone is, he doesn't need to be overpowered by the rhythm section, even when it's playing as complicitly as here.

Jari Perkiomaki (born 1961)

ALTO AND SOPRANO SAXOPHONES, BASS CLARINET

Contemporary Finnish saxophonist.

****(*) Shades**
Jazzweaver SAJCD 97001 *Perkiomaki; Samuli Mikkonen (p); Pekka Luukka (g); Jorma Ojanpera (b); Markus Ketola, Mikko Hassinen (d); Kristiina Ilmonen (urdu).* 96.

Perkiomaki is a perfectly accomplished player, basing himself mainly around the alto, and his shrewd analysis of Ornette Coleman's 'Invisible' makes for a convincing essay in the context of this record. Alas, though, for the rest: most of the originals are colourless pegs for some pithy but hardly overwhelming improvising, from the leader and the rest. There are a couple of changes of pace with the mildly funky 'Teddy Bear' and the closing 'Picasso', where Perkiomaki picks up the bass clarinet for the first time.

Rich Perry

TENOR SAXOPHONE

Born in Cleveland, Perry was touring with the Glenn Miller Orchestra in 1975 and then moved to New York, where he has since performed in a wide range of small- and big-band settings. One notable recent gig has been as one of the principal soloists in the Maria Schneider Orchestra.

***** To Start Again**
Steeplechase SCCD 31331 *Perry; Harold Danko (p); Scott Colley (b); Jeff Hirshfield (d).* 4/93.

****** Beautiful Love**
Steeplechase SCCD 31360 *Perry; Jay Anderson (b); Victor Lewis (d).* 10/94.

*****(*) What is This?**
Steeplechase SCCD 31374 *Perry; Fred Hersch (p); Jay Anderson (b); Tom Rainey (d).* 4/95.

***** Left Alone**
Steeplechase SCCD 31421 *Perry; Frank Kimbrough (p); Jay Anderson (b); Billy Drummond (d).* 4/97.

We were rather cool about Perry's debut on his first appearance in this *Guide*, but the subsequent records and a greater familiarity with his work have proved that to be an over-cautious judgement. Previously hidden in big-band sections and sideman roles for some 20 years, the tenorman's absolute command goes with a soft-edged tone and an undemonstrative delivery that creates a paradox at the centre of his style. Other commentators have cited Getz, Marsh, Rollins and other forebears as his models, yet Perry doesn't sound much like anyone else, while at the same time not quite standing out as an individual. The main characteristic of such a player is consistency, and there is very little to choose between his work on each of these four records. Instead, more depends on the context. *Beautiful Love* is easily the pick of the four since without a piano the skill and judicious intensity of the sax playing comes through more clearly. There are truly marvellous improvisations on 'Prisoner Of Love', 'All The Things You Are' and 'I Fall In Love Too Easily' at the heart of the record, and for once eight quite lengthy tracks don't seem a moment too long. Anderson and the superb Lewis are also in good order. The debut *To Start Again* still sounds a little ordinary, despite some exemplary work from Danko; we prefer *What is This?*, which drafts in Hersch, whose playing is at its liveliest. They take the Thad Jones line, 'What Is This?', at a terrific clip, and there is some exceptionally genuine interplay between piano and tenor on the ballads. *Left Alone* is a shade behind again, perhaps because Kimbrough is no real match for either Danko or Hersch. The set-list, which includes tunes by Bley, Coleman, Shorter, Waldron and Andrew Hill, is typical of Perry's imagination. Although we have ranked the four discs a notch apart from each other, nobody who wants to hear the leader will be disappointed by any of them.

*****(*) So In Love**
Steeplechase SCCD 31447 *Perry; Renee Rosnes (p); Peter Washington (b); Billy Drummond (d).* 9/97.

***** Canções Do Brasil**
Steeplechase SCCD 31463 *Perry; Harold Danko (p).* 4/98.

*****(*) Doxy**
Steeplechase SCCD 31473 *Perry; George Mraz (b); Billy Hart (d).* 11/98.

Perry's albums continue to work thoughtful variations on the blowing date. The duet album with Danko consists of Brazilian songs, but beyond that the discs are focused around the players and their abilities, rather than any overriding concepts. *So In Love* benefits hugely from Rosnes, Washington and Drummond as the supporting team. The pianist is going through a purple patch with recording, and she sounds as lucid and imaginative as she does on her own records. Perry picks excellent tunes – Steve Swallow's 'Eiderdown', Ron Carter's 'Little Waltz', Alec Wilder's 'Moon And Sand' – and he noses round them, looking for counter-melodies and improvisations that seem to run in a sort of parallel with the theme.

The collaboration with Danko invites comparison with Stan Getz–Kenny Barron and similarly minded duos. Perry and Danko aren't looking for that kind of comparison; if anything, this takes an opposite stance to the view of Brazilian music as sweetly romantic and sensuous. Their quiet and introspective path through the nine themes – nothing obvious here, either, with no Jobim but Gismonti, Francis Hime and Toninho Horta all represented – has a mournful and sometimes abstracted air. The results are a little dry, but not unpleasurable.

The return to a trio format produces another fine session for Perry. He is not a great communicator on the saxophone, in the way that a master of this trio situation like Rollins is, but that is more a matter of his preference for a sound and a manner that never buttonholes the listener. It is intriguing to hear him improvising on 'Blue In Green', Bill Evans's oblique classic, where he finds an almost chilly peacefulness. Much of this music has a take-it-or-leave-it quality, but it's not a bad change from the in-your-face tactics of many modern saxophonists.

Charli Persip (born 1929)

DRUMS, PERCUSSION

Charli – who really does favour that spelling – worked in big bands under Tadd Dameron, Dizzy Gillespie and Harry James, before forming his own group, the Jazz Statesmen. Since then, with the exception of his Superband project, he has worked mainly as a jobbing sideman. He has an unfailing sense of time and can work in complex metres while maintaining a forceful, even physical presence.

***** In Case You Missed It**
Soul Note 121079 *Persip; Eddie E.J Allen, Frank Gordon, Ambrose Jackson, Ron Tooley, Jack Walrath (t); Clarence Banks, Jason Forsythe, David Graf (tb); Carl Kleinsteuber (tba); Bobby Watson (as); Monty Waters (as); Orpheus Gaitanopoulos, Alan Givens, Bill Saxton (ts); Fred Houn (bs); Richard Clements (p); Anthony Cox (b); Eli Fountain (perc).* 9/84.

*****(*) No Dummies Allowed**
Soul Note 121179 *Persip; Tony Barrero, Ambrose Jackson, Genghis Nor, Jack Walrath (t); Nathan Duncan, Jason Forsythe, Matt Haviland, Herb Huvel (tb); Sue Terry, Sayyd Abdul Al-Khabyyr (as, f); Orpheus Gaitanopoulos, Craig Rivers (ts, f); Pablo Calajero (bs); Darrell Grant (p); Melissa Slocum (b); Eli Fountain (perc).* 11/87.

Drummer Persip and his Superband have attempted to maintain a collectivist, internationalist and (intermittently) non-sexist approach without any of the pomposity that has marred some otherwise excellent work by the Afro-Asian Ensemble, a broadly similar outfit co-led by baritonist Fred Houn. Houn also appears on the brawling *In Case You Missed It*.

Persip's track record is quite extraordinary and his technique is now honed to perfection. He's something of a hybrid of Blakey and Big Sid Catlett, but he has also paid attention to Cozy Cole and Shadow Wilson. They're all performance players, big sounds but with sufficient sense of space (compare Rich or Krupa) to let things happen around them. Persip's inspirational qualities (mustn't say leadership) are evident in *No Dummies Allowed*, a dumb title for such a spanking set of big-band arrangements. Alto saxophonist Sue Terry's work on the Billie Holiday medley, 'Strange Crazy Heartache', suggests that she has a formidable musical intelligence; her solo statement catches something of Lady's voice, and Jack Walrath does some terrific back-of-the-stand stuff. 'Vital Seconds' and 'Desert Ship' are both composed by saxophonist Orpheus Gaitanopoulos, a robust player who occasionally disrupts the band's surprising finesse. Both albums are worth finding, but the later set is the better by some distance.

Eric Person (born 1964)

ALTO SAXOPHONE, SOPRANO SAXOPHONE

Hailing from St Louis, Person got his start in the business in a band that has been a key proving-ground for adventurous young players. Chico Hamilton gave him permission to experiment, but with the proviso that the basics had to be in place, a balance amply in evidence in Eric's first records as leader.

***** Arrival**

Soul Note 121237 *Person; Michael Cain (p, ky); Cary DeNigris (g); Kenny Davis (b); Ronnie Burrage (d).* 93.

***** Prophecy**

Soul Note 121287 *As above, except omit Cain and Burrage.* 3/92.

Like his father Thomas (a well-respected figure in their home town), he has a strong blues inflexion, but his experience with funk bands, and more recently with the rejuvenated Chico Hamilton, attests to his range. Burrage (another Missourian) is the ideal drummer for the first session. He has a big sound but manages to avoid undue busyness. The same is true of another Hamilton employee, guitarist DeNigris. He guests on just two tracks, but his duet with Person on 'Every Time I Smile' is one of the highlights. There are rough edges aplenty, but almost all of them come out of boldness rather than lack of technique. Person recalls no one more than the young 'Black' Arthur Blythe. If he can steer clear of the lucrative but unrewarding distractions that held Blythe back, he has the makings of a very considerable contender. (None of the reviewers failed to note that, a generation before, Chico Hamilton had recruited another saxophone-playing Eric.)

Disappointingly at first glance, instead of rising to that challenge in his second record, Person chooses to backtrack the well-trodden path opened up by John Coltrane. There are two Coltrane pieces on the record, 'Up Against The Wall' and parts of 'Interstellar Space'; but what Person is attempting to do is to give his own sound a recognizable shape within the confines of long-form or relatively open-ended improvisational pieces, and that above all is the function the Coltrane pieces serve. In terms of sound pure and simple, he is emphatically not a Trane disciple. The inclusion of Wayne Shorter's 'Delores', and the arrangement of it for this drummerless group, suggests that his interests lie mainly in certain aspects of post-bop writing that have still not been fully explored. A promising follow-up.

*****(*) More Tales To Tell**

Soul Note 121307 *Person; Jim Finn (bcl, f); Michael Rabinowitz (bsn); John Esposito (p); Cary DeNigris (g); Dave Holland, Calvin Jones (b); Gene Jackson (d, perc).* 6/96.

Person really starts to blossom. All but two of the tracks are originals, and the quality of writing is a quantum jump ahead of its predecessors. The tales he has to tell are mostly quite terse in conception, unfussy and not overly embellished, but with lots of scope for texture. The bulk of the material is concentrated in the middle of the set with the restless 'On The Verge' (one of a brace featuring Holland), 'Knee Deep (In The Gene Pool)' and 'Survival Instincts'. The rest of the set is a little less focused, though there are some strong ideas at work on both the repertory pieces, a vivid arrangement of Miles's 'Little Church' (best known from *Live Evil*) and, rather more unexpected, a jazz interpretation of Terence Trent d'Arby's 'If You Should Go Before Me'. The other personnel make strong contributions. DeNigris is an old friend and partner and he likes to work away at ideas of his own, initially some distance from the leader's, but always consistent in tone and destination. Holland doesn't sound as if he's in anything other than cruise mode, but he certainly lifts the pace on his two appearances, and the extra horn is very effective.

Houston Person (born 1934)

TENOR SAXOPHONE

Born in Florence, South Carolina, Person was a relatively late starter. He worked for a time with Johnny Hammond before establishing his own guitar- and organ-based groups, with whom he has recorded extensively. Person is in the Coleman Hawkins mould, a fine ballad player with a low, urgent tone.

***** Goodness!**

Original Jazz Classics OJCCD 332 *Person; Sonny Phillips (org); Billy Butler (g); Bob Bushnell (b); Frankie Jones (d).* 8/69.

***** Legends Of Acid Jazz**

Prestige 24179 *As above, except add Cecil Bridgewater, Thad Jones, Virgil Jones, Ernie Royal (t), Garnett Brown (tb), Harold Vick (ts), Grant Green (g), Idris Muhammad, Bernard Purdie (d).* 10/70–4/71.

Though Person's Muse catalogue has not yet come back on line, his stock remains high as a forefather of the acid jazz movement, a lineage explicitly celebrated on the Prestige compilation. It's pretty straightahead stuff: blaring brass, chugging organ, square-four rhythm and the beefy sound of Houston's tenor over the top, inexhaustible, reliable, seldom anything other than squarely on the beat and on the case. The gospelly side of his playing personality is surprisingly much in evidence on these two dance-orientated sets. 'Lift Every Voice And Sing' on *Legends* has the power to bring a lump to the throat, and there are moments on both discs when Person, sounding like a latter-day Ike Quebec, negotiates some quite subtle interchanges with the rhythm players. One either goes for this aural equivalent of soul food or one doesn't.

***** Person-ified**

HighNote HCD 7004 *Person; Richard Wyands (p); Ray Drummond (b); Kenny Washington (d).* 11/96.

*****(*) My Romance**

HighNote HCD 7033 *As above.* 6/98.

Having taken his A&R and production nous from Muse to HighNote, Person turned in some of the best recorded work of his career, a pungent mix of jazz, gospel and blues with a first-rate rhythm section. Person the balladeer has often tended to the gruff and heavy-handed, but here he is convincingly romantic on 'Stranger On The Shore' and 'Gentle Rain', and when he says 'I'll Never Stop Loving You', one is inclined to believe him. Wyands is excellent in support and the Van Gelder sound flatters the pianist more than the rest of the group. Richard sounds uneasy only on the Ammons-inspired 'Blue Jug', which isn't his speed or style. Elsewhere he's immaculate, and it's hard to fault the other two either; Washington always gives of his best and Drummond could probably carry a whole orchestra on those broad shoulders.

The same group reconvened 18 months later to record a slightly quieter but even better album. Right from the opening 'But Beautiful' it is obvious that Person is completely in command of his idiom. The pace is very gentle and determinedly romantic, and 'Laura' and 'Stairway To The Stars' are both superlative performances. Wyands occasionally chafes at the pace, but he too is a natural balladeer and it is hard to fault his exquisitely tailored solos or his rhythm work with Drummond and Washington.

***** The Opening Round**
Savant SCD 2005 *Person; Joey DeFrancesco (org); Rodney Jones (g); Tracy Wormworth (b); Bernard Purdie (d). 2/97.*

From the same group of labels, Savant is devoted to a rootsier sound and this boisterous album comes in its 'Groove Masters' series. It's been some little while since Houston went back to the saxophone–organ–guitar format but it still fits him like a glove, and his solos on 'Sweet Sucker' and 'When A Man Loves A Woman' are pure delight. The band has a tight R&B feel to it, but also considerable intelligence, and DeFrancesco is adept at shifting registers within a couple of measures, keeping the music open and stimulating.

Ake Persson (1932–75)

TROMBONE

Born in Hässleholm, Persson was something of a prodigy on trombone, and he soon acquired a reputation for excellence in big-band work. He played with German radio bands, the Quincy Jones orchestra, the Clarke–Boland band and even with Duke Ellington on one of his European tours. He took his own life in 1975.

***** 'The Great' Ake Persson**
Four Leaf Clover FLC CD 127 *Persson; Frank Rosolino, Bob Burgess (tb); Carl-Erik Lindgren, Hacke Bjorksten (ts); Arne Domnérus (as); Lars Gullin (bs); Ingemar Westberg, Gosta Theselius, Bengt Hallberg, Rob Pronk, Reinhold Svensson, Claes-Goran Fagerstadt (p); Bengt Carlsson, Gunnar Johnson, Simon Brehm, Don Bagley, Georg Riedel (b); Nils-Bertil Dahlander, Egil Johansen, Sven Bollhem, Jack Noren, Kenneth Fagerlund, Stan Levey (d). 8/51–1/57.*

A welcome homage to one of the greatest of European trombonists. Persson was still a teenager when he made the earliest tracks here, and his mellifluous sound and effortless phrasing were already in place. The CD gathers together small-group dates with Domnérus and Hallberg, a three-trombone front-line with Rosolino and Burgess, two very fine tracks by The Modern Swedes – Persson quite outstanding on 'Penta' – and the better part of a 1957 quintet date with Gullin in which Persson is overdubbed into a trombone section. Most of this is vintage Swedish cool and much of it seems relatively slight in stature, the tracks coming off EPs and the like, with many of the tunes coming in at under three minutes apiece. But it pays tribute to the earlier work of an impeccable musician who virtually disappeared into big bands and orchestras for much of the remainder of his career. Hans Fridlund's note offers a poignant appreciation of the man who died by his own hand in 1975.

Bent Persson (born 1947)

TRUMPET

Born in Karlskrona, Persson has worked with many European groups who need a trumpeter playing in the classic style. He has an uncanny ability to evoke the sounds of stylists long gone.

***** Swinging Straight**
Sittel SITCD 9218 *Persson; Dicken Hedrenius (tb); John Högman (ts); Ulf Johansson (p); Göran Lind (b); Ronnie Gardiner (d). 12/94.*

Persson can sound like any bygone trumpeter he cares to – and he's been asked to play in just that way, on a number of revivalist projects – and perhaps that tells against his own session having a character of its own. Instead, this is purely pleasurable mainstream, buoyed up by a sense of enjoyment that is often hard to find on equivalent American dates. Persson here comes on like one of the great Basie trumpeters, and Hedrenius's rascally trombone and Högman's burly tenor merely add to the fun.

Edward Petersen

TENOR SAXOPHONE

Chicagoan saxophonist leading sessions of post-bop with home-grown bands.

***** Upward Spiral**
Delmark 445 *Petersen; Brad Williams (p); Fareed Haque (g); Rob Amster (b); Jeff Stitely (d). 6/89.*

*****(*) The Haint**
Delmark 474 *Petersen; Odies Williams III, Billy Brimfield (t); Willie Pickens (p); Brian Sandstrom (b); Robert Shy (d). 94.*

Upward Spiral is a part-studio, part-live account of a band that has worked regularly on the contemporary Chicago scene. Petersen is the dominant voice, walking the line between bop form and a freer conception with an unfussy confidence, and his solos contrast with the cloudier effects of Haque. Williams, Amster and Stitely provide competent support, but the extra grit and swing of the first four tracks – which were cut live in Chicago – suggest that the band has yet to find its feet in the studio. Since comparatively little is heard of Chicago's newer jazz, a welcome document.

So is *The Haint*. Though Petersen has apparently moved to New Orleans, this is still a Chicago band, and they play with a gutsy finesse that is different from the slick virtuosity of contemporary New York. Not that the playing sounds rough: Petersen has toughened his personal sound, and he has a fierce grip on material ranging from 'Jitterbug Waltz' to the near-free piece, 'Walking In The Sky'. Brimfield and Williams bring contrasting trumpet styles, and Pickens plays with fine authority.

Oscar Peterson (born 1925)

PIANO, ORGAN, ELECTRIC PIANO, CLAVICHORD

Few musicians have done more to popularize jazz – real jazz as opposed to a dilution – than Oscar Peterson. The big Canadian has been a stalwart on the scene for longer than half a century. Spotted by Norman Granz, he became a regular at Jazz At The Philharmonic events and has always been a big festival draw. His occasionally showy multi-note approach owes much to Art Tatum, but it was Nat Cole who was the most powerful and lasting influence. In recent years, Peterson's playing career was hampered by ill-health, but with characteristic patience and application he has returned to the studio and to performance.

****(*) The First Recordings**

Indigo IGOCD 2070 *Peterson; Armand Samson (g); Bert Brown (b); Russ Dufort, Franck Gariepy, Roland Verdon (d).* 4/45–7/46.

***** Oscar Peterson, 1945–1947**

Classics 1084 *As above, except add Albert King, Auston Roberts (b), Clarence Jones, Mark Wilkinson (d).* 4/45–12/47.

According to Lalo Schifrin, Oscar Peterson is the Liszt of modern jazz, Bill Evans its Chopin; this refers back to the much-quoted assertion that the Hungarian conquered the piano, while the Pole seduced it. Certainly, all through his career Peterson has seemed to have all the technical bases covered, working in styles from Tatum-derived swing to bebop, stride to near-classical ideas. What is extraordinary about him is how quickly and completely he matured as a stylist and how consistently he has been able to sustain piano jazz of the highest quality right through his career. Peterson left his native Canada in 1949 at the behest of Norman Granz, who became his main sponsor. However, he had already established a successful recording career before that, signing for RCA Victor in Montreal. Peterson was already known round the city as the Brown Bomber of Boogie Woogie, and it is that style which dominates these early sides. There are clinkers aplenty on the faster tracks, though buried so deep in the precocious rush of notes that they scarcely register as anything other than slubs and craquelure on what is already a fantastically rich canvas. 'Blue Moon', recorded in April 1946, is hugely accomplished, as is 'China Boy' and the somewhat later 'East Of The Sun'. A bass-playing Brown would play a huge role in his later career, but it was Bert Brown who supported on these early sides and, though he's not well registered even in these remasterings, it's obvious that Peterson relied heavily on him. The Tatum influence is less evident than one might have expected, given the consensus about Oscar's sources, but it is undeniably and unmissably present, and on tracks like 'I Got Rhythm' and 'The Sheik Of Araby' it is the dominant voice. Peterson had not yet quite attained an expressive personality of his own, but it is waiting in the wings.

The Classics compilation – and somehow it seems odd to find Oscar covered by the French label – pushes the story on into 1947 and some further recordings for Victor in Canada. There is a fine 'Ghost Of A Chance' from April and a wonderful version of 'Stairway To The Stars', taped just before Christmas. Deft and virtuosic as they are, these early sessions are likely to be of interest to committed fans only.

***** The President Plays With The Oscar Peterson Trio**

Verve 521451-2 *Peterson; Lester Young (ts); Barney Kessel (g); Ray Brown (b); J.C Heard (d).* 52.

Flawlessly lyrical piano-playing, but nothing much from Pres but the shards and fragments of a musical mind that had very little left to say. Some of the tunes are stunning. 'Tea For Two' is a revelation and 'On The Sunny Side Of The Street' is as fresh and uncomplicated as a spring morning. Much of the rest, though, is as empty as after-dinner conversation between generations who aren't at odds but who don't quite understand each other.

***** Jazz Masters 37: Oscar Peterson Plays Broadway**

Verve 516893-2 *Peterson; Clark Terry (t); Irving Ashby, Herb Ellis, Barney Kessel (g); Ray Brown (b); Gene Gammage, Alvin Stoller, Ed Thigpen (d).* 3/50–8/64.

*****(*) Jazz Masters 16: Oscar Peterson**

Verve 516320-2 *Peterson; Roy Eldridge (t); Sonny Stitt (as); Stan Getz, Flip Phillips, Ben Webster, Lester Young (ts); Lionel Hampton (vib); Milt Jackson (vib); Herb Ellis, Barney Kessel (g); Ray Brown (b); J.C Heard, John Poole, Buddy Rich, Alvin Stoller, Ed Thigpen (d); Fred Astaire, Ella Fitzgerald, Anita O'Day (v).* 52–61.

***** The Duke Ellington Songbook**

Verve 559785-2 *Peterson; Barney Kessel (g); Ray Brown (b); Ed Thigpen (d).* 52, 59.

***** The George Gershwin Songbook**

Verve 529698-2 *As above, except omit Thigpen.* 11 & 12/52.

***** Jazz At The Philharmonic, Hartford 1953**

Pablo 2308240 *Peterson; Roy Eldridge, Charlie Shavers (t); Bill Harris (tb); Benny Carter, Willie Smith (as); Flip Phillips, Ben Webster, Lester Young (ts); Herb Ellis (g); Ray Brown (b); J.C Heard, Gene Krupa (d).* 5/53.

*****(*) At Zardi's**

Pablo Live 2620118 2CD *Peterson; Herb Ellis (g); Ray Brown (b).* 55.

No single moment ever gave a clearer impression of Oscar Peterson's fabled technique than a tiny incident on one of those all-star Jazz At The Philharmonic events released in rafts by the Pablo label. Count Basie has just stated the opening notes of a theme in his inimitable elided style when there is a pause and then – presto! – showers of sparkling notes. Any suspicions about what the Count might have ingested during his few bars of silence are allayed by the liner-note. What had happened, quite simply, was that Basie had spotted Oscar Peterson standing in the wings and had dragged him on for an unscheduled 'spot'.

Peterson has been almost as prolific as he is effusive at the piano. He appears on literally dozens of albums in solo and trio settings, but also with horn-led groups and orchestras. He is one of the finest accompanists in swing-orientated jazz, despite which he served no real apprenticeship as a sideman, being introduced to an American audience (he was born and raised in Canada) by impresario and record producer Norman Granz in 1949. He has ridden on the extraordinary momentum of that debut ever since, recording almost exclusively for Granz's labels, Verve and, later, Pablo. The earliest material available here suggests how complete he was as an artist, even at the very beginning. He quickly became a favourite at JATP events and the *Hartford 1953* sessions anticipate the walk-on/walk-off sensation he was to become in the 1970s.

Peterson is perhaps best as a trio performer. During the 1950s these tended to be drummerless, and with a guitarist. Barney Kessel sounds rather colourless and Herb Ellis is much more responsive to Peterson's technique, as was his much later replacement, Joe Pass. After 1960, the stalwart Ray Brown was joined by a drummer, first by Ed Thigpen then by Louis Hayes. This coincided with Peterson's consolidation as a major concert and recording star; his early work, influenced primarily by Nat Cole, is now rather less well known. Of the mid-1950s sets, *At Zardi's* and the excellent *Jazz Masters* compilation (which covers the early years of the later trio as well) are certainly the best.

There has long been a critical knee-jerk about Peterson's Tatum influence. This was very much a later development. Tatum died in 1956 and only then does Peterson seem to have taken a close interest in his work. Even then it overlay the smoothed-out, ambidextrous quality he had found in Cole. With the turn of the 1960s and international stardom, Peterson's style changes only in accordance with the context of specific performances, particularly between the big, grandstanding 'all star' events and more intimate occasions with his own trio, where he demonstrates an occasional resemblance to Hampton Hawes and, more contentiously, to Bill Evans.

His debt to Duke Ellington is less obvious, but something of Duke's urbane phrasing crept into Oscar's playing in the '50s and one can hear him both surrender to it and resist it strongly on the Ducal songbook, one of the best of the sequence but also one of the most exposed. Oscar's solo on 'Prelude To A Kiss' is about as raw-nerved as he gets. Peterson's powerfully swinging style does on occasion tend to overpower his melodic sense and he is apt to become repetitious and, less often, banal. After four decades in the business, though, he understands its workings better than anyone. Above all, Peterson *delivers*.

*****(*) At The Stratford Shakespearean Festival**
Verve 513752-2 *Peterson; Herb Ellis (g); Ray Brown (b).* 8/56.

*****(*) At The Concertgebouw**
Verve 521649-2 *As above.* 9 & 10/57.

Unlike the Ahmad Jamal and Nat Cole trios, which also dispensed with drummers in favour of piano, guitar and bass, the Peterson group never sounded spacious or open-textured – the pianist's hyperactive fingers saw to that. Here, though, for once Peterson seemed able to lie back a little and let the music flow under its own weight, rather than constantly pushing it along. Peterson has described how during the daytime Brown and Ellis sat and practised all the harmonic variables that might come up during a performance. A sensible precaution, one might have thought, given a player with Peterson's hand-speed. The irony is that his vertical mobility, in and out of key, was never as rapid as all that, and there are occasions here, as on 'How High The Moon' and the closing 'Daisy's Dream' (both from Stratford), where it appears that Ellis and Brown manage to anticipate his moves and push him into configurations he hadn't apparently thought of.

The other concert is augmented with material from Los Angeles a fortnight later, suggesting a quick return to the United States. However, the 'Concertgebouw' material was actually recorded in Chicago. The Dutch concert given by the trio earlier in 1957 was never actually taped, but presumably it sounded classier on the sleeve to pretend that it had. One other mistake has been corrected from the CD. The track originally labelled 'Bag's Groove' clearly wasn't and has now been retitled 'Bluesology'.

*****(*) The Ultimate Oscar Peterson**
Verve 539786-2 *Peterson; Clark Terry (t, v); Milt Jackson (vib); Herb Ellis (g); Ray Brown (b); Ed Thigpen (d); Ernie Wilkins Orchestra.* 8/56–8/64.

Like Penguin's own classic 'Poets on Poets' series, these *Ultimate* compilations are selected by the musicians' peers, in this case not another piano player but the man who has anchored Peterson's groups over so many years, bassist Ray Brown. Given the range of material he has to select from, any choice is going to be controversial, but it's hard to argue with these ten tracks from *The Trio* ('Sometimes I'm Happy', 'In The Wee Small Hours Of The Morning' and 'Chicago'), *At The Stratford Shakespeare Festival* ('Love You Madly' and 'Noreen's Nocturne'), *Very Tall* ('Reunion Blues'), *The Jazz Soul* ('Waltz For Debby'), the big-band *Bursting Out* with Ernie Wilkins ('Blues For Big Scotia'), *West Side Story* ('Jet Song'), and *Trio + 1* ('Mumbles' with Clark Terry, inevitably). Tomorrow, asked again, you might well pick ten different tracks but, as these things go, this is a nicely balanced and not altogether predictable selection, and if you had never previously made Peterson's acquaintance it would at least take you some way towards a rounded picture of the artist.

*****(*) Plays My Fair Lady & The Music From Fiorello**
Verve 521677-2 *Peterson; Ray Brown (b); Gene Gammage (d).* 11/58, 1/60.

*****(*) A Jazz Portrait Of Frank Sinatra**
Verve 825769-2 *Peterson; Ray Brown (b); Ed Thigpen (d).* 5/59.

***** Plays The Cole Porter Songbook**
Verve 821987-2 *As above.* 7 & 8/59.

*****(*) The Jazz Soul Of Oscar Peterson**
Verve 533100-2 *As above.* 7 & 8/59, 9/62.

****** Plays Porgy & Bess**
Verve 519807-2 *As above.* 10/59.

Not to be confused with the later duo interpretation featuring Joe Pass, the Gershwin set is brilliantly spontaneous jazz, apparently recorded after the sketchiest of run-throughs. Peterson has played 'I Wants To Stay Here' (or 'I Loves You, Porgy', as it is more commonly known) many times in his career (see *Tristeza*, below), but nowhere with the pure feeling and simplicity he gives it on this disc. The two apostrophes to Bess at the end are heartfelt and utterly compelling, with liquid left-hand figures and an unstoppable flow of melody ideas. As pianist (Benny Green indicates in a special introductory note to the reissue), Ray Brown gets less solo space here than on many of the trio's records, unlikely to be a symptom of unfamiliarity with the material, more probably because Peterson makes the session so forcibly his own. Brown's contribution to the fiery 'There's A Boat Dat's Leavin' Soon For New York' is beyond reproach, however, and his intro to 'I Got Plenty O' Nuttin'' is masterful.

With Peterson, nothing fundamental rests on the quality of the material he has to work with. His almost alchemical transformation of the songs from *Fiorello* beggars belief. *My Fair Lady* offers more familiar melodies and the element of surprise is proportionately less. However, these are some of his most lyrical and melody-centred interpretations, often sticking quite close to the line. The Porter and Sinatra records are slightly odd in that Peterson does very little more than run through the songs, chorus by chorus, adding very little in the way of improvisational embellishment. The shortest track on the Sinatra is under two minutes, the longest on either just three and a half, the average about two minutes forty-five. This gives the performances a slightly abrupt air that's only partly mitigated by the sheer empathy the pianist feels with the tunes. Though Peterson's admiration for Sinatra comes through strongly, the Porter tribute isn't a great record, and there are signs that it was made to order as part of a burgeoning catalogue of 'songbook' projects; but its value lies precisely in its terseness, Peterson's brilliant feel for song form.

The Jazz Soul rounds out the picture and completes CD coverage of this classic period, pairing the disc of that name with a later session called *Affinity*. The latter is fairly adventurous for the time, including 'Waltz For Debby' and a complex, freighted version of 'Tangerine'. The pace drops thereafter, but these are special tracks and it's a wonder that they weren't made available to a new generation of listeners sooner.

****** The Song Is You: Best Of The Verve Songbooks**
Verve 531558-2 2CD *Peterson; Herb Ellis, Barney Kessel (g); Ray Brown (b); Ed Thigpen (d).* 52, 53, 54, 59.

An absolute joy and delight, whether as an introduction to the work of this period or as a spare copy for car or personal stereo. A Verve Take 2 compilation which really does bring together the best of these years. 'Lover', 'Tea For Two', 'Come Rain Or Come Shine': everyone will have favourites, and most tastes will be catered for. Excellent value.

***** Live At CBC Studios, 1960**
Just A Memory 9507 *Peterson; Ray Brown (b); Ed Thigpen (d).* 60.

For some reason, this session wasn't released on disc for almost 40 years, doubly odd in that it comes amid an otherwise quiet moment in Oscar's output. The performances are disciplined and swinging. 'Dancing On The Ceiling' and 'Blues For Big Scotia' stand out, but the real importance of this late release is historical rather than strictly aesthetic, filling in another stage in OP's development.

*****(*) The London House Sessions**
Verve 531766-2 5CD *As above.* 61.

Five CDs of quality live performance, beautifully registered, remastered and packaged and effortlessly musical from start to finish – but, given the price, for the hardcore Peterson fan only. It would be pointless to unpick a set as densely filled with extraordinary music, but 'Whisper Not' on disc one, 'On Green Dolphin Street' on two and four, 'I Remember Clifford' on three, and the closing 'Confirmation' on the final disc would be our desert island pick. *The Trio*, listed below, is one disc of highlights.

***** En Concert Avec Europe 1**
RTE 1002 *Peterson; Roy Eldridge (t); Sam Jones (b); Bobby Durham, Louis Hayes, Ed Thigpen (d).* 2/61–11/69.

A rather oddly spaced-out compilation of radio sessions. The opening 'Daahoud' is masterful and the two tracks with Eldridge are worth adding to their other confrontations, particularly 'Mainstem'. For the most part, though, this is a collector's item only.

***** The Silver Collection**
Verve 823447-2 *Peterson; Ray Brown (b); Ed Thigpen (d); Nelson Riddle Orchestra.* 8/59 & 63.

***** The Trio – Live From Chicago**
Verve 539063-2 *As above, except omit orchestra.* 9 & 10/61.

*****(*) Very Tall**
Verve 827821-2 *As above, except add Milt Jackson (vib).* 9/61.

***** West Side Story**
Verve 821575-2 *As above, except omit Jackson.* 1/62.

****** Night Train**
Verve 521440-2 *As above.* 12/62.

***** Plus One**
Emarcy 818 840 *As above, except add Clark Terry (t, flhn).* 8/64.

***** We Get Requests**
Verve 810047-2 *As above, except omit Terry.* 10 & 11/64.

After 30 years, *Night Train* is well established as a hardy perennial and is certainly Peterson's best-known record. Dedicated to his father, who was a sleeping-car attendant on Canadian Pacific Railways, it isn't the dark and moody suite of nocturnal blues many listeners expect but a lively and varied programme of material covering 'C-Jam Blues', 'Georgia On My Mind', 'Bag's Groove', 'Honey Dripper', 'Things Ain't What They Used To Be', 'Band Call', 'Hymn To Freedom' and a couple of others. Though by no means a 'concept album', it's one of the best-constructed long-players of the period and its durability is testimony to that as much as to the quality of Peterson's playing, which is tight and uncharacteristically emotional. The beautifully remastered reissue has six extra tracks, including a fascinating rehearsal take of 'Moten Swing' and an alternative of 'Night Train', which is called 'Happy Go Lucky Local'.

We Get Requests and *Live* reverse the polarity totally. Cool but technically effusive, Peterson gets all over two sets of (mostly) romantic ballads, played with a portrait of Nat Cole perched on the soundboard in front of him. *The Silver Collection* has four excellent trio tracks fighting for their lives among nine syrupy orchestrations that might have worked for another pianist but which are emphatically not in Peterson's line of sight. The *West Side Story* covers are interesting because they put the weight of emphasis on all the unlikeliest tunes. The 'Jet Song' receives the most developed interpretation but, while 'Maria' and 'Somewhere' are both consummately polished performances, they lack the commitment and graceful intelligence Peterson normally brings to romantic ballads. As a whole, and even upgraded to the highest standard of digital remastering, the record is a little lightweight and uninvolving.

So different is Peterson from John Lewis's unemphatic keyboard approach that there's not the remotest chance that *Very Tall* might be mistaken for an MJQ record. One of the great improvisers in modern jazz, Jackson is the undoubted star of the session, finessing 'On Green Dolphin Street' with a subtle counterpoint and adding a tripping bounce to 'A Wonderful

Guy'. Excellent stuff. Watch out for *Reunion Blues*, not currently around, which saw Peterson and the vibist get together again.

Plus One is aptly named. Terry never gets more involved than his guest star role would imply, and there are occasions when (to be frank) he sounds more like a revelling gatecrasher. He slides into a sombre, almost remorseful mood on 'They Didn't Believe Me', giving his flugelhorn that celebrated bone china fragility, before bouncing back with a second wind on a Peterson original (averaging one or two per disc around this time) called 'Squakay's Blues', dedicated to the redoubtable Joanie Spears, who managed the big man's career at this time.

Almost all these records are now available as 20-bit digital transfers, filling out the sound, sometimes subliminally, but sometimes, as in quieter moments on *Night Train*, quite dramatically. Anyone who hasn't yet upgraded from vinyl will be delighted with the difference. Anyone who already has a CD copy may wonder if it's really worth the outlay.

***** Paris Jazz Concert**

Malaco Jazz 1208 *Peterson; Roy Eldridge (t); Ray Brown, Sam Jones (b); Louis Hayes, Ed Thigpen (d).* 61–69.

The title is misleading because this isn't a tape of a single concert but of a sequence of Paris appearances in the '60s. The mastering is pretty suspect and, though some of the performances are above average, it's not a record that casual Peterson listeners need bother about.

***** Girl Talk**

MPS 821 842 2 *Peterson; Ray Brown, Sam Jones (b); Bobby Durham, Louis Hayes (d).* 64, 66.

More material from Oscar's sojourns in Villingen. 'On A Clear Day You Can See Forever' and 'Moon River' are the outstanding tracks, but both rhythm sections perform with ease and confidence, with Hayes getting the nod in the percussion department, an astonishingly lyrical player when he has material like this to work with.

***** With Respect To Nat**

Verve 557486-2 *Peterson; John Frosk, Joe Newman (t); Ernie Royal, Danny Stiles (t, flhn); Wayne Andre, Jimmy Cleveland, J.J Johnson (tb); Tony Studd (btb); Seldon Powell, Jerome Richardson (f); Jerry Dodgion, Phil Woods (as); Mervin Halladay (bs); Hank Jones (p); Herb Ellis, Barry Galbraith (g); Ray Brown, Richard Davis (b); Mel Lewis (d).* 65.

Nat Cole was always Peterson's biggest influence and his approach to the trio format was very much in the Cole template. This, then, is both a very sincere tribute and an example of the anxiety of influence. Oscar's vocal stylings are rougher and more abrupt than Nat's, but his piano playing is right in the groove and performances like 'When My Sugar Walks Down The Street' and 'What Can I Say After I Say I'm Sorry?' are first rate. The various backgrounds and arrangements, largely organized by the redoubtable Manny Albam, could hardly be bettered.

****** Exclusively For My Friends**

MPS 513830 4CD *Peterson; Ray Brown, Sam Jones (b); Bobby Durham, Louis Hayes, Ed Thigpen (d).* 63–68.

***** Exclusively For My Friends: The Lost Tapes**

MPS 529096 *As above, except omit Hayes.* 5/65, 11/67, 10/68.

Between 1963 and 1968 Peterson recorded a series of six LPs for the MPS label in the Villingen home of German producer, Hans Georg Brunner-Schwer. It's not quite the same sort of relationship as existed between Bud Powell and Francis Paudras. Peterson was successful, fit and hip to the realities of the music business. What is different about these recordings is the degree of relaxation (and, to a certain degree, of risk) in the performances. 'Love Is Here To Stay' on Volume 2 is one of the most interesting performances Peterson ever put on disc. Essentially a tribute to Tatum, it is full of harmonic ambiguities and stretched-out metres, and there is more musical meat in it than in the over-long 'I'm In The Mood For Love' on the first volume, which at 17 minutes begins to pall slightly. The highlight there is 'Like Someone In Love', which Peterson turns into a grand romantic concerto, closing with quotes from *Rhapsody In Blue*. The sessions were played before a small invited audience of friends and admirers, and the recordings are clearly aimed at connoisseurs, offering the nearest thing to a candid portrayal of Peterson musing on his art. There are unexpected touches of modernity, as in 'Nica's Dream' with Sam Jones and Bobby Durham on Volume 2, and there are perhaps too many knowing quotes (mostly from Ellington, but also from Basie's single-finger intros and even, less obviously, from Monk on 'Lulu's Back In Town'). The piano sounds big and resonant and the recordings are immediate and appropriately intimate.

By 1968, the magic of these sessions had perhaps worn a little thin and the *Lost Tapes* material suggests that it may be possible to have too much of a good thing. The solo pieces on Volumes 3 and 4 are rarely as acute as the group tracks, and there are signs that Peterson is simply not concentrating on 'Someone To Watch Over Me', which opens the last disc. A hint of self-indulgence at last? It should be noted that the six MPS LPs were: *Action, Girl Talk, The Way I Really Play, My Favourite Instrument, Mellow Mood* and *Travelin' On*. The reappearance of the missing tapes wasn't quite drama of Watergate proportions and doesn't add significantly to the tally on this handsome compilation. Peterson aficionados will be delighted with an 11-minute version of 'Tenderly', played with Brown and Thigpen, and with an unexpected run-through of Bobby Timmons's 'Moanin'' from a later session with Jones and Durham. For the most part, though, this is an item for completists, though of course it stands up on its own quite respectably as a Peterson record. If there were fewer of them around, it would be most desirable.

****(*) Motions And Emotions**

MPS 821289 *Peterson; Sam Jones (b); Bobby Durham (d); orchestra; Claus Ogerman (cond).* 69.

***** Hello Herbie**

MPS 821846 *As above, except add Herb Ellis (g); omit orchestra and Ogerman.* 11/69.

***** Tristeza On Piano**

MPS 817489 *As above, except omit Ellis.* 70.

***** Three Originals**

MPS 521059 2CD *As for above three discs.* 69–70.

***** Tracks**

MPS 523498 *Peterson (p solo).* 11/70.

Later sessions for Brunner-Schwer, though *Tristeza* was recorded in a New York studio. What's lost there, and in the others to an extent, is the gentle experimentalism of the private sessions. Peterson sounds as if he's on auto-pilot, and it's probably no coincidence that the track-listing veers strongly away from the earthbound, 'Down Here On The Ground' notwithstanding. 'Nightingale' is a rare self-written piece; 'Tristeza' and 'You Stepped Out Of A Dream' are equally moody.

Motions And Emotions is disappointing because the repertoire is so bland. The mixture of Lennon–McCartney, Mancini, Jim Webb, Bobby Gentry and Bacharach needs more leavening than even Peterson can give it; though professionally rehearsed and recorded, the strings are as gooey as always. As such, it represents a serious stumbling-block to any unqualified recommendation for the two-CD compilation, *Three Originals*. Most listeners might be prepared for two, rather better, originals. *Hello Herbie* is certainly worth having, if only for Peterson's great reading of Hampton Hawes's 'Hamp's Blues' and the Wes Montgomery tune, 'Naptown Blues', both of which catch him at his best. The reunion with Ellis is also a happy one; their interplay on 'Seven Come Eleven', a theme associated with Benny Goodman and Charlie Christian, is spot on.

The solo performances on the oddly titled *Tracks* have the musing, unselfconscious quality that was the other side of Peterson's prodigious keyboard showmanship. Things like 'A Little Jazz Exercise' and the reworkings of 'Basin Street Blues' and 'Honeysuckle Rose' are so chock-full of ideas that any aspirant jazz pianist will want to study them. For more casual listeners, these are valuable as solo performances, of which there are surprisingly few, relative to the huge mass of issued trios.

***(*) Two Originals

MPS 533549 *Peterson; Jiri Mraz (b); Ray Price (d). 70.*

Omitting just one track, 'Just Friends', for reasons of space (though it's hard to see how it would have caused problems), this is a compilation of *Walking The Line* and *Another Day*, two of the better Peterson albums of the early '70s. The line-up is slightly unfamiliar, but Mraz, who would become an American citizen and plain George in just a couple of years, brings his usual lyrical touch to the sessions, and he plays like a dream on 'I Didn't Know What Time It Was' and 'It Never Entered My Mind', two of the outstanding tracks, one from each album. Peterson himself is somewhat reflective and seems on occasion to be deliberately restricting the onrush of notes, not out of tiredness or diffidence but perhaps just to open up a little space. The piano sounds immaculately cared for and responsive and is perhaps a touch closer-miked than usual, unless this is just a side-effect of remastering. Whatever the reason, it's very attractive.

***(*) The Will To Swing

Verve 847203-2 *Peterson; Herb Ellis, Barney Kessel (g); Ray Brown, Sam Jones, Niels-Henning Orsted Pedersen (b); Louis Hayes, Buddy Rich, Ed Thigpen (d). 54–71.*

Another compilation drawn from Verve's vast holding of Oscar material. This is a good one, covering a vintage period and with an emphasis very strongly on jazz rather than popular entertainment. The version of 'Waltz For Debby' opening the second disc should be played to anyone who doubts OP's serious credentials as a modernist. Drawn from studio performances and live concerts, the sound is quite mixed and the levels seem unusually ill-adjusted, but as an introduction to Peterson's pianism this is hard to beat.

*** Swinging Cooperations

MPS 539085 *Peterson; Milt Jackson (vib); Ray Brown, Niels-Henning Orsted Pedersen (b); Louis Hayes (d). 7 & 10/71.*

The first astonishment here is that the first track of *Reunion Blues*, the first of two MPS discs compiled on this reissue, should be the Jagger–Richards rocker, 'Satisfaction'. The second is the way in which Oscar dispatches it. Everything else is pretty much by the book. Milt Jackson's 'Reunion Blues', written for the occasion, is unfamiliar, but scarcely a surprise. The better material is from the other LP, which reappears shorn of one track for space reasons. Charles Chaplin's 'Smile' has always been a favourite tune of Oscar's, and the trio with NHOP and Louis Hayes gives it a delicacy and warmth which sometimes disappear when jazz musicians try to make the tune swing. Oscar's 'Wheatland' is a delight, and versions of 'Younger Than Springtime' and 'Soft Winds' find the old romantic in top form.

**(*) Oscar Peterson–Stéphane Grappelli Quartet

Accord 403292 *Peterson; Stéphane Grappelli (vn); Niels-Henning Orsted Pedersen (b); Kenny Clarke (d). 2/72, 2/73.*

Likeable, uncomplicated, undemanding; what more can one say? The duo, 'Them There Eyes', was just one of a whole batch of such encounters that Grappelli (and Peterson) logged during the 1970s. It's no better or worse than the rest of them. Unfortunately, the recording quality on this one isn't up to scratch, with a very poor balance in the rhythm section. This is particularly dismaying because Clarke is one of the session's unambiguous assets.

***(*) History Of An Artist

Pablo 2625702 2CD *Peterson; Irving Ashby, Herb Ellis, Barney Kessel, Joe Pass (g); Ray Brown, Sam Jones, George Mraz, Niels-Henning Orsted Pedersen (b); Bobby Durham, Louis Hayes (d). 12/72–5/74.*

This collects some of Oscar's earliest trio dates for Pablo, and the original double-LP of *History Of An Artist* served notice of what would amount to a fine comeback on record during the '70s. Some great music here.

*** The Trio

Original Jazz Classics OJC 992 *Peterson; Joe Pass (g); Niels-Henning Orsted Pedersen (b). 73.*

*** The Good Life

Original Jazz Classics OJC 627 *As above. 73.*

For some fans this is Peterson's best vintage and most effective partnership. *The Trio* concentrates largely on blues material, with a withers-wringing 'Secret Love' as a curtain-piece. On the other album, 'Wheatland' needs the rhythmic drive that Ed Thigpen brought to the tune on *Compact Jazz*; but by and large the drummerless trio is a setting that suits Peterson's Tatumesque delivery. Only five tracks, and little sense of significant development on any of them as Peterson's technique becomes increasingly pleased with itself.

*** Oscar Peterson In Russia

Pablo 2625711 2CD *Peterson; Niels-Henning Orsted Pedersen (b); Jake Hanna (d). 11/74.*

The real meat of this journey was the duos with NHOP. Their trip down Green Dolphin Street is a revelation, one of the partnership's genuinely shining moments. Hanna is a rather pushy, forceful drummer for this context, but he has his strengths and, with temperatures outside doubtless plummeting, his push through 'Take The "A" Train' and 'Do You Know What It Means To Miss New Orleans' must surely have been welcome. Oscar redresses the balance with lovely readings of 'Someone To Watch Over Me' (solo) and 'Georgia On My Mind' (trio).

*** Oscar Peterson & Dizzy Gillespie

Pablo 2310740 *Peterson; Dizzy Gillespie (t). 11/74.*

***(*) Oscar Peterson & Roy Eldridge

Original Jazz Classics OJC 727 *Peterson; Roy Eldridge (t). 12/74.*

***(*) Oscar Peterson & Harry Edison

Original Jazz Classics OJC 738 *Peterson; Harry 'Sweets' Edison (t). 12/74.*

*** Oscar Peterson & Clark Terry

Original Jazz Classics OJCCD 806 *Peterson; Clark Terry (t). 5/75.*

*** Jousts

Original Jazz Classics OJCCD 857 *As the four discs above, except add Jon Faddis (t). 11/74–6/75.*

This instrumentation goes all the way back to 1928, when Louis Armstrong and Earl Hines recorded 'Weather Bird'. There are, inevitably, hints of a later Bird in Gillespie's blues style, but there is also a slackness of conception similar to what overtook Armstrong in later years, and Peterson's overblown accompaniments don't help. The ballads are better, but only because they're prettier.

Eldridge pushes a little harder (and, incidentally, sounds prettier than Diz), and the slightly later session is on balance the more compelling. There is still a feeling of Buggins's turn and mix-and-match about a lot of these sessions, but the two players' artistry does show through. Peterson's switch to organ was a happy stroke and might have been usefully extended to the album as a whole, rather than to selected tracks. The closing 'Blues For Chu' is a small master-stroke.

Of the three, Sweets is closest in conception to Armstrong, and the opening 'Easy Living' reverberates back and forth across almost half a century of the music. There are some lovely things later on in the set as well: 'Willow Weep For Me', where Sweets squeezes low, throaty tones out of his trumpet, and 'The Man I Love', a straight, unabashed performance.

The Clark Terry sequence as a whole seems the drabbest of the bunch. There's surprisingly little feeling of communication between two men who must have worked together literally dozens of times – or perhaps that's the problem. Oscar breezes away delightedly at 'Makin' Whoopee', 'Satin Doll' and 'Slow Boat To China', but there's not much in the way of bonhomie from Clark, who's had better days in the studio and seems intent on shouting his partner down.

Jousts brings together additional material from all four sessions, and from a date with Dizzy's spiritual son, Jon Faddis, who'd certainly pass for J.B. Gillespie on his tracks. A good buy for anyone who wants to sample the sequence, or who simply doesn't want to shell out for the set; needless to say, genuine enthusiasts will have other reasons for wanting it.

*** At The Montreux Jazz Festival 1975

Original Jazz Classics OJCCD 931 *Peterson; Milt Jackson (vib); Toots Thielemans (hca); Joe Pass (g); Niels-Henning Orsted Pedersen (b); Louie Bellson (d). 7/75.*

Notable for the inclusion of Parker's 'Au Privave', a bebop classic that has been a favourite of the pianist's but which still sits rather awkwardly alongside Peterson's usual diet of blues and swing. In the event, it's an effective enough performance, though the logic of his solo is rather lost in the showers of notes he plays. Thielemans underlines how good an improviser he can be, but Pass is very muted.

*** Porgy And Bess

Original Jazz Classics OJC 829 *Peterson; Joe Pass (g). 1/76.*

Peterson's choice of clavichord for the *Porgy And Bess* session looked initially promising but ultimately suggests nothing more than a way of freshening up rather stale performances. It's perhaps the least known of the keyboard family, covering between three and five octaves (Peterson seems to be using the larger model) and distinguished from the piano and harpsichord by the fact that the strings are struck (rather than plucked, as with the harpsichord) by metal tangents which can be left in contact with the string rather than rebounding, altering its distinctive vibrato. Peterson certainly hasn't mastered that aspect of the instrument and plays it with a pianist's 'clean' touch that loses him the delicious, bluesy wavers and bends it could have brought to these rather stolid Gershwin interpretations.

*** Montreux '77

Original Jazz Classics OJC 383 *Peterson; Ray Brown, Niels-Henning Orsted Pedersen (b). 7/77.*

*** Montreux '77

Original Jazz Classics OJC 378 *Peterson; Dizzy Gillespie, Clark Terry (t); Eddie 'Lockjaw' Davis (ts); Niels-Henning Orsted Pedersen (b); Bobby Durham (d). 7/77.*

The first of these is an intriguing two-bass experiment from the much-documented 1977 festival, where Peterson had become a recognized draw. Brown tends to take on some of the responsibilities of a guitarist, alternating his familiar 'walk' with clipped strums reminiscent of Herb Ellis's guitar and leaving the darker sonorities to the great Dane. The material, with the exception of 'There Is No Greater Love', is perhaps not ideally suited to the two string-players and they're often left with a rather subsidiary role. Peterson was just about blown out of sight by Tommy Flanagan's excellent performance earlier in the weekend, but he's generally in good if undemanding form. He can also be heard on other sets from the same event: with Roy Eldridge (OJC 373), Eddie 'Lockjaw' Davis (OJC 384) and on an *All-Star Jam* (OJC 380); there are festival highlights on OJC 385.

***(*) The London Concert

Pablo 2620111 2CD *Peterson; John Heard (b); Louie Bellson (d).*

A delight to hear Peterson and the ebullient Bellson in this context and away from the crowded stages they occupied at festivals. Above all, and despite his occasional flash grandstanding, Bellson is a great accompanist, and for much of the time here he happily restricts himself to that role, just laying off the odd deadly fill and take that! riposte as the mood hits him. Heard is a quieter partner but, as always in a Peterson group, absolutely central to the sound. A great evening, marked by more fireworks than usual for this vintage.

*** The Paris Concert

Pablo 2620112 2CD *Peterson; Niels-Henning Orsted Pedersen (b); Joe Pass (g).* 10/78.

Again, much of the interest focuses on two Parker tracks, 'Donna Lee' and 'Ornithology', both of which receive the kind of scalping treatment meted out by the army barber at boot camp. There's a 'who's next?' feel to the succession of tracks that makes you wish someone had shouted out 'Excursion On A Wobbly Rail' or 'Three Blind Mice' … *anything* to wrong-foot the man. Playing without drums, as he did a lot around this time, Peterson seems rhythmically yet more commanding, but he also opens up his phrasing quite noticeably, highlighting the stresses and accents.

***(*) Skol

Original Jazz Classics OJC 496 *Peterson; Stéphane Grappelli (vn); Joe Pass (g); Niels-Henning Orsted Pedersen (b); Mickey Roker (d).* 7/79.

Peterson as group player. He defers more than usual to his colleagues – 'Nuages' and 'Making Whoopee' have Grappelli's thumbprint on them, after all – and contributes to a surprisingly rounded performance. The music is still on the soft side, but Peterson is as unfailingly sensitive as an accompanist as he is as a leader, and his solo spots are all the more striking for being tightly marshalled. A good choice for anyone who prefers the pianist in smaller doses, or who enjoys Grappelli. The fiddler suffers broadly similar critical problems. A player of consummate skill and considerable improvisational gifts, he has been somewhat hijacked by television and has come (quite wrongly) to seem a middle-of-the-road entertainer rather than a 'legitimate' jazzman. There is still probably more thought and enterprise in just one Grappelli solo than in a whole raft of albums by Young Turk tenor saxophone players.

**(*) Digital At Montreux

Pablo 2308224 *Peterson; Niels-Henning Orsted Pedersen (b).* 7/79.

Very much a middle-market package for the hi-fi enthusiast who wants to watch the dials glow and twitch. This is a rather dead spell in Peterson's career, and listening to him negotiate 'Caravan' or 'Satin Doll' for the umpteenth time is a little like watching a snooker professional clear the table according to the book. One longs for a few near-misses. Collectors and dial-twitchers only.

**(*) The Personal Touch

Pablo 2312135 *Peterson; Clark Terry (t, flhn); Ed Bickert, Peter Leitch (g); Dave Young (b); Jerry Fuller (d); orchestra conducted by Rick Wilkins.* 1 & 2/80.

Rick Wilkins's orchestrations aren't as drowningly fulsome as one might have feared, and both Peterson and Clark Terry are forceful enough players to rise above them. All the same, it's hard to see how a fairly unenterprising set would have been much different for quintet alone. Peterson's brief switch to electric piano (listen to 'The World Is Waiting For The Sunrise' for a quick sample) underlines the instrument's limitations rather than the player's.

*** Live At The Northsea Jazz Festival

Pablo 2620115 *Peterson; Toots Thielemans (hca); Joe Pass (g); Niels-Henning Orsted Pedersen (b).* 7/80.

The sprawling Northsea Festival has some of the chaotic glamour of the old JATP packages. Though not a pianist who generally sounds good around horns, Peterson gives Thielemans a lot of space and respect, weaving counterlines round his plangent figures on 'Like Someone In Love' and 'Caravan' (a gorgeously exotic performance). It's a quieter, less dynamic set than many of the festival albums from the period (which suits Thielemans) but isn't particularly reflective. The Nat Cole references are well to the forefront if you care to look for them.

***(*) Nigerian Marketplace

Pablo 2308231 *Peterson; Niels-Henning Orsted Pedersen (b); Terry Clark (d).* 7/81.

The title-track has a vivid 'live from Lagos' bustle about it that carries on into 'Au Privave', by now established as Peterson's favourite Charlie Parker item. The middle of the programme is on much more familiar turf with 'Nancy', 'Misty' and, perhaps more surprisingly, Bill Evans's lovely 'Waltz For Debby'. Peterson hasn't shown a great deal of interest in Evans's book (and it's difficult to judge whether his occasional Hawes and Evans touches show a direct influence), but he handles this theme with characteristic amplitude and not too much depth. Newcomer Clark performs well if rather busily.

*** Freedom Song

Pablo 26401001 *Peterson; Joe Pass (g); Niels-Henning Orsted Pedersen (b); Martin Drew (d).* 2/82.

There are few places in the world where Peterson has not recorded, but there are no fans more vociferous in their support than the Japanese. These dates were recorded in Tokyo and they find him in cracking good form. 'Now's The Time' reinforces his attachment to bebop, and the medley 'Hymn To Freedom'/'The Fallen Warrior'/'Nigerian Marketplace' is one of his grandest conceptions. Reservations? Two. The sound is not all it might be, a little muffled and indistinct; and the band is not playing anything like as well as the leader's performance requires. Two cheers.

*** Two Of The Few

Original Jazz Classics OJC 689 *Peterson; Milt Jackson (vib).* 1/83.

We are declared sceptics when it comes to piano/vibraphone duos, but this one is a winner from start to finish. Perhaps because the session was run down and recorded at short notice, there's not much originality in the material, which consists entirely of well-worn standards. The closing 'Here's Two Of The Few' is great, though, and worth the price on its own. CD certainly brings out the definition of both instruments, so perhaps we're slowly being converted.

****(*) A Tribute To My Friends**

Pablo 2310902 *Peterson; Joe Pass (g); Niels-Henning Orsted Pedersen (b); Martin Drew (d).* 11/83.

***** If You Could See Me Now**

Pablo 2310918 *As above.* 11/83.

The tribute album nods in the direction of Fats Domino, Dizzy Gillespie, Ella and others who've crossed the big man's path over the years. There's a slight air of the end-of-contract, A&R meeting about it: how do we find a new wrinkle? *If You Could See Me Now* includes 'Limehouse Blues' and the bassist's feature, 'On Danish Shore'. These are about the best things on offer, but it's a thin set altogether.

****(*) Oscar Peterson Live!**

Pablo 2310940 *Peterson; Joe Pass (g); Dave Young (b); Martin Drew (d).* 11/86.

*****(*) Time After Time**

Pablo 2310947 *As above.* 11/86.

***** Oscar Peterson + Harry Edison + Eddie Cleanhead Vinson**

Pablo 2310927 *As above, except add Harry 'Sweets' Edison (t); Eddie Cleanhead Vinson (as).* 11/86.

The first of these related sessions consists largely of the deutero-classical 'Bach Suite', a more gainly and authentic pastiche than anything of Jacques Loussier's, but with an awful predictability about it as well. 'City Lights', 'Perdido' and 'Caravan' are tacked on at the end to keep the strict-constructionists happy. Better on harpsichord? *Time After Time* restores the balance considerably. An original 'Love Ballade' revives Peterson's reputation as a melodist, and the closing 'On The Trail' allays any doubts about failing stamina. The material with Edison and Vinson fails to live up to past encounters with the trumpeter, and there are odd occasions when Vinson seems to get in the way. It is, though, a hard session to fault on any more serious ground, and the 'Stuffy' and 'Satin Doll' work-outs are top class.

***** Oscar Peterson Plays Duke Ellington**

Pablo 2310966 *As above.* 67–86.

Apart from the inclusion of 'The Lady Of The Lavender Mist', a real Ellington obscurity, the material here is quite predictable. Oscar's interest in Duke's music for piano was scarcely a surprise, and Pablo had plenty to trawl for this elegant compilation. The tracks also include items written by Strayhorn and Mercer but, given the quality of the playing and the authority with which Oscar approaches the Ellington songbook, no one is going quibble about copyrights.

****** Piano Moods: The Very Best Of Oscar Peterson**

Polygram 557462 2CD *Peterson; Milt Jackson (vib); Ray Brown, Sam Jones, Jiri Mraz (b); Bobby Durham, Gene Gammage, Louis Hayes, Ray Price, Ed Thigpen (d).*

An impeccable 33-track compilation, questionable only for the absence of anything with guitarists Ellis or Kessel, but good enough on its own terms to overcome any quibbles or cavils. Piano jazz of the very highest order. Strongly recommended, even if you have most of the constituent records.

*****(*) Live At The Blue Note**

Telarc CD 83304 *Peterson; Herb Ellis (g); Ray Brown (b); Bobby Durham (d).* 3/90.

***** Saturday Night At The Blue Note**

Telarc CD 83306 *As above.* 3/90.

***** At The Blue Note: Last Call**

Telarc CD 83314 *As above.* 3/90.

***** Encore At The Blue Note**

Telarc CD 83356 *As above.* 3/90.

Whatever stiffness has crept into Peterson's fingers over the last few years has served only to increase the feeling he injects into his playing. It's hard to relate 'Peace For South Africa' on the first volume to the torrents of sound he conjured up in his big-hall Pablo days. This is quieter, more intimate and more thoughtful, and the ballad medley at its centre shows genuine melodic inventiveness. A must for Peterson fans, and 'Honeysuckle Rose' offers a good – albeit second-gear – impression of the Tatum-derived technique which overlaid his earlier commitment to Nat Cole.

The second volume was recorded the following night. It's a more varied, less familiar programme, but the playing is pretty much by the numbers. The 'final' visit and the almost inevitable *Encore* are even more subdued and formal. The elegance of Peterson's segues begins to pall long before the end. Fans will value 'It Never Entered My Mind' on the last but one, but more casual purchasers might want to plump for the first volume and leave it at that, even if it means missing the *Encore* performance of 'I Wished On The Moon' which, though brief, is exquisite.

***** Side By Side**

Telarc 83341 *Peterson; Itzhak Perlman (vn).* 94.

These jazz-meets-classical encounters hardly ever work, usually because many accomplished classical players couldn't swing even if you hanged them. Perlman, though, has always had a mischievous streak, even when the context is otherwise solemn, and on this *tête-à-tête* he brings his own catchy humour and bright musical intelligence to staples like 'Makin' Whoopee' and 'Mack The Knife'. Perhaps inevitably, it's most effective when Oscar is looking after the bottom end, but there's plenty to enjoy throughout.

*****(*) The More I See You**

Telarc CD 83370 *Peterson; Clark Terry (t, flhn); Benny Carter (as); Lorne Lofsky (g); Ray Brown (b); Lewis Nash (d).* 1/95.

Leaving aside the guitarist and the drummer, who are mere boys, the collective age here is 295. That's a lot of jazz experience to squeeze on to one disc. Peterson was still battling his way back to health and playing at this time, and the presence of even older men must have been some sort of stimulus to fold up his bed and play. There are some extraordinary moments, as when Terry duets with himself, trumpet and flugelhorn in opposite hands, in an episode from Ferde Grofé's *Grand Canyon Suite*, and the interplay between Peterson and Brown on 'In A Mellow Tone', but it's hard to make invidious comparisons. Lofsky is a young Canadian guitarist who has been generously sponsored by Oscar over the last few years. This was a summit conference and, while there is a certain amount of polite jockeying (these are not small egos on display), most of it is generously good-natured and no one can question the veracity of the music played. That it should have followed so swiftly on the heels of serious illness just makes it more special.

*****(*) Oscar Peterson Meets Roy Hargrove And Ralph Moore**
Telarc 83399 *Peterson; Roy Hargrove (t); Ralph Moore (ts); Niels-Henning Orsted Pedersen (b); Lewis Nash (d).* 96.

Moore has previously guested as 'fourth leg' to the Ray Brown trio and, though Telarc artist Brown isn't present on this occasion (we gather he was touring), it's a further chance to hear Peterson once again in the company of the big Viking who anchored his band for so many years. The two horn men occupy a good deal of the foreground, perhaps still compensating a little for Oscar's post-stroke change of pace. Hargrove isn't articulating at his best and a couple of times on 'My Foolish Heart' drifts perilously close to playing flat. 'Here's That Rainy Day' conjures up an extraordinary range of ghosts, from Miles to Bill Evans, and Oscar seems to quote someone's idea, some half-remembered phrase in the middle of his statement. A lovely album.

*****(*) Oscar & Benny**
Telarc 83406 *Peterson; Benny Green (p); Ray Brown (b); Greg Hutchinson (d).* 97.

Old cats teach young cats how it's done. This was, in effect, Oscar guesting with the current Ray Brown trio, and the two seniors steal the show in almost every department. There's never been any doubt that Benny Green learned a good deal from Peterson (and more directly from Peterson than from *his* sources, as is often suggested) and here there are moments when you might almost be listening to overdubs of the old man. Brown's huge, emphatic tone and crisp high-note runs are a perfect complement and the rhythmic profile is so full that there isn't much for Hutchinson, one of the best young mainstreamers on the scene at the moment, to do with his time, other than keep it. 'Scrapple From The Apple' is the stand-out track, confirming that Oscar is back from his brush with the Reaper and playing as well as ever. That doesn't necessarily mean as fast or as fluently, but with bags of feeling, which was the only question mark over him in the past.

***** A Tribute To Oscar Peterson: Live At Town Hall**
Telarc 83401 2CD *Peterson; Clark Terry (t, v); Stanley Turrentine (ts); Benny Green (p); Milt Jackson (vib); Herb Ellis (g); Ray Brown, Niels-Henning Orsted Pedersen (b); Greg Hutchinson (d); Shirley Horn, (v).* 97.

More interesting as an event than as music. This is one of those feel-good moments it would be churlish to quibble over. Few people in the business are regarded with such genuine affection as Oscar Peterson, and it is no surprise that so many were prepared to turn out and pay tribute in this way. The unlikely inclusion is Turrentine, but he turns out to be one of the stars of the show, alongside the two bassists and the redoubtable Shirley Horn, who gets better every time she opens her mouth.

***** Oscar In Paris**
Telarc 83414 2CD *Peterson; Lorne Lofsky (g); Niels-Henning Orsted Pedersen (b); Martin Drew (d).* 97.

Back to business. Recorded live at the Salle Pleyel, on a piano that classical players purr over. Good to hear the effortlessly swinging Martin Drew bring his very distinctive touch to the group. He and NHOP have always performed well together and with the addition of an in-form Lofsky, whose career seems to be taking off, they create a well-balanced group performance. The emphasis is still on ensembles and there are a couple of points when Oscar sounds tired and lacklustre. Generally, though, he is playing with precision and formidable hand-speed. We'd question that this Telarc was worth a double CD, but with a treasure like Peterson on your hands you'd probably want to release his warm-ups as well.

*****(*) A Summer Night In Munich**
Telarc 83450 *Peterson; Ulf Wakenius (g); Niels-Henning Orsted Pedersen (b); Martin Drew (d).* 7/98.

Oscar rather tastelessly described this as his 'NATO Quartet'. The actual performances are a good deal more harmonious than that antagonistic title suggests and the latter-day versions of things like 'Nigerian Marketplace', 'Hymn To Freedom' and 'When Summer Comes' are very good. Wakenius fills the shoes of Ellis and Kessel very well indeed, and it would have been interesting to hear piano and guitar duet more spaciously. Drummer Martin Drew takes a well-earned solo on the closing 'Sushi'.

*****(*) The Very Tall Band Live At The Blue Note**
Telarc 83443 *Peterson; Milt Jackson (vib); Ray Brown (b); Karriem Riggins (d).* 11/98.

Almost four decades after he recorded *Very Tall*, Oscar, Milt and Ray (and the title could have referred to the bassist only ironically) met up again for an old pals night at the Blue Note, which was becoming Oscar's second home. Peterson's technique is still far from being as florid and fiery-paced as it used to be, but he retains his ability to communicate a melody and to invest tunes as various as 'I Remember Clifford' and 'Nature Boy' with his unmistakable character. As if making up for his shorter stature, Brown is the hero of the session, claiming a wonderful bass solo medley which doesn't pall at seven and a half minutes and playing a wonderful introduction to 'Blues For Jr'. Milt Jackson's health was causing serious concern at the time and he sounds unusually inward and clenched, rarely cutting loose with those long, rippling, piano-like lines. Drummer Karriem Riggins comes on for the closing 'Caravan' and brings a thoroughly satisfying record to an appropriate climax. Life in the old dog(s) yet.

Ralph Peterson (born 1962)

DRUMS, TRUMPET

Peterson emerged as one of the busiest and most inventive drummers on the New York scene of the 1980s. He made several records for Blue Note as a leader, all currently out of print, and has since gone on to lead various editions of his group, The Fo' Tet

***** The Reclamation Project**
Evidence 22113-2 *Peterson; Steve Wilson (ss); Bryan Carrott (vib); Belden Bullock (b).* 11/94.

*****(*) The Fo'tet Plays Monk**
Evidence 22174-2 *As above.* 11–12/95.

Peterson is a very fine drummer, wonderful to hear live, and challenging and provocative as a leader. While peripherally associated with the black hard bop of the 1980s, he is more often thought of as a musician who can move from inside to out in New York's avant-garde company. A fireball of energy on any recording, he isn't so much noisy as determined to make something happen from the kit at every moment in the music.

There are a bundle of earlier Blue Note albums in the deletions file, but Peterson has since started recording for Evidence with the group he calls The Fo'tet. *Reclamation Project* takes the sombre theme of recovery from substance abuse and turns it into a thematic thread. Peterson is back in his more demanding groove here, delivering tunes in 9/8 and 14/8, setting Carrott and Wilson hugely difficult rhythmic tasks as improvisers – and somehow making it click. His innate sense of swing sees him through even the most potentially awkward situations. That said, this is a dark and sometimes introverted record, and some may find it hard to find a way inside.

The Fo'tet Plays Monk is a more prosaic project, but Peterson was clearly keen to take this out of the normal tribute furrow. Of the 11 tunes, only 'Epistrophy' and 'Well You Needn't' are obvious. Songo and second-line rhythms add some multicultural spice, and the sheer sizzle of the playing is exciting: Wilson's serpentine playing is worth a close listen, but the star improviser is Carrott, who seems as imaginatively at home in these settings as Milt Jackson was with Monk himself. 'Played Twice', 'Light Blue' and 'Brilliant Corners' are peerless. Only the two originals, one apiece by the leader and Carrott, seem less than absorbing.

*****(*) Back To Stay**

Sirocco SLJ 1006 *Peterson; Ralph Bowen (ss); Michael Brecker (ts); Bryan Carrott (vib, marim); Beldon Bullock (b).* 5–6/99.

A new edition of the band (Brecker plays only a cameo role), but the leader's energy remains unstinting, the tunes are full of detail, and Carrott, by now almost as important to this group as Peterson, blends solo and ensemble roles with unassuming panache. The instrumentation continues to offer a strikingly different sonic palette, and the approach to repertory pieces such as 'Soul Eyes' and 'Miles' Mode' is similarly unclichéd.

Le Petit Jazzband de Mr Morel

GROUP

A band of French revivalists led by Jean-Pierre Morel.

*****(*) Farewell Blues**

Stomp Off CD1343 *Jean-Pierre Morel (c); Alain Marquet (cl); Daniel Huck (ss, as, v); Michel Bescont (ts); Bernard Thévin (p); François Fournet (bj); Gérard Gervois (tba).* 3/97.

***** Delta Bound**

Stomp Off CD1344 *As above, except add Gabriel Conesa (tb).* 3–10/98.

The group is actually a reassembling of a band named Charquet & Co which Morel had run in Paris in the early '80s. They're expert revivalists, perfectly at home in idiomatic 1920s-style playing but with sufficient personality to make the music swing to their own beats. *Farewell Blues* is a very rare item in the Stomp Off catalogue since it's a reissue of a record from another label, in this case Morel's own operation. A smart mix of familiar material such as Ellington's 'Stevedore Stomp' and 'Shout 'Em Aunt Tillie' with more obscure pieces, the record is tight, hot and graceful in turn. Each of the players makes a strong contribution, but we might single out the superbly heated playing of tenor saxophonist Bescont, who sounds like himself without moving even a step beyond the saxophone language of the '20s. Tied to the beat but rocking with it, this is a very enjoyable set.

We don't find the follow-up, *Delta Bound*, quite so good, though it's not easy to say why: the band is almost the same (trombonist Conesa substitutes for Huck on a few tracks) and the material is of the same stripe. This time, though, some of the ensembles seem a little congested, and in at least one case – Morton's 'Grandpa's Spells' – the performance doesn't do the best justice to the subject-matter. An entertaining set nevertheless, and hopefully the band will stick around to do more.

Umberto Petrin

PIANO

Contemporary Italian pianist, in the post-bop idiom but brushing up against the avant-garde.

***** Ooze**

Splasc(h) 384-2 *Petrin; Guido Mazzon (t); Tiziano Tononi (d).* 4–5/92.

Petrin has taken a long, hard look at jazz piano history and synthesized a very idiosyncratic method. Many of these 15 tracks are miniatures, several last only a minute or two, but the opening treatment of Ornette Coleman's 'Street Woman' – which sounds like Earl Hines playing a Coleman tune – or the bleak, ghostly farewell of Donald Ayler's 'Our Prayer', with Mazzon making a guest appearance, display real understated authority. Though there are avant-garde flourishes here and there, Petrin has more conservative manners and, in reflective, almost rhapsodic pieces such as 'Mesty' or the slow but incisive look at 'Round Midnight', he approaches the serene radicalism of Paul Bley. Tononi adds very spare percussion parts to four tracks. The record has a disjointed and sometimes half-realized feel, but how many pianists making their debut would offer such an uncompromising programme?

*****(*) Wirrwarr**

Splasc(h) 481-2 *Petrin; Giancarlo Schiaffini (tb); Daniele Patumi (b); Tiziano Tononi (d).* 2/96.

*****(*) Monk's World**

Splasc(h) 619-2 *Petrin (p solo).* 3/97.

Petrin's progress is fascinating to hear. *Wirrwarr* is a programme of originals, aside from two surprising choices of Coltrane tunes – 'Ogunde' and 'After The Rain'. The long title-track is a fiercely argued creation, pianist and drummer engaging in a multi-layered dialogue over a steadying bass vamp. Schiaffini makes a cameo appearance on two tracks only, with 'Contiene Une Linea Di Lunghezza Infinita' about as far out as Petrin will ever go. If he is following the Varèsean doctrine of 'intelligent structures of sound moving freely in space', as the sleeve-note suggests, they remain sometimes hard to fathom. Which may be why, anchored by the familiarity of the tunes, his Monk recital stands out as his most clearly satisfying record. His own tune, 'Inscape', reappears from *Wirrwarr* along with two other originals, but otherwise these are gentle but inquiring treatments of several of the less frequently encountered themes from the Monk repertory: 'Brilliant Corners', 'Introspection', 'Green Chimneys', played to elicit not so much the quirks in Monk's music as its underlying, almost shy embrace of the ballad form.

Michel Petrucciani (1962–99)

PIANO

Born in Montpellier, he played in his father's band and began recording after moving to Paris, aged seventeen. Moved to the USA in 1982 and recorded for Blue Note, later for Dreyfus. A diminutive man handicapped by an obscure bone disease, he triumphed over any disability and became one of the most popular of concert performers, playing in a romantic post-bop style.

****** 100 Hearts**

Concord CCD 43001 *Petrucciani (p solo).* 83.

****** Live At The Village Vanguard**

Concord CCD 43006 2CD *Petrucciani; Palle Danielsson (b); Eliot Zigmund (d).* 3/84.

There's a freshness and quicksilver virtuosity about Michel Petrucciani's early records which is entirely captivating, and they still sound terrific. While he is an adoring admirer of Bill Evans – 'Call me Bill,' he once suggested to Jim Hall, who demurred – his extrovert attack places Evans's harmonic profundity in a setting that will energize listeners who find Evans too slow and quiet to respond to. Petrucciani was already a formidable talent when he began recording and, while some of these discs have been criticized for being the work of a pasticheur, that seems a curmudgeonly verdict on someone who enjoys the keyboard so much. *100 Hearts* is arguably the best of the early sessions, if only for the marvellous title-tune which skips and leaps around its tone centre: in themes like this, Petrucciani stakes a claim to be one of the great romantic virtuosos in contemporary jazz. *Live At The Village Vanguard* captures a typically rumbustious concert set by Petrucciani's trio of the day: 'Nardis' and 'Oleo' offer fresh annotations on well-worn classics and there are sparkling revisions of his own originals, 'To Erlinda' and 'Three Forgotten Magic Words'.

***** Pianism**

Blue Note 746295-2 *As above.* 12/85.

*****(*) Power Of Three**

Blue Note 846427-2 *Petrucciani; Wayne Shorter (ss, ts); Jim Hall (g).* 7/86.

***** Michel Plays Petrucciani**

Blue Note 848679-2 *Petrucciani; John Abercrombie (g); Gary Peacock, Eddie Gomez (b); Roy Haynes, Al Foster (d); Steve Thornton (perc).* 9–12/87.

Petrucciani's first three albums for Blue Note provided a variety of challenges. *Pianism* is another excellent batch of six workouts by the trio who made the earlier live album, and if Zigmund and Danielsson sometimes sound a little underwhelming, that's partly due to the leader's brimming improvisations. *Power Of Three* is a slightly fragmented but absorbing concert meeting of three masters, skittish on 'Bimini' and solemnly appealing on 'In A Sentimental Mood'.

Plays Petrucciani is an all-original set which lines the pianist up against two magisterial rhythm sections, with Abercrombie adding some spruce counterpoint to two pieces. The smart hooks of 'She Did It Again' suggest that the pianist would have had a good living as a pop writer if he had decided to quit the piano, but the more considered pieces show no drop in imagination, even if some of the themes seem to be curtailed before the improvisations really start moving.

***** Promenade With Duke**

Blue Note 780590-2 *Petrucciani (p solo).*

***** Marvellous**

Dreyfus FDM 36564-2 *Petrucciani; Dave Holland (b); Tony Williams (d); Graffiti String Quartet. n.d.*

Michel's promenade is more with Strayhorn and Petrucciani than with Ellington. Beautifully played and recorded, but it's rather sombre after the elated feel of his earlier sessions. Although some of his other Blue Note albums have disappeared, there is a French edition which boxes all seven of them together, but availability is somewhat limited.

Marvellous matches him with the formidable team of Holland and Williams, who play up the music's dramatic qualities to the hilt: a graceful tune like the 3/4 'Even Mice Dance' gets thumped open by Williams's awesome drumming. The pianist revels in the situation, though, and produces some of his most joyful playing. Yet it hardly squares with the string quartet parts, arranged by Petrucciani but more of a distraction than an integral part of such fierce playing.

*****(*) Au Théâtre Des Champs-Elysées**

Dreyfus FDM 36570-2 2CD *Petrucciani (p solo).* 11/94.

The opening 'Medley Of My Favourite Songs' might be a quintessential Petrucciani performance, 40 unbroken minutes of a piano master in full flow, lightning flashes of humour illuminating an otherwise seamless sequence. Maybe he will never quite recapture the effortless excitement of the early discs, and to that extent the energy of his playing is mitigated somewhat by his sense of proportion; but there's a great deal to enjoy across these two discs: a lovely, thoughtful 'Night Sun In Blois', a finger-busting Monk medley, and a beautifully distilled 'Besame Mucho' to close on.

***** Both Worlds**

Dreyfus FDM 36590-2 *Petrucciani; Flavio Boltro (t); Bob Brookmeyer (vtb); Stefano Di Battista (ts, ss); Anthony Jackson (b); Steve Gadd (d).* 96.

Almost a complete departure from his other work, this rather mysteriously seemed to set out to tame Petrucciani by placing him squarely in a band format, where he flourishes only intermittently as a soloist, and even then without his usual *brio*. He wrote all nine tunes but the arrangements are all Brookmeyer's, who brings his trademark quirks to a nevertheless very interesting line-up. The soloists are all strong enough, and there's a particularly appealing piano–soprano duet on 'Petite Louise', yet this could all use a shot of Michel letting go.

*****(*) Concerts Inédits**

Dreyfus FDM 36607-2 3CD *Petrucciani; Niels-Henning Orsted Pedersen, Louis Petrucciani (b); Lenny White (d).* 7/93–8/94.

****** Solo Live**

Dreyfus FDM 36597-2 *Petrucciani (p solo).* 2/97.

Petrucciani's passing robbed jazz of one of its most charismatic spirits, especially in performance, and these sets are reminders of how much an audience would respond to him. The three-disc set offers him in solo, duo and trio settings: it's somewhat patchy, since the solo disc has a rather hard and unattractive piano sound, and the trio set (with Louis Petrucciani and White, cut at a Japanese concert) doesn't entirely benefit from the drummer's energies. But the duo record with NHOP is a delight, two virtuosos at the top of their game without overpowering the listeners with how much they can play.

Solo Live is a marvellous Frankfurt concert recording. Michel warms up with a sequence of shorter pieces before stretching out on 'Trilogy In Blois' and 'Caravan'. He was always rethinking material: the 'Besame Mucho' here is entirely different from the treatment on *Concerts Inédits*. The final 'She Did It Again/Take The "A" Train' medley is showstopping, but each note seems to matter as part of the flow. This great communicator will be sorely missed.

John Petters

DRUMS

Essex-based drummer working in the traditional idiom.

***** Mixed Salad**

Jazzology JCD-176 *Petters; Ben Cohen (t); Len Baldwin (tb); Wally Fawkes (cl, ss); Martin Litton (p); Paul Sealey (g); Annie Hawkins (b).* 11/85–7/86.

****(*) Boogie Woogie And All That Jazz**

Rose RRCD003 *Petters; Neville Dickie (p); Mickey Ashman (b).* 7/93.

There's nothing very 'authentic' about these records, but how much authenticity can a chubby young drummer from Harlow give to traditional jazz? In fact Petters brings a great sense of fun to these sessions, and it's disappointing that both should be let down by their circumstances. The Jazzology date features some memorable playing on both 'Shim-Me-Sha-Wabble' and 'Out Of The Galleon', with the veteran Cohen sounding wonderfully lyrical, and Fawkes and Baldwin playing their part. The music never seems to hit quite the same high after those two tracks, and Litton's 'Wolverine Blues' is perfunctory; but the music is excellent trad, and it's a pity that the tinny sound and poor balance detract. *Boogie Woogie And All That Jazz* is a session of rag, boogie and novelty piano in which Dickie does all the playing and Ashman and Petters keep straight, simple time. Some of it sounds more like B Bumble And The Stingers than James P. Johnson, and the tunes are often ones that many will never want to hear again, but it's righteous. Recorded in Eastleigh.

Andreas Pettersson (born 1964)

GUITAR

Contemporary Swedish guitarist who took up the instrument after winning 1,000 krona from a slot machine and buying one! After several years of rock and fusion, he turned to a more straight-ahead style when joining a group led by Lars Lystedt in 1984.

***** Live In Finland**

Dragon DRCD 238 *Pettersson; Putte Wickman (cl); Jörgen Smeby (b); Martin Löfgren (d).* 7/92.

*****(*) Joyrider**

Sittel SITCD 9219 *Pettersson; Hector Bingert (as, ts, f); Kjell Ohman (p, org); Jörgen Smeby (b); Ronnie Gardiner (d).* 1–2/95.

***** Cookie & The Hawk**

Sittel SITCD 9248 *As above, except Ohman also plays accordion.* 10/97.

Pettersson's style is a synthesis of old-fashioned bebop guitar, *à la* Tal Farlow, and a few licks of a more modern import. He favours a clean, liquid tone which softens the tonalities he uses just enough to suggest a wider harmonic frame of reference, but his solos imply that his heart remains tied to playing on changes. His melodies are similarly long, tricksy lines, from which he then takes off, but, for all its fleetness and fluency, it's not groundbreaking jazz.

These are nevertheless enjoyable records. The Dragon album catches a one-off Baltic Jazz Festival appearance with the ageless Wickman, whose playing is more *outré* than anyone else's in the quartet. A typical festival set: spontaneous, energetic blowing on a bunch of standards, empathetic but hardly intimate. The Sittel albums are by a genuine band, and the playing has substantial impact. *Joyrider* brims with enjoyable excitement from the boisterous title-track onwards. Three standards, a blues and a group of worthwhile originals are rattled through without seeming rushed; a key to the record's success is Gardiner's unfussy but unfailingly swinging drumming. Pettersson's unselfish presence – he gives as much space to the others as he does to himself and refuses to push himself to the front of the mix – gives the album a nicely democratic feel, and Bingert, on a variety of reeds, is a useful player to have on hand, as is Ohman.

The follow-up, *Cookie & The Hawk*, is pitched as a more individual album, all of it written by Pettersson, but some of the material seems almost contrived. Ohman picks up an accordion for 'Tango For The Brave' and 'Maradona', and the freewheeling exuberance of the earlier disc seems to have trickled away. Although there is much crafty playing, there's little that genuinely stands out.

Oscar Pettiford (1922–60)

BASS, CELLO

Like Charlie Haden's, Pettiford's playing career began in a family orchestra, under the tutelage of his father, Harry 'Doc' Pettiford. As with his contemporary, Charles Mingus (who was also of mixed blood), there was an undercurrent of anger and frustration. Pettiford's wonderfully propulsive bass-playing marks a middle point between Mingus and Jimmy Blanton. Had he lived longer, he might now be acknowledged the more influential player, but he didn't live to see forty and spent his last years as a European exile.

****(*) Bass Hits**

Topaz TPZ 1071 *Pettiford; Cat Anderson, Harold Shorty Baker, Emmett Berry, Bill Coleman, Vic Coulson, Karl George, Dizzy Gillespie, Benny Harris, Shelton Hemphill, Taft Jordan, Al Killian, Shorty McConnell, Howard McGhee, Rex Stewart, Ed Vandever, Freddy Webster, Cootie Williams, Francis Williams (t); Ray Nance (t, vn); Lawrence Brown, Vic Dickenson, Claude Jones, Joe 'Tricky Sam' Nanton, Wilbur De Paris, Howard Scott, Trummy Young (tb); Ed Hall (cl); Jimmy Hamilton (cl, ts); Johnny Bothwell, Joe Eldridge, Jewell Grant, Johnny Hodges, Leonard Lowry, Leo Parker, Jimmy Powell, Russell Procope (as); Herbie Fields, Walter Thomas (as, ts); Ray Adams, Don Byas, Thomas Crump, Wardell Gray, Coleman Hawkins, Ike Quebec, Al Sears, Lucky Thompson (ts); Budd Johnson (ts, bs, cl); L Beck, Rudy Rutherford (bs); Wilbert Baranco, Duke Ellington, Johnny Guarnieri, Clyde Hart, Eddie Heywood, Sammy Price, Art Tatum, Sir Charles Thompson (p); Al Casey, Fred Guy, Charlie Norris, Allan Reuss, Connie Wainwright, Chuck Wayne (g); Denzil Best, David Booth, Big Sid Catlett, Cozy Cole, Sonny Greer, Shelly Manne, Roy Porter, Max Roach, Harold Doc West, Shadow Wilson (d); Estelle Edson (v).* 12/43–10/46.

Only two tracks out of 23 on *Bass Hits* were recorded under Pettiford's leadership. The remainder come from sessions fronted by Ben Webster, Coleman Hawkins, Dizzy Gillespie and Duke Ellington, but they have been selected to highlight the bassist's considerable skills. The opening track comes from a Leonard Feather-organized supergroup session with Tatum and Hawkins in attendance, but the real killer is the one that follows it. Recorded 19 days later, and under Hawkins's leadership, 'The Man I Love' is a classic of its time, and it's Oscar's solo as much as the saxophonist's that makes the piece so special. On a Billy Eckstine date from April 1944, he grabs a sensational solo on 'I Got A Date With Rhythm', and on 'Blue Skies' with Ben Webster's group he creates a brief statement that is perfectly weighted. Given the diversity and range of material on display, this is a primer record, valuable for highlighting Pettiford's skills, but not altogether satisfying as it stands. Pettiford's few moments as leader with the January 1945 All Stars are poorly documented, with about half the personnel unknown on 'Something For You', while the only other occasion he gets an above-the-title credit is as accompanist to the bluesy Estelle Edson on the closing 'Don't Drive This Jive Away'. Slim pickings.

***** The New Oscar Pettiford Sextet**

Original Jazz Classics OJCCD 1926 2 *Pettiford; Red Rodney (t); Earl Swope (tb); Julius Watkins (frhn); Al Cohn, Phil Urso (ts); Serge Chaloff (bs); Walter Bishop, Barbara Carroll, Jan Johansson (p); Terry Gibbs, Louis Hjulmand (vib); Charles Mingus (b); Denzil Best, Percy Brice (d).* 3/49–12/53.

It may seem faint or even sarcastic praise to say that these 1953 recordings mark the high-water mark of the cello as a jazz instrument, but not so. Pettiford's facility on the instrument is unparalleled, even by such gifted doublers as Ron Carter, and the freedom and fluency of his solo line on 'Pendulum At Falcon's Lair' is genuinely exhilarating. Oscar's placing of notes, his unfailing harmonic awareness and sheer musicality will win over all but the hardest-hearted sceptics. Oscar switches to bass for the lovely 'Tamalpais Love Song', a stately and rather mysterious composition on which what would have been the cello part is taken by french horn. 'Low And Behold' and the boppish 'Jack The Fieldstalker' are both virtuosic displays, but the album is leavened by a bright and pungent version of Quincy Jones's 'Stockholm Sweet'nin''. Two of the tracks feature Louis Hjulmand on vibes and Jan Johansson on piano; Hjulmand's originals, 'Fru Buel' and 'I Succumb To Temptation', are not the strongest things on the record and were excluded from the original Debut Records 10-inch release. The CD also includes four tracks recorded in 1949 under the leadership of Serge Chaloff and arranged by Shorty Rogers.

***** Vienna Blues: The Complete Session**

Black Lion BLCD 760104 *Pettiford; Hans Koller (ts); Attila Zoller (g, b); Jimmy Pratt (d).* 1/59.

*****(*) Montmartre Blues**

Black Lion BLCD 760124 *Pettiford; Allan Botschinsky (t); Erik Nordstrom (ts); Louis Hjulmand (vib); Jan Johansson (p); Jorn Elniff (d).* 8/59–7/60.

Pettiford's work with Monk and Ellington (who recognized both the break and the continuity with Blanton) survives on disc, and it's worth concentrating on the bassist's performances. It should also be noted that, though credited to Bud Powell, Black Lion's *The Complete Essen Jazz Festival Concert* documents a performance by the Oscar Pettiford Trio and (with Coleman Hawkins) Quartet from April 1960. The material on *Montmartre Blues* is every bit as good, suggesting that Pettiford's decline was not an artistic one, whatever else it was. Only weeks later, Pettiford died in his adoptive city of Copenhagen of what was then still called 'infantile paralysis'.

Jack Pettis (1902–?)

C-MELODY AND TENOR SAXOPHONES, CLARINET

Played saxophone in Chicago in his teens and was a member of the prototype New Orleans Rhythm Kings before it recorded. Went to New York and led several bands there, but disappeared from music in the '30s; is said to have married an heiress.

***** Jack Pettis His Pets, Band And Orchestra 1924–1929**

Kings Cross KCM 005 2CD *Pettis; Bill Moore, Phil Napoleon, Donald Bryan, Phil Hart, Manny Klein, Mike Mosiello (t); Frank Sarlo, Tommy Dorsey, Paul Weigan, Miff Mole, Jack Teagarden, Glenn Miller (tb); Len Kavash, Phil Sharp, Dick Stabile, Jimmy Dorsey, Don Murray, Benny Goodman, Tony Parenti, Harry Carney (cl, as); Spencer Clark (bsx); Al Goering, Frank Signorelli, Lennie Hayton, Jack Cornell (p); Joe Venuti, Matty Malneck, Nat Brusiloff, Nicky Gerfach (vn); Dick McDonough (bj, g, uke); Clay Bryson (bj, g); Eddie Lang, Carl Kress (g); Paul Nito (bj); Max Rosen, Joe Tarto (tba); Merrill Klein, Harry Goodman (b); Dillon Ober, Sam Fink (d); Scrappy Lambert, Billy Hillpot, Irving*

Kaufman, Frank Luther, Eugene Ramey, Erwin McGee, Irving Mills (v). 11/24–5/29.

The mysterious Pettis was a minor light in the New York scene of the 1920s. This fine two-disc edition builds on the Retrieval LP we listed in our first edition. The first disc is a somewhat motley collection of tracks from various groups, often roughly recorded, and even John R.T. Davies can't do that much with the remastering. This is mainly sound but unenterprising hot-dance music of the period. All the important music is on disc two, with some splendid sessions for Victor in 1929: there are some unmissable things in 'Freshman Hop', 'Bag O'Blues' and 'Campus Crawl', and opportunities which Goodman, Teagarden and Parenti jump on. Even Pettis himself, a rare champion of the C-melody saxophone, acquits himself well in several solos. The first disc lets the overall rating down, but at bargain price for the set this is a valuable way to get to hear and know some of the backwaters of early white jazz. As for Pettis himself, nobody seems to know what happened to him. There are some entertaining sleeve-notes by Warren Vaché Sr.

Barre Phillips (born 1934)

DOUBLE BASS, ELECTRONICS

Inspired by Ornette Coleman, the young San Fransciscan moved east in 1962, and six years later he recorded the first-ever solo-bass jazz record, Journal Violone, a discipline which has been a staple of his work ever since.

****** Mountainscapes**

ECM 843167-2 *Phillips; John Surman (bs, ss, bcl, syn); John Abercrombie (g); Dieter Feichtener (syn); Stu Martin (d).* 3/76.

****** Three Day Moon**

ECM 847326-2 *Phillips; Terje Rypdal (g, g syn, org); Dieter Feichtener (syn); Trilok Gurtu (perc).* 3/78.

***** Journal Violone II**

ECM 847328-2 *Phillips; John Surman (ss, bs, bcl, syn); Aina Kemanis (v).* 6/79.

*****(*) Camouflage**

Victo 08 *Phillips (solo).* 5/89.

***** Aquarian Rain**

ECM 511513-2 *Phillips; Alain Joule (perc).* 5/91.

*****(*) Uzu**

PSF CD 75 *Phillips; Yoshizawa Motoharu (b).* 96.

Phillips's first album of solo bass improvisations was originally intended as material for an electronic score, but composer Max Schubel thought the bass parts stood more than adequately on their own. Nearly 25 years later, Phillips produced an album which does make significant use of electronic processing of instrumental performance. The effect suggests that Schubel's instincts were sound, for *Aquarian Rain* is the most diffuse and least focused album the bassist has released. Phillips's own description of the process of 'collective composition', by which tapes were sent back and forth between his French home in Puget-Ville and the Studio Grame in Lyon where Jean-François Estager and James Giroudon worked the filters and gates, may have yielded exemplary music for live performance (a suite called 'Brick On Brick' was created, incorporating pieces like 'Inbetween I And E' and 'Promenade de Mémoire'), but it sounds rather stilted and contrived when digitalized and fixed. Enthusiasts for the bassist's work will find much of value but, compared to the duos with Guy, these interchanges with percussionist Joule lack even that tiny spark of electricity which rescues processed improvisation of this sort from becoming acoustic set-dressing.

It's galling to note that Phillips's very best record is *still* out of the ECM catalogue. The solo *Call Me When You Get There* from 1983, with its lyrical journeyings and unfussy philosophical musings, covers similar musical territory to the much earlier but almost equally fine *Mountainscapes*, a suite of subliminally interrelated pieces which demonstrate the astonishing transformations visited on basic musical perspectives by very slight changes in the angle of vision. Almost all of Phillips's output operates in that way. Whatever is being hidden on the recent solo, *Camouflage*, it can scarcely be the artist himself. Recorded in almost disturbing close-up (an effect necessarily heightened by CD reproduction), one can almost hear the bassist thinking as he investigates the sometimes fugitive tonalities of his instrument. Something of the same relationship between *Call Me* and *Mountainscapes* applies (recognizing the lapse in time) between *Camouflage* and *Journal Violone II*. The 1979 trio again makes use of Surman's melancholy soliloquizing, but in a rather more colouristic way that is reminiscent of *Three Day Moon*. This is Phillips's most accessible work on record but is by no means unrepresentative. Rypdal is an intelligent partner and Feichtener adds (as he had on *Mountainscapes*) some highly individual flourishes. One questions Gurtu's role, though: too effusive and individual a player, surely, for this selfless idiom.

Looking at Phillips's career only in the context of his recent solo work or of his improvisational activities with Derek Bailey's Company collective tends to cast it as something rarefied and dauntingly inward of gaze (the duo *Figuring* with Bailey (*q.v.*), Incus CD05, might attract that charge) but it's as well to remember that Phillips was Archie Shepp's bass player at the 1965 Newport Festival and that, with Surman and the late Stu Martin, also on *Mountainscapes*, he was a member of The Trio, one of the most dynamic free-jazz units of the late 1960s. There is a dancer's grace and concentration in Phillips's playing, an internal balance and rhythm that, as on *Camouflage*'s 'You And Me', make it virtually impossible to separate man and instrument.

There are problems on *Uzu*. Motoharu has so thoroughly wired himself up to what is described as a 'homemade electric vertical five string bass' that it is genuinely difficult to work out what one is listening to. This is a problem only if you take a close interest in the technical dimensions of music like this. For most people, the album will be a vivid, arresting experience, well worth a bit of patience.

Flip Phillips (born 1915)

TENOR SAXOPHONE

Born in Brooklyn, Joseph Phillips had a rather uneventful time in big bands, before joining Woody Herman in 1944. He then became closely identified with the travelling Jazz At The

Philharmonic concerts, jousting with the likes of Illinois Jacquet and playing in the shouting style which was the opposite of the cooler Lester Young method towards which younger tenormen were moving. From 1960 he was living and working outside music in Florida, although he still played gigs. In his old age, he is a grand survivor.

***** A Sound Investment**
Concord CCD 4334 *Phillips; Scott Hamilton (ts); John Bunch (p); Chris Flory (g); Phil Flanigan (b); Chuck Riggs (d).* 3/87.

***** A Real Swinger**
Concord CCD 4358 *Phillips; Dick Hyman (p); Howard Alden, Wayne Wright (g); Jack Lesberg (b); Butch Morris (d).* 5–6/88.

The spotlight has seldom been turned on this accomplished tenorman in more reflective mood. Recent years have seen him assume a comfortable elder-statesman role, but in his original prime he was only rarely recorded as a leader. In what's been an Indian summer for him, Phillips sounds warmly charismatic, pacing his solos with some flair and digging in just when he has to: the session in which he is the sole horn sounds fine, with 'September Song' and 'Poor Butterfly' to remind one of his authoritative ballad-playing. The set with Hamilton is sometimes too much of a good thing, with both tenors thickening the romantic broth a little over-generously at times, but one can't deny the heartiness of it all.

****(*) The Claw**
Chiaroscuro CR(D) 314 *Phillips; Clark Terry (t); Buddy Tate, Al Cohn, Scott Hamilton (ts); John Bunch (p); Chris Flory (g); Major Holley (b); Chuck Riggs (d).* 10/86.

***** Try A Little Tenderness**
Chiaroscuro CR(D) 321 *Phillips; Dick Hyman (p); Howard Alden, Bucky Pizzarelli (g); Bob Haggart (b); Ronnie Traxler (d); strings.* 6–7/92.

Flip is in good spirits for both these disparate sessions for Chiaroscuro. *The Claw* is a tenors-all-out jam session on board the SS *Norway* during the 1986 Floating Jazz Festival: they didn't look too far afield for the material ('Topsy', 'Flying Home', and so forth) and in the end it sounds too much like a parade of tenor solos to make for a satisfying record. But Flip and Al Cohn especially come up with a few remarks that evade the rules of the tenor extravaganza. Phillips gets to make his strings album on *Try A Little Tenderness* and, with canny arrangements by Dick Hyman and the saxophonist in his ripest form, the music is sly enough to sidestep most of the clichés of the situation – or, at least, to make them enjoyable anyway. A nice indulgence for the old warrior.

***** Swing Is The Thing!**
Verve 543477-2 *Phillips; James Carter, Joe Lovano (ts); Benny Green (p); Howard Alden (g); Christian McBride (b); Kenny Washington (d).* 10/99.

At almost 85, Flip is back home at Verve with this enjoyable stroll through tunes and music he knows well. There are inevitable shortcomings in his control, but the big tone is pretty much still there and none of this is giving him much trouble. Having Carter and Lovano come in on a few tracks does little other than introduce unfair contrast, though, even if Carter's exuberant sprint through his 'Where Or When' solo is nicely countered by Flip's deliberate shifting down a gear.

Harry Pickens

PIANO

Gainfully employed as lecturer and teacher as much as he is as a sideman, Pickens seems to be in residence at Louisville University, where this solo recital was recorded.

****(*) Passionate Ballads**
Double-Time DTRCD-146 *Pickens (p solo).* 2/98.

Eleven very familiar standards, all done at a steady ballad tempo: doesn't sound like a terribly enthralling record. Pickens often plays the tunes in a notably eloquent manner, though. He sounds like the teacher he is – harmonies and structures are laid systematically bare and, since we know just where the melodies are going to go, the ear is focused on how he gets there. But the consistently ponderous tempos have little to mitigate them in terms of touch or ingenuity. There is some explosive coughing in the audience which the microphones catch all too vividly.

Enrico Pieranunzi (born 1949)

PIANO

The Italian is an elegant performer and an often unexpected composer, a storyteller who very seldom lapses into abstraction. His piano style is a hybrid of Bill Evans and Herbie Hancock, with boppish accents that recall Bud Powell rather than Monk.

*****(*) Isis**
Soul Note 121021 *Pieranunzi; Art Farmer (flhn); Massimo Urbani (as); Furio Di Castri (b); Roberto Gatto (d).* 81.

***** Deep Down**
Soul Note 121121 *Pieranunzi; Marc Johnson (b); Joey Baron (d).* 2/86.

*****(*) What's What**
yvp 3006 *Pieranunzi (p solo).* 6/85.

****(*) Moon Pie**
yvp 3011 *Pieranunzi; Enzo Pietropaoli (b); Roberto Gatto (d).* 5–6/87.

*****(*) No Man's Land**
Soul Note 121221 *Pieranunzi; Marc Johnson (b); Steve Houghton (d).* 5/89.

***** Seaward**
Soul Note 121272 *Pieranunzi; Hein Van de Geyn (b); André Ceccarelli (d).* 3/94.

***** Trioscape**
yvp 3050 *Pieranunzi; Piero Leveratto (b); Mauro Beggio (d); Francesco Petreni (d, perc).* 2 & 5/95.

***** Flux And Change**
Soul Note 121242 *Pieranunzi; Paul Motian (d).* 95.

***** Ma L'Amore No**

Soul Note 121321 *Pieranunzi; Enrico Rava (t); Lee Konitz (ss); Piero Leveratto (b); Mauro Begio (d); Ada Montellanico (v).* 2/97.

***** Don't Forget The Poet**

Challenge CHR 70065 *Pieranunzi; Bert Joris (t, flhn); Stefano D'Anna (ss, ts); Hein Van de Geyn (b); Hans Van Oosterhout (d).* 3/99.

Pieranunzi is not an extravagant virtuoso; his self-effacing manner recalls something of Hancock, but he uses all the groundbreaking modern discoveries in modality, rhythm and the broadening of pianistic devices to his own ends. As with the Space Jazz trio, which he apparently leads with bassist Pietropaoli, he is an exponent of post-modern jazz, sounding perfectly self-aware yet concerned to introduce elements of abstraction and emotional flow alike. Perhaps the two discs to seek out are the ruminative but pointedly argued solo set, *What's What*, and the excellent trio session, *No Man's Land.*

Seaward is perhaps the straightest blowing album of Pieranunzi's current catalogue and thus the most welcoming for listeners who don't know his work. There are a few originals on the set, but it is dominated by standards and jazz tunes: 'Stardust', 'I Hear A Rhapsody', Wayne Shorter's joyous 'Footprints'. Van de Geyn and Ceccarelli are a dream rhythm-section, loose, disciplined and responsive.

Isis is transformed by the presence of Farmer and by a couple of gorgeous solos from the ill-fated Urbani, who provided Pieranunzi with a solo voice that chimes perfectly with his own. The duo album with Motian contains no fewer than 23 standard and original songs arranged into two long suites. It's a persuasive combination and is handled with imagination and skill.

Ma l'amore no is essentially a collaboration with the singer, Ada Montellanico, but it is also graced by two fine guest instrumentalists in Rava and Konitz, both of them playing as beautifully and elegantly as ever. Most of the songs are Italian, though universally communicable; but the addition of the neglected Gershwin classic, 'Who Can I Turn To', and the Beatles' 'Fool On The Hill' adds a special dimension. The quintet session from 1999 was the first of its kind for some years, and Enrico takes the opportunity to showcase 11 compositions which range from the gently ironic lyricism of 'With My Heart In A Song' to the more acerbic language of the title-piece.

Billy Pierce (born 1948)

TENOR AND SOPRANO SAXOPHONES

A one-time Jazz Messenger, Pierce emerged from the Boston scene in the early '80s to play a part in the new New York jazz of that era.

****(*) The Complete William The Conqueror Sessions**

Sunnyside SSC 9013D *Pierce; James Williams, James 'Sid' Simmons (p); John Lockwood (b); Keith Copeland (d).* 5/85.

**** Give And Take**

Sunnyside SSC 1026 D *Pierce; Terence Blanchard (t); Mulgrew Miller (p); Ira Coleman (b); Tony Reedus (d).* 6-10/87.

***** Equilateral**

Sunnyside SSC 1037 D *Pierce; Hank Jones (p); Roy Haynes (d).* 1/88.

***** One For Chuck**

Sunnyside 1053 *Pierce; Bill Mobley (t, flhn); Mulgrew Miller (p); Ira Coleman (b); Alan Dawson (d).* 4/91.

Pierce, who made these rather mixed dates for Sunnyside, seems to be slipping back into the margins of late. He is a workmanlike player not much given to grand statements, and this gives his records an unpretentious feel but makes it hard for them to stand out from the throng. Nothing memorable happens on either of the two earlier discs: it's especially disappointing with regard to *Give And Take*, which from moment to moment suggests a genuinely heavyweight encounter but over the long stretch delivers nothing much at all. *Equilateral* starts out with two advantages: the presence of Jones and Haynes, still among the best props a musician could hope to find alongside him, and the unusual bass-less instrumentation, which isn't intrusive but at least proposes a different balance from the usual. The programme is nearly all standards, and on some of them – particularly 'You Don't Know What Love Is' and 'Come Rain Or Come Shine' – Pierce summons the gravitas of greater players without surrendering too much of himself.

One For Chuck sets Pierce in front of another top-flight rhythm section, and with the useful if undemonstrative Mobley beside him he shoulders the weight of the session impressively enough, even dismissing the others for a couple of *a cappella* solos. In the end, though, it makes no deeper impression than the other Sunnyside dates.

Billie Pierce (1907–74)

PIANO, VOCAL and

De De Pierce (1904–73)

CORNET

Billie was a touring pianist in the '20s, but she settled in New Orleans with her husband, De De, and they worked frequently as a duo, securing a measure of fame in revivalist circles in the '60s and early '70s.

***** Billie Pierce (With Raymond Burke)**

American Music AMCD-76 *Billie Pierce; Jack Delany (tb); Raymond Burke (cl); Roy Zimmerman (p); Chink Martin (b); Paul Barbarin (d).* 7/50–3/54.

**** With Kid Thomas Valentine 1960**

504 CD 36 *Pierce; Pierce; Kid Thomas Valentine (t).* 60.

****(*) In Binghamton, N.Y.**

American Music AMCD-80 *Pierce; Pierce.* 10/62.

****(*) In Binghamton, N.Y. Vol. 2**

American Music AMCD-81 *Pierce; Pierce; Albert Warner (tb); Willie Humphrey (cl); Cie Frazier (d).* 10/62.

****(*) In Binghamton, N.Y. Vol. 3**

American Music AMCD-82 *As above.* 10/62.

***** New Orleans: The Living Legends**

Original Blues Classics OBC 534 *Pierce; Pierce; Albert Jiles (d).* 1/61.

The Pierces were a familiar husband-and-wife team in New Orleans dance-halls for many years. Though De De also worked in the Preservation Hall Jazz Band, it's his recordings with Billie that remain his best legacy; so far, these have made it to CD. The session with Kid Thomas sitting in as guest is very ramshackle-sounding, but the spirit abides, and it's a curiously moving document even with all the fluffs and effortful playing. The Binghamton discs were cut at a college concert. The music is often all over the place, and De De is so unpredictable that Willie Humphrey, who arrives in time for the second volume, seems to be trying to watch him all the time; but, for all the rackety playing, it becomes oddly exhilarating after a while.

On the OBC, the programme is nearly all simple, slow blues, taken at a stately tempo by Billie's piano, with cornet elaborations by De De that are modestly ambitious: he plays a much more improvised line than the standard New Orleans lead horns and, though he cracks a lot of notes and sometimes loses his way, he works hard at his playing. Billie's high vocals are sometimes hard to take, since she hardly varies her delivery (she once accompanied Bessie Smith, but sounds more like Clara Smith). This is deep New Orleans music.

On her own – or, at least, without De De – Billie's earlier recordings are something of a surprise. She sounds stronger and more individual, a blend of classic-blues singer and the more songful voice that she used for the likes of 'When The Saints'. The 1950 session, a private recording, features her in the sole company of Raymond Burke, who's in playful form, and the 1954 band date has her fronting a capable group with everyone in high spirits. None of these tracks was issued before and the sound in this first mastering is more than good enough – a pleasing discovery.

Nat Pierce (1925–1992)

PIANO

Pierce was working in Boston as an arranger when he joined Woody Herman in 1951; he then moved to New York and did much session-work as an arranger and led rehearsal bands. He returned to the Herman fold in the '60s, and in the '70s he co-led the Juggernaut orchestra with Frank Capp. He was a frequent dep for pianist-bandleaders like Kenton and Basie, who trusted his style implicitly.

***** The Ballad Of Jazz Street**

Hep 2009 *Pierce; Clark Terry, Burt Collins, Danny Stiles, Jerry Kail (t); Eddie Bert, Jim Dahl, Jimmy Cleveland, Bill Elton (tb); Dick Meldonian (cl, as); Keith Zaharia (as); Paul Gonsalves, Paul Quinichette (ts); Marty Flax (bs); Turk Van Lake (g); Sonny Dallas (b); Mousie Alexander (d).* 3/61.

****(*) 5400 North**

Hep 2004 *Pierce; Dick Collins (t); Bill Perkins (ts); Bob Saravia (b); Frank Capp (d); Mary Anne McCall (v).* 5/78.

Currently a rather dowdy showing for this much-liked arranger and pianist who depped for Basie and MD'd for Woody Herman. He led many rehearsal bands in New York around the early '60s and one of them was recorded in March 1961, though not originally for commercial release. Five agreeable flag-wavers, with good spots for Gonsalves, Bert and the others, lead to the three-part title-theme, a very effective Ellington pastiche. The sound is rather dusty and it's a comment on the quality of the music that it stands up so well.

The 1978 set comes from an open-air concert and is a bit of a filler. Collins and Perkins are sound enough, and Pierce's piano is sunny, but this sort of thing wasn't what he did best, and McCall's vocals are a struggle.

Dominique Pifarély

VIOLIN

Familiar as a sideman with Louis Sclavis, the violinist here works in a modern duo context.

***** Poros**

ECM 539724-2 *Pifarély; François Couturier (p).* 4/97.

This one turned up in a thoroughly marine and watery batch from ECM, released at the same time as episode two of Ketil Bjornstad's *The Sea*. It suffers from the same lack of focus. *Poros* is defined in an essay by Sarah Kofman as a kind of existentially indistinct course across water, a means of blazing a trail where none exists, 'a space where any way that has been traced is immediately obliterated, which transforms any journey into a voyage of exploration, which is always unprecedented, dangerous and uncertain'. That isn't what one hears from Pifarély and Couturier. Any suggestion that this is a tough and exploratory exercise in free improvisation is quickly dispelled. Though working further out than in his long-standing association with Louis Sclavis, Pifarély still sounds very anchored in a style and an idiom. The title-piece throws up ideas that could usefully have been explored further and may yet be, but it seems to confound its own premisses by building in familiar reference-points, tags and phrases which keep players and listener on course. Significantly, the best thing on the record is a performance of 'Warm Canto', composed by the man who kicked off ECM, Mal Waldron.

Dave Pike (born 1938)

VIBRAPHONE, MARIMBA

Born in Detroit, Pike began on drums and later switched to vibes. West Coast work in the '50s preceded a move to New York in 1960 and three years with Herbie Mann. His band, The Dave Pike Set, became popular in Germany, where he lived for several years, and then he toured South America. Pike returned to California in the mid-'70s.

***** Masterpieces**

MPS 531 848 *Pike; Volker Kriegel (g, sitar); J.A Rettenbacher (b, clo); Eberhard Weber (b); Peter Baumeister, Marc Hellman (d); Onias Carmadell, Djalma Correa, Edson Emetario De Santana (perc).* 1 & 8/69, 6/70, 3/71, 6/72.

(*) **Pike's Groove

Criss Cross CRISS 1021 *Pike; Cedar Walton (p); David Williams (b); Billy Higgins (d).* 2/86.

*** **Bluebird**

Timeless SJP 302 *Pike; Charles McPherson (as); Rein De Graaff (p); Koos Serierse (b); Eric Ineke (d).* 10 & 11/88.

A 1961 album declared *It's Time For Dave Pike*. It was and it wasn't. Pike's approach was both backward-looking, to the styles of Milt Jackson and Hamp, and also irretrievably time-locked, and though he returned to the States and to favour after an increasingly barren sojourn in Europe he's never quite recovered from the feeling that he's merely a bebop copyist on a lumpy and stiff-jointed instrument.

While in Europe, where he settled in 1968, he formed the Dave Pike Set, of which Kriegel was the effective co-leader and -writer. *Masterpieces* is putting it a touch optimistically, though there's plenty to enjoy on these 13 selections from *Noisy Silence – Gentle Noise, Four Reasons, Live At The Philharmonie, Infra Red, Album* and *Salomao*, and if you have any of the originals, then you probably also have a droopy moustache and a line in crushed-velvet jackets. Tunes like 'Mathar' (a sitar epic from Kriegel) and 'Walkin' Down The Highway In a Raw Red Egg' are entertainingly datelined. The live 'Nobody's Afraid Of Howard Monster' (written by bassist Rettenbacher) is good value, and only the closing 'Salomao' palls at 13-plus minutes.

Following his return to the United States, Pike mainstreamed himself to a degree, threw off some of the trendier accessories and addressed his undoubted talent to straight, swinging jazz. *Pike's Groove* is lifted almost bodily by a superb rhythm section. The eight Parker themes on *Bluebird* are delivered with great professionalism but without much understanding. McPherson has always been one of the more convincing copyists, but here he seems hampered by a rather drab approach. A curiosity.

Roberta Piket (born 1965)

PIANO

The daughter of a composer who studied in Vienna, Piket is a composer–pianist in a familiar post-bop style.

*** **Unbroken Line**

Criss Cross CRISS 1140 *Piket; Scott Wendholt (t); Donny McCaslin (ts, ss); Javon Jackson (ts); Michael Formanek (b); Jeff Williams (d).* 4/96.

Piket's father took part in the Spanish Civil War and then emigrated to America after the great War Against Fascism. Roberta imbibed a solid classical training from him and she retains a capacious understanding of all sorts of modern music. Her compositional gifts are evident from the very start of *Unbroken Line*. 'Brookland' sounds derivative of too many things for it to be indebted to any of them. 'The Long, Long Wait' was seemingly inspired by a session Piket heard involving her premier jazz influence, Richie Beirach; it's a meditation on *ars longa, vita brevis*, heartfelt and touched by a proper humility. 'Daily Affirmation' is based on Charlie Parker's 'Confirmation', though it develops in directions Bird hadn't dreamt of. The closing 'Unbroken Line' is a fierce blowing tune, and belated evidence that the composer isn't overly hung-up on her classical training. Only two standard treatments, but Irving Berlin's 'Always' and the pairing of 'You'll Never Walk Alone' and 'Some Enchanted Evening' are sensitively reworked. The supporting cast are excellent, almost all of them veterans of Criss Cross's superb catalogue. Jackson brings the most, in terms of ideas, but this is a showcase for the leader.

Charles Pillow

TENOR SAXOPHONE, SOPRANO SAXOPHONE, OBOE

Reed-playing all-rounder, with big-band experience and classical study already under his belt.

***(*) **Currents**

A Records AL713108 *Pillow; Tim Hagans (t); Ben Monder (g); Michael Holober (p); Chuck Bergeron (b); Adam Nussbaum, Matt Wilson (d).* 5/96.

'Giant Steps' on oboe; this, as they say, is protesting one's originality a little too much, except that the talented Pillow has worked out a convincing language for the double-reeded horn. His interplay with drummer Matt Wilson (who steps in for the able Nussbaum on two cuts) is fascinating. The interest was developed in a classical context at the Eastman School, but Pillow, a native of Baton Rouge and now a seasoned professional, cut his jazz teeth on the road with the Woody Herman Orchestra and Maria Schneider's big band. Like bassist Bergeron, he has become a key player in A's burgeoning catalogue. Perhaps the most impressive aspect of this first shot as leader is Pillow's skill as a composer and arranger. Somewhat predictably, he airs all three of his horns over the first three numbers, but what catches the ear more readily than the faintly eldritch wail of the oboe on 'The Trouble With Camelot' or indeed his tightly controlled and accurately pitched soprano on 'Matchmaker Matchmaker' is the sheer imagination that has gone into his arrangement of the standard. The same applies to 'I Only Have Eyes For You', which comes at the end of this fine set, just before 'Giant Steps'. The key men apart from the leader are Monder and Nussbaum, but Tim Hagans's appearance on three tracks lifts the dynamics considerably. A genuinely innovative player with a wonderful bugler's simplicity, he can also bring an acidulous edge, a little rub of lemon and salt round the edge of the glass. 'Your Eyes' is a beautiful piece, but for bravura front-line playing 'Even Steven' is the key track.

Courtney Pine (born 1964)

TENOR, ALTO AND SOPRANO SAXOPHONES, BASS CLARINET, FLUTE, ALTO FLUTE, KEYBOARDS

Born in London, Pine played funk and reggae as a teenage saxophonist, then became interested in John Coltrane. Always an organizer, he became a focal point for young London musicians in the '80s, helped form the Jazz Warriors big band and had an unprecedented hit album with his debut release. He has since investigated various jazz and popular black-music forms and remains among the most widely known of British jazz musicians.

****(*) Journey To The Urge Within**

Island 842687 *Pine; Kevin Robinson (t); Ray Carless (bs); Julian Joseph (p); Roy Carter (ky); Orphy Robinson (vib); Martin Taylor (g); Gary Crosby (b); Mark Mondesir (d); Ian Mussington (perc); Susaye Greene, Cleveland Watkiss (v).* 7–8/86.

***** The Vision's Tale**

Island 842373 *Pine; Ellis Marsalis (p); Delbert Felix (b); Jeff Tain Watts (d).* 1/89.

***** Within The Realms Of Our Dreams**

Island 848244 *Pine; Kenny Kirkland (p); Charnett Moffett (b); Jeff Tain Watts (d).* 1/90.

***** To The Eyes Of Creation**

Island 514044 *Pine; Dennis Rollins (tb); Keith Waite (f, perc); Bheki Mseleku (p); Julian Joseph (ky); Tony Rémy, Cameron Pierre (g); Wayne Batchelor (b); Mark Mondesir, Frank Tontoh, Brian Abrahams (d); Thomas Dyani, Mamadi Kamara (perc); Cleveland Watkiss, Linda Muriel (v).* 92.

***** Modern Day Jazz Stories**

Antilles/Talkin' Loud 529 428 *Pine; Eddie Henderson (t); Geri Allen (p, org); Mark Whitfield (g); Charnett Moffett (b); Ronnie Burrage (d, perc); D.J Pogo (turntables); Cassandra Wilson (v).* 95.

British readers will have had a difficult time of it separating Pine the musician from Pine the marketing phenomenon since, starting around the time of the first record above, he was fruitfully presented as the face of young British jazz in the 1980s. It was a move that brought unprecedented attention to the music in the UK, but the fall-out has been a certain suspicion among many who are wary of media hype, as well as a problem in evaluating the records purely on their musical worth. Fortunately, Pine himself is a saxophonist of clear and outstanding capabilities: whatever flaws these records may have, his own contributions are of a consistently high standard. *Journey To The Urge Within*, his hit debut, emerges as a sampler for young British talent, with Joseph, Mondesir, Crosby, Robinson and Watkiss all making interesting debut appearances and Pine leading the pack. There are good moments, and the sense of a group of players seizing their time is palpable, but inexperience and fragmentation take their toll on the record's impact and it tends to work out as a series of half-fulfilled gestures. The follow-up set is currently deleted, but both that and *The Vision's Tale* hinted at a talent that was taking a long time to work out what it wants to do. *The Vision's Tale* (a penchant for obfuscatory titles shouldn't put listeners off) put Pine in the hands of an American rhythm section, with Marsalis at his wiliest in accompaniment, and if a reading of 'I'm An Old Cowhand' seems to be asking for trouble – Pine has often been accused of balling together a host of unassimilated influences, though Coltrane rather than Rollins is the leading name involved – it's dealt with in enough good humour to lend a self-deprecatory note.

Within The Realms Of Our Dreams puts him back with a formidable American rhythm section, and there's no hint of difficulty for the leader. Originals such as 'Zaire', which features a double-time passage on soprano which is quite breathtaking in its technical aplomb, and 'The Sepia Love Song' show a maturing sense of detail as a composer, and 'Una Muy Bonita' and 'Donna Lee' sweep through Coleman and Parker with ferocious accomplishment. There are still too many notes, and too few ideas channelled down a single route to resolution, but this multifariousness of idea and delivery is clearly Pine's way.

To The Eyes Of Creation marks another change – Pine must be among the most restless talents of his generation – by bringing in a fresh interest in electronics, texture and timeless folk arcana, as in the bells, flutes and shakers of the closing 'The Holy Grail'. This set is something of a pan-global journey, taking in Africa, ska ('Eastern Standard Time'), a universal soul ballad ('Children Hold On'), bridging interludes, and a fair amount of intense saxophone. With a widescreen-soul production, the music sounds big and impressive but, like most travelogues, it's more a patchwork of interesting sights and sounds than a convincingly resolved statement.

Modern Day Jazz Stories finds Pine consolidating and developing this strain. He has the experience of Geri Allen to guide him and 'hook up the chords' and, with guest contributions from Eddie Henderson and Mark Whitfield and the ferocious bass of Charnett Moffett to root the whole session, it has a powerfully evocative quality. Pine keeps the turntable manipulations relatively far back in the mix, and places himself just left of centre. Interestingly, the most effective single track on the album is a setting of Langston Hughes's poem, 'The Negro Speaks Of Rivers', which Pine originally heard on a Gary Bartz album of the early 1970s. He has made something very contemporary and immediate out of Hughes's timeless lines.

***** Underground**

Talkin' Loud 537745-2 *Pine; Nicholas Payton (t); Cyrus Chestnut (ky); Mark Whitfield (g); Reginald Veal (b); Jeff Tain Watts (d); DJ Pogo (turntables); Jhelisa (v).* 3/97.

His vision is so populous and rich in its ambition that the plain truth is that Pine doesn't make enough records. Eight albums in nearly 15 years is simply an inadequate showing for a man who should be as prolific as David Murray in his pomp. That way we could rack one like this in his enjoyable second division, instead of having to settle for it as his premier set in a five-year period (a new album was due as we went to press). 'All the tracks started off as breaks or loops from classic records from the period 1964–1997' – but to get the consent would have been cripplingly difficult and expensive, so Pine reharmonized them and re-created them in real time. It was taking the long way round, but the results are often exciting, even thrilling – listen to what they're getting into on 'Oneness Of Mind'. Yet the track fades just as it's getting going. That sense of the cup being dashed from the lips recurs throughout *Underground*. There are sublime pop melodies like 'Invisible (Higher Vibe)', fragments of impressive solos. DJ Pogo putters around in the background, creating his own underfelt of scratched voices and sounds. Every so often, Pine gets off a head-turning solo. But the album never establishes its own world. Jazz, hip hop, soundtrack music, hip easy-listening – it's all part of Courtney's multi-kulti aesthetic, and you can hear him straining to make it all synthesize. Give this talented man his own label and let him keep on doing it – it might be the only way he'll make his masterpiece.

Armand Piron (1888–1943)

VIOLIN, VOCAL, BANDLEADER

Piron was born in New Orleans and began leading bands there in the first decade of the new century. He joined forces with Clarence Williams in music publishing and only rarely left his native city, continuing to work there until his death.

***** Piron's New Orleans Orchestra**
Azure AZ-CD-13 *Piron; Peter Bocage (t); John Lindsay (tb); Lorenzo Tio Jr (cl, ts); Louis Warnecke (as); Steve Lewis (p); Charles Bocage (bj, v); Bob Ysaguirre (tba); Louis Cottrell (d); Esther Bigeou, Ida G Brown, Lela Bolden, Willie Lewis, Willie Jackson (v).* 12/23–4/26.

For the most part they were recorded in New York, but Piron's band was a New Orleans outfit and as such was one of the few to be documented in the 1920s. This splendid reissue is a model of its kind: the sleeve-notes sum up years of research into the performers' activities, and the remastering of a set of terrifically rare originals is excellent, though a few of the 78s were obviously rather beaten up. That said, the disc isn't a revelation on a par with Azure's Papa Celestin/Sam Morgan disc. Piron's group was a more genteel, proper orchestra, pitching itself somewhere between ragtime, society music and the glimmers of early jazz: though 1923 is early in jazz recording history, they still sound a much less modern band next to Oliver or Fletcher Henderson from the same year (one should compare their treatment of 'Doo Doodle Oom' with Henderson's 1923 Vocalion version). A few tracks, including the very first, 'Bouncing Around', brew up a potent mix of syncopation, with Tio's wriggling clarinet-breaks and Bocage's urbane lead making their mark over an ensemble rhythm that is almost swinging. But there is surprisingly little development between the earliest and the latest tracks by the orchestra. The CD is beefed up with four tracks in which pianist Lewis accompanies blues singer Willie Jackson, and it closes on the charming discovery of a Lewis piano-roll of a title from their second session, 'Mama's Gone, Goodbye'.

John Pisano

GUITAR

Although born in New York, Pisano has played mostly on the West Coast, beginning with the Chico Hamilton group in the 1950s. He did lots of session work, made some duo albums with fellow guitarist Billy Bean (for Decca, so far unreissued) and was closely associated with Joe Pass for many years.

***** Among Friends**
Pablo 2310-956-2 *Pisano; Dori Caymmi (g, v); Joe Pass, Lee Ritenour, Ron Affif, Ted Greene, Phil Upchurch (g); Chuck Berghofer, Andy Simpkins, Jim Hughart, Jose Marino (b); Claudio Slon, Joe LaBarbera, Colin Bailey (d); Jeanne Pisano (v).* 2/91–12/94.

***** Conversation Pieces**
Pablo 2310-963-2 *As above, except add Joe Diorio, Gene Bertoncini (g), Chuck Domanico (b); omit Pass, Affif, Jeanne Pisano.* 6/94–6/95.

A good middleweight in heavyweight company, Pisano is an unassuming can-do kind of a player, perhaps previously best known for his duet work on some of Joe Pass's Pablo albums. Pass himself turns up on a couple of 1991 duets on the first disc, including a lovely 'Take The "A" Train', and the several other duet situations (with or without a rhythm section) all have their pleasing moments. Maybe the best is the simple, almost beatific treatment of 'Over The Rainbow' with Greene. Yet Pisano's reticence in taking the limelight lends a touch of blandness to the disc.

Somehow, even though it uses several other tracks from the same sessions, *Conversation Pieces* is an ounce more lively. Three tracks with Diorio, Domanico and Bailey are a good deal more urgent, and there are two fizzing acoustic turns with Bertoncini. On the minus side are comparatively anonymous conversations with Ritenour and Upchurch. Both discs are likely to find most appeal among guitarists: there's plenty for any aspiring student to study on.

Steve Pistorius (born 1954)

PIANO, VOCAL

Born in New Orleans, Pistorius recorded his first album – of piano ragtime – at the age of twenty, and is an expert on that style and on the various traditional idioms. He has been playing full-time since 1979.

*****(*) T'Ain't No Sin**
GHB BCD-289 *Pistorius; Scott Black (c, v); Jacques Gauthe (cl, as); John Gill (bsx, bj, v); Chris Tyle (d, v).* 89.

*****(*) Kiss Me Sweet**
Stomp Off CD-1221 *Pistorius; Chris Tyle (c, v); Tom Fischer (cl, as); Tim Laughlin (cl); Hal Smith (d); Suzy Malone (v).* 7/90.

In addition to his records with Tyle and Smith as leaders, Steve Pistorius has made these two excellent small-group records of his own. The quintet of the GHB record has a thinnish sound and some of the rhythms get close to the clockwork beat that trad parodists deploy, but much of the music is hot, affectionate, oddly lyrical. There are perhaps too many vocals, shared around the band, although Pistorius's own voice is a likeable one, something akin to Leon Redbone minus the mumbling. The material is a fascinating stack of 1920s' arcana, with items from the repertoires of Louis Armstrong, New Orleans Willie Jackson, Natty Dominique, Don Redman and Jelly Roll Morton, and the horn-playing – Black plays a sweetly strong lead, and Gauthe is all over the clarinet, with a whinnying alto as second string – is perfectly apposite. *Kiss Me Sweet* mixes trio, quartet and quintet tracks on another cheering programme of oddities and faithful trad vehicles. Pistorius himself is a frisky player, clearly out to enjoy himself but aware that this is delicate as well as rude music.

John Pizzarelli (born 1960)

GUITAR, VOCAL

Performed with his father as a guitar duo, then began working as a solo and with his own trio from 1990, gaining extra recognition as a vocalist.

(*) **Hit That Jive Jack!

Stash STB 2508 *Pizzarelli; Dave McKenna (p); Bucky Pizzarelli (g); Hugh McCracken (hca); Jerry Bruno, Gary Hasse (b); Butch Miles, Steven Ferrera (d).* 6/85.

*** **My Blue Heaven**

Chesky JD38 *Pizzarelli; Clark Terry (t, v); Dave McKenna (p); Bucky Pizzarelli (g); Milt Hinton (b); Connie Kay (d).* 2/90.

*** **All Of Me**

Novus PD 90619 *Pizzarelli; Randy Sandke, John Frosk, Anthony Kadleck, Michael Ponella (t); Jim Pugh, Rock Ciccarone, Michael Davis (tb); Paul Faulise (btb); Walt Levinsky, Phil Bodner (as); Scott Robinson (ss, ts, f); Frank Griffith (ts); Sol Schlinger (bs); William Kerr, Lawrence Feldman (f); Ken Levinsky (p); Bucky Pizzarelli (g); Martin Pizzarelli (b); Joe Cocuzzo (d); Gordon Gottlieb (perc, vib); strings.* 91.

***(*) **Naturally**

Novus 63151-2 *As above, except add Clark Terry (t, flhn), Jim Hynes (t), Bob Alexander, Mark Patterson, Wayne Andre (tb), Frank Wess, Harry Allen (ts), Jack Stuckey (bs), Dominic Cortese (acc); omit Sandke, Pugh, Ciccarone, Davis, Bodner, Schlinger, Kerr, Feldman and Gottlieb.* 92.

***(*) **New Standards**

Novus 63172-2 *Pizzarelli; Ted Nash (ts); Ray Kennedy (p, org); Bucky Pizzarelli (g); Jim Saporito (vib, perc); Martin Pizzarelli (b); Tony Corbiscello, Joe Cocuzzo (d); horns, strings, voices.* 93.

*** **Dear Mr Cole**

Novus 63182-2 *Pizzarelli; Benny Green, Ray Kennedy (p); Christian McBride, Martin Pizzarelli (b); John Guerin (d).* 94.

*** **After Hours**

Novus 63191-2 *Pizzarelli; Randy Sandke (t); Harry Allen (ts); Ray Kennedy (p); Bucky Pizzarelli (g); Martin Pizzarelli (b); Joe Cocuzzo (d).* 95.

John Pizzarelli follows in father's footsteps by using a guitar style that owes an obvious debt to paternal influence: quick, clean picking, a Django-like tone and a penchant for the humorous aside in the middle of otherwise terse improvisations. While this makes for solid, gratifying mainstream, Pizzarelli isn't really a young fogey: there's a coolness about his manner which detaches him a little from the material and, while some of his song choices are as neo-classic as one can get, he sounds a little dreamier than the Concord crew of mainstreamers. Besides, he sings – and this is what has determined his career in recent years. Pizzarelli was doing this sort of thing long before the likes of Harry Connick, and his singing and playing are accomplished in their own right; but the tenor of the later records is unmistakably tuned to seeking an audience that likes singers rather than players.

The Stash album is a reissue of an early vocal outing. Pizzarelli and the band have fun with the likes of 'The Frim Fram Sauce', but the manner and production sound elementary next to the sophistication of the Novus records. *My Blue Heaven* is beautifully recorded and shrewdly programmed, with Clark Terry tossing in some characteristic obbligatos and the instrumental pieces – including a very sharp-witted 'Don't Get Around Much Any More' – finding a real, spontaneous zest. *All Of Me* is Pizzarelli's initial stab at the big time: cleverly pitched between the big-band charts and the nucleus of the singer and the rhythm section, it's an artfully realized but legitimate musical success by dint of Pizzarelli's trust of the material. His three original songs are, though, no special achievement. *Naturally* continues the run with splendid results. An unlikely choice such as 'When I Grow Too Old To Dream' is beautifully pitched, 'I'm Confessin' is as delicate a ballad as one could wish for, and 'Nuages' receives a clever update. Pizzarelli sounds self-effacing instead of self-satisfied. But his originals are still a long way behind the standards.

That problem is solved in part on *New Standards*, where Pizzarelli elects to base a programme around new or unfamiliar songs. His own pieces are only so-so, but the others – especially 'Fools Fall In Love', 'I'm Your Guy' (which he at least had a hand in), 'I'm Alright Now' and 'Look At Us' – suit his persona to a 't': smart, hip, but an easy-going romantic under the skin. The arrangements are again nicely poised between small groups and horn and string embellishments, and the warm but not too foggy studio sound is ideal. Probably his best record.

Dear Mr Cole looks promising: with the nucleus of Green, McBride and Pizzarelli himself as a dream trio, Nat Cole tunes as the repertoire, and a perfectly intimate studio-mix, this was set up to be a classic. But the opening 'Style Is Coming Back In Style' with the other rhythm section is so blissful that the rest is almost a disappointment and, as cleverly as the trio plays, it's just a shade too neo-classic to wholly convince, despite some lovely moments.

After Hours moves the concept to a full-fledged ballad album. Sandke and Allen blow sweetly apposite obbligatos and John's working trio play with intuitive rightness: on a couple of less obvious choices such as 'Coquette' and 'Mam'selle', the pitch is flawlessly right. Because he's singing so quietly and without undue emphasis, it's easy to miss how effective Pizzarelli has become at this music, too. Yet the album still seems to slip uneventfully by – through its very nature, perhaps. If some of these gradings look harsh, it should be noted that in many ways this is the best sequence of vocal records of recent times, even though the individual albums miss out on masterpiece status.

*** **Our Love Is Here To Stay**

RCA 67501-2 *Pizzarelli; Tony Kadleck, Ron Tooley, Jim O'Connor, Glenn Drewes (t); Jim Pugh, John Mosca, Wayne Andre, Alan Raph, Ed Neumeister (tb); Andy Fusco, Chuck Wilson, Gary Keller, Scott Robinson, Kenny Berger, Tom Christiansen (reeds); Peter Gordon, John Clark (frhn); Ray Kennedy (p); Martin Pizzarelli (b); Dennis Mackrel, Danny D'Imperio (d).* 2/97.

Another good one, another not-quite-great one, and, while some have ridiculed Pizzarelli's discography, his class and poise seem unfazed. Don Sebesky's arrangements return him to a big-band setting and it's a kick to hear them go at 'Avalon' and

'Kalamazoo'. Some of the charts, though, are as rote as they come. Again, much more voice than guitar, but we like the singing, too.

***** Meets The Beatles**

RCA Victor 74321 61432-2 *Pizzarelli; Ray Kennedy (p); Martin Pizzarelli (b); Tony Tedesco (d); Sammy Figueroa (perc); strings, brass, woodwind.* 98.

It's no use, it can't be done – The Beatles simply can't become jazz, or even swing-styled pop. There's just too much baggage, too much freight of expectation and received memory. But all that said, Pizzarelli makes the best go of jazzing John 'n' Paul that anyone ever has. From the sambafied smooch of 'Here Comes The Sun' to the swinging four of 'Things We Said Today', it's very playable indeed, and the singer approaches the material without condescension or incomprehension. He's feeling it. But it still can't be done.

*****(*) P.S. Mr Cole**

RCA Victor 09026-63563-2 *Pizzarelli; Harry Allen (ts); Ray Kennedy (p); Martin Pizzarelli (b).* 1/96–97.

Recorded before the Beatles project, for the Japanese market, this has subsequently received a wider release. It's Pizzarelli's last word on Nat Cole, from 'Walkin' My Baby Back Home' to 'Embraceable You' (with a live favourite, 'I Like Jersey Best', slipped in at the end). Harry Allen strolls in for two solos. Pizzarelli and his pals can probably play this in their sleep by now, and the mood is suitably horizontal – but it's luxury-class music-making, so impeccable (and so trusting in the great material) that you soak in it like it's a warm bath. Which doesn't seem too bad.

****** Kisses In The Rain**

Telarc 83491 *As above, except omit Allen.* 6/99.

A new label, but nothing new in the music – John's dusting off more old standards, coming up with new ones of his own, and they're trying to get the feel of how the band do a live set in the context of a studio session. But nothing has to be new, anyway, since the pleasure in the record is how good this group have become at making such repertory their own. Pizzarelli's getting a bit old to be a young smoothie at this point, but fogeydom doesn't beckon either. It's character and wit that rule this music. Aw, give the man four stars – he's earned them.

King Pleasure (1922–1981)

VOCALS

Born plain Clarence Beeks, Pleasure won an amateur night at the Apollo in 1951 and went on to scoop enormous success with 'Moody's Mood For Love', a vocalese version of James Moody's saxophone solo on 'I'm In The Mood For Love'. But his career didn't last long and there are no records after the '50s.

*****(*) King Pleasure Sings**

Original Jazz Classics OJC 217 *Pleasure; Ed Lewis (t); J.J Johnson, Kai Winding (tb); Charles Ferguson, Lucky Thompson (ts); Danny Bank (bs); Jimmy Jones, John Lewis, Ed Swanston (p); Paul Chambers, Percy Heath, Peck Morrison (b); Kenny Clarke, Joe Harris, Herbie Lovelle (d); Betty Carter, Jon Hendricks, Eddie Jefferson, The Dave Lambert Singers, The Three Riffs (v).* 12/52, 9/53, 12/54.

***** Golden Days**

Original Jazz Classics OJC 1772 *Pleasure; Matthew Gee (tb); Teddy Edwards, Harold Land (ts); Gerald Wiggins (p); Wilfred Middlebrooks (b); Earl Palmer (d).*

Eddie Jefferson claimed to have invented the practice of fitting lyrics to bop solos, but it was Pleasure who garnered the praise and what cash was going. (Just to confirm Jefferson's luck, he was blown away outside a Detroit club in 1979, just as his career was reviving; Jefferson, Jon Hendricks and The Three Riffs all feature on two 1954 tracks from *Sings*.) The earlier of the two OJCs is shared with Annie Ross, who sings the classic vocalization of Wardell Gray's 'Twisted', along with 'Moody's Mood For Love' and Pleasure's 'Parker's Mood' the best-known vocalese performance. Pleasure has something of Ross's honeyed smoothness of tone but combines it with a more biting articulation that can sound remarkably like Charlie Parker's alto saxophone (or, more frequently, the smooth tenor sound of Teddy Edwards and Lucky Thompson). Using less sophisticated arrangements and generally less witty lyrics than Jon Hendricks's for Lambert, Hendricks and Ross, Pleasure more often relies on the quality of the voice alone. The accompaniments are generally good, but the Quincy Jones backings to 'Don't Get Scared' and 'I'm Gone' are exceptional.

Golden Days is a fine record, marked out by some adventurous improvisation from Pleasure and rugged solos from both Land and Edwards. Vocalese has always been something of an acquired taste, though interest in it has grown over the last few years. These two records are key texts in the revival.

Paul Plimley

PIANO, MARIMBA

Canadian pianist. Studied classical music in his youth, but since the late '70s has been immersed in Canada's free-music scene and has toured and performed internationally with a wide range of players. Also composes; has led an octet.

***** Both Sides Of The Same Mirror**

Nine Winds 0135 *Plimley; Lisle Ellis (b).* 11/89.

Although the tune titles ('Moving The Twin Entrances Of Light', 'Reflections Of A Persistent Mirage') suggest a trip into New Age wonderland, Plimley's music – he is a veteran of Canada's free-jazz movement – is a good deal thornier than that. He and Ellis have worked together for many years, and a thread of experience runs through all the playing here. Plimley's employment of clusters suggests Cecil Taylor or Don Pullen without really bowing to either man, and when he picks up the marimba mallets for 'Mirage' he expands on the percussiveness of his approach with a fine understanding of his own strengths. Ellis counterpoints with *arco* or guitar-like lines, and on a version of Jimi Hendrix's 'Third Stone From The Sun' he sounds as impressive a soloist as Plimley. The CD seems a little long at almost an hour – a concentrated 40 minutes might have made a better impression – but it's a solid introduction to these players.

*****(*) Noir**

Victo CD 022 *As above, except add Bruce Freedman (ss, as), Gregg Bendian (d).* 10/92.

A bristling contrast to the previous set, but hardly less absorbing. Basically a trio record – Freedman adds lyrical alto to one track, harsher soprano to another – the music is driven as much by Bendian as by the other two: his disruptive attacks on 'Noir' and 'Jill Cyborg' shatter any introversion between piano and bass. But all three fashion a free-thinking trio music that climaxes with the intense eloquence of the closing 'Fade To Grey Then Blue'. Plimley's music continues to demand a wider audience.

****** Density Of The Lovestruck Demons**

Music & Arts CD 9906 *Plimley; Lisle Ellis (b); Donald Robinson (d).* 6/94.

*****(*) Everything In Stages**

Songlines SGL 1503-2 *Plimley (p solo).* 4/95.

Plimley continues to create a formidable body of work. The trio set is a very accomplished manifesto from another Plimley group: besides the usual crop of originals, there are new meditations on Coleman's music, and the level of interaction among the three men is astonishingly vivid and sophisticated, from the quietest moment to the loudest. *Everything In Stages* is another contrast: 17 pieces, many very brief episodes, many examining one, often minute, aspect of the piano – technique, vocabulary, structure. Plimley makes one think about the whole nature of the instrument here, its physicality and resonances, and though it can be tough going it's many times more absorbing than the typical piano record.

*****(*) Sensology**

Maya MCD9701 *Plimley; Barry Guy (b).* 1/95.

****** Ivory Ganesh Meets Doctor Drums**

Songlines SGL 1523-2 *Plimley; Trichy Sankaran (perc).* 4/86–4/98.

*****(*) Safecrackers**

Victor 066 *Plimley; Lisle Ellis (b); Scott Amendola (d).* 1/99.

The meeting with Guy (at a Vancouver concert) is a joyful occasion, for all the high-velocity counterpoint. Both players can touch on the academy when they want to, and that introduces such elegant episodes as the beginning of 'Short Steps Until It Finally Dawned', but the impression of brief, snatched-up tracks such as 'Hand Held Hot Coals' is of sheer high spirits. There is an excellent gag at the end of the record, too, luckily explained in the sleeve-notes.

Ivory Ganesh Meets Doctor Drums is world jazz of a high order. Sankaran brings the almost courtly grace of his tabla rhythms to a platform which Plimley builds and demolishes and rebuilds with his usual ebullience, and the miracle is that this is one (ahem) fusion which doesn't seem forced, overcooked or blighted by mutual incomprehension. It helps that Plimley thinks hard about the piano's status as a percussion instrument, but he's helped enormously by Ganesh's superb responsiveness to each situation. Each man also gets some intriguing solos and, aside from the enormous 'Jhampalaya II', most of the tracks are actually quite short and resolved in very specific ways.

His latest trio debuts on *Safecrackers*. New drummer Amendola fits right in, and this is probably also the best sound Plimley's had in a studio. A surprising bit of audio-vérité at the end of 'An Exhilaration Of Larks, And Their Discovery Of Fire' (yes, his titles are becoming too arch for their own good) and an unexpected sign-off with Claude Thornhill's 'Snowfall'. Plimley likes to surprise, and he's still doing it.

Mika Pohjola (born 1972)

PIANO, HARPSICHORD

Finnish pianist who divides his time between a base in New York and European work.

***** On The Move**

MikaMusik MMK97 *Pohjola; Chris Cheek (ss, ts); Matt Penman (b); Roberto Dani (d).* 11/96.

The young Finn's music adapts well to this otherwise international quartet (recorded in New York). 'A Farmer's Dream' is the kind of pastorale that could only come from European backgrounds and, although Cheek's normal province is as US as apple pie, his soft articulation and graceful phrasing suit the setting to a 't'. The record is wonderfully sustained as far as the mischievous tango, 'Muistoja Torkkelinmaelta', but the last 20 minutes are something of an anti-climax, a typical CD-era problem. Pohjola himself plays in a musing post-bop style and he clearly gets on well with Dani and the excellent Penman, whose many subtleties are well captured in the intimate mix.

***** Announcement**

YLE/Radio Vega CDY-628 *As above.* 4/98.

Pohjola has some smart ideas. Into what is essentially a thoughtful post-bop date he stirs quite a few surprises. The most peculiar is the tape loop of some background noise from an Indian eating-house which frames the rich harmonies of 'Indian Resturant' over this oddly effective, clanking beat. The title-piece is an impression of a tribal chant, and 'Hair, Scarf And Fragrance' seems to work off a reggae-like vamp. 'Kids' Song' is also something unexpected. This is all quite modestly presented and, if there's nothing outstandingly memorable in the results, it's a pleasingly quirky attempt at going his own way. Cheek, a reliable voice to have on hand, is also in solid form.

Herb Pomeroy (born 1930)

TRUMPET, FLUGELHORN

Pomeroy worked on the Berklee faculty for 40 years from 1955, and his educational work probably denied him a wider career on record. Early big-band records for Transition, Roulette and United Artists are now rarely sighted. In retirement, he seems ready to do more.

***** This Is Always**

Daring DR 3021 *Pomeroy; Billy Novick (cl, as); Paul Schmeling (p); Jon Wheatley (g); Marshall Wood (b); Joe Hunt (d).* 11/96.

****(*) Walking On Air**

Arbors ARCD 19176 *Pomeroy; Dave McKenna (p); Gray Sargent (g); Marshall Wood (b); Jim Gwin (d); Donna Byrne (v).* 11/96.

Pomeroy is probably still best remembered as a big-band man, having led such a group in Boston for some years in the 1950s. These are easy-going small groups which offer him a modest showing. *This Is Always* is shared with Novick: eight slow pieces, with some nice rarities – Harry Warren's 'I Remember You', for instance, not the famous one by Schertzinger/Mercer. Novick's alto can sound a little like Johnny Hodges on a very low flame, and he and Pomeroy vary the pace fractionally to maintain interest, which they *just* do. *Walking On Air* is rather flat, mainly because Byrne's vocals are unconvincing. She's very good on a dead-slow 'Ill Wind', but the up-tempo tunes are undercharacterized and the band sound indifferent to the situation. Pomeroy himself handles both situations with a sometimes genteel grace.

Valery Ponomarev (born 1943)

TRUMPET, FLUGELHORN

A Muscovite under Clifford Brown's spell, Ponomarev defected in 1973 and joined Art Blakey in 1977. His group, Universal Language, was an interesting hard-bop band of the '80s and '90s.

*****(*) Means Of Identification**

Reservoir RSR 101 *Ponomarev; Ralph Moore (ts); Hideki Takao (p); Dennis Irwin (b); Kenny Washington (d).* 4/85.

***** Trip To Moscow**

Reservoir RSR CD 107 *As above.* 4/85.

Universal Language is a rather wonderful band name for a man who left Russia during the deep freeze of the Brezhnev years in order to play jazz in the West. A version of the story was adapted for the movies in a Robin Williams vehicle called *Moscow on the Hudson*. Less manic than Williams, the trumpeter nevertheless shares a great sense of humour and a palpable joy at being able to play and play freely. *Means Of Identification* is certainly the place to begin with him. As will be seen from the names, Universal Language is a multiracial outfit – black, white, Japanese, Slavic – united by the Esperanto of hard bop. When Ponomarev was with the Messengers, Art let him loose on 'I Remember Clifford' night after night. It's the outstanding performance here, a flowing, feeling solo on what the trumpeter considers to be one of the greatest jazz compositions ever. His admiration is evident, as it is for Art Blakey himself in 'Envoy', a fresh and soulful original. The opening 'Dialogue' pits him against Moore, an exciting duel which recalls the great Blue Note recordings. No surprise that this session was made at the Van Gelder studio in Englewood Cliffs. Originally the group included guitarist Kevin Eubanks, but Takao came in at short notice, apparently sight-read the charts with ease and kept his place. Irwin is a former Messenger, beautifully featured on 'Mirage'. Washington has his moment on 'Dialogue' and keeps things tight throughout.

Almost inevitably, the follow-up isn't quite so forceful. 'For You Only' combines sinew and tenderness, and much of the second album seems devoted to underlining the point that Ponomarev isn't just a fast-valve showman but a player of real expressive range. The point is well made, but one could have done with a little variation in the pace and content.

*****(*) Profile**

Reservoir RSR CD 117 *Ponomarev; Joe Henderson (ts); Kenny Barron (p); Essiet Essiet (b); Victor Jones (d).* 5/91.

Henderson makes an enormous difference to *Profile*, as you'd expect, and his shrewd exchanges with the trumpeter are marked by the kind of wry humour and playfulness that sometimes gets lost in his more brooding work. Ponomarev may switch to flugelhorn once or twice here; either that or his tone has become broader and more resonant in Henderson's company. He also seems inclined to follow the saxophonist and let lines spin out and unravel at very much greater length, notably on a superb version of 'I Concentrate On You', which is one of his key recorded moments. The rhythm section are flawless and the sound very rich and responsive. An excellent disc all round.

****** Live At Sweet Basil**

Reservoir RSR CD 131 *Ponomarev; Don Braden (ts); John Hicks (p); Peter Washington (b); Victor Jones (d).* 7/93.

The trumpeter's love affair with the language of jazz has shown no signs of cooling. This version of Universal Language – though this time the name doesn't actually appear on the disc – is still absolutely in line with its predecessors. What has changed is the subtlety of Ponomarev's conception. 'Friend Or Foe' has a totally surprising twist which everyone concerned negotiates with ease but which might well throw less seasoned players than Hicks or such carefully listening youngsters as Braden. The pianist is a key element on every cut of this crisply registered live session, but he excels himself on 'Be Careful Of Dreams' and the Coltrane-inspired 'Theme For Ernie'. Jones turned out to be a key recruitment. The trumpet/drums duo at the start of 'My Alter Ego' sounds like the Blakey days are back, but with new wrinkles and an even subtler trade on the Russian's heart-on-sleeve Clifford Brown influence. 'My Alter Ego' could mean almost anything or anyone but, like 'Valery's Changes', which kicks off the record, it also points to a shift in his approach, a quiet flirtation with free jazz. He never quite leaves the chords behind, but they are interpreted with a much freer hand and within a much less regular pulse. Intriguing stuff.

***** Live At Vartan Jazz**

Vartan Jazz VJ 006 *Ponomarev; Francesco Bearsetti (ts); Sid Simmons (p); Ken Walker (b); Ben Riley (d).* 2/95.

Vartan Jazz is a club in Denver, Colorado, founded and run by Vartan Tonoian, and broadcasting on the local radio network, KUVO. Hence a series of strong, well-recorded live sets from the label, featuring the likes of Milcho Leviev, Lew Tabackin and Hal Galper. Ponomarev's is the best to date. Apparently he had seen Ben Riley performing in Gorky Park in 1972, shortly before leaving for the States. Having Monk's former sideman in the band must have been a great thrill, and the trumpeter rises to the occasion with some storming playing. 'Long Way From Gorky Park' is an explicit reminder of the moment. The weak links in the group are Bearsetti and Simmons. The former grandstands shamelessly with not a great deal to say, while Simmons is rather too one-dimensional for Ponomarev's subtle themes. The opening 'One For Morgans' is very strong and the two tracks which follow, 'For Better Or For Worse' and 'To Waltz With You', continue in very much the same vein. Apart, though, from a fine reading of Kenny Dorham's 'NY Theme' and the excellent 'Unfinished Business', the set falls into cliché and repetition. One hears Ponomarev trying to get things going in new directions, but it isn't the happiest of blends.

****** A Star For You**

Reservoir RSR CD 150 *Ponomarev; Bob Berg (ts); Sid Simmons (p); Ken Walker (b); Billy Hart (d).* 4/97.

Perhaps the vintage Universal Language to date. Hart is as revelatory as ever, a hugely musical drummer who always has ideas to impart and energy in superfluity. Ponomarev makes it clear that this is a set very much dedicated to the spirit and memory of Art Blakey, perhaps because the 25th anniversary of his arrival in America wasn't so far away. The opening 'Commandments From A Higher Authority' is absolutely in the spirit of the Messengers' great days, a wheeling, driving theme which never quite comes to rest but exudes authority in every measure. 'Uh Oh' was apparently a Blakey vocal mannerism. It's a more jocular idea, and the trumpeter has fun trading figures with Hart. Bob Berg is the key addition to this group, superb on 'Dance Intoxicant' and the long standard, 'We'll be Together Again', adding a warm-toned confidence to every track. Simmons and Walker get to show why they got the call, playing with intelligence and taste, never over-fussy, but subtle when the tune calls for another dimension. Back at Van Gelder's place, the band gets exactly the sound it deserves: rich and ringing, with plenty of space round the horns and kit, but not so much that you feel the guys are working in parallel rather than as a unit. Highly recommended.

Jean-Luc Ponty (born 1942)

VIOLIN, ELECTRIC VIOLIN, KEYBOARDS

Classically trained, Ponty was a violin prodigy who found himself sidetracked by jazz. By the end of the 1960s he had made an international name for himself with festival and club work. Playing with Frank Zappa and the Mahavishnu Orchestra led him into fusion, and his own '70s recordings were pioneer efforts in the idiom. His star waned somewhat in the '80s and '90s, and he has dabbled in a jazz-inflected world music.

****(*) Live At Donte's**

Pacific Jazz 35635-2 *Ponty; George Duke (p); John Heard (b); Al Cecchi (d).* 3/69.

Ponty's earlier work should be better represented than it currently is. He was a pioneer of the violin in both a modern straight-ahead format and in the fusion of the 1970s and '80s. While he acknowledges Stuff Smith and Grappelli as inescapable influences, it's clear from these dusty 1969 tracks that he was more specifically in thrall to Coltrane and the long-form soloists of the decade. His solos have a spiralling excitement and a surprisingly far-sighted feel that suggests he is challenging his formidable technical prowess as he goes. The problem with the record is a very flat sound that does the musicians no favours. Interesting to hear subsequent fusion kingpin Duke as a Tynerish pianist, too, but in truth the rhythm section isn't up to all that much.

***** Aurora**

Atlantic 19158-2 *Ponty; Patrice Rushen (ky); Daryl Stuermer (g); Tom Fowler (b); Norman Fearington (d).* 12/75.

***** Imaginary Voyage**

Atlantic 19136-2 *Ponty; Allan Zavod (ky); Daryl Stuermer (g); Tom Fowler (b); Mark Craney (d).* 7–8/76.

**** Enigmatic Ocean**

Atlantic 19110-2 *Ponty; Allan Zavod (ky); Allan Holdsworth, Daryl Stuermer (g); Ralphe Armstrong (b); Steve Smith (d).* 6–7/77.

***** Cosmic Messenger**

Atlantic 19189-2 *Ponty; Allan Zavod (ky); Peter Maunu, Joaquin Lievano (g); Ralphe Armstrong (b); Casey Scheuerell (d).* 78.

****(*) Mystical Adventures**

Atlantic 19333-2 *Ponty; Chris Rhyne (p); Jamie Glaser (g); Randy Jackson (b); Rayford Griffin (d); Paulinho Da Costa (perc).* 8–9/81.

**** Fables**

Atlantic 81276-2 *Ponty; Scott Henderson (g); Baron Browne (b); Rayford Griffin (d).* 7–8/85.

****(*) Tchokola**

Columbia 468522-2 *Ponty; Yves Ndjock (g); Guy Nsangue (b); Brice Wassy (d); Abdou M'Boup (perc, v).* 91.

*****(*) No Absolute Time**

Atlantic 82500 *Ponty; Wally Minko (ky); Martin Atangana, Kevin Eubanks (g); Guy Nsangue (b); Moktar Samba (d); Abdou M'Boup, Sydney Thiam (perc).* 12/92–3/93.

*****(*) Le Voyage**

Rhino/Atlantic 72155-2 2CD *As Atlantic albums above.* 75–85.

Ponty had always amplified his violin, but by the 1970s he was making it a major part of his aesthetic, trying out echo and other effects to colour an approach which had fundamentally changed little since his earliest recordings. He had recorded a session with Frank Zappa, *King Kong*, in 1969, and Zappa's punishingly difficult kind of instrumental rock was a significant influence on the sort of fusion that Ponty recorded once he signed with Atlantic in 1975. Tunes were built out of complicated riffs or trance-like harmonic patterns, with modal solos played at blistering speed to create the excitement. Unusually, though, the music is more interesting than the average fusion band of the period allows, since the lyrical tang of the leader's violin sustains the mood of most of the records.

The earlier records, especially *Aurora* and *Imaginary Voyage*, are the best, if only because the sound of the group is at its freshest. Players like Stuermer and Zavod are capable technicians, but it's always Ponty whose fire ignites the music. Some of the Atlantics from this period are currently out of print, and after *Mystical Adventures* the music grew a little stale. *Fables* returns to a quartet format, but Ponty seems uninterested in the overall sound. A label switch brought him to Columbia, with mixed consequences: *Tchokola* was an attempt at a new kind of fusion, with Afropop players from different schools, and the results were an interesting but uneasy alliance. *No Absolute Time*, though, was his best record for years. Jazz-rock is cast aside in favour of a glittering kind of electric world-music: all the tracks simmer over a polyrhythmic base, drawn equally from human hands and drum machines, and Ponty's violin and keyboard effects are hummably rich and pleasing.

Atlantic have gone back to their vaults and compiled *Le Voyage*, an excellent two-disc set with several of the highlights from his many albums for the label. Hard to better this for a cross-section of Ponty's particular kind of fusion over the years.

****(*) Live At Chene Park**

Atlantic 82964-2 *Ponty; Chris Rhyne (ky); Jamie Glaser (g); Baron Browne (b); Michael Barsimanto (d).* 6/96.

Ponty returns to Atlantic with a solid if basically uneventful live set, the kind of thing that comes in the middle of a contract rather than at the beginning. The material's a nice blend of nuggets from the various parts of a fruitful career, but its rather old-fashioned feel is a step backwards. We await more from this likeable and gifted musician.

Odean Pope (born 1938)

TENOR SAXOPHONE

Pope was born in the intriguingly named Ninety Six, North Carolina, but moved to Philadelphia as a child. He worked with Max Roach and in an inventive band called Catalyst before forming his own Saxophone Choir.

*****(*) The Saxophone Choir**

Soul Note 121129 *Pope; Robert Landham (f); Julian Pressley, Sam Reed (as); Bootsie Barnes, Arthur Daniel, Bob Howell (ts); Joe Sudler (bs); Eddie Green (p); Gerald Veasley (b); Dave Gibson (d).* 10/85.

****** The Ponderer**

Soul Note 121229 *Pope; Byard Lancaster, Julian Pressley, Sam Reed (as); Glenn Guidone, Bob Howell, Middy Middleton, John Simon (ts); Joe Sudler (bs); Eddie Green (p); Tyrone Brown, Gerald Veasley (b); Cornell Rochester (d).* 3/90.

***** Epitome**

Soul Note 121279 *As above, except omit Lancaster, Veasley, Rochester; add Robert Landham (as); Dave Burrell (p); Craig McIver (d).* 10/93.

'I tried to imagine what it would sound like if I played at the bottom range of my instrument like Coltrane played at the top.' This is pretty much what Odean Pope has done. If he sounds less like his fellow-Philadelphian (the City of Brotherly Love shaped Trane, even if he wasn't born there) and more like Sam Rivers or even Jimmy Heath, Pope is nevertheless profoundly influenced by some less exposed aspects of Coltrane's approach: its concern with ensembles rather than its torrential outpouring of personal feelings, its rootedness rather than its God-bothering excursions. Pope is a profoundly modest individual who aligns himself with the pianist Ibn Hassan Ali's belief that Coltrane's music is a not-quite-conscious expression of some higher state. Behind Pope's Saxophone Choir is the fiery, inchoate music of *Ascension*, but also something of the voicing of the later Ellington orchestras, as they negotiated with 'world music'.

Pope has not been prolific. He rehearses the Choir meticulously and then records live in the studio with no overdubs. The charts are intricate and demanding, a broad orchestral sound punctuated with episodes from a roster of players who, like the leader himself, are not well known outside this context. Byard Lancaster, also a Philadelphian, has an earthy wail redolent of Jackie McLean and Ornette Coleman, and he blends perfectly with Pope's multiphonics on 'The Ponderer', title-piece on the best of the Choir albums. Like the others, it has a strong internal consistency and is almost written like a continuous symphonic work, from 'Overture' to the Spanish-tinged 'Phrygian Love Theme'. Eddie Brown's 'One For Bubba' serves as an encore piece and a chance for the rhythm section to do its stuff.

Pope has tremendous gifts as a composer, layering rhythmic figures and harmonies in a way that parallels some of Ornette's 'harmolodic' experiments, but still making sense; Ellington again doesn't seem far away on 'The Saxophone Shop', the slightly ragged opener on the 1985 album. *Epitome* is the most ambitious but also the weakest of the bunch. The addition of Dave Burrell was inspired, opening up a rich, almost gospelly vein, and the recruitment of Craig McIver, in place of Rochester, was to be a particularly fruitful one for Pope. 'Zanzibar Blue' is the outstanding track.

*****(*) Collective Voices**

CIMP 124 *Pope; Tyrone Brown (b); Craig McIver (d).* 8/96.

Unexpected to hear Pope in this context after years with the Choir. Brown and McIver are alumni, but Pope's association with the bassist goes all the way back to a criminally undervalued band called Catalyst which they founded in 1972 (vinyl browsers might be lucky enough to turn up their stuff even now). Brown was the inspiration for the Eddie Brown original, 'One For Bubba', which ends *The Ponderer*, and his funky, loose-shouldered bass-lines are the foundation of this small group. He contributes three strong originals to this session: one of them a tribute to classical bassist Gary Karr, and another, 'El Monte', arranged as a duo for bass and saxophone.

Pope has worked in various Max Roach groups in recent years, but he is not immediately thought of as a small-group player. The Coltrane influence is ever more deeply and inextricably enmeshed in a very personal idiom. On 'Collective Voices' and the two takes of 'You And Me' one can chart the extremes, the one dry and quite abstract, the other keeningly immediate and expressive. The overall impression, as ever, is of music that has been very carefully thought out. There are no throwaway gestures and, if one occasionally longs for a more unfettered and spontaneous expression, it's worth being reminded that there are bins full of cut-price free-for-all jazz in every store, but very little that reflects as much care and perspicacity as this.

***** Changes & Chances**

CIMP 191 *Pope; Dave Burrell (p).* 1/99.

Two fascinating individualists who seem to come from opposite ends of the musical spectrum, yet find a great deal of common territory. If the history of jazz really is 'Three Four vs. Four Four' as the opening cut suggests, then the result is an amicable and thoroughly stimulating draw. 'Changes' and 'Chances' are no less thoughtful exercises, but a touch academic in conception. The really expressive writing is by Burrell, who is restricted to just two numbers, 'Full Moon In The Village' and 'Early On'. Interesting to put this disc on after one of Burrell's duets with David Murray, a saxophonist with a more groove-driven concept. This, by contrast, is rather esoteric and in places rather forbidding. Unusually, it was recorded away from CIMP's home base (the Spirit Room at Rossie, New York), down in Chester, Pennsylvania. The sound is rather different but still bare-bones and unadorned.

Krzysztof Popek

ALTO FLUTE

The talented Pole has made something of a speciality of the lower- and warmer-pitched alto flute and he makes of it a convincing solo voice. He favours colour over complexity and expressiveness over speed.

***** Places**

Power Bros PB 00115 *Popek; Piotr Wojtasik (t, flhn); Volker Greve (vib); Paul Imm (b); Cezary Konrad (d).* 97.

***** Letters & Leaves**

Power Bros PB 00139 *Popek; Piotr Wojtasik (flhn); Wojciech Niedziela (p); Jacek Niedziela (b); Adam Buczek (d).* 98.

The slow, watercolour blend of alto flute and flugelhorn gives *Letters & Leaves* a lovely tonality. Popek's two originals are further reminder of what a hold Miles Davis has on the musical imagination in Poland, but one suspects that he has also been listening to Joe Farrell's still underrated work with Chick Corea. There is tremendous communication with Wojtasik, who has also emerged as a formidable artist in his own right, and their ability to trade and pass on solo ideas is worthy of a relay team. 'Estate' and 'Black Narcissus' get the album off to a deceptively understated start, and it's only as the set advances that one realizes how effortlessly this group swings as well.

Popek's ability to play within and across more challenging time-signatures is a key aspect of *Places*. Strictly speaking, this is a joint release with vibist Greve, who doubles on synth instruments as well, but it still feels like the flautist's record. 'In Search Of A Quiet Place' is gorgeous, and there is a lovely version of 'The Peacocks' as well. The recording again puts the emphasis on colour and subtle gradations of dynamics, but there is no mistaking the jazz credentials of all these players.

Michel Portal (born 1935)

SAXOPHONES, CLARINET, BASS CLARINET, BANDONEON

Portal grew up in Bayonne, France, and earned his reputation working with visiting Americans in Paris, ranging stylistically from swing and bop to the avant-garde. He is also a highly accomplished classical musician, with a very pure and controlled tone on all his instruments. He is the favourite clarinettist of composers like Pierre Boulez and Luciano Berio.

*****(*) ¡Dejarme Solo!**

Dreyfus Jazz Line 849231 *Portal (solo saxophones, clarinets, percussion, accordion).* 79.

In 1970 Portal was working with John Surman, and a decade later he too was exploring solo performance. The solo record will certainly recall some of Surman's work, not least in its confident incorporation of folk themes, but there is a jaggedness and angularity to Portal's attack that are very different from the Englishman's softer and more accommodating accents. The record and the individual tracks are quite brief and enigmatically poetic. There are no wasted gestures. Portal has a remarkable ability to make even extremes of sonority, as from sopranino to contrabass clarinet, sound perfectly natural and idiomatic. It is a great pity that he did not release more material in this vein.

***** Cinémas**

Label Bleu LBLC 6576 *Portal; Paolo Fresu (t); Laurent Dehors, Guillaume Orti (sax); Rita Marcotulli (p, syn); Andy Emler (syn); Ralph Towner (g); Nguyen Lê (g, syn); Richard Galliano (acc); Michel Benita, Linley Marthe, François Moutin (b); Tony Rabeson, Aldo Romano (d, perc); Mino Cinelu, Doudou N'Diaye Rose (perc); Juan Jose Mosalini et son Grand Orchestre de Tango.* 95.

Portal describes this project as 'various kinds of music for the cinema outplayed with jazz musician friends'. *Out*playing may distort a little in the translation, but it is clear that Portal has given his chums free rein to reinterpret these seven movie themes and one television score, the music for Michel Polac's much-admired *Droit de réponse*. This is played with just Mino Cinelu in accompaniment. Other tracks, like 'Champ d'honneur', find Portal in a horn-led sextet, or backed by Doudou N'Diaye Rose's tambours, or indeed, on 'Docteur Petio', with a whole tango orchestra. The results are beguiling and thoroughly unexpected, though the sheer range of styles may be bewildering for anyone who hasn't encountered Portal's brand of stylistic eclecticism before.

****** Dockings**

Label Bleu LBLC 6604 *Portal; Markus Stockhausen (t); Bojan Zulfikarpasic (p); Bruno Chevillon, Steve Swallow (b); Joey Baron (d).* 6/97.

A quiet masterpiece from an all-star band. Portal's daring in using such strong musical personalities so delicately and sparingly more than pays dividends, and it would be hard to imagine a record of such poise and grace. Baron and Swallow happily move between insistent ostinato figures and more or less free time, leaving Chevillon to anchor the basic metre. Bojan Z is as usual tasteful and responsive, and the two horns are deployed with great subtlety. Though there isn't a vibraphone, the most obvious model for the sound is the Dolphy group of *Out To Lunch!* (Eric is the dedicatee of the second track) but rendered ever more abstractly lyrical. Stockhausen has the penetrating intensity of a Freddie Hubbard, but with a softer and more plangent quality. The mourning dove timbre of Portal's clarinet on 'Dolphy', building in intensity over Baron's pattering accompaniment, is matched only by their interaction on 'Ida Lupino', this time with Portal on bandoneon. A truly marvellous record, thoughtfully swinging and emotionally focused.

Position Alpha

GROUP

Swedish all-sax quartet/quintet of the 1980s and '90s, a European pioneer of the form.

♛ ** The Great Sound Of Sound**

Dragon DRCD 307 *Mats Eklof (bs, bsx, cl, tb); Sture Ericson (as, ts, ss, f); Thomas Jaderlund (as, ss, bcl, f); Jonny Wartel (sno, ss, as, ts, cl, t); Jonas Akerblom (ss, as, bs, alto horn).* 10/84.

***** Greetings From The Rats**

Dragon DRCD 199 *As above, except add Erik Balke (saxes, v), Per Ekblad (d); omit Eklof, Wartel.* 6/90.

****(*) Titbits**

Dragon DRCD 252 *As above, except Eklof and Wartel return; add Jonny Axelsson (perc); omit Balke and Akerblom.* 8/93.

One of the great saxophone-band records, *The Great Sound Of Sound* is welcome at last on CD. By going one better than the host of saxophone quartets – and having a fifth member – Position Alpha created a huge sonority that is employed to devastating effect on a set recorded live in Gothenburg. Vast pieces like 'The Dada Zone' (and 'The Mama Zone') are comical in one way, disturbing in another: when one of their knees-up tempos dissolves into a flaring argument between the horns, it sounds like jazz tradition going sour before us. The tango, 'Riviera II', shows they can beat the big-band-section imitations beloved of the American sax groups with their eyes shut, and their two Mingus pieces are madly exhilarating, as bleakly humorous as the composer's own. There are stunning individual contributions when one of them gets hold of a solo, but it's the great sound of their sound that counts, recorded with raw immediacy and perfectly surviving the transfer from vinyl. A great favourite of ours which should be rescued from obscurity.

The rest of their output is inexplicably disappointing. Almost immediately, they began to move away from their first format, with very mixed results. *Greetings From The Rats* interspersed recitations by band members into the music and introduced a drummer, to no great purpose; there are a few real successes, such as 'Lexikon', but not enough. *Titbits* finds the group a shadow of its old self. Another live set, and this time the drummers often threaten to take over altogether; the saxophones sound distant and uninvolved.

Chris Potter (born 1970)

TENOR, ALTO AND SOPRANO SAXOPHONES, BASS CLARINET, ALTO FLUTE

Born in Columbia, South Carolina, Potter studied at Manhattan School and was gigging with Red Rodney when barely into his twenties. He has since become a prolific sideman and has already made many discs under his own name.

*****(*) Presenting Chris Potter**

Criss Cross Jazz 1067 *Potter; John Swana (t, flhn); Kevin Hays (p); Christian McBride (b); Lewis Nash (d).* 12/92.

*****(*) Sundiata**

Criss Cross Jazz 1107 *Potter; Kevin Hays (p); Doug Weiss (b); Al Foster (d).* 12/93.

***** Concentric Circles**

Concord CCD 4595 *Potter; Kenny Werner (p); John Hart (g); Scott Colley (b); Bill Stewart (d).* 12/93.

***** Pure**

Concord CCD 4637 *Potter; Larry Goldings (p, org); John Hart (g); Larry Grenadier (b); Al Foster (d).* 6/94.

Potter is growing into one of the major saxophonists of today. The astonishingly confident and full-blooded debut shows his prowess with any one of his chosen horns – there's amazingly little to choose between his alto (which he's subsequently given up) and tenor playing, both of them muscular in the post-bop manner but full of surprising stylistic twists that make one think of the artists of both Parker's generation and the elegant elaborations of a Benny Carter or a Hodges. The breakneck opener, 'Juggernaut', is a typical young man's manifesto, but just as impressive are the various approaches to Monk's 'Reflections', Davis's 'Solar' and the five originals by the leader. One could single out Potter's consistently powerful tone, his reluctance to go too far out for effect or the thematic weight applied to all his improvisations; it's the way all this is combined that is impressive. He also gets the best out of the sometimes erratic Swana as a front-line partner, and Hays, McBride and Nash are a superb team. *Sundiata* is a shade behind: a little of Potter's playing exuberance seems to have been held back, and on a set-piece like 'Body And Soul' his lines of thinking are a mite too calculated to convince. That said, there's still plenty of terrific music. Foster, Weiss and Hays don't miss any tricks, and when the group take on another immortal tenor situation by tackling Rollins's 'Airegin' there's a sense of new adventure to go with Potter's insistent classicism.

The first Concord albums, though, remain somewhat disappointing. Despite Potter's best intentions and obvious hard work, both seem over-produced and smothered. Good compositions like 'Lonely Moon' and 'Bad Guys' suffer from surroundings in which the arrangements and tempos sound airless and effortful. Where Potter gives himself some space, as on 'El Morocco', the opener on *Concentric Circles*, the fluency and detail of his playing are still a marvel; and both discs are worth hearing just for his own good spots. But the doubled-up horns, doubtful tunes (there's a particularly unfortunate take on 'Fool On The Hill' on *Pure*) and general feeling of weightiness tell against both discs. One longs to hear Potter in an unencumbered *Newk's Time* sort of setting.

****** Chris Potter / Kenny Werner: Concord Duo Series Vol. 10**

Concord CCD 4695 *Potter; Kenny Werner (p).* 10/94.

And here it is. Potter and Werner go at some of these duos like a couple of boy racers. 'Istanbul (Not Constantinople)' is very fast and funny. But the main point here – with due respect to Werner, who plays excellent things – is to hear Potter at full stretch and in clear space, surprisingly freeish at some points, always concerned with the weight of his sound, and eliding bar lines and turning handsome phrases much in the manner of the young Rollins. He plays soprano on two and bass clarinet on one, but the tenor's the thing, and it's interesting to hear how *much* he plays – rather than soloing and resting, both men are playing together almost constantly. The results are witty, full-blooded and with a serious 'modern' bent, since the tunes are either originals, tough jazz pieces or oddball standards.

*****(*) Moving In**

Concord CCD 4723 *Potter; Brad Mehldau (p); Larry Grenadier (b); Billy Hart (d).* 2/96.

Although Mehldau was a hired gun for the date, this is an intriguing meeting between two of the sharpest players of their generation. The pianist leaves centre-stage to Potter but manages to get in some of the most telling solos, distilling his usual inquiring lyricism into brief, intense passages. Potter sounds very fine and, though some of his writing (the only non-original is 'A Kiss To Build A Dream On') is a trifle cryptic, the delivery is grand and powerful enough to spin a convincing whole out of a disjunctive collection of pieces.

*****(*) Unspoken**

Concord CCD 4775 *Potter; John Scofield (g); Dave Holland (b); Jack DeJohnette (d).* 5/97.

Potter does his inevitable all-star date and makes it sound easy. 'Seven Eleven' and 'Et Tu Brute?' are brainy blowing vehicles which sum up an aspect of the saxophonist's approach: he likes form but always finds ways to get round it. One could argue that his bandmates are close to the record-too-far zone: sometimes there's the feeling that we've heard Sco, Dave and Jack do this groove so often that it's a comfortable stroll where it should be an urgent sprint. As quartet music, though, this is cut and delivered at a very high level, and the two tunes which the guitarist sits out give Potter the chance to seal his stature.

*****(*) Vertigo**

Concord CCD 4843-2 *Potter; Joe Lovano (ts); Kurt Rosenwinkel (g); Scott Colley (b); Billy Drummond (d).* 4/98.

Potter's latest for Concord is another step in 'helping me get to the next level'. As fine as many of the records under his own name are, nothing feels like a flat-out masterpiece so far, and his numerous sideman appearances betoken a player who loves to take gigs but is in some ways shy of asserting himself as the major personality on a record. Rosenwinkel (who worked with Potter in the Paul Motian Electric Bebop Band) is one of the most challenging players he's recorded with, and he makes more sense in this context than the ubiquitous Lovano, whose appearance on three tracks is more of a distraction than a help to the leader. Potter's solo intro to 'Act III, Scene I' sets out his stall, but the subsequent piece itself is an undeveloped episode. Better – outstanding, in fact – are the knotty improvisations he conjures out of the likes of 'Fishy'. There's still a studiedly cool quality to Potter's writing and group arranging, but the improvising he spins out of it remains rich and satisfying.

Bud Powell (1924–66)

PIANO

It was a life and career clouded by physical and mental illness, and by the death of a brother, Richie, in the same car accident that took Clifford Brown, but during its short, troubled span Bud Powell created some of the most intense piano jazz in the literature. He grew up in New York City and from the age of six-teen, sponsored by Thelonious Monk, was jamming at Minton's Playhouse, the crucible of bebop. Though he adopted certain devices of older piano-players Art Tatum and Teddy Wilson, Monk was his main influence. Powell attempted to extend his linear, horn-derived, but still thoroughly pianistic approach by using unfamiliar intervals. At its greatest and also at its most troubled, his music is dark and alienated. Much of this is purely harmonic, but it also reflects the chronic mental disturbance Bud suffered after receiving a beating – racially motivated – in 1945, from which he never entirely recovered.

****** The Complete Bud Powell On Verve**

Verve 521669-2 5CD *Powell; Ray Brown, George Duvivier, Percy Heath, Curley Russell, Lloyd Trotman (b); Art Blakey, Kenny Clarke, Osie Johnson, Max Roach, Art Taylor (d).* 5/49–2/51, 54–56.

****** The Ultimate Bud Powell**

Verve 539788-2 *As above.* 49–56.

*****(*) The Best Of Bud Powell On Verve**

Verve 523392-2 *As above.* 49–55.

The chronology of Bud Powell's issued records is slightly complex, and some of his very earliest work is documented at the end of this entry because it belongs with the material collected by his friend and protector, Francis Paudras. It was, in any case, an intermittent career and, more than most of his peers – certainly more than Parker – Bud suffered on the stand. Good and bad, 'early' and 'late' are inextricably mixed. However, the sheer erratic brilliance of his Blue Note recordings has tended to cloud the remarkable work that Powell did for Norman Granz. The Verve set documents his solo playing just before that catastrophic breakdown of 1951, and takes him through to rather calmer waters. There is no indication that neglect was ever part of Powell's problem. He was well looked after by Verve and they have done him proud with this magnificent five-CD package.

Powell's virtuosity shines through the bustling 'Parisian Thoroughfare' (a piece which, like 'Un Poco Loco', always precisely reflects his mood at the moment of playing) and 'A Nightingale Sang In Berkeley Square', which draws heavily on a Tatum influence. No single sesssion on this set really outweighs the Blue Notes below, but cumulatively and collectively this sits beside them, one of the pillars of this most complex man's lifework.

Selected by fellow pianist Chick Corea, the *Ultimate* compilation is an excellent introduction to Bud's Verve output and an ideal purchase for anyone who doesn't want to shell out for the (inevitably pricey) full set. The best-of set contains a lot of overlap – 'Dance Of The Infidels', 'Parisian Thoroughfare', 'Tempus Fugue-It' – but perhaps inevitably gives more emphasis to standards than to Bud originals.

****** The Amazing Bud Powell: Volume 1**

Blue Note 781503 *Powell; Fats Navarro (t); Sonny Rollins (ts); Tommy Potter (b); Roy Haynes (d).* 8/49, 5/51.

****** The Amazing Bud Powell: Volume 2**

Blue Note 781504 *Powell (p solo), and with George Duvivier, Curley Russell (b); Max Roach, Art Taylor (d).* 5/51 & 8/53.

***** Birdland '53**

Fresh Sound FSCD 1017 *Powell; Oscar Pettiford, Frank Skeete, Charles Mingus (b); Sonny Payne, Roy Haynes (d).* 2 & 3/53.

*****(*) Jazz At Massey Hall**

Original Jazz Classics OJC 111 *Powell; Charles Mingus (b); Max Roach (d).* 5/53.

****** The Complete Blue Note And Roost Recordings**

Blue Note 830083 4CD *Powell; Fats Navarro (t); Curtis Fuller (tb); Sonny Rollins (ts); Curley Russell, Tommy Potter, George Duvivier, Paul Chambers, Sam Jones, Pierre Michelot (b); Max Roach, Roy Haynes, Art Taylor, Philly Joe Jones, Kenny Clarke (d).* 47–63.

Despite the linking name and numbered format, the four Blue Note CD transfers can quite comfortably be bought separately; indeed *Volume One* – with its multiple takes of 'Bouncing With Bud' (one of which was previously on *The Fabulous Fats Navarro: Volume 1*), the bebop classic, 'Ornithology', and Powell's own barometric 'Un Poco Loco' – was out of print for some time, and the fourth volume was issued only in 1987, after which the whole series was made available again at a very acceptable mid-price. *Three* and *Four* have now disappeared again, but they have to some extent been superseded by the magnificent *Complete* which is a must for every Powell enthusiast in the land and is denied a crown only because it does have its dark and troublous moments and isn't perhaps the kind of thing you'd want to spend extended periods of time with. The multiple takes of 'Un Poco Loco' are perhaps the best place for more detailed study of Powell's restless pursuit of an increasingly fugitive musical epiphany. 'Parisian Thoroughfare' contrasts sharply with the unaccompanied version, above, and is much tighter; Powell had a more-than-adequate left hand; however, since he conceived of his music in a complex, multi-linear way, bass and drums were usually required – not for support, but to help proliferate lines of attack. The quintet tracks are harshly tempered, but with hints of both joy and melancholy from all three frontmen; Navarro's almost hysterical edge is at its most effective, and Powell plays as if possessed.

Volume 2 contains one of the most famous Powell performances: the bizarre, self-penned 'Glass Enclosure', a brief but almost schizophrenically changeable piece. There are also alternative takes of 'A Night In Tunisia', 'It Could Happen To You', 'Reets And I' and 'Collard Greens And Black Eyed Peas' (better known as 'Blues In The Closet', see below). *Jazz At Massey Hall* is the rhythm section's spot from the classic Parker/Gillespie concert in Toronto, which has become a trig point for bop fans. (Any lucky dog who owns the 12-CD compilation of Mingus on Debut will already have it.) If for no other reason, these tracks redirect attention to the enormous influence all three players had on bebop. Powell's schizophrenic opposition of delicate, high-register lines and thudding chords is most obvious on 'Cherokee'. He displaces 'Embraceable You' entirely, losing his two colleagues in the middle choruses as he works out his own romantic agony.

***** From Birdland (New York City 1956)**

[*sic*] Musidisc 550202 *Powell; Oscar Pettiford (b); Roy Haynes (d).* 2/53.

Some mistake surely? Well, yes. These live tracks, confidently attributed to Birdland and three years later, are identical to the dates of 7 and 14 February, which were taped at the Royal Roost. Even the personnel is wrong and it shouldn't take a seasoned bebop listener too long to work out that they're not listening to Paul Chambers and to a much lighter and busier drummer than Art Taylor. Not the best recording of the period. Some of those below are better; but an interesting set, and the two longish standards performances – 'Tea For Two' and 'Lover Come Back To Me' – throw light on Bud's debt to Tatum and Teddy Wilson.

****** Inner Fires**

Discovery 71007 *Powell; Charles Mingus (b); Roy Haynes (d).* 53.

A better bet all round. These tapes, made at Club Kavakos in Washington, DC, were in the private collection of Bill Potts until 1982, when they were released on Elektra Musician. The great bonus of the CD set is a brief five-minute interview with Bud, but it doesn't need that to make it a compelling session. He plays out of his skin for most of the hour, and the long versions of 'Little Willie Leaps' and 'Salt Peanuts' are simply masterful, a genius at the office.

***** Strictly Powell**

RCA 51423 *Powell; George Duvivier (b); Art Taylor (d).* 10/56.

*****(*) Swingin' With Bud**

RCA 13041 *As above.* 2/57.

The RCA recordings with Duvivier and Taylor are, by contrast to the Blue Notes, much lighter, less inward and, as the title rightly claims, more conventionally swinging. There was a tour in between the two sessions which may account for the more expansive mood of the later set. The first of the pair has an oddly mawkish quality in places and a strangely abject dependency on phrases borrowed from Tatum, Wilson and even George Shearing. For anyone who looks to Powell for bleak and unyielding intensity, these albums may turn out to be a disappointment, but there are interesting originals, like 'Croscrane' on *Strictly*, and cuts like 'Almost Like Being In Love' and 'In The Blue Of The Evening' on *Swingin'* suggest the kind of artist he might have been, had the shadows not crowded him. There's even a lighter edge to 'Oblivion' and 'Another Dozen', both of which are peppered with tiny, mock-classical quotes.

****** Bud Plays Bird**

Roulette 8 37137 *As above.* 10 & 12/57, 1/58.

Roulette was the label associated with Birdland, and these newly discovered masters, uncovered by the tireless Michael Cuscuna, are the most significant addition to the Powell discography since the release of Francis Paudras's extensive memorial album of Powelliana. Appropriately enough, given the provenance, all the material (except for 'Salt Peanuts') is a Parker composition. This is one of the most allusive and far-reaching of all Powell's recordings. He has rarely demonstrated his sheer musical intelligence so clearly, freely associating between harmonically or melodically similar materials, at times almost eliding passages which are too familiar and replacing them with new ideas, as on 'Relaxing At Camarillo' and the finger-breaking 'Shaw 'Nuff'. His introduction to 'Yardbird Suite' is actually the opening of Tadd Dameron's 'Our Delight'; 'Big Foot' (aka 'Drifting On A Reed') invokes

Dizzy's 'Oop-Pop-A-Da' and (as Ira Gitler very perceptively notes) Allen Eager's 'Meeskite' as well. 'Ornithology' and 'Scrapple From The Apple' are both magnificent, coming from the later and better December and January sessions, by which time the trio seems to have got its balance back. Powell plays inspired piano throughout, but it seems to have taken time to get Duvivier and Taylor, and particularly the bassist's characteristic low-end lines, accurately recorded. There are a number of incomplete and rejected takes from this session. Perhaps they will be issued in future in a more compendious issue, but for the moment applause to Cuscuna and Roulette for releasing a well-balanced album, and not an unedited slice of archive. All Bud Powell fans will want this record.

****** The Amazing Bud Powell: The Scene Changes**
Blue Note 46529 *Powell; Paul Chambers (b); Art Taylor (d).* 12/58.

The cover photograph is heartbreakingly symbolic: a lowering Bud looks down at sheet music on the piano in front of him, rapt, private, shut away with his thoughts, while round his left shoulder a little boy peers guardedly, like his own lost younger self. These 1958 performances for Blue Note were an attempt to rekindle the fires. All the material is original and, though most of it harks back to the bop idiom rather than forward to anything new, it contains some of his most significant statements of any period. 'Comin Up', of which there is also an alternative take, is in the released version his longest studio performance, and one of his most exuberant and playful, almost Latinate in feel. 'Down With It' is generic bebop and not a particularly effective idea, a long melody-line over orthodox changes, and only really distinguished for Chambers's fine *arco* solo. There was an earlier tune called 'Crossin' The Channel'; this, though, is Bud's alone and is the most formally constructed piece in the set, the one item that marks him down as a significant composer. 'The Scene Changes' is the final track on the original LP. It's a curious piece in that it looks back more than forward, almost as if the next scene were fated to be like the last. So it was to prove in Bud's life.

***** The Complete Essen Jazz Festival Concert**
Black Lion BLCD 760105 *Powell; Coleman Hawkins (ts); Oscar Pettiford (p); Kenny Clarke (d).* 4/60.

Announced by MC Joachim Berendt as the Oscar Pettiford Trio, it's not until the third track and Pettiford's superb introduction to 'Willow Weep For Me' that the nominal leader begins to assert himself. Powell has already got in two brisk solos, with only a couple of misfingerings on the hectic 'Shaw 'Nuff'. A few minutes later, the bassist is referring to Powell, putative composer of 'John's Abbey', as 'your favourite'. Hawkins (the other claimant for that credit) comes in for the last three tracks. He'd played 'Stuffy' many times before, but it's rare to hear him on 'All The Things You Are', which gets an unusually jaunty reading and some nice stretching of tempo on later choruses, closing with the familiar bop arrangement. The sound is well balanced and clean, and Powell seems to have lucked out on a decent instrument for a change.

*****(*) Round About Midnight At The Blue Note**
Dreyfus Jazz Line 849227 *Powell; Pierre Michelot (b); Kenny Clarke (d).* 4/61.

Michelot and fellow-exile Clarke are as attentive as courtiers, and Bud himself sounds unusually focused and responsive to what they in turn are doing, frequently making space for Michelot's miniature counter-melodies. Very much a straight bebop gig, it also points strongly to Bud's debt to Thelonious Monk, which is evident on 'Monk's Mood', 'Round Midnight' and 'Thelonious'. Was God in the house that night?

***** A Tribute To Cannonball Adderley**
Columbia CK 65186 *Powell; Idrees Sulieman (t); Cannonball Adderley (as); Don Byas (ts); Pierre Michelot (b); Kenny Clarke (d).* 12/61.

*****(*) A Portrait Of Thelonious**
Columbia CK 65187 *Powell; Pierre Michelot (b); Kenny Clarke (d).* 12/61.

Two sessions produced in Paris by Cannonball Adderley. His role was more complicated than the average producer's for, in addition, the first record is a tribute to him, and he also plays on one previously unheard track. The collaboration with Byas was a happy one for Bud, who was in better shape at this time than he had been in a couple of years, and certainly he is playing with confidence and passion. The trumpeter plays on only a few of the tracks and the quartets are frankly better. Byas's pre-bop stylings and instinct for the blues don't always sit entirely easily with Bud's approach, but they manage to broker some common ground and Bud puts more blues feel into his playing than usual. 'Jackie, My Little Cat' appears in an alternative take which is actually better than the release version, and there is a previously unissued retake of 'Cherokee' which has a lot going for it as well, not least that cameo by Cannonball. Sulieman makes his most significant intervention on the Dameron tune, 'Good Bait', tackling it with aplomb. 'All The Things You Are' is awash with memories of days with Bird and Dizzy, as saxophonist and piano player swap quotes, and doubtless reminiscences as well.

Recorded two days later, the Monk record is no less accomplished. Powell had been in on this particular story almost from the beginning; at nineteen, as a member of the Cootie Williams Orchestra he performed on the first recorded version of 'Round Midnight' and had subsequently gone on to become the other major piano innovator in the bebop revolution. The eight tunes recorded (there is also an unreleased take of 'Squatty') come from pretty much across the spectrum of Monk's output. 'Monk's Mood' is the longest track and one of the very best, with feeling support from Michelot, who it is known practised and rehearsed on his own for some time before these sessions and who certainly sounds absolutely on song for them. Clarke is his usual relaxed but hard-driving self and on 'Ruby, My Dear' he excels himself, playing with taste and imagination. These were rather special moments in Powell's life. In the city which had become his other home, with sensitive playing companions and a producer who knew the material inside out as well, he could hardly fail, though in the past equally well-starred sessions had come to nought. A shame we have had to wait so long for this stuff, but we're glad it's here now.

****(*) At The Golden Circle: Volume 1**
Steeplechase SCCD 36001 *Powell; Torbjørn Hultcranz (b); Sune Spangberg (d).* 4/62.

(*) **At The Golden Circle: Volume 2

Steeplechase SCCD 36002 *As above.*

(*) **At The Golden Circle: Volume 3

Steeplechase SCCD 36009 *As above.*

** **At The Golden Circle: Volume 4**

Steeplechase SCCD 36014 *As above.*

*** **Budism**

Steeplechase SCCD 30007/9 3CD *As above.* 4 & 9/62.

We're now firmly in the era of an important discographical subgenre: the Bud Powell-live-in-Europe album. There are a great many of these. Some are good, others awful, but the majority don't really stand up on their own terms. Steeplechase have long been guilty of excessive documentation. One sharply edited disc from the 19 April 1962 gig would have been more than adequate. The Copenhagen session finds Powell wavering between the hesitant and the near-brilliant, without ever quite capturing the quality of the previous decade. The rhythm section play about as much part in the music as Rosencrantz and Guildenstern do in *Hamlet* – though, like most Scandinavian players, they seem well enough versed in the idiom. Volume 3 has a second version of 'I Remember Clifford' from later in the residency; the last three all come from 23 April and are of more than passing interest, but by this stage the whole exercise seems rather redundant. Four volumes of Powell at his *best* would still call for stamina.

There is no certainty about the dating of the material on *Budism*. With the exception of ten tracks which are known to come from the autumn residency, there is no firm dating; however, listening to the tracks one by one, instinct suggests that they may well all come from the later period. There are a few small rhythmic devices which don't seem to be audible on the earlier sessions, most notably a sharp trill near the start of 'Dance Of The Infidels' on disc three (one of the definite September tracks), which crops up again on 'Epistrophy' and 'Off Minor' on the uncertainly provenanced disc one. Amorphous as the changes are, one might fudge it by saying that *Budism* is a more 'Monkish' selection, stylistically speaking, than the earlier Steeplechases. That may well recommend it.

*** **Bouncing With Bud**

Delmark DD 406 *Powell; Niels-Henning Orsted Pedersen (b); William Schiopffe (d).* 4/62.

Recorded three days after the later Golden Circle session, this has the pianist nosing again at 'I Remember Clifford', apparently dissatisfied with something in the theme. Otherwise it's quite predictable fare, played with discipline but not much passion. This material was originally issued on Sonet, with just one track ('Ruby My Dear', absent from this issue) released on Delmark.

*** **Bud Powell In Paris**

Discovery 70830 *Powell; Gilbert Rovère (b); Kansas Fields (d).* 2/63.

Reissued with two additional tracks, this is a solid, uncomplicated Bud performance. The only improvisations of any length are 'Body And Soul' and 'I Can't Get Started'. All the other cuts are quite short and in some cases almost sketchy, but Bud is capable of firing off phrases and runs which do sound like the work of a man in a state of grace, as his friend Francis Paudras suggested.

***(*) **Salt Peanuts**

Black Lion BLCD 760121 *Powell; Johnny Griffin (ts); Guy Hayat (b); Jacques Gervais (d).* 8/64.

You can almost smell the garlic and the sweat. Wonderfully authentic club jazz from the latter end of Powell's career, with Johnny Griffin doing his familiar unexpected sit-in on 'Wee', 'Hot House' and 'Straight, No Chaser'. Powell has an awful piano to play and the rhythm section isn't up to much, but (odd though the analogy may sound) much like Keith Jarrett in years to come, Powell always played best at moments of greatest adversity, and here he sounds supercharged. The title-track, 'Move' and '52nd Street Theme', for trio, bring France to Harlem. If 'Bean And The Boys' is familiar, the reason is explained above, apropos *Time Waits*. Wonderful, but don't expect audiophile sound.

(*) **Blues For Bouffemont

Black Lion BLCD 760135 *Powell; Michel Gaudray, Guy Hayat (b); Jacques Gervais, Art Taylor (d).* 7/64, 8/64.

Johnny Griffin doesn't sweep in like the 7th Cavalry to rescue *Bouffemont* and Powell is left to plod his lonely course on the July session. Bouffemont was the convalescent equivalent of Charlie Parker's Camarillo, but there's nothing very relaxed about these tracks. Further material from the *Salt Peanuts* line-up is enough to convince anyone that Black Lion got it right first time. Second rank, even by the rather relative standards of late Powell recordings.

André Previn (born 1929)

PIANO

A transplanted Berliner, like Marty Grosz, Previn is slightly better known as a conductor than as a jazz pianist. He's useful, though.

*** **Previn At Sunset**

Black Lion BLCD 760189 *Previn; Buddy Childers, Howard McGhee (t); Willie Smith (as); Vido Musso (ts); Dave Barbour, Irving Ashby (g); Red Callender, Eddie Safranski, John Simmons (b); Lee Young (d).* 10/45–5/46.

An enigmatic fellow, André Previn. Intensely private, yet given to scandal and something of a showman (heroically refusing to corpse when twitted as 'Andy Preview' by Morecambe and Wise on British television), one of the most thoughtful and sensitive classical conductors of his day yet widely assumed to be a sell-out populist, the finest interpreter of Gershwin's piano music with orchestra, and yet almost completely forgotten for his first love, not Dory Previn, but jazz. Only in the last few years has the sheer generosity and quality of his output begun to be recognized. Previn first recorded as a teenager, and the sessions on *At Sunset* find him confident and accomplished, certainly showing no signs of being overawed by the horns on 'All The Things You Are' and 'I Found A New Baby'. The unaccompanied tracks are a little lacking in meat and substance, but they're still creditable. It would be almost a decade before he did anything of real substance, however.

***** Double Play!**

Original Jazz Classics OJC 157 *Previn; Russ Freeman (p); Shelly Manne (d).* 4 & 5/57.

***** Pal Joey**

Original Jazz Classics OJC 637 *Previn; Red Mitchell (b); Shelly Manne (d).* 10/57.

***** Gigi**

Original Jazz Classics OJC 407 *As above.* 4/58.

***** Like Previn!**

Original Jazz Classics OJCCD 170 *Previn; Red Mitchell (b); Frank Capp (d).* 58.

***** André Previn And His Pals**

Fresh Sound FSR CD 106 *As above, except add Leroy Vinnegar (b), Shelly Manne (d).* 6 & 8/58.

***** Plays Songs By Vernon Duke**

Original Jazz Classics OJC 1769 *Previn (p solo).* 8/58.

***** King Size!**

Original Jazz Classics OJC 691 *Previn; Red Mitchell (b); Frank Capp (d).* 11/58.

A concentrated period of activity for Contemporary, and what a gift he must have been for the label, turning up immaculately rehearsed, straight, clean, unimpeachably professional, and then laying down first-take performances one after the other. One suspects there never will be a box of André Previn out-takes and alternatives, and yet there's nothing unswinging or unspontaneous about any of these performances. 'No Words For Dory', on *Like Previn!* touches an expressiveness one would not expect from him in this context.

The label quickly cottoned on to the show-based and songbook approaches as quick and effective ways of selecting and theming material. *Gigi* is predictably skittish and playful, though not without its moments of tenderness. *Pal Joey* offers more of real musical substance, including the deathless 'I Could Write A Book' and the less well-known 'What Is A Man?'. The Duke portfolio is the only one on which the pianist's classical training becomes evident, turning 'Cabin In The Sky' and 'Autumn In New York' into tiny symphonic statements and 'April In Paris' into an elegant, impressionistic tone-poem.

Double Play! had cast him in a more straightahead formula and repertoire, and in retrospect it almost seems the best of the bunch, because the most uncomplicatedly jazz-driven. Ever after, a Previn & His Pals album always seemed to need an angle or a spin, though, as the Fresh Sound compilation suggests, he could deliver the goods in a live context without strain or self-consciousness.

***** Plays Songs By Jerome Kern**

Original Jazz Classics OJC 1787 *Previn (p solo).* 2 & 3/59.

***** West Side Story**

Original Jazz Classics OJC 422 *As for Pal Joey.* 8/59.

*****(*) Plays Songs By Harold Arlen**

Original Jazz Classics OJC 1840 *Previn (p solo).* 5/60.

The pace didn't slacken into 1959 and 1960, though increasingly the approach seems deliberate and even over-programmed. Previn dropped the '& Pals' tag, and went out for a time as Trio Jazz, though he was also increasingly committed to the idea of solo performance. His minimal opening statements on 'Something's Coming' on *West Side Story* give way to a brash and tightly belted solo which exactly suits the emotional temper. Typically, though, it degenerates into rather technical figuring, octave jumps and altered chords which are impressive without being very involving. *King Size!* suffers in much the same way, almost too clever, and the fact that Red Mitchell also had a formidable musical brain only reinforced the impression, as the two attempt to outdo one another.

The songbook albums are again most impressive, though interestingly here there is now more unvarnished jazz than in the trios. The Kerns are magnificent. 'All The Things You Are' is little less than a summation of everything Previn had learned about jazz piano, though it's the harmonic shifts on 'Why Do I Love You?' and on Arlen's 'For Every Man There's A Woman' that tug at the heart-strings.

***** After Hours**

Telarc 83002 *Previn; Joe Pass (g); Ray Brown (b).* 3/89.

****(*) Uptown**

Telarc 83303 *As above, except Mundell Lowe (g) replaces Pass.* 3/90.

****(*) Old Friends**

Telarc 83309 *As above, except omit Lowe.* 8/91.

Previn's renaissance as a jazz pianist was hailed as a return to an old love, but it was also, of course, the resort of a man who had been bruised by orchestral politics more subtly cut-throat than anything the Medicis would have dared. These don't quite have the bounce and the freshness of old and very quickly sound formulaic. Listening back after a gap of some years doesn't change the impression, though Lowe's long-neglected gifts are a source of delight and interest on *Uptown*. Best to stick with the Contemporarys.

*****(*) Jazz At The Musikverein**

Verve 537704 *Previn; Mundell Lowe (g); Ray Brown (b).* 6/95.

*****(*) Show Boat**

Deutsche Grammophon 453 860 *As above, except add Grady Tate (d).* 96.

*****(*) We Got Rhythm: A Gershwin Songbook**

Deutsche Grammophon 453 493 *Previn; David Finck (b).*

A long way from the club in *The Subterraneans* where a very young Previn played himself soundtracking Kerouac's troglodyte hipsters to the Musikverein in Vienna. Listening to him tackle 'What Is This Thing Called Love?' revives the complaint that he was never called on or never willing to do a Cole Porter songbook for Contemporary. It's an exquisite, feeling performance, like everything on this record. 'Hi Blondie' is an original, but a tune that might have sprung unbidden out of some forgotten 1930s show. 'Satin Doll' is equally lovely and the medley that begins with 'Prelude To A Kiss' is a fitting end to the set, just to be followed by a roistering 'Sweet Georgia Brown'. Where Red Mitchell might have tinkered with the harmonics, and Mundell Lowe has had his own bout of experimentalism, Brown plays it straight and true, pushing along the beat with that huge, authoritative tone. We can vouch for the impact of this group live; engineer Andrew Wedman and producers Elizabeth Onstrow and Alison Ames (how often are we able to credit two women in the role, even in the late '90s?) deliver a rich, authentic sound, full of atmosphere and not missing a single detail.

We're not aware of ever having listed any Deutsche Grammophon releases, either, and it's nice to welcome the blue-chip classical label. *Show Boat* contains some wonderful music, and this group (especially with the addition of the utterly musical Tate) does it every justice. This is Lowe's big moment; recorded strong and very full, he leaves no doubt what we all missed when he was out of the picture.

The Gershwin date is interesting in that it followed an all-Mozart programme Previn was conducting at Tanglewood. The next day he and that fine bassist David Finck simply wandered down to the Florence Gould Auditorium in Seiji Ozawa Hall, Lenox, Massachusetts, got up a pot of coffee and started running through some tunes. Here and there Previn doesn't sound note-perfect, but he has the musical nous to profit from occasional slips, and the best of these tracks are quite exceptional. Edward Jablonski's liner-notes on the individual songs are an added plus (little details like the three-times failure of 'The Man I Love', the best track here, but a flop initially and canned from *Lady Be Good!* and *Strike Up The Band*), but the real delight is the simple lyricism and creative sophistication Previn brings to a composer whose work he seems to understand with his very nerve-ends.

Bobby Previte (born 1957)

DRUMS, PERCUSSION

Previte arrived in New York in the early '80s and quickly established himself as a versatile bandsman, composer and leader, most closely associated with the downtown circle, but up and ready for anything in music. His own bands have included Weather Clear, Track Fast and Latin For Travelers.

*** Claude's Late Morning

Gramavision R2 79448 *Previte; Ray Anderson (tb, tba); Wayne Horvitz (p, org, hca); Bill Frisell (g, bj); Josh Dubin (pedal steel g); Guy Klucevesek (acc); Carol Emmanuel (hp); Joey Baron (d); Jim Mussen (elec).* 88.

**** Empty Suits

Gramavision GV 79447 *Previte; Robin Eubanks (tb); Marty Ehrlich (as); Steve Gaboury (ky); Alan Jaffe, Elliott Sharp (g); Skip Krevens (pedal steel g); Jerome Harris (b, g, lap steel g, v); Carol Emmanuel (hp); Roberta Baum (v); David Shea (turntables).* 5/90.

**** Weather Clear, Track Fast

Enja 6082 *Previte; Graham Haynes (c); Robin Eubanks (tb); Don Byron (cl, bcl); Marty Ehrlich (as, f, cl, bcl); Anthony Davis, Steve Gaboury (p); Anthony Cox (b).* 1/91.

***(*) Hue And Cry

Enja ENJ 8064 *Previte; Eddie E.J Allen (t); Robin Eubanks (tb); Don Byron (cl, bs); Marty Ehrlich (as, ss, f, cl); Anthony Davis (p); Larry Goldings (org); Anthony Cox (b).* 12/94.

Previte's drumming has a strangely loose, unfettered quality that sometimes camouflages very effectively the absolute steadiness of the beat he is laying down. In the decade or so since he started recording under his own name, he has shown an ability to function in all sorts of contexts, drawing on musics outside jazz, stamping everything with a wry, slightly mischievous personality. The records often sound like soundtracks to an imaginary movie, with a multiplicity of characters, an enigmatic story-line, and no particular axe to grind. Moody reprises loom out of nowhere and disappear again. Despite the richness and diversity of its materials, *Claude's Late Morning* has a tremendous unity of feel that marks it out very distinctly. Frisell's guitar is an important element but, as with Tim Berne (for whom Previte has regularly played), there are no hot solos or featured spots as such, just a continuous flow of music, out of which performers emerge briefly before being drawn back into the fabric again.

Empty Suits is a joyous, all-in set that touches all the bases. Previte's compositions and arrangements are absolutely spot on and the guitars are used to maximum effect. 'Great Wall' is a dedication to the minimalist composer, John Adams, who may well have had an impact on Previte's repetitive but shifting structures. As a drummer, he combines the swing era with latter-day power *à la* Ronald Shannon Jackson, but he never overpowers an intelligently balanced mix. On the jazzier *Weather Clear, Track Fast*, the tunes are more stretched out and developed, leaving more space than usual for improvised passages. Don Byron plays an expansive role, but he's slightly overshadowed by the always resourceful Ehrlich, who has a bewildering array of voices at his disposal, and always manages to sound like a 40-a-day man, ranging from raw bop saxophone to bronchial bass clarinet and breathless flute. Haynes and Eubanks complete a most impressive front line. Davis is a bit stiff and there's a big difference when Steve Gaboury, regular pianist with the Empty Suits band, comes in to play the speciality, 'Quinella'.

Hue And Cry is one of the most satisfyingly rounded Previte albums. As more and more solo space is devolved to sidemen, he works ever harder to imprint himself on the music. The result is some of the rhythmically most subtle and fluent music of its idiom.

***(*) Too Close To the Pole

Enja 9306-2 *Previte; Cuong Vu (t, v); Curtis Hasselbring (tb, v); Andrew D'Angelo (as, bcl, v); Jamie Saft (ky); Lindsey Horner (b, v).* 96.

This is Previte's racetrack band (Weather Clear, Track Fast) coming through for a determined late challenge – probably from a position one or two off the stands rail, although the leader's five originals are as idiomatic as anything in this well-spoken milieu of free bop and beyond. Vu and Hasselbring are well drawn, and the lesser-known D'Angelo is running well off a light weight; but it's Previte himself, clearly a long way from being in the handicapper's grip, who is the paciest runner.

*** Euclid's Nightmare

Depth Of Field DOF 1-2 *Previte; John Zorn (as).* 3/97.

A nostalgic back-to-the-roots exercise by two now-venerable mandarins of their (ahem) scene. Few of these 27 miniatures manage to breast the two-minute barrier and perhaps that's a pity, since they often seem to be starting something which then stops. Or maybe we should just hear the thing as a continuous piece with its interstices decided on at random. Zorn is often a lot quieter and sweeter than one expects. Previte taps out one swinging tattoo after another.

*****(*) My Man In Sydney**
Enja 9348-2 *Previte; Jamie Saft (ky); Marc Ducret (g); Jerome Harris (b, g, v).* 1/97.

Boisterous good fun from a warm-to-hot quartet, coming to you from the sun-soaked pleasure zone of Sydney, Australia, in high summer (actually, it was cut in a place called The Basement Club). Saft's little battery of keyboards – Hammond, Fender Rhodes and Mini-Moog – induce a nicely nostalgic feel of late-'70s fusion, which Harris and Ducret undercut with their howlin' guitars; all the while, Previte is drumming up a storm of varied rhythms from the back, the side, anywhere he feels like he can roll it forward. The sound-mix is appropriately thick and humid. As brainy bar-bands go, there can't be many to touch this one.

Eddie Prévost (born 1942)

DRUMS, PERCUSSION

Conventional start in British trad and bebop, then co-founded AMM in 1965 and has been among the leaders of British improv since. Writings suggest his position as a foremost theoretician of the scene, and his own Matchless label has documented a broad range of work.

****** Live: Volumes 1 & 2**
Matchless MRCD 01/02 *Prévost; Gerry Gold (t); Geoff Hawkins (ts); Marcio Mattos (b).* 77.

*****(*) Continuum + 1983/84**
Matchless MRCD 07 *Prévost; Larry Stabbins (ts, ss); Veryan Weston (p); Marcio Mattos (b).*

****** Supersession**
Matchless MR 17 *Prévost; Evan Parker (ss, ts); Keith Rowe (g, elec); Barry Guy (b, elec).* 9/84.

Eddie Prévost was once nicknamed 'the Art Blakey of Brixton', and though he has long since outstretched his early jazz influences – Roach rather than Blakey, and above all Ed Blackwell – he still has deeper roots in jazz drumming than almost any of his free-music peers. The only arguable exception is his exact contemporary, Han Bennink, but Prévost has also explored traditions like Korean court music and, in recent years, the further reaches of noise-rock with groups like God.

His main area of activity remains the long-standing collective, AMM, and Supersession has to be heard in a similar context, one in which individual expression is less important – indeed almost irrelevant – against the interactions of the ensemble. Prévost's jazz origins are still quite clearly audible on *Live*, the album which inaugurated his own Matchless label, and one on which he delivers, as an obstetrician might, one of the best recordings of this period of British free jazz.

Gold and Hawkins make a marvellous partnership, ranging from austere fury to jovial rave-ups which occasionally recall the more experimental of Mingus's workshop bands. Gold in particular has a clear, emphatic signature, idiosyncratic enough to make one wonder why he hasn't been recorded more often.

Prévost is one of the most articulate exponents of the music. He is the author of a book called *No Sound Is Innocent* in which he argues the existence of an aesthetic in which music is inseparable from the realm of ideas and social exchanges. The quartet might seem conventionally distant from what he has done with AMM and with other groups, but it does illustrate how generously he opens himself to situations in which hierarchies collapse. There is no 'front line' here, no 'rhythm section'. It is the musical equivalent of total football, everyone contributing at every level.

That is presumably also the aim of Supersession, a punning name which combines the idea of the supergroup – the core of AMM plus two of the leading British improvisers of recent years – with a Hegelian concept in which thought constantly 'supersedes' the last level of organization. Some will say this is meta-jazz, too rarefied to bother with. Unfortunately (for them) it is as viscerally exciting as anything Art Blakey ever did.

The quartet with Stabbins and Mattos is not unrepresentative, but it certainly touches on different interests and loyalties. Stabbins is an undeservedly neglected player. He is a fascinating player who has learned much from Coltrane and earlier tenor players, but who has a sound and an approach to phrasing which is entirely his own. Mattos is a giant, a player of great spirituality. Prévost himself is in great form, crisp, disciplined, but wild as well.

*****(*) Loci Of Change – Sound And Sensibility**
Matchless MRCD 32 *Prévost (solo).* 9/96.

Evan Parker describes this as 'social music', while simultaneously suggesting that it is both 'lonely' and 'intimate'. This is just about right. Prévost gives no sense, and almost certainly wouldn't welcome the notion of expressive, let alone confessional music, but *Loci Of Change* does presuppose a very direct involvement on the listener's part. It is necessary to surrender oneself to Prévost's music, to its particular language. This does not require a suspension of all other associations, nor does it require a technically literate understanding of the instrumentarium – idiophones, membraphones, harmonics, overtones. It simply calls for a level of responsiveness which allows these six very different pieces to make their undogmatic point.

****** Touch – The Weight, Measure And Feel Of Things**
Matchless MRCD 34 *Prévost; Tom Chant (ss); John Edwards (b).* 3/97.

This is Prévost's most interesting project outside AMM, a mostly quiet and very centred trio which harks back to the free jazz of the 1960s (groups like Trevor Watts's Amalgam) but which also touches on the expanded language and dissolved categories of the '90s. Chant's curious birdcall effects and Steve Lacy-influenced chirrups and yelps are never foregrounded to the detriment of the other two instruments. Edwards is a hugely underrated player, perhaps damned to the shadow of the showier and more histrionic Paul Rogers, but absolutely critical to the disciplines of this music. Prévost himself is better than ever, hinting at a pulse, refusing to allow it to be taken. Ten years ago, there was some reason to fear that music of this kind had outlived its natural span. This makes it relevant again.

***** Concert, v.**
Matchless MRCD 37 *Prévost; Veryan Weston (p).* 98.

The first reaction to this music might be that it is private, inward and uncommunicative, but both these experienced players have the ability to make any performance sound eavesdropped.

Weston has a touch that at first hearing seems formal, almost constrained, but also fraught and strange. Prévost has dabbled in other musics over the last few years and plays with eclectic authority. For us, though, this is an instance of the law of diminishing returns. What must have been a riveting concert performance palls rather quickly.

Sam Price (1908–92)

PIANO, VOCAL

Played piano in his native Texas before going to Kansas, Chicago and New York. House pianist for Decca from 1938, playing blues and boogie styles, then worked in clubs, Europe, Texas again, and back in New York. Often visited Europe in later years and also ran his own clubs and commercial companies.

***** Sam Price 1929–1941**

Classics 696 *Price; Douglas Finnell, Joe Brown, Eddie 'Moon' Mullens, Shad Collins, Bill Johnston, Chester Boone, Emmett Berry (t); Bert Johnson, Floyd Brady, Ray Hogan (tb); Fess Williams (cl, as); Lem Fowler (cl, v); Don Stovall (as); Ray Hill, Lester Young, Skippy Williams (ts); Percy Darensbourg (bj); Duke Jones, Ernest 'Bass' Hill, Billy Taylor (b); Wilbert Kirk, Harold 'Doc' West, Herb Cowens, J.C Heard (d); Yank Taylor, Ruby Smith, Jack Meredith (v).* 9/29–12/41.

Aside from two 1929 tracks, all this material dates from 1940–41, when Price was recording regularly for Decca with his 'Texas Bluesicians'. It might have been recorded in New York, but the music is authentic southern swing, fronted by the pianist from Honey Grove, Texas. Many of the 24 tracks are features for his simple, blues-to-boogie playing and amiable vocals, which tend to predominate as the sessions go by, but there's also some fine playing from the horns. 'Sweepin' The Blues Away' includes excellent work by Brown and Stovall, and a 1941 session actually features the Lester Young band, though Young himself has only a few bars here and there in the limelight. Remastering is quite good, though the two 1929 tracks are noisy and some surface hiss is intrusive on a couple of later tracks.

***** Barrelhouse And Blues**

Black Lion BLCD 760159 *Price; Keith Smith (t); Roy Williams (tb); Sandy Brown (cl); Ruan O'Lochlainn (g); Harvey Weston (b); Lennie Hastings (d).* 12/69.

Busy to the end of his long life, Price turns up as sideman on many other records, and only occasionally under his own leadership (his records with Doc Cheatham are especially fine). He is well served by this enjoyable occasion on which he was recorded in London with a British band. The music is split between solo and ensemble tracks and, although the pianist is rather less glib than usual on the reflective 'Honey Grove Blues', the numbers with the full band turn out rather better: O'Lochlainn's oddball solos are a neat touch of local colour, and the lamented Brown contributes deep-set solos to each of two takes of Leroy Carr's 'In the Evening'. The CD runs to nearly 73 minutes and the remastering is fine.

Julian Priester (born 1935)

TROMBONE

A Chicagoan, Priester worked in R&B and big bands before coming to New York in 1958, joining the Max Roach group until the early '60s and subsequently freelancing. Moved to California in the '70s and is sighted occasionally; a couple of scarce ECM albums await reissue.

*****(*) Keep Swingin'**

Original Jazz Classics OJCCD 1863 *Priester; Jimmy Heath (ts); Tommy Flanagan (p); Sam Jones (b); Elvin Jones (d).* 1/60.

Priester has always been scarce as a leader. Apart from his 1977 ECM record, *Polarization*, which has acquired almost cult status with vinyl collectors, he remains virtually unknown in that capacity. To some extent, the eclipse must be due to the instrument he plays, which has almost always been B-list. Priester's apprenticeship was with Muddy Waters and Bo Diddley, playing blues and R&B, but in 1954 he was recruited by Sun Ra, which must have helped to reinforce his distinctive combination of swing with a dark, sometimes almost fey abstraction. Though the debut album is edged with shadows, it's basically a straightahead blowing set, short, well-crafted tunes with nicely defined shapes. The three on which Heath sits out give the leader a little more space. The closing 'Julian's Tune' is perhaps the clearest indication, though here more recent associations with Lionel Hampton and Max Roach are evident as well. They open with Heath's '24-Hour Leave', which establishes the atmosphere. 'The End' is a Priester original, strongly vocalized and with the blues running through it. Charles Davis is the composer of '1239A', which, though brief, is as strong on atmosphere as the rest of the set. Priester's own other originals are 'Bob T's Blues', which sounds like a studio run-down, and 'Under The Surface', another that plumbs his darker side. An excellent debut. Jimmy Heath had to change his horn to avoid being saddled with the nickname 'Little Bird'. Had Priester switched to another horn, perhaps he might have had a string of albums after this. As it was, he was condemned to spear-carrying – albeit to great effect – on other people's records.

*****(*) Hints On Light And Shadow**

Postcards POST 1017 *Priester; Sam Rivers (ts, ss, f, p); Tucker Martine (elec).* 11/96.

Priester spent a fruitful period in Herbie Hancock's band, during which time, like his colleagues, he adopted a Swahili name, Pepe Moto. More lastingly, he also acquired a facility in playing on top of moody electronic contexts, and there are moments on *Hints On Light And Shadow*, notably 'Zone' (actually a Rivers composition) and 'Autumnal Influences: The Book Of Beauty', where one can hear echoes of the Hancock years return to his playing. The redoubtable Rivers, playing here with grace and fire, was just entering the purple patch which he is still enjoying. His tenor playing is as robust as ever, and it blends well with the deep-down sound of the trombone. Tucker Martine's electronic backgrounds are mostly just that, a subtle canvas on which these two masters execute their art. He is also composer of the opening 'Heads Of The People' and here and there breaks through with a delicately judged idea, contributing to a fine, unexpected album.

Brian Priestley (born 1946)

PIANO

Born in Manchester, he is rather better known for his journalism and broadcasting than as a performer, but he is a skilful small-group leader, arranger and mainstream-modern pianist, with a special interest in the music of Duke Ellington.

***** You Taught My Heart To Sing**
Spirit of Jazz CD09-0995 *Priestley; Don Rendell (ss, ts, f).* 7/94.

A connoisseur's recital. Priestley, by now a veteran commentator and performer on the British scene, knows jazz piano history inside out, and this series of dedications to 15 keyboard masters eschews the obvious at almost every turn – only Bill Evans's 'Waltz For Debby' could be called over-familiar. His Ellington is 'Heaven', his Monk is 'In Walked Bud' and his Bud is 'Dance Of The Infidels', and each has a personal wrinkle in it. Priestley's delivery isn't exactly springheeled but his measured approach lets him map out ideas with a useful clarity, and the thick voicings add density rather than excess weight. He's also meticulous about avoiding bathos on the slower pieces.

***** Love You Madly**
32 Jazz 048 *Priestley; Tony Coe (ss, ts, cl); Gibbs (v).* 4/99.

An inevitable but mostly delightful homage from one of the master's most diligent followers, this set of duos and trios features Priestley browsing through his Ellington book while Gibbs does the singing and Coe chimes in with the occasional solo. The singer comes across as a bit too British for some of these lyrics, and some of us may have had enough of 'Squeeze Me' by now, but actually Priestley has characteristically looked for the byways of Ellingtonia and come up with some less obvious vehicles – 'Rhuum Bop', 'Everything But You', 'Go Away Blues'.

Marcus Printup

TRUMPET

Studied at Georgia State, then played with Marcus Roberts and the Lincoln Center Jazz Orchestra, before making these solos for Blue Note.

***** Song For The Beautiful Woman**
Blue Note 830790-2 *Printup; Walter Blanding (ts); Eric Reed (p); Reuben Rogers (b); Brian Blade (d).* 12/94.

***** Unveiled**
Blue Note 837302-2 *Printup; Stephen Riley (ts); Marcus Roberts (p); Reuben Rogers (b); Jason Marsalis (d).* 2/96.

Printup is a trumpeter to admire, and sometimes he's a very likeable one, too. He has a broad, generous vibrato which gives a romantic buff to music that's otherwise in the hard, modern manner of the day. Much is made in the sleeve-notes of the debut album about how he came to write the title-piece, but it makes no profound impression, and this goes for most of the original composing here. He plays a tight, crisp 'Speak Low' with the mute in, and the band finishes with Coltrane's 'Dahomey Dance': Blanding plays respectable second fiddle throughout, and Reed performs with less flash than he does in some other sideman situations.

Unveiled is a little looser, but only a little. The band's take on the Miles Davis chestnut, 'Dig', is handled at a very quick tempo, but it's simultaneously so precise that one thinks of a *dressage* team in action. While Riley, only a teenager when he recorded this session, is an interesting recruit, and Roberts as usual slips between portentousness and genuine invention, Printup still has the élan to be the most interesting man on the date. Some of the slow tunes are a bit drab, but he has a very pretty sound on the horn, and on a quirky piece like 'Leave Your Name And Number' it all comes together delightfully.

Don Pullen (1944–95)

PIANO, ORGAN, COMPOSER

Born in Roanoke, Virginia, Pullen was associated with avant-gardists such as Giuseppe Logan and Milford Graves in the '60s, and also worked in soul groups. Worked in the Charles Mingus groups in the '70s, before forming a band co-led with fellow Mingusian George Adams. His final records sought a synthesis of African, American and Brazilian musics. A great technician and a passionate composer-improviser.

***** Capricorn Rising**
Black Saint 120004 *Pullen; Sam Rivers (ts, ss, f); Alex Blake (b); Bobby Battle (d).* 10/75.

***** Healing Force**
Black Saint 120010 *Pullen (p solo).* 76.

*****(*) Warriors**
Black Saint 120019 *Pullen; Chico Freeman (ts); Fred Hopkins (b); Bobby Battle (d).* 4/78.

***** Milano Strut**
Black Saint 120028 *Pullen; Famoudou Don Moye (d, perc).* 12/78.

****** Evidence Of Things Unseen**
Black Saint 120080 *Pullen (p solo).* 9/83.

*****(*) The Sixth Sense**
Black Saint 120088 *Pullen; Olu Dara (t); Donald Harrison (as); Fred Hopkins (b); Bobby Battle (d).* 6/85.

****** New Beginnings**
Blue Note 791785 *Pullen; Gary Peacock (b); Tony Williams (d).* 12/88.

****** Random Thoughts**
Blue Note 794347 *Pullen; James Genus (b); Lewis Nash (d).* 3/90.

Don Pullen's solo records demand comparison with Cecil Taylor's. Pullen's traditionalism is more obvious, but the apparent structural conservatism is more appearance than fact, a function of his interest in boogie rather than Bartók, and he routinely subverted expected patterns. Some of the earlier solo discs are no longer available, but they tend to reinforce an impression of

Pullen as a performer interested in large masses of sound, sometimes to the detriment of forward progress. That in turn has led him back to the organ, on which he created huge, sustained chords and swirling textures, as on the duo record with Moye. *Evidence Of Things Unseen* is by far the best of the solo discs, though the recently reissued *Healing Force* will have its supporters as well. *Evidence* bespeaks the same dark-and-light opposition as Andrew Hill or Ran Blake, though Pullen was more of a free player than either, and certainly less of an ironist than Blake.

He favoured exotic dissonances within relatively conventional chordal progressions and, to that extent, was a descendant of Monk. His tribute album is very uneven, with completely wrong-headed effects on ''Round Midnight' and some of the aimlessness that creeps into his duos with George Adams.

Of the groups with horns, the best are those fronted by Freeman and Dara, where Pullen develops spiky, almost spasmodic graph-lines of improvisational material in the midst of inventive and often rather Ivesian structures; the technique is reminiscent of Mingus, with whom Pullen played in the mid-1970s. Rivers is too floaty and ethereal to be entirely effective in this context, though he noticeably tailors his approach to Pullen's cues.

The best work of all is in the two late-1980s trios. The first, with its big-name rhythm section, explodes in the fury of 'Reap The Whirlwind', where Williams's scything cymbal-lines and almost military patterns give a very fair taste of apocalypse. Though less revelatory than *Evidence*, Pullen's piano-playing seems trance-like, rooted in voodoo, pentecostalism and the Old Religion. By contrast, *Random Thoughts*, with its less experienced bass player and drummer, is calmer and less intense (though Pullen's right-hand swirls on 'Andre's Ups And Downs' and 'Endangered Species: African American Youth', which makes its thematic point by systematically eliding beats, are absolutely characteristic). The closing 'Ode To Life' is unaccompanied and almost child-like, with echoes of 'Falling In Love Again' and 'Lili Marlene' in the first and second halves of the brief phrase out of which it's constructed.

***** Kele Mou Bana**

Blue Note CDP 798166 *Pullen; Carlos Ward (as); Nilsson Matta (b); Mor Thiam, Guilherme Franco (perc); Keith Pullen, Taneka Pullen (v). 9/91.*

****** Ode To Life**

Blue Note CDP 789233 *As above, except omit Keith and Taneka Pullen. 2/93.*

Both *Kele Mou Bana* and *Ode To Life* are credited to Pullen's Afro-Brazilian Connection, a highly rhythmic unit that has prompted some of the pianist's more full-hearted and light-toned playing. The later of the records is by far the more pleasing. The title-piece becomes a memorial to the late George Adams, a gorgeous chorale that builds steadily into a set of complex variations. Ward's distinctive, soaring voice is an important component of the overall sound. The vocal elements on *Kele Mou Bana* are not sufficiently well done to be very interesting, and the later record scores again, but it is also uncluttered and direct.

***** Sacred Common Ground**

Blue Note CDP 832800 *Pullen; Joseph Bowie (tb); Carlos Ward (as); Santi Debriano (b); J.T Lewis (d); Mor Thiam (perc); Chief Cliff Singers. 95.*

One might wish for a better send-off for Pullen than *Sacred Common Ground*. His desire to find ever broader bases for the Afro-American music that is jazz was immensely laudable, but in casting about for new roots he dissipates much of the energy that made him such a distinctive presence on the scene. Pullen's death at the age of 51 left a hole, and one has to wonder what his state of health was when he completed this final record. Such considerations ought to be illegitimate, but it is such a strange piece of work in so many ways that an explanation is desirable. Only two of the longer tracks seem to cohere in any organic way, and these, significantly enough, are the tracks on which Pullen himself is dominant. For the rest, the record is a curious mish-mash of influences, with little imaginative centre. An ambiguous legacy.

Alton Purnell (1911–87)

PIANO, VOCAL

A New Orleans man, Purnell played with Bunk Johnson and George Lewis in the 1940s, Kid Ory and Teddy Buckner in the '50s, and thereafter as a solo. Often visited Europe in the '60s and '70s.

***** Alton Purnell In Japan 1976**

GHB BCD-243 *Purnell; Yoshio Toyama (t); Yoshizaku Yokomizo (tb); Masahiro Gotah (cl); Keiko Toyama (bj); Akio Tada (b); Yoshizo Nakajima (d). 7/76.*

This veteran of the Bunk Johnson and George Lewis bands was born in a room over Preservation Hall, so New Orleans music came naturally to him. There is very little under his own nominal leadership on record, but this cheerful, noisy live date from 1976 catches him in good fettle. Purnell's clattery, strange piano isn't well served by the sound-mix, but his singing comes through well enough – he is surprisingly affecting on 'You've Changed', for example – and the Japanese team with him carry off their parts with enthusiasm and a fair amount of panache. Trumpeter Toyama is especially fine at playing a Louisiana-via-Tokyo lead, and Gotah is very nimble. Rough-and-ready sound, but it doesn't spoil the fun.

Quartett

GROUP

A one-off record by a foursome who worked frequently in the 1980s.

****** No Secrets**

New Albion NA017 *Julian Priester (tb); Gary Peacock (b); Jerry Granelli (d, perc); Jay Clayton (v, elec). 1/88.*

Music of rare and delicate beauty from a group of friends who had been working together for half a decade when this record was cut, live to two-track, in a Seattle studio. The instrumentation is unusual, but Priester and Peacock have a special ability to work with singers, creating a soft vocal counterpoint which is unique in modern jazz. The trombonist's delicate, mournful sound is often heard shadowing Clayton, while the bass picks out a second, improvised melody line. 'Duality' is played by just Priester (sounding like an alphornist) and Peacock, whose grasp of complex harmonics is as sound and as tasteful as ever. Elsewhere, much of the surface detail is left to Granelli who, freed from strict timekeeping duties, demonstrates a melodic touch rare among drummers. His use of electronics on 'Entrances and Exits' recalls Tony Oxley's work of the early 1970s.

Clayton deploys a range of delay and chorus effects which extend her capacity considerably, but the real moments of beauty come when the group is playing freely and acoustically. A heartbreaking version of Horace Silver and Leonard Bernstein's 'Lonely Woman' is the only repertory piece. Tracks follow almost without a break, creating the impression of a continuous suite.

Ike Quebec (1918–63)

TENOR SAXOPHONE

Quebec began his career as a dancer but developed a tenor style that was somewhat influenced by Basie's creative alter ego, Herschel Evans. His recording career came in two phases, early and late, though 'late' was to be depressingly early. Ike succumbed to lung cancer at 45 and left behind a small but significant legacy of recordings, plus a creative thumbprint on many of Blue Note's most distinctive bop recordings.

***(*) Ike Quebec, 1944–1946

Classics 957 *Quebec; Buck Clayton, Jonah Jones (t); Tyree Glenn, Keg Johnson (tb); Johnny Guarnieri, Roger Ram Ramirez, Dave Rivera (p); Napoleon Allen, Bill De Arango, Tiny Grimes (g); Milt Hinton, Grachan Moncur, Oscar Pettiford (b); J.C Heard (d).* 7/44–8/45.

*** The Strong Tenor Of Mister Quebec, 1943–1946

EPM Musique 159602 *Similar to above.* 43–46.

Blue Note's last recording date in Hackensack and first in its new headquarters at Englewood Cliffs were both by Ike Quebec. Little known to younger fans, the saxophonist was nevertheless a figure of considerable influence at the label, acting as musical director, A&R man and talent scout (Dexter Gordon and Leo Parker were two of his 'finds'). He was also an important Blue Note recording artist, producing some marvellous sessions for the label just after the war and steering the label in the direction of a more contemporary repertoire. Mosaic had already issued a compilation of mid-1940s work by Quebec and John Hardee. *The Complete Blue Note 45 Sessions* brought together 27 popular sides Quebec made for the thriving jukebox market. By no means wholly organ-dominated, as such 45s tended to be, the sessions strongly featured Quebec's still-underrated tenor style, which sounds like a cross between Evans, Wardell Gray and Dexter Gordon. 'Blue Harlem', recorded for Blue Note in July 1944 in the company of Roger 'Ram' Ramirez, creator of 'Lover Man', was a jukebox hit and pretty much sums up the Quebec sound. The early cuts were made in collaboration with guitarist Tiny Grimes, who was also much involved in Charlie Parker's early career. The compilation includes a couple of rejected takes, of 'Blue Turnin' Grey Over You' and 'The Day You Came Along', alongside the released singles, of which 'Topsy'/'Cup Mute Clayton' (featuring Buck, of course) and 'Mad About You' and 'Facin' The Face' (which features Oscar Pettiford in an early appearance) are by far the best.

Much of the same material is covered on the EPM compilation, which reached us at the eleventh hour but is certainly worth investigation.

***(*) It Might As Well Be Spring

Blue Note 21736 *Quebec; Freddie Roach (org); Milt Hinton (b); Al Harewood (d).* 12/61.

*** Blue And Sentimental

Blue Note 784098 *Quebec; Sonny Clark (p); Grant Green (g); Paul Chambers (b); Philly Joe Jones (d).* 12/61.

*** Ballads

Blue Note 56690 *Quebec; Sonny Clark (p); Earl Van Dyke, Freddie Roach, Sir Charles Thompson (org); Grant Green, Willie Jones (g); Milt Hinton, Sam Jones (b); Art Blakey, Al Harewood, Louis Hayes, J.C Heard, Wilbert G. T Hogan (d).* 9/60–3/62.

It Might As Well Be Spring is pretty squarely in the tenor–organ tradition, except that Quebec has opted to record some gently expressive standards, not just the title-track but also 'Lover Man', 'Ol' Man River' and 'Willow Weep For Me', as well as his own compositions, 'A Light Reprieve' and 'Easy – Don't Hurt'. Digital remastering has restored a bit of detail to the sound, and Roach is the one who benefits most, a surprisingly subtle player who always has plenty to say and doesn't sound as if he's merely stoking up a fairground calliope. Much to enjoy, and probably spot-on at this length. We're not sure that extra material would make a substantial difference.

Quebec has several times teetered on the brink of major rediscovery, but each time interest has flagged. He is, admittedly, a rather limited performer when set beside Gordon or any of the other younger tenor players emerging at the time, but he has a beautiful, sinuous tone and an innate melodic sense that negotiates standards with a simplicity and lack of arrogance that are refreshing and even therapeutic. *Blue And Sentimental*, with fine performances on 'Minor Impulse', 'Don't Take Your Love From Me' and 'Count Every Star', is an excellent place to make his acquaintance, and once again sophisticated remastering has made a world of difference to the accessibility of the music.

Ballads is a fairly predictable compilation of laid-back themes drawn from four of Quebec's later albums for Blue Note, padded out with a single track, 'Born To Be Blue', which was recorded under Grant Green's leadership. An attractive package, and very welcome when these sessions are still only patchily available.

*** Bossa Nova Soul Samba

Blue Note 52443 *Quebec; Kenny Burrell (g); Wendell Marshall (b); Willie Bobo (d); Garvin Masseaux (shekere).* 10/62.

Recorded a matter of months before Ike's death from lung cancer and when he was already showing signs of waning powers, this was made at a time when 'Latin' albums – and particularly *bossa nova* sessions – were more or less *de rigueur*. Almost uniquely for the time, there is nothing by Jobim in the programme, and the range of material is quite broad and imaginative. 'Me'N'You' and 'Blue Samba' are both strong originals, suggesting that Ike might well have moved fruitfully in this direction, had he been granted a little more time. One to cherish, even if it isn't unduly innovative.

Alvin Queen (born 1950)

DRUMS

Alvin has spent much of his career in Europe and for a time ran his own record label, Nilva. He sounds like an inter-generational hybrid of swingers and bebop drummers, sometimes a little too metronomic, but consistently exciting.

*** Nishville

Moju 003 *Queen; Stepko Gut (t, flhn); Peter Mihelich (p); Reggie Johnson (b); Willie Kotoun (perc); RTS Big Band and String Ensemble.* 2–3/98.

Alvin's little benediction and prayer at the start of 'Michaela' is just one of the odder elements of this curious and very old-fashioned record. *Nishville* might have been conceived as soundtrack music for some gentle dramatic comedy. Co-led by Jugoslav trumpeter Gut, it was recorded in Belgrade with the radio big band and strings, and it explores a range of Balkan moods and landscapes. Gut is the main composer, though a good deal of his material comes from traditional sources. Alvin drives the band along with loose-wristed power and carves out some delicate solo spaces as well, like the middle section of 'Michaela'. The strings are nicely integrated with the horns and imaginatively voiced, but the album as a whole remains something of an oddity, albeit an attractive one.

Queen Mab

GROUP

Named for the duo of these two Canadian musicians.

***(*) Barbie's Other Shoe

Nine Winds 0198 *Lori Freedman (cl, bcl); Marilyn Lerner (p).* 3/97.

A moot point as to how much jazz there is in this, but there's no gainsaying the crackling quality of the playing, which is about a kind of brittle interconnecting of lines. The sparseness of the duo is made even more intense by the frequency with which one or other player drops out, or the way Lerner plays in isolated areas of the keyboard. The 11 tracks range from a long, wide-ranging piece such as 'Happy Ass' to the subverted boogie of the title-track, to the huge bass clarinet shapes set against solemn piano figures in 'Mab Roots'. Cool-headed, yet starkly intense, this feels like rather remorseless and unwelcoming music, but the vivid intensity of it all – even when the playing is stealthy and deliberate – will startle and surprise many more adventurous listeners.

Paul Quinichette (1916–83)

TENOR SAXOPHONE

His nickname was the Vice Pres, and Quinichette was one of the very few who, without turning into a slavish Lester Young copyist, managed to convey something of the great man's tone and spirit. He was out of the business for many years, working as an electrical engineer, but he left behind some strong and individual albums.

*** Complete Dawn Sessions

Blue Moon/Dawn DCD 106 *Quinichette; John Carisi, Renauld Jones, Thad Jones, Joe Newman, Gene Roland (t); Henry Cooker, Bob Swope (tb); Dick Meldonian (as); Bill Graham (as, bs); Nat Pierce (p); Freddie Green, Doyle Salathiel (g); Eddie Jones, Wendell Marshall, Oscar Pettiford, Dudley Watson (b); Osier Johnson, Walter Nolan, Sonny Payne (d); Sylvia Pierce (v).* 7/56, 8/57.

*** On The Sunny Side

Original Jazz Classics OJCCD 076 2 *Quinichette; Curtis Fuller (tb); John Jenkins, Sonny Red Kyner (as); Mal Waldron (p); Doug Watkins (b); Ed Thigpen (d).* 57.

***(*) For Basie

Original Jazz Classics OJCCD 978 2 *Quinichette; Shad Collins (t); Nat Pierce (p); Freddie Green (g); Walter Page (b); Jo Jones (d).* 10/57.

Very much a middle-order batsman, Quinichette was best in the loose, jam-session format that Prestige favoured in the later 1950s, and in the easy, open-ended cuts for Dawn. More often than is entirely comfortable, the man from Denver sounds overpowered by his colleagues. Trumpeter Gene Roland, hardly the most dominant of presences, is in great form on the August 1957 sets on the Dawn compilation. The larger formats consign Paul entirely to the shadows. He is more convincing on the Prestige dates. The eponymous 'On The Sunny Side Of The Street' and the Basie material on the other OJC are quite strong, but on both occasions the band is more impressive than the leader. On the former, he is paired with just Jenkins and rhythm, and he shapes some elegant and persuasive solos, but there isn't much to chew on here.

Michael Rabinowitz

BASSOON

Virtuoso performer on an instrument rare in jazz.

*** Gabrielle's Balloon

Jazz Focus JFCD 011 *Rabinowitz; John Hicks (p); Ira Coleman (b); Steve Johns (d).* 11/95.

Illinois Jacquet used to play a bit of bassoon, just for colour. Yusef Lateef and Oregon's Paul McCandless went some way towards overturning the Orwellian premiss: one reed, good; two reeds, bad. Michael Rabinowitz, though, is a man with a mission, who campaigns passionately on behalf of an instrument with no real presence in jazz. Purely in terms of colour, the bassoon can't be faulted; a rich, slightly fruity voice, a little careworn and chastened, and so, you might think, a perfect vehicle for the blues. Unfortunately, like the oboe, it's not an instrument that projects very strongly and there are problems with speed of articulation.

Rabinowitz has recorded before, a disc with the optimistic title *Bassoon On Fire*. At best, it's a slow smoulder. Constrained in tonality and unable to articulate as freely as a saxophone or clarinet, Rabinowitz might reasonably have played to his strengths, but so convinced is he that the bassoon can cut it with the rest of the band that he pushes it in uncomfortable directions. 'Nica's Blues' – like the title-piece a tribute to a daughter – sounds awkward and unidiomatic. There are two Monk tunes, 'Eronel' and 'Monk's Mood', which work better than they decently should, but it's only when the tonality is fitted to the instrument, as on 'Bernie's Tune' – in D minor – that Rabinowitz really sounds on the case. A curiosity.

John Rae

DRUMS

Edinburgh-based drummer with a blend of post-bop and Scottish music.

*** Celtic Feet

Caber 010 *Rae; Phil Bancroft (sax); Brian Kellock (p); Eilidh Shaw (vn); Simon Thoumire (concertina); Mario Caribé (b).* 6/99.

Mr Rae used to run a jazz collective round Edinburgh which at times seemed the only bulwark north of the border against trad, funk and lite jazz. Edinburghers – and Irvine Welsh readers – will understand a title like 'Power Of The Radge', a celebration of in-your-face, up-front *thrawn*-ness. No one will mistake the sheer rhythmic power of Rae's small band. Anchored by pianist Kellock and light-toned bassist Caribé, it weaves a complex rhythmic and textural spell, from the unexpected stride opening to the astonishing rhythmic coup of the closing 'Slumber Jack' – 17/16, indeed!

Thoumire's mournful concertina and the now patented saxophone sound of Phil Bancroft, who is more familiar in company with drummer brother Tom behind him, provide the spot colour, but it's Rae's ideas and sheer punch that make this such an engaging record. Hard to categorize (as is probably the intention) but, as the election celebration of 'May 7th' underlines, full of the confidence of a country and a music reinventing itself.

Boyd Raeburn (1913–66)

BASS, TENOR AND BARITONE SAXOPHONES

Began bandleading at twenty, and by the 1940s was in charge of a challenging group with many prominent modernists and some innovative arrangers. But the records weren't hits and he reverted to sweeter fare, leaving music altogether in 1957.

*** More 1944–1945

Circle CCD 113 *Louis Cles, Ewell Payne, Pincus Stavitt, Benny Harris, Stan Fishillsen, T.D Allison, Dizzy Gillespie (t); Earl Swope, Pullman Pederson, Bob Swift, Trummy Young, J.K Corman, O.C Wilson, W.C Robertson (tb); John Bothwell, Hal McKusick (as); Angelo Tompros, Joe Megro, Al Cohn (ts); Serge Chaloff (bs); George Handy, George Hendelman, Ike Carpenter (p); Dennis Sandole, John Payuo, Steve P Jordan (g); Andy Delmar, Mort Oliver, Oscar Pettiford (b); Don Lamond, Shelly Manne (d); Don Darcy, Marjorie Wood Hoffman (v).* 6/44–1/45.

*** The Transcription Performances 1946

Hep CD 42 *Similar to above.* 45–46.

In 1944 an unexplained fire at the Palisades Pleasure Park in New Jersey destroyed the instruments and music of one of the most challenging big bands of the period. Typically of Boyd Raeburn, his re-formed band and new book were even more adventurous than what had gone before. Musically, the Circle material from the apocalyptic year is typical of the leader's adventurous spirit and of the willingness of his players to push the boat out a little and take risks. Often exhilarating stuff. Raeburn's was a musicians' band, held in the highest esteem by his peers, regarded with some suspicion by those who believed that bands were for dancing. Raeburn had an intelligent awareness of classical and twentieth-century forms and was as comfortable with Bartók and Debussy as he was with Ellington and Basie. The bands were clangorous, neither 'sweet' nor 'hot', but a curious admixture of the two, and arrangements were full of awkward time-signatures and tonalities. Tunes such as 'Tonsilectomy', 'Rip Van Winkle' and 'Yerxa', from earlier and (as yet) not reissued sessions, are among the most remarkable of modern-band pieces. Hal McKusick was a featured soloist and the Raeburn bands of the time (like Kirk's or McShann's) are well worth scouring for the early work of prominent modernists. It may be that simple market forces pushed Raeburn back in the direction of the swing mainstream.

Hep's set of transcriptions comes in decent sound and is something of a mixed bag: vocal features for David Allyn and Ginny Powell blend in with some of the maverick arranger George Handy's outlandish work. 'Cartaphilius' is a typically extraordinary Handy piece, the sort of thing Stan Kenton must have enjoyed. In sum, this is an inconsistent body of work, but Raeburn deserves a better shake than jazz history has so far given him. More Raeburn material on Hep was due to appear as we went to press.

Ane Ramlose

VOICE

Swedish vocalist working in an impressionist style of contemporary modal jazz.

*** Days Without Makeup

Storyville STCD 4195 *Ramlose; Flemming Agerskov (t); Fredrik Lundin (ss, ts, bf); Hans Ulrik (ss, ts); Thomas Clausen (p); Hans Andersson (b); Peter Danemo (d).* 12/92–5/93.

Ramlose's small voice and soft articulation set the tone for this chamberish and not unpleasing set of dreamy modal themes. With Agerskov coming on like a Kenny Wheeler disciple and Clausen's smoothly lyrical piano underneath, the music offers an inevitable variation on Azimuth, though Ramlose is scarcely a match for Norma Winstone. Lundin and Ulrik put in harsher notes with some quite terse and involved improvising on their appearances. One for an autumn afternoon.

Lee Ranaldo

GUITAR, SYNTHESIZER, ELECTRONICS

Contemporary inside-outside guitarist.

***** Clouds**

Victo CD 054 *Ranaldo; Gianni Gebbia (as, sno); Jim O'Rourke (org, elec); William Hooker (d, v).* 5/97.

Recorded live at Victoriaville, a loudly compelling set which mixes guitar and drum duos with three quartet tracks and a further two involving O'Rourke (not on guitar on this occasion) and Gebbia. Interesting as these augmented numbers are, one wouldn't want too much of them. The interplay between Ranaldo and Hooker is what the record is really about; whether at length, as on '25 Views Of Florence', or highly condensed, as on 'Junkyard Language', the music is intelligent and unexpectedly brisk, without a whisper of self-indulgence. Not for every taste, but well worth sampling.

Freddy Randall (1921–99)

TRUMPET

A Londoner, Randall started out with a comedy group but formed his own traditional band in the late 1940s. He recorded extensively for Parlophone in the '50s but, after a spell of illness, faded from the scene. He returned to more active duty in the '70s but continued to work sparingly and, away from music, he ran an old people's home.

****** Freddy Randall And His Band**

Lake LACD123 *Randall; Roy Crimmins, Norman Cave, Dave Keir (tb); Archie Semple, Dave Shepherd, Al Gay (cl); Betty Smith (ts); Dave Fraser, Harry Smith (p); Ron Stone, Ken Ingerfield, Jack Peberdy (b); Lennie Hastings, Stan Bourne (d).* 3/53–7/55.

A record to convert unbelievers to the energy and vitality of the best British trad. Randall's groups weren't rough-and-ready outfits. He led by example, his trumpet playing crackling with conviction and imagination alike, and his groups were hard-bitten but swinging in their doughty way. Randall liked the sound of the Chicagoan brassmen rather than the New Orleans strain beloved by Ken Colyer, and his jazz has an incendiary quality to it which eluded many of his contemporaries. Not that there isn't a sense of fun in these tracks, chosen by Paul Lake from the 70-odd sides he made for Parlophone between 1953 and 1955. 'Professor Jazz' still raises a smile, and anyone who calls one of his originals 'My Tiny Band Is Chosen' has a reserve of wit as well as commitment. A model reissue, in excellent sound, and it is a pity that Randall himself did not live to see it happen.

Doug Raney (born 1957)

GUITAR

Doug's career kicked off at the age of eighteen when he worked with his dad, Jimmy Raney, and pianist Al Haig. A couple of years further on, Doug and Jimmy formed what was to be a longstanding duo. Both have recorded extensively, a substantial body of swinging, thoughtful and emotionally understated but unmistakably powerful jazz.

***** Introducing Doug Raney**

Steeplechase SCCD 1082 *Raney; Duke Jordan (p); Hugo Rasmussen (b); Billy Hart (d).* 9/77.

***** Cuttin' Loose**

Steeplechase SCCD 31105 *Raney; Bernt Rosengren (ts); Horace Parlan (p); Niels-Henning Orsted Pedersen (b); Billy Hart (d).* 8/78.

***** Listen**

Steeplechase SCCD 31144 *As above, except omit Parlan; replace NHOP with Jesper Lundgaard (b).* 12/80.

Raised to the family craft, Doug Raney quickly established his own identity and a more contemporary idiom that also seemed to draw on swing guitar (missing out, that is, much of the bebop influence his father has sustained). Less robust rhythmically than his father, Raney slots more conventionally into a horn-and-rhythm set-up. CD doesn't always flatter his technique, which sounds slightly scratchy and lacks Jimmy Raney's smooth, Jim Hall-like legato. However, now that the Steeplechase catalogue is back in better shape, fine early records like *Introducing* are back in circulation, broadening the picture considerably; with Raney Junior, bulk is what it's about, fewer moments of sheer glory than the old man, but in their stead a dogged brilliance that begins to impinge only over many records. He's an artist who needs to be listened to steadily and whole.

The closing 'Moment's Notice' on *Listen* is one of Raney's best performances on record. There is a steady modal shift on his theme statements, and the soloing is robust without losing the tune's innate romanticism. Rosengren's Coltraneisms are reasonably well assimilated, and he modulates well, as on *Cuttin' Loose*, between a smooth swing and a more aggressive modernism.

***** I'll Close My Eyes**

Steeplechase SCCD 1166 *Raney; Bernt Rosengren (ts, af); Horace Parlan (p); Jesper Lundgaard (b); Ole Jacob Hansen (d).* 7/82.

***** Meeting The Tenors**

Criss Cross Criss 1006 *Raney; Bernt Rosengren (ts, f); Ferdinand Povel (ts); Horace Parlan (p); Jesper Lundgaard (b); Ole Jacob Hansen (d).* 4/83.

***** Lazy Bird**

Steeplechase SCCD 31200 *Raney; Bernt Rosengren (ts); Ben Besiakov (p); Jesper Lundgaard (b); Ole Jacob Hansen (d).* 4/84.

*****(*) Blue And White**

Steeplechase SCD 31191 *Raney; Ben Besiakov (p); Jesper Lundgaard (b); Aage Tanggaard (d).* 4/84.

The first few years of the '80s saw Raney trying to consolidate and managing only to mark time. These are not very compelling albums if one comes to them first and without an awareness of the robust thinking that lies beneath their rather bland surfaces. *Blue And White* is probably the best of them, dominated by titanic performances of Jimmy Heath's 'Gingerbread Boy' and John Coltrane's 'Straight Street'. The three previous records are only exceptional for the contributions of Bernt Rosengren, one of the great unsung heroes of European jazz and at this period a somewhat dark and brooding performer, even on relatively lightweight material. Raney understandably defers to him more often than not, taking more of a back-seat role on these discs than he had before and would subsequently.

*****(*) Something's Up**
Steeplechase SCCD 31235 *As above, except replace Tanggaard with Billy Hart (d).* 2/88.

***** Guitar Guitar Guitar**
Steeplechase SCCD 31212 *Raney; Mads Vinding (b); Billy Hart (d).* 7/85.

*****(*) The Doug Raney Quintet**
Steeplechase SCCD 31249 *Raney; Tomas Franck (as); Bernt Rosengren (ts); Jesper Lundgard (b); Jukkis Uotila (d).* 8/88.

Things pick up sharply again with the neutrally titled 1988 album, which is intended to give the signal that here is a working band, under the command of its leader, playing full-on and undistractable. It's certainly a major lift on the rather shambolic essays of the early part of the decade. Besiakov is nowhere near as commanding a player as Parlan, but he has sharpened considerably over the four years since his last recording with Raney and lends a genuine presence to 'Good Morning Heartache' and 'Upper Manhattan Medical Group'.

The '88 quintet album is excellent in every department. There is another fine version of 'Speedy Recovery' (also on *Something's Up*). The extra horn and the absence of piano restores certain harmonic responsibilities to the guitar, but it also generates a very different texture through which he has to play with just a little more force than usual. It's difficult to know where else to start with Raney. The late-1980s albums are completely accomplished. Follow the stars.

***** Blues On A Par**
Steeplechase SCCD 31341 *Raney; George Cables (p); Steve LaSpina (b); Adam Nussbaum (d).*

It's always tricky to pitch two harmony instruments together, but Cables is such a subtle and swinging player that guitar and piano sound like two aspects of a single personality. The programme is more predictable than usual, with just the title-track as an original. 'When Sunny Gets Blue' is stretched out very much longer than usual, and it offers space to the whole group. Kenny Dorham's 'La Mesha' is delivered crisply and without fuss, setting up Charlie Rouse's 'Pumpkin's Delight' as a strong and big-voiced ending. Doug's delight in melody is most evident in the opening pair of tracks, 'I Concentrate On You' and 'Estate', which in a scant quarter of an hour run a remarkable range of ideas. He sounds more than usually relaxed and the guitar is nicely mixed with the rest of the group.

***** Back In New York**
Steeplechase SCCD 31409 *Raney; Kenny Barron (p); Peter Washington (b); Kenny Washington (d).* 95.

*****(*) Raney '96**
Steeplechase SCCD 31397 *Raney; Ben Besiakov (p); Lennart Ginman (b); Herlin Riley (d).* 7/96.

Rising forty, Raney was perhaps anxious to show that he hadn't got ring-rusty working in exile over in Europe, so the Manhattan session was something of a confidence-boosting exercise. It's certainly not as good a record as the four-oh celebration that is *Raney '96*, one of his strongest group albums yet, opening uncompromisingly with 'Giant Steps' and closing on 'Afro Blue', with material by Pat Martino, Wes Montgomery, Charlie Parker (an unexpected 'Moose The Mooche') and Bill Evans (a graceful 'Re: Person I Knew'). We've no technical reason for it, but Raney has become fuller-voiced and more resonant in recent years, and most noticeably on this album. The guitar seems to be the same favoured Gibson, but there are perhaps more upstroke notes and harmonics, filling in the background sound and creating harmonic shadows, where before all was sunlight and space. Whatever the reason, we like it; our favourite Raney album to date.

*****(*) The Backbeat**
Steeplechase SCCD 31456 *Raney; Joey DeFrancesco (org); Billy Hart (d).*

Raney hasn't previously experimented with the traditional guitar/organ funk format, but this delicious set, named after the Horace Silver tune, suggests he can do the Wes Montgomery/Grant Green stuff with the best of them. Unlike *Raney '96*, the recording is flatter and less detailed, but with lots of extra bass, which suits the material perfectly. Duke's 'Prelude To A Kiss' is exquisite, a trio performance of near-perfect balance. Nothing else quite comes up to this standard and the record could possibly seem one-dimensional ... but only to cheerless cynics.

***** You Go To My Head**
Steeplechase SCCD 31474 *Raney; Jay Anderson (b); Billy Hart (d).*

Steeplechase have always erred on the side of generosity in recording and issuing favoured artists. This is an album straight off the house production-line, a confident and uncomplicated performance that might sound a touch drab on second and subsequent hearings. All eight tracks kick in at about the same length and it might have been better to have given the trio its head on a couple of the stronger items – 'I Hear A Rhapsody', 'Triste', say – which suggest that there was much more to be said than is delivered. Never less than competent, Raney has been more arresting.

Jimmy Raney (1927–95)

GUITAR

Kentucky-born, Raney synthesized Charlie Christian with Lester Young to create long, cool, improvisational lines which have been hugely influential on guitarists of a later generation. Though now overtaken in terms of sheer quantity by his son Doug, with whom he has performed in duo and group contexts, Jimmy's work demands the closest attention.

****** A**

Original Jazz Classics OJC 1706 *Raney; John Wilson (t); Hall Overton (p); Teddy Kotick (b); Art Mardigan, Nick Stabulas (d).* 5/54–3/55.

Of the bop-inspired guitarists Raney perhaps best combined lyricism with great underlying strength. Essentially a group player, he sounds good at almost any tempo but is most immediately appealing on ballads. *A*, which contains some of his loveliest performances, remains an overlooked classic. Overton anticipates some of the harmonic devices employed by Hank Jones (below), and bebop bassist Kotick plays with a firm authority that synchronizes nicely with Raney's rather spacious and elided lower string work. Wilson adds a dimension to the lovely 'For The Mode' and to four more romantic numbers, including 'A Foggy Day' and 'Someone To Watch Over Me'.

*****(*) Raney '81**

Criss Cross Criss 1001 *Raney; Doug Raney (g); Jesper Lundgaard (b); Eric Ineke (d).* 2/81.

*****(*) The Master**

Criss Cross Criss 1009 *Raney; Kirk Lightsey (p); Jesper Lundgaard (b); Eddie Gladden (d).* 2/83.

****** Wisteria**

Criss Cross Criss 1019 *Raney; Tommy Flanagan (p); George Mraz (b).* 12/85.

The early 1980s saw some vintage Raney on record. The quartet with Hank Jones is valuable largely for the inclusion of alternative takes that give a clearer idea of how subtly the guitarist can shift the dynamic of a piece by holding or eliding notes, shuffling the rhythm and increasing the metrical stress. *'81* includes some rejected takes, of 'Sweet And Lovely', 'If I Should Lose You' and 'My Shining Hour' most obviously, which offer convincing demonstration of his speed of thought and suggest once again what an underrated player he was by all except jazz guitar groupies, who presumably know their way round this stuff already.

The Master offers second takes of 'The Song Is You' and 'Tangerine' (but not, unfortunately, the vibrant 'Billie's Bounce'), revealing how thoughtful an accompanist Lightsey is. The rhythm players are slightly too stiff for him, but he compensates by breaking up their less elastic figures with single-note stabs and scurrying runs at the next bar-line.

Flanagan's right hand is lost in a rather woolly mix, but the material on the marvellous *Wisteria* more than makes up for any purely technical shortcomings. From the opening 'Hassan's Dream', with its big, dramatic gestures, to 'I Could Write A Book', the drummer-less group plays at the highest level and 'Out Of The Past' is very special indeed.

*****(*) Duets**

Steeplechase SCCD 31134 *Raney; Doug Raney (g).* 4/79.

***** Stolen Moments**

Steeplechase SCCD 31118 *Raney; Doug Raney (g); Michael Moore (b); Billy Hart (d).* 4/79.

*****(*) Nardis**

Steeplechase SCCD 31184 *As Duets, above.*

If you can't hire 'em, breed 'em. Raney's partnership with his son, Doug, has been one of the most productive and sympathetic of his career. Their duos are masterpieces of guitar interplay, free of the dismal call-and-response clichés that afflict such pairings, and often unexpectedly sophisticated in direction. Generally, the repertoire is restricted to standards, but Jimmy is also an impressive composer and frequently surprises with an unfamiliar melody.

Duets is probably still the best available performance. The closing 'My Funny Valentine' would melt a heart of stone, and Doug Raney, with the lighter, less strongly accented style that was so responsive to Chet Baker's needs, is particularly good on 'My One And Only Love' and 'Have You Met Miss Jones'. The addition of rhythm doesn't alter the basic conformation of the music, but it does increase the tempo and spices up the slightly unlikely samba. The curtain number is that old duo warhorse, 'Alone Together'. *Nardis* is a tribute to the late Bill Evans. Elegantly crafted and wisely paced, it is perhaps the best representation of how he and Doug have created a rich and vigorous language almost by swapping generational roles. Doug sounds like the traditionalist and Jimmy like the radical, and on 'I Can't Get Started' the dialogue is intensely absorbing. Recommended.

*****(*) But Beautiful**

Criss Cross Criss 1065 *Raney; George Mraz (b); Lewis Nash (d).* 12/90.

This is the master at work, to be sure. Raney plays with consummate ease and elegance, as perfectly balanced and utterly tasteful as ever. It's a great pity that he hasn't recorded more in this format. Mraz and Nash are both excellent, as always, and contribute considerably to the direction of Raney's solos, which do still have a tendency to drift and turn hazy at the edges. Mraz is formidably disciplined without losing expressiveness. The recording is very close and soft, picking up all the overtones in both sets of strings. By contrast, Nash is a little recessed.

John Rangecroft

CLARINET

Veteran British free improviser, rarely heard from on record of late.

*****(*) Blythe Hill**

Slam 228 *Rangecroft; Marcio Mattos (b); Stu Butterfield (d).* 10/96.

Cultivated free playing by three old hands who know each other well – Butterfield and Rangecroft played together in Cirrus in the late 1960s, and Mattos joined them in the '70s. This is a rare sighting of the trio on record. It's chamberish, British free – Rangecroft is well known as a saxophonist, but he sticks to clarinet here, getting a rather cultured sound and seldom looking for extremes. The title-piece is a soberly beautiful exploration, and perhaps only on the long 'Altair' does the music show signs of sagging.

John Rapson

TROMBONE

Californian free-bop player with an interest in improvising to set structures.

***** Dances And Orations**

Music & Arts CD-923 *Rapson; Bobby Bradford (c); Anthony Braxton (ss, as, cl, f, cbcl); Wayne Peet (ky); Bill Roper (tba); Alex Cline (d).* 1–7/94.

Rapson is a member of the Californian avant-garde whose records are more usually found on Nine Winds. *Dances And Orations* started from a series of duo improvisations by Rapson and Braxton, which were subsequently overdubbed and otherwise altered by the other musicians. In some cases, Peet even sampled Braxton's playing to extend or otherwise revise the original sounds. They are best experienced cold: Rapson's sleeve-notes are so intimidatingly detailed that they take a lot of the mystery out of the music, which is sometimes compressed or otherwise tampered with to the extent that it seems like a mere exercise in ingenuity. Yet some of it, like the perfect miniature of 'Hold The Fort', is so refined in both delivery and texture that it secures just the kind of magic it aspires to.

Enrico Rava (born 1943)

TRUMPET, FLUGELHORN

Rava was born in the international city of Trieste and grew up in Turin, which in the '60s was to be a meeting-place for American musicians. Deeply influenced by Miles Davis, he gravitated towards the avant-garde with Gato Barbieri's group, and later with Steve Lacy; Rava was also a member of the Globe Unity Orchestra. His interest in free jazz has, though, always been tempered by an awareness of other genres and styles, anything from classical music and pop to electronics.

****** The Pilgrim And The Stars**

ECM 847322-2 *Rava; John Abercrombie (g); Palle Danielsson (b); Jon Christensen (d).* 6/75.

*****(*) The Plot**

ECM 523282-2 *As above.* 8/76.

****** Enrico Rava Quartet**

ECM 523283-2 *Rava; Roswell Rudd (tb); Jean-François Jenny-Clark (b); Aldo Romano (d).* 3/78.

Rava's finest recordings are these sessions from the later '70s, culminating in the eerily beautiful *The Pilgrim And The Stars*. The trumpeter's distinctive manner is a combination of sustained, curving notes, unmistakably coloured, with sudden rhythmic tangents. In combination with Abercrombie's guitar and the top-flight Scandinavian rhythm section, he creates a sound-world all his own. Reconvening the same band two years later yielded a more subtle album, structurally and compositionally, but *The Plot*'s narrative sophistication ('Amici', 'The Plot' itself) consistently yields to the sheer pictorial poetry evident on 'Foto Di Famiglia', a Rava/Abercrombie collaboration that might have come from the same sessions as the earlier record. Anyone interested in the progress of European jazz should take notice of it at least.

The eponymous Quartet album paired him – often literally – with the waywardly brilliant Rudd. Their unison lines on the upbeat 'The Fearless Five' would be useful evidence for anyone wanting to disprove the old *canard* about ECM's supposed New Ageist failings. Both men are in cracking form, but they save their most expressive and lyrical statements for the long 'Lavori Casalinghi', co-written with Graciela Rava, which opens the set. There are strong things on 'Tramps' as well, but here it's the remarkable rhythm section of Jenny-Clark and Romano which catches the ear; their interaction could hardly be bettered on either side of the Atlantic, and the bassist in particular is given a lot to do, covering for the absence of a harmony instrument. 'Round About Midnight' is a hokey party-piece for the two horns on their own.

***** Rava String Band**

Soul Note 121114 *Rava; Augusto Mancinelli (g); Giovanni Tommaso (b); Tony Oxley (d); Nana Vasconcelos (perc); string quartet.* 4/84.

*****(*) Secrets**

Soul Note 121164 *Rava; Augusto Mancinelli (g, g syn); John Taylor (p); Furio Di Castri (b); Bruce Ditmas (d).* 7/86.

***** Enrico Rava Quintet**

Nabel 4632 *Rava; Ullmann Gebhard (ts, ss, bf); Andreas Willers (g); Martin Willichy (b); Niko Schauble (d).* 3/89.

*****(*) Bella**

Philology W 64 *Rava; Enrico Pieranunzi (p); Enzo Pietropaoli (b); Roberto Gatto (d).* 5/90.

*****(*) Noir**

Label Bleu LBLC 6595 *Rava; Stefano Di Battista (sax); Roberto Ceccheto, Domenico Caliri (g); Maier Giovanni Girolamo (b); Umberto Trombetta (d).* 6/96.

In the early 1980s, Rava worked with (mainly) Italian bands, relying heavily on Mancinelli's Abercrombie-derived guitar. Tony Oxley's recorded contribution is restricted to the less than wholly successful *String Band* project, which reflects Rava's growing interest in formal composition for orchestral groups. *Secrets* gains immeasurably from the presence of another Englishman, John Taylor, whose cultured accompaniments and understated soloing are probably more widely recognized outside the British Isles.

The Nabel underlines how much a player of Rava's warmth and sensitivity owes to CD. The band is less interesting than any he has previously mustered (and Gebhard is a rather bland colourist), but the leader's tone and invention on two takes of 'Fourteen Days' are impressive indeed. *Bella* is a small gem. The chemistry between Rava and Pieranunzi, that most sensitive of accompanists, is enrapturing on 'My Funny Valentine' and, if the session as a whole rests a little heavily on Chet references, they're done with enough imagination for it not to matter. The electric group on *Noir* is vibrant, if a little overcooked. The better tracks are when di Battista plays and the pace is a little less frenetic. Rava's model is obviously the Miles Davis of the early '70s, and to that extent he does a good job, but it is an old-fashioned sound.

The CD comes with a comic book – or 'graphic novel' – which may delight some purchasers.

***(*) D.N.A.

Giants Of Jazz CD 53302 *Rava; Mario Rusca (p); Lucio Terzano (b); Tony Arco (d).* 12/96.

Though associated with budget reissue, the Italian-based Giants of Jazz has also started to issue newly recorded sessions, and it seems appropriate that Rava should be one of the first artists so documented. With the exception of four themes by pianist Rusca, who is reminiscent of compatriot Enrico Pieranunzi, all the tunes are standards, and it's fascinating to hear Rava, now 35 years into his career, return to the repertoire he must first have heard on Miles Davis records. The phrasing and articulation still betray an influence, but the voice is entirely the Italian's own. Play 'Out Of Nowhere' or 'My Foolish Heart' back to back with Prestige-era Miles, and the differences are marked.

**** Duo En Noir

Between The Lines btl 004 *Rava; Ran Blake (p).* 9/99.

A tribute to the late Art Farmer, recorded live in Frankfurt and issued on Franz Koglmann's new label, *Duo En Noir* represents one of the most creative pairings of Rava's career. The material is astonishingly varied, in the first ten minutes ranging from 'Nature Boy' to Bernard Hermann film music, and taking in modern themes like Al Green's gospelly love song, 'Let's Stay Together', as well as 'There's A Small Hotel'. Needless to say, given the instincts of both musicians, none of the material is played entirely straight. Blake can occasionally sound brittle and abstract, but there is real warmth to his playing here, while Rava sounds as if he uses best extra-virgin instead of valve oil, a lovely, compelling tone that recalls the great swing trumpeters and, of course, Art Farmer himself. Delightful.

Jason Rebello (born 1970)

PIANO

One of the young leading lights of the British 'jazz revival' of the 1980s, Rebello made some albums for BMG Novus but didn't make a tremendous international impact. After a spell of self-imposed seclusion, he returned to regular activity in 1998 and cut a new record. He has lately been working in Sting's touring ensemble.

*** Next Time Round

Onion ONR1003 *Rebello; Mark Turner (ts, ss); Orlando Le Fleming (b); Jeff Tain Watts, Jeremy Stacey (d). n.d.*

A fine comeback for the precocious (and no longer so young) pianist whose thoughtful music it was a pleasure to encounter a decade and more ago. Rebello's compositions have a touch of the abstruse about them, and that well suits a musician such as Turner, whose own playing never comes at you from an obvious vantage-point. Watts (Stacey deps on a single track) might have approached this as a cutting context ten years earlier, but he plays for the group; on 'Kenny's Song' (a dedication to the late Kirkland, who once produced a Rebello album) the trio finds an intense but clear-headed kind of group improvising. But there are things that still let the record down. Too much music was let on to the disc, which detracts from its overall impact – we could have done without yet another 'Round Midnight', surely – and there are moments when the musicians seem to be playing for themselves, adrift from listeners who are presumably meant to sit back and be impressed by some of the complexities. The producer needed to find a way to, say, throw Rebello's version of 'Jerusalem' into a more meaningful light. But welcome back.

The Recyclers

GROUP

Organized by drummer Steve Arguëlles, this is a multinational group of a fairly free-spirited nature.

***(*) Rhymes

ZZ 84111 *Noel Akchoté (g); Benoit Delbecq (p); Steve Arguëlles (d).* 93.

**** Visit

Babel BDV 9716 *As above, except add Wolter Wierbos (tb), François Houle (acl), Billy Jenkins (g), Kenneth Newby (suling).* 95.

The product of Steve Arguëlles's move to France, this is a group that has defined its own territory very quickly: mid-way between the tricky and ironic theatricals of Loose Tubes and the eclectic free bop that reigns on the Paris scene. Recorded on the fly over the summer of 1995, *Visit* documents a series of visits with guest performers. Jenkins has been a friend for years and is as waywardly brilliant as ever. The real delight is an encounter in Vancouver with the superb Canadian saxophonist Houle. Much of the material is rough and unpolished, home recording at its best, and yet it has a consistency of purpose and of quality that is deeply impressive. Akchoté is a player to watch, mercurial and sometimes almost perverse, but never less than interesting. Arguëlles's own progress is steady, quiet and unflusterable. He will find his own way whatever the context.

Red Records All Stars

GROUP

Convened under Victor Lewis's apparent leadership, the All Stars repay a long-standing debt of gratitude to the Italian-based label.

***(*) Together Again For The First Time

Red RR123275-2 *Bobby Watson (ss, as); Jerry Bergonzi (ts); Kenny Barron (p); David Finck, Curtis Lundy (b); Victor Lewis (d).* 6/96.

The album title doesn't quite make sense, but it conveys the right impression. This sounds like a reunion rather than a one-off recording. Lewis, who always sounded uneasy in the presence of Ray Mantilla (another Red loyalist), is very much in charge here and, teamed with the resourceful and unflappable Barron, he creates an expansive groove for the two very contrasting front men. Watson's sharp-edged wail and Latin feel are intriguingly juxtaposed with Bergonzi's more plangent and emotionally restless sound. Jerry's entry on bassist Finck's 'Look At You' is an example. Obviously influenced by early-period Coltrane, it's a well-organized statement but nothing like as well-shaped as Watson's response. As always with these ventures, writing credits are evenly distributed. It's not clear whether Lundy was unavailable for part of the session or whether Finck was always part of the game-plan. Curtis is such a distinctive player that his arrival makes a quantum difference, but David has plenty of ideas and a broad, nimble sound. A fine album and a must for Red collectors.

Freddie Redd (born 1927)

PIANO

Still best remembered for his Blue Note set of music from The Connection, Redd is a journeyman hard-bopper of honest service, with a modest showing on record.

***** Piano: East / West**

Original Jazz Classics OJC 1705 *Redd; John Ore (b); Ron Jefferson (d).* 2/55.

***** San Francisco Suite**

Original Jazz Classics OJC 1748 *Redd; George Tucker (b); Al Dreares (d).* 10/57.

***** Live At The Studio Grill**

Triloka 182 2 *Redd; Al McKibbon (b); Billy Higgins (d).* 5/88.

***** Everybody Loves A Winner**

Milestone MCD 9187 *Redd; Curtis Peagler (as); Teddy Edwards (ts); Phil Ranelin (tb); Bill Langlois (b); Larry Hancock (d).* 90.

Redd's amiable West Coast bop soundtracks an unscripted (but you've seen it) Bay Area movie: bustling streetcars, pretty girls flashing their legs, sudden fogs and alarms, an apology for a narrative. The *San Francisco Suite* is cliché from start to finish but, like the very much later *Winner* (Redd has been only a sporadic recorder in recent years), the hackneyed moods are done unpretentiously and engagingly. He was a lot more coherent when there was a real narrative to deal with. Redd was one of several jazzmen drawn to Jack Gelber's drugs drama, *The Connection*, and in Jackie McLean he had a player who knew both the music and the life inside out, the one illuminating and shadowing the other; but the Blue Note album which documents the music has once again been cut from the catalogue.

Redd is a player who hasn't been able to fall back on an absolutely secure playing technique. The younger Redd certainly gave Hampton Hawes no frights on the double-header *Piano: East/West* disc, and his biggest strength has always been the kind of terse writing the Gelber play inspired and which the San Francisco skyline unfortunately didn't. The Studio Grill sessions document a career-reviving residency in the Santa Monica Boulevard restaurant. 'I'll Remember April' has a vivid bounce that contrasts well with the blunt block-chords Redd favours in his own compositions. It and the closing 'All The Things You Are' are the two longest cuts of the set, suggesting perhaps a degree of Redd's frustration at the lack of sympathetic recording opportunities over the years. 'Waltzin' In' is the best of the originals, a bright, hummable melody that, like 'Don't Lose The Blues', sounds as if it ought to be a long-serving standard. 'Round Midnight' (credited to Monk, Bernice Hanighan and Cootie Williams) is beautifully executed, with just a hint of Redd's impressionism creeping back in.

Everybody Loves A Winner again highlights his talent as a composer (and some of his limitations as a performer). The addition of horns gives him some room for experiment, certainly more than with a conventional piano trio, but only Curtis Peagler's youthful alto in any way attempts to break the mould. An interesting figure, but by no means a 'neglected genius'. His critical standing is just about right.

Rob Reddy

ALTO AND SOPRANO SAXOPHONES

New York saxman with his boisterous little big band.

***** Post-War Euphoria**

Songlines SGL 1512-2 *Reddy; Eddie E.J Allen (t); Josh Roseman (tb); Jef Lee Johnson (g); Dom Richards (b); Pheeroan akLaff (d).* 1/96.

Reddy calls his group the Honor System; their album, recorded in New Jersey, is a rumbustious event, almost a party record if you think recent downtown New York jazz should be played at parties. Tracks like 'The Pipe Smoker' and 'Same Old' rattle and roll along, the ensemble making a lot of noise and driven by AkLaff's falling-downstairs drum parts which are as exuberant as they should be. Rather than handing out solos, Reddy breaks his group down into twos and threes and fours, so there's a broad range of duets and ensembles scattered through a lot of music (over 70 minutes) and they're all playing to the max. The drawback is that nothing peaks or stands out, which makes the disc, for all its spirited blowing (and Reddy himself, while not the most renowned name here, is probably the most vivid voice), fade into the background when it should collar the attention.

*****(*) Songs That You Can Trust**

Koch 7876 *As above.* 2/99.

The glib judgement (a route we never countenance, of course) is that this is more of the same. Reddy has assembled exactly the same group, a feat in itself in these peripatetic circles, and they're called on to blast their way through material which calls for the group to create its own relentless dynamic, rather than following by-the-numbers structures. The results, though, are as enlivening as the first record, and endowed with extra wit, grace and point. 'Prayer 1' is a genuinely affecting dirge. 'Count Your Blessings', which takes an age to get going and makes it worthwhile in the end, shows that Reddy's prepared to take his time. The best of this proposes an ensemble music worthy to stand beside Threadgill and Shannon Jackson, which in this book is high praise.

Dewey Redman (born 1931)

TENOR SAXOPHONE, ALTO SAXOPHONE, CLARINET, MUSETTE

Redman grew up in Ornette Coleman's home town and was the anchor member of one of Ornette's most incendiary bands. Dewey was almost thirty before he opted for a full-time musical career, and to some extent has never quite caught up with the slow start. His output as leader is quite small but has filled up in recent years. He has also been a member of Keith Jarrett's American quartet and of the Ornette repertory band, Old and New Dreams.

**** Ear Of The Behearer

Impulse! IMP 12712 *Redman; Ted Daniel (t, Moroccan bugle); Leroy Jenkins (vn); Jane Robertson (clo); Sirone (b, wood f); Eddie Moore (d, perc); Danny Johnson (perc).* 6/73, 9/74.

Redman's career has been notably erratic. The 1966 album *Look For The Black Star* has long been deleted, but the reappearance of *Ear*, repackaged with much of the later and much underrated *Coincide*, is a cause for rejoicing. Dewey's intense, vocalized tone was like nothing else around, but it drew on elements of Coltrane, Ayler and Ornette, as well as the once-dishonoured tradition of Texan honkers and wailers.

Redman enjoyed a long and very fruitful association with drummer Eddie Moore, who has something of the power and visceral impact of Charles Moffett and Eric Gravátt but with a gentler and more softly articulated quality underlying it. Dewey plays three pieces on alto during the *Ear* session, with just one track, 'Image (In Disguise)', on musette, but he switches to tenor for the darker-toned *Coincide*. Daniel returns on the later session and there is a cameo appearance by Leroy Jenkins on 'Seeds And Deeds'. For our money, the closing piece, 'Qow', is definitive Redman. A remarkable pair of albums, too long out of circulation. A shame that there wasn't room for more material from these fiery sessions.

*** Redman And Blackwell In Willisau

Black Saint 120093 *Redman; Ed Blackwell (d).* 8/80.

***(*) Musics

Original Jazz Classics OJCCD 1860-2 *Redman; Fred Simmons (tb); Mark Helias (b); Eddie Moore (d).* 10/78.

***(*) Living On The Edge

Black Saint 120123 *Redman; Geri Allen (p); Cameron Brown (b); Eddie Moore (d).* 9/89.

*** Choices

Enja ENJ 7073 *Redman; Joshua Redman (ts); Cameron Brown (b); Leon Parker (d).* 7/92.

Redman's strong Middle Eastern influence is perhaps most evident on the duets with Blackwell, where the musette introduces a subtle microtonal dimension which builds on Dewey's vocalized approach on single-reeded horns. Blackwell's chops are so finely attuned in contexts like this that it is hard at moments to imagine that there are two musical personalities at work. It is also hard, though, to avoid the impression that this is a sheared and foreshortened Ornette session.

At the opposite end of the decade, *Living On The Edge* preserves much of the menace Redman generated on the Impulse! sessions but with a new simplicity of emotion and with a tone notably less forced than on previous outings. There are strong parallels between Redman's quiet accommodation and Pharoah Sanders, though the Texan has retained more of the fire and fight of his youth. Allen is an ideal partner in that she is willing to examine intervals that fall outside the usual geometry of blues and bebop, but she also has an unfailing rhythmic awareness that keeps Redman within bounds.

The OJC set, originally recorded for Galaxy, features the band which Redman alternated with the Ornette repertory group, Old and New Dreams. *Musics* combines a samba, a stirring march, interludes on musette and autoharp and a totally unexpected version of Gilbert O'Sullivan's 'Alone Again (Naturally)'. Moore has a whale of a time, and the rich harmonic landscape introduced by Simmons (a very underrated musician) stands duty for piano and sometimes a whole horn section. An unexpected and highly enjoyable record.

Choices received more than usual attention because of the presence of Redman Jr. He had just graduated from Harvard and was being wooed and profiled right across the business. Pointless to listen for ancestral influences. Joshua grew up away from Dad and doesn't sound remotely like him. Dewey sticks with alto for all but 'Everything Happens To Me', a big, soft, tenor ballad perhaps included to show the kid – who sits this one out – that playing the sorrow songs still requires more than a Harvard scroll. Dewey plays it cool and spare and well this side of mawkishness. Joshua takes his turn with a slower theme on 'Imagination' and cuts an elegant solo. He gets some room again on 'O'Besso' when Dewey switches to musette. This is one of his less successful Eastern ideas and at 14 minutes is way too long. The final track, dedicated to the memory of drummer Eddie Moore, is a stormer, with an expansive free section in the middle that pits the Redmen against each other in what initially sounds like a stand-off and which develops steadily into a shoulder-to-shoulder surge which the old guy wins by a whisker. Just as it should be.

***(*) In London

Palmetto PM 2030 *Redman; Rita Marcotulli (p); Cameron Brown (b); Matt Wilson (d).* 10/96.

Recorded live at Ronnie Scott's club, Redman sounds rejuvenated and adventuresome with a band that splits down naturally into two pairs, himself and long-standing oppo Brown up against the young Italian Marcotulli and Wilson. The Mid-Westerner is the first white drummer to be hired by the saxophonist, and he repays the confidence handsomely. The band actually work from a different axis on 'Tu-Inns', the most adventurous tune on the set. Piano and bass take off darkly, building up a steady, brooding ostinato against which saxophone and drums enter with an explosion of sound. As ever, Redman mixes outside and relatively mainstream styles, giving 'The Very Thought Of You', his tribute to Dexter Gordon, a loose, swinging energy and Sammy Cahn's 'I Should Care' an easy, melodic interpretation. 'Portrait In Black And White' is an unexpectedly straightforward Jobim cover, but what's interesting about each of these middle-of-the-road numbers is how carefully they're juxtaposed with the more adventurous material. Tunes like 'I-Pimp', 'Kleerwine' and 'Elevens' suggest that Redman hasn't abandoned his loyalty to the avant-garde. A remarkable record, characterized by some daring group-interaction. The sound is a bit uninflected, but the performances more than make up for any technical insufficiency.

****(*) Momentum Space**
Verve 559944-2 *Redman; Cecil Taylor (p); Elvin Jones (d).* 98.

After all this time, they must have been astonished to be asked, or perhaps mildly peeved. The result is a flat, chaotic sampling of deutero-radical approaches with most of the power sucked out. Cecil at least sounds as though he's having fun here and there, but Dewey and Elvin honk and thrash away without much purpose, and 'Life', 'As', 'It', 'Is' is as ungainly a sequence as these remarkable gentlemen can ever have consigned to record. That said, the sound is very good indeed, well up to the standard you'd hope for and expect, and it's wonderful to hear the supertrio at all, even if they are crashing gears much of the time.

Don Redman (1900–64)

ALTO AND SOPRANO SAXOPHONES, OTHER INSTRUMENTS, BANDLEADER

Joined Fletcher Henderson in 1923 as arranger and reed player, then was lured away to McKinney's Cotton Pickers. Led own band, 1931–40, before writing for other bandleaders. Toured with a post-war big band in 1946, and later freelanced for New York orchestras in the '50s. One of the pioneer jazz arrangers and a fine multi-instrumentalist.

*****(*) Don Redman, 1931–1933**
Classics 543 *Redman; Henry Allen, Shirley Clay, Bill Coleman, Langston Curl, Reunald Jones, Sidney De Paris (t); Claude Jones, Benny Morton, Fred Robinson, Gene Simon (tb); Jerry Blake (cl, as, bs); Robert Cole, Edward Inge (cl, as); Harvey Boone (as, bs); Robert Carroll (ts); Horace Henderson, Don Kirkpatrick (p); Talcott Reeves (bj, g); Bob Ysaguirre (bb, b); Manzie Johnson (d, vib); Chick Bullock, Cab Calloway, Harlan Lattimore, The Mills Brothers (v); Bill Robinson (tap dancing).* 9/31–5/36.

***** Don Redman, 1933–1936**
Classics 553 *As above.*

***** Chant Of The Weed**
Topaz TPZ 1043 *As above, except add Tom Stevenson, Robert Williams (t), Quentin Jackson (tb), Carl Frye, Edward Inge (cl, as, bs), Eddie Williams, Gene Sedric (ts).* 28–38.

Redman remains one of the essential figures of the pre-war jazz period. He started out as lead saxophonist and staff arranger with Fletcher Henderson's band, infusing the charts with a breathtaking simplicity and confidence, eventually leaving in 1928 to front the highly successful McKinney's Cotton Pickers. This was his most celebrated music, but some of the music under his own leadership in the '30s surpassed his earlier charts, even if the recordings are inconsistent. The material on the two Classics discs is the core of Redman's output. The earlier of the pair features the band's remarkable theme-tune, 'Chant Of The Weed', Redman's brilliant and justly celebrated arrangement of 'I Got Rhythm' and two cuts of the title-track. The band at this time also featured Harlan Lattimore, one of the few genuinely challenging singers of the era, who was once described by George T. Simon as sounding like a rather hip Bing Crosby; one man or the other is spinning in his coffin even now. The arrangements are well up to scratch, and there is more impressive work from Lattimore. Bojangles Robinson tip-taps on one version of the title-piece, but the better cut features the Mills Brothers and Cab Calloway.

The Topaz compilation is, as they always are, a useful fast run-through of the career, without much depth of focus at any point. The obvious things are there – 'Chant Of The Weed', 'Shakin' The African', 'Nagasaki' – and there aren't any glaring chronological gaps. A very worthwhile purchase.

Joshua Redman (born 1969)

TENOR, ALTO AND SOPRANO SAXOPHONES

Dewey Redman's son became a figurehead for the young American jazz movement of the '90s. After winning the 1991 Thelonious Monk Competition, he began making a series of high-profile albums for Warner Bros. Despite an eclectic choice of material, Redman has so far preferred to work in straight-ahead settings and he brings an almost purist approach to his own recording.

****** Joshua Redman**
Warner Bros 945242-2 *Redman; Kevin Hays, Mike LeDonne (p); Christian McBride, Paul LaDuca (b); Gregory Hutchinson, Clarence Penn, Kenny Washington (d).* 5–9/92.

****** Wish**
Warner Bros 945365-2 *Redman; Pat Metheny (g); Charlie Haden (b); Billy Higgins (d).* 93.

*****(*) Mood Swing**
Warner Bros 9362-45643-2 *Redman; Brad Mehldau (p); Christian McBride (b); Brian Blade (d).* 3/94.

***** Spirit Of The Moment – Live At The Village Vanguard**
Warner Bros 945923-2 2CD *Redman; Peter Martin (p); Christopher Thomas (b); Brian Blade (d).* 3/95.

Joshua Redman's first albums caused a sensation, and their commercial success is deserved: few discs in recent years have communicated such sheer joy in playing as these. Although he had already made some interesting sideman appearances, the saxophonist's eponymous set was a stunning debut: a canny blend of bop, standards, the odd tricky choice (Monk's 'Trinkle Tinkle') and young man's fancy (James Brown's 'I Got You (I Feel Good)'), all of it buoyed up on the kind of playing that suggests an instant maturity. His lean tone turned out to be as limber or as weighty as he wished, his phrasing had plenty of spaces but could cruise at any bebop height, and his invention sounded unquenchable. The euphoric but controlled feeling extends to his sidemen, Hays, McBride and Hutchinson (two odd tracks were drafted in from other sessions). Beautifully recorded, too.

Wish was an equally splendid follow-up: a little more self-conscious with the starry support group, and a couple of the tunes (Eric Clapton's 'Tears In Heaven'?) seemed a little too modish; but the more open harmonics of Metheny's guitar and the gravitas of Haden and Higgins framed the younger man's improvisations with great eloquence. The bonus live versions of 'Wish' (from the first album) and a roughly sketched 'Blues

For Pat' add a further dimension and extend the joyousness of Redman's playing.

After such a start, *Mood Swing* had huge expectations to live up to. It's still a very impressive record, but it's just arguable that the sheer *joie de vivre* of the playing on the first two records has been suspended in favour of a more considered, careful methodology. Not that Redman holds much back in his solos, or that his group are any less imposing. Mehldau, in fact, gives notice that he is a star in the making himself: his contributions, allusive, mischievous and profound by turns, are as substantial as the leader's own. And McBride and Blade are superfine. But here and there are traces of a self-conscious eloquence that suggest a spirit in transition.

Spirit Of The Moment might also be a snapshot analysis of work in progress. There are inevitable recalls of the great Rollins records of nearly 40 years before, especially when Redman tackles 'My One And Only Love' and 'St Thomas'. But this is more exhaustive – two CDs of close to 80 minutes apiece – and more prone to longueurs. As good as the group is, it doesn't really match either the quartet on *Mood Swing* or Redman's previous touring band of McBride, Blade and Eric Reed. Perhaps, too, the days of a new voice setting down an instantaneous great document, as Rollins once did, are as long gone for jazz as is, say, the idea of rock giants cutting their debut set in an afternoon (cf. the Beatles). Gripes aside – and when a man makes a start as powerful as Redman's, one can't help but be anticipatory – there's still much great jazz here.

***(*) Freedom In The Groove

Warner Bros 46330-2 *Redman; Peter Martin (p); Peter Bernstein (g); Christopher Thomas (b); Brian Blade (d).* 4/96.

It's hard to imagine Redman making a less than enjoyable record at this point. He has such a fine sound, fertile imagination and ambitious delivery that he is a kind of celebration of the core jazz language in himself. But his stance is inevitably becoming more mediated and arranged as he goes on. His own sleeve-note essay, which details the background to his musical tastes and his viewpoint on eclecticism, may be entirely from the heart, but in the context of a major-label jazz disc it can't help but read like a press flak's handout. The ten originals on the disc are a catchy set of variations on various forms – a touch of the blues, a couple of groove tunes, a modal blow, a Coltraneish prayer – that he has absorbed along the way. The solos are uniformly (perhaps *too* uniformly – the odd stumble might humanize him a little) handsome and eloquent, and of course his group is a talented one. He benefits further from Matt Pierson's shrewd production and a really splendid studio sound from James Farbar. At this point, Redman can't surprise us; he can only play his best strokes. For many, that will be enough.

***(*) Timeless Tales For Changing Times

Warner Bros 9362-47052-2 *Redman; Brad Mehldau (p); Larry Grenadier (b); Brian Blade (d).* 98.

It was a good idea for Redman to do an album of modern-day cover-versions: he's young enough to empathize with an audience that knows about Prince and Stevie Wonder (although his choices of pop material are actually rather old-fashioned and conservative, with names like Joni Mitchell and Bob Dylan in the composer credits) but determined enough to make them part of an uncompromised jazz record. Mehldau especially is a like-minded conspirator in this. The result is an intelligent and incisive repertory record. Wonder's 'Visions' and Mitchell's 'I Had A King' are vehicles in which the improvisations grow plausibly out of the song structure. There's no sense that the players use some motif from the song as a peg on which to hang increasingly remote solos: Redman has arranged the material too assiduously for that. He plants 'Summertime' and 'Yesterdays' in there as if to democratize the set-list, too. This record didn't excite as much attention as his earlier sets, but it feels like a genuine step forward for him.

*** Beyond

Warner Bros 9362-47465-2 *Redman; Mark Turner (ts); Aaron Goldberg (p); Reuben Rogers (b); Gregory Hutchinson (d).* 5/99.

The one entirely satisfying piece here is 'Leap Of Faith', where guest tenor Turner engages in a thinkers' duel with the leader, a compelling interchange of views that turns a neat circle across nine minutes. The other pieces, though, never break out of their cryptic skin. 'Balance' and the very long 'Twilight ... And Beyond' are particularly perverse in the way that they turn into mere bombast after their careful development, as if Redman felt that he had to reach catharsis of some kind. In the circumstances, his new group makes no definite impression on music that needs to provide listeners with more of a map than Redman has here.

Dizzy Reece (born 1931)

TRUMPET

A Jamaican, Reece was working in Europe from 1949, basing himself in London from 1954, then settling in New York from 1959. Though a frequently encountered name in bop circles, he recorded comparatively little.

***(*) Asia Minor

Original Jazz Classics OJC 1806 *Reece; Joe Farrell (ts, f); Cecil Payne (bs); Hank Jones (p); Ron Carter (b); Charli Persip (d).* 62.

Reece established his base of operations in Europe for a long while and became a regular partner of British players like Tubby Hayes and Victor Feldman. One of his rare British sessions was *Progress Report* for Tempo, which someone should revive, and his Blue Note dates, *Star Bright* and *Blues In Trinity*, are both tough to find. Even at a somewhat later stage, Reece is slightly difficult to pin down stylistically. Though he can play skyrocketing top-note lines, there's something curiously melancholy about his work on *Asia Minor*, an all-too-rare solo recording which recalls some of the South African players. His trump card here is, of course, the marvellous band he has round him, all of whom contribute to this very welcome calling-card from a dedicated practitioner who has been unjustly neglected in recent years.

Eric Reed (born 1970)

PIANO

Reed came to prominence as a member of the Wynton Marsalis group, with whom he still plays. Born in Philadelphia, he moved to Los Angeles at eleven and was playing with Gerald Wilson when still only sixteen.

****(*) Soldier's Hymn**
Candid CCD 79511 *Reed; Dwayne Burno (b); Gregory Hutchinson (d).* 11/90.

Although intended as a showcase debut for Reed, *Soldier's Hymn* is much more of a trio record. Originals like the title-piece (present in two different versions) and 'Coup De Cone' are conscious evaluations of the manner of a Jazz Messengers rhythm section (Art Blakey is the album's dedicatee), and elsewhere Reed's chord-based solos and call-and-response interplay suggest the influence of Ahmad Jamal or even Ramsey Lewis. This works out well on the less ambitious pieces – 'Soft Winds' is an impressive update of the old Benny Goodman tune – but on the more portentous tracks, such as 'Things Hoped For' or the half-baked medley which Reed does as a solo turn, the music sounds more like a demo session than a finished record.

****(*) Musicale**
Impulse! 11962 *Reed; Nicholas Payton (t); Wycliffe Gordon (tb); Wessell Anderson (as); Ben Wolfe, Ron Carter (b); Karriem Riggins, Gregory Hutchinson (d).* 3–4/96.

***** Pure Imagination**
Impulse! 12592 *Reed; Reginald Veal, Reuben Rogers (b); Gregory Hutchinson, Carl Allen (d).* 7/97.

Reed had a couple of albums for the MoJazz label which are now in limbo, so it's a bit of a jump from the Candid debut to *Musicale*, which was a disappointment, fussily conceived and executed. 'Black, As In Buhaina' is a strong opening tribute to Art Blakey, but thereafter the record never seems to settle, several of the pieces stopping just as they're getting started, and only on the closing blues, where Gordon sits in, does the music find a relaxed groove. *Pure Imagination*, a sequence of show tunes book-ended by an opening and closing piece by Reed, feels much stronger, even if the playing has an air of self-regard which some may find annoying. Reed has a congratulatory touch that isn't always agreeable, but when he lets the songs breathe he finds a very lyrical note, and Veal and Hutchinson (the other two arrive for the last track only) swing.

*****(*) Manhattan Melodies**
Impulse! 129242 *Reed; Reginald Veal (b); Gregory Hutchinson (d); Renato Thoms (perc); Diana Reeves (v).* 99.

Immensely confident, as ever, this time Reed delivers a mightily impressive set, based around songs associated with New York. The thunderous assault on 'The 59th Street Bridge Song (Feelin' Groovy)' makes for an intimidating opener, but it's carried off with aplomb, and that mix of grandstanding and assurance sets the tone for the record. 'Blues Five Spot', with its simultaneous multiple time, is Monk rewritten in the most virtuosic terms. This is solo, but most of the record is Reed, Veal and Hutchinson working as one, massively swinging and steely with determination. Not that they can't be cool when they want: 'An Englishman In New York' is fetchingly attired, and the closing ballad treatment of 'New York, New York' is four minutes of utter serenity. Some may find Reed's power-packed delivery too bombastic by half, but it's hard to shut out his command of what he's doing.

Ruben Reeves (1905–55)

TRUMPET, BANDLEADER

Reeves was a Chicagoan who taught music during the day. He led his own recording band for a brief period at the end of the 1920s, but the records were indifferently received and he later joined the Cab Calloway band. He played as section-man for various leaders after the war, but quit the busienss in 1952.

***** The Complete Vocalions 1928–1933**
Timeless CBC 1-039 *Reeves; Fats Robins, James Tate, Cicero Thomas (t); Eddie Atkins, William Franklin, Gerald Reeves, John Thomas (tb); Darnell Howard, Fred Brown (cl, as); Fess Williams, Omer Simeon (cl); Ralph Brown (as); Franz Jackson, Norval Morton (ts, f); Clarence Lee, Bobby Wall, Joe McCutchin (vn); Jimmy Prince, Eddie King (p); Cecil White (g); Lawrence Dixon (bj, v); Elliott Washington (bj); Harry Gray (tba); Sudie Reynaud (b); Jasper Taylor, Richard Barnes (d); Blanche Calloway (v).* 4/28–12/33.

Ruben 'River' Reeves was seen by Vocalion as a rival to Louis Armstrong, and the 15 titles he made in 1929 are a sort of riposte to Armstrong's Hot Seven and Five sides. As with Jabbo Smith, Reeves was both like and unlike Armstrong: a similar *brio* but not quite the same mastery of execution, and he stumbles at moments when Louis would simply soar. But he was still a very good trumpet player and, with bandsmen like Simeon and Howard also on hand, the music is a splendid evocation of small-group Chicago jazz at a great moment in time. The records sold poorly and Reeves returned to the studios as a leader on only one further occasion, to cut the four 1933 titles which close the disc. The band is much bigger, but the leader still sounds commanding and fiery. He spent the rest of his career doing section work before becoming a bank guard. This is his story (aside from one lost master, 'Bottoms Up') and, judged on solos like those in 'Papa Skag Stomp' and 'Head Low', it bears plenty of re-telling. Excellent remastering in what is one of the best-presented reissue series of the period.

Hans Reichel (born 1949)

GUITAR, PREPARED GUITAR, DAXOPHONE/DACHSOPHON, OTHER INSTRUMENTS

Some rock background, but basically a free-music specialist on guitar and his invented 'daxophone', as well as on other customized string instruments. Can be as melodious and pretty as he is dissonant in his music.

****** The Death Of The Rare Bird Ymir / Bonobo Beach**
FMP CD 54 *Reichel (g solo).* 2/79–4/81.

***** The Dawn Of Dachsmann (Plus)**
FMP 60 *Reichel (g, daxophone solo).* 5–7/87.

***** Angel Carver**
FMP CD 15 *Reichel; Tom Cora (clo, cellodax).* 10/88.

***** Coco Bolo Nights**
FMP CD 10 *Reichel (g solo).* 12/88.

*****(*) Stop Complaining / Sundown**
FMP CD 36 *Reichel; Fred Frith, Kazuhisa Uchihashi (g).* 6/90–1/91.

*****(*) Shanghaied On Tor Road**
FMP CD 46 *Reichel (daxophone solo).* 2–3/92.

*****(*) Lower Lurum**
CD BRD 016 *As above.* 94.

Riveting free-form guitar with a strong narrative flavour and a complete absence of the 'I've suffered for my art, now it's your turn' aggression of much solo improvised music. Reichel clearly desires to communicate and to convey a story, however notionally and abstractly. His playing is unfussy and uncluttered and he's generally best heard solo, though Cora offers stimulating support. The 'prepared' effects on some of the earlier records (which have disappeared with FMP's vinyl catalogue) are less effective than his admirably disciplined real-time performances, though he coaxes intriguing sounds from a group of personalized instruments which have some connection to the life and life-philosophy of Herr Dachsmann. The marvellous *Death Of The Rare Bird Ymir* (now slightly edited and paired on CD with *Bonobo Beach*) is probably the best of the albums. Recorded in real time, it features Reichel using such challenging devices as playing two guitars simultaneously (something Derek Bailey had done on Gavin Bryars's piece, *The Squirrel And The Rickety-Rackety Bridge*), playing fretless guitars and picking below the bridge on an electric instrument. Reichel has also pioneered a group of instruments associated with Dachsmann, his imaginary version of Adolphe Sax. *Shanghaied* is devoted entirely to one of these, and a pretty strange sound it makes, too.

The long duet with Frith is curiously jazzy in places, almost as if he and Reichel were spoofing those chummy two-guitar sessions the catalogue is littered with. The Japanese is an interesting player and the live set from Kobe is starkly involving. Later material begins to sound rather similar, but a great deal depends from which end you are approaching this original and offbeat entertainer. Anyone stumbling across *Lower Lurum* (billed as an 'operetta' for guitar and daxophone) will be bowled over. Those who have followed Reichel's course over the years may need the aural equivalent of a sorbet before appreciating yet another weirdly rich course.

Django Reinhardt (1910–53)

GUITAR, VIOLIN

One of the few genuine legends of the music, Jean Baptiste Reinhardt was born at Liverchies in Belgium. He was something of a prodigy and played professionally before his teens. When he was eighteen, though, a fire in his caravan seriously damaged his hand and for the rest of his life he had to negotiate two clawed fingers on his fretting hand. The Django legend developed between the wars with the success of the Quintette du Hot Club de France. As a gypsy, he survived the Second World War only through the patronage of a Luftwaffe officer who admired his music. After the Liberation, Django became an international hero, travelling to America to work with Duke Ellington. As erratic as he was brilliant, he seemed foredoomed to a short and glittering career, and he died aged just 43 at Samois, near Paris.

*****(*) Django Reinhardt, 1934–1935**
Classics 703 *Reinhardt; Pierre Allier, Gaston Lapeyronnie, Alphonse Cox, Maurice Moufflard, Alex Renard (t); Marcel Dumont, Isidore Bassard, Pierre Deck, René Weiss, Guy Paquinet (tb); André Ekyan (cl, as); Amédée Charles (as); Charles Lisée (as, bs); Andy Foster (as, cl, bsx); Maurice Cizeron (as, cl, f); Noël Chiboust, Alix Combelle (ts); Stéphane Grappelli (vn, p); Michel Warlop (vn); Jean Chabaud (p); Roger Chaput, Joseph Reinhardt (g); Roger Chomer (vib); Juan Fernandez, Roger Grasset, Louis Pecqueux, Louis Volas (b); Maurice Chaillou (d, v); Bert Marshall (v).* 3/34–3/35.

****** Django Reinhardt, 1935–1936**
Classics 739 *Reinhardt; Bill Coleman, Alex Renard (t); George Johnson (cl); Maurice Cizeron (as, f); Alix Combelle (ts); Garnet Clark (p); Stéphane Grappelli (vn); Pierre Feret, Joseph Reinhardt (g); June Cole, Lucien Simoens, Louis Vola (b); Freddy Taylor (v).* 9/35–10/36.

****** Swing From Paris**
ASV CD AJA 5070 *Reinhardt; Stéphane Grappelli (vn); Roger Chaput, Pierre Ferret, Joseph Reinhardt, Eugène Vées (g); Robert Grassnet, Tony Rovira, Emmanuel Soudieux, Louis Vola (b).* 9/35–8/39.

***** Swingin' With Django**
Pro Arte CDD 549 *Reinhardt; Stéphane Grappelli (vn); Joseph Reinhardt, Pierre Ferret, Marcel Bianchi, Eugène Vées (g); Louis Vola (d).* 35–43.

***** Welcome To Jazz: Django Reinhardt**
Koch 322 074 *As above.*

*****(*) Django Reinhardt**
Koch CD 399 533 *As above; no personnels listed.* 36–39.

***** Django Reinhardt, 1937**
Classics 748 *Reinhardt; Stéphane Grappelli (vn); André Ekyan (as); Marcel Bianchi, Pierre Ferret (g); Louis Vola (b).* 4–7/37.

*****(*) Django Reinhardt, 1937 – Volume 2**
Classics 762 *Reinhardt; Stéphane Grappelli, Paul Bartel, Josef Schwetsin, Michel Warlop (vn); Philippe Brun, Gus Deloof, André Cornille, André Pico (t); Guy Paquinet, Josse Breyère (tb); Jean Magnien (cl); Charles Blanc, Max Lisée, André Lamory (as); Charles Shaaf (ts); Maurice Cizeron (f); Georges Paquay (f, d); Pierre Zepilli (p); Louis Gaste, Joseph Reinhardt, Eugène Vées (g); Eugène D'Hellemes (b); Maurice Chaillou (d).* 9–12/37.

*****(*) Django Reinhardt, 1937–1938**
Classics 777 *Similar (i.e. Hot Club de France) to Classics above, except add Jean-Louis Jeanson (tb, vn), André Lluis (as, cl), John Arslanian (cl, bcl, ts, bs), Adrien Mareze, Noël Chiboust (ts), Larry Adler (hca), Roger Pirenet, Roger Du Hautbourg (vn), Bob*

Vaz (p), André Taylor (d), Gregoire Coco Aslan (perc), André Dassary (v). 12/37–6/38.

*****(*) Jazz Masters 38: Django Reinhardt**

Verve 516393-2 *Similar to above.* 38–53.

****** Bruxelles / Paris**

Musidisc 403222 *As above, except add Raymond Fol (p).*

***** Django Reinhardt, 1938–1939**

Classics 793 *Similar to above, except add Bob Stewart (c), Barney Bigard (cl, d), Billy Taylor (b).* 6/38–4/39.

*****(*) Django Reinhardt, 1939–1940**

Classics 813 *Similar to above, except add Frank Big Boy Goudie (t), André Ekyan (as), Charles Lewis, Joe Turner (p), Marceau Sarbib, Lucien Simoens (b), Tommy Benford, Charles Delaunay (d).* 5/39–8/40.

One of the Christian-name-only mythical figures of jazz, Django embodies much of the nonsense that surrounds the physically and emotionally damaged who nevertheless manage to parlay their disabilities and irresponsibilities into great music. Django's technical compass, apparently unhampered by loss of movement in two fingers of his left hand (result of a burn which had ended his apprenticeship as a violinist), was colossal, ranging from dazzling high-speed runs to ballad-playing of aching intensity.

Pity the poor discographer who has to approach this material. The Reinhardt discography is now as mountainous as his native Belgium is flat. All we can hope to do is point out a few accessible passes. There is also a problem with titles: the principle seems to be that anything with 'Paris' or 'swing', either in conjunction or separately, will sell records; and there is the additional problem that Django's name has become so iconic that it alone is often deemed enough. There are huge numbers of compilations on the market, some of them of questionable authority and quality, often inaccurately dated and provenanced and with only notional stabs at accurate personnels. But this is a glass house we are entering ...

Classics – who do their usual thorough job – devote a whole CD to the output of just one month in 1937; the tally for the year as a whole is staggering. Unusually for this label, there is quite a bit of material which strictly belongs to other artists, prominently trumpeter Brun, but which features significant amounts of Django and so is included. The series begins with Django's first recordings with the Michel Warlop orchestra in 1934, reaching on into the classic Hot Club sessions over the next couple of years. In bulk, though, the music begins to sound slightly tired and dated, and Django's astonishing technique almost *too* perfect.

The other Classics are no less exhaustive, and the 1938–9 volume, with its roster of guests, is a most valuable indicator of his standing *vis-à-vis* the original begetters of a music he had graced for several years not fully appreciated outside Europe. Other curiosities in the run include four tracks with harmonica genius Larry Adler (who's still around to tell the stories of that day, 60 years ago).

The Koch compilation brings together some excellent material but is severely hampered by the lack of any information beyond year of recording. Most of the songs are very familiar indeed and, as a back-up CD of early favourites, or perhaps as an introduction to Django's work, this would do very well. Shame not to offer a bit of context, though.

The Verve is valuable for the breadth of its coverage. Some will quibble at the lack of earlier material, but the fact that it carries the story right up to the year of Django's death gives the picture a certain valuable symmetry, and the music is, of course, quite wonderful. The Hot Club reunion of 1946 in London is well represented, and some care has been taken to give a reasonable balance of material over the final years, including the poignant 'Night And Day' of March 1953, when the shadows were beginning to draw in.

The ASV is beautifully remastered by Colin Brown, an example of how historical recordings can be restored without intrusive sweetening or inauthentic balances. At 66 minutes, it's also excellent value. It's good to be reminded how extraordinarily forceful the drummerless Hot Club could sound. Even with the chugging background, 'Appel Direct' is remarkably modern, and it's easy to see why Django continues to exert such an influence on guitarists of later, technically more sophisticated generations. The titles are confusingly similar, but this is the best single-volume option.

Most of the other volumes scoot ahead in time and are not as coherent, either artistically or technically, for that reason. The Musidisc offers a more extensive sample of the important sessions of 21 May 1947 (with Hubert Rostaing and the reconstituted Hot Club; the albums share 'Just One Of Those Things') and of 8 April 1953, the month before his death (with Martial Solal; they share a marvellous 'I Cover The Waterfront'), as well as good-quality material from 1951: 'Nuits De St Germain-Des-Prés', 'Crazy Rhythm', 'Fine And Dandy'.

Bruxelles/Paris has a marginally tougher version of 'Nuages'. In 1947, Django was battling with amplification (not always successfully), coping with the repercussions of a not entirely ecstatic reception with Ellington in the USA (ditto), and slipping backwards into the moral vagrancy that undoubtedly shortened his life. On the better tracks, on 'Blues For Barclay', 'Manoir De Mes Rêves', 'Mélodie Du Crépuscule', and 'Nuages', his instincts seem to be intact. He picks off clusters of notes with tremendous compression, holds and bends top notes like a singer and keeps a deep, insistent throb on the bottom string that, when it makes it up through the lo-fi hiss and drop-out, is hugely effective.

****** The Classic Early Recordings In Chronological Order**

JSP Jazz Box JSPCD 901 5CD *As for the above, with some variations.* 34–39.

The first thing to note about this marvellous and superbly priced compilation is that it is not strictly chronological at all, but 'piecewise continuous'. Prompted by the poor quality of the existing reissues (and the shortcomings of the Classics volumes are well documented), remastering engineer Ted Kendall, who learned his craft under the tutelage of the great John R.T. Davies, has cleaned away the 'audio rubble' and restored these great recordings to something like pristine condition. All but the first two tracks on Volume 1, of which there are no original pressings, have been taken from excellent-quality 78s. We have compared in detail 15 tracks from various Classics volumes with their equivalents here, and it is clear that a whole generation of Django listeners have grown up with insecurely pitched renditions, with problems ranging from intermittent flattening of tone to consistently slow transfers, often resulting in tunes being heard a quarter-tone adrift. It would be redundant simply to detail the tracks we have sampled with very close attention. Even a cursory listen suggests that the JSP box, which is issued at a bargain price, is a much more attractive proposition. The arrangement of material is logical enough. Volume 1 consists of the Hot Club recordings of 1934 and 1935, with Stéphane Grappelli strongly featured. Volume 2 corrals the London Deccas and, though Kendall has had to compromise here and there with vinyl and one corroded metal master (only the sharpest ears will notice), the quality remains very high indeed. Volume 3 is discographically trickier since some of the material was never issued on 78. Kendall has clarified a few troublesome points, confirming for instance that a supposed alternative take of 'Time On My Hands' from March 1939 is simply a dub of the original release. Volume 4 steps back in time to the Decca and HMV recordings made between March 1935 (the earliest of them with Coleman Hawkins) and the first Swing label releases of 1937. The last disc rounds up some additional material from 1935 along with the fine 1937 HMVs. The detail shouldn't put anyone off. These are quite splendid jazz records which belong in every collection, and Ted Kendall has done a demanding job with taste and precision.

***** Django Reinhardt, 1940**

Classics 831 *Reinhardt; Philippe Brun, Pierre Allier, Aimé Barelli, Christian Bellest, Alex Renard, Al Piguillem (t); Guy Paquinet, Gaston Moat, Pierre Deck (tb); Hubert Rostaing (cl, ts); Alix Combelle (bs); André Ekyan (as); Charles Lewis, Raymond Wraskoff (p); Pierre Ferret, Joseph Reinhardt (g); Emmanuel Soudieux, Francis Luca (b); Pierre Fouad (d).* 2–10/40.

***** Django Reinhardt, 1940-1941**

Classics 852 *Reinhardt; Pierre Allier, Aimé Barelli, Christian Bellest, Jean Heutchel, Severin Luino, Georges Wallez (t); André Cauzard, Maurice Gladieu, Guy Paquinet (tb); Hubert Rostaing, Christian Wagner (cl); Alix Combelle (cl, ts, glock); Max Blanc, Charles Lisée, Pierre Martineau (as); Roger Allier, Noël Chiboust, Georges Jacquemont (ts); Léo Chauliac, Paul Colot (p); Joseph Reinhardt (g); Tony Rovira (b); Pierre Fouad (d); Charles Trenet (v).* 12/40–3/41.

***** Django Reinhardt, 1941–1942**

Classics 877 *Similar to above, except add Raymond Chantrain, Georges Clais, Paul D'Hondt (t), Sus Van Camp, Jean Damm (tb), Louis Billen, Jo Magis (cl, as), Jeff Van Herswingels (ts), Arthur Saguet (ts, bs, cl), Jack Demany (ts), John Ouwerckx (p), Jim Vanderjeught (p), Arthur Peeters (b), Josse Aerts (d).* 4/41–3/42.

***** Django Reinhardt, 1942–1943**

Classics 905 *Similar to above, except add Alex Caturegli, Lucien Devroye, Maurice Giegas, Janot Morales, Maurice Moufflard, Alex Renard (t), Nick Ferrar, Maurice Gladieu, Louis Melon, Pierre Remy (tb), Gérard Léveque (cl), Bobby Naret, Guy Plum (cl, ts), Robert Mavounzy, Robert Merchez (as), Charles Hary, Benny Pauwels (f, cl, ts), André Lluis, Fud Candrix (cl, ts), Emile Deltour, Chas Dolne, Jean Douillez, Walter Feron, Raymond Goutard, Paulette Izoird, Sylvio Schmidt (vn), Eugène Vées (g), Jean Storne (b), Pierre Fouad, Gaston Léonard (d), Nelly Kay (v).* 5/42–7/43.

***** Django Reinhardt, 1944–1946**

Classics 945 *Reinhardt; Alex Caturegli, Herb Bass, Christian Bellest, Robin Gould, Roger Hubert, Bernie Privin, Jerry Stephan, Lonnie Wilfong (t); Bill Decker, Don Gardner, Shelton Heath, John Kirkpatrick, Marcel Librecht, Pierre Remy (tb); Jim Hayes, Hubert Rostaing (cl, as); Desiré Duriez, Roger JeanJean, André Lluis, Joe Moser (as); Bernie Cavalière, Noël Chiboust, Peanuts Hucko, Gaston Rahier, Bill Zickefoose (ts); Ken Lowther, Yves Raynal (bs); Stéphane Grappelli (vn); Leo Chauliac, Larry Man, Mel Powell (p); Roger Chaput, Alan Hodgkiss, Jack Llewellyn, Joseph Reinhardt (g); Bob Decker, Coleridge Goode, Josz Schulman, Lucien Simoens (b); Bill Bethel, Ray McKinley, Jerry Mengo (d); Sgt Jack Platt (cond).* 11/44–5/46.

The war years obviously brought a certain non-musical poignancy to the story, but the coldest and most detached audition still reveals a shift in Django's playing towards something altogether more inward, secretive, less joyous, and, even when there are no obvious shadows gathering, there is a hint of darkness and doubt. Again there is a good deal of non-Django (or non-lead) material included, largely stuff by Ekyan and Brun; and the latter's session from February 1940, recorded in Paris, has the fascinating discographical footnote of a playing role for Charles Delaunay, who was operating under the aka of H.P. Chadel.

With the war in progress, Django was cut off from many of his greatest sources of inspiration, Grappelli only most obviously, but it also caught him at his peak of popularity and on 13 December 1941 he made the recording of 'Nuages' that was to cement him in jazz history for ever. Even after more than half a century, and the despoliation of a thousand buskers, it's still a wonderful performance. Django had recorded the piece earlier, but he was dissatisfied with the result – and his judgement, as ever, was sound. It's certainly the highlight of the 1940 and 1941 Classics volume. The dating is a little misleading, because only one item from March 1941 is included, a Charles Trenet song – 'La Cigale Et La Fourmi' – with the Quintette du Hot Club de France accompanying. A track credited to 'Festival Swing 1941', a Charles Delaunay-sponsored event, was actually recorded on Boxing Day 1940, as was the celebratory 'Django's Music' line-up originally issued on Swing 95. Most of the remaining material is under the nominal leadership of trumpeter Pierre Allier or clarinettist Christian Wagner and, though Django's personality shines through every time, these are more workaday sessions and not strictly part of the core discography.

The end of 1942 saw Django's behaviour becoming ever more erratic. On another Delaunay tour in the south and Algiers, he refused to play matinees and simply left the party. Delaunay managed to get the remaining players back to the mainland just before the Allied invasion of 8 November 1942. Django had been recording with the Stan Brenders orchestra, an undemanding gig that in no way stretched or challenged him. In the spring of 1943, though, he made some Hot Club sides with Léveque and Lluis sharing the front line, and he also recorded a trio and a couple of improvised solos for the Swing label. The remainder of the year was taken up with collaborations with Fud Candrix and a few sides with a big band, never Django's strongest suit.

The Liberation of Paris was a key moment in the early autumn of 1944 and immediately opened up the jazz and swing scene. The first recordings represented are a session by Noël Chiboust's orchestra, appropriately enough entitled 'Welcome' (Django doesn't play on the first part), but the real delights had to wait until 1945, the beginning and end of the year, when Django recorded with a 'mystery' Hot Club featuring Peanuts Hucko,

Mel Powell and Ray McKinley, and then in November with an American swing band under the direction of Sergeant Jack Platt. 'Djangology' and 'Manoir De Mes Rêves' from the latter session are professional enough, but it's interesting to hear Django playing American standards on the January 1945 session, including a wonderful 'How High The Moon'.

Sentimentally, if not always musically, the reunion with Grappelli was always going to be an important moment. They met up in London in January 1946 and recorded four sides for Swing and another four (including a reworked and extremely disappointing 'Nuages') for Decca the following day. The old magic simply wasn't there, though everyone seems upbeat and keen to play. The British rhythm section had been well versed in Hot Club idiom, but they lack the Gauloise-wreathed cool and sophistication of their cross-Channel counterparts, and the songs never quite come off. Back in Paris in May, there was a date with Rostaing. Again, Django sounds jaded and almost indifferent, and he even fluffs a couple of chord changes on 'Yours And Mine' and 'On The Sunny Side Of The Street'. It had been a long war, but with its passing went the last tension and urgency in Django's playing. Thereafter, he was to become a replica of himself, capable of extraordinary things, but with a critical element missing. Listening to the span of the Classics issues to date, one can't help hearing a fall.

***** Swing Guitar**

Jass J CD 628 *Reinhardt; Herb Bass, Robin Gould, Jerry Stephan, Lonnie Wilfong (t); Bill Decker, Don Gardner, Shelton Heath, John Kirkpatrick (tb); Jim Hayes (cl, as); Joe Moser (as); Bernie Calaliere, Bill Zickefoose (ts); Ken Lowther (bs); Larry Mann (p); Bob Decker (b); Red Lacky (d).* 10/45–3/46.

Django and the European Division Band of the Air Transport Command recorded from the American Forces Network *Bandstand* and *Beaucoup De Music* (*sic*) broadcasts, in rehearsal and live at the Salle Pleyel in the months immediately following the end of the war in Europe. Eric Bogart likens the ATC band to one of the 'scrapping, blues-heavy' territory bands of the inter-war years, of which only Basie's made it to the big time. They certainly have a tougher feel than one normally associates with such outfits, and the opening 'Djangology' gets more than a run for its money, with an altered bridge by arranger Lonnie Wilfong. There is a fine interpretation of 'Belleville', with the first really classy guitar solo. Django excels himself on the unaccompanied 'Improvisation No. 6', taken from a slightly later small-group session, after which the group returns for rather more routine runs through 'Honeysuckle Rose' and 'Sweet Sue', the latter featuring a surprisingly effective penny-whistle solo. There's a second 'Djangology' and, rounding out the session, six cuts without the guitarist but including spirited readings of 'Swing Guitars' and 'Manoir De Mes Rêves' and other tunes not immediately associated with Django, of which 'Perdido' and Strayhorn's 'Midriff' are the most impressive. As Django sessions go, this is about beta-plus, but the ATC outfit are consistently impressive and are well worth checking out. Jack Towers's 'audio restoration' has been done with common sense and good taste.

***** Django Reinhardt, 1947**

Classics 1001 *Reinhardt; Jo Boyer, Vincent Casino, Louis Ménardi (t); André Lafosse, Guy Paquinet (tb); Hubert Rostaing, Michel De Villers (as, cl); Jean-Claude Fohrenbach (ts); Stéphane Grappelli (vn); Eddie Bernard (p); Joseph Reinhardt, Eugène Vées (g); Ladislas Czabancyk, Willie Lockwood, Emmanuel Soudieux (b); Al Craig, Pierre Fouad (d).* 3–7/47.

***** Django Reinhardt, 1947 – Volume 2**

Classics 1046 *Reinhardt; Gérard Léveque, Maurice Meunier, Hubert Rostaing (cl); Stéphane Grappelli (vn); Eddie Bernard (p); Joseph Reinhardt, Eugène Vées (g); Emmanuel Soudieux (b); Fred Ermelin, André Jourdan, Jacques Martinon (d).* 7–11/47.

*****(*) Swing De Paris**

Arco 3 ARC 110 *Reinhardt; Gérard Léveque, Maurice Meunier, Hubert Rostaing (cl); Joseph Reinhardt, Eugène Vées (g); Eddie Bernard (p); Ladislas Czabancyk, Emmanuel Soudieux (b); André Jourdan, Jacques Martinon (d).* 7–11/47.

*****(*) Pêche A La Mouche**

Verve 835419-2 *Reinhardt; Vincent Casino, Jo Boyer, Louis Menardi, Rex Stewart (t); André Lafosse, Guy Paquinet (tb); Michel De Villers (as, cl); Hubert Rostaing (cl); Jean-Claude Forenbach (ts); Eddie Bernard, Maurice Vander (p); Joseph Reinhardt, Eugène Vées (g); Will Lockwood, Ladislas Czabancyk, Pierre Michelot, Emmanuel Soudieux (b); Al Craig, Ted Curry, André Jourdan, Jean-Louis Viale (d).* 4/47–3/53.

Django's visit to the United States made a big impact on him, both positive and negative. It certainly reinforced the feeling of isolation and aggressive independence that increasingly became part of his character. It may also have reminded him that jazz was, after all, an American music. However, it did expose him to a whole raft of new influences – not least bebop – which henceforward were to play a part in his music. Though there is nothing that definitively points to a bebop influence, the phrasing is terser and the attack more forceful. Also the grouping of phrases on tunes such as 'Lover Man' (March), 'Just One Of Those Things' (May) and 'Blues For Barclay' (July, all Classics 1001) points to a more modern idiom.

The most pressing business of all was to record a reunion of the Hot Club after Grappelli's return from wartime exile in England. The violinist had often pronounced himself irritated by Django's 'monkey business', and the reunion did not seem likely to be long-standing. In the spring, Django reconvened his wartime quintet with Hubert Rostaing and recorded a score of sides in Paris and Brussels. There was a further meeting with Grappelli in November, but it's a strangely flat-footed and unamiable encounter which might have waited for more complete coverage in a later Classics volume.

Prefaced by a track each – 'Pêche A La Mouche' and 'Minor Blues' – from Django's quintet and orchestra, the 1947 sessions for Blue Star with the re-formed Hot Club are not classics like the great sides of the previous decade, but they have a spontaneity and ease that are both attractive and aesthetically satisfying. Producer Eddie Barclay gave Django a free hand to play what he wanted, and the music that emerged was bright, flowing and often thoughtful, with a rough edge that is only partially explained by the technical limitations of the recording.

There is one further session from 1947, under the leadership of Rex Stewart, which again might have served to remind Django of the huge cultural distance between him and the Americans. He plays with immense elegance on 'Night And Day' but never sounds as though he's on top of what Stewart is doing harmonically.

The later recording, which was issued as a 10-inch LP, not as 78s, saw the shadows move a little closer round the guitarist, but Django's solo on 'Brazil' is, as noted by Pierre Michelot, quite astonishing in its fiery grace, and he seems to have overcome some of the amplification problems he had been having since the war. He tackles 'Night And Day' again, on his own terms this time, and there are beautiful versions of 'Nuages' and 'Manoir De Mes Rêves'. He isn't a musician whose work divides easily into 'early' and 'late', but it's clear that the period between these two recordings was one of personal and artistic change and, in some respects, retrenchment. Django had made a great many miscalculations and had to spend too much time compensating for them.

As ever, the Classics are hard to beat for literal chronology and completeness, but the sound is very much better on the other compilations and, unless exhaustive documentation is required and pure sound is at a discount, these are the priority purchases.

*****(*) Djangology 1949**

Bluebird/BMG ND90448 *Reinhardt; Stéphane Grappelli (vn); Gianni Safred (p); Carlo Recori (b); Aurelio De Carolis (d).* 1–2/49.

A final opportunity to hear Reinhardt and Grappelli playing together, albeit with a dud rhythm section. In an intelligent sleeve-note (which includes useful track-by-track comments on all 20 CD items), guitarist Frank Vignola warns against making comparisons between these rather edgy and competitive sessions and the great days of the pre-war Quintette du Hot Club. The most evident token of changing musical times, and a legacy of Django's relatively unsuccessful American trip, is a boppish cast to several of the tracks, most significantly the Ur-text of bebop, 'I Got Rhythm'. Fortunately for the session, both Django and Grappelli got rhythm to spare, for the local musicians are a positive hindrance. On 'All The Things You Are' Safred chords morosely in the background while Recori and de Carolis go off for a *grappa*. Django's frustration comes through in places, but it's clear that at least some of the aggression is directed at his one-time junior partner who now claims his full share of the foreground. For all its shortcomings, this is a worthwhile addition to the discography.

Emily Remler (1957–90)

GUITAR

Studied at Berklee from 1974, then spent three years in New Orleans before returning to NYC and playing in her own small group. Also worked in a duo with Larry Coryell.

***** Firefly**

Concord CCD 4162 *Remler; Hank Jones (p); Bob Maize (b); Jake Hanna (d).* 4/81.

***** Take Two**

Concord CCD 4195 *Remler; James Williams (p); Don Thompson (b); Terry Clarke (d).* 6/82.

***** Transitions**

Concord CCD 4236 *Remler; John D'Earth (t); Eddie Gomez (b); Bob Moses (d).* 10/83.

***** Catwalk**

Concord CCD 4265 *As above.* 8/84.

****** East To Wes**

Concord CCD 4356 *Remler; Hank Jones (p); Buster Williams (b); Marvin 'Smitty' Smith (d).* 5/88.

Remler's senseless early death (from heart failure while on tour in Australia) deprived us of a talent that seemed on the point of breakthrough. While her early role-models were conservative ones in terms of her instrument – Christian and Montgomery, specifically – her tough-minded improvising and affinity with hard-hitting rhythm sections let her push a mainstream style to its logical limits. *Firefly* was her debut for the label and is fluent if a little anonymous, although she handles the diversity of 'Strollin'' and 'In A Sentimental Mood' without any hesitation. *Take Two* puts on an extra layer of assurance: Williams is a sympathetic pianist, and the improvising on 'In Your Own Sweet Way' and 'For Regulars Only' shows new resource. *Transitions* and *Catwalk* were made in a somewhat unusual partnership with D'Earth, whose crisp, pinchy solos make an interesting foil to the leader's more expansive lines. The best single disc, though, is the impeccable Montgomery tribute, *East To Wes*. Smith proves to be an ideal drummer for the guitarist, his busy cymbals and polyrhythmic variations on the bebop pulse perfectly cast to push Remler into her best form: 'Daahoud' and 'Hot House' are unbeatable updates of each tune. Jones, imperturbable as ever, takes a cool middle course. While conceived as a Montgomery homage, Remler's playing actually shows how unlike Wes she really was: harder of tone, her solos more fragmented yet equally lucid.

****** Retrospective, Vol. One: Standards**

Concord CCD 4453

***** Retrospective, Vol. Two: Compositions**

Concord CCD 4463 *As above records, except add Larry Coryell (g), James Williams (p), Don Thompson (b), Terry Clarke (d).* 81–88.

Two excellent compilations of Remler's Concord years. The first volume is superior, with an intelligent choice of standards, two beautiful duets with Larry Coryell and an unaccompanied solo on 'Afro Blue'. Her original themes are rather less memorable, but the playing on the second volume remains enticing throughout.

The Remote Viewers

GROUP

British explorers previously associated with B Shops For The Poor.

****(*) Low Shapes In Dark Heat**

Leo Lab CD 049 *Adrian Northover (ss, as); Louise Petts (as, syn, v); David Petts (ts, syn).* 2 & 7/98.

***** Obliques Before Pale Skin**

Leo Lab 061 *As above, except add theremins to instrumentation for Northover, Petts and Petts.* 6 & 7/99.

The CIA and NASA still, we understand, take remote sensing very seriously, but what are we to make of these enigmatic trios? At moments, we might be dealing with a conventional saxophone quartet who, in the absence of the senior and most sensible member, muck about in the studio for a couple of afternoons, but then Louise Petts's remarkable voice and strange, associative lyrics kick in and the spell is cast.

This is music of great privacy. Even when a familiar theme does emerge – and *Low Shapes* includes a tender version of the theme from television's *Callan* – the associations are not necessarily shared. The effect is somewhat akin to a session by Bristol's lamented Startled Insects, but produced by and guesting John Zorn and the sound-crew of *The X-Files*.

The second album opens with a minimally unaccompanied reading of Jimmy Van Heusen's 'It Could Happen To You', continues with Madonna's 'Secret' and ends with a gorgeous version of Dmitri Tiomkin's 'Wild Is The Wind'. What happens in between defies straightforward description, beyond the fact that it is a richer acoustic mix, with few of the London Saxophone Quartet mannerisms that made the debut so quirkily old-fashioned in places.

Don Rendell (born 1926)

TENOR SAXOPHONE, SOPRANO SAXOPHONE, FLUTES

Played with John Dankworth from 1950, then in big bands and with his own group. The Rendell–Carr Quintet of the '60s is a much-remembered outfit, and he has been an avuncular presence since, teaching rather more than performing live.

***(*) Space Walk

Redial 538 806-2 *Rendell; Stan Robinson (ts, cl, f); Peter Shade (vib, f); Jack Thorncroft (b); Trevor Tomkins (d).* 72.

Though many who know and appreciate his work will think of Rendell as a mainstream player, he was also deeply influenced by John Coltrane's 'sheets of sound' period, this long before Trane became the orthodoxy in jazz saxophone. That is immediately evident on the opening 'On The Way', though it is Stan Robinson who takes the first – and equally Coltrane-inspired – solo, leaving Don to come in later, sounding rather distant and as yet uncertain. The opening number segues into 'Antibes', a remembrance of the Rendell–Carr Quintet's appearance at the south of France festival. The key component here, and just one of the album's many brilliant instrumental twists, is the trio of flautists. Rendell is one of those rare saxophone players who are equally and in some lights more convincing on flute.

'Street Called Straight' is an example of how expressive he can be on what is usually treated as a 'double' or colour instrument. It's one of two tracks here inspired, unlikely as it sounds, by St Paul's wanderings in the Mediterranean. The other is Stan Robinson's 'Earoaquilo', which evokes the stormy wind that brings in cold air from the continent.

No one has ever quite explained Britain's ability to produce convincing and expressive vibes players, but Peter Shade belongs up there with Bill LeSage, Frank Ricotti and Tubby Hayes, and he makes an important contribution to this imaginative and unusual record, not least the title-track, which is almost a vibraphone feature.

Arthur Rhames (1957–89)

TENOR SAXOPHONE

Grew up in Brooklyn and acquired a formidable reputation as saxophonist, pianist and guitarist. His death from an AIDS-related illness in 1989 and a lack of any official recordings have contributed to a posthumous legend.

*** Live From Soundscape

DIW 401 *Rhames; Jeff Esposito (p); Jeff Siegel (d).* 10/81.

Those whom the gods destroy, they first make 'promising'. Arthur Rhames was being talked up on both sides of the Atlantic, almost from his very first club appearances. Despite never having been signed by any record company, Rhames had an almost mythical reputation on the New York music scene. In addition to saxophone playing that seemed to take Coltrane-derived harmonics way past the far-out busking of Charles Gayle, he was a brilliant pianist in a version of McCoy Tyner's idiom, and he played scorching electric guitar. How great was he? Many musicians claim him as an important influence, young as he was, and there is much eloquent testimony to Rhames's disciplined business sense (so why no deal?) and obsession with health and fitness, all of which seems doubly ironic in view of his early death and the almost total absence of recordings. A club session, recorded on a reel-to-reel machine with just two mikes, *Live From Soundscape* is a pretty raw document of a raw blowing gig. Sticking to tenor (an insert picture shows him playing soprano on the subway), Rhames provides exhaustive readings of both 'Giant Steps' and 'Moment's Notice', as well as a slightly terser rendition of 'Bessie's Blues'. That he had mastered Coltrane's language there can be no doubt; that he managed to take it even a modest step onward is more questionable. 'I Got Rhythm' underlines the surefootedness of his vertical improvisation, but there is nothing here that would cause a second-generation bebopper to blush. 'I Want Jesus To Walk With Me' suggests an additional kinship to Ayler. The remaining track, '42nd Street', is essentially a feature for Esposito, who acquits himself very well when fully audible over a drummer who is clearly trying to out-do his ancestors Elvin and Rashied. Any ultimate judgement, of course, has to be suspended. It is important to recognize not just the technical limitations of this disc but also the fact that it consists of performances made when Rhames was only 24, with almost another decade of his short life to go. Where had he gone by the summer of 1989, when his health failed irrevocably? Without a sense of that, he may have to rest with those, like Buddy Bolden, whose legends are larger than the surviving record.

Melvin Rhyne (born 1936)

ORGAN

Rhyne's reputation stems from his work with Wes Montgomery for Riverside. It took some considerable time to establish a separate identity, but in his mid-fifties things started to happen and since then there has been a steady procession of strong, idiosyncratic albums.

***** The Legend**

Criss Cross Criss 1059 *Rhyne; Brian Lynch (t); Don Braden (ts); Peter Bernstein (g); Kenny Washington (d).* 12/91.

***** Boss Organ**

Criss Cross Criss 1080 *Rhyne; Joshua Redman (ts); Peter Bernstein (g); Kenny Washington (d).* 1/93.

The Legend was Rhyne's first recording as a leader, done impromptu after the organist had finished a Criss Cross session for trumpeter Brian Lynch. Whether the title is entirely deserved is a matter for debate, but Mel certainly enjoyed an enviable reputation among fellow players and he plays with a robustly insouciant confidence. Rhyne immediately sounds different from the prevailing Jimmy Smith school of organ players. Instead of swirling, bluesy chords, he favours sharp, almost staccato figures and lyrical single-note runs that often don't go quite where expected. The format for the session is the same as that for the classic Montgomery recordings, and Kenny Washington makes a particularly strong impact. The set opens with Eddie 'Lockjaw' Davis's 'Licks A-Plenty', kicks along with 'Stompin' At The Savoy', Wes Montgomery's 'The Trick Bag' and Dizzy Gillespie's 'Groovin' High'; there are two evocative ballads, 'Serenata' and 'Old Folks', and the session closes with a long 'Blues For Wes', with Lynch and saxophonist Braden sitting in.

Another young horn player makes a vital contribution to the later *Boss Organ*. Few saxophonists have been more comprehensively hyped than Joshua Redman. He lives pretty much up to billing on this set, swanking through tunes by Stevie Wonder and Wes Montgomery as if he grew up playing them. Rhyne sounds relaxed and laid back – almost too unhurried since, as the set advances, it begins to drag ever so slightly. Enjoyable, though, and a convincing consolidation of the fine form of *The Legend*.

*****(*) Stick To The Kick**

Criss Cross Criss 1137 *Rhyne; Ryan Kisor (t); Eric Alexander (ts); Peter Bernstein (g); Kenny Washington (d).* 12/94, 12/95.

***** Mel's Spell**

Criss Cross Criss 1118 *Rhyne; Peter Bernstein (g); Kenny Washington (d); Daniel G Sadownick (perc).* 12/94, 12/95.

*****(*) Kojo**

Criss Cross Criss 1164 *As above.* 12/97.

By the latter half of the 1990s, a Melvin Rhyne record was as predictable and as reliable as a No. 12 bus, and these must have delighted existing fans. The band on *Stick* ... offers a scaled-down version of a big-band sound and it would be intriguing to hear Mel working with a full-size ensemble. Apart from Dameron's 'Lady Bird' and Bud Powell's 'Wail', all the material is by Rhyne himself. He writes themes rather than songs, but themes with a very definite shape and structure. The other two albums are much looser in concept and feature considerably more standards material. Mel shows how readily he can switch between bebop ('Blue'N'Boogie') and a swing ballad like 'In A Sentimental Mood', both on *Kojo*; on *Mel's Spell* he weaves a delicious programme of tunes, from Bird's 'Billy's Bounce' to Frank Sinatra's 'This Love Of Mine'. As ever, Gerry Teekens gives Mel a big and very natural sound. The organ/guitar/drums trio is not difficult to record, technically speaking, but it calls for a measure of taste and balance which isn't always on call.

Buddy Rich (1917–87)

DRUMS, VOCAL

A child performer in vaudeville, Rich was a bandleader by the time he was eleven. He worked in many of the big swing bands of the 1930s and spent six years with Tommy Dorsey before leading his own group in the late '40s (it foundered financially). He freelanced through the '50s, sang and did some acting, and spent five years with Harry James, before re-forming a big band in 1966. Against the run of the time, it was an international success, and he toured with it for the rest of his life, although heart problems interrupted an otherwise tireless working schedule. A ruthless man, peerless in his technique, Rich has been idolized by many as the archetypal swinging jazz drummer.

***** His Legendary 1947–48 Orchestra**

Hep CD 12 *Rich; Tommy Allison, Stan Fischelson, Phil Gilbert, Charlie Shavers, Charlie Walp, Dale Pearce, Frank LePinto, Doug Mettome (t); Mario Daone, Bob Ascher, Chunky Koenigsberger, Rob Swope, Jack Carmen, Lou McGarity (tb); Peanuts Hucko (cl); Hal McKusick, Eddie Caine, Jerry Therkeld (as); Allen Eager, Mickey Rich, Ben Larry, Warne Marsh, Al Sears, Jimmy Giuffre (ts); Harvey Levine (bs); Harvey Leonard, Jerry Schwarz, Buddy Weed (p); Joe Mooney (acc); Terry Gibbs (vib); Gene Dell, Remo Palmieri (g); Trigger Alpert, Tubby Phillips, Charlie Leeds, Nick Stagg (b); Stan Kay, Big Sid Catlett (d); Ella Fitzgerald (v).* 10/45–10/48.

***** The Legendary 46–48 Orchestras Vol. 2**

Hep CD 56 *As above, except add Bitsy Mullens, Pinky Savitt, Louis Oles (t), Earl Swope, Johnny Mandel, Al Lorraine (tb), Les Clarke, Jerry Thirkeld (as), George Berg, Mickey Rich (ts), Sid Brown (bs), Tony Nichols (p), Jimmy Johnston (b), Stan Kay (d), Dottie Reid (v).* 3/46–10/48.

***** Buddy Rich 1946–1948**

Classics 1099 *Similar to above discs, except add Red Rodney (t).* 1/46–10/48.

Rich, probably the most renowned big-band drummer of all time, had a rough time as a bandleader in the late 1940s, but somehow he held on until 1949. Hep's sets of airshots, V-Discs and the like find various editions of the group in vigorous form. Some of the charts are routine, but others make the most of the impressive sections, and there are some fine soloists on the first disc, particularly Allen Eager on 'Daily Double' and 'Nellie's Nightmare'. There is one small-group track with Charlie Shavers on trumpet and a fairly hilarious 'Blue Skies' where Rich scats along with Ella Fitzgerald. The second disc leans more towards the 1948 orchestra, which is more commercially directed, with vocals and ballads tending to take over; but the opening 'Let's Blow' is prototypical of the excitement that Rich was after in a big band. The sound is fair to good on both discs, but the clout of the orchestra still comes through when they hit hard enough.

Classics bring together three sessions for V-Disc and three for Mercury. It duplicates eight titles with Hep 56, but the balance of the Mercury titles is well worth having: 'Dateless Brown' and 'Desperate Desmond' are flag-wavers of real excitement. Rich shows how appealing a vocalist he could be on 'Baby, Baby All The Time', and bop gets a modest look-in on 'Oop-Bop-Sha-

Bam'. An interesting cross-section of titles, with a few soloists – such as Red Rodney – to surprise.

***(*) Swingin' New Big Band

Pacific Jazz 835232-2 *Rich; Bobby Shew, John Sottile, Yoshito Murakami, Walter Battagello (t); Jim Trimble, John Boice (tb); Dennis Good, Mike Waverley (btb); Gene Quill (as, cl); Pete Yellin (as, f); Jay Corre, Marty Flax (ts, cl, f); Steve Perlow (bs, bcl); John Bunch (p); Barry Zweig (g); Carson Smith (b).* 9–10/66.

*** Big Swing Face

Pacific Jazz 837989-2 *As above, except add Chuck Findley (t), Ron Myers (tb), Ernie Watts (as, f), Quin Davis (as), Robert Keller (bs), Ray Starling (p), Richard Resnicoff (g), James Gannon (b), Cathy Rich (v); omit Boice, Quill, Yellin, Perlow, Bunch, Zweig and Smith.* 2–3/67.

***(*) The New One!

Pacific Jazz 494507-2 *Rich; Chuck Findley, Russell Iverson, John Sottile, Yoshito Murakami (t); Jim Trimble, John Boice, Robert Brawn, Jack Spurlock, Sam Burtis (tb); Ernie Watts, James Mosher (as, cl, f); Robert Keller, Pat LaBarbera (ts, cl, f); Jay Corre (ts, cl); Meyer Hirsh, Frank Capi (bs, bcl); Ray Starling, Russell Turner Jr (p); Richie Resnicoff (g); James Gannon, Ronald Funoldi (b).* 6–12/67.

***(*) Mercy, Mercy

Pacific Jazz 854331-2 *Rich; Al Porcino, Bill Prince, Ken Faulk, Dave Culp (t); Jim Trimble, Rick Stepton, Peter Graves (tb); Art Pepper, Charles Owens, Don Menza, Pat LaBarbera, John Laws (reeds); Walt Namuth (g); Gary Walters (b); Tony Bennett (v).* 7/68.

*** Swingin' New Big Band / Keep The Customer Satisfied

BGO BGOCD169 *Rich; Bobby Shew, John Sottile, Yoshito Murakami, Walter Battagello, John Giorgani, John Madrid, Mike Price, George Zonce (t); Jim Trimble, John Boice, Rick Stepton, Tony Lada (tb); Larry Fisher, Mike Waverley (btb); Gene Quill (cl, as); Richie Cole, Jimmy Mosher, Pete Yellin (as, f); Jay Corre, Marty Flax (cl, ts, f); Pat LaBarbera (ss, ts, f); Don Englert (ts, f); Steve Perlow (bs, bcl); Bob Suchoski (bs); John Bunch, Meredith McClain (p); Barry Zweig (g); Rick Laird, Carson Smith (b).* 9/66–2/70.

The late 1960s were scarcely vintage times for big bands, but Rich, who was used to stopping at nothing, drove a limousine outfit through the period with concessions that didn't really bother him much. They had items like 'Uptight' and 'Ode To Billie Joe' in the book, but they still played the likes of 'In A Mellotone' and 'Sister Sadie', and among the technique-laden sections there were players who could step out and play an individualist's solo: Don Menza, Jay Corre, Bobby Shew, and – on *Mercy, Mercy* – Art Pepper, who has a wounded feature on 'Chelsea Bridge'. The Pacific albums are nearly all taken from live dates, from Hollywood or Las Vegas, and since the band thrived in performance they are among Rich's most characteristic testaments. There's nothing subtle about the arranging or the musicianship: all is speed, bravado, intensity. Not to say that the band didn't have different strokes at its disposal: some of the charts on *Swingin' New Big Band* (by a variety of hands, including Oliver Nelson, Bill Holman and Phil Wilson) are as elegant as they are assertive. But Rich's rule meant that the band had to fire on all cylinders and there were no pastel shades involved. He even makes 'Ode To Billie Joe' (*Mercy, Mercy*) into a stormer. There's little to choose between the discs, which have been handsomely reshaped by Pacific with numerous unissued bonus tracks on each disc and some fine discoveries among them. We especially like *Mercy, Mercy* for the stunning treatment of Joe Zawinul's title-track and for the contributions of Pepper and Menza. *The New One!* includes material written for a TV series, *Away We Go*, that Rich worked on during 1967: the theme-tune is a typical barnstormer and, although the sound seems compressed on this reissue, there's plenty to hear, with Watts taking some storming solos – listen to the preposterously over-fast but thrilling treatment of Wes Montgomery's 'Naptown Blues'. In sum, these are probably the necessary Rich albums for the library – considering that his catalogue is still neglected on CD and there is perhaps no obvious classic album in it. The BGO set couples the original *Swingin' New Big Band* with a lesser effort from 1970, and we prefer the Pacific edition.

*** Buddy And Soul

BGO BGOCD 23 *Rich; Sal Marquez, Nat Pavone, Dave Culp, Bob Yance, Mike Price, Darryl Eaton, Ken Faulk, Oliver Mitchell (t); Rick Stepton, Vince Diaz, Don Switzer (tb); Ernie Watts, Joe Romano, Richie Cole, Don Menza, Pat LaBarbera, Joe Calo, Don Englert (reeds); Dave Lahm (ky); Herb Ellis, Dave Dana, Freddie Robinson (g); Bob Magnusson (b); Victor Feldman (perc).* 1–6/69.

Live or in the studio, Rich's band hit very hard. Anachronistic in the age of Hendrix and Jefferson Airplane (Rich's choice of a tune called 'Love And Peace' probably didn't express what he thought about rock's ascendance), they made up in personal firepower what they lacked in stage amplification. There's some dreadful, modish material and some things which Rich made into valid vehicles through sheer force of will. Big-band jazz out of its time, and presumably for ever.

**(*) Lionel Hampton Presents Buddy Rich

Kingdom GATE 7011 *Rich; Steve Marcus (ss, ts); Gary Pribek, Paul Moen (ts); Barry Kiener (p); Lionel Hampton (vib); Tom Warrington (b); Candido Camero (perc).* 77.

An engaging reunion for Hampton and Rich, with Marcus and Pribek coming from Rich's big band and Moen arriving from Hamp's. Two Coltrane themes give the tenors a chance to smoke, and the vibes and rhythm section trade plenty of fours. Nothing surprising happens, but all concerned seemed to enjoy the date.

Tim Richards (born 1952)

PIANO

A familiar presence on the British contemporary scene, most of Richards's work can be found under the listing for his band, Spirit Level; this is an outing under his own name.

***(*) The Other Side

33 JAZZ 037 *Richards; Kubryk Townsend (b); Kenrick Rowe, Andreas Trillo (d).* 97.

... but the other side of what? This is Richards's other project, working apart from the horn-fronted Spirit Level, and interestingly he gravitates to a mostly standards repertoire, or rather to a body of jazz tunes which take their cues in turn from standards material, things like Miles Davis's and Victor Feldman's 'Seven Steps To Heaven', Hampton Hawes's 'Blues The Most' and Big John Patton's 'String Bean'. Rowe (a Spirit Level regular) is used only on seven of the 15 tracks, a very different percussionist from the stylish but forceful Trillo, about whom we know very little, except that his roots seem to be in the swing era, reminiscent of Shelly Manne rather than anything more recent. Richards switches to electric keyboard for Eddie Harris's 'Freedom Jazz Dance' and demonstrates once again the ability to give amplified piano considerable personality. His blues phrasing and sense of harmonic structures are hugely impressive, here and elsewhere.

Jerome Richardson (born 1920)

SAXOPHONES, WOODWINDS, FLUTES

Richardson started working in his teens, and has rarely stopped since. He worked with Marshall Jones, Quincy Jones, led his own group at Minton's, and was a charter member of the Thad Jones–Mel Lewis band. He has recorded only rather rarely under his own name.

***** Midnight Oil**

Original Jazz Classics OJC 1815 *Richardson; Jimmy Cleveland (tb); Hank Jones (p); Kenny Burrell (g); Joe Benjamin (b); Charli Persip (d).* 11/58.

*****(*) Roamin' With Richardson**

Original Jazz Classics OJC 1849 *Richardson; Richard Wyands (p); George Tucker (b); Charli Persip (d).* 11/59.

The quiet Texan was always more than a journeyman multi-instrumentalist. It took him some time to assert himself in his own voice. He became a leader only on moving to New York City in 1953, having served an apprenticeship with Jimmy Lunceford, Lionel Hampton and Earl Hines. *Oil* was an earlier session on New Jazz, predating *Roamin'* by a few months, as rare as hen's teeth and reissued without fanfare. The interesting thing about the 1959 band is that all four are individualists, and each is encouraged to bring something to the session. Wyands in particular asserts himself on tracks like 'Warm Valley' and 'Poinciana', the latter a solitary outing on flute, the former with his very distinctive, Mulligan-influenced baritone. His only other horn this time out is tenor saxophone ('Friar Tuck' and 'Candied Sweets').

In the past, we've argued that Richardson's one great stock-in-trade has been the simple variety of his resources. Certainly on both records he can rely on an absolutely solid band and indulge a little decorative work here and there. Further acquaintance, though, confirms that he is an able, often thoughtful soloist, and his traded lines with Cleveland and the more boppish Burrell will be a revelation to those who have heard him only as a utility band player.

***** Jazz Station Runaway**

TCB 97402 *Richardson; David Hazeltine (p); Howard Alden, Russell Malone (g); George Mraz (b); Denis Mackrel (d); Frank Colon (perc).* 97.

An infrequent leader in recent years, Richardson sounds a touch anonymous. Concentrating on alto saxophone, he finds an interesting line through material like 'Warm Valley' and 'Freedom And Salvation' but rarely comes up with anything larger and more capacious than the basic material. The recording is very clear and animated and the balance of instruments is admirable, with guitars and piano situated front and centre and horn punched in above.

Kim Richmond

ALTO SAXOPHONE

California-based post-bop saxophonist with a broad range of stylistic sympathies.

***** Looking In Looking Out**

USA 630 *Richmond; Mike Fahn (vtb); John Gross (ts, f); Tad Weed, Wayne Peet (p); Ken Filiano (b); Billy Mintz (d).* 6–11/88.

****** Passages**

Sea Breeze CDSB-2043 *Richmond; Wayne Bergeron, Ron King, Clay Jenkins, Dave Scott (t); Rick Culver, George McMullen, Charlie Morillas, Morris Repass (tb); Suzette Moriarity, John Dickson (frhn); Sal Lonzano, Phil Feather, Glen Berger, John Yoakum, John Mitchell, Bob Carr, John Gross (reeds); Bill Cunliffe (p); Tom Hynes (g); Bill Roper (tba); Trey Henry (b); Ralph Razze (d); Mike Turner, Dave Johnson (perc).* 5/92.

*****(*) Range**

Nine Winds NWCD 0172 *Richmond; Clay Jenkins (t); Joey Sellars (tb); Dave Scott (p); Trey Henry (b); Joe LaBarbera (d).* 9/94.

Richmond has performed in many jazz and rock settings, and his debut as a leader reflects catholic and well-informed preferences. There are six good originals on *Looking In Looking Out*, with flavoursome tone-colours and a harried rhythmic undertow that won't let the music settle into mere mainstream blowing. Try the clever use of valve trombone against flute in 'Specifico Americano' or the straggling, vaguely inebriated treatment of 'Nardis'. Richmond takes some acerbic solos but is smart enough to give Fahn, Gross and Weed – all interesting soloists – the same measure of space. The leader's sleeve-note speaks of 'simultaneous improvisation' and, while this is of a comparatively ordered nature, it brings off a fine record. Moving up to the scale of a big band seems to have held no terrors for him: *Passages* is a gutsy, songful record that makes the most of the sleek power of an orchestra without turning to mere glibness. There are excellent soloists – Gross, Cunliffe, McMullen and the leader's own alto – but what matters is the sonority of the orchestra as a unit. Richmond makes 'My Funny Valentine' lush and uplifting instead of wounded and sad (and still introduces an unexpected dissonance at the climax), writes a vast fantasy out of 'Street Of Dreams' and pours an awful lot into the two minutes or so of

'Image And Likeness'. Sea Breeze have made a speciality of recording this kind of album, and the studio sound is superb.

Range continues an impressive sequence. Back in a small-group format, Richmond co-leads this ensemble with Jenkins, and the music is an inquiring update on various West Coast traditions. The music's essential reserve – freely though the musicians play, underlying harmonic/rhythmic principles remain firm – serves to underline the virtues of each man's improvisational thinking and, with the excellent Sellars contributing just as much as the other two horns, the eight themes unfold with a sort of compelling inevitability.

Mike Richmond (born 1948)

BASS

Emerged in the '70s as a versatile rhythm-section sideman, playing in fusion and post-bop bands, latterly in a more straight-ahead vein.

***** On The Edge**

Steeplechase SCCD 31237 *Richmond; Larry Schneider (ss, ts, f); Adam Nussbaum (d).* 88.

*****(*) Dance For Andy**

Steeplechase SCCD 31267 *Richmond; Larry Schneider (ss, ts); Jim McNeely (p); Keith Copeland (d).* 89.

The title-track which opens *On The Edge* is a superb trio improvisation that has Schneider and Richmond almost locking horns before Nussbaum's resolving solo. The rest of the record doesn't quite match up, but the leader – whose wide experience with leaders such as DeJohnette, Getz and Silver has granted him a steadfast mainstream-modern reputation – pilots the trio with great enthusiasm. *Dance For Andy* is one of those rare CDs that sustain interest through a 70-minute-plus duration. Richmond's four originals are nothing special – aside, perhaps, from the witty, sanctified licks of 'Gospel' – but there is a serene trio reading of 'I Remember Clifford', a fast and swinging 'You And The Night And The Music' and a reading of Jim Pepper's 'Witchi-Tai-To' which manages to supplant Jan Garbarek's glorious version in the memory. Schneider deploys his Brecker influence to gripping effect on both records.

***** Blue In Green**

Steeplechase SCCD 31296 *Richmond; Larry Schneider (ts); Richie Beirach (p); Jeff Williams (d).* 8/91.

A bit disappointing, perhaps, after the last two. Schneider sounds a little more diffident this time and, though Beirach compensates by being more driving than he sometimes is, there's comparatively little of the freewheeling energy that made *On The Edge* exciting. It's still a solid and enjoyable traversal of some good jazz and show tunes by four expert players.

Frank Ricotti (born 1949)

VIBRAPHONE, ALTO SAXOPHONE

British vibesman and occasional saxophonist, prominent in the early '70s.

***** Our Point Of View**

CBS 49440 2 *Ricotti; Chris Spedding (g); Chris Laurence (b); Bryan Spring (d).* 69.

It's slightly sad to read Frank Ricotti looking back over thirty years and running down the insufficiencies of an album that was made in more innocent times. Lacking the cosmetic technologies of later years, it is marked by occasional slips of articulation that could now easily be eliminated, but it has a freshness that would be ruined by crisper production values.

The presence of a Gary Burton composition may have reinforced a prejudice that this was a group modelled on Burton's rock-influenced group with Larry Coryell, but Ricotti had already teamed up with Chris Spedding before the American group came on the scene, so a direct influence can be ruled out. Spedding's erratic subsequent career has blurred the sheer emotional power of his playing at this time. Encountered afresh, his was a remarkable talent and a perfect counterbalance to Ricotti's lightness of touch. The rhythm section was one of the finest Britain could offer. Laurence has long been acknowledged, but Spring is still better known to British club audiences than to the record-buying public. His touch on his regular boss Stan Tracey's 'Three Time Loser, Three Times Blueser' is sure and exact.

Ricotti's saxophone playing on 'Dark Though Sun Shines', one of three Brian Miller compositions, is unspectacular but strangely affecting, rising above its technical flaws, much like the record itself. Welcome back to an old favourite.

Georg Riedel

BASS

A senior figure in Swedish jazz after 1945, Riedel is the rock-solid presence on countless mainstream-to-modern sessions, and has occasionally led dates of his own, starting as far back as 1954: his Jazz Ballet album of 1964 was released in the USA.

*****(*) Kirbitz**

Phontastic PHONTCD 9511 *Riedel; Jan Allan (t); Arne Domnérus (as, cl); Putte Wickman (cl); Claes Rosendahl (ts, f); Bengt Hallberg (p); Lars Erstrand (vib); Rune Gustafsson (g); Egil Johansen (d).* 6/80–6/81.

What is more or less the royal family of Swedish mainstream jazz, assembled for a few sessions in 1980–81, playing standards, John Kirby, Bengt Hallberg – and Georg Riedel. The bassist is king for a day in this setting, even though he scarcely even takes a solo. What counts is the ensemble playing, the witty compositions, the almost balletic little solos, all recorded in the kind of close, crisp sound that makes the music dance. It's appropriate that Kirby's ghost is evoked specifically (though in a tune actually by Charlie

Shavers, 'Opus 5'), since most of these pieces effect a wry, humorous variation on his old Sextet recordings. Riedel's 'Knickedick' and title-track, and Hallberg's 'Chance To Dance', are as clever and accomplished as this kind of jazz ought to be, and musicians like Wickman and Domnérus are inevitably right at home. So is Jan Allan, though he plays rather more forcefully, and at times he even rescues the situation when it threatens to get too mimsy: listen to what he does with 'A Child Is Born'.

Tim Ries (born 1959)

TENOR SAXOPHONE, SOPRANO SAXOPHONE

Born in Detroit, Ries started on trumpet but is now playing post-bop saxophone.

*****(*) Universal Spirits**

Criss Cross CRISS 1144 *Ries; Scott Wendholt (t); Ben Monder (g); Scott Colley (b); Billy Drummond (d).* 10/97.

One afternoon in Paris, Tim Ries saw Ornette Coleman being interviewed in a hotel lobby. Not knowing a better way to introduce himself, he took out his soprano and played the early Coleman tune, 'Jayne'. Ornette stood up and applauded, as well he might have done, for the version included here is excellent. Ries's kinship with trumpeter Wendholt is almost twin-like, a mutual understanding that beams out from the very first number, a deceptively simple circle-of-fifths thing called 'Indeed', which has been in his book for many years. Other pieces on the set are derived from his classical side as well, most obviously the Bach 'Sonata No. 2: Siciliano', which is something he has played on flute with his wife, harpist Stacey Shames. A strongly personal record, almost every tune seems – and feels – associated with some strong emotion. 'Guardian Angel' relates to his mother's recovery from life-threatening illness, 'St Michel' to a chance escape from a terrorist bomb in Paris; 'When I'm Through' is a lullaby for his daughter, and again shows indications of being written for a chamber group rather than a jazz band. It's difficult to pin down Ries's influences. He has worked with Phil Woods and Joe Henderson, and he obviously admires Ornette. His playing style, though, doesn't come from any of these contacts but from a deep and very serious familiarity with his instrument and from the dictates of each individual theme. As ever on Criss Cross, the band is tailor-made. Monder and Colley are friends, and Billy Drummond has the ability to fall in with almost any line-up thrown at him.

Yannick Rieu

TENOR SAXOPHONE

Canadian saxophonist playing hard-bop material with a more free-thinking approach.

*****(*) Sweet Geom**

Victo CD030 *Rieu; Frederik Alarie (b); Paul Leger (d).* 5/94.

The Canadian tenorman could do with a wider exposure, and this seems to be all he has in the racks at the moment. The sheer audacity of doing a full-scale treatment of Rollins's 'Freedom Suite' is mitigated by the thoughtful, unflashy interpretation. Rieu *does* sound like Rollins here – and throughout – but his own themes (the title-piece, itself a three-part suite, spreads across a 25-minute span) have a shape which was missing on an earlier record. This trio is a genuinely integrated unit, and Rieu's generous allowance of space to the others pays off in a music that works its tension-and-release with real intelligence and the proper intensity.

Knut Riisnaes (born 1945)

TENOR AND SOPRANO SAXOPHONES

Norwegian post-bop saxophonist of wide experience, one of the two Riisnaes sax-playing brothers.

*****(*) Confessin' The Blues**

Gemini GMCD 63 *Riisnaes; Red Holloway (as, ts); Kjell Ohman (p, org); Terje Venaas (b); Egil Johansen (d).* 8/89.

***** The Gemini Twins**

Gemini GMCD 75 *As above.* 1/92.

***** Knut Riisnaes / Jon Christensen**

Odin 4040 *Riisnaes; John Scofield (g); Palle Danielsson (b); Jon Christensen (d).* 10/91–5/92.

Gifted with a huskily rich and weighty tone, Riisnaes is an Oslo-born jazzman who, like so many musicians from northern Europe, deserves a far wider reputation than he has (his brother, Odd, is also a fine tenorman). His celebrated *Flukt* LP won a Norwegian Grammy award but it's currently *still* out of print. *Confessin' The Blues* is a fine place to start, though. The session was organized to document Red Holloway's visit to the Oslo Jazz Festival in 1989, and the sympathetic interplay among all five men belies the hasty circumstances of the occasion. While there are some straightforward blowing tracks, such as an ebullient 'Billie's Bounce', the highlight is probably the almost indecently languorous stroll through 'All Blues' at the beginning, which is paced out by both tenormen to sumptuous effect. If Holloway is the more perkily bluesy of the two saxophonists, Riisnaes emerges as at least his equal, taking a solo 'My Romance' which methodically opens out the melody to superb effect. The rhythm section, with Ohman playing mostly organ, is absolutely on top of things, and the digital sound is excellent. They have a return match on *The Gemini Twins*, which is a mild disappointment since nothing hits the peaks of the previous record. Riisnaes's solo ballad treatment of 'Tribute To Melvin' and the ultra-slow 'Yesterdays' still make the record substantial.

The quartet with Scofield, Danielsson and Christensen puts Riisnaes into a more contemporary context and, while Scofield's status as a top hired-gun means that his sound has become a commonplace in this setting, Riisnaes and Christensen carry on a serious dialogue of their own. No standards, but ten interesting originals, firmly if not definitively characterized.

Odd Riisnaes (born 1953)

TENOR AND SOPRANO SAXOPHONES, PIANO

The younger of the tenor-playing Riisnaes brothers, working in a similar post-bop style.

***** Thoughts**

Taurus TRCD 828 *Riisnaes; Dag Arnesen (ky); Kare Garnes (b); Tom Olstad (d).* 8/89.

***** Another Version**

Taurus TRCD 831 *Riisnaes; Iver Kleive (org); Steinar Larsen (g); Terje Gewelt (b); Tom Olstad (d).* 10/93.

Odd Riisnaes manages to be powerful and self-effacing at the same time. His rounded, full tone carries over from tenor to soprano, and he's fond of measuring out a melody, giving weight to every part of the line. But he seems reticent about asserting his own personality on the music, which is still an absorbing essay on the various options for sax and rhythm section. *Thoughts* has a number of mood pieces resolved in the partnership with Arnesen (on synthesizer as often as not): improvisation takes a back seat, but there's compensation in the brisk 'Somehow' and 'Modern And Larsen'. *Another Version* changes tack again. Several pieces were recorded in the Helgerud church in Baerum, Kleive playing the organ and Riisnaes standing in the nave; as meditative sketches they carry plenty of substance. But one misses the brighter moments of some of Riisnaes's earlier playing: only Gewelt's 'One Side' impresses as a jazz piece.

*****(*) Your Ship**

Taurus TRCD 835 *Riisnaes; Svein Gjermundrod, Roy Nikolaisen (t); Harald Halvorsen, Steffan Stokland (tb); Jan Olav Martinsen, Rigmor Heisto Strand (frhn); Steinar Larsen (g); Bjorn Kjellemyr (b); Pal Thowsen (d).* 11/95.

An imposing and surprising departure for Riisnaes, yet one entirely in character: ambitiously shaped and delivered yet introspective and small-scale at the same time. Nine compositions follow a theme of a journey by sea, based around the quartet of Riisnaes, Larsen, Kjellemyr and Thowsen, and the leader has also scored several passages for the glowering brass section, who are not called upon to improvise but make the most telling contribution to the result. On the title-track, where they offset the sound of Riisnaes's soprano, the chill timbre of the horns adds a formidable power to the solo saxophone line. 'Embarkation', where Riisnaes overdubs himself into a tenor section, is just as fine. Not every piece seems completely effective, and Larsen's guitars don't always chime in with everything else, but this is a striking programme that deserves much study and reflection.

Ben Riley (born 1933)

DRUMS

A rare leadership outing for the veteran drummer: sideman for leaders from Thelonious Monk to Alice Coltrane, his most recent association has been with the band Sphere.

*****(*) Weaver Of Dreams**

Joken BK 105 *Riley; Ralph Moore (ts); Buster Williams (b).* 8/93.

What do you mean, *No harmony instrument?* Any group that includes Buster Williams is already grounded on a bedrock of harmony and can also count on the quickened pulse the little magician brings to all his sessions. Williams is, of course, a seasoned recording star, with several fine records as leader. Despite his seniority, Ben Riley hasn't hitherto thought to make the jump from engine-room to bridge. It was, ironically, his stint as locum to the ailing Art Blakey in the Messengers that gave him the notion; ironic, because everyone thought Ben's light, melodic approach was completely wrong for jazz's equivalent of the Navy Seals.

Never underestimate Riley, though. He started out in the real service as a paratrooper with the famous 188th Airborne and, for all his delicacy of touch, he's never been a player to mess with. Listen to the parade-ground accuracy and bayonet-sharp accents he brings to his solo on 'Sweet And Lovely'. The outstanding cuts, though, are a version of Williams's now well-covered 'Tokudo' and a stripped-down arrangement of 'Witchcraft' on which Moore's mournful, almost-out-of-tune tenor does little more than state the melody, leaving the rest of the action to his seniors. The album sets its agenda with Wayne Shorter's challengingly free-form 'Black Nile'. It checks out with a solitary Riley original, 'Doonda', which is elegant but unsurprising. The real surprise is that we haven't heard stuff like this from Ben before. One of the rankers goes point at last.

Howard Riley (born 1943)

PIANO

Born in Huddersfield, Riley played in local clubs before moving south and finding his own way to completely free playing. A long and distinguished discography charts this direction and his occasional glances back into bebop repertory.

*****(*) Angle**

Columbia 494433-2 *Riley; Barbara Thompson (f); Barry Guy (b); Alan Jackson (d).* 12/68–1/69.

♛ ** The Day Will Come**

Columbia 494434-2 *As above, except omit Thompson.* 3–4/70.

****** Flight**

Future Music FMR CD 26 *Riley; Barry Guy (b); Tony Oxley (d).* 3/71.

We take a great deal of pleasure – and claim no credit whatever – in the long-belated reissue of Howard Riley's two CBS recordings. Along with the three-LP *Facets* on Impetus, which may yet see the light of day again, they established the then 25-year-old as a major presence on the British scene. Would that major labels showed such generosity again.

For Riley himself, the key thing about these recordings was that they represented a working band. Other improvising musicians of the time were happy to issue what were effectively public rehearsals. By contrast, these records by the Howard Riley Trio contain a remarkable 20 tracks, none of them longer than eight and a half minutes, all but one – the fully notated flute and piano duets, 'Three Fragments', on *Angle* – the product of terse, focused improvisation on written themes. Riley is the only credited composer on the earlier album, which perhaps accounts for its thoughtful and rather reserved character.

The introduction of Barry Guy as co-composer on the brilliant *The Day Will Come* is the key factor in our very high rating for this record. It is worth noting that, whatever the public persona Guy has now, in 1969 Chris Wellard thought nothing of describing him in his liner-note as 'rumbustious and violent'. It is he who balances the rather tender and melancholic cast of Riley's playing. His *arco* solo on 'Angle' is astonishing, and he drives the following track, 'Aftermath', into territory new in British jazz at the time. On the later album Guy tunes like 'Sad Was The Song', 'Playtime' and the title-track present genuine improvisational challenges.

Of the trio members, Jackson is the one who seems to have been eclipsed by the passing years. He is a drummer of great control and precision, inch-perfect on fast numbers like 'Angle' without compromising a robustly swinging presence which recalls Phil Seamen but also has ties right back to the days of Dave Tough.

We're thrilled to see both records back in circulation, even if to some extent they eclipse some of the work that followed. Some months on from *The Day Will Come*, *Flight* represents a development of Riley's trio language, expanded considerably through the use of Guy's pedal and amplifier and drummer Oxley's astonishing range of amplified percussion effects. Even playing acoustically, his trademark device of exchanging sticks and mallets for knitting needles generates a light, skittering sound that blends perfectly with the piano.

All three men contribute material. Oxley's 'Cirrus' is a personal *tour de force*; Riley's opening 'Motion' is a fair representation of his parallel interest in 'legitimate' composition. Pianist and bassist are jointly credited for 'Two Ballads'. Riley's technique is utterly assured, his sense of time is gnomic rather than metronomic, and his dynamics – ranging from huge clusters to the tiniest mosaic effects – bring a constantly shifting intellectual drama.

*****(*) Feathers With Jaki**

Slam CD 215 *Riley; Jaki Byard (p); Mario Castronari (b); Tony Marsh (d).* 81–91.

The idea of Riley playing Monk in the company of Jaki Byard would have struck even sympathetic fans as an unlikely one. This, though, is one of the forgotten classics of jazz in Britain, an anomalous but highly creative encounter somewhat akin to the fabled meeting of Cecil Taylor and Mary Lou Williams, though far less acrimonious.

Byard is the more obviously Monk-like in conception and execution, and is far more deeply rooted in blues tonality. However, it's Riley who tends to keep the music on line and within touching distance of the original. The sound-quality isn't all that good, and no better – as we remember it – than the original LP. Released by Leo Records, it's now been compiled with a later Spotlite recording by Riley's Feathers Trio. Some good stuff on that, but people will want this one for the Riley/Byard encounter.

*****(*) Procession**

Wondrous WM 0101 *Riley (p solo).* 4/90.

***** The Heat Of Moments**

Wondrous WM 0103 *As above.* 4/91–4/92.

*****(*) Beyond Category**

Wondrous WM 0104 *As above.* 2/93.

You might well ask what has happened to the work of the mid- and later 1970s and of the '80s. Familiar story: neglect and deletion. Riley has been indebted to Brian Miller of Wondrous for issuing these well-recorded, highly atmospheric sessions which, though taped in studio, somehow suggest a live ambience. The first two consist of nothing but originals, though as ever written with a strong awareness of the jazz-piano tradition; we wonder how many listeners ambushed by 'April Again', the lead item on *Procession*, would guess who the player was. Similarly 'Inseparable' and the long 'Tell Me', while 'Striding' hints at a different tradition again.

It was some time before Riley committed himself wholeheartedly to solo performance. There is no discomfort in any of these, but nor is there the muscly, overdetermining sweep of some who have tackled the discipline. Instead, a rigorous and almost deliberate approach, which becomes a touch enervated on *The Heat Of Moments*. This is a much more abstract performance. Apart from the title-track and 'Zig Zag' (which inescapably recalls Byard), most of the pieces are short and introspective. 'Mirror Image' has nothing to do with the Zawinul composition, but coincidentally reflects the Austrian's combination of 'correctness' and an earthy, folksy groove.

Beyond Category is devoted to the music of Monk and Ellington, two of the obvious jazz influences on Riley's work. This came along at a time when he was placing greater emphasis on form and less on freedom, and one can hear him working inside the songs, pushing at their boundaries, appending footnotes and marking sources. Of the 17 tracks only two are over five minutes long, suggesting a considerable concentration of effort and thought.

*****(*) The Bern Concert: Interchange**

Future Music FMR CD 08 *Riley; Keith Tippett (p).* 8/93.

Riley mentions that the first piano duo he remembers hearing was an old 78 of James P. Johnson and Clarence Williams, and he points to the combination of subtlety and 'orchestral' power the instrumentation yields. Though Johnson and Williams are mostly replaced by latter-day mentors, that same combination of virtues is audible all the way through this.

Riley and Tippett had recorded together before, *First Encounter* for Impetus and *In Focus* for Affinity. It's difficult to say how this later album differs, except as a function of how both men have changed as individuals over the years. Tippett probably allows more space than he did; Riley has a more forcible attack. However, only someone particularly anxious to separate two voices as closely entwined as strands of DNA is going to worry about who is playing what line at a particular moment. The status of the subtitle isn't entirely clear, but what one hears is almost an hour of continuous creative interchange, highly responsive and respectful. The digital recording is of very high quality, though perhaps a little intimately miked for some tastes.

*****(*) Wishing On The Moon**

Future Music FMR CD 14 *Riley; Mario Castronari (b); Tony Marsh (d).* 95.

****** Descending Circles**

Blueprint BP221 *Riley; Elton Dean (as, saxello); Mario Castronari (b); Mark Sanders (d).* 10/95.

The mid-'90s saw Riley perhaps shifting emphasis back to group playing (often with Dean as co-leader, but also with Art Themen) and at the same time taking a greater interest in composition. There is a more tightly reined and briskly registered attack, a more straightforward approach to the chords, and a freely melodic approach that often suggests a standard lies somewhere behind the theme, an enigma being subjected to fresh variation, but never openly declared.

The trio with Castronari and Marsh is as different from the early-'70s group as its very different personnel would suggest. Both are forceful players who are also capable of sitting out when required, or heading off on parallel courses of their own. The integrity and cohesion of the older group isn't there, but in its place there's a sparkle and lightness of touch which carries over into the quartets as well. Dean is marvellous in these contexts, and his writing for the group is different enough from Riley's to maintain interest. 'Descending Circles' is an almost definitive Riley composition: sturdy, well rooted, harmonically fascinating, but with a usefully problematic shape and direction. The group sound less secure on two spontaneous improvisations. This isn't Castronari's bag, one suspects, though he throws himself into it with a will. Playing with a horn pushes Riley further than usual into a chords mode, but with no sign that he feels constrained or uncomfortable. An earlier record, *All The Tradition*, is listed under Dean's leadership.

Sammy Rimington (born 1942)

CLARINET, ALTO AND TENOR SAXOPHONES, VOCAL

Born in London, he began playing with Ken Colyer and other trad stalwarts around 1960. Moved to the USA in 1965, subsequently to New Orleans, and played and recorded with many masters of the New Orleans style. Returned to Europe in the '70s and investigated jazz-rock, but stayed mainly with traditional jazz styles and by the '90s was as eminent as many of his former heroes.

***** Clarinet King In Norway**

Herman HJCD 1001 *Rimington; Andy Finch (p); Ole Olen (b); Søren Houlind (d).* 12/77.

***** The Exciting Sax Of Sammy Rimington**

Progressive PCD-7077 *Rimington; David Paquette (p, v); Walter Payton (b); Placide Adams, Stanley Stephens, Ernest Elly (d).* 4/86–4/91.

****(*) One Swiss Night**

Music Mecca 1021-2 *Rimington; Freddy John (tb); Jon Marks (p); Koen De Cauter (g, bj); Karl-Ake Kronquist (b); Sven Stahlberg (d).* 11/91.

***** More Exciting Sax Of Sammy Rimington**

Progressive PCD 7088 *Rimington; Phamous Lambert (p); Lloyd Lambert (b); Ernie Elly (d).* 5/94.

****(*) Watering The Roots**

Jazz Crusade JCCD-3011 *Rimington; Big Bill Bissonnette (tb); Sarah Bissonnette (ts); Eric Webster (bj); Ken Matthews (b); Colin Bowden (d).* 1/95.

Rimington has had a strange career: a stalwart with Ken Colyer, a transplantation to Louisiana where he became a bosom friend of Capt. John Handy, a flirtation with jazz-rock and now occasional sightings in sundry pick-up groups, like these. The two Progressive albums feature him exclusively on alto, where he sounds like Handy but phrases as if he were brother to Johnny Hodges: the result is a queer hybrid, soaked in a woozy kind of romanticism. Engagingly done, although the sound-mix (with the piano in the distance, the drums right up front) doesn't assist on the earlier disc. The second sounds better and goes along at a jollier pace, with Rimington this time sounding more like a jump-band hornman on a featured night of his own. *One Swiss Night* catches him with a second-rate band (John's trombone is especially unhealthy) on dull material, but there is one real surprise, a very Websterish reading of 'My Funny Valentine' on tenor. *Watering The Roots* finds Sammy back in England. Bissonnette organized and sponsored the recording, and it's fair enough that he plays on it, but he can't summon the authority to stand in the front line and is painfully outclassed by the clarinettist. The material this time goes back to New Orleans purism, and the only one earning stars is Rimington. He deserves a break in better company and on a proper budget.

The Herman album resuscitates a set made by Rimington's quartet at the end of a 1977 tour. He sticks to clarinet, and his own playing, from the beautifully inflected 'Hymn For George Lewis' to the bodacious 'Lou-Easy-An-I-A', is excellent. But the rhythm section is hamfisted, and Rimington needs another horn as some kind of context.

***** Live 'In Store' At The Louisiana Music Factory**

504 CDS 74 *Rimington; Clive Wilson (t); Lester Caliste (tb); Bob Broockman (p); Les Muscutt (bj); Gerald Adams (b); Frank Oxley (d).* 1/98.

Recorded at one of the leading record stores in the French Quarter, here's a recent Rimington crew tackling a dozen favourites from the NO book. Broockman has been playing in the city since the '40s, but this was his first record date; Caliste works for the Post Office but plays nights. Wilson and Rimington are old playing companions from many years before, in the Barry Martyn band. Inevitably, the feel is good-natured fun, and any blemishes are easily forgiven. Not the record Rimington fans have necessarily been waiting for, but good-hearted.

Per Ringkjøbing

FLUGELHORN, TRUMPET

Born in Denmark but a veteran who's played all over Europe – he was with Acker Bilk in 1962 – and taught extensively, Ringkjøbing plays a solid mainstream horn.

*****(*) Everything Happens To Me**

Olufsen DOCD 5166 *Ringkjøbing; Erling Kroner (tb); Lennart Wallin (p); Jens Melgaard (b); George Cole (d).* 3/92.

A Danish villager making a belated stab at his own record, Ringkjøbing has been around – a two-year gig at a US Air Force base in Iceland was 'the top of the iceberg', he notes – and knows his jazz. If he's a Dixieland veteran, you'd hardly know it from the long lines, serpentine melodic sense and lovely mellifluous tone he gets from the flugelhorn, which he uses as his first instrument. The wry, Dickenson-like trombone of Kroner is an ideal sparring-partner on this programme of standards. If it's reminiscent of the Hackett–Dickenson team, that makes it a rare strain indeed among today's records. Melgaard is stunningly quick and fluent in his solos, but Wallin is a bit clunky and Cole a little four-square. Otherwise, an exceptional brew of contemporary mainstream.

***** An Individual Thing**

Olufsen DOCD 5181 *Ringkjøbing; Erling Kroner (tb); Morten Hojring (g); Ole Skipper Mosgaard (b); Lars Beijbom (d); Helene Johnsson (v); strings and woodwinds.* 3/93.

Ringkjøbing was ill, recuperating from a car accident, when he made this record, and it shows in some involuntary frailties – but that makes the fine ballad treatment of the title-track all the more impressive, and throughout this gentle programme the playing has a blush of sincerity that draws the listener in. Kroner sounds a bit offhand here and there but has a splendid feature of his own on 'Chelsea Bridge', and Johnsson – otherwise booked as one of the string players – does a decent job on 'Day Dream'.

Rinneradio

GROUP

Finnish saxophonist Tapan Rinne and his groups in a provocative mix of jazz, rock and other strains of the avant-garde.

***** Dance And Visions**

Pyramid 3035 *Mika Myllari (t); Jari Hongisto (tb); Tapani Rinne (ss, ts, bs, cl, bcl); Tommi Lindell, Seppo Kantonen (ky); Seppo Tyni (g); Jari Kokkonen (b); Keimo Hirvonen (d); Jan Noponen (perc); Leeva Rinne, Wimme Saari (v).* 90.

***** Unik**

Aani AA-X-005 *As above, except add Kajasto, Pauli Saastamoinen, Matti Wallenius, Iliro Rantala, Sami Kuoppamaki, Judge Bean Jr (unidentified instruments); omit Myllari, Hongisto, Hirvonen, Noponen, Leeva Rinne. n.d.*

***** Pfft**

Rockadillo 2054 *Tapani Rinne (reeds); Kajasto (ky, elec); Jari Kokkonen (b); Mika Vainio (elec).* 3/95.

***** Rok**

Rockadillo 2047 *Tapani Rinne (reeds); Kajasto, Pauli Saastamoinen (ky, elec); Jari Kokkonen (b); Keimo Hirvonen, Freakmaster K. One (d); Malang Cissokho (perc).* 96.

Rinneradio is basically saxophonist Rinne teamed with various collaborators, particularly Kajasto, who began by creating a ferocious but not nihilistic barrage of violent but not crude jazz-rock gestures nailed on to wayward but not anarchistic rhythm- or sound-beds. The early *Dance And Visions* is conventional: using horns and real rhythm-sections, they approximate synthetic beats and soundscapes by treating the instruments in ways that remind one of early Eno albums. Rinne's sax parts are the more unsettling for being placed right at the front of the mix, but he's not afraid to pause for a moment of prettiness, as in 'Pelakuu'. Actually, a sweetness tends to prevail in the subsequent discs. *Unik* relies more specifically on the electronics and, by the time of *Rok*, the textures created by Kajasto and Saastamoinen are the predominant substance, with Rinne apparently content to decorate them, most often with soprano or bass clarinet. There are some surprisingly gorgeous passages on all the records, and *Rok* ends on three long tracks which owe as much to ambient and trance musics as they do to any jazz beginnings. *Pfft* is a live album where the group played in one room and Mika Vainio simultaneously remixed the music in another. The result is a kind of aural heat-haze, although again the group itself seems in danger of disappearing inside its own sonic image. Not the future of jazz, or anything else; just some interesting moments in late-twentieth-century music.

Sam Rivers (born 1923)

TENOR SAXOPHONE, SOPRANO SAXOPHONE, FLUTE, PIANO, VOCAL

Born in El Reno, Oklahoma, he studied composition and viola in Boston and played sax in local bands. Backed R&B singers and show groups, but also worked with Miles Davis (1964) and Cecil Taylor (1968–73), composed, and led his own occasional bands and sessions. Ran Studio RivBea, a focal point for New York jazz in the '70s, and has been one of the major teachers in American jazz. In the '90s, as an honoured veteran, he finally began recording more frequently, especially his big-band writing.

*****(*) Trio Live**

Impulse! IMP 12682 *Rivers; Arild Andersen, Cecil McBee (b); Barry Altschul (d).* 8 & 10/73.

Rivers was content to leave a significant measure of freedom in his trio performances. Larger units tended to have more structure, but these recordings, albeit highly developed, are the sketch-pads on which he worked out ideas. Even so, there is a clear continuity between these multi-sectioned works and the long-form compositions showcased on the much later big-band *Inspiration*, the same blend of structure and freedom. Most of this material, recorded weeks apart at the Molde Jazz Festival in Norway and at Yale University, has been heard before, but on a bizarre range of Impulse! compilations. Presented as performed, it reveals the organization even in Sam's most free-floating work. The two sets, 'Suite For Molde' and the Yale piece, 'Hues For Melanin', are subdivided according to the leader's choice of horn. The long soprano section of 'Hues' was formerly available on *Impulse! Artists On Tour*; the flute section was issued on *The Drums*; the remainder, and the soprano and flute sections of *Suite For Molde* were issued on a Rivers record called *Hues*, with the remainder released as *No Energy Crisis*.

These are now collectors' items. The beauty of having the material on one format is that it is possible to track the progress of improvisations. Rivers characteristically trades ideas from one instrument to another. The most obvious traffic is between the tenor and flute. Sam often recasts a phrase many minutes later, allowing it to resettle into a new instrumental idiom. It's a fascinating process, and anyone with the technical wherewithal to scoot back and forth from one track to another will learn a great deal about his musical thinking.

Altschul is, as ever, the most musical of drummers. Of the two bassists, Andersen more than holds his own. His bowed work on the *Suite For Molde* is rich and suggestive, while his more straightforwardly rhythmic drive manages to suggest a synthesis between metre and harmony. It's a hybrid that is unique to Sam Rivers. He is arguably the missing link between the innovations of John Coltrane and Ornette Coleman, and the sharp geometries of Anthony Braxton and the M-Base Collective. He dabbles in elements of atonality but retains the purest instinct for melody.

*****(*) Colors**

Black Saint 120064 *Rivers; Marvin Blackman (ts, f, ss); Talib Kibwe (f, cl, ts, ss); Chris Roberts (ss, f); Steve Coleman (as, f); Bobby Watson (as, f); Nat Dixon (ts, cl, f); Eddie Alex (ts, picc); Jimmy Cozier, Patience Higgins (bs, f).* 9/82.

This spectacular convocation of New York reed-playing talent went under the name Winds of Manhattan. Dominated by flutes and without a rhythm section, it creates a sound that is absolutely consistent with everything Rivers had been doing over the previous 20 years, but scaled up dramatically. The usual interest in wave-forms, flux and unity, dispersement and integration, come together again in these complex charts. Rivers is unmistakably the leader, in that he determines the basic concepts, but the music as a whole is democratic and very broadly based. Those familiar with Coleman or Watson or even with the distinctive Kibwe may well be able to pick out their voices, but this is not the point of the exercise, and *Colors* is best listened to as an orchestral piece, relatively undifferentiated and a long way removed from conventional theme-and-solos jazz.

***** Lazuli**

Timeless CD SJP 291 *Rivers; Darryll Thompson (g); Rael Wesley Grant (b); Steve McCraven (d).* 10/89.

Rivers has never been drawn with any enthusiasm to conventional structures and this must be accounted his most straight-ahead project on record. The use of a guitar player keeps the surface shifting, and Thompson, while not a virtuoso, is a formidably intelligent player who would be worth following up. The basic concept is familiar, though this time Sam seems to have abandoned water as a metaphor in favour of the swimming blue of a semi-precious stone. Far be it from us to say that his usual radicalism has ossified on *Lazuli*, but it's certainly a less than overwhelming record.

****** Portrait**

FMP CD 82 *Rivers (ts, ss, f, p, v solo).* 6/95.

A self-portrait presumably and of the artist at over 70, espousing what he describes in a notably effusive liner-note as an 'uninhibited emotion-driven free-flowing river of vibrant, bold, melodic inventions'. It's a piece of text that runs dangerously close to self-review: 'dazzling', 'musical perfection', 'eloquently phrased' and so on. What saves it is there is hardly a word with which one might disagree. These unaccompanied essays, with their characteristic one-word titles – 'Image', 'Reflection', 'Shadow' and overlong 'Cameo' – are magnificently crafted and thoroughly imbued with the creator's personality. Full attributions are given for all the instruments used, Keilwerth saxophones, a Bosendorfer Imperial and a Gemeinhardt flute, while under 'voice' it says laconically 'Sam Rivers', which is a version of 'model's own' on the fashion pages. Again, it makes complete sense, for this is the most thoroughly individual thing he has done for many years, a magnificent testament to his creative range, his generosity of spirit, and his great, great intelligence.

*****(*) Concept**

RivBea 50101 *Rivers; Doug Mathews (b); Anthony Cole (d).* 2–7/96.

A mixture of studio material recorded at the bassist/producer's homebase and live tracks from Florida, this is a tightly constructed record which has presumably been selected from a wide range of available material. The playing is consistently fascinating. The sound is underpowered and there are occasions when Rivers disappears into the background for no readily discernible reason. Interesting to note that the track titles here are entirely abstract – 'Aspect', 'Concept', 'Notion' – and the music has something of that quality as well, certainly nothing like as personalized, even confessional as on the FMP session. If that stands as Rivers's highest achievement of recent times, this must be accounted a more tentative project. Though clearly drawing on the shared experience of a working trio, it lacks the intimacy and the quickfire response one might expect from such a unit, working over a six-month period. It would be fascinating to hear some of the material that wasn't released; perhaps over the course of a live set or a day in the studio the logic and the dynamics would make more sense. A fine achievement nevertheless.

*****(*) Configuration**

Nato 777 711 *Rivers; Tony Hymas (p); Noël Akchoté (g); Paul Rogers (b); Jacques Thollot (d).* 97.

****** Eight Day Journal**

Nato 777 726 *Rivers; Henry Lowther (t, bugle); François Corneloup (ss, bs); Carol Robinson (cl, bcl); Sylvain Kassap (ss, bcl, basset hn); Tony Hymas (p); Noël Akchoté (g); Rita Manning (vn); Philip Dukes (vla); Sophie Harris (clo); Chris Laurence (b); Paul Clarvis (perc).* 1/98.

****** Winter Garden**

Nato 777 769 *Rivers; Tony Hymas (p).* 12/98.

Sam's association with pianist and composer Tony Hymas (and with the Nato label) has been a particularly happy one, albeit signalling a change of direction which some Rivers enthusiasts might find puzzling. *Eight Day Journal* is a long-form ensemble composition with a solo part for saxophone. Written entirely by Hymas, it casts Sam as a slightly mournful outsider, and one can't help thinking of Black American novelist James Baldwin's meditations on his own first appearance in a remote Swiss village, facing no overt hostility or even suspicion, but simply an existential detachment.

Hymas's writing is always exquisitely mournful and troubled, interweaving lyrical passages with sections of musical *bande dessiné*, like the images which accompany the CD. The second section, devoted to Sunday, 5 March 1984, and whatever happened then, is the key to the piece. Sam's tenor growls and mumbles give way to a passage of stilled harmony before he returns – on soprano – with a high note figure of heart-stopping purity. The dance section which follows is no less beautiful, a proudly tragic tango that includes some of Sam's most open and melodic playing on record, and just possibly a sly nod in the direction of Gato Barbieri's *Last Tango In Paris* theme. Akchoté's guitar and Hymas's rippling accompaniments are the other prominent voices; otherwise, the ensemble is just that, a well-marshalled unit with genuine personality but no ego.

The duos with Hymas are certainly not recorded to favour the pianist. Sam is recorded in vivid close-up, just the comfortable side of distortion, while Hymas sounds tucked in tight behind, a rather odd, one-dimensional mix that muffles some sensitive interaction. When he shifts to soprano for his own 'Sunset', the resemblance to Mal Waldron's duo records with Steve Lacy is confirmed. Like them, these are highly intimate encounters, song-based but with opportunities for free playing as well. The four numbered improvisations are obviously late takes; it would be wonderful to hear the earlier pieces some time. Sam has been more sparing with his flute in recent years, but 'Iris' is a reminder of how brilliant a practitioner he can be. Much like its immediate predecessor, the album is best heard as a continuous conversation.

Configuration is a minor miracle, a small-group record which is completely different in approach from the composition-led *Eight Day Journal*. It opens with 'Beatrice', a wholehearted love song to the co-founder of Rivbea. Sam plights his troth with a delicate vulnerability, and the mood of the session remains lightly lyrical. Akchoté and Rogers are the other main composers. The guitarist's 'Cheshire Hotel' is a more angular piece; there may be plush carpet, but there are the echoes of nightmares in the old walls. A tiny folder of flute 'Etchings' with Rogers in support gives way to the improvised title-piece, which is initially dominated by Hymas's signature trills and arpeggios. 'Rififi' and 'Zing' confirm the saxophonist's close relationship with the British bassist, a player who has imbibed and understood the lessons of Jimmy Garrison and Paul Chambers and grafted them on to something new and unprecedented. Thollot is something of an unknown quantity, but he establishes a presence from the opening measures and plays both inside and outside the metre with impressive authority. We have also found *Configuration* as a Pelican Sound CD (PSR 9803). Whatever the imprint, it's worth having and hearing.

****** Inspiration**

RCA Victor 7432 164717 2 *Rivers; Ralph Alessi, Ravi Best, Baikida Carroll, James Zollar (t); Ray Anderson, Art Baron, Joseph Bowie (tb); Joseph Daley (bhn); Bob Stewart (tba); Steve Coleman, Greg Osby (as); Chico Freeman, Gary Thomas (ts); Hamiet Bluiett (bs); Doug Matthews (b); Anthony Cole (d).* 9–10/98.

Sam regards this project as nothing more than a sample of his compositional/improvisational approach, pointing out that each of the pieces – which are selected from a worklist of more than 100 titles – was intended for performance at upwards of three-quarters of an hour and thus would require a CD each to do them full justice.

We beg leave to wonder. Trimmed of backgrounds and presumably many of the possible solos, these quarter-scale representations are powerful and convincing, and it's difficult to imagine some of them – and most obviously the atonal cluster pieces, 'Nebula' and 'Whirlwind' – sustaining interest and coherence over the full duration. The oldest piece represented is, almost inevitably, 'Beatrice', in which the main theme has always come garlanded with secondary subjects. Thirty years after its composition, this is its definitive incarnation, an anniversary tribute.

Rivers explains the enormous impact Dizzy Gillespie's solo work with the Eckstine orchestra made on him when he was in the Navy, listening to USO discs between watches. 'Inspiration' is a set of variations on Dizzy's 'Tanga', written while Sam was a member of the Gillespie touring orchestra. By contrast, 'Vines' is an exercise in harmonic minimalism, all the activity taking place over one admittedly ambiguous chord. 'Solace' is a later poem to Bea, no less lyrical, but more quietly accepting.

The all-star band consists largely of players who, individually and severally, have worked with Rivers before. Our only quibble is with the use of an electric bassist; Doug Matthews is an immaculate technician, but he doesn't seem to create quite the right sound for this ensemble. There are fine solo statements by tubist Stewart and the ever-distinguished Bluiett. No indication is given as to who the other soloists are. Sam, of course, is distinctive and prominently featured, but it may take a moment or two to decide whether Bowie or Anderson, Freeman or Thomas, Osby or album producer Coleman are occupying front-of-stage. That in part is testimony to the sheer originality of Rivers's concept: that he can mould a orchestra of highly individual performers so that it sounds like the expression of a single, idiosyncratic imagination. *Inspiration* is one of the finest big-band records of recent times. It joins a long tradition, one that links together such unlikely bedmates as the Eckstine orchestra and Trane's *Ascension* group, the classic Ellington bands and the great improvising collectives of the 1960s and '70s. It also cements Sam Rivers's place in the history of the music.

Max Roach (born 1924)

DRUMS, PERCUSSION

All revolutions in jazz are, on closer inspection, revolutions in the rhythm section. The fierce metres of bebop, with the accent taken away from the bass drum and given to the hi-hat instead, were created by Kenny Clarke, Art Blakey and Max Roach. In terms of long-term influence, Roach may be the most important of the three and he has continued to create a radical, often politically engaged brand of jazz in which the drum is primal and at the centre of the action. His group, M'Boom, took this to the extreme, but it is also true of Roach's more conventional personnels.

***** Max Roach**

Original Jazz Classics OJCCD 202 *Roach; Idrees Sulieman (t); Leon Comeghys (tb); Gigi Gryce (as); Hank Mobley (ts); Walter Davis Jr (p); Frank Skeete (b).* 4 & 10/53.

*****(*) Brownie Lives!**

Fresh Sound FSRCD 1012 *Roach; Clifford Brown (t); Sonny Rollins (ts); Richie Powell (p); George Morrow (b).* 4 & 5/56.

Almost half a century of extraordinary music-making. With Kenny Clarke and Art Blakey, Roach was in at the birth of the revolution that was bebop but, unlike either of them, he continued to develop a language for the drums that took account of melody and – more obviously than either of his contemporaries – of sound-colour as well. Stylistically, he stands mid-way between swing drummers like Jo Jones, Dave Tough, Gene Krupa and Big Sid Catlett and the avant-garde of the 1960s. If Krupa made the drummer a 'high-price guy', as he claimed with some justification, Roach set jazz percussionists free as instrumentalists in their own right. Some of his best solo performances now have to be dug out of samplers, but there is plenty around from the early days.

The eponymous 1953 session gives little indication of what is to follow and there are spells where Roach sounds oddly unlike himself. No mistaking the flashes of originality in the writing, even though most of the themes are orthodox bebop. Even at this juncture, the horns sound carefully arranged, almost orchestral in timbre – though, as he was to do later, Roach also breaks the band up into constituent parts. Six of the tracks are for quartet only, though brass and a second saxophone bring a rather special extra dimension to 'Sfax' and 'Orientation'.

Roach's career as leader really took flight only when he formed the now legendary – though, in the event, tragically short-lived – quintet with Clifford Brown. Their rapport was immediate and, for much of the period after Brownie's death, one senses Roach searching for a trumpeter to take his place, something he achieved briefly with the equally short-lived Booker Little. Roach himself missed the road accident which killed Brown and Richie Powell, but his career faltered badly. The live *Brownie Lives!* comes from a residency at Basin Street in New York, just six weeks before the tragic events of that summer. Understandably billed as a tribute to the trumpeter, it's arresting for what it tells us about the co-leader. Roach is magnificent throughout and, with digital remastering, occupies his proper place in the mix. He improvises constantly, shifting and re-calibrating the rhythms on 'I Get A Kick Out Of You' and on his brilliant young colleague's 'Daahoud'; the energy passing between the two is palpable. A very exciting set, though one probably has to look under Brown's name for the best of their association.

**** Alone Together

Verve 526373-2 2CD *Roach; Clifford Brown, Kenny Dorham, Booker Little, Tommy Turrentine (t); Julian Priester (tb); Ray Draper (tba); George Coleman, Harold Land, Hank Mobley, Paul Quinichette, Sonny Rollins, Stanley Turrentine (ts); Herbie Mann (f); Ray Bryant, Jimmy Jones, Richie Powell, Bill Wallace (p); Barry Galbraith (g); Joe Benjamin, Bob Boswell, Nelson Boyd, Art Davis, Milt Hinton, George Morrow (b); Boston Percussion Ensemble; Abbey Lincoln (v).* 9/56–10/60.

A very valuable compilation both with and, later, without Brownie, and an excellent introduction for anyone who hasn't caught up with Roach. Fans of the drummer may well feel that it's better representative of his work than of the trumpeter's – which seems fair, given the relative weight of material. There are two tracks from *Max Roach + 4* and just one from *Jazz In 3/4 Time*. Most of the rest is later, some of it from less well-known records like *The Many Sides Of Max* (1959, with Little, Priester and Coleman) and *Quiet As It's Kept* (1960, with the Turrentines and Priester again). 'Max's Variations' is based on 'Pop Goes The Weasel' and is performed with the Boston Percussion Ensemble, a foreshadowing of later drum orchestra projects like M'Boom. On balance, a very good record indeed, pointing the way to most of the directions Roach was to take over the next few years. Serious enthusiasts should not settle for anything less than the full run of original albums, but for almost everyone else there can't be any better place to start.

***(*) Plays Charlie Parker

Verve 512448-2 *Roach; Kenny Dorham (t); George Coleman, Hank Mobley (ts); Nelson Boyd, George Morrow (b).* 12/57, 4/58.

*** Max

GRP 051 825 2 *Roach; Kenny Dorham (t); Hank Mobley (ts); Ramsey Lewis (p); George Morrow (b).* 1/58.

**** Deeds, Not Words

Original Jazz Classics OJCCD 304 *Roach; Booker Little (t); Ray Draper (tba); George Coleman (ts); Art Davis, Oscar Pettiford (b).* 9/58.

A mere couple of years after Bird's death, the heritage industry was only just gearing up. Nobody had more right to claim a slice of it than Roach, who plays with a warmth and engagement that is audible on every track. The Coleman/Dorham front line is consistently more interesting than the April 1958 replacement on which Mobley sounds blustery and sometimes poorly rehearsed, taking a long time to settle on 'Parker's Mood'; but there is enough excellent musicianship around to make up any slight deficit. Four previously unissued tracks turned up in 1984 and are included on the CD. Nothing of earth-shaking importance, but 'Raoul' and 'This Time The Dream's On Me' are well worth having. Coleman is the secret weapon here, a superb harmonic improviser, constantly surprising, shapeshifting and rejigging the lines.

Max is something of a transitional album – as if it wasn't possible to say that of every record Max Roach has ever issued. In some respects, it has a very old-fashioned, orthodox hard-bop sound; in others, it looks forward to the open-ended ensembles of the '60s avant-garde in which the distinction between 'front line' and 'rhythm section' was largely, if temporarily, suspended. There are moments when the two horns and pianist Ramsey Lewis (still in his straight-jazz incarnation) vamp for several measures, while Roach and the consistently underrated Morrow improvise freely. 'Audio Blues' works like that, though Dorham's 'Speculate' and Mobley's tough-tenor 'C.M.' are straightahead and in the groove.

Roach was bruisingly committed again on *Deeds, Not Words*, a superb statement that makes a nonsense of generic pigeonholes like 'hard bop' but which also feels like the apotheosis of that often derided style. Draper's chesty valvings are not much more than a footnote in recent jazz, but he has booked his place and this is one of his more successful appearances, fulfilling an important role in this piano-less group that was to stay together successfully for two years. The CD also includes a duo featuring Roach with Oscar Pettiford which was made during a Sonny Rollins session; no idea why it turns up, unrelated, here.

*** Drum Conversation

Enja ENJ 4074 *Roach; Tommy Turrentine (t); Julian Priester (tb); Bobby Boswell (b).* 60.

For some reason, Roach had always seemed more comfortable with brass players than with reeds. Priester fills the gap to some degree, playing smooth *legato* lines on 'Lotus Blossom' and 'A Night In Tunisia', but the overall effect is very sparse and unfussy, with considerable emphasis on the drum-kit. Boswell never sounds quite up to what is required of him, and the sound is very poorly balanced.

♛ **** We Insist! Freedom Now Suite

Candid CCD 79002 *Roach; Booker Little (t); Julian Priester (tb); Walter Benton, Coleman Hawkins (ts); James Schenck (b); Ray Mantilla, Thomas Du Vall (perc); Abbey Lincoln (v).* 8 & 9/60.

Some works of art are inseparable from the social and cultural conditions which spawned them, and *We Insist!* is certainly one of these, a record that seems rooted in its moment. Within a few short years, the civil rights movement in the USA was to acquire a more obdurate countenance. On the threshold of the Kennedy years, though, this was as ferocious as it got. The opening 'Driva' Man' (one of Oscar Brown Jr's finest moments as a lyricist) is wry and sarcastic, enunciated over Roach's deliberately mechanical work rhythms and Coleman Hawkins's blearily proud solo, just the kind of thing you might expect from a working stiff at the end of the longest shift in history. It's followed by 'Freedom Day' which, with 'All Africa', was to be part of a large choral work targeted on the centenary of the Emancipation Proclamation. 'Freedom Day' follows Roach's typically swinging address, but is distinguished by a Booker Little solo of bursting, youthful emotion, and a contribution from the little-regarded Walter Benton that matches Hawkins's for sheer simplicity of diction.

The central 'Triptych' – originally conceived as a dance piece – is a duo for Roach and Lincoln. 'Prayer', 'Protest' and 'Peace' was not a trajectory acceptable to a later generation of militants, but there is more than enough power in Lincoln's inchoate roars of rage in the central part, and more than enough ambiguity in the ensuing 'Peace', to allay thoughts that her or Roach's politics were blandly liberal. The closing 'Tears For Johannesburg' has more classic Little, and also good things from Priester and Benton. It follows 'All Africa', which begins in a vein reminiscent of Billie Holiday, briefly degenerates into a litany of tribal names and slogans, and hinges on a 'middle passage' of drum music embodying the three main Black drum traditions of the West: African, Afro-Cuban and Afro-American. Its influence on subsequent jazz percussion is incalculable, and this extraordinary record remains listenable even across four decades of outwardly far more radical experimentation.

*** Members, Don't Git Weary

Koch International 8514 *Roach; Charles Tolliver (t); Gary Bartz (as); Stanley Cowell (p); Jymie Merritt (b); Andy Bey (v).* 10/60.

Coming so soon after *Freedom Now!*, this is inevitably something of an anti-climax, and it's perhaps more interesting in parts than as a whole. As a showcase for the burgeoning talents of Tolliver, Bartz and Merritt, it's almost an extended audition. Gary is trenchant and intense in his solo spots and Tolliver's bright, metallic tone has rarely since been heard to such advantage, even though his solo building is rather predictable. Andy Bey's vocal on the title-track takes a bit of getting used to, but it's attractively hokey. Roach plays his familiar 3/4s and 6/8s against a straight backbeat, giving the album, as so often with this transitional artist, a feeling of belonging to two generations simultaneously.

**** It's Time

Impulse! IMP 11852 *Roach; Richard Williams (t); Julian Priester (tb); Clifford Jordan (ts); Mal Waldron (p); Art Davis (b).* 62.

It's Time was always a magnificent-*sounding* record, bright and brash and very accurately balanced. Poor Richard Williams has long been destined for the footnotes, recording just one impressive record under his own name but contributing to some remarkable sessions for other leaders. Here he sounds at his best, picking off clean, single-note lines when out front, blurring his sound most attractively when in the ensembles, and contributing a steady run of ideas. Priester also has one of his finest moments, a wonderful solo on 'Another Valley' which modulates between A major and A minor and carries an almost biblical authority. In contrast to his rather laid-back approach on *Speak, Brother, Speak*, Waldron is taut and ambiguous. A fine group record in every way. Only Roach's feature sounds padded, and perhaps a little too discursive.

***(*) Speak, Brother, Speak

Original Jazz Classics OJCCD 646 *Roach; Clifford Jordan (ts); Mal Waldron (p); Eddie Khan (b).* 10/62.

Driven by the same impulse as *We Insist! Freedom Now*, this is even more explicitly hooked into the civil rights movement of the time. The four band members are credited as co-composers of the long title-piece, a 25-minute epic based on a blues progression with a suspended interlude which serves to introduce each of the soloists in turn; they then preach on a 'text' suggested by the change in metre. It's a fascinating exercise, though not perhaps the band to have tried it out with. Waldron sounds diffident and uncomfortable, and Khan has little of substance to offer. 'A Variation' is more conventionally driven by a harmonic idea, and both the pianist and Jordan immediately seem easier with it. It must have been fascinating to have been at the Jazz Workshop in San Francisco when this was being recorded. How much more material was taped that day? Will we ever be able to hear it?

*** The Max Roach Trio Featuring The Legendary Hasaan

Atlantic 82273 *Roach; Hasaan (p); Art Davis (b).* 12/64.

The legend of Hasaan – who was also known as Ibn Ali, and who comes out as a strange hybrid of Abdullah Ibrahim and Ahmad Jamal – hasn't really stretched much beyond this record. This was a time when Atlantic were anxious to graft any amount of marketable exotica on to jazz performances and, while the familiar 3/4 and 6/8 variations are intriguingly varied with unfamiliar intervals and metres, the result is never much more than interesting, and only mildly so.

***(*) Drums Unlimited

Atlantic 7567 81361 *Roach (d solo) and with Freddie Hubbard (t); Roland Alexander (ss); James Spaulding (as); Ronnie Mathews (p); Jymie Merritt (b).* 10/65, 4/66.

The group tracks are little more than a change of pace around Roach's three solo features. The title-track is a meticulously structured and executed essay in rhythmic polyvalence that puts Sunny Murray's and Andrew Cyrille's more ambitious works in context; the second is a further exploration of the inner algebra of 3/4, adding nothing much more than further curlicues; while the last of the pieces is a heart-felt tribute to one of the swing-era drummers who has exerted a strong pull on Roach, Big Sid Catlett. Some of that era also creeps into the writing on 'In The Red', a fascinating idea performed by the group in a rather lack-lustre way. Of the additional players, only Hubbard seems sufficiently relaxed, with an autonomous and often implicit pulse. Spaulding and Alexander are inclined to fall into rather mechanical cadences, almost as if afraid of losing a count that is already so capacious and undogmatic that one could claim any amount of freedom in it.

*** Lift Every Voice And Sing

Koch Jazz 8516 *Roach; Cecil Bridgewater (t); Billy Harper (ts); George Cables (p); Ruby McClure (b, v); Eddie Mathias (b); Ralph McDonald (perc); J.C. White Singers (v).* 71.

This lost Atlantic classic might well have come from the legendary Stax label with the Staples Singers. Roach and former wife Abbey Lincoln have always been interested in the power of gospel and spirituals, and these arrangements of traditional material, some of them by William Bell, some by Lincoln, some by Roach, come at the end of a period in which the music business was rediscovering some of the lost dimensions of Black American music. Billy Harper is or should have been a storefront preacher, and Bridgewater, a longtime Roach collaborator, could dep for the Archangel Gabriel. 'Motherless Child', 'Troubled Waters' and 'Joshua' are the strongest and most developed tracks, with the voices beautifully arranged and recorded. Koch have done sterling service of late, bringing sets like this back from oblivion.

**** Birth And Rebirth

Black Saint 120024 *Roach; Anthony Braxton (as, ss, sno, f, cl, cbcl).* 9/78.

**** Historic Concerts

Soul Note 121100 2CD *Roach; Cecil Taylor (p).* 12/79.

In 1972 Roach wrote an article in the journal, *Black Scholar*, called 'What Jazz Means To Me'. It's a curious piece in retrospect, half confident and assertive, half elegiac. Users of this book will be well used to finding hiatuses in the careers even of major figures and will be aware that gaps in the discography usually have more to do with industry values or vicissitudes in the reissue programme than with prison sentences, decades spent in the shadow of junk or (though it happens) spells away from the music. Roach founded his percussion ensemble, M'Boom, in 1970 and it occupied much of his time in the coming years. However, the 12-year gap in the discographical record at this point does seem excessive for a musician of his stature.

The duets with Braxton are a key point. In their anxiety to sort-code music, critics couldn't decide who was climbing into whose pigeonhole, whether *Birth And Rebirth* was a better example of the reedman's accommodation to the mainstream, or of Roach's avant-garde credentials. In the event, of course, they met exactly head-to-head. Braxton, even of this vintage, is still making respectful gestures towards bop, and Roach is constantly looking for points beyond orthodox time-signatures. The sound is mainly very good, not as sharp and present as the hat ART set (deleted), but musically far superior. The reunion has a more contrived, less spontaneous quality. A suite of four notionally connected arguments, used as the basis for extended improvisation, it calls on a wider range of sounds, not least from Braxton's flute and contrabass clarinet. The prevailing mood is combative rather than genuinely dialectical, abrasive rather than organic and coherent.

By contrast, the summit with Taylor, recorded at the McMillin Theatre at Columbia University, is still exhilarating. Both men warm up in their respective corners, before launching into a huge, 40-minute fantasy that sees neither surrendering a whit of individuality. As was noted at the time, it was the perfect occasion to test the cliché about Roach the melodic percussionist and Taylor the percussive pianist and, like all successful sound-bites, it proves to be both helpful and misleading. For much of the opening duet, Roach fulfils a conventional drummer's role, sustaining a time-feel, accelerating and arresting the pace of development, filling and embellishing; it is Taylor who creates the grandly insane melodies that spring away for whole minutes at a time. The second segment unravels more than a little, and there are symptoms of weariness in Roach's soloing. A recorded interview with the participants makes this a valuable historical document.

***(*) M'Boom

Sony 57886 *Roach; Kenyatte Abdur-Rayhman, Roy Brooks, Joe Chambers, Omar Clay, Fred King, Warren Smith, Freddie Waits (perc).* 7/79.

The prospect of eight percussionists banging away in consort either appeals instantly or inspires dread. The reality is far more intriguing and approachable than the more pessimistic might expect and, if there are doubters out there, a couple of moments with the group's gorgeous multi-instrumental version of Monk's 'Epistrophy' should be enough to win them over. We tend not to dwell on the technical aspects of jazz recording, but miking and balancing a consort of this kind is no simple exercise, and so hats off to all those involved in the original session and in an immaculate remastering for CD. We have not listed the instruments separately, but suffice it to say that 'percussion' covers everything from powered vibraphone and orchestral bells down to musical saws, claves and whistles (which aren't strictly percussive or concussive, but never mind). The compositions are evenly spread across the personnel, but we especially like Max's 'Glorious Monster' and Omar Clay's 'Rumble In The Jungle', which constitute the central pillar of the album. It's fair to say that this isn't the kind of music you put on and then forget. Roach is always involving and highly dramatic, and that is multiplied several times over in this context. It would have been good to hear, as was possible in concert performance, more subdivisions of the group. For the purposes of an album, group performance was more in order. We've been listening to this off and on for twenty years; it still stands up today.

*** Pictures In A Frame

Soul Note 121003 *Roach; Cecil Bridgewater (t, flhn); Odean Pope (ts, f, ob); Calvin Hill (b).* 1 & 9/79.

*** In The Light

Soul Note 121053 *As above.* 7/82.

This was to be the basis of Roach's working band in the 1980s, a period during which he turned back once again to standards. At this stage, though, the writing is still strong and rather sombre, accurately pitched – or they were well recruited – to meet the players' sensibilities. The arrangements almost sound as if they were intended for a much larger group with a wider array of timbres at its disposal. Some of the pieces have an almost vestigial quality, as if there are horn lines still be overlaid, and a good many are for subdivisions of the group, as if Roach is still experimenting with the constituents of the jazz ensemble. Through it all pulses a strength and determination one immediately recognizes as Roach's artistic signature.

The later of this pair already sounds less tentative and a good deal more straightforwardly linear. Pope concentrates on tenor, less on the oboe and flute doubles which give the earlier disc much of its tone-colour. Bridgewater favours a more open sound than before or since. The key tracks are two Monk covers – 'Ruby, My Dear' and 'Straight, No Chaser' – with Roach repositioning the rhythmic commas like the master he is.

***** Swish**

New Artists NA 1001 *Roach; Connie Crothers (p).* 2/82.

We can't offer any information as to how this outwardly unlikely combination came about but can only speculate that Crothers wanted a star name to help launch the New Artists imprint. Both are listed as producers, which makes one wonder why Roach was content to hear himself represented so inadequately on record. The microphones are poorly positioned and may not have been up to the task of recording a drummer. Fortunately the playing is generally very good; none of the high dramas of the *Historic Concerts* with Taylor, of course, but plenty to listen to, even if some of it veers towards the inconsequential. 'Let 'Em Roll' has a much-needed touch of drama and tension; far and away the best thing on the set.

****(*) Collage**

Soul Note 121059 *Roach; Kenyatte Abdur-Rahman (xyl, cabassa, perc); Eddie Allen (woodblocks, perc, cym); Roy Brooks (steel d, slapstick, musical saw, perc); Joe Chambers (xyl, mar, vib, b mar); Eli Fountain (cowbell, xyl, crotales, orchestral bells); Fred King (tym, concert bells, vib); Ray Mantilla (bells, chimes, perc); Warren Smith (b, mar, perc); Freddie Waits (concert tom-toms, gongs, bass d, shaker).* 10/84.

We can vouch for the sheer vitality and exuberance, and for the sheer thoughtfulness of M'Boom's live output. Unfortunately, though perhaps not surprisingly, it does not transfer easily to record. Roach is not very prominent, restricting himself to snare, bass and marimba for much of the time and leaving it to the ever-inventive Chambers, Waits and Mantilla (each of whom can confidently be picked out of the mix on occasion) to add the substance and flesh to what is otherwise a rather sparse document.

***** Live At Vielharmonie**

Soul Note 121073 *Roach; Cecil Bridgewater (t, flhn); Dwayne Armstrong (ts); Phil Bower (b); string quartet.* 11/83.

*****(*) Easy Winners**

Soul Note 121109 *Roach; Cecil Bridgewater (t, flhn); Odean Pope (ts); Tyrone Brown (b); Ray Mantilla (perc); string quartet.* 1/85.

Roach was much interested at this point in doubling a basic horn-and-rhythm jazz group with the acme of classical ensembles, the string quartet. At the same time, he seemed particularly concerned with exploring aspects of his own personal history, and the 1983 German concert celebrates two of his most important collaborators, Booker Little and, on 'Bird Says', Charlie Parker. The sound isn't absolutely *comme il faut* and there are problems in the balance of the strings, something that was later taken care of in studio settings. Armstrong has a rather blunt and wearying tone when compared to the assertive Pope, and Bower's electric bass was an unhappy compromise, especially when placed in front of acoustic strings.

Roach's daughter Maxine plays viola with the Uptown String Quartet on *Easy Winners*. The album contains a further memorial to Little and a later, much tougher and more coherent version of 'Bird Says'. The reappearance of Mantilla, who'd performed on *We Insist!* and with M'Boom seems a little surprising, but our initial prejudice has been overcome: he does add an extra dimension. The balance between the two quartets is very much better this time, with lots of space round the strings, who lift their game and establish a real presence.

***** Scott Free**

Soul Note 121103 *Roach; Cecil Bridgewater (t, flhn); Odean Pope (ts); Tyrone Brown (b).* 5/84.

***** It's Christmas Again**

Soul Note 121153 *As above, except add Lee Konitz (as), Tony Scott (cl), Tommaso Lana (g).* 6/84.

Scott LaFaro also died in a motor accident in 1961, within four months of Booker Little, and doubtless reviving memories of the wasted promise of Clifford Brown, whose departure left an unfillable gap in Roach's life. *Scott Free* is a hefty two-part suite which sustains interest, not just for Roach's astonishing ability to give even minute changes in the metre all the drama of major instrumental statements, but because his partners are by now so well attuned to what he is doing. Bridgewater and Pope play with considerable dash and eloquence, weaving strong contrapuntal lines and trading ideas at a high rate of resolution.

It's Christmas Again stands up very well. The guest performers appear only on a single track and, even if it weren't included, this would be a successful record. The only reason we can't rate them any higher is that both discs have a curiously unmemorable quality. So absorbed and inward is the playing that it doesn't always communicate very openly, and many listeners will struggle to remember the music, even if they remember having been impressed by it. A measure perhaps of the extent to which Roach was re-examining his procedures during this fertile and prolific period.

*****(*) Survivors**

Soul Note 121093 *Roach; Donald Bauch, Guillermo Figueroa (vn); Louise Schulman (vla); Christopher Finckel (clo).* 10/84.

*****(*) Bright Moments**

Soul Note 121159 *Roach; Odean Pope (ts); Tyrone Brown (b); Uptown String Quartet.* 10/86.

Survivors continues the strings experiment and takes it a step further by dispensing with a jazz group altogether. This is territory the Kronos Quartet were exploring around the same time, and they must have kicked themselves that they didn't follow up a collaboration with Ron Carter by setting up an encounter with a drummer who sounds more and more as if he is moving away from jazz strictly conceived and out into new territory. 'The Drum Also Waltzes' is an old idea given fresh impetus and a very unexpected sound, but the best of the material is in the vibrant

'Billy The Kid' and the African-influenced 'Smoke That Thunders'. Roach experiments with dotted rhythms and stretched-out passages of suspended harmony in which he is the only active presence. This was to become a regular feature of his work in the '90s.

Bright Moments is necessarily something of a compromise, a step back towards a more conventional jazz idiom and line-up, but by this stage Roach has worked out exactly how and where the two instrumentations clash and merge, and he has devised a language conducive to maximizing their respective strengths. A fine record.

****** To The Max!**

Enja ENJ 7021/22 2CD *Roach; Cecil Bridgewater (t); Odean Pope (ts); George Cables (p); Tyrone Brown (b); Uptown String Quartet; M'Boom (perc); The John Motley Singers (v).* 11/90–6/91.

A complete newcomer to Roach's music might do very well to start with this generous tribute record which finds him working in a number of current contexts. The first disc is dominated by 'Ghost Dance', a three-part composition for orchestra and chorus, with a remarkable central section from M'Boom. The piece has a formal elegance, and a shift of pace that we have been suspected in the past of comparing to Philip Glass's Hopi-influenced *Koyaanisqatsi*. Comparing: yes, and favourably. Likening: no. The root material is still the blues, but Roach has come a long way with that language since the 1950s. The closing section, marked by a loudspeaker-threatening recording of an atomic blast, balances choral precision with some fiercely beautiful passages from Pope and Cables.

M'Boom are up again for 'A Quiet Place', one of the strongest performances they have ever recorded. There are touches here of 'La Cathédrale Engloutie', though whether Roach intends a reference to Debussy – or, indeed, to Leonard Bernstein, who wrote an opera of the same name – isn't at all clear. Certainly there is a lulled, underwater quality to the writing which suggests both: soft chimes and a swaying marimba pulse. 'The Profit' is the first of four quartet tracks which underline the point that Roach's jazz drumming is as urgent as ever, pushing along Bridgewater's Clifford Brown-influenced solo. 'Tricotism' is an Oscar Pettiford tune – perhaps *the* Pettiford tune – and stands appropriately enough as a feature for Tyrone Brown, who has become Roach's Chambers and Garrison in recent years. 'Tears' is an instrumental version of an Abbey Lincoln performance from *We Insist!* – and how wonderful it would have been if Abbey could have come on at this point to do the whole thing again. 'A Little Booker' reworks another tribute piece and involves the Uptown String Quartet.

Roach takes two solo slots. 'Drums Unlimited' was first recorded back in the 1960s. It's audibly an older man who's playing now, but also a wiser player, finding angles and routes through the music that simply wouldn't have occurred to someone still programmed by bebop. 'Self Portrait' is more of a showpiece, and less engaging for that reason. But the recording is of excellent quality and one can spend a very great deal of time – practising drummer or not – working out the crissing-crossing energies of the work.

****** With The New Orchestra Of Boston And The So What Brass Quintet**

Blue Note 34813 *Roach; Cecil Bridgewater, Frank Gordon (t); Marshall Sealy (frhn); Steve Turre (tb); Bob Stewart (tba); Fred C Tillis (cond).* 12/93–10/95.

The long 'Festival Journey' casts Roach as an orchestral soloist, a sweeping 50-minute work composed by Galveston-born Fred Tillis. It isn't the first piece they have worked on together; Roach was also the soloist on *Ring Shout Concerto* some time before. The new work has no obvious programme, though the dynamic seems to be a reassertion of jazz's centrality in American culture. That seems to be the upshot of the closing movement, 'Strutting', though it's harder to work out the exact direction of its two predecessors, 'Bells, Drones And Spiritual Fantasy' and the opening 'Outbursts, Thunder, Clouds And Mists'. One stops worrying too much about meanings as the music becomes steadily more absorbing. Roach plays with utter authority and control, and is recorded with precision.

The second and much shorter piece is a reworking of 'Ghost Dance' – see *To The Max!* – with a top-drawer brass quintet and a much better sound. It's full of vivid atmospheres, lights and shades and, unlike the other work on the disc, does seem to have a logical dramatic destination.

*****(*) Beijing Trio**

Asian Improv 0044 *Roach; Jon Jang (p); Jiebing Chen (erhu).* 98.

There have been previous attempts to synthesize jazz with Asian musics, but this brilliant trio scores highly in exploring common ground rather than exotic differences. Jang is a superb player, deeply grounded in the music of both traditions, and Roach is as responsive to new rhythms as ever. The *erhu* – a kind of two-stringed fiddle – has to stand in for a double bass, which it does with surprising fidelity, and Jiebing Chen deliberately lowers the register of the instrument in places to yield a sound that is surprisingly close (a chance resemblance that rehearings have only confirmed) to *Money Jungle*, a trio with Duke Ellngton and Charles Mingus, on which Roach also played. This is a very challenging and unexpected record, more than just a blandly diplomatic meeting of cultures, a piece of genuine improvisation and experiment. Mostly highly recommended.

Gino Robair

DRUMS, PERCUSSION, THEREMIN

Drummer and percussionist basing himself in spontaneous improvisation, working mostly in and around California.

***** Singular Pleasures**

Rastascan 23 *Robair (d, perc solo).* 2/95.

*****(*) Buddy Systems**

Meniscus MNSCS 003 *Robair; Dan Plonsey (cl); Dave Barrett (saxes, saxello); Oluyemi Thomas (ss, acl, perc); John Butcher (ts); Tim Perkis (syn, computer); LaDonna Smith (vla, vn, v); Carla Kihlstedt (vn); Myles Boisen (g, b, CD player); Matthew Sperry (b); Otomo Yoshihide (turntables, CD players).* 3/96–1/98.

Robair's solo album has all the usual reservations about such things – is a record of solo drumming, no matter how varied and ingenious texturally and sonically, the sort of thing that one wants to return to? – but he makes the most of his situation and, by carving the disc into 14 episodes, there's little opportunity for any one procedure to outstay its welcome. He thinks orchestrally for much of the time, so the canvas is suitably grand, but some of his concentrated displays of technique – on bowed cymbals, say – will be of as much appeal, though non-specialist tastes may cavil.

Little to dismay on the Meniscus disc, though. One or two of these improvisations, with various pals in differing combinations, are on the dour side, but there are far more bullseye hits than targets missed. The skirmishes with Otomo Yoshihide in particular are deliciously nutty, and the burblings of Tim Perkis's computer seem to spur Robair into hyperactive creativity. At the other extreme is the acute and almost stately 'Tonal Vibrations' with Oluyemi Thomas. Should repay close study.

George Robert

ALTO AND SOPRANO SAXOPHONES, CLARINET

Swiss saxophonist devoted to bebop styles.

***** Featuring Mr Clark Terry**

TCB 90802 *Robert; Clark Terry (flhn, v); Dado Moroni (p); Isla Eckinger (b); Peter Schmidlin (d).* 12/90.

****(*) Youngbloods**

Mons CD 1987 *Robert; Dado Moroni (p).* 10/92.

***** Tribute**

Jazz Focus JFCD004 *Robert; Dado Moroni (p); Oliver Gannon (g); Reggie Johnson (b); George Ursan (d).* 7/94.

****(*) Voyage**

TCB 95102 *Robert; Dado Moroni (p); Isla Eckinger (b); Peter Schmidlin (d).* 12/94.

Robert plays bebop alto, pure and straightahead. His solos are collections of licks which he can reel off at impressive speed, and as an executant he's completely at ease with whatever tune is on the book. He likes the classic repertoire, and though he doesn't write that much he sometimes comes up with a pleasing line: 'Remembering Henri', a requiem for his brother, turns up in two strong versions on *Tribute* and *Voyage*. Moroni is clearly a favourite partner, and the groups on these various records seem to enjoy having him in the front line. Yet none of the discs really cuts a very deep impression. Clark Terry has plenty of fun on his guest appearance, which includes one of the most surreal versions of 'Mumbles' yet put on record, and the enthusiasm is infectious. *Youngbloods* is all right, but Moroni's heavyweight manner seems to crowd Robert for a lot of the time, and the very upfront piano sound doesn't assist.

Tribute was recorded straight after a brief tour, and the band are well on their toes: 'The Village' has some genuinely impassioned alto, and Gannon's tart playing is a nice contrast. This is probably Robert's best record. *Voyage* re-runs some of this material with a different band at a club set in Lausanne: accomplished as usual, but there are predictable longueurs and *Tribute* is a better bet.

David Thomas Roberts

PIANO

A ragtime scholar and practitioner at work in California.

*****(*) Folk Ragtime: 1899–1914**

Stomp Off 1317 *Roberts (p solo).* 94–96.

The title sounds like a college thesis, but the contents are thoroughly delightful. These are ragtime strains from areas long since left to archivists, and Roberts (and Trebor Tichenor, whose superb notes help to bring the history of the music to life) does us a service by performing them with such elegance and particularity. The composers represented include Charles H. Hunter, Thomas E. Broady, Calvin Lee Woolsey and John William 'Blind' Boone, and the tunes have titles like 'A Bran Dance Shuffle', 'Felix Rag (A Phenomenal Double Ragtime Two Step)' and 'A Tennessee Tantalizer'. For those who know only the likes of Joplin, these embroidered trifles from a neglected treasure-chest of American music will be almost shocking. Roberts honours their composers by playing them with a seemingly flawless touch. Nothing is too fast or heavy, tempos are judged to the finest degree and the recording is excellent. Our only hesitation is that 72 minutes of this kind of music is a lot at a single sitting: you may prefer to sample these a few rags at a time.

Hank Roberts

CELLO, FIDDLE, 12-STRING GUITAR, VOICE

Though somewhat removed from the scratch-and-scrabble of more avant improvising cellists, Roberts has a style that identifiably owes something to post-Hendrix guitarists like Bill Frisell. He is a member of the string group, Arcado, but has also recorded quite extensively as leader.

***** I'll Always Remember**

Level Green 22002 *Roberts; Peter Chwazik (b, elec); Bill King (d).* 5/97.

All of Roberts's recordings for JMT having been deleted, there are thin pickings at present. This trio album sounds as if much of the material was spontaneously composed in rehearsal or in the studio – which is not to denigrate it, but to suggest that this feels more of a blowing band than previous units. Certainly the middle tracks, leading up to the wonderfully titled 'Our Meeting With Other Worldly Spirit Creatures At The Campfire' must have been worked on collectively. Longer items, 'Living Bicycles/Jersey Devil' and 'Trees', are more formally structured, but without losing the fresh and responsive cast of the short tracks. The sound isn't top notch, with some distortion on Hank's cello here and there, but it captures the group as it is, and as it does.

Luckey Roberts (1887–1968)

PIANO

Started as a child performer in vaudeville, then played piano in Baltimore bars and began writing ragtime-to-jazz pieces which were popular in New York, where he set the pace for Harlem pianists from around 1912. Led his own band and wrote prolifically, with many show scores being produced. Figured in the revival of the '40s but never recorded much, and eventually ran his own bar in the city.

*****(*) The Circle Recordings**
Solo Art SACD-10 *Roberts (p solo).* 5/46.

***** Luckey & The Lion – Harlem Piano**
Good Time Jazz GTJCD-10035 *Roberts; Willie 'The Lion' Smith (p).* 58.

Charles Luckeyeth Roberts was a giant of Harlem stride piano, and he was also one of its least-documented performers, at least so far as records are concerned. One of the titles on the Circle session, 'Shy And Sly', was cut for Columbia as far back as 1916 but was never issued; aside from a few cameo appearances, it wasn't until the 1940s that he got himself properly on record. The six tracks on the Solo Art CD sound like a man making up for lost time: they explode with sheer bravado, rhythms taken at a helter-skelter pace, trills and runs and horn-like outbursts folded into each of the pieces. 'Pork And Beans', which Willie The Lion Smith also liked to play, is the one to try first. But this is all there is of Roberts on this CD: the rest is devoted to early tracks by Ralph Sutton.

Luckey joined forces with The Lion for the 1958 album: they share the date rather than playing together. It's a piquant contrast. Roberts was already an old man, but much of his particular flair is intact on the splendid locomotive piece, 'Railroad Blues', and 'Complainin'' is a chuckle. Not much evidence, in sum, for a piano legend but, given the extravagances of Luckey's style, maybe that's all for the best.

Marcus Roberts (born 1963)

PIANO

Learned piano from the age of eight, studied in his native Florida, then joined the Wynton Marsalis group in 1985 and stayed until '91, although he continues to be closely identified with the Marsalis 'clan'. Recorded extensively by BMG, then by Columbia.

****(*) Gershwin For Lovers**
Columbia 477752-2 *Roberts; Reginald Veal (b); Herlin Riley (d).* 93.

Roberts was first acknowledged as the gifted pianist in the Wynton Marsalis group, but he has long since gone on to making his own way as a thoughtful and accomplished pianist-composer – even if the association with Marsalis still sticks to him like a limpet. Perhaps he exacerbates the situation by using musicians closely associated with the Marsalis axis, and by following tenets that the trumpeter has particularly espoused. Either way, Roberts has been in thrall to a specific notion about the jazz tradition all through an interesting if rather studied career on record. His several albums for Novus have been supplanted by a more recent association with Columbia. His first for the label is 'intended to be part of a romantic evening', says the artist, but there's an awful lot of foreplay here. While there may be some of the pianist's best work – in a fine solo on 'They Can't Take That Away From Me' and a closing trot through 'But Not For Me', where the tempo finally picks up – there's some terribly serious music to get through as well. The intractably slow delivery of the earlier tunes on the record isn't just a matter of ballad tempos. It's a conceptual trudge, too. For all the interesting touches here and there, the bald reality is that Roberts and company don't even swing for much of the time.

***** Time And Circumstance**
Columbia 484451-2 *Roberts; David Grossman (b); Jason Marsalis (d).* 3/96.

***** Blues For The New Millenium**
Columbia CK 68637 *Roberts; Marcus Printup, Randall Haywood (t); Ronald Westray, Vincent Gardner (tb); Richard Brown (ts, ss); Stephen Riley (ts); Ted Nash (cl, f, bs); Sherman Irby (as); Roland Guerin, Thaddeus Expose (b); Ali Jackson, Jason Marsalis (d).* 10/96–5/97.

Time And Circumstance is a suite of 14 pieces concerning a personal relationship, and with its various imbalances – some of the extracts are suffocatingly long, others perplexingly brief, and there is a great deal of space allotted to bass and drums – Roberts can scarcely be accused of avoiding a personal touch. Yet he seems too generous in handing out space to musicians who are less interesting than he is, and Grossman in particular gets more than his share. Thelonious Monk haunts Roberts's composing, but that's an awkward shade to assimilate without seeming like a copyist, and Marcus doesn't quite avoid the difficulty. As always, it seems, the disc is simply too long, and could have usefully lost 20 minutes; but there remains a lot of interesting playing.

Blues For The New Millenium is Roberts's most specific homage to old times, with covers of Jelly Roll Morton and Robert Johnson along with his own musings on past and present jazz. The musicianship is impeccable and the delivery impressive, but Roberts's most familiar problem surfaces again: he's studied this stuff so hard that there's no sense of spontaneity left in it, and there are numerous bands on labels like Stomp Off that have all the freshness and unforced energy which the pianist can't quite extract from his forces. Recorded and mixed with fine clarity and zing, the music has a polish that evades many a smaller-budget project, but it's hardly any more convincing.

*****(*) In Honor Of Duke**
Columbia CK 63630 *Roberts; Roland Guerin (b); Jason Marsalis (d); Antonio Sanchez (perc).* 4/99.

Since he is in many respects a conservative, Roberts's penchant for organizing his records in difficult, almost abstruse ways is surprising. This sequence of originals, gathered together as an Ellington homage, resists expectation most of the way through. Bass and drum parts are granted an almost cussed independence. Swinging passages suddenly fall away into near-silence. Rather than programming it in a fast-mid-slow-mid-fast style, it feels like a single, varied pulse, and Roberts musters an appealing lightness much of the way. His records have rarely been fun and they have often sunk under the weight of their pretensions, but that never happens here. His bag of Ellington quotations is effectively rustled and will tempt knowledgeable listeners into a spot-the-lick parlour game, but he doesn't forget about Monk and Coltrane either. Earnest support from Guerin and Marsalis on what sounds like Roberts's best record.

Herb Robertson (born 1951)

TRUMPET, FLUGELHORN, POSTHORN, OTHER INSTRUMENTS

A familiar figure on New York's so-called downtown scene in the 1980s and '90s, Robertson is on many of the key records from that movement and has a few of his own too.

***** Falling In Flat Space**
Cadence CJR 1065 *Robertson; Dominic Duval (b); Jay Rosen (perc, v, etc.).* 2/96.

*****(*) Sound Implosion**
CIMP110 *As above.* 3/96.

A maverick presence on a whole range of downtown projects, Robertson often gives the impression that he took up the trumpet only that afternoon, discovered an aptitude for it and has been having fun playing ever since. His tone is raw, breathy and of a sort to make orthodox brass teachers throw themselves out of upper-storey windows. However, he's never less than wholly musical, and his tight, almost pinched sound, which often sounds as if coming from a pocket or piccolo trumpet, is instantly attractive.

The story of these two discs is that *Falling In Flat Space* was sent in to Cadence on spec. Producer Bob Rusch offered the trio a recording and subsequently decided to release the first session as well. It has to be said that, given CIMP's *audio vérité* approach, there isn't much to choose between actual session and presumed demo. Like all the label's output, the sound is raw and very immediate. Strictly, this is a collaborative trio. *Sound Implosion* begins with a long solo statement from Duval, an expert craftsman who seems unfettered by the example of any previous bass player and who sounds much more European (Peter Kowald and Paul Rogers spring to mind) than any North American. Rosen and Robertson both call on a huge range of ancillary sounds – whistles, posthorns, voice, toys, and so on – to vary the weave.

On *Falling In Flat Space* the main interest lies in three long improvisations in the middle of the set. Almost everything else is preparatory or somehow unachieved. Of the three, 'The Double Stop' is most impressive, but there is also 'We Can't Get Started', an uncredited standard which nods to Mingus here and there. *Sound Implosion* follows the same course: long and short pieces (the latter more successful here) and a wholly unexpected re-creation of Jimmy Van Heusen's 'Deep Purple'. Two excellent free-jazz records which trumpet enthusiasts will want to compare with recent projects by Dave Douglas and Paul Smoker.

Jim Robinson (1892–1976)

TROMBONE

Robinson took up the trombone while serving with the US army in France. He played in and around New Orleans for most of his long life, and was a favourite with most of the bandleaders for his old-fashioned style, rarely playing anything that sounded like a solo, and hitting his notes hard. Much of his best work is with George Lewis or Bunk Johnson, but he led some sessions at least nominally.

***** Jim Robinson's New Orleans Band**
Original Jazz Classics OJC 1844 *Robinson; Ernest Cagnolotti (t); Louis Cottrell (cl); George Guesnon (g); Alcide 'Slow Drag' Pavageau (b); Alfred Williams (d).* 1/61.

***** Plays Spirituals And Blues**
Original Jazz Classics OJC 1846 *As above, except add Annie Pavageau (v).* 1/61.

***** Classic New Orleans Jazz Vol. 2**
Biograph BCD 128 *Robinson; Kid Thomas Valentine, Ernest Cagnolotti, Tony Fougerat (t); John Handy (as); Sammy Rimington, Albert Burbank, Orange Kellin (cl); Dick Griffith, George Guesnon, Al Lewis (bj); Dick McCarthy, Alcide 'Slow Drag' Pavageau, James Prevost (b); Sammy Penn, Cie Frazier, Louis Barbarin (d).* 8/64–12/74.

***** Birthday Memorial Session**
GHB BCD-276 *Robinson; Yoshio Toyama (t); Paul 'Polo' Barnes (cl); James Miller (p, v); Keiko Toyama (bj); Chester Zardis (b); Cie Frazier (d).* 73.

The doyen of New Orleans trombonists – along with Louis Nelson – Robinson had turned eighty by the time the last of these records was made, but his simple, perfectly appropriate playing wasn't too bothered by the passing of time, and he performs much as he did on all the sessions he appeared on over a space of some 35 years. The two OJCs were originally a part of Riverside's New Orleans Living Legends series and were among the first occasions when Robinson had been asked to perform as a leader. Cagnolotti and Cottrell weren't much more interested than Jim in taking a lead, and as a result the front line sounds reserved here and there; but the two discs – neatly split between NO standards on the first and gospel and blues tunes on the second – are as tough and genuine as most such sessions from this period. The Biograph disc puts together three sessions stretching across ten years. The first is a noisy and quite exciting gathering of generations – Valentine and Robinson on one side, Rimington and Handy on another – with boisterous music resulting, and the four tracks from the following year are in the same mould; but it's on the closing 'Gasket Street Blues', which features one of Robinson's rare, unaffected solos, that the man himself stands out most clearly.

On *Birthday Memorial* the band play with undimmed enjoyment of the occasion. The presence of the Toyamas, the Japanese couple who lived and worked on Bourbon Street for a spell in the late 1960s, invigorates the other old-timers involved on the date, with Yoshio's admiration for Bunk Johnson letting him fit into the group without any sense of strain.

Reginald R. Robinson (born 1973)

PIANO

As a teenager in 1980s Chicago, Robinson heard some ragtime and fell under its spell. He is that rarity, a contemporary ragtime composer-performer.

***** The Strongman**

Delmark DE-662 *Robinson (p solo).* 93.

***** Sounds In Silhouette**

Delmark DE-670 *Robinson (p solo).* 94.

His name even sounds like that of a ragtime composer. Yet Robinson was born in Chicago in the early 1970s and, though he wrote 40 of the 43 compositions on these two discs, he is a self-taught prodigy who only found out about ragtime from his local library. 'Ragtime seems mysterious to me,' he says, and it's the enigmatic, allusive strain in the music that Robinson fastens on and develops. He also likes Chopin, and some of his writing suggests a dignified balance of that composer with Joplin and Charles L. Johnson. The only non-originals he plays are 'Maple Leaf Rag' and a medley of three tunes by Johnson, but these fit alongside his own vignettes without any awkwardness. Whether suggesting a waltz or a cakewalk, the rhythms of his playing seem to light on exactly the syncopation that provided the heartbeat of a typical rag: what one hears isn't quite swing, it's the jauntiness of ragtime movement. He is well recorded (though his sprightly right hand is sometimes overlit in the studio mix) and apparently without any self-consciousness about his art. Rare and fascinating music.

Scott Robinson (born 1959)

CLARINET, BASS CLARINET, SOPRANO, ALTO, C-MELODY, TENOR, BARITONE, BASS AND CONTRABASS SAXOPHONES, CONTRABASS SARRUSOPHONE, THEREMIN

An eclectic stylist, Robinson grew up in Virginia but was born to be a scholar: at twenty-two he was the youngest-ever member of the Berklee faculty. He specializes in the oddest intruments of the reed family, even more than Anthony Braxton, but his straight-ahead playing is good enough to have got him on to many mainstream sessions.

***** Thinking Big**

Arbors ARCD 19179 *Robinson; David Robinson (t, c); Dan Barrett (tb); Mark Shane (p, cel); Richard Wyands (p); Bucky Pizzarelli (g); Pat O'Leary (b); Klaus Suonsaari (d).* 12/96.

We are delighted to welcome another record featuring the contrabass sarrusophone, and Robinson tops all previous multiple-reed efforts by also having virtually every member of the sax family involved as well, including the contrabass monster. He leads a typical Arbors band through an eclectic bunch of tunes: rare Ellington, the Hot Five's 'My Heart' and some other whiskery pieces. It's all in good humour, and the bizarre croaking and thundering of the big horns is fairly extraordinary, but it tends to underline their hopelessness as jazz instruments. Braxton used the contrabass sax to some purpose; Robinson just makes it sound like the novelty instrument it is. By contrast, his bass sax features (four here) seem light and lyrical. At times he seems overawed by the situation, since he's sounded better on other people's records, though there are still some pungent slices of revivalism.

Spike Robinson (born 1930)

TENOR SAXOPHONE

An American who came to Britain on a navy posting in 1951, Robinson is a frequent visitor to the UK and has made most of the records under his own name under British auspices. He started on alto but is a cool midstreamer in the style of the Lester Young school.

*****(*) At Chesters Vol. 1**

Hep CD 2028 *Robinson; Eddie Thompson (p); Len Skeat (b); James Hall (d).* 7/84.

***** At Chesters Vol. 2**

Hep CD 2031 *As above.* 7/84.

Although he plays tenor now, Robinson was an altoman entirely under Parker's spell when he made some early tracks in London in 1951. Robinson's switch to tenor may have deprived us of a fine Bird-man, but his command of the bigger horn is scarcely less impressive on what were comeback recordings. His models now are Getz, Sims and – at the insistence of some – Brew Moore, but Robinson is deft enough to make the comparisons sound fully absorbed. These two live records, made in Southend on a 1984 British visit, are wonderfully light and swinging, as if the tenor were an alto in his hands. *Volume 1* has the edge for a couple of ethereal ballads and the swing which is piled into 'Please Don't Talk About Me When I'm Gone'. Vivid location recording.

***** In Town**

Hep CD 2035 *Robinson; Brian Lemon (p); Len Skeat (b); Allan Ganley (d); Elaine Delmar (v).* 10/86.

***** The Odd Couple**

Capri 74008 *Robinson; Rob Mullins (ky); Fred Hamilton (b); Jill Fredericsen (d).* 8/88.

***** Jusa Bit O'Blues**

Capri 74012 *Robinson; Harry 'Sweets' Edison (t); Ross Tompkins (p); Monty Budwig (b); Paul Humphrey (d).* 9/88.

***** Jusa Bit O'Blues Vol. 2**

Capri 74013 *As above.* 9/88.

The Capri records provide Robinson with some of his most encouraging settings. All three find Robinson drifting through a clutch of standards with carefree ease, and any preference among them might depend on the choice of songs on each. Edison is reliably lyrical, and both rhythm sections play their part without complaint; the only qualm might be the essential sameness which accompanies such seasoned and professional music-making. In other words, they're more satisfying than exciting. The Hep CD is much the same.

***** Three For The Road**
Hep CD 2045 *Robinson; Janusz Carmello (t); David Newton (p); Louis Stewart (g); Paul Morgan (b); Mark Taylor (d).* 7/89.

****(*) Stairway To The Stars**
Hep CD 2049 *Robinson; Brian Kellock (p); Ronnie Rae (b); John Rae (d).* 10/90.

Robinson continues on his steady way. *Three For The Road* makes for an amiable blowing match between a seasoned cast: nothing fancy, and nothing untoward. *Stairway To The Stars*, though, is a trifle dull – Robinson never plays with less than a professional commitment, but on this occasion he sounds as though he might have been a bit tired. What he may be in need of now is context and a hands-on producer: there are enough off-the-cuff live dates in his discography already.

***** A Real Corker**
Capri 74-43 *Robinson; Louis Stewart (g); Red Mitchell (b); Martin Drew (d).* 10/91.

***** Reminiscin'**
Capri 74029C *Robinson; Mundell Lowe (g); Monty Budwig (b); Jake Hanna (d).* 12/91.

Reminiscin' is ... another off-the-cuff live date. But at least it presents Spike back in his local town of Denver and playing with three knowing veterans (it was one of Monty Budwig's last dates). A bit special: 'Dream Dancing', which floats like smoke over water, and its unspoken companion-piece, 'Dancing In The Dark'.

A Real Corker is fortuitous. Robinson and Mitchell were in Cork to play the festival together and, with Stewart on hand, they did – but they also found time to do a studio date, and the results, if less than immortal, have a genial twist to them that makes the occasion worth keeping. The setlist has some sweet things in it, too: 'Under A Blanket Of Blue', 'I Don't Want To Walk Without You', 'It Seems To Me I've Heard This Song Before'.

***** Spike Robinson And George Masso Play Arlen**
Hep CD 2053 *Robinson; George Masso (tb); Ken Peplowski (cl, ts); John Pearce (p); Dave Green (b); Martin Drew (d).* 10/91.

Consistency has become Robinson's most obvious virtue: this is another dependable, likeable record, with Masso and Peplowski (who's on only two tracks) as foils. The trombonist plays quirkily enough to make one think of Bill Harris, and it's a strong counterpoint to Spike's gentlemanly playing. 'This Time The Dream's On Me' and 'My Shining Hour' work particularly well. But the snug, tasteful rhythm section keep dragging the music back into formulaic mainstream.

***** Plays Harry Warren**
Hep 2056 *Robinson; Victor Feldman, Pete Jolly (p); Ray Brown, John Leitham (b); John Guerin, Paul Kreibich (d).* 12/81–8/93.

Spike's 'modern' career comes full circle with this release, which couples a reissue of his 1981 set for Discovery with a new date made in 1993 with a different American rhythm section. There's an almost seamless transition between the two dates and the playing is as handsome as one might expect – though, without another horn out front, Robinson sometimes lets himself drift off – as charmingly as ever. At nearly 80 minutes, another overloaded CD.

***** Tenor Madness**
Essential Jazz ESJCD 600 *Robinson; Alan Barnes, John Barnes (ts, bs); Bobby Wellins (ts); John Pearce (p); Leon Clayton (b); Bobby Worth (d).* 3/97.

More amiable, harmless jazz, with Spike in allegiance with a group of British foot-soldiers. The feel here is either Four Brothers or Tenor Madness, depending on one's own sympathies, and the players have plenty of fun with it. Listeners may feel that they've had enough of this kind of indulgence at this point in jazz history, but it's a reasonable enough excuse to make another record, and Al Cohn's tunes (7 out of the 14 on show here) are always worth hearing.

Andrew Robson

ALTO SAXOPHONE

Young Australian saxophonist making his debut.

***** Scrum**
Rufus RF031 *Robson; Steve Elphick (b); Hamish Stuart (d).* 5/96.

Continuing Rufus's excellent documentation of contemporary Australian jazz, Robson's fierce trio plays a tough and tender variation on post-bop sax-and-rhythm. He's closer to the hard-bop masters than to the free school, even when the music nudges at tonality, and there's a clever interplay between the musicians on the title-track, which epitomizes the co-operative feel of the date. Robson isn't shy with his writing – there are ten originals here – but perhaps a familiar melody or two might have thrown the rest of the music into slightly sharper relief. 'Margaret Island' is an evocative and pensively lyrical farewell.

Betty Roche (born 1920)

VOCAL

Originally from Wilmington, Delaware, Roche sang in Harlem with the Savoy Sultans and Hot Lips Page and enjoyed two spells with the Duke Ellington orchestra – though she made no studio records with Duke. Her LP career was confined to three albums.

***** Singin' And Swingin'**
Original Jazz Classics OJC 1718 *Roche; Jimmy Forrest (ts); Jack McDuff (org); Bill Jennings (g); Wendell Marshall (b); Roy Haynes (d).* 1/61.

***** Lightly And Politely**
Original Jazz Classics OJC 1802-2 *Roche; Jimmy Neeley (p); Wally Richardson (g); Michael Mulia (b); Rudy Lawless (d).* 1/61.

Roche had two separate spells with Duke Ellington, in the 1940s and again in the early '50s, but she made only a handful of sides with the orchestra: her set-piece was a version of 'Take The "A" Train' which incorporated a long scat episode. Duke liked her style: 'she had a soul inflexion in a bop state of intrigue'. Her Bethlehem tracks of the 1950s have been available but are now out of print (although, with the Bethelehem catalogue currently enjoying one of its several reissue programmes, that may change soon enough). These 1961 sessions are a modest but enjoyable memento of her art. Bop appears on *Singin' And Swingin'* with 'Billie's Bounce', but her huskier ballad delivery takes some of the slush out of 'When I Fall In Love', and her Anita O'Day influence shows through in a certain wry sidelong delivery of some of the lyrics. That trait is more exposed on the cooler, slower *Lightly And Politely*. Some of the lyrics she seems to phrase in abruptly chopped sections, a little like Abbey Lincoln, and it lends a curious detachment to heartbroken stuff like 'Jim'. By the end of the record, however, one feels that she has made the songs her own in an odd sort of way.

Bob Rockwell (born 1945)

TENOR AND SOPRANO SAXOPHONES

Grew up in Minneapolis and went on to tour with many kinds of bands, including a spell in Las Vegas in the late '60s. In New York from 1978, in many sideman situations, then moved to Copenhagen in 1983, where he bases himself, playing there and in Europe.

***** After Hours**

Go Jazz 6029-2 *Rockwell; David Hazeltine, Bobby Peterson (p); Billy Peterson (b); Kenny Horst (d).* 85–87.

Caught on a couple of club dates in the mid-'80s, this is a survival brought back by Ben Sidran's Go Jazz label. 'You Stepped Out Of A Dream', which rolls and tumbles forward for nearly ten minutes, is a fine trio performance. 'Dominator' is actually rather reserved. It's an enjoyable blowing date, although the saxophonist seems at times to be behind Horst's very loud kit.

****(*) No Rush**

Steeplechase SCCD 1219 *Rockwell; Butch Lacy (p); Jesper Lundgaard (b); Jukkis Uotila (d).* 11/85–2/86.

***** On The Natch**

Steeplechase SCCD 1229 *As above.* 87.

***** The Bob Rockwell Trio**

Steeplechase SCCD 1242 *Rockwell; Rufus Reid (b); Victor Lewis (d).* 1/89.

***** Reconstruction**

Steeplechase SCCD 31270 *As above, except add Joe Locke (vib).* 3/90.

Rockwell is an assured player who can create exciting music without suggesting a singular vision. He touches on freedom and tonal exploration in the manner of Sonny Rollins – and he seldom goes further than touching – but there's no special adherence to the Rollins sound, or to any slavish worship of Coltrane, though Rockwell's facility (particularly on soprano) again recalls that towering influence. His solos are often about momentum rather than melody, and he can get knotted up in the twists and turns of a theme, but it makes it more interesting to see how he'll extricate himself. Which he usually does. *No Rush* is a composite of various sessions at the Café Montmartre, and the similarly constructed *On The Natch* goes off at the same pitch, although the later session seems slightly more energetic. Aside from a ballad on each disc, the material is all originals by Rockwell and Lacy, and they run into the familiar problem of faceless modal themes, useful enough as lift-off points but not very absorbing for a listener. At its best – on 'Nightrider' from *On The Natch* – the quartet push and challenge one another into a dense and plausible group music, but in isolation the improvising sounds a trifle introverted and uptight.

The two later records give Rockwell a better chance to shine. The trio set has some notably powerful tenor, the leader pacing himself over the long haul with fine assurance and winding up with the feeling that he has more to say yet; Reid and Lewis, two outstanding talents in themselves, add to the lustre. *Reconstruction* brings in the vibes of Joe Locke on a rarely encountered instrumentation, faintly reminiscent of the Milt Jackson–Lucky Thompson sessions of the 1950s, and while the playing here is much more studied in its intensity, all four men avoid meaningless blowing for most of the date.

*****(*) Light Blue**

Steeplechase SCCD 31326 *Rockwell; Jesper Lundgaard (b).* 1–12/92.

***** Ballads And Cocktails**

Olufsen DOCD 5156 *Rockwell; Jan Kaspersen (p).* 1/92.

Rockwell in dialogue with two Danish homeboys. With Lundgaard, he's amiable, conciliatory: without drums or keyboards the leanness of the sound suggests the interplay of two horns and, with the bassist's wide range yet traditional inflexions, there's a classic feel to the improvising. They start with a rare Parker blues, 'Bird Feathers', stroll on through a neat range of standards and jazz themes, and end on a whipcrack treatment of 'After You've Gone'. Most of the tunes are dispatched tightly enough – only 'Sweet Lorraine' ambles up to nearly eight minutes – and the saxophonist's tone warms all the melody lines a treat.

With the mercurial and slightly zany Kaspersen, the music is rather different. There are five originals by the pianist as well as new thoughts on his beloved Monk, and it is really much more his record than Rockwell's, since the saxophonist tends to comment a little distractedly on the galumphing rhythms and blocked-out chords, a Charlie Rouse to Kaspersen's eccentric chief. Engaging, nevertheless.

***** Born To Be Blue**

Steeplechase SCCD 31333 *Rockwell; Andy LaVerne (p); Jesper Lundgaard (b).* 2/93.

Another good one, though a little compromised by material and context. Rockwell has preferred to be in dialogue with pianists rather than drummers of late, and it doesn't always suit him: some of the tracks, notably Charlie Haden's 'The First Song' and 'A Nightingale Sang In Berkeley Square', lumber along a bit and could use some propulsion. But the title-piece is a thoughtful meditation, assertively done, and Monk's 'Bye-Ya' is excellent.

Claudio Roditi (born 1946)

TRUMPET, FLUGELHORN, VOCAL

Born in Rio, he studied at Berklee in 1970, then moved to New York in 1976. Worked frequently with Paquito D'Rivera, but is also heard in numerous sideman roles and big-band duties, playing a mix of Latin and unadorned hard-bop styles.

****(*) Gemini Man**

Milestone M 9158 *Roditi; Daniel Freiberg (ky); Roger Kellaway (p); Nilson Matta (b); Ignacio Berroa, Akira Tana (d); Rafael Cruz (perc).* 3/88.

***** Slow Fire**

Milestone M 9175 *Roditi; Jay Ashby (tb); Ralph Moore (ts); Danilo Perez (p); David Finck (b); Akira Tana, Ignacio Berroa (d); Rafael Cruz (perc).* 89.

Roditi's bright tone and fizzing delivery have served him well in several bands, and these dates of his own are intermittently exciting. His Brazilian roots turn up in the various samba-derived rhythmic bases which account for several of the tunes but, like so many of the current wave of Latin-American jazz musicians, he owes a great stylistic debt to Dizzy Gillespie. Neither date has perhaps quite the final ounce of weight that would make it outstanding, but the first has Kellaway's astute comping and the second adds Ashby and Moore to beef up the sound of the band, which otherwise tends to resolve itself in the percussion section.

**** Two Of Swords**

Candid CCD 79504 *Roditi; Jay Ashby (tb); Edward Simon, Danilo Perez (p); Nilsson Matta, David Finck (b); Duduka Fonseca, Akira Tana (d).* 9/90.

Not terrible, but this is just a potboiler. Roditi splits the session between a 'jazz' and a 'Brazilian' group, and both perform in much the same direction, although the Brazilian band has Ashby in the front line to add some tonal colour. Roditi's fat-toned flugelhorn gets a little more exposure than usual, but the music lacks much character. Another CD which doesn't really justify its 72-minute length.

****(*) Milestones**

Candid CCD 79515 *Roditi; Paquito D'Rivera (cl, as); Kenny Barron (p); Ray Drummond (b); Ben Riley (d).* 11/90.

An absolutely top-class band with everybody feeling fine and playing hard – yet the results are, as with the records above, vaguely disappointing. One can't fault the virtuosity of either of the horn players – D'Rivera, especially, gets off some breathtaking flights on both alto and clarinet – but the final impression is of too many notes and too much said. The jam-session material doesn't assist matters much – the ballad, 'Brussels In The Rain', is the only departure from familiarity – and with playing time at almost 70 minutes it does start to sound like too much of a good thing. The live recording is clear if a little dry.

*****(*) Free Wheelin'**

Reservoir RSRCD 136 *Roditi; Andres Boiarsky (ss, ts); Nick Brignola (ss, bs); Mark Soskin (p); Buster Williams (b); Chip White (d).* 7/94.

***** Samba – Manhattan Style**

Reservoir RSRCD 139 *Roditi; Jay Ashby (tb); Greg Abate (as); Andres Boiarsky (ss, ts); Helio Alves (p); John Lee (b); Duduka Fonseca (d).* 5/95.

Roditi doing a tribute to Lee Morgan sounds like a recipe for overcooking it. Yet *Free Wheelin'* comes close to being exactly the classic album the trumpeter must have in him. This is the best band he's had in the studio: Boiarsky is a heavyweight, and the rhythm section, especially the inimitable Williams, are right there with the horns. But it's Roditi's concentration of his own powers that impresses here. Without trading in any of his fire, he keeps all his solos tight and impeccable, which makes flare-ups like those on 'Trapped' and 'The Joker' all the more exciting. 'The Sidewinder' follows the original arrangement – in his notes Roditi confesses that he couldn't see any point in messing around with the original charts – and still sounds entirely different from Morgan's original. Nine of the ten tunes are from Morgan's own pen, but the new twist on 'A Night In Tunisia' – with trumpet overdubs and a two-soprano section – is a startling departure. Brignola guests on three and is a welcome visitor. Still slightly exhausting at 70 minutes, but a good one.

Samba – Manhattan Style is a notch lower, with a less impressive cast. The gentler aspects of Roditi's playing bring lustre to pretty melodies such as 'Fone Da Saudade', and the sweetness of samba infects the best of the music, although one feels that there's too much padding, and the studio sound does nothing for the lower frequencies.

****(*) Double Standards**

Reservoir RSR 148 *As above, except add Hendrik Meurkens (hca), Gil Goldstein (p), Marty Ashby (g), David Finck (b), Chip White (d).* 9–10/96.

***** Claudio, Rio And Friends**

Groovin' High 529858-2 *Roditi; Guillerme Dias Gomez (t, flhn); Mauro Senise (as, f); Nivaldo Ornellas (ts); Jota Moraes (ky); Guinga, Rodrigo Campello, Lula Galvao (g); Arthur Maia (b); Pascoal Meirelles (d); Leila Pinheiro (v).* 2/95.

Double Standards is a disappointment after the last couple of records. Cut as a pure blowing session in the studio, with stand-bys like 'Bye Bye Blackbird' and 'So What' in the programme, there's nothing wrong with the music but it has no pressing need to exist; only Roditi's shy vocal on 'Desafinado' breaks out of the general blandness. *Claudio, Rio And Friends* may lack the finesse of a New York situation, but it's a lot more interesting. Made on a visit home and featuring the Cama de Gato quartet, this is a genuine blend of jazz and Braziliana that finds the right sort of balance between the gentle *brio* of the local music and Roditi's stronger streak. 'Romanza' is the best of some pleasing originals, and the players perform with deferential charm behind the trumpeter.

Red Rodney (1927–94)

TRUMPET

His given name was Robert Chudnick, which wasn't quite the right handle, nor was his shock of ginger hair quite the right look, for the early days of bebop. And yet Red was one of the most responsive trumpeters Charlie Parker worked with. Unfortunately he also responded to and imitated Bird's other habits, and Rodney's career was punctuated with narcotics problems. To his credit, he put these behind him and sustained a second career right through to his death in the mid '90s.

***** First Sessions: Volume 3**
Prestige PCD 24116 *Rodney; Jimmy Ford (as); Phil Raphael (p); Phil Leshin (b); Phil Brown (d).* 9/51.

Rodney was the red-haired Jewish boy in Charlie Parker's happiest band. Though diffident about his own talents, the young Philadelphian had done his learning up on the stand, playing with the likes of Jimmy Dorsey while still a teenager. Rodney was perhaps the first white trumpeter to take up the challenge of bebop, which he played with a crackling, slightly nervy quality. It sat well with Parker, and Rodney was an integral part of Bird's quintet in 1950 and 1951, having first worked with him slightly earlier than that. Not a prolific recording artist, Rodney's career succumbed from time to time to one of the more common jeopardies of life on the road, but there is some excellent stuff on disc. The early Prestige material dates from Rodney's time in the Parker band, and it has the nervy exuberance you'd expect. Ford is a very average player, and each number seems to mark time when he solos. Rodney's best work, the 1955 *Modern Music From Chicago*, is increasingly scarce.

*****(*) Bluebird**
Camden 74321 61081-2 2CD *Rodney; Ira Sullivan (t); Bill Watrous (tb); Richie Cole, Charles McPherson (as); George Young (ts, f); David Schnitter (ts); Garry Dial, Roland Hanna, Barry Harris (p); Sam Jones, Barry Smith, Buster Williams (b); Steve Bagby, Roy Brooks, Eddie Gladen, Billy Higgins (d).* 7/73–81.

Licensed from 32 Jazz Records, this is a valuable reissue of 21 tracks culled from five albums made for Muse in the '70s. The best of these were unquestionably *Bird Lives* and *Home Free* from 1973 and 1977 respectively, and more than half of the material is taken from them. With Charles McPherson on alto, this was as close to the sound of Bird's original groups as you could to find at the time and, though Richie Cole (why won't Camden spell artists' names correctly?) was to take his place later, McPherson was a wonderfully responsive partner. Rodney also found a sympathetic spirit in trumpeter Ira Sullivan, with whom he led a two-horn front line for a while, though there is just one track from *Night & Day* here, the latest recording on the set. The slightly earlier groups with Cole are very good indeed, and their interplay on 'All The Things You Are', Cole's 'Red Rodney Rides Again' and the definitive 'Bluebird' were lapped up by bebop purists and nostalgists.

*****(*) Red Giant**
Steeplechase SCCD 31233 *Rodney; Butch Lacy (p); Hugo Rasmussen (b); Aage Tanggaard (d).* 4/88.

***** One For Bird**
Steeplechase SCCD 31238 *Rodney; Dick Oatts (as); Gary Dial (p); Jay Anderson (b); John Riley (d).* 7/88.

****(*) Red Snapper**
Steeplechase SCCD 31252 *As above.* 7/88.

Nowhere was bebop accorded higher sentimental status than in Scandinavia. House bands and rhythm sections have excellent chops (the same is true of Japanese players) but with a strongly authentic 'feel' as well. Of these 1988 sessions *Red Giant* is undoubtedly the best, with Rasmussen, Tanggaard and the rough-diamond Lacy all contributing substantially. Compare the versions of 'Greensleeves' and a curiously but effectively tempoed 'Giant Steps' with those on *Red Snapper*, which seem merely curious. The original material on *Red Snapper* is perhaps more interesting, but there's very little doubt where Rodney's heart lies. At sixty-plus, he sounded chastened but undeterred, and his playing reveals a depth of reference that was seldom there previously.

***** Then And Now**
Chesky JD 79 *Rodney; Chris Potter (as, ts); Gary Dial (p); Jay Anderson (b); Jimmy Madison (d).* 5/92.

Flugelhorn soaks all the individuality out of Rodney's playing and, were it not for an able and committed young band, this would be little more than an exercise in nostalgic re-creation. The disc also includes an interview, which will be of interest to anyone who follows the trumpeter or the original bebop movement.

Bob Rodriguez

PIANO

Contemporary pianist-composer, based in New York but also at work with the West Coast avant garde.

*****(*) Mist**
Nine Winds NWCD 0177 *Rodriguez; Ken Filiano (b); Ron Glick (d).* 94.

A rewarding and idiosyncratic addition to the piano-trio literature. Rodriguez is known for some scoring for the Creative Opportunity Orchestra led by Tina Marsh, but this CD reveals a thoughtful pianist easily bored by conventional trio methods. The four standards are all dramatically revised without destructiveness. 'Dolphin Dance' is almost unrecognizable with its harmonic structure gone and its rhythmic language dispersed: what emerges is a slow reharmonization of the theme, beautifully achieved. 'Waltz For Debby' is also done slow, and its harmonies are similarly altered. 'A Polovetzian [*sic*] Dance', which most would prefer to recognize as 'Stranger In Paradise', emerges as a fast piece of hard bop, and Legrand's 'I Will Say Goodbye' is motionlessly lyrical. The originals aren't quite so strong, and 'Constellation' rambles a bit, but Rodriguez has a lovely touch and he involves the other two as equals: hear Filiano's impeccable solo on 'Debby' or the suavely done free piece, 'Loose And Open'.

***** Reinventions**
CreOp Muse 006 *Rodriguez; Cathy Campbell (p).* 11/98.

Solo this time (Campbell appears on only two duet pieces), Rodriguez approaches these eight standards and two Chopin pieces with a specifically revisionist brief. Most of it involves altered chords, which are placed so as to make the melody quickly recognizable but its framework sometimes startlingly unfamiliar. Two or three of these are intriguing but, since he does it on every piece, the results are sometimes arch: it might have been better to play some of them, er, straight. 'I'll Take Romance', for instance, is hard to identify at all, but what's replacing the original form isn't all that interesting either. Rodriguez still has a fine touch, but a little more blood in the recital wouldn't have hurt.

Paul Rogers

BASS

British free-music bassist and improviser.

*** Heron Moon

Rare Music RM 025 *Rogers (b solo).* 10/95.

Rogers stands squarely in a formidable tradition of European bass improvisers, enormously skilful with and without the bow; and there is some fine virtuosity on show in the four-part title-piece and the five-part 'Song Time'. Judged against the colossal standards of, say, Peter Kowald's *Was Der Ist?*, though, this is not such a compelling disc. A few sections sound a little like exercises and one misses the sheer physicality of sound which Rogers brings to bear in a live performance (the studio mix, while faithful enough, seems a little genteel for such a passionate artist). But an hour of music still passes quickly, and committed listeners in this field will find his range of expression constructs an absorbing train of thought.

Shorty Rogers (1924–94)

TRUMPET, FLUGELHORN

Milton Rogers came from Massachusetts, but he is for ever seen as a kingpin figure in the West Coast jazz of the 1950s and after, scoring several of the classic big-band dates of the period and subsequently writing a lot of music for TV and Hollywood. His own playing was lithe if unremarkable, but his love for jazz was demonstrated by his final years, spent in various reunion editions of his old outfits.

**** The Big Shorty Rogers Express

RCA 218519 *Rogers; Conte Candoli, Pete Candoli, Harry 'Sweets' Edison, Maynard Ferguson, Conrad Gozzo, John Howell (t); Harry Betts, John Haliburton, Frank Rosolino (tb); Bob Enevoldsen (vtb); John Graas (frhn); George Roberts (btb); Gene Englund, Paul Sarmento (tba); Charlie Mariano (as); Art Pepper (as, ts, bs); Bill Holman, Jack Montrose (ts); Jimmy Giuffre (ts, bs, cl); Bob Cooper (ts, bs); Lou Levy, Marty Paich (p); Curtis Counce, Ralph Pena (b); Stan Levey, Shelly Manne (d).* 53–56.

Much influenced by the Davis–Mulligan–Lewis *Birth Of The Cool*, and even claiming a revisionist role in the creation of that movement, Shorty Rogers turned its basic instrumentation and lapidary arranging into a vehicle for relaxedly swinging jazz of a high order. *Express* includes all the material from the classic 1953 date, *Cool And Crazy*. The material is consistently dramatic and varied, though after a while one does begin to wonder whether Rogers's talent isn't being spread a little too thinly. The cover photograph has him sitting on the cow-catcher of a locomotive, and again there is the suspicion that sheer momentum and steam-power carry these charts forward, a long way past the more refined modulations of mood. Rogers himself was never a memorable soloist. His arrangements, though, are among the best of the time. If they lack the gelid precision that Lewis and Mulligan brought to *Birth Of The Cool*, Rogers's charts combine the same intricate texture with an altogether looser jazz feel; 'Boar-Jibu' exactly bridges the distance between Giuffre's 'Four Brothers' for Woody Herman and *Birth*. 'Sweetheart Of Sigmund Freud', 'Coop De Graas' and 'Infinity Promenade' are big-band swingers of unrivalled class and excitement. Indispensable.

***(*) Shorty Rogers And His Giants

RCA 74321 60989-2 *Rogers; Milt Bernhart (tb); John Graas (frhn); Art Pepper (as); Jimmy Giuffre (ts); Hampton Hawes (p); Joe Mondragon (b); Gene England (tba); Shelly Manne (d).* 1/53.

**** Shorty Rogers Courts The Count

RCA 74321 63818-2 *Rogers; Conrad Gozzo, Maynard Ferguson, Harry 'Sweets' Edison, Clyde Reasinger, Pete Candoli (t); Milt Bernhart, Harry Betts, Bob Enevoldsen (tb); John Graas (frhn); Herb Geller, Bud Shank (as); Bob Cooper, Jimmy Giuffre (ts, bs); Zoot Sims, Bill Holman (ts); Bob Gordon (bs); Marty Paich (p); Curtis Counce (b); Shelly Manne (d).* 2–3/54.

*** Collaboration

RCA ND 74398 *Rogers; Milt Bernhart (tb); Bud Shank (as, f); Bob Cooper (ts, ob); Jimmy Giuffre (bs); André Previn (p); Al Hendrickson (g); Joe Mondragon (b); Shelly Manne (d).* 3–6/54.

***(*) Wherever The Five Winds Blow

RCA ND 74399 *Rogers; Jimmy Giuffre (ts); Lou Levy (p); Ralph Pena (b); Larry Bunker (d).* 7/56.

***(*) Plays Richard Rogers

RCA 74321 433882 *Rogers; Conte Candoli, Pete Candoli, Harry 'Sweets' Edison, Maynard Ferguson, Al Porcino (t); Milt Bernhart, George Roberts, Bob Burgess, John Haliburton, Frank Rosolino (tb); Jimmy Giuffre (cl, bs); Herb Geller (as); Bill Holman, Jack Montrose, Bill Perkins (ts); Pepper Adams (bs); Pete Jolly (p); Sam Rica (tba); Red Mitchell (b); Stan Levey (d).* 1–4/57.

*** Portrait Of Shorty

RCA 74321 61105-2 *Rogers; Al Porcino, Conrad Gozzo, Don Fagerquist, Conte Candoli, Pete Candoli (t); Frank Rosolino, George Roberts, Harry Betts, Bob Enevoldsen (tb); Herb Geller (as); Bob Cooper (ts, bs); Richie Kamuca, Jack Montrose (ts); Pepper Adams (bs); Lou Levy (p); Monty Budwig (b); Stan Levey (d).* 7–8/57.

*** Gigi In Jazz

RCA 74321 125882 *Rogers; Bill Holman (ts); Larry Bunker (vib); Pete Jolly (p); Buddy Clark, Ralph Pena (b); Mel Lewis (d).* 1/58.

*** Chances Are, It Swings

RCA 74321 433902 *Rogers; Don Fagerquist, Pete Candoli, Conte Candoli, Ollie Mitchell, Ray Triscari, Al Porcino (t); Bob Enevoldsen (vtb); Harry Betts, Dick Nash, Kenny Shroyer (tb); Paul Horn, Bud Shank (cl, as, f); Bill Holman, Richie Kamuca (ts); Chuck Gentry (bs); Gene Estes, Red Norvo (vib); Pete Jolly (p); Howard Roberts, Barney Kessel (g); Joe Mondragon, Monty Budwig (b); Mel Lewis (d).* 12/58.

*** The Wizard Of Oz

RCA 74321 453792 *Rogers; Don Fagerquist, Al Porcino, Conte Candoli (t); Harry Betts, Kenny Shroyer, Frank Rosolino (tb);*

Bob Enevoldsen (vtb); Bud Shank (f, as); Herb Geller (as, ts); Bill Holman (ts); Jimmy Giuffre (bs, cl); Larry Bunker (vib); Pete Jolly (p); Barney Kessel (g); Joe Mondragon (b); Mel Lewis (d). 2/59.

***** The Swinging Nutcracker**

RCA 74321 421212 *Rogers; John Audino, Conte Candoli, Ray Triscari, Jimmy Zito (t); Harry Betts, Frank Rosolino, Kenny Shroyer (tb); Art Pepper (as); Jimmy Giuffre (cl); Bud Shank (as, f); Richie Kamuca, Harold Land, Bill Perkins, Bill Holman (ts); Chuck Gentry (bs); Pete Jolly, Lou Levy (p); Joe Mondragon (b); Frank Capp, Mel Lewis (d).* 5/60.

*****(*) An Invisible Orchard**

RCA 74321 49560-2 *Rogers; Ray Triscari, Ollie Mitchell, Stu Williamson, Conte Candoli, Al Porcino (t); Harry Betts, Frank Rosolino (tb); Kenny Shroyer, Marshall Cran, George Roberts (btb); Bud Shank, Paul Horn (as); Bill Perkins, Harold Land (ts); Bill Hood, Chuck Gentry (bs); Pete Jolly (p); Emil Richards (vib); Red Mitchell (b); Mel Lewis (d).* 2–4/61.

Rogers seemed to be in the studios all the time in the 1950s and early '60s and, although his Atlantic albums are currently out of circulation, several of his RCA sets have made a comeback lately via these European reissues. There is frankly little to choose between them, each built around some sort of concept, most of them obvious from the titles. The *Collaboration* was with André Previn, who is co-credited. *Wherever The Five Winds Blow* is a small-group date of sheer finesse, the quintet breezing over the material like a polished sailboat. *Chances Are, It Swings* is a mixed bag of orchestral charts, while *Gigi In Jazz* returns to the small-group format. We have so far been spared (shame!) the reappearance of *Shorty Rogers Meets Tarzan* from the same period. In a way, this music was as much cursed as illuminated by its Californian sunshine. Revisionist critics looked down their noses at it for many years, claiming all sorts of outrages: clinical, studio-bound playing, smoothness over passion, the suppression of more radical Californian jazz, etc. At this distance, the virtues of the music now seem more apparent, as they are in the New York jazz of three decades earlier. Rogers had the wit to turn many of the less promising tunes into tongue-in-cheek set-pieces that are not so far from the more irreverent repertory excursions of more recent years. Rather than creating a climate for memorable improvising, Rogers stitched the solos into a detailed fabric. Each man was usually called on for no more than a few appropriate bars, and the result was a language of excellence in miniature. In players such as Shank, Holman, the Candolis, Bernhart and Cooper, Rogers had performers who could eat up these opportunities, and it spawned a discipline which today's West Coast jazz – via the numerous 'occasional' big bands that still record for labels such as Sea Breeze – continues to work from. While the music has some period feel, its vitality survives. To complete the picture, Atlantic should look into reviving some of their excellent material of the same vintage.

Recent additions to the range have all but completed RCA's Rogers output in reissue form (we're still waiting for *Tarzan* though!). The original *Shorty Rogers And His Giants* is by a fresh-sounding nonet, and Shorty sounds like he's raring to go with his charts. *Courts The Count*, though, is better still, a great favourite of ours, and sounding better than ever in this transfer. Shorty scored nine Basie chestnuts, such as 'Taps Miller', 'Tickle Toe' and 'Jump For Me', and somehow managed to pay homage without once sounding like the Basie band itself. Check, for instance, the brooding 'Topsy', a brilliant bit of recasting. *Portrait Of Shorty* is more routine, but the playing remains full of sparkle.

An Invisible Orchard collects three sessions for an album that was never released at the time: an ambitious suite of compositions that remain in the Rogers pocket but find him clearly looking for new directions within his accustomed style. The opening 'Inner Space' is certainly one of his most challenging efforts, a maze of interwoven lines that still hold the trademark Rogers clarity and lightness. Most of the eight pieces feel like transitional music, between the sun-soaked optimism of his earlier charts and a darker – or at least more abstruse – feel. There are hints, for instance, of a John Lewis influence, most obviously in the MJQ-like opening of 'La Valse'. An intriguing departure which RCA shelved at the time of its production.

***** Yesterday Today And Forever**

Concord CCD 4223 *Rogers; Bud Shank (as, f); George Cables (p); Bob Magnusson (b); Roy McCurdy (d).* 6/83.

*****(*) America The Beautiful**

Candid CCD 79510 *Rogers; Bud Shank (as); Conte Candoli (t); Bill Perkins (bs, ts, ss); Bob Cooper (ts); Pete Jolly (p): Monty Budwig (b); Lawrence Marable (d).* 8/91.

***** Eight Brothers**

Candid CCD 79521 *Rogers; Conte Candoli (t, flhn); Bud Shank (as); Bill Perkins (ts, ss, bs); Bob Cooper (ts); Pete Jolly (p); Monty Budwig (b); Lawrence Marable (d).* 1/92.

For much of the intervening period, Rogers concentrated on film music. His 1980s comeback found him in strong voice and, alongside Bud Shank, in musically conducive company. *America The Beautiful* is certainly the pick of these three. Shank takes 'Lotus Bud' on alto saxophone rather than alto flute this time. The solo intro is huskily beautiful and is surpassed only by Bill Perkins's eerily cadenced soprano solo on another Bud's 'Un Poco Loco'. 'Here's That Old Martian Again' continues a series of similar conceits, done in reassuringly un-alien blue rather than green, but with a hint of 'Blue In Green' in the shift across the line. The Lighthouse All Stars play beyond themselves, with big credits to drummer Marable. Recommended.

The other two are rather less interesting. Rogers doesn't sound a naturally confident player alongside the other Lighthouse chapter members, and his solos on these latter-day recordings are genial but rarely memorable. Better, perhaps, to look on both as Bud Shank discs (he shares top billing) and concentrate on his terse expressions instead.

Adrian Rollini (1904–56)

BASS SAXOPHONE, GOOFUS, VIBRAPHONE, KAZOO, PIANO, DRUMS

A child prodigy on piano, Rollini took up the leviathan bass saxophone when only eighteen. He had no peers on the instrument, and was a busy sessionman in the 1920s and early '30s, before opening his own New York club. As the instrument became passé, he switched to vibes and eventually drifted into light music. At the time of his death, he was running his own hotel in Florida.

***** Bouncin' In Rhythm**

Topaz TPZ 1027 *Rollini; Wingy Manone (t, v); Manny Klein, Dave Klein, Roy Johnson, Chelsea Quealey, Freddy Jenkins (t); Bix Beiderbecke, Bobby Hackett, Red Nichols (c); Jack Teagarden, Abe Lincoln, Bill Rank, Miff Mole (tb); Benny Goodman, Paul Ricci, Pee Wee Russell, Albert Nicholas (cl); Jimmy Dorsey (cl, as, t); Joe Marsala (cl, as); Fud Livingston (cl, ts); Don Murray (cl, bs); Frankie Trumbauer (Cmel); Arthur Rollini, Sam Ruby (ts); Putney Dandridge (p, v); Howard Smith, Fulton McGrath, Jack Russin, Frank Signorelli, Joe Turner (p); Joe Venuti (vn); Eddie Lang, George Van Eps, Dick McDonough, Carmen Mastren, Bernard Addison (g); Tommy Felline (bj); Artie Bernstein, Sid Weiss, Joe Watts (b); Vic Berton, Herb Weil, Stan King, Sam Weiss, Chauncey Morehouse (d).* 10/34–1/38.

There are few instruments which can claim a single performer as their undisputed master, but it's true of the bass saxophone and Adrian Rollini. He played bass and melody lines with equal facility, could move through an ensemble with disarming ease, and never gave the impression that the instrument was anything but light and easy in his hands. Still, it remained a sound rooted in the 1920s and, with the onset of the swing era, Rollini found himself more gainfully employed on vibes and – on the last session here, with a Freddy Jenkins group – drums. With the disappearance of an Affinity CD featuring Rollini's own bands, all that remains is this hotchpotch of sessions with various masters – Beiderbecke, Trumbauer, Venuti and Lang, Mole and Jenkins – plus six from the few sessions under Rollini's leadership. It's a decent sampler of his methods, though anyone who collects jazz from the 1920s will probably have many of the tracks already. Remastering is cleanly done.

Sonny Rollins (born 1930)

TENOR AND SOPRANO SAXOPHONE

Born Theodore Walter Rollins, the New York saxophonist recorded as a teenager with Bud Powell and J.J. Johnson, later with Miles Davis and Thelonious Monk, before working in Max Roach's group for two years. Since 1957 he has been his own leader. Recording associations have been with Prestige, Blue Note, RCA, Impulse! and, since, 1972, Milestone. Two famous sabbaticals from public appearances (1959–61 and 1968–71) have been the only interruptions in a prolific and inspirational career in concert and on record. Although famously inscrutable at times, Rollins's music has been – in its virtuoso command of the horn and in the calibre of his improvising – enormously influential.

****(*) Sonny Rollins With The Modern Jazz Quartet**

Original Jazz Classics OJC 011 *Rollins; Miles Davis, Kenny Drew, John Lewis (p); Percy Heath (b); Art Blakey, Kenny Clarke, Roy Haynes (d).* 1/51–10/53.

***** Moving Out**

Original Jazz Classics OJC 058 *Rollins; Kenny Dorham (t); Thelonious Monk, Elmo Hope (p); Percy Heath, Tommy Potter (b); Art Blakey, Art Taylor (d).* 8–10/54.

Rollins's most important early session is with Miles Davis on *Bags' Groove* (OJC 245). The nine 1951 tracks on OJC 011 are cursory bop singles, and the MJQ – despite the headline billing – appear on only three tracks, in a meeting that took place a second time on an Atlantic album some years later. One track, 'I Know', has the novelty of Miles Davis on piano. *Moving Out* is more substantial, though it still stands as a stereotypical blowing date, even with a single track – 'More Than You Know' – from a session with Monk. The most interesting contributor here is probably Hope, whose off-centre lyricism still turns heads.

*****(*) Work Time**

Original Jazz Classics OJC 007 *Rollins; Ray Bryant (p); George Morrow (b); Max Roach (d).* 12/55.

*****(*) Sonny Rollins Plus 4**

Original Jazz Classics OJC 243 *Rollins; Clifford Brown (t); Richie Powell (p); George Morrow (b); Max Roach (d).* 3/56.

****** Tenor Madness**

Original Jazz Classics OJC 124 *Rollins; John Coltrane (ts); Red Garland (p); Paul Chambers (b); Philly Joe Jones (d).* 5/56.

♛ ** Saxophone Colossus**

Original Jazz Classics OJC 291 *Rollins; Tommy Flanagan (p); Doug Watkins (b); Max Roach (d).*

*****(*) Sonny Rollins Plays For Bird**

Original Jazz Classics OJC 214 *Rollins; Kenny Dorham (t); Wade Legge (p); George Morrow (b); Max Roach (d).* 10/56.

****** Tour De Force**

Original Jazz Classics OJC 095 *Rollins; Kenny Drew (p); George Morrow (b); Max Roach (d); Earl Coleman (v).* 12/56.

***** Sonny Rollins Volume 1**

Blue Note 81542 *Rollins; Donald Byrd (t); Wynton Kelly (p); Gene Ramey (b); Max Roach (d).* 12/56.

An astounding year's work on record. Rollins was still a new and relatively unheralded star when he was working through this series of sessions, and – in the aftermath of Parker's death – jazz itself had an open throne. There was a vast distance between Rollins and the tenorman who was winning most of the polls of the period, Stan Getz, but though Sonny evaded the open-faced romanticism and woozy melancholy associated with the Lester Young school, he wasn't much of a Parkerite, either. Rollins used the headlong virtuosity of bop to more detached, ironical ends. The opening track on *Work Time* is a blast through 'There's No Business Like Show Business', which prefigures many of his future choices of material. Parker would have smiled, but he'd never have played it this way. Still, Rollins's mastery of the tenor was already complete by this time, with a wide range of tones and half-tones, a confident variation of dynamics, and an ability to phrase with equal strength of line in any part of a solo. If he is often tense, as if in witness to the power of his own creative flow, then the force of the music is multiplied by this tension. The most notable thing about the records is how dependent they are on Rollins himself: Roach aside, whose magnificent drum parts offer a pre-echo of what Elvin Jones would start to develop with John Coltrane, the sidemen are often almost dispensable. It is Rollins who has to be heard.

If *Work Time* is just a little sketchy in parts, that is only in comparison with what follows. *Plus 4* is one of Rollins's happiest sessions. With both horn players in mercurial form, and Roach sensing the greatness of the band he is basically in charge of, the music unfolds at a terrific clip but has a sense of relaxation which the tenorman would seldom approach later in the decade. His own piece, 'Pent-Up House', has an improvisation which sets the stage for some of his next advances: unhurried, thoughtful, he nevertheless plays it with biting immediacy. *Tenor Madness* features Coltrane on, alas, only one track, the title-tune, and it isn't quite the grand encounter one might have wished for: but the rest of the record, with Miles Davis's rhythm section, includes surging Rollins on 'Paul's Pal' and 'The Most Beautiful Girl In The World'. The undisputed masterpiece from this period is *Saxophone Colossus* and, although Rollins plays with brilliant invention throughout these albums, he's at his most consistent on this disc. 'St Thomas', his irresistible calypso melody, appears here for the first time, and there is a ballad of unusual bleakness in 'You Don't Know What Love Is', as well as a rather sardonic walk through 'Moritat' (alias 'Mack The Knife'). But 'Blue Seven', as analysed in a contemporary piece by Gunther Schuller, became celebrated as a thematic masterpiece, where all the joints and moving parts of a spontaneous improvisation attain the pristine logic of a composition. If the actual performance is much less forbidding than this suggests, thanks in part to the simplicity of the theme, it surely justifies Schuller's acclaim. *Plays For Bird*, though it includes a medley of tunes associated with Parker, is no more Bird-like than the other records, and a reading of 'I've Grown Accustomed To Her Face' establishes Rollins's oddly reluctant penchant for a tender ballad. *Sonny Rollins* ended the year in somewhat more desultory fashion – the session seems to return to more conventional horns-and-rhythm bebop – but *Tour De Force*, recorded two weeks earlier, is almost as good as *Colossus*, with the ferocious abstractions of 'B Swift' and 'B Quick' contrasting with the methodical, almost surgical destruction of 'Sonny Boy'. The OJC reissues are all remastered in splendid sound.

*****(*) Way Out West**

Original Jazz Classics OJC 337 *Rollins; Ray Brown (b); Shelly Manne (d).* 3/57.

*****(*) Sonny Rollins Vol. 2**

Blue Note 97809 *Rollins; J.J Johnson (tb); Horace Silver, Thelonious Monk (p); Percy Heath (b); Art Blakey (d).* 4/57.

*****(*) The Sound Of Sonny**

Original Jazz Classics OJC 029 *Rollins; Sonny Clark (p); Percy Heath (b); Roy Haynes (d).* 6/57.

****** Newk's Time**

Blue Note 84001 *Rollins; Wynton Kelly (p); Doug Watkins (b); Philly Joe Jones (d).* 9/57.

♛ ** A Night At The Village Vanguard**

Blue Note 99795 2CD *Rollins; Donald Bailey, Wilbur Ware (b); Pete LaRoca, Elvin Jones (d).* 11/57.

Rollins continued his astonishing run of records with scarcely a pause for breath. A visit to Los Angeles paired him with Brown and Manne on a session which, if it occasionally dips into a kind of arch cleverness, features some superb interplay between the three men, with Rollins turning 'I'm An Old Cowhand' into a jovial invention. The CD edition includes three alternative takes. One of the compelling things about this sequence is the difference in drummer from session to session: Blakey's inimitable pattern of rolls and giant cymbal strokes sounds, for once, a little inappropriate, with Philly Joe Jones using the same kind of drama to far more effect on *Newk's Time*. Elvin Jones, still in his formative phase, matches all of Rollins's most imperial gestures, and 'Striver's Row' and 'Sonnymoon For Two' become tenor–drums dialogues which must have directed the drummer towards his later confrontations with Coltrane. The undervalued player here, though, is Haynes, whose playing on *The Sound Of Sonny* is ingeniously poised and crisp. The Blue Note *Vol. 2* finds Rollins a little cramped by his surroundings, but Johnson's sober playing is a far more apposite accompaniment than Byrd's was, its deadpan line a wry rejoinder to the tenor parts. The new RVG edition is very punchy. *The Sound Of Sonny* is unexpectedly cursory in its treatment of some of the themes: after the longer disquisitions which Rollins had accustomed himself to making, these three- and four-minute tracks sound bitten off. But the grandeur of Rollins's improvisations on 'Just In Time' and 'Toot-Toot-Tootsie' is compressed rather than reduced, and a solo 'It Could Happen To You', though a little snatched at, celebrates the breadth of his sound. We are somewhat divided on the merits of *Newk's Time*. If Rollins is arguably self-absorbed on some of the studio session, the extraordinary motivic development of 'Surrey With The Fringe On Top' is one of his most powerful creations, and 'Blues For Philly Joe' takes the work done on 'Blue Seven' a step further.

The live material, originally cherry-picked for a single peerless LP, has now been stretched across two CDs, and in its latest incarnation the in-person feel is heightened by the addition of some more of Sonny's announcements. In the past we felt that the abundance of this material slightly checked the power-packed feel of the original LP, but in the new RVG edition the sound is extraordinarily deep and immediate, and the sheer impact of Rollins on top form is close to overwhelming – hence our upgrading to crown status, since this is a model example of a classic record given its proper treatment. Working with only bass and drums throughout leads Rollins into areas of freedom which bop never allowed and, while his free-spiritedness is checked by his ruthless self-examination, its rigour makes his music uniquely powerful in jazz. On the two versions of 'Softly As In A Morning Sunrise' or in the muscular exuberance of 'Old Devil Moon', traditional bop-orientated improvising reaches a peak of expressive power and imagination. Overall, these are records which demand a place in any collection.

***** The Essential Sonny Rollins On Riverside**

Riverside FCD-60-020 *Rollins; Kenny Dorham (t); Ernie Henry (as); Sonny Clark, Thelonious Monk, Hank Jones, Wynton Kelly (p); Percy Heath, Paul Chambers, Oscar Pettiford (b); Max Roach, Roy Haynes (d); Abbey Lincoln (v).* 56–58.

***** The Best Of: The Blue Note Years**

Blue Note 93203 *As the Blue Note albums above.* 56–57.

****** The Complete Prestige Recordings**

Prestige 4407 7CD *As the appropriate discs above.* 51–56.

Each of the two best-ofs score lower marks only because the original albums are indispensable. But the Riverside set does include tracks which are otherwise under the leadership of Dorham or Monk. The *Complete Prestige* set, on the other hand, is an abundant feast for those who'd prefer to have the nine original albums compressed to a seven-disc edition.

*****(*) The Freedom Suite**

Original Jazz Classics OJC 067 *Rollins; Oscar Pettiford (b); Max Roach (d).* 2/58.

*****(*) The Sound Of Sonny / Freedom Suite**

Riverside CDJZD 008 *Rollins; Sonny Clark (p); Percy Heath, Paul Chambers, Oscar Pettiford (b); Roy Haynes, Max Roach (d).* 6/57–2/58.

***** Sonny Rollins And The Contemporary Leaders**

Original Jazz Classics OJC 340 *Rollins; Hampton Hawes (p); Victor Feldman (vib); Barney Kessel (g); Leroy Vinnegar (b); Shelly Manne (d).* 10/58.

Although we have been taken to task over this assertion, we still aver that Rollins hasn't shown a great deal of interest in composition. Some of his early bop-oreintated themes remain in the repertory, but he has based most of his improvising around other people's tunes for much of the past 40 years. Nevertheless, 'The Freedom Suite' takes a stab at an extended work, although its simple structure makes it more of a sketch for an improvisation than anything else. The engineers caught his sound with particular immediacy on this date, and it's more a celebration of his tone and dynamic variation than a coherent, programmatic statement (Orrin Keepnews's sleeve-notes seem deliberately to fudge the directness of whatever Rollins was trying to say about black freedom). A somewhat neglected record, and one worth further pondering as regards its importance in the Rollins canon. The (British) Riverside CD usefully couples both *The Freedom Suite* and *The Sound Of Sonny*. Despite a self-conscious clustering of stars for the 'Contemporary Leaders' date, Rollins takes a determined path through one of his most bizarre programmes: 'Rock-A-Bye Your Baby', 'In The Chapel In The Moonlight', 'I've Told Ev'ry Little Star'.

*****(*) Sonny Rollins And The Big Brass**

Verve 557545-2 *Rollins; Nat Adderley (c); Clark Terry, Reunald Jones, Ernie Royal (t); Frank Rehak, Billy Byers, Jimmy Cleveland (tb); Dick Katz, John Lewis (p); Don Butterfield (tba); Henry Grimes, Percy Heath (b); Roy Haynes, Connie Kay, Specs Wright (d).* 7–8/58.

A rare sighting on Verve (actually the original edition came out on Metrojazz), this is coupled with the even more unfamiliar tracks cut with John Lewis, Percy Heath and Connie Kay, which was once a shared LP with a Teddy Edwards session on MGM. Ernie Wilkins's charts are lively and chrome-laden (with no softening reeds and in this very bright transfer, this is sometimes metal-machine music) and, while Rollins responds to them, it's not really the kind of thing he does best. But there are three good trio tracks with Grimes and Wright, and Sonny even essays a solo 'Body And Soul, though it seems comparatively unadventurous.

Rollins had already worked with the MJQ, on a 1953 Prestige date, but these four live tracks are memorably effective – Lewis might be temperamentally very different from Rollins, but his obliquities are so subtly apt and resourceful that it makes one wish they had worked together much more often. And the saxophonist is in huge, hearty voice on each track, 'I'll Follow My Secret Heart' (which Lewis sits out) and 'You Are Too Beautiful' offering almost indecently full-bodied oratory.

*****(*) St Thomas**

Dragon DRCD 229 *Rollins; Henry Grimes (b); Pete LaRoca (d).* 3/59.

Rollins's European tour of 1959 brought about no 'official' recordings, but some radio and concert material has survived. The Dragon set is formidable, although the studio programme which makes up most of the record isn't quite up to the storming concert recording of 'St Thomas' which opens it. A feeling persists throughout these 1959 records that Rollins is coming to the end of a great period, having balanced his own achievements within a straight-bop milieu and realized that, as a singular figure, he is remote from the ideas of interplay within a group (and particularly between horns) which almost everyone else in jazz was pursuing.

*****(*) The Bridge**

RCA 0902 668518-2 *Rollins; Jim Hall (g); Bob Cranshaw (b); Mickey Roker, Ben Riley, Harry T Saunders (d).* 1–5/62.

***** Our Man In Jazz**

RCA 74321 19256-2 *Rollins; Don Cherry (t); Bob Cranshaw, Henry Grimes (b); Billy Higgins (d).* 7/62–2/63.

***** Sonny Meets Hawk**

RCA 74321 22107-2 *Rollins; Coleman Hawkins (ts); Paul Bley (p); Bob Cranshaw (b); Roy McCurdy (d).* 7/63.

***** The Standard Sonny Rollins**

RCA 74321 22109-2 *Rollins; Herbie Hancock (p); Jim Hall (g); David Izenson, Teddy Smith, Bob Cranshaw (b); Stu Martin, Mickey Roker (d).* 6–7/64.

***** All The Things You Are**

Bluebird ND 82179 *As above two discs.* 7/63–7/64.

*****(*) Sonny Rollins & Co**

Bluebird 7863 66530-2 *Similar to above discs.* 63–64.

****** The Complete RCA Victor Recordings**

RCA 09026 68675-2 6CD *As above discs; add Thad Jones (c), (perc).* 1/62–9/64.

The saxophonist disappeared for two years, before returning to the studio with a new contract from RCA. The CD era has seen this music emerging in a confusing series of editions and, while RCA have reverted to some of the original LPs for their programming, several earlier CDs are still available to complicate matters.

The Bridge started him off. On the face of it, little had changed: though Ornette Coleman's revolution had taken place in the interim, the music sounded much like the old Rollins. But this is his most troubled and troubling period on record. The treatment of 'God Bless The Child' is starkly desolate in feeling; although there are lighter moments in such pieces as a shuffle-beat version of 'If Ever I Would Leave You', Rollins plays with a puzzling melancholy throughout. Hall, though, is an unexpectedly fine partner, moving between rhythm and front-line duties with great aplomb and actually finding ways to communicate with the most lofty of soloists. It's an often compelling record as a result.

The meetings with Cherry and Hawkins are much less successful. *Our Man In Jazz* was hailed as Rollins's head-on collision with the new thing, as exemplified by Cherry, but hardly anything the two men play bears any relation to the other's music: recorded live, they might as well be on separate stages. On an exhaustively long 'Oleo', the tenorman's pent-up outburst could almost be an expression of rage at the situation. Cherry, peculiarly, sounds like a pre-echo of the older Rollins in his crabby, buzzing solo on 'Doxy'. Three brief studio tracks at the end are an almost irrelevant postscript.

The encounter with Hawkins is much more respectful, even if Rollins seems to be satirizing the older man at some points, notably in his weirdly trilling solo on 'Yesterdays'. Again, though, there's relatively little real interplay, aside from a beautifully modulated 'Summertime'. *The Standard Sonny Rollins* sets him alongside either Jim Hall or Herbie Hancock plus rhythm section: aimless, encumbered by his own genius, Rollins sounds bored with whatever tune he's playing but can't help throwing in the occasional brilliant stroke. It's a fascinating if frustrating experience to hear. *Sonny Rollins & Co*, if still available, includes all of the original *The Standard Sonny Rollins* along with remaining alternative takes and oddments: a brief look at 'Three Little Words' explodes the tune, for instance. A contrasting 'Now's The Time' is elongated into a 16-minute essay in which the bruised, broken-up style of the 'new' Rollins takes apart the old bebop blues. As always, a compelling insight into a master's methods.

The *Complete* edition spreads all the above music across six CDs, together with the unissued fragments which went to make up *Alternatives* (now seemingly in limbo) and a few other stray items. Awkward though some of the music often is, few sets document a major artist in both triumph and adversity as scrupulously as this; along with the Prestige and Blue Note editions, this is essential to Rollins followers. The original sessions always sounded particularly handsome on original vinyl; as clean as this edition is, it seems to have lost some warmth in the transition.

***(*) **On Impulse!**
Impulse! 12232 *Rollins; Ray Bryant (p); Walter Booker (b); Mickey Roker (d).* 7/65.

***(*) **Alfie**
Impulse! 12242 *Rollins; Jimmy Cleveland, J.J Johnson (tb); Phil Woods (as); Oliver Nelson, Bob Ashton (ts); Roger Kellaway (p); Kenny Burrell (g); Walter Booker (b); Frankie Dunlop (d).* 1/66.

(*) **East Broadway Rundown
Impulse! 33120 *Rollins; Freddie Hubbard (t); Jimmy Garrison (b); Elvin Jones (d).* 5/66.

Rollins's Impulse! records numbered only a handful and they tend to be somewhat overlooked. The new editions of *On Impulse!* and *Alfie*, while not quite demanding a re-evaluation, sound better than ever, and the former in particular, with 'On Green Dolphin Street' and especially 'Three Little Words' transformed into great Rollins set-pieces, is a must. *Alfie* is arguably slighter stuff, with only the main theme – a swaggering line in the tradition of 'Sonnymoon For Two' – offering much meat to the soloist. But this unusual situation for Rollins is one he seems to have enjoyed, and there are some surprisingly unencumbered and witty solos. Nelson, who arranged, had to do little more than keep the horns out of Sonny's way, but it's interesting to conjecture what impact Kellaway – who contributes a handful of intriguing remarks – might have had on the situation. *East Broadway Rundown* still sounds disappointing, with Garrison and Jones no kind of dream match for the leader. The long title-track spends a lot of time going nowhere: only a gnarled 'We Kiss In A Shadow' approaches the real Rollins.

*** **Next Album**
Original Jazz Classics OJC 312 *Rollins; George Cables (p); Bob Cranshaw (b); David Lee (d); Arthur Jenkins (perc).* 7/72.

** **Horn Culture**
Original Jazz Classics OJC 314 *Rollins; Walter Davis Jr (p); Yoshiaki Masuo (g); Bob Cranshaw (b); David Lee (d); James Mtume (perc).* 6–7/73.

(*) **The Cutting Edge
Original Jazz Classics OJC 468 *Rollins; Rufus Harley (bagpipes); Stanley Cowell (p); Yoshiaki Masuo (g); Bob Cranshaw (b); David Lee (d); James Mtume (perc).* 7/74.

** **Nucleus**
Original Jazz Classics OJC 620 *Rollins; Raul De Souza (tb); Bennie Maupin (ts, bcl, lyr); George Duke (p); Bob Cranshaw, Chuck Rainey (b); Roy McCurdy, Eddie Moore (d); James Mtume (perc).* 9/75.

*(*) **The Way I Feel**
Original Jazz Classics OJC 666 *Rollins; Oscar Brashear, Chuck Findley, Gene Coe (t); George Bohannon, Lew McCreary (tb); Marilyn Robinson, Alan Robinson (frhn); Bill Green (ss, f, picc); Patrice Rushen (ky); Lee Ritenour (g); Don Waldrop (tba); Alex Blake, Charles Meeks (b); Billy Cobham (d); Bill Summers (perc).* 8–10/76.

*** **Easy Living**
Original Jazz Classics 893 *Rollins; George Duke (ky); Charles Icarus Johnson (g); Paul Jackson, Byron Miller (b); Tony Williams (d); Bill Summers (perc).* 8/77.

(*) **Don't Stop The Carnival
Milestone 55005 *Rollins; Donald Byrd (t, flhn); Mark Soskin (p); Aurell Ray (g); Jerry Harris (b); Tony Williams (d).* 4/78.

(*) **Milestone Jazzstars In Concert
Milestone 55006 *Rollins; McCoy Tyner (p); Ron Carter (b); Al Foster (d).* 9–10/78.

*** **Don't Ask**
Original Jazz Classics OJC 915 *Rollins; Mark Soskin (ky); Jerome Harris (b); Al Foster (d); Bill Summers (perc).* 5/79.

Rollins returned to action with *Next Album*, a very happy album which sounded much more contented than anything he'd recorded in over a decade. 'Playin' In The Yard' and 'The Everywhere Calypso' were taken at a joyous swagger, 'Poinciana' showcased his debut on soprano, and 'Skylark' was the tenor *tour de force* of the record, the saxophonist locking into a persuasively argued cadenza which shook the melody hard. But at root the album lacks the sheer nerve of his early music. This reining-in of his darker side affects all of his 1970s records to some degree. *Horn Culture* makes a more oppressive use of the electric rhythm section, none of whom plays to Rollins's level, and while the two ballads are pleasing, elsewhere the music gets either pointlessly ugly ('Sais') or messy with overdubs and overblowing ('Pictures In The Reflection Of A Golden Horn'). *The Cutting Edge*, recorded at Montreux, is a muddle, with only a lovely reading of 'To A Wild Rose' to save it.

Nucleus and *The Way I Feel* both court outright disaster. The former has at least some interesting material, and Rollins's very slow path through 'My Reverie' is perversely compelling; but the band have his feet chained, and none of the tracks takes off. The latter, with its dubbed-in horn section, is plain feeble. The best of *Easy Living* – 'My One And Only Love', a merry treatment of Stevie Wonder's 'Isn't She Lovely' and the bleak title-piece – earns a better rating, but Rollins is still surrounded by players who don't belong with him, even Williams.

Don't Stop The Carnival has two great set-pieces, a ravishing 'Autumn Nocturne' and a fine display of virtuosity on 'Silver City', but the mismatched band – Williams tending towards extravagance, and Byrd prefiguring his astonishing total decline of the 1980s – let him down. The *Jazzstars* live session is another disappointment, with the all-star group playing well but to no special purpose and with nothing to show at the end of the record. The almost sublime frustration of this period was provided by reports of (unrecorded) concerts where Rollins was reputedly playing better than ever. *Don't Ask* is initially a groaner – with a track called 'Disco Monk' and the boogaloo thump of 'Harlem Boys' – but there are some unpredictably enjoyable moments since Rollins is actively enjoying what seem to be inappropriate situations for him. 'My Ideal' is another of his peculiarly bitter ballads. These are curmudgeonly ratings – but we're talking about Sonny Rollins and, next to his masterpieces, these are intensely disappointing records.

*** Love At First Sight

Original Jazz Classics OJC 753 *Rollins; George Duke (p); Stanley Clarke (b); Al Foster (d); Bill Summers (perc).*

*** Sunny Days, Starry Nights

Milestone 9122 *Rollins; Clifton Anderson (tb); Mark Soskin (p); Russel Blake (b); Tommy Campbell (d).* 1/84.

Rollins began the 1980s with a session that intercut some of his old philosophies with supposed modernists like Duke and Clarke, though both are called on to perform in neo-traditional roles. The result is a diffident rather than a genuinely contrary record: not bad, with a nice 'The Very Thought Of You' and a sweet original called 'Little Lu', but the perfunctory retread of the ancient Rollins classic, 'Strode Rode', shows up the lightweight cast and situation. *Sunny Days, Starry Nights* features the nucleus of the band he kept for many years, built around Soskin and Anderson. Nobody else is remotely on Rollins's level, and he seems to prefer it that way: certainly his best performances have arisen out of a certain creative isolation. This is another good-humoured date, with the melody of 'I'll See You Again' coming in waves of overdubbed tenor and jolly themes such as 'Kilauea' and 'Mava Mava' tempting the leader out of himself; it's as enjoyable as any of his later records.

**(*) The Solo Album

Original Jazz Classics OJC 956 *Rollins (ts solo).* 7/85.

This still sounds like a curious failure. Since Rollins's solo cadenzas had always been luminous moments in his best concerts, hopes were high that this one-man recital would be a classic. Yet so much of it seems like aimless wool-gathering, the very opposite of Rollins at his best, that one assumes it was an occasion he didn't really want to take part in. A good opportunity to study his tonal characteristics at length, but on a purely musical level this was a great disappointment.

***(*) G Man

Milestone 9150 *Rollins; Clifton Anderson (tb); Mark Soskin (p); Bob Cranshaw (b); Marvin 'Smitty' Smith (d).* 8/86–4/87.

*** Dancing In The Dark

Milestone 9155 *As above, except Jerome Harris (b, g) replaces Cranshaw.* 9/87.

*** Falling In Love With Jazz

Milestone 9179 *As above, except add Branford Marsalis (ts), Tommy Flanagan (p), Bob Cranshaw (b), Jeff Tain Watts, Jack DeJohnette (d); omit Smith.* 6–9/89.

*** Here's To The People

Milestone 9194 *As above, except add Roy Hargrove (t), Al Foster (d), Steve Jordan (perc); omit Marsalis and Flanagan.* 91.

The live show which produced the title-track of *G Man* caught Rollins in his most communicative form: it might not be his most profound playing, but the sheer exuberance and tumbling impetus of his improvising sweeps the listener along. *Dancing In The Dark* seems tame in comparison, though the leader plays with plenty of bite: tracks such as 'Just Once', though, seem to have been designed more for radio-play than anything else, and the band's snappy delivery of 'Duke Of Iron' is a well-crafted routine, not a spontaneous flourish. The two studio sessions follow a similar pattern, with the guest horn player on each date doing no more than blowing a few gratuitous notes. *Falling In Love With Jazz* has a quite irresistible version of 'Tennessee Waltz', and there are two Rollins flights through 'Why Was I Born?' and 'I Wish I Knew' on *Here's To The People*, where his tone seems grouchier and less tractable than ever before. Both discs, though, sound excessively studio-bound, suggesting that Rollins could use a change of scene here. In his sixties, though, he is probably content to work at his own whim, which – on the basis of the extraordinary catalogue listed above – he has surely earned.

*** Old Flames

Milestone MCD-9215-2 *Rollins; Jon Faddis, Byron Sterling (flhn); Clifton Anderson (tb); Alex Brofsky (frhn); Tommy Flanagan (p); Bob Stewart (tba); Bob Cranshaw (b); Jack DeJohnette (d).* 7–8/93.

This is a sombre record after the sequence of mostly cheerful Milestones that Rollins delivered in the previous ten years or so. The only upbeat piece is 'Times Slimes', a title directed at corporate greed and its effect on the environment; the major set-pieces, 'I See Your Face Before Me' and Franz Lehár's 'Delia', are wrenchingly slow, tragic laments. Rollins is in magisterial voice, his tone veering between exasperation and wistfulness; but the session still lacks the urgency and incisiveness he once brought to even his most wayward playing. He is a different musician now. Jimmy Heath's stentorian brass charts on two tracks lend a little variation, and Flanagan's thoughtful presence is an unobtrusive bonus.

*** + 3

Milestone 9250 *Rollins; Tommy Flanagan, Stephen Scott (p); Bob Cranshaw (b); Jack DeJohnette, Al Foster (d).* 8–10/95.

Another strange one. Sonny's tone has never been grainier or more fogbound, he uses repetitions obsessively, cracks some notes as wilfully as Miles Davis, and states a written melody with seemingly intentional cruelty. The two different rhythm sections – Cranshaw is common to both – adopt a mediatory role, yet both manage to sound relatively faceless, imposing though these players are. Rollins turns 'Cabin In The Sky' into one of his tragic vehicles, complete with roving cadenza, and he defaces 'Mona

Lisa'; but some of these pieces sound merely charmless – especially the two originals, which purport to be funky in an elephantine way. The most enigmatic figure in jazz continues to go his own way.

*****(*) Global Warming**

Milestone 9280 *Rollins; Clifton Anderson (tb); Stephen Scott (p); Bob Cranshaw (b); Idris Muhammad, Perry Wilson (d); Victor See Yuen (perc).* 1–2/98.

The good-humoured 'Island Lady' and the sunny-sounding title-track militate against a mood which is meant to be about planetary crisis: '*Global Warming* is my *Freedom Suite* of 1998,' says Rollins. One turns instead to an elaborate 'Mother Nature's Blues' and a strangely queasy ballad called 'Echo-Side Blue' for the leader's darkest thoughts; with 'Change Partners' as the sole standard, this is an unbalanced and rather enigmatic set altogether. Anderson gets more space than he has ever had on a Rollins record and makes quite assertive use of it; Scott, now a Rollins regular, is the most inventive band pianist he's had for a long time. The result is a fractious and unpredictable album which sometimes has Rollins straining on the horn – some of his forays into a false register sound like a real effort – yet which has a greater share of inspirational tenor than any other disc he's put his name on in ten years.

****** Silver City**

Milestone 2501-2 2CD *As Milestone albums above.* 72–95.

Rollins has been fortunate in his repackaging, and this two-disc set – with a revealing interview essay – is a notably effective round-up of the pick of many mixed albums. His inconsistency and contrariness are part of what makes Rollins great, and to that extent the many individual Milestone albums, for all their faults, will remain in most collections. For less committed Rollins acolytes, this should be a first choice: there's nothing amiss here and, while a third disc would surely have covered the remaining high spots, this one stands very fairly by itself.

Aldo Romano (born 1941)

DRUMS

Italian-born, Romano moved to France as a child and began on guitar before moving to drums. Now a respected modernist and group leader with a bagful of distinguished credits.

*****(*) Non Dimenticar**

MLP 518264-2 *Romano; Paolo Fresu (t); Franco D'Andrea (p); Furio Di Castri (b).* 2/93.

***** Prosodie**

Verve 526854-2 *Romano; Paolo Fresu (t, flhn); Stefano Di Battista (as, ss); Olivier Ker Ourio (hca); Franco D'Andrea (p); Jean Michel Pilc (p, whistle); Michel Benita, Furio Di Castri (b).* 1/95.

Romano's stylistic development has been, by some standards, back to front, beginning with free drumming and only later adopting the more mainstream, time-keeping role that can be sampled on the second record, a belated recognition of his gifts by a major label. The compositions are certainly not mainstream, except in the sense that there is now a recognizable Franco-Italian style in jazz, compounded of bebop elements with a folk strain, dance and formal concert music. 'Nat Eyes' and the pugnacious 'Folk Off' are pretty clear examples, but these are mixed in with less pulse-driven items, including some featuring Romano reciting lyric poems by his wife. The relaxed, insouciant swing that made him such a favourite with players like Enrico Rava and Michel Petrucciani is in evidence throughout.

The slightly earlier *Non Dimenticar* is a dreamily beautiful exploration of ten favourite Italian songs. Lucio Dalla's 'Caruso', done at a wonderful dead-slow tempo, and a gorgeous 'Estate' stand out, with Fresu milking his Miles allegiance to superb effect. D'Andrea sounds in good fettle, and Di Castri and Romano play as if feeling every measure of their homeland's weepy romanticism – but who cares, when it sounds this good?

Furio Romano

ALTO SAXOPHONE

Italian saxophonist playing his own variation on post-bop styles.

***** Danza Delle Streghe**

Splasc(h) H 318-2 *Romano; Rudy Migliardi (tb, tba); Donato Scolese (vib); Piero Di Rienzo (b); Massimo Pintori (d).* 6/90.

*****(*) Inside Out**

Splasc(h) H 362-2 *As above, except Roberto Della Grotta (b) replaces Di Rienzo; add Tom Harrell (t, flhn).* 9/91.

Romano rings many changes on hard-bop expectations with his remarkable quintet. The four long tracks straggle through continuously evolving shapes and colours: there are conversations between instruments rather than themes and solos, and when they play 'Goodbye Pork Pie Hat' it emerges only after a fanciful dialogue between alto sax and tuba. Scolese's vibes are a key element, replacing the firm ground of a piano with an allusive shimmer that tends to avoid harmonic ties. Rhythmically, Romano also eludes anything very boppish: if anything, Pintori is more inclined to choose a rock-orientated beat, which is certainly what drives 'Ombre Di Luna'.

The second record is just as challenging, and it is improved by the addition of the versatile Harrell, whose vigorous playing is always tempered by the feeling that fundamentally he's a cool stylist. There's a marvellous revision of Monk's 'Epistrophy', but they don't really get rude enough with another Mingus tune, 'Jelly Roll'. 'Iter', though, begins with a superb discussion between the horns before turning on a boogaloo beat. The leader's own playing is rather spiny and raw at times, but it suits the balance of the music. More, please!

Wallace Roney

TRUMPET, FLUGELHORN

In the 1980s, three young trumpeters seemed to divide the known world between them. While Wynton Marsalis and Terence Blanchard parcelled out the mainstream tradition, Roney estab-

lished himself as the eclectic heir of Miles Davis. He is married to, and has regularly recorded with, pianist Geri Allen.

*****(*) No Job Too Big Or Too Small**
32 Jazz 32140 *Roney; Kenny Garrett (as); Ravi Coltrane, Antoine Roney (ts); Gary Thomas (ts, f); Geri Allen, Donald Brown, Mulgrew Miller, Jacky Terrasson (p); Ron Carter, Christian McBride, Charnett Moffett, Peter Washington (b); Eric Allen, Cindy Blackman, Kenny Washington, Tony Williams (d).* 2/87–6/93.

****** According To Mr Roney**
32 Jazz 32044 *Roney; Antoine Roney (ts); Kenny Garrett (as); Gary Thomas (ts); Mulgrew Miller, Jacky Terrasson (p); Ron Carter, Peter Washington (b); Eric Allen, Cindy Blackman (d).* 1/88, 9/91.

Roney plays with an edgy subtlety and a willingness to drift obliquely across and behind the beat. This led to inevitable and mostly negative comparisons to Miles Davis. The fact is that Roney quickly mastered his own idiom; Miles-tinged it may be, but it is emphatically individual as well. The first of the 32 Jazz discs packages the 1991 *Seth Air* with the slightly earlier *Intuition*. Its open, modal charts and strong independent rhythm recall the Davis bands of the early '60s (not least because Ron Carter is there and in such strong voice), but Roney's phrasing is far more dynamic, recalling Fats Navarro and Howard McGhee rather than Miles. Only on 'Willow, Weep For Me', arranged for quartet with no reeds, does the comparison really hold. *Seth Air* featured a rather different band. Carter's wise old head was no longer in evidence and Roney had replaced Cindy Blackman, the drummer who had played on all the previous Muses except the debut, which was chaperoned by the late Tony Williams. Antoine Roney isn't as articulate a stylist as his brother and some of his soloing veers towards the inconsequential. Terrasson is a player who divides opinion; technically astute, he often lacks real bottom weight. Here, he is superb, and his detailed comping on 'Taberah' and 'Sometimes My Heart Cries' is exemplary. Roney himself plays with a lighter and less physical delivery, almost as if he has changed mouthpiece and embouchure. The change gives the album a slightly two-toned effect, but it is an excellent sampling of the Muse period and with any luck signals a comprehensive reissue programme to come.

Top marks to 32 Jazz for putting together such an intelligent and attractive selection from Roney's work for Muse as *No Job* turns out to be. Given the reissue of *Seth Air* and *Intuition*, it makes sense that these are downplayed in favour of 1993's *Munchin'*. No one will argue with the balance and quality of the inclusions. Roney's debt to Miles Davis is again evident throughout, most obviously on Wayne Shorter's 'Lost', Bill Evans's 'Blue In Green' and of course on Miles's 'Solar'. Yet there are also nods to Clifford Brown and to Fats Navarro as well, and here and there Roney seems to personalize phrases and harmonic devices from the great recordings of the past. His own composition, 'For Duke', one of only two by Wallace, though the record opens with brother Antoine's 'Melchizedek', suggests his debt to the jazz of a pre-bop generation as well. If *No Job* was conceived as a way of showing Roney in as many different moods as possible, then the job has been done well. Here he is an incendiary front man, romantic balladeer and enigmatic brass poet. It would have been good to have the rest of the Muse material back in circulation, but this is a more than welcome return from one of the brightest players of his day.

***** Misterios**
Warner Bros 245641 *Roney; Ravi Coltrane, Antoine Roney (ts); Geri Allen (p); Gil Goldstein (ky); Clarence Seay (b); Eric Allen (d); Waltinho Anastacio, Steve Barrios, Steve Thornton (perc); woodwinds; strings.* 93.

****** The Wallace Roney Quintet**
Warner Bros 45914 *Roney; Antoine Roney (ts); Carlos McKinney (p); Clarence Seay (b); Eric Allen (d).* 2/95.

*****(*) Village**
Warner Bros 46649 *Roney; Michael Brecker, Pharoah Sanders (ts); Antoine Roney (ts, ss, bcl); Geri Allen, Chick Corea (p); Robert Irving III (syn); Clarence Seay (b); Lenny White (d); Steve Berrios (perc).* 12/96.

Roney's contract with Warner Bros opened him up to bigger-budget production and glossier packaging. Inevitably, this did blunt the urgency of his work to a degree. *Misterios* is swamped in superfluous sound but does contain some beautiful playing. 'Michelle', the Lennon/McCartney staple, is an unexpected choice but one which works well with just horn and rhythm. Brother Antoine appears on three cuts, including Jaco Pastorius's '71+' and Pat Metheny's 'Last To Know', one of a pair of compositions by the guitarist. Coltrane Jr makes a guest appearance on Astor Piazzolla's 'Muerte', which is medleyed with an excerpt from Bach's *Art Of The Fugue*, but does nothing of any great consequence. What a burden he carries. By contrast, Roney seems to have settled comfortably into being Miles's most eloquent heir.

The follow-up album on WB might almost be a Davis album of a bygone age. This time all the material is by the group, with compositions from Antoine (in Wayne Shorter mode on 'Spyra', and 'Ultra-Axis'), McKinney and Seay, as well as the closing 'Geri' and 'Northern Lights' from Roney himself. *Village* very much picks up where *Quintet* left off, though, in an effort to boost sales and profile, Warners have teamed him up with an all-star band which doesn't really do him any great favours. Two of the tracks, the title-piece and 'Oshiririke', are collectively composed, and they suggest that some attempt was made to loosen the constraints of what had become a rather formulaic session. Guest pianist Chick Corea's 'Affinity' is the lead-off tune and Chick gives way to Mrs Roney only mid-set, though he turns up as second keyboard on Fender Rhodes on Lenny White's 'EBO'. The drummer is a revelation, playing wonderful cross-patterns and fills and setting up grooves you could launch ships down. Brecker and Sanders have cameo parts, though Pharoah makes full use of the spotlight on a theme dedicated to him. An excellent record, but less coherent and focused than its plainly named predecessor.

Room

GROUP

A group of contemporary composer-improvisers.

***** Hall Of Mirrors**

Music & Arts 700 *Larry Ochs (sno, ts); Chris Brown (p, elec); William Winant (vib, perc); Scott Gresham-Lancaster (elec).* 5–8/91.

Room's second album (there is an earlier record for Sound Aspects) offers an ambiguous set of compositions that sound like almost total improvisations. If Ochs is the dominant voice, casting typically intense tenor and sopranino solos over the music, then Brown is the likely Svengali, playing piano like a percussion instrument and introducing samples and keyboard programmes seamlessly into the mix. Gresham-Lancaster also plays somewhere in the shadows: unlike George Lewis or Richard Teitelbaum, he seems to want electronics to simulate natural sounds, or at least to behave 'naturally'. Winant's ghostly vibes and pattering drums complete a chamberish line-up. Two long pieces and two fillers, and it might say something about the looseness of the group that it's the two briefer pieces which sound the most interesting.

Adonis Rose (born 1974)

DRUMS

Young drummer entering the vanguard of today's post-bop.

***** Song For Donise**

Criss Cross Criss 1146 *Rose; Nicholas Payton (t); Tim Warfield (ts); Anthony Wonsey (p); Reuben Rogers (b).* 12/97.

***** The Unity**

Criss Cross 1173 *As above.* 6/99.

Rose first came to notice with Nicholas Payton's band on the trumpeter's *Gumbo Nouveau* disc for Verve. This session returns the compliment: more or less the same line-up and with Payton and Wonsey the main composers. One might suspect that Payton, a Wayne Shorter devotee, also brought in 'E.S.P.', but this is the best pointer to Rose's own debt to the late Tony Williams. He has the same dry, rippling delivery, and a generous amount of the same innate musicality. On 'Love Walked In', which is for piano trio only, he cements the connection with a beautifully crafted performance. Perhaps inevitably, the session is dominated by the two horn men. The cast returns for another go on *The Unity* and, while this is perhaps just another good day at the office, the music continues to breathe and expand as these young performers become ever more masterful in their skills. Payton gets a huge sound on 'I Remember You', which sounds as if it must be an uncredited flugelhorn, and Wonsey, who plays modestly for much of the way, digs in hard on his own mockingly titled 'Smooth Jazz'.

Bernt Rosengren (born 1937)

TENOR AND ALTO SAXOPHONES, FLUTE, TAROGATO, PIANO

Rosengren led Swedish hard bop as its premier young tenorman in the late '50s. He acquired some international exposure in the '60s with George Russell and others, but he has basically remained tied to his native scene as a player and bandleader, and a fair spread of his career is currently available on CD.

***** Stockholm Dues**

EMI 792428-2 (Swed.) *Rosengren; Lalle Svensson (t); Claes-Goran Fagerstadt, Lars Sjøsten (p); Bjorn Alke, Torbjørn Hultcrantz (b); Bo Skoglund (d); Nannie Porres (v).* 3–4/65.

****** Notes From Underground**

EMI 136462-2 (Swed.) *Rosengren; Maffy Falay (t, darbuka); Bertil Strandberg (tb); Tommy Koverhult (ss, ts, f); Gunnar Bergsten (bs); Bobo Stenson (p); Torbjørn Hultcrantz, Bjorn Alke (b); Leif Wennerstrom (d); Okay Temiz, Bengt Berger (perc); Salih Baysal (v, vn).* 9/73.

***** Surprise Party**

Steeplechase SCCD 31177 *Rosengren; Horace Parlan (p); Doug Raney (g); Jesper Lundgaard (b); Aage Tanggaard (d).* 3/83.

***** The Hug**

Dragon DRCD 211 *Rosengren; Carl Fredrik Orrje (p); Anders Ullberg (g); Torbjørn Hultcrantz (b); Leif Wennerstrom (d).* 5/92.

*****(*) Full Of Life**

Dragon DRCD 205 *Rosengren; Krister Andersson (ts, cl); Goran Lindberg (p); Sture Nordin (b); Bengt Stark (d).* 3/91.

*****(*) Bent's Jump: Summit Meeting Live At Bent J**

Dragon DRCD 233 *As above.* 7/93.

Rosengren has been a force in Swedish jazz for some 40 years and is still undervalued on the world stage. Wider availability of his earlier records would still be welcome, though at least the two EMI issues are in the racks, albeit as Swedish-only issues. *Stockholm Dues* is a decent approximation of a genre hard-bop record, but it's let down by the thick, clattery sound and some occasionally scrappy playing; Porres's singing on some tracks is also an uneasily acquired taste. But Rosengren's muscular, assured playing stands out when he takes centre stage, with Svensson a solid partner. There are several tracks added to what was the original LP issue.

Notes From Underground is far superior and stands as an important record of its time. Rosengren varies the tracks from 11 players down to quartet, with the members of the Turkish-Swedish group Sevda also on hand – an early example of a jazz-world fusion that retains its potency. The big group plays with enormous gusto on Rosengren's charts, the rhythms roiling underneath, and the points of reference – Coltrane/Sanders and the McCoy Tyner groups of the early '70s – are subsumed in the force of Rosengren's delivery. Crucial is his partnership with Koverhult, the latter now entirely neglected but a tenorman capable of the force and intensity of the leader's own best playing. The Rachmaninov arrangement which opened the original double-album has been lost, but that means all the music can now be fitted on to a single CD. Splendid remastering, and the title is a somewhat ironic comment on the state of live jazz in Stockholm at the time.

The Steeplechase session, rather glibly dismissed in our first edition, is standing up rather better than we previously allowed. Admittedly not much more than one of the label's in-house blowing dates, the calibre of the band is nevertheless considerable and the easy-going authority of the playing is hardly disappointing.

The Hug is an agreeable, lightly swinging programme of standards and a few originals which all involved take affably enough, though scrutiny of any passage reveals that nobody's asleep. Rosengren's tone and phrasing are a nice balance of strength and a certain vulnerability which can sometimes give his solos a dozing quality they don't deserve. He is in more commanding form on the two albums by the band Summit Meeting. *Full Of Life* is a studio date, while *Bent's Jump* was recorded at the establishment squired by Bent J. Jensen, one of the great jazz-club owners. The live session has an ounce more snap to it, although the sound is somewhat documentary-standard. The music is a sinewy variation on midstream hard bop, and the two saxophonists – neither exactly a pugilist – forge an amicable front line that transcends jam-session clichés.

***** Porgy And Bess**

Liphone 3167 *Rosengren; Carl Fredrik Orrje (p); Per-Ola Gadd (b); Bengt Stark (d).* 1/96.

*****(*) Plays Evert Taube**

Arietta ADCD 19 *Rosengren; Håkan Nyqvist (t, flhn, frhn); Sven Berggren (tb); Tommy Koverhult (ss, f); Gunnar Bergsten (bs); Peter Nordahl (p); Patrik Boman (b); Jesper Kviberg (d).* 99.

In the light of Joe Henderson's take on the Gershwin score, Rosengren's *Porgy And Bess* seems a much more modest affair, tenor and rhythm section working patiently through the score – taken surprisingly literally by the leader – with no grand set-pieces. But the saxophonist's maturity is as considerable as Henderson's and, even when he sounds comparatively diffident, he makes one hear fresh things in what is now a thoroughly jazzed piece of Americana. As a bonus there is some particularly thoughtful playing by Orrje.

Taube's name may not be too familiar to non-Swedish audiences, but he was the country's national poet and a songwriter who dominated Swedish radio for many years. Rosengren has arranged 12 of Taube's songs, chosen from 40 years of the composer's work. A graceful rather than a memorable melodist, Taube seems somewhat hidden in Rosengren's arrangements, an elusive simplicity built over by the saxophonist's writing. He is keen to give everyone something to do, even when there's a soloist out front, and the horns are almost continuously involved. The waltz metre of 'Personligt Samtal' is decorated by some intense solos, but one never feels that the music has lost its founding character. A strong and typically individual set by a true individualist.

Ted Rosenthal (born 1959)

PIANO

A New York pianist with several albums to his name but no current label affiliation, Rosenthal plays post-bop piano with a strong Monk influence.

***** Images Of Monk**

Jazz Alliance TJA-10023 *Rosenthal; Brian Lynch (t); Dick Oatts (ss, as); Mark Feldman (vn); Scott Colley (b); Marvin 'Smitty' Smith (d).* 12/92.

***** At Maybeck Recital Hall Vol. 38**

Concord CCD 4648 *Rosenthal (p solo).* 10/94.

Rosenthal, a winner of the Monk Piano Competition in 1988, is very much under Thelonious's spell. *Images Of Monk* is based around half a dozen Monk tunes, with the horns and rhythm section otherwise standing tall as a fierce hard-bop outfit. Rosenthal himself suffers a little from the duties of leadership: he imposes only a modest amount of himself on the music. Lynch and Oatts make more of an impression.

His turn in the Maybeck spotlight is slightly marred by a tendency to show off. Since he has a go at everything from 'Jesu, Joy Of Man's Desiring' to 'You've Got To Be Modernistic', there's no denying the catholicity of his taste, but some of the treatments sound a bit pleased with themselves. His own tunes, where our familiarity is taken less for granted, tend to turn out the best.

Kurt Rosenwinkel

GUITAR, VOCAL

A ubiquitous presence on the New York club scene of the late '90s, Rosenwinkel has progressed rapidly from sideman to leader status with these sets.

*****(*) East Coast Love Affair**

Fresh Sound FSNT 016 *Rosenwinkel; Avishai Cohen (b); Jorge Rossy (d).* 7/96.

***** Intuit**

Criss Cross 1160 *Rosenwinkel; Michael Kanan (p); Joe Martin (b); Tim Pleasant (d).* 8/98.

***** The Enemies Of Energy**

Verve 543042-2 *Rosenwinkel; Mark Turner (ts); Scott Kinsey (ky); Ben Street (b); Jeff Ballard (d).* 99.

The debut has a beautiful feel – the three men were recorded in Small's Club, where Rosenwinkel has had a regular gig, and the sound of the record is close, almost humid. The interplay lifts the material to a high level of invention – when they fade 'All Or Nothing At All', it sounds as though they could have gone on in that groove for hours yet. Rosenwinkel plays with a clean, almost classical sound and his melody lines are spacious and paced to suit whatever tempo they've chosen – he never seems to feel he has to rush through his phrases. Cohen and Rossy are just as generous of spirit on a very enjoyable set. It's certainly more successful than the subsequent Criss Cross, which is all right but basically uneventful. The bebop tunes are given a going-over which sounds like a lot of other records, and it feels like routine.

The Enemies Of Energy is by Rosenwinkel's regular band. The music's a curious blend of straight-ahead, fusion, prog-rock instrumentals and even folk music, with Rosenwinkel accompanyng his own vocal on 'The Polish Song'. Kinsey's keyboards bring in what sound like clavinet and analogue synthesizers. Rosenwinkel and Turner have their moments, but this feels like a patchwork in search of a clear pattern, and what might sound a lot more vivid and convincing in a live situation seems very tame in the studio.

Michele Rosewoman (born 1953)

PIANO, PERCUSSION

Californian pianist bridging post-bop with traces of Cuban music and her own take on the tradition.

**** The Source

Soul Note 121072 *Rosewoman; Baikida Carroll (t); Roberto Miranda (b); Pheeroan akLaff (d).* 4/83.

Like many musicians from the Oakland scene, Rosewoman owes her greatest debt to Ed Kelly, a teacher and pianist who unfortunately has made little impact on record but who is remembered with warmth and respect by many younger-generation Californian players. Rosewoman's style also owes much to Cecil Taylor, though her interest in Cuban music means that she never goes quite as far as Taylor in the direction of abstraction. *The Source* was out of print for some time and is a welcome addition to Rosewoman's small catalogue. Carroll is a remarkable player with an incendiary solo style, and his contributions to the long title-track, to 'To Be Cont ...' and to 'For Monk' (another obvious source for the pianist) are genuinely exciting. Here and there, Rosewoman's playing is reminiscent of Geri Allen, but she has a more pungent attack and – perhaps as a consequence – a more convincing ballad style.

***(*) Quintessence

Enja 5039-2 *Rosewoman; Steve Coleman (as); Greg Osby (as, ss); Anthony Cox (b); Terri Lyne Carrington (d).* 1/87.

*** Contrast High

Enja 5091-2 *Rosewoman; Greg Osby (as, ss); Gary Thomas (ts, f); Lonnie Plaxico (b); Cecil Brooks III (d).* 7/88.

With *The Source* back in circulation, *Quintessence* doesn't sound quite so exciting. Rosewoman has worked with groups of every size. She probably sounds best in the context of a medium-sized group, where her writing and playing are equally highlighted. 'For Now And Forever' is an exceptional piece of work, reminiscent of the stop-start themes Ornette Coleman was writing in the mid-'60s. The composer's Cecil Taylor debt is obliquely registered in 'Lyons' (written in homage to saxophonist Jimmy) and 'Springular And Springle', while the ballad, 'The Thrill-Of-Real-Love', is wonderfully sardonic. Gary Thomas gives *Contrast High* a lower and richer tonality and, while his phrasing is often wayward, he always seems to have something to say. This is a more straightforward, groove-driven record, and none the worse for that, except that Rosewoman perhaps settles too readily into straight-ahead mode and finds fewer opportunities to touch on the African and Cuban inflexions that made *The Source* and *Quintessence* such strong statements.

***(*) Occasion To Rise

Evidence ECD 22042 *Rosewoman; Rufus Reid (b); Ralph Peterson (d).* 9/90.

*** Harvest

Enja 7069 *Rosewoman; Steve Wilson (as, ss); Gary Thomas (ts, f); Kenny Davis (b); Gene Jackson (d); Eddie Bobe (perc).* 93.

By the turn of the '90s Rosewoman sounded like a player who was trying to relocate herself in the tradition. *Harvest*, and in particular the powerful 'Warriors', found her renegotiating some of the Afro-jazz idiom of the 1960s and in some ways reinventing the wheel as well. *Occasion To Rise* is much more confident in its appropriation of ancestral notions; the Ellington of *Money Jungle* isn't so far in the background. There are five originals, including the Mingus-influenced 'Sweet Eye Of Hurricane Sally', but one might have wanted to hear more developed versions of Coltrane's 'Lazy Bird', Lee Morgan's 'Nite Flite' and Mingus's own 'Weird Nightmare'. Rosewoman's interpretation of 'Prelude To A Kiss' deserves mention, not least for the interplay between piano and bassist Rufus Reid, who positively sings his part. The closing 'Eee-Yaa' and 'West Africa Blue' and almost the whole of *Harvest* suggest that at this stage in her career Rosewoman would benefit from a spell of study in Africa. She understands instinctively which components of jazz come from the old continent but doesn't yet seem quite aware how they impact on what she is doing.

***(*) Guardians Of The Light

Enja 9378-2 *Rosewoman; Steve Wilson (as, ss); Craig Handy (ts); Kenny Davis (b); Gene Jackson (d).* 3/99.

Something of a stopgap live album for Rosewoman and Quintessence, with several old pieces such as 'West Africa Blue' and 'The Thrill Of Real Love' reappearing from older records. That said, the quintet play them beautifully, the latter in particular a sumptuous treatment of the melody, and with the leader's piano growing more confident in its idiosyncrasies this Sweet Basil gig is full of music. Wilson and Handy are assertive without overcooking it, and in any case this is a big and tough-sounding rhythm section, even when it's handling melodious material. 'Ask Me Now' is as individual a Monk interpretation as one could hope to hear.

Renee Rosnes (born 1962)

PIANO

Canadian-born Rosnes has maintained a consistent output for Blue Note throughout the 1990s and is one of the most reliable names on the current roster, an adventurous player and composer who maintains close links with the label's classic repertoire.

*** Renee Rosnes

Blue Note CDP 7 93561 *Rosnes; Branford Marsalis (ts, ss); Wayne Shorter (ss); Ralph Bowen (ts); Herbie Hancock (p); Ron Carter (b); Lewis Nash (d).* 4/88–2/89.

Blue Note have never got out of the habit of signing up promising talent and then throwing as many big names at it as they can. It almost torpedoed Canadian-born Rosnes on her debut. She had shown her capabilities with Joe Henderson's touring group and was certainly in no need of the rather glib star vehicles provided by Marsalis and Shorter.

She switches to synthesizers for a spot with Wayne, recorded live to DAT at the legendary Club Montmartre in Copenhagen. It's something of a false note on the record, which mixes three Rosnes originals with Monk's rarely covered 'Bright Mississippi',

Joe Henderson's 'Punjab' and a couple of standards. Her playing is bright and shrewd, and the sound is mostly very good, though there is an inconsistency of register between the two main studio sessions.

*****(*) For The Moment**

Blue Note 94859 *Rosnes; Steve Wilson (ss, as); Joe Henderson (ts); Ira Coleman (b); Billy Drummond (d).* 2/90.

With Henderson himself on hand, together with husband Billy Drummond (that's Renee's husband, not Joe's, lest we set tongues wagging) and the ever-responsive Wilson, she sounds much more comfortable. Both saxophones are featured on three tracks, Joe alone on four, and Steve on one. The older man is superb on another unfamiliar Monk, 'Four In One', and on Woody Shaw's 'The Organ Grinder'. The change of tonality with Wilson on alto and soprano is just what the record needs, for the trio is a little too unvaried. The two originals bring out some of the most adventurous playing that had been heard to date from Rosnes, still a touch light in articulation but very inventive.

***** Without Words**

Blue Note/Somethin' Else 98168 *Rosnes; Buster Williams (b); Billy Drummond (d); strings.* 1/92.

Why this wasn't left uncluttered we can't imagine. Robert Freedman's string arrangements are note-perfect and beautifully played, but they were hardly required on this session, and Rosnes might have been tempted to stretch out more on these standards if producer Matt Pierson had allowed her a bit more room. 'You And The Night And The Music', 'Estate' and Duke's 'In A Sentimental Mood' are the outstanding tracks. Buster Williams was an inspired choice to make up the *ménage à trois*.

*****(*) Ancestors**

Blue Note 34634 *Rosnes; Nicholas Payton (t); Chris Potter (ts, ss, af); Peter Washington (b); Al Foster (d); Don Alias (perc).* 10/95.

This is the record that marks Rosnes's maturity as a composer. In 1994, she had met her biological mother and learnt more about her Indian heritage; at almost the same moment her adoptive mother succumbed to a late-diagnosed cancer. These extremes of joy and pain are reflected in 'Ancestors' itself, a swinging, confident piece with a measure of tragedy at its centre, and also in 'The Ache Of The Absence', 'Lifewish', 'The Gift' and 'Chasing Spirits', which give the latter stages of this fine record the feel of a loosely connected suite.

This is the first time she has recorded with a brass instrument. Payton's solo on 'The Ache' is immaculate, only matched by Potter's restless idea on 'Chasing Spirits'. Washington and Foster (the latter another stalwart of the Henderson band) cannot be faulted on any count, and the sound, masterminded by Bob Belden, is pristine.

****** As We Are Now**

Blue Note 56810 *Rosnes; Chris Potter (ts, ss); Christian McBride (b); Jack DeJohnette (d).* 3/97.

This time, Rosnes has few items of personal agenda on show. 'The Land Of Five Rivers' is a small exception, a portrait of the northern Indian landscape her ancestors left to go to Canada. The disc gets off to a roaring start with 'Black Holes', an original that sits well for both piano and horn. Nothing could be of greater contrast than the haunted title-piece, named after a May Sarton novel and almost as beautiful. Tony Williams's 'Pee Wee' was written for the Miles Davis album, *Sorcerer*, and was included on the album just a couple of weeks after the drummer's untimely death. Rosnes has the gift of turning strong emotion into compelling music. No mistaking the strength of her feelings, or the ability to convert and transform it.

****** Art & Soul**

Blue Note 99997 2 *Rosnes; Scott Colley (b); Billy Drummond (d); Richard Bona (perc); Dianne Reeves (v).* 2/99.

As ever, Rosnes draws on the past and makes it sound fresh, friendly and contemporary. Beginning with 'Blues Connotation' (a clever, eleven-and-a-half-bar blues by Ornette Coleman) was a master stroke, for its off-centre phrasing and hectic pace leave the listener slightly winded and pleasantly punchy for the rest of a fine set. Following it up with a romantic reading 'With A Little Help From My Friends' was even more clever. Rosnes has the gift of taking shop-worn tunes and making them sound as if they were being written on the spot, and the musing quality she brings to the Beatles song, this time with minimal accompaniment from Colley and Drummond, is spot-on.

Wyane Shorter's 'Footprints' features lyrics by Kitty Margolis and a strong vocal by Dianne Reeves, who also features on 'Fleurette Africaine', a Duke Ellington tune first recorded on the *Money Jungle* session with Charles Mingus and Max Roach. Richard Bona's *kalimba* adds a delightful and unexpected dimension. 'Little Spirit' is a love-song for Renee's baby son, and the closing piece is an arrangement of a Bartók children's song (though you might have guessed Chick Corea), a reflection of the only thing likely to distract this fine performer from music, now or in the future. Rosnes is playing at her very best.

Frank Rosolino (1926–78)

TROMBONE

Though he was also fondly remembered as a comic vocalist, it's Rosolino's fast, responsive trombone playing which established his reputation. He worked in an array of big bands, including Gene Krupa's, before joining Howard Rumsey's Lighthouse All Stars, with whom he worked during the latter half of the 1950s. His eventual suicide was all the more poignant for seeming so totally out of character.

****** Frank Rosolino / 5**

V.S.O.P. #16 *Rosolino; Richie Kamuca (ts); Vince Guaraldi (p); Monty Budwig (b); Stan Levey (d).* 6/57.

*****(*) Free For All**

Original Jazz Classics OJC 1763 *Rosolino; Harold Land (ts); Victor Feldman (p); Leroy Vinnegar (b); Stan Levey (d).*

*****(*) Fond Memories Of ...**

Double-Time Records DTRCD 113 *Rosolino; Louis Van Dyke (p); Jacques Schols (b); John Engels (d); Metropole Orchestra.* 6/73, 5/75.

***(*) Frank Talks

Storyville 8284 *Rosolino; Thomas Clausen (p); Bo Stief (b); Bjarne Rostvold (d).* 78.

Coming of age in Gene Krupa's post-war band, Rosolino developed a style that seemed to combine elements of bop harmony with the more durable virtues of swing. A wonderfully agile player with a tone that could be broad and humane, almost vocalized one moment, thinly abstract the next, Rosolino brings a twist of humour to almost everything he plays.

Rosolino/5 is close to the best of the available records: three Rosolino standards, mostly in modified blues forms, together with 'Thou Swell', 'They Say', the old groaner 'Cherry' and Bill Holman's topically titled 'Fallout'. Typically, almost every track involves some manipulation of time or harmony, with 'Thou Swell' falling unexpectedly in threes, and 'How Long' cast in a long, yearning line that puts maximum emphasis on the interplay between Rosolino and the superlative Kamuca, who has rarely sounded better on disc.

The OJC rounds out a fine session done for the Speciality label with some valuable alternative takes ('There Is No Greater Love', 'Chrisdee' and 'Don't Take Your Love From Me') and some great performances from the band that belie the undisciplined mood suggested by the title. Land is a more muscular soloist than Kamuca, but no less responsive to the mood of the session, and capable of some extremely delicate and detailed passage-work.

The Dutch session was recorded at the radio studios in Hilversum at a time when Rosolino was spending most of his time on this side of the Atlantic, often working with Conte Candoli. The Metropole Orchestra are featured on only three tracks, including the superlative 'Corcovado', and though there are no real quibbles about the rhythm section, they aren't entirely well adapted to Rosolino's fast, elegant later style. *Fond Memories* was a limited-edition pressing, but copies should still be in circulation, and they are well worth snapping up.

The Storvyville session, recorded less than three months before his death, finds him buoyant and persuasive on a Copenhagen club date. Ably supported by Thomas Clausen, who takes some very effective solos, he strolls through five long tunes of which the first and last, the poignantly named 'Blue Daniel' and 'Waltz For Diane', are originals. The middle cuts are probably longer than is strictly effective, with something of the Buggins's turn of solos one tends to find on sessions like this; but there is plenty for fans of the trombonist to enjoy in a record that seems to have surfaced only in 1998. Rosolino's end could hardly have been grimmer or more bitterly ironic for a man who had played on a record called *The Most Happy Fella* and who is remembered above all for his good humour; in the liner-note to *Fond Memories of* ..., J.J. Johnson speaks of his 'infectious giggle'. In the autumn of 1978, suffering from depression, he murdered his children, then took his own life.

Billy Ross

TENOR, ALTO AND SOPRANO SAXOPHONES, CLARINET

West Coast reedsman with range of big-band and studio experience.

**(*) The Sound

Milestone MCD-9227-2 *Ross; Roger Ingram (t); Dana Teboe (tb); Nick Brignola (bs); Mike Levine (p); Don Coffman (b); Duffy Jackson, Archie Pena (d); Nelson Pedron (perc); Wendy Peterson (v).* 6/94.

*** Woody

Contemporary 14079-2 *Ross; Tony Concepcion, Jeff Kievit, Ira Sullivan, Barry Ries (t); Pete Minger (flhn); John Allred, Dana Teboe (tb); Joe Barodi (btb); Ed Calle, Turk Mauro, Flip Phillips, Frank Tiberi (ts); Mike Brignola (bs); Nestor Torres (f); Mike Levine (ky); Dan Warner (g); Dennis Marks, Julio Hernandez, Rafael Valencia (b); James Martin, Ed Metz, Lee Levin, Archie Pena (d); Flaco Padron, Richard Bravo (perc); Wendy Peterson (v).* 1–3/96.

Conceived as a tribute to Stan Getz, *The Sound* struggles to come to life. Ross is an able and sincere player, but he can't do much more than try to emulate Getz's high cry – quite effective on the title-track, but earthbound elsewhere. There is a redundant xeroxing of 'Four Brothers', with Ross overdubbing all but the baritone part, and when they get to the clip-clop rhythm of 'My Old Flame' it sounds more like Getz's fusion phase than anything. A few other nice spots, but otherwise a less than distinguished return for producer Bob Weinstock, back in the studios after a 35-year break.

After Stan Getz, Woody Herman. At least Ross has the credentials, as an ex-Hermanite himself, and with Phillips and Tiberi guesting, along with a decent cast of studio pros, the tunes come off with good clout. As a record it feels like there's too much show-biz gloss and too little genuine feel, but the best of it has a stirring energy.

Florian Ross

PIANO, BANDLEADER

German pianist and composer, making records for the fledgling Naxos label.

***(*) Seasons And Places

Naxos Jazz 86029-2 *Ross; Nils Wogram (tb); Matthias Erlewein (ts); Dietmar Fuhr (b); Jochen Råckert (d).* 3/98.

*** Suite For Soprano Sax And String Orchestra

Naxos Jazz 86037 *As above, except omit Wogram, Erlewein; add David Liebman (ss), Event String Ensemble, Manfred Knaak (cond).* 3/98.

It's too early in the label's history to talk about 'Naxos' artists, but the German label has already – and wisely – invested some faith in Florian Ross. It could prove to be a key signing. One only rarely encounters a young composer as fully formed and technically assured. A student of British pianist John Taylor in Cologne, he has already garnered a string of composition prizes and commissions, many of them for large-scale pieces. The first test of his talents, though, was the small-group *Seasons And Places*.

It demonstrates both musical intelligence and swing. 'Let Me Do It (Not You)' is the kind of idea which can very rapidly descend into academic self-indulgence. Ross's short piano statements immediately make it clear that it isn't going to be another arid example of '12-tone jazz', but a genuinely idiomatic idea. Trombonist Wogram puts down the first of several strong solo statements on the album. He returns again on 'Ology Elegy / Neck Tied', and to even greater effect. Ross features himself on 'Sea Greene', one of several tunes which imply a Latin feel without slipping into south-of-the-border cliché. A debt to Taylor is repaid in 'Winteraire', an idea of exquisite delicacy that touches bases as far afield as Schubert and Bill Evans; the only solo statements are by bassist Dietmar Fuhr, who isn't particularly well recorded but sounds a formdable talent in his own right. The closing 'Hymnus (for a Sailor)' is genuinely touching.

On 'Clapham Junction', Ross shows how comfortably he has absorbed the lessons of the '60s avant-garde without surrendering to them. His ability to synthesize them with large-scale forms is evident on the *Suite For Soprano Sax And String Orchestra*. Basically a concertante piece for Liebman, it consists of an overture and seven main parts, interspersed with short instrumental interludes, which make little sense in isolation but gradually reveal a coherent relationship to the whole. Liebman is, as ever, thoughtful, slightly inward, but with enough colour and muscle in his tone to prevent his solo cadenzas from sounding fey or self-indulgent. Again Dietmar Fuhr provides strong support, and is brought forward enough in front of the strings to cement his presence. The long closing section is weaker than the 'Band Interlude' which precedes it, and though harmonically a reversed order wouldn't have made sense, there might have been some virtue in closing the album differently. Even so, this is a very impressive achievement which reveals more of itself with every hearing.

Ned Rothenberg

ALTO SAXOPHONE, BASS CLARINET, SHAKUHACHI

A charter member of the New Winds ensemble, Rothenberg has embraced many branches of the music, from Dolphy-influenced post-bop to formal composition and improvisation on solo horn. A versatile instrumentalist and one of the few Westerners to sound convincing on shakuhachi, the traditional Japanese bamboo flute.

*****(*) The Crux: Selected Solo Wind Works (1989–1992)**
Leo CD LR 187 *Rothenberg.* 12/91, 6 & 8/92.

*****(*) Port Of Entry**
Intuition INT 3249 2 *Rothenberg; Jerome Harris (g, b); Samir Chatterjee (tabla, perc).* 10/97, 3/98.

The Crux is not the first solo record Rothenberg has released. During the 1980s unaccompanied performance became what he himself calls 'home base', the *crux* at which he reassessed both technique and philosophy. His alto saxophone playing – particularly unaccompanied – bears some comparison with Anthony Braxton's but is much more precise in articulation, just as its content is rather more diffuse. By the same token, his solo bass clarinet performances have to be compared to Eric Dolphy's, and much the same judgements apply. At the centre of this recital is a meditative piece for *shakuhachi*, an instrument on which linear development is rather difficult, and sound colours, which vary with the pitches, are of paramount importance. Beautiful as it is, the significance of 'Do Omoi' lies in the extent to which these factors have influenced Rothenberg's saxophone work. The long closing item, 'Sokaku Reibo', is performed on alto and strongly suggests new approaches to the instrument. In sharp contrast, 'Maceo' is dedicated to soul singer James Brown's long-standing partner and is as brief and punchy as 'Sokaku Reibo' (which means 'the cranes in their nest') is ethereal and impressionistic. The most jazz-orientated of the pieces is 'Epistrophical Notions', dedicated to Thelonious Monk and clearly inspired by his deliberately lumpish harmonies and spasmodic rhythms.

Though *Port Of Entry* is strictly credited to the group, Sync, it is very much a Rothenberg project. His basic idea, inspired by Pat Metheny, is that creative musicians are stretched only by working in contexts, modes and idioms in which they are not adept. In this trio, he has to pit himself against the kind of complex Carnatic rhythms which are basic ABC to a player like Chatterjee but which sit oddly for a Westerner. Jerome Harris is a natural-born blues player whose work falls naturally into blues forms, and yet on 'Lost In A Blue Forest', Rothenberg has him work out of normal range by playing an acoustic bass guitar with bottleneck and pick; very effectively, too.

Jim Rotondi (born 1962)

TRUMPET, FLUGELHORN

From Butte, Montana, Rotondi played in high school jazz groups and graduated in music from North Texas State. He moved to New York in 1987, toured with Ray Charles, and started recording.

***** Introducing Jim Rotondi**
Criss Cross 1128 *Rotondi; Eric Alexander (ts); Larry Goldings (p, org); Dwayne Burno (b); Billy Drummond (d).* 12/96.

*****(*) Jim's Bop**
Criss Cross 1156 *Rotondi; Eric Alexander (ts); Harold Mabern (p); John Webber (b); Joe Farnsworth (d).* 10/97.

***** Excursions**
Criss Cross 1184 *Rotondi; Steve Davis (tb); Eric Alexander (ts); David Hazeltine (p); Peter Washington (b); Kenny Washington (d).* 12/98.

No more and no less than three excellent Criss Cross hard-bop dates. Whether such a prospect quickens the pulse or induces a yawn will be up to individual readers, since there's nothing in Rotondi's music that is either strikingly new or very different from his label companions. He doesn't write much – only six of the 24 compositions across the three discs are his, and two of those share a credit with Alexander – and his methods are based around clean, graceful improvising, with a flugelhorn sound much like Freddie Hubbard's on ballads. Alexander, his front-line cohort on all three dates, is always a fail-safe partner in the studios and three different rhythm sections each do their swinging duty – interesting to spot old-timer Mabern in fast company on *Jim's Bop*. Farnsworth really kicks the fast ones along on that date, and it's full of spark. *Excursions* is just slightly disappointing in that Davis doesn't seem to add much except extra weight (and another solo) to all of the tunes.

Charlie Rouse (1924–88)

TENOR SAXOPHONE

Rouse spent the 1960s in the company of Thelonious Monk and remained a devoted interpreter of the great man's work. He began his career with Billy Eckstine and Dizzy Gillespie and played for some time in R&B bands as well. Rouse is an immediately identifiable soloist, but his legacy of recordings as leader is patchy.

***** Jazz Modes**

Biograph 134/135 *Rouse; Julius Watkins (frhn); Gildo Mahones (p); Janet Putnam (hp); Paul Chambers, Oscar Pettiford, Martin Rivera, Paul West (b); Ron Jefferson, Art Taylor (d); Chano Pozo (perc); Eileen Gilbert (v).* 7–12/56.

*****(*) Takin' Care Of Business**

Original Jazz Classics OJC 491 *Rouse; Blue Mitchell (t); Walter Bishop (p); Earl May (b); Art Taylor (d).* 5/60.

***** Two Is One**

Strata East 660.51.012 *Rouse; George Davis, Paul Metzke (g); Calo Scott (clo); Stanley Clarke, Martin Rivera (b); David Lee (d); Airto Moreira, Azzedin Weston (perc).* 74.

****** Moment's Notice**

Storyville STCD 8268 *Rouse; Hugh Lawson (p); Bob Cranshaw (b); Ben Riley (d).* 10/77.

*****(*) Epistrophy**

32 Records 32029 *Rouse; Don Cherry (t); George Cables (p); Buddy Montgomery (vib); Jeff Chambers (b); Ralph Penland (d); Jessica Williams (p).* 10/88.

Rouse always played saxophone as if he had a cold in the head. There were those who questioned whether his slightly adenoidal, wuffling tone was ever appropriate to Thelonious Monk's music. However, Rouse became one of Monk's most loyal and stalwart supporters, and an essential part of some of Monk's finest quartet recordings. Rouse also carried the banner posthumously in his band, Sphere, and in such tribute recordings as the not entirely successful *Epistrophy*, recorded just a month before his death.

For a time in the late 1950s Rouse co-led a group called Les Jazz Modes with french horn master, Julius Watkins. The material, available again on Biograph, is more interesting as a historical artefact than as a listenable record, but there are episodes and occasional tracks which recommend it.

A decade on, it's easier to reach at least tentative conclusions. No, he wasn't the most individual player or the most trenchant soloist around but, as *Moment's Notice* amply bears out, he had a capacity for straightforward expression and built into it some thoughtful and unexpected harmonic ideas that made him, contrary to outward appearance, an ideal partner for Monk. United with Ben Riley, and with the like-minded Lawson and Cranshaw, he is a formidable leader, confidently steering the group through material by Monk (two takes of 'Well, You Needn't'), Thad Jones ('A Child Is Born', inevitably) and Shirley Scott ('Royal Love'), as well as Lawson's 'The Clucker' (also two takes) and 'The Joobobie'.

Two Is One is a pretty startling performance, and most listeners would be hard pressed to identify the source. Using two guitars and the pungent timbre of Calo Scott's cello, Rouse creates a most unusual background for solos that are weighted differently and contain fewer overt bebop references. It's a difficult performance to locate within Rouse's overall output, but there is no denying its effectiveness.

Epistrophy was his final throw, even if no one knew that at the time. It has a magisterial calm that belies the restless intensity of the material covered: 'Nutty', 'Ruby, My Dear', 'Blue Monk', 'In Walked Bud'. Rouse invests them all with the rhythmic slant that is part of the Monk inheritance. Montgomery seems to understand what is going on and plays delicious spikey vibes. Williams, still undiscovered as an artist in her own right, adds a compelling ambiguity. No one could possibly deny the little man his curtain-call. Charlie was gone by the end of the year; as these things go, *Epistrophy* was a decent send-off.

ROVA

GROUP

An American all-saxophone group, its name derived from the surname initials of the players, although Andrew Voigt has been replaced by Steve Adams (ROAA would be harder to pronounce). Though their music seeks an exact balance between composition and improvisation, they have lately been written for extensively by many different composers.

***** Favourite Street**

Black Saint 120076-2 *Larry Ochs, Bruce Ackley, Andrew Voigt, Jon Raskin (reeds).* 11/83.

*****(*) Beat Kennel**

Black Saint 120176-2 *As above.* 4/87.

ROVA's first five albums were cut over a period of 12 months, but all – save *The Bay*, listed under Andrea Centazzo's entry – are still missing in action. Along with the World Saxophone Quartet, they pioneered the all-sax ensemble as a regular and conceptually wide-ranging unit. Whereas WSQ were more concerned with updating the swinging vitality of the big-band sax section, though, ROVA sought out remoter climes, specifically building on the discoveries of the Chicago avant-garde and claiming such composer-performers as Steve Lacy and Roscoe Mitchell as major influences. Their early work can be rather hard-going: deliberately eschewing conventional notions about swing, prodding at the boundaries of sound and space, many of their 1980s records are notebooks which frequently throw up as many failures as successes.

Steve Lacy was only belatedly recognized as a major patrician influence on a wide spectrum of modern players, and ROVA's homage to him on *Favourite Street* paid overdue tribute. The bony rigour of Lacy's themes focuses ROVA's meandering, no matter how adventurous their earlier trips had been: Lacy's music is a good way to clear the head of distractions, either as listener or as performer, and in their thoughtful elaborations on seven favourite themes they clear away some of the more baroque elements of their work. The subsequent *Beat Kennel* appears to build on this: in 'The Aggregate' and 'Sportspeak', their assured rhythms and tone-colours pull them closer to a jazz tradition, and in their vibrant reading of a Braxton composition they create distinctive jazz repertory.

***** Long On Logic**

Sound Aspects SAS CD 037 *As above, except Steve Adams (reeds) replaces Voigt.* 3/89.

***** Electric Rags II**

New Albion NA027 *As above.* 3/89

***** This Time We Are Both**

New Albion NA 041 *As above.* 11/89.

***** For The Bureau Of Both**

Black Saint 120135-2 *As above.* 2–9/92.

Steve Adams replaced Andrew Voigt, but otherwise ROVA's universe remained constant: a teeming cosmos of saxophone sounds. It's still a sometimes unfriendly place, and these programmes offer little respite: the Sound Aspects session starts with tunes by Fred Frith and Henry Kaiser, but the four originals by members of the group are the most concentrated offerings, hard and effortful exercises in saxophone oratory.

Electric Rags II is properly co-credited with the composer, Alvin Curran, who devised a 30-section work, designed to be performed in a random order and played in tandem with a computerized system of electronics that makes various adaptations to each man's playing. This can work in real and deferred time. The concept, one of many such which grew up as computers and electronics were increasingly brought into new music, is absorbing but the results often seem like a jumble which the players may or may not be in charge of. There are many rich and even funny moments, but it seems like little more than an entertaining (and, at this distance, already somewhat dated) one-off.

Now that Hat's *Saxophone Diplomacy* is deleted, *This Time We Are Both* is the only evidence of ROVA's work in the former Soviet Union. A snapshot of their second excursion into the era of *glasnost*, the six pieces make up a typical concert of that time – the frolicsome 'Third Terrain', the sombre 'The Freedom Of Information' and their epic 'The Unquestioned Answer'. Held back somewhat by the fair but less than ideal sound – this is a group that needs all the sonic detail in place.

For The Bureau Of Both seems like a transitional record. Pieces such as 'Streak' take off from energetic riffs, but again one feels that their hearts are more involved in a big work like the 18-minute 'The Floater'.

*****(*) The Works Vol. 1**

Soul Note 120176-2 *As above.* 7–9/94.

This seemed like a breakthrough record which their subsequent albums have built on. Like any group of long-standing experience, ROVA knew themselves well enough by now to discover new things in old chapters. There are just three compositions here, each a lengthy exploration and each concerned with both minutiae – of timbre, tempo, texture – and long-form considerations, such as the progressive weight of a piece, its sustainable intensities and its capacity to decay. Ochs's 'When The Nation Was Sound' is both one of their most ambitious and most approachable pieces, while the themes by Jack DeJohnette and John Carter are exemplary pieces of repertory and revisionism, ROVA-style.

*****(*) The Works Vol. 2**

Black Saint 120186-2 *As above.* 8/95.

*****(*) John Coltrane's Ascension**

Black Saint 120180-2 *As above, except add Dave Douglas, Raphe Malik (t); Glenn Spearman (ts); Chris Brown (p); Lisle Ellis (b); Donald Robinson (d).* 12/95.

It might seem churlish to deny the group their unreserved fourth star, but the quality of their records keeps going up and it's more an encouraging sign that a group of some 20 years' standing can still suggest their best is yet to come. *The Works Volume Two* consists of three long works: Tim Berne's 'The Visible Man' is solid sax-band repertory, but the two stronger pieces are Fred Ho's indignant-to-explosive 'Beyond Columbus And Capitalism', an intensely vivid piece of revolutionary rhetoric in sound, and Jon Raskin's fairly monumental 'Appearances Aren't Always What They Seem'. While the Ho piece has its fallibilities, Raskin knows the virtues of the band so well that his piece musters an almost visionary sweep, passing from bright contrapuntalism to fantastical convolutions to a moving coda that is among their most sheerly beautiful moments.

The sheer audacity of trying to re-create 'Ascension' in its entirety is justified by the uplifting result. Augmented by a rhythm section (Ochs takes a solo spin with them on 'Welcome', to introduce the record), the group employ Coltrane's theme but take the inevitable departures with both the solos and what seems to be spontaneous counterpoint. Trane and his men were taking early steps in a new world; these players have a fund of preconceived knowledge. The result is a realization which makes up in assured power what it might lack in 'pure' freedom. Douglas is a crucial element, injecting a lyrical passage before Raskin's almost brutal alto solo, but everyone plays their part. Bravo!

****** Bingo**

Victo CD 056 *Bruce Ackley, Steve Adams, Larry Ochs, Jon Raskin (saxes).* 9/96.

They've become a great repertory group – the five pieces here are from commissions involving Lindsay Cooper, Barry Guy and Fred Frith, plus one of Larry Ochs's most colourful originals – and they are, if not exactly reinventing themselves, at least reconsidering how they respond to each other, how the balance of their group can change, how they sound when they play soft or loud, how they start and end a piece, and what they can do to make their music new *and* better. The result is a considered and exceptionally satisfying record which has as much freshness in it as detail and maturity. Who's to say they won't be even better, twenty years hence?

*****(*) The Works Vol. 3**

Black Saint 120196-2 *As above.* 3–7/97.

Studio commissions from Muhal Richard Abrams and Robin Holcomb and a live-in-Turkey original by Steve Adams make up this third volume. Holcomb's 'Laredo' is in the Copland tradition and Abrams's 'Quartet #1' is in the modern Chicagoan tradition. Adams's 'The Gene Pool' is a classic ROVA situation, initiatives and responsibilities passed around the quartet quickly and creatively. More than good enough to stand beside the others.

Keith Rowe

GUITAR

Guitarist and founder-member of AMM, Rowe is as much a sound-sculptor as an improviser.

****** A Dimension Of Perfectly Ordinary Reality**
Matchless MRCD19 *Rowe (g solo).* 89.

***** Dial: Log-Rhythm**
Matchless MRCD36 *Rose; Jeffrey Morgan (as).* 97.

There has been an intermittent but often heated debate in British improvisation about 'instrumentalism', about whether music is a function of specific and idiomatically delimited technical resources or whether musical instruments should be an invisible and ultimately dispensable conduit for sound. Keith Rowe – and his colleagues in AMM – work at the sharp end of the debate. To describe him as a 'guitarist' is misleadingly simplistic. Rowe's deconstruction and reinvention of the guitar is one of the most radical sound strategies in contemporary music. He plays the instrument flat on a table and uses a range of articulation devices and electronic interventions to shape the sound – or, rather, to let the sound shape itself.

It's virtually impossible to describe what he does in terms of conventional technique, beyond saying that both these performances are thoughtful, intense and often very beautiful; above all, like the music of AMM, it is quite without expressive ego. The duo with Morgan doesn't strike us as the best starting-point for listeners who have no previous history with either Rowe or AMM. The saxophonist is emphatically his own man and the record is very much a meeting of equals. For a more revealing insight into how Keith Rowe functions, the earlier album is definitive, a whirling, almost violent foray into pure sound. Make some time for it.

Jimmy Rowles (1918–96)

PIANO, VOCAL

He arrived in Los Angeles in 1940 and worked in big bands and then as an accompanist, to singers such as Billie Holiday and Peggy Lee. A great deal of session-work, often uncredited, before a move to New York in 1973, where he became better known as a soloist and trio leader. Returned to California in the '80s but made occasional appearances elsewhere.

***** Our Delight**
VSOP 99 *Rowles; Max Bennett, Chuck Berghofer (b); Nick Martinis, Larry Bunker (d).* 4/68.

*****(*) Subtle Legend Vol. 1**
Storyville STCD *Rowles; Monty Budwig (b); Donald Bailey (d).* 1–10/72.

*****(*) Subtle Legend Vol. 2**
Storyville STCD 8295 *As above.* 1/72.

*****(*) Music's The Only Thing That's On My Mind**
Audiophile ACD-188 *Rowles; George Mraz (b).* 11/76.

****** Grandpa's Vibrato**
Black & Blue BB 200.2 *Rowles; Jimmy Woode (b); Bobby Durham (d).* 7/79.

His vast experience with both big bands and vocalists gave Rowles a matchless repertoire of songs, and since the early 1970s he appeared as a significant figure in his own right. For a man who appeared on so many recording dates, there is still very little Rowles in visible print, and Columbia have deleted his classic *The Peacocks* with Stan Getz. But some reissues and discoveries have appeared since our last edition, and everything by this humorous, profound musician is welcome. *Our Delight* resurrects a tape of some old sessions at The Carriage House in Burbank with a couple of sympathetic rhythm sections. Jimmy is in prime mischief-making form, turning 'You Say You Care' into 'Straight No Chaser', making an oddball bossa nova out of 'America The Beautiful' and lavishing affection on 'Moon Of Manakoora'. The sound is pretty variable and the crowd occasionally break in, but it's a delicious record if you can listen through the distractions.

The two volumes of *Subtle Legend* are in much better sound, emanating from sets in Glendale and Los Angeles. The second disc has more vocals ('Nina Never Knew' and 'That Sunday, That Summer' are particularly hard to resist) and Rowles visits Shorter, Strayhorn and his other favourites. Budwig and Bailey are reserved, compared to the rhythm section on the Black & Blue disc, but they suit the acquiescent mood of the music.

Music's The Only Thing That's On My Mind is a delightful duo with Mraz, who plays respectfully but with appropriate sass. Rowles liked Wayne Shorter's tunes and he does four of them here – with 'Tell It Like It Is' and 'Running Brook' two notable rarities. His own waltz, 'The Lady In The Corner', is given the perfect reading. His vocals may be an acquired taste but don't take much acquiring.

Grandpa's Vibrato is a candidate for Rowles's best trio record. Woode and Durham are unfussily swinging and the bassist's big sound is a fine assist. The whole trio get well treated by the microphones – which is a surprise since it was recorded in an open-air studio. Rowles's idiosyncratic way with time, chords and dynamics makes every one of these tracks a head-turning surprise, from the marvellous opening treatment of Mitchell Parish's 'Evenin'' to the lubricious rendition of Jimmie Lunceford's 'Honey Keep Your Mind On Me'.

***** Sometimes I'm Happy, Sometimes I'm Blue**
Orange Blue 003 *Rowles; Harry 'Sweets' Edison (t); Stacey Rowles (t, flhn); Ray Brown (b); Donald Bailey (d); Clementine (v).* 6/88.

***** Trio**
Capri 74009 *Rowles; Red Mitchell (b); Donald Bailey (d).* 8/89.

***** Remember When**
Mastermix CHECD 11 *Rowles; Eric Von Essen (b).* 89.

***** Lilac Time**
Kokopelli 1297 *As above.* 4/94.

Rowles recorded through the 1980s and, while none of these records is less than good, it must be said that the energy level on some of them is occasionally negligible. The pianist's talent for reordering tunes and imparting felicities hadn't diminished, but he took things much easier. His trumpet-playing daughter, Stacey, takes a useful guest-role on some sessions, playing agreeable solos which recall a more boppish Harry 'Sweets' Edison, whose own appearance on the Orange Blue CD underlines the comparison, although the two never play together. *Trio* restores some of the impishness that is an essential in Rowles's best music, as he investigates such hoary themes as 'Dreamer's Lullaby' and 'You People Need Music'. Red Mitchell, who plays on three of the above sessions, was a favourite companion, and his voluminous sound is a wry partner for Rowles's particular tale-spinning; Bailey, though, is less in tune and occasionally sounds indifferent to the conversation.

Remember When has some delightful music. The forgotten gem this time is 'Just Like A Butterfly'; the voice comes out on 'Looking Back', and there is a version of Carl Perkins's 'Grooveyard' which is an object-lesson in swinging at a slow tempo. It's mostly just Jimmy browsing through some old memories, and making them worth remembering. Despite indifferent health, he continued to play into the 1990s, and *Lilac Time* is a typical Rowles date: gentle, reflective, with a little iron running through it and a nostalgic's taste for buried treasure.

Gonzalo Rubalcaba (born 1963)

PIANO, KEYBOARDS

A young Cuban émigré pianist, Rubalcaba created a minor sensation with his early appearances and was quickly signed up by Blue Note, for whom he has recorded through the 1990s.

****(*) Discovery: Live At Montreux**

Blue Note 795478-2 *Rubalcaba; Charlie Haden (b); Paul Motian (d).* 7/90.

****** The Blessing**

Blue Note 797197-2 *As above, except Jack DeJohnette (d) replaces Motian.* 5/91.

***** Diz**

Blue Note 830490-2 *Rubalcaba; Ron Carter (b); Julio Barreto (d).* 12/93.

***** Antiguo**

Blue Note 837717-2 *Rubalcaba; Reynaldo Melian (t); Felipe Cabrera (b); Julio Barreto (d); Giovanni Hidalgo, Dagoberto Gonzalez (perc); Lazaro Ros, Maridalia Hernandez (v).* 6/95–7/96.

***** Inner Voyage**

Blue Note 499241-2 *Rubalacaba; Michael Brecker (ts); Jeff Chambers (b); Ignacio Berroa (d).* 11/98.

Rubalcaba is among the most recent and perhaps the most singular of those Cuban musicians who have made an impact on the American jazz scene of late. While he plays with as much grandstanding power as his countrymen, there is also a compensating lightness of touch which one sometimes misses in the perpetually ebullient tone of most Cuban jazz. However, *Discovery*, a record of his sensational debut appearance at the Montreux Festival of 1990, suffers from an excess of tumult which finally makes the record wearisome, impressively played though it all is. From the first terrifically overheated workout on Monk's 'Well You Needn't', it sounds as if Rubalcaba is out to impress at any cost, and Motian and Haden can only anchor him as best they can. Much exhilaration, but not a record to play often.

The subsequent studio record, *The Blessing*, is a huge step forward. The pianist rations his outbursts to a handful and instead negotiates a thoughtful but no less compelling way through a delightful programme: Haden's 'Sandino' emerges with just the right note of troubled dignity, 'Giant Steps' is reharmonized and made new through brilliant use of repetition, DeJohnette's charming 'Silver Hollow' rivals the composer's own version, and 'The Blessing' and 'Blue In Green' remodel Coleman and Evans. Best of all, perhaps, is a beautifully chiselled treatment of 'Besame Mucho' which eliminates all sense of kitsch that the tune may possess, suggesting instead a flinty sort of romanticism. Rubalcaba's touch and finesse are marvellous throughout, and DeJohnette is clearly the ideal drummer for the situation, his unassuming virtuosity meeting all the challenges head on.

Diz is Rubalcaba's 'pure' bebop album, nine themes from the heartland of the repertory done partly as a tribute to Dizzy Gillespie. Appropriately enough, perhaps, it is not much like any traditional bebop record, infused with suggestions of Latin polyrhythms even when those rhythms aren't always directly stated. The dark colours of, say, 'Bouncing With Bud' are the elements that dominate. Yet this is all too knowing a record: Carter's elegant lines work well, but Barreto's drumming is aggravatingly ingenious, and it spurs the pianist on to some pointlessly clever improvising. For all his dazzle, Rubalcaba can be hard to warm to.

Some of his Blue Notes have been deleted since our last edition, but there are a couple of new ones, too. *Antiguo* is another mightily ambitious undertaking, this time a fusion of his core Cuban-American jazz, a trio of bata drummers, an Afro-Cuban choir, the Dominican pop diva, Maridalia Hernandez, and the almost shamanic chanting of Lazaro Ros. A heady mixture, which Rubalacaba's battery of keyboards – 11 synths and samplers are credited – adds even more spice and/or bulk to. Some of this is reminiscent of Chick Corea's *My Spanish Heart* (from 1976 – hardly a forward-looking music to cite!), with the babble of synths mixed with the voices to often unconvincing effect, and it's hard to comprehend which principles Rubalcaba is being faithful to: it doesn't sound like any useful development out of the ingredients which he is stirring together. That said, the record is undeniably very pretty and songful a lot of the time.

Inner Voyage is yet another side of this interesting if frustrating talent. Played often at a slow-to-mid tempo, this is trio jazz of surpassing restraint, a somewhat surprising feat of concentration from this frequently explosive musician. Brecker comes in on two tracks and puts matters on edge somewhat, but more typical is the almost tortoise-like pace chosen for 'Here's That Rainy Day'.

Roy Rubenstein

TROMBONE

English traditional trombonist working with contemporaries from both sides of the Atlantic in his Chicago Hot Six.

***** Shout 'Em!**

Delmark DE-227 *Rubenstein; Bob Nabors (c); Norrie Cox (cl); Jack Kuncl (bj); Dick Pierre (b); Ken Lowenstine (d); Katherine Davis (v).* 12/93–1/94.

Somehow this expatriate 'bone man has ended up leading his Chicago Hot Six on that city's most eminent local label. Traditional music played without a trace of self-consciousness, though not necessarily the better for it: the dynamic is unvaryingly even and some of the tempos are a bit too gentlemanly. 'Shout 'Em Aunt Tillie', a choice piece of early Ellington, gets a splendid treatment, and 'Pontchartrain Blues' counts as rarely-heard Jelly Roll Morton. Katherine Davis sings on four numbers and her surprisingly small, intimate voice suits the situation. Excellent recording.

Roswell Rudd (born 1935)

TROMBONE, TRUMPET, FRENCH HORN, VOCALS

Born in Connecticut, Rudd made his professional debut with Eli's Chosen Six and, despite his adherence to the avant-garde, his approach always suggested a return to the primordial simplicities of early jazz. His trombone style recalls the more expressionist methods of an earlier age, using slurs and growls, blustering swing and a big, sultry tone.

**** Flexible Flyer

Black Lion BLCD 760215 *Rudd; Hod O'Brien (p); Arild Andersen (b); Barry Altschul (d); Sheila Jordan (v).* 3/74.

It has been a matter of intense frustration that Rudd has made so few records since his work with the New York Art Quartet and Archie Shepp in the 1960s announced a marvellously vivid and unpredictable spirit in the new jazz of the period, and certainly one of the most imaginative trombone players since J.J. Johnson. Only the German, Albert Mangelsdorff, has made a comparable impact on the unfashionable horn, though Mangelsdorff's star is, if anything, more securely positioned above the horizon. One of the difficulties with Rudd is that he has often preferred to work with other leaders, such as Cecil Taylor, or the 'comeback' recordings made under the leadership of Allen Lowe. Much of his best work of recent years has been in the company of the British saxophonist, Elton Dean.

The wonderful *Flexible Flyer* returned to catalogue just too late for our last edition, which was a matter of great regret, for this has long been one of our favourite modern-jazz records. It begins, memorably, with low, chesty rumbles from Rudd, pitched against Jordan's almost whispered vocal on 'What Are You Doing The Rest Of Your Life?' and it isn't until two and a half minutes have passed that the rest of the band come in, lending the Michel Legrand classic an unexpected emotional pitch somewhere between despair and euphoria. Herbie Hancock's 'Maiden Voyage' uses the doubled front line to equally powerful effect. Jordan's wordless singing is reminiscent of Norma Winstone's but less pure in tonality and closer to the swaying, pitch-bending passion of Omme Kholsoum. As throughout the set, Hod O'Brien's comping is mixed very far up, almost swamping the trombone entirely. Rudd is more prominent on his own 'Suh Blah Blah Buh Sibi' (on which he also sings the Arabic-sounding title-phrase), but it's his slide work over the staccato, two-part beat which really catches the attention. It's only from this point on the album onwards that he can be said to solo in the conventional sense. Dedicated to producer Moselle Galbraith, 'Moselle Variations' is a weird stop-start trilogy of free-jazz gestures courageously blended with orthodox swing. The remaining track is O'Brien's mournful 'Waltzing In The Sagebrush', a tune that may well draw on long-gone nights in front of the radio. The pianist was a boyhood friend of Rudd's, reunited years later to create this astonishing record, which looks forward as recklessly as it indulges a gentle nostalgia.

***(*) Regeneration

Soul Note 121054 *Rudd; Steve Lacy (ss); Misha Mengelberg (p); Kent Carter (b); Han Bennink (d).* 6/82.

Regeneration is very satisfying although, for a demonstration of Rudd's latter-day style, Enrico Rava's *Quartet* album for ECM is a more representative and comprehensive example. Like the two CIMP sessions (titles self-explanatory), it's a tribute to the pianist and composer with whom Rudd worked in the early 1960s. For 35 years since Nichols's death in 1963, Rudd has been the keeper of the spirit, campaigning with Steve Lacy and an increasing constituency of players against Nichols's marginalization. Lacy and Rudd used to work together in a unit which performed only Thelonious Monk material, and so it's no surprise to hear three Monk tunes here alongside the same number of Nichols pieces.

**** The Unheard Herbie Nichols: Volume 1

CIMP 133 *Rudd; Greg Millar (g, perc); John Bacon Jr (d, vib).* 11/96.

***(*) The Unheard Herbie Nichols: Volume 2

CIMP 146 *As above.* 11/96.

The CIMP session was a chance to concentrate on Nichols entirely, and to dig out some of the most obscure material in his legacy. There are some surprises in instrumentation as well. On 'Some Wandering Bushmen', Rudd played trumpet on the initial take before reprising the same tune on his more familiar horn. On the long 'Jamaica' (Volume 1) he plays percussion, and elsewhere on the same disc gets out the little-used mellophone. The biggest surprise of all, though, comes at the end of Volume 2, when Roswell sings the lyric to 'Vacation Blues'.

Most of this material is genuinely unknown and unheard, even to those who do know 'Shuffle Montgomery' and 'Lady Sings The Blues'. It seems extraordinary that tunes like 'Freudian Frolics', the far from lightweight 'Tee Dum Tee Dee', 'Prancin' Pretty Woman', and 'Karna Kanji' are not in the wider repertoire. The trio is well balanced and very responsive, with Millar taking part at least of the accompanist's role. He and Bacon duet on 'Dream Time', leaving Rudd to play 'One Twilight' and 'Passing Thoughts' unaccompanied, the latter a long, virtuosic performance that must count as one of his most extraordinary statements on record. These are important statements, largely because of the slighted legacy of one of the great jazz composers, but also because Rudd himself is so badly under-represented in the catalogues. Anyone who has admired either man will be drawn to these and, while we favour the first volume, both are strongly recommended.

Hilton Ruiz (born 1952)

PIANO, ORGAN, KEYBOARDS

Ruiz got an early start: he was playing at Carnegie Hall at the age of eight. He played in Latin and soul groups as a teenager and spent four years with Roland Kirk from 1973, as well as stints with a wide range of leaders. His own groups and records began to be noticed in the 1980s, via his charismatic blending of Latin feel with undiluted post-bop.

*****(*) Piano Man**

Steeplechase SCCD 31036 *Ruiz; Buster Williams (b); Billy Higgins (d).* 7/75.

***** New York Hilton**

Steeplechase SCCD 31094 *Ruiz; Hakim Jamil, Steve Solder (d).* 2/77.

*****(*) Manhattan Mambo**

Telarc CD 83322 *Ruiz; Charlie Sepulveda (t); Papo Vasquez (tb); David Sanchez (ts, perc); Andy Gonzalez (b, bell); Ignacio Berroa (d, perc); Joe Gonzalez, Giovanni Hidalgo (perc).* 4/92.

*****(*) Heroes**

Telarc CD 83338 *As above, except add Steve Turre (tb), Carlos Patato Valdes, Tito Puente (perc); omit Vasquez.* 11/93.

***** Live At Birdland**

Candid CCD 79532 *Ruiz; David Sanchez, Peter Brainin (ts); Andy Gonzalez (b); Steve Berrios (d); Giovanni Hidalgo (perc).* 6/92.

Ruiz's desire to give jazz a Latin accent runs a little deeper than the usual South-of-the-Border trimmings. Born in Puerto Rico, he has a profound understanding of an impressive range of popular forms – samba, *soca*, *clave* – and makes them an integral element in his writing and reworking of standards and classics. *Piano Man* is perhaps Ruiz's best album; it's certainly his most impressive trio group, with Williams's singing bass and Higgins's tuneful drums complementing his own two-handed style. 'Straight Street' and 'Giant Steps' are the most ambitious (and successful) tracks. Strongly recommended. *New York Hilton* is solid but basically nothing like as good, lacking the finesse of the earlier disc.

There is a bit of a hiatus in the middle of the story here, because Ruiz's fine series of Novus albums has been lost with his departure from the label: check remaindered racks for the excellent likes of *Doin' It Right* and *A Moment's Notice*. His two albums for Telarc carry on in a similar vein. *Manhattan Mambo* – the title is a typical Ruiz nod to his background blending in with his professional foreground – lines up three incandescent horn players, all steeped in the idiom, to duck and dive over the rhythms and the thump of Ruiz's piano. *Heroes* offers a series of nods to Rollins, Parker, Roach, Davis and the like, although one of the champs in question, Tito Puente, actually plays on the date. The music is more obviously in bebop heartland as far as the material's concerned, but Ruiz manages to make it a convincing small-group extension of Dizzy Gillespie's Afro-Cuban music and, with Turre arriving to bolster the horns further, the group has enormous panache from the blistering 'Sonny's Mood' onwards.

What the band on *Live At Birdland* cries out for is a brass player to replace one of the two rather anonymous saxophones – for some reason, Sanchez seems to have been having an off-night. They are really effective only on the last two tunes, 'On Green Dolphin Street' and Wayne Shorter's 'Footprints'. Even the specially written 'Blues For Two Tenors' doesn't have much punch. Ruiz himself is playing very well, with lots of fire, and the recording is very expertly balanced.

***** Island Eyes**

RMM Tropijazz RMD 82042 *Ruiz; Jon Faddis (t); John Stubblefield (ts); Dave Valentin (f); Bernd Schoenhart (g); Tito Puente (vib, perc); John Benitez (b); Ignacio Berroa (d); Milton Cardona, Richie Flores (perc).* 97.

**** Rhythm In The House**

RMM Tropijazz RMD 82255 *Ruiz; Ruben Rodriguez (b); Tito Puente (vib, perc); Richie Flores (perc).* 97–98.

Island Eyes has its moments – a fierce treatment of Sam Jones's 'Unit Seven', a lushly extravagant 'Body And Soul' – but the glossy production and ill-judged treatments of 'Stand By Me' and 'Gee Baby Ain't I Good To You' suggest that Ruiz was stuck for a way to go with this one. It goes almost disastrously wrong on the next one, *Rhythm In The House*. This sounds like Hilton's bid for the smooth-jazz playlist, all electric keyboards, static rhythms and a failed attempt to bring Latin polyrhythm to synthetic situations. When Puente comes in for the very last track, 'Michael's Mambo', and Ruiz goes back to the piano, they nearly salvage something – but much too late.

Howard Rumsey (born 1917)

BASS

Studied in Los Angeles, then formed a small group with Stan Kenton and subsequently joined the Kenton orchestra. Formed the Lighthouse All Stars, a revolving group of West Coast leading lights, which performed regularly at the Hermosa Beach Lighthouse Club, then promoted other Californian concerts in the '50s and '60s.

*****(*) Sunday Jazz A La Lighthouse**

Original Jazz Classics OJC 151 *Rumsey; Shorty Rogers (t); Milt Bernhart (tb); Jimmy Giuffre, Bob Cooper (ts); Hampton Hawes, Frank Patchen (p); Shelly Manne (d).* 7/52–2/53.

***** Volume 3**

Original Jazz Classics OJC 266 *As above, except add Rolf Ericson (t), Frank Rosolino (tb), Bud Shank (as, f), Herb Geller (as), Max Roach, Stan Levey (d), Carlos Vidal, Jack Costanza (perc).* 7/52–8/56.

****** Sunday Jazz A La Lighthouse Vol. 2**

Original Jazz Classics OJC 972 *As above, except add Chet Baker (t), Russ Freeman, Lorraine Geller, Claude Williamson (p); omit Rosolino, Levey, Vidal, Costanza, Geller, Hawes, Patchen.* 3–9/53.

***** Oboe / Flute**

Original Jazz Classics OJC 154 *Rumsey; Bob Cooper (ob, cor); Bud Shank (f, af); Buddy Collette (f); Claude Williamson, Sonny Clark (p); Max Roach, Stan Levey (d).* 2/54–9/56.

***** In The Solo Spotlight**

Original Jazz Classics OJC 451 *Rumsey; Conte Candoli, Stu Williamson (t); Frank Rosolino (tb); Bob Enevoldsen (vtb); Bud Shank, Lennie Niehaus (as); Bob Cooper, Richie Kamuca (ts); Bob Gordon, Pepper Adams (bs); Claude Williamson, Dick Shreve (p); Stan Levey (d).* 8/54–3/57.

***** Volume 6**

Original Jazz Classics OJC 386 *Rumsey; Conte Candoli (t); Frank Rosolino (tb); Stu Williamson (vtb); Bud Shank (as); Bob Cooper (ts); Claude Williamson (p); Stan Levey (d).* 12/54–3/55.

***** Lighthouse At Laguna**

Original Jazz Classics OJC 406 *Rumsey; Frank Rosolino (tb); Bud Shank (as, f); Bob Cooper (ts); Claude Williamson, Hampton Hawes (p); Barney Kessel (g); Red Mitchell (b); Shelly Manne, Stan Levey (d).* 6/55.

***** Music For Lighthousekeeping**

Original Jazz Classics OJC 636 *Rumsey; Conte Candoli (t); Frank Rosolino (tb); Bob Cooper (ts); Sonny Clark (p); Stan Levey (d).* 10/56.

***** Mexican Passport**

Contemporary 14077-2 *As for OJC 151, 266, 406 and 636 above.* 52–56.

Rumsey was of no major significance as a bassist, but he was a canny organizer, and his Lighthouse All Stars – the name which all these CDs go under – offered the pick of the West's best in the mid-'50s. Their Sunday afternoon concerts are still talked about by veterans of the Hermosa Beach scene, effectively 12-hour jam sessions that started in the afternoon and went on into the small hours. There are live sessions on OJCs 151, 972 and 406 (though the latter was cut at Laguna Beach) and part of OJC 154; the rest are studio dates. To catch the excitement of these sessions, the best is the recent arrival, *Sunday Jazz A La Lighthouse Vol. 2*: a buzzing crowd, bandstands full of the hottest players; with 25 minutes of previously unreleased material, this one's a best buy. Sound is at times more atmospheric than accurate, but it's a terrific document of those sessions. The first volume is also excellent, with some fine work by Hawes, but the *Laguna* set is more like a formal concert, with a guest spot by Kessel and two tracks by the Hawes–Mitchell–Manne trio.

The studio dates are more in the familiar West Coast language and are rather more efficiently styled. Considering the stellar line-up, *In The Solo Spotlight* is a shade disappointing, with too many of the features emerging as glib showcases. While none of the others really stands out, followers of the style will find much to satisfy, not least in the consistently superb drumming by Manne and Levey. *Mexican Passport* compiles the various Latinesque tracks which the band made across their albums.

Gösta Rundqvist

PIANO

From Iggesund, in northern Sweden, Rundqvist worked in local bands, formed a jazz-rock outfit called Splash and joined the Sandvik Big Band in 1979. His current direction seems to be in a modal post-bop setting.

***** Until We Have Faces**

Sittel SITCD 9212 *Rundqvist; Krister Andersson (ts); Sture Akerberg, Yasuhito Mori (b); Peter Ostlund (d).* 5/94.

Rundqvist's playing is a gracious synthesis of modern styles – Evans, Jarrett, Corea – touched by a vein of introspection that sounds like his own, best heard here on his pensive original 'Northern Light', done as a piano solo. The long programme is divided between solos, duo with bass, trios and the rhythm section with Andersson, nicely varied and unpretentiously delivered. Sometimes the music ambles along without much consequence; but an interpretation like 'Tenderly', shimmeringly delivered at a very slow tempo, ought to delight anyone with ears. Impeccable studio sound.

Jimmy Rushing (1903–72)

VOCAL

Raised in Oklahoma, Rushing started as a pianist, but began singing and making a name for himself in that capacity around the South-West of the USA in the mid-'20s. His greatest successes were with the Count Basie orchestra of the '30s and '40s, his huge physical presence partnering the great voice. A gentle and genial man, he worked right up until his death from leukaemia in 1972.

***** Mr Five By Five**

Topaz TPZ 1019 *Rushing; orchestras of Walter Page, Bennie Moten and Count Basie.* 11/29–4/42.

Jimmy Rushing began recording in 1929, with Bennie Moten, and carried on for 40-plus years. Many of his finest performances are with Count Basie and are listed under the bandleader's name, but this collection creams off some of his best features for Bennie Moten and Basie. It's useful to have the original takes of Rushing favourites like 'Sent For You Yesterday' and 'Harvard Blues' all in one place. That said, the remastering is erratic – not one of the best discs in the usually solid Topaz series – and the formulaic nature of his Basie discs makes an unbroken sequence less appetizing. With his Vanguard recordings back out in the cold, though, this is as good a place as any to start hearing this great blues–jazz man. *Jimmy Rushing Swings The Blues* (CDS RPCD 637) covers similar ground.

****** Rushing Lullabies**

Columbia CK 6511 *Rushing; Buck Clayton, Emmett Berry, Bernie Glow, Mel Davis, Doc Cheatham (t); Dicky Wells, Vic Dickenson, Urbie Green, Frank Rehak (tb); Rudy Powell, Earl Warren (as); Coleman Hawkins, Buddy Tate (ts); Danny Bank (bs); Nat Pierce, Ray Bryant (p); Sir Charles Thompson (org);*

Danny Barker, Skeeter Best (g); Milt Hinton, Gene Ramey (b); Jo Jones, Osie Johnson (d). 2/58–6/59.

Coupling the original albums *Rushing Lullabies* and *Little Jimmy Rushing And The Big Brass*, this is a connoisseur's set of jazz singing, one of the ripest and most enjoyable examples of Rushing on record from what should have been a period of great success for him. These albums have never been widely known, but they date from a vintage period of mainstream playing, the band almost peerless in its personnel with a host of strong soloists headed by Hawkins and Tate. Some of the material dates back to the original jazz age, some – 'Good Rockin' Tonight', handled with a sort of smiling tolerance – a nod to rock'n'roll, but Rushing sings all of it with his singular blend of blues and jazz in a serene counterpoint that survives the years. A model reissue in excellent sound.

***** Who Was It Sang That Song?**
New World 80510-2 *Rushing; Buck Clayton (t); Dickie Wells (tb); Julian Dash (ts); Sir Charles Thompson (p); Eugene Ramey (b); Jo Jones (d).* 10/67.

***** Gee Baby, Ain't I Good To You?**
New World 80530-2 *As above.* 10/67.

Recorded in a studio that had once been a hotel ballroom, this 'jazz party' is a boisterous affair. The stellar personnel suggest a special occasion, but the pretty awful recording (not helped by the fact that the original stereo masters were destroyed, and the tracks were reconstructed from indifferent mono tapes) and the sometimes ramshackle playing are discouraging. Even so, Rushing is indomitable, Clayton is elegant, Wells idiosyncratic and the unlikely presence of Dash is a surprising plus. The best of it could have been boiled down to a single CD, but there is little enough of LP-era Rushing available to make every surviving disc worth having.

***** Every Day I Have The Blues**
Impulse! 547967-2 *Rushing; Clark Terry (t); Dickie Wells (tb); Buddy Tate, Bob Ashton (ts); Hank Jones, Shirley Scott (org); Dave Frishberg (p); Hugh McCracken, Wally Richardson, Kenny Burrell (g); George Duvivier, Bob Bushnell (b); Grady Tate, Joe Marshall (d).* 67–68.

Although Jimmy himself remains in fine voice, this is a misconceived Bob Thiele production. It couples two Impulse! albums which mixed together some genuine blues with faddish tunes such as 'Berkeley Campus Blues' (which complains about student sit-ins) and some attempted funky stuff from the guitarists. The imperturbable Rushing carries on regardless, but this was hardly his ideal setting, although there are compensations in the cameos from Terry, Wells and Tate.

George Russell (born 1923)

COMPOSER, BANDLEADER, PIANO, ORGAN

George Russell's significance within jazz is rather tough to evaluate. For many years he was almost entirely marginalized by the critical and commercial establishment. After graduating in his native Cincinnati, he suffered a long illness during which he overturned much of what he and his teachers had thought about harmonics. Russell is responsible for what remains the most significant single theoretical treatise written about the music. The Lydian Chromatic Concept of Tonal Organization, completed in the early 1950s, was the direct source of the modal or scalar experiments of John Coltrane and Miles Davis. Russell spent most of the 1960s in Europe, reworking his treatise and writing little music. Recognition has been slow and hard-won.

****** Jazz Workshop**
RCA Victor 74321 591422 *Russell; Art Farmer (t); Hal McKusick (as, f); Bill Evans (p); Barry Galbraith (g); Milt Hinton (b); Teddy Kotick (b); Joe Harris, Osie Johnson, Paul Motian (d).* 3–12/56.

****** Stratusphunk**
Original Jazz Classics OJC 232 *Russell; Alan Kiger (t); Dave Baker (tb); Dave Young (as); Chuck Israels (b); Joe Hunt (d).* 10/60.

****** Ezz-thetics**
Original Jazz Classics OJC 070 *Russell; Don Ellis (t); Dave Baker (tb); Eric Dolphy (as, bcl); Steve Swallow (b); Joe Hunt (d).* 5/61.

*****(*) The Stratus Seekers**
Original Jazz Classics OJC 365 *Russell; Dave Baker, Don Ellis (t); John Pierce (as); Paul Plummer (ts); Steve Swallow (b); Joe Hunt (d).* 1/62.

***** The Outer View**
Original Jazz Classics OJC 616 *Russell; Garnett Brown (tb); Paul Plummer (ts); Steve Swallow (b); Pete LaRoca (d); Sheila Jordan (v).* 8/62.

However important Russell's theories are, they are even now not securely understood. Sometimes falsely identified with the original Greek Lydian mode, *The Lydian Chromatic Concept* is not the same at all. In diatonic terms, it represents the progression F to F on the piano's white keys; it also confronts the diabolic tritone, the *diabolus in musica*, which had haunted Western composers from Bach to Beethoven. Russell's conception assimilated modal writing to the extreme chromaticism of modern music. By converting chords into scales and overlaying one scale on another, it allowed improvisers to work in the hard-to-define area between non-tonality and polytonality. Like all great theoreticians, Russell worked analytically rather than synthetically, basing his ideas on how jazz *actually was*, not on how it could be made to conform with traditional principles of Western harmony. Working from within jazz's often tacit organizational principles, Russell's fundamental concern was the relationship between formal scoring and improvisation, giving the first the freedom of the second, freeing the second from being literally esoteric, 'outside' some supposed norm.

Russell's theories also influenced his own composition. 'A Bird In Igor's Yard' , a celebrated early piece, was a (rather too) self-conscious attempt to ally bebop and Stravinsky – it was also a young and slightly immature work – but it pointed the way forward. Russell's music always sounds both familiar and unsettlingly alien. His versions of staples like Charlie Parker's 'Au Privave', Thelonious Monk's equally precocious 'Round Midnight', and Miles Davis's almost oriental 'Nardis' on *Ezzthetics* create new areas for the soloists to explore; in Don Ellis and Eric Dolphy he has players particularly responsive to expansions of the harmonic language (Dolphy in particular preferred to work the inner space of a piece, rather than to go 'out'). 'Ezz-thetic' first appeared on the classic 1956 *Jazz Workshop* sessions, now restored to CD. It is one of the key pieces in an astonishing collection, including several pieces that stand as almost unique avenues of thought in the jazz language: 'Night Sound', 'Round Johnny Rondo', 'Knights Of The Steamtable' and 'Concerto For Billy The Kid', the latter including one of Bill Evans's most remarkable solos on record.

As a very good start to a Russell collection there's a strong case to be made for *Ezz-thetics*, with its fine Dolphy contributions (coincidentally or not, the year of the saxophonist's death also marked the beginning of Russell's long exile in Europe and a mutual alienation from the American scene). But all these early Russells, with the exception of the slightly less achieved *The Outer View*, are indispensable. His regular sextet is responsible for most of the music on the various OJCs, and the improvising on *Stratusphunk* and *The Stratus Seekers* matches the composing and arranging in terms of insight and creativity. Disappointingly, we still await *At The Five Spot* on CD.

****(*) Othello Ballet Suite / Electronic Organ Sonata No. 1**

Soul Note 121014 *Russell; Rolf Ericson (t); Arne Domnérus (as); Bernt Rosengren (ts); Jan Garbarek (ts); Jon Christensen (d); others unknown.* 1/67.

Conducting the exuberant big bands of the 1980s, Russell bore a striking physical resemblance to the choreographer, Merce Cunningham. There was a dancemaster's precision to his gestures that was communicated through his music as well. Russell's conception of harmonic space is somewhat like a modern choreographer's. The *Othello Ballet Suite* is only the most obvious example of how his imagination turns on movement – in this case, the curiously inward movements of Shakespeare's play – and on the formation of black identity in the West. The music is more stately than passionate, with an almost ritualistic quality to its development. Russell's orchestration is curiously reminiscent of Ravel, and it cloys in consequence; the saxophones sound slightly out of pitch. The *Electronic Organ Sonata* is rather superficial, too obvious an essay in Russell's harmonic and structural ideas to be entirely involving. The sound on both pieces, though, is good, and both are highly significant in his development of a non-canonical but systematic musical language.

*****(*) The Essence Of George Russell**

Soul Note 121044/5 2CD *Russell; Maffy Falay, Bertil Lövgren, Palle Mikkelborg, Palle Boldtvig, Jan Allan, Lars Samuelsson, Stanton Davis (t); George Vernon, Gunnar Medberg (tb); Runo Ericksson, Olle Lind (btb); Arne Domnérus (as, cl); Claes Rosendahl (ts, ss, as, f); Lennart Aberg (ts, ss, f); Bernt Rosengren (ts); Erik Nilson (bs, bcl); Bengt Egerblad (vib); Rune Gustafsson, Terje Rypdal (g); Bengt Hallberg (p); Arild Andersen, Roman Dylag (b); Jon Christensen (d); Rupert Clemendore (perc).* 66, 67.

***** Electronic Sonata For Souls Loved By Nature**

Soul Note 121034 *Russell; Manfred Schoof (t); Jan Garbarek (ts); Terje Rypdal (g); Red Mitchell (b); Jon Christensen (d).* 4/69.

***** Electronic Sonata For Souls Loved By Nature 1980**

Soul Note 121009 *Russell; Lew Soloff (t); Robert Moore (ts, ss); Victor Gomer (g); Jean-François Jenny-Clark (b); Keith Copeland (d, perc).* 6/80.

****(*) Trip To Prillargui**

Soul Note 121029 *Russell; Stanton Davis (t); Jan Garbarek (ts); Terje Rypdal (g); Arild Andersen (b); Jon Christensen (d).* 3/70.

For all the quality of the performances, these are conceptually woolly and rather abstract works that add no more than grace-notes to Russell's remarkable compositional output. In the triumvirate of great arrangers, Russell is closer to the open texture of Gil Evans than to Quincy Jones's lacquered surface. There is a sense, though, with these performances that surface is all that matters. The original *Electronic Sonata*, which is included on the big-band *Essence* as well as on the self-titled small-group recording, has a depth of perspective and firmness of execution that the still-puzzling 1980 revision totally lacks. Conceived for tapes and ensemble, the piece is again chiefly concerned with the relationship between scored and improvised materials. *Trip To Prillargui* is beautifully played but sounds curiously emptied of significance, and it yields no more on repeated hearings; the transfer to CD has made a big difference, but it's still less than compelling.

***** Listen To The Silence**

Soul Note 121024 *Russell; Stanton Davis Jr (t); Jan Garbarek (ts); Bobo Stenson (p); Webster Lewis (org); Bjornar Andresen, Terje Rypdal (g); Arild Andersen (b); Jon Christensen (perc); Sue Auclair, Gailanne Cummings, Kay Dunlap, David Dusing, Joyce Gippo, Ray Hardin, Don Hovey, Don Kendrick, Dan Windham (v).* 6/71.

Episodically fascinating, this series of otherwise untitled 'Events I–IV' has something of the feel of rehearsal material worked up quickly for performance. The harmonics are unmistakably Russell's and as challenging as ever, but the players are left with little opportunity to swing the ideas or to invest them with any kind of expressive presence, and they remain as neutrally beautiful as snapshots inside a cloud chamber or of cultures in a Petri dish. Significantly, the main interest is in the developing voices of particular soloists, Garbarek, Rypdal and Christensen, all of whom would learn much from the experience with Russell, but who already seemed to be chafing. The project does underline how brilliant a writer for voices Russell was (a gift even he seems to have underestimated) and how exceptional an engineer Jan Erik Kongshaug was and was to be in the coming decade when he became the man more or less directly responsible for another chimera of new music, the 'ECM sound'.

****(*) Vertical Form VI**

Soul Note 121019 *Russell; Americo Bellotto, Bertil Lövgren (t, flhn); Hakan Hyquist (t, flhn, frhn); Jan Allan (t, frhn); Ivar Olsen (frhn); Bengt Edvarsson, Jorgen Johansson, Lars Olofsson (tb); Sven Larsson (btb, tba); Arne Domnérus (cl, as, ss); Jan Uling (f, as, ts); Lennart Aberg, Bernt Rosengren (f, as, ts, ss); Erik Nilsson (f, bcl, bs); Rune Gustafsson (g); Bjorn Lind (electric p); Vlodek Gulgowski (electric p, syn); Monica Dominique (electric p, cel, org, clavinet); Stefan Brolund, Bronislaw Suchanek, Lars-Urban Helje (b); Lars Beijbom, Leroy Lowe (d); Sabu Martinez (perc).* 3/77.

If we're looking for appropriate visual analogies, *Vertical Form VI* is less like an upright menhir than another kind of standing stone. The dolmen has a huge, slabby top perched on unfeasibly skinny supports. By that analogy Russell's piece has considerable mass and gravitational force, but seems to rest on nothing more than the bare uprights of theory, with little or no emotional engagement. The band is well drilled and produces a big, generous sound. Once encountered, though, the music seems just to sit there, much involved with its own enigma and a few intelligent guesses about its origins. Towards the end of the 1970s and during the following decade, Russell began to receive some of the attention he had long deserved.

*****(*) New York Big Band**

Soul Note 121039 *Russell; as above, plus: Stanton Davis, Terumasa Hino, Lew Soloff (t); Gary Valente (tb); Dave Taylor (btb); John Clark (frhn); Marty Ehrlich (as); Ricky Ford (ts); Roger Rosenberg (ts); Carl Atkins (bs, bcl); Mark Slifstein (g); Stanley Cowell, Gotz Tangerding (p); Ricky Martinez (electric p, org); Cameron Brown (b); Warren Smith (d); Babafumi Akunyon (perc); Lee Genesis (v).* 77–78.

*****(*) Live In An American Time Spiral**

Soul Note 121049 *Russell; Stanton Davis, Tom Harrell, Brian Leach, Ron Tooley (t); Ray Anderson, Earl McIntyre (tb); Marty Ehrlich (as, f); Doug Miller (ts, f); Bob Hanlon (bs); Jerome Harris (g); Jack Reilly, Mark Soskin (ky); Ron McClure (b); Victor Lewis (d).* 7/82.

New York Big Band includes a vital (in every sense) performance of the epochal 'Cubana Be, Cubana Bop', written in collaboration with Dizzy Gillespie and first performed in 1947. With its structural and not just decorative use of African and Caribbean metres, the piece opened out a whole new direction for jazz writing, paving the way for *The African Game* 25 years later. *Big Band* also includes two sections from *Listen To The Silence* and a wonderful and unexpected 'God Bless The Child' that derives something from Dolphy's long engagement with the piece.

The main piece on *Live* is a concert performance of 'Time Spiral'. Concerned again with the larger, almost meta-historical movements of human life, the charts have a slightly dense philosophical feel on the studio album, but they open up considerably in a live setting. The album also includes a fine reading of 'Ezz-thetic' and the faintly ironic 'D.C. Divertimento', given force by a (mostly) young and enthusiastic band.

***** The London Concerts: Volumes 1 & 2**

Label Bleu 6527 2CD *Russell; Stuart Brooks, Ian Carr, Mark Chandler (t); Pete Beachill, Ashley Slater (tb); Andy Sheppard, Chris Biscoe, Pete Hurt (reeds); Brad Hatfield, Steve Lodder (ky); David Fiuczynski (g); Bill Urmson (b); Steve Johns (d).* 89.

Somewhat as he had in Scandinavia two decades earlier, Russell found young British players (and some of their elders) hanging on his every compositional idea, and more than willing to work with him. These recordings, originally on Stash, were the first discs since the early part of the decade, a bizarre neglect of the man some would consider one of the half-dozen most important composers to have graced the music. Whether that valuation stands up to these oddly confected discs, which contain another performance of the 'Electronic Sonata', is very much a matter of personal judgement. We tend to think rather not. The band is absolutely on the case, but the material sounds either diffuse or ridiculously knotty, needing something of the looseness and relaxation that Gil Evans got out of British players. It is rather baffling to look back on the Russell discography, since it seems to suggest a brilliant early phase that has almost completely disintegrated into unsuitable and unproductive music. While there are worthwhile things among the later records, as noted, Russell's dazzling small-group music of the 1950s and early '60s now seems like a prematurely closed chapter which jazz would do well to take another look at.

Hal Russell (1926–92)

SAXOPHONES, TRUMPET, VIBRAPHONE, DRUMS, BANDLEADER

Born in Detroit, Russell played drums in big bands before spending most of the 1950s and '60s in Chicago, playing behind numerous visitors and forming a pioneer free-jazz group with Joe Daley. Later applied himself to trumpet, sax and vibes and formed the NRG Ensemble in the late '70s, which performed his music until his sudden death, five weeks after cutting The Hal Russell Story.

***** Generation**

Chief 5 *Russell; Chuck Burdelik (cl, as, ts); Charles Tyler (as, cl, bs); Brian Sandstrom (g, b, t); Curt Bley (b); Steve Hunt (d, vib).* 9/82.

*****(*) Conserving NRG**

Principally Jazz PJP CD 02 *Russell; Brian Sandstrom (t, g, b, perc); Chuck Burdelik (ts, as, perc); Curt Bley (b); Steve Hunt (d, vib, perc).* 3/84.

There was nothing else in the jazz of its period quite like Hal Russell's NRG Ensemble. Playing just one instrument is considered rather wimpish, especially when the old man drifts back and forth between vibes, cornet and high-register, Ayler-influenced saxophone. Arguably, no one made a comparable impact so late in his career, other than Joe Maneri, who trod similar territory. Russell actually set out as a drummer; he was recruited by Miles Davis in 1950 and by the radical Chicagoan, Joe Daley (now little known outside free-jazz circles in the United States), a decade later. Towards the end of the 1970s he took up trumpet again for the first time since his student days and learned to play the saxophone. Given the band's fierce underground reputation, *Generation* and *Conserving NRG* are slightly disappointing, sounding forced where the later *Finnish/Swiss Tour* appears spontaneous, disorderly where the later things conform to some logic. Nevertheless it's powerful stuff, the sound is better, and there isn't that much of Russell available. Watch out for 'Generation' itself, and the scissorhands 'Poodle Cut'. The sound on both records is rather slipshod, presumably due to the exigencies of performance, but both are perfectly listenable.

*****(*) The Finnish / Swiss Tour**

ECM 511261-2 *Russell; Mars Williams (ts, ss, didgeridoo); Brian Sandstrom (b, t, g); Kent Kessler (b, didgeridoo); Steve Hunt (d, vib, didgeridoo).* 11/90.

***** Naked Colours**

Silkheart SHCD 135 *Russell; Joel Futterman (p, rec); Jay Oliver (b); Robert Adkins (d).* 91.

***** Hal's Bells**

ECM 513781-2 *Russell (all instruments).* 5/92.

*****(*) The Hal Russell Story**

ECM 517364-2 *Russell; Mars Williams (ts, as, bsx, f, didgeridoo, bells, v); Brian Sandstrom (b, g, t, toys, perc); Kent Kessler (b, tb); Steve Hunt (d, tim, vib, perc).* 7/92.

In its blend of forceful, rock-inflected ostinati, extreme dynamics and broadly satirical approach, the NRG Ensemble bears some kinship to Frank Zappa's Mothers of Invention; in his liner-note to *The Finnish/Swiss Tour*, Steve Lake also notes Russell's physical resemblance to Charles Ives, which isn't so far away, either. A record of the Ensemble's first and rather surreal European itinerary, the leader quotes from Keith Jarrett, and for 'Linda's Rock Vamp' dons Prince of Darkness shades over his prescription specs, as the liner booklet shows, in dubious homage to his former employer. The band have the huge, dark sound of the mid-1970s Miles Davis units, the days when Miles was Abstract Expressionist rather than Neo-Figurative. 'Compositions' are treated as reference points, and performances frequently develop into all-out jams which nevertheless give off a strong aura of control. The sheer *size* of the sound suggests a much larger outfit. Sandstrom's stripped guitar-playing, Steve Hunt's ferocious time-keeping and the occasional use of twinned basses generate astonishing volume, with Mars Williams (formerly of the rock band, Psychedelic Furs) overblowing furiously beside the leader on the powerful 'Temporarily'. 'For MC' is for didgeridoos, electric guitar and cornet; the Zappa-sounding 'Hal The Weenie' is also an Aylerish invocation of ghosts and spirits.

His final legacy was two quite extraordinary 'concept' albums for ECM, the first a multi-tracked solo effort, the second a potted autobiography in music and cartoon narrations shouted through a paper megaphone. The tunes on both are a mixture of reworked standards and themes worked out on the spot for the session. Those in *Hal's Bells* range from vibraphone solos – the lovely 'I Need You Know' – to 'group' pieces like 'Kenny G', a curious name-check for Bill Clinton's favourite saxophonist, arranged for tenor, vibes and drums, to the more radical 'For Free' (saxophones, trumpets, vibes and drums) which harks back to his days with the Joe Daley group. Some of these tracks plod a little. Certainly, few of them have the all-out energy of the material on *Story*, a record which compresses 40 years of music-making into a standard-length CD. Russell's biography is no more linear and sequential than anything else he ever did, but it takes him from childhood fantasies right through to middle-aged fantasies of moving 'beyond the barlines / beyond the changes / beyond the time / tiptoeing in some wild and lonely space'. Underneath all the clamour, it is the loneliness and isolation that show through. Though the NRG ensemble had become Russell's mouthpiece, it is on the solo session that his curiously vulnerable personality emerges with greatest clarity. It comes through again on the quartet co-led with Futterman, a loyal supporter and interpreter who provides all the compositional material for the session, though Russell wholly dominates it. A figure to put alongside Ives and Ruggles, Nancarrow and Moondog and Harry Partch, Russell is a genuine American original.

Luis Russell (1902–63)

PIANO, BANDLEADER

Born in Panama, Russell was working in New Orleans in the early 1920s, but his major break came as the resident bandleader at the Saratoga Club in New York in 1928. In 1935 his band became the full-time backing group for Louis Armstrong, but they were sacked in 1940 and Russell led a band of diminishing importance thereafter. At the time of his death he was driving cars and teaching piano.

****** The Luis Russell Collection, 1926–1934**

Collector's Classics COCD-7 *Russell; Louis Metcalf, Henry 'Red' Allen, Bill Coleman, Otis Johnson, George Mitchell, Leonard Davis, Gus Aiken (t); Bob Shoffner (c); Kid Ory, J.C Higginbotham, Vic Dickenson, Preston Jackson, Dicky Wells, Nathaniel Story, Jimmy Archey (tb); Albert Nicholas (cl, ss, as); Charlie Holmes (ss, as); Darnell Howard, Henry Jones (cl, as); Bingie Madison (cl, ts); Barney Bigard, Teddy Hill, Greely Walton (ts); Will Johnson (g, bj); Lee Blair (g); Johnny St Cyr (bj); Bass Moore (tba); Pops Foster (b); Paul Barbarin (d); Walter Pichon, Sonny Woods, Chick Bullock, Palmer Brothers (v).* 3/26–8/34.

****** Luis Russell 1926–1929**

Classics 588 *Similar to above.* 3/26–12/29.

****** Luis Russell 1930–1931**

Classics 606 *Similar to above.* 1/30–8/31.

****** Luis Russell & His Orchestra**

Topaz TPZ 1039 *As above discs, except add Louis Armstrong (t, v), Eddie Condon (bj), Lonnie Johnson (g).* 1/29–8/34.

Russell led one of the great orchestras of its period, having originally put it together in New Orleans in 1927, with such young local stars as Allen, Nicholas and Barbarin in attendance. Their 18 essential sides from seven remarkable sessions in New York are variously available on the Classics and Topaz CDs. The band had secured a prime Harlem residency at the Saratoga Club. This was a sophisticated outfit: first, in its soloists, with Higginbotham dominating the earlier sides and Allen, Nicholas and Holmes adding their own variations to the later ones; and, secondly, in its increasing stature as an ensemble. 'Louisiana Swing', 'High Tension', 'Panama' and 'Case On Dawn' all show the orchestra swinging through the more advanced new ideas of counterpoint and unison variation while still offering chances for Allen and the others to shine as soloists.

The Collector's Classics CD fills in various gaps in the Russell discography. There are two small-group sessions from 1926, the first having a Mortonesque sound through the presence of Mitchell, Ory and Nicholas in the front line, the second a fine example of Chicago music moving out of the barrelhouse and into the front parlour. 'Broadway Rhythm' and two takes of 'The Way He Loves Is Just Too Bad' come from a Banner session of 1929 featuring the full band, and the final two sessions for Victor (1931) and Banner (1934) appear in full: if the ten tracks suggest Russell's hard-bitten swing was softening a little with the era of smooth big bands just around the corner, there is still some memorable playing on the likes of 'Hokus Pokus'. Superlative remastering by John R.T. Davies. The Classics discs cover similar ground, although remastering seems to be spottier. Whatever the choice, the music is very highly recommended, especially to any who feel this era of jazz is too far away for them.

Topaz's compilation cherrypicks the best of Russell's orchestral sides but stirs in two tracks when the band backed Louis Armstrong and also adds Armstrong's Savoy Ballroom Five classic, 'Mahogany Hall Stomp'. A strong single disc.

****(*) Luis Russell 1945–1946**

Classics 1066 *Russell; Chester Boone, {f}John {l}Swan, Emory Thompson, James Mitchell, Rex Kearney, George Scott, Bernard Flood (t); Luther Brown, Austin Lawrence, Charles Williams, Charles Stocvall, Thomas Brown, Nathaniel Allen (tb); Sam Lee, Clarence Grimes (as); Esmond Samuels, Andy Martin, Troy Stowe (ts); Howard Robertson (bs); Howard Biggs, John Motley (p); Ernest Lee Williams (g); Don Richmond, Nathan Wodley, Leslie Bartlet (b); Roy Haynes (d); Milton Biggs, Lee Richardson (v).* 45–46.

Russell's later sides are all but unknown, and deservedly so on this evidence. An unidentified Eckstine-styled vocalist pours himself over four tracks, there are some strictly routine big-band shouters, and a general feeling of pointlessness pervades. For hardcore collectors only!

Pee Wee Russell (1906–69)

CLARINET, TENOR SAXOPHONE

Charles Ellsworth Russell, a jazz original, came from Missouri and played in the New York school of hot music in the 1920s, with Nichols, Mole and the others. From the '30s he was better known as a member of the Eddie Condon gang, but his later playing suggested his disaffection for that style of jazz, and in his final decade he played in increasingly mainstream-to-modern settings, though by the end of the '60s he was largely back with traditonal music. Alcoholism, illness and depression prevented him from ever making a more solid base for his career.

***** The Land Of Jazz**

Topaz TPZ 1018 *Russell; Red Nichols (t, c); Leo McConville, Manny Klein, Henry 'Red' Allen, Max Kaminsky, Marty Marsala (t); Bobby Hackett (c); Miff Mole, Tommy Dorsey, George Brunies, Vernon Brown (tb); Brad Gowans (vtb); Fud Livingston (cl, ts); Jimmy Lord (cl); Happy Caldwell, Bud Freeman, Gene Sedric (ts); Adrian Rollini (bsx); Lennie Hayton, Fats Waller, Arthur Schutt, Jess Stacy, Joe Bushkin, Teddy Wilson, Frank Froeba (p); Jack Bland, Eddie Condon, Allan Reuss, Dick McDonough, Eddie Lang (g); Al Morgan, Pops Foster, Artie Shapiro, Sid Weiss (b); Vic Berton, Zutty Singleton, George Wettling, Johnny Blowers, Lionel Hampton (d); Billy Banks (v).* 8/27–9/44.

*****(*) Jazz Original**

Commodore CMD 14042 Mostly similar to above, with some omissions; 1/38–1/45.

***** Jack Teagarden / Pee Wee Russell**

Original Jazz Classics OJC 1708 *Russell; Max Kaminsky (t); Dicky Wells (tb); Al Gold (ts); James P Johnson (p); Freddie Green (g); Wellman Braud (b); Zutty Singleton (d, v).* 8/38.

Russell's music is tyremarked by his many years in Dixieland, which he came to hate, with the Condon gang, who sent him up for much of the time, and by his own fatalism and poor habits. There's a danger in patronizing his home-made approach to playing, and he *was* inconsistent, but his best music is exceptional. He began with the New York players of the 1920s – Nichols, Mole, Beiderbecke – but was more readily linked with Condon's Chicagoans in the 1930s and '40s. The Topaz compilation starts with Nichols, adds four tracks with Billy Banks, including the immortal 'Oh Peter', but bulks up with various Condon line-ups for Commodore from 1938. Pee Wee sounds fine on 'Tappin' The Commodore Till' and a lovely slow solo on 'Sunday'. But the four outstanding items are by a quartet with Russell, Jess Stacy, Sid Weiss and George Wettling, culminating in the almost gargled 'D.A. Blues'. Sound is variable – some of the Commodores have a low-fi resonance – but mostly good.

The 1938 session (the rest of the CD features a Teagarden-led group) features a surprising line-up on five standards and a blues, two tracks featuring Russell and the rhythm section alone. Kaminsky and Wells are the most confident-sounding voices, but it's Russell's queer sense of line and wobbly pitch that take the ear. His partnership with Johnson is just one of a series of unlikely alliances he formed with pianists on record, which would later include George Wein and Thelonious Monk.

Jazz Original is all Commodore material and there is some crossover with the Topaz disc. The 1944 quartet date is complete with four alternative takes, and there are also four 1941 titles by 'The Three Deuces' – Russell, Joe Sullivan and Zutty Singleton. The rest of the disc features Russell with the usual suspects and the transfers are rather better overall than the Topaz set: it's the best single bet for early Pee Wee.

*****(*) We're In The Money**

Black Lion BLCD 760909 *Russell; Doc Cheatham, Wild Bill Davison (t); Vic Dickenson (tb); George Wein (p); John Field, Stan Wheeler (b); Buzzy Drootin (d); Al Bandini (v).* 53–54.

*****(*) Jazz Reunion**

Candid CS 9020 *Russell; Emmett Berry (t); Bob Brookmeyer (vtb); Coleman Hawkins (ts); Nat Pierce (p); Milt Hinton (b); Jo Jones (d).* 2/61.

Russell's quixotic progress is still inadequately represented on CD. *We're In The Money* includes two dates by basically the same band, although the substitution of Davison for Cheatham lends a different feel: the former's irascible, barking playing is a startling contrast to Cheatham's politely hot phrasing. Russell listens to each man and pitches his remarks for due contrast himself. Dickenson, a kindred spirit, kibitzes from the sidelines and the recording is fine. The *Reunion* was with Hawkins – one of the tracks, 'If I Could Be With You One Hour Tonight', they'd recorded together as far back as 1929 – and it caught both men in excellent form, Hawkins's solos delivered in his most leathery, autumnal manner which makes Russell's nagging at notes sound minimalist. Jones, in particular, reads everybody's moves superbly, although Berry and Brookmeyer especially seem rather irrelevant.

****** Swingin' With Pee Wee**

Prestige 24213-2 *Russell; Buck Clayton, Ruby Braff (t); Vic Dickenson (tb); Bud Freeman (ts); Tommy Flanagan, Nat Pierce (p); Wendell Marshall, Tommy Potter (b); Osie Johnson, Karl Kiffe (d).* 2/58–3/60.

A valuable and long-awaited reissue of a classic Russell session, *Swingin' With Pee Wee* is one of his best latter-day records. Clayton handled the arranging duties, and the rhythm section, with Flanagan, Marshall and Johnson, was about the most modernistic Russell had had behind him at this point. The result is a stylish and triumphant assimilation of his clarinet into a vibrant mainstream setting. His dissertation on his great blues, 'Englewood', is but one example of Pee Wee at his best – and Clayton matches him in the calibre of his playing. Even more of a bonus are the tracks from the 1958 date for Counterpoint, *Portrait Of Pee Wee*, with Braff and Dickenson – not quite as good, but it only adds to the merits of an excellent reissue.

Ray Russell

GUITAR

British guitarist prominent at the end of the '60s, exploring a wide-ranging rock and jazz alliance.

***** Dragon Hill**

Columbia 494435 2 *Russell; Harry Beckett (t, flhn); Bud Parkes (t); Donald Beichtol (tb); Lyn Dobson (ts); Roy Fry (p); Ron Mathewson (b); Alan Rushton (d).* 69.

***** Rites And Rituals**

Columbia 494436 2 *Russell; Harry Beckett (t, flhn); Nick Evans (tb); Tony Roberts (sax); Daryl Runswick (b); Alan Rushton (d).* 69.

At the time, he seemed the most excitingly experimental of them all, a wild, clever presence who combined the intellectual challenge of the avant-garde with the waist-level thump of rock and roll. A live album from the same period suggested that Russell needed the presence of an audience to produce his best work, but, like Howard Riley and Tony Oxley, fellow avant-gardists of the time, he benefited from the sudden and unexpected interest of CBS in the British free scene and produced two albums of lasting fascination, only recently returned to circulation from the rarity bins at record fairs.

Russell's squally tone and out-of-tempo articulation are unique – compare his work with that of Chris Spedding – but like the other British free guitarist of the time, Derek Bailey, he has the ability to imply a settled groove without settling into metrical tramlines. His phrasing on the long 'Dragon Hill' is fascinating, horn-like lines underpinned with a percussive attack that allows the rest of the group to drift out of conventional character. *Rites And Rituals* lacks the sheer surprise of *Dragon Hill* but is perhaps a more sophisticated conception. Its brass and wind components are more convincingly thought out and generally better played than on the two expanded-group tracks on *Dragon Hill*. Russell still awaits rediscovery; his is a bright and unexpected talent and one that should have been more generously sponsored when it counted.

Charles Rutherford Jazz Pacific Orchestra

GROUP

A characteristically accomplished and powerhouse modern big band from California.

***** Reunion**

Sea Breeze CDSB-2044 *Joe Davis, Bob Bennett, Kevin Mayes, Tim Wendt, Charlie Peterson, Kai Palmer, Gary Roll, Bob Allen, Ron Stout (t, flhn); Regan Wickman, Mike Johnson, Corey Wicks, Mike Fahn (tb); Everett Carroll, Tom Smith, Chris Abernathy, Larry Jagiello, Dave Arrollado, Eric Marienthal, Doug Webb, Tom Kubic, Brian Williams (saxes); Alan Rowe (p); Todd Oliver (g); Eric Stiller, Ernie Nunez (b); Ray Price (d); Christine Rosander (v).* 9/91.

***** Groovin' Hard**

Sea Breeze CDSB-2050 *Joe Davis, Gary Roll, Ron Stout, Kai Palmer, Matt Fronke (t, flhn); Regan Wickman, Mike Fahn, Corey Wicks, John Ward, Len Wicks (tb); Everett Carroll, Paul Bastin, Jeff Jorgenson, Jerry Pinter, Brian Williams (saxes); Alan Rowe (p); Todd Oliver (g); Ernie Nunez (b); Ray Price (d).* n.d.

***** Note Walker**

Sea Breeze CDSB-2064 *As above, except Don Clark, Bob Bennett (t), Benjamin Olariu, Jim Boltinghouse, Mike Zelazo, Francisco Torres (tb), Bob Swaaley, Sy Eubank (p), Eric Stiller, Valerie Sullivan (b) replace Davis, Roll, Wickman, Fahn, Ward, Rowe, Oliver and Nunez; add Christine Rosander (v).* n.d.

Three irreproachable releases by a varying team of West Coasters. Rutherford leads, directs and produces but doesn't play and leaves most of the arranging to other hands, most notably Don Menza, to whom the third CD is dedicated. There's little enough between the three records that some of the routines crop up more than once: the flag-waver 'Shaw Nuff' on *Reunion* is a showcase for the trumpet section, and just the same thing happens with 'Ornithology' on *Note Walker*. But they're good routines, proficiently dispatched. Certain guest soloists – Marienthal, Kubic – liven up the first disc somewhat; the second settles around the excellent reed section, while the third rises on its absorbing sequence of scores by Menza, notably the title-piece, 'Tenor Time' and the Latin bustle of 'Sambiana'. Each of them also has a share of rote passages and mere cliché. Hard to fault them, but difficult to see anyone wanting more than one.

Paul Rutherford (born 1940)

TROMBONE

A Londoner, Rutherford played in RAF bands, then studied at Guildhall. A prime mover in both Spontaneous Music Ensemble, Iskra 1903 and London Jazz Composers Orchestra, as well as playing solo, Rutherford is a major part of British free music.

***** Sequences 72 & 73**

Emanem 4018 *Rutherford; Kenny Wheeler (t, flhn); Malcolm Griffiths, Paul Nieman, Geoff Perkins (tb); Dick Hart (tba);*

Dave White (ss, as, bs, bcl, cbcl); Trevor Watts (ss, as); Evan Parker (ss, ts); Howard Riley (p); Derek Bailey (g); Barry Guy (b); Tony Oxley (elec); Maggie Nicols, Norma Winstone (v). 9/72–5/74.

****** The Gentle Harm Of The Bourgeoisie**

Emanem 4019 *Rutherford (tb solo).* 7–12/74.

The trombone is said to be the musical instrument closest to the human voice. When Paul Rutherford spoke or sang through his horn, it sounded like no instrument anyone had ever heard, a sound as lyrically potent and as expressively stressed and freighted as a whole ensemble. Rutherford was part of some of the most important improvising groups of the 1960s, co-founding the Little Theatre Club with Trevor Watts and John Stevens and joining their Spontaneous Music Ensemble, as well as Watts's Amalgam, the London Jazz Composers' Orchestra, and founding his own electro-acoustic trio with LJCO bassist and composer Barry Guy and guitarist Derek Bailey; Iskra 1903, which re-formed in 1980 with violinist Philip Wachsmann, was named after Lenin's revolutionary newspaper. It's worth labouring the genealogy to underline just how central Rutherford has been to the scene and to point up just how important recent reissues have been.

Rutherford's solo performances, documented on *The Gentle Harm Of The Bourgeoisie*, are as wryly subversive as the title suggests. Devotedly recorded by Martin Davidson at the Unity Theatre, it's now infinitely more listenable than on muddy LP. Rutherford's grasp of multiphonics is already assured; additional sounds and overtones come from mutes, microphone knocks and from spittle in the horn, part and parcel of the process. The two long tracks, 'Elaqust' from July 1974 and 'Osirac Senol' from the week before Christmas, are definitive.

Sequences 72 & 73 is a historic release, a first chance to hear Rutherford's work as composer/conductor. Iskra 1912 never performed in public and these studio recordings were never released. The two 'Sequences' were recorded a year apart, while Rutherford recorded the short solo 'Non-Sequence' in the late spring of 1974. The main difference between the main pieces is that Derek Bailey's stereo guitar was overdubbed on to the latter, which also featured Tony Oxley on live electronics, replacing the saxophones of Trevor Watts, who was one of the main soloists on the 1972 session, duetting with Guy. The brass players are sometimes required to play chorally, sometimes improvising freely. The other main soloist in 1972 was Evan Parker, who is heard on tenor a year later.

With no drummer, there is no definite pulse and, as so often in Rutherford's music, it is the human voice, wordless on this occasion, which provides the unifying principle. Quite why these extraordnary works have had to wait until now for release is a mystery only if one chooses to forget how marginalized this music has been, and how little critical press its creator has had, since they were recorded.

***** Rogues**

Emanem 4007 *Rutherford; Paul Rogers (b).* 11/88.

*****(*) ISKRA / NCKA 1903**

Maya MCD 9502 *Rutherford; Phil Wachsmann (vn); Barry Guy (b).* 10/92.

Rogues involves two-thirds of a trio that also included drummer Nigel Morris. The involvement of a percussionist meant that this was a very different set-up from Iskra 1903, in either of its incarnations, and Morris's absence on the 1988 disc changes the language quite considerably. None of this material appeared on LP and it was finally issued almost a decade after the performances, which were recorded at a pub called the Cannonball in Adderley Street, Birmingham. Debates about documenting such music still rage, but the opening 'Rogues 1' is as riveting as it must have been on the night. The rest of the disc is less compelling.

The Iskra 1903 disc was also recorded live, in Vancouver. It once again underlines Rutherford's genius for creating contexts in which fellow-musicians thrive. His own playing is calm, positive and completely tuneful, if by that one means a basic musicality that goes beyond mere melodism. The sound is quite crisp, for a concert recording, and though Wachsmann's amplified violin tends to dominate, the basic unity of the trio is always evident.

Terje Rypdal (born 1947)

ELECTRIC GUITAR, GUITAR, SOPRANO SAXOPHONE, FLUTE, OTHER INSTRUMENTS AND EFFECTS

Born in Oslo, Rypdal played rock in the '60s before teaming with George Russell and Jan Garbarek. A pioneer of electric-guitar 'impressionism', he's spent almost 30 years with the ECM label and recorded there in a range of settings, with several (unlisted) recent records in particular more concerned with contemporary composition than jazz.

***** Terje Rypdal**

ECM 527645-2 *Rypdal; Sveinung Hovensjo (b); Jon Christensen (d).* 72.

***** What Comes After**

ECM 839306-2 *Rypdal; Erik Niord Larsen (ob, eng hn); Sveinung Hovensjo, Barre Phillips (b); Jon Christensen (perc, org).* 8/73.

***** Whenever I Seem To Be Far Away**

ECM 843166-2 *Rypdal; Odd Ulleberg (frhn); Erik Niord Larsen (ob); Pete Knutsen (p, mellotron); Sveinung Hovensjo (b); Jon Christensen (perc); Helmut Geiger (vn); Christian Hedrich (vla); strings of Südfunk Symphony Orchestra, conducted by Mladen Gutesha.* 74.

*****(*) Odyssey**

ECM 835355-2 *Rypdal; Torbjørn Sunde (tb); Brynjulf Blix (b); Svein Christiansen (d).* 8/75.

*****(*) After The Rain**

ECM 523159-2 *Rypdal; Inger Lise Rypdal (v).* 76.

*****(*) Waves**

ECM 827419-2 *Rypdal; Palle Mikkelborg (t, flhn, elec); Sveinung Hovensjo (b); Jon Christensen (d, perc).* 9/77.

In the later 1980s, Terje Rypdal was increasingly seen at the head of an impressive train of opus numbers; two classical releases, *Undisonus* and *Q.E.D.*, appeared on ECM in the '90s. 'Straight' composition was, in fact, his third string. His professional career had begun as a rock performer, in the pit band at a Scandinavian production of *Hair!* (chilblains were doubtless a problem) and as accompanist to his sister, Inger Lise Rypdal (who added soft vocal colours to the otherwise solo *After The Rain*). In the 1970s, under the influence of George Russell (directly) and of Jimi Hendrix (less so), Rypdal made a series of highly atmospheric guitar-led albums which combined elements of classical form with a distinctive high-register sound and an improvisational approach that drew more from rock music than from orthodox jazz technique. (It's worth noting that *After The Rain* refers to a Rypdal composition, not Coltrane's.)

If there is an 'ECM sound', in either a positive or a more sceptical sense, it may be found in the echo-y passages of these albums. Rypdal's music is highly textural and harmonically static, its imagery kaleidoscopic rather than cinematic. At worst, Rypdal's solo excursions sound merely vacuous. The debut is pretty typical of his combination of power and lyricism, though in future years the two strands were increasingly separate, carried in different works and by different kinds of ensemble. In the 1970s, Rypdal had more or less single-handedly pioneered a style of guitar playing which grafted a rock attack over large-scale orchestral washes. 'Silver Bird Is Heading For The Sun' on *Whenever I Seem To Be Far Away* is reminiscent of Pink Floyd's woollier moments, yet it has a harmonic outline that is almost worthy of Bill Evans, and that is true to Rypdal's range of sources. The long title-track (which Rypdal calls an 'image', a useful generic description of his work) is, on the other hand, highly effective in its balance of winds, guitar and strings. ('Live' strings are more effective than the cumbersome and now outmoded mellotrons and 'string ensembles' that the guitarist uses elsewhere.)

Waves and *Odyssey* are the most interesting of this group, although we are still rather partial to *After The Rain*, which evokes a particular time in record-making and has some shamelessly pretty moments. Rypdal favours brass with an almost medieval quality and, despite Mikkelborg's baroque embellishments, the trumpeter fits that prescription surprisingly well. Hovensjo and Christensen don't play as an orthodox rhythm section but as a shifting backdrop of tones and pulses; the bassist doubles on a six-stringed instrument which is effectively a rhythm guitar. Despite being technically dated in some ways, these albums seem to have come round again, addressing a post-modernist desire to embrace the last-but-one technology and a gentler, more sentimental range.

*****(*) Descendere**

ECM 829118-2 *Rypdal; Palle Mikkelborg (t, flhn, ky); Jon Christensen (d, perc).* 3/79.

*****(*) Terje Rypdal / Miroslav Vitous / Jack DeJohnette**

ECM 825470-2 *Rypdal; Miroslav Vitous (b, p); Jack DeJohnette (d).* 6/78.

***** To Be Continued**

ECM 847333-2 *As above.* 1/81.

There have always been charges that Rypdal is not 'really' an improviser, just a high-powered effects man. At the root of the misconception is a prevailing belief that improvisation takes place only on a vertical axis, up and down through chord progressions and changes. Rypdal's genius is for juxtapositions of textures, overlays of sound that act as polarizing lenses to what his companions are doing. A broad, open chord laid close over a drum pattern takes the 'percussive' stringency out of DeJohnette's line, making him sound as if he were playing piano (as in other and later company he might well be) or adding harmonics to Vitous's huge bass-notes. There is also, of course, a great deal of straightforward interplay which in itself helps refute the charge that Rypdal is a mere techno-freak.

The other trio is less conventional in format, though Mikkelborg's palette-knife keyboard effects mean that there's very little sense of 'missing' piano or bass. The trumpeter, who has an approach broadly similar to Rypdal's, tends to lay it on a little thick, and there is a suspicion of either muddle or overkill on a couple of tracks. That apart, *Descendere* still sounds fresh and vital and stands out as a high point in Rypdal's output.

***** Eos**

ECM 815333-2 *Rypdal; David Darling (clo, 8-string electric clo).* 5/83.

The scorching power chords of the opening 'Laser' tend to mislead, for this is a remarkably subtle and sophisticated record, making the fullest use of the players' astonishing range of tone-colours and effects. Darling conjures anything from Vitous-like bass strums to high, wailing lines that are remarkably close in timbre to Rypdal's souped-up guitar. He is still mostly reliant on rock-influenced figures played with maximum sustain and distortion, but his rhythm counts are consistently challenging, and the pairing of instruments sets up an often ambiguous bitonality. The title-track wavers a bit at over 14 minutes, but the two closing numbers, 'Mirage' and 'Adagietto', are particularly beautiful.

*** Chaser**

ECM 827256-2 *Rypdal; Born Kjellmyr (b); Audun Kleive (d).* 5/85.

**** Blue**

ECM 831516-2 *As above.* 11/86.

***** The Singles Collection**

ECM 837749-2 *As above, except add Allan Dangerfield (ky).* 8/88.

It may say something about Rypdal's psychic economy that, at a time when his scored, formal music was achieving new heights of sophistication and beauty, he should have gone on the road and on record with a power trio of minimum finesse. *Chaser* is a harsh, clunking slice of nonsense that does Rypdal no credit at all. *Blue* at least shows signs of thought, notably on 'The Curse' and 'Om Bare'. How many people have been thrown by the ironically titled *Singles Collection*? It's not utterly improbable that Rypdal might have been sneaking out the odd seven-incher over the years, but this is a wholly new album of wry, generic samples. Basically, it's a tissue of rock guitar styles, with the changing of stylistic season marked by Dangerfield's progress from apoplectic Hammond to a rather under-programmed synth. Rypdal has expressed interest in Prince's music (and 'U.'N.I.' is presumably a reference to the Small One's trademark elision of titles) but it isn't clear whether he is drawn more to Paisley Park production techniques or to Prince's Carlos Santana-derived (rather than Hendrix-derived) guitar playing. Rypdal emerges as a surprisingly good *pasticheur*, and there is plenty to think about in this slightly odd, deliberately regressive set. It's certainly the best of these three.

***** If Mountains Could Sing**
ECM 523987-2 *Rypdal; Born Kjellemyr (b); Audun Kleive (d); Terje Tonnesen (vn); Lars Anders Tomter (vla); Oystein Birkeland (clo); Christian Eggen (cond).* 1 & 6/94.

Half a dozen tracks by the shortly to be disbanded Chaser trio, and five more augmented by strings. As one might expect by this stage in the game, the whole is elegant and richly textured, though the specifics are less than compelling. Rypdal's full-on guitar is over-emphatic when in company with the strings, and Manfred Eicher's fabled production values are less secure than they might be. No indication when individual tracks were made, though it must be assumed that the strings sessions were recorded at a separate session. Whatever the case, Rypdal sounds very different, somewhat dry and percussive. There is some lovely material, though. The title-track and the wry 'But On The Other Hand' stand out, and 'Foran Peisen', for trio alone, is as good as Rypdal has done with this line-up.

*****(*) Skywards**
ECM 533768-2 *Rypdal; Palle Mikkelborg (t); Terje Tonnesen (vn); David Darling (clo); Christian Eggen (p, ky); Paolo Vinaccia (d, perc); Jon Christensen (d).* 2/96.

Skywards was made to mark Rypdal's 25-year association with ECM. In a rare liner-note, Rypdal concedes that *If Mountains Could Sing* had not been an easy album to record and repeats his weariness with the increasingly formulaic Chasers. The idea was to put together a celebration orchestra of old colleagues and create an album that would illustrate both continuity and progress. The main piece is a specially written 'Sinfonietta', subtitled 'Out Of This World', and a couple of the other works – 'Remember To Remember' and 'Shining' – bear a close relation to pieces in Rypdal's classical catalogue. 'Into The Wilderness' was originally written for a film soundtrack. Though a much more disparate album, it is also more successful than its predecessor. The larger group, with Mikkelborg a key component, is superb on 'Shining', the trumpeter's main feature. The reunion with Darling is also a fruitful one, and on 'Remember To Remember' the combination of string sounds finally comes right in the small-group context. Not quite the epochal retrospective it might have been, but a fine album nevertheless.

Stefano Sabatini

PIANO

Italian post-bop pianist in the Bill Evans mould.

****(*) Wonderland**
Splasc(h) H 360-2 *Sabatini; Flavio Boltro (t); Stefano Di Battista (ss, as); Maurizio Giammarco (ts); Francesco Puglisi, Furio Di Castri (b); Maurizio Dei Lazzaretti, Roberto Gatto (d).* 4/91.

Sabatini's graceful music comes and goes, leaving barely a trace. His lyrical kind of midstream bop is nicely unpretentious, but it also tends to be featherlight in impact and, charming though the themes and solos are, they don't have any kind of impact, least of all his deferential piano solos. The best improvising comes from the reliable if occasionally sleepy Giammarco.

***** Waiting**
Splasc(h) H 451-2 *Sabatini; Stefano D'Anna (ts, ss); Francesco Puglisi, Dario Deidda (b); Amedeo Ariano, Pietro Iodice (d).* 6/95.

A shade tougher and more convincing, courtesy in the main of D'Anna, whose tenor solos line Sabatini's themes with a layer of muscle they might otherwise miss. It's difficult to be immune to the warmth of 'Baja Del Sol', 'Daydream' and his other, mostly lyrical, pieces, although the pianist's own playing remains uneventful. Some pleasing Roman sunshine.

Helmut Joe Sachse

GUITAR, FLUTE

Veteran German guitarist-improviser with a handful of solo sets to his name.

*****(*) Berlin Tango**
ITM 1448 *Sachse; George Lewis (tb); David Moss (d, perc, elec, v).* 12/86, 10/87.

*****(*) European House**
FMP CD41 *Sachse solo.* 90.

Sachse thinks nothing of cutting across a chaotically abstract passage with a sudden rock riff or Wes Montgomery-style octave run. An eclectic of a fairly radical sort, he has synthesized whole tracts of modern and contemporary guitar playing. The solo record is rather thinly recorded and misses much of Sachse's quieter gestures. An earlier solo record on FMP had included a modestly reconstructed standard, 'Round About Midnight'; *European House* is rather less respectful of 'Epistrophy' and Coltrane's 'Impressions'. It's this element one misses on the anarchic *Berlin Tango*; 'Lover Man' may mislead, for it's actually a bizarre parody of all-stops-out soul, with Moss's surreal falsetto scats alternated with sexy murmurs and Sachse's lead guitarist posturing. Lewis plays a rather diffident role throughout and was presumably present on only one or other of the dates. The better disc is undoubtedly the solo set; without Moss's clatteringly intrusive effects, Sachse improvises percussion on the guitar body and carrying case.

Ed Saindon

VIBRAPHONE

Mainstream-modernist vibesman working with some veterans of that style.

***** Swing On The Sunnyside**
A Records AL 73068 *Saindon; Herb Pomeroy (t, flhn); Dick Johnson (cl); Barry Smith (b); Matt Gordy (d).* 4 & 5/95.

Saindon is something of a throwback to those vibes players who treated the instrument as a kissing cousin of the piano. Not much that has happened since Milt Jackson impinges, but this tribute to the classics of the swing era nevertheless swings. A four-mallet performer, he produces rippling melody lines and resonant chords, sustaining an almost orchestral sound on the unaccompanied 'I Found A New Baby'. You know you're in for something a bit special when the label makes a point of insisting that there is no doubletracking on the vibe parts. Virtuosic playing apart (and if that sounds dismissive, it could pall at length), what makes the record interesting is that Saindon works permutations of five further instrumentations, ranging upward from a duo with Smith, a trio with Gordy and three different line-ups with horns. The set opens and closes with the full personnel, 'On The Sunny Side Of The Street' and 'Sweet Georgia Brown'. Wonderful to hear the saintly Herb Pomeroy on four tracks, including a superb performance of the Jimmy Van Heusen song, 'It Could Happen To You', and also Dick Johnson, who is the anointed successor to Artie Shaw.

Salty Dogs Jazz Band

GROUP

Originating in Lafayette, Indiana, this revivalist band is a dynasty in itself, having been first formed in 1947, and with several members who can boast decades of service.

***** Long, Deep And Wide**

GHB BCD-237 *Lew Green (c); Tom Bartlett (tb); Kim Cusack (cl, as); John Cooper (p); Mike Walbridge (tba); Jack Kuncl (bj, g); Wayne Jones (d); Carol Leigh (v).* 6/89.

***** Joy, Joy, Joy**

Stomp Off CD1233 *As above, except add John Otto (as, cl, v).* 12/89–2/92.

The Salty Dogs are grand foot-soldiers. John Cooper, who has been with them since 1953, is the longest-serving member, but even Carol Leigh has sung with them for 20 years, and they're hardly troubled by questions of 'authenticity'. There have been many records over the years, but these two CDs show their current form. Given their experience, it's a pity that the Salty Dogs don't take a few more chances with some of their treatments. The GHB disc is a very obvious gathering of warhorses, while *Joy, Joy, Joy* is a fascinating collection of material by or associated with Banjo Ikey Robinson, much of it unrecorded for decades. Yet there's little to choose between these records in terms of their persuasively chugging beat, the tight, neat solos and Leigh's engaging vocals, which are on the matronly side of bawdy. The second record is probably the more worthwhile, but their version of, say, 'Alexander's Ragtime Band' on the earlier set has a fine zest. They enjoy their jazz.

Dino Saluzzi (born 1935)

BANDONEON, FLUTE, PERCUSSION, VOICE

Saluzzi was born in Argentina, in Salta province. He worked for the house orchestra of the national radio station, Radio El Mundo, in the 1950s, and worked for a time with Gato Barbieri. His interest has ranged between tango, folkloric music, jazz and classical forms, and he uses the bandoneon in a markedly orchestral way, conjuring everything from single voices to whole sections and infusing the whole with tremendous longing and nostalgia.

***** Kultrum**

ECM 457854-2 *Saluzzi (solo).* 11/82.

*****(*) Andina**

ECM 837186-2 *As above.* 5/88.

Though it was the Argentinian master, Astor Piazzolla, who sparked a revival of interest in bandoneon and accordion, it has been Dino Saluzzi who has performed some of the most significant new music on an instrument that has always held a peculiar fascination for the avant-garde; this partly because of its slightly kitsch image, but also because it permits an astonishing range of harmonic and extra-harmonic devices (wheezes, clicks, terminal rattles) that lend themselves very readily to improvisational contexts.

Saluzzi's compositions and performances (and he is usually best heard solo) cover a wide spectrum of styles, from sombre, almost sacred pieces (like 'Choral' on *Andina*, his best record), to a semi-abstract tone-poem like 'Winter' on the same album, which takes him much closer to the exploratory work of radical accordionist, Pauline Oliveros. *Kultrum* is well worth hearing, and sets the agenda for what is to be a life's work, a whole album of pieces united by the composer's cross-cultural philosophy, but it is also a very inward work, darkly private and not always as communicative as one might like. As a first exposure to Saluzzi, *Andina* is the one to plump for; richly and intimately recorded, although doubtless less authentic in idiom, it has infinitely greater presence than the later album.

*****(*) Once Upon A Time ... Far Away In The South**

ECM 827768-2 *Saluzzi; Palle Mikkelborg (t, flhn); Charlie Haden (b); Pierre Favre (d).* 7/85.

***** Volver**

ECM 831395-2 *Saluzzi; Enrico Rava (t); Harry Pepl (g); Furio Di Castri (b); Bruce Ditmas (d).* 10/86.

***** Mojotoro**

ECM 511952-2 *Saluzzi; Celso Saluzzi (bandoneon, perc, v); Felix Cuchara Saluzzi (ts, ss, cl); Armando Alonso (g, v); Guillermo Vadalá (b, v); José Maria Saluzzi (d, perc, v); Arto Tuncboyaciyan (perc, v).* 5/91.

***** Cité de la Musique**

ECM 533316-2 *Saluzzi; Jose M Saluzzi (g); Marc Johnson (b).* 95.

Saluzzi tends to recede a little in a group setting, perhaps because European ears have not been conditioned to listen to button accordion as anything other than a bland portable organ useful for dancing and local colour. Both Rava and (especially) Mikkelborg are rather dominant players and occupy more than their fair share of the foreground. *Once Upon A Time* is better because Haden and Favre are so responsive; *Volver* takes a bit of getting used to.

At first hearing, remarkably similar to one of Edward Vesala's accordion-led pieces, 'Mojotoro' is dedicated to the universalization of musical culture. It draws on tango, Bolivian *Andina* music, Uruguayan *Candombe* and other folk forms, travelling between deceptively spacious but highly intricate bandoneon figures and passionate saxophone outcries which suggest a hybrid of Gato Barbieri with another ECM alumnus, Jan Garbarek. The multi-part 'Mundos' is less effective than the title-piece, and the strongest performances are on the more conventionally structured pieces, 'Tango A Mi Padre' and Pintin Castellanos's wonderful *milonga*, 'La Punalada'. Instrumental colours are expertly handled, but the main drama comes from the interaction between Saluzzi and his kinsman, 'Cuchara', who is a marvellously evocative clarinettist.

Cité de la Musique is big on atmosphere, but a disc with no real centre, and one finds oneself wandering through it, a little disorientated culturally, not at all clear what idiom one's dealing with and where one's being led. Johnson is superb as ever, but no sense of engagement beyond a pro's refusal to be thrown or wrongfooted.

***** Kultrum – Rosamunde Quartet**

ECM 457854-2 *Saluzzi; Andreas Reimer, Simon Fordham (vn); Helmut Nicolai (vla); Anja Lechner (clo).*

The original *Kultrum* (above) was for unaccompanied bandoneon, but Saluzzi has always regarded the work as an ongoing and ever-expanding project rather than as a fixed opus number, and on this beautifully modulated album he emphasizes the orchestral dimensions of the piece with the addition – or, rather, the integration – of the Rosamunde Quartet. These are experienced practitioners of modern and contemporary repertoire and, like their colleagues, Kronos, are untroubled by non-Western rhythms. Easy to assume that Saluzzi uncritically embraces the tango tradition, but in 'Salon de tango', he suggests that his country's national form is escapist and passive. 'Milonga de los morenos' touches on the genre's African influences while 'Miserere', now almost a repertory piece, touches on a wider range of emotions than grief. Indeed, on this version it seems closer to anger. The development of *Kultrum* continues apace and deepens every time Saluzzi returns to it.

Perico Sambeat (born 1962)

ALTO SAXOPHONE, FLUTE

Played in his local scene in the '80s before visiting and performing in London and New York, subsequently associating with several major players; regular sideman in the Guy Barker group.

***** Uptown Dance**

EGT 565 *Sambeat; Michael Philip Mossman (t, picc t, tb); David Kikoski (p); Bill Morning (b); Keith Copeland (d).* 5/92.

***** Dual Force**

Jazz House JHCD 031 *Sambeat; Steve Melling (p); Dave Green (b); Stephen Keogh (d).* 12/93.

The Spaniard plays with unstinting energy. He loves the sound of bebop alto to the extent that he could have stepped on to a bandstand with Stitt or Cannonball and come off just fine. The tightly packed solo on 'The Menace', on the earlier of these two sessions, shows what he can do. But the context, on this date in particular, is more modern and prickly than that: the compositions by the underrated Mossman establish a lean, angular world of unusual shapes and harmonies, and Sambeat seems to thrive on them. The brassman is in excellent voice himself, Kikoski is bright and alert, and the result is a cut above the average. The Jazz House disc, recorded during a season at Ronnie Scott's, is more cursory: as sole horn, Sambeat carries it and, though his colleagues play well, it's no more than a workmanlike result.

*****(*) Ademuz**

Fresh Sound FSNT 041 *Sambeat; Mike Leonhart (t); Mark Turner (ts); Brad Mehldau (p); Kurt Rosenwinkel (g); Joe Martin (b); Jorge Rossy (d); Guillermo McGill, Enric Canada (perc); Enrique Morente (v).* 8–11/95.

Sambeat was associated early on with new majors such as Mehldau, Turner and Rosenwinkel, and they're all here on this simmering, thickly textured session, excitingly delivered, if over-crowded with detail and noise. The percussion team is involved most of the way through and they set much of the feel of the music, from the polyrhythmic undergrowth of the title-track to the more closely argued layers of 'Expedición'. The leader makes as much of an impression as anyone in his solos, often sailing out of the hyperactivity in the rhythm section with aplomb. The other players are sometimes crowded for space and never make the impression they do on their later records, but this is still a charismatic and frequently exciting record.

David Sanborn (born 1945)

ALTO AND SOPRANO SAXOPHONE

Sanborn is one of the most widely known instrumentalists of today, principally through his signature alto saxophone sound, which has appeared on hundreds of recordings in the past three decades. He took up the horn partly as therapy for a polio condition which he went through as a child. He worked with rock and rhythm-and-blues bands in the 1960s before leading a long series of albums which bridged jazz with instrumental pop and R&B. He has expressed his distate for the 'smooth jazz' school of recording and tries to distance himself from being considered an influence on it.

****(*) Taking Off**

Warner Bros 927295-2 *Sanborn; Randy Brecker (t); Tom Malone (tb); Peter Gordon, John Clark (frhn); Michael Brecker (ts); Howard Johnson (bs, tba); Don Grolnick (ky); Steve Khan, Buzzy Feiten, Joe Beck (g); Will Lee (b); Chris Parker, Rick Marotta (d); Ralph Macdonald (perc); strings.* 75.

**** Heart To Heart**

Warner Bros 3189-2 *Sanborn; Jon Faddis, Lew Soloff, Randy Brecker (t); Michael Brecker (ts); Mike Mainieri (vib).* 1/78.

***** Voyeur**

Warner Bros 256900-2 *Sanborn; Tom Scott (ts, f); Michael Colina (ky); Hiram Bullock, Buzzy Feiten (g); Marcus Miller (b, g, ky, d); Buddy Williams, Steve Gadd (d); Lenny Castro, Ralph Macdonald (perc).* 81.

**** As We Speak**

Warner Bros 923650-2 *Sanborn; Bill Evans (ss); Bob Mintzer (bcl); Robert Martin (frhn); Don Freeman, Lance Ong, George Duke (ky); James Skelton (org); Michael Sembello (g, v); Buzzy*

Feiten (g); Marcus Miller (b); Omar Hakim (d); Paulinho Da Costa (perc). 82.

Whatever palatable, easy-listening trimmings are applied to David Sanborn's records, his own contributions always cut deeper than that. 'I'm pushing for the limit,' he always says about his playing, whether in the studio or on the concert stage. He had a particular sound by the time of *Taking Off*, having already worked in rock and blues bands for ten years, and, while he is shy of jazz as a basis for his own music, his high, skirling tone and succinct phrasing have inspired countless other players. The problem with *Taking Off* and *Heart To Heart* is context: other than delivering a vague format of funky instrumentals, there's little for Sanborn to bite on here, and the original tunes aren't much more than 1970s funk clichés. *Voyeur* is the album that raises the game a notch: the sound assumes a hard gleam, and a tightness that would be constricting for most players replaces any sense of a loose gait. The altoman thrives in the context, cutting sharp circular patterns like a skater on ice, with the prettiness of 'It's You' and 'All I Need Is You' balancing the bright, airless funk of 'Wake Me When It's Over'. *As We Speak*, though, was a disappointing repeat run, with sentimental fluff courtesy of guitarist-singer Sembello taking up too much room.

***** Backstreet**

Warner Bros 923906-2 *Sanborn; Marcus Miller (ky, g, b, perc); Michael Colina (ky); Hiram Bullock (ky, g); Buzzy Feiten (g); Steve Gadd (d); Ralph Macdonald (perc).* 83.

***** Straight To The Heart**

Warner Bros 925150-2 *Sanborn; Randy Brecker, Jon Faddis (t); Michael Brecker (ts); Don Grolnick (ky); Hiram Bullock (g); Marcus Miller (b, ky); Buddy Williams (d); Errol Bennett (perc).* 84.

**** A Change Of Heart**

Warner Bros 925479-2 *Sanborn; Michael Brecker (EWI); Marcus Miller (ky, g, b); Don Grolnick, Rob Mounsey, Michael Colina, John Mahoney, Michael Sembello, Bernard Wright, Philippe Saisse, Ronnie Foster, Randy Waldman (ky); Mac Rebennack (p); Hiram Bullock, Hugh McCracken, Nicky Moroch, Carlos Rios (g); Anthony Jackson (b); Mickey Curry, John Robinson (d); Paulinho Da Costa, Mino Cinelu (perc).* 87.

*****(*) Close-Up**

Reprise 925715-2 *Sanborn; Marcus Miller (ky, g, b); Richard Tee, Ricky Peterson (p); Hiram Bullock, Nile Rodgers, Steve Jordan, Jeff Mironov, G.E Smith, Paul Jackson (g); Andy Newmark, Vinnie Colaiuta, William House (d); Paulinho Da Costa, Don Alias (perc); Michael Ruff (v).* 88.

Marcus Miller had been playing and composing for Sanborn's records before, but with *Backstreet* he began producing as well, intensifying further the almost abstract neo-funk which the saxophonist had behind him in the mix. *Backstreet* featured some agreeable tunes as well as the beat, though, and in the title-piece, 'A Tear For Crystal' and 'Blue Beach' Sanborn wrung the most out of each situation. His sound was sometimes almost frozen in the still space of the studio but his tone remained uniquely capable of emoting in this context. Cut before a studio audience, *A Change Of Heart* simulated one of Sanborn's live shows and, while it has some tedious features, it's a rare chance to hear the leader in more extended solos than usual, and they are strong enough to belie his insistence that a jazz context is inappropriate for him.

A Change Of Heart was a false step. Four different producers handle the eight tracks, and the result is a mish-mash of styles where each man tries to affix Sanborn's trademark wail in his own setting. Only Miller's work is truly effective, although Michael Sembello gave Sanborn one of his most insistently catchy melodies in 'The Dream'; the rest is over-produced pop-jazz. *Close-Up*, however, was a brilliant return to form. This time Miller handled the whole project and turned in tunes and arrangements which took Sanborn to the very limit of this direction. Having experimented with different keyboard and drum-programme sounds on the earlier records, Miller built backing tracks of maze-like complexity which barely gave the saxophonist room to breathe, yet the exciting riff-tune, 'Slam', the sweet melodies of 'So Far Away' and 'Lesley Ann' and the staccato snap of 'Tough' squeezed Sanborn into delivering some of his smartest ideas. It's a little like a modernization of West Coast jazz, where soloists were required to put a personal stamp on 16 bars in the middle of a skin-tight arrangement. The sound is artificially brilliant but entirely suitable for the music.

***** Another Hand**

Elektra 61088-2 *Sanborn; Art Baron (tb, btb); Lenny Pickett (cl, ts); Terry Adams, Mulgrew Miller (p); Leon Pendarvis (org); Bill Frisell, Marc Ribot, Al Anderson, Dave Tronzo (g); Greg Cohen, Charlie Haden, Marcus Miller (b); Joey Baron, Steve Jordan, Jack DeJohnette (d); Don Alias (perc); Syd Straw (v).* 90.

A striking if sometimes uneasy change of direction. After working with a wide range of players on his American TV series, *Night Music*, Sanborn (and producer Hal Willner) sought out less familiar territory and came up with this curious fusion of jazz, R&B and the kind of instrumental impressionism which participants Frisell and Ribot have been associated with. Sanborn sounds interested but not entirely sure of himself at some points, and seems happiest on the rhythmically less taxing pieces such as the infectious lope of 'Hobbies' and two tracks with the Millers and DeJohnette. The film-music medley arranged by Greg Cohen emerges as a queer pastiche. Possibly more important to its maker than to his audience, but well worth hearing.

*****(*) Upfront**

Elektra 61272-2 *Sanborn; Earl Gardner, Laurie Frink, Randy Brecker, Paul Litteral, Herb Roberston (t); Dave Bargeron, Art Baron (tb); Stan Harrison (as); Lenny Pickett, Arno Hecht (ts); Crispin Cioe (bs); Richard Tee (org); John Purcell (ts, saxello); William Patterson, Eric Clapton (g); Marcus Miller (b, ky, g, bcl); Steve Jordan (d); Don Alias, Nana Vasconcelos (perc).* 91.

Looser, funkier, free-flowing where the last one was bound up in itself, this is Sanborn sounding comfortable and in charge. His own playing doesn't change so much from record to record, but he sounds a lot happier back here in Marcus Miller's grooves than he did on Hal Willner's on the previous disc. The hip, updated treatment of Ornette's 'Ramblin'' works out a treat, with Herb Robertson adding squittery trumpet, but the whole record has a lot of fine playing – in a live-in-the-studio atmosphere – that stands up to plenty of listening.

***** Hearsay**

Elektra 61620-2 *Sanborn; Earl Gardner, Michael Stewart (t); John Purcell, Lenny Pickett (ts); Marcus Miller (bcl, ky, g, b); Ricky Peterson (org, p); William Patterson, Dean Brown, Robben Ford (g); Steve Jordan (d); Don Alias (perc).* 93.

Still seeking a live-in-the-studio sound, Miller produces a great set of grooves here for Sanborn to blow over; a revision of Marvin Gaye's 'Got To Give It Up' and a gorgeous 'The Long Goodbye' are two highlights among many. But the man himself sounds merely capable. One longs for a single killer solo, or for one of the other horns to step up and push him into his best form.

***** Pearls**

Elektra 61759-2 *Sanborn; Don Grolnick (ky); Kenny Barron (p); Marcus Miller, Christian McBride, Mark Egan (b); Steve Gadd (d); Don Alias (perc); Oleta Adams, Jimmy Scott (v); strings.* 94.

Sanborn's strings album is an elegant vehicle for his sound. The choice of material is safe rather than surprising, but it's interesting that the old-fashioned pieces – 'Willow Weep For Me' or 'Come Rain Or Come Shine' – don't suit him nearly as well as the 'mature' modern pop of Sade's title-tune – where he gets a nice note of menace in – or Leon Russell's 'Superstar'. Scott and Adams take a vocal apiece, to no great effect, and the sound is glassy rather than warm, but the overall effect is pleasing enough.

***** The Best Of David Sanborn**

Warner Bros 9362-45768-2 *As various discs above.* 75–93.

Sanborn's hits collection covers seven of his Warners albums and is a neat survey of his most commercially successful years. As a pocket primer on the most copied and insidiously influential sax sound of its era, very effective.

***** Songs From The Night Before**

Elektra 61950-2 *Sanborn; Randy Brecker (t); John Purcell (bcl, f); George Young (ss, cl, f); Dave Tofani (ts, f); Ricky Peterson (ky); Paul Peterson, Phil Upchurch, Dean Brown (g); Pino Palladino (b); Steve Jordan (d); Don Alias (perc).* 96.

Ricky Peterson has worked with Sanborn before, but here he produces a whole set for the nominal leader. The results are just sweet enough for the radio and sufficiently gritty for Sanborn to get creative. An affecting melody like 'Rikke' sits next to a tersely funky take on Eddie Harris's 'Listen Here', and further down the list is Wayne Shorter's 'Infant Eyes'. Sanborn remains peerless at grafting a serious player's heart and soul on to moves that would otherwise be mere fluff: his kind of urban night music, shrewdly suggested by this disc's packaging, can pass by unnoticed but still present an authoritative and lived-in hinterland to 'real' jazz. Like his other recent records, though, this one misses a pressing reason to exist.

*****(*) Inside**

Elektra 7559-62346-2 *Sanborn; Wallace Roney (t); Michael Brecker, Lennie Pickett (ts); Ronnie Cuber (bs); Gil Goldstein (p); Ricky Peterson (org); Marvin Sewell, Dean Brown, Bill Frisell, Fareed Haque (g); Hank Roberts (clo); Marcus Miller (b, bcl, ky, v); Gene Lake (d); Don Alias (perc); Cassandra Wilson, Sting, Lalah Hathaway, Eric Benet (v).* 98.

Sanborn has another go at making heavyweight music that they'll still play on the radio. Back with Marcus Miller at the desk, he gets close to delivering his best record. Warm, without the phoney radiance of smooth jazz, the settings which Miller devises are just idiosyncratic enough to refuse to let the record slip into the background and, if Sanborn himself sometimes drifts through the music rather than commanding it, he plays his parts with real sensitivity and effort. His own tune, 'Lisa', one of two writing credits, is the prettiest thing on the record. Miller writes in real horns – Brecker and Cuber play only charts, but they're easy to spot – and plays his brainy-sidekick role just right.

David Sanchez (born 1969)

TENOR SAXOPHONE, SOPRANO SAXOPHONE

Born in Guaynabo, Puerto Rico, Sanchez played salsa before turning to jazz, and he studied with Kenny Barron. Encouraged by Dizzy Gillespie, he won a contract with Columbia.

***** Sketches Of Dreams**

Columbia 480325 *Sanchez; Roy Hargrove (t); Danilo Perez, David Kikoski (p); Larry Grenadier (b); Adam Cruz (d); Milton Cardona, Jerry Gonzalez, Leon Parker (perc).* 94.

When he made his first record, (*Departure*, currently deleted), Sanchez was already in his mid-twenties, still young but not a raw and untamed stripling, and there was a callowness in it which is only briefly engaging. Sanchez has a big, broad, old-fashioned sound that some have likened to Johnny Griffin but which in approach borrows much from Rollins and very little from Coltrane, unusually for a player of his generation. Once again on *Sketches Of Dreams* what makes this album is the sterling support from Perez, Grenadier and Cruz, who turn what might have been an exercise in individualist showmanship into a jazz album.

*****(*) Street Scenes**

Columbia 485137 *Sanchez; Kenny Garrett (as); Danilo Perez (p); John Benitez, Larry Grenadier, Charnett Moffett (b); Horacio Hernandez, Clarence Penn (d); Milton Cardona, Richie Flores (perc); Cassandra Wilson (v).* 2–3/96.

On *Street Scenes* Sanchez concentrates more on his tenor playing and on constructing well-shaped and logical solos, a little less on texturing and ornamentation. It's all the better for it. Effective guest slots from Kenny Garrett and Cassandra Wilson (on 'Dee Like The Breeze'), but a slightly more functional role for Perez, whose own career was moving apace. This throws more light on the leader himself, and Sanchez sounds like a man comfortably in control of his thing. His exchanges with Garrett on 'Los Cronopios' are both traditional saxophone-duel stuff and highly contemporary, almost ironic. It may or may not be significant that the best track of all is the only unadorned quartet, 'Four In One', just Sanchez, Perez and rhythm. Moffett and Hernandez are used only on the title-track, subtitled 'Downtown', a strong rhythmic idea that outstays its welcome by a couple of minutes.

*****(*) Obsession**

Columbia CK 69116 *Sanchez; John Clark (frhn); George Young (as, ff); Dale Kreps (as, af); Tom Christensen (ts, ob); Andres*

Boiarsky (ss, ts, cl); Roger Rosenberg (bs, bcl); Edsel Gomez (p); John Benitez (b); Adam Cruz (d); Richie Flores, Jose Gutierrez, Hector Matos, Pernell Saturnino (perc); strings. 12/97–1/98.

Branford and Delfeayo Marsalis were on hand to produce what turns out to be Sanchez's most wholly Latin date of the bunch, and a first attempt to deal with other composers' work. Four of the tracks are from Puerto Rican musicians, two from Brazil (including Jobim's 'Omorro nao tem vez'), and the set is rounded out with Ray Bryant's 'Cuban Fantasy', arranged for big band. The overall sound is very big, almost grandiose; but here and there Sanchez sounds slightly pinched, almost as if playing on a borrowed horn. His solo development, though, has never been better and there is a depth of focus which hasn't been evident on previous records. With extra woodwinds and strings in the mix, the arrangements are both capacious and nicely detailed. The focus, though, remains on Sanchez himself.

Tommy Sancton

CLARINET, VOCAL

A revivalist clarinettist, Sancton grew up only 30 blocks away from Preservation Hall in New Orleans. Although he played in the city in 1970, he subsequently gave up music, and he returned to it only in the late '80s, since when he has been a more regular participant in the music associated with the city.

*****(*) New Orleans Reunion**

GHB BC-283 *Sancton; David Paquette (p, v); Cornelis 'Pam' Pameijer (d).* 10/89.

The title suggests a homecoming of ancients, but these not-so-old veterans have a wonderful time on this almost impromptu studio date. All three men worked in New Orleans in revivalist outfits in the 1970s, but here they touch on an intimacy and unaffected warmth rare in much of this kind of music. Sancton is a careful, unflashy player, stately in the manner of the old masters of New Orleans clarinet but gifted with a smooth, beguiling tone that graces all of his lines. He seldom plays in the high register and that gives his solos a flowing ease of delivery on ballads and stompers alike. Paquette is a cheerful, two-fisted player, a fine partner, and Pameijer is as proper as a New Orleans drummer should be. Although most of the tunes are familiar enough, they picked some lovely rarities in Claude Hopkins's 'Crying My Eyes Out Over You' and Ellington's 'A Lull At Dawn'. The recording is very close-miked and friendly.

Pharoah Sanders (born 1940)

TENOR SAXOPHONE

Originally Farrell Sanders (and persuaded to make the change by none other than Sun Ra), John Coltrane's latter-day playing partner has run the gamut, from stretched-out bop to high-intensity trance music to a late and unexpected role as a disco hero. A powerful soloist and something of an enigma in the recent history of the music.

***** Pharoah's First**

ESP Disk 1003 *Sanders; Stan Foster (t); Jane Getz (p); William Bennett (b); Marvin Patillo (d, perc).* 9/64.

*****(*) Izipho Zam**

Charly CDGR 226 *Sanders; Sonny Fortune (as); Lonnie Liston Smith (p); Sonny Sharrock (g); Cecil McBee, Sirone (b); Howard Johnson (tba); Billy Hart, Majid Shabazz (d); Chief Bey (African d); Tony Wylie (perc); Leon Thomas (v, perc).* 1/69.

***** Karma**

Impulse! IMP 11532 *Sanders; Julius Watkins (frhn); James Spaulding (f); Lonnie Liston Smith (p); Ron Carter, Richard Davis, Reggie Workman (b); William Hart, Freddie Waits (d); Nathaniel Bettis (perc); Leon Thomas (v, perc).* 2/69.

**** Jewels Of Thought**

Impulse! IMP12472 *Sanders; Lonnie Liston Smith (p, f, perc); Richard Davis, Cecil McBee (b, perc); Roy Haynes (d); Idris Muhammad (d, perc).* 10/69.

****(*) Deaf, Dumb, Blind, Summun, Bukmun, Umyun**

Impulse! AS 9199 *Sanders; Woody Shaw (t, perc, v); Gary Bartz (as, perc); Lonnie Liston Smith (p, perc); Cecil McBee (b); Clifford Jarvis (d); Nathaniel Bettis (perc, v); Anthony Wiles (perc).* 7/70.

****(*) Thembi**

Impulse! IMP 12532 *Sanders; Michael White (vn, perc); Lonnie Liston Smith (p, perc); Cecil McBee (b, perc); Roy Haynes (d); Clifford Jarvis (d, perc); Nat Bettis, Chief Bey, James Jordan, Majid Shabazz, Anthony Wiles (perc).* 11/70, 1/71.

If the Creator does, indeed, have a master plan, then the role he has written for Pharoah Sanders is a complex one. Like those other great saxophonists, Snub Mosley and Bill Clinton, he hails from Little Rock, Arkansas, and in the 1960s, while Snub was getting by and Bill was obstinately refusing to inhale, Sanders was swallowing great draughts of air to produce some of the most raucously beautiful saxophone sounds of the decade. Having worked with John Coltrane during the latter's last years, he had acquired licence to stretch harmonics to the utmost, but always, unlike Coltrane, over a hypnotically simple ground, which is why in later years Sanders was able to reinvent himself as the wicked uncle of the club and dance scene.

An ESP Disk recording was almost *de rigueur* for anyone in the New York avant-garde. Sanders's is better than most, though it suffers from a very anonymous band. As usual, the leader plays with enough intensity to weld metal, albeit with a softer and broader tone than Coltrane's. Like his sometime employer, he was taken up by Impulse! and given a freer hand than was strictly good for him. Unlike the admirably disciplined Trane, Pharoah never knows when an idea has run its course, and the half-hour plus of 'The Creator Has A Master Plan' (which is basically all there is of *Karma*) palls rather quickly. The saxophone part is pretty much front and centre throughout and, though Bob Thiele's production gives due weight to the other instruments, there is no mistaking that it's Pharoah's gig. The short 'Colors' is a makeweight, but on reflection contains as much of promise as the main event. Like other Impulse! products of the time, it feels like slim pickings at less than 40 minutes; surprising that there wasn't at least some out-take material to pad it out.

Summun, Bukmun, Umyun consists of just two pieces, and it is pretty short measure in contemporary CD terms. Lonnie Liston Smith's adaptation of 'Let Us Go Into The House Of The

Lord' is altogether more engaging than the title-piece, which is overstocked with yodelling cries and aimless percussion. Bartz sounds in good voice and it is intriguing to hear Woody Shaw in this company; not his usual turf, though as ever he responds very positively to a free environment.

Izipho Zam is interesting but timelocked, a shambolic and rather undisciplined group performance which doesn't really give any of the soloists except Fortune and the irrepressible Sharrock much room to express themselves. Even well re-mastered, *Thembi* obstinately refuses to move us, a bland and strangely mechanical run-through of the familiar ethnic/free clichés of the period, with an over-emphasis on small instruments and not enough on straight playing. This was more about wearing funny hats than making music. *Jewels Of Thought* is even weaker still, two great slabs of ambient sound which again bear the stamp of Lonnie Liston Smith as co-composer. Perhaps it was his influence that blunted these early records. Certainly Sanders seems all too willing to shed the ferocity and sheer strength of his work with Coltrane.

***** Pharoah**

India Navigation IN 3421 *Sanders; Jiggs Chase (org); Dierdre Sanders (harmonium); Munoz (g); Steve Neil (b); Gregg Bundy, Lawrence Killian (d).* 71.

Just as an ESP-Disk session seemed *de rigueur* for the avant-garde, so too did a record for India Navigation. Depending on your point of view, this is either where Pharoah set off looking for new musical directions, new points of crossover in the black music continuum, *or* the moment when the rot set in. A live album featuring what was briefly the working band, it all too readily degenerates into fuzzy electric blues, most obviously on 'Harvest Time', a title which now rattles with ironies. The sound is no better and no worse than you'd expect, given the club provenance, but this was certainly not the last time that Pharoah found himself tacked on to the front of a bland pop unit. David Murray was to pull it off in future years with his R&B projects, but here the dissociation of styles is still too jarring. Seven years later, Pharoah made a pop record called *Love Will Find A Way*, never to our knowledge released on CD. It had at least the merit of blatancy and unpretentiousness.

*****(*) Black Unity**

Impulse! IMP 12192 *Sanders; Hannibal Marvin Peterson (t); Carlos Garnett (ts); Joe Bonner (p); Stanley Clarke, Cecil McBee (b); Norman Connors, Billy Hart (d); Lawrence Killian (perc).* 11/71.

Skimpy as to length, but packed with interest. The line-up alone should be tweaking interest already; Garnett, Bonner, McBee and Hart have never enjoyed the celebrity they deserve, and here they contribute to a fascinating collage of sound, dark splashes of colour which never sound virtuosic but which contribute to an intensely vivid and dramatic canvas. Garnett in particular is stunning, a lighter sound almost in alto range. Again, it's tempting to wonder how much material from the session was left on the cutting-room floor. We have two versions of Coltrane's 'Ascension' and a first draft of Ornette's 'Free Jazz' and, though the differences are not critical in either case, the fascination remains.

***** Journey To The One**

Evidence ECD 22016 *Sanders; Eddie Henderson (flhn); Joe Bonner, John Hicks (p); Paul Arslanian, Bedria Sanders (harmonium); Mark Isham (syn); Chris Hayes, Carl Lockett (g); James Pomerantz (sitar); Yoko Ito Gates (koto); Ray Drummond, Joy Julks (b); Randy Merrit, Idris Muhammad (d); Phil Ford (tabla); Babatunde (perc); Claudette Allen, Donna Dickerson, Bobby McFerrin, Vicki Randle, Ngoh Spencer (v).* 80.

A club classic. In purely artistic terms, this was something of a false start. Learning that he was to make an album of ballads was a little like learning – and we're struggling now for a suitably bathetic comparison – that Carlos the Jackal was doing voluntary work with the elderly. What's quickly apparent is that the gentler, more linear and melodic Sanders is not fundamentally different from the high-octane screamer, just differently modulated. As was to be the norm from here on in, the key track is a Coltrane cover, in this case 'After The Rain'. Players of the quality of Bonner, Hicks and Henderson add materially to the mix. The piano players are required to generate an almost tranced quality, bedding Sanders's breathy excursions. This is such a well-trodden set now that it's hard to reach an objective conclusion; strong, vibrant jazz.

***** Rejoice**

Evidence ECD 22020 *Sanders; Danny Moore (t); Steve Turre (tb); Bobby Hutcherson (vib); John Hicks (p); Joe Bonner (p, v); Peter Fujii (g, v); Lois Colin (hp); Art Davis (b); Jorge Pomar (b, v); Billy Higgins, Elvin Jones (d); Babatunde, Big Black (perc); Flame Braithwaite, William S Fischer, Mira Ishida, B Kazuko, Bobby London, Sakinah Muhammad, Carol Wilson Scott, Yvette S Vanterpool (v).* 81.

Cluttered by spurious vocals, but packed with interesting episodes. The basic group is hard to fault, but it's rarely heard in isolation and there is always someone running interference. The brasses aren't heard to advantage; a pity, because one can imagine someone like Eddie Henderson thriving in this company. The two Coltrane items are 'Moments Notice' and 'Central Park West', the latter interesting for being one of the few originals on which Trane did not solo. Sanders turns it into a moody, brooding excursion.

***** Shukuru**

Evidence ECD 22022 *Sanders; William Henderson (p); Ray Drummond (b); Idris Muhammad (d); Leon Thomas (v).*

****(*) Heart Is A Melody**

Evidence ECD 22063 *Sanders; William Henderson (p); John Heard (b); Idris Muhammad (d); Paul Arslanian (bells, whistle); Andy Bey, Flame Braithwaite, Cort Cheek, Janie Cook, William S Fischer, Mira Hadar, Debra McGriffe, Jes Muir, Kris Wyn (v).* 1/82.

Henderson becomes a key player in the early 1980s, an able and fluent player with a touch of the Herbie Hancocks. Sanders appears to be rethinking his strategy around this time, turning back to standards playing for the first time in many years. That tenor saxophonist's shibboleth, 'Body And Soul', on *Shukuru* is intelligently performed, with few new ideas, but a sympathetic synthesis of much of what has gone on between Byas and

Coltrane concentrated into a relatively straightforward melodic response.

*****(*) Africa**

Timeless SJP 253 *Sanders; John Hicks (p); Curtis Lundy (b); Idris Muhammad (d).* 3/87.

A change of label and a deliciously stripped-down personnel. 'Naima' is the key track here, with Hicks – who independently wrote 'Naima's Love Song' – giving the familiar, yearning melody his own almost private spin. Lundy is a master in his own right and he fits in with Hicks like jigsaw pieces, a rich, contoured sound that prompts the wonder that Sanders ever wants to work in any other context. Lovely, lovely stuff.

***** A Prayer Before Dawn**

Evidence ECD 22047 *Sanders; William Henderson (p, syn); John Hicks (p); Lynn Taussig (sarod, chandrasarang); Alvin Queen (d); Brian McLaughlin (tabla).* 9/87.

The cover of *A Prayer Before Dawn* shows the middle-aged Sanders with white fringe beard and anomalously black hair framing a benevolently owlish expression far removed from the contorted scowl of former years. With accommodation has come productivity, a steady string of unscary and mostly very palatable records. The sound is drier and less physical than Timeless had started to give him, but very effective on its own terms. Coltrane cover: 'After The Rain' again, torrential, fresh, brand-new.

***** Moon Child**

Timeless SJP 326 *Sanders; William Henderson (p); Stafford James (b); Eddie Moore (d); Cheikh Tidiane Fale (perc).* 10/89.

*****(*) Welcome To Love**

Timeless SJP 358 *Sanders; William Henderson (p); Stafford James (b); Eccleston W Wainwright (d).* 7/90.

Henderson and James aren't quite in the Hicks/Lundy mould, but you can readily hear the kind of thing Sanders is after, a hypnotic groove that allows the horn to float almost at will. Interestingly, the saxophonist stays very much on the comfortable side of the chords; even given all the leeway in the world, Sanders no longer wants to tread the outside edge. *Moon Child* is the straightest jazz album he'd made for years, anticipating the trim, angular contours of the later *Crescent With Love*. At this juncture, though, he sounds almost restrained, holding out if not holding back. *Welcome To Love* is more elaborate, embellished, and much of the credit has to go to the estimable Eccleston W. Wainwright, who ought to be executive vice president of his own firm with a name like that, but certainly can't be short of work playing as he does.

*****(*) On Timeless**

CD SJP 253/326/358 3CD *As for Africa, Moon Child, Welcome To Love.*

A valuable gathering-in of Pharoah's work for the Dutch label, though on the face of it it seems odd that they should have opted for this approach, with no additional tracks or out-takes, rather than a more conventional compilation or best-of. Hearing these albums back-to-back doesn't significantly relocate them. The 'Timeless years' were strong but relatively uneventful in terms of big stylistic shifts.

****** Crescent With Love**

Evidence ECD 22099 2CD *Sanders; William Henderson (p); Charles Fambrough (b); Sherman Ferguson (d).* 10/92.

The 25th anniversary of Coltrane's death spawned a rash of tribute albums, few of them as apostolically convincing as this. A perfectly balanced band, with Henderson growing in stature almost as you listen to him and Fambrough showing once again what a responsive and intelligent player he can be in the right company. Five Coltrane tunes, opening with 'Lonnie's Lament', 'Wise One', 'Naima', 'Crescent' and closing disc two with 'After The Rain', these interspersed with 'Misty', 'Too Young To Go Steady', 'Feeling Good', Pietro Piccioni's 'Light At The Edge Of The World' and one original, Henderson's 'Softly For Shyla'. Sanders sounds thoughtful and even a little wistful, as befits a tribute to his friend, but he never lets his playing drift into sentiment. A strong, creative record, perhaps the only one of the recent batch that can be considered essential.

****(*) Message From Home**

Verve 529578-2 *Sanders; Michael White (vn); William Henderson (p, ky, v); Bernie Worrell (ky, v); Jeff Bova (ky); Dominic Kanza (g); Steve Neil (b); Hamid Drake (d, perc); Aiyb Dieng (perc).* 95.

Another change of label and a noticeably sharper sound, not matched by the quality of the playing. Sanders sounds almost flabby and, because he has surrounded himself with a mechanical, electronic sound, the weakness of the front line sinks in with every repeat hearing. A disappointment after the high of *Crescent With Love*.

****(*) Save Our Children**

Verve 557297-2 *Sanders; William Henderson (p, harmonium); Bernie Worrell (org, electric p, syn); Tony Cedras (harmonium); Jeff Bova (syn); Alex Blake (b); Zakir Hussain (tabla, mbira, v); Trilok Gurtu (d, tabla, perc); Abdou Mboup (talking d, v); Asante, Abiodun Oyewole (v).* 98.

Not even the devoted Mr Horst who runs a very useful Pharoah Sanders webpage has a good word to say about this, and he's a fan of *Love Will Find A Way*. Producer Bill Laswell may have (OK, has) done some important work in a jazz context, but his besetting sin of over-production really comes to the fore here: a treacly, over-rich sound that leaves Pharoah sounding as if he's busking to some obscure white-label club track. The pity is that the leader is in rather good form, leaner and more to the point than of late and with fewer of the irritating mannerisms – acidic grace-notes, slowed-down and speeded-up versions of the same phrase – that have crept in and out of his work down the years. How intriguing it would be to hear this remixed with a basic acoustic quartet – but then that's not where the money lies these days. The title-track is a shocker, and only later (on 'Kazuko' and 'The Ancient Sounds') does this approach anything like the quality you'd expect of the great man. Time to *really* get back to those roots he's always banging on about.

Randy Sandke (born 1949)

TRUMPET, CORNET, GUITAR

Born in Chicago, he learned trumpet and followed the music of idols like Bix and Louis. Worked for ASCAP in New York but began playing jazz again and found himself in demand in swing-mainstream circles. In the '90s he took on an ambassadorial role for the styles he loved, playing at repertory concerts but also recording more outré material on his own records.

***** The Sandke Brothers**

Stash ST-CD-575 *Sandke; Jordan Sandke (t, c); Joel Helleny (tb); Michael Brecker, Tad Shull (ts); Jaki Byard, Jim McNeely (p); John Goldsby, Milt Hinton (b); Charles Braugham, Kenny Washington (d).* 5–6/85.

***** Stampede**

Jazzology JCD-211 *Sandke; Dan Barrett (tb, c); Ken Peplowski (cl); Scott Robinson (bsx, c); Ray Kennedy (p); Marty Grosz (g); Linc Milliman (tba); Dave Ratajczak (d).* 12/90.

***** Wild Cats**

Jazzology JCD-222 *As above, except Mark Shane (p), James Chirillo (g), Jack Lesberg (b) replace Robinson, Kennedy, Grosz and Milliman.* 7/92.

***** I Hear Music**

Concord CCD-4566 *Sandke; Ken Peplowski (ts, cl); Ray Kennedy (p); John Goldsby (b); Terry Clarke (d).* 2/93.

*****(*) Get Happy**

Concord CCD-4598 *As above, except Kenny Barron (p) replaces Kennedy; add Robert Trowers (tb).* 9/93.

*****(*) The Chase**

Concord CCD-4642 *Sandke; Ray Anderson (tb); Chris Potter (as, ts, ss); Michael Brecker (ts); Ted Rosenthal (p); John Goldsby (b); Marvin 'Smitty' Smith (d).* 3/94.

*****(*) Calling All Cats**

Concord CCD 4717 *Sandke; Joel Helleny (tb); Chuck Wilson (as); Gary Keller (ts); Scott Robinson (ss, ts, bs); Howard Alden (g); Michael Moore (b); Dennis Mackrel (d).* 12/95.

When it comes to versatility, Sandke's the man, and it lines him up alongside Guy Barker, Wynton Marsalis and a select few in a trumpet section that could play more or less anything in pretty much any style. As ever, the problem with that skill lies in how to sound like yourself. Sandke is getting there, but on some of the earlier records his accomplishments can sound hollow. The Stash CD reissues two LPs, one under the leadership of each Sandke brother: there's little to choose between them in terms of the improvising, but Randy's tunes have a more interesting bent – 'Bix's Place' is very pretty, and so is the ballad, 'Brownstones'. Jordan plays well, but he seems to have faded from the scene somewhat. Sandke's New Yorkers account for the next four discs. This is a repertory group in the manner of those helmed by Marty Grosz and Keith Ingham, and with a similar cast of performers, so there's little to surprise anyone who's heard the many records in this burgeoning genre. *Stampede* is a bit brisker than *Wild Cats*, but the latter gives the soloists some extra room and Sandke sounds more relaxed: he constructs a very fetching solo out of 'Wild Cat' itself, for instance. On all four discs there is first-class support from both Peplowski and Barrett, spirits in close kinship to the leader. Sandke himself is rather variable: some of his solos sound almost pernickety in their attempts to please period feel, others better their environment.

The Concords are more ambitious. *I Hear Music* mixes old songs with six originals by Sandke, and if his tunes aren't so impressive here they serve as sound vehicles for a deepening mastery of the trumpet: his high notes are cleaner and tougher, and his fast lines have a hard-bitten confidence. *Get Happy*, though, introduces an intriguing set-list: Monk's 'Humph', Ellington's 'Black Beauty' (done as an exquisite trio for trumpet, clarinet and piano), Miles Davis's 'Deception' and Mingus's 'Boogie Stop Shuffle'. There's also a somewhat odd affection for Al Jolson's repertoire. Barron's expert accompaniment is a further bonus, and Trowers adds extra colour to five tracks, while Sandke excels on a winsome arrangement of Fauré's 'Sicilienne'. *The Chase* continues what's by now an impressive sequence. Anderson and the splendid Potter add muscle and élan to the front line, while Robinson and Brecker lend further gravitas. The material stretches from Don Redman to Duke Jordan, and Sandke sounds in control of all of it. *Calling All Cats* continues what is an admirable sequence. By now, the line between repertory and Sandke's originals is blurring enough to make his music sound all of a multifarious piece. The title-tune is an especially frisky original, the 7/4 treatment of 'Mr Snow' is a delight, tunes by Cootie Williams and Buck Clayton make a pleasing homage to trumpeters-who-compose, the band are all warmth and polish – Alden is a very welcome contributor this time – and Sandke himself hits every note on the button.

****** The Re-Discovered Louis And Bix**

Nagel-Heyer CD 058 *Sandke; Jon-Erik Kellso, Nicholas Payton (t); Wycliffe Gordon, Dan Barrett (tb); Ken Peplowski (cl, ts); Kenny Davern (cl); Chuck Wilson (as); Scott Robinson (ts, Cmel, bsx); Dick Hyman (p, cel); Howard Alden, James Chirillo (g, bj); David Ostwald (tba); Peter Washington, Greg Cohen (b); Joe Ascione (d).* 6–9/99.

Other albums by the New York All Stars are listed under that name, but Sandke gets top billing here – as well he might. A stunning bit of revivalism, this aligns eight Armstrong pieces – some little-heard, others virtually unknown and unrecorded – and seven similarly associated with Beiderbecke. It starts with a bristling piece in the Oliver Jazz Band style called 'Papa What Are You Trying To Do To Me I've Been Doing It For Years', moves through Hot Seven and big-band styles to something in the manner of the All Stars. The Bix material (abetted by Hyman's scholarship) is at least as fascinating, with Goldkette and Venuti material of varying stripes. The playing is little short of superlative by all hands: outside of the great Keith Nichols projects, this kind of living-history has seldom been presented with this mix of individual panache and proper homage. One of the best projects this label's realized to date, going several notches above their frequently polite mainstream manners.

Arturo Sandoval (born 1949)

TRUMPET, FLUGELHORN, KEYBOARDS, PERCUSSION, VOCAL

A Cuban expatriate, Sandoval created a storm of interest in the 1980s, seeming to ride in on a fresh wave of Latin jazz creativity. His subsequent progress has been much less interesting.

****(*) No Problem**

Jazz House JHCD 001 *Sandoval; Hilario Duran Torres (p); Jorge Chicoy (g); Jorge Reyes Hernandes (b); Bernardo Garcia Carreras (d); Reinaldo Valera Del Monte (perc).* 8/86.

****(*) Straight Ahead**

Jazz House JHCD 007 *Sandoval; Chucho Valdes (p); Ron Matthewson (b); Martin Drew (d).* 8/88.

****(*) Just Music**

Jazz House JHCD 008 *Sandoval; Hilario Duran Torres (ky); Jorge Chicoy (g); Jorge Reyes Hernandes (b); Bernardo Garcia Carreras (d); Reinaldo Valera Del Monte (perc).* 8/88.

**** Flight To Freedom**

GRP 059634-2 *Sandoval; Ed Calle (ts, f); Chick Corea, Mike Orta, Danilo Perez, Richard Eddy (ky); Rene Luis Toledo (g); Anthony Jackson, Nicky Orta (b); Dave Weckl, Orlando Hernandez (d); Long John, Portinho (perc).* 91.

In person, Sandoval is one of the most ebullient trumpet ambassadors since Dizzy Gillespie, his great mentor. On record, this Cuban exile and scintillating virtuoso is a less convincing figure. The live record is a fair sample of the kind of music he serves up at Ronnie Scott's on his regular visits and, while the playing bubbles with Latin fire and brilliance, battle fatigue tends to overtake the listener. Sandoval may be a great technician, but it's often hard to detect any reason for the galloping runs other than a love of showmanship. The band provide zesty accompaniment. In the studio, with Valdes and a British rhythm section, the atmosphere seems calmer until they go into the trumpet machismo of 'Mambo Influenciado', which shows that Sandoval doesn't need a live audience to prod him into going over the top. *Just Music* was recorded around the same time and is another mixed bag of kitsch and genuine music-making. The GRP set was his first 'American' statement after defecting to the USA, and the irony is that it often falls into international muzak: GRP house-bands provide faceless backing tracks which the trumpeter dances over with a sometimes light but more often crashingly heavy footfall.

***** I Remember Clifford**

GRP GRP-96682 *Sandoval; Ernie Watts, David Sanchez, Ed Calle (ts); Felix Gomez (ky); Kenny Kirkland (p); Charnett Moffett (b); Kenny Washington (d).* 91.

Tribute albums are becoming a bore, but this is easily the best record under Sandoval's name. The material is all in dedication to Clifford Brown, and most of it emanates from Brownie's own repertoire, including 'Joy Spring', 'Daahoud' and the like. The up-tempo pieces are as thrilling as Sandoval can make them: 'Cherokee' is taken at a preposterously fast tempo, and the trumpeter still pulls off a solo which outpaces everybody else. Watts and Sanchez also fire off some exciting solos of their own, and the rhythm section is absolutely on top of it, with Kirkland at his most dazzling. Yet there remains a gloss of routine on the music, which can sound utterly unyielding, and the production decision to create some trumpet parts by feeding them through a harmonizer only adds to the sense of a spirit tamed by the demands of making successful records.

**** Dream Come True**

GRP 059702-2 *Sandoval; Bill Watrous (tb); Ernie Watts (ts); Michel Legrand, Otmaro Ruiz (ky); Brian Bromberg (b); Peter Erskine, Aaron Sefarty (d); Carlos Gomez, Mitchell Sanchez (perc); strings.* 93.

**** The Latin Train**

GRP 059820-2 *Sandoval; Dana Teboe (tb); Ed Calle (ts, bs, f); Kenny Anderson (as); Otmaro Ruiz (p); Rene Toledo (g); David Enos (b); Aaron Sefarty (d); Manuel Castrillo, Luis Enrique, Edwin Bonilla, Carl Valldejuli (perc); Joe Williams, Celia Cruz, Oscar D'Leon, Luis Enrique, Vicente Rojas, Laura Pifferrer, Cheito Quinones (v).* 1/95.

Gimcracked around Sandoval's prodigious but exhausting talents, these albums are a stifling bore, and they show Sandoval already with nowhere interesting to go. *Dreams Come True* just about gets by on the basis of 'Dahomey Dance', which at least gives Watts and Watrous something useful to do; the rest, heavingly arranged by Legrand, is charmless. So is most of *The Latin Train*, which seems about as feelingful and sincere as a Las Vegas wedding. The frantic high-note playing and souped-up arrangements go nowhere fast. For diehard fans only.

****(*) Swingin'**

GRP 059846-2 *Sandoval; Clark Terry (t); Dana Teboe (tb); Michael Brecker, Ed Calle (ts); Eddie Daniels (cl); Joey Calderazzo (p); Mike Stern (g); John Patitucci (b); Gregory Hutchinson (d).* 1/96.

Well, the supporting cast is terrific, and Sandoval probably stands as tall as any of them on this set of bebop and hard-bop covers and copies. But it's hard to see why anyone would want to invest in this kind of xeroxed imitation.

**** Americana**

N-Coded Music NC-4205-2 *Sandoval; Jason Carder (flhn); Dana Teboe (tb); Ed Calle (as, ts, ss, cl); Charles McNeill (ts); Doug Bickel (p); Richard Eddy Martinez, Jim Gasior (ky); Dan Warner, Danny Toledo (g); Dennis Marks (b); Ernesto Simpson (d); Luis Enrique (perc). n.d.*

Smooth jazz in all but name, this set of pop tunes from the songbooks of Sting, Janet Jackson and so forth musters some respectable music – 'Englishman In New York' not bad, 'All Night Long' good enough to compete with Herb Alpert. But the ballads are melted slush. Likely to be Arturo's final listing in this book.

Nisse Sandström

TENOR SAXOPHONE

Although he was playing a kind of free jazz in the early '60s, Sandström eventually focused on a mainstream bop style and was a familiar presence in Swedish studios in the '70s and '80s.

***** Home Cooking**

Phontastic PHONTCD 9309 *Sandström; Tommy Flanagan (p); Red Mitchell (b).* 10/80.

***** For Lester And Billie**

Phontastic PHONTCD 7562 *Sandström; Horace Parlan (p); Red Mitchell (b); Monica Zetterlund (v).* 8/83.

Sandström's congenial style gives him the aura of the Fifth Brother, and all the other musicians on these records obviously feel right at home in such affable company. Cut in Red Mitchell's Stockholm apartment, *Home Cooking* offers plenty of fun, warming up with 'I Remember You' and proceeding past a definitively swinging version of Flanagan's 'Minor Mishap'. Mitchell plays with his usual teetering playfulness, every solo almost-but-not-quite dropping out of time, and there is plenty of humour between piano and tenor. Some may not like the home-made sound, but it does suit the informality of the occasion.

The *Lester And Billie* collection marked Zetterlund's return to active duty in a jazz context and, though she sounds a little off here and there, the gentle complexion of the music cushions any problems. Sandström wears his Lester on his sleeve, as one might expect, only he doesn't flub the opportunity on the likes of 'I Wished On The Moon' the way his mentor might have done. Two worthwhile reissues.

Marit Sandvik (born 1956)

VOCAL

Norwegian vocalist from the far north of Europe.

****** Song, Fall Soft**

Taurus TRCD 834 *Sandvik; Oystein Blix (tb); Jorn Oien (p); Konrad Kaspersen (b); Trond Svarre Hansen (d).* 3/95.

Jazz from Tromsø, at the northern tip of Norway, an unlikely home for bebop for many years and a self-sufficient community of players, many of whom have passed into local legend. Sandvik's strong, lean voice is perfectly at ease, whether torching 'Cry Me A River' (her startling entrance takes the breath away), scatting the melody of Jimmy Raney's 'Motion' or duetting with Hansen on a beautiful 'Up Jumped Spring'. She never struggles for a note, has a perfectly clear sense of where a melody's going and uses the most subtle dynamics in all her vocals. She writes lyrics for Wayne Shorter's 'Fall' (transmogrified into the title-piece) and three graceful originals by Oien, whose exquisite touch and insight stand in a fine tradition of Norwegian jazz. Blix is a surprise choice for a front-line partner, but his sober agility works superbly in the context, and Kaspersen and Hansen do everything they have to. Jan Erik Kongshaug also gives them all a wonderful sound. A quite marvellous record.

San Francisco Starlight Orchestra

GROUP

A band of devotees of the more 'orchestral' style of '20s dance music, sometimes hot, sometimes in a sweeter vein. They play regularly in their home town and are meticulous about period detail.

***** Doin' The Raccoon**

Stomp Off CD1271 *Bob Schulz (c, v); Bruce Vermazen (c); Brent Bergman, Gene Isaeff (tb); John Howard (cl, as, bs); John Pedone (as, cl); Robert Young (ts, ss, bsx, cl, c); Alan Hall (p); Ray Landsberg, Ed Rosenback (vn, v); Jeremy Cohen, Su Jacobsen, Pamela Carey (vn); Dave Frey (bj); Jim Brennan (tba); Hugh O'Donnell (d).* 12/92–7/93.

***** Cheerful Little Earful**

Stomp Off CD1296 *As above, except add Gloria Isaeff (vn), Janine-Marie Braddock (v); omit Bergman, Jacobsen.* 2–4/95.

***** Rose Colored Glasses**

Stomp Off CD1334 *As above, except omit Young and Cohen; add Brian Campbell (cl, ts, bsx).* 9/97–3/98.

An institution in the city, this contentedly time-locked outfit re-creates the symphonic jazz of Paul Whiteman, blending hot-dance arrangements of period material with the sweetness of a violin section. They are stricter and more genteel than most of the Stomp Off repertory bands and, with their specific commitment which goes as far as using period instruments when possible (Schulz even blows on Bix Beiderbecke's cornet on the first disc), probably unique. Since they go as far as including a Rudy Wiedoeft number, jazz listeners may find it all a bit much, but the second disc's quota of hot tunes includes 'Bessie Couldn't Help It' and 'Baltimore'. *Rose Colored Glasses* continues in more or less identical fashion, with a few licks of the exotic: 'Rumba Negro', 'Maori (A Samoan Dance)'. Play one of these in the car and shock your fellow drivers.

Kent Sangster

TENOR SAXOPHONE, SOPRANO SAXOPHONE

The young Canadian is firmly grounded in modern saxophone idiom but is already individual enough to resist pigeon-holing.

*****(*) Adventures**

Jazz Focus JFCD 006 *Sangster; David Liebman (ss); Mick Goodrick (g); Jon Ballantyne (p); Drew Gress (b); Owen Howard (d).* 1/95.

In any decent, well-ordered society, there should be a moment when, in all due maturity, you confront an old teacher. Musicians probably have more opportunity than most and here, on 'Mr B', Kent Sangster locks sopranos with David Liebman. This isn't just one more for the Gipper, but a meeting of minds, the one still forming, still taking in and processing possible trajectories, the other gently magisterial. It's right that they should have had such an encounter, but Liebman is also right in saying that Kent has already acquired his own voice.

The soprano playing is mellifluous and assured. On 'Ballad For Wayne' (presumably Shorter, another obvious influence) and 'Border Crossing', he phrases confidently and builds solos with a logic that isn't merely harmonic brickwork but genuinely expressive. The tenor is maybe less individual but is thoroughly idiomatic, and it would be fascinating to hear the one standard of the set – 'Night And Day' – done on the bigger horn as well. Recommended.

Eivin Sannes (born 1937)

PIANO

Born in Hønefoss, Sannes turned pro in 1957. His regular gig as the house pianist in Bergen's Hotel Neptun during the '60s was a focal point for Norwegian jazz.

*** Sandu

Gemini GMCD 67 *Sannes; Sture Janson (b); Ronnie Gardiner (d).* 5/90.

*** Jubilee

Gemini GMCD 93 *Sannes; Atle Hammer (t); Harald Gundhus (ts, f); Jesper Thilo (ts); Arvid Genius (vib, v); Sture Janson, Niels Pallesen (b); Edward Olsen (d); Sven Erik Nørregaard, Sergio Gonzalez (perc).* 6–7/97.

Sannes comes from, in his own words, 'the generation that will always be grateful to the great composers – Duke Ellington, Van Heusen, Benny Golson and many others'. The veteran Norwegian pianist plays 15 standards on *Sandu* with a lot of engaging sparkle. His manner is poised between swing and the cooler end of bebop – one of his early inspirations was Pete Jolly – and, while there's nothing to startle a casual listener here, the tracks are delivered with fine, unassuming candour. A duet with Janson on 'Lulu's Back In Town' is particularly crisp and witty, but there's something good in all the tracks and, though he can be a little too fond of arpeggios and the occasional commonplace, some unusual tunes – Buster Bailey's 'Peruvian Nights' and Victor Feldman's 'Azule Serape', which bookend the record – add fresh interest.

Sannes celebrates 40 years of playing on *Jubilee*, with plenty of old friends on hand, four new originals and some Monk, Dameron and standards. A nice stroll through his back pages, nothing fancy, much to enjoy.

Mongo Santamaria (born 1922)

PERCUSSION

Born in a poor quarter of Havana, Santamaria came to the USA in 1950, originally to work with Cal Tjader, and became a hugely influential force in hybridizing the rhythms of Latin American music with jazz. In his own groups he adapted the charanga line-up to accommodate saxophones and brasses. His composition, 'Afro Blue', still occasionally credited in error to John Coltrane, is a modern classic.

*** Sabroso

Original Jazz Classics OJCCD 281 *Santamaria; Louis Valizán (t); Jose Chombo Silva (ts); Rolando Lozano (f); Vince Guaraldi (p); Cal Tjader (vib); Felix Pupi Legarreta (vn); Al McKibbon, Victor Venegas (b); Willie Bobo (perc); Pete Escovedo, Bayardo Velarde (v).* 59.

*** Arriba!

Fantasy 24738 *Santamaria; Rolando Lozano (f); Jose Chombo Silvo (ts); Joao Donato (p); Felix Pupi Legarreta (vn); Victor Venegas (b); Cuco Martinez (perc); Rudy Calzado (v).* 59.

*** Our Man In Havana

Fantasy FCD 24729 2 *Santamaria; Armandito El Fine (t); Julio (f); Paquito (f, p); Nino Rivera (tres); Willie Bobo (perc); Bol, Pepito (b); Gustavito (guiro); Yeyito (perc); Mario Arenas, Carlos Embales, Cheo Junco, Macuchu, Armando Raymact, Luis Santamaria, Merceditas Valdés (v); Cuban All Stars.* 60.

Santamaria is now regarded more as a catalyst than as a significant performer in his own right, but his work is well worth hearing, and he has stuck to his last over the years. *Sabroso*, which includes in the line-up Santamaria's old boss, Cal Tjader, is nicely balanced between traditional *charanga* with its flute-and-violin front line and a more contemporary jazz sound. Bobo and vocalist Escovedo are effectively co-leaders, providing a lot of the drama of the set.

Arriba! sticks doggedly to the same formula, a generous array of 22 themes by the leader, band members Lozano and Legarreta, with the Gillespie/Pozo classic, 'Manteca', thrown in as an example of reciprocal influence.

The personnel on *Our Man In Havana* remains somewhat obscure, largely because many of the players are identified only by their first names. It's remotely possible that political pressures have something to do with this. The music is certainly very much on first-name terms: hot, intimate and joyous, with a greater admixture than before of traditional elements. The two main vocalists, Embales and Valdés, are classic exponents of the repertoire and flautist Julio and *tres* player Nino Rivera add to the chemistry.

*** Watermelon Man

Milestone 47075 *Santamaria; Marty Sheller (t); Mauricio Smith (f); Bobby Capers, Pat Patrick (f, sax); Jose Chombo Silva (ts); Rodgers Grand (p); Felix Pupi Legarreta (vn); Victor Venegas (b); Frank Hernandez, Ray Lucas (d); Willie Bobo, Joseph Gorgas, Kako (perc); Rudy Calzado, La Lupe, Osvaldo Chihuahua Martinez (v).* 12/62, 9/63.

By the first years of the '60s, Santamaria was working in what was identifiably a jazz idiom, with strong Latin inflexions, rather than the other way round. Herbie Hancock's 'Watermelon Man', played very much in the spirit of the original but rhythmically much looser and more elaborate, delivered the percussionist his first major hit. From this point on, his reputation was firmly established. The horn voicings are very jazz-orientated and the track lengths were carefully tailored to radio and jukebox requirements. It would be good to hear longer versions of almost all of these tunes, not least the Cannonball Adderley/Joe Zawinul collaboration, 'Cut That Cane'. The reissue includes six previously unissued tracks from a live Californian set recorded in 1962. These don't add much to a record that is already classic Santamaria.

*** At The Black Hawk

Fantasy FCD 24734 *Santamaria; Jose Chombo Silva (ts); Pat Patrick (sax, f); Rolando Lozano (f); Joao Donato (p, tb); Victor Venegas (b); Willie Bobo (perc); Rudy Calzado (v).* 62.

There was still something of a split in Santamaria's market placing at this time, so Fantasy divided the material from the Black Hawk into two slightly different album packages. The jazz-inflected *Mighty Mongo* and the more Cuban *Viva Mongo!* are paired up on this fine CD reissue. Santamaria's sidemen were also getting used to the idea of playing like jazz musicians, and saxophonist Jose Chombo Silva unveils a range of influences from Hawkins to John Coltrane, which makes slightly more sense when you see tunes like 'Body And Soul' and 'All The Things You Are' slipped into the programme for the first time.

*** Mongo At The Village Gate

Original Jazz Classics OJCCD 490 *Santamaria; Marty Sheller (t); Pat Patrick (as, f); Bobby Capers (ts, f); Rodgers Grand (p); Victor Venegas (b); Frank Hernandez (d); Julian Cabrera, Osvaldo Chihuahua Martinez (perc).* 9/63.

The live records have always been the best measure of Santamaria's work and, even though the registration on this Symphony Sid-hosted event isn't of the absolute best, the whole disc is shot through with a sense of excitement and the tunes are allowed to find their own length rather than be tailored for radio and jukebox. Santamaria's feature on 'My Sound' was the sort of thing that American players from Dizzy Gillespie onward were to find so inspirational.

**(*) Mongo Introduces La Lupe

Milestone MCD 9210-2 *Santamaria; Alfredo Chocolate Armenteros, Marty Sheller (t); Pat Patrick (as, f); Bobby Capers (ts, f); Rodgers Grand, Rene Hernandez (p); Victor Venegas (b); Kako, Osvaldo Martinez, Frank Valerino (perc, v); La Lupe (v).* 63.

La Lupe is a bit of an acquired taste and just a touch overdone. She features on only half the tracks, leaving the rest to a rather generic and formulaic instrumental recording which Santamaria fans will treasure and most others find irritatingly inconsequential. This was the band's high-water mark and it was overproducing furiously. Marty Sheller and Chocolate Armenteros exchange some high-note stuff that would have done Dizzy Gillespie proud, and the usual range of saxophonists and percussionists, not forgetting the ever-present Rodgers Grand, provide deft accompaniment. For enthusiasts only, though.

*** Greatest Hits

Fantasy 24753 *As above.* 58–63.

The first of a series of anthologies and compilations which manage, big hits apart, not to step on each others' toes. This rounds up Mongo's first records for Fantasy, up to the point when 'Watermelon Man' propelled him into the pop charts. It's worth having if you don't own or wouldn't find the occasion to play the original releases. There are no new or unissued selections, just a nicely packaged and well-sequenced choice.

*** Skins

Milestone 47038 *Santamaria; Paul Serrano, Marty Sheller (t); Nat Adderley (c); Hubert Laws (f, picc, ts); Al Abreu, Pat Patrick (sax, f); Bob Capers (as, bs); Chick Corea, Rodgers Grand (p); Jose De Paulo (g, perc); Victor Venegas (b); Ray Lucas (d); Julio Collazo, Carmelo Garcia, Wito Kortwright, Osvaldo Chihuahua Martinez, To-Tiko (perc); Carmen Costa, Marcellina Guerra, Elliott Romero (v); chorus.* 64, 72.

Skins has always been the best place to start for those who are not ready for the undiluted Santamaria of earlier years. The album still has a lot to recommend it, and the presence of Adderley and Chick Corea, who learned a great deal from Santamaria's music, will recommend it to jazz fans. There is a preponderance of vocal music on the later set which is rather wearing when mixed up as loud as it is; very much in the style of the time but unnatural to contemporary tastes.

*** Summertime

Original Jazz Classics OJCCD 626 *Santamaria; Dizzy Gillespie (t); Tommy Villarini (t, perc); Doug Harris (ts, f); Toots Thielemans (hca); Milton Hamilton (p); Lee Smith (b); Steve Berrios (d, perc).* 7/80.

Coming back to this record after several years, we find our enthusiasm somewhat diminished by what now seems an overlong and indulgent set on which Mongo, Dizzy and Toots stretch out over four tunes, including the percussionist's otherwise evergreen 'Afro Blue' and the title-piece. Dizzy has articulation problems throughout and yet seems bent on hitting the heights every time he takes a solo. The opening tune, Alphonse Mouzon's 'Virtue', is the best thing on the album, its crisp promise unfulfilled.

*** Soy Yo

Concord CCD 4327 *Santamaria; Eddie E.J Allen (t); Sam Furnace (as, bs, f); Tony Hinson (ts, f); Bob Quaranta (p, ky); Ray Martinez (b); John Andrews (d, perc); Pablo Rosario, Steve Thornton, Valentino (perc); Ada Chabrier, Denice Nortez Wiener (v).* 4/87.

**(*) Soca Me Nice

Concord CCD 4362 *Santamaria; Ray Vega (t, flhn); Bobby Porcelli (as, bs, f); Mitch Frohman (ts, f); Bob Quaranta (p); Ray Martinez (b); Johnny Almendra Andreu, Humberto Nengue Hernandez (perc); Angelo-Mark Pagen (v).* 5/88.

**(*) Ole Ola

Concord CCD 4387 *As above, except omit Martinez, Pagen; add Bernie Minoso (b), Jil Armsbury, Bobbi Cespedes, Claudia Gomez (v).* 5/89.

*** Live At Jazz Alley

Concord CCD 4427 *As above, except omit Armsbury, Cespedes, Gomez; add Eddie Rodriguez (perc).* 3/90.

Concord label boss Carl Jefferson was always interested in Latin jazz, and so Santamaria was a not unexpected signing. It's difficult to avoid the impression that by this stage the Cuban's creativity was at something of a discount and that he was merely reworking successful formulae. It was also some time since the huge chart success of 'Watermelon Man' and Mongo could have used another hit. Sade's 'Smooth Operator' makes it into the final cut on *Soy Yo*, as does the then rather dated 'Day Tripper' on *Soca Me Nice*, which suggests how anxious he was to update and broaden his fan base. The first of the records is probably the best, even so, though there are some very good things on *Live At Jazz Alley* as well, Mongo as ever responding to the challenge of a live date. At nearly seventy, Santamaria plays with undiminished energy, and there is a fine, shuffling rendition of 'Afro Blue' which will be of interest to those who heard John Coltrane do the same tune, also in Seattle, a quarter of a century earlier.

***** Afro Blue: The Picante Collection**
Concord CCD 4781 *As for Concord records above.* 87–90.

An enjoyable reduction of Santamaria's time with the label, though interestingly his releases for Concord were originally on the main imprint rather than the specialist Picante. All the obvious favourites are included: 'Manteca', 'Para Ti' and a long, live version of 'Afro Blue'.

***** Mambo Mongo**
Chesky 100 *Santamaria; Eddie Allen (t); Jimmy Cozier (as); Craig Rivers (ss, as, ts); Hubert Laws, Dave Valentin (f); Dario Eskenazi (p); Johnny Almendra Andreu (perc); Eddie Rodriguez (perc, v).* 3–92.
Later Santamaria albums were arranged and conducted by trumpeter Marty Sheller, who had been part of the early American bands. Here, having switched to a new label, he seems to have captured something like the feel of the old group, but only very episodically and with no consistency, and the record jumps in and out of focus on almost every number. William Allen and Hilton Ruiz are also credited as composer/ arrangers, and it is Ruiz's 'Caribbean Sunrise' which gives the first half of the record its optimistic bounce. The group also tackles a composition by Onaje Allan Gumbs, 'Are They Only Dreams', a softly dreamlike theme with an edgy second subject which is darker than Santamaria's usual fare.

*****(*) Mongo Returns**
Milestone 9245 *Santamaria; Eddie Allen (t, flhn, as, bs, f); Roger Byam (ss, ts, f); Robert DeBellis (as, bs, f); Mel Martin (picc, f, af, bf); Oscar Hernandez (p, ky); Hilton Ruiz (p); John Benitez (b); Robert Ameen (d); Greg Askew (d, shekere); Johnny Almendra Andreu (d, perc); Louis Bauzo, Steve Berrios (perc, g).* 6/95.

... and returns to Fantasy Records in some triumph with one of his most vivid sets for some considerable time. Once again, Marty Sheller is in charge of the arrangements and, with Hilton Ruiz on board as pianist, and bringing with him the charts for 'Free World Mambo', the stage was set for something quite special. The nods in the direction of pop music are still evident in Stevie Wonder's 'You've Got It Bad, Girl' and Marvin Gaye's 'When Did You Stop Loving Me', but these sound entirely consistent with the style and working practice of the band. A cracking record, recommendable to fans and newcomers alike.

***** Brazilian Sunset**
Candid 79703 *Santamaria; Eddie Allen (t, flhn); Jimmy Cozier (as, bs, f); Craig Rivers (ts, f); Ricardo Gonzalez (p); Johnny Almendra Andreu (d, perc); Eddie Rodriguez (perc).* 2/96.

Santamaria's 75th birthday was already behind him when this lovely, low-key record was made. The reprise of 'Watermelon Man' was a forgivable indulgence and 'Summertime' might well have been segued into 'Autumn Leaves', so thoroughly is the record suffused with a ripe nostalgia. Immaculately produced by Alan Bates and Mark Morganelli, it's flawless product, even if a long way removed from the excitement of the early years.

*****(*) Skin On Skin: The Mongo Santamaria Anthology, 1958–1995**
Rhino 75689 *As for many of the above.* 58–95.
A skilfully selected compilation that picks its way round existing anthologies and makes light of a 15-year gap covering most of the '70s and '80s. As a one-stop introduction to 'Afro Blue', 'Summertime', 'Para Ti', 'Manteca' and 30 others you really couldn't hope to do better.

Michel Sardaby

PIANO

French pianist who made some striking music in the 1970s with American players before doing most of his recording in his own country.

****** Night Cap**
Sound Hills SCCD 8004 *Sardaby; Percy Heath (b); Connie Kay (d).* 70.

*****(*) Straight On**
Sound Hills SCD 8003 *Sardaby; Louis Smith (t); Ralph Moore (ts); Peter Washington (b); Tony Reedus (d).* 5/92.

For most listeners, these two widely spaced sessions will be a first introduction to the Frenchman's work. An artist and architect by training, Sardaby has the structural awareness one associates with Martial Solal or John Lewis, allied to a resonant left hand. Melody lines tend to be quite fast and detailed, with few non-functional notes.

The 1970 trios are a revelation. The presence of Heath and Kay is a reminder of the Lewis connection, and several of Sardaby's originals could almost have been by the great American. There are, however, signature devices and favourite chord progressions which give the game away. The originality of Sardaby's style is premissed on a relatively small set of idiosyncrasies, but they are followed through so elegantly and unabashedly that they acquire considerable charm from their very repetition. All the material on *Night Cap* and *Straight On* is by Sardaby, except for 'Satin Doll', which concludes the trios. The band seem comfortable with the charts. Moore is unflappable and exact, Smith more edgy and intense, but they combine very effectively and, with Sardaby chording more heavily than in the past, give the ensembles the weight of a much larger group. Two themes stand out: the appropriately elegant 'Smoothie', which has touches of Ahmad Jamal, and the slighter but no less beautiful 'Ballad For Roni', which initiates the leader's best solo. It's a pity there's no overlap between the two sessions to check Sardaby's progress. He's made many other albums, but most have a very limited availability and it would be good to see him more generously exposed.

Satchmo Legacy Band

GROUP

A one-off tribuite band, put together in 1987 by Freddie Hubbard for a European tour.

***** Salute to Pops: Volume 1**

Soul Note 121116-2 *Freddie Hubbard (t, flhn, v); Curtis Fuller (tb, v); Alvin Batiste (cl, v); Al Casey (g, v); Kirk Lightsey (p, v); Red Callender (b, tba, v); Alan Dawson (d, v).* 6/87.

*****(*) Salute to Pops: Volume 2**

Soul Note 121166-2 *As above.* 6/87.

The purpose of the Satchmo Legacy was not to produce identikit versions of the Hot Fives and Sevens but to give some of the classic Armstrong repertoire and associated material a respectful but thoroughly contemporary airing. That's immediately evident in the boppish inflexion Hubbard gives to 'Struttin' With Some Barbecue'. Lightsey's contribution to this opening track on *Volume 1* is thoroughly distinctive, and in a curious way the pianist dominates the session, constantly pushing familiar themes and progressions off in unexpected directions. The combination of Lightsey, Hubbard and Fuller acts as a guarantee against revivalist pastiche. Batiste's 'Blues For Pops' is heartfelt but essentially undemanding, setting up a relaxed but slightly shambolic ending that takes in 'Ory's Creole Trombone' (a feature for Fuller), 'Stardust', 'Wild Man Blues' and 'Saints'.

Volume 2 is, if anything, stronger, with just enough focus to shave an extra half-star. The opening 'Muskrat Ramble' is the best thing on the session and the most interesting with regard to the continuity between Armstrong and the bebop style which dominates the brass solos; Fuller takes his in the style of the tune's composer, Kid Ory, but tips his hat to J.J. Johnson as well. Batiste's reaction is slightly eccentric: low-toned and almost gloomy; but there is nothing to match the sheer oddity of Lightsey's vocal antics.

Tom Saunders

CORNET, VOCAL

A Wild Bill Davison disciple who recorded with his mentor on several occasions, Saunders follows in that fiery tradition of hot cornet playing.

***** Call Of The Wild**

Arbors ARCD 19146 *Saunders; Bill Allred (tb); Chuck Hedges (cl); Rick Fay (ts); Johnny Varro (p); Paul Keller (b); Warren Sauer (d).* 4/95.

***** Exactly Like You**

Nagel-Heyer 023 *Saunders; Dick Sudhalter (c, t, flhn); Bill Allred, Roy Williams (tb); Chuck Hedges (cl); Danny Moss (ts); John Barnes (bs, cl); Johnny Varro (p); Marty Grosz (g, v); Isla Eckinger (b); Butch Miles (d); Jeanie Lambe (v).* 9/95.

Saunders calls his group the Wild Bill Davison Legacy Band, since much of their material pays tribute to the cornetist. The Arbors date is a studio session brimming with boisterous *joie de vivre*, running through (and over) some of Bill's favourite tunes, from 'Running Wild' to 'On The Alamo'. There's nothing fancy here, and the band have the chops and the know-how to keep it short of mere Dixieland blarney. *Exactly Like You* captures a concert from Hamburg in which the band was joined by guests Sudhalter, Williams, Barnes and Grosz for a run-through of some more Davison chestnuts (plus Grosz doing one of his Fats Waller numbers). This is a notch above the usual mainstream jam since most of the players are genuine virtuosos and there is some terrific playing on several of the tunes. 'Exactly Like You' is a strong feature for the reedmen, and the other horns take it in turns in the front line before an all-hands-on-deck finale. Lambe comes on only for, oddly enough, 'Milenberg Joys'. In a close call for individual honours, Allred just takes them ahead of Hedges, but acolytes of the genre will enjoy the whole show.

Savannah Jazz Band

GROUP

British trad from the north of England.

****(*) Savannah Jazz Band**

Lake LACD29 *Tony Smith (t, v); Brian Ellis (tb); Martin Fox (cl); Jack Cooper (bj); Tony Pollitt (b); John Meehan (d).* 6/92–1/93.

****(*) It's Only A Beautiful Picture ...**

Lake LACD51 *As above.* 1/95.

***** Out In The Cold**

Lake LACD82 *As above, except add Dave Morrell (tb); Ellis plays (p).* 1/97.

***** Nothing Blues**

Lake LACD112 *As above, except omit Morrell; Ellis plays (tb).* 11/98.

Based in Huddersfield, which is some way from Savannah, the SJB play unreconstructed trad somewhat in the Ken Colyer tradition: absolutely no frills, not many solos, and no shame about the vocals. Smith cracks too many notes to provide a really purposeful lead, and it's left to the bustling clarinet of Fox to make the biggest impression. These aren't bad records, but they sound pretty ramshackle when compared with the best of the new American traditionalists. The first has a more acidic sound-mix, but at least that has some fizz, which the second is a little short on.

The two later records emerge rather better, partly owing to a more sympathetic sound, particularly on *Nothing Blues*, and partly through what must be a course of pep pills for whoever decides the tempos. Ellis was too ill to blow trombone on the earlier date, and he adds some clattery piano instead. However, we really must ask Mr Smith to give someone else a go at the vocals, if there have to be any!

Jarmo Savolainen (born 1961)

PIANO

Contemporary Finnish pianist at work both on his home patch and on American turf.

*****(*) Songs For Solo Piano**

Beta BECD 4023 *Savolainen (p solo).* 12/89–6/90.

When Savolainen first turned up in the USA, one seasoned critic refused to accept that somewhere in his east Finnish ancestry there wasn't at least one antecedent from south of the

Mason–Dixon line. This is perhaps slightly overstating the case, but there certainly isn't much of your copywriter's 'Nordic chill' about this gifted piano stylist. He comes from the same quarter of country as percussionist Edward Vesala, but he is much more obviously steeped in jazz and in a wide range of idioms, from blues and swing to bebop and the fringes of the avant-garde. The solo record provides an ideal opportunity to sample him at close quarters. First records always invite questions about 'influences'. The two improvisations and 'Song No. 1' recall a spectrum of American players from Chick Corea to Keith Jarrett, though here and there one can hear the impact of other, perhaps less prominent stylists: Hampton Hawes, Wynton Kelly, even a touch of Teddy Wilson. 'Lowlands', 'The Word' and the opening 'Ode For Opportunists' are all well-crafted originals. The piano – apparently a model-D Steinway – is superb and has been given the sort of presence, reserved but by no means distant, that a classical player would be delighted with.

***** First Sight**

Timeless CD SJP 380 *Savolainen; Wallace Roney (t); Rick Margitza (as); Ron McClure (b); Billy Hart (d).* 5/91.

Savolainen seems totally at home with the Americans on the New York session for Timeless. The writing is broadly conceived, not too busy and always directed towards maximizing solo space. The pianist yields precedence to the hornmen, restricting himself to brisk and uncluttered interventions that always concentrate on reasserting the basic structures. Rhythmically, he stays pretty much inside but has the kind of time feel that implies all manner of alternative counts, playing threes against fours and dropping into brief but effective *rubato* passages. McClure solos brilliantly on 'The Word', taking his cue from the chords, but by no means constrained by them. A couple of tracks later on, 'Inner Modes' and 'Thoughts' drift towards a Garbarek conception, but Margitza's bluesy sound and an unusually raw mix by Jan Erik Kongshaug, at the Oslo studio favoured by ECM, prevent it from setting like aspic. Almost as a corrective, at this point Savolainen chips in with the one standard of the set, 'How My Heart Sings'. A strong album, executed with vigour and freshness.

****** True Image**

A Records AL 73031 *Savolainen; Tim Hagans (t); David Liebman (ss); Kari Heinila (ts); Ron McClure (b); Billy Hart (d).* 3/94.

*****(*) Another Story**

A Records AL 73112 *Savolainen; Tim Hagans (t); Kari Heinila (ts); Anders Jormin (b); Markku Ounaskari (d).* 8/97.

True Image was also made in New York and is packed with solid, four-square jazz. There are two groups involved, a larger group fronted by Hagans and Heinila and a quartet with Liebman which represented the first time for three years he had played with old Quest colleagues McClure and Hart; 'smooth as glass' was his delighted estimate of the reunion. The soprano coaxes the pianist out of his relative reserve and there are some lovely exchanges on the cleverly constructed 'Things Are The Way They Are', which may be related to 'All The Things You Are', albeit distantly.

The follow-up was taped in Helsinki and is altogether more relaxed, though less tautly focused. For the first time, Savolainen relies almost entirely on originals. Just one standard, and one composition by Heinila among the 11 that make up this generously proportioned set. This sounds like a working group, though it seems clear that some of the material hasn't been fully assimilated. One would like to hear a tighter and more focused performance of 'Another Story' and 'Rapids', which blunt an otherwise impressive opening section. Nicely balanced and mixed, and a positive sign that Savolainen is growing in stature as both composer and performer.

The Savoy Sultans

GROUP

Cooper was a modest saxophonist, but he led the very popular Savoy Sultans for many years, including a residency at New York's Savoy Ballroom from 1937 to 1946.

***** Al Cooper's Savoy Sultans 1938–1941**

Classics 728 *Cooper; Pat Jenkins (t, v); Sam Massenberg (t); Rudy Williams (as); Ed McNeil, Sam Simmons, Irving 'Skinny' Brown, George Kelley (ts); Oliver Richardson, Cyril Haynes (p); Paul Chapman (g, v); Grachan Moncur (b); Alex 'Razz' Mitchell (d); Helen Procter, Evelyn White (v).* 7/38–2/41.

The Sultans usually played opposite the Chick Webb band at Harlem's Savoy Ballroom, and visiting bands were wary of competing with them, since they were so popular with the dancers. The records are another matter: simple head arrangements, average solos and merely capable playing make one wonder why they were held in such high regard. However, playing through these 24 tracks, one can hear some of the simple appeal of what wasn't really a big band but a small, mobile, flexible unit which covered whatever base the customers wanted. Pat Jenkins is the best soloist. Transfers start out very clean, but some of the tracks have plenty of original surface noise.

Ken Schaphorst

COMPOSER, ARRANGER

Wrote and studied in the Boston area during the '80s, co-founding the Jazz Composers Alliance in 1985 and forming his own big band. Since 1991 has directed jazz studies at Lawrence University, Wisconsin.

****** Purple**

Naxos Jazz 86030-2 *Schaphorst; Dave Ballou, John Carlson, Andy Gravish, Cuong Vu (t, flhn); Jose Roseman, Curtis Hasselbring (tb); Dave Taylor, Chris Cresswell (btb); Doug Yates (as, cl, bcl); Jay Brandford (as, cl); Donny McCaslin, Seamus Blake (ts); Andy Laster (bs, cl); John Medeski (ky); Uri Caine (p); Brad Shepik (g); Drew Gress (b); Jamey Haddad, Dane Richeson (d).* 1/98.

Schaphorst's four earlier big-band records have been tough to find, and this one certainly deserves a wider hearing. He's a conservative radical, hewing to familiar forms and techniques – blues lines, writing with Ellingtonian concern for individuals, making the band a big swinging entity when it has to be – but insisting that there are fresh wrinkles on the old language. So he uses Caine and Medeski as a double-act, bolsters the rhythm section as an independent entity by having two drummers much of the way, and makes sure that the band works on several levels, players constantly called on to switch roles as soloists, ensemble foot-soldiers, accompanists and section-shouters. The soloists are a very talented team – any band that can boast Blake, Caine, Medeski, Ballou and Shepik in its number is never going to be starved of improvisers – and, rather than stepping out to assert themselves, they serve to heighten the contrast of individual voices within this hugely impressive outfit. Each of the nine pieces sets up its own world without seeming to stand aside from its siblings, which suggests that Schaphorst's writing and scoring is, for all its multiplicity of elements, very definitely on one track. David Baker's excellent studio sound will be the envy of many other big-band leaders. This is one of the jewels in the Naxos list so far.

Niko Schauble (born 1962)

DRUMS, PERCUSSION

Contemporary drummer leading an international group based in Australia.

***** On The Other Hand**

Naxos Jazz 86011 *Schauble; Stephen Grant (c, flhn); Paul Grabowsky (p); Ren Walters (g); Chris Bekker (b).* 6/97.

Naxos have cast their net far and wide for new and promising talent, but few bands are as thoroughly international as this (notionally) Australian outfit. Schauble was born in Germany and is a nephew of bass virtuoso Eberhard Weber. He has a 'European' sound, quite light and complex, but he can swing as well. Of the other players, only Grabowsky is well known, and he is the key player in a line-up that sounds bursting with energy but often a little wayward. All the compositions are credited to the group, which seems a little surprising. They alternate between terse, pungent items which come in at less than three minutes and longer blowing tunes like 'Jazz Jungle' (the best), 'Waiter Waiter' and 'Why Do We Want To Know?' A strong, very detailed recording, made in the studios of ABC Radio in Melbourne, who are getting behind contemporary music in a big way. Schauble, we see, is also responsible for the cover art. Talented guy.

Mario Schiano

ALTO AND SOPRANO SAXOPHONES, SHEKERE, ORGAN

A pioneer of Italian free music, Schiano recorded with Gruppo Romano in the 1960s but spent much of the next two decades in comparative obscurity. In the '90s he recorded frequently and now holds a singular place in his country's contemporary jazz and improvising doctrine.

***** Gruppo Romano Free Jazz 1966/67 Schiano Trio 1969/70**

Splasc(h) H 509-2 *Schiano; Giancarlo Schiaffini (tb, bari-flhn, ocarina); Bruno Tommaso (b, p); Marcello Melis (b); Franco Pecori (d).* 6/67–4/70.

***** Original Sins**

Splasc(h) H 502-2 *Schiano; Giancarlo Schiaffini (tb); Franco D'Andrea (p); Marcello Melis, Bruno Tommaso (b); Franco Pecori, Paul Goldfield, Franco Tonani, Marco Cristofolini (d).* 3/67–4/70.

*****(*) Sud**

Splasc(h) H 501-2 *Schiano; Massimo Bartoletti, Roberto Antinolfi, Gaitano Delfini (t); Guido Anelli, Ruggero Pastore (tb); Eugenio Colombo, Tommaso Vittorini, Massimo Urbani, Maurizio Giammarco, Toni Formichella (reeds); Domenico Guaccero (ky); Bruno Tommaso, Roberto Della Grotta (b); Alfonso Alcantara Vieira, Michele Iannacone (d); Mandrake (perc).* 1/73–5/78.

Schiano is a weathered veteran of Italy's tiny and often nearly invisible free-jazz movement. His uncompromising but fundamentally lyrical and persuasive alto playing is relatively unstartling, but persistence and a readiness to meet and collaborate with improvisers from other territories has resulted in what's now an extensive discography. Splasc(h) have taken up his cause of late, and these reissues of previously obscure early works fill in a number of details of prehistoric Italian free playing. The earliest CD covers the pioneering Gruppo Romano Free Jazz, originally a trio, then a quartet with Schiaffini, then back to a trio with Tommaso replacing Melis. 'No going back,' says Pecori (now a journalist) in his sleeve-notes, but the scratchy, exuberant music smacks of an excitement which is worth rekindling. The 1967 session is blemished by very poor sound; the 1970 date has something of a free-bop feel, with Schiano even turning in a performance of 'Moonlight In Vermont' along the way. A worthwhile piece of history. *Original Sins* is an interesting patchwork of bits and pieces – 'Beat Suite' is the best excerpt, a dynamically varied trio work-out by Schiano, Tommaso and Pecori – *Sud* is of more consistent quality. A mix of quick-fire quintet pieces and rolling, blustering sketches for a big band, the record finds a fine and spontaneous balance between its elements, uses the synthesizer with rare integrity for the period, and is a valuable glimpse of some important players (apart from Schiano, there are major contributions by Vittorini and Giammarco) from a largely 'unavailable' period of Italian jazz.

*****(*) Unlike**

Splasc(h) H 309-2 *Schiano; Co Strieff (as); Evan Parker (ts); Alex Von Schlippenbach (p); Jean-Marc Montera (g); Maarten Altena, Joelle Léandre (b); Paul Lovens (d).* 3/90.

*****(*) Uncaged**

Splasc(h) H 357-2 *Schiano; Giancarlo Schiaffini (tb); Marcello Melis (b); Famoudou Don Moye (d); Mauro Orselli (bells).* 4/91.

***** And So On**

Splasc(h) H 368-2 *Schiano; Paul Rutherford (tb); Ernst Reisjeger (clo); Leon Francioli (b); Gunter Sommer (d, etc.).* 10/91.

Uncaged and *And So On* are full-length sessions by groups assembled for the occasion, with old friend Moye in usefully alert form on the former date, binding together the memorable interplay between Schiano and the perennially undervalued Schiaffini, whose mix of trombone grotesqueries and hard-bitten commentary is something to treasure. The live date, recorded at Rome's Alpheus Club, features a sober but intensely active group with

Reisjeger and Sommer the wild cards, countering the more meditative work of the two horns (Reisjeger gets a suitably demented solo piece as an encore). *Unlike* finds Schiano in three group-settings: there are two brief duets with Strieff and two numbers apiece with a quartet and a quintet, the latter the Von Schlippenbach Trio with Léandre as a further guest. Perhaps surprisingly, it's the quintet pieces which turn out for the best: Altena's brilliant yet discreet responses to Schiano and Lovens mitigate the more glaring noises made by Montera on guitar. The group with Léandre, Parker, Von Schlippenbach and Lovens follows the vocabulary laid down by the nucleus of that group, and Schiano has a harder time making himself felt. But all of these records have points of absorbing interest.

***** Meetings**

Splasc(h) H 418 *Schiano; Irène Schweizer, Giorgio Gaslini (p); Phil Wachsmann (vn); Clenert Ford (g, v); Bruno Tommaso, Barry Guy (b); Paul Lovens (d); Archie Savage, Pamela Fries (v).* 1/80–10/93.

*****(*) Blue Memories**

Splasc(h) H 449-2 *Schiano; Renato Geremia (ts, cl, f, vn, p); Joelle Léandre (b, v).* 10/94.

*****(*) Used To Be Friends**

Splasc(h) H 452-2 *Schiano; Paul Rutherford (tb); Ernst Reijseger (clo); Peter Kowald (b); Paul Lovens (d).* 10/95.

****** Social Security**

Victo 043 *Schiano; Sebi Tramontana (tb); Evan Parker (ss, ts); Barry Guy (b); Paul Lovens (d).* 5/96.

***** The Friendship Of Walnuts**

Splasc(h) H 611-2 *Schiano; Connie Bauer (tb); Pasquale Innarella (frhn); Roberto Ottaviano (ss, ts); Ernst-Ludwig Petrowsky (cl, as); Vittorino Curci (ts, v, tape); Giuseppe Guarrella (b); Fabrizio Spera (d).* 6/96.

Plenty of music and most of it more than worthwhile. Schiano's own playing remains an element rather than a premier voice in all these ensembles and sometimes he seems like an anti-virtuoso when in company with the likes of Parker and Rutherford. With the smaller groups of *Meetings* and *Blue Memories* this is more problematic, but only in so far as the music occasionally misses a lead when it needs one to be taken. *Meetings* sweeps together a jittery set by the Action Trio of Schiano, Gaslini and Tommaso, two sextet pieces from a Rome concert ('Three Little Songs' part two is particularly effective) and two peculiar gospel tracks on which Schiano plays organ and Archie Savage vocalizes. *Blue Memories* is a friendly joust with Geremia (switching instruments all the time) and Léandre – not bad, if prone to meandering.

Used To Be Friends brings together a superb group for five improvisations where Schiano's good humour seems to set the tone. This is a vivid and often lighthearted encounter. A phone message from Evan Parker interrupts part two, but the man himself is present at the Victoriaville Festival set on *Social Security*, a surpassingly powerful quintet in very fine voice, with the unexpected power and breadth of the little-known Tramontana matching the other four all the way. These two sets are something of a match, but the Victo one has the edge, and the sound is slightly better. *The Friendship Of Walnuts* assembles a bigger ensemble for a single, dense collective. Schiano is something of a bystander here, with such power-players as Ottaviano, Petrowsky and Curci on hand, but the principal music comes from the inimitable Bauer, hugely inventive and accomplished. Another disc where the sound is less than ideal, although improv veterans won't be too troubled by it.

Lalo Schifrin (born 1932)

PIANO, ARRANGER

Born in Buenos Aires, Schifrin studied music in Paris in the '50s, then began film soundtrack work and moved to New York. Wrote for and toured with Dizzy Gillespie in the early '60s, then with Quincy Jones, and eventually focused entirely on film and TV scoring; many famous signature-themes are his. Back with big-band work in the '90s, seemingly for his own amusement.

**** Black Widow**

CTI ZK 65128 *Schifrin; Jon Faddis (t); Wayne Andre, Billy Campbell, Barry Rogers (tb); Dave Taylor (btb); Pepper Adams, Joe Farrell (saxes); Hubert Laws, George Marge (f); Clark Spangler (ky); Eric Gale (g); Andy Newmark (d); Don Alias, Carlos Martin, Carter Collins, Sue Evans (perc); Patti Austin (v); strings.* 3/76.

***** Jazz Meets The Symphony**

Atlantic 782506-2 *Schifrin; Ray Brown (b); Grady Tate (d); London Philharmonic Orchestra.* 11/92.

***** More Jazz Meets The Symphony**

East West/Atlantic 95589-2 *As above, except add Jon Faddis, James Morrison (t), Paquito D'Rivera (as).* 12/93.

Schifrin has spent most of his career in Hollywood, but his arrangements have made a mark on some fine albums, none more so than Dizzy Gillespie's *Gillespiana*. These engaging records aren't so much any kind of Third Stream as sumptuous examples of high-grade jazz schmaltz. *Black Widow* is a survival from a grim period for jazz, but Schifrin's charts have a grain of wit about them that manages to just about peek through the discofied situations, mewling solos and general inconsequentiality (this was 1976, after all). The recent Atlantics don't show his aesthetic changing much. The LPO gamely play their way through charts that won't tax any intellects, while Schifrin and the wily team of Brown and Tate noodle over the top. The second disc is a little more high-powered, with two long suites in dedication to Miles Davis and Louis Armstrong and the noted guest soloists in attendance, but it's really more of the same – impeccably recorded, feather-bedded easy listening.

Alexander Von Schlippenbach (born 1938)

PIANO

The founder of the vast collective, Globe Unity, was born in Berlin and studied music there under the composer, Bernd Alois Zimmerman. He played with trumpeter Manfred Schoof and recorded extensively with other improvisers. The Schlippenbach Trio has been making music for nearly 30 years, though Globe Unity now seems to be in abeyance. Schlippenbach is percussive and intense, but also aware of structure and responsive to traditional jazz piano as well as free music.

****** Smoke**

FMP CD 23 *Schlippenbach; Sunny Murray (d).* 10/89.

Schlippenbach's clean, atonal lines are far more reminiscent of Thelonious Monk than of Cecil Taylor, the figure who is usually adduced as ancestor for this kind of free music. By 1970 Schlippenbach had to some extent turned away from total abstraction and was showing an interest not only in formal compositional principles (serialism, orthodox sonata form, aspects of *ricercare*) but also in renewing his own initial contact with early and modern jazz, blues and boogie-woogie. These interests were still obvious even underneath the radical freedoms of his influential collective, Globe Unity Orchestra, but they became much clearer in his work with the later Berlin Contemporary Jazz Orchestra, where he uses the conventionally swinging drummer, Ed Thigpen, and trumpeter Benny Bailey in among the free men. Schlippenbach's conception of freedom has nearly always resulted in densely layered explorations of tonality, with a pronounced rhythmic slant. It's this that renders him surprisingly accessible as a performer.

Despite being tossed with insulting casualness into that overstuffed category, Schlippenbach is a very different kind of player from Taylor. By the same token, Sunny Murray is a very different kind of player *now* from what he was when he played with Taylor back in 1960. *Smoke* is an intriguing collaboration, in which both men hang up their 'free music' armour and get down to what sounds like a set of phantom standards. There are a dozen or more teasing echoes, more elusive than allusive, but only one outwardly identifiable theme, Monk's 'Trinkle Tinkle'. Beautifully recorded and superbly played, it warms slowly from a rather misterioso opening. Only on 'Down The Mission' does the Taylor parallel make complete sense. Elsewhere, Monk and even Herbie Nichols seem more valid points of reference. Murray's 'Angel Voice' uses material that he has developed over two decades; cymbal overtones create an illusion of choral effects, studded by tight accents and the familiar poly-directional lines.

****** Elf Bagatellen**

FMP CD 27 *Schlippenbach; Evan Parker (ss, ts); Paul Lovens (d).* 5/90.

*****(*) Physics**

FMP CD 50 *As above.* 6/91.

The Schlippenbach Trio with Parker and Lovens has been one of the most lasting and creative associations in European free jazz. Schlippenbach's catalogue has slumped with the disappearance of FMP's vinyl catalogue; two other great records, *Detto Fra Di Noi* and *Das Höhe Lied*, were released on Paul Lovens's small Po Torch label, which may now be difficult to find, and have not been on CD. Missing and mourned is the magnificent *Pakistani Pomade*, garlanded with top rating in our first edition. *Elf Bagatellen* almost merits *Pakistani Pomade*'s crown, not just for its markedly improved sound-quality, but also for the sheer untrifling intensity of the trio's performances. Like the earlier record, this is a studio performance rather than a live set, and it acts as a very conscious summation of the trio's near-two-decade career. It is, inevitably, rather more predetermined than a more spontaneous performance, and there are shards of melody scattered throughout. 'Sun-Luck: Revisited' refers to 'Sun-Luck Night-Rain', one of the finest pieces on the 1972 album, while 'Yarak: Reforged' provides a similar gloss on a piece from *Payan*, a rare recording for a label other than FMP, in this case Enja. Parker and Lovens have rarely played better together and, if Schlippenbach seems a trifle mild-mannered in places, the richness of the sound more than compensates for a slight drop in pulse-rate. Tremendous stuff.

The more recent *Physics* by the same trio doesn't quite rise to the heights of its predecessors, but it is a dramatic performance all the same. Taped at the 1991 free-music workshops at the Akademie der Künst in Berlin, it has a freewheeling, exploratory quality which is one of the graces of European improvised music. Schlippenbach structures 'The Coefficient Of Linear Expansion' with magisterial control. At nearly 45 minutes, it has the compression and exactitude of a work a tenth that length, and yet it seems to imply all sorts of realities that lie outside the confines of the work.

*****(*) The Morlocks**

FMP CD 61 *Schlippenbach; Henry Lowther, Thomas Heberer, Axel Dorner (t); Jörg Huke, Marc Boukouya, Sören Fischer (tb); Utz Zimmermann (btb); Tilman Denhard (ts, f, picc); Darcy Hepner (as); Evan Parker (ts, ss); Walter Gauchel (ts); Claas Willecke (bs, f); Aki Takase (p); Nobuyoshi Ino (b); Paul Lovens (d, perc).* 7/93.

This is perhaps more strictly a Berlin Contemporary Jazz Orchestra record but, since it consists entirely of Schlippenbach pieces and bears his signature all over it, there is some justification for covering it here. Unlike many of his contemporaries, Schlippenbach has never let go of the term 'free jazz', and it is interesting to compare the harmonic language of many of the pieces here, not least the opening dedication to his companion, Aki Takase, with the work of Ornette Coleman. There are moments in 'The Morlocks' itself when he seems to be playing with the parameters of pitch, duration and attack in a way that is very similar to Ornette's. Elsewhere, as on 'Rigaudon Nr 2 Aus Der Wassertoffmusik', he uses graphic scores and a much more gestural approach that now sounds slightly old-fashioned. On the magnificent 'Marcia Di Saturno', though, he constructs a dense landscape that is much closer to the neo-tonality of his American contemporaries; bassist Nobuyoshi Ino introduces it with a brooding grace before saxophonist Gauchel develops the difficult central elements. This record establishes Schlippenbach much more clearly as a composer. It is worth comparing its language to that of the London Jazz Composers Orchestra under Barry Guy, which is simultaneously more abstract but also more orthodoxly jazz-centred.

*****(*) Complete Combustion**

FMP CD 106 *Schlippenbach; Evan Parker (ss, ts); Paul Lovens (d, perc).* 4/98.

The Schlippenbach Trio is still the best response to the rather trite suggestion that the only improvised music that 'really' works comes as a result of chance encounters. In point of fact, the Trio has recorded only very rarely down the years, but the players' familiarity and understanding is a key element in the process of creation. To suggest that the relationship is telepathic is to multiply concepts unnecessarily and to drift into the metaphysical. As this remarkable live recording underlines, the real key is dialectic, a testing and synthesis of ideas in the crucible of live performance. Having dabbled with something close to Webernian organization on *Elf Bagatellen*, the group has gone back to its former freedom but with a new dynamic implicit in Evan Parker's opening and the slow involvement of the other players. The ability of individual players to drop back and listen, to maintain silence and wise counsel has always been one of the group's great strengths. It is evident here on 'Complete Combustion', less so on 'Fuels 1–7', a sequence of shorter pieces that explore other areas of the group's shared language. Taken together, and lest anyone doubt its vitality, they reaffirm the creative energy of free music.

****** Digger's Harvest**
FMP CD 013 *Schlippenbach; Tony Oxley (d).* 11/98.

Fascinating to compare this with the Schlippenbach/Murray duo that made *Smoke* a decade before. All but the first and last tracks are very short and highly focused. The titles are all drawn from the names of poisonous plants and there is a sharp and sometimes toxic edge to these improvisations. Oxley is the dominant presence almost throughout, not because he filibusters a more prominent place than his playing partner but quite simply because what he plays is more immediately compelling. Yet Schlippenbach is worth listening to with some care as well. His phrasing on 'Digger's Harvest' and on a couple of the short tracks is quite without precedent in this music: taut, elegant, and persuasive without undue rhetoric. A fine record, whoever you buy it for.

Larry Schneider (born 1950)

TENOR, ALTO AND SOPRANO SAXOPHONES

Born in New York, Schneider came up as one of the post-bop tenors of the 1970s, working with Horace Silver and others, but he decamped to San Francisco, where the weather is better for his other passion, tennis.

***** So Easy**
Label Bleu LBLC 6516 *Schneider; David Friedman (vib); Marc Ducret (g); Henri Texier (b); Daniel Humair (d).* 3/88.

*****(*) Just Cole Porter**
Steeplechase SCCD 31291 *Schneider; Andy LaVerne (p); Mike Richmond (b); Keith Copeland (d).* 8/91.

*****(*) Blind Date**
Steeplechase SCCD 31317 *As above.* 4/92.

Schneider has played a sideman role in many situations, and these albums commence a belated recognition of an accomplished saxophonist. He's emblematic of a generation of hard-bop tenor players who came of age in the 1970s, before the fashionable new interest in the form, which leaves his playing untainted by technical strivings and nicely weathered by his experience. *So Easy* finds him in a slightly less convincing situation, with Friedman's vibes an unusual partner and the rhythm section going their own way at times, fine though that often is. It's the Steeplechase albums, with long-time cohort LaVerne, that feature him best. The album of Cole Porter tunes is close to being a definitive gallery of standards, with Schneider in riveting voice on 'What Is This Thing Called Love?', knowingly tender on 'Every Time We Say Goodbye'. *Blind Date* brings the quartet together again on four standards, two originals by LaVerne and Charles Mingus's 'Peggy's Blue Skylight'. Schneider likes long improvisations and, more often than not, makes them work: the best solos here, such as the grand, sprawling oratory on the title-tune and the flaring urgency that grows out of 'Autumn Leaves', are usefully anchored by a rhythm section that hears him very clearly, with LaVerne a comparably mature voice.

***** Bill Evans ... Person We Knew**
Steeplechase SCCD 31307 *Schneider; Andy LaVerne (p).* 3/92.

***** Mohawk**
Steeplechase SCCD 31347 *As above, except add Steve LaSpina (b), Anton Fig (d).*

A couple of concept albums. Schneider and LaVerne duet on the Evans legacy with considerable potency at times, although the record runs aground a bit on the bare concept. 'Dream Gypsy' is the outstanding performance, evocative of the kind of hushed intensity Evans used to create with Jim Hall, and some of the other pieces are ingenious: the tense contrapuntal lines of 'Israel' and the unfolding melodies of 'Show Type Tune' in particular. Some of the other pieces seem half-done, and Schneider's tone takes on a querulous edge that doesn't always seem right for the music. *Mohawk* tackles nine Charlie Parker tunes, and Schneider turns to the alto for the whole date. He sounds more like Lee Konitz at many moments, especially on the solo version of 'Donna Lee', and, while this is an enjoyable repertory record, some of the settings come out as rather cute; the dead-slow tempo for 'Yardbird Suite' or the Latin temperament of 'Scrapple From The Apple' are two such.

***** Ali Girl**
Steeplechase SCCD 31429 *Schneider; Alexander Sipiagin (flhn); Dave Stryker (g); Jay Anderson (b); Billy Drummond (d).* 9/97.

Back after a break, Schneider delivers something of a hotchpotch date. Four of the six tunes are done on soprano, on which he again suggests a Konitzian bent: try the first chorus of his solo on 'I'm Old Fashioned'. The tracks extend into long, somewhat rambling excursions, with good work by all hands, but without cutting a deep impression. Sipiagin sits in on two tunes, one of which, 'The Way You Look Tonight', brings out the tenor and the best solo of the session.

***** Ornettology**
Steeplechase SCCD 31461 *Schneider; Scott Wendholt (t); Mike Richmond (b); Billy Drummond (d).* 4/98.

Eight Ornette Coleman tunes, making an interesting pendant to the Charlie Parker record, although this doesn't convince as something that Schneider had any pressing need to record. If anything, the quartet take a rather glib and unruffled path through the likes of 'The Disguise' and 'When Will the Blues Leave'. Energetic playing and creative improvising, but the uncommitted might ask why the record had to be made.

Maria Schneider (born 1960)

COMPOSER, ARRANGER, BANDLEADER

After lessons from Bob Brookmeyer and a stint as assistant to Gil Evans, the lady from Windom, Minnesota, had the best possible grounding in big-band jazz – and yet setting out on her own, as she did in 1989, was brave in the extreme, but a Monday night residency at Visiones in New York gave her the platform she needed.

***** Evanescence**

Enja ENJ 8048-2 *Schneider; Laurie Frink, Greg Gisbert, Tim Hagans, Tony Kadleck (t); Larry Farrell, John Fedchock, George Flynn, Keith O'Quinn (tb); Rick Margitza (ts); Rich Perry (ts, f); Mark Vinci (picc, f, cl); Tim Ries (ss, f, cl); Scott Robinson (bsx, bcl); Bill Hayes (flexatone); Kenny Werner (p); Jay Monder (g); Jay Anderson (b); Dennis Mackrel (d); Emedin Rivera (perc).* 10/92.

*****(*) Coming About**

Enja ENJ 9069-2 *As above, except omit Anderson, Hayes, Mackrel, Rivera; add Rock Ciccarone (tb); Charles Pillow (eng hn, cl); Frank Kimbrough (p); Tony Scherr (b); Tim Horner (d).* 11/95.

Schneider's characteristic voice is closer to Brookmeyer's than to the more obvious Svengali, a rich fabric of sound that is alert to nuance but still capable of great power. Her use of a relatively straightforward rhythm section belies the sophistication of the metre, and often the horns are playing improbable counts over a basic 4/4. Schneider was blessed from the very start by a team of time-served craftsmen with enough musical individuality to temper the slightly too accurate placing of the charts.

By the time the second album appeared – and this may be implicit in the title – Schneider had the confidence to turn her vessel into the wind and let it go. Her suite, 'Scenes From Childhood', is largely written and works well on its own terms, but it is tracks like 'Love Theme From "Spartacus"' and 'Giant Steps' which really show her mettle.

Whether Schneider can sustain her early promise is likely to be a question of economics and logistics rather than talent, which she has by the basket.

Rob Schneiderman (born 1957)

PIANO

Born In Boston, Schneiderman grew up in California and moved to New York in 1982, influenced by old-school beboppers. He also has a doctorate in mathematics and teaches the subject at Berkeley.

****(*) New Outlook**

Reservoir RSR 106 *Schneiderman; Slide Hampton (tb); Rufus Reid (b); Akira Tana (d).* 1/88.

***** Smooth Sailing**

Reservoir 114 *As above, except add Billy Higgins (d); omit Hampton and Tana.* 2/90.

***** Radio Waves**

Reservoir 120 *Schneiderman; Brian Lynch (t); Ralph Moore (ts); Gary Smulyan (bs); Todd Coolman (b); Jeff Hirshfield (d).* 5/91.

***** Standards**

Reservoir 126 *Schneiderman; Rufus Reid (b); Ben Riley (d).* 3–8/92.

***** Dark Blue**

Reservoir 132 *Schneiderman; Brian Lynch (t); Ralph Moore (ss, ts); Peter Washington (b); Lewis Nash (d).* 5/94.

*****(*) Keepin' In The Groove**

Reservoir 144 *Schneiderman; Rufus Reid (b); Akira Tana (d).* 1/96.

*****(*) Dancing In The Dark**

Reservoir 152 *Schneiderman; Brian Lynch (t); Gary Smulyan (bs); Rufus Reid (b); Billy Hart (d).* 5/97.

'Beautiful and abstract and I'm curious about it.' Rob Schneiderman was talking about mathematics – more specifically his specialist subject of Low Dimensional Topology, not much investigated by jazz musicians – and making the comparison with music. He is up to seven albums in his series for Reservoir now and, while there's no masterwork here, they offer a genuine kind of modern bop that can be very satisfying. Slide Hampton was an unusual choice as the sole horn on *New Outlook*, and his mild-mannered fluency suits Schneiderman's approach perhaps a little too well: the music tends to settle down into blandishments of the kind that have been committed to record many times before. Despite a couple of interesting ideas – such as the prickly waltz tempo chosen for Alec Wilder's 'While We're Young' – the music never quite lifts off the ground. Maybe the pianist just prefers the kind of knowing, grooving accompaniment that's second nature to Reid and Higgins, because they all sound much happier on *Smooth Sailing*, a blithe mix of standards and new tunes.

Good spirits also prevail on the next date, with three horns in the front line. Lynch is a little overwhelmed by the beguiling Moore and the big, tough sound of Smulyan's baritone, but Schneiderman resolves any difficulties with intelligent if sketchy arrangements. But then it's back to the trio for the rather aristocratic treatment of *Standards*, in which Schneiderman gives up on his own writing for a day at least. Riley is such a wily drummer – very different from Higgins – that he's often barely there, but it suits the occasion. Schneiderman plays interesting things, as he does on all these records, without making one think that it's of great consequence. *Dark Blue* is soundly professional without generating much excitement, and the preponderance of themes based on blues doesn't lift it far enough out of routine; Lynch and Moore, though, guarantee good value. A beguiling 'People Will Say We're In Love' is the highlight.

The next two are a point ahead. Nothing extraordinary about *Keepin' In The Groove*, with only one original amidst a clever choice of jazz tunes, but it's played with such enjoyment that the feel is infectious. Reid and Tana are an absolutely grooving team – hear the drummer's wonderful brushwork on 'Four' and 'Bebop' – and they light up a trio music which Schneiderman refuses to clutter with awkward lines or mere verbosity. The good form carries on into *Dancing In The Dark*. The horns make an impeccable duo, and Lynch is at his best – catch his fabulous solo on 'Broken Dreams'. Smulyan doesn't miss out, and Schneiderman brought some of his best writing to the date in 'Broken Dreams', 'Oval Essence' and 'Late Breakthrough'.

Daniel Schnyder

TENOR AND SOPRANO SAXOPHONES

Swiss saxophonist whose ambitious approach seems to be concerned primarily with adapting a jazz aesthetic to a composer's needs.

***** Secret Cosmos**

Enja 5055-2 *Schnyder; Max Helfenstein (t); Hugo Helfenstein (tb); Hans Peter Hass (btb); Han Bergstrom (frhn); Matthias Ziegler (f); Urs Hammerli (b).*

***** The City**

Enja 6002-2 *Schnyder; Lew Soloff, Michael Philip Mossman (t); Ray Anderson (tb); Vladislaw Sendecki (p); Michael Formanek (b); Ronnie Burrage (d).* 9/88.

***** Decoding The Message**

Enja 6036 *As above, except add Matthias Ziegler (f), Daniel Pezzotti (clo), Robert Mark (perc).* 5/89.

***** Mythology**

Enja 7003 *As above, except add Mark Feldman, Mary Rowell (vn), Lois Martin (vla), Erik Friedlander (clo), Jeff Hirshfield (d); omit Anderson, Sendecki, Burrage, Ziegler, Pezzotti and Mark.* 4/91.

****(*) Nucleus**

Enja 8068-2 *Schnyder; Michael Philip Mossman (t, flhn, picc t, tb); Kenny Drew Jr (p); Michael Formanek (b); Marvin 'Smitty' Smith (d).* 1/94.

****(*) Tarantula**

Enja 9302-2 *Schnyder; Michael Philip Mossman (t, flhn); Jim Pugh (tb); Dave Taylor (btb); John Clark (frhn); Hubert Laws (f, picc); Thomas Chapin (f); Alejandro Rutkauskas, Adam Taubitz (vn); Akiko Hasegawa, Juerg Daehler (vla); Daniel Pezzotti (clo); Michael Formanek, Andy McKee (b); Bobby Sanabria (perc); NDR Radio-Philharmonie Hannover.* 94–96.

While he plays on all these discs, Schnyder's real interest is in composing and arranging, and he has attracted some imposing names for his Enja albums. Post-bop orthodoxy is ignored in favour of a wide-ranging approach which is often as close to contemporary European composition as it is to jazz: Schnyder tinkers with textures and lines, tries tone-rows and motivic variations as bases for themes, and generally asks a lot of his musicians. There's something good on all the earlier records, and perhaps the third, with a couple of impeccably scored pieces in 'The Sound Of The Desert' and 'A Call From Outer Space', is the best. But nothing ever quite manifests itself as a genuinely heavyweight piece, and the substance of some of the themes is dissipated by what might be a low boredom threshold: the shortness of several of the pieces isn't so much a refreshing brevity as a hint that Schnyder could be a bit of a gadfly. He brings in a string quartet for *Mythology*, which adds textural variation – though not so much that the surfaces of his writing are especially disturbed. No real change or improvement with *Nucleus*: in some ways, with titles like 'The Mystified Churchgoer' and throwaway, almost soundbite-like episodes such as 'Retrogradus Ex Machina', Schnyder is getting more arch and less tractable. The trend, if such it be, continues on the pompous-sounding *Tarantula*, which comes in four parts: brass-heavy group, sax and string quartet, sax with orchestra and a second brass-heavy group. 'Memoires' with the NDR Orchestra is undeniably pretty, and there are cameos for Laws and some of the others that work well enough, but a lot of it is plain boring.

Loren Schoenberg (born 1958)

TENOR SAXOPHONE

Though unremarkable as a soloist, Schoenberg is an energetic figure in American jazz: manager and archivist for Benny Goodman in his last years, big-band leader, author and broadcaster, and a considerable authority on the music's swing years especially.

***** Out Of This World**

TCB 98902 *Schoenberg; Bob Millikan, John Eckert, Tony Kadleck, Greg Gisbert, Scott Robinson, Richard Sudhalter (t); Mike Christianson (tb, vtb, tba); Eddie Bert, Bobby Pring, Rafi Malkiel, Matt Finders (tb); Steve Wilson, Jon Gordon (as, ss, f, cl); Doug Lawrence (ts, cl); Mark Lopeman (ts, cl, f); Danny Bank (bs, bcl, cl); Dick Katz (p); James Chirillo (g); Dennis Irwin, John Goldsby (b); Danny Gottlieb (d); Chuck Redd (d, vib); Barbara Lea (v).* 12/97.

Schoenberg's own-name records have never made much of an impact, but this recent set for TCB, with its alliance of grand old names such as Eddie Bert and Danny Bank along with young fogeys like Robinson and Schoenberg himself, is a good-natured and enjoyable outing. Divided between orchestral and small-group tracks, the charts are actually by several hands, and Schoenberg himself does only the charming 'Close As Pages In A Book', with a lovely vocal by Barbara Lea. The programme strikes an astute balance between musicianly rarities like Strayhorn's 'Bittersweet' and twists on the familiar, such as Bill Holman's arrangement for 'Lover Man'. A very fair effort, though it seldom really grabs the attention.

Mathias Schubert (born 1960)

TENOR SAXOPHONE

German saxophonist of fierce contemporary demeanour.

****** Blue And Grey Suite**

Enja ENJ 9045 *Schubert; Simon Nabatov (p); Lindsey Horner (b); Tom Rainey (d).* 12/94.

Schubert – and what a start in musical life *that* surname must have been – is a player of excoriating power and intensity. If one can imagine compatriot Christof Lauer at his most intense, and then go up a gear and keep the pedal down for the duration of a CD, that's close to the impact. In addition, Schubert is almost as strongly influenced by modern art music as by jazz. 'Le Maître' is inspired by Olivier Messiaen's 'La Nativité du Seigneur', not exactly a contrafact, but a fascinating gloss on an important modern work whose use of tone-colours and intervals is virtuosic in the extreme. 'Nichols' Dime', by contrast, is dedicated to the great jazz pianist, an attempt to write a conventional AABA song-structure, but with a serial melody and an odd rhythmic variation that betrays its origins in a concert piece for saxophone duo. 'The Blue And Grey Suite' is a long and complex multi-part work built round a tango-ish theme which Schubert calls 'Fantankow'. It also includes another 12-note theme called 'The Stopper', the love-child of Anton Webern and Lee Morgan; and a glorious ballad theme called 'Malincolia', which is as gentle as this extraordinary player ever allows himself to be. In Simon Nabatov he has a playing partner who is almost as fiery, one of those pianists who generate overtones all over the sound-box, great harmonic ripples which boom on and on, colliding with the next line or phrase. Schubert has strong views on the role of the 'rhythm section', often regarding himself as an accompanist rather than a 'front-line' player. He lays elegant counter-lines against the bass and sharp, percussive figures in the path of Tom Rainey's drumming. All in all, an immensely powerful record which should be approached with some caution. We are disappointed that Schubert has brought forth nothing new as yet.

Ed Schuller

DOUBLE BASS

Schuller comes from good musical stock, the son of composer and conductor Gunter Schuller. His Eleventh Hour band has been impressively adventurous and thoughtful, constantly nudging at the limits of genre and convention.

*** The Eleventh Hour

Tutu CD 888 124 *Schuller; Greg Osby (as, ss); Gary Valente (tb); Bill Bickford (g); Victor Jones (d); Arto Tuncboyaciyan (perc).* 2/91.

***(*) Snake Dancing

Tutu CD 888 188 *Schuller; Gary Valente (tb); Mark Goldsbury (sax); Bill Bickford (g); Ronnie Burrage (d, perc); Nat Irving (elec); Nicole Kampgen (v).* 98.

'PM In The AM' is a tribute to Ed's time with Paul Motian, and there's a slight sense that for *The Eleventh Hour* he was trying to put together something like that mid-'80s line-up which included Joe Lovano, the late Jim Pepper and Bill Frisell. Schuller limits solo bass experiments to the very last track, a multi-tracked poem to a friend called 'For Dodo'. It's a surprisingly affecting piece and it gives some opportunity to assess Schuller's approach, which is influenced severally by Mingus (most prominently), rock guitar and Eastern drones. The two-part title-piece has an urgent impetus but tries to cram too much cleverness (no less than a miniature history of the world) into too short a space. 'Keeping Still/Mountain' is essentially a rhythmic exercise, pushed just a little too far; the material doesn't really stand up to the pasting it receives. The long 'Shamal' leads the group into promising overtone territory but gets rather stranded there.

Snake Dancing is both more coherent and more positively swinging. Schuller is still very much involved in advanced ideas, but there is a clarity of line and purpose that is new and refreshing. 'Qualify Your Funk' might be a Ray Anderson composition, except that Gary Valente's trombone is many decibels louder than anything Ray would attempt. 'Wave Forms 1 & 2' are more abstract, while 'Koch's Curve' make use of computer sequencing by Nat Irving and an effective vocal by Nicole Kampgen. Bill Bickford is an consistently inventive player and is well up to form here, but the revelation, apart from Schuller himself, is saxophonist Mark Goldsbury, who delivers beautifully structured solos at high speed with no loss of resolution.

Bob Schulz

CORNET, VOCALS

Schulz is under the spell of Bob Scobey, as both a cornetist and a bandleader, and his Frisco Jazz Band play very much in a modern-day styling of the Californian revivalists.

**(*) Thanks Turk!

Stomp Off 1288 *Schulz; Tom Bartlett (tb, v); Kim Cusack (cl); Ray Skjelbred (p); Scott Anthony (bj); Bill Carroll (tba); Wayne Jones (d).* 5–6/94.

*** Travelin' Shoes

Stomp Off 1315 *As above, except Steve Pistorius (p) and John Gill (bj, v) replace Skjelbred and Anthony.* 5/96.

Schulz and his men are a sound team of Turk Murphy/Bob Scobey followers, and they hardly put a foot wrong here on *Thanks Turk!* – keen, well-rounded interpretations of many Murphy favourites. Plenty of it goes back to the original masters of the 1920s, and there are some rag tunes like 'Smokey Mokes' and 'Swipsey Cake Walk'. Twenty numbers done in this vigorous and chanceless way are a bit of a bore, though, and one eventually longs for one of the players to take the session by the scruff of its neck. It never happens, although Bartlett's rather crabby trombone has a go here and there.

Travelin' Shoes gets off on the good foot with a knockout treatment of 'Pretty Baby' and, while this is another disc that trades heavily on the Scobey–Murphy style (to the extent of using several of their original charts), it's an ounce more personal, and Mike Cogan engineers an excellent sound for the band. Even Bob's vocals are in the spirit.

Manfred Schulze (born 1934)

BARITONE SAXOPHONE

Schulze worked out of the GDR and formed his first Brass Quintet as early as 1969. Interested as much in the writing of Hindemith, Schoenberg and Bach as in free improvisation, he brought a striking mix of disciplines to bear on what was original and surprising music.

***(*) Viertens : Nummer 12

FMP CD 87 *Schulze; Johannes Bauer (tb); Manfred Hering, Dietmar Diesner, Heiner Reinhardt (reeds).* 5/85–7/86.

*****(*) Konzertino**

FMP CD 70 *Paul Schwingenschlögl (t); Johannes Bauer (tb); Manfred Hering (ss, as, cl); Heiner Reinhardt (ss, ts); Gert Anklam (bs).* 9/94.

To call Schulze underrated would be an understatement. He worked in comparative isolation in the GDR, rarely recorded or travelled, and worked patiently at a synthesis of improvising with quite specific and formal structures for reeds and brass. The 1980s recordings are marvellously choleric, the stiff, severe textures peeling open to reveal powerful improvisatory ideas. 'Nummer 12' is a long concert-piece, but rather better and more focused are the two studio tracks, 'Viertens' and the sly 'B-A-C-H'. Bauer aside, these players are not often encountered, but they give the music their all.

The later disc is a Berlin concert performed almost as a tribute to Schulze, who by this time was too ill to play himself. The group has a somewhat jazzier feel, the solos emerging more conventionally out of the group's interaction, and some of the dour distinction of the earlier disc has dissipated; but there's a compensating verve to the playing, and Schwingenschlögl adds some useful brassy fizz.

Irène Schweizer (born 1941)

PIANO

Still seriously neglected, Irène Schweizer is a pioneering figure in European free jazz. She founded her innovative trio as long ago as 1963 and since then has worked with most of the major figures of European modernism. Her style is complex, dense and intellectually generous, and on her day few pianists in the world can equal her for sheer drama.

****** The Storming Of The Winter Palace**

Intakt CD 03/2000 *Schweizer; George Lewis (tb); Joelle Léandre (b); Gunter Sommer (d, perc); Maggie Nicols (v).* 5/86, 3/88.

The great Mary Lou Williams asserted that 'working with men ... you automatically become strong, though this doesn't mean you're not feminine'. Schweizer has almost inevitably been saddled with a 'female Cecil Taylor' tag, one that has been harder to shift as a result of her series of duets with drummers, encounters which invite all manner of yin–yang nonsense. As a sometime percussionist herself, Schweizer makes instinctive guesses as to how her own keyboard language might meld with untuned instruments. That is evident in her important sequence of recordings with percussionists, but it is also a component of her other work in a variety of groups and as a solo pianist.

The Storming Of The Winter Palace is a welcome reissue of a classic LP. Recorded at the Moers Festival in 1986 and at the Taktlos Festival in Zurich two years later, it documents a group with formidable powers. Schweizer is very much the key element, assembling and unpicking a series of small-scale themes and ideas like some intellectual *tricoteuse*. Maggie Nicols's ability to break down narrative song into its constituent elements, semantic nonsense, and still leave you feeling that you've heard a story and been serenaded as well continues to amaze, as does George Lewis's ability to make even a disassembled trombone sound like the most musical thing on the planet. The two 'rhythm' players are supreme craftspersons and crafty supremos of free music. Sommer is not so much a minimalist as a miniaturist, able to invest tiny ideas with enormous significance, as effective in what he does not do as most drummers are in a full-scale assault on the kit. Léandre rumbles away in the background – and, to be truthful, too much in the background acoustically to represent fully her part in this music.

The earlier Moers piece is the most developed of the three included. 'Now And Never' makes few references to any musical forms outside itself, but it quickly establishes its own internal logic and Schweizer sustains a high level of concentration, contention and flow, reinforcing the impression that everything she does is a miniature concerto for piano, like 'Theoria', the piece written for her by Barry Guy and performed with the London Jazz Composers Orchestra. 'The Storming Of The Winter Palace' is dominated to a degree by Nicols, who is at her most angrily playful. A relatively short piece, it is also highly condensed and impacted, with a great deal of musical information to absorb. 'Living On The Edge', which follows, is more intense but also more verbose and with a few flat moments. Taken together, though, this represents a wonderful documentation of an important group.

***** Irène Schweizer / Louis Moholo**

Intakt CD 006 *Schweizer; Louis Moholo (d).* 11/86.

****** Irène Schweizer / Gunter Sommer**

Intakt CD 007 *Schweizer; Gunter Sommer (d).* 2/87.

*****(*) Irène Schweizer / Andrew Cyrille**

Intakt CD 008 *Schweizer; Andrew Cyrille (d).* 9/88.

****** Irène Schweizer / Pierre Favre**

Intakt CD 009 *Schweizer; Pierre Favre (d).* 2/90.

It is enormously difficult to make qualitative judgements among these superb sets. They are extraordinarily various in approach, though it seems clear that the Europeans are much closer in basic conception to Schweizer than the two Americans, as one might expect. Sommer and Favre are melodic players, moving round the kit much as she moves across the keyboard. Moholo creates a network of cross-rhythms that Schweizer herself likens to Elvin Jones's playing with Coltrane, but there is nothing to build on it, and one is left with an impression of two artists working at right angles, making beautiful sounds but in isolation one from the other. With Favre, the level of interaction is such that one almost seems to be hearing a meta-instrument, a source of sound which is neither one voice nor the other, but a genuine synthesis of the two. With Sommer, the connection is more dialectical, but the result is still entirely sympathetic: two voices in conjunction, mutually responsive. Andrew Cyrille was a long-standing collaborator of Cecil Taylor's and is a leader in his own right. It is difficult to gauge what is wrong on this session. One senses that Schweizer is very aware of the Taylor lineage and deliberately tries to steer away from it, though the clusters and clumped runs she falls into are immediately and inescapably redolent of the American pianist. This remarkable series of duets was not finished in 1990. A later record with Han Bennink was still to come and is reviewed below, but the bulk of the series was in place by the end of the '80s. Hearing it somewhat later, and transferred to CD, suggests more consistency than difference. Schweizer never for a moment diverges from her robust, assured approach. It is her playing partners who are required to rethink their language.

****** Piano Solo: Volume 1**
Intakt CD 020 *Schweizer (p).* 5/90.

*****(*) Piano Solo: Volume 2**
Intakt CD 021 *As above.*

Schweizer is not a natural unaccompanied performer. The most communicative of players, she needs no one to play against, but she simply functions better in an environment where there is an element of interchange and reciprocity. That having been said, these are excellent discs. Brief and apparently inconsequential structures are delivered without elaboration and there is a meditative stillness to much of the music. 'The Ballad Of The Sad Café', a title derived from Carson McCullers's soft-tough story, is a masterpiece of unsentimental expression, played with an affecting combination of gentleness and ironclad certainty. 'Sisterhood Of Spit' is a name that refers to an all-female collective of the 1970s. It's dedicated to the late Chris McGregor, whose Brotherhood of Breath was a lasting example of the possibility of reconciling lyrical expressiveness and hard-edged improvisational freedom, and also to saxophonist Dudu Pukwana. It both reflects and ironizes the spirit they evoked. Recorded at home in Switzerland, both records are faithfully and accurately registered, picking up Schweizer's softest figures and sustains, and handling the loudest and most impactful moments without distortion.

***** Les Diaboliques**
Intakt CD 03 *Schweizer; Joelle Léandre (b); Maggie Nicols (v).* 4/93.

***** Spliting Image**
Intakt CD 048 *As above.*

Three of the most consistently neglected figures on the European scene, united on one powerful record. Schweizer is the centre of gravity to which Léandre and Nicols lean and steer. Her touch is softer and more spacious than on the solo discs, deliberately leaving space open, not packing the time with information but allowing her playing partners room to breathe. Nicols, so often acerbic, gives herself the chance to unpack her sometimes cluttered ideas. Unfortunately, she loses impetus as a consequence. Léandre is well recorded and has a good deal to say, but is inclined to repeat herself. The second record from the same group, who subsequently called themselves Les Diaboliques, is every bit as good. Some evidence that Léandre is jockeying for prominence in what is already a tightly constructed group, but generally the level of interaction is as close and responsive as one might wish. Another intriguing disc, though on balance we'd probably just plump for the first one by the trio.

****** Irène Schweizer / Han Bennink**
Intakt CD 010 *Schweizer; Han Bennink (d).* 1/95.

Our admiration for Bennink is probably in breach of the Second and Third Commandments. On this, he is supreme, the ideal foil to Schweizer's full-voiced and pointed delivery. Recorded live, as is much of this remarkable series, it shows two artists of markedly different temperament – and Schweizer is both more 'serious' and more unaffectedly playful – negotiating a comfortable middle ground. Of all the piano/drums duets, this is the one that sounds as if it might be the result of prior negotiation.

*****(*) Many And One Direction**
Intakt CD 044 *Schweizer (p).* 4/96.

The title says it all: a critical moment in a career which seems to have combined an eclectic range of ideas with an absolute solidity of purpose. The latest solo record is beautifully engineered and is played with an immaculate touch. One wonders a little how much Schweizer is attempting to say and how much she simply wants her listeners to luxuriate in the sound. Either way, this is an immensely strong performance, marred only by a reliance on predetermined outlines which she does a good deal to disguise and hide, to no real purpose.

Louis Sclavis (born 1953)

BASS CLARINET, TENOR AND SOPRANO SAXOPHONES

Born in Lyons, Sclavis studied there and toured with the Workshop of Lyons improvising group. His playing is a blend of free forms, contemporary-compositional structures, theatre music and folk strains, a mix which has grown increasingly personal.

****** Clarinettes**
IDA 004 *Sclavis (solo), and with Christian Rollet, Christian Ville (perc).* 9/84–1/85.

*****(*) Chine**
IDA 012 *Sclavis; François Raulin (p, syn, perc); Dominique Pifarély (vn); Bruno Chevillon (b); Christian Ville (d, perc).* 7–9/87.

*****(*) Chamber Music**
IDA 022 *Sclavis; Yves Robert (tb); Michel Godard (tba); Dominique Pifarély (vn); Philippe De Schepper (g); François Raulin (p, syn); Bruno Chevillon (b).* 7–9/89.

Louis Sclavis has attempted to create an 'imaginary folklore' that combines familiar jazz procedures with North African and Mediterranean music, French folk themes and music from the *bal musette.* Early exposure on the mostly solo *Clarinettes* confirmed word-of-mouth reports from France that he was a performer to be reckoned with. Unlike Sidney Bechet, who may have been a dim ancestral influence, his clarinet work is a great deal more forceful than his soprano saxophone playing, and Sclavis is one of the foremost of a growing number of younger jazz musicians who have rescued the clarinet from desuetude as an improvising instrument. His bass clarinet work is particularly original, drawing little or nothing from the obvious model and condensing most of Sclavis's virtues: melodic invention, timbral variation, rhythmic sophistication. Perhaps the most striking track on *Clarinettes* is 'Le Chien Aboie Et La Clarinette Basse' a husky duo with percussionist Ville which puns on a French gypsy saying: the dog barks '*et le caravane passe*'. For all his interest in European folk and popular themes, Sclavis considers himself unequivocally a jazz musician. A duo version of 'Black And Tan Fantasy' on the same album suggests he has much to contribute to standards playing. Most of his work, however, has been original and this, coupled with his obvious straining at the conventions of the orthodox jazz ensemble (particularly as regards the drummer, whom Sclavis considers to be excessively dominant), seemed at first to hold back his development as a soloist. *Chine* is a fine and original set of pieces, but its unfamiliar tonal components only partially mitigate an overall lack of development. *Chamber Music*, as the title implies, throws still more weight on compositional values, but there are signs that Sclavis was working through his dilemmas. In Chevillon he has an understanding and highly effective foil whose rhythmic awareness makes light of settings without a part for a drummer or percussionist.

*****(*) Rouge**
ECM 511929-2 *Sclavis; Dominique Pifarély (vn); François Raulin (p, syn); Bruno Chevillon (b); Christian Ville (d).* 9/91.

****** Ellington On The Air**
IDA 032 *As for Chamber Music, except omit de Schepper; add Francis Lassus (d, perc).* 12/91–2/92.

*****(*) Acoustic Quartet**
ECM 521349-2 *As for Rouge, except omit Raulin, Ville; add Marc Ducret (g).* 93.

****** Les Violences De Rameau**
ECM 533128-2 *As for Rouge, except add Yves Robert (tb), Ferdinand Lassus (perc).* 96.

Sclavis's ECM debut is a challenging and surprisingly abstract set that rarely allows itself to settle into a jazz groove. *Rouge* establishes Sclavis as an enterprising and thought-provoking composer. If it does so at the expense of rhythmic energy (a strategy consistent with his ambivalence about jazz percussion), it doesn't short-change in other departments. The first four tracks are moodily atmospheric, with a strong suggestion of North African music; 'Nacht' is particularly effective, with dissonant flashes of multi-tracked clarinet echoed by the softly bouncing thunder of Ville's bass drum, before giving way to an evocative solo by Chevillon. Pifarély comes into his own on 'Reeves', teasing out a long unison statement with Sclavis and then soloing on his own 'Moment Donné'. Several tracks sound as if they are through-composed and, apart from the later stages of 'Les Bouteilles' and a delicious waltz-tag on the title-piece, the emphasis is all on textures and rather brooding melodic outlines rather than on linear development. The longest track, 'Face Nord', echoes 'Reflet' in the way it suspends Sclavis's high, swooping clarinet-lines over a dense chordal background (that on 'Face Nord' suddenly erupts into a convincing simulacrum of a flat-out electric guitar solo, all done on Raulin's imaginatively programmed synth).

The ECM follow-up is once again impressionistic rather than dynamic. The drummerless *Acoustic Quartet* is listed as co-led by Pifarély, and he certainly plays an increasingly prominent role in the music, as does Chevillon, another long-standing accomplice. Ducret has a less functional role and is used for broad (and not always very subtle) background effects, where a more adventurous leader and/or producer might have preferred a starker profile. Pifarély contributes three compositions, including the long 'Seconde', and the violinist's writing has matured very quickly. However, Sclavis's touch on 'Sensible' and 'Rhinoceros' is flawless, and the brief 'Beata' is incomparably lovely. Attractive as it all is, one misses the edgy, improvisational sound that energizes the Ellington session. The interplay between Sclavis and the admirable Robert adds a dimension that has been missing for some time. The programme is an imaginative exercise in re-creation. Ellington themes are interleaved with associated originals by Sclavis, Chevillon, Raulin and others. 'Jubilee Stomp' yields 'J'Oublie'; though not itself included, 'Mood Indigo' suggests Chevillon's 'Indigofera Tinctoria' and Andy Emler's 'Mode Andy Go'; a snatch of 'Caravan' introduces 'Caravalse'; and so on. The verbal puns aren't screamingly witty, but the music is always intelligently allusive and manages to suggest new angles on Ellington without lapsing into pastiche. Indeed, it's very clear that Sclavis has picked precisely those themes which most emphatically suit his own compositional style.

Nothing could have prepared anyone, though, for his turn to the mysterious music of Rameau for the next record. This is a perfect illustration of his eclectic, omnivorous approach to French music, a virtuosic appropriation of a composer who has never been warmly appreciated outside France but who reveals on closer inspection an almost Gothic concentration of expression which is, yes, violent. A now familiar line-up, augmented significantly by the wonderful Robert, broods through fascinating charts which are neither obscure nor transparent.

*****(*) Trio De Clarinettes Live**
FMP CD 39 *Sclavis; Jacques Di Donato (cl, bcl); Armand Angster (cl, bcl, cbcl).* 11/90.

*****(*) Et On Ne Parle Du Temps**
FMP CD 66 *Sclavis; Ernst Reijseger (clo).* 7/94.

Sclavis on free ground, although the trio of clarinets is actually quite strictly worked out: there is even a Pierre Boulez piece, 'Domaines', to go with the five-part 'Berliner Suite' which otherwise comprises the record. Timbral exercises, counterpoint, call-and-response: their materials are classic, even if the feel of the record is, perhaps inevitably, more reminiscent of European chamber music than the style once evoked by Clarinet Summit. For specialist tastes, a delightful record.

With Reijseger, Sclavis has some of the clearest space he's ever had on record to demonstrate what a master he is of the clarinet family. The music is brimful of great technique from both men, without (much) resorting to show-off proficiency. Here and there are either dead spots or bits of machismo, but mostly this is a witty and often thrilling duel between top players.

John Scofield (born 1951)

GUITAR

Studied at Berklee 1970–73, then with Billy Cobham and Charles Mingus on record. With Dave Liebman and under his own leadership, he began recording regularly, then joined Miles Davis in 1982, staying until 1985. Subsequently he has recorded many discs for Blue Note and Verve and has been in huge demand as a sideman. Seen by many as the quintessential, most widely read and flexible contemporary jazz guitarist.

***** Live**
Enja 3013 *Scofield; Richie Beirach (p); George Mraz (b); Joe LaBarbera (d).* 11/77.

***** Rough House**
Enja 3033 *Scofield; Hal Galper (p); Stafford James (b); Adam Nussbaum (d).* 11/78.

John Scofield was perhaps the last of Miles Davis's sidemen to break through to a major career, but the records listed above, all made prior to his joining Davis in 1982, bespeak a substantial talent already making waves. He had played with a diverse group of leaders – Charles Mingus, Lee Konitz, Gary Burton, Billy Cobham – before forming the band that made the 1977 live album. Beirach is a little too cool to suit Scofield's needs and Gomez is all tight virtuosity rather than loosely funky, but the music is still impressive, since the leader's own playing is an intriguing mix of a classic, open-toned bop style and a blues-rock affiliation. He gets the same sound on the studio date with Galper, but this is a tougher record, with the pianist flying directly alongside the guitarist on tunes which unreel at a uniformly fast tempo: Nussbaum gives them both plenty of push.

*****(*) Shinola**
Enja 4004 *Scofield; Steve Swallow (b); Adam Nussbaum (d).* 12/81.

*****(*) Out Like A Light**
Enja 4038 *As above.* 12/81.

Scofield's final Enja albums were recorded at a live date in Munich. Good though the earlier records are, these loose, exploratory tracks are his most interesting so far: the trio functions as a single probing unit, Swallow's fat sound counterpointing the guitar, and the space and drift of such as 'Yawn' from *Shinola* opens Scofield's horizon. With pianists, he was putting in as many notes as Coltrane on occasion, but here – with Nussbaum restlessly decorating the pulse – the guitarist sounds as if he doesn't see the need to cover every harmonic area. Good digital sound.

**** Electric Outlet**
Gramavision GR 8045 *Scofield; Ray Anderson (tb); David Sanborn (as); Pete Levin (ky); Steve Jordan (d).* 4–5/84.

****** Still Warm**
Gramavision GR 8508 *Scofield; Don Grolnick (ky); Darryl Jones (b); Omar Hakim (d).* 6/85.

***** Blue Matter**
Gramavision 18-8702 *Scofield; Mitch Forman (ky); Hiram Bullock (g); Gary Grainger (b); Dennis Chambers (d); Don Alias (perc).* 9/86.

***** Loud Jazz**
Gramavision 18-8801 *As above, except Robert Aries, George Duke (ky) replace Forman; Bullock omitted.* 12/87.

***** Pick Hits Live**
Gramavision 18-8805 *As above, except omit Duke and Alias.* 10/87.

*****(*) Flat Out**
Gramavision 18-8903 *Scofield; Don Grolnick (org); Anthony Cox (b); Johnny Vidacovich, Terri Lyne Carrington (d).* 12/88.

Scofield's six Gramavision albums are a coherent and highly enjoyable body of work. *Electric Outlet* was a false start: the band seems gimcracked around a dubious idea of highbrow pop-jazz, Sanborn and Anderson are there only for colour, and the attempted grooves are stiff and unyielding. But *Still Warm* solved matters at a stroke. Steve Swallow's production clarified the sound without overpowering the fluidity of Scofield's arrangements, Grolnick added thoughtful keyboard textures, and Jones and Hakim (colleagues from the Miles Davis band) were tight and funky without being relentlessly so. Scofield's own playing here assumes a new authority: tones are richer, the hint of fuzz and sustain is perfectly integrated, and his solos are unflaggingly inventive: for a single sample, listen to the sharp, hotly articulated solo on 'Picks And Pans'.

The band which the guitarist then formed with Grainger and Chambers bolstered the funk-fusion side of his playing: the drummer, especially, is a thunderous virtuoso in the manner of Billy Cobham, and the next three albums are all fired up with his rhythms. Scofield's writing revolves around ear-catching melodic hooks and a favourite device of a riff repeated over a shifting harmonic base, and the two studio albums are full of naggingly memorable themes. But the music was formulaic in the end: the live record is a feast of hard-nut jazz-funk showmanship, but it starts to sound clenched by the end. *Flat Out* comes as a welcome change of pace: Vidacovich and Carrington, who split chores between them through the record, are swinging but no less busy drummers: hear the consummately controlled rave-up on 'The Boss's Car' (a cheeky rip-off of Bruce Springsteen's 'Pink Cadillac'). Two standards, a Meters tune and a rollicking turn through 'Rockin' Pneumonia' also lighten the programme.

****** Time On My Hands**
Blue Note 792894-2 *Scofield; Joe Lovano (ts); Charlie Haden (b); Jack DeJohnette (d).* 11/89.

*****(*) Meant To Be**
Blue Note 795479-2 *Scofield; Joe Lovano (ts, cl); Marc Johnson (b); Bill Stewart (d).* 12/90.

Scofield's transfer to Blue Note has moved his career and his music substantially forward. Lovano is an inspired choice of front-line partner, renegotiating the jazz roots of Sco's approach without surrendering the feisty attack which he amplified through his Gramavision records. *Time On My Hands* provides some of his best writing, including the lovely ballad of 'Let's Say We Did' and the twining melodies of 'Since You Asked'. 'Fat Lip' is acoustic jazz-rock which Haden and DeJohnette jump on with brilliant ferocity. Superb studio sound throughout. If *Meant To Be* seems a shade less invigorating, it's only because it seems like a second run through the same territory. Both are very highly recommended.

*****(*) Grace Under Pressure**
Blue Note 7981672 *Scofield; Randy Brecker (flhn); Jim Pugh (tb); John Clark (frhn); Bill Frisell (g); Charlie Haden (b); Joey Baron (d).* 12/91.

Though given a mixed reception on its release, this is a strong and thoughtfully realized continuation of Scofield's work for Blue Note. If he's starting to seem over-exposed as a player, turning up in countless guest roles as well as on his own records, the ten themes here display a consistent strength as a writer: variations on the blues, slow modal ballads, riffs worked into melodies, Scofield makes them all come up fresh, and he creates situations where the rhythm players can line the music with intensities and colours of their own. There are hard, swinging solos on the title-track and 'Twang', and if the interplay with Frisell can sometimes seem more like cheese and chalk, there are piquant contrasts which sometimes blend with surprising effectiveness: 'Honest I Do' is the kind of haunting, downbeat melody that Scofield has made his own. The brass are used very sparingly to underscore a few tracks.

*****(*) I Can See Your House From Here**
Blue Note 827765-2 *Scofield; Pat Metheny (g); Steve Swallow (b); Bill Stewart (d).* 12/93.

For his second meeting with another leading guitarist, Scofield uncorked some more of his best writing: the title-piece and 'No Matter What' are typically serpentine, elegant, feelingful tunes to which the slick playing only adds. This is far more collaborative than the record with Frisell, with Metheny taking several writing credits himself, and, while it occasionally softens in the face of Pat's tendency to turn to marshmallow, it's good.

***** Hand Jive**
Blue Note 827327-2 *Scofield; Eddie Harris (ts); Larry Goldings (p, org); Dennis Irwin (b); Bill Stewart (d); Don Alias (perc).* 10/93.

Scofield's final Blue Note albums (he has since signed to Verve) round off the most enjoyable run of guitar records in recent years. Perhaps no genuinely fresh ground is broken here, but just by shuffling his options the guitarist finds new ways of walking over old paths. The fashion to turn back to the guitar/organ combos of the 1960s has already grown stale, but Scofield's take on the genre turns the emphasis around: not surprisingly, it's the guitar player who takes the limelight rather than a licks-bound organist, and in any case Goldings is the most interesting new organ man on the scene. *Hand Jive* blends the chugging groove beloved of the old school with the leaner rhythms of Irwin and Stewart, Sco's pop-tune sensibility, Goldings's feel for line and colour and the surprise choice of maverick tenorman Harris. The result is excellent fun. His final date for the label, *Groove Elation*, which we slightly preferred of these two, has apparently gone to the dead-letter office.

****** Quiet**
Verve 533185-2 *Scofield; Randy Brecker (t, flhn); Wayne Shorter (ts); Charles Pillow (f, cor, ts); Lawrence Feldman (f, ts); John Clark, Fred Griffin (frhn); Roger Rosenberg (bcl); Howard Johnson (bs, tba); Steve Swallow (b); Bill Stewart, Duduka Fonseca (d).* 4/96.

Having already tried numerous settings for Blue Note, Scofield's Verve debut was different again. Playing acoustic guitar exclusively is one departure; setting it against the mournful sound of low brass and woodsy reeds is another. The horn charts are just witty enough to inject a certain wryness and just eerie enough to lend a sometimes other-worldly air to the likes of 'After The Fact'. The addition of Shorter, playing his now unaccustomed tenor on three tracks, seems like an unlikely bonus, but he fits in uncannily well. Scofield's own playing is made to seem less conspicuous by his playing acoustic, yet it lends a certain piquancy to his improvising. And then there is Swallow, co-producing and seeming to direct much of the playing with high, light bass-lines of the utmost ingenuity and relevance. The result comes close to Scofield's finest hour.

*****(*) A Go Go**
Verve 539979-2 *Scofield; John Medeski (ky); Billy Martin (b); Chris Wood (d).* 97.

Opportunism, maybe, but this is a shrewd match, and if the MM&W trio sometimes seem at a loss for substance on their own records, Scofield hands it to them on a plate with his ten originals here. The difference between tunes such as 'Green Tea' and 'Hottentot' and any other organ blues or Bo Diddley shuffle is the degree of harmonic/melodic sophistication which Scofield has slid in. *A Go Go* emerges as not so much a fun record with brains as a loosely intense essay on the common ground in jazz, rock and funk. The dead drum sound and buzzing keyboards which are the trio's trademarks remain. It's a 'fusion' which suggests that neither side is merely buying in to the other.

***** Bump**
Verve 543430-2 *Scofield; Mark Degli Antoni (ky); David Livolsi, Tony Scherr (b); Kenny Wollesen, Eric Klab (d); Johnny Durkin, Johnny Almendra (perc).* 99.

Not bad, but Scofield's edging away from jazz and into a hinterland of rock does seem vaguely disappointing. As his tone gets more clotted and the phrasing more hook-orientated, the results are bitty and insubstantial over the course of a CD. For all the cleverness of the playing – and there is plenty – this feels fundamentally lightweight, even if his intentions seem more honourable than many who are seeking a way out of their niche.

Jimmy Scott (born 1925)

VOCAL

A hormone problem kept Scott's voice unusually high-pitched as he grew up. He sang around Cleveland in the 1940s and joined Lionel Hampton in 1950, hob-nobbing with the boppers and recording plenty of songs, but after 1960 he was plagued with contractual difficulties and lost his way. Returned in the late '80s, and finally achieved cult eminence with a string of records in the '90s.

***** Everybody's Somebody's Fool**
Decca/GRP 050669-2 *Scott; orchestras led by Lionel Hampton, Billy Taylor, Lucky Thompson.* 1/50–8/52.

Scott's early records had been almost forgotten by all but a handful of vocal followers, but his return to prominence in the 1990s has awakened enough interest for these sides to be trawled out of the Decca vaults. His high but unmannered voice will remind you of many female singers, but there's a musing quality to his style at this point which sets delicacy alongside a pleading, contrite sensibility. He made a speciality out of ballads full of entreaties, such as the title-track, his first hit with Lionel Hampton, and not all of this material is worthwhile raw matter for his extraordinary voice. The last four tracks, with an octet led by Thompson, open on a heart-sick 'Why Was I Born?', but he doesn't do too badly by 'The Bluest Blues', an unreleased track from the same session.

****** All The Way**
Sire/Warner Bros 926955-2 *Scott; David Fathead Newman (ts); Kenny Barron (p); John Pisano (g); Ron Carter (b); Grady Tate (d); strings.* 92.

****** Dreams**

Sire/Warner Bros 9362-45629-2 *Scott; Patience Higgins, Red Holloway (ts); Mitchell Froom (org); Junior Mance (p); Milt Jackson (vib); Rick Zunigar (g); Ron Carter (b); Peyton Crossley (d).* 2/94.

*****(*) Heaven**

Warner Bros 9362-46211-2 *Scott; Jacky Terrasson (p); Hill Greene (b); Joseph Bonadio (d).* 4/96.

***** Holding Back The Years**

Birdology 3984-27577-2 *Scott; Pamela Fleming (t); Bruce Kirby (ts); Gregorie Maret (hca); Michael Kanan (p); Matt Muniseri (g); Ghill Green (b); Victor Jones (d); strings.* 98.

Absent from recording studios for many years, Scott's comeback was little short of astounding. *All The Way* presents the voice as withered but strong, stretched and vibrato-laden but peculiarly youthful, even as it suggests a lifetime's experience and the wear of many disappointments. Some notes he grabs at, shouting them, but his control seldom falters and even a bar of struggle seems to be part of a song's overall plan. It can be a sometimes exhausting listen, since Scott either compels the attention or drives you away, but there's no singing like it listed elsewhere in this book. Both *All The Way* and *Dreams* can boast blue-chip accompanists and the most handsome of standards in the song-list. We slightly prefer the second, with impeccable cameos from Jackson and a quiet, nocturnal feel to the occasion, but the string arrangements on the first will appeal to many, and the emotion of Scott's return feels palpable throughout this one.

Heaven is a surprise match with Terrasson, and one which works far better than the pianist's deluded encounter with Cassandra Wilson, although even here Jacky can't always resist his impulse to overplay. The material is a curious mix of secular pop (the Talking Heads title-track), gospel-soul, folk themes and spirituals, all of it one way or the other about heaven. Very bare-bones in presentation, and the most exposed Scott has ever left himself, it's hard to be unmoved, often by his frailties as much as by his vocal powers. By now the voice is becoming thinner and less able to do its owner's bidding, and the idea of *Holding Back The Years* was unreasonable. Against a sort of soft-rock/lounge backing, Jimmy takes on ten songs from contemporary rock writers. It's not that the likes of Elvis Costello, Mick Hucknall and Bryan Ferry songs are beyond him, but he doesn't have the kind of narcissism which those performers invest in their own material to make it work for them. Against the odds, he still makes more of this project than anybody might have expected. A new album for a new label, Fantasy, was due as we went to press.

Ronnie Scott (1927–97)

TENOR SAXOPHONE

There have been musician-run jazz clubs before – Shelly's Manne Hole, Ali's Alley, Fred Anderson's Velvet Lounge – but none with quite the charisma of Ronnie Scott's in London's Soho. Unlike the others, Ronnie's career as proprietor and MC eclipsed his playing, which is a shame because he was a fine tenor player and, in the opinion of Charles Mingus, quite the best and bluesiest of the 'white boys'.

****** When I Want Your Opinion, I'll Give It To You**

Ronnie Scott's Jazz House JHAS 610 *Scott; Stan Tracey (p); Ernest Ranglin (g); Malcolm Cecil, Rick Laird (b); Jackie Dougan, Chris Karan, Ronnie Stephenson (d).* 12/63–4/65.

*****(*) The Night Has A Thousand Eyes**

Ronnie Scott's Jazz House JCAS 614 *Scott; Sonny Stitt (ts); Stan Tracey (p); Malcolm Cecil (b); Jackie Dougan, Ronnie Stephenson (d).* 5/64.

Poor old Ronnie. Latterly the jokes covered for a lot of pain. It was always ironic that he should have become a virtual brand name, and a substantial proportion of the Japanese and American tourists who filed into the Frith Street club never got a chance to hear him play. Originally Ronald Schatt, he was a past-master at the chewish chive, but also a musician soaked in the blues and capable of compelling emotion in a solo. He recorded only sparingly, though a couple of his records have acquired almost iconic status in Britain and on the Continent. *When I Want Your Opinion* (a typical Scott line) brings together material from the early to mid-'60s when the club really was the crucible of modern jazz in Britain. The various groups, with either Malcolm Cecil or Rick Laird (later to join the Mahavishnu Orchestra and then to give up music for photography) were boppish in idiom, but closer in feel to the swing era. If there is a saxophonist Scott resembles on these tracks, then it must be the Janus-faced Don Byas, who also recorded at the club towards the end of his life. The presence of Ernest Ranglin brings a bouncy playfulness to 'Ronnie's Blues' from December 1963. A couple of months later, he's missing, and Chris Karan has been replaced by Jackie Dougan. Stan Tracey is the piano player on all the tracks with keyboard (there are two trios, with just Laird and Dougan or Stephenson) and he brings his usual abrupt lyricism to 'Bye Bye Blackbird' (recorded in 1965) and a touch of deadpan humour to 'I'm Sick And Tired Of Waking Up Tired And Sick', a Scott original that in 1997 seemed unbearably ironic.

The great joy of being Ronnie Scott was, of course, being allowed to cry *and* sing at your own party. The 1964 encounters with Sonny Stitt are the first of his encounters with visiting Americans to be released by Les Tomkins and Jazz House. Just three long tracks, but some roaring Scott performances, which show him to be no slouch in any company. 'The Night Has A Thousand Eyes' kicks off with Sonny's bright, exuberant solo, switches to Scott for a long, beautifully shaped statement which feeds off the American's in the wittiest and most sardonic way, leaving it to Stitt to round out the solos. Unfortunately, tape problems mean that the number has to be faded at the end. Scott takes the initiative on 'A Sonny Day For Ronnie', recorded later in the month, and leaves Stitt eating dust; honours are even again in the exchange of eights, but it's definitely the club owner's moment. Perhaps rightly, Stitt takes charge on 'Bye Bye Blackbird', a performance that throws in some classic bebop phrasing along the way.

*****(*) The Night Is Scott And You're So Swingable**

Redial 558 888-2 Scott; Stan Tracey (*p*); Ernest Ranglin (*g*); Lennie Bush, Rick Laird (*b*); Tony Crombie, Bill Eyden (*d*); strings/ 7/64, 11/65.

Redial's archaeology of classic British jazz has thrown up few more welcome sets than this one. Just a few choruses of 'Baubles, Bangles And Beads' are enough to confirm why these '60s bands, with Tracey threatening the house piano or Ranglin grooving away on his own thing, are regarded with such nostalgia. The guitarist features on the tracks with strings, which is an interesting combination of sounds, but it's the piano quartet tracks which are of real value. 'The Night Has A Thousand Eyes' has touches of Coltrane's extended harmony but, for all its ambition, this is a cracking interpretation of a wonderful song. As so often in later years, Scott plays the melody with a vocalized tone, as if hearing the words in his head. No less a personage than composer Richard Rodney Bennett did the string arrangements and, as expected, they're swingingly idiomatic, with no saccharine or stodge.

****** Live At Ronnie Scott's**

Columbia 494439 2 *Scott; Kenny Wheeler (t, flhn); Chris Pyne (tb); Ray Warleigh (as); John Surman (ss, bs); Gordon Beck (p, org); Ron Mathewson (b); Kenny Clare, Tony Oxley (d).* 69.

This was the group known simply as The Band, a kind of house outfit that had the time to develop some pretty sophisticated charts and an enviable level of empathy on the stand. Ronnie himself is in great form in front of the home crowd (most of whom, needless to say, had travelled a good way to be there). His solo on the opening 'Recorda Me' is up there with any of composer Joe Henderson's and his long, burning statement on the closing 'Macumba' bracket the album beautifully. Warleigh plays with his usual headlong appetite and Surman blisters the paintwork on Laurie Holloway's 'King Pete', which sees him shift to soprano. Wheeler is as calmly tasteful as ever but, even in this congenial company, manages to suggest a great deal of passion under the unflustered exterior. The rhythm section is fascinating. Beck has never received due credit and remains something of a figure apart. His comping is as solid as railway sleepers, underpinning solos of terse originality. Mathewson switches between upright and electric bass, the latter sounding rather dated in this context. The real key to the band's headlong pace is the twinned drumming of Clare and Oxley; Tony cut his jazz teeth at Ronnie's and provides the turbulent, swirling groove on which the set is constructed. It's possible to hear Kenny laying accents and paradiddles in the middle of Tony's sweeping runs, content to let him do the assault course and to stay laid back and cool himself. A final word for Chris Pyne, who blows dour and strong on Kenny Wheeler's 'Second Question', using a big virile tone that sounds deeper in pitch than it is just because the tone is so broad. A strong album from a band in top form.

*****(*) Never Pat A Burning Dog**

Ronnie Scott's Jazz House JC 012 *Scott; Dick Pearce (t); Mornington Lockett (ts); John Critchinson (p); Ron Mathewson (b); Martin Drew (d).* 10 & 11/90.

Never Pat A Burning Dog (seems obvious, but you never know) will appeal to those who have worn out their copy of *Serious Gold*, his late-'70s Pye album, though they may also be surprised at how far his harmonic thinking has developed since then. A muted, almost elegiac set (recorded live at Ronnie Scott's Club in Soho) begins with a stunning version of McCoy Tyner's 'Contemplation', full of glassy harmonies and tender, dissonant flourishes. Scott's choice of material is typically adventurous and tasteful: Jimmy Dorsey's 'I'm Glad There Is You', David Sanborn's 'White Caps', Cedar Walton's 'When Love Is New', a slightly unsatisfactory reading of Freddie Hubbard's 'Little Sunflower' with the less than inspiring Lockett in for Pearce, and two standards, 'All The Things You Are' and the still-under-recorded 'This Love Of Mine'. Scott's tone is deep and subtly modulated and his phrasing has the kind of relaxed precision and inner heat one associates with Paul Gonsalves or Zoot Sims. Despite the variety of material, it's a remarkably consistent set, perhaps even a little unvaried in treatment.

The records will never quite make up for the loss of his presence. Scott was an original, a wise old business head whose love of the music was the best excuse for occasional peevishness and an unsmilingly literal approach to the small print on a contract. We grew up there; we'll miss him.

Shirley Scott (born 1934)

ORGAN, PIANO

Born in Philadelphia, she studied trumpet and piano, then began working with Lockjaw Davis and switched to organ. Formed her own trio in 1960, often working with Stanley Turrentine, who was her husband for a time. Visible in the '90s on TV with Bill Cosby, and still playing organ and piano.

***** Workin'**

Prestige 24126-2 *Scott; Eddie 'Lockjaw' Davis (ts); Ronnell Bright (p); Wally Richardson (g); George Duvivier, Peck Morrison (b); Arthur Edgehill, Roy Haynes (d); Ray Barretto (perc).* 5/58–3/61.

***** Legends Of Acid Jazz**

Prestige 24200-2 *Scott; Stanley Turrentine (ts); Herb Lewis, George Tucker (b); Roy Brooks, Otis Finch (d).* 6–11/61.

***** Legends Of Acid Jazz – Soul Sister**

Prestige 24233-2 *Scott; Lem Winchester (vib); Kenny Burrell (g); George Duvivier, Eddie Khan (b); Otis Finch, Arthur Edgehill (d).* 6/60–2/64.

*****(*) Soul Shoutin'**

Prestige 24142-2 *Scott; Stanley Turrentine (ts); Major Holley, Earl May (b); Grassella Oliphant (d).* 1–10/63.

***** Blue Flames**

Original Jazz Classics OJC 328 *As above.* 8/65.

Scott has been used to heavy company. In 1955, in her native Philadelphia, she was working in a trio with John Coltrane. Wider recognition came with her association with Eddie 'Lockjaw' Davis, which led to dozens of albums for Prestige, Impulse!, Atlantic and Cadet through the 1970s. There are currently only a few CD revivals of this prodigious output, and surely Impulse! have something to schedule. Scott wasn't a knockabout swinger like Jimmy Smith and didn't have the bebop attack of Don Patterson, but there's an authority and an unusual sense of power in reserve which keep her music simmering somewhere near the boil. She is a strong blues player and a fine accompanist, and her right-hand lines have a percussive feel that utilizes space more than most organ players ever did. She was also married to Stanley Turrentine, and they made a number of records together: *Soul Shoutin'* brings together the contents of the original albums *The Soul Is Willing* and *Soul Shoutin'*, and this one gets the nod as the pick of the reissues. The title-track off *The Soul Is Willing* is the near-perfect example of what this combination could do, a fuming Turrentine solo followed by a deftly swinging one by Scott. In comparison, *Blue Flames* seems like short measure, but this kind of jazz is perhaps best sampled a few tracks at a time in any case, including these two – nothing more nor less than some cooking tenor and organ on some blues and a ballad or two. *Workin'* is a compilation of four sessions that cover some of Shirley's earlier dates and includes one bruiser with Lockjaw Davis – good stuff, if a notch below *Soul Shoutin'*. The two *Acid Jazz* sets bring back four more of the two dozen or so original LPs that Scott made for Prestige: the first couples *Hip Soul* and *Hip Twist*, the second brings together *Soul Sister* and, oddly, the much later *Travelin' Light*. The first one has another heaping helping of Turrentine, while the second relies on the not terribly interesting Winchester and the admirable Burrell. Little to choose, really, since while her cast-list varied Scott herself played with unshakeable consistency.

***** Blues Everywhere**

Candid CCD79525 *Scott; Arthur Harper (b); Mickey Roker (d).* 11/91.

***** Skylark**

Candid CCD 79705-2 *As above.* 11/91.

For once Scotty handles the acoustic keyboard for an entire date, and what comes out is a fat, funky, authoritative trio date somewhat in the style of Red Garland. Harper and Roker can sleepwalk through this kind of music and, since it keeps on swinging for nearly an hour, it's a tribute to Shirley that they stayed awake. Their second set is laid down on the subsequent *Skylark*, and one can safely say it's more of the same: two enjoyable records, but only a relative will need both of them. Fine, live recording from Birdland in New York.

***** A Walkin' Thing**

Candid CCD79719 *Scott; Terell Stafford (t); Tim Warfield (ts); Arthur Harper (b); Aaron Walker (d).* 11/92.

Harper survives from the last two trio records, but otherwise this is a hot young group that Shirley's in charge of. The feel is vintage Prestige/Blue Note (done at Van Gelder's, unsurprisingly) and if some of the tracks are a bit of a long stretch nobody sounds unhappy about it. It suits Warfield and Stafford to take their time on the title-piece especially. Scott presides with unblinking authority.

Stephen Scott (born 1969)

PIANO

At seventeen, Scott won the National Association of Jazz Educators' Young Talent Award. Apprenticed with Betty Carter and Bobby Watson, before recording his own albums for Verve. Currently with Sonny Rollins.

*****(*) Vision Guest**

Enja ENJ 9347-2 *Scott; Ron Carter (b); Victor Lewis (d): Steve Kroon (perc).* 3/98.

Not yet thirty, but Scott already sounds like a veteran. The switch of labels (his Verve records are out of print already) seems to have relaxed him and opened up conduits to all sorts of corners of his personal history. Scott has often spoken about his debt to Wynton Kelly and here and there on this album, and notably on the interludes that separate the main tracks, he seems to be drawing on Wynton's funky blues idiom.

The most interesting single thing on this session is called – significantly enough – 'A Work In Progress' – an intelligent slice of modern jazz that quite explicitly allies itself to the tradition. Carter is the ideal playing partner for this kind of set. He adapts cheerfully to almost any situation but retains a rich integrity of voice that is as commanding as anything in contemporary jazz. Lewis likewise is on top of whatever is thrown his way. A pity that the material isn't more stretching, but one suspects that Scott wants to play inside his game for the next little while.

Tony Scott (born 1921)

CLARINET, BARITONE SAXOPHONE, PIANO, ELECTRONICS

Born A.J. Sciacca, he worked as a New York sideman in the 1940s and '50s and led his own groups from 1953, playing his own version of bop on the clarinet. Left for Europe and Asia in 1959, and turned to investigating various ethnic musics, although jazz remains in his make-up. Now based in Italy, though his activities rarely reach international audiences.

*****(*) The Complete Tony Scott**

RCA 74321 421322 *Scott; John Carisi, Thad Jones, Jimmy Nottingham, Clark Terry, Wendell Culley, Jimmy Maxwell, Joe Newman, Bernie Glow (t); Henry Coker, Quentin Jackson, Benny Powell, Sonny Truitt, Bill Hughes (tb); Gigi Gryce (as); Frank Foster, Zoot Sims, Frank Wess (ts); Danny Bank, Sahib Shihab, Charlie Fowlkes (bs); Bill Evans (p); Freddie Green (g); Les Grinage, Milt Hinton (b); Osie Johnson, Paul Motian (d).* 12/56.

Scott's position as a master of his instrument has never been in question, but it was that instrument's own status which bebop and after was disputing, and excellent records like this one have been comparatively lost as a result. A dozen miniatures handsomely crafted for a crack studio band, with Scott incisively making his way through and around the music, never encumbered by the task but going at it with a degree more passion than these situations would customarily demand.

****** A Day In New York**

Fresh Sound FSR CD 160/2 2CD *Scott; Clark Terry (t); Jimmy Knepper (tb); Sahib Shihab (bs); Bill Evans (p); Henry Grimes, Milt Hinton (b); Paul Motian (d).* 11/57.

*****(*) Dedications**

Core COCD 9.00803 *Scott; Bill Evans, Horst Jankowski (p); Juan Suastre (g); Shinichi Yuizi (koto); Scott LaFaro, Peter Witte (b); Paul Motian, Herman Mutschler (d).* 57–59.

*****(*) Sung Heroes**

Sunnyside SSC 1015 *As above, except omit Jankowski, Witte, Mutschler, Yuizi.* 10/59.

In 1959 Tony Scott turned his back on America, wounded by the death of several friends (Hot Lips Page, Billie Holiday, Charlie Parker, Lester Young) and by what he considered the 'death' of the clarinet in jazz terms. Since then he has been a wanderer, exploring the culture and music of the East, trading in the sometimes aggressive assertions of bebop for a meditative approach to harmony that at its best is deeply moving, at its least disciplined a weak ambient decoration.

These beautiful *Dedications* (some of which were available under the title *Sung Heroes* on Sunnyside and can still be found in that format) record Scott's reactions to a group who have figured iconically in his life: Billie Holiday (the dedicatee of a delicate quartet, 'Misery'); Anne Frank (an overdubbed duet with himself on clarinet and baritone saxophone that might seem inept were it not so moving); Art Tatum; Hot Lips Page; an unnamed African friend; the Schoenbergian composer, Stefan Wolpe (who receives the homage of an atonal blues); his father; Israel; the bullfighter, Manolete; and Charlie Parker. There are also Japanese-influenced pieces, based on traditional verse and images. The high clarinet protestations of 'Blues For An African Friend' and the succeeding 'Atonal Ad Lib Blues' suggest what a remarkable talent Scott's was, giving the instrument the power and immediacy of soprano saxophone without sacrificing its distinctive timbre. Influenced primarily by Ben Webster, he seems to condense and process an enormous acreage of jazz history in his enticingly miniaturist structures.

Scott enjoyed a close and fruitful relationship with Bill Evans, and perhaps his best recorded work is the session of 16 November 1957 with the Evans trio and guests, tackling a copious roster of originals and well-worn standards (including a lovely 'Lullaby Of The Leaves' with Knepper). The clarinettist's opening statements on Evans's 'Five' are almost neurotically brilliant and a perfect illustration of how loud Scott could play. 'Portrait Of Ravi' and 'The Explorer' are Scott originals, directed towards the concerns that were increasingly to occupy him. Evans's light touch and immense harmonic sophistication suited his approach ideally. Scott was at the top of his professional tree and enjoyed great critical acclaim. More recent years have found him a relatively forgotten figure. But he is unmistakably an original.

***** Music For Zen Meditation**

Verve 521444-2 *Scott; Hozan Yamamoto (shakuhachi); Shinichi Yuizi (koto).* 2/64.

***** Music For Yoga Meditation And Other Joys**

Verve 835371-2 *Scott; Collin Walcott (sitar).* 68.

Scott's absorption in Buddhist thinking ultimately resulted in some intriguing cross-cultural experiments like this one. His interest in Indian *raga* (as in his ahead-of-the-pack dedication to Ravi Shankar on the Fresh Sound, above) and in African musics, below, bespeaks certain philosophical premisses which are rather difficult to judge on purely artistic grounds. How efficacious *Music For Zen Meditation* may be for its professed purpose is beyond the scope of this book to determine, but it's slightly disappointing to note how quickly Scott seemed prepared to abandon the taut harmonic arguments of his work with Evans, LaFaro and Motian in favour of the bland affirmations here. Nevertheless these discs – the second, with the then virtually unknown Collin Walcott, is a recent revival – have remained hugely popular in their way over the years, Verve even placing *Zen Meditation* in their Master Edition series. An early crossover into world music which must have seemed potent in their day; now they're charming period-pieces for hippie reminiscence.

*****(*) African Bird**

Soul Note 121083 *Scott; Glenn Ferris (tb); Giancarlo Barigozzi (f, bf); Chris Hunter (as, f); Duncan Kinnel (mar); Rex Reason (kalimba); Robin Jones, Karl Potter (perc); Jacqui Benar (v).* 81–5/84.

Conceived and performed before 'World Music' had become a sneer, *African Bird* is a largely convincing synthesis of Scott's African and Afro-American concerns into a suite of songs with an impressive level of coherence and developmental logic. To all intents and purposes it is a solo record, with largely incidental colorations from all but Barigozzi and Kinnel, who both play beautifully. For a flavour of where Scott has been since 1960, this is ideal.

Al Sears (1910–90)

TENOR SAXOPHONE

Joined the Chick Webb band in 1928, then led his own group for much of the '30s. A famous spell with Ellington, 1944–9, then in the '50s he started his own publishing house and played in rock'n'roll shows.

****(*) Swing's The Thing**

Original Jazz Classics OJC 838 *Sears; Don Abney (p); Wally Richardson (g); Wendell Marshall (b); Joe Marshall (d).* 11/60.

A minor Ellingtonian, Sears did rather better out of music publishing and became one of the few jazzmen to make money out of rock'n'roll. His Websterish sound is seldom more than a fair copy of the master, and on this plain and unremarkable date he ambles through some blues, some Ellington, and quite a decent take on 'Out Of Nowhere'. The band are very ordinary, and perhaps the curious should go to some of Ellington's 1940s records to hear Sears at his most effective.

Amanda Sedgwick

ALTO AND SOPRANO SAXOPHONES, CLARINET

A young saxophonist-composer based in Sweden.

***** Volt**

Caprice CAP 21491 *Sedgwick; Magnus Broo (t); Johan Söderlund (cl, bcl); Susanne Hörberg (f); Anders Inge, Torsten Nilsson (vn); Mikael Sjögren (vla); Per Blendulf (clo); Filip Augustson (b); Jesper Kviberg (d).* 5/96.

Sedgwick's ambitious record is an interesting attempt at integrating a jazz-based quartet with a chamber ensemble. The long three-part title-piece is full of enterprising writing which does its best to marry the two groups, often to entertaining if seldom provocative ends. The results are more lightweight than large scale, but perhaps that stops the music from succumbing to the kind of pretentiousness which accompanies many such ventures.

Occasionally the writing is reminiscent of some of Ornette Coleman's chamber pieces, which makes the concluding 'encore' of Coleman's 'Round Trip' a suitable closer. The quartet also play Roland Kirk's 'Now Please Don't You Cry Beautiful Edith', in which Sedgwick's soprano is a rather more striking voice than it is in her big work.

Joey Sellars

TROMBONE

California-based trombonist and arranger-composer, with his own take on the post-bop tradition.

***** Something For Nothing**
Nine Winds NWCD 136 *Sellars; Greg Varlotta, Clay Jenkins (t, flhn); Alex Iles, Bruce Fowler (tb); Danny Hemwall (btb); Kim Richmond (ss, as, cl, f); John Schroeder (ss, ts, cl, f); Rob Verdi (bs, bcl, f); Kei Akagi (p); Ken Filiano (b); Billy Mintz (d).* 2/89.

Although some of the big-band music on Nine Winds has been of a free-spirited nature, Sellars here leads a band of pros who could sit comfortably with any studio chores on the Los Angeles session-scene. The one cursory nod to any kind of dissembled structure on 'American Standard' is the least convincing moment on the record; the rest is sharply drilled and punchily phrased, modern big-band music, with Sellars throwing opportunities to soloists who can eat up changes and modal settings alike. His own trombone improvisations are as strong as anybody's, but a special mention to the splendid baritone of Verdi on the title-tune. Some measure of the success of the arrangements comes in the point that, although only five themes stretch across some 70 minutes of music, no track runs right out of steam.

****** Pastels, Ashes**
Nine Winds NWCD 0153 *Sellars; Clay Jenkins, Ron King (t, flhn); Bruce Fowler, Alex Iles (tb); Dan Hemwall (btb); Kim Richmond (ss, as, cl, f); Jerry Pinter (ss, ts, cl, f); Rob Verdi (bs, bcl, f); Kei Akagi (p); Ken Filiano (b); Billy Mintz (d).* 10/91.

Cut live to two-track in a single day in the studio, this is a brilliant effort by Sellars. Still there are only six tunes, covering 70 minutes of music, but the brimming arrangements make use of every musician almost continuously. There are superb improvisations from Pinter, Jenkins and Fowler in particular, and Sellars blends structure and surprise with a deftness that should have other arrangers genuflecting. Rather than recycling patterns or mixing together clichés, his scores actually develop and press ideas into new shapes, and he's one of the few current composers to require a long form to be at his most effective. The only disappointment is that there's been nothing new from Sellars since our last edition.

Bernie Senensky

PIANO

Born In Winnipeg, Senensky began recording as a leader in 1975, following several years as part of the local rhythm section for visiting players.

***** Homeland**
Timeless SJP 426 *Senensky; Gary Bartz (ss, as); Harvie Swartz (b); Akira Tana (d).* 1/91.

***** Wheel Within A Wheel**
Timeless SJP 410 *Senensky; Bobby Watson (ss, as); Ray Drummond (b); Marvin 'Smitty' Smith (d).* 2/91.

***** Rhapsody**
Timeless SJP 434 *Senensky; Jim Vivian (b); Bob Moses (d).* 7/93.

We have been a while catching up with Senensky. He is a Canadian (all three albums were cut in Toronto) with extensive local experience but, aside from these Timeless albums, he hasn't had much international exposure. Despite the heavy company on the first two discs in particular, Senensky more than holds his own. He likes the music brisk, eventful and quick-witted, and his solos are full of fast, long lines that bed down in solid post-bop language with some Tristano-ish obliqueness. 'Bop-Be', on *Wheel Within A Wheel*, is a typical original, a winding line over changes that Watson eats up in his thrilling solo. This is the pick of the three dates: Watson is only rarely heard as a sideman on someone else's originals, and he's sufficiently engaged to be thinking hard while spinning out his usual effortless lines. *Homeland* isn't quite so good, partly because Bartz, though hardly coasting, doesn't really make his bleary sound at home in the music, and partly because the album simply runs out of steam: at 75 minutes, there are too many long solos from all hands.

By himself, or at least with only bass and drums to hand, Senensky takes a confident course through *Rhapsody*. Only three originals in nine tracks, and the closely miked trio work up a lot of steam on the up-tempo pieces; but one misses the fillip which Watson brought to the earlier disc.

Boyd Senter (1897–?)

CLARINET, ALTO AND TENOR SAXOPHONES

Born in Nebraska, Senter first learned piano, then switched to clarinet. He made many records as a soloist in the 1920s and worked in Detroit during the '30s, eventually selling sports equipment and hardware items as well as playing.

***** Jazzologist Supreme 1928–1930**
Timeless CBC 1-032 *Senter; Phil Napoleon, Mickey Bloom, James Migliore (t); Bill Haukenheiser (c); Tommy Dorsey, Charlie Butterfield, Ray Stilwell, Herb Winfield (tb); Fud Livingston (cl, ts); Jimmy Dorsey (as); Jack Russell, Frank Signorelli (p); Eddie Lang, Carl Kress (g); Dan Calker (bj, g); Ward Lay (b); Vic Berton, Stan King, Walter Meyer (d).* 3/28–6/30.

Senter is a wryly beloved figure among collectors of early jazz. The 'Jazzologist Supreme' was shameless in producing some horrible sounds on the clarinet, and his most outlandish playing makes even Ted Lewis sound like Artie Shaw. Yet even in the midst of his barnyard phrasing and jackass effects, one can often discern a surprisingly tough and hard-bitten musician. He must have had some sense of humour about his music – why else would he name his band The Senterpedes? – and on the sessions where he's joined by the likes of Napoleon, Lang and the Dorseys there is the obvious compensation of some hot and classy New York jazz to set beside Senter's vaudevillian routines. In any case, tracks like 'Prickly Heat' and 'Mobile Blues' muster their own peculiar intensity. This is by no means a comprehensive edition of Senter's music (he even recorded several masters for Paramount) but it is a useful and excellently remastered group of his OKeh recordings. Brian Rust's sleeve-notes reveal that The Boss Of The Stomps eventually retired to selling saw blades and fishing tackle in Mio, Michigan.

Sextet of Orchestra USA

GROUP

A small group drawn from John Lewis's Orchestra USA project, here for the purposes of playing Kurt Weill.

*****(*) Mack The Knife**

RCA Victor 159162 2 *Nick Travis (t); Thad Jones (c); Mike Zwerin (bass t); Eric Dolphy (as, bcl, f); Jerome Richardson (as, bcl); John Lewis (p); Jimmy Raney (g); Richard Davis (b); Connie Kay (d).* 1/64–6/65.

Mike Zwerin tells a good story, but even he would surely concede that his version of how this record was inspired constitutes what Mark Twain called a 'stretcher'. Bass trumpeter and journalist Zwerin reckons that his desire to make a jazz album of Kurt Weill songs was spurred on by hearing Doors vocalist Jim Morrison singing 'Alabama Song' on the radio. Correct us if we're wrong, but the Doors' first album appeared in 1967, by which time Zwerin's pet project was long since in the can.

A pet project which bordered on obsession. Zwerin financed the first side of the record, which was produced by Phil Ramone, and then RCA paid Tom Dowd to direct the later session, probably the only occasion when these legends of music production appeared on the same disc. By the time the second date was arranged, two of the stars of the first were dead. Eric Dolphy died in 1964, not far from where some of Weill's great Berlin songs were written. Nick Travis was also gone, robbing the album of players who instinctively grasped Zwerin's hectic, un-showbizzy arrangements. He hadn't wanted to include 'Mack The Knife', which was already a show singers' staple after versions by Louis Armstrong and Bobby Darin, but RCA insisted and exacted a further toll by using it as the title-piece of the original release. One wonders what Dolphy would have made of it had he survived. By contrast Richardson is more of an 'inside' player, working within the chords and rarely challenging orthodoxy.

John Lewis is the dominant presence on the first session, playing with typical intelligence and a shrewd humour on 'Alabama Song' and the often overlooked 'As You Make Your Bed'. He was replaced later by guitarist Jimmy Raney, a fascinating player but not necessarily the obvious choice for this material. Weill has never sounded woollier or more abrasively satirical. Zwerin's forgotten classic is a welcome reissue.

Bud Shank (born 1926)

ALTO SAXOPHONE, FLUTE, PENNY WHISTLE

Originally a tenor player, Shank switched to the smaller horn while working with Charlie Barnet and Stan Kenton, adding the flute to his armoury. The Ohioan's light, tender touch was a significant component of the Lighthouse All Stars sound, and Shank was the founder of the LA Four. Like many of the cool West Coast school, he turned to bebop rather late in his career.

***** Jazz In Hollywood**

Original Jazz Classics OJC 1890 *Shank; Shorty Rogers (flhn); Jimmy Rowles, Lou Levy (p); Harry Babasin (b); Roy Harte, Larry Bunker (d).* 3/54–9/54.

***** Bud Shank & Bill Perkins**

Blue Note 93159 *Shank; Bill Perkins (as, ts, f); Hampton Hawes, Jimmy Rowles (p); Red Mitchell, Carson Smith, Ben Tucker, Leroy Vinnegar (b); Mel Lewis, Shelly Manne (d).* 5/55–58.

***** Blowin' Country**

Blue Note 94846 *Shank; Bob Cooper (ts, bcl, ob); Claude Williamson (p); Don Prell (b); Chuck Flores (d).* 11/56–6/57.

***** Bud Shank Quartet**

Fresh Sound FSR CD 129 *Shank; Claude Williamson (p); Don Prell (b); Chuck Flores, Jimmy Pratt (d).* 11/56–4/58.

Bud Shank has been the quintessential West Coast altoman for more than 40 years. He has appeared on numberless sessions but his playing has remained sharp, piercingly thoughtful and swinging in a lean, persuasive way. For a long spell he was considered cool to the point of frigidity, and his later work has grown fiercer and more inclined to collar the listener; but the early albums have a kind of snake-eyed ingenuity which has its own appeal. *Jazz In Hollywood* is an interesting find, two rather rare albums for the Nocturne label combined on one disc. One was Shank's debut, with a quintet including frequent partner Rogers; the other features a trio date for Lou Levy. *Quartet* rounds up some stray TV and South African dates, including one where Shank tries out the penny whistle. Neither of these is exactly vintage Bud.

The two Blue Notes, originally on Pacific, were reissued in 1998. Both are effectively co-led sessions with Bill Perkins and Bob Cooper respectively, though the Perkins material is drawn from a number of mid- to late-'50s dates and includes a trio version of 'I Hear Music' with just Hampton Hawes and rhythm. Though bitty, it's a fine record. Bob Cooper brings his usual range of alternative horns to his session. The title comes from a Shank tune and doesn't refer to country and western music. Most of the tunes are familiar enough, but the set includes the lovely 'Two Lost Souls', the Steve Allen theme, and a delightful short version of 'I've Grown Accustomed To Her Face'.

***** Sunshine Express**

Concord CCD 6020 *Shank; Bobby Shew (t, flhn, c); Mike Wofford (p); Fred Atwood (b); Larry Bunker (d).* 1/76.

Shank spent a large part of the 1960s covering pop tunes for World Pacific, before cutting a string of albums with the LA4 for Concord in the following decade. *Sunshine Express* is more obviously jazz-driven than the LA4 material approach, which borrowed substantially from Shank's light, Latinate pop. Shew is a wonderful player on his day; returning to this album after some time, it is the trumpeter's clean-milled middle-register choruses which stand out. Wofford is also first rate, especially when tracking Shank's spacious, delicately phrased flute lines.

***** Crystal Comments**
Concord CCD 4126 *Shank; Alan Broadbent, Bill Mays (p).* 10/79.

Shank and Bill Mays recorded a set of classically inspired duets called *Explorations: 1980*. The tunes on this CD were recorded at the same time, but with the unusual instrumentation of flute, piano and Fender Rhodes piano, with Mays and Alan Broadbent taking it in turns at the electric instrument. However unlikely the line-up sounds, the trio functions pretty much like an orthodox bop group, with the rhythm parts largely handled by the acoustic keyboard, broad bass ostinati from Mays, more percussive devices in the left hand from Broadbent. The tunes are all fairly orthodox as well, 'Scrapple From The Apple' initially unfamiliar in this form, 'How Are Things In Glocca Morra?', 'Body And Soul', 'On Green Dolphin Street' and 'Solar' rounding out an enjoyable but rather lightweight set.

*****(*) This Bud's For You**
32 Jazz 32164 *Shank; Kenny Barron (p); Ron Carter (b); Al Foster (d).* 11/84.

Another phoenix from the slowly reviving Muse catalogue, and a very fine one. Shank is in top form and the group could hardly be more generously configured. Comparing the new issue with the original LP is interesting. Unless we are mistaken, the balance of bass to piano has been shifted to bring Barron forward a touch though without relegating big Ron to the wings. Walter Norris's lovely 'Space Maker' is an interesting inclusion.

***** California Concert**
Original Jazz Classics OJC 948 *Shank; Shorty Rogers (flhn); George Cables (p); Monty Budwig (b); Sherman Ferguson (d).* 5/85.

***** Serious Swingers**
Contemporary C 14031 *Shank; Bill Perkins (ts); Alan Broadbent (p); John Heard (b); Sherman Ferguson (d).* 12/86.

***** Tomorrow's Rainbow**
Contemporary C 14048 *Shank; Marco Silva (ky); Ricardo Peixoto (g); Gary Brown (b); Michael Spiro (d).* 9/88.

In more recent years Shank has deployed a tougher bebop idiom, still with the same lyrical edge and softness of tone but with sharper and more incisive phrasing, and a shorter line. *Sunshine Express* and *California Concert* are relatively tame but, starting with *Serious Swingers*, co-led with Perkins, the music begins to turn up the heat. *Tomorrow's Rainbow* teams him with Marco Silva's fusion group, Intersection, for a lively Latin set that keeps the temperature well up.

***** A Flower Is A Lovesome Thing**
Koch International 6912 *Shank; Bob Cooper (ts, f); Metropole Orchestra.* 88.

One of the last occasions on which Shank can also be heard on flute, this half-and-half collaboration with Bob Cooper and the well-schooled Dutch orchestra has few real moments of drama but is solidly executed and elegantly produced. The two saxophonists unfortunately don't play together, but the contrast of voices and approaches – by this stage, Shank was by far the more passionate and emphatic performer – makes for a nicely balanced set, and Bud's solo on 'Like Someone In Love' is one of his best of the period.

***** Tales Of The Pilot: The Music Of David Peck**
Capri 74025-2 *Shank; David Peck (p); David Peterson (g); Chuck Deardorf (b); Dave Coleman (d).* 12/89.

David Peck (and Chuck Deardorf) worked in Shank's group for a time; here the saxophonist returns the compliment, playing a selection of Peck compositions with the pianist's group, Syzygy. The writing is interestingly varied. 'Why Tell Me Now' has a mournful, almost hymn-like quality, and 'Bouquet of Fires' crackles through some unexpected changes. Impressive stuff and a must for Shank fans.

****(*) Drifting Timelessly**
Capri 75001-2 *Shank; Roumanis String Quartet.* 90.

Drifting aimlessly would be the obvious retort, but for the fact that some of Shank's solo work is absolutely sterling. Working with material by producer George Roumanis, Bud soars gracefully and places his notes with real care. The accompaniments are overdone, but flawlessly accurate in execution.

****** Lost In The Stars**
Fresh Sound FSRCD 18 *Shank; Lou Levy (p).* 12/90.

***** The Doctor Is In!**
Concord CCD 79520 *Shank; Mike Wofford (p); Bob Magnusson (b); Sherman Ferguson (d).* 9/91.

*****(*) I Told You So!**
Candid CCD 79533 *Shank; Kenny Barron (p); Lonnie Plaxico (b); Victor Lewis (d).* 6/92.

*****(*) New Gold!**
Candid CCD 79707 *Shank; Conte Candoli (t); Bill Perkins (ts, ss); Jack Nimitz (bs); John Clayton (b); Sherman Ferguson (d).* 12/93.

Lost In The Stars is a Sinatra songbook, marked by the quirky brilliance of Levy (an accompanist's accompanist) and by Shank's attractive alto sound which sounds as if it's been in and out of retirement as often as the man himself. 'This Love Of Mine', a much-overlooked standard, is played masterfully, with just the right balance of sentiment and cynicism.

The recent *New Gold!* sees him steering comfortably towards his seventieth birthday. Shank's own playing is exemplary, but it is Perkins who shapes the music round himself on this date and, though the varied package of songs suits Shank perfectly, he doesn't shine quite as brightly as he had on the previous *I Told You So!*, a splendidly gritty performance with a fine rhythm section.

*****(*) By Request**
Milestone 9273 *Shank; Cyrus Chestnut (p); George Mraz (b); Lewis Nash (d).* 97.

The veteran altoman is still in formidable form on this meeting with another top-flight trio. Eleven picked standards are dealt with minus fuss or circumstance and, if he substitutes a rough intensity for some of the guile of his younger self, the music seems very alive.

***** After You, Jeru**

Fresh Sound FSRCD 5028 *Shank; Mike Wofford (p); Bob Magnusson (b); Joe LaBarbera (d).* 12/98.

With the exception of the title-piece, which closes the record, the whole album is devoted to Mulligan compositions. Shank's tenderest statement for years will appeal even to those who are unconvinced by his light and undramatic playing. The album strengthens as it advances and the closing sequence, with 'Night Lights', 'Theme For Jobim' and the title-piece in close proximity, is very fine indeed. Otherwise, rather low key.

Lakshminarayana Shankar (born 1950)

VIOLIN, DOUBLE VIOLIN

Born in Madras, he learned violin as a boy and studied the Indian classical tradition before going to the USA in 1969. Co-founded Shakti with John McLaughlin and pursued his own fusions in the '80s, although he remains best known in his own country, where he still plays 'authentically'. Adrift from ECM, he has tended to slip away from jazz listeners of late.

***** Who's To Know (M.R.C.S.)**

ECM 827269-2 *Shankar; Umayalpuram K Sivaraman (mridangam); Zakir Hussain (tabla); V Lakshminarayana (tala keeping).* 11/80.

***** Vision**

ECM 811969-2 *Shankar; Jan Garbarek (ts, ss, bsx, perc); Palle Mikkelborg (t, flhn).* 4/83.

***** Song For Everyone**

ECM 823795-2 *Shankar; Jan Garbarek (ts, ss); Zakir Hussain, Trilok Gurtu (perc).* 84.

****(*) The Epidemics**

ECM 827522-2 *Shankar; Caroline (syn, tamboura, v); Steve Vai (g); Gilbert Kaufman (syn); Percy Jones (b).* 85.

*****(*) Nobody Told Me**

ECM 839623-2 *Shankar; V Lakshminarayana (vn, v); Zakir Hussain (tabla); Vikku Vinayakram (ghatam); Ganam Rao, Caroline (v).* 87.

***** M.R.C.S.**

ECM 841642-2 *Shankar; Zakir Hussain (tabla); Vikku Vinayakram (ghatam); Jon Christensen (d).* 88.

***** Pancha Nadal Pallavi**

ECM 841641-2 *Shankar; Zakir Hussain (tabla); Vikku Vinayakram (ghatam); Caroline (talam, sruthi).* 7/89.

Subheaded 'Indian classical music' (a designation that has caused some controversy in quarters unamused by Shankar's syncretism of subcontinental idioms), *Who's To Know* poses a sly challenge to the Western listener. Is this 'authentic' Indian music? How would we know even if it wasn't? ECM's initial resistance to liner-notes and tendency to throw uncontextualized music at purchasers has changed in recent years (not least with the advent of the classically orientated New Series), but if Shankar's music is to be saved from a reductive categorization with 'ethnic', 'World Music' or 'New Age' materials, then more needs to be known about its rhythmic and harmonic premisses than is usually forthcoming.

Shankar's performing style is clearly not authentic in the sense that it is not constrained by traditional formulae and proscriptions. Shankar has played with saxophonist Jan Garbarek, and with Eastward-stepping guitarist John McLaughlin, in Shakti, the group that introduced him to a wider European audience. The association with Garbarek and Mikkelborg was a particularly fruitful one, demonstrating how readily Shankar's idiosyncratic ten-string double violin (whose twin necks can be played separately or simultaneously) and largely microtonal language translate to a Western improvisational idiom. There is nothing floatingly 'ethnic' about the music on *Vision*, which contains unprecedented bass saxophone work from Garbarek; it is a thoroughly contemporary and extremely intense performance from all three participants. The enigmatically titled *M.R.C.S.* is a re-recording of a solo project, with tabla master Zakir Hussain more than taking the place of the original rhythm box, and the other musicians helping to create a taut rhythmic web that trades up Shankar's almost pedestrian melodic notions into music of extravagant dimensions.

Pancha Nadal Pallavi is very much closer to Indian classical idiom and is consequently less penetrable from a Western point of view. Like the excellent *Nobody Told Me*, these are American sessions centred on the interplay between Shankar's remarkable double-necked instrument (dimly reminiscent of John McLaughlin's trademark double-neck guitar in Mahavishnu days) and Zakir Hussain's virtuosic tabla. The singing is intricate and insistently rhythmic. The latter album also features the acoustic violin of Shankar's father, V. Lakshminarayana, and the drones (a technical device, no slur intended) of his wife Caroline (who seems to have shed a surname). She also appears on *The Epidemics*, a title used for Shankar's touring band, albeit with different personnel. This is the weakest of the albums, too far removed from the tradition that nourishes the best of them.

Jack Sharpe

BARITONE SAXOPHONE

Experienced British arranger, broadly in a swing–mainstream style.

****(*) Roarin'**

Jazz House JHCD 016 *Sharpe; Derek Watkins, Jimmy Deuchar, Mark Chandler, Stuart Brooks, Simon Gardner (t); Geoff Wright, Chris Pyne, Pete Beachill, Dave Stewart (tb); Andy Mackintosh (as); Jamie Talbot, Dave Bishop (ts); Dave Hartley (p); Chris Laurence (b); Harold Fisher (d).* 5/89.

Although the sleevenote-writer's claim that this 'may be the best big band ever put together outside America' is pretty laughable, it is actually an impressive outfit, creaming off some of the most proficient of British players to execute a sequence of tough and forceful scores. Mackintosh and Bishop are the two major soloists and they have virtuoso features on 'Old Folks' and Tubby Hayes's

'100% Proof' respectively; while Mackintosh, in particular, may aspire to the kind of thing Chris Hunter or David Sanborn would do with the Gil Evans orchestra, it sounds more like routine pyrotechnics here. The only soloist who makes any real impression is Jimmy Deuchar, who sounds halting and imprecise on 'I'm Beginning To See The Light' beside the others, yet still seems to be more his own man than any of them. The band sound as if they need to relax more: only the closing 'J And B', a Deuchar theme, achieves a less forced take-off. Recorded live at Ronnie Scott's club, the sound is constricted but clear enough.

Sonny Sharrock (1940–94)

GUITAR

Sonny started out in doo-wop groups in the 1950s, before making the switch to jazz. He appeared on Pharoah Sanders's Tauhid and was a member of Herbie Mann's group for several years, recording a couple of fiery albums under his own name, including the long-deleted Monkey Pocky Boo. Later years brought him a measure of celebrity with noise group, Last Exit, but Sonny is still poorly represented on record.

****** Guitar**

Enemy EMY 102 *Sharrock.* 86.

Sharrock might have remained a lost legend if Bill Laswell hadn't provided him with a new context in Last Exit and egged him into this solo album, which shatters a former reputation for avant-garde 'weirdness'. *Guitar* is a textbook of what the electric instrument can be made to do in the hands of a master: Sharrock eschews fast picking in favour of blizzards of chords, walls of noise on the edge of feedback, drones that create a sort of violent timelessness and the first serious use of slide guitar in a 'jazz' context. 'Blind Willie', a dark nod to blues'n'gospel masters, Johnson and McTell, is as severe as 'Like Voices Of Sleeping Birds' is beautiful.

****(*) Seize The Rainbow**

Enemy EMY 104 *Sharrock; Melvin Gibbs, Bill Laswell (b); Abe Speller, Pheeroan akLaff (d).* 5/87.

***** Live In New York**

Enemy EMY 108 *Sharrock; Dave Snyder (ky); Melvin Gibbs (b); Pheeroan akLaff (d); Ron 'The Burglar' Cartel (v).* 7/89.

***** Highlife**

Enemy EMY 119 *Sharrock; Dave Snyder (ky); Charles Baldwin (b); Abe Speller, Lance Carter (d).* 10/90.

After the opening-round knockout of *Guitar*, these band albums were a mite disappointing. *Seize The Rainbow* rationalizes rather than extends Sharrock's ideas within a brawny blues-rock format with hints of exotica. The live album unleashes a little more ferocity without surrendering Sharrock's oft-obscured romantic streak, which peeks through on 'My Song'. Gibbs and akLaff play relatively straight but concentrated rhythms behind him. *Highlife* returns to polish rather than spit for its nine tracks – the guitarist is never one for rambling, unending solos – but gruff, clenched workouts like 'Chumpy' suggest that Sharrock's kind of fusion could work on more than one level. Bass-heavy recordings on all these records, but crystalline clarity isn't what one should be looking for with music like this.

****** Ask The Ages**

Axiom 848957-2 *Sharrock; Pharoah Sanders (ss, ts); Charnett Moffett (b); Elvin Jones (d).* 91.

Ask The Ages is of a high order. Here Sharrock uncorks some of his most ecstatic playing, and there are no more suitable players to accompany such a flight than Sanders and Jones, who quickly move in on the guitarist's space and both exalt and liberate his electric waving and crying. Moffett is a bit of a helpless bystander, but the interplay of the other three men is magnificently evocative of some kind of bliss. At the time of his death, Sharrock was about to sign a new contract; it wasn't to be.

Charlie Shavers (1917–71)

TRUMPET, VOCALS

Born in New York, Shavers made an extraordinary impact at the age of nineteen when he joined John Kirby's sextet. His vertiginous high-note playing, unstaunchable humour and deep sense of the history of jazz saw him through from the swing era to bebop and beyond. Shavers went from Kirby to Tommy Dorsey, and thence to a career as the eternal sideman, entertaining and vivid, but somehow not a leader.

***** The Complete Charlie Shavers With Maxine Sullivan**

Avenue Jazz R2 75819 *Shavers; Bennie Moten (tb); Hank D'Amico, Buster Bailey (cl); Russell Procope (as); Ken Kersey, Billy Kyle (p); Aaron Bell (b); Panama Francis, Specs Powell (d); Al Jazzbo Collins, Maxine Sullivan (v).* 57.

***** Live**

Black & Blue 59.302 *Shavers; Budd Johnson (ss, ts); André Persianny (p); Roland Lobligeois (b); Oliver Jackson (d).* 2/70.

There is so little around of Shavers as leader that any returns to catalogue are valuable. The 1957 sessions with Maxine Sullivan were recorded at a time when she had more or less withdrawn from music to work as a community nurse. Her voice is the antithesis of Shavers's, pure, elided and without vibrato. The other dominant personality is Bennie Moten, and 'Moten Swing', while not a definitive performance, is certainly a highlight. Shavers responds with some pungent but tender playing. The original first side is dominated by an eight-minute 'Story Of The Jazz Trumpet', a stand-up routine narrated by Al Jazzbo Collins, but dominated by Charlie's shrewd impersonation of his musical ancestors: Pops, Dizzy, Eldridge, Harry James and others. After John Kirby's death in 1952, Shavers was asked by Leonard Feather if he would be interested in reviving the line-up for a recording. The final five tracks of the record are from that group. His solo spot on 'If I Had A Ribbon Bow' is breathtakingly lyrical and intense.

By 1970, he was suffering the early stages of thoracic cancer, and he sounds curiously disconsolate in the company of a a plodding French rhythm-section, leaving much of the work to saxophonist Johnson. There are still flashes of the old Shavers on 'Lester Leaps In', 'Prelude To A Kiss' and a couple of untitled blues, but this is a thin and indifferently recorded legacy from the man whose mouthpiece was placed in Louis Armstrong's casket and who was delighted to find that British razor sockets were dedicated to his name: For Shavers Only.

Artie Shaw (born 1910)

CLARINET

Arthur Arshawsky was born in New York and was a dance band musician who formed his own band in 1936. His orchestra became one of the major swing-era big bands, and his use of strings and arrangements blending commercialism with interesting musical values was almost unique of its kind. But Shaw was a contrary soul, critical of any pandering to audiences, and he formed and disbanded several orchestras during the period 1939–44. As a clarinettist, he was as accomplished as Benny Goodman and, like Goodman, was the major soloist in his own band. He had several marriages, became a gifted writer of fiction and was interested in psychoanalysis – but he was entirely disillusioned with the business of music, and after 1949 he rarely performed again. In the 1980s and '90s, though, he returned to conducting, although he himself no longer played.

****(*) Artie Shaw 1936**
Classics 855 *Shaw; Willie Kelly, Lee Castaldo, Dave Wade, Zeke Zarchy (t); Mark Bennett, Mike Michaels, Buddy Morrow (tb); Tony Zimmers, Tony Pastor (ts); Fulton McGrath, Joe Lippman (p); Wes Vaughan, Tony Gottuso, Gene Stultz (g); Hank Wayland, Ben Ginsberg (b); Sammy Weiss, George Wettling (d); Peg La Centra (v); Julie Schechter, Lou Klaymann, Sam Persoff, Jimmy Oderich, Jerry Gray, Frank Siegfield, Bill Schumann, Ben Plotkin (strings).* 6–11/36.

***** In The Beginning**
Hep CD 1024 *As above.* 6–12/36.

***** Artie Shaw 1936–1937**
Classics 886 *Shaw; Lee Castle, Zeke Zarchy, John Best, Malcolm Crain, Tom Di Carlo (t); Buddy Morrow, Harry Rodgers, George Arus (tb); Les Robinson, Art Masters, Harry Freeman (as); Tony Pastor (ts, v); Fred Petry (ts); Joe Lippman, Les Burness (p); Tony Gottuso, Al Avola (g); Ben Ginsberg (b); Sam Weiss, Cliff Leeman (d); Peg La Centra (v); Jerry Gray, Sam Persoff, Bill Schumann (strings).* 12/36–7/37.

***** The Chant**
Hep 1046 *As above.* 12/36–8/37.

***** Artie Shaw 1937**
Classics 929 *As above, except add Jules Rubin (ts), Dolores O'Neil, Nita Bradley, Bea Wain, Leo Watson (v); omit Castle, Zarchy, Morrow, Masters, Petry, Lippman, Gottuso, Weiss, Gray, Persoff, Schumann, La Cetra.* 8–12/37.

***** Non-Stop Flight**
Hep 1048 *As above.* 8–12/37.

Among the most picaresque of jazz figures, Shaw's amazing life makes his records seem tame. They form a unique part of the jazz literature, although his real successes were comparatively few and his ambitions always outran his achievements. One problem was having relatively lightweight bands. Certainly his sessions for Brunswick, which represent the start of his story on record and which are collected here, have only himself as any kind of soloist and, with haphazard material and the oddly backward rhythm section, it's unsurprising that Shaw was considered minor league at the start of the swing era. But there are glimmers of light, and there is the then extraordinary sound of the string section meeting the band on numbers like 'Sugar Foot Stomp' and 'Sobbin' Blues'. Shaw's second band (his 'New Music') arrived in 1937 and soon sounded like a sleeker and more powerful unit, though the great finesse of the Victor sides was yet to become apparent – even Shaw's own playing is hit and miss. 'Nightmare', which would later be his first theme, showed a more interesting direction and, with the hiring of Leo Watson as vocalist, the band seemed a much hipper outfit.

The Classics and Hep releases follow a very similar course but, while Hep's transfers are usually clean and clear, the Classics tracks are another motley lot – some with huge amounts of surface noise, some very loud, others muddy. None of this is deathless material, but the Hep records are clearly the ones to get.

***** Artie Shaw And His Rhythm Makers 1938**
Tax 3709-2 *Shaw; John Best, Malcolm Crain, Tom Di Carlo (t); Harry Rogers, George Arus (tb); Les Robinson, Harry Freeman (as); Tony Pastor, Jules Rubin (ts); Les Burness (p); Al Avola (g); Ben Ginsberg (b); Cliff Leeman (d); Nita Bradley (v).* 2/38.

*****(*) Artie Shaw 1938**
Classics 965 *Shaw; Chuck Peterson, John Best, Claude Bowen, Bernie Privin (t); George Arus, Ted Vesley, Harry Rodgers, Russell Brown, Les Jenkins (tb); Les Robinson, Hank Freeman, George Koenig (as); Tony Pastor (ts, v); Ronnie Perry, Georgie Auld (ts); Les Burness, Bob Kitsis (p); Al Avola (g); Sid Weiss (b); Cliff Leeman, George Wettling (d); Billie Holiday, Helen Forrest (v).* 7–12/38.

****** Artie Shaw 1939**
Classics 1007 *As above, except add Buddy Rich (d); omit Bowen, Vesley, Brown, Koenig, Burness, Leeman, Wettling and Holiday.* 1–3/59.

*****(*) Artie Shaw 1939 Vol. 2**
Classics 1045 *Similar to above.* 3–8/39.

*****(*) Artie Shaw 1939-1940**
Classics 1087 *Shaw; Chuck Peterson, Billy Butterfield, Harry Geller, Bernie Privin, Charles Margulis, Manny Klein, George Thow (t); George Arus, Les Jenkins, Harry Rogers, Randall Miller, Bill Rank, Babe Bowman (tb); Jack Cave (frhn); Les Robinson, Hank Freeman, Blake Reynolds, Bud Carlton, Jack Stacey, Ben Kanter, Lyle Bowen (as); Tony Pastor (ts, v); Georgie Auld, Dick Clark, Happy Lawson (ts); Joe Krechter (bcl); Morton Ruderman (f); Phil Nemoli (ob); Bob Kitsis, Stan Wrightsman, Lyle Henderson (p); Al Avola, Bobby Sherwood (g); Sid Weiss, Jud DeNaut (b); Buddy Rich, Carl Maus, Spencer Prinz (d); Helen Forrest, Pauline Byrne, Martha Tilton (v); strings.* 8/39–5/40.

*****(*) Begin The Beguine**
RCA Bluebird ND 82432 *Basically as Classics discs above.* 7/38–1/41.

Although 'Begin The Beguine' made him a success – Shaw switched the original beguine beat to a modified 4/4, and its lilting pulse was irresistible – the huge hit he scored with it was greeted with loathing when it dawned on him what it meant in terms of fawning fans and general notoriety. He never seemed satisfied with his bands, and the four different orchestras on the Bluebird compilation played through a series of break-ups and disbandments by the leader. The second band, with arrangements by Jerry Gray and with Buddy Rich powering the rhythm section, was a harder-hitting outfit than the original Shaw 'New Music'. But their best sides are still scattered. *Begin The Beguine* includes such hits as the title-piece, 'Nightmare', 'Traffic Jam' and 'Frenesi', as well as sides with Helen Forrest handling vocals and two tracks by Shaw's small group, The Gramercy Five. The 1940 band includes Billy Butterfield and Johnny Guarnieri, and 'Star Dust' and 'Moonglow' hint at Shaw's romantic-symphonic aspirations, which troubled him at a time when listeners might have preferred to jitterbug. The remastering has been smartly done, though the NoNoise system is, as usual, not to all tastes.

Classics have the first four Victor sessions with their first disc (in reasonable if sometimes rather brutal-sounding remasters). A generous 24 tracks makes an impressive disc. It starts with 'Begin the Beguine' and goes on through many of Shaw's most enterprising records. Billie Holiday turns in her one Shaw appearance on 'Any Old Time' and there are ten appealing vocals by Helen Forrest: but it's the gusto of the band and Shaw's piercing solos one remembers, a quite astonishing advance on the music of only a little over a year earlier. This sounds like a swing master close to full command.

Classics 1007 carries on the story in style – these are good-sounding transfers. One is impressed with how often Shaw got a musical result of one sort or another. Listen to the way the band makes the melody line of 'The Man I Love' sing, or how Shaw makes the most of even a bit of hokum like 'The Donkey Serenade'. Only 10 of the 22 tracks sport a vocal – a very low strike-rate compared to most other white bands of the day – and even then Shaw could boast the admirable Helen Forrest as his singer. It's sometimes disappointing that there weren't more interesting soloists to emerge from the band, but Shaw by himself is always worth listening to. Track for track, this is a marvellous portrait of a swing band.

Classics 1045 sees a slackening in the quality of the material, but Shaw still delivers some excellent individual records such as 'One Foot In the Groove' and 'Out Of Nowhere', as well as the hit coupling of 'Traffic Jam' and 'Serenade To A Savage'. Even on the more routine songs, the band's accomplished playing draws its own rewards, and Forrest's singing is a further bonus. Classics 1087 has its own share of indifferent material – despite featuring 'Oh! Lady Be Good', a terrific chart and one of Shaw's biggest hits – and Forrest has to sing some real fluff on the first four sessions, after which Shaw broke up the band and retreated to Mexico. He was back in Los Angeles only months later with a new band, this time with strings attached. It was a recording outfit only and never appeared live; but the experiment worked, since it gave Shaw another big hit in 'Frenesi'. Mainly good transfers again, although here and there we detected a strange hint of speed wobble in the sound.

They weren't quite there yet on the radio transcriptions on the Tax CD, but this is still an entertaining disc and in fine sound, considering the sources.

***** Live In 1938–39 Vol. One**

Phontastic CD 7609 *Shaw; Chuck Peterson, Claude Bowen, John Best, Bernie Privin (t); George Arus, Russell Brown, Harry Rodgers, Les Jenkins (tb); Les Robinson, Hank Freeman, Tony Pastor, Ronnie Perry, Georgie Auld (reeds); Les Burness, Bob Kitsis (p); Al Avola (g); Sid Weiss (b); Cliff Leeman, Buddy Rich, George Wettling (d); Helen Forrest (v).* 11/38–1/39.

***** Live In 1938–39 Vol. Two**

Phontastic CD 7613 *As above, except omit Bowen, Brown, Burness, Perry, Wettling and Leeman.* 1–3/39.

***** Live In 1939 Vol. Three**

Phontastic CD 7628 *As above.* 2–5/39.

*****(*) In The Blue Room / In The Café Rouge**

RCA Victor 74321 18527-2 2CD *As above, except add Harry Geller (t), Dave Barbour (g).* 11/38–11/39.

*****(*) King Of The Clarinet 1938–39**

Hindsight HBCD-502 3CD *As above discs.* 11/38–11/39.

***** 1938–39 Old Gold Shows**

Jazz Hour 1009 *Probably as above discs.* 38–39.

Airshots by the 1938–9 band. The Phontastics offer a broad survey. Like all such ancient history, there is period charm (the announcements, the hysterical applause) as well as period dross and even a decent amount of good music. Some of the tracks are too short to have much impact, but there are some more extended pieces that show the band at full stretch: a fast and sassy 'Carioca' and a long treatment of 'The Chant' that prefigures something of 'Concerto For Clarinet'. These are both on *Volume Three*, but there are interesting things on the first two discs as well, notably otherwise unrecorded items such as 'The Yam' (*Volume One*), Shaw playing Ellington with 'Diga Diga Doo' (*Volume Two*) and some alternative versions of hits like 'Back Bay Shuffle' (also *Volume Two*). The sound is very mixed: quite sharp and clear on some pieces, very fusty on others. These are mainly for Shaw specialists. RCA's own *Blue Room/Café Rouge* set is a little more appealing since the sound is fine and the performances are of a more consistent standard. Shaw adds a little spoken introduction himself (recorded in the 1950s, when the LPs were originally released) and the live versions of the band's hits are played with great enthusiasm. Most notable, though, is the finesse Shaw could get from his musicians on even regular radio and dancing engagements. His own solos have their usual steely calm as well as an extra bite for the occasion. Hindsight's three-disc set may be a first choice for those wanting a generous survey: splendidly packaged and annotated, with interesting comments on most of these versions by Shaw himself, they underline how this band's airshots throw a strikingly different light on how a big band worked outside the studios. The sound isn't as bright as on some of these reissues, but there's a lot to enjoy across the three discs. Jazz Hour's compilation is another good one, if a notch behind Victor's, and it has some more strong material: 'In The Mood', 'Back Bay Shuffle' and 'Copenhagen', among others. Very clean sound for the period.

***** Hollywood Palladium 1941**

Hep 19 *Shaw; Billy Butterfield, George Wendt, Jack Cathcart, Steve Lipkins, Lee Castle, Hot Lips Page, Max Kaminsky, Bobby Hackett (t); Vernon Brown, Bruce Squires, Morey Samuel, Ray Conniff, Jack Jenney, Elmer Smithers (tb); Charlie DiMaggio, Les Robinson, Neely Plumb (as); Jerry Jerome, Bus Bassey, Georgie Auld, Mickey Folus (ts); Johnny Guarnieri (p); Al Hendrickson, Mike Bryan (g); Jud DeNaut, Ed McKimmey (b); Nick Fatool, Dave Tough (d); strings.* 7/40–9/41.

***** In Hollywood 1940–41 Vol. 2**
Hep 55 *Similar to above.* 9/40–3/41.

Two further discs of airshots, culled from numerous Hollywood broadcasts, where Shaw was working on films and the Burns And Allen show. Most of the arrangements are by either Lennie Hayton or Ray Conniff, and the various bands on display – some with strings, some not – make light work of them. The first disc is slightly more interesting, with an alternative version of 'Concerto For Clarinet' and some rousing work by Hot Lips Page and Georgie Auld on the final tracks. The second, though, has a very fine treatment of 'Star Dust'. The material is taken from surviving acetates, and some of those on the first disc haven't worn as well as they might. Interesting footnotes for the Shaw specialist.

***** Mixed Bag**
Musicmasters 65119-2 *Shaw; Roy Eldridge, Stan Fishelson, Bernie Glow, George Schwartz, Manny Klein, Ray Linn, Clyde Harley (t); Harry Rogers, Gus Dixon, Ollie Wilson, Bob Swift, Si Zentner (tb); Rudy Tanza, Lou Prisby, Skeets Herfurt (as); Herbie Steward, Jon Walon (ts); Chuck Gentry (bs); Dodo Marmarosa, Milt Raskin, Hank Jones (p); Barney Kessel, Tal Farlow, Dave Barbour (g); Morris Rayman, Artie Shapiro, Tommy Potter (b); Lou Fromm, Nick Fatool, Irv Kluger (d); Mel Torme, The Mel-Tones, Lillian Lane, Ralph Blane, Kitty Kallen (v).* 8/45–3/54.

What it says – sessions for Musicraft from the mid-'40s, plus a stray Gramercy Five track with Hank Jones and Tal Farlow from 1954. Shaw admits in the notes that this was a comparatively unadventurous period for him, with the band sticking to simple charts and lusher frameworks than he might have liked. The Shaw trademark of precision remains a given. As smooth big-band music from an era on the wane, this serves well and, though some of the masters sound a bit scratchy, sound is mostly clean enough.

****(*) The Artistry Of Artie Shaw**
Fresh Sound FSCD 2012 *Shaw; Don Fagerquist, Dale Pierce, Vic Ford (t); Sonny Russo, Fred Zito, Angie Callea, Zoltan Cohen (tb); Herbie Steward, Frank Socolow (as); Al Cohn, Zoot Sims (ts); Danny Bank (bs); Gil Barrios (p); Jimmy Raney (g); Dick Nivison (b); Irv Kluger (d).* 12/49.

Considering the personnel and the possibilities – of Shaw meeting the early cool movement, if not bebop – this is a disappointment. Yet more radio transcriptions, these make a so-so fist out of charts that include pieces from the hands of Johnny Mandel and Tadd Dameron. Shaw is his impeccable self as soloist but the others don't get much room, and the rhythm section's dour.

*****(*) The Last Recordings**
Musicmasters 65071-2 2CD *Shaw; Hank Jones (p); Tal Farlow (g); Joe Roland (vib); Tommy Potter (b); Irv Kluger (d).* 54.

This was Shaw's last document and it's valuable to have it back in circulation, with ten new tracks. The music is poised somewhere between the swing principles that Shaw remained faithful to and the faintest wisp of bop-styled modernism which such fellow crossovers as Farlow and Jones also make the most of. Lithe and piercing, but fundamentally relaxed and even-tempered, this is high-calibre chamber-jazz which left the Shaw story tantalizingly unfinished.

Ian Shaw (born 1962)

VOCAL

Born in Wales, Shaw studied music in London and since the late '80s has worked almost constantly in the city, performing in musicals as well as clubs, and generally gaining recognition as one of the leading British vocalists of his day, though he prefers to drift betweeen categories rather than be called a jazz singer per se.

*****(*) In A New York Minute**
Milestone 9297-2 *Shaw; Iain Ballamy (as, ts); Cedar Walton (p); David Williams (b).* 9/98.

Shaw has recorded other albums in Britain, but this is the only one likely to receive international distribution. Luckily, it's also his most accomplished and compelling work. The bare-bones accompaniment of Walton and Williams is a setting which would make almost any singer sound good; it takes Shaw close to greatness. Though he's flirted with soul, pop and supper-club styles in the past, he folds all his expertise into a bullseye delivery in these songs. He doesn't really swing in the manner of a Torme descendant, and he tends to fashion his own tightrope relationship with the beat, which in the past has often seemed jerky. But the urgent mannerisms of 'Standing In the Dark' have taken on a conviction which presents an artist in his maturity, and his prime; and the passionate embrace of many of these lyrics recalls a cadre of singers (Mark Murphy is the obvious reference-point) who could mix beat-poetry slickness with torch-song sensuality. The songs are beautifully chosen, from the title-piece (thankfully, Fran Landesmann's song, not Don Henley's lugubrious effort of the same title) to a graceful 'Wouldn't It Be Loverly', to a slow, chastening 'Last Night When We Were Young'. Icing on this cake: Iain Ballamy's sax contributions, which are marvellous.

Lee Shaw

PIANO

Contemporary American pianist drawing mostly on the virtuoso end of bop language.

***** Essence**
CIMP 125 *Shaw; Mike DeMicco (g); Rich Syracuse (b).* 9/96.

While we are happy to applaud CIMP's unvarnished recording procedures in principle, this is one that could have beneficially used a little sweetening. Shaw and her group were recorded live in a club setting, and it does tend to sound as if somebody's pro-Walkman captured the gig. Which is a pity, since the pianist is a gifted and rather intense performer. Art Tatum is cited in the sleeve-notes, which isn't too fanciful, and, allied with a bopper like DeMicco, the music has a virtuosic flavour which is sublimated in tunes like the fast, exhilarating 'Holiday'. Shaw's fundamental lyricism is another plus: she seldom sounds like she's running through the material with anything less than full commitment. A very interesting encounter.

Woody Shaw (1944–89)

TRUMPET

Father sang gospel music, and young Woody studied trumpet at eleven. Worked with the Eric Dolphy band until 1964, then played in Europe, with Horace Silver, Max Roach and eventually, in the '70s, his own regular bands. Despite his talent and influence on many younger players, his career never really had much luck, and nor did he.

***** Last Of The Line**

32 Jazz 32024 *Shaw; Garnett Brown (tb); Steve Turre (tb, btb); René McLean (ss, ts); Billy Harper, Joe Henderson (ts); Harold Vick (ts, f); Joe Bonner, George Cables, Herbie Hancock, Larry Young (p); Ron Carter, Paul Chambers, Cecil McBee (b); Joe Chambers (d).* 12/65–11/75.

****** Dark Journey**

32 Jazz 32039 *Similar to above, and as for The Moontrane below, except add Arthur Blythe, Kenny Garrett (as); Anthony Braxton (as, ss, cl); Muhal Richard Abrams, Kenny Barron, Kirk Lightsey, Horace Silver, Cedar Walton (p); Peter Leitch (g); Ray Drummond, Neil Swainson, Buster Williams (b); Carl Allen, Roger Humphries, Victor Jones, Victor Lewis (d).* 10/65–3/86.

*****(*) Song Of Songs**

Original Jazz Classics OJCCD 1893-2 *Shaw; Emmanuel Boyd (ts, f); Bennie Maupin, Ramon Morris (ts); George Cables (p); Henry Franklin (b); Woodrow Theus II (d).* 9/72.

****** The Moontrane**

32 Jazz 32019 *Shaw; Steve Turre (tb); Azar Lawrence (ts); Onaje Allan Gumbs (p); Cecil McBee, Buster Williams (b); Victor Lewis (d); Guilherme Franco, Tony Waters (perc).* 12/74.

****** Solid**

Camden 74321 610792 2CD *As above, except add Kenny Garrett (as); Kenny Barron (p); Kirk (p); Peter Leitch (g); Ray Drummond, Neil Swainson (b); Carl Allen, Victor Jones (d).* 12/74–6/87.

Woody Shaw's career judgement was almost as clouded as his actual vision. A classic under-achiever, his relatively lowly critical standing is a function partly of his musical purism (which was thoroughgoing and admirable) but also more largely of his refusal or inability to get his long-term act together. A sufferer from *retinitis pigmentosa* (which severely restricted his sight-reading), he fell under a subway train in the spring of 1989 and died of his injuries.

Woody made his recording debut with Eric Dolphy at the age of nineteen in what are usually thought of as the *Iron Man/Jitterbug Waltz* sessions. One reviewer was convinced that 'Woody Sho" was a *nom de session* for Freddie Hubbard, inexpicably when you listen to his Navarro- and Morgan-inspired attack and phrasing. It was Dolphy who taught Woody to play 'inside and outside at the same time', but it was listening to the classics that awakened a player with perfect pitch to the subtler nuances of harmony. Like all imaginative Americans, Woody was violently stretched between opposites and inexorably drawn to the things and the places that would destroy him. Europe drew him for all the usual non-musical reasons, but there is a sense, too, that Woody's foreshortened career represented a sustained fugue from the racially constrained job-description of the 'jazz musician'.

However hardly won, Woody's technique sounded effortless, which disguised the awful disquiet at the root of his music. His influences were not settling ones: at the one extreme Debussy, the most inside-and-outside of the pre-Schoenberg composers; at the other his Newark friend, the organist Larry Young, with whom he recorded the superb *Unity* and who taught him, across the grain of the earlier Hubbardly aggression and linearity, the value of accepting a measure of chaos in music.

Shaw's catalogue of work has not been in better shape at any moment since this *Guide* began publication. The restoration of his recordings for Muse – now on 32 – is a key factor, but so too is the reappearance of things like *Song Of Songs* and *Rosewood*. Most welcome of all is the reappearance of *The Moontrane*.

Woody's best-known composition was actually premiered on Larry Young's Blue Note classic, *Unity*, which has also since reappeared in the catalogue. The 1974 album which bears its name is the work of a settled and sympathetic group. Turre's later dalliance with conches and with world music styles hadn't yet blunted a fine, straightahead trombone style, and his own composition, 'Sanyas', which features some outrageous bass from Cecil McBee, is a high point of the record. The CD version includes alternative takes of 'Katrina Ballerina' and Azar Lawrence's 'Tapscott's Blues', both of which demonstrate once again how subtly Woody could vary his solo material. 'The Moontrane' itself is a modern classic, a piece of such refreshing originality that it seems to reinvent itself in line with every stylistic shift on the scene.

There are still some discographical problems surrounding Woody's material from this period. Tracks have been distributed across a number of compilations, valuable in themselves but somewhat muddled in chronology. We have listed them here rather than at the end of the entry because many more casual listeners may simply want a sampling of the trumpeter's work. *Last Of The Line* is basically a conflation of two albums called *Cassandranite* and *Love Dance*, grouping together the work of four sessions spread over a decade. The Camden twofer, *Solid*, starts with a hefty sampling of *The Moontrane* and then hops forward more than a decade to include tracks from the 1986 and 1987 *Solid* and *Imagination*, the latter of which is also noted below. Unfortunately, the technical details are less than pristine, with 'Ken Lightsey' and 'Roy Drummond' both listed.

Dark Journey is even more mixed, though chronologically much more representative of the passage from Woody's experimentalism of the mid-'60s through to his later, more authoritatively mainstream work. Of the earlier material, the demo session cut in New York City in December 1965 in the hope of attracting big-label notice and, in no small measure, of breaking free from Horace Silver's funk-orientated band, is perhaps the most interesting. Teamed with Henderson and old friend Young, who contributes 'Obsequious', Woody lets fly and utilizes a range of articulations he calls on only rarely elsewhere. Henderson was breaking through to a new conception of his own at this period, and whenever he takes the spotlight the current changes palpably.

A good example of a creative mismatch that briefly paid great dividends.

Other good material includes a single track, 'Spiderman Blues', from a December 1983 encounter with Cedar Walton and Buster Williams, both strong supporters of Woody's conception. Of the two tracks selected from the original *Solid*, 'The Woody Woodpecker Song' has the look of a filler, but 'Speak Low' is a superb example of how lyrically Woody was playing at the time, even quoting a tiny tag from Chet Baker's by then oft-reworked version of the song. 'Imagination' comes from the late disc of that name, as does 'Dat Dere', two more examples of how calmly expressive Woody could be in later years.

Interesting at this point to swing back and reconsider *Song Of Songs*, his second record as leader. Wonderful it is, but also undeniably timelocked, heavily dependent on Allan Gumbs's electric piano effects, but also swinging and propulsive. Woody's four compositions are still not fully assimilated, and not many contemporary players would attempt something as sardonic as 'The Goat And The Archer'. Redundant as it may be to make the point again, had Shaw been picked up by a sensitive label and producer at this point, afforded the players and the studio time his exacting concept demanded, then who knows what he might have achieved. As it is, these two albums are among the best he did until the brief starburst of the '80s.

**** Little Red's Fantasy

32 Jazz 32126 *Shaw; Frank Strozier (as); Ronnie Mathews (p); Stafford James (b); Eddie Moore (d).* 6/76.

When Shaw recorded this much-neglected record, his day job was regulation hard bop as a member of the Louis Hayes Quintet. Mathews and James were also members of that outfit, but the replacement of Hayes with the freer metre of Eddie Moore and the more adventurous, George Coleman-influenced harmonics of Frank Strozier, resulted in a much more open sound.

Talking about this album, Woody aligned himself technically – that is, as a trumpet player – with the traditionalists, but musically at some solitary mid-point between the mainstream and the avant-garde. Much of the material was or was to become familiar, but rarely was it played better on a recorded performance. The title-tune is a dedication to Maxine Shaw, Woody's wife and manager, who did so much to support and encourage his career. It is a delicate blend of passion and tenderness, rigorous discipline and freedom. The ensemble plays brilliantly on the long 'Sashianova' and the only question mark hangs over the closing track, 'Tomorrow's Destiny', on which Eddie Moore's drum solo seems to come from some other session. No amount of quibbling will dampen our enthusiasm for this record. Of the reissued originals – as opposed to compilations – this is the one to go for after *The Moontrane*.

***(*) Two More Pieces Of The Puzzle

32 Jazz 32069 *Shaw; Slide Hampton (tb, perc); Anthony Braxton (cl, as, ss); Arthur Blythe (as); René McLean (as, f, perc); Frank Foster (ss, ts, perc); Muhal Richard Abrams, Ronnie Mathews (p); Stafford James, Cecil McBee (b); Joe Chambers, Louis Hayes, Victor Lewis (d).* 6/76, 4/77.

A fascinating conflation of two very different sessions, but one which – as its title suggests – further opens up the picture. Woody and his Concert Ensemble played at the Berliner Jazztage in 1976, turning in a powerful festival set largely based on amiably traded choruses between the horns, clever pastiche and quotation, but all of it grounded in superbly disciplined ensemble work. Woody's own phrasing on 'Jean Marie', one of the tracks which marked out *Little Red's Fantasy*, is immaculate, and he even seems to make reference, as he was to do with Steve Turre on occasion, to the trombone's portamentos and slurs. Larry Young's 'Obsequious' sounds very different, performed by a larger and more textured ensemble. The opening and closing tracks, 'Hello To The Wind' and McLean's 'In The Land Of The Blacks', are overlong and subject to some lapses of focus, but in sum the set is – as we remember from being present at the festival – crackling with ideas and energy.

The remainder of this disc is even more astonishing. As we noted above, Woody began his recording career with Eric Dolphy and in 1977 he recorded a tribute in the company of two of Dolphy's living disciples, Arthur Blythe and Anthony Braxton. This is probably as close as he was to come to the avant-garde; but Braxton, as ever, shows himself to be responsive to mainstream idiom as well as more 'outside' conceptions. The set opened with 'Iron Man' and 'Jitterbug Waltz', played pretty much as a *homage* to Dolphy. Following these, a fine version of Andrew Hill's 'Symmetry', suggesting how much of a common source Hill was for all these players. Later still, a relaxed and inventive interpretation of Woody's staple 'Song Of Songs', but wedged in between two of the most extraordinary pieces in his entire canon. Brief they may be, but 'Diversion I & II', freely improvised trios with Abrams and McBee, show what a gifted improviser Shaw was. A slightly difficult record to judge as a whole, except that the quality is consistently high throughout. Thoroughly recommended to anyone who wants to explore the extremes of the trumpeter's career.

**** Rosewood

Columbia CK 65519 *Shaw; Steve Turre (tb, btb); Janice Robinson (tb); Carter Jefferson (ss, ts); James Vass (ss, as); Joe Henderson (ts); Frank Wes (f, picc); Art Webb (f); Onaje Allan Gumbs (p); Lois Colin (hp); Clint Houston (b); Victor Lewis (d); Sammy Figueroa, Armen Halburian (perc).* 12/77.

Not for nothing was *Rosewood* voted Best Jazz Album of 1978 in *Down Beat*. It is one of the most ambitious projects Shaw was ever involved in, and though he wrote only one of the pieces performed by the large-scale Concert Ensemble, his hand is evident throughout a well-balanced and expansive set.

Woody's sole writing credit is the title-piece, an idea to set alongside 'The Moontrane' and 'Song Of Songs' as among his very best. The other titles are Victor Lewis's intriguing 'The Legend Of Cheops', Allan Gumbs's 'Every Time I See You' and Clint Houston's nondescript 'Sunshowers'. Significantly, this last is the only track not to feature the splendid Joe Henderson, who graces both the larger ensemble and the small group which delivers 'Rahsaan's Run' and 'Theme For Maxine', another tribute to Mrs Shaw. In Joe's company, Shaw sounds blithe and thoughtful at the same time, riveting bright points of sound into Joe's leathery tone.

A less thoroughly compelling statement than *Song Of Songs*, this immaculately produced CBS session underlines what Shaw might have done if health and inclination had lent his career more shape and consistency.

***** Lotus Flower**

Enja ENJ 4018 *Shaw; Steve Turre (tb, perc); Mulgrew Miller (p); Stafford James (b); Tony Reedus (d).* 1/82.

***** Time Is Right**

Red RR 123168 *Shaw; Steve (tb, shell); Mulgrew Miller (p); Stafford James (b); Tony Reedus (d).* 1/83.

Shaw's bands of the 1980s were either the product of good luck, sympathetic label handling, or else they belie the received image of a guy perpetually nodding out on the practicalities, lost in a world of immaterial musical purity. (The only place he ever *sounded* that other-worldly was in his heavily Echoplexed work on *Zawinul*, the Weather Report keyboard man's Atlantic solo.) The Red *Time Is Right* is a concert recording from Bologna. Turre is disappointingly muffled during a couple of his solos and there is not much definition to the rhythm section. The two originals are strongly played, though, and the set ends with a very powerful reading of 'We'll Be Together Again'.

The big trombonist is effectively co-leader on *Lotus Flower*, though the title-track is his only composition credit. Mulgrew Miller's 'Eastern Joy Dance' isn't a tune that sits particularly easily for Woody's articulation, but he turns in a fine solo, a little less joyous than other interpreters might have been, but full of gentle fire. His own 'Rahsaan's Run' is a fascinating study piece for brass players, transcription revealing the sleek modal contours Miles Davis so much admired. There is also a wonderful reinterpretation of 'Song Of Songs'.

****(*) Woody Shaw With The Tone Jansa Quartet**

Timeless SJP 221 *Shaw; Tone Jansa (ts, ss, fl); Renato Chicco (p); Peter Herbert (b); Dragan Gajic (d).* 4/85.

Now that some of Shaw's best material is available again, this lacklustre Timeless set seems even less compelling than before. The band are competent and supportive, but they don't naturally speak in Woody's idiom, which creates the impression that he is playing rather eccentrically. Some listeners find Jansa's compositions intriguing. On their own terms, they may very well be, but they are not the right fuel.

***** Bemsha Swing Live**

Blue Note CDP 7243 8 29029 2 *Shaw; Geri Allen (p); Robert Hurst (b); Roy Brooks (d).* 2/86.

Ten years after his death, Shaw sounds more than ever like a lost genius, someone whose career was never adequately steered or sufficiently appreciated. These live sessions from Baker's Keyboard Lounge in Detroit are dominated by Monk tunes, and it is fascinating to compare Woody's handling of the bebop keyboard legacy with his reinterpretations of Sonny Clark material at the Mount Fuji Jazz Festival later on that same summer. Fascinating, too, to hear him in the presence of a player of Geri Allen's sensibilities. The long unravelling of 'Well, You Needn't' exposes a few longueurs and what seem to be repetitions in Woody's playing. Closer examination, though, suggests that he was deliberately exploring tiny modulations. His improvisations have a shifting, almost fugitive quality by this stage, but it is still easy to overlook their subtleties.

Allen was probably doing some of her most interesting work at this stage, harmonically adventurous, percussive and rhythmically very tight. There are moments when Hurst and Brooks disappear into the background, leaving the piano to carry the load. 'Bemsha Swing' itself is a cracking opener, and there are also strong interpretations of Wayne Shorter's rarely covered 'United', Woody's own 'Ginseng People' and 'In A Capricornian Way', and a closing reading of 'Star Eyes' that shows how much Shaw learned from earlier boppers like Fats Navarro and Howard McGhee. A strong live set.

*****(*) Imagination**

32 Jazz 32090 *Shaw; Steve Turre (tb); Kirk Lightsey (p); Ray Drummond (b); Carl Allen (d).* 6/87.

Almost as if they realized that time was short and future opportunities limited, Woody's fellow-players rallied round over the last couple of years of his life. Where in the past they had often merely kept up with the traffic, more and more often in these late sessions it is possible to hear them trying to think their way into Woody's mind. 'Dat Dere' and the Burke/Van Heusen title-piece are among our favourites in his whole output, flowing, graceful improvisations with a good deal of thought in the development of the chords and the song structure.

Lightsey, Drummond and Allen are all in inspired form and the CD transfer has lifted the bassist out of the acoustic liftshaft where he seemed to be working on the first release. Doubtless there will be more Shaw reissues before our next edition. For the moment, though, it is satisfying to pause with his catalogue so generously restored. A compelling musician who seems more valuable with the passing years.

George Shearing (born 1919)

PIANO, ACCORDION, VOCAL

Born blind to a poor London family, Shearing trained as a classical pianist but turned to jazz, partly on the advice of his teacher. He played dance-band gigs before settling in the USA in 1946. His quintet, first formed in 1949, lasted for many years and won a huge following for its many albums, all of them in a light music-smooth jazz mould. He later worked extensively with Mel Torme and still plays in solo and small-group situations.

***** The London Years**

Hep CD 1042 *Shearing; Leonard Feather (p); Carlo Krahmer (d).* 3/39–12/43.

Shearing's early recordings are in some ways slight, given that he glossed over bop's passion with a tinkling niceness that suggested a clever pianist merely toying with the music. But the occasional parallels with Lennie Tristano suggest the more profound direction Shearing could have gone in; that he chose a more temperate kind of commercial climate leaves one of those might-have-beens that jazz is full of. His very earliest records are in any case a showcase of swing piano, recorded in London in the early years of the war. The Hep CD collects 25 tracks and is an enjoyable, witty sequence of solos (there are two early tracks with Krahmer and one with Feather on piano, where Shearing squeezes a few dolorous blues chords out of the accordion). There are many entertaining bits of Tatum, Waller and Wilson in the pianist's style, and these tracks might surprise anyone unfamiliar with his first period.

*****(*) Verve Jazz Masters: George Shearing**
Verve 529900-2 *Shearing; Marjorie Hyams, Cal Tjader, Joe Roland, Don Elliott (vib); Chuck Wayne, Dick Garcia (g); John Levy, Al McKibbon (b); Denzil Best, Marquis Foster, Bill Clark (d); Armando Peraza (perc).* 49–54.

These are the MGM recordings which established the Shearing Quintet as a commercial force. Clever rather than profound, appealing rather than attention-grabbing, the front line of piano, vibes and guitar was a refreshing sound which, when allied to memorable themes such as 'Lullaby Of Birdland', proved immensely popular. Shearing had been listening closely to bebop and synthesized what he needed from it to make a cool, modern sound. At this distance, away from any controversy about its standing, the results are smoothly enjoyable on any level. This compilation brings together the expected hits and the slightly more challenging material such as 'Conception', which was once covered by Miles Davis (although Shearing has recently complained that Miles got the bridge wrong!).

***** Three Originals**
MPS 523522-2 2CD *Shearing; Sigi Schwab, Louis Stewart (g); Herbert Thusek (vib); Andy Simpkins, Niels-Henning (b); Rusty Jones, Stix Hooper (d); Chino Valdes, Carmelo Garcia (perc).* 10/73–9/79.

Shearing's Capitol albums are blue-chip easy listening rather than jazz. So it's a somewhat extended leap to the next entry. The contents of three original MPS albums – *Light, Airy And Swinging, Continental Experience* and *On Target* – in a two-disc package. The first is the best, eight tunes with the smart rhythm section of Simpkins and Hooper, and nothing outdoes the opening skip through 'Love Walked In'. The second gets bogged down in sluggish Latin percussion. The third is soaked in Robert Farnon's strings – nice, though the Telarc album, below, sounds better.

****(*) Blues Alley Jazz**
Concord CCD 4110 *Shearing; Brian Torff (b).* 10/79.

***** Two For The Road**
Concord CCD 4128 *Shearing; Carmen McRae (v).* 80.

***** Alone Together**
Concord CCD 4171 *Shearing; Marian McPartland (p).* 3/81.

***** First Edition**
Concord CCD 4177 *Shearing; Jim Hall (g).* 9/81.

**** Live At The Café Carlyle**
Concord CCD 4246 *Shearing; Don Thompson (b).* 1/84.

**** Grand Piano**
Concord CCD 4281 *Shearing (p solo).* 5/85.

**** Plays The Music Of Cole Porter**
Concord CCD 42010 *Shearing; Barry Tuckwell (frhn); strings.* 1/86.

****(*) More Grand Piano**
Concord CCD 4318 *Shearing (p solo).* 10/86.

***** Breakin' Out**
Concord CCD 4335 *Shearing; Ray Brown (b); Marvin 'Smitty' Smith (d).* 5/87.

****(*) Dexterity**
Concord CCD 4346 *Shearing; Neil Swainson (b); Ernestine Anderson (v).* 11/87.

****(*) A Perfect Match**
Concord CCD 4357 *Shearing; Neil Swainson (b); Jeff Hamilton (d); Ernestine Anderson (v).* 5/88.

***** The Spirit Of '76**
Concord CCD 4371 *Shearing; Hank Jones (p).* 3/88.

****(*) George Shearing In Dixieland**
Concord CCD 4388 *Shearing; Warren Vaché (c); George Masso (tb); Kenny Davern (cl); Ken Peplowski (ts); Neil Swainson (b); Jerry Fuller (d).* 2/89.

***** Piano**
Concord CCD 4400 *Shearing (p solo).* 5/89.

Shearing has always been on the periphery of jazz rather than anywhere inside it, even when he's been making records with genuine jazz musicians. In the 1980s, his many records for Concord put some focus on his work and have drummed up a few more worthwhile situations. Some of his best playing will be found on records under Mel Torme's name, but a few others listed here are also worth hearing. When Shearing sets aside his incessant borrowings from other players and eschews middlebrow ideas of what's tasteful to play in the jazz idiom, he can come up with some nice ideas: the partnerships with McPartland and Jones find him adapting to the far greater range of both those players with some success, and he even holds his own in the trio with Brown and Smith. Carmen McRae's recital finds her in good, typically grouchy form, and Shearing accompanies with deference and good humour. The meeting with Ernestine Anderson is all right, but Anderson isn't the singer that McRae is.

The albums that lose their way are those where he has to provide most of the musical interest himself: the solo sets and duos with bassists usually have one or two clever or gracious reworkings of standards, but they don't really sustain or repay close attention. Having said that, the solo disc, *Piano*, finds him in an unusually effective, ruminative mood. The 'Dixieland' album is routine but pleasing enough, while the Cole Porter set is MOR prettiness.

***** I Hear A Rhapsody**
Telarc 83310 *Shearing; Neil Swainson (b); Grady Tate (d).* 2/92.

A new label and a live album from New York's Blue Note must have galvanized the expatriate Englishman a little. The boppish moments he essays on 'Birdfeathers' and 'Wail' are some of his most convincing in years. Swainson and Tate are right there with him, too.

***** Walkin'**
Telarc 83333 *As above.* 2/92.

***** How Beautiful Is Night**
Telarc 83325 *Shearing; Robert Farnon Orchestra.* 93.

***** That Shearing Sound**
Telarc 83347 *Shearing; Steve Nelson (vib); Louis Stewart (g); Neil Swainson (b); Dennis Mackrel (d).* 2/94.

It seems almost impertinent to say it, but Shearing seems to be getting better, at least as far as the calibre of his records is concerned. Certainly Telarc are eliciting some of his most enjoyable music in years. None of these is a masterpiece exactly, but each shows the man's persuasive craftsmanship at its best. *Walkin'* is a second helping from the Blue Note engagement which produced the earlier disc, and the programme is intriguing – 'That's Earl Brother', 'Pensativa', 'Celia' and, above all, 'Subconscious-Lee', which is dark enough to be genuinely Tristano-esque. Measure for measure, this must be one of his best records. *How Beautiful Is Night* recalls his Capitol days, although Farnon's arrangements are so luxurious and so sumptuously recorded that one surrenders to the sheer comfort. *That Shearing Sound* debuts a new band, and with Nelson and Stewart in the line-up it looks very promising. That said, they both bow amiably enough to Shearing's sometimes tyrannical arrangements, which in the main elongate the style of his 1940s quintet to double-length tunes. On its own terms, smartly enjoyable.

***** Paper Moon**

Telarc CD-83375 *Shearing; Louis Stewart (g); Neil Swainson (b).* 3/95.

***** Favorite Things**

Telarc CD-83398 *Shearing (p solo).* 3/96.

Paper Moon is in dedication to Nat Cole, and when they start 'Straighten Up And Fly Right' with the kind of rocking swing that Shearing enjoys, one looks forward to a felicitous occasion. Somehow, though, as graciously as it's done, the disc in the end falls victim to the routine which is the other side of Shearing's jazz. Stewart seems a bit subdued in support. *Favorite Things* has a parlour-piece where a touch of Scarlatti turns into the title-song, and when 'Angel Eyes' turns up as a dark and mysterious creature, it again seems like something special's happening. This time, though, there are too many slow ones, and when George gets Garneresque on the penultimate 'P.S. I Love You' it's almost a shock.

Jack Sheldon (born 1931)

TRUMPET, VOCAL

Florida-born, Sheldon moved to Los Angeles as a teenager and has been there ever since. He was an anchorman trumpeter in much of the West Coast jazz of the 1950s, and in the '60s he did both acting and stand-up comedy as well as jazz. He has latterly returned to a modest jazz career, though his onstage persona is that of a Hollywood man.

***** The Entertainers**

VSOP 90 *Sheldon; Frank Rosolino (tb); Howard Roberts (g); Joe Mondragon (b); Shelly Manne, Stan Levey (d); Johnny Mercer (v).* 3/64–3/65.

***** Live At Don Mupo's Gold Nugget**

VSOP 101 *As above, except omit Rosolino, Manne, Mercer.* 4/65.

***** Playing For Change**

Uptown 2743 *Sheldon; Don Sickler (flhn); Jerry Dodgion (as); Barry Harris (p); Rufus Reid (b); Ben Riley (d).* 5/86.

****(*) Hollywood Heroes**

Concord CCD 4339 *Sheldon; Ray Sherman (p); Doug McDonald (g); Dave Stone (b); Gene Estes (d).* 9/87.

****(*) On My Own**

Concord CCD 4529 *Sheldon; Ross Tompkins (p).* 8–9/91.

***** Jack Sheldon Sings**

Butterfly BCD 7701 *Sheldon; George Graham, Wayne Bergeron, Ron Stout, Stan Martin (t); Alex Iles, Andy Martin, Mike Fahn, Bruce Wagner (tb); Sal Lozano, Danny House, Tom Kubic, Jennifer Hall, Jerry Pinter (reeds); Tom Rainey (p); Troy Henry (b); Ray Brinker (d).* 9/92.

Sheldon has been something of a polymath: an ingenious comedian, a very hot cool-school trumpeter, a slight but charming vocalist – and for two of those attributes he owes something to Chet Baker. But he works best with a straight man, or at least a foil – in the Curtis Counce group of the 1950s, or on an early Jimmy Giuffre LP, he fires up on the challenge of the other horns. Still, the two VSOP albums are a truthful record of Sheldon's stage routine in his prime – a probably unique blend of proper bebop, crooning (Johnny Mercer helps out on one disc) and comic patter. The latter is still best sampled on his old LP, *Ooo – But It's Good!*, even though it's impossible to find. But the Richard Burton parody on 'Creamfinger' on *Golden Nugget* may still raise a smile, and there is actually some more than capable instrumental work from Sheldon and Howard Roberts on *The Entertainers*. For an even earlier taste of Sheldon, try to find *The Quartet And The Quintet* (Pacific Jazz 93160-2), released in 1998 in a 'Connoisseur' limited edition. It picks up his 1955 sessions for Jazz:West (very rare in their vinyl form) but disappeared from most racks in a flash.

Playing For Change is no-nonsense small-band bop and, with Dodgion going through the gears and the rhythm section in prime shape, this is crisply cooked and flavoursome playing. The two Concords are slighter and Sheldon seems restrained. *Hollywood Heroes* is lively, yet Sheldon has no real context, and the result sounds too much like a nice trumpet–voice–rhythm-section date to make any deep impression. He is in talespinning mood in *On My Own*, though it's done with trumpet and singing rather than with one of his deadpan routines. A better wager is *Sings*, where the vocals and the spit-and-polish trumpet-playing are in ideal balance in front of a sleek Hollywood big band.

Archie Shepp (born 1937)

TENOR SAXOPHONE, SOPRANO SAXOPHONE, ALTO SAXOPHONE, PIANO, VOICE

Archie Shepp is one of the major intellectuals of modern jazz. A passionate and articulate spokesman for the music and its ethnic-national ramifications, he is also a significant playwright. His early saxophone style resembled Ben Webster with a carborundum edge, but – like another sometime Trane associate, Pharoah Sanders – Shepp's approach has grown gentler and more lyrical down the years; he also plays piano and sings.

****** New York Contemporary Five**

Storyville 8209 *Shepp; Don Cherry (c); John Tchicai (as); Don Moore (b); J. C Moses (d).* 11/63.

Archie Shepp once declared himself something 'worse than a romantic, I'm a sentimentalist'. Shepp has tended to be a theoretician of his own work, often expressing his intentions and motivations in off-puttingly glib and aphoristic language. He has, though, consistently seen himself as an educator and communicator rather than an entertainer (or even an Artist) and is one of the few Afro-American artists who has effected any sort of convincing synthesis between black music (with its tendency to be depoliticized and repackaged for a white audience) and the less comfortable verbal experiments of poets like LeRoi Jones (Imamu Amiri Baraka). The dialectic between sentiment and protest in Shepp's work is matched by an interplay between music and words which, though more obvious, is also harder to assess. A playwright who also wrote a good deal of influential stage music, Shepp devised a musical style that might be called dramatic or, at worst and later in his career, histrionic.

Though strongly associated in most people's minds with John Coltrane (he worked on the augmented *Love Supreme* sessions and on *Ascension*), Shepp's most potent influence among the modernists was the radical populism of Ornette Coleman. Unlike Coltrane, the Texan saw no need to dismantle or subvert the tradition in order to use it, and Shepp was much affected by Ornette's rediscovery of the freedoms inherent in earlier forms. Fortunately, early work with The New York Contemporary Five (which grew out of a Coleman-influenced quartet co-led with trumpeter Bill Dixon) is now available on CD. The group had an influence out of all proportion to its brief life-span. As often with Shepp projects, there was no piano player. The longest piece on the album is non-member Bill Dixon's elaborate 'Trio', but all the front men are credited composers – Tchicai with 'Mick' and 'Wo Wo', Cherry with 'Consequences' and Shepp himself with 'Funeral' – but the twin presences which define this almost complete reissue of the band's studio work are Ornette Coleman and Thelonious Monk. The horns tackle 'O.C.' and 'When Will The Blues Leave' with aching intensity, and the absence of a harmonic centre leaves both open to the wildest flights. Shepp establishes himself as the *de facto* leader with towering solos; Storyville have his name and picture, as they say in Hollywood, 'over the title'. The Monk tunes are treated almost as throwaways, but their influence, melodic, lyrical and nakedly expressive, permeates the album as a whole and points out the direction Shepp would take in later years.

*** The House I Live In

Steeplechase SCC 6013 *Shepp; Lars Gullin (bs); Tete Montoliu (p); Niels-Henning Orsted Pedersen (b); Alex Riel (d).* 11/63.

The tenor on *The House I Live In* is very different from what people normally think of as the Shepp of the 1960s. Pre-radical, though, he sounds like a player long steeped in swing and blues. Though primarily of historical interest, this hasn't made the much-needed transition to CD in step with a Gullin rediscovery or a comprehensive reassessment of Shepp's career, and may therefore sound like a rather enigmatic one-off. The opening 'You Stepped Out Of A Dream' is perhaps the best of the set, the closing 'Sweet Georgia Brown' giving off the air of a hastily agreed encore. Shepp and NHOP met again on record in 1980, below.

**** Four For Trane

Impulse! IMP 12182 *Shepp; Alan Shorter (t); Roswell Rudd (tb); John Tchicai (as); Reggie Workman (b); Charles Moffett (d).* 8/64.

One of the classic jazz albums of the 1960s, and a fascinating glimpse into how thoroughly different what was already thought of as the Coltrane revolution might sound. Shepp immediately sounds more deeply soaked in the blues than the man he is paying tribute to here; Shepp's interpretation of 'Cousin Mary' is stunningly good, and his entry on 'Syeeda's Song Flute' is one of those musical moments that stay embedded in the skin like a bee-sting, painful and pleasurable by turns. Without a harmony instrument, the group has a loose, floating quality which Coltrane himself would never have attempted. The sound is totally open and without walls. Shorter, Rudd and Tchicai (who was to play such a significant part on Trane's *Ascension*) are all in spanking form, and the altoist's solo on the unforgettably titled 'Rufus (swung; his face at last to the wind, then his neck snapped)' has a raw urgency that recalls the very roots of this music. This is Shepp's only composition of the set and, following the love ballad, 'Naima', it makes a dramatic end to a set of powerful and committed music, as if Coltrane's dark twin had risen up and gained speech.

***(*) Fire Music

Impulse! 051158-2 *Shepp; Ted Curson (t); Joseph Orange (tb); Marion Brown (as); David Izenzon, Reggie Johnson (b); Joe Chambers, J.C Moses (d).* 2 & 3/65.

One of the best of Shepp's albums (though sounding rather brittle on CD), *Fire Music* is the saxophonist's most balanced synthesis of *agitprop* and lyricism, avant-gardism and traditionalist deference. 'Hambone', the long opening track, is a blues-rooted but unconventional theme, cast in irregular time-signatures, tough and citified. At the opposite extreme, there is a slightly kitsch 'Girl From Ipanema' with a reworked bridge; Shepp's colonization of pop tunes is less subversive than Coltrane's (for the most obvious comparison, see 'My Favorite Things' on *New Thing*, below) because he always remains half sold on the sentiments therein, but he makes a persuasive job of the Jobim tune. 'Los Olvidados' is dedicated to the youthful underclass of the city, the 'forgotten ones', those who will not be beguiled by Sandy Becker's 'Hambone' television character. The main focus of the piece is on Marion Brown's desolate middle passage, conjuring up thwarted promise in a hectic but unheeding environment; Shepp's own solo, as became his norm, is a rather pat summing-up, musical Method-acting, that slightly detracts from the sophistication of the composition. 'Malcolm, Malcolm – Semper Malcolm', scored for just Shepp, Izenzon and Moses and dominated by Shepp's sonorous recitation, is a brief foretaste of the later but no more convincing 'Poem For Malcolm', below. Clipped and re-dedicated from a longer and more ambitious work, it runs a slight risk of being ironized by 'Prelude To A Kiss' and the Jobim tune that follow; Shepp's ironies, though, are maintained not just between but also within compositions. It's interesting to note that the trajectory of the album is (roughly) from populist experimentalism to a kind of experimental populism. The absence of piano is significant because it prevents the music (and particularly the two familiar themes) from sinking into comfortable tone-centres, thus maintaining its ambiguous, questing nature.

***(*) On This Night

Impulse! GRP 11252 *Shepp; Bobby Hutcherson (vib); Henry Grimes, David Izenzon (b); Rashied Ali, Joe Chambers, J.C Moses (d); Ed Blackwell (perc); Christine Spencer (v).* 3 & 8/65.

On This Night has a slightly complicated discographical history, explained by a laudable desire to get Impulse! releases back into some semblance of chronological order. 'Malcolm' is repeated from *Fire Music*, a slightly unnecessary duplication; two takes of 'The Chase' and the alternative take of 'The Mac Man' were originally released on a sequel called *Further Fire Music*; a further take of 'The Chase' was around for some time on a compilation called *The Definitive Jazz Scene: Volume Three.* Anyone who has a vinyl copy of *On This Night* will now look in vain for 'Gingerbread, Gingerbread Boy', which has been moved, quite logically, to the *New Thing At Newport* document (again, below).

So much for the background. Having the March and August 1965 sessions together on one CD makes good sense, even though they are presented in reverse chronological order. It's a big, brawling record, announced by Shepp's out-of-kilter piano and Christine Spencer's churchy voice on the opening 'On This Night (If That Great Day Would Come)'. As well as those items mentioned above, there is a brief excursion on Ellington's 'In A Sentimental Mood', a fine 'The Original Mr Sonny Boy Williamson' and, one of Shepp's quirkily poetic titles, 'The Pickaninny (Picked Clean – No More – Or Can You Back Back Doodlebug)' ... and your guess is probably as good as ours. Hutcherson makes an important contribution, as do the various drummers, with Moses making his presence felt very strongly on the five trio tracks with Izenzon from the March session which yielded the classic 'Malcolm'. The sound-quality is much improved from LP, with due weight given to the sidemen, but some of Shepp's high-register stuff sounds brittle and harsh to no obvious purpose. Mostly, though, this can be tempered on a home hi-fi, so no permanent damage done.

*** New Thing At Newport

Impulse! 543414-2 *Shepp; Bobby Hutcherson (vib); Barre Phillips (b); Joe Chambers (d).* 7/65.

With the classic Coltrane Quartet on the other side of the original album, this gave an explicit and, in the circumstances, slightly ironic blessing to Shepp's emergence as one of the leading lights of the New Thing. Again, the balance of apparently contradictory motivations is just about right, with a less than wholly subversive 'My Favorite Things' set against the inner furies of 'Call Me By My Rightful Name' and 'Skag', and the surreal 'Rufus (Swung His Face To The Wind ...)' from *Four For Trane.* On the whole, though, the music is far from radical in impact, and Shepp's spoken interpolations serve, as throughout his career, to mitigate any slight shift towards abstraction at this stage. Perhaps because of the circumstances and the eventual packaging of the music, Shepp's Newport performance has been somewhat overrated. Again piano-less, the quartet takes a sharp, percussive edge from Hutcherson's tightly pedalled vibes. Phillips fares deservedly better on the CD and can be heard for the remarkable influence he was on the group. Shepp sounds quite self-consciously like a latter-day descendant of Webster and Hawkins, aggravating swing rhythms and phraseology with devices borrowed from R&B and early rock (and, more immediately, from the unabashed populist radicalism of Ornette Coleman). On the other side, Coltrane already sounds tired, but with the understandable weariness of a man whose path would be hard to follow.

**** Live In San Francisco

Impulse! IMP 12542 *Shepp; Roswell Rudd (tb); Donald Garrett, Lewis Worrell (b); Beaver Harris (d).* 2/66.

Recorded at the Both/And Club on Divisadero Street, this is a measure of how ambitous and creative an artist Shepp could be. 'The Wedding' is a recitation, accompanied by Worrell on bowed bass, while 'Wherever June Bugs Go' is drawn from his play, *June Bugs Graduate Tonight.* Proof of his instrumental capability comes with his piano playing on 'Sylvia', a solo feature with just bass and drums, and on the brass solo section of 'Three For A Quarter, One For A Dime', at more than half an hour in duration a generous bonus track excluded from the original LP release. Otherwise, the Shepp of this vintage prefers to stick to tenor and to work without piano or guitar. Doubling the basses affords him a measure of harmonic depth and shade, but for the most part it is the solo horn, with legato changes on trombone, which makes all the running. The recording is near perfect for its time and in the context of a live set, and it sounds very much as though the best of a longer engagement has been selected. The set ends with 'In a Sentimental Mood' and another bonus, 'Things Ain't What They Used To Be', played with the same emotional rigour Shepp brings to Herbie Nichols's 'Lady Sings The Blues'. A glorious album, very near Shepp's best.

***(*) Mama Too Tight

Impulse! IMP 12482 *Shepp; Tommy Turrentine (t); Grachan Moncur III, Roswell Rudd (tb); Howard Johnson (tba); Perry Robinson (cl); Charlie Haden (b); Beaver Harris (d).* 8/66.

'I play music out of an overwhelming need to play ...', and yet *Mama Too Tight* is also the best possible illustration of Shepp the control freak, the master-musician who needs to retain his hold on the reins. The largish ensemble, with brasses and clarinet, allows him to develop orchestral textures at the same time as he pushes forward his increasingly lyrical approach. The overlapping trombones on 'Basheer' (one of a group of portraits of black artists) suggest twin preachers, exegete and commentator, and on 'Mama Too Tight' itself the two slide-men could almost be prophets crying in the wilderness, not quite in agreement, but united in adversity. Turrentine's high, chiming sound (which Shepp himself rightly likens to that of Fats Navarro) cuts through the ensembles. The rhythm section, again minus piano, is utterly musical, fulfilling an orchestral function, and Johnson's part on 'A Portrait Of Robert Thompson (as a young man)', a suite of pieces which begins with Ellington's 'Prelude To A Kiss', elevates the tuba to the front rank of horns. This is one of Shepp's quieter albums, one on which he is content to take a back seat to the ensemble. In direct ratio, it is also one of his most impressive as a composer, a disc that demands – and repays – a bit of work.

**** The Way Ahead

Impulse! 051 272 2 *Shepp; Jimmy Owens (t); Grachan Moncur III (tb); Charles Davis (bs); Dave Burrell, Walter Davis Jr (p);*

Walter Booker, Ron Carter (b); Beaver Harris, Roy Haynes (d). 1/68.

A great deal of fuss was made when in the '90s Ornette Coleman used a piano player for the first time in decades. No less significant was Sheep's reintroduction of a keyboard here, and typically he opts for the maverick traditionalism of Dave Burrell, who brings his usual intelligence and sense of history to the blues, 'Damn If I Know'.

This 1998 reissue includes the whole of *The Way Ahead* with a couple of tracks from the relatively obscure *Kwanza*, which pitched Shepp up against baritone saxophonist Charles Davis, a somewhat ungainly encounter. The main album stands at a curious point in the career, looking as much back as it does ahead, and Shepp seems to be exploring the potential of free soloing over quite settled harmonic foundations, even if in Burrell's hands and given the heterodoxy of Moncur and Jimmy Owens, these are more challenging than usual. The trombonist contributes two fine compositions, 'Frankenstein' and 'New Africa', one from each album. And there is also a long version of Cal Massey's 'Bakai'. Historically, this is an important release, filling in a missing part of the picture. Anyone who knows only the later, romantic/sentimental Shepp will certainly recognize the voice, if not its particular mood. Anyone who still prefers to regard him as a Coltrane epigone might be gently persuaded that Archie was always about different things.

***** Yasmina, A Black Woman**

Le Jazz 51 *Shepp; Lester Bowie (t); Clifford Thornton (c); Arthur Jones (as); Hank Mobley (ts); Roscoe Mitchell (bs, bsx); Dave Burrell (p); Malachi Favors, Earl Freeman (b); Philly Joe Jones, Sunny Murray, Art Taylor (d); Laurence Devereaux (balafon).* 8/69.

Originally issued on Affinity, this intriguing set brings together members of the Art Ensemble, radical drummer Sunny Murray and, most improbably, hard-bop tenor Hank Mobley, whose driving approach complements Shepp unexpectedly well on 'Sonny's Back'. It's a slightly schizophrenic album. The title-piece, at 20 minutes, is ambitious in both structure and development and is full of avant-garde gestures, some of which will seem a little dated at this distance. At the opposite extreme, 'Body And Soul' is a generic tenor work-out, and yet Shepp manages to stamp a measure of individuality on both ends of the spectrum. The CD should not be too difficult to find and, while it takes some time to adjust the ear to a mix of styles, it's a rewarding experience.

*****(*) Steam**

Enja 2076 *Shepp; Cameron Brown (b); Philly Joe Jones (d).* 76.

Perhaps the last point in his career at which Shepp can truly be considered a contender. The heavyweight 'Message For Trane' almost sounds like a gesture of farewell, a turning back once again from the trailing edge of the avant-garde to explore the roots, but also a slightly sorrowful recognition that the astral channels have grown too congested for many more such messages to get through. 'Steam' is brash and open, infinitely better here than the awful vocal version on the deleted *Attica Blues*, one of Shepp's worst and most ill-judged albums. 'Solitude' has the romantic quietly closing the door on the sentimentalist. Shepp doubles on piano but, given the space to develop his ideas (there are only those three tracks), the album is notable for the unwonted coherence of his saxophone solos.

*****(*) Looking At Bird**

Steeplechase SCCD 31149 *Shepp; Niels-Henning Orsted Pedersen (b).* 2/80.

Never short of a handy phrase and ever mindful of a need to resist the condescending nomenclature of 'jazz', Shepp prefers to consider bebop as the baroque period of Afro-American classical music. Given the brutal accretions of his approach, it's an accurate but still slightly misleading designation. His Parker readings are irregular pearls with a raw, slightly meretricious beauty but with only questionable currency as serious re-examinations of the tradition. There is a rather better version of 'Now's The Time' (one of Parker's most traditionally rooted tunes and the one to which Shepp seems to be drawn) on the later *I Didn't Know About You*. The great NHOP cut his teeth on this repertoire and sounds completely at home with it, bouncing and singing through a more or less predictable roster of bebop anthems. It's probably easier for bass players who don't have to negotiate a dense and anxiety-inducing archaeology of previous readings to make their own statements, but the Dane does seem to encourage Shepp to some of his most relaxed and probing performances in the bebop canon. (It's worth listening to this in the context of two saxophone–bass duo takes of 'Davis' with Buell Neidlinger on Cecil Taylor's *Cell Walk For Celeste*, Candid 9034.)

*****(*) Goin' Home**

Steeplechase SCCD 31079 *Shepp; Horace Parlan (p).* 4/77.

***** Trouble In Mind**

Steeplechase SCCD 31139 *As above.* 2/80.

Parlan's slightly raw, bluesy style suits Shepp almost perfectly. The earlier of these, a moving compilation of gospel tunes, is by far the better and more concentrated. *Trouble In Mind*, which takes the same line on 11 blues staples, is perhaps a little too earnest in its pursuit of authenticity but achieves a chastened dignity.

****(*) I Know About The Life**

Sackville SK 3062 *Shepp; Ken Werner (p); Santi Wilson Debriano (b); John Betsch (d).* 2/81.

***** Soul Song**

Enja 4050 *As above, except omit Betsch; add Marvin 'Smitty' Smith (d).* 12/82.

****(*) Down Home New York**

Soul Note 121102 *Shepp; Charles McGhee (t, v); Ken Werner (p, v); Saheb Sarbib (b); Marvin 'Smitty' Smith (d, v); Bartholomew Gray (v).* 2/84.

****(*) Live On Broadway**

Soul Note 121122 *Shepp; George Cables (p); Herbie Lewis (b); Eddie Marshall (d); Royal Blue (v).* 5/85.

After about 1975, Shepp's reputation held up more robustly in Europe than in the USA, in part because it may have been easier to sustain the mien of cool, magisterial fury when removed from the company of younger black Americans who either did it better or who rejected the premisses and methodology. Smith takes a more pragmatic line on American racism, and he plays on *Down Home New York* (as on the earlier *Soul Song*) with a brisk self-confidence that rather shames the leader's dull rhythmic sense and increasingly formulaic phrasing. On both albums, it's the group rather than the leader that impresses.

Perhaps because the rhythm section is less ebullient, Shepp plays better on *Live On Broadway*, but 'My Romance', 'A Night In Tunisia', 'Giant Steps' and a vocal 'St James Infirmary' still leave the residual impression of an illustrated lecture. *I Know About The Life*, the earliest of the group, is simply drab.

**** Mama Rose**

Steeplechase SCCD 31169 *Shepp; Jasper Van't Hof (ky).* 2/82.

Successive recordings of 'Mama Rose' (and there seem to be droves of them) are probably the most useful gauge of Shepp's progress or decline. The version with van't Hof is vulgarly overblown and recorded in horrible close-up. Nothing here on a par with Shepp's longer-standing partnership with Horace Parlan.

*****(*) California Meeting**

Soul Note 121122 *Shepp; George Cables (p); Herbie Lewis (b); Eddie Marshall (d); Royal Blue (v).* 5/85.

An intriguing live programme with a very good band. Cables is the co-star, negotiating 'Giant Steps' with what sounds like a bow to Tommy Flanagan along the way. Marshall and Lewis do a very respectable job and, though the vocals won't be to everyone's taste, Shepp is blowing strongly on both tenor and soprano. 'A Night In Tunisia' is one of his strongest performances of the '80s, a reaffirmation of his belief that bop is the Baroque phase of modern jazz.

****(*) Little Red Moon**

Soul Note 121112 *Shepp; Enrico Rava (t, flhn); Siegfried Kessler (p, syn); Wilbur Little (b); Clifford Jarvis (d).* 11/85.

A mystifyingly dull record, which many will be attracted to on the prospect of hearing Shepp do 'Naima' and 'Whisper Not' in the company of the ever-inventive Rava. The individual components, and not least Shepp's solos on the title-track and the Benny Golson tune, are absolutely fine, but the parts certainly don't add up to anything of substance. Serious collectors and devoted Sheppherds only.

**** Lover Man**

Timeless SJP 287 *Shepp; Dave Burrell (p); Herman Wright (b); Steve McCraven (d); Annette Lowman (v).* 1/88.

Shepp's previous approaches to the song give no hint of the tragic associations that still hover round 'Lover Man' as a result of Charlie Parker's catastrophic breakdown while attempting to record it. Here, he simply manages to sound inept. 'Lover Man' and 'Lush Life' are robbed of all pathos (and, what's worse, dignity), while 'My Funny Valentine' is full-choked sentimentality of a no longer appealing sort. Avoid.

***** Art Of The Duo**

Enja 7007 *Shepp; Richard Davis (p).* 10/89.

Both Shepp and Davis are experienced duo performers; they know the tricks and the pitfalls, and both are able to work their way out of difficulties with considerable aplomb. Both 'Body And Soul' and 'Round Midnight' are models of seat-of-the-pants jazz playing – but this is where the problems also begin. There's a prevailing sense of observing two guys playing one-on-one, doing it for real but without much respect for rules, taste or onlookers. Recorded in a Boston club, the sound is rather messy. A pity there wasn't a studio available the following morning.

*****(*) I Didn't Know About You**

Timeless CD SJP 370 *Shepp; Horace Parlan (p); Wayne Dockery (b); George Brown (d).* 11/90.

****(*) Black Ballad**

Timeless CD SJP 386 *As above, except replace Brown with Steve McCraven (d).* 1/92.

There have long been signs that Shepp regards himself as one of the last surviving heirs of the bop tradition. He switches to alto here for 'Hot House' and the title-track, sounding rather closer to Hodges than to Charlie Parker but not, at first hearing of these tracks, instantly recognizable as himself. He opens, after a brief historical excursus, with 'Go Down Moses (Let My People Go)', vocalizing through his horn before singing the verse with quiet passion. Shepp has always had problems coming to terms with Monk's output, but Parlan (here, as on their duo encounters) coaches him along; this time it's 'Ask Me Now', one of their very best recordings. The sound is bright and closely recorded, favouring saxophone and piano, and the album represents an encouraging return to form.

Temporary, alas, since *Black Ballad* is little more than a weary plod through one of those 'in the tradition' sets that allow contemporary players to work out of character without significantly rethinking the source material. Shepp doesn't have anything to say on 'Do You Know What It Means To Miss New Orleans' or 'Ain't Misbehavin'', and both sound rather stiff and professorial. In contrast, on 'Lush Life' he whips out an onion and emotes shamelessly. It might have been OK in a club setting but, done like this, it comes across very forced and contrived.

Andy Sheppard (born 1957)

TENOR SAXOPHONE, SOPRANO SAXOPHONE, FLUTE

Born in Warminster, Wiltshire, he came to some prominence in the '70s bands Sphere and Spirit Level, before spending time in Paris, returning in time to catch star-status in the '80s jazz boom and recording for Antilles and Blue Note. His reputation settled down in the '90s and he pursued a career as film and TV composer along with his small-group work with Steve Lodder.

***** Inclassifiable**

Label Bleu LBLC 6583 *Sheppard; Steve Lodder (syn); Nana Vasconcelos (perc).* 10/94.

Sheppard is a British saxophonist who had a fruitful time in the 1980s and early '90s. Unfortunately, his Antilles and Blue Note albums are currently out of print. Sheppard lasted no longer with Blue Note than most of his European contemporaries, but one has to pause to wonder, before lambasting the label for shortsightedness, whether such a response is anything more than a knee-jerk. This is a troublingly diffuse album by an artist too mature to speak about in terms of 'promise'. Anyone who has heard a version of the group in concert will realize that the record is no more than a shadowy version of the live act, and should perhaps be comforted by that. This might have been an ideal occasion for a festival or concert recording. In the studio it sounds thin and stilted and Sheppard's unmistakable gifts are short-sold.

***(*) Moving Image

Verve 533875-2 *Sheppard; Steve Lodder (ky); Johnny Ice Taylor (vn); Dudley Phillips (b); Mark Mondesir (d); Richard Ajileye, Bosco D'Olivera (perc).* 1/95, 8/96.

Again based on the Small Co-Motion axis of Sheppard and the ever more assertive Lodder, this intriguing session was originally recorded as incidental music to a television documentary series on comedian Peter Sellers. Inevitably, the dominant tone is bittersweet and even elegiac, with Sheppard laying mostly abstract colours over firm keyboard patterns. The rhythm section keeps things very tight and organized, and there is a complex consistency running through the music which justifies its separate release in this form. The closing two tracks are taken from another television project, a film about the late eighteenth-century African violinist, cellist and composer, Joseph Emidy. An attractive, unexpected record which, though it fails to answer recent questions about Sheppard's progress, doesn't disappoint either.

*** Learning To Wave

Provocateur PVC 1016 *Sheppard; Steve Lodder (ky); John Parricelli (g); Chris Laurence (b); Paul Clarvis (d, perc, tabla); Shalda Sahai (tabla).* 6/98.

A decade adrift stylistically, *Learning To Wave* is by no means the revelatory shift of direction Sheppard implies. The title refers to a trip to Africa where children would appear out of nowhere to wave at passing cars. Some of that relaxed spontaneity is evident in Andy's contemplative playing, which nowadays is muzzled by a broad fusion reverb. Relaxed as it is obviously meant to sound, there is a tense quality to the album, too much of the embattled, isolated individualist in Sheppard's playing and writing. A few more – and rawer – sessions with strangers might work wonders at this stage. The impression is of a man comfortable with his sound and playing entirely within himself. As previously, his soprano is the more convincing horn, delicately balanced between Wayne Shorter's minimalist gestures and Grover Washington's light, funky groove.

Lodder is loyalty itself, a craftsman who just occasionally rises above himself and does something of real moment. Sheppard has said that he wrote much of the material on guitar, which puts Parricelli's role in a different light. The guitarist is easily overlooked in a group setting, sometimes too tasteful for his own good; here, he doesn't put a foot wrong. *Learning To Wave* is a *nice* record; only a curmudgeon would snipe at it. Sadly, that's the business we're in.

Joya Sherrill (born 1927)

VOCALS

The New Jersey-born singer was a precocious talent, greatly admired by Duke Ellington, for whom she wrote the lyrics for 'Take The "A" Train'. Her solo career never really took off, and she is best remembered as an agile, precise interpreter of the great man's music.

*** Sings Duke

Verve 547266-2 *Sherrill; Ray Nance (c, v); Cootie Williams (t); Johnny Hodges (as); Paul Gonsalves (ts); Ernie Harper, Billy Strayhorn (p); Joe Benjamin, John Lamb (b); Shep Shepherd (d).* 65.

Billy Strayhorn's presence at the piano determines the emotional temperature of this smooth and oddly unemphatic set. How different it might have been if Duke himself had been around on the day, except that Joya was never the most rhythmic and harmonically astute of singers. Her great strength was an ability to pitch a song and to invest even the slightest of lyrics with tough, terse emotion. Inevitably and unfairly, much of the interest comes from the players. Gentlemen that they are, Nance and Hodges and Gonsalves pay court with the deepest seriousness, but with a slight reserve. The better material comes early on, with 'Mood Indigo' and 'Prelude To A Kiss', but once Sherrill's voice becomes familiar the impact is lost, and attention switches to the background. An attractive set, and a convincing tribute to Duke's songwriting skills.

Bobby Shew (born 1941)

TRUMPET, FLUGELHORN

Worked in several big bands and Las Vegas groups in the '60s, then settled in California and has since taught, done session-work and played in occasional small-group settings.

***(*) Playing With Fire

MAMA MMF 1017 *Shew; Tom Harrell (t, flhn); Kei Akagi (p); John Patitucci (b); Roy McCurdy (d).* 9/86.

*** Heavyweights

MAMA MMF 1013 *Shew; Carl Fontana (tb); George Cables (p); Bob Magnusson (b); Joe LaBarbera (d).* 95.

A pro's pro, Shew has spent much of his career in top-notch big bands and studio work. These records for MAMA are brimming with virtuoso playing without resorting to soulless cliché. The session with Harrell sat on the shelf for many years until Shew persuaded MAMA to release it. Hastily prepared, the music crackles with ebullience and spontaneity: the choruses on the opener, 'Prelude And Blues', are so exciting that the rest of the date struggles to match up. It does, although here and there one wishes they'd had time to finesse the situation a little more. Still, the two brassmen are as *simpatico* as blood brothers, and this should go down as a great two-trumpet record.

The meeting with trombonist Fontana is more considered all round: a less explosive rhythm section, and the interplay between the two horns is more about warmth and elegance than fireworks. To that extent it's a less compelling record, but some may prefer the sonorities which Shew and Fontana create almost without trying.

Sahib Shihab (born 1925)

SOPRANO, ALTO AND BARITONE SAXOPHONES, FLUTE

Born Edmund Gregory in Savannah, Shihab adopted his Muslim name after the war, after a stint with Fletcher Henderson, with whom he was primarily an altoist. Later years saw him specialize rather more in baritone and flute. He recorded little as a leader, but he is an individual stylist with a foot in mainstream jazz and the avant-garde.

***** Conversations**

Black Lion BLCD 760169 *Shihab; Allan Botschinsky (flhn); Ole Molin (g); Niels-Henning Orsted Pedersen (b); Alex Riel, Bjarne Rostvold (d).* 63.

****(*) All Those Cats**

Ubiquity 19302 *Shihab; Benny Bailey (t); Jimmy Woode (b); Kenny Clarke (d); a.o.*

Shihab is probably still best remembered for his work on some of Thelonious Monk's Blue Note sessions. Since relocating to Europe in the 1960s, though, he has turned up on many a continental big-band date. Shihab played alto with Monk some years earlier but had switched to baritone as his first instrument by the time he made his first records for Savoy.

The Black Lion set was recorded in Copenhagen with a decent bebop-influenced group which is most interesting for the appearance of a teenage NHOP. 'Conversations' comes in three distinct parts and is as thoughtful and original as one would expect from the saxophonist. *All Those Cats* was received immediately before press time, with scant opportunity to judge a set somewhat packed with Jimmy Woode compositions, but Shihab seems to be in fine form; more on this welcome release in our next edition.

Mark Shim (born 1973)

TENOR AND SOPRANO SAXOPHONES

Born in Jamaica, eventually moving to Virginia, Shim studied alto, then tenor. Moved to Brooklyn and played in David Murray's Big Band and the Mingus Big Band; also toured in one of Betty Carter's final groups.

*****(*) Mind Over Matter**

Blue Note 37628-2 *Shim; Geri Allen (p); David Fiuczynski (g, v); Curtis Lundy (b); Ralph Peterson (d, t); Eric Harland (d).* 2/97.

*****(*) Turbulent Flow**

Blue Note 23392-2 *Shim; Edward Simon (p); Stefon Harris (vib, mar); Drew Gress (b); Eric Harland (d).* 99.

Shim's music feels classic and modern, absolutely of today. He gets a giant, growling sound out of the tenor – hard to imagine that he was once an alto player, so naturally does he fit into the big horn's timbres – and he writes twisty, unguessable lines, as if setting himself and his bandmates a challenge before they've even started improvising ('all my tunes have crazy chords'). Peterson (on three tracks of the first disc) and Harland (all the others) are drummers who relish that kind of set-up and, while the music doesn't have the deep-set swing of a classic Blue Note record, the tone has as much gravitas – these are players who are looking for a result. Allen is a keen contributor to the first record, but Simon is hardly any less impressive on the second, which benefits further from the catalytic Harris, a thrilling contributor as sideman as much as he is when leading his own discs.

If anything, Shim is just a little too generous in handing out solo space on *Mind Over Matter*: we want to hear what this powerful young voice can do over more extended and all-conquering solos. 'Oveida' is a ballad with a baronial touch. Fiuczynski is a surprise element: he seems far too rocky in tone, but his playing fits in well enough to suggest how strong Shim's settings are. *Turbulent Flow* sees the interaction of Simon and Harris making a knotty but propulsive backdrop for the leader. No doubt he'll be heard someday in a more exposed and exposing situation: either way, these discs are a pretty tremendous start.

Matthew Shipp (born 1961)

PIANO

Born in Wilmington, Delaware, he began on piano at the age of five. Studied at Berklee and New England Conservatory but didn't begin recording until the '90s. A musician who has absorbed a great deal of music, Shipp is situated in the avant-garde but can probably be a principal in whatever area of improvisation he chooses.

***** Points**

Silkheart SHCD 129 *Shipp; Rob Brown (as); William Parker (b); Whit Dickey (d).* 90.

*****(*) Circular Temple**

Infinite Zero 32758-2 *As above, except omit Brown.* 10/90.

***** Zo**

2 13 61 21315-2 *Shipp; William Parker (b).* 93.

***** Critical Mass**

213 CD003 *Shipp; Mat Maneri (vn); William Parker (b); Whit Dickey (d).* 9/94.

***** Before The World**

FMP CD 81 *Shipp (p solo).* 6/95.

****(*) Thesis**

hatOLOGY 506 *Shipp; Joe Morris (g).* 11/97.

Already in his late thirties, Shipp has been around long enough to know what he's about, yet these records show a steady progress of discovery that suggests he is taking his time in a productive and rather exciting way. The FMP date, for instance, is a record of his first solo concert (in Berlin) and he clearly came to it as a mature yet naturally open player. He has assembled a repertory cast of companions as the personnels suggest and the players clearly know each other's moves pretty well. The two 1990 albums take some cues from the avant-garde past – Taylor, Bley, and Shipp's personal favourite, Andrew Hill – while going their own way in a quite dramatic fashion from moment to moment. Shipp likes to worry at individual motifs or gradually to open out blocks and progressions which can take a long and absorbing time in yielding their numerous details. Dickey's light but propulsive rhythms scurry the music along and Brown's fundamentally lyrical lines add further nuances. *Points* is just a shade behind the trio date since it just runs out of steam here and there, while the second disc could if anything be even longer.

Zo seems more specifically experimental in that Shipp and Parker seem to want to plunge into the darkest (and sometimes the dreariest) corners they can find, deep left-hand chords set on top of juddering bass vamps: their version of 'Summertime' is a bit excruciating, but some of the improvisations are full of a kind of slow, concentrated energy. *Critical Mass* takes a similar form, though this one is divided into a tripartite meditation on a church mass, components developed into a quartet music that seems to be both slow and stately and densely churning. Shipp never sprints through his music the way Taylor does, and his decision to use players like Parker and Maneri rather than saxophonists lends a somewhat baroque feel to his ensembles. An interesting record but rather dour work for the listener.

Wayne Shorter (born 1933)

TENOR SAXOPHONE, SOPRANO SAXOPHONE

Shorter worked with Art Blakey and Miles Davis and recorded on his own account, but it was an association he made while working with Maynard Ferguson that led to one of his most significant creative relationships. For more than a decade, with Joe Zawinul, he was half of the central axis of the profoundly influential Weather Report. Shorter has something in common with John Coltrane, but his characteristic approach is more staccato and elided, and with a more delicately lyrical tone on soprano saxophone.

*****(*) Introducing Wayne Shorter**

Vee Jay VJ 007 *Shorter; Lee Morgan (t); Wynton Kelly (p); Paul Chambers (b); Jimmy Cobb (d).* 11/59.

***** Second Genesis**

Vee Jay 016 *Shorter; Cedar Walton (p); Bob Cranshaw (b); Art Blakey (d).* 10/60.

***** Wayning Moments**

Vee Jay 014 *Shorter; Freddie Hubbard (t); Eddie Higgins (p); Jymie Merritt (b); Marshall Thompson (d).* 62.

Anyone who has encountered Shorter only as co-leader of Weather Report will know him primarily as a colourist, contributing short and often enigmatic brush-strokes to the group's carefully textured canvases. They may not recognize him as the formidable heir of Rollins and Coltrane (scale up and repitch those brief soprano saxophone statements, and the lineage becomes clear). They will emphatically not know him as a composer. As Weather Report's musical identity consolidated, Joe Zawinul largely took over as writer. However, much as Shorter's elided 'solos' (in a group that didn't really believe in solos) still retained the imprint of a more developed idiom, so his compositions for the early records – 'Tears' and 'Eurydice' in particular – convey in essence the virtues that make him one of the most significant composers in modern jazz, whose merits have been recognized by fellow-players as far apart as Art Blakey, Miles Davis ('ESP', 'Dolores', 'Pee Wee', 'Nefertiti') and Kirk Lightsey (a challenging tribute album).

Known as 'Mr Weird' in high school, Shorter cultivated an oblique and typically asymmetrical approach to the bop idiom. His five years with the Jazz Messengers are marked by an aggressive synthesis of his two main models, but with an increasingly noticeable tendency to break down his phrasing and solo construction into unfamiliar mathematical subdivisions. Working with Miles Davis between 1964 and 1970 (a period that coincides with his most productive phase as a solo recording artist), he moved towards a more meditative and melancholy style – with an increasing dependence on the soprano saxophone – which is consolidated on the fine *Super Nova* (below), where he also makes unusually inventive use of the Jekyll–Hyde guitar partnership of McLaughlin and Sharrock. Shorter's recordings at this time relate directly to his work on Miles's *In A Silent Way* and to his work with Weather Report over the following decade.

Shorter's earliest recordings, for Vee Jay, have been available only rather intermittently over the years. The current issue, though, has restored them and re-established their place in the canon, correcting a number of mistakes which surrounded previous releases. On *Introducing*, he sounds in thrall to the Coltrane of the time, and possibly John Gilmore as well. The 26-year-old, who had seriously considered giving up music altogether, turns in five strong originals and a short but blistering version of Weill's 'Mack The Knife'. This CD version includes four alternatives, which add little to the picture but helpfully reinforce the impression of a searching performer who has sufficient lateral vision to keep himself one step ahead of the game. Morgan was at his best in 1959, playing with punch and fire and, like Kelly, with a grasp of the blues which was never vouchsafed to the session leader.

Second Genesis is unfortunately titled, for it is all too obviously another visit to a well that has already been drained. The band, anchored by the Chief Messenger, is superb, but Shorter himself has little enough to say, pushing through his five originals with nervy attention, a detailed, almost deliberate style very different from later work. He's at his best, interestingly, on the two Richard Rodgers compositions which close the album, 'Getting To Know You' and 'I Didn't Know What Time It Was', the latter almost serving as self-definition for a player who works across the bar-lines and, as often as not, ignores the basic count and tonality.

Wayning Moments catches him on the brink of what was to be a purple patch for Blue Note. Hubbard is a lesser performer than Morgan on this material, though he does bring an occasional flicker of ambiguity which does the music no harm. The original album is padded out with alternative takes for every (very short) track, a rather dull reduplication of effort that will excite only those who are already firmly wedded to this period. Higgins is a drab pianist whose approach to the changes is signalled with lights, flags and telegrams, robbing even these short tracks of any drama whatsoever. Listeners would be well advised to stick to the earlier discs, or to hold fire for the classic Blue Notes.

*****(*) Night Dreamer**

Blue Note 84173 *Shorter; Lee Morgan (t); McCoy Tyner (p); Reggie Workman (b); Elvin Jones (d).* 4/64.

*****(*) Juju**

Blue Note 99005 *As above, except omit Morgan.* 8/64.

Shorter's most individual work remains the group of albums made for Blue Note in the mid-1960s, ending in 1970 with the low-key *Odyssey Of Iska*. *Juju* and undervalued and compositionally daring *Night Dreamer* pit him with one version of the classic Coltrane quartet. This is Shorter at his most Coltrane-like, and happening across these records again is a slightly startling experience. The lines are much fuller than typical Wayne, with lots of accidentals and grace notes. 'Virgo' on the first record is an object lesson in how Trane influenced slightly younger players but, even on the debut for Blue Note, the emphasis falls very much on Shorter the composer. 'Charcoal Blues' and 'Armageddon' are instantly identifiable as from his hand, and the little exotic accent of 'Oriental Folk Song' is a touch that was to be reproduced in almost all the records which followed.

New takes of 'JuJu' and 'House Of Jade' on the second album (available in a Rudy van Gelder tribute edition) offer valuable insights into how thoughtful and experimental a player Shorter was at this period, already trying to marry the sheer energy and drive of hard bop with something altogether more lateral and evocative. The Coltrane influence seems less evident four months later, and the absence of Lee Morgan emphasizes a more brooding and melancholy strain which was to become the Shorter signature.

****** Speak No Evil**
Blue Note 99001 *Shorter; Freddie Hubbard (t); Herbie Hancock (p); Ron Carter (b); Elvin Jones (d).* 12/64.

*****(*) The Soothsayer**
Blue Note 84443 *Shorter; Freddie Hubbard (t); James Spaulding (ss, as); McCoy Tyner (p); Ron Carter (b); Tony Williams (d).* 3/65.

*****(*) Etcetera**
Blue Note 33581 *Shorter; Herbie Hancock (p); Cecil McBee (b); Joe Chambers (d).* 6/65.

****** Adam's Apple**
Blue Note 46403 *Shorter; Herbie Hancock (p); Reggie Workman (b); Joe Chambers (d).* 2/66.

For us, the first and last of these are by far Shorter's most satisfying records. Oddly, the middle pair are probably the most obscure, not released until some time later. The understanding with Hancock was total and telepathic, two harmonic adventurers on the loose at a moment when, with John Coltrane still around as a tutelary genius, the rules of jazz improvisation were susceptible to almost endless interrogation.

Speak No Evil created a template for a host of imitators, but so far no one has ever produced a like album with such strength *and* internal balance. There has always been some controversy about Freddie Hubbard's role on the session, with detractors claiming that, unlike Shorter, the trumpeter was still working the hand dealt him in the Messengers and was too hot and urgent to suit Shorter's growing structural sophistication. In fact, the two blend astonishingly well, combining Hubbard's own instinctive exuberance on 'Fee-Fi-Fo-Fum' with something of the leader's own darker conception; interestingly, Shorter responds in kind, adding curious timbral effects to one of his most straight-ahead solos on the record. As with *Adam's Apple*, much of the interest lies in the writing. Shorter has suggested that 'Dance Cadaverous' was suggested by Sibelius's 'Valse Triste', which he plays on *The Soothsayer*; 'Infant Eyes' is compounded of disconcerting nine-measure phrases that suggest a fractured nursery rhyme; the title-piece pushes the soloists into degrees of harmonic and rhythmic freedom that would not normally have been tolerated in a hard-bop context. Set *Speak No Evil* alongside Eric Dolphy's more obviously 'revolutionary' *Out To Lunch!*, recorded by Blue Note earlier the same year, and it's clear that Shorter claims the same freedoms, giving his rhythm section licence to work counter to the line of the melody and freeing the melodic Hancock from merely chordal duties. It's harder to reconstruct how alien some of Shorter's procedures were because, by and large, he does remain within the bounds of post-bop harmony, but it's still clear that *Speak No Evil* is one of the most important jazz records of the period.

Adam's Apple would be remembered for 'Footprints' if for nothing else. It's Wayne's one deathless contribution to the repertory and it still pops up in delightful surprise on the CD. In fact, the 1966 record is a series of surprises. Shorter's interest in Latino styles – supposedly 'a departure' when *Native Dancer* came along – is already well in place with 'El Gaucho', but there is another side on show as well, in the rollicking, head-back laddishness of Jimmy Rowles's '502 Blues'. It takes a moment or two to register who is playing.

The Soothsayer and *Etcetera* weren't released until the end of the 1970s, a sign perhaps that interest in Shorter had switched over almost entirely to his work with Weather Report. Though certainly not of the same quality as the two albums that bracketed them, both are strong and challenging sets. It's no surprise that *Etcetera* might have frightened the corporate horses; it's certainly Shorter's freest recorded session, powerfully argued and vividly recorded, but demanding when set up against 'Footprints' and 'Fee-Fi-Foe-Fum'. With no extra horns, the emphasis falls squarely on saxophone and piano, though McBee and the redoubtable Chambers go about their work with admirable focus and concentration. As so often, Shorter includes one piece by another composer, this time, intriguingly, Gil Evans's 'Barracudas'.

The sextet also makes for compelling listening. 'Angola' (included in two versions) and 'Lady Day' are definitive Shorter compositions, and the closing arrangement of Sibelius's 'Valse Triste' demonstrates yet again how wide and attentive was his awareness of other musics.

***** Schizophrenia**
Blue Note 32096 *Shorter; Curtis Fuller (tb); James Spaulding (ss, as, f); Herbie Hancock (p); Ron Carter (b); Joe Chambers (d).* 3/67.

***** Super Nova**
Blue Note 84332 *Shorter; Walter Booker, John McLaughlin, Sonny Sharrock (g); Miroslav Vitous (b); Chick Corea (vib, d); Jack DeJohnette (d, perc); Airto Moreira (perc); Maria Booker (v).* 9/69.

Schizophrenia is a title that has come back to haunt Wayne Shorter. It's easy and largely pointless to underscore his eccentricity as a performer. He can be gnomic to the point of uncommunicativeness, but the opening 'Tom Thumb' does show him continuing to tread a path between straightforward hard bop and freer elements. With Hancock and Carter again on board, the balance of forces is rock solid, and the two extra horns are used pretty much in that capacity, filling out ensembles and filling in short, accented statements. Spaulding contributes one original to an album that isn't marked by any of the highs of past discs, though 'Miyako' is a beautiful thing.

****** The Best Of Wayne Shorter**
Blue Note 91141 *Shorter; Freddie Hubbard (t); Curtis Fuller (tb); James Spaulding (as); Herbie Hancock (p); Ron Carter, Reggie Workman (b); Joe Chambers, Elvin Jones, Tony Williams (d); collective personnel.* 12/64–3/67.

Earlier versions reflected the rather enigmatic valuation Blue Note placed on one of the label's most brilliant but complex talents. As an introduction, or simply as a distillation of the Capitol years, it's hard to fault now. The track-listing runs in full: 'Speak No Evil', 'Infant Eyes', 'Tim Thumb', 'Lost', 'Adam's Apple', 'Footprints' (of course!), 'Virgo', 'JuJu' and, another of the tunes that appealed so much to Miles Davis, 'Water Babies'. Hard to fault and a truly excellent buy.

****(*) Native Dancer**
Columbia 467095 *Shorter; Milton Nascimento (g, v); Herbie Hancock (p); Airto Moreira (perc); with Dave McDaniel, Roberto Silva, Wagner Tiso, Jay Graydon, Dave Amaro (instrumentation not listed).* 12/74.

A decade to the month after *Speak No Evil* finds Shorter in a bland samba setting which does more to highlight Nascimento's vague and uncommitted vocal delivery than the leader's saxophone playing. There is a hint of the old Shorter in the oblique introduction to 'Lilia' and some fine tenor work on 'Miracle Of The Fishes', but much of the rest could have been put together by a competent session *pasticheur*. Reviewers tended to go one way or the other on *Native Dancer*, but the consensus was that it was a 'surprise' and a 'new departure'. In fact, Shorter had long shown an interest in Latin-American rhythms and progressions; 'El Gaucho' on *Adam's Apple*, above, is one of his finest compositions, and *Native Dancer* is almost exactly contemporary with Weather Report's Pan-American *Tale Spinnin'*. The 'surprise' lay in the lush, choking arrangements and unnecessary verbiage. Shorter encountered similar resistance when his 1980s band flirted with discofied funk-jazz, stripped-down settings that pushed his distinctive tenor sound to the forefront again.

***** Atlantis**
Columbia 481617-2 *Shorter; Jim Walker (picc, f); Yaron Gershovksy, Michiko Hill (p); Larry Klein (g, ky, b); Joseph Vitarelli (ky, synclavier); Michael Hoenig (synclavier); Ralph Humphrey (d); Alex Acuna (d, perc); Lenny Castro (perc); Diana Acuna, Dee Dee Bellson, Nain Brunel, Troye Davenport, Sanaa Lathan, Edgy Lee, Kathy Lucien (v).* 85.

Shorter hadn't recorded under his own name for nearly a decade, and his return was something of a shock. *Atlantis* was marked out by wacky funk rhythms and a dense electronic sound that was at odds with Shorter's spare, elided sound. Almost all the material is written by the leader, but it takes a couple of listens to cut through the incidentals and hear how consistent the strategies are with Shorter's classic work for Blue Note. The band isn't so much undistinguished as determinedly anonymous, delivering a highly processed sound that stands at the apex of a weirdly extended stylistic triangle embracing those early acoustic sets and Wayne's work with Weather Report. The studio sound is sharp and clinical, and often intriguingly at odds with the emotional temperature of the writing.

***** High Life**
Verve 529224-2 *Shorter; Rachel Z (ky); David Gilmore (g); Marcus Miller (b, bcl); Will Calhoun, Terri Lyne Carrington (d); Lenny Castro, Airto Moreira, Munyungo Jackson, Kevin Ricard (perc); brass and strings.* 95.

Shorter's return to active duty is a solid, colourful, gregarious session. Marcus Miller's production is characteristically multi-textured and inventive, and there are plenty of spots for Shorter the soloist to make a mark on what are generally more flexible fusion settings than he's enjoyed for some years. But the lack of either compositional depth or attention-grabbing melodies tells against the record making a deeper impact, and there's nothing here to challenge the best of the Weather Report era.

Tad Shull (born 1955)

TENOR SAXOPHONE

Took up sax at eleven, studied with Dave Liebman and then in Boston, moving to New York in 1978, playing more with swing stylists than with hard boppers.

*****(*) Deep Passion**
Criss Cross Criss 1047 *Shull; Irving Stokes (t); Mike LeDonne (p); Dennis Irwin (b); Kenny Washington (d).* 11/90.

***** In The Land Of The Tenor**
Criss Cross Criss 1071 *As above, except omit Stokes.* 12/91.

Shull is a big-toned tenor specialist out of Norwalk, Connecticut. His first models were Don Byas and Coleman Hawkins, moving on to Johnny Griffin and Lockjaw Davis. Having taken the trouble to get himself a decent sound and to learn the changes inside out, he's not afraid to tackle ungarnished D flat blues. 'The Eldorado Shuffle' brings *Deep Passion* to a rambunctious, shouting close and *In The Land Of The Tenor* ends in much the same way, with another elastic blues, Lucky Thompson's little-heard 'Prey-loot'.

Thompson also makes his mark on the quieter side of Shull's playing, but he's shown no sign of picking up the soprano, even for tunes which might seem to lie comfortably for the small horn. There's plenty of evidence that Shull keeps his ears open. Though an unabashed traditionalist, he doesn't look the kind of guy who's going to be prepared to grind out 'Body And Soul' every night. On *Deep Passion* (the title-track is another Thompson song) he digs out Mary Lou Williams's 'Why' and Babs Gonzales's 'Soul Stirrin''. A year later, he's working equally enterprising material: Kurt Weill's lovely 'This Is New', Hank Jones's 'Angel Face' and Ellington's 'Portrait Of Bojangles'. The band fits him like an old jacket. LeDonne's a great player who also writes a decent tune; 'Tadpole' and 'Big Ears' on the first record are down to him. Irwin and Washington can't be faulted. It's a pity, though, that Stokes was dropped or couldn't make it to the 1991 session. Despite a tendency to drift into a Wynton-as-Pops mode at inopportune moments, he adds a dimension that's missed the second time around.

Janis Siegel

VOCAL

A member of Manhattan Transfer, this is a rare 'solo' outing for the singer.

***** Slow Hot Wind**

Varèse Sarabande VSD-5552 *Siegel; Fred Hersch (p); Tony Dumas (b); Ralph Penland (d).* 95.

Siegel's fresh, open, unaffected singing makes this duet record (Dumas and Penland assist on 4 of the 12 tracks) a disarming confection. In keeping with her background in the vocal group, Manhattan Transfer, she sounds more like a Broadway singer, or at least a cabaret stylist, than an out-and-out jazz performer: lyrics are granted a steady, respectful delivery and her uncomplicated phrasing and sunny timbre give the lyrics a clear-headed beauty that is the hallmark of a performer with few pretensions. It's Hersch who supplies the ornamentation, the textural weight, and he's in good form. One or two dislikeable choices of song let the disc down here and there, but the whole is good enough to have one awaiting the reissue of Siegel and Hersch's *Short Stories* (Atlantic, currently out of print).

David Sills (born 1969)

TENOR SAXOPHONE

Contemporary American saxophonist, making his debut.

***** Journey Together**

Naxos 86023 2 *Sills; Alkan Broadbent (p); Larry Koonse (g); Darek Oles (b); Joe LaBarbera (d).* 11/97.

The Jazz School of Hard Knocks is a little undersubscribed these days. Sills has a degree in classical saxophone from California State University, but not even his tutors could think he was throwing away his education, so natural is his instinct for inspiration. In approach, it resembles that of his mentor, Joe Henderson, who provides the key title here, 'Inner Urge', a generously proportioned blowing theme with enough subtlety to test the young man's harmonic skills.

Opening with a Tristano track – '317 East 32nd Street' – was a bold move, but Sills makes it sound like his own, and guitarist Koonse adds an extra dimension. As ever, Broadbent is a flawless accompanist, and Joe LaBarbera is one of the most swinging and responsive drummers on the circuit. All in all, a very auspicious label debut.

Alan Silva (born 1939)

DOUBLE BASS, VIOLIN, CELLO, PIANO, SYNTHESIZERS

Silva's CV is a relatively unusual one. He was born in Bermuda and raised in New York, where he took lessons in piano and violin, before showing an interest in jazz trumpet. Led into jazz by Donald Byrd, he eventually took up double bass at the late age of twenty-three.

***** Take Some Risks**

In Situ 011 *Silva; Misha Lobko (cl); Bruno Girard (vn); Didier Petit (clo).* 11/86.

Recorded live in Paris, *Take Some Risks* features an ensemble that sounds very much like an extension of Silva's own musical personality and perhaps consequently rather too private and uncommunicative. It consists of a single multi-part suite under the general title, *Standard Equipment*. The piece breaks down only rather awkwardly and is probably best heard as a continuous process with only contingent breaks. The language is typical of Silva: softly fractured but with an almost formal elegance.

*****(*) In The Tradition**

In Situ 166 *Silva; Johannes Bauer (tb); Roger Turner (d, perc).* 4/93.

Silva's discovery of synthesizers was an important moment in his career. This wonderful trio shows how musically and inventively he embraced technology. His wry understanding of what 'standard' means in a jazz context is reflected in the track listing: 'Standards 1–9'. Silva deals with neither orthodox tunes nor straightforward chord sequences, but manages to sound as if he has absorbed the Broadway songbook as well as the solo sequences of *Free Jazz* and *Ascension*.

Turner and Bauer are utterly *simpatico* and any reservations we have about this record stem from an unlovely mix and from a tendency to repeat ideas with irrelevant embellishment rather than moving on.

*****(*) A Hero's Welcome: Pieces For Rare Occasions – Volume 1**

Eremite MTE 017 *Silva; William Parker (b).* 3/98.

Two modern giants of the bull fiddle, united in a project of awesome power. Silva's ambitions to write orchestrally have finally been fulfilled. He uses MIDI keyboards and old-fashioned acoustic piano to create a body of sound that occupies a mid-territory between Duke Ellington or Charles Mingus and Edgard Varèse. The five relatively brief sections might almost be movements in a romantic symphony, were the language and articulation not so unmistakably American.

Parker is by now beyond reproach and beyond categorization; but what is surprising is how thoroughly and how completely Silva still thinks/plays like a bass player, even if nowadays his imagination ranges right across the strings and beyond. The good news is that this is just the first release in a sequence featuring a remarkable modern duo.

Horace Silver (born 1928)

PIANO

Born in Norwalk, Connecticut, he toured with Stan Getz in 1950, then moved to New York and worked with Art Blakey from 1952. Formed own quintet from 1956 and he has largely worked in that format ever since. Spent nearly 30 years with Blue Note, then stints with Columbia and now Impulse!. The defining stylist of hard-bop piano, mixing bebop licks with gospel influences, and an influential composer, as well as one of the most enduring of small-group leaders.

*****(*) Horace Silver Trio**

Blue Note 81520-2 *Silver; Percy Heath, Gene Ramey, Curley Russell (b); Art Blakey (d); Sabu Martinez (perc).* 10/53.

*****(*) Horace Silver And The Jazz Messengers**

Blue Note 46140-2 *Silver; Kenny Dorham (t); Hank Mobley (ts); Doug Watkins (b); Art Blakey (d).* 11/54.

Horace Silver's records present the quintessence of hard bop. He not only defined the first steps in the style, he also wrote several of its most durable staples, ran bands that both embodied and transcended the idiom and perfected a piano manner which summed up hard bop's wit and trenchancy and popular appeal. The first outcroppings of that can be heard in the *Trio* album, with its first versions of 'Horacescope', 'Opus de Funk' and 'Ecaroh' – funkier and less many-noted than the preceding wave of bop pianists. Silver's borrowings from the swing masters are still in evidence here.

The Blue Note *Jazz Messengers* album might be the one that started it all: two sessions, originally issued as a brace of ten-inch LPs, with a definitive hard-bop cast. While the finest music by this edition of the original Jazz Messengers was probably recorded at the Café Bohemia the following year (listed in Art Blakey's entry), this one is still fresh, smart but properly versed in the new language (or, rather, the new setting for the old language). The album sets out Silver's own expertise: a crisp, chipper but slightly wayward style, idiosyncratic enough to take him out of the increasingly stratified realms of bebop piano. Blues and gospel-tinged devices and percussive attacks give his methods a more colourful style, and a generous good humour gives all his records an upbeat feel.

*****(*) Further Explorations**

Blue Note 56583-2 *Silver; Art Farmer (t); Clifford Jordan (ts); Teddy Kotick (b); Louis Hayes (d).* 5/57.

*****(*) Blowin' The Blues Away**

Blue Note 95342-2 *Silver; Blue Mitchell (t); Junior Cook (ts); Gene Taylor (b); Louis Hayes (d).* 8/59.

***** Horace-Scope**

Blue Note 84042-2 *As above, except Roy Brooks (d) replaces Hayes.* 7/60.

*****(*) The Tokyo Blues**

Blue Note 53355-2 *As above, except Joe Harris (d) replaces Brooks.* 7/62.

***** Silver's Serenade**

Blue Note 21288-2 *As above, except Roy Brooks (d) replaces Harris.* 5/63.

****** Song For My Father**

Blue Note 99002-2 *As above, except add Carmell Jones (t), Joe Henderson (ts), Teddy Smith (b), Roger Humphries (d).* 10/64.

*****(*) Cape Verdean Blues**

Blue Note 84220-2 *Silver; Woody Shaw (t); J.J Johnson (tb); Joe Henderson (ts); Bob Cranshaw (b); Roger Humphries (d).* 10/65.

****** The Jody Grind**

Blue Note 84250-2 *Silver; Woody Shaw (t); James Spaulding (as, f); Tyrone Washington (ts); Larry Ridley (b); Roger Humphries (d).* 11/66.

Although Silver went on to record some 25 further albums for Blue Note, only the above are currently available as CD reissues. It's hard to pick the best of the albums since Silver's consistency is unarguable: each album yields one or two themes that haunt the mind, each usually has a particularly pretty ballad, and they all lay back on a deep pile of solid riffs and workmanlike solos. Silver's own are strong enough, but he was good at choosing sidemen who weren't so characterful that the band would overbalance: Cook, Mitchell, Mobley, Shaw, Jones and Spaulding are all typical Silver horns, and only Johnson (who was guesting anyway) and Henderson on the above records threaten to be something rather more special. The two choicest records, though, are surely *Song For My Father*, with its memorable title-tune, the superb interplay of Jones and Henderson, and the exceptionally fine trio ballad, 'Lonely Woman', and *The Jody Grind*, which hits some sort of apex of finger-snapping intensity on the title-tune and 'Mexican Hip Dance'. *Blowin' The Blues Away* includes the soul-jazz classic, 'Sister Sadie', sounding very hot in its new RVG Edition; and although this and the two subsequent albums with this line-up each have their merits, our favourite of the three is *The Tokyo Blues*, with its material inspired by a trip to Japan and the band playing at the top of their game. The somewhat earlier *Further Explorations* marks the start of the long association between Farmer and Jordan, who were still recording together with memorable results in the '80s.

The Cape Verdean Blues presents Henderson, Shaw and Johnson on three tracks for one of Silver's most full-bodied front lines. A recent reappearance is *Silver's Serenade*, a typically solid if unremarkable set of Silverisms. His piano solo on the title-piece is a compendium of quotes and licks that he shapes with a kind of diffident aplomb, as if he knows that this stuff comes so easily he could do it in his sleep. The rougher 'Let's Get To The Nitty Gritty' is a more wholehearted groover. In the end, Silver's albums miss the intensity that came as second nature to Blakey's Jazz Messengers: his blues are chirpier, less driven, and to that extent the records feel less significant.

****** Re-Entry**

32 Jazz 32005 *Silver; Carmell Jones, Woody Shaw (t); Joe Henderson (ts); Larry Ridley, Teddy Smith (b); Roger Humphries (d).* 4/65–2/66.

These broadcasts from The Half Note previously popped up briefly on Silver's Silveto label, but this looks like their CD debut. Two excellent editions of the quintet in extended workouts of 'Song For My Father', 'The African Queen', 'The Natives Are Restless Tonight' and 'Que Pasa'. Henderson's tremendous solo on 'Song For My Father', which climaxes on a series of startling hollers, is enough by itself to make the disc worth having, but this is altogether excellent music.

****** Retrospective**

Blue Note 495576-2 4CD *As Blue Note albums above, plus Randy Brecker, Charles Tolliver, Cecil Bridgewater, Tom Harrell (t); Tyrone Washington, Stanley Turrentine, Michael Brecker, Harold Vick, Bennie Maupin, George Coleman, Bob Berg, Larry*

Schneider (ts); David Friedman (vib); Bob Cranshaw, John Williams, Larry Ridley, Ron Carter (b); John Harris Jr, Mickey Roker, Al Foster (d); Bill Henderson, Andy Bey, Gail Nelson (v); brass, chorus. 10/52–11/78.

A superbly chosen anthology of Silver's many albums for Blue Note, with the first three discs full of peerless stuff and the fourth making the most of his patchy and often misdirected later work. It samples many otherwise out-of-print records and introduces several players whose Silver age is often forgotten, such as Harrell, Berg and Schneider. The booklet has some glorious Frank Wolff photography as a bonus. The perfect introduction to the master.

****(*) It's Got To Be Funky**
Columbia 473877-2 *Silver; Oscar Brashear, Bob Summers, Ron Stout (t, flhn); Bob McChesney (tb); Maurice Spears (btb); Suzette Moriarty (frhn); Red Holloway (as, ts); Eddie Harris, Branford Marsalis (ts); Bob Maize (b); Carl Burnett (d); Andy Bey (v).* 2/93.

***** Pencil Packin' Papa**
Columbia 476979-2 *As above, except Jeff Bernell (t), George Bohannon (tb), James Moody (ts), Rickey Woodard (ts), O.C Smith (v) replace Summers, McChesney, Marsalis and Bey.* 10–11/94.

These were very disappointing. Silver at last returned to a major label, but the over-produced, impersonal set of brass-dominated charts on *It's Got To Be Funky* sounds like a designer's idea of the man's funky language. Andy Bey's over-ripe vocals on four tunes ('The Hillbilly Bebopper' is a bit much, even for Silver) are rotten, and it's the more frustrating because the music does sometimes really work out: 'Funky Bunky' is smart, the leader's own piano is still worth a taste, and Harris takes solo honours by simply sounding like himself in an otherwise colourless ensemble. There's a slight upswing on *Pencil Packin' Papa.* Old soulman Smith is a respectable replacement for Bey, and the brass team sound looser and more in keeping with the Silver ethos. That said, this is still no more than a competent set of tunes, the new 'Senor Blues' is no match for the old, and only the tenormen make the most of their solo chances.

***** The Hardbop Grandpop**
Impulse! IMP 11922 *Silver; Claudio Roditi (t); Steve Turre (tb); Michael Brecker (ts); Ronnie Cuber (bs); Ron Carter (b); Lewis Nash (d).* 2–3/96.

This is more like it, although the all-star band lends a muscle-bound quality to the music which Silver's usual impishness doesn't quite mitigate. At least the soloists take their chances and there's a decent set of originals, even if a lot of it feels like revisiting old glories.

***** A Prescription For The Blues**
Impulse! 051238-2 *Silver; Randy Brecker (t); Michael Brecker (ts); Ron Carter (b); Louis Hayes (d).* 5/97.

*****(*) Jazz Has A Sense Of Humor**
Verve 050293-2 *Silver; Ryan Kisor (t); Jimmy Greene (ss, ts); John Webber (b); Willie Jones III (d).* 12/98.

The heavyweight line-up for *A Prescription For The Blues* is again a bit too heavy to suit Silver's music best: he sounds as if he's trying to undercut those big bruisers the Breckers, and the trio number, 'Brother John And Brother Gene', is the most beguiling piece on show.

Informally dedicated to Fats Waller, the music on the Verve album looks from the titles and the lyrics printed on the sleeve (mercifully they are not sung, by anyone) as if they are harbingers of a comedy album. But that's just Horace kidding us around. Actually, the music is as sprightly and righteous as many of his better old records. Solo for solo, Kisor and Greene may not be up to their premier forebears, but this feels more like a genuine Horace Silver band than any of his last few efforts. Some of the faster tempos seem too quick – a gutbucket mid-tempo was usually the ideal Silver pace – but never mind, the band clicks.

Silver Leaf Jazz Band

GROUP

Led by trumpeter Chris Tyle, this is a modern group playing New Orleans and vintage Chicago styles.

****(*) Streets And Scenes Of Old New Orleans**
Good Time Jazz GTJCD-15001-2 *Chris Tyle (t, v); Dave Sager (tb); Jacques Gauthe (cl); Tom Roberts (p); John Gill (d, v).* 5/93.

***** Jelly's Best Jam**
Good Time Jazz GTJCD-15002-2 *Chris Tyle (t); John Gill (tb); Orange Kellin (cl); Tom Roberts, Jelly Roll Morton (p); Vince Giordano (b); Hal Smith (d).* 10/93.

*****(*) Sugar Blues**
Stomp Off CD1298 *Chris Tyle, Leon Oakley (c); John Gill (tb); Mike Baird (cl); Steve Pistorius (p); Clint Baker (bj); Marty Eggers (b); Hal Smith (d).* 4/95.

***** Here Comes The Hot Tamale Man**
Stomp Off CD1311 *Chris Tyle (c, v); Mike Owen (tb); Orange Kellin (cl); Tom Fischer (as); Steve Pistorius (p); Craig Ventresco (g, bj); Mike Eggers (b); Hal Smith (d).* 3/96.

Chris Tyle leads this group of New Orleans wannabees. Even though the group is based in the city, few of them are authentic NO musicians, and followers of this axis of traditional players will recognize many of the names. They got off to a somewhat ordinary start with *Streets And Scenes Of Old New Orleans*: the best numbers are the more obscure pieces, including several by Johnny Wiggs. Tunes as hoary as 'Perdido Street Blues' and 'Tin Roof Blues' have been done more vividly elsewhere. But the subsequent Jelly Roll Morton set, *Jelly's Best Jam*, is much more like the right thing: a shrewd blend of familiar and less hackneyed Morton titles is arranged with enough élan to sidestep mere copycat tactics, and the inclusion of four of Morton's 1938 piano solos offers a ghostly echo of the master's presence.

The two Stomp Off discs follow a similar line of homage without artifice. *Sugar Blues* is a tribute to King Oliver that walks a very difficult line. Tyle's aim was to fashion the sound of the Oliver Creole Jazz Band and put it to use not only on Oliver's repertoire but also on contemporary tunes that he might have played. It's fascinating to hear them tackle 'If You Want My Heart' and 'That Sweet Something, Dear', two famous 'lost' Oliver records, as well as the cornet–piano duet on 'The Pearls' and set-pieces like 'Eccentric'. Tyle is a shrewd judge of tempos and he gets amazingly close to a hi-fi treatment of Oliver's band sound. Not everything convinces, but this is a mostly splendid record.

Even tougher to pull off is the Freddie Keppard homage, *Here Comes The Hot Tamale Man*. With so little surviving evidence to go on, Tyle has still managed to weave together 19 tracks and a sound that seems like a plausible echo of Keppard's terse, often relentless music. His own cornet playing certainly seems to catch much of the blaring intensity of Keppard himself, and though the rest of the band seem rather less characterful they create convincing treatments of the likes of the title-piece and 'Messin' Around'. Tyle's vocals aren't quite so effective, but he's surely allowed some indulgence.

Sonny Simmons (born 1933)

ALTO AND TENOR SAXOPHONES, COR ANGLAIS

Born Huey Simmons in Louisiana, he moved to California as a boy and took up alto sax. Worked with Prince Lasha for many years and made his recording debut with Lasha's group. Associated with the '60s avant-garde but made only a handful of records and dropped from sight in the '70s, reappearing in the '90s with a string of new records.

*****(*) Ancient Ritual**

Qwest/Reprise 945623-2 *Simmons; Charnett Moffett (b); Zarak Simmons (d).* 12/92.

Isolated from the main currents of the music, Sonny Simmons never really built on the interest he created with a handful of records in the 1960s and '70s, which revealed a liaison between Ornette Coleman's freedoms and a terse, bop-orientated lyricism. There are two excellent albums for Arhoolie and Contemporary which have been missing for years, and his early ESPs have yet to be made available again in the catalogue's latest edition. *Ancient Ritual*, though, was really a marvellous comeback for Simmons, and a surprisingly uncompromised record from a major label. The old authority remains, coupled with a skirling fluency that makes simple themes like 'Country Parson' and 'Theme For Linda' resonate with a master's eloquence. He manages to make reiterative statements hypnotic without sounding repetitive, and when the music ignites behind him he refuses to resort to hyperbole. The studio sound catches an embattled but lyrical alto tone beautifully, but it does no favours at all to either Moffett (almost inaudible at times) or Zarak Simmons. The bassist is, in any case, hardly the right man for this situation, his excessive ornamentation a distraction when you can hear it.

***** American Jungle**

Qwest/Reprise 946543-2 *Simmons; Travis Shook (p); Reggie Workman (b); Cindy Blackman (d).* 12/95.

A passionate continuation, but this one doesn't go well, with a number of uncertainties in its realization. Shook seems an odd choice for the group, delivering a rather pallid version of McCoy Tyner to the leader's various nods to Coltrane (specifically 'My Favorite Things'). Workman and Blackman play up the expected storm and Simmons takes most of the solo limelight, yet the mediated feel of the album seems at odds with the saxophonist's concerns, which he makes clear on the title-track.

****** Transcendence**

CIMP 113 *Simmons; Michael Marcus (stritch, manzello); Charles Moffett (d).* 4/96.

*****(*) Judgement Day**

CIMP 117 *Simmons; Michael Marcus (manzello, Cmel); Steve Neil (b); Charles Moffett (d).* 5/96.

Two almost desperately powerful records by an angry man. The sleeve-notes say something about the saxophonist's resolve and intensity, revealing the strained circumstances of both sessions, and the bloody virulence of the playing can at times seem as exhausting to listen to as it was to perform. Moffett's swing and jazz time are one leavening agent; the lovely sound of Marcus's horns intertwining with Simmons is another. But these are severely beautiful records altogether, which CIMP's unadulterated sound enhances. The second gets a marginally lower rating if only because Neil sometimes seems an unnecessary addition to the other three. Simmons plays alto on the first, a very dark tenor on the second, and, despite evident problems, he is awesome.

Ken Simon

TENOR SAXOPHONE

American saxophonist moving in an uncompromising free-jazz direction.

****(*) The Twilight Of Time**

Cadence CJR 1082 *Simon; Vattel Cherry (b); David Pleasant (d).* 7/97.

The cover photo looks like Monument Valley, and Simon and his team are like high plains drifters, free-jazz outlaws in an otherwise lawbound time. Romanticism apart, this isn't all that good: the saxophonist doesn't so much build on Albert Ayler's legacy (specifically recalled in 'Albert's Ladder') as flatten it. He's a brutally aggressive player and, since he doesn't have a great deal to say, it's wearisome. Cherry and Pleasant do their best to illuminate, but it's difficult work.

Ralph Simon

TENOR, ALTO AND SOPRANO SAXOPHONES, SYNTHESIZER

New York saxophonist working in a wide-ranging post-bop and fusion environment.

***** As**

Postcards 1004 *Simon; Gene Adler (p, kalimba); Jeff Berman (vib); Dan Rose (g); Marc Johnson, David Dunaway (b); Billy Hart, Chip White (d); Tom Beyer (perc).* 5/81.

***** Music For The Millenium**

Postcards 1015 *Simon; Michael DiSibio (t); Julian Priester (tb); Paul Bley (ky); Alan Pasqua (p); Jeff Berman (vib); Elizabeth Panzer (hp); Gary Peacock (b); Bruce Ditmas (d, syn); Tom Beyer (perc).* 9–11/95.

Simon has been working as A&R man for Postcards and he has had the leeway both to release an old on-the-shelf session of his own and to cut an entirely new one. Recorded in 1981 but unreleased until 1994, *As* is a colourful session, rich with the sound of kalimba, vibes and percussion, over which the saxophonist and Adler (who died in 1992 and is the dedicatee) float attractive modal improvisations. Each tune tends to find its own level, so 'Gepetto' and 'Julie And Julius' are brief episodes while 'Skin On Skin' drifts on for 20 minutes. It sometimes evaporates into high-calibre background music; and much the same thing happens on the altogether more modern-sounding *Music For The Millenium*, which enables the leader to bring in many of the performers he has been engaging on records of their own. The result is an interesting, if ultimately rather shapeless, sequence of what aspire to be sound-pictures rather than jazz pieces. Simon sticks to soprano and a breath-controlled synthesizer and, with Bley and Ditmas also adding various electronics, the synthetic soundscapes tend to dominate: Priester and the superb Peacock play their hearts out (listen to the bassist's driving patterns on 'Are You Ready?', where he seems oblivious to the surrounding paraphernalia) but they tend to end up as bit players. Still, this is demonstrably more absorbing a record than most such ventures, and the closing tilt at 'Blue In Green' (where DiSibio and Pasqua make their only appearance) is like an oblique memory of jazz in another world.

Pete (La Roca) Sims (born 1938)

DRUMS

A New Yorker, Sims – he got his nickname through playing in timbale bands – was an accomplished hard-bop drummer who came to prominence in the late-'50s Sonny Rollins group. Dismayed at the decline of jazz in the late '60s, he left music and studied as an attorney; but he has since returned, although not to full-time performing.

*** Turkish Women At The Bath

32 Jazz 32052 *Sims; John Gilmore (ts); Chick Corea (p); Walter Booker (b).* 5/67.

*** SwingTime

Blue Note 854876-2 *Sims; Jimmy Owens (t); Dave Liebman, Lance Bryant (ss); Ricky Ford (ts); George Cables (p); Santi Debriano (b).* 2–3/97.

Blue Note collectors will always remember him as Pete La Roca, the nickname he picked up through his expertise as a *timbale* player in Latin bands, 40 years ago; but he prefers plain Pete Sims. The unsung hero of many a hard-bop date, with only the much-liked *Basra* to his name on Blue Note (recently available again briefly as a Connoisseur Edition), Sims has had something of a minor resurgence, with records appearing from different ends of his career. The 32 Jazz date is a curious oddity that was out of circulation for many years after being incorrectly attributed to Chick Corea's leadership. Sims actually composed all seven themes. It's not, though, a terribly interesting rediscovery: the mix is clattery and unflattering to each of the players in turn, Corea seems to have his mind on something else, and Gilmore does little but blow lustily at the front, as if not sure what's going on.

The drummer has bided his time between occasional gigs and work as an attorney. The return to the studios on *SwingTime* offers a set of likeable, splashy hard bop, something of a contradiction in terms, given the strictness of the genre, but convincing enough. Though he has to split soprano duties with Bryant, Liebman is easily the outstanding player, getting an especially pithy solo into 'Susan's Waltz'. Owens is all right and Ford sounds almost outlandishly larger-than-life on tenor. Sims himself ('I'm really a kettle drummer') isn't shy about leading, although the Newley–Bricusse tune, 'The Candyman', perhaps wasn't his best idea.

Zoot Sims (1925–85)

TENOR, ALTO, SOPRANO AND BARITONE SAXOPHONES, VOCAL

A Californian, and one of Woody Herman's 'Four Brothers' saxophonists in the 1940s, Sims continued to work in big-band situations on several tours, but from 1950 was primarily a solo artist who worked in almost countless studio and live situations. One of his most frequent collaborators was fellow tenorman, Al Cohn. Instantly recognizable, and among the most consistently inventive and swinging of musicians, Sims was a paradigmatic jazzman. He died of cancer in 1985, having played for as long as he was able.

***(*) Quartet And Sextet

RCA Vogue 74321 511522 *Sims; Frank Rosolino (tb); Gerry Wiggins, Henri Renaud (p); Jimmy Gourley (g); Pierre Michelot, Don Bagley (b); Kenny Clarke, Jean-Louis Viale (d).* 6/50–9/53.

*** Quartets

Original Jazz Classics OJC 242 *Sims; John Lewis, Harry Biss (p); Curley Russell, Clyde Lombardi (b); Don Lamond, Art Blakey (d).* 9/50–8/51.

***(*) Zoot!

Original Jazz Classics OJC 228 *Sims; Nick Travis (t); George Handy (p); Wilbur Ware (b); Osie Johnson (d).* 12/56.

Like Jack Teagarden, Zoot Sims started out mature and hardly wavered from a plateau of excellence throughout a long and prolific career (oddly enough, Sims's singing voice sounded much like Teagarden's). As one of Woody Herman's 'Four Brothers' sax section, he didn't quite secure the early acclaim of Stan Getz, but by the time of these sessions he was completely himself: a rich tone emboldened by a sense of swing which didn't falter at any tempo. He sounded as if he enjoyed every solo, and if he really was much influenced by Lester Young – as was the norm for the 'light' tenors of the day – it was at a far remove in emotional terms. *Quartet And Sextet* catches Zoot in Paris on two separate occasions; the 1950 tracks, with a heap of alternative takes, find him strolling through some themeless chord changes along with 'Night And Day' and a couple of other standards. The sound has much improved over the previous edition (which we listed as *Tenorly*) and Zoot's swinging lines are infectiously electric. The 1953 tracks offer a fine glimpse of the excellent Rosolino, as well as Jimmy Gourley, and are rather more relaxed. *Quartets* sets up the kind of session Sims would record for the next 35 years:

standards, a couple of ballads, and the blues, all comprehensively negotiated with a rhythm section that strolls alongside the leader: neither side ever masters the other. 'Zoot Swings The Blues' has Sims peeling off one chorus after another in top gear, while a seemingly endless 'East Of The Sun' shares the solos around without losing impetus. The original Prestige recording is grainy. *Zoot!* goes up a notch for the inspirational pairing of Sims and Travis, a minor figure who probably never played as well on record as he does here: 'Taking A Chance On Love' is a near-masterpiece, and Ware and Johnson play superb bass and drums.

***** Tonite's Music Today**

Black Lion BLCD 760907 *Sims; Bob Brookmeyer (vtb); Hank Jones (p); Wyatt Reuther (b); Gus Johnson (d).* 1/56.

*****(*) Morning Fun**

Black Lion BLCD 760914 *As above, except Bill Crow (b), Jo Jones (d) replace Reuther and Johnson.* 8/56.

The albums with Brookmeyer and Eardley were recorded while they were in Gerry Mulligan's Sextet: 'Lullaby Of The Leaves', included on *Morning Fun*, was one of the staples in Mulligan's repertoire, and the mood here (and throughout the sessions with Brookmeyer) owes much to him. But the atmosphere on both dates is of an utterly relaxed, good-pals jam session, refereed by the eternally sweet-natured Jones. *Morning Fun* just has the edge, perhaps, for the knockout tempo of 'The King' and a couple of lovely ballads (Zoot also sings 'I Can't Get Started').

*****(*) The Modern Art Of Jazz**

Dawn DCD 101 *Sims;Bob Brookmeyer (vtb); John Williams (p); Milt Hinton (b); Gus Johnson (d).* 1/56.

***** Zoot Sims Goes To Jazzville**

Dawn DCD 103 *Sims; Jerry Lloyd (t); John Williams (p); Bill Anthony, Knobby Totah (b); Gus Johnson (d).* 8–9/56.

*****(*) That Old Feeling**

Chess GRP 18072 *Sims; John Williams (p); Knobby Totah (b); Gus Johnson (d).* 10–11/56.

***** Down Home**

Bethlehem BET 6022-2 *Sims; Dave McKenna (p); George Tucker (b); Dannie Richmond (d).* 7/60.

The Dawn material has been out in various incarnations, often compiled as one CD, but these are surely the definitive editions, with previously unreleased tracks as a bonus. *The Modern Art Of Jazz* is a cracking session with Brookmeyer, both horns ebullient throughout, and though the sound is a bit cavernous it's very listenable. *Zoot Sims Goes To Jazzville* sets him alongside the little-known Lloyd, who does nothing to disgrace himself and has a light though rather short-breathed style. Zoot plays alto on four tracks, and a surprise choice is Monk's 'Bye-Ya'. The original LP programme is bolstered by six extra tracks, four of them 'new'.

That Old Feeling collects two sessions originally released on Argo and ABC-Paramount, including a date where Zoot overdubbed alto and baritone to make a one-man sax section. Unlike other such experiments, this one worked out well: Zoot's utter professionalism, coupled with his easygoing style, seems to have transcended the artifice of the situation, and a couple of tunes – 'Minor Minor' and 'Pegasus' – are lucid gems. But there is also a sumptuous ballad feature on 'The Trouble With Me Is You'. *Down Home* sets him up with a very interesting rhythm section, but Zoot doesn't quite have enough space: McKenna gets equal time in the front line, and he hadn't yet secured the authority of his later work.

***** Either Way**

Evidence ECD 22007-2 *Sims; Al Cohn (ts); Mose Allison (p); Bill Crow (b); Gus Johnson (d); Cecil 'Kid Haffey' Collier (v).* 2/61.

One of the earlier collaborations between these two tenor masters, *Either Way* suffers from a foggy sound-mix and the less-than-desirable presence of Collier, whose singing on three tunes wastes valuable saxophone time (on what is a short CD anyway). But there is still some great duelling on 'The Thing', 'I'm Tellin' Ya' and a honeyed 'Autumn Leaves', plus the bonus of Allison at the piano.

***** Recado Bossa Nova**

Fresh Sound FSR-CD 198 *Sims; Spencer Sinatra (f, picc); Phil Woods (cl); Gene Quill (cl, bcl); Sol Schlinger (bcl); Ronnie Odrich, Phil Bodner, Jerry Sanfino (reeds, f); Jim Hall, Kenny Burrell, Barry Galbraith (g); Milt Hinton, Art Davis (b); Sol Gubin (d); Ted Sommer, Willie Rodriguez, Tommy Lopez (perc).* 8/62–63.

Zoot's entry in the bossa nova craze. Al Cohn and Manny Albam did a perfect pro's job in arranging everything from 'Bernie's Tune' to 'Cano Canoe' for Sims to blow on, and the results are finely manicured without encumbering the saxophonist. He takes some typically swinging, unruffled solos.

***** Zoot Sims In Copenhagen**

Storyville STCD 8244 *Sims; Kenny Drew (p); Niels-Henning Orsted Pedersen (b); Ed Thigpen (d).* 8/78.

A characteristic club date with Zoot. Drawbacks: the rhythm section play well but are too generously featured; the material is stuff Zoot did many times over; the sound is a bit rough here and there. The plus is that Sims is playing close to the top of his latter-day game, which ought to be good enough for anybody.

****** Zoot Sims And The Gershwin Brothers**

Original Jazz Classics OJC 444 *Sims; Oscar Peterson (p); Joe Pass (g); George Mraz (b); Grady Tate (d).* 6/75.

***** Soprano Sax**

Original Jazz Classics OJC 902 *Sims; Ray Bryant (p); George Mraz (b); Grady Tate (d).* 1/76.

****(*) Hawthorne Nights**

Original Jazz Classics OJC 830 *Sims; Oscar Brashear (t); Snooky Young (t, flhn); Frank Rosolino (tb); Bill Hood, Richie Kamuca, Jerome Richardson (reeds); Ross Tompkins (p); Monty Budwig (b); Nick Ceroli (d); Bill Holman (arr).* 9/76.

****** If I'm Lucky**

Original Jazz Classics OJC 683 *Sims; Jimmy Rowles (p); George Mraz (b); Mousie Alexander (d).* 10/77.

*****(*) Warm Tenor**

Pablo 2310-831 *As above.* 9/78.

*****(*) For Lady Day**

Pablo 2310-942 *As above, except Jackie Williams (d) replaces Alexander.* 4/78.

***** Just Friends**

Original Jazz Classics OJC 499 *Sims; Harry 'Sweets' Edison (t); Roger Kellaway (p); John Heard (b); Jimmie Smith (d).* 12/78.

***** The Swinger**

Original Jazz Classics OJC 855 *Sims; Ray Sims (tb, v); Jimmy Rowles (p); John Heard, Michael Moore (b); Shelly Manne, John Clay (d).* 11/79–5/80.

***** Passion Flower**

Original Jazz Classics OJC 939 *Sims; Bobby Bryant, Al Aarons, Oscar Brashear, Earl Gardner (t); J.J Johnson, Britt Woodman, Grover Mitchell, Benny Powell (tb); Frank Wess (as, f); Marshal Royal (as); Plas Johnson, Buddy Collette (ts); Jimmy Rowles (p); John Collins (g); Andy Simpkins, John Heard, Michael Moore (b); Grady Tate, Shelly Manne, John Clay (d).* 8/79–5/80.

****** I Wish I Were Twins**

Original Jazz Classics OJC 976 *Sims; Jimmy Rowles (p); Frank Tate (b); Akira Tana (d).* 7/81.

*****(*) The Innocent Years**

Original Jazz Classics OJC 860 *Sims; Richard Wyands (p); Frank Tate (b); Akira Tana (d).* 3/82.

***** Blues For Two**

Original Jazz Classics OJC 635 *Sims; Joe Pass (g).* 3–6/82.

***** On The Korner**

Pablo 2310-953 *Sims; Frank Colett (p); Monty Budwig (b); Shelly Manne (d).* 3/83.

*****(*) Suddenly It's Spring**

Original Jazz Classics OJC 742-2 *Sims; Jimmy Rowles (p); George Mraz (b); Akira Tana (d).* 5/83.

***** Quietly There**

Original Jazz Classics OJC 787 *Sims; Mike Wofford (p); Chuck Berghofer (b); Nick Ceroli (d); Victor Feldman (perc).* 3/84.

**** The Best Of Zoot Sims**

Pablo 2405-406 *As above Pablo albums.*

When Sims signed to Norman Granz's Pablo operation, he wasn't so much at a crossroads as contentedly strolling down an uneventful path. For a man who could fit effortlessly into any situation he chose – admittedly, he never chose a situation that might cause much trouble – Sims could have spent his final years as a nebulous figure. But his Pablo albums set the seal on his stature, sympathetically produced, thoughtfully programmed and with enough challenge to prod Zoot into his best form. *Gershwin Brothers* is a glorious sparring match with Peterson, rising to an almost overpowering charge through 'I Got Rhythm' via a simmering 'Embraceable You' and a variation on Coltrane's approach to 'Summertime'. It's the ravishing tone which makes the session with Pass so attractive: with drums and bass cleared away, the tenor sound is swooningly beautiful. A pity, though, that Pass sounds so perfunctory throughout. The sessions with Jimmy Rowles at the piano, though, are indispensable examples of Zoot at his best. *If I'm Lucky* is, narrowly, the pick, for its ingenious choice of material – '(I Wonder Where) Our Love Has Gone' counts as one of Sims's most affecting performances – and the uncanny communication between saxophonist and pianist throughout. *Warm Tenor* is only a shade behind, and the recently discovered set of tunes associated with Billie Holiday, *For Lady Day*, is another plum choice, with an amble through 'You Go To My Head' that dispels the happy-sad clouds of Holiday's *œuvre* with a smouldering lyricism. *Suddenly It's Spring* is another that betrays Rowles's affection for unlikely material – 'In The Middle Of A Kiss', 'Emaline', even Woody Guthrie's 'So Long' – and, though the playing seems a shade too relaxed in parts, it's still delightful music. *The Swinger* reunites Zoot with brother Ray and they make a joshing, harmless team: 'Now I Lay Me Down To Dream Of You' is sweetness personified. *I Wish I Were Twins* is at last on CD, and it's another great one: perhaps new rhythm section Frank Tate and Akira Tana push Rowles a little too much, but there is a little masterpiece in their version of 'Georgia'. *The Innocent Years* substitutes Wyands for Rowles, and this is a swinging session: Zoot does an earthy blues on soprano, plays 'Over The Rainbow' as a fast samba and takes 'The Very Thought Of You', which was one of his favourite vehicles for soprano, at his patented easy lope.

Soprano Sax was one of his earliest Pablos but is only recently on CD. Zoot grew to like his second horn and he sounds just like himself on it, a pinchier, tinier Zoot but still a perfect lyricist on 'Baubles, Bangles And Beads' and his favourite 'Bloos For Louise'. *Passion Flower* features him with a big band scored by Benny Carter on nine Ellington tunes. The charts are frankly functional rather than inspiring, but Zoot tended to find his inspirations from within anyway and he seems chipper enough.

The only real disappointment is *Hawthorne Nights*, which finds Zoot a tad perfunctory for once on a generally uninspiring set of Bill Holman charts. *On The Korner* finds him in a San Francisco club, still enjoying himself, with 'Dream Dancing' and the surprisingly urgent soprano rendition of 'Tonight I Shall Sleep' of special interest; Frank Colett plays fine supporting piano. Although only a year away from his death when he made *Quietly There*, a set of Johnny Mandel themes, Sims was still in absolute command. Feldman's percussion adds a little extra fillip to the likes of 'Cinnamon And Clove', although Sims himself sounds undistracted by anything: his winding, tactile improvisation on the melody of 'A Time For Love', to pick a single instance, bespeaks a lifetime's preparation. The *Best Of* is a mysteriously ill-chosen retrospective: better to pick any one of the albums with Rowles if a single disc is all that's required.

***** Elegiac**

Storyville STCD 8238 *Sims; Bucky Pizzarelli (g).* 11/80.

***** 'Live' In Philly**

32 Jazz 2056 *Sims; Ben Aronov (p); Major Holley (b); Mickey Roker (d). n.d. (c. 81).*

***** In A Mellow Tone**

JLR 103.604 2CD *Sims; Rick Bell (ts); Yancey Korosi (p); Dewey Sampson (b); James Martin (d).* 8/81.

Three live dates come out of the shadows of a large discography. *Elegiac* follows the same format as *Blues For Two*, this time with the more muscular style of Pizzarelli in the partnership. Some of the playing is nearly ferocious, such as the whipcrack treatment of 'Limehouse Blues', and it's interesting to hear Sims blow on some of his latter-day favourites in this context. But it has to be docked a point for the very grey sound of what must have been an amateur recording.

Only so-so sound again on the JLR set, where Zoot guested with the house band at e.j.'s in Atlanta. Bell is clearly delighted at the chance to blow alongside and the first disc has them sharing the front line, efficacious on 'All The Things You Are' and 'Lester Leaps In' in particular. Zoot is on his own with the rhythm section for the rest and he sounds in bumptious form. If the sound were better it would be a splendid discovery, but again we must restrict the rating, given the sometimes brutal acoustics.

The session from Philadelphia is a nice discovery from 32 Jazz, in pretty decent sound. A typical Zoot programme – three Ellington tunes, 'That Ole Devil Called Love', a soprano feature – and he and the band play through it with the expected enjoyment, although some of Aronov's solos overdo it a bit.

Jae Sinnett

DRUMS

A radio station director in Norfolk, Virginia, Sinnett is also a post-bop drummer with two discs to his name.

*** House And Sinnett

Positive PMD78020-2 *Sinnett; Steve Wilson (ss, as); Cyrus Chestnut (p); Clarence Seay (b).* 8/93.

*** Listen

Heart Music 20 *Sinnett; John D'Earth (t); Jesse Davis (as); Billy Pierce (ts); Cyrus Chestnut, Allen Farnham (p); Clarence Seay, Kiyoshi Kitagawa (b).* 7/96.

The first album is a light, swinging slice of modern jazz, tailored by the leader to fit this quartet and achieving its modest aim. Sinnett is a bright but never overpowering drummer, and he's content to let Wilson and Chestnut take the major space: the pianist confirms his growing reputation, though Wilson doesn't have a great deal to say. The second splits the music between a surprisingly hard-hitting trio with Farnham and Kitagawa and a drilled, best-behaviour sextet in which the horns seem to be working under orders, crisply though they play. Nicely done, and no reason to withhold any plaudits, although in the end it's likely to be considered another also-ran hard-bop outing.

The Six Winds

GROUP

Founded by Ad Peijnenburg in 1976 as Four Winds, the group later expanded to a sextet of composer-performers, all based in the Netherlands.

*** Man Met Muts

Bvhaast 9004 *Mariëtte Rouppe Van der Voort (sno); Dies Le Duc (ss); Frans Vermeerssen (as); John Tchicai (ts); Ad Peijnenburg (bs); Klaas Hekman (bsx).* 10/89.

*** Anger Dance

Bvhaast 9305 *As above.* 12/92.

***(*) Manestraal

Bvhaast 9706 *As above.* 3/97.

This band seems to qualify as an 'occasional' outfit, with only three records in a decade, but they're one of the most distinctive of the all-sax groups. They work in ensemble terms, exploring particular stretches of saxophone sound within a single piece. 'Fluitketel' and 'Kies Van Tien', both on the first record, suggest a mulling-over of chords and harmonic variations. Each of the saxophonists sticks to only one horn, none displays an extrovert personality as an improviser (not even Tchicai), and the music tends to be solid, thoughtful, and possessing of a dusky, hypnotic quality over the course of a CD. *Man Met Muts* suffers from a drab sound-mix; *Anger Dance* is brighter and displays some lushness as well as depth. But the best of the trio is the most recent, *Manestraal.* The music has moved inexorably towards structure and composition, with solos a seeming irrelevance, or at least important only as counterpoint to the rest of the music. Several of these pieces, especially the quite beautiful 'Atono', outstrip anything on the earlier records. The sound is still less than imposing, the horns placed in a middle-distance, but perhaps it suits the feel of the music.

Lars Sjøsten (born 1941)

PIANO

He came up with the Swedish post-bop of the 1960s onwards and has been quietly recording and playing ever since, though his presence is scarcely known outside his native land.

*** In Confidence

Dragon DRCD 197 *Sjøsten; Jan Kohlin (t); Bertil Strandberg (tb); Dave Castle (as); Krister Andersson (ts); Gunnar Bergsten (bs); Petter Carlsson (frhn); Oystein Baadsvik (tba); Patrik Boman (b); Nils Danell (d).* 11–12/90.

Sjøsten is a deft, economical pianist, conservative as a composer – he might build an idea round a rhythmic oddity or an unusual tonality – but good with groups of any size. He's been recording as a leader since 1971 but this is still his only CD in print. These are pleasing, good-natured compositions, deftly arranged, without hidden depths but not short on imagination. The ten pieces are arranged for trio, quartet (with Bergsten), sextet and a ten-piece band and, while the theme statements by the horns could be tighter, the casual complexion suits the music rather well. Bergsten, Strandberg and Castle are the most inventive soloists, and Sjøsten rounds matters off with a thoughtful trio version of 'You'd Be So Nice To Come Home To'.

Alan Skidmore (born 1942)

TENOR SAXOPHONE

Son of saxophonist Jimmy, he played with big bands and blues groups in the '60s. Formed his own band at the end of the '60s, but has since followed a journeyman route, playing with many leaders; an accomplished stylist with his influences fully assimilated.

***(*) Tribute To 'Trane

Miles Music MMCD 075 *Skidmore; Jason Rebello (p); Dave Green (b); Stephen Keogh (d).* 2/88.

***** East To West**

Miles Music MMCD 081 *Skidmore; Stan Tracey, Steve Melling (p); Mick Hutton, Roy Babbington (b); Clark Tracey, Bryan Spring (d).* 11/89–2/92.

****** After The Rain**

Miles Music MMCD 084 *Skidmore; Colin Towns Mask Symphonic; Radio-Philharmonie Hannover des NDR; individual personnels not listed.* 98.

Like his saxophonist father, Jimmy, who was a stalwart of the British mainstream scene in the 1950s and early '60s, Alan Skidmore is much less well known than he ought to be. In a wilderness of clones, he stands out – admittedly older and therefore wiser – as one of the few who have submitted the Coltrane legacy to thoughtful consideration, rather than taking it as licence for frenzied harmonic activity and emotional streaking. Skidmore is rather poorly represented on record, though he can also be heard on a growing range of reissued British jazz records from the Golden Age of the late '60s and early '70s.

At least one of his own small-label releases featured an interpretation of Coltrane's 'Lonnie's Lament', a theme he returns to on *Tribute To 'Trane*. With typical self-effacement, Skidmore asks that the album, one of a flood marking the twentieth anniversary of the great saxophonist's death, be regarded as a 'thank you' rather than as another god-bothering ritual by a disciple. The choice of material is interesting. 'Naima' and 'Mr P.C.' represent a more predictable closing sequence, but 'Resolution', 'Bessie's Blues', 'Crescent' and 'Dear Lord', together with the outstanding 'Lonnie's Lament' (on which Rebello and Keogh are both superb, incidentally), suggest the depth of Skidmore's understanding of the music. The performances are not in themselves self-consciously *de profundis*, and there are no overpowering histrionics. Well recorded in medium close-up, this takes its place behind McCoy Tyner *et al.*'s *Blues For 'Trane* as the best of the twentieth-anniversary votes of thanks.

East To West represents a solid continuation of the work documented on the previous disc. There are three tracks from a Hong Kong club date of 1989, with Tracey's trio in support, and three more from the Scott club in 1992. Skidmore's tenor oratory is as mighty and full-blooded as before, with even Tracey's own 'Funky Day In Tiger Bay' transformed into a thunderous outpouring of saxophone. The later session brings further gifts to the Coltrane shrine with 'Crescent', 'Wise One' and as thumping a take on 'Mr P.C.' as you'll find outside the master's own work. But docked a notch for the indifferent sound, which isn't much above bootleg quality on the Hong Kong material.

Coltrane is once again the dominant presence on the extraordinary big-band album as well. Three of the pieces are Trane compositions ('After The Rain', 'Naima' and 'Central Park West'), and four more ('Nature Boy', 'Nancy', Fred Lacey's 'Theme For Ernie' and 'In A Sentimental Mood') were recorded by him at one time or another. Any doubts about putting jazz improvisers in strings settings should by now have been thoroughly dispelled. Here the backgrounds are as unobtrusive and subtly shaded as one could wish for, giving the album an intimate, quietly reflective feel rather than syrupy excess. The German orchestra's underpainting on 'Nature Boy' is breathtaking, a brief overture to an unaccompanied statement of Eden Ahbez's haunting melody. Palle Mikkelborg is the conductor and he organizes the sound with his usual deft touch. Engineer Manfred Kietzke has Skidmore well out in front and slightly off-centre, which gives his solos even greater presence.

Though Colin Towns is the arranger of eight out of 13 tracks, his Mask Symphonic performs on only three. The sound here is more compressed, and it might seem leaden were it not for Towns's remarkable touch with points of orchestral colour. Comparisons with Gil Evans are now perfectly valid. The closing 'Central Park West', a tune on which Trane never soloed but which Joe Lovano revived a few years ago, is exquisite. A beautiful, very moving record, not to be dismissed as soft-centred easy listening.

***** The Call**

Provocateur Records PVC 1018 *Skidmore; Colin Towns (ky); Steve Melling (p); Arnie Somogyi (b); Gary Husband (d); Madosini Manqineni (mouth bow); Mandla Lande, Nkululeko Ludonga, Simpawe Matole, Zandisile Mbizela, Dizu Zungula Plaatjies, Mzwandile Qotoyi (perc, v); Dizu Kudu Horn Band.* 4 & 5/99.

Back in the days of SOS, his saxophone trio with John Surman and Mike Osborne, Skidmore liked nothing more than getting in behind the drumkit for a couple of numbers. Though his playing career has been almost entirely focused on the saxophone, Skid professes to be a drummer at heart and *The Call* sees him reunited with South African group, Amampondo, whom he first met on a trip to the Cape in 1994.

Five years later, Colin Towns of Provocateur Records organized a return trip and a recording session. Skidmore fits into the distinctive triplet rhythm of the African group with consummate ease. Years of standing on bandstands with the late Dudu Pukwana presumably alerted him to the possibilities of this kind of music and, though the dedication of the record is once again to John Coltrane, it is Dudu's spirit which shines through at every turn. Trane's ballad playing informs 'Bridges Of Sand', a delicate duo with Towns, and the strangely moving 'Migration', which also features Arnie Somogyi's sonorous bass; but it is the numbers with Amampondo and on 'Rwakanembe' the Dizu Kudu Horn Band which catch the attention. Kudu horn is one of your more recherché jazz instrumental categories – but what an infectious sound, and what a delightful album.

Steve Slagle

ALTO AND SOPRANO SAXOPHONES

Born in Los Angeles, Slagle's family moved east in the '60s and he studied at Berklee from 1970. Early work included lead alto with Lionel Hampton, Woody Herman (on tenor), the Jack McDuff group and the Carla Bley Band.

***** The Steve Slagle Quartet**

Steeplechase SCCD 31323 *Slagle; Tim Hagans (t); Scott Colley (b); Jeff Hirshfield (d).* 11/92.

*****(*) Spread The Word**

Steeplechase SCCD 31354 *As above.* 4/94.

*****(*) Reincarnation**

Steeplechase SCCD 31367 *Slagle; Kenny Drew Jr (p); Cameron Brown (b); Jeff Hirshfield (d).* 10/94.

Slagle has hitherto been best known by association – as a sideman with Carla Bley and in the Mingus Big Band, for instance – but his several albums as a leader deserve a hearing. *Quartet* features some difficult writing by the leader: 'Leadbelly Sez' is a tricky eight-bar blues, and 'Mondo' might suggest a leaning towards the original Ornette Coleman quartet. Colley and Hirshfield work very capably behind the horns, and Hagans plays thoughtfully. The quartet returns for *Spread The Word*, and this time they manage to suggest an eloquent kind of free playing that actually owes little to Coleman's quartet. The improvising has an air of long-breathed virtuosity about it, the many-noted solos rooted in bebop but coloured by the freedoms of what came after. If the leader's convolutions suggest a struggle with form, Hagans's calm and lucid playing reconciles structure with freedom, and the contrast between the two styles makes the music compelling and rounded at the same time.

Slagle's own work suggests a link between hard-bop stylists and the free players of a generation later, which some of his own sleeve-notes on *Reincarnation* also allude to. The opening track here is a long, sinewy extemporization on Charles Mingus's 'Reincarnation Of A Lovebird', and Slagle recalls how it struck him as a link between Parker and Dolphy. If you add Jackie McLean to the mixture, it could almost come up as Slagle himself, and this twisting solo is certainly one of the best things he's done on record. There are fine ballads in 'Soultrane' and 'Bess, You Is My Woman Now' and, though one misses some of the interaction which Hagans created on the other discs, Slagle takes the weight on his own shoulders very convincingly. In the circumstances, Drew's excellent work is something of a bonus.

***** Our Sound!**

Double-Time DTRCD-107 *Slagle; Dave Stryker (g); Bill Moring (b); Tony Reedus (d). 4/95.*

*****(*) Alto Blue**

Steeplechase SCCD 31416 *Slagle; Ryan Kisor (t); Scott Colley (b); Gene Jackson (d). 4/97.*

The Double-Time session, taken down more or less on the hoof, is a swinging, genuine date with plenty to listen to – Stryker is a good partner, offering harmonic leads without tying the leader down, and Reedus stokes the rhythms with a good deal of fire. 'Theme For Ernie' is a persuasive rendering of the dedication to Ernie Henry. But a couple of choices seem less effective: Mingus's 'Haitian Fight Song' doesn't really convince as a quartet tune and 'Little Rootie Tootie' seems arbitrarily done. Keeper: the duet on 'Lush Life'.

Alto Blue is more like it, and arguably Slagle's best to date. The music is all blues, either in form or feeling, and with Kisor matching or even outplaying the leader on some pieces the content is way up. Slagle's three originals work beautifully and his flute feature on 'Detour Ahead' is clean as a whistle. Colley and Jackson vary the rhythms and sponsor the horns without getting in their way, and the studio sound catches them all to a 't'.

Carol Sloane

VOCAL

American vocalist who made some Columbia albums in the early 1960s, re-emerging in the '80s as a more jazz-directed singer, recording for independent labels.

***** Love You Madly**

Contemporary 14049-2 *Sloane; Art Farmer (flhn); Clifford Jordan (ts); Kenny Barron, Richard Rodney Bennett (p); Kenny Burrell (g); Rufus Reid, Akira Tana (d). 10/88.*

***** The Real Thing**

Contemporary 14060-2 *Sloane; Phil Woods (as); Mike Rienzi (p); Rufus Reid (b); Grady Tate (d, v). 5/90.*

***** Heart's Desire**

Concord CCD 4503 *Sloane; Stefan Scaggiari (p); John Lockwood (b); Colin Bailey (d). 9/91.*

*****(*) Sweet And Slow**

Concord CCD 4564 *As above, except add Frank Wess (ts, f). 4/93.*

***** When I Look In Your Eyes**

Concord CCD 4619 *Sloane; Bill Charlap (p); Howard Alden (g); Steve Gilmore (b); Ron Vincent (d). 6/94.*

Carol Sloane's quiet, considered style of singing isn't so much conversational as conspiratorial. She takes as many liberties with a melody as many a more flamboyant singer and she has the ability to swing in her easeful way; but since her voice often resembles a sung whisper, one could mistake her delicacy for reserve. She actually rises to the challenge of the material with consistent aplomb. These are not especially varied albums and it's hard to pick out a singular gem, but consistency is her long suit. Like many such singers, she has been around long enough to be a veteran but has built up a significant catalogue in the CD era only by dint of sympathetic labels such as Concord. The two Contemporary albums, though, are just as strong. *Love You Madly* has the support of the Art Farmer group which made some superb sets for Contemporary and, while they stay in the background, there are some lovely moments – especially when Burrell does a couple of softly-softly duets with Sloane. Bennett does a turn only on 'Norwegian Wood', which seems to have strayed in from another record altogether. *The Real Thing* is handsomely arranged by Rienzi and has Woods turning in five typically flawless solos in support; Tate sings a duet on 'Makin' Whoopee'.

The three Concords are similarly fine. Some of the material on *Heart's Desire* is a bit hit-and-miss, but the trio's exemplary support adds a hushed eloquence to the occasion, and Sloane's introspective qualities carry the record through. *Sweet And Slow* repeats the trick with Wess for extra company, and this might be the best place to hear her. *When I Look In Your Eyes* is shrewdly shaped around ballads, swingers, obvious tunes and unfamiliar ones – Ellington's 'Tulip Or Turnip' is a bit of a surprise – but the greater emphasis on pace is a shade less productive.

***** The Songs Carmen Sang**

Concord CCD 4663 *Sloane; Phil Woods (as, cl); Bill Charlap (p); Michael Moore (b); Ron Vincent (d). 4/95.*

***** The Songs Sinatra Sang**

Concord CCD 4725 *Sloane; Byron Stripling, Greg Gisbert (t); Steve Turre (tb); Bill Easley (ss, as, ts); Scott Robinson (bs, bcl, bsx); Frank Wess (ts, f); Bill Charlap (p); Ben Brown, Sean Smith (b); Dennis Mackrel, Ron Vincent (d).* 3/96.

***** The Songs Ella & Louis Sang**

Concord CCD 4787 *Sloane; Clark Terry (t, flhn, v); Bill Charlap (p); Marcus McLaurine (b); Dennis Mackrel (d).* 5/97.

Sloane's very own songbook series. These are records to admire, gracefully achieved, although they're never much more than the sum of their parts. The *Carmen* collection is strong on the ballads, especially McRae's two great 'Moon' songs, 'If The Moon Turns Green' and 'It's Like Reaching For The Moon'. *Sinatra* is a little burdened by its horn charts which sound a bit tacked on: Sloane does best by a very long and slow but successful 'One For My Baby' and the gentle coda of 'Young At Heart'. She obviously likes Charlap, and he does good service on both discs. *Ella & Louis* is a tailor-made opportunity for Terry to do his thing, with horn and with voice, and they clearly had fun on chestnuts like 'I Won't Dance' and 'Blueberry Hill' – although both principals, without being uncharitable, don't have quite the chops that they once did.

Hal Smith (born 1953)

DRUMS

A pro since the late '70s, Smith is from Indiana but is associated with many West Coast revivalist groups and New Orleans bands of today, leading the Frisco Syncopators and the Down Home Jazz Band.

***** Milneburg Joys**

GHB BCD-277 *Smith; Chris Tyle (c); David Sager (tb); Jacques Gauthe (cl, ss); Steve Pistorius (p); Amy Sharpe (bj); Bernie Attridge (b).* 6/89.

Smith and Tyle are co-leaders of the Frisco Syncopators, one of the several fine American trad groups currently revisiting the classic repertoire with unusual aplomb. Though they take their cue from Bob Scobey's original Frisco Jazz Band, the group is actually New Orleans-based, and their approach seasons chestnuts such as 'Skid-Dat-De-Dat' and 'Panama' with enough sharpness to lend a fresh point of view. The rhythm of the group attains a nice blend of sleekness and ragged drive, and in the clean-toned Tyle and the adept Pistorius they have two excellent soloists. The studio sound eschews the accustomed murk of trad recordings in favour of a crisp and punchy attack that gives the record extra zip, although most of the vocals are the usual acquired taste in this setting.

Harrison Smith

TENOR SAXOPHONE, SOPRANO SAXOPHONE, BASS CLARINET

British bop-to-free saxophonist with a wide CV.

***** Outside Inside**

Slam CD 231 *Smith; Liam Noble (p); Jeremy Brown (b); Winston Clifford (d).* 3/98.

Smith belongs to a generation of British players for whom rapid transition between free music and a settled groove presents no difficulty. Sparingly recorded for a musician of his experience, he plays with maturity and presence on this session as leader. Opening with bass clarinet on 'Inside Outside' was a bold stroke, but his long unfolding statement holds the attention throughout. He switches to soprano for 'Adventures With DP', a more tuneful and expressive horn for Smith than the tenor, on which he always sounds a little forced.

A freer conception informs the two-part 'Cliffhanger/For U', and Smith revels in the space to develop a raw-textured but sensitive solo that instantly identifies itself as British and of a certain vintage. The supporting band is always on hand with a complementary idea. Noble has a thoughtful touch and Clifford is unfailingly musical.

Jabbo Smith (1908–90)

TRUMPET, VOCAL

Born Cladys Smith in Pembroke, Georgia, Smith was a dashing figure in late-'20s Chicago and was signed by Brunswick as a rival to Louis Armstrong. His career was damaged by drink and a poor attendance record at his own gigs, and by 1940 he was barely visible, subsequently taking jobs outside music. Came back in the '70s and was on Broadway in New York in the '80s, reformed and intact.

****** Jabbo Smith 1929–1938**

Classics 669 *Smith; Omer Simeon, Willard Brown (cl, as); Leslie Johnakins, Ben Smith (as); Sam Simmons (ts); Millard Robins (bsx); Cassino Simpson, Kenneth Anderson, Alex Hill, William Barbee, James Reynolds (p); Ikey Robinson (bj); Connie Wainwright (g); Hayes Alvis, Lawson Buford (tba); Elmer James (b); Alfred Taylor (d).* 1/29–2/38.

****** Ace Of Rhythm**

Topaz TPZ 1072 *Similar to above, except add Louis Metcalf (t), Joe Nanton (tb), Otto Hardwick (ss, as, bs), Garvin Bushell (as, bsn), Harry Carney (cl, bs), Rudy Jackson (cl, ts), James P Johnson, Duke Ellington (p), Fats Waller (org), Wellman Braud (b), Sonny Greer, Walter Bishop (d).* 11/27–2/38.

Until his rediscovery in the 1960s, Smith was legendary as Armstrong's most significant rival in the 1920s, a reputation built almost entirely on the records reissued on these discs. He had already made a name for himself with Charlie Johnson's orchestra, but it was the 20 sides he cut with his Rhythm Aces that have endured as Smith's contribution to jazz. The Classics CD includes all of them, together with four tracks from a single 1938 session by Smith's then-eight-strong group. Smith's style is like a thinner, wilder variation on Armstrong's. He takes even more risks in his solos – or, at least, makes it seem that way, since he's less assured at pulling them off than Louis was. Some passages he seems to play entirely in his highest register; others are composed of handfuls of notes, phrased in such a scattershot way that he seems to have snatched them out of the air. If it makes the music something of a mess, it's a consistently exciting one. Organized round Smith's own stop-time solos and dialogue with the rhythm, with the occasional vocal – a quizzical mix of Armstrong and Don Redman – thrown in too, the records seem like a conscious attempt at duplicating the Hot Five sessions, although in the event they sold poorly. Simeon is curiously reticent, much as Dodds was on the Hot Fives, and alto players Brown and James do no more than behave themselves. The livewire foil is, instead, the extraordinary Robinson, whose tireless strumming and rare, knockout solo (as on 'Michigander Blues') keep everything simmering. Shrill and half focused, these are still lively and brilliant reminders of a poorly documented talent (who reappeared in his seventies as a festival and stage performer).

The Topaz CD isn't a clear-cut alternative, since it substitutes eight tracks where Smith was a sideman for three of the 1938 cuts and five of the lesser Rhythm Aces pieces. There are two appearances with Ellington (odd to hear Smith doing the Miley part on 'Black And Tan Fantasy') and two rollicking pieces with an Ikey Robinson group. Specialists may prefer to have the Rhythm Aces sides complete, but measure for measure *Ace Of Rhythm* offers a better portrait of Jabbo in his prime.

Jeffrey Smith

VOCALS

Cinnamon-voiced and technically astute, Smith is somewhat reminiscent of a cross between Johnny Hartman and Al Hibbler. He has dabbled in pop material but comes across most strongly on swing standards, where the harmonic changes are more familiar.

***** A Little Sweeter**

Verve 537790-2 *Smith; Terell Stafford (t, flhn); Justin Robertson (as); Kenny Barron (p); Ray Drummond (b); Ben Riley (d).* 9/96.

****(*) Down Here Below**

Verve 547273-2 *Smith; Kamal Abdul Alim (t); Talib Kibwe (as, f); Justin Robinson (as); Charles Davis (ts); Rodney Kendrick (p, org); James Hurt, James Weidman (p, syn); John Peters (org, syn); Regina Carter (vn); Curtis Lundy (b); Dion Parson (d); Guilherme Franco (perc); Dianne Reeves (v); Assitan Mama Keita (v, perc).* 97.

Like other recent Verve signings before him, Smith seems to have been groomed for crossover appeal, with a toehold in a light-jazz version of world music. Our strong preference (not surprisingly, given the line-up) is for the earlier record. Opening with 'Eleanor Rigby' and then 'Lush Life' was a canny stroke, for Jeffrey's slight mournfulness wears off as the album progresses and it ends much more up-beat than it begins. Barron is masterly throughout, clearly enjoying his recent time in the major-label sun. His accompaniment on 'Love For Sale' and 'Polka Dots And Monbeams' is exactly what a singer of this description cries out for.

The follow-up record is rather densely produced but is infectious enough in its way. Rodney Kendrick arranged the songs, and his hand is strongly evident throughout. Smith seems to have narrowed the range of his voice, sticking to an amiable high baritone. 'Afro Blue' and 'Love On A Two-Way Street' are admirable and the larger band is full of surprises and devices.

Jimmy Smith (born 1925)

ORGAN

Studied piano and bass in Philadelphia, but he switched to organ in the early '50s and arrived in New York with a trio in 1956. Many albums for Blue Note, 1957–61, and Verve, 1962–73. Opened his own club in 1975 and quit touring, but returned to it in the '80s and is still performing. His style – bebop lines rooted in the blues, punchily delivered – set the tone for all the organists who came after him, and helped create the soul-jazz genre.

*****(*) A New Sound ... A New Star ... Jimmy Smith At The Organ Vols 1–3**

Blue Note 57191-2 2CD *Smith; Thornel Schwartz (g); Bay Perry, Donald Bailey (d).* 2–6/56.

****** Groovin' At Smalls' Paradise**

Blue Note 99777-2 2CD *Smith; Eddie McFadden (g); Donald Bailey (d).* 11/57.

***** Home Cookin'**

Blue Note 53360-2 *Smith; Percy France (ts); Kenny Burrell (g); Donald Bailey (d).* 7/58–6/59.

***** Standards**

Blue Note 21282-2 *Smith; Kenny Burrell (g); Donald Bailey (d).* 8/57–5/59.

****(*) Crazy Baby**

Blue Note 84030-2 *Smith; Quentin Warren (g); Donald Bailey (d).* 3/60.

*****(*) Open House / Plain Talk**

Blue Note 84269-2 *Smith; Blue Mitchell (t); Jackie McLean (as); Ike Quebec (ts); Quentin Warren (g); Donald Bailey (d).* 3/60.

***** Back At The Chicken Shack**

Blue Note 46402-2 *As above.* 4/60.

****(*) Midnight Special**

Blue Note 84078-2 *Smith; Stanley Turrentine (ts); Kenny Burrell (g); Donald Bailey (d).* 4/60.

***** I'm Movin' On**

Blue Note 32750-2 *Smith; Grant Green (g); Donald Bailey (d).* 1/63.

***** Prayer Meetin'**

Blue Note 84164-2 *Smith; Stanley Turrentine (ts); Quentin Warren (g); Sam Jones (b); Donald Bailey (d).* 6/60–2/63.

Jimmy Smith got going rather late as a jazz organist. Astonishingly enough, he allegedly didn't even touch the instrument until he was 28, but he quickly established and personified a jazz vocabulary for the organ: tireless walking bass in the pedals, thick chords with the left hand, quick-fire melodic lines with the right. It was a formula almost from the start, and Smith has never strayed from it, but he so completely mastered the approach that he is inimitable. At his best he creates a peerless excitement, which is seldom sustained across an entire album but which makes every record he's on something to be reckoned with.

Smith made a great stack of albums for Blue Note. As with all the long-serving artists on the label, their availability has been frustratingly inconsistent. This seems to be what's around at the moment. His first three albums have been collected on the twofer, *A New Sound ...*, and welcome it is since it catches much of the initial raw excitement that Smith was after. Pet licks and his familar great flourishes, delighting in the noise-making capacity of the organ, still sound at their most fresh and swinging here. But better yet is *Groovin' At Smalls' Paradise*, Smith in his element in a club setting and, while McFadden also gets plenty of space (and doesn't do badly, in his modest way), the master's big, sprawling solos are definitive: 'After Hours' is perhaps the classic Smith blues performance, although the entire record works to a kind of bluesy slow burn. The original albums have been turned into a double-CD and, in the Rudy Van Gelder Edition remastering, the years fall away. This is the Smith album to get.

It was disappointing, though, to hear how quickly Smith's albums became formulaic. *Home Cookin'* has the little-known Percy France on tenor, but more significant is the presence of Burrell, the organist's favourite partner. A solid one, with five bonus tracks on the CD edition. *Crazy Baby* is discouragingly rational. *Back At The Chicken Shack* has Turrentine confronting Smith to periodically powerful effect – the title blues in particular blows very warmly – but, for all its 'classic' status, this is an album we've never really been impressed by. *Midnight Special* was recorded at the same session and is ... more of the same. *I'm Movin' On* is notable mainly for the sole recorded appearance of Smith with guitarist Grant Green – though the programme never quite gets off the ground and what should have been the big steamer, 'Back Talk', resolves itself into a series of clichés.

Smith rarely recorded with more than one horn in attendance, and the front line on *Open House/Plain Talk* marked a welcome change of pace. Regulation hard bop, perhaps, but plenty of smoke and cinders, and just as an alternative to the usual Smith programme this is one to hear. *Prayer Meetin'* is more secular blues than sanctified gospel, but either way Turrentine gets in a righteous blow. Two extra tracks from an abandoned 1960 session fill out the CD.

Standards is a new discovery, seven cuts from a previously unheard 1959 date plus five from earlier sessions, all with Burrell and Bailey. With the tempos mostly idling and the emphasis on ballads, this is almost as much Burrell's album as it is Smith's, and it underlines how fine a partner for the organist the guitarist has always been: economical, bluesy, adroit. A sleeper but a good one.

****** Bashin'**

Verve 539061-2 *Smith; Joe Newman, Ernie Royal, Doc Severinsen, Joe Wilder (t); Jimmy Cleveland, Urbie Green, Britt Woodman (tb); Tom Mitchell (btb); Jerry Dodgion, Phil Woods (as); Bob Ashton, Babe Clark (ts); George Barrow (bs); Barry Galbraith, Quentin Warren (g); George Duvivier (b); Donald Bailey, Ed Shaughnessy (d).* 3/62.

***** Any Number Can Win**

Verve 557447-2 *Smith; Jimmy Maxwell, Joe Newman, James Sedlar, Charlie Shavers, Snooky Young (t); Jimmy Cleveland, Paul Faulise, Melba Liston, Kai Winding (tb); Jerry Dodgion, Marvin Halladay, Budd Johnson, Seldon Powell, Jerome Richardson, Phil Woods (reeds); Kenny Burrell, Vince Gambella, Billy Mure (g); Bob Bushnell, Art Davis, George Duvivier, Milt Hinton (b); Bobby Donaldson, Ed Shaughnessy (d); Doug Allen, George Devens, Art Marotti (perc).* 7/63.

***** The Cat**

Verve 810046-2 *Smith; Ernie Royal, Bernie Glow, Jimmy Maxwell, Marky Markowitz, Snooky Young, Thad Jones (t); Bill Byers, Jimmy Cleveland, Urbie Green (tb); Ray Alonge, Jimmy Buffington, Earl Chapin, Bill Correa (frhn); Tony Studd (btb); Kenny Burrell (g); George Duvivier (b); Don Butterfield (tba); Grady Tate (d); Phil Kraus (perc).* 4/64.

***** Got My Mojo Workin' / Hoochie Coochie Man**

Verve 533828-2 *Smith; Joe Newman, Ernie Royal, Richard Williams, Snooky Young (t); Quentin Jackson, Melba Liston, Tom McIntosh, Britt Woodman (tb); Donald Corrado, Willie Ruff (frhn); Jack Agee, Romeo Penque, Phil Woods, Jerome Richardson, Jerry Dodgion, Bob Ashton (reeds); Buddy Lucas (hca); Kenny Burrell, Billy Butler, Barry Galbraith, Bill Suyker (g); Don Butterfield (tba); George Duvivier, Bob Cranshaw, Ron Carter, Ben Tucker, Richard Davis (b); Grady Tate (d); Bobby Rosengarden (perc).* 12/65–2/66.

****(*) Peter And The Wolf**

Verve 547264-2 *Smith; Joe Newman, Ernie Royal, Snooky Young, Richard Williams (t); Quentin Jackson, Britt Woodman, Tom McIntosh (tb); Dick Hixson, Tony Studd (btb); Jimmy Buffington, Willie Ruff (frhn); Bob Ashton, Danny Bank, Jerry Dodgion, Jerome Richardson, Stan Webb (reeds); Billy Butler, Barry Galbraith (g); Richard Davis (b); Harry Breuer, Bobby Rosengarden, Grady Tate (d); Oliver Nelson (cond).* 5/66.

Smith might have felt, after 20 albums or so, that he'd done all he could do at Blue Note. But one thing he hadn't done was act as a soloist within a big band. Verve's first step with him was to set up just such a situation, and with Oliver Nelson's sinister chart for 'Walk On The Wild Side' Smith immediately struck into exciting new terrain. It's actually only one of four witty and successful charts on the *Bashin'* album. Just as good is the wryly engaging lope through 'Ol' Man River', for instance, which gives Smith's sardonic humour full rein. The rest of the album is more ordinary small-group workouts, and it's a pity that Nelson, clearly in top form, couldn't have scored the whole thing. In its Master Edition form, this is an essential Smith record.

Somehow, the feel and freshness of this set was never recaptured at Verve. *The Cat* pits him against Lalo Schifrin charts, which are interesting but never as good; and the pop-to-blues material which makes up the two albums, *Got My Mojo Workin'* and *Hoochie Coochie Man*, is more notable for Smith's grunted approximations of the lyrics than the sometimes cheesy arrangements. Nelson didn't click with it this time. Nor did he fare especially well with the preposterous idea of re-creating Prokofiev's *Peter And The Wolf*, one of Creed Taylor's inspirations. At least it only runs for some 33 minutes.

The odd one out here is *Any Number Can Win*. The charts this time were by Billy Byers and Claus Ogerman, and they did a decent job: 'The Ape Woman'(!) is genuinely menacing and 'Georgia On My Mind' played with much feeling, though the title-track is a pinball-arcade jingle.

(*) **Christmas Cookin'

Verve 513711-2 *Smith; Quentin Warren, Kenny Burrell, Wes Montgomery (g); Bill Hart, Grady Tate (d); orchestra directed by Bill Byers.* 6/64–9/66.

***(*) **The Dynamic Duo**

Verve 521445-2 *Smith; Wes Montgomery (g); Grady Tate (d); Ray Barretto (perc); Oliver Nelson orchestra.* 9/66.

*** **Further Adventures Of Jimmy And Wes**

Verve 519802-2 *As above.* 9/66.

***(*) **Walk On The Wild Side: The Best Of The Verve Years**

Verve 527950-2 2CD *As above discs, plus Steve Williams (hca), George Benson, Arthur Adams, Quentin Warren, Eric Gale, Thornel Schwartz, Vince Gambella (g), Wilton Felder, Ron Carter, Bob Bushnell (b), Buck Clarke (perc), Paul Humphrey, Billy Hart, Bernard Purdie, Mel Lewis (d), orchestras directed by Oliver Nelson, Johnny Pate and Thad Jones, strings.* 3/62–2/73.

The Christmas album is one of the best in a hapless genre: great cover-art, and the music isn't too hopeless. Smith's meeting with Montgomery isn't so much a battle of the giants as a genial bit of backslapping. The sessions produced enough for two albums and although some of the material is a bit thin – 'Baby It's Cold Outside' and 'King Of The Road' – the sound of the group, Montgomery's funky lyricism matched with Smith's extravagant blues, is a delight and, with Oliver Nelson charts abetting a few tracks, they rekindle some of the excitement of the early Smith Verve dates.

Verve's two-disc best-of is a very useful sweep through what is a very mixed catalogue and, as far as this period is concerned, this should satisfy all but the most obsessive Smith devotee. Aside from obvious choices like the title-tune, the compilers choose a smart mix of small groups and big bands. One or two nuggets, such as an alternative take of 'OGD' from the date with Montgomery, will tempt collectors and there are a few rescued obscurities: two tracks from the orchestral collaboration with Thad Jones, *Portuguese Soul*; a live blues from 1972, 'Sagg Shootin' His Arrow', with a band including Arthur Adams and Wilton Felder; the title-track off Johnny Pate's set of charts, *Groove Drops*; and 'The Boss' with George Benson and Donald Bailey. Good stuff, and a slightly superior choice to the *Verve Jazz Masters 29* compilation from the same source (Verve 521855-2).

*** **Live At Salle Pleyel 1965**

RTE 710379-380 2CD *Smith; Quentin Warren (g); Billy Hart (d).* 65.

With the many live sets for Blue Note mostly out of print, Smith acolytes will welcome this concert, recorded by French radio, which features nearly two hours of the man's stage show of the period. Loud, noisy and ineffably vigorous, this is how Smith will probably be best remembered and, though one disc might be enough for most tastes, it's useful to have a complete show in one package.

***(*) **All The Way Live**

Milestone 9251-2 *Smith; Eddie Harris (ts); Kenny Dixon (d).* 8/81.

An off-the-cuff meeting between Smith and Harris at San Francisco's Keystone Korner produced some delightful music. They stuck to the blues and some standards, and Harris couldn't resist turning on his swaggering circular lines and lexicon of bebop licks. They suit Smith just fine – although, since he plays as imperturbably as ever, one wonders whether he'd change his style even if the ghost of Buddy Petit got up on stage to jam.

*** **Prime Time**

Milestone M 9176 *Smith; Curtis Peagler (as, ts); Herman Riley, Rickey Woodard (ts); Phil Upchurch, Terry Evans (g); Andy Simpkins (b); Michael Baker, Frank Wilson (d); Barbara Morrison (v).* 8/89.

*** **Fourmost**

Milestone MCD 9184-2 *Smith; Stanley Turrentine (ts); Kenny Burrell (g); Grady Tate (d, v).* 11/90.

(*) **Sum Serious Blues

Milestone MCD-9207-2 *Smith; Oscar Brashear (t); George Bohannon (tb); Maurice Spears (btb); Buddy Collette (as); Herman Riley (ts); Ernie Fields (bs); Mick Martin (hca); Phil Upchurch (g); Andy Simpkins (b); Michael Baker (d); Marlena Shaw, Bernard Ighner (v).* 1/93.

Smith has adapted rather cautiously to changing times. He still sticks to straight-ahead Hammond, but he or his producers vary the other ground rules, with mixed results. *Prime Time* and *Fourmost* are simple blowing records with muscular solos by the horns on the former and a rather more stately contribution from Turrentine on the latter. *Sum Serious Blues* is produced by Johnny Pate as a throwback to some of Smith's Verve sessions of the 1960s – some blues, a new version of 'The Sermon', a couple of vocals from Shaw and Ighner. Probably no more systematized than any of the older records, but it doesn't sound as spontaneous, either.

*** **Damn!**

Verve 527631-2 *Smith; Roy Hargrove, Nicholas Payton (t); Abraham Burton (as); Tim Warfield, Mark Turner, Ron Blake (ts); Mark Whitfield (g); Christian McBride (b); Bernard Purdie, Art Taylor (d).* 1/95.

*** **Angel Eyes**

Verve 527632-2 *As above, except add Gregory Hutchinson (d); omit Burton, Warfield, Turner, Blake, Purdie, Taylor.* 1/95.

Having gone back to Blue Note, Smith then returned to Verve with *Damn!*, an enjoyable if finally somewhat programmed session in which the old man spars alongside rather than with a bulging personnel of young Turks. The chosen themes blend bebop and funk, but it's a little stiff in the joints. *Angel Eyes* is a re-run with the dials set on 'ballad'. Thoughtfully programmed, with the instrumentation carefully varied between solos, duos, trios and one performance by the whole sextet, this is a genuine piece of work that has much appeal, if finally succumbing a little to the same conceptual fatigue that besets the other record: Smith's best music has always had more spit in it than this can muster.

Johnny 'Hammond' Smith (1933–1997)

ORGAN

Began on piano but switched to Hammond organ in the '50s and was one of the school of Chicago organ-combo leaders, popular in the '60s, quiet in the '70s, popular again in the '80s and '90s.

****(*) That Good Feelin' / Talk That Talk**

BGP 0612 *Smith; Oliver Nelson (ts); Thornel Schwartz (g); George Tucker (b); Arthur Taylor, Leo Stevens (d); Ray Barretto (perc).* 11/59–4/60.

****(*) That Good Feelin'**

Prestige 24164 *Smith; Thornel Schwartz (g); George Tucker (b); Leo Stevens (d).* 9–11/59.

****(*) Talk That Talk**

Prestige 24151 *Smith; Oliver Nelson (ts); Lem Winchester (vib); Eddie McFadden (g); George Tucker, Wendell Marshall (b); Art Taylor, Bill Erskine (d); Ray Barretto (perc).* 4–10/60.

***** Black Coffee**

Milestone 47072 *Smith; Sonny Williams (t); Seldon Powell, Houston Person (ts); Eddie McFadden (g); Leo Stevens (d).* 11/62–63.

****(*) Soul Flowers**

Prestige 24235 *Smith; Earl Edwards, Houston Person (ts); Wally Richardson (g); Jimmy Lewis (b); John Harris (d); Richard Landrum (perc).* 9/67–1/68.

**** Legends Of Acid Jazz**

Prestige 24177 *Smith; Virgil Jones (t); Rusty Bryant (as, ts); Wally Richardson (g); Bob Bushnell, Jimmy Lewis (b); Bernard Purdie (d).* 5–12/69.

Smith (who actually changed his name to Johnny Hammond at one point) has made dozens of albums, yet he is one of the least followed of the organists who came in the wake of Jimmy Smith. These reissues mostly couple up his various albums for Prestige to convenient if hardly compelling effect. For the record: *Black Coffee* puts that original alongside *Mr Wonderful*; *Talk That Talk* is next to *Gettin' The Message*; *That Good Feelin'* is that album plus his debut, *All Soul*; *Legends Of Acid Jazz* doubles up *Soul Talk* and *Black Feeling*; and *Soul Flowers* couples that one with *Dirty Grape*. The (British) BGP set puts together the two albums of its title. All good-value packages, but Smith is strictly second-division in the Hammond league. To be fair, Prestige didn't give him much of a chance at making any kind of classic. The material is all blues or obvious standards, the sidemen are scarcely a scintillating lot (Nelson hardly bothers to stick the horn in his mouth on the three tracks he plays on) and Smith himself is a decent but undemonstrative player on an instrument where one has to be indecent and extremely demonstrative. The soulful clichés of the 1969 sessions are no more and no less discouraging than the earlier ones, really, and our preference is for the *Black Coffee* set, which has two good saxophone players and some of the best material.

Keith Smith (born 1940)

TRUMPET, VOCAL

London-born, Smith spent time in New Orleans, California and New York, in traditional and mainstream company, before returning to Britain. His Hefty Jazz group was the backbone of many jazz-package shows which he ran in the 1980s and '90s.

****(*) Keith Smith And His Climax Jazz Band**

GHB BCD-27 *Smith; Mike Sherbourne (tb); Frank Brooker (cl, ts); Jon Marks (p); Brian Turnock (b); Barry Martyn (d).* 65.

****(*) Mr Hefty Jazz**

Lake LACD 67 *Smith; Jimmy Archey, Hugh Watts (tb); George Lewis (cl); John Handy (as); Alton Purnell, Lars Edegran (p); George Guesnon, Ron Simpson (bj); Pops Foster, Alcide Slow Drag Pavageau (b); Freddy Moore (d, v); Cie Frazier (d).* 4/65–9/66.

****(*) Keith Smith & Jimmy Archey**

GHB BCD-217 *Smith; Jimmy Archey (tb); Dranell Howard (cl); Captain John Handy (as); Lars Edegran, Alton Purnell (p); Ron Simpson (bj); Pops Foster (b); Freddy Moore (d, v); Cie Frazier (d).* 3–9/66.

***** Swing Is Here Again**

Lake LACD 80 *Smith; Vic Dickenson, Bob Havens, Tom Artin, Johnny Mortimer, Russell Moore (tb); Peanuts Hucko, Johnny Mince (cl); Bruce Turner (as, cl); Benny Waters, Al Gay (ts); Barney Bates, Stan Greig, Dick Cary, Nat Pierce, Johnny Guarnieri (p); Jim Douglas (g); Peter Ind, Major Holley, Arvell Shaw, Harvey Weston (b); Barrett Deems, John Cox, Bobby Worth, Oliver Jackson (d).* 11/78–10/83.

Unrepresented on CD until recently, Smith is a British trad-to-swing trumpeter who has often found himself in exalted company, as a look at the personnels of the two Lake compilations will attest. He has had a rather picaresque career (Lake's sleeve-notes tell how he was hustled out of a successsful fish-and-chip-shop operation in New Orleans by the local Mafia) and the records are a somewhat motley gathering of tracks. GHB's session by his Climax Jazz Band is very average British trad of the day, enlivened somewhat by guest drummer Martyn, who insists on playing New Orleans style even on inappropriate pieces like 'West End Blues'. Some boisterous playing is sabotaged by a complete lack of finesse. Smith's trumpet-style – originally an Anglophile version of Henry Allen, but also soaked in Armstrong and others – is decent enough, but the interest on the other discs is sparked by his companions. *Mr Hefty Jazz* features three sessions in which Smith was the unlikely kibitzer on dates with Lewis, Archey, Handy and others – in Canada, New Orleans and an attic in Plaistow! Quite good fun, but the recording quality (especially on the five tracks recorded at San Jacinto Hall in New Orleans) is sometimes dreadful. There's more from the Canadian session on *Keith Smith & Jimmy Archey*, along with five titles cut with a different back line in London the same year. Better sound overall and quite lusty playing, but it doesn't amount to much for a general listener. *Swing Is Here Again* is a better bet, pulling together 16 tracks from six different dates, and the pearls are the five pieces with the irresistible Dickenson from a session in Nice. At least these are all in good sound, although the remainder of the CD offers little more than a group of mementoes from a busy life.

Marvin 'Smitty' Smith (born 1961)

DRUMS

Playing in clubs as a teenager before turning pro with Jon Faddis. Recorded a huge number of sessions in the '80s and early '90s, but lately too busy with TV work to do much jazz playing.

***** Keeper Of The Drums**

Concord CCD 4325 *Smith; Wallace Roney (t); Robin Eubanks (tb); Steve Coleman (as); Ralph Moore (ts); Mulgrew Miller (p); Lonnie Plaxico (b).* 3/87.

***** The Road Less Travelled**

Concord CCD 4379 *As above, except James Williams (p), Robert Hurst (b) replace Miller, Plaxico; add Kenyatte Abdur-Rahman (perc).* 2/89.

One wonders if this is how Max Roach or Philly Joe Jones might have sounded on their own albums if recording techniques in the 1950s had been up to present-day standards. Drummer albums, even by some of the masters, used to be vulnerable to the Tedious Solo Syndrome, overlong and overmiked excursions that rattled the fillings. In a sense, Smitty Smith never stops soloing. His is the most insistent voice throughout almost every track, a maelstrom of furiously paced percussion that seems out of all proportion to the relatively modest bop-to-M-Base foregrounds. The debut *Keeper Of The Drums* is marginally the better of the two because the themes seem fresher. 'Miss Ann', not the Dolphy classic of that name, works a variation on the classic Spanish interval. 'Just Have Fun' and 'Song Of Joy' are directly reminiscent of 1950s models, and most people, offered a sample of 'The Creeper', will claim they've got it on a Blue Note somewhere. The writing is less varied and more predictable on *The Road Less Travelled.* There's no significant difference between the line-ups, except that Miller and Plaxico are marginally more sensitive, but the later set is brittle where the earlier album bends and moulds to the context. Smith's off-beats and compressed rolls are technically impressive but ultimately rather wearing. In his backwash one tends to lose sight of some excellent work from Moore and Roney in particular.

Smith is too busy working on *The Tonight Show* to do many sessions these days, and these albums are starting to seem remote, very much of their late-'80s time. He once looked set to be a champion, but Smitty has been overtaken by the rash of fine drummers who emerged in the '90s.

Mike Smith

ALTO AND SOPRANO SAXOPHONES

Chicago-based saxophonist, working primarily in a modern, hard-bop style. Also spent time in sax section of the Frank Sinatra orchestra in the 1980s.

****(*) Unit 7 A Tribute To Cannonball Adderley**

Delmark DE 444 *Smith; Ron Friedman (t, flhn); Jodie Christian (p); John Whitfield (b); Robert Shy (d).* 90.

***** On A Cool Night**

Delmark DE 448 *As above, except Jim Ryan (p), Bob Rummage (d) replace Christian and Shy.* 91.

***** The Traveler**

Delmark DE-462 *Smith; Ron Friedman (flhn); Jim Ryan (p); John Whitfield (b); Julian Smith, Bob Rummage (d).* 92.

***** Sinatra Songbook**

Delmark DE-480 *As above, except omit Friedman and Julian Smith. n.d.*

Hard bop from contemporary Chicago. Smith is frankly under the spell of Cannonball Adderley: he doesn't have the rasping, bluesy timbre down as well as Vincent Herring does, but the line of descent is clear from a few bars of any solo, and *Unit 7* is a proper genuflection in the direction of Cannon's work. But Smith looks a little further out, too: he organizes his bands with pithy discretion and seeks contrast in his choice and arrangement of material. 'Don't Scare Me None', for instance, the opening track on *On A Cool Night*, is a nicely measured bebop variation with a cunning tempo change to keep everyone awake. The first record begs direct comparison with the source of inspiration, and it takes only a goodish second place as a result, but *On A Cool Night* is more personal and hints at an emerging voice. Friedman is the more unusual player, though, if only for his curiously ingested tone – as if he were an avant-gardist trying to play it relatively straight.

Smith shows an increasing penchant for the soprano on *The Traveler* and the band seem to be growing in confidence as a unit, with Ryan's sparely searching accompaniments and the compatibility of the horns lending further assurance. This is hardly a ground-breaking band, but it plays decent jazz. Smith has spent some time playing lead alto in Sinatra's backing orchestra, so his *Songbook* features material he must know well, and there are a couple of tunes jazz players rarely touch, 'Only The Lonely' especially. Otherwise this is another unsurprising but enjoyable blow from Mike.

Roger Smith

GUITAR

An improviser of uncompromising dedication, Smith was a member of the Spontaneous Music Ensemble for longer than its co-founder, Trevor Watts, and yet is still often referred to as a relative newcomer. He employs a distinctive scrabbled attack and softly percussive tone.

*****(*) Unexpected Turns**

Emanem 4014 *Smith (g solo).* 12/93–7/96.

***** Extended Plays**

Emanem 4032 *As above.* 93–97.

***** S&M**

Incus CD 24 *Smith; Neil Metcalfe (f).* 7–12/95.

Not even the most cursory listener would mistake Roger Smith for fellow free guitarist Derek Bailey. Though Smith has studied with the acknowledged master of free-form guitar improvisation and has performed alongside Bailey in one version of the Spontaneous Music Ensemble, they could hardly be more different in approach. For a start, Smith favours a gut-strung Spanish guitar, rejects amplification and approaches the music with a good deal more stylistic baggage; where Bailey sets out with no pre-set formulae or destination, Smith often seems to be deconstructing something, albeit remote rather than familiar. Occasionally he will seem to be winding up towards some melancholy flamenco theme; elsewhere there is almost an African tinge; quite often, it sounds as though he is picking his way through something heard only fragmentarily and in an unknown idiom, but still recognizably a song.

The solo records give the best available account of his approach to date, though some will argue that his best work was within the confines of the SME, where he worked for nearly 20 years under the tutelage of John Stevens and made an often undervalued contribution to that remarkable group. Heard alone, Smith sounds remarkably delicate, creating lines of considerable delicacy which seem to head for some point of resolution. Most of the pieces are short, and only on the 11-minute 'Guitar In Top [sic]', one of half-a-dozen tracks recorded around Christmas 1994, does he seem to ramble. One suspects that Smith is by instinct a miniaturist, which is why the ironically titled *Extended Plays* both is and is not a good representation of his work.

The duos with Metcalfe see him paired with another unsung acoustic player and fellow member of the SME. Stevens coached his playing colleagues to listen to one another with a particular kind of *in*attention (he used the analogy of peripheral vision) and it sounds very much as though Metcalfe and Smith have taken that lesson to heart. These are not monologues, but neither are they conversations in any strict sense. Their reactions to each other suggest a melancholy abstraction, like Beckett's tramps. Though in both cases the sound is very faithful, these are lo-fi recordings. *Unexpected Turns* includes a whole range of ambient effects, from bird chatter to domestic clanks and rumbles. *S&M* is a little drier, which suits it quite well. This music, though, is not about production values. These records deserve much wider currency.

Stuff Smith (1909–67)

VIOLIN, VOCALS

Played with Alphonso Trent in the '20s, then in a band with Jonah Jones which was a big success on 52nd Street. Career petered out in the '40s, although musicians were still impressed; and from the '50s he based himself in California and Europe. A capricious temper and a liking for alcohol did him few favours.

*****(*) Stuff Smith & His Onyx Club Boys 1936**
Classics 706 *Smith; Jonah Jones (t, v); Buster Bailey (cl); George Clark (ts); Sam Allen, James Sherman, Clyde Hart, Raymond Smith (p); Bernard Addison, Bobby Bennett (g); John Brown, Mack Walker (b); Cozy Cole, Herbert Cowens, John Washington (d).* 2/36.

*****(*) Onyx Club Spree**
Topaz TPZ 1061 *Smith; Jonah Jones (t); Buster Bailey (cl); George Clarke, Lucky Thompson (ts); Sam Allen, Errol Garner, Clyde Hart, Jimmy Jones, James Sherman, Raymond Smith (p); Bernard Addison, Bobby Bennett, Luke Stewart (g); John Levy, Mack Walker (b); Cozy Cole, John Washington, George Wettling (d).* 2/36–10/45.

***** Stuff Smith 1939–1944**
Classics 1054 *Smith; Jonah Jones (t); George Clarke (ts); Sam Allen, Eric Henry, Jimmy Jones (p); Bernard Addison, Luke Stewart (g); Mary Osborne (g, v); John Brown (b); Herbert Cowens, John Levy (d); Stella Brooks (v).* 6/39–9/44.

***** The Stuff Smith Trio – 1943**
Progressive PCD 7053 *Smith; Jimmy Jones (p); John Levy (b).* 11/43.

*****(*) Stuff Smith / Dizzy Gillespie / Oscar Peterson**
Verve 521676-2 2CD *Smith; Dizzy Gillespie (t); Wynton Kelly, Carl Perkins, Oscar Peterson (p); Red Callender, Curtis Counce, Paul West (b); Oscar Bradley, Frank Butler, J.C Heard, Alvin Stoller (d); Gordon Family (v).* 1–4/57.

*****(*) Live At The Montmartre**
Storyville STCD 4142 *Smith; Kenny Drew (p); Niels-Henning Orsted Pedersen (b); Alex Riel (d).* 3/65.

***** Hot Violins**
Storyville STCD 4170 *Smith; Poul Olsen (vn); Svend Asmussen (vn, v); Kenny Drew, Jorgen Borch (p); Erik Molbach, Niels-Henning Orsted Pedersen (b); Makaya Ntoshko, Alex Riel, Bjarne Rostvold (d).* 3/65–2/67.

Hezekiah Leroy Gordon Smith's ninetieth birthday prompted a certain reassessment of his work. Those who remember his final performances in Scandinavia are themselves fewer on the ground these days, and emphasis has fallen on the earlier and better work. It's hard to imagine how Billy Bang's or Leroy Jenkins's mordant new wave fiddling would have come about had it not been for his example. Initially influenced by Joe Venuti, Smith devised a style based on heavy bow-weight, with sharply percussive semiquaver runs up towards the top end of his range. His facility and ease on a swinging 1943 version of Dvorák's 'Humoresque', included on Classics 1054, is jaw-dropping. Like many 1920s players, Smith found himself overtaken by the swing era and re-emerged as a recording and concert artist only after the war, when his upfront style and comic stage persona attracted renewed attention. Even so, he had a thriving club career in the meantime, most famously at the Onyx Club on 52nd Street, and managed to hold his ground while the bebop revolution, which he either anticipated, or was left untouched by, depending on your point of view, went on around him.

The Classics disc covers some important early material. This is when Smith's talent was at its most buoyant. 'I'se A Muggin'' and the associated musical numbers game are pretty corny (corny enough to be omitted from the Topaz compilation, which warns that the song 'goes on a bit'), but they retain their appeal over five decades like all the Vocalion sides, and Smith's astonishing fiddle technique lifts them up out of the mere novelty class. Jonah Jones makes a big impact, with a slithery, burping style that's hard to categorize and which shouldn't fit these sessions as well as it seems to. Sensibly, Classics have restricted this first volume to things Smith made under his own name. Future releases will include sessions for Alphonso Trent which are much less typical, though the second item here from the French label includes some excellent small-group sessions made after Smith's return east from the Coast.

Inevitably, there is a good deal of overlap between the Classics and Topaz discs, though the latter, unconstrained by completism, mentions but does not include a debunking version of 'I've Got You Under My Skin', made with the seven-piece Smith 'orchestra' of 1940. Both include the remarkable 'Crescendo In Drums' and a sample of the two versions underlines the technical superiority of the Topaz. Given that it is also a selection aimed at pointing up Smith's technical brilliance rather than his novelty performances, it should be the disc of choice.

The 1943 trio is a good representation of what he was about in the pre-war years, an exhaustive documentation of the session of 17 November with incomplete takes and false starts included alongside the release versions. Three full versions of 'Minuet In Swing' suggest that Smith went at a solo in a fairly deliberate way, attempting to maintain an energy level rather than rethinking his approach every time. On the other hand, an unissued 'Bugle Call Rag' – or 'Rage', as here – shows that he could be thoughtful even on lighter material.

Verve have, of course, always had a gift for picking up artists relatively late in their career and injecting new life into them. The sessions with Diz and Oscar are beautifully recorded, if not sublimely musical, and one values the record – a generously filled two-CD set – for the glimpses of the under-recorded Perkins as much as anything.

The later European sessions, recorded within a couple of years of Smith's death in Munich, are very much better. *Hot Violins* was made shortly before 'the cat that took the apron strings off the fiddle' was taken back into the fold. They're pretty tired, and it gets a bit dispiriting listening to Smith being cut by guys who're doing no more than playing his licks back at him. Asmussen does a party piece with a tenor violin on 'Caravan'; pitched somewhere between viola and cello, it makes a pretty noise, but it's hard not to feel so-what-ish about it.

Tab Smith (1909–71)

ALTO AND TENOR SAXOPHONES

Talmadge Smith's first break came in joining Lucky Millinder in 1936, before moving to Count Basie in 1940. Ran his own small groups at the end of the '40s and became involved in early R&B. Moved from music to real-estate development in the '60s.

***** Jump Time**

Delmark DD-447 *Smith; Sonny Cohn (t); Leon Washington (ts); Lavern Dillon, Teddy Brannon (p); Wilfred Middlebrooks (b); Walter Johnson (d); Louis Blackwell (v).* 8/51–2/52.

***** Ace High**

Delmark DD-455 *As above, except add Irving Woods (t), Charlie Wright (ts).* 2/52–4/53.

Smith jobbed around the Harlem big bands of the 1930s and eventually found a niche with Count Basie. But he won his wider fame as an R&B soloist in the 1950s and for a while jockeyed with Earl Bostic on the nation's jukeboxes. This pair of CDs collects a stack of such performances, offering a chronological survey of his output for the United label. Backed by an unobtrusive small group, Smith works through ballads, the blues and more roisterous outings. His sound is more graceful than Bostic's: he always seems to have something in reserve, and the hollow sound he sometimes gets in the alto's upper register reminds that he often made use of the soprano, too, although not here. Given the sameness of the format and the repetitive formulas Smith had to apply, these are surprisingly engaging CDs, although one or the other will be more than enough for all but the most devout followers. Very clean remastering.

Tommy Smith (born 1967)

TENOR SAXOPHONE

In Scotland and beyond, Smith was something of a legend before he left his teens. Since then, he has processed influences – Rollins, Garbarek, George Coleman, Michael Brecker, Branford Marsalis – faster than the critical establishment has been able to typecast him. These days, he writes complex long-form tunes and plays like nobody but himself: intense, lyrical and thoroughly versed in more of the tradition than most saxophonists manage in a lifetime.

***** Reminiscence**

Linn AKD 024 *Smith; Terje Gewelt (b); Ian Froman (d).* 7/93.

With a perversity that went all the way round to inevitable, Blue Note dispensed with Tommy Smith as soon as he had made one wonderful album – *Paris* – for them. As with Stan Tracey, it was too hard to market an 'Englishman' in North America. The confusion over accent isn't altogether risible for, in performance as in speech, Smith tends to shift between Scottish, American and Scandinavian tonalities. His highly individual sound, heard in his precocious teens on small-label sets like *Taking Off* and *Giant Strides*, has been replaced in more recent years by a simulacrum of Jan Garbarek's tense, keening sound, and then even more recently by a seeming return to the classic voices: Webster, Hawkins and Pres.

For the moment, though, on these his first records for Glasgow-based Linn, he simply sounds glad to be home, relaxed in the company of Gewelt and Froman, former colleagues in Forward Motion, and able to take some pleasure in his playing. There are still moments which suggest an ambition that outstrips not technique but the maturity to make it count, as on 'Emancipation Of Dissonance', and the awkward 'Ally' (which refers back to an earlier composition). In this rather spare and unforgiving context he can be a little dry and discursive, and his colleagues are no more expansive. However, one does constantly feel that Smith is on the brink of a new direction, and that this curiously titled disc (curious for a 27-year-old to be retreading and rethinking his own career) is a clearing of the ground for something new.

*****(*) Misty Morning And No Time**

Linn AKD 040 *Smith; Guy Barker (t, monette); Julian Arguëlles (sax); Steve Hamilton (p); Terje Gewelt (b); Ian Froman (d).* 12/94.

The trio is significantly augmented for the next record, which is certainly the most ambitious thing Smith had attempted thus far in terms of composition. *Misty Morning* was made in collaboration with the veteran Scottish poet, Norman MacCaig (since deceased), a notably plain-spoken and unfussy craftsman with a bottomless humanity and humour. Though the level of direct contact seems to have been quite slight, less than with Edwin Morgan on *Beasts Of Scotland* later, it seems also to have made a significant impact on Smith, allowing him to mix complexity (and the band baulked anxiously when they first saw these charts) with a directness of expression that is immediately appealing.

Barker is inspirational, tackling each of the compositions as if they were familiar standards and bringing a very individual sound to 'Memorial', a threnody for the poet's dead daughter, and one of the most directly emotional pieces Smith has yet written. Argüelles grows in stature every time one hears him, and his interplay with the leader on 'Estuary', a dappled theme which also makes use of Barker's liquid-sounding monette (an instrument not unlike Art Farmer's flumpet), is quite exceptional in its tact and taste. This was the breakthrough album. Afterwards, Smith has sounded less self-conscious, less driven, more focused and expressive.

***(*) **Beasts Of Scotland**

Linn AKD 054 *Smith; Guy Barker (t, flhn); Andy Panayi (as, f); Steve Hamilton (p, syn); Alec Dankworth (b); Tom Gordon (d, perc).* 96.

Playfully conceived, but revealing a core of solid invention, this was another poetic collaboration. Edwin Morgan is no less direct and unliterary than MacCaig, but he is also more immediately responsive to the music of his words, and this has allowed Smith to work at a new level again, creating tunes that are miniature tone-poems, evocative of the supposed subject-matter and at the same time utterly separate from it without ever sounding abstract.

He makes no attempt to evoke the fauna and avifauna of Scotland in sound-effects. 'Seal' has a slippery harmonic structure, but no more of it than that relates to the title. By the same token, 'Salmon' and 'Conger Eel' swim free of any programme, taut, elegant structures from Smith that throw up few opportunities for extended improvisation. 'Midge' may require a small gloss for non-Scottish listeners: a tiny insect, troublesome only in the plural and in the female gender, which has a healthy summer appetite for human blood. It's the most appealing idea and music of the set, though we rather liked Morgan's inclusion of the wolf as a beast of Scotland; there is a lobby for its reintroduction, and if it is as heroic as Smith makes it sound, then the sooner the better ...

***(*) **Azure**

Linn AKD 059 *Smith; Kenny Wheeler (t, flhn); Lars Danielsson (b); Jon Christensen (d).* 96.

A collaborative album, with compositions by the ever-tougher Christensen and some wonderful playing by Wheeler. As on the early Blue Note sessions, Smith is in some danger of being eclipsed by his 'sidemen', and the album is at some risk of disappearing into sub-ECM impressionism, but the rigour of compositions like the opening 'The Gold Of The Azure' and 'The Calculation' lift the set.

If this band could be kept together long term, it would become legendary. Smith's Garbarek years are probably behind him. He goes back into that mode once or twice on *Azure*, but the bulk of the record sees him exploring a more pointed harmonic direction that restores the earnest and unselfconscious drive of the early records.

**** **The Sound Of Love**

Linn AKD 084 *Smith; Kenny Barron (p); Peter Washington (b); Billy Drummond (d).* 97.

Who can this wise old man be, with the deep, breathy delivery, the chastened romanticism and the ability to combine passion and introspection? Whatever bruises Smith picked up during the Blue Note days are put right here. A top-drawer American band, seemingly almost unrehearsed, and a bag of songs by Ellington and Strayhorn, from the opening 'Johnny Come Lately', through 'Chelsea Bridge', 'Isfahan', 'Prelude To A Kiss' to a delightful closing 'Cottontail'. Crowd-pleasing romance and a more naked and unaffected Smith than we've ever had a chance to hear before. Barron is a giant of the music, and should be knighted, sanctified and nationalized without delay. His playing on 'Duke Ellington's Sound Of Love' (a Mingus composition and the only non-Duke and Sweet Pea tune on the album) is jaw-dropping: profound, lyrical and totally in tune with both the piece and the saxophonist. Marvellous album. If you can make room for only one by T. Smith, this should be it.

**** **Blue Smith**

Linn AKD 110 *Smith; John Scofield (g); James Genus (b); Clarence Penn (d).* 1/99.

... But then again, you wouldn't want to be without this one, either. Smith has spoken warmly about working with Scofield: the absolute distinctiveness of his guitar playing; the complete musicality; the sheer intelligence. Nevertheless, all the compositions here are his own. The liner-photos of the band are time-coded a quarter past midnight and there's a late-night feel to these splendid performances: nothing wee-small-hours and either over-mellow or frenetic; just relaxed, fluent and adult.

Smith's growing stature as a composer is evidenced above all in the relative simplicity of these tunes. Whereas in the past his besetting vice was an over-elaboration of the line, here the emphasis is on the scaffolding rather than the curlicues. 'Eany Meany Miny Mo', 'Blacken' Blue' and 'Hubba Hubba' are convincingly personal but unfussy and clean-limbed. Scofield's driving lines and rich harmonics are an essential ingredient, but Smith has rarely played better. Genus and Penn are magnificent, not so laid back as to suggest the horizontal but certainly not in a hurry for the last subway train.

Smith throws in one standard, 'Amazing Grace', and gives that weary old tune – Scottish? Virginian? – a remarkable dignity. Graceful and amazing.

Wadada Leo Smith (born 1941)

TRUMPET, FLUGELHORN, PERCUSSION

Born in Mississippi, Smith became part of the radical AACM group before founding the Creative Construction Company with Anthony Braxton and Leroy Jenkins. A subtle theoretician, he has rarely enjoyed adequate opportunity to put his ideas into practice and remains undervalued.

**** **Divine Love**

ECM 529126-2 *Smith; Lester Bowie, Kenny Wheeler (t); Dwight Andrews (af, bcl, ts, perc); Bobby Naughton (vib, mar, perc); Charlie Haden (b).* 9/78.

***(*) Go In Numbers

Black Saint 120053 *As above, except omit Bowie, Haden, Wheeler; add Wes Brown (b, odurgyaba f).* 1/80.

Heard the one about the Rastafarian trumpeter who went to live in Iceland? There's no punchline, because it isn't a joke. It seems an unlikely destination for Smith, except that his conception of jazz as a world music seems to need no definite cultural location, but shifts steadily from one to the next. Given the level of indifference at home, Iceland seemed as good a berth as any for a while.

Since the 1970s Smith has organized his music according to the principles of 'rhythm-units', which seem to call for a mystical equivalence of sound and silence, and of 'ahkreanvention', a method of notating improvised music. 'Tastalun' on *Divine Love* is the first of these pieces Smith had an opportunity to record, three muted trumpets weaving an extraordinary extended spell. So closely integrated is the playing by Smith and guests Wheeler and Bowie that it is difficult – and probably pointless – trying to sort out who is playing which line.

The basic group on both these records is Smith with Naughton and Andrews. *Divine Love* opens on a long meditation for alto flute, Andrews at his atmopsheric best, before Smith's tight, compressed sound comes through. The title-piece is another of his ritual works, like the earlier *Mass For The World* and *Budding Of A Rose*, issued on Moers but sadly no longer available. Naughton's vibes are a key element on these records, not least because there is no conventional percussion part. He opens the last track on *Divine Love*, pitched against Charlie Haden's bass, marking the pauses that constitute the work's stately rhythm unit. Andrews's bass clarinet intones ancient wisdoms while Smith sounds elevated, rapt, almost tranced.

Go In Numbers depends even more thoroughly on Naughton. This is a live recording, from the Kitchen in New York, of the group Smith called New Dalta Ahkri. In pure duration terms, it's better value for money than the decidedly skimpy *Divine Love*, which was reissued on CD with no extra tracks. However, neither the performances nor the recording are of the same quality, and no one should be put off by seeming short measure. The ECM album is a small masterpiece.

The two major statements on the Black Saint album occupy most of its length. Naughton and Wes Brown open 'Go In Numbers' with a desolate meditation that sounds like the funeral march of some lost leader. Smith's opening figures seem to contain half-remembered elements of Ives's *The Unanswered Question*. Elsewhere he sounds uncannily like a slowed-up version of Don Cherry, an influence that was to seem ever more pressing in years to come.

***(*) Procession Of The Great Ancestry

Chief CD6 *Smith; John Powell (ts); Bobby Naughton (vib); Louis Myers (g); Joe Fonda, Mchaka Uba (b); Kahil El'Zabar (d, perc).* 2/83.

'Seven mystical poems of jazz in 17 links', dedicated to some of the honoured shades of Afro-America, including fellow-trumpeters Miles, Dizzy, Roy Eldridge and Booker Little, with a special paean to Gabriel's right-hand man, the Rev. Martin Luther King Jr. As in *The Mass On The World*, this is conceived as a long seamless ritual, much of it conducted in duet with Naughton, whose vibes have never sounded more like mystical bells.

Smith makes no attempt to pastiche any of his musical ancestors. Stylistically, it would be difficult to determine merely by listening who was being celebrated in which piece, except that there is probably more of Miles in the title-track, which begins the procession proper. What Diz would have thought of a title like 'Celestial Sparks In The Sanctuary Of Redemption' is fortunately not recorded. A wonderful record, despite its slightly overcooked poetics. May be difficult to find, but well worth the search.

**(*) Kulture Jazz

ECM 519074-2 *Smith (solo).* 10/92.

Another attempt to commune with the ancestors. This time the honour'd shades are Billie Holiday, Trane, Ayler and Pops, but this time there is much greater emphasis on Smith's poetic writing, which, like Cecil Taylor's, has become ever more important relative to pure instrumentalism. One longs for more trumpet in place of the barrage of percussion and little instruments that clogs the album.

Interestingly, Smith's name is one that often comes up when supporters are (rightly) trying to debunk the notion of ECM as purveyors of nothing but pastelly Nordic chamber music. It was brave of them to go back to him after a gap of almost 25 years, but sadly this one dates far more quickly than *Divine Love*, which was a welcome reissue, seeming to coincide with quarter-centenary celebrations.

***(*) Tao-Njia

Tzadik TZ 7017 *Smith; Dorothy Stone (f, af, picc); Martin Walker (cl, bcl); Vicky Ray (p, cel); Mika Noda (vib, perc); Robin Lorentz (vn); Erika Duke (clo); David Philipson (bansuri, perc); Harumi Makino Smith (v).* 11 & 12/95.

In the spring of 1995 Smith unveiled a large-scale, multi-ensemble piece called *Odwira*. It was the clearest sign of how far he has moved from small-group improvisation to a new conception of himself as a composer, albeit a heterodox one. In this regard, and in some respects only, his career closely parallels that of Anthony Braxton.

Recent years have seen Smith personally and musically involved with Oriental culture, and this is strongly reflected in *Tao-Njia*. Acoustically, it is one of his most remarkable records, a rich montage of sounds that are at once new and immediately familiar, bearing Smith's stamp from the very first overdubbed passages of 'Another Wave More Waves'. Here, once again, the dominant exchange is between trumpet and vibraphone, no longer Bobby Naughton but Mika Noda, and pairs of low drums performed by David Philipson, two members of his Nda-Kulture Ensemble. They are augmented by members of new music and crossover specialists California E.A.R. for 'Tao-Njia' itself. As on *Kulture Jazz*, this is essentially a text piece, recited by Harumi Makino Smith against a wind-and-string ensemble, Smith's trumpet and pre-recorded *mbira*. It's the only questionable part of the record, over-long, slightly indulgent and not always very clearly articulated.

The remainder is taken up by 'Double Thunderbolt', one of many recent memorials to the late Don Cherry. It borrows his 'Symphony For Improvisers' tag for the second and fifth movements, opening with Smith on bamboo flute and ending – 'A Falcon Ascends In A Moonbow Lightbeam' – with magnificent solo muted trumpet. A piece to cherish, utterly true to Cherry's great gifts, and to Smith's.

***** Condor, Autumn Wind**

Wobbly Rail WOB 001 *Smith; Harumi Makimo Smith (v).* 11/97.

A very intimate, almost private musical experience that will either command or repel. So much of Smith's creative energy has gone into tributes to other musicians – and here again Dizzy Gillespie, Marion Brown and Albert Ayler are honoured – that one wonders whether he makes such obeisances with all due self-confidence or whether something like that old American principle, the 'anxiety of influence', is at work.

'Condor' is a further gesture of respect to Diz and is very fine, but the real meat of the album – and the most positive answer to the question above – is in the first three tracks. Haiku-simple and unfussily played, they show the Smiths at their unaffected best.

*****(*) Yo Miles!**

Shanachie 5046 2CD *Smith; Bruce Ackley, Steve Adams, George Brooks, Lary Ochs, Jon Raskin (sax); Oluyemi Thomas (bcl); Paul Plimley (p, org); John Medeski (org); Bob Bralove (ky); Nels Cline, Henry Kaiser, Freddy Roulette, Elliott Sharp (g); Chris Muir (g, elec); Michael (b, g); Wally Ingram, Lukas Ligeti (d, perc).* 1/98.

Why listen to reprocessed Miles when there is a whole shelfload of the real thing? If the answer seems self-evident, it might be worth spending an hour with Smith, guitarist Henry Kaiser and band on this generous two-CD pastiche of Miles's electric phase. Smith's trumpet playing is rawer and more intense than anything Miles ever attempted. One is tempted to say it is also more harmonically astute. What it lacks is the eggshell fragility of the original, which is what most fans will instinctively value most.

The material is predictable enough, mostly Jack Johnson and *Big Fun* vintage funk. Smith turns 'Calypso Frelimo' into a dark, squally ride, and ABC groove of 'Ife', perhaps the most ubiquitous staple of the electric years, into a sprawling essay in time-changes and minimal harmonics. 'Miles Dewey Davis III – Great Ancestor' is an original and in some respects the most stretching piece on the record.

Kaiser's part is harder to quantify and assess. Unlike John McLaughlin and later guitarists, he doesn't command much of a front role, but he underpins the ensembles with real understanding. The guest musicians, who include the members of the ROVA Saxophone Quartet, are used to great effect, and Kaiser and fellow-guitarist Chris Muir produce with a feel for the grooves and timbres that Teo Macero would enjoy.

Willie 'The Lion' Smith (1895–1973)

PIANO, VOCAL

A founder-member of the New York stride pianists, Smith served in the First World War, then haunted the toughest New York clubs. He led occasional bands, toured, and became a self-appointed living historian and raconteur in his old age. He wrote Echoes of Spring.

*****(*) Willie 'The Lion' Smith 1925–1937**

Classics 662 *Smith; Dave Nelson, Frankie Newton (t); June Clark, Jabbo Smith, Ed Allen (c); Jimmy Harrison (tb); Buster Bailey (cl, ss, as); Cecil Scott, Herschel Brassfield (cl); Prince Robinson, Robert Carroll (ts); Edgar Sampson (as, vn); Pete Brown (as); Buddy Christian, Gus Horsley (bj); Jimmy McLin (g); Bill Benford, Harry Hull (tba); Ellsworth Reynolds, John Kirby (b); O'Neil Spencer (d, v); Eric Henry (d); Willie Williams (wbd); Perry Bradford (v).* 11/25–9/37.

****** Willie 'The Lion' Smith And His Cubs**

Timeless CBC 1-012 *As above, except omit Clark, Harrison, Robinson, Christian, Benford, Jabbo Smith, Brassfield, Sampson, Horsley and Hull.* 4/35–9/37.

***** Willie 'The Lion' Smith 1937–1938**

Classics 677 *Smith; Frank Newton (t); Pete Brown (as); Buster Bailey (cl); Milt Herth (org); Jimmy McLin (g); Teddy Bunn (g, v); John Kirby (b); O'Neil Spencer (d, v).* 9/37–11/38.

*****(*) Willie 'The Lion' Smith 1938–1940**

Classics 692 *Smith; Sidney De Paris (t); Jimmy Lane, Johnny Mullins (as); Perry Smith (ts); Joe Bushkin, Jess Stacy (p); Bernard Addison (g); Richard Fulbright (b); George Wettling, Puss Johnson (d); Joe Turner, Naomi Price (v).* 11/38–11/40.

One of the great Harlem pianists and an unrivalled raconteur, Willie Smith came into his own when an old man, reminiscing from the keyboard. But these more youthful sessions stand up very well and are surprisingly little known. Classics 662 opens with two of his very few appearances on record in the 1920s: each of the pair of sessions is by a pick-up group, both with Jimmy Harrison and one with Jabbo Smith in the front line. Typical small-group Harlem jazz of the period, with Perry Bradford shouting the odds on two titles. The remainder – and all of the Timeless CD – is devoted to sessions by Smith's Cubs, an excellent outfit: with Ed Allen, Cecil Scott and Willie Williams on washboard on the first eight titles, they can't help but sound like a Clarence Williams group, but the next three sessions include Dave Nelson (sounding better than he ever did on the King Oliver Victor records), Buster Bailey, Pete Brown and Frankie Newton, effecting a bridge between older hot music and the sharper small-band swing of the late '30s. Smith plays a lot of dextrous piano – he also has a 1934 solo, 'Finger Buster', a typical parlour show-off piece of the day – and the music has a wonderful lilt and sprightliness. The Timeless transfers are clearly superior and include a lot of alternative takes: this is the disc to get if you just want the Cubs tracks, but the other tunes on the Classics disc are also worth hearing. Classics 677 is made up mostly of tracks by Milt Herth, a Hammond organist who had Smith, Spencer and Bunn making up his group. Herth is always getting in the way, but The Lion usually pushes some decent stride piano into the tunes, and there are two fine 1938 solos, 'Passionette' and 'Morning Air', which show something of his penchant for novelty piano of the Roy Bargy genre. Classics 692 starts with a three-piano date featuring Smith, Stacy and Bushkin, before a marathon session that produced 14 piano solos in one day: originals and show tunes, done in the manner of courteous syncopation that trademarks Smith's style. The rest of the disc includes a rare small-band session and a pair of blues, partnering Smith with Joe Turner. Exemplary, although docked a notch for less-than-ideal remastering.

***** Pork And Beans**

Black Lion BLCD 760144 *Smith (p, v).* 11/66.

The Lion's irrepressible showmanship often got in the way of his piano playing when it came to his later records. Most of them were done for whatever label would have him, and as a result most of them are now out of print. In Germany, in 1966, he played 15 tunes from memory – Luckey Roberts, Eubie Blake, Irving Berlin, Fats Waller, Willie Smith. Boisterous music in good sound.

Paul Smoker (born 1941)

TRUMPET

Paul Smoker is a Mid-West academic who plays free-form jazz of surpassing thoughtfulness. Though by no means averse to tackling standards, he creates a lot of his own material, cleaving to quasi-classical forms which, coupled with a tight, rather correct diction, sometimes recall Don Ellis.

***** Halloween 96**

CIMP 129 *Smoker; Vinny Golia (bs); Ken Filiano (b); Phil Haynes (d).* 10/96.

****** Halloween – The Sequel**

Nine Winds NWCD 0207 *As above.* 4/97.

***** Standard Deviation**

CIMP 186 *Smoker; Steve Salerno (g); Thomas Ulrich (clo); Jay Rosen (d).* 9/98.

Interesting that the liner-notes to the later record document some difficulties getting the sound right and the group properly balanced. Smoker has always depended on a very careful spatial distribution and a rather subtle internal balance. We're not convinced he got it with Golia, but we're not convinced that the baritonist is his natural playing partner. This is an entirely free-form set, five longish improvisations played at high temperature but lacking the analytical poise of Smoker's attack on standard material. Golia always has interesting things to say, as does Smoker, but this too often sounds like an amiable encounter between two men who really have nothing musical in common.

The return fixture is once again largely based on composition rather than free improvisation. The exceptions are two brief takes of 'That Was For Albert', a collective composition that bears some wispy traces of Ayler's own open-formed melodies. The sound is much better than on the CIMP, a label that prides itself on rough-hewn immediacy and no polish. The smoother surface does this music no disservice at all.

Smoker subtly adjusts the tonalities on *Standard Deviation*, which is really what the title is about. 'Speak Low' is shifted into a very unbluesy B major and 'Stormy Weather' into G flat. He also overturns the usual order of head and solo, placing rubato melody statements over strict-time accompaniments and vice versa. All four group members introduce songs and Rosen, who is among the most ubiquitous performers in the CIMP catalogue, is especially good in his introduction to 'Stormy Weather'. Unlike the earlier set with Golia, Smoker modulates the dynamics and expressive range with genuine mastery. 'Speak Low' is as delicate a version as you'll ever hear, and his approach to 'Beyond The Blue Horizon' is exquisitely weighted. Smoker's recent engagement with jazz harmonics is similar to that of Franz Koglmann (another who has suffered from the deletion of hat ART's 6000 catalogue) but is unmistakably more American in emphasis and, one almost hesitates to say, more expressive as well.

Gary Smulyan

BARITONE SAXOPHONE

Already a veteran of big-band section-playing, Smulyan worked with Woody Herman and Mel Lewis before making these leadership dates in the '90s.

***** The Lure Of Beauty**

Criss Cross 1049 *Smulyan; Jimmy Knepper (tb); Mulgrew Miller (b); Ray Drummond (b); Kenny Washington (d).* 12/90.

A staunch section-player, Smulyan has as good a grasp of baritone technique as any of the younger players of what's still a rare instrument. It was a smart idea to bring Jimmy Knepper to this session, a frequent associate of Pepper Adams and a player whose manner is individual enough to lift the music out of the hard-bop rut which several Criss Cross sessions have fallen into. The group work up a great head of steam on 'Canto Fiesta', the rhythm section grooving hard enough to sustain the feel over more than ten minutes, and there are a couple of pretty (if functional) ballad performances; but at 74 minutes the record could have lost a couple of items and been none the worse for it.

***** Homage**

Criss Cross 1068 *Smulyan; Tommy Flanagan (p); Ray Drummond (b); Kenny Washington (d).* 12/91.

It was a pleasing notion to pay tribute to another baritone master, Pepper Adams, who wrote all eight themes here. Having Flanagan, an old Detroit friend of Adams's, along as well was another good idea. Smulyan is both similar to and different from the older player, less ornery than Adams but given to a comparable stoniness and scepticism with the tender approach: on a ballad such as 'Civilization And Its Discontents' his refusal to turn to a sanctimonious vibrato adds to the power of the improvising, even with Flanagan's featherbed chords to hand. The hard-bop lines of 'Claudette's Way' are reeled off with unassuming strength: this is a baritone man who understands the weight and gravitas of the instrument without having to insist on it. Smulyan doesn't always convince one that the tunes are that good, but it's an impressively substantial record.

***** Saxophone Mosaic**

Criss Cross 1092 *Smulyan; Dick Oatts (ss, as, f); Billy Drewes (as, cl, f); Ralph Lalama (ts, cl, f); Rich Perry (ts); Scott Robinson (bs, bcl); Mike LeDonne (p); Dennis Irwin (b); Kenny Washington (d).* 12/93.

George Coleman's 'Apache Dance', which opens the record, features all the horns, but it's the exception. For the most part, Bob Belden's arrangements use this six-sax team for colour, and for something which Smulyan himself can bed down in. He peels off long, heated solos on every track, as if under pressure to make the baritone dominate the line-up, and it's an effective strategy. But here and there one wishes the other horns had taken a greater part, though everyone comes back in again on the closing 'Fingers'.

***** With Strings**

Criss Cross 1129 *Smulyan; Mike LeDonne (p); Peter Washington (b); Kenny Washington (d); strings.* 12/96.

Baritone plus strings is a rare arrangement. Bob Belden's charts are sound and gracious, and Smulyan does well enough by them, although he hardly strikes one as the ideal player for the situation: Chaloff or Mulligan, perhaps, but Smulyan is more out of the impassive Pepper Adams end of the horn. The programme is mostly built around originals, too, which gives the listener few enough footholds in coming to terms with the tunes. It's appealingly done, but one feels that Criss Cross (on their debut session with strings) might have gone all out for the emotional ticket and handed Smulyan a programme of familiar ballads.

Jim Snidero

ALTO SAXOPHONE

Snidero is a talented musician and a passionate musical advocate and educator who has created his own latter-day synthesis of hard bop. A seasoned player with an impressive track record working for everyone from Toshiko Akiyoshi to Frank Sinatra, he now has an extensive discography as leader as well.

****(*) Mixed Bag**

Criss Cross Criss 1032 *Snidero; Brian Lynch (t); Benny Green (p); Peter Washington (b); Jeff Tain Watts (d).* 12/87.

*****(*) Blue Afternoon**

Criss Cross Criss 1072 *As above, except replace Watts with Marvin 'Smitty' Smith (d).* 12/89.

Washington-born Snidero has never quite managed to locate himself stylistically. An immensely able player who seems to have processed a good deal of the jazz history of preceding generations, he is not yet a man with a definite voice and presence. We were assured that *Mixed Bag*, the title, shouldn't be taken too literally, but that is exactly what it is. 'Pannonica' lacks the sort of ironic detachment that Monk requires, and Snidero's introductory cadenza on 'Blood Count', a haunting Strayhorn theme, is one of the very best things he has done, but it stands somewhat apart among this material.

Blue Afternoon is better, not just because it features the splendid Smith, but also because the material is better judged. Wayne Shorter's 'Infant Eyes' and Mal Waldron's 'Soul Eyes' are key peformances, and Snidero's occasional Coltraneisms are reasonably in keeping with the music being played. Briskly played and well recorded.

*****(*) Time Out: Live**

Red Records RR 123228 *Snidero; Marc Copland (p); Peter Washington (b); Victor Lewis (d).* 7/89.

Recorded live and no better than it ought to be, technically speaking at least. Snidero is fiery enough but he generates more heat than light, and one can't avoid the impression that he has very little of any substance to say; Lester Young's 'What's your story, kid?' comment is relevant here, though on further hearings it's easier to see what Jim might be striving for, some version of hard-bop idiom that builds on but doesn't repeat the work of the Blue Note masters, the Blakeys and Morgans and Donaldsons.

With the passage of time, it seems a stronger and more thoughtful set, and of course the band is first rate. Lewis is endlessly resoureful and the loyal Washington doesn't miss a note.

*****(*) While Your Here**

Red Records RR 123241 *Snidero; Benny Green (p); Peter Washington (b); Tony Reedus (d).* 1/91.

Snidero had been around the New York scene for a decade by the time this was cut and the band – apart from a sitting tenant on bass – had seen some of the top talent of the day pass through without making any definite impression on the leader's style. As with Miller, though, he does seem to take a cue from Green. The tone is still hard, but there's a more exuberant bounce, a fresher-faced delivery, *and* there's a deepening of emotion in the slower and more *misterioso* numbers, which never before seemed to be a strong suit. *While Your Here* may yet be considered a transitional album on the way to something richer and more expansive. Had we been A&R men, this is the one that might have made us think Jim Snidero was worthy of long-term investment.

*****(*) San Juan**

Red Records 123265 *Snidero; Steve Nelson (vib); Kevin Hayes (p); Dennis Irwin (b); Billy Hart (d).* 10/94.

Nineteen ninety-four was something of a breakthrough year for Snidero. There is a sharpness and precision about his playing which wasn't always or consistently in evidence before, and the standard of writing seems to be on a new plane. All tracks, except for a sensitive reading of Kenny Dorham's 'La Mesha', are by him, and they're very good indeed. It's remarkable that music written in an idiom that was already probably 30 years past its sell-by should sound so fresh and immediate, and so well paced. Though no one is likely to mistake it for a period piece, this is the kind of album Blue Note was turning out in its heyday. 'Introspect', 'Mystery' and 'The Web' are bold and intelligent conceptions, and only with the closing 'To Whom It May Concern' does either conception or execution start to seem a little formulaic. A word of recognition for Steve Nelson, a Red stalwart who provides much of the impetus on these cuts. He is a player worthy of closer attention, but also perhaps still in need of a broader stage.

*****(*) Vertigo**

Criss Cross Criss 1112 *Snidero; Walt Weiskopf (ts); David Hazeltine (p); Peter Washington (b); Tony Reedus (d).* 12/94.

Opportunity knocked, as for so many interesting players of this generation, in the shape of Gerry Teekens and Criss Cross. The result is both engaging and challenging. Snidero kicks off with some new material, including the excellent original 'A.S.A.P.', before switching to standards, cracking interpretations of 'Ah-Leu-cha' and 'Skylark' which open up the band and allow them and tenorist Weiskopf (who has already established a presence on the label) to show their paces as a collective. Hazeltine isn't the most confident soloist on the planet, but he has Washington to lean on, and he turns in a more than competent set. The group sounds well rehearsed and sympathetic.

*****(*) Standards + Plus**
Double Time Records DTRCD 139 *Snidero; Mike LeDonne (p); Dennis Irwin (b); Kenny Washington (d).* 97.

Not clear what is intended by the 'Plus', other than entirely warranted enthusiasm for a strong, vibrant set. All nine tracks – it's a generously proportioned record – are based on standard material, to which Snidero or the label have interestingly and usefully attached dates of composition, ranging from 1929 for Vincent Youmans's 'Without A Song' to Sylvester Kynor's 'Bluesville', penned 30 years later.

He opens with 'You And The Night And The Music', handled in a manner that suggests Coltrane's deconstruction of 'My Favorite Things', the original Atlantic version rather than the more radical live performances which followed on. 'Round Midnight' and Benny Golson's 'Along Came Betty' are almost as good. LeDonne is a very talented accompanist without being distinctive as a solo voice. Confusingly, this time out it's the other (unrelated) Washington on drums – and what a strong and confidence-inspiring presence he is. Snidero is certainly going places. One wonders whether it would be so very hard to assemble a regular recording band. He certainly has the cachet and the experience now to call in a few favours. If not, it's a harder world than we thought.

****** The Music Of Joe Henderson**
Double Time Records DTRCD 152 Snidero; Joe Magnarelli (*t*); Conrad Herwig (*tb*); David Hazeltine (*p*); Dennis Irwin (*b*); Kenny Washington (*d*) 12/98.

Jim Snidero the jazz scholar comes to the fore on this fine disc, which is none the worse and none the less individual for being devoted to the great Joe H. There is every sign that Snidero has analysed these remarkable compositions in close detail and not just blandly covered them. He delves into rarely explored territory like the maverick blues, 'If', which Joe recorded on the 1967 Milestone album, *The Kicker*, and he brings no less insight to the more familiar 'Recorda-Me' and 'Punjab', which have become more or less repertory pieces. The band is sympathetic and sounds exceedingly well prepared to tackle challenging material. Magnarelli and Herwig have the combined precision and big tone one expects of good ensemble players and the rhythm section does its job fluently. Snidero's solos are considered but in no way pat or pre-formed. Interestingly, it is Henderson's rhythmic complexity rather than his harmonics which seem to intrigue the altoist. Henderson has a very distinctive way of splitting perfectly ordinary time-signatures up into unexpected fractions and, equally, making very complex metres sound as basic as four-to-the-floor. Snidero picks up those cues on the closing 'Black Narcissus' and 'Afro-Centric' in particular, two tunes which open him up to new and fascinating opportunities.

Ann-Sofi Soderqvist

TRUMPET, FLUGELHORN and

The Soegaard Ensemble

GROUP

Danish composers from Niels Viggo Bentzon to Bengt Hambraeus have long taken an interest in improvisation and electronics. The Soegaard Ensemble work at the free end of the spectrum, creating a light and very detailed sound that is almost classical in mood.

****(*) Chronox**
Leo Lab CD 040 *Jan Krogh (t); Steffan Poulsen (as, elec); Fredrik Soegaard (g, elec); Frank Jensen (p); Lars Juul (d).* 5 & 6/97.

Deriving its name from the Greek words *chronos* and *paradox*, the Ensemble's first widely available record examines the movement of sound in time. Soegaard himself is the dominant voice and the group's intellectual leader, exploring the musical application of Mandelbrot sets and fractals. There are two versions of 'Position', one studio, the other live and double the length; essentially, the piece involves eight cells or modules of sound deployed horizontally and then stacked into a great mass of sound. On this showing, a live recording might have been more interesting; both Soegaard and Poulsen know how to make their computers sing.

Martial Solal (born 1927)

PIANO

Born in Algiers, Solal came to France in his early twenties, worked with Django Reinhardt and became a valued accompanist for visiting or exiled Americans such as Sidney Bechet and Don Byas. He is a remarkable composer, creating complex themes out of simple intervals and brief melodic cells. At times, Solal has headed big bands and has written for film, but his main contribution is as a small-group and solo performer

*****(*) The Complete Vogue Recordings, Volume 1**
Vogue 74321 40932 2 *Solal; Joe Benjamin, Jean-Marie Ingrand, Pierre Michelot, Benoît Quersin (b); Roy Haynes, Pierre Lemarchand, Jean-Louis Viale (d).* 5/53–4/55.

***** The Complete Vogue Recordings, Volume 2**
Vogue 74321 40933 2 *Solal; Fats Sadi (vib); Jean-Marie Ingrand, Benoît Quersin (b); Christian Garrios (b); Jean-Louis Viale (d).* 1–11/56.

Solal's reputation rests largely on his solo and trio work; these early sessions, made after he had been working in Paris for about a decade, underline the excitement the young Algerian caused there. He swings effortlessly on standard and bebop material, but also subjects tunes like 'Ramona', 'Poinciana' and Dizzy's 'The Champ', all on Volume 1, to the most rigorous examination, breaking them down into parts and reassembling them, subtly transformed. The only thing missing in any bulk at this stage is Solal's own writing, though 'Farniente', 'Midi' and 'Ridikiool' give some notice of the subtlety and range of later work.

Volume 2 contains material recorded with the popular vibraphonist, Fats Sadi; unfortunately, he tends to overpower Solal's subtler ideas. For quick comparison, try the later version of 'Ridikiool' with vibes. Much of its wry humour has been lost. Wonderfully, though, the record includes no fewer than 15 unaccompanied Solal solos, including an astonishing 'I Can't Get Started', taped in Paris in November 1956.

*****(*) Sans Tambour Ni Trompette**
RCA 7432 137511 *Solal; Gilbert Rovere, Jean-François Jenny-Clark (b).* 10/70.

As the title suggests, Solal dispensed with the services of both horn player and drummer to experiment with a new kind of trio: virile, calm but searching, and at every turn indicative of a technique that was still uncovering new areas of concern and ever-wider circles of capability. There was nothing else quite like this in 1970 and, had it been performed or recorded in New York, it would have caused a sensation. The two long tracks, 'Sequence Tenante' and 'Unisson', might almost be Debussy dancing with Art Tatum. The two bass players anchor the harmonies, often at some remove one from the other, while Solal dances on top. By any standards these are astonishing performances, and recognition is long overdue for them.

***** En Solo**
RCA Victor 74321 47789 2 *Solal (p solo).* 11/71.

Beautifully remastered from a slightly muddy and indefinite recording, this offers yet more testimony to Solal's multi-faceted gifts as an improviser. All but two of the pieces are originals. 'Ah! Non!', 'Mercredi 13' and 'Jazz Antagoniste' are typical Solal ideas, fitted together like mosaic or cloisonné out of tiny shards of melody or sometimes, as on 'Fa Mi Re Do', out of minimal harmonic material. The two standards, 'What Is This Thing Called Love' and 'Darn That Dream', are played with a mixture of reserve and impressive emotion, particularly the latter, which must count as one of Solal's most focused and convincing interpretations of another composer's work.

***** Duo In Paris**
Dreyfus Jazz Line 19016 *Solal; Joachim Kühn (p).* 10/75.

*****(*) Bluesine**
Soul Note 121060 *Solal (p solo).* 1/83.

Bluesine is a lovely record, and an excellent place to sample Solal's solo style. Though he remains something of a specialized taste, he is utterly distinctive as a piano player, owing much to Monk and Bud and even, in some lights, to Oscar Peterson as well, but remaining absolutely his own man. The recording quality here is impeccable: very full and resonant, but with lots of attention to detail as well. A good place to start, with a mixture of original and standard material.

The earlier record with Kühn is more difficult to pin down, largely because these are both players with a markedly individual, not to say idiosyncratic, approach, and hearing them in conjunction can be slightly disconcerting. Kühn is more obviously a romantic; or perhaps that should be a more obvious romantic. He is also, on occasion, an obfuscator. Solal's romanticism is more strait-laced and unaffected, and he comes out of these duos well ahead.

****** Plays Hodeir**
OMDCD 5008 *Solal; Roger Guérin, Eric Le Lann, Tony Russo, Bernard Marchais (t); Jacques Bolognesi, Christian Guizien (tb); Marc Steckar (tba); Jacques Di Donato (cl); François Jeanneau (cl, ts, ss); Jean-Pierre Debarbat (ts, ss); Jean-Louis Chautemps (bcl, as, ss); Pierre Gossez (bs, cl); Pierre Blanchard (vn); Hervé Derrien (clo); Philippe Mace (vib); Christian Escoudé (g); Césarius Alvim (b); André Ceccarelli (d).* 3 & 4/84.

*****(*) Martial Solal Big Band**
Dreyfus Jazz Line 849230 *As above, except add Patrick Artero (t), Hamid Belhocine, Glenn Ferris, Denis Deloup (tb), Patrice Petitdidier (frhn), Philip Legris (tba), Pierre Mimran, Roger Simon, Jean-Pierre Solves (sax, f), Philippe Nadal (clo), Frédéric Sylvestre (g).* 12/83, 5/84.

****(*) Triptyque**
Adda 590067 *Solal; François Mechali (b); Jean-Louis Mechali (d); A Piacere Saxophone Quartet: Jean-Pierre Caens (ss), Jean-Marc Larché (as), Philippe Bouveret (ts); Yves Gerbelot (bs).* 3/90.

It's the larger ensembles of the 1980s that really stand out in Solal's recording career: the Gaumont *Big Band* session of 1981 (long deleted) and the truly superb Hodeir set, recorded at Radio France three years later. Trumpeter Roger Guérin is there of course and is, as always, striking, notably on the closing Monk tribute, 'Comin' On The Hudson'. 'Transplantation I' is a companion-piece to 'Flautando' (not included here) and features Debarbat's ringing tenor. 'D Or No' is for sextet and, like the full-band 'Le Désert Recommence', highlights Solal at his most ironically Gallic. The Verve *Big Band* (now deleted, but look out for remaindered copies) hinges on a long, elaborate suite, which is similar in construction to 'Et c'était si vrai' on the more richly voiced Dreyfus set. It is difficult to judge whether Solal is more effective with the larger unit or whether the angular movement of his compositions sounds better with a small ensemble. Simple preference will probably dictate future choices; both should certainly be sampled if at all possible.

Triptyque is something of an oddity, a suite of themes and solo spots with a slightly ragged saxophone quartet. Solal has sounded very much better, and the two Mechalis are so eye-droopingly dull in their features one wonders why they weren't re-taken or edited out.

*****(*) Solal–Lockwood**
JMS 067 *Solal; Didier Lockwood (vn).* 6/93.

The duos with Lockwood are very attractive. There is something so inescapably Gallic about the whole conception of the set that it prompts a smile with the very first violin phrases of Solal's 'Difficult Blues'. These fade to wonder with the quiet beauty of Miles's 'Solar'. 'Nuages' is fluffy and insubstantial, but Lockwood's original 'Amusette 2' and the closing 'Some Day My Prince Will Come' go right back to the non-European roots both men call on in this fine performance.

****** Improvisie Pour France Musique**
JMS 18638 2CD *Solal (p solo).* 93–94.

These radio recitals were awesome enough when they first went out. Given the chance to study them at close quarters and with the repeat button, one is simply astonished at the range of Solal's talents. In recent years he has begun to explore specific areas of jazz piano history. His debt to Bud Powell has long been recognized (an influence symbiotically received during Bud's sojourn in France) but his take on Garner and Tatum is less expected, and the version on this disc of 'Tea For Two' merits comparison with the great man's. We do not exaggerate, nor is it possible to overestimate, the sheer artistry of this astonishing record. Anyone interested in jazz piano should make it a priority.

****** Triangle**

JMS 18674 *Solal; Marc Johnson (b); Peter Erskine (d).* 95.

There can be few better straight piano improvisers anywhere in the world at the moment, and this is a spanking trio. After this, one almost wonders if Erskine and Johnson have been wasting their time on some of their own projects, so good are they as accompanists to the Frenchman. Individual tracks are kept relatively short, still with the outline of a song-form in their structure. 'Round About Twelve' (geddit?) plays games with the chromatic scale, while 'Anathème' (another pun on 'Thème pour Anna') alternates sour–sweet, dissonant–consonant passages in the most subtle way. Very fine indeed, and an ideal complement to *Improvisie*.

*****(*) Just Friends**

Dreyfus FDM 36592 *Solal; Gary Peacock (b); Paul Motian (d).* 7/97.

****** Balade du 10 Mars**

Soul Note 121340 2 *As above, except omit Peaock; add Marc Johnson (b).* 3/98.

When Solal made his American debut in 1963 at the Newport Jazz Festival, Paul Motian was in the group. Over the last couple of years, the association has been revived and has produced some of the best music of the pianist's career. Martial celebrated his seventieth birthday with Paul and Gary Peacock and has rarely sounded more blues-based and swinging, eliding at least some of his subtler, 'European' configurations to produce what is arguably his most straightahead album ever. This is not to say that it lacks individuality. No one who has listened to him with any attention will mistake who the soloist is on 'Willow Weep For Me' or 'You Stepped Out Of A Dream', though it is not until halfway through the record, and a markedly original 'Hommage A Frédéric Chopin', that something of a more familiar Solal comes through.

Balade du 10 Mars is even better. The free-form improvisation on Motian's 'Gang Of Five' is the most outside playing Solal has done on record for many years. 'Round Midnight' is a duet for piano and drums, recalling the same piece on the Newport record, which RCA should think hard about reissuing. Johnson stands in for Gary Peacock on this occasion and, as might be expected, the rhythm is looser and less rugged. As before, echoes of the classic Bill Evans trio are everywhere and it would be wonderful to hear either version of this group tackle 'Gloria's Step' or 'Waltz For Debby'. Martial's touch is as deft and lyrical as ever, but there is a new and welcome hint of wildness to the playing, as if finally he feels relaxed enough in his own technique to cut loose and challenge the harmonic rules. Unusual to hear Solal concentrate so absolutely on standards and jazz repertory. 'Night And Day', 'Softly, As In A Morning Sunrise', 'Almost Like Being In Love', 'The Lady Is A Tramp' and 'My Old Flame' round out the programme, with a fine, unhackneyed interpretation of 'Round Midnight' and just one other original, 'The Newest Old Waltz' coming in right at the end. A marvellous modern-jazz record by one of the masters.

***** Jazz'n (e)motion**

BMG/RCA 74321 55935 2 *Solal (p solo).* 1/98.

A wonderful writer of film music himself, Martial here explores the screen fantasies of fellow composers, from Charles Trenet's music for the Truffaut classic, *Baisers volés*, to 'Over The Rainbow' and 'The Shadow Of Your Smile' from *The Sandpiper*. He caresses the melodies and in some cases improvises only rather sparingly, preferring to stay within the confines of the original conception. There are exceptions: 'Carioca' from *Flying Down To Rio* is jazzed up considerably and 'Strike Up The Band' is inspired more by Busby Berkeley than by the Gershwins. Fine, moody stuff, but if anyone wants examples of Solal's own film-writing, they will need to look elsewhere. Apart from 'Hommage à Tex Avery', written for an imaginary movie, there is nothing.

*****(*) Contrastes**

Storyville STCD 4242 *Solal; Henrik Bolberg, Thomas Fryland, Lars Lindgren, Benny Rosenfeld (t); Steen Hansen, Peter Jensen, Klaus Lohrer, Vincent Nilsson (tb); Janus Mogensen (tba); Thomas Franck, Michael Hove, Flemming Madsen, Uffe Markussen, Nicolai Schultz (reeds); Anders Chico Lundvall (g); Morten Grønvad (mar); Thomas Ovesen, Mads Vinding (b); Jonas Hohansen, Daniel Humair (d).* 3/99.

The tenth anniversary of the Jazzpar Prize saw the committee make another critically popular selection; this kind of recognition for Solal has been long overdue. The formula remains the same, with music by the laureate's own group interspersed with commissioned performances involving the Danish Radio Jazz Orchestra. The main orchestral component of Solal's Jazzpar commission was the large-scale 'Mythe Décisif', a typically multi-layered and ambitious piece of composition that reminds us how fine a big-band writer he is. Jim McNeely has the band well drilled and precise, but not at the expense of real jazz feel. The three other band works are less dramatically proportioned, but 'En Coulisse', 'Monster Piece' and the richly textured 'Contrastes' are unmistakably Solal creations.

Good as these works are, what we wouldn't have given for a separate disc devoted to the playing of the Solal Trio. Mads Vinding and Daniel Humair (who also supplied the cover art) play out of their skins on two thematically similar versions of 'Ritournelle' and a lovely, crisp version of 'Summertime' which lays bare the bones of the song once again. An important staging-point in Solal's career which we earnestly hope will bring him an ever widening audience.

Lew Soloff (born 1944)

TRUMPET, FLUGELHORN

Classically trained at the Juilliard and Eastman schools, Soloff has become a first-call trumpeter for big bands and smaller ensembles, offering anything from nimble negotiation of complex charts to old-fashioned high-note pyrotechnics. He spent a fruitful time as a member of R&B band, Blood, Sweat & Tears. Influenced by that, and by leaders as diverse as Gil Evans and Thad Jones, he has devised a style of his own, terse, well structured and, underneath the toughness, very affecting.

***** With A Song In My Heart**

Milestone MCD 9290 *Soloff; Mulgrew Miller (p); Emily Mitchell (hp); George Mraz (b); Victor Lewis (d).* 1/98.

*****(*) Rainbow Mountain**

Enja/Tiptoe TIP 888 838 2 *Soloff; Miles Evans (t); Lou Marini (sax, f); Delmar Brown (ky); Joe Beck, Hiram Bullock (g); Mark Egan (b); Danny Gottlieb (d).* 1 & 2/99.

Soloff's mid-'80s records for Paddle Wheel are no longer available, which is a shame, but there has been some renewed activity over the past decade. As the years go by, Soloff takes on more and more of the easy lyrical style of his sometime boss, Clark Terry. That influence, direct or unconscious, is dominant on *With A Song In My Heart*. Lew's soloing has a featherlight mobility but delivered with a full, brassy tone. The choice of material is also challenging, with standards like the Andantino from Tchaikovsky's Fourth Symphony set against standards like 'Come Rain Or Come Shine' and 'With A Song In My Heart', Soloff originals 'Istanbul' and 'One For Emily', and film composer Dmitri Tiomkin's 'Deguello', one of two tracks on which the selfsame Emily Mitchell plays.

Rainbow Mountain is once again much closer to the sound and the ethos of the Evans band, and the addition of Delmar Brown, Miles Evans and Hiram Bullock on the title-track. 'Up From The Skies' is a further dip into the Hendrix catalogue, but the real surprise is a jazz arrangement of a rock song so cliché'd that it has been banned as a test piece in guitar stores (reference: *Wayne's World*), Led Zeppelin's 'Stairway To Heaven'. And yes, it works fine. They also do Credence Clearwater Revival's 'Born On The Bayou'. The band is a touch bland and unleavened, but guitarist Joe Beck and drummer Danny Gottlieb both have something of the leader's mercurial personality. The Paddle Wheels may become available again one day, but for the time being these are well worth having.

Sonny Clark Memorial Quartet

GROUP

One-off project dedicated to the late pianist's music.

***** Voodoo**

Black Saint BSR 120109 *John Zorn (as); Wayne Horvitz (p); Ray Drummond (b); Bobby Previte (d).* 11/85.

John Zorn's enthusiasm for the adventurously simple bop of Sonny Clark surfaced in his News for Lulu group. This, though, was a more sustained homage, seven Clark originals played with real feeling and attention to detail. Zorn himself gets a sound that at moments might recall Jackie McLean, but with a drier edge. It, coupled with Previte's drumming, is the giveaway. It's pretty obvious you're not listening to a period performance but to a latter-day version of Sonny's music. No great surprises in the selection of covers: 'Cool Struttin'', 'Minor Meeting', 'Nicely', 'Something Special', a heroic 'Voodoo', 'Sonia' and, ending as emphatically as it begins, 'Sonny's Crib'. A fascinating disc for anyone interested in the Blue Note diaspora.

Eddie South (1904–62)

VIOLIN

South learned violin as a child and received a considerable music education before playing in Chicago and New York in the 1920s. Worked on the black theatre circuit in the early '30s as a chamber-jazz act before touring Europe. On radio and even TV in the '40s and '50s, but gradually drifted from sight.

***** Eddie South 1923–1937**

Classics 707 *South; Jimmy Wade (c); Williams Dover (tb); Clifford King (cl, bcl, as); Arnett Nelson (cl, as); Vernon Roulette (cl, ts); Teddy Weatherford, Antonia Spaulding (p); Walter Wright, Stéphane Grappelli, Michel Warlop (vn); Everett Barksdale (g, bj, v); Django Reinhardt, Mike McKendrick, Roger Chaput, Sterling Conaway (g); Louis Gross (bb); Wilson Myers, Milt Hinton, Paul Cordonnier (b); Edwin Jackson, Jimmy Bertrand, Jerome Burke (d).* 12/23–11/37.

***** Eddie South 1937–1941**

Classics 737 *South; Charlie Shavers (t); Buster Bailey (cl); Russell Procope (as); David Martin, Stanley Facey (p); Stéphane Grappelli (vn); Django Reinhardt, Isadore Langlois, Eddie Gibbs, Eugene Fields (g); Paul Cordonnier, Doles Dickens, Ernest Hill (b); Specs Powell, Tommy Benford (d); Ginny Sims (v).* 11/37–3/41.

South wasn't simply one of the most accomplished of jazz violinists; he might have been one of the best-schooled of all jazz musicians of his time, given a thorough classical grounding that, unusually, blossomed into a hot rather than a cool improviser's stance. If his reputation rests on his Paris recordings of 1937 (available on Classics 707), there are some interesting footnotes to an unfulfilled career in the other tracks listed here. The first Classics disc starts with a very rare 1923 track by Jimmy Wade's Moulin Rouge Orchestra: awful sound (it was recorded for Paramount) but South's intensely blue violin still cuts through the ensembles. His slightly later Chicago and New York sessions are well played if comparatively lightweight – on songs such as 'Nagasaki' or 'Marcheta' he sounds almost like a vaudevillian – but the three sessions with Grappelli and Reinhardt are fascinating, the guitarist driven into his best form, the violinist playing his finest solos on 'Sweet Georgia Brown' and 'Eddie's Blues', and the date culminating in the extraordinary improvisation on Bach's D Minor Concerto for two violins by South, Grappelli and Reinhardt together. A further 1938 session in Hilversum has some more strong playing by South's regular quintet, but his final titles from 1940–41 belabour the material, which seems designed to cast South as a romantic black gypsy and sends him back to vaudeville. He seldom recorded again, despite a fair amount of broadcasting, and must be accounted as a talent out of his time.

South Frisco Jazz Band

GROUP

A clan of Californian followers of the Murphy–Watters methods, this great institution of its scene began playing in the late 1950s and has just recently elected to go into voluntary retirement.

****** Sage Hen Strut**

Stomp Off 1143 *Dan Comins, Leon Oakley (c); Jim Snyder (tb); Mike Baird (cl, ss, as); Bob Helm (cl, as); Robbie Rhodes (p); Vince Saunders (bj); Bob Rann (tba); Bob Raggio (d, wbd).* 11/84.

*****(*) Broken Promises**

Stomp Off 1180 *As above, except omit Helm.* 9/87.

*****(*) Got Everything**

Stomp Off 1240 *As above, except add Bob Helm (cl, ss, v), Jack Mangan (d).* 11/89–9/91.

*****(*) Big Bear Stomp**

Stomp Off 1307 *As above, except add Lloyd Byassee (d); omit Helm, Raggio and Mangan.* 10/95.

*****(*) Emperor Norton's Hunch**

Stomp Off 1342 *As above, except Brian Shaw (t), Charlie Bornemann (tb), John Gill (d, v) replace Comins, Snyder and Byassee.* 2–3/98.

The South Frisco Jazz Band (and by South Frisco they usually mean Los Angeles) have been playing as a group, on and off, since around 1960. Formed in the spirit of the Lu Watters and Turk Murphy groups, they approach traditional material with a zest, flair and ingenuity that shame most British trad groups and they manage to combine a faithful feel with a certain irreverence: this isn't corny or the work of pasticheurs, but it's very good fun. The band has made a fair number of records over the years and these CDs are a good representation of what the line-up can do. The two-cornet front line plays a fiercely hot lead on most of the tunes, and they're abetted by Snyder's choleric trombone and Baird's authentically quivering reed parts (Helm, an original Turk Murphy sideman, sits in on two of the discs). The material is all original archaeology: when they play Jelly Roll Morton, it's 'Little Lawrence' or 'If Someone Would Only Love Me' rather than 'Wolverine Blues', and there are tiny tributes scattered through the discs to the likes of Roy Palmer, Richard M. Jones and Natty Dominique. There are plenty of rags, too. Of these discs, *Sage Hen Strut* takes a very narrow lead for the choice of material and the complete absence of vocals (not quite the group's strong point, though they don't do much singing). *Big Bear Stomp* doesn't sound like one of their absolute best, but they still turn in enough winners – try Lovie Austin's 'Rampart Street Blues' – to please admirers of the other records.

Emperor Norton's Hunch features three personnel changes, although Gill is a very familiar name to these sorts of surroundings, and sadly it is likely to be their final record: the band members live too far apart to be able to play regularly, and after 42 years they deserve a bit of a rest. So this is a typically spirited farewell – not their greatest, but again liberally sprinkled with hotter-than-that playing. Until the Sage Hen struts again!

Sune Spångberg

DRUMS

Part of the community of young Turks who made up Swedish modernism in the '50s, Spångberg played on many important dates and has been a significant presence in that scene ever since. He worked extensively with the group, ISKRA, in music education.

****(*) Two Absent Friends**

Dragon DRCD316 *Spångberg; Arne Forsen (p); Ulf Akerhielm (b).* 2/96.

***** Live At Café Aguéli**

Dragon DRCD 328 *Spångberg; Johan Setterlind (t); Carl Fredrik Orrje, Göran Strandberg, Claes-Göran Fagerstadt, Ake Johansson (p); Ludvig Girdland (vn); Ivar Lidell, Owe Gustavsson (b); Nannie Porres (v).* 9/97–8/98.

Spångberg has been a singular witness in the music. He was with Bud Powell at The Golden Circle and he drummed on Albert Ayler's first record. His sleeve-notes to *Two Absent Friends* muse on a broad vista of Swedish jazz history but pay special note to the two dedicatees who provided the music here, Lasse Werner and Kurt Lindgren. Both composers had much inspiration in them and these 12 tunes are an attractive lot. More than that, one feels the music is haunted by a number of ghosts, not just Werner and Lindgren but also Torbjorn Hultcrantz, Jan Wallgren and Allan Olsson. It's a pity, then, that the results are finally not so distinguished. The trio muster only a rather clumsy empathy which detracts from the occasion, and Akerhielm's several *arco* solos seem insecure; nor is the balance, with Spångberg sounding too crisp and upfront in the mix, properly effective. Some fine material is deposited here, but it's not as well served as it might have been.

The live CD, cut at various sessions at the small Café Aguéli, is much more like it. The sound is rough, close-up and atmospheric, and the various combinations of musicians make an interesting match, old-timers such as Johansson and Fagerstadt next to young players like Orrje and Setterlind. Roots music as it's being played today.

Muggsy Spanier (1906–67)

CORNET

Recording as a teenager, Francis Spanier was off to a quick start in his native Chicago. He worked with Ted Lewis and Ben Pollack in the 1920s and '30s, before forming his Ragtime Band in 1939. The records are classics but the band was a commercial failure. He stuck with Dixieland through the '40s and '50s, moving west to join Earl Hines in 1957 and leading modest small groups up until his death.

*****(*) Pocket Giant**

Verve 531695-2 *Spanier; Dick Fierge, Dave Klein (c); Max Connett, Lloyd Wallen (t); Jules Fasthoff, George Brunies, Harry Raderman, Guy Carey, Sam Blank, Ted Vesley (tb); Volly De*

Faut, Frank Teschemacher, Jim Cannon, Benny Goodman, Ted Lewis, Ben Kanler (cl); Jimmy Dorsey (cl, as, bs); Louis Martin, Don Murray, Charles Pierce (as); Coleman Hawkins, Mezz Mezzrow, Hymie Wolfson, King Guion, Ralph Rudder (ts); Maurice Morse, Lyle Smith (bs, bsx); Mel Stitzel, Fats Waller, Jack Russin, Dan Lipscomb, Bob Laine, Jack Aaronson, Joe Sullivan, Frank Ross, Art Gronwall (p); Al Carsella (acc); Paul Lyman, Sol Klein (vn); Tony Gerhardi, Eddie Condon, Garry McAdams, Leon Kaplan (g); Marvin Saxbe, Stuart Branch (bj); Jim Lannigan, Bob Escamilla, Harry Barth (bb); Johnny Mueller, Jules Cassard, Alan Morgan, Francis Palmer (b); Paul Kettler, John Lucas, Ben Pollack, Gene Krupa, Josh Billings (d); Red McKenzie, The Four Dusty Travellers, Harry Maxfield (v). 2/24–9/37.

Spanier was only seventeen when he made the earliest music here – by the Bucktown Five, in Richmond, Indiana – but he was already a confident lead player, if less impressive as a soloist (his chorus on 'Hot Mittens' is a well-meaning near-disaster). 'Mobile Blues' is nevertheless a thoroughgoing jazz performance by a young group which had absorbed many of the latest developments in the music. After these early appearances, the CD follows Spanier's dance-band career in the 1920s, with a stray Ben Pollack track from 1937 to close on. The valuable tracks here are the round dozen from the Ted Lewis Band which are otherwise unavailable at present: Lewis had a hot band and Spanier was one of its warmest ingredients. Ray Miller's 1929 'That's A Plenty' has a blistering cornet solo too. Remastering is clean, and this French Verve edition is a much better bet than the similar *Muggshot* on ASV which we have previously listed.

**** The Great Sixteen

RCA 13039-2 *Spanier; George Brunies (tb, v); Rod Kless (cl); Ray McKinstrey, Bernie Billings, Nick Caizza (ts); George Zack, Joe Bushkin (p); Bob Casey (g, b); Pat Pattison (b); Marty Greenberg, Don Carter, Al Sidell (d).* 6–12/39.

**** Muggsy Spanier 1939–1942

Classics 709 *As above two discs, except add Ruby Weinstein, Elmer O'Brien (t), Ford Leary (tb, v), Karl Kates, Joe Forchetti, Ed Caine (as), Charlie Queener (p), Al Hammer (d), Dottie Reid (v).* 7/39–6/42.

Spanier's 1939 Ragtime Band recordings are among the classic statements in the traditional-jazz idiom. Bob Crosby's Bob Cats had helped to initiate a modest vogue for small Dixieland bands in what was already a kind of revivalism at the height of the big-band era, and Spanier's group had audiences flocking to Chicago clubs, although by December, with a move to New York, they were forced to break up for lack of work. Their recordings have been dubbed 'The Great Sixteen' ever since. While there are many fine solos scattered through the sides – mostly by Spanier and the little-remembered Rod Kless – it's as an ensemble that the band impresses: allied to a boisterous rhythm section, the informal counterpoint among the four horns (the tenor sax perfectly integrated, just as Eddie Miller was in the Bob Cats) swings through every performance. The repertoire re-established the norm for Dixieland bands and, even though the material goes back to Oliver and the ODJB, there's no hint of fustiness, even in the rollicking effects of 'Barnyard Blues'. 'Someday Sweetheart', with its sequence of elegant solos, is a masterpiece of cumulative tension, and Spanier himself secures two finest hours in the storming finish to 'Big Butter And Egg Man' and the wah-wah blues-playing on 'Relaxin' At The Touro', a poetic tribute to convalescence (he had been ill the previous year) the way Parker's 'Relaxin' At Camarillo' would subsequently be. His own playing is masterful throughout – the hot Chicago cornet-sound refined and seared away to sometimes the simplest but most telling of phrases.

The RCA set, *The Great Sixteen*, includes eight alternative takes which, if anything, detract from the perfect feel of the issued masters. Programme them in only if you're in a mood for scholarship. The Classics CD adds eight tracks to the definitive 16 by Muggsy's big band, none of them outstanding but all grist to the Spanier collector's mill. Whatever the choice, no collection is complete without some representation of this great music!

***(*) Muggsy Spanier 1944

Classics 907 *Spanier; Miff Mole, Lou McGarity (tb); Pee Wee Russell (cl); Boomie Richman (ts); Ernie Caceres (bs); Gene Schroeder, Dick Cary, Jess Stacy (p); Eddie Condon, Hy White (g); Bob Casey, Bob Haggart, Sid Weiss (b); Joe Grauso, George Wettling (d).* 4–10/44.

*** Muggsy Spanier 1944–1946

Classics 967 *Spanier; Lou McGarity, Vernon Brown (tb); Pee Wee Russell, Peanuts Hucko (cl); Bud Freeman, Nick Caizza (ts); Ernie Caceres (bs); Gene Schroeder, Dave Bowman, Nick Rongetti (p); Eddie Condon, Carl Kress, Hy White (g); Bob Haggart, Bob Casey, Trigger Alpert (b); Joe Grauso, Charlie Carroll, George Wettling (d).* 12/44–9/46.

***(*) Manhattan Masters

Storyville STCD 60-51 *Spanier; Lou McGarity, Miff Mole (tb); Pee Wee Russell (cl); Ernie Caceres (bs); Gene Schroeder, Nick Rongetti (p); Carl Kress, Fred Sharp, Allan Hanlon (g); Bob Casey, Jack Lesberg, Bob Haggart (b); Joe Grauso, Charles Carroll (d).* 3/45.

Muggsy's sessions for Commodore, V-Disc, Disc and an almost unknown date for Manhattan make a very welcome addition to his CD listing. The Commodores could probably sound better than they do here, but at present this is their only accessible edition. All the music on Classics 907 is vintage Spanier, with standouts including 'Lady Be Good', a superb 'Snag It' and a very fine 'Sweet Sue', with a solo by Miff Mole on the latter that proves he was far from the lost soul his post-1920s reputation would have one think. Besides Spanier, the standout player is Pee Wee Russell: connoisseurs of the bizarre will relish his vocal on the V-Disc, 'Pee Wee Speaks'. The subsequent volume is just a shade behind, perhaps, although there is so little surviving Spanier that it's a necessary disc for followers. Both docked a notch for unpleasing sound: they should be better than this.

The six Manhattan tracks reappear on the Storyville edition, along with a dozen other pieces which were done at the same sessions, although under the nominal leadership of either Miff Mole or Pee Wee Russell. The tracks were made at the instigation of Nick Rongetti of Nick's in Greenwich Village (he even gets to play a solo on 'That's A Plenty'!). It's Condonesque Dixieland without Condon and, although the principals are all in hearty fettle, it doesn't have the spark of greatness about it. But always good to hear Spanier and the excellent Mole, who was well out of the limelight at this stage: his fine solo on 'I Can't Give You Anything But Love' makes one regret his later decline all the more.

***** At Club Hangover 1953–54**

Storyville STCD 6033 *Spanier; Ralph Hutchinson (tb); Darnell Howard, Chico Gomez (cl); Mel Grant, Red Richards (p); Truck Parham (b); Barrett Deems, Cuz Couzineau (d).* 4/53–11/54.

Not a great time for Dixieland, but Spanier kept the faith and these were serviceable bands. Like the pro that he was, he plays and leads with assurance, and the only real disappointment is the choice of tunes which lines up warhorse after warhorse. The lovely playing on 'Moonglow' and 'If I Had You' makes one wish that they had other tunes on the set-list.

Martin Speake (born 1958)

ALTO SAXOPHONE

Speake studied in London and came to prominence with the all-sax group, Itchy Fingers; he has subsequently tried a variety of settings but seems most at home in a quartet, like this one.

***** Trust**

33 Records 33 JAZZ 035 *Speake; John Parricelli (g); Steve Watts (b); Julian Arguëlles (d).* 11/96.

Speake's recording debut as leader was in 1994 with a disc called *In Our Time*, which was released on Danny Thompson's The Jazz Label, which as far as we can gather is now in abeyance. *Trust* almost seems like back to square one. It features the same group, sounding very much in sympathy, but cleaving to essentially the same concept. As before, Arguëlles is the bedrock for Speake's muscular but tuneful ideas, playing with a bright, clean articulation that comes across very strongly. Tunes like 'Golden Rooster', 'The Heron' and 'The Accidental Flamboyant' are colourful and witty. The ballad forms are less secure, but only because Speake seems inclined to be reserved. It makes sense with this music to have guitar rather than piano. Parricelli's chiming, slightly edgy sound works very well indeed and contrasts nicely with Watts's dark, woody bass-lines. Speake toured in 2000 with a group including Bobo Stenson and Paul Motian.

Glenn Spearman (1947–98)

TENOR SAXOPHONE

Spearman's death from liver cancer in 1998 was not unexpected, but it left a sense of things undone and of a major talent not yet properly recognized. The late recordings have a quiet intensity which is comparable to Coltrane's.

***** Utterance**

Cadence CJR 1103 *Spearman; John Heward (d, kalimba, v).* 10/90.

*****(*) Mystery Project**

Black Saint 120147 *Spearman; Larry Ochs (ts, sno); Chris Brown (p, DX7); Ben Lindgren (b); Donald Robinson, William Winant (d).* 8/92.

****** Smokehouse**

Black Saint 120157 *As above.* 11/93.

Spearman was over forty before the first of these was recorded, so not surprisingly he already sounds settled into a strong and individual voice. He started out as a Coltrane-influenced screamer but quickly recognized that a more thoughtful delivery might well bear dividends. A 1981 duo with drummer Donald Robinson has been compared to Trane and Rashied Ali's *Interstellar Space*, and Spearman was to return to the same format with *Utterance*, a sequence of duos with drummer John Heward. By that time Spearman had come under the tutelage of Frank Wright, with whom he had bunked and woodshedded in France, and it was clear that he was striking out in a new direction. The Coltrane influence is still there, but it has been subsumed into something altogether more linear. After a period with trumpeter Raphe Malik's sextet, Spearman founded his Double Trio.

Dedicated to Ornette Coleman (and to the structured freedom on Ornette's *Free Jazz*), *Mystery Project* consists of a large three-part suite, in which the direction of the music is dictated not so much by notated passages as by the distribution of the personnel. As in Rova man Larry Ochs's 'Double Image', the basic group is a palette from which various colours and shadings can be drawn. Spearman's personal colour-code would seem to be black and red. He's a fierce player, overblowing in the upper register and virtually incapable of anything less than full throttle. He never sacrifices subtlety to power, though. This is intelligent music that never palls or sounds dated.

The follow-up record has the same line-up and makes similarly effective use of doubled instruments. It's a long – 75-minute – suite with an intermission built in, not because an LP version required a break, but because the music is so unremittingly present that one couldn't absorb any more without some surcease. Spearman's time in Europe opened up many interesting compositional ideas to him, but these performances are squarely in the tradition of the 1960s avant-garde, and their strength comes from Spearman's profound conviction that the ideas adumbrated at that time are far from exhausted but still constitute a *lingua franca* for improvisation. The 'in-take' and 'out-take' of 'Axe, Beautiful Acts' exude a fierce poetry that is worthy of Cecil Taylor.

*****(*) th**

CIMP 148 *Spearman; Christopher Cauley (as); David Prentice (vn, vla); Dominic Duval (b); John Heward (d, perc, v).* 5/97.

It was no surprise when Spearman turned up on CIMP. It's a label whose blunt, unvarnished ethos entirely matches his own. This group is co-led with drummer Heward, who duets with the saxophonist (and on this occasion kalimba player and vocalist) on the extraordinary 'Summoning', which has no precedent in either's work to date. Prentice sits out a couple of tracks and 'Initiation' is a trio with Spearman, Duval and Heward, thus varying the sound of this remarkable group.

The long 'Irreversible Blues' which opens the set has a fascinating asymmetrical structure, while '3 For John' (Heward? Coltrane?) is more of an exercise in extended harmonics and sprung rhythm. The other long track, 'Moment In Time', has a more conventional structure, but is no less challenging as an idea. As with everything else recorded at the Spirit Room in Rossie, the sound makes no compromises. One wishes there had been a few tucks and stitches here, though once again no complaints that the label has failed to deliver on its promise: 'what you hear is exactly what was played'.

***** Working With The Elements**

CIMP 181 *Spearman; Dominic Duval (b). 7/98.*

***** First And Last**

Eremite MTE015 *Spearman; Matthew Goodheart (p); Rashid Bakr (d). 7/98.*

Spearman died less than three months after these sessions and, to be frank, his failing health is all too evident. The live Eremite record is the saxophonist's last earthly word and it is an unhappy affair, dominated by Goodheart and at moments barely coherent. Recorded at the 1998 Fire in the Valley, it weaves awkwardly between intense insight, notably on the opening 'Intertextual Reference', and a prosy banality.

On the studio set for CIMP, Duval holds things together as often as not, and even his meandering personal feature, 'Sass Bolo', is more focused and articulate than a lot of the music involving Glenn. There are flashes here and there of the player who made *Smokehouse*, but they are few and far between.

Apart from 'Series Series' and 'Augh Oh', most of the pieces are very short. Some of them almost seem abortive, as if Spearman is unable or unwilling to follow through on his own premisses. A sad end to a remarkable career, but things to cherish even as the curtain falls.

Chris Speed

TENOR SAXOPHONE, CLARINET

Studied classical piano and clarinet, then added sax in high school. Worked with Jim Black in Boston, and formed the bands Humna Feel and Pachora. Based in New York since 1992.

***** Yeah No**

Songlines SGL 1517-2 *Speed; Cuong Vu (t); Skuli Sverrisson (b); Jim Black (d). 7–12/96.*

*****(*) Deviantics**

Songlines SGL 1524-2 *As above. 10/98.*

Speed has been a valuable and provocative presence on other people's records. His own set tends towards the fragmentary and emerges as an entertaining collection of, well, fragments. The frantic 'Scribble Bliss', the ghostly 'The Dream And Memory Store', the intense and purposeful 'Merge' – each uses the resources of the quartet to good ends without quite suggesting a particular vision. On its own terms, this is a sharp, funny exploration of some of the musics that Speed's come across – jazz and everything else. In many ways the key player is Black, whose nutty rhythms are what really bring the group to life, as boisterous as the horns are.

Deviantics pushes the ideas a little harder into a more coherent shape. This has elements of post-bop in it, but Vu is a strange player, as likely to play against the grain of whatever's going on as follow it, and the stew of influences is getting thicker and richer. Sverrisson's odd 'Tulip' is a very curious melange, and the following 'Wheatstone' is a storming modal blow. 'Valya' has an East European feel. An unpredictable but often genuinely exciting set.

Loz Speyer

TRUMPET, FLUGELHORN

Contemporary British brassman, here debuting his own quartet.

***** Two Kinds Of Blue**

33 Jazz 043 *Speyer; Andy Jones (g); Richard Jeffries (b); Tony Bianco (d). 6/98.*

A likeable hour or so of music from an easygoing quartet. Speyer's unflashy and patient playing may be short on finesse and chopsmanship but he knows what he can do, and he thinks up some practical settings for his modal playing, such as the long and cleverly organized 'Dodman Dance'. Jones is a big assist, whether comping melodiously or countering with his own solos, and Jeffries and Bianco don't slouch. Recorded after their 1998 tour, from the Isle of Dogs to Aberdeen.

Sphere

GROUP

Formed as a Monk repertory band, and named after the great man – his middle name – Sphere was a good festival draw and a less secure recording outfit. Though Rouse and Riley could claim apostolic connection to the great man, Williams became the de facto leader.

*****(*) On Tour**

Red RR 123191 *Charlie Rouse (ts); Kenny Barron (p); Buster Williams (b); Ben Riley (d). 85.*

***** Pumpkin's Delight**

Red RR 123207 *As above. 86.*

****** Sphere**

Verve 557796-2 *As above, except omit Rouse; add Gary Bartz (ss, as). 10/97.*

The spooky thing about Sphere is that the very day the band went into the studio to fulfil a long-standing arrangement to record an album of Monk tunes the great man's death was announced. He had been living in effective retirement for some time, but his work was slowly leaching into the jazz mainstream. The group made no attempt to pastiche his sound. Barron wisely sticks to what he knows best and only very rarely throws in a direct quote; unconsciously, one suspects. Rouse's slightly adenoidal sound is always attractive, and in some respects this is among his very best recordings. The two Reds were recorded in Italy, in Umbria and Bologna. The earlier of the pair is slightly surprising in including only one Monk composition. Williams and Barron are represented by two compositions each, the strongest of which are Williams's 'Dual Force' and the pianist's thoroughly Monkian 'Spiral'. The Umbrian set is recorded roughly but is very immediate and faithful to the live experience. Not a great record, but a thoroughly enjoyable one.

After Rouse's death, the rejuvenated Gary Bartz took over, a lighter, faster sound, but equally soaked in the blues. He makes a mark with two originals, 'Uncle Bubba' and 'Buck And Wing', and plays a lovely solo on Strayhorn's 'Isfahan', but it's the longer-standing members who make the greatest mark. Williams's sound is colossal and Barron contributes not just his usual dark tonality but also the wonderfully mournful 'Twilight'. Sphere may be an occasional project, but marvellous things happen when they get together.

Spirit Level

GROUP

Founded in 1979, Spirit Level went through personnel changes over the years but managed to maintain a consistency of direction, based on clever writing, impeccable ensemble work and soloists who always had things to say.

***** New Year**

Future Music FMR CD 03 1290 *Tim Richards (p); Jerry Underwood (ts); Ernest Mothle (b); Mark Sanders (d). 9/90.*

****** On The Level**

33 Records 33JAZZ026 *As above, except replace Mothle with Kubryk Townsend (b), Sanders with Kenrick Rowe (d). 94.*

*****(*) Great Spirit: Best Of Spirit Level**

33JAZZ051a/b 2CD *As above, except add Dave Holdsworth, Dick Pearce, Jack Walrath (t); Gilad Atzmon (ss, as); Denys Baptiste, Paul Dunmall (ts); Tony Kofi (as, bs); Roger Beaujolais (vib); Dave Colton (g); Paul Anstey, Davide Mantovani (b); Tony Marsh, Dave Ohm, Tony Orrell (d). 79–99.*

Tim Richards's group is in the anomalous position of being better known abroad than in the United Kingdom. Richards is a strong, sometimes idiosyncratic writer, with the ability to give his musicians exactly the kind of material they need without ever sounding as though he is compromising his own vision, and being prepared to allow others to contribute as both writers and players to that vision. The group has been through a number of personnel changes over the years and the process of change has continued until recently without ever seeming to affect the underlying character of a group which is more than Richards's personal vehicle.

Great Spirit is a wonderful sampling of the group at its best, coupled with a brand-new composition written to mark the twentieth anniversary. It includes tracks from the original Spotlite release, *Mice In The Wallet*, the later *Proud Owners* and *Killer Bunnies*, the latter featuring the irrepressible Jack Walrath on trumpet, a single track from *The Swiss Radio Tapes* and 1990's *New Year*, which is the only one of the batch currently available. It's not necessarily the best way of taking a measure of Richards as a composer; of the 15 tracks included, he wrote only six; most of *Killer Bunnies* was down to Walrath and there are contributions from Holdsworth, Dunmall and Underwood. What is clear, though, is the extent to which his blues-based playing and strongly individual leadership shape the material.

One of the authors wrote the liner-notes to *On The Level*, so our enthusiasm for it can be taken as read, and read *in situ*. The earlier record is not quite so compelling, though it shows off facets of the group – its melodism, its ability to sustain extended grooves in relatively short compass, its dynamic logic – which are slightly diffused on the more polished later disc.

The new twentieth anniversary piece, 'Suite For The Shed', is marked by the same characteristics. Its concluding segment, 'Ticket To Tomorrow', is intriguingly pitched and suggests that even if the Spirit Level story is officially at an end or in abeyance, the venturesome qualities of the band live on. It's a remarkable piece, full of emotion and generously proportioned. Richards's own work, which is covered elsewhere, has its great strengths, but the different versions of Spirit Level occupy a special place in recent British jazz.

The Spirits Of Rhythm

GROUP

Originally the Sepia Nephews and the Five Cousins, the group was expanded in the early 1930s with the arrival of Teddy Bunn. Favouring humorous or nonsense lyrics with use of the tiple (a kind of small Latin-American guitar with variable tuning), the group were still formidable musicians and sustained a career right through the '30s and the war years before disbanding.

***** The Spirits Of Rhythm, 1933–34**

JSP JSPCD 307 *Teddy Bunn (g); Leo Watson, Wilbur Daniels, Douglas Daniels (tiple, v); Wilson Myers (b); Virgil Scroggins (d, v); Red McKenzie (v). 33–34.*

The Spirits are now treasured largely for nurturing the extraordinary guitar-playing of Teddy Bunn, one of the undoubted giants of the instrument in jazz before Charlie Christian and Wes Montgomery revolutionized it, often ironically smoothing out the very features which made it different from the horns and piano. No less a musician than Derek Bailey has pointed to Bunn as an early influence. The Spirits were, however, essentially a singing group, not quite a novelty act but not a million miles from it. Watson and the two Daniels boys sang jovial scat lines, accompanying themselves on tiples, while Bunn kept up a solid but ever-changing background. The sound is light and delicate, an almost harp-like backing for voices. Like Freddy Guy, for whom he once depped in the Ellington band, and Freddie Green, who did a similar job for Basie, Bunn understood the workings of a group instinctively and, despite being wholly self-taught, had the uncanny ability to anticipate even non-standard changes.

The JSP set contains material from six sessions over a single twelve-month period. There are two versions of 'I Got Rhythm', both of them featuring Bunn quite strongly; but the outstanding track is 'I'll Be Ready' on which be plays crisp melodic breaks without a single excess gesture. The last few tracks come from a September 1934 session dominated by the doubtful talents of Red McKenzie. These are eminently dispensable.

Spontaneous Music Ensemble

GROUP

One of the most radical and thoughtful improvisation groups to emerge on the British scene in the '60s, SME (sometimes changed to Orchestra) evolved, like AMM, out of free jazz and quickly developed a performance philosophy that eschewed any predetermined structure or materials and any of the familiar supports of melody, harmony or rhythm. That said, at the heart of the group were a melodist and a master of rhythmical pulse, co-founders Trevor Watts and John Stevens. In later years, Watts's central position fell to Roger Smith and saxophonist John Butcher, but Stevens stayed at the helm until his untimely death.

***** Withdrawal**

Emanem 4020 *Kenny Wheeler (t, flhn, perc); Paul Rutherford (tb, perc); Trevor Watts (as, f, ob, perc, v); Evan Parker (ss, ts, perc); Derek Bailey (g); Barry Guy (b, p); John Stevens (d).* 9 & 10/66, 3/67.

*****(*) Summer 1967**

Emanem 4005 *Evan Parker (ts, ss); Peter Kowald (b); John Stevens (d).* 67.

****** Karyobin**

Chronoscope CPE 2001 *Kenny Wheeler (t, flhn); Evan Parker (ss); Derek Bailey (g); Dave Holland (b); John Stevens (d).* 2/68.

Asked to say what had been important to him about 1968, Derek Bailey made the typically perceptive and clear-sighted point that the year of revolutions had really made much less difference to the way things were, in either politics or culture, than a whole string of dates in the previous decade. For admirers of British improvised music, though, 1968 saw the emergence of the SME from the rather constricting cocoon of 'free jazz' into an approach that placed all its weight on a collectively generated, non-hierarchical sound with no preconceived structures of any sort.

The publication of 11 previously unissued SME tracks in 1997 was something of a nostalgia trip for anyone who has followed the British improvisation scene with affection. What is instantly noticeable is that the personnel then corresponds exactly to the front rank of senior players now, with the sad exception of the late John Stevens. Even more striking is that all of them, with the partial exception of Watts, have continued to mine the same musical lode for most of the intervening 30 years. *Withdrawal*, though, does catch them on the cusp. The group had made an LP for the now extinct Eyemark label in the spring of 1966, working in a vein that was unmistakably free jazz. A matter of months later, creating music for a 35-minute film made by George Paul Solomos, they seem to have moved out into new and more abstract territory. (How often has it happened, as is often noted of Miles Davis and *L'Ascenseur pour l'échafaud*, that a film or theatre project allows artists to explore new territory, new sounds, by yoking the music to another artistic artefact?) Part One is very much a feature for Kenny Wheeler, who had been sceptical about becoming involved in free music. It is far from dry, this startling sound, but it is already a long way removed from even a distant memory of bebop or swing. Guy provides dark shifting drones; Parker is not yet quite the skyscraping genius of later years, and it is the still-undervalued Rutherford and Watts (who took over the running of the SME during Stevens's sojourn on the continent) who dominate the ensembles. Bailey performs on some of the later tracks only, having been invited to join SME after its inception. Remarkable as the music is, the photographs (by Evan Parker and Jack Kilby) are a delight. Parker was reportedly overawed by his playing companions; it may be that he was also having second thoughts about the Zapatisto moustache.

Summer 1967 is significant not just in documenting one of Evan Parker's earliest recordings; it also preserves his and Stevens's first meeting with a player whom both were later to credit with opening up whole new areas of improvisational language to them. Kowald is a central figure in the European free movement, a generous, open-minded player who never for a moment stops listening to what is going on around him. This doesn't happen in a confrontational-conversational way, but with a constant awareness of what is going on in what Stevens was later to describe, using an analogy from his other art-form, as 'peripheral vision', an ability to pick up fleeting clues and render them as significant as the apparent focal point. That to a degree is what the SME has always been about, whatever its exact personnel and instrumentation.

Until Martin Davidson's excavations in the tape archive, the first significant product of the SME's change in philosophy was *Karyobin*, a strikingly light-toned and unaggressive exploration of group identity that lasts 49 minutes but contains within it arrays and patterns of musical sound which suggest infinity. The title is the collective name of the birds which inhabit paradise, living in harmony with one another. *Karyobin* has been a collectors' item on vinyl for many years. It transfers to CD pretty well, de-emphasizing the horns and drums slightly and letting Holland and Bailey come through with a bit more definition.

***** For You To Share**

Emanem 4023 *Trevor Watts (ss, v); John Stevens (perc, v); audience members perform various instruments.* 1 & 5/70.

****** Face To Face**

Emanem 4003 *Trevor Watts (as); John Stevens (d).* 73.

A few years further on, SME was functioning as a duo. Stevens and Watts were later to part company, somewhat acrimoniously, but for the duration of their partnership they created music of astonishing harmoniousness; 'harmony' would be the wrong word. *For You To Share* is interesting in that audience members join the two musicians in the collaborative, non-virtuosic philosophy of the AACM in Chicago. This isn't one of their strongest encounters, and is something of a timepiece (the CND symbol on the cover is a giveaway). Again, though, it is the delicacy of Stevens's percussion that is notable, while Watts's keening cries have an emotional pull that makes nonsense of attempts to re-label this sort of music 'abstract'. Small wonder that so many of these players were profoundly affected by the work of Samuel Beckett, in whom abstraction and the most passionate humanitarianism were wedded.

***** Mouthpiece**

Emanem 4039 *Stevens; no personnel listed.* 5–11/73.

These performances are credited to the Spontaneous Music Orchestra, which was essentially SME plus the members of a larger workshop group known as Free Space. No definite details about the musicians involved are known or given, but anyone familiar with this period in British improvisation will be able to make informed guesses about at least some of the players. As with much of Emanem's recent catalogue, all these performances are previously unissued, so they strike with something of the force of the original concerts, which were all in and around London; the two most substantial works were recorded at the SME's spiritual home, the Little Theatre Club, and at Ealing Technical College.

Since much of the music was workshopped, there is on occasion a faintly tentative air, and sometimes, as in the two versions of 'Sustained Piece', too dogged an application to a single informing idea, on this occasion quite literally the sustaining of blown or sung tones. 'One Two' is the closest the group came to a fixed beat or groove, with players opting whether to play on the first or second count. 'Mouthpiece' required the orchestra to begin with unvoiced mouth sounds, move on to vocalized sounds and only then to their instruments. This is perhaps the least involving part of the disc, but even here it offers a marvellous insight into how the SME functioned and how thoughtful a musician, teacher and catalyst the late John Stevens could be.

***(*) **Quintessence 1**

Emanem 4015 *Evan Parker, Trevor Watts (ss); Derek Bailey (g); Kent Carter (clo, b); John Stevens (perc, v).* 10/73, 2/74.

*** **Quintessence 2**

Emanem 4016 *As above.* 10/73–2/74.

Kent Carter first came to Britain in 1973 with Steve Lacy (who was himself to become an important overseas player in Derek Bailey's Company project). Despite coming from a radically different musical background, Carter fitted into the SME concept quite seamlessly. He recorded with Stevens and Watts at the Little Theatre Club in October of that year, and then joined the quintet (hence the title) form of the SME for the Institute of Contemporary Arts concert held the following February. *Quintessence 1* contains the first set from that occasion, together with three trios from the Little Theatre. The remainder of the ICA date is on Emanem 4016. The stereo separation of the two sopranos, cello and guitar leaves Stevens's kit very much in the foreground, and there are moments when the performance sounds almost like a concerto for percussion. His lifelong interest in the aural equivalent of 'peripheral vision' seems already to be in play here, and it makes for fascinating listening. His awareness of his colleagues' playing is instinctive, but it is not studied. He seems to respond to them almost as someone might who is reading during conversation, not rudely or detachedly, but because he is able to. The trio sessions, which have not previously been issued, don't quite match up in quality and are rather disappointing, though once again not because Carter is out of sympathy with the music.

*** **Low Profile**

Emanem 4031 *Nigel Coombes (vn); Colin Wood (clo); Roger Smith (g); John Stevens (d, c, v).* 11/77, 2/84, 10/88.

A mixed bag of SME performances, recorded in performance over a decade. Wood is heard only on the 1977 gig from Derby College of Further Education, which consists of the fragmentary 'Immediate Past Present' and a half-hour set rejoicing in the title, 'The Only Geezer An American Soldier Shot Was Anton Webern'. Like the much later 'Kitless With Elbow', it features Stevens's often very effective cornet (often it was bugle instead) and voice. Unusually, Smith uses an amplified guitar on the title-piece, a rare resort to electricity by a player who has almost always prepared a soft and unprocessed sound. This is by no means a major SME document, but it adds to the documentation and fills in the story from a time when the group was not heavily documented.

*** **Hot And Cold Heroes**

Emanem 4008 *As above, except omit Wood.* 80, 91.

**** **A New Distance**

Acta 8 *As above, except add John Butcher (ts, ss); omit Coombes.* 1 & 5/94.

There is at this point something of a jump in the documentation, and the final two items belong to a rather later SME. If the Stevens–Parker, Stevens–Watts axes were critical to earlier incarnations, those roles have more recently been taken by another saxophonist, John Butcher, and by guitarist Roger Smith, a musician of intense focus and awareness. They appear together on *A New Distance*, the most recent of the batch, which includes two London performances just a few months apart and in the last months of Stevens's life. Butcher's playing on both occasions is exceptional, gleaming with intelligence and a wonderful reserve.

Of all the players associated with the group, the one who seems most wholly defined by the experience, and yet the one constitutionally least adjusted to its collectivist, ego-less philosophy, is Coombes. The material on *Hot And Cold Heroes*, unlike the other records, has not been available before. Despite its obvious importance, it lacks their sheer impact and should perhaps not be considered a priority find. *Karyobin* and *A New Distance* are, in our view, essential.

Johnny St Cyr (1890–1966)

GUITAR, BANJO

Born in New Orleans, St Cyr is on many of the classic 1920s records by Armstrong and Morton. Thereafter he mixed music with working as a plasterer, though in the last decade of his life he played with many revivalist groups on the West Coast.

*** **Johnny St Cyr**

American Music AMCD-78 *St Cyr; Thomas Jefferson (t, v); Percy Humphrey (t); Jim Robinson, Joe Avery (tb); George Lewis (cl); Jeanette Kimball (p, v); Leo Thompson (p); Ernest McLean (g); Richard McLean, Fran Fields (b); Paul Barbarin, Sidney Montague (d); Jack Delany, Sister Elizabeth Eustis (v).* 7/54–5/55.

The doyen of New Orleans rhythm guitarists was seldom noted as a group leader, but American Music have pieced together a CD's worth of material. The first two tracks are rather dowdy treatments of 'Someday You'll Be Sorry' by a band with Percy Humphrey, Lewis and Robinson; but more interesting are the five previously unheard pieces by a quintet in which protégé Ernest McLean is featured rather more generously than Johnny himself, both men playing electric. The rest of the disc is jovial New Orleans music, fronted by the hearty Jefferson and the imperturbable Percy Humphrey. St Cyr, as always, is no more inclined to take any limelight than Freddie Green ever was, so it's nice to have a disc under his name. Remastering is from sources that were a lot cleaner than AM often have access to, so sound is good.

St Louis Ragtimers

GROUP

Dedicated to the earliest ragtime and associated music.

***** Full Steam Ahead And Loaded Up!**
Stomp Off CD1267 *Bill Mason (c, hca, jaw hp, wbd); Eric Sager (cl, ss); Trebor Tichenor (p); Al Strickler (bj, v); Don Franz (tba, jaw hp).* 12/92.

More good fun from the Stomp Off stable of revivalists, this time an ensemble who don't stop at the 1920s but go right back to nineteenth-century ragtime and minstrelsy. Trebor Tichenor's superb notes identify such pieces of arcana as 'Blind Boone's Southern Rag Medley No. 2 – Strains From The Flat Branch' and, though some of these ancient cakewalks, rags and intermezzos are probably deservedly forgotten, the high spirits and vivacity of this little group bring it all back to life. A few fruity vocals by Al Strickler and a fine show of multi-instrumentalism by Mason complete the circle.

Jess Stacy (1904–94)

PIANO

Born in Missouri, Stacy went to Chicago in the '20s and was a fixture on the scene until he joined Benny Goodman in 1935, with whom – aside from a spell with Bob Crosby – he stayed for a decade, an association he is best remembered for. He later became a Condonite and, after a gradual decline in work, left music to sell cosmetics in 1961. He returned to the festival circuit in the '70s.

****** Jess Stacy 1935–1939**
Classics 795 *Stacy; Billy Butterfield (t); Les Jenkins (tb); Hank D'Amico, Irving Fazola (cl); Eddie Miller, Bud Freeman (ts); Allen Hanlon (g); Israel Crosby, Sid Weiss (b); Gene Krupa, Don Carter (d); Carlotta Dale (v).* 11/35–11/39.

****** Ec-Stacy**
ASV AJA 5172 *Stacy; Bobby Hackett, Muggsy Spanier (c); Charlie Teagarden, Harry James, Ziggy Elman, Chris Griffin, Yank Lawson, Lyman Vunk, Max Herman, Billy Butterfield, Pee Wee Irwin, Anthony Natoli, Nate Kazebier, Bunny Berigan, Ralph Muzillo (t); Floyd O'Brien, Red Ballard, Joe Harris, Murray McEachern, Elmer Smithers, Buddy Morrow, Will Bradley, Jack Satterfield (tb); Benny Goodman, Johnny Hodges, Pee Wee Russell, Danny Polo, Hymie Schertzer, Bill De Pew, Dick Clark, Arthur Rollini, George Koenig, Vido Musso, Bud Freeman, Dave Mathews, Noni Bernardi, Matty Matlock, Art Mendelsohn, Eddie Miller, Gil Rodin, Sal Franzella, Henry Ross, Larry Binyon, Julius Bradley, Arthur Rando (reeds); Nappy Lamare, Allan Reuss, Frank Worrell, Ben Heller (g); Israel Crosby, Sid Wess, Artie Shapiro, Harry Goodman, Bob Haggart (b); Specs Powell, Gene Krupa, George Wettling, Ray Bauduc, Mario Toscarelli, Buddy Schutz (d); Lee Wiley (v).* 11/35–6/45.

One of the great piano masters of the 1930s gets his due at last with these two very strong compilations of his early work. There is a duplication of three of the early solo pieces, but the chronological Classics compilation concentrates on Commodore and Varsity material from 1938–9, while the ASV disc covers sideman work with Benny Goodman, Bob Crosby, Lionel Hampton, Bud Freeman and Pee Wee Russell for an exceptionally well-rounded portrait of a man who appeared in many interesting situations. His unassuming virtuosity went with a deceptively romantic streak – 'the intensity of Hines with the logic of Bix', as Vic Bellerby puts it – and his impeccable touch and undercurrent of blues feeling, even if tempered by a rather civilized irony, give him a rare position among the piano players of the era. The Classics set includes two splendid blues-based fantasies in 'Ramblin'' and 'Complainin'', the excellent solo session from 1939 and two engaging band dates, while the ASV offers several rarities, including an aircheck version of Beiderbecke's 'In A Mist', three 1944 duets with Specs Powell and the beautiful 'Down To Steamboat Tennessee' with Muggsy Spanier and Lee Wiley. Transfers are mostly very fair. Both discs are a strongly recommended portrait of a remarkable personality.

***** Stacy Still Swings**
Chiaroscuro CR(D) 133 *Stacy (p solo).* 7/74–7/77.

The veteran Condonite (as he later became) quit professional music in the 1950s but came back to festivals and studios very occasionally. This congenial, easy-going set of solos was among the last he made: nothing much has changed over the years except the tempos, and even then he was never exactly a tornado at the keyboard. His own tunes, such as 'Lookout Mountain Squirrels', are charming but robust; his standards are an old-fashioned choice.

Terell Stafford

TRUMPET, FLUGELHORN

American trumpeter with his own take on the post-bop vernacular.

***** Time To Let Go**
Candid CACD 79702 *Stafford; Tim Warfield (ts); Steve Wilson (as, ss); Edward Simon (p); Steve Nelson (vib); Michael Bowie (b); Victor Lewis (d); Victor See-Yuen (perc).* 95.

****** Centripetal Force**
Candid CACD 79718 *Stafford; John Clark (frhn); Ron Blake, Tim Warfield (ts); Russell Malone (g); Stefon Harris (vib); Stephen Scott (p); Ed Howard (b); Victor Lewis (d); Daniel Moreno (perc).* 10/96.

Stafford was a regular member of Bobby Watson's group, Horizon, which also numbered Simon and Lewis, and he comes to this debut project with a sensibility very much marked by Watson's small-group/big-sound idea. The opening 'Time To Let Go' is an emphatic statement of intent, and the other two originals, 'Qui Qui' and 'Why?', are in the same bag. Stafford isn't just another latter-day run-of-the-mill bopper. Though he draws on a range of influences running from Fats Navarro and Clifford Brown to mid-period Miles and Lee Morgan, he already has a distinctive personal inflexion and on Stephen Scott's lovely 'Was It Meant To Be', he carves out a very personal phraseology which points onward to the follow-up disc.

Centripetal Force is exactly what's at work here, a group which is working very closely and sympathetically. Again Tim Warfield brings his clean, youthful sound, but on just one track this time. Second time out, Stafford has at his disposal two of the brightest young guys on the scene, vibist Stefon Harris and pianist Stephen Scott, who sounds more comfortable on this session than he has on a couple of recent things under his own name. A version of 'Daahoud' is a special dedication, but it also points up the Brown influence again. Though the whole band is never heard together, the richer palette suits the trumpeter admirably and he produces some magnificent statements on 'I'll Wait' and 'Skylark', a back-to-back pair that are as sheerly refreshing as anything from the last few years. Thad Jones's 'A Child Is Born' is for trumpet and guitar and 'My Romance' is an elegant trumpet solo. Fine stuff from a highly intelligent young musician.

Jim Staley

TROMBONE, DIDGERIDOO

New York new-musician and improviser.

*****(*) Northern Dancer**

Einstein 006 *Staley; John Zorn (as); Zeena Parkins (hp); Davey Williams (g); Elliott Sharp (b, cl); Ikue Mori (drum machines); Shelley Hirsch (v).* 3/94–11/95.

*****(*) Blind Pursuits**

Einstein 011 *Staley; Borah Bergman (p); Phoebe Legere (v, acc).* 2–9/95.

Staley's collection of improvisations on *Northern Dancer* is an unusually sharp and effective showcase for the talents involved. Self-effacing as a participant himself, he seems to encourage his companions into creating some of their most vital work. The three principal groupings are Staley/Hirsch/Sharp, Staley/Williams/Mori and Staley/Parkins/Mori: the first offers two compelling pieces, with the trombonist's muted conversation a perfect foil for Hirsch over the rumblings of Sharp. In the other groups, it's Mori's deftly inventive use of his drum machines, as both colour and rhythmic propulsion, which marks out the music. Zorn barks his way through a brief duet and Staley finally stands alone at the end for a few minutes of melodious improvising: he seems to like the brassiness of the horn in particular.

Blind Pursuits puts Jim into two duo situations: half the disc is with vocalist Legere (she picks up the accordion for 'Tennessee Waltz'), half with the more familiar Bergman. Staley's full range of expression on the trombone lets him hold his own even with a combative personality like Bergman, and with the song-speech of Legere he creates dialogue which is quirkily like real conversation. If you have the taste for it, a model display of this kind of improvisation.

Tomasz Stańko (born 1942)

TRUMPET

One of the central figures and influences in Polish jazz, leading his own groups since 1962 and effecting his own blend of inside and out, mainstream and avant-garde.

***** Music For K**

Power Bros 00131 *Stańko; Zbigniew Seifert (as); Janusz Muniak (ts); Bronislaw Suchanek (b); Janusz Stefanski (d).* 1/70.

*****(*) Balladyna**

ECM 519289-2 *Stańko; Tomasz Szukalski (ts, ss); Dave Holland (b); Edward Vesala (d).* 12/75.

It may seem an odd thing to say, but Tomasz Stańko is an artist first and a musician only second. He is a man whose imagination is fired as much by words – Joyce, Lautréamont – and by visual images as by music. He is certainly not confined to jazz formulae, and at first hearing his music might seem to have more kinship with the abstract experimentalism of the Polish avant-garde than with orthodox or even free jazz. This is deceptive, for the trumpeter is deeply versed in the defining elements of jazz. His first big influence was Chet Baker, he says, though subsequently Miles Davis (who was to play an important part in the creative breakthrough of Stańko's generation of musicians) would become almost as important.

Totally free playing has never played a large part on the Polish scene and even when the setting is abstract there is still an underlying jazz 'feel', expressible both as a pulse and as dimly familiar harmonies and structures. Though some important records for Edward Vesala's Leo Records in Finland (not to be confused with Leo Feigin's London-based imprint) have not appeared on CD, the even earlier *Music For K* is still around, a forceful, sometimes inchoate session, with as much emphasis on Seifert's raw, emotive alto (this is before the ill-fated young genius made his shift to violin) as there is on Stańko's own rather fragile sound. The rhythm section is not really up to the task, though Stefanski is an accurate and unfussy percussionist, always absolutely on the beat. 'Cry' is the closest thing to American jazz of the time, but it is 'Music For K', dedicated to the late Krzysztof Komeda (who would be the inspiration for the later *Litania*) which really establishes Stańko's credentials as composer and *auteur*. He dominates this piece entirely, even when not in the foreground, and it points forward to the quieter, slower conception that he shares with the Finnish percussionist who joins him on the 1975 disc.

Stańko had jammed with Vesala some time previously and shyly revealed himself as a composer. It was to be some time, though, before his quality as both writer and performer became more widely known. *Balladyna* was his breakthrough album, a very personal statement given a high production gloss by ECM. Szukalski is a workmanlike player with, one suspects, a somewhat limited range. Stańko was fortunate in his other colleagues, however. Vesala is cautious in his approach to free music, but Holland seems to move between freedom and structure without a blink. The collectively written 'Tale' is rather weak, but Vesala's 'Num', three more Stańko compositions and an improvised duet with Holland give the record a solid impact and set the scene for the masterful ECM sessions of the 1990s.

*****(*) Bluish**

Power Bros 00113 *Stańko; Arild Andersen (b); Jon Christensen (d).* 10/91.

There is a gap in the story which accounts for most of the 1980s. When this superb record appeared, Stańko was still largely unavailable, with *Balladyna* not yet on CD and little available on widely distributed labels. The Rybnik-based Power Bros did manage to broker some distribution outside Poland, and *Bluish* awakened many listeners to the buried treasure that awaited them in Stańko. Working with northern Europe's premier rhythm section, he sounds more effusive than ever before, though with the same melancholy edge that made him such a haunting successor to both Chet and Miles.

The opening 'Dialogue' with Andersen recalls the duo with Holland on the earlier record. Stańko is not playing entirely free but is certainly not working within a fixed metre and his long, meditative lines are very compelling. The title-piece begins in a more straightforward idiom, before breaking down into a superb solo from Christensen which is marked by hesitations and silences.

Part two of 'If You Look Enough' (it comes first for some reason) is an eerie, out-of-tempo meditation, punctuated by brass smears and growls. The first part (placed last in the set) has the same chordal structure with a nagging insect-like chitter from Christensen. The drummer creates remarkable effects with damped cymbals on the long 'Bosanetta', a tune that recalls one of Vesala's tango pastiches, as does the succeeding 'Third Heavy Ballad', on which Stańko plays with a quiet lyricism that is reminiscent of Kenny Wheeler's work for ECM, the label that would shortly transform the enigmatic Pole's career.

***** Caoma**

Konnex KCD 5053 *Stańko; Sigi Finkel (ts, ss, f, p); Ed Schuller (b); Billy Elgart (d).* 12/91.

An oddity, disappointing after *Bluish* and showing little of the class and poise that would come with the ECM albums. Finkel is too boisterous a player for Stańko, and Schuller and Elgart both seem tuned to a more orthodox idiom than the trumpeter, leaving the session awkwardly suspended between Stańko's usual cool detachment and more propulsive sound. His trumpet playing is as good as ever, albeit in an unfamiliar context, and Stańko enthusiasts will doubtless find much to ponder and enjoy.

****** Bossanossa And Other Ballads**

GOWI CDG 08 *Stańko; Bobo Stenson (p); Anders Jormin (b); Tony Oxley (d).* 3 & 4/93.

This group was the highlight of the 1993 Jazz Jamboree in Warsaw, playing the material recorded on this record. Most of the material had been around for some time. 'Sunia' had been a staple of sets with Freelectronic, Stańko's free/fusion group. This is the definitive version, with wonderful interplay between Stańko's frail lead line and Oxley's metallic patterns. The Englishman resembles Vesala in his ability to register strong pulse in an otherwise free setting, but he is a lighter, more abstract player and ideal for this material, which is both unremittingly sombre and more playful.

Stenson was to become a key element in Stańko's musical thinking. Here he brings an uneasy cast to 'Maldoror's Love Song' and 'Die Weisheit von Isidor Ducasse', two pieces which reflect Stańko's fascination with the proto-surrealist and arch-decadent Lautréamont. The trumpeter uses a big, unfettered tone and long sinuous lines that anticipate and overlap the pianist's statements by several bars, creating a shifting surface across which the group lays out its sound. A wonderful record that caused a sensation when it was released, it stands up absolutely with passing time.

***** Matka Joanna**

ECM 1544 *Stańko; Bobo Stenson (p); Anders Jormin (b); Tony Oxley (d).* 5/94.

♛ ** Leosia**

ECM 1603 *As above.* 1/96.

Leosia is one of the finest jazz records of recent times, a work of immense creative concentration made by a band at the peak of its powers. Stańko has probably played better, but never with such instinctive support from his colleagues. As was the norm with ECM sessions at this time, considerable emphasis is put on the component members of the ensemble and on subdivisions of the basic group. Oxley, Jormin and Stenson are the begetters of 'Trinity' and bassist and drummer collaborate on the similarly constructed 'Brace'. 'No Bass Trio' is self-explanatory, and very fine, but the real action comes around these tracks, on the numbers drawn from *Bossanossa* and on the long title-piece which ends the album on a creative high, a long, perfectly weighted theme that seems to have no beginning or end.

The earlier ECM was less compelling, music written for a 1960 film by Jerzy Kawalerowicz, *Matka Joanna od Aniolow* ('and the Angels'). Stańko uses this found text as a basis to create 'images' for the group. Whether these turned out to be constraining rather than liberating isn't entirely clear, but the impression is of a less than wholehearted performance from all except Oxley, who steals the record with his focused abstractions. Stenson doesn't have his best day and often does little more than shadow the leader's keening monologues.

****** Litania**

ECM 1636 *Stańko; Bernt Rosengren (ts); Joakim Milder (ts, ss); Bobo Stenson (p); Terje Rypdal (g); Palle Danielsson (b); Jon Christensen (d).* 96.

Stańko had been a key member of Krzysztof Komeda's group in the 1960s and, given an increasing awareness of the pianist's eminence as a composer, some kind of tribute record had long seemed on the cards. For *Litania*, he summoned up a remarkable septet, co-fronted by the veteran Rosengren (one of the giants of European jazz) and the younger Milder, who is perhaps the weak link on the session.

They kick off with Komeda's 'Svantetic', one of his most lateral ideas and one of his best. There are three versions of 'Sleep Safe And Warm' from the soundtrack to *Rosemary's Baby* (only two of them involving Rypdal) and a striking performance of 'Ballada' from *Knife In The Water*, another Roman Polanski film for which Komeda wrote music. No room for 'Crazy Girl' or 'Astigmatic', which may be held in reserve for a follow-up session. What we have, though, is the clearest evidence both of Komeda's skill as a composer and of Stańko's ability to convey both the atmospherics of this neglected music and its ironclad structure. He is playing with absolute conviction and immense authority, and with a tone that conveys technical mastery coupled with total self-confidence.

Milder earns his place as a second-string soloist. Stenson and Christensen make one another play harder and with a more abrupt attack. Little of the pianist's tendency to drift off the pace, and certainly a very emphatic performance from Christensen. As a now legendary London performance amply proved, the absence of Rypdal would make very little difference. He is included as a colourist and, while he makes some lovely shapes on 'The Witch' and 'Sleep Safe And Warm', he is by no means integral to the music. Stańko's finest hour came with *Leosia*, but this is still an important, even historic record.

****** From The Green Hill**

ECM 1680 *Stańko; John Surman (bs, bcl); Dino Saluzzi (bandoneon); Michelle Makarski (vn); Anders Jormin (b); Jon Christensen (d).* 8/98.

Leosia was Stańko's apotheosis as composer and bandleader. *Litania* was a full-hearted tribute to his great mentor and friend. *From The Green Hill* is quite simply the most beautiful record he has ever made, a fragile, almost folkish disc, which is also a wonderful group performance. Reprising Komeda's 'Litania' as a bandoneon solo, with Saluzzi playing organ chords, was a stroke of genius, emphasizing the suite-like nature of the record and its continuity with Stańko's recent work.

The association with Surman is particularly happy. The saxophonist opens and signals the end of the album with his own theme 'Domino', which takes him back to a signature hybrid of folk and church music. He also leads into Stańko's 'Quintet Time' with a bass clarinet figure which recalls the old days with The Trio, before the track opens out into a restless free form that allows Christensen to express a quiet fury. The trumpeter plays some mournful high notes and smears reminiscent of the classic cornet players, though the dynamic of the piece is his usual brooding synthesis of Miles and Chet. 'Pantronic' sees Stańko donning Komeda's compositional mantle, while the title-piece might almost be a nod of appreciation in Surman's direction, so similar is it to some of the saxophonist's own themes.

Makarski is used rather sparingly, which is a pity, but probably wise. Her role in the group is episodic rather than structural and, if anything, she gains from being slightly marginalized. Jormin has emerged as a considerable player and composer, but he has a quieter time as well, some of his strengths cancelled out by the presence of Saluzzi.

Bobo Stenson (born 1944)

PIANO

Born in Västerås, Sweden, Stenson has been a major figure on the Stockholm post-bop scene since 1966. Work with Jan Garbarek and Charles Lloyd has been the prelude to his own considerable ECM albums.

****** Reflections**

ECM 523160-2 *Stenson; Anders Jormin (b); Jon Christensen (d).* 5/93.

These days, Stenson is virtually the house pianist at ECM, adding his effortlessly eclectic touch to the groups of Charles Lloyd, Tomasz Stańko and others. If this isn't quite the mainstream, it's certainly closer to it than seemed likely at one time. As co-founder of Rena Rama in 1971, he seemed embarked on an effort to hybridize jazz with Balkan and Indian folk music, a somewhat quixotic enterprise in the event, but one which coloured his work for many years, and which can still be heard on *Dansere*, on which he co-leads with Jan Garbarek.

Stenson's career began with Borje Frederiksson and, after a brief apprenticeship under the Swedish tenor saxophonist, he branched out with high-profile gigs for Stan Getz (in Africa, of all places) and Red Mitchell. Increasingly in the last ten years, he has been associated with ECM's efforts to reshape and redefine modal jazz. *Reflections* is as fine a performance as one would have expected, given the more than telepathic understanding between these players. Stenson and Jormin are termperamentally so close as to function almost like a single creative organism, an effect perhaps most noticeable on the bassist's two compositions, 'NOT' and 'Q', enigmatic titles which reflect his rather oblique musical personality. The title actually refers to Duke Ellington's 'Reflections In D'. The only other non-original is 'My Man's Gone Now', played as if through the prism of Miles and Gil Evans.

Stenson's two main compositions are 'The Enlightener', a shape-shifting meditation erected on a tricky mode which oddly (and not just the title) recalls recent work by Geri Allen, and '12 Tones Old', a clever reworking of age-old harmonic ideas. The final and longest piece, 'Mindiatyr', is the closest to how this group might sound in a club context. It's to be hoped that it might be possible to hear such a recording in the not too distant future.

Leni Stern

GUITAR, VOCAL

The most significant female jazz guitarist since the late Emily Remler, Mike Stern's wife is a strongly individual stylist who has now recorded many times as leader. Always recognizable, she favours a clean, ringing line, but likes to experiment with other sonorities as well.

*****(*) Secrets**

Enja 5093 *Stern; Bob Berg (ts); Wayne Krantz, Dave Tronzo (g); Lincoln Goines, Harvie Swartz (g); Dennis Chambers (d); Don Alias (perc).* 9–10/88.

*****(*) Closer To The Light**

Enja 6034 *Stern; David Sanborn (as); Wayne Krantz (g); Lincoln Goines, Paul Socolow (b); Dennis Chambers, Zachary Danziger (d); Don Alias (perc).* 11–12/89.

Stern quickly backed out of the fusion *cul-de-sac* to create albums of subtle presence that depend on interplay rather than very sophisticated themes. Perhaps oddly (or perhaps because she rejects conventional axe-man *machismo*), she has preferred to surround herself with other, often more dominant guitarists. Krantz's title-track on *Secrets* is one of the few false notes: a busy, hectic theme that overpowers the band. Stern herself works best with easy-paced melodies and settings that leave room for delicate, spontaneous touches. Sanborn, perhaps surprisingly, fits in particularly well on his two tracks on the well-balanced *Closer* (which also seems to have been released as *Phoenix*). Stern's duos with Krantz and the two-guitar quartets (with Goines and Chambers or Socolow and Danziger backing them) are the best she's committed to record so far.

**** Ten Songs**

Lipstick LIP 890092 *Stern; Bob Malach (ts); Billy Drewes (ss); Gil Goldstein (ky); Wayne Krantz (g); Alain Caron, Michael*

Formanek, Lincoln Goines (b); Dennis Chambers, Rodney Holmes (d); Don Alias (perc); Badal Roy (tablas, perc). 10/91.

Stern was a more interesting player on her earlier, bare-faced sessions, with their scrubbed-down sound. For the Lipstick set, she's given herself a rather blowsy funk sound, with every instrument puffed up and over-loud. The two best tunes are credited to Wayne Krantz; 'Our Man's Gone Now' sounds as if it might be a tribute to Miles, who is (or, rather, Marcus Miller is) the main influence on the arrangements; 'If Anything' features Stern on her Spanish and slide guitars, which are consistently her most effective instruments (only Sonny Sharrock has made a more developed use of slide guitar in a jazz context). A rather inconsequential set that somehow reflects the slightly throwaway title.

***** Like One**

Lipstick LIP 89017 2 *Stern; Bob Malach (ts); Didier Lockwood (vn); Russel Ferrante (ky); Alain Caron (b); Dennis Chambers (d).* 2–5/93.

****(*) Words**

Lipstick LIP 89076 2 *Stern; David Mann (as); Joy Askew (ky, v); George Whitty (ky); Lincoln Goines (b); Billy Ward (d); Lionel Cordew (d, perc).* 12/94–2/95.

A welcome return to form. *Like One* is very nearly hijacked by Malach's plangent saxophone and Caron's deep-chested bass, but Leni is playing very economically and it's as well to pay attention to her brief but beautifully constructed solos. She is subtlety itself on the earlier record and she drifts just a little back towards fusion postures on *Words*. As ever, the material is mostly original. 'Jessie's Song' bears more than a passing resemblance to Miles's 'Jean Pierre', with its stop–start theme, but it opens out into an easy swinger that leaves plenty of room for saxohone and guitar. Leni also includes two pop songs, Joni Mitchell's 'Court And Spark' and Sting's 'Every Breath You Take', which work well in this format. *Words* lacks a big tune and the vocal tracks are merely distracting. It's good to see her in such form, though, and nice to see that she's revived the uke-like tiple, which hasn't been much seen in jazz since the days of Teddy Bunn and the Spirits of Rhythm.

Mike Stern (born 1954)

GUITAR

Stern came to prominence as the guitarist in one of Miles Davis's 'comeback' bands of the early 1980s. He often seemed loud and unsubtle in that context, but he was probably no worse than any other fusion-directed guitarist of the day. He has since expanded his range through a long series of albums for Atlantic, and for much of the late 1980s and early '90s he co-led a popular touring band with Bob Berg.

***** Time In Place**

Atlantic 781840-2 *Stern; Bob Berg, Michael Brecker (ts); Don Grolnick (org); Jim Beard (ky); Jeff Andrews (b); Peter Erskine (d); Don Alias (perc).* 12/87.

****(*) Jigsaw**

Atlantic 782027-2 *Stern; Bob Berg (ts); Jim Beard (ky); Jeff Andrews (b); Peter Erskine, Dennis Chambers (d); Manolo Badrena (perc).* 2/89.

***** Odds And Ends**

Atlantic 82297-2 *As above, except add Lincoln Goines, Anthony Jackson (b), Ben Perowsky (d), Don Alias (perc); omit Andrews, Erskine and Badrena.* 91.

*****(*) Standards (And Other Songs)**

Atlantic 782419-2 *Stern; Randy Brecker (t); Bob Berg (ts); Gil Goldstein (ky); Jay Anderson, Larry Grenadier (b); Ben Perowsky (d).* 92.

*****(*) Is What It Is**

Atlantic 82571-2 *Stern; Michael Brecker, Bob Malach (ts); Jim Beard (ky); Will Lee, Harvie Swartz (b); Ben Perowsky, Dennis Chambers (d).* 93.

***** Between The Lines**

Atlantic 82835-2 *Stern; Bob Malach (ts); Jim Beard (ky); Lincoln Goines, Jeff Andrews (b); Dave Weckl, Dennis Chambers (d).* 95.

***** Give And Take**

Atlantic 83036-2 *Stern; David Sanborn (as); Michael Brecker (ts); Gil Goldstein (ky); John Patitucci (b); Jack DeJohnette (d); Don Alias (perc).* 97.

Perhaps Stern has still not quite shaken off his association with Miles Davis, where he created a mixed impression as something of a metalhead guitarist in the early 1980s. But his own discography is considerable by now, even if he still lags some way behind those inveterate recording artists, John Scofield and Bill Frisell, in first-call credibility. Mostly his Atlantic albums offer a musicianly, muscular style of fusion which is tougher than the smooth-jazz format, but not quite challenging enough to interest a wider constituency.

The problem on several of the earlier albums is the material, which can be little more than a springboard for solos – and these are tidy and intermittently powerful (especially Berg's) on the earlier sets. Chambers and Erskine provide other interest with their interactive parts but, while the band acquired a substantial reputation on the live circuit, it's too much a rational and unsurprising group in the studios. *Time In Place*, *Jigsaw* and *Odds And Ends* all followed a similar brief – commendably turned out, but nothing to get really excited about. The following *Standards (And Other Songs)* recast Stern as a 'serious' improviser at the moment when he might have drifted back towards jazz-metal. Instead, with seven standard jazz or show tunes dominating the programme, Stern cooled off the pace without surrendering all his fire-power. His best solos here have a fluency and resonance that might have got him his job with Davis in the first place.

At this point, though, Stern's music begins to sound more assured and whole, to go with the inventiveness of the solos. *Is What It Is* returns to original themes: Jim Beard's production orchestrates the keyboards and rhythm instruments into a thick, almost juicy, studio mix, which Stern's guitar noses through and occasionally screams over. Brecker and Malach lend heavyweight sax support, but the fundamental text is attractively lyrical in tunes such as 'What I Meant To Say'. *Between The Lines*, again produced by Beard, follows a similar path, though there's a sense of diminishing returns and, while the record scores big on texture, this time individual parts don't always impress beyond a surface attraction. It also goes on for too long, at 70 minutes. But 'Wing And A Prayer' at least is among the prettiest tunes Stern has given us.

For *Give And Take*, Stern enlisted Gil Goldstein as producer and another starry cast of performers. This time the music turns back to straight-ahead, with tunes like 'Giant Steps' and 'Oleo' in the set-list, and the sparse production floats the guitarist to a central point, where he peels off some of his most lucid solos. Brecker has a couple of cameos and Sanborn turns up to blow on a blues; but the record never seems like more than the sum of its parts, for all the virtuous playing.

*****(*) Play**
Atlantic 7567-83219-2 *Stern; Bob Malach (ts); John Scofield, Bill Frisell (g); Jim Beard (ky); Lincoln Goines (b); Ben Perowsky, Dennis Chambers (d).*

Both tougher and more colourful than many of its predecesors, this is a candidate for Stern's very best at Atlantic. Jim Beard returns as producer, and with his shrewd keyboard touches he puts aside any wispiness in Stern's writing besides getting a real presence out of all the players on each track. The first three have the leader swapping punches with Scofield, and four of the next seven have Frisell as conversationalist. Stern has continued to hone his knack for coming up with fetching, hooky tunes, and pieces such as 'All Heart' can double as smart mood-music as well as players' vehicles. Malach gets off some burning solos on 'Tipatina's' and 'Link' which in the context seem like an unlooked-for bonus.

Peggy Stern

PIANO

American pianist with a very broad range of influences and a taste for diverse playing situations.

***** Pleiades**
Philology W 82 *Stern; Ben Allison (b); Jeff Williams (d).* 4/93.

*****(*) The Fuchsia**
Koch 3 78372 2H1 *Stern; Thomas Chapin (as, f); Drew Gress (b); Bobby Previte (d).* 6/95.

A vast spectrum of ethnic and stylistic influences feed into Stern's music. If there is an Ur-text, then it is probably the Tristano school (confirmed by recent associations with Lee Konitz), but African, Jewish and Latin tinges are there as well. The trio record is a strong introduction to Stern the composer and player. The opening 'Mourning Dove' is reminiscent of Bill Evans, as is the lovely title-track. The three standards are nicely placed and confidently dispatched, with altered chords and subtle changes of pace and pitch.

The disc with Chapin is less abstract, and a good deal funkier. Previte's drumming is the key element, mathematical and shrewd and the perfect jumping-off point for some vivid wind-and-piano interchanges that suggest a duo album will some day be desirable. 'Win Slow' covers her classical side, a gorgeous theme with acres of space around the line. 'Bar Flies' and 'Not Since Bud' are more open-ended, suggesting that Stern is also a fine improviser. Neither album has a particularly flattering sound, with some distortion at the upper end on *Pleiades*.

John Stevens (1940–94)

DRUMS, PERCUSSION, BUGLE

Worked in RAF bands, 1958–64, and then worked in London's modern scene, becoming interested in completely free playing and co-founding Spontaneous Music Ensemble. Led other bands – Splinters, Dance Orchestra, Away, Freebop, Folkus – in the '70s and '80s and was tireless in his encouragement of young players. A difficult and tempestuous man but one of the most significant figures of his age.

***** A Luta Continua**
Konnex LC 5056 *Stevens; Jon Corbett (t, tb); Alan Tomlinson (tb); Paul Rutherford (tb, euph); Robert Calvert (ts); Trevor Watts (as, ss); Lol Coxhill (ss); Elton Dean (saxello); Dave Cole, Nigel Moyse, Martin Holder, Tim Stone, Mark Hewins (g); John Martyn (g, v); Jeff Young (org); Paul Rogers, Nick Stephens, Ron Herman, Andre Holmes (b); Francis Dixon, Richie Stevens (perc); Pepi Lemer, John Martyn (v).* 5/77–12/81.

***** Mutual Benefit**
Konnex LC 8718 *Stevens; Jon Corbett (t); Robert Calvert (ts, ss); Nigel Moyse, Tim Stone (g); Jeff Young (p, org); Ron Herman, Nick Stephens (b).* 5/77–5/80.

***** Touching On**
Konnex KCD 5023 *Stevens; John Calvin (sax); Dave Cole, Allan Holdsworth, Nigel Moyse (g); Jeff Young (p); Ron Mathewson, Nick Stephens (b). n.d.*

****** New Cool**
The Jazz Label TJL 006 *Stevens; Byron Wallen (t); Ed Jones (ts); Gary Crosby (b).* 8/92.

Stevens was an agile and forceful drummer, a protean figure who seemed at ease in a bewildering range of musics, from hard-edged free improvisation, through semi-rock and traditional jazz, and even latterly encompassing classical composition. He was also a gifted educator, who has left his mark on a whole generation of young British players. He came from an art school background, and several CD covers bear witness to his skill as a graphic artist. Initially inspired by Phil Seamen, his most obvious stylistic debts are to Kenny Clarke's proto-bop and to Elvin Jones. His Spontaneous Music Ensemble/Orchestra (see separate entry) was one of the most influential improvising groups of the period, while other Stevens groups, Splinters, the rock-defined Away and the Dance Orchestra, were more concerned with pre-structured forms. Stevens, it has to be said, claimed never to see any difference.

The Dance Orchestra tracks on *A Luta Continua* (the war-cry of the Portuguese anti-fascist movement) embrace groups of very different sizes; like SME, the Orchestra was always intended to be a flexible ensemble, the only constants being Stevens, trumpeter Jon Corbett and saxophonist Trevor Watts, who was co-leader of SME. As always, and unusually in free-jazz circles, Stevens put considerable emphasis on vocals, and the October 1979 tracks that make up about half the disc even include parts by folk-rocker John Martyn. There is also an unexpected emphasis on guitar, sometimes used as a conventional harmony instrument (Stevens only rarely called on a piano player, though he liked to feature Jeff Young on organ), sometimes (as on 'Birds') used quite abstractly.

Though *Mutual Benefit* is nominally an Away record, there is considerable overlap between the two, both in style and in personnel (and two tracks from the same May 1977 recording session). Stevens's crisp, almost militaristic accents create passages of dissipated melody over which the other players are relatively free to improvise. The striking thing about his playing is that he was always able to give the sense – or illusion – of a regular metre or pulse, even when it was clear from the most casual listening that what Stevens was playing was anything but regular. It is easy to be seduced by parts of *Mutual Benefit* into thinking that not much is going on, but, like Ornette Coleman's experiments with electric groups, there is a great deal of complexity behind the rather one-dimensional exterior.

Touching On is a free-ish jazz-rock session that reflects Stevens's talents only inadequately. Perhaps the most interesting tracks are those featuring Allan Holdsworth, one of many artists who receive a dedication on *Mutual Benefit*. This process was far from incidental or *ex post facto* to Stevens. Almost everything he did, whether it was with long-standing colleagues like Trevor Watts or with college students, was specifically designed with individuals in mind. To the very end of his life, Stevens continued to bring forward gifted young players. The SME evolved constantly, as its specific ethos demanded, but so too did his other groups, and *New Cool*, recorded at the Crawley Jazz Festival, is an excellent example of how seriously he took his mission to lead younger musicians at an accelerated pace through some of the major epiphanies of his own career. Of the four tracks, two are reworkings of Ornette and John Coltrane material, 'Ramblin'' and 'Lonnie's Lament' respectively. The listener doesn't need to be aware of this to enjoy or appreciate this music, which is immensely accessible, but it adds a significant dimension once the connection becomes obvious. As always, Stevens is thinking about old friends as well, in this case the two South Africans, Johnny Mbizo Dyani and Dudu Pukwana, whose own early deaths he was to echo all too soon thereafter. He is dotted through this book, but this is at present a very inadequate showing for one of the most influential men in British jazz history, and we must hope that more of John's music is restored to the catalogues soon.

Michael Jefry Stevens (born 1951)

PIANO

Post-bop American pianist, skirting – or brushing up against – free playing.

****** Elements**

Leo CD LR 241 *Stevens; Dominic Duval (b); Mark Whitecage (as, ss); Dom Minasi (g); Jay Rosen (d).* 3/94.

****(*) Haiku**

Leo CD LR 225 *Stevens; Mark Feldman (vn).* 4/95.

The language of bebop – rhythm, blues and syncopation apart – is already contained in the language of J.S. Bach. That, at least, is what Stevens was told by Sir Roland Hanna. It isn't quite true, but it allowed a young man whose listening experience seemed to be divided equally between Bill Evans and Bartók, and whose playing experience had been grounded on a stint playing Farfisa organ in a rock band, to get a purchase on jazz and improvisation.

Both of these records are unusually jazz-based for Leo Records. *Elements* in particular keeps throwing up echoes of everyone, from Evans and Monk to Andrew Hill and, an occasional Leo artist, to Cecil Taylor as well. It isn't clear whether the five performers have been assigned elemental personalities along the lines of earth, air, fire, water and ether/resist. If so, there seems little doubt that Stevens conceives himself as the fifth element, the binding principle that makes matter and action possible. He is by no means the dominant personality on a record that is nominally co-led by Duval. Often Stevens drops out altogether, as he does on the central 'Fire', and only on the last-but-one track, 'Coda (Resist)', does he push forward expressively. For the remainder, this is an admirably ego-free session, reminiscent in structure of some recent ECM releases where the basic group breaks down into its components almost track by track.

Whitecage and Rosen have both recorded for CIMP in recent times, the saxophonist as leader, Rosen in trumpeter Herb Robertson's trio. Both sound like men who have got their ideas and their ambitions in order, and it seems likely that both will produce interesting work in future.

Stevens has worked (and recorded) with Whitecage before (in a band called Liquid Time) and also with Mark Feldman in the Mosaic Sextet, who have released a record on Konnex – see above. The duos with the violinist are slightly disappointing. Though as beautiful as the group pieces on *Elements*, they are curiously inconsequential when heard more than once. The sound lacks the breathy, elevated quality of Whitecage's soprano and alto (almost an oboe or heckelphone tone) and the delicate figuring of Minasi's guitar. Feldman plays less idiomatically than usual, often producing what sound almost like saxophone lines. Almost all the pieces seem to struggle to sustain their ideas or, more often, idea.

Grant Stewart (born 1971)

TENOR SAXOPHONE

Candian tenorman ploughing the hard-bop furrow.

***** Downtown Sounds**

Criss Cross CRISS 1085 *Stewart; Joe Magnarelli (t); Brad Mehldau (p); Peter Washington (b); Kenny Washington (d).* 12/92.

Stewart was raised in Toronto and influenced in the main by Pat LaBarbera and Bob Mover. At 21 he sounds very confident but in no hurry to force his own interpretations too hard. This is a solid repertoire session with an interesting spin. One doesn't hear Rollins's 'Audobahn', Strayhorn's 'Smada', 'Daydream' and 'Intimacy Of The Blues', or Cole Porter's 'From This Moment On' on a young man's record. He tackles them all with modesty and some aplomb, unfazed by the twists and turns of Parker's 'Ko-Ko', but more at ease with medium-tempo pieces that sit more comfortably for his relaxed, Wardell Gray-like tenor sound.

Louis Stewart (born 1944)

GUITAR

Born in Waterford, Stewart worked in Irish showbands before backing visiting Americans in Dublin. Later toured with Tubby Hayes and Benny Goodman, and joined Ronnie Scott in the late '70s. Now a familiar if unassuming figure on the European circuit.

***** Out On His Own**

Jardis 9612 *Stewart (g solo).* 11/76–1/77.

***** Acoustic Guitar Duets**

Jardis 9613 *Stewart; Martin Taylor (g).* 7/85.

***** Winter Song**

Jardis 9005 *Stewart; Heiner Franz (g).*

***** In A Mellow Tone**

Jardis 9206 *As above.* 6/92.

*****(*) Overdrive**

Hep 2057 *Stewart; Ronnie Rae (b); Tony McLennan (d).* 2/93.

Formidably accomplished yet completely unassuming, Stewart is a pro's pro on the guitar. He can play with the speed and technical assurance of, say, John McLaughlin when he wants to; yet his customary soft tone, quiet pitch and introverted emotional agenda take him far away from the kind of showmanship one associates with the (ahem) guitar hero. An Irishman with many years in jazz behind him, he has had few opportunities to head up records of any limelight status, but what he has done has been unfailingly fine. The Jardis records all seem to be reissues of one sort or another. The all-solo outing, *Out On His Own*, and the three albums of duets are all much the same in terms of their impact. Stewart defers either to himself or to his playing partners: his comprehensive range of devices – Wes-like sweetness of tone, bebop velocity, double-time passages next to articulate single-note trellises, gently persuasive melodic twists – is used to keep his music genuine rather than to set out to impress listeners. But the quiescent environment makes these records pleasing but finally lacking in the ingredient that would make them essential.

The live album from Hep is in some ways no better, since Rae and McLennan are a prosaic team who do little to sting Stewart into more vital form. That said, the best of this music is so impeccable that it's impossible not to enjoy. Nine well-worn standards don't hold a lot of promise, yet Stewart's flow of ideas seems improbably fresh and enlivening.

Rex Stewart (1907–67)

CORNET, KAZOO, VOCALS

The good-natured Philadelphian had two stints with Fletcher Henderson, interrupted by doubts about his own ability to fill the shoes of Louis Armstrong, who was his greatest influence. A pioneer of half-valving and of a loquacious, vocalized style, Stewart was a persuasive and engaging soloist.

***** An Introduction To Rex Stewart: His Best Recordings, 1926-1941**

Best of Jazz 4005 *Stewart; Langston Curl, Joe Smith, Russell Smith, Bobby Stark (t); Ed Cuffee, Jimmy Harrison, Claude Jones, Benny Morton (tb); Don Redman (cl, as); Benny Carter, Edward Inge (as); Coleman Hawkins (cl, ts); Prince Robinson (ts); Fletcher Henderson (p); Todd Rhodes (p, cel); Charlie Dixon, Dave Wilborn (bj); Ralph Escudero, Billy Taylor (b); Cuba Austin, Kaiser Marshall (d).* 5/26–11/30.

*****(*) Rex Stewart: 1934-46**

Classics 931 *Stewart; Stafford Simon (t); Lawrence Brown, George Stevenson, Sandy Williams (tb); Tyree Glenn (tb, vib); Earl Bostic, Tab Smith (as); Barney Bigard, Rudy Powell (cl, as); Pete Clarke, Bingie Madison, Al Sears (ts); Cecil Scott (ts, bs); Harry Carney (bs, cl); Mike Colucchio, Johnny Guarnieri, Eddie Heywood, Billy Kyle, Roger Ramirez, Dave Rivera (p); Brick Fleagle, Ulysses Livingston (g); Wellman Braud, Wilson Myers, Junior Raglin, Billy Taylor, Sid Weiss (b); J.C Heard, Jack Maisel, Bazeley Perry, Keg Purnell, Dave Tough (d).* 12/34–2/46.

*****(*) Rex Stewart And The Ellingtonians**

Original Jazz Classics OJC 1710 *Stewart; Lawrence (tb); Barney Bigard (cl); Billy Kyle (p); Brick Fleagle (g); Wellman Braud, John Levy (b); Cozy Cole, Dave Tough (d).* 7/40–46.

*****(*) Rex Stewart: 1946-1947**

Classics 1016 *Stewart; Lawrence Brown, Sandy Williams (tb); John Harris (cl, as); Al Sears, Vernon Story (ts); Harry Carney (bs); Don Gais, Eddie Heywood, Jimmy Jones, Billy Kyle (p); Ulysses Livingston (g); Simon Brehm, Fred Ermelin, John Levy, Junior Raglin (b); Uffe Baagh, Cozy Cole, Ted Curry, Keg Purnell (d); Honey Johnson, Joya Sherrill (v).* 1/45–12/47.

*****(*) Rex Stewart: 1947-1948**

Classics 1057 *Stewart; Sandy Williams (tb); Hubert Rostaing (cl); John Harris (cl, as); Vernon Story (ts); Don Gais (p, cel); Django Reinhardt, Jean-Jacques Tilché (g); Ladislas Czabanyck, Lucien Simoens (b); Ted Curry (d); Honey Johnson, Louie Williams (v).* 12/47–1/48.

***** Trumpet Jive!**

Prestige PCD 24119 *Stewart; Tyree Glenn (tb, vib); Earl Bostic (as); Cecil Scott (ts, bs); John Dengler (bsx, wbd, kazoo); Wilbert Kirk (hca, perc); Dave Rivera (p); Jerome Darr, Brick Fleagle, Chauncey Westbrook (g); Junior Raglin (b); J.C Heard, Charles Lampkin (d).* 7/45–3/60.

****** Chatter Jazz**

RCA 2118525 *Stewart; Dicky Wells (tb); John Bunch (p); Leonard Gaskin (b); Charles Master Paolo (d).* 1/59.

The poet John Keats once wrote about the way very great artists erect a Great Wall across their respective genres, Shakespeare in the drama, Milton in the poetic epic. For trumpeters of the 1920s, Louis Armstrong fell into that category. His achievement was so primal and so pre-eminent that it was extraordinarily difficult to see a way round or over it. Rex Stewart, a self-confessed Armstrong slave (though he also loved Bix), experienced the problem more directly than most when he took over Armstrong's chair in the Fletcher Henderson orchestra.

The early material on Best of Jazz gives little real impression of what was to come, except that Stewart's solo forays are bright and peppy, with a chattery, button-holing quality that makes them stick out from the ensemble. Other cuts have him with McKinney's Cotton Pickers and the Ellington band, before the cornetist began to make records under his own name in the mid-'30s. There are inevitable overlaps in the compilations which follow, but this is a decent introduction to his work over a relatively long period, and it is more evenly remastered than the Classics discs, which are, as usual, somewhat rough and ready.

In reaction to the inevitable but invidious comparisons, Stewart developed his distinctive 'half-valving' technique. By depressing the trumpet keys to mid-positions, he was able to generate an astonishing and sometimes surreal chromaticism which, though much imitated, has only really resurfaced with the avant-garde of the 1960s. As a maverick, Stewart was ideal for the Ellington orchestra of the mid-'30s, though the Black and Blue sessions seem, despite the august company, to step back a generation to the sound of the Hot Sevens. Stewart was never to lose that loyalty. On the Prestige, he can be heard singing in obvious (and authentic) imitation of Pops, but also taking in a good deal of what he had learnt with Henderson.

The early Classics disc brings together all the material Stewart recorded under his own name over a busy decade in which he spent most of his time working for other leaders. The very earliest cuts, with George Stevenson and Rudy Powell, were made for Vocalion just before Christmas 1934. There is no mistaking Stewart, even at this early period and even before he developed the harmonic richness of later years. It's only somewhat later, in the recordings of the mid-'40s, that he manages to combine it with the fullness of tone that was to be his trademark. Recording in turn for Keynote, Capitol, Parlophone and Mercury, Stewart created a body of work that was tantalizingly individual, out of all proportion to its actual amount.

As an original Ellingtonian, Stewart was revered in Europe and in 1947 went back to France and Scandinavia, where he laid down sessions for Blue Star, Cupol and Baronet. These represent the greater bulk of the two later Classics sets, credited to Rex Stewarts Orkester and other groups. The only additional material consists of four cuts done in New York for the short-lived HRS, and anomalously on the volume dated 1946/1947, a single, rejected take of 'Blue Jay' for Capitol recorded with the Big Eight in Los Angeles in January 1945. Half a dozen effective standards included on the same disc were recorded at the Salle Pleyel in Paris and originally released on three 78-r.p.m. discs. On these Rex sounds in buoyant and enthusiastic form, punching out the notes like a stapler. Generally, though, the voice was mellower, and the December 1947 tracks on Classics 1057 are the most relaxed and conversational work yet heard from him on record. Difficult to pick out individual tracks, largely because these sessions work best by accretion, piling on anecdotal detail at a leisurely pace rather than going for the big dramatic finish or large-scale romancing. Hard not to pick out his encounter with Django Reinhardt on 10 December 1947 for a brace of matey cuts. With Hubert Rostaing also on board, 'Confessin'' and 'Night And Day' are minor classics of post-war swing.

After Paris, Rex moved on through Europe, making some important recordings in London; these will presumably form the bulk of the next Classics issue. It was probably from Django Reinhardt, though, that he first heard the Hot Club staple, 'Nagasaki'; the cornetist returned to it in 1960, as part of the *Happy Jazz* session repackaged with Wingy Manone material on Prestige. (*Trumpet Jive!* was the name of a Manone LP.)

The RCA comes pretty late in the story, but Rex had developed a seemingly effortless route round his own limitations and could still put on a show. The chemistry with Wells was spot on, and this is one of his most engaging records of any period.

Stewart's vocalized style had few imitators, though Clark Terry gave it a more contemporary slant, bridging the gap with the modernists. In later life, Stewart became one of the most persuasive writers on jazz and his *Jazz Masters of the '30s* is required reading for students of the period. His ability to give convincing demonstrations of changes in trumpet playing became a component of his act, and the later, Rudy van Gelder-recorded session on *Trumpet Jive!* is just such a date, with Stewart sending himself up on his own 'Rasputin' and 'Tell Me'.

Slam Stewart (1914–87)

DOUBLE BASS, VOICE

Studied in Boston and heard violinist Ray Perry singing along to his own lines; Slam adapted that to his bass playing. Worked in a duo with Slim Gaillard and with Art Tatum and many others. Keeping busy to the end.

**(*) Slam Stewart 1945–1946

Classics 939 *Stewart; Erroll Garner, Billy Taylor, Johnny Guarnieri (p); Red Norvo (vib); Bill D'Arango, Mike Bryan, Chuck Wayne, John Collins (g); Harold Doc West, Morey Feld (d).* 1/45–4/46.

Stewart was already a star when he appeared in the movie, *Stormy Weather*, in 1943. During the 1930s he had been a stalwart of the New York scene, playing with Art Tatum and forming an evergreen partnership (love it, hate it; it sold records) with Slim Gaillard which exploited the less serious side of Stewart's virtuosic self-harmonizing on bass and vocals. However corny he now seems, few modern bass players have taken up the technical challenge Stewart posed (though Major Holley had a stab), and the purely musical aspects of his work are of abiding value. The Classics disc shuffles together five early sessions under his own name. Erroll Garner was working for Slam at The Three Deuces when they made the January 1945 date which has its apotheosis in the absurd 'Dark-Eyesky'. There are a dozen tracks with a quintet including Red Norvo, and Stewart is relatively back-seat on these for at least some of the time. For the most part, these sessions impart a harmless kind of chamber-jazz which is frankly boring after a few tracks. The very oddity of Stewart's technique is initially off-putting, but on repeated listening its complexities begin to make an impact. It's perhaps a shame that Stewart wasn't able – or didn't choose – to record with more of the younger modern bassists. If Mingus and Pettiford are now thought to have set the instrument free, much of what they did was already implicit in Stewart's work of the 1930s.

Loren Stillman (born 1980)

ALTO SAXOPHONE

A very young man starting out in jazz.

***** Cosmos**

Soul Note 121310-2 *Stillman; Russ Lossing (p); Scott Lee (b); Bob Meyer (d). 2/96.*

The novelty here is Stillman's age, with only 15 birthdays behind him when he made the session. The tunes, five of them originals, are probably more interesting than the playing. Stillman can certainly get around the horn, and his tone has a newly wrought pallor which isn't a bad change from the sleek confidence of many of the newer saxophonists. But his solos go nowhere particularly productive, and there are always passages of experimental filler in there somewhere. The arpeggiated melody of 'Wishbone', though, is neatly developed, and the other three men know their stuff: the title-piece is a free episode which hangs together surprisingly well.

G.E. Stinson

GUITAR

California-based guitarist with experience in rock, soft fusion (Shadowfax) and more demanding settings. He seems quite at home in all of them.

*****(*) The Same Without You**

Nine Winds NWCD 0154 *Stinson; John Fumo (t); Steuart Liebig (b); Alex Cline (d). 2/92.*

Stinson bolsters his guitar sound with a battery of effects – his favourite setting seems to be hugely reverberant sustain, washed down with a variety of fuzz tones. But hardnose improvisers like Fumo and Cline leaven any suggestion that this might be an ersatz rock record. The quartet sometimes get lost in the long, rambling structures, especially the massive 'Oklahoma Elegy', but four-way improvisations like 'Mr Spoonful' and 'Goin' For The Jar' have real substance and none of the post-mod posturings this kind of instrumentation has recently lost out to elsewhere. Cline has never supplied a rockier beat, but he's as much a master of that as he is of jazz time.

Sonny Stitt (1924–82)

ALTO, TENOR AND BARITONE SAXOPHONES

A quick learner of the bebop vernacular, it is open to dispute as to how much Stitt absorbed from Charlie Parker – they met early on – and how much he developed for himself. He played tenor in a band he co-led with Gene Ammons from 1950, and thereafter drifted between that and the alto, very occasionally picking up the baritone. A definitive example of the 'road' musician, always available to play with local rhythm sections or jam with Jazz At The Philharmonic, Stitt made scores of records and, arguably, diluted his reputation with an approach that was simultaneously dedicated and careless.

***** Sonny Stitt / Bud Powell / J.J. Johnson**

Original Jazz Classics OJC 009 *Stitt; J.J Johnson (tb); Bud Powell, John Lewis (p); Curley Russell, Nelson Boyd (b); Max Roach (d). 10/49–1/50.*

****(*) Prestige First Sessions Vol. 2**

Prestige 24115 *Stitt; Al Outcalt, Matthew Gee (tb); Gene Ammons (bs); Kenny Drew, Duke Jordan, Junior Mance, Clarence Anderson (p); Tommy Potter, Earl May, Gene Wright (b); Art Blakey, Teddy Stewart, Wesley Landers, Jo Jones (d); Larry Townsend (v). 2/50–8/51.*

***** Kaleidoscope**

Original Jazz Classics OJC 060 *Stitt; Bill Massey, Joe Newman (t); Kenny Drew, Charles Bateman, Junior Mance, John Houston (p); Tommy Potter, Gene Wright, Ernie Shepard (b); Art Blakey, Teddy Stewart, Shadow Wilson (d); Humberto Morales (perc). 2/50–2/52.*

Considering the size of his discography – there are at least 100 albums under Stitt's own name – the saxophonist still has relatively little left in the catalogue, although the desultory nature of many of his records suggests that perhaps it is better this way. Stitt took every opportunity to record, often with undistinguished pick-up groups, and while his impassive professionalism meant that he seldom sounded less than strong, his records need careful sifting to find him genuinely at his best. Originally, he was acclaimed as a rival to Charlie Parker, and the derivation of his style – which may have been arrived at quite independently of Bird – is a famously moot point. Whatever the case, by the time of the 1949 sessions on OJC 009, he was in complete command of the bop vocabulary and playing with quite as much skill as any man in the milieu. This disc finds him exclusively on tenor, which he plays with a rather stony tone but no lack of energy. Powell contributes some superb playing on such up-tempo pieces as 'All God's Children Got Rhythm', and the 1950 group with Johnson and Lewis, though less obviously hot, finds Stitt at his best on the urgent improvisation on 'Afternoon In Paris'. Both the Prestige collection and *Kaleidoscope* bring together bits and pieces from the early days of the label and, though some of the tracks sound foreshortened, Stitt dominates throughout both discs. He occasionally played baritone, too, and there's a surprisingly full-blooded ballad treatment of 'P.S. I Love You' on *Kaleidoscope* which suggests that his use of the bigger horn was by no means offhand. The boxy sound of the originals carries over into all the CD issues.

***** Jazz Masters 50**

Verve 527651-2 *Stitt; Lee Katzman, Jack Sheldon, Dizzy Gillespie (t); Frank Rosolino (tb); Sonny Rollins (ts); Amos Trice, John Lewis, Jimmy Jones, Lou Levy, Oscar Peterson, Bobby Timmons, Jimmy Rowles (p); Skeeter Best, Paul Weeden, Herb Ellis (g); Al Pollan (tba); George Morrow, Percy Heath, Ray Brown, Paul Chambers, Leroy Vinnegar, Edgar Willis, Buddy Clark, Tommy Bryant (b); Lennie McBrowne, Charli Persip, Billy James, Stan Levey, Ed Thigpen, Kenny Dennis, Lawrence Marable (d); strings. 1/56–2/62.*

Verve's compilation series reached number 50 with this useful Stitt collection, picking a dozen tracks, no fewer than nine of which come from out-of-print Stitt albums. But all the best moments here – save perhaps the lovely ballad-with-strings, 'Time After Time', from 1961 – are from familiar records: *Sonny Side Up* with Gillespie and Rollins and *Sits In With The Oscar Peterson Trio*. Stitt's own-name dates weren't any more commanding then than his later sets for Prestige. Of course there's still much exemplary alto and tenor, and the remastering gets the most out of Sonny's impeccable tone and delivery.

*****(*) Sonny Stitt Sits In With The Oscar Peterson Trio**
Verve 849396-2 *Stitt; Oscar Peterson (p); Herb Ellis (g); Ray Brown (b); Ed Thigpen, Stan Levey (d).* 10/57–5/58.

A memorable meeting. Stitt plays alto and tenor here, and sounds unusually at ease with a pianist who might have brought out his most sparring side: instead, on the likes of 'Moten Swing' and 'Blues For Pres', they intermingle their respective many-noted approaches as plausibly as if this were a regular band (in fact, they never recorded together again). The CD includes three tracks from a session a year earlier, previously unreleased, with a storming 'I Know That You Know' emerging as the highlight. Excellent CD remastering.

***** Salt And Pepper**
Impulse! 12102 *Stitt; Paul Gonsalves (ts); Hank Jones (p); Milt Hinton, Al Lucas (b); Osie Johnson (d).* 6–9/63.

This couples the original *Salt And Pepper* together with Stitt's other Impulse! album, *Now!*. Neither was exactly a masterpiece but they have their moments. The tracks with Gonsalves find the saxophonists running themselves ragged on the blues and, when they finally get to a really rather gorgeous 'Star Dust', it makes the rest of the date seem like a waste. *Now!* is at its best on simple little pieces like 'Estralita', and Jones adds his usually seigneurial presence.

****(*) Sonny Stitt Meets Brother Jack**
Original Jazz Classics OJC 703 *Stitt; Jack McDuff (org); Eddie Diehl (g); Art Taylor (d); Ray Barretto (perc).* 2/62.

****(*) Autumn In New York**
Black Lion BLCD 760130 *Stitt; Howard McGhee (t); Walter Bishop (p); Tommy Potter (b); Kenny Clarke (d).* 10/67.

***** Soul Classics**
Original Jazz Classics OJC 6003 *Stitt; Virgil Jones (t); Jack McDuff, Don Patterson, Gene Ludwig, Leon Spencer (org); Hank Jones (p); Pat Martino, Grant Green, Billy Butler, Melvin Sparks, Eddie Diehl (g); Leonard Gaskin, George Duvivier (b); Idris Muhammad, Art Taylor, Billy James, Randy Gillespie (d).* 2/62–2/72.

***** Soul People**
Prestige 24127-2 *Stitt; Booker Ervin (ts); Grant Green, Vinnie Corrao (g); Don Patterson (org); Billy James (d).* 8/64–9/69.

***** Night Letter**
Prestige 24165-2 *Stitt; Jack McDuff, Gene Ludwig (org); Pat Martino (g); Leonard Gaskin (b); Herbie Lovelle, Randy Gillespie (d).* 9/63–10/69.

**** Made For Each Other**
Delmark DD-426 *Stitt; Don Patterson (org); Billy James (d).* 7/68.

****(*) Legends Of Acid Jazz**
Prestige 24169-2 *Stitt; Virgil Jones (t); Don Patterson, Leon Spencer (org); Melvin Sparks (g); Idris Muhammad (d).* 1/71.

***** Legends Of Acid Jazz Vol. 2**
Prestige 24236 *Stitt; Charles McPherson (as); Don Patterson (org); Pat Martino (g); Bill James (d).* 9/68.

Whatever the state of jazz's declining fortunes in the 1960s, Stitt worked and recorded incessantly, if often carelessly. A lot of run-of-the-mill albums for Roulette and Cadet are currently unavailable; these Prestige dates scarcely break the mould. With McDuff in tow, Stitt strolls unblinkingly through a programme of rootless blues. *Soul People* has some natty sparring with Booker Ervin, never one to shirk some cheerful sax fisticuffs, and, though the ballad medley is a bit dragging, 'Flying Home' isn't. A 1969 'Tune Up' and one track with Patterson in the chair fills up the disc. *Soul Classics* collects tracks from eight sessions over a decade and is a truthful picture of Stitt's ups and downs. Four tracks feature the saxophonist with his varitone horn, a gimmick which didn't last; but more encouraging is the tough 'Night Crawler' with Patterson and a dark-blue 'Goin' Down Slow' with a surprise guest-slot by Hank Jones.

The Black Lion quintet, recorded in Switzerland, is about as authentic as bebop bands get, though these four tracks spark only intermittently; the earlier tracks with an unknown group are a little more exciting. *Made For Each Other* is a desperately routine set of tracks that Stitt plays his varitone sax on throughout: missable. *Night Letter* and the two *Legends Of Acid Jazz* discs, though they sound like compilations, actually put together six complete original albums. The first couples a spunky 1963 date with Jack McDuff, *Soul Shack*, with the 1969 *Night Letter*, where Martino's guitar sneaks in some of the best licks. The second fits together *Turn It On!* with the modishly titled *Black Vibrations*, each by more or less the same group (Patterson comes in for two titles). *Acid Jazz Vol. 2* pairs a Stitt date with Patterson, *Soul Electricity!*, and a Patterson date with Stitt, *Funk You*, which also brings in Charles McPherson. They were recorded only a day apart! Stitt is still using the varitone on 'his' session, but the other one has some nicely struck sparks. Not much really changes across the seven years the discs span, although the later group is the more self-consciously funky and garners a lower mark as a result. Stitt himself never had to pretend about soul.

*****(*) Keepers Of The Flame**
Camden 74321 610762 2CD *Stitt; Barry Harris (p); Sam Jones (b); Roy Brooks, Alan Dawson (d).* 6/71–2/72.

*****(*) Endgame Brilliance**
32 Jazz 32009 *As above.* 6/71–2/72.

***** The Champ**
32 Jazz 32084 *Stitt; Joe Newman (t); Duke Jordan (p); Sam Jones (b); Roy Brooks (d).* 4/73.

***** Constellation**
Camden 74321 610912 2CD *Stitt; Ricky Ford (ts); Jimmy Heath (ts, ss, f); Barry Harris (p); Sam Jones, George Duvivier, Richard Davis (b); Billy Higgins, Roy Haynes, Leroy Williams (d).* 75–80.

Stitt began recording for Muse (or, to be accurate, for Cobblestone, the logo under which the first albums appeared) in 1971, and he seemed ready to reassert his eminence. The original albums, *Tune Up!* and *Constellation*, were received at the time as if they were reminding the jazz audience that bebop hadn't gone away. Stitt was in his very best late form, flying through the changes as always but doing so with an extra pinch of determination and inspiration, brought on by his favourite accompanist, Barry Harris (who appears on so many of Stitt's '70s records). The material was the inevitable and the obvious, yet the musicians respond to it with phenomenal spark. Perhaps, with so many sax-

and-rhythm records having been cut in between, the music sounds less vibrant now, but these are still among Stitt's finest. They have now been reissued in the USA on *Endgame Brilliance*, but European readers may prefer to seek out the British Camden release, which at budget price offers the same music plus a second disc featuring two Lou Donaldson sessions (discussed under his name).

Constellation is in the same bargain series, and this presents four Stitt sessions from the period: *Blues For Duke*, *Mellow*, *My Buddy* and *Sonny's Back*. A pity that the first two are very tired-sounding: Stitt is really ambling through these, and even Jimmy Heath's guesting on the second date doesn't perk him up (the piano sound too is pretty cold). The two later sessions, though, are much livelier, and Ricky Ford turns up for a shooting match on 'Sonny's Bounce'.

The Champ is Stitt and Harris again, this time with Joe Newman as second horn. Good, honest work, but the earlier records are the ones to have.

****(*) Back To My Own Home Town**

Black & Blue 59574-2 *Stitt; Gerald Price (p); Don Mosley (b); Bobby Durham (d).* 11/79.

***** The Good Life**

Evidence ECD 22088-2 *Stitt; Hank Jones (p); George Duvivier (b); Grady Tate (d, v).* 11/80.

*****(*) Just In Case You Forgot How Bad He Really Was**

32 Jazz 32051 *Stitt; Richie Cole (as); John Handy (ts, as); Cedar Walton (p); Bobby Hutcherson (vib); Herbie Lewis (b); Billy Higgins (d).* 9/81.

Stitt died in 1982 from cancer, but he betrayed only a few signs of failing powers up to the end. The pick-up date in France (Black & Blue) is as rote as one might imagine. *The Good Life* was recorded in Japan and works out better. Stitt could hardly have felt more comfortable than with this rhythm section; it's a pity, given his vast knowledge of standards, that they couldn't have chosen a more interesting set of tunes to play on. 'Angel Eyes' is a splendid tenor performance and with the title ballad it makes up a pleasing valediction.

He sounds, though, even better on the subsequent *Just In Case You Forgot How Bad He Really Was*. Something of a summit meeting between the three saxophonists, it brings out Stitt's combative qualities without anything sounding bad-tempered. Cole's snappy improvising makes a teasing foil, the rhythm section is terrific, and Hutcherson drifts in as a useful extra guest. Excellent live sound on a previously unreleased date. Stitt's opening blues (dedicated to his dentist, since new bridgework had revitalized his playing) should be enough to convince those sceptical about the album title's machismo.

Markus Stockhausen

TRUMPET, FLUGELHORN, SYNTHESIZER

Son of Karlheinz, he has pursued a career as a fusionesque trumpeter and sound-scaper, creating a kind of brainy mood-music with an improvisational edge.

****(*) Cosi Lontano ... Quasi Dentro**

ECM 837111-2 *Stockhausen; Fabrizio Ottaviucci (p); Gary Peacock (b); Zoro Babel (d).* 3/88.

***** Aparis**

ECM 841774-2 *Stockhausen; Simon Stockhausen (sax, syn); Jo Thones (d, electric d).* 8/89.

*****(*) Despite The Fire-Fighters' Efforts ...**

ECM 517717-2 *As above.* 7/92.

***** Sol Mestizo**

Act 9222 *Stockhausen; Philip Catherine (g); Chano Dominguez (p); Simon Stockhausen (ky, ss); Jochen Schmidt (b); Enrique Diaz (b, v); Thomas Alkier (d); Filipe Mandingo (perc); Juanita Lascarro, Alexandra Naumann, Pia Miranda (v).* 2/95.

Markus Stockhausen came to prominence as Michael, the main soloist in his father's opera, *Donnerstag*, the first part of the colossal *Licht* cycle, which bids fair to become the twenty-first century's *Ring*. As an improvising performer he has the same purity of tone all through the range but lacks entirely the dramatic force he draws from his father's global conception on 'Michaels Reise um die Erde'. Though the material is quite impressive, the conventional quartet set-up on *Cosi Lontano* ... suits his approach not one bit. His solos are vague and unanchored and, without Peacock's patient figuring, it would all fall apart.

In recent years, Stockhausen has continued to experiment with his own brand of theatricality and world music. *Sol Mestizo* is a set of pieces written by the Chilean, Enrique Diaz. On the face of it a strange project for Stockhausen, it actually works very well, and his trumpet playing (minus the quarter-tone effects of the earlier record) is quite straightforward and often very upbeat, reminiscent of some early bebopper experimenting with free rhythms.

Markus and half-brother Simon have also constituted two-thirds of a group called Aparis. The eponymous record and the very impressive *Despite The Fire-Fighters' Efforts* ... are more straightforwardly impressionistic and altogether more successful. Neo-funk tracks like 'High Ride' on the former sit rather uneasily, but Thones's acoustic and electric drums and Simon's intelligent sequencing bring a propulsive energy to even the quieter, watercoloured pieces. No clear indication why they've used a shot of Windsor Castle ablaze on the cover of the second group record, and there's a persistent avoidance of the dramatic climaxes individual pieces seem to promise, as if every piece, not just the album title, ends with a string of ellipses. Increasingly impressive, though it's hard to shake off the feeling that this is just relaxation from working in the old man's shop.

Stockholm Jazz Orchestra

GROUP

Founded in 1983 to showcase some of the best straight-ahead musicians in Sweden's capital, under the general leadership of Fredrik Norén, the SJO frequently invites guest conductors and soloists to work with them.

***** Dreams**

Dragon DRCD 169 *Jan Kohlin, Fredrik Norén, Lars Lindgren, Stig Persson, Gustavo Bergalli (t, flhn); Bob Brookmeyer (vtb); Mikael Råberg, Bertil Strandberg, Mats Hermansson (tb); Sven Larsson (btb); Dave Castle (ss, as, cl); Håkan Bröstrom (ss, as, f); Ulf Andersson, Johan Alenius (ss, ts, cl); Hans Arktoft (bs, bcl); Anders Widmark (ky); Jan Adefeldt (b); Johan Dielemans (d).* 8/88.

***** Jigsaw**

Dragon DRCD 213 *As above, except Peter Asplund (t, flhn), Anders Wiborg (tb), Johan Hörlén (ss, as, cl, f), Jan Levander (ts, cl, f), Joakim Milder (ts), Jim McNeely (p), Martin Lofgren (d) replace Lindgren, Brookmeyer, Larsson, Bröstrom, Alenius, Widmark and Dielemans.* 3/91.

***** Live At Jazz Club Fasching**

Dragon DRCD 269 *As above, except add Bob Mintzer, Per Johansson (ts), Neta Norén (bs), Göran Strandberg (p), Jukkis Uotila (d), Rafael Sida (perc); omit Milder, McNeely, Löfgren.* 4/94.

***** Sound Bites**

Dragon DRCD 311 *As above, except add Patrik Skogh (t, flhn), Dick Oatts (as), Hector Bingert, Marcus Lindgren (ts), Alberto Pinton (bs, bcl), Jim McNeely (p); omit Mintzer, Johansson, Norén, Strandberg, Sida, Levander, Kohlin, Persson, Andersson, Arktoft.* 9/95.

Originally a rehearsal band, and now an occasional enterprise under a nominal leadership from Fredrik Norén, the SJO recorded the first two CDs to celebrate working with guest arrangers: *Dreams* with Bob Brookmeyer and *Jigsaw* with Jim McNeely. While the two sessions are unalike in tone and delivery, each is rewarding. Brookmeyer, who spends much time as a resident composer with West German Radio, knows European orchestras, and his themes make the most of the prowess of the band: difficult scoring in 'Missing Monk' and 'Cats' is dispatched without much effort by the group, and while the soloists take a lesser role they're perfectly in tune with Brookmeyer's quirkily structured pieces. Some of them resemble no more than eccentrically linked episodes, but there are many striking passages – the first three tracks are an informal suite, with 'Lies' a particularly intriguing patchwork – which deserve a close listen.

Jigsaw is a more conventional record. One gets the feeling that McNeely is a more meticulous and thoroughgoing composer than Brookmeyer, but a less inspirational one. The modern orchestral bop of 'Off The Cuff', for instance, or the concerto for Milder in 'The Decision' are convincing and tersely wound set-pieces, but the freewheeling demeanour of the earlier record is missed. Still, it may suit some tastes better. *Sound Bites* is a second turn for McNeely, and with guest soloist Oatts the orchestra sounds in vigorous spirits at a Stockholm concert. Although McNeely brought four of his own themes to the concert – the opening 'Pete's Feet' is probably the best – the most interesting scores are 'Yesterdays', scored with accumulating power around Oatts's soprano, and 'In A Sentimental Mood', something of a concerto for Hörlén. Oatts aside, there are few soloists: this is one band where the ensemble itself is what counts.

The live album has Bob Mintzer as guest conductor-soloist. The stays are a bit looser and there's a frolicsome feel to some of the music, although Mintzer's scores are rather tough and sometimes unyielding; so it winds up as much like their studio work. Star soloist: Peter Asplund on 'Elvin's Mambo'.

Irvin Stokes (born 1926)

TRUMPET

Although he came along in the bop era, Stokes was a section-man in swing orchestras when they were in decline. His later prominence was mainly in Panama Francis's Savoy Sultans.

**** Just Friends**

Arbors ARCD 19199 *Stokes; Lloyd Mayers (p); Earl May (b); Eddie Locke (d).* 12/97.

Another old-timer rediscovered by Arbors, Stokes plays this session with old-fashioned gentility: Phil Schaap compares him to Doc Cheatham in the sleeve-notes, and it's not unfair to either man. But Stokes has little of Doc's ebullience and he is clearly taking it pretty easy on this set of standards, a blues and one mildly interesting choice which the sleeve lists as Kenny Durham's 'Blue Basso' (*sic* – it's Kenny Dorham's 'Blue Bossa'!). This is Stokes trying bebop, and frankly it defeats him.

Stolen Van

GROUP

Australian piano–bass–drums trio weaned as much on rock as on jazz.

*****(*) Stolen Van**

Rufus RF035 *Sean Wayland (p); Michel Rose (g); Maria Zivkovic, Peter Garritty (vn); Jane Brownley (vla); Nick Dobosi (clo); Adam Armstrong (b); Simon Barker (d); Hamish Stuart (v).* 4/96.

The trouble with jazz musicians covering modern pop tunes is that they seem to treat them as interludes, breaks from the hard stuff, and there's always – faint or otherwise – an air of patronizing the music. Witness Herbie Hancock's interesting if openly sowhat *The New Standard*. The difference with this Australian trio (Wayland, Armstrong and Barker – the others are along for the ride at various points) is that they obviously love tunes by Steely Dan (especially) and others, and want to play them because they like them. The result is a lightweight but extremely enjoyable walk through the thickets of 'Rose Darling', 'The Caves Of Altamira', 'Babylon Sisters' and other Dan favourites, plus bits from John Lennon, Elvis Costello, Suzanne Vega and Jimmy Webb's pristine 'Witchita Lineman'. It comes out as the most refreshing of nods to a vast area of songwriting which jazz still deigns largely to ignore – for a complex string of reasons, it's true. But this fun-yet-serious group points a way forward which a number of other musicians are now also starting to follow. And just in case you think they don't even know the words, there's a vocal reprise of 'Witchita Lineman'.

Billy Strayhorn (1915–67)

PIANO, COMPOSER, ARRANGER

He began writing for Duke Ellington in 1939, first as lyricist, then as collaborator. He occasionally played piano while Duke directed, and made some own-name band recordings in the '50s and '60s, but the importance of 'Swee' Pea' was as a composer and right-hand man to Ellington.

*****(*) Great Times!**

Original Jazz Classics OJC 108 *Strayhorn; Duke Ellington (p); Wendell Marshall, Lloyd Trottman (b); Oscar Pettiford (b, clo); Jo Jones (d).* 9–11/50.

They were like two aspects of a single complex self. Where Duke Ellington was immodest, priapic and thumpingly egocentric, his longtime writing and arranging partner, Billy Strayhorn, was shy, gay and self-effacing. It's now very difficult, given the closeness of their relationship and their inevitable tendency to draw on aspects of the other's style and method, to separate which elements of an 'Ellington–Strayhorn' composition belong to each; but there is no doubt that Swee' Pea, as Ellington called him, made an immense impact on his boss's music. Even if he had done no more than write 'Lush Life' (see below) and 'Take The "A" Train', Strayhorn would still have been guaranteed a place in jazz history.

The ground-rules have shifted a little since the publication of David Hajdu's 1997 biography of Strayhorn, a book which intends no disrespect to the genius of Duke Ellington but which relocates some significant emphases and suggests that Strayhorn may have had a greater part in creating the Ellington sound than is usually acknowledged. Indeed, it may be that association with Ellington significantly redirected aspects of Strayhorn's own talent; whether to his benefit or loss remains ambiguous. Either way, there is so little available under Strayhorn's own name at present that one has to go to the Ellington shelf to get any sense of his work – which is as it should be. Still, it's about time that the excellent small-group session, *Cue For Saxophone*, was back on CD.

Strayhorn was not an outstanding pianist by himself and he wasn't, of course, an instinctive performer. In fairness, the 1950 *Great Times!* may be credited to Strayhorn's account. In performance terms he's overshadowed by his boss, playing much more 'correctly' and inside the key than the Duke found comfortable. It's easier to separate them on the inevitable '"A" Train' and 'Oscalypso', when Strayhorn switches to celeste.

Frank Strazzeri (born 1930)

PIANO

Originally a reed player, Strazzeri is thought of as a veteran of the West Coast school of the 1960s, but he had already worked in New York, spent three years in New Orleans Dixieland groups, and been on the road with Woody Herman. He has since remained based in Los Angeles, doing session-work and leading his own groups on occasional records.

***** Little Giant**

Fresh Sound FSR-CD 184 *Strazzeri; Horacio Fumero (b); Peer Wyboris (d).* 11/89.

***** Wood Winds West**

Jazz Mark 111 *Strazzeri; Bill Perkins (ss, as, f, af); Bob Cooper (ts, cl); Jack Nimitz (bs, bcl); Dave Stone (b); Paul Kreibich (d).* 2/92.

A journeyman pianist who's worked under many a famous leader, Strazzeri's kind of jazz glides off surfaces rather than cutting deep, and these sunny, cool, rounded sessions are as close to definitive as he'll ever find himself on record. Conservative in terms of harmony and rhythm, his distinctiveness comes out in his touch: he plays with a delicacy that makes all his solos flow evenly across each chorus, with nothing struck very hard and no phrase emerging out of kilter with the others. In other situations it might result in merely dull music, but Strazzeri picks tunes like a man who's easily bored. *Little Giant* was a session organized at a few hours' notice, and the temptation to go for easy old warhorses must have been hard to resist; instead, there's scarcely anything which isn't out of the ordinary, including 'Don'cha Go 'Way Mad', Carl Perkins's 'Grooveyard', George Shearing's 'Conception' and Ellington's 'I'm Gonna Go Fishin''. Fumero and Wyboris keep spontaneously good time. The *Wood Winds West* date is more about Strazzeri's talents as an arranger for the multiple horns of Perkins, Cooper and Nimitz and, on a straight, lush theme like 'Nocturne', it can seem like an exercise in mood music rather than a jazzman's undertaking. But these old pros find serendipitous routes to many nice touches.

String Trio Of New York

GROUP

Led by bassist Lindberg, the Trio represents a dogged refusal to accept the casual consensus that a jazz group necessarily includes a horn, a piano and a set of drums. The personnel has changed and changed very successfully, but the group's future was threatened when Lindberg suffered serious wrist damage, now successfully overcome.

***** Common Goal**

Black Saint 120058 *Billy Bang (vn, yokobue, f); James Emery (g, soprano g, mand): John Lindberg (b).* 11/81.

*****(*) Rebirth Of A Feeling**

Black Saint 120068 *As above.* 11/83.

In the interests of neatness it would be convenient to shorthand these albums: 'with Billy Bang – good; without – not'. Despite a general critical consensus to that effect, the reality isn't so simple. Though Bang's ducks-and-drakes approach to tonality was a vital component of the STNY's first four albums, Burnham is a perfectly adequate replacement, and it's clear that much of the impetus of the band comes from the bassist, who is also an impressive writer and emerges with a bang of his own on *Time Never Lies* with the fascinating 'Middle Eastern Essay'.

Rebirth Of A Feeling claims the attention more than any of the later discs. Centred round Bang's 'Penguins An' Other Strange Birds' (a gloriously wacky piece) and the long, rather more brooding 'Utility Grey', which was written by Lindberg, it's a superb record which can be recommended warmly to anyone who hasn't yet encountered the STNY. Whatever the merits of the post-Bang STNY (and they are considerable), there's no doubt that their best albums are those involving him; unfortunately, there's scarcely any of it left around to clinch the point.

***(*) **Intermobility**
Arabesque AJ018 *As above, except replace Burnham with Regina Carter (vn).* 7/92.

***(*) **Octagon**
Black Saint 120131 *As above.* 11/92.

There was a further change of personnel after 1990, with Regina Carter coming in for Burnham. She's not a particularly imaginative player (certainly not when placed against someone like Britain's Sylvia Hallett), but *Intermobility* restored a little of the buzz and fire, a few of the raw edges; and *Octagon* is an ambitious record nevertheless, covering a startling range of contemporary compositions (Marty Ehrlich, Muhal Richard Abrams, Mark Helias, Leo Smith and Bobby Previte are all credited), and Carter's own 'Forever February' is one of the loveliest things they've done, which bodes well for future projects.

***(*) **With Anthony Davis**
Music & Arts CD 994 *As above, except add Anthony Davis (p).* 97.

In common with just about everyone else at the time, the trio decided to dig back into recent jazz history. That they picked Anthony Davis, a noted composer of avant-garde works, to accompany them on this project bespeaks a certain unwillingness to take the obvious course. Davis brings in one long tune of his own, 'Happy Valley Blues' (imagine what it would sound like if Frederic Rzewski were Duke's lovechild), but for the rest the music is all by Monk, Ellington and Mingus, beginning and ending with the Duke on 'Caravan' and the less-known 'Heaven' and wedging in 'Peggy's Blue Skylight' (one of Mingus's most adventurous deconstructions of popular song) between 'Eronel', a wonderful 'Ruby, My Dear' and 'Evidence'. The playing is impeccable throughout, with Carter finally sounding as if she is an integral part of the group.

***(*) **Blues ...?**
Black Saint 120148-2 *As above, except omit Davis.* 10/93.

Not clear what the question mark is about, except that the Trio seems to be interrogating the blues rather than merely rehashing them. 'Cobalt Blue', 'Red Shift' and 'Speedball' represent a toughening of the band's sound, while an intriguing montage of Charlie Parker tunes suggests how readily this personnel adapts to bebop as well. The addition of 'Freddy Freeloader', Miles's relaxed blowing theme from *Kind Of Blue*, adds a further dimension to a thoroughly unexpected and highly attractive record.

**** **Faze Phour**
Black Saint 120168 *As above, except omit Carter; add Diane Monroe (vn).* 11/97.

Another change of personnel, but – more important – a token of successful recovery from Lindberg's career-threatening arm injury. The idea of *Phaze Four* is a retrospective of what is now two decades of activity, with re-recordings of three earlier pieces alongside new material. As ever, the group also covers some repertory material, on this occasion Monk's 'Straight, No Chaser' (highly successful), Duke's 'In A Sentimental Mood' (oddly not), and Mingus's rise-and-fall tone-poem, 'Pithecanthropus Erectus' (which succeeds on pure cheek). Monroe fits very comfortably into a now settled partnership. By no means a player of Bang's dramatic presence, she is none the less capable of fireworks, on the opening 'Frozen Ropes' and her own 'Groovin' Roots'. As ever, the sound is very strong, nicely balanced and richly textured.

Jan Strinnholm (born 1936)

PIANO

Born in Stockholm, he started playing boogie piano in school, then was inspired by Coltrane and Bill Evans. He has worked modestly in the leading mainstream-modern circles of Swedish jazz since.

*** **Strinnholm – 95**
Sittel SITCD 9224 *Strinnholm (p solo).* 3/95.

A rare CD for the Swedish veteran. Most of these are originals, sprightly or ruminative as the fancy takes him, and the long, thoughtful but quite pointed improvisation, 'Step By Step', which starts the record, is characteristic of his style, romantic but with a lean streak. He's managed to filter bebop, Coltrane, Evans and Jarrett (all honoured in his sleeve-note) into a manner which isn't so much distinctively individual as gracious in the way it displays his experience. Well done.

Dave Stryker (born 1957)

GUITAR

Born in Omaha, Stryker took up guitar at ten and began playing in local rock bands. Moved to Los Angeles, then to New York in 1980. Worked with Jack McDuff, Lonnie Smith, Jimmy Smith and Stanley Turrentine, then led his own dates.

*** **Stryke Zone**
Steeplechase SCCD 31277 *Stryker; Marc Cohen (p); Ron McClure (b); Ronnie Burrage (d).* 10/90.

**** **Passage**
Steeplechase SCCD 31330 *Stryker; Steve Slagle (ss, as); Joey Calderazzo (p); Jay Anderson (b); Adam Nussbaum (d).* 3/91.

***(*) **Blue Degrees**
Steeplechase SCCD 31315 *Stryker; Rick Margitza (ts); Larry Goldings (org); Jeff Hirshfield (d).* 4/92.

*** **Full Moon**
Steeplechase SCCD 31345 *Stryker; Steve Slagle (as, f); Jay Anderson (b); Jeff Hirshfield (d).* 10/93.

Stryker did long service in the pressure-cooker atmosphere of Jack McDuff and Jimmy Smith groups and, while he prefers a slightly blurred tone over the crisp lines of many modern guitarists, he has a knack for cutting through any ensemble. 'Jungle' on *Passage* is an example of how he digs into a solo – the leering bent notes and swaggering delivery are a startling display; but the fast bop lines of 'It's You Or No One' on the same record show he has the necessary language down pat. Consistently energetic and persuasive, there's little to choose between these records as regards his own playing. *Stryke Zone* is a shade behind for a rhythm section that doesn't quite strike best sparks, and the next two Steeplechases are the place to start. *Passage* is an all-round programme – there's a brief, pretty 'I Fall In Love Too Easily' as a nice change of pace – with both intensity and finesse. *Blue Degrees* is just a touch cooler – Goldings, the only organ player ever to feature on a Steeplechase date at that point, is more of a pastel player than a bar-burner – but the undervalued Margitza is a welcome presence, and Stryker is full of ideas again.

Full Moon is perhaps a mite disappointing as the next in the sequence. Ornette Coleman's 'The Sphinx' makes a hurried, splashy opening, Coltrane's 'Wise One' is mush for flute and acoustic guitar, and not till Slagle's 'Leadbelly Sez' do they really dig in. But there's still some marvellous playing on Wayne Shorter's 'Deluge' and two slow-to-mid blues.

*** **Stardust**

Steeplechase SCCD 31362 *Stryker; Joey DeFrancesco (org); Adam Nussbaum (d).* 10/94.

*** **Nomad**

Steeplechase SCCD 31371 *Stryker; Randy Brecker, Bill Warfield, Bob Millikan, John Eckert, Tony Kadleck, Bud Burridge (t); Tim Sessions, Jeff Nelson (tb); Steve Slagle, Andy Fusco, Bob Hanlon, Alex Stewart, Walt Weiskopf, Bob Parsons (reeds); Joel Weiskopf (p); Scott Colley, Lynn Seaton (b); Jeff Hirshfield, Grisha Alexiev (d).* 8/94.

***(*) **The Greeting**

Steeplechase SCCD 31387 *Stryker; Bruce Barth (p); Scott Colley (b); Tony Reedus (d); Daniel Sadownick (perc).* 11/95.

*** **Blue To The Bone**

Steeplechase SCCD 31371 *Stryker; Brian Lynch (t); Conrad Herwig (tb); Rich Perry (ts); Bob Parsons (bs); Bruce Barth (p, org); Jay Anderson (b); Billy Drummond (d).* 3/96.

Stryker's good run continues on these latest Steeplechases, though there's a certain sense of diminishing returns, and not many will want to own all of these. *Stardust* sets him up with Joey DeFrancesco on the kind of gig he cut his teeth on and, with the organist in his usual bumptious form, the session slips by in friendly style, though it presses few demands on the listener. *Nomad* is perhaps the most disappointing record, given that this was a rare opportunity to be a featured soloist with a big band. There's nothing wrong with the record, yet there seems so little to remember: the arrangements feel perfunctory, if not exactly hurried, and soloists like Brecker and Slagle do no more than they have to. Stryker plays handsomely enough, but it feels like a mishandled project. *The Greeting* is more satisfying in every way: Stryker's originals are a sound lot, Barth is a good new companion, and the guitarist finds his most melodic and purposefully aggressive form, though the closing cover of a Sonny Sharrock tune scarcely competes with that departed master.

Blue To The Bone tries another variation by sticking to straight-up blues with a horn section and Barth turning to the organ. Again, Stryker knows this terrain well, and there's no lack of feeling or grit in the delivery: his bottleneck intro to 'Bayou Blues' is an arresting touch, and Slagle's chart for 'Messenger' is very sharp. In the end, though, this feels like an LP-length project getting tuckered out over a CD's duration.

*** **All The Way**

Steeplechase SCCD 31455 *Stryker; Scott Colley (b); Bill Stewart (d).* 4/97.

Stryker grasps the nettle of a trio session (mystifyingly described as 'a seldom-explored milieu' in the sleeve-notes). The playing is comely and expansive rather than particularly biting – Stewart plays much more delicately here than he does with Pat Metheny – and each of the eight standards receives a good-natured interpretation. Stryker concentrates on little details, like his paraphrases of the melody of 'All The Way', sweetly done.

John Stubblefield (born 1945)

TENOR SAXOPHONE, SOPRANO SAXOPHONE

Born in Little Rock, Arkansas, he started on piano, then took up tenor and moved to Chicago, working for a spell with the AACM. In New York from 1971 and worked for many leaders, from Mingus to McCoy Tyner.

*** **Confessin'**

Soul Note 121095 *Stubblefield; Cecil Bridgewater (t, flhn); Mulgrew Miller (p); Rufus Reid (b); Eddie Gladden (d).* 9/84.

***(*) **Bushman Song**

Enja 5015 *Stubblefield; Geri Allen (p, syn); Charnett Moffett (b); Victor Lewis (d, perc); Mino Cinelu (perc, v).* 4/86.

**** **Countin' The Blues**

Enja 5051 *Stubblefield; Hamiet Bluiett (bs); Mulgrew Miller (p); Charnett Moffett (b); Victor Lewis (d).* 5/87.

*** **Morning Song**

Enja 8036 *Stubblefield; George Cables (p); Clint Houston (b); Victor Lewis (d).* 5/93.

Despite a similar concern for the jazz tradition, Stubblefield attracted far less critical attention as a solo recording artist than David Murray, for whom he has occasionally depped in the World Saxophone Quartet. The Arkansas man is a more narrowly focused player, without Murray's extraordinary fluency in almost every dialect of the jazz tradition; but he has a strongly individual voice, constructs solos with impeccable logic, and his own music has a rootsy immediacy and appeal.

Confessin' is a strongly worded testament from a player who has always clung to the notion of tenor saxophone as essentially a vocalized instrument. 'Spiral Dance' and 'Waltz For Duke Pearson' (dedicated to the now-underrated pianist) are well constructed, with something of the WSQ's emphasis on improvisation *within* the basic structure of the piece (compare some of the Art Ensemble of Chicago references on *Bushman Song*, which traces Stubblefield's engagement with a wider than usual spectrum of black music), and 'Confessin'' brings the set to a fine climax.

The more recent *Countin' The Blues* reunites Stubblefield with his WSQ colleague, Bluiett. Unlike Murray, who left the smaller horn aside in favour of tenor and bass clarinet, Stubblefield has worked steadily on soprano saxophone. Pitched 'parallel' to Bluiett's baritone, it heightens the tonal impact of both horns. Miller is excellent (as he is on *Confessin'*), but it's left to Moffett and the increasingly confident Lewis to give the arrangements the forward thrust they get on *Bushman Song* from a rock-tinged Geri Allen and from Moffett.

The most recent of the records lacks the urgency and sheer inventiveness of its predecessor. With more of the weight thrown on Stubblefield himself, it gets a shade discursive in places, particularly on the long(ish) originals. There is, though, a brilliant reading of drummer Lewis's 'Shaw Of Newark' to savour. Nothing new from Stubblefield in recent years, and it may be that teaching is taking up most of his time.

Dick Sudhalter (born 1938)

CORNET, TRUMPET, FLUGELHORN

A jazz writer of great acumen and distinction, Sudhalter is a cornetist and trumpeter whose wily lyricism owes much to the school suggested by Bix Beiderbecke, of whom he has written the definitive biography.

***** With Pleasure**

Audiophile ACD-159 *Sudhalter; Dan Barrett (tb); Bob Reitmeier (cl, as, ts); Dan Levinson (cl, ts); Joe Muranyi (cl); Dave Frishberg (p, v); James Cirillo (g); Howard Alden (g, bj); Putter Smith (tba, b); Bill Crow (b); Eddie Locke, Dick Berk (d).* 3/81–4/94.

***** After Awhile**

Challenge 70014 *Sudhalter; Roy Williams (tb); Jim Shepherd (tb, bsx); John R.T Davies (as); Al Gay (ts); Keith Nichols (p, tb); Mick Pyne (p); Nevil Skrimshire, Paul Sealey (g); Dave Green, Jack Fallon (b); Allan Ganley, Jack Parnell (d); Chris Ellis (v).* 5–6/94.

Sudhalter's Bixian brass stylings have tended to take a back seat to his jazz scholarship, but he is a lyrical player and a rare example of a musician-historian who can make his enthusiasms take on a personal cast when he plays. These good-natured sessions make no great demands on the listener, but they're enjoyable for all that. The first reissues a 1981 date with eight extra, subsequent tracks, and it blends the echoes of a vanished Chicago with a few more modern licks: Sudhalter cuts from such ancient cloth as 'Madame Dynamite' and 'Boneyard Shuffle' and reshapes a Beiderbecke legacy such as 'Slow River' into a winsome duet with Frishberg. The Challenge album goes to the other side of the Atlantic – to the Bull's Head in Barnes, in fact – and brings on an English team for a similarly inclined session. The material isn't quite so arcane here, but the playing probably isn't quite as vivacious either.

***** Melodies Heard ... Melodies Sweet**

Challenge CHR 70055 *Sudhalter; Roger Kellaway, Sy Johnson (p); Frank Vignola, James Chirillo (g); Ed Saindon (vib); Marshall Wood (b); Joe Cocuzzo (d); Barbara Lea (v).* 5–8/98.

It is, indeed, sweet and melodious music, and Sudhalter's own playing has never sounded better. Six duets with his old friend Kellaway are good enough to wish for an entire album by the duo, and the concept – songs by jazzmen – is lightly worn, since the tunes are an unhackneyed and likeable lot. But it never feels like much more than an amiable time-passer, graciously though everyone plays – perhaps too graciously. Lea sings two lyrics, and the others come and go at the leader's suggestion.

Idrees Sulieman (born 1923)

TRUMPET, FLUGELHORN

Veteran bebop trumpeter who was a presence on the first-generation New York scene, recording with Monk and Mary Lou Williams. He decamped for Europe in the '60s and later took up alto sax as a second horn.

****(*) Now Is The Time**

Steeplechase SCCD 31052 *Sulieman; Cedar Walton (p); Sam Jones (b); Billy Higgins (d).* 2/76.

****(*) Bird's Grass**

Steeplechase SCCD 31202 *Sulieman; Per Goldschmidt (ts); Horace Parlan (p); Niels-Henning Orsted Pedersen (b); Kenny Clarke (d).* 12/76.

**** Groovin'**

Steeplechase SCCD 31218 *Sulieman; Per Goldschmidt (ts, bs); Horace Parlan (p); Mads Vinding (b); Billy Hart (d).* 8/85.

Sulieman seems destined to be a forgotten man of bebop trumpet, even though he recorded with Monk in the 1940s and appeared with many leading boppers. His subsequent career found him buried in big bands and he was spied only intermittently by an international audience. These three Steeplechase albums find him only a shadow of his former self. The articulation sounds blurred – badly so by the time of the 1985 date – and the ideas are unremarkable; he struggles at fast tempos and does no more than hold his own on ballads, though 'The Summer Knows', from *Bird's Grass*, is prettily done. Exposed on the first album, he needs Goldschmidt's support on the second, and by the third, in which the saxophonist divides his time between tenor and baritone, one feels that these are sessions best left alone by posterity.

Ira Sullivan (born 1931)

TRUMPET, FLUGELHORN, PECKHORN, SAXOPHONES

Sullivan is something of an enigma, a transitional figure between bop and free music whose restless style and intriguing multi-instrumentalism may well have had an impact on the nascent AACM generation in Chicago. Sullivan's reluctance to travel restricted him to Florida for much of his career.

***(*) **Nicky's Tune**
Delmark DD 422 *Sullivan; Nicky Hill (sax); Jodie Christian (p); Vic Sproles (b); Wilbur Campbell (d).* 58.

*** **Blue Stroll**
Delmark DD 602 *As above, except omit Hill; add Johnny Griffin (ts).* 59.

Sullivan started out as a bopper, but one who assiduously avoided the basic, standards-based repertoire in favour of new material; this, it seems, was the condition he imposed when he went on the road with Red Rodney. Much of his recorded output was on the now-deleted Muse label, which is now making a comeback thank to Joel Dorn and 32 Records; so far, though, nothing of Ira's has come through and these two albums for Delmark are all that's generally available.

The earlier of the pair is dedicated to the equally enigmatic Nicky Hill, one of those catalytic players who remained little known outside a small circle. Like all of Ira's output, it's a slightly puzzling and forbidding experience if you approach it expecting basic changes and contrafacts on 'I Got Rhythm', 'Cherokee' and 'How High The Moon'. Ira's harmonic sense is unimpeachable and his understanding with the excellent Christian is intuitive and sympathetic. Trumpet is the dominant voice on both records, but the saxophones and peckhorn are deployed to excellent effect. This was the period when Ira was losing patience with the formulae of bebop, even his own individual brand, and was striking out in the direction of free jazz. There are atonal and polytonal episodes on *Nicky's Tune*, fewer on the set with Griff, who barges and blusters his way through his solos, tossing out tags and quotes as if to remind the others what else was going on in the world. Two powerful records by an almost forgotten figure; let's hope that next time out some more of Ira's work has been returned from the Dead Letter Office.

Joe Sullivan (1906–71)

PIANO

Studied in Chicago and then worked in the local scene during the 1920s and early '30s. Joined Bob Crosby in 1936 but was sidelined by illness. Worked in group and solo situations in the '40s, but was playing solo in San Francisco in the '50s and, despite a couple of modest comebacks, finally drifted into obscurity.

*** **Joe Sullivan 1933–1941**
Classics 821 *Sullivan; Ed Anderson (t); Benny Morton (tb); Edmond Hall, Pee Wee Russell (cl); Danny Polo (ts, cl); Freddie Green (g); Billy Taylor, Henry Turner (b); Yank Porter, Zutty Singleton, Johnny Wells (d); Joe Turner, Helen Ward (v).* 9/33–3/41.

This collects all of Sullivan's piano solos of the period, plus the two dates by his Café Society Orchestra and a 1941 trio date for Commodore with Pee Wee Russell and Zutty Singleton. Sullivan had a terrific left hand and his style was a personal blend of boogie-woogie and stride language, imbued with a shot of local Chicago blues. Not a great melodist, perhaps, which gives some of the dozen solos here a certain sameness, and the band tracks are nothing very special; but the intensity of Sullivan's style has weathered the years well enough and his bluff passion gives the music bite. Transfers are variable, but the music survives the surface noise and boomy bass patterns.

***(*) **Joe Sullivan 1944–1945**
Classics 1070 *Sullivan; Archie Rosatie (cl); Ulysses Livingston (g); Artie Shapiro (b); Zutty Singleton (d).* 11/44–12/45.

Twenty of these 24 tracks are solos, and they're some of Sullivan's best work. Two obscure tracks for Sunset are rocking boogie-woogie pieces. There are eight tracks made for Capitol EPs and an undated session that was later issued on Folkways. Sullivan's virtues shine through – his almost violent swing, the Irish humour, the no-nonsense improvising – and it's an enjoyable disc. Four quintet tracks are nothing special. This sound isn't terrible, but don't expect hi-fi.

(*) **Piano Solo
Storyville STCD 8234 *Sullivan (p solo).* 8/53–11/73.

Richard Hadlock's notes detail Sullivan's last years in a touching and funny way. He worked regularly at San Francisco's Club Hangover in the '50s but, after that closed, he worked rarely, and basically he drifted away. This collects 18 tracks, many from the Hangover, and some from a session which Hadlock recorded privately. Sullivan's ornery playing strikes sparks, but there are stumbles too, and the sound is often pretty awful, with crowd noise at times close to overpowering. A characterful memento, but it needs a tolerant ear.

Maxine Sullivan (1911–87)

VOCAL

Born Marietta Williams, Sullivan was singing in New York when Claude Thornhill did arrangements of a couple of Scottish songs for her and started a craze for jazzing folk material. She worked with John Kirby, Benny Goodman and others, then as a solo, before retiring to be a nurse during the 1950s. She came back around 1960 and thereafter sang (and sometimes played valve-trombone) in a career which stretched into the '80s.

*** **Maxine Sullivan 1937–1938**
Classics 963 *Sullivan; Manny Klein, Charlie Spivak, Frank Newton, Charlie Shavers (t); Bobby Hackett (c); Jack Lacey (tb); Buster Bailey (cl); Jimmy Lytell, Paul Ricci (cl, as); Toots Mondello, Jess Carneol, Pete Brown (as); Babe Russin (ts); Eddie Powell (bs, f); Claude Thornhill (p); Artie Bernstein, John Kirby (b); Chauncey Morehouse, O'Neil Spencer, Buddy Rich (d).* 6/37–6/38.

***(*) **Maxine Sullivan 1938–1941**
Classsics 991 *Sullivan; Bobby Hackett (c); Lloyd Reese, Charlie Shavers, Doc Cheatham, Lincoln Mills, Sidney De Paris (t); Vic Dickenson, Jimmy Archey, Joe Britton (tb); Slats Long, Chester Hazlett (cl, as); Buster Bailey, Leo Trammel, Reggie Merrill, Eddie Powell (cl); Benny Carter (t, as); Floyd Turnham, Russell Procope, Ernie Purce, Eddie Barefield (as); Bud Freeman, Buddy Banks, Fred Williams, Ernie Powell (ts); Carl Prager (bcl); Harold Goltzer (bsn); Mitch Miller (ob); Milt Rettenberg, Eddie Beal, Walter Gross, Billy Kyle, Sonny White (p); Ken Binford, Herb Thomas (g); Ed Brader, Red Callender, Frank Carroll, John*

Kirby, Charles Drayton (b); Ed Rubsam, Oscar Bradley, Cary Gillis, O'Neil Spencer, Al Taylor (d). 12/38–4/41.

***** More 1940–1941**

Circle CCD-125 *Sullivan; Charlie Shavers (t); Buster Bailey (cl); Russell Procope (as); Billy Kyle (p); John Kirby (b); O'Neil Spencer (d).* 10/40–11/41.

*****(*) Maxine Sullivan 1941–1946**

Classics 1020 *Sullivan; Charlie Shavers, Emmett Berry, Shorty Rogers, Joe Newman, Neal Hefti (t); Al Grey, Trummy Young, Alton Moore, Sandy Williams (tb); Buster Bailey, Hank D'Amico (cl); Russell Procope (as); Willard Brown (as, bs); Tony Scott (cl, as); Dexter Gordon, Don Byas (ts); Billy Kyle, Kenneth Billings, Teddy Wilson, Sonny White (p); Samuel Persoff, Samuel Rand, Joseph Breen (vn); Laura Newell (hp); Everett Barksdale, Freddie Green, Tony Colucci (g); Red Norvo (vib); John Kirby, Cedric Wallace, Billy Taylor, John Simmons, Harry Patent (b); O'Neil Spencer, Morey Feld, Specs Powell, J.C Heard (d); strings.* 6/41–46.

*****(*) The 'Le Ruban Bleu' Years**

Baldwin Street BJH-303 *Similar to above, except add Ellis Larkins (p), Everett Barksdale (g), Beverley Peer (b), Jimmy Lunceford Orchestra (personnel unidentified).* 44–49.

'Loch Lomond' was the novelty hit which launched Maxine Sullivan's career, part of a faintly ludicrous vogue for turning folk tunes and 'light music' into swing vehicles. The song (and 'Darling Nellie Gray', 'It Was A Lover And His Lass' and so forth) still works, though, because of Sullivan's transparent, almost ghostly singing. She didn't really swing her material so much as give it a lilting quality, floating it on phrasing that was measured and controlled without sounding excessively polite. Her version of 'St Louis Blues' sounds mousy next to a voice like Bessie Smith's, but the demure melancholy with which she invests it is surprisingly compelling. She also finds a particular tranquil beauty in 'Easy To Love', 'Moments Like This' and 'Spring Is Here'. All these are on Classics 963, which covers her successful first years in the studios. A disc's worth of this is a lot in one go, though, and we find the Classics transfers inconsistent and surely muddier than they should be.

Classics 991 picks up the story and starts with three sessions for Victor, then two with John Kirby's small group which was an almost ideal setting for Max. There are some good, forgotten songs here such as 'I'm Happy About The Whole Thing' and 'Kinda Lonesome', as well as the expected updates of such as 'Drink To Me Only With Thine Eyes'. But the Kirby dates, with their gentle jig-jog rhythms and pastel tones, suit her wonderfully well. 'If I Had A Ribbon Bow' is a definitive piece of Sullivan. Classics 1020 carries on with ten more charming titles with Kirby, before an interesting and obscure date for Beacon, two titles with Teddy Wilson, four with a Benny Carter band and six with a chamberish group that remade several of her earlier successes. The sound on these last titles is very muddy, on the rest average-to-good. Sullivan's singing remains rather demure and unconfected but, taken a few tracks at a time, she is irresistible.

The Baldwin Street release (Le Ruban Bleu was a supper club where Sullivan sang for several seasons from 1943) duplicates many of the tracks with Classics 1020 but also adds six splendid tracks with an Ellis Larkins trio (in surfacey sound), a pair of songs with a 1949 studio orchestra ('Cry, Buttercup, Cry' a choice rarity) and some AFRS transcriptions with the Lunceford orchestra. A collector's delight!

The Circle CD collects a series of transcriptions by the John Kirby group, six of which feature Sullivan. Some of them continue the folk-towards-jazz theme, and Kirby's willowy band are perhaps all too suitable as a backing group, but the music exudes an undeniable period charm. Excellent sound, given the source.

****** Close As Pages In A Book**

Audiophile 203 *Sullivan; Bob Wilber (ss, cl); Bernie Leighton (p); George Duvivier (b); Gus Johnson Jr (d).* 6/69.

***** Shakespeare**

Audiophile 250 *Sullivan; Rusty Dedrick (t, flhn); Dick Hyman (p, hpd); Bucky Pizzarelli (g); Milt Hinton (b); Don Lamond (d).* 6/71.

***** The Queen: Like Someone In Love**

Kenneth CKS 3402 *Sullivam; Bent Persson (t); Jens Lindgren (tb); Goran Eriksson (as); Erik Persson, Claes Brodda (ts); Bjorn Milder (p); Mikael Selander (vn, g); Ronnie Holmqvist, Anders Rabe (g); Olle Brostedt (b, g); Goran Lind (b); Sigge Dellert (d).* 10/78–5/83.

*****(*) The Queen: Something To Remember Her By**

Kenneth CKS 3406 *Sullivan; Bent Persson (t); George Vernon (tb); Claes Brodda (cl, ts); Goran Eriksson (as); Erik Persson (ts, bs); Bjorn Milder (p); Mikael Selander (g); Olle Brostedt (g, b); Goran Lind (b); Sigge Dellert (d).* 10/78–7/84.

Sullivan retired in the 1950s but later returned to regular singing (she also played flugelhorn and valve-trombone) and by the 1980s was as widely admired as she had ever been. Her manner didn't change much but, as recording improved, her intimate style and meticulous delivery sounded as classic as any of the great jazz singers. In her seventies there was inevitably a decline in the strength of her voice, but careful production ensured that her albums sounded very good.

Close As Pages In A Book was long a collectors' favourite, and it makes a welcome return on CD. The dozen songs are perfectly delivered – thoughtful, graceful, introspective without being introverted, this is peerless jazz singing, and the accompaniments by Wilber and his team are as *simpatico* as one could wish. The Shakespeare collection was the last word on Sullivan's 'Elizabethan' direction and it sounds better, at least, than Cleo Laine's efforts in this field. The pick of these, though, may be the beautiful *Something To Remember Her By* collection on Kenneth, cut in Sweden with local players. The sessions cover a six-year period, but Maxine sounds entirely at ease throughout, whether swinging on 'You Were Meant For Me' or strolling through 'Thanks For The Memory'. The band are very fine, too, with Brodda's Websterish tenor and Eriksson's sinuous alto particularly impressive. The recording is rather dry but otherwise sounds very good. This was meant to be the first of five such volumes (and is numbered five!) but so far only *Like Someone In Love* (numbered one in the sequence) has emerged as a follow-up. Not quite so good, this one, suggesting that the best tunes had already been cherrypicked for the previous release.

***** Great Songs From The Cotton Club**

Mobile Fidelity MFCD 836 *Sullivan; Keith Ingham (p).* 11/84.

***** Uptown**

Concord CCD 4288 *Sullivan; Scott Hamilton (ts); John Bunch (p); Chris Flory (g); Phil Flanigan (b); Chuck Riggs (d). 1/85.*

***** Swingin' Street**

Concord CCD 4351 *As above. 9/86.*

*****(*) Love ... Always**

Baldwin Street BJC-201 *Sullivan; Seldon Powell (ts, f); Dick Hyman (p); Major Holley (b); Mel Lewis (d). 12/85.*

****(*) Spring Isn't Everything**

Audiophile 229 *Sullivan; Loonis McGlohon (p); Jim Stack (vib); Terry Peoples (b); Bill Stowe (d). 7/86.*

***** Highlights In Jazz**

Storyville STCD 8276 *Sullivan; Doc Cheatham (t); Bill Watrous (tb); Phil Bodner (cl); Buddy Tate (ts); Derek Smith (p); Milt Hinton (b); Butch Miles (d). 3/87.*

Max never slowed down: she recorded 16 albums in the 1980s, and *Spring Isn't Everything*, one of her last sessions, features a 'song-book' recital (the tracks are all by Harry Warren) which finds her still in excellent shape. Unfortunately the studio balance doesn't favour her at all. Better to turn to the two Concord dates with Hamilton's smooth neo-classic band, which do as fine a job for her as they do for Rosemary Clooney, and what was an award-winning album with Keith Ingham, dedicated to tunes associated with the Cotton Club. A couple of new reissues have added to the pile. She's given marvellous support on *Love ... Always*, with Hyman in top form and the admirable and unjustly neglected Seldon Powell filling in many of the backgrounds. She makes as much of more modern songs like 'He's Got Away' and 'Two For The Road' as she does of the more familiar standards: a fine example of latter-day Sullivan. The Storyville set is a New York concert, cut only weeks before she died. The studio records are better, but it's hard to listen to this set and not be moved by her still-indomitable artistry, which here closes with a ten-minute 'St Louis Blues'.

Stan Sulzmann (born 1948)

TENOR SAXOPHONE, ALTO SAXOPHONE, SOPRANO SAXOPHONE, ALTO FLUTE

Worked on the London scene in the '60s and formed a long-standing quartet in 1970. Lately a frequent partner of pianists John Taylor and Marc Copland, and composing for larger groups.

*****(*) Feudal Rabbits**

Ah Um 011 *Sulzmann; Patrick Bettison, Mick Hutton (b); Steve Arguëlles (d). 12/90.*

****(*) Never At All**

Future FMR CD 05 28193 *Sulzmann; Marc Copland (p, syn). 2/92.*

***** Treasure Trove**

ASC CD 7 *Sulzmann; Nikki Iles (p); Martin Pyne (perc). 10/95.*

A classic case of a Talent Deserving Wider Recognition who has consistently failed to break through to the audiences his ability and commitment would seem to merit. Chronically under-recorded, Sulzmann made what looked like a promising return to his late-1970s form (*Krark* was a much-underrated record) with the curiously titled *Feudal Rabbits*. In the event, it's electric bassist Bettison who steals most of the honours, heavily featured on a number of tracks and name-checked on 'Feeling Bettison'. Sulzmann's delivery is introspective and melancholic and there's hardly an up-tempo track on the record. The best single piece is a version of Kenny Wheeler's delicate '3/4 In The Afternoon'. Pleasantly downbeat jazz that asks to be played late at night. One feels there ought to be a more challenging context for one of Britain's unsung instrumentalists.

Unfortunately, *Never At All* isn't it. American keyboard man Copland had worked with Sulzmann off and on for years, following a chance encounter in the 1970s. They've clearly built up a level of mutual understanding, but it tends to drain the music of tension rather than activating it. Sulzmann's flute is sharply etched over clouds of synthesizer tones on the lovely 'Phobos And Deimos', but only Copland's long 'Never At All' and 'Guinevere' offer much evidence of thoughtful interchange rather than merely companionable conversation.

Pianist and composer Nikki Iles has long been recognized as an artist of special promise. She has something of Geri Allen's richness of texture and rhythmic awareness and, good as she is in a larger group setting (most notably in Emanon with her husband, trumpeter Richard Iles), she comes across most formidably in settings like *Treasure Trove*. Pyne is restricted to just one number, on which Sulzmann also airs his beautifully toned alto flute, and it was a good notion not to clutter this partnership with any other guest slots. The range of Sulzmann's reeds and Iles's intelligently varied attack, in combination with fascinating material (all originals, except Paul Simon's 'I Do It For Your Love' and Bill Evans's 'Since We Met'), contribute to a thoroughly satisfying set that could perhaps have done with a bit more studio presence.

***** Birthdays, Birthdays**

Village Life 99108VL *Sulzmann; Patrick White, Henry Lowther, Noel Langley, Kenny Wheeler, Derek Watkins (t); Mark Bassey, Pete Beachill, Jeremy Price, Nichol Thomson, Richard Henry, Sarah Williams (tb); Ray Warleigh, Martin Hathaway, Julian Siegel, Pete Hurt, Mick Foster (saxes); Pete Saberton (p); Frank Ricotti (vib); John Parricelli (g); Tim Wells (b); Paul Clarvis (d). 7–8/99.*

Sulzmann conducts and composes but plays very little on this record (he's credited only with 'toy saxophone' on a single track). Played with great gusto by a strong team of British pros, the music is expertly put across if somewhat hard to follow at times: 'Little Dog' seems like a bundle of bits and pieces, and the bebop line of 'Newness' searches for a context for itself. Some of the scores sound overcrowded with incident. But when, as on the ingenious 'Midnight', everything locks into place, the results are impressive. Stan should have given himself more to do as a player, too.

Sun Ra (1914–93)

PIANO, CLAVIOLINE, CELESTE, ORGAN, SYNTHESIZER

The most mysterious figure in the history of jazz was, depending on your angle of vision, either a fearsome avant-gardist or a traditionalist in the line of Fletcher Henderson, for whom he wrote many arrangements early in his career. The truth about Sun Ra

was that he was both those things. The man born Herman 'Sonny' Blount in Alabama grew up steeped in the blues. Even when he founded his famous Arkestra, with its theatrical approach to jazz, and became a leading presence on the Chicago improvisation scene, his work was always grounded in melody and in blues changes. Sun Ra's claim to come from Saturn was doggedly sustained, one of the great metaphors of Black American music.

*****(*) Sound Sun Pleasure!!**

Evidence ECD 22014 *Sun Ra; Hobart Dotson, Ahk Tal Ebah, Art Hoyle (t); Bob Northern (flhn); Marshall Allen, Danny Davis (as); John Gilmore (ts); Charles Davis, Pat Patrick (bs); Danny Ray Thompson (reeds); Stuff Smith (vn); Ronnie Boykins, Victor Sproles (b); Robert Barry, Nimrod Hunt, James Jackson, Clifford Jarvis (d); Hatty Randolph, Clyde Williams (v).* ?53–60.

*****(*) Supersonic Jazz**

Evidence ECD 22015 *Sun Ra; Art Hoyle (t); Julian Priester (tb); James Scales (as); Pat Patrick (as, bs); John Gilmore (ts); Charles Davis (bs); Wilburn Green, Victor Sproles (b); Robert Barry, William Bugs Cochran (d); Jim Herndon (perc).* 56.

*****(*) Visits Planet Earth / Interstellar Low Ways**

Evidence ECD 22039 *Sun Ra; Phil Cohran, Art Hoyle, George Hudson, Lucious Randolph, Dave Young (t); Julian Priester, Nate Pryor (tb); James Spaulding (as); Marshall Allen (as, f); Pat Patrick (as, bs, space f, bells, solar d); John Gilmore (ts, bells, solar d); Charles Davis (bs); Ronnie Boykins, Victor Sproles (b); Robert Barry, William Bugs Cochran, Edward Skinner (d); Jim Herndon (perc).* 56, 58, 60.

****** We Travel The Spaceways / Bad And Beautiful**

Evidence ECD 22038 *Sun Ra; Art Hoyle, Walter Strickland (t); Phil Cohran (t, space harp, perc); Julian Priester, Nate Pryor (tb); James Scales, James Spaulding (as); Marshall Allen (as, bells, flying saucer, perc); John Gilmore (ts, cosmic bells, perc); Pat Patrick (bs, perc); Ronnie Boykins, Wilburn Green (b); Tommy Hunter (d); Robert Barry (d, perc); Edward Skinner (perc).* 56, 58 or 59, 59 or 60, 61.

***** Angels And Demons At Play / The Nubians Of Plutonia**

Evidence ECD 22066 *Sun Ra; Bill Fielder, Lucious Randolph (t); Phil Cohran (t, zither); Bob Bailey, Julian Priester, Nate Pryor (tb); James Spaulding (as); Marshall Allen (as, f); Pat Patrick (as, bs); John Gilmore (ts, cl, bells); Charles Davis (bs); Ronnie Boykins, Wilburn Green (b); Robert Barry, Jon Hardy (d); Jim Herndon (perc).* 56, 60.

♛ ** Jazz In Silhouette**

Evidence ECD 22012 *Sun Ra; Hobart Dotson (t); Julian Priester (tb); Marshall Allen, James Spaulding (as, f); John Gilmore (ts); Charles Davis (bs); Pat Patrick (bs, f); Ronnie Boykins (b); William Bugs Cochran (d).* 58.

A much-maligned and hugely influential figure, Sun Ra was either born in Chicago under the earth-name Herman Poole 'Sonny' Blount, as the birth-roll insists, or on Saturn, as the man himself often claimed. Uncertainty about his seriousness (and sanity) tended to divert attention from a considerable three-decade output, which included well over 100 LPs. Because much of it remained inaccessible during his lifetime, critical responses were apt to concentrate on the paraphernalia associated with his Arkestra big band, rather than on the music. Nevertheless, he was one of the most significant band-leaders of the post-war period. He drew on Ellington and Fletcher Henderson (for whom he did arrangements after the war), but also on the bop-derived avant-garde, and was a pioneer of collective improvisation. Though rarely acknowledged as an instrumentalist, he developed a convincing role for the synthesizer and was a strong rather than subtle piano player. The solo recordings, some of which have been reissued (see below), are only now being appreciated.

Above all, Sun Ra maintained a solitary independence from the music industry, a principled stance that certainly cost him dear in critical and commercial terms. For the first time in many years, it's possible again to get hold of important material self-released on the El Saturn label. These discs are being re-issued *in toto* by Evidence (who work out of Conshohocken, Pennsylvania), a colossal project that will presumably take several years. Sound-quality is remarkably good, given the often shaky balance of the original masters and the fact that they've been subjected to uncertain storage conditions. The original El Saturn titles have been preserved wherever possible, even when this has led to rather cumbersome doubling up. One of the drawbacks of Evidence's programme is the out-of-sequence pairing of sessions, rendering a strictly chronological review impossible. A more orderly approach or a separate chronological listing might have been helpful, even though exact recording dates remain a matter of controversy.

The 1950s were in many respects a golden age for Sun Ra and the Arkestra. The music is frankly experimental (in the sense that both leaders and players are clearly working through ideas on the stand) and the sci-fi apparatus was already part and parcel of American culture through the latter half of the decade. Chants like 'We Travel The Spaceways' began to sound more artful and mannered as the years went by, but for now they manage to sound almost spontaneous. There was always a suspicion that titles like 'Rocket Number Nine Take Off For The Planet Venus' were simply a diversionary addition to a fairly conventional jazz tune.

The bands themselves are terrific, of course. The marvellous *Jazz In Silhouette* will surely some day be recognized as one of the most important jazz records since the war. The closing 'Blues At Midnight' is sheer excitement. The baritone solo on the short 'Saturn', most probably Patrick, is an extension of Sun Ra's brilliantly individual voicings. The leader makes considerable use of the baritone and flutes, but also includes a specialist flugelhorn player on *Sound Sun Pleasure!!*, and elsewhere he makes distinctive use of electric bass, tympani and log drums. The great surprise of these recordings (though presumably no surprise to those who have taken the Saturnian aesthetic fully on board) is their *timelessness*. Listening to 'Enlightenment', given an uncharacteristically straightforward reading on *Jazz In Silhouette*, it's very difficult to guess a date for the performance. As Francis Davis suggests in a useful liner-note, the *Jazz In Silhouette* 'Enlightenment' is ideal 'blindfold test' material that might have been recorded at any point from the 1940s to the late 1980s. Only the long drum passage on 'Ancient Aiethopia' and the astonishing Dotson solo and chants that follow sound unequivocally 'modern'. Inevitably, the next track, 'Hours After', is orthodox swing.

The original *Sound Sun Pleasure!!* has been filled out for CD by material from the 1950s which was released in 1973 as *Deep Purple*. The earliest material appears to come from as early as 1953, a useful round-number indicator of Sun Ra's remarkable longevity, and features violinist Stuff Smith on the lo-fi, home-recorded title-track. *Supersonic Jazz* comes from the same period. Again, it is a set of originals combining conventional harmony and orchestrations with a thoroughly individual 'voice' (conveyed in occasional devices like Wilburn Green's use of electric bass on 'Super Blonde' and the closing 'Medicine For A Nightmare') and a striking gentleness that contrast sharply with the often brutal aspect of contemporaneous hard bop. So good is Julian Priester's own brief 'Soft Talk' (the only non-Sun Ra composition) that one immediately wishes for more. All the Evidence reissues have original cover-art, crude by present standards but wildly unconventional in the late 1950s and '60s when a pretty girl with a low-IQ expression was generally considered essential to successful music marketing.

Bad And Beautiful, recorded during 1961, is thought to be the first Arkestra disc to be made in New York City. Chronologically it belongs after the last of the Chicago discs, *Fate In A Pleasant Mood*, which is discussed below. There is no doubt that the pace slackened somewhat after this point, allowing greater concentration on detail and on refining the Arkestra sound. Compare the version of Sun Ra's bluesy 'Ankh' here with a harder-edged performance on *Art Forms For Dimensions Tomorrow*, below. There are three standards on the session, the Previn/Raksin title-track, 'And This Is My Beloved' and 'Just In Time', played in a rather more mannered and deliberate style than later in his career, but with no outer-space embellishments.

(A word about personnels. There may seem a degree of redundancy in listing every player on every available Arkestra recording, except, of course, those which offer no breakdown. Despite the improbable but common misconception that Sun Ra commanded the loyalty of a single group of musicians for nearly four decades, personnels changed very rapidly. Instrumentations are also remarkably capricious. Most players doubled on percussion and vocals at some time or other; at various stages, others may be credited with a secondary instrument only: Gilmore on bass clarinet, Allen on oboe, and so on. We have tried to note these in accordance with the details given on the disc, recognizing all the while that these are often unreliable in the extreme. It is sometimes possible to hear uncredited instruments, and former Arkestra members have taken convincing issue with specific attributions. These, however, are matters for the specialist. Apart from normalizing inconsistent spelling, details above and below are as given.)

**** The Singles

Evidence ECD 22164 2CD *Sun Ra; The Nu Sounds; The Cosmic Rays; Mr V's Five Joys; Arkestra/Arkistra, including: Fred Adams, Phil Cohran, Akh Tal Ebah, Art Hoyle, Lucious Randolph, Michael Ray, Walter Strickland, E.J Turner (t); Jothan Collins (flhn, v); Tyrone Hill, Julian Priester (tb); Marshall Allen (as, ob); James Spaulding (as); Danny Davis (f, acl, d, perc, v); Mickey Boss, John Gilmore (ts); Pat Patrick, Danny Ray Thompson (bs); Buddy Guy, Sam Thomas (g); Ronnie Boykins, Wilburn Green, Victor Sproles (b); Luqman Ali, Robert Barry, William Bugs Cochran, Alvin Fielder, Clifford Jarvis, C. Scoby Stroman (d); Jim Herndon (perc); Lacy Gibson (v, g); Sam Bankhead, David Henderson, Little Mack, Juanita Rogers, Yochanan (v); other personnel unidentified or uncertain.* 54–82.

An eye-opening title to be sure, but from the early 1950s to the mid-'70s Sun Ra issued a huge array of singles, aiming to some extent for a jukebox market and airing his never-to-fade enthusiasm for doo-wop, R&B and funk (an affection echoed by Anthony Braxton, another who is often thought of as an ultra-modernist, but who claims Frankie Lymon and the Teenagers as an influence). This is a key document in African-American music, underlining how much of a continuum there is between popular forms and the avant-garde, even during a period when separatist tendencies seemed to dominate. Included are sessions made in the later 1960s with the 'space age vocalist' Yochanan, with early groups like the Nu Sounds and the Cosmic Rays (a sort of club version of the early Arkestra), and for vocalists like Lacy Gibson. Everyone will find favourites. Ours include a 1968-ish basement recording (without Sun Ra himself) and then a later radio station recording of 'I'm Gona Unmask The Batman', a glorious piano–drums duo with Luqman Ali on 'Rough-House Blues', 'Great Balls Of Fire' with the Arkestra in 1958, and the outrageously hokey 'Daddy's Gonna Tell You No Lie' with the Rays a couple of years earlier. Sound quality is as variable as elsewhere in the Saturn canon, but the sheer energy and verve of the performances more than make up for technical deficiencies. *Jazz In Silhouette* still remains our recommended Sun Ra record, but this runs it a close second, and it has the sterling advantage of tracing the Arkestra's and its leader's progress over more than two decades. There is some padding out with live and rehearsal material, but for the most part it documents one of the most extraordinary and unexpected creative adventures of recent times.

*** Monorails And Satellites

Evidence ECD 22013 2 *Sun Ra (p solo).* 66.

Before considering the Arkestra recordings of the 1960s, it is worth interpolating a comment about the solo material. There has always been a convention that Sun Ra's 'real' instrument was the collective sound of the Arkestra itself and, while it has been contextualized with reference to the Henderson and Ellington orchestras or, looking forward, to Gil Evans and AACM, it's very rare to find the leader's piano playing contextualized in the same way. With that in mind, it's worth noting that in the year *Monorails And Satellites* was made, Andrew Hill released *Andrew!* and Cecil Taylor *Unit Structures* on Blue Note; Chick Corea released his debut, *Tones For Joans Bones*; *Solo Monk* had appeared the year before, fellow-Chicagoan Muhal Richard Abrams's *Levels And Degrees Of Light* was still some months away. How does Sun Ra fare, compared to these? The immediate and obvious response is that *Monorails And Satellites* sounds rather old-fashioned, but at a second hearing there are aspects which are entirely unprecedented: great blocks of pure sound, a tonal richness and uncertainty that suggest Scriabin rather than James P. Johnson. There are few warp-speed runs on *Monorails*; rather, a gently spacey version of 'arranger's piano' that always seems to suggest cues for an absent band. The title-track certainly sounds like a direct transcription of Arkestra charts, as does the opening 'Space Towers'. 'The Galaxy Way', though, is entirely pianistic, a remarkable performance by any measure. Only one standard this time around: a surprisingly smooth version of 'East Street'.

*** Fate In A Pleasant Mood / When Sun Comes Out

Evidence ECD 22068 *Sun Ra; Phil Cohran, George Hudson, Walter Miller, Lucious Randolph (t); Teddy Nance, Bernhard*

Pettaway, Nate Pryor (tb); Danny Davis (as); Marshall (as, f, bells, perc); John Gilmore (ts); Pat Patrick (bs); Ronnie Boykins (b); Jon Hardy (d); Clifford Jarvis (d, perc); Tommy Hunter (gong, perc); Theda Barbara (v). 60, 62–63.

****** Cosmic Tones For Mental Therapy / Art Forms For Dimensions Tomorrow**

Evidence ECD 22036 *Sun Ra; Manny Smith (t); Ali Hassan (tb); John Gilmore (ts, bcl, dragon d, sky d); Pat Patrick (bs, f); Marshall Allen (as, ob, astro space d); Danny Davis (as, f); Robert Cummings (bcl); James Jackson (f, log d); Ronnie Boykins, John Ore (b); Clifford Jarvis, C. Scoby Stroman (d, perc); Thomas Hunter (perc).* 61–62, 63.

****** Other Planes Of There**

Evidence ECD 22037 *Sun Ra; Walter Miller (t); Ali Hassan, Teddy Nance (tb); Bernhard Pettaway (btb); Marshall Allen (as, ob, f); Danny Davis (as, f); John Gilmore (ts); Robert Cummings (bcl); Pat Patrick (bs); Ronnie Boykins (b); Roger Blank, Lex Humphries (d).* 64.

This is where the outer-space stuff begins with a vengeance. Sun Ra briefly experimented with the Hammond, producing huge, blocky areas of sound. Curiously, it wasn't an instrument that greatly attracted him, and recorded instances are surprisingly rare; there is another on *We Travel The Spaceways*. He coaxes extraordinary percussive effects from it on 'Moon Dance', the first highlight of *Cosmic Tones*. The other, unquestionably, is John Gilmore's long solo on 'Adventure-Equation'. It's a rare outing for Gilmore on bass clarinet (duties normally assigned to Robert Cummings), the only instrument he's credited with on this album. There has to be some doubt about this, as about most of these personnel details; but there is no doubt about the quality of the solo, which is his most compelling on record until 'Body And Soul' on *Holiday For Soul Dance*, several years later. The album is awash with echo effects and thunderous reverb, apparently devised by drummer Thomas Hunter, who claimed production and engineering credits. The 1961–2 *Art Forms* material is a good deal more straightforward in terms of pure sound, and the playing is absolutely up to standard. The band turns in a sterling performance of 'Ankh' (see *Bad And Beautiful*, above) which includes steaming solos from Patrick and trombonist Ali Hassan. Highly recommended.

Fate/Sun is a less appealing compilation but it does catch the Arkestra at a critical juncture. *Fate In A Pleasant Mood* documents the last Arkestra to be based in Chicago; it therefore strictly precedes the first of the New York sessions, *Bad And Beautiful*, which is listed above. Following a trip to Canada in the spring of 1961, a long-standing Arkestra began to break up, leaving only a rump of loyal adherents: Gilmore, Allen, Boykins and, despite having set out on a solo course, Pat Patrick, who signed up for a second term. Sun Ra began recruiting new members, including the teenage Danny Davis, who makes a solid impact on *When Sun Comes Out*. Gilmore sounds jaded and tentative on this record, and there is little of the spark of the earlier band, less still of its inspired weirdness. The appearance of Theda Barbara on 'Circe' is a foretaste of how important singers like June Tyson were to become in years to come.

Other Planes Of There is a long-overlooked masterpiece, but certainly also an oddity in the canon. In effect, it is Sun Ra's concerto for Arkestra. His own piano introduction touches bases all the way from Bud Powell to Cecil Taylor, and there are wonderful solos from Danny Davis, Gilmore and Marshall Allen (on oboe). The rest of the record consists of shorter, jazzier segments, with another thoughtful solo from Gilmore on 'Sketch' and a more sensuous statement from Patrick on 'Pleasure'. *Other Planes* stands apart from the other recordings in this group. The instrumentation is straighter and the structures more obviously polyphonic. It shows how adaptable Sun Ra's concept still was in the mid-'60s.

****** The Magic City**

Evidence ECD 22069 *Sun Ra; Walter Miller (t); Chris Capers (t, perc); Ali Hassan, Teddy Nance (tb); Bernhard Pettaway (btb); Marshall Allen (as, f, picc); Danny Davis (as, f); Harry Spencer (as); John Gilmore (ts); Pat Patrick (bs, f); Robert Cummings (bcl); Ronnie Boykins (b); Roger Blank, Jimhmi Johnson (d); James Jackson (perc).* 65.

****** Atlantis**

Evidence ECD 22067 *Sun Ra; Akh Tal Ebah, Wayne Harris (t); Ali Hassan, Charles Stephens (tb); Robert Northern (frhn); Marshall Allen (as, ob, Jupiter f, perc); Danny Davis (as); John Gilmore (ts, perc); Robert Cummings (bcl); Pat Patrick (bs, f, perc); Robert Barry, Clifford Jarvis (d, perc); James Jackson (perc).* 67, 69.

As befits its majestic programme, the 22-minute 'Atlantis' is for the biggest Arkestra yet. Only the similarly conceived 'Magic City' matches it for sheer power, but it is about a futuristic place trapped in the present, rather than a past civilization swallowed up by history. 'The Magic City' was a promotional slogan for Birmingham, Alabama, to boost it as a commercial centre. References to slavery and race in an accompanying poem are bound up with imagery borrowed from the Bible or *Paradise Lost*, suggesting the rootedness of Sun Ra's fantastical vision in contemporary reality and in Afro-American tradition. The piece itself was collectively improvised, though the confident synchronization of small-group sections within the main piece strongly suggests either an element of 'conduction' or of predetermined sequences. This was the period of Ornette's *Free Jazz* and, more to the point, of Coltrane's huge *Ascension*, and 'The Magic City' stands up remarkably well in that company.

Sun Ra himself plays (often simultaneously) both piano and clavioline. He claimed the latter gave him the 'purest' sound he'd ever had from an electric instrument. Oddly, though economics may have had something to do with it (the Arkestra was still a shoestring operation and busted instruments were not always repaired or replaced), by the time of *Atlantis* he's using squeaky little keyboards like the Hohner Clavinet or the Gibson Kalamazoo organ (a sound immortalized by Ray Manzarek of The Doors). By this time, though, the sound is very much better, and *Atlantis* gained wider than usual currency, following reissue on the Impulse! label. Four tracks are for Sun Ra with Gilmore, Robert Barry and Clifford Jarvis only. A fifth, 'Bimini', adds Allen, Patrick and Jackson on percussion. These were supposed by some observers to be Sun Ra's nod in the direction of Thelonious Monk, but Cecil Taylor seems a more likely point of reference. The main piece starts *in media res* (just like *Paradise Lost*) and rumbles hellishly before Sun Ra kicks in with a quite extraordinary organ solo that must count as one of his most significant instrumental passages. Ali Hassan plays a dadaist trombone solo before the piece is turned on its head with a skittish beat and the chant: 'Sun Ra and band from outer space have entertained you here.' It's an odd gesture, given the emotional temperature of what goes before, but that was Sun Ra ...

****** Outer Spaceways Incorporated**

Black Lion BLCD 760191 *Sun Ra; Akh Tal Ebah, Kwame Hadi (t, d); Ali Hassan, Teddy Nance (tb, d); Bernhard Pettaway (tb); Marshall Allen (as, f, ob, d); Danny Davis (as, f); Robert Cummings (bcl); Pat Patrick (bs, f, d); John Gilmore (ts, d); Ronnie Boykins (b); Nimrod Hunt (d); James Jackson (d, f); Clifford Jarvis (perc).* 68.

*****(*) Calling Planet Earth**

Freedom 7612 3CD *As above, except add Larry Northington (as, d), Robert Barry, Lex Humphries, Tommy Hunter (d), June Tyson (v).* 66–71.

The most startling thing about *Outer Spaceways Incorporated* was the label it was on. Black Lion was more commonly identified with the conservative end of mainstream, but Alan Bates (also known for his work with Candid) was admirably open-eared and pluralistic in his tastes and came up with left-field sets like this for the label more often than is commonly supposed. *Outer Spaceways Inc.* is notable for one of the most measured and sympathetic sleeve-notes ever written for a Sun Ra record. Victor Schonfield had been an ardent champion of the free scene in the United Kingdom and was instinctively drawn to the Arkestra's collectivist ethos (enlightened despotism might be a more accurate description). His description of the leader's 'spavined piano, and the carefully controlled clanking dissonance of the horns' is just about right, too. Whatever the exact occasion of its recording, *Outer Spaceways Inc.* seemed to draw together aspects of the Arkestra's music from the previous decade while simultaneously pointing forward. 'Somewhere There' gets things going in an atmosphere of whirling chaos which gradually resolves into a semblance of order on the title-track and the previously unreleased 'Intergalactic Motion'. The second half of the record is very different. 'Saturn' is, as Schonfield points out, a relatively straightforward big-band piece, constructed round a timeless Gilmore solo. 'Song Of The Sparer' (a theme that anticipates 'I Am The Alter-Destiny' on *Space Is The Place*) is hauntingly beautiful, while 'Spontaneous Simplicity', dominated by flutes and Latin-American drum patterns, sounds like a later version of the Arkestra's 'here to entertain you' tail-piece on *Atlantis*. For a good many people who hadn't caught up with *Heliocentric Worlds*, this was a first introduction to the Arkestra's music. In Britain certainly, it was for some time the best-known Sun Ra record. The augmented CD, with Schonfield's original notes reproduced intact, is still an excellent buy.

Much of the same material is also available on the three-CD Freedom set, which also includes two live New York performances from the later '60s and a Danish date from 1971. The repertoire and quality on these are pretty consistent with most of Sun Ra's work of the period, and the package makes a very good introduction to the Arkestra of the time.

*****(*) Holiday For Soul Dance**

Evidence ECD 22011 *Sun Ra; Phil Cohran (c); Danny Davis, Hobart Dotson, Akh Tal Ebah, Wayne Harris (t); Ali Hassan (tb); Marshall Allen, Danny Ray Thompson (as); John Gilmore (ts); Pat Patrick (bs, b); Robert Cummings (bcl); Bob Barry (d); James Jackson, Carl Nimrod (perc); Ricky Murray (v).* 68–69.

***** My Brother The Wind, Volume II**

Evidence ECD 22040 *Sun Ra; Akh Tal Ebah, Kwame Hadi (t); Marshall Allen (as, ob, f); Danny Davis (as, acl, f); John Gilmore (ts, perc); Pat Patrick, Danny Ray Thompson (bs, f); James Jackson (ob, perc); Alejandro Blake (b); Clifford Jarvis, Lex Humphries (d); Nimrod Hunt (hand d); William Brister, Robert Cummings (perc).* 69, 70.

Predictably, *My Brother The Wind, Volume II* was followed many moons later by Volume One. Sun Ra's organ really does sound 'intergalactic' on this one, but he also checks out that ubiquitous squealer of the late '60s, the Mini-Moog. His approach, inevitably, is heterodox in the extreme. Instead of making the synth sound like anything else, he homes in unerringly on its 'own' sound – shrill, with loads of vibrato – and then pushes all the buttons to get right into its uptight psyche: angry bleeps, TV shutdown hiss, off-station crackles. The band, unfortunately, have begun to plod a bit, though the (uncredited) appearance of June Tyson on 'Walking On The Moon' – no relation to the pop hit – marks a hitherto undocumented association that was to last until the 1990s; Tyson died shortly after Sun Ra in 1993.

Holiday is a more appealing album, largely because the band get their act together. It's entirely a standards set, but for the brief snippet of cornetist Cohran's 'Dorothy's Dance', which may have been conceived in homage to Oz. Sun Ra's opening solos on 'Holiday For Strings' and 'I Loves You, Porgy' amply confirm his *bona fides* as a 'straight' swing soloist. He shows a surprisingly light touch and gently alternates emphasis on left- and right-hand figures which again bear only a fleeting and misleading resemblance to Monk's. Gilmore's solo on 'Body And Soul', the tenor saxophonist's proving-ground, suggests something of what Coltrane found in his work. Much less well-known, Hobart Dotson also emerges strongly as an underrated player deserving of reassessment. Boykins's unexplained absence leaves the bottom end a bit straggly. Alejandro Blake is at best only a stop-gap replacement; at several points he's audibly flummoxed by what's going on and chugs out bland ostinato figures or else – what the hell! – goes quietly mad.

***** Black Myth / Out In Space**

MPS 557656-2 2CD *Sun Ra; Marshall Allen (as, f, picc, ob); John Gilmore (ts, perc, v); Pat Patrick (as, ts, bs, cl, bcl, f, perc); Robert Cummings (bcl); James Jackson (f, ob, d, perc); Alan Silva (b, vn, vla, clo); Alejandro Blake (b); Lex Humphries (d, perc); June Tyson (v).* 10–11/70.

Like a good deal of Sun Ra's live work from the '70s, this material has been heard before in different formats, not least on a record with the apocalyptic title *It's After The End Of The World*, but the early tracks, taped at the Donaueschingen Festival, are the most valuable portions of a two-CD set, including a lot of material that seems to have been written recently and perhaps rehearsed with the festival in mind. The remaining tracks are well performed, but 'We Travel The Spaceways' is now so familiar that only exceptional performances will find a place in any but completist collections; this certainly isn't of that calibre. Even so, anyone wanting a representation of what Sun Ra was about at the cusp of his third decade of music-making will be reasonably satisfied.

*****(*) Space Is The Place**

Evidence ECD 22070 *Sun Ra; Kwame Hadi (t, vib, perc); Wayne Harris (t); Marshall Allen (as, f, ob, bsn, kora, perc); Danny Davis (as, f, acl, perc); Larry Northington (as, perc); John Gilmore (ts, perc, v); Eloe Omoe (bcl, perc); Danny Ray Thompson (bs, perc); Lex Humphries (d); Ken Moshesh (perc); June Tyson (v).* 72.

In 1968, the year of upheaval in America as elsewhere, Sun Ra and the Arkestra made their first trip to the West Coast. Perhaps surprisingly, they were met with a wholly lukewarm response. Three years later, Sun Ra taught a course entitled 'The Black Man in the Cosmos' at the University of California, Berkeley, developing ideas that were to influence Anthony Braxton; Braxton wasn't on the course – but, then, hardly anyone was. Sun Ra felt rejected by the university and by California in general, and he returned east in high dudgeon. It was a repeat of the stormy Montreal trip.

However, Sun Ra had been spotted by producer Jim Newman, who suggested making a feature film loosely based on the mythology implicit in the Berkeley course. *Space Is The Place* cast Sun Ra as a cosmic equalizer, John Shaft in an even more outrageous suit, locked in combat with The Overseer, an interplanetary super-pimp who symbolizes the exploitation of the black races. As with a lot of experimental cinema of the time (a good example is Conrad Rooks's ill-fated *Chappaqua*, for which Ornette Coleman wrote the music), the soundtrack was far more interesting than the film itself. Using material from the previous few years – 'Outer Spaceways Incorporated', 'Calling Planet Earth', 'Space Is The Place' – Sun Ra compiled a brisk montage of Arkestra music. Sixteen tracks was unusually quick turnover, but it works remarkably well and the playing is tight and enigmatic. Tracks like 'Mysterious Crystal' were almost unprecedented in the Arkestra canon, combining a huge array of elements into something that simply cannot be characterized by reference to any other music. A setting like this was tailor-made for June Tyson, who sings hypnotically on 'Blackman'. Marshall Allen switches from his occasional oboe to bassoon to suggest the creaking evil of 'The Overseer', while Danny Davis switches to alto clarinet (anticipating Hamiet Bluiett's experiments on that unfamiliar horn by many years). The movie may still be circulating in obscure art-houses. Whatever the case, the music stands up amazingly well.

*****(*) Space Is The Place**

Impulse! IMP 12492 *Sun Ra; Akh Tal Ebah (t, flhn); Kwame Hadi (t); Marshall Allen, Danny Davis (as, f); John Gilmore (ts, v); Danny Ray Thompson (bs, v); Pat Patrick (bs, b, v); Eloe Omoe (bcl, f); Lex Humphries (d); Atakatune, Odun (perc); Cheryl Banks, Judith Holton, June Tyson, Ruth Wright (v); all Arkestra members also play percussion.* 10/72.

There is inevitable confusion over Sun Ra album titles, with so many overlaps and elsewhere a relatively limited permutation of space-related concepts. This one, entirely different from the record above, was engineered by Baker Bigsby for the Blue Thumb label and issued under those auspices in 1972, at a moment when Sun Ra seemed on the brink of mainstream recognition. It's a rather smooth performance by Arkestra standards, and almost too formulaically representative of what the group was about. Sun Ra plays piano only on 'Images', a small-group performance with Tal Ebah and Gilmore in close attendance, but with Patrick on bass. Elsewhere he plays the Farfisa 'Space' organ, and perhaps what is lacking on the album as a whole is the range of sounds that he might have been able to add with a Mini-Moog or some other synth of the time. To describe a Sun Ra album as 'spacious' is to risk being misunderstood, but that is how it comes across, open textured, uncluttered and rather proper. A good point of entry for anyone who really doesn't want to fight their way past the hiss and crackle of the classic El Saturns, and there is much to enjoy on the title-track which dominates the set; but not one of his greatest moments.

***** Life Is Splendid**

Total Energy 3026 *Sun Ra; Ahk Tal Ebah (t, flhn, v); Lamont McLamb (t); Marshall Allen, Danny Davis (as, f); Larry Worthington (as); John Gilmore (ts, perc); Pat Patrick (bs); Danny Ray Thompson (bs, f); Leroy Taylor (bcl); Lex Humphries, Robert Underwood, Alzo Wright (d); Russell Branch, Stanley Morgan (perc); Cheryl Bank, Judith Holton, June Tyson, Ruth Wright (v).* 9/72.

****(*) Outer Space Employment Agency**

Total Energy 3021 *Sun Ra; Intergalactic Orchestra.* 9/73.

These were recorded in successive years at the Ann Arbor Blues And Jazz Festival. This was the town in Michigan where Sun Ra had had his first, uneasy encounter with the student hippie movement, an aspect of his fan-base he found troubling and unsatisfactory. In 1972, Slug's saloon in New York City, a regular Arkestra location, had closed its doors and, over the next few years, the ensemble was more mobile and in some respects more responsive to changes of mood. The pity is that the opening of the 1972 Ann Arbor performance is missing. Proper balances were achieved only some minutes into a 40-minute suite of Arkestra staples. June Tyson and the leader are the dominant voices, and the huge swoops and wails of Sun Ra's organ are as exciting as any in the documentation, and it's a shame that the whole continuous performance can't be heard in its (doubtless dramatic) entirety. Memory may be deceptive, but we seem to recall that an edit of 'Life Is Splendid' was once included on an Atlantic sampler of performances from Ann Arbor. It would have hurt less if the meters had failed to calibrate the following year. This shaky recording is no less typical of the Arkestra's performances of the period and as such is valuable as a document of Sun Ra's work of the early '70s. He and June Tyson are the main elements, with the band behind producing a wild and often chaotic backdrop of pure sound, often according to no discernible harmonic or rhythmic logic. The long closing medley, which includes the title-piece, is more accessible than the rest of the record and the sound is inexplicably better in the middle section, following a rather obvious edit point. Were there multiple tape sources, or can it be that tapes of another performance have been collaged?

***** A Quiet Place In The Universe**

Leo CD LR 198 *Sun Ra; probably Ahmed Abdullah (t); Akh Tal Ebah (t, v); Craig Harris (tb); Vincent Chauncey (frhn); Marshall Allen (as, picc); Pat Patrick (as); John Gilmore (ts); Danny Ray Thompson (bs, f) Luqman Ali (d); Atakatune, Eddie Thomas (perc); Eloe Omoe (bcl, f); James Jackson (bsn, f, perc); June Tyson (v).* 76–77.

We have to declare ourselves a touch confused about this one. According to a liner-note, tracks 3–6 ('Images', 'Love In Outer Space', 'I'll Never Be The Same' and 'Space Is The Place') have already been released on *A Night In East Berlin*, CD LR 149. The last of these four is ubiquitous, but none of the other tracks matches, and the listed personnels differ, and the suggested dates differ, so we are in the dark. This tape was no more illuminating than usual, found with just a number but believed (by expert Chris Trent) to be 1976 or 1977. If so, and it seems likely, this fills a long gap in the current discography. The sound is murky and congested and there is considerable to-ing and fro-ing even though it does appear to be a concert documentation. 'I Pharoah' is a slice of music-theatre which homes in close on the leader and sounds to us as if it may not have been recorded at the same time or from the same position as the rest ...? The plus, as always, is the Gilmore solo, this time on the title-track, which is unusually arranged and followed by a french horn solo from Vincent Chauncey. Some good music, then, but outstanding questions about the exact provenance.

*** Strange Celestial Road

Rounder 3035 *Sun Ra; Walter Miller, Curt Pulliam, Michael Ray (t); Tony Bethel, Craig Harris (tb); Vincent Chauncey (frhn); Marshall Allen, Sylvester Baton, Eloe Omoe, John Gilmore, James Jackson, Noel Scott, Danny Ray Thompson, Kenny Williams (reeds); Skeeter McFarland, Taylor Richardson (g); Damon Choice, Harry Wilson (vib); Steve Clarke, Richard Williams (b); Luqman Ali, Reg McDonald (d); Atakatune (perc); Rhoda Blount, June Tyson (v).* 6/79.

/* Live From Soundscape

DIW 388 *As above, except omit Pulliam, Harris, Scott, Kenny Williams, Richardson, Richard Williams, McDonald, Blount; add Charles Stephens (tb), Danny Davis (reeds).* 11/79.

Though the music was fairly routine, a limited edition of the Soundscape disc offered an extra CD containing a 72-minute unedited lecture by Sun Ra, recorded the night before the Soundscape concert. Though it might have been more effective as a 30-minute edited lecture, it offers a unique insight into Sun Ra's thinking as it had developed since *Space Is The Place*, which was, after all, only a B-movie version of his basic mythology, heavily compromised by 'blaxploitation' clichés. The limited edition was issued in numbers that guaranteed it would become a collectors' item, but some copies are bound to turn up second-hand. These merit four-star rating (and may well command five-star prices).

The earlier record from 1979, probably recorded in June and presumably in New York City, contains just three tracks, 'Celestial Road', 'Say' and 'I'll Wait For You'. Musically more compelling than the Soundscape session, it's still generic Arkestra, with big-band swing, total freedom and ritual all intermingled. The sound is not bad and the definition of individual instruments in the ensembles probably better than average.

***(*) Cosmo Sun Connection

Recommended ReR SR1 *Sun Ra; Tyrone Hill (tb); Marshall Allen (as, f); Eloe Omoe (as, bcl); John Gilmore (ts, perc); Danny Ray Thompson (bs, f); Rollo Radford (b); Atakatune (perc); other personnel unidentified.* 84.

The story on this undated but apparently 1984 recording is an interesting one. Recommended imported a good deal of Sun Ra material into Europe during the 1970s and '80s. Pressings were paid for up front, but on one occasion money had been so tight in the Arkestra that ReR's front man, Chris Cutler, arrived to find his advance had been spent and no discs were forthcoming. To purge his debt, Sun Ra gave Cutler the master-tape of *Cosmo Sun Connection*; Cutler in turn is turning over proceeds to the Arkestra as a gesture of respect and to help a group which now finds itself leaderless and in no small debt.

Musically, it isn't a classic, though performances of 'Fate In A Pleasant Mood' and the title-track are absolutely typical of what the group was doing in this period. Gilmore makes a commanding figure throughout, though it's Marshall Allen (better recorded and sounding full of beans) who steals his thunder on occasion. Hints of funk and rock-influenced, straight-eight patterns give the record an immediate impact that will recommend (no pun intended) it to those who find some of the floatier, ritual stuff hard to swallow.

*** The Sun Ra Arkestra Meets Salah Ragab In Egypt

Leo/Golden Years of New Jazz GY 1 *Sun Ra; Tyrone Hill (tb); Marshall Allen (as, f); Danny Ray Thompson (as, bs, perc); John Gilmore (ts, perc); Eloe Omoe (as, bcl, perc); James Jackson (bsn); Rollo Radford (b, perc); Claude Broche, Chris Henderson, Clifford Jarvis (d); Matthew Brown, Salah Ragab (perc).* 71, 72–74, 75, 83, 84.

Given how thoroughly his philosophy was based on the ancient Egyptian civilizations and their thought-practice, the prospect of playing in Egypt was obviously a very beguiling one for Sun Ra. The Arkestra played at the Ballon Theatre in Cairo in 1971, a performance documented on a rare Thoth Intergalactic LP, but, despite the confusing dates on the disc, all of the Sun Ra material comes from two further visits in 1983 and 1984 when he played in the company of drummer (and later head of Egypt's military music) Salah Ragab. The remainder of the album consists of much earlier material by Ragab and his small group ('Oriental Mood') and by the Cairo Jazz Band ('Ramadan', 'A Farewell Theme') and the Cairo Free Jazz Ensemble ('Music For Angela Davis'), performances which do not involve either Sun Ra or any Arkestra members. Like the item below, this was originally released on Praxis but has now been licensed to Leo Feigin's new Golden Years of New Jazz imprint. The Egyptian players seem to be as much impressed by American innovations as Sun Ra was by ancient Nilotic culture; the final piece at least, but for some unexpected tonalities, might be the work of an American or even European improvising ensemble of the time. The Arkestra was so completely *sui generis* that it's hard to be surprised by any variation in its 'usual' practice. Ragab certainly brings a fresh rhythmic awareness to the tracks where he is featured, and one can imagine American musicians heading home with unsuspected subdivisions of 13/8 and 11/8 ringing in their ears.

***(*) Live At Praxis '84

Leo/Golden Years of New Jazz GY 5 2CD *Sun Ra; Ronnie Brown (t, flhn, perc); Marshall Allen (as, cl, f, ob, kora, perc); Eloe Omoe (as, bcl, contra-acl, f, perc); John Gilmore (ts, cl, perc, v); Danny Ray Thompson (bs, as, f, perc); James Jackson (bsn, f, ob, perc, v); Rollo Radford (b); Don Mumford (d, perc); Matthew Brown, Salah Ragab (perc).* 2/84.

Trimmed down from a triple LP recorded in concert in Athens, Greece, this double set is one of the best live recordings of the Arkestra at any period, certainly in terms of giving an accurate impression of how a set developed round swing standards, free-for-all improvisation and ritual chanting. The ability to swing from 'Mack The Knife', 'Cocktails For Two' and 'Satin Doll' back to 'Theme Of the Stargazers' is consistently jaw-dropping and the band had rarely sounded as exuberant, with some of the more intriguing textures coming from what are described as 'electric valve instruments'. There is less emphasis than even five years before on Sun Ra himself as an instrumentalist. Increasingly, he seemed to be the dramaturge and guiding spirit who held the whole remarkable thing together.

*****(*) A Night In East Berlin / My Brothers The Wind And Sun No. 9**

Leo CD LR 149 *Sun Ra; Michael Ray, Ahmed Abdullah (t); Tyrone Hill (tb); Pat Patrick (as); Marshall Allen (as, f); John Gilmore (ts, perc, v); Danny Ray Thompson (bs, perc); Kenny Williams (bs); Eloe Omoe (as, bcl); James Jackson (bsn, perc); Bruce Edwards (g); Billy Bang, Owen Brown Jr (vn); June Tyson (vn, v); John Ore, Rollo Radford (b); Luqman Ali, Earl Buster Smith (d); ?Pharoah Abdullah (perc); Art Jenkins (v).* 6/86, 1/88 or 90.

In true Leo Records style, the origins of these tapes are shrouded in uncertainty, and the disc fades in on the opening of the East Berlin set, as if the mikes weren't on quick enough. Whatever the technical shortcomings, there's no mistaking the quality or beauty of the music. 'Mystic Prophecy' highlights two of the Arkestra's pillars, Marshall Allen and John Gilmore, and Gilmore is pressed into vocal duty with his boss in the absence of June Tyson, who seems not to have made the trip on this occasion.

The material on *My Brothers The Wind And Sun No. 9* was originally released in an extremely limited edition on an El Saturn white-label release with just a number and (in some cases) a few hand-written comments. Like the East German material, titles weren't known till later. It's thought this may have been recorded at the Knitting Factory in New York City, and there is apparently further material from that time. Good news, because this is a steamingly good band, fierce and propulsive in the slipstream of Sun Ra's synth and with the additional bonus of Billy Bang in the ensembles and soloing. Regrettably, this being *samizdat*-land, it's interrupted by the end of the tape. The most valuable single item on the disc is the quasi-atonal 'The Shadow World', a most unexpected conception even for this most unexpected of groups. No surprise that it should again feature Allen and Gilmore.

***** Reflections In Blue**

Black Saint 120101 *Sun Ra; Randall Murray (t); Tyrone Hill (tb); Pat Patrick (as, cl); Marshall Allen (as, f, ob, picc); Danny Ray Thompson (as, cl, bcl); John Gilmore, Ronald Wilson (ts); James Jackson (bsn, African d); Carl LeBlanc (g); Tyler Mitchell (b); Thomas Hunter, Earl Buster Smith (d).* 12/86.

****(*) Hours After**

Black Saint 120111 *As above.* 12/86.

***** Love In Outer Space**

Leo CD LR 180 *Sun Ra and his Arkestra; no personnel details.* 12/83.

***** Cosmo Omnibus Imaginable Illusion**

DIW 824 *Sun Ra; Michael Ray (t, v); Ahmed Abdullah (t); Tyrone Hill (tb); Marshall Allen (as); John Gilmore (ts, perc); Danny Ray Thompson (bs); Leroy Taylor (cl, bcl); Bruce Edwards (g); Rollo Radford (b); Eric Walter (b); Earl Buster Smith (d); June Tyson (v, vn); Judith Holton (dancer).* 8/88.

The 1980s were a period of steady and often unimaginative consolidation. Sun Ra's music had, at last, become a *style*. Even so, the Arkestra were still able to create an astonishing impact in performance. There are powerful moments on *Love In Outer Space*, which was recorded at a concert in Utrecht. The closing 'Space Is The Place' still sounds positive and challenging, and there are outrageous versions of 'Big John's Special' and 'Round Midnight'.

Of later 1980s performances, the DIW, recorded in Tokyo, combines a suite of mythic themes with a surprisingly straight 'Prelude To A Kiss'. Edit out the chants and some of the more self-conscious FX, and it sounds like one of Sun Ra's most complete and convincing recordings of the last 15 years. *Reflections In Blue* and, from the same sessions, *Hours After* concentrate exclusively on mainstream composition (though the latter is punctuated by a chaotic 'Dance Of The Extra Terrestrians' and 'Love On A Far Away Planet', which are more typical of past snippets from the Arkestra's anarchic shows).

***** Second Star To The Right: Salute To Walt Disney**

Leo CD LR 230 *Sun Ra; Michael Ray (t, v); Tyrone Hill, Julian Priester (tb); Marshall Allen (as, cl, f); Eloe Omoe (as, cl, bcl); Noel Scott (as, cl, f); James Jackson (bsn, ob, v); Bruce Edwards (g); Arthur Joonie Booth (b); June Tyson (vn, v); Earl Buster Smith (d); Elson Nascimento Santos (perc).* 4/89.

***** Stardust From Tomorrow**

Leo CDLR 235/236 2CD *As above.* 4/89.

Sun Ra plays Disney. Of course. Initially this sounds so perverse as to go all the way round to being inevitable. A&M had done an album of Disney covers which included the Arkestra doing 'Pink Elephants On Parade' from *Dumbo*, but this Austrian concert goes the whole hog. Marshall Allen provides alto solos of surreal beauty in the opening chant on 'Forest Of No Return' and to the Sun Ra-introduced 'Someday My Prince Will Come'. The leader even quotes a couple of Miles Davis tags on his long, delicate opening, before horns, vocalists June Tyson and a falsetto Michael Ray, and then the rhythm come in behind him. 'Frisco Fog' isn't Disney and, perversely, it's the best band track on the date, a driving, train-time number that gets the sections properly worked out. 'I'm Wishing' is pretty good but takes an age to get under way. The title-tune gives Hill a lot of space, and 'Hi Ho! Hi Ho!' features Scott on alto and clarinet. Sun Ra expert seems to think 'Zip-A-Dee-Doo-Dah' is from *Sleeping Beauty* but, apart from that, it's good to have what is effectively a private bootleg recording so fully documented. The sound is awful; someone coughs right in the mike at one point and there is only a rather artificial balance on some tracks. The piano is clearly audible, though, and no complaints about the quality of the music.

Stardust From Tomorrow was recorded in concert at the Jazzatelier in Ulrichsberg, Austria. It's a fascinating document of the Arkestra at work and in its pomp. The mix of material is breathtaking: untitled composition/improvisations by the leader, 'Prelude To A Kiss', Noble Sissle and Fletcher Henderson's 'Yeah, Man' and the crowd-pleasing 'We Travel The Spaceways' to round off the night. It sounds as if it has been recorded through the mixing desk and, while the balance is pretty decent, there's too much emphasis on horns and percussion and not nearly enough on the main man. Otherwise, though, a fine set.

****** Mayan Temples**

Black Saint 120121 *Sun Ra; Ahmed Abdullah, Michael Ray (t, v); Tyrone Hill (tb); Noel Scott (as); Marshall Allen (as, f); John Gilmore (ts, perc); James Jackson (bsn, perc); Jothan Callins (b); Clifford Barbaro, Earl Buster Smith (d); Ron McBee, Elson Nascimento Santos, Jorge Silva (perc); June Tyson (v).* 7/90.

As Francis Davis points out in his liner-note, this studio session restores the emphasis to Sun Ra's piano playing. Illness would shortly curtail his ability to play acoustic keyboards this crisply. His introductions and leads are absolutely in the line of Ellington, and the voicings are supple, open-ended and often quietly ambiguous, leaving considerable emphasis on the soloists. As always, Gilmore is a giant and Marshall Allen's searing solo on 'Prelude To Stargazers' is a model of controlled fury. He re-records 'El Is A Sound Of Joy' (see *Supersonic Jazz*, above), a late-1950s theme that sounds completely contemporary and brings a freshness and simplicity to 'Alone Together' that is quite breath-taking. 'Discipline No. 1' is a lovely ballad, illustrating Sun Ra's ability to give simple material an unexpected rhythmic profile (Davis rightly points to the example of Mingus in this case) and the closing 'Sunset On The Night On The River Nile' is one of his very best space anthems. Few Sun Ra albums give a better sense of his extraordinary versatility; this is far preferable to the majority of recent live sets.

*****(*) Live At The Hackney Empire**

Leo CD LR 214/215 2CD *Sun Ra; Michael Ray (t, v); Jothan Callins (t); Tyrone Hill (tb); Marshall Allen (as, f, picc, ob); Noel Scott (as, bcl); John Gilmore (ts, cl, perc, v); Charles Davis (bs); James Jackson (bsn, perc); India Cooke (vn); Kash Killion (clo); John Ore (b); Clifford Barbaro, Earl Buster Smith (d); Talvin Singh (perc, v); Elson Nascimento Santos (perc); June Tyson (v).* 10/90.

This concert was recorded as part of a documentary project originally for Britain's Channel 4. Originally, there was a projected backdrop and other effects, but so far the finished work – by Chris Foster and Dave Hayes – has not materialized. It has nevertheless bequeathed us some excellent music, if unsurprising in content by Arkestra standards, until the second set, at any rate. All the familiar names are present and all in good form: Gilmore, Allen (glorious on 'Prelude To A Kiss') and Tyson. Disc two begins with a violin improvisation, before Davis, Cooke, Allen and others solo over 'Discipline 27-II'. There is then a version of 'East Of The Sun' (vocalist, Gilmore), a beautiful rendition of a Sun Ra favourite, 'Somewhere Over The Rainbow', and a rapid charge through the Sissle/Henderson anthem, 'Yeah Man!', and 'Frisco Fog'. A now-familiar mixture of the strange and the traditional, this is a highly attractive set. It will be good to see the film when funds make it possible but, for now, this is recommended. One of the best later Arkestra recordings.

(***) Pleiades

Leo CD LR 210/211 2CD *Sun Ra; Jothan Callins, Michael Ray (t); Tyrone Hill (tb); Marshall Allen (as); John Gilmore, Noel Scott (ts); Charles Davis (bs); James Jackson (ob, d); India Cooke (vn); Kash Killion (clo); John Ore (b); Clifford Barbaro, Earl Chinna Smith (d); Elson Nascimento Santos (perc); T Singh (tabla); June Tyson (v, vn); unidentified symphony orchestra.* 10/90.

It is a measure of Sun Ra's belatedly growing reputation that this concert was able to take place at all. Recorded in Paris, it features a mainly unfamiliar Arkestra and all-too-familiar repertoire (with the exception of Chopin's 'Prelude in A major'!) in an acoustic that is Jupiterian in resonance. The recording falls so far below acceptable standards that *Pleiades* seems to represent a return to the snap, crackle and pop of the old El Saturns (and of Leo's original, *samizdat* catalogue). One wonders how good and faithful servants like Gilmore and Allen viewed the music by this stage; Tyson's enthusiasm, though, is undimmed, and it is significant that she should have survived Sun Ra by such a short time.

****(*) Friendly Galaxy**

Leo CD LR 188 *Sun Ra Arkestra; no personnel details.* 4/91.

***** At The Village Vanguard**

Rounder 12125 *Sun Ra; John Gilmore (ts); Chris Anderson (p); Bruce Edwards (g); John Ore (b); Earl Chinna Smith (d).* 91.

****(*) Destination Unknown**

Enja 7071 *Sun Ra; Ahmed Abdullah, Michael Ray (t); Tyrone Hill (tb); Marshall Allen (as); James Jackson (bsn, d); Bruce Edwards (g); Jothan Callins (b); Earl Buster Smith (d); Elson Nascimento Santos, Stanley Morgan (perc).* 3/92.

The rest should have been silence, but just as the concert appearances (and the word is used advisedly) continued to the bitter end, so too will offcuts and live sessions continue to emerge. Few of the later dates do Sun Ra's memory any credit. Ill and tired, he plays a largely symbolic role in the proceedings, fronting shrunken ensembles that no longer seem to have the concentration to play ensemble music. The absence of Gilmore on the last session, whatever the reason, has to be seen as symbolic. He is present on the Rounder Records disc, which documents the moment when Sun Ra led a sextet at the Village Vanguard. The leader is doing little more than adding shades and gestures to the group, and the presence of guitarist Bruce Edwards probably renders most of them irrelevant. The plaudits go to Chris Anderson, who sounds very much as Sun Ra must have done in the Fletcher Henderson years, hooked confidently into swing, but looking ever outward for something new. Gilmore makes his presence known in brief flashes, but the old dark fire has gone.

There will be other releases, and continued debate about the enigma that was Sun Ra. As for his place in history, one must conclude that, for the moment at least ... destination unknown.

Monty Sunshine (born 1928)

CLARINET

Born in London, Sunshine is a key figure in British trad of the '50s and onwards. He was a featured soloist in the Chris Barber band,

and his departure in 1960 to form his own group and play in a relatively strict New Orleans style was a minor sensation at the time. In the past four decades he has pursued his own take on this music, and he found a big following in Europe, especially Germany.

***** In London**
Black Lion BLCD 760508 *Sunshine; Alan Gresty (t); Eddie Blashfield (tb); Ken Barton (bj, g, v); Mickey Ashman (b); Geoff Downs (d).* 7/79.

***** Just A Little While To Stay Here**
Lake LACD 70 *As above, except add Ken Colyer (t, v), John Beecham, Ron Brown (tb), Barry Dew, Lonnie Donegan (bj, v), Pete Sayers (g, v), Tony Bagot (b), Geoff Downs (d).* 80–87.

An auld licht traditionalist, Sunshine stood firm when the Chris Barber band began to shift its ground in the late 1950s to accommodate the growing vogue for skiffle and the blues. Sunshine had contributed materially to the group's success and was the featured soloist on the big hit, 'Petite Fleur'. Leaving Barber certainly punched holes in his marketability, but he has commanded a loyal following in both Britain and continental Europe throughout the past three decades.

The earlier Sunshine is well represented on Chris Barber records and on some useful trad compilations, but to some extent he has remained in the shadow of more eminent colleagues. The obvious fillip on *Just A Little While* ... is the presence of Colyer and Donegan (and perhaps, for some tastes, country singer Pete Sayers as well) on a couple of tracks each. But for them, this would be a slightly pedestrian set. There are live tracks from London, Hamburg and Cologne, and all of the material was previously issued on the German Pinorrekk label.

In London sounds a little shrill transferred to CD and doesn't offer an entirely accurate representation of Sunshine's Bechet-influenced tone. It does, though, give a fair sense of his approach to standard material. The arrangements of 'Just A Closer Walk With Thee' and 'Careless Love' are nicely personalized. Gresty knows the stuff inside out and chips in with some forceful statements of his own on both sets.

****(*) Gotta Travel On**
Timeless TTD 570 *Sunshine; Alan Gresty (t); John Beecham (tb); Barry Dew (bj, g, v); Tony Bagot (b); Geoff Downs (d, v).* 7/91.

***** South**
Timeless CD TTD 583 *As above, except Tony Scriven (d) replaces Downs.* 8/93.

By the turn of the 1990s, Sunshine found himself in the position of many of the older British trad players: increasingly preaching to the converted. The solos are by the book and even a little leg-weary on the 1991 session, which was recorded live at The Bull's Head in Barnes, London, a long-standing jazz haunt. *South* is a very decent set from the line-up who've stuck with Sunshine during his latter-day resurgence. Again, no great surprises or revelations, just good, strong, revivalist jazz, articulated clearly and without fuss.

***** Live At The Worker's Museum, Copenhagen**
Music Mecca CD 1096 *Sunshine; Arne Mathiesen (t, v); Finn Frosig (tb, v); Preben Danielsson (cl, as, ss); Jorgen Juncker (bj); Ebbe Wettlaufer (b); Morten Pedersen (d).* 3/96.

Sunshine has been as much admired in Scandinavia as the other British traditionalists, and this lively set catches him with 'Pee Dee' Danielsson's group playing Kid Ory tunes (a fine version of 'Savoy Blues') and some traditional gospel, ending unexpectedly with 'When I Grow Too Old To Dream', which has a delightful elegiac quality that has crept back into Sunshine's work over the past half-decade. The sound is a bit cavernous, but decent enough for all but the fussiest of purchasers, and a bit of lift in the bass helps a good deal.

***** You Are My Sunshine**
Timeless TTD 609 *Sunshine; Alan Gresty (t); John Beecham (tb); Barry Dew (bj, v); Tony Bagot (b); Tony Scriven (d).* 4/96.

***** Live At The BP Studienhaus**
Timeless TTD 620 *As above.* 9/97.

This line-up has acquired plenty of seasoning by now, and they sound as comfortable as you'd expect; but there's a degree of literacy and easy-going determination which set the Sunshine band apart from many traditional outfits: they're less drilled than Barber's group but won't submit to the sloppiness of weekend trad. There are too many obvious tunes on both these discs – surely Sunshine must be exhausted with the likes of 'Just A Little While To Stay Here' and 'Put On Your Old Grey Bonnet'? – and the singing won't really do. But the group are still enjoying themselves, and the live album has a genuine *joie de vivre* rare in this often glum, relentless genre. Sunshine's clarinet is still finding unexpected paths, too: listen to his pretty outrageous solo on 'Yellow Dog Blues' from *You Are My Sunshine.*

Klaus Suonsaari (born 1959)

DRUMS

Suonsaari is a Finn who led one of his country's leading groups, Blue Train, in the '80s, before these leadership dates.

*****(*) Reflecting Times**
Storyville STCD 4157 *Suonsaari; Tom Harrell (t, flhn); Bob Berg (ts); Niels Lan Doky (p); Ray Drummond (b).* 3/87.

***** Inside Out**
Soul Note 121274 *Suonsaari; Scott Wendholt (t, flhn); Scott Robinson (ts, ss, f); Renee Rosnes (p); Steve Nelson (vib); Ray Drummond (b).* 3/94.

A Finnish drummer who sounds not a bit like Edward Vesala (but is a physical ringer for Bill Frisell). The Storyville record obviously gains visibility from the other band members, but it is the leader's clean, unaffected swing, reminiscent of Billy Hart or Billy Higgins, that strikes even the casual listener straight away, and it has become clear that he is not just a facile time-keeper but is also a very thoughtful musician, contributing several numbers to *Inside Out*, a very polished record which is disappointing only relative to earlier promise. Something doesn't quite gel about it.

Despite the bright opening, we have not heard the best from him yet, but at present no recent follow-up.

Surge

GROUP

Trio playing electric music, based around modal fusion, with some freebop stirred in.

*** **Surge**

Dragon DRCD 216 *Staffan Svensson (t); Bo Wiklund (ky); Per Ekland (d). 9/91.*

(*) **For The Time Being

LJ LJCD 5213 *As above. 95–96.*

If only everything on the LJ record had turned out as well as 'Ode', a long and impeccable piece which sets up a series of melodic drifts that are eventually resolved in the haunting use of an extract from a traditional gypsy song. As it is, too much of the rest falls into the unfocused category of sketchwork. Wiklund draws out various mildly interesting electronic textures which Svensson noodles over; Ekland does his best to create a meaningful rhythmic base. But the record never adds up to much, and the live track, 'Perpetual Motion', suggests that as a working trio they have the same problems on stage as they do in the studio.

The earlier disc is actually rather better. Much of it seems like a hangover from some of the more modish styles of fusion in the '80s, Svensson's trumpet played through various attachments, the keyboards setting up broody echoes of Jon Hassell and Eno tracks. Fair play if it's to your taste.

John Surman (born 1944)

BARITONE AND SOPRANO SAXOPHONES, BASS CLARINET, ALTO CLARINET, SYNTHESIZERS, PIANO, RECORDER

Born in Tavistock, Devon, he studied in London and quickly came into prominence as a leading force in the new British jazz of that period. Major associations with Mike Westbrook, Mike Gibbs, John McLaughlin and SOS, as well as his own solo records, before the sequence of ECM albums which has brought him further renown in the '80s and '90s.

*** **John Surman**

Deram 844 884-2 *Surman; Kenny Wheeler (t, flhn); Malcolm Griffiths, Paul Rutherford (tb); Tom Bennellick (frhn); Mike Osborne (as); Russell Henderson (p, b); Dave Holland, Harry Miller (b); Stirling Betancourt, Alan Jackson (d); Errol Phillip (perc). 69.*

***(*) **How Many Clouds Can You See?**

Deram 844 882-2 *Surman; Harry Beckett (t, flhn); Malcolm Griffiths, Chris Pyne (tb); George Smith (tba); Mike Osborne (as); Alan Skidmore (ts); John Warren (bs, f); John Taylor (p); Harry Miller, Barre Phillips (b); Alan Jackson, Tony Oxley (d). 70.*

♛ **** **Tales Of The Algonquin**

Deram 844 883-2 *Surman; Harry Beckett, Martin Drover, Kenny Wheeler (t, flhn); Danny Almark, Malcolm Griffiths, Ed Harvey (tb); Mike Osborne (as, cl); Alan Skidmore (ts, af); Stan Sulzman (as, ss, f); John Warren (b, f); John Taylor (p); Harry Miller, Barre Phillips (b); Alan Jackson, Stu Martin (d). 71.*

John Surman first came to notice in Mike Westbrook's group, and it was a direct result of his performances on the Westbrook albums *Celebration* and *Marching Song* that persuaded producer Peter Eden to record him for Deram. The first of these makes slightly unexpected listening, being largely devoted to calypso jazz in the Sonny Rollins mode, played accurately and with some exuberance but hardly representative of what are now thought to be Surman's great strengths: his ability to combine power with a fragile delicacy on both baritone and soprano, and his ability to move between sophisticated vertical improvisation and diatonic folk.

At the same time Surman was developing a more individual style in a trio with Dave Holland and Alan Jackson, and the second half of the debut record was devoted to large-scale arrangements of trio material. Unfortunately that is very much the impression the album creates. The ensembles sound padded-out rather than organic, though by the closing 'Dance', inspired by Coltrane's *Africa/Brass*, the mix is a good deal richer and more coherent.

How Many Clouds Can You See? marks a dramatic step forward. The slow, brooding opening track, 'Galata Bridge', builds steadily to a climax of frenzied energy before calming and then building again to a more measured peak, almost as if the ensemble have crossed the bridge in question, which is in Istanbul and straddles two very different cultures. The Middle Eastern influence is replaced by a folksy Celticism on 'Caractacus', the name of the Pictish chieftain who faced down the Romans; this is a feature for Surman and drummer Jackson. After that comes a first Surman collaboration with the Canadian composer John Warren, who was to play an important part on the third and last Deram recording. 'Premonition' is a powerful trade-off between free jazz and more classically orientated structures, and was an important pointer to what was to come later.

The final two tracks, the multi-part 'Event' and the title-piece, are small-group pieces, reflecting the kind of work Surman was doing with The Trio. The closing part of 'Event', 'Circle Dance', is powered along by drummer Oxley's vivid use of dynamics and his ability to combine a strong pulse with apparent freedom from steady metre. It is another key moment, and one regrets that Surman was to have few chances in future years to work in this vein with players of Oxley's and Phillips's stature.

With a perversity that goes all the way round to predictability, Surman's time with Deram ended with his very best album to date, a full-scale collaboration with Warren. *Tales Of The Algonquin* is a masterpiece, conceived on a grand scale, meticulously executed and marked by superb soloing from Surman, Skidmore and the always wonderful Osborne. The set opens with four unrelated themes by Warren. Surman produces a boiling soprano solo on the up-tempo 'With Terry's Help', which exploits double time and displaced harmonies. 'The Dandelion' is perhaps the stand-out track of the album, though it is Mike Osborne's plaintive, keening solo which gives it its power. By contrast, the connected pieces which give the album its title are slightly too fey and impressionistic. 'Shingebis And The North Wind' is adventurous even by the standards of those blithely experimental days. Again Surman takes a back seat, this time to trumpeter Harry Beckett, who solos with an elemental sadness. Surman sounds most sure-footed in the immediate company of his Trio colleagues Phillips and Martin and produces his own most effective playing with them on 'The Adventures Of Manabush'. *Tales* is a record that has enjoyed almost legendary status among British jazz fans. It is one of the most welcome re-issues of the last half-decade and a must for admirers of British modern jazz.

****** Where Fortune Smiles / Live At Woodstock Town Hall**
Sequel Records NED CD 302 2CD *Surman; John McLaughlin (g); Karl Berger (vib); Dave Holland (b); Stu Martin (d).* 71–76.

In 1971, Surman left Europe for the USA, apparently exhausted by his touring schedule with The Trio and anxious to break new creative ground. He had already worked with Dave Holland and had been an important presence on John McLaughlin's debut recording, *Extrapolation*. He had also met and worked with Karl Berger, who makes such a significant contribution to *Where Fortune Smiles*. Once, this album was spoken of in the same breath as McLaughlin's *My Goal's Beyond*, which documented the guitarist's commitment to Sri Chinmoy and his philosophy, but *Extrapolation* is a far better point of comparison. It has the same mix of torrential intensity and sweet, song-like gentleness. The opening two tracks are the best point of comparison. Surman's 'Glancing Backwards' is a fiery twelve-note figure, traded between saxophone, guitar and vibes, marked by the feedback-laden rock sound of Jimi Hendrix and his followers. Ironically, McLaughlin's 'Earth Bound Hearts' is a gentle, semi-acoustic feature for Surman's soprano.

The album never quite regains its initial intensity. Much of its energy is burnt out in the first nine minutes. The title-piece is introduced by Berger, whose solo sounds like Fender Rhodes, and developed by a laid-back McLaughlin; no Surman at all. As on the opening track, Holland is masterly and is now mixed very far forward for CD. The closing 'Hope' is a solemn chorale for baritone and accompaniment, a fitting end to an oddly balanced but still entrancing record.

The brief second half of this budget-priced twofer is a duo session which technically belongs to drummer Stu Martin and is derived from music he wrote for radio. We have covered it in more detail under Martin's name. The two discs don't quite sit comfortably together. If we were bound for a desert island – and with rising sea levels who knows where the next edition will be datelined? – a two-CD set of *Where Fortune Smiles* with *Extrapolation* would be a priority purchase.

***** Westering Home**
FMR CD 19 *Surman (all instruments).* 72.

*****(*) Morning Glory**
FMR CD 21 *Surman; Malcolm Griffiths (tb); John Taylor (p); Terje Rypdal (g); Chris Laurence (b); John Marshall (d).* 73.

Westering Home was an early and only intermittently convincing version of the multi-tracked solo projects that Surman was to make his staple in the 1970s and '80s. He uses a variety of horns, piano and percussion to construct an evocative collage which, despite the pibroch and hornpipe elements, remains centred in jazz. It is a record that should perhaps be dusted down only now and again, as a reminder of the many and complex elements that go into the making of this very gifted artist.

Morning Glory was the name of and sole release by an unfortunately short-lived group that could and should have been allowed to develop further. Surman is both front man and chief composer, though he seems to have gone through some sort of creative crisis at this time, abandoning his signature baritone in favour of soprano and bass clarinet. Rypdal is the colourist and decorator, providing great washes of sound. Griffiths's brass tones seemed unfashionable in 1973 but sound much more idiomatic and relevant now. As so often, Laurence and Marshall – two absurdly underrated players – provide the dynamism. One wonders how warmly Surman himself looks back on this record; whatever his feelings, it remains one of the classics of its day.

***** Upon Reflection**
ECM 825472-2 *Surman (ss, bs, bcl, syn).* 5/79.

*****(*) The Amazing Adventures Of Simon Simon**
ECM 829160-2 *Surman; Jack DeJohnette (d, perc, p).* 1/81.

*****(*) Such Winters Of Memory**
ECM 810621-2 *Surman; Karin Krog (v, ring modulator, tambura); Pierre Favre (d).* 12/82.

***** Withholding Pattern**
ECM 825407-2 *Surman (ss, bs, bcl, rec, p, syn).* 12/84.

****(*) Private City**
ECM 835780-2 *As above.* 12/87.

*****(*) Road To St Ives**
ECM 843849-2 *As above.* 4/90.

****** Adventure Playground**
ECM 511981-2 *Surman; Paul Bley (p); Gary Peacock (b); Tony Oxley (d).* 9/91.

*****(*) The Brass Project**
ECM 517362-2 *Surman; Henry Lowther, Stephen Waterman, Stuart Brooks (t); Malcolm Griffiths, Chris Pyne (tb); David Stewart, Richard Edwards (btb); Chris Laurence (b); John Marshall (d); John Warren (cond).* 4/92.

Surman turned an absence of satisfying commissions to (creative) advantage on a series of multi-tracked solo projects on which he improvised horn lines over his own synthesizer accompaniments. In the early 1960s, he had modernized baritone saxophone playing, giving an apparently cumbersome horn an agile grace that belied its daunting bulk and adding an upper register much beyond its notional range (somewhat as Eric Dolphy had done with Surman's second instrument, the bass clarinet, and Albert Mangelsdorff with the trombone).

Upon Reflection quickly established the rather withdrawn, inward mood that became almost a vice on *Withholding Pattern* (it's hard not to read too much into the titles), but it also revived the folkish mode of Surman's solo *Westering Home*, which had mixed free passages with piano songs and even a sailor's dance on what sounds like harmonica. Surman's work of the 1980s under the aegis of ECM has updated that experiment and allied it to the stark and unadorned 'Northern' sound associated with Jan Garbarek and the better parts of Rypdal. This is at its coolest and most detached on *Secret City*, which was based on dance scores and sounds rather inconsequential outside that context.

Withholding Pattern is a curious combination of mock jauntiness ('All Cat's Whiskers And Bee's Knees') and similar untypical abstraction, with some of his best baritone playing for years, marred by bland waterdrop synthesizer patterns. 'Doxology' reflects an early interest in church music which re-emerges in the 'organ' opening to 'Tintagel' on *Road To St Ives*. The 1990 album isn't intended to be directly evocative of places, but it is one of Surman's warmest and most humane performances, in which the absence of 'live' accompaniment seems less constricting. Surman is a highly rhythmic player, but his multi-tracked backgrounds are often very unresponsive.

This wasn't a problem on Surman's live and studio collaborations with percussionist and keyboard player, Jack DeJohnette. *The Adventures Of Simon Simon* re-creates the quasi-narrative style of Surman's 1970s duo collaborations with The Trio drummer, Stu Martin, who died suddenly in 1980 (*Live At Woodstock Town Hall* has apparently reappeared on CD). DeJohnette's more explicit jazz background gives the music a more linear thrust, and less of the '(with)holding pattern' stasis that sometimes creeps into it, and creeps again into the otherwise excellent collaboration with singer Sheila Jordan and percussionist Pierre Favre.

Much of Surman's compositional energy in recent years has been directed towards his Brass Project, and a record was long overdue. It represented his first opportunity to work in the studio with Canadian composer-arranger John Warren since they recorded the magnificent *Tales Of The Algonquin* at the end of the 1960s. Unfortunately, comparison between the two records doesn't reflect all that positively on *The Brass Project*. Nevertheless it's a fine record; Surman's gently bucolic themes are played with just the right mixture of exuberance and reserve, and the voicings are often very subtle.

A faint sense that Surman has spent the last decade profitably marking time in an idiom that suited ECM's high-shine production had been shattered by the previous year's *Adventure Playground*, not so much a Surman album as a series of intimate collaborations in a freer mode than has been the saxophonist's norm over the past few years. The standard of playing is very high indeed (most noticeably from Bley and Oxley) and strongly suggests that Surman has still got a great deal to contribute at the sharper end of the music.

*****(*) Stranger Than Fiction**

ECM 521850-2 *Surman; John Taylor (p); Chris Laurence (b); John Marshall (d).* 12/93.

This was very nearly a re-formation of the Morning Glory group. Without a second horn or Rypdal's clangorous guitar playing, the emphasis is very squarely on Surman and Taylor and on light-footed country airs with a countervailing shadow. The long 'Triptych' with which the record closes is a masterpiece of abstract invention, relieving any doubt that they are content merely to spin out uncomplicated melodies. Careful listening suggests that Laurence and Marshall are much more important to the group than appears at first sight, supplying an unshakeable foundation and a subtle hint to the frontmen that stopping to muse is tempting but ultimately insufficient.

****** Nordic Quartet**

ECM 527120-2 *Surman; Vigleik Storaas (p); Terje Rypdal (g); Karin Krog (v).* 8/94.

Surman and long-time partner Krog are a gifted team. The interesting thing about this record is how much of the emphasis is devolved to the little-known Storaas (an elegant stylist with a few forgivable Keith Jarrett touches) and to even-handed group improvisation. Krog's voice is much jazzier than the setting strictly suggests, and her phrasing imposes a certain discipline on the opening 'Traces', 'Unwritten Letter' and 'Wild Bird'. Surman often functions as her accompanist and commentator, working off the vocal line. Rypdal is, as usual, more detached and abstract, but there is a compelling logic to the music that overcomes its cool detachment and draws the listener into its world.

*****(*) A Biography Of The Rev. Absalom Dawe**

ECM 523749-2 *Surman (solo).* 10/94.

Dawe was an ancestor of Surman's and his part in this is limited to providing a certain thematic glue to a further set of solo improvisations which nowadays place less emphasis on synthesized ostinati and much more on the detailed interplay of horn lines. Adding alto clarinet to his armoury has given Surman an important new timbre and pitch, and many of these pieces seem – at first hearing and without undue thought – to be lighter and more plain-spoken than some of the earlier ECMs. It is the same mix of jazz, folk and church themes, however, the only difference lying in the more relaxed, less stressed opposition of tension and release, and in the significance accorded to individual lead-lines. Surman is now a master of this demanding craft.

***** Proverbs And Songs**

ECM 537799-2 *Surman; John Taylor (org); Salisbury Festival Chorus; Howard Moody (cond).* 1/96.

Richly and resonantly recorded in the magnificent acoustic of Salisbury Cathedral, but flat and desiccated for all that. Surman's exchanges with Taylor are episodically involving, but the vocal settings have an overpowering quality that neutralizes some iron-hard instrumental ideas. It has always been understood that Surman's writing drew much from the Anglican tradition, and here is the proof. Unfortunately, in making the influence explicit he loses much of the subtlety that informed earlier records.

Ralph Sutton (born 1922)

PIANO

Sutton played with Jack Teagarden while still a college student, and after the war worked for many years as Eddie Condon's intermission pianist. Turned up in Dixieland and trad groups of varying kinds and was a founder member of The World's Greatest Jazz Band in 1968. Has enjoyed an Indian summer of recording and gigging in the '80s and '90s, and is recognized as perhaps the last original master of stride piano.

***** Quartet With Ruby Braff**

Storyville STCD 8243 *Sutton; Ruby Braff (c); Milt Hinton (b); Mousie Alexander (d).* 2/68.

***** Live At Sunnie's Rendezvous 1969**

Storyville STCD 8286 *Sutton; Al Hall (b); Cliff Leeman (d).* 2/69.

*****(*) Live At Sunnie's Rendezvous Vol. 2**
Storyville STCD 8281 *As above, except add Bob Wilber (ss, cl).* 2/69.

Sutton has been one of the premier stride and swing-piano players in jazz for 50 years, although it's only comparatively recently that he's got on record as a leader in a big way. These sessions date from a period when he performed at a club run by his wife in Aspen. The sound is imperfect on each, and the relaxations of a club set mean that they lack the focus of his studio dates. Nevertheless this is swinging music. Braff sounds typically forthright and unpretentious on his appearance, tersely handling the dozen repertory tunes with his hard-bitten lyricism. There are too many solo spots for Hinton, but the rhythm section do well. The trio date is marginally better for Sutton himself: a lot of Waller tunes here, though the best thing is the suitably aggressive 'Dog Ass Blues'. The second helping from Sunnie's adds Bob Wilber to the fun, and he is in excellent enough form to hitch this one up a notch: 'Dardanella' is divine.

****(*) Live At Haywards Heath**
Flyright 204 *Sutton (p solo).* 11/75.

***** Trio And Quartet**
Storyville STCD 8210 *Sutton; Lars Blach (g); Hugo Rasmussen (b); Svend Erik Norregaard (d).* 5/77.

***** Last Of The Whorehouse Piano Players: The Original Sessions**
Chiaroscuro CR(D) 206 *Sutton; Jay McShann (p); Milt Hinton (b); Gus Johnson (d).* 12/79.

*****(*) Partners In Crime**
Sackville SKCD 2-2023 *Sutton; Bob Barnard (t); Milt Hinton (b); Len Barnard (d).* 8/83.

****** At Café Des Copains**
Sackville SKCD 2-2019 *Sutton (p solo).* 6/83–1/87.

*****(*) More At Café Des Copains**
Sackville SKCD2-2036 *Sutton (p solo).* 1/88–1/89.

*****(*) Eye Opener**
Solo Art SACD 122 *Sutton (p solo).* 4/90.

***** Easy Street**
Sackville SKCD2-2040 *Sutton; Bob Barnard (t); Len Barnard (d).* 5/91.

Sutton is a great favourite with British audiences and two of the solo albums were cut in England. The Flyright record finds him in relaxed, ambling form, and there is his usual mixture of romping stride and tinkling, wayward balladry, but the piano is in bad shape and the sound isn't much of an improvement on what was a rotten LP issue. Much better to go to either the Sackville or the Solo Art sessions. *Eye Opener* was recorded (on a Steinway) at a church hall in Woking, and besides Sutton chestnuts like the title-piece (a famous piece of virtuosity) there is a charming Willard Robison medley and mothballed stride fantasies such as 'Rippling Waters' and 'Clothes Line Ballet'. This one was last listed on J&M but has been reissued on Solo Art.

The quartet date with the Barnard brothers has a timeless feel, since the trumpeter seems wholly unselfconscious about an Armstrong influence, and their opening romp through 'Swing That Music' shows how beautifully swing repertory can turn out when delivered in the right hands. Sutton's accompaniments are as sharp as his solos: when he leans in and clears the decks, his huge two-handed manner gives the clearest impression of what stride masters such as Waller and Johnson would have sounded like if they'd been recorded on contemporary equipment. *Easy Street* is a rematch with perhaps just the slightest shine taken off: there's some handsome playing, but a vague sense of routine about some of the tunes. The solo record from Café Des Copains, drawn from a series of broadcasts over a five-year period, uses scarce material – 'Russian Lullaby', 'Laugh Clown Laugh' and a rollicking 'Somebody Stole My Gal', with its rhythms cunningly displaced – which Sutton relishes, acknowledging the melodies but steamrollering past them into areas of what might be called 'pure' stride piano. The second helping on *More* concentrates on two shows a year apart and gets a slightly lower mark since the material is rather more familiar this time.

The 1979 date was originally issued as two LPs on ChazJazz and it also includes two previously unreleased tracks. The meeting of Sutton and McShann is the occasion for much musical backslapping and, while their styles aren't exactly complementary, Sutton tones down enough to make McShann's wry kind of blues seep through. They both sing, although Ralph sticks to Fats Waller ham on 'Truckin''. Lots of fun.

Storyville have reissued *Trio And Quartet* after several years in the vinyl scrapyard. Recorded on one of Ralph's Scandinavian tours, this is a typically amiable encounter which finds Blach, Rasmussen and Norregaard as capable if not especially effective bystanders. Sutton tends to go his own way.

*****(*) Maybeck Recital Hall Vol. 30**
Concord CCD 4586 *Sutton (p solo).* 8/93.

The main point here is that Sutton gets a decent piano-sound on record, something that has eluded him many times in the past. The programme is nothing more or less than a typical Sutton beanfeast – Waller, The Lion, Bix.

***** Sunday Session**
Sackville SKCS2-2044 *Sutton; Milt Hinton (b); Butch Miles (d).* 12/92.

***** Echoes Of Swing**
Nagel-Heyer CD 038 2CD *Sutton; Jon-Erik Kellso (t); Bill Allred (tb); Antti Sarpila (cl, ss); Jack Lesberg (b); Gregor Beck (d).* 3/97.

Sackville's disc was done in Switzerland, and it sets the trio to work on another familiar programme of jazz tunes and standards. Good stuff but, even though Miles is a surprise choice of drummer (and he does fine), there's much that is polished routine about the occasion. At this point Sutton's never going to do anything startling but, with so many CDs of his around, this is really just another one. So too the Nagel-Heyer concert disc, even though recording Sutton with a band is something of a rarity now. The horns play handsomely and good spirits abide across both discs but, with so much mainstream being recorded, again this falls into the middleweight bracket.

***** Sweet Sue**
Nagel-Heyer CD 057 *Sutton; Jon-Erik Kellso (t); Brian Ogilvie (cl, ts); Marty Grosz (g, v); Dave Green (b); Frank Capp (d).* 10/99.

A set of Waller tunes given a good going-over in one of the regular Nagel-Heyer concerts/record dates. Sutton takes a relatively minor role as band pianist and the spirited work of Kellso and Ogilvie takes precedence, although Grosz does his usual scene-stealing, dedicating 'It's A Sin To Tell A Lie' to Kenneth Starr (historians will be scratching their heads over that one soon enough).

Tierney Sutton

VOCALS

Singer trying to mix standards with genuine jazz material.

***** Introducing Tierney Sutton**

A Records AL 73111 *Sutton; Buddy Childers (flhn); Christian Jacob, Michael Lang (p); Trey Henry (b); Ray Brinker (d).* 8/95–4/96.

Ms Sutton's star potential doesn't seem to have developed much since this release: long hair, long legs, big, rangy voice and, on this showing, limited only by a fairly conservative approach to some reasonably adventurous material. That she has the capacity to tackle it more imaginatively is hinted at at every turn. A medley of Wayne Shorter's 'Footprints' and 'My Favorite Things', coming late in the set, was an opportunity to cut loose and try something different. Chick Corea's 'High Wire' was another strong choice, though probably the best two things are the closing 'If I Were A Bell' and 'In The Wee Small Hours Of The Morning', on which Lang co-stars. Definitely a singer to watch, by which, of course, we mean listen to. But this is at present still a one-off.

Esbjörn Svensson (born 1964)

KEYBOARDS

Born in Västeras, Svensson studied music in Stockholm and began working in the local scene from the mid-'80s. He formed his current trio in 1993.

***** When Everyone Has Gone**

Dragon DRCD 248 *Svensson; Dan Berglund (b, whistle); Magnus Oström (d, v).* 7–9/93.

***** Mr And Mrs Handkerchief**

Prophone PCD 028 *As above.* 3/95.

****** Trio Plays Monk**

Superstudio 76802 *As above, except add Ulf Forsberg, Ulrika Jansson, Elisabeth Arnberg, Ulrika Edstrom (strings).* 96.

Svensson's early records are comparatively modest, but he was already telling an attractive story at the piano. The sound of *When Everyone Has Gone* is lightly impressionistic post-bop, nodding at Keith Jarrett's Standards Trio but scaling down the grand gestures to a more manageable size. The trio play together in a loose but cleanly focused way that gives a degree of relaxation to themes which might sound merely uptight. 'Mohammed Goes To New York Part Two' is a catchy piece of Scandinavian funk, much in the style of Niels Lan Doky, but Svensson's heart is probably more in the ballads: 'Waltz For The Lonely Ones' is particularly charming. He also uses the electronic keyboards with such restraint that they acquire an almost ghostly quality at the back of the music. *Mr And Mrs Handkerchief* dispenses with the electronics, but this time Svensson alternates between upright and grand pianos: the homely quality of the upright lends an oddly clattery quality to his work, an almost perverse note when one hears the delicacy of his touch on, say, 'The Day After'. As if in compensation, Berglund plays with a degree more urgency this time.

Any reservations about the trio's calibre are brushed aside by the superlative Monk tribute album. Svensson chooses nothing unusual from the canon – only 'Eronel', given a beautifully lyrical turn, might be deemed scarce – so it's all the more astonishing what freshness and urgency he and his partners bring to the material. The secret is in the rhythmic frameworks, each of them unexpected to some degree: march, funk or parade times are introduced to melodies which have otherwise grown stale in the jazz repertory, and it's amazing what this does to the likes of 'I Mean You' and 'Rhythm-A-Ning'. There is a choice string arrangement lent to 'Round Midnight' which is in all ways wholly unhackneyed, while they even manage to find a right-sounding pulse for the intractable 'Little Rootie Tootie'. Svensson is no genius at the keyboard, but he comes up with some glorious ideas: he seems to think no further ahead than the next note in every part of the extended 'Bemsha Swing', yet so spontaneous is the improvisation that it carries all before it. Berglund and Oström, recorded in a kind of hot close-up, are just as fine. An outstanding disc.

****** Winter In Venice**

Superstudio 74321 539612 *Svensson; Dan Berglund (b); Magnus Oström (d).* 10/97.

****** From Gagarin's Point Of View**

ACT 9005-2 *As above.* 5–11/98.

Did we say no genius? Svensson may be out to prove us wrong. Working in comparative isolation in Stockholm, he's producing piano-trio records ready to take on the best of whatever the rest of the jazz world can retaliate with. *Winter In Venice* is a radiant set. The Jarrett comparison comes up again (in one way unfortunately so, as Svensson has some of the singalong bug) since the meditative beauty of the title-piece, for one, recalls the pared-away melodicism of the old master's mid-period improvising. And a track such as 'At Saturday' even suggests a smidgen of gospel-funk. But Svensson is content to adopt a less-is-more position almost throughout. Many would have taken the opportunity to turn several of these pieces into marathon shows of rhetoric, but the trio let only one track break the six-minute barrier. Berglund and Oström are by now fully in tune with the group conception and they're superbly responsive, the drummer finding almost pinpoint details in his playing.

From Gagarin's Point Of View continues in the same vein, perhaps even more inventively. If jazz musicians are going to effect any kind of rapprochement with rock or dance music, then one way might be via the kind of fusion which the trio suggests in 'Dodge The Dodo', where Oström plays a sort of hip-hop beat at the kit and Svensson still lets the melodious theme determine the end result. It's just one of 11 diverse, ingenious compositions. The shaping of these episodes into a sequence may strike some as a bit too artful, but it's the act of musicians who are of a generation that knows about their vast range of options and still want to play acoustic jazz. At any rate, Svensson does more than enough here to show why, along with such performers as Guus Janssen and Brad Mehldau, he's helping to keep the piano-trio situation full of new music.

Ewan Svensson

GUITAR, GUITAR-SYNTHESIZER

Contemporary Swedish guitarist, seeking his own path through the fusion and modal-bop fields which are currently the instrument's main areas.

***** Present Directions**

Dragon DRCD 218 *Svensson; Palle Danielsson (b); Magnus Gran (d).* 9/90–6/91.

Anyone fluent in the vocabulary of Scofield and Abercrombie will find Svensson's conversation easy to follow. If he seldom sounds strikingly individual, he follows the language with great skill. Across 12 compositions and over an hour of music on *Present Directions*, he alternates between fast, neatly picked solos and broader, expressive washes via the guitar-synthesizer. What makes the difference is the exacting support offered by Danielsson, as strong a bassist as one could ask for in this setting, and Gran's busy and intelligent drumming.

***** Reflections**

Dragon DRCD 239 *Svensson; Ove Ingemarsson (ts, EWI); Harald Svensson (p); Matz Nilsson (b); Magnus Gran (d).* 11/92–1/93.

***** Next Step**

Dragon DRCD 284 *As above, except omit Harald Svensson.* 11/94.

More mood(y) electric jazz from Svensson, this time abetted by the severe-sounding Ingemarsson, who plays the EWI with rather more sensitivity than some practitioners. The compositions are thoughtful, if rather lacking in melody, but the duet with Harald Svensson on 'Boat Trip' is very pretty, and the leader has plenty to say beyond the usual unreeling of fast licks. The subsequent *Next Step* pares the music back to a quartet, Ingemarsson sticking to straight-ahead tenor; and his bluff authority cuts through any chaff that Svensson might have been tempted by. They move very easily through the 11 tunes. Nothing special to make the record stand out from its predecessors, though.

***** Streams**

Dragon DRCD 291 *Svensson; Yasuhito Mori (b); Magnus Gran (d).* 9/95–2/96.

In his unemphatic way, Svensson has put together a strong catalogue of records, even if none of them stands out as an essential. Back in the trio format, and alternating only between a cool-toned electric and (on two tracks) an acoustic instrument, he patiently explores another 13 tunes with Mori's lines shadowing his and with Gran the soul of discretion. The writing, however, sounds particularly enticing: anonymous though it sounds, 'Piece IV' is ingeniously memorable, and some of the mood pieces are done at precisely the right temperature.

Steve Swallow (born 1940)

BASS GUITAR

Early work with Paul Bley and Jimmy Giuffre, then with Stan Getz and Gary Burton for the rest of the '60s. Spent some time in California before returning east, and switched to bass guitar as his sole instrument. Latterly a central figure in the Carla Bley circle. His own records are musicianly but often suggest that he's not that bothered about them.

*****(*) Home**

ECM 513424-2 *Swallow; David Liebman (ss, ts); Steve Kuhn (p); Lyle Mays (syn); Bob Moses (d); Sheila Jordan (v).* 9/79.

***** Carla**

XtraWatt 833492-2 *Swallow; Carla Bley (org); Larry Willis (p); Hiram Bullock (g); Victor Lewis (d); Don Alias (perc); Ida Kavafian (vn); Ikwhan Bae (vla); Fred Sherry (clo).* 86–87.

*****(*) Swallow**

XtraWatt 511960-2 *Swallow; Steve Kuhn (p); Carla Bley (org); Karen Mantler (ky, hca); Gary Burton (vib); Hiram Bullock, John Scofield (g); Robby Ameen (d); Don Alias (perc).* 9–11/91.

***** Real Book**

XtraWatt 521637-2 *Swallow; Tom Harrell (t, flhn); Joe Lovano (ts); Mulgrew Miller (p); Jack DeJohnette (d).* 12/93.

***** Deconstructed**

XtraWatt 537119-2 *Swallow; Ryan Kisor (t); Chris Potter (sax); Mick Goodrick (g); Adam Nussbaum (b).* 95.

Swallow is one of the most accomplished bassists of recent times. A man of real generosity of spirit, he has largely sublimated his own ambitions in the service of others, not least his partner, Carla Bley. The writing on *Carla* barely reflects the quality of classics like 'Arise Her Eyes' and 'Hotel Hello', which represent Swallow's other main contribution to modern jazz. But for the absence of the dedicatee's abrasive melodic mannerisms, this might just as well be a Carla Bley album (which will be sufficient recommendation for Bley fans).

For *Home*, Swallow set a group of poems by Robert Creeley, tiny snapshots of ordinariness that deliver their meanings precisely and without embellishment. Much the way Swallow plays. It might be that these pieces would work better with a less developed accompaniment, perhaps just voice, bass and piano, but the scoring is never allowed to overpower the lyric.

There's a touch of sameness about the writing on the eponymous *Swallow*, but the bassist's arrangements are impeccable and he's seldom sounded better. The tunes are mostly mid-tempo Latino grooves with plenty of solo scope. Guest players Burton and Scofield don't figure all that prominently and the most arresting voice is Karen Mantler's harmonica; her brief solo on 'Slender Thread' sets the bassist up for one of his delicate, single-note constructions, built up over Bley's organ chords and a soft shuffle beat. It could do with just one ripping tune, but that isn't Swallow's forte. On its own perfectly respectable terms, this is a beauty.

Real Book is a modest adventure for an all-star (though arguably over-familiar) band of heroes. Harrell and Lovano are dependably excellent, and the session has class and aplomb from moment to moment; but this kind of meeting of heavyweights isn't necessarily Swallow's best thing, and the music misses some of his most interesting quirks.

Deconstructed is an attempt to strike some new chords. Using a trumpeter and saxophonist of airier bent makes a difference to the shape of the songs, and spreading the harmonic business across two guitars gives the music a spacious quality which is very appealing. However, nothing develops and there is hardly a tune which goes anywhere more interesting than its own initial premisses.

John Swana

TRUMPET, FLUGELHORN

Raised in Philadelphia, where he still lives, Swana began listening to jazz in high school, then sat in at the local clubs. His experience is with big bands, organ combos and the current post-bop mainstream.

***** Introducing John Swana**
Criss Cross 1045 *Swana; Billy Pierce (ts); Benny Green (p); Peter Washington (b); Kenny Washington (d).* 12/90.

***** John Swana And Friends**
Criss Cross 1055 *Swana; Tom Harrell (t, flhn); Billy Pierce (ts); Mulgrew Miller (p); Ira Coleman (b); Billy Drummond (d).* 12/91.

*****(*) The Feeling's Mutual**
Criss Cross 1090 *Swana; Chris Potter (ts, as, f); Dave Posmontier (org); Steve Giordano (g); Billy Drummond (d).* 12/93.

Swana is a staunch modern traditionalist, firmly in the mould of such bygone masters as Lee Morgan and Kenny Dorham, and though he also cites Tom Harrell as a key influence it's his silvery tone and ready fluency that mark him out as an accomplished player. These are meaty, enjoyable records that just miss out on indispensability: little about the first two lingers long in the mind. *Introducing* pairs him with a near-perfect companion in the useful Pierce, who manages to play muscular tenor without quite falling into muscle-bound moves. The rhythm section are characteristically full of *brio*, but the material comes out sounding the same, even with such diverse composers as Wayne Shorter, Kenny Dorham and Swana himself. *John Swana And Friends* adds Harrell to the front line, and his arrangements of some of the jazz tunes – a tart reharmonization of 'Oleo', for instance – introduce a fresh twist. Yet the music never quite catches fire as it might, and Harrell's lovely playing on 'Darn That Dream' puts Swana in the shade.

The Feeling's Mutual is a more relaxed and convincing step forward. With the estimable Potter turning in fine support, Swana takes some of his best solos on his originals here, but more important is the way he's organized the group: Posmontier and Giordano (friends from Philadelphia) steer well clear of organ/guitar-band clichés, and instead the music has an open, modal feel that material like Chick Corea's 'Litha' seems tailored for. A surprising 'When Johnny Comes Marching Home' and a yearning ballad called 'Autumn Landscape' use the same virtues for different results. A very good Criss Cross.

*****(*) In The Moment**
Criss Cross 1119 *Swana; Steve Davis (tb); Eric Alexander (ts); Kenny Barron (p); Peter Washington (b); Kenny Washington (d).* 12/95.

Swana has been lucky in his sidemen, and that proves true again here: the rumbustious Davis and Alexander are a sound contrast in styles to the leader's more wistful and cajoling manner, and the rhythm section is absolutely blue-chip. The originals are a quite characterful lot, particularly the very engaging ballad, 'Martha', and the muted set-piece for the leader on 'Ballad Of The Sad Young Men' has genuine class about it.

*****(*) Philly–New York Junction**
Criss Cross 1150 *Swana; Joe Magnarelli (t, flhn); Eric Alexander (ts); Joel Weiskopf (p); Peter Washington (b); Kenny Washington (d).* 6/98.

*****(*) Tug Of War**
Criss Cross 1163 *Swana; Chris Potter (ts, ss, f); David Hazeltine (p); Dwayne Burno (b); Byron Landham (d).* 12/97–12/98.

Both of these are, in their way, no more than massively confident genre entries, rendered skilful by the great expertise of the players and informed by their pleasure at playing together; but the lack of a grand concept – which is the Criss Cross 'what you hear is what you get' trademark – adds to rather than subtracts from the results. The sextet session benefits from the piquancy of having Swana and Magnarelli together in the front line, and the horns are used in some interesting ways across the course of the date; but the quality of the solos, plangent but relaxed, is what you remember. Sample the title-track to hear how much they extract out of a relatively straightforward blowing tune.

Tug Of War is distinguished not only by the partnership of Swana and Potter, five years on from *The Feeling's Mutual*, but also by the excellent original material, idiomatic within a fairly conservative hard-bop tack, but fresh and imaginative, too. For once a 70-minute record doesn't seem too long – it's neatly paced and, even though the two halves of the record were made almost exactly a year apart, there's nothing disjointed between the dates. Swana and Potter both play some beautiful solos, but they are often almost aced out of it by Hazeltine's ability to surprise.

Swedish Swing Society

GROUP

A band formed by Lars Erstrand to play the repertoire of Benny Goodman.

*****(*) Winter Swing**
Sittel SITCD 9213 *Antti Sarpila (cl); Ulf Johansson (p, tb, v); Lars Erstrand (vib); Bjorn Sjodin (d).* 2/94.

***** What's New?**
Sittel SITCD 9235 *As above.* 5/96.

The SSS make an excellent case for their repertory music on both of these discs. The first, cut live at a concert in Uppsala, is properly high-spirited: 'Air Mail Special' goes like a rocket and, by avoiding too many of the most obvious chestnuts, the group make it all seem fresh. The three more familiar names in the band each do well, but not least of the music's merits is the swinging beat laid down by Sjodin. *What's New?* is mildly disappointing as a follow-up, though. Many interesting choices among the tunes, but the whiff of excitement which the live record latched on to seems absent: what one hears is merely a very good run-through of the material.

Steve Swell (born 1954)

TROMBONE

Born in Newark, Swell is a contemporary trombonist, going his own way through free and post-bop styles of playing.

*****(*) Observations**

CIMP 108 *Swell; Chris Kelsey (ss).* 2/96.

*****(*) Out And About**

CIMP 116 *Swell; Roswell Rudd (tb); Ken Filiano (b); Lou Grassi (d).* 6/96.

***** Moons Of Jupiter**

CIMP 149 *Swell; Mark Whitecage (as, cl); Dominic Duval (b); Jay Rosen (d).* 5/97.

Superb records helmed by a distinctive and impassioned improviser. Swell isn't a virtuoso trombonist in the manner of Rutherford or Christmann, but he's a powerful, vocal player whose energies ignite each of these occasions. The duo with Kelsey is a long-standing rehearsal partnership, and they read each other's moves with brilliant empathy. These are long, almost Tristano-like lines of counterpoint, each following a determined plan that has the feel of extemporization, and if the format is a little monochromatic there's nothing routine in their conversation. *Out And About* sets up an encounter with a godfather of free trombone. Rudd seems less than the force he was, and Swell is clearly the stronger participant, but the music is more an affectionate, collaborative joust than a cutting contest. Swell's tone has a raucous, overheated timbre when he warms up and, set beside Rudd's more constricted delivery, the results are more reminiscent of a couple of old Dixieland tailgaters going at it than anything 'avant-garde'. Filiano and Grassi enter into the spirit with the necessary gusto.

Moons Of Jupiter gets off to a tumultuous start with the overwhelmingly powerful 'For Henry Darger'. The rest of the record never quite measures up to the opening: as good as the horns are, they don't quite click with the long-standing partnership of Duval and Rosen, and it turns out as a free-bop date with flashes of brilliance. As so often with CIMP releases, both Duval and Filiano, on the previous disc, suffer from inaudibility – these records simply don't give the bassist a chance.

***** Atmospheels**

CIMP 184 *Swell; Will Connell (as, cl, bcl); Lou Grassi (d).* 8/98.

***** Flurries Warm And Clear**

CIMP 203 *Swell; Ned Rothenberg (as, cl, bcl); Tomas Ulrich (clo).* 7/99.

Two different trios. Connell is an unexposed veteran – now in his sixties, he came up through the Horace Tapscott groups of the 1960s and has recorded only rarely – and he plays buzzsaw solos on alto which are rampant in a not very purposeful way. With no bassist, Grassi seems unsure of how to make the music go forward, and it tends to clump around his bass-drum pedal. That said, there are still some corking improvisations from the leader, such as his long, blaring take on 'Folk Tune'.

Track three, 'Acoustic Rumble', pretty much sums up the second disc. It's chamber-jazz of a growly, unbeautiful temperament. Ulrich drones and slides around the other two, and a lot of the music is a dense weave. Three duos lighten the texture, and briefer, snappier pieces such as 'Consume This' perk the listener up.

Duncan Swift (1943–97)

PIANO

Born in Rotherham, Swift became a trad band pianist in the '70s and doubled this up with running a pub. He recorded two albums as a stride soloist but was taken by cancer in 1997.

****(*) The Broadwood Concert**

Big Bear BEARCD 34 *Swift (p solo).* 90.

****(*) The Key Of D Is Daffodil Yellow**

Duncan Swift Records 1 *Swift (p solo).* 12/92–6/93.

In the somewhat rare category of British stride, Duncan Swift worked as idiomatically as anyone this side of Keith Ingham. *The Broadwood Concert* is an entertaining live show, with the pianist hammering through a lengthy programme of mostly fast showcase pieces; but its impact is diminished by the lack of light and shade – the great stride players knew when to cool off, and Swift is less convincing in the more placid moments. Contrarily, the second album, this time on his own label, tends to linger in its quiet moments a little too much, and his guying of 'Maple Leaf Rag' as 'Maple Leaf Tatters' (as Thelonious Monk might have played it, apparently) is too clever by half.

Jorge Sylvester

ALTO AND SOPRANO SAXOPHONES

American saxophonist bridging US and Latin musics.

***** MusiCollage**

Postcards POST 1011 *Sylvester; Claudio Roditi (t, flhn); Marvin Sewell (g); Monte Croft (vib); Santi Debriano (b); Gene Jackson (d); Bobby Sanabria (perc).* 7/95.

Sylvester's assertive sax-playing is but one interesting element here. The opening track, 'Token', explodes off a polyrhythmic base that suggests both Latin and African pulses without neglecting an American jazz doctrine. The subsequent pieces, which rely more on Jackson than on the remarkable Sanabria, are more conventionally attuned and, to that degree, are a little less exciting; but Sylvester's fierce alto and the reliable Roditi – for once content with second spot – brighten all the tracks, and substituting vibes for piano was a shrewd textural move. Not all of it's memorable, but the tracks that work offer some real excitement.

Lew Tabackin (born 1940)

TENOR SAXOPHONE, FLUTE

Born and educated in Philadelphia, Tabackin's approach to tenor derives little from Philly's greatest saxophonist. Where others of his type have taken the Coltrane style as read, Lew harks back to an earlier generation, a breathy, slightly sour tone that is intriguingly mirrored and inverted in his flute playing. Perhaps best known for his big-band association with his wife, Toshiko Akiyoshi, he is also an able solo performer.

*****(*) Desert Lady**

Concord CCD 4411 *Tabackin; Hank Jones (p); Dave Holland (b); Victor Lewis (d).* 12/89.

****** I'll Be Seeing You**

Concord CCD 4528 *Tabackin; Benny Green (p); Peter Washington (b); Lewis Nash (d).* 4/92.

****** What A Little Moonlight Can Do**

Concord CCD 4617 *As above.* 4/94.

The Akiyoshi–Tabackin band flourished for almost a decade before being disbanded to allow husband and wife to concentrate on individual projects. Tabackin is a stylish and greatly underrated small-group saxophone player who inclines towards Sonny Rollins's melodic improvisation. His solos sound both expertly structured and wholly spontaneous, and he is an able and effective flautist, with an attractively orientalized tone, picked up by osmosis (so he claims) from his wife. Both sides of his playing style are evident on *Desert Lady*, on which he is supported by an absolutely first-rate rhythm section. 'Chelsea Bridge' and Strayhorn's 'Johnny Come Lately' are constructed in such a way that the melody is implicit in each phrase and the harmonic progressions, though quite daring, are impeccably logical and thought out. Tabackin's tone isn't particularly distinctive and his flute playing is often more immediately arresting. 'Desert Lady' and 'Yesterdays' are worth investigating on an album that doesn't pall on repeated hearings.

I'll Be Seeing You and *Moonlight* are almost perfectly balanced jazz records. Tabackin has rarely been heard to such advantage on disc. His solos on 'Isfahan' and 'I Surrender Dear' and 'Poinciana' and Jimmy Knepper's 'Leave Of Absinthe' are elegance personified, and the group rise to the occasion magnificently. Green carries enormous authority on his deceptively narrow shoulders, a player of great character and authority who these days sounds like no one but himself.

*****(*) Pyramid**

Koch International 6917 *Tabackin; Metropole Orchestra; Rob Pronk (cond).* 88–94.

Since the disbanding of the Akiyoshi–Tabackin big band, Lew has worked intermittently with the generously resourced Metropole Orchestra in the Netherlands, a size and type of band which is now almost inconceivable in the USA. Rob Pronk's arrangements are generously proportioned and thoroughly swinging, and even his violins seem to know how to play jazz. Tabackin, as ever, alternates flute and tenor and pumps out terse, growly solos on a range of standard material, including just one composition of his own on this occasion, 'Broken Dreams', which also featured a delicate oboe solo from Martin de Ruiter of the Metropole woodwind section. The tracks in the main are short and very symmetrically structured, and it might have been interesting to hear the pace varied more, but 'Yesterdays', 'Speak Low' and 'Sweet And Lovely', all of them from a 1988 session, stand out strongly.

***** Live At Vartan Jazz**

Vartan Jazz 003 *Tabackin; Kenny Walker (b); Bill Goodwin (d).* 8/94.

There are a number of good live sets from the '90s. (We have also heard one on Camerata called *In A Sentimental Mood*, with a Japanese rhythm section, but have no idea whether it is generally available.) This is a powerful and uncompromising trio, with something of an emphasis on Thelonious Monk compositions. Walker and Goodwin are more than competent players but, lacking a second horn or piano player, the emphasis falls almost exclusively on Lew's saxophone. His solo on 'Bemsha Swing' is superbly organized and very thoughtful and, despite occasional distortions in the sound – unless they are deliberately overblown notes – the package works very well indeed.

****** Tenority**

Concord CCD 4753 *Tabackin; Randy Brecker (t); Don Friedman (p); Peter Washington (b); Mark Taylor (d).* 6/96.

What an intriguing album. With Randy Brecker sitting in for the middle of the session and Friedman dipping out after 'Chasin' The Carrot', the group is as variously constituted as could be with this personnel. Gershwin's 'Soon' is transformed; even though the melody remains intact, the changes are significantly reorganized. Tabackin's own 'Fashion's Flower' is a delicate waltz, the sort of thing that he might in other circumstances have also tackled on flute, which isn't used here at all. After five tunes, Brecker is in place and the piano falls silent, meaning that the harmonic background is much less conventional. The trumpeter makes Monk's 'Trinkle Tinkle' his curtain-call, delivering a solo of pungent simplicity. 'The Best Thing For You' and 'You Stepped Out Of A Dream' are for saxophone, bass and drums only, always a challenging configuration; but, as if to demonstrate his mastery still more unambiguously, Lew takes the closing 'You Don't Know What Love Is' as an unaccompanied tenor solo. It's a fitting end to a remarkable record, one that refocuses the leader's quiet ambition.

Richard Tabnik

ALTO SAXOPHONE

Part of the New York circle of Tristano-ites, Tabnik works his own variations on that cool idiom.

*****(*) Solo Journey**

New Artists NA 1011 *Tabnik (as solo).* 9/90.

*****(*) In The Moment**

New Artists NA 1015 *Tabnik; Cameron Brown (b); Carol Tristano (d).* 10/92.

***** Life At The Core**

New Artists NA 1016 *Tabnik; Andy Fite (g); Calvin Hill (b); Roger Mancuso (d).* 11/92.

Tabnik has a cool, slightly nervy approach, like a cross between early Lee Konitz and some of the drier avant-gardists of the 1960s. The solo record invites an obvious comparison to Braxton, and in many ways it's a perfectly valid comparison, since so many of the source players (Lester Young, Warne Marsh, Paul Desmond) are the same. At just over the hour and 40 separate cuts, *Solo Journey* palls slightly in the later stages, though the bulk of it is crisply and imaginatively done, Tabnik finding things to say in the short sound-bites as well as in the longer and more developed tracks. His attempt to re-create Pres's clarinet solo on 'Countless Blues' is an indication of how thoroughly Tabnik has scried the canon.

He does something similar *à propos* 'Shoe Shine Boy' on the trio record, and this is perhaps his most effective setting. Cameron Brown's bass is mixed up very strong and chocolatey and sometimes overpowers the speakers, but Tabnik and Carol Tristano find plenty to do across those textures. The saxophonist's work on the long 'Butterflies And Universes' is among his most individual, and a long way ahead of the rather prosey material on *Life At The Core*, where he seems constrained by the presence of a harmony instrument.

As on the unaccompanied record, Tabnik doesn't mind having people eavesdrop on his rough drafts (the New Artists label seems dedicated to this approach) and includes two takes of 'It's Just A Feeling' on *In The Moment*. Set side by side, they say more about this developing artist than umpteen pages of critical text. Well worth a serious listen.

Aki Takase

PIANO

Once a student of Yosuke Yamashita, Takase emerged in the 1980s as a pianist working in an area which touched on post-bop but more often looked towards an entirely free vocabulary.

****** Shima Shoka**

Enja 6062-2 *Takase (p solo).* 6/90.

*****(*) Blue Monk**

Enja 7039-2 *Takase; David Murray (ts, bcl).* 4/91.

***** Close Up Of Japan**

Enja 7075-2 *Takase; Nobuyoshi Ino (b); Toki String Quartet.* 6/92.

*****(*) Piano Duets Live In Berlin 93/94**

FMP OWN-90002 *Takase; Alex Von Schlippenbach (p).* 3/93–12/94.

Takase rises out of jazz piano history with unique intensity and panache. Her earlier music (there are two vinyl-only releases from the beginning of the 1980s on Enja) suggested a pianist who was involving herself in earlier methods only reluctantly – most of the music leapt into the darkness of free playing at the earliest opportunity. Her CD releases offer a somewhat lopsided view of what she can do, but the solo record is a triumph. With Murray, these are real duets: a fat, fulsome 'Ellingtonia' and a galumphing 'Body And Soul' are highlights, but four excellent declensions of Monk form the heart of the record, which is almost as strong and accomplished as any of Murray's discs with Dave Burrell.

The solo record is where Takase makes her real mark. Her own tunes number seven, and range from the Monk derivation of 'Meraviglioso' to the brief, lightning-struck 'A.V.S.'. But her covers of other composers are the most remarkable things here: her treatment of Carla Bley's 'Ida Lupino' is even more deliberate, weighty and substantial than a Paul Bley reading; 'Giant Steps' is complex and superbly distilled; and her treatment of Ellington's 'Rockin' In Rhythm' is the *tour de force* of the disc, a fantasy imbued with such simultaneous drive and elegance that the composer himself – far removed though it is from any Ellington interpretation – would surely have applauded.

Close Up Of Japan is an interesting if mixed attempt at blending improvisation with meticulous written parts for the Toki String Quartet. 'Milestones' seems a bit self-consciously third-stream in feel, and the title-piece is a rather effortful attempt at blending East and West. But the arrangement of Astor Piazzolla's 'Winter In Buenos Aires' is sonorously effective, and Takase and Ino work well together on Charlie Haden's 'Song For Che'.

The record with Schlippenbach is meticulously balanced, opening with two long pieces by AVS, centred with four Monk tunes and ending with two extended variations on Takase themes. Even the two pairs of compositions share affinities: 'Na, Na, Na, Na ... Ist Das Der Weg?' and 'Tales Of Something' both come out of overlapping, building-block figures that achieve a terse complexity, and 'The Morlocks' (recorded before the orchestral version on the FMP CD of that title) and 'Chapelure Japonaise' are whirlwinds of prepared-piano turbulence. The Monk tunes – each pianist takes one solo – are like a breathing space, and Frank Zappa's 'You Are What You Is' is like a roistering encore. For catholic tastes, perhaps, but an impressive record.

*****(*) Duet For Eric Dolphy**

Enja 91209-2 *Takase; Rudi Mahall (bcl).* 5/97.

Mahall is by no means intimidated by the fact that David Murray has already played this duettist role on a Takase record. He's a mercurial player, making light of the lumbering reputation of the bass clarinet, with a slightly pinched tone and a quacking approach to a line. Ten Dolphy tunes – a big chunk of his *œuvre*, in fact – are whistled through, along with three originals and a peg-leg treatment of 'I'm Confessin''. Miniaturized into briefly explosive or bittersweet episodes, it's an inventive, droll record.

Natsuki Tamura

TRUMPET

Japanese trumpeter with a taste for solo work.

*****(*) How Many?**

Leo Lab CD 029 *Tamura; Satoko Fujii (p).* 11/96.

***** A Song For Jyaki**

Leo Lab CD 039 *Tamura (t solo).* 7/97.

Solo brass playing is a pretty rugged discipline. Tamura handles it with grace and elegance, and creates a wonderful sound all on his own. The recording is pretty much unsweetened, and on tunes like 'Blues For Myself' and the closing 'My Folk Song' the horn has a raw, almost vocal quality which is instantly appealing. The duos with Fujii are more obviously accessible but are, ironically, further from conventional jazz idiom. Virtually all the pieces are short and song-like, with echoes of traditional Japanese music throughout. An unexpected record, marked by melodic twists and turns and an unprecedented density of harmony for this kind of setting.

Akira Tana (born 1952)

DRUMS

Co-leader of the group TanaReid, with bassist Rufus Reid, Tana is based in New York and has long experience of the local scene.

****(*) Yours And Mine**

Concord CCD 4440 *Tana; Jesse Davis (as); Ralph Moore (ss, ts); Rob Schneiderman (p); Rufus Reid (b).* 9/90.

***** Passing Thoughts**

Concord CCD 4505 *As above, except Craig Bailey (as, f), Dan Faulk (ss, ts) replace Davis and Moore; add Guilherme Franco (perc).* 1/92.

*****(*) Looking Forward**

Evidence ECD 22114-2 *Tana; Tom Harrell (t, flhn); Craig Bailey (as, f); Mark Turner (ts, ss); John Stetch (p); Rufus Reid (b).* 11/94.

Though we have listed them under Tana's name, these discs are all by TanaReid, the group co-led by the drummer and Rufus Reid. Since neither man is an idiosyncratic stylist, the music tends to run along familiar boppish lines: it's a nice repertory band with a few new wrinkles. Schneiderman, the only other player common to the first two records, is a telling presence, contributing 'Day And Night' and 'Blue Motion' to the book, two of their best tunes. The first album is let down a little by the horns: Moore seems below par, and Davis, though he plays enthusiastically, isn't as powerful as he is on his own Concord dates. Bailey and Faulk, though both a little raw, play with a sharper focus on *Passing Thoughts*.

Looking Forward isn't so much a breakthrough as a progressive record. Without being unduly demonstrative, the band sounds like a much more sophisticated outfit. Kenny Barron's 'The Third Eye' is a startling revision, resembling a through-composed chunk of free-bop, and a standard piece like 'The Duke' is carefully sifted for textures, provided most effectively by Bailey's use of flute. There's an agreeably tart contrast between his sinewy alto and Turner's full-bodied tenor, the latter quite beautiful on Victor Feldman's ballad, 'Falling In Love'. Harrell guests on four tracks and is typically marvellous. Without resorting to variety for its own sake, the group has created a diverse and convincing set.

John Tank

TENOR AND SOPRANO SAXOPHONES

Born in Canada, Tank was schooled in music and studied with George Coleman and Junior Cook. He recorded with Mingus and leads his own groups in his home base.

*****(*) So In Love**

TCB 95602 *Tank; Jack Walrath (t); Kenny Drew Jr (p); Ron McClure (b); Marvin 'Smitty' Smith (d).* 2/95.

Tank is a Canadian and he cut this set during a long weekend in New York. No quarter is given by the local team, and it would have done the nominal leader an injustice, anyway: he is perfectly composed and delivers five good originals – check out 'Address This Issue' and 'Uptown Lex' in particular – along with a big, dark sound on tenor and a hard and fearless one on soprano. He's a veteran of his local scene and clearly there's nothing missing in a style that sounds at home either in Cole Porter's title-tune or in the quirky confines of Walrath's tune, 'Vengeance'. The others are all on top form and Smith, who seldom does this kind of gig any more, sounds particularly good.

Horace Tapscott (1934–99)

PIANO

Tapscott's music and his views on integration and racial equality cannot be separated, and yet he rarely composed anything resembling programme or agit-prop music, preferring to let the free flow of creativity do the job of discourse for him. Inevitably, given his views, he was held apart from the critical mainstream and, despite a substantial body of recording from the time of his comeback in 1978 onwards, most of it was for his own label. He remains, perversely, best known for the compositions and arrangements on Sonny Criss's 1968 album, Sonny's Dream.

♛ ** The Dark Tree**

hatOLOGY 2-2053 2CD *Tapscott; John Carter (cl); Cecil McBee (b); Andrew Cyrille (d).* 12/89.

There was, inevitably, a darker side to the cool 'West Coast sound' and to the conventionally sunny image of California. One hardly thinks of Eric Dolphy or Charles Mingus as 'West Coast' players, yet that is what they were, and they conveyed a fundamental truth about the region's culture that is reflected in Horace Tapscott's still painfully unrecognized work. His death in February 1999 will doubtless spark a belated critical enthusiasm; too little and too late. Tapscott was first and always a community musician. His decision to remain in Los Angeles as a performer–activist undoubtedly thwarted wider recognition, but so too did the fact that he conformed to no readily marketable pigeonhole; 'West Coast Hot' was considered something of a pleonasm in the business, and there was a measure of suspicion regarding Tapscott's political agenda. In 1961 he helped establish the Union of God's Musicians and Artists Ascension, out of which grew the Pan-Afrikan People's Arkestra, both attempts to find uncompromised work for talented, young, black musicians. Their work is fiercely disciplined, built up out of deceptively simple elements, but with subtle polychordal shadings that reflect Tapscott's solo work and his intriguing duos and trios with members of the PAPA. Much of this work has been issued on his own Nimbus label, but its status and availability have always been troublingly hard to pin down. Readers should refer to our first (1992) edition for a listing of LP releases.

Tapscott characteristically builds pieces over sustained *ostinati* in the bass clef (he features McBee very strongly in his late-1980s band), building solos out of simple but often enigmatic themes. The most obvious influence is Monk and there are clear parallels with Randy Weston and Dollar Brand (Abdullah Ibrahim), but there is also a 'correctness' of touch and development that recalls classical technique in its purest form, not a Third Stream dilution. Over this, Tapscott likes to place a freer-sounding horn, Arthur Blythe in the late 1960s and the more abstract John Carter two decades later.

The Dark Tree is special in having two neglected giants of modern jazz working with instinctive sympathy, intelligence and bottomless expression. Both pianist and clarinettist are entirely at ease with brusque, angular melodies and more sweepingly lyrical passages. Tunes like 'Lino's Pad' exploit unusual and often difficult time-signatures, combinations of metre which present no problems to players as deft as McBee and Cyrille. Alternative versions of 'The Dark Tree' can be found elsewhere, notably on a valuable Novus/BMG compilation called *West Coast Hot* which pops up every now and then and is well worth the search. These two versions, though, are the key statements; one can't say 'definitive' of a piece that is defined by its fugitive, experimental quality, but the interplay between Carter and Tapscott is astonishing and one's only regret is that they didn't choose to tape or release a duo version as well. According *The Dark Tree* the clinching accolade of a crown might seem belated enthusiasm, but the record has been out of circulation for some time and returns now, in the wake of Horace's death, with redoubled impact. The recording sounds as fresh and densely textured as ever. A genuinely important reissue.

*****(*) aiee! The Phantom**
Arabesque AJ0119 *Tapscott; Marcus Belgrave (t); Abraham Burton (as); Reggie Workman (b); Andrew Cyrille (d).* 6/95.

****** Among Friends**
Jazz Friends Productions JFP 004 *Tapscott; Sonny Simmons (as); James Lewis (b); John Betsch (d).* 7/95.

*****(*) Thoughts Of Dar Es Salaam**
Arabesque AJ 0128 *Tapscott; Ray Drummond (b); Billy Hart (d).* 96.

Arabesque took on Tapscott in the mid-'90s, perhaps conscious that time might be slipping away for one of the sleeping giants of the music. The oddly named *aiee! The Phantom* is unmistakable Tapscott: big, pounding motifs, with horns punching away over the top. The long pieces, 'Mothership' and a reprise of an older theme 'Drunken Mary/Mary On Sunday', are very impressively voiced and crafted, almost like scaled-down versions of big-band arrangements. The only quibble relates to Burton, who usually punches his weight but sounds out of place here. It isn't that he can't keep pace with Tapscott's slewing harmonics and rapid-rotation rhythm; it's simply that he doesn't have much to add in his own voice.

The contrast with the frail, wavering eloquence of Sonny Simmons on the live Paris set is too obvious to overstate. Interestingly, all the material is straight from repertory – 'Milestones', 'Body And Soul', 'So What' and a version of 'Caravan' that underlines how much Horace had built on Duke's pianism – but is played with surpassing thoughtfulness. There is not a casual gesture in 50 minutes of music, and 'Body And Soul' stands alongside some of the great performances of the old chestnut, all the way from Horace's fast, hypnotic opening to Sonny's elaborate restatement. 'Caravan' becomes a showcase for Betsch, a long, crisp solo heralded by Sonny's Rahsaan-like whistle. The bass is a touch distant, but otherwise all the music is beautifully registered.

Tapscott had never shied away from standards but he rarely played them in common times. The slightly strange thing about *Thoughts Of Dar Es Salaam* is that there is scarcely an oblique or asymmetrical time-signature to be heard. Despite a trio perfectly capable of tackling anything he threw at them, Horace stays in ordinary metres throughout, leaving Hart and Drummond to embellish and vary at will, but not straying on his own account. Recent years had seen him re-examining aspects of bebop. 'So What' on *Among Friends* is a vivid example, and 'Now's The Time' on the trio record is a powerful restatement of how much unexplored acreage Horace had found in bop. Some of the tunes would seem pointlessly cranky when executed in any way other than straightforwardly, and Tapscott seems to have wakened to the potential of clear and clean-edged melody. For many listeners, *Thoughts* will be a first exposure to his work. As such, it's potentially misleading, and they should certainly not neglect to follow through with *The Dark Tree.*

Gregory Tardy

TENOR SAXOPHONE

Debut date for the young American tenorman, working in the modern tradition.

*****(*) Serendipity**
Impulse! 12582 *Tardy; Russell Gunn, Tom Harrell (t); Mulgrew Miller, Aaron Goldberg (p); Reginald Veal (b); Eric Harland (d).* 9/97.

The young tenorman has a lovely sound on the horn: furry, vocalized but classically full-bodied. This debut session is cleverly varied, from the oblique-in-the-modern-style originals to 'Ask Me Now' and the burnished balladry of 'Prisoner Of Love'. Nothing feels very substantial, but it's all played with such love for the idiom that it's impossible not to enjoy. Guest spots for Gunn and Harrell (two apiece) are well taken, but the key player is probably Miller, whose graceful presence adds the most solid of foundations to Tardy's fresh improvising.

Buddy Tate (born 1915)

TENOR SAXOPHONE, CLARINET

Tate was the replacement for the late Herschel Evans in the Basie band, which shows how much faith the Count placed in him. Born in Sherman, Texas, he'd worked with the Clouds of Joy before that and was later to become a solo artist, though most of Buddy's solos are scattered over recordings by others. He has formidable control in the upper register of his instrument and can frequently sound as if he is playing something other than a tenor.

**** Jumping On The West Coast**

Black Lion BLCD760175 *Tate; Emmett Berry, Forest Powell (t); Teddy Donnelly (tb); Charles Q Price (as, v); Frank Sleet (as); Charlie Thomas (ts); Bill Doggett, Frank Whyte (p); Louis Speiginer (g); Benny Booker (b); Edward Smith, Chico Hamilton, Pete McShann (d); Jimmy Witherspoon (v).* 4/47–5/49.

Buddy Tate is one of the greatest and most durable of swing tenormen, a major performer for over half a century and a much-loved and amiable man; but the records under his own name are perhaps a little disappointing in the light of his grand reputation, and his reticent standing as a leader may account for the reason why he's never quite secured the wider fame of some of his peers. His great records were made with Basie – whom he joined following Herschel Evans's death in 1939 – and his old friend from the band, Buck Clayton; in 1947, when the motley collection of tracks on the Black Lion CD were made, he was still with the band but did some moonlighting in an anonymous ensemble which cut 12 of the 18 tracks here (the others are by even less identifiable groups, though there's a nice early blues from Witherspoon). The music is unpretentious but forgettable jump-band music, typical of the day.

***** Swinging Scorpio**

Black Lion BLCD760165 *Tate; Humphrey Lyttelton (t, cl); Bruce Turner (cl, as); Kathy Stobart (cl, ts, bs); Mick Pyne (p); Dave Green (b); Tony Mann (d).* 7/74.

****(*) The Texas Twister**

New World 352 *Tate; Paul Quinichette (ts); Cliff Smalls (p); Major Holley (b); Jackie Williams (d).* 75.

*****(*) Jive At Five**

Storyville STCD 5010 *Tate; Doc Cheatham (t); Vic Dickenson (tb, v); Johnny Guarnieri (p); George Duvivier (b); Oliver Jackson (d).* 7/75.

Tate's records in the 1970s have a desultory, pick-up feel to them, but there's still plenty of ingratiating music here. Tate does some singing on *The Texas Twister*, and at least he sounds better than Zoot Sims or Phil Woods in this role. It otherwise interrupts an attractive two-tenor workout for the leads which offers a scarce glimpse of Quinichette in his later days. *Swinging Scorpio* is more of a Humphrey Lyttelton session with Tate as guest: the band are playing charts by Tate's old chum, Buck Clayton, though, and he fits snugly if a little shakily here and there into the British ensemble. The charts could use a rather more swinging rhythm section, but otherwise the music is well handled, with Humph playing the Clayton role with some aplomb. The best of these records, though, is the all-star date on *Jive At Five*, which benefits from a perfectly balanced front line: the upright, proper Cheatham, the louche Tate, the almost lascivious-sounding Dickenson. Each man's ballad feature is a treat, and Guarnieri supports and embellishes beautifully.

*****(*) The Ballad Artistry Of Buddy Tate**

Sackville SKCD-3034 *Tate; Ed Bickert (g); Don Thompson (b); Terry Clarke (d).* 6/81.

****(*) Just Jazz**

Reservoir RSR CD 110 *Tate; Al Grey (tb); Richard Wyands (p); Major Holley (b, v); Al Harewood (d).* 4/84.

The Ballad Artistry is surely Tate's best latter-day record. By sticking mostly to slow tempos and never forcing the pace, the supporting trio provides just the right sort of intimacy and cushioning detail to let Tate relax and, though he still has his doubtful moments, most of his solos are controlled, ruminative, nicely eloquent. It's much like a vintage Ben Webster date. Bickert is in excellent form, unobtrusively filling all the harmonic space round the saxophonist, and Thompson and Clarke both play well. An immaculate 'Darn That Dream' and the pleasing choice of Ellington's 'Isfahan' provide the highlights. The Reservoir disc is a reissue of an earlier LP with a couple of alternative takes to beef up playing time. Nothing very exciting here, but dependable playing from the principals, and Grey in particular taking a witty role.

Art Tatum (1910–56)

PIANO, CELESTE

Born in Toledo, Ohio, and almost sightless from birth, Tatum travelled widely in the 1930s on the club circuit. He recorded as a soloist and accompanist until he formed a trio in 1943. A master of every kind of jazz piano style, he nevertheless was not interested in composing himself and preferred to work endless variations on standard material, often following a formula on familiar tunes but varying it to infinitesimal degrees. He influenced pianists and other instrumentalists alike, all of them impressed by the depth of his rhythmic and harmonic thinking within his self-imposed boundaries. He died from uraemia in 1956.

*****(*) Art Tatum 1932–1934**

Classics 507 *Tatum (p solo).* 3/33–10/34.

*****(*) Art Tatum 1934–1940**

Classics 560 *Tatum; Lloyd Reese (t); Marshal Royal (cl); Bill Perkins (g); Joe Bailey (b); Oscar Bradley (d); Adelaide Hall (v).* 10/34–7/40.

The enormity of Tatum's achievements makes approaching him a daunting proposition even now. His very first session, cut in New York in 1933, must have astonished every piano player who heard any of the four tracks (only available on Classics 507). 'Tiger Rag', for instance, becomes transformed from a rather old-fashioned hot novelty tune into a furious series of variations, thrown off with abandon but as closely argued and formally precise as any rag or stomp at one-quarter of the tempo. If Tatum had only recorded what is on these first CDs, he would be assured of immortality; yet, like Morton's early solos, they are both achievements in their own right and sketchbooks for the great works of his later years.

There are just a few distractions in the music leading up to 1940: Adelaide Hall sings a couple of vocals on one session, and

Tatum's Swingsters record one 1937 session (which also includes Tatum on celeste).

****** The Standard Transcriptions**
Music & Arts CD-919 2CD *Tatum (p solo).* 35–45.

****** The Standard Transcriptions 1935–1945**
Storyville STCD 8260/1 2CD *Tatum (p solo).* 35–45.

(***) Standards
Black Lion BLCD 760143 *Tatum (p solo).* 35–43.

Tatum's transcription discs for radio were made at different sessions over a period of several years and have survived as rather indifferently stored acetates. They are as valuable in their way as the later sessions for Norman Granz: briefer, many solos almost casually tossed off, and some blemished by the poor recording (Tatum never finally received the kind of studio sound which his work demanded), but it's a magnificent archive, spread over two lengthy CDs. Some of them, such as 'I Wish I Were Twins', have the melody abstracted into a monstrously fast chunk of stride piano; others, like 'The Man I Love', become tender but firm ballads, while others begin at a medium tempo before hurtling forward in double-time. Trifles such as Dvorák's 'Humoresque' are treated with Tatum's peculiar knowing gaucheness, while his treatment of such as 'I'm Gonna Sit Right Down And Write Myself A Letter' are like destructive tributes to such colleagues as Waller and Johnson: immensely superior in terms of technique, Tatum nevertheless pays them a kind of offhand homage by adopting elements of their manner to his own vast vocabulary. 'All God's Chillun Got Rhythm', meanwhile, prefigures Powell and bebop intensity. Highly recommended ... however, collectors are now posed a tricky choice between the Music & Arts set and a new Storyville edition of the same music. It's complicated by what seems to be an inconsistency between the sets. The earlier solos seem to be better served by the Storyvillle set but, after that, honours are difficult to award and, while Don Asher's essay on the Music & Arts set is highly entertaining, some may prefer the more scholarly Storyville notes. In the end, either set should provide much pleasure to Tatum admirers, although those expecting hi-fi should be warned that many of the tracks (on each set!) still suffer from inferior sound.

Both sets completely supersede the Black Lion disc, which includes 20 solos in inferior mastering and with what seem to be some pitching problems created by uncertain speeds.

*****(*) Art Tatum 1940–1944**
Classics 800 *Tatum; Joe Thomas (t); Edmond Hall (cl); Oscar Moore, John Collins, Tiny Grimes (g); Billy Taylor, Slam Stewart (b); Eddie Dougherty, Yank Porter (d); Joe Turner (v).* 7/40–44.

***** Art Tatum 1944**
Classics 825 *Tatum; Tiny Grimes (g); Slam Stewart (b).* 5–12/44.

***** On the Sunny Side**
Topaz TPZ 1066 *As above.* 5/44–5/45.

*****(*) Art Tatum 1945–1947**
Classics 982 *Tatum (p solo).* 5/45–1/47.

Tatum's 1940 solos are another superb sequence. There is a first revision of 'Tiger Rag', which first appeared at his debut session, and particularly imaginative interpretations of 'Lullaby Of The Leaves', 'Moon Glow' and, improbably enough, 'Begin The Beguine'. The Classics *1940–1944* disc goes on to take in ten trio tracks with Grimes and Stewart, a format that took up much of the pianist's time in the 1940s. It didn't so much cramp his style as push it into a formula to a degree that some will be dissatisfied by. In a sense, though, it was characteristic of the man. Grimes and Stewart were mere mortals next to the pianist, but their earthbound playing kept Tatum within reach of a paying audience. The *1944* Classics disc covers trio sessions for the Asch and Comet labels, in rather murky sound, and goes on to a single solo date for Asch – including a version of 'Sweet And Lovely', one tune he never recorded commercially again. The low-fi sound keeps this one within specialist realms. *On The Sunny Side* follows similar ground but adds eight characteristic solos from the following May.

These are also on Classics 982, which is otherwise filled out by 11 solos for V-Disc and a January 1947 session for Victor. It is oddly moving to hear Tatum himself introduce his V-Disc solos and hope that the servicemen enjoy hearing the tunes, whatever they may think of the piano playing. One or two unusual choices, such as '9.20 Special' and 'I'm Beginning To See The Light', make these solos of extra interest, and the Victor date is valuable because Tatum was recorded this well only rarely.

*****(*) The Art Of Tatum**
ASV AJA 5164 *Tatum; Oscar Pettiford (b); Big Sid Catlett (d).* 8/32–10/44.

A useful collection of early Tatum solos, with a single concert track with Pettiford and Catlett to round it off. The compilers have taken a generous sample and, though some will still find ASV's remastering rather fudgy, this may appeal to any who want only a single example of the man's earlier work.

***** The V Discs**
Black Lion BLCD 760114 *Tatum; Tiny Grimes (g); Oscar Pettiford, Slam Stewart (b); Big Sid Catlett (d).* 44–46.

*****(*) In Private**
Fresh Sound FSR-CD 127 *Tatum (p solo). c.* 48.

***** The Complete Capitol Recordings Of Art Tatum**
Capitol 821325-2 2CD *Tatum; Everett Barksdale (g); Slam Stewart (b).* 7/49–12/52.

The V Discs is an interesting supplement rather than an essential part of the Tatum discography. Mostly solos, with the other musicians sitting in on only three tracks, these sessions for American forces overseas include some typically accomplished Tatum, but the variable sound-quality – some tracks are quite clean, others are badly marked by surface noise – makes listening through the disc a sometimes jolting experience. 'Lover', 'I'm Beginning To See The Light' and a Gershwin medley are, though, top-class Tatum. *In Private* comes from a tape allegedly made at Buddy Cole's house around 1948. There are many stories of Tatum doing even more impossible things at after-hours sessions, but he must have felt he was being watched at this one, since there is nothing strikingly different from his everyday genius here. But the disc comes in unusually clean sound, there is a notably fine 'Over The Rainbow', and a couple of tunes – 'You're Driving Me Crazy' and 'Sittin' And A Rockin'' – are ones he didn't often record.

The Capitol sessions date from the period when Tatum was working with a trio, but Barksdale and Stewart actually appear on only some of the tracks. These are mostly fine rather than great

Tatum performances: from most other pianists they would be astonishing work but, ranked next to his other recordings, these are, comparatively speaking, on a lower flame. There are hints of the routine which he would often settle into on particular tunes, and one or two tracks where he sounds relatively indifferent to the occasion. On others – 'Someone To Watch Over Me' or 'Somebody Loves Me', both on the first disc – he is the great Tatum.

*****(*) Masters Of Jazz Vol. 8: Art Tatum**
Storyville STCD 4108 *Tatum (p solo).* 8/32–1/46.

The Storyville disc is a hotchpotch of solos covering the 1930s and '40s. The music is unimpeachable but it makes little sense as a chronological compilation.

***** Piano Starts Here**
Columbia 476546-2 *Tatum (p solo).* 33–49.

Tatum's debut solo session turns up again here, this time as a prelude to nine solos from a 1949 Gene Norman concert. There is one unusual choice in 'The Kerry Dance'. Valuable as always, but probably for completists only, since sound is again no better than fair.

****** The Art Tatum Solo Masterpieces Vol. 1**
Pablo 2405-432 *Tatum (p solo).* 12/53.

****** The Art Tatum Solo Masterpieces Vol. 2**
Pablo 2405-433 *Tatum (p solo).* 12/53.

****** The Art Tatum Solo Masterpieces Vol. 3**
Pablo 2405-434 *Tatum (p solo).* 12/53.

****** The Art Tatum Solo Masterpieces Vol. 4**
Pablo 2405-435 *Tatum (p solo).* 4/54.

****** The Art Tatum Solo Masterpieces Vol. 5**
Pablo 2405-436 *Tatum (p solo).* 4/54.

****** The Art Tatum Solo Masterpieces Vol. 6**
Pablo 2405-437 *Tatum (p solo).* 1/55.

****** The Art Tatum Solo Masterpieces Vol. 7**
Pablo 2405-438 *Tatum (p solo).* 1/55–56.

<Crown>Q ****** The Complete Pablo Solo Masterpieces**
Pablo 4404 7CD *As above seven discs.* 12/53–1/55.

Tatum's extraordinary achievement was set down in no more than four separate sessions over the course of a little over a year. Twenty years after his first solo records, this abundance of music does in some ways show comparatively little in the way of 'progression': he had established a pattern for playing many of the tunes in his repertoire, and changes of inflexion, nuance and touch may be the only telling differences between these and earlier variations on the theme. But there are countless small revisions of this kind, enough to make each solo a fresh experience, and mostly he is more expansive (freed from playing-time restrictions, he is still comparatively brief, but there can be a major difference between a two-and-a-half-minute and a four-minute solo) and more able to provide dynamic contrast and rhythmic variation. He still chooses Broadway tunes over any kind of jazz material and seems to care little for formal emotional commitments: a ballad is just as likely to be dismantled as it is to be made to evoke tenderness, while a feeble tune such as 'Taboo' (Vol. 7) may be transformed into something that communicates with great power and urgency. Tatum's genius (these records were originally known as 'The Genius Of Art Tatum') was a peculiar combination of carelessness – even at his most daring and virtuosic he can sometimes suggest a throwaway manner – and searching commitment to his art, and those contradictory qualities (which in some ways exemplify something of the jazz artist's lot) heighten the power of these superb solos.

While it is invidious to single out particular discs, we suggest that the uncommitted start with discs four and six. The boxed-set edition includes all the music, and demands a fifth star. It is tantalizing to conjecture what Tatum might have done in contemporary studios, for his whole discography is marred by inadequate recording – even these later solos are comparatively unrefined by the studio – but the CD versions are probably the best to date.

****** The Tatum Group Masterpieces Vol. 1**
Pablo 2405-424 *Tatum; Benny Carter (as); Louie Bellson (d).* 6/54.

*****(*) The Tatum Group Masterpieces Vol. 2**
Pablo 2405-425 *Tatum; Roy Eldridge (t); Larry Simmons (b); Alvin Stoller (d).* 3/55.

*****(*) The Tatum Group Masterpieces Vol. 3**
Pablo 2405-426 *Tatum; Lionel Hampton (vib); Buddy Rich (d).* 8/55.

*****(*) The Tatum Group Masterpieces Vol. 4**
Pablo 2405-427 *As above.* 8/55.

*****(*) The Tatum Group Masterpieces Vol. 5**
Pablo 2405-428 *Tatum; Harry 'Sweets' Edison (t); Lionel Hampton (vib); Barney Kessel (g); Red Callender (b); Buddy Rich (d).* 9/55.

****** The Tatum Group Masterpieces Vol. 6**
Pablo 2405-429 *Tatum; Red Callender (b); Jo Jones (d).* 1/56.

****** The Tatum Group Masterpieces Vol. 7**
Pablo 2405-430 *Tatum; Buddy DeFranco (cl); Red Callender (b); Bill Douglass (d).* 2/56.

****** The Tatum Group Masterpieces Vol. 8**
Pablo 2405-431 *Tatum; Ben Webster (ts); Red Callender (b); Bill Douglass (d).* 9/56.

****** The Complete Pablo Group Masterpieces**
Pablo 4401 6CD *As above eight discs.* 6/54–8/56.

Even after the awesome achievement of the solo sessions, Tatum wasn't finished yet. Norman Granz recorded him in eight different group-settings as well. The overall quality isn't so consistently intense, since Tatum's partners are sometimes either relatively incompatible or simply looking another way: the cheery Hampton and Rich, for instance, work well enough in their trio record, but it seems to lighten the music to an inappropriate degree. Yet some of this music is actually undervalued, particularly the trio session with Callender and Douglass, the group working in beautiful accord. The sextet date with Edison, Hampton and Kessel is comparatively slight, and the meeting with Eldridge, while it has moments of excitement, again sounds like two virtuosos of somewhat contrary methods in the same room.

The meetings with Carter, DeFranco and Webster, though, are unqualified masterpieces: the Carter session is worth having just for the astonishing 'Blues In C', and elsewhere Carter's aristocratic elegance chimes perfectly with Tatum's grand manner, their differing attitudes to jazz eloquence a rare match. With DeFranco, whose virtuosity is not so different from Tatum's own, the way the ingenuities of each man unfold can make one chuckle out loud: Tatum must have loved this session. The meeting with Webster might on the face of it have been unlikely, but this time the contrasts in their styles create a moving alliance, the heavy, emotional tenor floating poignantly over the surging piano below. As music to study, live with and simply enjoy, this is the most approachable of all of Tatum's series of recordings: he finds the company stimulating and manages to vary his approach on each occasion without surrendering anything of himself. All the music sounds good in this remastering.

****** 20th Century Piano Genius**

Verve 531763-2 2CD *Tatum (p solo).* 4/50–7/55.

***** Ultimate Art Tatum**

Verve 559877-2 *Tatum (p solo).* 4/50–7/55.

Even though these were privately recorded at the home of Tatum admirer Ray Heindorf, the sound is a lot better than on many of his regular sessions – a reminder of one of the most unfortunate aspects of jazz on record, that we cannot hear Tatum in hi-fi on a good piano. Out of 39 performances, 13 come from a 1950 occasion and the rest date from July 1955, late in the pianist's life, though he shows no lessening of his powers. The quite crisp fidelity lets one hear the precision and exactness of Tatum's runs, his mercurial fingerings and his almost offhand genius rather better than usual, and in, say, 'Yesterdays' he seems to be thinking, creating and moving on so quickly that one understands anew all the disbelieving praise that has helped to build his legend. For all its informality, this isn't a bad place to start hearing Tatum – though the Pablo discs remain the cornerstones. The *Ultimate* collection is well chosen by Hank Jones, but it's somewhat pointless, given that the two-disc set gives everything here plus plenty more.

Art Taylor (1929–94)

DRUMS

Taylor began working on the New York scene in 1950 and became one of the most prolific drummers of the hard-bop movement. He moved to Europe in 1963 and later began interviewing musicians, resulting in the book, Notes and Tones. He returned to New York in the 1980s and became a senior figure and group leader until his death.

***** Taylor's Wailers**

Original Jazz Classics OJC 094 *Taylor; Donald Byrd (t); Jackie McLean (as); John Coltrane, Charlie Rouse (ts); Ray Bryant, Red Garland (p); Wendell Marshall, Paul Chambers (b).* 2–3/57.

*****(*) Taylor's Tenors**

Original Jazz Classics OJC 1852 *Taylor; Charlie Rouse, Frank Foster (ts); Walter Davis (p); Sam Jones (b).* 6/59.

Art Taylor was a prolific visitor to the studios in the 1950s, drumming for Red Garland, John Coltrane, Miles Davis and many others on countless sessions, most of them for Prestige. The company gave him a few shots at a leadership date and, while the first is a well-cooked hard-bop session, it doesn't go much further than that. The album is actually compiled from two sessions, one with Coltrane, who works up his patented head of steam on 'C.T.A.', and another with Rouse, whose more circumspect passions are rather well caught in his solo on 'Batland'. 'Off Minor' and 'Well You Needn't' feature in Thelonious Monk's own arrangements, but the band sound no more committed here than elsewhere, with Byrd his usual blandly confident self. The leader's own playing is authoritative, although some of his mannerisms leave him a degree short of the single-minded drive of Art Blakey.

Taylor's Tenors is a cracker. Rouse didn't often have to play in two-tenor situations, but he acquits himself with honour against Foster, who moves like a particularly dangerous big cat through Taylor's flashing rhythms. 'Rhythm-A-Ning' and 'Little Chico' both go off like a rocket, 'Cape Millie' and 'Straight No Chaser' cool off, but the pots are on again for 'Dacor'. Forty minutes or so of this sort of thing is enough; and this is just right.

***** Mr A.T.**

Enja 7017-2 *Taylor; Abraham Burton (as); Willie Williams (ts); Marc Cary (p); Tyler Mitchell (b).* 12/91.

With the demise of Art Blakey, Taylor's Wailers looked set to be one of the principal training grounds for younger players in the manner of the Messengers, but sadly the leader himself has now passed on. *Mr A.T.* premieres the final edition of the band, with Williams and Burton striking sparks in the front line on worthwhile staples such as 'Gingerbread Boy' and 'Soul Eyes': both are big, burly players and, though Taylor still has an aristocrat's touch, he kicks the group along with real gusto, even if the music is formulaic.

Billy Taylor (born 1921)

PIANO

Born in North Carolina but moved to New York in the 1940s and worked in various contexts, eventually running a trio for most of the '50s. From the '60s he was more involved in teaching and generally broadcasting the good word about jazz, a role he has followed with peerless energy.

****(*) Cross-Section**

Original Jazz Classics OJC 1730 *Taylor; Earl May (b); Percy Brice (d); Charlie Smith, Jose Mangual, Ubaldo Nieto, Machito (perc).* 5/53–7/54.

***** The Billy Taylor Trio With Candido**

Original Jazz Classics OJC 015 *Taylor; Earl May (b); Percy Brice (d); Candido (perc).* 9/54.

****(*) Billy Taylor With Four Flutes**

Original Jazz Classics OJC 1830 *Taylor; Phil Bodner, Herbie Mann, Frank Wess, Jerome Richardson, Bill Slapin, Jerry Sanfino, Seldon Powell (f); Tom Williams (b); Albert 'Tootie' Heath, Dave Bailey (d); Chano Pozo (perc).* 7/59.

***** Custom Taylored**

Fresh Sound FSR-CD 205 *Taylor; Henry Grimes (b); Ray Mosca (d).* 3/60.

While he has become best known as one of the most experienced and respected forces in jazz education in America, Billy Taylor's talents as a piano player should be recognized more than they are. He played with everyone from Stuff Smith to Charlie Parker on 52nd Street in the 1940s, and having worked with Machito stood him in good enough stead to make these Latin-flavoured outings sound plausible. Taylor's affinities are essentially with bop, but his sensibility is akin to Teddy Wilson's: cultivated, gentlemanly, his improvisations take a leisurely route through his surroundings, alighting only on points which are germane to the setting, but managing to suggest a complete grasp of the material and task at hand. *Cross-Section* features eight tracks by his trio with May and Brice and four with Machito's rhythm section: daintily cast, the music is very engaging and, although the second session is transparently fixed to feature Candido – whose conga and bongo solos tend to bore when heard at length – the slow and almost luxuriant reading of 'Love For Sale' and the swinging 'Mambo Inn' suggest Taylor's careful preparation for the date. There is no dramatic sense of Latin-jazz fusion on either of these records, just a calm and logical pairing of one genre with another. *With Four Flutes* dates from five years later and counts as one of the sillier ideas of the day, given that the massed flutes on each track do little more than try to outwhistle one another. Even so, they get up a fair head of steam on 'St Thomas', and Taylor himself keeps urbane order.

The trio fly through the dozen originals on *Custom Taylored* with fine aplomb. Originally done for a radio transcription service, and curtailed in running time, the crispness and snap of these blues and riff pieces comes fizzing through. Lightweight, maybe, but one of Billy's most enjoyable sessions.

***** You Tempt Me**

Taylor-Made 1003 *Taylor; Victor Gaskin (b); Curtis Boyd (d).* 6/85.

***** White Nights And Jazz In Leningrad**

Taylor-Made 1001 *Taylor; Victor Gaskin (b); Bobby Thomas (d).* 88.

***** Solo**

Taylor-Made 1002 *Taylor (p solo).* 8/88.

***** Billy Taylor And The Jazzmobile All Stars**

Taylor-Made 1004 *Taylor; Jimmy Owens (t, flhn); Frank Wess (ss, ts, f); Ted Dunbar (g); Victor Gaskin (b); Bobby Thomas (d).* 4/89.

***** Dr T**

GRP 9692 *Taylor; Gerry Mulligan (bs); Victor Gaskin (b); Bobby Thomas (d).* 92.

***** It's A Matter Of Pride**

GRP 9753 *Taylor; Stanley Turrentine (ts); Christian McBride (b); Marvin 'Smitty' Smith (d); Ray Mantilla (perc); Grady Tate (v).* 93.

****(*) Homage**

GRP 9806 *Taylor; Chip Jackson (b); Steve Johns (d); Jim Saporito (perc); Turtle Island String Quartet.* 10/94.

Taylor's move into education has left his back-catalogue in some disrepair, and we must await the reappearance of such as the fine *Billy Taylor At The London House* from 1956. Establishing his own label in the 1980s has, though, made Taylor more available now than for many years. Of the four discs so far released, *White Nights* is an attempt to re-create the experience of a visit to Leningrad, and the earlier *You Tempt Me* is largely made up of a sequence of themes from the pianist's suite, 'Let Us Make A Joyful Noise', intended to evoke something of the spirit of Ellington's Sacred Concerts: although the most interesting piece is his unexpected reworking of 'Take The "A" Train' which reharmonizes Strayhorn's melody at a steady, compelling gait. Both sessions are good, but the *Solo* date is a better (or at least more comprehensive) display of Taylor's powers. There are perhaps two tunes too many in a long (72 minutes) CD, but Taylor's exact, finely wrought treatments make durable new statements out of the likes of 'Old Folks' and 'More Than You Know', as well as some of his own originals. The sextet session is distinguished by Taylor's uncompromising choice of material: there's nothing familiar, aside perhaps from Lee Morgan's 'Ceora', and the carefully positioned features for Owens and Wess are thoughtfully handled by the hornmen.

His first album for GRP shows no break with his recent tradition and continues Taylor's very even line. Mulligan sits in on three tracks and sounds in very happy form on his own 'Line For Lyons', while Taylor brushes up his bebop on the familiar tunes. Nothing to shake the earth – and probably the better for it. *It's A Matter Of Pride* sets him up with quite a team: Turrentine adds some preaching tenor to three tracks, Tate does his surprising vocal piece on two others, and McBride and Smith don't seem to be coasting. Very graciously done, though the excerpts from Taylor's suite in dedication to Luther King are a bit ponderous. *Homage* mixes rap, dance and string quartet contributions, and all the extra-curricular stuff tends to obscure Taylor himself, who remains bouncily creative in his swing-to-bop way. Not one of his best, but the catalogue's looking stronger now anyway. The GRPs are out of print in Europe, but American collectors should have more luck.

***** Music Keeps Us Young**

Arkadia 71601 *Taylor; Chip Jackson (b); Steve Johns (d).* 8/96.

Back to straight-ahead for this trio date, and Taylor gives no suspicion of boredom, even when he gets to his old favourite, 'I Wish I Knew How It Would Feel To Be Free'. A couple of tracks find him wandering to no special purpose, but when given a melody like 'Wouldn't It Be Loverly' he knows how to make it sing.

***** Ten Fingers – One Voice**

Arkadia 71602 *Taylor (p solo).* 8/96.

Billy celebrated his 75th by delivering a rare solo album. He's such a genial, big-hearted player that even when he's doing little more than ornament a melody, he's very listenable. There's not much to get excited about with 'Tea For Two' or 'Laura', but the original ballad, 'Can You Tell By Looking At Me?', could charm a statue.

Cecil Taylor (born 1930)

PIANO, VOICE

Taylor learned piano at six and went on to study at New York College and New England Conservatory. Worked in R&B and swing-styled small groups in the early '50s, then led his own band with Steve Lacy from 1956. Although he had few opportunities to work in either clubs or concerts, Taylor acquired a reputation as the most daring of artists, with his music leaving tonality and jazz rhythm and structure behind (meanwhile he was still frequently working as a dishwasher). Occasional records, trips to Europe and finally, from 1969, a steady group with more international bookings allowed him more exposure. Academia began to recognize him and he taught in colleges. In the late '70s and '80s his work was steadily more admired and acknowledged, and his poetry and writing also came to the fore. By century's end he had built up a much more substantial discography, numerous awards of various kinds, and the reputation properly due a grandmaster of the music. Throughout his career, both on and off record, there has been no suspicion of any compromises at any point on his most singular path.

****** Jazz Advance**

Blue Note 84462-2 *Taylor; Steve Lacy (ss); Buell Neidlinger (b); Dennis Charles (d). 9/56.*

Taylor's first record remains one of the most extraordinary debuts in jazz, and for 1956 it's an incredible effort. The pianist's 1950s music is even more radical than Ornette Coleman's, though it has seldom been recognized as such, and, while Coleman has acquired the plaudits, it is Taylor's achievement which now seems the most impressive and uncompromised. While there are still many nods to conventional post-bop form in this set, it already points to the freedoms in which the pianist would later immerse himself. The interpretation of 'Bemsha Swing' reveals an approach to time that makes Monk seem utterly straightforward; 'Charge 'Em' is a blues with an entirely fresh slant on the form; Ellington's 'Azure' is a searching tribute from one keyboard master to another. 'Sweet And Lovely' and 'You'd Be So Nice To Come Home To' are standards taken to the cleaners by the pianist, yet his elaborations on the melodies will fascinate any who respond to Monk's comparable treatment of the likes of 'There's Danger In Your Eyes, Cherie'. Lacy appears on two tracks and sounds amazingly comfortable for a musician who was playing Dixieland a few years earlier. And Neidlinger and Charles ensure that, contrary to what some may claim, Taylor's music swings. The CD reissue sounds very well.

*****(*) Looking Ahead!**

Original Jazz Classics OJC 452 *As above, except Earl Griffith (vib) replaces Lacy. 6/58.*

The most pensive of Taylor's early records may be the best place to start in appreciating his music. The A minor blues of 'Luyah! The Glorious Step', Griffith's charming 'African Violet' and the remarkable fantasy on 'Take The "A" Train', 'Excursion On A Wobbly Rail' mark the pianist's transitional explorations of jazz form, while 'Toll' embarks on a new journey towards his own territory. 'Wallering', named in tribute to Fats Waller, is a wonderfully constructed improvisation on 'two improvised figures that are simultaneous', as Taylor says in the sleeve-note. Griffith combines edginess with inborn lyricism, which works surprisingly well in context, and Neidlinger and Charles swing the music without inhibiting Taylor's search for rhythmical freedom.

*****(*) Love For Sale**

Blue Note 94107-2 *Taylor; Ted Curson (t); Bill Barron (ts); Buell Neidlinger (b); Denis Charles (d). 4/59.*

The three Cole Porter songs that open the record are starting-points for interpretations which are as radical as any standard had been subjected to at this point in jazz. Taylor keeps a toehold on melody or harmony, but no more than that and, as his phrase-lengths become ever more unpredictable, his shaping of the material transforms not just the songs but the way jazz after bop could improvise on received forms. Even Coleman's version of 'Embraceable You' is nothing like as dramatic as what Taylor does with 'Get Out Of Town'. The three originals that close the disc, with Curson and Barron joining the group, are in some ways less striking, since the horns remain tied to hard-bop language, even though Curson is clearly more responsive than the awkward Barron. Another fascinating stop in the patient transition from jazz orthodoxy to Taylor's mature music.

****** The World Of Cecil Taylor**

Candid CCD 79006 *As above, except Archie Shepp (ts) replaces Griffith. 10/60.*

*****(*) Air**

Candid CCD 79046 *As above. 1/61.*

****** Jumpin' Punkins**

Candid CCD 79013 *As above, except add Clark Terry (t), Roswell Rudd (tb), Steve Lacy (ss), Charles Davis (bs), Billy Higgins (d). 1/61.*

*****(*) New York City R&B**

Candid CCD 79017 *As above. 1/61.*

*****(*) Cell Walk For Celeste**

Candid CCD 79034 *As above. 1/61.*

The 1961 recordings for Candid – some of them under the nominal leadership of Neidlinger – secure a final balance between Taylor's insistent unshackling of familiar organization and his interest in standard material. *The World Of Cecil Taylor* introduced Shepp into the pianist's difficult universe, and it is a memorable encounter: Shepp's scrawling tenor battles through 'Air' with courageous determination, but it's clear that he has little real idea what's going on, and Taylor's own superbly eloquent improvisation makes the saxophonist seem like a beginner. It's even more apparent on the alternative takes of the piece (there were 18 attempts at it in the studio), many of which are on the Mosaic boxed set of this music (now out of print) and three of which are on *Air* (a collection of alternatives which includes two different takes of 'Number One' and one of 'Port Of Call'). But the same sessions also included the lovely and (for Taylor) surprisingly impressionistic 'Lazy Afternoon' and the blues fantasy of 'O.P.'. The larger band tackles only two tunes, both by Ellington, 'Things Ain't What They Used To Be' and 'Jumpin' Punkins', though they sound more like the Monk ensembles of *Monk's Music* than any Ellington band. Finally, there are the trio pieces: 'E.B.', which approximates a sonata and includes a superb piano improvisation, and the wholly improvised yet seemingly finished 'Cindy's Main Mood' are outstanding. The original records are *The World* and *New York City R&B*, but the various collections of out-takes are equally revealing.

*****(*) Mixed**

Impulse! 12702 *Taylor; Ted Curson (t); Roswell Rudd (tb); Jimmy Lyons (as); Archie Shepp (ts); Henry Grimes (b); Sunny Murray (d).* 10/61.

The three pieces here (the rest of the disc is given over to a Roswell Rudd session which Taylor is not involved in) were originally released under Gil Evans's name on the LP, *Into The Hot*. Still poised between some measure of hard-bop language and his own developments, the music has a somewhat jolted feel, as if three tracks and 22 minutes simply wasn't sufficient to project the wealth of ideas Taylor had going on; even though this is the first disc to feature such collaborators as Lyons and Murray, everything is still trying to fall into place. The outstanding track, though, is 'Mixed', the only one to feature Curson and Rudd as well as the rest of the group. With its cross-ply of riffing, intense variations in dynamics, richness of voicing and juggernaut momentum, this proposes a group music very different from what would come later. As with the John Carisi music which made up the rest of the original *Into The Hot* LP, it feels like an unexplored nook in the music.

♛ ** Nefertiti, The Beautiful One Has Come**

Revenant 202 2CD *Taylor; Jimmy Lyons (as); Sunny Murray (d).* 11/62.

(****) Trance

Black Lion BLCD 760220 *As above.* 11/62.

It's taken a long time for these recordings to appear on CD, and many newcomers to the music may wonder why they caused such fascination. The drawbacks are numerous: the original recording was never very effective; Taylor seems to be playing one of the poorest pianos Copenhagen had to offer; Murray's drums sound thin and rattly a lot of the time. Nevertheless, these sessions from the Café Montmartre should be accounted among the greatest live recordings in jazz. Taylor is still working his way out of jazz tradition and, with Murray at his heels, the playing has an irresistible momentum that creates its own kind of rocking swing, the pulse indefinable but palpable, the rhythm moving in waves from the drummer's kit. Lyons shapes his bebopper's vocabulary into gritty flurries of notes, a man caught in a squall and fighting his way through it and over it. He would become Taylor's most dedicated interpretative colleague, but here he is sharing in the discovery of a fierce new world. Melody has a part to play: the two versions of 'Lena' measure out a beleaguered lyricism, for instance. Group interaction is a matter, sometimes, of clinging tight and hanging on, but this was a trio that had already done a lot of work together, and in the multiple layers of the monumental 'D Trad, That's What' and 'Call' the musicians seem to touch on an inner calm to go with the outward intensity. The Revenant release runs to two discs and includes some previously unheard extra material (admittedly in even more terrible sound!). Black Lion's *Trance* covers a lot of the same ground but is incomplete: clearly the Revenant set is the one to go for, although it is not so widely distributed.

*****(*) Unit Structures**

Blue Note 84237-2 *Taylor; Gale Stevens Jr (t); Jimmy Lyons (as); Ken McIntyre (as, bcl, ob); Henry Grimes, Alan Silva (b); Andrew Cyrille (d).* 5/66.

Unit Structures is both as mathematically complex as its title suggests and as rich in colour and sound as the ensemble proposes, with the orchestrally varied sounds of the two bassists – Grimes a strong, elemental driving force, Silva tonally fugitive and mysterious – while Stevens and McIntyre add other hues and Lyons improvises with and against them. The title-piece is a highly refined but naturally flowing aggregation of various cells which create or propose directions for improvisation, combinations of players and tonal and rhythmical variations. Unfortunately, the equally fine *Conquistador* has been deleted. Blue Note's recording wasn't ideal for this music, but it's good enough.

*****(*) Akisakila**

Konnex KCD 5039 *Taylor; Jimmy Lyons (as); Andrew Cyrille (d).* 5/73.

*****(*) Akisakila Vol. 2**

Konnex KCD 5040 *As above.* 5/73.

Originally released on vinyl in Japan, this documents a titanic Tokyo concert by the trio. The group piece lasts for some 80 minutes (somewhat awkwardly spread over the two discs) and there are 30 minutes of solo piano. 'Bulu Akisakila Kutala' is all thunder from start to finish: Lyons is sometimes lost in the mix between piano and drums, and this gives his work an even more keening quality than usual. But he stands his ground. Taylor's solos reprise some of the ideas in the solo records above; but his solo work is, of course, all of a piece. Less than ideal sound.

*****(*) Dark To Themselves**

Enja 2084-2 *Taylor; Raphe Malik (t); Jimmy Lyons (as); David S Ware (ts); Marc Edwards (d).* 6/76.

Originally edited to fit LP length, this is a complete set from the 1976 Lubljana Festival. With no bassist, Taylor supplied all the bottom end himself, and the horns parade themselves over his figures. Edwards works hard, although he is scarcely a match for the drummers who've held down this role before and since. More than in many of Taylor's concert recordings, the music here suggests not darkness but incandescence – the flaring trumpet of Malik has a prominent role in the first 20 minutes, and the brilliance of Taylor's playing in this section is radiant.

****** Cecil Taylor Unit**

New World NW 201 *Taylor; Raphe Malik (t); Jimmy Lyons (as); Ramsey Ameen (vn); Sirone (b); Ronald Shannon Jackson (d).* 4/78.

****** 3 Phasis**

New World NW 203 *As above.* 4/78.

This was a superb group, full of contrast but bursting with the spirit of Taylor's music and exultant in its ability to make it work. The two New World albums are studio recordings, but they're performed with the intensity of a live set. These are colourful records: Ameen is a key member of the group, his fiddling vaguely reminiscent of Michael Sampson with Albert Ayler (a group which Jackson also played in), and there are moments when he aspires to a very close kinship with the pianist. But textures are only one part of this music. Malik and Lyons play bright or wounded or bitingly intense lines, and they play their part in a group chemistry which sometimes has the players contrasting with one another, sometimes combining to push the music forward, sometimes providing a textured background to Taylor's own sustained flights of invention. After the ferocity of his playing and organization in the late 1960s, there is more obvious light and shade here, the freedoms more generously stated, the underlying lyricism more apparent. If there's a slight problem, it's with Jackson, who – ingenious and masterful though he is – hasn't quite the same grasp of Taylor's designs as Sunny Murray or Andrew Cyrille.

****** Winged Serpent (Sliding Quadrants)**
Soul Note 121089 *Taylor; Enrico Rava, Tomasz Stankon (t); Jimmy Lyons (as); Frank Wright (ts); John Tchicai (ts, bcl); Gunter Hampel (bs, bcl); Karen Borca (bsn); William Parker (b); Rashid Bakr (d); Andre Martinez (d).* 10/84.

An important and insufficiently recognized record. Taylor's four compositions here begin from melodic cells: an eight-note motif starts 'Taht', a sort of riff (which at one point seems ready to turn into a locomotive piece, very much in an Ellingtonian tradition!) emerges in 'Womb Waters', but mainly these are exploding, brilliantly coloured ensemble improvisations where the horns (all very well caught by the recording) make superbly euphoric collective statements. Densely characterized though Taylor's music is, these musicians make their way into it with the highest courage, and the results are extraordinarily compelling.

****** For Olim**
Soul Note 121150 *Taylor (p solo).* 4/86.

By now, Taylor had built an impressive discography of solo recordings and there is nothing rote in this further addition to it. 'Olim' is the only long piece at some 18 minutes in duration; the others are sometimes only a couple of minutes long, isolating an idea, delivering it up, and then closing it down. What emerges most clearly from such a session is the refinement of his touch, sometimes obscured by the messier live mixes he's had to contend with, the absolute integration of favourite devices – clusters, call-and-response – into a peerless mastery of the techniques available to the pianist, and his communicative abilities: nothing here does anything but speak directly to an attentive listener.

***** Live In Bologna**
Leo LR 100 *Taylor; Carlos Ward (as, f); Leroy Jenkins (vn); William Parker (b); Thurman Barker (d, mar).* 11/87.

***** Live In Vienna**
Leo LR 174 *As above.* 11/87.

(***) Chinampas
Leo LR 153 *Taylor (speech).* 11/87.

Carlos Ward is hardly the man one thinks of when citing Taylor's saxophonists, and he is scarcely a match for Jimmy Lyons; but his more directly responsive and familiar lines make an agreeable change in their way, and Jenkins is a formidable presence on both records, adding rustic colours and primeval textures to the mix, which also includes marimba and bell sounds from Barker. Frankly, though, these concert sets haven't worn well, and we must admit that there are many better examples of Taylor's work in this entry.

Chinampas may appeal only to hardcore Taylor devotees, since there is no piano, simply the man reading some of his poetry. It's a fascinating adjunct to a monumental body of work; but, inevitably, it's of limited appeal.

****** Erzulie Maketh Scent**
FMP CD 18 *Taylor (p solo).* 7/88.

****** Pleistozaen Mit Wasser**
FMP CD 16 *Taylor; Derek Bailey (g).* 7/88.

****** Leaf Palm Hand**
FMP CD 6 *Taylor; Tony Oxley (d).* 7/88.

****** Spots, Circles And Fantasy**
FMP CD 5 *Taylor; Han Bennink (perc, etc.).* 7/88.

****** Regalia**
FMP CD 3 *Taylor; Paul Lovens (perc).* 7/88.

****** Remembrance**
FMP CD 4 *Taylor; Louis Moholo (d).* 7/88.

****** The Hearth**
FMP CD 11 *Taylor; Evan Parker (ss, ts); Tristan Honsinger (clo).* 7/88.

****** Riobec**
FMP CD 2 *Taylor; Gunter Sommer (d).* 7/88.

***** Legba Crossing**
FMP CD 0 *Heinz-Erich Godecke (tb); Ove Volquartz (ss, ts, bcl); Joachim Gies (as); Brigitte Vinkeloe (as, ss, f); Daniel Werts (ob); Sabine Kopf (f); Harald Kimmig (vn); Paul Plimley (p); Alexander Frangenheim, Uwe Martin, George Wolf (b); Lukas Lindenmaier, Peeter Uuskyla, Trudy Morse (v).* 7/88.

****** Alms / Tiergarten (Spree)**
FMP CD 8/9. *Taylor; Enrico Rava (t, flhn); Tomasz Stankon (t); Peter Van Bergen (ts); Peter Brötzmann (as, ts); Hans Koch (ss, ts, bcl); Evan Parker (ss, ts); Louis Sclavis (ss, cl, bcl); Hannes Bauer, Wolter Wierbos, Christian Radovan (tb); Martin Mayes (frhn); Gunter Hampel (vib); Tristan Honsinger (clo); Peter Kowald, William Parker (b); Han Bennink (d).* 7/88.

This unprecedented set of records still seems like a towering achievement, and it may stand as the apex of Taylor's latter-day work, creating resonances and establishing links and influences which may reverberate through European free playing for years to come. A document of his visit to a celebratory festival of his music in Berlin, it matches him with several of the finest European improvisers in a series of meetings that had, at that time, relatively few precedents. Although groupings such as Derek Bailey's Company had allowed a certain amount of Euro-American co-operation among improvisers, it was rare indeed for a player of Taylor's magnitude to be involved in such a celebration. An unparalleled inspiration to all these players, the fact of his presence seems to make most of them play above themselves.

Originally issued as a single boxed set, and now available as individual records, no collection should be without at least some of these, as examples of the expressive power and liberating energy which this central figure has introduced into jazz and twentieth-century music in general. We would single out the encounters with Bailey, Parker/Honsinger, Oxley, Moholo and

Bennink as particularly brilliant examples of Taylor's adaptive capabilities and his partners' own contributions, but every one of these records is both thought-provoking and individually inspiring to any listener prepared to give themselves over to Taylor's music.

Only the Workshop record, *Legba Crossing*, which Taylor merely directs, is in any way less than essential, although even here it is absorbing to follow how Taylor's methodology is brought to bear on the situation. The climactic concert with the full orchestra, *Alms/Tiergarten*, is a monumental event, the colossal sonic impact tempered by Taylor's own unflinching, instinctual control and a grasp of dynamics and dramatic possibility which is breathtaking. It is also, in the circumstances, deeply moving. So often in this area of jazz, above all others, the rewards for the players are minimal beyond the satisfaction in the music itself. The force of Taylor's presence in this situation has a legitimizing power which will remain an emotional matter to both the musicians and the hardy followers of this neck of the jazz woods, for ever off the familiar, accepted paths. As a collective achievement this stands as one of the major jazz recording projects and, were the original boxed set still available (it is now a prized collectors' item in its original form), we would have no hesitation in awarding it a crown.

**** In East Berlin

FMP CD 13/14 2CD *Taylor; Gunter Sommer (perc).* 6/88.

**** Looking (Berlin Version)

FMP CD 28 *Taylor (p solo).* 11/89.

***(*) Looking (Berlin Version)

Corona FMP CD 31 *Taylor; Harald Kimmig (vn); Muneer Abdul Fataah (clo); William Parker (b); Tony Oxley (d).* 11/89.

**** Looking (The Feel Trio)

FMP CD 35 *Taylor; William Parker (b); Tony Oxley (d).* 11/89.

The duets with Sommer were recorded a month prior to the Berlin sessions: thunder and lightning, light and shade, and brimful of music, even across two long CDs. The three editions of *Looking* take a *Rashomon*-style look at the same piece of music, one solo (dense, heavily contoured, lots of pedal-sustain), one trio (magnificent interplay with Parker and Oxley, who became a frequent Taylor confrère), and one with the somewhat more awkward string stylings of Kimmig and Fataah, the latter meshing unconvincingly with Parker. The incredible richness of event continues, with barely a pause, in what was a remarkable period for the man.

**** Celebrated Blazons

FMP CD 58 *Taylor; William Parker (b); Tony Oxley (d).* 6/90.

Does Taylor swing? The old litmus test comes to mind, since Taylor's ever-widening horizons sound more in touch and touched by jazz tradition than ever. Oxley's drumming is a more European flavour than anything Taylor's other regular drummers have created, yet it only serves to emphasize the huge rhythmic resources of the leader's own playing. Where Cyrille's magnificent breakers would sometimes obscure the keyboard, Oxley's playing – a unique blend of lumpen momentum and detailed percussive colour – reveals more of it. Parker, too, is coming into his own, deflecting off what the others do while speaking his own piece. Nearly an hour of music, and it swings.

**** Double Holy House

FMP CD 55 *Taylor (p, v, perc).* 9/90.

Taylor's quietest, most beguiling record ever is a profound meditation on some of the well-springs of what he does. It starts with a beautiful prelude at the piano before an extended recitation of poetry, accompanied by tiny splashes of percussion, and eventually a return to the piano – although the voice and percussion were actually recorded later, the act seems spontaneously whole. Eventually the accustomed intensity of Taylor in full flow breaks through and with his accompanying cries the music searches through vocal and non-vocal tradition with a master's aptitude. Outstanding, again.

**** Olu Iwa

Soul Note 121139-2 *Taylor; Earl McIntyre (tb); Peter Brötzmann (ts, targato); Frank Wright (ts); Thurman Barker (mar, perc); William Parker (b); Steve McCall (d).* 4/86.

On the shelf for eight years before release, and with Wright and McCall both gone in the interim, this already has the feel of history about it. Some of the music, too, has one reflecting on Taylor's own history: the presence of Barker's marimba harks back to Earl Griffith on the ancient *Looking Ahead!*, and the small group with horns reminds one of *Unit Structures*. But the two sprawling pieces here (the first is almost 50 minutes; the second, where the horns depart, is nearly 30) have moved far on from those days. Alternately hymnal, purgatorial, intensely concentrated and wildly abandoned, the first theme is a carefully organized yet unfettered piece that again disproves Taylor's isolation (it's firmly within free-jazz traditions, yet sounds like something no one else could have delivered). The second, despite the absence of the towering Brötzmann, superb in the first half, is if anything even more fervent, with the quartet – a one-time appearance for this band on record – playing at full stretch. Another great one.

*** Iwontunwonsi – Live At Sweet Basil

Sound Hills SSCD-8065 *Taylor (p solo).* 2/86.

Another one from the archives, and perhaps less than essential, given that Taylor's 1980s music is relatively widespread and in circulation. Basically a piano solo of some 45 minutes, this unspools some of the master's favourite methods into a typically Byzantine exploration of the keyboard. In the heavy company of some of the above discs, though, this one's a middleweight.

***(*) Melancholy

FMP CD 104 *Taylor; Tobias Netta (t); Jorg Huke, Thomas Wiederman (tb); Wolfgang Fuchs (sno, bcl); Harri Sjöström (ss); Volker Schott (as); Evan Parker (ts, ss); Thomas Klemm (ts); Barry Guy (b); Tony Oxley (d).* 9/90.

A performance by the 'Workshop Ensemble', and to that extent perhaps only a rough cut of the kind of big-scale group music which Taylor might achieve, given limitless time and resources. But it is still enough to have other composers and arrangers slack-jawed, with three pieces that put an evolving structure through complex changes and developments. If the middle section, 'Sphere No. 2', seems like a bonding of improvisers, then 'Sphere No. 3' expands to a glorious reconciliation of free solos and composed and implicit structures. Besides Taylor himself, superb contributions from Guy, Parker and Klemm – but it's as a group performance that this works best.

****** The Tree Of Life**
FMP CD 98 *Taylor (p solo). 3/91.*

A gorgeously lyrical and handsomely realized recital, decently recorded, and one of Taylor's most sheerly enjoyable records. For readers who aren't prepared to entertain the pianist on the basis of the sheer amount of work involved – and it's a viewpoint which even we have some sympathy with – this might even be the record to start with. It's no great departure for the man, 70 minutes or so of often rapt and sometimes even quizzical playing, and it tends towards the distilled feel of much of his latter-day music: having got much of the thunder behind him, or having the means to explore it via his various larger groupings, by himself he seems more content to sit and muse on aspects of a voluminous art. And this is the result.

***** Always A Pleasure**
FMP CD 69 *Taylor; Longineau Parsons (t); Harri Sjöström (ss); Charles Gayle (ts); Tristan Honsinger (clo); Sirone (b); Rashid Bakr (d). 4/93.*

As always, there are marvellous moments. But we would count this among Taylor's less successful group concerts (Berlin, again, in 1993). While Honsinger, Sirone, Bakr and – surprisingly – Parsons seem right in tune, Sjöström isn't, and Gayle is frankly completely in the wrong world for this occasion. He simply can't get through the way he does on his own records, and he's reduced to what seems like ranting from the sidelines. The closing segment lets the group find a sort of peaceful reconciliation with itself, and it's nearly worth sorting through some of the prior confusion to get to the coda.

*****(*) Qu'a: Live At The Iridium Vol. 1**
Cadence CJR 1092 *Taylor; Harri Sjöström (ss); Dominic Duval (b); Jackson Krall(d). 3/98.*

***** Qu'a Yuba: Live At The Iridium Vol. 2**
Cadence CJR 1098 *As above. 3/98.*

The instrumentation for these New York club sets goes back to Taylor's first group with Steve Lacy. Sjöström at times seems to be thinking about that, some of his remarks having a playful irony that suggests his illustrious forebear, but in other respects the music is inevitably a long, long way distant from such ancient history. The saxophonist does better here than he did on the earlier, FMP session without finally making a convincing case for his presence. Duval isn't particularly well placed in the mix, and his *arco* playing has an unpleasant buzz which suggests a tinny bass amplifier. Krall, though, is inventive and often delicately propulsive: his brushwork halfway through the first set is impeccable. Taylor's intensity seems as trenchant as ever. Whatever the shortcomings of the two discs in either musical or recording terms, his own contributions remain worthy of the listener's best attention.

John Taylor (born 1942)

PIANO

A Mancunian, Taylor arrived in London in 1964 and was soon in the thick of the local scene. Led his own groups in the late '60s and '70s and co-formed Azimuth in 1977. An internationalist as a performer, much admired overseas, his most notable partnerships have been with vocalist Norma Winstone and trumpeter Kenny Wheeler.

*****(*) Pause, And Think Again**
FMR CD 24 *Taylor; Kenny Wheeler (t); Chris Pyne (tb); Stan Sulzmann (as); John Surman (ss); Chris Laurence (b); Tony Levin (d); Norma Winstone (v). 71.*

***** Ambleside Days**
Ah Um 013 *Taylor; John Surman (ss, bs, bcl, syn).*

***** Blue Glass**
Jazz House JHCD 020 *Taylor; Mick Hutton (b); Steve Arguëlles (d). 6/91.*

Much admired, Taylor is under-recorded as a leader, though one should also weigh his work with Azimuth in the balance. He started out as an accompanist, established and sustained a reputation with his first wife, Norma Winstone, and is still routinely described as if his gifts are best suited to a supportive role. In fact, Taylor is a riveting solo performer and an exceptional writer. Typically, he likes to spin out long lines of melody, braced by a firm but flexible rhythmic base. He sounds effortlessly fluent but never less than thoughtful. It's ironic that the most immediately arresting of these records was made a quarter of a century ago. Anyone familiar with Azimuth will hear powerful echoes throughout *Pause, And Think Again*, particularly when Winstone and Wheeler occupy the foreground. Even more impressive than the soloing, though, are the tightly marshalled but intriguingly open-ended ensembles, especially on the two title-pieces, which sandwich a thing called 'White Magic'.

The record with Surman belongs every bit as much to the saxophonist. The two men share an interest in pastoral ideas, and it is fascinating to listen to them both steer as close as could be to mere prettiness before pulling suddenly away with something arresting and unexpected but also entirely appropriate. Much the same applies to the live set from Ronnie Scott's jazz club. Like 'White Magic', 'Blue Glass' is a good example of Taylor's gifts as a sound-painter, but it is his treatment of standards – 'Spring Is Here', 'How Deep Is The Ocean' – that catches the attention first time around. There is also a new version of 'Clapperclowe' from *Ambleside Days*, cast very differently for the trio format.

Mark Taylor (born 1969)

TENOR, ALTO AND SOPRANO SAXOPHONES, BASS CLARINET

Australian post-bop saxophonist, seemingly at home with any instrument in the family.

***** Shakedown**

Rufus RF034 *Taylor; Scott Tinkler (t); Alister Spence (p); Jeremy Sawkins (g); Adam Armstrong (b); Toby Hall (d).* 5–6/97.

A resourceful set that ends up just the right side of slickness. Taylor's an authoritative presence on his four horns and, in what's basically a set that runs along hard-bop lines, the players come up with some nicely subversive touches: Spence has a habit of slipping head-turning phrases into his solos, Sawkins takes steady, stinging improvisations on his four appearances. It could use a genuine surprise here and there, but we can't fault the gutsiness of the band.

Martin Taylor (born 1956)

GUITAR

Taylor was closely associated with Stéphane Grappelli in his pomp and has shown an instinctive feel for the Hot Club de France idiom while simultaneously carving out a richly expressive solo sound that draws on every aspect of the jazz guitar tradition, up to (but probably not including) the electric fusion of the 1970s. He veers between unaccompanied performance and a more spacious group sound.

****(*) Taylor Made**

Wave CD 17 *Taylor; Peter Ind (b); John Richardson (d).* 79.

***** Triple Libra**

Wave CD 24 *Taylor; Peter Ind (b).* 81.

Awesomely but unassumingly gifted, Taylor is the kind of artist who gives the music a good name. In straightforward technical terms, he is probably a match for any guitarist of today. His lines seem so cleanly articulated that there is no distance between thought and execution. Perhaps too much so. These aren't very exciting records; the studio sound is as blemish-free as the playing, and one never quite gets that little flicker of danger that would lift them up a notch. The debut album confirms all of that. Precocious, able, even facile, but not yet with a story to tell. Taylor tackles 'On Green Dolphin Street' with an assurance that is uncanny and brings a crisp precision to George Benson's 'My Latin Brother', a more contemporary sound. Taylor only really begins to sound like himself on the follow-up *Triple Libra*, where he chips in with 'Green Eyes', an early sign of compositional gifts, along with a superb version of Chick Corea's 'Windows'. Long out of circulation, these records are a welcome addition to the catalogue, though – relative to what follows – they should be considered a priority only for confirmed Taylor fans.

***** Don't Fret**

Linn AKD 014 *Taylor; David Newton (p); Dave Green (b); Allan Ganley (d).* 9/90.

***** Change Of Heart**

Linn AKD 016 *Taylor; David Newton (p); Brian Shiels (b); John Rae (d).* 6/91.

Change Of Heart includes a blues, 'You Don't Know Me', that Taylor takes to the cleaners, but the anodyne brilliance of the playing takes some of the pith out of the playing, and certainly undermines the conviction of the rock-orientated 'Angel's Camp'. The earlier record is more solidly in the jazz camp, thanks mostly to Ganley's civil adaptation of Art Blakey's beat; but the more four-square Rae does no harm to the second session. Taylor was advancing by leaps and bounds all through the '80s and the contrast between these and the Wave sessions above is breathtaking. Technically there isn't much in it. Expressively, he's already on a different plane.

***** Artistry**

Linn AKD 020 *Taylor (g solo).* 5/92.

Recorded with superb polish and clarity, this solo recital is almost too good to be true. The title is exactly right, for one feels that the main aim isn't so much musical as technical, a chance to show off untarnishable gifts rather than to make anything more personal of these songs. Taylor is an endlessly expressive player in a live context, but a chill descends whenever he enters a studio. Not all the tunes are ballads, yet they all seem to come out that way: sensitive, shimmering and rhythmically so even that the notes fold into one another with little apparent variation. Other guitarists will love and treasure it. We've found it hard to sustain interest.

***** The Linn Box**

Linn AKD 115 *Taylor; as for Don't Fret, Change Of Heart, Artistry.*

A nicely repackaged three-volume set that brings together Martin's first three records for Linn. There's no new material on offer, so Taylor collectors are unlikely to be attracted, but newcomers will find the box an invaluable primer.

***** Reunion**

Linn AKD 022 *Taylor; Stéphane Grappelli (vn).* 92.

Or: *Old Art and Young Hector*. This fascinating creative friendship has been closely documented in a couple of rather moving television programmes. It's difficult to tell which moves most, the youthful exuberance of an old fiddle-player who worked with Django and has long passed his Biblical span, or the improbably coiffed young man who seems to understand and appreciate the older language almost as well as Grappelli himself. The best of this is wonderful, but it's a little bit unrelieved unless you buy wholeheartedly into the idiom, Grappelli is as flagrantly inventive as ever; it's impossible to stop and wonder if what he just did was legitimate or even possible, because he's done another half-dozen unexpected things in the meantime. Taylor is fleet-fingered and wise, and on tunes like 'It's Only A Paper Moon' and 'Hotel Splendid' demonstrates how fast his own harmonic intelligence operates.

****** Spirit Of Django**

Linn AKD 030 *Taylor; Dave O'Higgins (ts, ss); John Goldie (g); Jack Emblow (acc); Alec Dankworth (b, cabassa); James Taylor (perc).* 6–8/94.

Given the association with Grappelli, the naming of this group was no surprise, and nor was much of the repertoire. Taylor had decided to give up unaccompanied performance for a while and concentrate on a group sound. It must have been difficult to sustain the level of highly exposed creativity he was bringing to solo concerts. What the group allows him to do is work within a much bigger harmonic and timbral framework, allow his guitar to thread together ideas rather than sustain them all. In Dave

O'Higgins (one of the best of the younger generation of British saxophonists) and the seasoned Jack Emblow, he has partners who are absolutely in sympathy with what he is doing. In Dankworth, he has a bass player who can sustain the tempo in a drummerless group (son James has only a bit part at this stage) but who can also lend himself to the other parameters of the music as well. On 'Night And Day' and 'Honeysuckle Rose', he is creating as much of the musical movement as anyone else. Taylor intended the record to be a tribute to his own father, as well as to the artistic parent namechecked in the title. Playing acoustically and in a setting that juxtaposes Django material ('Nuages', 'Minor Swing', 'Swing 42') against originals and Taylor's own celebrated reworking of Robert Parker's 'Johnny And Mary' theme, he sounds very different from the solo artist, less busy and layered, but instantly identifiable as himself. A masterly record, and probably his best to date.

*****(*) Portraits**

Linn AKD 048 *Taylor; Chet Atkins (g).* 7–12/95.

Notwithstanding Taylor's apparent desire to leave this kind of thing aside for a while, this is an excellent record, and the chance to play with another of the great legends of modern music must have been irresistible. Atkins went around afterwards saying what a privilege it had been for him to play with Martin, when everyone might have supposed the gratitude flowed the other way. They're first heard together on 'Sweet Lorraine' and one can hear at once where some of Taylor's clean-picked lines come from – not from Django after all. He tries a couple of interesting overdubs, but as before it is the solo tracks where the real action lies. A version of Earl Klugh's 'Kiko' and a closing version of Bill Evans's lovely 'Very Early' are the real gems.

*****(*) Years Apart**

Linn AKD 058 *Taylor; Gerard Presencer (flhn); Dave O'Higgins (sax); John Goldie (g); Stéphane Grappelli (vn); Jack Emblow (acc); Terry Gregory (b); James Taylor (perc); Claire Martin (v).* 96.

The second Spirit of Django album lacks the impact of the first, but it's still a highly appealing and beautifully crafted performance. The basic group plays wonderfully well, but one wonders if, Grappelli aside, the guest performances from Presencer and Martin (and a further cameo from son James) don't dilute the whole rather than enhance it. 'Manoir de mes rêves' is worth waiting for, sealing a habit of finishing albums with the strongest number. The title-piece is wonderful, too, with one of Taylor's most nakedly expressive lines.

***** Two's Company**

Linn AKD 081 *Taylor; duets with Bob Barnard, Ian Date, George Golla, James Morrison, Johnny Nicol, Jim Pennell, Suzanne Wyllie, Peter Zog.* 97.

To all intents and purposes another solo album. The motley assortment of guests don't add very much to what Martin himself is doing. If the album signals anything – and, with no fewer than 17 tracks, it signals it with great insistence – it is that Taylor may be moving away from swing and closer to a more mainstream jazz style, at least for this project. That's suggested in 'Royal Garden Blues' as much as in the following 'You Stepped Out Of A Dream' and 'Willow Weep For Me'. As ever, the closing track is the killer, a glorious rendition of 'My Foolish Heart'.

****** Gold**

Linn AKD 064 *Taylor; as for the above.* 90–97.

We're not usually enthusiastic about 'best of' compilations, but this magnificently remastered career retrospective on special, gold-coated pressings offers a good selection of tunes (14 of them, with all the obvious ones included) and pristine, shiny sound. Kicking off with 'Johnny And Mary' was inevitable, given its prominence as an advertising theme, and Linn have wisely gone for a pretty straightforward sample thereafter, including 'Minor Swing', 'Paper Moon', 'Nuages' and 'I Got Rhythm.' A perfect starter for anyone who hasn't any of Taylor's previous albums. We should note that up to *Two's Company* Linn have also issued high-quality cassettes of all the albums, and that there is a memorial disc of Martin's association with the late Stéphane Grappelli; that we have covered under the violinist's entry.

***** Gypsy**

Linn AKD 090 *Taylor; Dave O'Higgins (sax); Jack Emblow (acc); John Goldie, Terry Gregory (g); James Taylor (perc).* 96–97.

The most recent disc from Spirit of Django has a steady-as-she-goes feel. The group is now well enough established to have struck off in some new directions, but *Gypsy*, which was recorded on tour in England with three studio tracks added, has a faintly recycled quality. Taylor is as good as always, and these cuts have presumably been selected to show him at his best. However, the group doesn't always gel and the two subsidiary guitarists go about their business with a slightly grim determination, as if they were being paid by the chord.

***** Kiss And Tell**

Columbia 495387 2 *Taylor; Randy Brecker (flhn); Jay Ashby (tb, v); Kirk Whalum (ss, ts); George Garzone (ts); Matt Rollings (p, org); Brian Siewert (ky); Pat Bergeson (g); John Catchings (vn); Kristin Wilkinson (vla); David Davidson (clo); Eddie Gomez, Chris Kent (b); Al Foster (d); Eric Darken (perc).* 99.

Major-label interest was long overdue, but Taylor wastes no time in flash grandstanding and instead delivers a musical set that covers just about every aspect of his playing approach. His solo style is represented on 'Mona Lisa', a performance that would have made his dad proud. There are ancestral influences, too, on the guitar/piano duet, 'Ginger', an old tune written for his great-grandfather, the boxer Ginger Stewart, and on 'The Nearness Of You', a duet with tenor saxophonist Kirk Whalum, who played it with the dying Arnett Cobb. And there is a hint of godparental influence on 'Sunstep', which revives memories of the association with Grappelli.

As often when an established artist makes the jump to major league status, the album feels like an eclectic showcase, with every track worthy of expansion into a full session. Rumour suggests that Al Foster was second-call drummer for the group tracks, which is a slightly frightening thought. The decision to add strings was an odd one; it works on 'The Odd Couple', a theme which Taylor has used before, but falls flat on 'The Nearness of You'. Including the movie theme obviously sparked off a line of thought, because Taylor also includes the signature-tune of

Hawaii Five-O, recorded with the other band. The real delight of the album, though, and his wittiest cover since 'Johnny And Mary', is a reading of Maria Muldaur's 'Midnight At The Oasis', prefaced by a minute-long solo reading of 'What A Friend We Have In Jesus'. Next time, it would be good to hear Taylor with a settled band and less of the special pleading that big labels bring to albums by Brits and Europeans who can't be assumed to make a dent on the American market.

John Tchicai (born 1936)

ALTO, SOPRANO AND TENOR SAXOPHONES, FLUTES, BASS CLARINET

It is often assumed that Tchicai is African-American, an impression cemented by his part in John Coltrane's masterpiece of new jazz, Ascension, but the saxophonist is half-Danish, half-Congolese. He started out on violin and, after switching to saxophone, was noticed by Archie Shepp and others on the European festival circuit. Originally rather dry and papery in tone, Tchicai has become more emotionally nuanced over the years and nowadays recalls no one more than Sidney Bechet.

***** The Real Tchicai**

Steeplechase SCCD 31075 *Tchicai; Pierre Dørge (g); Niels-Henning Orsted Pedersen (b).* 3/77.

***** Ball At Louisiana**

Steeplechase SCCD 31174 *Tchicai; Pierre Dørge (g).* 11/81.

***** Timo's Message**

Black Saint 120094 *Tchicai; Thomas Dürst, Christian Kuntner (b); Timo Fleig (d, perc).* 2/84.

***** Satisfaction**

Enja 7033 *Tchicai; Vitold Rek (b).* 3/91.

****** Grandpa's Spells**

Storyville STCD 4182 *Tchicai; Misha Mengelberg (p); Margriet Nabrier (syn); Peter Danstrup (b); Gilbert Matthews (d).* 3/92.

Tchicai moved to the United States in the early 1960s and joined Archie Shepp and Bill Dixon in the New York Contemporary Five; but he went on to lead a more significant, if less well-known, group with percussionist Milford Graves and trombonist Roswell Rudd, known as the New York Art Quartet. In the following year he played alongside fellow altoist Marion Brown (whom he somewhat resembles in approach) on John Coltrane's epic *Ascension*, before returning to Europe to work on a number of individual projects.

Tchicai has now been a presence in the European avant-garde for more than a quarter of a century, although his few records and occasional appearances have marginalized him more than somewhat. Though most obviously influenced by Ornette Coleman and, to a lesser extent, Eric Dolphy, Tchicai's very individual tonality has more often been likened to that of Lee Konitz, and his performing style has followed a similar trajectory, turning away from a rather cool and dry approach towards a rootsier and more forceful delivery. The two Steeplechases are rather dry affairs in which the moments of beauty feel as forced as hothouse blooms. Dørge and NHOP try to eke some energy out of the saxophonist, but he often seems curiously ill at ease. That said, there are some striking moments, especially on some of the ballads on the later disc, on which NHOP is absent.

The 1980s saw Tchicai shift away from alto saxophone. His tenor and soprano work was initially competent but rather anonymous, and it really came into its own only during the following decade, as on the excellent *Grandpa's Spells*. For the most part, the 1970s had been a time of consolidation, of teaching and of research into Eastern musics, but he returned to performance with a group called Strange Brothers. Among the more recent material, there is a fine 'Stella By Starlight' on *Timo's Message*, but again the weight of interest falls largely on Tchicai's now quite varied compositional style, which included calypso and rock elements. The duos on *Satisfaction* are fascinating but unvaried, and it's not clear why Tchicai, a consummate organizer and arranger, should prefer to record in this very exposing format.

Grandpa's Spells foreshadows Tchicai's growing interest in electronics. The basic quartet is augmented with intelligently deployed sequences that give pieces like 'Community Bells' a rich, almost orchestral texture. There are two old-fashioned improvisations from the group, with Mengelberg well to the fore, a hint of the 'fusion' direction on 'Heksehyl', some folky stuff using traditional melodies ('Fran Engeland Till Skottland'), a touch of Carl Nielsen, and two Jelly Roll Morton compositions.

***** Love Notes From The Madhouse**

8thhb 80001 *Tchicai; Aaron Getsug (bs, v); Margriet Naber-Tchicai (ky, v); Jeff Parker (g, v); Fred Hopkins (b); Benita Haastrup (d, perc, v); Yusef Komunyakaa (v).* 9/97.

Jazz and poetry have been long-standing bedfellows, but this remarkable collaboration between Tchicai and poet Yusef Komunyakaa redefines the relationship. With the exception of Billy Strayhorn's 'Bloodcount', everything is conceived by the players. 'Dolphy's Aviary' is a remarkable musical and verbal history of recent jazz, and the terse, allusive lyrics are wonderfully complementary to the music. Not suited to every taste, but worth exploring.

Jack Teagarden (1905–64)

TROMBONE, VOCAL

A Texan, Teagarden took the trombone to new levels, with his impeccable technique, fluency and gorgeous sound, allied to a feel for blues playing which eluded many of his white contemporaries. He was also a fine, idiosyncratic singer. He was with Ben Pollack for five years from 1928, with Paul Whiteman in the '30s, and finally led his own swing orchestra, though it left him broke in the end. He joined the Louis Armstrong All Stars in 1946, stayed till 1951, then led small groups of his own and toured for the rest of his life. He died in New Orleans, worn out by drink.

***** I Gotta Right To Sing The Blues**

ASV AJA 5059 *Teagarden; Leonard Davis, Red Nichols, Ray Lodwig, Manny Klein, Charlie Teagarden, Ruby Weinstein, Sterling Bose, Dave Klein, Harry Goldfield, Nat Natoli, Frank Guarente, Leo McConville, Charlie Spivak (t); Jack Fulton, Glenn Miller, Ralph Copsey, Bill Rank (tb); Benny Goodman (cl); Mezz Mezzrow, Arthur Rollini, Charles Strickfadden, Benny Bonaccio, John Cordaro, Chester Hazlett, Jimmy Dorsey, Art Karle, Eddie

Miller, Matty Matlock, Joe Catalyne, Pee Wee Russell, Max Farley, Happy Caldwell, Arnold Brilhart, Bernie Day, Sid Stoneburn, Babe Russin, Larry Binyon, Gil Rodin, Irving Friedman, Adrian Rollini, Min Leibrook (reeds); Red McKenzie (kz, v); Fats Waller (p, v); Joe Sullivan, Jack Russin, Lennie Hayton, Arthur Schutt, Gil Bowers, Joe Moresco, Roy Bargy, Vincent Pirro, Howard Smith (p); Joe Venuti, Matty Malneck, Mischa Russell, Harry Struble, Walt Edelstein, Alex Beller, Ray Cohen (vn); Carl Kress, Jack Bland, Nappy Lamare, Eddie Lang, Dick McDonough, Perry Botkin, Mike Pingitore, George Van Eps (g); Treg Brown (bj, v); Eddie Condon (bj); Artie Bernstein, Art Miller, Jerry Johnson, Harry Goodman, Al Morgan (b); Norman McPherson (tba); Ray Bauduc, George Stafford, Herb Quigley, Stan King, Gene Krupa, Josh Billings, Larry Gomar (d). 2/29–10/34.

Teagarden's star is somehow in decline, since all his greatest work predates the LP era and at this distance it's difficult to hear how completely he changed the role of the trombone. In Tea's hands, this awkward barnyard instrument became majestic, sonorous and handsome. By the time he began recording in 1926 he was already a mature and easeful player whose feel for blues and nonchalant rhythmic drive made him stand out on the dance-band records he was making.

This compilation features 12 different bands and 18 tracks, which points up how easily Teagarden could make himself at home in bands of the period. One celebrated example is the treatment meted out to a waltz called 'Dancing With Tears In My Eyes', under Joe Venuti's leadership: Teagarden contravenes everything to do with the material and charges through his solo. Two early sessions under his own name have him trading retorts with Fats Waller on 'You Rascal You' and delivering his original reading of what became a greatest hit, 'A Hundred Years From Today'. Stricter jazz material such as two tracks by The Charleston Chasers is fine, but no less enjoyable are such as Ben Pollack's 'Two Tickets To Georgia', where Teagarden's swinging outburst suggests that he treated every setting as a chance to blow. One or two of the transfers are noisy, but most of the remastering is agreeably done.

***** A Hundred Years >From Today**

Conifer 153 *Teagarden; Charlie Teagarden, Claude Whiteman, Sterling Bose, Frank Guarente (t); Pee Wee Russell, Benny Goodman (cl); Chester Hazlett, Jimmy Dorsey, Rod Cless (cl, as); Joe Catalyne, Max Farley, Dale Skinner, Mutt Hayes (cl, ts); Frankie Trumbauer (Cmel); Bud Freeman (ts); Adrian Rollini (bsx); Casper Reardon (hp); Fats Waller (p, v); Joe Meresco, Terry Shand, Charlie LaVere (p); Walt Edelstein, Joe Venuti, Lou Kosloff (vn); Nappy Lamare (g, v); Dick McPartland, Perry Botkin, Frank Worrell (g); Artie Bernstein, Eddie Gilbert, Art Miller (b); Stan King, Bob Conselman, Larry Gomar, Herb Quigley (d).* 10/31–9/34.

***** Jack Teagarden 1930–1934**

Classics 698 *As above, except add Gene Austin (v).* 10/30–3/34.

***** Jack Teagarden 1934–1939**

Classics 729 *Teagarden; Charlie Teagarden, Charlie Spivak, Carl Garvin, Alec Fila, Lee Castaldo (t); Jose Gutierrez, Mark Bennett, Charles McCamish, Red Bone (tb); Benny Goodman (cl); Clint Garvin, Art St John (cl, as); John Van Eps, Hub Lytle (cl, ts); Ernie Caceres (cl, ts, bs); Frankie Trumbauer (Cmel); Terry Shand, John Anderson (p); Casper Reardon (hp); Allan Reuss (g); Art Miller (b); Herb Quigley, Cubby Teagarden (d); Meredith Blake, Linda Keene (v).* 9/34–7/39.

The two Classics discs take their usual chronological survey of Teagarden's work up to the middle of 1939. The tracks by the 1931 band are mostly spirited stuff: a hot 'Tiger Rag', a couple of items in which Fats Waller and Tea swap banter – and some feeble tracks with Gene Austin singing. The 1933 date is another heated one, with a front-rank group of Chicagoans on hand, although Classics 698 ends on a couple of dreary sessions. Classics 729 opens with Casper Reardon's famous harp party-piece, 'Junk Man', before moving to the first sessions by the big band Teagarden formed after leaving Paul Whiteman. He never had much luck as a bandleader, but this wasn't a bad group: decent if second-division swing, always suddenly illuminated when the leader took a solo. The Conifer disc is a mixed bag of 17 tracks, all issued under Teagarden's leadership. Some of the tunes are more vocal than instrumental and reveal the leader's peculiar ability to swing even at indolent tempos. Adequate sound.

****(*) Jack Teagarden 1939–1940**

Classics 758 *Teagarden; Charlie Spivak, Carl Garvin, Lee Castle, John Fallstitch, Tom Gonsoulin, Frank Ryerson (t); Jose Gutierrez, Mark Bennett, Charles McCamish, Eddie Dudley, Seymour Goldfinger, Joe Ferrall (tb); Clint Garvin, Art St John (cl, as); John Van Eps, Hub Lytle (cl, ts); Jack Goldie, Tony Antonelli, Joe Ferdinando (as); Larry Walsh (ts); Ernie Caceres (bs); John Anderson, Jack Russin, Nat Jaffe (p); Allan Reuss, Dan Perri (g); Art Miller, Arnold Fishkind, Benny Pottle (b); Cubby Teagarden, Dave Tough, Ed Naquin (d); Kitty Kallen (v).* 3/39–2/40.

***** Jack Teagarden 1940–1941**

Classics 839 *Teagarden; John Fallstitch, Tom Gonsoulin, Sid Feller, Pokey Carriere (t); Rex Stewart (c); Jose Gutierrez, Seymour Goldfinger, Joe Ferrall (tb); Art St John, Jack Goldie, Danny Polo, Tony Antonelli, Joe Ferdinando, Larry Walsh, Benny Lagasse, Art Moore, Art Beck (reeds); Barney Bigard (cl); Ben Webster (ts); Billy Kyle, Ernie Hughes, Nat Jaffe (p); Dan Perri, Brick Fleagle (g); Arnold Fishkind, Billy Taylor (b); Ed Naquin, Paul Collins, Dave Tough (d); Lynn Clark, David Allen, Marianne Dunne, Kitty Kallen (v).* 2/40–1/41.

Teagarden was struggling to find success with this band. Most of the records tend towards undemanding, commercial swing, vocalists Kallen and Allen begin to dominate, and even the leader's peerless phrasing was starting to figure less. The first disc is brightened by a mere handful of instrumentals, though there is a fine 'Wolverine Blues' and 'The Blues' is vintage Tea. Classics 839 gets its stars mainly from the session by the Teagarden Big Eight, a small group which featured the trombonist sparring with Rex Stewart on four good (if hardly earthquaking) titles. The rest is pretty dreary, with the likes of 'Fatima's Drummer Boy' plumbing the depths of material. Transfers are clean but not very lively.

**** It's Time For Tea**

Jass J-CD-624 *Teagarden; John Fallstitch, Pokey Carriere, Sid Feller, Truman Quigley (t); Jose Gutierrez, Joe Ferrall, Seymour Goldfinger (tb); Danny Polo, Tony Antonelli, Joe Ferdinando, Art Moore, Art Beck (reeds); Ernie Hughes (p); Arnold Fishkind (b);*

Paul Collins (d); David Allen, Lynn Clark, Marianne Dunne (v). 1–6/41.

Teagarden had started leading a big band in 1939, but it wasn't until 1941 – as revealed in the excellent notes here – that it achieved much commercial success. On the evidence of the 24 sides collected here, it was done at the expense of much jazz content. Most of the tracks work politely through forgettable pop material of the day, along with leaning on a fashionable penchant for jazzing the classics: there are charts for 'Anitra's Dance' and Debussy's 'Afternoon Of A Faun' here, as well as 'Casey Jones'. It isn't until 'Harlem Jump' (number 21) that we get a thorough-going swing performance. There are glimmers of Teagarden – who, after all, was the band's only feasible soloist apart from Polo – but not nearly enough. For collectors only, though the remastering is painstakingly done.

*****(*) Jack Teagarden 1941–1943**

Classics 874 *Similar to above, except add Billy May, Art Gold (t), Jimmie Noone, Heinie Beau (cl), Dave Matthews (ts), Joe Sullivan (p), Dave Barbour (g), Art Shapiro (b), Zutty Singleton (d), Bing Crosby, Mary Martin (v).* 1/41–11/43.

Three more sessions by the big band, a couple of tracks with Bing Crosby and two small-group dates for Capitol make up this CD. It's a curious jump from 'Prelude In C Sharp Minor' to 'Chicks Is Wonderful', but the three Decca sessions are among the best vehicles for Teagarden, who plays and sings with serene authority on 'Blue River', 'Black And Blue', 'The Blues Have Got Me' and especially 'Nobody Knows The Trouble I've Seen'. The seven titles by The Capitol International Jazzmen bring together an unlikely band – May, Teagarden, Noone (making his farewell on record), Matthews, Sullivan – but it worked out very well, with the various soloists shining in different degrees. One of the best of the Classics Teas.

***** Has Anybody Here Seen Jackson?**

Jass J-CD-637 *Teagarden; Jimmy Simms, Pokey Carriere, Truman Quigley, Roy Peters, Jimmy McPartland, Chuck Tonti, Clair Jones, Val Salata, Tex Williamson, Bob McLaughlin (t); Jose Gutierrez, Joe Ferrall, Fred Keller, Wally Wells, Ray Olsen (tb); Danny Polo, Tony Antonelli, Clint Garvin, Art Moore, Art Beck, Dale Stoddard, Gish Gilbertson, Vic Rosi, Ken Harpster, Clark Crandell (reeds); Ernie Hughes, Don Seidel (p); Myron Shapler, Don Tosti (b); Paul Collins, Frank Horrington (d); David Allen, Kitty Kallen (v).* 10/41–8/44.

A second volume of Standard Transcriptions. This one comes off rather better: 'Bashful Baby Blues' is a great one, 'Sherman Shout' and 'Dig The Groove' dig in, and Tea's vocals – as well as those of the ultra-smooth David Allen, an underrated band singer – sound good. Excellent remastering and fine documentation. This covers much the same material as Masters of Jazz Vol. 10 (Storyville STCD 4110 CD), but this is the superior issue. The above pair of discs are now also available in a two-disc edition.

*****(*) Jack Teagarden 1944–1947**

Classics 1032 *Teagarden; Bobby Hackett (c); Clair Jones, Bob McLaughlin, Val Salata, Tex Williamson, Max Kaminsky, Ray Norden, Jerry Rosen, Andy Marchese, Jerry Redmond, Nyles Davis, Lee Castle, Carl Garvin, Frank Ryerson (t); Fred Keller, Ray Olsen, Wally Wells, Palmer Combatelli, Jack Lantz, Chuck Smith, Kenny Martin, Mark Bennett, Eddie Dudley, Jose Gutierrez (tb); Art Lyons, Peanuts Hucko (cl); Ernie Caceres, Vic Rosi, Clint Garvin (cl, as); Dale Stoddard, Bob Derry, Dale Jolley, Bert Noah, Merton Smith, Ray Skieraski, Leon Radcliffe, Ray Tucci (as); Howard Gilbertson, Ken Harpster, Nick Caiazza, Johnny McDonald, Cliff Strickland, Hub Lytle, John Van Eps (ts); Clark Crandall, Art St John (bs); Don Seidel, Bill Clifton, Norma Teagarden, Bob Carter, Nick Tagg, Gene Schroeder, Jack Russin (p); Herb Ellis, Charles Gilruth, Eddie Critchlow, Chuck Wayne, Allan Reuss (g); Jimmy Lynch, Felix Giobbe, Pops Foster, Lloyd Springer, Jim Hearne, Jack Lesberg, Bonnie Pottle (b); Frank Harrington, Cozy Cole, George Wettling, Bobby Fisher, Dave Tough (d); Wingy Manone, Christine Martin (v).* 11/39–10/47.

Starting with a couple of 1939 V-Discs that were missed off an earlier volume, this is a mix of rare and familiar Teagarden. His 1944 session for Commodore includes a duet with Wingy Manone on 'Rockin' Chair'. There are six sides from his own label, Teagarden Presents, two Dixieland titles and four by his latest big band. A V-Disc of 'Body And Soul', with a largely unknown rhythm section, is classic Tea. Four Victor titles by Teagarden's Big Eight, including Kaminsky and Hucko, swagger along, and Tea sounds in good heart. A hotchpotch but an excellent one.

***** Club Hangover Broadcasts**

Arbors ARCD 19150/1 2CD *Teagarden; Jackie Coon (t); Jay St John (cl); Norma Teagarden, Lil Armstrong, Don Ewell (p); Kas Malone (b); Ray Bauduc (d).* 4/54.

Four broadcasts by a Teagarden small group in San Francisco. With the big band and the Armstrong All Stars behind him, Tea sounds settled enough, though there are no vocals from him – a by-product of an old cabaret tax law. The material is all Dixieland chestnuts and the band suffers a little under Ray Bauduc's crashing drums, but there are some nice glimpses of the leader at his best, even if they are only glimpses (and often ones where Tea isn't very well miked). Clean sound, though Coon and Bauduc (and Malone) usually sound louder than everyone else. Ewell and Armstrong are the intermission pianists and get a couple of solos each.

**** Jack Teagarden And His All Stars**

Jazzology 199 *Teagarden; Dick Oakley (c); Jerry Fuller (cl); Don Ewell (p); Stan Puls (b); Ronnie Greb (d).* 58.

Teagarden drifted through his final years in a way that looks as careless and slipshod as some of Armstrong's later efforts: the numerous renditions of 'St James Infirmary' and 'Rockin' Chair' (both included here) eventually sound as fatigued as his perennially tired voice. The Jazzology release is a well-recorded club date, made in Cleveland in 1958, but it features a dusty band and a leader content to amble along. There is much better Teagarden from the 1950s still awaiting reissue. Verve briefly reissued his Willard Robison collection in their Elite Edition, and admirers who missed it should check out the Teagarden bins to see if any copies remain.

Joe Temperley (born 1929)

BARITONE AND SOPRANO SAXOPHONES, BASS CLARINET

Born in Fife, he played in dance-band sax sections in the 1950s, before spending seven years with Humphrey Lyttelton from 1958. In 1965 he moved to New York and became familiar in American big bands as well as doing much session-work. He has enjoyed an Indian summer with his stay in the Lincoln Center Jazz Orchestra in the '90s.

***** Nightingale**
Hep CD 2052 *Temperley; Brian Lemon (p); Dave Green (b); Martin Drew (d).* 4/91.

***** Concerto For Joe**
Hep CD 2062 *As above, except add Steve Sidwell, Eddie Severn, Gerard Presencer (t); Gordon Campbell, Nichol Thomson (tb); Peter King (as); Duncan Lamont (ts); Brian Kellock (p); Alec Dankworth (b); Jack Parnell (d).* 9/93–7/94.

Temperley has seldom figured in record sessions in the UK since his move to America and there has been very little under his own leadership, but *Nightingale* was an opportune session. A seamless, singing manner belies the difficulties of the instrument and, though his sometimes bubbly timbre at fast tempos may not be to all tastes, there's a genuineness about his improvisations. There's a beautiful Ellington rarity in 'Sunset And A Mocking Bird', in which Temperley's sound never makes one think of Harry Carney. He ends on an *a cappella* 'My Love Is Like A Red, Red Rose' that sums up the sound he can get from the horn. The weakness lies in the rhythm section: nothing very wrong, but the sheer ordinariness of the playing is unfortunate. *Concerto For Joe* is an agreeable continuation. Jimmy Deuchar's composition for Temperley is the centrepiece of the record, performed by the saxophonist with the big group, and it's a substantial if not quite deathless performance. Elsewhere there are more quartet tracks with the previous group. Temperley sounds well enough but, in the end, as with the previous disc, a certain flavour of routine militates against its acquiring essential status.

***** Double Duke**
Naxos 86032-2 *Temperley; Wycliff Gordon (tb); Eric Reed (p); Rodney Whitaker (b); Herlin Riley (d).* 10/98.

Naxos have snared an impressive line-up for this one, an Ellington homage with Temperley supported by several of the Marsalis teamsters. It's a good blow, but frankly the leader is outdone by his fellow players, and Gordon's ripe range of styles with both open horn and plunger mute borders on the cartoonish at times (notably in an outrageous handling of 'Black And Tan Fantasy' and the closing 'Danny Boy'). 'Creole Love Call' is played so slowly that it's below a crawl.

Jacky Terrasson (born 1966)

PIANO

Born in Berlin, of French and American parents, Terrasson grew up in Paris and attended the Lycée Lamartine. He moved to New York in 1990 and won the Thelonious Monk Competition in 1993, thereafter signing to Blue Note.

***** Jacky Terrasson**
Blue Note 829351-2 *Terrasson; Ugonna Okegwo (b); Leon Parker (d).* 7–8/94.

***** Reach**
Blue Note 835739-2 *As above.* 95.

Terrasson has been gathering much acclaim, and these debut records as a leader are notably single-minded efforts. He never approaches a tune from any predictable point: on the first disc, there are versions of 'I Love Paris', 'My Funny Valentine' and 'Bye Bye Blackbird' which are so revisionist as to be almost unrecognizable at times. Yet he sticks to otherwise familiar paths of harmony and rhythmic patterns which call to mind influences ranging from Ahmad Jamal to Bill Evans. The problem with both discs is a slightly exasperating ingenuity which seems less at the service of the music and more about creating a sensation. Terrasson's writing has a greater showing on the second set, *Reach*, though it often sounds to be more about motifs and vamps than full-scale structures. Okegwo and Parker perform well, but theirs is a largely subsidiary role, rather than one where a true trio music is called for.

****(*) Rendezvous**
Blue Note 855484-2 *Terrasson; Lonnie Plaxico, Kenny Davis (b); Mino Cinelu (perc); Cassandra Wilson (v).* 1–4/97.

Anyone expecting something of the order of, say, *The Intimate Ella* from this collaboration is likely to be sorely disappointed. Perhaps it's inevitable, with two such self-regarding artists as Terrasson and Wilson, that their shared record is simultaneously inflated and introverted, to the virtual exclusion of an audience. There are quite preposterous versions of 'It Might As Well Be Spring' and 'If Ever I Would Leave You' which take melodic and rhythmic displacement to extraordinary lengths and, while they get away with 'Old Devil Moon' and 'Tennessee Waltz', the rest of the record is pretty much a trudge, including Terrasson's own features. Wilson's following may find this a lot more entertaining than we do, possibly, but this isn't a record to convert anybody.

***** Alive**
Blue Note 859651-2 *Terrasson; Ugonna Okegwo (b); Leon Parker (d).* 6/97.

Caught live at New York's Iridium Club, the Terrasson trio deliver a typically larger-than-life set. The music has much presence and numerous surprising moments, but again we are unconvinced by Terrasson's musical decisions. His attractive original 'Cumba's Dance' is gradually speeded up to a nonsensical tempo. Tony Williams's 'Sister Cheryl' goes from quiet reflection to great intensity, but with no real logic, and 'Nature Boy' is made merely eccentric. At its best, as on the opening 'Things Ain't What They Used To

Be', the trio offer a persuasive revision of their materials. But for a lot of the time Terrasson appears to be such a crowd-pleaser, conscious or otherwise, that the uncommitted will be bewildered by his music.

Clark Terry (born 1920)

TRUMPET, FLUGELHORN

Also known as 'Mumbles' after his famously indistinct scat style, Terry was born in St Louis and managed to hold down a seat in both the Basie and Ellington bands, before disappearing into the studios and broadcasting, like many of his generation. He re-appeared in the '70s and added flugelhorn to his armoury as he became an ever more expressive soloist, widely featured at festivals and capable of sustaining interest entirely on his own.

*** Serenade To A Bus Seat

Original Jazz Classics OJC 066 *Terry; Johnny Griffin (ts); Wynton Kelly (p); Paul Chambers (b); Philly Joe Jones (d).* 4/57.

Though not reducible to his 'influences', Terry hybridizes Dizzy Gillespie's hot, fluent lines and witty abandon with Rex Stewart's distinctive half-valving and Charlie Shavers's high-register lyricism; he is also a master of the mute, an aspect of his work that had a discernible impact on Miles Davis. Miles, though, remained unconvinced by Terry's pioneering development of the flugelhorn as a solo instrument; later in his career he traded four-bar phrases with himself, holding a horn in each hand. An irrepressible showman with a sly sense of humour, Terry often fared better when performing under other leaders. His encounter with the Oscar Peterson Trio in 1964 is often judged his best work, and it's hard to see where and when he played better. The 'early' – he was 37 – *Serenade To A Bus Seat* combines a tribute to civil-rights activist Rosa Parks with pungent versions of 'Stardust' and Parker's 'Donna Lee'. Terry isn't an altogether convincing bopper, but he's working with a fine, funky band, and they carry him through some slightly unresolved moments.

**** Daylight Express

Chess GRP 18192 *Terry; Paul Gonsalves (ts); Mike Simpson (sax, f); Willie Jones (p); Remo Biondi (g); Jimmy Woode (b); Sam Woodyard (d).* 7 & 8/57.

Slotted into the middle of his contract with Riverside (which yielded most of the OJCs) these insecurely dated sessions from the summer of 1957 yielded two LPs for Argo: *Out On A Limb* and (under Gonsalves's name) *Cookin'*. The ten tracks with the saxophonist, which include the previously unissued 'The Girl That I Call Baby', are far and away the most interesting things on the record. Clark sounds rather restrained in his presence, concentrating on a quietly lateral lyricism, whereas on the early session, which was produced, you'll be glad to know, by Daddy-O Daylie, he goes for broke every time, demonstrating an iron lip on 'Trumpet Mouthpiece Blues' and positively ripping up tunes like 'Daylight Express' and 'Taking A Chance On Love'. The songs are all very short, with the exception of the 'Mouthpiece' feature, and the impact is not dissimilar to having an express train shoot past in front of you. Interesting to compare with the more measured approach on the Gonsalves session. A very welcome reissue, which comes as part of GRP's bid to restore all the Leonard Chess 'Legendary Masters'.

*** Duke With A Difference

Original Jazz Classics OJC 229 *Terry; Quentin Jackson, Britt Woodman (tb); Tyree Glenn (tb, vib); Johnny Hodges (as); Paul Gonsalves (ts); Jimmy Jones, Billy Strayhorn (p); Luther Henderson (cel); Jimmy Woode (b); Sam Woodyard (d); Marion Bruce (v).* 7 & 9/57.

In 1957 Terry was most of the way through his eight-year stint with Ellington (he'd already worked with Charlie Barnet and Count Basie and was bound for a staff job with NBC, the first black man to get his feet under that rather clubby table) and a successful partnership with trombonist Bob Brookmeyer. It's the slide-brass men he cleaves to on this mildly impertinent tribute to his boss. He undercuts both Jackson and Hodges on a beautifully arranged 'In A Sentimental Mood' (which features Strayhorn on piano and Luther Henderson on celeste) and cheerfully wrecks 'Take The "A" Train' in spite of Gonsalves's best efforts to keep it hurtling along the rails. Marion Bruce's vocals are nothing to write home about, but the band is as good as the form book says it ought to be.

**** In Orbit

Original Jazz Classics OJC 302 *Terry; Thelonious Monk (p); Sam Jones (b); Philly Joe Jones (d).* 5/58.

Terry's solitary excursion on Monk's *Brilliant Corners*, a vivid 'Bemsha Swing', underlined the degree to which Monk himself still drew sustenance from swing. *In Orbit* is firmly Terry's album. If the material is less stretching, the arrangements are surprisingly demanding, and the interplay between flugelhorn (used throughout) and piano on 'One Foot In The Gutter' and the contrasting 'Moonlight Fiesta' is highly inventive.

*** Top And Bottom Brass

Original Jazz Classics OJC 764 *Terry; Don Butterfield (tba); Jimmy Jones, Sam Jones (b); Art Taylor (d).* 2/59.

The title is self-explanatory, the results patchy. Terry's own ability to dive down into lower registers means that this bold attempt at chiaroscuro is both likely to work and also unnecessary, indeed it might almost seem as if it neutralizes one of the trumpeter's great assets. The material is kept pretty simple and straightforward: 'Mardi Gras Waltz' is delightful and some of the interchanges on 'Top'N'Bottom' are well worth hearing again. A sidebar rather than a classic Terry album.

*** Yes, The Blues

Original Jazz Classics OJC 856 *Terry; Eddie Cleanhead Vinson (as); Harmonica George Smith (hca); Art Hillery (b); J.C Heard, Roy McCurdy (d).*

Somewhat dominated by Vinson's raw blues line (especially on the closing 'Kidney Stew', the saxophonist's signature-tune), this isn't the best place to catch up with Terry, but it is a hugely entertaining album which sounds as if it might have originated in a spontaneous jam and certainly benefits from a live ambience. Vinson may require reassessment in the years ahead, for here he has certainly negotiated an intriguing path between country blues and orthodox swing, a route mastered by very few others.

****** Color Changes**

Candid CCD 79009 *Terry; Jimmy Knepper (tb); Julius Watkins (frhn); Yusef Lateef (ts, f, eng hn, ob); Seldon Powell (ts, f); Tommy Flanagan, Budd Johnson (p); Joe Benjamin (b); Ed Shaughnessy (d).* 11/60.

Terry's best record, and ample evidence that swing was still viable on the cusp of the decade that was to see its demise as anything but an exercise in nostalgia. What is immediately striking is the extraordinary, almost kaleidoscopic variation of tone-colour through the seven tracks. Given Lateef's inventive multi-instrumentalism, Powell's doubling on flute and Terry's use of flugelhorn and his mutes, the permutations on horn voicings seem almost infinite. 'Brother Terry' opens with a deep growl from Terry, a weaving oboe theme by composer Lateef and some beautiful harmony work from Watkins (who a matter of days later was to make such a contribution to Benny Bailey's superb Candid session, *Big Brass*) who interacts imaginatively with Knepper on Terry's 'Flutin' And Fluglin''. Again arranged by Lateef, this is a straightforward exploration of the relation between their two horns; Terry has written several 'odes' to his second instrument, and this is perhaps the most inventive. 'Nahstye Blues', written by and featuring Johnson, in for the unsuitably limpid Flanagan, comes close to Horace Silver's funk. Terry is slightly disappointing, but Lateef turns in a majestic solo that turns his own cor anglais introduction completely on its head. The closing 'Chat Qui Pêche' is an all-in, solo-apiece affair that would have sounded wonderful in the Parisian *boîte* it celebrates and brings a marvellous, expertly recorded record to a powerful finish. Needless to say, it comes highly recommended.

*****(*) Mellow Moods**

Prestige PCD 24136 *Terry; Lester Robertson (tb); Budd Johnson (ts); George Barrow (bs); Junior Mance (p); Eddie Costa (p, vib); Joe Benjamin, Art Davis (b); Charli Persip, Ed Shaughnessy (d).* 7/61, 5/62.

Following on from the last item, this confirms that a purple patch was in progress. A calmer, less frantic record all round, it showed off Terry's abilities as a balladeer as well as a fast action man. Mance is a good accompanist on the earlier session, a quartet with just Terry and rhythm. Inevitably there is slightly less of him on the other date, but this almost-big band generates an impressive body of noise when it gets going, and the settings laid out for him on 'If I Were You' and 'It's Fun To Think' are completely irresistible.

***** Live At The Wichita Jazz Festival**

Vanguard 79335 *Terry; Greg Bobulinski, Dave Carley, Paul Cohen, Oscar Gamby, Jimmy Nottingham (t); Chuck Connors, Sonny Costanzo, Janice Robinson, Jimmy Wilkins (tb); Jack Jeffers (tb, btb, tba); Frank Wess, Chris Woods (as); Jimmy Heath, Ron Odrich, Ernie Wilkins (ts); Charles Davis (bs); Arnie Lawrence, Phil Woods (reeds); Duke Jordan, Ronnie Matthews (p); Wilbur Little, Victor Sproles (b); Ed Soph (d, perc).* 74.

A surprisingly modern programme from the revitalized Terry. He includes Kenny Dorham's 'Una Mas' and, even more unexpectedly, Wayne Shorter's complex 'Nefertiti', alongside the easy swing of 'Take The "A" Train' and the delightful 'Mumbles'. The arrangements are by Ernie Wilkins, Phil Woods, Jimmy Heath and Allan Foust, and the latter also contributes the long curtain-piece, 'Cold 'Tater Stomp'. The section aren't always entirely together and there is some definite slackness in the horns but, like many a festival gig, it relies more on atmosphere than on formal accuracy.

***** Live In Chicago: Volume 1**

Monad 803 *Terry; Ernie Wilkins (as, ts); Marty Harris (p); Victor Sproles (b); Ed Soph (d).* 76.

*****(*) Live In Chicago: Volume 2**

Monad 804 *As above.* 76.

Not released for almost 20 years, these live dates come from Ratso's club in Chicago. The atmosphere is brisk and business-like, and it's Wilkins rather than CT who gives himself the space to develop some interesting ideas on tunes like 'Secret Love' (a Terry favourite) and 'Mood Indigo'. Despite a sparkling performance on 'One Foot In The Gutter' on the first disc, The trumpeter is much better on the second, which includes 'I Want A Little Girl', a moody 'Autumn Leaves', and the evergreen 'Mumbles'.

***** Clark After Dark**

MPS 529 088 *Terry; Eddie Blair, Tony Fisher, Dave Hancock, Derek Watkins, Kenny Wheeler (t); Cliff Hardy, Dave Horler, Nat Peck, Ray Premru (tb); Terry Jones (frhn); Roy Willox (as, f, cl); Al Newman (as, bcl); Stan Sulzmann (ts, f, af); Tony Coe (ts, f, cl); Ronnie Ross (bs, cl); Gordon Beck (p); Martin Kershaw (g); Chris Laurence (b); Tristan Fry (d, perc); strings.* 9/77.

A first-class British band accompany Clark on an oddly autumnal stroll. No 'Autumn Leaves', but browns and deep blues for the main part. He's playing wonderfully, and the engineering does all the right and tactful things for him. 'Nature Boy' and 'Willow Weep For Me' are gems.

****** Memories Of Duke**

Original Jazz Classics OJC 604 *Terry; Joe Pass (g); Jack Wilson (p); Ray Brown (b); Frank Severino (d).* 3/80.

Obvious, really, but exquisitely done. The interplay between Pass and Brown touches unsuspected areas of 'Cotton Tail' and 'Sophisticated Lady' (compare the version with Red Mitchell, below) and, though Severino might have been dispensed with for at least a couple of the softer tracks, the overall sound is excellent.

****(*) Squeeze Me**

Chiaroscuro CRD 309 *Terry; Virgil Jones (t); Al Grey, Britt Woodman (tb); Haywood Henry, Red Holloway, Phil Woods (reeds); John Campbell (p); Marcus McLaurine (b); Butch Ballard (d).*

Good arrangements, but a rather knotted sound that strips some fine horn-players of any real individuality. The rhythm section sounds under-rehearsed and the tempo is always either lagging behind or rushing to catch up. Disappointing.

*****(*) Ow Live at E.J.'s**

JLR 103.601 2CD *Terry; Johnny O'Neal (p); Dewey Sampson (b); James Martin (d).* 12/81.

Terry working out with what is presumably the house band at the Atlanta club who have issued the record. It's a fairly unadventurous programme of material and the band sound as if they are watching their fingers here and there. The curios are Redman's

'Just An Old Manuscript' (how often is it covered?), a surprisingly boppish version of 'Shaw 'Nuff', and Terry's own 'Rebecca', which closes the set on a high. There is also a strong sequence centred on Green Dolphin Street but including Miles's 'All Blues' and Monk's 'Straight, No Chaser', which suggests how easily and confidently Clark kept up with developments past his usual timeline. As so often with these things, we'd question that there really was enough top-quality material for a double CD, but it was clearly a great night for E.J.'s, and we'd hardly begrudge them the pat on the back.

*** Clark Terry–Red Mitchell

Enja 5011 *Terry; Red Mitchell (b, p, v).* 2/86.

***(*) Jive At Five

Enja 6042 *As above.* 7/88.

Jive At Five is the more musicianly of these rather knockabout sets by one frustrated crooner and one master of verbal salad, whose 'Hey Mr Mumbles' gets its 5,000th airing on the earlier album. As a purely musical dialogue, these have no right to work half as well as they do, but Terry is in excellent lip on the later version of 'Big'n And The Bear' and the Ellington material. Mitchell's comping skills come into their own on 'Cotton Tail' (two nicely varied takes), 'Sophisticated Lady' and 'Prelude To A Kiss'.

***(*) Portraits

Chesky JD 2 *Terry; Don Friedman (p); Victor Gaskin (b); Lewis Nash (d).* 12/88.

*** Having Fun

Delos DE 4021 *Terry; Bunky Green (as); Red Holloway (as, ts); John Campbell (p); Major Holley (b, tba); Lewis Nash (d).* 4/90.

By the 1980s, Terry was more than satisfied with his billing as an elder statesman and trotted out all his tricks with almost indulgent ease. The big production numbers like 'Ciribiribin' sound good on *Portraits*, but the album overall almost sounds like an audiophile test disc, so exact and limpid is the reproduction. *Having Fun* means what it says, with jokey-straight versions of the Flintstones theme (one of the most irritating melodies ever committed) and 'It's Not Easy Being Green'. Holley is a marvellous partner; a duo record, with the two men vocalizing at full throttle, would be something to hear.

***(*) Live At The Village Gate

Chesky JD 49 *Terry; Jimmy Heath (ts, ss); Paquito D'Rivera (as); Don Friedman (p); Marcus McLaurine (b); Kenny Washington (d).* 11/90.

Recorded three weeks short of Terry's seventieth birthday, this is a good-natured set of uncomplicated jazz. Terry alternates his trumpet ('my driver') and flugelhorn ('putter'), favouring a soft, blurred-edge tone that in no way compromises the clarity of his bop-influenced lines. Jimmy Heath is dry without being sterile and takes a lovely solo on 'Pint Of Bitter', a dedication to the late Tubby Hayes. D'Rivera shows up for only a single track, the appealing 'Silly Samba'. The recording is impeccably handled, with a light sound that still captures the live ambience; on 'Keep, Keep, Keep On Keepin' On', Terry has the entire audience singing along, and so he can't resist throwing them 'Hey Mr Mumbles' at the end. 'If Sylvester Stallone can make *Rocky* 3, 4, 5, I don't see why I can't make Mumbles 8, 9 and 10.'

*** Shades Of Blues

Challenge 70007 *Terry; Al Grey (tb); Charles Fox (p); Marcus McLaurine (b).* 5/94.

Apart from the closing trilogy ('Parker's Mood', McShann's 'Hottie's Blues' and Handy's 'St Louis Blues') and a mostly polite early inclusion of Al Grey's 'Salty Mama', all of the themes are original blues, simple and unpretentious but played with maximum variation. Clark's vocal on 'Whispering The Blues' is very much in the 'Mumbles' tradition, light, buoyant and deceptively clever. The interplay with Grey is more challenging than might at first appear, with every conceivable variation on conventional blues changes.

*** Reunion

D'Note Classics 2001 *Terry; Brian Gould (tb, v); Howard Dudune (as, ts, cl); PeeWee Claybrook (ts); Dean Reilly (b); Harold Jones (d).* 95.

And you didn't know that they'd ever been apart. Clark and tenorman Claybrook go back many years, and this friendly, uncomplicated session is pitched square in the middle of common musical ground. Duke and Strayhorn's 'Isfahan' has an unfamiliar cast but works well, and there is a lively version of 'Jitterbug Waltz'.

*** Top And Bottom Brass

Chiaroscuro 347 *Terry; Don Butterfield (tba); David Glasser (as); Red Holloway (ts); Jimmy Jones, Willie Pickens (p); Sam Jones, Marcus McLaurine (b); Sylvia Cuenca, Art Taylor (d).* 11/95.

Red Holloway can't spent much time ashore these days, having tapped into the jazz cruise sector. In a curious way, though, the key element here is the 'bottom brass' of tubist Don Butterfield. Clark's chocolatey flugelhorn is the main voice, and his quarter-hour ballad medley will be a constant source of delight. Recorded on the SS *Norway*, the music seems brisk and oxygenated – or ozoned – and Terry is in cracking form.

*** Express

Reference 73 *Terry; Bob Lark (t); Jason Aspinwall, Amir El-Saffar, Eric Nelson, Vance Thompson, Gil Wukitsch (t, flhn); Steve Bradley (tb); Dave Hutten (as, f); Mark Colby (ts); Rob Denty (ts, cl); Jeff Erikson (bs, cl); Michael Stryker (p); Sharay Reed (b); Tom Hipskind, James Ward (d).* 12/95.

Amiable big-band swing with a few modern touches from Terry and the well-drilled DePaul University Big Band under the direction of Bob Lark. The programme is dominated by Ellington and Strayhorn tunes, of which 'Star-Crossed Lovers' and the closing 'Something To Live For' are by far the most vivid. Clark's warm tone isn't always matched by the band, which can sound a touch mechanical when the tempo drops; but the faster tunes are pitch-perfect and the disc is enjoyable from start to finish.

***(*) One On One

Chesky 198 *Terry; Monty Alexander, Geri Allen, Kenny Barron, Tommy Flanagan, Don Friedman, Eric Lewis, Marian McPartland, Junior Mance (p).* 99.

Something of the range and sophistication of this lovely album of trumpet and piano duets can be gauged from the roster of accompanists. A word of advice. Buy it, stick it in the machine and sit back without the notes. Second time around, you can start to work out who's at the piano. Given that at least two of Clark's partners are – seemingly deliberately – playing out of character, it won't be as easy as you might think. And that's all the help you're getting.

TEST

GROUP

New York improvisers playing hardcore free jazz.

*****(*) TEST**

AUM Fidelity AUM012 *Daniel Carter (as, ts, f, t); Sabir Mateen (cl, as, ts, f); Matthew Heyner (b); Tom Bruno (d).* 8/98.

*****(*) Live / TEST**

Eremite MTE021 *As above.* 11/98.

This quartet seem ready to spearhead a back-to-the-roots exercise in New York free jazz, playing long and loud (though not unlyrical) sets of unfettered improvisation. The notes to the AUM Fidelity release suggest that TEST can be heard at the corner of 57th and 5th, and they've also been known to do subway gigs; this is classic street music: tough, sweepingly passionate, but informed and articulate playing. The Eremite disc has one long set from Baltimore and a brief postscript for a Boston show which is a riotous coda to the disc. Rough, live sound, but the spirit is unquenchable and there is some feelingful and exciting interplay among the four players, each of whom suggests that he has a good grasp of long form in improvising. *TEST* isn't much less intense, although there's a serene interlude called 'Alen's Flight Preparation' where the horn players pick up flutes and play a whispery dialogue. Carter, who occasionally turns to the trumpet but is more often on sax, and Mateen are both driven but not without their melodious side, and it sweetens or at least lightens what might otherwise have been an overdose of grim.

Tethered Moon

GROUP

Three major individual performers in a trio which has been working together since the mid-'80s.

***** Play Kurt Weill**

JMT 514021-2 *Masabumi Kikuchi (p); Gary Peacock (b); Paul Motian (d).* 94.

***** Chansons De Piaf**

Winter & Winter 910048-2 *As above.* 5/99.

While Peacock and Motian are familiar names, Kikuchi may still be relatively obscure to a wider audience. Yet he is as experienced as his colleagues: he was working with Lionel Hampton as far back as 1962, and he later toured with Sonny Rollins and Joe Henderson. He formed this trio for a number of sessions for Paddlewheel, Evidence and JMT, some of which we have listed in earlier editions, although those records have long since gone – with the exception of the Weill record, still listed as of spring 2000, but this is likely to be your last chance to get it (also worth seeking out is Kikuchi's beautiful solo date, *After Hours*, released on Verve for about five minutes in 1995).

On the Winter & Winter record, the trio investigates songs associated with Edith Piaf, an ingenious and hitherto unexplored idiom for a jazz record. 'L'Accordéoniste' is a thrilling start, the pianist setting up the theme and melody before bass and drums storm in, but the melody emerges only at the very end of the track. 'Sous Le Ciel De Paris' is heavy with tears, and the full-flushing emotion which was Piaf's calling-card seems to be present there too, even as Kikuchi and his colleagues also seek out some darker abstractions. But the pianist's penchant for singing along with his playing (a mannerism borrowed from Jarrett, and one of his least useful bequests) is at times so intrusive that we find the results as often exasperating as uplifting.

Henri Texier (born 1945)

DOUBLE BASS

'It's a sound you feel safe with, like you could lie down on it and go to sleep'; and there is a pillowing security and strength in Texier's sound which amply confirms his fellow-player's assessment. Influenced by the great Wilbur Ware, Texier has a strong, full sound that nearly always sounds better at lower tempos, when its sheer weight and fullness become more evident. Like Charlie Haden, though, he can also play nimbly and melodically.

***** La Companera**

Label Bleu LBLC 6525 *Texier; Michael Marre (t, flhn); Louis Sclavis (cl, ts); Philippe Deschepper (g); Jacques Mahieux (d).* 2/83.

***** Paris-Batignolles**

Label Bleu LBLC 6506 *As above, except replace Marre with Joe Lovano (ts).* 5/86.

The earlier of these records was noted as much for Sclavis's contribution as for the leader's. In 1983, he was not much known outside France, but there were already mutterings about his ingenious and fiery, folk-based improvisations. Interesting as he was at this stage, it's only when Marre makes up the complement that the record really catches light. *Paris-Batignolles* is higher-octane stuff from the start. Lovano's remarkably traditional sound melds perfectly with this group, both on the faster dance-tunes and on the brooding laments. Texier isn't caught so well or so fully on this live recording from the Amiens Jazz Festival, but his presence is consistently evident in the reactions of fellow-players, who always seem easier and open-hearted in his presence.

****** Izlaz**

Label Bleu LBLC 6515 *Texier; Joe Lovano (ts, ss, cl, f, perc); Steve Swallow (b); Aldo Romano (d).* 5/88.

***** Colonel Skopje**

Label Bleu LBLC 6523 *As above, except add John Abercrombie (g).* 7/88.

Texier's Transatlantik Quartet allowed a promising relationship with Lovano to cement and brought in the rock-tinged, free-swinging bass guitar of Steve Swallow. The sound is wonderfully open and unstuffy. 'Ups And Downs' is superb, though it bears no relation to Bud Powell's composition of that name, and the only quibble about this set is that the sound-mix is awry, pushing up bass and drums too far and making Lovano sound as if he's out back somewhere, waiting to get in. *Colonel Skopje* is a ragbag, too various to hang together convincingly, though Abercrombie's presence guarantees some interesting moments, as always.

*****(*) Respect**

Label Bleu LBLC 6612 *Texier; Bob Brookmeyer (vtb); Lee Konitz (as); Steve Swallow (b); Paul Motian (d).* 4–5/97.

Superior, beautifully crafted jazz from a dream line-up. The interplay between Texier and Motian is immaculate, particularly on the drummer's own 'In The Year Of The Dragon', and the blend of horns has a dreamy precision. Konitz is well settled into a purple patch, spinning off quicksilver lines on his own 'Thingin'', which manages to sound as if it was made up on the spot. Brookmeyer's cool, slightly reserved approach probably won't appeal to everybody, but it's combined with a flawless sense of structure and a certain wry humour. Certainly the pairing of voices on 'Lee And Me' is as tongue-in-cheek as 'Idyll', Bob's other composition, is sincere and unalloyed. Texier himself has seldom been heard to greater advantage. The acoustic in Amiens's Studio Gil Evans is both intimate and capacious, and the bass, which never calls for much in the way of electronic boosting, is as resonant and present as if he were standing between your speaker cabinets, playing live.

***** Mosaic Man**

Label Bleu LBLC 6608 *Texier; Glenn Ferris (tb); Sebastien Texier (as, cl); Bohan Zulfikarpasic (p); Tony Rabeson (d).* 9/98.

This is the Azur Quintet, nowadays very much centred on Texier and his son, Sebastien. The bass still remains the axis on which the music turns, freeing up Bojan Z's role considerably and allowing the two horns to range quite widely. Apart from 'Mosaic Man' itself and 'Cap d'Espérance', the songs are mainly quite short. As ever, Henri doesn't indulge himself in long solo features, preferring to register a presence with rich, double-stopped chords and fleet, muscular melody-lines. Not our favourite to date of his own recordings, but a fine showing nevertheless.

Eje Thelin (1938–90)

TROMBONE

Starting with Dixieland, Thelin worked his way through jazz styles. His Swedish quintet of the early '60s was widely acclaimed. In the '70s he became increasingly interested in large-scale composition. He remains disgracefully neglected by CD reissues.

***** Raggruppamento**

Phono Suecia PSCD 56 *Jan Kohlin, Bertil Lövgren, Håkan Nyqvist (t); Olle Holmquist, Nils Landgren, Jorgen Johansson (tb); Sven Larsson (btb); David Wilczewski, Ulf Andersson, Jan Kling, Lennart Aberg, Erik Nilsson (reeds); Bobo Stenson (p); Stefan Blomquist (ky); Goran Klinghagen (g); Per-Ake Holmlander (tba); Teddy Walter (b); Anders Kjellberg (d); Andre Ferrari (perc).* 4/89.

Thelin was an important Swedish musician who worked his way from Dixieland to free playing with an entirely plausible logic, having developed a formidable agility on the trombone early on. There is, regrettably, still nothing under his own name at present which features his playing: this concert of his extended suite, 'Raggruppamento', was his final achievement, completed when he was already ill with cancer and unable himself to play. It's a pity in some ways that his solo parts are performed by guitarist Klinghagen rather than one of the trombonists: Klinghagen does a decent job, but one misses the rigour of Thelin's own playing. The Swedish Radio Jazz group is a formidable ensemble, though, and they translate all the sonorities of Thelin's score into a shimmering whole. The 11 parts are typically catholic in their breadth of sympathies: Thelin's interest in electronics is reflected by Blomquist's sensitive keyboards, but the rumbustious section-work is as important as the more translucent moments. There are also fine solos from Wilczewski, though disappointingly few from the other horns, considering the stellar personnel. Excellent concert recording.

Toots Thielemans (born 1922)

HARMONICA, GUITAR, WHISTLING

If you were a young Belgian jazz fanatic in the early 1940s, you took up guitar in emulation of Django. Thielemans recorded 'Bluesette' in 1961, after working with George Shearing; his first hit had him playing guitar and whistling, but he subsequently became the pre-eminent harmonica player in jazz, with a facility and depth of expression that rivals any conventional horn players. A festival favourite, Thielemans tended to avoid the studio in later years.

*****(*) Man Bites Harmonica**

Original Jazz Classics OJC 1738 *Thielemans; Pepper Adams (bs); Kenny Drew (p); Wilbur Ware (b); Art Taylor (d).* 12/57.

Thielemans frequently finds himself in the awkward and unsatisfactory position of coming first in a category of one or consigned to 'miscellaneous instruments'. Though ubiquitous in the blues, the harmonica has made remarkably little impact in jazz, and there are no recognized critical standards for his extraordinary facility as a whistler. Thielemans's pop and movie work has tended further to downgrade his very considerable jazz credentials. Surprisingly, to those who know him primarily as a performer of moodily atmospheric soundtrack pieces (*Midnight Cowboy* pre-eminently) or as composer of the undemanding 'Bluesette', his roots are in bebop and in the kind of harmonically liberated improvisation associated with John Coltrane. That's perhaps most obvious in the dark, Chicago-influenced sound of *Man Bites Harmonica*, which includes a wonderful 'Don't Blame Me'. The rather dark-toned group is not the setting one expects for him, but it is wonderfully effective.

***** Aquarela Do Brasil**

Verve 830391-2 *Thielemans; Elis Regina (v); Orquesta Elis Cinco.* 69.

This belongs as much to the singer as to Toots, but for lovers of Latin jazz it's a jewel of an album, lush and overproduced, but full of enchanting moments, from the inevitable Jobim ('Wave') to Toots's little posy, 'Five For Elis'. There is a light and joyous touch to everything the two principals attempt and it's almost a pity that this couldn't have been recorded with just a couple of guitarists and a melodic bass player. 'Honeysuckle Rose' is robbed of much of its intimacy by the big sound.

***** The Silver Collection: Toots Thielemans**

Polydor 825086 *Thielemans; Ferdinand Povel (ts); Rob Franken (ky); Wim Overgaauw, Joop Scholten (g); Victor Kaihatu, Niels-Henning Orsted Pedersen (b); Bruno Castellucci, Evert Overweg (d); Ruud Boos Orchestra; collective personnel, other details unknown.* 4/74–4/75.

In addition to the inevitable 'Bluesette', there are good solo performances of 'Muskrat Ramble', 'The Mooche' and a slightly off-beam 'You're My Blues Machine' on *The Silver Collection*, a useful sample which establishes his bop *bona fides* with 'My Little Suede Shoes' and is marred only by a set of rather dreary band arrangements by Boos.

*****(*) Images**

Candid 71007 *Thielemans; Joanne Brackeen (p); Cecil McBee (b); Freddie Waits (d).* 9/74.

****(*) Live**

Polydor 831694 *Thielemans; Wim Overgaauw, Joop Scholten (g); Rob Franken (electric p); Victor Kaihatu, Rob Langereis (b); Bruno Castellucci (d); Cees Schrama (perc).* 4/75.

***** Live In The Netherlands**

Original Jazz Classics OJC 930 *Thielemans; Joe Pass (g); Niels-Henning Orsted Pedersen (b).* 7/80.

These live sets appear to confirm a long-standing belief that Thielemans is not always a successful studio performer but needs the resistance and charge of a live audience. *Images* is one of the best records he ever made. The group is stunningly inventive and the version of 'Giant Steps' is all the proof anyone will ever need of the chromatic harmonica's place in the jazz canon. Other compositions are by Toots and pianist Brackeen, who is in very good form. The Netherlands trio is a record that grows in stature with every hearing, and Toots's bop-tinged solos on 'Thriving On A Riff' and 'Someday My Prince Will Come' are a revelation. NHOP and Pass are both in splendid form and the interplay of melodic lines creates entirely new contrafacts out of familiar materials. Ellington's 'The Mooche' is a guitar solo, brief but evocative and with a steely edge.

The third of the group stands up less well as the years go by, largely because the accompanying musicians are so sturdy and unresponsive. Toots delivers his usual unflappable set, but the backgrounds could certainly be more exuberant.

****** Do Not Leave Me**

Stash ST CD 12 *Thielemans; Fred Hersch (p); Marc Johnson (b); Joey Baron (d).* 6/86.

Do Not Leave Me was recorded in Brussels a year or two earlier and has all the qualities of a sentimental homecoming. The opening 'Ne Me Quitte Pas', by Jacques Brel, another native of the city, is drenched with emotion. 'Stardust' is dedicated to Benny Goodman, who had died a few days previously. It follows a long medleyed version of Miles Davis's 'All Blues' and 'Blue 'N' Green', the latter co-written with Bill Evans. Thielemans had played with the pianist in 1978, at which session he met Marc Johnson. 'Autumn Leaves' is a bass-and-drums feature, with an astonishing solo from Baron that brings up the temperature for the samba rhythms of 'Velas', which Thielemans takes on guitar. A fine set closes with 'Bluesette', which he calls his 'calling card or, better yet, social security number'. Everyone whistles along.

****** Only Trust Your Heart**

Concord CCD 4355 *Thielemans; Fred Hersch (p); Marc Johnson, Harvie Swartz (b); Joey Baron (d).* 4–5/88.

*****(*) Footprints**

Emarcy 846650 *Thielemans; Mulgrew Miller (p); Rufus Reid (b); Lewis Nash (d).* 89.

The later '80s marked a considerable revival of Thielemans's jazz playing. A studio jazz recording led by Thielemans was by then a rarity, but *Only Trust Your Heart* is his masterpiece. Restricted on this occasion to harmonica, the playing is superb. The choice of material (and Fred Hersch's arranging) is impeccable and challenging and the production first rate, with Thielemans front and centre and the band spread out very evenly behind him. The set kicks off with a marvellous reading of Wayne Shorter's 'Speak No Evil', includes 'Sophisticated Lady', Monk's 'Little Rootie Tootie' and Thad Jones's 'Three And One', transposed unfamiliarly high to bring it within the range of Thielemans's instrument, which takes on the slightly yodelling timbre of soprano saxophone. Throughout, Thielemans's solo development merits the closest attention, particularly on the original 'Sarabande', the better of two duets with Hersch. The pianist's other composition, 'Rain Waltz', deserves wider distribution. Allegedly nearly all first takes, each of the dozen tracks represents Thielemans's undervalued art at its finest.

*****(*) For My Lady**

Emarcy 510133 *Thielemans; Shirley Horn (p, v); Charles Ables (b); Steve Williams (d).* 4/91.

This attractive collaboration with Shirley Horn yields an album of impeccable performances that sound completely spontaneous and uncontrived. Horn's piano playing (which in recent years has tended to take a back seat to her singing) is the ideal accompaniment, and Thielemans responds by echoing the contours of her unmistakable vocal phrasing. There are several entrances which, for a note or two, could be either of them.

*****(*) East Coast West Coast**

Private Music 01005 82120 2 *Thielemans; Terence Blanchard (t); Joshua Redman, Ernie Watts (ts); Bruce Barth, Alan Broadbent, Michael Lang, Lyle Mays (p); Robben Ford, John Scofield (g); Mike Maineri (vib); Jerry Goodman (vn); Dave Carpenter, Charlie Haden, Christian McBride (b); Troy Davis, Peter Erskine (d).* 94.

Recorded in New York and Los Angeles, this was Toots's tribute to some of his musical heroes, Coltrane, Monk, Diz, Brubeck and Desmond, Bill Evans and Miles Davis. The musicianship is exceptional throughout and some of the performances, notably 'Waltz For Debby' with Charlie Haden and Alan Broadbent (West Coast), 'Groovin' High' with Troy Davis and Chris McBride and the fabulous closing sequence of 'Ornithology' and 'Blue In Green' (the latter a back East quartet performance with Dave Carpenter, Mike Lang and the endlessly inventive Peter Erskine) are among the best studio sides Toots has made in 30 years. The duet with Herbie Hancock on 'A Child Is Born' is – forgive the tasteless analogy – to die for. The sound-quality is consistently excellent right through the album, and the only possible quibble is the sheer array of talent assembled for just one or two tracks. Especially good to hear Jerry Goodman, formerly of The Flock and Mahavishnu Orchestra, back in action. With names and talent like that around, the session tapes must be gold dust.

***** Concerto For Harmonica**
TCB 94802 *Thielemans; Matthie Michel (t, flhn); Michel Weber (as, cl); Yvan Ischer (ss, ts); Christian Gavillet (bs, bcl); Fred Hersch (p); Antoine Ogay (b); Big Band de Lausanne.* 12/95.

Christian Gavillet's 'concerto' for Toots is really just a suite of thematically connected melodies with very little structural logic beyond that. That, though, is sufficient to conjure one of the Belgian's finest performances, though he saves the really good stuff for a couple of encores with just Hersch in accompaniment. As ever, the sound of the harmonica floats away above the well-drilled Swiss band, which is under the direction of Charles Papasoff. Other featured soloists include Gavillet himself, a fine baritonist in a pre-Mulligan style, and trumpeter Michel, who has a soft, almost liquid tone. A delightful evening's music.

***** Chez Toots**
Private Music 82160 *Thielemans; Oscar Castro-Nueves, Philip Catherine (g); Marcel Azzola (acc); Hein Van de Geyn (b); André Ceccarelli (d); Chip, Shirley Horn, Diane Krall, Dianne Reeves, Johnny Mathis (v); strings; backing vocalists.*

A tribute to the music of France, with tunes by Brel, Piaf and Trenet. Toots is paired with each of the guest vocalists in what appear to be overdubbed recordings. The voices are each and all individual and assured, but there is a touch of gimmickry about the set as a whole which confounds its jazz feel. Krall is very good on 'La Vie en rose' and of course Shirley Horn wrote the book on this kind of thing, but Mathis is a bit too Las Vegas for the setting. The best tracks are those on which Thielemans simply stretches out with his harmonica and plays some jazz.

Jesper Thilo (born 1941)

TENOR SAXOPHONE, CLARINET, TRUMPET

From Copenhagen, Thilo was working in the Danish mainstream from the early '60s and is a big-sounding player, almost equally influenced by swing and bop styles.

***** Jesper Thilo Quartet With Clark Terry**
Storyville STCD 8204 *Thilo; Clark Terry (t); Kenny Drew (p); Jesper Lundgaard, Mads Vinding (b); Svend-Erik Norregaard, Billy Hart (d).* 12/80.

***** Jesper Thilo Quintet Featuring Harry Edison**
Storyville STC-CD 4120 *Thilo; Harry 'Sweets' Edison (t); Ole Kock Hansen (p); Ole Ousen (g); Jesper Lundgaard (b); Svend-Erik Norregaard (d).* 2/86.

****(*) Shufflin'**
Music Mecca CD 1015 2 *Thilo; Ole Kock Hansen, Søren Kristiansen (p); Henrik Bay (g); Jesper Lundgaard, Hugo Rasmussen (b); Svend-Erik Norregaard (d); Ann Farholt (v).* 9/90.

*****(*) Jesper Thilo Quintet Featuring Hank Jones**
Storyville STCD 4178 *Thilo; Hank Jones (p); Doug Raney (g); Hugo Rasmussen (b); Svend-Erik Norregaard (d).* 3/91.

***** Plays Duke Ellington**
Music Mecca CD 1025-2 *Thilo; Søren Kristiansen (p); Hugo Rasmussen (b); Svend-Erik Norregaard (d); Ann Farholt (v).* 4/92.

***** Don't Count Him Out**
Music Mecca CD 1035-2 *As above.* 3/93.

*****(*) Movin' Out**
Music Mecca 1045-2 *Thilo; Ben Besiakov (p); Jesper Lundgaard (b).* 4/94.

***** Together**
Music Mecca 1975-2 *Thilo; Søren Kristiansen (p); Niels Pallesen (b); Svend-Erik Norregaard (d).* 10/95.

***** Jesper Thilo / Ann Farholt Meets Thomas Clausen**
Music Mecca 2025-2 *Thilo; Thomas Clausen (p); Henrik Bay (g); Mads Vinding (b); Svend-Erik Norregaard (d); Ann Farholt (v).* 10/96.

*****(*) Thank You Mr Hat!**
Music Mecca 2045-2 *Thilo; Henrik Bolberg (t); Søren Kristiansen (p); Niels Pallesen (b); Svend-Erik Norregaard (d).* 11/97.

Thilo plays the kind of straight-ahead swing that the Scandinavians have now virtually patented: he's a tenorman in the noble tradition, a plain speaker and a reliable journeyman. The early session with Terry is coupled with a quartet date from the same month, and though this is no more than a friendly chug through a familiar programme the front line has real class. The set with Edison would be by far the more impressive were it not for the dullness of the accompaniments; however, the trumpeter does kick-start 'There Will Never Be Another You' and there are some graceful moments on a romantic medley recorded on a later – and better – night. *Shufflin'* is very much in the same vein, a professional club set that doesn't really bear frequent repetition at home. The bebop flourishes on 'How High The Moon', with Ann Farholt's rather strained voice acting as second horn, are quite dramatic, and there are enough imaginative flourishes on a long roster of standards to sustain interest; but, again, nothing to write home about.

The more recent records count among his best. The meeting with Hank Jones benefits hugely from Hank's benign but slyly alert presence, whether prodding a soloist or taking a typically suave improvisation of his own. Raney, too, plays very well. The first two Music Mecca albums are focused round Ellington and Basie repertoire and, though some of the choices are a little too familiar in each case, the quintet plays them with fine enthusiasm and Thilo musters some of his sharpest improvising (his clarinet playing on 'Duke's Place' is also a neat surprise). Farholt's singing is much more assured and the studio sound is very crisp on each record.

It seems almost cheeky to suggest that Thilo is improving. But it's hard to avoid the feeling that *Movin' Out* is his best record. The lighter feel of a drummerless trio suits him and, though he stands in a mainstream tenor tradition, he has a more airy approach to an improvisation than some masters of the style; boppish without really sounding 'modern', his solos have a fleetness which defies cliché. 'Blue Monk' turns a contemporary blues into a masterclass of the style. Besiakov is perhaps no more than a good prop, but this is a cracker of a record.

There is some flab on *Together* – too many bass solos and perhaps too many tracks overall – but otherwise Thilo is still in top form. 'Donna' is full-on bebop, still synthesized through a swing man's dedications, and it's intriguing to hear how he makes Joe Henderson's 'Recorda-Me' into the kind of full-blooded declamation which the more oblique hard-boppers would shy away from. The rhythm section is good, if not quite in the front rank, and it may be time to hear Thilo trading punches with an all-American band.

Thank You Mr Hat! is by the same group, with a couple of years' worth of extra seasoning and trumpeter Bolberg stepping in on the final four tracks. They're all in great shape, too. Jesper sweeps all before him – cop the wondrous invention on a long, luxuriant 'Sweet Lorraine' – but the others are swinging like champions too. The ten tracks are all in the old-favourite category, but it's conceived as a tribute to the wonderful Arnvid Meyer (or 'Mr Hat', as J.C. Higginbotham christened him) and the days when Arnvid's small-group swing dominated the Danish jazz scene (with Thilo in the band). A warm tribute to a great man.

A surprise to hear Thilo taking out the trumpet for 'September Song' on *Meets Thomas Clausen*. But he's soon back on tenor for the cheeky 'Five Bebop Tunes', a beefy 'It Might As Well Be Spring', a grouchy 'Svinninge Blues'. Clausen follows keenly, but one's reaction may depend on how much Farholt appeals – she's all over the record and sometimes seems over-confident.

*****(*) 40th Anniversary Collection**

Music Mecca CD 2105-2 2CD *As Music Mecca discs listed above.* 92–97.

The best of Jesper, or at least the pick of his Music Mecca albums, generously pillaged for a little over two hours of music in this double-disc compilation. Arguably too much from the Ellington and Basie discs, but if you wanted one Thilo record for the collection we wouldn't dissuade you from snapping this one up.

Frode Thingnaes (born 1940)

TROMBONE

A veteran trombonist of the Norwegian swing-to-bop school, usually encountered in a sideman role.

***** Watch What Happens!**

Gemini GMCD 85 *Thingnaes; Steffan Stokland (btb); Henryk Lysiak (p); Pete Knutsen, Jan Erik Kongshaug (g); Terje Gewelt (b); Svein Christiansen (d).* 11/93–1/94.

A veteran Norwegian trombonist, Frode Thingnaes doesn't stint on this rare outing as a leader – overdubbing accounts for up to six horns on each track, and with his light, singing tone he gets a very pleasing sound out of his one-man section. Some of the arrangements opt for a light-music feel rather than anything more demanding, though often the sonorities are their own reward, and when he clears the decks and gives himself a straight-ahead solo he shows himself to be a capable jazzman. Genial swing-to-bop stuff.

The XIII Ghosts

GROUP

A one-off recording project featuring several London-based improvisers.

***** Giganti Reptilicus Destructo Beam**

Scatter 04 *Alex Ward (as, cl, v); Tim Hill (reeds, perc, junk); Nick Couldry (ky); Jim Denley (f, as, picc); Pat Thomas (p, elec); Evan Thomas (g); Andru Clare (g, toys); Switch (elec, v). n.d.*

Ranging from mere seconds to a minute or two, these 45 (not 46, as per the sleeve!) tracks are a juicy jumble of Ward's sax and clarinet blasts, assisted by various pals, and defaced or otherwise by sampler/electronics person Switch. There's plenty of fun to be had by setting the CD to random play; alternatively, one can follow the slightly Zappa-esque trail that The Ghosts pursue by putting it in and pressing 'play'. The sleeve dedications are all to noted horror film directors, from William Castle to Jose (Coffin Joe) Marins. These guys want to be in the soundtrack business.

Gary Thomas (born 1961)

TENOR SAXOPHONE, FLUTE

Thomas was one of the most assertive and acerbic of the M-Base musicians, with a punchy, insistent tone that is most forceful on his own records but which has also contributed materially to records by other leaders, including Uri Caine, Peter Herborn and John McLaughlin.

***** Seventh Quadrant**

Enja 5047 *Thomas; Paul Bollenback (g, syn); Renee Rosnes (p); Anthony Cox (b); Jeff Tain Watts (d).* 4/87.

***** Code Violations**

Enja 5085 *Thomas; Paul Bollenback (g, syn); Tim Murphy (p, ky); Anthony Cox, Geoff Harper (b); Dennis Chambers, Steve Williams (d).* 7/88.

Of the streets streety, as Dickens might have said. Actually did say, except that he wasn't talking about Gary Thomas. The young saxophonist quit a paying gig with Miles Davis because the music was too simplistic for him. Since then, he's carved out a tough and uncompromising course for himself with music that is as ruggedly contemporary as the latest front page and as hard as a very hard thing. The debut of Seventh Quadrant was pretty auspicious. Some have argued (and Thomas has vehemently denied) that the major influence is Coltrane. However, the rugged atonality and the tense, centrifugal rhythms have to have come from somewhere; Trane's language, fast-forwarded to the late '80s, sounds as likely a root-source as any. Bollenback was to become a regular partner and, one suspects, an important influence on the overall sound. Thomas himself comes on like a latter-day Wayne Shorter, drawing something from the Afro-mystical mode Wayne developed in *Ju-Ju* and *Odyssey Of Iska*. The tone is acidulous, hard-edged and pungent, always upfront and quite dry in the mix. The best things are 'Foresight, Preparation And Subterfuge', 'No' and 'The Eternal Present'.

Code Violations has never been a big favourite of ours. Titles like 'Maxthink', 'Traf', 'Zylog', 'Sybase' and 'Adax' suggest Thomas is searching for some grounding in black urban sci-fi, claiming to be the bastard son of Samuel Delany and only succeeding in turning himself into the H.G. Wells of modern New York.

***** Found On Sordid Streets**
Winter & Winter 910 002 *Thomas; George Colligan (org); Paul Bollenback (g); Howard Curtis (d); Steve Moss (perc); Pork Chop, No Name (v)*. 2/96.

***** Pariah's Pariah**
Winter & Winter 910 033 *As above, except omit Moss, Pork Chop, No Name.* 99.

Thomas's first record for the newly founded W&W label wisely attempted to do no more than consolidate the sound he had been trading in for years at JMT. He reworks 'Exile's Gate' and includes Terri Lyne Carrington's 'The Eternal Present', a tune that sounds as if it's been around longer than any of these guys. The raps are still pretty hokey and not entirely convincing, but this is a solid performance from all concerned.

The follow up album is no less tough and uncompromising, but without the raps Thomas's tenor comes through stronger than ever, and on 'Zero Tolerance' and 'Vanishing Time', which represent the real climax of the album, he is playing at his peak, phrasing fast and with real control and definition.

Luther Thomas

ALTO SAXOPHONE

Originally associated with new jazz in St Louis in the 1970s and early '80s, Thomas has only rarely been heard from on record since.

***(*) Don't Tell**
Creative Consciousness CD 1000A *Thomas; Ted Daniel (t); Charles Eubanks (ky); Wilber Morris (b); Dennis Charles (d). n.d.*

****(*) BAGin' It**
CIMP 112 *As above, except omit Eubanks.* 4/96.

**** Saxcrobatic Fanatic**
CIMP 145 *Thomas; Kelvyn Bell (g); Ronnie Burrage (d).* 4/97.

Thomas was a member of the St Louis co-operative, BAG, and his subsequent course has been difficult to follow: one album for Moers, many years ago, and little else. These recent records are a dispiriting testament. *Don't Tell* is a ludicrous shambles: swamped by a deafening keyboard line and Charles turned up to stadium levels, the horns struggle with a bizarre kind of avant-fusion that doesn't bear even the most casual scrutiny. CIMP has since sponsored a couple of albums, but they're the weakest things in their catalogue. *BAGin' It* earns its stars for the heroic efforts of Daniel, Wilber Morris and Charles, who would be a fine trio by themselves. Luther's noisy and directionless playing seems at once dated and self-consciously far out. *Saxcrobatic Fanatic* has a few flourishes which the trio manage to put over, but this isn't the kind of record this label should be making; it needs a souped-up production to hide the thinness of Bell's sound and ideas, and something to temper the repetitive bluster which Thomas relies on. Seventy minutes of this sort of thing is several bridges too far.

René Thomas (1927–75)

GUITAR

Though Belgian, Thomas made his mark on the Parisian scene of the 1950s, before spells in New York and Canada. His later stint with Stan Getz and Eddie Louiss brought him his widest exposure.

*****(*) Guitar Groove**
Original Jazz Classics OJC 1725 *Thomas; J.R Monterose (ts); Hod O'Brien (p); Teddy Kotick (b); Albert 'Tootie' Heath (d).* 9/60.

A fatal heart attack cut short a career that was already rather overshadowed by a more colourful and charismatic guitarist, Thomas's Belgian compatriot, Django Reinhardt. Though Django must have been the unavoidable comparison when Thomas moved to North America, there really wasn't very much in common between them and Thomas's modernist credentials allowed him to fit into the American scene more comfortably than his illustrious predecessor. *Guitar Groove* is a fine product of his American sojourn and is one of the high points of a poorly documented career. The original, 'Spontaneous Effort', combines firm, boppish melody with an easy swing. Monterose is too raw-throated for 'Milestones' but slots into 'Ruby My Dear' with impressive ease. He sits out for 'Like Someone In Love' and O'Brien joins him on the bench for the duration of 'How Long Has This Been Going On?'. The sound is better balanced on these tracks than when the horn is present, but overall it sounds very good indeed.

Barbara Thompson (born 1944)

SAXOPHONES, FLUTES, SOPRANINO RECORDER, KEYBOARDS

At twenty, Thompson joined Neil Ardley's orchestra, where she met future husband, Jon Hiseman. They, together with Colin Dudman, have been the basic line-up of Paraphernalia, a band that has now lasted for nearly three decades in different forms.

***** Mother Earth**
VeraBra CDVBR 2005 *Thompson; Anthony Oldridge (vn, electric vn); Colin Dudman (ky); Dill Katz (b); Jon Hiseman (d, perc).* 82.

***** Barbara Thompson's Special Edition**
VeraBra CDVBR 2017 *Thompson; Rod Argent, Clem Clempson, Colin Dudman, Steve Melling, Bill Worrall (ky); Rod*

Dorothy, Anthony Oldridge (vn); Dave Ball, Dill Katz, John Mole (b); Jon Hiseman (d); Gary Kettel (perc). 6/85.

*****(*) Heavenly Bodies**
VeraBra CDVBR 2015 *Thompson; Guy Barker, Stuart Brooks, John Thirkell (t); Bill Geldard (btb); David Cullen, Pete Lemer, Steve Melling (ky); Paul Dunne (g); Rod Dorothy, Patrick Halling, Robin Williams (vn); Tony Harris (vla); Quentin Williams (clo); Dave Ball, Andy Paak (b); Jon Hiseman (d, perc).* 8/86.

***** A Cry From The Heart**
VeraBra CDVBR 2021 *Thompson; Pete Lemer (ky); Paul Dunne (g); Phil Mulford (b); Jon Hiseman (d, perc).* 11/87.

*****(*) Breathless**
VeraBra CDVBR 2057 *Thompson; Pete Lemer (ky); Malcolm MacFarlane (g); Jon Hiseman (d).* 90.

***** Everlasting Flame**
VeraBra CDVBR 2058 *Thompson; Pete Lemer (ky); Malcolm MacFarlane (g); Paul Westwood (b); Jon Hiseman (d); Hossam Ramzy (perc); Anna Gracey Hiseman, London Community Gospel Singers (v).* 93.

***** Shifting Sands**
Intuition INT 3174 2 *Thompson; Pete Lemer (ky); Billy Thompson (vn); Paul Westwood (b); Jon Hiseman (d).* 98.

An astonishingly talented multi-instrumentalist, Thompson encompasses straight-ahead jazz, rock and fusion, but she incorporates an interest in ethnic, formal and elements of ambient and 'New Age' music. She is difficult to categorize and has therefore rarely received the critical attention she merits. Thompson is a forceful soloist who regularly introduces unusual harmonic juxtapositions by playing two instruments simultaneously. Thompson's band, Paraphernalia, has never perhaps been as effective in the studio as in a live setting. Earlier recordings such as *Mother Earth* (originally released in Britain on her own Temple Music label) demonstrate her facility for synthesis of quite eclectic materials. It combines quite orthodox jazz structures (albeit influenced by rock) with an underlying formal 'programme' that conforms thematically to her concern with quasi-theosophical connections between human beings and the planet they inhabit. This is done most effectively on *Heavenly Bodies*, her best record currently available, in which the musical surface and the improvisational logic are both much more highly developed.

Special Edition is a rather messy compilation of live materials by three different versions of Thompson's band, one of them including rockers Clem Clempson and Rod Argent (the latter can at least claim to have taken rock ideas into imaginative territory). The band featured on both *Breathless* and *Everlasting Flame* also has a strong rock tinge, but it provides Thompson with a solid platform for some of her most evocative solos on record and some of her most imaginative writing. 'The Night Before Culloden' and 'Tatami' on the later disc identify how far away from orthodox jazz she has felt able to work. They also, less encouragingly, help identify the essential bittiness of the records. Paraphernalia's live performances tend to be much more focused.

Shifting Sands is ever more of a family affair, with Billy Thompson joining the line-up and acquitting himself extremely well. As often, Barbara has assembled a loosely themed programme, concerned with change and decay, illusion and continuity. The last of these at least is the key to her work, a steady and clear-sighted application to creative music.

Danny Thompson (born 1943)

DOUBLE BASS

Ubiquitous in all strands and styles of British music – from the jazz-tinged folk of Pentangle to pop and soul – Thompson remains a jazz player at heart. He has a big, generous tone, improvises with a melodic freedom reminiscent of Scott LaFaro, and never fails to communicate generous personality and spiritual strength.

****** Live 1967**
What Disc WHAT3CD *Thompson; Tony Roberts (ts, bcl, f); John McLaughlin (g).* 67.

The last couple of years have been critically important in the re-assessment of British jazz of the 1960s and '70s. Alongside the reissues of Tony Oxley and Howard Riley, Joe Harriott and Ray Russell, this newly discovered tape stands out strongly. Not much is known about where the recording was made, but it is of remarkably good quality and it captures the drummerless trio running through an eclectic bag of material with enthusiasm and verve. Tony Roberts still hasn't received due recognition. This will only help. His bass clarinet work on 'Naima' (which, as Wally Houser points out in his liner-note, was far from being a chestnut in 1967, the year of Trane's death) is quite magnificent, topped only by a solo from John McLaughlin who here shows the kind of player he was before he went off to work with Miles Davis. McLaughlin's obvious understanding of bebop prompts a reassessment of his later career and of the remarkable *Extrapolation*, which came less than two years after this. The trio make a wonderful job of Brubeck's 'In Your Own Sweet Way' and Miles's 'All Blues', on which Thompson himself is supreme: lyrical, dead-centre and effortlessly rhythmic. Any one of these players might have got the call from the great man, but it was McLaughlin who went and his life course changed radically. It's fascinating to hear him in this unexpected context. An excellent album from what looks like being a very strong series. Some problems of attribution – Bud Powell's 'Celia' is credited to Charlie Parker, and Wally talks about Dizzy Gilespie's 'Anthropology' – but otherwise a very welcome and endlessly fascinating package.

Don Thompson (born 1940)

VIBRAPHONE, PIANO, BASS

Frequently encountered as a bassist, Thompson is a Canadian who was first noticed in the John Handy group in the '60s. He has made many sideman appearances and had long associations with Jim Hall and George Shearing.

****(*) Winter Mist**
Jazz Alliance TJA-10004 *Thompson; Reg Schwager (g); Pat Collins (b); Barry Elmes (d).* 4/90.

Surprisingly, Thompson plays vibes exclusively on this disc, recorded at a Toronto club. The impressionism of the title and cover-art extends to the music, which is predominantly vague, not helped much by a foggy sound-quality that relegates Collins in particular to the shadows. Schwager, though, comes up with some pleasing solos and, while there's far too much music at 74 minutes, the best of it passes agreeably enough.

*** Celebration

Jazz Focus JFCD024 *Thompson; Kevin Turcotte (t, flhn); Josh Brown (tb); Roy Styffe (as); Pat LaBarbera (ss, ts); Perry White (bs); Jim Vivian (b); Ted Warren, Mark McLean (d).* 12/96.

And here he's on piano, leading his Banff Jazz All Stars (a band grown out of past members of a month-long workshop curriculum, here playing at a Toronto festival) through four of his themes and a couple of Kenny Wheeler charts. They're well played, and melodically attractive, but the soloists seldom make a significant mark and it does tend to sound like a festival occasion. The one track which breaks away a little, 'For Dave Holland', engenders the most striking set of solos and has rather more spontaneous fizz than the rest.

Gail Thompson

COMPOSER, BANDLEADER, FLUTE

Emerged as part of the new wave of young instrumentalists on the London jazz scene of the mid-'80s, playing a key role in forming the Jazz Warriors and subsequently writing for and directing her own big band, although illness has curtailed her own work on sax, flute and bass.

*** Gail Force

EFZ 1005 *Gerard Presencer, Martin Shaw (t, flhn); Winston Rollins (tb); Andy McIntosh (as, ss, f); Scott Garland, Dave O'Higgins (ts); Mark Lockheart (ts, ss); Adrian York (ky); Jim Mullen (g); Laurence Cottle (b); Ian Thomas (d); Gary Hammond (perc); Ian Shaw (v).* 1/94.

*** Jazz Africa

Enja ENJ 9053 *Thompson; Harry Beckett, Claude Deppa (t, flhn); Patrick Hartley (tb); Tom Harris (ts, ss, f); Jerry Underwood (ts, ss); Mike Parlett (as, f); Jim McKay (WX7); Mervyn Africa (p, syn); Lucky Ranku (g); Mario Castronari (b); Cheryl Alleyne (d); Joe Legwabe (perc).* 5/95.

Gail Thompson's story is both sad and salutary. Less than a day after playing with Art Blakey in London, she suffered a spasm of the facial muscles that left her unable to play. Thompson had been a founding member with Courtney Pine of the Jazz Warriors and had fronted her own Gail Force on baritone saxophone, a big, rousing sound that seemed exactly commensurate with her larger-than-life personality. Thompson absorbed herself in jazz education for some time and gamely plugged away at writing. *Gail Force* might seem a little padded with two radio edits thrown in to make up the duration, but it's still a strong record, with Dave O'Higgins filling the gap left by Gail's horn on 'Maybe It's Me', perhaps the strongest single track. The arrangements, by Fayyaz Virji and Mike Hornet, are very good indeed, though guitarist Jim Mullen, who solos magnificently on 'The Big Picture', is left to do a good deal of the journeywork in the sections.

Jazz Africa was largely the result of a trip to the continent, an experience that seems to have reshaped Thompson's thinking quite significantly. The good news was that she was playing again, contributing a long flute introduction to 'Long Time In Togo'. There are moments when the music will be reminiscent of Afro-British groups like Jabula and Zila, and the presence of veteran Harry Beckett will conjure up memories of Ogun records from the 1970s. However, the conception is anything but anachronistic. Thompson has pared down the sound considerably. 'Burkina Faso' is stripped to the bone, opening up feature spots for trombonist Patrick Hartley and guitarist Lucky Ranku, though this time the flute part is taken by Tom Harris. Other soloists worth noting are the redoubtable Mervyn Africa on 'Expedition' and the exuberant 'Finale', Claude Deppa, bassist Castronari on 'Kamara River' and altoist Mike Parlett on a couple of numbers. Thompson seems keen on wind synthesizers and gives Jim McKay more than his fair share of space. Sound-quality from a live recording in Duisburg isn't too special with all the horns sounding a bit distant, but there's no mistaking the reaction of the crowd to vigorous, soulful music. A new record from Thompson was due as we went to press.

Lucky Thompson (born 1924)

TENOR SAXOPHONE, SOPRANO SAXOPHONE

Legend has the young South Carolinan obsessively practising saxophone fingerings on a broom handle before he had a proper horn. Thompson has always seemed an outsider, drawing on the swing era, involved in bebop, but also prefiguring much of what went on in the 1960s and '70s, after his playing career was effectively over.

*** Smooth Sailing

Indigo IGO CD 2104 *Thompson; John Best, Buck Clayton, Karl George, Conrad Gozzo (t); J.J Johnson, Shorty Rogers, Dickie Wells, Gerald Wilson (tb); Marshall Royal (as, cl); Jewell Grant, Herb Hoise, Dick Norris (as); Gordon Reeder (ts); Leon Beck (bs); Stuff Smith (vn); Wilbert Baranco, Eddie Beal, Sammy Benskin, Bill Doggett, Errol Garner, Bob Mosley, G Styles (p); Irving Ashby, Frank Davenport, Freddie Green, Al Hendrickson, Barney Kessel, Charlie Norris, Gene Phillips (g); Red Callender, Al Hall, John Kitzmiler, Charles Mingus, Oscar Pettiford, Rodney Richardson, Bob Stone (b); Edward Hall, Bob Hummell, Jackie Mills, Roy Porter, Alvin Stoller, George Wettling, Shadow Wilson, Lee Young (d); David Allyn, Ernie Andrews, Marion Abernathy, Sylvia Sims (v).* 12/44–6/47.

*** The Beginning Years

IAJRC CD 1001 *Thompson; Frank Beach, Karl George, Al Killian, Chuck Peterson, Charlie Shavers (t); Lyle Griffin, Sidney Harris, J.J Johnson, Charles Maxon, Si Zentner (tb); Rudy Rutherford (cl); Marshal Royal (as, cl); Jewell Grant, Hal McKusick, Clint Meagley, Eddie Rosa (as); Stan Getz (as, ts); L Beck, Butch Stone (bs); Wilbert Baranco, Eddie Beal, Bill Doggett, Dodo Marmarosa, Bob Mosley, Jimmy Rowles (p); Frank Davenport (cel); Irving Ashby, Freddie Green, Al Hendrickson, Barney Kessel, Charles Norris, Gene Phillips, Tony*

Rizzi (g); Harry Babasin, Red Callender, Arnold Fishkind, Charles Mingus, Oscar Pettiford, Rodney Richardson, Bob Stone (b); Edward Hall, Don Lamond, Roy Porter, Alvin Stoller, Shadow Wilson, Lee Young (d); Marion Abernathy, David Allyn, Ernie Andrews, Estelle Edson (v); other personal uncertain. 45–47.

****** Accent On Tenor Sax**

Fresh Sound FSCD 2001 *Thompson; Ernie Royal (t); Jimmy Hamilton (cl); Earl Knight, Billy Taylor (p); Sidney Gross (g); Oscar Pettiford (b); Osie Johnson (d).* 54.

***** Lucky Thompson With Gerard Pochonet & His Quartet**

Fresh Sound FSR CD 86 *Thompson; Martial Solal (p); Michel Hausser (vib); Jean-Pierre Sasson (g); Pierre Michelot, Benoît Quersin (b); Gérard Pochonet (d).* 3/56.

Thompson's disappearance from the jazz scene in the 1970s was only the latest (but apparently the last) of a strangely contoured career. A highly philosophical, almost mystical man, he reacted against the values of the music industry and in the end turned his back on it without seeming regret. The beginning was garlanded with promise. He recorded with Charlie Parker just after the war (a rare example of that chimera, the bebop tenor player), but then returned to his native Detroit, where he became involved in R&B and publishing. Like Don Byas, whom he most resembles in tone and in his development of solos, he has a slightly oblique and uneasy stance on bop, cleaving to a kind of accelerated swing idiom with a distinctive 'snap' to his softly enunciated phrases and an advanced harmonic language that occasionally moves into areas of surprising freedom.

The material on *The Beginning Years* includes Thompson's debut as leader, an autumn 1945 session with J.J. Johnson in the line-up and a magnificent performance of 'Irresistible You' which is the earliest indication of Lucky's skills as a balladeer. Everything else on the disc is for other leaders, much of it straightforward accompaniment for singers, with just occasional flashes of saxophone brilliance. It's an album that is more interesting than genuinely enjoyable, worth picking up by anyone who's been intrigued by the later, more individual sessions and who wants to see where Lucky is coming from. Nicely detailed session notes help the listener navigate a rather bitty disc.

The Indigo compilation mostly features Thompson under other leaders – Freddie Green, Oscar Pettiford, Bob Mosley, Karl George, Frank Davenport and Ike Carpenter – but does also include 'Test Pilots' from 1944 with Stuff Smith and Errol Garner, a September 1945 all-stars session with J.J. Johnson, and six tracks recorded for Down Beat with the equally fugitive Dodo Marmarosa on piano. The sound quality is generally pretty poor, but there are enough glimpses of Thompson as a solo voice to make this a valuable documentation of a career that has yet to be fully assessed.

Thompson's best performances as leader are always when he has first-rate partners to bounce off, as with *Accent On Tenor Sax*. Thompson's rich, driving style coaxes some astonishing playing out of Jimmy Hamilton, who contributes 'Mr E-Z' to the session. Thompson's tenor has a smooth, clarinet quality on 'Where Or When', gliding over the changes with total ease. One curious characteristic is Thompson's preference for soloing at least a couple of choruses without harmonic accompaniment, a device that is most obvious on *Lord, Lord* ... but is common to all the records to some degree. Though very far back in the mix, Pettiford and Johnson play superbly, and the bassist checks in with one fine composition, 'Kamman's A'Comin''. For the last four tracks, including a superb 'Mood Indigo', Ernie Royal comes in on trumpet and Earl Knight replaces the guesting Billy Taylor.

*****(*) Lucky In Paris**

High Note HJCD 7045 *Thompson; Martial Solal (p); Michel Hausser (vib); Gilbert Gassin (b); Gérard Pochonet (d); Gana M'Bow (perc).* 1/59.

Originally released in France and France only on Symphonium Records, this catches Lucky in a transitional phase, sounding broody and reflective but also revelling in the company of Martial Solal and Gérard Pochonet, and still playing his soprano in the limber, expressive way that sets his approach to the instrument apart from what would become the orthodoxy of John Coltrane's style. Thompson sounds much closer to Johnny Hodges and, in places, to Lester Young, as in his wonderfully lyrical intepretation of 'We'll Be Together Again'. This was, strictly speaking, Pochonet's group and he commands his fair share and more of the spotlight, even on a short track like 'Tea For Two'. The interplay of piano and saxophone on 'Pennies From Heaven' is exquisite. Why this record was never released internationally seems incomprehensible. It catches Lucky ranging more freely than ever over the chords and reshaping melodies like that of 'Have You Met Miss Jones?' but already betraying a reticence that would all too shortly become permanent.

****** Lord, Lord, Am I Ever Going To Know?**

Candid CCD 79035 *Thompson; Martial Solal (p); Peter Trunk (b); Kenny Clarke (d).* 61.

This is the Lucky Thompson record to have, eight originals recorded in Paris with musicians who understood his wants and shared his musical and spiritual values. It is astonishing that this material has lain unheard for so long; only the title-track had been issued before and the other song titles were chosen by Alan Bates and Mark Gardner for release in 1997. The title-track is a loping tenor blues, crafted with great care and sophistication. The ballad that follows, 'Love And Respect', is the first of the soprano numbers, light-toned and limber. The real *tour de force* is the unaccompanied 'Choose Your Own', which has Lucky switching back and forth between tenor and soprano with seamless precision. As Gardner points out, with great justice, Thompson never believed he had even scratched the surface in his career, a statement denied by the vivid and intense improvisation on the final number which Bates and Gardner have called 'Scratching The Surface'. It's an extraordinary piece, and one that it would be interesting to play blindfold to some jazz commentators. Almost all will guess at a later date than 1961 and suggest someone in the nascent avant-garde, though it's by no means an 'outside' performance itself. The CD opens with a recording made in 1968, a message from Thompson to delegates at what was to have been a symposium in Coventry (ironic location, in the circumstances) dedicated to Lucky's work. What we hear is a man of surpassing modesty, but with a burning conviction as well. He asks us to rethink our priorities and take a more careful look at some of our idols' feet. He offers blessings and warm wishes and the the next thing we hear is 'Lord, Lord, Am I Ever Gonna Know?'. Presumably he found his own answer to that. The sorry tailpiece to the story is that the planned symposium was cancelled for lack of interest. Thompson took himself outside little more than a decade after this, and what followed was silence.

****** Lucky Strikes**

Original Jazz Classics OJC 194 *Thompson; Hank Jones (p); Richard Davis (b); Connie Kay (d).* 9/64.

Lucky Strikes is tighter and more precise. In the meantime Thompson had made significant bounds in his understanding of harmonic theory, and he attempts transitions that would have been quite alien to him a decade earlier. All his characteristic virtues of tone and smooth development are in place, though. He subtly blurs the melodic surface of 'In A Sentimental Mood' (a curious opener) and adjusts his tone significantly for the intriguing 'Reminiscent', 'Midnite Oil' and 'Prey Loot'. The Swiss concert material is far more conventional, perhaps in deference to the ticket office, but more probably because the group is so stiffly unswinging.

*****(*) Happy Days**

Prestige PRCD 24144 *Thompson; Tommy Flanagan, Hank Jones (p); Wendell Marshall, George Tucker (b); Dave Bailey, Jack Melady, Walter Perkins (d).*

***** Lucky Meets Tommy**

Fresh Sound FSRCD 199 *Thompson; Tommy Flanagan (p); Frank Anderson (org); Wally Richardson (g); Willie Ruff (b); Oliver Jackson, Walter Perkins (d).* 65.

Flanagan was the ideal piano partner for Thompson, a fluent melodist who doesn't lack for rhythmic drive and who constantly flirts with harmonic freedom. He's easily the more convincing of the two piano players on *Happy Days*, as upbeat and joyous a session as the name suggests, but with a softer and more poignant side as well. 'Long Ago And Far Away' and 'Dearly Beloved' are among the best things Thompson recorded; his own solos are crafted with intelligence and taste and he's never less than wholly responsive to those around him. The Fresh Sound is, as usual for this imprint, better musically than it is technically.

***** Soul's Nite Out**

Ensayo ENYCD 3471 *Thompson; Tete Montoliu (p); Eric Peter (b); Peer Wyboris (d).* 5/70.

Thompson has something of a cult following, not least in Barcelona, where local fans and musicians have long regarded him as up there with the very greats. That is where *Soul's Nite Out* was recorded, on a symbolically potent May Day in 1970. Thompson concentrates very largely on soprano, as so often at this time, switching to his tenor for Duke's 'I Got It Bad' and three other numbers. The tunes are all surprisingly short and solos rarely run to more than a few choruses, but there is no mistaking the inventiveness and sophistication of his playing. Montoliu and the locally celebrated rhythm section provide a fertile base.

Malachi Thompson (born 1941)

TRUMPET, VOICE

A player who mixed hard bop with free playing in about equal measure, Thompson is of the generation which fuelled the new music of Chicago in the 1960s, although his fundamentally more conservative line is at a tangent to those explorers. He overcame a serious illness to begin a long series of Delmark recordings, and his two principal bands are Freebop and Africa Brass.

***** Spirit**

Delmark DD-442 *Thompson; Carter Jefferson (ts); Albert Dailey (p); James King (b); Nasar Abeday (d); Randy Abbott (perc); Leon Thomas, Arnae Burton (v).*

***** The Jaz Life**

Delmark DD-453 *Thompson; Joe Ford (ss, as); Carter Jefferson (ts); Kirk Brown (p); Harrison Bankhead (b); Nasar Abeday (d); Richard Lawrence (perc).* 6/91.

***** Lift Every Voice**

Delmark DE-463 *Thompson; David Spencer, Kenny Anderson, Bob Griffin, Elmer Brown (t); Edwin Williams, Bill McFarland, Ray Riperton (tb); Steve Berry (btb); Carter Jefferson (ts); Kirk Brown (p); Harrison Bankhead (b); Ayreeayl Ra (d); Richard Lawrence, Enoch (perc); voices.* 8/92.

***** New Standards**

Delmark DE-473 *Thompson; Steve Berry (tb); Joe Ford (as); Ron Bridgewater, Sonny Seals, Carter Jefferson (ts); Kirk Brown (p); Yosef Ben Israel, John Whitfield (b); Ayreeayl Ra, Nasar Abeday (d); Dr Cuz (perc).* 4/93.

***** Buddy Bolden's Rag**

Delmark DE-484 *Thompson; David Spencer, Kenny Anderson, Phillip Perkins, Lester Bowie, Zane Massey (t); Edwin Williams, Bill McFarland, Ray Riperton, Steve Berry (tb); Ari Brown (ts); Harrison Bankhead (b); Darryl Ervin (d); Richard Lawrence, Dr Cuz (perc).* 94.

***** 47th Street**

Delmark DE-497 *Thompson; Steve Berry (tb); Joe Ford (ss, as); Carter Jefferson, Billy Harper, Ron Bridgewater (ts); Kirk Brown (p); Harrison Bankhead, John Whitfield (b); Dana Hall, Nasar Abadey (d); Dr Cuz (perc); Marian Hayes, Mae Koen, Dianne Madison, Byron Woods, Dan Porter (v).* 4/93–9/96.

With 20 years of recording behind him and no real recognition on a world stage, Thompson has been quietly building up a catalogue of records for Delmark in his home base of Chicago. Despite a serious illness diagnosed as lymphoma in 1989, he has come back with a personal take on new Chicagoan developments which bespeaks a courageous outlook. If he is not an especially outstanding technician or any kind of innovator, his music is a skilled synthesis of several threads from the Chicagoan repertory.

That said, none of these discs really marks itself out from the others, and each has its share of disappointments as well as successes. *Spirit* dates from the early 1980s and is relatively sketchy, but his long association with Carter Jefferson provides a confident front line and Dailey's dignified piano parts lend extra weight. *The Jaz Life* was almost a comeback album after his illness and peaks on the splendid swagger of Thompson's arrangement of the Ray Charles chestnut, 'Drown In My Own Tears'. *Lift Every Voice* is the first album to feature his big brass ensemble, which shares duties with his regular Freebop Band, and 'Elephantine Island' and 'Old Man River' make sonorous waves. Sometimes, though, it seems as if Thompson isn't sure what to do with the orchestra. He is back on safer ground with *New Standards*, which looks at some choice pieces of modern repertory. Freebop's slightly ragged edges are at least a change from the smart orthodoxy of most modern revivalists, but they could use a grain of extra finesse here and there. This was Jefferson's last album (he died in 1993) and his fine tenor improvisation on Booker Little's 'We Speak' is a poignant farewell.

Buddy Bolden's Rag brings back Africa Brass, with Bowie, Massey and Ari Brown as guests: Brown gets off a knockout solo on 'Harold The Great', Bowie makes some mysterious noises on a revised 'Nubian Call' and the brass play with real enthusiasm. Though one still feels that Thompson's collaring of this genre misses some of the visionary clout which Brass Fantasy has brought to this kind of big-band music, and the leader's own solos miss the ripe authority of Bowie himself, it's an entertaining set. *47th Street* is a dedication to Chicago's black community and the title-piece and 'Mystery Of Jaaz [sic] Suite' feature the singers, to rather merry effect. Thompson has a strong band here – though there are four tracks left over from 1993, including Jefferson's final recordings – and even if, as before, there's a faulty, sometimes unkempt feel to the ensembles, the music has spirit. Thompson's own playing seems to have got slower and more thoughtful, and hence more effective. His little chorus with the mute on 'CJ's Blues' is very beguiling.

*** Freebop Now!

Delmark DE-506 *Thompson; Steve Berry (tb); Billy Harper, Sonny Seals, Carter Jefferson (ts); Oliver Lake (as); Kirk Brown (p); Harrison Bankhead, John Whitfield, James Cammack (b); Richard 'Drahseer' Smith, Nasar Abadey, Hamid Drake (d); Tony Carpenter (perc); Amiri Baraka, Larry Smith, Sharese Locke (v).* 4/93–5/98.

*** Rising Daystar

Delmark DE-518 *Thompson; Steve Berry (tb); Gary Bartz (as, ss); Sonny Seals (ts); Kirk Brown (p); Harrison Bankhead, John Whitfield, James Cammack, Fred Hopkins (b); Dana Hall, Nasar Abadey (d); Tony Carpenter (perc); Dee Alexander (v).* 8/97–6/99.

Thompson continues an interesting if erratic series of discs. *Freebop Now!* is half good, and the good's mostly in the first half, with Berry and Harper turning in some spirited work in celebration of some 20 years of the Freebop Band. But the record turns awkward in the latter stages, with a long piece based around a science-fiction story which in turn is based on an Amiri Baraka poem. It's not something to return to.

Rising Daystar is a more conventional date, but Thompson should resist the temptation to try too many things over the course of a record. There are basically three different groups here, a quintet, a septet, and a trio in which Thompson flexes his bardic (and scat) chops over rhythms by Hopkins and Hall. 'Surrender Your Love' is a fairly hopeless stab at jazzing a pop-soul tune, vocalized by Alexander. Otherwise, playing honours are again taken by Bartz, Berry and Kirk Brown. Thompson himself leads from the front but, in a long solo like the one he takes on the title-tune, it suggests that he needs to pace himself better.

Claude Thornhill (1909–65)

PIANO, ARRANGER

Formally trained, Thornhill began working for New York bands in the mid-'30s and led some groups of his own, before touring with his orchestra from 1940. After war service, he re-formed the orchestra in 1946, having already had an association with Gil Evans since the late '30s, hiring him and Gerry Mulligan to write many of the band's arrangements. Worked through the '50s, with various-size groups, though playing dance music rather than jazz.

*** Snowfall

Hep CD 1058 *Thornhill; Joe Ahuano, Ralph Harden, Bob Sprentall, Rusty Dedrick, Conrad Gozzo (t); Bob Jenney (tb, v); Tasso Harris (tb); Vincent Jacons, Dick Hall (frhn); Irving Fazola (cl); Dale Brown, George Paulsen, Jack Ferrier, Bill Motley (cl, as); Hammond Russum, John Nelson (cl, ts); Hal Tennyson, Ted Goddard (cl, as, bs); Allen Hanlon (g); Don Whitaker, Harvey Sell (b); Gene Lemen, Ray Hagan, Nick Fatool (d); Dick Harding, Jane Essex, Kay Doyle (v).* 9/40–7/41.

***(*) The Transcription Performances 1947

Hep CD 60 *Thornhill; Ed Zandy, Emil Terry, Louis Mucci, Paul Cohen, Red Rodney (t); Tak Takvorian, Allan Langstaff, John Torick (tb); Walt Weschler, Sandy Siegelstein, Al Anthony (frhn); Danny Polo, Lee Konitz (cl, as); Mickey Folus (cl, ts, bs); Mario Rollo (cl, ts); Bill Bushey (cl, bs); Barry Galbraith (g); Bill Barber (tba); Joe Schulman (b); Billy Exiner (d); Fran Warren, Gene Williams (v).* 9–12/47.

*** The 1948 Transcription Performances

Hep CD 17 *Thornhill; Louis Mucci, Emil Terry, Ed Zandy, Johnny Vohs, Bob Peck, Johnny Carisi, Gene Roland (t); Allan Langstaff, Johnny Torick, Leon Cox (tb); Walter Weschler, Sandy Siegelstein, Al Antonucci, Addison Collins (frhn); Danny Polo, Lee Konitz, Gerry Mulligan, Mickey Folus, Jerry Sanfino, Brew Moore, Jet Rollo (reeds); Barry Galbraith, Joe Derise (g); Bill Barber (tba); Russ Saunders, Joe Shulman (b); Bill Exiner (d); The Snowflakes (v).* 4–10/48.

With the revival of interest in mood-music mandarins like Martin Denny and Arthur Lyman, it's not inconceivable that Thornhill's work could catch the ear of those seeking something in the classic easy-listening style. He was a pianist and arranger who formed a band in 1939, struggled with it for three years, then re-formed it after his war service. Never a striking commercial success, Thornhill's interest in a meticulousness of sound – subtle section-work, carefully filtered reed textures, the static bass harmony provided by Barber's tuba parts – resulted in little classics like his theme, 'Snowfall'. But his relationship to jazz is rather hazy, given the formalized tone of the band, and though there were major cool-school players in the orchestra and it features much of the early work of Gil Evans and Mulligan as arrangers, many of the recordings are exotically ephemeral.

The earlier studio recordings have been restored to print by Hep's excellent compilation, *Snowfall*, and from the first tracks it's clear why Thornhill was so popular with audiences seeking sweet music. There seems to be the scent of freesias and the feel of lace-work around such scores as 'Alt Wein' and 'Love Tales', dappled by the leader's piano. He stacks up clarinets, quietly, or threads the reed section around simple brass comments which can't even be called riffs. A piece such as 'Portrait Of A Guinea Farm' is as exotic as society music would ever get. 'Snowfall' itself is a flawless miniature. But there are also numerous vocal features, such as 'Mandy is Two', which may bring on impatience in the listener. The sleeve-note suggests that Thornhill's band was 'too musical' to secure wider success, but that was not a problem which bothered such musical orchestras as those of Ellington or Goodman.

The first volume of transcriptions is the best place to follow Thornhill's placid truce between jazz – either late swing or early bebop – and a more circumspect kind of orchestration. 'Robbins' Nest' is Basie done by stealth; 'Anthropology' is bebop tied up in a chocolate box. These are 2 of the 11 Gil Evans charts on the CD, intriguing examples of his early work and already showing departures from everyone else's thinking. There are also a couple of Gerry Mulligan arrangements, though these are somewhat green, and the rather raffish version of 'Oh You Beautiful Doll' shows that Thornhill had a sense of humour too. Hep CD 17 continues the story, with further transcriptions in excellent sound (better than that on the 1947 disc). There is a further treatment of 'Anthropology', Mulligan's first take on 'Godchild', and a number of standards relayed through the veils of sound which continued to be Thornhill's speciality. One feels, though, that the pieces he liked best were things like 'Spanish Dance', 'Adios' and 'La Paloma', where his aspirations to have a unique-sounding group weren't troubled by any mild leanings towards bop terminology. 'Royal Garden Blues' is a jazz standard almost as Mantovani might have played it. In the end, Thornhill's benign music is little more than an entertaining *cul de sac*.

Teri Thornton (1936–2000)

VOCAL

An 'overnight sensation' when she won the 1998 Thelonious Monk Jazz Vocal Award, Thornton was embarking on a second career that had begun some 40 years earlier. She was presented as a new star in the early '60s and seemed set for a successful career after three albums, but illness and personal problems intervened and she was all but forgotten until her rediscovery by Suzi Reynolds, who produced her comeback record.

***** Devil May Care**

Original Jazz Classics OJC 1017 *Thornton; Clark Terry (t); Britt Woodman (tb); Earl Warren (as); Seldon Powell (ts); Wynton Kelly (p); Freddie Green, Sam Herman (g); Sam Jones (b); Jimmy Cobb (d).* 12/60–1/61.

***** I'll Be Seeing You**

Verve 547755-2 *Thornton; Howard Johnson (c, cbcl, bs, tba); Dave Bargeron (tb); Jerome Richardson (as, f, bf); Ray Chew, Norman Simmons (p); Lonnie Plaxico, Michael Bowie (b); J.T Lewis, Grady Tate (d).* 6/97–98.

Thornton's debut was re-released in the light of her re-emergence. It's a decent if largely unremarkable 'girl singer' record of its day, with a dozen interpretations capably dispatched. Her return to active duty on Verve is a pleasingly eccentric record, but it won't be to all tastes. She has a big, rangy voice, similar in style (though not in tone) to Carmen Macrae's, and the programme here is a mix of blues, standards, originals and an oddly effective treatment of 'The Lord's Prayer'. At its most laid-back, on 'I Believe In You' and 'Where Are You Running?', the music holds a simple appeal which Thornton makes the most of by relying on the natural strength of her voice. When she overcooks it, as on the six-course meal she makes out of 'Knee Deep In The Blues', some will be tempted to shut the record off. Howard Johnson is responsible for some of the equally off-centre charts, and the record ends with a live track from her competition-winning performance. Alas, she was unable to enjoy her renewed career for long, since she was taken by cancer early in 2000.

Henry Threadgill (born 1944)

ALTO SAXOPHONE, TENOR SAXOPHONE, CLARINET, BASS FLUTE

Describing an artist as 'uncategorizable' is both a feeble shorthand and a truism, but in the case of Henry Threadgill it's also an inevitable recourse, because the Chicagoan's dense, chewy music really is sui generis. Formerly leader of Air and New Air, he started to create denser and more carefully structured compositions in the 1980s, using bizarre instrumentations and voicings, and yet his playing is always visceral and compelling.

*****(*) Spirit Of Nuff ... Nuff**

Black Saint 120134 *Threadgill; Curtis Fowlkes (tb); Edwin Rodriguez, Marcus Rojas (tba); Masujaa, Brandon Ross (g); Gene Lake (d).* 11/90.

***** Live At Koncepts**

Taylor Made TMR 10292 *As above, except omit Fowlkes, Lake; add Mark Taylor (frhn), Larry Bright (d).* 5/91.

Threadgill's Very Very Circus appears to be the culmination of a cycle in his work. *Spirit of Nuff ... Nuff* (his titles are nothing if not enigmatic) deploys the band in a way that recalls 1960s' experiments with structures and free improvisation, but with far more discipline. Threadgill's writing has been quite muted in emotional timbre; 'Unrealistic Love', in which Threadgill's solo is announced by a long guitar passage, is typical. The arrangements on 'First Church Of This' (on which he plays flute) and 'Driving You Slow And Crazy' (which opens with a fractured chorale from the brasses) are consistently inventive, but it's increasingly clear that Threadgill, like Anthony Braxton, has now almost reached the limits of what he can do with a more or less conventional jazz instrumentation. It will be interesting to see whether he is able to develop a new instrumental idiom or whether he will choose – or be forced – to remain within the conventions.

Live At Koncepts suggests that there is still considerable mileage in this transitional period. Very Very Circus sounds entirely individual but still with some ties back into jazz. The group blends very skilfully, with three low brasses and two electric guitars ranged across the back of the mix, leaving lots of room for Threadgill's now strangely familiar saxophone to speak in its unmistakable accent.

***(*) **Song Out Of My Trees**
Black Saint 120 154 *Threadgill; Ted Daniel (t); Myra Melford (p); Amina Claudine Myers (org, hpd); James Emery, Ed Cherry, Brandon Ross (g); Dierdre Murray, Michelle Kinney (clo); Jerome Richardson (b); Gene Lake, Reggie Nicholson (d).* 8/93.

***(*) **Too Much Sugar For A Dime**
Axiom 514258 *Threadgill; Mark Taylor (frhn); Edwin Rodriguez, Dorian L Parreott II, Marcus Roja (tba); Masujaa, Brandon Ross (g); Jason Hwang, Leroy Jenkins (vn); Simon Shaheen (vn, oud); Larry Bright, Gene Lake (d, perc); Johnny Rudas, Miguel Urvina (culo, fulia, puya); Arenae, Mossa Bildner (v).* 93.

**** **Carry The Day**
Columbia CK 66995 *Threadgill; Mark Taylor (frhn); Edwin Rodriguez, Marcus Roja (tba); Brandon Ross, Masujaa (g); Tony Cedras (acc); Jason Hwang (vn); Wu Man (pipa); Johnny Rudas, Miguel Urbina (perc, v); Sentienla Toy, Mossa Bildner (v).* 94.

Song Out Of My Trees is for the most part dominated by strings, though the title-track is played over organ (Amina in testifyin' mood) and guitar. By using soprano and alto guitars in addition, tracks like 'Crea' take on a rich harmonic coloration that is quite difficult to pin down. On the superb 'Grief', Threadgill switches to a line-up of accordion, harpsichord and two cellos, a dazzling mixture of sounds and textures. Perhaps structural concerns have been downplayed to some extent here in the search for a new timbral language. It's a fascinating process to watch at close quarters, but slightly wearying after a few listens.

No one writes or orchestrates like Threadgill. *Too Much Sugar* ... is a mad, glorious romp which explores some very dark timbres and tonalities and yet remains witty, fresh and consistently exciting. We can't in conscience recommend it to anyone who draws hard-and-fast borderlines round the Republic of Jazz, but if your tastes are liberal and elastic, it's a marvellous experience, and Henry's voicings for horn and tuba are masterly.

Carry The Day is dizzyingly wonderful. Threadgill throws together disparate elements – African pop, salsa, Andalusian chant, tuba, *pipa*, accordion – with a master surrealist's touch, and he comes up with something that on the title-piece makes its own weird and incommunicable sense. Almost every track sounds as if poised on the brink of entropic noise yet manages (precariously on 'Growing A Big Banana') to pull it all together and save the day.

***(*) **Makin' A Move**
Columbia 481131 *Threadgill; Mark Taylor (frhn); Edwin Rodriguez, Marcus Roja (tba); Myra Melford (p); Ayodele Aubert, James Emery, Ed Cherry, Brandon Ross (g); Michelle Kinney, Dierdre Murray, Akua Dixon Turre (clo); Pheeroan akLaff (d).* 95.

**** **Where's Your Cup**
Columbia CK 67617 *Threadgill; Brandon Ross (g); Tony Cedras (acc, harmonium); Stomu Takeishi (b); J.T Lewis (d).* 8/96.

Makin' A Move is a last word (for the time being at least) from Very Very Circus, who are rotated with a guitar-driven band fronted by Myra Melford (which doesn't include Threadgill at all) and, on 'Refined Poverty', a line-up that has the leader working against three cellos. The range of sounds and styles is less perplexing on subsequent hearings, for the initial impression is of slightly baffling diversity with no consistent focus. In fact, this is one of the most organized of Threadgill records, not quite thematic or programmatic, but linked by Bill Laswell's production and by a carefully restricted spectrum of musical ideas. Very definitely a record that needs time and patience.

The most recent record is much less varied in sound, homing in tight on the working unit the saxophonist now calls Make A Move. The philosophy is as enigmatic as ever, but this is Threadgill's Prime Time, a tough, terse, pulse-driven group which eschews the multi-dimensional approach of earlier ensembles and records. '100 Year Old Game' and 'Where's Your Cup?' are unmistakable Threadgill, which isn't to say that he has settled into a 'style', just that there is no one else on the planet who thinks as laterally as this. Ross is again an important part of the equation, but the addition of Tony Cedras is a key dimension, a creakily acoustic sound that trades on harmonic ambiguity. Lewis is akLaff without the fiery, almost rock-tinged drive.

The Three Sounds

GROUP

Formed in 1955, the group lasted until the '70s, playing light variations on bop and the blues and recording dozens of albums.

*** **Black Orchid**
Blue Note 821289-2 *Gene Harris (p); Andrew Simpkins (b); Bill Dowdy (d).* 2–6/62.

*** **Standards**
Blue Note 821281-2 *As above.* 10/59–6/62.

At one time, every jazz label had a piano trio like this – Red Garland at Prestige, Erroll Garner at Columbia, Ramsey Lewis at Chess. Harris, Simpkins and Dowdy were the Blue Note version. Standards, simple variations on the blues or mild gospelesque outings, a steady, steady tempo that the drummer simply ticked off on number after number, and the pianist never letting the melody get too far away from the listener. This is as easy-going as jazz after bebop has ever been, and it's undeniably pleasant on the ear. But it's hard to imagine anyone wanting more than one Three Sounds album, as popular as they were; and even though vintage Blue Note vinyl remains in high demand among collectors, this is the group that nobody much collects. One reason is, they recorded an awful lot of sessions for the label. The original programme for *Black Orchid* has been expanded with seven previously unissued tracks, doubling the length of the disc, while *Standards* has nearly an hour of never-before-released. It is all much the same as everything else they did, and Harris carried on in much the same vein for Concord.

Steve Tibbetts

GUITAR, MANDOLIN, SITAR, KEYBOARDS, KALIMBA

Based in St Paul, Minnesota, Tibbetts is a guitar-impressionist, creating big aural landscapes using electronic and studio enhancements, with regular collaborator Marc Anderson doing rhythmic duties.

****(*) Northern Song**
ECM 829378-2 *Tibbetts; Marc Anderson (perc).* 10/81.

***** Bye Bye Safe Journey**
ECM 817438-2 *Tibbetts; Bob Hughes (b); Marc Anderson, Steve Cochrane, Tim Wienhold (perc).* 83.

***** Yr**
ECM 835245-2 *As above.* 80.

***** Exploded View**
ECM 831109-2 *As above, except add Marcus Hughes (perc), Claudia Schmidt, Bruce Henry, Jan Reimer (v); omit Cochrane and Wienhold.* 85–86.

***** Big Map Idea**
ECM 839253-2 *Tibbetts; Michelle Kinney (clo); Marc Anderson, Marcus Wise (perc).* 87–88.

*****(*) The Fall Of Us All**
ECM 521144-2 *As above, except add Mike Olson (syn), Jim Anton, Eric Anderson (b), Claudia Schmidt, Rhea Valentine (v); omit Kinney.* 93.

Steve Tibbetts and Marc Anderson are musicians whose methodical, dreamy patchworks of guitars and percussion are surprisingly invigorating, taken a record at a time. Tibbetts's favourite device is to lay long, skirling electric solos over a bed of congas and acoustic guitars; at its best, the music attains a genuinely mesmeric quality. While their pieces are mostly short in duration, an interview included in the notes to *Big Map Idea* reveals that many are excerpts from much longer jamming situations, and Tibbetts's self-deprecating stance – 'When I tape four hours of sound, only ten minutes have any potential, and only 30 seconds ends up being used' – is refreshing. Anderson is clearly as important an influence in the music, and his pattering, insinuating rhythms are an appealing change from the usual indiscriminate throb of world-music situations. *Bye Bye Safe Journey* is perhaps the best of the earlier albums: Tibbetts plays at his most forceful and there's very little slack in the music. 'Running', which features the ingenious use of a tape of a child running, shows how inventively Tibbetts can use found sound. *Yr* is a re-issue of his first album, previously available on an independent label, and *Northern Song* is a bit too quiet and rarefied. *Big Map Idea* opens with a charming treatment of Led Zeppelin's 'Black Dog' and, although some of the tracks suggest that Tibbetts has been listening to Bill Frisell – dreaminess overtaking the rhythmic impetus at times – it is a landscape of his own.

In a way, Tibbetts and Anderson are as consistent as a hard-bop band: the differences between their records are more a matter of nuance and small variation than of any dramatic development. *Exploded View* and *Big Map Idea* continued the run of their 1980s work with patient inevitability, the tracks following one another like a sequence of snapshots or episodes from work in progress. The only striking difference was a greater interest in the use of (wordless) voices. *The Fall Of Us All*, Tibbetts's first album of the '90s, sounds bigger and more powerful than anything that went before. Rhythm is the presiding element for much of the record, Anderson playing a grander role than ever before, and the big, digital soundstage is nearly overwhelming at times. This is large-scale impressionism, and in 'Full Moon Dogs' or 'All For Nothing' Tibbetts has created some of his most imposing and vivid music.

***** A**
Hannibal HNCD 1438 *Tibbetts; Knut Hamre (hardingfele); Turid Spildo (hardingfele, v); John Siegfried (hp, b); Steve Hassett (psaltrey); Ray Gilles (jublang, suling); Karla Ackerman (vn); Amy Morton (vla); Emily Khorana (clo); Anthony Cox (b); Marc Anderson (d).* 99.

Tibbetts on his travels again, this time to Norway for a meeting with the Hardanger fiddle-player, Knut Hamre. The droning sound of the two hardingfele players is austerely beguiling, and for once Tibbetts is rather outdone in terms of texture: these multi-string instruments really do muster orchestral sonority by themselves. That said, the record could use a little injection of pace, or something to outflank the fiddles, since they will eventually weary any who are less than devoted to the style.

Jerry Tilitz

TROMBONE

A New Yorker, Tilitz studied with Lennie Tristano and trombonist Curtis Fuller. Much of his activity has been in education, but he is also a persuasive writer, arranger and performer.

***** The New York Tapes**
Both Feet BF 1001-2 *Tilitz; Tom Harrell, Valery Ponomarev (t); Arnie Lawrence (ss, as); Bob Kindred (ts); Gary Smulyan (bs); Harold Danko, Armen Donelian, Jim McNeely (p); Jon Burr (b); Wayne Dockery, Jerome Harris (b); Jeff Brillinger, Billy Hart, Bob Moses (d).*

After many years, Tilitz finally got around to mastering and releasing some of the music he recorded with New York friends round the end of the 1970s and beginning of the '80s. He writes strong, muscly themes, and 'Pathological', included here, actually won him a composer's grant from the National Endowment for the Arts. It and an outstanding reworking of Duke's 'It Don't Mean A Thing' are the outstanding performances, but 'Calamity Jane' is delightful in its stop/start way, and the calibre of the band is some sort of imprimatur to Tilitz's quality.

Bobby Timmons (1935–74)

PIANO, ORGAN, VIBRAPHONE

If he had done nothing else in his short career, Timmons would have been guaranteed immortality for writing 'Moanin'', the gospelly tune that became a Jazz Messengers hit. Otherwise a permanent underachiever, haunted by self-doubt and alcoholism, the Philadelphian rarely lived up to his potential.

*****(*) This Here Is Bobby Timmons**
Original Jazz Classics OJC 104 *Timmons; Sam Jones (b); Jimmy Cobb (d).* 1/60.

***** Easy Does It**

Original Jazz Classics OJC 722 *As above.* 3/61.

***** Soul Time**

Original Jazz Classics OJC 820 *Timmons; Blue Mitchell (t); Sam Jones (b); Art Blakey (d).* 8/60.

****** In Person**

Original Jazz Classics OJC 364 *Timmons; Ron Carter (b); Albert 'Tootie' Heath (d).* 10/61.

***** Sweet And Soulful Sounds**

Original Jazz Classics OJCCD 928 *Timmons; Sam Jones (b); Roy McCurdy (d).* 6 & 7/62.

*****(*) Born To Be Blue**

Original Jazz Classics OJC 873 *Timmons; Ron Carter, Sam Jones (b); Connie Kay (d).* 8–9/63.

***** Workin' Out**

Prestige 24143 *Timmons; Wayne Shorter (ts); Johnny Lytle (vib); Keter Betts, Ron Carter (b); Jimmy Cobb, William Peppy Hinnant (d).* 10/64–1/66.

***** From The Bottom**

Original Jazz Classics OJCCD 1032 *Timmons; Sam Jones (b); Jimmy Cobb (d).* 64.

This Here is a pun on 'Dat Dere', Timmons's second-best-known tune, to which Oscar Brown Jr subsequently added a lyric. Timmons will for ever be remembered, though, as the composer of 'Moanin'', recorded by the Jazz Messengers in 1958 on a marvellous album of that name and a staple of live performances thereafter. *This Here* was recorded two years later, just before his second stint with Art Blakey. It features both the hit tracks; as a disc, it is probably less good value than a now-deleted Milestone compilation, also called *Moanin'*, which includes material from the January 1960 session, together with excellent tracks recorded over the next three years. *Easy Does It* is slightly shop-soiled and untidy round the edges, though 'Groovin' High' is splendid. Only those who really appreciate Timmons's piano playing need consider it a priority purchase.

Timmons's characteristic style was a rolling, gospelly funk, perhaps longer on sheer energy than on harmonic sophistication. The live *In Person* is surprisingly restrained, though Timmons takes 'Autumn Leaves' and 'Softly, As In A Morning Sunrise' at an unfamiliar tempo. The drummer is probably better suited to Timmons's style than Cobb, but there's nothing between Carter and Jones. Timmons's handling of more delicate material here is rather better than expected and certainly better than on *This Here*; there, 'My Funny Valentine' (also on the Milestone *Moanin'*) and 'Prelude To A Kiss' leave a lot to be desired, and the unaccompanied 'Lush Life' (a song whose subject-matter was rather close to home) is uncomfortably slewed. Traces of Bud Powell in his approach at this time slowly disappeared over the next few years. 'Sometimes I Feel Like A Motherless Child', from an August 1963 session on the Milestone *Moanin'*, is perhaps the most typical if not the best trio performance on record.

Timmons never sounds quite right in a group with horns, which is why *Soul Time* and the Prestige material with a young Wayne Shorter seem so unsatisfactory. There are excellent things on *Born To Be Blue* and on *Sweet And Soulful Sounds*, and there are even things to take out of *From The Bottom* where Bobby turns to organ for a retread of 'Moanin'' and to vibes for the delightfully paced 'Quiet Nights' and 'Someone To Watch Over Me'. These were recordings made late in the Riverside story and not released until some time later; they have had to wait even longer for CD reissue.

Keith Tippett (born 1947)

PIANO, OTHER INSTRUMENTS

Bristol-born Tippett has been a key figure of the British avant-garde for more than 30 years. He played bebop and traditional jazz before attempting a more experimental course with his own groups, Ovary Lodge, Ark and the huge Centipede; more recently he has been a key member of the improvising group, Mujician. He also worked with Amalgam, Ninesense and other leaders' groups, but gradually his distinctive approach came to be focused on solo performance, using spontaneous 'preparations' to turn his piano into a whole orchestra of effects. Some of his work has veered towards classical composition, but his basic language is undetermined by any organizing principle except his unfailing sense of beauty.

*****(*) Frames: Music For An Imaginary Film**

Ogun 010/011 2CD *Tippett; Marc Charig (t, thn, thumb p); Henry Lowther (t); Dave Amis, Nick Evans (tb); Elton Dean (as, saxello); Trevor Watts (as, ss); Brian Smith (ts, ss, af); Larry Stabbins (ts, ss, f); Stan Tracey (p); Steve Levine, Rod Skeaping, Phil Wachsmann, Geoffrey Wharton (vn); Tim Kramer, Alexandra Robinson (clo); Peter Kowald (b, tba); Harry Miller (b); Louis Moholo (d); Frank Perry (perc); Maggie Nicols, Julie Tippetts (v).* 5/78.

Though routinely likened to Cecil Taylor (he actually *sounds* much more like Jaki Byard), Tippett is unique among contemporary piano improvisers. He shows little interest in linear or thematic development but creates huge, athematic improvisations which juxtapose darks and lights, open-textured single-note passages and huge, triple-*f ostinati* in the lowest register. On *Mujician III*, his most accomplished work, these sustained rumbles persist so long that the mind is drawn inexorably towards tiny chinks in the darkness, like points of light in a night sky.

The reappearance of *Frames* restores some balance to Tippett's discography, which in recent years has depended almost entirely on his solo recordings. Like Centipede, the big band he called Ark went in pairs of players, a huge, warm-hearted sound which has been expertly remastered by Steve Beresford. This vast soundtrack in four parts has the seamless, orchestral quality of the solo performances, but with a vastly enlarged palette of sound. Pointless to identify soloists in music as selfless as this, but a word for the twinned basses of Peter Kowald and the late Harry Miller near the beginning, and for the astonishing percussion-plus-electric-violin passage that begins Part Two, originally the second side of the LP release. All in all a staggering record, one of the very finest large-scale projects to be released in Britain in the craven, cowardly '70s.

****** Mujician I / II**

FMP CD 56 *Tippett (p solo).* 12/81, 6/86.

****** Mujician III (August Air)**
FMP CD 12 *As above.* 6/87.

*****(*) Une Croix Dans L'Océan**
Victo CD 046 *As above.* 95.

Though he is still remembered for such quixotic projects as the 50-strong Centipede band, for whom he wrote *Septober Energy*, and for the later Ark, Tippett is still best heard as a solo and duo performer. It may turn out that the three *Mujician* albums made for FMP during the 1980s (the word was his daughter's childish version of her father's vocation) will be regarded as among the most self-consistent and beautiful solo improvisations of the decade and a significant reprogramming of the language of piano. Though there are unmistakable gestures to the presence of Cecil Taylor (especially on the first album), the differences of basic conception could hardly be greater.

Tippett has always insisted that listeners should not concern themselves with *how* particular sounds are made in his performances, but absorb themselves in what he clearly sees as a highly emotional and spontaneous process in which 'technique' is not separable from the more instinctual aspects of the music. In addition to now relatively conventional practices like playing 'inside', he makes use of distinctive sound-altering devices, such as laying wood blocks and metal bars on the strings, producing zither and koto effects. Though there are similarities, this is very different from John Cage's use of 'prepared piano'. Cage's effects, once installed, are immutable; Tippett's are spontaneous and flexible.

The long 'August Air' is one of the essential performances of the decade. It seems to complete a cycle whose development can only be experienced and intuited, not rationalized. The transfer of the two first *Mujician* discs to CD allows the sequence to be heard as a whole and, though a goodly span of time separates the three records, they make sense heard as a continuous sequence, an extended dialogue with the piano and with Tippett's musical sources. These are beautiful records, unaffected and sincere, though not so laden with ego that they make sense only as confessionals.

*****(*) Twilight Etchings**
FMP CD 65 *Tippett; Willi Kellers (d); Julie Tippetts (v).* 10/93.

***** Couple In Spirit II**
ASC CD 12 *Tippett; Julie Tippetts (v).* 96.

Though the British label ASC have finally done something to redress the scandalous lack of interest in Tippett's work back home, it should be said that both of these records were recorded in Germany, at the Total Music Meeting in Berlin in 1993 and at the Stadtgarten in Cologne, now a key venue for new music, three years later. Tippett's performances with Julie are always rather special, and both of these records bespeak the closest empathy and understanding. The addition of Kellers does nothing to blunt it, and indeed he seems to have an intuitive grasp of what drives these two deeply committed musicians, adding his own commentaries, his wilfully insistent pulse and his unfailing instinct for the appropriate gesture. Two very good records; not Tippett at his best or most characteristic, but well worth having.

Cal Tjader (1925–82)

VIBRAPHONE, PERCUSSION, VOCAL

Though originally from St Louis, Tjader based himself in California and, after high-profile stints with Dave Brubeck and George Shearing, led his own groups from 1954. His essentially lightweight blend of Latin, Cuban and bebop styles became very successful in the late 1950s and '60s, and he helped pioneer the salsa idiom, at least from a jazz perspective. His many records kept him in the public ear, but he died in Manila at only 56.

***** Mambo With Tjader**
Original Jazz Classics OJC 271 *Tjader; Manuel Duran (p); Carlos Duran (b); Edgard Rosalies, Bayardo Velarde (perc).* 9/54.

***** Tjader Plays Mambo**
Original Jazz Classics OJC 274 *Tjader; Dick Collins, John Howell, Al Porcino, Charlie Walp (t); Manuel Duran (p); Carlos Duran (b); Edgard Rosalies, Bayardo Verlade (perc).* 8–9/54.

***** Tjader Plays Tjazz**
Original Jazz Classics OJC 988 *Tjader; Bob Collins (tb); Brew Moore (ts); Sonny Clark (p); Eddie Duran (g); Al McKibbon (b); Eugene Wright (vib); Bobby White (d).* 12/54–6/55.

***** Los Ritmos Calientes**
Fantasy FCD-24712-2 *Tjader; Joe Silva (ts); Jerry Sanfino, Jerome Richardson (f); Vince Guaraldi, Richard Wyands, Manuel Duran (p); Al McKibbon, Bob Rodriguez, Eugene Wright (b); Roy Haynes, Al Torres (d); Willie Bobo, Armando Peraza, Luis Kant, Armando Sanchez, Mongo Santamaria, Bayardo Velarde (perc).* 54–57.

***** Black Orchid**
Fantasy FCD-24730-2 *Similar to above, except add Paul Horn (f), Luis Miranda (perc).* 54–57.

***** Cal Tjader Quartet**
Original Jazz Classics OJC 891 *Tjader; Gerald Wiggins (p); Eugene Wright (b); Bill Douglass (d).* 5/56.

***** Latin Kick**
Original Jazz Classics OJC 642 *Tjader; Brew Moore (ts); Manuel Duran (p); Carlos Duran (b); Luis Miranda, Bayardo Velarde (perc).* 56.

****(*) Jazz At The Blackhawk**
Original Jazz Classics OJC 436 *Tjader; Vince Guaraldi (p); Gene Wright (b); Al Torres (d).* 1/57.

**** Latin Concert**
Original Jazz Classics OJC 643 *Tjader; Vince Guaraldi (p); Al McKibbon (b); Willie Bobo, Mongo Santamaria (perc); strings.* 9/58.

***** Monterey Concerts**
Prestige P24026 *Tjader; Paul Horn (f); Lonnie Hewitt (p); Al McKibbon (b); Willie Bobo, Mongo Santamaria (perc).* 4/59.

Cal Tjader was a great popularizer whose musical mind ran rather deeper than some have allowed. As a vibes player, he was an able and not quite outstanding soloist, but his interest in Latin rhythms and their potential for blending with West Coast jazz was a genuine one, and his best records have a jaunty and informed atmosphere which denigrates neither side of the fusion. He made a lot of records, and many of them have been awarded reissue, which makes it difficult to choose particular winners. Tjader helped to break Willie Bobo and Mongo Santamaria to wider audiences, and the steps towards an almost pure salsa sound are documented on most of the records listed above. The earlier records are feet-finding, in a way, but they have a freshness which later became more of a routine. Tjader plays either vibes or percussion, but he's the kit drummer on *Tjader Plays Tjazz*, which has four very flat ballad features for quartet but sparkles a bit more on six quintet tunes with Sonny Clark and Brew Moore. Tjader's excellent solo on 'Jeepers Creepers' shows how good he could be in a straight-ahead small band, but that was not his destiny. *Cal Tjader Quartet* is the most conventional of all his records, but in the end it's little more than a capable vibes-plus-rhythm date.

Latin Kick, which has Brew Moore again guesting on tenor, is a good one, and *Jazz At The Blackhawk* is another unLatin event in which Tjader sounds at ease on standard material. *Latin Concert*, though, starts to run the formula down, and the intrusion of strings marks the inevitable move towards wallpaper which Tjader seemed shameless enough about. Two recent compilations, *Los Ritmos Calientes* and *Black Orchid*, collect the residue of Tjader's Fantasy sessions from the period, and they're effectively split between authentic Latin themes (on Fantasy 24712) and Tjaderized jazz and show-tune standards (Fantasy 24730). Not bad.

***** El Sonido Nuevo**

Verve 519812-2 *Tjader; Barry Rogers (tb, perc); Julian Priester, Jose Rodriguez, Mark Weinstein (tb); George Castro (f, perc); Jerry Dodgion (f); Derek Smith (org); Lonnie Hewitt, Chick Corea, Eddie Palmieri, Al Zulaica (p); unknown (g); Stan Appelbaum (cel); Bobby Rodriguez, Stan Gilbert, George Duvivier (b); Tommy Lopez, Manny Oquendo, Carl Burnett, Grady Tate (d); Armando Peraza, Ismael Quintana, Ray Barretto (perc).* 11/63–3/67.

Held in high esteem as the album which commenced the real fusion of Latin and jazz called salsa, *El Sonido Nuevo* (here with six extra tracks, picked from *Breeze From The East* and the otherwise unavailable *Along Comes Cal*) draws its power more from pianist Eddie Palmieri and his arrangements than anything Tjader does. The title-track illustrates the difference: Tjader embellishes the percussive onslaught below with pretty figures, then Palmieri comes in and intensifies it with his hard, percussive piano parts. Too many of the tracks are still too short, in the fashon of the day, and one longs for a decisive blast from the ensemble but, next to much of Tjader's work, it's impressive. The bonus tracks are softer and a good deal sweeter.

***** Several Shades Of Jade / Breeze From The East**

Verve 537083-2 *Tjader; Jerry Dodgion (f); Lonnie Hewitt (p); Dick Hyman (org); George Duvivier (b); Ed Shaughnessy (d); Lalo Schifrin Orchestra.* 4–12/63.

***** Soul Sauce**

Verve 521668-2 *Tjader; Donald Byrd (t); Jimmy Heath (ts); Lonnie Hewitt (p); Kenny Burrell (g); Bob Bushnell, Richard Davis, John Hilliard (b); Johnny Rae, Grady Tate (d); Armando Peraza, Alberto Valdes, Willie Bobo (perc).* 11/64.

***** Soul Burst**

Verve 57446-2 *Tjader; Jerry Dodgion, Seldon Powell, Jerome Richardson (f); Chick Corea (p); Attila Zoller (g); Richard Davis, Bobby Rodriguez (b); Grady Tate (d); Carlos Patato Valdez, Jose Mangual, Victor Pantoja (perc).* 2/66.

***** Jazz Masters 39**

Verve 521858-2 *Tjader; various studio groups arranged by Lalo Schifrin, Claus Ogerman, Bobby Bryant.* 61–67.

***** Talkin' Verve: Cal Tjader**

Verve 531562-2 *Similar to above Verve discs.* 8/61–9/67.

Soul Sauce is good fun – Creed Taylor reins in any freewheeling approach Tjader might have thought about, and the situations are about as formularized as this music would ever be, but it's smart and crisp enough to remain very playable. Byrd and Heath squeeze out a bit of interest in their solo spots. *Several Shades Of Jade/Breeze From The East* couples two characteristic Tjader exercises in vaguely exotic, mildly titillating kitsch. This music has about as much to do with the mystic East as a trip to Aldgate East tube station, but Schifrin's scoring has a certain low-rent fascination and Tjader and the others play up to the situation gamely enough. The second album, *Breeze From The East*, is pretty ludicrous (it even includes the theme from *Burke's Law!*) but it's a nice antidote after listening to a series of Walt Dickerson and Gary Burton albums. *Soul Burst* is another helping of light froth, with the three flautists strutting around the busy percussion section, and it features the mildest 'Manteca' on record. But it will fill an easy-going gap in your schedule. The Jazz Masters disc is a useful trawl through eight Verve albums, several of them out of print, and the settings range from Schifrin-directed orchestras to small groups. The *Talkin' Verve* set is about the same but packaged with a more self-conscious hipness.

**** Amazonas**

Original Jazz Classics OJC 840 *Tjader; Raul De Souza (tb); Hermeto Pascoal (f); Egberto Gismonti, Dawilli Gonga (ky); Aloisio Milanez (p); David Amaro (g); Lis Alves (b); Roberto Silva (d).* 6/75.

****(*) The Grace Cathedral Concert**

Fantasy 9677 *Tjader; Lonnie Hewitt (p); Rob Fisher (b); Pete Riso (d); Poncho Sanchez (perc).* 5/76.

***** Here And There**

Fantasy 24743 *Tjader; Clare Fischer (p); Bob Redfield (g); Rob Fisher (b); Pete Riso (d); Poncho Sanchez, Carmelo Garcia (perc).* 9/76–6/77.

****(*) La Onda Va Bien**

Concord CCD 4113 *Tjader; Roger Glenn (f, perc); Mark Levine (p); Rob Fisher (b); Vince Lateano (d); Poncho Sanchez (perc).* 7/79.

**** Gozame! Pero Ya ...**

Concord CCD 4133 *As above, except add Mundell Lowe (g).* 6/80.

***** The Shining Sea**

Concord CCD 4159 *Tjader; Scott Hamilton (ts); Hank Jones (p); Dean Reilly (b); Vince Lateano (d).* 3/81.

(*) **A Fuego Viva

Concord CCD 4176 *Tjader; Gary Foster (ss, as, f); Mark Levine (p); Rob Fisher (b); Vince Lateano (d); Poncho Sanchez, Ramon Banda (perc).* 8/81.

** **Good Vibes**

Concord CCD 4247 *As above, except omit Banda.* 82.

Tjader returned to Fantasy in 1970, after his spell with Verve, and pretty much picked up where he'd left off. *Amazonas* includes heavyweights like Pascoal and Gismonti in the group, but it's flimsy stuff. *Here And There* couples the original LPs *Guarabe* and *Here*, the former studio, the latter live, and this was an effective partnership with Fischer, even if the material sticks to Tjader's preference for the soft option. The Cathedral concert is another lightweight match.

Tjader had something of a comeback when he joined Concord, though the music wasn't very different from what he'd been doing 20 years earlier. Cleaner, crisper recording and highly schooled musicianship put a patina of class on these records, but it still emerges as high-octane muzak from track to track. *Good Vibes* in particular is an unseemly farewell. The best things happen on *The Shining Sea* and *A Fuego Viva*: the former introduces Hamilton and Jones and can't really fail from that point, while Gary Foster's experience with Clare Fischer stands him in useful stead for the latter record. Too softcore for real Latin aficionados, too lightweight for a sterner jazz audience, Tjader fell between stools to the end, but, if one can take the trouble to sift through his records, there are rewards to be found.

***(*) **Cal Tjader's Greatest Hits**

Fantasy 24736 *Tjader, plus personnel as Fantasy and OJC albums listed above.* 54–76.

Purists may prefer *El Sonido Nuevo*, but for us this is the Tjader album to have, 20 of his most characteristic pieces covering the modest spectrum of his work.

Christine Tobin

VOCALS

Blending folkish material with a convincing jazz feel, Tobin's is a unique talent.

*** **Aililu**

Babel BDV 9501 *Tobin; Steve Buckley (penny whistle); Huw Warren (p, acc); Phil Robson (g); Ben Davis (clo); Steve Watts (b); Roy Dodds, Mike Pickering (d).* 94.

*** **Yell Of The Gazelle**

Babel BDV 9613 *As above, except omit Davis, Pickering; add Django Bates (thn), Don Paterson (g).* 12/95.

***(*) **House Of Women**

Babel BDV 9820 *As above, except omit Bates, Paterson; add Mike Pickering (d), Paul Clarvis (d, perc).* 98.

Anyone who remembers Norma Winstone's remarkable *Edge Of Time* (now urgently in need of revival) will have some sense of what Tobin is about. It would be wrong, though, to overstate the resemblance or to imply a strong influence. Whereas Winstone developed out of standards jazz, Tobin comes out of the jazz-inflected tradition of Pentangle and June Tabor. The presence of guitarist Don Paterson on 'The Generous Lover' (*Yell Of The Gazelle*) also suggests a kinship with Ken Hyder's pioneering crossover band, Talisker. She has also paid attention to the song-writing techniques of Leonard Cohen and Joni Mitchell, particularly Joni's reworking of Mingus themes, and 'Chair In The Sky' is one of the highpoints of *Yell*. Elsewhere, she puts her own lyrics to themes by guitarists John Abercrombie and John Scofield. The defining sound of these records is as much down to the band, Warren, Watts and Dodds, as to the singer herself. Theirs are unobtrusive presences and are as often used to provide musical interludes and episodes as for straightforward accompaniment. The voice is slightly frail, cautious in range, and rarely rises above a soulful middle register. Her own material (a solitary song, 'Promised Land', on the first album, increasingly evident on its successors) is extremely intelligent and requires some work. Tobin makes very simple ideas go some distance.

The third album is the best so far. The opening song, 'House Of Women', has an epical quality that she hadn't before attempted, and it bespeaks a new ambition. It pays off in the sequence of three new songs – 'Acts Of Obscenity', 'Echoes' and 'Seneca' – which dominates the middle section of the record. Here at least, the comparison with Tabor (and, at moments, with Joni as well) is entirely justified. A fascinating performer, somewhat remote from the jazz mainstream, but entirely in the spirit of the music.

Skeets Tolbert (1910–?)

CLARINET, ALTO SAXOPHONE, VOCAL

Born in Charlotte, North Carolina, Tolbert came to New York and gigged around during the early 1930s. He formed his 'Gentlemen Of Swing' in 1939 and made a success of the group until he decided to move to Houston, Texas, in the mid-'40s, when he became involved in union work and teaching rather than playing.

*** **Skeets Tolbert 1931–1940**

Classics 978 *Tolbert; Lester Mitchell, Joe Jordan, Carl Smith (t); Leslie Johnakins (as, bs); Lem Johnson (ts, cl); Otis Hicks, Ernest Parham (ts); Freddy Jefferson, Jimmy Gunn, Clarence Easter, Red Richards (p); Guy Harrington (bj, v); Harry Prather (tba, b); Bill Hart, Hubert Pettaway (d); Babe Hines, Babe Wallace (v).* 5/31–3/40.

*** **Skeets Tolbert 1940–1942**

Classics 993 *As above, except add Wingy Carpenter (t, v), Buddy Johnson, Herbert Goodwin (p), John Drummond (b), Larry Hinton (d), Nora Lee King, Jean Eldridge, Yack Taylor (v); omit Johnakins, Mitchell, Jordan, Jefferson, Gunn, Easter, Harrington, Prather, Hart, Hines and Wallace.* 10/40–7/42.

An interesting footnote in New York's swing era, Tolbert's career on record began with the territory band of Dave Taylor, who cut the two early tracks which start the first Classics CD. The remaining sides on both CDs are very different: up-market, black, small-group swing. Tolbert's style is a polished variation on the kind of material that might otherwise have gone to Fats Waller or Louis Jordan. His groups were drilled but relaxed outfits and they featured some good players: the outstanding one is probably trumpeter Carl 'Tatti' Smith, but Tolbert himself was no slouch on alto, and the rhythm sections are able, swinging teams. Wingy Carpenter turns up on two later sessions and Buddy Johnson is on one. When they play a blues, as on 'Harlem Ain't What It Used To Be' (an ironic title, since Tolbert never played in Harlem), they do it with some sensitivity, not slickness. Most of the material is made up of relatively undistinguished novelty songs, but nothing descends to any sort of embarrassment and Tolbert's music had no mugging in it. Taken a few tracks at a time, these are very enjoyable records and, since the originals are rather rare and little-known, this is an excellent initiative by Classics.

Charles Tolliver (born 1942)

TRUMPET, FLUGELHORN

Florida-born Tolliver began his recording career with Jackie McLean and ever since has created a kind of augmented bop which, with versions of his co-operative group, Music Inc, he has tried to scale up for larger ensembles. A bright, fierce brass player, he is significantly underexposed on record.

*****(*) The Ringer**

Black Lion BLCD 760174 *Tolliver; Stanley Cowell (p); Steve Novosel (b); Jimmy Hopps (d).* 6/69.

*****(*) Live at Historic Slugs**

Charly CDGR 232 *As above, except omit Novosel; add Cecil McBee (b).* 5/70.

***** Grand Max**

Black Lion BLCD 760145 *Tolliver; John Hicks (p); Reggie Workman (b); Alvin Queen (d).* 8/72.

*****(*) Live In Tokyo**

Charly CDGR 248 *Tolliver; Stanley Cowell (p); Clint Houston (b); Clifford Barbaro (d).* 12/73.

The particular challenge of Tolliver's music is its dramatic simplicity. In place of the complex chord-sequences favoured by most composers of his generation, he favours very basic motifs, often consisting of only four or five notes, repeated in *ostinato*. It's very much harder to play inventively over such a background than where the chords offer endless permutations of 'changes', but Tolliver develops solo material apparently without limit in a highly lyrical mainstream style that recalls Clifford Brown. *The Ringer* is the most swingingly straightforward of the available records, though Cowell's chords are never quite orthodox and many of the leader's solos seem to float in with less support than a Mexican bank.

The main problem with Tolliver is visibility. Early albums like *Paper Man* are collectors' items. The label he co-founded, Strata East, has been in and out of availability so often that its twilight status now seems a given. Recently, though, Tolliver has licensed the back-catalogue to Charly, allowing sets like the 1970 Slugs performance to be released. It's a good example of the challenge the trumpeter set himself with his Music Inc band. As the only horn, he was left very exposed out front, having to play longer and more intensely than usual and with a tough-minded rhythm section who were not inclined to let him off the hook. The closing dedication to 'Our Second Father' (John Coltrane) offers some idea of where the band aesthetic comes from, though Tolliver's basic conception is more straightforwardly modal than the classic Trane quartet. His experiments in clusters and pantonal harmony surface here and there, notably on the lovely ballad, 'Felicite', but for the most part he floats long scalar ideas over relatively static accompaniments. Cowell is, of course, a master at this kind of thing and plays with consummate skill, rippling strange oriental lines and churchy vamps more or less side by side. The big difference between this album and the 1969 disc is McBee. Mixed up prominently, he comes across as the real bedrock.

The Ringer seems to lack some of the bite of earlier and later albums, and it might have benefited from a saxophone player of Coleman's or Bartz's skills; but it's Tolliver who occupies the foreground, a superb technician with an utterly distinctive voice.

Some measure of his stature as a player can be gleaned from the 1973 live session with Music Inc. The opening 'Drought' is perfectly representative of his radical simplicities, a long, urgent solo delivered in an intense, parched tone, held together by Barbaro's insistent time-keeping and Houston's characteristically furious bass-playing, which is a consistent feature of the set. We've been dismissive of Clint on occasion in the past, but on form, he is a wonderfully exciting and witty player, as on his opening to 'Stretch'. Tolliver rarely puts a note out of place and the only point at which the album flags is a throwaway 'Round Midnight', which was presumably an encore. The live sound is good, though Cowell isn't recorded to best advantage.

Tolvan Big Band

GROUP

Contemporary Swedish big band, drawing its personnel mainly from the region around Malmö; directed since 1979 by saxophonist Helge Albin.

***** Colours**

Phono Suecia PSCD 47 *Roy Wall, Anders Gustavsson, Sten Ingel, Fredrik Davidsson, Anders Bergcrantz (t, flhn); Vincent Nilsson, Olle Tull, Ola Akerman, Stefan Wikstrom (tb); Bjorn Hangsel (btb); Helge Albin (as, f); Per Backer (as, syn); Cennet Jonsson (ss, ts, syn); Inge Petersson (ts); Bernt Sjunnesson (bs, f); Lars Jansson (ky); Anders Lindvall (g); Lars Danielsson (b); Lennart Gruvstedt (d); Bjarne Hansen (perc).* 12/89.

Under the direction of altoman Helge Albin, this Swedish big band has made some superb records. Albin's arrangements are highly personal and colouristic: he gets a strikingly individual sound out of the reed section in particular, with extensive use of flutes in the tonal palette and a gripping demonstration of contrast with the brass. But this is in some ways a disappointing set after three excellent albums for Dragon (all yet to appear on CD). All ten themes are by Albin and, while he's an interesting composer, it's his variations on other standards which are compelling on the earlier records. Some of these pieces fail to muster a genuine melodic weight. But there are still marvellous moments – the five-way saxophone rumpus on 'Gold Ochre', Danielsson's thoughtful bass pattern on 'Zinnober', the cut-and-thrust of 'Kobolt' – and Jansson and Petersson are worthy new members of the band. The recording is perhaps a shade too bright on CD.

*****(*) The Touch**

Pep Pop PPP0415 *As above, except Christer Gustavsson (t), Ola Nordqvist (tb), Ronny Stensson (ss, as), Jorgen Emborg (ky) replace Ingel, Wikstrom, Backer, Jansson and Hansen.* 2/95.

Back to their best. Albin cajoles some superlative playing from the band on these eight charts – six originals plus a terrific revitalization of Coltrane's 'Mr Syms' and an ingenious 'I Remember You' – which show off the flair and snap of the section-work as never before. There are starring solos from Bergcrantz, Lindvall, Petersson and others, but it's the responsiveness of the orchestra which impresses, and the studio mix lets one hear every element in their sound.

****** Plays The Music Of Helge Albin**

Naxos Jazz 86025-2 *Peter Asplund (t, flhn); Roy Wall, Anders Gustavsson, Christer Ghustavsson, Fredrik Davidsson (t); Vincent Nilsson, Olle Tull, Ola Akerman, Ole Nordqvist (tb); Björn Hängsel (btb); Per Bäcker, Helge Albin (as, f); Cennet Jönsson (ss, ts, bcl); Inge Petersson (ts, f); Bernt Sjunnesson (bs, f); Jörgen Emborg (p); Lars Danielsson (b); Lennart Gruvstedt (d).* 11/97.

Anyone ever caught raising an eyebrow at the idea of Swedish big bands competing with the rest of the jazz world might do well to ponder the attention-grabber slipped into these sleeve-notes: that Sweden, a country with fewer people than New York City, is home to 500 big bands. Hard to say where the Tolvan crew rank in the list, but it must be pretty close to the top, and Naxos have here snapped up a terrific session for their burgeoning jazz label. Albin wrote everything here and it is as rich, eventful and satisfying an orchestral record as you could wish to find in the current jazz environment. Albin keeps everyone on their toes by involving the orchestra as a constantly shifting entity, sections working together or in contrast, brass and reeds in sumptuous counterpoint or brawling opposition and, though he is missing a couple of the best soloists from the earlier records, there is ample compensation in the presence of Asplund. At Naxos price, an outrageous bargain!

Jim Tomlinson

TENOR SAXOPHONE

Young British tenorman whose style is bound up in the cool, post-Lester saxophone manner.

***** Only Trust Your Heart**

Candid CCD 79758 *Tomlinson; Guy Barker (t); John Pearce (p); Colin Oxley (g); Simon Thorpe (b); Steve Brown (d); Stacey Kent (v).* 10/98.

Humphrey Lyttelton's sleeve-note describes Tomlinson's sound as 'softly articulated but capable of becoming steely at moments, in a way reminiscent of Stan Getz'; and that Getzian feel is the saxophonist's entire starting point. Some may feel it's where he finishes up, too, since he seldom departs from the shadow of the inspiration, and the programme is based around a ballad feel that rarely moves above mid-tempo. Tomlinson's comely sound is so unwavering that the entire record is a pleasure, but it could arguably use a little more of that steel. His group plays with impeccable discretion, Oxley having a more central role than Pearce, but when Guy Barker comes in on three tracks his more experienced demeanour adds a fresh dimension: the outstanding track features their collected thoughts on a Johnny Mandel tune called 'Just A Child'. Stacey Kent's three vocals are suavely accomplished, although she tends to distract from the balance of the record. Tomlinson will be proud of this, but he surely has more ambitious records to come.

Ross Tompkins (born 1938)

PIANO

Known as a fixture on piano in mainstream circles, the Detroit-born Tompkins was nevertheless modernist enough to have played with both Eric Dolphy and Wes Montgomery as a young man. Solo discs of his have been rare, but Progressive has been remedying that.

*****(*) Celebrates The Music Of Jule Styne**

Progressive PCD-7103 *Tompkins (p solo).* 10/95.

*****(*) Celebrates The Music Of Harold Arlen**

Progressive PCD-7107 *Tompkins (p solo).* 7/97.

Tompkins is a scrupulous interpreter: he often plays verse as well as chorus on many of the songs selected for each of these recitals, and he has the gentlemanly habit of keeping the composer's melody within easy reach. Jim Mooney's excellent sound enriches the weighty chords with which Tompkins likes to signpost his way forward, and his sometimes startling interpolations – a nippy double-time flourish or a billowing left-hand rumble that's suddenly quelled by a retort in the treble – keep one listening. He also chooses songs that are among the less expected parts of each composer's canon: 'The Christmas Waltz', 'It's Been A Long, Long Time', 'Right As Rain'. Very enjoyable.

Pietro Tonolo

SOPRANINO, SOPRANO AND TENOR SAXOPHONES

Studied classical violin, then switched to saxophone, and has since become a principal in the contemporaty Italian movement.

***** Slowly**

Splasc(h) 327-2 *Tonolo; Roberto Rossi (tb, shells); Piero Leveratto (b); Alfred Kramer (d).* 5/90.

*****(*) Tresse**

Splasc(h) 386-2 *Tonolo; Henri Texier (b); Aldo Romano (d).* 5/92.

Tonolo's accomplished midstream tenor works a creditable contemporary groove across both these sessions. *Slowly* features tight, almost disciplined interplay between trombone and tenor, while bass and drums cut a neoclassic hard-bop groove on tunes such as 'Misterioso' and 'Introspection'. *Tresse* is a further step forward in that Tonolo (on tenor exclusively this time) creates a wide range of settings with his distinguished partners without really stepping far from familiar signposts. They are conventionally swinging on 'You're The Top', thrillingly intense on

'Gammon', airily lyrical on 'For Heaven's Sake'. Tonolo doesn't seem like a grandly ambitious spirit – several of these pieces are finished inside five minutes – but he has a hip, versatile mind.

***** Simbiosi**

Splasc(h) 431-2 *Tonolo; Paolo Birro, Rita Marcotulli, Danilo Rea, Riccardo Zegna (p).* 6/94.

***** Disguise**

Splasc(h) 492-2 *Tonolo; Giampaolo Casati (c, t); Roberto Rossi (tb); Gianluigi Trovesi (as, picc, bcl); Riccardo Zegna (p, d); Pietro Ciancaglini (b); Alfred Kramer, Luigi Bonafede (d).* 12/96.

Simbiosi is an album of duets with four different pianists. The readiest empathy comes with Marcotulli, with the simply gorgeous soprano–piano duet on 'Finestre', but there are several productive combinations throughout the record. Sometimes, though, as in the effortful version of 'The Fool On The Hill', one feels that Tonolo is trying too hard to make his point, and a more judicious hand on the tiller might have made the record more effective. *Disguise* also seems, at times, like too ponderous an exercise, with Tonolo drawing on famous melodies by Satie, Beethoven, Handel, Prokoviev and others for his 'disguised' material. While there are some interesting developments out of the themes, some of it emerges as merely cute, and the ensembles seem needlessly wayward and lacking in focus.

Sumi Tonooka (born 1956)

PIANO

American pianist working from a bebop base.

*****(*) Secret Places**

Joken BK 103 *Tonooka; Rufus Reid (b); Lewis Nash (d).* 12/89.

***** Taking Time**

Candid CCD 79502 *Tonooka; Craig Handy (ss, ts); Rufus Reid (b); Akira Tana (d).* 11/90.

***** Here Comes Kai**

Candid CCD 79516 *As for Secret Places.* 3/91.

Sumi Tonooka made a couple of small-label albums in the 1980s to little response. It's somewhat ironic that the one new disc in her entry for this edition should be the earliest set of the three. Joken is the label run by fellow-pianist Kenny Barron and the sessions were recorded by the indefatigable Rudy Van Gelder. The technical quality is unimpeachable, the music very fine indeed. Five years after her move from Detroit to New York, Tonooka was still hypnotized by her musical studies, reprising ideas that had turned up in academic exercises, like the strange Egyptian scale on 'Phantom Carousel', or the rather inward logic of the title-track. Inevitably, the best measure of her talent is a pair of standards. 'Round Midnight' is a rather laboured tribute to the composer and performer who turned her on to jazz. 'Over The Rainbow' is a simpler and less mannered performance, and it's here that Tonooka's distinctive touch – tender, formal, but effortlessly rhythmic – is most clearly profiled. Reid and Nash are impeccable.

They turn up again on the second of the Candid records, two strong, intelligent statements which build on the debut discs quite significantly, even if they lack the spontaneity and freshness of *Secret Places. Taking Time* has its impact dispersed a little by the presence of Handy, who plays well enough but tends to distract from the trio, Tonooka's most productive setting. She has an assertive touch which lacks nothing in technique, but her interest in breaking up her phrasing into horn-like lines clears away a lot of the excess. She writes good tunes, too: 'It Must Be Real' and 'In The Void', both from the second record, have their melodies integrated into arrangements which involve Reid and Nash closely enough to make this a real group at work.

Mel Torme (1925–99)

VOCAL, DRUMS

A child performer, Torme graduated from radio work to touring, and his group, the Mel-Tones, were popular in the '40s. Had solo hits and became a nightclub performer in the '50s. A gifted songwriter, passable drummer and capable arranger, Torme was a versatile man, and he was enduringly popular and prolific until a stroke stopped him performing in 1997.

***** The Best Of The Capitol Years**

Capitol 799426-2 *Torme; Red Norvo (vib); Howard Roberts, Tal Farlow (g); Peggy Lee (v); studio orchestras.* 1/49–5/52.

The young Torme's voice was honey-smooth, light, limber, ineffably romantic and boyish; and it's amazing how many of those qualities he kept, even into old age. His 1940s material for Musicraft seems to be back in the deletion racks, but this is a pleasing miscellany from his tenure with Capitol, very cleanly remastered. There are four previously unreleased tracks with Norvo and Farlow in support and a couple of duets with Peggy Lee, as well as two songs that find Mel himself at the piano. Some of the material is less than top-of-the-line, and most of the arrangements heave rather than glide, but Torme's rhythmic panache and tonal sweetness turn back the years.

****** Mel Torme Swings Shubert Alley**

Verve 821581 *Torme; Al Porcino, Stu Williamson (tb); Frank Rosolino (tb); Vince DeRosa (frhn); Art Pepper (as); Bill Perkins (ts); Bill Hood (bs); Marty Paich (p); Red Callender (tba); Joe Mondragon (b); Mel Lewis (d).* 1–2/60.

*****(*) Swingin' On The Moon**

Verve 511385-2 *Torme; Russell Garcia Orchestra.* 60.

This is arguably Torme's greatest period on record, and it captures the singer in full flight. His range had grown a shade tougher since his 1940s records, but the voice is also more flexible, his phrasing infinitely assured, and the essential lightness of timbre is used to suggest a unique kind of tenderness. Marty Paich's arrangements are beautifully polished and rich-toned, the french horns lending a distinctive colour to ensembles which sound brassy without being metallic. There may be only a few spots for soloists but they're all made to count, in the West Coast manner of the day. It's loaded with note-perfect scores from Paich and a couple of pinnacles of sheer swing in 'Too Darn Hot' (a treatment Torme kept in his set to the end) and 'Just In Time', as well as a definitive 'A Sleepin' Bee'. Deleted, shamefully enough, in Europe, but it should still be in American print.

At least they've brought back *Swingin' On The Moon*. This is a more rote affair and a record of one 'moon' song after another may strike some as a concept that belongs in outer space; but everything Torme did in this period was delightful, and so is this.

***** Round Midnight**

Stash ST-CD-4 *Torme; Pete Candoli, Don Fagerquist, Don Rader, Joe Newman, Sonny Cohn, Flip Richard, Al Aarons (t); Shorty Rogers (flhn); Bob Enevoldsen (vtb); Ken Shroyer (bt); Henry Coker, Benny Powell, Grover Mitchell, Urbie Green, Jerry Collins, Carl Fontana, Henry Southall (tb); Paul Horn (cl, as, f); Marshal Royal, Woody Herman (cl, as); Bud Shank (as, f); Eric Dixon, Frank Wess, Frank Foster (as, ts); Bob Cooper, Bob Pierson, Louis Orenstein, Sal Nistico (ts); Arthur Herfert, Buddy Collette (reeds); Bill Hood (bcl, bsx, tba); Tom Anastos, Charlie Fowlkes, Jack DuLong (bs); Count Basie, Don Trenner, Marty Paich, Lou Levy, Nat Pierce (p); Allan Reuss, Freddie Green (g); Verlye Mills (hp); Albert Pollan (tba); Red Mitchell, Perry Lind, Monty Budwig, Buddy Catlett, Tony Leonardi (b); Ronnie Zito, Sonny Payne, Mel Lewis, Larry Bunker, Benny Barth (d); Chester Ricord, Ralph Hansell (perc); Mort Lindsay Orchestra.* 56–68.

Pieced together from various off-the-air recordings, this is an intriguing stroll through a dozen years of Torme's career. He plays drums with Woody Herman on 'Four Brothers', joshes through 'Lil' Darlin'' with Basie's band, and accompanies himself elsewhere on both piano and baritone ukulele. There are 27 songs here, many of them unavailable on any other Torme record, and on such as 'Don't Let That Moon Get Away' and 'Lonely Girl' the singer sounds at his most thoughtful and determined, wasting nothing in the lyrics. The sound-quality is often indifferent, and there are some merely throwaway pieces, so this might be for hardened Torme collectors rather than a casual listener; but it's hard not to enjoy such a surprising set. Admirable sleeve-notes by Will Friedwald.

***** Prelude To A Kiss**

Fresh Sound FSR-CD 109 *Torme; Don Fagerquist (t); Vince DeRosa (frhn); Hynie Gunker (as, cl); Ronnie Lang (as, bs, cl); Bob Enevoldsen (ts, bcl); Stella Castellucci (hp); Bill Pilman (g); Joe Mondragon (b); Mel Lewis (d); strings.*

Vinyl collectors will remember this one with some affection, issued on minor labels at budget price for several years. Originally interspersed with dialogue between Mel and an unnamed female admirer (sadly expunged from this release, though a little of it survives before the final track), the music and singing are actually pretty marvellous, arranged by Marty Paich in the style of the great Bethlehem and Verve sessions. Mel sounds terrific on the likes of 'One Morning In May' and 'I'm Getting Sentimental Over You'. Docked a notch for brevity, and for cutting the chat.

***** Sunday In New York**

Atlantic 780078-2 *Torme; studio orchestras directed by Shorty Rogers, Dick Hazard and Johnny Williams.* 12/63.

Not a classic Torme session, but it's nice that Atlantic have kept something from his tenure with them in circulation. The tunes are all to do with New York, and it's not a bad concept with 'Autumn In New York', 'Harlem Nocturne' and a charming rarity, 'There's A Broken Heart For Every Light In Broadway', in the set-list.

***** That's All**

Columbia CK 65165 *Torme; studio orchestras directed by Robert Mersey, Dick Hazard, Mort Garson, Pat Williams.* 64–66.

****(*) Right Now!**

Columbia CK 65164 *Torme; studio orchestras directed by Mort Garson, Shorty Rogers, Ernie Freeman, Arnold Goland.* 66–67.

Torme didn't look back kindly on his '60s recordings, and there's an apologetic air about both these packages; even so, there's a lot of very appealing singing. *That's All* was a ballad album of some distinction, with lovely versions of 'P.S. I Love You' and 'The Nearness Of You', and it is extended by various singles and rarities to a 24-track disc. 'I Remember Suzanne' is a pretty period-piece and there's one of his sweetest readings of 'The Christmas Song'; the rest shows quality-control thinning a little. *Right Now!* is less distinguished, a set of contemporary pop covers to which Torme brings his customary care and diligence; in the end one wonders why anyone thought such a refined singer should be trying to make a go of the likes of 'Secret Agent Man'. Worth keeping, though, are 'All That Jazz' and 'Wait Until Dark'.

***** An Evening With George Shearing And Mel Torme**

Concord CCD 4190 *Torme; George Shearing (p); Brian Torff (b).* 4/82.

***** Top Drawer**

Concord CCD 4219 *Torme; George Shearing (p); Don Thompson (b).* 3/83.

***** An Evening At Charlie's**

Concord CCD 4248 *As above, except add Donny Osborne (d).* 10/83.

****(*) Mel Torme–Rob McConnell And The Boss Brass**

Concord CCD 4306 *Torme; Arnie Chycoski, Erich Traugott, Guido Basso, Dave Woods, John McLeod (t, flhn); Rob McConnell, Ian McDougall, Bob Livingston, Dave McMurdo (tb); Ron Hughes (btb); George Stimpson, Jim McDonald (frhn); Moe Koffman (ss, as, cl, f); Jerry Toth (as, cl, f); Eugene Amaro (ts, f); Rick Wilkins (ts, cl); Robert Leonard (bs, bcl, f); Jimmy Dale (p); Ed Bickert (g); Steve Wallace (b); Jerry Fuller (d); Brian Leonard (perc).* 5/86.

***** A Vintage Year**

Concord CCD 4341 *Torme; George Shearing (p); John Leitham (b); Donny Osborne (d).* 8/87.

***** Reunion**

Concord CCD 4360 *Torme; Warren Luening, Jack Sheldon (t); Bob Enevoldsen (vtb); Lou McCreary (tb); Gary Foster (as); Ken Peplowski (ts); Bob Efford (bs); Pete Jolly (p); Jim Self (tba); Chuck Berghofer (b); Jeff Hamilton (d); Joe Porcaro, Efrain Toro (perc).* 8/88.

****(*) In Concert Tokyo**

Concord CCD 4382 *As above, except add Dan Barrett (tb), Allen Farnham (p), John Von Ohlen (d); omit Jolly, Hamilton, Porcaro and Toro.* 12/88.

***** Night At The Concord Pavilion**

Concord CCD 4433 *Torme; John Campbell (p); Bob Maize (b); Donny Osborne (d); Frank Wess Orchestra.* 8/90.

***** Fujitsu–Concord Jazz Festival 1990**

Concord CCD 4481 *As above.* 11/90.

**** Mel And George Do World War Two**

Concord CCD 4471 *Torme; George Shearing (p); John Leitham (b).* 90.

Torme's contract with Concord gave him the chance to record a long run of albums that should provide his final legacy as a singer. Even though most singers would be thinking about easing up at this stage, Torme's workload and enthusiasm both seemed limitless. The voice has throttled back a little, and there is a greyness at the edges, but he still makes his way to high notes very sweetly and will sometimes cap a song with an extraordinary, long-held note that defies the rules on senior singers.

If there's a problem with these records, it's the formulaic settings which Concord tend to encourage for some of their regulars. The duo setting with Shearing is actually a good one, since both men seem to admire each other's work to the point where some of the sessions threaten to slip into mutual congratulations; and context is given to both Shearing's sometimes dinky playing and Torme's romantic sweeps. Of their records together, both *Top Drawer* and *An Evening With* are splendid, and *An Evening At Charlie's* isn't far behind; but there are too many live albums here, when Torme can slip into an ingratiating showmanship and an intrusive audience distracts from what is really a close and intimate kind of jazz singing. The World War Two disc founders on the terrible material, charmingly though the principals deal with it.

Of the other discs, the meeting with Rob McConnell's band is marred by a certain glibness on both sides; the two albums with Paich don't quite recapture their great collaborative feel of the 1950s, but *Reunion* sparkles, with a lovely 'Bossa Nova Potpourri' and a hip reading of Donald Fagen's 'The Goodbye Look'; and the two 1990 concert sessions find Torme in ebullient form, delivering a gorgeous 'Early Autumn' on *Concord Pavilion* and two equally distinctive ballads in 'Wave' and 'Star Dust' on *Fujitsu–Concord*.

**** Nothing Without You**

Concord CCD 4516 *Torme; Guy Barker (t, flhn); Chris Smith (tb); John Dankworth (ss, as, cl); Ray Swinfield (as, cl); Ray Loeckle (ts, f, bcl); David Roach (ts, f); Jamie Talbot (bs, bcl, cl); John Colianni (p); Larry Koonse (g); John Leitham (b); Donny Osborne (d); Martyn David (perc); Cleo Laine (v).* 3/91.

****(*) Christmas Songs**

Telarc CD-83315 *Torme; John Colianni (p); John Leitham (b); Donny Osborne (d).* 4/92.

****(*) Sing, Sing, Sing**

Concord CCD 4542 *As above, except add Ken Peplowski (cl), Peter Appleyard (vib).* 11/92.

These records are a disappointing set. *Nothing Without You* is shared with Cleo Laine, whose voice isn't quite the come-hither instrument it once was, and the mawkish atmosphere and overcute situations make this one dispensable to all but obsessive devotees of either singer. The Christmas album is fair game for a man who wrote 'The Christmas Song' but otherwise it goes the seasonal way of all such projects. *Sing, Sing, Sing* finds Mel with two Concord regulars sitting in with his rhythm section at the 1992 Fujitsu Festival, with a 14-minute Benny Goodman medley as the centrepiece. Fair enough, but there are already plenty of live Torme albums in the catalogue and this adds little to the list.

****(*) The Great American Songbook**

Telarc 83328 *Torme; Bob Milikan, Ross Konikoff, John Walsh, Frank London (t); Tom Artin, Rich Willey, Timothy Newman (tb); Jack Stuckey (as, cl, f); Adam Brenner (as, cl); Jerry Weidon, Jeff Rupert (ts, cl); David Schumacher (bs, bcl); John Colianni (p); John Leitham (b); Donny Osborne (d).* 10/92.

***** Velvet And Brass**

Concord CCD 4667 *Torme; Arnie Chycoski, Steve McDade, John MacLeod, Guido Basso, Kevin Turcotte (t, flhn); Alastair Kay, Bob Livingston, Jerry Johnson (tb); Ernie Pattison (btb); Rob McConnell (vtb); Gary Pattison, James MacDonald (frhn); Moe Koffman, John Johnson, Rick Wilkins, Alex Dean, Bob Leonard (reeds); David Restivo (p); Reg Schwager (g); Jim Vivian (b); Ted Warren (d); Brian Leonard (perc).* 7/95.

The Telarc album is yet another live offering from Torme: he retains his usual high standards without suggesting that the record demands a place in any but the most devoted admirer's archive. There is a very fine 'Stardust', as good a version as he's ever done, but the medleys and more routine moments don't amount to much. The Concord set offers a return bout with Rob McConnell's Boss Brass, a group he loves to sing with, and this time the record is a keeper. Torme is in remarkably good shape for a seventy-year-old and, though one tends to credit singers with the mere ability to keep singing at such a stage in their careers, this is a project with some challenge in it. McConnell's band play with some discernment and several of the songs depart from convention: 'Autumn Serenade', 'High And Low' and, especially, 'If You Could See Me Now'.

****** The Mel Torme Collection**

Rhino R2 71589 4CD Torme; various orchestras and small groups; 44–85.

Rhino's four-disc retrospective of one of the most accomplished of vocalists is so consistently enjoyable that one overlooks the sometimes spotty remastering and occasionally idiosyncratic selection. It starts with mid-'40s work with the Mel-Tones, picks some of his best Musicraft sides, then follows with some of the finest of his Capitol, Bethlehem and Verve sides, before going choosily through the 1960s. The '70s are largely ignored altogether, while the '80s are covered by a handful of cameo appearances. There are many delights along the way, including a lovely 1947 transcription of 'Three Little Words', the singer at his youthful peak; some of his best work with Marty Paich; three tracks from the disgracefully ignored *Torme Meets The British* Philips album of 1957; a previously unheard 'Walkin' Shoes' with Shorty Rogers; a virtuoso live Gershwin medley from 1975; and his extraordinary guest appearance with Was (Not Was) on 'Zaz Turned Blue'. One is impressed over and over again by Torme's musicianship, but the most agreeable aspect of the set is his enjoyment of the singer's art, an effortless pleasure that he insists we share.

Jean Toussaint (born 1957)

TENOR AND SOPRANO SAXOPHONES

Born in St Thomas, Toussaint learned saxophone there before going to Berklee in the US, joining Art Blakey in 1982. He moved to London in 1986 and teaches at Guildhall School.

*** What Goes Around

World Circuit WCD 029 *Toussaint; Tony Remy (g); Julian Joseph, Jason Rebello, Bheki Mseleku (p); Wayne Batchelor, Alec Dankworth (b); Mark Mondesir, Clifford Jarvis (d); Cleveland Watkiss (v).* 9/91.

**(*) Life I Want

New Note NNCD 1001 *Toussaint; Dennis Rollins (tb); Jason Rebello (ky); Jean Michel Pilc, Christian Vaughan (p); Tony Rémy, Ciyo Brown (g); Wayne Batchelor (b); Darren Abraham, Mark Mondesir, Winston Clifford (d); Karl Vanden Bossche, Nana Tsiboe (perc); Cleveland Watkiss (v).* 95.

Toussaint's leadership debut is finally let down a little by its eclecticism. The various combinations of rhythm section – a clutch of contemporary British stars – are all worthwhile in themselves, but the three tracks with Joseph, Dankworth and Mondesir are concentrated and direct in a way that makes one wish Toussaint had stuck to this quartet for the entire record. He's generous in allotting solo space to others and, as a result, the impact of his own playing is diminished, but his firm tone and picked phrasing suggest a player not much interested in bluster. Two Monk tunes put his own original material in a poorer light, but the title-piece is a curt, nicely weighted theme that hangs in the mind, and only Watkiss's feature, 'Lower Bridge Level', sounds misplaced.

Life I Want is also let down by lightweight material. Toussaint has assembled a crew of smart British players but they haven't the force of character to put anything dramatic into the tunes. What comes out is a solid, enjoyable but quickly forgettable set of themes.

Ralph Towner (born 1940)

CLASSICAL GUITAR, 12-STRING GUITAR, PIANO, SYNTHESIZER

Studied music at Oregon University and guitar in Vienna in the '60s; then in New York from 1969, playing in various groups, coming to prominence in Oregon. Has also pursued solo career as stand-alone acoustic guitarist and occasional pianist, with a long sequence of ECM discs to his name.

***(*) Trios / Solos

ECM 833328-2 *Towner (solo) and with Paul McCandless (ob); Glen Moore (b); Collin Walcott (tabla).* 11/72.

**** Diary

ECM 829157-2 *Towner (solo).* 4/73.

'Only tenuously connected with jazz', it says in *Grove*, so what's he doing here, and at this length? Two things cement Towner firmly to this music, both of them occurring at the start of the 1970s. The first was an astonishing 12-string solo on 'The Moors', a stunning guest spot by the 31-year-old on Weather Report's *I Sing The Body Electric*, still one of the finest fusion records ever made. The second was the formation of Oregon, a group which brought to a jaded scene a fresh acoustic sound – not unmixed with technical awareness – and a hint of other improvising traditions. There had never been (and probably never again will be) a group quite like it: four earnest, professorial types from the far North-West, playing oboe, cor anglais, french horn, gut-strung guitar, stand-up bass, tablas and sitar; indeed *Grove* suggests some '60 to 80' instruments in all (why the imprecision in the count isn't clear).

The other important thing that happened to Ralph Towner was the emergence of the ECM label. If anyone creates what has sometimes been parodied as 'the ECM sound' – cool, acoustic, European, very spacious and classical in intent – then it's surely Towner. *Trios/Solos* was effectively an Oregon record, documenting some of the sub-pairings that presumably went on in the rehearsal room and certainly featured in concerts. Though not usually standards or jazz repertory players, Towner and Moore give a persuasive reading of Bill Evans's 'Re: Person I Knew', though curiously it's Moore who almost steals the album with his solo 'Belt Of Asteroids', a fantastic unaccompanied performance.

The other album is a genuine solo performance. Like the abstract blues '1 × 12' and 'Suite: 3 × 12' on *Trios/Solos*, it finds him trying to cut a trail between the two great 'twelves' of modern music: the blues and Viennese dodecaphony, which he studied in Europe in 1963 and 1967; the addition of 12-string guitar gives the mix an almost mystical quality. *Diary* is for some fans *the* Ralph Towner record. It is certainly very beautiful and, as with Oregon, there is no anxiety about using studio effects (apart from the churchy ECM acoustic) when required; 'Icarus' is a highly effective overdub. 'Silence Of A Candle', though, one of the genuine classics from the early days of Oregon, is almost thrown away on piano, a little too heavy-handed for such a glorious piece. This is odd, because Towner aims to play guitar 'pianistically'. He once told Joachim Berendt that his aim was to treat his first instrument as if it was a piano trio – not piano, violin, and cello, presumably, but a trio like Evans's. His ability to work simultaneous lines, sustain rich harmonics and drones (especially on the 12-string) and even get a percussive counterpoint out of the snap of the strings and the thud of the sound-box is what makes his solo playing so rich and multi-dimensional.

**** Solstice

ECM 825458-2 *Towner; Jan Garbarek (ts, ss, f); Eberhard Weber (b, clo); Jon Christensen (d).* 12/74.

*** Sound And Shadows

ECM 829386-2 *As above.* 2/77.

Solstice was an attempt to hybridize the Oregon aesthetic, unmistakably American, with the new European jazz that ECM was sponsoring. Almost every separate element was both in place and subtly transformed: Paul McCandless's keening oboe into Garbarek's taut, stressed soprano sound; Moore's huge, woody bass into Weber's multiphonic sound; Walcott's unusual counts into Christensen's uninterruptable flow.

'Distant Hills', on the later and rather disappointing *Sound and Shadows*, is the best point of comparison between the groups, and one surely has to come down in favour of the original. It's only really when Weber and Christensen are given their head, as on the bassist's marvellous 'Piscean Dance', that the pace exceeds the most accommodating medium tempo, but this isn't theme-and-solos jazz, but a new and still not quite secure hybrid. Garbarek sounds wonderful throughout, alternating tenor and soprano, as Towner moves between guitar and piano. This must have been a riveting group live.

***** Matchbook**
ECM 835014-2 *Towner; Gary Burton (vib).* 75.

Odd title for a record #1. What resonances do book matches have? ... throwaway advertisement, fugitive memories, perhaps of far-away places, a touch of something illicit, a spark of flame? There is nothing of that here. It's been suggested that some of the best material on the session was ditched because it was too raw. If so, then some pungent bathwater was thrown away to rescue a very douce baby indeed. Towner often does little more than accompany Burton's nagging, slightly troubled melodies, and even these fail to catch light. A decade later, the sparks still wouldn't fly ...

*****(*) Batik**
ECM 847325-2 *Towner; Eddie Gomez (b); Jack DeJohnette (d).* 78.

As a title this was equally unfortunate, for quite clearly the aim was to relocate Towner in what was unmistakably a jazz context, much as was to happen to Jan Garbarek with Star in 1991. The results are patchy but good. DeJohnette has some difficulty adjusting to the minimalist approach and he sounds impatient here and there, before his impeccable musicianship reasserts itself. It's meat and drink to Gomez, however, who sounds closer to Glen Moore than anyone might have expected, recalling some of their finest moments together. 'Batik' itself is overlong and slightly shapeless, but it does maximize the space for improvisation, and it includes some strong exchanges between Towner and Gomez in particular. We had quibbles about the original sound, but the balance is ideal on CD, with Towner pushed well forward.

***** Old Friends, New Friends**
ECM 829196-2 *Towner; Kenny Wheeler (t, flhn); David Darling (clo); Eddie Gomez (b); Michael DiPasqua (d, perc).* 7/79.

Friends either grow closer with age, or they disappear altogether. This collaboration has fared rather better than expected. Gomez is again the star, but Kenny Wheeler's unexpectedly forceful soloing catches the attention early on and becomes the most obvious focus. Towner tries out some slightly unusual articulations, and at a couple of points sounds as if he's detuned a top string. This time around, we'll skip the obvious comparison and not mention Oregon at all.

*****(*) Solo Concert**
ECM 827268-2 *Towner (g solo).* 10/79.

****(*) Blue Sun**
ECM 829162-2 *As above.* 12/82.

Towner never seemed to be a natural stage performer, certainly not without the mutual-support mechanism of the group. Working alone, he could seem and sound diffident and introverted. Not so on the 1979 disc, recorded at concerts in Munich and Zurich. There is fire and some passion in the playing. Miles Davis's 'Nardis', a rare jazz piece, is idiomatic but also unmistakably Towner's conception, and one can almost hear the trumpet-line come floating in over the top at a couple of points. 'Ralph's Piano Waltz', written for Towner by John Abercrombie, has rarely sounded better. None of the tracks outstays its welcome, with the possible exception of the opening 'Spirit Lake', not one of his stronger ideas; don't be put off by it, for what follows is very good indeed. *Blue Sun* is a frank disappointment, an album with almost no character and none of the intensity of the earlier solo disc.

****(*) Slide Show**
ECM 827257-2 *Towner; Gary Burton (vib, mar).* 5/85.

Odd title for a record #2. What resonances do slide shows have? ... fleeting images, rather personalized memories, no real narrative flow or development. Yes, pretty much the same again, a decade on, from this highly talented but seriously inward-looking duo. This may have been involving, even moving, to play. As a listening experience, unfortunately it never gets anywhere.

***** City Of Eyes**
ECM 827754-2 *Towner; Markus Stockhausen (t, picc t); Paul McCandless (ob, eng hn); Gary Peacock (b); Jerry Granelli (d).* 90.

At first blush, this is very close to *Old Friends, New Friends.* Stockhausen is a masterful performer, with instinctive taste and a greatly under-appreciated ability to bury himself in other people's ideas (perhaps a legacy of his apprenticeship with Papa Karlheinz). The blending of wind sounds is often quite exceptional, unfamiliar as they are in this sort of context. Peacock is very much in the same mould as Gomez, and they are probably the two double-bassists who give Glen Moore his sound. Granelli remains the weak point, a formulaic player who either hasn't a clue what is expected of him here or else who chooses to stick to his own tried-and-tested patterns, irrespective of what's going on around him.

***** Open Letter**
ECM 511980-2 *Towner; Peter Erskine (d).* 7/91.

We were unduly hard on this one in the distant past. The point at issue was a track like 'Infection', a duo between Towner and Erskine which seemed to trade in everything each is good at, in favour a drab 'jazz' style which suits neither. Towner never sounds convincing playing heavyweight lines, and the percussion doesn't do much more than accentuate the fact. However, his own increasingly confident use of the Prophet synth adds a very significant dimension to much of this. If it seems slightly pointless at this stage in Towner's career to push him out into darker and deeper waters – the cover seems to feature a pall of volcanic ash, maybe an ironic reference back to the peaceful seascape of *Diary* – then perhaps it has to be asked who is doing the pushing, artist or label?

*****(*) Lost And Found**
ECM 529347-2 *Towner; Denny Goodhew (ss, sno, bs, bcl); Marc Johnson (b); Jon Christensen (d).* 5/95.

Sorry, but look at that line-up. If this isn't another attempt to recapture – forget about 'the ECM sound' – 'the Oregon sound', then frankly we give up. It's even constructed very much the way early Oregon records were, with tiny carved images (one track is called 'Scrimshaw') interspersing longer, almost narrative pieces. And as has become ECM's practice in recent years, the leader opens the set himself, a solo 'Harbinger' that doesn't quite prepare one for the astonishing 'Trill Ride' with Johnson, a duo which avoids all the pitfalls of *Open Letter* and which yet manages to make the guitarist sound tough and aware. Johnson himself is simply masterful, and if anyone wants a crash course in one branch of modern bass-playing Towner's discography affords some valuable reference points. Goodhew and Christensen don't put in an appearance until 'Elan Vital', but they make an immediate difference to the sound. Goodhew is a bright, propulsive player with a delightful touch on the higher horns and a nice judgement of space on the baritone and bass clarinet. He leads off the collaborative 'Soft Landing' on sopranino and contributes two strong pieces elsewhere, 'Flying Cows' (a baritone feature and quite the jazziest thing Towner's been involved with for years) and 'Midnight Blue ... Red Shift', which deserve to be covered. 'Soft Landing' is one of the freer things Towner has done in recent years, and he should be reassured that it's an experiment worth repeating. As so often before, though, the real drama is what passes between guitar and bass. No piano these days; in the presence of a player like Johnson, it really isn't necessary.

****** A Closer View**

ECM 531623-2 *Towner; Gary Peacock (b).* 12/95.

A wholly involving and deeply resonant set, two great string players meditating on their instruments. Peacock has an immense tone, but it's the *detail* that one notices primarily, shakes, soft strums (as on 'Moor'), delicate harmonics and bent tones (on 'Infrared' and the seemingly improvised 'From Branch To Branch' and 'Postcard To Salta'). As with much of ECM's recent output, this is a genuinely collaborative project, and Towner often sounds as though he is playing accompaniment to the contrabass. He is also playing with firmer attack and a greater use of dissonance than usual, and there are signs too that he may have been listening to classical flamenco, evidenced not so much in the harmonic shapes he uses as in the overall shape and texture of his performances. A fine album.

*****(*) Ana**

ECM 537023-2 *Towner (solo).* 3/96.

To mark 25 years with the label – an astonishing achievement in itself – a quietly magisterial release that will delight anyone who enjoys Towner's music and will surprise no one, whether they admire him or not. Again, there is no piano part and no overdubs, simply a recital of virtuosic guitar-playing. The set closes with a sequence, 'Seven Pieces for Twelve Strings', which sums up much of what Towner has done over the years. Phrase-shapes reminiscent of 'The Moors' with Weather Report swap places with rich passages entirely in harmonics and, on 'Sage Brush Rider', an almost country feel. There is, to be fair, one suprise: 'Veldt', a strummed, percussive piece which might almost be something by South African composer Kevin Volans. It rounds off the first half of a highly effective record. Towner's ability to tell stories, and tell them quietly and without rhetoric, remains unchecked.

Colin Towns (born 1948)

KEYBOARDS, ARRANGER

Born in London, Towns taught himself music and began writing as a teenager. Worked in rehearsal bands and jazz-rock groups, but began writing for film in the late '70s, a career which has brough him wider eminence and many commissions. Founded his own Mask Orchestra in 1991 to play his big-band compositions, and has recently started his own label, Provocateur.

****** Nowhere And Heaven**

Provocateur PVC 1013 2CD *Towns; John Barclay, Graham Russell, Henry Lowther, Guy Barker, Gerard Presencer (t); Mark Nightingale, Richard Edwards, Peter Beachill, Pat Hartley (tb); Roger Williams (btb); Peter King (as); Jamie Talbot (as, ss, cl); Alan Skidmore, Nigel Hitchcock (ts, ss); Alan Barnes (bs); Julian Arguëlles (bs, ss); Phil Todd (bcl); Andrea Hess (clo); Dudley Phillips (b); Clark Tracey (d); Maria Pia De Vito (v).* 96.

***** Still Life**

Provocateur PVC 1015 *Towns; Julian Arguëlles (ts, ss); John Parricelli (g); Dudley Phillips (b); Ralph Salmins (d).* 98.

*****(*) Dreaming Man With Blue Suede Shoes**

Provocateur PVC 1017 *As above discs, except add Dave Hartley (p), Norma Winstone (v); strings, brass, woodwind.* 97–98.

Towns has been so busy with film and TV work that most will have missed his jazz credentials – at least until the formation of the Mask Orchestra and these superb albums. The Orchestra collects many of the best London-based players and they're given some tremendous challenges by these imaginative and uncompromising scores. The simple charge would be that Towns is writing jazz-film-music, something meant to accompany something else, but even if that were true it would be a welcome departure from the familiarities of modern big-band albums. Instead, an example such as the title-track to *Nowhere And Heaven* is a fully formed and stand-alone score for a team of jazz players working within a strikingly personalized idiom. Towns constantly involves the orchestra, rather than resigning it to a subsidiary role behind soloists or making it a trained animal going through practised tricks. He subtly differentiates tonal colour and space, balances the weight of different sections within a composition, and has a fine grasp of dynamics – the ear is constantly teased, without any recourse to avant-garde flourishes (he keeps an absolute grip on what he wants his players to do – there's nothing 'free' in this music).

Perhaps most telling of all is his understanding of modern studios: the ingenious *recording* of all of this music is shaped as often by his way with a studio desk as much as it is by the inflexions of the players, with occasional keyboard flavourings and mixes that throw fresh light on what can sound quite different in a live context. The two-disc *Nowhere And Heaven* is a huge sprawl of almost two and a half hours of music, not all of it of similar calibre, but there's enough here to fascinate and return to time and again for fresh listening. *Still Life* is more song-based and features Maria Pia De Vito throughout: the appeal may depend on how one responds to her voice, and this is a less ambitious undertaking for Towns; but the quintet's playing is full of character, Arguëlles and Parricelli both outstanding.

Dreaming Man With Blue Suede Shoes is different again, introducing The Mask Symphonic with a full orchestral complement as well as the basic Mask Orchestra. The title-track is a self-portrait, the least this generous entrepreneur can allow himself: it's also an extraordinarily complex and big-scale integration of soloists, jazz rhythm-section, rock electricity and improvising soloists, a theme which to a greater or lesser degree is followed throughout the record. Most such projects founder on hubris. Just slightly, here and there, the ambitions of the project threaten to topple it over, but what other composer-arranger is trying anything like this (as well as paying for it himself)? Bravo!

Tino Tracanna

SOPRANO, ALTO AND TENOR SAXOPHONES

Studied in Bologna, then joined the Franco D'Andrea group in 1981 and stayed 13 years. Also a regular in the Paolo Fresu Quintet, and leader of his own groups and projects.

***** 292**

Splasc(h) 322-2 *Tracanna; Paolo Fresu (t, flhn); Massimo Colombo (ky); Marco Micheli (b); Francesco Sotgiu (d); Naco (perc); Mariapia De Vito, Marti Robertson (v).* 6/90.

***** Arcadia**

Modern Times 30118 *Tracanna; Paolo Fresu (t); Emilio Gallante (f); Massimo Colombo (p); Bebo Ferra (g); Paolino Dalla Porta (b); Francesco Petrini (d); Naco (perc). n.d.*

Tracanna is another member of Italy's contemporary jazz vanguard, and he debuted with two briskly entertaining albums for Splasc(h) (the first, *Mr Frankenstein Blues*, isn't yet on CD). The second record is more considered than his first and more confidently finished. Tracanna plays soprano as his first horn here, although there's a startling, helter-skelter alto solo on 'P.F.C. Concept', and his meditations on 'Argomenti Persuasivi' and the pretty ballad, 'Notti Eluse Ed Attese Deluse' (which also appears as a song, delivered by De Vito), are very well done. Fresu and Colombo are suitably challenging partners. Several of the same team reappear on *Arcadia*, which carries on the good and eclectic work, with the merest tinges of funk creeping into 'Mitologie Metropolitane' as opposed to the ECM feel of '23.5'. Tracanna himself continues to develop the soprano as his main horn and he gets a lucid, lyrical timbre out of it.

***** Quartetto**

Splasc(h) 618-2 *Tracanna; Massimo Colombo (p); Paolino Dalla Porta (b); Francesco Petreni (d).* 7/96.

A dozen originals by the leader, here dividing his time equally between tenor and soprano, each thoughtfully dispatched by his regular quartet. The record as a whole is somewhat unstartling, rather careful, and to that extent one could count it as slightly disappointing: there's nothing to denote the individuality Tracanna has sounded on the earlier discs, or with Paolo Fresu. But the playing has a fine polish to it.

*****(*) Gesualdo**

Splasc(h) 677-2 *Tracanna; Claudio Pontiggia (frhn); Riccardo Parrucci (f); Glorioa Merani (vn); Alessandro Franconi (vla); Filippo Burchietti (clo); Paolino Dalla Porta (b); Francisco Petreni (d); Fulvio Maras (perc); Maria Pia De Vito (v); Corrado Guarino (cond).* 4/98.

Five madrigals by Gesualdo, from the late sixteenth century, plus some in-the-spirit originals by Tracanna and Guarino. The composer is very far away from jazz in all senses, but his melodies endure and Guarino, who did most of the arranging, takes care not to manhandle him. Pontiggia and Tracanna get plenty of space to improvise in the appropriate passages and the latter is almost as imposing a presence as the co-leader, getting a sound like a frisky crumhorn. De Vito (familiar from Colin Towns's records) was an inspired choice for the vocal role, idiomatic but open to a freer expression.

***** Nudes**

Splasc(h) 703-2 *Tracanna; Paolino Dalla Porta (b).* 10/99.

A demanding format, which Tracanna approaches on soprano and tenor. Gracefully played, the performers working from compositions rather than a free form, the situation is not quite as exposed as the title suggests. The playing has style, but it's not the most engaging of records.

Clark Tracey (born 1961)

DRUMS

The younger Tracey began playing drums in his father's group from 1978, and over many years and thousands of gigs he's developed into a failsafe and superbly accomplished drummer in a tough, straight-ahead style.

*****(*) Full Speed Sideways**

33 Jazz 018 *Tracey; Mark Nightingale (tb); Nigel Hitchcock (as); Dave O'Higgins (ts); John Donaldson (p); Arnie Somogyi (b).* 2/94.

An exciting straight-ahead record by a group abrim with talent. Tracey's tunes are meaty enough to give the players plenty to chew on, and they set up one knockout solo after another from the three horns, with the more studious Donaldson acting as the cool drink of water. It's unfancy, and some would call it routine, but it would take a real sourpuss to sneer at the likes of 'The Revenge Of Sam Tacet', even if Hitchcock gets so over-excited in his fast solos that he sounds like he's about to fall off the stand. Clark's own playing is copybook, refining a Blakey influence to the point where inessentials are banished and the remaining tools are sharp, cutting and wholly right for the job.

Stan Tracey (born 1926)

PIANO, SYNTHESIZER

Worked in dance bands before playing jazz in the 1950s and working with Ted Heath, 1957–9. House pianist at London's Ronnie Scott Club 1960–67, backing many visiting players, and then a group leader of numerous units, from trio and quartet to big band. The pioneer modernist and composer-leader in post-war British jazz, and one of its most significant figures for close on five decades.

****** Under Milk Wood**

Jazzizit 9815 *Tracey; Bobby Wellins (ts); Jeff Clyne (b); Jackie Dougan (d).* 5/65.

Stan Tracey is one of Britain's few genuinely original contributions to world jazz. The persistent notion that Tracey only plays a rather second-hand, olde-worlde version of his original mentors, Duke Ellington and Thelonious Monk (or what one critic called 'white man's blues'), is completely misleading. While elements of Monk's style – the insistent, percussive left hand, the quirky melodism – and of Duke's capacious structural understanding remain components of Tracey's work in all its various forms and outlets, he has brought something entirely original to the music.

Tracey has recorded extensively, but he has never been well represented in the CD era and much of his work is on scarce and out-of-print vinyl. We are pleased to welcome back *Under Milk Wood*, though, in what is its latest incarnation. It remains one of the most distinctive records of its era, a setting of Dylan Thomas which uses spare, unadorned jazz materials to somehow evoke the eccentric light of the original play. A pioneering work which is a rare instance of jazz accommodating an outside inspiration in a way that honours the qualities of each side of the equation. Its leanness is a Tracey characteristic which has sometimes been dissipated by his big-scale orchestrations. Wellins's somewhat legendary solo on 'Starless And Bible Black' remains compelling, but it shouldn't overpower the impact of the rest of a record which should be listened to in its entirety.

***** Genesis**

Steam SJCD 114 *Tracey; Guy Barker, Steve Sidwell, John Barclay, Henry Lowther, Alan Downey (t); Malcolm Griffiths, Geoff Perkins, Pete Smith, Pete Beechel (tb); Peter King, Jamie Talbot (as); Tony Coe (ts, cl); Art Themen (ts); Phil Todd (bs); Roy Babbington (b); Clark Tracey (d).* 1/87–8/89.

***** We Still Love You Madly**

TAA 004 2CD *As above, except add Chris Pyne (tb), Alan Skidmore (ss, ts); omit Downey, Smith, Beechel, Coe.* 7/86–12/88.

Genesis is still the only one of Tracey's large-scale suites to be available on CD at this juncture. Unlike *Milk Wood*, which makes no obvious attempt to be programme-music (a re-recorded vocal version with a later band was signally unsuccessful), to a large extent *Genesis* is constrained by its attempt to express the Creation myth as sound. There are moments of pure invention, as on 'The Sun, Moon & Stars', with Themen and Guy Barker to the fore, but there is something slightly plodding about the rest, and one wonders, if Tracey had simply been writing nine discontinuous pieces with no overarching theme, whether they would not have been executed more successfully.

The Ellington set reissues two albums, one of orchestral treatments and the other of solo and (with Roy Babbington) duo interpretations. The orchestral pieces are played with fine spirit but sometimes get bogged down in too many long solos by the horns. The playing has a rackety quality which Duke might have enjoyed more than many a more pompous homage, although there are arguably too many over-familiar choices from the canon. The duo record is more personal, and on the solos in particular (especially 'Prelude To A Kiss'), Stan and Duke work closely together. But the session is sabotaged by a pretty awful piano sound which the CD remastering has done little to improve. The producers should have done better than this.

*****(*) For Heaven's Sake**

Cadillac SGCCD 04 *Tracey; Gerard Presencer (t); Andrew Cleyndert (b); Clark Tracey (d).* 9/95.

Billed as 'The New Stan Tracey Quartet', this set was cut before they'd played any gigs, and its freshness, even on a set made up largely of standards and Monk tunes, is very appealing. As ever, it's the spareness in Tracey's music which makes the deepest impression; Monk is winnowed down to his essence in 'Crepuscule With Nellie' and 'Bright Mississippi', and the pianist sets out standards such as 'Just Friends' as skeletal keyboard blueprints, which the other players decorate to give the music its light. Presencer, then 23, is mercurial but already mature, his own 'Blah De Blah De Blah' a modest but intriguing original, and his solos beautifully toned and supple. Cleyndert and Clark read the old man's moves handsomely. Very little waste, and one can only regret that the quartet didn't make another record when they'd played some more.

*****(*) Solo: Trio**

Cadillac SGCCD 06 *Tracey; Andrew Cleyndert (b); Clark Tracey (d).* 1–6/97.

When you get right down to it, the only true way to hear Stan Tracey is solo. He does the bass; he does the percussion; he does the rip-note, blue-edge melody lines. He does the lot. The solo tracks here are the best available example of Tracey's rough and chunky style. Monk's 'Ask Me Know' bruises lesser players and the harmonic permutations of 'Body And Soul' are so deeply stacked that only someone of Tracey's individuality can seem to work something entirely new. The trios aren't quite as compelling and there are a couple of tracks – the original 'Lover's Freeway' and a duff 'Round Midnight' (on which we have declared a moratorium) – which really don't cut the mustard. No fault of the rhythm players, who are spot-on. It would just have been good to have had more of the main man.

Theo Travis (born 1964)

TENOR AND SOPRANO SAXOPHONES, FLUTE

British saxophonist moving easily between post-bop, fusion and, most recently, free idioms.

***** 2 a.m.**

33 Records 33JAZZ 011 *Travis; David Gordon (p); Mark Wood (g); Rob Statham (b); Ichiro Tatsuhara (d); Robin Jones (perc).*

***** View From The Edge**

33 Records 33JAZZ 019 *Travis; Tony Coe (ts, bcl); David Gordon (p); Mark Wood (g); Jeff Clyne, Rob Statham (b); John Marshall, Ichiro Tatsuhara (d).* 6/94.

*****(*) Secret Island**

33 Records 33JAZZ 033 *Travis; David Gordon (p); John Etheridge (g); Rob Statham, Dave Sturt (b); Marc Parnell, Andrew Small (d); Gary Hammond (perc).* 5 & 6/96.

'Brummagem' used to be the cant for anything shoddily built, ersatz or second-hand, but there is nothing but cleanly smelted strength and quality in the work of this Birmingham-born saxophonist. An able composer as well as improviser, Travis contributes all but one tune to his debut recording; there was an earlier cassette release, but this may be hard to track down now. He plays the eclecticism card a little too forcefully but impresses with tunes which range from the hectic clatter of 'Sex, Food And Money (Part Two)' and 'Nightmare In New York' to the calmer lyricism of 'Shore Thing', a strain which comes out more strongly on *Secret Island*.

The two follow-up albums are poised and confident and allow Travis to settle down to making well-rounded sets rather than showcasing as many disparate aspects of his talent as possible. *View From The Edge* is closer to the dynamic of the first album. Guest appearances from Coe, Clyne and Marshall are an additional fillip, and the addition of guitarist Wood points forward to a later trio for the same label. With the exception of 'Love For Sale', all the pieces are by Travis, and the set is dominated by the long, opening 'Fort Dunlop' (the great tyre factory in Birmingham), 'Freedom' and the closing 'The Purple Sky', which includes all the guest performers except Coe.

Secret Island is a mellower and less abrasive record than the other two. John Etheridge is a key presence, with a folksy approach to jazz playing. None of the other guests, Hammond, Sturt or Small, makes anything like the same impact. As with all of 33's catalogue, the sound is good, slightly over-emphatic and mixed as if a rock or pop session, with too much emphasis on volume at the expense of subtlety.

***** Bodywork**

33 JAZZ 036 *Travis; Mark Wood (g); John Marshall (d).* 9/97.

Thirteen 'wholly spontaneous' improvisations, as the sleeve-notes state: it's conservative but often exciting playing. Travis can't shake off the forms of late-Coltrane improvising, and Marshall is a drummer who has a clock in his head, so even if they're making these up, it's really only Wood who sounds genuinely unfettered, and even he bows to the overall sense of preordained resolution. Nevertheless, these are clever and attractive pieces, reminiscent of much British experimentation of the '70s – and none the worse for revisiting that modest alcove.

The Trio

GROUP

A group of brief but significant life, who galvanized British listeners with their 1970 debut and became a 'power trio' benchmark.

****** The Trio**

BGO BGOCD 231 *John Surman (bs, ss, bcl); Barre Phillips (b); Stu Martin (d).* 3/70.

***** Conflagration**

Sequel Records NED CD 303 *As above, except add Harry Beckett, Kenny Wheeler (t, flhn); Marc (c); Nick Evans, Malcolm Griffiths (tb); Mike Osborne (as, cl); Stan Sulzmann (as, f); Alan Skidmore (ts, ss); Chick Corea, John Taylor (p); Dave Holland (b); John Marshall (d).* 71.

For years, aficionados of British jazz have misted over at the mere mention of this 1970 record. Like John McLaughlin's *Extrapolation*, on which Surman also played, it was a salutary reminder of how good that scene could be when it got its act together. Though occasionally discussed as if it was a Surman record, this was a genuinely collaborative group, with all three members contributing material. (In point of fact, it is Phillips who can claim the lion's share of credits.)

A wonderfully welcome CD reissue, it will captivate new listeners as well as those who spent the early 1970s nodding sagely to 'Incantation' and 'Caracticus', the evergreen 'Green Walnut' and '6's And 7's', 'Silvercloud' and 'Dee Tune'. Surman's multi-instrumentalism isn't overdone and Phillips's melodic bass is always tasteful. The late Stu Martin is the least-known member of the group, his career cut short by a fatal heart attack. This wasn't necessarily his personal finest hour, but he contributes in full measure to a classic recording.

If a big-band version of The Trio sounds like a bad Irish joke, things had gone seriously awry by the time *Conflagration* was recorded. The album was billed as 'featuring' John Surman, and whether it was his own project, a trio encounter or a collaborative big band remains unclear. It has always been a record that yields slightly less than the sum of its admittedly impressive parts. The presence of Chick Corea, whose name is bafflingly dropped on promotional stickers for the two-CD Surman compilation of *Where Fortune Smiles* and *Live At Woodstock Town Hall*, was a sign of the saxophonist's growing international reputation, but Corea's addition adds little light and not much heat. The British improvisers represented are not having the best of days either, though honourable mentions to the brilliant Mike Osborne, trumpeter Harry Beckett and drummer John Marshall, all of whom shine through the heat-haze.

The Trio (Norway)

GROUP

Cheekily appropriating a famous appellation, three young gentlemen from Norway play their brand of post-bop.

****** Meet The Locals**

Resonant RM3-2 *Petter Wettre (ts, as); Ingebrigt H Flaten (b); Jarle Vespestad (d).* 98.

*****(*) In Color**

Resonant RM 5-2 *As above, except add David Liebman (ss, ts).* 10/99.

Meet The Locals must go down as one of the most attention-grabbing debuts in years and, played blindfold, should have listeners everywhere demanding to know who this is. That it actually emerges from Oslo, where the most internationally familiar tone has been set by Jan Garbarek's plaintive wail, is all the more startling. This is clipped, tough, overdriven saxophone trio music, deriving from quite closely wrought hard-bop structures yet all but bodily hurled into free space by the fantastic impetus which the threesome work up on 'Meet The Locals', 'Chasing The Girl' (a scarcely recognizable derivative of Joe Henderson's 'Inner Urge') and 'Cold Turkey'. Vespestad is the most swinging drummer imaginable for the situation, pushing the other two as hard as he can possibly go (and that includes when he's going at a simply brushed four) while the supremely assured Wettre peels off line after line. It may sometimes be pattern-playing at this kind of velocity, but Wettre keeps his cool to an amazing degree, the tone utterly secure and the breath-control phenomenal. Flaten stands his ground in the middle and even gets in a growling feature of sorts with 'A Bored Broad Abroad'. Maybe the concluding 'The Epidemic Of Self-Pity' is, at 32 minutes, an ounce overweight, but the record has already earned its four stars.

If *In Color* seems like a disappointment, that may be because the livid excitement of the debut is too much mollified by the presence of Liebman. Always the consummate professional, the American digs the situation, but he adds little to the occasion except extra weight and sometimes even gets in the way. That proviso aside (and Liebman is only on five of ten tracks anyway), it's another hothouse of excitement. The very close-up sound which the group favours puts an intimacy on a style of playing which too often now is recorded with a festival-stadium respectability: it works best if the band feels as if they're on top of you; on, say, 'Next Level', the crispness and deep bottom of the sound involve the listener as few such records do. These are fabulous records: get them.

Trio AAB

GROUP

One of the several bands involving the Bancroft brothers.

***** Cold Fusion**

Caber 004 *Phil Bancroft (sax); Kevin MacKenzie (g, syn); John Speirs (b); Tom (d, perc, elec); Gina Rae (v).* 8/97–4/98.

An early release on the talented Scottish brothers' own label, this is a relaxed and free-flowing expression of their musical interests. Like the physical process that gives the album its title, it's room-temperature modern jazz that doesn't aspire to the structural complexities of Tom Bancroft's big-band writing (also available on a Caber CD) or to the more driven and rock-tinged approach of MacKenzie's own projects.

Phil Bancroft's 'Untitled' is a musing saxophone solo that confirms his developing expressiveness. There is a fine version – albeit mistitled – of Ornette's 'When Will The Blues Leave' and an unexpected reading of murdered hip-hopper Tupac Shakur's 'I Ain't Mad Atcha'. 'Abstract' is a delightful tone-poem seemingly built on a traditional melody, which surfaces at the close. Speirs and singer Gina Rae (who comes from Scotland's other musical dynasty) appear on only two numbers, Rae providing a backing vocal for the Tupac piece. Trio AAB are certainly a more commanding outfit in a live setting. One danger of producing and releasing your own records is a lack of distance and perspective. It would have been interesting to see what Manfred Eicher or Steve Lake might have made of these sessions.

Trio Nueva Finlandia

GROUP

The individual members of TNF have seen considerable mainstream jazz action with the likes of Johnny Griffin and Dexter Gordon, as well as more adventurously with Anthony Braxton and Cecil Taylor. Founded in 1993, the group is devoted to what they prefer to call 'unique music', freely improvised but tautly disciplined.

***** Ha! – What's Going On?**

Leo Lab CD 046 *Baron Paakkunainen (ss, ts, bs, f, af); Eero Ojanen (p); Teppo Hauta-aho (b, clo, siren).* 95, 96, 97.

From the opening 'Ha!' you are in the presence of something bold and epic, a story spun out in performance like the traditional tales of the Finnish *Kalevala*. Paakkunainen remains on flute for much of the time, which ensures that the basic sound-world is ethereal, intimate and harmonically shifting. 'Prelude Just In Tones' and some aspects of the 'Suite No. 17258' (which surely isn't an oblique reference to the Electric Light Orchestra?) may suggest a workshop rehearsal rather than a finished performance, and there are generic aspects to a couple of other tracks; otherwise this is fine and often very beautiful music, not perhaps as unique in voice as the Trio might like to think, but memorable enough.

Trio Time

GROUP

The long-standing rhythm section whose members have served 5, 17 and 18 years respectively with the Humphrey Lyttelton Band.

****(*) How Beautiful Is Night**

Calligraph CLGCD036 *Ted Beament (p); Paul Bridge (b); Adrian Macintosh (d).* 11/98.

Kind of their boss to let his rhythm section have an album of their own on Humph's Calligraph label, but the results, while entirely amiable, are no more than that. A blues, a bunch of standards and a delivery which is so mild as to be almost anaesthetic. They sneak in Sam Rivers's 'Beatrice' and Miles Davis's 'Solar', but otherwise this is old-fashioned and featherweight.

Lennie Tristano (1919–78)

PIANO

Blind as a child, Tristano learned piano, saxophone and cello and studied music in Chicago. Worked in trios in New York in the '40s, then with a sextet, but gradually abandoned live work for full-time teaching from 1951. Created a doctrinal school of thought which placed rigorous thought and construction ahead of mere emoting in jazz; once controversial, now a part of the language.

****** The Complete Lennie Tristano**
Mercury 830921-2 *Tristano; Billy Bauer (g); Clyde Lombardi, Bob Leininger (b).* 10/46–5/47.

(***) Live At Birdland 1952
Jazz Records JR-1CD *Tristano; Lee Konitz (as); Warne Marsh (ts); Billy Bauer (g); Arnold Fishkind (b); Jeff Morton (d).* 45–52.

(***) Wow
Jazz Records JR-9 *As above, except omit Fishkin and Morton.* 50.

*****(*) Live In Toronto**
Jazz Records JR-5 *As above, except add Peter Ind (b), Al Levitt (d).* 6/52.

*****(*) Manhattan Studio**
Jazz Records JR-11 *Tristano; Peter Ind (b); Tom Weyburn (d).* 55–56.

****** Lennie Tristano / The New Tristano**
Rhino/Atlantic R2 71595 *Tristano; Lee Konitz (as); Gene Ramey, Peter Ind (b); Jeff Morton, Art Taylor (d).* 55–61.

***** Continuity**
Jazz Records JR-6 *Tristano; Lee Konitz (as); Warne Marsh (ts); Henry Grimes, Sonny Dallas (b); Paul Motian, Nick Stabulas (d).* 10/58–6/64.

***** Note To Note**
Jazz Records JR-10 *Tristano; Sonny Dallas (b); Carol Tristano (d).* 64–65.

If Charlie Parker can be made to seem the Schoenberg of modern jazz, then Tristano is certainly its Webern; he represents its 'difficult' phase. Whereas most horn-led post-bop delved into uncomfortable psychic regions and cultivated a scouring intensity, Tristano ruthlessly purged his music of uncontrolled emotion, in sharp contrast to the highly expressive playing of Bill Evans. Perhaps because his basic instruction to his horn players – the best-known of whom were, of course, Lee Konitz and Warne Marsh – was that they should use a deliberately uninflected and neutral tone, concentrating instead on the structure of a solo, Tristano has remained a minority taste, and a rather intellectual one. This is a pity, because Tristano's music is always vital and usually exciting. Though he abandoned the rhythmic eccentricities of bop in favour of an even background count, his playing is far from conventional, deploying long sequences of even semiquavers in subtly shifting time-signatures, adding sophisticated dissonances to quite basic chordal progressions. If his emphasis on structural rigour and technical (rather than emotional) virtuosity still alienates some listeners, there is a problem for the beginner in the nature of the Tristano discography, much of which involves indifferent live recordings and posthumously released private tapes. However, far from being the cerebral purist of legend, the blind Tristano was fascinated by every possibility of music-making and was a pioneer in studio overdubbing and in speeding up half-speed recordings to give them a cool, almost synthesized timbre.

The key track in this regard was 'Requiem', perhaps the most striking item on the 1955 Atlantic sessions, reissued on the indispensable Rhino CD. His overdubbing and multi-tracking would influence the Bill Evans of *Conversations With Myself*. But the latter part of the album offers a rare club date with Lee Konitz: the saxophonist sounds dry and slightly prosaic on 'If I Had You' and much more like his normal self on a beautiful 'Ghost Of A Chance'. Tristano's own solos are derived, as usual, from the refined and twice-distilled code of standard material.

This is the essential Tristano CD, but the early sessions on the Mercury disc are almost as important. They catch Tristano just before bebop – specifically, Powell and Parker – had had a significant impact on his playing, so his style, refracted through Tatum and Hines, is like a mysterious, charged yet inscrutable distillation of swing piano's most elaborate settings. One is sometimes reminded of Tatum's (or Nat Cole's) trio recordings, yet Tristano's ideas, while harmonically dense, adapt bop's irresistible spontaneity better than either of those peers. Eleven of the 19 tracks are previously unreleased alternative takes, and the five versions of 'Interlude' (alias 'A Night In Tunisia') are as varied as Parker's Dials. In Bauer he had one of his most sympathetic partners: often lost to jazz history, the guitarist's lines are unfailingly apt yet fresh. Comparison between each take shows how insistent Tristano already was on making his music new from moment to moment. Some of the surviving masters were in imperfect shape, with occasional high-note distortions, but it won't trouble anyone used to music from this period.

The New Tristano is an essential record. The multiple time-patterns secured on most of the tracks suggest a vertiginous, almost mathematical piano music that moves beyond its scientific sheen to a point where the ingenuities acquire their own beauty: 'I can never think and play at the same time. It's emotionally impossible.' Howsoever the conjoining of technique, interpretation and feeling may work for the listener, this is remarkable piano-jazz, and the contrasting ballads of 'You Don't Know What Love Is' and 'Love Lines' suggest a world of expression which jazz has seldom looked at since.

The Jazz Records releases are from tapes kept in the Tristano family archive. Both *Live At Birdland 1952* (which also includes four early piano solos from 1945) and *Wow* are tarnished by terrible sound, the discs apparently made from wire recordings: more's the pity, since both feature the musicians in what is, even through the detritus of the flawed sound, masterful music. That becomes clearer on the considerably superior (if still imperfect) sound of the 1952 Toronto concert. Any who might doubt Tristano's ability to outswing any of the regular bebop pianists should lend an ear to the astonishing solo on the first piece, his favourite 'Lennie's Pennies'. Throughout, the group work with uncanny accord, improvisations moving seamlessly from one man to the next, yet set within a palpable groove by Ind (though he's nearly inaudible) and Levitt.

Manhattan Studio derives from worktapes from Tristano's New York studio over a year or two. Much of this is prime Tristano, the up-tempo pieces especially: 'Momentum', 'I'll Remember April' and, above all, 'All The Things You Are', which is like a working primer on bebop piano, are riveting examples of the man's artistry, and he's assisted by Ind's simply melodic solos and Weyburn's steady beat. This was previously available on an Elektra LP, *New York Improvisations*, and it has to be said that the indifferent sound hasn't been much improved by the CD transfer.

The concert fragments on *Continuity* are in better sound. There are four pieces from 1958 with Marsh, Grimes and Motian, including an 'Everything Happens To Me' which fades after 50 tantalizing seconds, and some 24 minutes from 1964 with Marsh, Konitz, Dallas and Stabulas. The playing is of a typically high order, with a fine '317 East 32nd', but the snapshot documentation is finally rather frustrating, and the Konitz *Live At The Half Note* set on Verve, even with Bill Evans in for Tristano, may appease less specialist appetites.

The duos with Dallas date from the early 1960s. Five improvisations cover 40 minutes, and the overdubbed drums (hardly sacrilege – Carol Tristano merely centres the rhythm, never doing more than mark time) fill out an otherwise rather dry recording. Like all the Jazz releases, there's a half-finished quality: rigorous though Tristano was, such notebook survivals inevitably lack the precise brilliance of such as *The New Tristano*. But there are insights enough here to make this a valuable pendant to the other solo music.

Gianluigi Trovesi (born 1944)

ALTO AND SOPRANO SAXOPHONES, ALTO AND BASS CLARINET, PICCOLO

Studied at Bergamo from 1960 and in a jazz environment was first noticed as a member of Giorgio Gaslini's groups in the 1970s. He has become a familiar name in many European jazz situations since then, although his own music is a deeply personalized take on jazz, classical and native Italian music of several sorts.

*****(*) Roccellanea**

Splasc(h) H 506-2 *Trovesi; Paolo Fresu (t, flhn); Giancarlo Schiaffini (tb); Paolo Damiani (b); Ettore Fioravanti (d).* 12/83.

****(*) Dances**

Red 181 *Trovesi; Paolo Damiani (b, clo); Ettore Fioravanti (d).* 1/85.

****(*) Les Boites A Musique**

Splasc(h) H 152 *Trovesi; Luciano Mirto (elec); Tiziano Tononi (perc).* 3/88.

Trovesi is a key figure in Italy's new jazz, as performer, composer and organizer. *Roccellanea*, for instance, came about as part of a research project into jazz and its relationship with indigenous Mediterranean culture. That issue has been largely taken up since by the splendid efforts of Peppo Spagnoli's Splasc(h) label to document the Italian scene in all its variety, and it's appropriate that the session in question appears in the label's 'Italian Jazz Classics' series. Co-credited to Trovesi and Damiani, the disc consists of two long-form pieces in which the quintet explore a score that offers a superbly vivid blend of writing and improvising. Originally played by the two leaders with Manfred Schoof, Connie Bauer and Gunter Sommer, the three locals who substituted on the recording session are more than up to the job. Since Damiani uses an amplified bass that sounds rather like one of Eberhard Weber's old set-ups, the music has a pleasantly dated feel which the playing refutes: the three horn players criss-cross to great effect, Fresu's more conventional lines ameliorating the expressionism of the other two.

This is a more useful survival than the other two projects, which gave a somewhat misleading impression of Trovesi as a lugubrious stylist. Luciano Mirto is credited as 'computer operator', and he establishes harsh, jangling washes of sound which Trovesi decorates with a mirthless sort of intensity while Tononi patters away in the background. Interesting, but the genre has been handled with better results elsewhere. *Dances* ends on the track 'Sorry I Can't Dance', which suggests a sense of humour, though the playing here often seems curiously effortful – even though bass and drums employ a wide variety of rhythms.

****** From G To G**

Soul Note 121231-2 *Trovesi; Pino Minafra (t, flhn, didjeridoo, v); Rodolfo Migliardi (tb, tba); Marco Remondini (clo); Roberto Bonati, Marco Micheli (b); Vittorio Marinoni (d); Fulvio Maras (perc).* 5/92.

From G To G is a small classic. Without sacrificing any of his intensities, Trovesi has created a colourful, unpredictable, brilliant marshalling of devices drawn from jazz and far beyond. While there are hints of Italian folk music and remote echoes of ancient masters of Italian composition, the synthesis leads inexorably to a real Italian jazz. 'Herbop' uses two themes which are split and reshaped continuously through 18 minutes of music, soloists and ensemble set in perfect balance. 'Now I Can' and 'Hercab' are satirical without being heavy-handed and without losing an underlying severity which Trovesi uses to pare off any fat in the music. But the finest piece is probably 'From G To G' itself, a long, serenely effective dirge in memory of a friend, with a memorable solo from Minafra. The brass player turns in some of his most lucid work here, Migliardi is rumbustious on tuba and urgently expressive on trombone; but it's Trovesi himself who leads from the front, his alto solos elegantly moving forward from Dolphy and Coleman into a sonority that again suggests the tradition of Italian song. Very fine indeed.

***** Let**

Splasc(h) H 429 *Trovesi; Giancarlo Schiaffini (tb, euph, elec); Walter Prati (elec); Fulvio Maras (perc, elec).* 1/92.

This deconstructivist free-with-electronics session isn't really Trovesi's forte, and he plays more of a willing second fiddle to Sciaffini, whose short-breathed monologues and wheezing electronics (abetted by Prati) fill in most of the space. Pitched somewhere between improvisation and shapeless sound-blocks, the music aspires to dialogue here and there – notably in the horn conversation of 'Allegro, Adagio, Quasi Vivo' – and climaxes in the epic 'Canzona Duodecima', which seems to reprise everything else that's happened in 11 packed minutes.

*****(*) Radici**

Egea SCA 050 *Trovesi; Gianni Coscia (acc).* 95.

A gently harmonious collaboration, Trovesi sticking to clarinets, with Coscia's accordion creating both a lovely harmonic undertow and rippling breakers of arpeggios that counterpoint all the reed player's lines. Some of it is café society, some classical rigour, some folk-tune, some dance: 'Antica Mazurka' is a little of all of that, sonorously spread across eight minutes. A tough record to find, on this Italian independent, but worth the effort!

*****(*) Les Hommes Armés**

Soul Note 121311-2 *As for From G To G.* 5/96.

For all its ingenuities, this is just a degree less welcoming and appealing than its predecessor. Much of it revolves around the ancient European melody of 'L'Homme Armé', out of which came pieces by numerous composers (and Trovesi makes direct reference to the *Kyrie* from Dufay's Mass on the theme at one point). Five tunes – 'Tango', 'Tengo', 'Tingo', 'Tongo' and 'T'Ungo' – are used to interlude the big pieces, which are themselves broken up into diverse fragments; and then there's a crackpot version of 'Mood Indigo' and a tribute to Eric Dolphy, based on a reharmonization of 'Miss Ann'. Trovesi's team play with their usual aplomb but, as delightful as it often is from moment to moment, the record never quite coheres or compels the way *From G To G* did.

****** Around Small Fairy Tales**
Soul Note 121341-2 *Trovesi; Emilio Soana (t); Andrea Dulbecco (vib); Marco Esposito (b); Vittorio Marinoni (d); Orchestra di Camera di Nembro Enea Salmeggia; Bruno Tommaso (cond).* 1/98.

Wonderfully vivid and colourful music, informed by jazz but just as much in debt to the strains he associates with his birthplace of Nembro, this is fashioned somewhat as a suite, the eight pieces arranged by Bruno Tommaso to feature the orchestra alongside rhythm section and Trovesi's own solos. Swooningly romantic in places, but usually with a hint of tartness underneath via Trovesi's own parts, this is enjoyable as soundtrack escapism or as an intelligent and highly crafted blending of consonant ingredients.

Alain Trudel (born 1966)

TROMBONE

Contemporary Canadian trombonist.

***** Jericho's Legacy**
Naxos 86021 2 *Trudel; John Stetch (p); Eric Legacé (b); Jim Hillman (d).* 3/98.

Canadian Trudel is a much more interesting musician than he is a jazz trombone player. His technical facility is undoubted and his Monk-influenced compositional approach is packed with promising ideas, but he lacks convincing presence as a performer. His chops are tested to the maximum on the closing 'Anthropology', but a better measure of his skills can be taken from the group of Monk tunes, including the ubiquitous 'Round Midnight' which occupies the middle section of the record.

His own compositions are a mixed bunch. The opening 'Right Of Way' is somewhat abstract and the title-track perhaps carries too much programmatic baggage, but the mid-tempo ballad, 'What After', is worthy of Curtis Fuller at his best. Pianist Stetch has recorded with the 29th Street Saxophone Quartet's Ed Jackson and seems to thrive in unusual instrumental contexts. He makes an excellent contribution to a thoughtful and sometimes provocative album.

Erik Truffaz

TRUMPET

Born on the Franco-Swiss border, Truffaz has often worked in Geneva but counts himself a French musician. Began in a modal post-bop style, but has more recently experimented with electronic textures and is a rare European signing to Blue Note.

***** Nina Valéria**
Plainisphare PL 1267-79 *Truffaz; Maurice Magnoni (ss, ts); Pierre-Luc Vallet (ky); Marcello Giuliani (b); Marc Erbetta (d).* 92.

***** Out Of A Dream**
Blue Note 855855-2 *Truffaz; Cyrille Bugnon (as, ts); Patrick Muller (p); Marcello Giuliani (b); Marc Erbetta (d).* 97.

***** The Dawn**
Blue Note 493916-2 *As above, except add Nya (v); omit Bugnon.* 12/97.

*****(*) Bending New Corners**
Blue Note 522123-2 *As above.* 4/99.

The rather dreamy and attractively melodic acoustic music of the Plainisphare set didn't altogether suggest that Truffaz was going to go the way he has – although even there he investigated a dance-directed beat in 'Paysage D'Ombres'. More typical was the pretty ballad feel of 'Patience D'Azur' and the title-track, his own muted playing having a Milesian introversion. The Blue Note debut, *Out Of A Dream*, carried on in this vein. If anything, it isn't quite as strong compositionally as *Nina Valéria*, although the sound is undeniably fuller and brighter. But there's nothing here that marks much of an advance on the earlier set, and Bugnon makes little impression. *The Dawn* is altogether different. The album is barely under way before in comes Nya, a self-conscious (and sometimes embarrassing) mix of rapper, beat poet and talk-over artist. The words are the expected blend of hipsterese, which listeners raised on Lord Buckley and Eddie Jefferson will find strictly old hat, and a more contemporary outlook, although litle dates as quickly as a recorded rapper. The music, though, is an often strikingly effective translation of mild hip-hop beats – played in real time by the rhythm section – to a fundamentally acoustic small-group sound. What makes it work is the starkness of the sound: there's no distracting keyboard clutter, Truffaz has to play the sole horn, and his own delivery is quite skinned-back and pointed. The improvised groove of 'Round-Trip' is bleakly effective. It doesn't feel like a very substantial record, but it's starting something.

Bending New Corners carries it on. Muller makes more extensive use of Fender Rhodes, often with thick sustain and wah wah to grant it an even more fashionably retro sound. All but one of the themes are credited as group compositions, and there's a sense that the band grow these tracks out of collective blowing on simple motifs. If anything, Truffaz himself takes an even lower profile as soloist-leader and, although some of the music sounds like a cleaner, sweeter edition of a lot of old electric Miles Davis stuff, the abstractions of 'More' – followed by the beatbox noodling of 'Less' – are looking towards something else. Even Nya sounds more confident and genuine on his four appearances. Difficult to see how this music will develop without either descending into self-parody or changing into dance music (the group have already been playing at rock festivals), but that's for Truffaz to figure out.

Assif Tsahar

TENOR SAXOPHONE

Contemporary free-form saxophonist.

****(*) Shekhina**

Eremite MTE04 *Tsahar; William Parker (b); Susie Ibarra (d). 7/96.*

Passionate free playing that runs dry on Tsahar's lack of variation. His delivery is all post-Ayler howling and wailing – the relatively pacific 'Hidden Heart' is a piece of bruised lyricism and a welcome change – and he does it well enough, but the constant overblowing turns into what seems like the same phrase in gruelling rotation. The redoubtable Parker and the interesting Ibarra do their best to shift the scenes around him, but it's heavy going. Recorded at Fire In The Valley festival in Amherst, Massachusetts.

Gust William Tsilis

VIBRAPHONE, MARIMBA

Tsilis plays an unfashionable instrument as if no one had ever used it in a jazz context before. He always seems to be inventing his own language rather than merely using a phrasebook prepared by predecessors like Milt Jackson and Bobby Hutcherson.

***** Pale Fire**

Enja ENJ 5061 *Tsilis; Arthur Blythe (as); Allan Farnham (ky); Anthony Cox (b); Horace Arnold (d); Arto Tuncboyaciyan (perc, v).*

*****(*) Sequestered Days**

Enja ENJ 6094 *Tsilis; Joe Lovano (ts, f); Peter Madsen (p); Anthony Cox (b); Billy Hart (d). 3/91.*

*****(*) Wood Music**

Enja ENJ 7093-2 *Tsilis; David Paterson (ts); Uri Caine (p); Serge Gubelman (didjeridu); Lonnie Plaxico (b); Tony Reedus (d). 1/93.*

Tsilis's Enja debut is a curious mixture of earthly modern jazz and slightly awkward post-Weather Report atmospheric pieces that never quite took shape. His use of marimba veered towards an ironic imitation of electronic blips and waterdrops, a device that recurs on 'Not Ever Quite', one of the less dynamic tracks on the altogether better *Sequestered Days*. Even in fine form, Blythe is a rather one-dimensional player when compared to Lovano, who can conjure up anything from smooth swing insinuations, as on the opening 'Mahalia', to a more brittle sound over freer passages. On 'Lisa Robin', he opens on flute over Tsilis's marimba in what sounds like one of Joe Zawinul's folksier themes; the piece develops into an evocative solo from Cox, who underpins the long 'Crazy Horse'. Tsilis's vibraphone work on 'Evening In Paris' is less than wholly convincing, but elsewhere he lets the rhythm prod him towards a livelier delivery, as on 'Medger Evers', which is perhaps the best tune of the set. Its real find is the fluent Madsen, who takes over from the leader and punches out a fine, two-handed solo over Hart's clattering, swishing percussion, before handing over to Lovano wearing his Coltrane hat to take it out. The title-track is a strong modal theme one would like to see tackled by a much bigger band, for, as on *Pale Fire*, it's clear that Tsilis knows what he wants from his musicians, the arrangements are full of promise.

Wood Music marks an intriguing shift of tonality and timbre. Tsilis opts for marimba, and the disc concentrates on dark and brooding sounds, punctuated by didjeridu and riveted together by Plaxico's grainy bass sounds, which are as convincingly authentic on electric bass as on upright. A fine album, well up to the quality of its predecessors.

Mickey Tucker (born 1941)

PIANO

Tucker studied piano in Pittsburgh, became a high school teacher, then worked as an accompanist in New York. Did much sideman work in the 1970s and '80s, but eventually moved to Australia.

***** Blues In Five Dimensions**

Steeplechase SCCD 31258 *Tucker; Ted Dunbar (g); Rufus Reid (b); David Jones (d). 6/89.*

***** Hang In There**

Steeplechase SCCD 31302 *Tucker; Greg Gisbert (t); Donald Harrison (as); Javon Jackson (ts); Ray Drummond (b); Marvin 'Smitty' Smith (d). 12/91.*

****(*) Getting There**

Steeplechase SCCD 31365 *Tucker (p solo). 4/94.*

Tucker led a journeyman career in the 1960s and '70s with only a handful of dates under his own name. His return to leading his own sessions is celebrated on these pleasing if inessential efforts. The first album is primarily a collaboration between Tucker and Dunbar: Reid and Jones provide pulse and flow, but the most creative thinking comes from piano and guitar, the lines intersecting and parrying each other with consummate empathy. Tucker contributes only the title-track, while Dunbar's 'A Nice Clean Machine For Pedro' makes light work of a testing piece. The fine recording serves Tucker better than any of his previous records, his subtle touch and expressive facility clear at last. He had moved to Australia, but a 1991 trip to New York resulted in the pick-up date captured on *Hang In There*. A strong line-up is let down slightly by Gisbert, who's defeated by the superfast tempo for 'Happy'; but Harrison and Jackson are fine, Smith is utterly mercurial, and Tucker stands as tall as the rest of them. 'Hook-Turns And Hectares' is as smartly convoluted as its title. The solo album, though, is sometimes disappointing. Tucker seems to have decided to invest the occasion with some pomp and ceremony: Shorter's 'Paraphernalia' and Strayhorn's 'Lush Life' are heavy and airless, the three-part dedication to Coltrane is nothing special, and 'Jitterbug Waltz' is unnecessarily prolix.

Bertram Turetzky

BASS

A noted teacher and composer, Tureztky is somewhat more renowned in the contemporary-classical field but here works as an improviser.

****(*) Intersections**

Nine Winds NWCD 0129 *Turetzky; Vinny Golia (reeds, f, picc). 8–12/86.*

Eleven duets – although four of them involve multiple overdubs – between Turetzky's irreproachably solemn bass and Golia's arsenal of clarinets and flutes. This is slow, grain-by-grain music, with both men insisting on the lower frequencies for much of the record and the interplay more a matter of harmonization than of line countering line. It's interesting, even compelling at times, but the weight of the music can just as often be oppressive. Hard work.

Bruce Turner (1922–93)

CLARINET, ALTO SAXOPHONE

Born in Saltburn, Turner joined the Humphrey Lyttelton Band in 1953, which outraged trad purists. He formed his own Jump Band in 1957 (the recordings are all out of print), then disbanded it and joined Acker Bilk in 1966. He rejoined Lyttelton in 1970.

*** That's The Blues, Dad

Lake LACD49 *Turner; Kenny Baker, Terry Brown (t); Keith Christie (tb); Wally Fawkes (cl); Jimmy Skidmore (ts); Harry Klein (bs); Dill Jones, Lennie Felix, Al Mead (p); Ike Isaacs, Cedric West, Fitzroy Coleman (g); Frank Clarke, Jim Bray, Major Holley, Danny Haggerty (b); Benny Goodman, Stan Greig, Don Lawson, Phil Seamen, Billy Loch (d).* 2/55–1/58.

A pleasing memorial to the reedman who was a much-loved fixture in British trad-to-swing circles. In later years he became more like the modernist that trad fans were afraid had been imported into the Humphrey Lyttelton band in the early '50s, but here his affection for Hodges, Carter and other masters of swing alto is more obvious. Paul Adams's meticulous compilation puts together tracks by groups co-led by Turner and Fawkes, the Jazz Today group with Kenny Baker and Keith Christie, and Turner's own Jump Band. None of these bands was destined for immortality, and Fawkes and Turner stand out like beacons of inventiveness, but they all made light, amiable work out of a small corner of the music. Adams has done his best with a mix of surviving vinyl and master tapes, and the sound is as good as one can hope for.

Joe Turner (1907–90)

PIANO, VOCAL

Born in Baltimore, Turner played piano in New York in the '20s but spent much of the '30s in Europe. After military service he returned to Europe and seldom went back.

***(*) Stride By Stride Vol. 1

Solo Art SACD 106 *Turner (p, v).* 12/60.

Turner was one of the least well-known of the great Harlem stride pianists, since he did very little recording in the USA and decamped for Europe in the 1940s. His albums reveal an often self-effacing, gentlemanly stylist, fond of an occasional vocal but concentrating on the keyboard, playing the tunes with a modest amount of elaboration and voicing his lines with a certain restraint: he seldom goes for the hurricane kind of stride, and when he plays something like 'Boogie' (on *Stride By Stride Vol. 1*) it's relatively perfunctory. 'Tea For Two' was one of his favourites: there's a memorable version on *Stride By Stride Vol. 1* (once issued on vinyl on 77, and emanating from a Swiss club session), and this is the best place to hear him. Actually, until some of his later recordings are repackaged, it's more or less the only place.

Mark Turner (born 1965)

TENOR SAXOPHONE

Raised in California, Turner took up alto in high school and switched to tenor before attending Berklee, where he met such current colleagues as Kurt Rosenwinkel. He moved to New York in 1990.

**** Yam Yam

Criss Cross 1094 *Turner; Seamus Blake, Terence Dean (ts); Brad Mehldau (p); Kurt Rosenwinkel (g); Larry Grenadier (b); Jorge Rossy (d).* 12/94.

***(*) Consenting Adults

Criss Cross 1177 *Turner; Brad Mehldau (p); Peter Bernstein (g); Larry Grenadier (b); Leon Parker (d).* 12/94.

***(*) Two Tenor Ballads

Criss Cross 1182 *Turner; Tad Shull (ts); Kevin Hays (p); Larry Grenadier (b); Billy Drummond (d).* 12/94.

Turner's debut album was almost nothing like the traditional tenor/rhythm date and he has the character to make such a contrary effort almost entirely successful. Warne Marsh is his most acknowledged influence, and the sinuous lines of most of his improvisations are both like and unlike that tenor master. His own tunes are off-centred, oblique, never quite going the way one expects; with the equally unpredictable Rosenwinkel as the other main horn – if one discounts the superlative Mehldau, that is – the music emerges as a seamless yet intriguingly episodic sequence. In one striking departure, the tenors of Blake and Dean join in on 'Zurich' in a remarkable, almost ghostly interweaving of saxophone sound. This was certainly a very impressive start.

Recorded during the same week but both unreleased until 2000, the other Criss Cross discs are a welcome addition to the Turner canon. *Consenting Adults* is credited to MTB and, while its pick-up nature places it behind both the debut and the discs listed below, there's still much impressively achieved playing here. Parker introduces some unexpected touches, such as the rocking pulse with which he underpins the second version of 'Little Melonae', and Mehldau squeezes in a coolly spacious trio ballad. *Two Tenor Ballads* is more like a typical Criss Cross blowing date, even if pitched at a deliberately laid-back level, but Turner and Shull make a surprisingly compatible team, the more classic sound of the latter a piquant counter to Turner's timbre.

**** Mark Turner

Warner Bros 9 46701-2 *Turner; Joshua Redman (ts); Edward Simon (p); Christopher Thomas (b); Brian Blade (d).* 12/95.

Turner's first for a major (though it was produced by Gerry Teekens, like the last one – so was originally meant for Criss Cross?) is not quite the departure the debut was: it's more in a specific tenor-plus-rhythm vocabulary, perhaps. But what a vocabulary! Redman guests on three tracks and creates a quite sublime contrapuntalism, complementary rather than competitive, though some terrific sparks are struck on the fade to the opening 'Mr Brown'. Maybe the solos on this one reach a tad self-consciously for the limits, but these are players who know what they're doing. Tristano's '327 East 32nd Street' is another fine pair-off, but the grandest set-piece is on a rather obscure Ornette Coleman tune, 'Kathelin Gray'. Simon contributes a gorgeous solo to this one and the tenors work together like their operatic counterparts, stately, full-throated and in rapturous counterpoint.

Turner has the rest of the date to himself – though Simon, Thomas and Blade are the most resourceful of teams behind him – and, while there's no more of his own writing, the improvisations on 'Autumn In New York' and Coltrane's '26-2' are proof of his composer's mind. He has one of the most appealing tenor sounds of recent times, flitting around the highest reaches of the horn without sounding thin or stretched, and hearing him nourish a melody line with it is very satisfying.

****** In This World**
Warner Bros 9362-47074-2 *Turner; Brad Mehldau (p); Kurt Rosenwinkel (g); Larry Grenadier (b); Brian Blade, George Rossy (d).* 6/98.

A superb continuation, with Turner and Mehldau seemingly reading each other's minds at some points. An original such as 'Lennie Groove' is straight out of its inspiration, yet settled squarely into a more contemporary, multi-levelled climate of expression. Turner's confidence in his altissimo range is growing all the time, his tone lean but never under strain, and when he improvises at speed the absence of cliché can be thrilling, even as he projects an implacable sense of calm. Rossy sits alongside Blade on the final pair of tracks while Rosenwinkel is on only three tracks but is also a telling contributor. Quite a dense and demanding record, but immensely satisfying.

*****(*) Ballad Session**
Warner Bros 9362-47631-2 *Turner; Kevin Hays (p); Kurt Rosenwinkel (g); Larry Grenadier (b); Brian Blade (d).* 10/99.

Disappointing at this stage to find Turner being asked to make a record like this, since it is (on the face of it) a passive retreat from the concerns of the previous two. Ten ballads of varying pedigree, impeccably played; but it's not until the second half of the record that it really makes an impression, starting with a haunting recitation of Bobby Hutcherson's 'Visions', then into three further jazz themes. Here Turner's winsome tone and Rosenwinkel's nimble counterpoint come into their own. But the opening standards seem merely droopy, for all the finesse of the playing.

Matt Turner

CELLO, PIANO, VOICE

Improviser specializing in cello and working in a broad range of settings, here sampled in two very different situations.

****(*) The Mouse That Roared**
Meniscus 002 *Turner (clo solo).* 6/97.

***** Never, Never Now**
Stellar! Sound Productions 1005 *Turner; Jeff Song (b, v); John Mettam (d, v).* 6–10/97.

Turner has made a number of records, though we feel that some of them – particularly with bassist Song – are rather outside our field of activity, being more concerned with ethnic improvisation. The solo record is interesting but somewhat unconvincing: some of the seven improvisations don't go anywhere much and Turner struggles to sustain interest at times. The other disc is completely different, a set of modest power-trio improvisations (with later, overdubbed vocals, some of which are pretty silly) which sometimes hit the spot very effectively. Turner has also essayed a record of solo piano improvisation.

Steve Turre (born 1948)

TROMBONE, SHELLS

An in-demand brassman throughout the '70s, '80s and '90s, Turre has made occasional records as leader, where his prowess on both trombone and sea-shells has brought about a somewhat unique crossover.

*****(*) Viewpoints And Vibrations**
Stash STCD 2 *Turre; Jon Faddis, Bill Hardman (t); Bob Stewart (tba); Haywood Henry (cl); Junior Cook (ts); Mulgrew Miller, Hilton Ruiz (p); Akua Dixon (clo); Paul Brown, Andy Gonzalez, Peter Washington (b); Idris Muhammad, Leroy Williams (d); Manny Oquendo, Charlie Santiago (perc); Suzanne Klewan, Timmy Shepherd (v).* 1/86–2/87.

*****(*) Fire And Ice**
Stash STCD 7 *Turre; Cedar Walton (p); John Blake, Gayle Dixon (vn); Melvyn Roundtree (vla); Akua Dixon Turre (clo); Buster Williams (b); Billy Higgins (d); Jerry Gonsales (perc).* 2/88.

It helps in this life to have a gimmick, and Steve Turre's effective cornering of the market in conch-blowing is as good an example as any in the business. Their lonely, slightly eldritch sound, plus a hair, beard and moustache rig that falls between Fu Manchu and Ming the Merciless, *plus* a place in the excellent house-band on *Saturday Night Live*, have given this leading contemporary trombonist a shrewd purchase on how to give a slightly problematic horn a fresh set of accessories. Born in Nebraska, Turre grew up in California and quickly forged a career with an eclectic range of leaders, including Ray Charles, Max Roach, Woody Shaw and, perhaps most influential of all, Rahsaan Roland Kirk.

The sound itself isn't that original. What sets Turre apart is his gift for drama and his instinctive sense of what makes for a strong set. *Viewpoints And Vibrations* is a CD compilation of an LP called *Viewpoint* and some bonus material from a tribute to Rahsaan. Turre kicks off with a superb quartet version of J.J. Johnson's 'Lament', tipping his hat to an obvious role-model along the way, but it's the Kirk material that really catches light: 'A Handful Of Fives' and 'Steppin' Into Beauty' are exceptional, and the Vibration Society front line of Hardman and Cook can't be faulted.

Fire And Ice benefits immeasurably from the Walton–Williams–Higgins rhythm section, and the quartet numbers are first rate. The track with strings palls slightly with hindsight, but

'Mood Indigo' is undeniably beautiful and Turre's big, broad tone might well have graced an Ellington brass section in years gone by. As a technician (and conches aside) he lacks idiosyncrasies, concentrating on melodic detail and on wonderfully exact slides between pitches. Great ears. Fine player. Two impressive records.

***(*) **Right There**

Antilles ANCD 510040 *Turre; Wynton Marsalis (t); Benny Golson (ts); Dave Valentin (f); John Blake (vn); Benny Green, Willie Rodriguez (p); Akua Dixon Turre (clo, v); Buster Williams (b); Billy Higgins (d); George Delgado, Herman Olivera, Manny Oquendo (perc).* 3/91.

(*) **Sanctified Shells

Antilles 514 186 *Turre; Dizzy Gillespie, Charlie Sepulveda (t); Robin Eubanks (shells, tb); Clifton Anderson (tb); Douglas Purviance (btb); Reynaldo Jorge (shells, perc); Andy Gonzalez (b); Ignacio Berroa, Herlin Riley (d, perc); Milton Cardona, Kimati Dinizulu, Badal Roy, Claude Thomas, Carmen Turre (perc).* 1/92.

Turre was always going to be a difficult act to develop and promote, and a contract with PolyGram didn't immediately solve the problem. *Right There* is in some respects his best record, certainly as far as straight trombone playing is concerned; comparisons with Curtis Fuller and, even more appositely, Julian Priester seemed entirely legitmate. Then came the nonsense of *Sanctified Shells*, on which Turre's unique and initially fascinating double is indulged way past its deserts. The idea of a conch choir sounds great for a world music festival, or perhaps for a track on a CD. It certainly doesn't sustain for most of a CD. Singificantly, it's 'Macho (Para Machito)' and 'Toreador' one remembers, the former because the trombone choir is impressive, the latter because it has a guest spot from Dizzy Gillespie.

The guest cameos lift *Right There* as well. Wynton Marsalis and Benny Golson kick right in on 'Woody And Bu' and the top-drawer rhythm section produce some moments of magic on their own account. One of the things that has dogged Turre, though, is the need to unveil all the tricks, frill and furbelows on every record. Akua Dixon Turre's voice is a lot better than her old man's lyric, but one wonders what 'Duke's Mountain' is doing on the record at all, an error of judgement only slightly mitigated by an interesting version of Duke's 'Echoes Of Harlem'.

**** **Steve Turre**

Verve 537133-2 *Turre; Alfredo Chocolate Armenteros (t); Randy Brecker, Jon Faddis (t, flhn); Jimmy Bosch, Robin Eubanks, Frank Lacy, Douglas Purviance (tb, shells); J.J Johnson, Britt Woodman (tb); Willie Rodriguez, Steven Scott (p); Stefon Harris (vib, mar, balifone); Romero Lubambo (g); Andy Gonzalez (b); Horacio Negro Hernandez, Victor Lewis, Portinho (d); Milton Cardona, Kimati Dimizulu, Herculano Federici, Mongo Santamaria (perc); Carlos Baptiste, Regina Carter (vn); Ron Lawrence (vla); Akua Dixon Turre (clo); Graciela Perez, Cassandra Wilson (v).* 5 & 6/96.

A triumph, but a slightly puzzling one. The eponymous title suggests that Verve wanted to relaunch Turre. Anyone familiar with his earlier output would immediately recognize the rarangements, with blurting shells and low brass figures. Anyone who hadn't experienced Turre before might think he was too comprehensively upstaged by his guests, not least the great J.J., who turns in a magnificent solo on the processional 'The Emperor' and the gloriously swinging 'Steve's Blues', where he plays open against Turre's muted solo. Placing a Cassandra Wilson vocal first was a slightly odd decision, while 'Ayer Lo Vi Llorar' seems to belong on another album celebrating Graciela Perez. It takes a couple of hearings to realize just how much Turre really does contribute to the overall sound. His plunger mute solo is exemplary.

The other star of the session is vibist Stefon Harris, who has been a mainstay of Buster Williams's recent group. His balifone passage on 'The Emperor' and his feature on the Hutcherson-inspired 'Coastin' With Bobby' are among the strongest things on a record which is full to capacity with arresting sounds.

As ever, Turre makes intelligent and tasteful use of strings, especially on 'Let It Go'. The ony quibble is that a record intended to refocus critical attention on the leader seems to downplay his manifold talents. Time, perhaps, for a quartet album with a rhythm section of world-beating potential. And, yes, he can bring along his shells if he wants.

Stanley Turrentine (born 1934)

TENOR AND SOPRANO SAXOPHONES

Father Thomas played with the Savoy Sultans, and brother Tommy was a hard-bop trumpeter. 'Mr T' worked in R&B bands in the '50s before joining Max Roach and then cutting albums for Blue Note from 1960, and with Shirley Scott for Prestige. Had crossover success in the '70s but moved back to more straightahead playing and now divides his time between both situations.

***(*) **Up At Minton's**

Blue Note 28885-2 2CD *Turrentine; Horace Parlan (p); Grant Green (g); George Tucker (b); Al Harewood (d).* 2/61.

*** **Rough 'N' Tumble**

Blue Note 24552-2 *Turrentine; Blue Mitchell (t); James Spaulding (as); Pepper Adams (bs); McCoy Tyner (p); Bob Cranshaw (b); Mickey Roker (d).* 7/66.

***(*) **The Best Of Stanley Turrentine: The Blue Note Years**

Blue Note 93201-2 *Turrentine; Blue Mitchell (t); Curtis Fuller, Julian Priester (tb); James Spaulding (as); Pepper Adams (bs); Herbie Hancock, Gene Harris, Les McCann, Horace Parlan, McCoy Tyner (p); Shirley Scott, Jimmy Smith (org); George Benson, Kenny Burrell, Grant Green (g); Ron Carter, Bob Cranshaw, Major Holley, Herbie Lewis, Andy Simpkins, George Tucker (b); Bill Dowdy, Otis Finch, Al Harewood, Clarence Johnston, Jimmy Madison, Mickey Roker, Grady Tate (d).* 60–84.

Turrentine's bluesy soul-jazz enjoyed considerable commercial success in the 1960s and after. His forte was the mid-tempo blues, often in minor keys, played with a vibrato as broad as his grin. A long sequence of Blue Note albums started as far back as 1960 (*Look Out!*) and ended in 1969 with *Ain't No Way*, but their availability seems to confound expectation, and Stan The Man's records seem to come and go from that catalogue with bemusing rapidity. So snap up *Rough 'N' Tumble* quickly if you want it. Typical Turrentine, the big blue sound sailed over Duke Pearson's functional but effective horn charts, with Green and

Tyner getting in some artful fills here and there. Very enjoyable, if scarcely any kind of classic.

At least the twofer *Up At Minton's* seems to be more of a fixture, the original pair of albums spread across a mid-price double-CD. A pity that brother Tommy, who'd been on *Jubilee Shout* a month earlier, didn't make the date, but it's a fine opportunity to hear Stan stretching out with a willing team, as well as some splendid work from Green, whose star seems to have risen dramatically again in the last few years – sad that it had to be a posthumous acclaim. The Blue Note *Best Of* is thoroughly recommended, picking nine longish tracks (the shortest are a lovely, brief 'God Bless The Child' from the excellent *Never Let Me Go* and the previously unreleased 'Lonesome Lover', a Max Roach composition). Worth searching out.

**** Pieces Of Dreams**
Original Jazz Classics OJC 831 *Turrentine; Sonny Burke, John Miller, Gene Page (ky); Ray Parker, Dean Parks, David T Walker (g); Ron Brown (b); Ed Moore, Ed Greene (d); Gary Coleman, Joe Clayton (perc); strings, voices.* 7/74.

**** Everybody Come On Out**
Original Jazz Classics OJC 911 *Turrentine; Oscar Brashear, Paul Hubinon, Bob Findley (t); George Bohannon, Charley Loper (tb); Lew McRearey (btb); Buddy Collette, Bill Green (reeds); Joe Sample (ky); Lee Ritenour, Craig McMullen (g); Paul Jackson (b); Harvey Mason (d); Bill Summers (perc); strings.* 3/76.

****(*) The Best Of Mr T**
Fantasy 7708 *Turrentine; Freddie Hubbard (t); Cedar Walton (p); Paul Griffin, Patrice Rushen, Joe Sample (ky); Cornell Dupree, Eric Gale, Ray Parker Jr, Lee Ritenour (g); Ron Carter (b); Jack DeJohnette, Harvey Mason (d).*

***** More Than A Mood**
MusicMasters 65079-2 *Turrentine; Freddie Hubbard (t, flhn); Cedar Walton (p); Ron Carter (b); Billy Higgins (d).* 92.

**** If I Could**
MusicMasters 518444 *Turrentine; Hubert Laws (f, picc); Sir Roland Hanna (p); Gloria Agostini (hp); Ron Carter (b); Grady Tate (d); Steve Kroon, Vincent Leroy Evans (perc); strings conducted by Matthew Raimondi.* 5/93.

Despite a partial return to jazz structures in subsequent decades, Turrentine appears to have moved over almost permanently to pop, like his collaborator on the thumping *Straight Ahead*, George Benson. His albums for Fantasy in the 1970s are a dull and dated lot, with only a few phrases poking through the candied, synthetic gloom to suggest that Mr T. is actually in there somewhere. In the '90s, he has gone back to his original strengths, perhaps only to find that his voice has faded away more than he realized. *More Than A Mood*, with the similarly exhausted Hubbard, has its moments and, when Turrentine gets worked up over the rhythm section, it can seem like his old self in the stirrups. But a year later he had already gone back on to the soft stuff. *If I Could* is close to useless.

Richard Twardzik (1931–55)

PIANO

Born in Danvers, Massachusetts, Twardzik made only a handful of recordings. He worked in the Boston area and was on tour with Chet Baker in Paris when he died of a heroin overdose.

(****) 1954 Improvisations
New Artists NA 1006 *Twardzik; Jack Lawlor (b); Peter Littman (perc).* 54.

Much cited but seldom heard, Twardzik was a precociously brilliant young player who recorded with Serge Chaloff, Charlie Mariano and Chet Baker and accompanied Charlie Parker on a radio broadcast, before succumbing to the same problem that had stained Parker's life. Apart from 'Yellow Waltz', he left nothing behind with his name on it. That itself justified the release after more than 30 years of these oddly haunting recordings. Do not be misled: these are not professional recordings but the results of amateur taping. There is little significant drop-out, though once or twice some slowing does seem to occur. Acoustically, though, no worse than many a treasured Bud Powell set. What compounds and complicates the problem is that Twardzik is playing a bar-room upright so out of tune (until the seventh track, 'Yesterdays', by which time the Man with the Dog has been summoned) that he almost sounds as if he's using a 'prepared' instrument. All the same, his attention to originals like 'All The Things You Are', 'Nice Work If You Can Get It' and a wonderfully bizarre 'Get Happy' demands the closest attention, even if prolonged listening induces an effect rather like being tapped on the forehead with a spoon. Twardzik's warm-up is as interesting a piece of musicianly actuality as anything since Brownie's practice tapes were released, and track by track one can almost hear him thinking out, rejecting, revising and refining his strategy, note by thoughtful note. Jazz-piano enthusiasts will be fascinated; jazz pianists will want to give it the closest study.

29th Street Saxophone Quartet

GROUP

Four New York-based saxophonists of different backgrounds, who rehearsed at Jim Hartog's apartment on … 29th Street.

*****(*) Live**
Red RR 123223 *Ed Jackson, Bobby Watson (as); Rich Rothenberg (ts); Jim Hartog (bs).* 7/88.

***** Milano New York Bridge**
Red 123262-2 *As above.* 11/92–12/93.

At once the most fun and the most coherent and self-challenging of the saxophone quartets, 29th Street was first put together at the behest of Jackson and Hartog, who both met Rich Rothenberg independently of each other and then persuaded Bobby Watson to enlist. If Watson was in many ways the key member of the group – his are the most distinctive improvisations, and his romantic streak softens the edges of some of their repertoire to beneficial effect – there's an exceptional uniformity of ideas and abilities in this band. Since they never double on other instruments, there's a special concentration on individual and collective timbre, which has been raised to a very high level, and their interaction became so advanced that they're close to that fabled point where improvisation and structure merge into one. Yet it's a high-spirited, funky and contagiously exciting group to listen to.

At present the group seems to have fallen into abeyance and there isn't much in the catalogue. *Live* is arguably their most vivid record. While there are occasional flaws – at least by their own prodigiously high standards – the sheer exuberance of the playing is phenomenal. Hartog's 'New Moon' must be the prettiest of all their ballads, and the way Jackson's yelping alto leads into the collective barnstorming of Kevin Eubanks's 'Sundance' is enough to elicit cheers from any listener. *Milano New York Bridge* is not quite one of their best: mostly jazz standards, tightly arranged and a bit airless in parts.

Charles Tyler (1941–92)

ALTO AND BARITONE SAXOPHONES

Worked with Albert Ayler as a teenager in Cleveland, and subseqently with him in New York. Moved to California in 1969 and recorded occasionally, though he began to drift from view and was living in Paris at the time of his death.

****(*) Autumn In Paris**

Silkheart SH 118 *Tyler; Arne Forsen (p); Ulf Akerhielm (b); Gilbert Matthews (d). 6/88.*

After the 1960s, Tyler never sounded as distinctive on anything bearing his own name as he does on Billy Bang's fine *Rainbow Gladiator*. A 1981 Storyville session called *Definite* was made slightly earlier than the seething Bang session, and Tyler comes across as uncertain in tone and unclear about his own stance on the tradition. *Autumn In Paris* is more settled in tone, but inescapably dull, with Tyler's free tonal approach significantly narrowed down; 'Legend Of The Lawman' is the specific point of comparison, its rooted, black sound considerably diluted by the European group. The album also includes none of his fierce, Hamiet Bluiett-influenced baritone. A very modest showing for a once-significant voice.

McCoy Tyner (born 1938)

PIANO, KOTO, FLUTE, PERCUSSION

Born in Philadelphia, Tyner worked with local players until meeting John Coltrane in 1959. He joined the Coltrane quartet in 1960 and stayed for six years, simultaneously making his own records for Impulse!. After a spell with Blue Note, he commenced a long association with Milestone and began leading medium-sized groups as well as working in a trio situation. In the '80s and '90s he made records for several labels, in solo, small-group and big-band settings. His grand style, uncompromisingly based around familiar tonalities and all the qualities of the acoustic piano, remains a major influence on contemporary pianists.

*****(*) Inception**

Impulse! 12202 *Tyner; Art Davis (b); Elvin Jones (d). 1/62.*

***** Reaching Fourth**

Impulse! 12552 *Tyner; Henry Grimes (b); Roy Haynes (d). 11/62.*

***** Nights Of Ballads And Blues**

Impulse! 12212 *Tyner; Steve Davis (b); Lex Humphries (d). 3/63.*

****(*) Plays Ellington**

Impulse! 12162 *Tyner; Jimmy Garrison (b); Elvin Jones (d); Willie Rodriguez, Johnny Pacheco (perc). 12/64.*

Tyner was still with John Coltrane's group when he started making records under his own name and, while these early sessions add little to what he was doing with the saxophonist, they do reveal what the pianist was doing more clearly than the engine-room of the Coltrane band could allow. Impulse! have now reorganized his output into a clear sequence of single-disc reissues. *Inception* was Tyner's debut as a leader. He had yet to build his playing into the massive, orchestral concept which came later, and his variations on his own 'Inception' and 'Blues For Gwen' are beautifully bright and lively, echoing Coltrane's own comment in the sleeve-note on how the pianist would use unusual clusters to illuminate his structures. *Reaching Fourth* is a welcome return for an almost forgotten album. Though the programme is more conventional, Tyner finds an imaginative format for 'Old Devil Moon' and 'Have You Met Miss Jones', and Grimes and Haynes are a wonderful team, incisive and swinging in perfect accord with the pianist. *Nights Of Ballads And Blues* is all jazz standards or pop tunes, and it is perhaps a degree more ordinary, yet the playing is unfailingly strong. The Ellington album is disappointing: Tyner's romanticism emerges, but his interpretative bent seems untested by the likes of 'Satin Doll' – it works better on the *Ballads And Blues* version – and the addition of the percussionists on four tracks seems like nothing but a gimmick. This is a very attractive sequence in Impulse!'s digipak format and, though we find that Rudy van Gelder's piano sound remains cloudy and unsympathetic, the records probably sound as good as they ever will.

****** The Real McCoy**

Blue Note 97807-2 *Tyner; Joe Henderson (ts); Ron Carter (b); Elvin Jones (d). 4/67.*

A key album in Tyner's discography. On the face of it, the music might be a direct extension of the Coltrane group, with Henderson substituting for Trane. But, with Tyner calling the tunes, it sounds quite different: dynamics are much more varied, form is more finely articulated and, while the band pushes at limits of tonality and metre alike, it never quite breaches them. The opening 'Passion Dance' is a definitive Tyner composition: structured round a single key but pounding through a metre which the leader noted as 'evoking ritual and trance-like states', it gathers power through the piano and saxophone statements until it sounds ready to explode, yet the concluding regrouping and subsequent variations are resolved immaculately. 'Contemplation', 'Four By Five' and 'Search For Peace' explore this brinkmanship further, through 3/4, 4/4 and 5/4 rhythms and fragments of melody which are enough to fuel all of the band's manoeuvres. Henderson is superbly resolute in avoiding cliché, Carter and

Jones work with dramatic compatibility, and Tyner's own playing exults in some of his discoveries learnt over the previous three years: his grand pedal-chords and fluttering right-hand lines establish the classic patterns of call-and-response which have dominated his manner ever since, and the sound he gets is peculiarly translucent, enabling one to hear through the clusters and follow all of his complex lines. Very highly recommended. It has been remastered as part of the Rudy van Gelder Edition and sounds better than ever.

***** Asante**

Blue Note 93384-2 *Tyner; Gary Bartz (ss, as); Andrew White (as, ob); Hubert Laws (f, af); Ted Dunbar (g); Buster Williams, Herbie Lewis (b); Billy Hart, Freddie Waits (d); Mtume (perc); Songai (v).* 7–9/70.

This sounds like a transitional record, two 1970 sessions (originally withheld for release until later in the decade) which see Tyner feeling his way towards the pan-cultural feel of his best music of the coming decade. Songai's wordless vocals are the most dated element, and some of the percussion parts seem like tacked-on polyrhythms, but the three earlier tracks with Laws, White and Bartz making a vividly colourful front line are more encouraging, especially the bright weave of interdependent lines in 'Forbidden Land'. Exoticism from a more innocent time.

***** Sahara**

Original Jazz Classics OJC 311 *Tyner; Sonny Fortune (ss, as, f); Calvin Hill (b, perc); Alphonse Mouzon (d, t, f).* 1/72.

Another important record for Tyner. After leaving Blue Note (several of his last sessions for them are currently missing), his career floundered until he was signed by Milestone: his first release, *Sahara*, was a poll-winning record which established his course for the 1970s. Mouzon couldn't have played the way he does but for Elvin Jones, yet his choked cymbals and relentless emphasis of the beat are very different from Jones's polyrhythmic swells. Fortune plays with uproarious power and velocity, and his solo on 'Rebirth' is electrifying, but his is essentially a decorative role, while the pianist drives and dominates the music. The group acts as the opposing face to Cecil Taylor's brand of energy music: controlled by harmonic and metrical ground-rules, nobody flies for freedom, but there is a compensating jubilation in the leader's mighty utterance. 'Sahara' and 'Ebony Queen' best express that here, although the piano solo, 'A Prayer For My Family', is a useful oasis of calm. Later Tyner records would be better engineered and realized, but this one remains excitingly fresh.

***** Song For My Lady**

Original Jazz Classics OJC 313 *As above, except add Charles Tolliver (flhn), Michael White (vn), Mtume (perc).* 9–11/72.

*****(*) Echoes Of A Friend**

Original Jazz Classics OJC 650 *Tyner.* 11/72.

****(*) Song Of The New World**

Original Jazz Classics OJC 618 *Tyner; Virgil Jones, Cecil Bridgewater, Jon Faddis (t); Garnett Brown, Dick Griffin (tb); Julius Watkins, Willie Ruff, William Warnick III (frhn); Hubert Laws (picc, f); Sonny Fortune (ss, as, f); Harry Smyles (ob); Kiane Zawadi (euph); Bob Stewart (tba); Juni Booth (b); Alphonse Mouzon (d); Sonny Morgan (perc); strings.* 4/73.

*****(*) Enlightenment**

Milestone MCD-55001-2 *Tyner; Azar Lawrence (ss, ts); Juni Booth (b); Alphonse Mouzon (d).* 7/73.

*****(*) Atlantis**

Milestone MCD-55002-2 *Tyner; Azar Lawrence (ss, ts); Juni Booth (b); Willy Fletcher (d); Guilherme Franco (perc).* 8–9/74.

***** Trident**

Original Jazz Classics OJC 720 *Tyner; Ron Carter (b); Elvin Jones (d).* 2/75.

**** Fly With The Wind**

Original Jazz Classics OJC 699 *Tyner; Hubert Laws (f, af); Paul Renzi (picc, f); Raymond Duste (ob); Linda Wood (hp); Ron Carter (b); Billy Cobham (d); strings.* 1/76.

Following the success of *Sahara*, Tyner embarked on a regular schedule of recording and found himself a popular concert draw at last. The music certainly sounded at home among 'progressive' trends in rock and beyond, although the pianist's beefy romanticism had a lot more profundity in it than most such music-making. *Song For My Lady* varied the cast of the previous disc by adding Michael White and Charles Tolliver to two open-ended pieces, but it was the lyricism of the title-track and Tyner's solo outing, 'A Silent Tear', which were most impressive. *Echoes Of A Friend* is a solo tribute to John Coltrane which resounds with all the grand exhortation which the pianist can wring from the keyboard. *Atlantis* and *Enlightenment* are two huge, sprawling concert recordings which will drain most listeners: Tyner's piano outpourings seem unstoppable, and Lawrence comes on as an even fierier spirit than Fortune, even if both are in thrall to Coltrane. The *Enlightenment* set, cut at Montreux, is marginally superior, if only for the pile-driving 'Walk Spirit, Talk Spirit'; but *Atlantis* is still very strong, with a majestic turn through 'My One And Only Love' and another torrential group-performance on the title-piece.

It was this kind of incantatory concert form which began to make Tyner's output sound overcrowded with effort: without the ability to soar away from structure, the music could seem bloated, as if packed with steroids. His other Milestone records of the period compensate with varied settings: *Song Of The New World* adds brass and string sections, *Fly With The Wind* sets up an orchestra behind him. But the latter seems to have its energy papered over with the strings, and *Song Of The New World* uses the extra musicians to no very bountiful purpose. *Trident* reunited him with Elvin Jones, but the results were genial rather than passionate. Some fine albums from the period are currently deleted – including *Sama Layuca*, *The Greeting* and *Passion Dance* – and, though they all contain music of lesser power than *Enlightenment*, Tyner's search for strength and tenderness in equal measure remains compelling.

*****(*) Supertrios**

Milestone MCD 55003-2 *Tyner; Ron Carter, Eddie Gomez (b); Tony Williams, Jack DeJohnette (d).* 4/77.

***** Quartets 4 × 4**

Milestone MCD-55007-2 *Tyner; Freddie Hubbard (t); Arthur Blythe (as); Bobby Hutcherson (vib); John Abercrombie (g); Cecil McBee (b); Al Foster (d).* 3–5/80.

Shrewdly balanced between show-tunes, jazz standards and Tyner originals, the double-trio event, with Tyner meeting

Gomez and DeJohnette on one date and Carter and Williams on the other, is a memorable one. Almost 15 years after his first trio records, Tyner's methods have taken on an invincible assurance, and with musicians like these he is working at his highest level. The session with Carter and Williams is slightly the more invigorating, with pianist and drummer working trenchantly through 'I Mean You' and 'A Moment's Notice', which stands out among many versions the pianist has played.

The album of quartets, with Abercrombie, Hubbard, Blythe and Hutcherson taking turns as the star guest, is pretty disappointing, given the personnel. Everyone plays politely rather than with any pressing need to communicate anything, and as a result it's perhaps the meeting with Hutcherson, most thoughtful of musicians, which comes off best.

*** Bon Voyage

Timeless SJP 260 *Tyner; Avery Sharpe (b); Louis Hayes (d).* 6/87.

Moving from a larger unit back to a trio as his regular working line-up stymied Tyner's progress to some degree. There's little here which he hasn't done better on previous records. *Bon Voyage* features mainly standards. Sharpe and Hayes do what they can to shadow the great boxing presence of the leader, even if at times that seems to mean merely crashing alongside, and, while this would be an excellent effort from lesser men, for Tyner it's relatively ordinary.

***(*) Uptown / Downtown

Milestone M 9167 *Tyner; Virgil Jones, Earl Gardner, Kamau Adilifu (t); Robin Eubanks (tb); Steve Turre (tb, dijeridu); John Clark (frhn); Joe Ford, Doug Harris (ss, as); Ricky Ford, Junior Cook (ts); Howard Johnson (tba); Avery Sharpe (b); Louis Hayes (d); Steve Thornton (perc).* 11/88.

A memorable departure for Tyner, which he has built on with his recent Birdology albums. The six charts here amplify the sweep of his groups of the 1970s, and the miracle is that it comes across as expansive and uncongested. Although he hardly seems like a big-band pianist, his own solos seem able to raise the already grand sound of the orchestra to an even higher level, and the choice of horn soloists – Joe Ford, Turre, Cook, Ricky Ford – makes for a thrillingly coloured and barnstorming effect. Five of the pieces are Tyner originals, the sixth is by Steve Turre, and nothing misfires; even the live sound is good enough to expose the few touches of under-rehearsal which slip through.

***(*) Things Ain't What They Used To Be

Blue Note B21Y-935982 *Tyner; George Adams (ts); John Scofield (g).* 89.

Tyner returned to Blue Note as a solo artist, and the albums are prized examples of a great player in his late prime. Alas, the splendid *Revelations*, a solo 'studio' recital in New York's Merkin Hall, has been deleted for the moment. *Things Ain't What They Used To Be* is more of the same, although Scofield and Adams duet on some tracks. Tyner sees no reason to check his regular flow, and as a result the three pieces with Scofield sound too full, but the duet with Adams on 'My One And Only Love' is gloriously realized, and some of the solos – particularly his latest thoughts on 'Naima' – are Tyner at his finest.

*** New York Reunion

Chesky JD 51 *Tyner; Joe Henderson (ts); Ron Carter (b); Al Foster (d).* 4/91.

Tyner often seems to find himself heading up all-star sessions, and this one is predictably enjoyable if not quite indispensable. Henderson doesn't know how to be boring, but his occasional diffidence on such as 'What Is This Thing Called Love?' suggests he isn't fully involved, and even the duet with Tyner on 'Ask Me Now', which starts with four minutes of unaccompanied tenor, is finally more interesting as an exercise than as a piece of music one wants to return to.

**** Soliloquy

Blue Note CDP 796429-2 *Tyner (p solo).* 2/91.

Tyner's third solo outing for Blue Note completes a triptych that sums up his art: rushing, open-hearted, grand of gesture, ineffably romantic, muscular, florid. He still takes every chance to overplay his hand, but that is his way: 'Willow Weep For Me', for instance, is about as aggressive a version of this tune as has ever been recorded. Yet his best melodies – either written or improvised out of tunes by Powell, Coltrane and, surprisingly, Dexter Gordon – are as communicative as they are powerful. He has written for long enough to make his own choices of tune a reflection on his own dynasty: 'Effendi' dates back to his earliest Impulse! sessions, 'Española' – a haunting use of the Spanish tinge – is brand new, and both are performed with fine evocative skill. The piano sound (the album was, like its predecessors, recorded at Merkin Hall in New York) is superb.

***(*) Remembering John

Enja 6080-2 *Tyner; Avery Sharpe (b); Aaron Scott (d).* 2/91.

Tyner's latest look at Coltrane is by turns restless, impetuous and profoundly considered. He avoids most of the obvious choices: only 'Giant Steps', punched out in a relentless two minutes twenty seconds, could be called an old chestnut. 'One And Four', bounced off its bass vamp, and 'Pursuance' are Tyner at his loosest and most exciting, while 'Up 'Gainst The Wall' is a more structured but no less intense sequence. 'Good Morning Heartache' is unusually delicate. 'In Walked Bud' seems to have drifted in from another session, but no matter: it merely makes one want to hear Tyner take on Monk more often than he does. Sharpe and Scott, too, are assuming a stature of their own beyond their status as long-serving disciples.

***(*) Warsaw Concert 1991

Fresh Sound FSR-CD 185 *Tyner (p solo).* 10/91.

Tyner's solo concerts are a blessed mix of the reverential and the powerhouse. He goes at 'Giant Steps' hammer-and-tongs, but on a charming original such as 'Lady From Caracas' he gets a melting kind of romanticism out of the keyboard. A round dozen interpretations offer Tyner, Monk, Coltrane and two standards as source material and, if everything is as expected, nothing is quite predictable. Good concert sound.

***(*) Journey

Birdology 519941-2 *Tyner; Earl Gardner, Virgil Jones, Eddie Henderson (t); Steve Turre, Slide Hampton, Frank Lacy (tb); John Clark (frhn); Doug Harris (ss, f); Joe Ford (as); John Stubblefield, Billy Harper (ts); Ronnie Cuber (bs); Tony

Underwood (tba); Avery Sharpe (b); Aaron Scott (d); Jerry Gonzalez, Waltinho Anastacio (perc); Dianne Reeves (v). 5/93.

Tyner's big band is making music that can stand with any of his mightiest records from the 1970s. While the very fine *The Turning Point* has been deleted, *Journey* is a repeat run at a slightly lower voltage overall. Dianne Reeves's feature on 'You Taught My Heart To Sing' is an inappropriately sentimental gesture, but there's compensation with one of the best tracks from both sessions in the tumultuous reading of 'Peresina'. A valuable development from this remarkable jazzman.

****** Manhattan Moods**

Blue Note 828423-2 *Tyner; Bobby Hutcherson (vib, mar).* 12/93.

They've met before with auspicious results, but this encounter is pure bliss from first to last. Instead of the instruments cancelling each other out, as is often the case in this kind of situation, keyboard and vibes entwine to create textures of ecstatic beauty: limpid, resonant, revealing. Tyner allows Hutcherson centre stage for much of the time, even if the piano is slightly the more forward in the mix, and Bobby responds with some of his most rapt playing. One could complain that they might have chosen some fresher tunes to play, but the results tend to sweep aside reservations, and the closing look at 'For Heaven's Sake' is on a par with Hutcherson's superlative version with Kenny Barron (discussed under the pianist's name).

***** Infinity**

Impulse! 11712 *Tyner; Michael Brecker (ts); Avery Sharpe (b); Aaron Scott (d); Waltinho Anastacio (perc).* 94.

***** Prelude And Sonata**

Milestone MCD-9244-2 *Tyner; Joshua Redman (ts); Antonio Hart (as); Christian McBride (b); Marvin 'Smitty' Smith (d).* 11/94.

Infinity marks the return of Impulse! as a 'new' jazz label, and it's fitting that it should be Tyner who starts it off. This isn't one of his greatest: Brecker could have been the fall-guy here, cast in the Coltrane role, but he manages to sidestep too many of the comparisons without finally convincing that he needn't walk in giant steps. *Prelude And Sonata* is basically a ballad album, bookended with pieces of Chopin and Beethoven, and it's interesting to note that McBride and Smith – for all their star status – are no more an appropriate match for Tyner than the undervalued Sharpe and Scott. The saxophonists play well, but this kind of session has become a commonplace which Tyner doesn't especially respond to. He plays professionally on both records without ever getting into his top gear.

***** What The World Needs Now**

Impulse! 11972 *Tyner; Christian McBride (b); Lewis Nash (d); strings.* 5/96.

The concept looks like a groaner, with Tyner engaged to embellish the compositions of Burt Bacharach, arranged by John Clayton. But it offers the promise of an intriguing truce between Tyner's full-on romanticism and his jazz instincts, and even the possibility of a middle-of-the-road music of genuine depth and subtlety, rather than the phoney narcotics of smooth jazz. The result, though, is a near-miss. Too much of it follows the same pattern: lovely out-of-tempo intro by the strings, followed by Tyner's theme statement, a gentle improvisation on the material by the trio, and a few interpolations by the orchestra. There's disappointingly little dialogue between the large and small groups, and Clayton seems keen to simply stay out of Tyner's way. The result is high-calibre mood-jazz – these are beautiful original songs, after all – and nothing much more.

*****(*) McCoy Tyner And The Latin All-Stars**

Telarc CD-83462 *Tyner; Claudio Roditi (t, flhn); Steve Turre (tb, shells); Gary Bartz (ss, as); Dave Valentin (f); Avery Sharpe (b); Ignacio Berroa (d); Giovanni Hidalgo, Johnny Almendra (perc).* 7/98.

He's gone to yet another new label, and it's amusing to find that this fresh start has found him, if anything, returning to his glory days of the 1970s Milestone bands. Bartz goes all the way back to *Asante*, and the rest of the group know better than to try and upstage the master. If anyone can make a 'Latin Jazz' album without submitting to the tyranny of that rhythm, it's Tyner – all he really does is fit the expected sunshine-shuffle into his own thunderous drive, and the result is his most characteristic set for years. Valentin plays a few silly solos, but he's largely rendered harmless by the situation, and there's some excellent work from the other horns, especially Turre. Tyner's latest thoughts on 'Afro Blue' are a highlight and the farewell parade through 'Blue Bossa' sends us out with a cheer.

*****(*) McCoy Tyner With Stanley Clarke And Al Foster**

Telarc CD-83488 *Tyner; Stanley Clarke (b); Al Foster (d).* 4/99.

All-star again, underlined by all three names appearing in the album title. Clarke divides his time between electric and stand-up instrument, and one piece, 'I Want To Tell You 'Bout That', gets a version with each option (predictably, the 'electric' rendition is zippier). These are three individual stylists still in top fettle and the record is no disappointment, even if it's clear that at this point McCoy is going to spend the rest of his career musing on what he's already achieved.

Gebhard Ullmann

TENOR AND SOPRANO SAXOPHONES, BASS CLARINET, FLUTE, BASS FLUTE, ALTO FLUTE, PICCOLO

An eclectic reed specialist who shuttles between Berlin and New York, Ullmann is at home in many contemporary settings and works regularly with several different groups, working mainly from his own prolific composer's book.

***** Per-Dee-Doo**

Nabel 4640 *Ullmann; Michael Rodach (g); Martin Lillich (b); Niko Schauble (d).* 7/89.

***** Suite Noire**

Nabel 4649 *Ullmann; Andreas Willers (g); Bob Stewart (tba); Marvin 'Smitty' Smith (d).* 1–8/90.

*****(*) Basement Research**

Soul Note 12171-2 *Ullmann; Ellery Eskelin (ts); Drew Gress (b); Phil Haynes (d).* 11/93.

Ullmann's records are fascinating essays on various aspects of tradition and the avant-garde and how they intertwine. *Per-Dee-Doo* is a revisionist look at ten jazz standards – from Miles Davis's 'Fall' all the way back to Benny Goodman's 'Seven Come Eleven' – cut up and creatively damaged by Rodach's guitar, Ullmann's woodwind arsenal and the broken rhythms of the other two. The recording sometimes gets too muddy for the good of the music, but there is much intriguing turmoil, without too much obvious desecration along the way. *Suite Noire* tracks the duo work of Ullmann and Willers over ten years of performing together. Smith is on two tracks, including a quite pulverizing 'medley' of 'Lonely Woman' and 'Double Density', while Stewart adds human-breath bass-lines to another two. Essentially, though, this is a duo record, overlapping lines and densely coloured textures dominating the music.

The meeting with the Eskelin/Gress/Haynes trio on *Basement Research* is different again. Ullmann is stepping into a trio environment where the players already know one another well, and he's welcomed cautiously, though there's some provocative duelling for space. If Eskelin is the further out of the two players, Ullmann's primarily cool extremism is still cutting-edge, and the tracks in which the two both play tenor have a splendidly combative element. A fine disc, well recorded.

***** Ta Lam**

Songlines SGL 1520-2 *Ullmann; Dirk Engelhardt (ss, ts, bcl); Thomas Klemm (ts, f); Jurgen Kupke (cl); Joachim Litty (acl, bcl, as); Heiner Reinhardt (bcl); Volker Schlott (ss, as, f); Hans Hassler (acc).* 8/91–3/94.

*****(*) Trad Corrosion**

Nabel 4673 *Ullmann; Andreas Willers (g); Phil Haynes (d).* 4/95.

What an extraordinary record *Ta Lam* is. Ullmann summons a great phalanx of reed players (and overdubs himself on five other tracks, playing nine different horns) in a collection of pieces that blend free-for-all uproar with a lumbering, symphonic delivery that is sometimes too weighty for its own good. A bizarre arrrangement of 'Mack The Knife' will turn enough heads, but what about the rising crescendo (and diminuendo) of 'Think Tank', or the way odd-man-out Hassler scampers in and around the saxophone army? Beautifully recorded, this is an intriguing disc, and its ration of near-misses shouldn't stop the curious from investigating.

Trad Corrosion is entirely different. Here the trio try to play as quietly and minimalistically as possible, squeezing 19 pieces into less than 50 minutes, some of them no more than the briefest idea, quickly dispatched. Hyper-sensitive to space, sound and silence – Haynes especially is a marvel at playing a lot of music without making a lot of noise – this one succeeds in creating an intensity without any bluster.

*****(*) Kreuzberg Park East**

Soul Note 121371-2 *Ullmann; Ellery Eskelin (ts); Drew Gress (b); Phil Haynes (d).* 5/97.

A return match for this quartet. Stylistically, this is a more diverse record, with Ullmann the composer keen to display his range, which stretches from the stealthy whisperings of 'Flutist With Hat And Shoe' to the vertiginous contrapuntal melodies of 'Almost Twenty-Eight'. It's all meat and drink to Eskelin and the others, who remain unfazed by whatever the leader throws their way. Good-humoured and rarely without an abosorbing moment.

James Blood Ulmer (born 1942)

GUITAR, VOCALS

Born in South Carolina, Ulmer sang gospel, played in funk groups, and then studied with Art Blakey and Ornette Coleman in turn; the former influence is often understated by commentators on his music, but it is certainly there. Some of the guitarist's work borders on the hard-edged black rock sound of bands like Living Color, but his jazz and blues chops are undeniable.

*****(*) Tales Of Captain Black**

DIW 403 *Ulmer; Ornette Coleman (as); Jamaaladeen Tacuma (b); Denardo Coleman (d).* 12/78.

***** Are You Glad To Be In America?**

DIW 400 *Ulmer; Olu Dara (t); Oliver Lake (as); David Murray (ts); William Patterson (g); Amin Ali (b); Ronald Shannon Jackson (d).* 1/80.

Often described as a student of Ornette Coleman's still-unassimilated 'harmolodics' – a theory which dispenses with the normal hierarchy of 'lead' and 'rhythm' instruments, allowing free harmonic interchange at all levels of a group – Ulmer had actually started to devise similar ideas independently. In the late 1960s he played with organists Hank Marr and Big John Patton, promoting a harsh modern derivative of soul-jazz. His work with drummer Rashied Ali (who rejoined one of the more abstract of Ulmer's late-1980s bands, Original Phalanx/Phalanx) brought him to the attention of Ornette Coleman.

Tales Of Captain Black is in many ways as much Coleman's album as Ulmer's, even if the saxophonist doesn't play all that much. His signature twirls and twists on the horn are inimitable and, with Denardo on drums, this was clearly a direction he wanted to explore further (as he has indeed gone on to do). But Ulmer is the most powerful presence, driving a ferocious course with jazz, rock and funk phrases that he makes into a visceral and convincing whole. Tacuma, too, plays a radically innovative role on electric bass, sometimes twinned with the guitarist, often fighting everything that Ulmer does. It's boiling, thrilling music, and if it seems less astonishing than it did on release (the original LP was on Artists House) it's basically worn well.

Are You Glad To Be In America?, with a cast of loft-jazz heroes taking cameo roles, is just as impressive but is let down by the indifferent studio mix. The title-track is one of Ulmer's enduring hits, and listening to it now is an almost nostalgic experience: it was once released as a single in the UK on the Rough Trade label, aligning Ulmer and his gang with a punk experimentalism that seems amusing at this distance.

****** Odyssey**

Columbia 485101 *Ulmer; Charles Burnham (vn); Warren Benbow (d).* 3–5/83.

Ulmer's contract with Columbia petered out after three albums, and so far only the final one has made it to CD. It's a classic New York record of the period. Given a beefy, up-front sound (at last),

Ulmer slimmed his group down to a bass-less trio, added the almost shamanistic sound of Charles Burnham's fiddle, and set the group to rock and roll over eight rootsy chunks of American music. 'Church' and 'Little Red House' reach back to gospel, blues and country dance as transmogrified into electrical storms, the whine of the violin mingling with the bite and twang of Ulmer's chording to superb effect. 'Are You Glad To Be In America?' reappears as a kind of slow lament. The essential Ulmer record.

***** Original Phalanx**

DIW 8013 *Ulmer; George Adams (ts, ss, f); Sirone (b); Rashied Ali (d).* 2/87.

***** In Touch**

DIW 8026 *As above.* 2/88.

**** Black And Blues**

DIW 845 *Ulmer; Ronnie Drayton (g, v); Amin Ali (b, v); Grant Calvin Weston (d, v).* 91.

'Harmolodics' started to seem like a millstone round Ulmer's neck. Partly in reaction, he turned towards the less outwardly complex, funk-based approach which is evident on most of his later releases. As with Coleman's music, this emphasized the extent to which the guitarist's 'radicalism' was based on traditional procedures. Most of Ulmer's characteristic distortions of pitch and loud riffing are part of a long-established electric blues idiom; what distinguishes Ulmer is the extremity to which he pushes such devices (to the point of tonal abstraction) and the bitter, inchoate quality of his playing. *Original Phalanx* and *In Touch* are good examples of the band he co-led with Adams, but some of his more recent stuff shows a falling-off. Try as we have to find something more positive to say about it, *Black And Blues* is just dull.

***** Harmolodic Guitar With Strings**

DIW 878 *Ulmer; John Blake, Gayle Dixon, Ron Lawrence, Akua Dixon Turre (strings).* 93.

As a British DIY commercial goes: It does exactly what it says on the tin. This DIW release is clearly inspired first and foremost by Ornette Coleman's experiments with a string group and it's mostly a very interesting essay, though there is too much of a mismatch between the two main components, sometimes reducing the ensemble to a mere backdrop. 'Theme From Captain Black' unaccountably comes at the very end; perhaps because of its familiarity, it's the best thing on the album.

****** Music Speaks Louder Than Words**

Koch Jazz 7833 *Ulmer; Amin Ali, Calvin Fuzz Jones (b); Rashied Ali, Aubrey Dale (d).* 4/97.

***** Forbidden Blues**

DIW 932 *Ulmer; Charles Burnham (vn); Amin Ali, Calvin Fuzz Jones (b); Grant Calvin Weston (d, v).* 10/98.

Something of a return to form. Just when it looked as though James was too insecure or too self-directed to play anyone's stuff but his own, he came out with a brilliant album of Ornette Coleman compositions, repaying his first and still greatest inspiration. The opening 'Lonely Woman' is wonderful and sets the pace and tone for an album of brooding majesty. 'Elizabeth' and 'Sphinx', 'Street News' and the *Skies Of America* theme make up the bulk of the remainder, and there are three Ulmer originals in the mix as well. Rashied Ali is an honoured guest – though, to be honest, he adds little of consequence.

The songs on *Forbidden Blues* are mostly short and well structured, and Ulmer's maverick approach to the blues has once again started to yield surprises, mostly from asymmetrical forms and unexpected tonalities, as on 'Eviction' and the fine 'High Yellow'. The record palls well before the end; though it's well under an hour in duration, it feels like longer. Burnham is always a valuable presence and he makes some powerful interventions here. Time, surely, to let his compositional gifts loose in this context.

UMO Jazz Orchestra

ENSEMBLE

Founded in 1975, and with a range that embraces everything from light standard swing to the avant-garde, UMO is one of the world's great jazz orchestras. The key to its success has been a careful blend of inch-perfect section-work, some genuinely individual solo voices, and an intriguing leaven of guest musicians.

*****(*) Kalevala Fantasy**

Finlandia 1576 59936-2 *Heiki Haimila, Esko Heikkinen, Timo Paasonen, Jörgen Petersen, Simo Salminen (t); Juhani Aalto, Mikael Långbacka, Pekka Laukkanen, Mircea Stan (tb); Juhani Aaltonen, Eero Koivistoinen, Pentti Lahti, Pertti Päivinen, Teemu Salminen (reeds); Heikki Sarmato (p, elp); Otto (g); Pekka Sarmanto (b); Esko Rosnbell (d, perc).* 11/86.

Few countries are so thoroughly defined by a single work as Finland is by the *Kalevala*. It pervades the literary, dramatic, visual and musical culture with an overdetermining grip that still doesn't seem to be oppressive. Heikki Sarmanto's meditation on the national epic was written to mark its 150th anniversary and is in every measure commensurate with its themes.

The story of Lemminkainen provides a threading continuity to a rich array of themes and ideas. Sarmanto draws on folk themes, blues shapes and stray echoes of Finnish classical music, from Sibelius onwards. 'Maiden Of The River' is the most substantial track, a glorious, shapely theme that picks up on harmonic devices in some of the earlier pieces: 'Fairest One Of All' and 'The Promise Broken'.

Most of the soloists later became familiar, but guitarist Otto Berger has a fine moment on 'The Three Tasks'. The music was choreographed by Boris Eifman of St Petersburg, but it works perfectly well as an aural experience.

***** UMO Plays The Music Of Muhal Richard Abrams**

UMO CD 101 *Anders Bergcrantz, Chuck Findley, Heiki Haimila, Esko Heikkinen, Simo Salminen (t); Juhani Aaltonen, Mikael Långbacka, Mircea Stan, Markku Veijonsuo (tb); Kari Heinila, Eero Koivistoinen, Pentti Lahti, Pertti Paivinen, Teemu Salminen (sax); Seppo Kantonen (p); Kirmo Lintinen (syn); Lars Danielsson (b); Klaus Suonsaari (d); Mongo Aaltonen (perc).* 5/88.

This, it hardly needs saying, exemplifies the chewier and more adventurous side of UMO's remit. Since the composer himself supervised the sessions, we have to assume that he was relatively pleased with the results, but the results are rather flat and mechanical and without the fire that a Chicago outfit might have brought to the proceedings. But then, the Windy City hasn't been in any rush to offer Abrams recording opportunities of this sort. Among the pieces included are 'Ritob', 'Fotex', 'Melancholia' and 'Symtre' and there is a fine Abrams arrangement of Duke's 'Melancholy' for contrast.

As ever, the section-work is impeccable and there are some good solo spots from the likes of Lahti (a genuine national treasure) and Bergkrantz. The rhythm section could do with a more relaxed approach, but all credit to the recording engineers in Helsinki and to remix wizard Dave Baker who gave the record its undeniable gloss.

***(*) UMO Jazz Orchestra

Naxos Jazz 86010 *Anders Bergcrantz, Esko Heikkinen, Teemu Mattsson, Timo Paasonen, Mikko Pettinen (t, flhn); Markku Veijonsuo (tb); Mikko Mustonen (tb, euph); Pekka Laukkanen (tb, tba); Mikael Långbacka (btb); Eero Koivistoinen (ts, ss); Manuel Dunkel (ts, f); Jouni Jarvela (as, ss, cl); Pentti Lahti (as, ss, f); Pertti Paivinen (bs, bcl, f); Teemu Salminen (ts, bcl, cl, f); Seppo Kantonen (p); Kirmo Lintinen (syn); Markku Kanerva, Jarmo Saari (g); Hannu Rantanen, Pekka Sarmanto (b); Markus Ketola (d); Mongo Aaltonen (perc); Bino Nkwazi, Jarmo Saari (v); Kari Heinila, Kirmo Lintinen (cond).* 5/97.

All credit to the team at Naxos Jazz as well. This was an enterprising signing and it could prove to be good business for both Naxos and UMO. Most of the material is original, with compositions from conductor Heinila and saxophonist Koivistoinen the most prominent. There are two arrangements of jazz tunes, Miles's 'All Blues' (a feature for excellent trumpeter Bergcrantz and vocalist Nkwazi) and a more unexpected version of John Coltrane's 'Equinox' on which Koivistoinen manages to avoid the remotest hint of pastiche Trane.

Nicely paced, with a well-judged selection of tunes, this makes for an ideal introduction to what the band do and do best. And at a throwaway price, it should be pretty nearly irrestistible to big-band fans.

**** Electrifying Miles

A Records AL 73153 *Tim Hagans (t); Esko Heikkinen, Teemu Mattsson, Timo Paasonen, Mikko Pettinen (t, flhn); Pekka Laukkanen, Mikko Mustonen, Marku Veijonsuo (tb); Mikael Långbacka (btb); Pentti Lahti (ss, as, f); Jouni Jarvela (ss, as, cl); Teemu Salminen (ts, cl, bcl, f); Janne Murto (ts, f); Pertti Paivinen (bs, bcl, f); Jukka Hakokongas, (elp, org); Jarmo Savolainen (p, elp, syn); Raoul Björkenheim (g); Harri Rantanen, Pekka Sarmanto (b); Markus Ketola, Aussi Nykanen (d); Mongo Aaltonen (perc); Eero Koivistoinen (cond).* 4/97.

Guest soloist Tim Hagans did his apprenticeship in the Stan Kenton band, and if this Miles Davis tribute has another stylistic source it is the Kenton orchestra. The most effective aspect of the project is that Hagans is able to suggest enough of Miles's spirit without sounding like a slavish acolyte. He solos on every track, most effectively on 'Spanish Key' and 'Sanctuary', where he shares the front line with the second tune's arranger, Raoul Björkenheim. It, of course, is a Wayne Shorter composition, as are 'Prince Of Darkness' and 'Nefertiti', and it seems that conductor Eero Koivistoinen (a trumpeter himself) was drawn rather to these more complex, long-lined items in the Miles oeuvre than to the trumpeter's own rather less elaborate themes. 'What It Is' is a Miles/John Scofield collaboration, played briefly and simply as a feature for Hagans.

Other soloists acquit themselves well. The Olympic Rhythm Section, led by Björkenheim and the two keyboard players, is a fair simulacrum of the *Bitches Brew* band. Pertti Paivinen's Maupin-influenced bass clarinet on 'Spanish Key' is very effective, and he returns with fresh ideas on 'Calypso Frelimo' right at the end of this fine album, which is one of the very best large-scale Miles tributes on the shelves.

***(*) Ellington Tribute

Finlandia 3984 27857-2 *Esko Heikkinen, Teemu Mattsson, Timo Paasonen, Tero Saart (t); Pekka Laukkanen, Vesa-Matti Mattsson, Mikko Mustonen, Markku Veijonsuo (tb); Jouni Jarvela, Mikko Jarvinen, Pentti Lahti, Janne Murto, Pepa Paivinen, Teemu Salminen (reeds); Kirmo Lintinen (p); Pekka Sarmanto (b); Mikko Hassinen, Markus Ketola (d).* 7 & 8/97.

In 1985, UMO performed a programme of Ellington compositions with Mercer Ellington wielding the baton, an association which he repeated in 1995, not long before his death. UMO's grip on the charts is hard to fault, though again there is a soulless clank to some of the playing, relieved only by sterling solos from Lahti, Heikkinen and the underrated Mustonen. Taking the Williams part in 'Concerto For Cootie', the trumpeter shows his true mettle and his thoughtful absorption of the classic recordings.

The overture blends together 'Things Ain't What They Used To Be', 'Sophisticated Lady', and a great reading of 'Perdido'. They save '"A" Train' for last, which confirms an upbeat tone for this early and prescient centenary tribute. Concentrating on the more rhythmic side of Duke's legacy is no bad thing, but it would have been good to have had a greater admixture of moodier themes and solos.

*** Selected Standards

Beta BECD 4029 *Esko Heikkinen, Timo Paasonen, Antero Priha, Simo Salminen (t, flhn); Markku Johanson (flhn); Pekka Laukkanen, Mikael Långbacka, Mikko Mustonen, Markku Veijonsuo (tb); Pentti (ss, as, picc, f); Jukka Perko (ss, as, cl); Sonny Heinila (ts, f); Teemu Salminen (ts, f, cl); Pertti Paivinen (bs, bsx, bcl); Kirmo Lintinen (p); Jarno Kukkonen (g); Pekka Sarmanto (b); Markko Timonen (d); Mongo Aaltonen (perc); Bill Carson (v).*

It does exactly what it says on the spec. A set of bright, elegantly executed standard themes, somewhat lacking in surprises but marked out by fine musicianship right through the band. Paivinen's baritone solo on 'My Shining Hour' is a revelation, and Kukkonen's complementary solo makes this the outstanding track of the set, though a rascally 'Love For Sale' (complete with rap) and a feeling interpretation of 'Darn That Dream' round out an excellent album.

By this stage in the game, one looks for somewhat more from UMO. This is motor show jazz: sleek, shiny and somewhat mechnical.

***(*) Day Dreamin'

FSR FSRCD 02 *Esko Heikkinen, Timo Paasonen, Mikko Pettinen, Tero Saarti (t); Mikael Långbacka, Pekka Laukkanen,*

Mikko Mustonen (tb); Ulf (tb, p, v); Jouni Jarvela, Pentti Lahti, Janne Murto, Pepa Paivinen, Teemu Salminen (reeds); Mikael Jakobsson (p); Larry Coryell (g); Pekka Sarmanto (b); Markus Ketola (d); Ricardo Padilla, Yamar Thiam (perc); Annika Hultman (v); Kirmo Lintinen (cond). 4/98.

Never slow to capitalize on a winning formula, UMO followed up the fine Ellington tribute with a set devoted to Billy Strayhorn. Larry Coryell isn't the first and most obvious guest soloist, but he fits into place with almost casual ease, playing beautiful solos on 'Day Dream', 'Absinthe' and 'Blood Count', and in duo with fellow-soloist Johansson on 'Lotus Blossom', the trombonist momentarily switching to piano.

The other important element is the vocal styling of Annika Hultman. A slightly characterless singer when intense emotion is called for, she has an elegant and buoyant approach to harmony, which makes her an exceptional band vocalist. Drifting back and forth across the beat doesn't always do her favours and occasionally makes her seem mannered, but there is no doubting her musicianship.

Fans of Coryell will welcome the chance to hear him in this context but, as ever, the real hero is the ensemble, this time out under the direction of Kirmo Lintinen, one of at least half a dozen conductors from the ranks of UMO.

University Of Wisconsin–Eau Claire Jazz Ensemble

GROUP

The big band made up of students from the Jazz Studies Area at University of Wisconsin–Eau Claire, under the direction of Bob Baca.

**** Jazz In Clear Water**

Walrus CDWR-4507 *Jeremy Miloszewicz, Pat Phalen, Dan Julson, James Simmons, Todd Walker (t); Doug Williams, Kevin Loughney, Adam Bever, Chris Fulton, Eric Olson (tb); Kristin Bucholz, Jason Gillette (as); Drew Disher, Donald Pashby, Chad Walker (ts); Chris Campbell (bs); Tom Benz (g); Michael Weiser, Matt Harris (p); Chris Bates, Scott Pingel (b); Williams Wood, Andy Algire (d).* 3/93.

***** In Transit**

Sea Breeze SBV-4509 *As above, except add Dennis Luginbill, Kyle Newmaster (t), Scott Busse (tb), Bill Voltz (ts), Adi Yeshaya (p), Matt Neesley (d); omit Phalen, Walker, Williams, Olson, Bucholz, Pashby, Harris, Bates and Wood.* 94.

***** Brilliant Corners**

Sea Breeze SBV-4515 *Jeremy Miloszewicz, Tim Hoffman, Matt Mealy, James Simmons, Kyle Newmaster (t); Jeff Ilse, Adam Bever, Eric Songer, Matt Franko, Tim Roddel (tb); Andy Parks, Becky Weber, Susan Page, Amanda Flosbach (frhn); Jason Gillette, Tom Luer (as); Clay Pufahl, Ryan Lehman (ts); Chris Gumz (bs); Derek Machan, Jason Craft (p); Scott Pingel, Aaron Doty (b); Andy Algire, Jamie Andrews, Tony Mazzone (d).* 95.

As usual with American college bands, standards here are set very high, with not many notes out of place. As so often, though, precision tends to steamroller flair and excitement into a somewhat flat pancake. The first disc, admittedly, is sabotaged by the sound-mix: recorded live, all the pointed ensemble-work sounds indistinct, and Pingel's awful bass showcase 'Chop Suey' is a marathon the record could have done without. The succeeding studio album works out much better (even though Pingel has another tedious solo outing). Greg Hopkins's arrangement of 'What Are You Doing The Rest Of Your Life' is a properly arresting setting for Gillette's alto, the opening 'Body And Soul' finds some interesting folds in a faded bloom and, if the flag-wavers are typically overdone, they're still big on impact. Excellent sound this time. *Brilliant Corners* is another outing for the next year's edition of the band. Pingel is still there, and he gets two more features, but the charts are executed with the expected panache – 'Nardis' and Geoff Keezer's 'Leilani's Mirror' are both particularly effective vehicles – and, if the soloists rarely do anything memorable, the band's the thing.

Uppsala Big Band

GROUP

Swedish big band staffed primarily by young contemporary players.

****(*) In Progress**

Sittel SITCD 9208 *Per Onnerud, Jonas Wiklund, Anders Nystrom, Jonas Andersson (t, flhn); Jerk Eriksson (t); Claes Agren, Lennart Lind, Istvan Domonkos, Ulf Johansson (tb); Nils Mannerfeldt (btb); Mats Nyfjall, Mats Bengtsson, Bengt Gustavsson, Tore Berglund, Hakan Dahlgren, Stefan Nyhem (reeds); Micael Zingmark, Anders Bromander, Anders Goransson (ky); Ulf Holmberg (g); Mats Ejesjo, Per Johansson (b); Mats Engstrom (d); Claes Janson (v); MeMera (v group).* 12/92–9/93.

Purists may fume, but there's a case to be made that this kind of big band – young, modish, loaded with keyboards, electric guitar and bass, and tackling Donald Fagen alongside Horace Silver – will convert contemporary ears more easily than any Basie revivalists. And they know their stuff: 'The Jody Grind' is delivered with enormous clout, 'Lady Bird' swings, 'EG Blues' sizzles. On the down side, soloists make little impression (Ulf Johansson, sitting in on two tracks, shows them how it's done) while the vocal features for Janson and cooing male group MeMera are for the very tolerant. The digital sound is bright enough to cut glass, too.

Massimo Urbani (1957–93)

ALTO SAXOPHONE

A brilliant prodigy, Urbani was working at seventeen with Giorgio Gaslini's quartet. He subsequently played in whatever context he fancied. A Roman who was careless about taking care of himself or his career, he died following a heroin overdose, and his surviving recordings are now precious mementoes of one of the most masterful bebop saxophonists to have emerged from Europe.

***** 360 Degrees Aeutopia**

Red RR 123146-2 *Urbani; Ron Burton (p); Cameron Brown (b); Beaver Harris (d).* 6/79.

*****(*) Dedications To Albert Ayler And John Coltrane**

Red RR 123160-2 *Urbani; Luigi Bonafede (p); Furio Di Castri (b); Paolo Pellegatti (d).* 6/80.

*****(*) Easy To Love**

Red RR 123208-2 *Urbani; Luca Flores (as); Furio Di Castri (b); Roberto Gatto (d).* 1/87.

*****(*) Out Of Nowhere**

Splasc(h) H 336-2 *Urbani; Paul Rodberg (tb); Giuseppe Emmanuele (p); Nello Toscano (b); Pucci Nicosia (d).* 4/90.

****** The Blessing**

Red RR 123257-2 *Urbani; Maurizio Urbani (ts); Danilo Rea (p); Giovanni Tommaso (b); Roberto Gatto (d).* 2/93.

Urbani's senseless death robbed Europe of a player whose records are a flawed testament to a bopper of enormous guts and facility. Marcello Piras describes him as a 'wastrel genius' in his notes to the Splasc(h) issue. Certainly Urbani's earlier records sometimes failed to live up to the reputation he had as a wunderkind in the 1970s, but these recent reissues still make an impressive group. The opening of the first Red album consists of an astonishing outburst of alto on 'Cherokee', at a suitably hectic tempo, and though matters cool off somewhat from that point, Urbani's grip seldom lets go. Cameron Brown is superb at the bass, but Beaver Harris's splashy drumming isn't right for the group. The *Dedications* set poses an intriguing premiss, although Urbani never really tackles Ayler head-on, except in some of his distortions. It's more about linking Parker and Coltrane. There is a lustrous, acerbic 'Naima' as well as one of his fighting bebop miniatures in 'Scrapple From The Apple'. *Easy To Love* is a relatively straightforward programme of standards, apart from the opening 'A Trane From The East'; Urbani burns through them.

The final offerings, both taken down almost by chance, are a memorable and even chastening last statement. The Splasc(h) record, cut at Rodberg's studio with the trombonist sitting in on two tunes, is simple, standard fare, with a very modest rhythm section, but Urbani's herculean playing comes through all the more strongly as a result, utterly tempestuous on 'There Is No Greater Love' and surprisingly lyrical on 'Alfie'. Highly recommended; but the final session for Red is even stronger. For all the glances in the direction of Coltrane, Urbani was a diehard bopper to the end; but his brother, Maurizio, looked forward in other directions, and his two appearances offer a tart contrast in styles on a pair of originals by Tommaso. Otherwise Urbani's coruscating tone and energy command all the attention, even with the impressive Rea in the group: two takes of 'What's New' are brimming with ideas, and a solo 'Blues For Bird' is an astonishing tribute to Parker.

***** Urlo**

Elicona 3343-2 *Urbani; Carlo Atti (ts); Massimo Farao (p); Piero Leveratto (b); Gianni Cazzola (d).* 10/88.

***** Round About ... Max**

Sentemo SNT 30392 *Urbani; Gianni Lenoci (p); Pasquale Gadaleat (b); Antonio Di Lorenzo (d); strings.* 11/91.

Urbani's passing has made remaining documents of his work more precious, so these two otherwise unexceptional discs are welcome. *Urlo* is a brief quartet date with three originals by Farao and Leveratto balanced by three standards and a blues. Urbani coasts here and there, but there is the unpredictable launching into sheer passion that makes his music so exhilarating from moment to moment. *Round About ... Max* includes two tracks with a string section, along with five other standards. The recording is pretty atrocious for something made in the 1990s – the bass frequencies are negligible, and even Urbani sounds thin at times – but his outlandish solo treatment of 'Days Of Wine And Roses' is a gem, and a duet with Lenoci on 'Invitation' was worth preserving.

Michal Urbaniak (born 1943)

ELECTRIC VIOLIN

Like his tragic fellow-countryman and -instrumentalist, Zbigniew Seifert, Urbaniak began his career as a Coltrane-influenced saxophonist, concentrating increasingly on violin as he found an individual voice. Like Jean-Luc Ponty, he experimented with fusion, but in more recent years he has returned to a much straighter jazz direction, playing violin with a strong horn feel.

***** Fusion**

Columbia/Legacy CK 65525 *Urbaniak; Wojciech Karolak, Adam Makowicz (ky); Czeslaw Bartkowski (d); Urszula Dudziak (v).* 6/73.

In contrast to Seifert, who died in his early thirties in 1979, Urbaniak has shown less interest in free music than in accommodating conventional jazz structures and those folk elements which seem most adaptable to his instrument; very recently, he has been recording in a more or less straight folk idiom, though these records may be difficult to find outside Poland. In the 1970s he also showed a strong interest in electronics, experimented with the wind-generated lyricon and made a number of successful albums with his singer wife, Ursula Dudziak.

Of these, only the self-identifying *Fusion* currently survives the cull. Blending Coltrane's harmonics with folk themes and a more than commonly sophisticated rock beat, it's a deceptive package, more sophisticated than at first appears, but also funkier than the rather lumpen production might suggest. Dudziak is a very special singer and even manages to invest her Echoplexed episodes with genuine emotion. The two keyboard players create shifting patterns which are immediately reminiscent of Miles's post-*Bitches Brew* groups, though less subtle and still obviously jazz-derived. Makowicz was undergoing strange transformations at the time, but his quality shines through. Without a strong bass line, the songs are floaty and vagrant, but strongly anchored in melody. A fusion classic, a little worn and attractively distressed.

***** My One And Only Love**

Steeplechase SCCD 31159 *Urbaniak; Gene Bertoncini (g); Michael Moore (b).* 7/81.

***** Take Good Care Of My Heart**

Steeplechase SCCD 31195 *Urbaniak; Horace Parlan (p); Jesper Lundgaard (b); Aage Tanggaard, (d).* 8/84.

****** Songbird**

Steeplechase SCCD 31278 *Urbaniak; Kenny Barron (p); Peter Washington (b); Kenny Washington (d).* 10/90.

Songbird is quite the most impressive of this bunch, a mature set of originals that see the violinist finally come into his own as a wholly convincing harmonic and melodic improviser. His tone on the amplified instrument is cleaner and less raw-edged than previously, but he clearly knows how to vary bow-weight and left-hand stopping in order to create a range of articulations which do not so much mimic the saxophone as raise the violin to the same expressive level in this context.

The earlier sets are pretty much of a piece. The drummerless trio with Bertoncini and Moore suggests some interesting continuities with other aspects of Urbaniak's playing career. 'Folky/Mazurka' develops his traditional idiom in a jazz direction. 'Apology' might almost be an idea left over from the fusion years and 'Summertime' is handled in very much that way. There are originals from guitar player and bassist as well, but these are polite inclusions and somehow slow the progress of the album. *Take Good Care* is graced by the presence of Horace Parlan, who is always highly responsive to context. His phrasing is weightier than usual in places, and there are a couple of occasions when he develops a solo idea almost like a string player, firing off rapid triplets that sit invitingly across the 4/4 count. In response, Urbaniak sounds ever more like a saxophonist. Good albums, but certainly not up to the quality and authority of the *Songbird* band.

*****(*) Some Other Blues**

Steeplechase SCCD 31338 *Urbaniak; David Kikoski (p); Peter Washington (b); Kenny Washington (d).*

***** Ask Me Now**

Steeplechase SCCD 31454 *Urbaniak; Jim Pryor (p); Dwayne Burno (b); Billy Drummond (d).*

Urbaniak was something of a latecomer to bebop, but *Ask Me Now* suggests that he instinctively hipped to the legacy of Parker and Monk. It's entirely a repertory album, with no originals. 'Ornithology' and 'Moose The Mooche' bracket a strong set, but it's clear that Urbaniak's Bird is mediated by Coltrane. That's certainly clear on *Some Other Blues*, which kicks off with the Trane tune and closes with the 'Rosemary's Baby' theme by compatriot, Krzytsztof Komeda. Its language is both complex and clean-limbed and features some of the most direct playing the violinist has put on record.

Ask Me Now is only compromised by a band who don't seem to know what Urbaniak is trying to do. Pryor is interesting when the spotlight falls on him, but a lumpy accompanist. Burno has a sleepy insouciance that doesn't charm in this context. Urbaniak's tone has grown ever more relaxed, but also more precise in tonality. What he loses in expressiveness he gains in structure.

Allan Vaché (born 1953)

CLARINET

The younger of the two Vaché brothers is a clarinettist of great facility whose work as a sideman in mainstream situations has recently been built on by a plentiful supply of leadership dates.

***** Jazz Im Amerika Haus Vol. 3**

Nagel-Heyer 013 *Vaché; Warren Vaché (c); Johnny Varro (p); Jim Douglas (g); Frank Tate (b); Mike Masessa (d).* 8/94.

***** Swing Is Here**

Nagel-Heyer 026 *Vaché; Antti Sarpila (cl, ss); Mark Sahen (p); Len Skeat (b); Joe Ascione (d).* 10/95.

***** Summit Meeting**

Nagel-Heyer 027 *As above, except add Ken Peplowski (cl, ts).* 10/95.

***** Allan Vaché's Florida Jazz Allstars**

Nagel-Heyer 032 *Vaché; David Jones (c); John Allred (tb); Johnny Varro (p); Bob Leary (g); Bob Haggart (b); Ed Metz Jr (d).* 3/96.

***** Swing And Other Things**

Arbors ARCD 19171 *Vaché; Warren Vaché (c); Johnny Varro (p); John Cocuzzi (vib); Bucky Pizzarelli (g); Frank Tate (b); Ed Metz Jr (d).* 6/96.

Hitherto less well-known than his brother Warren, Allan Vaché seems to be taking his place in the fold of mainstreamers looked after by Nagel-Heyer and Arbors. A fluent technician, he gets all over the clarinet with indecent rapidity and can handle the most overheated of tempos with no apparent trouble. If anything, his playing seems to egg on the rhythm section into going ever faster. On the first, live album above, it helps him to hit a few clinkers along the way, but even when he gargles a note it just gets swallowed up in the flow. The songbook of the 1920s and '30s (with the occasional later tune) is what he loves and, while he sometimes chooses a comparative rarity, most of these tunes will be well known to even the uninitiated.

There's very little to choose among the five discs. *Jazz Im Amerika Haus Vol. 3* is perhaps the weakest, if only because of characteristic live-album longueurs; but it's still a good blow and is the one chance to hear the brothers together at length. *Florida Jazz Allstars* is our favourite, if only for a quite beautiful treatment of Bob Haggart's 'My Inspiration': Vaché should work at this tempo more often. Jones and Allred have their own moments of exultation, too. *Swing Is Here* is rather exhaustingly full of clarinet, and a problem with both this and *Summit Meeting* is the sound, which has very little bottom (Skeat often disappears altogether). The latter, though, has the bonus of Peplowski joining in, sometimes on tenor, to add further piquancy to the front line: his gorgeous solo treatment of 'These Foolish Things' smokes the other two. The tempos are sometimes almost manically fast and the record's too long at almost 80 minutes, but there's lots to enjoy.

Perhaps the Arbors disc is the best place to hear Vaché as the featured man (Warren sits in on only 'Cheek To Cheek'). His penchant for noodling around the very highest register can be annoying: he gets the notes all right, but the tone goes as thin as a pencil. Some agreeable choices of tune and a charming ballad in 'Nancy With The Laughing Face'.

*****(*) Revisited!**

Nagel Heyer 044 *Vaché; David Jones (c); Bob Leary (g, v); Phil Flanigan (b).* 6/97.

***** Raisin' The Roof**

Nagel Heyer 054 *Vaché; Jim Galloway (ss); John Bunch (p); Howard Alden (g); Michael Moore (b); Jake Hanna (d).* 12/98.

The group subject to the revisitation is the Bechet–Spanier Big Four, and this is one re-creation which works out exceedingly well. For once, Vaché's full-flushing manner doesn't seem overpowering, even in this slimmed-down context: Bechet himself was no shrinking violet, and he might have approved of some of the clarinet fusillades on offer. Jones plays the Muggsy role very well. Neither man is a ringer for their respective forebears, so the record is more than just a slavish homage.

Raisin' The Roof is another good one, but again there's an impression that there's just too much playing going on here, and a little restraint wouldn't have hurt. Galloway gets caught up in it and his normally more relaxed style gets squeezed, while the otherwise imperturbable campaigners in the rhythm section sail serenely on. 'Dream' is nice, but at nine minutes it's far too long.

Warren Vaché (born 1951)

CORNET

Born in Rahway, New Jersey, Vaché was deeply influenced by Louis Armstrong. He has worked with the Benny Goodman Band and in the house band at Eddie Condon's, but his most enduring association has been with like-minded saxophonist Scott Hamilton. Vaché's slightly dry, pungent tone is estimably controlled; even when he opts to play slightly sharp, it is always with dramatic intent.

***** First Time Out And Encore '93**

Audiophile ACD 196 *Vaché; Kenny Davern (ss); Bucky Pizzarelli, Wayne Wright (g); Michael Moore (b); Connie Kay (d).* 11 & 12/76, 4/93.

Warren Vaché came to prominence re-creating the solos of Bix Beiderbecke and ever since has been addicted to the backward glance. He is one of the leading swing players of the last couple of decades and is arguably the first cornetist since Ruby Braff (with whom he has shared a couple of labels over the years) to try to build on the example of Pops. But whereas Ruby is always incisive, pugnacious and sometimes downright filthy, Vaché has a curiously mild approach to swing which consistently fails to excite. He has the facility to play extremes of pitch very quietly and with estimable control, but this is not the same as being equipped to play great jazz. For us, he remains a triumph of technique over content.

'Nepotism be damned!' cried his father, writing the sleeve-note for young Warren's debut. Paired with an 'encore' from a decade and a half later, the 1976 session presents a calm and competent young brass player with a thoroughly old-fashioned delivery. It doesn't suggest much more than that. The duo tracks with Bucky Pizzarelli stem from both dates, and there is nothing to choose between the two. 'When It's Sleepy Time Down South' from 1993 is a brilliant closer, but by then it's hard to be excited. The group tracks with Davern, Moore and Kay, recorded a fortnight after the debut, are more adventurous, and Davern is in splendid form, but there is little to get the teeth into.

***** Midtown Jazz**

Concord CCD 4203 *Vaché; John Bunch (p); Phil Flanigan (b).* 2/82.

***** Easy Going**

Concord CCD 4323 *Vaché; Dan Barrett (tb); Howard Alden (g); John Harkins (p); Jack Lesberg (b); Chuck Riggs (d).* 12/86.

Midtown Jazz and *Easy Going* seem just about the right description. The earlier of these is probably his most straight-ahead session, and it has unmistakable strengths. Bunch and Flanigan are formidable players, with plenty to say on their own account. Both are known for their work with Scott Hamilton, who is perhaps the better known of the Concord 'young fogeys', but with Vaché they seem tighter, less effusive. *Easy Going* is mannerly enough to be completely ignorable. It cries out for some modulation of mood and attack. The tunes are almost all brief and relatively undeveloped and, while there is no intrisnic objection to Vaché's concentration on melody ('playing the changes' can be as arid as integral serialism) he seems unwilling to stamp his personality on the music. Porter's 'You'd Be So Nice To Come Home To' and the closing 'Moon Song' (significantly the longest track) suggest some willingness to put himself on the line, but not enough to save the set. Dan Barrett is an unexpected revelation.

**** Warm Evenings**

Concord CCD 4392 *Vaché; Ben Aronov (p); Lincoln Milliman (b); Giampaolo Biagi (d); Beaux Arts String Quartet.* 6/89.

Warm baths would be more like it. Vaché sounds rather constrained by Jack Gale's string arrangements and he manages to make them sound much more banal than they actually are, which is quite subtle and responsive to the tunes. On 'A Flower Is A Lovesome Thing', it is Gale who seems to get inside the dynamic and the emotion of the tune, leaving Vaché to embellish and embroider, but adding nothing of substance. The four tracks simply for jazz quartet aren't strong enough to redeem a very dull and craven album that begs for someone to kick over the traces and go for broke, just the once.

****** An Affair To Remember**

Zephyr ZECD 8 *Vaché; Brian Lemon (p).* 12/95.

*****(*) Warren Plays Warren**

Nagel Heyer CD 033 *Vaché; Randy Sandke (t); Kenny Drew Jr (p); Murray Wall (b); Jimmy Cobb (d).* 5/96.

Vaché's love affair with the music of Harry Warren has now been documented twice over. The Zephyr disc is superb, largely because Lemon is in crisply brilliant form. There is an inevitable overlap of material – 'Nagasaki', 'I Only Have Eyes For You', 'September In The Rain', and others – but the difference of setting and the imaginative settings by fellow trumpeter Sandke on the German recording mean that almost nothing sounds repetitive or trite. Vaché's tone has broadened, but is also much sharper and more emphatic in attack than it was. With Lemon, he is able to indulge that long-standing ability to soften the dynamic even while exploring the outer reaches of his range. His tone is fat and fruity and the close miking on the Zephyr set gives a very immediate and authentic version of what he's about.

****** Shine**

Zephyr ZECD24 *Vaché; Tony Coe (ts, ss, cl); Alan Barnes (as, bs, cl); Brian Lemon (p); Dave Cliff (g); Dave Green (b); Allan Ganley, Clark Tracey (d).* 1 & 5/97.

***** Memories Of You**

Zephyr ZECD 21 *As above, except omit Coe.* 5/97.

Glorious stuff, though mostly because Barnes and Coe are in such good form. *Shine* begins and ends with versions of 'Shine' itself, and Zephyr's recent practice of including alternatives makes complete sense. Vaché's tone seems particularly relaxed and conversational in this company, and his soloing on 'Stella By Starlight', 'Pee Wee's Blues' (the great Erwin was his teacher), and 'Don't Get Around Much Any More' are exemplary. We have emoted sufficiently elsewhere about this rhythm section. They are hard to beat on a session of this kind but, with a front line of genuinely international quality, even they have to take a back seat. Coe is missed on the second album but the chemistry with Barnes is sufficient to see it through, and rarities like 'You're Mine, You' from two of the creators of 'Body And Soul' and 'Serenata' make this an intriguing listen for students of traditional jazz and swing.

***** Swingtime!**

Nagel-Heyer CD 059 *Vaché; Randy Reinhart (t); John Allred, Matt Bilyk (tb); Chuck Wilson (as, cl); Harry Allen, Rickey Woodard (ts); Alan Barnes (bs, as, cl); Steve Ash (p); Murray Wall (b); Jake Hanna (d).* 1/00.

Vaché ushered in the new century with an unashamed exercise in swing nostalgia. This is a beautifully balanced band, with a lot of middle weight and players who are prepared to improvise in the middle register rather than skyscrape. 'Jumpin' At The Woodside' is a delight and Harry Allen's arrangement of 'Stompin' At The Savoy' would have had the original creators nodding with delight. Vaché is the main soloist, but Barnes and Woodard are featured, as is the very good John Allred.

Warren Vaché Sr

BASS

Better known as the patriarch of the Vaché clan, Warren Senior is no mean bass-player himself, with plenty of swing-to-mainstream experience. He also writes (books on Pee Wee Erwin and Claude Hopkins) and edits a jazz magazine.

***** Swingin' And Singin'**

Jazzology JCD-202 *Vaché; Larry Weiss (c); Nick Capella (tb); Nick Sassone (cl, ts); Lou Carter (p); Dawes Thompson (g); Mike Burgevin (d).* 2/90.

The senior Vaché takes an unassuming role as bassist and MD in this engaging set by a group of seasoned old-timers ('There are no kids in this band', he says proudly in the sleeve-note). On the plus side is an interesting programme of material, deliberately avoiding too many Dixieland warhorses; Weiss's poised and full-toned cornet, a voice firmly in the great tradition; and the air of easy-going enjoyment that the band generates. The minuses are minor, but they would include the two vocals and tempos that occasionally get a little too restful to hold the attention. The recording is soft-focused and sometimes rather remote.

Kid Thomas Valentine (1896–1987)

TRUMPET

Although originally from elsewhere in Louisiana, Valentine became one of New Orleans's most characteristic trumpeters, leading his own Algiers Stompers from 1926, working extensively with George Lewis, then playing at home and on tour for the rest of a very long and busy life.

****** Kid Thomas And His Algiers Stompers**

American Music AMCD-10 *Valentine; Bob Thomas, Harrison Barnes (tb); Emile Barnes (cl); George Guesnon (g, bj); Joseph Phillips (b); George Henderson (d).* 9/51.

***** Larry Borenstein Collection Vol. 8**

504 CD 37 *Valentine; Louis Nelson (tb); Edmund Washington (as, v); Joe James (p); Burke Stevenson (b); Sammy Penn (d, v).* 57.

***** The Dance Hall Years**

American Music AMCD-48 *Valentine; Louis Nelson (tb); Emanuel Paul (cl, ts); Joe James, James 'Sing' Miller (p); Burke Stevenson, Joseph Butler (b); Sammy Penn (d); 'Pa' (v).* 59–3/64.

*****(*) Sonnets From Algiers**

American Music AMCD 53 *Valentine; Louis Nelson (tb); Paul Barnes (cl); Emanuel Paul (ts); Joe James (p); George Guesnon (bj); Sammy Penn (d, v).* 7/60.

****(*) Kid Thomas' Dixieland Band 1960 With Emanuel Paul**

504 CD33 *Valentine; Louis Nelson (tb); Emanuel Paul (ts); Joe James (p, v); Joseph Butler (b); Sammy Penn (d, v).* 9/60.

***** Kid Thomas And His Algiers Stompers**

Original Jazz Classics OJC 1833 *As above, except add Emile Barnes, Albert Burbank (cl), Homer Eugene (p).* 8/60–1/61.

****(*) Kid Thomas And His Algiers Stompers**

Original Jazz Classics OJC 1845 *As above, except omit Burbank, Eugene.* 1/61.

***** Kid Thomas And Emanuel Paul With Barry Martyn's Band**

GHB BCD-257 *Valentine; Cuff Billett (t); Pete Dyer (tb); Emanuel Paul, Bill Greenow (ts); Richard Simmons (p); Terry Knight (b); Barry Martyn (d).* 64.

Thomas Valentine arrived in New Orleans rather late – in 1922. By the time he made his first records, almost 30 years later, he had led bands all over Louisiana but remained based in the city, where he continued to play for a further 35 years. He approached this awesome career with a Zen-like simplicity, reducing the New Orleans sound to its essentials and creating a lifetime's work from them. A fascinating lead-trumpeter, his methods – including a severe observance of the melody, a blunt, jabbing attack and a vibrato that sounds like an angry trill – manage to create high drama and lyrical depth alike, and though he seldom took solos he was such a strong lead voice that he tended to dominate every band he played in.

He made a lot of records during his long life. The first (1951) sessions have survived in excellent sound and find Valentine and Barnes in their first prime: there are two trombonists, since Bob Thomas had to leave after three numbers, and the changed balance of the front line tells much about the sensitivity of the New Orleans ensemble. Alden Ashforth's excellent notes chronicle the whole session in detail. The most characteristic is *The Dance Hall Years*, where Thomas plays with his regular working band (usually called The Algiers Stompers) at a couple of dance sessions, one identified only to the late '50s, the other dated precisely to March 1964. The material is familiar New Orleans stuff and a few blues. The seven earlier tracks are dustily recorded but the remainder sound good, although there seems to be no audience present. Nelson and Paul are in strong form and the band drives along with the ramshackle but perfectly appropriate rhythm that makes this music tick. The 504 CDs are drawn from the Larry Borenstein archives. The 1957 set is notable for Ed Washington's full-on style, with its scattershot approach to pitch, and on a typical set of staples he puts some nervous energy into the occasion. The later disc is a less significant survival: the band sound shop-worn in parts and the sound is rather dusty, though Thomas rouses them on occasion.

The two OJCs are more from Riverside's *New Orleans; The Living Legends* series, and they're surprisingly disappointing in some ways. Though clearly recorded, the band sound shrill – especially the clarinets – and some of the tempos seem either too hurried or down to a crawl. OJC 1833 is the better of the two. Better still, though, is the almost contemporaneous *Sonnets from Algiers*. This time the slightly acid and very up-front sound catches the raw charisma of the group, and the familiar set-list includes some particularly characterful takes on 'Ballin' The Jack' and 'Milenberg Joys'. The session with Barry Martyn and his British team is a spirited, affectionate meeting between men of vastly different backgrounds and, while Martyn anchors the pulse, his colleagues don't do so well, with Dyer especially blasting all before him to no real purpose. Thomas and Paul, though, fashion a more graceful partnership.

♛ ** Kid Thomas–George Lewis Ragtime Stompers**
GHB BCD-5 *Thomas; Jim Robinson (tb); George Lewis (cl); Emanuel Sayles (bj); Alcide Slow Drag Pavageau (b); Sammy Penn (d).* 11/61.

This wonderful session could stand as the perfect introduction to classic New Orleans playing. For one thing the sound is superb, better than on most of Valentine's other records, and it lets us hear the balance of the front line – Valentine's curt lead, Lewis's lovely rococo embellishments, Robinson's doughty support. The rhythm team is unimpeachable. The tunes are obvious, but just what was needed for the day. As a group, the sextet swing along with the indefinable rightness which this music, at its best, delivers like no other style of jazz. Essential!

*****(*) The December Band Vol. 1**
GHB BCD-197 *Valentine; Jim Robinson (tb); Sammy Rimington (cl); Captain John Handy (as); Bill Sinclair (p); Dick Griffith (bj); Dick McCarthy (b); Sammy Penn (d).* 12/65.

*****(*) The December Band Vol. 2**
GHB BCD-198 *As above.* 12/65.

*****(*) Kid Thomas At Moose Hall**
GHB BCD-305 *Valentine; Bill Connell (cl); Dick Griffith (bj); Dick McCarthy (b); Bill Bissonnette (d).* 67.

***** Same Old Soupbone!**
Jazz Crusade JC-3001 *Valentine; Louis Nelson (tb); Emanuel Paul (ts); Charlie Hamilton (p); Joe Butler (b); Sammy Penn (d).* 10/68.

****** Kid Thomas In California**
GHB BCD-296 *Valentine; Bill Bissonnette (tb, v); Captain John Handy (as); Cyril Bennett (p); Jim Tutunjian (b); Sammy Penn (d); Carol Leigh (v).* 2–3/69.

*****(*) Spirit Of New Orleans 4**
Music Mecca 1059-2 *Valentine; Percy Humphrey (t); Louis Nelson, Jim Robinson (tb); Orange Kellin, Albert Burbank (cl); Emanuel Paul (ts); Charlie Hamilton (p); Niels Richard Hansen (bj); Chester Zardis, Joseph Hutler (b); Cie Frazier, Alonzo Stewart (d).* 71–72.

It was quite an occasion at Moose Lodge Hall in December 1965 when Valentine and cohorts took to the stage. From the 23-year-old Rimington to the venerable Valentine and Robinson, the band swung mightily through their sets, spread rather generously across two CDs. Handy especially seems in unquenchably high spirits, Rimington isn't overawed once, and the comparatively youthful rhythm section sound as if they were prepared to play all night. As one example, listen to the tempo that develops on 'Ice Cream'. Great New Orleans music, and we regretfully hold back a single notch due to the sometimes disappointing sound-quality, which often has soloists disappearing off-mike.

At Moose Hall and *In California* were both recorded by Bissonnette, a stalwart crusader for New Orleans jazz who usually worked out of Connecticut. Forced to switch from his usual trombone to drums for the earlier session, he drafted in local hero Connell and booked Thomas to play the session, which suffers from an imperfect location sound and plenty of clinkers by the players, yet still offers much great Thomas. He was obliged to play more solos than usual, which he never liked doing, but somehow he took to the task with great relish, even though the rhythm section plays a lot faster and with more bounce than he was used to. As Bissonnette notes, there is more Kid Thomas on this one record than on two or three of his regular dates.

In California is one of the best available discs. Bissonnette secured a very good sound, recording mostly at Earthquake McGoon's, and the front-line partnership of Thomas and Handy strikes many sparks. 'Say Si Si' and 'Rose Room' are tunes less often encountered in the Thomas discography, and Penn's drumming is an outstanding show of maverick New Orleans timekeeping. Carol Leigh contributes two sweet-toned but convincing vocals. Highly recommended.

Jazz Crusade is Bissonnette's own label and *Same Old Soupbone!* is salvaged from a local TV appearance by Thomas's band. A good if comparatively routine Thomas date by his standard band, playing much of their usual material. The title is a favourite saying of the leader's, the sort of thing he would say to shrug off compliments or questions.

Music Mecca's compilation of two different LPs (plus four previously unreleased tracks) has Thomas sharing the billing with a

Percy Humphrey-led band. The Humphrey tracks are slightly better since he is in great form, but Thomas's tunes fare well, with the Europeans, Kellin and Hansen, fitting in without a murmur. Bright but effective sound.

***** Kid Thomas & Earl Humphrey With Orange Kellin's New Orleans Joymakers**
GHB BCD-353 *Valentine; Earl Humphrey (tb); Orange Kellin (cl); Lars Edegran (p); Sylvester Handy (b); Lester Alexis (d).* 70.

***** Live In Denmark Vol. 1**
Storyville STCD 6026 *Valentine; Louis Nelson (tb); Soren Sorenson (ts); Erik Hansen, Jon Marks (p); Niels Richard Hansen (bj); Derek Cook (b); Keith Minter (d).* 12/72–1/74.

***** Live In Denmark Vol. 2**
Storyville STCD 6027 *As above.* 12/72–1/74.

Kid Thomas was an inveterate traveller to the end of his life, and there are plenty of surviving tour recordings. The GHB disc was cut in South Carolina and is the only opportunity to hear Valentine with the third of the famous Humphrey brothers, trombonist Earl. Perhaps not the most immortal of sessions but, with Thomas away from his usual sidemen, he plays a little more sideways than normal and, with Humphrey responding, there's plenty of interest. The Danish session is selected from five nights of recording in Copenhagen and has Valentine and Nelson together with a European outfit. Sorenson sounds like he learned to play at Emanuel Paul's knee, and he helps make up a boisterous front line; but listen to Valentine's circumspect playing on 'Yellow Dog Blues' to hear how, at 77, he was still formidably inventive. The second volume, new to this edition, includes eight previously unheard tracks. Excellent sound and, though so far only these two have been issued, Storyville have scheduled four more from the same sessions!

Eric Van der Westen (born 1963)

BASS

Dutch bassist leading a substantial, local post-bop outfit.

*****(*) Working Dreamer**
Bvhaast CD 9212 *Van der Westen; Chris Abelen, Hans Sparla (tb); Erwin Vann (ss, ts, bcl); Paul Van Kamenade (as); Paul De Leest (cl, ts); Ge Bijvoet (p); Pieter Bast (d). n.d.*

Van der Westen might have been listening to David Murray's Octet when he made this – his own musters a lot of the same *brio*, with rollicking counterpoint and horns-answering-horns music. His 'Ballad For John Carter' is a dirge Murray would be proud of; the conflation of Mingus melodies in 'The Underdog' is prime jazz repertory; and the five-part 'Out Of Time, Out Of Space' gets the most out of a little big band. But he puts, naturally, a Europeanized spin on it, too. The record may be on Bvhaast and these might be Dutchmen at work, but it's tellingly different from, say, a Willem Breuker band: more streamlined, less soberly comic. A nice absence of trumpets, a lot of good reeds, and a very good record.

Joe Van Enkhuizen

TENOR SAXOPHONE

Dutch mainstream-modern saxophonist with a penchant for Ellington tunes.

***** Joe Meets The Rhythm Section**
Timeless SJP 249 *Van Enkhuizen; Horace Parlan (p); Rufus Reid (b); Al Harewood (d).* 7/86.

***** Ellington Ballads**
Timeless SJP 288 *Van Enkhuizen; Horace Parlan (p).* 88.

***** Ellington My Way**
Timeless SJP 419 *Van Enkhuizen; Frits Landesbergen (vib); Hein Van Der Gein (b); Doug Sides (d).* 3/88–11/91.

***** Blues Ahead**
Timeless SJP 356 *Van Enkhuizen; Carlo Dewys (org); Han Bennink (d).* 12/88–4/89.

He has a great sound and plenty of élan – southern-styled tenor, full of bullish good humour, homeboy swing and a bearhug tenderness on the slow ones. He is, though, from Holland. *Joe Meets The Rhythm Section* is hard-bop repertory enlivened by some out-of-the-way choices of material. *Blues Ahead* offers a rare glimpse of Bennink on a straight-ahead kind of session and, with Dewys enthusiastically copying Jack McDuff and Shirley Scott, the leader's fuming solos emerge with gutsy vividness. *Ellington My Way* was recorded at four sessions over three years, yet is all of a piece – 11 choice chunks of Ellingtonia given a bluff, no-nonsense interpretation, with the surprise choice of Landesbergen's vibes to add colour on four tracks. *Ellington Ballads* is obvious, and as comforting as a plate of shepherd's pie. Non-British readers, please excuse us.

Fred Van Hove (born 1937)

PIANO

Classical studies in his native Antwerp, then he played in dance orchestras before becoming interested in free jazz, playing extensively with Peter Brötzmann in the 1960s and early '70s. Many associations across the spectrum of free playing since then, although discs under his own nominal leadership are comparatively few in number.

***** Passing Waves**
Nuscope CD 1001 *Van Hove (p solo).* 5/97.

*****(*) Flux**
Potlatch P 2398 2CD *Van Hove (p solo).* 1/98.

Van Hove's almost ancestral status in European free music isn't acknowledged by his available discography: a stack of vinyl from the '70s and '80s has yet to get even a sniff of CD reissue, and recent sightings (in front of microphones, at least) have been rare. These two solo sets arrived almost simultaneously. The scarcity of his records is compensated for by their dense, sometimes super-concentrated content. Interesting to conjecture on what he learned from Taylor, or if – as with his early collaborator, Peter

Brötzmann – he arrived at his style mostly independently of American influence. Either way, as far back as the earliest FMPs he was projecting a fiercely individual aesthetic on free-jazz piano, and by now it is quite his own, while inevitably steeped in the unorthodoxies of the style. The two sets are quite unalike, since the Potlatch (live) is made up of two long, continuous sets while the Nuscope is a more prepared set of ten studio pieces. The latter takes a specific starting-point for most of the tracks – a billiard ball on the strings, or the qualities of an arpeggio – and fashions it quite deliberately. The former simply lets Fred go at the keyboard, and he works through big structures with the kind of block-follows-block linearity that marks him out, perhaps, as old school. That said, his pianism (which Georg Graewe comments on admiringly in a sleeve-note to *Passing Waves*) is so refined that the concert disc in particular is mostly spellbinding. Some of *Passing Waves* is more interesting for its formal ideas than for their execution, but *Flux* is often as exciting as it is profound and enriching.

Marc Van Roon

PIANO

Dutch pianist leading a regular trio in post-bop explorations, here with an American guest.

***(*) **Falling Stones**

Mons 874 669 *Van Roon; Dave Liebman (ss); Joshua Samson (ts); Tony Overwater (b); Wim Kegel (d); Jasper Blom (perc).* 4/94.

Although Van Roon's name is at the top, this is dominated by Dave Liebman, who heard this rhythm section on a trip to Amsterdam and decided to record with them on his next visit. The results are splendidly forceful and imaginative and mark another fine entry from the saxophonist. Tranquil tone-poems such as the title-track mingle with all-out energy pieces such as 'Get Me Back To The Apple', and the improvising has a clarity that always lets one hear the form beneath. If he more or less has the date hijacked by Liebman, Van Roon nevertheless contributes three of the best themes. Blom sits in on two tracks, Samson on one.

Ken Vandermark (born 1964)

SAXOPHONES, CLARINETS

Born in Warwick, Rhode Island, Vandermark played trumpet into his teens, then switched to saxophone. Studied and led bands in Boston and Montreal, then relocated to Chicago and spent the '90s working in that local scene, running a string of bands, organizing gigs and generally making significant waves.

*** **Big Head Eddie**

Platypus PP 001 *Vandermark; Todd Colburn (g); Kent Kessler (b); Michael Zerang (d).* 2/93.

***(*) **Solid Action**

Platypus PP 002 *As above, except Daniel Scanlan (c, g, vn) replaces Colburn.* 5/94.

***(*) **Standards**

Quinnah Q08 *Vandermark; Mars Williams (saxes); Kevin Drumm (g); Jim Baker (p, syn); Daniel Scanlan (g, vn); Kent Kessler (b); Steve Hunt, Hamid Drake (d).* 7/94.

*** **Caffeine**

Okkadisk 12002 *Vandermark; Jim Baker (p); Steve Hunt (d).* 94.

***(*) **International Front**

Okkadisk 12005 *Vandermark; Kent Kessler (b); Curt Newton (d).* 9/94.

*** **Blow Horn**

Okkadisk OD12019 *Vandermark; Mats Gustafsson (ts, bs, flageolet); Kent Kessler (b); Steve Hunt (d).* 10/95.

**** **Utility Hitter**

Quinnah Q09 *Vandermark; Mars Williams (reeds); Kent Kessler, Nate McBride (b); Hamid Drake, Curt Newton (d).* 9/95.

***(*) **Hoofbeats Of The Snorting Swine**

Eighth Day Music EDM 80001 *Vandermark; Mars Williams (ss, as, ts, cl).* 3/95–2/96.

***(*) **Single Piece Flow**

Atavistic ALP47 *Vandermark; Jeb Bishop (tb, g); Mars Williams (saxes); Kent Kessler (b); Tim Mulvenna (d).* 8/96.

Vandermark has charged straight to the front of free music in America – and not from New York, either. One could call him an archetypal post-modernist, working in rock, R&B and jazz alike, except with Vandermark there's nothing cool or once-removed about his expressiveness. He's a full-on energy player a lot of the time, a canny organizer of groups and musical forms, a man perhaps destined to make things happen. While he's primarily a tenor saxophonist, he often picks up both bass and B-flat clarinets, and he espouses European models as readily as American ones – Evan Parker arabesques might invade a solo as plausibly as Dolphyesque skirlings and Lockjaw Davis-like pugilistics. Vandermark likes structure – most of these records start off from compositions, sometimes of considerable complexity – but his music can take off into the most provocative and open-ended byways. He also knows a lot of great players, most of them stalwarts of a scene which Vandermark himself has been crucial in documenting and bringing to wider attention.

Names are often dropped all over these records but, when someone like George Clinton or Witold Lutoslawski is cited, it never means that Vandermark is about to get either funky or neoclassical. What he loves is jazz language in the raw, and this is how the earlier discs sound. *Big Head Eddie* is a nifty set of tunes, sparked by Colburn's scrawling guitar lines, lurid and alive if not quite focused yet. *Solid Action* is Vandermark's first shot at greatness, with Scanlan a tremendously exciting figure on all three of his instruments, and the wild landscaping of 'Bucket' and 'Catch 22' balanced by the fuming, rocked-over 'Leadfoot'. An exciting disc.

Standards is experimental in that it sets Vandermark up as a member of four different trios: sax with (respectively) bass/drums, saxes/drums, keyboards/guitar and guitar/drums. Each has something interesting to yield and some of it sounds almost glaringly new and alive. *Caffeine* and *International Front* are by two trios, one named Caffeine, the other Steelwool. With Baker and Hunt, Vandermark is just slightly too exposed and, for all the interesting music here, this doesn't quite have the vividness of some of his other discs. The Steelwool Trio, with long-time compadre Kessler (also a colleague in the NRG Ensemble) in great fettle, is a roughly shod power trio that finds each man vying for attention: muscular, exhilarating, unrepentant.

Our favourite of these earlier discs is the monumental *Utility Hitter* by the Barrage Double Trio: three guys from Chicago meet three from Boston, and it's a mutual slugfest of sensitivity and ingenuity. The dedications to Mingus, Andrew Hill, Ornette, Cherry and Ayler (the latter a huge, brawling outrage) are marvellous, but so is the revisionist hard-bop-as-raging-fury of their tribute to Griffin and Lockjaw, 'Over And Both'.

Blow Horn is a day at Uberstudio in Chicago. Gustafsson more usually crosses horns with Vandermark from his position in the AALY Trio, and 'Dedication' carries on that shouting tradition. Hunt and Kessler sometimes get drowned out (not something one can often say about a drummer going full tilt), although they're good enough to listen to by themselves, which happens on the first two minutes of 'Blow Horn For Service' at least. Not our favourite of these records, but still plenty of action.

Hoofbeats Of The Snorting Swine finds Vandermark locking horns with frequent sparring-partner Williams (the record is credited to Cinghiale). Typical Vandermark in that it feels as if the duo is running (or careering) down composed lines, even as they blow right away from them. Williams is at least an equal partner here, sharing the writing duties and matching the other man at every step. A dialogue for two epic sensibilities.

Single Piece Flow debuts The Vandermark Five, with Jeb Bishop an intriguing booking. Almost temperate in parts, there's some exemplary use of the group as a unit, with a piece like 'The Mark Inside' offering a sort of jaundiced twist on jazz tradition. When Vandermark offers dedications to the likes of Johnny Hodges and Gil Evans, it's the tribute of a fan, but one isn't always sure what homage he's paying. As prolific as he has already been in a short space of time, there's little to suggest a man who'll be content to be a career jazz musician.

*****(*) The DKV Trio With Fred Anderson**
Okkadisk OD12014 *Vandermark; Fred Anderson (ts); Kent Kessler (b); Hamid Drake (d).* 12/96.

*****(*) Baraka**
Okkadisk OK 12012 *As above, except omit Anderson.* 2/97.

***** Deep Telling**
Okkadisk OD12027 *As above, except add Joe Morris (g).* 4/98.

*****(*) Live In Wels & Chicago 1998**
Okkadisk OD12030 2CD *As above, except omit Morris.* 11/98.

This is the DKV Trio, one of Vandermark's most regularly assembled projects. The album with Anderson is beautifully focused. The older man is a less multi-faceted player than either Vandermark or some of the other horn men on these records, but he fits gracefully into the trio's set-up and there is some muscleman playing which doesn't descend into posturing. *Baraka* has its moments of stasis – the title-track runs for more than 35 minutes, and it needs plenty of resources to sustain that – but there is still an awful lot to listen to. Morris guests on *Deep Telling* and the results are quieter and more inward-looking in feel: there are three quartet tracks and five by differing combinations of the four players. *Wels & Chicago* features two concerts, recorded in the same month but geographically a continent apart – and the music is sometimes prone to traversing a great distance without saying a great deal. The 30-minute 'Open Door' is out of steam well before the end. But the Wels set, basically framed around Don Cherry's 'Complete Communion Suite', is a stunning example of free repertory, the original materials ingeniously transplanted to this situation.

***** Straight Lines**
Atavistic ALP115 *Vandermark; Jeb Bishop (tb); Kent Kessler (b); Tim Mulvenna (d).* 9/98.

Vandermark's Joe Harriott Project is an overdue salute to that departed master, but the record is under-rehearsed and unfinished in feel. It could be that the group are a shade too respectful of Harriott's themes, since their playing feels a bit stiff and uncertain, something that a Vandermark record has never been in the past. Bishop is arguably the strongest voice and some of his solos are cracklingly inventive responses to the material.

*****(*) Target Or Flag**
Atavistic ALP106 *Vandermark; Jeb Bishop (tb, g); Mars Williams (saxes); Kent Kessler (b); Tim Mulvenna (d).* 10/97.

****** Simpatico**
Atavistic ALP107 *As above, except Dave Rempis (as) replaces Williams.* 12/98.

The latest reports from The Vandermark Five. This seems to be Vandermark's principal outlet as far as writing and arranging are concerned. Dedications to the likes of Shelly Manne, Jack Montrose and Curtis Counce betray his affection for the urbane precision of prime West Coast jazz, and his own pieces make the point of following some of the precepts (counterpoint, tonal contrast) which that school lived by. Except they're channelled through a combative and inclusive perspective which takes in all the more expected freedoms. Obsessive work is making the band (and its leader) into ever more expressive and capable players, so a tough slice of free bop such as 'Attempted, Not Known' on *Target Or Flag* holds no terrors. Bishop seems to be as at home on guitar as he is on trombone (one of the less frequently encountered examples of doubling). Rempis is a surprise substitute for Williams on *Simpatico* and, since he plays only alto, it slightly narrows the tonal palette – though this supercharged and superbly focused set is surely their best to date.

*****(*) Design In Time**
Delmark DE-516 *Vandermark; Robert Barry, Tim Mulvenna (d).* 99.

Vandermark goes through the card here, playing jump-band tenor on 'Green Chimneys', unchained howling on 'Angels', even New Orleans clarinet on 'Cut To Fit'. Barry and Mulvenna make an unapologetically swinging team, playing at least as much time as they do free, and with Coleman, Monk and Ayler among the composer-credits this is an amenable place to acquaint a newcomer with Vandermark's methods.

Jasper Van't Hof (born 1947)

PIANO, KEYBOARDS, DRUMS

The gifted Dutchman worked with flautist Chris Hinze and with Archie Shepp, and has had a special fondness for working with violinists, most obviously Jean-Luc Ponty and the late Zbigniew Seifert. Sometimes showy and over-effusive, Van't Hof has a powerful sense of structure and writes challenging charts reminiscent of Chick Corea in more formal mode.

***** Eyeball**

Limetree FCD 0002 *Van't Hof; Wim Overgaauw (g, bj); Zbigniew Seifert (vn); John Lee (b); Gerry Brown (d).* 3/74.

Van't Hof's approach to fusion was typically adventurous and sophisticated. This group is largely memorable for the inclusion of Seifert, one of the lost figures of modern European jazz and a dazzling player, and much of the limelight is claimed by him and the guitarist; but it's the Dutchman's solid mechanics and clear-eyed logic which makes the music sing. Bassist Lee is credited with two of the compositions but, for the most part, the emphasis is squarely on Van't Hof himself as he switches between acoustic piano, Fender Rhodes and organ, on which he sounds not unlike a less elemental Larry Young. The studio recording has a good, live feel, though there do seem to be overdubs and edits here and there, and the disc affords an interesting introduction to the pianist's early work. The album shouldn't be confused with another *Eyeball*, released on CMP and featuring another fine jazz violinist, Didier Lockwood; to the best of our knowledge, that one is still out of catalogue.

***** Solo Piano**

Timeless SJP 286 *Van't Hof (p solo).* 10/87.

Dominated by two tunes that would figure throughout his recording career, these sessions for Timeless grow with familiarity. Though showy and overpacked and, on occasion, downright florid, Van't Hof's keyboard style is by this stage very much his own. 'Dinner For Two' and Duke's 'Prelude To A Kiss' are sweepingly romantic and edged with subtle chromaticism. If there are still influences at work, then McCoy Tyner perhaps has the edge over Chick Corea this time, but there is no mistaking the individuality of the approach.

***** Dinner For Two**

MA Music International A 803 *Van't Hof; Bob Malach (ts).*

****(*) The Prague Concert**

P & J 102 *As above.* 1/92.

****(*) Blau**

ACT 9203 *As above, except add Wayne Krantz (g), Nicholas Fiszman (b), Philippe Allaert (d).*

Malach turned out to be a highly responsive partner. The duets are less effective live than in the studio, largely because the sound is so grating and uninflected, but there is no mistaking the rapport between the two musicians. Malach is even more dominant in the group with Krantz, an imaginatively constituted outfit that should have recorded more. Van't Hof favours long, ripplingly arpeggiated lines and richly augmented chords, but he is also capable of playing spare, funky lines. It may seem like a very long shot, but play these duets back to back with David Murray's collaborations with Dave Burrell. There is the same stark melody combined with all the harmonic elegance and daring that one could ask for.

*****(*) At The Concertgebuow – Solo**

Challenge CHR 70010 *Van't Hof (p solo).* 12/93.

Boxing Day 1993 and the most prestigious concert venue in the Netherlands. Jasper rises to the occasion grandly. His rippling opening statement on 'Equivalent' (which may have been written for the occasion) establishes a mood for the rest of the evening: lyrical, gracious and not a bit self-indulgent. Interesting to compare the versions here of 'Prelude To A Kiss' and 'Dinner For Two' with those on the earlier solo album. The first and obvious point is that the Concertgebuow piano is a better and more responsive instrument, but the hushed expectancy with which Jasper invests the Ellington melody is quite entrancing. He ends with a wonderful reading of Horace Silver's 'Peace', rounding off a thoroughly satisfying performance. Why, then, the rather hesitant valuation? Simply because there is little texture to the set, no highs and lows, no light and shade, and no drama. Technically accomplished, but not vital enough for most listeners.

*****(*) Tomorrowland**

Challenge CHR 70040 *Van't Hof; Bob Malach (ts); Jean-François Jenny-Clark (b).* 9/96.

Jasper made very substantial claims for this record, suggesting that it represented a new genre, related to but different from African-American jazz. Bold as the writing is, and splendidly as it is executed, it's hard to swallow his claim that VOJ – as he chooses to call this new style – has made a qualitative step beyond bebop. The writing is, as one would expect, both thoughtful and intense, and three longish tracks space through the record – 'Wildcard', 'Round About' (which may have been influenced by Monk) and 'The Quiet American' are all markedly individual. Jenny-Clark and Malach are admirably responsive. The bassist has never enjoyed the kind of attention his attentive, detailed playing deserves. Like Barre Phillips, he is able to combine an old-fashioned sound (reminiscent of Wilbur Ware) and unfailing swing with what often sounds like complete freedom. Malach, too, follows no known school, and the drummerless trio has a marked independence of direction that is consistently fascinating. The harmonic language and experimental metres are certainly food for thought – but as to founding a new idiom, we don't think so.

*****(*) Face To Face**

Canossa INT 3238 2 *Van't Hof; Ernie Watts (ts); Bo Stief (b); Nippie Noya (perc).* 98.

Again confusingly, there was a veraBra release called *Face To Face* with pretty much the same line-up as this, except that here, instead of Aldo Romano on drums, Jasper takes to the kit himself on two tracks. As it turns out, he's a more than functional drummer and his playing on 'First Day' is extremely creditable. We disliked the recording on the other album of this title; Ernie Watts is a saxophonist who needs no flattering but deserves the kind of resonant, slightly soft acoustic he gets here. His composition, 'On The Border', is elegantly conceived and executed, with a prominent place for the saxophone, but the plaudits have to be reserved for the closing pair of tracks, Charlie Mariano's 'Pink Lady' and Jasper's own 'Cogito Ergo Sum', on which again he takes to the sticks. His piano and organ playing is consistently stimulating, and (this) *Face To Face* is consistently enjoyable.

***(*) **Un Mondo Illusorio**
Challenge CHR 70059 *Van't Hof (org solo).* 8/98.

Completely *sui generis*, this astonishing record is certainly at the boundaries of jazz, VOJ, or any other identifiable idiom. Van't Hof has long included organ in his armoury, but these performances on the instrument at Chiesa di Santa Maria delle Rose in Bonefro, Italy, are unique, provocative and sometimes bewilderingly idiosyncratic. Consisting of 17 short études or thematic improvisations, the album explores an astonishing range of tonalities and timbres, from the percussive snaps and clicks of 'Dimenarsi da maniaco' to huge, shimmering tone-clusters reminiscent of classical composer-organists Jehan Alain and Olivier Messiaen. The mood of the recording is almost entirely thoughtful and reflective, with little in the way of dynamic variation. Van't Hof's concentration is palpable, but so too is his shrewd sense of humour. While these are far from lightweight pieces, there is a sense of play about them. We are, it hardly needs to be said, a long way from Art Tatum, and anyone who demands an element of swing will be put off from the outset; but, should you like to think you have open ears and mind, *Un Mondo Illusorio* is a very worthwhile experience.

Tom Varner

FRENCH HORN

At work in the New York scene for some 20 years, Varner, whose background is Missourian, specializes in what is still a rarity on jazz terms, the french horn.

*** **Tom Varner Quartet**
Soul Note 121017-2 *Varner; Ed Jackson (as); Fred Hopkins (b); Billy Hart (d).* 8/80.

*** **Long Night Big Day**
New World NW 80410-2 *Varner; Frank London (t); Steve Swell (tb); Ed Jackson, Thomas Chapin (as); Rich Rothenberg (ts); Lindsey Horner (b); Phil Haynes (d).* 3/90.

**** **The Mystery Of Compassion**
Soul Note 121217-2 *Varner; Steve Swell (tb); Dave Taylor (btb); Matt Darriau, Ed Jackson (as); Rich Rothenberg, Ellery Eskelin (ts); Jim Hartog (bs); Mark Feldman (vn); Mike Richmond (b); Tom Rainey (d).* 3/92.

**** **Martian Heartache**
Soul Note 121286-2 *Varner; Ed Jackson (as); Ellery Eskelin (ts); Pete McCann (g); Drew Gress (b); Tom Rainey (d); Dominique Eade (v).* 3/96.

Varner's decision to apply french horn as a weapon in the New York avant-garde might once have seemed improbable but, with every kind of instrument pressed into service in that milieu, no longer. There is the inevitable feel from time to time that it's a trombonist we're listening to, but Varner has taken pains to develop his own vocabulary on an often intractable brass instrument. The *Quartet* album is more like uneventful free bop, depending on satisfying solos to make its modest impact. The New World album was much more ambitious: the basic unit is three horns, bass and drums (London, Swell and Chapin appear only on 'Wind Trio +') and, if the earlier disc was meant to display Varner's improvisational prowess, it's his sense of structure which calls the shots here. 'Big Day', 'Search For Sanity' and especially 'Prince Of Jamaica' (Queens)' transcend their compositional complexities, but 'Art And Leisure' is a terribly unconvincing mix of tone rows and twelve-bar blues. A mixed effort, but worth a listen.

The later Soul Note records are something else entirely. On *The Mystery Of Compassion*, Varner's alarming juxtapositions make coherent sense without losing their capacity to surprise, and the players involved respond with a passionate intensity which is rare even among these driven musicians. The central group is a quintet made up of Varner, Jackson, Rothenberg, Richmond and Rainey. On all-out barnstormers like 'How Does Power Work?' and '$1000 Hat' they play with unstinting panache. 'The Well' is a concerto-like piece for Feldman, and 'Death At The Right Time' uses a tentet to create a bemusing recall of Coltrane's 'Ascension'. Varner's own improvising has never been better – he actually makes the instrument assert its personal qualities – and he closes the record on a sombre antiphonal piece for low brass called 'Prayer' which makes a moving coda to the rest.

Martian Heartache is probably even better. Varner packs 15 pieces into the record, again based around the core quintet, with McCann arriving only for the fascinating 'Erva Etc'. Sculpted with absolute precision but loose and swinging in feel, Varner refuses to allow the music to turn fragmentary or episodic: even the shortest pieces are fully realized, composed and uncluttered. He plays a gracious role as leader, offering terrific opportunities for the horns to make characterful statements, without letting anybody blemish their book by spinning out rhetoric. Jackson and Eskelin are more than equal to the task.

**** **The Window Up Above**
New World 80552-2 *Varner; Dave Ballou (c); Mark Feldman (vn); Pete McCann (g); Steve Alcott, Lindsey Horner (b); George Schuller (d); Thirsty Dave Hansen (v).* 5/98.

A complete departure for Tom, but just as powerful and surprising a record. It's a ramble through 200 or so years of American songwriting, going as far back as the earliest public-domain folk-tunes and as far forward as Ellington, George Jones and Hank Williams (the latter two voiced by Thirsty Dave Hansen). If he treats 'I Got It Bad' relatively straight, it's to emphasize the lieder element in the tune. 'Kingdom Coming' gets a blues injected into it, and 'When Jesus Wept' is gradually, but logically, broken down into a strange lament. 'Abide With Me' gets its first jazz treatment, as a sweet waltz, since Monk's horn arrangement. And so on: no track seems silly or forced, and Varner makes every melody count. Excellent work from the little-known McCann, playing a Frisell-like role a lot of the way, and cameos from Feldman and Ballou add to the pleasure of a mature and beautifully sustained record.

Nana Vasconcelos (born 1944)

BERIMBAU, PERCUSSION, VOICE

Raised in the heartland of Brazilian music, Recife, Vasconcelos started his career as a drummer, but then came within the orbit of, first, Gato Barbieri and Don Cherry, who encouraged him to experiment with free jazz. Nana was a member of the short-lived Codona, but since its disbandment on the death of Collin Walcott he has worked with other groups in parallel with a solo career, singing and playing berimbau.

****(*) Saudades**

ECM 829380-2 *Vasconcelos solo, and with Egberto Gismonti (8-string g); strings.* 3/79.

***** Lester**

Soul Note 121157 *Vasconcelos; Antonello Salis (g, acc, v).* 12/85.

Unlike his slightly older compatriot, Airto Moreira, who was propelled into independent stardom by a stint with Miles Davis and on the strength of his wife Flora Purim's astonishing voice, Vasconcelos has largely suffered from the old and patronizing Hollywood syndrome of 'specialist extra' recruitment: 'Six Chinees for a street scene in Kowloon!' … 'One Lascar and a Hottentot!' Vasconcelos has played bit-parts on countless Latin-modern sessions, bringing a distinctive range of sounds largely based on the Afro-Latin *berimbau*, a bow with a wire string plucked with a coin or stroked with a stick, its sound modified by a gourd or shell resonator pressed against the player's abdomen. Whereas Moreira was inclined to put together a rhythmic background like a pizza chef, throwing in aural ingredients with more sense of drama than of taste, Vasconcelos is a much more concentrated musician, capable of sustained performance on his own and as a full member of improvising groups; some of his best work is with guitarist Egberto Gismonti, who guests on *Saudades*, but also with Codona (*q.v.*). The problem has been how to make Vasconcelos's intensely rhythmic but rather specialized music accessible to a Western audience. *Saudades* is, alas, not the solution. In addition to overdubbing his vocal parts (which seems completely redundant), the album places him in highly chromatic string-settings which are utterly European in conception. Vasconcelos's Tarzan cry on the opening 'O Berimbau' appears to startle the orchestral players for a moment; it certainly throws the whole set into perspective.

Lester is very much truer to the Brazilian's enormous talents, though Salis is a surprisingly passive partner, following rather than confronting. There is an interesting Antilles set, *Bush Dance*, but this is not currently available, and Vasconcelos still, regrettably, has to be sought on other leaders' albums. The three Codona sets probably remain the best bet.

Sarah Vaughan (1924–90)

VOCAL, PIANO

Studied piano as a child, then joined the Earl Hines band in 1943 as vocalist. Left with Billy Eckstine to sing in his new band, then solo from the late '40s, usually working live with a trio or small group, but on record mostly with orchestras, especially from the mid-'50s. Had many crossover hits during that decade but was always seen as a jazz vocalist, and one of the most gifted, with a multi-octave range, a wide variety of tone, a bopper's way with scat – though she rarely used it – and the stage presence of a forbidding diva. Never as popular as Holiday or Fitzgerald – and, some would say, better than either.

***** Sarah Vaughan 1944–1946**

Classics 958 *Vaughan; Dizzy Gillespie, Freddy Webster, Shorty McConnell, Gail Brockman, Boonie Hazel, Clarence Brereton, George Treadwell, Al Aaron, Danny Blue, Art House, Al Porcino, Neal Hefti, Sonny Rich, George Schwartz (t); Gerald Valentine, Trummy Young, Tracy Allen, Mike Datz, Rude De Luca, Gus Dixon, Johnny Mandel, Taswell Baird, Howard Scott, Chippy Outcalt, Dicky Wells (tb); Aaron Sachs, Buster Bailey, Tony Scott (cl); Charlie Parker, Scoville Brown, Leroy Harris, John Jackson, Bill Frazier, Russell Procope, Lou Prisby, Gene Zanoni, Leroy Harris, Sam Zittman (as); Don Byas, Dexter Gordon, Gene Ammons, Flip Phillips, Ben Webster, Al Cohn, Irv Roth (ts); Cecil Payne, Serge Chaloff, Leo Parker, Cecil Scott (bs); Al Haig, Jimmy Jones, Bud Powell, Leonard Feather, John Malachi, Billy Kyle, Freddy Jefferson, Roy Kral, Harvey Leonard, Tadd Dameron (p); John Collins, Remo Palmieri, Bill D'Arango, Connie Wainwright, Chuck Wayne, Barry Galbraith (g); Al McKibbon, Curley Russell, Ted Sturgis, Tommy Potter, Jack Lesberg, John Kirby, Gene Ramey, Ted Sturgis, Joe Pillicane, Ed Cunningham (b); Pete Glover, Big Sid Catlett, Kenny Clarke, Art Blakey, Morey Feld, Max Roach, Bill Beason, Ed Nicholson, Art Madigan (d).* 9/44–7/46.

*****(*) The Divine Sarah Vaughan: The Columbia Years 1949–1953**

Columbia 465597 2CD *Vaughan; Miles Davis, Billy Butterfield, Taft Jordan, Andrew Ferretti, Bernie Privin, Yank Lawson, Carl Poole, Ziggy Elman (t); Will Bradley, Jack Satterfield, William Rausch, Benny Green, John D'Agostino, William Pritchard (tb); Tony Scott (cl); Hymie Schertzer, Art Drelinger, George Kelly, Toots Mondello, Al Klink, Bill Versaci, Richard Banzer, Bill Hitz, Budd Johnson (saxes); Jimmy Jones (p); Freddie Green, Al Caiola, Mundell Lowe (g); Frank Carroll, Eddie Safranski, Jack Lesberg, Billy Taylor, Bob Haggart (b); J.C Heard, Terry Snyder, Norris Shawker, Bill Coles (d); strings; studio orchestras led by Percy Faith, Paul Weston and Norman Leyden.* 1/49–1/53.

****** 16 Most Requested Songs**

Columbia 474399-2 *As above.* 1/49–1/53.

Her vocal on the 1946 Dizzy Gillespie Sextet record of 'Lover Man' was Sarah Vaughan's banner arrival. Yet she'd already cut several fine sides, four with a Dizzy Gillespie small group, including a fine vocal version of 'Night In Tunisia', and there were several other scattered appearances, all of which seem to have been gathered up on the intriguing if finally slightly disappointing Classics CD. A later session with Bird and Dizzy includes a terrific 'Mean To Me', with Parker shadowing her almost like Lester with Billie, but the remaining sessions are motley in nature and Vaughan seems to get only doleful ballads to sing. 'All Too Soon', with a Tony Scott group, is a nice one, with some lovely Ben Webster, and overall the best performances earn the stars – although remastering seems very spotty. But her sessions for Musicraft and Columbia were her first significant body of records, following her stint with the Billy Eckstine Orchestra. The next Classics volume will no doubt start on her Musicraft sessions.

The bulk of the Columbias are scarcely jazz-orientated sessions, with full orchestras and hefty ballads, but two sessions from May 1950 put Vaughan in front of a small band including Miles Davis, Tony Scott and Budd Johnson for eight fine tracks. Vaughan's musical insight – she was a more than capable pianist – and involvement with bop's early days gave her a hip awareness that went with a voice of vast range and power, and her early Billy Eckstine influence – both singers use vibrato to the same enormously ripe effect – makes her sound like a close relation of Eckstine on all these tracks. Far from disguising the operatic qualities of her voice, Vaughan insists on them, sometimes dispersing the sense of a lyric while luxuriating in the depth of her own voice. Luckily, the material on the Columbia sessions is good enough to withstand such indulgence, and it's a very enjoyable double set, acceptably if not outstandingly remastered. But less committed souls will prefer the useful single-disc compilation, *16 Most Requested Songs*, which luckily includes four of the tracks with the small group.

♛ ** Sarah Vaughan**

Verve 543305-2 *Vaughan; Clifford Brown (t); Paul Quinichette (ts); Herbie Mann (f); Jimmy Jones (p); Joe Benjamin (b); Roy Haynes (d).* 12/54.

****** Swingin' Easy**

Emarcy 514072-2 *Vaughan; Jimmy Jones, John Malachi (p); Richard Davis, Joe Benjamin (b); Roy Haynes (d).* 54–57.

The session with Clifford Brown was a glorious occasion, and the kind of date that occurred far too infrequently during the rest of Sarah's career. A blue-chip band (even Mann doesn't disgrace himself) on a slow-burning set of standards that Vaughan lingers over and details with all the finesse of her early-mature voice: 'Lullaby Of Birdland' (the master take is a composite, and there is a 'partial alternative' take here too) is taken at a pace that suspends or lets time drift, and the very slow pace for 'Embraceable You' and 'Bill' doesn't falter into a trudge. In the past we have wondered if the many slow tempos were perhaps *too* many, but in this superb new remastering it is very difficult to find any flaw in what should be recognized as one of the great jazz vocal records. We are upgrading it to crown status as a result.

Swingin' Easy isn't far behind, though. With just a rhythm section in support, Vaughan is at her freest and most good-humoured: it's worth having just for the cheeky, sublime 'Shulie A Bop', but there's also a gorgeous 'Lover Man' and a shivery 'Linger Awhile'.

*****(*) Sings George Gershwin**

Verve 557567-2 2CD *Vaughan; Hal Mooney Orchestra.* 57.

***** Golden Hits**

Mercury 824891-2 *Vaughan; Hal Mooney Orchestra.* 58.

*****(*) Sings Broadway: Great Songs From Great Shows**

Verve 526464-2 2CD *As above discs.* 3/54–1/56.

*****(*) Jazz Masters 42: The Jazz Sides**

Verve 526817-2 *As above.*

Vaughan's later Mercury sessions are sometimes a shade self-conscious – not in any sense an embarrassment to Vaughan but in the way that she can get hung up on the sound of her own voice, the criticism most often levelled at her. Musicality and the comparative brevity of each piece usually win through, though, and while her 'songbook' collections miss some of the simple swing and infectiousness of the contemporaneous Ella Fitzgerald records in the same style, Vaughan's grandness and the lavish Mercury recording make these rich sonic experiences. At the moment, Universal seem to be rethinking their Vaughan holdings, and the individual albums which are out there are few in number. The Gershwin set competes but loses out to the Fitzgerald counterpart, though that is scarcely a disgrace. *Golden Hits* offers a fine cross-section of material, although the occasional stuffiness of the studio orchestra discourages any hint that Vaughan might use the occasions as springboards for more idiomatic jazz singing. Her coloratura tones and sweeping phrasing work instead to a different aesthetic, and one that is as individually creative.

Sings Broadway is an intelligent compilation from this era, with a 'songbook' approach to the material, and scarcely a dud track among it all. Some may prefer the *Jazz Masters* choice from her more jazz-directed sessions, but it's still no substitute for the four-star discs listed above.

*****(*) At Mister Kelly's**

Emarcy 832791-2 *Vaughan; Jimmy Jones (p); Richard Davis (b); Roy Haynes (d).* 57.

*****(*) Sassy Swings The Tivoli**

Mercury 832788-2 2CD *Vaughan; Kirk Stuart (p); Charles Williams (b); Georges Hughes (d).* 7/63.

The best of these live sessions is the earliest, *At Mister Kelly's*. Most singers can't wait to get out of clubs and into concert halls, but the 'intimacy' of the situation can be a boon, and with this excellent trio Vaughan sounds completely relaxed. Nineteen songs, some of them dashed off, but she dashes better than most. The later date is very good rather than great. *Tivoli* is a solid balance between the unbridled grandeur of her range and the more loose-limbed jazz-musician stance – despite the grandiloquence of her voice, most of her best records have been done with small groups rather than orchestras.

*****(*) Ultimate Sarah Vaughan**

Verve 539052-2 *Vaughan; various groups.* 54–67.

*****(*) 'Round Midnight: Sarah Vaughan**

Verve 510086-2 *As above.*

*****(*) Verve Jazz Masters: Sarah Vaughan**

Verve 518199-2 *As above.*

None of these compilations holds a candle to either *Sarah Vaughan* or *Swingin' Easy*, even though they take tracks from both. But each has enough classics – 'Shulie A Bop', 'Dreamsville' on *Ultimate*, 'April In Paris', 'Jim', 'Darn That Dream' on *'Round Midnight*, 'Say It Isn't So' and 'Lonely Woman' on *Jazz Masters* – to satisfy a seeker after a run-through of Sarah's Emarcy/ Mercury period.

****** After Hours**

Roulette 855468-2 *Vaughan; Mundell Lowe (g); George Duvivier (b).* 7/61.

A comparatively little-known record, yet one of her finest. With the skeletal accompaniment of Lowe (who plays only a single solo on the date) and Duvivier, Vaughan muses over 11 standards (there is a previously unheard try-out take on 'Through The Years') which find her by turns playful and profound. A light, gorgeous 'Easy To Love' looks back to her bebop days, there's a starkly effective 'My Favorite Things', and 'Vanity' – just one among several fascinating choices of song – is immaculately modulated. The remastering gets the most out of the great voice.

*****(*) Snowbound / The Lonely Hours**
EMI 855394-2 *Vaughan; orchestras arranged and conducted by Don Costa and Benny Carter.* 63–64.

The first album has Vaughan getting indecently comfortable in Costa's very deep-pile orchestrations; the second has her finding a soupçon of civilized blues in Benny Carter's charts. Carter is scarcely trying too hard here, but he still finds a few interesting quirks, such as the low brass for 'You're Driving Me Crazy', and Vaughan is at her most perfectly controlled on 'Look For Me, I'll Be Around'. The Costa tracks are a shameless wallow by all concerned. As a coupling, this works rather well in showing off Vaughan's two sides of the time.

*****(*) How Long Has This Been Going On?**
Pablo 2310-821 *Vaughan; Oscar Peterson (p); Joe Pass (g); Ray Brown (b); Louie Bellson (d).* 4/78.

*****(*) Duke Ellington Song Book One**
Pablo 2312-111 *Vaughan; Waymon Reed (t, flhn); J.J Johnson (tb); Eddie Vinson (as, v); Frank Wess (ts, f); Frank Foster, Zoot Sims (ts); Jimmy Rowles, Mike Wofford (p); Joe Pass, Bucky Pizzarelli, Pee Wee Crayton (g); Andy Simpkins, Bill Walker (b); Grady Tate, Charles Randell (d); big band.* 8–9/79.

*****(*) Duke Ellington Song Book Two**
Pablo 2312-116 *As above.* 8–9/79.

****** Copacabana**
Pablo 2312-125 Vaughan; Helio Delmiro (*g*); Andy Simpkins (*b*); Grady Tate (*d*) 10/79.

***** Send In The Clowns**
Pablo 2312-230 *Vaughan; Sonny Cohn, Frank Szabo, Willie Cook, Bob Summers, Dale Carley (t); Booty Wood, Bill Hughes, Denis Wilson, Grover Mitchell (tb); Kenny Hing, Eric Dixon, Bobby Plater, Danny Turner, Johnny Williams (saxes); George Gaffney (p); Freddie Green (g); Andy Simpkins (b); Harold Jones (d).* 2–5/81.

****** Crazy And Mixed Up**
Pablo 2312-137 *Vaughan; Sir Roland Hanna (p); Joe Pass (g); Andy Simpkins (b); Harold Jones (d).* 3/82.

Vaughan's Pablo albums will endure as some of her most finely crafted music. *How Long Has This Been Going On?* introduced a new note of seriousness into her recording career after several years of indifferent efforts and a seemingly careless approach to the studios. The voice has never been better or more closely recorded, and the picked session players and uniformly strong material make these albums the most consistent of her career. *How Long* has the odd flaw, but there are beautiful readings of 'I've Got The World On A String' and the title-tune, and when Vaughan takes it in turns to do a duo with each member of the band it's a marvellous display of her ability. The Ellington albums gave her – at last – the opportunity to stamp her identity on the greatest of jazz songbooks, and while again there are a few disappointments – a second-class 'Solitude' that should have been a classic, the sometimes overbearing heft of Bill Byers's arrangements and the slightly problematical balance – there are some exceptionally bountiful treatments, of 'In A Sentimental Mood', 'I'm Just A Lucky So-And-So' and 'Chelsea Bridge' to cite three. Both discs stand as a worthy counterpoint to Fitzgerald's celebrated Ellington collaboration.

Send In The Clowns features the Basie orchestra minus Basie and, while it's good – the gliding 'All The Things You Are' and a lovely 'Indian Summer' especially – the hard power of the band and Vaughan's own superhuman technique sometimes secure a coldness rather than any warmth of interpretation. *Copacabana* is the neglected album of the bunch, with the sparest of accompaniments to support the great, glowing voice, and the bossa/samba material proving unexpectedly strong material for Vaughan. Best of all, perhaps, is *Crazy And Mixed Up*, a disappointingly short (about 32 minutes) but ideally paced and delivered set of standards with the most sympathetic of accompaniments.

*****(*) Linger Awhile**
Pablo 2312-144-2 Vaughan; Waymon Reed (*t*); Frank Foster (*ts*); Jimmy Jones, Roland Hanna, Mike Wofford, Jimmy Rowles, Oscar Peterson (*p*); Joe Pass, Bucky Pizzarelli (*g*); Richard Davis, Andy Simpkins, Ray Brown (*b*); Roy Haynes, Grady Tate, Louie Bellson (*d*); Count Basie Orchestra 7/57–2/81.

The first eight tracks are quite a discovery, Vaughan live at the 1957 Newport Festival. Girlish and almost flirtatious at some points, the dark mocha tones are there on 'Black Coffee' and the virtuosity of 'All Of Me' is inimitable. The rest offers eight alternative takes from her Pablo albums, many of them fine enough to make one want to return to the neglected original albums. As an album it doesn't really hang together, but as a feast of rare Vaughan for devotees it's excellent.

**** Brazilian Romance**
Columbia 496856-2 *Vaughan; Marcio Montarroyos (flhn); Ernie Watts (as); Tom Scott (ts, lyricon); Hubert Laws (f); George Duke (ky); Dan Huff, Dori Caymmi (g); Alphonso Johnson, Chuck Domanico (b); Carlos Vega (d); Paulinho Da Costa (perc); strings.* 1–2/87.

One of her last records, and it makes a pitiful comparison with her glory days. Sergio Mendes produces what might as well be elevator music, and it's a tribute to the great singer that she's still able to get something out of these songs – often only for a line or two, but enough to let you know she was still Sarah Vaughan.

Charlie Ventura (1916–92)

TENOR SAXOPHONE

Born Charles Venturo in Philadelphia, worked a day job in a navy yard but jammed after hours with local players. Joined Gene Krupa, 1942–6, then ran own big band and small group, as well as JATP appearances. Led a 'Bop For The People' group from the late '40s but, despite a later spell with Krupa, drifted from sight in the '60s.

***** Charlie Ventura 1945–1946**

Classics 1044 *Ventura; Howard McGhee, Red Rodney, Buck Clayton (t); Barney Bigard (cl); Willie Smith (as); Arnold Ross, Bill Rowland, Harry Fields (p); Barney Kessel, Dave Barbour, Eddie Yance (g); Art Shapiro, Red Callender, Billy Hadnott, Al Hall, John Levy (b); Specs Powell, Nick Fatool, Gene Krupa (d).* 3/45–3/46.

Ventura was very popular in his day, but has since been entirely marginalized in the music's history. Unfairly so, on the evidence of these early sessions, since his playing had chutzpah and skill, even if he was entirely derivative of Coleman Hawkins and took on the bop vernacular as only a sideline to his main swing language. This CD collects five sessions for Sunset, Black & White, Savoy and Lamplighter and, while his own playing is enjoyable, there is rather more interesting playing from McGhee, Rodney and even the young Barney Kessel. The first Black & White session sounds rough, but otherwise the transfers seem good. Later Classics CDs should show him in his popular phase.

Joe Venuti (1903–78)

VIOLIN, PIANO

Born in Philadelphia (he once claimed it was on board a ship bound for the USA), he befriended Eddie Lang as a boy and they worked together on the New York dance-band and small-group jazz recording scene until Lang's death. Formed his own band in the '30s, then returned from war service to feature regularly on radio. Out of favour in the '60s but made a great comeback in 1967–8, and then regular appearances and records until his death. A legendary practical joker and a pioneer of jazz violin.

***** Stringin' The Blues**

Topaz TPZ 1015 *Venuti; Tommy Dorsey (t, tb); Charlie Margulis, Leo McConville, Charlie Teagarden, Red Nichols (t); Bix Beiderbecke, Andy Secrest (c); Jack Teagarden (tb, v); Miff Mole, Bill Rank (tb); Jimmy Dorsey (cl, as, bs, t); Benny Goodman (cl); Charles Strickfadden, Bobby Davis (as); Frankie Trumbauer (Cmel, bsn); Pete Pumiglio (cl, bs); Issy Friedman (cl, ts); Don Barrigo (ts); Adrian Rollini (bsx, gfs, hot fountain pen); Min Leibrook (bsx); Red McKenzie (kz, v); Lennie Hayton (p, cel); Rube Bloom, Arthur Young, Frank Signorelli, Itzy Riskin, Phil Ward, Fulton McGrath, Arthur Schutt (p); Eddie Lang, Dick McDonough, Frank Victor (g); Eddie Condon (bj); Joe Tarto, Ward Lay, Doug Lees (b); Stan King, Justin Ring, Paul Graselli, Neil Marshall, Vic Berton, Chauncey Morehouse (d).* 11/26–9/34.

*****(*) Violin Jazz 1927–1934**

Yazoo 1062 *Similar to above.* 27–34.

***** Pretty Trix**

IAJRC 1003 *Venuti; Jerry Colonna (tb); Fulton McGrath, Joe White (p); Red Norvo (xy); Neil Marshall (d); Louis Prima (v); rest unknown.* 12/34.

Venuti wasn't the only violinist to play jazz in the 1920s, but he established the style for the instrument as surely as Coleman Hawkins did for the saxophone. He was a key figure on the New York session scene of the era and he appears on many dance-band records alongside Beiderbecke, Trumbauer and the Dorseys; but his most important association was with Eddie Lang and, although their partnership was curtailed by Lang's death in 1933, it was a pairing which has endured like few other jazz double-acts. With the two JSP CDs, which collected all their duets and the tracks by Venuti's Blue Four, currently out of print, we at present have to make do with these various compilations. Some of the tracks – 'Wild Cat', 'Doin' Things' – are like spontaneous bursts of virtuosity, Venuti's reeling melody-lines counterpointed by Lang's driving accompaniment and subtle variations of dynamic; others, especially the Blue Four tracks, feature oddball instruments – Trumbauer on bassoon on 'Running Ragged', Jimmy Dorsey on trumpet on 'My Honey's Lovin' Arms', Rollini on everything he plays on – to create a kind of jazz chamber music of improbable zip and bravado. There are also touches of kitsch in the style, and the occasional indifferent vocal (even if the singer on one session was none other than Harold Arlen!), but Venuti's irascible swing makes sure that every record is an event.

The Yazoo disc is a splendid compilation and there are a few rare alternative takes – of 'Raggin' The Scale', 'Hey! Young Fella' and 'Jig-Saw Puzzle Blues' – included among the 14 tracks. Remastering leaves a lot of the surface hiss alone, but the music itself comes through very brightly. The Topaz disc is half in the 1920s and half out: useful to have some of the later Blue Six titles together, and the final session from 1934 is unusual, though some of the transfers from (British) Columbia 78s are occasionally noisy, and the overall standard is weaker than it might be.

The *Pretty Trix* date is a pendant to the other records, a set of rare radio transcriptions featuring Venuti, Prima and Norvo with a 1934 band of largely unknown personnel. The playing is sometimes sloppy and the sound mixed, but Venuti's best moments have all the flash of old and it's a scarce glimpse of a musician who wouldn't have any limelight again for decades.

*****(*) Joe Venuti And Zoot Sims**

Chiaroscuro CRD 142 *Venuti; Spiegel Wilcox (tb); Zoot Sims (ts); Dick Hyman, John Bunch (p); Bucky Pizzarelli (g); Milt Hinton (b); Cliff Leeman, Bobby Rosengarden (d).* 5/74–5/75.

****** Alone At The Palace**

Chiaroscuro CRD 160 *Venuti; Dave McKenna (p).* 4/77.

****(*) Joe In Chicago, 1978**

Flying Fish FF-70077 *Venuti; John Young (p); Jethro Burns (mand); Mike Dowling, Steve Goodman, Curley Chalker, Eldon Shamblin (g); John Vany, Jim Tullio (b); Barrett Deems, Angie Vartas (d).* 76–78.

Venuti's Indian summer in the studios is currently represented by only a few records. He remained in such good form to the end of his playing life that all his final records are worth hearing at least. Perhaps the partnership with Zoot Sims has been a shade overrated, since Sims's bluff swing is no different from anything he plays on his own records and occasionally sounds a little glib, whereas Venuti's own playing – coloured by unexpected bursts of pizzicato, oddball kinds of bowing and resinous streams of melody that seem to go on for ever – is of a different order. *Sliding By* (now deleted) continued a profitable association with Dick

Hyman, but it's *Alone At The Palace* which is Venuti's valedictory masterpiece. McKenna's granitic swing and authority are just the kind of bedrock the violinist loved and, whether they play 'At The Jazz Band Ball' or 'Runnin' Ragged' (almost exactly 50 years after Venuti's original version) or a slush-free 'Send In The Clowns', it's all superbly achieved. The CD reissue of the original LP includes four new tracks and three alternative takes, all equally welcome, and the sound is admirably clear. The Flying Fish session is missable, though: studio sound is amateurish, with Joe sounding like he's miles away, and the accompaniments are terribly lame. Even so, the old man jousts through two numbers from *My Fair Lady* with great finesse, and it's worth hearing for those alone.

Edward Vesala (1945–99)

DRUMS, PERCUSSION, OTHER INSTRUMENTS

Grew up in a remote part of Finland, taking up drums at twenty. Played rock and studied music before travelling through Asia and returning to the local Finnish jazz-scene. Toured with Tomasz Stanko, 1975–80, then with own Sound And Fury Ensemble. His death at the end of the century was a severe loss to European music.

*****(*) Nan Madol**

ECM 829376-2 *Vesala; Kaj Backlund (t); Mircea Stan (tb); Charlie Mariano (as, f, nagaswaram); Juhani Aaltonen (ts, ss, f); Pentti Lahti (ss, bcl); Seppo Paakkunainen (ss, f); Sakari Kukko (f); Elisabeth Leistola (hp); Juhani Poutanen (vn, alto vn); Teppo Hauta-aho (b).* 4/74.

♛ ** Lumi**

ECM 831517-2 *Vesala; Esko Heikkinen (t, picc t); Tom Bildo (tb, tba); Pentti Lahti (as, bs, f); Jorma Tapio (as, cl, bcl, f); Tapani Rinne (ts, ss, cl, bcl); Kari Heinilä (ts, ss, f); Raoul Björkenheim (g); Taito Vainio (acc); Iro Haarla (hp); Häkä (b).* 6/86.

****** Ode To The Death Of Jazz**

ECM 843196-2 *Vesala; Matti Rikonen (t); Jorma Tapio (as, bcl, f); Jouni Kannisto (ts, f); Pepa Päivinen (ts, ss, bs, f, cl, bcl); Tim Ferchen (mar, bells); Taito Vainio (acc); Iro Haarla (p, hp, ky); Jimi Sumen (g); Uffe Krokfors (b).* 4 & 5/89.

****** Invisible Storm**

ECM 511928-2 *Vesala; Matti Riikonen (t); Jorma Tapio (as, bcl, f, bf, perc); Jouni Kannisto (ts, f); Pepa Päivinen (ts, ss, bs, f, af); Jimi Sumen (g); Pekka Sarmanto (b); Marko Ylönen (clo); Mark Nauseef (perc).*

***** Nordic Gallery**

ECM 523294-2 *Vesala; Matti Riikonen (t); Tapani Rinne (cl); Jorma Tapio (as, bcl, acl, bf); Jouni Kannisto (ts, f); Pepa Päivinen (ts, ss, bs, bsx, f, af, picc); Iro Haarla (hp, p, ky, acc, koto); Petri Ikkela (acc); Jimi Sumen (g); Pekka Sarmanto (b); Kari Linsted (clo).* 93–94.

Edward Vesala bore an uncanny physical resemblance to Richard Brautigan and wove narratives and textures which, like the late American novelist's, are magically suffused, wry and tender by turns. Vesala was one of very few percussionists capable of sustaining interest as a solo performer (an early-1980s recording of extracts from the Finnish epic, *Kalevala*, rivets the attention despite the minimalist accompaniment and the fact that no English translation is provided); despite this, Vesala has been sparing of solo tracks on his records (the brief 'Call From The Sea' on *Nan Madol* is an exception), preferring to elevate his light, pulse-driven but often non-metrical drumming until it occupies the forefront of a piece. Recording with ECM greatly enhanced his capacity in this regard. Vesala's groups have a unique sound, compounded of folk and popular references, but with a grasp of orchestration that, for all his commitment to themes and solos, is more typical of through-composed concert music. He favours extremes of timbre, alternating very dark themes exploiting sombre modes and tonalities with light, airy arrangements of flutes, soprano saxophones and harp; typically, though, he reverses the expressive polarity, investing light-toned pieces like 'The Wind' (on *Nan Madol*, re-recorded later) with a sinister quality, often reserving darker instrumentation for tongue-in-cheek compositions based on popular forms.

Vesala produced one unqualified masterpiece, *Lumi*. Even its cover, of a shrouded, Golem-like figure on an empty road under a threatening sky, suggests something of Vesala's distinctive combination of almost Gothic intensity and sheer playfulness. A re-recording of 'The Wind' shows how much he has advanced since 1974. It is spare, subtly voiced, less dependent on literal reference than its predecessor, but not a whit less evocative. 'Frozen Melody' is a superb exercise in static harmony; Vesala works variations on a descending repetition of four notes of the same pitch, gradually unpicking the rhythmic implications. 'Fingo', like 'A Glimmer Of Sepal' on *Ode To The Death Of Jazz*, is based on tango rhythms and illustrates Vesala's interest in extreme stylistic repetitions. This is evident on the later album too, in 'Winds Of Sahara', which begins in spooky 'ethnic' mode, wobbles a bit, and then breaks into a camel-racing flag-waver of Maynard Ferguson proportions; 'Calypso Bulbosa' evokes similar incongruities.

Vesala worked slowly and was never a prolific recorder, although a lack of resources to prepare and create his music also took its toll. Each of his records was a superb balance of careful organization and arrangment and all-out freedom. Though not too much should be invested in chance resemblances and coincidences, it's interesting to note a parallel between Vesala's method on 'The Way Of ...' (*Nan Madol*) and that of British drummer Tony Oxley on his 1969 album, *The Baptised Traveller*, notably the extraordinary 'Stone Garden', composed by Charlie Mariano, who appears on two tracks on Vesala's album. The descending sequences are, though, entirely characteristic of Vesala and owe no apparent debt to anyone else.

The opening four tracks of *Invisible Storm* represent the most powerfully dramatic work Vesala committed to record. It opens with an extraordinary recitation, 'Sheets And Shrouds', a cracked voice in an unfamiliar tongue (and Finnish has a quality that is both ancient and curiously Asian) before giving way to 'Murmuring Morning', a slow chorale highlit by Ylönen's cello, and then exploding in the thudding fury of 'Gordion's Flashes'. The fourth piece – and each is successively longer – also features a spoken vocal; 'Shadows On The Frontier' is in English but preserves the tranced quality of the opening. Though there is no explicit reason to connect them, they do seem to cohere in a way that later tracks do not. Of these, 'Somnamblues' is another of Vesala's brilliant generic parodies, and the closing 'Caccaroo

Boohoo' is drily witty. The longest single item, 'The Wedding Of All Essential Parts', and the title-track are less impressive – but only relative to Vesala's now absurdly high standard. His melodic inventiveness grows apace, concentrating on sinuously extended figures that evade conventional rhythmic resolution but underneath which there beats a powerful, even dramatic, pulse. *Lumi* remains the record of choice, but it's hard to put *Invisible Storm* lower than essential in terms of contemporary recording. Needless to say, the studio work and mastering are impeccable.

The final disc of the group was the only real disappointment. Newcomers may well still be entranced by the sheer unexpectedness of Vesala's sound-world in this series of still landscapes and wry portraits, but anyone who has followed his course over a few discs will surely find *Nordic Gallery* formulaic and repetitive, a reworking of elements rather than anything new. Vesala's passing is a blow to the music, and the restoration of several, at present vinyl-only, albums would be some consolation.

Andrea Vicari

PIANO, KEYBOARDS

Born in America and raised in the United Kingdom, Vicari is a prodigiously talented pianist and composer whose debut recording has enough poise and maturity to pass for the fruit of a decade rather than half-a-decade's professional music-making.

***** Suburban Gorillas**

33 Records 33JAZZ016 *Vicari; Simon Da Silva (t); Malcolm Earle Smith (tb); Martin Dunsdon (ts, ss, f); Leigh Etherington (as, ss); Mornington Lockett (ts, perc); Hilary Cameron (ky, v); Mark Ridout (g); Dorian Lockett (b); Simon Pearson (d, perc); Rony Barrak (tabla).* 1/94.

*****(*) Lunar Spell**

33 Records 33JAZZ026 *Vicari; Mornington Lockett (ts, ss); Phil Robson (g); Dorian Lockett (b); Tristan Maillot (d).* 2–3/95.

The large-scale debut reflects her ambition. It was put together to fulfil an Arts Council commission, the 'French Suite' which concludes the disc. Here Vicari allows her interest in classical harmonies and ethnic rhythms – largely Arabic, but with further hints of salsa and samba – to collide without embarrassment. The result is exhilarating on 'L'Orchestre Des Fous' and strangely moving on the more thoughtful 'Dance Verdange'. The strength of the album lies almost entirely in the writing. Though there are impressive statements by Leigh Etherington on 'Southern Comfort', a Keith Jarrett-influenced country tune, from Malcolm Smith on 'Pegasus', and from Mornington Lockett throughout, it is the youthful, fresh-voiced ensembles that mainly catch the ear.

Opportunities for Suburban Gorillas to play live have been predictably rare, but the quintet on *Lunar Spell* has a seasoned, well-travelled feel. This record is a big step forward in performance terms. Vicari's muscular chords, almost obsessively repeated in the opening 'You're Reported', set up a powerful blowing groove for her band. Robson provides a lot of the harmonic colour, allowing her to thump away in the left hand and to spin long, attractive solo lines up in the treble. The long title-piece is hugely impressive, as are the generous contours of the Latin '¡Vay a Tomar!' Both Locketts are in sharp form, and the only question mark about Maillot's performance relates to his place in a slightly off-balance studio-mix. With its monochrome cover and straight look from Ms Vicari, this is a plain-spoken declaration of independence and of intent. The follow-up has been slow to come, but Vicari is a shrewd and patient enough musician not to raise the stakes prematurely.

Vienna Art Orchestra

ENSEMBLE

The brainchild of composer and arranger Matthias Ruegg, and founded in 1977, the VAO attempt to forge a synthesis between jazz and twentieth-century compositional language, between the avant-garde and popular music. Not a conventional big band in section terms, the ensemble favour an open, improvisational sound rather than massed instruments. Five years into the VAO's history, Ruegg also formed the Vienna Art Choir.

****** Nightride Of A Lonely Saxophoneplayer**

Moers 02054/5 2CD *Ruegg; Karl Bumi Fian, Hannes Kottek (t, flhn); Herbert Joos (t, flhn, bhn, alphorn); Christian Radovan (tb); John Sass (tba); Wolfgang Puschnig (as, sno, bcl, f, picc); Harry Sokal (ts, ss, f); Roman Schwaller (ts); Woody Schabata (vib); Uli Scherer (ky, perc); Heiri Kaenzig (b); Wolfgang Reisinger (d); Ima (tamboura); Andy Manndorff (g); Tom Nicholas (perc); Erich Dorfinger (sound effects); Lauren Newton (v).* 10/85.

*****(*) Swiss Swing**

Moers 02060 *Ruegg; Karl Bumi Fian (t); Woody Schabata (vib); Hans Hassler (acc); Uli Scherer (ky); Heiri Kaenzig (b); Wolfgang Reisinger (d); Elfi Aichinger, Sarah Barrett, Maria Bayer, Renate Bochdansky, Lauren Newton (v).* 3/86.

***** Two Little Animals**

Moers 02066 *As for Minimalism, except omit Strieff; add Andy Mandorff (g).* 10/87.

*****(*) Inside Out**

Moers 02062/3 2CD *As above.* 11/87.

The VAO discography has been seriously mauled since our last edition, with the disappearance of the hat ART catalogue (including the crowned *Minimalism Of Eric Satie)* and some pretty severe rationalization of the ensemble's output on what were Polygram, now Universal, labels. Some sense that the VAO and Ruegg, having delivered one unquestioned masterpiece, were marking time in the later '80s. It became difficult to tell on occasion whether a piece was being deconstructed, reworked or debunked. That's somewhat the feeling with 'Cry Me A River' on *Inside Out*, or the ragtime ideas on the superbly titled *Nightride Of A Lonely Saxophoneplayer* (how could you *not* admire an album called that?). The shift of label didn't do any favours as far as sound was concerned, and it was only when the VAO signed up to Polygram a year or two further on that the full range of colours and dynamics was again available to listeners. *Swiss Swing* is closer in some respects to the work of the Vienna Art Choir, but it's the hand-picked small group which generates most of the musical interest.

****** The Original Charts**
Verve 551928-2 *Ruegg; Theodore Benkenstein, Karl Bumi Fian, Matthieu Michel (t); Herbert Joos (flhn); Christian Radovan, Danilo Terenzi (tb); Charly Wagner (btb); Claudio Pontiggia (frhn); Florian Brambock, Klaus Dickbauer, Herwig Gradischnig, Andy Scherrer, Harry Sokal (reeds); Frank Tortiller (vib); Uli Scherer (p); Heiri Kaenzig (b); Thomas Alkier (d); Corin Cuschellas (v).* 10/93.

A slightly unfamiliar look to the VAO for its first outing on the flagship label, but a programme that seems absolutely heaven-sent for Ruegg and his players, the masterworks of Duke Ellington and Charles Mingus. Where one might have expected a deconstructive spin, he has gone back to the original charts – or to subsequent arrangements transcribed from discs – and built an impressive concert programme. Recorded live at the Five Spot in New York City, this is arguably the best representation of how rigorously but tolerantly Ruegg controls his players. The performances are bright, very together and almost always at the service of the music. Whatever order was originally followed, there is a clear logic to the progression, from greater freedom and uncertainty (kicking off with Mingus, 'Hobo Ho', 'The Shoes of the Fisherman's Wife' and 'Don't Be Afraid, The Clown's Afraid, Too') and moving towards great order with the Ellington material. Towards the end there are two versions of 'Anitra's Dance', Duke's version of a piece by Grieg, arranged by Strayhorn and then transcribed by Dave Berger. As Ruegg says, 'That sounds more post-modern than it really is'; though this record clearly falls into a rich new vein of tradition-bending, it is more respectfully traditional than most, more straightforwardly directed to the masters.

****** Nine Immortal Nonevergreens For Eric Dolphy**
Amadeo 537 096 2 *Ruegg; Karl Bumi Fian, Herbert Joos, Matthieu Michel (t); Christian Muthspiel (tb); Claudio Pontiggia (frhn); Florian Brambock, Klaus Dickbauer, Andy Scherrer (reeds); Uli Scherer (p); Frank Tortiller (vib); Heiri Kaenzig (b); Thomas Alkier (d).* 95–96.

*****(*) Ballads**
Amadeo 537 097 2 *As above, except add Rudi Pilz (t), Dominique Stoger, Charly Wagner (tb), Herwig Gradischnig, Heinrich Von Kalnein, Harry Sokal (reeds), Sascha Otto (f), Vasile Marian (ob), Wolfgang Muthspiel (g), Chris Laurence, Angelika Riedl (b), Betty Carter, Corin Curschellas, Urszula Dudziak, Sheila Jordan, Anna Lauvergnac, Helen Merrill, Yvonne Moore, Linda Sharrock, Monika Trotz (v).* 96.

Originally issued together as part of a three-CD set to mark the VAO's twentieth anniversary, the two subdivisions marked 'Powerful Ways', 'Quiet Ways' are now available as *Nine Immortal Evergreens*, a sequence of Eric Dolphy themes given the Ruegg treatment, and an album of standard *Ballads*. Predictably, given market pressures, 'Unexpected Ways', *M: Concerto For Voice and Silence* has not lasted the course. Listening back to these beautiful records, we have not particularly missed their rather airless sibling. The ballad album is closer to expectation, with a fascinating range of guest vocalists. Helen Merrill is spine-tinglingly good on the opening 'What's New', and only when Sheila Jordan comes in with 'If You Could See Me Now' and Urszula Dudziak with 'You've Changed' is it as good again. Betty Carter is frankly disappointing, sounding as though she's not fully engaged with the project, and Linda Sharrock overcooks 'Lush Life'; but the less well-known singers – Yvonne Moore on 'Innocence of Clichés' and Anna Lauvergnac on two tracks, one a duet with Monika Trotz – all promise much. The orchestrations are flawless and beautifully played, but it's the third item in the set, the Dolphy registrations, which really lift the roof off. Recorded live in Zurich, Vienna and New York, these concentrate pretty heavily on material from *Out To Lunch*. Scherrer, Fian and Muthspiel are the soloists on 'Hat And Beard', Michel and Pontiggia more unexpectedly on 'Gazelloni', originally a flute feature, and Brambock, Fian and Muthspiel again are to the fore on 'Straight Up And Down'. Joos and Scherrer are the soloists on 'Something Sweet – Something Tender', which vies with the glorious 'Miss Ann' as the outstanding track. Other material comes from earlier in Dolphy's career: the haunted 'Out There' and the outwardly simple '245' are both splendidly done, made to sound almost majestic. The one slight quibble concerns Waller's 'Jitterbug Waltz' which, though Dolphy recorded it, isn't in character for this set, particularly with two versions of it to choose from. Last time out, we piously hoped that these records wouldn't just mark a successful anniversary but would point the way forward as well. That, so far, has proved not to be the case; but we remain optimistic that these musicians will still create something remarkable.

Frank Vignola (born 1965)

GUITAR, BANJO

Frank is one of the latest in Concord's stable of smoothly accomplished guitar players. There is only a slight and subtle rock influence on his playing style, which is immediately identifiable while hard to define, drawing on the fusion guitarists of an earlier generation, notably Al DiMeola, while retaining its individuality.

***** Appel Direct**
Concord CCD 4576 *Vignola; John Goldsby (b); Joseph Ascione (d, perc).* 4/93.

*****(*) Let It Happen**
Concord CCD 4625 *As above, except add Ken Peplowski (cl), Arnie Lawrence (as, ss), Dave Grisman (mand).* 4/94.

Vignola's smooth and unstressed sound disguises a wealth of subtlety that emerges only over time. Don't dismiss these records too quickly. We'll have to take Concord's word for it that the two sessions were recorded a year apart. The second of the pair might almost have been a guest walk-up on the same day, so seamlessly do they fit together. The guests certainly lift things. Peplowski's contribution to 'Flèche D'Or' is typically graceful, and the addition of a second stringed instrument, Grisman's mandolin, on four Latin numbers brings a further range of sounds to the date.

*****(*) Look Right, Jog Left**
Concord Vista CCD 4718 2 *Vignola; Allen Farnham (ky); John Goldsby (b); Joseph Ascione (d, perc).* 12/95.

***** Déjà Vu**
Concord Vista CCD 4802 2 *Vignola; Marty Kirshner (sax); Allen Farnham, Mark Portman, Ken Wallace (ky); John Burk, Alan Hinds (g); Jerry Brooks, Jon Decatur, Neil Stubenhaus (b);*

Vinnie Colaiuta, Steve Hauss (d); Joe Ascione (d prog); Rafael Padilla (perc); Melanie Daniels, Shannon Rae, Ken Wallace (v). 98.

Frank self-mockingly defines the word 'vignolette' as everything from a late-night thought to a slice of pie and, as the album reveals, a musical interlude, punctuating a strong set of originals (mostly) and covers. The songs are mainly very brief and to the point, almost none of them over five minutes in duration, and they put the emphasis very squarely on basic melodic invention rather than abstract improvisation. 'Desert Moon Blues' is ideally suited to the electric ambience of Unit Four, though some of the arrangements are rather too lumpy even for these forces.

The same melodism shines through on *Déjà Vu*, an unexpected programme of rock interpretations. To say the selection is eclectic is to understate the case considerably. It begins with Cream's 'White Room', continues with songs by Carole King, Bob Marley, Foreigner's 'Waiting For A Girl Like You', Sting's 'Walkin' On The Moon', Elvis Costello's 'Alison' and John Lennon's 'Imagine'. It at least has been subject to jazz interpretation before, but the others emerge freshly and with considerable imagination. David Crosby's 'Déjà Vu' gives the album its title and a kind of melodic leitmotif; of all the tunes included, it seems both furthest from and most faithful to the sources. Ironically, the only jazz composition on the set – Chick Corea's 'Spain' – is the least convincingly handled. The vocals where they feature are mostly pretty dud and surplus, but otherwise the album is great fun and immaculately recorded, lending slightly dry electronic resources a genuine warmth and presence.

Biggi Vinkeloe

ALTO SAXOPHONE, FLUTE

Born in Germany, raised in France, and now seemingly based in Sweden, Vinkeloe is a free-bop saxophonist.

***** Mbat**

LJ 5209 *Vinkeloe; Barre Phillips (b); Peeter Uuskyla (d).* 4/93.

***** One Way Out**

Slask 8433 *As above.* 7/97.

*****(*) Slowdrags And Interludes**

LJ LJCD5219 *As above, except Peter Kowald (b) replaces Phillips.* 1/99.

Vinkeloe's sparse delivery and pierced tone recall Jimmy Lyons, and her compositions are more like dissembled bits of melody than anything else ('Fragments' is one of them). So Phillips, who plays free but never surrenders a melodic line, is a good partner for her on *Mbat*. When they find their way to counterpoint on the title-track, the music feels like it's reached its reward. Some of the eight pieces wind on rather aimlessly, but it's pleasing music in its benign, muted way. *One Way Out* is a more pointed and more confident continuation, peaking on the long title-piece.

Carved up into 19 sections, the music on *Slowdrags And Interludes* has a more ritualistic feel to it, with 12 brief 'Interludes' interspersing the handful of longer pieces. They sound like improvisations with a splash of preordained structure (and, since there are individual composer-credits, that may be the case), and with Uuskyla's rhythms – more often tattoos or cymbal-crashes in stark, open space – as simple and open as the leader's melodies, it's left to the incomparable Kowald to provide the textural density, which he does, superbly. Kowald may not be the humorist that Phillips is, but he has far more in the way of technique and ideas. Concentrated, without sounding dense, the record rewards patient study.

Leroy Vinnegar (1928–99)

DOUBLE BASS

Moved to California in the '50s and became one of the most in-demand sessionmen in Los Angeles studios, playing on a vast number of jazz and pop sessions alike.

*****(*) Leroy Walks!**

Original Jazz Classics OJJCD 160 *Vinnegar; Gerald Wilson (t); Teddy Edwards (ts); Victor Feldman (vib); Carl Perkins (p); Tony Bazley (d).* 6–9/57.

***** Leroy Walks Again!**

Original Jazz Classics OJCCD 454 *Vinnegar; Teddy Edwards (ts); Mike Melvoin (p); Victor Feldman (p, vib); Roy Ayers (vib); Ron Jefferson, Milton Turner (d).* 8/62.

***** Jazz's Great 'Walker'**

Vee Jay VJ 022 *Vinnegar; Mike Melvoin (p); Bill Goodwin (d).* 64.

****(*) Walkin' The Basses**

Contemporary 14068 *Vinnegar; Geoff Lee (p); Mel Brown (g); Curtis Craft (d).* 92.

***** Integrity: The Walker Live At Lairmont**

Jazz Focus JFCD009 *Vinnegar; Gary Harris (ss, ts); Dan Faehnle (g); Mel Brown (d).* 5/95.

Given the unimaginative range of titles, it seems almost redundant to say that Vinnegar was one of the great exponents of walking bass, his talent an ability to invest a solid four beats to the bar with a seeming infinity of harmonic and rhythmic variations. Indianapolis-born, he moved to Los Angeles 45 years ago and established himself as first-call bass player for jazz and even the occasional rock gig; he even once did sessions for the bass-less Doors.

The Vee Jay album opens with a textbook demonstration of Vinnegar's double-stopping, playing two notes simultaneously. Merely doing this is impressive enough; investing it with a degree of musicality is something else entirely. Because he rarely solos, here or on the OJCs, much of the interest rests on what his band members are doing, but CD has been generous to him, pushing the bass up in the mix.

The earliest of the albums is probably still the most appealing. Gerald Wilson went on to find his forte in bandleading and large-scale arrangement, but, compared to the bland cut-outs which pass for solos from Hill on the 1962 session, his solos are well crafted and full of ideas and Edwards is as urbane and funky – if you can be both urbane and funky – as ever.

Vinnegar returned to recording as leader in 1992 with *Walkin' The Basses*. There had been stories of ill-health, perhaps even of retirement, but the Lairmont set, recorded in Bellingham, Washington, sees those lines pumping out with the regularity of a Stairmaster. It's basically a bebop set, with Bird's 'Segment', Hampton Hawes's 'Me Ho' and a cracking version of Freddie Hubbard's 'Little Sunflower'. Our index will point readers to many more sessions featuring Vinnegar, but these few discs are persuasive testimony to one of the unsung giants of the music.

Eddie 'Cleanhead' Vinson (1917–88)

ALTO SAXOPHONE, VOCALS

Played in swing bands in the 1930s and '40s, but later best known as an R&B-directed altoman and singer, although he wrote several bop staples such as 'Tune Up'. A memorable live face at the festivals of the '70s and '80s.

***** Jamming The Blues**
Black Lion BLCD 760188 *Vinson; Hal Singer (ts); Peter Wingfield (p); Joe Wright (g); Jerome Rinson (b); Peter Van Hooke (d). 7/74.*

***** I Want A Little Girl**
Original Jazz Classics OJC 868 *Vinson; Martin Banks (t); Rashied Jamal Ali (ts); Cal Green (g); Art Hillery (p, org); John Heard (b); Roy McCurdy (d). 2/81.*

A hugely entertaining singer/saxophonist, Vinson became a festival favourite in the 1970s, guesting with anyone who thought they could take his pace, playing Parker-tinged R&B with disconcerting self-possession. Some claim to find a Louis Jordan influence in Vinson's work, but this may have more to do with his performing personality than with any stylistic borrowing. The Montreux Festival set on *Jamming The Blues* includes a terrific 'Now's The Time' and some smoothly Parkerish solos on themes of his own and Ellington's 'C Jam Blues'.

The OJC features Vinson the festival personality with slightly heavy-fisted bands. *I Want A Little Girl* runs through a bag of blues numbers and contains a surprising 'Straight, No Chaser' and an excellent version of Pettiford's 'Blues In The Closet'.

Giulio Visibelli

TENOR AND SOPRANO SAXOPHONES, FLUTE

Contemporary Italian saxophonist-composer.

***** Il Grande Cerchio**
Splasc(h) 367-2 *Visibelli; Mitch Forman (ky); Marco Micheli (b); Bill Elgart (d). 3/92.*

***** Senza Parole**
Splasc(h) 499-2 *Visibelli; Sandro Gibellini (g); Franco Testa (b); Mauro Beggio (d). 4/96.*

Confident, if finally lightweight, these are dependable entries from a musician who's perhaps more interested in the writing and the overall result than in his own playing voice. The first disc is entirely self-composed and emerges as a series of thoughtful and carefully prepared set-pieces, each rising to a particular climax or making a textural or harmonic point before fading away. The emphasis on flute and soprano over the tenor suggests Visibelli's stance as an articulator rather than an improviser, and themes such as 'Sleeping Mice' are satisfying rather than intriguing. *Senza Parole* offers ten themes by contemporary Italian writers and, with the interesting Gibellini on board, the harmonies open out a little more. There's a rather surprising finale in 'Lontano Lontano', where guitar and saxophone go out on a limb, but otherwise this is mediated, polished, literate playing that certain tastes will find particularly agreeable.

Miroslav Vitous (born 1947)

DOUBLE BASS

Vitous studied classical music in his native Prague before going to America to study at Berklee. He worked with a variety of leaders, including Art Farmer and Miles Davis, before joining Weather Report as founding bassist. A professor and sometime head of jazz at the New England Conservatory, Vitous has maintained a quiet career, recording somewhat sporadically in later years.

***** Miroslav**
Freedom FCD 741040 *Vitous; Don Alias, Armen Halburian (perc). 76, 77.*

****(*) Guardian Angels**
Evidence 22055 *Vitous; Mabumi Yamaguchi (ss); Kenny Kirkland (p, syn, ky, g); John Scofield (g); George Ohtsuke (d). 11/78.*

After leaving Weather Report in 1973, having recorded three classic albums (he appears only briefly on *Mysterious Traveller*, the group's fourth release), Vitous experimented with various 'lead' and 'piccolo' basses, but he doesn't seem to have acquired the confidence in their use that made Stanley Clarke and a later Weather Report member, Jaco Pastorius, such charismatic figures (compare Vitous's and Pastorius's work with guitarist Bireli Lagrene, and that becomes clear). It took Vitous some time to re-establish the musical identity stamped all over his marvellous pre-Weather Report solo debut, *Infinite Search* (later re-released on Atlantic as *Mountain In The Clouds* (out of print)). The eponymous Freedom disc is packed with fascinating textures and makes clever use of overdubbing techniques. 'Pictures From Moravia' makes a first recorded appearance and there is a rather pretentiously titled 'Concerto In E Minor' which, at five and a half minutes, is scarcely more than a brief tone poem. 'Tiger In The Rain' is delightful, though, one of the most sophisticated concepts in the bassist's entire workbook. There's again a hint of awkwardness to the fusion idiom of *Guardian Angels*, which alternates rather ineffectually between jazz rock and softer, more impressionistic pieces. There are some delightful and unexpected sonorities, not least from the use of baritone guitar, but it's a patchy project, only of interest as a pointer to later work.

*****(*) First Meeting**
ECM 519280-2 *Vitous; John Surman (ss, bcl); Kenny Kirkland (p); Jon Christensen (d). 5/79.*

****** Journey's End**
ECM 843171-2 *As above, except add (bs) to Surman; omit Kirkland; add John Taylor (p). 7/82.*

***(*) **Emergence**

ECM 827855-2 *Vitous solo.* 9/85.

The first of the ECMs is a return to the thoughtful music-making of *Mountain In The Clouds*. Once again Vitous attempts to reintegrate the classical and folk-impressionistic elements on the earlier record into a much more coherent performance. Kirkland sets aside his electronic keyboards and turns in a performance of rippling grace. No problems with the recording-quality on *Journey's End* – the sound is rich and warm. That's also true of *First Meeting*, except that Kirkland's approach doesn't seem altogether appropriate for tunes like 'Silver Lake' and 'Beautiful Place To', too obviously jazz-based and funky and lacking Taylor's floating lyricism. Surman still wasn't playing any baritone when the first record was made, and its deep rich sound is much missed. *Emergence* is both a step forward and a summation. 'Morning Lake Forever' relates back to a composition on the first Weather Report record, and there's a new solo version of 'When Face Gets Pale' from *Miroslav Vitous Group*, which still hasn't appeared on CD. It begins with an 'Epilogue', which suggests a degree of self-reassessment, and though the 'Atlantis Suite' is rather too floating in conception (like the pretentiously titled 'Concerto in Three Parts' on *First Meeting*) there is a new solidity of purpose to his playing. Originally influenced by Scott LaFaro's remarkable performances with the Bill Evans Trio, Vitous has returned to something close to those singing lines. Though *Emergence* is a triumph, Vitous's best work still has to be sought out on the albums of other leaders, notably Chick Corea and Jack DeJohnette. Vitous also features prominently on two recent discs featuring Jan Garbarek: the duo, *Atmos*, and *Star*, widely hailed as the saxophonist's 'return to jazz'. Both are listed under Garbarek's name.

Eric Vloeimans (born 1963)

TRUMPET

Vloeimans is a talented young Dutchman who makes music of considerable individuality and presence. His credits include stints with Charlie Mariano, Jasper van't Hof, Ernst Reijseger and Aldo Romano.

*** **First Floor**

Challenge CHR 70011 *Vloeimans; Anton Goudsmit (g); Arnold Dooyeweerd (b); Pieter Bast (d).* 94.

*** **Bestiarium**

Challenge CHR 70038 *As above, except add Peter Weniger (ts, ss).* 6/96.

*** **Bitches And Fairy Tales**

Challenge A 59134-2 *Vloeimans; John Taylor (p); Marc Johnson (b); Joey Baron (d).* 98.

Vloeimans has the ability to hit you between the eyes with a single trumpet tone, to invest it with more sheer presence and personality than most players can muster in an evening. The debut album for Challenge, with whom he has developed across half a decade, was deft, expressive and attractively uncautious. Eric plays with a kind of controlled abandon. He has something in common with the critics' darling, Dave Douglas, in that he can deliver a free and complex idea with the simplicity and earthy tone of a conventional blues line.

He's a pretty decent writer as well, and on *Bestiarium* he unveils ten themes of memorable range and intensity. Apart from 'The Rabbit, The Fox, The Hunter And The Hole' and 'Elephant Walk', the album doesn't have much to do with critters. Weniger, who guests on six tracks, is a bit of an animal, but an ideal foil to Vloeimans's own rather contained approach. Interestingly for a player of his temperament, he isn't inclined to cut loose, and one frequently wants to hear the same material in a live context. The long 'For Jacq' – without saxophone – is a joy and perhaps the strongest single thing on the set, which is nicely paced, if a little arch. Hein Van De Geyn, one of the mainstays of the Dutch jazz scene, produces with a sure touch, combining good separation with the impact of a rock group.

The most recent album was recorded in New York and teamed Eric with a formidable band. John Taylor's credentials hardly need restating, and Marc Johnson is taste and elegance personified. The driving force behind the group, though, is Baron, whose electrifying percussion is the main force after the trumpet. Apart from the short duet with Taylor, 'Subway Closing Time', all the material is original, and Vloeimans confirms his standing with a set of tunes that sound deceptively familiar and at the same time fugitive and enigmatic. Surely 'Lightning And Twinkling' has been around for ever? On a Wayne Shorter or Herbie Hancock record maybe? Except that its core theme is reminiscent of the opening of a classical overture by Willem Pijper. Given Vloeimans's openness to ideas, that isn't such an unlikely source.

Petras Vysniauskias

SOPRANO SAXOPHONE, ALTO SAXOPHONE, BASS CLARINET, FLUTE

Lithuanian saxophonist blending a local folk heritage with free-jazz language.

*** **Viennese Concert**

Leo CDLR 172 *Vysniauskias; Vyacheslav Ganelin, Kestutis Lusas (p, syn); Mika Markovich (d); Gediminas Laurinavicius (perc).* 6/89.

(*) **Lithuania

ITM 1449 *Vysniauskias; Arkadij Gotesman (d, perc).* 6/90.

Vysniauskias is a gifted Lithuanian who demonstrates extraordinary command of all the saxophones, clarinets and flute. Like the Ganelin Trio, he favours what has been called a 'mixed composition technique', combining free improvisation with predetermined structures. In performance, he has a disconcerting habit of concentrating on the upper registers of the low-pitched instruments, and the lower register of his soprano saxophone and flute. This creates a very distinctive timbre that bears an unmistakable echo of folk music, and Vysniauskias has made significant use of Lithuanian forms in his compositions and performances.

Both of his available recordings suffer from considerable *longueurs* where the music doesn't seem to be going anywhere. The opening item of the *Viennese Concert* is a rather wistful soprano saxophone solo called 'Plunge' that has an inconsequential, practice-tape quality. The long – and presumably partly scored – 'Salto Mortale Op. 8' is a collage of free tonal, abstract and quasi-bop passages, all played with considerable restraint. Kestutis Lusas, who can also be heard in extended improvisation with the saxophonist on Leo's enormous eight-CD *Document* (Leo 801/8), is a much more effective collaborator than Ganelin, who has become increasingly mannered and self-conscious in settings other than those which he completely dominates. Lusas's solemn, hymnic synthesizer accompaniment to the saxophonist's distracted wailing on 'Salto Mortale' gives the piece some shape and restores interest in an album that really could have done with an early change of pace and intensity.

The duos with Gotesman are more obviously folkish. The opening 'Sonet' is dedicated to Lithuania and includes apparent references to pre-war anthems and popular songs. Like Markovich, Gotesman is quite prepared to make use of silence and of acoustically minimal gestures, tiny fragments of sound that barely register on the hearer. Vysniauskias plays bass clarinet and flute in addition to his saxophone, following his normal practice of concentrating on extremes of pitch. Ironically, this is something he avoids on the *Viennese Concert*, where his soprano playing is strikingly reminiscent of the rather dry tonality one associates with Steve Lacy.

Philipp Wachsmann (born 1944)

VIOLIN, VIOLA, ELECTRONICS

Ugandan-born Wachsmann studied with Nadia Boulanger and went on to devise his own form of neo-classicism within free music. A brilliant sound-sculptor, he has mainly been heard in other leaders' improvising ensembles, like the London Jazz Composers' Orchestra, Iskra 1903 and, more recently, Gush and Evan Parker's Electro-Acoustic Ensemble. Wachsmann also runs his own label, Bead Records.

***(*) Eleven Years From Yesterday

FMR CD-2-100988/Bead CD 01 *Wachsmann; Peter Jacobsen (p, hpd, syn); Ian Brighton (g); Marcio Mattos (b, clo); Trevor Taylor (perc). 10/88.*

Typical of the violinist's intrepid synthesis of neo-classicism and pure sound, a tightrope walk between Stravinsky and Varèse, these group improvisations are delicately executed by a highly sympathetic group of musicians who share many of Wachsmann's concerns. Jacobsen's keyboard work is astonishing, combining formality with the most unhierarchical approach imaginable.

Wachsmann deploys his electronics with virtuosic precision, never introducing an effect merely for its own sake, much as Georg Trakl, from whose death-songs all the titles are derived, never used a word but for maximum expressive impact. The three central pieces – 'On sombre boat he rode', 'Down the shimmering torrents' and 'Full of purple stars' – are exquisite group creations and it's only during the very last track that the pace and expression seem to flag, an example of more not necessarily being a good thing.

*** Icarus

FMR CD15 V1298 *Wachsmann; Mark Wastell (clo); Roger Curphy (b); Trevor Taylor (perc, elec); Carol Ann Jackson (v). 8/95.*

*** Chathuna

Bead CD 03 *Wachsmann (solo). 10/96.*

Icarus flies a little too close to the sun of pure abstraction. The wax melts and eventually the music takes a disappointing tumble. The five improvisations seem to call for some stronger structural rationale than each receives. Wachsmann's playing is as focused and provocative as ever, and there are a couple of occasions, notably on the two long closing tracks, where one would like to extract his playing and hear the violinist on his own, as he is on *Chathuna.*

It was conceived in collaboration with artist Sarah Eckel, whose work is shown on the cover, and was recorded in the Synagogue at Oerlinghausen. In recent times, Wachsmann has talked about a hidden pulse in his music. That is clearly audible here. 'Point Of Departure', the opening piece, has nothing to do with Andrew Hill's jazz masterpiece; but the underlying metre and the carefully layered harmonics come from broadly the same tradition. Though Wachsmann has seemed the least jazz-based and most academic of the British-based free-music specialists, that may now be changing, or it may always have been illusory.

Easy to hear from this how readily he would fit into saxophonist Evan Parker's electronic project. Wachsmann shares Evan's interest in complex mathematical procedures and high-harmonic improvisation, where the calculus of sound is the key concern.

**** Some Other Season

ECM 557366-2 *Wachsmann; Paul Lytton (perc, elec). 10/97.*

The two brightest sparks in Parker's Electro-Acoustic Ensemble went back into the studio as a duo. Lytton dusted off a lot of his old percussion and together they cut a modern masterpiece. The unexpected jazz feel creeps in again, notably on 'Shuffle' and 'Whispering Chambers', though it's the latter (and not 'Shuffle', as producer Steve Lake suggests) which bears the obvious kinship to Monk.

As expected, and as is now very much part of the ECM ethos, both solos and duos were recorded. Lytton does some wonderful things, 'Leonardo's Spoon', 'Nu Shu' and 'Shell', while Wachsmann seems more comfortable this time out working in partnership, though he saves his very best and straightest playing of the set for the penultimate solo, 'From The Chalk Cliffs'.

Impeccably played and recorded, this will appeal to new-music listeners and jazz fans as well as to those devoted to the European improvisation scene.

Steve Waddell

TROMBONE, VOCAL

Aussie trombonist and bandleader, a relative youngster among the seasoned pros of the game; his Creole Bells band plays in the trad style that mixes Lu Watters and Graeme Bell.

***** Egyptian Ella**

Stomp Off CD 1230 *Waddell; Bob Pattie (c); Dafydd Wisner-Ellix (cl, ss, perc, v); Doug Rawson (p); John Brown (bj); Fred Clark (tba).* 12/90–2/91.

***** Along The Road**

Stomp Off CD 1301 *As above, except Eric Holroyd (c), Mike Edwards (cl, as, v), Tony Orr (bj) replace Wisner-Ellix and Brown.* 6/95.

*****(*) Waltzing Matilda**

Stomp Off CD 1348 *As above, except add Hans Karssemeyer (p), Richard Opat (d, wbd); omit Rawson.* 3/98.

Steve Waddell's Creole Bells come from Melbourne, Australia, and they offer an amiable continuation of the kind of down-under trad that Graeme Bell initiated some 40 years earlier. The absence of a drummer on the first two discs frees the group from the tyranny of the trad beat to some degree, although Fred Clark's gruff bass-lines are suitably ponderous. Waddell's noisy trombone and the scratchily hot solos by Pattie give the group its character, and the material is inventively chosen; on the minus side, at times the vocals are close to hopeless, though the later discs fare better in this regard! *Along The Road* focuses on local composers like Roger Bell and Ian Pearce and is a nice change of menu, but it's *Waltzing Matilda* which shows them at their best. The two-cornet front line (Holroyd is still listed only as a guest – when's he joining full time?) is in cracking form, Karssemeyer (who died in 1999) plays excellent piano, but above all the arrival of Richard Opat really lights a fire under the group's collective tail.

Harvey Wainapel

ALTO SAXOPHONE, TENOR SAXOPHONE, SOPRANO SAXOPHONE, CLARINET

Contemporary saxophonist here delivering a tribute to Kenny Barron.

*****(*) Ambrosia – The Music Of Kenny Barron**

A Records AL 73060 *Wainapel; Ilja Reijngoud (tb); Cor Bakker (p); Marco Silva (ky, perc); Carlos Oliveira (g, zabumba); Rich Kuhns (acc); Jeff Buenz, Rob Langereis (b); Celso Alberty, Kees Kranenburg (d); Mark Lamson, Michael Spiro (perc); Metropole Orchestra; Rob Pronk (cond).* 4 & 12/95, 1/96.

Only someone who hasn't been collecting jazz records over the last 20–30 years could possibly wonder at the idea of a tribute to Kenny Barron. He has been one of the great accompanists and also one of the most idiomatic jazz composers of recent times, and saxophonist Wainapel's devotion is wholly justified, if not by track record, then certainly by these nine elegantly crafted tracks. The first five are with the Metropole Orchestra, a suite of arrangements by Jeff Beal. The title-piece is a dialogue between Wainapel and bassist Langereis, an exquisitely flavoured theme with endless potential for both soloists. 'Lullaby' is for alto alone, a long, weaving melody which is perhaps the leader's best moment on the disc. The final four tracks reflect Barron's Latin side. These are less successful, largely because Wainapel isn't obviously at home in this territory, preferring a more abstract and less pulse-driven idiom. Silva is the key collaborator, though Rich Kuhns makes a delicious noise on 'Sambao', which almost everyone – collector or casual listener – will recognize.

Ulf Wakenius

GUITAR

Swedish guitarist moving between mainstream and more fusion-orientated situations.

***** Venture**

L + R CDLR 45052 *Wakenius; Randy Brecker (t); Bob Berg, Bill Evans (ts); Lars Danielsson, Niels Lan Doky (ky); Lars Danielsson, Christian Minh Doky (b); Jack DeJohnette (d).* 1/91.

***** First Step**

Imogena IGCD 034 *Wakenius; Ove Ingmarsson (ts); Lars Jansson (ky); Lars Danielsson (b); Raymond Karlsson (d).* 10/92.

****(*) Enchanted Moments**

Dragon DRCD 278 *As above, except omit Ingmarsson.* 10/95–3/96.

***** Live**

Dragon DRCD 347 *Wakenius; Ake Johansson (p); Yasuhito Mori (b); Magnus Gran (d).* 4/99.

It's taken us time to catch up with Wakenius, whose playing impresses without quite suggesting a recording artist of striking originality. As a technician, he plays the electric instrument with a precision and attention to tone that imply a cool head no matter what the situation. There's a good example on the opening track of *Venture*, where a full-on blow-out for all hands is mastered by the leader: his own playing is as heated as Bob Berg's, but with a sense of symmetry and control which the saxophonist's more intemperate playing seems oblivious to. The 'local' band on the Imogena session surrenders nothing to the all-star outfit on the first date, and each has its share of invigorating music, but the first Dragon date specifically turns down the intensity with Wakenius sticking to acoustic over a series of sometimes anodyne backings. His treatment of 'Blame It On My Youth' on *First Step* presaged the quiescent music of this third disc, but some of it is all too pretty and unembellished. Yet when he gives himself the space to improvise a chorus, as on the translucent version of 'Cry Me A River', one wonders why he bothers with the smooth-jazz prettiness of much of the rest.

Live opens with a dedication to Wes Montgomery, 'The Greatest Of Them All', and by himself Wakenius creates a benign pastorale. But that's quickly displaced by 'Notes To J.C.', some 20 minutes of full-on hard-bop quartet music. Wakenius doesn't really sustain these long solos beyond their sheer momentum, but it's exciting to hear when propelled by Mori and the bullish Gran. Plenty to enjoy.

Collin Walcott (1945–84)

TABLAS, SITAR, PERCUSSION INSTRUMENTS, VOICE

Studied violin, percussion and – with Ravi Shankar – sitar, joining the Paul Winter Consort in 1970 and Oregon in 1971.

Remained with that group until his death. A pioneer 'world' jazz musician.

***(*) **Cloud Dance**

ECM 825469-2 *Walcott; John Abercrombie (g); Dave Holland (b); Jack DeJohnette (d).* 3/75.

***(*) **Grazing Dreams**

ECM 827866-2 *Walcott; Don Cherry (t, f, doussn'gouni); John Abercrombie (g, electric mand); Palle Danielsson (b); Dom Um Romao (perc).* 2/77.

*** **Dawn Dance**

ECM 829375-2 *Walcott; Steve Eliovson (g).* 1/81.

Walcott's sudden death in a road accident in (then) East Germany robbed contemporary music of a remarkable player who, more than any other individual of his generation (except, perhaps, his friend and Codona colleague, Don Cherry), was possessed of a genuinely global understanding. It's significant that the classically trained Walcott, who also studied tabla under Alla Rakha and sitar under Ravi Shankar, should have spent some professional time with clarinettist Tony Scott, one of the first American musicians to understand and explore the trade-off between Eastern and Western musics. What is often forgotten about Walcott is that, for all his occasionally ethereal effects, he is capable of a thumpingly compelling beat on tablas and robust bass-lines on the normally 'atmospheric' sitar. Like most musicians of his generation, Walcott was much influenced by the John Coltrane quartet. However, few have so thoroughly explored the implications of Coltrane's masterful rhythm section. Walcott was instrumental in inviting drummer Elvin Jones to colla-borate on a (long-deleted) recording by Oregon, a venture which emphasized and reinforced the group's solid rhythmic foundation.

Though *Grazing Dreams* has much to recommend it, *Cloud Dance* has a freshness and originality that sustain its appeal. 'Prancing', for just tablas and double bass, is one of the most exciting performances in the ECM catalogue and convincing evidence of Walcott's desire to extend the idiom of the Garrison/Jones rhythm section. Of the other duos, 'Padma', for sitar and guitar, works less well; but the album as a whole can quite reasonably be heard as a suite of related pieces that dance towards their thematic source in the closing title-piece. The quartet format on *Grazing Dreams* inevitably anticipates Walcott's and Cherry's work with Codona, and the long 'Song Of The Morrow' is a perfect encapsulation of the group's idiom.

Walcott's duo record with guitarist Eliovson is undeservedly little known and is well worth investigating, opening up just another corner of this extraordinary talent, an almost folksy sound, cool and fresh. In retrospect, Walcott's best and most characteristic work was with Oregon (and to a lesser extent Codona). The surviving members have pointed out how fundamental he was to the philosophy of both groups and, in the case of Oregon, genuinely irreplaceable.

Mal Waldron (born 1926)

PIANO

Waldron has effectively had two careers, divided by a catastrophic nervous breakdown in 1963. Up to that point, he had worked with Ike Quebec, Charles Mingus and, most memorably, Billie Holiday, with whom he stayed until her death in 1959. He also established himself as a distinctive recording artist with a darkly lyrical style. After his illness he had to begin afresh, and he emerged from the shadows with a new sound: percussive, minor-keyed and often long-lined, and much influenced by his move to Europe.

***(*) **Update**

Soul Note 121130-2 *Waldron (p solo).* 3/86.

An immensely gifted and prolific player whose professional roots are in the raw soul-jazz of Big Nick Nicholas and Ike Quebec, Waldron typically builds up solos from relatively simple ideas (his classic, much-covered 'Soul Eyes' could hardly be less elaborate), paying great attention to colour and shading, and to space. He favours block chords rather than rapid single-note runs, a style which has lent itself equally to large ensembles and smaller blowing groups (he worked with Mingus and Coltrane in the mid-1950s and early 1960s), sensitive accompaniment (he spent more than two years with Billie Holiday), and free playing. Though it's clear that Waldron's main influences are Bud Powell and Thelonious Monk, he has developed independently and sounds quite unlike either. Until relatively recently he has not been a prolific solo performer, and this record is by no means hisbest music; but it does allow closer inspection of his compositional and improvising style and it helps establish the brand identity of one of the labels which have consistently supported his work, Enja giving him a darker and more lugubrious sound, Soul Note a sunnier, clearer focus. Unfortunately, the Enja vinyl catalogue has taken a pasting and, while it may be possible to find vinyl copies like *Mingus Lives*, recorded one week after the great bassist's death, *Black Glory, A Touch Of The Blues, Hard Talk, One-Upmanship* and *What It Is* (all of which are reviewed in the first edition of the *Guide*), there is as yet no sign of them on compact disc.

Update is unusual in including a standard (in addition to 'Night In Tunisia', there is a very individual gloss on a Frank Loesser tune); Waldron has generally preferred to spin his own material out of dark, minor intervals and from an area in the centre of the keyboard, using extremes of pitch only for dramatic contrast and colour effects. *Update* also further adjusts Waldron's polite reserve *vis-à-vis* free playing, which he explored with the 1969 *Free At Last* trio, below. Taken together, 'Free For C.T.' and 'Variations On A Theme By Cecil Taylor' firmly underscore Waldron's rugged individualism and refusal to be colonized by what has become the most invasive of contemporary piano styles. The variations are subtly rhythmic and beautifully proportioned. This is an important album in Waldron's career, coming at a time when his group performances were also at a peak. It merits the closest attention.

***** Mal – 1**

Original Jazz Classics OJC 611 *Waldron; Idrees Sulieman (t); Gigi Gryce (as); Julian Euell (b); Arthur Edgehill (d).* 11/56.

***** Mal – 2**

Original Jazz Classics OJC 671 *Waldron; Bill Hardman (t); Jackie McLean, Sahib Shihab (as); John Coltrane (ts); Julian Euell (b); Art Taylor, Ed Thigpen (d).* 4 & 5/57.

***** Mal – 3: Sounds**

Original Jazz Classics OJC 1814 *Waldron; Art Farmer (t); Eric Dixon (ts); Calo Scott (clo); Julian Euell (b); Elvin Jones (d).* 58.

*****(*) Mal – 4**

Original Jazz Classics OJC 1856 *Waldron; Addison Farmer (b); Kenny Dennis (d).* 9/58.

****** Impressions**

Original Jazz Classics OJC 132 *Waldron; Addison Farmer (b); Albert 'Tootie' Heath (d).* 59.

***** Left Alone**

Bethlehem BET 6024-2 *Waldron; Jackie McLean (as); Julian Euell (b); Al Dreares (d).* 2/59.

Despite Sulieman's and Gryce's bursting expressiveness, the first OJC is a low-key selection from Waldron's Prestige period, which saw the pianist concentrating on sophisticated harmonic patterns and cross-rhythms. The sound – as they used to say about serving girls – is no better than it ought to be, but, given the anonymity of the rhythm section, not much is lost. A fine 'Yesterdays' picks things up a bit at the end. All the same material can also be found on a high-gloss Coltrane on Prestige set (16 CDs for Gold Card types) and, if anything, sounds rather sharper there.

The later tracks with Coltrane and McLean are inevitably of greatest interest. Waldron made substantial strides as a composer towards the end of the 1950s and that's reflected in his solo construction, too. In 1957, Coltrane had finally decided to rid himself of a deeply rooted drug and alcohol dependency. It isn't reading too much into basically conventional performances to suggest that his solos have a new maturity, coupled with an emotional vulnerability, which McLean seems to comprehend better than the rather single-minded Shihab, but round which Waldron steals with unfailing tact and supportive ease. No classic tracks, though 'Don't Explain' (with McLean) and 'The Way You Look Tonight' (with Shihab) are a cut above the rest.

Mal – 3 already shows signs of the tremendous stresses and tensions that make *Impressions* such a darkly wonderful record; there is even a track at the beginning of the 1958 disc called 'Tension', as if to signal what's coming. There is something extremely uncomfortable about listening to Waldron at this period. The echoes of Bud Powell are unmistakable and faintly sinister, given the breakdown in Waldron's health just a couple of years later. 'Champs Elysées' and 'With A Song In My Heart' are both outwardly sanguine but, all the way through, Waldron is inverting harmonies, throwing in minor-key variations, generally changing the emotional temper. It's a stern experience, but a rewarding and chastening one. *Mal – 4* skins the line-up back to a trio and is again rather Janus-faced in its delivery: compare the opening 'Splidium-Dow' with the subsequent 'Get Happy' (!), interestingly enough another favourite of Powell's. These are scarce and rather little-known records in their original form and deserve to be in wider currency. The Bethlehem reissue comes on like a footnote to the OJCs and is relatively slight, but collectors will welcome McLean's guest appearance on the title-piece, and there is also a spoken reminiscence from Mal regarding the then lately-deceased Billie Holiday.

*****(*) Free At Last**

ECM 831332-2 *Waldron; Isla Eckinger (b); Clarence Beckton (d).* 11/69.

To call Waldron 'unmelodic' is a description, not a criticism. He has rarely written memorable tunes, concentrating instead on subtly coded tonal cells out of which, as his career has continued, longer and longer improvisations can be developed. *Free At Last* was a conscious attempt to come to terms with free jazz; in Waldron's own words, it represented his desire to play 'rhythmically instead of soloing on chord changes'. At the same time, Waldron utterly rejects any notion of free jazz as 'complete anarchy or disorganized sound'. At first glance, these half-dozen tracks are disappointingly constrained and modest in scope. The long 'Rat Now' (a typical Waldron pun) and 'Rock My Soul' point a way forward for extended improvisation that does not depend on chord sequences; but, interestingly, both have the same 'feel' as more conventionally harmonic music because Waldron's clusters always seem to gravitate towards specific resolutions. A useful trivia question, especially for anyone who wields the 'ECM sound' *canard* too freely, is to ask what the label's very first release was. If one quality characterizes ECM's output, it has been a search for new principles of organization in jazz, its only constraint a rejection of anarchic disorganization. *Free At Last* was a fine send-off.

*****(*) Blues For Lady Day**

Black Lion BLCD 760193 *Waldron; Henk Haverhoek (b); Pierre Courbois (d).* 2/72.

Bassist and drummer figure on only the last two tracks, recorded a few days later, down the road from Baarn in Leiden. They're interesting pieces: after the brooding intro, 'A.L.B.O.M.' (or 'A Little Bit Of Miles'), is thoroughly untypical Waldron, distributed all over the keyboard and with considerable dynamic variation; 'Here, There And Everywhere' (*not* the Beatles tune) is an arresting exercise in pace and variation, constantly speeding up and retarding the beat. He fares pretty well with the rhythm section, who seem to understand what he's about, but the meat of the record is still the solo stuff, a vintage selection of tunes associated with his one-time boss, Billie Holiday. On 'Strange Fruit' he goes off into territory darker than Billie ever trod, and his version of 'The Man I Love' is convincingly anguished.

****** One-Upmanship**

Enja ENJ 2092 *Waldron; Steve Lacy (ss); Jimmy Woode (b); Makaya Ntoshko (d).* 2/77.

Waldron also kicked off the Enja label with *Black Glory*, recorded a couple of years after he helped launch ECM with *Free At Last*. His most important recording for the Ludwigsburg label, though, was the one he made with Steve Lacy in 1977. It has been out of circulation for a long time and its return is most welcome as Waldron approaches his 75th birthday. *One-Upmanship* alternates group tracks with solo performances. All the material is original and it includes two Waldron classics, 'Hooray For Herbie' and the extraordinary 'Seagulls of Kristiansund', a theme that was to become a staple of his live gigs in subsequent years.

Not surprisingly, it's Lacy who provides the birdsong, while Mal nudges away at the dark, minor tonality of the piece. Woode and Ntoshko don't on the face of it seem likely partners in the rhythm section, but the chemistry has rarely been bettered and Jimmy's solid support is a valuable counterweight to Waldron's melancholic side.

*****(*) Moods**

Enja 3021 *Waldron solo, and with Terumasa Hino (t); Hermann Breuer (tb); Steve Lacy (ss); Cameron Brown (b); Cameron Ntoshko (d).* 5/78.

The mid- to late 1970s was a vintage spell in Waldron's career. With perverse predictability, it's here that the biggest hole in the current discography (apart from the gap in the '60s when the pianist's health collapsed almost fatally) should occur. His improvisations were stretching out and growing more adventurous as he absorbed the lessons of free playing. In this regard, the association with Lacy was of paramount importance. Though they seem fundamentally opposed in basic aesthetics, it's clear that Lacy's dry abstraction is only a continual refinement of his Dixieland roots. He swings with absolute conviction on all these sides. The absent *Hard Talk* remains the most compelling. *Moods* is much more varied, with an extra horn in the ensembles and a valuable sample of Waldron's rather mournful solo style; 'Soul Eyes' and 'I Thought About You' are beautiful and serve as reminders of the pianist's contact with Coltrane; but 'Anxiety','Lonely', 'Thoughtful' and 'Happiness' sound like 'face-pulling' exercises; and the soft, Monkish figurations of 'Duquility' are rather too elliptical. Waldron hits the keys with uncommon firmness, perhaps unused to or unsatisfied with the piano, perhaps merely trying new levels of attack.

***** Dedication**

Soul Note 121178-2 *Waldron; David Friesen (b).* 11/85.

Something of an oddity, but an enjoyable one. Friesen's floating, soft-edged bass-lines (played on an amplified, bodyless instrument, credited as 'Oregon bass') actually work rather well over Waldron's dark mutterings, and the set as a whole has a coherence and unity that begin to sound slightly repetitive only on subsequent hearings.

****** Songs Of Love And Regret**

Freelance FRL CD006 *Waldron; Marion Brown (as).* 11/85.

*****(*) Much More!**

Freelance FRL CD010 *As above.* 11/88.

****** Sempre Amore**

Soul Note 121170-2 *Waldron; Steve Lacy (ss).* 2/86.

*****(*) Art Of The Duo**

Tutu 888106 *Waldron; Jim Pepper (ts, ss).* 88.

For straightforward beauty these are unsurpassed in Waldron's output. Clearly there is a sharp difference between Brown's waveringly pitched emotionalism and Lacy's dry phrasing (and between either and Jim Pepper's almost folksy delivery); but in all cases the two saxophonists get inside the song, concentrating in a manner one doesn't normally associate with Waldron on developing the melody. *Sempre Amore* is dedicated to Ellington–Strayhorn material, which must have made an intriguing change from Lacy's specialized diet of Monk. The two Freelances are more eclectic, taking in 'All God's Chillun Got Rhythm' and 'Now's The Time' (*Much More!*), McCoy Tyner's 'Contemplation' and (for comparison with the Lacy set) 'A Flower Is A Lovesome Thing' (*Love And Regret*). The earlier set opens with a slightly hesitant 'Blue Monk' (the CD reissue includes a rejected take that comes in at double the length and is far superior), which is then glossed in Waldron's own 'A Cause De Monk' and Brown's own 'To The Golden Lady In Her Graham Cracker Window', a typically delicate tune. Pepper gets a hold of 'Somewhere Over The Rainbow' and gives it the kind of gruff bear-hug that he often brought to ballads. A reading of 'Ruby My Dear' is less successful, though Waldron clearly has no worries about the tonality. The originals favour the saxophonist's relaxed blues phrasing. A vintage selection. Not for hardened cynics.

*****(*) The Git Go**

Soul Note 121118-2 *Waldron; Woody Shaw (t, flhn); Charlie Rouse (ts, f); Reggie Workman (b); Ed Blackwell (d).* 9/86.

****** The Seagulls Of Kristiansund**

Soul Note 121148-2 *As above.* 9/86.

Two top-flight sets from a single night of a fine week's engagement at the Village Vanguard in New York City. All six compositions are Waldron's and his playing is supremely economical, sketching in tonal centres with a minimum of elaboration, soloing on the faster tracks with a positive touch, shading beautifully on the slow 'Seagulls Of Kristiansund'. This shows a side of Waldron's work which some critics have likened to American minimalism: a slow accretion of almost subliminal harmonic and rhythmic shifts steadily pile up until the music seems ready to overbalance. Perhaps oddly – for subsequent releases from live or studio sessions rarely match up to the original albums – the second album is more appealing. *The Git Go* consists of no more than the title-piece and an overlong 'Status Seeking', which seems to have lost much of the terse discipline Waldron brought to it on *The Quest*. On the second album, Waldron kicks off 'Snake Out' with a menacing bass pulse that builds up almost unbearable tension before loosing Woody Shaw on one of his most unfettered solos. Rouse's solo is more compact and provides a taut bridge between Shaw and Waldron, who plays lyrically over a bleak vamp. Blackwell and Workman both solo effectively, though the drummer's finest moment comes at the end of 'Judy', the middle track of the set and a tribute to Waldron's great supporter, Judy Sneed. Shaw's solo is astonishing. Blackwell shines again on 'Seagulls', producing non-metrical effects on his splash cymbal; Workman's foghorn and seabird effects are straight out of Mingus's bag. *The Git Go* has some *longueurs*, but its successor is thoroughly and straightforwardly enjoyable, and should be tried for size.

****** Our Colline's A Tresure**

Soul Note 121198-2 *Waldron; Leonard Jones (b); Sangoma Everett (d).* 4/87.

Still on a high. Waldron's handling of 'The Git Go' is markedly different from that on the Village Vanguard sessions, tighter in conception, if not in length, and with most of the solo space inevitably restored to the composer. The opening 'Spaces' is a superb example of direct motivic improvisation and lets in Jones for the first of several fine contributions. Everett, a neighbour of Waldron's in Munich, is less well known but sounds more than competent. The title-piece (and the mis-spelt word is probably deliberate) is dedicated to a young French friend of Waldron's, who may grow up to tresure the beautiful waltz-tune better than she will the picture on the cover.

*** Mal Dance And Soul

Tutu 888102 *Waldron; Jim Pepper (ts); Ed Schuller (b); John Betsch (d).* 11/87.

***(*) Quadrologue At Utopia

Tutu 888118 *As above.* 10/89.

***(*) The Git-Go At Utopia, Volume 2

Tutu 888148 *As above.* 10/89.

Good, mostly new material from Waldron's late-1980s band. As with Clifford Jordan, above, it is Pepper's peculiar tonality that fits him for this context. The saxophonist, who is of American-Indian descent, appears only on 'Soulmates' in the 1987 session, but he is a full-blooded presence on the aptly named *Quadrologue* and is especially good on the atmospheric 'Mistral Breeze'. Though less versatile than Joe Lovano (with whom he used to work in the Paul Motian group), Pepper has an enormous emotional range and the kind of innate rhythmic sophistication that Waldron requires. The leader sounds faintly muted on 'Ticket To Utopia' but warms towards an excellent finish on 'Funny Glasses & A Moustache'.

The second volume (and as a pairing these are interestingly comparable to the 1986 Soul Notes, one of which shares the title) maintains the standard, with – if anything – a stronger showing from Waldron himself. 'The Git-Go' now sounds so well worn as to have been around for ever. Even so, the leader still finds new things to do with it, reversing the changes in a later section and transposing his own accompaniment down through the keys in weird minor intervals that suggest the whole thing is suddenly going to come apart.

*** No More Tears (For Lady Day)

Timeless SJP 328 *Waldron; Joey Cardoso (b); John Betsch (d).* 11/88.

Unlike *You And The Night And The Music*, this one doesn't really get off the ground. Waldron has clearly reached a point in his career where he is prepared to re-examine a more traditional jazz repertoire, and it would be cynical to suggest that the choice of material was conditioned by his sidemen's limitations. Betsch is one of the finest European-based drummers, but Cardoso is a plodding fellow whose solo on the opening 'Yesterdays' begins to pall before he has got himself properly warmed up. This comes from a Timeless series dedicated to the preservation of the traditional piano trio (almost as if they were steam engines or an endangered species). Fortunately, Waldron does a fine conservation job on his own, injecting new life into warhorses like 'Smoke Gets In Your Eyes' and 'Alone Together', which used to be as plentiful in the catalogue as buffalo on the plains of Wisconsin but which seem to have been exploited to death and appear much more rarely on standards sets of late.

**** Crowd Scene

Soul Note 121218 *Waldron; Sonny Fortune (as); Ricky Ford (ts); Reggie Workman (b); Eddie Moore (d).* 6/89.

***(*) Where Are You?

Soul Note 121248 *As above.* 6/89.

'Crowd Scene' is a large-scale piece that attempts to capture the point at which individual elements begin to cohere and act in unison, as a collectivity. Waldron has always liked to describe himself as a parcel of disparate elements, held together by chance, everyday necessities, good luck, rather than by any pressing philosophy; and something of that seems to underline this piece. 'Yin And Yang', the other long track, perhaps represents a more specific and settled viewpoint, but one that in no way contradicts the first. Like 'Crowd Scene', it's held together by riffs and *ostinati*, rather than by any single principle of development. The two saxophonists, who managed to dramatize a sense of diversity and questioning plurality in the first piece, are not so much opposites as two sides of a single reality in the second, playing in close intervals but with markedly different timbres. The effect is very powerful, and engineer Kazunori Sugiyama has done a marvellous job capturing it so accurately. For once, it's good to have Waldron in the studio. Much would have been lost in a club or concert hall. There's a bit of padding on the second disc; only a second and longer take of 'Where Are You?' takes it up over the 50-minute mark. However, what there is is so good that no casual purchaser will feel short-changed. 'Waltz For Marianne' is gorgeous, with Workman playing a prominent role. One feels that, with a little judicious editing, an absolutely top-flight single CD could have been made out of these.

***(*) Waldron–Haslam

Slam 305 *Waldron; George Haslam (bs).* 2/94.

*** Two New

Slam 306 *Waldron; George Haslam (bs, tarogato).* 4/95.

Spells of indifferent health have slowed up Waldron's recording regimen of late. These engaging duet records with British baritone man Haslam don't have the gravitas and sheer monumentality of the best Waldron, but their friendly dialogue has its own rewards and at some moments – especially in the two improvised pieces on the first disc, 'Catch As Catch Should' and 'Motion In Order' – there is the trademark dry, lyrical intensity which is in all of the pianist's best work. Though Haslam might have been outclassed, especially in having to step into the shoes of some of Waldron's other horn partners, his light, flexible lines make an attractively serene counterpoint. Excellent recording on both discs.

**** Soul Eyes

RCA 74321 538872 *Waldron; Steve Coleman (as); Joe Henderson (ts); Reggie Workman (b); Andrew Cyrille (d); Abbey Lincoln (v).* 96.

A glorious set, celebrating a master musician. The band is exactly the kind of line-up he thrives on. Cyrille's polyphonic drumming, Reggie Workman's dark bass, the two saxophonists, a generation apart but taking a similar line on 'The Git Go' (Joe Henderson) and 'Soul Eyes' (Steve Coleman), while last but not least the singer brings a touch of magic to this set by an artist for whom songs have always been a central component of his musical thinking. 'God Bless The Child' and 'Straight Ahead' are magnificent features for Abbey Lincoln, who emotes a course through the songs without a hint of excess. A lovely album from a master who may at last be finding his moment in the mainstream.

***** Travellin' In Soul-Time**

BVHaast CD 9701 *Waldron; Toru Tenda (f); Jeanne Lee (v).* 96.

Recorded live in Tokyo, Nagasaki and Kobuchizawa, this remarkable trio combine traditional Japanese material with some of Mal's most culturally ambiguous work, pieces like 'Black Rain' (who could guess at its provenance?) and the perennial 'The Seagulls of Kristiansund', which has never sounded fresher or more unexpected. Jeanne Lee is not just a wonderful singer but a masterful musician, and her contribution to this album is bound to invite comparison with Mal's interaction with Billie Holiday. The additional element of Toru Tenda's delicate but piercing flute (serving a similar role to Steve Lacy's soprano saxophone in past encounters) makes for a fresh and unexpected collection of performances that suggest Waldron still refuses to stand still but continues to explore fresh musical and cultural territory.

Dan Wall

ORGAN

Best known for his work with guitarist John Abercrombie's trio, Wall is very much his own man, influenced by – but independent of – the example of Jimmy Smith and Larry Young.

***** Off The Wall**

Enja ENJ 9310-2 *Wall; Ingrid Jensen (t); Lester Larue, Karl Ratzer (g); Adam Nussbaum (d).* 7/96.

Wall works some interesting wrinkles on the old guitar-trio format, adding the gifted Jensen and giving her an open, breezy context. His own playing is right, funky and full of unexpected ideas. 'The End Of A Love Affair' is the most substantial statement, but 'The Electric Ballroom' is a fascinating piece, too. Hard to believe that Wall hasn't listened to Weather Report. His bass lines are irresistibly reminiscent of Joe Zawinul's, but the melodies are very different, folky and North American, without Joe's odd synthesis of classical forms and the blues.

Ratzer is by no means the subtle stylist John Abercrombie is. He plays clipped but elaborate lines, strung out into long forms that fit the organ shapes and the percussion track (oddly recorded) almost perfectly. Much as with the Abercrombie trio (who always sounded more convincing in a club setting), a live album would be good.

Bennie Wallace (born 1946)

TENOR SAXOPHONE

Born in Chattanooga, he studied clarinet in college and arrived in New York in the '70s. Kept a swing-era perspective on his playing while still aware of the Rollins–Coltrane tradition. Departed for California in 1990 and has written much film music since.

***** The Fourteen Bar Blues**

Enja 3029 *Wallace; Eddie Gomez (b); Eddie Moore (d).* 1/78.

***** The Free Will**

Enja 3063 *Wallace; Tommy Flanagan (p); Eddie Gomez (b); Dannie Richmond (d).* 1–2/80.

***** The Bennie Wallace Trio And Chick Corea**

Enja 4028 *As above, except Chick Corea (p) replaces Flanagan.* 5/82.

*****(*) Plays Monk**

Enja 3091 *Wallace; Jimmy Knepper (tb); Eddie Gomez (b); Dannie Richmond (d).* 3/81.

*****(*) Big Jim's Tango**

Enja 4046 *Wallace; Dave Holland (b); Elvin Jones (d).* 11–12/82.

***** Sweeping Through The City**

Enja 4078 *Wallace; Ray Anderson (tb); Pat Conley (p); John Scofield (g); Mike Richmond, Dennis Irwin (b); Tom Whaley (d); The Wings of Song (v).* 3/84.

A traditionalist of the best kind, Bennie Wallace has made a lot of highly entertaining records without quite finding the bigger audience his populist music might reach. His trio albums give him the space he enjoys and set up his Sonny Rollins influence to its most effective ends: the grand, swaggering rhythms and tonal exaggerations buttress an improvising style which owes much to R&B and roadhouse music, a greasiness which can distract from the intense structures that Wallace can work together. He isn't a licks player, doesn't dawdle in clichés, and the essential heartiness of his music is deceptive, for he provides greater rewards for listeners who are prepared to work with him. The first trio albums suffer just a little from a slightly awkward mix of personalities: Gomez's rubbery virtuosity doesn't always suit Wallace's moves, even if they clearly enjoy playing together, and the following *The Free Will* is also too gentlemanly, through Flanagan's characteristically professorial touch. Chick Corea's guest appearance doesn't do anything much for the trio – only Corea could contribute a tune called 'Mystic Bridge' to follow a Wallace original entitled 'The Bob Crosby Blues' – and, while Gomez follows the pianist, Richmond tends to stick with the tenorman. The Monk collection ups the ante: Wallace likes these tunes, he picks a couple of the less obvious ones, and Jimmy Knepper sits in on three tracks for a typically quizzical dialogue. The line-up for *Big Jim's Tango* is another formidable one – Wallace has never been shy of playing with his peers – and the extravagant terpsichorea of 'Big Jim Does The Tango For You' is in some ways the definitive Wallace performance. Holland and Jones are their unimpeachable selves, here and elsewhere. *Sweeping Through The City* invents some gospel roots for Bennie via the roistering contribution of The Wings of Song on two tracks; the rest is neo-bop and blues, with Anderson and Scofield adding their own characteristic thoughts to the mixture.

*****(*) The Old Songs**

Audioquest 1017 *Wallace; Lou Levy (p); Bill Huntington (b); Alvin Queen (d).* 1/93.

***** The Talk Of The Town**

Enja 7091-2 *As above, except Jerry Hahn (g) replaces Levy.* 1/93.

Left out in the cold by Blue Note, for whom he cut a couple of typically enjoyable albums, Wallace made a welcome return with two records for different labels (he has in the meantime been busy on film-score work). Cut live to two-track, *The Old Songs* finds

Bennie rumbling through a bunch of standards with one original tune, 'At Lulu Whitte's', to keep his composing hand in. Levy appears on only three tracks and the freely spaced rhythms of Huntington and Queen give Wallace plenty of space to break the melodies open: 'When You Wish Upon A Star' is a classic revision, 'Love Letters' a vintage piece of Wallace frowsiness. The same kind of set-up prevails on *The Talk Of The Town*, though here five of the eight tunes are Wallace originals. The tenorman scrubs his way through 'The Best Things In Life Are Free' and 'I Concentrate On You', but the best moments come on his movie ballad, 'If I Lose', and the closing tribute to Lockjaw Davis, 'Blues Velvet', a screamer of a blues. If the record is a shade below par for this fine musician, it may be because Hahn isn't much of a sparring partner.

Thomas 'Fats' Waller (1904–43)

PIANO, ORGAN, VOCAL

The son of a clergyman, Waller worked in vaudeville until the mid-'1920s and began composing with lyricist Andy Razaf, as well as making occasional sideman appearances with bands like the Ted Lewis group. His fame came with the 'Fats Waller And His Rhythm' sessions for Victor, which began in 1934 and proceeded through hundreds of titles. A nonpareil humorist and lampooner of trite pop tunes, Waller's own best songs were strong enough to have remained in the standard repertory. His piano style, which emerged from stride, was percussive and swinging, yet often delicate or even whimsical. He died of pneumonia while on an overnight train.

****(*) Classic Jazz From Rare Piano Rolls**

Biograph BCD 104 *Waller; James P Johnson, Lawrence J Cook (piano rolls).* 3/23–1/29.

***** Low Down Papa**

Biograph BCD 114 *Waller; James P Johnson (piano rolls).* 5/23–6/31.

Thomas Waller was already deputizing for James P. Johnson and playing film and stage-show accompaniments when he started making piano-rolls for the QRS company in 1923. These two discs transfer some of his many rolls to CD. Most of the tunes are typical light blues novelties of the day, and they're played with a crisp, courtly demeanour, although individuality is to some extent suppressed by the machinery of the roll system: certainly Waller's first piano records show much more idiosyncrasy than any of these tracks. There are a couple of items with Johnson, Waller's great mentor, and one on the earlier disc which was credited to Waller but is actually by Lawrence Cook. Ebullience and good humour are persistent here to the point of becoming exasperating, and perhaps these pieces are best sampled a few at a time: there are only a few genuinely Walleresque touches, such as the abrupt doubling of tempo in 'Your Time Now', on *Low Down Papa*. The rolls have been brightly recorded, although *Low Down Papa* is less glassy and generally has the better selection of themes.

***(*) Fats At The Organ**

ASV AJA 5007R *Waller (org).* 23–27.

A unique record, if a bizarre one. Waller made several pipe-organ solos early in his career, but this set consists of organ transcriptions of piano-roll solos: Waller is heard twice-removed. If the piano-roll discs listed above sound artificial, it's hard to hear much of Waller in here except in the merry rhythmic gait of the original rolls: all the choices of registration are made by Ronald Curtis – admittedly after studying Waller's original organ records – and any authenticity that remains comes off a second-best to whatever a 78 can produce.

****(*) Fats Waller 1922–1926**

Classics 664 *Waller; Clarence Williams (kz, v); Clarence Todd (kz); Justin Ring (perc); Sara Martin, Alberta Hunter, Anna Jones, Porter Grainger, Rosa Henderson, Alta Browne, Bertha Powell, Caroline Johnson (v).* 10/22–4/26.

This is fantastically obscure music, 19 tracks of classic blues and vaudeville singers accompanied by Waller, plus two 1922 solos and two tracks with the Jamaica Jazzers (Clarence Williams and Clarence Todd blowing through their kazoos). Those accustomed to listening to the earliest blues reissues will know what to expect in terms of sound-quality; everyone else may be in for a shock (and even Classics themselves have apologized for it on the sleeve). On its own terms, fascinating, with the almost unknown titles by Alta Browne, Bertha Powell and Anna Jones especially interesting.

**** The Complete Early Band Works 1927–29**

Halcyon HDL 115 *Waller; Tom Morris (c); Charlie Gaines, Henry Allen, Leonard Davis (t); Jack Teagarden, Jimmy Archey, J.C Higginbotham (tb); Arville Harris (cl, as, ts); Albert Nicholas, Charlie Holmes (cl, as); Larry Binyon (ts); Bobbie Leecan (g); Will Johnson, Eddie Condon (bj); Pops Foster, Al Morgan (b); Eddie King, Gene Krupa, Kaiser Marshall (d); The Four Wanderers (v).* 5/27–12/29.

****(*) Fats Waller 1926–1927**

Classics 674 *As above discs, except add Alberta Hunter, Maude Mills (v).* 11/26–6/27.

***** Fats Waller 1927–1929**

Classics 689 *As above discs, except add Bert Howell (vn, v), Lou Raderman, Howard Nelson (vn), David Martin (clo), Chuck Campbell (tb), J Lapitino (hp), Gene Austin, Andy Razaf, Juanita Chappelle (v).* 11/27–6/29.

*****(*) Fats Waller 1929**

Classics 702 *As above discs.* 6–12/29.

Waller doesn't sing anywhere on the Halcyon disc and, given the nightmarish vocals by The Four Wanderers on two tracks, perhaps he was numbed into silence. The seven tracks by Fats with Tom Morris's Hot Babies are a garish mismatch of pipe organ and cornet-led hot band and, since the resonances and overtones of the organ tamp down everything the other players do, it's hard to imagine how anyone could have thought that the group would work. The eight tracks by Fats Waller & His Buddies are merely loose-knit New York jazz of the period (1929).

The Classics discs go forward with Waller's 1926–7 organ solos, beautiful, lilting creations, as well as some of the Morris Hot Babies tracks and more accompaniments to Mills and Hunter. There is some very strange stuff on Classics 689 – three tearful tributes to the lately departed Florence Mills, where Waller plays respectful piano, and a version of 'Chloe' with violin, organ and piano. It ends with Gene Austin singing 'Maybe – Who Knows?'. In between, though, are several classic piano solos and 'I Ain't Got Nobody', one of the best of his organ records. Remastering on all these is mixed but quite an improvement over Classics 664. The 1929 disc offers a great run of his finest piano solos (see below): still not the best sound, but it's a strong one-disc primer on early Waller.

****(*) You Rascal You**

ASV AJA 5040 *Waller; Henry 'Red' Allen, Len Davis, Bill Coleman, Herman Autrey, Charlie Gains, Charlie Teagarden, Sterling Bose (t); Jack Teagarden (tb, v); Charlie Irvis, Tommy Dorsey, J.C Higginbotham, Charlie Green (tb); Arville Harris, Ben Whittet, Artie Shaw, Albert Nicholas, Larry Binyon (cl, as); Gene Sedric, Larry Binyon (cl, ts); Bud Freeman (ts); Al Casey, Dick McDonough (g); Eddie Condon (bj); Billy Taylor, Pops Foster, Artie Bernstein (b); Stan King, Kaiser Marshall, Harry Dial (d).* 3/29–11/34.

***** Fats Waller 1929–1934**

Classics 720 *As above.* 12/29–11/34.

Waller's early band sides, picked out in this ASV cross-section of 1929–34 sessions, suggested a mercurial talent pondering on its ultimate direction. The two sides by Fats Waller's Buddies are frantic small-band New York jazz of the day (1929), with little of the slyness of the Rhythm sides represented by seven 1934 tracks, and the guest-star role he takes on a Jack Teagarden version of 'You Rascal You' offers little more than inspired mugging, entertaining as it is. A few solos, including the enchanting 'My Fate Is In Your Hands', suggest the other side of Waller's art, and the complexity of his personality. Mixed reproduction again, alas: some sides sound very dull, others are clear and strong. Much the same applies to the Classics version of this material.

***** Fats Waller 1934–35**

Classics 732 *Waller; Herman Autrey, Bill Coleman (t); Floyd O'Brien (tb); Gene Sedric (cl, ts); Mezz Mezzrow (cl, as); Al Casey (g); Billy Taylor, Charles Turner (b); Harry Dial (d, vib).* 9/34–1/35.

*****(*) Fats Waller 1935**

Classics 746 *As above, except add Rudy Powell (cl, as), James Smith (g), Arnold Bolling (d); omit Mezzrow and Taylor.* 1/35–6/35.

*****(*) Fats Waller 1935 Vol. 2**

Classics 760 *As above, except omit Coleman, Sedric, Dial.* 6–8/35.

*****(*) Fats Waller 1935–1936**

Classics 776 *As above, except add Benny Morton (tb), Emmett Matthews (ss), Bob Caroll, Gene Sedric (ts), Hank Duncan (p), Yank Porter (d); omit Powell, Smith.* 11/35–2/36.

***** Fats Waller 1936**

Classics 797 *As above, except add Slick Jones (d); omit Morton, Matthews, Caroll, Duncan.* 6–9/36.

***** Fats Waller 1936–1937**

Classics 816 *As above, except omit Bolling, Porter.* 11/36–3/37.

***** Fats Waller 1937**

Classics 838 *As above, except add Bunny Berigan (t), Tommy Dorsey (tb), Dick McDonough (g), George Wettling (d).* 3–6/37.

***** The Early Years Vol. 1**

RCA Bluebird 66618-2 2CD *As appropriate discs above.* 34–35.

***** The Early Years Vol. 2**

RCA Bluebird 66640-2 *As appropriate discs above.* 35–36.

***** The Early Years Vol. 3**

RCA Bluebird 66747-2 2CD *As appropriate discs above.* 36.

Waller worked hard in the studios and, though his material has been traditionally looked down upon, he did usually make the most of it, even if the relentless clowning, yelled asides, importuning of soloists and general mayhem obscured much of what his hands were doing at the keyboard. This is often knockabout music, but whenever he gets to a good melody or does one of his own better tunes – such as the 12-inch master of 'Blue Turning Grey Over You' – its underlying seriousness rises to the surface. Autry and Sedric, the most ubiquitous yet least recognized of horn players, are always ready to heat things up. Bill Coleman's presence on a few early sessions introduces some of his elegant horn, and the almost forgotten Rudy Powell replaced Sedric on several of the 1935 dates.

Much order has now been imposed on these sessions. Both RCA and Classics have set out comprehensive surveys of Waller's Rhythm recordings and his various solos, although Bluebird include alternative takes (which Classics don't) while Classics find some non-Bluebird material along the way. The Classics CDs are the easiest to follow, but the RCA sets are attractively packaged and the remastering (much improved on the earlier standards of the Bluebird reissues) is generally better.

Classics 732 includes four piano solos as well as the session which produced 'Serenade For A Wealthy Widow'; 'Baby Brown' is another good one. Classics 746 has 'Rosetta', 'I'm Gonna Sit Right Down And Write Myself A Letter', the outstanding 'Dinah' and 'Sweet And Slow'. Either this or the following Classics 760 might be a good one to sample: the latter includes several more of the best Rhythm tracks, with one of the best ever versions of 'Somebody Stole My Gal'. Classics 776 has the fruits of a session involving a 12-piece band, which even has a second pianist, Hank Duncan, who brings on a joshing cutting contest on 'I Got Rhythm'. Also on this disc is a particularly fine session that produced 'The Panic Is On', 'Sugar Rose' and 'West Wind'. There is still a decent quota of good music on Classics 797, but this and the next two see the Rhythm formula wearing dangerously thin and some truly dreadful material coming under assault. There are many pickings here, but they're camouflaged by a lot of nonsense. By the time the Classics sequence reaches its end, this will be a fairly monumental set, but follow the stars in the mean time for Waller's better moments. The Bluebird discs, as noted, are at least as good a bet.

*****(*) The Middle Years Part 1 (1936–38)**

Bluebird 07863 66083-2 3CD *Waller; Herman Autrey, Paul Campbell, John Hamilton, Nat Williams (t); George Robinson, John Haughton (tb); Gene Sedric (cl, ts); Caughey Roberts, Lonnie Simmons, William Alsop, Alfred Skerritt, James Powell (reeds); Ceele Burke, Al Casey (g); Charles Turner, Al Morgan,*

Cedric Wallace (b); Slick Jones, Lee Young (d, vib); Peggy Dade (v). 12/36–4/38.

*****(*) Fats Waller 1937 Vol. 2**

Classics 857 *Waller; Herman Autrey, Paul Campbell (t); Gene Sedric, Caughey Roberts (cl, ts); Al Casey, Ceele Burke (g); Charles Turner, Al Morgan (b); Slick Jones, Lee Young (d).* 6–12/37.

***** Fats Waller 1937–1938**

Classics 875 *As above, except add John 'Bugs' Hamilton, Courtney Williams (t), George Robinson, John Haughton (tb), William Alsop, James Powell, Fred Skerritt (as), Lonnie Simmons (ts), Cedric Wallace (b).* 12/37–7/38.

***** Fats Waller 1938**

Classics 913 *Waller; Dave Wilkins, Herman Autrey (t); George Chisholm (tb); Alfie Kahn, Gene Sedric (cl, ts); Ian Sheppard (ts, vn); Al Casey, Alan Ferguson (g); Len Harrison, Cedric Wallace (b); Hymie Schneider, Edmundo Ros, Slick Jones (d); Adelaide Hall (v).* 8–12/38.

***** Fats Waller 1938–1939**

Classics 943 *Waller; Herman Autrey (t); Gene Sedric (cl, ts); Coco Heimel, Al Casey (g); Candy Hall, Cedric Wallace (b); Slick Jones, Johnny Marks (d).* 12/38–4/39.

***** Fats Waller 1939**

Classics 973 *As above, except add John 'Bugs' Hamilton (t), Chauncey Graham (ts), John Smith (g), Larry Hinton, Max Lewin (d); omit Heimel, Hall, Marks.* 6/39–11/39.

*****(*) The Middle Years Part 2 (1938–1940)**

Bluebird 07863 66552-2 3CD *As appropriate discs above.* 38–40.

Waller's progress with his Rhythm is documented further here, as before, on both Classics and RCA Bluebird. The humour grows less manic, more formulaic, and sometimes even gentle in its delivery; the material continues to be a mix of worthy and throwaway; and the tenor of each session is usually rather light and fresh, since Waller disliked doing more than the minimum rehearsal before setting down a take. Classics 857 starts with five rather sweetly engaging solos, including 'Keepin' Out Of Mischief Now' (an almost definitive version), and some excellent Rhythm tracks make this one a very good entry in the series. Classics 875 includes eight titles where the Rhythm group was augmented into an orchestra: Waller is uncharacteristically reserved on some of his vocals but there are fine versions of 'Skrontch' and 'The Sheik Of Araby'. There's also a curious date where Ceele Burke plays steel guitar and Waller sings 'Why Do Hawaiians Sing Aloha?'

Waller visited Europe twice in the late 1930s, and he recorded in London on both trips. Two sessions in 1938 found him handling organ and piano with a British band, cutting six organ solos (including a surprisingly bleak and unsettling 'Deep River') and backing Adelaide Hall for two further songs (all on Classics 913). Two Rhythm dates back in New York round off the disc. Next year, he worked alone or with drum-only support. There are six wistful miniatures, the 'London Suite', and a rather mournful 'Smoke Dreams Of You', which go to suggest the reflective side of Waller's art which rarely made it to record yet which is always touted by supporters as his shamefully overlooked inner self. Whatever the case, these are slight but charming pieces, and they're on Classics 973, along with three more dates with the Rhythm. On one, they do a polite remake of 'Bond Street' from the London Suite. Classics 943 includes a bizarre two-title date where Waller plays electric organ behind Gene Austin, who sounds like he's doing a Waller impersonation. It also offers three very rare tracks from his 1939 London visit, including 'Cottage In The Rain' – unfortunately dubbed from a very poor master. Transfers tend to be respectable rather than outstanding, and the Bluebird sets, which cover a lot of similar ground, on the whole are better.

***** The Definitive Fats Waller, His Rhythm, His Piano**

Stash ST-CD-528 *Waller; Herman Autrey (t); Rudy Powell (cl, as); Gene Sedric (cl, ts); Al Casey (g); Cedric Wallace, Charles Turner (b); Slick Jones, Harry Dial (d).* 35–39.

A generous (76 minutes) helping of Waller and the Rhythm from broadcasts in 1935 and 1939. The material is staple Waller fare and the exuberance is as expected, in surprisingly good sound for the period and the sources. While the 'new' versions aren't strikingly revelatory of any different side to Waller, they confirm his ability to create happy music out of the thinnest of tunes.

***** Fats Waller 1939-1940**

Classics 1002 *Waller; John Hamilton (t); Gene Sedric (cl, ts); John Smith, Al Casey (g); Cedric Wallace (b); Slick Jones (d); Una Mae Carlisle (v).*

***** Fats Waller 1940-1941**

Classics 1030 *As above, except omit Smith and Carlisle; add Catherine Perry (v).* 7/40–3/41.

*****(*) Fats Waller 1941**

Classics 1068 *As above, except add Herman Autrey, Bob Williams (t), George Wilson, Ray Hogan (tb), Jimmy Powell, Dave McRae (as), Bob Caroll (ts), Charles Turner (b), Arthur Trappier (d); omit Perry.* 5–12/41.

***** Fats Waller 1942-1943**

Classics 1097 *Waller; Herman Autrey, John Hamilton, Joe Thomas, Nathaniel Williams, Benny Carter (t); Herb Flemming, George Wilson, Slim Moore (tb); Gene Sedric, Gene Porter (cl, ts); Jackie Fields, George James (as); Bob Caroll (ts); Al Casey, Irving Ashby (g); Cedric Wallace, Slam Stewart (b); Arthur Trappier, Zutty Singleton (d); The Deep River Boys, Ada Brown (v).* 3/42–9/43.

If Waller was ultimately trapped by his non-stop funny-man image, the routine of his 'Fats Waller And His Rhythm' records at least helped to focus a talent that was sometimes in danger of merely running ragged. The dozens of throwaway tunes he lampooned may have had little intrinsic merit, and he often falls back on favourite lines and devices, but – like Armstrong in the same period – Waller remains an inimitable talent, and the space limitations of the records often result in performances full of compressed excitement. The later sessions are unpredictable in this respect, since he often goes gentle when one expects a shot of uproar. It is certainly untrue to say that the Rhythm recordings declined in quality: the 1941–2 sessions include some of the finest sides the band made, and Hamilton, Sedric and Autrey, all minor figures who nevertheless played handsomely at the right moment, lend a more urgently swinging touch to the music than anything provided by, say, the Louis Jordan band (compare Waller's 'Your Socks Don't Match' or 'Don't Give Me That Jive' (both on Classics 1068), two very Jordanesque tunes, with any of the altoman's records – next to Jordan's calculating burlesques, Waller's wit sounds wholly spontaneous).

Since RCA's multi-disc overview seems to be gone for the moment, these Classics volumes – which finally complete the Waller story after 21 CDs! – take first place. The pick of the four is surely Classics 1068, which has the Rhythm augmented by horns for one session which produced the terrific 'Chant Of The Groove', five piano solo tracks, and superior singles such as 'Buck Jumpin'' and 'Clarinet Marmalade'. Classics 1097 offers the final four Victor dates, including Fats singing 'That's What The Well Dressed Man In Harlem Will Wear' in front of the Victor First Nighter Orchestra, and Benny Carter playing trumpet on the last session. Ten titles for V-Disc, Fats alone at the piano or the organ, make a fine conclusion to the series, with the chilling farewell of 'Sometimes I Feel Like A Motherless Child' making an eerie finale to his career on record. Sound is mostly more than acceptable on all four discs.

Jan Wallgren (1935–96)

PIANO

Originally from Norway, Wallgren spent most of his life in Sweden. A bopper in the 1950s and '60s, he was an eclectic who turned to prolific composing and brought a dedicated knowledge of classical and folk forms to his writing and playing.

***(*) Standards And Blueprints

Dragon DRCD 246 *Wallgren (p solo).* 4/87–2/93.

**** Raga, Bebop And Anything

Dragon DRCD 303 *Wallgren; Magnus Broo (t); Nils Landgren (tb); Hakan Brostrom (ss, as); Jonas Knutsson (ss, as, bs); Lennart Aberg (ss, ts); Christian Spering (b); Anders Kjellberg (d).* 4/95.

Wallgren's *Blueprints*, listed in our first edition in its vinyl form, is an album we have returned to often, and its CD incarnation adds six standards and a conflation of Monk and Powell. The veteran bebopper-turned-composer wore his heart on his sleeve here, with the jazz pieces sitting beside dedications to Berg, Webern and Schoenberg, and while it is principally a recital of tiny miniatures – some of which might blow away on a puff of wind – the beauty of his touch brings most of it to life, with the dozen 'Hints And Suggestions' particularly fine. His version of the Lennon–McCartney tune, 'Blackbird', is about as eloquent as the Beatles have ever been in a jazz setting.

The group record takes its title from an advertisement once placed to advertise a Wallgren concert ('Wallgren: Raga, bebop and anything'). Like so many Scandinavian composers, his music is inseparable from a heritage that a jazz vocabulary has only tempered. Chorale and passacaglia forms are as prevalent here as the blues, and in company with a front-rank band the leader sets out a rich programme of nine themes, none of them alike with each other. Cancer took him in the summer of 1996, and this stands as a memorial to a rare imagination.

Per Henrik Wallin (born 1946)

PIANO

An explosive post-bop stylist, the Swede led many record dates during the 1970s and early '80s but was badly injured in a 1988 accident and has since recorded only occasionally.

**** Coyote

Dragon DRCD 320 *Wallin; Tørbjörn Hultcrantz (b); Erik Dahbäck (d).* 8/86–10/87.

***(*) Dolphins, Dolphins, Dolphins

Dragon DRCD 215 *Wallin; Mats Gustafsson (ss, ts, bs); Kjell Nordeson (d).* 8/91.

Wallin's extensive discography has been seriously depleted by the disappearance of vinyl. He is a fascinating pianist, taking whatever he wants from free- and post-bop piano language: a bravado delivery, involving tumultuous climaxes and moment-by-moment contrast, makes him hard to follow or even like at times, but he is surely a European original. *Coyote* documents some radio sessions by his power trio of the '80s. Massive pieces like 'The Strange Adventures Of Jesper Klint' go through lightning changes of mood, spinning through amazing pyrotechnics from the keyboard but always under precarious but particular control. Compared to some of his other groups, the bassist and drummer are much in tune with his style and help rather than hinder. A belated but splendid release.

Hospitalized after a crippling accident in 1988, Wallin astonishingly came back with seemingly none of his power depleted. The shade most closely evoked here is Thelonious Monk, since 'Nu Nu Och Då Nu Går Då Och Nu' sounds like a perversion of 'Round Midnight', and other Monkish melodies drift through the remaining tunes. But the level of interplay here – confrontational and conspiratorial in equal proportion – goes against the impression given by much of his earlier work, that Wallin is best by himself, although his long solo, 'J.W.', is a wonderfully expressive tribute to a painter friend. Gustafsson is gothically powerful and jagged, Nordeson works with military intensity, and it's all splendidly recorded.

*** Blues For Allan

Flash Music FLCD-8 *Wallin; Peter Janson (b); Leif Wennerström (d).* 4–12/98.

His second record of the '90s finds Wallin at Club Fasching with a new trio – Janson, who plays in the Aaly Trio, is a great find. 'Thelonious' is so dramatically reharmonized that Monk himself might have raised an eyebrow. For once, Wallin's playing is too relentless: the pair of blues pieces are almost teeth-grindingly tensed up. 'Ryssland' is a desolate tribute to the Russian people. 'Sweet And Lovely' is neither, although the record as a whole is a good antidote to too many perfumed piano recitals.

George Wallington (1924–93)

PIANO

Born in Sicily, Wallington was involved in the first wave of bebop, working with Gillespie and others. Though he made a series of recordings between then and 1957, he subsequently left the music business altogether and returned for one album and a few concerts in the mid-'1980s.

*****(*) The George Wallington Trios**
Original Jazz Classics OJC 1754 *Wallington; Chuck Wayne (mandola); Charles Mingus, Oscar Pettiford, Curley Russell (b); Max Roach (d).* 9/52–5/53.

***** Trios**
RCA Vogue 74321 11504 2 *Wallington; Pierre Michelot (b); Jean-Louis Viale (d).* 9/54.

More so even than Joe Albany or Dodo Marmarosa, George Wallington is the underrated master of bebop piano: his name is still best known for his composing 'Lemon Drop' and 'Godchild'. His speed is breathtaking, his melodies unspooling in long, unbroken lines, and he writes tunes which are rather more than the customary convoluted riffs on familiar chord-changes. The OJC *Trios* disc is all piano, bass and drums, and there are marvellous, flashing virtuoso pieces like the ultrafast 'Cuckoo Around The Clock', although the elegance of 'I Married An Angel' is a harbinger of Wallington's later work. The eight tracks on the Vogue disc (there are a further six by Jimmy Jones) are cooler, more reflective treatments, including a definitive version of one of his own favourite compositions, 'Ny'. The sound here is clear enough, though bass and drums aren't served well.

***** Live! At Café Bohemia**
Original Jazz Classics OJC 1813 *Wallington; Donald Byrd (t); Jackie McLean (as); Paul Chambers (b); Art Taylor (d).* 9/55.

***** Jazz For The Carriage Trade**
Original Jazz Classics OJC 1704 *As above, except Phil Woods (as), Teddy Kotick (b) replace McLean and Chambers.* 1/56.

*****(*) The New York Scene**
Original Jazz Classics OJC 1805 *As above, except Nick Stabulas (d) replaces Taylor.* 3/57.

Some of these are merely serviceable hard-bop entries, prosaic stuff after the fine fierceness of the earlier records; but some of the music takes exception. Wallington's playing seemed to turn inwards and his improvisations are at an altogether cooler temperature. Byrd muddles through the first two dates and is approaching his faceless self on the later one, yet this anonymity throws some of Wallington's own contributions into sharper relief – almost like Freddie Hubbard on some of the more outré Blue Notes of the next decade. Woods hits every note he needs to with his usual accuracy on his appearances; McLean is his customary tart mid-'50s self on the earliest date. *Café Bohemia* and *Carriage Trade* are tough and darting but finally straightahead in their demeanour; it's *The New York Scene* that looks a little further out, thanks to Wallington's material and his own solos, which have begun to skin bebop language back to something more elemental. A shame that he chose at this point to quit jazz altogether.

***** The Pleasure Of A Jazz Inspiration**
VSOP 84 *Wallington (p solo).* 8/85.

Tempted back into the studios, Wallington created this 'jazz tone poem' in eight parts. Bebop figures drift through some of the themes: 'Writing In The Sand' is very like Powell's 'Parisian Thoroughfare'. But the slower pieces are unusually dark, with the harmonies of 'Memory Of The Heart' almost impenetrably dense, and there's a hint of sourness that goes with the pleasure. Wallington sounds rusty here and there, and much of the old exhilaration has dissipated, but it's an interesting if eccentric postscript to a frustrating career.

Jack Walrath (born 1946)

TRUMPET, FLUGELHORN, VOCALS

Montana-born, Walrath worked in Charles Mingus's group during the '70s, having attended Berklee and worked in a variety of R&B units. Strongly influenced by bebop, he has a clear-edged and intense sound and great humour, which comes across on many of his recordings.

***** In Montana**
Jazz Alliance 10030 *Walrath; Chuck Florence (ss, ts, perc); Bob Nell (p, perc); Kelly Roberty (b, perc); Jim Honaker (d, perc); Jon Lodge (perc).* 80.

In a period dominated largely by the saxophone and by the muted, melted edges of Miles Davis's trumpet style, it's good to find a player who restores some of brass's authentic ring and bite. Walrath is a hugely talented player with a tough, almost percussive sound. A high-note man in several contemporary big bands (Charles Mingus's *Cumbia And Jazz Fusion* and *Three Or Four Shades Of Blues* spring immediately to mind, but he has also done sterling service with Charli Persip Superbands), Walrath has so far not made his deserved impact as a leader. Two good Blue Notes (look particularly for *Neohippus*) are still out of the catalogue, but just before going to press there was news that some at least of Jack's work for Muse was scheduled for reissue on 32 Jazz Records. More on that, we hope, next time.

This is a brisk and unaffected set from an unfamiliar band, and there is no mistaking that Jack himself is very firmly in the driving seat. Though Nell and Roberty are strongly represented, it's the trumpeter's dry, sardonic sound which dominates from start to finish. Not the easiest of records to get hold of, but in our opinion well worth the effort.

*****(*) In Europe**
Steeplechase SCCD 31172 *Walrath; Glenn Ferris (tb); Michael Cochran (p); Anthony Cox (b); Jimmy Madison (d).* 7/82.

The brass front line on the Steeplechase is ringingly present, and Ferris's old-fashioned tone is a huge asset on 'Duesin' In Dusseldorf' and 'At Home In Rome', two of four Walrath originals on a relatively short-measured release that will leave most purchasers calling for more. Cox and Madison make an interesting partnership, not always absolutely squarely on the metre, but lateral enough to keep a step ahead of a notably capricious leader.

***** Portraits In Ivory And Brass**

Mapleshade 2032 *Walrath; Larry Willis (p); Steve Novosel (b).* 6/92.

A subtler and more sophisticated side of Jack emerges on this delicately nuanced record. Apart from the opening 'Bess, You Is My Woman Now', all the tunes are credited to Walrath and Willis, but it's some testimony to their writing skills that they all sound familiar. Jack's phrasing has never been more exquisite and his theme development on 'Kirsten' and 'Road To Sophia' is logical and expressive. Willis has long been a skilled arranger and, though less widely appreciated as a player, he claims a full share in this attractive album, majoring on his own 'Shadows' and 'Green Eyes'.

***** Hi Jinx**

Stash 576 *Walrath; Ricky Ford (ss, ts); Michael Cochrane (p); Cameron Brown, Anthony Cox (b); Mike Clark (d).* 2/94.

Ford, Cochrane and Clark are all leaders in their own right and this is a record strong on ego and personality. Cochrane is represented as a composer, and he continues to impress. The central section of the record, from Walrath's 'Revenge Of The Fat People', Mingus's 'Duke Ellington's Sound Of Love' and 'Beer!', pretty much covers the spectrum of Jack's work as composer and performer. His solo on the Mingus tune is delightful, and the ale-inspired tune is one of his most joyous.

***** Hipgnosis**

TCB 01062 *Walrath; David Fiuczynski (g); Hill Green (b); Cecil Brooks III (d); Dean Bowman (v).* 3/95.

****** Solidarity**

ACT 9241 *Walrath; Ralph Reichert (sax); Buggy Braune (p); Christian Havel (g, v); Andreas Henze (b); Joris Dudli (d).* 8/95.

Walrath's long-standing passion for horror films is reflected in the name of his working band, The Masters of Suspense. They are featured on *Hipgnosis*, an unusual set in that it puts considerable emphasis on lyrics and vocal performance. These suggest that Walrath remains under the influence of the great Charles Mingus, at whose former home he wrote the piece, 'Mingus Piano'. The 'Sweet Hip Gnosis' suite which it brings to an end is much involved with Walrath's other fascination in esoteric philosophy, a rich and complex group of distantly related pieces that cohere more and more securely each time they are heard. The Mingus association is cemented by 'Eclipse' but is omnipresent, detectable even on a Walrath original like 'Blues Sinistra'.

Solidarity is the closest of the surviving records to the Muses, a blues-soaked and – as Jack points out – very American-sounding recording that could again almost be a Mingus offshoot. Reichert's father owns the Hamburg club where the recording was made; it's an atmospheric place and a strong, smouldering set. The two-part 'Hamburg Concerto' and the title-track bespeak anew Walrath's ability to give long forms the immediacy and the visceral punch of a simple blues, while 'Hot-Dog For Lunch', 'Political Suicide' and 'Psychotic Indifference' underline his more capricious and satirical side. Reichert claims joint honours, and his father's production yields up a sound which favours the horns over the rest of the group – not overwhelmingly so, but with a definite edge. Good stuff.

*****(*) Journey, Man!**

Evidence 22150 *Walrath; Bobby Watson (as); Craig Handy (ss, ts); Kenny Drew Jr (p); Ray Drummond (b); Victor Lewis (d).* 11/95.

Jack called this band Hard Corps and used it to mark a return to pretty orthodox hard bop. Whether this was out of frustration or a genuine desire to explore that slightly tired idiom is hard to determine, but the playing on *Journey, Man!* – from the horns in particular – suggests an exuberant embrace of the old style. 'Butt! (Tails From The Backside)' veers close to parody, but 'Pete's Steps', derived from Coltrane's 'Giant Steps', is both generic and spot on. 'Bouncin' With Ballholzka' flirts with elements of freedom, while 'When Love Has Gone (It Comes Out Like This)' is an exquisite ballad, pitched in a middle register and showing a side of Walrath's playing that is all too rarely highlighted.

*****(*) Get Hit In Your Soul**

ACT 9246 2 *Walrath; Bill Bickford (g); Miles Griffith (v); WDR Big Band.* 96–98.

A joyous celebration of the music and the spirit of Charles Mingus, which of course Walrath experienced at first hand. Miles Griffith serves to remind us that Mingus's recitations and songs were never an incidental aspect of what he was about but were absolutely central to it, and 'Oh Lord, Don't Let Them Drop That Atomic Bomb On Me' is the proof: passionate, wry and intense. However, the real surprises on the album are Jack's compositions. The opening 'Motley As An Amorphous Hangdown' is brassy and roiling, while his arrangement of the famous Egyptian 'Hymn To Aten' alongside Psalm CIV touches new areas of expression for the trumpeter.

Craig Walters

TENOR AND SOPRANO SAXOPHONES

Sydney-based Australian saxophonist.

***** First Light Aspiring**

Rufus RF016 *Walters; Alister Spence (ky); Adam Armstrong (b); Toby Hall (d).* 1/95.

Post-bop from Sydney, and played with impressive energy to go with the expected chops. Walters is no great individualist, but he writes decisive, attention-grabbing themes and this quartet play them with fine relish. Spence uses synthesizer on a couple of tunes, but it's for atmospherics – especially on the long centre-piece, 'Mount Aspiring' – rather than any kind of fusion concession. The mix tends to shove everybody to the front, but at least nobody's shy about being there.

Cedar Walton (born 1934)

PIANO

Dallas-born Walton has impressive credentials. After a stint in the military, he worked with Kenny Dorham and J.J. Johnson before joining the Jazz Messengers (and, unusually, rejoined the outfit a few years later). He also served a tour as house pianist for the Prestige label. He has a confident feel for the blues but favours a kind of angular lyricism.

*****(*) Cedar!**

Original Jazz Classics OJCCD 462 *Walton; Kenny Dorham (t); Junior Cook (ts); Leroy Vinnegar (b); Billy Higgins (d). 7/67.*

*****(*) Soul Cycle**

Original Jazz Classics OJCCD 847-2 *Walton; James Moody (ts, f); Rudy Stevenson (bs); Reggie Workman (b); Albert 'Tootie' Heath (d).* 68.

*****(*) Cedar Walton Plays Cedar Walton**

Original Jazz Classics OJC 6002 *As Cedar!, plus Blue Mitchell (t), Clifford Jordan (ts), Bob Cranshaw, Richard Davis (b), Jack DeJohnette, Mickey Roker (d). 7/67–1/69.*

***** Spectrum**

Prestige PRCD 24145-2 *As above. 7/67–1/69.*

Walton has only slowly been recognized as a significant jazz composer. Tunes like 'Bolivia', 'Ojos De Rojo', 'Maestro' and 'Ugetsu' rival McCoy Tyner's work for sophisticated inventiveness. During the 1970s Walton was anchoring Clifford Jordan's Magic Triangle band. They seem to have struck up an immediate rapport on these earlier sessions, made for Prestige, for which label Cedar was house pianist for a time. *Plays* contains a useful sample of the earlier quartet and quintet stuff with Dorham and Cook, but the compilation misses a fine trio, 'My Ship'. Paired with the characteristically blunt Mitchell, Jordan takes the direct route to goal, with no sign of his irritating tendency to mark time in mid-solo. 'Higgins Holler' and 'Jakes Milkshakes' also feature sterling work by DeJohnette, who still sounds rather eager to please. There's an excellent trio performance of Walton's 'Fantasy In D', related to 'Ugetsu', with Roker and Cranshaw. Though there's good stuff on OJC 462, the compilation has to be a better bet. By and large *Spectrum* runs a few variants on the same sessions and the same material and, heard afresh, it has much to recommend it; but the reappearance of *Soul Cycle*, with Moody and Stevenson, is the real find, a brisk, expressive session which is paced just about perfectly and contains one gem of a performance in 'My Cherie Amour'.

*****(*) Breakthrough**

32 Jazz 32102 *Walton; Hank Mobley (ts); Charles Davis (ss, bs); Sam Jones (b); Billy Higgins (d).* 72.

*****(*) Naima**

32 Jazz 32046 *Walton; Clifford Jordan (ts); Sam Jones (b); Louis Hayes (d).* 73.

***** Firm Roots**

Camden 74321 61074 2 2CD *As above, except add Terence Blanchard (t), Jesse Davis (as), David Williams (b), Billy Higgins (d).* 72–90.

Between 1972 and 1990, Walton recorded a series of albums for Muse, whose back catalogue is once again available on 32 Jazz and Camden. The earliest session was recorded live in a band co-led by Hank Mobley, fairly orthodox hard bop leavened with some interesting work from Davis. Walton occasionally sounds rather crude, as if trying to pump some action out of a dodgy club piano, but he also creates some delicate ballad shapes on 'Theme From Love Story'.

Naima was, as far as we are aware, originally released as *Live From Boomer's*, which is probably a more apt title for a hard-driving and rather acid set. Jordan's tenor work on 'The Highest Mountain', perhaps his best-known composition, is worthy of notice, but there are more approachable things on offer as well, notably Rollins's 'St Thomas' and the Coltrane ballad which gives the album its title. Jones and Hayes are in superb form and Sam's peerless bass work is now fully audible.

The Camden selection is slightly odd. Five tracks, including 'Love Story', from the 1972 album, four from *Naima/Boomer's*, but omitting the Rollins and Coltrane themes, two from a 1974 Muse called *Firm Roots*, a trio set with Jones and Hayes, and the whole of the 1990 session, *As Long As There's Music*. Oddly balanced, but a good-value compilation for anyone who doesn't want the stuff entire or in its original configuration.

The 1970s material has Walton alternating between grand and electric piano and between grandness and bathos, though it shouldn't be assumed that his amplified work is in any way anticlimactic. He is one of the few around at the time who made the Fender Rhodes sound as individual and expressive as a Steinway, and his electric playing on *Breakthrough* is occasionally revelatory.

*****(*) First Set**

Steeplechase SCCD 31085 *Walton; Bob Berg (ts); Sam Jones (b); Billy Higgins (d).* 1 & 10/77.

*****(*) Second Set**

Steeplechase SCCD 31113 *As above.* 1 & 10/77.

***** Third Set**

Steeplechase SCCD 31179 *As above.* 1 & 10/77.

This was a vintage period for Walton, who was beginning to shake off a tendency to blend with his surroundings. This is the band that went out as Eastern Rebellion, documented on Timeless and elsewhere, though these discs seem to be credited to Walton alone. His European gigs were models of tough contemporary bop and, though the incidence of covers is higher than one might expect, given the strength of his writing, the standard of performance is consistently high, and for once Steeplechase's exhaustive documentation seems justified. Berg, who replaced George Coleman in the group, turns in an excellent performance of Coltrane's 'Blue Train' on *Second Set*, avoiding the usual pastiche of Trane's lonesome solo and turning the theme into something altogether tougher and more locomotive. There are several good Monk performances, but the opening 'Off Minor' on *First Set* is the most dynamic. There certainly wasn't enough strong material for three discs, and these sessions suggest an obvious occasion for editing and repackaging.

*****(*) Among Friends**

Evidence ECD 2023 *Walton; Bobby Hutcherson (vib); Buster Williams (b); Billy Higgins (d).* 7/82.

The Keystone Korner in San Francisco became a regular resort for recording companies in search of cheap, atmospheric recordings. This was recorded during the final months of its existence. In July 1982 vibist Hutcherson was there with his group, a residency documented on *Farewell Keystone*. Walton's trio was the warm-up act and was playing so well that a decision was taken to record them as well. Perhaps the most valuable part of the session is the solo medley from the pianist at the end, a rippling segue from 'Ruby My Dear' to 'My Old Flame' and 'I've Grown Accustomed To Her Face', played with great feeling and understanding. Hutcherson appears as a guest on only one track, the long 'My Foolish Heart', but he raises the ante considerably. Williams and Higgins are impeccable – but then, aren't they always?

*****(*) Cedar Walton–Ron Carter–Jack DeJohnette**
Limetree MCD 0021 *Walton; Ron Carter (b); Jack DeJohnette (d).* 12/83.

The young DeJohnette had proved his value to Walton on the 1968 Prestige sessions; 15 years made a substantial difference to the drummer's chops. In 1983 he's confident enough to play less and quieter, and all three players are intuitively musical in approach, which encourages a tight, unembellished style. Walton's own 'Rubber Man' is the outstanding track, but there are also worthwhile performances of 'Alone Together' and 'All The Things You Are', tunes which can sound thoroughly shop-soiled when accorded only routine treatment.

***** Bluesville Time**
Criss Cross Criss 1017 *Walton; Dale Barlow (ts); David Williams (b); Billy Higgins (d).* 4/85.

***** Cedar**
Timeless SJP 223 *As above, except omit Barlow.* 4/85.

Williams and Higgins were the ground floor of Walton's fine 1980s groups. The drummer's ability to sustain and develop a pattern became increasingly important to the pianist as he simplified and reduced his delivery. Barlow compares very favourably with the inventive Bob Berg, who had played for a time in Walton's other group, Eastern Rebellion (see above). The material is excellent – 'Naima' and 'I Remember Clifford' alongside distinctive originals like 'Rubber Man' and 'Ojos De Rojo' – but the playing, Higgins apart, isn't quite crisp enough. The drummer sounds great on *Cedar*, but the material doesn't give anyone enough to bite down on and there's too much filling for too little substance.

*****(*) The Trio: Volume 1**
Red 123192 *Walton; David Williams (b); Billy Higgins (d).* 3/85.

***** The Trio: Volume 2**
Red 123193 *As above.* 3/85.

***** The Trio: Volume 3**
Red 123194 *As above.* 3/85.

Recorded live in Bologna, these represent a compelling mixture of originals ('Ojos De Rojo', 'Jacob's Ladder', 'Holy Land'), standards ('Lover Man', 'Every Time We Say Goodbye') and challenging repertoire pieces (Ellington's 'Satin Doll', Fred Lacey's 'Theme For Ernie', S.R. Kyner's 'Bluesville'). Walton's brilliant phrasing and inbuilt harmonic awareness keep thematic material in view at all times, and his solos and accompaniments are always entirely logical and consistently developed. About Higgins there is very little more to add but that he has inherited and fully deserved the mantle of Elvin Jones. Williams offers firm, unobtrusive support but isn't a very exciting soloist.

*****(*) Blues For Myself**
Red RR 123205-2 *Walton (p solo).* 2/86.

***** Live At Maybeck: Volume 25**
Concord CCD 8234 *As above.* 90.

The Maybeck set is something of a missed opportunity. Walton's usual self-possession seems to have deserted him. The piano is as well behaved as ever and the Maybeck acoustic is as flattering as could be, but the results fall well short both of the series as a whole and of Cedar's own output.

By contrast, the Red session is relaxed, stylish and more than competent, with a fascinating mixture of new and standard material. Neal Hefti's 'Little Darlin'' is a high point and there are excellent versions of Monk's 'Let's Call This' and Duke's 'Sophisticated Lady', but the weight of emphasis falls on Walton originals, including 'Bridge Work', 'Sixth Avenue' and the title-song, which reasserts his commitment to the blues. The recording is a bit unvarnished and clattery, but the standard of playing can't be faulted on any count.

****** Manhattan Afternoon**
Criss Cross 1082 *Walton; David Williams (b); Billy Higgins (d).* 12/92.

*****(*) Cedar's Blues**
Red Records RR 123179 2 *As above, except add Curtis Fuller (tb), Bob Berg (ts).* 93.

***** Off Minor**
Red Records RR 123242 2 *Walton; David Williams (b).* 93.

Manhattan Afternoon is a tremendous record. With just two originals tucked away in the middle of the set, Walton sticks to a programme of fairly routine standards and repertoire pieces – Monk's 'I Mean You' isn't his most played piece, though – and dispatches them all with consummate skill. His very first solo, on 'There Is No Greater Love', is replete with unexpected angles, and the soft harmonic displacements recur later on John Lewis's 'Afternoon In Paris'. Williams and Higgins fit the music like a glove. Strongly recommended.

The quintet record was recorded live in Bologna. It showcases four Walton themes, including a brief but powerful take of 'Ugetsu' and an unexpectedly romping 'Fiesta Espanola'. The only standard of the session is 'Over The Rainbow', executed without a shred of sentimentality. Berg is on fine form, but it's Fuller, so often the bridesmaid, who captures the attention, even when slightly off-mic.

The duos with Williams are strongly tinged with Monk's angular harmonics. The bass player is a rich source of harmonic ideas as well as being a strong, rhythmic anchor. A highly effective record, though probably only of interest to converts.

****** The Composer**
Astor Place TCD 4001 *Walton; Roy Hargrove (t); Vincent Herring (as); Ralph Moore (ts, ss); Christian McBride (b); Victor Lewis (d).* 1/96.

Not since *Cedar Plays Cedar* has there been such a full-blooded attempt to establish Walton's credentials as a writer, and yet what one remembers from this crisply recorded set isn't the writing at all but some fantastic playing from a band that sounds as if it works together every week. 'Hindsight' and 'Underground Memoirs' are both crafted and well scaffolded, but it's the horns that make it, and often on the record Walton lies back and comps while the youngsters flutter about in the foreground. It's well worth concentrating on his line for a moment or two, doing what he does and filtering out any extraneous signal in favour of a direct line to the chords.

****** Roots**

Astor Place TCD 4010 *Walton; Terence Blanchard (t); Scott Whitfield (tb); Don Sickler (t, flhn); Bobby Porcelli (as); Joshua Redman (ts); Willie Williams (ss, ts); Gary Smulyan (bs); Ron Carter (b); Lewis Nash (d); Ray Mantilla (perc).* 1/97.

As on the previous Astor Place set, Walton sticks to original material, confident now that his pianism is not just a technical resource but the basis of a broad musical vision. Unlike the previous album, though, this is a retrospective of compositions that go back many years. 'Mode For Joe', 'Ojas De Rojo' (which features Josh Redman in great form), and 'Fantasy In D' (which includes one of three fine contributions from Whitfield) are all well known from previous records, but here they have a fresh and incisive quality that makes them sound new-minted. The larger ensemble is of the highest quality, building on the strengths of a magnificent trio. Carter is allowed to come forward strongly in the mix and Nash, kept off to the side, is less intrusive than on some of his recorded appearances. Walton's arrangements are sure-footed and confidently shaped and, even when fully voiced, sound as stark and raw-boned as any blues. A fine album from a master composer.

Wanderlust

GROUP

Australian group touching on more worldly musics to spice up their approach.

****(*) Wanderlust**

ABC Jazz 518650-2 *Miroslav Bukovsky (t, flhn); Charles Greening (tb); Tony Gorman (as, cl); Alan Dargin (dijeridu); Alister Spence (ky); Carl Orr (g); Adam Armstrong (b); Fabian Hevia (d); Greg Sheehan (perc, v).* 93.

***** Border Crossing**

Rufus RF018 *As above, except Julian Gough (ts) replaces Gorman; add Renée Geyer (v); omit Sheehan and Dargin.* 5/95.

Miroslav Bukovsky leads this entertaining if lightweight Australian group, working an area that blends jazz chops and solos with a setting that has more to do with a mood/world music. Spence's keyboards set up hazy harmonic backdrops for horn and percussion workouts that tend to roll amiably on without making too great a dent on the listener. The first album is more arranged and suffers from a reticent production, but the second is stronger, Greening in particular emerging as a maverick voice, tailgating his way through his surroundings. Bukovsky himself sounds like an eclectic – which does suit the music. Both records run close to 80 minutes apiece; they could have trimmed away some of the noodling.

David S. Ware (born 1949)

TENOR SAXOPHONE, SAXELLO, STRITCH

Studied in Boston but settled in New York and played with Cecil Taylor in the '70s. Drove taxis in the '80s before a comeback with European recordings which over the next decade led to something like star status in the American avant-garde, culminating in a record deal with Columbia.

*****(*) Passage To Music**

Silkheart SHCD 113 *Ware; William Parker (b); Marc Edwards (d).* 4/88.

*****(*) Great Bliss: Volume 1**

Silkheart SHCD 127 *As above, except add Matthew Shipp (p).* 1/90.

***** Great Bliss: Volume 2**

Silkheart SHCD 128 *As above.* 1/90.

****** Flight of I**

DIW 856 *As above.* 12/91.

Ware grew up in New Jersey, attended Berklee for a couple of years at the end of the 1960s and then formed his own group, Apogee, before moving to New York City. He has worked extensively with drummer Andrew Cyrille and with Cyrille's mentor, Cecil Taylor. Other leaders have included trumpeter Raphe Malik and pianist Barry Harris. Since the late '80s, though, Ware has recorded a good many albums under his own name, all of them in a fierce, modernist style that makes much use of overblowing and multiphonics. Though he once carried alto and baritone as well as his tenor, he seems to have abandoned the big horn. Albert Ayler is only the most obvious source for the sound; Pharoah Sanders is unmistakably another, and Ware seems to have borrowed more than the alto-related stritch from Roland Kirk.

Passage To Music has something of Ayler's and Sanders's Afro-mysticism and constitutes something of a personal initiation, from 'The Ancient Formula', down 'The Elders Path', to the final 'Mystery'. Personal, but by no means solitary. Ware's comradeship with bassist William Parker, one of the true keepers of the avant-garde flame, is more than usually evident here in the absence of a harmony instrument. The addition of Matthew Shipp isn't in any way normative or conventional; most of what the leader does is still utterly 'outside'. The pianist produces some superbly throbbing open chords on *Great Bliss*, allowing Edwards to experiment with tymps and bells, reminiscent of Rashied Ali's explorations with Coltrane.

The drummer takes a more straightforwardly rhythmic role on the first of the DIW sessions, perhaps in response to Ware's own seeming decision to adopt a more linear and, unlikely as it sounds, melodic approach. 'There Will Never Be Another You' unmistakably recalls Sonny Rollins in wayward mood. Ware at least momentarily abandons the two 'novelty' horns to concentrate on tenor. 'Flight Of I' and 'Infi-Rhythms' are soaring, prayerful meditations; the saxophone roars and declaims like a storefront preacher, and Shipp plays like a man possessed.

By contrast, the two volumes of *Great Bliss* are slightly disappointing, except if seen as Shipp's coming-out ball. He's certainly the star and at 29 had, surprisingly, recorded only once previously, in a duo format with saxophonist Rob Brown. There's a degree of padding to get two full CDs out of this material. 'Saxelloscape One', on the first volume, is entirely forgettable, though the additional flute piece, 'Mind Time', is definitely worth having, a reminder of Ware's other, no less full-blast, horn.

*****(*) Third Ear Recitation**
DIW 870 *As above, except replace Edwards with Whit Dickey (d).* 93.

****** Earthquation**
DIW 892 *As above.* 5/94.

*****(*) Dao**
Homestead Records HMS230 *As above.* 9/95.

♛ ** Godspellized**
DIW 916 *As above, except replace Dickey with Susie Ibarra (d).* 5/96.

****** Go See The World**
Columbia *As above.* 12/97.

Opening (and closing) *Third Ear Recitation* with 'Autumn Leaves', albeit in hectic flight from the enchanter, and following it with Rollins's 'East Broadway Run Down' was some sort of confirmation of Ware's growing interest in a more linear and at the same time harmonically refined approach to jazz. The music on this CD was painstakingly rehearsed. The rhythmic shifts were not left to accident and, with new drummer Whit Dickey in the chair, are much closer to Cyrille's multi-rhythmic approach than Edwards's.

The real pay-off comes with *Earthquation* and the towering *Godspellized*, though on the latter the percussionist has changed again. The 1994 album is the most visceral to date, and the first that really begins to push through the envelope; Coltrane, Ayler and Sanders suddenly do seem like a generation back. Ware brackets his own 'Ideational Blue' and 'Cococana' with two raw, unadorned versions of 'Tenderly'. Again Shipp's role is critical. He nudges at chord shapes until they seem to distort, then knocks them back into shape again. How he does it isn't clear, a matter of attack dynamics and pedalling, perhaps; but it has the effect on 'Ideational Blue' of pitching Ware against a shifting background that refuses to resolve even momentarily.

Dao is primarily interesting because it may be Ware's attempt to create his own *A Love Supreme*, a connected sequence of highly spiritual themes for what was rapidly becoming a 'classic quartet'. 'Dao Forms' and the closing 'Dao' itself are the two major statements, internally linked as much by harmonic gesture as by common material, but coaxed into life by tremendous performances from all four players. Parker's intuitions are increasingly impressive and his turbulent contribution to 'Rhythm Dao' points in directions he has not yet explored on disc.

The addition of Susie Ibarra on *Godspellized* adds yet another dimension. She is both wonderfully direct and almost perversely oblique. Like a lot of female drummers (Cindy Blackman, Marilyn Mazur), she combines assertiveness with an unexpected delicacy and, in Ibarra's case, an authentically Oriental insistence that within the simplest of rhythms, mathematically speaking, there are huge chasms of ambiguity. These Ware, Parker and Shipp vault ever more confidently. This time the cover is Sun Ra's 'Stargazers', and though one can't quite see Ware in the Arkestra hopping from Lunceford arrangements to Disney tunes, you can hear why he's hooked into at least one song from Saturn. As has become the norm, there are two versions of the title-piece, one long, one a terse but definite Amen to close the set. Only Charles Gayle, another William Parker associate, has managed to push the Coltrane idiom further out.

If *Godspellized* seems essential, *Go See The World* (which was Mrs Ware's blessing/mission to her son at birth) is a gentle consummation. More accommodating than its predecessor, it is no less compelling, and is exquisitely recorded. This is the John Coltrane Quartet of the late '90s, the only difference being that the Jimmy Garrison role has been upgraded dramatically. Ware's post-post-bop improvisations on 'Esthetimetric' and 'Rapturelodic' are riveting, but the highlight is his meditation on the Hamlisch/Bergman crooner, 'The Way We Were'. Think back to the moment Trane deconstructed 'My Favorite Things' or 'The Inch Worm' and join us in a moment when jazz reinvents itself, forthrightly, humbly and with absolute conviction.

Wilbur Ware (1923–79)

DOUBLE BASS

Self-taught, he played in swing and bop groups in the 1940s, and with hard-boppers in the '50s, most famously with Thelonious Monk (1957–8). He influenced a school of bassists exemplified by Charlie Haden. Records as leader are very few in number.

*****(*) The Chicago Sound**
Original Jazz Classics OJC 1737 *Ware; John Jenkins (as); Johnny Griffin (ts); Junior Mance (p); Wilbur Campbell, Frank Dunlop (d).* 10 & 11/57.

Though much of what Ware did stemmed directly from Jimmy Blanton's 'Jack The Bear', he developed into a highly individual performer whose unmistakable sound lives on in the low-register work of contemporary bassists like Charlie Haden. Ware's technique has been questioned but seems to have been a conscious development, a way of hearing the chord rather than a way of skirting his own supposed shortcomings. He could solo at speed, shifting the time-signature from bar to bar while retaining an absolutely reliable pulse. Significantly, one of his most important employers was Thelonious Monk, who valued displacements of that sort within an essentially four-square rhythm and traditional (but not European-traditional) tonality; the bassist also contributed substantially to one of Sonny Rollins's finest recordings. He grew up in the sanctified church and there is a gospelly quality to 'Mamma-Daddy', a relatively rare original, on *The Chicago Sound*. The only other Ware composition on the record, '31st And State', might have come from Johnny Griffin's head; the saxophonist roars in over the beat and entirely swamps Jenkins, whose main contribution to the session is a composition credit on two good tracks.

Though the Ware discography is huge (with numerous credits for Riverside in the 1950s), his solo technique is at its most developed on his own record. 'Lullaby Of The Leaves' is almost entirely for bass, and there are magnificent solos on 'Body And Soul' (where he sounds *huge*) and 'The Man I Love'. One wonders if a couple of alternative takes mightn't have been included on the

CD. Ware's impact was enormous, and one record (albeit a fine one) seems a poor trawl.

Tim Warfield

TENOR SAXOPHONE

Like other Criss Cross artists, Warfield has managed to bring a classic hard-bop style up to date. He has a full, emphatic tone which oscillates between terse R&B and a more loquacious version of Wayne Shorter's gnomic approach.

***** A Cool Blue**

Criss Cross 1102 *Warfield; Terell Stafford (t); Cyrus Chestnut (p); Tarus Mateen (b); Clarence Penn (d).* 12/94.

*****(*) A Whisper In The Night**

Criss Cross 1122 *As above, except add Stefon Harris (vib).* 12/95.

***** Gentle Warrior**

Criss Cross 1149 *As above, except omit Harris; add Nicholas Payton (t).* 12/97.

Warfield's three Criss Cross records are as solidly accomplished as anything on the label but are also rather lacking in personality. If the label is the '90s equivalent of Blue Note – and we have argued that point often enough – these records partake of some of the classic imprint's incidental shortcomings: formulaic repetition, reliance on generic writing, and over-reliance on a narrowly collegiate personnel.

Stafford always sounds like a man who wishes he were in charge of things and his contributions have an impatient quality that is briefly engaging on *A Cool Blue*, less effective subsequently. The middle record is by some way the shortest and most concentrated of the three, and one feels that quality control has won out. The two standards – 'Speak Low' and 'Bye Bye Blackbird' – give the set a balance that isn't reflected elsewhere, but it also benefits from two of Warfield's best compositions, 'Tin Soldier' and 'I've Never Been Blue Before', which are definitive of his approach.

While we like *Gentle Warrior* and admire its softer and more subtly inflected approach, it cries out for an reprise of Harris's wonderful vibes-playing, and the alternation of trumpet players is less than effective, largely because Payton and Stafford are too similar in approach. Time will tell whether Tim Warfield has the stamina and the change of pace to sustain a career as a solo artist. These are valuable records but rarely as exciting as one might have hoped.

Washboard Rhythm Kings

GROUP

Although the name suggests some early rural blues outfit, they were actually a New York-based group who recorded many sessions in the city during the early 1930s, styling themselves in the manner of early small-band swing.

***** Washboard Rhythm Kings Vol. 1**

Collectors Classics COCD-17 *Dave Page (t); Ben Smith (as); Jimmy Shine (as, v); Carl Wade (ts); Eddie Miles (p, v); Steve Washington (bj, g); Teddy Bunn (g); Jimmy Spencer (wbd); Jake Fenderson, The Melody Four (v).* 4/31–3/32.

***** Washboard Rhythm Kings Vol. 2**

Collectors Classics COCD-18 *As above, except add Taft Jordan (t), Wilbur Daniels (bj), Leo Watson, George 'Ghost' Howell (b, v), H Smith (wbd).* 32.

***** Washboard Rhythm Kings Vol. 3**

Collectors Classics COCD-19 *As above, except add Valaida Snow (t), John 'Shorty' Haughton (tb), Jerome Carrington (as), Bella Benson, Lavada Carter (v).* 10/32–8/33.

There are plenty of unidentified names to add to the various personnel listed above, which gives some idea of how little is known about this group, which recorded around New York for a period of a couple of years at the beginning of the 1930s. Smith, Wade and Miles seem to have been the mainstays of the band, which otherwise fluctuated between a quartet and a group running to ten pieces. While a washboard may have been appropriate for the earlier tracks, which sounded about as down-home as a band working in New Jersey could be, by the time of the final session in August 1933 it was anachronistic for a group that was playing quite a tough and respectable small-group swing. The material is a peculiar blend of blues, jazz themes and pop tunes: 'Please Tell Me' (*Vol. 1*), for instance, is a mixture of Ellington's 'Stevedore Stomp' and Blind Blake's 'Diddy Wah Diddy'. The earlier stuff is attractively rough and unpretentious, the later tracks more ambitious; but all of it makes up a valuable backwater in the recording of jazz at the end of the first golden age. John R.T. Davies has done the transfers on all three discs and they are from mainly superb originals.

Dinah Washington (1924–63)

VOCAL

Born Ruth Lee Jones in Tuscaloosa, Alabama, Washington joined Lionel Hampton in 1943, then went solo as an R&B artist, finally aspiring to a grand torch singer role in the '50s, making many records for Emarcy, Mercury and Roulette. She finally referred to herself as 'The Queen', and her gospel-and-blues methodology undeniably influenced a generation of soul singers who followed her. Married nine times, she died from an accidental pill overdose.

***** Mellow Mama**

Delmark DD 451 *Washington; Karl George (t); Jewell Grant (as); Lucky Thompson (ts); Milt Jackson (vib); Wilbert Baranco (p); Charles Mingus (b); Lee Young (d).* 12/45.

Whether or not she counts as a 'jazz singer', Washington frequently appeared in the company of the finest jazz musicians and, while she was no improviser and stood slightly apart from such contemporaries as Fitzgerald or Vaughan, she could drill through blues and ballads with a huge, sometimes slightly terrifying delivery. Her start came with the Lionel Hampton band, and after leaving him she made these dozen tracks for Apollo Records in the company of a band organized by Lucky

Thompson. While Washington herself sounds comparatively raw and unformed, the jump-blues material doesn't demand a great range, and she swings through the likes of 'My Voot Is Really Vout' as well as the more traditional 'Beggin' Mama Blues'. Thompson's team sound as if they're having fun, and the remastering is quite clear.

*****(*) Dinah Jams**
Emarcy 814639-2 *Washington; Clifford Brown, Clark Terry, Maynard Ferguson (t); Herb Geller (as); Harold Land (ts); Junior Mance, Richie Powell (p); Keter Betts, George Morrow (b); Max Roach (d).* 8/54.

Washington's sole 'jazz' record is fine, but not as fine as the closely contemporary Sarah Vaughan record with a similar backing group, and therein lies a tale about Washington's abilities. She claimed she could sing anything – which was probably true – but her big, bluesy voice is no more comfortable in this stratum of Tin Pan Alley than was Joe Turner's. Still, the long and luxuriant jams on 'You Go To My Head' and 'Lover Come Back To Me' are rather wonderful in their way, and there is always Clifford Brown to listen to.

*****(*) For Those In Love**
Emarcy 514073-2 *Washington; Clark Terry (t); Jimmy Cleveland (tb); Paul Quinichette (ts); Cecil Payne (bs); Wynton Kelly (p); Barry Galbraith (g); Keter Betts (b); Jimmy Cobb (d).* 55.

***** Dinah!**
Emarcy 842139-2 *Washington; Hal Mooney Orchestra.* 55.

*****(*) The Swingin' Miss D**
Verve 558074-2 *Washington; Quincy Jones Orchestra.* 55.

***** In The Land Of Hi-Fi**
Emarcy 826453-2 *Washington; Hal Mooney Orchestra.* 4/56.

***** The Fats Waller Songbook**
Emarcy 818930-2 *Washington; Ernie Royal, Johnny Coles, Joe Newman, Clark Terry (t); Melba Liston, Julian Priester, Rod Levitt (tb); Eddie Chamblee, Jerome Richardson, Benny Golson, Frank Wess, Sahib Shihab (reeds); Jack Wilson (p); Freddie Green (g); Richard Evans (b); Charli Persip (d).* 10/57.

***** Sings Bessie Smith**
Verve 538635-2 *Washington; Blue Mitchell, Fip Ricard, Clark Terry (t); Melba Liston, Quentin Jackson, Julian Priester (tb); Eddie Chamblee, Harold Ousley (ts); Charles Davis, McKinley Easton, Sahib Shihab (bs); Wynton Kelly, James Craig, Jack Easton (p); Paul West, Robert Lee Wilson (b); Max Roach, James Slaughter (d).* 12/57–7/58.

***** What A Diff'rence A Day Makes!**
Verve 543300-2 *Washington; studio orchestra, including Jerome Richardson (reeds), Charles Davis (bs), Joe Zawinul (p), Milt Hinton (b), Panama Francis (d).* 59.

***** Unforgettable**
Mercury 510602-2 *Washington; studio orchestra.* 59–1/61.

*****(*) Verve Jazz Masters: Dinah Washington**
Verve 518200-2 *As above Emarcy discs, plus Quincy Jones Orchestra.* 55–61.

***** Verve Jazz Masters: Sings Standards**
Verve 522055-2 *As above.* 52–58.

***** 'Round Midnight: Dinah Washington**
Verve 510087 *As above, except add Nook Shrier Orchestra, Eddie Chamblee Orchestra, Tab Smith Orchestra, Jimmy Cobb Orchestra.* 10/46–12/61.

***** Ultimate Divas: Dinah Washington**
Verve 539053-2 *As above.* 52–61.

****** The Dinah Washington Story**
Mercury 514841-2 2CD *As above discs.* 43–59.

Washington's studio albums for Emarcy are a good if fairly interchangeable lot: the quality of the backing doesn't much affect the calibre of her singing, and a frowsy studio orchestra is as likely to generate a great vocal as a smoking jazz ensemble. *For Those In Love* is a stand-out from this pack, since the accompaniment is as classy as that on the *Dinah Jams* session, and at least one track – a perfectly realized 'I Could Write A Book' – is a stone classic. The new edition of *What A Diff'rence A Day Makes!* sounds particularly glowing, in audio terms, but the usual problems with Washington's albums apply: a fine performance of 'I Thought About You' is marred by the cooing backing vocals, and Belford Hendricks's arrangements are little more than feebly functional. Fewer problems with *The Swingin' Miss D*, since Jones uses a crack jazz orchestra, and though Dinah doesn't seem to be any more excited by them than by any of her other accompanists, it's a record full of classy, genuine music-making. *Sings Bessie Smith*, which couples a studio date with an Eddie Chamblee orchestra and three live tracks from a Newport session, is something of a curio. It's never as good as the similarly directed session by Lavern Baker for Atlantic, and as ever Washington seems ambiguous about her material: as if singing blues is beneath her, she almost camps it up at times. But there are some dark, truthful moments too.

The Dinah Washington Story still sweeps the board as a first choice from this area: a 40-track double set that creams off all the most interesting songs from the period, with a few from her earliest days to round out the picture. The other compilations will do fine for anyone wanting a one-disc representation of Dinah's albums from this period. Anyone wanting a complete Washington collection from her Mercury years is directed to the several multi-disc sets available in the USA comprising *The Complete Dinah Washington On Mercury Volumes 1–7*. Each is a three-disc set, and in total they cover the period 1952–61 as comprehensively as anyone would wish.

****(*) In Love**
Roulette 797273-2 *Washington; studio orchestra.* 62.

****(*) Back To The Blues**
Roulette 854334-2 *Washington; studio orchestras.* 7–11/62.

***** The Best Of Dinah Washington**
Roulette 799114-2 *Washington; studio orchestras.* 62–63.

The Roulette albums merely continue what was a disappointing decline on record, even though it's hard to define exactly where the problem lies. Washington sings mightily and with no lack of attention throughout all these records, and an improvisational gleam resides at the heart of many of these songs, especially 'Do Nothin' Til You Hear From Me' (*In Love*). But the relentlessly tasteful orchestrations by Don Costa and Fred Norman turn down the heat all the way through, and Washington can sound curiously alone and friendless on a lot of the tracks. *Back To The*

Blues is arguably the most disappointing, since she makes so little out of promising vehicles such as 'How Long, How Long Blues' and 'Don't Come Running Back To Me' – although when abetted by harps and cooing vocal support, perhaps it's no surprise. Washington's legacy is something of a conundrum: a great pop singer with a dilettante's touch, she is difficult to see clearly.

*****(*) Live At Birdland 1962**

Baldwin Street BJH 301 *Washington; Joe Zawinul (p); Jimmy Rouser (b); Al Jones (d).* 61–62.

A fascinating postscript to the Washington discography, this collects three Birdland broadcasts, two with the listed trio, one with unknown tenor, organ and drums. The great voice is scaled down, more intimate and more moving. There are several medleys – she liked to talk to friends when working Birdland, so she would try to shorten sets by stringing as many songs together as possible! – and Zawinul is clearly keeping his ears wide open so as not to miss any cues. Symphony Sid jumps in here and there with announcements. One of her most likeable entries and something that will surely delight Washington admirers: sound is a bit boxy and flat, but very listenable.

Grover Washington Jr (1943–99)

ALTO, SOPRANO, TENOR AND BARITONE SAXOPHONES

The early death of Grover Washington was a shock. Grover's joyous, soaring saxophone had turned up in some unexpected contexts over the years but the man from Buffalo was an underrated improviser whose abilities were perhaps critically eclipsed by the million-selling success of records like Mister Magic. Sadly, one of Grover's early R&B employers, organist Charles Earland, died within weeks of him, further underlining how untimely a loss it was.

*****(*) Inner City Blues**

Motown 530577 *Washington; Bob James (arr); collective personnel.* 9/71.

****** Mister Magic**

Motown 530103 *Washington; Randy Brecker, Jon Faddis, Marvin Stamm (t); Eric Gale (g); Gary King, Ralph Upchurch (b); Harvey Mason Sr (d); Ralph MacDonald (perc).* 11/74.

Much exploited for television signature tunes, programme stings and advertising, Washington's brand of smooth, contemporary soul-jazz has rarely won over the more sober jazz critics, who like to think he's just another pop musician. There is, however, no getting away from Washington's consummate musicianship and taste. He has a lovely, melting tone, even on the treacherous soprano, and is capable of writing simple, beautiful ballads, like the Grammy-winning 'Just The Two Of Us', which appeal to pop and jazz fans alike.

The Marvin Gaye covers on *Inner City Blues* (including the title-track) and a delicate interpretation of Bill Withers's 'Ain't No Sunshine' pushed the album in the direction of a younger pop and soul audience, but there is no mistaking the leader's jazz background. Washington derives much from Cannonball Adderley – and sometimes from Earl Bostic in his gentler mode – and his solos are logically shaped and suffused with the blues.

Mister Magic is pure pleasure. The title-track has a soaring, timeless quality that still makes people smile. The theme is held suspended just so long and then it's as if someone has shaken a storm of butterflies out of a basket. It was a staple on British television for many years as signature-tune to a current affairs programme. Billy Strayhorn's 'Passion Flower' is the other key performance and a sign that Washington could bring some-thing special and individual to repertory material; one wishes passionately that he had made more records in this vein.

***** Live At The Bijou**

Motown 37463 0239 2 *Washington; Leslie Burrs (f); James Sid Simmons (ky); Tyrone Brown (b); Millard Vinson (d); Doc Gibbs (perc).* 78.

Live albums by Grover Washington are rare indeed, and this one offers what is presumably a pretty accurate impression of how the band sounded in a club context. 'Mr Magic' doesn't have the same airborne quality as on the original, studio set. The double-LP format is over-generous and a spot of judicious editing wouldn't have gone amiss.

****(*) Paradise**

Elektra 60537 *Washington; James Sid Simmons (p); Tyrone Brown, Richard Lee Steacker (g); John Blake (vn); Millard Vinson (d); Doc Gibbs (perc).* 79.

***** Winelight**

Elektra 60338 *Washington; Paul Griffin, Richard Tee (p); Bill Eaton, Ed Walsh, Raymond Chew (syn); Eric Gale (g); Marcus Miller (b); Steve Gadd (d); Robert Grenidge, Ralph MacDonald (perc); Bill Withers, Hilda Harris, Yvonne Lewis, Ullanda McCullough (v).* 6–7/80.

***** Come Morning**

Elektra 60337 *Washington; Richard Tee (p); Paul Griffin (syn); Eric Gale (g); Marcus Miller (b); Steve Gadd (d); Ralph MacDonald (perc); Grady Tate, Yvonne Lewis, Vivian Cherry, Ullanda McCullough, Frank Floyd, Zack Sanders, William Eaton (v).* 6–9/81.

***** The Best Is Yet To Come**

Elektra 60215 *Washington; Jon Faddis (t); Frank Wess, Alex Foster (ts); Mona Goldman-Yoskin (f); Teddi Schlossman, Richard Tee (p); James Lloyd, Paul Griffin, Billy Childs, Dexter Wansel (ky); James Herb Smith, Eric Gale, Lee Ritenour, Richard Lee Steacker (g); Marcus Miller, Cedric Napoleon, Abe Laboriel (b); Yogi Horton, Harvey Mason, Darryl Washington (d); Victor Feldman, Kevin Johnson, Leonard Gibbs, Ralph MacDonald (perc); Patti Labelle, Bobby McFerrin, Carla Benson, Evette Benton, Lucille Jones (v).* 82.

***** Anthology Of Grover Washington Jr**

Elektra 60415 *As above discs.*

***** The Best Of Grover Washington**

Motown 530260 *Washington; Randy Brecker, Jon Faddis, John Frosk, Bernie Glow, Thad Jones, Irwin Markowitz, Bob Millikan, Alexander Otey, Ernie Royal, Alan Rubin, Marvin Stamm (t, flhn); Paul Faulise, Santo Russo (tb); Alan Raph (btb); Ray Alonge, James Buffington, Fred Klein (frhn); Gerry Niewood (as); Jerry Dodgion (ts); Pepper Adams, Don Ashworth, Phil Bodner (bs); Arthur Clarke (bs, f); Hubert Laws (f, picc); Romeo Penque (woodwinds); Hilary James (p, ky); Jorge Dalto (p); Jay Berliner, Gene Bertoncini, Cornell Dupree, Eric Gale, Steve Khan (g); John Blake (vn); Ron Carter, Richard Davis, Anthony Jackson, Marcus Miller, George Mraz, Idris Muhammad (b); Billy Cobham, Pretty Purdie (d); Phil Kraus, Ralph MacDonald, Airto Moreira (perc); additional instruments; strings.*

A time-served session-man with Prestige, Washington tends to make albums the way American football is played. Players are called on for cameo performances in highly specialized roles and are then dispensed with. The sound is teased and plucked and sprayed into shape but manages, unlike most commercial pop product, to sound relatively unconfected and even, on some of the earlier discs, quite spontaneous. We've never warmed to *Paradise*, which is thinly arranged and produced. *Winelight* and *Come Morning* at least sound as if they have had some money spent on them, though not necessarily in the most tasteful way possible. The only real constant is Washington himself. He phrases a little like Cannonball Adderley, who was the main inspiration behind 1975's wonderful *Mister Magic*. There's nothing that good in the present batch, and newcomers might do worse than try out the interestingly titled *Anthology*, which, though it does cover obvious things like 'The Best Is Yet To Come', 'East River Drive' and (of course) 'Just The Two Of Us', is also quite sensitively programmed.

**** Inside Moves**

Elektra 60318 2 *Washington; Richard Tee (ky); Eric Gale (g); Anthony Jackson (b); Marcus Miller (b, syn); Steve Gadd, Buddy Williams (d); Anthony MacDonald, Ralph MacDonald (perc); vocals, strings.* 3/84.

A fallow period for the saxophonist, and only the most devoted fans are likely to find much to arrest them on an album that almost uniquely yielded no obvious big hit number. The material is as drab as any in Grover's catalogue and the playing also seems perfunctory.

****(*) Strawberry Moon**

Columbia CK 40510 *Washington; Joey DeFrancesco (p); James Lloyd (p); Jason Miles (syn); B.B King (g, v); Michael J Powell, Richard Lee Steacker (g); Tyrone Brown, Gerald Veasley (b); Jim Salamone, Darryl Washington (d, perc); Doc Gibbs (perc); Jean Carne, Elizabeth Hague, Spencer Harrison (v).* 87.

****(*) Then And Now**

Columbia CK 44256 *Washington; Igor Butman (ts); Tommy Flanagan, Herbie Hancock, James Sid Simmons (p); Richard Lee Steacker (g); Ron Carter, Gerald Veasley (b); Marvin 'Smitty' Smith, Grady Tate, Darryl Washington (d); Miguel Fuentes (perc).* 88.

**** Time Out Of Mind**

Columbia CK 45253 *Washington; Bill Jolly, Donald Robinson, Jim Salamone, James Sid Simmons, Philip Woo (ky); Richard Lee Steacker (g); Ronnie Foster (g, ky, etc.); Gerald Veasley (b); Darryl Washington (d); Daryl Burgee, Miguel Fuentes, Doc Gibbs (perc); Spencer Harrison, Paula Holloway, Phyllis Hyman (v).* 89.

There are parallels between Washington's move to Columbia and Miles Davis's move *from* Columbia to Warner Bros. In both cases, the logic seemed to be to throw as much production as possible at the album, get as much of the personnel plugged in as the studio boards would take and then crank up all the levels.

Strawberry Moon has an interesting vignette from B.B. King ('Caught A Touch Of Your Love') and some typically smooth playing from the leader, who excels on 'The Look Of Love'. Otherwise, there isn't much that's genuinely arresting. A year later, *Then And Now* suggested possibilities which no one seemed inclined to pick up on. The addition of Flanagan and Hancock (not to forget big Ron Carter and the two distinguished drummers) plus the inclusion of jazz and standard material seemed to signal some desire to return to the jazz mainstream. Performances of 'Stella By Starlight' and Hancock's 'Just Enough' are encouraging, though Grover for once seems a little constrained by his sidemen and fails to take flight.

It wasn't to be repeated. *Time Out Of Mind* is the most disappointing of all Washington's later records, an overspiced gumbo of funk and fusion gestures, for once unredeemed by the leader's trademark saxophone.

****(*) Next Exit**

Columbia CK 48530 / 469088-2 *Washington; Ite Jerez (t); Lewis Khan (tb); John Bolden, Terry Bolden (ky, perc); Curtis Dowd Jr, Sergio George (ky); Randy Bowland, Rodney Millon, Richard Lee Steacker (g); Reuben Rodriguez, Gerald Veasley (b); Darryl Washington (d); Lalah Hathaway, Nancy Wilson, The Four Tops (v); additional vocals; strings.* 92.

Much of the emphasis is on guest vocalists, but there is enough instrumental interest on 'Take Five (Take Another Five)', the disarming opener, on Grover's 'Next Exit' and 'Summer Chill' to sustain attention and, as ever, the orchestrations are gorgeous. After his death, Grover's album titles all suddenly seemed ironic, except maybe this one which hinted (as does the music) that the road ahead might not be infinite.

***** All My Tomorrows**

Columbia 474553-2 *Washington; Eddie Henderson, Earl Gardner (t, flhn); Robin Eubanks (tb); Bobby Watson (as); Bobby La Vell (ts); Jimmy Cozier (bs); Hank Jones (p); Romero Lubambo (g); George Mraz (b); Billy Hart, Lewis Nash (d); Freddy Cole, Jeanie Bryson (v).* 94.

A look at that personnel is enough to make one think that Washington had recanted. Mostly these are sensible, lush (well, we'd hardly expect 'harsh') charts by dependable hands such as Slide Hampton, placing Grover in a more jazzed environment than usual but not doing anything to trip him up or let him come to harm. It merely underlines the smooth appeal of his saxophone playing, here displayed on soprano, alto and tenor alike. And we wouldn't wish anything else: we have enough hard-bop saxmen as it is. If Grover can put even a drop of soul into the smooth-jazz scenario, don't stand in his way.

***** Soulful Strut**

Columbia 485142-2 *Washington; Mac Gallohon, Andy Gravish, Tim Ouimelte, Jimmy Powell (t); Herb Hubel (tb); Aaron Heick (sax, f); Dale Kelps (as, bcl, f); Rick DePofi (ts); Donald Robinson (p); Charlie Ernst, George Whitty (ky); Dan Shea (ky, b, d); Steve Bargonetti, Bob Ward (g, ky); Randy Bowland, Dan Huff, Ray Obiedo, Paul Pimsler, Richard Lee*

Steacker, Chris Taylor (g); Gary Haase (b, d, arr); Gerald Veasley (b); Steve Gadd, Omar Hakim, Peter Michael, Richie Morales (d); Cyro Baptista, Pablo Baptista, Joe Bonadio, Norberto Goldberg, Roger Squitero (perc); Lindiwe Diamini, NtombKhona Diamini, Sandy Griffith, Wayne Hernandez, Amanda Homi, Bakithi Khumalo, Claytoven Richardson, Katherine Russell, Wincy Terry, Jeanie Tracy (v). 96.

Just because classic Blue Notes didn't carry credits for 'grooming' doesn't mean we should be too snooty about this one, which does. The ten tracks, which lean heavily on arranger Gary Haase, are a touch too primped and correct, but the authority of Grover's saxophone cuts through even the most viscous of background arrangements and 'I Can Count The Times' and 'Mystical Force' are positively honeyed. As so often, he is the only truly individual solo voice, though Washington and Haase have attempted to pull some of the horns up through the mix. The sheer size of personnel suggests how meticulously this and similar albums have been assembled, a dot-and-wash approach to production which is also a long way removed from live recording round a stereo pair. A delight for anyone who appreciates professionally executed soul-jazz, and a goldmine – surely? – for any remix artist and sampler on the lookout for instrumental nuggets.

Sadao Watanabe (born 1933)

ALTO SAXOPHONE, SOPRANINO SAXOPHONE, SOPRANO SAXOPHONE, FLUTE

Born in Tochohi, he joined the Toshiko Akiyoshi band in 1953 and took it over when she left for Berklee. Studied in the USA and founded the first Japanese jazz school in 1965. A patrician figure at home, he divides his playing time between a version of soft Brazilian fusion and more firmly centred bebop.

*****(*) Parker's Mood**

Elektra 60475 *Watanabe; James Williams (p); Charnett Moffett (b); Jeff Tain Watts (d).* 7/85.

*****(*) Tokyo Dating**

Elektra WPCP 4327 *As above.* 7/85.

****(*) Good Time For Love**

Elektra 60945 *Watanabe; Kenji Nishiyama (tb); Ansel Collins, Onaje Allan Gumbs, Rob Monsey, Sohichi Noriki (ky); Keiichi Gotoh (syn); Bobby Broom, Radcliffe Bryan, Takayuki Hijikata, Tsunehide Matsuki, Jeff Mironov, Earl Smith, Tohru Tatsuki (g); Victor Bailey, Bertram McLean, Kenji Takamizu, Ken Watanabe (b); Will Lee (b, v); Poogie Bell, Carton Davis, Shuichi Murakami, Chris Parker, Hideo Yamaki (d); Mino Cinelu, Sue Evans, Sydoney Wolfe (perc); Eve (v); collective personnel.* 2–3/86.

***** Birds Of Passage**

Elektra 60748 *Watanabe; Freddie Hubbard (flhn); Hubert Laws (f); George Duke, Russell Errante (ky); Dan Huff, Paul Jackson (g); Abraham Laboriel (b); Vinnie Colaiuta, John Robinson, Carlos Vega (d); Alex Acuna, Paulinho Da Costa (perc); collective personnel.* 87.

***** Elis**

Elektra 60816 *Watanabe; Cesar Camargo Mariano (ky); Heitor Teixeira Pereira (g); Nico Assumpção (b); Paulo Braga (d); Papeti (perc); Toquinho (v, g).* 2/88.

***** Made In Coracao**

Elektra WPCP 4331 *Watanabe; Toquinho (v, g); Amilson Godoy (ky); Edson Jose Alves (g); Ivani Sabino (b); William Caram (d); Osvaldo Batto, Papeti (perc).* 3–4/88.

Like most Japanese of his generation (the composer Toru Takemitsu told a very similar story), Sadao Watanabe heard nothing but Japanese traditional and German martial music during his teens, and was exposed to Western popular music only through American forces radio; he also cites Norman Granz's Jazz At The Philharmonic broadcasts as a big influence. Watanabe had already largely rejected Japanese music (his father was a teacher of *biwa*, a lute-like instrument). By the time he was twenty, he was sufficiently adept on the alto saxophone to join Toshiko Akiyoshi and perform in America.

He subsequently recorded with both Chico Hamilton (who was always on the look-out for unusual tonalities) and Gary McFarland, who turned Watanabe on to the fashionable sound of *bossa nova*. Perhaps because he encountered jazz at a relatively advanced stage in its development, Watanabe seemed able to take virtually any of its stylistic variants (swing, bop, Latin, Afro and, later, fusion) on their own terms. Though his recent recordings have tended to be heavily produced, middle-market fusion, Watanabe has recorded with an impressive array of American heavyweights including (to mention only the piano players) Chick Corea, Herbie Hancock, Cedar Walton and Richard Tee. In 1967 he collaborated with Toshiko Akiyoshi's ex-husband, Charlie Mariano, producing three fine albums of standards and oriental themes.

These, like most of Watanabe's output, were released only in Japan. Between 1961 and 1980, he made a total of 36 albums. The best of them are the more swinging, 'American' sets. Watanabe's Japanese bands have tended to be correct but rather stiff, a criticism that might be levelled at his own playing but for the surpassing beauty of his tone.

Of the Elektra albums, the most interesting from a straight jazz point of view are the live Parker set and the subsequent studio album with Williams, Moffett and Watts. The recent Brazilian sets will appeal to Latin fans, and these probably have a sharper rhythmic edge than the drifting studio fusion of most of the others.

****(*) Go Straight Ahead 'N Make A Left**

Verve 537944-2 *Watanabe; Bernard Wright (ky); Stephen Teele (b); Mike Flythe, Hassan Flythe, Charley Drayton (d); Steve Thornton (perc).* 1–2/97.

****(*) Viajando**

Verve 557859-2 *Watanabe; Cesar Mariano (ky); Romero Lubambo (g); Nilsson Matta (b); Paulo Braga (d); Cafe (perc, v); Meninas Do Brasil, Pamela Driggs (v).* 1–2/98.

These barely pass muster as serious jazz records; but they're not meant to be that. As a sweet, harmonious confection of sax solos over lite-fusion backdrops, they play agreeably enough. *Go Straight Ahead* is more urbanized (Wright has at least as much to do as Watanabe) and *Viajando* works from a synthetic Latin base.

It's all harmless fluff, but time and again Watanabe finds a notably trim or elegant turn of phrase in his solos.

*****(*) Remembrance**

Verve 547440-2 *Watanabe; Nicholas Payton (t, flhn); Robin Eubanks (tb); Cyrus Chestnut (p); Romero Lubambo (g); Christian McBride (b); Billy Drummond (d).* 1/99.

By the sharpest contrast with the 1997 and 1998 discs, *Remembrance* teams Watanabe with ranking jazz players and strong improvising charts, all of them originals. The real hero of the set (as so often where he is present) is McBride. He rattles off titanic solos on 'Dim Blue' and 'Forest Song' but, more importantly, provides a solid architecture for the whole set.

Watanabe's chops are still in excellent shape. Never a profound soloist, he nevertheless manages to shape elegant statements over blues chords and mid-tempo boppish themes. His tone has always sounded slightly sharp, less than a quarter-tone, but enough to sustain its exotic character. On 'Aquarian Groove' and 'Going Back Home', he is reminiscent of Sonny Fortune, elsewhere of the largely forgotten Carlos Garnett.

Benny Waters (1902–98)

ALTO AND TENOR SAXOPHONES, CLARINET, VOCAL

He studied in Boston before spending several years from 1925 with Charlie Johnson, then with Henderson, Hopkins, Lunceford and others through the 1930s and '40s. From 1955 he was mostly in Europe, touring relentlessly, and he carried on doing this into a charismatic old age.

***** When You're Smiling**

Hep 2010 *Waters; Roy Williams (tb); Joe Temperley (bs); Alex Shaw (p); Ron Mathewson (b); Martin Drew (d).* 8/80.

****(*) Hurry On Down**

Storyville STCD 8264 *Waters; Paul Sealey (g); Erica Howard (b); John Cox (d).* 4/81.

***** Benny Waters–Freddy Randall Jazz Band**

Jazzology JCD-124 *Waters; Freddy Randall (t); Jim Shepherd (tb); Stan Greig (p); Paul Sealey (g, bj); Tiny Winters, Mike Durrell (b); Laurie Chescoe (d).* 12/82.

Waters was an indomitable personality, among the oldest practising jazzmen, and though his recent records tend to be too accommodating for a man who doesn't like to act his age, there is much vigorous work on clarinet and alto. Like Benny Carter or Doc Cheatham, he sounds like a survivor from another age, raising his voice among us with few concessions to his surroundings. His tone, vibrato and delivery are antiquarian, but none of this suggests frailty, more an enduring style.

These British recordings, made when Waters was a mere lad and only pushing eighty, are likeable stuff. *When You're Smiling* is prime British mainstream, courtesy of Williams, Temperley and the rhythm section, and even without Waters there would be plenty to listen to. Benny is in grand spirits on the title-piece and Williams has three features where he makes trombone playing seem like the easiest thing on earth. *Hurry On Down*, with respectable if sometimes charmless backing from Paul Sealey's trio, is all right, but Waters usually sounds better with another hornman standing at his elbow. The meeting with Freddy Randall and a more trad-orientated crew is good enough, though some of the rhythms plod and there's too much solo space given to the sidemen; Randall's brusquely hot solos and Waters's sometimes impish humour are the reasons to listen.

***** Swinging Again**

Jazz Point 1037 *Waters; Thilo Wagner (p); Jan Jankeje (b); Gregor Beck (d).* 5/93.

****(*) Plays Songs Of Love**

Jazz Point 1039 *Waters; Red Richards (p); Vic Juris (g); Johnny Williams Jr (b); Jackie Williams (d).* 7/93.

In his nineties, Waters was a phenomenon. That doesn't guarantee that his records would be anything more than a novelty from someone who makes Benny Carter seem like a youngster, but *Swinging Again* is a creditable effort from any saxman and, if the support from the European rhythm section is a bit faceless, Waters has character enough to go around. Ten more tunes, three vocals. The second album is slush of a high order by what's mostly a team of oldtimers, and the material runs the gamut from 'Always' (which creaks a bit, even if Waters was born before it was written) to 'You Are The Sunshine Of My Life'.

Matt Wates

ALTO SAXOPHONE

Studied at Berklee and is now at work on the British contemporary scene.

***** Smallbills Garage**

AB ABCD 9 *Wates; Martin Shaw (t, flhn); Andy Panayi (ts, f); John Pearce (p); Malcolm Creese (b); Steve Brown (d).* 11/98.

Crisp, good-natured and under-cooked, this is something like the jazz equivalent of a New Age salad. Wates writes perky, sweetly resolved tunes which he arranges for this group like exercises in structural economy and deftness. The band handle every tricky little contour. It's all very amiable, but it tends to be forgotten the moment it's over. It's also far too long at almost 74 minutes: better to have let one or two of these tunes get out of hand and muscle a few of the lamer pieces out of the way.

Mitch Watkins

GUITAR, GUITAR SYNTHESIZER, KEYBOARDS

Guitarist who can play fusion or straight-ahead situations and who follows the eclectic path of most contemporary jazz-based guitarists.

****(*) Underneath It All**

Enja 5099-2 *Watkins; Stephen Zirkel (t, flhn); Paul Ostermayer (ss); Rob Lockart (ts, syn); Anthony Cox (b); Dennis Chambers (d); Arto Tuncboyacian (perc, v).* 1/89.

***** Curves**

Enja 6054-2 *Watkins; Bob Berg (ts); Jay Anderson (b); Dennis Chambers (d).* 5/90.

*****(*) Strings With Wings**

Tiptoe 888814-2 *Watkins; Bill Ginn (ky); Gene Elders (vn); Marty Muse (pedal steel g); Chris Maresh (b); Paul Glasse (mand); Brannen Temple, Scott Laningham (d); James Fenner (perc).* 1/92.

****(*) Humhead**

Dos Jazz 7501 *Watkins; John Mills (saxes); Doug Hall, Darryl Dunn (ky); Chris Maresh (b); Brannen Temple (d); Chris Searles (perc); Abra Moore (v).* 95.

Mitch Watkins plays in almost every guitar style one can think of, which lends inevitable identity problems to these records. He has a caseful of jazz-rock licks when the amps are turned up and the fuzzbox is on, but he's rather better served by the countrified twang that ties him to his native Texas. *Underneath It All* is an excessively modish debut that suffers from some overheated and tuneless tunes, but the sinuous line he draws out of the title-track makes up for matters like the merely silly version of 'Lester Leaps In'. *Curves* sets him up in a quartet where he plays Mike Stern to Bob Berg's Bob Berg – he does it very well, but it seems a tad pointless. The breakthrough comes with the surprisingly light and charming *Strings With Wings*, where he records with a crew of fellow Texans and comes up with a fusion of styles that makes for heartbreaking ballads such as 'One Lost Love' and simple, picturesque miniatures that let his thoughtful improvisations resonate through a clean, wiry sound-mix.

It's clear from the follow-up *Humhead* that this is a fine line that Watkins walks. Here and there one finds the lyricism which buoyed up the previous records, as in 'Solitude' and 'When Sadie Sings', but much of the disc gets caught up in anonymous rock instrumentalism that could have come off any one of a thousand such albums.

Bill Watrous (born 1939)

TROMBONE

One of the great trombone technicians, Watrous can play extraordinarily fast, prefers a steady pace, and produces a tone so smooth it could be spread on toast. He worked in swing groups and show bands in the 1970s before moving to California and majoring in studio work and arranging.

***** Bone-ified**

GNP Crescendo GNPD 2211 *Watrous; Shelly Berg (ky); Lou Fischer (b); Randy Drake, Tom Cummings (d).* 92.

****(*) A Time For Love**

GNP Crescendo GNPD 2222 *As above, except add Dennis Farias, Wayne Bergeron, Ron Stout (t), Doug Inman, Bob McChesney, Rich Bullock (tb), Sal Lozano, Phil Feather, Bill Liston, Bruce Eskovitz, Bob Carr (saxes), Dave Carpenter (b); omit Cummings.* 93.

***** Space Available**

Double-Time DTRCD-124 *Watrous; Dennis Farias, Wayne Bergeron, Bob Summers, Darrel Gardiner, Steve Huffsteter (t); Doug Inman, Bob McChesney, Wendell Kelly, Rich Bullock (tb); Sal Lozano, Phil Feather, Bill Liston, Gene Burkurt, Bob Carr (reeds); Shelly Berg (p); Trey Henry (b); Randy Drake (d).* 12/96.

Watrous remains among the most accomplished trombonists alive. His occasional albums, though, are almost too classy for their own good. The main thing he needs is context, and the GNP albums don't really pull this one off. Berg's flashy piano and frequent recourse to string-synthesizer parts make a much too fulsome contribution out of what he has to do and, despite some typically fluent and thoughtful solos by the trombonist, the album makes only a modest impression. *A Time For Love* is all Johnny Mandel tunes. The big band appears only here and there, Berg goes back to the synthesizer, and the mood is more like light music than a jazz situation. Watrous salvages something, but maybe he just wants to treat these projects as extensions of his studio routine.

Space Available puts him in the surroundings of the Refuge West Big Band, an institution in Sherman Oaks, California, for a number of years and an awesomely proficient machine when it comes to tackling difficult scores and multi-storeyed frameworks. Watrous loves this kind of situation and he has a solo on every tune, his familiar style – a plummy, fat tone, phrasing that seems to have no discernible joins in it and a way of getting from one end of an improvisation to the other without any hint of faltering – still intact. In a way it's a pity that more members of the band aren't heard from in a solo capacity, since it could use a jolt of surprise here and there: one sometimes feels that proficiency is everything here and, if nothing sounds soulless, there's nothing to set the heart on fire either. 'The Road Goes Ever Onward' has some rather extraordinary textures in it and Watrous will always make jaws drop with some of his playing: try the way he turns 'My Foolish Heart' into a *bel canto* aria for the horn.

Bobby Watson (born 1953)

ALTO SAXOPHONE, SOPRANO SAXOPHONE

Watson learned his trade as saxophonist and musical director with the Jazz Messengers, establishing himself as a soloist of real authority, with a keening, blues-drenched sound. Most of his recording has been for European labels.

***** Advance**

Enja ENJ 9075 *Watson; Jim McNeely (p); Todd Coolman (b); Adam Nussbaum (d).* 84.

***** Round Trip**

Red RR 123187-2 *Watson; Pietro Bassini (p); Attilio Zanchio (b); Giampiero Prina (d).* 2/85.

♛ ** Love Remains**

Red CD 123212 *Watson; John Hicks (p); Curtis Lundy (b); Marvin 'Smitty' Smith (d).* 11/86.

***** Beatitudes**

Evidence ECD 22178 *As above.* 87

****** The Year Of The Rabbit**

Evidence ECD 22210 *Watson; Irving Stokes (t); Art Baron (tb); Bill Easley (ts, cl); Jim Hartog (bs); Mulgrew Miller (p); Lawrence Lucie (g); Curtis Lundy (b); Kenny Washington (d).* 2/87.

Few contemporary saxophonists are more instantly recognizable than the brilliant Kansan. Watson's hard, bright sound and trademark descending wail (a device that seems increasingly mannered as years go by) were first acclaimed in a vintage Jazz Messengers line-up. Watson went on to work in Charli Persip's Superband and to co-found the 29th Street Saxophone Quartet. Though the quartet has been internationally successful, Watson's recording career has been intermittent to say the least. Most of his best work has been for the Italian Red label. Most of Watson's titles from the late 1970s to mid-'80s have so far failed to make the transition to CD (the loss of *Estimated Time Of Arrival*, named after his theme-tune, and 1984's *Perpetual Groove* leaves a bit of a hole). However, the very good *Beatitudes*, co-led with Lundy, is still around. With typical perversity, both his Blue Note discs with Horizon have disappeared from the catalogue, which makes the Red catalogue all the more important.

For some perverse reason we omitted *Round Trip* last time. It's a slightly disappointing record and certainly contains no inkling of the majesty of *Love Remains*, but hindsight invests it with an impressive confidence. The Ornette-composed title-track kicks off a set which contains almost nothing of Watson's own – only the closing 'All The Thing Of Jo Maka' bears his name – and not enough of his signature blues. Miles's and Bill Evans's 'Blue In Green' and Lee Morgan's 'Ceora' don't seem quite the right repertoire for this group, however confidently they're played.

Love Remains is Watson's one certain masterpiece, a startlingly poised performance. From the Parker-influenced 'Mystery Of Ebop' to the solemnly funky 'Dark Days (Against Apartheid)', it has a complete unity of purpose. The title-piece, jointly credited to Bobby and Pamela Watson, is built round a three-note motif which means the same thing in any language. Hicks's solo is a perfect foil for Watson's slightly plangent second entry, while Lundy and Smitty Smith sustain a dark bass pulse. Lundy's 'Sho Thang' is the only non-Watson composition, a weak interlude before Pam Watson's 'The Love We Had Yesterday' rounds off the set. If the 1980s threw up maybe a baker's dozen of essential jazz albums, *Love Remains* comes in somewhere near the top.

The earlier *Advance* is a live recording, noisy and appreciative, but not quite the Watson who was to emerge in the next couple of years. Much more like the real thing is *The Year Of The Rabbit*, a heartfelt, beautifully disciplined tribute to Johnny Hodges. All the great songs are there and, not surprisingly, it's 'Isfahan' that steals the show, one of the most evocative and sympathetic accounts of that great song *not* performed by Rabbit himself.

*****(*) This Little Light Of Mine**

Red RR 123250 *Watson (as solo).* 93.

The solo saxophone album was a challenge Watson had resisted for many years. The results are inevitably patchy, and it isn't the kind of set that makes for comfortable listening straight through. Better to concentrate on one track at a time and savour Watson's deft phrasing and sinuous developments. A few of the pieces are little more than work-outs: 'These Foolish Things', 'Body And Soul', and a quick run through the 'Giant Steps' changes. 'Misterioso', 'Donna Lee' and Joe Henderson's 'Recorda Me' are more developed, but some of the most interesting ideas emerge out of traditional material; there are two takes of Apostoloy Kaldara's 'Mes'Tou Bosporou' and the title-track is an old spiritual Watson's preacher grandfather used to sing. *This Little Light* doesn't quite take him full circle, but it sets out certain agenda that he could usefully spend the next ten years addressing.

****** Quiet As It's Kept**

Red RR123284-2 *Watson; Terell Stafford (t); Orrin Evans (p); Lenny Argese, Greg Skaff (g); Curtis Lundy (b); Ralph Peterson (d); Marlon Simon (perc); Pamela Watson (v).* 98.

The hair is grizzled these days but, a decade on from *Love Remains*, Watson is playing with the same maturity and grace. He was never a turbulent player, but the distinctive keening swoop which used to punctuate solos has given way to a mellower and more measured slide down the scale. The calm reflection of 'Always A Friend' represents a new dimension in his music. The title-track is vintage Watson, identifiable from the very first bars and as ably constructed as ever. 'Nubian Breakdown' is a more fragmentary and alienated piece, and perhaps a nod in the direction of Arthyur Blythe, though it also resembles some of Sonny Fortune's African-inspired pieces. The mood of 'Back Home Again With You' and 'Watch The Children Play' is touchingly sombre. Stafford is used on only three tracks, including 'Nubian Breakdown' and the intriguing folk-song arrangement, 'Nanatsu-No-Ko'. For balance, that seems about right, for Terell is a dominant presence wherever he plays and this is an album which truly belongs to Bobby Watson. The use of guitar is something of a departure, and it's elegantly done; Skaff's rapid articulation on the first track is revelatory. As in the past, Pamela Watson shares in the plaudits, credited as co-composer on 'Concentric Circles' and adding a vocal to 'Afternoon in Ottobrun'. A remarkable musical partnership. *Quiet* isn't a classic, but it is a very special record, easily Watson's best for years.

Eric Watson

PIANO

Expatriate American pianist working from France.

***** The Amiens Concert**

Label Bleu 6512 *Watson; Steve Lacy (ss); John Lindberg (b).* 11/87.

****(*) Broadway By Twilight**

Musidisc 500482 *Watson (p solo).* 2/92.

***** Soundpost**

Music & Arts 920 *Watson; John Lindberg (b).* 9/90–5/95.

Watson is an interesting player, but he's hard to characterize: influences such as Monk, John Lewis and Mal Waldron seem to drift in and out of his music, and his composing favours dark, sluggish structures that mysteriously relax into moments of pure lyricism. Intriguing – but sometimes hard to take over the course of a record, and the hint of gallows humour suggested by his titles ('New Canaan Con Man', 'Substance Abuse') never really surfaces. Steve Lacy seems to have been attracted by Watson's grainy intensity, and he makes a fist of the settings on the Label Bleu album without quite invading Watson's world. *The Amiens Concert* is a bleak, unsmiling recital, with four Watson themes and one apiece by the others: again, when Lacy absconds on 'Substance Abuse', Watson and Lindberg reach a scowling truce. The duo record, *Soundpost*, is just as demanding, recorded mainly in 1995 with two stray solo tracks from earlier sessions. Watson's thick left-hand sonorities allow Lindberg to roam over his instrument and, when they toil implacably through the pianist's five-part 'The Twisted Suite', the players create a dense thunder of sound. Stern but absorbing.

Broadway By Twilight is just on the far side of agreeable. Watson milks all the sweetness out of seven standards and leaves each one a dark, cauterized corpse. The funereal tempos and brooding development aren't very nice, though that's hardly Watson's style. Trouble is, each theme ends up sounding the same, perhaps.

*****(*) Silent Hearts**

Free Flight 1434 *Watson; Mark Dresser (b); Ed Thigpen (d).* 10/98.

Watson's best record by a mile. Centred by the swinging rhythms of Dresser and Thigpen – an unlikely but superb combination – the pianist comes up with eight strong originals and allows himself the indulgence of memorable melodies and considerable amounts of light and shade. That renders the thunderous explosion which takes place halfway through the one marathon performance, 'Punchin Paich Patch', all the more effective. A terrific piano trio record.

Ernie Watts

TENOR SAXOPHONE, ALTO SAXOPHONE, SOPRANO SAXOPHONE

Watts's moment in the spotlight came when he won a Grammy for his playing on the Chariots of Fire soundtrack. A stalwart of the West Coast big bands, he'd worked as staff arranger on The Tonight Show and seemed content to remain off to the side of things until he began recording under his own name for JVC in the '80s. Watts has a mellow, understated delivery, but is capable of great emotional compression.

*****(*) Ernie Watts Quartet**

JVC 3309-2 *Watts; Pat Coil (p); Joel Di Bartolo (b); Bob Leatherbarrow (d).* 12/87.

****** Reaching Up**

JVC 2031-2 *Watts; Arturo Sandoval (t); Mulgrew Miller (p); Charles Fambrough (b); Jack DeJohnette (d).* 93.

***** Unity**

JVC 2045-2 *Watts; Geri Allen (p); Eddie Gomez, Steve Swallow (b); Jack DeJohnette (d).* 12/94.

*****(*) The Long Road Home**

JVC 2059-2 *Watts; Kenny Barron (p); Mark Whitfield (g); Reggie Workman (b); Carmen Lundy (v).* 96.

One of the real delights of Charlie Haden's Quartet West has been Watts's tender-muscular sax patterns, looming and shimmering out of Haden's Angelean fogs. Watts's solo career has been slow in getting under way, but the last few years have seen some interesting activity, after probably thousands of studio dates as an often anonymous soloist. The eponymous *Quartet* features his rawer-sounding alto and positively desolate soprano (which might have sounded good in Quartet West) in a broadly romantic set of themes. The rhythm section are nothing to write home about and Watts is left with most of the work on 'Body And Soul', but as a package it's very accomplished.

Reaching Up is an unambiguous jazz album, albeit with other inputs hovering round the edges. DeJohnette provides the fuel for a driving, energetic work-out that highlights the leader's solo construction perfectly. Arturo Sandoval turns up on two tracks, bringing his usual fierce integrity, but the stage is Watts's and he uses it to the full. *The Long Road Home* is a more brooding, almost *misterioso* affair, with the central trio of Watts, Barron and Workman apparently searching for a proper desolation in the midst of some quite fierce playing. Mingus's 'Nostalgia In Times Square' has seldom seemed so chilling and, if the Carmen Lundy tracks lighten the mood somewhat, it ends on the cold-fingered caress of 'Moonlight And Shadows'.

Unity was unusual in featuring two bass players – though, with Steve Swallow on the strength, one is really dealing with a second, harmonically challenging, harmony instrument. Allen and DeJohnette were inspired recruitments and Jack's 'Silver Hollow' is one of the highlights of the set; by that token, it's surprising that nothing of Geri's was included. The set ends with a vividly expressive interpretation of Mal Waldron's 'Soul Eyes', a jazz classic which sits as well for Watts's tenor as it did for Coltrane's.

****(*) Project: Activation Earth**

Amherst AMH 93320 *Watts; Pete Levin (p, syn); Paul Mariconda (syn); Bruce Brucato, George Puleo (g); Ted Reinhardt (d); Rick Galloway (perc).* 89.

An oddity; Watts in collaboration with a group called Gamalon, who specialize in an inventive brand of jazz-fusion. Inevitably, the sound-world is very different from what one normally expects of Watts, but tunes like 'Activation' and 'Other Side' bespeak an imaginative use of electronic resources.

****** Classic Moods**

JVC 2072 *Watts; Mulgrew Miller (p); George Mraz (b); Jimmy Cobb (d).* 98.

An utterly delightful jazz record, beautiful, intelligent and impossible to pigeon-hole. Individually, each of the four players is known for full-voiced, lyrical playing. What is interesting when they come together is how much space they leave. Mraz is masterly on 'Round Midnight', conjuring unsuspected new paces from that overworked steed. Watts himself has the ability to make a classic sound entirely fresh and contemporary. His solo on 'It Never Entered My Mind' is redolent of the younger John Coltrane, as is the long ballad form of 'Lush Life'. Both are among the most feeling and intense recordings he has made and they grace an album that genuinely does merit the classic label. No amount of rhetoric will flatter it; *Classic Moods* deserves to be heard.

Jeff Tain Watts

DRUMS

Watts emerged from the group of players centred around the Marsalis brothers in the 1980s, an association which continues, although he has also subsequently worked in a wider circle.

***** Megawatts**

Sunnyside SSC 1055D *Watts; Kenny Kirkland (p); Charles Fambrough (b).* 7/91.

Watts emerged as one of the leading drummers of his time when he worked in the first Wynton Marsalis Quintet, and this debut set under his own name reunites the original rhythm section from that band. His two original tunes have no special interest: Watts makes noise as a player, not as a composer, and his favourite devices – thumping interpolations on the toms, crash-cymbal strokes that seem to linger in their own time, and an iron-faced swing – are well in evidence here. Kirkland is gregariously on top of the material. It's a good record, if rather charmless: there is some light-and-shade, but the trio are really interested only when they have the burners up full.

*****(*) Citizen Tain**

Columbia CK 69551 *Watts; Wynton Marsalis (t); Delfeayo Marsalis (tb); Kenny Garrett (as); Branford Marsalis (ss, ts); Kenny Kirkland (p); Eric Revis, Reginald Veal (b).* 6–8/98.

A somewhat belated follow-up was well worth the wait. Watts not only manages to reassemble the Marsalis family for the final track (when producer Delfeayo also sits in), he writes some good tunes, has Wynton and Branford recalling the explosive excitement of their original quintet on 'The Impaler', and provides settings for Kirkland that make one regret that fine player's early death. Some of the music is a shade too keen to impress the listener, but this is in most respects a powerful and assured document of these players at this time.

Trevor Watts (born 1939)

ALTO SAXOPHONE, SOPRANO SAXOPHONE

Played in RAF bands in the early '60s, then moved in London free-music circles and co-founded SME. More recently, in his Moiré Music group, has investigated fusions of jazz with other musics.

***** A Wider Embrace**

ECM 521351-2 *Watts; Colin McKenzie (b); Nana Tsiboe, Nee-Daku Patato, Jojo Yates, Nana Appiah, Paapa J Mensah (perc).* 4/93.

*****(*) Moiré**

Intakt CD 039 Watts; Colin McKenzie *(b)*; Paapa J Mensah *(d, perc, v)*; 3/95.

A stalwart of the British free-jazz scene, Watts has to some extent turned his back entirely on abstract music in order to explore the strongly rhythmic, non-European language of his two main groups of the 1980s, the Drum Orchestra and (as on the first record) Moiré Music. The word 'moiré' refers to the shimmering patterns one sees in watered silk, and what Watts was trying to do was to create such patterns musically by overlaying rhythmic patterns and textures in live performance.

Moiré Music performances have tended to be either entrancing or dull. The ECM album inclines to the latter but is still eminently listenable, and techno buffs can marvel at the way engineer Gary Thomas and Steve Lake at ECM managed to get so many drums sounding good. Watts's studies in African percussion music have occasionally resulted in illustrated lectures. While there is a wealth of ethnomusicological detail attached to this recording, it is altogether more flowing, and Watts is playing singingly and with passion. Unfashionable he may be, even as a negative example, but this is territory opened up by Ginger Baker in the years after Cream. Though some aspects of the music have still not been thought through, it's a significant performance.

The tight, fierce trio on the Intakt disc gives a better sense of how his current work relates back to British free-movement projects like Amalgam. Mensah is a big presence, bringing a pungent vocal attack as well as wild percussion, and McKenzie's bass lines weave to and fro like oiled rope.

Weather Report

GROUP

Along with Miles's electric band, of which Joe Zawinul was a member, the Mahavishnu Orchestra and Return To Forever, Weather Report were key players in the development of fusion music. The spare atmospherics of the early albums gave way to a funkier and more dance-based approach, largely determined by Joe's rock-solid, harmonically subtle bass-lines and chord progressions and by Wayne Shorter's minimal approach. The personnel kept changing, but the basic concept remained consistent and strong for 15 years.

***** Weather Report**

Columbia 468212 *Joe Zawinul (ky); Wayne Shorter (ts, ss); Miroslav Vitous (b); Alphonse Mouzon (d); Airto Moreira (perc).* 71.

****** I Sing The Body Electric**

Columbia 468207 *Joe Zawinul (ky); Wayne Shorter (ts, ss); Miroslav Vitous (b); Eric Gravátt (d); Dom Um Romao (perc); with Ralph Towner (g); Wilmer Wise (t, picc t); Hubert Laws (f); Andrew White (eng hn); Joshie Armstrong, Yolande Bavan, Chapman Roberts (v).* 72.

****** Live In Tokyo**

Columbia 489208 2CD *Joe Zawinul (ky); Wayne Shorter (ts, ss); Miroslav Vitous (b); Eric Gravátt (d); Dom Um Romao (perc).* 1/72.

Weather Report are one of the great contemporary jazz groups. 'Birdland' on *Heavy Weather* (below) is one of only a tiny handful of contemporary jazz tunes that everyone seems to have heard. Though it has tended to overshadow the rest of the group's output, it encapsulates perfectly the formula that has made the group so successful: solid part-writing from Joe Zawinul, Wayne Shorter's enigmatic saxophone sound, a free-floating personnel round the Zawinul–Shorter cadre, and great product marketing (Weather Report covers have been consistently eye-catching and aesthetically pleasing). In 1990 Columbia withdrew the whole Weather Report catalogue on vinyl and embarked on a programme of CD reissues. That programme has been very welcome, though the packaging leaves something to be desired; in line with other Columbia reissues, newcomers have to look long and hard to sort out personnels. Reprinting old liner-notes and running self-serving and misleading puffs in place of clear and straightforward information is something of a dereliction (though absolutely in line with CBS's famously cavalier attitude to musicians and fans alike). A much-talked-about boxed set of all the group's Columbia recordings seems to have been delayed yet again. Perhaps by the time of our next edition ...

From its inception until its demise in 1986, Weather Report was a flexible ensemble. After the first album, it was unmistakably Zawinul's flexible ensemble. From that point, Zawinul claimed the majority of composition credits (though Shorter, Pastorius and others chipped in) and steered the band's increasingly rhythm-orientated conception. Zawinul compositions are typically riff-centred bass-clef ideas, built up in layers by the rest of the band. Those who had followed Shorter's developing career were alternately baffled and horrified by the exiguous squeaks and tonal smears that suddenly were passing for solos (solos, it had been pointed out, were not the Weather Report way; 'we always solo and we never solo'). The first album was a set of fey acrylic sketches, clearly derived from the pastel side of the 1969–70 Miles Davis band (in which both Zawinul and Shorter saw service) but much rawer in tone. The opening 'Milky Way' is a pleased-with-itself set of FX on electric piano and soprano saxophone; 'it has to do with overtones and the way one uses the piano pedals?' Yeah? That's great, man. Most of the rest is in similar vein. Many years later, Vitous rejigged his folksy 'Morning Lake' and made something of it. The recording is thin and erratic, which is a shame, for Shorter's closing 'Eurydice' introduces some promise.

Everything about *I Sing The Body Electric* was very 1972: the title lifted from Whitman via Ray Bradbury, the brilliant sci-fi artwork (an overdue hand, please, for Ed Lee, Jack Trompetter and Fred Swanson), the psychobabble liner-note ('There is flow. There is selflessness'). There was also a band on the brink of premature extinction. Side one is more or less an extension of the debut album. The (presumably) anti-war 'Unknown Soldier' is almost prettified. The only thing that redeems it from banality is a tense cymbal pulse that on the live second side erupts into some of the most torrential and threatening percussion of the period. Zawinul is on record as thinking that Gravátt was the finest drummer the group ever had. On 'Vertical Invader' he plays with a clubbing hostility that somehow intensifies the impression that the group was heading off in four or five (Dom Um Romao was only a part-timer) directions at once. These days, Gravátt works as a prison guard. *Plus ça change.*

The live material from Japan had been known from the second side of *I Sing The Body Electric* but, as anyone who managed to catch the group at this time knows (and they played memorable gigs in Europe as well, not least at Ronnie Scott's in London), the live impact was fearsome and cumulative. Listening to *Live In Tokyo* over the span of two whole discs confirms for sure and for good that this was not merely a studio-confected band, good on atmospheres but lacking in sheer fire and funk. The ferocity of Gravátt's drumming, the soaring brilliance of Vitous's bass playing, and (as always) the Zawinul–Shorter axis made this one of the great groups of the time. Much of the second disc was drawn from the group's first album, and though 'The Moors', medleyed with 'Eurydice', hasn't the frail beauty of the studio version it has certainly acquired a new strength and gravitas. One for collectors, and by far the most important new release on the Report front for many years.

***(*) **Sweetnighter**

Columbia 485102-2 *Joe Zawinul (ky); Wayne Shorter (ts, ss); Miroslav Vitous (b); Alphonso Johnson, Eric Gravátt (d); Dom Um Romao (perc).* 73.

**** **Mysterious Traveller**

Columbia 471860-2 *Joe Zawinul (ky); Wayne Shorter (ts, ss); Miroslav Vitous (b); Ismael Wilburn (d); Dom Um Romao (perc).* 73–74.

Sweetnighter was never likely to be much more than a consolidating record, though nowadays it yields up considerable treasures, not least the stunning 'Boogie Woogie Waltz', which is the band's single most accessible track before 'Birdland'.

Mysterious Traveller is still perhaps the most sheerly beautiful of the records, from the wild joy of 'Nubian Sundance' with its synthed crowd-noises to the quietness of 'Blackthorn Rose', a lyrical, delicate piece of music that suggests this may have been the point of maximum closeness between the band's onlie begetters, Zawinul and Shorter. Some of the material was recorded at Zawinul's home, with his kids romping in the background, and only later put together in the studio, and it is this balance between improvisational immediacy and brilliantly crafted overdubbing that gives the record its lasting freshness and power.

*** **Tale Spinnin'**

Columbia 476907 *As above, except Alphonso Johnson (b) replaces Vitous; omit Romao, Wilburn; add Leon Ndugu Chancler (d), Alyrio Lima (perc).* 74.

***(*) **Black Market**

Columbia 468210 *Joe Zawinul (ky); Wayne Shorter (ts, ss); Alphonso Johnson, Jaco Pastorius (b); Chester Thompson, Narada Michael Walden (d); Alejandro Neciosup Acuna, Don Alias (perc).* 76.

***(*) **Heavy Weather**

Columbia CK 65108 *Joe Zawinul (ky); Wayne Shorter (ts, ss); Jaco Pastorius (b); Alejandro Neciosup Acuna (d, perc); Manolo Badrena (perc).* 76.

(*) **Mr Gone

Columbia 468208 *Joe Zawinul (ky); Wayne Shorter (ts, ss); Jaco Pastorius (b); Tony Williams, Steve Gadd, Pete Erskine (d); Manolo Badrena (perc); Denice Williams, Jon Lucien (v).* 78.

*** **Night Passage**

Columbia 468211 *Joe Zawinul (ky); Wayne Shorter (ts, ss); Jaco Pastorius (b); Peter Erskine (d); Robert Thomas Jr (perc).* 80.

*** **Weather Report**

Columbia CK 48824 *As above.* 82.

*** **8:30**

Columbia 476908 2CD *As above.* 83.

*** **Procession**

Columbia CK 65453 *Joe Zawinul (ky); Wayne Shorter (ss, ts); Victor Bailey (b); Omar Hakim (d); Jose Rossy (perc).*

*** **Domino Theory**

Columbia 25839 *As above.* 84.

*** **Sportin' Life**

Columbia CK 39908 *As above.* 84.

Ever afterwards, Weather Report albums were inclined to look like audition sessions for new drummers. Steve Gadd, Tony

Williams and Peter Erskine all played on *Mr Gone*, suggesting (in that correctly) a band that was going in too many directions at once. *Black Market* seems to combine the virtues of earlier albums: atmospheric tone-poetry, thudding, joyous rhythms. With Pastorius arriving in time to cut the funky 'Barbary Coast', Zawinul has the engine-room tuned to his obvious satisfaction. 'Black Market' is a wonderful, thunderous tune that completely blows out Shorter's rather wimpy 'Three Clowns' and utterly wimpy lyricon figures; galling, because on 'Cannon Ball', dedicated to Julian Cannonball Adderley, for whom Zawinul played and wrote 'Country Preacher' and 'Mercy, Mercy, Mercy', Shorter signs in again with some chunky tenor.

The decision to repeat the eponymous title of the first album for the eleventh was, on the face of it, puzzling; but in some ways this overlooked record does hark back to the first couple, where atmosphere and degree of abstraction were still very much the key.

Heavy Weather was the breakthrough album in market terms. It allegedly shifted in excess of 400,000, largely on the strength of 'Birdland', a whistleable, riffy tune dedicated to the New York jazz club. No one had ever danced to 'Orange Lady' or 'Surucucú'; suddenly, Weather Report were big – a fact that comfortably disguised the detail that, 'Birdland' and 'A Remark You Made' apart, *Heavy Weather* was nothing much. Onstage, the band went decidedly *nouveau riche*, tossing around techno-nonsense, indulging in pointless virtuosity.

All except Shorter. He is widely taken to be *Mr Gone* (at high school, they'd called him 'Mr Weird'), but he shows his taste, maintaining virtual silence on the band's worst record, lower than which it took them some time to dive. *Night Passage* was better, but it was already obvious that a decade was more than enough, the band had done its best work; the rest was for the fans and for CBS, not for the players, and that makes an important and unhappy difference.

The final settled line-up created some exceptionally good work. *Procession* is particularly good, though often overlooked, and the electronically distorted voices of Manhattan Transfer on 'Where The Moon Goes' reprises their imaginative and still stirring intepretation of 'Birdland'. *Domino Theory* has one signature Zawinul piece, 'The Peasant', which earns the stars, but that's about it.

***(*) This Is This

Columbia CD 57052 *Joe Zawinul (ky); Wayne Shorter (ss); Carlos Santana (g); Victor Bailey (b); Peter Erskine, Omar Hakim (d); Mino Cinelu (perc).* 85.

A curtain call and a slightly sad farewell to one of the most influential groups of recent times. The photo of Zawinul and Shorter shaking hands on the back cover underlined the strong impression that this was a farewell project. For most of the album, Joe's keyboard and wind-synth figures replace much of the saxophone work of the past, while guest performer Santana creates some astonishing effects on 'The Man With The Copper Fingers', a track that anticipates much of what Zawinul was to do with his future groups. Erskine is also on the fringes, though his hand is also evident in the production, and he hands over drumming responsibilities to the much less expressive Hakim.

*** The Jaco Years

Columbia CK 65451 *As above.* 75–80.

As a survey of Pastorius's contribution as a composer, this makes some sense, but Weather Report and Jaco fans will almost certainly have the material already. The solo workout on 'Slang' is a predictable curtain-call, but as a whole *The Jaco Years* merely underlines the impression that WR was Zawinul's band, with Shorter as his secret sharer, and all other participants, even Pastorius, as bit-players.

Chick Webb (1909–39)

DRUMS

Born in Baltimore, the diminutive Webb had already been bandleading for some time in New York when he took over at the Savoy ballroom in 1933. He kept the most competitive band in the city there for six years, hiring Ella Fitzgerald as his band singer in 1935, but TB of the spine eventually killed him. Fitzgerald took over his band after his death.

**** Chick Webb 1929–1934

Classics 502 *Webb; Ward Pinkett, Louis Bacon, Taft Jordan (t, v); Edwin Swayzee, Mario Bauza, Reunald Jones, Bobby Stark, Shelton Hemphill, Louis Hunt (t); Robert Horton, Jimmy Harrison, Sandy Williams, Ferdinand Arbello, Claude Jones (tb); Hilton Jefferson, Louis Jordan, Benny Carter (cl, as); Pete Clark, Edgar Sampson (as); Elmer Williams (cl, ts); Wayman Carver (ts, f); Don Kirkpatrick, Joe Steele (p); John Trueheart (bj, g); Elmer James (bb, b); John Kirby (b); Chuck Richards, Charles Linton (v).* 6/29–11/34.

***(*) Rhythm Man 1931–1934

Hep CD 1023 *As above.* 31–34.

***(*) Chick Webb 1935–1938

Classics 517 *As above, except add Nat Story, George Matthews (tb), Chauncey Houghton (cl, as), Ted McRae (ts), Tommy Fulford (p), Bill Thomas, Beverley Peer (b); omit Bacon, Swayzee, Jones, Hemphill, Hunt, Horton, Harrison, Arbello, Carter, Kirkpatrick, Richards, Linton.* 6/35–8/38.

Between them, these CDs include virtually all of Webb's studio recordings aside from those with vocals by Ella Fitzgerald, which Classics have released under her name. The two tracks by The Jungle Band of 1929 sound almost primitive in comparison to the ensuing sessions, driven as much by Trueheart's machine-like banjo-strumming as by Webb; but its use of the reeds and Webb's already exciting playing point a way out of the 1920s and, by the time of the 1931 session – which includes a memorable arrangement by Benny Carter of his own 'Blues In My Heart' and a valedictory appearance by Jimmy Harrison, who died not long afterwards – Webb was running a great band, which eventually (in 1933) won him a long-running residency at Harlem's Savoy Ballroom. Edgar Sampson handled the best of the earlier arrangements, and the leader could boast fine soloists in Taft Jordan (later to join Ellington), Sandy Williams, Bobby Stark and Elmer Williams, as well as a rhythm section that was almost unrivalled for attack and swing. Webb's own mastery of an enormous drum-kit allowed him to pack a whole range of percussive effects into breaks and solos which never upset the momentum of the band. His distance from the showmanship of Gene Krupa, who would far surpass him in acclaim, was complete. Some of the best examples of what he could do are on the second Classics disc, including the terrific drive of 'Go Harlem' and the breaks in 'Clap Hands! Here Comes Charley'. Once Fitzgerald had started singing with the band and began to secure a wider fame, though, some of the zip went out of their playing and, although the weakest material is confined to the Fitzgerald CDs, the closing tracks on Classics 517 show them cooling off.

Choosing among these discs is a matter of individual taste. The two Classics CDs offer uninterrupted coverage, but their reproduction, though quite listenable, is second-best to the Hep disc. Hep's excellent survey covers only the period 1931–4 and misses many of the best tracks, but it is still a fine set in excellent sound.

*****(*) Chick Webb And His Savoy Ballroom Orchestra 1939**

Tax 3706-2 *Webb; Dick Vance, Bobby Stark, Taft Jordan (t); Sandy Williams, Nat Story, George Matthews (tb); Garvin Bushell, Hilton Jefferson (cl, as); Wayman Carver (ts, f); Ted McRae (ts); Tommy Fulford (p); Bobby Johnson (g); Beverley Peer (b); Ella Fitzgerald (v).* 1–5/39.

The swing which Webb and the orchestra generate on these broadcasts, made not long before the drummer's death, belies any hint that the band was getting fatigued. Twenty-two tracks from two sessions, the first with Fitzgerald absent, find all concerned in top form. Stark, Jordan and Williams are again the outstanding soloists, but Webb's own playing is certainly the most powerful thing on the second date, where he combines with the excellent Peer to turn unlikely tunes such as 'My Wild Irish Rose' into battlegrounds. The slightly superior sound gives it an advantage over the first session, but both are very listenable, and the treatment of Count Basie's showcase 'One O'Clock Jump' on the earlier set reminds that Webb managed to defeat Basie's orchestra in a 'battle of the bands' at the Savoy almost exactly a year before.

Eberhard Weber (born 1940)

BASS, CELLO, OCARINA, KEYBOARDS

Learned cello as a boy but soon switched to bass and played many gigs in the '60s, although only as a part-timer, since he also worked in film and television. Early associations with Wolfgang Dauner and Volker Kriegel led to his own composing and bandleading, and a long tenure with ECM beginning in 1973. He was a pioneer in using bass with electronics, playing an adapted upright model.

*****(*) The Colours Of Chloe**

ECM 833331-2 *Weber; Ack Van Rooyen (flhn); Rainer Bruninghaus (ky); Peter Giger, Ralf Hubner (d); strings.* 12/73.

Having played straight-ahead jazz bass through the 1960s, Weber delivered this uncannily beautiful album to Manfred Eicher's ECM operation and won himself an award or two. If some passages now suggest a cooler version of *Tubular Bells*, with the overlapping themes of 'No Motion Picture' hinting at the tranquillizing pomposity of progressive rock, the singular beauty of the textures and Weber's discovery of a new world based around massed cellos and subtle electronic treatments remains insidiously affecting. While the improvisational content is carefully rationed against the measure of the themes, Bruninghaus and Weber himself emerge as thoughtful and surprisingly vigorous virtuosos. If the CD offers few improvements over the excellent original vinyl edition, the recording itself still sounds splendid.

****** Yellow Fields**

ECM 843205-2 *Weber; Charlie Mariano (ss, shenai); Rainer Bruninghaus (ky); Jon Christensen (d).* 9/75.

Weber's masterpiece is essentially a period piece which nevertheless still seems modern. The sound of it seems almost absurdly opulent: bass passages and swimming keyboard textures that reverberate from the speakers, chords that seem to hum with huge overtones. The keyboard textures in particular are of a kind that will probably never be heard on record again. But there's little prolixity or meandering in this music. Weber builds very keenly around riffs and rhythmical figures, and solos – Mariano sounding piercingly exotic on the shenai, heartbreakingly intense on soprano – are perfectly ensconced within the soundfield. The key element, though, is the inspirational series of cross-rhythms and accents which Christensen delivers, rising to an extraordinary crescendo towards the close of 'Sand-Glass', a sprawling performance built from simple materials. And the leader's own bass never sounded better.

**** The Following Morning**

ECM 829116-2 *Weber; Rainer Bruninghaus (ky); Oslo Philharmonic Orchestra.* 8/76.

***** Silent Feet**

ECM 835017-2 *Weber; Charlie Mariano (ss, shenai); Rainer Bruninghaus (ky); John Marshall (d).* 11/77.

****(*) Fluid / Rustle**

ECM 829381-2 *Weber; Gary Burton (vib, mar); Bill Frisell (g, bal); Bonnie Herman, Norma Winstone (v).* 1/79.

The anchorless drifting of *The Following Morning* was an inexplicably disappointing continuation, rhythmically dead and texturally thin, with Weber and Bruninghaus circling dolefully through their material and badly missing a drummer. *Silent Feet* introduced John Marshall, formerly of Soft Machine, into the Colours band which Weber was touring with and, while his stiffer virtuosity wasn't the same thing as Christensen's sober flair, he restored some of the punch to Weber's music. The record hasn't the memorable tunes and perfect empathy of the earlier discs, though. Nor is *Fluid/Rustle* much more than enervating, with Burton's blandly effortful playing and Frisell's as-yet-unfocused contributions adding little to Weber's pretty but uninvolving pieces.

****(*) Later That Evening**

ECM 829382-2 *Weber; Paul McCandless (ss, cor, ob, bcl); Lyle Mays (p); Bill Frisell (g); Michael DiPasqua (d).* 3/82.

Two new bands provided Weber with better results. *Little Movements* was his best since *Yellow Fields*, but unfortunately it has still to appear on CD and Weberites will have to search for remaining vinyl copies. *Later That Evening* isn't quite so good, with Mays a poor substitute for Bruninghaus and McCandless missing Mariano's acute sense of context, but it has its moments.

****(*) Chorus**
ECM 823844-2 *Weber; Jan Garbarek (ss, ts); Manfred Hoffbauer (cl, f); Martin Kunstner (ob, cor); Ralf Hubner (d).* 9/84.

***** Orchestra**
ECM 837343-2 *Weber; Herbert Joos, Anton Jillich, Wolfgang Czelusta, Andreas Richter (tb); Winfried Rapp (btb); Rudolf Diebetsberger, Thomas Hauschild (frhn); Franz Stagl (tba).* 5–8/88.

Weber has lacked a valuable context in recent years: having patented one of the most gorgeous of bass sounds, he doesn't seem to have much else to say with it. *Chorus* is heavy on the brooding-spirit element, with Garbarek delivering some of his most stentorian commentaries on what are less than riveting themes, as Weber and Hubner toil away in the background. As a sequence of mood-music cameos, it may appeal strongly to some, but it's a depressing listen over the course of an entire record. *Orchestra* may disappoint any who've attended Weber's highly entertaining solo concerts. He splits the album between bass soliloquies and counterpoint with a chilly brass section, yet the prettiest piece on the disc is the synthesizer tune, 'On A Summer's Evening'.

****** Pendulum**
ECM 519707-2 *Weber (b solo).*

Weber's second solo record is all bass this time and finds much of the beguiling and unexpectedly light-hearted feel of his one-man concerts. Ironically, it is much more studio-orientated: where *Orchestra* was overdub-free and essentially live, *Pendulum*, while remaining a solo meditation, is carefully edited for maximum effect. Weber's bass remains a unique sound in the music, and here he finds an almost perfect balance between the mixed blessing of bass opulence and the sing-song quality of his best melodies. Overlapping riffs or vamps counter the steady onward flow of the improviser's ideas, and in 'Street Scenes', 'Children's Song No. 1' or 'Pendulum' itself he secures a marvellous, patient equilibrium. His sleeve-notes are remarkably self-aware and offer some useful signposts for working through this encounter with 'my life-long preoccupation – also my old adversary'. Weber's best for many years: we're still waiting for the encore.

***** Works**
ECM 825429-2

A solid selection of Weber highlights, all but one of the pieces dating back to his music from the 1970s, with the memorable 'Touch' from *Yellow Fields* and 'Sand' from Ralph Towner's *Solstice* album particularly fine.

Ben Webster (1909–73)

TENOR SAXOPHONE

Born in Kansas City, he started on violin, then piano, before taking up sax at Budd Johnson's suggestion. Joined Bennie Moten in 1931and worked with many bands before gaining his greatest eminence with Duke Ellington from 1940. Left in 1944, rejoined 1948–9, then worked as a freelance through the '50s. Settled in Europe from 1964 and eventually died in Amsterdam, having long since been an unpredictable if beloved character. His unique timbre on the tenor – breathy, swooningly romantic – is high on most lists of favourite sounds in jazz.

***** The Horn**
Progressive PCD-7001 *Webster; Hot Lips Page (t); Clyde Hart (p); Charlie Drayton (b); Denzil Best (d).* 2/44.

***** Ben Webster 1944–1946**
Classics 1017 *As above, except add Emmet Berry, Dick Vance (t), Walter 'Foots' Thomas, Budd Johnson (ts), Marlowe Morris, Johnny Guarnieri, Jimmy Jones (p), Oscar Pettiford, Al Hall, John Simmons (b), Big Sid Catlett, Cozy Cole, David Booth (d).* 2/44–1/46.

****** King Of The Tenors**
Verve 519806-2 *Webster; Harry 'Sweets' Edison (t); Benny Carter (as); Oscar Peterson (p); Barney Kessel, Herb Ellis (g); Ray Brown (b); Alvin Stoller, J.C Heard (d).* 5–12/53.

****** Soulville**
Verve 833551-2 *Webster; Oscar Peterson (p); Barney Kessel, Herb Ellis (g); Ray Brown (b); J.C Heard, Stan Levey (d).* 5/53–10/57.

****** Ben Webster Meets Oscar Peterson**
Verve 521448-2 *Webster; Oscar Peterson (p); Ray Brown (b); Ed Thigpen (d).* 59.

A quarter-century after his death, his sound still haunts every tenor saxophonist who tackles a ballad. Ben Webster, often identifiable via a single, signature note, played jazz like few other musicians ever have. As he got older and less partial to any tempo above a very slow lope, he pared his manner back to essentials which still, no matter how often one hears them, remain uniquely affecting. Sometimes, all he does is play the notes of a melody, in a time that is entirely of his own choosing, and still he makes it uniquely absorbing. The best of his early work is with Duke Ellington – he remained, along with Paul Gonsalves, one of only two tenormen to make a genuine impression on Ducal history – but his records as a solo player, from the early 1950s onwards, are a formidable legacy.

The Horn is a collection of WBC transcriptions featuring Ben as nominal leader of a quintet with Hot Lips Page: the flow of the music is somewhat jolted by the programme, which includes various false starts and alternatives for the sake of completeness, and Lips Page takes a subsidiary role; but Webster's playing is already graceful and creating its own time and space. The remastering is occasionally cloudy but mostly good. Classics 1017 starts with the same session, minus the various alternatives, then proceeds through some excellent small-group music. There's a rare glimpse of Marlowe Morris on two 1944 titles (with lots of surface noise), before four titles by Walter Thomas, nice jump-band music; four quartet titles for Savoy, including an 'I Surrender Dear' which prefigures the great ballad interpretations of the '50s; and four titles by an Al Hall quintet with Dick Vance on trumpet, not very remarkable. Webster collectors will want to hear this music, but the remastering isn't up to much.

By 1953, Webster was ready to make his mark on the LP era – 78-r.p.m. duration was too short for such a patient improviser – and Norman Granz began recording him for his labels. *King Of The Tenors* blends a date with Oscar Peterson plus rhythm section with another where Edison and Carter sit in too, though the spotlight is always on Webster. 'Tenderly' has never been more tender,

'That's All' is sheer heaven, but 'Jive At Six' is a good piece of studio knockabout. Peterson may seem an unlikely partner, but just as Webster played superbly next to Art Tatum, so he mastered the potentially open floodgates of Peterson's playing. On *Soulville* there are lustrous ballads in 'Where Are You' and an eerily desolate 'Ill Wind', while 'Boogie Woogie' brings out the raucous side of the tenorman. Three previously unissued tracks from the sessions are also included on the CD. *Meets Oscar Peterson* is just as fine, with two melting ballads in 'The Touch Of Your Lips' and 'In The Wee Small Hours Of The Morning' and a lissom 'This Can't Be Love'. In its latest incarnation, as a Verve Master Edition with excellent sound, it stands as one of the indispensable mainstream jazz albums of the '50s.

****** Music For Loving**

Verve 527774-2 2CD *Webster; Harry Carney (bs); Teddy Wilson, Billy Strayhorn, Leroy Lovett (p); Billy Bauer (g); Ray Brown, George Duvivier, Wendell Marshall (b); Jo Jones, Osie Johnson, Louie Bellson (d); horns and strings.* 3/54–9/55.

****** The Soul Of Ben Webster**

Verve 527475-2 2CD *Webster; Art Farmer, Harry 'Sweets' Edison, Roy Eldridge (t); Vic Dickenson (tb); Johnny Hodges (as); Harold Ashby (ts); Jimmy Jones, Oscar Peterson, Billy Strayhorn (p); Mundell Lowe, Barney Kessel, Herb Ellis (g); Milt Hinton, Ray Brown, Jimmy Woode (b); Dave Bailey, Alvin Stoller, Sam Woodyard (d).* 3/57–7/58.

Impeccably prepared, these two-disc reissues are among Webster's most handsome records. The strings sessions, mostly arranged by Ralph Burns, may sound a little thin to ears used to digital grandeur, but the writing is beguiling and Webster sweeps through what must have been an ideal setting for him. Hidden away at the end of the package, almost as a bonus, is the rare album which Harry Carney recorded with strings, a fine date in its own right.

The Soul Of Ben Webster puts together three original LPs: the title album, Harry Edison's *Gee Baby Ain't I Good To You*, and Johnny Hodges's *Blues A-Plenty*. With three superb bands on hand, the music is a blueprint for small-group swing, and Webster contributes some of his most rounded and accomplished playing: the mesmerizing drift through 'Chelsea Bridge', for instance. His own date featured Ashby as second tenor, and there's a palpable camaraderie. Some of the Hodges titles are a bit slight, but this is altogether an indispensable issue.

*****(*) Ben Webster And Associates**

Verve 543302-2 *Webster; Roy Eldridge (t); Coleman Hawkins, Budd Johnson (ts); Jimmy Jones (p); Les Spann (g); Ray Brown (b); Jo Jones (d).* 4/59.

A belated arrival for a blustery, swaggering jam session for Ben and some top-dog pals. Tempos such as those chosen for 'De-dar' and 'Young Bean' are much faster than he would have liked but, with Hawkins and Johnson on hand, he wasn't going to take anything lying down, and the playing is vociferous and full of splendour. 'Time After Time' is a peerless Ben ballad. The remastering has left a lot of tape-hiss intact, but the music has great presence.

*****(*) Verve Jazz Masters 43: Ben Webster**

Verve 525431-2 *As Verve records above, except add Ella Fitzgerald (v), Johnny Otis Orchestra.* 12/51–11/59.

A choice selection from Webster's Verve years. Besides some of the staples from the albums listed above, there's Ella doing 'In A Mellow Tone' from the *Ellington Songbook* sessions and a 1951 version of 'Star Dust' with Johnny Otis that seems to float skyward, star-dusted indeed.

***** At The Renaissance**

Original Jazz Classics OJC 390 *Webster; Jimmy Rowles (p); Jim Hall (g); Red Mitchell (b); Frank Butler (d).* 10/60.

*****(*) Ben And 'Sweets'**

Columbia 460613-2 *Webster; Harry 'Sweets' Edison (t); Hank Jones (p); George Duvivier (b); Clarence Johnston (d).* 6/62.

Among friends and feeling fine. Nobody ever played 'My Romance' like Ben, and the version on *Ben And 'Sweets'* is very close to definitive, a chorus of melody and another of improvisation which unfold with unerring logic. His treatment of melody remains a compulsory point of study for aspiring improvisers: he respects every part of each measure, yet makes it his own by eliminating a note, adding another, or taking breaths at moments when no one else would think of pausing lest the momentum fall down. Webster's inner clock never fails him. Edison, the wryest of sidekicks, noodles alongside in his happiest lazybones manner, and Jones takes a handful of princely solos. The remastering will sound a bit lifeless to those who've heard the original vinyl. *At The Renaissance* finds Webster in unusual company and, while Rowles reads him like a good book, the others sometimes sound a little too smartly present and correct. 'Gone With The Wind', though, is a beauty.

****(*) Live At Pio's**

Enja 2038 *Webster; Junior Mance (p); Bob Cranshaw (b); Mickey Roker (d).* 63.

****(*) Live! Providence, Rhode Island, 1963**

Storyville STCD 8237 *Webster; Mike Renzi (p); Bob Petterutti (b); Joe Veletri (d).* 12/63.

***** Soulmates**

Original Jazz Classics OJC 390 *Webster; Thad Jones (c); Joe Zawinul (p); Richard Davis (b); Philly Joe Jones (d).* 9–10/63.

Ben was already settling into a repertory of favourite tunes when he made the Enja live album: 'Sunday', 'How Long Has This Been Going On?' and 'Gone With The Wind' were three of them. Docked a notch for imperfect live sound and Mance's tiresome clichés at the piano, but Webster sounds well enough. He enjoyed himself in Providence, too: 'My Romance', 'Embraceable You', 'Danny Boy'. The local rhythm-section plays respectfully but the sound is from an average, amateur tape. *Soulmates* offered a strange pairing with the young Joe Zawinul, with Jones sitting in on four tracks, although Webster was happy with any pianist who stood his ground. Highlights include a poignant reflection on Billie Holiday's 'Trav'lin' Light' and the title blues.

*****(*) Stormy Weather**

Black Lion BLCD 760108 *Webster; Kenny Drew (p); Niels-Henning Orsted Pedersen (b); Alex Riel (d).* 1/65.

*****(*) Gone With The Wind**

Black Lion BLCD 760125 *As above.* 1/65.

Recorded on a single long, long night at Copenhagen's Café Montmartre, these glorious records commemorate the start of

Webster's lengthy European sojourn. Drew's scholarly blend of blues and bop phrasing lends gentlemanly support, while the two local youngsters on bass and drums behave respectfully without losing their enthusiasm. Ultimately, the music rests with Webster's now inimitable tone and delivery. Close to the microphone, he's often content barely to enunciate the melody in an exhalation which feathers down to a pitchless vibration as often as it hits an actual note. Up-tempo pieces tend to be throwaway bundles of phrases, but anything slower becomes a carefully orchestrated set-piece. Sometimes the pace becomes almost too stolid, and perhaps the records are best heard a few tracks at a time, but it's enormously characterful jazz.

***** There Is No Greater Love**

Black Lion BLCD 760151 *As above.* 9/65.

***** The Jeep Is Jumping**

Black Lion BLCD 760147 *Webster; Arnvid Mayer (t); John Darville (tb); Niels Jorgen Steen (p); Henrik Hartmann, Hugo Rasmussen (b); Hans Nymand (d).* 9/65.

Webster back at the Montmartre in September, with an only marginally less engaging set, including his latest thoughts on 'I Got It Bad And That Ain't Good'. The session with Arnvid Mayer's band hems the saxophonist in a little more, with the group plodding at points, although Webster himself is again serenely in charge.

***** Big Ben Time!**

Philips 814410-2 *Webster; Dick Katz (p); Alan Haven (org); Spike Heatley (b); Tony Crombie (d).* 1/67.

****(*) Ben Webster Meets Bill Coleman**

Black Lion BLCD 760141 *Webster; Bill Coleman (t, flhn, v); Fred Hunt (p); Jim Douglas (g); Ronnie Rae (b); Lennie Hastings (d).* 4/67.

Big Ben Time! found Webster with a British rhythm-section on a London visit. This isn't absolutely prime Webster, but admirers will relish 'How Deep Is The Ocean?', 'Where Or When?' and some characteristic musings on a few choice cuts of Ellington. The other date is a bit disappointing. Webster and Coleman were both in London (as was Buck Clayton, scheduled for the date but, in the event, indisposed) and they cut this session with Alex Welsh's rhythm section in support. It's pleasing enough, but something tired seems to have crept into the music: the tempos plod a little too much, holding back both hornmen – and, considering the quality of Webster's playing on 'For Max' (dedicated to Max Jones) and 'For All We Know', it's a shame.

***** Ben And Buck**

Storyville STCD 8245 *Webster; Buck Clayton (t); Camille De Ceunyck (p); Tony Vaes (b); Charlie Pauvels (d).* 6/67.

Webster and Clayton could have been a dream team, but they actually don't play together all that much here. Most of the set is a feature for one or other of them and, when they do work together, it's usually at the kind of tempo Webster didn't like (anything over slow). Still, the individual features are often wonderful, and it's a shame that the inadequate sound doesn't catch the range of Clayton's lovely tone.

***** Masters Of Jazz Vol. 5: Ben Webster**

Storyville 4105 *Webster; Palle Mikkelborg, Perry Knudsen, Palle Bolvig, Allan Botschinsky (t); Per Espersen, Torolf Moolgaard, Axel Windfeld, Ole Kurt Jensen (tb); Uffe Karskov, Jesper Thilo, Dexter Gordon, Sahib Shihab, Bent Nielsen (reeds); Ole Kock Hansen, Kenny Drew (p); Ole Molin (g); Niels-Henning Orsted Pedersen, Hugo Rasmussen (b); Ole Steenberg, Albert 'Tootie' Heath, Bjarne Rostvold (d); strings.* 68–70.

***** Plays Ballads**

Storyville STCD 4118 *As above, except add Erling Christensen, Flemming Madsen (reeds), William Schiopffe (d), John Steffensen (perc).* 7/67–11/71.

****(*) Live At The Haarlemse Jazz Club**

Limetree MCD 0040 *Webster; Tete Montoliu (p); Rob Langereis (b); Tony Inzalaco (d).* 5/72.

***** Gentle Ben**

Ensayo ENY-CD 3433 *Webster; Tete Montoliu (p); Eric Peter (b); Peer Wyboris (d).* 11/72.

***** Baden 1972**

TCB 02102 *Webster; Dexter Gordon (ts); Kenny Drew (p); Bo Stief (b); Ed Thigpen (d).* 11/72.

****(*) My Man**

Steeplechase SCCD 31008 *Webster; Ole Kock Hansen (p); Bo Stief (b); Alex Riel (d).* 4/73.

Webster's final years found him based in Copenhagen, and his manner was by now so *sui generis* that it's tempting to view the later work as a single, lachrymose meditation on the same handful of favourite ballads and Ellington tunes. But Ben's own subtle variations on himself create felicitous differences between each stately rendition of 'Prelude To A Kiss' or 'Old Folks'. He was lucky in his accompanists: while several of the rhythm sections sound anonymous in themselves, Webster's knack of helping them raise their game elicits some exceptionally sympathetic playing from almost everybody. The two Storyville albums collect scatterings from several sessions over a five-year period, including dates with strings, some heavenly ballads, and a couple of dates with Teddy Wilson at the piano: both mixed bags, but plenty of vintage Webster. *My Man* is a middling session, recorded on a typical late night at the Café Montmartre and a bit too relaxed. Sound on the Haarlemse club date is pretty dusty but there is a lovely 'Star Dust' to enjoy, and only Inzalaco's enthusiasms sometimes get the better of the music. Montoliu is on hand again for the Barcelona studio date, *Gentle Ben*, which catches Ben's sound beautifully. Peter and Wyboris are less than ideal, but otherwise this is a bountiful example of late Webster. The radio broadcast from Baden is a potboiler and, though Ben enjoyed Dexter's company, this probably wasn't his sort of thing at this stage. That said, there's some lovely playing on a 'Blues In F' and Gordon does a surprisingly bleak turn on 'Didn't We'. Ed Thigpen kicks off 'Sunday' at an insane tempo and Webster doesn't seem best pleased, but he gets through it. Anyone who loves the sound of Ben Webster will find something to enjoy in all these records.

Tad Weed

PIANO

California-based pianist, working as part of the community of players recorded by the Nine Winds operation.

***(*) Soloing

9 Winds NWCD 0148 *Weed; Ken Filiano (b); Joe LaBarbera, Billy Mintz (d).* 7/90–5/91.

Weed's broad stylistic range, sureness of touch and carefully controlled quirkiness give this record a real unaffected sparkle. Despite the title, only five of the 11 tracks are done as solos: his version of Gerry Niewood's flimsy 'Joy' lends the melody unexpected strength by introducing dark, thoughtful voicings without losing the sprightliness of the tune. Clifford Brown's 'Joyspring' is fast without sounding hectic, yet Weed has it down coolly enough to introduce some deft rhythmical risks. The trio pieces benefit from LaBarbera's excellent drumming (Mintz sits in on only two tracks), and in over an hour of music there are very few dull moments. The piano-sound is a little dry, though few will find it troubling.

Joel Weiskopf (born 1962)

PIANO

Syracuse-born, Weiskopf is a New York-based midstream-modernist with a wide range of experience, including a year with the Woody Herman orchestra and numerous sideman dates.

*** The Search

Criss Cross 1174 *Weiskopf; Peter Washington (b); Billy Drummond (d).* 12/98.

The younger of the two Weiskopf brothers is a sunny player. His treatments of Shorter ('Edda'), Gershwin ('Bess You Is My Woman Now') and Monk ('Criss Cross') aren't so much lightweight as light-filled, the melodies articulated with a free, zesty airiness. His original 'Song For The Lost', with its unusual melodic structure, is the most inventive of his own pieces: on the title-track he tends to get a bit lost in rhetoric, and the tune outstays its welcome. He has superb cohorts in Washington and Drummond, the latter's cymbal-play in 'Song For The Lost' being especially ear-catching.

Walt Weiskopf (born 1959)

TENOR SAXOPHONE

Weiskopf was an alto player until, aged twenty, he was offered a tenor chair in the Buddy Rich band. He has much other big-band and section experience and is based in New Jersey.

*** Exact Science

Iris ICD-1002 *Weiskopf; Joel Weiskopf (p); Jay Anderson (b); Jeff Hirshfield (d).* 89.

***(*) Mindwalking

Iris ICD-1003 *As above.* 6–9/90.

**** Simplicity

Criss Cross Jazz 1075 *Weiskopf; Conrad Herwig (tb); Andy Fusco (as); Joel Weiskopf (p); Peter Washington (b); Billy Drummond (d).* 12/92.

*** A World Away

Criss Cross 1100 *Weiskopf; Larry Goldings (org); Peter Bernstein (g); Bill Stewart (d).* 12/93.

Weiskopf is an experienced section-player (with Buddy Rich and Toshiko Akiyoshi) but these records are a lot more ambitious than the usual sideman-steps-out date. *Exact Science* is a carefully weighted set of tunes that place as much emphasis on the writing as on the improvising: Weiskopf's lean, slightly querulous tone might sound like Coltrane-lite, but his phrasing is scrupulously thoughtful and personal. Some of the themes are intriguingly paced – 'Mr Golyadkin' might have come off a Jan Garbarek/Bobo Stenson date – and others don't quite come off, while the sound of the record has a sometimes unflattering timbre. *Mindwalking* is better still, with a superior mix and scarcely a dud moment. The brevity of several tracks shows how little waste there is in Weiskopf's music, improvisations always in balance with themes, and the prevailing feel of intellectual surprise sets him quite apart from the midstream of modern hard bop. Yet the one standard, Alec Wilder's 'Blackberry Winter', is as deeply felt and fully achieved as any more obvious tenor rhapsody.

Both discs lead naturally to the splendid *Simplicity*. More than ever, Weiskopf chooses to assert his writing over his playing, with his own solos relatively discreet and deferential. The brimming, complex melodies of 'Subordination', the artfully overlapping horns of 'Brazilia' and the wholly original revision of 'Lazy Afternoon' are among the most interesting moments, but there's nothing here to disappoint. Fusco and Herwig are modest personalities too, but their relative mildness lets the calibre of Weiskopf's writing come through, and his rhythm section, ably led by brother Joel, is keenly alert.

A World Away puts the emphasis more keenly on Weiskopf's own playing, and for once the setting doesn't seem just right for him. Goldings, Bernstein and Stewart are old hands at the organ–guitar groove and, though clichés are displaced by the leader's typically penetrating writing, the music misses the firm centre of the previous discs. One compensation is another ingenious standard choice, 'The Long Hot Summer'.

***(*) Night Lights

Double Time DTRCD 106 *Weiskopf; Joel Weiskopf (p); Drew Gress (b); Steve Davis (d).* 10/95.

***(*) Song For My Mother

Criss Cross 1127 *Weiskopf; Joe Magnarelli (t); Conrad Herwig (tb); Jim Snidero (as, f, af); Anders Bostrom (f, af); Scott Robinson (bs, bcl, f); Joel Weiskopf (p); Peter Washington (b); Billy Drummond (d).* 12/95.

More excellent jazz. *Night Lights* has Weiskopf seeing what he can find within the confines of tenor, rhythm and standards. The trio seem to light on just the right tempo in all the tunes and, whether balladeering on 'Some Other Time' or taking a somewhat cryptic fast turn through 'You Go To My Head', Weiskopf uses his vibratoless tone and lean, twisty phrasing to fine effect. He also picks some intriguing tunes: 'Moonlight On The Ganges', 'Camelot', 'With The Wind And The Rain In Her Hair'.

Song For My Mother returns him to a nine-strong line-up. There's a surprise emphasis on Bostrom's flute, though he's not especially remarkable as a soloist; and it's the varied ways the leader marshals his horns that make the session well out of the ordinary for Criss Cross blowing. 'Where Is Love' is spine-tingling ballad-playing, and 'High Noon' a real head-turner.

*****(*) Anytown**
Criss Cross 1169 *Weiskopf; Renee Rosnes (p); Joe Locke (vib); Doug Weiss (b); Tony Reedus (d).* 12/98.

Weiskopf says that his aim this time was to try and sustain longer solos than on his previous records – a recipe for trouble, given the existential meanderings of too many saxophonists. But the seven originals are among his most absorbing work too, and the band is absolutely off the top shelf. The title-track is a furiously paced start which cools off only for the first part of Rosnes's solo. 'Blues In The Day' isn't a blues but a complex unison theme, 'Scottish Folk Song' is a folkish melody cleverly harmonized, and the 'Naima'-like 'Adrienne' is a tender but unsentimental ballad line. Here and there Reedus makes too much noise, but there is very little to find fault with on another great Weiskopf session, longer solos and all.

Jerry Weldon (born 1957)

TENOR SAXOPHONE

Undersung veteran section-player and sessionman, here in a featured setting.

*****(*) Head To Head**
Criss Cross CRISS 1159 *Weldon; Michael Karn (ts); Bruce Barth (p); Peter Washington (b); Billy Drummond (d).* 6/98.

If, as we've come to suspect, Criss Cross is the Blue Note of the '90s, this is the kind of session which confirms the lineage. Only Charlie Parker's 'Ko-Ko', which closes the set, degenerates into anything like an old-fashioned tenor battle. For the rest, two very different players: the elder Weldon as smooth as the rum which gives the opening 'Captain Morgan' its title, Karn providing the fire and incendiary spark.

The unisons are inch-perfect throughout and so thoroughly bathed in the kind of overtones you get when two very different tenormen line up together that it almost sounds as if a whole horn section is on hand. As well as being older, Weldon is the more convincing soloist. His statements on Dizzy Gillespie's 'Ow' are hard to fault, with a subtle variation on the restatement; but Karn has his moment on his own 'Big D', written in that usually unbluesy key but dedicated to bassist Dennis Irwin. He also features on 'Who Can I Turn To', reproducing Tony Bennett's lazy phrasing in the opening chorus. A hugely entertaining, old-fashioned jazz record, it really ought to come supplied with cigarette smoke and overpriced drinks.

Nick Weldon (born 1955)

PIANO

London-based pianist and accompanist, mainstream-to-bop in idiom.

***** Lavender's Blue**
Verge 001 *Weldon; Tim Garland (ts); Andrew Cleyndert (b); Paul Clarvis (d); Christine Tobin (v).* 94.

The son of novelist Fay Weldon, he'd been around the London scene for quite some time before recording in his own right. A sensitive accompanist who's worked with leading American instrumentalists and singers, Weldon also has a fine compositional gift. Wisely, though, he divides the album between new and more familiar stuff. Hampton Hawes's 'Sonora' is an interesting choice and may point to one of his less obvious influences as a player. 'Alone Together' and 'Softly, As In A Morning Sunrise' are more predictable, but they're given a promising spin as they go by. Of the new things, 'Mabs And Tucker' is inspired by characters in Mum's best book, 'Liffey' is a guest spot for Garland, and the title-track, which also unveils the man's literary talents, is an ambitious vocal for Christine Tobin, who sounds better here than on most of her own stuff. The trio numbers two of the brightest young players around; Clarvis could always do with leaving one or two of his gimmicks at home, but Cleyndert is a great find.

Bobby Wellins (born 1936)

TENOR SAXOPHONE

A veteran Glaswegian modernist, Wellins won renown with the Stan Tracey group of the '60s and has worked his personal variations on small-group hard bop since.

***** Nomad**
Hot House HHCD 1008 *Wellins; Jonathan Gee (p); Thad Kelly (b); Spike Wells (d); Claire Martin (v).* 4/92.

****** Don't Worry 'Bout Me**
Cadillac SGCCD 05 *Wellins; Graham Harvey (p); Alec Dankworth (b); Martin Drew (d).* 2/96.

****** The Satin Album**
Jazzizit JITCD 9607 *Wellins; Colin Purbrook (p); Dave Green (b); Clark Tracey (d).* 7/96.

As long ago as 1965, Bobby Wellins guaranteed his moment of jazz immortality with a solo on Stan Tracey's instrumental rendition of *Under Milk Wood*. 'Starless And Bible Black' remains the key reference-point for Wellins, a moment of brooding lyricism not without a hint of self-mockery, and it is a characteristic common to the residents of Llareggub and Glasgow that they don't take themselves too seriously, even when they are pouring their hearts out. Wellins is a consummate ballad player, breathy and very immediate, with, as fellow-Scot and fellow-saxophonist Tommy Smith has pointed out, a lot of 'air', not so much in his tone as in his shaping of a solo.

Unfortunately – though he himself now speaks of it with calm and some amusement – Wellins's health and career went off the grid for a good many years, and so the discography is startlingly thin. Comeback discs like *Birds Of Brazil*, reviewed in an earlier edition, are no longer available, and only with his sixtieth birthday did Wellins begin to establish himself as a recording artist. *Nomad* is frankly disappointing, not so much because the saxophonist is below par as because the group behind him lacks definition and a bit of colour in its cheeks. To be fair to them, Wellins has picked some fairly chewy material: Hank Mobley's 'This I Dig Of You', Brownie's 'Sandu' and Monk's 'Little Rootie Tootie'. He doesn't hang around waiting for stragglers on any of them.

The other two albums were recorded only months apart, indication that Wellins was marking his sixtieth year with a burst of activity. Some of the most impressive work on *Nomad* was with singer Claire Martin. Wellins has always had a particular affection for voices. What he does is almost vocalese in reverse, taking the words out of the line, but retaining their emotional as well as their more strictly musical significance. That is what lies behind *The Satin Album*, an extended gloss (no pun intended) on Billie Holiday's 1958 LP, *Lady In Satin*. This is an altogether stronger group than on the Hot House release, and Wellins's interplay with Green is remarkable. 'I Get Along Without You Very Well' has the familiar self-possession and humour; but what follows, 'For All We Know', a wry plea of *carpe diem*, lifts the album at mid-point to a new height of emotional and philosophical sophistication.

The Cadillac disc was recorded live at the Vortex in north London, and it has all the presence and intimacy of that upper room. No American player could map out any more of the side-tracks and by-ways of these seven standards (a Wellins original, 'Tracery', closes the set) with any more subtlety, and yet not lose contact with the song itself. 'How Deep Is The Ocean' is masterful: beauty, exhilaration and the abyss all compressed into 12 minutes; even 'Lover Man' has a kind of majesty.

Dicky Wells (1907-1985)

TROMBONE

Worked with various New York bands in the early 1930s – and made some memorable records in Paris – before spending eight years with Count Basie from 1938. Thereafter he turned up in various small groups, although alcohol troubled him and his playing was inconsistent. He was a gifted writer and was still playing in the '80s.

****** Dicky Wells 1927–1943**

Classics 937 *Wells; Bill Coleman, Shad Collins, Bill Dillard, Kenneth Roane, Gus McLung (t); Frankie Newton (t, v); John Williams, Fletcher Allen (cl, as); Cecil Scott (cl, ts, bs); Howard Johnson (as); Lester Young (ts); Don Frye, Ellis Larkins (p); Django Reinhardt, Roger Chaput, Freddie Green (g); Hubert Mann, Rudolph Williams (bj); Chester Campbell, Mack Walker (tba); Richard Fullbright, Al Hall (b); Lloyd Scott, Bill Beason, Jo Jones (d).* 1/27–12/43.

The important tracks here are the dozen Wells headed up in Paris on two memorable July days in 1937. The first two groups feature the trombonist with Bill Coleman and Django Reinhardt, with Dillard and Collins making up a three-man trumpet-section on three titles. With no piano and Reinhardt driving all before him, the ensembles have a sound at once mercurial and light and limber, with quite magnificent playing from Coleman and Wells. There isn't a note out of place on 'Between The Devil And The Deep Blue Sea', 'Sweet Sue', the blues 'Hangin' Around Boudon' and 'Japanese Sandman'. The next session is comparatively lightweight, but it ended on what were effectively two trombone solos with rhythm accompaniment, and Wells's seven choruses on 'Dicky Wells Blues' make up one of the great pieces of trombone improvisation on record. His sound introduces a sober gaiety into the instrument's lugubrious temperament, and his vibrato and colouristic use of sudden shouting notes make every chorus fresh and surprising.

The disc opens with seven tracks with which Wells made his debut, with Lloyd Scott and Cecil Scott: lively if unexceptional New York jazz of the 1920s. It ends on a septet date for Signature, from 1943, with Coleman, Young and Larkins (playing the Basie role). They take 'I Got Rhythm' far too fast, but there's compensation in the next three titles, with Dicky playing a beautiful slow introduction to 'I'm Fer It Too'. Wells can be heard to useful effect on many Basie records, but he seldom stepped out front again and he never surpassed those wonderful Paris dates.

Dick Wellstood (1927–87)

PIANO

Worked in Chicago and New York in the 1950s and became a young upholder of swing and mainstream values, prized as band player and accompanist. A witty writer and dry humourist, his early death when still in great form was a loss to the music.

***** The Blue Three At Hanratty's**

Chaz Jazz CJ 109 *Wellstood; Kenny Davern (ss, cl); Bob Rosengarden (d).* 81.

***** Dick Wellstood And His Famous Orchestra Featuring Kenny Davern**

Chiaroscuro CRD 128 *As above, except omit Rosengarden.*

***** Dick Wellstood And His All-Star Orchestra Featuring Kenny Davern**

Chiaroscuro CRD 129 *As above.* 81.

A jobbing musician who was content to play supper-club dates, parties and tribute recordings to great predecessors like Waller, James P. Johnson and Art Tatum, Dick Wellstood is easily underestimated. Always up for a gig though he may have been, he was also a practising lawyer, and his easy, engaging stride approach masks a steel-trap understanding of every wrinkle of piano jazz, an eclecticism that allows him to play in virtually every idiom, from early ragtime to quasi-modal compositions from the shores opposite bop. He has a decent touch with a Monk tune, as he shows on the third of the discs above. Regrettably, much of his work has bloomed and faded in highly unappreciative settings and company, and he is not well represented in the current catalogue. There is a distinct shortage of CD material for so active and undemanding a player.

At the keyboard, he sounds most like a younger version of James P. Johnson, setting up big and forceful alternations in the left hand against a characteristic tremolo in the melody line. He favours huge, raw bass-figures and counters their jagged outlines with wonderfully subtle fills and footnotes. The personnels above are not incomplete, despite the titles. The 'orchestra' business is one of Wellstood's jokes, as are originals like 'Fat As A Bastard'. In his late fifties he tempered his approach slightly, enough to admit an occasional ballad, though often in very improbable keys.

****** Live At The Sticky Wicket**
Arbors ARCD 19188 2CD *Wellstood (p solo).* 11/86.

How often do we manage to laugh aloud in the course of the lonely pilgrimage that is the *Penguin Jazz Guide*? Frankly, not that often, which makes this a particularly well-loved point in the journey. Wellstood's undentable good humour, lacking the sardonic bite of a Mose Allison or the surreal waywardness of a Slim Gaillard, has nevertheless warmed us many times over the past few years. Intended as a memorial and retrospective, this long set was recorded at the eponymous club in Hopkinton, Massachusetts, a location unknown to us, but graced by the great man's presence on this night. The programme is remorseless: 'St James Infirmary', 'Ain't Misbehavin'', 'The Entertainer', 'Maple Leaf Rag', 'Prelude To A Kiss', in fact, 32 tracks that cover a vast gamut of jazz history, played with unaffected exuberance. A sheer delight from start to finish.

Alex Welsh (1929–82)

CORNET, VOCALS

Despite the surname, Welsh was a Scot. He didn't entirely look the part but was nevertheless a fine cornetist, influenced by Wild Bill Davison (though he emphatically denied this). When he died in 1982, Humphrey Lyttelton described the Welsh band's impact as a combination of 'romanticism and rage', a near-perfect characterization of its leader's buttoned-up ferocity.

*****(*) Strike One**
Lake LACD 107 *Welsh; Roy Williams (tb); John Barnes (as, bs, cl, v); Fred Hunt (p); Jim Douglas (g, bj); Ron Mathewson (b); Lennie Hastings (d).* 6/66.

***** Music Of The Mauve Decade**
Lake LACD 62 *As above.*

***** Dixieland To Duke**
Lake LACD 92 *As above.*

*****(*) Classic Concert**
Black Lion BLCD 760503 *Welsh; Roy Williams (tb, v); John Barnes (cl, as, bs, f, v); Fred Hunt (p); Jim Douglas (bj, g); Harvey Weston (b); Lennie Hastings (d).* 10/71.

***** Doggin' Around**
Black Lion BLCD 760510 *Welsh; Roy Williams (tb); Johnny Barnes (as, bs, cl, f); Jim Douglas (g); Fred Hunt (p); Harvey Weston (b); Roger Nobes (d).* 7 & 8/73.

The band changed markedly in approach during the 1960s, a period during which the once teetotal Welsh acquired a famous thirst for vodka, moving away from the ragged, Chicagoan 'Condon style' towards a more orthodox swing approach. The band's enormous success at Antibes in 1967 and at later American festivals seemed to do no more than reinforce internal divisions. The Lake sets are pretty much definitive of what the band was about, and *Strike One* is a cracking listen by any standard. *Mauve Decade* and *Dixieland To Duke* are more diffuse and, though Welsh probably plays better and more confidently elsewhere, it is the first album which catches the Welsh alchemy at its finest.

The early 1970s were a period of relatively undemonstrative consolidation for the band. Though less limber than the 1960 front line of Roy Crimmins and the wounded Archie Semple, the 1971 line-up of Williams and the multi-talented Barnes was still capable of performing powerfully. Side by side, 'Sleepy Time Down South' and 'Maple Leaf Rag' confirm something of Lyttelton's description; set alongside the 'Clark And Randolph Blues', a previously unissued version of the Art Hodes tune on the Lake compilation, they're slightly wan. Welsh himself sounds tired but plays with great straightforwardness and a lovely tone.

The slightly later record is no less enjoyable, but there is something amiss with the sound-balance, which has everyone ricocheting around in what sounds like an aircraft hangar. Barnes is a great asset on his baritone sax and Roy Williams maintains his form on trombone, but a lot of the spark has gone out of the group, along with about 85 per cent of the rage. 'You Are The Sunshine Of My Life' has all the romantic urgency of a brisk handshake, and it's only on up-tempo traditional numbers like 'Limehouse Blues' that Welsh sounds at all committed to the gig.

Scott Wendholt (born 1965)

TRUMPET, FLUGELHORN

Contemporary post-bop trumpeter leading his own variations on a familiar theme.

***** The Scheme Of Things**
Criss Cross Jazz 1078 *Wendholt; Vincent Herring (ss, as); Kevin Hays (p); Dwayne Burno (b); Billy Drummond (d).* 1/93.

***** Through The Shadows**
Criss Cross 1101 *Wendholt; Don Braden (ts, f); Bruce Barth (p); Ira Coleman (b); Billy Drummond (d).* 12/94.

***** From Now On ...**
Criss Cross 1123 *Wendholt; Steve Armour (tb); Steve Wilson (as); Tim Ries (ts, ss); Bruce Barth (p); Larry Grenadier (b); Billy Drummond (d).* 12/95.

***** Beyond Thursday**
Double-Time DTRCD-128 *Wendholt; Dave Berkman (p); Tony Scherr (b); Adam Watson (d).* 6/97.

Wendholt has built up a solid little discography, even if none of the four discs really stands up as indispensable. In almost 70 minutes of good, substantial post-bop on *The Scheme Of Things* there is plenty to enjoy, yet not much to remember. The most striking thing is the contrast between Herring (who has had a working quintet with the trumpeter) and Wendholt: the saxophonist's sour, blue playing is a piquant alternative to the polished, processional manner of some of Wendholt's solos. The leader isn't terribly well served by the recording, and he sounds a bit thin on

Freddie Hubbard's 'Birdlike', the sort of tune where a trumpeter should stand tall. But there is some impressive improvising, and his favourite device, a fast trill, comes in for clever use.

The writing on *Through The Shadows* is one point of advance; the other is the band which, man for man, is arguably no stronger than the first but seems a more purposeful group for Wendholt's ideas. 'Totem' and the title-piece are especially strong, and the mid-tempo for Duke Pearson's 'You Know I Care' elicits a solo of real finesse and control by Wendholt. The third Criss Cross date is split between sextet tracks with Armour and Wilson and a quartet with Ries. Some of this sounds a bit rushed, as if the label's usual one-day-in-the-studio strategy put a strain on both groups, but there's little gainsaying the skill and crispness of the best playing.

Beyond Thursday is another one-day quickie, reuniting Wendholt with a rhythm section he used to play with at Augie's in New York. Being sole horn is a challenge he seems to rise to: this is probably his best showcase as a soloist, and the mix of clean, long notes and bubbling phrases which he pursues on 'The Party's Over' becomes the thematic thread of the date. Berkman plays Fender Rhodes, and its interesting sonorities work unexpectedly well, dark one moment, light and pneumatic the next. There's nothing extraordinary here, but it's handsomely done.

Jens Wendleboe

TROMBONE

Norwegian trombinist and arranger with these big-band sessions to his name.

****(*) 'Lone Attic**

NOPA 2905 *Wendleboe; Christian Beck, Fred Noddelund, Bernt Steen, Ole Antonsen (t); Tore Nilsen, Harald Halvorsen, Dag Eriksen, Oivind Westby (tb); Johan Bergli, Arild Stav (as); Knut Riisnaes, Odd Riisnaes (ts); Vidar Johansen (bs); Helge Iberg (ky); Frode Alnaes (g); Tom Antonsen (b); Svein Christiansen (d).* 85.

*****(*) Big Crazy Energy Band**

NOPA/NRK NN 1001-2 *Wendleboe; David Zalud, Petter Kateraas, Svein Gjermundrod, Jens Petter Antonsen (t, flhn); Anders Stengard, Harald Halvorsen, Helge Sunde, Oivind Westby (tb); Daniel Wilensky, Johan Bergli, Georg Reiss, Knut Riisnaes, Vidar Johansen, Rolf Malm (reeds); Bugge Wesseltoft (ky); Asbjorn Ruud (g); Bjorn Holta (b); Erik Smith (d); Frank Jakobsen (perc); Elisabeth Moberg (v).* 4–5/91.

Wendleboe loves to push his big bands through hair-raising charts that bounce between jazz, rock and anything else he can think of: kindred spirits might be Loose Tubes, Ornicar Big Band, Either/Orchestra. But Wendleboe seldom lets go as he might, and *'Lone Attic* in particular sounds stiff when it should really be taking off. Part of the problem is a penchant for tongue-in-cheek rock and disco rhythms that tie the band down to a tyrannical beat. Despite having such skilful improvisers in the earlier band as the Riisnaes brothers, Wendleboe also finds it difficult to frame soloists to their best advantage. But *Big Crazy Energy Band* is a major improvement. They belt through the opening 'The Night Of The 1990's' with stunning aplomb, and the ensuing 'Fanfare And Punk' and Wesseltoft's rippling Hammond organ transformation of 'Abide With Me' are tremendous set-pieces. It isn't quite sustained at that level, and Moberg's vocals are an unnecessary addition; but there's enough fine music to merit a strong rating.

Peter Weniger

SOPRANO AND TENOR SAXOPHONES

Swiss saxophonist working in a post-bop style which occasionally approaches free playing.

****(*) Hymn To Gobro**

Jazzline JL 11132-2 *Weniger; Conrad Herwig (tb); Hubert Nuss (p); Ingmar Heller (b); Hardy Fischotter (d).* 11/89.

***** Private Concert**

Mons 1878 *Weniger; Hubert Nuss (p).* 4/90.

***** The Point Of Presence**

Mons 1889 *As above, except add Conrad Herwig (tb).* 5/91.

***** Key Of The Moment**

Mons 1901 *Weniger; David Liebman (ss); John Abercrombie (g); Rufus Reid (b); Adam Nussbaum (d).* 2/93.

Weniger's approach to improvising is a conscientious balancing of traditional and nearly free form. The duo concert with Nuss is based round standards and three originals, but the wide-ranging interpretations of 'Stella By Starlight' and Dave Liebman's 'What It Is' alike suggest that both men – though Weniger especially – like the minimum of signposts for their playing. Weniger's full-bodied tone on both tenor and soprano seldom breaks into anything like a false register: he likes to stretch melody lines and structural experiments off into infinity as his way of being free.

The Point Of Presence is marginally superior, since Herwig's enlistment was an inspired piece of casting. He goes an inch further than Weniger by blowing chords on the horn and adapting other avant-garde techniques, but he also likes to stay within relatively contained boundaries. On the soprano/trombone duet piece, 'Blue Beauty', or the multifarious directions of 'The Point Of Presence' itself, the music acquires refinement and detail without losing spontaneity. The earlier quintet session is much more straightforward, a light, easy-going and not unpleasing group of originals – Herwig's 'Opalescent' is particularly engaging – and two jazz standards, with a capable if anonymous rhythm section.

Key Of The Moment directs Weniger towards more mainstream modernism. Liebman appears on only one track, 'Flatbush', where the two sopranos trade licks; the rest is polished, literate jazz of a high if not especially distinctive order. No reason to deny it three stars, but the best of Weniger is with Nuss.

Cecilia Wennerstrom (born 1947)

BARITONE SAXOPHONE

Swedish saxophonist who began playing at 27, having been a vocalist for several years previous to that.

***** Minor Stomp**
Four Leaf Clover FLCCD 157 *Wennerstrom; Ann Blom (p); Filip Augustson (b); Henrik Wartel (d).* 6/97.

Wennerstrom was a late starter on the horn, and this likeable quartet session must be accounted a belated turn in the spotlight. She has a rather chalky tone and her phrasing at tempo can be effortful, but it doesn't stop her putting her authority on five standards and a couple of original lines. The plain speaking extends to the rest of the quartet, and the unpretentiousness of the date is its own reward.

Kenny Werner (born 1951)

PIANO

A Brooklynite, Werner studied at Manhattan School and Berklee, then went to Brazil, before returning to gigs with Archie Shepp and, in the '80s, the Mel Lewis band. Led his own trio from 1981.

****(*) Introducing The Trio**
Sunnyside SSC 1038D *Werner; Ratzo Harris (b); Tom Rainey (d).* 3/89.

***** Uncovered Heart**
Sunnyside SSC 1048D *Werner; Randy Brecker (t, flhn); Joe Lovano (ss, ts); Eddie Gomez (b); John Riley (d).* 90.

*****(*) Press Enter**
Sunnyside SSC 1056D *Werner; Ratzo Harris (b); Tom Rainey (d).* 8/91.

Werner is a beguiling player, perfectly at home in either a solo, trio or rhythm-and-horns date, and if on his earlier discs he can seem a little becalmed in his playing it does gradually draw an attentive listener in. *Uncovered Heart* includes some good originals and, if the horns perform with mundane expertise, Werner himself stands up as a leader worthy of respect. The first trio album seems a little undercooked, with nods to Bill Evans that sometimes turn into slavish imitation; but the second, *Press Enter*, is beautifully handled and suggests a much stronger empathy among the three players. Werner's long out-of-tempo introduction to a very thoughtful 'Blue In Green' sets one of the keynotes for the record, an exploration of shifting rhythms, and Rainey's almost pointillistic stickwork is ideally directed. Certainly the best place to start listening to Werner.

****(*) Meditations**
Steeplechase SCCD 31327 *Werner (p solo).* 12/92.

Not bad, but Werner's return to the solo recital (there is a forgettable Enja record in the deletions pile) is prettily nondescript. There are three numbered 'Meditations' and a 'Contemplation Suite', all leaves from the same tree, judiciously played, charmingly articulated, but rhythmically and melodically mundane. The best interpretation is a dense revision of 'Giant Steps': Aki Takase and Dick Wellstood have done it, but piano-solo treatments are comparatively rare, and this one's a vivid nod to Coltrane. Monk and Debussy are mistakenly alluded to in the sleeve-notes: Werner is not in their league, but he's worth hearing.

***** Copenhagen Calypso**
Steeplechase SCCD 31346 *Werner (p solo).* 10/93.

***** Maybeck Recital Hall Vol. 34**
Concord CCD 4622 *Werner (p solo).* 2/94.

Two more solo dates, and not so much mixed successes as unexceptional recitals. The Copenhagen set has a vague air of Coltrane hovering around it, with 'Ballad For Trane' and 'Naima' in the programme, while the Maybeck set – in impeccable sound as always – mixes various strands of post-bop piano on a sequence of familiar pieces, along with another 'Naima' – though it must be said that Werner distils a very attractive lyricism out of the tune. Sound efforts, but it would be good to have Werner get back to his own writing, which has rather more character than he often invests in other people's works.

*****(*) Standards Live At Visiones**
Concord CCD-4675 *Werner; Ratzo Harris (b); Tom Rainey (d).* 8/95.

*****(*) A Delicate Balance**
RCA 516942 *Werner; Dave Holland (b); Jack DeJohnette (d).* 6/97.

Back with his favourite trio, Werner has great fun with a programme of standards this time. They approach the Visiones gig with complete irreverence: 'All The Things You Are' is taken entirely apart, 'There Will Never Be Another You' is delivered polytonally – yet they follow with an old-fashioned Blue Note blues in 'Blue Train'. It's a boring-looking set-list that comes to dramatic life on the stand. Sound isn't ideal, but there's plenty of atmosphere.

The RCA album is entirely different, self-composed (a clever reharmonization of 'Work Song' is the only exception) and paradoxically expansive where many of the tunes on the Concord disc are dispatched quickly. The opening Monk tribute, 'Amonkst', is a bit obvious, but thereafter Werner's lines impress for their fastidious search for the unexpected, swinging on 'Ivoronics' and 'Footsteps', blossoming on 'Lorraine' and ending cryptically on the themeless 'Melodies Of 1997'. It must be tempting to overplay with Holland and deJohnette behind you, but for the most part he tempers force with restraint. Bassist and drummer are a nonpareil partnership at this point and they don't disappoint.

*****(*) Unprotected Music**
Double-Time DTRCD –139 *Werner; Marc Johnson (b); Joey Baron (d).* 12/97.

A spare day of studio time brought forth this session of trio improvisations, new ground for Werner as far as an entire date is concerned, although there's one standard ('It's Alright With Me'), 'Greensleeves' is tailgunner for 'Hell Realm', and 'Tribute To Sonny' turns out to be akin to a Rollins calypso. Not free as in European improv, then; but these are more like wide-ranging thinkers than blank-canvas players anyway. Though titles such as 'Vague Wanderings' don't inspire confidence, Werner's lyricism resonates throughout, and it's a show of three considerable musicians enjoying themselves.

*****(*) Beauty Secrets**
RCA 74321 699042 *Werner; Dave Ballou (t); Joe Lovano, Toby Malaby (ts); Mark Feldman, Todd Reynolds, Victor Schulz, Heidi*

Stubner (vn); Mary Wooten (clo); Drew Gress, Johannes Weidenmuller (b); Billy Hart, Ari Hoenig (d); Betty Buckley (v). 4–5/99.

Werner's second for RCA is a sometimes bemusing mixture. It opens with four pieces for trio (Werner, Gress and Hart), one of which, the title-track, is distinguished by a piano introduction of sublime beauty. There's a duet with Lovano, a quintet track with Malaby, Weidenmuller, Ballou and Hoenig, a quartet with Feldman added to the core trio (the superb collective improvisation, 'Goblins'), then a version of 'Send In The Clowns' sung by theatre vocalist Betty Buckley. The finale is a 12-minute piece that seems like light concert-music, with extensive written parts for the strings and Werner reading out a poem. While some of this seems hugely overblown, full marks to Werner for ambitiousness, and the smaller and more concentrated tracks are fine enough to persuade that he's on an impressive streak.

Fred Wesley

TROMBONE

A frequent member of James Brown bands and other soul horn sections, Wesley plays in a style which stirs elements of hard bop into a stew of funk and soul rhythms.

****(*) New Friends**

Minor Music 801016 *Wesley; Stanton Davis (t, flhn); Steve Turre, Robin Eubanks (tb); Maceo Parker (as, perc); Tim Green (ts, perc); Geri Allen (ky); Anthony Cox (b); Bill Stewart (d); Carmen Lundy (v).* 90.

****(*) Comme ci comme ça**

Minor Music 801020 *Wesley; Hugh Ragin (t, flhn); Maceo Parker (as); Karl Denson (ss, ts, f); Peter Madsen (p); Rodney Jones (g); Anthony Cox (b); Bill Stewart (d); Teresa Carroll (v).* 8/91.

***** Swing And Be Funky**

Minor Music MM 801027 *As above, except Dwayne Dolphin (b, v), Bruce Cox (d, v) replace Cox and Stewart; omit Parker.* 5/92.

Wesley and his frequent collaborator, Maceo Parker, are showmen of a high order. Deprived of a groove – Stewart and Cox are good drummers, but they're coming from a hard-bop experience, not James Brown – they tend to falter on long solos and group interplay. The jazz set-pieces on the first record include 'Rockin' In Rhythm' and two Monk tunes, but they're no more than passable efforts, and the intended trombone summit meeting on 'For The Elders' isn't any more profound than a Kai Winding 'bone extravaganza. *Comme ci comme ça* is an ounce weightier, with the unexpected appearance of Ragin adding bite to the front line. The original material is lightweight – anything called 'Love In L.A.' sounds a sure candidate for oblivion – but the band work hard and the studio sound is bigger and sharper. *Swing And Be Funky* catches the band on a live show, which is probably the best place to hear it, but, as with so many hot live groups, much is lost in the transfer, and the closing 'Bop To The Boogie' is a useless piece of exhortation. Wesley himself is an adept and rather sonorous player, eschewing the horn's rasp in favour of fluency and sweetness, but he's scarcely a major figure on the instrument.

Frank Wess (born 1922)

TENOR SAXOPHONE, FLUTE

A native of Kansas City, Wess became a stalwart of the Basie woodwind section and an impressive solo star in his own right. His tenor approach is somewhat influenced by Lester Young, and perhaps by Don Byas as well, but Wess's real importance as an instrumentalist is in making the flute a valid solo voice. He plays with a strong, correct tone and is a nimble improviser.

*****(*) Dear Mr Basie**

Concord CCD 4420 *Wess; Joe Newman, Harry 'Sweets' Edison, Al Aarons, Snooky Young, Raymond Brown (t); Al Grey, Grover Mitchell, Benny Powell, Michael Grey (tb); Marshal Royal, Curtis Peagler (as); Billy Mitchell (ts); Bill Ramsay (bs); Ted Dunbar (g); Eddie Jones (b); Gregg Field (d).* 11/89.

****** Live At The 1990 Concord Jazz Festival: Second Set**

Concord CCD 4452 *Wess; Pete Minger (flhn); Marshal Royal (as); Rick Wilkins (ts); Gerry Wiggins (p); Lynn Seaton (b, v); Harold Jones (d).* 8/90.

*****(*) Entre Nous**

Concord CCD 4456 *Wess; Ron Tooley, Snooky Young (t); Joe Newman (t, v); Pete Minger (t, flhn); Art Baron, Grover Mitchell, Doug Purviance, Dennis Wilson (tb); Curtis Peagler, Bill Ramsay (as); Billy Mitchell (ts); Arthur Clarke (bs); Tee Carson (p); Ted Dunbar (g); Eddie Jones (b); Dennis Mackrel (d).* 11/90.

Wess's flute solo on the custom-built 'Entre Nous', title-piece of the fine 1990 concert album, recorded in Japan, shows off his burnished and now supremely confident tone to the utmost. Ironically, the live recording displays it better than the earlier Savoys, which are close-miked and rather brittle in sound (they are, in any case, currently out of print).

Wess capitalized on his long tenure in the Basie band with his own large ensemble. *Dear Mr Basie* is probably the more exciting of the two records and it represents a wholly successful homage to the great man, but it is *Entre Nous* that catches at the throat with moments of sheer beauty; and it is on the other Concord, recorded at the label's August 1990 showcase event, that Wess demonstrates that he has lost nothing of the sparky intelligence which made those early records as fascinating as they can be maddening.

***** Surprise! Surprise!**

Gemini GMCD 84 *Wess; Norman Simmons (p); Joe Cohn (g); Lynn Seaton (b); Jackie Williams (d).* 8/93.

*****(*) Tryin' To Make My Blues Turn Green**

Concord 4596 *Wess; Cecil Bridgewater, Greg Gisbert (t); Steve Turre (tb, shells); Scott Robinson (ts, acl); Richard Wyands (p); Lyn Seaton (b); Gregory Hutchinson (d).* 9/93.

***** Going Wess**

Town Crier 518 *Wess; Bobby Forrester (org); Clarence Tootsie Bean (d).* 9/93.

***** Surprise! Surprise!**

Chiaroscuro 350 2CD *Wess; Frank Foster, Jimmy Heath, Flip Phillips (ts); Richard Wyands (p); Lynn Seaton (b, v); Winard Harper (d).* 95.

Recent times have seen Wess working more comfortably in small-group settings and these, recorded within a month of one another during the man's 71st summer, are a good example of how he has turned a serviceable band style into an expressive and very personal voice. The Gemini disc was recorded at Oslo's Rainbow Studio and engineered by Jan Erik Kongshaug, who is responsible for most of ECM's output. Predictably, it sounds as good as they get, even though on this occasion the band Wess assembled has some creaking elements. It would be unfair to point to individuals, beyond saying that the rhythm section don't sound so much unrehearsed as rather stiff and unswinging. Wess switches to flute for the brand-new 'Equal Parts', but for once he fails to convince, and it is his tenor solo on Ettore Stratta's 'Forget The Woman' which takes the laurels. Joe Cohn, son of saxophonist Al, wins credit for his elegant soloing and solid accompaniment.

The Concord disc is a very different kettle of fish, much more confected. Teamed with players of the class of Turre, Bridgewater and the developing Gisbert, Wess has to go some to assert his leadership, but it's evident in the richness of the textures and in the overall configuration of the set, which is masterful. Seaton will be a revelation to some, a flawless timekeeper who solos persuasively, both pizzicato and with the bow.

Going Wess, one of several punning titles that have been round the block a couple of times, was Frank's first opportunity to record with an organ trio. Lest anyone fear that this most exact and light-toned of players should suddenly have descended into roiling funk or soul-jazz, Forrester is a notably delicate exponent of the Hammond. The set begins with Parker's 'Au Privave' and doesn't let up its brisk, confident swing from there to the close, which is another essay on one of Wess's favourite themes, 'Cottontail'.

Confusingly, the Chiaroscuro set has the same title as the earlier disc. This double set was recorded as part of a jazz cruise – nice work if you can get it – and the addition of a couple of guest stars lifts the gently relaxed mood up a notch. Among the walk-ons is Jimmy Heath on a long, long version of 'All The Things You Are', while the veteran Flip Phillips turns the engines back to full ahead for a steaming version of 'Cottontail'. The outstanding moment, though, is the renewed partnership with old Basie compadre Frank Foster for a powerfully sweeping version of 'My Funny Valentine', a showcase for Wess's flute. Seaton takes a couple of vocals and Wyands makes his presence felt with some excellent solo choruses, notably on 'Friendship' ... which is probably the keynote of the album. A lot of good music for your money.

Bugge Wesseltoft

PIANO, KEYBOARDS, ELECTRONICS, VOCALS

Active as a keyboard player in Norwegian jazz since the beginning of the '90s, Wesseltoft is seeking out new fusion forms with his own groups.

*****(*) New Conception Of Jazz**

Sonet 537251-2 *Wesseltoft; Jens Petter Antonsen, Erlend Gjerde, Sjur Miljeteig (t); Vidar Johansen (ss, bcl); Trude Eick (waldhorn); Ingebriht Flaten, Sveinung Hovensjø, Bjørn Kjellemyr (b); Audun Kleive (d, elec); Rune Arnesen, Anders Engen (d).* 1/95–8/96.

***** It's Snowing On My Piano**

ACT 9260-2 *Wesseltoft (p).* 10/97.

***** Sharing**

Jazzland 538278-2 *Wesseltoft; Erlend Gjerde, Nils Petter Molvaer (t); Vidar Johansen (ss); Ingebriht Flaten (b); Anders Engen, Paal Nilssen-Love (d); Olle Abstract, Pål Strangefruit (turntables); Jan Bang (d prog); Sidsel Endresen (v).* 98.

Wesseltoft first made an impact a decade ago when he recorded with Arild Andersen and Jan Garbarek. Those associations give only a partial impression of what he is about, for alongside the classically-tinged filigree he has created his own intriguing synthesis of jazz, funk and hip-hop, a project which goes out under the umbrella title, New Conception of Jazz.

There is nothing on either NCOJ record which would have astonished Miles Davis or perturbed the M-Base collective in its heyday. Wesseltoft's strength doesn't lie in the originality of the approach so much as in the distinctive character of the soundscapes he creates, intimate and lyrical with a strangely off-kilter quality which is either immediately beguiling or irritating. The earliest record is certainly the most adventurous, a sometimes edgy, questioning album that, in 'Spectre Supreme' and 'Modular' in particular, asks fascinating questions about where jazz is going at the end of the 1990s. Though the emphasis is largely on texture and pure sound, there is also some great linear playing, as on 'Trio' with Kjellemyr and Arnesen.

Sharing is content to rest on a settled formula – or, rather, a settled eclecticism. It's a much more polished record, technically assured and superbly cast. Sidsel Endresen, with whom Bugge has recorded before, contributes a delightful vocal to 'You Might Say', one of the less heavily treated items on the set. A bonus three-track disc came with the limited-edition first release. It included one all-acoustic track, 'Tune In', which underlines once again what a god Miles was and is to this generation of Scandinavian players. Not so much a matter of sound or syntax, more the confidence to place sounds and gestures and let them stand for nothing but themselves. Saxophonist Vidar Johansen is a sensitive and responsive partner with a very similar approach, but it would have been good to have heard more of Nils Petter Molvaer, who has gone on to make his own new synthesis of styles. The young trumpeter is magnificent on 'Breen'N'Glue'.

The other album is Wesseltoft's debut as a solo pianist. It is, ahem, a Christmas record, a mixture of traditional themes like 'Stille Nacht', 'O Little Town Of Bethlehem' and 'In Dulci Jubilo' and original compositions. Magnificently recorded by Jan Erik Kongshaug at Rainbow Studios in Oslo, it might just as readily belong in the catalogue of another, rather more celebrated label. If Erik Satie had known how to ski, this is how he would have sounded.

Kate Westbrook

VOCALS, TENOR HORN, PICCOLO

Although closely associated with her husband's work, Kate is a fine performer in her own right and has some recent records listed under her own name.

****(*) Goodbye, Peter Lorre**

Femme/Line FECD 9.01060 *Westbrook; John Alley, Mike Westbrook (p); Fine Trash (v).* 96.

*****(*) Love Or Infatuation**

ASC CD 20 *Westbrook; Mike Westbrook (p).* 5/97.

We have always been rather curmudgeonly about Kate Westbrook's highly theatrical vocal style. Out of context, it can jar. In its place, though, it is a powerful vehicle for strong lyrics, better at tough affirmation than at more reflective inscape. Kate has worked most frequently in the context of husband Mike's various groups, but she has run her own group, the Skirmishers, and these two albums find her working pretty much on her own account, albeit using material by other hands.

Goodbye, Peter Lorre is an odd, awkward hybrid, recommendable only to established fans, but Kate's interpretations of the songs of Friedrich Hollaender on *Love Or Infatuation* are absolutely first rate. Hollaender himself may be unfamiliar as a name, but everyone knows songs like 'Falling In Love Again' from *The Blue Angel* and 'You've Got That Look' and 'The Boys In The Backroom' from *Destry Rides Again*. Westbrook isn't Dietrich, and she doesn't attempt to be. What she does instead is a clever pastiche, relocating the songs both harmonically and dramatically for her own musical personality. As ever, Mike is a sympathetic and often arresting accompanist. Sadly, for the moment at least, this seems to be a limited-edition release. More, please.

Mike Westbrook (born 1936)

COMPOSER, PIANO, TUBA

Studied painting but turned to music and, on arriving in London in 1962, set about composing and arranging for groups of many different shapes and sizes: the Concert band, Cosmic Circus, Brass Band and others. Worked widely in theatre, occasionally in TV, and has frequently worked on major, revisionist settings of British icons from Blake to the Beatles. A man of many talents.

****** Celebration**

Deram 844 852-2 *Westbrook; Dave Holdsworth (t, flhn); Malcolm Griffiths (tb); Dave Perrottet (vtb); Tom Bennelick (frhn); George Smith (tba); John Surman (ss, bs, bcl); Mike Osborne (as); Bernie Living (as, f); Dave Chambers (ts, cl); Harry Miller (b); Alan Jackson (d).* 7–8/67.

*****(*) Release**

Deram 844 851-2 *As above, except omit Perrottet, Bennelick, Smith, Chambers; add Paul Rutherford (tb); (George) (ts).* 8/68.

*****(*) Marching Song**

Deram 844 853-2 2CD *As for both albums above, except omit Perrottet, Smith, Chambers; add Kenny Wheeler (t, flhn); Greg Bowen, Tony Fisher, Ronnie Hughes, Henry Lowther (t); Mike Gibbs, Eddie Harvey (tb); Martin Fry (tba); Alan Skidmore (ts, f); John Warren (as, bs, f); Brian Smith (ts); Barre Phillips (b); John Marshall (d).* 69.

It's tempting to suggest that, were Mike Westbrook American or German rather than English, his career might already have been garlanded with the praise it so conspicuously deserves. Britain's neglect of one of its most distinguished contemporary composers amounts to a national disgrace. Westbrook's regular groups – the early Concert Band, the mixed-media Cosmic Circus, the jazz-rock Solid Gold Cadillac and, most recently, the Brass Band – have drawn from a startling range of musical and performance backgrounds.

The Concert Band was probably the most straightforwardly jazz-influenced of all, Ellingtonian in sound and in intention, profoundly engaged and committed – as the anti-war agenda of these early discs underlines – and already theatrical in ways that suggested Westbrook had been listening to Charles Mingus's long-form works as well. Like both Mingus and Ellington, Westbrook has the ability to make what on paper look like relatively conventional horn voicings sound utterly original. The more abstract and expressionist tone-poems of subsequent years, and most notably *Metropolis*, retreated slightly from that dramatic premiss, but it has never been absent in 30 years' music-making.

Westbrook's early recordings for Deram have only just returned to the catalogue, sounding fresh and vigorous on CD. He had founded his original concert band as early as 1958, recruiting John Surman shortly thereafter, and then expanding the group to something like the ensemble that started giving concert performances of *Celebration* and *Marching Song*, both of which were shortened for recording.

Surman is the main soloist and co-composer on the first album, mostly on baritone, but checking in with a roiling soprano solo on 'Awakening', which also features Mike Osborne. Ossie, sounding close to his best on these recordings, is the main soloist on another Surman composition, 'Image'. Hints of Westbrook's later interest in the possibilities of rock rhythms surface on 'A Greeting'. By contrast, his limited exploration of free improvisation is evident on 'Echoes And Heroics', an intense ostinato over which Surman and Osborne, Malcolm Griffiths and Dave Holdsworth improvise at high intensity.

As the title hints, *Release* extended Westbrook's interest in freedom. Though hailed by his admirers as an advance on *Celebration*, it has always seemed to us a less accomplished album, rather bitty and perhaps rather too intent on dramatic impact. A continuous concert linked by cadenzas, it this time mixes in standards as well: 'Lover Man', 'Flying Home', 'Gee, Baby, Ain't I Good To You', 'Sugar' and, unexpectedly, 'The Girl From Ipanema'. It is almost as if Westbrook wants to ensure that, however far he ventures in the direction of the avant-garde, it will be clear where his root loyalties lie. Two versions of 'Folk Song' and 'Take Me Back' confirm the absolute importance of John Surman to the mission, and it's still the saxophone players who take the bulk of solo space.

As its military theme perhaps dictates, brass begins to dominate on *Marching Song*: a long, fraught exploration of how patriotism corrodes into horror and disillusion. First heard at the Camden Festival in the spring of 1969, it may well have been inspired by fiftieth anniversary commemorations the previous November of the end of the First World War. In the opening sequence, over a background of not altogether crowd noises, the band marches off round the stereo field while trumpeter Dave Holdsworth expresses the individual soldier's enthusiasm for the cause. A quieter section immediately follows, almost as if doubts and fears are already present. Bernie Living's overdubbed solo has a restless, almost schizophrenic quality. The twinned basses create a bed for Surman and Osborne, performing powerfully again. Huge ensemble chords signal a further change of mood, opening up a singing soprano feature by Surman which seems to nod in the direction of John Coltrane (though 'My Favorite Things' rather than 'Naima', as Mike Hennessey suggests in his sleeve-note). Paul Rutherford is the featured soloist on 'Other World', before the drums kick in with 'Marching Song' itself. The drama is kept balanced until, in 'Conflict', the apocalypse is unleashed. This is some of the most violent music you'll encounter within these pages, an angry, despairing statement which is all the more powerful for its sheer physicality. George Smith's tuba solo is completely *sui generis*, a quite remarkable statement. 'Requiem' and 'Memorial' document the inevitable aftermath, but with a weary, disillusioned tonality which is far more disturbing even than what has gone before.

These albums established Westbrook as a major presence on the European scene. In future years, recordings were harder to come by and much of his best work was limited to one-off festival performance and occasional broadcasts. That he was able to get such splendid results in the studio was testimony to his and the band's commitment.

***** Metropolis**

BGO CD 454 *Westbrook; Nigel Carter (t) Harry Beckett, Dave Holdsworth, Henry Lowther (t, flhn); Kenny Wheeler (t, flhn, mel); Malcolm Griffiths, Paul Nieman, Derek Wadsworth (tb); Paul Rutherford (tb, euph); Geoff Perkins (btb); Mike Osborne (as, cl); Ray Warleigh (as, f); Alan Skidmore (ts, ss); George Khan (ts); John Warren (bs); John Taylor (p); Gary Boyle (g); Harry Miller (b, clo); Chris Laurence (b); Alan Jackson, John Marshall (d); Norma Winstone (v).* 8/71.

We always considered this a modern classic, a near-perfect example of Westbrook's ability to create musical structures and contexts flexible enough to be performed by anything from a conventional small combo to the largest big band. The material that makes up *Metropolis* had been played by forces ranging from a quartet to 25 musicians by the time it was recorded. In retrospect, it sounds strangely bitty, fragmentary rather than cohesive, and much less securely rehearsed and performed than the Deram records above on which Westbrook's reputation rests.

Essentially, it is a further attempt on that modernist cliché, a sonic evocation of the urban dream/nightmare. It opens with a chaotic septet improvisation, two plangent trombones, two saxophones and rhythm, before kicking off into a driving, rock-tinged riff which surfaces here and there throughout the record, opposed to a softly questioning, rising figure which has always seemed to us a latter-day version of the nightingale in Berkeley Square.

The suite restarts with a second improvisation in which Ray Warleigh's flute segues seamlessly into Norma Winstone's voice, which is used instrumentally throughout. Malcolm Griffiths, Henry Lowther and, before them, Alan Skidmore and Dave Holdsworth all solo effectively in the early stages of the disc. Where Charles Mingus would have cheerfully mixed genres and juxtaposed elements, Westbrook tries to create a work out of whole cloth. Heard again after a gap of some years, *Metropolis* comes across as repetitive and episodic, an awkward hybrid of free jazz and fusion. Its moments of beauty – like Winstone's first entry, Skidmore's first solo and Harry Beckett's mournful coda – are breathtaking, but the album as a whole has lost its early impact. We would also draw attention to what sound like tape problems here and there. Westbrook's own solo on Part Seven is disconcertingly detuned and Mike Osborne's feature shortly afterward lacks Ossie's usual consistency of tone: presumably a problem that arose in remastering, for it is certainly not evident on the original LP.

***** Piano**

Impetus INT 17624 *Westbrook (solo p).* 78.

Recorded on a warm and responsive instrument in the Recital Room at South Hill Park, Bracknell, this is a rare chance to hear Westbrook unaccompanied and untheatrical. The immediate comparison is Charles Mingus again, a musing sample of ideas and exploratory gestures, almost as if leafing through the pages of a musical notebook. Westbrook has never been considered a virtuosic soloist, and the best way to listen to this album is *sans* notes, *sans* titles, *sans* everything except a sensitivity to the sources of his music. As an eavesdropped moment, it is both revealing and remarkably moving.

***** For The Record**

Transatlantic/Line TACD 9.00785 *Westbrook; Phil Minton (t, v); Kate Westbrook (thn, picc, v); Dave Chambers (reeds, v); Paul Rutherford (tb, euph, v).* 10/75.

*****(*) Love / Dream And Variations**

Transatlantic/Line TACD 9.00788 *Westbrook; Paul Cosh, Alan Downey, Henry Lowther (t); George Chisholm, Malcolm Griffiths, Geoff Perkins, Paul Rutherford (tb); Dave Chambers, John Holbrooke, Mike Page, John Warren (reeds); Dave MacRae (p); Brian Godding (g); John Mitchell (vib, perc); Chris Laurence (b); Alan Jackson (d, perc).* 2/76.

In a very real sense, Westbrook is not a jazz musician at all but a musical magpie; Rossini's 'La Gazza Ladra' and the '*Lone Ranger*' theme may have touched a chord of self-awareness (great artists thieve, after all, and Westbrook is certainly a masked loner).

If he is also an improviser, and there is no doubt that he is, it is not as an instrumentalist. Instead, he improvises with genre and with the boundaries of genre. Purely musical influences like Mingus and Ellington (whose 'Creole Love Call' is covered on the excellent *Love/Dream And Variations*) and Thelonious Monk are tempered by an interest in the boundaries of music and verse, theatre, the plastic arts and agit-prop, which has led Westbrook to reconsider the work of Brecht and Weill and the Beatles.

For The Record is marred by vocal histrionics, but it is a record that yields up more of interest with the passing years, not least in the way Westbrook has tried to re-integrate some of the large-scale harmonic strategies of the old Concert Band with a much-reduced instrumentation. It also includes four Blake settings, an early glimpse of the magnificent project that was to occupy Westbrook for much of the next period.

***(*) The Westbrook Blake

Impetus INT 8013 *Westbrook; Phil Minton (t, v); Kate Westbrook (thn, picc, v); Mike Davis (t, picc t); Dave Hancock (t); Malcolm Griffiths (tb); Nick Patrick (tba); Chris Biscoe, Alan Wakeman (sax); Georgie Born (clo); Chris Laurence (b); Dave Barry (perc).* 80.

The appearance in 1998 of *Glad Day* (see below), an extended version of this project, renders the original release something of a collectors' piece. It has its strengths, of course, not least a raw and somewhat unfinished character, as if Blake's inkblots and burin marks were still visible on the texts and images. Greatly impressive as it is, we would draw your attention to the reworked version.

**** The Cortège

Enja 7087 2CD *Westbrook; Phil Minton (t, v); Guy Barker, Dave Pearce, Dave Plews (t, flhn); Malcolm Griffiths (tb, btb); Kate Westbrook (thn, bamboo f, picc, v); Alan Sinclair, Dave Powell (tba); Chris Hunter (as, ss, ts, f); Phil Todd (ts, ss, as, cl, af); Lindsay Cooper (bsn, ob, sno); Chris Buscoe (bs, as, ss, acl, f); Brian Godding (g); Georgie Born (clo); Steve Cook (b); Dave Barry (d, perc).* 3–4/82.

***(*) Pierides

Core/Line COCD 9.00377 *Westbrook; Kate Westbrook (thn, picc, v); Peter Whyman (as, cl); Brian Godding (g, g syn).* 3/86.

Together with the former Kate Barnard, Westbrook has since devised a remarkable series of performances/entertainments which blend elements of jazz, popular song, verse and theatre. The finest of these are *The Cortège* and its dark thematic twin, *London Bridge Is Broken Down* (which represents the same drama of life-in-death-in-life but is currently out of circulation). *The Cortège* is a major composition by any standards. First performed at the Bracknell Jazz Festival in 1979 and released subsequently on Original Records, it has been a hole in Westbrook's discography for some time. Modelled loosely on a New Orleans funeral procession, it has the same fast-slow-fast rhythm. Westbrook has used the number '3' as the basic structural principle of the piece, which is full of three-note melodies and nine-note patterns raised on very small harmonic intervals with similarly invariant bass-lines. The texts are drawn from Lorca, Rimbaud, Hesse and elsewhere. Perhaps the most forceful integration of words and music occurs at the start of Rimbaud's '*Démocratie*', where Kate Westbrook sings over cello and bassoon, before the orchestra gradually enters and the piece builds towards the climactic '*En avant, route!*'. 'Erme Estuary', by contrast, is a threnody for Westbrook's father, who instilled in him a love of music and the theatre.

If *The Cortège* is the most dramatic of the large-scale suites, perhaps the purest and most straightforward is the trio, *Love For Sale* (now deleted), which weaves a remarkable range of sources (including an old Westbrook touchstone, William Blake, and a range of standard and traditional tunes) into a coherent performance that balances social anger, sentiment and purely formal control. The vocal and instrumental recipe works nearly as well on *Pierides*, where Godding's guitar adds a further dimension to music that was originally conceived as a dance/theatre piece known as *Pier Rides*, a wry Anglicization of the collective name of the Greek Muses; it's also (to give a sense of the serendipitous way Westbrook's imagination seems to work) the name given to the nine Thessalian maidens who, having challenged the Muses to a singing contest and lost, are turned into magpies.

*** The Orchestra Of Smith's Academy

Enja ENJ 9358-2 *Westbrook; Graham Russell, Stuart Brooks, Noel Langley, James McMillan, Lee Butler (t); Paul Nieman, Adrian Lane, Mike Kearsey (tb); Tracy Holloway (tb, euph); Chris Biscoe, Alan Barnes, Peter Whyman, Dave Bitelli, Alan Wakeman, Chris Caldwell (saxes); Pete Saberton (ky); David Maric (p); Anthony Kerr (vib); R Farrer (mar); Phil Boyden, Dominique Pifarély (vn); Frank Schaefer (clo); Tim Maple (g); Andy Grappy (tba); Malcolm Moore, Steve Berry (b); Peter Fairclough, Simon Pearson (d); Kate Westbrook (v).* 9/92–7/95.

In 1992 Westbrook was offered a retrospective at the Catania Festival in Sicily. This album represents the middle night of three and music all written round the matrix of what he calls the 'Smith's Hotel Chord', which Westbrook discovered at the hostelry of that name in Glasgow during a 1983 tour (although the set included on this CD was actually recorded some weeks later, in England). Developing materials out of the chord, Westbrook often liked to place different rhythmic cycles side by side, as on the innovative recreation of '*I.D.M.A.T. (It Don't Mean A Thing)*' and the exquisite harmonies of 'So We'll Go No More A-Roving', which reworks Westbrook's original 'Smith's Hotel Chord' as a feature for Chris Biscoe's emotive alto.

The most interesting aspect of the set is its dependence on the blues, albeit in heterodox forms. 'Checking In', a feature for Anthony Kerr, Dominique Pifarély and Pete Saberton, has a 24-bar structure. 'Measure For Measure' is a bizarre 12-bar form grafted on to classical sonata with free elements superadded. Very strange. 'Blighters' is another feature for Kate Westbrook, adapted from a text by Siegfried Sassoon.

Kerr and Pifarély are reunited to front 'Viennese Waltz'. As throughout the album, solos are recorded much less effectively than ensembles, and the violinist in particular sounds as if he is standing on the brink of a vast empty water tank. A valuable glimpse at an important moment in Westbrook's career.

(There is an additional track, 'Blues For Terenzi', written in memory of trombonist Danilo Terenzi, who worked in Westbrook's Orchestra and Brass Band but who died of cancer at the age of thirty. It was commissioned by Steve Martland and was played by the Martland Band at the Cheltenham Festival some three years later.)

**(*) Stage Set

ASC CD 9 *Westbrook; Kate Westbrook (v).* 11/95.

***(*) Bar Utopia

ASC CD 13 *Westbrook; Andy Bush, Noel Langley (t); Paul Edmonds, James McMillan (t, flhn); Mark Bassey, Tracy Holloway, Adrian Lane (tb); Andy Grappy (tba); Dave Bitelli (as, ts, cl); Peter Whyman (as, ss, cl); Chris Biscoe (as); Alan Wakeman (ts); Karen Street (ts, acc); Chris Caldwell (bs);*

Anthony Kerr (vib); Stanley Adler (clo); Steve Berry (b); Peter Fairclough (d); Kate Westbrook, John Winfield (v). 10/96.

The Westbrooks have continued to plough what seems a lonely furrow in the mid-1990s. Their particular brand of music theatre, whether miniaturized and personalized, as in *Stage Set*, or else scaled up ambitiously, as in *Bar Utopia*, consistently receives critical garlands ... and no support. The big-band set has all the Westbrook signatures: subtle ideas, bravura theatrical writing and ample space for improvisation. The overture is dedicated to Jelly Roll Morton and his 1926 recording, 'The Chant', a household god who doesn't entirely explain what happens subsequently. The three distinct groups who perform on 'Bar Utopia' itself are nicely distributed, and solo space throughout the record is always subordinate to structural dictates.

We are not great fans of *Stage Set*. Hampered by Kate Westbrook's increasingly mannered singing and by the rather sparse setting, it engages neither mind nor emotions, as *Bar Utopia* does on occasion.

****** Glad Day**

Enja ENJ 9376-2 2CD *Westbrook; Kate Westbrook (thn, picc, v); Peter Whyman (ss, as); Alan Wakeman (ss, ts, perc); Chris Biscoe (ss, as, bs); Brian Godding, Alan Hill, Paul Hirsh, Roger Potter (g); Steve Berry (b); Dave Barry (d, perc); Senior Girls' Choir of Blackheath Conservatoire of Music and the Arts.* 11/97.

This remarkable double set brings together freshly recorded performances of material which had been written for Adrian Mitchell's show *Tyger*, developed in *The Westbrook* Blake and then revived and augmented in 1996. There are items here which have been heard in different forms on *For The Record*, Mike's solo *Piano*, together with stray items from *Love For Sale*, *A Little Westbrook Music* and *Stage Set*. Hearing it as a whole confirms the centrality of the project to Westbrook's output. It is also a deeply moving musical experience, superbly arranged and with brilliantly marshalled choral parts.

The sequence opens with the instrumental 'Glad Day', a seeming self-portrait of the artist as the spirit of lightness and joy. It then immediately dips into the darkness with the famous 'London Song', in which Kate Westbrook's voice is pitched against wailing to evoke the piteous cries of the 'charter'd streets'. Phil Minton's vocal on 'For The Slave' is a powerful statement of libertarian passion, while Westbrook himself recites 'The Price'. The first disc ends with a powerful elaboration of 'Holy Thursday', opening with a reprise of the solo piano version on Mike's solo record, and then developing into a quarter-hour group performance.

Disc two begins with the opposition of Tyger and Lamb and the myth of the Upas-Tree and is in most regards darker and more intense, though Westbrook shifts harmonies to hint at lights and shades even in the bleakest places, just as he likes to point up the shadows that fall across innocence. 'The Human Abstract' was originally made by the Westbrook Trio as a single for CND and this, interestingly, is the performance which takes Mike back to the large-scale collective improvisation of the late 1960s and early '70s. It is a remarkable performance, to which the vocal is more than incidental but not quite an integral part. The closing pairing of 'The Fields' and 'I See Thy Form' hints at a chastened rapture, authentically Blakean. This may not be Westbrook's final word on Blake, but it represents at least a summation of a twenty-year obsession.

*****(*) Platterback**

PAO 10530 *Westbrook; Kate Westbrook, John Winfield (v); Karen Street (v, acc); Stanley Adler (v, clo).* 98.

A bittersweet tale of five travellers *en route* from Stiltsville to Platterback, this is the most engaging piece of music theatre the Westbrooks have created for years. It is also an intriguing shift in musical language, with accordion and cello (the latter always a Westbrook favourite) taking the place of horns and woodwinds.

As before, the piece draws on a whole range of styles, from Ellington-tinged jazz to cabaret song and quasi-serial structures. It evokes a landscape crowded with story and with cultural associations. John Winfield's voice is an engaging foil to Kate Westbrook's and, with three other vocalists in the line-up, the emphasis is very largely on texts and words; but it is their integration with an often minimalist backing that makes them so powerfully effective.

At the time of writing, *Platterback* was available only by mail order, but it seems to be scheduled for more orthodox distribution in due course.

Randy Weston (born 1926)

PIANO

Strongly influenced by Monk, from whom he had lessons, the impressively proportioned Weston – he is 6 foot 5 – spent the late '60s and early '70s in North Africa, an experience that coloured his playing from then on. His solo approach is a cross between Monk and Abdullah Ibrahim, but Weston is best known for the joyous 'Hi-Fly', a classic jazz tune.

***** Get Happy**

Original Jazz Classics OJCCD 1870 *Weston; Sam Gill (b); Wilbert Hogan (d).* 8/55.

***** With These Hands ...**

Original Jazz Classics OJCCD 1883 *Weston; Cecil Payne (bs, as); Ahmed Abdul-Malik (b); Wilbert Hogan (d).* 3/56.

*****(*) Jazz A La Bohemia**

Original Jazz Classics OJC 1747 *Weston; Sam Gill (b); Al Dreares (d).* 10/56.

***** The Modern Art Of Jazz**

Dawn DCD 107 *Weston; Ray Copeland (t); Cecil Payne (as, bs); Ahmed Abdul-Malik (b); Wilbert Hogan, Willie Jones (d).* 11/56.

Weston cuts such an impressive figure that his rather marginal critical standing remains an enigma. Though dozens of players every year turn to the joyous 'Hi-Fly' theme, few of them seem to have probed any deeper into Weston's output, which is considerable and impressive. Like many players of his generation, his main initial influence was Thelonious Monk. In later years, though, Weston was to explore African and Caribbean musics, somewhat in the manner of Dollar Brand/Abdullah Ibrahim and Andrew Hill, and to attempt larger-scale structures of a sort pioneered by James P. Johnson and Duke Ellington. Though a ruggedly beautiful performer, it is as a composer that he is most seriously underrated. For the clearest sense of what Weston gained – harmonically, rhythmically, spiritually – from his trip to Africa, it's necessary only to compare the excellent *Carnival* (currently deleted) with the much earlier *Jazz A La Bohemia* and *With These Hands*, which was recorded in the spring of the same year. It isn't the case that Weston passively 'discovered' African rhythms and tonalities on one of his early-1960s study trips. Art is seldom the product of accidents. As one can clearly hear from the Africanized inflexions of the Riverside sessions, Weston went in search of confirmation for what he was already doing. Abdul-Malik had a turn of phrase that was very different from anyone else of the time. 'You Go To My Head' on *A La Bohemia* has a quality quite unlike the average standards performance of the time, and Payne's rather solemn-sounding baritone here and on the other 1956 recordings can almost suggest the buzz and thump of Central African drones. Among younger-generation players, probably only Billy Harper had the right combination of traditionalism and modernist, post-bop technique, though later Weston was to record successfully with the new avant-traditionalist of tenor saxophone, David Murray.

After his Riverside contract expired, Weston recorded for Dawn with a somewhat augmented band. *The Modern Art of Jazz* was a valuable reissue for filling in a further aspect of the story. Both technically and artistically less appealing than the preceding discs, it does represent a very important step in Weston's development into the 'world' artist he became, and the originals, 'Loose Wig', 'A Theme For Teddy' and 'J.K. Blues', are all forestastes of a vein he was to refine in coming years.

*****(*) Monterey '66**

Verve 519698-2 *Weston; Ray Copeland (t, flhn); Booker Ervin (ts); Cecil Payne (bs); Bill Wood (b); Lennie McBrowne (d); Big Black (perc).* 9/66.

***** Nuit Africaine**

Enja ENJ 2086 *Weston (p solo).* 8/74.

It's clear that he was already attracted to African musics before he ever set foot on the continent. The 1966 Monterey sextet (Ervin was a guest artist) was well ahead of its time, extending the ideas of both Duke Ellington, who appeared on the same bill at Monterey, and Dizzy Gillespie. Weston had been working on a jazz programme in the public school system, and there is a didactic undercurrent to the music, even in a festival context. Big Black's drumming is of considerable significance and is much underrated, relative to people like Chano Pozo and the later modernists like Sunny Murray and Andrew Cyrille. This was actually the sextet's last appearance; it sounds like a band that has been together for some time. In those days, Weston was a rather diffident pianist, generally playing only accompaniments to the horns and concentrating on the shape of his compositions, of which the most important here is 'African Cookbook' at a sprawling 25 minutes. Almost all of Weston's later music and most of his important themes ('Little Niles' included) are already present at this period, and most of his later music draws directly on it. Though very well played in their way, the duos with Wood are a bit of an oddity. Weston isn't the most exciting pianist to listen to in this context, and he seems intent on delivering familiar themes – 'Body And Soul', 'Hi-Fly', 'African Cookbook' – with a minimum of additives. What it lacks, fatally, is colour and spice.

***** Khepera**

Verve 557821-2 *Weston; Benny Powell (tb); Talib Kibwe (as, f); Pharoah Sanders (ss, ts); Alex Blake (b); Victor Lewis (d); Chief Bey (perc, v); Neil Clark (perc); Min Xiao Fen (pipa, gong).* 2/98.

Weston's Verve albums have lately been under the axe. This augmented trio session with the emphasis very much on African sounds and rhythms, *Khepera* is more or less a world-music project, with very little space for jazz improvisation. 'Anu Anu' and 'The Shrine' are the tracks which maintain most connection with Weston's earlier career, but this time he seems self-consciously bent on an 'ethnic' sound and feel. The results are perfectly attractive and the record yields up new subtleties every time, but it's not the most compelling performance by the pianist himself, who sounds almost jaded here and there.

What We Live

GROUP

A striking improvisational group, driven by strong empathies and formidable technique. Later recordings see the group collaborate with a variety of guest instrumentalists.

***** What We Live**

DIW 909 *Larry Ochs (sno, ts); Lisle Ellis (b); Donald Robinson (d).* 4 & 6/94, 6/95.

****(*) What We Live Fo(u)r**

Black Saint 120156-2 *As above, except add Glenn Spearman (wood f), Ben Goldberg (bcl), Paul Plimley (p), William Winant (vib), India Cooke (vn), Miya Masaoka (koto).* 6/94.

*****(*) Never Was**

Black Saint 120169 *As for What We Live.* 6 & 7/96.

*****(*) Trumpets**

Black Saint 120189-2 *As above, except add Dave Douglas, Wadada Leo Smith (t).* 11/96, 3/98.

*****(*) Quintet For A Day**

New World 80553-2 *As above.* 4/98.

The trio was formed in 1994 in the Bay Area, always with the proviso that other participants would become involved as circumstances dictated. The first album and *Never Was* are the only two on which the founding members play without guest spots. The language is intense but surprisingly relaxed, as if the high intensity of East Coast free jazz were tempered with Californian sunshine. There is hardly a note on either album on which one feels the group is straining for effect.

Ellis is the main composer and his ideas sound very much like a milder version of Cecil Taylor's ferocious polytonality. Ochs is a much more impressive soloist than any of his colleagues in the ROVA saxophone quartet, and he is one of the very few contemporary players who has managed to make a decent fist of the treacherously pitched sopranino saxophone. The main pieces on *Never Was* are fierce and intense, but also compellingly lyrical. The understanding between Ochs and Ellis on 'Strength In Numbers' recalls some of the exchanges between Taylor and Jimmy Lyons, and Robinson has certainly listened carefully to the torrid playing of '60s innovators Sunny Murray, Andrew Cyrille and Milford Graves.

We find the guest-studded 1994 album shambolic and unfocused. It seems perverse to get the late Glenn Spearman in and then restrict him to wood flute. Few of the other cameos add a great deal to the sum. The two trumpet sessions are a different matter. On *Trumpets* the two horn men appear on alternate tracks, Smith's burning intensity chequered with Douglas's thoughtful cool; Dave's playing on 'Orbital' and 'Song Of Roland' is breathtaking. They play together on every track on *Quintet For A Day* and here there is a more measured texture, a combination of long and short, almost imagistic tracks. What We Live is a group that requires a measure of commitment and patience, not because the music is alienating or harsh, but precisely because it is so accessible that it can easily seem shallower and less mediated than it actually is. Give these fine records an early audition.

Ian Wheeler

CLARINET, ALTO SAXOPHONE, HARMONICA

A stalwart member of the Chris Barber band and occasional leader.

****(*) At Farnham Maltings**

Lake LACD 32 *Wheeler; Rod Mason (c, v); Ole 'Fessor' Lindgreen (tb); Ray Foxley (p); Vic Pitt (b); Colin Bowden (d).* 4/93.

Wheeler is an accomplished and sometimes rather sly clarinet player: on 'Higher Ground', for instance, he has George Lewis down to a faintly cruel 't'. But it also tends to mean that, as a leader at least, he doesn't impose a particularly individual stamp. Mason makes a suitable front-line partner with his Armstrong licks, but the excellent Lindgreen outplays both of them. They play it safe with the material and Mason's singing is ill-advised, but that is the norm for British trad records. In context, Ray Foxley's solo run through his own 'Liberia Rag' is quite charming.

Kenny Wheeler (born 1930)

TRUMPET, FLUGELHORN

The brilliant Canadian trumpeter and composer came to London in the 1960s and very quickly became associated with the avant-garde, playing in some of the most advanced groups of the day. It was clear, though, that his limpid, very pure tone was also amenable to other styles and that his interests veered to composition every bit as much as to free improvisation. Wheeler's body of work for the ECM label is definitive of its devotion to advanced musical language, great purity of sound and a constant trade-off between experimentalism and accessibility.

*****(*) Gnu High**

ECM 825591-2 *Wheeler; Keith Jarrett (p); Dave Holland (b); Jack DeJohnette (d).* 6/75.

****** Deer Wan**

ECM 829385-2 *Wheeler; Jan Garbarek (ts, ss); John Abercrombie (g, electric mand); Ralph Towner (12-string g); Dave Holland (b); Jack DeJohnette (d).* 7/77.

*****(*) Double, Double You**

ECM 815675-2 *Wheeler; Michael Brecker (ts); John Taylor (p); Dave Holland (b); Jack DeJohnette (d).* 5/83.

*****(*) Welcome**

Soul Note 121171 *Wheeler; Claudio Fasoli (t, flhn); Jean-François Jenny-Clark (b); Daniel Humair (d).* 3/86.

***** Flutter By, Butterfly**

Soul Note 121146 *Wheeler; Stan Sulzmann (ss, ts, f); John Taylor (p); Billy Elgart (d).* 5/87.

****** Music For Large And Small Ensembles**

ECM 843152-2 2CD *Wheeler; Alan Downey, Ian Hamer, Henry Lowther, Derek Watkins (t); Hugh Fraser, Dave Horler, Chris Pyne, Paul Rutherford (tb); Julian Arguëlles, Duncan Lamont, Evan Parker, Ray Warleigh (sax); Stan Sulzmann (ts, f); John Taylor (p); John Abercrombie (g); Dave Holland (b); Peter Erskine (d); Norma Winstone (v).* 1/90.

****** The Widow In The Window**

ECM 843198-2 *Wheeler; John Taylor (p); John Abercrombie (g); Dave Holland (b); Peter Erskine (d).* 2/90.

***** California Daydream**

Musidisc 50029 *Wheeler; Jeff Gardner (p); Hein Van Der Geyn (b); André Ceccarelli (d).* 12/91.

*****(*) Kayak**

Ah Um 012 *Wheeler; Dave Horler, Chris Pyne (tb); Dave Stewart (btb, tba); John Rook (frhn); Stan Sulzmann (ss, ts, f); Julian Arguëlles (ss, ts); John Horler, John Taylor (p); Chris Laurence (b); Peter Erskine (d).* 5/92.

Wheeler has been a fixture on the British jazz scene since 1952, when he emigrated from his native Canada and did section work with some of the best bandleaders of the time, joining John Dankworth in 1959 and staying until the mid-'60s. Initially influenced by the bop trumpet of Fats Navarro and his equally short-lived descendant, Booker Little, Wheeler also took on board the clipped abstractions and parched romanticism of trumpeter and flugelhorn player Art Farmer. Under this combination of interests, Wheeler turned towards free playing, joining John Stevens's influential Spontaneous Music Ensemble, Alexander von Schlippenbach's Globe Unity Orchestra and Anthony Braxton's superb early-1970s quartet. More recently, Wheeler has played with Norma Winstone and her pianist husband, John Taylor, in the impressionistic Azimuth, and he became the latest permanent recruit to the United Jazz + Rock Ensemble in 1979.

It was possible in 1990 to wonder at Wheeler's threescore years because he became a leader only rather late in his career. Famously self-critical, the trumpeter seemed to lack the basic ego-count required to front a working band. Association with Manfred Eicher's musician-friendly ECM made an enormous difference to Wheeler's self-perception, and since 1975 he has regularly recorded for the label whose painstaking technical virtues match his own. With ECM, Wheeler has also made enormous strides as a composer; standards are now very rare in his recorded work and the Dietz/Schwartz 'By Myself' on ECM 843152-2 seems a significant exception. 'Ana', on *The Widow In The Window*, had already been given a notable reading by the Berlin Contemporary Jazz Orchestra (ECM 841777-2).

Music For Large And Small Ensembles contains some of Wheeler's most distinctive scores and is perhaps the best place to gain an understanding of how Wheeler's particular grasp of tonality and instrumental colour works in a mixture of scored and improvised settings. As in Azimuth, he uses Norma Winstone's voice to increase the chromaticism of his arrangements and further humanize unwontedly personal and self-revealing pieces, full of folk echoes and deeply embedded North American themes (the 'Opening' to 'Sweet Time Suite' sounds like a variant on a cowboy tune, and there's a wide-open quality to the voicings that can be heard in fellow-Canadian Leonard Cohen's eclectic jazz–buckskin–*musette*–rock syntheses). The trios that conclude disc two (there are also three duets which do not involve Wheeler as a player) are closer to his free-abstract work than to the thematic improvisations on his best-known ECM records. Significantly, the most abstract of the albums he has made for the label, *Around 6*, is currently deleted. The best of those that remain is undoubtedly *Deer Wan*. It includes Wheeler's most atmospheric brass effects and some of his most unfettered playing. The opening 'Peace For Five' is a straightforward blowing theme, with fine solos by each of the players. The three remaining tracks are more elliptical but no less impressive, and only the relatively brief '3/4 In The Afternoon', featuring one of Ralph Towner's off-the-peg 12-string spots, is a mild disappointment.

Deer Wan's predecessor on ECM is distinguished by being Keith Jarrett's last session as a sideman. There is some evidence that the pianist was less than happy with the music, but he produces three startling performances that are matched by Wheeler's distinctive phraseology and impeccable tone. An important album for the trumpeter, it's still marked by a degree of diffidence which persists through the later work. The two Soul Notes suffer from a flatter acoustic, which seems to rob Wheeler's higher-register passages of their ringing strength. Musically, they're well up to scratch; 'Everybody's Song But My Own' (*Flutter By*) and 'Invisible Sound' and 'Emptiness' (*Silence*) utilize the softly falling figures one has heard in Wheeler's work from the outset but which increasingly play a structural role in the composition. *Widow In The Window* recaptures – but for Garbarek – the sound of *Deer Wan*, while adding a new solidity of conception. Taken in conjunction with the contemporaneous *Music For Large And Small Ensembles*, it signals Wheeler's emergence as a major jazz composer. Late in the day by some standards, but none the less welcome.

Kayak is marred by oddly balanced sound but is musically fascinating. The latter part of the set is taken up with a suite loosely centred on C: 'See Horse', the impressionistic 'Sea Lady' (with a fine flute solo from Sulzmann), 'C Man' (dedicated to bassist Laurence, who introduces the solos), and 'C.C. Signor!' (a rollicking tribute to Chick Corea that brings the album to a very effective close). Wheeler distributes the solo space very even-handedly, concentrating exclusively on flugelhorn for his carefully crafted explorations. The writing is consistently excellent, mixing older material like '5 4 6' and 'Gentle Piece – Old Ballad', the latter strongly recalling the Wheeler of *Deer Wan*. Despite reservations about the production, strongly recommended.

The Musidisc is a live session, recorded in Paris. Gardner and Van Der Geyn chip in with two pieces each, but they're so unsophisticated alongside Wheeler's 'The Imminent Immigrant' and 'Bethan' (which, quite properly, start and finish the set) that it's ridiculous. Sound is a bit echoey and overfull, but it's a nice record and one that Wheeler fans will definitely want to have.

****** Angel Song**

ECM 533098-2 *Wheeler; Lee Konitz (as); Bill Frisell, Dave Holland (b).* 95.

*****(*) Siren's Song**

Justin Time JTR 8465 *Wheeler; John Taylor (p); Norma Winstone (v); Maritime Jazz Orchestra.* 96.

Two misconceptions here. First, *Angel Song* was widely thought to be a co-led project with Konitz; while it is as collaborative as much of the label's recent output, with much emphasis on internal relationships within the group, it has Wheeler's stamp all over it: a delicate, floating sound with a sting and hard ideas scattered through it. By the same token, *Siren's Song* (a seeming paucity of album-title ideas at the moment) is not really an Azimuth project and is not so billed. What it is is a form of jazz *concerto grosso* with the trio ranged against a well-schooled and precise Canadian orchestra. They provide texture and depth of focus, but they also feed and re-feed Wheeler's more searching musical cues, creating a back and forth of ideas that is actually a lot more thoughtful than first appears. *Angel Song* is the one to have from this period, and it is probably the more accessible too. Frisell's soft-edged phrasing melds with Holland's unusually deep-rooted figures, creating a symmetry that fires both hornmen to some of their best recorded work in years.

Rodney Whitaker (born 1968)

DOUBLE BASS

Wynton Marsalis once autographed a fragment of score for Rodney with the words: 'Listen to Jimmy Blanton'. Whitaker, who teaches at Michigan State University, has been a member of the Marsalis-led Lincoln Center Orchestra for some time and has demonstrated that, subconsciously at least, he has already absorbed much of Blanton's language. A copper-bottomed soloist with a big tone, he is an asset to bands of any size.

***** Children Of The Light**

DIW 907 *Whitaker; Nicholas Payton, Wallace Roney (t); James Carter (ts); Alex Herding (bs); Cassius Richmond (f); Geri Allen, Cyrus Chestnut (p); Gregory Hutchinson, Karriem Riggins (d); Andrew Daniels II (perc).* 9/95.

***** Hidden Kingdom**

DIW 929 *Whitaker; Ron Blake (ss, ts); Mark Hynes (ss); Cassius Richmond (as, f); James Carter (ts, bs); JD, Peter Martin, Rich Roe (p); Gerald W Cleaver, Gregory Hutchinson, Kariem Riggins (d); Leonard King (v).* 96.

*****(*) The Brooklyn Session: Ballads And Blues**

Criss Cross 1167 *Whitaker; Wycliff Gordon (tb); Ron Blake (ss, ts); Stefon Harris (vib); Eric Reed (p); Carl Allan (d).* 12/98.

The Detroit jazz community is said to be one of the tightest in the United States, built on mutual support and respect. Rodney Whitaker was quickly picked out as a young man to watch and foster, and his early reputation won him a place in Donald Washington's group, Bird/Trane/Sco/Now!, a cumbersome handle for a working band, but a reasonable shorthand for the influences at work. Whitaker is quite open about his own biggest influence: the intense, short-lived genius of Paul Chambers informs much of what he does.

There are hints of Coltrane in his own writing. It's difficult to miss the link between 'Langman', a song for his young son, and 'Afro Blue', which Trane made his own. There's also a strong hint of 'Syeeda's Strong Flute' in the underlying structure of 'Woman Child', another Whitaker original. Most of the other material comes from the young man's growing circle of associates. Only 'On Green Dolphin Street', which features guests Geri Allen and her husband Wallace Roney, is a recognized standard. The pool of players is pretty extraordinary for a debut record. Carter is as fierce and assertive as ever on the opening 'Mandela's Muse' and, though Payton lacks Roney's urgency and precision, he's turning into an impressive soloist in a rather outmoded style. Chestnut increasingly plays like a veteran, with Kenny Barron's ability to blend into a band without losing his individuality. A word is due for flautist Cassius Richmond, who contributes a great deal to 'Mandela's Muse', Monzola Whitaker's 'One Silent Moment' and the Latinate 'El Morro'. Kariem Riggins and Gregory Hutchinson share drum duties, and Whitaker plays noticeably differently with each, emphasizing the beat with Hutchinson, who tends to lay off and outside the pace, nudging it along rather than propelling hard. Whitaker looks like being an important player for years to come.

If he hadn't yet garnered as many plaudits as Christian McBride, they surely couldn't be far away, and yet the follow-up album does little more than mark time and capitalize rather slackly on what had been a promising start. Whitaker falls into the tricky-second-album trap of trying to pack in too many different possible registers, including a vocal by Leonard King on 'The Promise Of You', which seems to have snuck in from another record.

Far better is the debut for Criss Cross, which is very much a tribute to Rodney's greatest single ancestral influence, the precocious but ever more impressive legacy of Paul Chambers. Mr PC is represented by three tracks, the ubiquitous 'Whims Of Chambers', which every bass player takes in with his mother's milk, 'Ease It', and 'The Hand Of Love', the last of which is a long way from the prevailing bebop idiom of the time, and a delicately phrased song which bears surprising kinship to the Motown material Rodney grew up with. Like many young players of his generation, he has kept an active lookout for new 'standards' and perhaps the most striking solo performance on the record is Whitaker *arco* phrasing on the Carly Simon song, 'The Way They Always Said It Should Be'. Miles would have approved. Crisply recorded with a nice live feel, *Ballads And Blues* is a sterling performance which represents a bright young talent at his very best.

Brian White

CLARINET

English clarinettist, in a trad-to-swing bag, but particularly devoted to the music of Muggsy Spanier and his groups.

***** Muggsy Remembered Vol. 1**
Jazzology JCD-116 *White; Alan Gresty (t); Geoff Cole (tb); Goff Dubber (ss, ts); Alan Root, Jonathan Vinten (p); Tony Bagot (b); Ian Castle (d).* 4/88–10/93.

***** Muggsy Remembered Vol. 2**
Jazzology JCD-200 *As above, except omit Vinten.* 4/88–4/89.

***** Pleasure Mad**
Jazzology JCD-178 *White; Ben Cohen (t, v); Geoff Cole (tb); Alan Thomas (p); Joe Becket, Gordon Davis (b); Ian Castle (d).*

***** Really The Blues**
GHB BCD-303 *White; Alan Elsdon (t); Goff Dubber (ss, cl, v); Neville Dickie, John Clarke (p); Malcolm Harrison (g); Gordon Davis (b); Colin Miller (d).* 5–8/90.

***** C'est Magnafique**
Jazzology JCD-248 *White; Ben Cohen (c); Geoff Cole (tb); Jonathan Vinten (p); Richard Lyons (b); Colin Miller (d).* 12/92.

***** Muggsy Remembered Vol. 3**
Jazzzology JCD-316 *White; Alan Gresty (c); Geoff Cole (tb); Goff Dubber (ts); Martin Litton (p); Tony Bagot (b); Tony Scriven (d).* 8–9/98.

The English clarinettist White takes repertory to a near-fanatical state on these affectionate, punctilious re-creations of bygone jazz. The Spanier albums mix Muggsy's 'Great Sixteen' tunes with a handful of other variations on the Ragtime Band style and, while there is some ingenious counterfeiting here, they do tend to make one think of playing the originals instead. Problematically, while the band try stretching out on a few of the previously 78-length arrangements, they add nothing of consequence. Gresty does a commendable job of ghosting for the original, but his nearly note-perfect takes on Muggsy's superb 'Someday Sweetheart' improvisation or the climactic 'I Want A Big Butter And Egg Man' hardly compete with the master. Volume One is enhanced by four tracks from 1993, recorded partly in tribute to pianist Root, who died earlier that year.

The re-creations of the King Jazz sessions on *Really The Blues* are rather more effective, but finally not much different in impact. Dubber and White make a more obviously compatible team than Bechet and Mezzrow, and they sound the more personal for it; but Elsdon's trumpet parts are merely derivative, and the rhythm section secure a somewhat hollow bounce. *Pleasure Mad* casts a wider net and reels in Hot Five tunes and '1919 March', among others. This set is by White's Magna Jazz Band, which he's led since 1951, and *C'est Magnafique* continues their tradition. It's some comment on the group's resilience that this is as good a disc as any they've made. The 16 tracks include an intelligent choice of rarities – from the books of Bechet, Don Redman, Jimmy Blythe and others – and all are dispatched with an enthusiasm that sounds to be second nature by now.

The third volume of Muggsy memorials comes a full ten years after the first, but the spirits are very willing. Although much of the material has only a tenuous link with Spanier, White's men – many of them drawn from the current Monty Sunshine group – still latch on to a decent echo of the Spanier Ragtimers, though even here there is revisionism: the thudding bass feature on 'The World Is Waiting For The Sunrise', as one instance.

****(*) Tribute To Kid Ory**

Lake LACD106 *White; Alan Elsdon (t); Geoff Cole (tb); Pat Hawes (p); Nevil Skrimshire (g); John Rodber (b); Colin Miller (d).* 6/98.

A disappointingly tame recording of what has become a popular touring group. Ory was scarcely a defining personality in his kind of music, and the material is all too familiar, but White's group make perfunctory work of this one. Elsdon and the leader play the best solos.

Chip White

DRUMS

Leadership debut for this contemporary drummer, also showcasing his writing.

***** Harlem Sunset**

Postcards POST1006 *White; Claudio Roditi (t, flhn); Robin Eubanks (tb); Gary Bartz (ss, as); Steve Nelson (vib); Buster Williams (b).* 6/94.

Beautiful playing, though the music tends to stand revealed after a single play: pleasing as White's tunes are, familiarity doesn't reveal any great profundities. He's a busy but not overpowering drummer, pushing the tunes along in straightforward time, embellished by deft use of the sticks, and he gets a light, sometimes haunting sound out of the horns, cushioned on Nelson's vibes which give a resonance to the chords that a piano might have dulled. 'Circle Dance' and 'Excuse Me Now' are particularly attractive. There's a nice contrast between Roditi's brimming style and Eubanks's more sober virtuosity, while Bartz is his usual strong self, if at a rather lower wattage than normal.

David White

GUITAR

Guitarist whose preference for a simple tone and no effects in a contemporay setting is a refreshing change from the norm.

***** All Stories Are True**

Cadence CJR 1057 *White; Valery Ponomarev (t); Tim Armacost (ts); Calvin Hill (b); Victor Jones (d).* 5/93.

***** Object Relations**

CIMP 117 *As above, except Shingo Okudaira (d) replaces Jones.* 6/96.

*****(*) Double Double**

CIMP 168 *White; George Garzone, Tim Armacost (ss, ts); John Lockwood (b); Joris Dudli (d).* 2/98.

Likeable, oddball neo-bop, but not without its problems. White's muffled, sometimes bluesy sound is a refreshing change from the standard Montgomery/Scofield options, and he has a Tristano-like sense of selflessness: some of his solos sound completely 'inside'. *All Stories Are True* takes on some interesting structures, too, such as the various metres of 'Iconoclasts' and the contrary 'Hot Issues In An Open House'. Ponomarev and Armacost come up with some strong improvisations in support. But the rhythm section often seem unaware of what's going on and where everybody's headed. Hill especially is very busy, yet oblivious to the rest of the music, and both he and Jones are given an unpleasant studio sound. *Object Relations* picks up the baton three years later, with Okudaira in for Jones, and the results are much the same, though the CIMP sound is just as unsuitable. Armacost and Ponomarev have their moments, although some of these pieces seem inflated beyond their useful length.

The latest album is a clear notch ahead. Garzone is a valuable addition to any band, and he seems to encourage Armacost to raise his game, too. The results are dominated by the two saxmen, who play generously but are part of a strong quintet which White, Lockwood and Dudli fill out more than dutifully. This time White takes more of a back seat as a soloist; but his tunes are fertile ground for the horns, and the one standard, 'Love Thy Neighbour', is beautifully handled.

Michael White (born 1954)

CLARINET

White is from a musical New Orleans family and is dedicated to the original music of his home, playing in the grand traditions of the city. He still brings a New Orleans band to New York's Village Vanguard every New Year for the celebration. At home, he also plays in brass bands as well as his own groups.

***** Shake It & Break It**

504 CDS 6 *White; Greg Stafford (c); Reginald Koeller (t); Freddie Lonzo (tb); Sadie Goodson Cola (p, v); Frank Moliere (p, v); Les Muscutt (g); Walter Payton Jr, Chester Zardis (b); Frank Parker, Stanley Stephens (d).* 1/81–5/87.

We were rather cool in our first edition on what was White's debut recording, and Frank Moliere's piano still sounds awful, but perhaps we've grown more tolerant of New Orleans 'idiosyncrasies' down the years. The music is played with undeniable spirit, and there is now the bonus of five tracks from a 1987 session, recorded in the cavernous-sounding Olivier House, with Cola and Zardis (who had played together in Buddy Petit's band, 60 years earlier!) in attendance. Stafford plays carefully and the stage belongs mostly to White, who sounds very good. It's a pity that we have no more recent records under his name.

Mark Whitecage (born 1937)

ALTO AND SOPRANO SAXOPHONES, CLARINET, ALTO CLARINET

A free-thinking alto saxophonist who made some discs in the 1970s with John Fisher, Bobby Naughton and Leo Smith, Whitecage has only recently resurfaced as a recording artist. His idiosyncratic methods move between chamber-like forms and entirely free improvisation.

*****(*) Free For Once**

CIMP 106 *Whitecage; Dominic Duval (b); Jay Rosen (d).* 1/96.

****** Caged No More**

CIMP 119 *As above, except add Tomas Ulrich (clo). 7/96.*

Whitecage is a somewhat reclusive figure whose appearances on record have been unfortunately rare. On alto he plays long, almost pure streams of melody which impart a graceful beauty to a free-bop methodology which makes these discs both exciting and serenely attractive. Even when he's playing at a heated full stretch, Whitecage seems to want to talk about agreeable things, and it makes these fundamentally uncompromising sessions temperate enough to avoid the raging exhaustion that sometimes afflicts this area of jazz. *Free For Once* is still a shade too long, but there's an almost terpsichorean feel to the music which Rosen and Duval pick up on (it's not only on 'Two Horn Tango' that they fall into a tango rhythm). Whitecage has so much to say on the horn that he sustains the date. *Caged No More* is a notch better, though, and Whitecage was right to feel proud of it. Ulrich's cello adds pith and sinew to the group's sound, and the players frequently hit a stride that balances lyricism, intensity and creative flux in an unusually harmonious accord.

***** 3 + 4 = 5**

CIMP 155 *As above, except add Joseph Scianni (p). 6/97.*

*****(*) Consensual Tension**

CIMP 157 *Whitecage; Sabir Mateen (as, ts, cl, f); Joe Fonda (b); Harvey Sorgen (d). 7/97.*

***** Research On The Edge**

CIMP 193 *Whitecage; Sabir Mateen (as, ts, cl, f); Chris Dahlgren (b); Jay Rosen (d). 2/99.*

Having found a patron in Robert Rusch of Cadence/CIMP, Whitecage seems to be making up for lost time as far as record-making is concerned. *3 + 4 = 5*, recorded at Dunn Hall in Potsdam, NY, continues the good work of the previous disc, but the balance of the group is sent slightly askew by the addition of Scianni and, for all its 'naturalness', the recording is unkind to both Ulrich and Duval, who simply can't be heard properly for much of the session.

Consensual Tension introduces Whitecage's 'Other Quartet', and a splendid one it is: Mateen is a more restless and argumentative soul and, while Whitecage adds lyrical and sometimes rococo flights to the mix, Mateen is gritty and cutting. Fonda and Sorgen – they manufacture a nice, slithering shuffle on 'Joe's Groove' – fill in the backgrounds and sometimes push their way to the front. It's very free, but the way they play 'Oleo', a spontaneous fancy in the studio, proves how this thinking has plenty of formal knowledge stirred into it.

Whitecage's 'Other Other Quartet' (we hardly dare guess what the next group will be called) picks up the baton for *Research On The Edge*. This is more like unvarnished energy music: the first three tracks are huge blow-outs ('Green St Rundown' runs almost half an hour) and, mightily as the four men play, there are passages when sound and fury stand in for communicable creativity, or so it seems. Not that they are playing full-tilt all the time: there is the usual cycle of attack and decay in each piece. When they do 'Well You Needn't' at the end, the music almost gets funky, and it freshens the listener up. Enjoyable, but probably not the best representation of Whitecage's work.

Tim Whitehead (born 1950)

TENOR SAXOPHONE

Born in Liverpool, he studied law but turned to music in the '70s. Early groups South Of The Border and Borderline brought him local renown, then a spell with Loose Tubes, followed by his own small bands in the '90s.

***** Silence Between Waves**

Jazz House JHCD 033 *Whitehead; Pete Jacobsen (ky); Arnie Somogyi, Steve Watts (b); Dave Barry (d). 1–4/94.*

*****(*) Personal Standards**

Home Made HMR047 *As above, except add Liam Noble (p), Davide Mantovani, Sam Burgess (b), Milo Fell (d); omit Watts. 98–99.*

Whitehead has fashioned a convincing and evocative English tone to his playing and writing. Although recorded in the less than pastoral surroundings of Ronnie Scott's Club, *Silence Between Waves* is quartet music that is redolent of Albion's greenest meadows as well as market-town England. Jacobsen is a willing collaborator, his hard-bitten solo on 'Southend' no less effective than his meditative introduction to 'The Sky Seas Me', but it's otherwise very much the saxophonist's show, traversing the range of the tenor saxophone with broad-shouldered ease and drawing long, melodic lines in his solos rather than falling back on licks. That said, the record is far too long and could comfortably have surrendered 20 of its 80 minutes, heightening the impact of the best playing.

Personal Standards suffers the same drawback, to a degree: Whitehead can sustain long solos persuasively enough, but some of these pieces still outstay their most effective duration. Nevertheless a very impressive record overall. The saxophonist selected pop material for the most part, 'My Girl', 'Dancing In The Street', 'Lovely Day' and 'What's Going On' being among the most familiar choices, and while these are conservative interpretations they showcase a magnificent saxophone timbre: the leader has never had a better sound in a studio. Although the other players give their best, Whitehead is an almost overpowering presence in this company, and the hallmark of the record is the way he personalizes what is sometimes unpromising material.

Mark Whitfield

GUITAR

Though superficially from the same mould as Kevin Eubanks and Hiram Bullock, Whitfield is much more deeply suffused with the blues. His phrasing is attractively old-fashioned without ever sounding like pastiche, and his arrangements are always absolutely contemporary.

***** True Blue**

Verve 523591-2 *Whitfield; Nicholas Payton (t); Branford Marsalis (ss, ts); Kenny Kirkland (p); Rodney Whitaker (b); Jeff Tain Watts (d). 94.*

*****(*) Forever Love**

Verve 533921-2 *Whitfield; Jim Pryor (p); Roland Guerin (b); Donald Edwards (d); Diana Krall (v).* 96.

These seem to be all that survives of Whitfield's run of albums for Verve, and they are superficially very different. The earlier album was recorded in Hollywood with a top-drawer roster of Polygram artists and a very definite emphasis on the blues. And yet it's the later album with its relatively unfamiliar line-up and more show-bizzy programme which has the jazz vibe.

True Blue made the classic corporate mistake of garlanding new and relatively untried talent with bankable names. Whitfield barely comes across at all, and his guests are able to offer only cameo contributions. Even so, some of the tracks – an unexpected 'Ba-Lue Bolivar Ba-Lues Are' and a cracking version of Trane's 'My Syms' – are strongly impressive and Whitfield makes his mark as a composer as well.

The later record is the one we'd recommend, even against the obvious draw of Marsalis, Kirkland and Payton. It's a gentler album, more thoughtful and less obviously bent on making an impact. It's also beautifully executed and having Diana Krall on board is never a disadvantage, though it would have been good to hear her on piano as well. Standout tracks: that mid-section which sequences 'My One And Only One', 'Nature Boy' and 'It Never Entered My Mind', the last respectfully aware of Miles and John Coltrane. Super stuff.

Wesla Whitfield

VOCAL

California-based vocalist, singing the great American songbook.

***** Seeker Of Wisdom And Truth**

Cabaret CACD 5012 *Whitfield; Mike Greensill (p); John Goldsby (b); Tim Horner (d).* 11/93.

***** Teach Me Tonight**

High Note HCD 7009 *Whitfield; Noel Jewkes (as, ts, bs, cl, bcl); Mike Greensill (p); Michael Moore (b); Joe LaBarbera (d).* 1/97.

Whitfield has a strong and clear voice – perhaps too strong, since it often feels like she's bearing down on a song, if not quite wrestling it to the ground. Her penchant for very long notes without vibrato can make a lyric seem enormously extended, and because she usually likes to sing the verse as well this can sometimes tell against her. Nor does she exactly strike one as a swinging vocalist. All this carping aside, she can often turn in uncommonly affecting performances on improbable tunes; if her style appeals, her records will appeal very strongly.

The discography is looking a bit foreshortened by the absence of her Landmark albums. *Seeker Of Wisdom And Truth* is a decent one – the Astaire medley is delightful, 'The Boy Next Door' has a nice ambiguity about it, and 'I Want To Talk About You' is very fine. *Teach Me Tonight* has an obvious benefit in the personnel: Jewkes is a master multi-instrumentalist, Moore and LaBarbera are unimpeachable, Greensill knows her better than anybody. Doubts about some of the interpretations will nag the uncommitted, but how about the rubato intro to 'Almost Like Being In Love', or the shoulder-shrug 'I Fall In Love Too Easily'?

*****(*) With A Song In My Heart**

High Note HCD 7040 *Whitfield; Mike Greensill (p); Michael Moore (b).* 5/99.

Whitfield (formerly Weslia, now Wesla, apparently due to confusion over how her name is pronounced) goes absolutely her own way. Her pronunciation has become even more idiosyncratic, swallowing some consonants, hitting long, loud notes when you expect a little leniency – listen to the curt ending of 'Spring Is Here' – and turning some songs into curiously abstract meditations. The result, in these Rodgers and Hart performances, is a set of 18 interpretations which stand resolutely aside from so many other versions of this familiar material. It helps that Greensill and Moore come up with unusual frameworks of their own, never merely comping; but it's Whitfield's show and she makes it her own.

Sebastian Whittaker

DRUMS

Post-bop drummer working in idiomatic hard-bop surroundings.

***** First Outing**

Justice JR 0201 *Whittaker; Dennis Dotson (t, flhn); James Lakey (tb); Shelley Carrol, John Gordon (ts); Stefan Karlsson (p); David Craig (b).* 90.

***** Searchin' For The Truth**

Justice JR 0202 *Whittaker; Barry Lee Hall (t); James Lakey (tb); Jesse Davis (as); Stefan Karlsson (p); David Craig (b).* 91.

Whittaker is a young man who has overcome considerable personal difficulties to become a musician. Sightless piano players are relatively common, but drumming requires a very different spatial sense and orientation, and this Whittaker seems to have acquired. His label goes out under the Green-ish slogan 'Recycle Paper, Not Music'; but there is a persistent sense that much of the Justice catalogue is recycled hard bop. Whittaker is a more honest practitioner than most, and the combination of his Blakey-derived technique (with rather individual bass accents) and a misty analogue sound frequently conjures up the impression that one is listening to some obscure corner of the late-'50s Blue Note catalogue.

First Outing is probably the better of the two discs by a whisker, though the appearance of Jesse Davis on *Searchin' For The Truth* in place of two barely individuated tenors is a step in the right direction. The first album offers a fine, abrupt arrangement of John Coltrane's 'Impressions', a blues theme which sometimes tempts young players into evening-long meanderings but which Whittaker handles quite briskly. It's somehow suggestive that he insists on calling individual numbers 'songs'; that's very much how he handles them. There's no sense that either he or The Creators are short on ideas, merely that he sees no virtue in scales and modal exercises. Pianist Karlsson, also a Justice recording artist, is an important influence, though surprisingly it's Lakey and Craig who between them dominate the writing credits on *First Outing*. Whittaker's own stuff is pretty basic, and only 'Searchin' For The Truth' (the longest track on either disc) overstretches itself. Whittaker isn't an altogether inspiring soloist, preferring to concentrate on small areas of sound before moving on to something else. Like the rest of the music, it's very focused, but in a relaxed, almost consciously undramatic way.

Tommy Whittle (born 1926)

TENOR SAXOPHONE

Veteran Scottish tenorman with long experience in dance orchestras and studio work; only rarely steps into the solo limelight.

****(*) Warm Glow**

Teejay 103 *Whittle; Brian Dee (p); Len Skeat (b); Bobby Orr (d).* 2/92.

This distinguished saxophonist has spent much of his time ensconced in various kinds of studio band, but he still does a good Websterish ballad and a cordial mid-tempo stroll. The title of the record sums it up, although there's a little more heat on a blues and 'Fascinating Rhythm'.

Putte Wickman (born 1924)

CLARINET

One of the godfathers of post-war Swedish jazz, Wickman styled himself a swing player at first but – despite the unfashionable nature of his instrument – he increasingly adopted a personal take on the cooler side of bebop language. Essentially he has worked in whatever context he liked for the past 40 years, though he led a dance band for a time in the 1960s.

***** Young, Searching And Swinging**

Phontastic CD 9304 *Wickman; Gosta Torner (t); George Vernon (tb); Arne Domnérus, S Gustafsson (as); G Bjorklund, Gosta Theselius (ts); Charlie Norman, Bob Laine, Reinhold Svensson, Gunnar Svensson (p); Johan Adolfsson (acc); Fred Eriksberg, Stan Carlberg, Kalle Lohr, Rolf Berg, Rune Gustafsson (g); Sune Svensson, Bo Kallstrom (vib); Thore Jederby, Simon Brehm, Roland Bengtsson, Yngve Akerberg, Hans Burman (b); Ake Brandes, B Frylmark, Georg Oddner, Jack Noren, S Bollhem, Robert Edman, Sture Kallin (d).* 3/45–2/55.

***** The Sound Of Surprise**

Dragon DRCD 289 *Wickman; Lars Sjøsten (p); Sture Nordin (b); Pelle Hulten (d).* 1/69.

***** Bewitched**

Bluebell ABCD 051 *Wickman; Claes Crona (p); Mads Vinding, Ove Stenberg (b); Bjarne Rostvold, Nils-Erik Slorner (d).* 9/80–7/82.

***** Desire / Mr Clarinet**

Four Leaf FLC-CD 101 *Wickman; Lars Samuelsson (t); Bjorn J-Son Lindh (ky, f); Janne Schaffer (g); Teddy Walter (b); Magnus Person, Per Lindvall (d).* 4/84–6/85.

*****(*) The Very Thought Of You**

Dragon DRCD 161 *Wickman; Red Mitchell (b).* 12/87–1/88.

****** Some O' This And Some O' That**

Dragon DRCD 187 *Wickman; Roger Kellaway (p); Red Mitchell (b).* 6/89.

Putte Wickman is still, after more than five decades, completely at home among Sweden's jazz masters. An impeccable swing player who followed cool developments in the 1950s, Wickman has spent time away from jazz but seems fully aware of every kind of development in the music. Some of his earlier recordings have been restored to circulation by *Young, Searching And Swinging*, which compiles 22 tracks from various playing situations – though all small groups – over his first ten years in the studio. Many are with pianist Reinhold Svensson, who partnered the clarinettist in a quartet for several years. The format doesn't move far beyond the small-band sides by Goodman and Shaw, and could even seem anachronistic at a time when bop had taken a grip, but Wickman's essentially cool stance allowed wrinkles of modernism to sidle into the music. By the time of the final sextet tracks that persona is firmly in place. Some of the earlier tracks sound a little grey, but remastering is mostly good.

The recent Dragon reissue goes some modest way towards filling in a large gap in the Wickman story on record. A snapshot of a quartet show at Stockholm's Pawnshop Club, in front of an irresponsibly noisy audience, this finds Wickman (at probably the least fashionable point in jazz history for his kind of music) in a rich vein of invention. Like his contemporary, Buddy DeFranco, he seems to have the gift of playing jazz on the instrument that transcends its time-frame. The surroundings are discouraging but the music has a doggedly creative spirit.

Bewitched covers two trio sessions – Crona plays on both – in which Putte investigates two sets of standards. The 1980 session is better by a whisker: Stenberg plays with real drive and there's an interesting version of Bernie Senensky's 'Another Gift' which makes one wish that Wickman would look at contemporary tunes more often. The music tends to be sleepy on melody statements, then gradually wakes up when the leader probes his way through a solo. The Four Leaf CD reissues a pair of albums in which the clarinettist works in a soft-fusion setting: it's slight stuff, the playing vitiated a little by the context, but Wickman finds things to say, and the music remains disarmingly pretty.

The two later Dragons find Wickman in splendid fettle. The duo set with Mitchell is momentarily troubled by the bassist's capricious streak: his fascination with the lowest register sometimes strays into indulgence, and the huffing momentum won't be to all tastes. But Wickman goes on spinning out memorable improvisations, and they devise some unexpected variations on the (standard) material: Basie's 'Topsy' becomes rather intense and brooding, and the Ellington themes have no sniff of routine in them. When Kellaway joins in, the music spreads itself out (eight pieces take 72 minutes here, whereas there are 13 in 68 minutes on the duo record), and Kellaway's extravagant imagination is perfectly checked by Wickman's insidious, wily lines. The recording is sometimes a little flat, since both discs were made in Red Mitchell's apartment rather than a studio, but it suits the intimacy of the music.

*****(*) Putte Wickman In Trombones**

Phontastic NCD 8826 *Wickman; Olle Holmquist, Bertil Strandberg, Anders Wiborg, Urban Wiborg, Nils Landgren (tb);*

Gosta Rundqvist (p); Sture Akerberg, Christian Spering (b); Peter Ostlund (d). 5–6/92.

***** In Silhouette**
Phontastic NCD 8848 *Wickman; Butch Lacy (p); Rune Gustafsson (g); Jesper Lundgaard (b); Arne Tangaard (d).* 6/94.

Putte likes trombones: they make a sound he 'can pull over himself like a comforting down quilt'. *In Trombones* is a little reminiscent of an oddball West Coast date of 40 years earlier, but the excellent charts – Strandberg, Rundqvist, Bo Sylven – create a leaner tone on some tracks; others have the clarinet bedding down in deep-pile trombone luxury. Wickman still sounds brilliantly zestful and alert: the clarinet solos on 'Ebony Dance' remind that, even when some have been talking about the clarinet finding its modern feet via Braxton and Byron, Putte Wickman's been here all the time.

In Silhouette is a mixed bag where Wickman again does his best work on the originals, and the relatively pale interpretations of some of the standards suggest that he should always be given fresh challenges. Gustafsson, another wily veteran by now, has his own ideas and gets just enough space to sneak them in.

***** Interchange**
Phontastic NCD 8852 *Wickman; Claes Crona (p); Olle Steinholtz (b); Rune Carlsson (d).* 6/84/–8/96.

These veterans were in good form on the June day in 1984 when the first dozen of these tracks were made, and it was a shrewd idea of Anders Ohman to recall Putte and Claes to the studios to cut five further duets for the CD reissue. As he says, they pick up from where they left off as if it was the same session. A nice mix of standards and jazz themes, each given a soft but incisive treatment, with the combination of clarinet and piano a particularly attractive one in timbral terms.

Gerald Wiggins (born 1922)

PIANO

Though born a New Yorker, Wiggins has made most of his music on the West Coast, particularly as an accompanist to singers or in piano-trio situations.

****(*) Music From Around The World In Eighty Days In Modern Jazz**
Original Jazz Classics OJC 1761 *Wiggins; Eugene Wright (b); Bill Douglass (d).* 56–57.

***** Wiggin' Out**
Original Jazz Classics OJC 1034 *Wiggins; Harold Land (ts); Jackie Mills (d).* 9/60.

***** Relax And Enjoy It!**
Original Jazz Classics OJC 173 *Wiggins; Joe Comfort (b); Jackie Mills (d).* 61.

Gerry Wiggins began with swing big bands, but he has pursued much of his career as an accompanist, originally with Lena Horne. On his own, with an appropriate rhythm section, he plays light, undemanding but beguiling swing-to-cool piano, rarely challenging the listener and preferring to make a few well-chosen remarks rather than refashioning a tune. The *Eighty Days* material is typical of many records that were worked up from popular contemporary film and show material and, while it's not bad, it sounds as perfunctory as most such genre entries. *Relax And Enjoy It!* is now on CD and has worn well enough, although this amiable recital of a few standards will probably appeal only to the piano-trio collector who must have everything.

Wiggin' Out is something different: Wig plays Hammond organ on this one, with the surprise presence of Harold Land. It's the tenorman who earns the stars, mostly, since Wiggins isn't exactly Jimmy Smith at the organ and the music is a bit lead-footed under Mills's stewardship. But some pleasing moments survive – catch Land's lean and pointed solo on 'A Night In Tunisia'.

*****(*) Live At Maybeck Recital Hall Volume Eight**
Concord CCD 4450 *Wiggins (p solo).* 8/90.

Wig's entry in this splendid ongoing series is arguably his best-ever record. On a good piano, with impeccable sound, the quality which Jimmy Rowles – very much a kindred stylistic spirit – refers to in his sleeve-note as 'natural relaxation' emerges in full bloom. It's not so much a matter of taking his time, since none of the pieces here runs to much more than five minutes in length; more a point of shaping a performance to precisely the right tempo and dynamic in order to set down the thoughts the pianist has in mind. Here, for instance, he treats 'I Should Care' as a kind of slow stride interpretation, and Ahmad Jamal's 'Night Mist Blues' has a rocking steadiness which even the composer has never quite realized. Some of the tunes are perhaps over-familiar, even to Wig himself, who has little of significance to add to 'Take The "A" Train' or 'Body And Soul', but that is the privilege of senior status. The recording is as truthful as usual in this fine sequence of records.

***** Soulidarity**
Concord CCD 4706 *Wiggins; Andy Simpkins (b); Paul Humphrey (d).* 8/95.

None of these men is exactly a youngster, but they take the opening 'The Way You Look Tonight' at a fearsome pace after Wiggins's out-of-tempo introduction. As if chastened, the following 'You're Mine You' is taken very slow. And so on, through a neat programme of standards which are familiar without seeming hackneyed. Wiggins plays some of them rather splashily, as if he's thinking more about the big picture than the detail, and Simpkins, who gets more space here than he ever did in The Three Sounds, is the one who centres the music. There are lots of nice little touches, although the record scarcely demands a hearing.

Bob Wilber (born 1928)

SOPRANO, ALTO AND TENOR SAXOPHONES, CLARINET

Born in New York, Wilber studied with both Sidney Bechet and Lennie Tristano as a teenager. He worked in various Dixieland–swing–bop situations in the 1950s and '60s, mostly as a freelance, before joining the World's Geatest Jazz Band in 1968 and forming Soprano Summit in 1973 with Kenny Davern. Other repertory projects connected with King Oliver and Bechet followed. He announced his retirement in 1995 but still seems to be recording.

*****(*) Soprano Summit In Concert**

Concord CCD 4029 *Wilber; Kenny Davern (ss, cl); Marty Grosz (g); Ray Brown (b); Jake Hanna (d).* 7/76.

***** Live At The Illiana Jazz Club**

Storyville STCD 8254 *As above, except add Eddie De Haas (b), Bob Cousins (d); omit Brown and Hanna.* 11/76.

***** Soprano Summit Live At Concord '77**

Concord CCD 4052 *As above, except add Monty Budwig (b), Jake Hanna (d); omit De Haas, Cousins.* 77.

*****(*) Summit Reunion**

Chiaroscuro CR(D) 311 *Wilber; Kenny Davern (cl); Dick Hyman (p); Bucky Pizzarelli (g); Milt Hinton (b); Bobby Rosengarden (d).* 5/90.

***** Summit Reunion – Jazz Im Amerika Haus Vol. 5**

Nagel-Heyer 015 *Wilber; Kenny Davern (cl); Dave Cliff (g); Dave Green (b); Bobby Worth (d).* 9/94.

*****(*) Yellow Dog Blues**

Chiaroscuro CR(D) 339 *As CR(D) 311 above.* 3/95.

Once upon a time everyone tried to play soprano sax like Sidney Bechet. Now that everyone tries to play soprano like either Coltrane or Steve Lacy, Bob Wilber seems like something of a throwback. Since he actually played with Bechet and has done more than anyone to keep that master's music in circulation, there's no 'authenticity' problem here. Wilber still seeks the wide, singing tone of his mentor, but he long since became his own man, and even where there is a specific homage – as in *On The Road* (below), which was made by his band, Bechet Legacy – he still sounds like himself. This is an impressive run of records. The *Soprano Summit* discs are by a popular double-act with Davern. Both Concord albums were recorded live and they suffer from a tad too much showmanship here and there, but the brimming energy of the up-tempo pieces is a marvel, and Wilber always knows when to cool things off: his gorgeous treatment of 'The Golden Rooster' on *In Concert* is as good as any Hodges showcase. *Live At Illiana* finds them on a good night in Chicago and, though it's another live album, there's still much fun.

The band was dissolved for a while, and in the interim Davern chose to give up soprano in favour of clarinet alone. Their reunion album is very strong, the more piquant since there's a regular contrast between the horns rather than a doppelgänger effect. The group carried on into the '90s, though the latest concert set from the Amerika Haus is a potboiler – Wilber and Davern seem to be jogging through this one rather than striking sparks. However, *Yellow Dog Blues* is much more like it; everyone seems in the highest of spirits and Davern and Wilber run good-natured rings round each other; listen also for the marvellous things Hyman is playing in the ensembles. Three perfect choices: 'I'll See You In C-U-B-A', 'Hindustan' and 'The Japanese Sandman'.

***** Bob Wilber And The Scott Hamilton Quartet**

Chiaroscuro CR(D) 171 *Wilber; Scott Hamilton (ts); Chris Flory (g); Phil Flanigan (b); Chuck Riggs (d).* 6–7/77.

*****(*) On The Road**

Jazzology JCD-214 *Wilber; Glenn Zottola (t); Mark Shane (p); Mike Peters (g, bj); Len Skeat (b); Butch Miles (d).* 11/81.

***** Ode To Bechet**

Jazzology JCD-142 *As above, except add Vic Dickenson (tb, v), Reggie Johnson (b), Joanne 'Pug' Horton (v); omit Skeat.* 8/82.

*****(*) The Duet**

Progressive PCD 7080 *Wilber; Dick Wellstood (p).* 3/84.

***** Bechet Legacy**

Challenge CHR 70018 *Wilber; Randy Sandke (t); Mike Peters (g); John Goldsby (b).* 1/84.

****** Dancing On A Rainbow**

Circle CCD-159 *Wilber; Wallace Davenport (t); Dave Sager (tb); Clarence Ford (cl, ts, bs); Dave Bodenhouse (p); Danny Barker (g); Dewey Sampson (b); Freddie Kohlman (d); Joanne 'Pug' Horton (v).* 12/89.

*****(*) Moments Like This**

Phontastic NCD 8811 *Wilber; Antti Sarpila (ss, ts, cl); Ulf Johansson (tb, p, v); Sture Akerberg (b); Ronnie Gardiner (d).* 5/91.

Wilber's other projects are perhaps rather more interesting. *On The Road* is a very fine salute to Bechet, uncovering many rarities in the material and with top-notch support from Zottola in particular. The CD remastering is a bit bright. *Ode To Bechet*, though it welcomes Vic Dickenson to the ranks in a guest role, is a slight disappointment: the material seems a bit taut, and Dickenson can't really find an effective way in. *Bechet Legacy* puts similar material into a concert situation and, though Sandke isn't much like Muggsy Spanier, the instrumentation inevitably evokes the Bechet–Spanier small group. Another astute piece of revivalism. Better still, though, is *Dancing On A Rainbow*. This is an exemplary mainstream outfit, with Sager's quirky trombone and Ford's ripe gallery of reeds lending character as well as precision, and Wilber's Ellington archaeology is spot-on: it was a shrewd idea to bring back 'Love In My Heart' and 'Charlie The Chulo', but all the material turns out well. The 1977 album with Scott Hamilton is merely OK mainstream, with the tenorman still in his copycat phase, but the recent *Moments Like This* sets up Wilber with another young disciple, the Swedish reedsman, Sarpila. Johansson does his usual trick of doubling trombone and piano, and it sounds like a happy occasion.

The 1984 duets with Dick Wellstood have made a welcome transition to CD. Wellstood's slightly macabre imagination might not be to all tastes, as in his transformation of 'I've Got You Under My Skin' into a stride showcase, but he was a thinking player and had the executive powers to match. Wilber, more of a literalist, makes a nice balance, and the disc has some superb moments.

***** Horns A-Plenty**

Arbors ARCD 19135 *Wilber; Johnny Varro (p); Phil Flanigan (b); Ed Metz Jr (d).* 3/94.

*****(*) Bean**

Arbors ARCD 19144 *Wilber; Harry Allen, Tommy Whittle, Antti Sarpila (ts); Mick Pyne (p); Dave Green (b); Clark Tracey (d).* 10/94.

****(*) Nostalgia**

Arbors ARCD 19145 *Wilber; Ralph Sutton (p); Bucky Pizzarelli (g); Bob Haggart (b); Butch Miles (d).* 3/95.

***** The Hamburg Concert – Tribute To A Legend**
Nagel-Heyer CD 028 *Wilber; Randy Sandke (t); Mark Shane (p, v); Dave Cliff (g); Dave Green (b); Butch Miles (d); Joanne 'Pug' Horton (v).* 10/95.

***** Bufadora Blow-Up**
Arbors ARCD 19187 *Wilber; Charlie Bertini, Wendell Brunious, Jon-Erik Kellso, Bob Merrill (t); Dan Barrett, George Masso, Paul O'Connor (tb); Shoeless Henry Aaron, Jerry Jerome, Brian Ogilvie, Scott Robinson, Chuck Wilson (saxes); Dick Hyman (p); Howard Alden (g); Phil Flanigan (b); Ed Metz Jr (d); Joanne 'Pug' Horton (v).* 3/96.

*****(*) What Swing Is All About**
Nagel-Heyer CD 035 *Wilber; Antti Sarpila (cl, ts); Mark Shane (p); Phil Flanigan (b); Joe Ascione (d); Joanne 'Pug' Horton (v).* 9/96.

Wilber has announced his retirement from active duty, and his records of the 1990s are presumably his farewell. His consistency is such that it's hard to imagine Wilber cutting a bad record, but these are nevertheless rather a mixed lot. *Horns A-Plenty* finds him switching between clarinet and four saxes on a typically arcane set of tunes, with a few lightweight originals floating in among the likes of 'Just A Rose In A Garden Of Weeds'. Not bad, but the music's pleasantries tend to leave no impression. *Bean* puts a four-man tenor team through their paces on a tribute to Coleman Hawkins. Wilber concentrates on Hawk's music from the 1930s and early '40s, and there are some ingenious reductions and embellishments on what are in several cases neglected originals. The team are recorded in a dry but very effective acoustic, and some of the unison passages are played wonderfully, with Wilber and Whittle emerging as the most Hawk-like. *Nostalgia* is mostly ballads and tunes from bygone albums. If Wilber were British, he might have thought twice about doing 'The Lambeth Walk' here; and a couple of the classical pieces recall the days of Rudy Wiedoft. Stately stuff. If Wellstood were still alive, he might have lent a Machiavellian touch at the piano, but Sutton, admirable though he is, is no such ironist.

The Hamburg Concert is another Bechet Legacy project, with a string of tunes associated with the great man and played with the expected brio by the band – a little too much brio, perhaps. Butch Miles is on his most bumptious form and, though that actually gives the music a sometimes welcome kick, it occasionally seems to egg the normally meticulous Sandke into overplaying what he seems to be hearing as a supercharged Armstrong role. It's still agreeable to hear a contemporary band playing 'Egyptian Fantasy' and 'Dans La Rue D'Antibes'.

The big-band date comes from Wilber's feature spot at the 1996 March of Jazz Festival in Florida. It falls easily on the ear and, as a soloist, Wilber works sunnily in this context, but his writing for the band is nothing very special – he likes the reed section, and that's about it. A better choice is *What Swing Is All About*, another concert set on Nagel-Heyer but measured with particular grace and balance by Wilber and cohorts. Sarpila proves to be very *simpatico* in the front line and the material, though saddled with a few overbaked chestnuts, comes up fresh.

***** A Perfect Match**
Arbors ARCD 189193 *Wilber; Britt Woodman (tb); Dick Hyman (org); James Chirillo (g); Phil Flanigan (b); Joe Ascione (d).* 8/97.

***** Everywhere You Go There's Jazz**
Arbors ARCD 19202 *Wilber; Bent Persson (t, c); Don Barrett (tb); Antti Sarpila (cl, ss, as, ts); Dick Hyman (p); Peter Appleyard, Lars Erstrand (vib); Dave Cliff (g); Dave Green (b); Ed Metz Jr (d); Joanne 'Pug' Horton (v).* 3/98.

Since Wilber and Hyman share the billing on *A Perfect Match*, hopes are raised of a sax–piano duet record. Instead, it's a Hodges tribute, with Hyman playing organ in the Wild Bill Davis style. A nice repertorial jog, and frankly not much more than that, although the surprise presence of Britt Woodman is a nostalgic note. The International March Of Jazz All-Stars tackle the other disc, and a formidable line-up it is, although some it is less than inspiring: 'Mood Indigo' is merely silly in three, and some of the pieces are too groomed to work up much interest. But this time Hyman gets in some apposite remarks, and Barrett and Horton are both very fine on 'Music Maestro Please'.

Barney Wilen (1937–96)

SOPRANO, ALTO, TENOR AND BARITONE SAXOPHONES

Born in Nice, Wilen made a big impact on Parisian audiences when still a teenager and played with Miles Davis in 1957. A stop-start career saw him working as an engineer and film-maker as much as playing sax. Toyed with free and jazz-rock but returned to straightahead playing in the '80s.

***** Newport '59**
Fresh Sound FSR-CD 165 *Wilen; Clark Terry (t); Toshiko Akiyoshi, Bud Powell, Ewald Heidepriem (p); Tommy Bryant, Eric Peter, Karl Theodor Geier (b); Roy Haynes, Kenny Clarke, Eberhardt Stengl (d).* 59.

Basically a tenor player, Wilen made his name when Miles Davis chose him to play in a group he was fronting in Europe in 1957. But Wilen had already garnered a reputation with visiting Americans for a considerably accomplished technique and a real mastery of hard-bop forms. Unfortunately, his French albums of the period are out of circulation. Wilen's subsequent visit to play at Newport in 1959 is commemorated by the Fresh Sound CD, although there's only 20 minutes of music from that occasion: Akiyoshi plays exuberant bebop piano in support and Wilen's even, supple tenor works patiently and impressively through 'Passport' and 'Barney's Tune', with what was then a rare appearance of the soprano on 'Round Midnight', in which his tonal control is impressive. Two other tracks of unclear date find him with Powell (very subdued), Terry and Clarke; Wilen's solo on 'No Problem' is typically artful – since the recording is subject to some vagaries of balance, he seems to emerge from the shadows here. There is also another 'Round Midnight' with a German rhythm-section. The sound is very mixed throughout but it's listenable enough.

****(*) La Note Bleue**
IDA 010 *Wilen; Alain Jean-Marie (p, org); Philippe Petit (g); Riccardo Del Frà (b); Sangoma Everett (d).* 12/86.

***** French Ballads**
IDA 014 *Wilen; Michel Graillier (p); Riccardo Del Frà (b); Sangoma Everett (d).* 87.

****** Wild Dogs Of The Ruwenzori**

IDA 020 *Wilen; Alain Jean-Marie (ky); Riccardo Del Frà (b); Sangoma Everett (d); Henri Guedon (perc).* 11/88.

****** Sanctuary**

IDA 029 *Wilen; Philip Catherine (g); Palle Danielsson (b).* 1/91.

Wilen's contract for IDA helped create a comeback for a fine musician. In the 1980s he tinkered with jazz–rock and African rhythms (he went to live in Africa in the late 1960s) and his return to a bop-inflected style has something of the full-circle maturity which Stan Getz came to in his later work; Wilen's tenor sound does, indeed, have something of the magisterial sweep which Getz delivered, but the main character of his playing continues to lie in his even trajectory. His solos have a serene assurance which eschews dynamic shifts in favour of a single flowing line. With his tone still exceptionally bright and refined, it grants his playing a rare, persuasive power.

La Note Bleue was a disappointing start, though, because the record is so bitty: what seem to be little fragments and codas from longer pieces are made into whole tracks, the material is drily over-familiar, and the pieces are cut short before the group can get going. With Wilen perfectly adept at long solos, this foreshortening sounds wrong. *French Ballads* is better, although some of the playing again seems proscribed, and Wilen dispatches a few of the themes with a too casual finesse. *Wild Dogs Of The Ruwenzori* finally establishes his second wind: it's beautifully programmed, with straight-ahead swingers, hints of calypso rhythm and a few deftly understated fusion pulses setting a delightful variation in tempos. The title-tune and 'Pauline Extended' bond Wilen's solos into a tight electronic framework, but his latest reflections on Rollins in 'Little Lu' and the two versions of 'Oh Johnny' are flawlessly paced and delivered. The rhythm section does well on all three records.

Sanctuary continued Wilen's good run. Catherine switches between acoustic and electric instruments and Wilen chooses classical rapture or firm, propulsive lines depending on the tempo. Danielsson's third voice is immensely rich and apposite. One might pick out the absolutely lovely reading of 'How Deep Is The Ocean', but there's scarcely a weak moment on the record.

*****(*) Movie Themes From France**

Timeless SJP 335 *Wilen; Mal Waldron (p); Stafford James (b); Eddie Moore (d).* 10/90.

Wilen is still in great voice here. Perhaps Waldron isn't an ideal choice, since his usual impassive stance dries out some of these romantic melodies to the point of desiccation: 'Les Parapluies de Cherbourg' sounds like a dirge at the start. But it pays off over the long haul, with a powerful 'Autumn Leaves' and a still, serene, ominous treatment of two of the 'Lift to the Scaffold' themes. The saxophonist breaks new melodies and ideas out of all this material and, though he sounds tired at some points, it adds to his gravitas.

***** Dream Time**

Deux Z 84108 *Wilen; Alain Jean-Marie (p).* 3/91.

***** New York Romance**

Sunnyside SSC 1067 *Wilen; Kenny Barron (p); Ira Coleman (b); Lewis Nash (d).* 6/94.

A certain waywardness crept into Wilen's playing; while it subverts some of the sax-meets-rhythm expectations, it isn't always comfortable. The duet with Jean-Marie comes from a 1991 festival appearance: Wilen sounds rusty on 'Latin Alley' and the exposed format doesn't always suit him, but the long, serpentine lines of 'No Problem' and 'Afternoon In Paris' have all his old mastery. His tone on tenor is taking on a foggy side which sounds even more pronounced on the rare baritone outing on 'Blues Walk' from *New York Romance*. This is one of several albums Wilen has recorded for the Japanese Venus label, this one then being licensed to Sunnyside. Compared to the super-sharp rhythm section, Barney sounds a little bleary here and there, and his imprecision isn't always beneficial: the rather taut and wound-up 'You'd Be So Nice To Come Home To' is disappointing. But the desolate soprano outing on 'Cry Me A River', with its wide dynamic contrasts, and an unexpectedly slow and bleak 'Mack The Knife' show his powers as yet undimmed. Wilen seems to have been much lionized by the Japanese since they sponsored several latter-day albums and have reissued much of his catalogue in domestic releases: admirers who have access to Japanese issues should make a point of seeking them out.

Ernie Wilkins (1922–99)

SAXOPHONE, ARRANGER

Wilkins won his spurs with Earl Hines (in Fatha's very last orchestra) and with Count Basie, before striking out as a freelance composer and arranger with a very distinctive ensemble sound: light, mobile and seemingly effortless. The Almost Big Band was his own most effective showcase.

****** Montreux**

Steeplechase SCCD 31190 *Wilkins; Allan Botschinsky, Willie Cook (t); Erling Kroner (tb); Richard Boone (tb, v); Vagn Elsberg (t, flhn); Sahib Shihab (as, f); Bernt Jadig, Jesper Thilo (ts); Per Goldschmidt (ts, bs); Kenny Drew (p); Mads Vinding (b); Aage Tanggaard (d).* 7/83.

*****(*) On the Roll**

Steeplechase SCCD 31225 *Wilkins; Benny Rosenfeldt, Jan Zum Vohrte, Jens Winther (t); Bent Jadig, Jesper Thilo (ts); Per Goldschmidt (ts, bs); Jesper Lundgaard (b); Ed Thigpen (d).* 86.

Wilkins was largely responsible for modernizing the post-war Basie band and tightening up its flagging charts. His gift was for fleet, uncomplicated section-work which combined speed with an often deceptive impression of weight. The 1960s were a bleak time for the saxophonist, with stories of drug problems and much less non-commercial work around for an arranger of his skill and imagination. As for so many players of his type and inclination, Europe proved to be a haven. The Almost Big Band was founded in 1980 and has remained the most effective outlet for Wilkins's music. The Montreux set is representative. 'Hurry Up and Wait', 'A Song For Ben Webster' and the long 'Bosco's Business' showcase Wilkins the composer, but it's the opening arrangement of Randy Weston's classic 'Hi-Fly' which grabs you by the lapels.

On The Roll is even more thoroughly dominated by originals, though here again many are in the spirit of other composers, notably Ellington and Strayhorn. Individually, the soloists are less riveting than on the earlier record, but the ensembles march like the Guards; and once again the opening track, another tribute, 'Almost Basie', guarantees attention. Ernie is unmistakably back in business.

Staffan William-Olsson

GUITAR

Open-toned guitarist leading groups of keen young (and some not-so-young) Scandinavians.

***** Three Shades Of Blue**

Real RT 104-2 *William-Olsson; Roy Nikolaisen (t); Egil Kapstad (p); Terje Venaas (b); Egil Johansen (d).* 5/95.

***** Smile!**

Real RT-108 *William-Olsson; Roy Nikolaisen (t, flhn); Petter Wettre (ts); Jørn Olen (p); Terje Gewelt (b); Børre Dalhaug (d).* 10/98.

Brimful of confidence, the young guitarist leads his veteran rhythm section (and fellow youngster Nikolaisen, present on five tracks) a merry bebopper's dance through this programme. He sounds a bit like a supercharged Kenny Burrell, skating over the blues and articulating his lines with a funky Gibson tone. The nine originals are punched out as blowing vehicles and everybody has a good time, although the record eventually flags a bit and one longs for Kapstad to get a bit more useful space.

Smile! has plenty more dash. 'Lover, Come Back To Me' goes off at a hurricane tempo and Wettre, for one, seems to be tapped for toe as a result. But these young Norwegians like the cut of cool and fast bop, and William-Olsson's seven originals are sound enough bases for some enjoyably blithe solos, even if the province of some of the writing isn't exactly brand new: 'Can You Spare A Dime?' sounds like an upside-down 'Sidewinder'. The leader's open tone and taste for very long lines suit his nimble playing and he gets zesty accompaniment from the others.

Buster Williams (born 1942)

DOUBLE BASS

One of the key sidemen in modern jazz, Williams was born in Camden, New Jersey. Originally coached in drums as well as bass, his eventual career was mapped out for him when he first heard Oscar Pettiford's bass improvisations. Williams has a rock-solid grounding in harmony, counterpoint and orchestration, gained at the Combs College of Music, Philadelphia, at the very end of the 1950s and aired on just about every recording he has made since then.

***** Crystal Reflections**

32 Records 32087 *Williams; Kenny Barron (ky); Jimmy Rowles (p); Roy Ayers (vib); Billy Hart, Nobu Urushiyama (d).* 76.

*****(*) Somewhere Along The Way**

TCB 97602 *Williams; Gary Bartz (as); Carlos McKinney (p); Stefon Harris (vib); Lenny White (d).* 11/96.

*****(*) Lost In A Memory**

TCB 99252 *As above, except omit Bartz, McKinney; add Geri Allen (p).* 97.

The little genius has graced many records over the years but, unlike many a gifted sideman, has also created a body of work under his own name. Buster's harmony is impeccable and he has a rhythmic sense that is unfailing, feeling and utterly original. Williams worked with singers for many years – Dakota Staton, Nancy Wilson, Betty Carter – and always shows an instinct for the dimensions of song. His own compositions, like 'Toku Do', call out for lyrics and a tough-but-tender singing voice.

Williams loves to play melody lines, scampering tunes almost too urgent for coherence. He over-indulges shamelessly on *Crystal Reflections*, but he also shows an instinct for form that is constantly suggestive. 'My Funny Valentine' is a masterpiece, but the familiarity of the theme shouldn't detract from the impact of the other tunes. Barron and Hart are magnificent, and having Jimmy Rowles on the strength is a guarantee of quality.

Somewhere Along The Way unveils the bones of a line-up that was to express Williams's music with real confidence. Vibist Stefon Harris cut his teeth in this band, filling the role that Roy Ayers had performed in the past. Gary Bartz had a similar background in Miles's band and is exceptional on 'Summertime' (*Somewhere*). Without a horn, the recent *Lost In A Memory* is even more focused and at times very intense. A couple of horn-led tracks might have made sense, but Buster's playing is so good that one wouldn't have it any other way.

Clarence Williams (1893–1965)

PIANO, JUG, VOCAL

Born outside New Orleans but playing there in his early days, Williams was a smart hustler who was already earning money from publishing by 1916. He later owned his own publishing house in New York, while organizing countless recording sessions as A&R man for OKeh and playing either piano or jug on his own dates (his wife, Eva Taylor, sang on many, too). His 'Blue Five' sessions ran on into the '30s, but he eventually left the business in 1943 and ran a shop in Harlem.

***** Complete Sessions Vol. 1 1923**

EPM/Hot 'N Sweet FDC 5107 *Williams; Thomas Morris (c); Charlie Irvis, John Mayfield (tb); Sidney Bechet (cl, ss); Buddy Christian (bj); Sara Martin, Eva Taylor, Lawrence Lomax, Rosetta Crawford, Mamie Smith, Margaret Johnson (v).* 7–11/23.

*****(*) Complete Sessions Vol. 2 1923–1925**

EPM/Hot 'N Sweet FDC 5109 *As above, except add Louis Armstrong, Bubber Miley (c), Aaron Thompson (tb), Buster Bailey, Lorenzo Tio (cl, ss), Don Redman (as), Virginia Liston, Maureen Englin, Sippie Wallace (v); omit Martin, Lomax, Crawford and Smith.* 11/23–3/25.

****(*) Clarence Williams 1921–1924**

Classics 679 *Similar to above two discs.* 10/21–11/24.

***** Complete Sessions Vol. 3 1925–26**

EPM/Hot 'N Sweet 15122 *As above, except add Johnny Dunn, Big Charlie Thomas, Edward Allen (c), Joe 'Tricky Sam' Nanton, Jimmy Harrison, Jake Frazier (tb), Bob Fuller (cl), Coleman Hawkins (cl, ts, bs), Leroy Harris (bj), Cyrus St Clair (tba), Clarence Todd (v); omit Thompson, Tio, Liston, Englin, Wallace.* 7/25–4/26.

***** Clarence Williams 1924–1926**

Classics 695 *Similar to above.* 12/24–1/26.

***** Clarence Williams 1926–27**

Classics 718 *Williams; Tommy Ladnier, Jabbo Smith, Ed Allen, Bubber Miley, Tom Morris, Louis Metcalf (c); Jimmy Harrison, Joe Nanton (tb); Buster Bailey (cl); Arville Harris, Don Redman (cl, as); Coleman Hawkins (ts); Fats Waller (p); Leroy Harris (bj); Cyrus St Clair (bb); Eva Taylor (v).* 3/26–4/27.

***** Clarence Williams 1927**

Classics 736 *Williams; Ed Allen (c); Henry Allen, Ed Anderson (t); Charlie Irvis (tb); Buster Bailey (ss, cl); Carmelo Jari, Arville Harris, Ben Whittet, Albert Socarras (cl, as); Leroy Harris (bj); Cyrus St Clair (bb); Floyd Casey (wbd); Clarence Lee, Evelyn Preer (v).* 3–9/27.

Williams was of negligible importance as a musician – he wasn't a great pianist, handled vocals with clumsy enthusiasm and often resorted to blowing a jug on his Jug Band records – but he was a brilliant hustler and a master at making record dates come together. At his very first session, on the first CD listed above, he secured the services of Sidney Bechet (also making his debut), and in fact Bechet appears on every track on this disc. Later sessions brought in Armstrong alongside Bechet, Bubber Miley, Lorenzo Tio and others. The material was mostly novelty tunes ('Who'll Chop Your Suey When I'm Gone?') or vaudeville blues, with the occasional tougher piece – such as Sippie Wallace's two tracks on Volume 2 – and some instrumentals by Clarence Williams's Blue Five.

Both Classics and Hot 'N Sweet have undertaken complete series, but the latter quickly came to a halt. The Classics discs got off to an indifferent start with the first two discs, which had very mixed reproduction, although Classics 718 and 736 are more consistent and quite lively. Musically, the later sides are hotter, though Bechet makes a striking impact throughout the first disc, and his partnership with Armstrong on 'Cake Walking Babies From Home', 'Mandy Make Up Your Mind' and a few others is exhilarating enough to cut through the acoustic recording. Hot 'N Sweet's Volume 2 is perhaps the best disc to sample; but the third volume introduces cornetist Ed Allen, Williams's most loyal sideman, who seldom recorded elsewhere, and it includes some rollicking band sides. The first Classics disc starts off with some ancient 1921 material in which Williams is basically a band singer on six tracks, historical curios more than anything. Classics 718 has several tracks where Williams and The Blue Five are accompanying the sweet-voiced Eva Taylor, but there is more jazz on Classics 736: three different versions of Williams's hit, 'Cushion Foot Stomp', the knockabout 'Old Folks Shuffle', a Brunswick date with Henry Allen and Ed Anderson as a two-trumpet front line, and two versions of another Williams favourite, 'Shootin' The Pistol'.

***** Clarence Williams 1927–1928**

Classics 752 *Williams; Ed Allen, King Oliver (c); Ed Cuffee (tb); Arville Harris, Benny Waters, Albert Socarras, Buster Bailey (cl, as); Coleman Hawkins (ts); James P Johnson (p); Leroy Harris (bj); Cyrus St Clair (tba); Floyd Casey (d, wbd).* 10/27–8/28.

*****(*) Clarence Williams 1928–1929**

Classics 771 *As above, except add Ed Anderson (c), Ben Whittet (cl, as), Ernest Elliott (cl), Claude Hopkins (p), Charlie Dixon (bj), Kaiser Marshall (d); omit Hawkins, Johnson.* 8/28–1/29.

***** Clarence Williams 1929**

Classics 791 *As above, except add James P Johnson (p), Russell Procope (cl, as); omit Anderson, Elliott, Hopkins, Dixon, Marshall.* 1/29–5/29.

*****(*) Clarence Williams 1929–1930**

Classics 810 *As above, except add Ed Anderson, Charlie Gaines, Leonard Davis, Henry Allen (t), Geechie Fields (tb), Frank Robinson (bsx, hca, v), Prince Robinson (cl, ts).* 6/29–4/30.

***** Clarence Williams 1930–1931**

Classics 832 *Williams; Ed Allen, Bill Dillard, Ward Pinkett, Henry Allen, Charlie Gaines (t); Jimmy Archey (tb); Albert Socarras (cl, as, f); Henry Jones (as); Arville Harris, Prince Robinson, Bingie Madison (cl, ts); Fred Skerritt (bs, as); Gene Rodgers, Herman Chittison (p); Lonnie Johnson (g); Goldie Lucas (g, bj); Ikey Robinson, Leroy Harris (bj); Cyrus St Clair (tba); Richard Fulbright (b); Bill Beason (d); Floyd Casey (wbd); Eva Taylor, Clarence Todd (v).* 5/30–2/31.

****** Dreaming The Hours Away**

Frog DGF14 *Similar to appropriate discs above.* 5/26–9/28.

*****(*) Whoop It Up**

Frog DGF17 *Similar to appropriate discs above.* 2/29–2/31.

Williams's music doesn't have any great variety in it: his basic configurations were the Washboard and Jug Bands, the Jazz Kings sides, a few stray piano solos, the occasional vocal where he's accompanied by another (James P. Johnson on one occasion) and some ensemble dates which are simply credited to the Williams Orchestra. The more knockabout material was reserved for the jug or washboard situations, but some of these also have a gentleness about them and, though Casey's irresistible beat and St Clair's parping lines provide a steady momentum, Williams could often find unexpected subtleties in some of his line-ups – pairing reeds together, or providing space for the faithful Ed Allen to play one of his tight, incisive solos. Allen is the unsung hero of most of these dates, unfailingly consistent and interesting, and though a few star names turn up here and there – notably King Oliver, Eddie Lang and James P. – it's Williams's repertory cast that make most of the music: Allen, Harris, St Clair, Casey, Whittet, Cuffee and a few others. Because the playing is fun and unpretentious, these tracks have often been undervalued over the years, but at the same time it's hard to pick out special highlights. We award a token extra notch for Classics 771 (some excellent individual tracks) and Classics 810 (a particularly nice variety of bands and approaches), but if you enjoy one of these discs, you'll enjoy them all. The transfers (from unlisted sources, as usual) vary almost from track to track, and some sound very sludgy, but the music shines through on the best of them.

However, Frog's two compilations of Williams's Columbia sessions completely outclass the Classics discs. Superb sound from what seem to be mint copies of the originals make these model reissues. *Dreaming The Hours Away* is particularly outstanding since it includes several of the best Jazz Kings sides and 11 tracks – mostly accompaniments to the likes of Ethel Waters, Lucille Hegamin and Lizzie Miles – which aren't included in the Classics sequence. The sound on *Whoop It Up* is just as good and, although the only 'new' tracks are a pair of accompaniments to singer Bertha Idaho, these sessions are again some of Clarence's best, and the Columbia studios were his most congenial home. These are certainly the discs to get if you want only a couple of Williams CDs.

***** Clarence Williams 1933**

Classics 845 *Williams; Ed Allen (c); Albert Nicholas, Cecil Scott (cl); Herman Chittison, Willie 'The Lion' Smith (p); Ikey Robinson (bj, g); Cyrus St Clair (tba); Willie Williams, Floyd Casey (d, wbd); Eva Taylor, Clarence Todd (v).* 5–11/33.

***** Clarence Williams 1933–1934**

Classics 871 *As above, except add Charlie Gaines (t, v), Louis Jordan (as, v), James P Johnson (p), Roy Smeck (bj, g), Dick Robertson, Chick Bullock, Little Buddy Farrior (v); omit Nicholas, Chittison, Smith, Robinson, Williams, Taylor, Todd.* 12/33–6/34.

***** Clarence Williams 1934**

Classics 891 *As above, except add Willie 'The Lion' Smith (p), Richard Fulbright (b), Ikey Robinson (bj, v), Eva Taylor, Clarence Todd (v); omit Gaines, Jordan, Robertson, Bullock, Farrior.* 7–10/34.

***** Clarence Williams 1934–1937**

Classics 918 *As above, except add Wilbur De Paris (tb), Prince Robinson (ts), Jimmy McLin (g), William Cooley, Chick Bullock (v); omit Smith, Robinson, Todd, Johnson.* 9/34–4/37.

****(*) Clarence Williams 1937–1941**

Classics 953 *Similar to above, except add James P Johnson (p), Cozy Cole (d), Babe Matthews (v).* 4/37–10/41.

The Depression cut down so many survivors of the 1920s that Williams's endurance seems remarkable. He actually made more records in 1934 than in some of his peak years. This is a very little-known sequence of sessions, many of the originals very rare, and, while nothing much changes from the earlier music, an almost repertorial feel takes over as one goes through the tracks. The principal voices remain those of Ed Allen and Cecil Scott, the most loyal of sidemen, whose respective styles grow more polished down the years without losing the old-fashioned heat that must have seemed anachronistic by the mid-'30s. Along with Casey (still playing washboard) and the similarly faithful St Clair, Williams went serenely on. There is the odd difference between dates: a 1934 Decca session with Willie The Lion Smith (Classics 891) is brighter and rather louder than the others. But as late as the final Vocalion session, of May 1935 (Classics 918), the group are still playing disciplined, impeccable small-group jazz in the manner of a decade earlier. Transfers are in the usual inconsistent Classics style.

The final disc is something of a curiosity. Most of it is taken up with radio transcriptions of uneventful gospel material from 1937. There's a 1938 trio date which Williams hardly seems to take part in, and a final pair of titles with James P. and Eva Taylor from 1941.

*****(*) Clarence Williams Vol. 1**

Collectors Classics COCD-19 *As above discs.* 27–28.

*****(*) Clarence Williams Vol. 2**

Collectors Classics COCD-20 *As above discs.* 28.

The Frog collections listed above are now a clear first choice for non-specialists, although these collections are good too, remastered by John R.T. Davies. Serious collectors should check the track listings – on the other hand, they will probably want the complete Classics edition anyway.

Cootie Williams (1910–85)

TRUMPET

Not many musicians can have had not one but two concertos written for them by as august an artist as Duke Ellington, but that was Cootie's good fortune, in 1940 and again in 1963, when he rejoined the Ellington orchestra. Having replaced Bubber Miley, he developed a solo style that seemed to cover every creative eventuality, grainy, intense, and making use of the mutes. Cootie's recordings as leader are less well known but are still the source of some wonderful jazz.

****** Duke Ellington's Trumpets**

Black & Blue BLE 59.231 *Williams; Joe 'Tricky Sam' Nanton (tb); Barney Bigard (cl); Johnny Hodges (as, ss); Otto Hardwick (as, bsx); Harry Carney (bs); Duke Ellington, Billy Strayhorn (p); Billy Taylor (b); Sonny Greer (d).* 3/37–2/40.

***** Echoes Of Harlem**

Topaz TPZ 1042 *As above and below, except add Lawrence Brown, Juan Tizol (tb), Benny Goodman, Mezz Mezzrow (cl), Georgie Auld (ts), Count Basie, Tommy Fulford, Jess Stacy (p), Bernard Addison, Allan Reuss (g), Hayes Alvis, Jimmy Blanton, John Kirby (b), Cozy Cole, Lionel Hampton, Harry Jaeger, Chick Webb (d).* 12/36–8/44.

*****(*) Cootie Williams, 1941–1944**

Classics 827 *Williams; Milton Fraser, Joe Guy, Harold Money Johnson, Ermit V Perry, George Treadwell (t); Louis Bacon (t, v); Ed Burke, Jonas Walker, Robert Horton, George Stevenson, Sandy Williams, Lou McGarity (tb); Charlie Holmes, Les Robinson (as); Eddie Cleanhead Vinson (as, v); Eddie 'Lockjaw' Davis, Bob Dorsey, Lee Pope, Greely Walters (ts); John Williams, Skippy Martin, Eddie De Verteuil (bs); Johnny Guarnieri, Kenny Kersey, Bud Powell (p); Artie Bernstein, Norman Keenan (b); Butch Ballard, Jo Jones, Vess Payne (d); Pearl Bailey (v).* 5/41–8/44.

****(*) Cootie Williams, 1945-1946**

Classics 981 *Williams; Billy Ford, Otis Gamble, Harold Money Johnson, Ermit V Perry, George Treadwell (t); Gene Redd (t, vib); Ed Burke, Robert Horton, Edward Johnson, Dan Logan, Julius Watson (tb); Rupert Cole, John Jackson, Frank Powell, Daniel Williams (as); Eddie Cleanhead Vinson (as, v); Chuck Clarke, Everett Gaines, Eddie Johnson, Lee Pope, Sam Taylor (ts); Bob Ashton, George Favors, Eddie De Verteuil (bs); Arnold Jarvis (p); Sam Allen, Leroy Kirkland, Pee Wee Tinney (g); Jimmy Glover, Norman Keenan, Carl Pruitt (b); Butch Ballard, Sylvester Payne (d); Johnny Mercer, Bob Merrill, Tony Warren (v).* 2/45–7/46.

(*) The Big Challenge

Fresh Sound FSRCD 77 *Williams; Rex Stewart (c); Bud Freeman, Lawrence Brown, J.C Higginbotham (tb); Coleman Hawkins (ts); Hank Jones (p); Milt Hinton (b); Gus Johnson (d).* 4 & 5/57.

Ellington wrote 'Do Nothing Till You Hear From Me' as a 'Concerto For Cootie', a feature for the young growler he recruited at nineteen as a replacement for Bubber Miley. During the 1930s Williams showed himself (as the sessions collected on Black & Blue prove) of all the Ellingtonians the one most capable of sustaining an independent career. His high, bright trumpet was to be replaced by even more agile players, but no one with the sheer musical intelligence of Cootie. The material here is all excellent and, though much of it is already quite well known, it is good to have it on the one disc. (The set also includes some tracks by Rex Stewart's pre-war bands.)

The Topaz and Classics compilations have a certain amount of overlap in the later sessions but, as per usual, the French strict-constructionists do not include material recorded under any other leader, so the tracks with Hamp's band or Barney Bigard's Jazzopators are not included on Classics. As so often in this very valuable and clearly documented series, one is apt to be distracted from the leader's achievement by early sightings of soon-to-be-important players. Bud Powell's appearance with the Williams Orchestra marked an important phase in his career, and the band also made the first recordings of two Thelonious Monk compositions, 'Fly Right' (aka 'Epistrophy') and 'Round Midnight', the latter from the August 1944 date covered on both discs. Cootie's own contributions go their growling, alternately chipper and sombre, way. Topaz usefully includes 'Concerto' and a 'Royal Garden Blues' with Benny Goodman's Sextet and, in terms of roundness and representativeness, this is by far the better option unless much of the material is owned already. Some will undoubtedly favour the Orchestra sides with Vinson playing and singing, and Lockjaw beginning to make his move. These are delightful recordings and even the rather muddy Classics sound can't blunt their appeal.

The second Classics volume is full of anticipations of Cootie's later swing to R&B. His bands of 1945 and 1946 are full of names who would play a part in a later chapter of American music: Gene Redd was the father of singer Sharon Redd and Gene Jr of Kool & The Gang; Sylvester Payne was the father of Basie's drummer; Eddie Vinson puts in an appearance as vocalist on 'Juice Head Baby' and 'When My Baby Left Me'. Excellent as many of these cuts are, they are far short of the quality of his work with Duke. 'Echoes Of Harlem' comes from a 1946 session with Johnny Mercer as vocalist; elsewhere Bob Merrill takes on vocal duties. We find these dates pall on subsequent hearings, but Cootie's admirers will find enough of the real thing to make this a worthwhile purchase.

By the late 1950s, when *The Big Challenge* was set up (and set up is the operative term), Williams was working with a rock'n'roll group, a drab routine that had significantly blunted the edge of his tough, brassy sound. Much of his most effective playing on the set seems to derive from the man in the opposite corner. He reduplicates Rex Stewart's half-valved style and gruff swoops authentically but also rather redundantly, because the cornetist is in excellent, pungent form. Williams plays most convincingly on 'Walkin' My Baby Back Home', where he throws in a muted solo even the Duke would have liked. The two tenors compare more straightforwardly, trading choruses on 'Alphonse And Gaston' with the polite brutality of a Larry Holmes fight. The closing 'I Knew You When' is a carefully matched head arrangement that allows Williams and Stewart to slug it out to a finish. Not altogether inspiring stuff, and a sorry reminder of the way in which Williams's independent career, thwarted by the draft and the recording ban, was short-circuited into blandly commercial sessions that offered little scope for his towering talent.

James Williams (born 1951)

PIANO, ORGAN

A Memphis piano-man, he studied theory there and played in clubs before turning to teaching himself at Berklee. With Art Blakey, 1977–81, then leading and freelancing in New York. A can-do personality who teaches, produces and organizes, he sometimes finds the time to record himself.

***** Progress Report**

Sunnyside SSC 1012D *Williams; Bill Easley (as); Bill Pierce (ts); Kevin Eubanks (g); Rufus Reid (b); Tony Reedus (d); Jerry Gonzalez (perc).* 85.

***** I Remember Clifford**

DIW 601 *Williams; Richard Davis (b); Ronnie Burrage (d).*

***** Meets The Saxophone Masters**

DIW 868 *Williams; George Coleman, Billy Pierce, Joe Henderson (ts); James Genus (b); Tony Reedus (d).* 9/91.

***** Talkin' Trash**

DIW 887 *Williams; Clark Terry (t, flhn, v); Billy Pierce (ss, ts); Steve Nelson (vib); Christian McBride (b); Tony Reedus (d).* 93.

*****(*) Awesome!**

DIW 623 *Williams; Ray Brown (b); Elvin Jones (d).* 99.

Williams made his first major mark with The Jazz Messengers, and the Sunnyside session – there are earlier discs for Concord which are out of print – certainly keeps Blakey's faith, with a typically muscular but lyrical approach. The horns, though, do little but go through well-practised motions: it's a workmanlike, intermittently sparking record. Williams is finally just a touch too diffident to characterize these otherwise pleasing records as best he might. There is authoritative leadership but not quite the last ounce of personal insight which might have taken these discs into the front rank. That said, the interplay on *I Remember Clifford* is admirable, with Davis in shining form and the studio sound glistening with class.

He's strongly challenged on the *Saxophone Masters* disc but holds his own, despite often losing out in sheer volume to a crowded front line. It might have been better to have broken up the band a bit. Henderson is so obviously out in front of the other two on this occasion that one wants to hear more of him and less of the other two, who come lumbering out of left and right channels like hungry linebackers. *Talkin' Trash* has a bit of a gospel flavour here and there, particularly on 'The Orator', and a cheery, energetic band offer one another good-natured support throughout. This kind of smiling music is what Williams does best.

There's a lot more high-stepping and joyous stuff on *Awesome!*. We are reminded of Erroll Garner, Ahmad Jamal, even Oscar Peterson – there's a similar broad-handed delivery which isn't undermined by any sense that the music's in any way 'difficult', as quick and intense as it often is. Ray and Elvin enjoy themselves as much as the boss at the piano, and the result is surely the Williams record to have, from an almost ecstatic 'Time After Time' to a rather incisive and surprising take on Mary Lou Williams's 'Stolen Moments'.

Jeff Williams (born 1950)

DRUMS

An experienced and prolific hard-bop drummer who began recording in the '70s; this seems to be his sole leadership entry to date.

*****(*) Coalescence**

Steeplechase SCCD 31308 *Williams; Tim Ries (ts, f); Pat Zimmerli (ts, bcl); Kevin Hays (p); Doug Weiss (b). 5/91.*

Williams has been very busy as a sideman since the early 1970s, but his leadership debut shows no sign of fatigue or routine. The eight themes here are resoundingly free of hard-bop cliché or empty rhetoric, and the decidedly unstarry band – Ries and Zimmerli have had little limelight thus far – makes light of a demanding occasion. The two-tenor pieces which open and close show the horns as darkly complementary rather than combative and, throughout, Williams works to make the music unpredictable: the sequence of duets in 'Dialogue', the timeless quality of 'Autonomy'. There are small flaws: the outward-bound bass clarinet and soprano of 'Skulduggery' is unconvincing, and 'Wondering' studies too hard on sounding gloomy. But Weiss and Williams make a fascinating rhythm section, and sometimes one listens past the others and into their endlessly inventive time. Excellent sound.

Jessica Williams (born 1948)

PIANO

Jessica Williams will one day tell her own remarkable story, which begins in Baltimore and stretches to the West Coast. Her style is very much her own, but is compounded of many elements of the jazz piano tradition, including Art Tatum, Dave Brubeck, Bill Evans and a lyrical edge reminiscent of Hampton Hawes. Prolific, perhaps over-prolific, Williams has astonishingly made 60 LPs and CDs.

***** The Next Step**

Hep CD 2054 *Williams (p solo). 4/93.*

***** In The Pocket**

Hep CD 2055 *Williams; Jeff Johnson (b); Dick Berk (d). 4 & 7/93.*

****(*) A Song That I Heard**

Hep CD 2061 *As above. 3/94.*

The first of the Hep records is called *The Next Step* with good reason. It is by no means a recording debut and catches a mature artist at work. Great plaudits to label boss Alastair Robertson for having the foresight to sign her up at a point in the story when Williams was not a well-known name outside Baltimore and California. Heard unaccompanied, her style is complex, clever and slightly overwrought, too laden with quotations and parallel ideas. Her experience as a drummer and Hammond player, and her long experimentation with synthesizers can be detected in a taste for dense chord-clusters overlain on a driving beat. Often, as on the second and third Hep discs, one wonders what is really required of the bassist and drummer, so ahead of the game does she seem.

Originals like 'The Quilt', inspired by the AIDS memorial quilt, and 'Bongo's Waltz', which is dedicated to her dog, suggest a strong compositional talent, though as time goes by one begins to detect a formulaic quality, too much dependence on certain harmonic quirks. 'A Gal In Calico' on *In The Pocket* is a *tour de force*; legacy of many years playing bars and clubs round Baltimore, it underlines her talent for spotting the interrelatedness of thematic material, because buried in the texture one can spot a whole procession of tiny, almost subliminal tags from Rodgers and Hammerstein, Porter and Gershwin songs. 'I Remember Bill', from the same set, is a tender memoir of another potent influence.

***** Arrival**

Jazz Focus JFCD 001 *Williams (p solo). 94.*

***** Momentum**

Jazz Focus JFCD 003 *Williams; Jeff Johnson (b); Dick Berk (d). 2/94.*

***** Inventions**

Jazz Focus JFCD 008 *As above. 1/95.*

An almost exact repetition of her recording pattern for Hep, Williams's first three records for Jazz Focus sound somewhat like more of the same. For our taste, the Canadian label gives her a warmer sound, with less space between the instruments, which helps to mitigate a feeling that the rhythm lines are merely superadded and are not integral.

Alarmingly, *Inventions* comes with the generic subtitle, 'Explorations in Music', which was to appear on some of the later Jazz Focus discs. Much of her 'exploration' involves nothing more than walking in the footsteps of those who have gone before. There is a foray into Coltrane's harmony on 'Last Trane' and a nod in the direction of Toshiko Akiyoshi (both *Inventions*), but where she is strongest is when the melody lines are simple and clearly directed and the harmonic language is her own.

On balance, the Hep album is probably the stronger of the two solos, but that may simply be the vestige of genuine surprise when it first emerged.

***** Encounters**

Jazz Focus JFCD 005 *Williams; Leroy Vinnegar (b); Mel Brown (d). 10/94.*

No nonsense about 'explorations', and for a change a rhythm section which really does offer Williams some challenges. Recorded live at Atwater's club in Portland, Oregon, *Encounters* kicks off with a wonderful version of John Coltrane's 'Equinox', not necessarily the kind of repertoire you'd associate with the veteran walker Vinnegar, but all grist to his mill. Randy Weston's 'Berkshire Blues' is equally unexpected but no less effective, and Brown really comes into his own at this point. We suspect that the tracks are not in the order played; there is a certain slackening of pace and a more tentative quality to the tunes after 'If I Were A Bell'. Williams's own 'The Sheikh' is very much a personal feature, but the two standards which follow, 'Wrap Your Troubles In Dreams' and 'Say It Over And Over Again', are quite nondescript and unfocused.

*****(*) Gratitude**
Candid CCD 79721 *Williams (p solo).* 6/95.

***** Live At Maybeck Hall: Volume 21**
Concord CCD 65721 *As above.* 95.

Williams's apotheosis at Berkeley's most famous recital hall was, in the event, a major disappointment, and something of a lost opportunity. It's a set that very rapidly degenerates into an illustrated lecture on modern jazz piano, pointlessly allusive and fragmentary, lacking any real expressive depth. Perhaps it is simply that Williams is such a seasoned club player that she found the more academic atmosphere of Maybeck unconducive.

We like *Gratitude* as much as anything she has committed to record. There are two Coltrane tunes in the programme – the blues 'Mr Syms' and 'Like Sonny' – and reprises of her own 'Last Trane' and 'The Sheikh'. She was presumably listening to Trane a good deal at the time, and also to Monk, who is represented again by 'Justice', a marvellous reading, and by a thoroughly individual interpretation of the tired old piano warhorse 'Round Midnight', which is suddenly fresh as a colt again. The two standards are 'I Cover The Waterfront' and 'Nice Work If You Can Get It', both of them dispatched briskly and without indulgence.

*****(*) Intuition**
Jazz Focus JFCD 010 *Williams (p solo).* 6/95.

****** The Victoria Concert**
Jazz Focus JFCD 015 *As above.* 9/95.

The studio album is more thoroughly suffused with the blues than Williams has seemed for a while, not just as a matter of strict harmony but in feel and emotional pressure as well. 'Holocaust Blues' is a dark, strong original, boldly placed first in the set. Billy Cobham's and George Duke's 'Heather' is an entirely unexpected inclusion, but a great find. Otherwise, Monk is the presiding deity, with both 'Green Chimneys' and 'Monk's Dream' covered.

The live album is joyous, open-hearted and at points quite intense. Opening with 'I Want To Be Happy' is some kind of statement of intent, and even blues material like 'Mr Syms', a theme which always seems to have the corners of its mouth slightly turned down, is given a buoyant and almost rambunctious feel. At a quarter of an hour, 'Straight, No Chaser' is a work-out of Marine Corps proportions, a real harmonic and rhythmic assault course. Williams, as ever, passes with flying colours (if that isn't mixing military services) but the likely reaction is going to be So what?; a lot of effort expended for very little real musical return. Even with that one quibble, a fine, beautifully styled album, though perversely Jessica looks more sombre on the cover than on any previous release.

***** Joy**
Jazz Focus JFCD 014 *Williams; Jay Thomas (t, ts, f); Hadley Caliman (ts); Jeff Johnson (b); Dick Berk, Mel Brown (d, perc).* 11/95, 1/96.

*****(*) Jessica's Blues**
Jazz Focus JFCD 018 *As above, except omit Caliman, Berk.* 10/96.

Williams's decision to record with horns wasn't altogether surprising, but it takes a moment or two to adjust to the sheer busyness of the sound. Thomas is a talented and adaptable player, shifting from trumpet on the opening 'Joy', which is retrospectively dedicated to the late Don Cherry, to flute on 'Infinite Circle', to trumpet and flute on a reworked 'The Quilt', and back to trumpet again on the Hancock-like 'Dharma Dance', which also features more straightahead tenor from Hadley Caliman.

Williams seems to thrive on these larger-scale arrangements, and she plays with an attractive simplicity that would not be out of place in more restricted settings as well. Unembellished melody statement is the key to *Jessica's Blues*. It is also a more coherent package, having been recorded in a single session rather than over a period of time and with slightly different personnel from its predecessor.

*****(*) Encounters II**
Jazz Focus JFCD *Williams; Leroy Vinnegar (b); Mel Brown (d).* 10/96.

A happy reunion with the veteran walker and at the same club in Portland that hosted their earlier meeting. By this stage in the game, nothing that Williams might choose to play should evince any surprise, but it's a little startling to come across Rahsaan Roland Kirk's 'Haunted Melody' upsides with Basie's 'The "M" Squad' and 'Mack The Knife'. 'Empathy' is a highly effective original, with a curious turn in the melody line which strongly suggests the Monk influence is still strong.

Someone had obviously done a bit of homework on the acoustic at Atwater's. The bass and drums are better balanced than on the original *Encounters*, and there's a bit more air round the piano. A fine record; certainly one to consider.

*****(*) Higher Standards**
Candid CCD 79736 *Williams; Dave Captein (b); Mel Brown (d).* 11/96.

*****(*) Jazz In The Afternoon**
Candid CCD 70750 *As above.* 2/98.

A pure standards album always seemed a likely bet. It's slightly surprising that it should have been so long in coming, but Williams has chosen to bide her time and craft it carefully. Our suspicion is that a very great deal more than is actually released was recorded, so technically secure is the playing and so well sequenced the results. Surely it wasn't all as good as this? The downside is that it comes across as an album of peaks and climaxes, with hardly any basic passage-work.

'Mack The Knife' is again very good indeed, but the high points of the album are 'A Night In Tunisia', which is recast as funky post-bop, and 'East Of The Sun (And West Of The Moon)', which can't be faulted on any count whatsoever. Captein is a less effusive and insistent player than either Vinnegar or Johnson, but he takes his place in the trio with great assurance.

By the time of *Jazz In The Afternoon*, which was recorded live at Chemekata College, Oregon, the trio is functioning like a band that has been working together for years. Williams is once again brilliant on 'Straight, No Chaser', though one wonders how often one would want to buy a record like this just to hear her *not* repeating ideas. Her own 'I Remember Dexter' is another slightly self-conscious attempt to write herself into jazz history, and a not entirely successful one.

***** In The Key Of Monk**
Jazz Focus JFCD 029 *Williams (p solo).* 5/97.

Emphatically not an album of Monk covers, but an attempt to create a seamless suite of meditations on the great pianist and composer. Williams's own pieces, like 'The House That Rouse Built' (a reference to Monk's saxophonist Charlie) and 'Monk's Hat', veer close to pastiche but are strong enough in themselves to sustain some rather over-the-top playing. The best of the album is in the opening ten minutes, with 'Bemsha Swing', 'Just A Gigolo' and 'Reflections' rattled off with drive, swing and great charm. The rest is a touch laboured and will probably appeal only to devoted Williams fans.

Joe Williams (1918–99)

VOCAL

Raised in Chicago, he sang in clubs in the city from the late '30s and later toured with Andy Kirk. His hit version of 'Every Day' made his reputation, then he joined Count Basie, 1954–60. After that, he worked as a solo, usually with a trio, including Junior Mance and latterly Norman Simmons.

***** A Swingin' Night In Birdland**
Roulette 95335-2 *Williams; Harry 'Sweets' Edison (t); Jimmy Forrest (ts); Hugh Lawson (p); Ike Isaacs (b); Clarence Johnston (d).* 6/62.

***** Ultimate Joe Williams**
Verve 559709-2 *Williams; Med Flory, Lanny Morgan (as); Ray Reed, Jay Migliorio (ts); Jack Nimitz (bs); Norman Simmons (p); Henry Johnson, Kenny Burrell, Ted Dunbar (g); Bob Badgley, Paul West, Charles Ables (b); Gerryck King, Dennis Mackrel, Steve Williams (d); Shirley Horn (v); Count Basie Orchestra.* 55–90.

Williams followed on from Billy Eckstine in bringing in a new sophistication to the black male singer's stance. Though he made his name singing blues with Count Basie (and their albums together are classics – turn to the Basie entry for details), Williams preferred superior standards and original material. His current CD showing is disappointing, with Verve having deleted most of their material and not much from either Roulette or RCA. The Birdland date sounds a bit scrappy, with Edison's group lowering rather than raising the tone, but Williams is in fine voice, and this is the only original from his prime years in circulation. The *Ultimate* compilation isn't bad, but compiler Kevin Mahogany didn't have much to work from, and most of his choices are from Williams's few latter-day Verve sets, including a Christmas album.

****(*) Joe Williams With The Count Basie Orchestra**
Telarc CD-83329 *Williams; Frank Foster (ts); Count Basie Orchestra.* 11/92.

***** Here's To Life**
Telarc 83357 *Williams; strings conducted by Robert Farnon.* 8/93.

Williams endured marvellously well, even into his seventies. The top end lost much of its old limber power and there might be a shake where once all was honey-smooth, but he still phrased with the assurance of a singer who knows where the pulse is all the time, and he could hit a note with the same regal potency. By the time of his Telarc dates, though, the voice was finally sounding a little frayed. His appearance with the Foster/Basie ensemble is a nostalgic one, and he handles himself with dignity and an almost Zen calm on the slower ones. Farnon's limousine of an orchestra is the most gorgeous thistledown for Joe to get comfortable in. He gives himself a few tough ones, several surprising high notes here and there, and generally makes a go of a situation that most singers approaching his age wouldn't even have thought about.

Mary Lou Williams (1910–81)

PIANO

Williams grew up in Pittsburgh and played professionally from her early teens. Along with her husband, John Williams, she joined Terrence Holder's Clouds of Joy orchestra, shortly to be taken over by Andy Kirk, for whom Mary Lou arranged and performed. Her later style shows a deep understanding of jazz history, a profound spiritual dimension and a grasp of structure and harmonic logic that bears comparison with Duke Ellington's.

*****(*) Mary Lou Williams 1927–1940**
Classics 630 *Williams; Harold Baker, Henry McCord, Earl Thompson (t); Bradley Bullett, Ted Donnelly (tb); Edward Inge (cl); Earl Buddy Miller (cl, as); Dick Wilson (ts); John Williams (as, bsx); Ted Robinson, Floyd Smith (g); Joe Williams (bj); Booker Collins (b); Robert Price, Ben Thigpen (d).* 1/27–11/40.

*****(*) Key Moments**
Topaz TPZ 1016 *Similar to above.* 29–40.

****** Mary Lou Williams 1944**
Classics 814 *Williams; Bill Coleman (t, v); Frankie Newton, Charlie Shavers, Dick Vance (t); Vic Dickenson, Trummy Young (tb); Claude Greene, Edmond Hall (cl); Remo Palmieri (g); Al Hall, Al Lucas (b); Jack Parker, Specs Powell (d); Nora Lee King (v).* 2–11/44.

****** Mary Lou Williams 1944-1945**
Classics 1021 *Williams; Bill Coleman (t); Claude Greene (cl); Joe Evans (as); Coleman Hawkins (ts); Margie Hyans (vib); Mary Osborne (g); Jimmy Butts, Al Lucas, Edie Robinson, Bea Taylor (b); Denzil Best, Eddie Dougherty, Bridget O'Flynn, Jack Parker (d); Josh White (v).* 11 & 12/44, 6/45.

*****(*) Mary Lou Williams 1945-1947**
Classics 1050 *Williams; Irving Kusting, Edward Sadowski, Leon Schwartz (t); Allan Feldman, Martin Glaser (ss); Mauricio Lopez (as, bs); Orlando Wright (ts); Frank Roth (p); John H Smith Jr (g); Mary Osborne (g, v); Margie Hyams, Bridget O' Flynn (vib,

d); Grachan Moncur, Milton Orent, June Rotenberg (b); Rose Gottesman, Jack Parker (d). 45, 2, 7 & 10/46, 47.

Duke Ellington described her as 'perpetually contemporary'. Mary Lou Williams's career encompassed weary days of travel with Andy Kirk's Clouds of Joy band (she began as a part-time arranger and only grudgingly won recognition as a piano player), staff arranging for Ellington, and band-leading. Having divorced John Williams, who had taken her on the road with Kirk, she married trumpeter Harold Baker and co-led a group with him.

The earlier Classics compilation covers some intriguing early stuff, including sides made with Jeanette's Synco Jazzers as Mary Leo Burley (her step-father's name) when she was only sixteen, and two good solo sides recorded for the Brunswick label in Chicago in 1930. There are also two useful solos from rather later; 'Mary's Special' from April 1936 has her doubling on celeste, and there's a fine 'Little Joe From Chicago', recorded for Columbia in October 1939. The next decade saw Mary move out as an artist in her own right, and the Classics compilation (1944) includes much of the best of that material, including 'Little Joe From Chicago', 'Roll 'Em' and a piece from a jam session organized by the photographer and film-maker, Gjon Mili. The disc includes some excellent solos as well as forgettable work accompanying singer Nora Lee King.

The appearance of further Classics volumes helps to fill out the story even more. In 1945, Mary Lou was completing work on her *Zodiac Suite* and also presenting a regular radio programme on which she performed excerpts from the extended work. They are included here under the generic title 'Signs of the Zodiac' and performed either solo ('Pisces', 'Capricorn', 'Sagittarius', 'Aquarius' and 'Libra') or with a quartet. Most of the material on this volume was recorded for the Asch label, the only exceptions being two *astronomically* inspired piano solos for Selmer in France and a fascinating single track, 'Timmie Time', recorded some time in 1945 with an all-female group. The remaining tracks were recorded just before Christmas 1944 with an orchestra co-fronted by trumpeter Bill Coleman.

The zodiac pieces mark the emergence of Williams as a more than usually ambitious composer, but there are signs of her breaking free of conventional swing harmonics in a piece like the alarmingly titled 'Carcinoma'. The remaining tracks from the session sound flat and uninflected and one wonders whether Williams and her players – Coleman apart – were at odds about the material. Even the closing 'Lady Be Good' sounds perfunctory, though it closely anticipates Coleman Hawkins's later and better-known 'Rifftide' variant.

The Girl Stars reappear at the start of Classics 1050, making one wonder why it was necessary to split off 'Timmie Time' on the previous issue. Dominated by Williams and Mary Osborne, who sounds superficially like Charlie Christian, the group had more than novelty appeal, and tunes like 'Rumba Rebop', 'Boogie Misterioso' and 'Fifth Dimension' (the latter pair from a July 1946 session for Victor) are full of musical interest. Later that year Williams was working in a trio with June Rotenberg and Bridget O'Flynn (who had swapped drums and vibes duties with Margie Hyams) and recorded a neat selection of standards, including the Dvorák 'Humoresque' and 'All God's Chillun Got Rhythm'. A couple of tracks find her not playing but directing the rather mournful Milton Orent and Frank Roth Orchestra; 'Lonely Moments' is rather effective, but again the band seem either baffled or resentful of some of Mary Lou's alternative changes. Two tracks from 1947 are with a drummerless group including the emergent Kenny Dorham and on bass Grachan Moncur Senior, the father of the '60s trombonist. The return to circulation of the original *Zodiac Suite* sections is an important development, especially when coupled with the live performance below. For the most part, though, these two issues show Williams working hard at expanding her jazz vocabulary into new areas and coming to terms with the rhythmic demands of bebop, a music which she embraced only somewhat cautiously.

*****(*) The Zodiac Suite**

Smithsonian Folkways SF CD 40810 *Williams; unidentified big band, featuring Ben Webster (ts); New York Philharmonic Orchestra.* 12/45.

On New Year's Eve 1945/6, Williams gave a remarkable performance of her *Zodiac Suite* with the New York Philharmonic at Town Hall. It's a sequence of dedications to fellow-musicians (identified by their astrological characteristics) and combines straight orchestral writing of a slightly bland, film-soundtrack sort with jazz interpolations and occasional sections ('Taurus' and 'Gemini', significantly) where the two seem to coincide. Williams had been profoundly dissatisfied with a partial reading of the music, recorded in 1957 for Norman Granz's Verve label, and the rediscovery of the 'lost' tapes from the Town Hall concert is a significant addition to the discography. The sound isn't always very reliable, with occasional crackles and some loss of resolution in the string parts, but Williams is caught in close-up and the piece remains a key moment in the recognition of jazz as an important twentieth-century music, not 'classical', but with its own history and logic.

****** The London Sessions**

Vogue/BMG 73214 09312 2 *Williams; Lennie Bush, Ken Napper (b); Allan Ganley, Tony Kinsey (d); Tony Scott (perc).* 1/53, 54.

There were self-imposed hiatuses in Williams's career, but these dates, recorded in London just over a year apart, help to fill a gap in the existing discography. Only four tracks are originals, presumably in deference to a pick-up band, and these are less stretching than the stuff Mary Lou had been doing a decade before. Even so, she reharmonizes freely with Bush and Kinsey in '54 on a brisk 'Flying Home', which sounds like a transcription of a novel big-band arrangement, and on the fine opening interpretation of 'Perdido', which was the first tune out of the bag the previous year. A valuable second take of 'Round About Midnight', recorded solo, offers an object lesson in pace and phrasing, and there are useful retakes of other tunes as well, mostly because the rhythm section isn't quite on the case. The bongos would be considered superfluous now and they do get irritating, even on 'Titoros' which has the excuse of a Latin feel. A valuable record and indispensable for anyone trying to assemble a broad picture of Williams's progress.

****** Zoning**

Smithsonian Folkways SF CD 40811 *Williams (p solo).* 74.

****** Free Spirits**

Steeplechase SCCD 31043 *Williams; Buster Williams (b); Mickey Roker (d).* 7/75.

*****(*) Live At The Cookery**

Chiaroscuro CRD 146 *Williams; Brian Torff (b).* 11/75.

***** Embraced**

Pablo 2620-108 *Williams; Cecil Taylor (p).* 77.

***** Solo Recital / Montreux Jazz Festival 1978**

Original Jazz Classics OJC 962 *Williams (p solo).* 78.

There followed a period away from the USA, living in France (where she recorded for Vogue), and then away from music altogether, during which time she worked with drug addicts. Renewed activity from the late 1950s onwards included lecture-recitals on the history of jazz, large-scale sacred compositions – *Mary Lou's Mass* and *Black Christ Of The Andes* – reflecting her conversion, and stormy contact with the new avant-garde, as on her remarkable if often bemusing collaboration with Cecil Taylor. *Embraced* gives off little sense of the hostilities behind the scenes, but it underlines her ability to play from almost any stance within the black-music tradition: gospel, blues, swing, bop, free.

Williams was treated dismissively by male colleagues for much of her career (Kirk finds room for only half-a-dozen references in his autobiography, and his acknowledgement of her 'tremendous influence' seems rather *pro forma*). In the 1970s she was releasing material on her own label, Mary Records, including the superb *Zoning* (since reissued on Smithsonian Folkways) and the huge *Mary Lou's Mass*. The *Solo Recital* from Montreux in 1978 is a defiant showcase performance and its extensive coverage of signature compositions is particularly valuable to have in one place, even if her own playing may not have been what it once was. The rather earlier *Live At The Cookery* is perhaps a better bet, though. Jon Bates has done an excellent job of bringing the sound up to current standards and there's a minimum of distortion and extraneous noise ('I'm recording. If you talk too loud, it'll be on the record'). It's not clear why she tolerated Brian Torff thudding away relentlessly in her left ear, but Williams had always tended to be a right-sided player and, here more than ever, concentrates on a middle and upper register. Her playing is superb throughout and there are vintage performances of 'Roll 'Em', 'The Surrey With The Fringe On Top' (an odd favourite of hers), 'The Man I Love' and Johnny Hodges's 'The Jeep Is Jumping'.

As a straightforward performance, *Free Spirits* is very much better. Williams's health was still robust (it began to break down towards the end of the 1970s) and her playing is much sharper and surer, also more relaxed and swinging. Typically, she mixes standards ('Temptation', 'Surrey With The Fringe On Top') with jazz staples (Miles's 'All Blues', Bobby Timmons's gospel-tinged 'Dat Dere') and her own work, 'Ode To Saint Cecilie', 'Gloria', 'Blues For Timme', unexpectedly adding two John Stubblefield compositions (two takes each of 'Baby Man' and 'Free Spirits') and a promising 'Pale Blue' by bassist Buster Williams, who provides a perfect complement to her light left hand.

****** At Rick's Café American**

Storyville STCD 8285 *Williams; Milton Suggs (b); Drashear Khalid (d).* 11/79.

There are few surviving records from Williams's last period, when she was playing not just with great majesty and grace, but with a return of her characteristic salty wit. This is a fairly standard programme, light on her own compositions – only 'What's The Story, Morning Glory' – but resolutely upbeat, even when the blues mood is strongest. 'Surrey With The Fringe On Top' and 'The Jeep Is Jumping' both make an appearance, buoyant and well thought out. 'St James Infirmary' is one of her best recorded performances, and the closing version of her friend Billy Taylor's 'A Grand Night For Swinging' must have sent the Chicago crowd smiling into the night. Competent as her young sidemen are, a greater admixture of solo playing would have been welcome, but an excellent record nevertheless: wise, witty and full of gentle experience.

Perhaps inevitably, Mary Lou Williams rejected the term 'jazz', not so much because it was a white construct as because it was a fundamentally reductive one. However swinging and jazz-based her solo and small-group output, Williams transcended the conventional bounds of jazz composition and performance. It's possible at last to see her life's work reasonably complete and rounded out, and an impressive achievement it is.

Roy Williams (born 1937)

TROMBONE

Born in Bolton, Williams played in different groups during the trad era but his stay with Alex Welsh (13 years, from 1965) made him more renowned. Currently freelances and can lay fair claim to being Britain's most distinctive mainstreamer on his instrument.

***** Gruesome Twosome**

Black Lion BLCD 760507 *Williams; John Barnes (ss, bs); Brian Lemon (p); Len Skeat (b); Stan Bourke (d).* 7/80.

***** Something Wonderful**

Hep CD 2015 *Williams; Eddie Thompson (ky); Len Skeat (b); Jim Hall (d).* 3/80–5/81.

***** Royal Trombone**

Phontastic 7556 *Williams; John McLevy (t); Arne Domnérus (as, cl); Putte Wickman (cl); Nisse Sandstrom (ts); Bengt Hallberg (p); Rune Gustafsson (g); Len Skeat, Georg Riedel (b); Rune Carlsson (d).* 12/83.

Williams emerged as a second-eleven man in British trad, but his stay with the Alex Welsh band of the 1960s (and, subsequently, with Humphrey Lyttelton) revealed a much more accomplished and versatile performer than anything most of his colleagues could aspire to. He has a lovely, creamy sound on the trombone which, with its relatively quiet dynamic and effortless delivery, has drawn comparisons with Jack Teagarden that are surprisingly near the mark. These albums are typically relaxed, almost indolent on the Black Lion date, but inimitably Williams. The trombonist and John McLevy were visiting Sweden for the Phontastic sessions and teamed up with an all-star group of locals. Standards make up most of the menu, although Hallberg pens a crafty twist on 'Exactly Like You' called 'Accurately Like You', and there's a lot of variation in voicings and instrumentations: 'I'm Old Fashioned' is a duet for trombone and piano. Wickman aces out Williams from time to time and has a serene 'I Remember Clifford' to himself, but the guest leader plays admirably throughout. The CD issue adds some tracks to the original LP release but leaves out some that were on the matching album, *Again!*.

The meeting with John Barnes on *Gruesome Twosome* is marked by British diffidence: the rhythm section scarcely rouse themselves above ticking off the time. But the two horns have some delicious moments: Barnes plays baritone for the most part, and some of the interplay with Williams is much like that between Mulligan and Brookmeyer at their best, with 'People Will Say We're In Love' particularly enjoyable. *Something Wonderful* relies on Williams's class to see it through, since the material is over-familiar and Thompson's trio uninvolving, although there's a serenely effective duo for piano and trombone on 'It Never Entered My Mind'.

*** **Standard Time**

Sine SND0021 *Williams; Bob Hudson (p); Pete Heron (b); Derek Bush (d).* 9/95.

***(*) **Interplay**

Sine SND0038 *As above, except add John Barnes (bs), Geoff Pearson (b); omit Heron.* 10/96.

Williams has seldom found himself in ideal recording situations: one wonders what records might have resulted from some pre-production and pairing him with a crack rhythm-section. These are pleasing enough without being startling. *Standard Time* has him mulling over 12 standards with Hudson's decent if workman-like trio, and it's an amiable hour or so of music, if slightly both-ered by the very loud bass. *Interplay* finds him back with old sparring partner Barnes, and this is a lot more energizing. The horns circle round each other like dancing masters and some of the dialogue has a gem-like sparkle to it. The material is, again, a trifle overworked but they do sound very good on the likes of 'Squatty Roo'.

(*) **Weavers Of Dreams

Raymer Sound RSCD684 *Williams; Frank Brooker (ts, ss); Billy Harper (p); Dave Turner (b); Nigel Cretney (d).* 9/98.

One night at the Falcon Hotel, Bude. Brooker's band (which has apparently played in Siberia) tend to get in Williams's way more than help him out and there are some distinctly wayward moments, as well as a sound that isn't handing out favours. Despite it all, the trombonist still manages some typically literate and persuasive solos.

Tom Williams (born 1962)

TRUMPET, FLUGELHORN

From Baltimore, Williams confesses to a Kenny Dorham influence, and here features as leader of some typical modern bop.

*** **Introducing Tom Williams**

Criss Cross CRISS 1064 *Williams; Javon Jackson (ts); Kenny Barron (p); Peter Washington (b); Kenny Washington (d).* 12/91.

**** **Straight Street**

Criss Cross CRISS 1091 *Williams; Gary Thomas (ts, ss); Kevin Hays (p); Peter Washington (b); Kenny Washington (d).* 12/93.

Williams is unusual among younger-generation horn players in not being unduly tinged by Miles. His debut recording followed a period with the Ellington orchestra under Mercer Ellington and regular gigs with such senior players as Hank Jones, Charlie Rouse and Jackie McLean. It's an unfussy start. As on the follow-up album, a Dorham composition, 'Windmill' (on *Straight Street* 'Short Story'), occupies an important position just past mid-way. His opening shot is the original 'Thursday The Twelfth', a slightly derivative piece that serves very well as a calling-card; Barron's solo steals the show. 'The Pursuit Of Happiness' is a long, thoughtful piece with a curious, militaristic quality that perhaps reflects his day job in US Army bands. He also does Horace Silver's 'Peace' as a companion work, which may confirm the point.

Straight Street brings together a very similar band. If Barron is missed, Thomas seems a more than acceptable substitute for the dark-toned and often lugubrious Jackson. The set opens with Woody Shaw's lyrical 'If', given a bright, more contemporary sound than the slightly routine bebop aspect of its predecessor. No Williams compositions this time around. Coltrane's 'Straight Street' is given a Latin treatment. 'Jitterbug Waltz' follows and tees up highly impressive renditions of Mingus's 'Duke Ellington's Sound Of Love' and then, played rather less straight, Wayne Shorter's 'Nefertiti', a challenging piece at the best of times. Williams doubles on flugelhorn second time around, and he makes telling use of the bigger, fatter tone. This is an impres-sive record, conscious of its own limitations but bold enough to ignore them when the pace heats up and Thomas calls for a more abrasive approach.

Tony Williams (1945–97)

DRUMS

A prodigy on drums, he was working with Miles Davis at seven-teen and played on key '60s dates such as Dolphy's Out To Lunch. Later investigated the wilder shores of fusion in Lifetime, but by the '80s he was a revered senior figure, increasingly interested in composing and investigating acoustic music again. He died suddenly at 52.

***(*) **Life Time**

Blue Note 8 56980 2 *Williams; Sam Rivers (ts); Herbie Hancock (p); Bobby Hutcherson (vib, mar); Ron Carter, Richard Davis, Gary Peacock (b).* 8/64.

***(*) **Spring**

Blue Note 746135 *Williams; Sam Rivers, Wayne Shorter (ts); Herbie Hancock (p); Gary Peacock (b).* 8/65.

Tony Williams's death following a relatively innocuous surgical procedure was doubly shocking, first for the unnecessary waste of life, and more importantly because it came at a time when his career was in marvellous resurgence. Williams had his baptism of fire in the Miles Davis band while still in his teens; everyone who owns it treasures the live recording from the south of France on which the MC announces '*Le jeune Tony Williams à la batterie ... il a dix-sept ans*'. Somewhat as Denardo Coleman did for his father, Tony gave Miles a raw and unfinished sound, one that didn't know it was breaking the rules. It was clear even then that he would go places, and recordings under his own name weren't slow in coming, even if they have slipped in and out of circulation ever since.

Williams's early Blue Notes are intense, sometimes rather inward-looking explorations of the rhythmic possibilities opened up by bebop. Much of what he had learnt to date was concentrated into *Life Time* (not to be confused with the later jazz-rock group, which we have listed separately this time). This album has now been issued in Blue Note's RVG edition, dedicated to the achievement of engineer Rudy Van Gelder. Compare the crisp attacks and precise, undistorted cymbal sound with what Williams had to put up with in later years and judge how worthy the tribute is on both sides. On 'Memory', Williams turns in a remarkable trio performance with Hancock and Hutcherson (and it should be remembered that his most shining moment before this point was on Eric Dolphy's *Out To Lunch!* session, on which Hutcherson and Davis both played). Rivers's angular approach was ideally suited to the young drummer's multidirectional approach and attack. The addition of Shorter on *Spring* underlines the impression that Williams was always happiest with a rather enigmatic lyricism. It's another delightful album and, while it lacks the resonance that comes with the doubled basses on *Life Time*, it has a big, rich sound that reverberates through the memory for many hours after every hearing.

Williams's own drumming at this period may have suffered slightly from a division of attention between playing, writing and bandleading, but one suspects that what he was after was a sound, rather than a mere outlet for virtuosity, and on these excellent records he found it.

****(*) The Joy Of Flying**

Sony SRCS 9171 *Williams; Michael Brecker (ts); Tom Scott (lyricon); Cecil Taylor (p); Brian Auger, Jan Hammer (ky, syn); George Benson, Ronnie Montrose (g); Mario Cipollina, Stanley Clarke, Paul Jackson (b); Ralph MacDonald (perc).* 79.

Atlas shrugs and Homer nods. Everyone is entitled to an off-day, and at this point in his career Williams was both marking time (in the other sense) and falling in with the presumed tastes of the times. This is an unlovely and inelegant record, heavily dependent on the creaky technology of the day, but ending with a bizarre acoustic duet with Cecil Taylor which seems to send the listener off in an entirely new direction.

What's going on? Perhaps not even the participants really understood. Williams himself was clearly searching for a new direction and was obviously still somewhat torn between the avant-garde and the more populist style that had taken hold of jazz. The opening duet with Hammer is pretty drab, as is the later 'Eris'. A track with Brian Auger goes nowhere and, though Benson is – as he always was – an attractive player, his contribution to this is cosmetic.

Williams's attempt to write himself into the simpler, blunter dialect of the time works up to a point. This is a record that only the most devoted of fans will treasure.

***** Wilderness**

Ark 21 8 54571 *Williams; Michael Brecker (ts); Herbie Hancock (p); John Van Tongeren (ky); Pat Metheny, Lyle Workman (g); Stanley Clarke (b); David Garibaldi (perc); orchestra.*

A curious record, though testimony to the obvious conclusion that in the last few years of his life Williams was going in almost as many directions musically as there were days in the week. *Wilderness* is a large-scale poem to the frontier, both the physical emptinesses of America and the spiritual richness that could be discovered through them. Alternating small-group (albeit supergroup) and orchestral pieces, it's a step on from the thematic approach of *The Story Of Neptune*.

The overture is 'Wilderness Rising', a Copland-influenced idea which outstays its promise by a couple of minutes. The first of the group tracks puts things into a more familiar context, but John Van Tongeren's co-compositions on some tracks take the music off in directions that one senses Williams finds fascinating but isn't entirely clear how to articulate.

Metheny always has the air of the young, well-off kid on the block who wants to play with the older, tougher guys and then somehow manages to shame them with a moment or two of pure grace. He did it with Ornette on *Song X*, and he pulls it off again here, adding such lovely orchestral effects that one wonders why the strings and woodwinds were needed at all. On the short 'Wilderness Island', he brings a wonderful touch to the climax of Williams's best solo feature. The only uncomfortable element is Clarke's very '70s-sounding bass, though Stan's to be applauded for a lovely, accomplished orchestration on 'Harlem Mist '55'.

****** Young At Heart**

Sony Columbia 4873132 *Williams; Mulgrew Miller (p); Ira Coleman (b).* 96.

In his last couple of years, Williams straddled extremes. He effectively reconvened Lifetime in the guise of Arcana, a boiling trio with Bill Laswell and Derek Bailey (and, later, other guitarists), and he at last got down to making a trio record in a straight jazz idiom. Given its place in the canon, *Young At Heart* has to seem replete with ironies. It is not Williams's greatest record, but it is ample reminder that he was first and foremost a jazz man and one of the very greatest of the last 30 years.

Sticking pretty much to standards, though a version of his own 'Neptune' stands out, this is as even-handed a project as one could wish. Miller is superb, efficient, lyrical and note-perfect, and Ira Coleman stamps his personality on the music more than he has to date. The best of the tracks are the most familiar themes: 'On Green Dolphin Street', 'Body And Soul' (a lovely contribution from Coleman) and 'You And The Night And The Music'. Williams hadn't been known as much of a standards player, but he caresses these as if they were second skin.

Williams's death was a grievous loss to jazz, and an unnecessary waste. His legacy is rich and complex. What is painful is the recognition that he was only just entering into a new phase, a new level of creativity.

Willie Williams

TENOR SAXOPHONE, SOPRANO SAXOPHONE

Philadelphia-born tenorman, becoming a familiar sideman and here as a post-bop leader.

***** Spirit Willie**

Enja ENJ 7045 *Williams; Geoff Keezer (p); Christian McBride (b); Victor Lewis (d).* 3/92.

*****(*) WW3**

Enja ENJ 8060 *Williams; Scott Colley (b); Harold Summey Jr (d).* 9/93.

Tenormen from Philadelphia are presumed to be influenced by John Coltrane, whether they sound like Trane or not. In reality, Willie Williams tends to sound like the last player he was thinking about, whether that be a deep-voiced Jackie McLean (whose 'Dr Jackle' is featured on *WW3*), or Hank Mobley, or Sonny Rollins. Williams spent some time working with Bobby Watson's Horizon and with Clifford Jordan's big band. An early album is not currently available, but *Spirit Willie* has the freshness and the name-dropping respectfulness of a debut. 'After All This Time' is very much in Watson's bag, while 'Song For Me' works some variations on the 'Giant Steps' changes, the one occasion when Philadelphia's finest is overtly referred to. Perhaps unfortunately for the leader, Keezer and McBride are on such spanking form that the earlier of these two albums is hijacked from the start.

WW3 is much more of a Williams feature. The title-suite – 'Armageddon', 'The Choice Is Yours' and 'Babylon Falls' – trips on its own ambition but contains some fine playing. Odean Pope's 'Out For A Walk' is superlative, as is Kenny Dorham's Latin-tinged 'La Mesha'. Williams is not an entirely convincing soprano player, but the cuts which feature the smaller horn are more convincing in a trio context, and Williams's harmonic awareness has come on in leaps and bounds. Working without a piano player can be tough in this idiom, but Colley insistently nudges at the chords and Williams never sounds less than sure where he is in his solo and where he is going.

Larry Willis (born 1940)

PIANO

Born in New York, he played hard bop with Jackie McLean in the '60s before trying fusion, soul-jazz and crossover in the '70s, spending a period with Blood Sweat & Tears. Moved back into straightahead in the '80s and has numerous sideman credits.

***** Just In Time**

Steeplechase SCCD 31251 *Willis; Bob Cranshaw (b); Kenny Washington (d).* 7/89.

***** Heavy Blue**

Steeplechase SCCD 31269 *Willis; Jerry Gonzalez (t, flhn); Joe Ford (ss, as); Don Pate (b); Jeff Tain Watts (d).* 12/89.

***** Let's Play**

Steeplechase SCCD 31283 *Willis; Santi Debriano (b); Victor Lewis (d).* 1/91.

***** Steal Away**

Audioquest AQ-CD1009 *Willis; Gary Bartz (as); Cecil McBee (b).* 12/91.

*****(*) How Do You Keep The Music Playing?**

Steeplechase SCCD 31312 *Willis; David Williams (b); Lewis Nash (d).* 4/92.

***** Solo Spirit**

Mapleshade 1432 *Willis (p solo).* 4/92.

****(*) Unforgettable**

Steeplechase SCCD 31318 *Willis (p solo).* 5/92.

*****(*) A Tribute To Someone**

Audioquest AQ 1022 *Willis; Tom Williams (t); Curtis Fuller (tb); John Stubblefield (ss, ts); David Williams (b); Ben Riley (d).* 7/93.

***** Serenade**

Sound Hills 8063 *Willis; Ray Drummond (b); Victor Lewis (d).* 5/94.

Something of a journeyman whose stints with Blood Sweat & Tears and numerous high-profile leaders have kept him involved but out of the spotlight, Willis has come into his own with the fine series of Steeplechase sessions. He plays at the gentler end of hard-bop piano, writes tunes that often wind up somewhere near the blues, and often picks compositions that have been neglected by others. *Just In Time* is a solid start, but *Heavy Blue* is a more interesting date for the contrasting horns: Gonzalez sounds handsomely lyrical on flugelhorn and is countered by Joe Ford's bruising alto solos, which are always bursting into double-time runs. Willis's five originals here are all worthwhile. The next two piano-trio albums, *Let's Play* and *How Do You Keep The Music Playing?*, are probably the best places to hear Willis's own playing. The first has lovely readings of 'Who Can I Turn To?' and 'Bess, You Is My Woman Now', and Lewis is in fine form, though Debriano is a bit overbearing at times. *How Do You Keep The Music Playing?* finds Willis distilling the lightest of tones out of Wayne Shorter's usually impenetrable 'Dance Cadaverous'; he throws in some gentlemanly funk on 'Slick Rick' and even makes 'Ezekiel Saw The Wheel' fit the programme. Williams and Nash are a near-perfect team. The trio with Bartz and McBee sounds a little too off-the-cuff, as if the participants were surprised to walk into the studio together, and the bassist can't always find the spaces between Bartz and Willis, except on his beloved 'D Bass-ic Blues'; but Bartz continues his renaissance, and it would be good to hear him with Willis and a full rhythm section.

The only disappointment in this stack is the Steeplechase solo disc, dedicated to Nat Cole ballads and, finally, a bit soporific. By himself, Willis expands his voicings and makes some of these tunes sound too weighty and formal, though there are still some pleasing variations. He seems much more at home, though, with the programme of gospel and sanctified themes on *Solo Spirit*. Some of the pieces are perhaps a bit heavy on the reverence – nine themes run to nearly 80 minutes – and Ellington's 'Come Sunday' suits him better than 'Take My Hand, Precious Lord'. But he sustains it as a contemplative solo recital.

The dedicatee of *A Tribute To Someone* is Herbie Hancock, who penned the title-tune and two others in the programme. It's agreeable to find a record with this instrumentation that doesn't sound too much like a Jazz Messengers date, and Willis's distinguished touch rubs off on his team: these are notably elegant group performances. The title-piece is done with both panache and power in reserve, and the trio number, 'Sensei', is a lovely tune, given a perfect reading by Willis, Williams and Riley. The only false notes are struck by Stubblefield, whose noisy playing sounds merely coarse here instead of exciting.

Serenade is neither more nor less than Larry Willis in good, gracious form, with two men he can trust and be comfortable with. It's no better or worse than his other trio records, simply offering an hour of aristocratic jazz from three worthy constituents. The very cordial opener is Benny Carter's 'Summer Serenade'.

Alex Wilson

PIANO, SYNTHESIZER

Wilson moved to London in 1993, already in possession of a highly individual blend of jazz and Afro-Cuban grooves and melodic ideas. He is a fine arranger and a volatile keyboard performer, destined to go places.

***** Afro-Saxon**

Candid BCCD 79201 *Wilson; Jesus Alemany, Sid Gauld, Paul Jayasinha (t); Mark Bassey (tb); Joe De Jesus (tb, f); Bobby Watson (as); Denys Baptiste, Paul Booth(ts); Toni Koffi (bs); Alfred Kari Banneman, Ciyo (g); Larry Bartley, Elpidio Caicedo, Nico Gomez, Neville Malcolm (b); Cheryl Alleyne, Robert Fordjour (d); Davide Giovannini (d, perc, v); Thomas Akuru-Dyani, Bill Bland, Dave Pattman, Roberto Pla, Emrys Solis (perc); Jonathan Shortaxn (d prog); Gwyn Jay Allen, Lauren Dalrymple (v).* 98.

Part of Candid's Big City showcase of new talent, *Afro-Saxon* introduces an extravagant young talent who is both a boilingly percussive player and a genuinely inventive arranger with a gift for complex metres and cross-rhythms. He also provides a launch platform for guest soloists like Bobby Watson, whose feature on 'My Little Suede Shoes' will melt your ceiling tiles, and Paul Jayasinha, whose flugelhorn on 'Africa Is Da Place' will bring a smile to the dourest face.

The only problem with this debut album is that it tries to do too much too quickly. Wilson has ideas in abundance, but perhaps he needs a more settled context to develop them. It's to be hoped that he will be allowed to grow at his own pace and not be put into a forcing-frame.

Bert Wilson

SOPRANO, ALTO AND TENOR SAXOPHONES, BASS CLARINET

Multi-instrumentalist who leads his regular band, Rebirth, through occasional recordings of rousing free bop.

***** Live At The Zoo**

Nine Winds 0138 *Wilson; Nancy Curtis (f); Allen Youngblood (p); Chuck Metcalf (b); Bob Meyer (d).* 8/88.

***** Further Adventures In Jazz**

FMO 004 *Wilson; Syd Potter (t); Nancy Curtis (f); Craig Hoyer (p); Peter Vinikow (b); Bob Meyer (d); Michael Olson (perc); Greta Matassa (v).* 1/92.

***** Endless Fingers**

Arabesque AJ0123 *As above, except add Chuck Stentz (ts), Dan Schulte (b); omit Potter, Olsson and Matassa.* 6–7/94.

Bert Wilson and his band, Rebirth, make cheerful, passionate jazz that is as life-affirming as it is questing. The leader's alto and tenor style is an extravagant symposium of hard-bop licks and wildly expressive effects, trademarked by a big, whinnying vibrato that harks back to classic free jazz without really planting its flag there: he prefers quite tight structures and a careful sifting of group sounds, as peppery as the group can become. The Nine Winds record (several LPs are in vinyl heaven) documents a fine edition of Rebirth, marked out as much by the intelligent work of the rhythm section as by Wilson's howling solos and Curtis's less free-wheeling but still interesting flute work. *Further Adventures In Jazz* offers a new line-up, though Curtis and Meyer continue, with guest spots for Potter and Matassa on two tracks apiece. Wilson's affection for hard-bop virtuosity is often worn on his sleeve: he describes 'Happy Pretty' as '12 keys in 12 bars in 12 seconds, though we play it somewhat faster here'. Some of the tunes on both records are a bit scrappy or ragged, even for such a roistering group, and a little more finesse in the production would have helped; that comes through on *Endless Fingers*, which is certainly their best-sounding record, and the band play with their customary gusto. Curtis comes into her own, stealing thunder with a high-velocity flute solo on 'Once Is Never Enough', and guest Chuck Stentz signs in for a couple of two-tenor blowouts. Wilson himself is as exuberant as ever. Yet the record finally seems no better or worse overall than its predecessors. Maybe the group simply has too much fun to think about making a masterpiece.

Cassandra Wilson (born 1955)

VOICE, GUITAR

Born in Jackson, Mississippi, Wilson's emergence in the 1980s was as a peripheral member of the so-called M-Base group of New York musicians. Following a number of records for JMT, she signed to Blue Note and scored major successes with her first releases for the label.

****(*) Days Aweigh**

JMT 834412-2 *Wilson; Steve Coleman (as); Rod Williams (ky); Jean-Paul Bourelly (g); Kevin Bruce Harris, Kenneth Davis (b); Marc Johnson (d).* 5/87.

*****(*) Blue Skies**

JMT 834419-2 *Wilson; Mulgrew Miller (p); Lonnie Plaxico (b); Terri Lyne Carrington (d).* 2/88.

***** Live**

JMT 849149-2 *Wilson; James Weidman (ky); Kevin Bruce Harris (b); Marc Johnson (d).* 90.

***** After The Beginning Again**

JMT 514001-2 *Wilson; James Weidman (ky); Kevin Bruce Harris (b); Marc Johnson (d); Jeff Haynes (perc).* 91.

***** Songbook**

JMT 514026-2. *As above JMT discs.* 85–91.

**** Dance To The Drums Again**

DIW/Columbia 472972-2 *As above, except add Jean-Paul Bourelly (g), Rod Williams (ky), Kevin Johnson, Bill McClellan (d). n.d.*

Wilson's early records contain all the seeds of the success she has enjoyed at Blue Note, but with one exception they rarely cohere as albums of any particularity or sustained success. Most are awkward compromises between a more traditional jazz singing role and the funk and rap influences which dominate today's commercial black music. Her own compositions were flavourless vehicles for her style, marked by rambling melodies, vaguely prescriptive lyrics and rhythmical staggers; the early records (up to *Blue Skies*) are an occasionally exciting but often unfocused attempt at finding a balance. She shows a marked Betty Carter influence rhythmically, but the timbre of her voice is cloudier, and it can throw an interesting spin on otherwise familiar songs. *Blue Skies* is the least typical but easily the best of her JMT records: though made up entirely of standards with a conventional rhythm section, the recital finds Wilson investing the likes of 'Shall We Dance?' with a wholly unfamiliar range of inflexions and melodic extensions which is captivating. Her third-person version of 'Sweet Lorraine' is peculiarly dark and compelling and, while some of the songs drift a little too far off base, it's a remarkable record, and it makes the ensuing *Jumpworld* (now deleted), a return to self-consciously 'modern' music, sound all the more contrived. The live session confirms that Wilson can sustain a concert set which is essentially a seamless, ongoing vocal improvisation, but the slipshod attention to quality-control, as far as the material is concerned, is a point which seems to afflict most of what she does. *After The Beginning Again* is one of her strongest studio dates – 'There She Goes' is a haunting tune, built round Wilson's yearning tag-line, and there's a memorably downcast treatment of 'Baubles, Bangles And Beads' – but *Dance To The Drums Again* sounds flat and tired, leaving Wilson apparently stranded in a creative impasse.

***** Blue Light 'Til Dawn**

Blue Note 781357-2 *Wilson; Olu Dara (c); Don Byron (cl); Tony Cedras (acc); Charles Burnham (vn); Gib Wharton (steel g); Brandon Ross, Chris Whitley (g); Lonnie Plaxico, Kenny Davis (b); Lance Carter, Bill McClellan (d); Cyro Baptista, Jeff Haynes, Kevin Johnson, Vinx (perc). n.d.*

Wilson's debut for Blue Note was hailed in many quarters (mostly by rock critics) as a masterpiece, and it's certainly a clear step forward from her recent records: Brandon Ross's production clarifies all the colours of her voice for the first time, and the inventive textures involving Dara, Byron, Burnham and Baptista create digital fantasies on country blues and string-band forms. Yet Wilson again makes peculiar labour out of some of the songs: Joni Mitchell and Robert Johnson tunes stagger under her mannerisms, and it's on the simpler, more straightforward arrangements, such as a lovely glide through Van Morrison's 'Tupelo Honey', that it all comes together.

***** New Moon Daughter**

Blue Note 837183-2 *As above, except add Graham Haynes, Butch Morris (c), Gary Breit (org), Kevin Breit (g), Mark Anthony Peterson (b), Dougie Bowne (d); omit Dara, Byron, Davis, Carter, McClellan, Johnson, Vinx.* 95.

The same again, only more polished, a shade more inventive, as well as a fraction more arch: 'Last Train To Clarksville' was a cute idea for a cover, and Wilson takes it over, but her improvisation on the fade suggests that she doesn't really know what to do with it. 'Strange Fruit' is harrowing in a deadpan, designerish way, and the Robert Johnson tunes again don't fit. Where she really puts her mark on the music is in her own writing: the calm, serenely pretty 'Until' is outstanding, and so are 'Memphis' and 'Find Him'. Jazz as art-song, and pretty damn accomplished.

*****(*) Traveling Miles**

Blue Note 54123-2 *Wilson; Olu Dara (c); Steve Coleman (as); Vincent Henry (hca); Eric Lewis (p); Regina Carter (vn); Doug Wamble, Marvin Sewell, Pat Metheny, Kevin Breit (g); Stefon Harris (vib); Cecilia Smith (mar); Dave Holland, Lonnie Plaxico (b); Marcus Baylor, Perry Wilson (d); Jeffrey Haynes, Mino Cinelu (perc); Angelique Kidjo (v).* 12/97–9/98.

There's always going to be a preening quality in Wilson's vocals, and non-believers will probably find it as hard to warm to this record as to her previous sets. But as a tribute to Miles Davis, this seems like the most creative and thought-through of the many genuflections to the master since his passing. For once – although even this seems self-conscious at times – Wilson seems less like the epicentre of the music and more like a graceful sound which drifts through a record that is, as usual, heavy on texture and feel and light on improvisational input. There is no trumpet on the record at all – Dara's cornet makes only a couple of ghostly appearances – and most of the weight is carried by the guitarists. It seems strange to hear the likes of 'Run The Voodoo Down' and 'Blue In Green' adorned with lyrics, although Wilson's poetry is more useful as atmosphere than as substance. But this is surely the best singing she has put down on record, wistful without becoming studied, and 'Time After Time' is a pop interpretation which surpasses any of those she tried on the previous Blue Note albums. Since the record was far from a runaway success in commercial terms, it'll be interesting to see what she tries next.

Gerald Wilson (born 1918)

TRUMPET, BANDLEADER

Studied in Detroit then joined Jimmie Lunceford, before forming own band. Has worked in Los Angeles music ever since, arranging, accompanying, bandleading in many kinds of music.

***** Gerald Wilson, 1945–1946**

Classics 976 *Wilson; James Anderson, Emmett Berry, Hobart Dotson, Red Kelly, Fred Trainor, Snooky Young (t); Ralph Bledsoe, Vic Dickenson, Robert Huerta, Melba Liston, Isaac Livingstone, Alton Moore (tb); Edward Hale, Leo Trammel, Floyd Turnham (as); Eddie Davis, Vernon Slater, Olis West (ts); Maurice Simon, Charles Waller (bs); Jimmy Bunn (p); Williams Edwards, Buddy Harper, Benny Sexton (g); Arthur Edwards, Robert Rudd (b); Henry Tucker Green (d); Estelle Edson, Dick Gray, Pat Kay, Betty Roché, Thrasher Sisters (v).* 5/45–46.

Gerald Wilson joined the Jimmie Lunceford Orchestra just around the time America joined the Second World War. After a stint in the Navy, the talented young trumpeter and composer decided to form his own band. It was a progressive outfit whose faintly experimental air has long since been eclipsed by Stan Kenton's more abrasive approach, but these early recordings are full of interest.

As often with Classics releases, much of the interest lies in identifying stars of the future in embryo. Melba Liston debuts as a soloist on a reading of 'Come Sunday', recorded for Excelsior in 1945, while the irrepressible Snooky Young features on a rather later 'One O'Clock Jump'. Wilson's own contributions as a player are less dramatic. He also features on 'Come Sunday', urbane, unflustered and conscientious but hardly incendiary. His main role is as arranger, turning in crisp, intelligent charts which anticipate the work of later years. There is already a signature Wilson sound: slightly dark, overtoned, regular without being robotic. Anyone who has turned on to the fine bands of the 1970s and '80s will find much of interest in these sides. Even where the sound is less than pristine, the content is always involving.

*****(*) State Street Sweet**

Mama MMF 1010 *Wilson; Ron Barrows, Bob Clark, George Graham, Tony Lujan, Bobby Shew, Frank Szabo, Snooky Young (t); Thurman Green, Alex Iles, Charlie Loper, Ira Nepus (tb); Maurice Spears (btb); John Stephens, Randall Willis (as); Plas Johnson, Carl Randall, Louis Taylor (ts); Jack Nimitz (bs); Brian O'Rourke (p); Eric Otis, Anthony Wilson (g); Trey Henry (b); Mel Lee (d).* 95.

Wilson's appearance at the Monterey Jazz Festival in 1963 was something of a revival meeting. After running a successful band during the 1940s, he more or less dropped out of jazz for a decade, returning to the fray only at the start of the '60s. Wilson had cut his teeth with the Jimmie Lunceford Orchestra, where he had replaced Sy Oliver as staff arranger. There he acquired skills which have lasted him to this day. One of the great orchestrators in jazz, he leans heavily on the blues, but integrates swing, bebop, rock and some classical influences. *State Street Sweet* is a lovely record marked out by well-honed skill and a sure hand at recruiting players. Bobby Shew is excellent on 'The Serpent' and guest Plas Johnson has a brief starring role on 'Come Back To Sorrento'.

****** Theme For Monterey**

MAMA MMF 1021 *Wilson; Ron Barrows, Oscar Brashear, David Krimsley, Carl Saunders, Snooky Young (t); Leslie Benedict, George Bohanon, Isaac Smith, Maurice Spears (tb); Scott Mayo, Jack Nimitz, Carl Randall, John Stephens, Louis Taylor, Randall Willis (sax); Brian O'Rourke (p); Eric Veliotes, Anthony Wilson (g); Trey Henry (b); Mel Lee (d).* 97.

Wilson was a natural choice for the keynote new work at the 40th anniversary Monterey Jazz Festival. Prestigious as such a commission is, no one could have expected a piece of such grave and joyous brilliance as *Theme For Monterey*. At more than three-quarters of an hour, it has a scope and simplicity of purpose which few contemporary players would have dared, and yet repeated listenings reveal a whole raft of subtle ideas, personal and musicological references. The 'encore' pieces, 'Summertime' and the brief bop exercise of 'Anthropology', offer just a glimpse of how a Wilson band attacks repertory material. Both arrangements were premiered at the Library of Congress in recognition of its archiving of Wilson's work.

The real interest lies in his suite of original themes. 'Lyons' Roar' is a dedication to Monterey Festival maven Jimmy Lyons; the main soloists are trumpeter Oscar Brashear, tenors Carl Randall and Randall Willis, and guitarist Anthony Wilson, who probably gets more space on the disc than he strictly deserves. It also features pianist Brian O'Rourke, who is the most effective presence on 'Cookin' On Cannery Row' and 'Spanish Bay'. The set is very nearly hijacked by the very first track, an exquisite thing called 'Romance', which highlights the bright, expressive soprano of Scott Mayo.

Glenn Wilson

BARITONE SAXOPHONE, BASS CLARINET, ALTO FLUTE

Contemporary saxophonist specializing in baritone, heard in big-band situations and occasional small-group leadership dates.

****(*) Elusive**

Sunnyside 1030 *Wilson; Jim Powell (t, flhn); Bob Belden (ts); Harold Danko (p); Dennis Irwin (b); Adam Nussbaum (d).* 12/87.

***** Bittersweet**

Sunnyside 1057 *Wilson; Rory Stuart (g).* 6/90–9/92.

***** Blue Porpoise Avenue**

Sunnyside 1074 *Wilson; Marc Copland (p); Rory Stuart (g); Jay Anderson (b); Jeff Hirshfield (d).* 10/90.

Although, like so many baritone specialists, Wilson seems doomed to recording mainly as a section sideman, he plays with fine gusto and thoughtful intelligence on the records made under his own leadership. *Elusive* is perhaps a little too civilized: the baritone blow-out on 'McCoy's Passion' is excitingly realized, 'Outformation' is a surprising on-the-spot four-way improvisation, and 'Adams Park' a well-sustained threnody for Pepper Adams. But the tracks where Wilson is joined by Belden and Powell emerge as routine post-bop, and the soft-edged production lacks the impact the music needs to collar attention. *Bittersweet* is an engaging duo album with the adept guitar of Stuart keeping Wilson company. Standing thus exposed holds few terrors for the saxophonist, whose melody lines seem to grow longer, more even, with individual notes softened by his delivery. A couple of pieces feature overdubbed bass clarinet and alto flute, which varies the pace a little. *Blue Porpoise Avenue* sat on the shelf for several years before release. The date would earn its merit for the opener alone, a trio version of 'Some Other Time' in which Wilson lives out the baritone's capacity for gentle-giant tenderness and melancholy. There's much more to enjoy, though, with the boppish writing suiting leader and rhythm section; Copland, though, can be a trifle too clever with some of his responses.

Steve Wilson (born 1961)

ALTO SAXOPHONE

Played in soul bands as a teenager, then arrived in jazz as a member of Blue Note's Out of the Blue Band in the 1980s. Since then has been a prolific New York sideman, with a few dates of his own.

*****(*) New York Summit**

Criss Cross Criss 1062 *Wilson; Tom Williams (t); Mulgrew Miller (p); James Genus (b); Carl Allen (d).* 12/91.

***** Blues For Marcus**

Criss Cross Criss 1073 *Wilson; Steve Nelson (vib); Bruce Barth (p); James Genus (b); Lewis Nash (d).* 1/93.

Wilson first surfaced in the mid-'80s with Out of the Blue, a group dedicated to the classic Blue Note sound. With a sound reminiscent of former Messenger Bobby Watson (a stylistic link confirmed by his sound-alike duets with vibraphonist Nelson on *Blues For Marcus*), the young Virginian acquitted himself more than respectably. Wilson is by no means an uncritical retro hard-bopper. His first two CDs as leader demonstrate impressive if marginally over-ambitious skills as a composer ('Diaspora' on the second record gets rather hung up on complex time-signatures) but also an instinct for unusual repertoire. The first record opens with Ted Curson's lovely 'Reava's Waltz' and includes material by Ron Carter, Duke Ellington, Eddie Harris, Thelonious Monk, Joe Sample and Bobby Timmons ('Damned If I Know', rather than the ubiquitous 'Moanin'') alongside a single original. By 1993, Wilson's confidence in his own work is more evident, but there is still room for Ornette Coleman's 'Jayne', Joe Chambers's 'Patterns' and Roland Kirk's 'The Haunted Melody'. Wilson hasn't as yet quite put together the band that suits his approach. Tom Williams is a competent rather than an exciting trumpeter in the Freddie Hubbard mould; he sounds clean and orderly in ensembles but lacks pep in his solos. An outing on the Wilson original, 'Ujima', is little more than a warm-up effort. Ironically, he's missed on the second album, which is rather light in sound. Barth contributes an original, 'Cornerstone', but as a player he lacks Mulgrew Miller's firmly anchored chords and easy switches of register. Genus is the only common element. He may have slipped the engineers a sawbuck before the later sessions, for he's much more clearly audible than on *Summit*.

***** Step Lively**

Criss Cross Criss 1096 *Wilson; Cyrus Chestnut (p); Freddie Bryant (g); Dennis Irwin (b); Gregory Hutchinson (d); Daniel Sadwonick (perc).* 12/93.

Wilson's third Criss Cross is not so much a progression as an affirmation of the sound impression of the previous two. His lean, unsentimental tone on the alto blends with a rather good-humoured approach, which makes for a somewhat unusual blend of lightness and intensity. He restricts himself to two self-penned originals, the complex blues of the title-track and the jaunty 'The Epicurean', and the presence of the admirable Chestnut lends further muscle. In the end, perhaps no more than another solid Criss Cross date, but there are plenty of rewarding things, and Wilson deserves attention.

***** Generations**

Stretch 9019 *Wilson; Mulgrew Miller (p); Ray Drummond (b); Ben Riley (d).* 2/98.

The 'generations' refer to the players of yore who have inspired Wilson, and he brought in three of them – Riley aside, not exactly names that were prominent long ago! – to back him up. The results are pleasing, if hardly outstanding. Miller and Drummond are such seasoned pros that even their routine work has an eminence to it, but they don't do much more than create a diplomatic framework for Wilson's solos. The leader sounds fine, although if he's to make an impact as a leader on record, he's going to need a more meaningful context than this.

Teddy Wilson (1912–86)

PIANO

Born in Austin, Texas, Wilson visited Chicago in 1928 and fell in love with the jazz there. He formed a duo with Art Tatum in 1931, then arrived in New York to join Benny Carter, thanks to John Hammond. His studio small-group work included classic sessions with Billie Holiday and Lester Young, and he then joined Benny Goodman. A brief spell with his own big band in 1939 was suspended in favour of more small-group work, then a staff job at CBS and teaching at Juilliard. He toured as a soloist in the '60s, '70s and '80s, always the most gracious and poised of performers.

*****(*) Teddy Wilson 1934–35**

Classics 508 *Wilson; Roy Eldridge, Dick Clark (t); Benny Morton (tb); Tom Macey, Benny Goodman, Cecil Scott (cl); Hilton Jefferson, Johnny Hodges (as); Chu Berry, Ben Webster (ts); John Trueheart, Lawrence Lucie, Dave Barbour (g); John Kirby, Grachan Moncur (b); Cozy Cole (d); Billie Holiday (v).* 5/34–12/35.

*****(*) Teddy Wilson Vol. 1: Too Hot For Words**

Hep 1012 *As above.* 1–10/35.

Few jazz records have endured quite as well as Teddy Wilson's 1930s music. Wilson arrived in New York as, on the basis of the four solo titles which open the first Classics CD, an enthusiastic young stride pianist, already under the spell of Earl Hines and of Art Tatum, with whom he worked as a two-man piano team. But even here there are the signs of an individual whose meticulous, dapper delivery and subtle reading of harmony would be hugely influential. Amazingly, everything is in place by the time of the first band session in July 1935: the initial line-up includes Eldridge, Goodman and Webster, and the singer is Billie Holiday, who would feature as vocalist on most of Wilson's pre-war records. Two classics were made immediately – 'What A Little Moonlight Can Do' and 'Miss Brown To You' – and the style was set: a band chorus, a vocal, and another chorus for the band, with solos and obbligatos in perfect accord with every other note and accent. All the others seem to take their cue from the leader's own poise, and even potentially unruly spirits such as Eldridge and Webster behave. The first of Classics' comprehensive seven-disc series includes 11 piano solos and 12 band sides, and it's a delight from start to finish, even though there was better to come.

The reissue of these records has been complicated by Holiday's presence, for all her tracks with Wilson are now also available on discs under her own name. Collectors will have to follow their own tastes, but we would opine that, of all the various transfers of this material, the Hep discs – which follow the Classics discs fairly closely in sequencing, if finally not quite so generously in the number of tracks on each disc – have the most truthful sound. Even so, the Classics CD, above, is consistently clean and enjoyable in sonic terms.

*****(*) Teddy Wilson 1935–36**

Classics 511 *Wilson; Dick Clark, Gordon Griffin, Frank Newton, Roy Eldridge, Jonah Jones (t); Benny Morton (tb); Benny Goodman, Buster Bailey, Rudy Powell, Tom Macey (cl); Jerry Blake (cl, as); Vido Musso (cl, ts); Harry Carney (cl, bs);*

Johnny Hodges (as); Ted McRae, Chu Berry (ts); Dave Barbour, John Trueheart, Allan Reuss, Bob Lessey, Lawrence Lucie (g); Lionel Hampton (vib); Israel Crosby, Harry Goodman, Leemie Stanfield, Grachan Moncur, John Kirby (b); Gene Krupa, Big Sid Catlett, Cozy Cole (d); Helen Ward, Ella Fitzgerald, Red Harper, Billie Holiday (v). 12/35–8/36.

****** Teddy Wilson Vol. 2: Warmin' Up**

Hep 1014 *As above.* 12/35–6/36.

***** Teddy Wilson 1936–37**

Classics 521 *Wilson; Gordon Griffin, Irving Randolph, Henry Allen, Jonah Jones, Buck Clayton, Cootie Williams (t); Cecil Scott (cl, as, ts); Vido Musso (cl, ts); Harry Carney (cl, bs); Benny Goodman (cl); Johnny Hodges (as); Ben Webster, Prince Robinson, Lester Young (ts); Allan Reuss, Freddie Green, James McLin (g); Harry Goodman, Milt Hinton, Walter Page, John Kirby (b); Cozy Cole, Jo Jones, Gene Krupa (d); Billie Holiday, Midge Williams, Red Harper (v).* 8/36–3/37.

****** Teddy Wilson Vol. 3: Of Thee I Swing**

Hep 1020 *Largely as above.* 8/36–2/37.

Wilson hit his stride as this long series of sessions proceeded. The next two Classics CDs are laden with fine music, and Billie Holiday's contributions assume greatness: the 16 tracks she sings on Classics 521 number among her finest records, and the mixed quality of the material seems to make no difference to her. Just as Lionel Hampton began pilfering men from local big bands for his Victor sessions, so Wilson organized similar contingents for his records, and some of these bands are drawn from either the Goodman or the Basie orchestra, although one offbeat session features Henry Allen, Cecil Scott and Prince Robinson. The spotlight is off Wilson to some extent, but one of the major reasons for the success of these dates is the light, singing fluency of the rhythm section, and the pianist's unemphatic but decisive lead is the prime reason for that. Ella Fitzgerald sings on one session on Classics 511 and Midge Williams, Helen Ward and Red Harper take their turns at the microphone, but it's Holiday one remembers. Lester Young's association with the singer also starts here, but his solos are really no more memorable than the offerings by Buck Clayton, Benny Goodman or Roy Eldridge. Those collecting the Classics CDs may be dismayed by the erratic sound-quality on Classics 521 in particular, and once again we prefer the Hep series.

****** Teddy Wilson 1937**

Classics 531 *Wilson; Cootie Williams, Harry James, Buck Clayton (t); Buster Bailey, Benny Goodman, Archie Rosati (cl); Harry Carney (cl, bs); Johnny Hodges (as); Vido Musso, Lester Young (ts); Red Norvo (xy); Allan Reuss, Freddie Green (g); John Kirby, John Simmons, Harry Goodman, Artie Bernstein, Walter Page (b); Cozy Cole, Jo Jones, Gene Krupa (d); Helen Ward, Billie Holiday, Frances Hunt, Boots Castle (v).* 3–8/37.

****** Teddy Wilson Vol. 4: Fine & Dandy**

Hep 1029 *Largely as above.* 3–7/37.

*****(*) Teddy Wilson 1937–1938**

Classics 548 *Wilson; Harry James, Buck Clayton (t); Bobby Hackett (c); Benny Morton (tb); Pee Wee Russell, Prince Robinson (cl); Johnny Hodges, Tab Smith (as); Gene Sedric, Lester Young, Chu Berry, Vido Musso (ts); Red Norvo (xy); Allan Reuss, Freddie Green (g); Walter Page, Al Hall, John Simmons (b); Johnny Blowers, Jo Jones, Cozy Cole (d); Billie Holiday, Nan Wynn (v).* 9/37–4/38.

****** Teddy Wilson Vol. 5: Blue Mood**

Hep 1035 *As above.* 8/37–1/38.

****** Teddy Wilson 1938**

Classics 556 *Wilson; Jonah Jones, Harry James (t); Bobby Hackett (c); Trummy Young, Benny Morton (tb); Pee Wee Russell (cl); Benny Carter, Johnny Hodges, Toots Mondello, Ted Buckner, Edgar Sampson (as); Lester Young, Herschel Evans, Bud Freeman, Chu Berry, Ben Webster (ts); Allan Reuss, Al Casey (g); Al Hall, John Kirby, Milt Hinton, Walter Page (b); Johnny Blowers, Cozy Cole, Jo Jones (d); Billie Holiday, Nan Wynn (v).* 4–11/38.

****** Moments Like This**

Hep CD 1043 *As above, except add Roy Eldridge (t), Ernie Powell (c).* 3/38–1/39.

This is jazz of such a consistently high level that it seems churlish to offer criticism. The Classics CDs are mainly in pretty good, clean sound, with the occasional track sounding a little starchier: the Hep transfers continue to be our first recommendation, though the Classics 'uniform' editions may appeal more to some collectors. The first 1937 CD is magnificent, the first five sessions as strong in material as they are in performances: 'Mean To Me', 'I'll Get By', 'How Am I To Know?' and more. These are also among Holiday's greatest records. The 1937–8 disc includes the September 1937 session which offered the memorable two-part 'Just A Mood' quartet with Harry James and Red Norvo, as well as a previously rejected date. The 1938 set sees Bobby Hackett arriving to play lead, as well as six solos originally made for the 'Teddy Wilson School For Pianists'. Wilson's mixture of lyricism and vigour is almost unique in the jazz of the period and it suggests a path which jazz doctrine has seldom explored since.

***** Teddy Wilson 1939**

Classics 571 *Wilson; Roy Eldridge, Karl George, Harold Baker (t); Floyd Brady (tb); Pete Clark (cl, as, bs); Rudy Powell (cl, as); Benny Carter (as, ts); Ben Webster, George Irish (ts); Danny Barker, Al Casey (g); Al Hall, Milt Hinton (b); Cozy Cole, J.C Heard (d); Billie Holiday, Thelma Carpenter, Jean Eldridge (v).* 1–9/39.

Inevitably, Wilson went on to lead his own big band, and musicians were more than impressed by its secure power and purposeful clarity of tone, a direct extension of Wilson's own manner. But it failed commercially, and its records don't quite match its reputation, largely through charts that are only so-so but which may have come alive in person. The 1939 sides are collected here, along with four more Wilson solos, including a sparkling 'China Boy'.

***** Teddy Wilson 1939–1941**

Classics 620 *Similar to above, except add Doc Cheatham, Bill Coleman (t), Floyd Brady, Benny Morton (tb), Jimmy Hamilton (cl), George James (bs), Eddie Gibbs (g), Yank Porter (d), Helen Ward (v); omit Roy Eldridge, Powell, Barker, Carter, Hinton, Cole, Carpenter, Holiday and Jean Eldridge.* 12/39–4/41.

After two more sessions with the big band, Wilson returned to small groups and then a trio as his last sessions for Columbia. Still not quite up to the impeccable calibre of the earlier dates, but a

1940 session with Bill Coleman and Benny Morton in the front line is fine, and Wilson's solos-with-rhythm maintain his own fierce standards.

***** The Keystone Transcriptions**
Storyville STCD 8258 *Wilson (p solo).* 39–40.

An hour's worth of solo Wilson taken off surviving acetates made for a transcription service. There are 26 pieces: Wilson fastens on to each in turn, polishes it, drops it in the slot, and moves on. His perfect economy gives a brittle, brilliant quality to the music: the pieces dissolve like ice in a glass. But if he gloves his emotions, there's still a strangely affecting quality to the more wistful melodies, as in 'You're My Favourite Memory'. A modest yet valuable survival.

*****(*) Teddy Wilson 1942–1945**
Classics 908 *Wilson; Emmett Berry, Joe Thomas, Charlie Shavers, Buck Clayton (t); Benny Morton (tb); Edmond Hall (cl); Ben Webster (ts); Remo Palmieri (g); Red Norvo (vib); Al Hall, Billy Taylor, Johnny Williams (b); J.C Heard, Big Sid Catlett, Specs Powell (d); Helen Ward, Maxine Sullivan (v).* 1/42–8/45.

It starts with a handsome solo on 'These Foolish Things', then moves through various small-group dates for Columbia, V-Disc and his first sessions for Musicraft. The instinctual chemistry of the great 1930s sessions is gone, but these are still groups full of fine players, and there are moments to savour: Berry and Morton on 'B Flat Swing', Red Norvo, Maxine Sullivan on 'This Heart Of Mine'. The final date includes Clayton and Webster on four excellent titles.

***** Teddy Wilson 1946**
Classics 997 *Wilson; Buck Clayton (t); Scoville Browne (as, cl); Don Byas, Charlie Ventura (ts); George James (bs); Remo Palmieri (g); Billy Taylor (b); J.C Heard (d); Sarah Vaughan (v).* 5–11/46.

Wilson's Musicraft sessions are tarnished by their indifferent piano-sound, and some of his subtlety is lost. But there are nevertheless 14 handsome solos collected here, four titles by an octet with Clayton and Byas, and four by a quartet with Ventura. Sarah Vaughan sings on four tracks: 'Penthouse Serenade' is gorgeous, and the horns are splendid on 'I Want To Be Happy'.

***** Central Avenue Blues**
VJC 1013 *Wilson; Charlie Shavers (t); Benny Morton (tb); Joe Thomas (reeds); Edmond Hall (cl); Red Norvo (vib); Remo Palmieri (g); Big Sid Catlett (d); Paul Baron Orchestra. c.* 48.

Central Avenue Blues is a collection of V-Disc masters in excellently refurbished sound: Shavers will sound as overbearing as usual to some ears, but the more considered methods of Hall and Norvo should counterbalance that, and Wilson is Wilson.

**** Air Mail Special**
Black Lion BLCD 760115 *Wilson; Dave Shepherd (cl); Ronnie Gleaves (vib); Peter Chapman (b); Johnny Richardson (d).* 6/67.

****(*) The Dutch Swing College Band Meet Teddy Wilson**
Timeless CDTTD 525 *Wilson; Ray Kaart (t); Bert De Kort (c); Dick Kaart (tb); Bob Kaper (cl); Peter Schilperoot (cl, ts, bs, p); Arie Ligthart (g); Henk Bosch Van Drakestein, Bob Van Oven, Fred Pronk (b); Huub Janssen, Louis De Lussanet (d).* 2/64–10/73.

**** Teddy Wilson Meets Eiji Kitamura**
Storyville STCD 4152 *Wilson; Eiji Kitamura (cl); Ichiro Masuda (vib); Masanaga Harada (b); Buffalo Bill Robinson (d).* 10/70.

***** With Billie In Mind**
Chiaroscuro CRD III *Wilson.* 5/72.

***** Runnin' Wild**
Black Lion BLCD 760184 *Wilson; Dave Shepherd (cl); Kenny Baldock (b); Johnny Richardson (d).* 7/73.

****(*) Blues For Thomas Waller**
Black Lion BLCD 760131 *Wilson (p solo).* 1/74.

***** Three Little Words**
Black & Blue 233 094 *Wilson; Milt Hinton (b); Oliver Jackson (d).* 7/76.

Columbia and Verve should be doing something about reissuing Wilson's late-'50s sessions (Mosaic have done a boxed set of some of them), since they're among his better latter-day efforts. Until then, there is a significant gap in the discography, which picks up with these various dates from the late '60s onwards. Wilson's later music is frequently disappointing in the light of his earlier achievements. Lacking any commitment from a major label, he seemed to wander from session to session with a sometimes cynical approach to the occasion, careless of the company and relying on an inner light which had long since burned down to a routine. Only when a sympathetic producer was on hand did Wilson raise his game, and the solo records listed above include some of the best music of his later albums. *With Billie In Mind* is devoted to material he had recorded with Holiday in the 1930s, and its graceful, characteristic atmosphere makes for a special occasion. Six titles are added to the original LP issue. The Waller collection is less happy; the mature Wilson was a very different pianist from Waller, and his brand of sober gaiety isn't well attuned to the bumptious themes here, although 'Black And Blue' is more like the familiar Wilson. *Three Little Words* is a fine trio date, Wilson very much at home with players he trusts. *Runnin' Wild* was recorded at the 1973 Montreux Festival and is an unusually muscular and hard-hitting occasion: Wilson almost storms into 'One O'Clock Jump', plays 'Mood Indigo' with something like abandon and seems to enjoy sparring with Shepherd on 'Runnin' Wild' itself. An interesting change of pace, and the recording is rather aggressive too.

The other records are eminently missable. *Air Mail Special* features dreary British mainstream, and Wilson doesn't bother to disguise his boredom. Eiji Kitamura and his companions do marginally better, but the music is mostly second-hand swing. The Dutch Swing College Band play with their customary zeal and Wilson sounds in good spirits on 'Limehouse Blues' in particular; but there's little to remark on, other than pleasant mainstream noodling (the tracks from the 1960s don't feature Wilson).

***** Teddy Wilson And His All Stars**
Chiaroscuro CR(D) 150 *Wilson; Harry 'Sweets' Edison (t); Vic Dickenson (tb); Bob Wilber (cl, ss); Major Holley (b); Oliver Jackson (d).* 6/76.

A rare example of Wilson leading an American small group. It might have been a little classic, but something's wrong. Bobby Hackett was supposed to play on the date, but he died, and Edison is the substitute: he's too louche for the occasion. Wilber's arrangements are a shade too clever, and some of the tempos are too fast. But on a few slow ones, where Dickenson can stretch out, and Wilson seems to peer through from the back (the studio sound isn't very good, either), it sounds much better.

***** Moonglow**

JLR 103.608 2CD *Wilson; Layman Jackson (b); Billy Daniels (d).* 8/80.

***** Masters Of Jazz Vol. 11: Teddy Wilson**

Storyville STCD 4111 *Wilson; Jesper Lundgaard, Niels-Henning Orsted Pedersen (b); Bjarne Rostvold, Ed Thigpen (d).* 12/68–6/80.

***** Alone**

Storyville STCD 8211 *Wilson (p solo).* 5/83.

Wilson carried on working into the 1980s, and these are among his final recordings. He still sounds much as he did nearly 50 years before – sometimes more professionally detached, occasionally quietly enjoying his own wisdom. The material on the *Masters Of Jazz* disc – drawn from two trio dates 12 years apart – is still heavily reliant on the 1930s standards which Wilson always stood by. As good as anything he recorded later in life. *Moonglow* is another in the series of two-disc sets cut live at Atlanta's E.J.'s club and, although the sound is, like others in this series, inadequate, Wilson sounds in generous form. *Alone* was cut at a Danish concert. The normally taciturn pianist talks between some of the tunes, and he sounds in amiable spirits on some of his favourites, though the location sound and the piano itself seem no more than adequate.

Lem Winchester (1928–61)

VIBRAPHONE

Of all jazz's casualties, Winchester is one of the saddest, not because he mortgaged his life to drugs or liquor, but because he died in a pointless firearm accident on the brink of success. A Delaware police officer, he had been only an amateur player until the first of these brought him both critical acclaim and awards.

**** Winchester Special**

Original Jazz Classics OJC 1719 *Winchester; Benny Golson (ts); Tommy Flanagan (p); Wendell Marshall (b); Art Taylor (d).* 9/59.

**** Lem's Beat**

Original Jazz Classics OJC 1785 *Winchester; Curtis Peagler (as); Oliver Nelson (ts); Billy Brown (g); Roy Johnson (p); Wendell Marshall (b); Art Taylor (d).* 60.

****(*) Another Opus**

Original Jazz Classics OJC 1816 *Winchester; Frank Wess (f); Hank Jones (p); Johnny Hammond Smith (org); Eddie McFadden (g); Eddie Jones, Wendell Marshall (b); Bill Erskine, Gus Johnson (d).* 6 & 10/60.

***** With Feeling**

Original Jazz Classics OJC 1900 *Winchester; Richard Wyands (p); George Duvivier (b); Roy Haynes (d).* 10/60.

Winchester's vibes playing is vigorous enough, if sometimes flat-footed, but he is one of those players who tend to be comprehensively upstaged by their sidemen. Golson's gruff, argumentative tenor on the first record and Nelson's loamy sound on the second create most of the interest, and Wess, a vastly underrated exponent of the flute, is as interesting as always on *Another Opus*. The rhythm section on *Lem's Beat* and the bonus 'Lid Flippin'' on the third record hint at some of the forthcoming extroversions of soul-jazz without quite leaving hard-bop routine behind. The leader's solo spots on 'Friendly Persuasion' and 'Lady Day' are exquisite, but it's always been a little hard to be excited about a player whose moment seemed to have passed almost before anyone registered he was there.

Only the final album in the group, the most recent to make the transfer to CD, prompts any substantial reassessment. Abandoning the larger-scale arrangements he got from Oliver Nelson, Lem concentrates on a small-group blowing session and generates a joyous mood on 'Skylark' and 'But Beautiful'. Wyands is as immaculate as ever, punching out solid, blocky chords round the vibes, while Duvivier and Haynes keep the boilers stoked. Winchester's death was a loss to the music and to the truncated history of jazz vibes, but even now he sounds like a minor talent.

Kai Winding (1922–83)

TROMBONE, TROMBONIUM

Winding was born in Denmark and came to America in his early teens. He was around to see the birth of bebop and helped to devise a fast, clear-toned delivery for the trombone, a development which also had an impact on how the horn sections of big bands could sound. His long partnership with J.J. Johnson is definitive of the modern history of the instrument.

***** Kai And Jay And Bennie Green With Strings**

Original Jazz Classics OJCCD 1727 *Winding; Bennie Green, J.J Johnson (tb); Dick Katz, John Malachi (p); Peck Morrison, Tommy Potter (b); Al Harewood, Osie Johnson (d); strings.* 8/52, 12/54.

*****(*) Nuf Said**

Rhino 75995 *Winding; J.J Johnson (tb); Dick Katz (p); Tommy Potter (b); Al Harewood (d).* 55.

***** Jive At Five**

Status DSTS 1012 *Winding; Carl Fontana, Wayne Andre (tb, trombonium); Dick Lieb (btb, trombonium); Roy Frazee (p); Kenny O'Brien (b); Tom Montgomery (d).* 6/57.

The success of Jay & Kai was, in the end, not altogether equitably shared. J.J. Johnson's unchallenged dominance on the trombone as a bop voice was always questionable. Where J.J. brought a saxophone-like articulation to the instrument, it was Winding who showed how it could follow the woodwind players' fast vibrato and percussive attack and still retain its distinctive character. While with the Kenton band, Winding worked out ways of producing a very tight vibrato with the lip rather than using the slide, and this had a marked impact on a younger generation of players. A lot of the surviving Winding material is on discs also featuring J.J., Bennie Green and others, and more can be found under J.J.'s entry. Early on, though, the balance of innovation seemed to fall to the Dane. The sessions from 1952 and 1954 are important not so much for the lush and overcooked tracks with strings as for the later pairing of Jay and Kai in a quintet format. These cuts established a formula which was to become uniquely successful, though it may have hampered both men subsequently. Winding's compositions, 'Wind Bag' and 'Don't Argue', suggest that he was also a deft composer with a quirky approach to harmony and a fuller understanding than most of his employers and colleagues of the value of his rapid-fire attack and clean-edged delivery.

Nuf Said is a valuable reissue, capturing the partnership at its most confident, but in this format also showing how much hard work went on in the studio to perfect the elegantly choreographed sound. There are seven alternative takes, including versions of 'Lover' and 'It's All Right With Me' which seriously rival the release numbers. The quintet had a settled sound by this point, but there is no mistaking that the main action lies with the two front men, and even the agile Katz is given little of moment to do except comp and fill.

The 1957 record is under Winding's sole leadership. His stint with Kenton had convinced him that massed trombones made the noise closest to the angels and he persisted with the choral approach. Here it works very well indeed; though some will be put off by what might be thought to be Kentonisms, they should be assured that the idiom and the arrangements are Winding's own. The key tracks are an original blues and a thoroughly wonderful version of 'In A Sentimental Mood' in which the voicings could hardly be bettered. There remains, to be sure, something a little cold about Winding's work. Certainly, compared to J.J., he couldn't give a ballad more than a gruff expressiveness, but that was not his forte. What he did, he did well, and he deserves more credit for it.

Norma Winstone (born 1941)

VOCALS

Studied in London and became associated with the new British jazz of the '60s, singing in a variety of mainstream-to-modern situations. Formed Azimuth with John Taylor and Kenny Wheeler in the '70s, and has continued to broaden her scope of associations. An unassuming virtuoso.

*****(*) Somewhere Called Home**

ECM 1337 *Winstone; Tony Coe (cl, ts); John Taylor (p).* 7/86.

*****(*) Well Kept Secret**

Hot House HHCD 1015 *Winstone; Stacey Rowles (flhn); Jimmy Rowles (p); George Mraz (b); Joe LaBarbera (d).* 10/93.

***** ... Like Song, Like Weather**

Enodoc ENOCD 002 *Winstone; John Taylor (p).* 3/96.

***** Manhattan In The Rain**

Enodoc ENOCD 001 *Winstone; Tony Coe (ts, cl); Steve Gray (p, syn); Chris Laurence (b).* 3/97.

Winstone's first entry on Mike Westbrook's remarkable road-movie of an album, *Metropolis*, is one of the most breathtaking in contemporary jazz, a pure, reed-like tone that suddenly rises up out of the growling 'male' horns. One of the things that makes Winstone so exceptional as a singer is her equal confidence with pure abstraction (as in much of her work with Azimuth) and the most straightforward vocal line; she has talked of a 'Radio 2' side to her work, the BBC's light music network in the UK, but this is unduly self-deprecating. Like Karin Krog in Norway, she is a fine musician in her own right, a sensitive lyricist as well as an imaginative standards singer.

In the absence of the now-rare *Edge Of Time* (released by Deram in 1971 and long overdue for reissue) *Somewhere Called Home* is a more-than-acceptable sample of Winstone's atmospheric approach. It takes a certain amount of brass neck to include 'Hi Lili Hi Lo' and 'Tea For Two' on a set like this. Coe and Taylor are able and sensitive partners, but one wonders whether it wouldn't have come off better with just Taylor's thoughtful accompaniments.

The title of *Well Kept Secret* just about says it all. This finds Winstone where she should be (no disrespect to Taylor *et al.*), working with an international musician of Rowles's quality. 'A Timeless Place' is gorgeous, with its Winstone lyric to the celebrated 'Peacocks' melody, and 'A Flower Is A Lovesome Thing' is fragile and delicate without giving any sense that it will be easy to pull apart.

The security of the secret is underlined by the fact that a couple of years have added little more to Winstone's catalogue. *Manhattan In The Rain* and ... *Like Song, Like Weather* stray perilously close to the Radio 2 strain. These seem to have been released out of chronological sequence. The duo album has a quiet grace but little dramatic tension. 'I Loves You Porgy' is perhaps too polite a reading to be quite convincing, and both Winstone and her playing partner sound easier when the material is slightly quirkier, as on 'Carla's Blues' (aka Carla Bley's 'Sing Me Softly Of The Blues') and 'Tango Beyond', the latter co-written with Tony Coe. *Manhattan* is another set of light-textured standards opening on a high with Lerner and Loewe's 'The Heather On The Hill', but rarely reaching such heights again. The album seems to be dedicated to the memory of Tom Jobim and Elis Regina; but there's little in a groove that would suggest they are a major influence, and Winstone's reading of 'Retrato em Branco e Petro' is very much in her own voice, and not a version of someone else's. Coe is underused (his clarinet line on 'The Heather' is breathtaking) and the absence of a percussionist softens the edges almost too much. Here and there a more emphatic attack might have helped.

Jens Winther (born 1960)

TRUMPET, FLUGELHORN

Danish trumpeter with wide international experience.

****(*) Looking Through**

Storyville STCD 4127 *Winther; Tomas Franck (ts); Thomas Clausen (p); Jesper Lundgaard (b); Alex Riel (d).* 4/88.

*****(*) Scorpio Dance**

Storyville STCD 4179 *Winther; Tomas Franck (ts); Ben Besiakov (p); Lennart Ginman (b); Al Foster (d).* 3/91.

*** **The Four Elements**
Stunt 19802 *Winther; Michael Molhede, Andreas Pesendorfer, Duncan Mackay, Kornel Kovacs, Rich Nichols, Justin Mullens, Mick Ball (t); Peter Dahlgren, Nichol Thomson, Werner Wurm, Aurelio Santoro (tb); Mattias Jacobson (btb); David Liebman (ss); James Knight, Hagai Amir (as); Felix Petry, Bruno Brochet (ts); Idrikis Veitners (bs); Pessi Levanto (p); Tadao Tsujikawa (syn); Jacco Griekspoor (vib); Carballo Serafin (g); Jacon Jensen (b); Eric Garland (d); Agnes Heginger, Eri Matsubara, Carolina Saboia, Waltraud Kottler, Dorothy Murphy (v).* 7/96.

Winther has the confidence to play either tight, modern, hard bop or a more free-thinking, if fundamentally conservative, kind of improvisation. He can sustain long solos, but his ballad statements or flugelhorn lead on the likes of 'Ubataba', on the first record, are just as revealing. The earlier session is solid Danish jazz, but it could have lost a couple of tracks and been the better for it: Lundgaard and Riel don't sound terribly interested for once, and Clausen's frequent use of a Fender Rhodes electric piano lends a somewhat dated feel to the sound. *Scorpio Dance* is sharper all round. The sound is crisper, if a little dry, and Foster's presence (at Winther's own invitation) is inspirational, with the drummer on tirelessly inventive form. The two long tracks, 'Scorpio Dance' and 'Tree Of Life', bring out terrific solos from Winther, and there is a probing trumpet–drums duet performance on 'Intimy'. Ginman is lost in the mix, but otherwise the group sound very alert, and Besiakow sensibly takes much more of a back seat than Clausen did on the earlier record.

The big-band record for Stunt is hugely ambitious. It features members of the International Association Of Schools Of Jazz Orchestra, founded by Dave Liebman, which rehearsed Winther's four-part work while working on a cruise ship, and they delivered this performance for the 1996 Copenhagen Festival. Winther is principal soloist, Liebman chips in with a terrific solo on 'Fire', and the music is a polymorphous assemblage of styles – Gil Evans veils of sound, Palle Mikkelborg funk, various odds and ends from the big-band tradition. The enthusiasm of the players seems boundless and, if it may not stand up to minute examination, it's surely an entertaining show.

Christine Wodrascka

PIANO

Improvising pianist drawing on free and composed forms alike.

***(*) **Live Au Petit Faucheux**
AA 312605 *Wodrascka; Jean-Marc Montera (g); Yves Romain (b); Youval Micenmacher (d).* 10/93.

**** **Vertical**
FMP CD 79 *Wodrascka (p solo).* 6/95.

From the interrupted cakewalk of 'Vocalises' to the prepared-piano harshness of 'Vaudevillesque', Wodrascka's 12 pieces for the keyboard have a bewitching variety and spontaneity about them, even as they seem composed and complete. Nothing here rambles or outstays its welcome: even the slow development of 'Voyage Intervisceral', full of glowering bass-register sonorities, seems to last as long as it ought to. Jazz is clearly only a part of her vocabulary, which suggests a synthesis of many strands of composition and improvisation, but Wodrascka moves confidently through her options; she can also be very funny.

Since our last edition, we have caught up with the group record, *Live Au Petit Faucheux*, which sees Wodrascka's solo playing in a convincing transfer to a group concept. There's the same interest in miniature form, event-packed but compressed pieces, and apparent anarchy suddenly framed and made coherent by a few moments of decisive structure. The others are all willing participants, although Wodrascka has both the first and last words.

Mike Wofford

PIANO

A frequent visitor to the Californian studios, Wofford cut his first album for Epic in 1966 and made many discs for Discovery in the 1970s and '80s. In the '90s he was much less conspicuous, though still active.

*** **At Maybeck Volume Eighteen**
Concord CCD 4514 *Wofford (p solo).* 9/91.

With all his albums for Revelation wiped off the racks, Wofford is served only by this solo session in Concord's Maybeck series. It's a good one, although the pianist's oblique manner won't be to all tastes. A funky theme like Ray Bryant's 'Tonk' is ingeniously broken down, but the results aren't exactly funky. Jazz standards such as 'Stablemates' and 'Main Stem' are run through an elaborate series of variations and, while some of them are intriguing, there are moments when it seems as if the journey is going to sound interesting only to the man who's creating it. He is perhaps at his best on the briefest track, 'Too Marvellous For Words', where the melody is referred to only periodically and the improvisation is tautly conceived.

Nils Wogram (born 1975)

TROMBONE

German trombonist who studied for three years in New York, 1992–4, now making records in various Euro-American situations.

*** **New York Conversations**
Mons 874658 *Wogram; Kenny Werner (p); Brad Shoeppach (g); Doug Weiss (b); Owen Howard (d).* 4/94.

*** **Speed Life**
Enja 9346-2 *Wogram; Simon Nabatov (p); Nicolas Thys (b); Jochen Rückert (d).* 12/97.

Wogram's music is like he sounds: big, brassy, confident. The groups on these dates follow as keenly as they can. He isn't afraid of free, open space: 'Newsed', on *Speed Life*, makes the most of a seemingly themeless environment, and the four-way contrapuntalism of 'Annoying Neighbour', later on the same record, is a complex idea delivered with punch and panache. His phrasing has a vocalist's touch, full of human colour, shouting interpolations, grunts and occasional snarls, but always pushing quickly onwards to the next idea: he doesn't hang around. Nabatov, who likes a challenge, is a more than suitable partner on the Enja album, and they have a rapport which is sometimes striking, sometimes a bit mysterious. The tunes here are rather oblique, though: Wogram's originals are clever, but perhaps not quite as personalized as they should be, and the record runs out of light here and there.

The Mons album was made when he was still only 21. His playing is full of zing, and the solos have a boppish zip to them that he seems to have subsequently toned down in favour of a more expressionist approach. His team are splendid: Werner, who doesn't know how to play indifferently, is full of ideas from his mercurial solo on the opening 'Brazil' onwards.

Piotr Wojtasik

TRUMPET, FLUGELHORN

Miles Davis is almost a national hero in Poland and Wojtasik is his most devoted disciple. Very different in approach from compatriot Tomasz Stanko, he has a slow, thoughtful delivery couched in a mournful tonality that favours the lower end of the range.

***** Lonely Town**
Power Bros PB 00137 *Wojtasik; Zbigniew Namyslowski (as); Krzysztof Popek (af); Maciej Sikala (ts); Jaroslaw Smietana (g); Leszek Mozdzer (p); Jacek Niedziela (b); Marcin Jahr (d); strings.* 11/94.

****** Escape**
Power Bros PB 00177 *Wojtasik; Maciej Sikala, Tomasz Szukalski (ss, ts); Slawomir Kurkiewicz (b); Krzysztof Dziedzic (d).* 5/96, 12/98.

*****(*) Quest**
Power Bros PB 00147 *Wojtasik; Billy Harper (ts); Leslaw Mozdzer (p); Buster Williams (b); Ben Riley (d).* 12/96.

Wojtasik's limpid delivery and sophisticated approach to harmonics are never at war. Often, the sheer beauty of what he is doing distracts the listener from the inventiveness of the composition. *Escape*, enhanced like many of Power Bros's recordings with a ten-minute CD-ROM interview, is dominated by the long, modal title-piece, its sections linked by percussion and bass cadenzas. Basically simple ideas are transformed and adapted in the course of the piece, a sequence of variations and solos that remain close to the source and rely heavily on shifts of dynamic and tone-colour rather than harmonic elaboration.

Wojtasik's association with tenor saxophonist Billy Harper has been a fruitful one. Billy is the star guest and main composer on *Quest*, a quintet record which draws its inspiration straight from Miles Davis's 1950s classics. The title-track requires extra percussion and a second saxophone and reaches out into new territory for the trumpeter. The remainder is more straightforward but is never less than adventurous.

Harper's 'Illumination' is also a key piece on *Escape*, the only live cut on an album put together immaculately at Polish Radio Bialystok. His dark and slightly forbidding swing has rarely found such a sympathetic interpreter as Wojtasik and the almost martial fanfare opening generates an immediate frisson of excitement. Two of the albums – *Escape* and *Quest* – feature John Coltrane compositions. Trane famously didn't solo on 'Central Park West', leaving the mournful theme as a torso for later performers. Tomasz Szukalski's meditation on its quiet, undulating scale is one of his most compelling solos on record.

Tempting to assume that the all-American band on *Quest* is superior to the home-grown product on the other two. Fine as Harper, Williams and Riley are, they never quite convey the passion of the Polish band. Wojtasik's solo on 'Escape' is a high point in recent jazz from Poland, and this slim but evocative body of work deserves wider recognition.

Anthony Wonsey (born 1972)

PIANO

A gifted performer and a fine writer, Wonsey belongs to a generation of well-educated and confidently eclectic players for whom jazz sounds like a definite choice among approaches rather than the only streetcar running.

***** Anthonyology**
Evidence/Alfa Jazz ECD 22151 *Wonsey; Christian McBride (b); Carl Allen (d).* 95.

***** Another Perspective**
Evidence/Alfa Jazz ECD 221288 *As above.* 96.

*****(*) Open The Gates**
Criss Cross 1162 *Wonsey; Nicholas Payton (t); Ron Blake (ts); Gerald Cannon, John Webber (b); Willie Jones, Nasheet Waits (d).* 5–12/98.

No surprise to learn that at Berklee the young Wonsey majored in film scoring. There is an atmospheric quality to his own writing, notably the wonky chords of 'Faces Of A Clown' and 'Black Fairy Tales' on the debut record and the excellent 'Wise Man Willis' on the follow-up. However, Wonsey isn't simply a pictorialist. He writes and plays idiomatically, having seemingly gobbled up whole tracts of the recent jazz-piano tradition, everything from Bill Evans and Bud Powell (who became a big influence through the offices of New York cabbie and Powell associate, Jimmy Weaver, dedicatee of 'Hey Jimmy' on *Anthonyology*) to Mulgrew Miller and Hank Jones.

Throughout both records there's a freshness of conception that is immediately appealing. McBride is already a master, but it's Allen who steals the plaudits on the debut record in particular, responding to the youngster's ideas with admirable open-mindedness.

The third album is more than consolidation but somewhat less than a significant step forward. Wonsey's writing is as bright and forthright as ever, but there is a hint of repetition in the harmonic ideas, which seem to rely on certain major/minor idiosyncrasies. 'Open The Gates' is oddly reminiscent of Andrew Hill's work, and the two approaches to 'My Heart Is With You' compress a good deal of the modern piano literature. The only repertory piece is Duke Pearson's 'Big Bertha', which might seem an unlikely choice, but Wonsey's absorption in bebop is intelligent enough to lift the tune up and away from Blue Note retro cliché. Blake and Payton (who contributes 'Into The Blacklight') are convincing in their parts, and Waits has the dark, copper-bottomed sound of his creative ancestors. A fine, accomplished record.

Rickey Woodard (born 1956)

TENOR AND ALTO SAXOPHONES

West Coast-based tenorman with an unfashionable but cheery mainstream-swing sound.

***** The Frank Capp Trio Presents Rickey Woodard**
Concord CCD 4469 *Woodard; Tom Ranier (p); Chuck Berghofer (b); Frank Capp (d).*

***** California Cooking!**
Candid CCD 79509 *Woodard; Dwight Dickerson (p); Tony Dumas (b); Harold Mason (d).* 2/91.

*****(*) The Tokyo Express**
Candid CCD 79527 *Woodard; James Williams (p); Christian McBride (b); Joe Chambers (d).* 6/92.

*****(*) Yazoo**
Concord CCD 4629 *Woodard; Ray Brown (t); Cedar Walton (p); Jeff Littleton (b); Ralph Penland (d).* 94.

*****(*) The Silver Strut**
Concord CCD 4716 *Woodard; Oscar Brashear (t); Cedar Walton (p); John Clayton (b); Jeff Hamilton (d).* 95.

Woodard is actually from Nashville but works in Los Angeles, and there's a flavour of West Coast sunshine about his music, which has a burnished, easy-going lilt to it without sacrificing anything in energy. Zoot Sims, surprisingly, is the stylist whose manner Woodard most closely resembles, but his tone is as close to unique as a tenorman's can be in an age of a thousand tenor players: lean but hard, with a dusky timbre that he sustains through all the registers. His alto playing is more in hock to soul–bop sax playing, but there's the same fluency and bite. Dickerson and the others keep up and take occasional solos on *California Cooking!*, but everything here is down to Woodard, and he completely dominates the 66 minutes which include fine readings of Hank Mobley's 'This I Dig Of You' and Duke Pearson's rare 'Jeannine'. The piano sounds a fraction recessed, but the sound is otherwise excellent.

The Tokyo Express, like so many of Candid's recent discs recorded live at Birdland in New York, is a significant step forward. Increased visibility means a better response-rate on the phone calls, and here Woodard has a first-rate band behind him. The leader's approach to standards grows more confident with every session and his solo on 'Polka Dots And Moonbeams' touches all sorts of unexpected bases, including an unmistakable quote from Paul Desmond, a player not always fully acknowledged by musicians of Woodard's generation. The sound is very good, letting the rhythm section come through truly and with good definition.

Woodard can also be heard with Frank Capp's trio on a showcase record designed to show off the young player. The problem here is that the rhythm section comes through like a Sherman tank, leaving Woodard sounding as if he was playing in a goods yard.

Yazoo is tantalizingly close to being something really special. Trumpeter Brown sits out two tracks and allows Woodard to try things that the more detailed arrangements rule out. His solo on 'September In The Rain' and 'Portrait Of Jennie' are exemplary, but the real stars of the disc are Walton and his composition 'Holy Land', a truly lovely thing that should be in everybody's bandbook.

More lovely music on *The Silver Strut*. Woodard always seems only a pace for two away from a classic, and this time it's the material that seems just a little stale. 'Stardust' and 'Loverman' are very gratifyingly done, but they're hardly the most inventive of choices. When he turns up something lke Hank Mobley's 'Take Your Pick', the interest is a little more piqued.

Chris Woods (1925–85)

ALTO AND BARITONE SAXOPHONES, FLUTE

Originally from Memphis, Woods worked mostly in and around St Louis before moving to New York in 1962. He was much in demand as a sideman and, of his few albums as a leader, most were cut in Europe in the mid-'70s.

***** Modus Operandi**
Delmark DE-437 *Woods; Greg Bobulinski (t); Jim McNeely (p); Roland Wilson (b); Curtis Boyd (d).* 1/78.

Woods's principal album as a leader is no more or less than a decent showcase for his impeccable bebop chops. His clean tone, quicksilver delivery and assured demeanour were ideal in his customary sideman role, and here his genial approach lights up the music but rarely dazzles the listener. A local team of Chicagoans includes the young Jim McNeely at the piano, and Bobulinski has an amusing show-off solo on the boogaloo piece, 'What That'; but otherwise Woods's professionalism sets the agenda. The rather tight and dry sound isn't ageing very gracefully.

Phil Woods (born 1931)

ALTO AND SOPRANO SAXOPHONES, CLARINET, BASS CLARINET, VOCAL

Toured with big bands before much small-group work in the 1950s, forming a two-alto band with Gene Quill in 1957. Then more big-band work and many, many studio sessions in the '60s. Formed European Rhythm Machine quartet while living in Paris. Returned to USA in early '70s and has since run his own quintet for many years, touring and recording regularly. A master of unadorned bebop alto, his unstinting allegiance to the Parker method has been deepened by persistence and a bottomless appetite for playing.

*****(*) Pot Pie**
Original Jazz Classics 1881 *Woods; Jon Eardley (t); George Syran (p); Teddy Kotick (b); Nick Stabulas (d).* 10/54–2/55.

***** Woodlore**
Original Jazz Classics OJC 052 *Woods; John Williams (p); Teddy Kotick (b); Nick Stabulas (d).* 11/55.

***** Pairing Off**
Original Jazz Classics OJC 092 *Woods; Donald Byrd, Kenny Dorham (t); Gene Quill (as); Tommy Flanagan (p); Doug Watkins (b); Philly Joe Jones (d).* 6/56.

****(*) The Young Bloods**

Original Jazz Classics OJC 1732 *Woods; Donald Byrd (t); Al Haig (p); Teddy Kotick (b); Charli Persip (d).* 11/56.

****(*) Four Altos**

Original Jazz Classics OJC 1734 *Woods; Gene Quill, Sahib Shihab, Hal Stein (as); Mal Waldron (p); Tommy Potter (b); Louis Hayes (d).* 2/57.

*****(*) Phil & Quill**

Original Jazz Classics OJC 215 *Woods; Gene Quill (as); George Syran (p); Teddy Kotick (b); Nick Stabulas (d).* 3/57.

***** Sugan**

Original Jazz Classics OJC 1841 *Woods; Ray Copeland (t); Red Garland (p); Teddy Kotick (b); Nick Stabulas (d).* 7/57.

Phil Woods has never seemed like a beginner. He sprang into his recording career. Tone, speed of execution and ideas were all first-hand borrowings from bebop and, inevitably, Parker; but he sounded like a mature player from the first, and he has often suffered from a degree of neglect, both as a young musician and as a senior one. A series of Prestige dates from the 1950s have never exactly been collectors' pieces, but they deserve a fresh appraisal in their OJC incarnations. *Pot Pie* was his first disc as a leader, and it wears very well. Eardley contributes three angular originals and his clean, clear sound is a pleasing foil for the altoman, who actually sounds rather less in debt to Bird than he sometimes did later. The solos on the title-track and 'Mad About The Boy' have an inquiring bent that belies Woods's rep as an inflexible speedster. *Woodlore* too is a relatively quiet business, and it's the prettiness of his sound that impresses on 'Be My Love' and 'Falling In Love All Over Again'; but 'Get Happy' is a burner. The rhythm section, with Williams sometimes barely in touch, is less impressive.

Pairing Off and *Four Altos* milk the jam-session format which was beloved by Prestige at the time, and both dates come off better than most. *Pairing Off* features a couple of crackerjack blues in the title-tune and 'Stanley The Steamer', and only Byrd's relative greenness lets the side down; Philly Joe is superbly inventive at the kit. *Four Altos* is an idea that ought to pall quickly, but the enthusiasm of Woods and Quill in particular elevates the make-shift charts into something worthwhile. They made a very fine team: *Phil & Quill* doesn't have an ounce of spare fat in the solos, and the spanking delivery on, say, 'A Night At St Nick's' is as compelling as anything Prestige were recording at the period. Quill's duskier tone and more extreme intensities are barely a beat behind Woods's in terms of quality of thought (they also have two tracks on the subsequent compilation, *Bird Feathers*, OJC 1735 CD). *The Young Bloods*, although interesting for a rare 1950s appearance by Al Haig, is beset by the familiar problem of Byrd's lack of authority, and sparks never fly between the horns the way Woods would probably have wished. *Sugan* is an attractive meeting with Red Garland and it has some gripping moments, although the reliance on bebop staples and occasionally rote delivery suggest that the date could have used more preparation.

***** Rights Of Swing**

Candid CCD79016 *Woods; Benny Bailey (t); Curtis Fuller, Willie Dennis (tb); Julius Watkins (frhn); Sahib Shihab (bs); Tommy Flanagan (p); Buddy Catlett (b); Osie Johnson, Mickey Roker (d).* 1–2/61.

Something of a one-off in the Woods lexicon, since he has seldom fronted self-composed arrangements for a larger group. The music rather self-consciously negotiates a five-part 'symphonic' structure and, perhaps inevitably, takes its real life from the improvising, which the leader blows through with his usual gumption.

***** Round Trip**

Verve 559804-2 *Woods; orchestra, including Thad Jones (t), Jimmy Cleveland (tb), Jerry Dodgion, Jerome Richardson (reeds, f); Herbie Hancock, Roland Hanna (p), Richard Davis (b), Grady Tate (d); strings.* 7/69.

At least this fills part of what is a huge gap in the Woods discography. Woods himself turned his hand to many of the arrangements and, although weighed down with strings and some questionable originals ('Love Song For Dead Ché'?), the record manages to be appealingly pretty as well as regularly torched by the unfettered Woods alto. Listen to his tumultuous solo on 'Here's That Rainy Day' as one example.

***** Quartet Volume One: A Live Recording**

Clean Cuts CCD 702 *Woods; Mike Melillo (p); Steve Gilmore (b); Bill Goodwin (d).* 5/79.

A huge jump in the discography: Woods was frequently in the studios in the 1960s but usually for other leaders, and his 1970s albums for RCA and Muse are out of print. This on-the-hoof live date from Austin, Texas, catches his then-current quartet in thoughtful form. A relaxed, almost pensive set features nearly as much Melillo and Gilmore as Woods, and the leader is a little more laid-back than usual.

****** Phil Woods / Lew Tabackin**

Evidence ECD 22209-2 *Woods; Lew Tabackin (ts); Jimmy Rowles (p); Michael Moore (b); Bill Goodwin (d).* 12/80.

Available briefly as a Japanese vinyl release, this is a great favourite of ours and we are delighted to see it on CD at last. There can be few more rambunctious jazz records made at that time: in what is a good-natured cutting contest between two masters of bebop saxophone, they have at it for a glorious 58 minutes (there's an alternative take of 'Theme Of No Repeat'). One could argue that everything that has to be said is said in the first eight minutes, a 'Limehouse Blues' that takes the roof off – but, for the sheer ebullience of blowing on the changes, there are few better records than this. The terrific rhythm-section is, in the circumstances, a delightful bonus.

****** Integrity**

Red 123177-2 2CD *Woods; Tom Harrell (t, flhn); Hal Galper (p); Steve Gilmore (b); Bill Goodwin (d).* 4/84.

This became a firm line-up, and any who heard the group in concert will surely want this live record. Harrell had worked for some years as a freelance in search of a context, and with Woods he secured a precise focus: the material here is a connoisseur's choice of jazz themes – including Neal Hefti's 'Repetition', Ellington's 'Azure', Wayne Shorter's 'Infant Eyes' and Sam Rivers's '222' – mediated through a very clear-headed approach to modern bop playing. Harrell's lucid tone and nimble, carefully sifted lines are as piquant a contrast with Woods as one could wish, without creating any clashes of temperament. Galper's pensiveness is occasionally a fraction too laid back, but he moves as one with bass and drums. Woods himself assumes a role both paternal and sporting, stating themes and directions with unswerving authority but still taking risky routes to resolving an idea: his solo on Charlie Mariano's 'Blue Walls', for instance, is rhythmically as daring as any of his early work. Good in-concert recording.

***(*) **Heaven**
Evidence ECD 22148-2 *As above.* 12/84.

***(*) **Bop Stew**
Concord CCD 4345 *As above.* 11/87.

***(*) **Bouquet**
Concord CCD 4377 *As above.* 11/87.

**** **Flash**
Concord CCD 4408 *As above, except add Hal Crook (tb).* 4/89.

This was one of the great touring and recording bands of the 1980s, Harrell and Woods inspiring each other and the rhythm section inquiring and swinging. Woods didn't need to change anything about his own style, but it blossoms anew in counterpoint with Harrell's lyrical fire, and each album is handsomely programmed and delivered. *Heaven* suffers just slightly from a clattery sound, but the material – two Ellington tunes, Brubeck's 'The Duke', another skintight treatment of Sam Rivers's '222' and a completely unorthodox 'I'm Getting Sentimental Over You' – overcomes. *Bop Stew* and *Bouquet* are from a fine Japanese concert and feature the band at its most expansive and inventive. *Flash*, the final album with Harrell (who has since been replaced by Hal Crook as the front-line horn), has the edge of some outstanding composing by the trumpeter – 'Weaver' and 'Rado' are particularly sound vehicles – and Crook's extra tones on a few tracks.

*** **All Bird's Children**
Concord CCD 4441 *As above, except omit Harrell.* 6/90.

As good as Crook is, with a sparkling fluency as a soloist and a canny arranger's ear, it's hard to avoid the feeling that Harrell was missed by the band. In other respects, it's another assured session by the Woods ensemble. Highlight: the lush 'Gotham Serenade' by Galper.

*** **Evolution**
Concord CCD 4361 *As above, except add Nelson Hill (ts), Nick Brignola (bs).* 5/88.

***(*) **Real Life**
Chesky JD 47 *As above, except Jim McNeely (p) replaces Galper.* 9/90.

*** **Here's To My Lady**
Chesky JD 3 *Woods; Tommy Flanagan (p); George Mraz (b); Kenny Washington (d).* 12/88.

Woods's Little Big Band builds on the virtues of the quintet with smart logic. Arrangements by Galper, Woods, Harrell and Crook leave the group without a specific identity, allowing it to shape a vocabulary through the charisma of the leader and the pro's pro feel of the ensemble. *Real Life* is the bigger and more confident record, with a couple of lovely ballad features for Woods and a burning memorial to his old sparring partner, 'Quill', in which Brignola takes the second alto part; but the somewhat eccentric Chesky studio sound, an attempt to secure analogue warmth and presence on digital equipment, may not be to all tastes. Similar remarks apply to the quartet Chesky session, although the blue-chip rhythm-section are so apposite to Woods's needs that it makes one wish he would take a vacation from his usual band a little more often. The mood here is rather more languid than usual, with nothing breaking into a gallop, and it's a useful appendix to his more full-blooded work in the 1980s.

*** **Embraceable You**
Philology 214 W 25 *Woods; Marco Tamburini, Flavio Boltro, Paolo Fresu (t, flhn); Danilo Terenzi, Hal Crook, Roberto Rossi (tb); Giancarlo Maurino (ss, as); Mario Raja (ss, ts); Maurizio Giammarco (ts); Roberto Ottini (bs); Danilo Rea (ky); Enzo Pietropaoli (b); Roberto Gatto (d).* 7/88.

A passionate mess. Nothing wrong with the calibre of the band – these are some of Italy's finest. Woods, too, is in strong form and occasionally reaches exalted heights: the reading of 'Embraceable You', characterized with the purplest of prose in the sleeve-notes, is almost as good as the producer makes out. But Mario Raja's arrangements are cumbersome, the band seem under-rehearsed, and the studio sound is hopelessly ill-focused: Paolo Piangiarelli may be a great fan, but he should entrust production duties to someone else.

*** **Phil On Etna**
Philology W 38/39 2CD *Woods; Giovanni La Ferlita, Mario Cavallaro, Giuseppe Privitera, Enzo Gulizia (t); Camillo Pavone, Paul Zelig Rodberg, Benvenuto Ramaci (tb); Salvo Di Stefano (btb); Carlo Cattano, Umberto Di Pietro (as); Salvo Famiani, Ercole Tringale (ts); Anthony Russo (bs); Giuseppe Emmanuele (p); Nello Toscano (b); Pucci Nicosia (d); Antonella Consolo (v).* 3/89.

Another extravagant set from Philology, compiling 100 minutes of music from a concert with the Catania City Brass Orkestra, a young big band following up a week's tuition under Woods's direction. They're eager to please, and Woods himself plays with astonishing commitment as featured soloist throughout: several of the improvisations here rank with anything he's recorded in recent years. But the band lack any notable finesse and, faced with a demanding chart such as 'Pink Sunrise', they're audibly struggling. The few other soloists play with the trepidation of keen but bashful students. Good live sound, though.

*** **Flowers For Hodges**
Concord CCD 4485 *Woods; Jim McNeely (ky).* 6/91.

*** **Elsa**
Philology W 206-2 *Woods; Enrico Pieranunzi (p).* 7/91.

Woods in two very different duo situations. He plays all his collection of reeds on the Concord album, which pairs him with McNeely on a set of tunes associated with Johnny Hodges. Soprano aside, it might have been more appropriate to have stuck to the alto, and McNeely's occasional synthesizer introduces a watery taste that Hodges might not have approved of; the familiar prickly romanticism endures, nevertheless. *Elsa* is from an Italian concert. While Pieranunzi listens and follows intently, Woods goes his own way, so the interactive elements are all in one direction. Philology's warts-and-all presentation, intent on capturing every note, also lets the impact of the music falter, since

78 minutes is really too much of a good thing in less than perfect sound. But there is still much vivid and inimitable playing: the title-tune and the following shift into 'Some Day My Prince Will Come' are full of great alto playing.

***** Phil's Mood**

Philology W 207-2 *Woods; Enrico Pieranunzi (p); Enzo Pietropaoli (b); Alfred Kramer (d).* 90.

****(*) Live At The Corridonia Jazz Festival**

Philology W 211-2 *As above, except Roberto Gatto (d) replaces Kramer.* 7/91.

Woods's partnership with Pieranunzi is a fruitful new step for him. The studio album, *Phil's Mood,* uses some of the same material as the live disc and, since there are also multiple takes – four altogether of 'New Lands' – they cover the ground with scrupulous intensity. A wider choice of material would have made the earlier record stronger, but it still stands as a persuasive Woods session, the rhythm section responding to his customary plangency. The live album is again blemished by too much material and indifferent sound: more festival versions of 'Lover Man' and 'Anthropology' are hardly the best way to encounter Woods on record today.

***** Full House**

Milestone 9196 *Woods; Hal Crook (tb); Jim McNeely (p); Steve Gilmore (b); Bill Goodwin (d).* 2/91.

Cut live at Hollywood's Catalina, this set shows no sign of energy flagging, though there are no special felicities – just a top band going through its sure-footed paces.

***** Just Friends**

Philology W 106 *Woods; Renato Sellani (p); Massimo Morriconi (b).* 6/94.

***** Our Monk**

Philology W 78 *Woods; Franco D'Andrea (p).* 11/94.

More of Phil's Italian adventures. *Just Friends* lets him loose on standards with fresh-faced support from Sellani and Morriconi and is merely an interim report from a musician in good shape. The Monk recital with D'Andrea is the more challenging occasion, and it is absorbing for the way an initially unlikely interpreter such as Woods handles the repertoire. Actually, one can go all the way back to *Pot Pie* to discover Monkian leanings in his style, and the contours of this material offer him few problems at any level. D'Andrea tends to buff away at the tunes and flatten them a little, but it's a fair match.

***** Plays The Music Of Jim McNeely**

TCB 95402 *Woods; Brian Lynch (t); Jim McNeely (p); Steve Gilmore (b); Bill Goodwin (d).* 2/95.

***** Mile High Jazz Live In Denver**

Concord CCD-4739 *As above, except Bill Charlap (p) replaces McNeely.* 4/96.

Less frequently recorded in the 1990s, the Woods quintet has been through some changes – McNeely has come and gone and Lynch has replaced Crook – while following a course faithful to the leader's stance. These are more good – if not quite outstanding – sessions of modern hard bop. McNeely had already left when the TCB album was made, but he returned to cut seven of his own tunes with the group. Fine material, and the performances are strong, if not quite as multifarious as the themes deserve. Concord's *Mile High Jazz* is a vigorous show, Lynch in good fettle and the leader showing that he's lost none of his chops. Perhaps the main interest is in hearing how inventive Gilmore and Goodwin are, more than 20 years after they started working with Woods. If the horns have the limelight, they're pushed and fed by a consistently imaginative rhythm that deserves more acclaim than it's received.

***** The Complete Concert**

JMS 083-2 2CD *Woods; Gordon Beck (p).* 5/96.

Almost two and a half hours of music. Woods and Beck have often worked together, and this is a gracious reunion. Beck indulges his admiration for Bill Evans in several of the tune choices, and Woods, for once, seems to prefer to be steered by his partner. The result is more recital than gig, and it brings out the lyric side of each man. There's much to enjoy and lots to listen to – and, perhaps inevitably, it's all a bit too much of a pleasant thing: one disc of the higher points would have been fine.

*****(*) Celebration!**

Concord CCD-4770 *Woods; Brian Lynch, Ken Brader, Jan Betz, Pat Dorian (t); Rick Chamberlain, Hal Crook, Keith O'Quinn (tb); Jim Daniels (btb); George Young (ss, as, f); Nelson Hill (as, f); Tom Hamilton, Lew Delgado (ts, cl); Jim Buckley (bs, bcl); Bill Charlap (p); Steve Gilmore (b); Bill Goodwin (d).* 1/97.

Despite the economics of it, it's surprising how many big-band dates are still made in America. This one grew out of a festival gig, and it's an excellent showcase for Woods. Using mainly his own material and all his own charts, the saxophonist gets a personalized sound that sets the occasion apart from the chrome and flash which many big bands strive for. The woodwinds sound properly fat and fulsome, the brass have the right bite and, rather than the sections rushing and darting at one another, Woods measures the sonorities of each. Kent Heckman's excellent studio sound makes the band sound big and warm without seeming monumental. Woods's tunes are a good lot, but he also does well with Wayne Shorter's 'Nefertiti' and the soloists leap out of the scores. Encore!

*****(*) The Rev And I**

Blue Note 494100-2 *Woods; Johnny Griffin (ts); Cedar Walton (p); Peter Washington (b); Ben Riley (d); Bill Goodwin (perc).* 1/98.

Woods loves two-sax encounters, and this session (he and Griffin, like so many other big-bandsmen who've played together, call each other 'Section') brims over with bonhomie and swagger. The old Hampton favourite, 'Red Top', is pure catnip. Griffin is no longer the terror he once was, but Woods still sounds like he could take on any comers. Producer Bill Goodwin has taken the trouble to make sure that there's enough pre-match preparation to take it above blowing-session status, and it all benefits from that finesse. And each saxophonist gets a gorgeous ballad feature.

Reggie Workman (born 1937)

DOUBLE BASS

Played R&B as a teenager, then worked in New York hard-bop groups in the '60s before moving towards the freer styles of Archie Shepp and John Coltrane. Heavily involved in education and has latterly begun leading his own groups.

*****(*) Synthesis**

Leo CDLR 131 *Workman; Oliver Lake (reeds); Marilyn Crispell (p); Andrew Cyrille (d).* 6/86.

***** Images**

Music & Arts CD 634 *Workman; Don Byron (cl); Marilyn Crispell (p); Michele Navazio (g); Gerry Hemingway (d); Jeanne Lee (v).* 1 & 7/89.

*****(*) Altered Spaces**

Leo CDLR 183 *As above, except omit Navazio, add Jason Hwang (vn).* 2/92.

As befits his name, Workman has clocked up an astonishing number and range of sideman credits: with Coltrane (*Olé*, the 1961 European tour, the *Africa/Brass* sessions) and with Wayne Shorter, Mal Waldron, Art Blakey, Archie Shepp and David Murray. Workman is also a forceful leader who has moved on to explore areas of musical freedom influenced by African idioms and frequently resembling the trance music of the *griots*. Of the available albums, *Synthesis*, a live performance from The Painted Bride in Philadelphia, is the most convincing. Workman bows, triple-stops and produces unreliably pitched sounds (presumably from below the bridge), leaving it to Crispell, as on *Images*, to give the performance its undoubted sense of coherence. Of the six tracks on *Synthesis*, it is her 'Chant' which sounds most like a fully articulated composition. Workman's ideas are developed less completely and, while they often lead to more adventurous solo excursions from the individual performers, they rarely do much more than peter out. 'Jus' Ole Mae' on *Synthesis* is '(Revisited)' on the later album, a brighter and more evocative performance but one that lacks the sheer daring and adventurous seat-of-the-pants logic of the Philadelphia version.

Altered Spaces is the most ambitious work the Ensemble has yet tackled. The long suite, 'Apart', explores territory very close to Don Byron's chilling *Tuskegee Experiments* yet seems closer in spirit to the revolutionary stoicism of Brecht's *Mother Courage*, which Jeanne Lee's vocal explicitly quotes. The bass-and-violin prelude serves as an introduction to Jason Hwang, author of the controversial play, *M. Butterfly*, and of the libretto for Philip Glass's *1000 Airplanes On The Roof*. A new member of the Ensemble, Hwang brings an oriental calm that takes the music ever further away from 'jazz'. Oddly, on this occasion it is Crispell who sounds locked into a formulaic sound that seems to be pushing for resolutions that the two string players' long lines and Hemingway's open-ended patters serve to resist. Impressive, all the same, for its sheer cross-grainedness.

****** Summit Conference**

Postcards POST1003 *Workman; Julian Priester (tb); Sam Rivers (ts, ss); Andrew Hill (p); Pheeroan akLaff (d).* 12/93.

****** Cerebral Caverns**

Postcards POST1010 *Workman; Julian Priester (tb); Sam Rivers (ts, ss, f); Elizabeth Panzer (hp); Geri Allen (p); Gerry Hemingway (d, elec); Al Foster (d); Tapan Modak (tablas).*

These are cracking records, made by top-flight players. The *Summit Conference* group has a wish-list quality and delivers from the very start. Rivers and Priester are in boilingly good form, and the younger akLaff keeps the pace up. Slight quibbles about Hill's audibility; he isn't a delicate player and it worried us that he didn't seem to be coming through. Though the bulk of the session is up-tempo, often in fractured metres, there's still room for a heart-on-sleeve ballad, Rivers's 'Solace', introduced by trombone, piano and sax (in that order) before the composer goes up a gear and delivers his most magisterial solo for years. Priester's 'Breath' is pitched in a distant, sharp-ridden key that would have most players twitching; this group brings it on exactly on the button and without a hesitant moment.

Almost inevitably, *Cerebral Caverns* (now isn't that an off-putting title?) doesn't quite match up, but it's hard to mark it down, given the quality of performances. Allen is always better on other people's dates, and here she's called on to do the sort of high-intensity stuff that Marilyn Crispell brought to previous Workman groups. She's featured in two trios with Workman, one with Hemingway (superb), one with harp (fascinating, but not quite there). 'Fast Forward' reunites the earlier group, without piano, and with the more experienced but no less passionate Foster on drums. The title-piece is the most ambitious in terms of sound, with harp again, flute, and Hemingway's electronically triggered drum-pads contributing to a complex mix of textures. All praise to Postcards producer Ralph Simon, who might just look at the way he mikes and mixes piano. Otherwise A1.

World Saxophone Quartet

GROUP

No permutation of instruments can be more sheerly tedious and yet more compelling than four saxophones together. The difference lies in the players involved and, for as many years as anyone cares to remember, the World Saxophone Quartet has been the market leader. Less self-consciously radical and avant-garde than ROVA and yet streets ahead of the average ensemble for sheer enterprise, they have always been riveting live and only slightly less compelling on record.

***** Steppin'**

Black Saint 120027 *Hamiet Bluiett (bs, f, af, acl); Julius Hemphill (f, ss, as); Oliver Lake (ss, ts, as, f); David Murray (ts, bcl).* 12/78.

****** W.S.Q.**

Black Saint 120046 *As above.* 3/80.

*****(*) Revue**

Black Saint 120056 *As above.* 10/80.

***** Live In Zurich**

Black Saint 120077 *As above.* 11/81.

*****(*) Plays Duke Ellington**

Elektra Musician 979137 *As above.* 4/86.

****** Dances And Ballads**
Elektra Musician 979164 *As above.* 4/87.

*****(*) Rhythm And Blues**
Elektra Musician 60864 *As above.* 11/88.

Market-leaders in the now well-attested saxophone-quartet format, the WSQ were founded in 1977. The debut album was not particularly well recorded but it helped establish the group's identity as adventurous composer-improvisers who could offer great swinging ensembles (not quite as hokey as those of the 29th Street Saxophone Quartet) and remarkable duo and trio divisions of the basic instrumentation. The armoury of reeds was pretty modest to begin with, but increasingly after 1978 all four members began to 'double' on more exotic specimens, with Bluiett's alto clarinet (rarely used in a jazz context) and Murray's bass clarinet both lending significant variations of tonality and texture. 'Scared Sheetless' from the first album gives a fair impression of its not altogether serious appropriation of free-jazz devices. 'R&B' on the second album plays with genre in a friendlier and more ironic way.

The best of the earlier records, *W.S.Q.* is dominated by a long suite that blends jazz and popular elements with considerable ingenuity and real improvisational fire. 'The Key' and 'Ballad For Eddie Jefferson' (dedicated to the inventor of jazz vocalese) are perhaps the most interesting elements, but the closing 'Fast Life' is as fine a curtain-piece as the group has recorded. With *Revue* (a significant pun), the centre of gravity shifts slightly towards rising star Murray and towards what looks like a reassessment of the group's development. Murray's 'Ming' is well known from his own records but has never been played with such fierce beauty.

The Ellington album marks a gentle, middle-market turn that did the group no harm at all. Opening and closing with 'Take The "A" Train', they check out 'Sophisticated Lady' and 'I Let A Song Go Out Of My Heart', do a wonderful 'Come Sunday', and add a raw lyricism to 'Lush Life' and 'Prelude To A Kiss'. The sound is better than usual, with no congestion round about the middle, as on some of the earlier sets. There's a broader big-band sound to *Dances And Ballads*, achieved without the addition of outsiders as on *Metamorphosis*, below, which seems to draw something from the Ellington set. Hemphill contributes only two tracks, but there's a fine version of David Murray's Prez tribute, 'For Lester' (later to appear on his octet, *HopeScope*), and Oliver Lake's 'West African Snap', 'Belly Up' and 'Adjacent' are among the best of his recorded compositions. The soul staples covered on *Rhythm And Blues* – including 'Let's Get It On', '(Sittin' On) The Dock Of The Bay' and, unforgettably, 'Try A Little Tenderness', with Murray's tenor going places Otis Redding never heard of – are done with absolute conviction and seriousness. Only *Steppin'* and the rather rough *Live In Zurich* are disappointments, though the latter has a fine reading of 'Steppin'' itself.

All four members developed highly individual careers apart, Murray most of all; along with Hemphill, he is the most distinctive and flexible composer. The durability of the group lay in the degree to which personal strengths were encouraged and exploited rather than subordinated. With so many instrumental permutations and the possibility of internal subdivisions, the WSQ's exploratory sound has never settled into a manner.

***** Metamorphosis**
Elektra Nonesuch 979258 *Oliver Lake (as, ss, f); David Murray (ts, bcl); Hamiet Bluiett (bs); Arthur Blythe (as); Melvin Gibbs (b); Chief Bey, Mar Gueye, Mor Thiam (perc).* 4/90.

The departure of Julius Hemphill and arrival of Arthur Blythe couldn't have looked altogether propitious, given (a) Hemphill's importance as a writer for the group, and (b) Blythe's stuttering fortunes in recent years. The title-track, though, is given over to the new boy and he fills the outgoing man's shoes with impressive confidence, checking in with a powerful contrapuntal weave that is lifted a notch by the (initially disturbing; the WSQ used always to go it alone) presence of the three African drummers. In the event, they add a great deal more than bassist Gibbs, who clocks on for three tracks only and might as well not have bothered. Murray's 'Ballad For The Black Man' is very much an individual feature and easily the most coherent single track; Lake's 'Love Like Sisters' has tremendous potential but might well sound better tackled by a more conventional horn-plus-inventive-rhythm outfit.

***** Breath Of Life**
Nonesuch 983124 *As above.* 92.

Even giants nod on occasion and this nondescript set has to be accounted an off-day in the WSQ's impressive progress. The playing is immaculate as ever, but there is a strange lack of focus in the writing, a bland equalization of voices, almost as if someone had called a truce on competing visions.

*****(*) Moving Right Along**
Black Saint 120127 *Oliver Lake, Eric Person (as, ss); James Spaulding (as); David Murray (ts, bcl); Hamiet Bluiett (bs, acl).* 10/93.

First indications were that the WSQ were going to be feeling their way around for some time. *Moving Right Along* sees the first recording of the group with Eric Person, who also contributes a fresh original, 'Antithesis'. He fits in immediately and well, and sounds closer to the group's overall conception than Spaulding. The emphasis this time is on sharp, tight arrangements. 'Giant Steps' is dispatched in less than three minutes and there is a superb two-part arrangement of 'Amazing Grace' by Bluiett, who also contributes 'N.T.', a hard-edged portrait of the Black insurrectionist. Bluiett's 'Astral Travels' are less convincing, but his alto clarinet has become an integral component of the group sound; opening up the lower registers previously led to the more romantically inclined Murray on his second horn.

*****(*) Four Now**
Justin Time JUST 83-2 *Hamiet Bluiett (bs, contra-acl); Oliver Lake (as); David Muray (ts, bcl); John Purcell (saxello, eng hn, f, af); Chief Bey, Mar Gueye, Mor Thiam (perc, v).* 95.

A reunion of the guest line-up that made the 1991 *Metamorphosis* record, this is the better album because the elements seem to work together rather than in strict parallel. Three of the tracks are written by Mar Gueye and the gifted Mor Thiam and one feels that the idiom is more suited to the Senegalese percussionists than was the case on the earlier record. There are also fewer avant-garde gestures from the WSQ itself, who last time out – and this is a view marked with 20/20 hindsight – seemed anxious to demonstrate their greater sophistication by playing rugged dissonances and hard-edged melodies that excluded rather than welcomed the Africans. Purcell has established himself as a key member of the group. His composition, 'Colors', may have originally been written for other forces (that is our guess) but it is beautifully arranged for the Quartet, and it coaxes some lovely playing from everyone concerned.

***** Takin' It 2 The Next Level**

Justin Time 93-2 *Oliver Lake (as); John Purcell (ts, saxello); David Murray (ts, bcl); Hamiet Bluiett (bs); Donald Blackman (ky); Calvin Jones (b); Ronnie Burrage (d).* 6/96.

Again the 'empty chair' went to John Purcell; in addition, a full-on rhythm section. The results are typically spirited and entirely within the WSQ tradition. 'Rio' blends the quartet's multiple voices with a percolating rhythm to fine effect, and big set-pieces like 'Blues For A Warrior Spirit' and 'The Desegregation Of Our Children' are as formidable as they should be. But it's hard to avoid the feeling that the group is not continuing out of any artistic necessity and, as propulsive as the rhythm players are, their principal contribution is perhaps to rationalize the WSQ into just another band.

***** M'Bizo**

Justin Time JUST123-2 *Hamiet Bluiett (bs, bsx, cbcl); Oliver Lake (as); David Murray (ts, bcl); John Purcell (saxello); Jimane Nelson (org); Mario Canonge, D.D Jackson (p); Jaribu Adhurahman, James Lewis (b); Ronnie Burrage (d); Mabeleng Moholo (makhoyane); Muzi Okhanyao Buthelezi, Klod Kiavue, Pule Molebatsi, Lolo Jafta Ntombela, Mosoeu Ketlele Sgubu (d, perc); John Diwele Lubi, Albert Mabena, Gilbert Masite, Sikmumbuzo Matsinya, Monde Ncqwebo, Sam Tshabalala (v).* 11/97, 6/98.

To all intents and purposes, this is a David Murray project, in the line of his albums, *Fo Deuk Revue* and *Creole Project*, which have seen him experiment with African and Afro-Caribbean syntheses. Two of the pieces were commissioned by the Banlieues Bleues festival for the World Cup and were conceived as a marching piece. The remaining tracks, which comprise the 'M'Bizo Suite', were recorded somewhat earlier. Murray's interest in African traditions is in many respects parallel to Miles Davis's discovery of a new culture of rhythm in the South Africa of the late apartheid years, when the patterns of marching feet, clapping and stamping seemed to sound out the death knell of a whole political system. The WSQ were to return to these discoveries in a later album. Here, though, Murray acts as catalyst to a multi-tribal collage of sound which is often strictly inauthentic and sometimes startlingly inept in musicological terms, but which never fails to capture the attention. The Quartet as such is more or less eclipsed on this record by Murray's interaction with his guest musicians. On its own terms, it's a success. As a measure even of the recent, collaboratively minded World Saxophone Quartet, it's less than a complete success.

****** Selim Sivad: A Tribute To Miles Davis**

Justin Time JUST 119-2 *Hamiet Bluiett (bs, contra-acl); Oliver Lake (as, f); David Murray (ts, bcl); John Purcell (saxello, af); Jack DeJohnette (d, p); Okyerema Asante, Chief Bey, Titos Sompa (perc).* 98.

The curse of tribute albums – of which there are in any case too many – is a craven literalism, a wannabe mimicry of voices which were unique or idiosyncratic or plain perverse. True to form, the WSQ's take on Miles Davis's long and epochal career is cast very much in the band's own idiom. From the delicate lyricism of 'Blue In Green' to the abstract attack of 'Selim' from the violent, palindromic *Live/Evil*, Miles's music is comprehensively re-thought rather than merely pastiched. Some tunes are barely recognizable, a shift that suggests creative response rather than ineptitude. 'Freddie Freeloader' becomes a sardonic African dance; 'Nefertiti', always a test-piece, is handed to kalimba and flute while the other horns spar and dodge; even the late 'Tutu' is recast and put back in time as if it were a contrafact on some forgotten theme of the 1960s avant-garde. If the purpose of a tribute is to recognize the genius of a forerunner, *Selim Sivad* underlines the great genius of its dedicatee, but does something more. It takes and inverts Miles's ideas and makes them work in a musical environment far away from any the great man physically inhabited. The presence of DeJohnette is important. He helped shape the basic metres of this most unbasic of musics. He himself has moved on, but he has retained enough of his rough schooling to think himself back into that revolutionary mind-set. A brilliant, beautiful record.

John Wright

PIANO

Veteran Chicagoan pianist whose sequence of albums for Prestige in the early '60s were a modest blend of hard bop and gentle soul-jazz.

***** South Side Soul**

Original Jazz Classics OJC 1743 *Wright; Wendell Marshall (b); Walter McCants (d).* 8/60.

***** Mr Soul**

Original Jazz Classics OJC 1876 *Wright; Wendell Marshall (b); Walter Perkins Jr (d).* 4/62.

These are pleasant, almost harmless reminders of pianist John Wright whose Prestige albums once attracted a small following. There's little here that didn't emerge just as readily on records by Ahmad Jamal and Junior Mance, and Wright's deferential side – his ballads are carefully weighted and closer to Bill Evans than anything – has perhaps told against these discs reaching a wider audience in more recent years. The album titles and tunes of the order of 'Strut' are of their period, and one wonders what Wright felt about the bag he ended up in. He certainly finds the possibilities of 'What's New' (*Mr Soul*) at least as appealing as any down-home clichés. On their own terms, these are agreeable survivals.

Richard Wyands (born 1928)

PIANO

A failsafe sideman, Wyands has been in countless bands and on numberless records, always in an easy-going but authoritative bop orthodoxy. He very occasionally gets his own gig in the studios.

***** Then, Here And Now**
Storyville STCD 8269 *Wyands; Lisle Atkinson (b); David Lee (d).* 78.

***** Reunited**
Criss Cross 1105 *Wyands; Peter Washington (b); Kenny Washington (d).* 95.

***** Get Out Of Town**
Steeplechase SCCD 31401 *As above.* 10/96.

Wyands is an evergreen who seems to have been around for ever. Most jazz fans will have seen or heard him with one group or another, in mainstream or post-bop environments, and been thankful that such a witty and apposite player has been on hand in the rhythm section. That he had turned fifty before making a first record under his own name may suggest that leadership isn't Richard's forte. He is a bright, clear-voiced technician, but by no means a compelling soloist. Wyands is in the venerable tradition of Wynton Kelly, Bobby Timmons and Sonny Clark and so offers few surprises – more a quietly swinging satisfaction. The brickwork is solid enough; one simply waits and hopes for something a little more rough-hewn than his symmetrical, chord-based statements.

The two later records are full of good music, but both seem rather deliberate and pre-set. It seems that the debut session, originally released on Jazzcraft, was squeezed into a hefty gigging schedule. If so, Wyands and his fans are the gainers. He sounds relaxed, not note-perfect but in tune with both material and sidemen. 'Yesterdays' is the most inventive cut, and a good example of Wyands's witty rhythmic experiments. It's a shame that there isn't an alternative of this number, as there is of Duke's 'Blue Rose' and the Latin-tinged original 'Leonora'. J.J. Johnson's 'Lament' and the show tune, 'As Long As There's Music', are both given expressive readings.

Of the later records – and note the gap in chronology – the Criss Cross set is our marginal preference, with a more imaginative programme of tunes and a more concentrated approach. Whereas Atkinson and Lee provide not much more than four-square support on the Storyville, Washington and Washington are more inventive on their own account.

Albert Wynn (1907–73)

TROMBONE

Born in New Orleans, Wynn accrued a wide range of experience: touring with Ma Rainey, then various stints in St Louis, Europe (for four years), New York and Chicago. He settled there in the '40s and worked with various revivalist bands in the city until ill-health slowed him down in the '60s.

***** Albert Wynn And His Gutbucket Seven**
Original Jazz Classics OJC 1826 *Wynn; Bill Martin (t, v); Darnell Howard (cl); Buster Moten, Blind John Davis (p, v); Mike McKendrick (g, bj); Robert Wilson (b); Booker Washington (d).* 9/61.

Wynn is on a fair number of Chicago records from the 1920s, but he was something of a forgotten man by the time he made this entry in Riverside's *Living Legends* series. His solos are rather careful and circumspect, which leaves the main limelight to the formidable Howard, whose bustling work leans towards the gaspipe manner at some points but is undeniably exciting. Martin's rather mannered trumpet is a nice balance, and the only time-wasting is from bluesman Davis, whose two vocals are dispensable. Wilson and Washington keep unobtrusive time. A worthwhile survival.

Gail Wynters

VOCALS

Young American singer making her name debut.

***** My Shining Hour**
Naxos 86027-2 *Wynters; Gordon Brisker (ts, f); Bill Cunliffe (p); Joe Puma (g); Ed Howard (b); Danny D'Imperio (d).* 7/98.

Daughter of a Nazarene preacher who collected Billie Holiday and Art Tatum records, Wynters served her apprenticeship in a family radio show, singing country gospel and blues. It's a background still evident in her delivery of more secular and popular material. She has recorded before, but not in a straight jazz format.

Her strength is an ability to recast familiar song forms rather than acrobatic improvisation, though a couple of scat choruses on 'Blues My Naughty Sweetie Gave To Me' suggest she is more than capable of this as well. 'Every Time We Say Goodbye' is hardly recognizable and the title-track has undergone its own, rather subtler transformation. It's all done with impeccable musical judgement and the band, dominated by producer Brisker, gives sterling support.

The ballads are less convincing than the faster-tempo songs, and the closing 'The Right To Love', co-written by Lalo Schifrin and Gene Lees, exposes her limitations rather pointlessly. Future plans should, though, definitely include an encounter with another former child radio star, Charlie Haden, and a bag of Jeri Southern songs.

Sam Yahel (born 1971)

ORGAN

Young New York-based organist, blending classic and more contemporary Hammond styles.

***** Searchin'**
Naxos Jazz 86004 *Yahel; Ryan Kisor (t); Eric Alexander (ts); Peter Bernstein (g); Joe Strasser (d).* 4/96.

*****(*) Trio**
Criss Cross 1158 *Yahel; Peter Bernstein (g); Brian Blade (d).* 12/97.

After a globe-trotting youth, Yahel came to study in New York and quickly established a credible presence. He's sensibly gone for a mix of standards for this debut, opening with Duke's organ-friendly 'Searchin'', including the beautiful Jobim 'Double Rainbow' and restricting the originals to the middle reaches of the record. That being said, 'A Suspicious Love Affair' and 'Hymn For Her' are both superb creations, not too self-consciously idiomatic, and highlighting a technique that recalls Barbara Dennerlein without all her MIDI gizmos. The horns are reserved for four of the nine tracks, a nicely judged modulation of pace. As with the rest of the early Naxos releases, engineer David Baker and producer Mike Nock get a good sound.

Trio is an almost introspective matter as far as this brand of jazz goes. The opening 'Blues For Bulgaria' is a thoughtful modal line. Bobby Hutcherson's 'Isn't This My Music Around Me?' and Ray Brown's 'Gravy Waltz' are the choices of a thinking and hip mind. Yahel plays beautifully as both soloist and accompanist, working through many of the pieces in a continuous dialogue with Bernstein, while the superb Blade is all butterfly elegance and sharply accented energy around the two of them. Very good indeed.

Yosuke Yamashita

PIANO

Along with Jon Jang, Yamashita is the most significant pianist of Asian background since Toshiko Akiyoshi. His approach embraces classic piano jazz and elements of oriental harmony and rhythm. Very much a group player, he is not so much a powerful soloist as a gifted conceptualist who controls many parameters of the music.

*****(*) It Don't Mean A Thing**

DIW 810 *Yamashita (p solo).* 2/84.

An intriguing stylist with a highly individual take on the modern-jazz tradition, Yamashita has explored bop and swing staples like those on *It Don't Mean A Thing*, and classic ballads like 'Round Midnight', but he has also delved into the turbulent sound-world of Albert Ayler, in the company of his compatriot, Sakata. With a sharp but curiously delicate touch, Yamashita prefers to play in short, apparently discontinuous blocks of sound that often do not connect in accordance with accepted harmonic or even rhythmic logic. His piano–shakuhachi duets with Hozan Yamamoto (one of a group of deleted Enjas) are particularly unusual in their approach to rhythm, and it's often the flute that holds a basic pulse while Yamashita ranges more freely.

***** Asian Games**

Verve Forecast 518344-2 *Yamashita; Ryuchi Sakamoto, Nicky Skopelitis (ky); Bill Laswell (b); Aiyb Dieng (perc).* 88.

*****(*) Dazzling Days**

Verve 521303-2 *Yamashita; Joe Lovano (ts); Cecil McBee (b); Pheeroan akLaff (d).* 5/93.

The *Asian Games* sessions were released outside Japan somewhat belatedly in 1994. The music is a typically off-centre Bill Laswell production, with Yamashita enthusiastically centring the whirling textures and for once sounding like the straight man of the team. A notebook of ideas rather than a fully fledged album, perhaps, but some intriguing music comes out. The return match with Lovano and his New York band is another exciting encounter: nothing quite as outstanding as the title-track on *Kurdish Dance* maybe, but 'Dazzling Cradle' is pretty stunning, and the extraordinary treatment of 'My Grandfather's Clock' would make anyone sit up.

*****(*) Canvas In Quiet**

Verve 537007-2 *Yamashita (p solo).* 95.

***** Wind Of The Age**

Verve 557008-2 *Yamashita; Ravi Coltrane (ts, ss); Cecil McBee (b); Pheeroan akLaff (d).* 97.

The first is quintessential Yamashita, swinging but restrained, impressionistic, but also powerfully detailed. The solo album includes some moments which border on the classical, like the 'Divertimento in F minor', but this is a generous selection of miniatures and it is almost better to treat the set as if it were a continuous suite. Yamashita's touch is as precise and evocative as ever, and the recording brings out every nuance.

The most recent offers the enticing prospect of Ravi soloing on 'My Favorite Things'. Needless to say, he takes it at a very different pace and with a less urgent harmonic edge than his father but, curiously enough, it is no less estranging and powerful all these years on and done as mildly as this. Wisely, it's kept to the end of an otherwise quite straitlaced session which demands some closeness of attention but which really catches light only with the first of the two closing standards, 'My One And Only Love'.

***** Dr Kanzo**

Verve 849447-2 *Yamashita; Kioichi Matsukaze (f); Dairo Miyamoto (cl, bcl); Toshihiko Katori (vib); Hideaki Mochizuki (b); Shota Koyama (d); Tomohiro Yahiro (perc); Aska Kaneko (v).* 97.

A moody, often very effective, imaginary soundtrack that places the greatest emphasis on atmosphere and texture. The Japanese players are mostly unknown in the West, but they play with considerable authority. Not perhaps one of Yamashita's best or most idiomatic records, but an intriguing curiosity nevertheless.

Keith Yaun

GUITAR

Boston-based improviser and free-bopper.

*****(*) Countersink**

Leo Lab CD 047 *Yaun; Nathan Cook (ts); Mat Maneri (vn); John Lockwood (b); Johnny McLellan (d).* 1/98.

A seasoned veteran of the Boston improvising scene, Yaun is a thoughtful, precise player who seems to regard improvisation as a dialectical process, advancing ideas, flatly contradicting them and then patiently synthesizing the two into musical statements of real substance. On this debut recording, an apparently new band sounds as if it has been working together for some time.

Much of the music comes from drummer McLellan, whose 'Durt Kolphy' opens the record. This is inspired by Kurt Cobain and an idea of Eric Dolphy's. It's very quiet and focused music, dominated by Yaun's reflective solo and a rather more stressed statement by Mat Maneri. 'Loner Inches' is credited to the violinist but sounds very much like a collective improvisation and is the weakest thing on the record. The group seem to play better when anchored to something even fleeting, as it is on the very beautiful 'Heavy Hand Of Love', the longest track on the record and one of the most compelling performances we've heard in this vein for years.

Two versions of 'Runup' show the group in a more free-blowing, jazz-influenced vein, reflecting the record's steady move back towards jazz idiom. 'Collide' is a waltz that might have come from the pen of Max Roach on a quiet day; no surprise that McLellan is again the composer. Saxophonist Nathan Cook doesn't establish much of a presence until the latter part of the album, but it's easy to overlook his rather dry delivery. He often sounds as if he were playing a C-melody or some other non-canonical saxophone, but in terms of development he is close cousin to Anthony Braxton in his Warne Marsh mode. Lockwood is someone we have heard and been impressed by before. His contribution here is always significant, and agreeably understated.

John Young (born 1922)

PIANO

A great veteran of the local scene in Chicago for decades, John Young is an unfussy and genuine master of the post-bebop language. His few records are modest statements with no pretensions to anything beyond his own solid form.

***** Serenata**

Delmark DD 403 *Young; Victor Sproles (b); Phil Thomas (d).* 2/59.

A local legend in Chicago, where he has worked and played his whole life, John Young has done little to put his name in the history books or discographies. This short, enjoyable session – three alternative takes carry it just past the 40-minute mark – makes no case for immortality, but it is a fine example of how the music is succoured by the craftsmanship of such an accomplished player. Young hits a soulful groove on some tunes, abetted by the alert but quite spacious rhythms of Sproles and Thomas, and his naturally dancing, infectious manner has enough of the blues in it to make his swing and bebop stylings stay close to the tradition. 'Cubana Chant' is as good as any Ray Bryant or Red Garland fingersnapper, and the title-piece has an unfussy lyricism which is very attractive. Excellent remastering for CD issue.

Larry Young (1940–79)

ORGAN

Born in Newark, he studied piano and began on organ, at seventeen, in his father's nightclub. Associated with hard bop in the '60s, then with fusion (Lifetime); but he made little public headway and was marginalized at the time of his death, from pneumonia.

*****(*) Testifying**

Original Jazz Classics OJCCD 1793 *Young; Thornel Schwartz (g); Jimmie Smith (d).*

*****(*) Young Blues**

Original Jazz Classics OJCCD 1831 *As above, except add Wendell Marshall (b).* 9/60.

***** Groove Street**

Original Jazz Classics OJCCD 1853 *As above, except omit Marshall; add Bill Leslie (ts).* 2/62.

Larry Young – later known as Khalid Yasin – was the first Hammond player to shake off the pervasive influence of Jimmy Smith (not to be confused with Jimmie the drummer on the earlier of these records) and begin the assimilation of John Coltrane's harmonics to the disputed border territory between jazz and nascent rock.

Young was to achieve almost legendary status with bands like Lifetime and Love Cry Want, and on Miles Davis's electronic masterpiece, *Bitches Brew*. On all three, and on one-off sessions like John McLaughlin's *Devotion*, he traded on a wild, abstract expressionist approach, creating great billowing sheets of sound. It's unfortunate that much of what survives of his work outside these groups is a throwback to the organ–guitar–drums jazz he was leaving behind at the end of the 1960s. *Testifying* and *Young Blues* are both pretty callow, squarely in the Jimmy McGriff mould; Schwartz played with Jimmy for a time. Even so, both sets show a measure of the tonal sophistication Young was to display in later years. James Blood Ulmer fans would sense a kindred spirit on tracks like 'Exercise For Chihuahuas' and 'Some Thorny Blues' and the title-number on *Testifying*.

Groove Street is a broodingly funky organ/guitar/saxophone workout that manages to make some convincing changes on what might have been a drab and over-exploited formula. It certainly isn't the most subtle of records, but it has great strengths and is well worth hearing.

*****(*) Into Something!**

Blue Note 543276-2 *Young; Sam Rivers (ts); Grant Green (g); Elvin Jones (d).* 11/64.

♛ ** Unity**

Blue Note 56416-2 *Young; Woody Shaw (t); Joe Henderson (ts); Elvin Jones (d).* 11/65.

The earlier of this pair promises somewhat more than it delivers. Sam Rivers plays with concentrated brilliance without engaging the emotions and Green is a good deal drier than usual, perhaps to compensate for a more than usually high-temperature group. Young and Jones keep the temperature well up. All the compositions are by the organist, and 'Plaza De Toros' and 'Tyrone' offer a useful encapsulation of his polytonal approach.

Unity is a masterpiece, whipped along by Jones's ferocious drumming and Henderson's meaty tenor, even on a soft-pedal tune like 'Softly As In A Morning Sunrise'. Young contributes nothing as a writer, which doesn't in any way diminish the impact of his performance. Woody Shaw's 'The Moontrane', 'Zoltan' and 'Beyond All Limits' are a measure of *his* under-regarded significance as a composer; the first of the three is the perfect test of Young's absorption of Coltrane's ideas, as he develops a rather obvious (if precocious – Shaw wrote it when he was just eighteen) sequence of harmonics into something that represents a genuine extension of the great saxophonist, not just a bland repetition. This is a record that has proved hard to track down over the years. Of all our highest-rated albums, it has been one of the most elusive, despite the label and Young's relative eminence. Its inclusion in Blue Note's recent Rudy Van Gelder edition is testimony to two great men of music.

Lester Young (1909–59)

TENOR SAXOPHONE, CLARINET, VOCAL

A profoundly sensitive individual, in terms both of aesthetics and of a deep capacity for hurt, Pres – as Billie Holiday dubbed him – is one of the most influential saxophonists ever to play jazz. He marks a point of transition from swing to bebop. Borrowing something from Frankie Trumbauer, he first developed a style which was dry and cool and which changed dramatically after Young's traumatic time in the military which occasioned a serious breakdown. He grew up near New Orleans and played in a family setting, but left home to start a professional career with Art Bronson and then with Walter Page's Blue Devils. Count Basie recruited the 25-year-old but Young soon left and joined Fletcher Henderson's band, where his unorthodox approach, so very different from the Coleman Hawkins orthodoxy, led him to be ostracized. He was soon back with Basie and started to record under his own name and as an accompanist for Billie Holiday, to whom he was the perfect foil. His improvisations grew ever more elegantly structured, built up from short, slightly staccato phrases, but stretched out and ambiguous. The draft was a nightmare for Young, who was court-martialled for drug abuse. The man who emerged in 1945 was at least partly broken and became increasingly dependent on drink and narcotics; his tone coarsened and his solos became ever more formulaic as the legend of Pres grew. The late recordings, like Billie Holiday's, have their admirers, but they are a pale shadow of the pre-war Young.

***** Lester – Amadeus!**

Phontastic CD 7639 *Young; Buck Clayton, Ed Lewis, Bobby Moore, Harry 'Sweets' Edison, Carl Smith (t); George Hunt, Dan Minor, Dicky Wells, Benny Morton (tb); Earl Warren (as, bs); Herschel Evans (ts); Jack Washington (bs); Count Basie (p); Eddie Durham, Freddie Green (g); Walter Page (b); Jo Jones (d); Helen Humes (v).* 36–38.

*****(*) The 'Kansas City' Sessions**

Commodore CMD 14022 *Young; Buck Clayton, Bill Coleman (t); Dicky Wells (tb); Eddie Durham (tb, g); Joe Bushkin (p); Freddie Green (g, v); Walter Page, John Simmons (b); Jo Jones (d).* 3/38, 3/44.

For every ten jazz fans who can whistle 'Goodbye, Pork Pie Hat', there's probably only one who can claim any real knowledge of Lester Young's music. Universally acknowledged as a major influence on the bop and post-bop schools, Young's own output is neglected and frequently misunderstood. Serious appraisal of his work is complicated by an irreconcilable controversy about the quality of Young's post-war work.

Despite the title, all the *Kansas City Sessions* were recorded in New York City, but with the Kansas City Six and Five. It's possible to see these cuts, not just arithmetically, as a decade-later equivalent of Armstgrong's Hot Fives and Sevens. They are almost as important to the development of the music. Many of the alternative takes from the September 1938 session have been issued on Tax, and this compilation puts them together with the release versions; 'Way Down Yonder In New Orleans', 'I Want A Little Girl', 'Them There Eyes', 'Countless Blues' and 'Pagin' The Devil' are among his best. The Commodore sides illustrate the vast difference between Pres's style and Coleman Hawkins's. Pres's solo on 'Them There Eyes', both versions, has a forlorn and lonesome quality that overturns the original song's dynamic completely. The final four tracks on the sessions do not feature Young.

****** The Complete Aladdin Sessions**

Blue Note 32787 2CD *Young; Shorty McConnell, Howard McGhee (t); Vic Dickenson (tb); Willie Smith (as); Maxwell Davis (ts); Joe Albany, Jimmy Bunn, Nat Cole, Gene DiNovi, Wesley Jones, Dodo Marmarosa, Argonne Thornton (p); Irving Ashby, Nasir Baraakat, Dave Barbour, Fred Lacey, Chuck Wayne (g); Ted Briscoe, Red Callender, Curtis Counce, Rodney Richardson, Junior Rudd, Curley Russell (b); Chico Hamilton, Roy Haynes, Tiny Kahn, Lyndell Marshall, Johnny Otis, Henry Tucker (d).* 7/42–12/47.

*****(*) Lester Young, 1943–1946**

Classics 932 *Young; Harry 'Sweets' Edison, Al Killian, Joe Newman (t); Ted Donnelly, Dicky Wells, Eli Robinson, Lewis Taylor (tb); Jimmy Powell, Earl Warren (as); Buddy Tate (ts); Rudy Rutherford (bs); Count Basie, Johnny Guarnieri, Clyde Hart (p); Freddie Green (g); Rodney Richardson, Slam Stewart (b); Big Sid Catlett, Jo Jones, Shadow Wilson (d); other personnel as for Aladdin sessions above.* 12/43–1/46.

Listeners who have heard Young's classic solos – the 1936 'Lady Be Good' with Jo Jones and Carson Smith, 'Jumpin' At The Woodside' and the later 'Lester Leaps In' with Basie – will have to judge how much of a falling-off is evident in the material on the Savoy sessions, which are marked by flashes of brilliance but not distributed consistently enough. The truth is that Young's best work was nearly all done for others. The Aladdin sessions do, however, cover some of his best work as a leader, though even some of these are for another singer, Helen Humes. Young's cool, wry approach still seems slightly out of synch with prevailing expectations, though he is absolutely *simpatico* with Willie Smith, another figure now routinely overlooked in accounts of how jazz developed into its modern phase. The big pluses on this generously proportioned compilation are a rare glimpse of the 1942 Los Angeles session with Nat Cole and an instrumental 'Riffin' Without Helen', recorded as part of the Humes session, presumably while she was off powdering her nose. Michael Cuscuna has made his usual impeccable job of bringing the sound-quality up to speed for CD. Carefully declicked and with background noise reduced to a minimum, these two discs provide optimum listening.

Not so the Classics compilation, which covers at least some of the same territory and includes the same instrumental from the Humes session, of which Blue Note were making much; Anatol Schenker suggests that it was actually released in small numbers under the title 'It's Better To Give Than To Receive'. The December 1945 and January 1946 sessions overlap both formats, but the Classics set also includes the Savoy dates of April and May 1944, the former under Earl Warren's leadership, the latter a small group with the Count and the Basie band rhythm-section.

*****(*) Lester Young & The Piano Giants**
Verve 835316-2 *Young; Harry 'Sweets' Edison, Roy Eldridge (t); Vic Dickenson (tb); Nat Cole, Hank Jones, John Lewis, Oscar Peterson, Teddy Wilson (p); Herb Ellis, Freddie Green (g); Ray Brown, Gene Ramey, Joe Shulman (b); Bill Clark, Jo Jones, Buddy Rich (d).* 3/46–1/56.

***** Lester Young Trio**
Verve 521650-2 *Young; Harry 'Sweets' Edison (t); Dexter Gordon (ts); Nat Cole (p); Red Callender (b); Juicy Owens, Buddy Rich (d).* 43, 4/46.

***** Lester Young 1946–1947**
Classics 987 *Young; Shorty McConnell (t); Joe Albany, Nat Cole, Argonne Thornton (p); Irving Ashby, Fred Lacey (g); Red Callender, Rodney Richardson (b); Chico Hamilton, Lyndell Marshall, Buddy Rich (d).* 3/46–2/47.

***** Prez Conferences**
Jass J CD 18 *Young; Buck Clayton (t); Coleman Hawkins (ts); Mike Caluccio, Nat Cole, Kenny Kersey, Nat Pierce, Bill Potts, Sinclair Raney (p); Irving Ashby, Oscar Moore, Mary Osborne (g); Billy Hadnott, Johnny Miller, Gene Ramey, Doug Watkins, Norman Williams (b); Jim Lucht, Buddy Rich, Willie Jones, Specs Powell, Shadow Wilson (d).* 46–58.

***** Masters Of Jazz: Lester Young**
Storyville STCD 4107 *Young; Jesse Drakes, Idrees Sulieman (t); John Lewis, Bill Potts, Horace Silver (p); Aaron Bell, Gene Ramey, Franklin Skeete, Norman Williams (b); Jo Jones, Connie Kay, Abram Lee, Jim Lucht (d).* 5/51–12/56.

*****(*) The President Plays**
Verve 521451-2 *Young; Oscar Peterson (p); Barney Kessel (g); Ray Brown (b); J.C Heard (d).* 11/52.

***** Pres & Sweets**
Verve 849391-2 *Young; Harry 'Sweets' Edison (t); Oscar Peterson (p); Herb Ellis (g); Ray Brown (b); Buddy Rich (d).* 12/55.

***** Pres & Teddy**
Verve 831270-2 *Young; Teddy Wilson (p); Gene Ramey (b); Jo Jones (d).* 1/56.

Immediately after the war there was evidence of some of the less desirable traits that crept into his 1950s work (a formulaic repetition and a self-conscious and histrionic distortion of tone and phrasing akin to his friend Billie Holiday's around the same time); it's clear that he is trying to rethink harmonic progression. A new device, much noted, is his use of an arpeggiated tonic triad in first inversion (i.e. with the third rather than the root in lowest position) which, whatever its technical niceties, smoothed out chordal progression from ever shorter phrases. Some of that is evident in the 1946 trios with Rich and Cole, and on other augmented line-ups from that time. There are extra versions of 'Back To The Land' and 'I Cover The Waterfront', illustrating Pres's ability to reshape a theme and send it off in a new direction, while still using the same basic roster of melodic devices.

The 1952 session for Norman Granz (now believed to have been made in November, not in August) includes the slightly bizarre sound of Young lewdly singing the lyric to 'It Takes Two To Tango': 'Drop your drawers, take them off ...' It's a curiosity, but the rest of the session is very good indeed. The Verve compilation includes some excellent material, recorded in January 1956, with Roy Eldridge, another stylistic bridge-builder, and Teddy Wilson, together with a 1950 version of 'Up'N'Adam' with Hank Jones. The Nat Cole material is available separately on the *Trio* album.

***** Lester Young In Washington, D.C. 1956: Volume 1**
Original Jazz Classics OJC 782 *Young; Bill Potts (p); Norman Williams (b); Jim Lucht (d).* 12/56.

***** Lester Young In Washington, D.C. 1956: Volume 2**
Original Jazz Classics OJCCD 881 *As above.* 12/56.

***** Lester Young In Washington, D.C. 1956: Volume 3**
Original Jazz Classics OJCCD 901 *As above.* 12/56.

***** Lester Young In Washington, D.C. 1956: Volume 4**
Original Jazz Classics OJCCD 1043 *As above.* 12/56.

****(*) Lester Young In Washington, D.C. 1956: Volume 5**
Original Jazz Classics OJCCD 1051 *As above.* 12/56.

***** The Best Of Lester Young**
Pablo 2405420 *As above.*

The 1956 OJCs further confound the notion of a man who had given up on life and art; though drastically reconceived and hardly abetted by Potts's backward-looking accompaniments (it was often Prez's sidemen who wanted to play in the 'old style' about which he became so painfully ambivalent), 'Lester Leaps In' and 'These Foolish Things' (both on the better Volume 2) are major jazz performances. Right to the very end Young was capable of quite extraordinary things. 'There Will Never Be Another You', with Kenny Clarke, Jimmy Gourley, Harold Kauffman and Jean-Marie Ingrand (with one exception, not the company he deserved) was recorded within a fortnight of his death and still sounds vital, moving and full of musical intelligence.

Young's later years have been unhelpfully coloured by too many sorry anecdotes (about his drinking, world-weariness, and increasingly restricted conversational code) and, more recently, by Bertrand Tavernier's composite anti-hero, Dale Turner, in *Round Midnight*, a character who is truer in spirit to the declining Bud Powell. Powell felt safe in the past and retreated into recreations of his best work. Throughout his life, Young had been brutally cut off from his own past; by its end the only direction he knew was uneasily forward.

*****(*) The Ultimate Lester Young**
Verve 539772-2 *As for Verve recordings above.* 44–55.

Another in Polygram's insightful series in which younger-generation musicians – in this case, Wayne Shorter – select material by their artistic forebears. Wayne suggests that it was Pres's tragedy that after the war he wasn't given much opportunity to play with younger musicians of a more advanced disposition. The strong implication is that the modernist hints and foreshadows which can be heard in his phrasing and his harmonics throughout this thoroughly enjoyable compilation might have flowered into something new and different. We are inclined to think that this was wishful thinking. Lester was a pretty broken man in terms of straightforward physical health, and he was certainly not agile enough to cope with much in the way of mental gymnastics.

***** Jazz Masters 30**
Verve 521859-2 *Young; Nat Cole, Hank Jones, John Lewis, Oscar Peterson, Teddy Wilson (p); Barney Kessel (g); Ray Brown, Gene*

Ramey, Slam Stewart (b); Big Sid Catlett, J.C Heard, Jo Jones, Buddy Rich (d). 43–56.

A very good introduction to Young's later work, faithfully and pleasingly remastered. The *Ultimate* collection is probably our favourite of the two and, given that there is a significant overlap, it is the one to opt for.

****(*) Laughin' To Keep From Cryin'**

Verve 543301-2 *Young; Harry 'Sweets' Edison, Roy Eldridge (t); Hank Jones (p); Herb Ellis (g); George Duvivier (b); Mickey Sheene (d).* 2/58.

Late in the day and a desperately tired act. There are moments, as when Pres switches to clarinet for 'Salute To Benny' and 'They Can't Take That Away From Me', when the music is as vivid and logical as one might hope but for the most part this is a drab curtain-call, and Young doesn't even appear on all the tracks, sitting out the first part of the 'Ballad Medley', which he finishes with the trio on 'Blue And Sentimental'. The remastering is very good, and something of the smothered passion of Pres's late recording does come across.

***** The Complete Lester Young Studio Sessions On Verve**

Verve 547087-2 8CD *Young; Harry Edison, Jesse Drakes, Roy Eldridge (t); Vic Dickenson (tb); Nat Cole, John Lewis, Oscar Peterson, Teddy Wilson, Gildo Mahones, Lou Stein, Hank Jones, Rene Urtreger (p); Barney Kessel, Herb Ellis, Freddie Green, Jimmy Gourley (g); Joe Shulman, Ray Brown, Gene Ramey, John Ore, George Duvivier, Jamil Nasser (b); Jo Jones, Bill Clark, Buddy Rich, J.C Heard, Connie Kay, Louie Bellson, Mickey Sheen, Kenny Clarke (d).* 3/46–3/59.

Here finally are Lester Young's closing years in all the close-up detail befitting such an important musician. Even as vinyl, these dates were scattered across many albums – the booklet reproduces no fewer than 21 different 'original' LP sleeves – and several of the tracks have been unavailable in any form for many years. A lot of it is, by the standards of most jazz, wretched music. All too often in these dates its principal is playing so poorly, with such lack of control, that if newcomers were to hear Young for the first time, in these dates, they would be astonished that he is as revered as he is. Some of the eight discs can be virtually written off altogether as pleasurable listening experiences. Others expose Young as a hollow, crippled voice surrounded by sympathetic but bewildered contemporaries, gamely trying either to hold him up or to cover him up with their own playing. The final session here, recorded in Paris in March 1959, finds Young so enfeebled that he can barely get the notes out of the horn, and to listen to this as entertainment is a stretch which we would rather not extend to.

Young's Verve story, as suggested already, is a lot more complex than mere inexorable decline. The first seven sessions are all tenor-plus-rhythm with, in succession, Nat Cole, Hank Jones, John Lewis and Oscar Peterson. The material is blues, a few workouts on familiar chords, and standards, some of them rather surprising choices. None of the performances is bad, and Young contributes something fine to each of them – an unpredictable curlicue, a pale flurry of melody, a bashful beeping on a single note. Yet, at the same time, there is something wrong with all of them. Sometimes a solo will seem ready to fold up and die, and he will have to pull it round at the last moment. Other passages find him strong and hale, only to tamely crack a note or suddenly stumble, a beach jogger tripping over driftwood. It wouldn't matter so much if it happened only here and there – but it happens on every tune, to some degree.

The exceptionally handsome booklet quotes a remark made by Coleman Hawkins, the earth to Lester's air sign: 'That Lester Young, how does he get away with it? He's stoned half the time, he's always late, and he can't play.' It was and it wasn't true.

Aziza Mustafa Zadeh (born 1969)

PIANO, VOCALS, PERCUSSION

Classically trained, this remarkable performer is the daughter of a leading Azeri composer and pianist and of a singing mother. Now settled in Germany, she works an idiosyncratic territory bounded – like Azerbaijan itself – with competing stylistic influences.

*****(*) Aziza Mustafa Zadeh**

Columbia 828622 *Zadeh (p, v solo).* 91.

***** Always**

Columbia 388521 *Zadeh; John Patitucci (b); Dave Weckl (d).* 93.

****(*) Dance Of Fire**

Columbia 035226 *Zadeh; Bill Evans (ss, ts); Kai E. Karpeh Camargo, Stanley Clarke (b); Omar Hakim (d).* 95.

***** Seventh Truth**

Columbia 423825 *Zadeh; Ludwig Jantzer (d); Ramesh Shotham (perc).* 96.

*****(*) Jazziza**

Columbia 789723 *Zadeh; Toots Thielemans (hca); Philip Catherine (g); Eduardo Contrera (perc).* 97.

Given what has happened in jazz in recent years, no one should betray too much surprise at the idea of an Azeri scat singer, or a pianist who combines Bill Evans with the musics of central Siberia. It would be easy to write Aziza Mustafa Zadeh off as a well-packaged beauty with an interesting musical gimmick; easy, but almost criminally misleading. She is a prodigally talented musician with deep roots in both jazz and classical music and able to draw confidently on other traditions as well. Her place in music was perhaps guaranteed when her father, the distinguished Vagif Mustafa-Zade, won the 1979 Monaco jazz competition with a piece called 'Expecting Aziza'.

It is equally misleading to speculate how she might handle a set of jazz standards, for this isn't where she is coming from at all. Zadeh's great skill, evident from the first album and ever more secure in its successors, is an ability to make asymmetrical themes and awkward vocal transactions swing like nobody's business, unless the name of your business is Shirley Horn plc. She has something of Shirley's piano touch and a good deal of her worldly-wise approach to singing, but with a freshness that manages to speak of wide-open steppes rather than crowded stoops.

The first album arrived with something of a splash, a very intimate and personal showcase, nicely balanced between piano playing and singing. The trio assembled for the follow-up could hardly have been more sympathetic, though some signs of

Zadeh's enthusiasm for fusion and jazz-rock rhythms creeps through when Patitucci switches to his six-string electric bass. This becomes the dominant strain on the next record – which, to our way of thinking, is the least original, albeit the most immediately arresting of the bunch. Unusual to hear Zadeh with a horn in the group, and not entirely a satisfactory balance of voices. There are, though, some very good songs on the record, most obviously the long 'Bana Bana Gel' and 'Spanish Picture', which are the most extended improvisations yet heard in her recorded output at least.

Seventh Truth and *Jazziza* represent something of a return to the delicate lyricism of the first album. Thielemans and Catherine are both exquisite players and find much to intrigue them in Zadeh's writing. Both concentrate on atmospherics, leaving the composer to develop her lines. The 1996 record incorporates Indian percussion seamlessly and with great taste, and it suggests that Zadeh has been studying subcontinental musics for some time, in addition to her other interests. Every sign that, having established and consolidated her strengths as a writer, Zadeh is now prepared to tackle jazz repertoire. *Jazziza* includes fine versions of 'Lover Man', 'Scrapple From The Apple', 'You've Changed', a very good 'Take Five' and an exceptional version of 'My Funny Valentine'. Expect more in this vein from a very gifted artist whose jazz credentials are now unimpeachable.

Bobby Zankel

ALTO SAXOPHONE

Based in Philadelphia, Zankel is a saxophonist and composer working in an area that moved between post-bop and a conservative kind of free playing.

***** Seeking Spirit**

Cadence CJR 1050 *Zankel; Stan Slotter (t, f); Johnny Coles (t); Odean Pope (ts); Ray Wright (bs); Sumi Tonooka, Uri Caine (p); Tyrone Brown (b); Craig McIver, David Gibson (d).* 3/91–1/92.

****(*) Emerging From The Earth**

Cadence CJR 1059 *As above, except add John Blake (vn), Ralph Peterson Jr (d), Ron Howerton (perc); omit Coles, Pope, Wright, Tonooka, McIver, Gibson.* 3/94.

****(*) Human Flowers**

CIMP 103 *Zankel; Marilyn Crispell (p); Newman Baker (d).* 11/95.

Zankel seems like a talented player-composer, and it's a pity that his debut album is let down by some unwarranted flaws. The record is evenly split between sessions for quartet and octet: the former blaze along on the back of Gibson's explosive drumming, and some clever touches in the writing – the layered rhythms of 'Something Up Her Sleeve', for instance – help to concentrate the intensity of the playing. The five octet pieces are a shade more ambitious, but the sometimes ragged ensembles distract from thoughtful improvising by Pope, Coles and Tonooka. The leader's own alto works off a strangulated tone and impassioned delivery, but he's badly served by the production, which should have him much nearer the front.

Emerging From The Earth is an ambitious continuation, involving the septet in all eight pieces, but again there are disappointing aspects. Even as Zankel crowds his compositions with incident, the sound of the group seems awry – Blake's violin doesn't really fit in, and some of the ensembles demand a coherence that eludes them – while the sound is again a drawback: too often the instruments sound like a muddle, and the rhythm section in particular is made to seem chaotic by the mix.

The trio session, *Human Flowers*, is entirely different. Performed as a continuous three-way conversation, with few changes in dynamics, this is rather wearying stuff over the long haul, and when Zankel's ingenuities are tested to the full he comes up a bit short at times. The CIMP philosophy of releasing unmixed live digital sound doesn't work very well here: piano and drums both sound too thin to give the music sufficient impact.

Joe Zawinul (born 1932)

PIANO, KEYBOARDS

Born in Vienna, he studied at the Conservatory there prior to wartime evacuation. Became interested in jazz and eventually went to the USA on a Berklee scholarship. Played for Dinah Washington, then with Cannonball Adderley for the rest of the '60s. Then with Miles Davis, subsequently forming the hugely successful Weather Report with Wayne Shorter and Miroslav Vitous, eventually disbanded in 1986. Later projects have been mixed successes, but he remains a major composer and few have been as creatively successful with electric keyboards.

***** And The Austrian All Stars / His Majesty Swinging Nephews, 1954–1957**

RST 91549 *Zawinul; Dick Murphy (t); Hans Salomon (as, ts); Karl Drewo (ts); Johnny Fischer, Rudolf Hansen (b); Victor Plasil (d).* 10/54–3/57.

***** The Beginning**

Fresh Sound FSRCD 142 *Zawinul; George Tucker (b); Frankie Dunlop (d); Ray Barretto (perc).* 9/59.

Creator of some of the classic jazz tunes of the last 40 years, from 'Mercy Mercy Mercy' and 'Country Preacher' to 'Birdland' and beyond, Joe Zawinul has managed to place himself where the action is since he arrived in the United States in 1959. These records straddle that moment of fruitful exile. In Austria, the young conservatory-trained pianist had worked with the legendary Friedrich Gulda, but he had also been involved with a number of inventive small groups who represented the accelerated development of jazz during the deNazification period. The RST disc covers what was probably the most advanced group in Austria at the time, formed in 1954 and sounding pretty much on a par with any similarly-aged and -inclined group from the United States. Originally recorded for Turicaphon's Elite Special label, it's a fascinating session for a first glimpse of Zawinul as jazz composer. Even this early, 'Mekka' is unmistakably his, a forceful pounding left hand holding the ideas together, exotic intervals and resolutions consigned to the top line. Elsewhere, Zawinul takes the least likely harmonic path, occasionally leaving the otherwise excellent Salomon and the less adroit Drewo at the starting gate.

By 1957, a trio with Fischer and Plasil, it's clear that he needs broader horizons for his playing. The move to America seemed inevitable. There, he gigged with Maynard Ferguson and Dinah Washington before falling in with Adderley and making a record, still to be found in the second-hand trays, with Ben Webster. The Fresh Sound – misleadingly titled, unless one chooses to think of the move Stateside as the start of his 'real' career – was made very soon after his arrival, testimony to the substantial word-of-mouth reputation Zawinul acquired on an already overcrowded scene. In what was then, mercifully, not the parlance, he really goes for it, obviously trying to make an impact with a set of lyrical standards. Given the instincts of Tucker and Dunlop, the pace is medium to up, but there are affecting ballad performances as well: 'My One And Only Love' is beautiful, only slightly marred by Barretto's intrusive percussion. These records shouldn't be overvalued. To a degree, they are curiosities, because they pose the question as to how a young man from the city of serialism and the waltz acquired sufficient jazz know-how to make himself indispensable to Cannonball Adderley, catch the eye of Ben Webster and, later, Miles Davis, and go on to found one of the most successful fusion groups ever.

*** The Rise And Fall Of The Third Stream / Money In The Pocket

Rhino R2 71675 *Zawinul; Blue Mitchell, Jimmy Owens (t); William Fischer, Joe Henderson, Clifford Jordan (ts); Pepper Adams (bs); Bob Cranshaw, Richard Davis, Sam Jones (b); Louis Hayes, Roy McCurdy, Freddie Waits (d); Warren Smith (perc); Alfred Brown, Selwart Clarke, Theodore Israel (vla); Kermit Moore (clo).* 4/66–12/67.

In 1967 the fusion revolution, in which Zawinul was to have a significant part, was still a year or two away. These two records are pretty much of their time, a mixture of funky soul-jazz on the earlier *Money* and then-fashionable classical/non-European crossovers on the '67 sessions. 'Third Stream' seems less risibly distant now than it once did and it was a movement that perfectly suited someone of Zawinul's background. The very opening track, 'Baptismal', underlines one very legitimate objection. A brooding cello solo with viola just behind (anticipating the tonality of later work like 'His Last Journey' on *Zawinul*) gives way to a medium-pace jazz tune which bears only the slightest relation to the introduction. The setting of the two-part 'Soul Of A Village' would seem, on the face of it, to be far to the east of the Tyrol (China, possibly), and the embellishments are a little intrusive. These are not Zawinul compositions; with the exception of 'From Vienna, With Love', everything is credited to William Fischer. (We take leave to doubt this; though Fischer certainly did the arrangements, surely at least some of these ideas are Zawinul's? If not, the resemblance is uncanny.)

The jazzier *Money* session is nicely done. Joel Dorn's hand at the controls was a guarantee of quality at this time and, while he sounds a bit heavy-handed when balancing the strings on *Third Stream*, the horn arrangements on the remaining tracks are brightly registered, with lots of room for Adams's rich tone and a clear vantage for the neglected Mitchell. Zawinul here shares the credits with Henderson (the thoughtful 'If') and two tunes by another musician who always gets the foundations right before he does the curlicues, bassist Sam Jones. It isn't a classic session, but whenever the horns give ground to Zawinul and the rhythm section, as on the closing 'Del Sasser', his playing is absolutely riveting.

**** Zawinul

Atlantic 7567 81375 *Zawinul; Jimmy Owens, Woody Shaw (t); Wayne Shorter, Earl Turbinton (ss); George Davis, Hubert Laws (f); Herbie Hancock (p); Walter Booker, Miroslav Vitous (b); Joe Chambers, Billy Hart, David Lee (d); Jack DeJohnette (hca, perc).* 70.

The eponymous Atlantic with its haunting sepia cover, a huge close-up of Zawinul's sombre face, was made the year that Weather Report was formed and a year after Zawinul took part in Miles Davis's epochal – or at very least transitional – *In A Silent Way*, for which the Austrian wrote the title-track, also included here. *Zawinul* is a lovely, lovely record. Somewhat pretentiously titled 'music for two electric pianos, jazz flute, trumpet, soprano saxophone, two contrabasses and percussion', it nods backwards in the direction of his conservatory past almost as much as it anticipates the coming experiments in fusion music. Woody Shaw's echoplexed trumpet strongly recalls Miles (who writes the liner-note) but with Vitous handling one of the bass parts and Shorter replacing the little-known Turbinton on 'Double Image', the original Weather Report is already in place. *I Sing The Body Electric*, the group's second disc, was to include a live-in-Japan version of 'Doctor Honoris Causa', a tribute to Zawinul's keyboard twin, Herbie Hancock. Here it gets a much more measured reading, less frenetic and intense, more floating and indefinite, as in 'His Last Journey', where the electric piano's ability to imitate tolling bells (another Weather Report favourite) is exploited to great effect. Not just because Shorter is present, 'Double Image' is the track that most clearly points forward. The brief 'Arrival In New York' is an aural impression of the immigrant wharves; not far removed from Mingus's 'Foggy Day' on *Pithecanthropus Erectus*, it underlines how important sheer sound was to Zawinul and his group. There is nothing here as completely abstract as on the first two Weather Report records, and there is much that harks back to the gospelly funk of his days with Cannonball. Even so, it is a disc that looks forward more securely than back.

**(*) Dialects

Columbia 489774 *Zawinul (ky solo).* 86.

For almost all of the 15 years from 1970 to 1985, Zawinul's attention was taken up with Weather Report. There were no side-projects of any note, and it was assumed that as chief writer and, with Shorter, only consistent member, the band reflected his musical interests pretty closely. As soon as the band folded, though, Zawinul seemed to take off on a new initiative that would take him ever further in the direction of world music. No personnel are listed for *Dialects*, his most developed exercise in multi-tracked, sample-based music, and probably the furthest he would go from his jazz roots. Some of the effects are anticipated on tracks like 'Nubian Sundance', the lead-off item on Weather Report's *Mysterious Traveller*, with shouting voices, rumbling percussion effects and a throbbing *moiré* of keyboard sounds. Nothing on this album has anything like that verve and exuberance, though. Much of it is weakly pedestrian and overwrought, hung up on effects rather than focused on musical performance. The old gift for powerful bass-lines is still there, but one looks for more.

*****(*) Black Water**

Columbia 465344 *Zawinul; Anthony Zawinul (ky, v); Scott Henderson (g); Gerald Veasley (b, v); Cornell Rochester (d); Munyungo Jackson (perc); Lynne Fidmont-Linsey (v, perc); Carl Anderson, Kevin Dorsey, Dorian Holly, Fred White (v).* 89.

Attributed to The Zawinul Syndicate, which was the working band title of the time, this is a much better record than *Dialects* because it sounds like real-time playing again. Veasley (who also does the narrations) and Rochester create a powerful beat that is worthy of any of the Weather Report incarnations, and Henderson's guitar and slide guitar, though never a component of the WR sound, have a similar logic. A vocal version of 'Monk's Mood', with a lyric by the bassist, and an instrumental version of 'Little Rootie Tootie' don't quite come off, but it's interesting to hear Zawinul turn to such themes at this stage in his career and in this way. 'Familial' is an imaginative version of a Jacques Prévert poem, the sort of thing Jacques Brel might have done had he moved to America. The family connection is maintained by handing young Anthony Zawinul the microphone for his own 'And So It Goes', a solo spot for the new generation that promises more than it delivers. The key track, in both vocal and musical terms, is the title-piece, a very strong idea which seems to refer to the Weather Report of *Heavy Weather* vintage, though how much of this is mere coincidence of theme remains difficult to gauge. 'They Had A Dream' is a moving dedication to Martin Luther King Jr, Malcolm X and Mahatma Gandhi, strange bedfellows and a curious combination of musical styles, but very effective and genuinely moving.

(***) Stories Of The Danube

Philips 454 143 *Zawinul; Amit Chatterjee (g, v); Burhan Ocal (oud, v, perc); Walter Grassman (d); Arto Tuncboyaciyan (perc, v); Czech State Philharmonic Orchestra, Brno; Caspar Richter (cond).* 11/95.

Billed as Zawinul's first symphony, this majestically proportioned progress from source to sea and through several centuries of bloody but replenishing history is certainly not a jazz record, nor is it intended to be. Zawinul's long-standing interest in orchestral writing and in finding neutral ground between improvisation and composition is well served, but the music fails to catch light. There are moments in 'Gipsy', which comes at the very heart of the piece, the middle one of its seven movements, when it all starts to make sense, but the pace is ponderous and the orchestrations far from convincing. 'Unknown Soldier' is very different from the haunting track on Weather Report's *I Sing The Body Electric*, and this is perhaps the best point of comparison with past work. Spectacularly mounted as a live piece, it may well have been impressive. As a recorded work, it simply fails to convince.

**** My People**

Escapade 03651 *Zawinul; Mike Mossman (t, tb); Bobby Malach (sax); Amit Chatterjee, Osmane Kouka, Gary Poulson (g); Burhan Ocal (oud); Richard Bona (b); Tal Bergmann (d, perc); Alex Acuna, Souleyman Doumbia, Trilok Gurtu, Michito Sanchez (perc); Lucho Avelleneda, Bolot, Assitan Dembele, Djeme Doumboouya, Duke Ellington, Salif Keita, Kenny O'Brien, Beto Sabala, Thomas Sanchez (v); Arto Tuncboyaciyan (v, perc).* 96.

Zawinul claims Czech, Hungarian and Sinti ancestry, and this is his attempt to create a personalized world music by bringing together as many different musical traditions as possible and watching them spark each other off. Except that they don't, leaving a drab residue of common riffs, rhythms and disharmonies. A hugely disappointing record.

***** World Tour**

ESC Records ESC/EFA 03656 2CD *Zawinul; Gary Poulson (g); Richard Bona, Victor Bailey (b); Paco Sery (d, kalimba, v); Manolo Badrena (perc, v, nolopipe); Frank Hoffman, Pape Abdou Sech (v).* 5–11/97.

Joe! Call home! Between 29 January and 14 December 1997, the Zawinul Syndicate played 126 concerts, 24 in October alone. Even by the overblown standards of stadium mega-rock, this is a pretty heroic endeavour. Sadly, the music documented is rarely more than mildly involving, a mixture of stretched-out world music jams and tighter song-forms. The best of the material, 'Lost Tribes' on disc two, the long 'Indiscretions' and the opening 'Patriots' on disc one, are close enough to Weather Report grooves to draw in the old fans. Much of the rest, though, falls into a rather bland and formulaic delivery which must have become ever more deeply entrenched as the caravan moved on. The live mixes are generally very good, though often percussion is allowed to dominate. Richard Bona is a less jazz-orientated bassist than Victor Bailey, but in a perverse way he fits more comfortably into the mix. Badrena is a star and occasionally outstars Zawinul himself, but this is unquestionably Joe's concept and the main man's gig.

Denny Zeitlin (born 1938)

PIANO

Studied with George Russell and has since operated parallel careers in jazz and psychiatry, though the latter seems to be the more dominant side of his work of late.

*****(*) Time Remembers Time Once**

ECM 837020-2 *Zeitlin; Charlie Haden (b).* 7/81.

*****(*) At Maybeck: Volume 27**

Concord CCD 4572 *Zeitlin (solo).* 10/92.

****** Denny Zeitlin / David Friesen: Concord Duo Series – Volume 8**

Concord CCD 4639 *Zeitlin; David Friesen (b).* 6/94.

Zeitlin is one of a select number of jazz musicians who have combined playing with a career in medicine or, in his case, psychiatry. While a student at Columbia University, he was signed by the legendary talent-spotter John Hammond and recorded a number of albums, including the excellent *Zeitgeist*, which showed off his ability to marry free improvisation with a strong sense of musical structure. Ironically, he's probably better known by film-music buffs (largely for a soundtrack to the remake of *Invasion of the Body Snatchers*) than by jazz fans. It's curious, too, given his undoubted facility as a composer, that he usually prefers to play standards. The Maybeck recital numbers just two originals in a dozen tracks, the opening 'Blues On The Side' and 'Country Fair'; good examples, though, in that they point to his ability to put seemingly inimical materials side by side and harmonize them in great rushes of sound. Even his version of 'Round Midnight' is markedly different from the norm, no longer a late-evening ballad heard, but a slightly austere and disciplined statement more suited to one of the more rigorous hours in the monastic day. 'My Man's Gone Now' has an almost tragic dimension while the medley of 'What Is This Thing Called Love?' and Coltrane's 'Fifth House' suggests a two-part classical structure pushed towards what Zeitlin likes to describe as the 'merger state', where piano, music, player, audience and performing space are almost indistinguishable one from the other. If that suggests Zeitlin is happiest in solo performance, he has also produced some wonderful small-group and duo work, notably with David Friesen. The set with Charlie Haden is also dominated by other composers' work – Cole Porter, Luiz Eca, Coltrane, Ornette, as well as Haden, and two standards, 'As Long As There's Music' and 'How High The Moon', the latter wittily segued on to Trane's 'Satellite'. The title-piece is in Zeitlin's robust philosophical voice, a piece too secure in itself to be labelled an exercise in nostalgia but one that certainly harks back to an earlier age.

The Maybeck duo with Friesen is a *tour de force*. His own 'Echo Of A Kiss' seems to be a distant relative of 'Prelude To a Kiss', its chords turned inside out, the stilled moment of expectation turned around by experience. He also includes another Ornette tune, 'Turnaround', which oddly enough also featured on Hampton Hawes's duo record with Charlie Haden. The key track here is 'The Night Has A Thousand Eyes'. It starts straightforwardly enough, nudging around the familiar melody, before opening up into a free meditation, driven along by Friesen's strummed chords and huge, revving sounds on the lower strings. The bassist distinguishes himself again on the final track, his own 'Signs & Wonders', and certainly establishes his ownership of the music as a whole.

Hannes Zerbe (born 1941)

PIANO

Dutch pianist who has led his Brass Band since 1979.

***** Rondo A La Fried**

Bvhaast CD 9207 *Zerbe; Jochen Gleichmann (t, flhn); Andreas Altenfelder, Harry Kuhn (t); Jorg Huke (tb); Gundolf Nandico, Wolfgang Stahl (frhn); Jurgen Kupke (cl); Willem Breuker (ss, as, bs, bcl); Manfred Hering (as); Helmut Forsthoff (ts); Gerhard Kubach (b); Wolfram Dix (d).* 3/92.

A rare sighting on record for Zerbe's group. Although they start with a piece by Eisler, the bulk of the disc features Zerbe's naggingly memorable title-piece, setting a poem by Erich Fried, and the 'Suite In Sieben Sätzen Aus Konig K', which starts with an oom-pah march and goes through progressive disintegrations. The music stands squarely in the Euro improv tradition – beer-hall music laced with composerly flourishes, goosed up with a free-form freak-out here and there – which makes Breuker's sponsorship (and guest appearance) logical. But it's all done with great gusto, and there is some terrific playing, though the sound-mix is rather harsh on the brass. Disappointingly, no follow-up so far.

Monica Zetterlund (born 1938)

VOCAL, PIANO

The leading jazz singer from Sweden – and, arguably, all of Scandinavia – Zetterlund made her first demos in 1957 and was dubbed the 'Swedish Sensation' by her first LP. Although she subsequently made some more pop-flavoured records and has followed a successful second career as an actress, she remains a jazz artist and continues to record with the Swedish jazz élite of several generations.

****** Swedish Sensation! The Complete Columbia Recordings, 1958–60**

EMI 475061-2 (Swed) 2CD *Zetterlund; Bengt-Arne Wallin, Allan Botschinsky, Pelle Bolvig, Erik Larsen, Jorgen Moller, Benny Bailey, Bernth Gustavsson, Gosta Nilsson, Donald Byrd, Sixten Erikkson, Weine Renliden, Arnold Johansson, Jan Allan (t); Ake Bjorkman (flhn); Ake Persson, Willy Clausen, John Lind, Bent Ronak, Kurt Jarnberg, Andreas Skjold, George Vernon, Jorgen Johansson, Gordon Ohlsson, Gunnar Medberg, Folke Rabe (tb); Arne Domnérus, Johannes Jorgenson, Uffe Karskov, Rolf Backman, Rolf Billberg (as); Rolf Blomqvist, Karl Leukowitz, Poul Moller, Georg Bjorklund, Johnny Ekh, Bjarne Nerem, Lennart Jansson, Carl-Henrik Noren (ts); Rune Falk (bs, bcl); Lars Gullin, Stig Gabrielsson, Gunnar Larsen (bs); Gunnar Svensson, Atli Bjorn, Lars Bagge, Bengt Hallberg, Thore Swanerud, Rolf Larsson (p); Christer Jagerhult (cel); Rune Gustaffsson, Bengt Hogberg (g); Georg Riedel, Finn Ziegler, Dan Jacobsen, Lars Pettersson, Arne Wilhelmsson, Gunnar Almstedt, Claes Rindroth (b); Joe Harris, William Schiopffe, Pedro Biker, Sture Kallin, Egil Johansen, Jack Noren (d); strings.*

****(*) Nu Ar Det Skont Att Leva**

EMI 136449-2 (Swed) *Zetterlund: Maffy Falay, Bernth Gustavsson, Weine Renliden, Jan Allan, Americo Bellotto, Gunnar Gunrup, Luciano Mosetti (t); Olle Holmqvist, Lars Olofsson, Torgny Nilsson, Bengt Edwardsson (tb); Sven Larsson (btb, tba); Christer Torge (btb); Solve Klingstedt, Hans Bergman, Olle Schill, Kjell-Inge Stevensson, Lars Ahman (cl); Leif Hellmann (as); Bjarne Nerem (ts); Erik Nilsson, Lars Gullin (bs); Ulf Bergstrom, Yngve Sandstrom, Jan Kling, Christer Persson, Jerker Hallden (f); Monica Dominique (p, org); Lasse Bagge (p, cel); Carl-Axel Dominique (vib); George Wadenius, Rune Gustafsson, Lennart Nyhlen (g); Palle Danielsson, Bosse Hagstrom, Sture Akerberg (b); Tommy Slim Borgudd, Egil Johansen, Johan Dielemans (d).* 71–75.

***** For Lester And Billie**

Phontastic PHONTCD 7562 *Zetterlund; Nisse Sandstrom (ts); Horace Parlan (p); Red Mitchell (b).* 8/83–1/84.

***** Topaz**

RCA 74321 164752 (Swed) *Zetterlund: Jan Allan (t); Bernt Rosengren (ts); Toots Thielemans (hmca); Lasse Bagge, Stefan Nilsson, Tommy Lydell (ky); Johan Norberg, Peter Ericson (g); Hasse Larsson, Sture Akerberg (b); Christer Jansson, Johan Dielemans (d); Titiyo Jah, Henry Gibson (perc).* 93.

There is now a decent representation of this coolest of cool stylists on CD – though, since these are all Swedish releases, it will take readers outside that country a bit more effort to track them down (there are other discs available in Sweden which we have not been able to hear so far). The EMI double-CD is still the perfect introduction to her early work, converting the *Swedish Sensation!* album along with the tracks from eight EPs into a handsomely documented package. Singing mostly in English (four tracks from an EP dedicated to *My Fair Lady* songs are sung in Swedish) Zetterlund has some of the slightly fey charm of Astrud Gilberto, but she's a much more accomplished vocalist. On ballads, she makes no attempt at any breathy charm but delivers lines with a clarity and restraint that can sound unforgettably poignant from moment to moment. An incomparably lovely 'Deep In A Dream', done almost as a duet with Arne Domnérus, is one special highlight, but there are many more, from the almost artless sincerity of the first two EPs to the fine work with arranger Lars Gullin on two late tracks. Along the way are many neat cameos by most of the famous names in Swedish jazz of the period, plus Bailey and Byrd as guest-star trumpeters.

Occupied with film and TV work, Zetterlund has had something of an on-and-off career since. The second EMI disc collects all the 1975 *Hey, Man!* album with five tracks from 1971's *Monica-Monica*, though some of these are bizarrely misguided: an arrangement of Albinoni's *Adagio* is set against Frank Zappa's 'Toads Of The Short Forest'! Superior are the 1975 tracks, with a fine 'If You Could See Me Now'. Monica was a little frail and out of practice for the Phontastic sessions, but her opening duet with Mitchell on 'I Should Care' is as beguiling as ever, and the three instrumentalists (Zetterlund sings on 6 of the 15 tracks) are in top form for their trio pieces, Sandstrom relishing the situation. *Topaz* is another gentle, reflective record. The settings are updated to the 1990s with keyboards and guitar, and the songs are mostly contemporary, but Zetterlund sings them with the peculiar kind of cool panache that has yet to desert her. Thielemans is a helpful presence, and Rosengren has a strong solo on 'The Zanzibar Song'.

****** Ett Lingonris Som Satts I Cocktailglas**

RCA 74321 32989-2 6CD Zetterlund; others as discs above, plus Bill Evans (*p*) and many more! 57–93.

Gorgeous packaging for this six-disc celebration of Zetterlund's career for RCA, starting with some scratchy 1957 demos and going as far as her 1993 *Topaz* set. There are many items which will surprise even dedicated Zetterlund collectors along the way, including alternative takes from her celebrated session with Bill Evans (and a TV show track with Evans for good measure), and the final disc is made up of rare concert and soundtrack recordings covering the breadth of her work. There are tracks from her London session of 1964, with Bill McGuffie and Jimmy Deuchar; a moving reading of Lars Gullin's 'Silhouette', with the Thad Jones–Mel Lewis Orchestra; several challenging songs by Povel Ramel, which she handles superbly; and plenty more besides. Excellent remastering of even the live tracks. There are 13 duplications with the *Swedish Sensation!* set, but that will surely not stop Monica's admirers from seeking out what is the outstanding collection of her work on the market (non-Swedish speakers should be warned, though, that the booklet is entirely and exclusively in her own language).

***** Det Finns Dagar**

RCA 74321 4174-2 *Zetterlund; Anders Bergcrantz (c, t, flhn); Gustavo Bergalli (t); Fredrik Norén (flhn); Bertil Strandberg, Nils Landgren (tb); Mattis Cederberg (btb); Gunnar Magnusson (cl); Ulf Andersson (ts, ss, f); Bernt Rosengren (ob); Sven Larson (tba); Helene Cort, Jerker Hallden (f); Jan Sigurd (p); Mats Asplen, Kjell Ohman (org); Hakan Andersson (acc); Magnus Persson (vib); Thomas Hallberg (g); Jan Adefelt, Per-Ola Gadd, Marcus Wikström, Hans Backenroth (b); Rune Carlsson, Christer Sjöström (d); strings.* 97.

This recent record from the *grande dame* of Swedish jazz is full of graceful music. She was never a big-sounding singer and the voice is growing more frail, but the understated way with lyrics is all her own, and this set of originals by pianist Jan Sigurd is tailored to suit her style. A glance through the personnel shows how she's kept the faith with jazz as the music which suits her, too.

James Zollar (born 1959)

TRUMPET

Born in Kansas, Zollar came to New York in 1984 and has become a familiar presence in larger groups there, with this somewhat belated leadership effort for the new Naxos label.

*****(*) Soaring With Bird**

Naxos Jazz 86008 *Zollar; Andy Martin (tb); Pete Christlieb (ts); Bill Cunliffe (p); Ron Eschete (g); John Clayton (b); Paul Kreibich (d).* 1/97.

This could be Naxos's first really significant signing. Zollar has been making a name for himself, gigging with David Murray (and recording with him on the saxophonist's Grateful Dead project) and working on Don Byron's quirky *Bug Music* set. His trademark muted sound harks back earlier than Miles, though he is the obvious influence on the Harmon sound Zollar gets on 'I Didn't Know What Time It Was'. His facility with the plunger mute is a legacy of a highly creative stint with the Duke Ellington Orchestra; it's heard to best effect on 'Parker's Mood'.

A native of Kansas City (and appearing in the Altman film of that name), Zollar is a natural for an album of Charlie Parker and ornithologically related items. He has assembled a bright, occasionally brash group and a strong programme of tunes. Apart from a group of standards in the middle of the set – 'I Didn't Know', 'The Song Is You' and 'If I Should Lose You' – all the material is by Parker. Christlieb, Martin and Eschete are guests; they don't overlap at all, so the impression is of subtly different groups for different songs. Martin plays a key role on 'Donna Lee' and Christlieb on 'Dewey Square'. Eschete is more reserved, but he makes some interesting noises on 'Chasing The Bird'.

Attila Zoller (1927–98)

GUITAR, BASS

The Hungarian began playing guitar in Budapest jazz groups in the late '40s, then moved to Vienna and later to Germany, before studying in the USA. A familiar name in European circles in the

'60s and '70s but sighted only occasionally as a leader on record, Zoller's own-name legacy is in the end rather slight.

*** **Common Cause**
Enja ENJ 3043 *Zoller; Ron Carter (b); Joe Chambers (d).* 5 & 10/79.

***(*) **Memories Of Pannonia**
Enja ENJ 5027 *Zoller; Michael Formanek (b); Daniel Humair (d).* 6/86.

*** **Overcome**
Enja ENJ 5055 *As above, except add Kirk Lightsey (p).* 11/86.

Like many quiet and understated players, Zoller rarely received his fair share of critical attention. Among fellow players, though, his stock remained very high. Recognized as a fine, romantic accompanist, he was also highly regarded as a solo player and small-group leader who has been part of the modern scene in Europe since the end of the war. The 1986 trio is one of Zoller's best records, graced with a lovely reading of 'Sophisticated Lady' which catches his restrained lyricism perfectly. The addition of Lightsey was a happy thought, and the two get on famously, intelligent musicians engaged in discussion of above-average sophistication. The record was made at the Leverkusen Festival and there are some technical deficiencies as well as a rather ponderous pace which unfortunately diminishes its impact and calls for more work than most listeners will consider worth the investment.

John Zorn (born 1954)

ALTO SAXOPHONE, DUCK CALLS

A lifelong New Yorker, Zorn studied briefly in St Louis but made his mark with the circle of improvisers based in New York in the mid-'70s. Steadily came to wider attention through relentless work, composing, performing, and eventually gaining major-label recognition, though this was soon sidelined in favour of his own label, Tzadik, which releases most of his work. Groups down the years include Naked City, Painkiller and Masada. Outspoken, furiously prolific but ruthless about quality control, Zorn has fashioned his own multiple-idiom music, of which jazz remains a buried but tangible part.

*** **First Recordings 1973**
Tzadik TZ 7304 *Zorn (all instruments).* 73.

***(*) **The Parachute Years 1977–1980**
Tzadik TZ-7316 7CD *Zorn; George Lewis (tb); Bruce Ackley (ss); Robert Dick (f, bf, picc); Anthony Coleman (ky); Wayne Horvitz (ky, hca, elec); Bob Ostertag (elec); Mark Miller (vib, perc); LaDonna Smith, Polly Bradfield (vn, vla); Eugene Chadbourne (g, tiple); Davey Williams (g, bj); Henry Kaiser, Bill Horvitz (g); Tom Cora (clo); David Moss, Charles Noyes (d, etc.).* 77–81.

Whatever path you take across contemporary jazz, contemporary improvisation, contemporary film music or any of the advanced sonics, it is likely that you will come across John Zorn. What follows cannot pretend to be anything more than a sketchy and partial discography and, even if the border patrols we have posted on the country called Jazz are now notoriously soporific and unvigilant, some at least of these records will offend purists.

Zorn's early work on record was for a long time available only on ultra-rare vinyl, or not at all. The debut recordings see him navigating a solitary course through the shattered columns of avant-garde jazz. 'Variations On A Theme By Albert Ayler' (as ever, difficult to be categorical about *what* Ayler theme it is) suggests where Zorn was artistically at the age of nineteen, but 'Wind Ko/La' and 'Automata Of Al-Jazari' offer useful pointers to the years ahead and their obsessions.

The seven-disc set documents his period with the independent Parachute label. There are four principal works: *Lacrosse*, in its original sextet version (1978) and in a previously unheard quartet format from a year earlier (Zorn, Chadbourne, Kaiser, Ackley); *Hockey*, played by two different trios, one acoustic, one electric; *Pool*, 50 minutes of music by the 1980 quintet of Zorn, Bradfield, Miller, Noyes and Ostertag; and *Archery*, dated 1979 but cut in 1981, with three long rehearsal-pieces as a bonus. These are all examples of the composer-leader's game of system-pieces, the mechanics of, say, an Avalon Hill wargame used as a suggestive basis for structuring an improvisation. While that sometimes oblique patterning implies a kindred music to those of Leo Smith or Anthony Braxton in the same time-frame, Zorn's meticulousness and intensity outdo even those Chicagoan masters. *Lacrosse* remains a stunning experience, the instruments recorded in glaring close-up, with the leader's squawking reeds in an almost brutal alignment with the sounds of the string players. While the free playing sometimes approximates the feel and grain of some of the more chamberish Company ensembles, the notes to some of the discs reveal how focused and fierce Zorn was about getting the results he wanted: as 'free' as this improvising is, very little is actually left to chance, at least in the accustomed manner of free playing. What is lost in spontaneity is made up for by the often furious grip which Zorn imposes on all the players and their contributions, an element which remains the constant in his discography.

Historically, this is arguably as important a set as any Blue Note or Prestige milestone, with Chadbourne, Williams, Bradfield, Smith, Kaiser, the Horvitzes and the rest all playing as significant a performing role as the leader in what was an unrepeatable slice of New York's music of that time. Burrowing through it some 20 years on, we find it a startling reminder of the small-scale earthquake which these performers instigated. Rather than mere 'prentice work, one can often hear things in this collection which echo more vividly than much of Zorn's more obviously 'outrageous' work with Naked City and the like. Remastered with great vitality, bringing the music right into the present, this is a model reissue.

***(*) **Locus Solus**
Tzadik TZ 7303 *Zorn; Wayne Horvitz (ky); Arto Lindsay (g); Anton Fier, Mark Miller, Ikue Mori (d); Christian Marclay (turntables); Whiz Kid (scratching); Peter Blegvad (v).* 83.

This is one of the sacred texts of '80s New York improv, a fierce, scrabbly set of associations that draw heavily on the power-trio aesthetic of rock bands like Hüsker Dü. Zorn favours the short, sharp shock approach to improvisation, steering sessions that are remarkably reminiscent of Billy Jenkins's 12 × 3-minute-round 'Big Fights', but for the fact that one player is always refereeing and sometimes even normalizing the music. *Locus Solus* is one of those records that, in one respect very much of its time, also seems to float freely without obvious stylistic or fashion anchors. It's impressively compact but sometimes rather too abrupt.

*** The Classic Guide To Strategy: Volumes 1 and 2

Tzadik TZ 7305 *Zorn (ss, as, cl, game calls).* 2/83–9/85.

Originally issued as a Lumina LP, Volume One of the *The Classic Guide* seems to have been the first chapter in a sequence of five records, all bearing the same title. There is some evidence that the history of American culture, and particularly Jewish-American culture, may be the history of huge, hubristic projects which never quite came to fruition: Norman Mailer's multi-decker novel of Hollywood, Alfred Kazin's history of the Jews, Saul Bellow's ever-receding *meisterwerk.* It becomes easier with the passing years to see Zorn in this company and this strange, wilful record, reminiscent in its way of Braxton's solo-sax monologues though utterly different in intent, feeds a growing impression of Zorn as a jazz traditionalist who has been let down by the idiom rather than turning his back on it.

As we will doubtless repeat *ad nauseam* to the end of this section, this surviving torso of a much larger project serves notice of what an inventive saxophone player Zorn is, a quality which is easy to overlook. The basic material is tuneful free bop, oddly soulful and full of character. The *faux*-oriental titles – 'Senki' and 'The Moon In The Cold Stream Like A Mirror' – are a diversion, as are the non-Western flourishes, though the material on Volume Two, almost all of which appears on the CD issue, seems closer to Japanese music than the first sessions. This is emphatically a jazz record.

**** Yankees

Charly CDGR 221 *Zorn; George Lewis (tb); Derek Bailey (g).* 83.

Though a collaborative effort, this more and more *feels* like a Zorn project. It is one of the great improvisation records of the decade and is a key item in what turned out to be a vintage year for the saxophonist. Pieces like 'The Legend Of Enos Slaughter' and 'On Golden Pond' confirmed Zorn's rising eminence and turned on a new generation of listeners to the brilliant Bailey as well. The trio's performances in London around the same time were revelatory, but it is important to note – *pace* a couple of recent comments – that these are not live performances but a studio session. Though doubtless run down without preconceived structures, the music is more deliberate, more formal in articulation if not in form than might be expected. The two tracks noted form the bulk of the material, but the sheer concentration of the shorter tracks, on which Lewis tends to play more literally and idiomatically, is breathtaking. A record to cherish.

♛ **** The Big Gundown

Elektra Nonesuch 979139 *Zorn; Jim Staley (tb, btb); Tim Berne (as); Vicki Bodner (ob, eng hn); Bill Frisell, Fred Frith, Jody Harris, Robert Quine, Vernon Reid (g); Arto Lindsay, Anthony Coleman (p, ky); Wayne Horvitz (p); Big John Patton (org); Orvin Acquart (hca); Toots Thielemans (hca, whistling); Ned Rothenberg (shakuhachi, etc.); Michihiro Sato (shamisen); Guy Klucevesek (acc); Carol Emanuel (hp); Polly Bradfield (vn); Melvin Gibbs (b); Anton Fier (d); Mark Miller, Bobby Previte (d, perc); Cyro Baptista, Reinaldo Fernandes, Duduka Fonseca, Claudio Silva, Jorge Silva (perc); David Weinstein (elec); Bob James (tapes); Christian Marclay (turntables); Laura Biscotto, Diamanda Galas, Shelley Hirsch (v).* 9/84–9/85.

Utterly remarkable in every way and one of the essential records of the 1980s. Ennio Morricone's soundtrack scores – to movies by Pontecorvo, Lelouch, Bertolucci, Petri and, most memorably, Sergio Leone – are among the most significant artistic collaborations of recent times, a simultaneous confirmation and dismantling of the *auteur* myth. Zorn appears to have been influenced every bit as much by Leone's weird pans, sustained close-ups and frozen poses (where a fly or a melting harmonica note on the soundtrack might command more attention than the actor), followed by bouts of violence which are ritualized rather than choreographed (as they would be in a Peckinpah movie).

Zorn assembles musicians with his usual puppet-master care, bringing on harmonica player Toots Thielemans to whistle plangently on 'Poverty' from *Once Upon A Time In America*, organist Big John Patton to grind out the 'Erotico' line from *The Burglars*, Diamanda Galas and Vernon Reid to lash up a storm on 'Metamorfosi', a theme from Petri's *La Classe Operaia Va In Paradiso.* Zorn's political concerns are engaged to the extent of his determination to raise preterite music to the gates of heaven, thereby overcoming what he considers the 'racist' compartmentalization of high and low, black and white, formal and improvised styles on which the music industry depends.

The Big Gundown establishes the pattern for much of Zorn's subsequent music. It is very much a 'studio' record, an artefact, and Zorn himself has adduced the example of George Martin and the Beatles, or the earlier works of another enormous, alphabetically and stylistically late-coming influence, Frank Zappa. Like Zappa, Zorn appears to trash the very musics he seems to be setting up as icons. The result is ambivalent, unsettling and utterly contemporary.

*** Ganryu Island

Tzadik TZ 7319 *Zorn; Michihiro Sato (shamisen).* 11/84.

Originally issued on Yukon Records, which allowed cynics to grumble that listening to *Ganryu Island* is like panning for gold: seeming eternities spent plodging through muddy dross in order to turn up just a few moments of pure gold. By the oddest perversity, the very best tracks seem to be those which were excluded from the vinyl release, unless it is simply the case that one needs some time with Zorn and Sato before the music delivers up its delights. *Shamisen* rarely avoid a generic, plinky-plonky sound, but Sato is genuinely interesting.

**** Spillane

Elektra Nonesuch 79172 *Zorn; Jim Staley (tb); Anthony Coleman, Wayne Horvitz (p, ky); Big John Patton (org); Dave Weinstein (ky); Carol Emanuel (hp); Albert Collins, Bill Frisell (g); Melvin Gibbs (b); David Hofstra (b, tba); Bob James (tapes, CDs); Ronald Shannon Jackson (d); Bobby Previte (d, perc); Christian Marclay (turntables); Kronos Quartet: David Harrington, John Sherba (vn); Hank Dutt (vla); Joan Jeanrenaud (clo); Ohta Hiromi (v).* 8/86–9/87.

Zorn's own liner-notes to *Spillane* offer immensely valuable insights into his work and philosophy: his interest in Carl

Stalling, composer of Bugs Bunny and other cartoon soundtracks; his Japan obsession (reflected here in 'Forbidden Fruit' for voice and string quartet); his conceptual-collage, file-card approach to 'Spillane' itself; the need for longer durations to accommodate Albert Collins's blues lines on 'Two-Lane Highway'; his overall conviction that 'the era of the composer as autonomous musical mind has just about come to an end'.

For all their apparent serendipity, Zorn's groups are selected with very great care. He approaches instrumental coloration much as a graphic artist might use a 'paintbox' package on a computer graphics screen, trying possibilities consecutively or even simultaneously, but making his gestures in a very precise, hard-edged way. 'Spillane' is a sequence of tiny sound-bites, evocative not so much of Mickey Spillane's fictional world (in the sense of dim bars, lonely roads, chalked outlines on the pavement) as of his language, which is notably fragmentary, clipped and elided, poised between literalism and the purest self-reference. Zorn has pointed to the fact that Schoenberg's earliest atonal works were given unity only by use of texts; and it's clear that Zorn's imagery works in much the same way, with Mickey Spillane's voices soundtracking the music rather than vice versa.

'Two-Lane Highway' follows a more systematic and structured groove, a concerto for bluesman and improvising orchestra, with Collins's guitar, voice, mere *presence* taking the part of the solo instrument. The final part, 'Forbidden Fruit', is actually more conventional and is by far the dullest thing Zorn has done on record, reminiscent of Ennio Morricone's non-film, squeaky-door compositions.

**** Spy Vs Spy

Elektra Musician 960844 *Zorn; Tim Berne (as); Mark Dresser (b); Joey Baron, Michael Vatcher (d).*

In some respects a more straightforward tribute than the Morricone set, Zorn's take on the music of Ornette Coleman is a headlong, hardcore thrash that approaches levels of sheer intensity never attempted by Coleman's own Prime Time band. Only one of the first dozen tracks is over three minutes in length. 'Chronology', from Coleman's classic Atlantic album, *The Shape Of Jazz To Come*, lasts exactly 68 seconds, and half a dozen others, drawn from Coleman's output between 1958 and the 1980s, occupy no more than 15 minutes between them. It is these, rather than the more measured performances, which seem most faithful to the originals. The twinned altos, sharply separated by channel, scribble all over the white-noise drumming, brutal graffito effects which almost miraculously preserve Coleman's melodic outlines.

*** Filmworks VII

Tzadik TZ 7315 *Zorn; Wayne Horvitz (ky); Bill Frisell (g, bj); Carol Emanuel (hp); Kermit Driscoll (b); Bobby Previte (d).* 10/88.

Zorn's submersion in the hectic aesthetics of Japanese comics and cartoons was confirmed when he created these tracks for a children's cartoon show. This is the soundbite culture *in excelsis*, a slew of tiny programmatic gestures, most of them too brief to register as anything other than sonic blips. Even if you are cynical about the opposite extreme, John Coltrane's hour-long meditations on standard tunes, this is hard going as a continuous listen. It would make sense to programme one track every 20–30 minutes for the course of the day and treat them as if they were radio interstitials. Zorn has relocated the terms of aesthetic debate, from production to consumption.

*** Filmworks III

Tzadik TZ 7309 *Zorn; Dave Douglas (t); Keith Underwood (f); Robert Quine (g); Marc Ribot (g, bj); Arto Lindsay (g, v); Anthony Coleman (org); Peter Scherer (ky); Guy Klucevesek (acc); Carol Emanuel (hp); Jill Jaffee (vla); Erik Friedlander (clo); Greg Cohen, Kermit Driscoll, Bill Laswell, Chris Wood (b); David Hofstra (b, tba); Miguel Frasconi (glass hca); Joey Baron, Sim Cain (d); Bobby Previte (d, perc); Ikue Mori (d machine); Cyro Baptista (perc, v); Christian Marclay (turntables); David Shea (samples).* 90–95.

Another eclectic slew of material intended to accompany images but just about self-determining enough – for the first two dozen tracks, at least – to stand alone as an aural experience. Half of that number are for Joe Chapelle's *Thieves Quartet* and are played by the Masada lineup of Zorn, Douglas, Cohen and Baron. These are riveting pieces, albeit only the end-title-piece is of any great length. For Mei-Juin Chen's *Hollywood Hotel*, Zorn is joined by Marc Ribot in a sequence of surreal musical encounters which don't work quite as well out of context. For our money, the remaining material, written for Weiden and Kennedy, is dispensable, too rapid-fire to be of lasting interest and on occasion almost deliberately perverse in bringing the most elaborate instrumentation to the least substantial musical ideas. One for serious collectors only, but worth hearing once.

** Guts Of A Virgin / Buried Secrets

Earache MOSH 198 *Zorn; Justin Broadrick (g, d machine); G.C Green, Bill Laswell (b); Mick Harris (d, v).* 4/91.

Gross-out cover; tiny, confrontational tracks; provocative titles like 'Handjob', 'Purgatory Of Fiery Vulvas' and 'One Eyed Pessary' ... like any genuinely major artist, Zorn reserves the right to pour out smoke and ash as well as genuinely creative magma; but these tracks, officially credited to Pain Killer, really do give off more heat than light. Needless to say, there are things which deserve attention. For the most part, though, *Guts/Secrets* is little more than a sequence of hostile gestures. Also released in CD single format on Zorn's own Tzadik, it perhaps makes more sense heard as random and discontinuous provocation. Genuine students and aficionados may find it profitable. Bystanders might usefully remain just that.

(***) Elegy

Tzadik TZ 7302 *Barbara Chaffe (af, bf); David Abel (vla); Scummy (g); William Winant (perc); David Shea (turntables); David Slusser (elec); Mike Patton (v).* 11/91.

(****) Kristallnacht

Tzadik TZ 7301 *Frank London (t); David Krakauer (cl, bcl); Mark Feldman (vn); Marc Ribot (g); Anthony Coleman (ky); Mark Dresser (b); William Winant (perc).* 11/92.

Zorn does not play on these remarkable records, but all the music is by him and they bear his stamp throughout. *Elegy* is a suite of four, inexplicably colour-coded pieces. The later album is a set of more expressive and more obviously programmatic ideas, from the opening 'Shtetl', with its startling echoes of Jewish folk forms, to the closing 'Gariin'. Here are the seeds of what was to be a wholesale engagement – or re-engagement – with Jewish musical culture, most clearly represented in the Masada project of future years, but retroactively evident throughout the work of the previous decade and more. A key moment, even if the man himself wasn't playing.

*****(*) Live At The Knitting Factory**

Knitting Factory Works KFW 124 *Zorn; Steven Bernstein (t, sampler); Frank London (t, perc); Curtis Fowlkes, Steve Swell (tb); Marcus Rojas (tba); Doug Wieselman (cl); Tim Smith (bcl); Leslie Ross (bsn, shawm, reeds); Roy Nathanson (ss, as, ts); Allan Chase, Margaret Lancaster (ss, as); Paul Shapiro (ss, ts, f); Jay Rodrigues (as); Blaise Siwula (as, t); Walter Thompson (as, bs, f); David Cast Castiglione (ts, bs, bcl); Paul Hoskin (bs); David Krakauer (cl, bcl); Evan Gallagher (ky, sample tb, c); Nick Balaban, Randy Hutton, Myra Melford, Matthew Ostrowski, Dan Rosengard (syn); Craig Flanagin, Marc Ribot, Vito Ricci, Adam Rogers, Rolf Sturm, Kiki Wada (g); David Watson (g, t); Bob Lipman (g, perc); John King (dobro); Bill Ware (vib); Andrea Parkins (acc); Zeena Parkins (hp); Fred Lonberg-Holm (hp, CD players, sampler); April Chung, Alicia Svigals (vn); Thomas Ulrich (clo); Michelle Kinney (clo, elec); Paul Morrissett (kaval, gaida, vn); Reg Anderson (strings); Ed Broms, Joe Gallant, K.J Grant, Brad Jones, Sebastian Steinberg, Chris Wood (b); (b, v); Steve Waxman (b, t, perc); Christine Bard, Louie Belogenis, Hollis Headrick, James Lo, James Perowsky (d); Michael Evans, E.J Rodriguez (d, perc); James Pugliese (d, perc, sampler); Billy Martin, Danny Sedownik, Jane Tomkiewicz (perc); Dawn Buckholz, Anthony Coleman, Mark Degliatoni, Lee Hyla, David Shea, David Weinstein (sampler); Tim Spelios (CD players); Gisburg (v, hca, whistle); Jeff Buckley, M Doughty, Judy Dunway, Mark Ettinger, Tamela Glen, Cassie Hoffman, Donna Jewell, Makigami Koichi, Nina Mankin, Chris Nelson, Juliet Palmer, Wilbur Pauley, Rick Porterfield, Eric Qin, Kevin Sharp, Sharon Topper (v).* 1–12/92.

Zorn plays Cecil B. DeMille. A cast of what seems like thousands wheeled on at New York's premier club over a year-long residency/workshop to generate a set of inventive variations on a snakey theme. As the personnel details should suggest, the emphasis is on multi-instrumentalism. No virtuosic playing but rather a gestural sound collage that puts the emphasis on process over product. Only Zorn could have conceived such a project and his presence as conductor, *auteur*, dramaturge is essential to its success. It isn't a record that will appeal to anyone who looks first for a settled groove or a hummable tune, but it is undoubtedly fascinating, abstract expressionism of a modern and compelling sort.

****(*) Filmworks II**

Tzadik TZ 7306 *Zorn; Anthony Coleman (prepared p, ky); Marc Ribot (g, bj); Carol Emanuel (hp); Andy Haas (didjeridu); Cyro Baptista, Jim Pugliese (perc); David Shea (turntables, perc).* 5 & 6/92.

This is Zorn's *Chappaqua Suite*, originally written and recorded for a film by Walter Hill, but rejected – as Ornette Coleman was in favour of Ravi Shankar – for a more accessible Ry Cooder soundtrack. *Chappaqua* remains a classic of its kind. This sounds like occasional music which has managed to miss its occasion, which is just about right.

****** Masada: Alef**

DIW 888 *Zorn; Dave Douglas (t); Greg Cohen (b); Joey Baron (d).* 2/94.

*****(*) Masada: Beit**

DIW 889 *As above.* 2/94

***** Masada: Gimel**

DIW 890 *As above.* 2 & 6/94.

(***) Masada: Dalet

DIW DIWS 3 *As above.* 2/94.

By the mid-'90s, the Zorn discography had become unmanageable. It is no less so now. There is in preparation a 100-CD set, marketed in Japan, where Zorn is something of a cult hero. Even a project like this one, in which the saxophonist often movingly explores aspects of his Judaism, raises questions about opportunism. Why was his interest in Hebrew culture not made known sooner? A desire for privacy? A slow awakening to his cultural roots? Or a more cynical reason?

There seems no reason to take the third course in approaching these records. They are beautifully played, folk themes with a contemporary cutting edge, performed by a razor-sharp band whose stylistic reach is almost unbelievably capacious. The first three, named after the A-B-C of the Hebrew alphabet, are almost required listening, but thereafter the series becomes almost indistinguishably repetitive, an impression reinforced by near-identical covers. Number four was not previously listed because it was issued only as a free record for those who had bought earlier CDs. Several letters, ranging from friendly to grumpy, suggest that it has since been made commercially available; not in our local emporia, alas, so we'll stick with the protective brackets.

As always, and even when ostensibly drawing his inspiration from the notorious mass suicide of the Zealots at Masada, a key moment in Jewish history, Zorn has an eye to the market strategy. He has become an ambiguous superstar of the avant-garde; the only artist one might compare him to is Laurie Anderson, except that he has never sought her brand of middle-market appeal. An astonishing musician, as these records confirm, his place in the music is no more clear-cut than before.

*****(*) Bar Kokhba**

Tzadik TZ 7108 *Zorn; Dave Douglas (t); David Krakauer, Chris Speed (cl); John Medeski (org, p); Anthony Coleman (p); Marc Ribot (g); Mark Feldman (vn); Erik Friedlander (clo); Greg Cohen, Mark Dresser (b); Kenny Wolleson (d).* 8/94–3/96.

Larger-scale versions of Masada's 'radical Jewish culture', these are exquisitely voiced folkloric essays, executed without strain. Zorn's own part in these ensembles is more distant. The music genuinely sounds as if it arises out of the culture intact and without mediation, which is considerable testimony to his powers of synthesis and persuasion. As ever, Douglas and Speed are the most effective solo performers, though Dresser's rich bass playing is a huge asset.

***** Art Of Memory**

Incus CD 20 *Zorn; Fred Frith (g).* 94.

Freely improvised, but packed with associations from both players' musical pasts. Frith is a romantic and a mnemonist, creating music like an old bluesman out of remembered shards and fragments. Zorn responds with some of his most rooted and responsive playing, and yet the music seems private, enclosed, elbows out to the world. Fascinating as it is to have such encounters on disc, it also seems intrusive. A record to hear once and then file away.

(***) Tokyo Operations '94

Avant AVAN 049 *Takei Makoto (shakuhachi); Tanaka Yumiko (gidayu); Uchihashi Kazuhisha (g); Nakamujra Hitomi (hichiriki); Maruta Miki (koto); Kinoshita Shinichi (shamisen); Isso Yukihiro (nokan, dengakubue); Ito Taeko (ortin doo); Mekken (b); Senba Kiyohiko, Uemura Masahiro (perc); Yamamoto Kyoko (v); Makigami Koichi (prompter).* 11/94.

You must have had that moment in an Oriental restaurant when your mother says, 'Yes, very nice, dear, but could I have a knife and fork?' The procedures here are at the sushi-and-fries end of the counter, a group of Japanese players working in a (non) genre which is neither idiomatic nor completely subversive. Zorn's Cobra was always an umbrella project and only intermittently successful. This is not one of the great moments.

***** Masada: Hei**

DIW 891 *Zorn; Dave Douglas (t); Greg Cohen (b); Joey Baron (d).* 7/95.

***** Masada: Vav**

DIW 892 *As above.* 7/95.

For all but the most attentive and committed listeners, Masada started to seem like late Miles Davis. The real fans were swapping C90s and DATs of live performances, and admitting that the issued sessions were getting seriously commonplace. There were a few live bootleg recordings doing the rounds with Kenny Wollesen on drums in place of Baron. It's immediately evident from these how important Joey is to the sound of the band, and how irreplaceable. By this stage, Masada recordings are both utterly original and by-the-yard, a disconcerting collision of critical opposites that rather closes down any effort of judgement.

***** Weird Little Boy**

Avant AVAN 043 *Zorn; Chris Cochrane (g); Trey Spruance (g, ky, d); Mike Patton (d, v); William Winant (perc).* 11/95.

An amplified unit with a strong rock influence, Weird Little Boy is thirled to Dennis Cooper's unsettling texts, but very much coloured by the Zorn aesthetic. Unlike Naked City or the Sonny Clark tribute group, it's very much the saxophonist's album. There has been too little of Zorn's saxophone on recent records, so it's good to have some to take a fix on. The distinctive alto sound is heard to good effect here, but has to vie for attention with keyboards and samplers and some clutter from the other players.

***** Filmworks V**

Tzadik TZ 7307 *Zorn; Robert Quine, Marc Ribot (g); Cyro Baptista (perc); Jason Baker (v).* 10/95.

***** Filmworks VI**

Tzadik TZ 7308 *Zorn; Marc Ribot (g); Mark Feldman (vn); Erik Friedlander (clo); Greg Cohen (b); Cyro Baptista (perc); Ikue (d machine); Jason Baker (v).* 1 & 7/96.

Written for Oki Hiroyuki's movie, *Tears Of Ecstasy*, forty-eight tiny musical moments of jewelled beauty and not much consequence make up Volume Five of the *Filmworks*. Baker figures on only one track and it would have been interesting to have heard more. He resurfaces, again only briefly, on Volume Six, which, unusually, includes more developed pieces – including a sonic landscape for Maria Beatty's *The Black Glove* – and rather more interesting films than some of its predecessors.

***** Masada: Zayin**

DIW 893 *As above.* 4/96.

***** Masada: Het**

DIW 894 *As above.* 8/96.

Still beautiful, often moving (as on the opening 'Schechem' on *Het*, aka *Masada 8*), but by this stage in the game desperately calling out for a sensible one- or two-CD compilation. Listening to this stuff in bulk has a hypnotic inconsequence. How great it would be to encounter even one of these later records out of the blue, and without the weight of the previous six or seven or eight pressing down on one's expectations.

***** Filmworks IV – S&M + More**

Tzadik TZ 7310 *Zorn; Robert Quine (g); Kuroda Kyoko (p); Anthony Coleman (org); Jim Pugliese (vib, perc); Carol Emanuel (hp); Jill Jaffee (vla); Erik Friedlander (clo); Joey Baron (d); Cyro Baptista (perc).*

A more scattered but also more concentrated set of film-related pieces. Two of the tracks – 'Elegant Spanking' and 'A Lot Of Fun For The Evil One' – are around the quarter-hour mark and are highly developed performances. The strings are restricted to the former of these tracks and they mark Zorn's most convincingly idiomatic use of fiddles and harp on record. The sound is pretty shaky, except on the two tracks where the leader is credited with what has become his other 'instrument' – 'sound design'. His grasp of the spatial dimensions of music, its shifting masses and inertias, is as impressive as his more linear writing and playing.

***** Euclid's Nightmare**

Depth of Field DOF 1 *Zorn; Bobby Previte (d).* 3/97.

Two superb improvisers locked into the circle and unable to break it. This is the most indulgent either man has ever been on record, hammering at ideas that seem stale and cold, firing out improvisations like spikes from a staple-gun. Fans of both performers will doubtless find their loyalties confirmed. We, on the other hand, were much disappointed.

(***) Angelus Novus

Tzadik TZ 7028 *Stephen Drury (p); Callithumpian Consort of New England Conservatory.* 97.

Another compositional by-way, easily overlooked but well worth hunting down. The playing is poised and confident and suggests that in future Zorn may well find himself in the same position as Anthony Braxton, making a move from improvised performance to a creator of interpretative composition.

***** Masada: Tet**

DIW 933 *Zorn; Dave Douglas (t); Greg Cohen (b); Joey Baron (d).* 4/97.

Volume Nine of the ongoing project and a few intriguing signs that the constituent personalities are beginning to secede from the original Zorn premiss, or perhaps it's simply that Masada has begun to acquire an identity as a band rather than as a Zorn concept. 'Meholalot' is magnificent and the closing 'Jachin' suggests there may yet be a few unrevealed facets to a group of real originality and expressiveness.

*** **Filmworks VIII**

DIW 7318 *Zorn; Anthony Coleman (p); Marc Ribot (g); Mark Feldman (vn); Erik Friedlander (clo); Min Xiao-Fen (pipa); Greg Cohen (b); Kenny Wollesen (d, perc); Cyro Baptista (perc).* 7 & 11/97.

Zorn's film writing has been fuller in texture and in development of late, and these two projects – recorded for *The Port Of Last Resort* and *Latin Boys Go To Hell*, two films we don't know – are very much of a piece with that. One of the themes for *Port* is heard in three different versions, for *pipa*, guitar and piano. Other tracks are retreads of things that have floated around the Zorn canon for years.

*** **Masada: Yod**

DIW 935 *Zorn; Dave Douglas (t); Greg Cohen (b); Joey Baron (d).* 97.

Volume Ten ends with 'Zevul' which – alphabetically at least – suggests that Masada may have reached a point of stasis, other than for the live performances which are sure to leak out, officially and unofficially, over the next few years. What a long, strange trip it has been; but, hand on heart, how often do you listen to these after the first spin?

**** **Live In Jerusalem**

Tzadik TZ 7234 2CD *As above.* 97.

***(*) **Live In Taipei**

Tzadik TZ 7235 2CD *As above.* 97.

Any few remaining doubts about the durability and creative freshness of Masada were blown apart by these extraordinary releases. The sound-quality is good, the performances as good as anything Zorn has ever done as a performing musician. Inevitably, given the group's tacit manifesto, the Jerusalem concert represented an emotional high which isn't sustained in the Taipei recording. Even so, it too is a very valuable document and, it seems, there are more live sets to come from this period; word of material from Mogador and from (where? what?) Castle Clinton.

(***) **The Circle Maker**

Tzadik 7122 2CD *Marc Ribot (g); Mark (vn); Erik Friedlander (clo); Greg Cohen (b); Joey Baron (d); Cyro Baptista (perc).* 12/97.

Two interrelated groups involved here: the Masada String Trio (Feldman, Friedlander and Cohen); and the Bar Kokhba Sextet, which adds Ribot, Baptista and Baron. Recorded over two days in New York City, and produced by Zorn, these are unexpectedly bright and affirmative pieces, as if the coming of Thanksgiving had lifted the darkness of other cultural associations. The trio tracks which occupy disc one are the more interesting. Zorn's writing for strings isn't entirely idiomatic; here and there, there are melodic lines for violin which sound as if they've been transcribed from saxophone, but this doesn't detract from the impact of almost 30 vigorously expressive pieces. Some have been heard before and Zorn/Masada enthusiasts can indulge comparative studies to their hearts' content.

**** **Downtown Lullaby**

Depth Of Field DOF 2 *Zorn; Elliott Sharp (g); Wayne Horvitz (p, org, ky); Bobby Previte (d).* 1/98.

A new year and a moment to plight a renewed troth to improvisation. Horvitz emerges as the key contributor, having been out of the picture, *vis-à-vis* Zorn's music, for a little while. Named after NY addresses, the seven tracks have the buzz and excitement of the city. Previte is a very different kind of drummer from Baron, and he fights against the rhythm and the idiosyncratic melody with a jolly, combative self-possession. For a change, certainly relative to recent projects, Zorn limits himself to alto, and some of his fragmentary solos are as good as anything he's done for years.

*** **Music Romance: Volume 1 – Music For Children**

Tzadik TZ 7321 *Zorn; Anthony Coleman (ky); Marc Ribot (g); Mark Feldman (vn); Erik Friedlander (clo); Greg Cohen (b); Cyro Baptista (perc); a.o.* 98.

Zorn for kids; well, why not? He remains our first choice as millennial MD to *Sesame Street* and the Children's Television Workshop. We have had only the scantest listen to this disc, which has had some production problems, but it's *echt* Zorn, another corner of his sound world revealed. A fuller discussion in our next edition.

Zubop

GROUP

Vigorous British post-bop outfit putting an Anglicized spin on some verities in the language.

*** **Cycle City**

33 Records JAZZ 006 *Will Embling/Wisbling/Embliss (t, vtb, v); Ricky Edwards (as, f, bcl, v); Jon Petters (ts, cl, v); Mark Allen (bs); Philip Clouts (p, acc, v); Duncan Noble (b, v); Lindon Donaldson, Cliff Venner (d).* 91.

*** **Freewheeling**

33 Records JAZZ 015 *As above, except omit Allen, Donaldson, Venner; add Sean Randle (d), Gary Hammond (perc).* 8/93.

*** **Hiptodisiac**

33 Records JAZZ 038 *As above, except add John Blackwell (g), Juldeh Camara (riti, v).* 96.

The only mystery here is why the trumpeter's name keeps changing. Zubop play vivacious and intelligent, Afro-tinged bop fusion with no obvious identity problems. All three albums have been marked out by strong, idiosyncratic writing, somewhere between Django Bates and Dudu Pukwana, and a vigorous group sound and, though the band conspicuously lacks a strong single soloist, there is always enough going on in the ensembles to sustain interest, though by *Hiptodisiac* one does begin to wonder where it's all leading.

The first album was a breath of fresh air, with room to stretch out on 'Cycle City', 'Bheki's Arrival' (co-written with pianist Mseleku) and 'Free Yourself', and a brash, almost callow sound that was instantly and lastingly appealing. On the well-named *Freewheeling*, '20,000 Leagues Above Peckham' is a combination of full-on jam and intricate structure, a quality that crops up again on the most recent and most playful of Zubop's discs, where 'Gamelanaskanabopolus', 'We Come From The Universe Like The Dolphins And Frogs' (two more tunes by Edwards) and the folksier 'Song Of Snape' suggest that the band may be moving in a new direction, somewhat closer to the territory carved out by Bill Bruford's Earthworks. It would demand a heart of stone not to enjoy what Zubop do, but it's hard to make too serious a case for them either. Clever, enjoyable jazz from a group that has matured year on year.

Index

A

B

D

H

K

L

M

N

P

S

T

U

X

Y